EUROPEAN RAIL TIMETABLE

SUMMER 202[illegible]

GENERAL INFORMATION

EXTRA FEATURE

TIMETABLES

* no timings shown

CONTACT DETAILS

Editor	Chris Woodcock
Deputy Editor	Reuben Turner
Editorial Team	John Potter Richard Stirk Peter Weller
Additional compiling	Brendan Fox
Commercial Manager	Gemma Donaldson

Printed and bound by CPI Group (UK) Ltd, Croydon, CR0 4YY

Front cover: An unidentified Slovenian Railways service crossing the spectacular stone bridge at Solkan, located approximately two kilometres north of Nova Gorica station on the scenic route between Sežana and Jesenice (Table **1302**). © Nicola Pulham / Dreamstime.com.

ISBN 978-1-7394786-4-3

European Rail Timetable Limited
6A George Street, Nottingham, NG1 3BE

For sales and editorial correspondence:
28 Monson Way, Oundle, Northamptonshire, PE8 4QG, United Kingdom

website: www.europeanrailtimetable.eu
e-mail: editorial@europeanrailtimetable.eu
sales: sales@europeanrailtimetable.eu
telephone: +44 (0)1832 270198 Mondays to Fridays 1000 - 1600

© European Rail Timetable Limited, 2025
Company Number 8590554

Every care has been taken to render the timetable correct in accordance with the latest advices, but changes are constantly being made by the administrations concerned and the publishers cannot hold themselves responsible for the consequences of either changes or inaccuracies.

CALENDAR

CALENDRIER CALENDARIO KALENDER CALENDARIO

2025

JANUARY

M	T	W	T	F	S	S
①	②	③	④	⑤	⑥	⑦
–	–	1	2	3	4	5
6	7	8	9	10	11	12
13	14	15	16	17	18	19
20	21	22	23	24	25	26
27	28	29	30	31	–	–

FEBRUARY

M	T	W	T	F	S	S
①	②	③	④	⑤	⑥	⑦
–	–	–	–	–	1	2
3	4	5	6	7	8	9
10	11	12	13	14	15	16
17	18	19	20	21	22	23
24	25	26	27	28	–	–

MARCH

M	T	W	T	F	S	S
①	②	③	④	⑤	⑥	⑦
31	–	–	–	–	1	2
3	4	5	6	7	8	9
10	11	12	13	14	15	16
17	18	19	20	21	22	23
24	25	26	27	28	29	30

APRIL

M	T	W	T	F	S	S
①	②	③	④	⑤	⑥	⑦
–	1	2	3	4	5	6
7	8	9	10	11	12	13
14	15	16	17	18	19	20
21	22	23	24	25	26	27
28	29	30	–	–	–	–

MAY

M	T	W	T	F	S	S
①	②	③	④	⑤	⑥	⑦
–	–	–	1	2	3	4
5	6	7	8	9	10	11
12	13	14	15	16	17	18
19	20	21	22	23	24	25
26	27	28	29	30	31	–

JUNE

M	T	W	T	F	S	S
①	②	③	④	⑤	⑥	⑦
30	–	–	–	–	–	1
2	3	4	5	6	7	8
9	10	11	12	13	14	15
16	17	18	19	20	21	22
23	24	25	26	27	28	29

JULY

M	T	W	T	F	S	S
①	②	③	④	⑤	⑥	⑦
–	1	2	3	4	5	6
7	8	9	10	11	12	13
14	15	16	17	18	19	20
21	22	23	24	25	26	27
28	29	30	31	–	–	–

AUGUST

M	T	W	T	F	S	S
①	②	③	④	⑤	⑥	⑦
–	–	–	–	1	2	3
4	5	6	7	8	9	10
11	12	13	14	15	16	17
18	19	20	21	22	23	24
25	26	27	28	29	30	31

SEPTEMBER

M	T	W	T	F	S	S
①	②	③	④	⑤	⑥	⑦
1	2	3	4	5	6	7
8	9	10	11	12	13	14
15	16	17	18	19	20	21
22	23	24	25	26	27	28
29	30	–	–	–	–	–

OCTOBER

M	T	W	T	F	S	S
①	②	③	④	⑤	⑥	⑦
–	–	1	2	3	4	5
6	7	8	9	10	11	12
13	14	15	16	17	18	19
20	21	22	23	24	25	26
27	28	29	30	31	–	–

NOVEMBER

M	T	W	T	F	S	S
①	②	③	④	⑤	⑥	⑦
–	–	–	–	–	1	2
3	4	5	6	7	8	9
10	11	12	13	14	15	16
17	18	19	20	21	22	23
24	25	26	27	28	29	30

DECEMBER

M	T	W	T	F	S	S
①	②	③	④	⑤	⑥	⑦
1	2	3	4	5	6	7
8	9	10	11	12	13	14
15	16	17	18	19	20	21
22	23	24	25	26	27	28
29	30	31	–	–	–	–

2026

JANUARY

M	T	W	T	F	S	S
①	②	③	④	⑤	⑥	⑦
–	–	–	1	2	3	4
5	6	7	8	9	10	11
12	13	14	15	16	17	18
19	20	21	22	23	24	25
26	27	28	29	30	31	–

FEBRUARY

M	T	W	T	F	S	S
①	②	③	④	⑤	⑥	⑦
–	–	–	–	–	–	1
2	3	4	5	6	7	8
9	10	11	12	13	14	15
16	17	18	19	20	21	22
23	24	25	26	27	28	–

MARCH

M	T	W	T	F	S	S
①	②	③	④	⑤	⑥	⑦
30	31	–	–	–	–	1
2	3	4	5	6	7	8
9	10	11	12	13	14	15
16	17	18	19	20	21	22
23	24	25	26	27	28	29

APRIL

M	T	W	T	F	S	S
①	②	③	④	⑤	⑥	⑦
–	–	1	2	3	4	5
6	7	8	9	10	11	12
13	14	15	16	17	18	19
20	21	22	23	24	25	26
27	28	29	30	–	–	–

MAY

M	T	W	T	F	S	S
①	②	③	④	⑤	⑥	⑦
–	–	–	–	1	2	3
4	5	6	7	8	9	10
11	12	13	14	15	16	17
18	19	20	21	22	23	24
25	26	27	28	29	30	31

JUNE

M	T	W	T	F	S	S
①	②	③	④	⑤	⑥	⑦
1	2	3	4	5	6	7
8	9	10	11	12	13	14
15	16	17	18	19	20	21
22	23	24	25	26	27	28
29	30	–	–	–	–	–

PUBLIC HOLIDAYS 2025

JOURS FÉRIÉS GIORNI FESTIVI FEIERTAGE DÍAS FESTIVOS

The dates given below are those of national public holidays. They do not include regional, half-day or unofficial holidays. Passengers intending to travel on public holidays, or on days immediately preceding or following them, are strongly recommended to reserve seats and to confirm timings locally. Further information regarding special transport conditions applying on holiday dates may be found in the introduction to each country.

Austria: Jan. 1, 6, Apr. 21, May 1, 29, June 9, 19, Aug. 15, Oct. 26, Nov. 1, Dec. 8, 25, 26.

Belgium: Jan. 1, Apr. 20, 21, May 1, 29, June 8, 9, July 21, Aug. 15, Nov. 1, 11, Dec. 25.

Bosnia-Herzegovina: Jan. 1, 2, Mar. 1, May 1, 2. *Other religious holidays are observed in certain areas.*

Bulgaria: Jan. 1, Mar. 3, Apr. 18 – 21, May 1, 6, 26, Sept. 8, 22, Dec. 24, 25, 26.

Croatia: Jan. 1, 6, Apr. 20, 21, May 1, 30, June 19, 22, Aug. 5, 15, Nov. 1, 18, Dec. 25, 26.

Czech Republic: Jan. 1, Apr. 18, 21, May 1, 8, July 5, 6, Sept. 28, Oct. 28, Nov. 17, Dec. 24, 25, 26.

Denmark: Jan. 1, Apr. 17, 18, 20, 21, May 29, June 8, 9, Dec. 25, 26.

Estonia: Jan. 1, Feb. 24, Apr. 18, 20, May 1, June 8, 23, 24, Aug. 20, Dec. 24, 25, 26.

Finland: Jan. 1, 6, Apr. 18, 21, May 1, 29, June 20, 21, Nov. 1, Dec. 6, 24, 25, 26.

France: Jan. 1, Apr. 21, May 1, 8, 29, June 9, July 14, Aug. 15, Nov. 1, 11, Dec. 25.

Germany: Jan. 1, 6*, Mar. 8*, Apr. 18, 21, May 1, 29, June 9, 19*, Aug. 15*, Sept. 20*, Oct. 3, 31*, Nov. 1*, 19*, Dec. 25, 26.
* *Observed in certain regions: see also page 372.*

Great Britain: *England & Wales*: Jan. 1, Apr. 18, 21, May 5, 26, Aug. 25, Dec. 25, 26.
Scotland: Jan. 1, 2, Apr. 18, May 5, 26, Aug. 4, Dec. 1, 25, 26.

Greece: Jan. 1, 6, Mar. 3, 25, Apr. 18, 21, May 1, June 9, Aug. 15, Oct. 28, Dec. 25, 26.

Hungary: Jan. 1, Mar. 15, Apr. 18, 21, May 1, 2, June 9, Aug. 20, Oct. 23, 24, Nov. 1, Dec. 24, 25, 26.

Iceland: Jan. 1, Apr. 17, 18, 20, 21, 24, May 1, 29, June 8, 9, 17, Aug. 4, Dec. 25, 26.

Ireland (Northern): Jan. 1, Mar. 17, Apr. 18, 21, May 5, 26, July 14, Aug. 25, Dec. 25, 26.

Ireland (Republic): Jan. 1, Feb. 3, Mar. 17, Apr. 21, May 5, June 2, Aug. 4, Oct. 27, Dec. 25, 26.

Italy: Jan. 1, 6, Apr. 20, 21, 25, May 1, June 2, Aug. 15, Nov. 1, Dec. 8, 25, 26.

Kosovo: Jan. 1, 2, 7, Feb. 17, Mar. 31, Apr. 9, 20, 21, May 1, 9, June 7, Dec. 25.

Latvia: Jan. 1, Apr. 18, 20, 21, May 1, 4, 5, 11, June 8, 23, 24, Nov. 18, Dec. 24, 25, 26, 31.

Lithuania: Jan. 1, Feb. 16, Mar. 11, Apr. 20, 21, May 1, 4, June 1, 24, July 6, Aug. 15, Nov. 1, 2, Dec. 24, 25, 26.

Luxembourg: Jan. 1, Apr. 21, May 1, 9, 29, June 9, 23, Aug. 15, Nov. 1, Dec. 25, 26.

Moldova: Jan. 1, 7, 8, Mar. 8, Apr. 20, 21, May 1, 9, June 1, Aug. 27, 31, Dec. 25.

Netherlands: Jan. 1, Apr. 18, 20, 21, 26, May 5, 29, June 8, 9, Dec. 25, 26.

North Macedonia: Jan. 1, 7, Mar. 31, Apr. 21, May 1, 24, Aug. 2, Sept. 8, Oct. 11, 23, Dec. 8. *Other religious holidays are observed in certain areas.*

Norway: Jan. 1, Apr. 17, 18, 20, 21, May 1, 17, 29, June 8, 9, Dec. 25, 26.

Poland: Jan. 1, 6, Apr. 20, 21, May 1, 3, June 8, 19, Aug. 15, Nov. 1, 11, Dec. 25, 26.

Portugal: Jan. 1, Apr. 18, 20, 25, May 1, June 10, 19, Aug. 15, Oct. 5, Nov. 1, Dec. 1, 8, 25.

Romania: Jan. 1, 2, 6, 7, 24, Apr. 18, 20, 21, May 1, June 1, 8, 9, Aug. 15, Nov. 30, Dec. 1, 25, 26.

Serbia: Jan. 1, 2, 7, Feb. 15, 17, Apr. 18 – 21, May 1, 2, Nov. 11.

Slovakia: Jan. 1, 6, Apr. 18, 21, May 1, 8, July 5, Aug. 29, Sept. 1, 15, Nov. 1, 17, Dec. 24, 25, 26.

Slovenia: Jan. 1, 2, Feb. 8, Apr. 20, 21, 27, May 1, 2, June 8, 25, Aug. 15, Oct. 31, Nov. 1, Dec. 25, 26.

Spain: Jan. 1, 6, Apr. 18, May 1, Aug. 15, Oct. 13, Nov. 1, Dec. 6, 8, 25. *Also many regional and local holidays.*

Sweden: Jan. 1, 6, Apr. 18, 20, 21, May 1, 29, June 6, 8, 21, Nov. 1, Dec. 25, 26.

Switzerland: Jan. 1, 2, 6*, Mar. 19*, Apr. 18, 21, May 1*, 29, June 9, 19*, Aug. 1, 15*, Nov. 1*, Dec. 8*, 25, 26. *Also some local holidays.*
* *Observed in certain regions.*

Turkey: Jan. 1, Apr. 23, May 1, 19, July 15, Aug. 30, Oct. 29 (also 2025 feast holiday periods Mar. 29 - Apr. 1 and June 5 – 9).

Ukraine: Jan. 1, Mar. 8, 10, Apr. 20, 21, May 1, 8, June 8, 9, 28, 30, July 15, Aug. 24, 25, Oct. 1, Dec. 25

MOVABLE HOLIDAYS

Fêtes mobiles – Feste mobile
Bewegliche Feste – Fiestas movibles

	2025	2026
Good Friday	Apr. 18	Apr. 3 *
Easter Monday	Apr. 21	Apr. 6 *
Ascension Day	May 29	May 14 *
Whit Monday (Pentecost)	June 9	May 25 *
Corpus Christi	June 19	June 4

* *One week later in the Orthodox calendar*

TIME COMPARISON

COMPARAISON DES HEURES COMPARAZIONE DELLE ORE ZEITVERGLEICH COMPARACIÓN DE LAS HORAS

West European Time	*WINTER: UTC* *SUMMER: UTC + 1*	Ireland, Portugal, United Kingdom Iceland *(UTC all year)*
Central European Time	*WINTER: UTC + 1* *SUMMER: UTC + 2*	Albania, Austria, Belgium, Bosnia, Croatia, Czech Rep., Denmark, France, Germany, Hungary, Italy, Luxembourg, North Macedonia, Malta, Montenegro, Netherlands, Norway, Poland, Serbia, Slovakia, Slovenia, Spain, Sweden, Switzerland
East European Time	*WINTER: UTC + 2* *SUMMER: UTC + 3*	Bulgaria, Estonia, Finland, Greece, Latvia, Lithuania, Moldova, Romania, Ukraine Belarus and Western Russia *(UTC + 3 all year)* Kaliningrad *(UTC + 2 all year)* Turkey *(UTC + 3 all year)*

Daylight Saving Time ('Summer Time') applies in 2025 between 0100 GMT on March 30 and 0100 GMT on October 26 *(GMT = Greenwich Mean Time = UTC*

NEWSLINES

WELCOME

Timings in this edition generally cover the period from June 15 to December 13, although there are many exceptions that apply to specific countries or tables. Readers are advised to consult the introductory text at the beginning of each country section for confirmation of the published timetable validity. Differing validity periods may also be indicated for individual tables.

Our fully updated *Rail Extra* feature will be found on pages 589 to 601. It contains useful transport based information presented on a country-by-country basis, including schedules for selected tourist railways that we do not normally show.

INTERNATIONAL

Timings of all Eurostar services are confirmed until September 6 (Tables **10** and **18**). Engineering work on the high-speed line between Brussels and Lille from August 16 to 31 will result in extended journey times of between 15 and 30 minutes with services diverted via alternative routes. The *Eurostar Sun* service Amsterdam – Brussels – Marseille has been withdrawn.

One *Ouigo* service per day between Paris and Brussels now calls at St Quentin (Table **18**).

The overnight seated service Stuttgart – München – Wien (*IC* **461**/**460**) has been withdrawn (Table **32**).

Train **301** *Berlin Night Express* Stockholm – Berlin is extended to Dresden on certain Fridays with return train **300** starting from Dresden on certain Sundays (Table **50**). On July 31 and September 19 the southbound train is extended further to Chemnitz, returning on August 3 and September 21. Chemnitz is one of two designated European Capitals of Culture for 2025, the other being Nova Gorica in Slovenia.

From July 1 *Railjet* **257**/**256** Berlin – Děčín – Praha – Graz will be withdrawn between Berlin and Děčín (Table **60**). Note that compulsory seat reservation will apply from June 15 to August 31 for all international journeys on the Berlin – Dresden – Praha corridor. An additional pair of *EuroCity* services will run between Berlin and Praha from June 15 to September 15. Departing from Berlin Hbf at 0007, *EC* **259** will call at Flughafen Berlin, Dresden and stations to Praha. Northbound *EC* **258** will depart Praha at 2028, arriving Berlin Hbf at 0057.

Two *ICE* services in each direction between Dortmund and Wien have been curtailed to only run between Frankfurt and Wien (Table **66**). The services affected are **29** / **23** southbound and **22** / **228** northbound.

Engineering work will affect international services via Brig on certain dates with journeys partially operated by bus (Table **82**).

A new through service between Zürich and Pisa via Genova will operate from June 8 to September 28 (Tables **82** and **610**). Southbound service *EC* **155** departs Zürich at 0633, arriving Pisa at 1600. The northbound train, numbered **156**, leaves Pisa at 1320 and arrives Zürich 2327.

Trains **1205**/**1204** *Adria* Budapest – Split and **1247**/**1246** *Istria* Budapest – Rijeka / Koper will run again for the summer season. Train **1205**/**1204** runs on even dates southbound returning on uneven dates, while train **1247**/**1246** runs daily for the duration of the season (Table **89**).

A new summer service between Poland and the Croatian coast will commence on June 27. *EN* **1277**/**1276** Warszawa – Wien – Rijeka will run four days a week until August 31. Between Warszawa and Wien it will run as a portion of the *Sobieski* (Tables **89** and **99**).

GREAT BRITAIN

On the Isle of Wight, the section of line between Ryde Esplanade and Ryde Pier Head has reopened following a lengthy closure period to allow essential maintenance work to be carried out (Table **106**). It will close again for another short period after the summer season for further track renewal.

Most through services between Cardiff and Penzance have been withdrawn and now operate as separate trains Cardiff – Exeter and Exeter – Penzance. As a result, the Cardiff to Exeter services have been transferred to a modified Table **115**.

The summer service on the West of England main line from London to Penzance, shown in Table **110**, is valid until September 14. As is usual during the summer, the popular seaside town of Newquay is served by a number of additional long distance through services (Table **110**). The local service from Par to Newquay in Table **113** is also completely revised during the summer season. An enhanced hourly service is expected to start running on the Newquay branch later this year following the completion of work to install a passing loop on this single-track line. The Liskeard to Looe branch line has a completely revised service with a slight reduction in the number of trains on Mondays to Saturdays (Table **111**).

Various CrossCountry services now make additional stops at Worcestershire Parkway station (Table **119**). Manchester to Bristol services call in the southbound direction, with the extra northbound stops being made by trains heading to Newcastle and Edinburgh.

Transport for Wales has introduced some major alterations for its summer Sunday services from August 3 to September 14. The most significant changes affect Tables **136** and **149** for which we have published separate versions on page 579. Enhanced summer Sunday services will also be found in Tables **145**, **146** and **148**.

Table **152**, which previously covered services from London to both Liverpool and Manchester, is now dedicated to the Liverpool route with services to Manchester transferred to a new Table **153**. The reason for this is the introduction of additional services between London and Liverpool which do not run at regular intervals and have a different stopping pattern. Further services are expected to be added from September 15.

LNER has extended a number of its Leeds services to and from Bradford Forster Square, made possible by the opening of an additional platform at Bradford (Table **180**).

CrossCountry now runs through trains to Stansted Airport on an hourly basis, rather than every two hours (Table **208**).

Scotrail has retimed the first train of the day from Kyle of Lochalsh to Inverness on Mondays to Saturdays, now departing 26 minutes earlier at 0545 (Table **226**). This enables a connection to be made with the 0841 service from Inverness to Glasgow.

The Scottish Citylink bus service now operates hourly between Inverness and Fort William with two services extended through to Oban. These additional through services double the number of journeys available between Fort William and Oban to four each way (Table **228**).

FRANCE

As is usual in our Summer edition, our tables covering northern and western France (Tables **250** to **329**) are valid for the high-summer period which this year is from July 5 to August 31. The service from September 1 will be broadly similar with some routes seeing additional trains. These tables will be fully updated in time for the September digital edition.

The Paris to Hendaye overnight service does not appear to be running this summer (Table **319**).

Media reports suggest that rail services on the branch line from Montréjeau to Luchon will be reinstated from June 22 (Table **325**). As we went to press the full timetable was not available but it is believed that trains will depart Montréjeau at 0812, 1044, 1351, 1551, 1851 and 2051, returning from Luchon at 0614, 0939, 1242, 1436, 1736 and 1936. Some services will run to and from Toulouse.

Trenitalia will introduce four daily return *Frecciarossa* services on the Paris to Marseille route from June 15; timings will be found in Table **350**. Most of these trains also serve Lyon St Exupéry, Avignon and Aix-en-Provence. Certain trains have quite complex variations, so readers are advised to carefully check their reservation for confirmed timings. From the same date Trenitalia will also introduce an additional service in both directions between Paris and Lyon, meaning there are six daily *Frecciarossa* journeys each way (Table **340**).

The regional *TER* service between Marseille and Nice will be enhanced from June 29 with trains running hourly throughout the day. Previously shown in Table **361**, these trains have now been transferred to a new dedicated table, numbered **362**.

Electrification work being carried out between Paris and Troyes from June 30 to August 31 will mean all trains are replaced by bus between Nogent and Troyes. A limited number of through trains will continue to run Paris – Chaumont – Belfort – Mulhouse, operating via Châlons en Champagne. A special version of Table **380** will be found on page 602 with amended timings during this period.

TGV services using the high-speed line heading east from Paris have some significant variations during the high-summer period. As a result we have included two versions of Table **390** with the service from July 5 to August 31 found on pages 603 and 604.

CONTINUED ON PAGE 610

EXPLANATION OF STANDARD SYMBOLS

	EXPLANATION OF SYMBOLS	*EXPLICATION DES SIGNES*	*DELUCIDAZIONE DEI SEGNI*	*ZEICHENERKLÄRUNG*	*EXPLICACIÓN DE LOS SIGNOS*
	SERVICES	**SERVICES**	**SERVIZI**	**DIENSTE**	**SERVICIOS**
🚃 12	Through service (1st and 2nd class seats)	Relation directe (places assises 1re et 2e classe)	Relazione diretta (con posti di 1a e 2a classe)	Direkte Verbindung (Sitzplätze 1. und 2. Klasse)	Relación directa (con asientos de 1a y 2a clase)
🛏	Sleeping car	Voiture-lits	Carrozza letti	Schlafwagen	Coche-camas
▬	Couchette car	Voiture-couchettes	Carrozza cuccette	Liegewagen	Coche-literas
✕	Restaurant car	Voiture-restaurant	Carrozza ristorante	Speisewagen	Coche-restaurante
🍸	Snacks and drinks available *(see page 10)*	Voiture-bar ou vente ambulante *(voir page 10)*	Carrozza bar o servizio di buffet *(vedere pagina 10)*	Imbiss und Getränke im Zug *(siehe Seite 10)*	Servicio de cafetería o bar móvil *(véase pág. 10)*
2	Second class only	Uniquement deuxième classe	Sola seconda classe	Nur zweite Klasse	Sólo segunda clase
🚌	Bus or coach service	Service routier	Servizio automobilistico	Buslinie	Servicio de autobuses
⛴	Ferry service	Service maritime	Servizio marittimo	Schifffahrtslinie	Servicio marítimo
	DAYS OF RUNNING	**JOURS DE CIRCULATION**	**GIORNI DI EFFETTUAZIONE**	**VERKEHRSTAGE**	**DÍAS DE CIRCULACIÓN**
⚒	Mondays to Saturdays except holidays*	Du lundi au samedi, sauf les fêtes*	Dal lunedì al sabato, salvo i giorni festivi*	Montag bis Samstag außer Feiertage*	De lunes a sábado, excepto festivos*
Ⓐ	Mondays to Fridays except holidays*	Du lundi au vendredi, sauf les fêtes*	Dal lunedì al venerdì, salvo i giorni festivi*	Montag bis Freitag außer Feiertage*	De lunes a viernes, excepto festivos*
Ⓑ	Daily except Saturdays	Tous les jours sauf les samedis	Giornalmente, salvo il sabato	Täglich außer Samstag	Diario excepto sábados
Ⓒ	Saturdays, Sundays and holidays*	Les samedis, dimanches et fêtes*	Sabato, domenica e giorni festivi*	Samstage, Sonn- und Feiertage*	Sábados, domingos y festivos*
†	Sundays and holidays*	Les dimanches et fêtes*	Domenica e giorni festivi*	Sonn- und Feiertage*	Domingos y festivos*
①②	Mondays, Tuesdays	Les lundis, mardis	Lunedì, martedì	Montag, Dienstag	Lunes, martes
③④	Wednesdays, Thursdays	Les mercredis, jeudis	Mercoledì, giovedì	Mittwoch, Donnerstag	Miércoles, jueves
⑤⑥	Fridays, Saturdays	Les vendredis, samedis	Venerdì, sabato	Freitag, Samstag	Viernes, sábados
⑦	Sundays	Les dimanches	Domenica	Sonntag	Domingos
①–④	Mondays to Thursdays	Des lundis aux jeudis	Dal lunedì al giovedì	Montag bis Donnerstag	De lunes a jueves
	OTHER SYMBOLS	**AUTRES SIGNES**	**ALTRI SIMBOLI**	**SONSTIGE SYMBOLE**	**OTROS SÍMBOLOS**
IC **29**	Train number (**bold figures** above train times)	Numéro du train (en **caractères gras** au-dessus de l'horaire du train)	Numero del treno (in **neretto** sopra gli orari del treno)	Zugnummer (über den Fahrplanzeiten in **fetter Schrift** gesetzt)	Número del tren (figura en **negrita** encima del horario del tren)
◆	See footnotes (listed by train number)	Renvoi aux notes données en bas de page (dans l'ordre numérique des trains)	Vedi in calce alla pagina l'annotazione corrispondente al numero del treno	Siehe die nach Zugnummern geordneten Fußnoten	Véase al pie de la página la nota correspondiente al número del tren
🅁	Reservation compulsory	Réservation obligatoire	Prenotazione obbligatoria	Reservierung erforderlich	Reserva obligatoria
🏛	Frontier station	Gare frontalière	Stazione di frontiera	Grenzbahnhof	Estación fronteriza
✈	Airport	Aéroport	Aeroporto	Flughafen	Aeropuerto
|	Train does not stop	Sans arrêt	Il treno non ferma qui	Zug hält nicht	El tren no para aquí
▬▬	Separates two trains in the same column between which no connection is possible	Sépare deux trains de la même colonne qui ne sont pas en correspondance	Separa due treni della stessa colonna che non sono in coincidenza	Trennt zwei in derselben Spalte angegebene Züge, zwischen denen kein Anschluß besteht	Separa dos trenes de la misma columna entre los cuales no hay enlace
→	Continued in later column	Suite dans une colonne à droite	Continuazione più avanti a destra	Fortsetzung weiter rechts	Continuación a la derecha
←	Continued from earlier column	Suite d'une colonne à gauche	Seguito di una colonna a sinistra	Fortsetzung von links	Continuación desde la izquierda
v.v.	Vice versa	Vice versa	Viceversa	Umgekehrt	A la inversa
	** Public holiday dates for each country are given on page 4.* *Other, special symbols are explained in table footnotes or in the introduction to each country.*	** Les dates des fêtes légales nationales sont données en page 4.* *D'autres signes particuliers sont expliqués dans les notes ou bien dans l'avant-propos relatif à chaque pays.*	** Per le date dei giorni festivi civili nei diversi paesi vedere pagina 4.* *Altri segni particolari vengono spiegati nelle note in calce ai quadri o nella introduzione attinente a ogni paese.*	** Gesetzlichen Feiertage der jeweiligen Länder finden Sie auf Seite 4.* *Besondere Symbole sind in den Fußnoten bzw. in der Einleitung zu den einzelnen Ländern erklärt.*	** Las fechas de los días festivos en cada país figuran en la página 4.* *La explicación de otros signos particulares se da en las notas o en el preámbulo correspondiente a cada país.*

What is the European Rail Timetable?

The European Rail Timetable is a concise guide to rail and ferry schedules throughout Europe, and also includes selected areas of the world outside Europe. Needless to say, it cannot be comprehensive (it would run into thousands of pages), but through our knowledge and experience, together with valuable feedback from our readers, we can select those services which we believe will satisfy the needs of most travellers.

When do the services change?

There is a major annual timetable change in mid-December affecting almost all European countries, with many countries having a second change in mid-June. There are, of course, exceptions. For example, the British summer timetable starts in late May. Many holiday areas also have separate timetables for the high-summer period, particularly areas of France, Italy and Hungary. In fact, changes can happen at any time of year, and railways issue amendments either on set dates or as and when necessary. Engineering work also causes frequent changes, and shipping schedules can change at any time.

How are the trains selected for inclusion?

People travel for many reasons, whether for leisure, business, sightseeing, visiting friends or relations, or just for the fun of it, and there are no hard and fast rules for selecting the services that we show. Naturally, major towns and inter-city services are shown as a matter of course, but the level of smaller places and local trains shown will depend on the country and even the area. It's surprising just how many minor lines we manage to squeeze in! Generally we will show a greater number of local trains in areas which are popular tourist destinations or where other services are sparse.

It is not possible to show suburban trains within cities or conurbations, or most outer-suburban routes to places close to large cities. However, where there are places of particular interest or importance in this category we do try to show brief details of frequency and journey time.

When should I use the International section?

The rail tables are divided into two sections - International (Tables **9** to **99**) and Country by Country (Tables **100** upwards). For some international services between adjacent countries (for example Stockholm - Oslo or Hamburg - Århus) it is necessary to use the relevant Country tables - the index or maps will guide you. Local trains which cross international frontiers will usually only be found in the Country sections.

Some international trains also carry passengers internally within each country and will therefore be found in the Country tables as well as the International section. Some services are primarily for international travel and will therefore only be found in the International section - this includes *Eurostar* trains (London - Paris / Brussels / Amsterdam) and *Thalys* services (Paris - Brussels - Amsterdam / Köln), as well as certain long-distance night trains.

What about places outside Europe?

The European Rail Timetable includes the whole of Turkey and Russia (although the Russian and Belarusian sections will not be updated until further notice owing to the conflict in Ukraine). Our **Beyond Europe** pages, previously published in our seasonal editions, are now only available as a separate digital download. The latest version (published in Autumn 2024) is available to purchase on our website. The areas covered are **India**, **South East Asia**, **Australia**, **New Zealand**, **China**, **Japan**, **South America**, **North America**, **South Korea**, **Africa and the Middle East**.

What else does it contain?

A summary of international sleeper services will be found on page 35, listing types of accommodation, operators and facilities on board. We also include a summary of European rail passes on pages 581 – 587.

Seasonal editions also include our *Rail Extra* feature containing useful transport based information on a country by country basis (including details of many popular tourist railways).

Our timetables and other products may be purchased from our website **www.europeanrailtimetable.eu**.

HOW TO USE THE TIMETABLE

Using the index

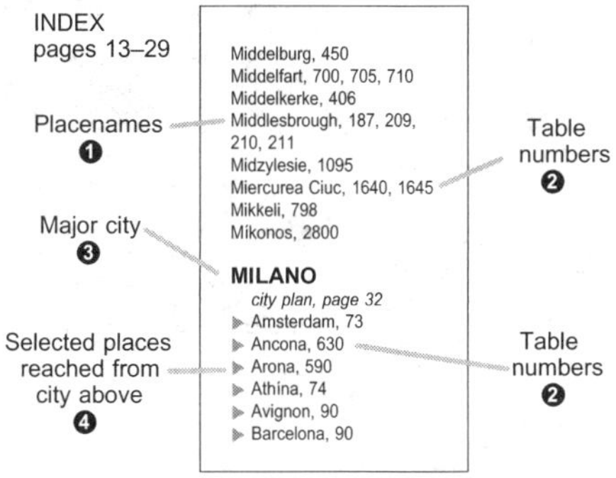

Look up the two places between which you are travelling. It can often be helpful to start your search from the *smaller* of the two locations. 5

Using the maps

The maps can be the quickest way of finding the required table number, if you already know the geographical location of the places required. 10

COMMENT TROUVER VOTRE TRAIN

1 Localité.
2 Numéros des tableaux.
3 Grande ville.
4 Localités sélectionnées à gagner de la grande ville en haut.
5 Cherchez les deux bouts du parcours désiré sur la liste des villes. Commencer par la ville de moindre importance peut faciliter la recherche.
6 Ligne principale.
7 Ligne secondaire.
8 Ligne à grande vitesse.
9 Liaison en autocar.
10 La consultation des cartes – si vous savez déjà la location géographique de vos points de départ et d'arrivée – est le moyen le plus rapide de repérer les numéros des tableaux relatifs à votre parcours.

COME TROVARE IL VOSTRO TRENO

1 Località.
2 Numeri dei quadri-orario.
3 Grandi città.
4 Principali destinazione raggiungibili dalla località in neretto sopra.
5 Cercate le localita' tra le quali dovrete viaggiare; spesso può essere di aiuto iniziare la ricerca dalla località più piccola.
6 Principale linea ferroviaria.
7 Linea ferroviaria secondaria.
8 Linea ad alta velocità.
9 Autobus.
10 Le mappe sono il metodo più rapido per trovare i numeri dei quadri-orario di cui avete bisogno, quando gia' siete a conoscenza della collocazione geografica delle localita' di partenza e arrivo del vostro viaggio.

WIE FINDE ICH MEINEN ZUG?

1 Ortsname.
2 Tabellennummer.
3 Großstadt.
4 Knotenpunkte erreichbar von der Großstadt oben.
5 Suchen Sie Ihre Start- und Endbahnhof im Ortsverzeichnis. Dazu empfehlen wir, Ihre Suche aus der Richtung des *kleineren* Ortes aufzunehmen.
6 Hauptstrecke.
7 Nebenstrecke.
8 Hochgeschwindigkeitsstrecke.
9 Busverbindung.
10 Kennen Sie die geographische Lage der Ausgangs- und Bestimmungsorte Ihrer Reise, dann empfehlen wir einen Blick in die im Kursbuch enthaltene Übersichtskarte.

COMO BUSCAR SU TREN

1 Localidad.
2 Números de los cuadros horarios.
3 Gran ciudad.
4 Principales destinos accesibles a través de esta localidad.
5 Busque los dos lugares a través de los cuales viaja. Normalmente facilita la búsqueda empezar por la localidad más pequeña.
6 Línea principal.
7 Línea secundaria.
8 Línea de alta velocidad.
9 Línea de autobuses.
10 Los mapas pueden ser la forma más rápida de encontrar los cuadros que debe consultar, si ya conoce el punto de inicio y conclusión de su viaje.

Numbers in circles refer to translations below

Reading the tables

Trains run daily unless otherwise shown by symbol or footnote ⓯

Table number and route ❶

Station names in local language ❷

Distance from Praha in km ❸

Important stations are shown in **bold** for clarity ❹

Indented station: shows a branch off the main route of the table ❺

d. = depart, a. = arrive (the first time in a column is always a departure time, the last is an arrival). ⓮

Train category (where shown) ⓭

Train number (where shown) ⓬

Standard symbols (e.g. Ⓐ, 🅁, ✕) are explained on page 6.

Other symbols (e.g. ⊖) and letters (**E**, **r**) are explained below the table.

♦ means footnotes are listed by train number. ⓫

1150 PRAHA - BRNO - WIEN / BRATISLAVA

km	*Sample table*										
			EC	*EC•*	*EC*	*SC**	*EC*	*EC*		*EC*	*EC*
		271	**71**	**131**	**345**	**15**	**273**	**73**	**475**	**275**	**103**
			✕			🍷	✕	✕			✕
		Ⓐ		♦	♦	🅁		⊖	♦	**E**	♦
	Praha Holešovice..........d.	...	...	...	...	...	0730	0830	...	0930	...
0	**Praha** hlavni .... ▷ d.	...	...	...	0528	0557	|	|	0918	|	...
62	Kolín .... ▷ d.	...	...	...	0613	|	0813	|	1013	1013	...
154	**Pardubice** .... ▷ d.	...	...	...	0636	0659	0836	0936	1036	1036	...
164	Česká Třebová......... ▷ d.	...	*0551*	...	0711	|	0911	|	1111	1111	...
255	**Brno** hlavní...................a.	...	*0711*	...	0814	0825	1014	1114	1214	1214	...
255	**Brno** hlavní.......... **1162** d.	...	0716	...	0816	0827	1016	1116	1216	1216	...
314	**Břeclav**................. **1162** a.	...	0751	...	0851	0900	1051	1151	1251	1251	...
314	**Břeclav**.................. **991** d.	0553	0802	0755	0855	0902	1055	1202	1255	1255	1302
	Wien Süd........... **991** a.	|	0902	|	|	1002	|	1302	|	|	1402
332	Kúty 🛃 ....d.	0610	...	0810	0910	...	1110	...	1310	1310	...
396	**Bratislava** Hlavná.........a.	0653r	...	0853	0947	...	1147	...	1347	1347	...
	Budapest Keleti **1170**.a.	...	...	...	1232	...	1432	...	...	...	...

🛃 indicates an international border (with or without controls) ❻

For other trains between Břeclav and Wien see Table **991** ❽

This is a train from Praha to Budapest. Timings read from top to bottom ❿

Station in *italics*: for stations between Bratislava and Budapest see Table **1170** ❼

Timings in *italics* are connections (change at Brno) ❾

Where two unconnected trains are shown in the same column, they are separated by a thick rule ⓱

1234
1306
▬
Ⓐ
1130
1153

CLASSES OF TRAVEL:
Trains have 1st and 2nd class seats unless otherwise shown. However, local trains may only have 2nd class seats. ⓯

TIME ZONES:
Times are in local time (Russian times are in Moscow time). For time zones see page 4. Timings are given in 24 hour clock (see page 11). ⓰

COMMENT LIRE LES TABLEAUX

❶ Numéro et parcours du tableau.
❷ Nom de la gare en langue locale.
❸ La distance en km de Praha.
❹ Les noms de gares importantes sont imprimés en **gras** pour faciliter la lecture.
❺ La mise en retrait des noms de gares indique une ligne d'embranchement.
❻ 🛃 indique une frontière internationale (avec ou sans le contrôle).
❼ Les noms de gares imprimés en *italique*: vous trouverez des gares sur le trajet Bratislava - Budapest en consultant le tableau **1170**.
❽ Consultez le tableau **991** pour trouver des trains supplémentaires de Břeclav à Wien.
❾ Les heures en *italique* indiquent une *correspondance* et supposent dans tous les cas un changement de train.
❿ Ici un train de Praha à Budapest. Lire de haut en bas.
⓫ Les signes conventionnels sont expliqués à la page 6. Les autres signes et lettres sont expliqués en bas du tableau. Le symbole ♦ à l'en-tête d'une colonne signifie qu'il faut consulter le note qui porte le numéro du train concerné.
⓬ Le numéro du train (en cas échéant).
⓭ Indication de catégorie (en cas échéant).
⓮ d. = départ, a. = arrivée. Pour chaque train la *première* mention est toujours une heure de *départ*, la *dernière* toujours une heure d'*arrivée*.
⓯ Sauf indication contraire, les trains circulent *tous les jours* et y compris des places assises de 1ère et 2ème classe.
⓰ Toutes les indications horaires sont données en heures locales (voir page 4). En Russie c'est à l'heure Moskva.
⓱ Deux trains de la même colonne qui ne sont pas en correspondance sont separés par une règle épaisse.

COME SI CONSULTA UN QUADRO ORARIO

❶ Numero del quadro e percorso.
❷ Nome della stazione nella lingua locale.
❸ Distanze in km da Praha.
❹ I nomi delle stazioni piu' importante sono stampati in **neretto** per renderne più facile la lettura.
❺ I nomi delle stazioni rientrati rispetto alla colonna principale indicano una diramazione dal percorso principale del quadro-orario in questione.
❻ 🛃 indica una stazione di confine (con o senza controllo).
❼ Stazioni in *corsivo*: per gli orari tra le stazione di Bratislava e Budapest bisogna consultare il quadro **1170**.
❽ Consultare il quadro **991** per ulteriori treni da Břeclav a Wien.
❾ Gli orari *in corsivo* si riferiscono a servizi *in coincidenza* che implicano un cambio di treno.
❿ Questo e' un treno da Praha a Budapest. La lettura viene fatta dall'alto verso il basso.
⓫ I simboli convenzionali sono spiegate a pagina 6. Altri simboli e lettere sono spiegati sotto il quadro-orario in questione. Il simbolo ♦ all'inizio di una colonna-orario significa che bisogna fare riferimento alla nota corrispondente al numero del treno in questione.
⓬ Numero del treno (quando indicato).
⓭ Classificazione del treno (quando indicato).
⓮ d. = partenza, a. = arrivo. Notare che l'orario che compare per *primo* nel quadro-orario è sempre un l'orario di *partenza*, mentre quello che compare per *ultimo* è sempre l'orario di *arrivo*.
⓯ Se non ci sono altre indicazioni i treni si intendono giornalieri, con prima e seconda classe di viaggio.
⓰ Gli orari sono sempre espressi in ora locale (in Russia e' utilizzati l'ora di Mosca). Per informazioni sui fusi orari vedere a pagina 4.
⓱ Quando nella colonna-orario ci sono due treni che non sono in coincidenza tra loro, questo e' indicato dalla linea in grassetto che li separa.

WIE LESE ICH DIE FAHRPLÄNE

❶ Tabellennummer und Strecke.
❷ Bahnhof in der Landessprache.
❸ Entfernungsangabe.
❹ Wichtige Bahnhöfe sind **fett** gedruckt um das Lesen zu vereinfachen.
❺ Eingerückte Bahnhöfe befinden sich auf einer abzweigenden Strecke.
❻ 🛃 Bezeichnet eine internationale Grenze (mit oder ohne Grenzkontrolle).
❼ *Kursiv* gedruckte Bahnhofsnamen: Bahnhöfe zwischen Bratislava und Budapest finden Sie in Tabelle **1170**.
❽ Zusätzliche Züge finden Sie in Tabelle **991**.
❾ *Kursiv* gedruckte Zeitangaben weisen immer auf das Umsteigen hin.
❿ Ein Zug von Praha nach Budapest. Sie lesen von oben nach unten.
⓫ Eine Erklärung der überall in dem Kursbuch verwendeten konventionellen Zeichen finden Sie auf Seite 6. Anderen Zeichen und Buchstaben finden Sie unter der Fahrplantabelle. Das Zeichen ♦ im Kopf der Zugspalte bedeutet: Sehen Sie bei der Fußnote des Zuges mit der betreffenden Zugnummer nach.
⓬ Zugnummer (wo zutreffend).
⓭ Zuggattung (wo zutreffend).
⓮ d. = Abfahrt, a. = Ankunft. Es handelt sich stets bei der ersten für einen Zug angegebenen Zeit um eine Abfahrtzeit, bei der letzten um eine Ankunftzeit.
⓯ Sofern nicht anders angemeldet, verkehren die Züge *täglich*. Im Allgemeinen führen die Züge die 1. und 2. Wagenklasse.
⓰ Fahrzeiten sind immer in der jeweiligen Landeszeit angegeben (Seite 4). Russische Fahrzeiten sind auf Moskauer Zeit.
⓱ Im Falle von zwei Züge in der gleichen Spalte ohne Anschlussmöglichkeit, liegt das Zeichen ▬ zwischen den Zügen.

COMO LEER LOS CUADROS

❶ Número y línea del cuadro.
❷ Nombre de las estaciones en el idioma local.
❸ Distancia en km de Praga.
❹ Los nombres de las estaciones más importantes están impresas en **negrita** facilitar la lectura.
❺ La impresión sangrada de los nombres de estas estaciones significa un ramal de la línea principal.
❻ 🛃 significa una frontera internacional (con o sin control de aduanas).
❼ Estaciones impresas en *cursiva*: para las estaciones entre Bratislava y Budapest debe consultar el cuadro **1170**.
❽ Consultar el cuadro **991** para encontrar más trenes desde Břeclav hasta Viena.
❾ Los horarios en cursiva, hacen referencia a servicios de enlace, que requieren un cambio de tren.
❿ Esto un tren desde Praga hasta Budapest. Leer de arriba a abajo.
⓫ La explicación de los signos convencionales se da en la página 6. Ostros símbolos y letras se explican al pie del cuadro. El símbolo ♦ en el encabezamiento de la columna quiere decir: consulte la nota que lleva el número del tren interesado.
⓬ Número de tren (si se indica).
⓭ Tipo de tren (si se indica).
⓮ d. = salida, a. = llegada. Nótese que el primer horario indicado en las columnas es siempre un horario de salida, y el último un horario de llegada.
⓯ Salvo indicación contraria, los trenes circulan *a diario* y llevan plazas sentadas de primera y segunda clases.
⓰ Todas las indicaciones horarias son en horario local (Para Rusia se utiliza la hora local de Moscú). Para comprobar las franjas horarias mirar la página 4. Los horarios utilizan el sistema horario de 24h (ver página 11).
⓱ Cuando dos trenes que no tienen conexión aparecen en la misma columna, estos se encuentran separados por el símbolo ▬.

Reading the footnotes

These footnotes relate to the sample table on page 8 ❶

In certain tables, footnotes are listed by train number, shown by ♦ on relevant trains ❷

♦ – **NOTES** (LISTED BY TRAIN NUMBERS)	**E** – SLOVAN, not June 19 - Sept. 4.
102/3 – POLONIA – [12] ✕ Warszawa - Ostrava - Břeclav - Wien and v.v.	**r** – 0659 on ©.
131 – MORAVIA – [12] Bohumin - Ostrava - Břeclav - Bratislava.	▷ – See also Table **1160**.
345 – AVALA – [12] ✕ Praha - Bratislava - Budapest - Beograd. Conveys on ⑤ June 12 - Sept. 18 ▬ 2 cl. Praha - Beograd (**335**) - Thessaloniki.	⊖ – Runs 10 mins later on Aug. 15.
475 – JADRAN – June 19 - Sept. 4. ▬ 1, 2 cl., ▬ 2 cl., [2] Praha - Bratislava - Zagreb - Split (Table **92**); [12] Praha - Bratislava.	• – *Ex* in Slovakia.
	* – Pendolino tilting train. Classified *EC* in Austria.
	OTHER TRAIN NAMES:
	71 – GUSTAV MAHLER
	73 – FRANZ SCHUBERT

Letters and symbols may be found above the timings (e.g. **E**) or against individual times (e.g. **r**). Symbols may also appear in the station column (e.g. ▷). ❻

Train names are sometimes listed separately. ❺

Train **345** is named 'AVALA' and runs daily from Praha to Beograd with 1st and 2nd class seats and a restaurant car. On Fridays June 12 to September 18, a through couchette car runs from Praha to Thessaloniki, attached to train **335** between Beograd and Thessaloniki. ❸

Train **475** is named 'JADRAN' and runs only from June 19 to September 4. It has a sleeper, couchettes and second class seats from Praha to Split via Bratislava and Zagreb, as well as first and second class seats only going as far as Bratislava. Further details will be found in Table **92**. ❹

Always read the footnotes; they may contain important information. Standard symbols are explained on page 6. ❼

Dates shown are where a train **starts** its journey (unless otherwise noted). Some notes show both directions of the train (e.g. **102/3**) with "and v.v." ❽

FURTHER HINTS ON READING THE TIMETABLE

- Refer to the introduction to each country for important information such as train types, supplements, compulsory reservation, and the dates of validity of the timings. Exceptions are noted in individual tables.
- For dates of public holidays see page 4.
- Please allow adequate time for changing trains, especially at large stations. Connections are not guaranteed, especially when late running occurs (connecting trains are sometimes held for late running trains).
- A Glossary of common terms appears on page 12.

LES NOTES EN BAS DU TABLEAU

❶ Ces notes se rapportent au example de tableau à la page 8.
❷ Dans certains tableaux, le symbole ♦ à l'en-tête d'une colonne signifie qu'il faut consulter le note qui porte le numéro du train concerné.
❸ Le train **345** s'appelle AVALA et circule tous les jours de Praha à Beograd avec des places assises de 1ère et 2ème classe et une voiture-restaurant. Tous les vendredis du 12 juin jusqu'au 18 sept il y a aussi une voiture-couchettes de Praha à Thessaloniki, qui se joint au train **335** entre Beograd et Thessaloniki.
❹ Le train **475** s'appelle JADRAN et circule seulement entre le 19 juin et le 4 septembre. Il compris des voitures-lits, couchettes et places assises de 2ème classe à Split via Zagreb, et des places assises de 1ère et 2ème classe jusqu'à Bratislava. Voir le tableau **92**.
❺ Les noms des trains sont parfois indiqués séparément.
❻ Les lettres et signes sont situés à l'en-tête d'une colonne ou à côté d'une heure dans la colonne. Une signe peut sortir également a côté d'un nom de gare.
❼ Les notes peuvent vous donner des informations importantes. Les signes conventionnels sont expliqués à la page 6.
❽ Sauf indication contraire, les jours et dates de circulation mentionnés sont ceux applicables à la *gare d'origine* du train (mentionnée si elle ne figure pas sur le tableau même dans les notes). Les notes peuvent expliquer les deux sens d'un train (e.g. **102/3**) utilisant "and v.v." (et vice versa).

PLUS DE CONSEILS

- Il vous est fortement recommandé de consulter aussi l'introduction à chaque section nationale: vous y trouverez des précisions concernant la classification des trains, les prestations offertes à bord des trains, les suppléments, la réservation des places, etc.
- Jours fériés - voir page 4.
- Aucune correspondance n'est garantie pourtant. N'oubliez pas non plus que dans les grandes gares les changements peuvent entraîner une longue marche et l'emprunt d'escaliers.
- Lexique - voir page 12.

NOTE ALLA FINE DEL QUADRO-ORARIO

❶ Queste note si riferiscono all' esempio a pagina 8.
❷ In certi quadri-orario, il simbolo ♦ nelle note di testa significa che bisogna fare riferimento alla nota con il numero di treno corrispondente.
❸ Il treno **345** si chiama AVALA ed e' giornaliero tra Praha a Beograd con posti di 1ª e 2ª classe e carrozza ristorante. Il venerdì dal 12 giugno fino al 18 settembre e' aggiunta a Beograd una carrozza cuccette diretta a Thessaloniki, combinandosi con il treno **335** tra Beograd e Thessaloniki.
❹ Il treno **475** si chiama JADRAN ed e' operativo solo dal 19 giugno al 4 settembre. Il treno si compone di carrozze letti, carrozze cuccette, e posti di 2ª classe tra Praha e Split, via Bratislava e Zagrabria; inoltre ci sono anche posti di 1ª e 2ª classe fino a Bratislava. Consultare anche il quadro-orario **92** al riguardo
❺ I nomi dei treni sono talvolta indicati separatamente.
❻ Lettere e simboli possono essere sia alla testa di una colonna-orario, che accanto all'orario del treno stesso. Un simbolo potrebbe anche essere accanto al nome di una stazione.
❼ E' importante leggere sempre le note a le informazioni a fine quadro. I segni convenzionali sono elencati e spiegati a pagina 6.
❽ Salvo casi in cui sia diversamente indicato, le date di circolazione dei treni si riferiscono sempre alla stazione dove il treno inizia il suo viaggio (come viene riportato nelle note a fine quadro, e Inoltre nel quadro stesso).

ALTRI CONSIGLI UTILI

- Vi consigliamo vivamente di consultare anche l'introduzione dedicata ad ogni nazione. Troverete importanti informazioni riguardanti i servizi di trasporto di ciascun paese, così come le categorie dei treni, la ristorazione, il pagamento di supplementi, le necessità di prenotazione, ecc.
- I giorni festivi suddivisi per paese sono elencati a pagina 4.
- Le coincidenze indicate non sono garantite. Tenete presente che che nelle grandi stazioni il trasferimento tra due binari potrebbe significare un lungo tratto da percorrere a piedi e con l'uso di scale.
- Il glossario si trova a pagina 12.

FUSSNOTEN

❶ Fußnoten beziehen sich auf die Beispieltabelle auf Seite 8.
❷ ♦ : Sehen Sie bei der Fußnote des Zuges mit der betreffenden Zugnummer nach.
❸ Zug **345** heißt AVALA und fährt täglich zwischen Praha und Beograd mit Sitzplätzen 1. und 2. Klasse. An Freitagen vom 12. Juni bis 18. September führt dieser Zug durchgehende Liegewagen von Praha nach Thessaloniki (mit Zug **335** vereinigt von Beograd nach Thessaloniki).
❹ Zug **475** heißt JADRAN und fährt nur von 19. Juni bis 4. September. Er führt Schlaf-, Liege und Sitzwagen 2. Klasse von Praha nach Split über Zagreb, auch Sitzwagen 1. und 2. Klasse, die nur bis Bratislava fahren. Auf Tabelle **92** finden Sie weitere Informationen.
❺ Zugnamen können besonders aufgeführt sein.
❻ Zeichen und Buchstaben finden sich im Kopf der Zugspalte oder neben einer bestimmten Zeitangabe. Zeichen sind auch in der Bahnhofsspalte möglich.
❼ In Fußnoten findet man wichtige Informationen. Standardzeichen sind auf Seite 6 erklärt.
❽ Die erwähnten Tage und Zeitabschnitte für Züge, die nicht täglich verkehren, gelten für den Ausgangsbahnhof des Zuges (wenn dieser nicht in der Tabelle steht, ist er in einer Fußnote erwähnt). Fußnoten dürfen beide Richtungen erklären (z.B. **102/3**), mit "and v.v." (und umgekehrt).

WEITERE HINWEISE

- Es ist zu empfehlen, die Einleitungen zu jedem einzelnen Land zu lesen. Darin werden Sie wichtige Informationen über die Besonderheiten jedes Landes finden: Zugcharakterisierung, Services an Bord der Züge, Zuschlagpflicht, Reservierungsbedingungen usw.
- Feiertage - siehe Seite 4.
- Anschlussversäumnisse durch Verspätung oder Ausfall von Zügen sind immer möglich. Bitte beachten Sie, dass auf Großstadtbahnhöfen häufig längere Fußwege zurückgelegt bzw. Treppen benutzen werden müssen.
- Glossar - siehe Seite 12.

LAS NOTAS AL PIE DEL CUADRO

❶ Estas notas hacen referencia al ejemplo de la página 8.
❷ El símbolo ♦ ciertas tablas horarias significa: que hay que consultar la nota a pie de página con el número correspondiente.
❸ El Tren **345** se llama AVALA y circula a diario entre Praga y Belgrado con plazas sentadas de 1ra y 2da clase, además de con coche-restaurante. Los Viernes del 12 de junio al 18 de septiembre el tren lleva coches litera desde Praga hasta Tesalónica que se combinan con el tren **335** entre Belgrado y Tesalónica.
❹ El Tren **475** se llama JADRAN y circula solamente del 19 de junio al 4 de septiembre. El Tren **475** se llama JADRAN y circula solamente del 19 de junio al 4 de sept. El tren dispone de lleva vagones de coches cama, litera, y plazas sentadas de 2da clase entre Praga y Split a través de Zagreb, también plazas sentadas de 1ra y 2da clase hasta Bratislava. Consulte el cuadro **92**.
❺ Los nombres de los Trenes a veces son enumerados por separado.
❻ Las letras y signos se encuentran en el encabezamiento de las distintas columnas horarias o adyacentes a horas de salida individuales. Los símbolos también pueden aparecer en la columna de la estación.
❼ Lea siempre las notas a pie de cuadro ya que pueden contener información importante. La explicación de los signos convencionales se da en la página 6.
❽ Salvo indicación contraria los días y fechas de circulación de los trenes son aquéllos mencionados en la estación de *origen* del tren. Algunas notas muestran ambas direcciones del tren mediante la nota "and v.v." (y viceversa).

INFORMACIÓN ADICIONAL

- Se recomienda vivamente que consulte también los preámbulos al comienzo de cada sección nacional: le proporcionarán datos importantes sobre las particularidades de cada país: tipos de trenes, restauración, pago de suplementos, y necesidades de reservación anticipada.
- Días festivos - cunsulte la página 4.
- Los trasbordos no se pueden garantizar, sobretodo en el caso de retrasos. Hay que ser consciente también que el trasbordo en las estaciones de grandes ciudades puede suponer un desplazamiento bastante largo a pie y el uso de escaleras.
- Glosario - cunsulte la página 12.

The following is designed to be an outline guide to travelling around Europe by train. For further details of types of accommodation available, catering, supplements etc., see the introduction to each country.

BUYING YOUR TICKET

Train tickets must be purchased before travelling, either from travel agents or at the station ticket office (or machine). Where a station has neither a ticket office nor a ticket machine, the ticket may usually be purchased on the train.

Tickets which are not dated when purchased (for example in France and Italy) must be validated before travel in one of the machines at the entrance to the platform.

Most countries in Europe offer two classes of rail accommodation, usually 1st and 2nd class. 1st class is more comfortable and therefore more expensive than 2nd class. Local trains are often 2nd class only. In Southern and Eastern Europe, 1st class travel is advisable for visitors as fares are reasonable and 2nd class can be very overcrowded.

RESERVATIONS

Many express trains in Europe are restricted to passengers holding advance seat reservations, particularly in France, Italy, Sweden and Spain. This is indicated by the symbol 🅁 in the tables, or by notes in the introduction to each country. All *TGV* and *Eurostar* trains require advance reservation, as do all long-distance trains in Italy and Spain.

Reservations can usually be made up to two months in advance. A small fee is charged, but where a supplement is payable the reservation fee is often included. Reservations can often be made on other long-distance services and this is recommended at busy times.

SUPPLEMENTS

Many countries have faster train services for which an extra charge is made. This supplement is payable when the ticket is purchased and often includes the price of a seat reservation. The supplement can sometimes be paid on the train, but usually at extra cost. The introduction to each country gives further information. On certain long-distance services, the first class fare includes the provision of a meal.

RAIL PASSES

Passes are available which give unlimited travel on most trains in a given area. These range from Interrail and Eurail passes which cover most of Europe for up to one month, to local passes which cover limited areas for one day. Further details of Interrail, Eurail and other passes will be found in our rail passes section on pages 581 – 587.

FINDING YOUR TRAIN

At most stations departures are listed on large paper sheets (often yellow), and / or on electronic departure indicators. These list trains by departure, giving principal stops, and indicate from which platform they leave.

On each platform of principal European stations, a display board can be found giving details of the main trains calling at that platform. This includes the location of individual coaches, together with their destinations and the type of accommodation provided.

A sign may be carried on the side of the carriage indicating the train name, principal stops and destination and a label or sign near the door will indicate the number allocated to the carriage, which is shown on reservation tickets. 1st class accommodation is usually indicated by a yellow band above the windows and doors and/or a figure '1' near the door or on the windows

A sign above the compartment door will indicate seat numbers and which seats are reserved. In non-compartment trains, reserved seats have labels on their headrests. In some countries reserved seats are not marked and occupants will be asked to move when the passenger who has reserved the seat boards the train.

LUGGAGE & BICYCLES

Luggage may be registered at many larger stations and sent separately by rail to your destination. In some countries, bicycles may also be registered in advance and certain local and some express trains will convey bicycles (there may be a charge). The relevant railways will advise exact details on request.

✕ CATERING 🍷

Many high-quality and long-distance trains in Europe have restaurant cars serving full meals, usually with waiter service. An at-seat service may also be provided to passengers in first class accommodation. Such trains are identified with the symbol ✕ in the tables. Full meals may only be available at set times, sometimes with separate sittings, and may only be available to passengers holding first class tickets. However, the restaurant car is often supplemented by a counter or trolley service offering light snacks and drinks.

Other types of catering are shown with the symbol 🍷. This varies from a self-service buffet car serving light meals (sometimes called bistro or café) to a trolley which is wheeled through the train, serving drinks and light refreshments. Where possible, the introduction to each country gives further information on the level of catering to be expected on particular types of train.

Please note that the catering shown may not be available throughout the journey and may be suspended or altered at weekends or on holidays.

SLEEPING CARS 🛏

Sleeping cars are indicated by the symobol 🛏 in the tables. Standard sleeping car types have bedroom style compartments with limited washing facilities and full bedding. Toilets are located at one or both ends of the coach. An attendant travels with each car or pair of cars and will serve drinks, snacks and breakfast at an extra charge. Traditionally, 1st class sleeping compartments have one or two berths (in Britain and Norway two berth compartments require only 2nd class tickets) and 2nd class compartments have three berths. Some trains convey special T2 cabins, shown as 🛏 (T2) in the tables, with one berth in 1st class and two berths in 2nd class. On certain routes it is now possible to reserve a single compartment with a 2nd class ticket.

Compartments are allocated for occupation exclusively by men or by women except when married couples or families occupy all berths. Children travelling alone, or who cannot be accommodated in the same compartment as their family, are placed in women's compartments. In Russia and other countries of the CIS, however, berths are allocated in strict order of booking and men and women often share the same compartments.

Some trains have communicating doors between sleeping compartments which can be opened to create a larger room if both compartments are occupied by the same family group. Berths can be reserved up to 2 months (3 months on certain trains) before the date of travel and early reservation is recommended as space is often limited. Berths should be claimed within 15 minutes of boarding the train or they may be resold.

Compartments with showers are also available on some domestic overnight services in Sweden and Italy, and on certain other international routes as indicated on our international overnight services summary on page 35.

COUCHETTES ━

Couchettes (━) are a more basic form of overnight accommodation consisting of simple bunk beds with a sheet, blanket and pillow. The couchettes are converted from ordinary seating cars for the night, and there are usually 4 berths per compartment in 1st class, 6 berths in 2nd class. On certain trains (e.g. in Austria and Italy), 4 berth compartments are available to 2nd class passengers, at a higher supplement. Washing and toilet facilities are provided at the ends of each coach. Men and women are booked into the same compartments and are expected to sleep in daytime clothes.

ÖBB nightjet

Many night trains radiating from Germany and Austria, are operated by Austrian Railways and are branded *ÖBB nightjet*. All services convey sleeping-car, couchette and seating accommodation. Standard sleeping-car compartments can be configured with one, two or three berths and have a washbasin (with toiletries provided). *Deluxe* sleeping-car compartments can also be configured with one, two or three berths and have an en-suite washroom with WC, washbasin and shower (shower gel and towels are provided). The sleeping-car fare includes a welcome drink, a bottle of water, a newspaper and a full breakfast served in the morning (including free hot drink refills). Four and six-berth couchettes are available, the price of which includes a bottle of water and a small breakfast. Women only, family and wheelchair couchette compartments are provided. Second class seating cars (with six-seat compartments) are also conveyed. Reservation is compulsory in all categories of accommodation and special all-inclusive fares are available. Brand new overnight rolling stock is gradually being introduced on *nightjet* routes which include a new style of couchette accommodation for single travellers in mini capsule style compartments (traditional four-berth couchette accommodation is also available, together with one and two-berth sleeping-car compartments). Please note that Interrail and Eurail pass holders must pay a special pass holders fare to travel on *nightjet* services.

INTERNATIONAL OVERNIGHT SERVICE SUMMARY

A summary of international overnight services will be found on page 35 which specifies the various types of accommodation and catering provided on each individual service (including details of the operator).

CAR-SLEEPERS

Trains which convey motor cars operate throughout much of Europe and are shown in Table **1** for international services and Table **2** for other services. The motor cars are conveyed in special wagons while passengers travel in sleeping cars or couchettes, usually (but not always) in the same train.

WHEELCHAIR ACCESS ♿

Most main-line domestic and international trains, together with an increasing number of local trains, are specially equipped to accommodate passengers in wheelchairs. Access ramps are available at many stations and some trains are fitted with special lifts. These trains have at least one wheelchair space, and are equipped with accessible toilets.

Most railways publish guides to accessibility, and many countries provide dedicated staff to assist disabled travellers. Wheelchair users normally need to reserve in advance, stating their requirements.

HEALTH REQUIREMENTS

It is not mandatory for visitors to Europe to be vaccinated against infectious diseases unless they are travelling from areas where these are endemic. For travellers' peace of mind, however, protection against the following diseases should be considered:

COVID-19	Measles / Rubella
Hepatitis A / B	Polio
HIV	Tetanus
Influenza	Tuberculosis

Full information is available from the manual published by the World Health Organisation, and travellers should seek advice from their Travel Agent.

DRINKING WATER

Tap water is usually safe to drink in most parts of Europe. The water in washrooms or toilets on trains is, however, not suitable for drinking. Those who doubt the purity of the tap water are recommended to boil it, to use sterilisation tablets, or to drink bottled water.

CLIMATE

Most of Europe lies within the temperate zone but there can be considerable differences between North and South, East and West, as illustrated in the table below. Local temperatures are also affected by altitude and the difference between summer and winter temperatures tends to be less marked in coastal regions than in areas far removed from the sea.

	Bucuresti	Dublin	Madrid	Moskva
JANUARY				
Highest	3°	8°	10°	−6°
Lowest	−5°	2°	3°	−12°
Rain days	9	13	8	11
APRIL				
Highest	18°	12°	18°	10°
Lowest	5°	5°	8°	2°
Rain days	10	11	10	9
JULY				
Highest	30°	20°	32°	23°
Lowest	15°	12°	19°	14°
Rain days	10	11	3	12
OCTOBER				
Highest	18°	14°	19°	8°
Lowest	5°	7°	11°	2°
Rain days	8	12	10	10

Highest = Average highest daily temperature in °C
Lowest = Average lowest daily temperature in °C
Rain days = Average number of days with recorded precipitation
Source: World Weather Information Service

FIND US ON FACEBOOK!

www.facebook.com/EuropeanRailTimetable

and on **Twitter** @EuropeanRailTT

METRIC CONVERSION TABLES

The Celsius system of temperature measurement, the metric system of distance measurement and the twenty-four hour clock are used throughout this book. The tables below give Fahrenheit, mile and twelve-hour clock equivalents.

CURRENCY CONVERSION

The information shown below is intended to be indicative only. Rates fluctuate from day to day and commercial exchange rates normally include a commission element.

Country	unit	code	1 GBP =	1 USD =	1 EUR =	100 JPY =
Euro zone (‡)	**euro**	**EUR**	**1.19**	**0.87**	**1.00**	**0.61**
Albania	lek	ALL	116.93	86.23	98.17	60.25
Belarus	rubl	BYN	4.44	3.27	3.72	2.28
Bosnia	marka	BAM	2.32	1.71	1.95	1.20
Bulgaria	lev	BGN	2.32	1.71	1.95	1.20
Czech Republic	koruna	CZK	29.64	21.86	24.88	15.27
Denmark	krone	DKK	8.88	6.55	7.45	4.57
Georgia	lari	GEL	3.70	2.73	3.11	1.91
Hungary	forint	HUF	481.03	354.76	403.86	247.87
Iceland	krona	ISK	171.84	126.73	144.27	88.55
Kazakhstan	tenge	KZT	694.78	512.40	583.32	358.02
Macedonia	denar	MKD	73.26	54.03	61.50	37.75
Moldova	leu	MDL	23.39	17.25	19.63	12.05
Norway	krone	NOK	13.69	10.10	11.50	7.05
Poland	złoty	PLN	5.05	3.72	4.24	2.60
Romania	leu	RON	6.03	4.45	5.06	3.10
Russia	ruble	RUB	108.21	79.80	90.85	55.76
Serbia	dinar	RSD	139.65	102.91	117.22	71.91
Sweden	krona	SEK	12.90	9.51	10.83	6.64
Switzerland	franc	CHF	1.11	0.82	0.93	0.57
Turkey	lira	TRY	52.82	38.93	44.33	27.20
Ukraine	hryvnya	UAH	56.44	41.59	47.36	29.06
United Kingdom	pound	GBP	1.00	0.73	0.83	0.51
United States	dollar	USD	1.35	1.00	1.13	0.69
Uzbekistan	som	UZS	17.513*	12.908*	14.699*	9.019*

‡ – Austria, Belgium, Croatia, Cyprus, Estonia, Finland, France, Germany, Greece, Ireland, Italy, Latvia, Lithuania, Luxembourg, Malta, the Netherlands, Portugal, Slovakia, Slovenia and Spain.

The euro is also legal tender in Andorra, Kosovo, Monaco, Montenegro, San Marino, and the Vatican City.

* – Expressed in thousands i.e. 17,513, 12,908, 14,699, 9,019

PASSPORTS AND VISAS

Nationals of one country intending to travel to or pass through another country normally require a valid passport and will also require a visa unless a special visa-abolition agreement has been made between the countries concerned. The limit of stay permitted in each country is usually 3 months.

Applications for visas should be made well in advance of the date of travel to the local consulate of the country concerned. Consuls usually make a charge for issuing a visa. Before issuing a transit visa, a consul normally requires to see the visa of the country of destination.

The possession of a valid passport or visa does not necessarily grant the holder automatic access to all areas of the country to be visited. Certain countries have zones which are restricted or prohibited to foreign nationals.

All border controls have been abolished, however, between those countries which have signed the **Schengen Agreement** (see list below), and a visa allowing entry to any of these countries is valid in all of them.

LIST OF SCHENGEN AREA COUNTRIES

Austria, Belgium, Bulgaria, Czech Republic, Croatia, Denmark, Estonia, Finland, France, Germany, Greece, Hungary, Iceland, Italy, Latvia, Lithuania, Luxembourg, Malta, Netherlands, Norway, Poland, Portugal, Romania, Slovakia, Slovenia, Spain, Sweden, Switzerland.

TEMPERATURE

°C	°F
−20	−4
−15	5
−10	14
−5	23
0	32
5	41
10	50
15	59
20	68
25	77
30	86
35	95
40	104

Conversion formulae :
°C = (°F − 32) x 5 / 9
°F = (°C x 9 / 5) + 32

DISTANCE

km	miles	km	miles	km	miles
1	0.62	45	27.96	300	186.41
2	1.24	50	31.07	400	248.55
3	1.86	55	34.18	500	310.69
4	2.49	60	37.28	600	372.82
5	3.11	65	40.39	700	434.96
6	3.73	70	43.50	800	497.10
7	4.35	75	46.60	900	559.23
8	4.97	80	49.71	1000	621.37
9	5.59	85	52.82	1100	683.51
10	6.21	90	55.92	1200	745.65
15	9.32	95	59.03	1300	807.78
20	12.43	100	62.14	1400	869.92
25	15.53	125	77.67	1500	932.06
30	18.64	150	93.21	2000	1242.74
35	21.75	175	108.74	3000	1864.11
40	24.85	200	124.27	4000	2485.48

TIME

Midnight departure	= 0000
1 am	= 0100
5 am	= 0500
5.30 am	= 0530
11 am	= 1100
12 noon	= 1200
1 pm	= 1300
3.45 pm	= 1545
Midnight arrival	= 2400

GLOSSARY

	FRANCAIS	*ITALIANO*	*DEUTSCH*	*ESPAÑOL*
additional trains	d'autres trains	ulteriori treni	weitere Züge	otros trenes
also	[circule] aussi	[si effettua] anche	[verkehrt] auch	[circula] también
alteration	modification	variazione	Änderung	modificación
approximately	environ	circa	ungefähr	aproximadamente
arrival, arrives (a.)	arrivée, arrive	arrivo, arriva	Ankunft, kommt an	llegada, llega
and at the same minutes past each hour until	puis toutes les heures aux mêmes minutes jusqu'à	poi ai stessi minuti di ogni ora fino a	und so weiter im Takt bis	luego a los mismos minutos de cada hora hasta
calls at	s'arrête à	ferma a	hält in	efectúa parada en
certain	déterminé	certo	bestimmt	determinado
change at	changer à	cambiare a	umsteigen in	cambiar en
composition	composition	composizione	Zugbildung	composición
confirmation	confirmation	conferma	Bestätigung	confirmación
connection	correspondance, relation	coincidenza, relazione	Anschluss, Verbindung	correspondencia, enlace
conveys	comporte, achemine	ha in composizione	befördert, führt	lleva
daily	tous les jours	giornalmente	täglich	diariamente
delay	retard	ritardo	Verspätung	retraso
departure, departs (d.)	départ, part	partenza, parte	Abfahrt, fährt ab	salida, sale
earlier	plus tôt	più presto	früher	más temprano
engineering work	travaux de voie	lavori sul binario	Bauarbeiten	obras de vía
even / uneven dates	jours pairs / impairs	giorni pari / dispari	gerade / ungerade Daten	fechas pares / impares
every 30 minutes	toutes les 30 minutes	ogni 30 minuti	alle 30 Minuten	cada 30 minutos
except	sauf	escluso	außer	excepto
fast(er)	(plus) rapide	(più) rapido	schnell(er)	(más) rápido
for	pour	per	für	para
from Rennes	(en provenance) de Rennes	(proviene) da Rennes	von Rennes	(procede) de Rennes
from Jan. 15	à partir du 15 janvier	dal 15 di gennaio	vom 15. Januar (an)	desde el 15 de enero
hourly	toutes les heures	ogni ora	stündlich	cada hora
hours (hrs)	heures	ore	Stunden	horas
journey	voyage, trajet	viaggio, percorso	Reise	viaje, trayecto
journey time	temps de parcours	tempo di tragitto	Reisezeit	duración del recorrido
later	plus tard	più tardi	später	más tarde
may	peut, peuvent	può, possono	kann, können	puede(n)
minutes (mins)	minutes	minuti	Minuten	minutos
not	ne [circule] pas	non [si effettua]	[verkehrt] nicht	no [circula]
not available	pas disponible	non disponibile	nicht erhältlich	no disponible
on the dates shown in Table **81**	les jours indiqués dans le tableau **81**	nei giorni indicati nel quadro **81**	an den in der Tabelle **81** angegebene Daten	los días indicados en el cuadro **81**
only	seulement	esclusivamente	nur	sólo
operator	entreprise de transports	azienda di trasporto	Verkehrsunternehmen	empresa de transportes
other	autre	altro	andere	otros
runs	circule	circola, si effettua	verkehrt	circula
sailing	traversée	traversata	Überfahrt	travesía
ship	bateau, navire	nave, battello	Schiff	barco
stopping trains	trains omnibus	treni regionali	Nahverkehrszüge	trenes regionales
stops	s'arrête	ferma	hält	efectúa parada
subject to	sous réserve de	soggetto a	vorbehaltlich	sujeto a
summer	été	estate	Sommer	verano
supplement payable	avec supplément	con pagamento di supplemento	zuschlagpflichtig	con pago de suplemento
then	puis	poi	dann	luego
through train	train direct	treno diretto	durchgehender Zug	tren directo
timings	horaires	orari	Zeitangaben	horarios
to York	vers, à destination de York	(diretto) a York	nach York	(continúa) a York
to / until July 23	jusqu'au 23 juillet	fino al 23 di luglio	bis zum 23. Juli	hasta el día 23 de julio
to pick up	pour laisser monter	per viaggiatori in partenza	zum Zusteigen	para recoger viajeros
to set down	pour laisser descendre	per viaggiatori in arrivo	zum Aussteigen	para dejar viajeros
unless otherwise shown	sauf indication contraire	salvo indicazione contraria	sofern nicht anders angezeigt	salvo indicación contraria
valid	valable	valido	gültig	válido
when train **44** runs	lors de la circulation du train **44**	quando circola il treno **44**	beim Verkehren des Zuges **44**	cuando circula el tren **44**
winter	hiver	inverno	Winter	invierno

2025 European Rail Timetable Price List

Printed seasonal edition (published two times a year in January and June): £24.99

Monthly digital edition: £14.99. Beyond Europe digital edition: £4.99.

Annual subscription for 12 digital editions: £135.00

Annual subscription for 12 digital editions, together with two printed copies: £179.99

Two year printed subscription (four consecutive printed editions): £94.99

Special bundle deal which includes an annual subscription for 12 digital editions and two printed timetables, together with the latest Rail Map Europe and the 18th edition of the Europe by Rail guide book: £199.99

Note: Prices quoted do not include postage and packaging.

For details of other products and to order on-line visit **www.europeanrailtimetable.eu**

By post to: 28 Monson Way, Oundle, Northamptonshire, PE8 4QG (cheques payable to European Rail Timetable Limited)

✆ +44 (0) 1832 270198 (Monday to Friday 1000 – 1600)

INDEX OF PLACES by table number

[train] Connection by train from the nearest station shown in this timetable.
[boat] Connection by boat from the nearest station shown in this timetable.
[bus] Connection by bus from the nearest station shown in this timetable.
10/355 Consult both indicated tables to find the best connecting services.

A

AMSTERDAM

city plan, page 30

AMSTERDAM ✈ SCHIPHOL

ANKARA

ATHÍNA

for [boat], see Pireás

B

BARCELONA

city plan, page 30

D

DEN HAAG

DIJON

DORTMUND

DRESDEN

DUBLIN

city plan, page 31

DUISBURG

DÜSSELDORF

CRUISE TRAINS

The services shown in the European Rail Timetable are the regular scheduled services of the railway companies concerned. However, a number of specialised operators also run luxurious cruise trains taking several days to complete their journey. Overnight accommodation is provided either on the train or in hotels. Cruise trains are bookable only through the operating company or its appointed agents and normal rail tickets are not valid on these trains. A selection of operators is shown below.

The Danube Express : Fully escorted holidays in central and eastern Europe by luxury private train based in Budapest. Operator: Danube Express, Offley Holes Farm, Charlton Road, Preston, Hitchin, SG4 7TD, UK; ✆ +44 (0)1462 441400. Website: www.danube-express.com

Belmond Royal Scotsman : Luxury tours of Scotland starting from Edinburgh. Operator: Belmond Royal Scotsman, Shackleton House, 4 Battle Bridge Lane, London, SE1 2HP, UK; ✆ 0845 217 0799 (UK only) or +44 (0) 20 3117 1300. Website: www.royalscotsman.com

El Transcantábrico and **El Expreso de La Robla** : Rail cruises along Spain's northern coast. Operator: Trenes Turísticos de Lujo, Plaza de los Ferroviarios s/n., 33012 Oviedo, Asturias, Spain; ✆ +34 902 555 902, fax +34 985 981 711. Website: www.trenesturisticosdelujo.com

Trans-Siberian Express : Tours by private hotel train along the Trans-Siberian Railway. Operator : Golden Eagle Luxury Trains, Denzell House, Denzell Gardens, Dunham Road, Altrincham, WA14 4QF, UK; ✆ +44 (0)16 1 928 9410, fax +44 (0)161 941 6101. Website: www.goldeneagleluxurytrains.com.

Venice Simplon-Orient-Express : This well-known luxury train runs once or twice weekly from late March to early November, mostly on its established London - Paris - Venezia route. Operator: Belmond VSOE, Shackleton House, 4 Battle Bridge Lane, London, SE1 2HP, UK; ✆ 0845 217 0799 (UK only) or +44 (0) 20 3117 1300. Website: www.vsoe.com

LIST OF ADVERTISERS

ECONEX	inside front cover
EUROPE BY RAIL	37
EUROPEAN RAIL TIMETABLE	36, inside back cover

LIST OF RETAILERS

The European Rail Timetable is available for purchase direct from the retailers listed below. Some also stock the Rail Map Europe.

Great Britain

Blackwell's Bookshop	Oxford
Daunt Books	Six stores in London
Foyles	London and Birmingham
Magazine Heaven	Rushden Lakes, Northamptonshire
Stanfords	London and Bristol
Tornado Books & Hobbies	Birmingham

Austria

Buchhandlung DerMauritz	Wien
Freytag & Berndt	Wien

Belgium

Press Shop/Relay	Brugge railway station

France

La Librairie du Voyage	Rennes
Smith&Son (formerly WHSmith)	Paris, 248 Rue de Rivoli

Germany

FachBuchZentrum & Antiquariat Stiletto	Schrobenhausen
Freytag & Berndt	Regensburg and Nürnberg
Gleisnost Reisebuero	Freiburg railway station
GVE-Verlag/BahnBuchShop	Berlin Lichtenberg railway station info@gve-verlag.de
Dussmann das Kulturkaufhaus	Berlin, Friedrichstraße 90
Schropp Maps	Berlin, Hardenbergstraße 9a
Dr.Götze Land & Karte	Hamburg

Netherlands

Stanley & Livingstone	Den Haag
The American Book Center	Amsterdam
Treinreiswinkel	Amsterdam and Leiden

Sweden

Kartbutiken	Stockholm

Switzerland

Rail Map Shop	Trogen

CITY STATION LOCATION PLANS

——	Passenger railway	■	Main station
- - - -	Metro	▪	Local station
······	Bus / tram line		Bus station
- - - -	Ferry		Airport

Only those metro, bus, and tram lines which provide inter-station links or connect outlying main stations to the city centre are shown.

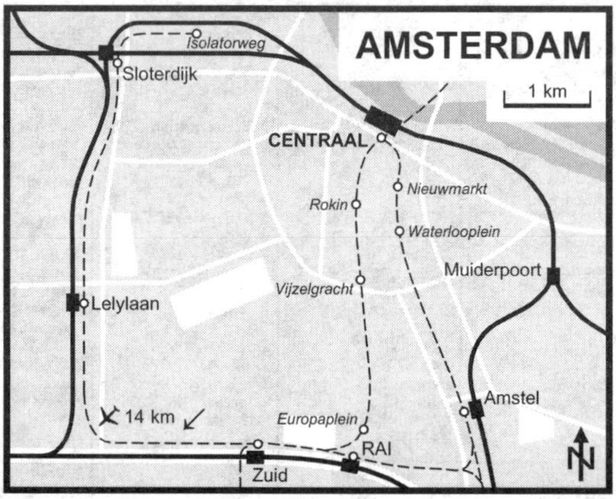

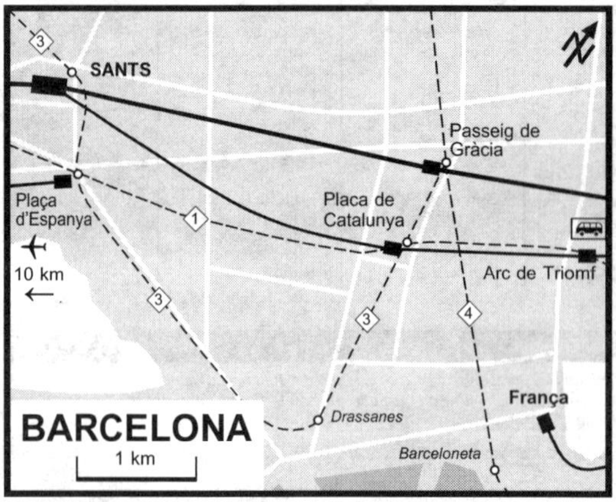

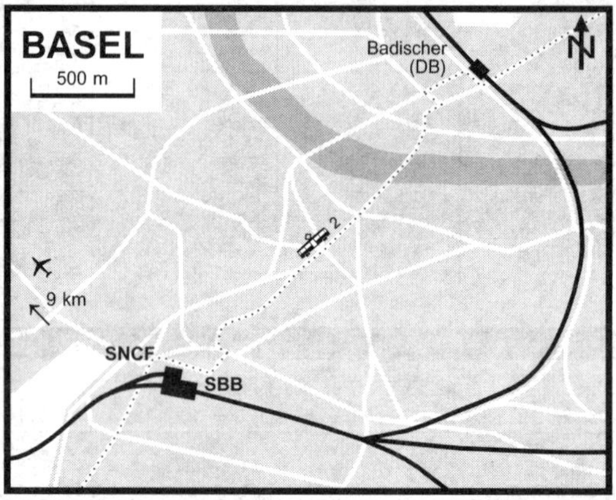

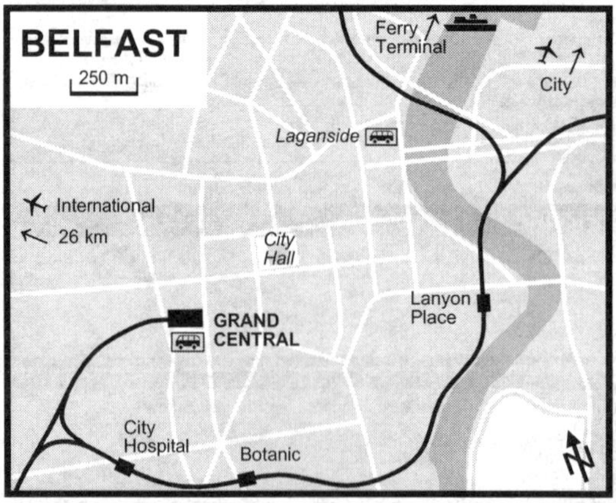

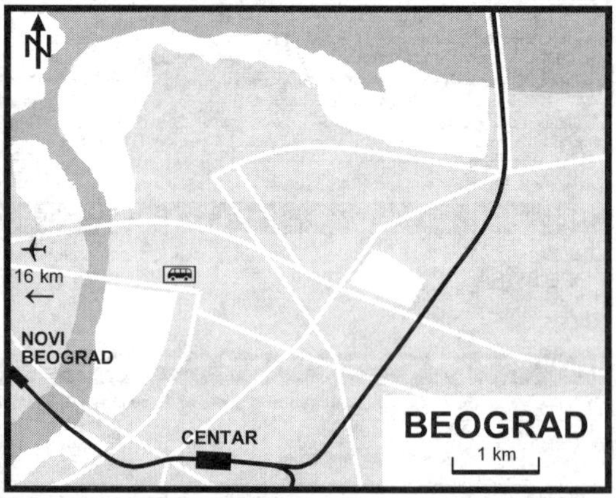

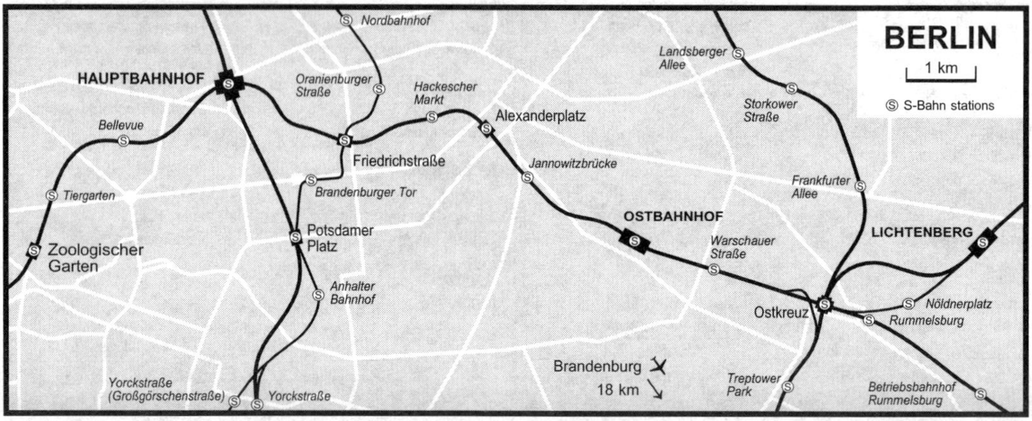

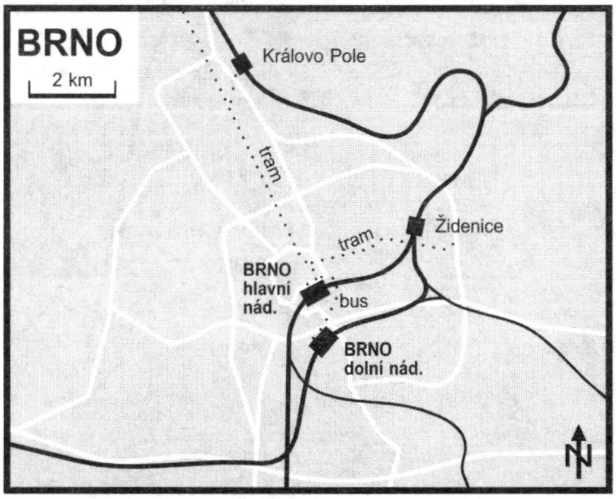
BRNO
2 km
Královo Pole
tram
Židenice
tram
BRNO
hlavní
nád.
bus
BRNO
dolní nád.

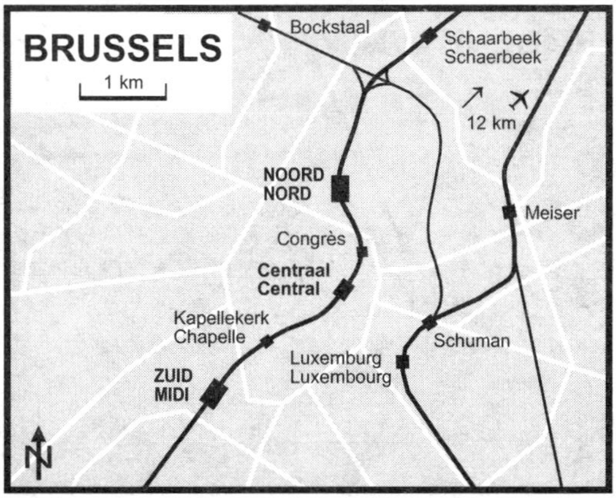
BRUSSELS
1 km
Bockstaal
Schaarbeek
Schaerbeek
12 km
NOORD
NORD
Congrès
Meiser
Centraal
Central
Kapellekerk
Chapelle
Schuman
Luxemburg
Luxembourg
ZUID
MIDI

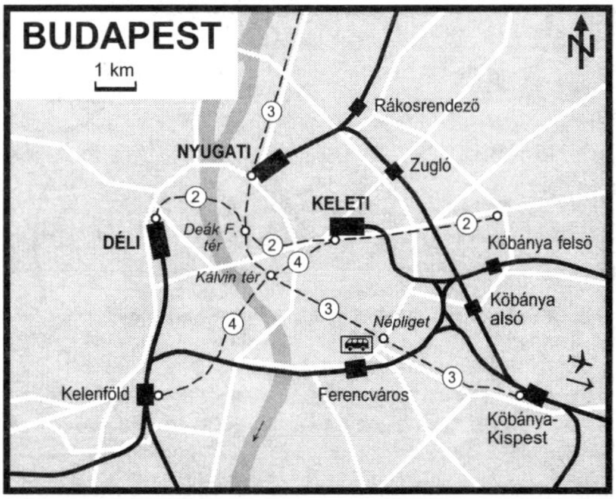
BUDAPEST
1 km
Rákosrendezö
NYUGATI
Zugló
KELETI
DÉLI
Deák F. tér
Kálvin tér
Köbánya felsö
Köbánya
alsó
Népliget
Kelenföld
Ferencváros
Köbánya-
Kispest

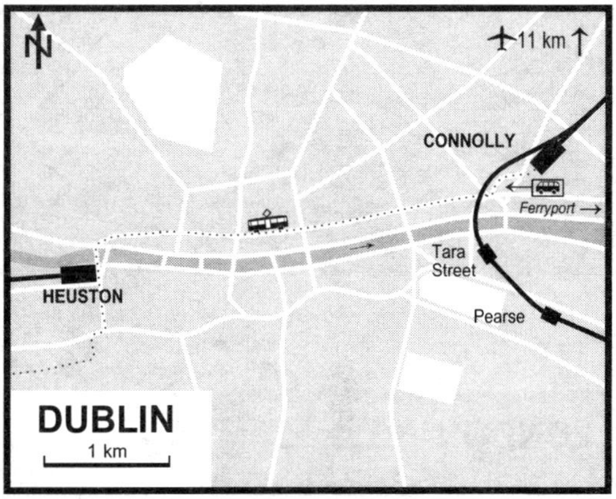
11 km
CONNOLLY
Ferryport
HEUSTON
Tara
Street
Pearse
DUBLIN
1 km

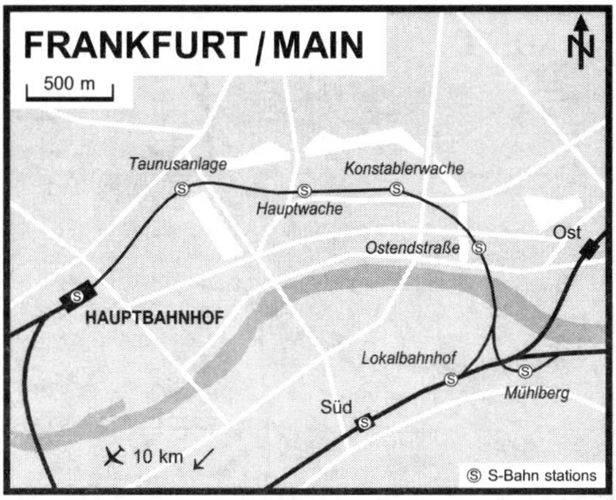
FRANKFURT / MAIN
500 m
Taunusanlage
Konstablerwache
Hauptwache
Ostendstraße
Ost
HAUPTBAHNHOF
Lokalbahnhof
Mühlberg
Süd
10 km
S-Bahn stations

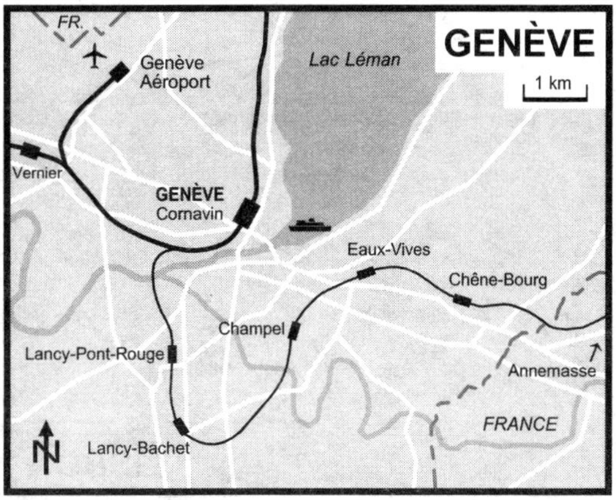
FR.
Genève
Aéroport
Lac Léman
GENÈVE
1 km
Vernier
GENÈVE
Cornavin
Eaux-Vives
Chêne-Bourg
Champel
Lancy-Pont-Rouge
Annemasse
FRANCE
Lancy-Bachet

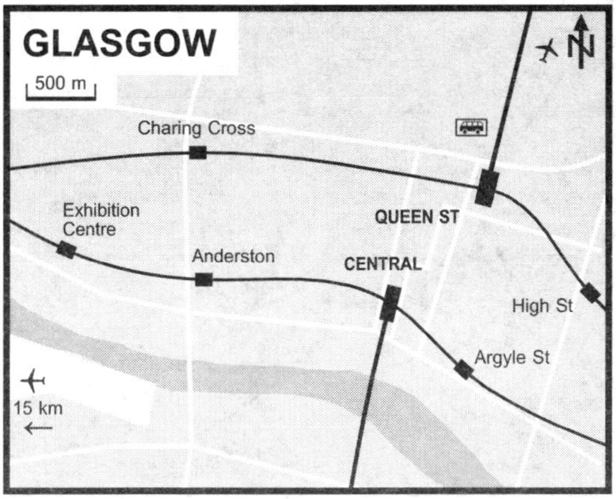
GLASGOW
500 m
Charing Cross
Exhibition
Centre
QUEEN ST
Anderston
CENTRAL
High St
Argyle St
15 km

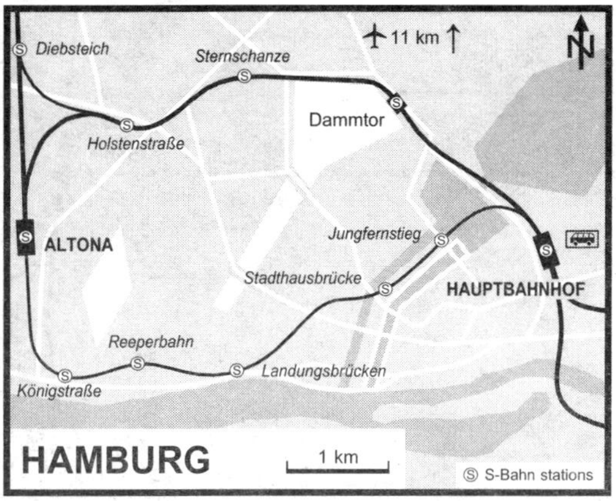
Diebsteich
Sternschanze
11 km
Dammtor
Holstenstraße
ALTONA
Jungfernstieg
Stadthausbrücke
HAUPTBAHNHOF
Reeperbahn
Landungsbrücken
Königstraße
HAMBURG
1 km
S-Bahn stations

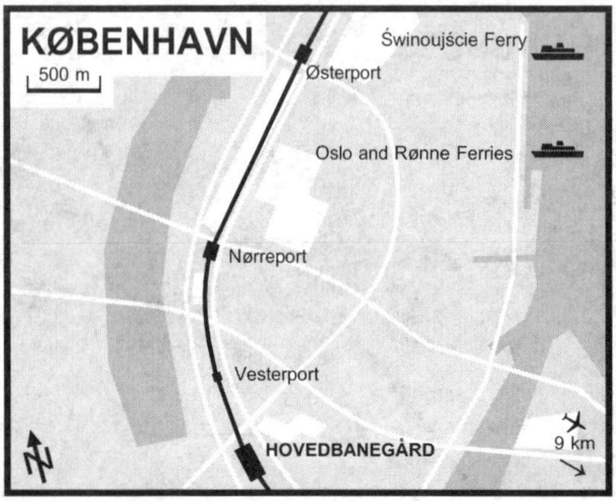
KØBENHAVN
500 m
Świnoujście Ferry
Østerport
Oslo and Rønne Ferries
Nørreport
Vesterport
HOVEDBANEGÅRD
9 km

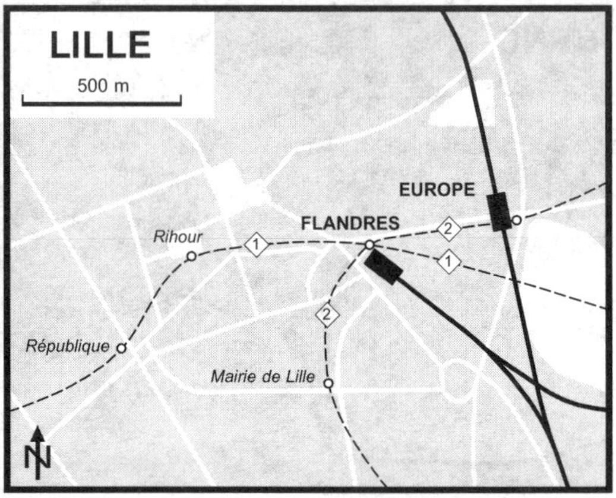
LILLE
500 m
EUROPE
FLANDRES
Rihour
1
2
République
Mairie de Lille

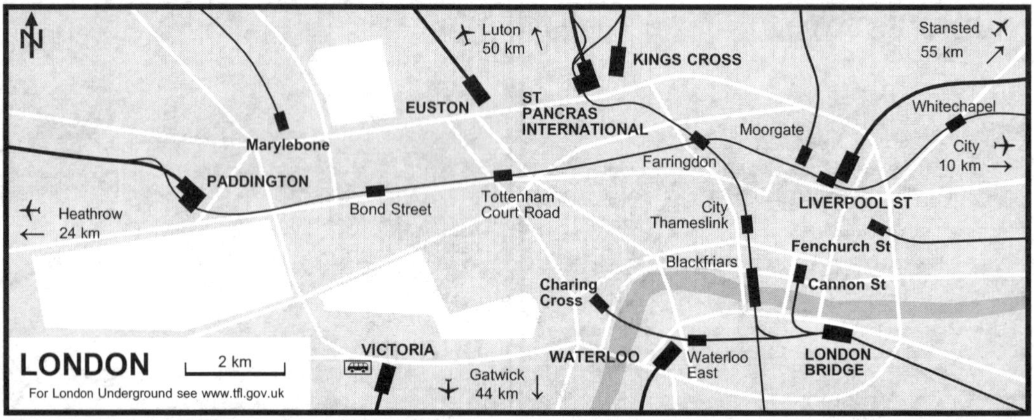
Luton
50 km
KINGS CROSS
Stansted
55 km
EUSTON
ST
PANCRAS
INTERNATIONAL
Whitechapel
Moorgate
Marylebone
Farringdon
City
10 km
PADDINGTON
LIVERPOOL ST
Heathrow
24 km
Bond Street
Tottenham
Court Road
City
Thameslink
Fenchurch St
Blackfriars
Charing
Cross
Cannon St
VICTORIA
WATERLOO
Waterloo
East
LONDON
BRIDGE
LONDON
2 km
For London Underground see www.tfl.gov.uk
Gatwick
44 km

Entrecampos
Roma
Sete Rios
Roma-Areeiro
Sintra
Oriente
Areeiro
Campolide
Alameda
São
Sebastião
Oriente
Marquês de
Pombal
Rato
Restauradores
Rossio
SANTA
APOLÓNIA
Baixa-Chiado
Rossio
Cascais
Cais do Sodré
Terreiro
do Paço
1 km
Barreiro
LISBOA

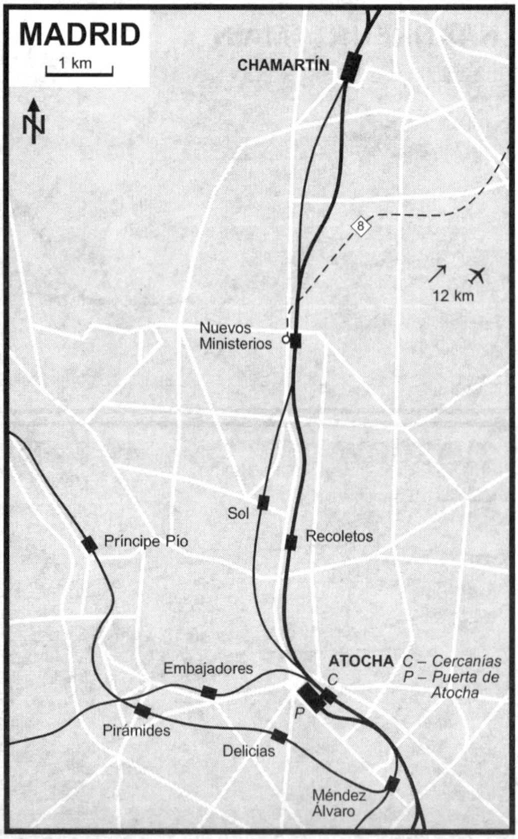
MADRID
1 km
CHAMARTÍN
8
12 km
Nuevos
Ministerios
Sol
Príncipe Pío
Recoletos
Embajadores
ATOCHA
C
C – Cercanías
P – Puerta de
Atocha
P
Pirámides
Delicias
Méndez
Álvaro

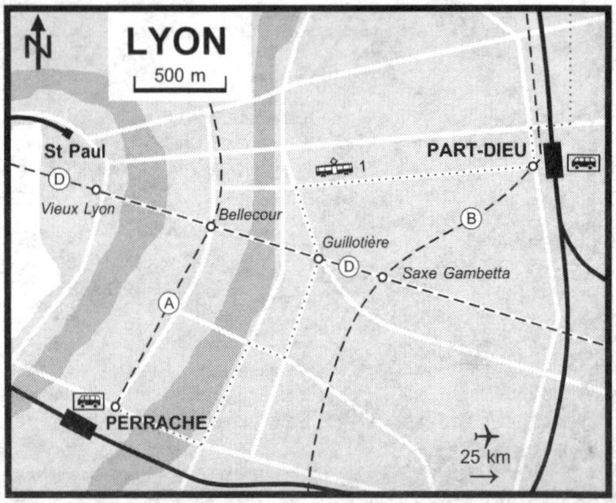
LYON
500 m
St Paul
PART-DIEU
1
D
Vieux Lyon
Bellecour
B
Guillotière
D
Saxe Gambetta
A
PERRACHE
25 km

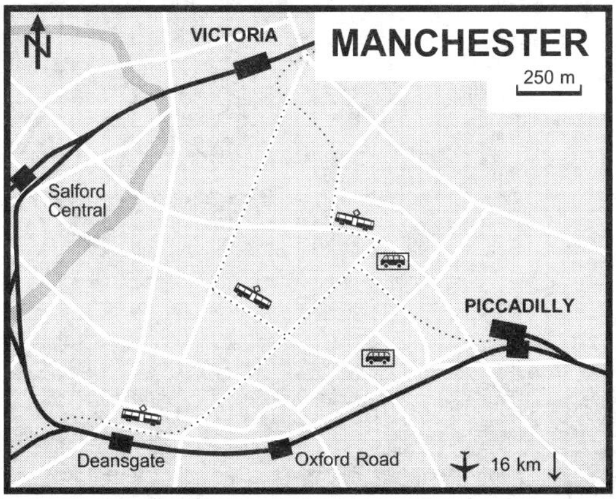
MANCHESTER
250 m
VICTORIA
Salford
Central
PICCADILLY
Deansgate
Oxford Road
16 km

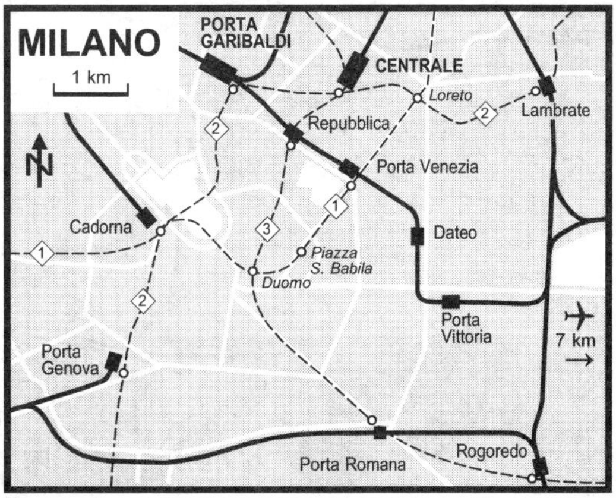
MILANO
1 km
PORTA
GARIBALDI
CENTRALE
Loreto
Lambrate
Repubblica
Porta Venezia
Cadorna
Dateo
Piazza
S. Babila
Duomo
Porta
Vittoria
7 km
Porta
Genova
Porta Romana
Rogoredo

27 km
Savyolovsky
Rizhskaya
Yaroslavskaya
BELORUSSKAYA
(Smolenskaya)
OKTYABRSKAYA
(Leningradski vokzal)
Komsomolskaya
Kazanskaya
Kurskaya
KIYEVSKAYA
Paveletskaya
MOSKVA
1 km

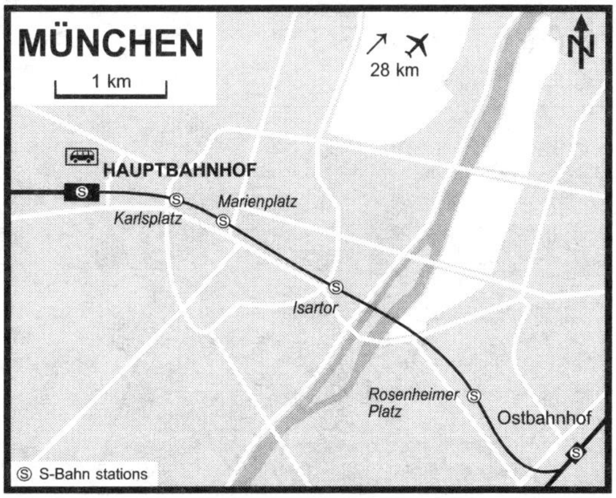
MÜNCHEN
1 km
28 km
HAUPTBAHNHOF
Marienplatz
Karlsplatz
Isartor
Rosenheimer
Platz
Ostbahnhof
Ⓢ S-Bahn stations

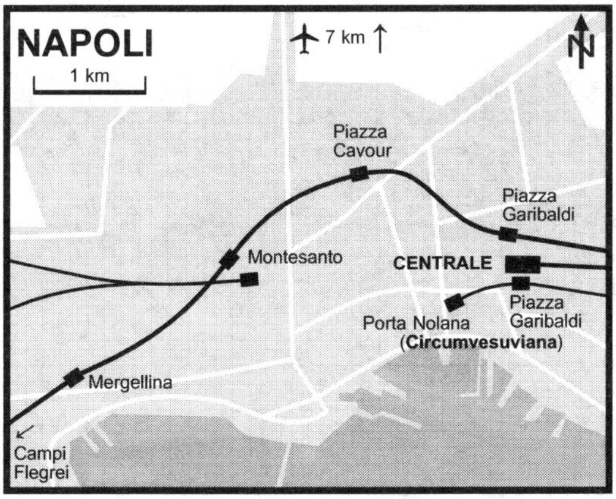
NAPOLI
1 km
7 km
Piazza
Cavour
Piazza
Garibaldi
Montesanto
CENTRALE
Piazza
Garibaldi
Porta Nolana
(Circumvesuviana)
Mergellina
Campi
Flegrei

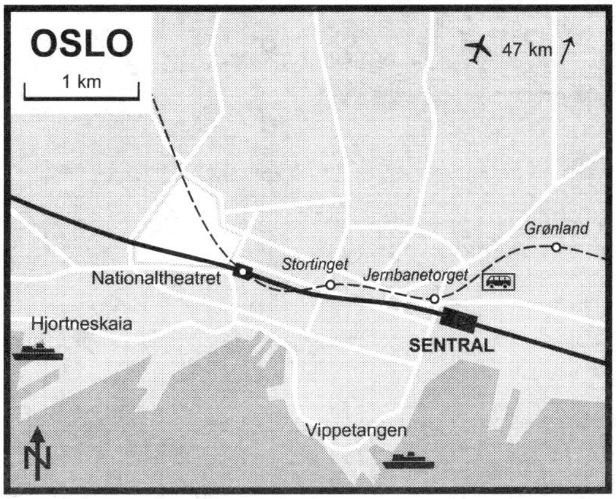
OSLO
1 km
47 km
Grønland
Nationaltheatret
Stortinget
Jernbanetorget
Hjortneskaia
SENTRAL
Vippetangen

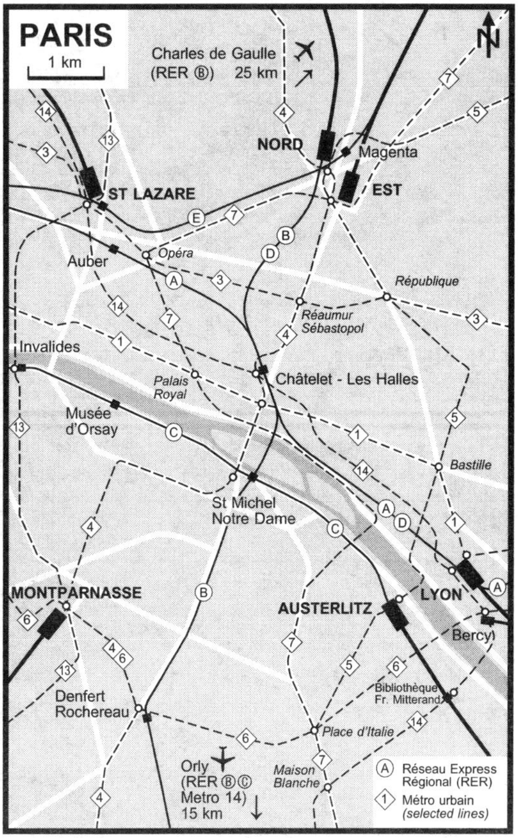
PARIS
1 km
Charles de Gaulle
(RER Ⓑ) 25 km
NORD
Magenta
ST LAZARE
EST
Opéra
Auber
République
Réaumur
Sébastopol
Invalides
Palais
Royal
Châtelet - Les Halles
Musée
d'Orsay
Bastille
St Michel
Notre Dame
MONTPARNASSE
AUSTERLITZ
LYON
Bercy
Bibliothèque
Fr. Mitterand
Denfert
Rochereau
Place d'Italie
Orly
(RER Ⓑ Ⓒ
Metro 14)
15 km
Maison
Blanche
Ⓐ Réseau Express
Régional (RER)
◇1 Métro urbain
(selected lines)

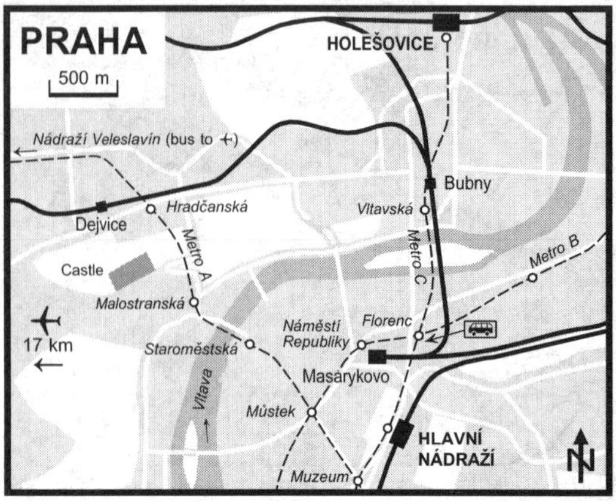
PRAHA
500 m
HOLEŠOVICE
Nádraží Veleslavín (bus to)
Bubny
Dejvice
Hradčanská
Vltavská
Metro A
Metro C
Metro B
Castle
Malostranská
17 km
Náměstí Republiky
Florenc
Staroměstská
Masarykovo
Vltava
Můstek
HLAVNÍ NÁDRAŽÍ
Muzeum

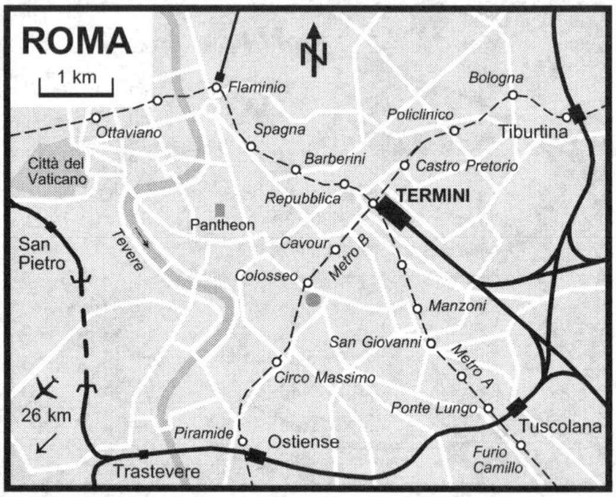
ROMA
1 km
Flaminio
Bologna
Ottaviano
Spagna
Policlinico
Tiburtina
Città del Vaticano
Barberini
Castro Pretorio
Repubblica
TERMINI
San Pietro
Pantheon
Tevere
Cavour
Metro B
Colosseo
Manzoni
San Giovanni
Metro A
Circo Massimo
26 km
Porta Lungo
Tuscolana
Piramide
Ostiense
Furio Camillo
Trastevere

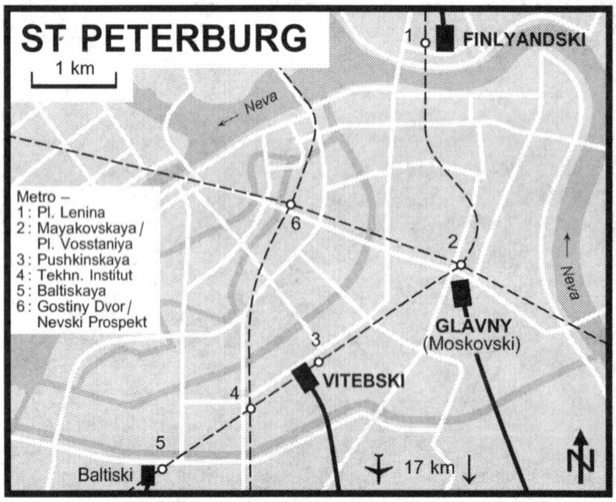
ST PETERBURG
1 km
1
FINLYANDSKI
Neva
Metro –
1 : Pl. Lenina
2 : Mayakovskaya / Pl. Vosstaniya
3 : Pushkinskaya
4 : Tekhn. Institut
5 : Baltiskaya
6 : Gostiny Dvor / Nevski Prospekt
6
2
Neva
GLAVNY (Moskovski)
3
VITEBSKI
4
5
Baltiski
17 km

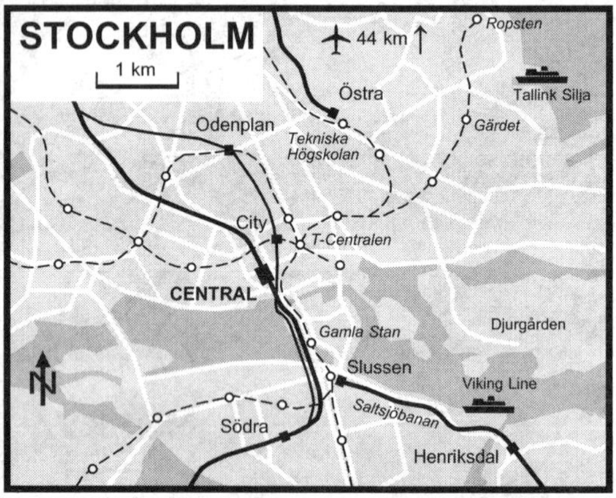
STOCKHOLM
1 km
44 km
Ropsten
Östra
Tallink Silja
Odenplan
Gärdet
Tekniska Högskolan
City
T-Centralen
CENTRAL
Gamla Stan
Djurgården
Slussen
Viking Line
Saltsjöbanan
Södra
Henriksdal

Marco Polo Airport
MESTRE
Murano
SANTA LUCIA
IC Bus
Tronchetto
Piazza S. Marco
Piazzale Roma
People mover
VENEZIA
2 km
Lido di Venezia

Gdańska
Wileńska
WSCHODNIA
Ratusz Arsenal
Stadion
Wisła
Świętokrzyska
CENTRALNA
Powiśle
10 km
Centrum
Śródmieście
Ochota
WARSZAWA
1 km

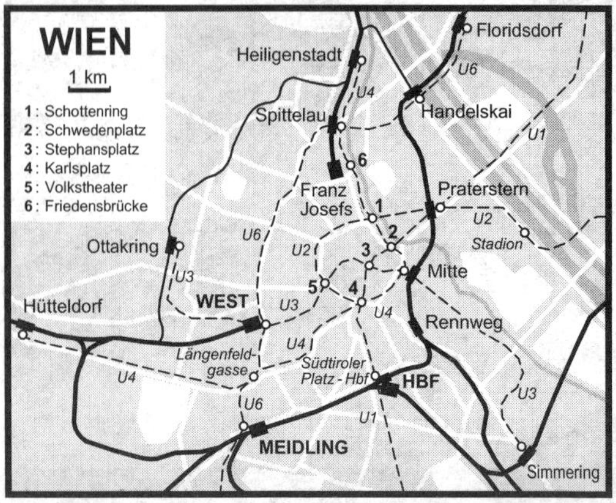
WIEN
1 km
1 : Schottenring
2 : Schwedenplatz
3 : Stephansplatz
4 : Karlsplatz
5 : Volkstheater
6 : Friedensbrücke
Floridsdorf
Heiligenstadt
U6
U4
Spittelau
Handelskai
U1
6
Franz Josefs
Praterstern
1
U2
2
Stadion
Ottakring
U6
U2
3
Mitte
U3
5
4
WEST
U3
U4
Hütteldorf
Rennweg
U4
Längenfeldgasse
Südtiroler Platz - Hbf
HBF
U4
U6
U3
U1
MEIDLING
Simmering

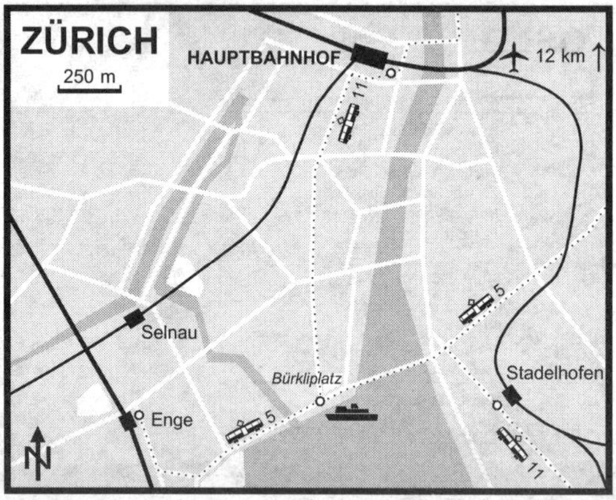
ZÜRICH
250 m
HAUPTBAHNHOF
12 km
11
Selnau
5
Stadelhofen
Bürkliplatz
Enge
5
11

SELECTED DAILY INTERNATIONAL SLEEPER SERVICES

From	To	Train no.	Brand	Facilities and owner	Train Name	International table no.
Amsterdam	Innsbruck	421/420	Nightjet	1, 2 cl. (öbb), 2 cl.(öbb)		21, 28, 53
Amsterdam	Wien	40421/40490	Nightjet	1, 2 cl. (öbb), 2 cl.(öbb)		28, 53
Stuttgart	Budapest	50237/50462	Euro Night	1, 2 cl.(mav), 2 cl.(mav)	Kálmán Imre	32, 65
Wien	Bucureşti	347/346	Euro Night	1, 2 cl.(cfr), 2 cl.(cfr), (cfr)	Dacia	32, 61
Budapest	Bucureşti	473/472	Euro Night	1, 2 cl.(cfr), 1, 2 cl.(cfr)	Ister	32, 61
Berlin	Stockholm	497/496	Euro Night	1, 2 cl., 2 cl.		50
Zürich	Praha	50467/50466	Euro Night	1, 2 cl. (čd)		52
Zürich	Praha	40458/40459	Euro Night	1, 2 cl. (čd)	Canopus	52, 54
Hamburg	Wien	491/490	Nightjet	1, 2 cl. (öbb), 2 cl.(öbb)		53, 64
Hamburg	Innsbruck	40491/40420	Nightjet	1, 2 cl. (öbb), 2 cl.(öbb)		53, 64
Zürich	Hamburg	471/470	Nightjet	1, 2 cl. (öbb), 2 cl.(öbb)		54, 73
Zürich	Berlin	409/408	Nightjet	1, 2 cl. (öbb), 2 cl.(öbb)		54, 73
Warszawa	Kyiv	68/67		1, 2 cl.(uz)	Kyiv Ekspres	59b
Berlin	Graz	457/456	Nightjet	1, 2 cl. (öbb), 2 cl.(öbb)	Metropol	60
Berlin	Budapest	40457 / 40476	Nightjet	1, 2 cl. (mav), 2 cl.(mav)	Metropol	60
Praha	Budapest	577/476	Euro Night	1, 2 cl. (čd), 2 cl.(čd)	Metropol	60
Stuttgart	Zagreb	40237/414	Euro Night	1, 2 cl.(hz), 2 cl.(hz)		62
Stuttgart	Rijeka	60237/480	Euro Night	1, 2 cl.(hz)		62
München	Roma	295/294	Nightjet	1, 2 cl. (db), 2 cl.(db)		71
Roma	Wien	40233/40294	Nightjet	1, 2 cl. (öbb), 2 cl.(öbb)		71
Stuttgart	Venezia	237/236	Nightjet	1, 2 cl. (db), 2 cl.(db)		71
Venezia	Wien	237/236	Nightjet	1, 2 cl. (öbb), 2 cl.(öbb)		71
La Spezia	München	40295/40235	Nightjet	1, 2 cl. (db), 2 cl.(db)		71
La Spezia	Wien	233/235	Nightjet	1, 2 cl.(ti), 2 cl.(ti)		71
Amsterdam	Zürich	403/402	Nightjet	1, 2 cl.(öbb), 2 cl.(öbb)		73
Zürich	Zagreb	40465/40414	Euro Night	1, 2 cl.(hz), 2 cl.(hz)		86
Zürich	Budapest	40467/40462	Euro Night	1, 2 cl.(mav), 2 cl.(mav)		86
Zürich	Graz	465/464	Nightjet	1, 2 cl. (öbb), 2 cl.(öbb)		86
Zürich	Wien	467/466	Nightjet	1, 2 cl. (öbb), 2 cl.(öbb)		86
Wien	Kyiv	40147/40749		1, 2 cl.(uz)	Hortobágy	96
Budapest	Warszawa	407/476		1, 2 cl.(pkp), 2 cl.(pkp)		99
München	Warszawa	409/406		1, 2 cl. (pkp)		99
Praha	Warszawa	407/443		1, 2 cl.(pkp), 2 cl.(pkp)		99
Non daily sleepers (other seasonal services operate):						
Brussels	Praha	453/452	European Sleeper	(1, 2, 3 berth) (es), (4, 6 berth) (es)	European Sleeper	20, 22, 55, 78
Brussels	Berlin	425/424	Nightjet	(1, 2, 3 berth), (4, 6 berth)(öbb)		20, 55
Brussels	Wien	425/50490	Nightjet	1, 2 cl. (öbb), 2 cl.(öbb)		21, 53
Paris	Berlin	40469/40424	Nightjet	(1, 2, 3 berth), (4, 6 berth)(öbb)		30, 55
Paris	Wien	469/468	Nightjet	1, 2 cl. (öbb), 2 cl.(öbb)		32
Berlin	Stockholm	301/300	Euro Night	2 cl.(bne)	Berlin Night Express	50
Bucuresti	istanbul	461/492		2 cl. 4-berth (tcdd)	Bosphor	61

Note: This list excludes trains not shown in our International section (e.g. Czech Republic to Slovakia).

– Shower.

Key to ownership of sleeping cars:
bne - Berlin Night Express; cd - Czech; cfr - Romanian; db - German; es - European Sleeper; hz - Croatian; mav - Hungarian; öbb - Austrian; pkp - Polish; tcdd - Turkish; ti - Italian; uz - Ukrainian; zs - Serbian.

Steam trains in the European Rail Timetable

There are numerous tourist and heritage lines operating around Europe, most of which operate a seasonal service using steam or heritage diesel traction. Unfortunately, space limitations mean that we are unable to show timings for most of these lines. However, there are a number of routes that offer a daily service throughout the year and for these we do include timings, together with a few services hauled by steam traction on main-line rail routes. The panel below lists tourist railway **steam** train schedules that are included in our regular timetable pages.

Readers should note that our expanded seasonal editions (published in March, June, September and December) provide details of many other tourist railways in our special ***Rail Extra*** feature, including a brief description of selected routes and an overview of the service provided. The feature also includes other useful rail travel information on a country by country basis.

COUNTRY	RAILWAY	TABLE	NOTES
GREAT BRITAIN	The Shakespeare Express	**123**	Regular summer Sunday main-line steam excursions between Stratford upon Avon and Birmingham
	Ffestiniog / Welsh Highland Railways	**145a**	Two narrow gauge railways linked at Porthmadog running through spectacular Welsh mountain landscapes
	North Yorkshire Moors Railway	**211**	Regular services run from spring to autumn, many steam-hauled through to Whitby via a link to the main line at Grosmont
	The Jacobite	**218**	A regular main-line steam excursion operating from spring to autumn over the spectacular West Highland line
FRANCE	Train des Pignes	**359**	A summer Sunday steam-hauled service running over part of the scenic Nice to Digne route
SWITZERLAND	Brienz Rothorn Bahn	**553**	A swiss mountain rack railway operating regular steam services from June to October
PORTUGAL	Comboio Historico	**694**	Enjoy a steam-hauled journey along the scenic Douro Valley between Régua and Tua at weekends from June to October
SWEDEN	Arvidsjaur Järnvägsförening	**766**	Operates twice a week from mid-July to early August over a section of the Inlandsbanan (Arvidsjaur - Slagnäs)
GERMANY	Rügensche Bäderbahn	**844a**	Daily steam services on the island of Rügen
	Lößnitzgrundbahn	**853**	Daily steam services between Radebeul Ost and Radeburg (near Dresden)
	Weißeritztalbahn	**853**	Daily steam services between Freital-Hainsberg and Kurort Kipsdorf (near Dresden)
	Zittauer Schmalspurbahn	**853**	Daily steam services between Zittau and Kurort Jonsdorf / Kurort Oybin
	Harzer Schmalspurbahnen	**867**	A famous narrow gauge network in central Germany with some services steam-hauled on a daily basis
	Fichtelbergbahn	**882**	Daily steam services between Cranzahl and Kurort Oberwiesenthal
AUSTRIA	Zillertalbahn	**955**	A single return steam service runs on selected days from May to October
	Achenseebahn	**956**	A narrow gauge steam rack railway with daily services running May to October
	Pinzgauer Lokalbahn	**957**	A single return steam service runs once or twice a week at certain times of the year
	Schneebergbahn	**984**	Most service are operated by modern diesel trains but a steam service also runs on Sundays during the summer
	Mariazellerbahn	**994**	An occasional steam service runs along this world famous mountain route (also a service hauled by heritage electric traction)
	Murtalbahn	**998**	Steam trains run between Murau and Tamsweg once or twice a week during the summer
POLAND	Koleje Wielkopolskie	**1099**	The popular scheduled steam services operating on the Wolsztyn to Poznań and Wolsztyn to Leszno routes
CZECH REPUBLIC	Jindřichohradecké Místní Dráhy	**1169**	A steam train runs on Saturdays from April to September (daily during July and August)

Products for sale from European Rail Timetable Limited

3rd Edition 3rd Revision of the
Rail Map Europe.
£12.99 + p&p

European Rail Timetable
Two seasonal editions.
£49.98 + p&p

18th Edition of the
Europe by Rail guidebook.
£20.99 + p&p

Autumn 2024 digital edition of the
Beyond Europe Timetable.
£4.99

Order on-line at **www.europeanrailtimetable.eu**
Telephone **01832 270198**

2025 European Rail Timetable Price List

Printed seasonal edition (published two times a year in January and June): £24.99

Monthly digital edition: £14.99. Beyond Europe digital edition: £4.99.

Annual subscription for 12 digital editions: £135.00

Annual subscription for 12 digital editions, together with two printed copies: £179.99

Two year printed subscription (four consecutive printed editions): £94.99

Special bundle deal which includes an annual subscription for 12 digital editions and two printed timetables, together with the latest Rail Map Europe and the 18th edition of the Europe by Rail guide book: £199.99

Note: Prices quoted do not include postage and packaging.

For details of other products and to order on-line visit **www.europeanrailtimetable.eu**

By post to: 28 Monson Way, Oundle, Northamptonshire, PE8 4QG (cheques payable to European Rail Timetable Limited)

✆ +44 (0) 1832 270198 (Monday to Friday 1000 – 1600)

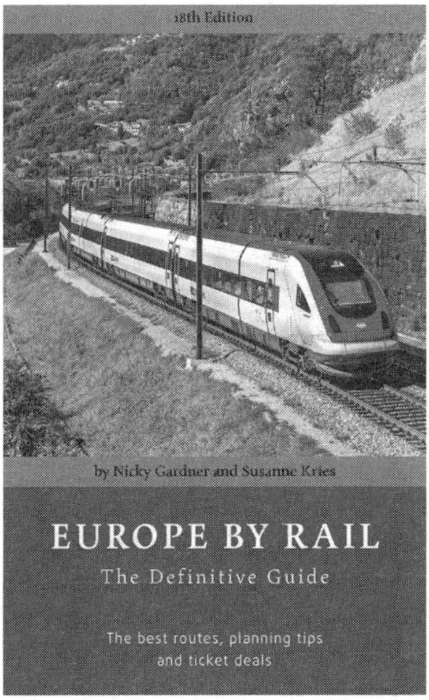

Exploring Europe by rail has never been easier. Written by Nicky Gardner and Susanne Kries, two highly experienced travellers, this guidebook contains all you need for planning your journey.

★ 50 routes
★ 544 pages
★ over 40,000 km of journeys
★ over 30 countries
★ tips on fares and ticketing
★ detailed route descriptions
★ sketch maps for each route
★ index maps which show all routes
★ suggestions for overnight stays

... and a very fine read!

The 18th edition of *Europe by Rail,* published in October 2024, has better coverage of France, Spain and Poland, improved ferry and bus connections, and a new section on travel apps. It is available directly from European Rail Timetable Ltd, all good bookshops and online retailers.

www.EuropeByRail.eu

Liège Guillemins station (photo © Erzsi Molnár / dreamstime.com)

AUTO-TRAIN, AUTOREISEZÜGE, MOTORAIL

Car-carrying trains are composed of special wagons or vans for the conveyance of motorcars usually with sleeping cars and couchettes enabling the driver and passengers to travel overnight in comfort in the same train. Some services convey vehicles separately allowing passengers a choice of trains for their own journey. Some shorter distance services run by day and convey seating coaches.

Cars are often loaded on the trains at separate stations from the passenger station and may be loaded some time before the passenger train departs. International car-carrying trains are shown in Table **1**, Domestic car-carrying trains in Table **2**. Some services also carry passengers without cars.

Details of Channel Tunnel shuttle services may be found on page 46. Details of domestic car-carrying shuttle trains may be found as follows: Austria (Table **969**), Germany (Table **821**), Italy (Table **589**), Slovenia (Table **1302**) and Switzerland (Tables **545** and **562**).

Services are for 2025 unless otherwise stated

Readers should be careful to check that dates refer to current schedules, as old dates may be left in the table until such time as current information is received. Loading and train times may vary on some dates, but will be confirmed by the agent when booking.

Contact details:

BahnTouristikExpress: ✆ +49 (0)911 240 388 22. www.rdc-deutschland.de

ÖBB Nightjet: ✆ +43 (0)5 1717. www.nightjet.com

Optima Tours: ✆ +49 (0)89 54 880 111. www.optimatours.de

Urlaubs-Express: ✆ +49 (0)22 18 002 0820. www.urlaubs-express.de

For the contact details of national operators please see the relevant country headings.

1 INTERNATIONAL CAR-CARRYING TRAINS

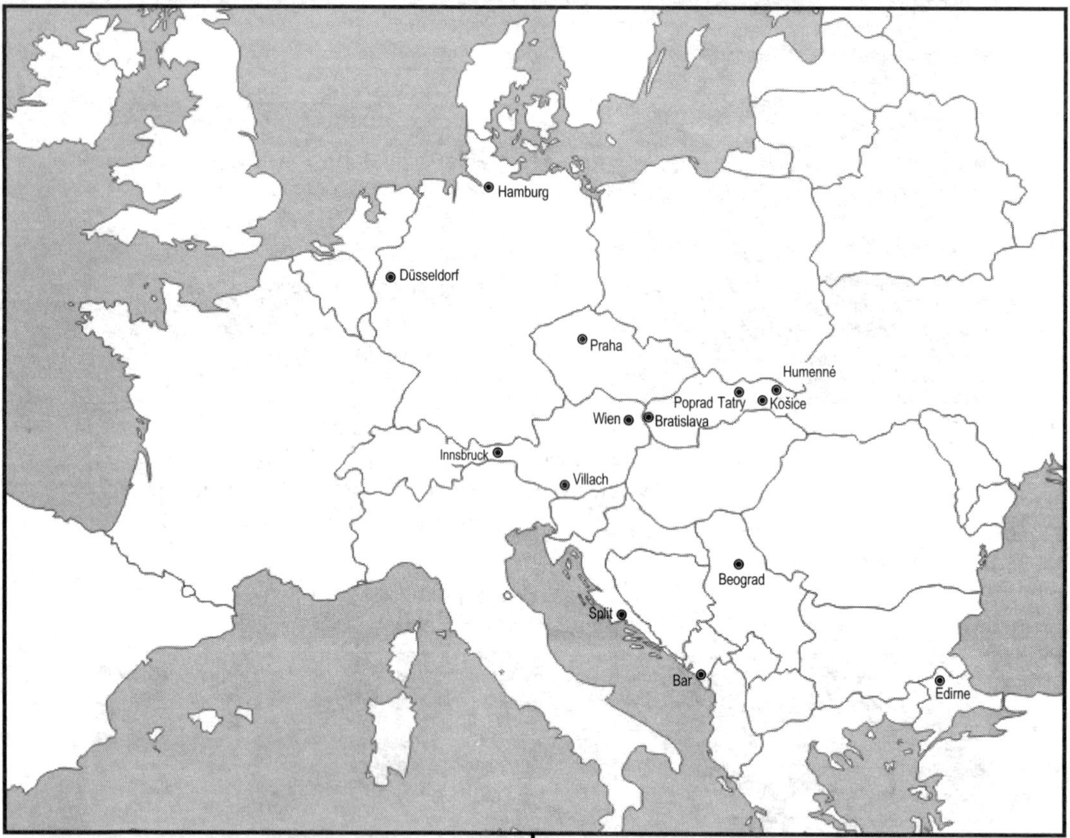

BAR

BEOGRAD: Železnice Srbije
Bar depart 2010, Beograd Centar arrive 0709.
Train **432**: 1, 2 cl., 2 cl., .

BEOGRAD

BAR: Železnice Srbije
Beograd Centar depart 2000, Bar arrive 0654.
Train **433**: 1, 2 cl., 2 cl., .

DÜSSELDORF

INNSBRUCK: *Urlaubs-Express*
May 9, 23, June 6, 18, July 2, 11, 27, Aug. 1, 15, 29, Sept. 12, 26, Oct. 3.
Düsseldorf Hbf depart 2044, arrive Innsbruck Hbf arrive 0823.
Train *UEX* **1388**: , .

VILLACH *Urlaubs-Express*
July 15, 29, Aug. 12, 19, 31, Sept. 7.
Düsseldorf Hbf depart 1953, arrive Villach ARZ arrive 0858.
Train *UEX* 1383: , .

EDIRNE

VILLACH: *Optima Tours*
Apr. 8, 15, 22, 29, May 6, 13, 20, 27, June 3, 10, 17, 24, July 1, 8, 15, 22, 29, Aug. 5, 15, 22, 29, Sept. 5, 12, 19, 26, Oct. 3, 10, 17, 24, 31, Nov. 7, 14.
Depart Edirne 1745, arrive Villach (two days later) 0811.
Train **154**: .

HAMBURG

VILLACH Urlaubs-Express
June 29, July 9, 30, Aug. 5, 12, 31, Sept. 7.
Hamburg-Altona depart 1900, arrive Villach ARZ 0858.
Train *UEX* **1393**: , .

INNSBRUCK Urlaubs-Express
May 9, 16, 23, 28, June 6, 13, 18, 27, July 2, 18, 25, 27, Aug. 1, 8, 15, 22, 29, Sept. 5, 12, 19, 26, Oct. 3.
Hamburg-Altona depart 2014, arrive Innsbruck 0823.
Train *UEX* **1399**: , .

HUMENNÉ

PRAHA: **Service suspened** *České Dráhy*
Daily (not Dec. 24, 31).
Humenné depart 1850, Praha hlavní nádraží arrive 0751.
Train *EN* **442**: 1, 2 cl., 2 cl. .

INNSBRUCK

DÜSSELDORF Urlaubs-Express
May 17, 29, June 14, 38, July 25, Aug. 9, 16, 23, 30, Sept. 20, 27, Oct. 4.
Innsbruck Hbf depart 2100. arrive Düsseldorf 0745.
Train *UEX* 1388: , .

INTERNATIONAL CAR-CARRYING TRAINS 1

INNSBRUCK

HAMBURG *Urlaubs-Express*
May 10, 17, 24, 29, June 7, 14, 19, 28, July 3, 12, 19, 26, 28, Aug. 2, 9, 16, 23, 30, Sept. 6, 13, 20, 27, Oct. 4.
Innsbruck Hbf load time not advised, depart 2100. arrive Hamburg-Altona 0828.
Train *UEX* **1398**: , .

KOŠICE

PRAHA: **Service expected to recommence from June 15** *České Dráhy*
Daily (not Dec. 24, 31).
Košice load 2005 - 2015, depart 2207, Praha hlavní nádraží arrive 0751.
Train *EN* **442**: 1, 2 cl., 2 cl. .

POPRAD TATRY

PRAHA: **Service expected to recommence from June 15** *České Dráhy*
①⑤⑥⑦ until Mar. 19; daily from Mar. 22
Poprad Tatry load 2215 - 2225, depart 2356, Praha hlavní nádraží arrive 0751.
Train *EN* **442**: 1, 2 cl., 2 cl. .

PRAHA

HUMENNÉ: **Service suspended** *České Dráhy*
Daily (not Dec. 24, 31).
Praha hlavní nádraží load 2045 - 2110, depart 2216, Humenné arrive 1114.
Train *EN* **443**: 1, 2 cl., 2 cl. .

KOŠICE: **Service expected to recommence from June 15** *České Dráhy*
Daily (not Dec. 24, 31).
Praha hlavní nádraží load 2045 - 2110, depart 2216, Košice arrive 0812.
Train *EN* **443**: 1, 2 cl., 2 cl. .

POPRAD TATRY: **Service expected to recommence from June 15** *České Dráhy*
④⑤⑥⑦ until Mar. 18; daily from Mar. 21
Praha hlavní nádraží load 2105 - 2125, depart 2216, Poprad Tatry arrive 0600.
Train *EN* **443**: 1, 2 cl., 2 cl. .

SPLIT

WIEN: *ÖBB Nightjet*
①④⑥ May 1 - Oct. 13.
Split depart 1722, Wien Hbf ARZ arrive 0938.
Train *EN* **1152**: , .

VILLACH

DÜSSELDORF: *Urlaubs-Express*
July 30, Aug. 13, Sept. 1, 8.
Villach load time not advised, depart 1900. arrive Düsseldorf 0823.
Train *UEX* **1382**: , .

EDIRNE: *Optima Tours*
Apr. 5, 12, 19, 26, May 3, 10, 17, 24, 31, June 7, 14, 21, 28, July 5, 12, 19, 26, Aug. 2, 9, 19, 26, Sept. 2, 9, 16, 23, 30, Oct. 7, 14, 21, 28, Nov. 4, 11.
Depart Villach 2132, arrive Edirne (two days later) 0603.
Train **141**: .

HAMBURG: *Urlaubs-Express*
July 16, 30, Aug. 6, 13, 20, Sept. 1, 8.
Load time Villach ARZ not advised, depart 1900, arrive Hamburg-Altona 0913.
Train *UEX* **1392**: , .

WIEN

SPLIT: *ÖBB Nightjet*
③⑤⑦ Apr. 30 - Oct. 12.
Wien Hbf ARZ depart 1857, Split arrive 1006.
Train *EN* **1153**: , , .

DOMESTIC LONG-DISTANCE CAR-CARRYING TRAINS 2

AUSTRIA

Wien Hbf ARZ - Feldkirch and v.v.
From Wien daily, depart 2243, arrive Feldkirch 0754.
Trains *NJ* **446**: 1, 2 cl., 2 cl., .
From Feldkirch daily, depart 2227, arrive Wien Hbf ARZ 0746.
Trains *NJ* **447**: 1, 2 cl., 2 cl., .

Graz - Feldkirch and v.v.
From Graz daily, depart 2225, arrive Feldkirch 0739.
Trains *NJ* **464**: 1, 2 cl., 2 cl., .
From Feldkirch daily, depart 2245, arrive Graz 0658.
Trains *NJ* **465**: 1, 2 cl., 2 cl., .

FINLAND

Services operate on the following routes - contact operator for schedules:

Helsinki - Kemijärvi and v.v.
Helsinki - Oulu and v.v.
Kolari - Tampere and v.v.
Rovaniemi - Turku and v.v.
Helsinki - Kolari and v.v.
Helsinki - Rovaniemi and v.v.
Rovaniemi - Tampere and v.v.

Note: Helsinki trains load and unload at Pasila station (3 km north of Helsinki station)

GERMANY

Düsseldorf Hbf - **München** Ost and v.v. Urlaubs-Express
From Düsseldorf May 9, 23, June 6, 18, July 2, 11, 15*, 27, 29*, Aug. 1, 12*, 16, 19*, 29, 31*, Sept. 7*, 12, 26, Oct. 3.
Depart 2044, arrive 0603. Train *UEX* **1383**: , (trains marked * depart 1953, arrive 0435 as *UEX* **1383**).

From München May 17, 29, June 14, 28, July 26, 30*, Aug. 9, 13*, 16, 23, 30, Sept. 1*, 8*, 20, 27, Oct. 4.
Depart 2247, arrive 0745. Train *UEX* **1388**: , (trains marked * depart 2357, arrive 0823 as *UEX* **1382**).

GERMANY (continued)

Hamburg Altona - **Lörrach** and v.v. BahnTouristikExpress
From Hamburg ④⑥ May 22 - Oct. 18 (also May 27, July 1, 15, 22, 29, Aug. 5, 12; not May 31). Depart 2140, arrive 0845. Train **1790**.
From Lörrach ⑤⑦ May 23 - Oct. 19 (also May 28, July 2, 16, 23, 30, Aug. 6, 13; not June 1). Depart 1950, arrive 0800. Train **1791**.

Hamburg Altona - **Lörrach** and v.v. Urlaubs-Express
From Hamburg May 21, 30, June 11, 25, July 4, 8, 11, 16, 18, 23, 25, Aug. 3, 17, Sept. 3. Depart 2132, arrive 0751. Train *UEX* **1849**: , .
From Lörrach May 22, 31, June 12, 26, July 5, 9, 12, 17, 19, 24, 26, Aug. 4, 18, Sept. 4. Depart 2049, arrive 0727. Train *UEX* **1848**: , .

Hamburg Altona - **München** Ost and v.v. Urlaubs-Express
From Hamburg May 9, 14§, 16, 23, 25§, 28, June 4§, 6, 11§, 13, 18, 20§, 27, July 2, 4§, 13§, 14, 20§, 25, 27, 29*, Aug. 1, 5*, 8, 10§, 12*, 15, 19*, 22, 26§, 29, 31*, Sept. 3§, 5, 7*, 10§, 12, 19, 26, Oct. 3, 10§, 17§.
Depart 2014, arrive 0603. Train *UEX* **1399**: , (trains marked * depart 1900, arrive 0435 as *UEX* **1393**; trains marked § depart 2132, arrive 0720 as *UEX* **1847**).

From München May 10, 15§, 17, 24, 26§, 29, June 5§, 7, 12§, 14, 19, 21§, 28, July 3, 5§, 12, 14§, 16*, 19, 21§, 28, 30*, Aug. 2, 6*, 9, 11§ 13*, 16, 20* 23, 27§, 30, Sept. 1*, 4§, 6, 8*, 11§, 13, 20, 27, Oct. 4, 11§, 18§.
Depart 2247, arrive 0828. Train *UEX* **1398**: , , (trains marked * depart 2359, arrive 0913 as *UEX* **1392**; trains marked § depart 2149, arrive 0736 as *UEX* **1846**).

SLOVAKIA

Bratislava - **Košice** and v.v.:
Bratislava load 2130 - 2140, depart 2255, Košice arrive 0441.
Košice load 2140 - 2150, depart 2345, Bratislava arrive 0533.
Daily (not Dec. 24, 31). Trains **681** / **680**: 1, 2 cl., 2 cl., .

Scenic Rail Routes of Europe

The following is a list of some of the most scenic rail routes of Europe, timings for most of which can be found within the timetable (the relevant table number has been specified in bold). Routes marked * are some of the editorial team's favourite journeys. Please note that this list does not include specialised mountain and tourist railways.

Types of scenery: C - Coastline, F - Forest, G - Gorge, L - Lake, M - Mountain, R - River

AUSTRIA

Bruck an der Mur - Villach	M R	**980**
Gmunden - Stainach Irdning*	M L	**961**
Innsbruck - Brennero	M	**595**
Innsbruck - Garmisch*	M	**895**
Innsbruck - Schwarzach-St Veit	M G	**960**
Krems - Emmersdorf	R	**991**
Landeck - Bludenz*	M	**951**
St Pölten - Mariazell*	M	**994**
Salzburg - Villach*	M G	**970**
Selzthal - Kleinreifling - Steyr	M G R	**976/977**
Wiener Neustadt - Graz	M	**980**

BELGIUM and LUXEMBOURG

Liège - Luxembourg*	R	**446**
Liège - Marloie	R	**447**
Namur - Dinant	R	**440**

BULGARIA

Septemvri - Dobrinishte	M	**1510**
Sofia - Burgas	M	**1500**
Tulovo - Gorna Orjahovica	M	**1525**

CROATIA and BOSNIA

Novi Grad - Sarajevo	M G R	**1350**
Ogulin - Split	M	**1330**
Rijeka - Ogulin	M	**1310**
Sarajevo - Ploče	M G R	**1355**

CZECH REPUBLIC

Karlovy Vary - Mariánské Lázně	R F	**1123**
Karlovy Vary - Chomutov	R	**1110**
Praha - Děčín	R	**1100**

DENMARK

Struer - Thisted	C	**716**

FINLAND

Kouvola - Joensuu	L F	**797**

FRANCE

Aurillac - Neussargues	M G	**331**
Bastia - Ajaccio	M	**369**
Bourg-en-Bresse - Bellegarde	M	**341**
Chambéry - Bourg St Maurice	M	**366**
Chambéry - Modane	M L	**367**
Chamonix - Martigny*	M G	**365a**
Clermont Ferrand - Béziers	M G	**332**
Clermont Ferrand - Nîmes*	M G R	**333**
Dole - St Claude	M G	**376**
Gap - Briançon	M L	**358**
Genève - Aix les Bains	M R	**364**
Grenoble - Veynes - Marseille	M	**358**
Marseille - Ventimiglia	C	**361**
Mouchard - Montbéliard	R	**378**
Nice - Digne	M	**359**
Nice - Cuneo*	M G	**581**
Perpignan - Latour de Carol*	M G	**354**
Portbou - Perpignan	C	**355**
Sarlat - Bergerac	R	**318**
Toulouse - Latour de Carol	M	**312**
Valence - Veynes	M	**358**

GERMANY

Arnstadt - Meiningen	M	**870**
Dresden - Děčín	G R	**1100**
Freiburg - Donaueschingen	G F	**938**
Garmisch - Reutte - Kempten	M	**888**
Heidelberg - Neckarelz	R	**923/924**
Koblenz - Mainz*	G R	**914**
München - Lindau	M	**935**
Murnau - Oberammergau	M L	**897**
Naumburg - Saalfeld	R	**849**
Niebüll - Westerland	C	**821**

GERMANY - continued

Nürnberg - Pegnitz	G R	**880**
Offenburg - Konstanz	M F	**916**
Pforzheim - Nagold / Wildbad	F	**941**
Plattling - Bayerisch Eisenstein	F	**929**
Rosenheim - Berchtesgaden	M L	**890/891**
Rosenheim - Wörgl	M	**951**
Siegburg/Bonn - Siegen	R	**807**
Stuttgart - Singen	F	**940**
Titisee - Seebrugg	L F	**938**
Trier - Koblenz - Giessen	R	**906/915**
Ulm - Göppingen	M	**933**
Ulm - Tuttlingen	R	**938**

GREAT BRITAIN and IRELAND

Alnmouth - Dunbar	C	**180/214**
Barrow in Furness - Maryport	C	**157**
Coleraine - Londonderry	C	**233**
Dun Laoghaire - Wicklow	C	**237**
Edinburgh - Aberdeen	C	**222**
Exeter - Newton Abbot	C	**110/112**
Glasgow - Oban / Mallaig*	M L	**218**
Inverness - Kyle of Lochalsh*	M C	**226**
Lancaster - Carlisle - Carstairs	M G R	**154**
Liskeard - Looe	R	**111**
Llanelli - Craven Arms	M	**145**
Machynlleth - Pwllheli	M C	**148**
Perth - Inverness	M	**223**
Plymouth - Gunnislake	R	**113a**
St Erth - St Ives	C	**111**
Sheffield - Chinley	M	**194/206**
Shrewsbury - Aberystwyth	M R	**147**
Skipton - Settle - Carlisle	M R	**173**

GREECE

Diakoftó - Kalávrita	M G	**1455**

HUNGARY

Budapest - Szob	R	**1255**
Eger - Szilvásvárad	M	**1299**
Székesfehérvár - Balatonszentgyörgy	L	**1220**
Székesfehérvár - Tapolca	L	**1225**

ITALY

Bolzano - Merano	M	**595**
Brennero - Verona*	M	**595**
Brig - Arona	M L	**590**
Catania - Randazzo	M	**644**
Domodossola - Locarno*	M G	**551**
Firenze - Viareggio	M	**614**
Fortezza - San Candido	M	**597**
Genova - Pisa	C	**610**
Genova - Ventimiglia	C	**580**
Lecco - Tirano	M L	**593**
Napoli - Palermo	C	**641**
Napoli - Sorrento	C	**639**
Porretta Terme - Pistoria	M	**583**
Roma - Pescara	M	**624**
Salerno - Reggio Calabria	C	**640**
Taranto - Reggio Calabria	C	**637**
Torino - Aosta	M	**586**
Ventimiglia - Cuneo*	M G	**581**

NORWAY

Bergen - Oslo*	M L	**780/781**
Bodø - Trondheim	M L	**787**
Dombås - Åndalsnes	M	**785**
Drammen - Larvik	C	**783**
Myrdal - Flåm*	M C	**781**
Oslo - Kongsvinger	R	**750**
Oslo / Røros - Trondheim	M L	**784/785**
Stavanger - Kristiansand	M	**775**

POLAND

Jelenia Góra - Walbrzych	M	**1084**
Kraków - Zakopane	M	**1066**
Olsztyn - Elk	L	**1035**

POLAND - continued

Tarnów - Krynica	M	**1078**

PORTUGAL

Covilhã - Entroncamento	M R	**691**
Pampilhosa - Guarda	M	**692**
Porto - Coimbra	C R	**690**
Porto - Pocinho*	R	**694**
Porto - Valença	M C	**696**

ROMANIA

Braşov - Ploeşti	M	**1600**
Caransebeş - Craiova	M G R	**1630**
Feteşti - Constanţa	R	**1680**
Oradea - Cluj Napoca	R	**1600**
Salva - Sighetu Marmaţiei	M R F	**1660**
Salva - Suceava	M F	**1660**

SERBIA and MONTENEGRO

Kraljevo - Mitrovica / Mitrovicë	M R	**1375**
Priboj - Bar	M L	**1370**

SLOVAKIA

Banská Bystrica - Brezno	M	**1188**
Žilina - Poprad Tatry	M	**1180**

SLOVENIA

Jesenice - Sežana	M G R	**1302**
Maribor - Zidani Most	M	**1315**
Maribor - Bleiburg	M G R	**1315**
Villa Opicina - Ljubljana	G R	**1305**
Zagreb - Ljubljana	G R	**1300**

SPAIN

Algeciras - Ronda	M R	**673**
Barcelona - Latour de Carol	M	**656**
Bilbao - San Sebastián	M	**686**
Bilbao - Santander	M	**687**
Ferrol - Gijón*	C	**681/85/87**
Granada - Almería	M	**673**
Huesca - Canfranc	M G R	**670**
León - Monforte de Lemos	M	**682**
León - Oviedo	M	**685**
Lleida - La Pobla de Segur	M L	**653**
Málaga - Bobadilla	G	**673**
Santander - Oviedo	M C	**687**
Zaragoza - València	M R	**670**

SWEDEN

Bollnäs - Ånge - Sundsvall	M L	**761**
Borlänge - Mora	M L F	**758**
Borlänge - Ludvika - Frövi	M L F	**755**
Narvik - Kiruna	M F	**765**
Östersund - Storlien	L F	**761**

SWITZERLAND

Andermatt - Göschenen	G	**576**
Basel - Delémont - Moutier	M R	**500a/515**
Basel / Luzern / Zurich - Chiasso	M L	**547/548**
Chur - Arosa	M G	**545**
Chur - Brig - Zermatt*	M	**575/576**
Chur - St Moritz*	M G	**545**
Davos - Filisur	M G	**545**
Davos - Landquart	M	**545**
Interlaken Ost - Jungfraujoch*	M	**564**
Interlaken Ost - Luzern	M L	**561**
Interlaken West - Spiez	L	**560**
Lausanne - Brig	M L R	**570**
Lausanne - Neuchâtel - Biel	M L	**500**
Montreux - Zweisimmen - Lenk	M L G	**566**
Rorschach - Kreuzlingen	L	**538**
St Moritz - Scuol Tarasp	M	**545**
St Moritz - Tirano*	M	**545**
Spiez - Zweisimmen	G	**563**
Thun - Kandersteg - Brig*	M L	**562**
Zürich - Chur	M L	**520**

City plans are on pages 30 – 34

AIRPORT → CITY CENTRE LINKS

Airport code and name	City	Distance	Journey	Transport ‡	City terminal	Table
AAL Aalborg	Aalborg	6 km	11 mins	Train 3 per hour	Main rail station	**701**
AAR Aarhus	Aarhus	37 km	50 mins	🚌 **925x** *Airport Express*: connects with flights	Banegårdspladsen, Central rail station	
ABZ Aberdeen, Dyce	Aberdeen	11 km	40 mins	🚌 **727**: ± 4 per hour	Union Square bus station.	
ALC Alacant	Alacant	12 km	30 mins	🚌 **C6**: every 20 minutes	Plaza Puerta del Mar	
MZH Amasya Merzifon	Amasya	18 km	25 mins	1) Train (limited service from Suluova) 2) Taxi	Amasya rail station	**1577**
AMS Amsterdam, Schiphol	Amsterdam	17 km	15 mins	Train: every 7 – 8 minutes	Centraal rail station	**451**
	Rotterdam	53 km	28 mins	Train: every 15 minutes	Centraal rail station	**460**
	Den Haag	43 km	32 mins	Train: every 30 minutes	Centraal rail station	**452**
AOI Ancona (also known as Marche)	Ancona	16 km	30 mins	1) 🚌 *Aerobus* 0700 - 2230 2) Train: 1 – 3 per hour	Main rail station	
ATH Athína, Elefthérios Venizélos	Athína	27 km	39 mins	Metro line **3** (blue line): 2 per hour	Syntagma	**1440**
	Pireás	41 km	90 mins	🚌 four regular services to Pireás (and Athína)	Platía Karaiskáki	
BCN Barcelona, Aeroport del Prat	Barcelona	14 km	19 mins	Train: 2 per hour	Sants. Also calls at Passeig de Gràcia rail station (26 mins)	**659**
BSL Basel - Mulhouse - Freiburg	Basel	9 km	20 mins	🚌 **50**: up to 8 per hour	SBB rail station / Kannenfeldplatz	
(also known as EuroAirport)	Freiburg	60 km	55 mins	🚌: every 1 – 2 hours	Rail station	
BHD Belfast, City, George Best	Belfast	2 km	15 mins	🚌 *Airport Express* **600**: every 20 minutes	Europa Buscentre. Also train from Sydenham rail station	
BFS Belfast, International	Belfast	26 km	40 mins	🚌 *Airport Express* **300**: every 15 minutes	Europa Buscentre (adjacent to Great Victoria St rail station)	
BEG Beograd, Nikola Tesla	Beograd	18 km	35 mins	🚌 **600**: every 30 minutes	Rail station	
BER Berlin, Brandenburg	Berlin	24 km	30 mins	Train *Regional* **RE7 / RB14 / FEX**: 4 per hour	Hbf, also Sudkreuz, Ostkreuz rail stations	**847a**
BIQ Biarritz - Anglet - Bayonne	Biarritz	3 km	15 mins	🚌 *Chronoplus* 36: regular services	Town centre	
	Bayonne	7 km	23 mins	🚌 *Chronoplus* **3, 4**: every 20 minutes	Rail station	
BIO Bilbao, Sondika	Bilbao	10 km	45 mins	🚌 Bizkaibus **A-3247**: every 20 minutes 0600 - 0000	Plaza Moyúa (Metro station Moyúa)	
BLL Billund	Vejle	25 km	34 mins	🚌 *Sydtrafik* **43**	Town centre	
BHX Birmingham, International	Birmingham	12 km	11 mins	Train: ①–⑥ ± 9 per hour, ⑦ 6 per hour	New Street rail station from International	**107, 141, 151**
BLQ Bologna, Guglielmo Marconi	Bologna	8 km	7 mins	Train *Marconi Express*: daily every 7 minutes 0540 - 2400	Centrale rail station	
BOD Bordeaux, Mérignac	Bordeaux	12 km	35 mins	**Tram:** Tramway line **A**, every 10 minutes 0500 - 2400	Mérignac Centre	
	Bordeaux	12 km	30 mins	🚌 *30' Direct*: 2 per hour	St Jean rail station	
	Bordeaux	12 km	45 mins	🚌 **Corol 39**: every 20 minutes (peak) 0600 - 2030	Tram A at Haillan Rostand, Tram B Pessac Alouette	
BOH Bournemouth, Hurn	Bournemouth	10 km	38 mins	🚌 **737** *MoreBus*: ①–⑤ only at 1335, 1620 and 1800	Rail station, Bus station (Travel Interchange)	
BTS Bratislava, Milan Rastislav Štefánika	Bratislava	10 km	25 mins	🚌 **61**: 4 per hour (additional services ①–⑤ peak hours)	Main rail station (Hlavná stanica)	
BRE Bremen	Bremen	3 km	16 mins	Tram **6**: ①–⑥ every 10 minutes, ⑦ every 30 minutes	Main rail station	
BRS Bristol, International	Bristol	13 km	45 mins	🚌 *Airport Flyer Exp*: 3 – 5 per hour	Temple Meads rail station, also bus station	
BRQ Brno	Brno	8 km	20 mins	🚌 **E76**: 2 per hour	Main rail station, also bus station	
BRU Brussels, Zaventem	Brussels	12 km	25 mins	Train: up to 8 per hour	Midi / Zuid rail station (also calls at Central and Nord)	**401**
	Antwerpen	38 km	34 mins	Train: 2 per hour	Centraal	**420, 432**
OTP Bucuresti, Henri Coanda	Bucuresti	16 km	45 mins	🚌 **100**: ①–⑤ every 15 – 30 mins, ⑥⑦ every 20 – 30 mins	Piata Victoriei (800m from Nord station or 1 stop on subway)	
	Bucuresti	23 km	25 mins	Train: every 40 minutes	Main rail station	
BUD Budapest, Ferenc Liszt	Budapest	16 km	40 mins	🚌 100E: every 10 – 20 minutes	Nagyvárad-tér metro station (metro connection to city centre)	
	Budapest	18 km	25 mins	Train: 2 – 6 per hour	🚌 **200E**, to Ferihegy station then train to Nyugati rail station.	
BZG Bydgoszcz	Bydgoszcz	4 km	20 mins	🚌 **80**: 2 per hour	Main rail station	
CCF Carcassonne, Salvaza	Carcassonne	5 km	10 mins	🚌: Airport shuttle (connects with flights)	Place Davilla and Carcassonne rail station	
CWL Cardiff	Cardiff	19 km	80 mins	🚌 **304**: hourly	Central rail station, city centre	
	Cardiff	19 km	50 mins	🚌 **905** to Rhoose, then train: hourly	Central rail station	
CTA Catania Fontanarossa	Catania	5 km	9 mins	Train: hourly ± 2 per hour, 🚌 shuttle to station	Main rail station Catania Centrale, also Messina and Syracuse	**642**
CRL Charleroi, Brussels South	Brussels	55 km	60 mins	🚌 *Brussels City Shuttle*: every 30 minutes	Brussels Midi (corner of Rue de France / Rue de l'Instruction)	
	Charleroi	11 km	18 mins	🚌 *Line* **A1**: 2 per hour	Main rail station	
ORK Cork	Cork	8 km	25 mins	🚌 **225** , **226**: ①–⑥ 2 per hour, ⑦ hourly	Rail station, also Parnell Place bus station	
LDY Derry (Londonderry)	Londonderry	11 km	30 mins	🚌 **234** (check locally); **145** hourly (check locally)	Foyle Street bus station	
DNR Dinard Bretagne	St Malo	14 km	20 mins	Taxis only. Dinard 6 km 10 minutes		
DTM Dortmund, Wickede	Dortmund	10 km	25 mins;	🚌 AirportExpress: every hour	Main rail station (Hbf). Also 🚌 to Holzwickede rail station	
DRS Dresden	Dresden	15 km	21 mins	Train (S-Bahn **S2**): every 30 minutes	Main rail stations (Hbf and Neustadt)	**857a**
DUB Dublin	Dublin	11 km	60 mins	🚌 **782, 783, 784**: every 15 minutes	Bus station (Busáras) 30min, O'Connell St.	
	Belfast	157 km	130 mins	🚌 **705X**: 17 per day (0050 - 2250)	Glengall Street (City Centre) also serves Dublin city centre.	
DBV Dubrovnik, Čilipi	Dubrovnik	21 km	30 mins	🚌 *Platanus* Shuttle Bus: connects with flights	Bus station	
				🚌 **11, 27, 38**: limited services (check locally)	Molunat, Vitaljina and Gruda	
DUS Düsseldorf, International	Düsseldorf	7 km	12 mins	Train (S - Bahn **S11**): every 20 minutes	Main rail station (Hauptbahnhof)	**800, 802**
EMA East Midlands, Nottingham -	East Midlands	10 km	10 mins	Nottsbus On Demand connects with rail station	East Midlands Parkway rail station	
Leicester - Derby	Nottingham	21 km	55 mins	🚌 *Skylink* 24/7: every 30 minutes	Broadmarsh bus station	
	Derby	19 km	45 mins	🚌 *Skylink* 24/7: every 15 minutes	Bus station	
	Loughborough	8 km	25 mins	🚌 *Skylink* 24/7: every 20 minutes	Lemyngton Street / High Street	
	Leicester	23 km	55 mins	🚌 *Skylink* 24/7: every 20 minutes	St Margaret's bus station	
EDI Edinburgh	Edinburgh	11 km	25 mins	🚌 *Airlink* **100**: every 10 minutes 0400 - 0100 (every 20 minutes at other times)	Haymarket rail station; St Andrew Square (for Waverley station)	
	Edinburgh	11 km	35 mins	Tram: every 7 minutes 0626 - 1900, then every 10 minutes until 2248	Haymarket rail station; St Andrew Square (for Waverley station)	
ERF Erfurt - Weimer	Erfurt	6 km	25 mins	Tram Line 4: 6 per hour	Main rail station (Hauptbahnhof)	
EBJ Esbjerg	Esbjerg	12 km	21 mins	🚌 **7c / 944X**: hourly	*Bybusterminal*	
EXT Exeter	Exeter	8 km	35 mins	🚌 **4A**: 2 – 3 per hour	St Davids rail station (also limited service **43** to Pinhoe rail station)	
FAO Faro	Faro	6 km	20 mins	🚌 *Proxima* **16**: hourly	Rail station, Bus station	
FLR Firenze, Amerigo Vespucci	Firenze	7 km	20 mins	**Tram T2** ⑦–④ 0500 - 0030, ⑤⑥ 0500 - 0200.	Santa Maria Novella rail station	
HHN Frankfurt, Hahn	Frankfurt	120 km	130 mins	🚌 **Flibco**: Shuttle 8 – 9 each way daily.	Frankfurt Hauptbahnhof	
Also 🚌 to: Bullay Bahnhof (50 minutes), Kirchberg (25 minutes), Koblenz Hbf (90 minutes), Mainz (70 minutes) and Saarbrücken (75 minutes).						
FRA Frankfurt	Frankfurt	10 km	15 mins	Train (S-Bahn **S8** or **S9**): 4 – 6 times hourly	Main rail station (Hauptbahnhof)	**917a**
FDH Friedrichshafen	Friedrichshafen	4 km	7 mins	Train: 1 – 2 trains per hour	Main rail station (Stadt) or Harbour (Hafen)	
GDN Gdańsk, Lech Walesa	Gdańsk	10 km	22 mins	Train *PKM*: Port Lotniczy, 3 – 4 per hour	Wrzeszcz rail station, then 3 stops (every 15 mins) to Gjówny	
GVA Genève	Genève	6 km	6 mins	Train: 5 per hour	Cornavin rail station	**500, 570**
GOA Genova, Cristoforo Colombo	Genova	7 km	30 mins	🚌 *Volabus*: 1 – 2 per hour	Principe rail station	

‡ – The frequencies shown apply during daytime on weekdays and are from the airport to the city centre. There may be fewer journeys in the evenings, at weekends and during the winter months. Extended 🚌 journey times could apply during peak hours.

5 AIRPORT → CITY CENTRE LINKS

City plans are on pages 30 – 34

Airport code and name	City	Distance	Journey	Transport ‡	City terminal	Table
GRO Girona	Girona	12 km	25 mins	🚌: hourly	Rail / Bus station (Estación autobuses)	
	Barcelona	102 km	75 mins	🚌: **602** connects with flights	Estacio del Nord, next to Arco de Trifunfo	
GLA Glasgow, International	Glasgow	15 km	15 mins	🚌 **500**: every 12 minutes	St Vincent Street near Central rail station	
PIK Glasgow, Prestwick	Glasgow	61 km	40 mins	Train: 2 per hour, 0600 - 0015	Central rail station	**216**
GOT Göteborg, Landvetter	Göteborg	25 km	35 mins	🚌: VY Airport Coach 3 – 4 per hour, 0735 - 0030	Nils Ericson Terminalen (bus station) / Central rail station	
GRZ Graz	Graz	9 km	9 mins	Train **S5**: 1 – 2 per hour 0438 - 2238.	Main rail station (Hauptbahnhof)	**980**
GNB Grenoble, St Geoirs	Grenoble	37 km	45 mins	🚌 **Actibus**: connects with flights	Main rail station, also bus station	
HAM Hamburg, Fuhlsbüttel	Hamburg	11 km	25 mins	Train (S-Bahn **S1**): every 10 minutes	Main rail station (Hauptbahnhof)	
HAJ Hannover, Langenhagen	Hannover	15 km	18 mins	Train (S-Bahn **S5**): every 30 minutes	Main rail station (Hauptbahnhof)	**809**
HEL Helsinki, Vantaa	Helsinki	19 km	35 mins	Train: 4 – 6 per hour	Main rail station	
NOC Ireland West Airport Knock	Ballyhaunis	22 km	30 mins	🚌 **64**: up to 6 a day. 🚌 **440**: up to 4 a day.	Rail station **64** Ballyhaunis, **440** Claremorris	**235**
IOM Isle of Man, Ronaldsway	Douglas	16 km	30 mins	🚌 hourly (every 30 minutes during peak periods)	Lord street	
IST istanbul International	istanbul	43 km	60 mins	Metro **M11**: every 20 mins; 🚌 *HAVAIST* **5** Airport Shuttle	Gayrettepe Metro Sta. Esenler Intercity Bus Terminal (city centre)	
SAW İstanbul, Sabiha Gökcen	İstanbul	32 km	60 mins	🚌: 1 – 2 per hour, 0540 - 2040	Bus station. Also Pendik rail station is 4km from airport	
XRY Jerez	Jerez	10 km	9 mins	Train **C-1**: 3 trains per day	Jerez de la Frontera, then to Cadiz	**671**
FKB Karlsruhe - Baden-Baden	Baden-Baden	8 km	15 mins	🚌 **215** hourly to Baden-Baden	Rail station; also **234, X34** to Rastatt rail station	
KTW Katowice, Pyrzowice	Katowice	34 km	50 mins	🚌 *ZTM*: **AP3** 1 – 2 per hour approx.	Katowice Dworzec (main rail station)	
KUN Kaunas	Kaunas	13 km	40 mins	🚌 **29G** 1 – 2 per hour 0521 - 0115	City centre, bus and railway stations	
	Vilnius	102 km	85 mins	🚌 connects with flights	Seinu Street, in front of McDonald's restaurant	
KLU Klagenfurt	Klagenfurt	5 km	25 mins	🚌 **4** (or walk to Annabichl rail station, then train or 🚌 **40**)	Main rail station and bus station	
CPH København, Kastrup	København	12 km	13 mins	Train: every 20 minutes	Main rail station (Hovedbanegård)	**700, 703**
	Malmö	36 km	26 mins	Train: every 20 minutes	Central rail station	**703**
CGN Köln / Bonn, Konrad Adenauer	Bonn	25 km	32 mins	🚌 **SB60**: 2 per hour	Main rail station (Hauptbahnhof)	
	Köln	15 km	16 mins	Train **S19**	Main rail station (Hbf). Also to Mönchengladbach, Koblenz	**802**
KRK Kraków John Paul II Airport (Balice)	Kraków	12 km	17 mins	Train: 2 per hour, from Lotnisko station	Kraków Gjówny	**1099**
KUT Kutaisi	Kutaisi	23 km	30 mins	Airport shuttle 🚌 to Kopitnari rail station, every 2 hours	Kopitnari rail station services to Kutaisi	**1590**
KBP Kyiv, Boryspil	Kyiv	34 km	40 mins	Train: 1 – 2 per hour	Main rail station **Airport Temporarily Closed**	
LBA Leeds - Bradford	Leeds	16 km	45 mins	🚌 *Flyer* **A1**: every 30 minutes	Main rail station and bus station	
	Bradford	11 km	40 mins	🚌 *Flyer* **A2, A3**: 1 per hour each service	Interchange rail station	
LEJ Leipzig - Halle	Leipzig	20 km	14 mins	Train: 2 per hour	Main rail station (Hauptbahnhof)	**866, 881**
	Halle	18 km	12 mins	Train: 2 per hour	Main rail station (Hauptbahnhof)	**866, 881**
LNZ Linz, Blue Danube	Linz	12 km	22 mins	🚌 **601:** 1 – 2 per hour 0530 - 2328	Main rail station. Also free 🚌 to Hörsching rail station, 3 mins	
LIS Lisboa, Portela	Lisboa	3 km	20 mins	Train (metro), Red (Vermelho) line: every 6 – 10 mins	Oriente rail station. For Santa Apolónia change at São Sebastião	
LPL Liverpool, John Lennon	Liverpool	11 km	37 mins	🚌 **500**: every 30 minutes 0400 - 2400	Lime Street rail station, Liverpool One bus station	
LJU Ljubljana, Jože Pučnik, Brnik	Ljubljana	26 km	45 mins	🚌: 1 – 2 per hour 0709 - 2100	Bus station (Avtobusna postaja)	
LCJ Jódź, Lublinek	Jódź	6 km	20 mins	🚌 **65A, 65B**	Kaliska rail station	
LCY London, City	London	12 km	25 mins	Train (Docklands Light Railway): every 7 – 10 mins	Bank underground (tube) station	**100**
LGW London, Gatwick	London	44 km	30 mins	Train *Gatwick Express*: every 15 minutes	Victoria rail station	**100, 102, 103, 185**
LHR London, Heathrow	London	24 km	15 mins	Train *Heathrow Express*: every 15 minutes	Paddington rail station	**100**
	London	24 km	26 mins	Train *Elizabeth Line*: every 15 minutes	Paddington and Liverpool Street rail stations	**100**
	London	24 km	58 mins	Underground train (tube): every 6 – 12 minutes	King's Cross St Pancras rail station	**100**
LTN London, Luton	London	50 km	35 mins	DART * to Parkway rail station, then train: 6 – 7 per hour	St Pancras International rail station	**100, 103, 170a**
SEN London, Southend	London	64 km	55 mins	Train: 3 per hour	Liverpool Street rail station	
STN London, Stansted	London	55 km	46 mins	Train *Stansted Express*: every 15 minutes	Liverpool Street rail station	**100**
LBC Lübeck, Blankensee	Lübeck	8 km	30 mins	Train: hourly 0500 - 0140, 🚌 **6**: 2 per hour.	Lübeck Hbf. Bus station (bus stop 5).	**827**
LUZ Lublin	Lublin	10 km	15 mins	Train: up to 14 per day	Main rail station	
LUX Luxembourg, Findel	Luxembourg	7 km	31 mins	Tram: Every 8 – 10 minutes	Central rail station	
LWO Lviv Danylo Halytskyi	Lviv	10 km	25 mins	Trolleybus **29**: every 9 – 16 minutes 0600 - 2215	City Centre **Airport Temporarily Closed**	
LYS Lyon, St Exupéry	Lyon	23 km	30 mins	Tram *RhôneExpress*: 2 per hour (4 per hour peak)	Part Dieu rail station	
	Chambéry	87 km	60 mins	🚌 Flixbus: 2 per day	Bus station (gare routière)	
	Grenoble	91 km	65 mins	🚌 Flixbus: hourly 0630 - 2330	Bus station (gare routière); Place de la Grenoble	
MAD Madrid, Barajas T4	Madrid	12 km	16 mins	Cercanías train from T4: every 15 – 20 minutes 0602 - 2225	Chamartín, also Atocha 29 mins. 🚌 from T4 to T1, T2 and T3.	
AGP Málaga	Málaga	8 km	12 mins	Train: every 30 minutes	María Zambrano (Renfe) and Centro-Alameda rail stations	**662**
MMX Malmö, Sturup	Malmö	30 km	40 mins	🚌 *flygbussarna*: 10 per day 0825 - 2300	Central rail station	
MAN Manchester	Manchester	16 km	20 mins	Train: every 10 minutes 0419 - 0038	Piccadilly rail station	**150, 154, 156, 163, 188, 193**
MRS Marseille, Provence	Marseille	28 km	25 mins	🚌 6: every 10 minutes (see also 🚌 / rail in Table **351**)	St Charles rail station; also 🚌 to Aix TGV station every 30 mins	
FMM Memmingen	Memmingen	5 km	10 mins	🚌 *Airport Shuttle* **2, 810A**	Bus station and rail station; also 🚌 to München (80 minutes)	
LIN Milano, Linate	Milano	9 km	20 mins	1) *Metro* **M4** 2) 🚌 *Starfly*: every 30 minutes	1) Central Milano 2) Centrale rail station	
MXP Milano, Malpensa	Milano	45 km	40 mins	Train: 1) Malpensa Express: every 30 mins 2) 1 – 2 per hour	1) Cadorna and Bovisa rail stations; 2) Centrale rail station	**606**
		45 km	50 mins	🚌 *Bus Express, Air Pullman, Terravision, Caronte*	Every 20 minutes to Centrale rail station.	
BGY Milano, Orio al Serio, Bergamo	Milano	45 km	60 mins	🚌 1 – 2 per hour	Centrale rail station (Air Terminal)	
	Bergamo	4 km	10 mins	🚌 **ATB 1**: 2 per hour	Rail station	
MSQ Minsk	Minsk	42 km	45 mins	🚌 *Aeroexpress* **1400, 1430**	Vostochniy and Moskovskiy bus stations	
DME Moskva, Domodedovo	Moskva	35 km	47 mins	Train, *Aeroexpress*: 1 – 2 per hour approx.	Paveletskaya rail station §	**1901**
SVO Moskva, Sheremetyevo	Moskva	35 km	35 mins	Train, *Aeroexpress*: 1 – 2 per hour approx.	Belorusskaya rail station §	**1901**
VKO Moskva, Vnukovo	Moskva	28 km	40 mins	Train, *Aeroexpress*: 1 per hour approx.	Kiyevskaya rail station §	**1901**
MUC München, International	München	37 km	40 mins	Train: **S1, S8** for Hbf every 10 mins; **S8** for Ost every 20 mins	Main rail stations (Hauptbahnhof, Ostbahnhof)	**892**
	Freising	6 km	10 mins	Train: hourly 0826 - 2247	Rail station for Regensburg and connections to Passau	**892, 878**
RMU Murcia, Corvera	Murcia	25km	30 mins	🚌 6 per day (seasonal service June - Oct.)	City centre	
NTE Nantes, Atlantique	Nantes	9 km	20 mins	🚌 *Shuttle*: 0515 - 0000	Main rail station	
NAP Napoli, Capodichino	Napoli	7 km	15 mins	🚌 *Alibus*: 2 per hour, 0530 - 0000	Piazza Garibaldi (Centrale rail station)	

‡ – The frequencies shown apply during daytime on weekdays and are from the airport to the city centre. There may be fewer journeys in the evenings, at weekends and during the winter months. Extended 🚌 journey times could apply during peak hours.

* – DART is an automated people mover operating between the airport terminal and Luton Airport Parkway station. Combined rail / DART tickets available.

¶ – Graz Airport - Feldkirchen rail station is located about 300 metres away from the airport.

§ – No updates until further notice.

City plans are on pages 30–34

AIRPORT → CITY CENTRE LINKS 5

Airport code and name	City	Distance	Journey	Transport ‡	City terminal	Table
NCL Newcastle, International	Newcastle	9 km	25 mins	Metro train: every 12 minutes	Main rail station	
NCE Nice, Côte d'Azur	Nice	5 km	7 mins	Train from Nice St Augustin (see note ◧)	SNCF station	361
		7 km	24 mins	Tram **2**: every 8–12 minutes	Magnan (Central Nice), Durandy (Nice Ville)	
FNI Nîmes-Arles-Camargue	Nîmes	12 km	25 mins	🚌 shuttle from Nîmes bus station 2–3 per day	Bus station	
NWI Norwich	Norwich	8 km	24 mins	🚌 **501**: 3 per hour; **35**: hourly	Bus station **501**; rail station **35**	
NUE Nürnberg	Nürnberg	6 km	12 mins	Train U-bahn **U2**: every 10 minutes	Main rail station (Hauptbahnhof)	
ODS Odesa	Odesa	9 km	50 mins	🚌 **117**: every 20 minutes; Trolleybus **14** (0700 - 2000)	Rail station **Airport Temporarily Closed**	
OSL Oslo, Gardermoen	Oslo	49 km	20 mins	Train *Flytoget*: 3 per hour	Central rail station	771
TRF Oslo, Sandefjord Torp	Oslo	123 km	116 mins	🚌 to Torp rail station (4 minutes), then train to Oslo	Also 🚌 to Oslo Bus terminal	783
OSR Ostrava, Leoš Janáček	Ostrava	31km	31 mins	Train **S4**: 7 per day, 🚌 Lines **AE, 333 670, 331, 632**	Ostrava hlavní	
PMO Palermo, Falcone-Borsellino	Palermo	24 km	45 mins	Train *Trinacria express*: 1–2 per hour	Centrale rail station	
PMI Palma, Mallorca	Palma	11 km	30 mins	🚌 **A1**: every 30 minutes	Paseo de Mallorca, Placa d'Espanya (for rail stations), the Port	
BVA Paris, Beauvais	Paris	80 km	30 mins	🚌 **6**: every hour; **A01**: 6 per day, also shuttle to Paris.	Beauvais rail station	
CDG Paris, Charles de Gaulle	Paris	25 km	35 mins	RER train (Line B): every 7–15 minutes	Nord, Châtelet Les Halles, and St Michel rail stations	398
	Disneyland	23 km	45 mins	🚌 **VEA** Magical Navette / Shuttle: every 20 minutes	Disneyland Resort, Disneyland hotels	
ORY Paris, Orly	Paris	15 km	31 mins	Metro train: (Line 14) every 6–15 minutes	Bercy, Gare de Lyon and Gare St Lazare rail stations	398
	Paris	15 km	35 mins	🚌 to Pont de Rungis, then RER train line **C**: 4 per hour	Austerlitz, St Michel, Musée d'Orsay and Invalides rail stations	
	Paris	15 km	35 mins	ORLYVAL shuttle to Antony then RER train line **B**: 4 per hour	Châlet-Les-Halles and Nord rail stations	398
PGF Perpignan, Rivesaltes	Perpignan	5 km	15 mins	🚌 hourly service	Rail station, bus station (gare routière)	
PSA Pisa, Galileo Galilei	Pisa	2 km	5 mins	People Mover: every 5–8 minutes 0600 - 0000	Centrale rail station	
OPO Porto	Porto	17 km	35 mins	Metro Train: Line E (Purple), 2–3 per hour	Campanhã rail station	
POZ Poznań, Jawica	Poznań	6 km	21 mins	🚌 **159** *MPK*: 2–4 per hour	Rail station (Gjówny)	
PRG Praha, Václav Havel	Praha	24 km	40 mins	🚌 **AE** *Airport Express*: every 20–30 mins 0530 - 2200	Hlavní rail station	
	Praha	17 km	60 mins	🚌 **59**: every 7–10 mins (0423 - 2332}	Nádraží Veleslavín metro station, then Metro line A to muzeum	
PUY Pula	Pula	6 km	15 mins	🚌 connects with flights	Main bus station	
REU Reus	Reus	6 km	11 mins	🚌 **L50** *Hispano Igualadina*: hourly 0800 - 2100	Rail station	652
	Barcelona	90 km	90 mins	🚌 *Hispano Igualadina* connects with flights	Sants rail station	
KEF Reykjavík, Keflavík	Reykjavík	50 km	45 mins	🚌 *flybus* connects with all flights	BSÍ bus terminal	
RIX Riga	Riga	13 km	30 mins	🚌 **22**: every 10–30 minutes	Abrenes iela (street) next to rail station	
RJK Rijeka	Rijeka	30 km	45 mins	🚌 *Olivari Bus* runs regular shuttle services	Bus stations at Rijeka, Omisalj and Kraljevica	
CIA Roma, Ciampino	Roma	15 km	35 mins	🚌 *Airlink*: 1–3 per hour, to Ciampino, then train	Termini rail station	622
FCO Roma, Fiumicino	Roma	26 km	42 mins	Train: 4 per hour	Ostiense and Tiburtina rail stations	622
(also known as Leonardo da Vinci)		26 km	32 mins	Train *Leonardo Express*: every 15 minutes (0608 - 2323)	Termini rail station	622
RTM Rotterdam The Hague	Rotterdam	5 km	30 mins	*Airport Shuttle* **33**: every 15 minutes	Groot Handelsgebouw (adjacent to Centraal rail station)	
RZE Rzeszów, Jasionka	Rzeszów	15 km	20 mins	🚌 ZTM **51**, PKS **224**, **MKS 224, 225**: connects with flights	Main rail station and bus station	
LED St Peterburg, Pulkovo II	St Peterburg	17 km	60 mins	🚌 **39, 39Ex** §	Moskovskaya Metro station, Line 2 for Nevski Pr. (see City Plans)	
SZG Salzburg, W. A. Mozart	Salzburg	5 km	22 mins	🚌 **2**: every 15–20 minutes	Main rail station	
SIP Simferopol	Simferopol	12 km	28 mins	🚌 **49a, 20** (trolleybus): every 10–15 minutes	Main rail station	
SKP Skopje, International	Skopje	14 km	25 mins	🚌 Airport Shuttle Service: 6–8 per day	Bus station	
SOF Sofia, International	Sofia	10 km	26 mins	Train Line **1**: from Terminal 2, every 10 minutes	City centre. Change at Serdika for Line **2**, for Central rail station	
SOU Southampton	Southampton	8 km	8 mins	Train: 50 metres from terminal, 4 trains per hour	Central rail station	105, 107
SPU Split, Kaštela	Split	16 km	50 mins	🚌: connects with flights (Croatia Airlines)	Bus station. Departs 200m from Airport terminal	
SVG Stavanger, Sola	Stavanger	14 km	40 mins	🚌: *Flybussen* every 20 minutes 0725–1905.	Bus station	
ARN Stockholm, Arlanda	Stockholm	44 km	20 mins	*Arlanda Express* train: every 15 minutes	Central rail station	747, 760
NYO Stockholm, Skavsta	Stockholm	103 km	80 mins	🚌: connects with flights	Cityterminal (bus station), also 🚌 to Nyköping rail station	
VST Stockholm, Västerås	Stockholm	107 km	75 mins	🚌: connects with flights	Cityterminal (bus station), also 🚌 **3** to Västerås rail station	
SXB Strasbourg, Entzheim	Strasbourg	10 km	8 mins	Train: from Entzheim Aéroport (300m walk) 1–5 per hour	Gare Centrale (Central rail station)	382
STR Stuttgart, Echterdingen	Stuttgart	20 km	27 mins	Train (S-Bahn **S2, S3**): 2–4 per hour	Main rail station (Hauptbahnhof)	936a
SZZ Szczecin, Goleniów	Szczecin	35 km	40 mins	Train: 14–20 per day.	Szczecin Gjówny.	
TLL Tallinn, Ülemiste	Tallinn	5 km	27 mins	🚌: various frequent services 0600 - 0000	Balti jaam (rail station)	
TMP Tampere, Pirkkala	Tampere	18 km	25 mins	🚌: **103** connects with flights	Main rail and bus station	
TBS Tbilisi	Tbilisi	19 km	35 mins	Train	Rail station	
TIA Tirana (Tiranë), Nënë Tereza	Tirana	12 km	45 mins	🚌 LU-NA shpk: every hour (24 hour service)	National Theatre of Opera	
TRN Torino, Caselle	Torino	16 km	20 mins	*GTT* train: every 30 minutes	Torino Porta Susa rail station. Change at Venaria for 🚌 **SF2**	
	Torino	16 km	25 mins	🚌: *Flibco* half-hourly 0430 - 2359,	Central Bus Station	
TLS Toulouse, Blagnac	Toulouse	8 km	38 mins	Tram **T2**: **closed until Dec. 2026** – until then use 🚌 **30** to	connect with tram line **T1** at Blagnac	
	Toulouse	8 km	20 mins	🚌: Shuttle Bus every 20 minutes	Place Jeanne d'Arc / Matabiau rail / bus station (gare routière)	
TRS Trieste, Ronchi dei Legionari	Trieste	33 km	29 mins	Train: hourly	Rail station	601
	Monfalcone	5 km	6 mins	Train: hourly	Rail station	601
TRD Trondheim, Værnes	Trondheim	33 km	37 mins	Train: hourly	Rail station. Værnes rail station is 220m from Airport terminal	787
VLC València	València	9 km	22 mins	Train Lines **3, 5**: every 15 minutes	Xátiva for Nord rail station	
VCE Venezia, Marco Polo	Venezia	12 km	25 mins	🚌 **5**: 3–4 per hour, **35**: 2 per hour	**35** Piazzale Roma (see city plans p32), **5**: Venezia Corsia	
	Venezia		80 mins	Waterbus *Alilaguna*: ± every 30 minutes	Lido 53-63 mins / Piazza S. Marco, 72-80 mins	
TSF Venezia, Treviso	Venezia	30 km	70 mins	🚌: *ATVO and Barzi connects* with flights	Mestre rail station, Piazzale Roma (see city plans p32)	
VRN Verona, Villafranca	Verona	12 km	15 mins	🚌 **199**: every 20 minutes 0535 - 2330	Rail station	
VNO Vilnius	Vilnius	4 km	7 mins	Train: every ± 40 minutes	Rail station	1815
WAW Warszawa, Frederic Chopin, Okęcie	Warszawa	13 km	23 mins	SKM / KM train: 3–5 per hour	Śródmieście (2–3 per hr) or Centralna (1–2 per hr)	1099
WMI Warszawa, Modlin	Warszawa	40 km	59 mins	🚌 to Modlin rail stn, then train: approx. 1–3 per hour	Centralna or Gdánska rail stations	1099
NRN Weeze, Niederhein	Düsseldorf	74 km	82 mins	🚌 **SW1**: to Weeze rail station, then train	Main rail station (Hauptbahnhof)	802
VIE Wien, Schwechat	Wien	21 km	16 mins	*City Airport Train (CAT)*: every 30 minutes (special fares)	Mitte rail station	985
	Wien	21 km	25 mins	S-bahn: every 30 minutes	Mitte rail station	985
	Bratislava	54 km	60 mins	🚌 *Slovak Lines*, hourly	AS Mlynské nivy (bus station) / Einsteinnova/Petrzalka	985
WRO Wrocjaw, Copernicus	Wrocjaw	10 km	50 mins	🚌 **106**: every 15 minutes	Rail station, bus station	
ZAG Zagreb	Zagreb	17 km	40 mins	🚌: 1–2 per hour connects with flights	Bus station (Autobusni kolodvor), Avenija Marina Drzica	
ZAZ Zaragoza	Zaragoza	10 km	30 mins	🚌: 1–2 per hour 0615 - 2315	Paseo María Agustín, 150m from Portillo rail station	
ZRH Zürich	Zürich	10 km	13 mins	Train: 7–8 per hour	Main rail station (HB)	500, 510, 530, 535, 555, 560

◧ – Nice St Augustin station is approximately 800m from Terminal 1.

‡ – The frequencies shown apply during daytime on weekdays and are from the airport to the city centre. There may be fewer journeys in the evenings, at weekends and during the winter months. Extended 🚌 journey times could apply during peak hours.

§ – No updates until further notice.

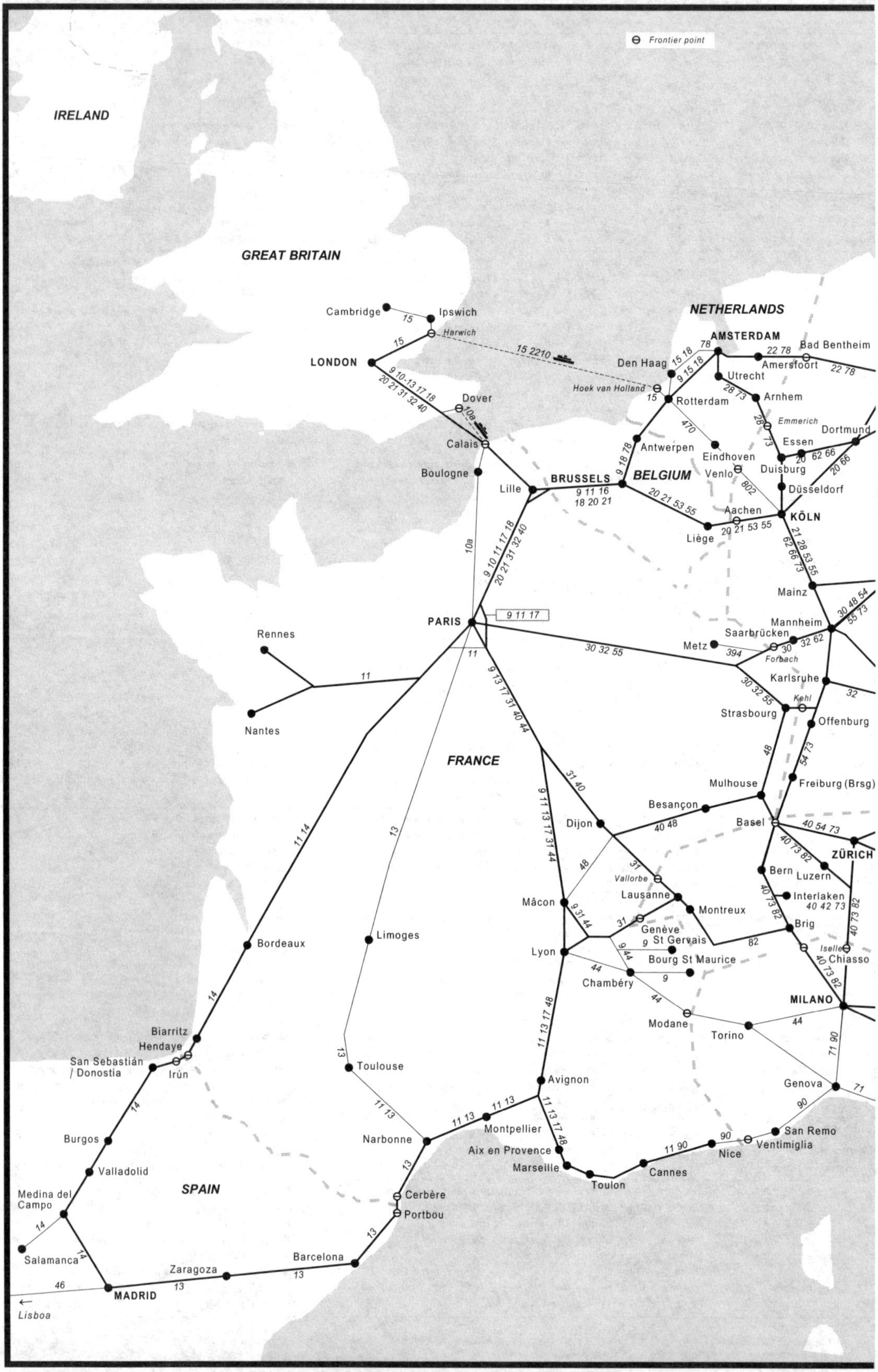
Frontier point
IRELAND
GREAT BRITAIN
NETHERLANDS
BELGIUM
FRANCE
SPAIN
Cambridge
Ipswich
Harwich
LONDON
Dover
Calais
Boulogne
Lille
BRUSSELS
Hoek van Holland
Den Haag
AMSTERDAM
Amersfoort
Bad Bentheim
Utrecht
Rotterdam
Arnhem
Emmerich
Antwerpen
Eindhoven
Venlo
Essen
Dortmund
Duisburg
Düsseldorf
Aachen
Liège
KÖLN
Mainz
Mannheim
Saarbrücken
Forbach
Metz
Karlsruhe
Kehl
Strasbourg
Offenburg
Freiburg (Brsg)
Mulhouse
Basel
ZÜRICH
Bern
Luzern
Interlaken
Brig
Iselle
Chiasso
MILANO
PARIS
Rennes
Nantes
Besançon
Dijon
Vallorbe
Lausanne
Montreux
Genève
St Gervais
Bourg St Maurice
Mâcon
Lyon
Chambéry
Modane
Torino
Genova
Avignon
Montpellier
Aix en Provence
Marseille
Toulon
Cannes
Nice
Ventimiglia
San Remo
Limoges
Bordeaux
Toulouse
Narbonne
Cerbère
Portbou
Biarritz
Hendaye
Irún
San Sebastián / Donostia
Burgos
Valladolid
Medina del Campo
Salamanca
MADRID
Zaragoza
Barcelona
Lisboa

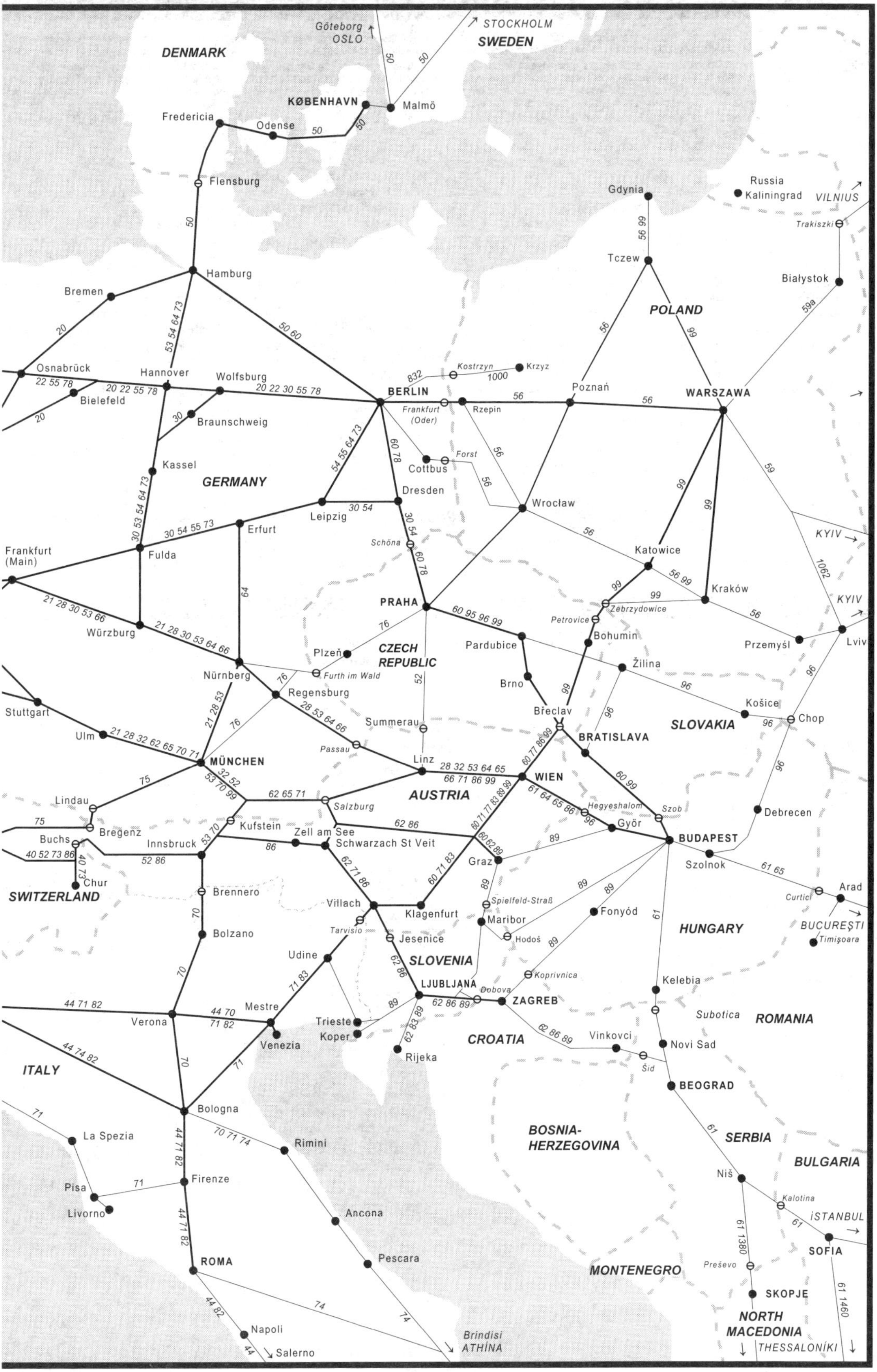
Göteborg
OSLO
STOCKHOLM
SWEDEN
DENMARK
KØBENHAVN
Malmö
Fredericia
Odense
Flensburg
Hamburg
Bremen
Osnabrück
Hannover
Wolfsburg
Bielefeld
Braunschweig
BERLIN
Kostrzyn
Krzyz
Frankfurt (Oder)
Rzepin
Forst
Cottbus
Kassel
GERMANY
Dresden
Leipzig
Erfurt
Fulda
Frankfurt (Main)
Schöna
Würzburg
PRAHA
CZECH REPUBLIC
Plzeň
Furth im Wald
Nürnberg
Regensburg
Stuttgart
Ulm
Summerau
Passau
Linz
MÜNCHEN
Salzburg
AUSTRIA
Lindau
Bregenz
Buchs
Chur
SWITZERLAND
Innsbruck
Kufstein
Zell am See
Schwarzach St Veit
WIEN
Graz
Villach
Klagenfurt
Brennero
Bolzano
Tarvisio
Jesenice
SLOVENIA
Udine
LJUBLJANA
Dobova
ZAGREB
Trieste
Koper
Rijeka
Verona
Mestre
Venezia
ITALY
Bologna
La Spezia
Pisa
Livorno
Firenze
Rimini
Ancona
Pescara
ROMA
Napoli
Salerno
Brindisi
ATHÍNA
CROATIA
Vinkovci
Šid
BOSNIA-HERZEGOVINA
MONTENEGRO
Gdynia
Russia
Kaliningrad
VILNIUS
Trakiszki
Tczew
Białystok
POLAND
Poznań
WARSZAWA
Wrocław
Katowice
Kraków
Zebrzydowice
Petrovice
Bohumin
Pardubice
Brno
Břeclav
Žilina
BRATISLAVA
SLOVAKIA
Košice
Chop
Przemyśl
Lviv
KYIV
Hegyeshalom
Szob
Győr
BUDAPEST
Szolnok
Debrecen
Curtici
Arad
BUCUREŞTI
Timişoara
HUNGARY
Spielfeld-Straß
Maribor
Hodoš
Fonyód
Koprivnica
Kelebia
Subotica
ROMANIA
Novi Sad
BEOGRAD
SERBIA
BULGARIA
Niš
Kalotina
İSTANBUL
SOFIA
Preševo
SKOPJE
NORTH MACEDONIA
THESSALONÍKI

INTERNATIONAL SERVICES

Services All trains convey first and second classes of seating accommodation unless otherwise noted. For information on types of sleeping car (🛏) and couchette car (🛏) see page 10. Restaurant (✕) and buffet (🍷) cars vary considerably from country to country in standard of service offered. The catering car may not be carried or open for the whole journey.

Timings **Valid June 15 - December 13, 2025, unless otherwise stated. Note that long-distance services in Germany are subject to frequent variations - please refer to the German section for more details.** Services can change at short notice and passengers are advised to consult the latest European Rail Timetable before travelling. International trains are not normally affected by public holidays, but may alter at Christmas and Easter - these changes (where known) are shown in the tables. Readers are advised to cross-check timings and days of running of services in the International section with the relevant country section.

Tickets **Seat reservations** are available for most international trains and are advisable as some trains can get very crowded. **Supplements** are payable on **EuroCity** (*EC*) trains in most countries and on most InterCity trains – consult the introduction at the start of each country to see which supplements apply.

AP	***Alfa Pendular***	Portuguese high-quality tilting express train.
Alvia	***Alvia***	Spanish high-speed train.
AVE	***Alta Velocidad Española***	Spanish high-speed train.
avlo	***avlo***	Spanish low-cost high-speed train.
D	***Durchgangszug*** or ***Schnellzug***	Overnight or international express. Some may only convey passengers to international destinations and are likely to be compulsory reservation, marked [R].
EC	***EuroCity***	Quality international express. Supplement may be payable.
ECD	***Eurocity Direct***	Dutch / Belgian international express.
Em	***Euromed***	Spanish 200 km/h train.
EN	***EuroNight***	International overnight express.
ES	***European Sleeper***	International overnight service.
☆	***Eurostar***	High-speed international train with three classes of service: Eurostar Premium, Eurostar Plus and Eurostar Standard.
FA	***Frecciargento***	Italian tilting trains using both high-speed and traditional lines.
FB	***Frecciabianca***	Italian fast premium fare services using traditional lines.
FR	***Frecciarossa***	Italian fast premium fare services using high-speed lines.
Ex	***Express***	Express between Czech Republic and Slovakia.
IC	***InterCity***	Express train. Supplement may be payable.
ICE	***InterCity Express***	German high-speed (230 - 320 km/h) service.
ICN	***InterCity Notte***	Italian overnight train, supplement payable.
IR	***InterRegio***	Inter-regional express usually with refurbished coaches.
IRE	***Interregio-Express***	German / Polish train.
ITA	***.italo***	Italian high-speed train. Supplement payable.
LE	***Leo Express***	Czech open-access quality international express with three classes of service (Premium, Business and Economy).
NJ	***ÖBB nightjet***	Austrian brand name covering international services. Facilities include *Comfortline Deluxe* sleeping cars and new generation sleeping cars and couchettes.
Ouigo	***Ouigo***	French or Spanish low-cost high-speed train.
RJ or *RJX*	***Railjet***	Austrian quality international express with three classes of service (Business, First and Economy).
RE	***Regional Express***	Regional semi-fast train.
REX	***Regional Express***	Austrian semi-fast train.
SC	***SuperCity***	Czech Pendolino tilting train, supplement payable.
ST	***Snälltåget***	Swedish open-access operator.
TGV	***Train à Grande Vitesse***	French high-speed train.
TLK	***Twoje Linie Kolejowe***	Polish long-distance train.
Sn	***Snabbtåg***	Swedish high-speed train.
♥	***Regiojet***	Czech open-access operator.

LeShuttle

The frequent car-carrying service between Folkestone and Calais through the **Channel Tunnel** is operated by Eurotunnel under the name of LeShuttle. The service operates up to four times hourly (hourly at night) and takes about 35 minutes. Passengers stay with their cars during the journey. Separate less-frequent trains operate for lorries, coaches, motorcycles, and cars with caravans. Reservations are advisable but passengers can buy tickets at the toll booths when they arrive at the terminal and board the next available shuttle. Book at www.leshuttle.com.

9 LONDON, AMSTERDAM, BRUSSELS and LILLE - ST GERVAIS and BOURG ST MAURICE

Eurostar trains Amsterdam, Brussels and Lille - Bourg St Maurice and v.v. are named EUROSTAR SNOW. Other connections are available by changing in Paris, or in Lille and Lyon. Timings may vary by a few minutes - please check your reservation.

Winter 2024/2025 service (except London - Bourg St Maurice service)

train type		*TGV*	*TGV*	*TGV*	☆	☆	☆	☆	☆	☆
train number		**5190**	**5116**	**5108**	**9904**	**9920**	**9920**	**9110**	**9116**	**9928**
train number					**9906**	**9924**	**9924**			**9929**
notes		[R] 🍷	[R] 🍷	[R] 🍷	[R] 🍷	[R] 🍷	[R] 🍷	[R] 🍷	[R] 🍷	[R] 🍷
notes		**A**	⑥**B**	⑥**C**	**D**	⑥**E**	⑥**F**	⑥**G**	⑥**H**	⑥**H**
London St Pancras	d.	...	...	...	...	...	...	0704	0901	...
Amsterdam Centraal	d.	...	...	...	...	0539	...	|	|	...
Schiphol ✈	d.	...	...	...	...	|	...	|	|	...
Rotterdam CS	d.	...	...	...	...	0625	...	|	|	...
Antwerpen Centraal	d.	...	...	...	...	0703	...	|	|	...
Brussels Midi / Zuid	d.	...	...	...	0709	0752	0752	|	|	...
Lille Europe	d.	...	...	0706	|	|	|	0926	1126	1150
Lille Flandres	d.	0520	0611	|	|	|	|	...	...	|
Douai	d.	0550	0633	|	|	|	|	...	...	|
Arras	d.	0611	0652	|	|	|	|	...	...	|
TGV Haute Picardie	d.	0631	0717	0743	|	|	|	...	...	|
Paris Charles de Gaulle ✈	d.	0708	0755	0833	|	|	|	...	...	|
Marne la Valleé Chessy	d.	0726	0812	0850	|	|	|	...	...	|
Cluses (Haute Savoie)	a.	|	|	1317	|	|	|	...	...	|
Salanches Megève	a.	|	|	1334	|	|	|	...	...	|
St Gervais ◧	a.	|	|	1346	|	|	|	...	...	|
Chambéry	a.	1030	1106	...	1154	1225	1225	...	...	1543
Albertville	a.	1106	1149	...	1236	1304	1304	...	...	1626
Moûtiers-Salins	a.	1147	1221	...	1317	1356	1356	...	...	1700
Aime la Plagne	a.	1208	1244	...	1338	1420	1420	...	...	1723
Landry	a.	1218	1256	...	1349	1431	1431	...	...	1734
Bourg St Maurice	a.	1231	1308	...	1406	1441	1441	...	...	1745

train type		☆	☆	*TGV*	☆	☆	*TGV*	☆	*TGV*	☆
train number		**9966**	**9153**	**5174**	**9982**	**9163**	**5196**	**9979**	**5178**	**9967**
train number		**9967**			**9983**			**9987**		**9969**
notes		[R] 🍷	[R] 🍷	[R] 🍷	[R] 🍷	[R] 🍷	[R] 🍷	[R] 🍷	[R] 🍷	[R] 🍷
notes		⑦**K**	⑦**K**	⑥**B**	⑥**P**	⑥**P**	**A**	⑥**L**	⑥**C**	**D**
Bourg St Maurice	d.	1109	...	1343	1400	...	1454	1530	...	1620
Landry	d.	1120	...	1352	1412	...	1503	1542	...	1631
Aime la Plagne	d.	1132	...	1403	1424	...	1513	1553	...	1642
Moûtiers-Salins	d.	1150	...	1419	1442	...	1535	1611	...	1705
Albertville	d.	1125	...	1457	1515	...	1609	1645	...	1748
Chambéry	d.	1315	...	1554	1610	...	1653	1740	...	1841
St Gervais ◧	d.	|	...	|	|	...	|	|	1600	|
Salanches Megève	d.	|	...	|	|	...	|	|	1610	|
Cluses (Haute Savoie)	d.	|	...	|	|	...	|	|	1630	|
Marne la Vallée Chessy	a.	|	...	1843	|	...	1947	|	2115	|
Paris Charles de Gaulle ✈	a.	|	...	1919	|	...	2003	|	2136	|
TGV Haute Picardie	a.	|	...	2007	|	...	2036	|	2212	|
Arras	a.	|	...	2030	|	...	2056	|	|	|
Douai	a.	|	...	2050	|	...	2112	|	|	|
Lille Flandres	a.	|	...	2117	|	...	2134	|	|	|
Lille Europe	a.	1718	1835	...	2000	2100	...	|	2242	|
Brussels Midi / Zuid	a.	...	|	...	...	|	...	2205	...	2306
Antwerpen Centraal	a.	...	|	...	...	|	...	2257	...	...
Rotterdam CS	a.	...	|	...	...	|	...	2333	...	...
Schiphol ✈	a.	...	|	...	...	|	...	|	...	...
Amsterdam Centraal	a.	...	|	...	...	|	...	0015	...	...
London St Pancras	a.	...	1900	...	...	2127	...	...	...	...

A – Dec. 21, 28, Jan. 4, Feb. 8, 15, 22.
B – ⑥ Dec. 21 - Mar. 29.
C – ⑥ Feb. 8 – 22.
D – Dec. 28, Jan. 4, Feb. 22, Mar. 1, 8.
E – ⑥ until Mar. 22 (also Apr. 5).
F – ⑥ Dec. 21 - Apr. 12.
G – ⑥ Jan. 11 - Mar. 1.
H – ⑥ Dec. 20, 2025 - Mar. 28, 2026.
J – ⑥ Dec. 21 - Mar. 1.
K – ⑦ Dec. 21, 2025 - Mar. 29, 2026.
L – ⑥ Dec. 28 - Apr. 12.
P – ⑥ Dec. 27, 2025 - Apr. 4, 2026.

◧ – Full name is St Gervais-les-Bains-le-Fayet.

☆ – *Eurostar* high-speed train. [R]. 🍷.
TGV – French high-speed train. [R]. 🍷.

LONDON - LILLE, PARIS, BRUSSELS and AMSTERDAM *by Eurostar* 10

All Eurostar services are 🅁 and special fares are payable. Three classes of service are available: Eurostar Premium, Eurostar Plus and Eurostar Standard.
All times shown are local times (France and Belgium are one hour ahead of Great Britain). ✕ available in Eurostar Premium and Eurostar Plus, 🍸 in Eurostar Standard.

SERVICE MAY 18 - JULY 19. See page 48 for service July 20 - September 6.

km																							
	train number	**9080**	**9106**		**9002**	**9004**	**9110**	**9006**	**9008**	**9114**		**9116**	**9014**	**9120**		**9018**	**9126**		**9022**	**9060**	**9130**	**9024**	
	train number																						
	notes	①–⑤	①–⑤		⑥	①–⑤	①–⑥	①–⑥		⑥⑦				⑥						①–⑤	⑥		
	notes	**A**	**A**			**B**	**B**	**B**	**C**				**C**							**D**			
0	**London** St Pancras .... d.	0601	0616	...	0631	0701	0704	0731	0801	0816	...	0901	0931	1001	...	1031	1104	...	1131	1201	1201	1231	...
35	Ebbsfleet International .... d.	|	|	...	|	|	|	|	|	|	...	|	|	|	...	|	|	...	|	|	|	|	...
90	Ashford International .... d.	|	|	...	|	|	|	|	|	|	...	|	|	|	...	|	|	...	|	|	|	|	...
166	Calais Fréthun .... a.	|	|	...	|	|	|	|	|	|	...	|	|	|	...	|	|	...	|	|	|	|	...
267	Lille Europe .... a.	|	|	...	|	|	0926	|	|	|	...	1124	|	1227	...	|	1326	...	|	|	1426	|	...
373	**Brussels** Midi / Zuid .... a.	|	0913	...	|	|	1005	|	|	1113	...	1205	|	1305	...	|	1405	...	|	|	1505	|	...
	Amsterdam Centraal .... a.	|	1120	...	|	|	...	|	|	1320	...	...	|	...	...	|	1620	...	|	|	...	|	...
492	**Paris** Nord .... a.	0922	...	...	0953	1022	...	1052	1127	...	...	...	1258	...	...	1353	...	...	1453	1527	...	1602	...

train number	**9132**	**9028**	**9030**	**9032**		**9142**	**9036**	**9038**	**9040**	**9148**	**9044**		**9046**	**9152**		**9050**	**9158**	**9054**		**9056**		
train number			②③																			
notes			⑤⑦					①④						Ⓑ						⑦		
notes			**E**					⑤⑦												**G**		
London St Pancras .... d.	1301	1331	1401	1431	...	1504	1531	1601	1631	1704	1731	...	1801	1804	...	1901	1934	2001	...	2031	...	...
Ebbsfleet International .... d.	|	|	|	|	...	|	|	|	|	|	|	...	|	|	...	|	|	|	...	|	...	...
Ashford International .... d.	|	|	|	|	...	|	|	|	|	|	|	...	|	|	...	|	|	|	...	|	...	...
Calais Fréthun .... a.	|	|	|	|	...	|	|	|	|	|	|	...	|	|	...	|	|	|	...	|	...	...
Lille Europe .... a.	1526	|	|	|	...	1726	|	|	|	1926	|	...	|	2026	...	|	2200	|	...	|	...	...
Brussels Midi / Zuid .... a.	1606	|	|	|	...	1805	|	|	|	2005	|	...	|	2109	...	|	2235	|	...	|	...	...
Amsterdam Centraal .... a.	...	|	|	|	...	...	|	|	|	...	|	...	|	2320	...	|	...	|	...	|	...	...
Paris Nord .... a.	...	1656	1735	1757	...	...	1902	1928	1951	...	2100	...	2124	...	...	2224	...	2330	...	2353	...	...

train number	**9007**	**9113**	**9009**	**9011**	**9115**	**9117**	**9013**	**9015**	**9121**	**9019**	**9125**	**9123**	**9023**	**9023**	**9129**	**9025**	**9027**	**9135**	**9031**	**9033**	**9035**	**9141**
train number																						
notes	①–⑥	①–⑥	①–⑤	⑥⑦	①–⑤	⑥⑦	①–⑤		⑥		⑥⑦	①–⑤	⑦	①–⑥	⑦	Ⓑ				⑦	⑥	
notes	**A**	**A**	**B**	**H**	**A**	**K**	**B**		**L**						**M**							
Paris Nord .... d.	0712	...	0742	0813	...	...	0842	0912	...	1012	...	...	1041	1112	...	1137	1212	...	1311	1340	1413	...
Amsterdam Centraal .... d.	|	...	|	|	0640	...	|	|	...	|	0840	...	|	|	...	|	|	...	|	|	|	...
Brussels Midi / Zuid .... d.	|	0756	|	|	0852	0852	|	|	0956	|	1056	1056	|	|	1156	|	|	1256	|	|	|	1452
Lille Europe .... d.	|	0835	|	|	0930	0930	|	|	1035	|	1135	1135	|	|	1235	|	|	1335	|	|	|	1530
Calais Fréthun .... d.	|	|	|	|	|	|	|	|	|	|	|	|	|	|	|	|	|	|	|	|	|	|
Ashford International .... a.	|	|	|	|	|	|	|	|	|	|	|	|	|	|	|	|	|	|	|	|	|	|
Ebbsfleet International .... a.	|	|	|	|	|	|	|	|	|	|	|	|	|	|	|	|	|	|	|	|	|	|
London St Pancras .... a.	0830	0857	0900	0930	0957	0957	1000	1030	1057	1130	1157	1157	1200	1230	1257	1300	1330	1357	1430	1500	1530	1557

train number	**9037**	**9039**	**9145**	**9043**	**9149**	**9045**	**9047**	**9153**	**9051**	**9157**	**9159**	**9053**	**9055**	**9161**	**9163**	**9059**		**9167**	**9061**	**9063**		
train number																						
notes	Ⓑ		①–⑤		⑥	①–⑤			Ⓑ	⑥⑦	①–⑤	⑤		⑦	⑥			Ⓑ	⑦	Ⓑ		
notes												**H**							**J**			
Paris Nord .... d.	1442	1512	...	1612	...	1640	1710	...	1810	...	...	1842	1911	...	...	2007	...	...	2033	2110	...	...
Amsterdam Centraal .... d.	|	|	1340	|	...	|	|	...	|	1640	...	|	|	...	...	|	...	1840	|	|	...	...
Brussels Midi / Zuid .... d.	|	|	1551	|	1656	|	|	1756	|	1851	1851	|	|	1956	2022	|	...	2056	|	|	...	...
Lille Europe .... d.	|	|	|	|	1735	|	|	1835	|	1930	1930	|	|	2035	2100	|	...	2135	|	|	...	...
Calais Fréthun .... d.	|	|	|	|	|	|	|	|	|	|	|	|	|	|	|	|	...	|	|	|	...	...
Ashford International .... a.	|	|	|	|	|	|	|	|	|	|	|	|	|	|	|	|	...	|	|	|	...	...
Ebbsfleet International .... a.	|	|	|	|	|	|	|	|	|	|	|	|	|	|	|	|	...	|	|	|	...	...
London St Pancras .... a.	1605	1630	1657	1735	1757	1809	1830	1900	1939	1957	1957	2000	2030	2057	2127	2130	...	2157	2200	2230	...	...

A – Not May 26, 29, June 9.
B – Not May 26.
C – Not June 15.
D – Also June 1, 15.
E – Also May 26; not June 13.
G – Not June 8.
H – Also May 26.
J – Also May 26, June 15.
K – Also May 26, 29, June 9.
L – Not June 28.
M – Not June 29.

EUROSTAR – WHEN SHOULD I ARRIVE AT THE STATION?

Figures shown below are minutes before scheduled departure, the first being the recommended arrival time with the second indicating when gates close. Connections at Paris, Lille and Brussels, shown in our international section, have been set to allow time to reach the check-in area before the gate closes. **NOTE**: We have set the minimum connecting time at Brussels to 60 minutes (allowing up to 15 minutes to transfer to the check-in area). For cross-Paris connections we have allowed a minimum of 120 minutes (60 minutes to transfer between Paris stations and 15 minutes to check-in before the gate closes). The check-in times apply to Standard and Plus travel classes. Shorter check-in times apply for Premium. In most cases longer connecting times are shown, but readers may still wish to consider booking earlier connecting services.

Station	*Recommended*	*Gates close*	*Station*	*Recommended*	*Gates close*
LONDON ST PANCRAS	90	30	**LILLE EUROPE**	90	30
PARIS NORD	90–120	45	**ROTTERDAM CENTRAAL**	60–90	45
BRUSSELS MIDI / ZUID	90–120	45	**AMSTERDAM CENTRAAL**	60–90	45

10 LONDON - LILLE, PARIS, BRUSSELS and AMSTERDAM *by Eurostar*

All Eurostar services are Ⓡ and special fares are payable. Three classes of service are available: Eurostar Premium, Eurostar Plus and Eurostar Standard.
All times shown are local times (France and Belgium are one hour ahead of Great Britain). ✕ available in Eurostar Premium and Eurostar Plus, 🍸 in Eurostar Standard.

SERVICE JULY 20 - SEPTEMBER 6. **See page 47 for service May 18 - July 19.**

Services marked ❖ arrive / depart Lille and arrive London 30 minutes later August 16 – 31.

km		9106	9002	9006	9110	9004	9006	9110	9110	9006	9114	9008	9114	9116	9116	9014	9120	9018	9126	9022	9060	9130	9024
	train number																						
	notes	①–⑤	⑥			①–⑤		①–⑥		①–⑥			⑥⑦				⑥				①–⑤	⑥	
	notes	**T**		**P**	**R**	**A**	**R**	**Q**	**P**	**Q**	**U**		**W**	**R**	**X**		**X**						
0	**London** St Pancras d.	0616	0631	0631	0634	0701	0701	0704	0704	0731	0734	0801	0816	0831	0901	0931	1001	1024	1104	1131	1201	1201	1231
35	Ebbsfleet International d.	│	│	│	│	│	│	│	│	│	│	│	│	│	│	│	│	│	│	│	│	│	│
90	Ashford International d.	│	│	│	│	│	│	│	│	│	│	│	│	│	│	│	│	│	│	│	│	│	│
166	Calais Fréthun a.	│	│	│	│	│	│	│	│	│	│	│	│	│	│	│	│	│	│	│	│	│	│
267	Lille Europe a.	│	│	│	0856	│	│	0926	0926	│	1002	│	│	1100	1124	│	1225	│	1326	│	│	1426	│
373	**Brussels** Midi / Zuid a.	0913	│	│	1005	│	│	1005	1020	│	1113	│	1113	1201	1205	│	1309	│	1405	│	│	1505	│
	Amsterdam Centraal a.	1120	│	│	...	│	│	...	...	│	1320	│	1320	...	...	│	...	│	1620	│	│	...	│
492	**Paris** Nord a.	...	0949	0949	...	1019	1019	...	...	1049	...	1119	...	...	...	1249	...	1349	...	1449	1520	...	1549

	9132	9028	9030	9032	9142	9036	9038	9040	9148	9044	9046	9152	9050	9158	9054	9056						
train number					9140																	
notes			⑤⑦				Ⓑ					Ⓑ				⑦						
notes			**H**																			
London St Pancras d.	1301	1331	1401	1431	1504	1531	1601	1631	1704	1731	1801	1804	1901	1934	2001	2031	...	...	...	...	...	...
Ebbsfleet International d.	│	│	│	│	│	│	│	│	│	│	│	│	│	│	│	│	...	...	...	...	...	...
Ashford International d.	│	│	│	│	│	│	│	│	│	│	│	│	│	│	│	│	...	...	...	...	...	...
Calais Fréthun a.	│	│	│	│	│	│	│	│	│	│	│	│	│	│	│	...	...	...	...	...	...
Lille Europe a.	1526	│	│	│	1726	│	│	│	1926	│	│	2026	│	2200	│	│	...	...	...	...	...	...
Brussels Midi / Zuid a.	1606**x**	│	│	│	1805	│	│	│	2005**x**	│	│	2109	│	2235	│	│	...	...	...	...	...	...
Amsterdam Centraal a.	...	│	│	│	...	│	│	│	...	│	│	2320	│	...	│	│	...	...	...	...	...	...
Paris Nord a.	...	1649	1720	1749	...	1850	1919	1949	...	2049	2119	...	2219	...	2319	2349	...	...	...	...	...	...

	9007	9113	9009	9011	9115	9117	9015	9121	9119	9019	9125	9123	9023	9023	9129	9025	9027	9135	9031	9033	9035	9141
train number																						
notes	①–⑥	①–⑥	①–⑤	⑥⑦	①–⑤	⑥⑦		⑥			⑥⑦	①–⑤	⑦	①–⑥	⑦	Ⓑ				⑦	⑥	
notes	**A**	**A** ❖	**A**	**H**	❖	❖		**X**	**R**		**W**	❖			**S**	**S**		❖				❖
Paris Nord d.	0712	...	0740	0812	...	...	0912	...	...	1011	...	...	1045	1112	...	1140	1212	...	1311	1340	1412	...
Amsterdam Centraal d.	│	...	│	│	0640	...	│	...	0740	│	0840	...	│	│	...	│	│	...	│	│	│	...
Brussels Midi / Zuid d.	│	0756	│	│	0852	0852	│	0956	0959	│	1056	1056	│	│	1156	│	│	1256	│	│	│	1452
Lille Europe d.	│	0835	│	│	0930	0930	│	1035	1105	│	1135	1135	│	│	1235	│	│	1335	│	│	│	1530
Calais Fréthun d.	│	│	│	│	│	│	│	│	│	│	│	│	│	│	│	│	│	│	│	│	│	│
Ashford International a.	│	│	│	│	│	│	│	│	│	│	│	│	│	│	│	│	│	│	│	│	│	│
Ebbsfleet International a.	│	│	│	│	│	│	│	│	│	│	│	│	│	│	│	│	│	│	│	│	│	│
London St Pancras a.	0830	0857	0900	0930	0957	0957	1030	1057	1127	1130	1157	1157	1200	1230	1257	1300	1330	1357	1430	1500	1530	1557

	9037	9039	9145	9043	9149	9045	9047	9153	9051	9157	9053	9159	9055	9161	9163	9059	9167	9061	9063			
train number																						
notes	Ⓑ		①–⑤		⑥	①–⑤			Ⓑ	⑥⑦	⑤	①–⑤		⑦	⑥		Ⓑ	⑦	Ⓑ			
notes					❖			❖		❖				❖	❖		❖	**C**				
Paris Nord d.	1442	1512	...	1612	...	1640	1712	...	1810	...	1840	...	1911	...	...	2012	...	2040	2112	...	...	...
Amsterdam Centraal d.	│	│	1340	│	...	│	│	...	│	1640	│	...	│	...	...	│	1840	│	│	...	...	...
Brussels Midi / Zuid d.	│	│	1551	│	1656	│	│	1756	│	1851	│	1926	│	1956	2022	│	2056	│	│	...	...	...
Lille Europe d.	│	│	│	│	1735	│	│	1835	│	1930	│	2005	│	2035	2100	│	2135	│	│	...	...	...
Calais Fréthun d.	│	│	│	│	│	│	│	│	│	│	│	│	│	│	│	│	│	│	│	...	...	...
Ashford International a.	│	│	│	│	│	│	│	│	│	│	│	│	│	│	│	│	│	│	...	...	...
Ebbsfleet International a.	│	│	│	│	│	│	│	│	│	│	│	│	│	│	│	│	│	│	...	...	...
London St Pancras a.	1600	1630	1657	1730	1757	1809	1830	1857	1939	1957	2000	2027	2030	2057	2127	2130	2157	2200	2230	...	...	...

A – Not Aug. 25.
C – Also Aug. 25; not Aug. 24.
H – Also Aug. 25.
P – Aug. 18 – 22, 26 – 29.
Q – Not Aug. 16 – 30.
R – Aug. 16, 23, 30.
S – Not Aug. 17, 24, 31.
T – Not Aug. 18 – 22, 25 – 29.
U – Aug. 16 – 31.
W – Not Aug. 16, 17, 23, 24, 30, 31.
X – Not Aug. 16, 23, 30.
x – 14 – 15 mins. later Aug. 16 - 31.

10a LONDON - DOVER - CALAIS - PARIS by RAIL - SEA - RAIL

Additional connections may be possible using other services: London - Dover and v.v. Tables **100** and **101**; Dover - Calais and v.v. Table **2110**; Calais - Paris and v.v. Tables **260** and **261**.
Passengers must make their own way Dover Priory - Dover Eastern Docks and v.v. (taxis available), and Calais Port - Calais Ville and v.v. (🚌 available). Allow 1 hour for connections.
⛴ operated by P & O Ferries (Ⓡ ✕ www.poferries.com). Check-in closes 90 minutes before departure. Foot passengers disembark 30 minutes after arrival in port.
Shipping schedules change frequently, please check with operator for latest information.

Service from May 18

				①–⑤	⑥	⑥⑦	①–⑤			Ⓒ	Ⓐ			⑥⑦	①–⑤							
	⛴					↯	↯		⛴					↯	↯	⛴						
London St Pancras d.	...	...	...	...	...	1004	1007	...	...	...	...	...	...	1304	1307	...	...	...	...	...	...	...
London Charing Cross d.	...	...	...	0902	0904	│	│	...	...	...	...	...	1204	│	│	...	...	...	...	...	...	...
Dover Priory ❦ a.	...	...	...	1055	1055	1113	1113	...	...	...	...	...	1355	1413	1413	...	...	...	...	...	...	...
Dover Eastern Docks 🏢 ❦ d.	0945	...	...	...	...	...	...	...	1340	...	...	...	...	...	...	1640	...	...	...	...	...	...
Calais Port 🏢 ❖ a.	1220	...	...	...	...	...	...	...	1615	...	...	...	...	...	...	1915	...	...	...	...	...	...
Calais Ville ❖ d.	...	1434	...	...	...	...	...	...	...	1735	1736	...	...	...	...	...	...	...	...	...	...	...
Boulogne Ville d.	...	1505	...	...	...	...	...	...	...	1806	1806	...	...	...	...	...	...	...	...	...	...	...
Amiens a.	...	1620	...	...	...	...	...	...	...	1921	1921	...	...	...	...	...	...	...	...	...	...	...
Paris Nord a.	...	1731	...	...	...	...	...	...	...	2031	2057	...	...	...	...	...	...	...	...	...	...	...

	⑥	①–⑤		⑦	①–⑥			⑥⑦		①–⑤	⑥		⑦		①–⑤	⑥						
			⛴	↯	↯				⛴			↯					⛴	↯				
Paris Nord d.	...	...	...	...	...	...	...	0928	...	...	...	...	...	...	1029	*1156*	...	...	...	...	...	...
Amiens d.	0526	0548	...	...	...	...	...	1037	...	...	...	...	...	...	1138	1337	...	...	...	...	...	...
Boulogne Ville d.	0654	0708	...	...	...	...	...	1159	...	...	...	...	...	...	1257	1502	...	...	...	...	...	...
Calais Ville ❖ a.	0738	0750	...	...	...	...	...	1240	...	...	...	...	...	...	1333	1545	...	...	...	...	...	...
Calais Port 🏢 ❖ d.	...	...	0945	...	...	...	...	...	1500	...	...	...	...	...	...	...	1845	...	...	...	...	...
Dover Eastern Docks 🏢 ❦ a.	...	...	1015	...	...	...	...	...	1530	...	...	...	...	...	...	...	1915	...	...	...	...	...
Dover Priory ❦ d.	...	...	...	1145	1148	1228	...	...	...	1724	1728	1745	1754	...	...	...	...	2048	2128	...	...	...
London Charing Cross a.	...	...	...	│	│	1421	...	...	...	1924	1921	│	2008	...	...	...	...	│	2324	...	...	...
London St Pancras a.	...	...	...	1254	1254	...	...	...	...	...	...	1854	...	...	...	...	...	2154	...	...	...	...

❦ – Passengers make their own way Dover Priory - Dover Eastern Docks and v.v.
❖ – Passengers make their own way Calais Port - Calais Ville and v.v. (🚌 available).
↯ – Supplement payable.

LONDON / BRUSSELS - LILLE - CHARLES DE GAULLE ✈ - WESTERN / SOUTHERN FRANCE 11

Supplements are payable on *TGV* trains. Connections at Lille are not guaranteed. Other connections are available by changing in Paris.

km	*train type*	*TGV*	*TGV*		*Ouigo*	*TGV*		*TGV*	*Ouigo*		*TGV*	*TGV*		*TGV*	*Ouigo*		*TGV*	*TGV*		*TGV*	*TGV*		*Ouigo*
	train number	**6821**	**6805**		**7831**	**5102**		**6823**	**7669**		**5202**	**9810**		**5210**	**7867**		**9870**	**9812**		**5113**	**6823**		**7897**
	train number																						
	notes	[R] 🍷	[R] 🍷		[R]	[R] 🍷		[R] 🍷	[R]		[R] 🍷	[R] 🍷		[R] 🍷	[R]		[R] 🍷	[R] 🍷		[R] 🍷	[R] 🍷		[R]
	notes				⊠			Ⓐ	⊠						⊠					⑥	Ⓒ		⊠
	notes					**A**																	
	London St Pancras d.	...	...	...	...	...	...	...	...	...	...	...	...	...	...	...	...	...	...	...	...	...	...
	Brussels Midi / Zuid d.	...	...	...	...	...	...	...	...	...	...	0627	...	...	...	...	0717	0817	...	...	...	...	...
	Tourcoing d.	...	...	...	...	...	...	...	0601	...	...	│	...	...	0744	...	│	│	...	...	...	...	...
	Lille Europe a.	...	...	...	...	...	...	...	│	...	...	0712	...	...	│	...	0751	0851	...	...	...	...	...
0	**Lille** Europe d.	...	...	...	...	0558	...	...	│	...	...	0722	...	0752	│	...	0802	0859	...	0859	...	...	...
	Lille Flandres d.	...	...	...	...	│	...	...	│	...	0611	│	...	│	│	...	│	│	...	│	...	...	...
	Douai d.	...	...	...	...	│	...	...	│	...	0633	│	...	│	│	...	│	│	...	│	...	...	...
	Arras d.	...	...	...	...	│	...	...	│	...	0652	│	...	│	│	...	│	│	...	│	...	...	...
99	TGV Haute Picardie d.	...	...	...	...	│	...	...	0642	...	0717	0751	...	│	│	...	│	│	...	│	...	...	...
203	Paris Charles de Gaulle ✈ a.	...	...	...	...	0651	...	...	0713	...	0754	0822	...	0843	0848	...	0855	0953	...	0953	...	...	...
203	Paris Charles de Gaulle ✈ d.	...	...	...	0659	0655	...	...	0718	...	0805	0827	...	0849	0855	...	0901	0959	...	0956	...	...	1100
227	Marne la Vallée (for Disneyland) d.	...	...	...	0716	0713	...	...	0732	...	0830	0843	...	0902	0912	...	│	1011	...	1011	...	...	1117
	Strasbourg a.	...	...	...	│	│	...	...	│	...	│	│	...	│	│	...	1105	│	...	│	...	...	│
289	Massy TGV d.	...	...	...	│	│	...	...	0808	...	0908	│	...	0942	│	...	...	│	...	│	...	...	│
	Le Mans a.	...	...	...	│	│	...	...	│	...	│	│	...	1029	│	...	...	│	...	│	...	...	│
	Rennes a.	...	...	...	│	│	...	...	│	...	│	│	...	1117	│	...	...	│	...	│	...	...	│
	St Pierre des Corps a.	...	...	...	│	│	...	...	0903	...	1003	│	...	...	│	...	...	│	...	│	...	...	│
	Angers St Laud a.	...	...	...	│	│	...	...	│	...	│	│	...	...	│	...	...	│	...	│	...	...	│
	Nantes a.	...	...	...	│	│	...	...	│	...	│	│	...	...	│	...	...	│	...	│	...	...	│
	Poitiers a.	...	...	...	│	│	...	...	0939	...	1039	│	...	...	│	...	...	│	...	│	...	...	│
	Angoulême a.	...	...	...	│	│	...	...	1022	...	1122	│	...	...	│	...	...	│	...	│	...	...	│
	Bordeaux a.	...	...	...	│	│	...	...	1105	...	1202	│	...	...	│	...	...	│	...	│	...	...	│
	Le Creusot TGV a.	...	...	...	│	│	...	...	...	...	...	│	...	...	│	...	...	│	...	│	...	...	│
521	**Lyon** Part Dieu a.	0640	0806	...	│	0900	...	1010	...	...	...	1030	...	...	1100	...	...	1200	...	1200	1210	...	│
	Lyon St Exupéry ✈ a.	│	│	...	│	│	...	│	...	...	...	│	...	...	│	...	...	│	...	│	│	...	1300
	Valence TGV a.	0714	0842	...	│	│	...	1045	...	...	...	1115	...	...	1146	...	...	1244	...	│	1245	...	│
	Avignon TGV a.	│	0925	...	0950	1009	...	│	...	...	...	1152	...	...	│	...	...	│	...	1309	│	...	│
	Nîmes a.	0803	│	...	│	│	...	1134	...	...	...	│	...	...	│	...	...	1335	...	│	1335	...	│
	Nîmes Pont-du-Gard a.	│	│	...	│	│	...	│	...	...	...	│	...	...	1228	...	...	│	...	│	│	...	│
	Montpellier Sud de France a.	│	│	...	│	│	...	│	...	...	...	│	...	...	1250	...	...	│	...	│	│	...	│
	Montpellier Saint-Roch a.	0836	│	...	│	│	...	1202	...	...	...	│	...	...	...	...	...	1403	...	│	1403	...	│
	Béziers a.	0921	│	...	│	│	...	1242	...	...	...	│	...	...	...	...	...	...	...	│	1446	...	│
	Narbonne a.	0937	│	...	│	│	...	1259	...	...	...	│	...	...	...	...	...	...	...	│	1502	...	│
	Toulouse Matabiau a.	1052	│	...	│	│	...	1415	...	...	...	│	...	...	...	...	...	...	...	│	1621	...	│
	Perpignan a.	...	│	...	│	│	...	...	...	...	...	│	...	...	...	...	...	...	...	│	...	...	│
	Aix en Provence TGV a.	...	0949	...	1013	1031	...	...	...	...	...	│	...	...	...	...	...	...	...	1331	...	...	1410
	Marseille St Charles a.	...	1004	...	1028	1050	...	...	...	...	...	1224	...	...	...	...	...	...	...	1346	...	...	│
	Toulon a.	...	1106	...	...	...	...	...	...	...	...	...	...	...	...	...	...	...	...	...	...	...	1507
	St Raphaël - Valescure a.	...	1201	...	...	...	...	...	...	...	...	...	...	...	...	...	...	...	...	...	...	...	...
	Cannes a.	...	1227	...	...	...	...	...	...	...	...	...	...	...	...	...	...	...	...	...	...	...	...
	Nice a.	...	1304	...	...	...	...	...	...	...	...	...	...	...	...	...	...	...	...	...	...	...	...

train type	*TGV*	*TGV*		☆	*TGV*		*Ouigo*	☆		☆	*Ouigo*		☆	*TGV*		*TGV*	*TGV*		*Ouigo*	*TGV*		
train number	**6813**	**5224**		**9110**	**9826**		**7841**	**9116**		**9120**	**7835**		**9126**	**9830**		**9874**	**6825**		**7845**	**5120**		
train number																						
notes	[R] 🍷	[R] 🍷		[R] 🍷	[R] 🍷		[R]	[R] 🍷		[R] 🍷	[R]		[R] 🍷	[R] 🍷		[R] 🍷	[R] 🍷		[R]	[R] 🍷		
notes				①–⑥			⊠			⑥	⊠								⊠	④⑤⑦		
notes																				**E**		
London St Pancras d.	...	...	...	0704	...	...	...	0901	...	1001	...	...	1104	...	...	...	...	...	...	...	...	...
Brussels Midi / Zuid d.	...	...	...	│	1017	...	...	│	...	│	...	...	│	1317	...	1317	...	...	...	...	...	...
Tourcoing d.	...	...	...	│	│	...	...	│	...	│	...	...	│	│	...	│	...	...	...	...	...	...
Lille Europe a.	...	...	...	0926	1051	...	...	1124	...	1227	...	...	1326	1351	...	1351	...	...	...	...	...	...
Lille Europe d.	...	...	...	...	1100	...	...	...	...	...	...	...	...	1401	...	1401	...	...	...	1526	...	...
Lille Flandres d.	...	0936	...	...	│	...	1130	...	...	...	1257	...	...	│	...	│	...	...	1520	│	...	...
Douai d.	...	1001	...	...	│	...	│	...	...	...	│	...	...	│	...	│	...	...	│	│	...	...
Arras d.	...	1019	...	...	│	...	│	...	...	...	│	...	...	│	...	│	...	...	│	│	...	...
TGV Haute Picardie d.	...	1040	...	...	│	...	│	...	...	...	│	...	...	│	...	│	...	...	1553	│	...	...
Paris Charles de Gaulle ✈ a.	...	1114	...	...	1153	...	1232	...	...	...	1353	...	...	1453	...	1453	...	...	1624	1619	...	...
Paris Charles de Gaulle ✈ d.	...	1115	...	...	1158	...	1233	...	...	...	1356	...	...	1458	...	1459	...	...	1631	1625	...	...
Marne la Vallée (for Disneyland Paris) d.	...	1132	...	...	1213	...	1250	...	...	...	1413	...	...	1515	...	1527	...	...	1648	1642	...	...
Strasbourg a.	...	│	...	...	│	...	│	...	...	...	│	...	...	│	...	1737	...	...	│	│	...	...
Massy TGV d.	...	1212	...	...	│	...	│	...	...	...	│	...	...	│	...	...	...	...	│	│	...	...
Le Mans a.	...	│	...	...	│	...	│	...	...	...	│	...	...	│	...	...	...	...	│	│	...	...
Rennes a.	...	│	...	...	│	...	│	...	...	...	│	...	...	│	...	...	...	...	│	│	...	...
St Pierre des Corps a.	...	1304	...	...	│	...	│	...	...	...	│	...	...	│	...	...	...	...	│	│	...	...
Angers St Laud a.	...	1402	...	...	│	...	│	...	...	...	│	...	...	│	...	...	...	...	│	│	...	...
Nantes a.	...	1444	...	...	│	...	│	...	...	...	│	...	...	│	...	...	...	...	│	│	...	...
Poitiers a.	...	...	...	...	│	...	│	...	...	...	│	...	...	│	...	...	...	...	│	│	...	...
Angoulême a.	...	...	...	...	│	...	│	...	...	...	│	...	...	│	...	...	...	...	│	│	...	...
Bordeaux a.	...	...	...	...	│	...	│	...	...	...	│	...	...	│	...	...	...	...	│	│	...	...
Le Creusot TGV a.	...	...	...	...	│	...	│	...	...	...	│	...	...	│	...	...	...	...	│	│	...	...
Lyon Part Dieu a.	1355	...	...	...	1401	...	│	...	...	...	1600	...	...	1700	...	...	1810	...	│	1830	...	...
Lyon St Exupéry ✈ a.	│	...	...	...	│	...	1433	...	...	...	│	...	...	│	...	...	│	...	1832	│	...	...
Valence TGV a.	│	...	...	...	1445	...	│	...	...	...	│	...	...	│	...	...	1844	...	1859	1921	...	...
Avignon TGV a.	1457	...	...	...	│	...	1527	...	...	...	1709	...	...	1809	...	...	│	...	1934	│	...	...
Nîmes a.	│	...	...	...	│	...	│	...	...	...	│	...	...	│	...	...	1934	...	│	2013	...	...
Nîmes Pont-du-Gard a.	│	...	...	...	1527	...	│	...	...	...	│	...	...	│	...	...	│	...	│	│	...	...
Montpellier Sud de France a.	│	...	...	...	1550	...	│	...	...	...	│	...	...	│	...	...	│	...	│	│	...	...
Montpellier Saint-Roch a.	│	...	...	...	...	...	│	...	...	...	│	...	...	│	...	...	2001	...	│	2050	...	...
Béziers a.	│	...	...	...	...	...	│	...	...	...	│	...	...	│	...	...	2047	...	│	...	...	...
Narbonne a.	│	...	...	...	...	...	│	...	...	...	│	...	...	│	...	...	2102	...	│	...	...	...
Toulouse Matabiau a.	│	...	...	...	...	...	│	...	...	...	│	...	...	│	...	...	2219	...	│	...	...	...
Perpignan a.	│	...	...	...	...	...	│	...	...	...	│	...	...	│	...	...	...	...	│	...	...	...
Aix en Provence TGV a.	1519	...	...	...	...	...	1549	...	...	...	│	...	...	1831	...	...	...	...	1958	...	...	...
Marseille St Charles a.	1534	...	...	...	...	...	1608	...	...	...	1742	...	...	1849	...	...	...	...	2016	...	...	...
Toulon a.	1636	...	...	...	...	...	...	...	...	...	...	...	...	...	...	...	...	...	...	...	...	...
St Raphaël - Valescure a.	...	...	...	...	...	...	...	...	...	...	...	...	...	...	...	...	...	...	...	...	...	...
Cannes a.	...	...	...	...	...	...	...	...	...	...	...	...	...	...	...	...	...	...	...	...	...	...
Nice a.	...	...	...	...	...	...	...	...	...	...	...	...	...	...	...	...	...	...	...	...	...	...

A – ①–⑥ (not June 6).

E – ④⑤⑦ (also May 7, 28, June 9; not June 8).

d – ⑧ (not May 1, 8, 29).

h – ⑦ (also June 9; not June 8).

TGV – French high-speed train. [R]. 🍷.

☆ – Eurostar high-speed train. [R]. Service May 18 - Sept. 6. See pages 47 and 48 for further information.

⊠ – *Ouigo* low-cost TGV service. Internet booking only at www.ouigo.com.

11 LONDON / BRUSSELS - LILLE - CHARLES DE GAULLE ✈ - WESTERN / SOUTHERN FRANCE

Supplements are payable on *TGV* trains. Connections at Lille are not guaranteed. Other connections are available by changing in Paris.

train type	☆	*TGV*	*TGV*		*TGV*	*TGV*		*TGV*	*TGV*		*TGV*	*TGV*		☆	*TGV*		*TGV*	*TGV*		*Ouigo*		
train number	**9132**	**9832**	**5135**		**9836**	**9836**		**9835**	**5240**		**9838**	**5235**		**9142**	**5124**		**5124**	**9844**		**7815**		
train number																						
notes	[R] 🍸	[R] 🍸	[R] 🍸		[R] 🍸	[R] 🍸		[R] 🍸	[R] 🍸		[R] 🍸	[R] 🍸		[R] 🍸	[R] 🍸		[R] 🍸	[R] 🍸		[R]		
notes			⑤					⑥				⑤			①–⑤		⑦			⊠		
notes			**F**			**G**		**H**				**F**			**K**		**L**					
London St Pancras d.	1301	...	...	...	...	...	...	...	...	...	...		...	1504	...	...	...	...	...	...	...	...
Brussels Midi / Zuid d.	|	1503	...	...	1617	1617	...	1617	...	...	1655	...	...	|	...	...	...	1817	...	...	...	...
Tourcoing d.	|	|	...	...	|	|	...	|	...	...	|	...	...	|	...	...	...	|	...	...	...	...
Lille Europe a.	1526	1538	...	...	1652	1652	...	1652	...	...	1729	...	...	1726	...	...	...	1851	...	...	...	...
Lille Europe d.	...	1548	1701	...	1701	1701	...	1701	...	...	1741	1741	...	...	1822	...	...	1901	...	...	...	...
Lille Flandres d.	...	|	|	...	|	|	...	|	1716	...	|	|	...	...	|	...	1822	|	...	1938	...	...
Douai d.	...	|	|	...	|	|	...	|	|	...	|	|	...	...	|	...	|	|	...	|	...	...
Arras d.	...	|	|	...	|	|	...	|	|	...	|	|	...	...	1846	...	1846	|	...	|	...	...
TGV Haute Picardie d.	...	|	|	...	|	|	...	|	|	...	1815	1815	...	...	1915	...	1915	|	...	|	...	...
Paris Charles de Gaulle ✈ a.	...	1643	1754	...	1754	1754	...	1754	1811	...	1844	1844	...	...	1945	...	1945	1954	...	2032	...	...
Paris Charles de Gaulle ✈ d.	...	1646	1758	...	1758	1758	...	1758	1816	...	1850	1850	...	...	1957	...	1957	1957	...	2037	...	...
Marne la Vallée (for Disneyland Paris) d.	...	1703	1812	...	1812	1812	...	1812	1833	...	1903	1903	...	...	2013	...	2013	2013	...	2056	...	...
Strasbourg a.	...	|	|	...	|	|	...	|	|	...	|	|	...	...	|	...	|	|	...	|	...	...
Massy TGV d.	...	1742	|	...	|	|	...	|	1912	...	1942	1942	...	...	|	...	|	|	...	|	...	...
Le Mans a.	...	1829	|	...	|	|	...	|	|	...	2029	2029	...	...	|	...	|	|	...	|	...	...
Rennes a.	...	|	|	...	|	|	...	|	|	...	2129	|	...	...	|	...	|	|	...	|	...	...
St Pierre des Corps a.	...	|	|	...	|	|	...	|	2003	...	...	|	...	...	|	...	|	|	...	|	...	...
Angers St Laud a.	...	1909	|	...	|	|	...	|	|	...	...	2129	...	...	|	...	|	|	...	|	...	...
Nantes a.	...	1950	|	...	|	|	...	|	|	...	...	2209	...	...	|	...	|	|	...	|	...	...
Poitiers a.	...	...	|	...	|	|	...	|	2040	...	...	...	...	...	|	...	|	|	...	|	...	...
Angoulême a.	...	...	|	...	|	|	...	|	2122	...	...	...	...	...	|	...	|	|	...	|	...	...
Bordeaux a.	...	...	|	...	|	|	...	|	2204	...	...	...	...	...	|	...	|	|	...	|	...	...
Le Creusot TGV a.	...	...	|	...	|	|	...	|	...	...	...	...	...	...	|	...	|	|	...	|	...	...
Lyon Part Dieu a.	...	...	2000	...	2000	2000	...	2000	...	...	...	...	...	...	2200	...	2200	2200	...	2254**p**	...	...
Lyon St Exupéry ✈ a.	...	...	|	...	|	|	...	|	...	...	...	...	...	...	|	...	|	...	...	...	...	...
Valence TGV a.	...	...	2045	...	2045	2045	...	2045	...	...	...	...	...	...	|	...	|	...	...	...	...	...
Avignon TGV a.	...	...	2126	...	|	|	...	2126	...	...	...	...	...	...	2309	...	2309	...	...	...	...	...
Nîmes a.	...	...	|	...	2136	2136	...	|	...	...	...	...	...	...	|	...	|	...	...	...	...	...
Nîmes Pont-du-Gard a.	...	...	|	...	|	|	...	|	...	...	...	...	...	...	|	...	|	...	...	...	...	...
Montpellier Sud de France a.	...	...	|	...	|	|	...	|	...	...	...	...	...	...	|	...	|	...	...	...	...	...
Montpellier Saint-Roch a.	...	...	|	...	2204	2204	...	|	...	...	...	...	...	...	|	...	|	...	...	...	...	...
Béziers a.	...	...	|	...	...	2255	...	|	...	...	...	...	...	...	|	...	|	...	...	...	...	...
Narbonne a.	...	...	|	...	...	2314	...	|	...	...	...	...	...	...	|	...	|	...	...	...	...	...
Toulouse Matabiau a.	...	...	|	...	...	|	...	|	...	...	...	...	...	...	|	...	|	...	...	...	...	...
Perpignan a.	...	...	|	...	...	2359	...	|	...	...	...	...	...	...	|	...	|	...	...	...	...	...
Aix en Provence TGV a.	...	...	2149	...	...	...	...	2149	...	...	...	...	...	...	2333	...	2333	...	...	...	...	...
Marseille St Charles a.	...	...	2204	...	...	...	...	2204	...	...	...	...	...	...	2352	...	2352	...	...	...	...	...
Toulon a.	...	...	...	...	...	...	...	...	...	...	...	...	...	...	...	...	...	...	...	...	...	...
St Raphaël - Valescure a.	...	...	...	...	...	...	...	...	...	...	...	...	...	...	...	...	...	...	...	...	...	...
Cannes a.	...	...	...	...	...	...	...	...	...	...	...	...	...	...	...	...	...	...	...	...	...	...
Nice a.	...	...	...	...	...	...	...	...	...	...	...	...	...	...	...	...	...	...	...	...	...	...

train type	*TGV*	*TGV*	*TGV*	☆	*TGV*	*TGV*	☆		*TGV*	*TGV*	*Ouigo*		*TGV*	☆	*TGV*		*Ouigo*	☆	*TGV*		*TGV*	☆
train number	**9809**	**9852**	**9890**	**9121**	**9886**	**9884**	**9123**		**5156**	**5260**	**7838**		**9854**	**9129**	**5276**		**7818**	**9135**	**9862**		**9862**	**9141**
train number							**9125**															
notes	[R] 🍸	[R] 🍸	[R] 🍸	[R] 🍸	[R] 🍸	[R] 🍸	[R] 🍸		[R] 🍸	[R] 🍸	[R]		[R] 🍸	[R] 🍸	[R] 🍸		[R]	[R] 🍸	[R] 🍸		[R] 🍸	[R] 🍸
notes	Ⓐ	①–⑥		⑥					①⑤		⊠			⑦	⑥		⊠		①–⑤		⑥⑦	
notes		**M**		**A**					**P**						**Q**				**S**			
Nice d.	...	...	...	...	...	...	...	...	...	...	...	...	...	...	...	...	...	...	...	...	...	...
Cannes d.	...	...	...	...	...	...	...	...	...	...	...	...	...	...	...	...	...	...	...	...	...	...
St Raphaël - Valescure d.	...	...	...	...	...	...	...	...	...	...	...	...	...	...	...	...	...	...	...	...	...	...
Toulon d.	...	...	...	...	...	...	...	...	...	...	...	...	...	...	...	...	...	...	...	...	...	...
Marseille St Charles d.	...	...	...	...	...	...	...	...	...	...	0613	...	0634	...	...	...	...	...	...	...	...	...
Aix en Provence TGV d.	...	...	...	...	...	...	...	...	...	...	0627	...	0650	...	...	...	...	...	...	...	...	...
Perpignan d.	...	...	...	...	...	...	...	...	...	...	|	...	|	...	...	...	...	...	...	...	0704	...
Toulouse Matabiau d.	...	...	...	...	...	...	...	...	...	...	|	...	|	...	...	...	...	...	...	...	|	...
Narbonne d.	...	...	...	...	...	...	...	...	...	...	|	...	|	...	...	...	...	...	...	...	0745	...
Béziers d.	...	...	...	...	...	...	...	...	...	...	|	...	|	...	...	...	...	...	...	...	0802	...
Montpellier Saint-Roch d.	...	...	...	...	...	...	...	...	0525	...	|	...	|	...	...	...	...	...	...	...	0857	...
Montpellier Sud de France d.	...	...	...	...	...	...	...	...	|	...	|	...	|	...	...	...	...	...	0912	...	|	...
Nîmes Pont-du-Gard d.	...	...	...	...	...	...	...	...	|	...	|	...	|	...	...	...	...	...	0933	...	|	...
Nîmes d.	...	...	...	...	...	...	...	...	0553	...	|	...	|	...	...	...	...	...	|	...	0925	...
Avignon TGV d.	...	...	...	...	...	...	...	...	|	...	0649	...	0715	...	...	...	...	...	|	...	|	...
Valence TGV d.	...	...	...	...	...	...	...	...	0644	...	|	...	|	...	...	...	...	...	1015	...	1015	...
Lyon St Exupéry ✈ d.	...	...	...	...	...	...	...	...	|	...	0745	...	|	...	...	...	...	...	|	...	|	...
Lyon Part Dieu d.	...	0550	...	...	...	...	...	...	0730	...	|	...	0825	...	...	...	0904**p**	...	1059	...	1059	...
Le Creusot TGV d.	...	0632	...	...	...	...	...	...	|	...	|	...	|	...	...	...	|	...	|	...	|	...
Bordeaux d.	...	|	...	...	...	...	...	...	|	0555	|	...	|	...	...	...	|	...	|	...	|	...
Angoulême d.	...	|	...	...	...	...	...	...	|	0634	|	...	|	...	...	...	|	...	|	...	|	...
Poitiers d.	...	|	...	...	...	...	...	...	|	0719	|	...	|	...	...	...	|	...	|	...	|	...
Nantes d.	...	|	...	...	0559	...	...	...	|	|	|	...	|	...	0808	...	|	...	|	...	|	...
Angers St Laud d.	...	|	...	...	0640	...	...	...	|	|	|	...	|	...	0843	...	|	...	|	...	|	...
St Pierre des Corps d.	...	|	...	...	|	...	...	...	|	0755	|	...	|	...	|	...	|	...	|	...	|	...
Rennes d.	...	|	...	...	|	0621	...	...	|	|	|	...	|	...	|	...	|	...	|	...	|	...
Le Mans d.	...	|	...	...	0726	0726	...	...	|	|	|	...	|	...	0930	...	|	...	|	...	|	...
Massy TGV d.	...	|	...	...	0826	0826	...	...	|	0855	|	...	|	...	1024	...	|	...	|	...	|	...
Strasbourg d.	...	|	0559	...	|	|	...	...	|	|	|	...	|	...	|	...	|	...	|	...	|	...
Marne la Vallée (for Disneyland Paris) d.	...	0748	|	...	0859	0859	...	...	0922	0930	0940	...	1018	...	1100	...	1110	...	1249	...	1249	...
Paris Charles de Gaulle ✈ a.	...	0802	0757	...	0910	0910	...	...	0934	0942	0950	...	1033	...	1109	...	1121	...	1304	...	1304	...
Paris Charles de Gaulle ✈ d.	...	0807	0807	...	0915	0915	...	...	0945	0945	0954	...	1036	...	1113	...	1126	...	1305	...	1305	...
TGV Haute Picardie d.	...	|	|	...	0950	0950	...	...	|	|	|	...	|	...	|	...	|	...	1338	...	1338	...
Arras a.	...	|	|	...	|	|	...	...	|	|	|	...	|	...	|	...	|	...	1358	...	1358	...
Douai a.	...	|	|	...	|	|	...	...	|	|	|	...	|	...	|	...	|	...	|	...	|	...
Lille Flandres a.	...	|	|	...	|	|	...	...	1042	1042	1050	...	|	...	|	...	1224	...	|	...	|	...
Lille Europe a.	...	0858	0858	...	1016	1016	...	...	...	...	...	...	1135	...	1210	...	...	...	1425	...	1425	...
Lille Europe d.	0710	0909	0909	1035	1027	1027	1135	...	...	...	...	...	1137	1235	...	...	...	1335	1451	...	1451	1530
Tourcoing a.	|	|	|	|	|	|	|	...	...	...	...	...	|	|	...	...	...	|	|	...	|	|
Brussels Midi / Zuid a.	0801	0943	0943	|	1101	1101	|	...	...	...	...	...	1211	|	...	...	...	|	1525	...	1525	|
London St Pancras a.	...	...	...	1057	...	...	1157	...	...	...	...	...	...	1257	...	...	...	1357	...	...	...	1557

A – Not June 28.
F – ⑤ (also May 7, 28; not May 2, 9, 30).
G – ⑤⑥ until June 14; ⑤ from June 20.
H – ⑥ (also May 1, 2, 8, 9, 29).
K – ①–⑤ (also June 8, 15).
L – ⑦ (not June 8, 15).

M – ①–⑥ (not June 9).
P – ①⑤ (also June 10; not May 2, 9, 30, June 9).
Q – ⑥ (also May 1, 2, 8, 9, 29, 30).
S – ①–⑤ (not May 1, 2, 8, 9, 29, 30).

p – Lyon **Perrache**.

TGV – French high-speed train. [R]. 🍸.
☆ – Eurostar high-speed train. [R]. Service May 18 - Sept. 6. See pages 47 and 48 for further information.
⊠ – *Ouigo* low-cost TGV service. Internet booking only at www.ouigo.com.

SOUTHERN / WESTERN FRANCE - CHARLES DE GAULLE ✈ - LILLE - BRUSSELS / LONDON 11

Supplements payable on all *TGV* services. Connections at Lille are not guaranteed. Other connections available via Paris.

train type	*Ouigo*	☆	*TGV*	*TGV*		*TGV*	*TGV*	☆		*TGV*	*TGV*	☆		*Ouigo*	☆	*TGV*		*TGV*	*TGV*	☆		
train number	**7842**	**9141**	**5080**	**6871**		**9866**	**5158**	**9149**		**5284**	**5278**	**9153**		**7860**	**9157**	**5192**		**5192**	**5288**	**9161**		
train number															**9159**							
notes	[R]	[R] 🍷	[R] 🍷	[R] 🍷		[R] 🍷	[R] 🍷	[R] 🍷		[R] 🍷	[R] 🍷	[R] 🍷		[R]	[R] 🍷	[R] 🍷		[R] 🍷	[R] 🍷	[R] 🍷		
notes	⊠						⑥	⑥			⑦			⊠		⑥		Ⓑ		⑦		
notes							**U**				**W**					**Z**		**d**				
Nice ... d.	...	...	...	...	...	...	...	...	...	...	...	...	...	...	...	...	...	...	...	...	...	...
Cannes ... d.	...	...	...	...	...	...	...	...	...	...	...	...	...	...	...	...	...	...	...	...	...	...
St Raphaël - Valescure ... d.	...	...	...	...	...	...	...	...	...	...	...	...	...	...	...	...	...	...	...	...	...	...
Toulon ... d.	...	...	...	...	...	...	...	...	...	...	...	...	...	...	...	...	...	...	...	...	...	...
Marseille St Charles ... d.	1002	...	...	...	...	1212	...	...	...	...	...	...	...	...	...	1334	...	...	...	...	...	...
Aix en Provence TGV ... d.	1017	...	...	...	...	1226	...	...	...	...	...	...	...	...	...	1348	...	...	...	...	...	...
Perpignan ... d.	|	...	...	...	...	|	...	...	...	...	...	...	...	...	...	|	...	...	...	...	...	...
Toulouse Matabiau ... d.	|	...	...	0739	...	|	...	...	...	...	...	...	...	...	...	|	...	...	...	...	...	...
Narbonne ... d.	|	...	...	0855	...	|	...	...	...	...	...	...	...	...	...	|	...	...	...	...	...	...
Béziers ... d.	|	...	...	0911	...	|	...	...	...	...	...	...	...	...	...	|	...	...	...	...	...	...
Montpellier Saint-Roch ... d.	|	...	...	|	...	|	1158	...	...	...	...	...	...	...	...	|	...	...	...	...	...	...
Montpellier Sud de France ... d.	|	...	...	1005	...	|	|	...	...	...	...	...	...	1359	...	|	...	...	...	...	...	...
Nîmes Pont-du-Gard ... d.	|	...	...	1029	...	|	|	...	...	...	...	...	...	1421	...	|	...	...	...	...	...	...
Nîmes ... d.	|	...	...	|	...	|	1225	...	...	...	...	...	...	|	...	|	...	...	...	...	...	...
Avignon TGV ... d.	1039	...	...	|	...	1249	|	...	...	...	...	...	...	|	...	1410	...	...	...	...	...	...
Valence TGV ... d.	|	...	...	1112	...	|	1314	...	...	...	...	...	...	|	...	|	...	...	...	...	...	...
Lyon St Exupéry ✈ ... d.	1134	...	...	|	...	|	|	...	...	...	...	...	...	1534	...	|	...	...	...	...	...	...
Lyon Part Dieu ... d.	|	...	...	1148	...	1359	1359	...	...	...	...	...	...	|	...	1519	...	1600	...	...	...	...
Le Creusot TGV ... d.	|	...	...	...	...	|	|	...	...	...	...	...	...	|	...	|	...	|	...	...	...	...
Bordeaux ... d.	|	...	...	...	...	|	|	...	...	1255	...	...	...	|	...	|	...	|	...	...	...	...
Angoulême ... d.	|	...	...	...	...	|	|	...	...	1336	...	...	...	|	...	|	...	|	...	...	...	...
Poitiers ... d.	|	...	...	...	...	|	|	...	...	1417	...	...	...	|	...	|	...	|	...	...	...	...
Nantes ... d.	|	...	...	...	...	|	|	...	...	|	1408	...	...	|	...	|	...	|	1517	...	...	...
Angers St Laud ... d.	|	...	...	...	...	|	|	...	...	|	1448	...	...	|	...	|	...	|	1602	...	...	...
St Pierre des Corps ... d.	|	...	...	...	...	|	|	...	...	1456	|	...	...	|	...	|	...	|	|	...	...	...
Rennes ... d.	|	...	1200	...	...	|	|	...	...	|	|	...	...	|	...	|	...	|	|	...	...	...
Le Mans ... d.	|	...	1259	...	...	|	|	...	...	|	1530	...	...	|	...	|	...	|	1658	...	...	...
Massy TGV ... d.	|	...	1355	...	...	|	|	...	...	1555	1826	...	...	|	...	|	...	|	1755	...	...	...
Strasbourg ... d.	|	...	|	...	...	|	|	...	...	|	|	...	...	|	...	|	...	|	|	...	...	...
Marne la Vallée (for Disneyland Paris) ... d.	1320	...	1430	...	...	1550	1550	...	...	1630	1701	...	...	1725	...	1709	...	1750	1829	...	...	...
Paris Charles de Gaulle ✈ ... a.	1332	...	1442	...	...	1603	1603	...	...	1643	1715	...	...	1738	...	1722	...	1803	1841	...	...	...
Paris Charles de Gaulle ✈ ... d.	1333	...	1457	...	...	1606	1606	...	...	1646	...	...	...	1743	...	1724	...	1806	1845	...	...	...
TGV Haute Picardie ... d.	|	...	|	...	...	|	|	...	...	1731	...	...	...	1814	...	1802	...	1837	|	...	...	...
Arras ... a.	|	...	|	...	...	|	|	...	...	|	...	...	...	|	...	1818	...	1857	|	...	...	...
Douai ... a.	|	...	|	...	...	|	|	...	...	|	...	...	...	|	...	1837	...	1915	|	...	...	...
Lille Flandres ... a.	1434	...	|	...	...	|	|	...	...	|	...	...	...	1844	...	1902	...	1944	|	...	...	...
Lille Europe ... a.	...	...	1554	...	...	1701	1701	...	...	1758	...	...	...	...	...	...	...	...	1939	...	...	...
Lille Europe ... d.	...	1530	...	...	...	1709	...	1735	...	...	...	1835	...	...	1930	...	...	...	...	2035	...	...
Tourcoing ... a.	...	|	...	...	...	|	...	|	...	...	...	|	...	...	|	...	...	...	...	|	...	...
Brussels Midi / Zuid ... a.	...	|	...	...	...	1744	...	|	...	...	...	|	...	...	|	...	...	...	...	|	...	...
London St Pancras ... a.	...	1557	...	...	...	...	...	1757	...	...	...	1900	...	...	1957	...	...	...	...	2057	...	...

train type	*TGV*	*TGV*	*TGV*	☆	☆	*Ouigo*		*Ouigo*	*Ouigo*		*TGV*	*TGV*		*TGV*	*TGV*		*Ouigo*	*TGV*				
train number	**9868**	**9864**	**9894**	**9163**	**9167**	**7898**		**7832**	**7660**		**5182**	**9882**		**5186**	**6866**		**7836**	**6852**				
train number																						
notes	[R] 🍷	[R] 🍷	[R] 🍷	[R] 🍷	[R] 🍷	[R]		[R]	[R]		[R] 🍷	[R] 🍷		[R] 🍷	[R] 🍷		[R]	[R] 🍷				
notes				⑥	Ⓑ	⊠		⊠	⊠					⑦			⊠					
notes														**h**								
Nice ... d.	...	...	...	...	...	...	...	...	...	...	...	...	...	...	1512	...	..◇.	...	...	...	...	...
Cannes ... d.	...	...	...	...	...	...	...	...	...	...	...	...	...	...	1547	...	...	...	...	...	...	...
St Raphaël - Valescure ... d.	...	...	...	...	...	...	...	...	...	...	...	...	...	...	1613	...	...	...	...	...	...	...
Toulon ... d.	...	...	...	...	...	1550	...	...	...	...	...	...	...	...	1712	...	...	1915	...	...	...	...
Marseille St Charles ... d.	1512	...	...	...	...	|	...	1646	...	...	...	1712	...	...	1814	...	1827	2012	...	...	...	...
Aix en Provence TGV ... d.	1526	...	...	...	...	1643	...	|	...	...	...	1726	...	...	1929	...	1842	2027	...	...	...	...
Perpignan ... d.	|	...	...	...	...	|	...	|	...	...	...	|	...	...	|	...	|	|	...	...	...	...
Toulouse Matabiau ... d.	|	...	...	...	...	|	...	|	...	...	...	|	...	...	|	...	|	|	...	...	...	...
Narbonne ... d.	|	...	...	...	...	|	...	|	...	...	...	|	...	...	|	...	|	|	...	...	...	...
Béziers ... d.	|	...	...	...	...	|	...	|	...	...	...	|	...	...	|	...	|	|	...	...	...	...
Montpellier Saint-Roch ... d.	|	1451	...	...	...	|	...	|	...	...	...	|	...	...	|	...	|	|	...	...	...	...
Montpellier Sud de France ... d.	|	|	...	...	...	|	...	|	...	...	1712	|	...	...	|	...	|	|	...	...	...	...
Nîmes Pont-du-Gard ... d.	|	|	...	...	...	|	...	|	...	...	1733	|	...	...	|	...	|	|	...	...	...	...
Nîmes ... d.	|	1519	...	...	...	|	...	|	...	...	|	|	...	...	|	...	|	|	...	...	...	...
Avignon TGV ... d.	1549	|	...	...	...	|	...	1719	...	...	|	1749	...	...	1851	...	1905	2049	...	...	...	...
Valence TGV ... d.	|	1615	...	...	...	|	...	|	...	...	1815	|	...	...	1926	...	|	2124	...	...	...	...
Lyon St Exupéry ✈ ... d.	|	|	...	...	...	1759	...	1815	...	...	|	|	...	...	|	...	2002	|	...	...	...	...
Lyon Part Dieu ... d.	1700	1700	...	...	...	|	...	|	...	...	1900	1900	...	1929	2002	...	|	2205	...	...	...	...
Le Creusot TGV ... d.	|	|	...	...	...	|	...	|	...	...	|	|	...	|	...	...	|	...	...	...	...	...
Bordeaux ... d.	|	|	...	...	...	|	...	|	1654	...	|	|	...	|	...	...	|	...	...	...	...	...
Angoulême ... d.	|	|	...	...	...	|	...	|	1736	...	|	|	...	|	...	...	|	...	...	...	...	...
Poitiers ... d.	|	|	...	...	...	|	...	|	1820	...	|	|	...	|	...	...	|	...	...	...	...	...
Nantes ... d.	|	|	...	...	...	|	...	|	|	...	|	|	...	|	...	...	|	...	...	...	...	...
Angers St Laud ... d.	|	|	...	...	...	|	...	|	|	...	|	|	...	|	...	...	|	...	...	...	...	...
St Pierre des Corps ... d.	|	|	...	...	...	|	...	|	1856	...	|	|	...	|	...	...	|	...	...	...	...	...
Rennes ... d.	|	|	...	...	...	|	...	|	|	...	|	|	...	|	...	...	|	...	...	...	...	...
Le Mans ... d.	|	|	...	...	...	|	...	|	|	...	|	|	...	|	...	...	|	...	...	...	...	...
Massy TGV ... d.	|	|	...	...	...	|	...	|	1949	...	|	|	...	|	...	...	|	...	...	...	...	...
Strasbourg ... d.	|	|	1701	...	...	|	...	|	|	...	|	|	...	|	...	...	|	...	...	...	...	...
Marne la Vallée (for Disneyland Paris) ... d.	1850	1850	|	...	...	1950	...	2010	2031	...	2050	2050	...	2131	...	...	2151	...	...	...	...	...
Paris Charles de Gaulle ✈ ... a.	1902	1902	1906	...	...	2005	...	2023	2041	...	2101	2101	...	2141	...	...	2203	...	...	...	...	...
Paris Charles de Gaulle ✈ ... d.	1906	1906	1912	...	...	...	...	...	2047	...	2106	2106	...	2147	...	...	2206	...	...	...	...	...
TGV Haute Picardie ... d.	|	|	1950	...	...	...	...	...	2118	...	|	|	...	|	...	...	|	...	...	...	...	...
Arras ... a.	|	|	|	...	...	...	...	...	|	...	|	|	...	|	...	...	|	...	...	...	...	...
Douai ... a.	|	|	|	...	...	...	...	...	|	...	|	|	...	|	...	...	|	...	...	...	...	...
Lille Flandres ... a.	|	|	|	...	...	...	...	...	2148	...	|	|	...	|	...	...	|	...	...	...	...	...
Lille Europe ... a.	1958	1958	2016	...	...	...	...	...	|	...	2159	2159	...	2328	...	...	|	...	...	...	...	...
Lille Europe ... d.	2009	2009	2027	2100	2135	...	...	...	|	...	...	2209	...	...	...	...	|	...	...	...	...	...
Tourcoing ... a.	|	|	|	|	|	...	...	...	2215	...	...	|	...	...	...	...	2326	...	...	...	...	...
Brussels Midi / Zuid ... a.	2043	2043	2101	|	|	...	...	...	...	...	...	2248	...	...	...	...	...	...	...	...	...	...
London St Pancras ... a.	...	...	...	2127	2157	...	...	...	...	...	...	...	...	...	...	...	...	...	...	...	...	...

U – ⑥ (also May 1, 8, 29; not May 3, 10, 31).
W – ⑦ (also June 9).
Z – ⑥ Apr. 5 - June 14 (also May 1, 8, 29).

d – Ⓑ (not May 1, 8, 29).
h – ⑦ (also June 9; not June 8).

TGV – French high-speed train. [R]. 🍷.
☆ – Eurostar high-speed train. [R]. Service May 18 - Sept. 6. See pages 47 and 48 for further information.
⊠ – *Ouigo* low-cost TGV service. Internet booking only at www.ouigo.com.

13 LONDON - PARIS - BARCELONA - MADRID

train type	☆		☆							*AVE*		*TGV*	*avlo*		*TGV*	*AVE*	*TGV*	*AVE*	*avlo*	☆	*TGV*	
train number	**9036**	**5741**	**9040**	**5737**			**3971**			**9730**		**9711**	**6308**		**9713**	**3152**	**6275**	**9742**	**6310**	**9014**	**9715**	
train number/notes	[R] 🍷	[R]	[R] 🍷	[R]	2		[R]	2		[R] 🍷		[R] 🍷	[R]		[R] 🍷	[R]	[R] 🍷	[R] 🍷	[R]	[R] 🍷	[R] 🍷	
notes		⑤⑦		⑤⑦																		
notes		**A d**		**A e**			**B f**					**C**								**D**		
London St Pancras d.	1531	...	1631	...	...	...	...	...	...	...	...	...	...	...	...	...	...	...	...	0931	...	...
Lille Europe d.	|	...	|	...	...	...	...	...	...	...	...	...	...	...	...	...	...	...	...	|	...	...
Paris Nord a.	1902	...	1951	...	...	...	...	...	...	...	...	...	...	...	...	...	...	...	...	1258	...	...
Paris Gare de Lyon d.	...	...	...	...	...	...	...	...	...	...	...	0638	...	...	0742	...	1055	...	...	...	1442	...
Paris Austerlitz d.	...	2008	...	2126	...	...	2213	...	...	...	...	|	...	...	|	...	|	...	...	...	|	...
Les Aubrais-Orléans d.	...	|	...	|	...	...	2322	...	...	...	...	|	...	...	|	...	|	...	...	...	|	...
Lyon Part Dieu d.	...	|	...	|	...	...	|	...	...	...	...	|	...	...	|	...	1308	1435	...	...	|	...
Valence TGV d.	...	|	...	|	...	...	|	...	...	...	...	0856	...	...	0958	...	|	1511	...	...	1656	...
Marseille St Charles d.	...	|	...	|	...	...	|	...	...	0804	...	|	...	...	|	...	|	|	...	...	|	...
Aix en Provence TGV d.	...	|	...	|	...	...	|	...	...	0818	...	|	...	...	|	...	|	|	...	...	|	...
Avignon TGV d.	...	|	...	|	...	...	|	...	...	0840	...	|	...	...	|	...	|	|	...	...	|	...
Nîmes Pont-du-Gard d.	...	|	...	|	...	...	|	...	...	|	...	|	...	...	1038	...	1349	|	...	...	|	...
Nîmes Centre d.	...	0600	...	0600	...	...	|	...	...	0902	...	0944	...	...	|	...	|	1600	...	...	1746	...
Montpellier Saint-Roch d.	...	0628	...	0628	...	...	|	...	...	0933	...	1016	...	...	|	...	|	1629	...	...	1817	...
Montpellier Sud de France d.	...	|	...	|	...	...	|	...	...	|	...	|	...	...	1116	...	1410	|	...	...	|	...
Béziers d.	...	0718	...	0718	...	...	|	...	...	|	...	1059	...	...	1207	...	...	|	...	...	1908	...
Toulouse Matabiau d.	...	|	...	|	...	...	|	...	...	|	...	|	...	...	|	...	...	|	...	...	|	...
Carcassonne d.	...	|	...	|	...	...	|	...	...	|	...	|	...	...	|	...	...	|	...	...	|	...
Narbonne d.	...	0741	...	0741	...	...	|	...	...	1034	...	1119	...	...	1224	...	...	1721	...	...	1924	...
Perpignan d.	...	0831	...	0831	...	...	|	...	...	1118	...	1206	...	...	1307	...	...	1811	...	...	2007	...
Latour de Carol 🏛 a.	...	|	...	|	...	...	1010	1030	...	|	...	|	...	...	|	...	...	|	...	...	|	...
Cerbère 🏛 a.	...	0916	...	0916	...	...	...	|	...	|	...	|	...	...	|	...	...	|	...	...	|	...
Portbou 🏛 a.	...	...	...	...	1035	...	...	|	...	|	...	|	...	...	|	...	...	|	...	...	|	...
Figueres Vilafant ◇ a.	...	...	...	...	1058**z**	...	...	|	...	1139	...	1229	...	...	1330	...	...	1835	...	...	2030	...
Girona a.	...	...	...	...	1138	...	...	|	...	1156	...	1246	...	...	1347	...	...	1852	...	...	2047	...
Barcelona Sants a.	...	...	...	...	1310	...	...	1355	...	1238	...	1328	...	...	1429	...	...	1934	...	...	2129	...
Barcelona Sants d.	...	...	...	...	...	...	...	...	...	1250	...	...	1400	...	...	1500	...	...	2000	...	...	...
Zaragoza Delicias a.	...	...	...	...	...	...	...	...	...	1422	...	...	1542	...	...	1624	...	...	2143	...	...	...
Madrid Puerta de Atocha a.	...	...	...	...	...	...	...	...	...	1552	...	...	1719	...	...	1752	...	...	2319	...	...	...

train type	*AVE*		*TGV*	☆	☆		*AVE*	*TGV*	*AVE*	*TGV*		*AVE*				☆				☆		
train number	**9737**		**9708**	**9051**	**9055**		**3113**	**9704**	**3123**	**9706**		**9725**			**5738**	**9015**	**5744**		**3970**	**9027**		
train number/notes	[R] 🍷		[R] 🍷	[R] 🍷	[R] 🍷		[R] 🍷	[R] 🍷	[R] 🍷	[R] 🍷		[R] 🍷		2	[R]	[R] 🍷	[R]	2	[R]	[R] 🍷		
notes				Ⓑ					Ⓑ						⑤⑦		⑤⑦					
notes								**C**							**A k**		**A m**		**B n**			
Madrid Puerta de Atocha d.	...	...	...	...	...	...	1127	...	1227	...	...	1318	...	...	...	...	...	...	...	...	...	...
Zaragoza Delicias d.	...	...	...	...	...	...	1252	...	1346	...	...	1446	...	...	...	...	...	...	...	...	...	...
Barcelona Sants a.	...	...	...	...	...	...	1446	...	1544	...	...	1622	...	...	...	...	...	...	...	...	...	...
Barcelona Sants d.	0819	...	0928	...	...	...	...	1520	...	1625	...	1634	...	1516	...	...	...	1431	...	...	...	...
Girona d.	0901	...	1010	...	...	...	...	1602	...	1707	...	1716	...	1648	...	...	...	|	...	...	...	...
Figueres Vilafant ◇ d.	0918	...	1027	...	...	...	...	1619	...	1724	...	1733	...	1727**z**	...	...	...	|	...	...	...	...
Portbou 🏛 d.	|	...	|	...	...	...	...	|	...	|	...	|	...	1752	...	...	...	|	...	...	...	...
Cerbère 🏛 d.	|	...	|	...	...	...	...	|	...	|	...	|	...	1804	1900	...	1900	|	...	...	...	...
Latour de Carol 🏛 d.	|	...	|	...	...	...	...	|	...	|	...	|	...	...	|	...	|	1756	1848	...	...	...
Perpignan d.	0952	...	1102	...	...	...	...	1702	...	1758	...	1806	...	...	1933	...	1945	...	|	...	...	...
Narbonne d.	1029	...	1140	...	...	...	...	1740	...	1837	...	1847	...	...	2041	...	2041	...	|	...	...	...
Carcassonne d.	|	...	|	...	...	...	...	|	...	|	...	|	...	...	|	...	|	...	|	...	...	...
Toulouse Matabiau d.	|	...	|	...	...	...	...	|	...	|	...	|	...	...	|	...	|	...	|	...	...	...
Béziers a.	|	...	1154	...	...	...	...	1757	...	1853	...	|	...	...	2058	...	2057	...	|	...	...	...
Montpellier Sud de France a.	|	...	1247	...	...	...	...	|	...	|	...	|	...	...	|	...	|	...	|	...	...	...
Montpellier Saint-Roch a.	1120	...	|	...	...	...	...	1845	...	1945	...	1952	...	...	2145	...	2145	...	|	...	...	...
Nîmes Centre a.	1156	...	|	...	...	...	...	1915	...	2016	...	2032	...	...	2210	...	2212	...	|	...	...	...
Nîmes Pont-du-Gard a.	|	...	1314	...	...	...	...	|	...	|	...	|	...	...	|	...	|	...	|	...	...	...
Avignon TGV a.	|	...	|	...	...	...	...	|	...	|	...	2054	...	...	|	...	|	...	|	...	...	...
Aix en Provence TGV a.	|	...	|	...	...	...	...	|	...	|	...	2117	...	...	|	...	|	...	|	...	...	...
Marseille St Charles a.	|	...	|	...	...	...	...	|	...	|	...	2132	...	...	|	...	|	...	|	...	...	...
Valence TGV a.	1243	...	1355	...	...	...	...	2003	...	2105	...	...	...	...	|	...	|	...	|	...	...	...
Lyon Part Dieu a.	1320	...	|	...	...	...	...	|	...	|	...	...	...	...	|	...	|	...	|	...	...	...
Les Aubrais-Orléans a.	...	...	|	...	...	...	...	|	...	|	...	...	...	...	|	...	|	...	|	...	...	...
Paris Austerlitz a.	...	...	|	...	...	...	...	|	...	|	...	...	...	...	0655	...	0903	...	0931	...	...	...
Paris Gare de Lyon a.	...	...	1612	...	...	...	...	2219	...	2318	...	...	...	...	...	...	...	...	...	...	...	...
Paris Nord d.	...	...	...	1810	1911	...	...	...	...	...	...	...	...	...	...	0912	...	...	...	1212	...	...
Lille Europe a.	...	...	...	|	|	...	...	...	...	...	...	...	...	...	...	|	...	...	...	|	...	...
London St Pancras a.	...	...	...	1939	2030	...	...	...	...	...	...	...	...	...	...	1030	...	...	...	1330	...	...

A – *INTERCITÉS DE NUIT* – 🛏 1, 2 cl., (2) Paris - Cerbère and v.v. Timings are subject to alteration.

B – *INTERCITÉS DE NUIT* – 🛏 1, 2 cl., (2) Paris - Latour de Carol and v.v. Timings are subject to alteration.

C – ⑥⑦ May 3 - June 29 (also May 9, 30). Daily July 5 - Aug. 31. ⑥⑦ Sept. 6 - Nov. 2.

D – Not June 15.

d – May 7, 28, June 6.

e – ⑤⑦ (also June 9; not May 2, 9, 30, June 6, 8).

f – ⑤⑥ until June 7; daily from June 9.

h – Not May 26.

k – ⑤⑦ (also May 7; not May 2, 4, 9, 11, 30, June 1, 6, 8).

m – May 4, 11, June 1, 6, 9. Arrives Paris 0810 on certain dates.

n – ⑥⑦ until June 8; daily from June 9. Arrives Paris up to 1 hour earlier on certain dates.

z – Figueres.

◇ – 🚌 connections available to Figueres bus station. (Table **657**).

TGV – French high-speed train. [R]. 🍷.

AVE – Spanish high-speed train. [R]. 🍷.

avlo – Spanish low-cost high-speed train. [R].

☆ – Eurostar high-speed train. [R]. Service May 18 - Sept. 6. See pages 47 and 48 for further information.

PARIS - HENDAYE - IRÚN - MADRID 14

train type / number		*TGV*	*MD*	*RE*	*Alvia*	*MD*			
train number		**8531**	**18014**	**18318**	**4176**	**18316**			
notes		🅁 🍷	2	2	🅁 🍷	2			
notes		①–⑥							
Paris Montparnasse d.	...	0711	...	...	...	...	...	...	...
Bordeaux St Jean d.	...	0920	...	...	...	...	...	...	...
Biarritz d.	...	1119	...	...	...	...	...	...	...
Hendaye d.	...	1147	...	...	...	...	...	...	...
Irún 🏛 d.	...	...	1318	...	1523	...	...	...	...
San Sebastián / Donostia d.	...	...	1400	...	1652	...	...	...	...
Vitoria / Gasteiz d.	...	...	1601	...	1846	...	...	...	...
Miranda de Ebro d.	...	...	1621	...	1912	...	...	...	...
Burgos Rosa de Lima d.	...	...	1720	...	2018	...	...	...	...
Valladolid Campo Grande d.	...	...	1850	1856	2106	2122	...	...	...
Medina del Campo d.	...	...	1915	1934	|	2201	...	...	...
Salamanca d.	...	...	|	2027	|	2241	...	...	...
Ávila d.	...	...	2001	...	|	...	...	...	...
Madrid Principe Pio a.	...	...	2142	...	|	...	...	...	...
Madrid Chamartín a.	...	...	...	...	2213	...	...	...	...

train type / number		*MD*	*Alvia*	*TGV*					
train number		**18310**	**4087**	**8544**					
notes		2	🅁 🍷	🅁 🍷					
notes		①–⑤							
Madrid Chamartín d.	...	...	0720	...	...	...	...	...	...
Madrid Principe Pio d.	...	...	|	...	...	...	...	...	...
Ávila d.	...	...	|	...	...	...	...	...	...
Salamanca d.	...	0600	|	...	...	...	...	...	...
Medina del Campo d.	...	0639	|	...	...	...	...	...	...
Valladolid Campo Grande d.	...	0705	0827	...	...	...	...	...	...
Burgos Rosa de Lima d.	...	...	0915	...	...	...	...	...	...
Miranda de Ebro d.	...	...	1030	...	...	...	...	...	...
Vitoria / Gasteiz d.	...	...	1051	...	...	...	...	...	...
San Sebastián / Donostia d.	...	...	1243	...	...	...	...	...	...
Irún a.	...	...	1409	...	...	...	...	...	...
Hendaye 🏛 d.	...	...	...	1611	...	...	...	...	...
Biarritz d.	...	...	...	1638	...	...	...	...	...
Bordeaux St Jean a.	...	...	...	1836	...	...	...	...	...
Paris Montparnasse a.	...	...	...	2100	...	...	...	...	...

Alvia – Spanish high-speed train. 🅁. 🍷.

LONDON - AMSTERDAM 15

BY RAIL – SEA – RAIL VIA HARWICH - HOEK VAN HOLLAND

notes	①–⑤	⑥	①–⑤	⑥	⑦	⑦		⑥⑦	①–⑤	①–⑤	⑥⑦		⑦		①–⑥		⑥⑦	①–⑤	①–⑤	⑥⑦		
notes							🚢	**B**	**B**							🚢	**B**	**B**				
London Liverpool Street d.	...	...	0630	0636	0645	...	...	...	...	...	...	...	2000	...	2036	...	...	...	...	...	...	...
Colchester d.	...	...	0730	0737	0748	...	...	...	...	...	...	...	2054	...	2137	...	...	...	...	...	...	...
Manningtree d.	...	...	0738	0745	0756	...	...	...	...	...	...	...	2102	...	2145	...	...	...	...	...	...	...
Cambridge d.	...	...	|	|	|	...	...	...	...	...	...	...	|	1946	|	...	...	...	...	...	...	...
Ipswich d.	0658	0659	|	|	|	0752	...	...	...	...	...	...	|	2103	|	...	...	...	...	...	...	...
Harwich International 🏛 d.	0725	0727	0752	0759	0811	0815	0900	...	...	...	...	...	2116	2129	2159	2300	...	...	...	...	...	...
Hoek van Holland Haven 🏛 a.	...	...	...	...	...	...	1715	1746	1757	...	...	...	...	...	...	0800	0847	0857	...	...	...	...
Schiedam Centrum ◧ a.	...	...	...	...	...	...	...	1812	1823	1845	1846	...	...	...	...	...	0913	0923	0945	0946	...	...
Rotterdam Centraal ◧ a.	...	...	...	...	...	...	...	...	...	|	|	...	...	...	...	...	...	...	|	|	...	...
Den Haag HS a.	...	...	...	...	...	...	...	...	...	1901	1901	...	...	...	...	...	...	...	1001	1003	...	...
Schiphol ✈ a.	...	...	...	...	...	...	...	...	...	|	|	...	...	...	...	...	...	...	|	|	...	...
Amsterdam Centraal a.	...	...	...	...	...	...	...	...	...	1955	1955	...	...	...	...	...	...	...	1055	1054	...	...

notes	⑥⑦	⑦	⑦	⑦	⑦			①–⑥	①–⑥	①–⑥	⑥	①–⑤			①–⑤		①–⑤	⑥	⑦	①–⑤	⑥	⑦
notes		**B**	🚢					**B**	🚢						**B**	🚢						
Amsterdam Centraal d.	1006	...	...	...	...	...	1036	...	...	...	...	...	...	1836	...	...	...	...	...	...	...	...
Schiphol ✈ d.	|	...	...	...	...	...	|	...	...	...	...	...	...	|	...	...	...	...	...	...	...	...
Den Haag HS d.	1100	...	...	...	...	...	1130	...	...	...	...	...	...	1930	...	...	...	...	...	...	...	...
Rotterdam Centraal ◧ d.	|	...	...	...	...	...	|	...	...	...	...	...	...	|	...	...	...	...	...	...	...	...
Schiedam Centrum ◧ d.	1114	1127	...	...	...	...	1144	1217	...	...	...	...	...	1944	2000	...	...	...	...	...	...	...
Hoek van Holland Haven 🏛 d.	...	1153	1345	...	...	...	...	1243	1415	...	...	...	...	...	2027	2200	...	...	...	...	...	...
Harwich International 🏛 a.	...	...	1945	2030	2138	...	...	...	1945	2045	2138	2147	...	...	...	0630	0709	0720	0720	0745	0750	0850
Ipswich a.	...	...	...	|	2204	...	...	...	...	|	2203	2213	...	...	...	...	|	|	|	0815	0817	0913
Cambridge a.	...	...	...	|	...	...	...	...	...	|	...	...	...	...	...	...	|	|	|	0941	0940	1039
Manningtree a.	...	...	...	2042	...	...	...	...	...	2058	...	...	...	...	...	...	0725	0733	0733	...	...	...
Colchester a.	...	...	...	2051	...	...	...	...	...	2107	...	...	...	...	...	...	0740	0742	*0753*	...	...	...
London Liverpool Street a.	...	...	...	2143	...	...	...	...	...	2214	...	...	...	...	...	...	0854	0844	*0857*	...	...	...

B – Rotterdam Metro line **B**.

◧ – Frequent trains available. Journey 5 minutes.

SEA CROSSING (for rail / sea / rail journeys): 🚢 – Ship operated by Stena Line. 🅁. Stena Plus lounge (supplement payable) and ✕ on ship. A cabin must be booked on night sailings.

LILLE - BRUSSELS (Summary Table) 16

WARNING! For dates of running of Eurostar services (☆) see Table **10** on pages 47 and 48.

train type	*TGV*	*TGV*	☆	*TGV*		☆	*TGV*	☆	☆	☆	*TGV*	☆		*TGV*	☆	☆	*TGV*		*TGV*	☆	☆	*TGV*
train number	**9809**	**9890**	**9110**	**9884**		**9116**	**9854**	**9120**	**9126**	**9130**	**9862**	**9132**		**9866**	**9142**	**9148**	**9864**		**9894**	**9152**	**9158**	**9882**
notes	Ⓐ		①–⑥					⑥												Ⓑ		
notes																						
Lille Europe d.	0710	0909	0930	1027	...	1128	1137	1231	1330	1430	1451	1530	...	1709	1730	1930	2009	...	2027	2030	2203	2209
Brussels Midi / Zuid a.	0801	0943	1005	1101	...	1205	1211	1305	1405	1505	1525	1606	...	1744	1805	2005	2043	...	2101	2105	2235	2248

train type	*TGV*	*TGV*	☆	*TGV*	☆	☆	*TGV*	☆	☆	☆	*TGV*	☆	*TGV*	☆	*TGV*	☆	*TGV*	☆	*TGV*	☆	☆	☆
train number	**9810**	**9870**	**9113**	**9812**	**9115**	**9121**	**9826**	**9123**	**9129**	**9135**	**9830**	**9141**	**9832**	**9149**	**9836**	**9153**	**9838**	**9157**	**9844**	**9161**	**9163**	**9167**
notes			①–⑥		**9117**	⑥		**9125**	⑦					⑥				**9159**		⑦	⑥	Ⓑ
notes						**L**			**M**													
Brussels Midi / Zuid d.	0627	0717	0756	0817	0852	0956	1017	1056	1156	1256	1317	1452	1503	1656	1617	1756	1655	1851	1817	1956	2022	2056
Lille Europe a.	0712	0751	0830	0851	0926	1030	1051	1130	1230	1330	1351	1526	1538	1730	1652	1830	1729	1925	1851	2030	2056	2130

L – Not June 28.
M – Not June 29.

☆ – Eurostar high-speed train. 🅁. Service May 18 - Sept. 6. See pages 47 and 48 for further information.

TGV – French high-speed train. 🅁. 🍷.

18 LONDON and PARIS - BRUSSELS - AMSTERDAM

For EUROSTAR SNOW trains see Table **9**. Connections at Brussels are not guaranteed.

train type	☆	*ECD*	☆	*ECD*	*ECD*		☆	*ECD*	☆	*ECD*	☆	☆	*ECD*	☆	☆	*ECD*		☆	☆	*ECD*	☆	
train number	**9301**	**9523**	**9397**	**9523**	**9527**		**9303**	**9527**	**9303**	**9531**	**9309**	**9309**	**9531**	**9106**	**9411**	**9535**		**9315**	**9315**	**9535**	**9110**	
notes	①–⑤	①–⑤	⑥	⑥⑦	①–⑤		⑦	⑥⑦	①–⑤	①–⑤	⑥	①–⑤	⑥⑦	①–⑤	①–⑥	①–⑤		⑦	①–⑥	⑥⑦	①–⑥	
notes	**A**						**B**		**A**			**A**			**A**			**B**	**A**			
London St Pancras d.	...	...	...	...	...	...	...	...	...	...	...	...	...	0616	...	...	...	...	...	...	0704	...
Paris Nord d.	...	...	...	...	...	...	...	...	0622	...	0708	0723	...	|	0755	...	...	0807	0825	...	|	...
Lille Europe d.	...	...	...	...	...	...	...	...	|	...	|	|	...	|	|	...	...	|	|	...	0930	...
Brussels Midi / Zuid a.	...	...	...	...	...	...	...	...	0747	...	0842	0845	...	0913	0917	...	...	0939	0947	...	1005	...
Brussels Midi / Zuid d.	0553	0649	0653	0657	0749	...	0753	0757	0753	0849	0853	0853	0857	0922	...	0949	...	0953	0953	0957	...	...
Antwerpen Centraal a.	0626	0723	0727	0731	0823	...	0827	0831	0827	0923	0927	0927	0931	|	...	1023	...	1027	1027	1031	...	...
Rotterdam Centraal a.	0702	0819	0802	0819	0919	...	0902	0919	0902	1019	1002	1002	1019	1032	...	1119	...	1102	1102	1119	...	...
Schiphol ✈ a.	0730	0848	0833	0848	0948	...	0930	0948	0930	1048	1030	1030	1048	|	...	1148	...	1133	1133	1148	...	...
Amsterdam Zuid a.	|	0856	|	0856	0956	...	|	0956	|	1056	|	|	1056	|	...	1156	...	|	|	1156	...	...
Amsterdam Centraal a.	0750	...	0850	...	...	...	0950	...	0950	...	1050	1050	...	1120	...	...	...	1150	1150	...	...	...

train type	☆	*ECD*	☆	☆	*ECD*	☆	☆	☆	*ECD*	*ECD*	☆	☆	☆	☆	☆	☆	☆	*ECD*	☆	*ECD*	☆	☆
train number	**9317**	**9539**	**9321**	**9321**	**9539**	**9114**	**9423**	**9327**	**9543**	**9543**	**9116**	**9329**	**9333**	**9333**	**9937**	**9120**	**9435**	**9551**	**9339**	**9551**	**9126**	**9341**
notes	①⑥	①–⑤	⑦	①–⑤	⑥⑦	⑥⑦			①–⑤	⑥⑦		⑥	①–④	⑤	⑤⑥⑦	⑥	**9335**	①–⑤		⑥⑦		
notes	**AD**		**E**	**A**									**AG**		**Q**							
London St Pancras d.	...	...	...	...	...	0816	...	...	...	...	0901	...	...	...	...	1001	...	...	...	...	1104	...
Paris Nord d.	0855	...	0922	0922	...	|	0955	1025	...	...	|	1055	1123	1123	...	|	1155	...	1222	...	|	1255
Lille Europe d.	|	...	|	|	...	|	|	|	...	...	1128	|	|	|	...	1231	|	...	|	...	1330	|
Brussels Midi / Zuid a.	1017	...	1044	1044	...	1113	1117	1147	...	...	1205	1217	1244	1244	...	1305	1317	...	1344	...	1405	1417
Brussels Midi / Zuid d.	...	1049	...	1053	1057	1122	...	1153	1149	1157	...	...	...	1253	1322	...	...	1349	1353	1357	1422	...
Antwerpen Centraal a.	...	1123	...	1127	1131	|	...	1227	1223	1231	...	...	...	1327	1357	...	...	1423	1427	1431	|	...
Rotterdam Centraal a.	...	1219	...	1202	1219	1232	...	1302	1319	1319	...	...	...	1402	1432	...	...	1519	1502	1519	1532	...
Schiphol ✈ a.	...	1248	...	1230	1248	|	...	1333	1348	1348	...	...	...	1430	1503	...	...	1548	1530	1548	|	...
Amsterdam Zuid a.	...	1256	...	|	1256	|	...	|	1356	1356	...	...	...	|	|	...	...	1556	|	1556	|	...
Amsterdam Centraal a.	...	...	...	1250	...	1320	...	1350	...	...	...	...	...	1450	1520	...	...	...	1550	...	1620	...

train type	*ECD*	☆	☆	*ECD*	*ECD*	☆	*ECD*	☆	*ECD*	☆	*ECD*		☆	*ECD*	☆	*ECD*	☆		☆	*ECD*	☆	*ECD*
train number	**9555**	**9447**	**9351**	**9555**	**9559**	**9130**	**9559**	**9132**	**9563**	**9357**	**9563**		**9459**	**9567**	**9363**	**9567**	**9142**		**9365**	**9571**	**9369**	**9571**
notes	①–⑤	⑥⑦		⑥⑦	①–⑤		⑥⑦		①–⑤	⑤⑦	⑥⑦			①–⑤		⑥⑦				①–⑤		⑥⑦
notes		**B**																	**H**		**JA**	
London St Pancras d.	...	...	...	...	...	1201	...	1301	...	...	...	...	...	...	...	...	1504	...	...	...	...	...
Paris Nord d.	...	1355	1422	...	...	|	...	|	...	1522	...	...	1555	...	1625	...	|	...	1655	...	1725	...
Lille Europe d.	...	|	|	...	...	1430	...	1530	...	|	...	...	|	...	|	...	1730	...	|	...	|	...
Brussels Midi / Zuid a.	...	1517	1544	...	...	1505	...	1606	...	1647	...	...	1717	...	1747	...	1805	...	1817	...	1847	...
Brussels Midi / Zuid d.	1449	...	1553	1457	1549	...	1557	...	1649	1653	1657	...	...	1749	1753	1757	...	...	...	1849	1853	1857
Antwerpen Centraal a.	1523	...	1627	1531	1623	...	1631	...	1723	1727	1731	...	...	1823	1827	1831	...	...	...	1923	1927	1931
Rotterdam Centraal a.	1619	...	1702	119	1719	...	1719	...	1819	1802	1819	...	...	1819	1902	1919	...	...	...	2019	2002	2019
Schiphol ✈ a.	1648	...	1730	1648	1748	...	1748	...	1848	1830	1848	...	...	1948	1933	1948	...	...	...	2048	2033	2048
Amsterdam Zuid a.	1656	...	|	1656	1756	...	1756	...	1856	|	1856	...	...	1956	|	1956	...	...	...	2056	|	2056
Amsterdam Centraal a.	...	...	1750	...	...	...	...	...	...	1850	...	...	...	...	1950	...	...	...	...	...	2050	...

train type	☆	*ECD*	☆	*ECD*	☆	☆	☆	*ECD*	☆		*ECD*	☆	☆	*ECD*	☆	☆	*ECD*	☆	☆	☆	☆	☆
train number	**9471**	**9575**	**9375**	**9575**	**9977**	**9148**	**9477**	**9579**	**9381**		**9579**	**9483**	**9152**	**9583**	**9387**	**9387**	**9583**	**9389**	**9158**	**9393**	**9395**	**9395**
notes		①–⑤	Ⓑ	⑥⑦	⑦		**9377**	①–⑤			⑥⑦		Ⓑ	①–⑤	①②③	④⑤⑦	⑥⑦	⑤⑥⑦		①–④	⑤	⑤⑦
notes					**R**		**C**					**K**									**E**	**K**
London St Pancras d.	...	...	...	...	...	1704	...	...	...	...	...	...	1804	...	...	...	...	...	1934	...	...	...
Paris Nord d.	1755	...	1825	...	...	|	1855	...	1925	...	...	1955	|	...	2022	2022	...	2053	|	2125	2134	2155
Lille Europe d.	|	...	|	...	...	1930	|	...	|	...	...	|	2030	...	|	|	...	|	2203	|	|	|
Brussels Midi / Zuid a.	1917	...	1947	...	...	2005	2017	...	2047	...	...	2117	2109	...	2144	2144	...	2217	2235	2247	2309	2317
Brussels Midi / Zuid d.	...	1949	1953	1957	2022	...	...	2049	2053	...	2057	...	2122	2149	...	2153	2157	...	...	...	...	...
Antwerpen Centraal a.	...	2023	2027	2031	2057	...	...	2123	2127	...	2131	...	|	2223	...	2227	2231	...	...	...	...	...
Rotterdam Centraal a.	...	2119	2102	2119	2132	...	...	2219	2202	...	2219	...	2232	2319	...	2302	2319	...	...	...	...	...
Schiphol ✈ a.	...	2148	2133	2148	2200	...	...	2248	2233	...	2248	...	|	2348	...	2333	2348	...	...	...	...	...
Amsterdam Zuid a.	...	2156	|	2156	|	...	...	2256	|	...	2256	...	|	2356	...	|	2356	...	...	...	...	...
Amsterdam Centraal a.	...	...	2150	...	2220	...	...	...	2250	...	...	...	2320	...	...	2350	...	...	...	...	...	...

OUIGO TRAINS PARIS - BRUSSELS

train type				*Ouigo*				*Ouigo*				*Ouigo*										
train number				**63**				**65**				**65**										
notes																						
notes				★				★				★										
Paris Nord d.	...	...	...	0818	...	...	...	1205	...	...	...	1914	...	...	...	...	...	...	...	...	...	...
Creil d.	...	...	...	0849	...	...	...	1245	...	...	...	1948	...	...	...	...	...	...	...	...	...	...
St Quentin d.	...	...	...	|	...	...	...	1348	...	...	...	|	...	...	...	...	...	...	...	...	...	...
Aulnoye Aymeries d.	...	...	...	1004	...	...	...	1417	...	...	...	2058	...	...	...	...	...	...	...	...	...	...
Mons a.	...	...	...	1042	...	...	...	1442	...	...	...	2142	...	...	...	...	...	...	...	...	...	...
Brussels Midi / Zuid a.	...	...	...	1121	...	...	...	1521	...	...	...	2221	...	...	...	...	...	...	...	...	...	...

A – Not July 14.
B – Also July 14.
C – ①④⑤⑦.
D – Not July 20 - Sept. 6.
E – July 20 - Sept. 6.
G – May 18 - July 19.
H – Ⓑ May 18 - July 19. ⑤ July 20 - Sept. 6.
J – Daily May 18 - July 19. Ⓑ July 20 - Sept. 6.
K – ⑤⑦ May 18 - July 19. ⑦ July 20 - Sept. 6.
Q – From Marne la Vallée (for Disneyland Paris) depart 1143.
R – From Marne la Vallée (for Disneyland Paris) depart 1840.
★ – Ouigo low-cost train. Internet booking only (www.ouigo.com). Outline service shown. For confirmed timings and running days please consult the Ouigo website.
☆ – Eurostar high-speed train. 🅁. Service May 18 - Sept. 6. See pages 47 and 48 for further information.

AMSTERDAM - BRUSSELS - PARIS and LONDON 18

For EUROSTAR SNOW trains see Table **9**. Connections at Brussels are not guaranteed.

train type	☆	☆	☆	☆	☆	*ECD*	☆	☆	*ECD*	☆	☆	☆	*ECD*	☆	☆	☆	*ECD*	☆	☆	*ECD*	☆	*ECD*	☆	
train number	**9300**	**9302**	**9304**	**9308**	**9113**	**9512**	**9310**	**9310**	**9512**	**9414**	**9115**	**9117**	**9516**	**9316**	**9316**	**9916**	**9516**	**9320**	**9121**	**9520**	**9322**	**9520**	**9426**	
notes	①–⑤	①	①–⑥	①–④	①–⑥	⑥⑦	①–⑤	⑥⑦	①–⑤	①–⑥	①–⑤	⑥⑦	⑥⑦	①–⑥	⑦	⑤⑥⑦	①–⑤		⑥	⑥⑦		①–⑤		
notes	**C A**	**D A**	**A**	**E A**			**A**	**B**		**A**				**A**	**B**	**G**		**J**	**L**					
Amsterdam Centraal d.	...	...	...	...	...	...	0610	...	...	...	0640	...	...	0710	...	0710	...	...	...	...	0810	...	...	...
Amsterdam Zuid d.	...	...	...	...	...	0603	|	...	0603	...	|	...	0703	|	...	|	0703	...	...	0803	|	0803	...	...
Schiphol ✈ d.	...	...	...	...	...	0611	|	...	0611	...	|	...	0711	0727	...	0727	0711	...	...	0811	0827	0811	...	...
Rotterdam Centraal d.	...	...	...	...	...	0641	0657	...	0641	...	0728	...	0741	0758	...	0758	0741	...	...	0841	0858	0841	...	...
Antwerpen Centraal d.	...	...	...	...	...	0729	0733	...	0737	...	|	...	0829	0833	...	0833	0837	...	...	0929	0933	0937	...	...
Brussels Midi / Zuid a.	...	...	...	...	...	0803	0806	...	0811	...	|	...	0903	0906	...	0906	0911	...	...	1003	1006	1011	...	...
Brussels Midi / Zuid d.	0603	0643	0713	0743	0756	...	0813	0813	...	0843	0852	0852	...	0913	0913	0920	...	0943	0956	...	1013	...	1043	...
Lille Europe a.	|	|	|	|	0830	...	|	|	...	|	0926	0926	...	|	|	...	...	|	1030	...	|	...	|	...
Paris Nord a.	0736	0805	0835	0905	|	...	0935	0935	...	1005	|	|	...	1040	1040	...	...	1105	|	...	1135	...	1205	...
London St Pancras a.	...	...	...	...	0857	...	...	...	...	...	0957	0957	...	...	...	...	...	...	1057	...	...	...	...	...

train type	☆	☆	*ECD*	☆	☆	*ECD*	☆	*ECD*	☆	*ECD*	☆	☆	*ECD*	☆	☆	*ECD*	*ECD*	☆	*ECD*	☆	☆	*ECD*	☆	☆
train number	**9125**	**9123**	**9524**	**9328**	**9328**	**9524**	**9129**	**9528**	**9334**	**9528**	**9438**	**9135**	**9532**	**9340**	**9340**	**9532**	**9536**	**9346**	**9528**	**9450**	**9141**	**9540**	**9352**	**9352**
notes	⑥⑦	①–⑤	⑥⑦	①–⑥	⑦	①–⑤	⑦	⑥⑦	⑥⑦	①–⑤	**9338**		⑥⑦	①–⑤	⑦	①–⑤	⑥⑦	⑥⑦	①–⑤			⑥⑦	①–⑤	⑥
notes				**A**	**K**				**B**					**A**	**K**			**B**					**A**	
Amsterdam Centraal d.	0840	...	...	0910	...	...	...	...	1010	...	...	...	...	1110	...	...	...	1210	...	...	...	...	1310	...
Amsterdam Zuid d.	|	...	0903	|	...	0903	...	1003	|	1003	...	...	1103	|	...	1103	1203	|	1203	...	...	1303	|	...
Schiphol ✈ d.	|	...	0911	0927	...	0911	...	1011	1027	1011	...	...	1111	1127	...	1111	1211	1227	1211	...	...	1311	1327	...
Rotterdam Centraal d.	0928	...	0941	0958	...	0941	...	1041	1058	1041	...	...	1141	1158	...	1141	1241	1258	1241	...	...	1341	1358	...
Antwerpen Centraal d.	|	...	1029	1033	...	1037	...	1129	1133	1137	...	...	1229	1233	...	1237	1329	1333	1337	...	...	1429	1433	...
Brussels Midi / Zuid a.	1038	...	1103	1106	...	1111	...	1203	1206	1211	...	...	1303	1306	...	1311	1403	1406	1411	...	...	1503	1506	...
Brussels Midi / Zuid d.	1056	1056	...	1113	1113	...	1156	...	1213	...	1243	1256	...	1313	1313	...	...	1416	...	1443	1452	...	1516	1516
Lille Europe a.	1130	1130	...	|	|	...	1230	...	|	...	|	1330	...	|	|	...	...	|	...	|	1526	...	|	|
Paris Nord a.	|	|	...	1235	1235	...	|	...	1335	...	1405	|	...	1435	1435	...	...	1538	...	1605	|	...	1638	1638
London St Pancras a.	1157	1157	...	...	...	...	1257	...	...	...	...	1357	...	...	...	...	...	...	...	...	1557	...	...	...

train type	*ECD*	☆	☆	*ECD*	☆	☆	☆	*ECD*	☆	☆	*ECD*	☆	*ECD*	☆	☆	*ECD*	☆	*ECD*	☆	☆	☆			
train number	**9540**	**9356**	**9145**	**9544**	**9358**	**9958**	**9358**	**9544**	**9462**	**9149**	**9548**	**9364**	**9548**	**9368**	**9153**	**9552**	**9370**	**9552**	**9474**	**9157**	**9159**			
notes	①–⑤	⑤⑦	①–⑤	⑥⑦	⑤⑥⑦	⑦	①–④	①–⑤	④⑤⑦	⑥	⑥⑦	Ⓑ	①–⑤			⑥⑦		①–⑤		⑥⑦	①–⑤			
notes		**B**			**B**	**B H**	**A**		**M B**					**P**										
Amsterdam Centraal d.	...	...	1340	...	1410	1410	...	...	...	...	...	1510	...	...	...	...	1610	...	...	1640	...	...	...	...
Amsterdam Zuid d.	1303	...	|	1403	|	|	...	1403	...	...	1503	|	1503	...	...	1603	|	1603	...	|	...	...	...	...
Schiphol ✈ d.	1311	...	|	1411	1427	1427	...	1411	...	...	1511	1527	1511	...	...	1611	1627	1611	...	|	...	...	...	...
Rotterdam Centraal d.	1341	...	1428	1441	1458	1458	...	1441	...	...	1541	1558	1541	...	...	1641	1658	1641	...	1728	...	...	...	...
Antwerpen Centraal d.	1437	...	|	1529	1533	1533	...	1537	...	...	1629	1633	1637	...	...	1729	1733	1737	...	|	...	...	...	...
Brussels Midi / Zuid a.	1511	...	1538	1603	1606	1606	...	1611	...	...	1703	1706	1711	...	...	1803	1806	1811	...	1838	...	...	...	...
Brussels Midi / Zuid d.	...	1543	1551	...	1613	1621	1613	...	1643	1656	...	1716	...	1743	1756	...	1813	...	1843	1851	1851	...	...	...
Lille Europe a.	...	|	|	...	|	...	|	...	|	1730	...	|	...	|	1830	...	|	...	|	1925	1925	...	...	...
Paris Nord a.	...	1705	|	...	1735	...	1735	...	1805	|	...	1838	...	1905	|	...	1935	...	2005	|	|	...	...	...
London St Pancras a.	...	...	1657	...	...	...	...	...	...	1757	...	...	...	...	1900	...	...	...	...	1957	1957	...	...	...

train type	*ECD*	☆	*ECD*	☆	☆	☆	*ECD*	☆	*ECD*	☆	☆	*ECD*	☆	☆	*ECD*	*ECD*	☆	☆	*ECD*	*ECD*	*ECD*	☆		
train number	**9556**	**9376**	**9556**	**9380**	**9161**	**9163**	**9560**	**9382**	**9560**	**9486**	**9167**	**9564**	**9388**	**9388**	**9564**	**9568**	**9394**	**9394**	**9568**	**9572**	**9572**	**9398**		
notes	⑥⑦	Ⓑ	①–⑤		⑦	⑥	⑥⑦		①–⑤	Ⓑ	Ⓑ	⑥⑦	Ⓑ	⑥	①–⑤	⑥⑦	⑤⑥	⑦	①–⑤	⑥⑦	①–⑤			
notes				**Q**																		**R**		
Amsterdam Centraal d.	...	1710	...	...	...	...	...	1810	...	...	1840	...	1910	...	...	...	2010	2010	...	...	...	2110	...	...
Amsterdam Zuid d.	1703	|	1703	...	...	...	1803	|	1803	...	|	1903	|	...	1903	2003	|	|	2003	2103	2103	|	...	...
Schiphol ✈ d.	1711	1727	1711	...	...	...	1811	1827	1811	...	|	1911	1926	...	1911	2011	2027	2027	2011	2111	2111	2127	...	...
Rotterdam Centraal d.	1741	1758	1741	...	...	...	1841	1858	1841	...	1928	1941	1958	...	1941	2041	2058	2058	2041	2141	2141	2158	...	...
Antwerpen Centraal d.	1829	1833	1837	...	...	...	1929	1933	1937	...	|	2029	2033	...	2037	2129	2133	2133	2137	2229	2237	2233	...	...
Brussels Midi / Zuid a.	1903	1906	1911	...	...	...	2003	2006	2011	...	2038	2103	2106	...	2111	2203	2206	2206	2211	2303	2311	2306	...	...
Brussels Midi / Zuid d.	...	1913	...	1943	1956	2022	...	2013	...	2043	2056	...	2113	2113	...	...	...	2213	...	...	...	...	...	...
Lille Europe a.	...	|	...	|	2030	2056	...	|	...	|	2130	...	|	|	...	...	...	|	...	...	...	...	...	...
Paris Nord a.	...	2035	...	2105	|	|	...	2139	...	2205	|	...	2240	2240	...	...	...	2340	...	...	...	...	...	...
London St Pancras a.	...	...	...	...	2057	2127	...	...	...	...	2157	...	...	...	...	...	...	...	...	...	...	...	...	...

OUIGO TRAINS BRUSSELS - PARIS

train type			*Ouigo*			*Ouigo*			*Ouigo*			*Ouigo*											
train number			**50**			**54**			**56**			**58**											
notes			**S**			**T**			**U**			**V**											
notes			★			★			★			★											
Brussels Midi / Zuid d.	...	...	0739	...	...	1338	...	...	1838	...	...	1938	...	...	...	...	...	...	...	...	...	...	...
Mons d.	...	...	0822	...	...	1422	...	...	1922	...	...	2022	...	...	...	...	...	...	...	...	...	...	...
Aulnoye Aymeries d.	...	...	0848	...	...	1448	...	...	1945	...	...	2046	...	...	...	...	...	...	...	...	...	...	...
St Quentin d.	...	...	|	...	...	1520	...	...	|	...	...	|	...	...	...	...	...	...	...	...	...	...	...
Creil a.	...	...	1003	...	...	1612	...	...	2103	...	...	2203	...	...	...	...	...	...	...	...	...	...	...
Paris Nord a.	...	...	1036	...	...	1645	...	...	2136	...	...	2236	...	...	...	...	...	...	...	...	...	...	...

A – Not July 14.
B – Also July 14.
C – ①–⑤ May 18 - July 19. ① July 20 - Sept. 6.
D – ① May 18 - July 19.
E – ①–④ May 18 - July 19.
G – To Marne la Vallée (for Disneyland Paris) arrive 1050.
H – To Marne la Vallée (for Disneyland Paris) arrive 1751.
J – ②③④⑤⑦ May 18 - July 19. ②③④⑤ July 20 - Sept. 6.
K – July 20 - Sept. 6.
L – Not June 28.
M – ④⑤⑦ May 18 - July 19. ⑦ July 20 - Sept. 6.
P – Ⓑ May 18 - July 19. ⑤ July 20 - Sept. 6.

Q – ④⑤⑦ May 18 - July 19.
R – Ⓑ May 18 - July 19. ⑤⑦ July 20 - Sept. 6.
S – ①–⑤ June 9 - Aug. 15 (not July 19, 20).
T – Daily June 9 - Aug. 15.
U – ①–⑥ June 9 - Aug. 15.
V – ⑦ June 8 - Aug. 10.

★ – Ouigo low-cost train. Internet booking only (www.ouigo.com). Outline service shown. For confirmed timings and running days please consult the Ouigo website.

☆ – Eurostar high-speed train. Ⓡ. Service May 18 - Sept. 6. See pages 47 and 48 for further information.

20 LONDON, PARIS and BRUSSELS - KÖLN, HAMBURG and BERLIN

For full service London - Brussels see Table 10. For full service Paris - Brussels see Table 18. Connections at Brussels are not guaranteed.

train type	ICE	ICE	ICE	ICE	☆	ICE	ICE	ICE	ICE	☆	ICE	ICE	ICE	☆	☆	☆	☆	ICE	ICE	ICE	☆	ICE
train number	11	545	555	206	9303	13	547	557	614	9411	849	859	612	9106	9315	9315	9110	15	559	200	9423	1051
notes					①-⑤		⑦			①-⑥	⑦			①-⑤	⑦	①-⑥	①-⑥					
notes			✣		D			✣		D		✣			E	D			✣		G	
London St Pancras d.	...	...	...	...	...	...	...	...	...	...	...	...	...	0616	...	...	0704	...	...	...	...	...
Paris Nord d.	...	...	...	...	0622	...	...	...	...	0755	...	...	...	|	0807	0825	|	...	...	...	0955	...
Brussels Midi/Zuid a.	...	...	...	...	0744	...	...	...	...	0917	...	...	...	0913	0939	0947	1005	...	...	...	1117	...
Brussels Midi/Zuid d.	0623	...	...	...	...	0825	...	...	...	0925	...	...	...	...	...	...	...	1025	...	...	1125	...
Brussels Nord d.	0631	...	...	...	...	0834	...	...	...	|	...	...	...	...	...	...	...	1034	...	...	|	...
Liège Guillemins d.	0712	...	...	...	...	0914	...	...	...	1013	...	...	...	...	...	...	...	1114	...	...	1213	...
Aachen 🏛 d.	0739	...	...	...	...	0939	...	...	...	1037	...	...	...	...	...	...	...	1139	...	...	1238	1247
Köln Hbf a.	0815	...	...	...	...	1015	...	...	...	1116	...	...	...	...	...	...	...	1215	...	...	1315	1331
Köln Hbf d.	...	0825	0845	0911	...	...	1026	1045	1011	...	1126	1145	1211	...	...	...	...	...	1245	1311	...	1335
Wuppertal Hbf d.	...	|	0916	0944	...	...	|	1116	1044	...	|	1216	1244	...	...	...	...	...	1316	|	...	|
Hagen Hbf d.	...	|	0933	1001	...	...	|	1133	1101	...	|	1232	1301	...	...	...	...	...	1333	|	...	|
Düsseldorf Hbf d.	...	0851	|	|	...	...	1051	|	|	...	1150	|	|	...	...	...	...	...	|	1334	...	1417
Duisburg Hbf d.	...	0910	|	|	...	...	1110	|	|	...	1209	|	|	...	...	...	...	...	|	1347	...	1431
Essen Hbf d.	...	0922	|	|	...	...	1122	|	|	...	1221	|	|	...	...	...	...	...	|	1400	...	1445
Bochum Hbf d.	...	0933	|	|	...	...	1133	|	|	...	1232	|	|	...	...	...	...	...	|	1410	...	1456
Dortmund Hbf d.	...	0947	|	1025	...	...	1147	|	1125	...	1245	|	1325	...	...	...	...	...	|	1425	...	1510
Hamm (Westf) d.	...	|	|	|	...	...	|	|	|	...	1311	1311	|	...	...	...	...	...	|	|	...	1534
Bielefeld Hbf d.	...	1035	|	|	...	...	1235	|	|	...	|	|	|	...	...	...	...	...	|	|	...	1605
Münster d.	...	|	|	1057	...	...	|	|	1157	...	|	|	1357	...	...	...	...	...	|	1457	...	|
Osnabrück Hbf d.	...	|	|	1123	...	...	|	|	1223	...	|	|	1423	...	...	...	...	...	|	1523	...	|
Bremen Hbf d.	...	|	|	1218	...	...	|	|	1317	...	|	|	1517	...	...	...	...	...	|	1617	...	|
Hannover Hbf a.	...	1128	1204	|	...	...	1328	1404	|	...	1428	1428	|	...	...	...	...	...	1604	|	...	1702
Hamburg Hbf a.	...	|	|	1314	...	...	|	|	1414	...	|	|	1614	...	...	...	...	...	|	1714	...	|
Berlin Hbf a.	...	1318	1400	...	...	...	1518	1549	...	...	1618	1618	...	...	...	...	...	...	1749	...	...	1851

train type	ICE	ICE	☆	ICE	ICE	ICE		☆	ICE	ICE	☆	☆	ICE	ICE	EC	☆	☆	ICE	☆	ICE	ICE	ICE
train number	951	610	9116	315	651	108		9435	953	518	9339	9126	17	653	8	9447	9351	317	9132	317	655	104
notes								Ⓑ								⑥⑦		Ⓐ		Ⓒ		
notes	✣				✣				✣					✣							✣	
London St Pancras d.	...	...	0901	...	...	...	...	...	...	...	...	1104	...	...	...	...	...	...	1301	...	...	...
Paris Nord d.	...	...	|	...	...	...	...	1155	...	...	1222	|	...	...	...	1355	1422	...	|	...	...	...
Brussels Midi/Zuid a.	...	...	1205	...	...	...	...	1317	...	...	1344	1405	...	...	...	1517	1544	...	1606	...	...	...
Brussels Midi/Zuid d.	...	...	...	1225	...	...	...	1325	...	...	...	...	1425	...	...	1525	...	1622	...	1625	...	...
Brussels Nord d.	...	...	...	1234	...	...	...	|	...	...	...	...	1434	...	...	|	...	1632	...	1634	...	...
Liège Guillemins d.	...	...	...	1314	...	...	...	1413	...	...	...	...	1514	...	...	1613	...	1714	...	1714	...	...
Aachen 🏛 d.	...	...	...	1339	...	...	...	1438	...	...	...	...	1539	...	...	1638	...	1739	...	1739	...	...
Köln Hbf a.	...	...	...	1415	...	...	...	1515	...	...	...	...	1615	...	...	1715	...	1815	...	1815	...	...
Köln Hbf d.	1345	1411	...	...	1445	1511	...	...	1545	1611	...	...	...	1645	1709	...	...	...	...	...	1845	1911
Wuppertal Hbf d.	1416	1444	...	...	1516	|	...	...	1616	|	...	...	...	1716	|	...	...	...	...	...	1916	|
Hagen Hbf d.	1432	1501	...	...	1533	|	...	...	1632	|	...	...	...	1733	|	...	...	...	...	...	1933	|
Düsseldorf Hbf d.	|	|	...	...	|	1534	...	...	|	1634	...	...	...	|	1733	...	...	...	...	...	|	1934
Duisburg Hbf d.	|	|	...	...	|	1547	...	...	|	1647	...	...	...	|	1747	...	...	...	...	...	|	1947
Essen Hbf d.	|	|	...	...	|	1600	...	...	|	1700	...	...	...	|	1800	...	...	...	...	...	|	2000
Bochum Hbf d.	|	|	...	...	|	1610	...	...	|	1710	...	...	...	|	1810	...	...	...	...	...	|	2010
Dortmund Hbf d.	|	1525	...	...	|	1625	...	...	|	1725	...	...	...	|	1825	...	...	...	...	...	|	2025
Hamm (Westf) d.	1511	|	...	...	|	|	...	...	1711	|	...	...	...	|	|	...	...	...	...	...	|	|
Bielefeld Hbf d.	|	|	...	...	|	|	...	...	|	|	...	...	...	|	|	...	...	...	...	...	|	|
Münster d.	|	1557	...	...	|	1657	...	...	|	1757	...	...	...	|	1857	...	...	...	...	...	|	2057
Osnabrück Hbf d.	|	1623	...	...	|	1723	...	...	|	1823	...	...	...	|	1923	...	...	...	...	...	|	2123
Bremen Hbf d.	|	1717	...	...	|	1817	...	...	|	1917	...	...	...	|	2017	...	...	...	...	...	|	2219
Hannover Hbf a.	1628	|	...	...	1804	|	...	...	1828	|	...	...	...	2004	|	...	...	...	...	...	2204	|
Hamburg Hbf a.	|	1814	...	...	|	1914	...	...	|	2014	...	...	...	|	2114	...	...	...	...	...	|	2316
Berlin Hbf a.	1818	...	...	...	1949	...	...	...	2018	...	...	...	...	2149	...	...	...	...	...	...	2349	...

train type	☆	ICE	ICE	ICE	☆	☆	ICE	ICE	ICE	NJ	ES	☆	ICE	☆	☆	☆	ICE	ICE	☆	☆		
train number	9459	947	957	514	9363	9142	19	657	102	425	453	9471	512	9375	9148	9477	319	100	9152	9483		
notes		①-④	⑤⑥					Ⓑ		①③⑤	①③⑤			Ⓑ		④⑤			Ⓑ	⑦		
notes										B	C											
London St Pancras d.	...	...	...	...	...	1504	...	...	...	...	...	...	...	...	1704	...	...	...	1804	...	...	...
Paris Nord d.	1555	...	...	...	1625	|	...	...	...	...	...	1755	...	1825	|	1855	...	...	|	1955	...	...
Brussels Midi/Zuid a.	1717	...	...	...	1747	1805	...	...	...	...	...	1917	...	1947	2005	2017	...	...	2109	2117	...	...
Brussels Midi/Zuid d.	1725	...	...	...	...	...	1825	...	...	1906	1922	1925	...	...	...	2022	2025	...	...	2125	...	...
Brussels Nord d.	|	...	...	...	...	...	1834	...	...	1916	|	|	...	...	...	|	2034	...	...	|	...	...
Liège Guillemins d.	1813	...	...	...	...	...	1914	...	...	2018	|	2013	...	...	...	2111	2114	...	...	2213	...	...
Aachen 🏛 d.	1837	...	...	...	...	...	1939	1957	...	2110	|	2037	...	...	...	2137	2139	...	...	2237	...	...
Köln Hbf a.	1915	...	...	...	...	...	2015	2044	...	2150	|	2115	...	...	...	2215	2222	...	...	2314	...	...
Köln Hbf d.	1918	1926	1946	2011	...	...	...	2047	2111	2201	|	2118	2212	...	...	...	...	2312	...	...	...	...
Wuppertal Hbf d.	|	|	2016	2044	...	...	...	2117	|	|	|	|	|	...	...	...	...	|	...	...	...	...
Hagen Hbf d.	|	|	2032	2101	...	...	...	2134	|	|	|	|	|	...	...	...	...	|	...	...	...	...
Düsseldorf Hbf d.	1943	1950	|	|	...	...	...	|	2134	|	|	2143	2235	...	...	...	...	2335	...	...	...	...
Duisburg Hbf d.	1956	2009	|	|	...	...	...	|	2147	|	|	2204	2248	...	...	...	...	2352	...	...	...	...
Essen Hbf d.	2010	2021	|	|	...	...	...	|	2200	|	|	2218	2308	...	...	...	...	0004	...	...	...	...
Bochum Hbf d.	|	2032	|	|	...	...	...	|	2210	|	|	|	|	...	...	...	...	0014	...	...	...	...
Dortmund Hbf d.	2038	2045	|	2125	...	...	...	|	2228	|	|	2241	|	...	...	...	...	0033	...	...	...	...
Hamm (Westf) d.	...	2111	2111	|	...	...	...	2205	...	|	|	...	|	...	...	...	...	0051	...	...	...	...
Bielefeld Hbf d.	...	|	|	|	...	...	...	2235	...	|	|	...	|	...	...	...	...	0123	...	...	...	...
Münster d.	...	|	|	2157	...	...	...	|	...	|	|	...	0001	...	...	...	...	|	...	...	...	...
Osnabrück Hbf d.	...	|	|	2223	...	...	...	|	...	|	|	...	...	...	...	...	...	|	...	...	...	...
Bremen Hbf d.	...	|	|	2317	...	...	...	|	...	|	|	...	...	...	...	...	...	|	...	...	...	...
Hannover Hbf a.	...	2228	2228	|	...	...	...	2328	...	|	|	...	...	...	...	...	...	0223	...	...	...	...
Hamburg Hbf a.	...	|	|	0014	...	...	...	|	...	|	|	...	...	...	...	...	...	|	...	...	...	...
Berlin Hbf a.	...	0018	0018	...	...	...	...	0114z	...	0826	0620	...	...	...	...	...	...	0536	...	...	...	...

B – **Suspended until further notice.** ①③⑤: *ÖBB nightjet* – 🛏 1, 2 cl., 🛌 2 cl. (4, 6 berth), (2) Brussels - Berlin (Table **55**).

C – ①③⑤. EUROPEAN SLEEPER – 🛏 (1, 2, 3 berth), 🛌 (5, 6 berth), (2) Brussels - Berlin - Praha (Table **78**).

D – Not July 14.

E – Also July 14.

G – ①②⑤⑥⑦ June 15 - July 19. Daily July 20 - Sept. 6.

z – ①⑥.

✣ – Subject to alteration from Aug. 9.

☆ – Eurostar high-speed train. 🅁. Service May 18 - Sept. 6. See pages 47 and 48 for further information.

BERLIN, HAMBURG and KÖLN - BRUSSELS, PARIS and LONDON 20

For full service Brussels - London see Table **10**. For full service Brussels - Paris see Table **18**. Connections at Brussels are not guaranteed.

train type	☆	*NJ*	*ES*	*ICE*	*ICE*	*ICE*	☆	☆	*ICE*	☆	☆	*EC*	*ICE*	*ICE*	*ICE*	☆	☆	*ICE*	*ICE*	☆	☆	
train number	**9414**	**424**	**452**	**101**	**813**	**18**	**9322**	**9123**	**513**	**9426**	**9426**	**7**	**656**	**656**	**316**	**9334**	**9135**	**515**	**956**	**9438**	**9438**	
notes	①–⑥	②④⑦	②④⑦		①–⑤			**9125**		①–⑥	⑦		②–⑤	①		⑥⑦				⑦	①⑤⑥	
notes	**C**	**A**	**B**										✣	✣								
Berlin Hbf d.	...	1906	2256	0022	...	...	...	...	...	...	...	...	...	0404	...	...	...	...	0527	...	...	...
Hamburg Hbf d.	...	|	|	|	...	...	...	...	...	...	...	0438	...	|	...	...	...	0546	|	...	...	...
Hannover Hbf d.	...	|	|	0313	...	...	...	...	...	...	...	|	0558	0558	...	...	...	|	0731	...	...	...
Bremen Hbf d.	...	|	|	|	...	...	...	...	...	...	...	0540	|	|	...	...	...	0644	|	...	...	...
Osnabrück Hbf d.	...	|	|	|	...	...	...	...	...	...	...	0637	|	|	...	...	...	0737	|	...	...	...
Münster d.	...	|	|	|	...	...	...	...	0603	...	...	0703	|	|	...	...	...	0803	|	...	...	...
Bielefeld Hbf d.	...	|	|	0428	...	...	...	...	|	...	...	|	|	|	...	...	...	|	|	...	...	...
Hamm (Westf) d.	...	|	|	0503	...	...	...	...	|	...	...	|	|	|	...	...	...	|	0856	...	...	...
Dortmund Hbf d.	0519	|	|	0536	0555	...	...	...	0636	0712	...	0736	|	|	...	...	...	0836	|	0910	...	...
Bochum Hbf d.	|	|	|	0548	|	...	...	...	0648	|	...	0748	|	|	...	...	...	|	|	|	...	...
Essen Hbf d.	0541	|	|	0600	|	...	...	...	0700	0736	...	0800	|	|	...	...	...	|	|	0933	...	...
Duisburg Hbf d.	0554	|	|	0613	|	...	...	...	|	0749	...	0813	|	|	...	...	...	|	|	0946	...	...
Düsseldorf Hbf d.	0614	|	|	0627	|	...	...	...	0727	0809	...	0827	|	|	...	...	...	|	|	1001	...	...
Hagen Hbf d.	|	|	|	|	0619	...	...	...	|	|	...	|	|	|	...	...	...	0858	0926	|	...	...
Wuppertal Hbf d.	|	|	|	|	0636	...	...	...	|	|	...	|	0844	0844	...	...	...	0915	0943	|	...	...
Köln Hbf a.	0641	0659	|	0649	0708	...	...	...	0749	0836	...	0849	0915	0915	...	...	...	0947	1012	1036	...	...
Köln Hbf d.	0645	0702	|	...	...	0742	...	...	...	0845	0845	...	...	...	0941	...	...	...	...	1045	1045	...
Aachen 🚉 d.	0723	0809	|	...	...	0820	...	...	...	0924	0924	...	...	...	1020	...	...	...	...	1123	1124	...
Liège Guillemins d.	0753	0851	|	...	...	0846	...	...	...	0951	0951	...	...	...	1046	...	...	...	...	1151	1151	...
Brussels Nord a.	|	0946	|	...	...	0926	...	...	...	|	|	...	...	...	1126	...	...	...	...	|	|	...
Brussels Midi/Zuid a.	0835	0955	0927	...	...	0935	...	...	...	1035	1035	...	...	...	1135	...	...	...	...	1235	1235	...
Brussels Midi/Zuid d.	0843	...	...	...	...	...	1013	1056	...	1043	1043	...	...	...	...	1213	1256	...	...	1243	1243	...
Paris Nord a.	1005	...	...	...	...	...	1135	|	...	1205	1205	...	...	...	...	1335	|	...	...	1405	1405	...
London St Pancras a.	...	...	...	...	...	...	...	1157	...	...	...	...	...	...	...	...	1357	...	...	...	...	...

train type	*ICE*	*ICE*	*ICE*	☆	*ICE*	*ICE*	☆	☆	*ICE*	*ICE*	*ICE*	☆	☆	*ICE*	*ICE*	☆	☆	*ICE*	*ICE*	*ICE*	☆	☆
train number	**105**	**654**	**16**	**9346**	**517**	**954**	**9450**	**9450**	**107**	**652**	**314**	**9358**	**9149**	**519**	**952**	**9462**	**9153**	**109**	**650**	**14**	**9370**	**9159**
notes				⑥⑦			⑦	①–⑥					⑥			⑦						**9157**
notes		✣								✣									✣			
Berlin Hbf d.	...	0608	...	...	...	0746	...	...	...	0807	...	...	...	...	0946	...	...	...	1007	...	...	...
Hamburg Hbf d.	0646	|	...	...	0746	|	...	...	0845	|	...	...	...	0946	|	...	...	1046	|	...	...	...
Hannover Hbf d.	|	0758	...	...	|	0931	...	...	|	0958	...	...	...	|	1131	...	...	|	1158	...	...	...
Bremen Hbf d.	0744	|	...	...	0844	|	...	...	0944	|	...	...	...	1044	|	...	...	1144	|	...	...	...
Osnabrück Hbf d.	0837	|	...	...	0937	|	...	...	1037	|	...	...	...	1137	|	...	...	1237	|	...	...	...
Münster d.	0903	|	...	...	1003	|	...	...	1103	|	...	...	...	1203	|	...	...	1303	|	...	...	...
Bielefeld Hbf d.	|	|	...	...	|	|	...	...	|	|	...	...	...	|	|	...	...	|	|	...	...	...
Hamm (Westf) d.	|	|	...	...	|	1056	...	...	|	|	...	...	...	|	1256	...	...	|	|	...	...	...
Dortmund Hbf d.	0936	|	...	...	1036	|	1058	...	1136	|	...	...	...	1236	|	...	...	1336	|	...	...	...
Bochum Hbf d.	0948	|	...	...	|	|	|	...	1148	|	...	...	...	1248	|	...	...	1348	|	...	...	...
Essen Hbf d.	1000	|	...	...	|	|	1125	...	1200	|	...	...	...	1300	|	...	...	1400	|	...	...	...
Duisburg Hbf d.	1013	|	...	...	|	|	1138	...	1213	|	...	...	...	1313	|	...	...	1413	|	...	...	...
Düsseldorf Hbf d.	1027	|	...	...	|	|	1154	...	1227	|	...	...	...	1327	|	...	...	1427	|	...	...	...
Hagen Hbf d.	|	1029	...	...	1058	1126	|	...	|	1229	...	...	...	|	1326	...	...	|	1429	...	...	...
Wuppertal Hbf d.	|	1046	...	...	1115	1143	|	...	|	1246	...	...	...	|	1343	...	...	|	1446	...	...	...
Köln Hbf a.	1049	1115	...	...	1147	1212	1226	...	1249	1319	...	...	...	1349	1412	...	...	1449	1515	...	...	...
Köln Hbf d.	...	...	1142	...	▬	...	1243	1243	▬	...	1342	...	...	...	...	1445	...	...	...	1541	...	...
Aachen 🚉 d.	...	...	1220	...	...	...	1324	1324	...	...	1420	...	...	...	...	1524	...	...	...	1620	...	...
Liège Guillemins d.	...	...	1246	...	...	...	1351	1351	☆	...	1446	...	...	...	...	1551	...	...	...	1646	...	...
Brussels Nord a.	...	...	1326	...	☆	...	|	|	**9145**	...	1526	...	...	...	...	|	...	...	...	1726	...	...
Brussels Midi/Zuid a.	...	...	1335	...	**9141**	...	1435	1435	①–⑤	...	1535	...	...	...	...	1635	...	...	...	1735	...	...
Brussels Midi/Zuid d.	...	...	...	1416	1452	...	1443	1443	1551	...	...	1613	1656	...	...	1643	1756	...	...	...	1813	1851
Paris Nord a.	...	...	...	1538	|	...	1605	1605	|	...	...	1735	|	...	...	1805	|	...	...	...	1935	|
London St Pancras a.	...	...	...	...	1557	...	...	...	1657	...	...	...	1757	...	...	...	1900	...	...	...	...	1957

train type	*ICE*	*ICE*	☆	*ICE*	*ICE*	*ICE*	☆	☆	*ICE*	*ICE*	*ICE*	☆		*ICE*	*ICE*	*ICE*	☆	*ICE*	*ICE*	*ICE*	*ICE*	
train number	**611**	**950**	**9474**	**201**	**558**	**12**	**9382**	**9167**	**613**	**858**	**848**	**9486**		**203**	**546**	**10**	**9394**	**205**	**554**	**544**	**318**	
notes								Ⓑ			①–④	Ⓑ					⑦					
notes					✣						⑦✣				✣							
Berlin Hbf d.	...	1146	...	...	1207	...	...	...	...	1346	1346	...	...	...	1448	...	...	...	1607	1646	...	...
Hamburg Hbf d.	1146	|	...	1246	|	...	...	...	1346	|	|	...	...	1445	|	...	...	1646	|	|	...	...
Hannover Hbf d.	|	1331	...	|	1358	...	...	...	|	1531	1531	...	...	|	1631	...	...	|	1758	1831	...	...
Bremen Hbf d.	1244	|	...	1344	|	...	...	...	1444	|	|	...	...	1544	|	...	...	1745	|	|	...	...
Osnabrück Hbf d.	1333	|	...	1437	|	...	...	...	1537	|	|	...	...	1637	|	...	...	1837	|	|	...	...
Münster d.	1403	|	...	1503	|	...	...	...	1603	|	|	...	...	1703	|	...	...	1902	|	|	...	...
Bielefeld Hbf d.	|	|	...	|	|	...	...	...	|	|	|	...	...	|	1728	...	...	|	|	1928	...	...
Hamm (Westf) d.	|	1456	...	|	|	...	...	...	|	1656	1654	...	...	|	|	...	...	|	|	|	...	...
Dortmund Hbf d.	1436	|	...	1536	|	...	...	...	1636	|	1713	...	...	1736	1814	...	...	1936	|	2014	...	...
Bochum Hbf d.	|	|	...	1548	|	...	...	...	|	|	1725	...	...	1748	1825	...	...	|	|	2025	...	...
Essen Hbf d.	|	|	...	1600	|	...	...	...	|	|	1737	...	...	1800	1837	...	...	|	|	2037	...	...
Duisburg Hbf d.	|	|	...	1613	|	...	...	...	|	|	1750	...	...	1813	1850	...	...	|	|	2050	...	...
Düsseldorf Hbf d.	|	|	...	1627	|	...	...	...	|	|	1809	...	...	1827	1912	...	...	|	|	2109	...	...
Hagen Hbf d.	1458	1526	...	|	1629	...	...	...	1658	1726	|	...	...	|	|	...	...	1958	2029	|	...	...
Wuppertal Hbf d.	1515	1543	...	|	1646	...	...	...	1715	1743	|	...	...	|	|	...	...	2015	2046	|	...	...
Köln Hbf a.	1547	1612	...	1649	1715	...	...	...	1747	1812	1832	...	...	1849	1936	...	...	2047	2114	2133	...	...
Köln Hbf d.	...	...	1645	...	...	1742	...	...	...	...	...	1845	...	...	...	1942	...	...	...	...	2142	...
Aachen 🚉 d.	...	...	1724	...	...	1820	...	...	...	...	...	1924	...	...	...	2020	...	...	...	...	2220	...
Liège Guillemins d.	...	...	1751	...	...	1846	...	...	...	...	...	1951	...	...	...	2046	...	...	...	...	2246	...
Brussels Nord a.	...	...	|	...	...	1926	...	...	...	...	...	|	...	...	...	2126	...	...	...	...	2326	...
Brussels Midi/Zuid a.	...	...	1835	...	...	1935	...	...	...	...	...	2035	...	...	...	2135	...	...	...	...	2335	...
Brussels Midi/Zuid d.	...	...	1843	...	...	...	2013	2056	...	...	...	2043	...	...	...	...	2213	...	...	...	...	...
Paris Nord a.	...	...	2005	...	...	...	2139	|	...	...	...	2205	...	...	...	...	2340	...	...	...	...	...
London St Pancras a.	...	...	...	...	...	...	...	2157	...	...	...	...	...	...	...	...	...	...	...	...	...	...

A – **Suspended until further notice.** ②④⑦: *ÖBB nightjet* – 🛏 1, 2 cl., ▬ 2 cl. (4, 6 berth), 🚃 Berlin - Brussels (Table **55**).

✣ – Subject to alteration from Aug. 9.

B – ②④⑦. EUROPEAN SLEEPER – 🛏 (1, 2, 3 berth), ▬ (5, 6 berth), 🚃 Praha - Berlin - Brussels (Table **78**).

C – Not July 14.

☆ – Eurostar high-speed train. Ⓡ. Service May 18 - Sept. 6. See pages 47 and 48 for further information.

21 LONDON, PARIS and BRUSSELS - FRANKFURT - MÜNCHEN and WIEN

For full service London - Brussels see Table **10**. For full service Paris - Brussels see Table **18**. Connections at Brussels are not guaranteed.

train type	*ICE*	*EC*	*ICE*	*ICE*	*ICE*	*ICE*	☆	*ICE*	*ICE*	*ICE*	*ICE*		☆	*ICE*	*ICE*	☆	☆	☆	☆	*ICE*	*ICE*	*ICE*	*ICE*	
train number	**11**	**7**	**571**	**529**	**915**	**27**	**9303**	**13**	**573**	**623**	**27**		**9411**	**625**	**517**	**9106**	**9315**	**9315**	**9110**	**15**	**575**	**627**	**29**	
notes							①–⑤						①–⑥			①–⑤	⑦	①–⑥	①–⑥					
notes													🅁											
notes							**A**						**A**				**B**	**A**						
London St Pancras d.	...	...	...	...	...	...	...	...	...	...	...	...	...	...	...	0616	...	...	0704	...	...	...	...	...
Paris Nord d.	...	...	...	...	...	...	0622	...	...	...	...	...	0755	...	...	|	0807	0825	|	...	...	...	...	...
Brussels Midi / Zuid a.	...	...	...	...	...	...	0744	...	...	...	...	...	0917	...	...	0913	0939	0947	1005	...	...	...	...	...
Brussels Midi / Zuid d.	0623	...	...	...	...	...	...	0825	...	...	...	...	0925	...	...	...	...	...	...	1025	...	...	...	...
Brussels Nord d.	0631	...	...	...	...	...	...	0834	...	...	...	...	|	...	...	...	...	...	...	1034	...	...	...	...
Liège Guillemins d.	0712	...	...	...	...	...	...	0914	...	...	...	...	1013	...	...	...	...	...	...	1114	...	...	...	...
Aachen Hbf 🏛 d.	0739	...	...	...	...	...	...	0939	...	...	...	...	1037	...	...	...	...	...	...	1139	...	...	...	...
Köln Hbf a.	0815	...	...	...	...	...	...	1015	...	...	...	...	1116	...	...	...	...	...	...	1215	...	...	...	...
Köln Hbf d.	0818	0853	...	...	...	0953	...	1020	...	...	...	...	...	...	1155	...	...	...	...	1220	...	...	...	...
Köln Messe / Deutz ◧ d.	|	|	...	...	...	|	...	|	...	...	...	...	...	1144	|	...	...	...	...	|	...	...	...	...
Bonn Hbf d.	|	0915	...	...	...	1015	...	|	...	...	...	...	...	|	|	...	...	...	...	|	...	...	...	...
Koblenz Hbf d.	|	0948	...	...	...	1048	...	|	...	...	←	...	...	|	|	...	...	...	...	|	...	...	...	...
Mainz Hbf d.	|	1039	...	...	...	1139	...	|	...	...	1142	...	...	|	|	...	...	...	...	|	...	...	...	...
Frankfurt Flughafen ✈ d.	0919	...	0924	0935	1008	→	...	1119	1124	1135	1201	...	...	1235	1251	...	...	...	...	1319	1324	1335	...	...
Frankfurt (Main) Hbf d.	0931	...	|	0954	|	...	...	1131	|	1154	1222	...	...	1254	|	...	...	...	...	1331	|	1354	1421	...
Würzburg Hbf d.	...	...	|	1103	|	...	...	...	|	1312	1334	...	...	1403	|	...	...	...	...	...	|	1503	1533	...
Nürnberg Hbf a.	...	...	|	1156	|	...	...	...	|	1404	1427	...	...	1500	|	...	...	...	...	...	|	1556	1628	...
Mannheim Hbf d.	...	...	0959	|	1039	...	...	...	1159	|	|	...	...	|	1331	...	...	...	...	...	1359	|	|	...
Stuttgart Hbf d.	...	...	1038	|	1122	...	...	...	1238	|	|	...	...	|	1414	...	...	...	...	...	1438	|	|	...
Ulm Hbf d.	...	...	...	|	1210	...	...	...	...	|	|	...	...	|	1512	...	...	...	...	...	...	|	|	...
Augsburg Hbf d.	...	...	...	|	1253	...	...	...	...	|	|	...	...	|	1555	...	...	...	...	...	...	|	|	...
München Hbf a.	...	...	...	1305	1326	...	...	...	...	1512	|	...	...	1607	1626	...	...	...	...	...	...	1706	|	...
Wien Hbf a.	...	...	...	...	...	...	...	...	...	...	1847	...	...	...	...	...	...	...	...	...	...	...	2047	...

train type	☆	*ICE*	*ICE*	*ICE*	☆	*ICE*	*IC*	*ICE*	*ICE*	*ICE*	☆	*ICE*	*ICE*	*ICE*	☆	*ICE*	*ICE*	*ICE*	*IC*	*ICE*	☆	*ICE*	*ICE*	*ICE*
train number	**9423**	**629**	**229**	**519**	**9116**	**315**	**2046**	**577**	**721**	**229**	**9435**	**723**	**927**	**611**	**9126**	**17**	**579**	**17**	**2048**	**725**	**9447**	**727**	**929**	**613**
notes											Ⓑ					⑥		Ⓑ			⑥⑦			
notes	🅁																				🅁			
notes	**G**																							
London St Pancras d.	...	...	...	...	0901	...	...	...	...	...	...	...	...	...	1104	...	...	...	...	...	...	...	...	...
Paris Nord d.	0955	...	...	...	|	...	...	...	...	...	1155	...	...	...	|	...	...	...	...	...	1355	...	...	...
Brussels Midi / Zuid a.	1117	...	...	...	1205	...	...	...	...	...	1317	...	...	...	1405	...	...	...	...	...	1517	...	...	...
Brussels Midi / Zuid d.	1125	...	...	...	...	1225	...	...	...	...	1325	...	...	...	...	1425	...	1425	...	...	1525	...	...	...
Brussels Nord d.	|	...	...	...	...	1234	...	...	...	...	|	...	...	...	...	1434	...	1434	...	...	|	...	...	...
Liège Guillemins d.	1213	...	...	...	...	1314	...	...	...	...	1413	...	...	...	...	1514	...	1514	...	...	1613	...	...	...
Aachen Hbf 🏛 d.	1238	...	...	...	...	1339	...	...	...	...	1438	...	...	...	...	1539	...	1539	...	...	1638	...	...	...
Köln Hbf a.	1315	...	...	...	...	1415	...	...	...	...	1515	...	...	...	...	1615	...	1615	...	...	1715	...	...	...
Köln Hbf d.	...	...	1353	1355	...	1427	1453	...	...	...	...	...	1553	1555	...	1620	...	1623	1653	...	...	...	1753	1755
Köln Messe / Deutz ◧ d.	...	1344	|	|	...	|	|	...	...	...	...	1544	|	|	...	|	...	|	|	...	...	1744	|	|
Bonn Hbf d.	...	|	1415	|	...	|	1515	...	...	...	...	|	1615	|	...	|	...	|	1715	...	...	|	1815	|
Koblenz Hbf d.	...	|	1448	|	...	|	1548	...	...	←	...	|	1648	|	...	|	...	|	1748	...	...	|	1848	|
Mainz Hbf d.	...	|	1539	|	...	|	1639	...	...	1542	...	|	1739	|	...	|	...	|	1839	...	...	|	1939	|
Frankfurt Flughafen ✈ d.	...	1435	→	1451	...	1519	...	1524	1535	1601	...	1635	...	1651	...	1719	1724	1728	...	1735	...	1835	...	1851
Frankfurt (Main) Hbf d.	...	1454	...	|	...	1531	...	|	1554	1621	...	1654	...	|	...	1731	|	1740	...	1754	...	1854	...	|
Würzburg Hbf d.	...	1603	...	|	...	...	...	|	1703	1733	...	1803	...	|	...	...	|	...	...	1903	...	2003	...	|
Nürnberg Hbf a.	...	1658	...	|	...	...	...	|	1756	1827	...	1859	...	|	...	...	|	...	...	1956	...	2100	...	|
Mannheim Hbf d.	...	|	...	1531	...	...	...	1559	|	|	...	|	...	1731	...	...	1759	...	...	|	...	|	...	1931
Stuttgart Hbf d.	...	|	...	1614	...	...	...	1638	|	|	...	|	...	1814	...	...	1838	...	...	|	...	|	...	2014
Ulm Hbf d.	...	|	...	1712	...	...	...	...	|	|	...	|	...	1912	...	...	...	...	...	|	...	|	...	2112
Augsburg Hbf d.	...	|	...	1755	...	...	...	...	|	|	...	|	...	1955	...	...	...	...	...	|	...	|	...	2155
München Hbf a.	...	1807	...	1826	...	...	...	...	1907	|	...	2006	...	2029	...	...	...	...	...	2107	...	2210	...	2226
Wien Hbf a.	...	...	...	...	...	...	...	...	...	2305	...	...	...	...	...	...	...	...	...	...	...	...	...	...

train type	☆	*ICE*	*ICE*	*IC*	*ICE*	*ICE*	☆	*ICE*	*ICE*	*ICE*	☆	*ICE*	*ICE*	*ICE*	*NJ*	☆	*ICE*		☆	☆	*ICE*	☆	☆	
train number	**9132**	**317**	**317**	**2440**	**771**	**729**	**9459**	**821**	**1021**	**615**	**9142**	**19**	**773**	**1021**	**40425**	**9471**	**617**		**9148**	**9477**	**319**	**9152**	**9483**	
notes		Ⓐ	Ⓒ												①③⑤					④⑤		Ⓑ	⑦	
notes							🅁									🅁				🅁			🅁	
notes															**C**									
London St Pancras d.	1301	...	...	...	...	...	...	...	...	...	1504	...	...	...	...	...	...	...	1704	...	...	1804	...	...
Paris Nord d.	|	...	...	...	...	...	1555	...	...	...	|	...	...	...	...	1755	...	...	|	1855	...	|	1955	...
Brussels Midi / Zuid a.	1606	...	...	...	...	...	1717	...	...	...	1805	...	...	...	...	1917	...	...	2005	2017	...	2109	2117	...
Brussels Midi / Zuid d.	...	1622	1625	...	...	...	1725	...	...	...	...	1825	...	...	1906	1925	...	...	...	2022	2025	...	2125	...
Brussels Nord d.	...	1632	1634	...	...	...	|	...	...	...	...	1834	...	...	1916	|	...	...	...	|	2034	...	|	...
Liège Guillemins d.	...	1714	1714	...	...	...	1813	...	...	...	...	1914	...	...	2018	2013	...	...	...	2111	2114	...	2213	...
Aachen Hbf 🏛 d.	...	1739	1739	...	...	...	1837	...	...	...	...	1939	...	...	2110	2037	...	...	...	2137	2139	...	2237	...
Köln Hbf a.	...	1815	1815	...	...	...	1915	...	...	...	...	2015	...	...	2150	2115	...	...	...	2215	2215	...	2314	...
Köln Hbf d.	...	1820	1820	1853	...	...	...	...	1953	1955	...	2020	...	...	2201	...	2155	...	...	...	2227	...	...	...
Köln Messe / Deutz ◧ d.	...	|	|	|	...	...	...	1933	|	|	...	|	...	...	|	...	|	...	...	...	|	...	...	...
Bonn Hbf d.	...	|	|	1915	...	...	...	|	2015	|	...	|	...	...	2226**b**	...	|	...	...	...	|	...	...	...
Koblenz Hbf d.	...	|	|	1948	...	...	...	|	2048	|	...	|	...	...	2325	...	|	...	...	...	|	...	...	...
Mainz Hbf d.	...	|	|	2042	...	...	...	|	2142	|	...	|	...	...	0036	...	|	...	...	...	|	...	...	...
Frankfurt Flughafen ✈ d.	...	1919	1919	...	1924	1935	...	2035	...	2051	...	2119	2124	...	|	...	2255	...	...	...	2342	...	...	...
Frankfurt (Main) Hbf d.	...	1931	1931	...	|	1954	...	2054	...	|	...	2131	|	2222	|	...	|	...	...	...	2356	...	...	...
Würzburg Hbf d.	...	...	...	...	|	2103	...	2203	...	|	...	...	|	2346	|	...	|	...	...	...	...	...	...	...
Nürnberg Hbf a.	...	...	...	...	|	2157	...	2300	...	|	...	...	|	0042	|	...	|	...	...	...	...	...	...	...
Mannheim Hbf d.	...	...	...	...	1959	|	...	|	...	2131	...	...	2158	...	|	...	2330	...	...	...	...	...	...	...
Stuttgart Hbf d.	...	...	...	...	2038	|	...	|	...	2214	...	...	2251	...	|	...	0008	...	...	...	...	...	...	...
Ulm Hbf d.	...	...	...	...	...	|	...	|	...	2312	...	...	...	...	|	...	...	...	...	...	...	...	...	...
Augsburg Hbf d.	...	...	...	...	...	|	...	|	...	2355	...	...	...	...	|	...	...	...	...	...	...	...	...	...
München Hbf a.	...	...	...	...	...	2318	...	0020	...	0026	...	...	...	...	0543**n**	...	...	...	...	...	...	...	...	...
Wien Hbf a.	...	...	...	...	...	...	...	...	...	...	...	...	...	...	1013	...	...	...	...	...	...	...	...	...

A – Not July 14.

B – Also July 14.

C – ①③⑤. *ÖBB nightjet* – 🛏 1, 2 cl., 🛌 2 cl. (4, 6 berth), (2) Brussels - Wien (Table **53**).

G – ①②⑤⑥⑦ June 15 - July 19. Daily July 20 - Sept. 6.

b – Bonn **Beuel**.

j – Frankfurt (Main) **Süd**.

n – München **Ost**.

◧ – Connections from Köln Hbf depart every 2 – 5 minutes (journey time 2 – 3 minutes).

☆ – Eurostar high-speed train. 🅁. Service May 18 - Sept. 6. See pages 47 and 48 for further information.

MÜNCHEN - FRANKFURT - BRUSSELS, PARIS and LONDON 21

For full service Brussels - London see Table **10**. For full service Brussels - Paris see Table **18**. Connections at Brussels are not guaranteed.

train type	*ICE*	☆	*ICE*	*ICE*	*NJ*	☆	☆	☆	*ICE*	*ICE*	*ICE*	☆	*ICE*	*ICE*	☆	*ICE*	*ICE*	*ICE*	*ICE*	*ICE*	☆		
train number	**618**	**9414**	**18**	**18**	**40468**	**9322**	**9123**	**9426**	**822**	**1014**	**316**	**9135**	**1022**	**820**	**9438**	**1012**	**728**	**770**	**2049**	**16**	**9141**		
notes		①–⑥	①–⑥	⑦	②④⑦		**9125**		①–⑥	①–⑥				①–⑥	①⑤	①–⑥							
notes															⑥⑦								
notes		**C**			**A**																		
Wien Hbf d.	...	...	...	...	1813	...	...	...	...	...	...	...	...	...	...	...	...	...	...	...	...	...	...
München Hbf d.	0000	...	...	...	2316**n**	...	...	...	0447	...	...	...	...	0553	...	0625	0647	...	...	...	...	...	...
Augsburg Hbf d.	0031	...	...	...	|	...	...	...	|	...	...	...	...	|	...	0700	|	...	...	...	...	...	...
Ulm Hbf d.	0116	...	...	...	|	...	...	...	|	...	...	...	...	|	...	0746	|	...	...	...	...	...	...
Stuttgart Hbf d.	0222	...	...	...	|	...	...	...	|	0636	...	...	...	|	...	0839	|	0923	...	...	...	...	...
Mannheim Hbf d.	0401	...	...	...	|	...	...	...	|	0720	...	...	...	|	...	0920	|	1004	...	...	...	...	...
Nürnberg Hbf d.	|	...	...	...	|	...	...	...	0600	|	...	...	...	0703	...	|	0757	|	...	...	...	...	...
Würzburg Hbf d.	|	...	...	...	|	...	...	...	0654	|	...	...	...	0755	...	|	0854	|	...	...	...	...	...
Frankfurt (Main) Hbf d.	0446	...	0627	0627	|	...	...	...	0804	|	0815	...	...	0909	...	|	1004	|	...	1025	...	...	...
Frankfurt Flughafen ✈ d.	0500	...	0641	0641	|	...	...	...	...	0751	0830	...	...	0923	...	0951	...	1035	...	1041	...	...	...
Mainz Hbf d.	|	...	|	|	0453	...	...	...	...	...	|	...	0820	|	...	...	...	...	0920	|	...	...	...
Koblenz Hbf d.	|	...	|	|	0547	...	...	...	...	...	|	...	0913	|	...	...	...	...	1013	|	...	...	...
Bonn Hbf d.	|	...	|	|	0633**b**	...	...	...	...	...	|	...	0945	|	...	...	...	...	1045	|	...	...	...
Köln Messe / Deutz ◧ a.	|	...	|	|	|	...	...	...	...	...	|	...	|	1015	...	...	...	...	|	|	...	...	...
Köln Hbf a.	0603	...	0733	0733	0659	...	...	...	...	...	0933	...	1006	...	...	...	...	...	1106	1133	...	...	...
Köln Hbf d.	...	0645	0742	0742	0702	...	...	0845	...	...	0941	...	...	...	1045	...	...	...	...	1142	...	...	...
Aachen Hbf 🏛 d.	...	0723	0820	0820	0809	...	...	0924	...	...	1020	...	...	...	1124	...	...	...	...	1220	...	...	...
Liège Guillemins d.	...	0753	0846	0849	0851	...	...	0951	...	...	1046	...	...	...	1151	...	...	...	...	1246	...	...	...
Brussels Nord a.	...	|	0926	0926	0946	...	...	|	...	...	1126	...	...	...	|	...	...	...	...	1326	...	...	...
Brussels Midi / Zuid a.	...	0835	0935	0935	0955	...	...	1035	...	...	1135	...	...	...	1235	...	...	...	...	1335	...	...	...
Brussels Midi / Zuid d.	...	0843	...	...	...	1013	1056	1043	...	...	...	1256	...	...	1243	...	...	...	...	...	1452	...	...
Paris Nord a.	...	1005	...	...	...	1135	|	1205	...	...	...	|	...	...	1405	...	...	...	...	...	|	...	...
London St Pancras a.	...	...	...	...	...	...	1157	...	...	...	...	1357	...	...	...	...	...	...	...	...	1557	...	...

train type	*ICE*	*ICE*	☆	☆	*ICE*	*ICE*	*ICE*	*ICE*	☆	*ICE*	*ICE*	*ICE*	☆	☆	*ICE*	*ICE*	*ICE*	*ICE*	*IC*	*ICE*	☆	☆	
train number	**1020**	**726**	**9450**	**9145**	**1010**	**724**	**578**	**314**	**9149**	**610**	**928**	**722**	**9462**	**9153**	**918**	**228**	**720**	**576**	**2045**	**14**	**9370**	**9159**	
notes				①–⑤					⑥				⑦									**9157**	
notes																							
notes																					...	...	
Wien Hbf d.	...	...	...	...	...	...	...	...	...	...	...	...	...	...	...	0713	...	...	...	...	...	...	...
München Hbf d.	...	0746	...	...	0827	0847	...	...	...	0927	...	0950	...	...	1029	|	1048	...	...	...	...	...	...
Augsburg Hbf d.	...	|	...	...	0901	|	...	...	...	1001	...	|	...	...	1101	|	|	...	...	...	...	...	...
Ulm Hbf d.	...	|	...	...	0946	|	...	...	...	1047	...	|	...	...	1146	|	|	...	...	...	...	...	...
Stuttgart Hbf d.	...	|	...	...	1039	|	1123	...	...	1151	...	|	...	...	1238	|	|	1323	...	...	...	...	...
Mannheim Hbf d.	...	|	...	...	1120	|	1203	...	...	1236	...	|	...	...	1320	|	|	1403	...	...	...	...	...
Nürnberg Hbf d.	...	0858	...	...	|	0957	|	...	...	|	...	1058	...	...	|	1129	1157	|	...	...	...	...	...
Würzburg Hbf d.	...	0954	...	...	|	1054	|	...	...	|	...	1154	...	...	|	1224	1256	|	...	...	...	...	...
Frankfurt (Main) Hbf d.	...	1109	...	...	|	1204	|	1225	...	|	...	1309	...	...	|	1336	1404	|	...	1427	...	...	...
Frankfurt Flughafen ✈ d.	...	1123	...	...	1151	...	1235	1241	...	1310	...	1323	...	...	1351	...	...	1435	...	1441	...	...	...
Mainz Hbf d.	1020	|	...	...	...	...	...	|	...	|	1220	|	...	...	...	...	...	...	1320	|	...	...	...
Koblenz Hbf d.	1113	|	...	...	...	...	...	|	...	|	1313	|	...	...	...	...	...	...	1413	|	...	...	...
Bonn Hbf d.	1145	|	...	...	...	...	...	|	...	|	1345	|	...	...	...	...	...	...	1445	|	...	...	...
Köln Messe / Deutz ◧ a.	|	1215	...	...	...	...	...	|	...	|	|	1415	...	...	...	...	...	...	|	|	...	...	...
Köln Hbf a.	1206	...	...	...	...	...	...	1333	...	1405	1406	...	...	...	...	...	...	...	1506	1533	...	...	...
Köln Hbf d.	...	...	1243	...	...	...	...	1342	...	...	...	...	1445	...	...	...	...	...	...	1541	...	...	...
Aachen Hbf 🏛 d.	...	...	1324	...	...	...	...	1420	...	...	...	...	1524	...	...	...	...	...	...	1620	...	...	...
Liège Guillemins d.	...	...	1351	...	...	...	...	1446	...	...	...	...	1551	...	...	...	...	...	...	1646	...	...	...
Brussels Nord a.	...	...	|	...	...	...	...	1526	...	...	...	...	|	...	...	...	...	...	...	1726	...	...	...
Brussels Midi / Zuid a.	...	...	1435	...	...	...	...	1535	...	...	...	...	1635	...	...	...	...	...	...	1735	...	...	...
Brussels Midi / Zuid d.	...	...	1443	1551	...	...	...	...	1656	...	...	...	1643	1756	...	...	...	...	...	...	1813	1851	...
Paris Nord a.	...	...	1605	|	...	...	...	...	|	...	...	...	1805	|	...	...	...	...	...	...	1935	|	...
London St Pancras a.	...	...	...	1657	...	...	...	...	1757	...	...	...	...	1900	...	...	...	...	...	...	...	1957	...

train type	*ICE*	*ICE*	☆	*EC*	*ICE*	*ICE*	*ICE*	*ICE*	☆	*ICE*	*ICE*	*ICE*	☆	*ICE*	*ICE*	*ICE*	*ICE*	*ICE*	☆	*ICE*	*ICE*	*ICE*	*ICE*
train number	**518**	**628**	**9474**	**8**	**28**	**626**	**1094**	**12**	**9382**	**516**	**28**	**624**	**9486**	**914**	**26**	**622**	**572**	**10**	**9394**	**26**	**1212**	**528**	**318**
notes													Ⓑ						⑦		**254**		
notes																							
notes																			...				
Wien Hbf d.	...	...	...	...	0913	...	...	...	...	...	...	...	...	...	1113	...	...	...	...	...	...	...	...
München Hbf d.	1127	1150	...	...	|	1247	...	...	...	1327	...	1350	...	1427	|	1447	...	...	...	...	1628	1648	...
Augsburg Hbf d.	1201	|	...	...	|	|	...	...	...	1401	...	|	...	1501	|	|	...	...	...	...	1701	|	...
Ulm Hbf d.	1247	|	...	...	|	|	...	...	...	1447	...	|	...	1546	|	|	...	...	...	...	1746	|	...
Stuttgart Hbf d.	1351	|	...	...	|	|	1523	...	...	1551	...	|	...	1637	|	|	1723	...	...	...	1838	|	...
Mannheim Hbf d.	1436	|	...	...	|	|	1604	...	...	1636	...	|	...	1720	|	|	1803	...	...	...	1921	|	...
Nürnberg Hbf d.	|	1258	...	...	1329	1357	|	...	...	|	...	1458	...	|	1530	1557	|	...	...	...	|	1757	...
Würzburg Hbf d.	|	1354	...	...	1424	1454	|	...	...	|	...	1554	...	|	1624	1654	|	...	...	...	|	1855	...
Frankfurt (Main) Hbf d.	|	1509	...	...	1541	1604	|	1627	...	|	...	1709	...	|	1741	1804	|	1827	...	...	|	2004	2015
Frankfurt Flughafen ✈ d.	1510	1523	...	...	1558	...	1635	1641	...	1710	←	1723	...	1751	1758	...	1835	1841	...	←	1951	...	2030
Mainz Hbf d.	|	|	...	1520	1618	...	...	|	...	|	1620	|	...	...	1818	...	...	|	...	1820	...	...	|
Koblenz Hbf d.	|	|	...	1613	→	...	...	|	...	|	1713	|	...	...	→	...	...	|	...	1913	...	...	|
Bonn Hbf d.	|	|	...	1645	...	...	...	|	...	|	1745	|	...	...	...	...	...	|	...	1945	...	...	|
Köln Messe / Deutz ◧ a.	|	1614	...	|	...	...	...	|	...	|	|	1814	...	...	...	...	...	|	...	|	...	...	|
Köln Hbf a.	1605	...	...	1706	...	...	...	1733	...	1805	1806	...	...	...	...	...	...	1933	...	2006	...	...	2139
Köln Hbf d.	...	...	1645	...	...	...	...	1742	...	▬	...	...	1845	...	...	...	...	1942	...	...	...	...	2142
Aachen Hbf 🏛 d.	...	...	1724	...	...	...	...	1820	...	...	...	...	1924	...	...	...	...	2020	...	...	...	...	2220
Liège Guillemins d.	...	...	1751	...	...	...	...	1846	...	☆	...	...	1951	...	...	...	...	2046	...	...	...	...	2246
Brussels Nord a.	...	...	|	...	...	...	...	1926	...	**9167**	...	...	|	...	...	...	...	2126	...	...	...	...	2326
Brussels Midi / Zuid a.	...	...	1835	...	...	...	...	1935	...	Ⓑ	...	...	2035	...	...	...	...	2135	...	...	...	...	2335
Brussels Midi / Zuid d.	...	...	1843	...	...	...	...	...	2013	2056	...	...	2043	...	...	...	...	...	2213	...	...	...	...
Paris Nord a.	...	...	2005	...	...	...	...	...	2139	|	...	...	2205	...	...	...	...	...	2340	...	...	...	...
London St Pancras a.	...	...	...	...	...	...	...	...	...	2157	...	...	...	...	...	...	...	...	...	...	...	...	...

A – ②④⑦. *ÖBB nightjet* – 🛏 1, 2 cl., ▬ 2 cl. (4, 6 berth), (2) Wien - Brussels (Table **53**).

C – Not July 14.

b – Bonn **Beuel**.

n – München **Ost**.

◧ – Connections from Köln Hbf depart every 2 – 5 minutes (journey time 2 – 3 minutes).

☆ – Eurostar high-speed train. 🅁. Service May 18 - Sept. 6. See pages 47 and 48 for further information.

22 AMSTERDAM - BERLIN

train type	IC	IC	IC	IC	IC	IC	IC	ES
train number	**141**	**143**	**145**	**147**	**149**	**241**	**243**	**453**
notes								①③⑤
notes								**A**
Amsterdam Centraal d.	0600	0800	1000	1200	1400	1600	1759	2234
Hilversum d.	0622	0822	1022	1222	1422	1622	1822	|
Amersfoort d.	0636	0836	1036	1236	1436	1636	1836	2313
Apeldoorn d.	0702	0902	1102	1302	1502	1702	1902	|
Deventer d.	0718	0918	1118	1318	1518	1718	1918	2352
Hengelo ▲ d.	0752	0952	1152	1352	1552	1752	1952	|
Bad Bentheim 🏛 ▲ d.	0812	1012	1212	1412	1612	1812	2012	|
Rheine ▲ d.	0826	1026	1226	1426	1626	1826	2026	|
Osnabrück Hbf ▲ d.	0854	1054	1254	1454	1654	1854	2054	|
Bünde (Westf) d.	0916	1116	1316	1516	1716	1916	2116	|
Hannover Hbf a.	1001	1201	1401	1601	1801	2001	2201	|
Berlin Hauptbahnhof a.	1151	1351	1551	1751	1951	2151	...	0620
Berlin Ostbahnhof a.	1202	1402	1602	1802	2002	2202	...	0629

train type	IC	IC	IC	IC	IC	IC	IC	ES
train number	**242**	**240**	**148**	**146**	**144**	**142**	**140**	**452**
notes								②④⑦
notes								**A**
Berlin Ostbahnhof d.	...	0553	0753	0953	1153	1353	1553	2244
Berlin Hauptbahnhof d.	...	0606	0806	1006	1206	1406	1606	2256
Hannover Hbf d.	0556	0756	0956	1156	1356	1556	1756	|
Bünde (Westf) d.	0643	0843	1043	1243	1443	1643	1843	|
Osnabrück Hbf ▲ d.	0706	0906	1106	1306	1506	1706	1906	|
Rheine ▲ d.	0736	0936	1136	1336	1536	1736	1936	|
Bad Bentheim 🏛 ▲ d.	0751	0951	1151	1351	1551	1751	1951	|
Hengelo ▲ d.	0809	1009	1209	1409	1609	1809	2009	|
Deventer d.	0847	1047	1247	1447	1647	1847	2047	0512
Apeldoorn d.	0859	1059	1259	1459	1659	1859	2058	|
Amersfoort d.	0926	1126	1326	1526	1726	1926	2126	0548
Hilversum d.	0939	1139	1339	1539	1739	1939	2138	|
Amsterdam Centraal a.	0959	1159	1359	1559	1759	1959	2159	0631

A – EUROPEAN SLEEPER – 🛏 (1, 2, 3 berth), 🛏 (5, 6 berth), (2) Brussels - Praha and v.v. (Table **78**).

▲ – For regional trains see Table **811**.

28 AMSTERDAM - FRANKFURT, WIEN and MÜNCHEN

Amended Amsterdam - Frankfurt service June 14, 15, June 28 - Aug. 24, Oct. 20 - Nov. 2, Dec. 6, 7. See pages 375, 376.

train type	ICE	ICE	ICE	ICE	ICE	ICE	ICE	ICE	ICE	ICE	ICE		ICE	ICE	ICE	ICE	ICE	ICE	ICE	ICE	NJ	NJ	
train number	**121**	**621**	**515**	**27**	**123**	**629**	**519**	**229**	**125**	**723**	**611**		**127**	**727**	**613**	**129**	**821**	**615**	**221**	**617**	**40421**	**421**	
notes																					**C**	**D**	
Amsterdam Centraal d.	0638	...	...	...	1037	...	...	...	1238	...	...	...	1438	...	...	1638	...	...	1838	...	1900	1900	...
Utrecht Centraal d.	0706	...	...	...	1104	...	...	...	1304	...	...	...	1504	...	...	1704	...	...	1904	...	1936	1936	...
Arnhem ◐ ▲ d.	0737	...	...	...	1137	...	...	...	1337	...	...	...	1537	...	...	1737	...	...	1937	...	|	|	...
Oberhausen Hbf ◐ ▲ d.	0833	...	...	...	1233	...	...	...	1433	...	...	...	1633	...	...	1833	...	...	2033	...	|	|	...
Duisburg Hbf ▲ d.	0841	...	...	...	1241	...	...	...	1441	...	...	...	1641	...	...	1841	...	...	2041	...	|	|	...
Düsseldorf Hbf ▲ d.	0855	...	...	...	1254	...	...	...	1455	...	...	...	1655	...	...	1855	...	...	2055	...	|	|	...
Köln Hbf a.	0918	...	...	...	1315	...	...	...	1518	...	...	...	1719	...	...	1918	...	...	2118	...	|	|	...
Köln Hbf d.	0928	...	...	0953	1321	...	...	1353	1528	...	...	...	1728	...	...	1928	...	...	2128	...	|	|	...
Frankfurt Flughafen ✈ a.	1017	...	1051	1158	1417	...	1451	1558	1617	...	1651	...	1817	...	1851	2017	...	2051	2217	2255	|	|	...
Frankfurt (Main) Hbf a.	1031	1054	|	1212	1431	1454	|	1613	1631	1654	|	...	1831	1854	|	2031	2054	|	2231	|	|	|	...
Würzburg a.	...	1201	|	1332	...	1601	|	1732	...	1801	|	...	...	2001	|	...	2201	|	...	|	0226	0226	...
Nürnberg a.	...	1258	|	1427	...	1658	|	1827	...	1859	|	...	...	2100	|	...	2300	|	...	|	0328	0328	...
Regensburg a.	...	|	|	1523	...	|	|	1923	...	|	|	...	...	|	|	...	|	|	...	|	0507	|	...
Mannheim a.	...	|	1123	|	...	|	1523	|	...	|	1723	...	...	|	1923	...	|	2124	...	2327	|	|	...
Stuttgart a.	...	|	1208	|	...	|	1608	|	...	|	1808	...	...	|	2008	...	|	2208	...	0008	|	|	...
Ulm a.	...	|	1310	|	...	|	1710	|	...	|	1910	...	...	|	2110	...	|	2310	...	...	|	|	...
Augsburg a.	...	|	1353	|	...	|	1753	|	...	|	1953	...	...	|	2153	...	|	2353	...	...	|	0624	...
München Hbf a.	...	1406	1426	|	...	1807	1826	|	...	2006	2029	...	...	2210	2226	...	0020	0026	...	...	|	0706	...
Innsbruck Hbf a.	...	...	...	|	...	...	...	|	...	...	...	...	...	...	...	...	...	...	...	...	|	0914	...
Passau 🏛 a.	...	...	...	1625	...	...	...	2026	...	...	...	...	...	...	...	...	...	...	...	...	0613	...	...
Linz Hbf a.	...	...	...	1726	...	...	...	2138	...	...	...	...	...	...	...	...	...	...	...	...	0743	...	...
Wien Hbf a.	...	...	...	1847	...	...	...	2305	...	...	...	...	...	...	...	...	...	...	...	...	0917	...	...

train type	ICE	ICE	ICE	ICE		ICE	ICE	ICE	ICE	ICE	ICE		ICE	ICE	ICE		ICE	ICE	ICE	ICE	NJ	NJ	
train number	**222**	**222**	**616**	**220**		**614**	**820**	**128**	**612**	**726**	**126**		**610**	**722**	**124**		**28**	**516**	**624**	**120**	**40490**	**420**	
notes	①–⑤	⑥⑦					①–⑥														**C**	**D**	
Wien Hbf d.	...	...	...	...	...	...	...	...	...	...	...	...	...	...	...	...	0913	...	...	...	2010	...	...
Linz Hbf d.	...	...	...	...	...	...	...	...	...	...	...	...	...	...	...	...	1034	...	...	...	2134	...	...
Passau 🏛 d.	...	...	...	...	...	...	...	...	...	...	...	...	...	...	...	...	1134	...	...	...	2253	...	...
Innsbruck Hbf d.	...	...	...	...	...	...	...	...	...	...	...	...	...	...	...	...	|	...	...	...	|	2046	...
München Hbf d.	...	...	0331	...	...	0532	0553	...	0727	0746	...	...	0927	0950	...	...	|	1327	1350	...	|	2252	...
Augsburg d.	...	...	0404	...	...	0604	|	...	0801	|	...	...	1001	|	...	...	|	1401	|	...	|	2325	...
Ulm d.	...	...	0447	...	...	0647	|	...	0847	|	...	...	1047	|	...	...	|	1447	|	...	|	|	...
Stuttgart d.	...	...	0551	...	...	0751	|	...	0951	|	...	...	1151	|	...	...	|	1551	|	...	|	|	...
Mannheim d.	...	...	0635	...	...	0836	|	...	1036	|	...	...	1236	|	...	...	|	1636	|	...	|	|	...
Regensburg d.	...	...	|	...	...	|	|	...	|	|	...	...	|	|	...	...	1235	|	|	...	2357	|	...
Nürnberg d.	...	...	|	...	...	|	0703	...	|	0858	...	...	|	1058	...	...	1329	|	1458	...	0136	0136	...
Würzburg d.	...	...	|	...	...	|	0755	...	|	0954	...	...	|	1154	...	...	1424	|	1554	...	0232	0232	...
Frankfurt (Main) Hbf d.	0526	...	|	0727	...	|	0904	0927	|	1104	1127	...	|	1304	1327	...	1536	|	1704	1727	|	|	...
Frankfurt Flughafen ✈ d.	0538	...	0707	0741	...	0907	...	0941	1107	...	1141	...	1307	...	1341	...	1555	1707	...	1741	|	|	...
Köln Hbf a.	0633	...	...	0833	...	...	...	1033	...	...	1233	...	...	...	1433	...	1806	...	...	1833	|	|	...
Köln Hbf d.	0641	0641	...	0841	...	...	...	1041	...	...	1241	...	...	...	1441	...	...	...	...	1841	|	|	...
Düsseldorf Hbf ▲ a.	0705	0705	...	0905	...	...	...	1105	...	...	1305	...	...	...	1505	...	...	...	...	1905	|	|	...
Duisburg Hbf ▲ a.	0723	0723	...	0923	...	...	...	1123	...	...	1323	...	...	...	1523	...	...	...	...	1923	|	|	...
Oberhausen Hbf ◐ ▲ a.	0731	0731	...	0931	...	...	...	1131	...	...	1331	...	...	...	1531	...	...	...	...	1931	|	|	...
Arnhem ◐ ▲ a.	0827	0827	...	1027	...	...	...	1227	...	...	1427	...	...	...	1627	...	...	...	...	2027	|	|	...
Utrecht Centraal a.	0859	0859	...	1059	...	...	...	1259	...	...	1459	...	...	...	1659	...	...	...	...	2059	|	|	...
Amsterdam Centraal a.	0929	0929	...	1129	...	...	...	1329	...	...	1529	...	...	...	1729	...	...	...	...	2129	0950	0950	...

C – *ÖBB nightjet* – 🛏 1, 2 cl., 🛏 2 cl. (4, 6 berth), (2) Amsterdam - Wien and v.v.
D – *ÖBB nightjet* – 🛏 1, 2 cl., 🛏 2 cl. (4, 6 berth), (2) Amsterdam - Innsbruck and v.v.

◐ – 🏛 between Arnhem and Oberhausen is Emmerich.
▲ – For regional trains see Table **802**.

PARIS - FRANKFURT - BERLIN, LEIPZIG, DRESDEN and PRAHA — 30

Services between Frankfurt and Dresden are subject to alteration June 24 - July 11.

Other trains: Paris - Karlsruhe Table **32**; Paris - Berlin via Brussels Table **20**; Paris - Frankfurt via Brussels Table **21**; Frankfurt - Berlin Tables **850** (via Erfurt) and **902** (via Kassel).

train type	*TGV*	*ICE*	*ICE*	*EC*	*TGV*	*ICE*	*EC*	*ICE*	*ICE*		*ICE*	*ICE*	*ICE*	*NJ*	*ICE*	*ICE*	*ICE*	*ICE*		*TGV*	*ICE*		*ICE*	*NJ*	
train number	**9561**	**372**	**1559**	**177**	**9551**	**1651**	**179**	**9591**	**1653**		**9553**	**276**	**1655**	**457**	**9563**	**274**	**1657**	**9555**		**9559**	**9557**		**674**	**40469**	
notes	Ⓡ★				Ⓡ★			Ⓡ★			Ⓡ★			Ⓡ	Ⓡ★			Ⓡ★		Ⓡ★	Ⓡ★				
notes	①–⑥																	Ⓑ		⑥	Ⓑ			①③⑤	
notes														C										D	
Paris Est d.	0715	...	...	...	0906	...	...	0955	...	...	1310	...	...	...	1521	...	...	1710	...	1903	1907	...	...	1912	...
Strasbourg d.	0908	...	...	...	|	...	...	1146	...	...	|	...	...	...	1713	...	...	|	...	|	|	...	...	2342	...
Forbach ⊞ d.	◧	...	...	...	1047	...	...	◧	...	...	|	...	...	...	◧	...	...	|	...	2049	2049	...	...	|	...
Saarbrücken d.	|	...	...	...	1058	...	...	|	...	...	1500	...	...	...	|	...	...	1900	...	2059	2059	...	...	|	...
Kaiserlautern d.	|	...	...	...	1137	...	...	|	...	...	1537	...	...	...	|	...	...	1937	...	2137	2137	...	...	|	...
Karlsruhe Hbf d.	0955	...	...	...	|	...	...	1236	...	...	|	...	...	...	1755	...	...	|	...	|	|	...	...	|	...
Mannheim d.	1020	...	...	...	1218	...	...	|	...	...	1618	...	...	...	1820	...	...	2018	...	2218	2218	...	...	|	...
Frankfurt (Main) Hbf a.	1059	...	...	...	1259	...	...	|	...	...	1659	...	...	...	1859	...	...	2059	...	2259	2259	...	...	|	...
Frankfurt (Main) Hbf d.	...	1114	1118	...	...	1318	...	|	1518	...	...	1714	1718	...	...	1914	1918	...	...	...	...	...	2335	|	...
Frankfurt (Main) Süd a.	...	|	|	...	...	|	...	1404	|	...	...	|	|	...	...	|	|	...	...	...	...	...	|	0316	...
Frankfurt (Main) Süd d.	...	|	|	...	...	|	...	1406	|	...	...	|	|	...	...	|	|	...	...	...	...	...	|	0319	...
Fulda a.	...	1212	1213	...	...	1413	...	|	1613	...	...	1812	1813	...	...	2012	2013	...	...	...	...	...	0113	|	...
Erfurt a.	...	|	1338	...	...	1538	...	|	1738	...	...	|	1938	...	...	|	2138	...	...	...	...	...	|	0547	...
Leipzig Hbf a.	...	|	1424	...	...	1624	...	|	1824	...	...	|	2024	...	...	|	2301	...	...	...	...	...	|	|	...
Dresden Hbf a.	...	|	1539	1710	...	1739	1910	|	1938	...	...	|	2140	2210	...	|	0016	...	...	...	...	...	|	|	...
Děčín (⊞ = Schöna) a.	...	|	...	1752	...	...	1952	|	...	...	...	|	...	2253	...	|	...	...	...	...	...	...	|	|	...
Praha Holešovice a.	...	|	...	1913	...	...	2113	|	...	...	...	|	...	0014	...	|	...	...	...	...	...	...	|	|	...
Praha hl. n. a.	...	|	...	1923	...	...	2123	|	...	...	...	|	...	0025	...	|	...	...	...	...	...	...	|	|	...
Kassel Wilhelmshöhe a.	...	1243	...	...	...	...	...	|	...	...	...	1843	...	...	...	2043	...	...	...	...	...	...	|	|	...
Göttingen a.	...	1303	...	...	...	...	...	|	...	...	...	1903	...	...	...	2103	...	...	...	...	...	...	0243	|	...
Braunschweig a.	...	1359	...	...	...	...	...	|	...	...	...	1959	...	...	...	2159	...	...	...	...	...	...	|	|	...
Wolfsburg a.	...	1418	...	...	...	...	...	|	...	...	...	2018	...	...	...	2218	...	...	...	...	...	...	0512	|	...
Berlin Hauptbahnhof a.	...	1531	...	...	...	...	...	1803	...	...	...	2133	...	...	...	2330	...	...	...	...	...	...	0649	0826	...

train type	*ICE*	*NJ*	*ICE*	*ICE*	*ICE*	*ICE*	*ICE*	*NJ*	*ICE*	*ICE*	*ICE*	*ICE*	*ICE*	*ICE*	*TGV*	*TGV*	*EC*	*ICE*	*ICE*	*EC*	*ICE*	*ICE*	*EC*	*ICE*	*ICE*
train number	**9558**	**40424**	**271**	**9568**	**9586**	**9566**	**9556**	**456**	**1654**	**277**	**9554**	**9554**	**1652**	**279**	**9552**	**9552**	**178**	**1650**	**9590**	**176**	**1558**	**9560**	**176**	**1556**	**9550**
notes	Ⓡ★			Ⓡ★	Ⓡ★	Ⓡ★	Ⓡ★	Ⓡ			Ⓡ★	Ⓡ★			Ⓡ★	Ⓡ★			Ⓡ★			Ⓡ★			Ⓡ★
notes	①–⑤	②④⑦		Ⓑ	⑥	⑥	①–⑤				⑥	⑦			Ⓑ	⑥									Ⓑ
notes		E						C																	
Berlin Hauptbahnhof d.	...	1906	2328	...	...	...	...	...	...	0629	...	...	...	0828	...	...	...	...	1155	...	...	...	...	...	...
Wolfsburg d.	...	|	0100	...	...	...	...	...	...	0738	...	...	...	0938	...	...	...	...	|	...	...	...	...	...	...
Braunschweig d.	...	|	|	...	...	...	...	...	...	0757	...	...	...	0957	...	...	...	...	|	...	...	...	...	...	...
Göttingen d.	...	2137	0308	...	...	...	...	...	...	0852	...	...	...	1052	...	...	...	...	|	...	...	...	...	...	...
Kassel Wilhelmshöhe d.	...	2208	|	...	...	...	...	...	...	0914	...	...	...	1114	...	...	...	...	|	...	...	...	...	...	...
Praha hl. n. d.	...	|	|	...	...	...	...	0308	...	|	...	...	...	|	...	...	0628	...	|	0828	...	...	1028	...	...
Praha Holešovice d.	...	|	|	...	...	...	...	0319	...	|	...	...	...	|	...	...	0639	...	|	0839	...	...	1039	...	...
Děčín (⊞ = Schöna) d.	...	|	|	...	...	...	...	0507	...	|	...	...	...	|	...	...	0807	...	|	1007	...	...	1207	...	...
Dresden Hbf d.	...	|	|	...	...	...	...	0550	0610	|	...	...	0810	|	...	...	0850	1010	|	1050	1210	...	1250	1410	...
Leipzig Hbf d.	...	|	|	...	...	...	...	...	0733	|	...	...	0933	|	...	...	...	1133	|	...	1333	...	...	1533	...
Erfurt d.	...	|	|	...	...	...	...	...	0818	|	...	...	1018	|	...	...	...	1218	|	...	1418	...	...	1618	...
Fulda d.	...	|	0433	...	...	...	...	...	0942	0946	...	...	1142	1147	...	...	...	1342	|	...	1542	...	...	1742	...
Frankfurt (Main) Süd a.	...	0022	|	...	...	...	...	...	|	|	...	...	|	|	...	...	...	|	1552	...	|	...	...	|	...
Frankfurt (Main) Süd d.	...	0026	|	...	...	...	...	...	|	|	...	...	|	|	...	...	...	|	1553	...	|	...	...	|	...
Frankfurt (Main) Hbf a.	...	|	0537	...	...	...	...	...	1036	1044	...	...	1236	1244	...	...	...	1436	|	...	1636	...	...	1836	...
Frankfurt (Main) Hbf d.	0556	|	...	0656	0656	0856	0856	...	...	...	1056	1056	...	...	1256	1256	...	...	|	...	...	1656	...	...	1856
Mannheim d.	0640	|	...	0737	0740	0938	0940	...	...	...	1140	1140	...	...	1342	1342	...	...	|	...	...	1738	...	...	1940
Karlsruhe Hbf d.	|	|	...	0806	|	1003	|	...	...	...	|	|	...	...	|	|	...	...	1707	...	...	1805	...	...	|
Kaiserlautern d.	0722	|	...	|	0822	|	1022	...	...	...	1222	1222	...	...	1424	1424	...	...	|	...	...	|	...	...	2022
Saarbrücken d.	0800	|	...	|	0900	|	1100	...	...	...	1300	1300	...	...	1500	1500	...	...	|	...	...	|	...	...	2100
Forbach ⊞ a.	0809	|	...	◧	0909	◧	|	...	...	...	|	1309	...	...	|	1509	...	...	◧	...	...	◧	...	...	2109
Strasbourg a.	|	0452	...	0847	|	1047	|	...	...	...	|	|	...	...	|	|	...	...	1753	...	...	1848	...	...	|
Paris Est a.	0950	0939	...	1038	1052	1238	1252	...	...	...	1452	1452	...	...	1652	1652	...	...	1955	...	...	2041	...	...	2252

C – *ÖBB nightjet* – 🛏 1,2 cl., 🛌 2 cl., (2) Berlin - Graz and v.v.
D – ①③⑤ *ÖBB nightjet* – 🛏 1,2 cl., 🛌 2 cl. (4, 6 berth), (2) Paris - Berlin.
E – ②④⑦ *ÖBB nightjet* – 🛏 1,2 cl., 🛌 2 cl. (4, 6 berth), (2) Berlin - Paris.

x – Frankfurt (Main) **Süd**.
◧ – ⊞ is Kehl.

★ – *Alleo* ICE / TGV service (a DB / SNCF joint enterprise).

LONDON - GENÈVE and LAUSANNE — 31

For full service Paris - Genève and v.v. see Table **341**.

train type		☆	☆	*TGV*	*TGV*		☆	*TGV*		☆	*TGV*		☆	*TGV*		☆	*TGV*		☆	*TGV*		
train number		**9002**	**9004**	**9269**	**9773**		**9014**	**9775**		**9022**	**9777**		**9024**	**9277**		**9028**	**9781**		**9036**	**9789**		
notes		⑥	①–⑤		**9783**												**9783**			⑤⑦		
notes				♣	♣		C	♣			♣			♣			♣			♣		
London St Pancras d.	...	0631	0701	...	...	...	0931	...	...	1131	...	...	1231	...	...	1331	...	...	1531	...	...	...
Paris Nord a.	...	0953	1022	...	...	...	1258	...	...	1453	...	...	1602	...	...	1656	...	...	1902	...	...	...
Paris Gare de Lyon d.	...	...	...	1156	1218	...	...	1418	...	...	1618	...	...	1756	...	...	1818	...	...	2018	...	...
Dijon d.	...	...	...	1334	|	...	...	|	...	...	|	...	...	1932	...	...	|	...	...	|	...	...
Bellegarde a.	...	...	...	|	1459	...	...	1659	...	...	1859	...	...	|	...	...	2100	...	...	2302	...	...
Genève Cornavin a.	...	...	...	|	1529	...	...	1729	...	...	1929	...	...	|	...	...	2129	...	...	2329	...	...
Frasne a.	...	...	...	1441	...	...	...	...	...	...	|	...	...	2042	...	...	...	...	...	...	...	...
Vallorbe ⊞ a.	...	...	...	1457	...	...	...	...	...	...	|	...	...	2057	...	...	...	...	...	...	...	...
Lausanne a.	...	...	...	1540	...	...	...	...	...	...	2012x	...	...	2140	...	...	...	...	...	...	...	...

train type		*TGV*	*TGV*	☆		*TGV*	☆	☆		*TGV*	☆		*TGV*	*TGV*	☆		*TGV*	☆				
train number		**9760**	**9264**	**9031**		**9764**	**9035**	**9037**		**9768**	**9043**		**9770**	**9268**	**9051**		**9774**	**9059**				
notes		①–⑥					⑥	Ⓑ						A	Ⓑ							
notes		♣	♣			♣				♣			♣	♣			♣					
Lausanne d.	...	...	0723	...	...	...	...	...	...	...	...	...	...	1219	...	...	...	...	...	...	...	...
Vallorbe ⊞ d.	...	...	0800	...	...	...	...	...	...	...	...	...	...	1258	...	...	...	...	...	...	...	...
Frasne d.	...	...	0814	...	...	...	...	...	...	...	...	...	...	1317	...	...	...	...	...	...	...	...
Genève Cornavin d.	...	0629	|	...	...	0829	...	...	...	1030	...	...	1229	|	...	...	1430	...	...	...	...	...
Bellegarde d.	...	0702	|	...	...	0900	...	...	...	1102	...	...	1302	|	...	...	1502	...	...	...	...	...
Dijon a.	...	|	0926	...	...	|	...	...	...	|	...	...	|	1425	...	...	|	...	...	...	...	...
Paris Gare de Lyon a.	...	0942	1104	...	...	1143	...	...	...	1342	...	...	1542	1604	...	...	1742	...	...	...	...	...
Paris Nord d.	...	...	...	1311	...	...	1413	1442	...	...	1612	...	...	...	1810	...	...	2007	...	...	...	...
London St Pancras a.	...	...	...	1430	...	...	1530	1605	...	...	1735	...	...	...	1939	...	...	2130	...	...	...	...

A – Daily June 15 - Aug. 17; ⑥⑦ Aug. 23 - Dec. 13.
C – Not June 15.
x – ①–⑤.
☆ – Eurostar high-speed train. Ⓡ. Service May 18 - Sept. 6. See pages 47 and 48 for further information.
♣ – *TGV Lyria* service. Ⓡ 🍷. Trains convey three classes of accommodation: Business 1ère, Standard 1ère and Standard. At-seat meal service in Business 1ère.

32 LONDON - PARIS - MÜNCHEN - WIEN

For other trains London and Paris - München and v.v. via Brussels see Table **21**.

train type	ICE	ICE	RJX	☆	ICE	TGV	ICE	RJX		☆	TGV	ICE	RJX	☆	TGV	EN	☆	TGV	IC	☆	NJ	
train number	**9571**	**563**	**67**	**9080**	**9573**	**9593**	**567**	**261**		**9014**	**9575**	**611**	**263**	**9022**	**9577**	**50237**	**9028**	**9579**	**461**	**9032**	**469**	
notes	🄡★				🄡★	🄡★					🄡★				🄡★			🄡★			①③⑤	
notes				①–⑤									⑤⑥⑦		Ⓑ			⑥				
notes					**J**	**K**				**D**			**F**			**A**			**H**		**B**	
London St Pancras d.	...	...	...	0601	...	...	...	...	...	0931	...	...	...	1131	...	...	1331	...	...	1431	...	...
Paris Nord a.	...	...	...	0922	...	...	...	...	...	1258	...	...	...	1453	...	...	1656	...	...	1757	...	...
Paris Est d.	0654	...	...	...	1054	1054	...	...	...	...	1354	...	...	...	1554	...	...	1754	...	...	1912	...
Strasbourg d.	0845	...	...	...	1245	1245	...	...	...	...	1545	...	...	...	1746	...	...	1945	...	...	2342	...
Kehl 🏛 d.	|	...	...	...	|	|	...	...	...	...	|	...	...	...	|	...	...	|	...	...	|	...
Karlsruhe Hbf d.	0928	...	...	...	1327	1327	...	...	...	...	1627	...	...	...	1828	...	...	2027	...	...	|	...
Mannheim Hbf d.	|	...	...	...	|	|	...	...	...	...	|	...	...	...	|	...	...	|	...	...	|	...
Stuttgart Hbf a.	1004	...	...	...	1404	1404	...	...	...	...	1704	...	...	...	1904	...	...	2104	...	...	|	...
Stuttgart Hbf d.	...	1051	...	...	...	...	1451	...	...	...	...	1814	...	...	1920	2029	...	2114	2246	...	|	...
Ulm Hbf d.	...	1136	...	...	...	...	1536	...	...	...	...	1912	...	...	2023	2153	...	2212	2335	...	|	...
Augsburg Hbf d.	...	1219	...	...	...	...	1619	...	...	...	...	1955	...	...	2107	2302	...	2258	0020	...	|	...
München Pasing a.	...	1240	...	...	...	...	1640	...	...	...	...	2017	...	...	|	|	...	|	0041	...	|	...
München Hbf a.	...	1249	...	...	...	...	1649	...	...	...	...	2029	...	...	2136	|	...	2326	0051	...	|	...
München Hbf d.	...	...	1328	...	...	...	...	1729	...	...	...	...	2116	...	...	|	...	...	0056	...	|	...
München Ost a.	...	...	|	...	...	...	...	|	...	...	...	...	2125	...	...	2352	...	...	0105	...	0543	...
München Ost d.	...	...	|	...	...	...	...	|	...	...	...	...	2125	...	...	2354	...	...	0107	...	0546	...
Salzburg Hbf 🏛 a.	...	...	1458	...	...	...	...	1858	...	...	...	...	2259	...	...	0128	...	...	0247	...	0726	...
Linz Hbf a.	...	...	1615	...	...	...	...	2015	...	...	...	...	0030	...	...	0504	...	...	0430	...	0846	...
St Pölten Hbf a.	...	...	1701	...	...	...	...	2101	...	...	...	...	0124	...	...	0558	...	...	0530	...	0936	...
Wien Hbf a.	...	...	1732	...	...	...	...	2132	...	...	...	...	0220	...	...	0632	...	...	0605	...	1013	...

train type	NJ	☆	IC	TGV	ICE	☆	EN	TGV	☆	☆		ICE	ICE	☆	RJX	ICE	ICE	TGV	☆	RJX	ICE	ICE
train number	**468**	**9023**	**460**	**9578**	**9596**	**9027**	**50462**	**9576**	**9037**	**9039**		**612**	**9574**	**9043**	**260**	**518**	**9572**	**9592**	**9059**	**60**	**514**	**9570**
notes				🄡★	🄡★			🄡★					🄡★				🄡★	🄡★				🄡★
notes	②④⑦	①–⑥							Ⓑ													
notes	**B**		**H**	**E**	**G**		**A**										**J**	**K**				
Wien Hbf d.	1813	...	2155	...	...	...	2328	...	...	...	...	...	...	...	0628	...	...	...	...	1028	...	...
St Pölten Hbf d.	1846	...	2230	...	...	...	0001	...	...	...	...	...	...	...	0659	...	...	...	...	1059	...	...
Linz Hbf d.	1936	...	2330	...	...	...	0051	...	...	...	...	...	...	...	0745	...	...	...	...	1145	...	...
Salzburg Hbf 🏛 d.	2118	...	0051	...	...	...	0405	...	...	...	...	...	...	...	0900	...	...	...	...	1300	...	...
München Ost a.	2314	...	0220	...	...	...	0550	...	...	...	...	...	...	...	|	...	...	...	...	|	...	...
München Ost d.	2317	...	0222	...	...	...	|	...	...	...	...	...	...	...	|	...	...	...	...	|	...	...
München Hbf a.	|	...	0231	...	...	...	|	...	...	...	...	...	...	...	1033	...	...	...	...	1432	...	...
München Hbf d.	|	...	0236	...	...	...	|	0651	...	...	...	0727	...	...	...	1127	...	...	...	...	1527	...
München Pasing d.	|	...	0245	...	...	...	|	|	...	...	...	0736	...	...	...	1136	...	...	...	...	1536	...
Augsburg Hbf d.	|	...	0309	...	...	...	0648	0720	...	...	...	0801	...	...	...	1201	...	...	...	...	1601	...
Ulm Hbf d.	|	...	0351	...	...	...	0738	0804	...	...	...	0847	...	...	...	1247	...	...	...	...	1647	...
Stuttgart Hbf a.	|	...	0502	...	...	...	0838	0901	...	...	...	0945	...	...	...	1345	...	...	...	...	1745	...
Stuttgart Hbf d.	|	...	...	0652	0652	...	...	0910	...	...	...	...	1052	...	...	...	1452	1452	...	...	...	1852
Mannheim Hbf d.	|	...	...	|	|	...	...	|	...	...	...	...	|	...	...	...	|	|	...	...	...	|
Karlsruhe Hbf d.	|	...	...	0732	0732	...	...	0953	...	...	...	...	1132	...	...	...	1532	1532	...	...	...	1932
Kehl 🏛 d.	|	...	...	|	|	...	...	|	...	...	...	...	|	...	...	...	|	|	...	...	...	|
Strasbourg a.	0452	...	...	0814	0814	...	...	1037	...	...	...	...	1215	...	...	...	1614	1614	...	...	...	2015
Paris Est a.	0939	...	...	1006	1005	...	...	1231	...	...	...	...	1406	...	...	...	1805	1805	...	...	...	2213
Paris Nord d.	...	1112	...	...	...	1212	...	...	1442	1512	...	...	...	1612	...	...	...	...	2007	...	...	...
London St Pancras a.	...	1230	...	...	...	1330	...	...	1605	1630	...	...	...	1735	...	...	...	...	2130	...	...	...

A – KÁLMÁN IMRE – 🛏 1, 2 cl., ▬ 2 cl. (4, 6 berth) (2) Stuttgart - Wien - Budapest and v.v.
B – Daily (not Apr. 25 - May 9, May 21 - 26) *ÖBB nightjet* – 🛏 1, 2 cl., ▬ 2 cl. (4, 6 berth), (2) Paris - Wien.
C – Daily (not Apr. 24 - May 8, May 20, 21, 22) *ÖBB nightjet* – 🛏 1, 2 cl., ▬ 2 cl. (4, 6 berth), (2) Wien - Paris.
D – Not June 15.
E – ①–⑥ (also July 19; not ⑥ July 5 - Aug. 30).
F – ⑤⑥⑦ (also June 18, 19, Aug. 14, Dec. 8).
G – ⑥ July 5 - Aug. 30 (not July 19).
H – Until June 14.
J – Ⓑ (also ⑥ July 5 - Aug. 30; not July 19).
K – ⑥ Sept. 6 - Dec. 13 (also June 21, 28, July 19).

TGV – French high-speed train. 🄡. 🍷.
RJX – ÖBB *Railjet* service.
★ – *Alleo* ICE / TGV service (a DB / SNCF joint enterprise).
☆ – Eurostar high-speed train. 🄡. Service May 18 - Sept. 6. See pages 47 and 48 for further information.

40 LONDON - PARIS - BASEL - ZÜRICH - MILANO

train type	TGV	EC		TGV	EC		☆	TGV	EC		☆	TGV	IC	TGV	EC		☆	TGV		☆	TGV	
train number	**9203**	**151**		**9211**	**19**		**9006**	**9213**	**21**		**9014**	**9215**	**583**	**9215**	**23**		**9022**	**9219**		**9028**	**9223**	
notes					**119**						**C**											
notes							①–⑥				①–⑤	①–⑤	①–⑤	⑥⑦								
notes	♣	⊗		♣	⊗			♣	⊗			♣		♣	⊗			♣			♣	
London St Pancras d.	...	...	...	...	...	...	0731	...	...	...	0931	...	...	...	...	...	1131	...	...	1331	...	...
Paris Nord a.	...	...	...	...	...	...	1052	...	...	...	1258	...	...	...	...	...	1453	...	...	1656	...	...
Paris Gare de Lyon d.	0722	...	...	1022	...	...	...	1222	...	...	...	1422	...	1422	...	...	...	1622	...	...	1822	...
Dijon d.	|	...	...	1201	...	...	...	1401	...	...	...	|	...	|	...	...	...	|	...	...	2001	...
Belfort Montbéliard TGV d.	0941	...	...	|	...	...	...	|	...	...	...	1641	...	1641	...	...	...	1841	...	...	|	...
Mulhouse d.	1006	...	...	1306	...	...	...	1506	...	...	...	1706	...	1706	...	...	...	1906	...	...	2106	...
Basel SBB a.	1026	...	...	1326	...	...	...	1526	...	...	...	1726	...	1726	...	...	...	1926	...	...	2126	...
Basel SBB d.	1033	...	...	1333	...	...	...	1531	...	...	...	...	1733	1733	...	...	...	1932	...	...	2133	...
Zürich HB d.	1126	1233	...	1426	1533	...	...	1626	1733	...	...	...	1826	1826	1933	...	...	2026	...	...	2226	...
Arth Goldau d.	...	1318	...	...	1618	...	...	...	1818	...	...	...	...	...	2018	...	...	...	...	...	...	...
Bellinzona d.	...	1414	...	...	1714	...	...	...	1914	...	...	...	...	...	2114	...	...	...	...	...	...	...
Lugano d.	...	1430	...	...	1730	...	...	...	1930	...	...	...	...	...	2130	...	...	...	...	...	...	...
Chiasso 🏛 d.	...	1502	...	...	1802	...	...	...	2002	...	...	...	...	...	2202	...	...	...	...	...	...	...
Como San Giovanni d.	...	1510	...	...	1810	...	...	...	2010	...	...	...	...	...	2210	...	...	...	...	...	...	...
Milano Centrale a.	...	1550	...	...	1850	...	...	...	2050	...	...	...	...	...	2250	...	...	...	...	...	...	...

C Not June 15.

⊗ – 🍷. Compulsory reservation for international journeys. Supplement payable for international journeys and for internal journeys within Italy
♣ – *TGV Lyria* service. 🄡 🍷. Trains convey three classes of accommodation: Business 1ère, Standard 1ère and Standard. At-seat meal service in Business 1ère.
☆ – Eurostar high-speed train. 🄡. Service May 18 - Sept. 6. See pages 47 and 48 for further information.

FOR RETURN SERVICE SEE NEXT PAGE →

MILANO - ZÜRICH - BASEL - PARIS - LONDON 40

train type	TGV	☆	☆		TGV	☆		EC	TGV	☆	☆		EC	TGV	☆		EC	TGV		EC	TGV	
train number	**9206**	**9035**	**9037**		**9210**	**9043**		**10**	**9218**	**9051**	**9055**		**14**	**9222**	**9059**		**150**	**9226**		**16**	**9234**	
train number										Ⓑ												
notes		⑥	Ⓑ																			
notes	♣				♣			⊗	♣				⊗	♣			⊗	♣		⊗	♣	
Milano Centrale d.	...	...	...	...	...	...	...	0710	...	...	...	...	0910	...	...	...	1110	...	...	1310	...	...
Como San Giovanni d.	...	...	...	...	...	...	...	0754	...	...	...	...	0950	...	...	...	1150	...	...	1350	...	...
Chiasso 🏛 d.	...	...	...	...	...	...	...	0805	...	...	...	...	1005	...	...	...	1205	...	...	1405	...	...
Lugano d.	...	...	...	...	...	...	...	0830	...	...	...	...	1030	...	...	...	1230	...	...	1430	...	...
Bellinzona d.	...	...	...	...	...	...	...	0847	...	...	...	...	1047	...	...	...	1247	...	...	1447	...	...
Arth Goldau d.	...	...	...	...	...	...	...	0945	...	...	...	...	1145	...	...	...	1345	...	...	1545	...	...
Zürich HB d.	0734	...	...	...	0934	...	...	1027	1134	...	...	...	1227	1334	...	...	1427	1534	...	1627	1834	...
Basel SBB a.	0828	...	...	...	1028	...	...	...	1228	...	...	...	...	1428	...	...	...	1628	...	...	1928	...
Basel SBB d.	0834	...	...	...	1034	...	...	...	1234	...	...	...	...	1434	...	...	...	1634	...	...	1934	...
Mulhouse d.	0853	...	...	...	1053	...	...	...	1253	...	...	...	...	1453	...	...	...	1653	...	...	1953	...
Belfort Montbéliard TGV d.	0920	...	...	...	|	...	...	...	1320	...	...	...	...	|	...	...	...	|	...	...	2020	...
Dijon d.	|	...	...	...	1200	...	...	...	|	...	...	...	...	1600	...	...	...	1800	...	...	|	...
Paris Gare de Lyon a.	1138	...	...	...	1338	...	...	...	1538	...	...	...	...	1730	...	...	...	1938	...	...	2242	...
Paris Nord d.	...	1413	1442	...	...	1612	...	...	...	1810	1911	...	...	...	2007	...	...	...	...	...	...	...
London St Pancras a.	...	1530	1605	...	...	1735	...	...	...	1939	2030	...	...	...	2130	...	...	...	...	...	...	...

⊗ – 🍷. Compulsory reservation for international journeys. Supplement payable for international journeys and for internal journeys within Italy

♣ – *TGV Lyria* service. Ⓡ 🍷. Trains convey three classes of accommodation: Business 1ère, Standard 1ère and Standard. At-seat meal service in Business 1ère.

☆ – Eurostar high-speed train. Ⓡ. Service May 18 - Sept. 6. See pages 47 and 48 for further information.

PARIS - TORINO - MILANO - VENEZIA and ROMA 44

For other connections from / to Torino and Milano see Tables **600** and **605**.

train type		FR		TGV	FR			FR	FR	FR		TGV		TGV	ICN			FR				
train number		**9281**		**9243**	**9543**			**9281**	**9735**	**9547**		**9247**		**9255**	**797**			**9287**				
notes		Ⓡ		Ⓡ	Ⓡ			Ⓡ	Ⓡ	Ⓡ		Ⓡ		Ⓡ	Ⓡ			Ⓡ				
notes																						
notes		**A**		♠				**B**				♠		♠								
Paris Gare de Lyon d.	...	0641	...	0645	...	...	...	0730	...	...	...	0945	...	1447	...	...	...	1518	...	...	...	...
Lyon Part Dieu d.	...	0851	...	|	...	...	...	0930	...	...	...	|	...	|	...	...	...	1720	...	...	...	...
Chambéry d.	...	1012	...	0944	...	...	...	1054	...	...	...	1244	...	1744	...	...	...	1846	...	...	...	...
St Jean de Maurienne d.	...	1053	...	|	...	...	...	1135	...	...	...	|	...	1827	...	...	...	1934	...	...	...	...
Modane 🏛 a.	...	1120	...	1048	...	...	...	1203	...	...	...	1346	...	1850	...	...	...	1959	...	...	...	...
Modane 🏛 d.	...	1130	...	1055	...	...	...	1210	...	...	...	1355	...	1855	...	...	...	2008	...	...	...	...
Oulx ▲ d.	...	1156	...	1125	...	...	...	1236	...	...	...	1425	...	1925	...	...	...	2034	...	...	...	...
Torino Porta Susa a.	...	1245	...	1223	1310	...	...	1320	...	...	...	1524	...	2024	2040	...	...	2120	...	...	...	...
Milano Porta Garibaldi ✣ a.	...	|	...	1350	|	...	...	|	...	...	...	1650	...	2150	2218**d**	...	...	|	...	...	...	...
Milano Centrale a.	...	1350	...	...	1402	...	...	1407	...	...	...	...	...	...	|	...	...	2207	...	...	...	...
Milano Centrale d.	...	...	...	...	1410	...	...	...	1445	1510	...	...	...	...	|	...	...	...	...	...	...	...
Verona Porta Nuova a.	...	...	...	...	|	...	...	...	1558	|	...	...	...	...	|	...	...	...	...	...	...	...
Venezia Mestre a.	...	...	...	...	|	...	...	...	1700	|	...	...	...	...	|	...	...	...	...	...	...	...
Venezia Santa Lucia a.	...	...	...	...	|	...	...	...	1712	|	...	...	...	...	|	...	...	...	...	...	...	...
Reggio Emilia AV a.	...	...	...	...	1454	...	...	...	...	1554	...	...	...	...	|	...	...	...	...	...	...	...
Bologna Centrale a.	...	...	...	...	1524	...	...	...	...	1624	...	...	...	...	|	...	...	...	...	...	...	...
Firenze SMN a.	...	...	...	...	1604	...	...	...	...	1704	...	...	...	...	|	...	...	...	...	...	...	...
Roma Termini a.	...	...	...	...	1749	...	...	...	...	1849	...	...	...	...	0552**t**	...	...	...	...	...	...	...
Napoli Centrale a.	...	...	...	...	1913	...	...	...	...	2005**f**	...	...	...	...	0846	...	...	...	...	...	...	...
Salerno a.	...	...	...	...	2010	...	...	...	...	2036	...	...	...	...	0946	...	...	...	...	...	...	...

train type			FR	TGV			FR	FR	TGV			FR	FR	FR			FR	TGV				
train number			**9292**	**9242**			**9716**	**9516**	**9246**			**9514**	**9732**	**9296**			**9532**	**9250**				
notes			Ⓡ	Ⓡ			Ⓡ	Ⓡ	Ⓡ			Ⓡ	Ⓡ	Ⓡ			Ⓡ	Ⓡ				
notes																						
notes				♠					♠									♠				
Salerno d.	...	...	...	...	...	...	...	0550	...	...	...	0923	...	...	...	...	...	...	...	...	...	...
Napoli Centrale d.	...	...	...	...	...	...	...	0640	...	...	...	0956**f**	...	...	...	...	1040	...	...	...	...	...
Roma Termini d.	...	...	...	...	...	...	...	0810	...	...	...	1110	...	...	...	...	1210	...	...	...	...	...
Firenze SMN d.	...	...	...	...	...	...	...	0955	...	...	...	1255	...	...	...	...	1355	...	...	...	...	...
Bologna Centrale d.	...	...	...	...	...	...	...	1036	...	...	...	1336	...	...	...	...	1436	...	...	...	...	...
Reggio Emilia AV d.	...	...	...	...	...	...	...	1100	...	...	...	1400	...	...	...	...	1500	...	...	...	...	...
Venezia Santa Lucia d.	...	...	...	...	...	...	0818	|	...	...	...	|	1248	...	...	...	|	...	...	...	...	...
Venezia Mestre d.	...	...	...	...	...	...	0830	|	...	...	...	|	1300	...	...	...	|	...	...	...	...	...
Verona Porta Nuova d.	...	...	...	...	...	...	0932	|	...	...	...	|	1402	...	...	...	|	...	...	...	...	...
Milano Centrale a.	...	...	...	...	...	...	|	1150	...	...	...	1450	1515	...	...	...	1550	...	...	...	...	...
Milano Centrale d.	...	...	0620	...	...	...	|	1202	...	...	...	...	...	1548	...	...	1602	...	...	...	...	...
Milano Porta Garibaldi d.	...	...	|	0600	...	...	1050	|	1210	...	...	...	...	|	...	...	|	1610	...	...	...	...
Torino Porta Susa d.	...	...	0711	0736	...	...	1143	1249	1341	...	...	...	...	1640	...	...	1649	1738	...	...	...	...
Oulx ▲ d.	...	...	0810	0836	...	...	...	...	1436	...	...	...	...	1728	...	...	...	1836	...	...	...	...
Modane 🏛 a.	...	...	0835	0903	...	...	...	...	1505	...	...	...	...	1752	...	...	...	1905	...	...	...	...
Modane 🏛 d.	...	...	0850	0918	...	...	...	...	1514	...	...	...	...	1812	...	...	...	1914	...	...	...	...
St Jean de Maurienne d.	...	...	0915	0943	...	...	...	...	1623	...	...	...	...	1837	...	...	...	|	...	...	...	...
Chambéry d.	...	...	0956	1028	...	...	...	...	|	...	...	...	...	1922	...	...	...	2022	...	...	...	...
Lyon Part Dieu a.	...	...	1115	|	...	...	...	...	|	...	...	...	...	2032	...	...	...	|	...	...	...	...
Paris Gare de Lyon a.	...	...	1323	1331	...	...	...	...	1914	...	...	...	...	2238	...	...	...	2324	...	...	...	...

A – ①–⑤ June 10 - July 4, Sept. 22 - Oct. 17.

B – Daily (not ①–⑤ June 10 - July 4, Sept. 22 - Oct. 17).

d – departure time.

f – Napoli **Afragola**.

t – Roma **Tiburtina**.

♠ – *TGV* France-Italy high-speed service.

▲ – Station for the resorts of Cesana, Claviere and Sestriere.

✣ – Change at Torino Porta Susa for stations beyond Milano.

46 MADRID - BADAJOZ - LISBOA / PORTO

train type		Alvia		IC	IC		MD				IC	IC				🚌	🚌	🚌	🚌		🚌	
train number		**190**	**482**	**512**	**523**		**17902**			**486**	**544**	**529**										
notes		2	2	R	R		2	2	2	2	R	R							①④⑤			
notes		①–⑥							⑧									②③	⑥⑦			
notes																A	A	A	A		A	
Madrid Chamartín-Clara Campoamor d.	...	0830	...	...	...	...	...	...	...	...	...	...	...	...	...	...	...	...	...	...	...	...
Madrid Atocha Cercanías d.	...	0851	...	...	...	...	1055	...	...	...	...	...	...	...	...	...	...	...	...	...	...	...
Madrid Estación Sur ✣ d.	...	│	...	...	...	...	│	...	...	...	...	...	...	...	...	1030	1330	1515	1615	...	2345	...
Talavera de la Reina d.	...	1017	...	...	...	...	1229	...	...	...	...	...	...	...	...	│	│	│	│	...	│	...
Navalmoral de La Mata d.	...	1100	...	...	...	...	1309	...	...	...	...	...	...	...	...	│	│	│	│	...	│	...
Monfragüe–Plasencia d.	...	1132	...	...	...	...	1337	...	...	...	...	...	...	...	...	│	│	│	│	...	│	...
Cáceres d.	...	1210	...	...	...	...	1437	...	...	...	...	...	...	...	...	│	│	│	│	...	│	...
Mérida a.	...	1242	...	...	...	...	1523	...	...	...	...	...	...	...	...	1429	│	1914	2014	...	│	...
Mérida d.	...	1247	...	...	...	...	...	1528	1824	...	...	...	...	...	...	1430	│	1915	2015	...	│	...
Badajoz 🏛 ⊠ ES d.	...	1326	1409	...	...	...	...	1605	1910	1941	...	...	...	...	...	│	│	2015	2115	...	│	...
Elvas 🏛 PT d.	...	...	1325	...	...	...	...	...	...	1857	...	...	...	...	...	│	│	│	│	...	│	...
Abrantes d.	...	...	1523	...	...	...	...	...	...	2054	...	...	...	...	...	│	│	│	│	...	│	...
Entroncamento a.	...	...	1555	1559	1633	...	...	...	...	2126	2143	2303	...	...	...	│	│	│	│	...	│	...
Lisboa Oriente a.	...	...	...	1652	│	...	...	...	...	...	2240	│	...	...	...	1724	1959	2214	2314	...	0614	...
Lisboa S Apolónia a.	...	...	...	1700	│	...	...	...	...	...	2250	│	...	...	...	...	...	...	...	...	...	...
Coimbra B a.	...	...	...	...	1734	...	...	...	...	...	...	0004	...	...	...	...	...	...	...	...	...	...
Aveiro a.	...	...	...	...	1805	...	...	...	...	...	...	0033	...	...	...	...	...	...	...	...	...	...
Porto Campanhã a.	...	...	...	...	1843	...	...	...	...	...	...	0113	...	...	...	...	...	...	...	...	...	...

train type		IC	AP	IC			MD		IC	IC		Alvia	Alvia			🚌	🚌	🚌		🚌		
train number		**511**	**121**	**520**	**481**		**17907**		**720**	**513**	**485**	**295**	**297**									
notes		R	R	R	2	2	2		R	R	2	2	2									
notes				⚒								⑧	⑥									
notes																A	A	A		A		
Porto Campanhã d.	...	...	...	0645	...	...	...	...	1045	...	...	...	...	...	...	...	...	...	...	...	...	...
Aveiro d.	...	...	...	0727	...	...	...	...	1125	...	...	...	...	...	...	...	...	...	...	...	...	...
Coimbra B d.	...	...	...	0757	...	...	...	...	1156	...	...	...	...	...	...	...	...	...	...	...	...	...
Lisboa S Apolónia d.	...	0730	0800	│	...	...	...	...	│	1230	...	...	...	...	...	...	...	...	...	...	...	...
Lisboa Oriente d.	...	0739	0809	│	...	...	...	...	│	1239	...	...	...	...	...	1015	1315	1515	...	2230	...	...
Entroncamento d.	...	0832	0857	0858	0906	...	...	...	1258	1332	1336	...	...	...	...	│	│	│	...	│	...	...
Abrantes d.	...	...	...	...	0938	...	...	...	...	...	1408	...	...	...	...	│	│	│	...	│	...	...
Elvas 🏛 PT d.	...	...	...	...	1140	...	...	...	...	...	1616	...	...	...	...	│	│	│	...	│	...	...
Badajoz 🏛 ⊠ ES d.	...	...	...	...	1254	1422	...	...	...	...	1726	1748	1810	...	...	│	1715	│	...	│	...	...
Mérida a.	...	...	...	...	...	1508	...	...	...	...	...	1823	│	...	...	1440	1800	│	...	│	...	...
Mérida d.	...	...	...	...	...	...	1521	...	...	...	...	1828	│	...	...	1510	1830	│	...	│	...	...
Cáceres d.	...	...	...	...	...	...	1602	...	...	...	...	1903	1859	...	...	│	│	│	...	│	...	...
Monfragüe–Plasencia d.	...	...	...	...	...	...	1703	...	...	...	...	1941	1938**p**	...	...	│	│	│	...	│	...	...
Navalmoral de La Mata d.	...	...	...	...	...	...	1737	...	...	...	...	2010	2017	...	...	│	│	│	...	│	...	...
Talavera de la Reina d.	...	...	...	...	...	...	1822	...	...	...	...	2055	2056	...	...	│	│	│	...	│	...	...
Madrid Estación Sur ✣ a.	...	...	...	...	...	...	│	...	...	...	...	│	│	...	...	1909	2214	2330	...	0659	...	...
Madrid Atocha Cercanías a.	...	...	...	...	...	...	2003	...	...	...	...	2218	2218	...	...	...	...	...	...	...	...	...
Madrid Chamartín-Clara Campoamor a.	...	...	...	...	...	...	...	...	...	...	...	2239	2239	...	...	...	...	...	...	...	...	...

A – Operated by Alsa (www.alsa.es). Rail tickets not valid.

p – Plasencia.

✣ – Madrid Estación Sur (south bus station) is close to Méndez Álvaro metro station (see Madrid city plan on page 32).

⊠ – Badajoz railway station is 1 km north of Badajoz city centre and Badajoz bus station is 2.5 km south of Badajoz city centre.

ES – Spain (Central European Time).

PT – Portugal (West European Time).

48 FRANKFURT - STRASBOURG - LYON - MARSEILLE

train type	ICE	TGV		TGV				
train number	**9568**	**9877**		**9580**				
notes		**2087**		R★				
	⑧	R						
Frankfurt (Main) Hbf d.	0656	...	...	1356	...	...	...	...
Mannheim d.	0737	...	...	1439	...	...	...	...
Karlsruhe d.	0806	...	...	1512	...	...	...	...
Baden-Baden d.	│	...	...	1535	...	...	...	...
Strasbourg a.	0847	...	...	1604	...	...	...	...
Strasbourg d.	...	0904	...	1616	...	...	...	...
Mulhouse d.	...	0957	...	1709	...	...	...	...
Belfort Montbéliard TGV d.	...	1021	...	1734	...	...	...	...
Besançon France-Comté TGV d.	...	1044	...	1758	...	...	...	...
Chalon sur Saône d.	...	│	...	1856	...	...	...	...
Lyon Part Dieu a.	...	1258	...	1956	...	...	...	...
Avignon TGV a.	...	1426	...	2109	...	...	...	...
Aix en Provence TGV a.	...	1449	...	2131	...	...	...	...
Marseille St Charles a.	...	1506	...	2146	...	...	...	...

train type	TGV		TGV	ICE				
train number	**9583**		**5516**	**9563**				
notes	R★		R					
Marseille St Charles d.	0812	...	0945	...	...	...	...	...
Aix en Provence TGV d.	0826	...	0959	...	...	...	...	...
Avignon TGV d.	0848	...	1022	...	...	...	...	...
Lyon Part Dieu d.	1004	...	1138	...	...	...	...	...
Chalon sur Saône d.	1106	...	│	...	...	...	...	...
Besançon France-Comté TGV d.	1204	...	1408	...	...	...	...	...
Belfort Montbéliard TGV d.	1227	...	1432	...	...	...	...	...
Mulhouse d.	1251	...	1458	...	...	...	...	...
Strasbourg a.	1343	...	1554	...	...	...	...	...
Strasbourg d.	1355	...	...	1713	...	...	...	...
Baden-Baden a.	1422	...	...	│	...	...	...	...
Karlsruhe a.	1446	...	...	1753	...	...	...	...
Mannheim a.	1518	...	...	1818	...	...	...	...
Frankfurt (Main) Hbf a.	1559	...	...	1859	...	...	...	...

★ – TGV service (A DB / SNCF joint enterprise).

49 VILNIUS - RIGA - TALLINN

train number		**872**	**335**		**889**	**339**		
train number / notes			**17**		**890**	**19**		
		⑤⑥⑦			**874**			
Vilnius d.	...	...	...	...	0700	...	...	...
Kaišiadorys d.	...	...	...	...	0741	...	...	...
Jonava d.	...	...	...	...	0759	...	...	...
Kèdainiai d.	...	...	...	...	0819	...	...	...
Radviliškis d.	...	...	...	...	0857	...	...	...
Šiauliai d.	...	...	...	...	0916	...	...	...
Joniškis 🏛 LT d.	...	...	...	...	0954	...	...	...
Jelgava 🏛 LV d.	...	...	...	...	1030	...	...	...
Riga d.	...	0926	...	...	1120	...	...	...
Sigulda d.	...	1033	...	...	1213	...	...	...
Cesis d.	...	1112	...	...	1245	...	...	...
Valmiera a.	...	1140	...	...	1311	...	...	...
Lugaži 🏛 LV d.	...	1215	...	...	1345	...	...	...
Valga 🏛 EE d.	...	1221	1224	...	1351	1410	...	...
Elva d.	...	...	1313	...	...	1447	...	...
Tartu d.	...	...	1347	...	...	1510	...	...
Jõgeva d.	...	...	1422	...	...	1553	...	...
Tamsalu d.	...	...	1452	...	...	1646	...	...
Tapa d.	...	...	1509	...	...	1704	...	...
Tallinn a.	...	...	1609	...	...	1804	...	...

train number		**16**	**873**		**14**	**871**		
trains number / notes		**338**	**892**		**332**			
			891			⑤⑥⑦		
Tallinn d.	...	1002	...	...	1341	...	...	...
Tapa d.	...	1100	...	...	1438	...	...	...
Tamsalu d.	...	1118	...	...	1454	...	...	...
Jõgeva d.	...	1203	...	...	1525	...	...	...
Tartu d.	...	1249	...	...	1608	...	...	...
Elva d.	...	1312	...	...	1638	...	...	...
Valga 🏛 EE d.	...	1349	1411	...	1724	1737	...	...
Lugaži 🏛 LV d.	...	...	1418	...	...	1744	...	...
Valmiera d.	...	...	1449	...	...	1817	...	...
Cesis d.	...	...	1514	...	...	1846	...	...
Sigulda d.	...	...	1544	...	...	1920	...	...
Riga d.	...	...	1655	...	...	2004	...	...
Jelgava 🏛 LV d.	...	...	1732	...	...	...	...	...
Joniškis 🏛 LT d.	...	...	1808	...	...	...	...	...
Šiauliai d.	...	...	1845	...	...	...	...	...
Radviliškis d.	...	...	1901	...	...	...	...	...
Kèdainiai d.	...	...	1942	...	...	...	...	...
Jonava d.	...	...	2004	...	...	...	...	...
Kaišiadorys **1809** d.	...	...	2024	...	...	...	...	...
Vilnius **1809** a.	...	...	2105	...	...	...	...	...

EE – Estonia. Operator: Elron.

LT – Lithuania. Operator: LTG Link.

LV – Latvia. Operator: Vivi / Pasažieru vilciens.

STOCKHOLM - KØBENHAVN - HAMBURG - BERLIN 50

Services between Stockholm and Malmö are subject to alteration from September 1. Services between Hamburg and Berlin are subject to alteration from August 2.

train type		EC	ICE			EC	ICE		EC	ICE	Sn		EC	ICE	Sn		EC	ICE	Sn		EC	ICE	
train number		**391**	**707**	**1** [R]		**393**	**709**		**395**	**801**	**523**		**1197**	**803**	**523**		**397**	**699**	**529**		**399**	**805**	
notes				Ⓑ							①–⑤												
notes				**A**									**G**										
Stockholm Central ... d.	...	...	...	2317	...	...	...	...	...	...	0519	...	...	...	0724	...	...	...	1025	...	...	...	...
Norrköping Central ... d.	...	...	...	0056	...	...	...	...	...	...	0639	...	...	...	0841	...	...	...	1140	...	...	...	...
Linköping Central ... d.	...	...	...	0127	...	...	...	...	...	...	0704	...	...	...	0906	...	...	...	1205	...	...	...	...
Nässjö Central ... d.	...	...	...	0316	...	...	...	...	...	...	0753	...	...	...	0958	...	...	...	1254	...	...	...	...
Alvesta ... d.	...	...	...	0404	...	...	...	...	...	...	0827	...	...	...	1032	...	...	...	1330	...	...	...	...
Hässleholm Central ... d.	...	...	...	|	...	...	...	...	...	...	0911	...	...	...	1112	...	...	...	1412	...	...	...	...
Lund Central ... d.	...	...	...	|	...	...	...	...	...	...	0940	...	...	...	1140	...	...	...	1441	...	...	...	...
Malmö Central ... a.	...	...	...	0659	...	...	...	...	...	...	0952	...	...	...	1152	...	...	...	1452	...	...	...	...
Malmö Central ... ⊡ d.	0505	...	...	...	0705	...	...	0905	...	...	...	1050	...	...	...	1250	...	...	...	1505	...	...	...
Københavns Lufthavn ✈ ... ⊡ d.	0527	...	...	...	0727	...	...	0927	...	...	...	1115	...	...	...	1315	...	...	...	1527	...	...	...
Ørestad ... ⊡ d.	0533	...	...	...	0733	...	...	0933	...	...	...	1121	...	...	...	1321	...	...	...	1533	...	...	...
København H. ... ⊡ d.	0539	0622	...	...	0743	0822	...	0939	1022	...	...	1127	1207	...	...	1327	1422	...	...	1539	1622	...	...
Odense ... d.	...	0735	...	...	...	0935	...	...	1135	...	...	...	1335	...	...	...	1535	...	...	...	1735	...	...
Kolding ... d.	...	0815	...	...	...	1015	...	...	1215	...	...	...	1415	...	...	...	1615	...	...	...	1815	...	...
Padborg 🛃 ... d.	...	0902	...	...	...	1102	...	...	1302	...	...	...	1502	...	...	...	1702	...	...	...	1902	...	...
Hamburg Hbf ... a.	...	1101	1136	...	...	1302	1336	...	1500	1536	...	...	1703	1735	...	...	1900	1937	...	...	2108	2151	...
Berlin Hbf ... a.	...	...	1322	...	...	...	1522	...	...	1722	...	...	...	1923	...	...	...	2122	...	...	...	2354	...

train type	Sn		EC		EN	EN	EN	EN	
train number	**533**		**1199**	**301**	**345**	**345**	**345**	**345**	
notes				**10301**	Ⓑ	⑥	Ⓑ	⑥	
notes			**H**	**DP**	**ER**	**ER**	**ES**	**ES**	
Stockholm Central ... d.	1225	...	...	1620	1735	1735	1735	1735	...
Norrköping Central ... d.	1340	...	...	1745	1900	1900	1900	1900	...
Linköping Central ... d.	1405	...	...	1810	1929	1929	1929	1929	...
Nässjö Central ... d.	1458	...	...	1905	2027	2027	2027	2027	...
Alvesta ... d.	1532	...	...	1942	2109	2109	2109	2109	...
Hässleholm Central ... d.	1612	...	...	2025	2156	2156	2156	2156	...
Lund Central ... d.	1641	...	...	2100	2231	2231	2231	2231	...
Malmö Central ... a.	1652	...	...	2208	2242	2242	|	|	...
Malmö Central ... ⊡ d.	...	1705	...	2210	2321	0111	|	|	...
Københavns Lufthavn ✈ ... ⊡ d.	...	1727	...	|	2356	0137	2356	0137	...
Ørestad ... ⊡ d.	...	1733	...	2244	|	|	|	|	...
København H. ... ⊡ d.	...	1739	1822	|	|	|	|	|	...
Odense ... d.	...	...	1935	|	|	|	|	|	...
Kolding ... d.	...	...	2015	|	|	|	|	|	...
Padborg 🛃 ... d.	...	...	2102	|	0352	0623	0352	0623	...
Hamburg Hbf ... a.	...	...	2318	0537	0600	0900	0558	0901	...
Berlin Hbf ... a.	...	...	...	0745	0924	1201**g**	1031	1317**g**	...

train type	EC		Sn	EC		ICE	EC		Sn
train number	**1194**		**528**	**1198**		**608**	**398**		**542**
notes						①–⑤			
notes	**L**			**J**					
Berlin Hbf ... d.	...	...	...	...	...	0530	...	...	...
Hamburg Hbf ... d.	2356	...	...	0703	...	0725	0850	...	...
Padborg 🛃 ... a.	0254	...	...	0853	...	▬	1053	...	...
Kolding ... a.	0458	...	...	0944	...	...	1144	...	...
Odense ... a.	0540	...	...	1040	...	...	1223	...	...
København H. ... ⊡ d.	0702	0714	...	1203	1214	...	1338	1359	...
Ørestad ... ⊡ d.	...	0721	...	...	1221	*Sn*	...	1406	...
Københavns Lufthavn ✈ ⊡ d.	...	0729	...	...	1229	**538**	...	1414	...
Malmö Central ... ⊡ a.	...	0755	...	...	1255		...	1440	...
Malmö Central ... d.	...	...	0807	...	...	1307	...	...	1507
Lund Central ... d.	...	...	0820	...	...	1320	...	...	1520
Hässleholm Central ... d.	...	...	0848	...	...	1348	...	...	1548
Alvesta ... d.	...	...	0929	...	...	1429	...	...	1629
Nässjö Central ... d.	...	...	1002	...	...	1502	...	...	1702
Linköping Central ... d.	...	...	1053	...	...	1557	...	...	1756
Norrköping Central ... d.	...	...	1116	...	...	1620	...	...	1819
Stockholm Central ... a.	...	...	1234	...	...	1733	...	...	1932

train type	ICE	EC		Sn	ICE	EC		Sn	ICE	EC			ICE	EC		ICE	EC		EN	EN	EN	EN	
train number	**806**	**396**		**546**	**804**	**394**		**550**	**802**	**392**		**2** [R]	**800**	**390**		**800**	**1190**		**346**	**346**	**346**	**346**	**300**
notes												Ⓑ							Ⓑ	⑥	Ⓑ	⑥	**10300**
notes												**A**					**K**		**EB**	**EB**	**EC**	**EC**	**DQ**
Berlin Hbf ... d.	0836	...	...	...	1036	...	...	...	1236	...	...	...	1436	...	...	1436	...	...	1834	1725	1731	1634	2110
Hamburg Hbf ... d.	1022	1053	...	...	1222	1253	...	...	1423	1456	...	...	1622	1655	...	1622	1844	...	2203	2137	2203	2053	2359
Padborg 🛃 ... a.	...	1253	...	...	...	1453	...	...	...	1653	...	...	...	1853	...	...	2053	...	2357	2357	2357	2357	|
Kolding ... a.	...	1344	...	...	...	1544	...	...	...	1744	...	...	...	1944	...	...	2144	...	|	|	|	|	|
Odense ... a.	...	1423	...	...	...	1623	...	...	...	1823	...	...	...	2023	...	...	2223	...	|	|	|	|	|
København H. ... ⊡ d.	...	1538	1559	...	...	1738	1759	...	...	1938	2014	...	...	2138	2214	...	2346	0014	|	|	|	|	|
Ørestad ... ⊡ d.	...	...	1606	...	...	...	1806	...	...	...	2021	...	...	...	2221	...	...	0021	|	|	|	|	0633
Københavns Lufthavn ✈ ... ⊡ d.	...	...	1614	...	...	...	1814	...	...	...	2029	...	...	...	2229	...	...	0029	0339	0339	0339	0339	|
Malmö Central ... ⊡ a.	...	...	1640	...	...	...	1840	...	...	...	2055	...	...	...	2255	...	...	0055	0359	0359	0359	0359	0658
Malmö Central ... d.	...	...	...	1707	...	...	...	1907	...	...	...	2217	...	...	...	...	...	...	0401	0401	0401	0401	0700
Lund Central ... d.	...	...	...	1720	...	...	...	1920	...	...	...	2231	...	...	...	...	...	...	0435	0435	0435	0435	0830
Hässleholm Central ... d.	...	...	...	1748	...	...	...	1948	...	...	...	0005	...	...	...	...	...	...	0509	0509	0509	0509	0905
Alvesta ... d.	...	...	...	1829	...	...	...	2029	...	...	...	0109	...	...	...	...	...	...	0602	0553	0602	0553	0946
Nässjö Central ... d.	...	...	...	1902	...	...	...	2102	...	...	...	0241	...	...	...	...	...	...	0645	0634	0645	0634	1025
Linköping Central ... d.	...	...	...	1957	...	...	...	2153	...	...	...	0348	...	...	...	...	...	...	0748	0736	0748	0736	1123
Norrköping Central ... d.	...	...	...	2021	...	...	...	2216	...	...	...	0417	...	...	...	...	...	...	0827	0805	0827	0805	1149
Stockholm Central ... a.	...	...	...	2133	...	...	...	2334	...	...	...	0553	...	...	...	...	...	...	0955	0933	0955	0933	1315

A – [couchette] 1, 2 cl., [sleeper] 2 cl., [2] 🍷 [R] Stockholm - Malmö and v.v.

B – June 7 - Aug. 1.

C – Aug. 2 - Dec. 13.

D – BERLIN NIGHT EXPRESS – [sleeper] 2 cl., 🍷 [R] Stockholm - Berlin and v.v. ✕ Stockholm - Malmö and v.v. Special fares apply.

E – SJ EURONIGHT – [couchette] 1, 2 cl., [sleeper] 2 cl. (6 berth), [2] 🍷 [R] Stockholm - Berlin and v.v.

G – Daily June 15 - Nov. 2 (not July 12 – 15, July 26 - Aug. 3).

H – Daily June 15 - Aug. 31 (not July 12 – 19, July 25 - Aug. 3).

J – Daily June 15 - Sept. 1 (not July 12 - Aug. 3).

K – Daily June 16 - Oct. 26 (not July 11 – 17, July 26 - Aug. 3).

L – Ⓑ June 15 - Aug. 31 (not July 11 – 19, July 25 - Aug. 3).

M – June 16 - Aug. 29.

P – Ⓑ until Oct. 31 (not July 3, 4, 10, 11, 14, 16, 17, 18, 24, 25, Aug. 1). Departures on ⑤ May 23 - June 27 and Aug. 8 - Oct. 31 (from Stockholm) continue to Dresden Hbf (a. 1030); departures on July 31, Sept. 19 continue to Chemnitz (on Aug. 1 a. 1129, on Sept. 20 a. 1255).

Q – Ⓑ until Nov. 2 (not July 4, 6, 11, 13, 15, 17, 18, 20, 25, 27, Aug. 1). Departures on ⑦ May 25 - June 29 and Aug. 10 - Nov. 2 start from Dresden Hbf (d. 1826); departures on Aug. 3, Sept. 21 start from Chemnitz (on Aug. 3 d. 1726, on Sept. 21 d. 1649).

R – June 7 - July 31.

S – Aug. 1 - Dec. 13.

g – Berlin Gesundbrunnen.

k – ⑤ Aug. 15 - Dec. 12 (not Aug. 22, Sept. 12, Oct. 10, Nov. 21, Dec. 5).

q – ①②③④⑦ Aug. 10 - Dec. 11 (not Sept. 22).

x – One hour later from Aug. 2 with altered train number.

y – Ⓑ Aug. 1 - Dec. 12 (not Aug. 24, Sept. 12 - 18, Oct. 12, Nov. 23, Dec. 7).

⊡ – Frequent additional services are available Malmö - København and v.v. (Table **703**).

Sn – *Snabbtåg* high-speed train. [R] ✕.

ST – Snälltåget (www.snalltaget.se).

PRAHA - LINZ - ZÜRICH 52

	EC	RJX	EC	RJX	EC	RJX	EC	EN	
	331	**162**	**333**	**166**	**335**	**760**	**337**	**40458**	
	✕	✕	✕	✕	✕	✕	✕		
								C	
Praha hl. n. ... d.	0620	...	1020	...	1420	...	1820	1828	...
Tábor ... d.	0723	...	1123	...	1523	...	1923	|	...
České Budějovice ... d.	0805	...	1205	...	1605	...	2005	|	...
Summerau 🛃 ... d.	0908	...	1308	...	1708	...	2108	|	...
Linz Hbf ... a.	1006	...	1406	...	1806	...	2206	|	...
Linz Hbf ... d.	...	1045	...	1445	...	1845	...	|	...
Salzburg ... a.	...	1153	...	1553	...	1953	...	|	...
Innsbruck Hbf ... a.	...	1344	...	1744	...	2144	...	|	...
Zürich HB ... a.	...	1720	...	2120	...	...	...	0904	...

	EN	EC	RJX	EC	RJX	EC	RJX	EC	
	40459	**330**	**765**	**332**	**161**	**334**	**165**	**336**	
		✕	✕	✕	✕	✕	✕	✕	
	C								
Zürich HB ... d.	1959	...	...	...	0640	...	1040	...	...
Innsbruck Hbf ... d.	|	...	0817	...	1016	...	1416	...	...
Salzburg ... d.	|	...	1007	...	1207	...	1607	...	...
Linz Hbf ... a.	|	...	1115	...	1315	...	1715	...	...
Linz Hbf ... d.	|	0652	...	1154	...	1554	...	1854	...
Summerau 🛃 ... a.	|	0750	...	1250	...	1652	...	1952	...
České Budějovice ... a.	|	0852	...	1352	...	1752	...	2052	...
Tábor ... a.	|	0937	...	1435	...	1835	...	2137	...
Praha hl. n. ... a.	0923	1039	...	1539	...	1939	...	2239	...

C – CANOPUS – [couchette] 1, 2 cl., [sleeper] 2 cl. (4, 6 berth), [2] Praha - Leipzig - Zürich and v.v. (Table **54**).

RJX – ÖBB *Railjet* service. [1] (premium class), [1] (first class), [2] (economy class), ✕.

53 HAMBURG, DÜSSELDORF and BRUSSELS - NÜRNBERG - INNSBRUCK and WIEN

		NJ	NJ	NJ	NJ		NJ		
		491	**40421**	**40491**	**421**		**40425**		
							①③⑤		
		A	**B**	**D**	**E**		**C**		
Hamburg Altona	d.	1956	...	1956	...	...	...	...	...
Hamburg Hbf	d.	2010	...	2010	...	...	...	...	...
Hannover Hbf	d.	2153	...	2153	...	...	...	...	...
Göttingen	d.	2239	...	2239	...	...	...	...	...
Amsterdam Centraal	d.	|	1900	|	1900	...	...	...	...
Utrecht Centraal	d.	|	|	|	|	...	...	...	...
Arnhem	d.	|	|	|	|	...	...	...	...
Duisburg Hbf	d.	|	|	|	|	...	...	...	...
Düsseldorf Hbf	d.	|	|	|	|	...	...	...	...
Brussels Midi/Zuid	d.	|	|	|	|	...	1906	...	...
Liège Guillemins	d.	|	|	|	|	...	2018	...	...
Aachen 🏛	d.	|	|	|	|	...	2110	...	...
Köln Hbf	d.	|	|	|	|	...	2201	...	...
Bonn Beuel	d.	|	|	|	|	...	2226	...	...
Koblenz Hbf	d.	|	|	|	|	...	2325	...	...
Mainz Hbf	d.	|	|	|	|	...	0036	...	...
Frankfurt Flughafen ✈	d.	|	|	|	|	...	|	...	...
Frankfurt (Main) Süd	d.	|	|	|	|	...	|	...	...
Würzburg Hbf	d.	0148	0229	0148	0229	...	|	...	...
Nürnberg Hbf	a.	0315	0328	0315	0328	...	|	...	...
Nürnberg Hbf	d.	0408	0408	0436	0436	...	|	...	...
Regensburg Hbf	a.	0507	0507	|	|	...	|	...	...
Augsburg Hbf	a.	|	|	0624	0624	...	|	...	...
München Ost	a.	|	|	|	|	...	0543	...	...
München Hbf	a.	|	|	0706	0706	...	|	...	...
Salzburg Hbf	a.	|	|	|	|	...	0726	...	...
Kufstein 🏛	a.	|	|	0826	0826	...	|	...	...
Wörgl Hbf	a.	|	|	0837	0837	...	|	...	...
Jenbach	a.	|	|	0853	0853	...	|	...	...
Innsbruck Hbf	a.	|	|	0914	0914	...	|	...	...
Passau 🏛	a.	0613	0613	...	...	...	|	...	...
Wels Hbf	a.	0714	0714	...	...	...	|	...	...
Linz Hbf	a.	0743	0743	...	...	...	0846	...	...
St Pölten Hbf	a.	0838	0838	...	...	...	0936	...	...
Wien Meidling	a.	0908	0908	...	...	...	1005	...	...
Wien Hbf	a.	0917	0917	...	...	...	1013	...	...

		NJ		NJ	NJ	NJ	NJ		
		40468		**420**	**40420**	**40490**	**490**		
		②④⑥							
		C		**E**	**D**	**B**	**A**		
Wien Hbf	d.	1813	...	...	...	2010	2010	...	...
Wien Meidling	d.	1820	...	...	...	2017	2017	...	...
St Pölten Hbf	d.	1846	...	...	...	2044	2044	...	...
Linz Hbf	d.	1936	...	...	...	2134	2134	...	...
Wels Hbf	d.	|	...	...	...	2151	2151	...	...
Passau 🏛	d.	|	...	...	...	2253	2253	...	...
Innsbruck Hbf	d.	|	...	2046	2046	|	|	...	...
Jenbach	d.	|	...	2106	2106	|	|	...	...
Wörgl Hbf	d.	|	...	2123	2123	|	|	...	...
Kufstein 🏛	d.	|	...	2135	2135	|	|	...	...
Salzburg Hbf	d.	2118	...	|	|	|	|	...	...
München Hbf	d.	|	...	2252	2252	|	|	...	...
München Ost	d.	2316	...	|	|	|	|	...	...
Augsburg Hbf	d.	|	...	2325	2325	|	|	...	...
Regensburg Hbf	d.	|	...	|	|	2357	2357	...	...
Nürnberg Hbf	a.	|	...	0053	0053	0057	0057	...	...
Nürnberg Hbf	d.	|	...	0136	0142	0136	0142	...	...
Würzburg Hbf	a.	|	...	0230	0234	0230	0234	...	...
Frankfurt (Main) Süd	a.	|	...	|	|	|	|	...	...
Frankfurt Flughafen ✈	a.	|	...	|	|	|	|	...	...
Mainz Hbf	a.	0451	...	|	|	|	|	...	...
Koblenz Hbf	a.	0545	...	|	|	|	|	...	...
Bonn Beuel	a.	0631	...	|	|	|	|	...	...
Köln Hbf	a.	0659	...	|	|	|	|	...	...
Aachen 🏛	a.	0747	...	|	|	|	|	...	...
Liège Guillemins	a.	0848	...	|	|	|	|	...	...
Brussels Midi/Zuid	a.	0955	...	|	|	|	|	...	...
Düsseldorf Hbf	a.	...	...	|	|	|	|	...	...
Duisburg Hbf	a.	...	...	|	|	|	|	...	...
Arnhem	a.	...	...	|	|	|	|	...	...
Utrecht Centraal	a.	...	...	|	|	|	|	...	...
Amsterdam Centraal	a.	...	...	0950	|	0950	|	...	...
Göttingen	a.	...	...	...	0605	...	0605	...	...
Hannover Hbf	a.	...	...	...	0650	...	0650	...	...
Hamburg Hbf	a.	...	...	...	0847	...	0847	...	...
Hamburg Altona	a.	...	...	...	0906	...	0906	...	...

A – *ÖBB nightjet* – 🛏 1, 2 cl., ━ 2 cl. (1, 4 berth), [2] 🍷 Hamburg - Wien and v.v.
B – *ÖBB nightjet* – 🛏 1, 2 cl., ━ 2 cl. (4, 6 berth), [2] Amsterdam - Wien and v.v.
C – *ÖBB nightjet* – 🛏 1, 2 cl., ━ 2 cl. (4, 6 berth), [2] Brussels - Wien and v.v.
D – *ÖBB nightjet* – 🛏 1, 2 cl., ━ 2 cl. (1, 4 berth), [2] 🍷 Hamburg - Innsbruck and v.v.
E – *ÖBB nightjet* – 🛏 1, 2 cl., ━ 2 cl. (4, 6 berth), [2] Amsterdam - Innsbruck and v.v.

54 PRAHA, HAMBURG and BERLIN - BASEL - ZÜRICH

		EN	NJ		NJ				
		40458	**408**		**471**				
		C	**G**		**H**				
Praha hl. n.	d.	1828	...	...	...	...	...	...	...
Dresden Hbf	d.	2102	...	...	...	...	...	...	...
Hamburg Altona	d.	|	...	...	2152	...	...	...	...
Hamburg Hbf	d.	|	...	...	2208	...	...	...	...
Berlin Hbf	d.	|	2057	...	|	...	...	...	...
Berlin Südkreuz	d.	|	2107	...	|	...	...	...	...
Halle (Salle) Hbf	d.	|	|	...	|	...	...	...	...
Leipzig Hbf	a.	2218	2345	...	|	...	...	...	...
Hannover Hbf	a.	|	|	...	0030	...	...	...	...
Frankfurt (Main) Süd	a.	0335	0335	...	|	...	...	...	...
Frankfurt (Main) Hbf	a.	|	|	...	|	...	...	...	...
Mannheim Hbf	a.	|	|	...	|	...	...	...	...
Karlsruhe Hbf	a.	0507	0507	...	0603	...	...	...	...
Baden-Baden	a.	0526	0526	...	|	...	...	...	...
Offenburg	a.	0546	0546	...	0637	...	...	...	...
Freiburg (Brsg) Hbf	a.	0617	0617	...	0721	...	...	...	...
Basel Bad Bf 🏛	a.	0656	0656	...	0759	...	...	...	...
Basel SBB	a.	0720	0720	...	0810	...	...	...	...
Zürich HB	a.	0904	0904	...	1005	...	...	...	...

		NJ	EN	NJ	NJ				
		409	**40459**	**470**	**470**				
				⑦	①–⑥				
		G	**C**	**H**	**H**				
Zürich HB	d.	1959	1959	1934	2059	...	...	...	...
Basel SBB	d.	2113	2113	2058	2213	...	...	...	...
Basel Bad Bf 🏛	d.	2122	2122	2129	2222	...	...	...	...
Freiburg (Brsg) Hbf	d.	2158	2158	2205	2258	...	...	...	...
Offenburg	d.	2231	2231	2240	2333	...	...	...	...
Baden-Baden	d.	|	|	2301	2354	...	...	...	...
Karlsruhe Hbf	d.	2307	2307	0019	0019	...	...	...	...
Mannheim Hbf	d.	|	2342	|	|	...	...	...	...
Frankfurt (Main) Hbf	d.	|	|	|	|	...	...	...	...
Frankfurt (Main) Süd	d.	0027	|	|	|	...	...	...	...
Hannover Hbf	a.	|	|	0529	0529	...	...	...	...
Leipzig Hbf	a.	0448	0448	|	|	...	...	...	...
Halle (Salle) Hbf	a.	0537	|	|	|	...	...	...	...
Berlin Südkreuz	a.	0711	|	|	|	...	...	...	...
Berlin Hbf	a.	0718	|	|	|	...	...	...	...
Hamburg Hbf	a.	...	|	0753	0753	...	...	...	...
Hamburg Altona	a.	...	|	0809	0809	...	...	...	...
Dresden Hbf	a.	...	0706	...	...	...	...	...	...
Praha hl. n.	a.	...	0923	...	...	...	...	...	...

C – CANOPUS – 🛏 1, 2 cl., ━ 2 cl. (4, 6 berth), [2] Praha - Zürich and v.v.
[1] 🍴 Praha - Leipzig and v.v.
G – *ÖBB nightjet* – 🛏 1, 2 cl., ━ 2 cl. (4, 6 berth), [2] Berlin - Zürich and v.v.
H – *ÖBB nightjet* – 🛏 1, 2 cl., ━ 2 cl. (4, 6 berth), [2] Hamburg - Zürich and v.v.

55 PARIS and BRUSSELS - BERLIN

train type			ICE		NJ	NJ	ES		
train number			**9591**		**40469**	**425**	**453**		
notes					①③⑤	①③⑤	①③⑤		
notes			**f**		**P**	**K**	**E**		
Paris Est	d.	...	0955	...	1912	...	...	...	...
Strasbourg	d.	...	1146	...	2342	...	...	...	...
Brussels Midi / Zuid	d.	...	|	...	|	1906	1922	...	...
Brussels Nord	d.	...	|	...	|	1916	|	...	...
Liège Guillemins	d.	...	|	...	|	2018	|	...	...
Aachen Hbf 🏛	d.	...	|	...	|	2110	|	...	...
Köln Hbf	d.	...	|	...	|	2201	|	...	...
Bonn Beuel	d.	...	|	...	|	2226	|	...	...
Koblenz Hbf	d.	...	|	...	|	2325	◧	...	...
Mainz Hbf	d.	...	|	...	|	0036	|	...	...
Frankfurt (Main) Süd	a.	...	1404	...	0316	0316	|	...	...
Erfurt	a.	...	|	...	0547	0547	|	...	...
Halle (Saale)	a.	...	|	...	0704	0704	|	...	...
Berlin Südkreuz	a.	...	|	...	0819	0819	|	...	...
Berlin Hbf.	a.	...	1803	...	0826	0826	0620	...	...

train type			ICE		NJ	NJ	ES		
train number			**9590**		**424**	**40424**	**452**		
notes					②④⑦	②④⑦	②④⑦		
notes			**g**		**M**	**N**	**E**		
Berlin Hbf	d.	...	1155	...	1906	1906	2256	...	...
Berlin Südkreuz	d.	...	|	...	|	|	|	...	...
Halle (Saale)	d.	...	|	...	|	|	|	...	...
Erfurt	d.	...	|	...	|	|	|	...	...
Frankfurt (Main) Süd	d.	...	1553	...	0026	0026	|	...	...
Mainz Hbf	a.	...	|	...	0451	|	◧	...	...
Koblenz Hbf	a.	...	|	...	0545	|	|	...	...
Bonn Beuel	a.	...	|	...	0631	|	|	...	...
Köln Hbf	a.	...	|	...	0659	|	|	...	...
Aachen Hbf 🏛	a.	...	|	...	0747	|	|	...	...
Liège Guillemins	a.	...	|	...	0848	|	|	...	...
Brussels Nord	a.	...	|	...	0946	|	|	...	...
Brussels Midi / Zuid	a.	...	|	...	0955	|	0927	...	...
Strasbourg	a.	...	1753	...	...	0452	...	...	...
Paris Est	a.	...	1955	...	...	0939	...	...	...

E – ①③⑤ EUROPEAN SLEEPER – 🛏 (1, 2, 3 berth), ━ (5, 6 berth), [2] Brussels - Berlin - Praha and v.v. (Table **78**).
K – **Suspended until further notice.** ①③⑤: *ÖBB nightjet* – 🛏 1, 2 cl., ━ 2 cl. (4, 6 berth), [2] Brussels - Berlin.
M – **Suspended until further notice.** ②④⑦: *ÖBB nightjet* – 🛏 1, 2 cl., ━ 2 cl. (4, 6 berth), [2] Berlin - Brussels.
N – ②④⑦ *ÖBB nightjet* – 🛏 1, 2 cl., ━ 2 cl. (4, 6 berth), [2] Berlin - Paris.
P – ①③⑤ *ÖBB nightjet* – 🛏 1, 2 cl., ━ 2 cl. (4, 6 berth), [2] Paris - Berlin.

f – Via Karlsruhe Hbf (a. 1234).
g – Via Karlsruhe Hbf (d. 1707).
◧ – Via Bad Bentheim 🏛 (Table **78**).

BERLIN - WARSZAWA, GDYNIA, WROCŁAW and PRZEMYŚL 56

train type	EC	EC/IC	EC	EC	EC/IC	EC	EC	EC	EC/IC	EC
train number	**41**	**59**	**45**	**47**	**57**	**49**	**231**	**247**	**55**	**249**
train number		**73000**			**73002**		**75000**		**73004**	
notes	①–⑥									⑧
notes	**A**	**B**	**A**	**A**	**C**	**A**	**D**	**A**	**E**	**A**
Berlin Hbf d.	0549**g**	0849**g**	0948**g**	1149**g**	1249**g**	1349**b**	1449**g**	1549**g**	1649**g**	1748**g**
Berlin Ostbahnhof d.	|	|	|	|	|	|	|	|	|	|
Frankfurt (Oder) 🏛 d.	0650	0950	1050	1250	1350	1450	1550	1650	1750	1850
Rzepin d.	0708	1012	1108	1308	1412	1508	1608	1708	1812	1908
Poznań Gł. a.	0832	|	1232	1432	|	1632	1732	1832	|	2032
Warszawa Centralna a.	1100	|	1500	1700	|	1900	|	2100	|	2300
Warszawa Wschodnia a.	1116	|	1516	1716	|	1916	|	2116	|	2316
Gniezno d.	...	|	...	...	|	...	1806	...	|	...
Inowrocław d.	...	|	...	...	|	...	1835	...	|	...
Bydgoszcz Gł. d.	...	|	...	...	|	...	1904	...	|	...
Tczew d.	...	|	...	...	|	...	2008	...	|	...
Gdańsk Gł. a.	...	|	...	...	|	...	2023	...	|	...
Sopot a.	...	|	...	...	|	...	2040	...	|	...
Gdynia Gł. a.	...	|	...	...	|	...	2050	...	|	...
Zielona Góra Gł. d.	...	1057	...	...	1457	...	...	...	1857	...
Glogów d.	...	1133	...	...	1533	...	...	...	1933	...
Wrocław Gł a.	...	1252	...	...	1653	...	...	...	2048	...
Wrocław Gł d.	...	1315	...	...	1715	...	...	...	2100	...
Opole Gł. d.	...	1356	...	...	1756	...	...	...	2141	...
Kedzierzyn-Koźle d.	...	1418	...	...	1818	...	...	...	2203	...
Gliwice d.	...	1446	...	...	1848	...	...	...	2233	...
Katowice a.	...	1509	...	...	1911	...	...	...	2255	...
Kraków Gł. a.	...	1609	...	...	2010	...	...	...	2350	...
Rzeszów Gł. a.	...	1739	...	...	2139	...	...	...	...	...
Przemyśl a.	...	1849	...	...	2245	...	...	...	...	...

train type	EC	EC/IC	EC	EC	EC	EC/IC	EC	EC	EC/IC	EC
train number	**248**	**37004**	**246**	**230**	**48**	**37002**	**46**	**44**	**37000**	**40**
train number		**54**		**57000**		**56**			**58**	
notes	①–⑥									⑧
notes	**A**	**E**	**A**	**D**	**A**	**C**	**A**	**A**	**B**	**A**
Przemyśl d.	...	...	...	...	...	0507	...	...	0920	...
Rzeszów Gł. d.	...	...	...	...	...	0609	...	...	1022	...
Kraków Gł. d.	...	0421	...	...	...	0753	...	...	1156	...
Katowice d.	...	0514	...	...	...	0851	...	...	1252	...
Gliwice d.	...	0539	...	...	...	0914	...	...	1315	...
Kedzierzyn-Koźle d.	...	0605	...	...	...	0940	...	...	1342	...
Opole Gł. d.	...	0628	...	...	...	1005	...	...	1405	...
Wrocław Gł a.	...	0708	...	...	...	1045	...	...	1445	...
Wrocław Gł d.	...	0713	...	...	...	1109	...	...	1510	...
Glogów d.	...	0830	...	...	...	1229	...	...	1629	...
Zielona Góra Gł. d.	...	0904	...	...	...	1304	...	...	1704	...
Gdynia Gł. d.	...	|	...	0706	...	|	...	...	|	...
Sopot d.	...	|	...	0716	...	|	...	...	|	...
Gdańsk Gł. d.	...	|	...	0735	...	|	...	...	|	...
Tczew d.	...	|	...	0751	...	|	...	...	|	...
Bydgoszcz Gł. d.	...	|	...	0857	...	|	...	...	|	...
Inowrocław d.	...	|	...	0924	...	|	...	...	|	...
Gniezno d.	...	|	...	1200	...	|	...	...	|	...
Warszawa Wschodnia d.	0444	|	0644	|	0844	|	1044	1244	|	1644
Warszawa Centralna d.	0500	|	0700	|	0900	|	1100	1300	|	1700
Poznań Gł. d.	0730	|	0930	1030	1130	|	1330	1530	|	1930
Rzepin d.	0857	0949	1057	1157	1257	1349	1457	1657	1749	2057
Frankfurt (Oder) 🏛 d.	0912	1012	1112	1212	1312	1412	1512	1712	1812	2112
Berlin Ostbahnhof a.	|	|	|	|	|	|	|	|	|	|
Berlin Hbf a.	1013**g**	1113**g**	1213**g**	1314**g**	1412**g**	1513**g**	1613**g**	1812**g**	1915**g**	2217**g**

KULTURZUG / POCIAG DO KULTURY

	IRE	IRE
	5461	**5463**
	F	**F**
	⑥	⑤**j**
Berlin Lichtenberg d.	0842	1442
Berlin Ostkreuz d.	0849	1449
Cottbus d.	1014	1613
Wegliniec a.	1130	1731
Bolesławiec a.	1146	1751
Legnica a.	1217	1822
Wrocław Gł. a.	1328	1927

	IRE	IRE
	5460	**5462**
	F	**F**
	⑦	⑤**j**
Wrocław Gł. d.	1636	1936
Legnica d.	1716	2019
Bolesławiec d.	1745	2048
Wegliniec d.	1802	2104
Cottbus a.	1925	2225
Berlin Ostkreuz a.	2122	2340
Berlin Lichtenberg a.	2131	2348

A – BERLIN WARSZAWA EXPRESS – (1,2) ✕ 🄡 Berlin - Poznan - Warszawa and v.v.
B – GALICJA – (1,2) ✕ Berlin - Zielona Góra - Kraków - Przemyśl and v.v.
C – WAWEL – (1,2) ✕ 🄡 Berlin - Zielona Góra - Wrocław - Krakow - Przemyśl and v.v.
D – GEDANIA (1,2) ✕ 🄡 Berlin - Poznań - Gdańsk - Gdynia and v.v.
E – ODER / ODRA – (1,2) ✕ 🄡 Berlin - Zielona Góra - Wrocław - Krakow and v.v.
F – KULTURZUG / POCIAG DO KULTURY - (2) Berlin - Wrocław and v.v. International journeys only. Special fares apply.

g – Berlin **Gesundbrunnen**. Depart / arrive Berlin Hbf and Berlin Ostbahnhof on certain dates.
j – Also Oct. 2; not Oct. 3.

KRAKÓW - WARSZAWA - VILNIUS 58

	IC	
	144	
	H	**24**
Kraków Gł.	0401	...
Warszawa Centralna d.	0755	...
Warszawa Wschodnia d.	0804	...
Białystok a.	0954	...
Białystok d.	1030	...
Suwałki a.	1210	...
Trakiszki 🏛 a.	1313	...
Mockava 🏛 ◐ § a.	1435	1515
Kaunas § a.	...	1626
Vilnius § a.	...	1729

		IC
		143
	23	**H**
Vilnius § d.	1235	...
Kaunas § d.	1339	...
Mockava 🏛 ◐ § d.	1452	1525
Trakiszki 🏛 d.	...	1448
Suwałki d.	...	1547
Białystok a.	...	1728
Białystok d.	...	1807
Warszawa Wschodnia a.	...	1956
Warszawa Centralna a.	...	2005
Kraków Gł. a.	...	2351

H – HAŃCZA – (1,2) ✕ 🄡 Kraków - Warszawa - Białystok - Mockava and v.v.
§ – Lithuanian time.
◐ – Ticketing point is Mockava.

WARSZAWA - KYIV 59

	52100	**12010**
	D24	**D20**
	c	**K**
Warszawa Wschodnia d.	1149	1749
Lublin d.	1331	2010
Chełm a.	1422	2105
Chełm 🏛 d.	1607	2256
Dorohusk	|	|
Kovel a.	2119	0401
Kyiv a.	0512	1045

	D19	**D23**
	21010	**25100**
	K	**c**
Kyiv d.	2021	2308
Kovel d.	0233	|
Dorohusk d.	|	|
Chełm 🏛 a.	0544	1116
Chełm d.	0700	1337
Lublin d.	0808	1434
Warszawa Wschodnia a.	1011	1611

K – KYIV EKSPRES / KIEV EXPRESS – 🛏 1, 2 cl. Warszawa - Kyiv and v.v. At Kyiv passengers may be required to board the train earlier for customs control.

c – A change of trains is required at Chełm.

60 HAMBURG - BERLIN - PRAHA - WIEN and BUDAPEST

Most *EC* and *RJ* trains convey ✕. Railjet (♥) trains convey 🍸. Compulsory reservation will apply from June 15 until August 31 for international journeys between Germany and Czech Republic. For *European Sleeper* trains Brussels - Berlin - Praha and v.v. see Table **78**. For other trains Praha - Bratislava - Wien and v.v. see Table **1150**.

train type	*EC*	*RJ*	*EC*	♥	*RJ*	*EC*	*RJ*	♥	*EC*	*EC*	*RJ*	*RJ*	*EC*	*EC*	*RJ*	*EC*		*EC*	*RJ*	*EC*	*EC*	*RJ*	*EC*	
train number	**271**	**71**	**273**	**1031**	**73**	**275**	**75**	**1033**	**459**	**277**	**257**	**257**	**171**	**279**	**79**	**131**	**1035**	**173**	**371**	**379**	**281**	**373**	**175**	
notes		①–⑥																						
notes									**A**		**P**	**Q**												
Hamburg Altona d.	...	...	...	...	...	...	...	...	...	...	...	...	...	...	...	...	...	0635**x**	...	...	...	...	...	...
Hamburg Hbf d.	...	...	...	...	...	...	...	...	...	...	...	...	...	...	...	...	...	0648**x**	...	0851**x**	...	...	1051**x**	...
Berlin Hbf d.	...	...	...	...	...	...	...	...	...	...	0615	...	0715**z**	...	...	...	...	0915**z**	...	1116**z**	...	...	1316**z**	...
Berlin Südkreuz d.	...	...	...	...	...	...	...	...	...	...	0620	...	0723**z**	...	...	...	...	0923**z**	...	1123**z**	...	...	1323**z**	...
Dresden Hbf d.	...	...	...	...	...	...	...	...	0708	...	0810	...	0910	...	...	...	...	1110	...	1310	...	...	1510	...
Bad Schandau ⊖ d.	...	...	...	...	...	...	...	...	0734	...	0836	...	0935	...	...	...	...	1135	...	1335	...	...	1535	...
Děčín d.	...	...	...	...	...	...	...	...	0757	...	0900	0900	0957	...	...	...	...	1157	...	1357	...	...	1557	...
Ústí nad Labem hl. n. d.	...	...	...	...	...	...	...	...	0813	...	0916	0916	1013	...	...	...	...	1213	...	1413	...	...	1613	...
Praha Holešovice d.	...	...	...	...	...	...	...	...	0913	...	1018	1018	1116	...	...	...	...	1315	...	1513	...	...	1713	...
Praha hl. n. a.	...	...	...	...	...	...	...	...	0923	...	1026	1026	1127	...	...	...	...	1323	...	1523	...	...	1723	...
Praha hl. n. d.	...	0439	0542	0616	0642	0742	0840	0916	...	0942	1035	1035	...	1142	1242	...	1316	1342	1442	...	1542	1642	...	...
Pardubice hl. n. d.	...	0540	0640	0713	0740	0840	0940	1013	...	1040	1140	1140	...	1240	1340	...	1413	1440	1540	...	1640	1740	...	...
Brno hl. n. d.	0622	0722	0822	0848	0922	1022	1122	1148	...	1222	1322	1322	...	1422	1522	...	1548	1622	1722	...	1822	1922	...	...
Břeclav a.	0652	0722	0852	0918	0952	1052	1152	1218	...	1252	1352	1352	...	1452	1552	...	1618	1652	1752	...	1852	1952	...	...
Břeclav d.	0655	0755	0855	0920	0955	1055	1155	1220	...	1255	1355	1355	...	1455	1555	1555	1620	1655	1755	...	1855	1955	...	...
Wien Hbf a.	|	0849	|	1021	1049	|	1249	1321	...	|	1449	1449	...	|	1649	|	1721	|	1849	...	|	2049	...	...
Wien Meidling a.	|	0903	|	1033	1103	|	1303	1333	...	|	1503	1503	...	|	1703	|	1733	|	1903	...	|	2103	...	...
Wiener Neustadt Hbf a.	|	0930	|	|	1130	|	1330	|	...	|	1530	1530	...	|	1730	|	|	|	1930	...	|	2130	...	...
Graz Hbf a.	|	1133	|	|	1333	|	1533	|	...	|	1733	1733	...	|	1933	|	|	|	2133	...	|	2333	...	...
Kúty a.	0711	...	0911	◐	...	1111	...	◐	...	1311	...	...	...	1511	...	1611	◐	1711	...	...	1911	...	...	...
Bratislava hl. st. a.	0802	...	1002	|	...	1202	...	|	...	1402	...	...	...	1602	...	1705	|	1802	...	...	2002	...	...	...
Štúrovo △ a.	0924	...	1124	|	...	1324	...	|	...	1524	...	...	...	1724	...	1834	|	1924	...	...	2126	...	...	...
Budapest Nyugati a.	1028	...	1228	|	...	1428	...	|	...	1628	...	...	...	1828	...	1949	|	2028	...	...	2230	...	...	...
Budapest Déli a.	...	...	...	1314	...	...	...	1614	...	...	...	...	...	...	...	...	2014	...	...	...	...	...	...	...

train type	*EC*	*RJ*	*EC*	*EC*	*EN*	*NJ*	*NJ*	*EC*	
train number	**283**	**375**	**177**	**179**	**577**	**40457**	**457**	**259**	
notes					**477**				
notes					**B**	**C**	**D**	**R**	
Hamburg Altona d.	...	...	1238**x**	...	...	...	...	...	...
Hamburg Hbf d.	...	...	1252**x**	...	...	...	...	...	...
Berlin Hbf d.	...	...	1516**z**	1716**z**	...	1921	1921	0007	...
Berlin Südkreuz d.	...	...	1523**z**	1723**z**	...	1928	1928	0043**f**	...
Dresden Hbf d.	...	...	1710	1910	...	2210	2210	0241	...
Bad Schandau ⊖ d.	...	...	1735	1935	...	2236	2236	0307	...
Děčín d.	...	...	1757	1957	...	2259	2259	0350	...
Ústí nad Labem hl. n. d.	...	...	1813	2013	...	2314	2314	0406	...
Praha Holešovice d.	...	...	1913	2113	...	0016	0016	0513	...
Praha hl. n. a.	...	...	1923	2123	...	0025	0025	0523	...
Praha hl. n. d.	1742	1842	...	...	2201	0036	0036	...	...
Pardubice hl. n. d.	1840	1940	...	...	2304	0140	0140	...	...
Brno hl. n. d.	2022	2122	...	...	0048	0314	0314	...	...
Břeclav a.	2052	2152	...	...	0118	0345	0345	...	...
Břeclav d.	2055	2155	...	...	0455	0455	0549	...	...
Wien Hbf a.	|	2249	...	...	|	|	0700	...	...
Wien Meidling a.	|	...	...	...	|	|	0710	...	...
Wiener Neustadt Hbf a.	|	...	...	...	|	|	0747	...	...
Graz Hbf a.	|	...	...	...	|	|	0959	...	...
Kúty a.	2111	...	...	...	0512	0512	...	...	...
Bratislava hl. st. a.	2203	...	...	...	0602	0602	...	...	...
Štúrovo △ a.	...	...	...	...	0724	0724	...	...	...
Budapest Nyugati a.	...	...	...	...	0829	0829	...	...	...
Budapest Déli a.	...	...	...	...	...	...	...	...	...

train type	*EC*	*EC*	*IC*	*EC*	*EC*	*RJ*	*EC*	*EC*	*EC*
train number	**178**	**176**	**284**	**174**	**282**	**70**	**106**	**378**	**280**
notes									
notes									
Budapest Déli d.	...	...	...	...	...	...	...	...	...
Budapest Nyugati d.	...	...	...	...	...	...	...	...	0530
Štúrovo △ d.	...	...	...	...	...	...	...	...	0636
Bratislava hl. st. d.	...	...	0458	...	0558	...	...	...	0758
Kúty d.	...	...	0549	...	0649	...	...	...	0849
Graz Hbf d.	...	...	|	...	|	...	0526	...	|
Wiener Neustadt Hbf d.	...	...	|	...	|	...	0728	...	|
Wien Meidling d.	...	...	|	...	|	...	0759	...	|
Wien Hbf d.	...	...	|	...	|	0710	0810	...	|
Břeclav a.	...	...	0604	...	0704	0804	0904	...	0904
Břeclav d.	...	...	0607	...	0707	0807	...	...	0907
Brno hl. n. d.	...	...	0639	...	0739	0838	...	...	0939
Pardubice d.	...	...	0813	...	0913	1013	...	...	1113
Praha hl. n. a.	...	...	0915	...	1015	1115	...	...	1215
Praha hl. n. d.	0628	0828	...	1028	...	...	...	1233	...
Praha Holešovice d.	0639	0839	...	1039	...	...	...	1243	...
Ústí nad Labem hl. n. d.	0745	0945	...	1145	...	...	...	1345	...
Děčín d.	0807	1007	...	1207	...	...	...	1407	...
Bad Schandau ⊖ a.	0824	1024	...	1224	...	...	...	1424	...
Dresden Hbf a.	0850	1050	...	1250	...	...	...	1450	...
Berlin Südkreuz a.	1035**y**	1236**y**	...	1436**y**	...	...	...	1636**y**	...
Berlin Hbf a.	1043**y**	1243**y**	...	1443**y**	...	...	...	1643**y**	...
Hamburg Hbf a.	1310**x**	1512**x**	...	1711**x**	...	...	...	1912**x**	...
Hamburg Altona a.	1323**x**	1524**x**	...	...	...	...	...	...	...

train type	*RJ*	*EC*	♥	*EC*	*RJ*	*EC*	*EC*	*RJ*	*RJ*	*EC*	*EC*	♥	*RJ*	*EC*	*EC*	*RJ*	♥	*EC*	*RJ*	*EC*	*RJ*	*NJ*	*NJ*	*EN*
train number	**72**	**172**	**1032**	**130**	**74**	**170**	**278**	**256**	**256**	**458**	**276**	**1034**	**78**	**274**	**258**	**370**	**1036**	**272**	**372**	**270**	**374**	**40476**	**456**	**476**
notes																						**456**		**576**
notes								**P**	**Q**	**A**					**R**							**E**	**D**	**F**
Budapest Déli d.	...	...	0745	...	...	...	...	...	...	...	...	1145	...	...	...	...	1445	...	...	...	...	...	...	...
Budapest Nyugati d.	...	0730	|	0812	...	...	0930	...	...	...	1130	|	...	1330	...	...	|	1530	...	1730	...	1930	...	1930
Štúrovo △ d.	...	0836	◐	0923	...	...	1036	...	...	...	1236	◐	...	1436	...	...	◐	1636	...	1836	...	2036	...	2036
Bratislava hl. st. d.	...	0958	|	1055	...	...	1158	...	...	...	1358	|	...	1558	...	...	|	1758	...	1958	...	2158	...	2158
Kúty d.	...	1049	|	1149	...	...	1249	...	...	...	1449	|	...	1649	...	...	|	1849	...	2049	...	2249	...	2249
Graz Hbf d.	0626	|	|	|	0826	...	|	1026	1026	...	|	|	1226	|	...	1426	|	|	1626	|	1826	|	1920	|
Wiener Neustadt Hbf d.	0830	|	|	|	1030	...	|	1230	1230	...	|	|	1430	|	...	1630	|	|	1830	|	2030	|	2132	|
Wien Meidling d.	0857	|	1026	|	1057	...	|	1257	1257	...	|	1426	1457	|	...	1657	1726	|	1857	|	2057	|	|	|
Wien Hbf d.	0910	|	1039	|	1110	...	|	1310	1310	...	|	1439	1510	|	...	1710	1736	|	1910	|	2110	|	2210	|
Břeclav a.	1004	1104	1136	1204	1204	...	1304	1404	1404	...	1504	1536	1604	1704	...	1804	1836	1904	2004	2104	2204	2304	2304	2304
Břeclav d.	1007	1107	1138	...	1207	...	1307	1407	1407	...	1507	1538	1607	1707	...	1807	1838	1907	2007	2107	2207	2357	2357	0507
Brno hl. n. d.	1039	1139	1209	...	1239	...	1339	1439	1439	...	1539	1609	1639	1739	...	1839	1909	1939	2039	2139	2236	0029	0029	0539
Pardubice d.	1213	1312	1344	...	1413	...	1513	1613	1613	...	1713	1744	1813	1913	...	2013	2044	2113	2221	2318	...	0200	0200	0713
Praha hl. n. a.	1315	1415	1439	...	1515	...	1615	1720	1720	...	1815	1839	1915	2015	...	2115	2139	2215	2319	0018	...	0301	0301	0815
Praha hl. n. d.	...	1433	...	...	...	1628	...	1728	1728	1828	...	...	...	...	2028	...	...	...	...	...	...	0308	0308	...
Praha Holešovice d.	...	1443	...	...	...	1639	...	1740	1740	1839	...	...	...	...	2039	...	...	...	...	...	...	0319	0319	...
Ústí nad Labem hl. n. d.	...	1545	...	...	...	1745	...	1842	1842	1943	...	...	...	...	2145	...	...	...	...	...	...	0420	0420	...
Děčín d.	...	1607	...	...	...	1807	...	1907	1857	2001	...	...	...	...	2207	...	...	...	...	...	...	0507	0507	...
Bad Schandau ⊖ a.	...	1624	...	...	...	1824	...	1924	...	2019	...	...	...	...	2224	...	...	...	...	...	...	0524	0524	...
Dresden Hbf a.	...	1650	...	...	...	1850	...	1950	...	2059	...	...	...	...	2250	...	...	...	...	...	...	0550	0550	...
Berlin Südkreuz a.	...	1836**y**	...	...	...	2036**y**	...	2137	...	...	...	...	...	...	0050	...	...	...	...	...	...	0805	0805	...
Berlin Hbf a.	...	1843**y**	...	...	...	2043**y**	...	2146	...	...	...	...	...	...	0057	...	...	...	...	...	...	0814	0814	...
Hamburg Hbf a.	...	2117**x**	...	...	...	...	...	...	...	...	...	...	...	...	...	...	...	...	...	...	...	...	...	...
Hamburg Altona a.	...	2135**x**	...	...	...	...	...	...	...	...	...	...	...	...	...	...	...	...	...	...	...	...	...	...

A – Conveys CANOPUS – 1, 2 cl., 2 cl. (4, 6 berth), 2 Zürich - Praha and v.v.

B – METROPOL – 1, 2 cl., 2 cl. 12 Praha (**577**) - Břeclav (**477**) - Budapest.

C – *ÖBB nightjet* METROPOL – 1, 2 cl., 2 cl., 2 Berlin (**40457**) - Břeclav (**477**) - Budapest.

D – *ÖBB nightjet* METROPOL – 1, 2 cl., 2 cl., 2 Berlin - Graz and v.v.

E – *ÖBB nightjet* METROPOL – 1, 2 cl., 2 cl., 2 Budapest (**40476**) - Břeclav (**456**) - Berlin.

F – METROPOL – 1, 2 cl., 2 cl. 12 Budapest (**476**) - Břeclav (**576**) - Praha.

P – May 31 - June 29.

Q – June 30 - Dec. 13.

R – June 15 - Sept. 15.

f – Flughafen Berlin.

x – Not Aug. 1, 2025 - Apr. 25, 2026.

y – Arrive 18–19 minutes later from Aug. 10.

z – Depart 20–22 minutes earlier from Aug. 10.

♥ – Operated by REGIOJET. Separate fares apply.

△ – Routeing point for international tickets is Szob.

⊖ – Routeing point for international tickets is Schöna.

◐ – Via Hegyeshalom. (Table **1250**).

RJ – ÖBB *Railjet* service. 1 (business class), 1 (first class), 2 (economy class), ✕.

WIEN - BUDAPEST - BUCUREŞTI, İSTANBUL, BEOGRAD, and THESSALONÍKI 61

WIEN - BUDAPEST - BRAŞOV - BUCUREŞTI

train type	IC*	IC*	IC*	IC 75	IC*	IC*	IC/D	D	
train number	367	73	75	IR 76	79	407	473	347	
notes	[R] ✕	[R] 🍸	[R]	[R]	2 [R]	[R] ✕	[R]	[R]	
notes	A	T	C	C	D	E	F	G	
Wien Hbf d.	...	...	...	...	...	...	...	1942	...
Budapest Keleti d.	0640	0710	0910	0910	1510	1740	1910	2305	...
Lökösháza 🏛 d.	|	1045	1245	1245	1845	|	2245	0239	...
Curtici 🏛 d.	|	1220	1420	1420	2020	|	0030	0419	...
Debrecen d.	0940	|	|	|	|	2040	|	|	...
Nyírábrány 🏛 d.	1049	|	|	|	|	2114	|	|	...
Valea lui Mihai 🏛 d.	1229	|	|	|	|	2249	|	|	...
Arad d.	|	1234	1434	1434	2057	|	0043	0451	...
Timişoara Nord d.	|	1411	|	|	2232	|	|	|	...
Craiova d.	|	2103	|	|	0537	|	|	|	...
Cluj Napoca a.	|	...	2052	|	|	|	|	|	...
Sighişoara d.	|	...	...	|	|	|	|	0922	...
Sibiu a.	|	...	...	1958	|	|	0547	|	...
Braşov a.	2306	...	...	2244	|	0946	0848	1250	...
Bucureşti Nord a.	...	...	...	...	0936	...	1135	1526	...

train type	IC*	IC/D	IC*	IC*	IR 77	IC*	IC*	D	
train number	406	472	78	74	IR 76*	72	366	346	
notes	[R] ✕	[R]	2 [R]	[R]	[R]	[R] 🍸	[R] ✕	[R]	
notes	E	F	D	C	C	T	A	G	
Bucureşti Nord d.	...	1758	1945	...	...	...	...	1507	...
Braşov d.	1905	2036	|	...	0700	...	0800	1746	...
Sibiu d.	|	2329	|	...	0953	...	|	|	...
Sighişoara d.	|	|	|	...	|	...	|	2112	...
Cluj Napoca d.	|	|	|	0836	|	...	|	|	...
Craiova d.	|	|	0008	|	|	0813	|	|	...
Timişoara Nord d.	|	|	0721	|	|	1539	|	|	...
Arad d.	|	0443	0857	1502	1502	1657	|	0128	...
Valea lui Mihai 🏛 d.	0608	|	|	|	|	|	1945	|	...
Nyírábrány 🏛 d.	0600	|	|	|	|	|	1920	|	...
Debrecen d.	0707	|	|	|	|	|	2015	|	...
Curtici 🏛 d.	|	0534	0934	1534	1534	1734	|	0210	...
Lököshaza 🏛 d.	|	0537	0942	1542	1542	1742	|	0200	...
Budapest Keleti a.	0955	0850	1250	1850	1850	2050	2300	0500	...
Wien Hbf a.	...	...	...	...	...	...	...	0820	...

WIEN - BUDAPEST - BUCUREŞTI - SOFIA - İSTANBUL

train type / number	RJX	IC*		461				493	
train number	61	79	461	465	1095	463	465	12501	
notes		2 [R]	2	493	2	2	2		
notes		D	V P	B P	Q	Q	Q	H	
Wien Hbf d.	1140	...	...	...	...	...	...	...	...
Budapest Keleti d.	1419	1510	...	...	...	...	...	...	...
Lökösháza 🏛 d.	...	1845	...	...	...	...	...	...	...
Curtici 🏛 d.	...	2020	...	...	...	...	...	...	...
Arad d.	...	2057	...	...	...	...	...	...	...
Timişoara Nord d.	...	2232	...	...	...	...	...	...	...
Craiova d.	...	0537	...	...	...	...	...	...	...
Videle d.	...	0833	...	...	...	...	...	...	...
Bucureşti Nord d.	...	0936	1011	1011	1011	...	...	...	...
Videle d.	...	...	1127	1127	1127	...	...	...	...
Giurgiu Nord 🏛 d.	...	...	1313	1313	1314	...	...	...	...
Ruse 🏛 a.	...	...	1340	1340	1339	...	...	...	...
Ruse 🏛 d.	...	...	1425	1425	...	1425	...	...	...
Gorna Orjahovica a.	...	...	1626	1610	...	1633	...	...	...
Gorna Orjahovica d.	...	...	1648	1735	...	1648	1735	...	...
Pleven a.	...	...	1754	|	...	1754	|	...	...
Mezdra d.	...	...	1910	|	...	1910	|	...	...
Sofia a.	...	...	2029**q**	|	...	2035	|	...	...
Sofia d.	...	...	...	|	...	...	|	1845	...
Plovdiv d.	...	...	...	|	...	...	|	2142	...
Veliko Tarnovo d.	...	...	...	1751	...	...	1751	|	...
Stara Zagora d.	...	...	...	2100	...	...	2053	|	...
Dimitrovgrad (Bulgaria) d.	...	...	...	2303	...	...	2158	2303	...
Svilengrad 🏛 d.	...	...	...	0045	...	...	...	0045	...
Kapikule 🏛 d.	...	...	...	0400	...	...	...	0400	...
Edirne d.	...	...	...	|	...	...	...	|	...
Çerkezköy d.	...	...	...	0813	...	...	...	0813	...
Halkalı (Istanbul) ◧ a.	...	...	...	0956	...	...	...	0956	...

train type / number	12502				2611	492	IC*	RJX	
train number	492	464	462	1094	460	464	78	66	
notes	§	2	2	2	2	460	2 [R]		
notes	H	S	S	S	B R	B R	D		
Halkalı (Istanbul) ◧ d.	2000	...	...	...	...	2000	...	...	...
Çerkezköy d.	2200	...	...	...	...	2200	...	...	...
Edirne d.	|	...	...	...	...	|	...	...	...
Kapikule 🏛 d.	0320	...	...	...	...	0320	...	...	...
Svilengrad 🏛 d.	0425	...	...	...	...	0425	...	...	...
Dimitrovgrad (Bulgaria) d.	0520	0710	...	...	...	0710	...	...	...
Stara Zagora d.	|	0840	...	...	...	0840	...	...	...
Veliko Tarnovo d.	|	1056	...	...	...	1056	...	...	...
Plovdiv d.	0655	|	...	...	...	|	...	...	...
Sofia a.	0948	|	...	...	...	|	...	...	...
Sofia d.	...	|	0700	...	0706**y**	|	...	...	...
Mezdra d.	...	|	0833	...	0836	|	...	...	...
Pleven d.	...	|	0951	...	0953	|	...	...	...
Gorna Orjahovica a.	...	1110	1105	...	1100	1110	...	...	...
Gorna Orjahovica d.	...	...	1135	...	1135	1135	...	...	...
Ruse 🏛 a.	...	...	1331	...	1331	1331	...	...	...
Ruse 🏛 d.	...	...	...	1415	1415	1415	...	...	...
Giurgiu Nord 🏛 d.	...	...	...	1500	1500	1500	...	...	...
Videle d.	...	...	...	1630	1630	1630	...	...	...
Bucureşti Nord d.	...	...	...	1732	1732	1732	1945	...	...
Videle d.	...	...	...	...	...	...	2046	...	...
Craiova d.	...	...	...	...	...	...	0008	...	...
Timişoara Nord d.	...	...	...	...	...	...	0721	...	...
Arad d.	...	...	...	...	...	...	0857	...	...
Curtici 🏛 d.	...	...	...	...	...	...	0934	...	...
Lököshaza 🏛 d.	...	...	...	...	...	...	0942	...	...
Budapest Keleti a.	...	...	...	...	...	...	1250	1340	...
Wien Hbf a.	...	...	...	...	...	...	...	1620	...

BUDAPEST - BEOGRAD - SKOPJE - THESSALONÍKI

train type	IC		IC		IC		IC		
train number	700	7302	714	7304	706	7306	708	7308	
notes	[R]	2	[R]	2	[R]	2	[R]	2	
notes									
Budapest Nyugati ⊡ d.	0550	...	1150	...	1450	...	1850	...	...
Szeged d.	0816	0851	1416	1451	1716	1751	2116	2143	...
Röszke 🏛 d.	...	0949	...	1549	...	1849	...	2242	...
Kelebia 🏛 ⊡ d.	...	|	...	|	...	|	...	|	...
Subotica 🏛 ♠ ⊡ a.	...	1024	...	1624	...	1924	...	2317	...
Novi Sad ♠ a.	...	...	...	...	...	...	...	...	...
Beograd Centar ♠ a.	...	...	...	...	...	...	...	...	...
Niš ¥ a.	...	...	...	...	...	...	...	...	...
Tabanovci 🏛 ¥ a.	...	...	...	...	...	...	...	...	...
Skopje ¥ a.	...	...	...	...	...	...	...	...	...
Gevgelija ¥ a.	...	...	...	...	...	...	...	...	...
Thessaloniki ♣ ¥ a.	...	...	...	...	...	...	...	...	...

train type		IC		IC		IC		IC	
train number	7301	717	7303	737	7305	713	7307	701	
notes	2	[R]	2	[R]	2	[R]	2	[R]	
notes									
Thessaloniki ♣ ¥ d.	...	...	...	...	...	...	...	...	...
Gevgelija 🏛 ¥ d.	...	...	...	...	...	...	...	...	...
Skopje ¥ d.	...	...	...	...	...	...	...	...	...
Tabanovci 🏛 ¥ d.	...	...	...	...	...	...	...	...	...
Niš ¥ d.	...	...	...	...	...	...	...	...	...
Beograd Centar ♠ d.	...	...	...	...	...	...	...	...	...
Novi Sad ♠ d.	...	...	...	...	...	...	...	...	...
Subotica 🏛 ♠ ⊡ d.	0603	...	0737	...	1337	...	1637	...	...
Kelebia 🏛 ⊡ d.	|	...	|	...	|	...	|	...	...
Röszke 🏛 d.	0707	...	0844	...	1444	...	1744	...	...
Szeged d.	0725	0744	0906	0944	1506	1544	1806	1844	...
Budapest Nyugati ⊡ a.	...	1009	...	1209	...	1809	...	2109	...

A – HARGHITA – 🚃12 Braşov - Debrecen - Budapest and v.v.

B – BOSPHOR – 🛏 2 cl. (4-berth) Bucureşti - Halkalı and v.v.

C – CLAUDIOPOLIS - FOGARAS – 🚃12 Budapest - Cluj Napoca and Budapest - Sibiu - Braşov and v.v.

D – MUNTENIA – 🛏 2 cl., 🚃2 Budapest - Timişoara - Craiova - Bucureşti and v.v.

E – CORONA – 🛌 1, 2 cl., 🛏 2 cl., 🚃2 Braşov - Debrecen - Budapest and v.v.

F – ISTER – 🛌 1, 2 cl., 🛏 1, 2 cl., 🚃2 Budapest - Sibiu - Braşov - Bucureşti and v.v.

G – DACIA - CORVIN – 🛌 1, 2 cl., 🛏 2 cl., 🚃2 Wien - Budapest - Braşov - Bucureşti and v.v.

H – SOFYA EXPRESS – 🛌 1, 2 cl., 🛏 2 cl. (4-berth) Sofia - Halkalı and v.v.

P – June 14 - Oct. 13.

Q – Oct. 14 - Dec. 13.

R – June 12 - Oct. 11.

S – Oct. 12 - Dec. 13.

T – TRAIANUS – 🚃2 Budapest - Timişoara - Craiova and v.v.

V – ROMANIA – 🛌 1, 2 cl., 🛏 2 cl. (4-berth) Sofia - Bucureşti and v.v.

q – Sofia **Sever**. Connection arrives Sofia 2035.

y – Sofia **Sever**. Connection departs Sofia 0650.

* – Classified *IR* within Romania.

§ – Attached to train **1620** between Plovdiv and Sofia.

◧ – Halkalı station is located *27 km* from central İstanbul, frequent **Marmaray** surburban services operate from / to Halkalı from central İstanbul and beyond, see Tables **1570 / 1573**.

⊡ – Engineering work is affecting all services between Budapest - Kelebia - Subotica, see Table **1295**. For additional journeys between Budapest and Szeged see Table **1290**.

♠ – Engineering work is affecting all services between Subotica - Novi Sad - (Beograd), see Table **1360.**

¥ – All international services on routes Beograd - Niš - Sofia and Beograd - Niš - Skopje - Thessaloniki are currently suspended due to long term engineering work.

♣ – For international 🚌 Sofia - Thessaloníki and v.v., see Table **1460**.

62 FRANKFURT - MÜNCHEN - LJUBLJANA - ZAGREB - BEOGRAD

Subject to confirmation. Services on this table are affected by the closure of the Tauern tunnel - for details see Table **970**.

train type	EN	D		RJ	D		D	EC		EC	EC		ICE	D		D	EC		ICE			
train number	**40237**	**315**		**111**	**211**		**317**	**217**		**113**	**213**		**115**	**215**		**319**	**219**		**117**			
notes											2											
notes	**B**				**C**																	
Dortmund Hbf d.	...	...	...	...	...	...	...	...	...	...	...	...	...	...	...	...	...	...	...	...	...	...
Münster Hbf d.	...	...	...	...	...	...	...	...	...	...	...	...	0631	...	...	...	...	...	...	...	...	...
Köln Messe/Deutz d.	...	...	...	...	...	...	...	...	...	...	...	...	0829	...	...	...	...	...	...	...	...	...
Frankfurt (Main) Hbf d.	...	...	...	...	...	...	...	...	...	0821	...	...	|	...	...	...	1220	...	1419	...	...	...
Saarbrücken d.	...	...	...	...	...	...	...	0536	...	|	...	...	|	...	...	...	|	...	|	...	...	...
Mannheim d.	...	...	...	...	...	...	...	0711	...	|	...	...	1102	...	...	...	|	...	|	...	...	...
Heidelberg d.	...	...	...	...	...	...	...	|	...	0913	...	...	|	...	...	...	1313	...	1513	...	...	...
Stuttgart Hbf d.	2029	...	...	...	...	...	...	0759	...	0958	...	...	1159	...	...	...	1358	...	1559	...	...	...
Ulm d.	2153	...	...	...	...	...	...	0855	...	1056	...	...	1256	...	...	...	1456	...	1657	...	...	...
Augsburg d.	2302	...	...	...	...	...	...	0941	...	1141	...	...	1341	...	...	...	1541	...	1741	...	...	...
München Hbf d.	|	...	...	0816	...	...	...	1016	...	1217	...	...	1417	...	...	...	1617	...	1817	...	...	...
München Ost d.	2354	...	...	0825	...	...	...	1025	...	1226	...	...	1426	...	...	...	1625	...	|	...	...	...
Salzburg Hbf 🏛 d.	0146	...	...	1012	...	...	...	1216	...	1412	...	...	1612	...	...	...	1816	...	2012	...	...	...
Bischofshofen d.	|	...	...	1054	...	...	...	1312	...	1454	...	...	1654	...	...	...	1912	...	2054	...	...	...
Selzthal a.	|	...	...	|	...	...	...	1439	...	|	...	...	|	...	...	...	2039	...	|	...	...	...
Graz a.	0732	...	...	|	...	...	...	1614	...	|	...	...	|	...	...	...	2214	...	|	...	...	...
Schwarzach St Veit d.	|	...	...	1109	...	...	...	...	...	1511	...	...	1709	...	...	...	...	...	2109	...	...	...
Bad Gastein d.	|	...	...	...	...	...	...	...	...	1541	...	...	...	...	...	...	...	...	...	...	...	...
Villach Hbf a.	|	0853	...	...	1253	...	1453	...	...	...	1653	...	...	1853	...	2053	...	...	...	...	...	...
Klagenfurt a.	|	|	...	...	|	...	|	...	...	...	|	...	...	|	...	|	...	...	...	...	...	...
Jesenice 🏛 a.	|	0929	...	...	1329	...	1529	...	...	...	1729	...	...	1929	...	2129	...	...	...	...	...	...
Ljubljana a.	|	1058	...	...	1431	...	1657	...	...	...	1832	...	...	2033	...	2230	...	...	...	...	...	...
Rijeka a.	|	...	...	...	|	...	...	...	...	...	|	...	...	|	...	...	...	...	...	...	...	...
Dobova 🏛 a.	1054	...	...	...	1623	...	...	...	...	...	2006	...	...	2241	...	...	...	...	...	...	...	...
Zagreb a.	1133	...	...	...	1710	...	...	...	...	...	2045	...	...	...	...	...	...	...	...	...	...	...
Zagreb d.	...	...	...	...	1737	...	...	...	...	...	...	...	...	...	...	...	...	...	...	...	...	...
Vinkovci a.	...	...	...	...	2138	...	...	...	...	...	...	...	...	...	...	...	...	...	...	...	...	...
Tovarnik 🏛 a.	...	...	...	...	...	...	...	...	...	...	...	...	...	...	...	...	...	...	...	...	...	...
Šid 🏛 a.	...	...	...	...	...	...	...	...	...	...	...	...	...	...	...	...	...	...	...	...	...	...
Beograd Centar a.	...	...	...	...	...	...	...	...	...	...	...	...	...	...	...	...	...	...	...	...	...	...

train type	EN	D		EC	IC		D	ICE		EC	EC		EC	D		D	RJ					
train number	**414**	**318**		**218**	**691**		**214**	**114**		**212**	**112**		**216**	**316**		**210**	**110**					
notes										2												
notes	**B**																					
Beograd Centar d.	...	...	...	...	...	...	...	...	...	...	...	...	...	...	...	...	...	...	...	...	...	...
Šid 🏛 d.	...	...	...	...	...	...	...	...	...	...	...	...	...	...	...	...	...	...	...	...	...	...
Tovarnik 🏛 d.	...	...	...	...	...	...	...	...	...	...	...	...	...	...	...	...	...	...	...	...	...	...
Vinkovci d.	...	...	...	...	...	...	...	...	...	...	...	...	...	...	...	0803	...	...	...	...	...	...
Zagreb a.	...	...	...	...	...	...	...	...	...	...	...	...	...	...	...	1235	...	...	...	...	...	...
Zagreb d.	1840	...	...	...	...	...	...	...	...	0705	...	...	...	...	...	1250	...	...	...	...	...	...
Dobova 🏛 d.	1921	...	...	...	...	...	0540	...	...	0745	...	...	...	...	...	1330	...	...	...	...	...	...
Rijeka d.	|	...	...	...	...	...	|	...	...	|	...	...	...	...	...	|	...	...	...	...	...	...
Ljubljana d.	|	0531	...	...	...	...	0726	...	...	0923	...	...	...	1131	...	1527	...	...	...	...	...	...
Jesenice 🏛 d.	|	0631	...	...	...	...	0831	...	...	1031	...	...	...	1231	...	1631	...	...	...	...	...	...
Klagenfurt d.	|	|	...	...	...	...	|	...	...	|	...	...	...	|	...	|	...	...	...	...	...	...
Villach Hbf d.	|	0707	...	...	...	...	0907	...	...	1107	...	...	...	1307	...	1707	...	...	...	...	...	...
Bad Gastein d.	|	...	...	...	0819	...	...	...	...	...	1219	...	...	...	...	...	1819	...	...	...	...	...
Schwarzach St Veit d.	|	...	...	...	0852	...	...	1052	...	...	1252	...	...	...	...	...	1852	...	...	...	...	...
Graz d.	2230	...	...	0545	|	...	...	|	...	...	|	...	1145	...	...	...	|	...	...	...	...	...
Selzthal d.	|	...	...	0719	|	...	...	|	...	...	|	...	1319	...	...	...	|	...	...	...	...	...
Bischofshofen a.	|	...	...	0848	0906	...	...	1106	...	...	1306	...	1448	...	...	...	1906	...	...	...	...	...
Salzburg Hbf 🏛 a.	0258	...	...	0944	0948	...	...	1148	...	...	1348	...	1544	...	...	...	1948	...	...	...	...	...
München Ost a.	0550	...	...	1131	...	...	...	1331	...	...	1530	...	1731	...	...	...	2131	...	...	...	...	...
München Hbf a.	|	...	...	1141	...	...	...	1341	...	...	1541	...	1741	...	...	...	2141	...	...	...	...	...
Augsburg a.	0645	...	...	1215	...	...	...	1414	...	...	1614	...	1814	...	...	...	...	...	...	...	...	...
Ulm a.	0736	...	...	1301	...	...	...	1501	...	...	1701	...	1901	...	...	...	...	...	...	...	...	...
Stuttgart Hbf a.	0838	...	...	1359	...	...	...	1559	...	...	1758	...	1958	...	...	...	...	...	...	...	...	...
Heidelberg a.	...	...	...	1444	...	...	...	|	...	...	1844	...	|	...	...	...	...	...	...	...	...	...
Mannheim a.	...	...	...	|	...	...	...	1655	...	...	|	...	2047	...	...	...	...	...	...	...	...	...
Saarbrücken a.	...	...	...	|	...	...	...	|	...	...	|	...	2216	...	...	...	...	...	...	...	...	...
Frankfurt (Main) Hbf a.	...	...	...	1540	...	...	...	|	...	...	1940	...	...	...	...	...	...	...	...	...	...	...
Köln Messe/Deutz a.	...	...	...	...	...	...	...	1927	...	...	...	...	...	...	...	...	...	...	...	...	...	...
Münster Hbf a.	...	...	...	...	...	...	...	|	...	...	...	...	...	...	...	...	...	...	...	...	...	...
Dortmund Hbf a.	...	...	...	...	...	...	...	2107	...	...	...	...	...	...	...	...	...	...	...	...	...	...

B – LISINSKI – 🛏 1, 2 cl., 🛏 2 cl. (4, 6 berth), (2) Stuttgart - Zagreb and v.v.

63 PRAHA - GDYNIA

train type		IC		IC		IC		IC	
train number		**264**		**262**		**260**		**460**	
notes		**A**		**A**		**A**		**B**	
notes		✕*		✕*		✕*			
Praha hl. n. d.	...	0651	...	1051	...	1450	...	1851	...
Pardubice d.	...	0754	...	1154	...	1554	...	1954	...
Ústí nad Orlici d.	...	0827	...	1227	...	1627	...	2027	...
Lichkov d.	...	0902	...	1302	...	1702	...	2102	...
Miedzylesie 🏛 d.	...	0917	...	1317	...	1717	...	2117	...
Klodzko Miasto d.	...	0943	...	1343	...	1743	...	2143	...
Wrocław Gł. a.	...	1047	...	1447	...	1847	...	2247	...
Wrocław Gł. d.	...	1110	...	1510	...	1910	...	2350	...
Poznań Gł. d.	...	1240	...	1640	...	2040	...	0141	...
Gniezno d.	...	1307	...	1707	...	2107	...	0208	...
Inowrocław d.	...	1336	...	1736	...	2136	...	0241	...
Bydgoszcz Gł. d.	...	1410	...	1809	...	2210	...	0320	...
Tczew d.	...	1517	...	1916	...	2317	...	0435	...
Gdańsk Gł. a.	...	1532	...	1932	...	2332	...	0451	...
Sopot a.	...	1548	...	1948	...	2348	...	0507	...
Gdynia Gł. a.	...	1558	...	1958	...	2358	...	0518	...

train type		IC		IC		IC		IC	
train number		**261**		**263**		**265**		**461**	
notes		**A**		**A**		**A**		**B**	
notes		✕*		✕*		✕*			
Gdynia Gł. d.	...	0400	...	0800	...	1200	...	2323	...
Sopot d.	...	0409	...	0809	...	1209	...	2333	...
Gdańsk Gł. d.	...	0425	...	0825	...	1225	...	2350	...
Tczew d.	...	0442	...	0842	...	1242	...	0007	...
Bydgoszcz Gł. d.	...	0555	...	0955	...	1355	...	0120	...
Inowrocław d.	...	0623	...	1023	...	1423	...	0149	...
Gniezno d.	...	0654	...	1054	...	1454	...	0223	...
Poznań Gł. d.	...	0731	...	1131	...	1531	...	0254	...
Wrocław Gł. a.	...	0849	...	1249	...	1649	...	0425	...
Wrocław Gł. d.	...	0915	...	1315	...	1715	...	0515	...
Klodzko Miasto d.	...	1019	...	1419	...	1819	...	0619	...
Miedzylesie 🏛 d.	...	1049	...	1449	...	1849	...	0649	...
Lichkov d.	...	1100	...	1500	...	1900	...	0700	...
Ústí nad Orlici d.	...	1134	...	1534	...	1934	...	0734	...
Pardubice d.	...	1203	...	1603	...	2003	...	0803	...
Praha hl. n. d.	...	1312	...	1712	...	2110	...	0906	...

A – BALTIC EXPRESS – (12) 🍷 Praha - Gdynia and v.v. Classified *EC* in Czech Republic.

B – BALTIC EXPRESS – (12) Praha - Gdynia and v.v. 🍷 Praha - Miedzylesie and v.v. Classified *EC* in Czech Republic.
Also conveys 🛏 1, 2 cl. (1, 2, 3 berth) as follows: Train **461** Apr. 14 - Aug. 30; train **460** Apr. 15 - Aug. 31.

* – ✕ Wrocław - Gdynia and v.v.

HAMBURG and BERLIN - WIEN - BUDAPEST 64

For services via Břeclav see Table 60.

train type		*NJ*	*RJX*			*IC*	*RJX*			*ICE*	*RJX*			*ICE*	*RJX*			*ICE*				
train number		**491**	**269**			**495**	**61**			**91**	**67**			**93**	**165**			**95**				
notes																						
notes		**A**												✣				✣				
Hamburg Altona ... d.	...	1956	...	...	...	...	...	...	...	0745	...	...	...	0751	...	...	...	1150	...	...	...	...
Hamburg Hbf ... d.	...	2010	...	...	...	...	...	...	...	0802	...	...	...	0805	...	...	...	1204	...	...	...	...
Hannover Hbf ... d.	...	2153	...	...	...	...	...	...	...	0926	...	...	...	|	...	...	...	|	...	...	...	...
Berlin Hbf ... d.	...	|	...	...	...	2228	...	...	...	|	...	...	...	1004	...	...	...	1404	...	...	...	...
Leipzig Hbf ... d.	...	|	...	...	...	0035	...	...	...	|	...	...	...	|	...	...	...	|	...	...	...	...
Nürnberg Hbf ... d.	...	0408	...	...	...	0600	...	...	...	1231	...	...	...	1332	...	...	...	1732	...	...	...	...
Passau ▦ ... d.	...	0615	...	...	...	0824	...	...	...	1429	...	...	...	1529	...	...	...	1926	...	...	...	...
Linz Hbf ... a.	...	0743	...	...	...	0926	...	...	...	1526	...	...	...	1626	...	...	...	2026	...	...	...	...
Wien Hbf ... a.	...	0917	0940	...	...	1047	1140	...	...	1647	1740	...	...	1747	1842	...	...	2147	...	...	...	...
Budapest Keleti § ... a.	...	...	1219	...	...	...	1419	...	...	...	2019	...	...	...	2119	...	...	...	...	...	...	...
train type		*ICE*			*RJX*	*ICE*			*RJX*	*ICE*			*RJX*	*IC*			*EC*	*NJ*				
train number		**94**			**162**	**92**			**62**	**90**			**68**	**494**			**148**	**490**				
notes																						
notes		✣				✣												**A**				
Budapest Keleti § ... d.	...	...	...	...	0640	...	...	...	0940	...	...	...	1540	...	...	...	1640	...	...	...	...	...
Wien Hbf ... d.	...	0613	...	...	0918	1013	...	...	1220	1313	...	...	1820	1913	...	...	1920	2010	...	...	...	...
Linz Hbf ... d.	...	0734	...	...	...	1134	...	...	...	1434	...	...	...	2034	...	...	...	2134	...	...	...	...
Passau ▦ ... d.	...	0836	...	...	...	1233	...	...	...	1537	...	...	...	2147	...	...	...	2235	...	...	...	...
Nürnberg Hbf ... a.	...	1030	...	...	...	1430	...	...	...	1729	...	...	...	2400	...	...	...	0057	...	...	...	...
Leipzig Hbf ... a.	...	|	...	...	...	|	...	...	...	|	...	...	...	0453	...	...	...	|	...	...	...	...
Berlin Hbf ... a.	...	1353	...	...	...	1752	...	...	...	|	...	...	...	0631	...	...	...	|	...	...	...	...
Hannover Hbf ... a.	...	|	...	...	...	|	...	...	...	2033	...	...	...	...	...	...	...	0650	...	...	...	...
Hamburg Hbf ... a.	...	1600	...	...	...	1951	...	...	...	2155	...	...	...	...	...	...	...	0847	...	...	...	...
Hamburg Altona ... a.	...	1620	...	...	...	2013	...	...	...	2211	...	...	...	...	...	...	...	0906	...	...	...	...

A – *ÖBB nightjet* – 1, 2 cl., 2 cl. (4, 6 berth), 2 Hamburg - Wien and v.v. (Table **53**). Special fares apply.

RJX – ÖBB *Railjet* service, ✕, 1 (business class), 1 (first class), 2 (economy class).

✣ – Subject to alteration from Aug. 2.

§ – ▦ is Hegyeshalom.

STUTTGART - MÜNCHEN - SALZBURG - WIEN - BUDAPEST - BUCUREŞTI 65

train type		*RJX*	*RJX*		*RJX*		*RJX*		*RJX*	*IC*		*RJX*	*RJX*		*RJX*	*D*		*RJX*		*EN*	*EN*	
train number		**269**	**265**		**61**		**63**		**65**	**473**		**67**	**165**		**69**	**347**		**261**		**406**	**50237**	
notes		①–⑥								R						R						
notes										**C**						**D**				**E**	**B**	
Stuttgart Hbf ... d.	...	...	...	...	...	...	...	...	...	...	...	...	...	...	...	...	...	...	...	...	2029	...
München Hbf ... d.	...	...	0621	...	0722	...	0928	...	1127	...	...	1328	...	...	1528	...	...	1729	...	1835	|	...
München Ost ... d.	...	...	0631	...	|	...	|	...	|	...	...	|	...	...	|	...	...	|	...	|	2354	...
Salzburg Hbf ▦ ... a.	...	...	0758	...	0858	...	1058	...	1258	...	...	1458	...	...	1658	...	...	1858	...	2026	0128	...
Salzburg Hbf ▦ ... d.	...	0707	0807	...	0907	...	1107	...	1307	...	...	1507	1607	...	1707	...	...	1907	...	2030	0353	...
Linz Hbf ... d.	...	0817	0917	...	1017	...	1217	...	1417	...	...	1617	1717	...	1817	...	...	2017	...	2146	0510	...
St Pölten Hbf ... d.	...	0903	1003	...	1103	...	1303	...	1503	...	...	1703	1803	...	1903	...	...	2103	...	2242	0600	...
Wien Meidling ... a.	...	0925	1025	...	1125	...	1325	...	1525	...	...	1725	1825	...	1925	...	...	2125	...	2309	0624	...
Wien Hbf ... a.	...	0932	1032	...	1132	...	1332	...	1532	...	...	1732	1832	...	1932	1942	...	2132	...	2316	0632	...
Györ ... a.	...	1054	...	...	1254	...	1454	...	1654	...	...	1854	1954	...	...	2056	...	2254	...	...	0754	...
Budapest Keleti ... a.	...	1219	...	...	1419	...	1619	...	1819	1910	...	2019	2119	...	...	2305	...	0019	...	...	0919	...
Bucureşti Nord ... a.	...	...	...	...	...	...	...	...	...	1135	...	...	...	...	...	1526	...	...	...	...	...	...
train type		*RJX*	*RJX*	*D*		*RJX*	*RJX*	*D*		*RJX*	*RJX*	*RJX*		*D*	*RJX*	*RJX*		*RJX*		*EN*	*EN*	
train number		**260**	**262**	**346**		**162**	**60**	**472**		**62**	**64**	**268**		**78**	**66**	**68**		**264**		**50462**	**407**	
notes				R				R										Ⓑ				
notes				**D**				**C**												**B**	**E**	
Bucureşti Nord ... d.	...	...	...	1507	...	...	...	1758	...	...	...	...	...	1945	...	...	...	...	...	...	...	...
Budapest Keleti ... d.	...	...	...	0500	...	0640	0740	0850	...	0940	1140	...	...	1250	1340	1540	...	1740	...	2040	...	...
Györ ... d.	...	...	...	0700	...	0802	0902	...	...	1102	1302	...	...	...	1502	1702	...	1902	...	2202	...	...
Wien Hbf ... d.	...	0628	0828	0820	...	0928	1028	...	...	1228	1428	1455	...	...	1628	1828	...	2028	...	2328	0539	...
Wien Meidling ... d.	...	0635	0835	...	...	0935	1035	...	...	1235	1435	1502	...	...	1635	1835	...	2035	...	2335	0546	...
St Pölten Hbf ... d.	...	0659	0859	...	...	0959	1059	...	...	1259	1459	1530	...	...	1659	1859	...	2059	...	0001	0615	...
Linz Hbf ... d.	...	0745	0945	...	...	1045	1145	...	...	1345	1545	1630	...	...	1745	1945	...	2145	...	0059	0715	...
Salzburg Hbf ▦ ... a.	...	0856	1053	...	...	1153	1253	...	...	1453	1653	1749	...	...	1853	2053	...	2259	...	0207	0830	...
Salzburg Hbf ▦ ... d.	...	0900	1100	...	...	...	1300	...	...	1500	1700	1800	...	...	1900	2100	...	...	...	0405	0833	...
München Ost ... a.	...	|	|	...	...	...	|	...	...	|	|	|	...	...	|	|	...	...	...	0550	1013	...
München Hbf ... a.	...	1033	1232	...	...	...	1432	...	...	1634	1831	1938	...	...	2031	2232	...	...	...	|	1024	...
Stuttgart Hbf ... a.	...	...	...	...	...	...	...	...	...	...	...	...	...	...	...	...	...	...	...	0838	...	...

B – KÁLMÁN IMRE – 1, 2 cl., 2 cl. (4, 6 berth) 2 Stuttgart - Budapest and v.v.

C – ISTER – 1, 2 cl., 1, 2 cl., 2 Budapest - Bucureşti and v.v.

D – DACIA – 1, 2 cl., 2 cl., 2 ✕ Wien - Budapest - Bucureşti and v.v.

E – CHOPIN – 1, 2 cl., 2 cl. 2 Warszawa - Wien - München and v.v. (Table **99**).

RJX – ÖBB *Railjet* service, ✕, 1 (business class), 1 (first class), 2 (economy class).

66 DORTMUND - KÖLN - FRANKFURT - WIEN

For connections Wien - Budapest see Table **1250**.

train type	NJ	IC	ICE	ICE	ICE	ICE	ICE	ICE
train number	**40421**	**495**	**21**	**23**	**91**	**27**	**29**	**229**
notes								
notes	**A**							
Dortmund Hbf d.	...	...	...	...	...	0835	...	1235
Düsseldorf Hbf d.	...	...	...	...	...	0927	...	|
Köln Hbf d.	...	...	...	...	...	0953	...	1353
Bonn Hbf d.	...	...	...	...	...	1015	...	1415
Koblenz Hbf d.	...	...	...	...	...	1048	...	1448
Mainz Hbf d.	...	...	...	...	...	1142	...	1542
Frankfurt Flughafen ✈ d.	...	...	...	...	...	1201	...	1601
Frankfurt (Main) Hbf d.	...	...	0619	0822	...	1222	1421	1621
Würzburg Hbf d.	0229	...	0734	0933	...	1334	1533	1733
Nürnberg Hbf d.	0408	0600	0831	1031	1231	1431	1631	1831
Regensburg Hbf d.	0509	0711	0925	1125	1325	1525	1725	1925
Passau Hbf 🛃 d.	0615	0824	1026	1229	1429	1629	1829	2031
Linz a.	0743	0926	1126	1326	1526	1726	1926	2138
Wien Hbf a.	0917	1047	1247	1447	1647	1847	2047	2305

train type	ICE	ICE	ICE	ICE	ICE	ICE	IC	NJ
train number	**228**	**28**	**26**	**90**	**22**	**20**	**494**	**40490**
notes								
notes								**A**
Wien Hbf d.	0713	0913	1113	1313	1513	1713	1913	2010
Linz d.	0834	1034	1234	1434	1634	1834	2034	2134
Passau Hbf 🛃 d.	0934	1134	1337	1537	1737	1937	2147	2253
Regensburg Hbf a.	1033	1233	1433	1633	1833	2033	2257	2355
Nürnberg Hbf a.	1127	1327	1528	1729	1928	2128	2400	0057
Würzburg Hbf a.	1222	1422	1622	...	2022	2222	...	0230
Frankfurt (Main) Hbf a.	1336	1536	1736	...	2136	2337	...	...
Frankfurt Flughafen ✈ a.	...	1555	1755	...	...	...	...	...
Mainz Hbf a.	...	1618	1818	...	...	...	...	...
Koblenz Hbf a.	...	1711	1911	...	...	...	...	...
Bonn Hbf a.	...	1743	1943	...	...	...	...	...
Köln Hbf a.	...	1806	2006	...	...	...	...	...
Düsseldorf Hbf a.	...	1832	2032	...	...	...	...	...
Dortmund Hbf a.	...	1921	2121	...	...	...	...	...

A – *ÖBB nightjet* – 🛏 1,2 cl., 🛏 2 cl. (4,6 berth), [2] Amsterdam - Düsseldorf - Wien and v.v. (Table **53**).

70 MÜNCHEN - INNSBRUCK - VENEZIA and BOLOGNA

For additional trains München - Innsbruck and v.v. see Table **951**. For overnight services see Table **71**.

train type	EC	EC	RJ	RJ	RJ	RJ	RJ	
train number	**1281**	**81**	**83**	**83**	**85**	**87**	**89**	
notes	♣	♣	♣	♣	♣	♣	♣	
notes	⑥⑦	①–⑤		**d**				
München Hbf d.	0732	0732	0933	0933	1132	1333	1533	...
München Ost d.	0744	0744	0944	0944	1144	1344	1544	...
Kufstein 🛃 a.	0834	0834	1034	1034	1234	1434	1634	...
Wörgl a.	0844	0844	1044	1044	1244	1444	1644	...
Jenbach a.	0858	0858	1058	1058	1258	1458	1658	...
Innsbruck Hbf a.	0918	0918	1118	1118	1318	1518	1718	...
Innsbruck Hbf d.	0924	0924	1124	1124	1324	1524	1724	...
Brennero / Brenner 🛃 a.	1000	1000	1200	1200	1400	1600	1800	...
Bolzano / Bozen a.	1127	1127	1327	1327	1527	1727	1927	...
Trento a.	1202	1202	1402	1402	1602	1802	2002	...
Verona Porta Nuova a.	1256	1258	1501	1501	1658	1901	2059	...
Padova a.	1357	1427	|	|	1756	|	|	...
Venezia Mestre a.	1413	1502	|	|	1812	|	|	...
Venezia Santa Lucia a.	1425	1514	|	|	1825	|	|	...
Bologna Centrale a.	...	...	1608	1608	...	2016	2211	...
Rimini a.	...	...	...	1730	...	...	...	...
Ancona a.	...	...	...	1910	...	...	...	...

	RJ	RJ	RJ	RJ	RJ	EC	EC	
	88	**86**	**84**	**82**	**82**	**80**	**80**	
	♣	♣	♣	♣	♣	♣	♣	
					e	①–⑤	⑥⑦	
Ancona d.	...	...	...	...	1130	...	...	...
Rimini d.	...	...	...	...	1234	...	...	...
Bologna Centrale d.	0745	0952	...	1352	1352	...	...	...
Venezia Santa Lucia d.	|	|	1135	|	|	1535	1535	...
Venezia Mestre d.	|	|	1147	|	|	1547	1547	...
Padova d.	|	|	1203	|	|	1603	1603	...
Verona Porta Nuova d.	0901	1101	1301	1458	1458	1701	1701	...
Trento d.	0959	1159	1359	1559	1559	1759	1759	...
Bolzano / Bozen d.	1036	1234	1434	1634	1634	1834	1834	...
Brennero / Brenner 🛃 d.	1200	1400	1600	1800	1800	2000	2000	...
Innsbruck Hbf a.	1236	1436	1636	1836	1836	2036	2036	...
Innsbruck Hbf d.	1242	1442	1642	1842	1842	2042	2042	...
Jenbach a.	1300	1500	1700	1900	1900	2100	2100	...
Wörgl a.	1314	1514	1714	1914	1914	2114	2114	...
Kufstein 🛃 a.	1324	1524	1724	1924	1924	2124	2124	...
München Ost a.	1416	1616	1816	2014	2014	2217	2217	...
München Hbf a.	1427	1627	1828	2026	2026	2228	2228	...

d – Apr. 17 - Oct. 5.

e – Apr. 18 - Oct. 6.

♣ – DB-ÖBB *RailJet* service. Conveys 🍴.

71 STUTTGART, MÜNCHEN and WIEN - VENEZIA, LA SPEZIA and ROMA

Due to the closure of the Tauern tunnel, services to and from Stuttgart and München are suspended until July 13. For service from July 14, see page 578.

train type	RJ	RJ		NJ	NJ	NJ	NJ	
train number	**131**	**133**		**40233**	**233**	**233**	**1237**	
notes								
notes	🍴	🍴		**B**	**C**	**E**	**D**	
Stuttgart Hbf d.	...	...	...	...	...	...	...	...
München Hbf d.	...	...	...	...	...	...	...	...
München Ost d.	...	...	...	...	...	...	...	...
Wien Hbf d.	0624	1224	...	1918	1918	1918	2149	...
Wien Meidling d.	0631	1231	...	1925	1925	1925	2156	...
Bruck an der Mur d.	0815	1415	...	2126	2126	2126	|	...
Linz Hbf d.	|	|	...	|	|	|	2325	...
Salzburg Hbf d.	|	|	...	|	|	|	|	...
Klagenfurt Hbf d.	1021	1621	...	2338	2338	2338	0412	...
Villach Hbf d.	1049	1649	...	0101	0134	0134	0500	...
Tarvisio 🛃 a.	1111	1711	...	0125	0157	0157	0523	...
Udine a.	1216	1816	...	|	|	|	0623	...
Venezia Mestre a.	1402	1952	...	|	|	|	0822	...
Venezia Santa Lucia a.	1414	2004	...	|	|	|	0834	...
Padova a.	...	...	...	|	0457	0457	...	...
Verona Porta Nuova a.	...	...	...	|	0551	0551	...	...
Milano Rogoredo a.	...	...	...	|	0742	0742	...	...
Genova Piazza Principe a.	...	...	...	|	0938	...	...	...
La Spezia Centrale a.	...	...	...	|	1110	...	...	...
Bologna Centrale a.	...	...	...	0538	...	...	...	...
Rimini a.	...	...	...	|	...	...	...	...
Ancona a.	...	...	...	|	...	...	...	...
Firenze Campo di Marte a.	...	...	...	0648	...	...	...	...
Pisa Centrale a.	...	...	...	|	...	...	...	...
Livorno Centrale a.	...	...	...	|	...	...	...	...
Roma Tiburtina a.	...	...	...	1005	...	...	...	...

train type	RJ	RJ	NJ	NJ	NJ	NJ	NJ	
train number	**132**	**130**	**1236**	**235**	**235**	**235**	**40294**	
notes				⑦–④	⑤⑥			
notes	🍴	🍴	**D**	**C**	**C**	**E**	**B**	
Roma Tiburtina d.	...	...	...	...	...	...	1810	...
Livorno Centrale d.	...	...	...	...	...	...	|	...
Pisa Centrale d.	...	...	...	...	...	...	|	...
Firenze Campo di Marte d.	...	...	...	...	...	...	2148	...
Ancona d.	...	...	...	...	...	...	|	...
Rimini d.	...	...	...	...	...	...	|	...
Bologna Centrale d.	...	...	...	...	...	...	2254	...
La Spezia Centrale d.	...	...	...	1646	1710	...	|	...
Genova Piazza Principe d.	...	...	...	1904	1950	...	|	...
Milano Rogoredo d.	...	...	...	2047	2126	2126	|	...
Verona Porta Nuova d.	...	...	...	2258	2258	2258	|	...
Padova d.	...	...	...	2343	2343	2343	|	...
Venezia Santa Lucia d.	0956	1552	2105	|	|	|	|	...
Venezia Mestre d.	1008	1604	2117	|	|	|	|	...
Udine d.	1028	1744	2247	|	|	|	|	...
Tarvisio 🛃 d.	1249	1849	0005	0300	0300	0300	0319	...
Villach Hbf a.	1311	1911	0027	0323	0323	0323	0357	...
Klagenfurt Hbf a.	1337	1937	0105	0438	0438	0438	0438	...
Salzburg Hbf a.	|	|	|	|	|	|	|	...
Linz Hbf a.	|	|	|	|	|	|	|	...
Bruck an der Mur a.	1543	2143	|	0639	0639	0639	0639	...
Wien Meidling a.	1729	2329	0810	0857	0857	0857	0857	...
Wien Hbf a.	1736	2336	0819	0904	0904	0904	0904	...
München Ost a.	...	...	...	...	...	...	...	...
München Hbf a.	...	...	...	...	...	...	...	...
Stuttgart Hbf a.	...	...	...	...	...	...	...	...

B – *ÖBB nightjet* – 🛏 1,2 cl., 🛏 2 cl. (4,6 berth), [2] 🍸 Wien - Roma and v.v. (not May 16, 30).

C – Daily until May 29 (not May 16). *ÖBB nightjet* – 🛏 1,2 cl., 🛏 2 cl. (4,6 berth), [2] 🍸 Wien - La Spezia and v.v.

D – *ÖBB nightjet* – 🛏 1,2 cl., 🛏 2 cl. (4,6 berth), [2] Wien - Venezia and v.v.

E – June 1 - July 13. *ÖBB nightjet* – 🛏 1,2 cl., 🛏 2 cl. (4,6 berth), [2] 🍸 Wien - Milano and v.v.

HAMBURG, BERLIN and AMSTERDAM - BASEL - ZÜRICH 73

Timings of *Nightjet* (*NJ*) services may vary - please check your reservation.

train type	NJ	ICE	NJ		NJ	ICE	EC		ICE	ICE	EC		ICE	EC	ICE		ICE	ICE	ICE		ICE	
train number	**403**	**3**	**408**		**471**	**271**	**151**		**275**	**275**	**7**		**73**	**9**	**75**		**371**	**77**	**373**		**79**	
notes		①–⑤							⑥⑦	①–⑤												
notes	**A**		**B**		**C**		**D**				**G**			**G**								
Hamburg Hbf d.	...	...	...	...	2208	...	...	...	...	...	0438	...	0824	...	1024	...	...	1224	...	...	1424	...
Bremen Hbf d.	...	...	...	...	│	...	...	...	...	...	0540	...	│	...	│	...	...	│	...	...	│	...
Berlin Hbf d.	...	...	2103	...	│	2328	...	...	...	0428	│	...	│	...	│	...	1028	│	1230	...	│	...
Hannover Hbf d.	...	...	│	...	0030	0210	...	...	...	│	│	...	0941	...	1141	...	│	1341	│	...	1541	...
Dortmund Hbf d.	...	...	│	...	│	│	...	...	...	│	│	...	│	0925	│	...	│	│	│	...	│	...
Essen Hbf d.	...	...	│	...	│	│	...	...	...	│	0800**y**	...	│	0951	│	...	│	│	│	...	│	...
Amsterdam Centraal d.	2015	...	│	...	│	│	...	...	...	│	│	...	│	│	│	...	│	│	│	...	│	...
Utrecht Centraal d.	2047	...	│	...	│	│	...	...	...	│	│	...	│	│	│	...	│	│	│	...	│	...
Arnhem ⊙ d.	│	...	│	...	│	│	...	...	...	│	│	...	│	│	│	...	│	│	│	...	│	...
Duisburg Hbf d.	│	...	│	...	│	│	...	...	...	│	0813	...	│	1005	│	...	│	│	│	...	│	...
Düsseldorf Hbf d.	│	...	│	...	│	│	...	...	...	│	0827	...	│	1020	│	...	│	│	│	...	│	...
Köln Hbf d.	2342	...	│	...	│	│	...	...	...	│	0853	...	│	1053	│	...	│	│	│	...	│	...
Bonn Hbf d.	│	...	│	...	│	│	...	...	...	│	0915	...	│	1115	│	...	│	│	│	...	│	...
Bonn Beuel d.	0004	...	│	...	│	│	...	...	...	│	│	...	│	│	│	...	│	│	│	...	│	...
Koblenz Hbf d.	│	...	│	...	│	│	...	...	...	│	0948	...	│	1148	│	...	│	│	│	...	│	...
Mainz Hbf d.	│	...	│	...	│	│	...	...	...	│	1042	...	│	1242	│	...	│	│	│	...	│	...
Frankfurt Flughafen ✈ d.	│	...	│	...	│	│	...	...	...	│	│	...	│	│	│	...	│	│	│	...	│	...
Frankfurt (Main) Hbf d.	│	...	│	...	│	0550	0805	...	0848	0850	│	...	1205	│	1405	...	1450	1605	1650	...	1805	...
Frankfurt (Main) Süd d.	│	...	0335	...	│	│	│	...	│	│	│	...	│	│	│	...	│	│	│	...	│	...
Mannheim Hbf d.	│	...	0420	...	│	0632	0847	...	0934	0934	1123	...	1246	1323	1446	...	1534	1646	1734	...	1846	...
Karlsruhe Hbf d.	│	0556	0507	...	0603	0658	0911	...	0959	0959	1149	...	1311	1349	1511	...	1559	1711	1800	...	1911	...
Freiburg (Brsg) Hbf d.	│	0702	0617	...	0721	0804	1015	...	1102	1102	1251	...	1414	1456	1614	...	1702	1814	1902	...	2014	...
Basel Bad Bf a.	0610	0736	0656	...	0759	0837	1045	...	1136	1136	1323	...	1445	1528	1645	...	1736	1845	1936	...	2045	...
Basel SBB a.	0620	0748	0720	...	0810	0848	1055	...	1148	1148	1333	...	1455	1536	1655	...	1748	1855	1948	...	2055	...
Basel SBB d.	0620	0806	0720	...	0810	0906	1106	...	1156	1156	1356	...	1506	1606	1706	...	1756	1906	1956	...	2106	...
Bern a.	│	│	│	...	│	│	│	...	1256	1256	1456	...	│	│	│	...	1856	│	2056	...	│	...
Interlaken Ost a.	│	│	│	...	│	│	│	...	1359	1359	1559	...	│	│	│	...	1959	│	2159	...	│	...
Zürich HB a.	0805	0900	0904	...	1005	1000	1200	...	...	...	...	...	1600	1700	1800	...	...	2000	...	...	2200	...
Chur a.	...	...	...	...	...	1122	...	...	...	...	...	...	...	...	...	...	...	...	...	...	...	...

train type	ICE	ICE	ICE	ICE	ICE	EC	EC	ICE	EC	ICE	ICE	ICE	ICE	ICE	ICE	NJ	NJ	NJ	NJ	NJ	NJ	NJ
train number	**78**	**372**	**76**	**74**	**278**	**8**	**6**	**70**	**150**	**376**	**376**	**272**	**272**	**292**	**4**	**470**	**402**	**409**	**470**	**402**	**402**	**402**
notes										Ⓑ	⑥	⑥	①–⑤	⑦		⑦	⑦		①–⑥	①–③	④⑤	⑥
notes									**D**							**C**	**A**	**B**	**C**	**A**	**A**	**A**
Chur d.	...	...	...	...	...	...	...	1238	...	...	...	...	...	...	...	...	...	...	...	...	...	...
Zürich HB d.	0559	...	0759	0959	...	1059	...	1359	1434	...	...	1659	1659	1659	1859	1934	1936	1959	2059	2134	2134	2159
Interlaken Ost d.	│	0559	│	│	0959	│	1159	│	│	1459	1459	│	│	│	│	│	│	│	│	│	│	│
Bern d.	│	0704	│	│	1104	│	1304	│	│	1604	1604	│	│	│	│	│	│	│	│	│	│	│
Basel SBB a.	0653	0801	0853	1053	1201	1153	1401	1453	1528	1701	1701	1753	1753	1753	1953	2028	2048	2053	2153	2228	2228	2253
Basel SBB d.	0706	0813	0906	1106	1212	1220	1427	1506	1538	1707	1707	1813	1813	1813	2013	2058	2117	2113	2213	2313	2313	2313
Basel Bad Bf d.	0714	0821	0914	1114	1222	1228	1435	1514	1552	1715	1715	1822	1822	1822	2021	2129	2137	2122	2222	2323	2323	2323
Freiburg (Brsg) Hbf d.	0747	0855	0948	1147	1255	1304	1506	1547	1624	1747	1747	1855	1855	1855	2055	2205	2213	2158	2258	0005	0005	0005
Karlsruhe Hbf d.	0851	1000	1051	1251	1400	1412	1612	1651	1731	1851	1851	2000	2000	2000	2202	0019	│	2307	0019	│	│	│
Mannheim Hbf d.	0917	1032	1117	1317	1432	1438	1639	1717	1800	1917	1917	2032	2032	2032	2232	│	│	│	│	│	│	│
Frankfurt (Main) Süd d.	│	│	│	│	│	│	│	│	│	│	│	│	│	│	│	│	│	0027	│	│	│	│
Frankfurt (Main) Hbf a.	0952	1108	1152	1352	1508	│	│	1752	1844	1952	1955	2108	2108	2108	2308	│	│	│	│	│	│	│
Frankfurt Flughafen ✈ a.	│	│	│	│	│	│	│	│	...	│	...	│	│	│	...	│	│	│	│	│	│	│
Mainz Hbf a.	│	│	│	│	│	1518	1718	│	...	│	...	│	│	│	...	│	│	│	│	│	│	│
Koblenz Hbf a.	│	│	│	│	│	1611	1811	│	...	│	...	│	│	│	...	│	│	│	│	│	│	│
Bonn Beuel a.	│	│	│	│	│	│	│	│	...	│	...	│	│	│	...	│	0528	│	│	0528	0528	0528
Bonn Hbf a.	│	│	│	│	│	1643	1843	│	...	│	...	│	│	│	...	│	│	│	│	│	│	│
Köln Hbf a.	│	│	│	│	│	1706	1906	│	...	│	...	│	│	│	...	│	0557	│	│	0557	0557	0557
Düsseldorf Hbf a.	│	│	│	│	│	1731	│	│	...	│	...	│	│	│	...	│	│	│	│	│	│	│
Duisburg Hbf a.	│	│	│	│	│	1745	│	│	...	│	...	│	│	│	...	│	│	│	│	│	│	│
Arnhem ⊙ a.	│	│	│	│	│	│	│	│	...	│	...	│	│	│	...	│	│	│	│	│	│	│
Utrecht Centraal a.	│	│	│	│	│	│	│	│	...	│	...	│	│	│	...	│	0852	│	│	0852	0913	0913
Amsterdam Centraal a.	│	│	│	│	│	│	│	│	...	│	...	│	│	│	...	│	0932	│	│	0932	0944	0944
Essen Hbf a.	│	│	│	│	│	1758	│	│	...	│	...	│	│	│	...	│	...	│	│	...	...	...
Dortmund Hbf a.	│	│	│	│	│	1821	2030	│	...	│	...	│	│	│	...	│	...	│	│	...	...	...
Hannover Hbf a.	1217	│	1417	1617	│	│	...	2017	...	2217	...	2341	0002	│	...	0529	...	│	0529	...	...	...
Berlin Hbf a.	│	1529	│	│	1930	│	...	│	...	│	...	│	│	0132	...	│	...	0718	│	...	...	...
Bremen Hbf a.	│	...	│	│	...	2015	...	│	...	│	...	│	│	...	...	│	...	...	│	...	...	...
Hamburg Hbf a.	1336	...	1536	1735	...	2114	...	2139	...	2339	...	0113	0136	...	...	0753	...	...	0753	...	...	...

A – *ÖBB nightjet* – 1, 2 cl., 2 cl. (4, 6 berth), [2] Amsterdam - Zürich and v.v.

B – *ÖBB nightjet* – 1, 2 cl., 2 cl. (4, 6 berth), [2] Berlin - Zürich and v.v. (Table **54**).

C – *ÖBB nightjet* – 1, 2 cl., 2 cl. (4, 6 berth), [2] Hamburg - Zürich and v.v. (Table **54**).

D – [12] Frankfurt - Zürich - Milano (Table **82**). Compulsory reservation for international journeys. Supplement payable for international journeys and for internal journeys within Italy.

G – From Sept. 1.

y – Sept. 1–5, Nov. 1 - Dec. 13.

⊙ – is at Emmerich.

CONNECTING SERVICES

Basel - Luzern - Chiasso: Table **550**. Basel - Bern - Interlaken and Brig: Table **560**.

Zürich - Landquart - Chur: Table **520**. Chur - St Moritz: Table **540**. Zürich - Bellinzona - Chiasso: Table **550**.

74 MILANO - PÁTRA - ATHÍNAI

For additional services Milano, Bologna and Roma - Ancona and Bari see Table **615**.

train type		*ICN*	*SF*		*IC*	*IC*	*SF*	*SF*		*IC*	*FA*	*FR*	*SF*	*SF*		*FR*	*SF*		*FR*	*SF*		
train number		**755**	⛴		**603**	**542**	⛴	⛴		**605**	**8311**	**9805**	⛴	⛴		**8807**	⛴		**8813**	⛴		
notes			⑦				⑤	②④			⑧		①–⑥	③			⑥			⑦		
notes		R ⁄			R ⁄	R ⁄	◧	◧		R ⁄	R ⁄	R ⁄		◧		R ⁄	◧		R ⁄	◧		
Milano Centrale d.	...	2150	...	...	0525	...	...	...	...	0705	...	1045p	...	...	...	1135	...	...	1435	...	...	...
Bologna Centrale d.	...	0010	...	...	0800	...	...	...	...	0958	...	1145	...	...	...	1245	...	...	1545	...	...	...
Roma Termini d.	...	|	...	...	|	0750	...	...	...	|	1315	|	...	...	...	|	...	...	|	...	...	...
Ancona d.	...	0250	...	...	1036	1125	...	...	...	1226	|	1337	...	...	...	1431	...	...	1734	...	...	...
Ancona Marittima d.	...	|	...	...	...	...	1300	1330	...	|	|	|	...	1530	...	...	1630	...	...	1930	...	...
Pescara Centrale d.	...	0413	...	...	...	...	|	|	...	1401	|	1447	...	|	...	...	|	...	...	|	...	...
Foggia d.	...	0609	...	...	...	...	|	|	...	1552	|	1622	...	|	...	...	|	...	...	|	...	...
Bari Centrale a.	...	0740	...	...	...	...	|	|	...	1705	1739	1727	...	|	...	...	|	...	...	|	...	...
Bari Marittima d.	...	...	1330	...	...	...	|	|	...	...	...	...	1930	|	...	...	|	...	...	|	...	...
Pátra a.	...	...	0700	...	...	...	1500	1530	...	...	...	...	1300	1730	...	...	1800	...	...	2200	...	...
Athína Lárisa a.	...	...	✣	...	...	...	✣	✣	...	...	...	...	✣	✣	...	...	✣	...	...	✣	...	...

train type		*SF*	*FR*	*FA*			*SF*	*SF*	*SF*	*IC*				*SF*	*SF*	*ICN*						
train number		⛴	**8820**	**8314**			⛴	⛴	⛴	**614**				⛴	⛴	**758**						
notes							⑥	⑤	②③		2			①	⑦							
notes			R ⁄	R ⁄			◧	◧	◧	R ⁄				◧	◧	R ⁄						
Athína Lárisa d.	...	✣	...	...	...	...	✣	✣	✣	...	...	...	...	✣	✣	...	...	...	...	...	...	...
Pátra d.	...	1730	...	...	...	...	1730	1730	1800	...	...	...	...	1730	2000	...	...	...	...	...	...	...
Bari Marittima a.	...	0900	...	...	...	...	|	|	|	...	...	...	...	|	|	...	...	...	...	...	...	...
Bari Centrale d.	...	...	1030	1240	...	...	|	|	|	1355	...	...	...	|	|	2128	...	...	...	...	...	...
Foggia a.	...	...	1133	1341	...	...	|	|	|	1507	...	...	...	|	|	2249	...	...	...	...	...	...
Pescara Centrale a.	...	...	1307	|	...	...	|	|	|	1700	...	...	...	|	|	0105	...	...	...	...	...	...
Ancona Marittima a.	...	...	|	|	...	...	1630	1730	1700	|	...	...	...	1900	1900	|	...	...	...	...	...	...
Ancona a.	...	...	1422	|	...	...	...	...	...	1835	1850	...	...	...	...	0256	...	...	...	...	...	...
Roma Termini a.	...	...	|	1705	...	...	...	...	...	|	2232	...	...	...	...	|	...	...	...	...	...	...
Bologna Centrale a.	...	...	1615	...	...	...	...	...	...	2100	...	...	...	...	...	0452	...	...	...	...	...	...
Milano Centrale a.	...	...	1810	...	...	...	...	...	...	2340	...	...	...	...	...	0705	...	...	...	...	...	...

p – Milano **Porta Garibaldi**.

⁄ – Supplement payable.

◧ – Journey 24–27 hours.

✣ – For connections Pátra - Athína and v.v. see Tables **1440** and **1450**.

SF – **Superfast Ferries** (www.superfast.com) see Tables **2716** and **2755**.

75 MÜNCHEN - ZÜRICH

train type	*EC*	*EC*	*EC*	*EC*	*EC*	*EC*	*EC*	*EC*	*EC*
train number	**290**	**198**	**196**	**194**	**192**	**190**	**98**	**96**	**296**
notes	✕	✕	✕	✕	✕	✕	✕	✕	✕
notes	①–⑥								⑧
München Hbf d.	...	0654	0853	1054	1254	1454	1653	1851	2055
Buchloe d.	...	0736	0936	1135	1336	1536	1736	1936	2136
Memmingen d.	...	0801	1001	1201	1401	1601	1801	2001	2201
Lindau Reutin 🏛 d.	0652	0852	1052	1252	1452	1652	1852	2052	2252
Bregenz 🏛 d.	0700	0900	1100	1300	1500	1700	1900	2100	2300
St Margrethen 🏛 d.	0710	0910	1110	1310	1510	1710	1910	2110	2310
St Gallen d.	0729	0929	1129	1329	1529	1729	1929	2129	2329
Winterthur d.	0803	1003	1203	1403	1603	1803	2003	2203	0003
Zürich Flughafen ✈ a.	0816	1016	1216	1416	1616	1816	2016	2216	0016
Zürich HB a.	0827	1027	1227	1427	1627	1827	2027	2227	0027

train type	*EC*	*EC*	*EC*	*EC*	*EC*	*EC*	*EC*	*EC*	
train number	**297**	**97**	**99**	**191**	**193**	**195**	**197**	**199**	
notes	✕	✕	✕	✕	✕	✕	✕	✕	
notes	①–⑥								
Zürich HB d.	0535	0733	0933	1133	1333	1533	1733	1933	...
Zürich Flughafen ✈ d.	|	0743	0943	1143	1343	1543	1743	1943	...
Winterthur d.	0558	0758	0958	1158	1358	1558	1758	1958	...
St Gallen d.	0632	0832	1032	1232	1432	1632	1832	2032	...
St Margrethen 🏛 d.	0651	0851	1051	1251	1451	1651	|	2051	...
Bregenz 🏛 d.	0702	0902	1102	1302	1502	1702	1902	2102	...
Lindau Reutin 🏛 d.	0710	0910	1110	1310	1510	1710	1910	2110	...
Memmingen d.	0802	1001	1201	1401	1601	1801	2001	2201	...
Buchloe d.	0825	1025	1225	1425	1625	1825	2025	2225	...
München Hbf a.	0905	1104	1304	1504	1704	1904	2105	2304	...

76 MÜNCHEN - PRAHA

train type	*ALX*	*ALX*	*ALX*	*ALX*	*ALX*	*ALX*	*ALX*		
train number	**365**	**353**	**355**	**357**	**359**	**361**	**363**		
notes									
notes	**A**	**A**	**A**	**A**	**A**	**A**	**A**		
München Hbf d.	0444	0644	0844	1044	1244	1444	1644	...	...
Regensburg d.	0617	0817	1017	1217	1417	1617	1817	...	...
Schwandorf d.	0653	0853	1053	1253	1453	1653	1853	...	...
Furth im Wald 🏛 d.	0740	0940	1140	1340	1540	1740	1940	...	...
Plzeň hl. n. a.	0847	1047	1247	1447	1647	1847	2047	...	...
Praha hl. n. a.	1022	1222	1422	1622	1822	2022	2222	...	...

train type	*ALX*	*ALX*	*ALX*	*ALX*	*ALX*	*ALX*	*ALX*		
train number	**362**	**360**	**358**	**356**	**354**	**352**	**364**		
notes									
notes	**A**	**A**	**A**	**A**	**A**	**A**	**A**		
Praha hl. n. d.	0535	0735	0935	1135	1335	1535	1735	...	...
Plzeň hl. n. d.	0711	0911	1111	1311	1511	1711	1911	...	...
Furth im Wald 🏛 a.	0820	1020	1220	1420	1620	1820	2020	...	...
Schwandorf a.	0905	1105	1305	1505	1705	1905	2105	...	...
Regensburg a.	0941	1141	1341	1541	1741	1941	2141	...	...
München Hbf a.	1118	1318	1518	1718	1918	2118	2318	...	...

A – BAVORSKÝ EXPRESS. Classified *EC* in the Czech Republic.

ALX – Arriva Länderbahn Express.

77 BRUSSELS - MÜNCHEN - VENEZIA

train type	*ES*	
train number	**1277**	
notes		
notes	**A**	
Brussels Midi / Zuid d.	1806	...
Köln Hbf a.	2328	...
Köln Hbf d.	2338	...
München Ost a.	0710	...
München Ost d.	0720	...
Kufstein 🏛 a.	0816	...
Wörgl a.	0900	...
Jenbach a.	0915	...
Innsbruck Hbf a.	1000	...
Innsbruck Hbf d.	1002	...
Brennero / Brenner 🏛 a.	1030	...
Bolzano / Bozen a.	1200	...
Verona Port Nuova a.	1345	...
Venezia Mestre a.	1500	...
Venezia Santa Lucia a.	...	...

train type	*ES*	
train number	**1278**	
notes		
notes	**B**	
Venezia Santa Lucia d.	...	...
Venezia Mestre d.	1615	...
Verona Port Nuova d.	1730	...
Bolzano / Bozen d.	1900	...
Brennero / Brenner 🏛 d.	2030	...
Innsbruck Hbf a.	2058	...
Innsbruck Hbf d.	2100	...
Jenbach d.	2130	...
Wörgl d.	2200	...
Kufstein 🏛 a.	2230	...
München Ost a.	2335	...
München Ost d.	2345	...
Köln Hbf a.	0700	...
Köln Hbf d.	0707	...
Brussels Midi / Zuid a.	1248	...

A – Feb. 5, 14, 23, Mar. 4, 12: EUROPEAN SLEEPER – 🛏 (1, 2, 3 berth), ▬ (5, 6 berth) ✕ Brussels - Venezia.

B – Feb. 9, 18, 27, Mar. 8, 16: EUROPEAN SLEEPER – 🛏 (1, 2, 3 berth), ▬ (5, 6 berth) ✕ Venezia - Brussels.

78 BRUSSELS - AMSTERDAM - BERLIN - PRAHA

train type	*ES*	
train number	**453**	
notes	①③⑤	
notes	**D**	
Brussels Midi / Zuid d.	1922	...
Antwerpen Centraal d.	2002	...
Roosendaal d.	2044	...
Rotterdam Centraal d.	2122	...
Den Haag HS d.	2142	...
Amsterdam Centraal d.	2234	...
Amersfoort Centraal d.	2313	...
Deventer d.	2352	...
Berlin Hbf a.	0620	...
Berlin Ost a.	0629	...
Dresden Hbf a.	0854	...
Bad Schandau 🏛 a.	0923	...
Děčín a.	0946	...
Praha hl. n. a.	1124	...

train type	*ES*	
train number	**452**	
notes	②④⑦	
notes	**D**	
Praha hl. n. d.	1802	...
Děčín d.	1938	...
Bad Schandau 🏛 d.	1955	...
Dresden Hbf d.	2030	...
Berlin Ost d.	2244	...
Berlin Hbf d.	2256	...
Deventer a.	0512	...
Amersfoort Centraal a.	0548	...
Amsterdam Centraal a.	0631	...
Den Haag HS a.	0711	...
Rotterdam Centraal a.	0732	...
Roosendaal a.	0816	...
Antwerpen Centraal a.	0847	...
Brussels Midi / Zuid a.	0927	...

D – EUROPEAN SLEEPER – 🛏 (1, 2, 3 berth), ▬ (5, 6 berth), (2.) Brussels - Praha and v.v.

GENÈVE, BASEL and ZÜRICH - MILANO and VENEZIA 82

All services in this table are subject to compulsory reservation for international journeys. Supplements are payable for international journeys and for internal journeys within Italy.

Engineering work on Genève - Brig - Milano and Basel - Brig - Milano routes will affect services with bus replacement services at certain locations on both routes

train type	EC	EC	EC	EC	EC	EC	EC	EC	EC	EC	IC	EC	EC	EC	EC	EC	EC	EC	EC	EC	EC	EC
train number	41	155	61	11	143	43	33	13	37	15	617	53	151	17	65	45	19	173	21	67	47	23
train number		A					133							117			119					
notes	🅁🍷	🅁🍷	🅁🍷	🅁🍷	🅁🍷	🅁🍷	🅁🍷	🅁🍷	🅁🍷	🅁🍷	🅁🍷	🅁🍷	🅁🍷	🅁🍷	🅁🍷	🅁🍷	🅁🍷	🅁🍷	🅁🍷	🅁🍷	🅁🍷	🅁🍷
notes					①–⑤	⑥⑦			X		①–⑤	⑥⑦	F									
Genève Cornavin d.	0527	...	...	...	0727	0727	...	...	...	...	...	...	...	...	...	1327	...	...	...	...	1827	...
Lausanne d.	0610	...	...	...	0810	0810	...	...	...	...	...	...	...	...	...	1410	...	...	...	...	1910	...
Montreux d.	0631	...	...	...	0831	0831	...	...	...	...	...	...	...	...	...	1431	...	...	...	...	1931	...
Sion d.	0709	...	...	...	0909	0909	...	...	...	...	...	...	...	...	...	1509	...	...	...	...	2009	...
Basel SBB d.	|	...	0628	...	|	|	...	...	...	...	1028	1028	1106	...	1228	|	...	1503	...	1728	|	...
Zürich HB d.	|	0633	|	0733	|	|	0833	0933	1033	1133	|	|	1233	1333	|	|	1533	|	1733	|	|	1933
Olten d.	|	|	0658	|	|	|	|	|	|	|	1058	1058	|	|	1258	|	|	1530	|	1758	|	|
Bern d.	|	|	0734	|	|	|	|	|	|	|	1134	1134	|	|	1334	|	|	|	|	1834	|	|
Spiez d.	|	|	0805	|	|	|	|	|	|	|	1205	1205	|	|	1405	|	|	|	|	1905	|	|
Luzern d.	|	|	|	|	|	|	|	|	|	|	|	|	|	|	|	|	|	1618	|	|	|	|
Arth-Goldau d.	|	0718	|	0818	|	|	0918	1018	1118	1218	|	|	1318	1418	|	|	1618	1649	1818	|	|	2018
Bellinzona d.	|	0814	|	0914	|	|	1014	1114	1214	1314	|	|	1414	1514	|	|	1714	1744	1914	|	|	2114
Lugano d.	|	0830	|	0930	|	|	1030	1130	1230	1330	|	|	1430	1530	|	|	1730	1810	1930	|	|	2130
Chiasso 🏛 d.	|	0902	|	1002	|	|	1102	1202	1302	1402	|	|	1502	1602	|	|	1802	1855	2002	|	|	2202
Como San Giovanni d.	|	0910	|	1010	|	|	1110	1210	1310	1410	|	|	1510	1610	|	|	1810	1903	2010	|	|	2210
Visp d.	|	|	0833	|	|	|	|	|	|	|	1233	1233	|	|	1433	|	|	|	|	1933	|	|
Brig d.	0741	|	0844	|	0941	0944	|	|	|	|	1241	1244	|	|	1444	1541	|	|	|	1944	2041	|
Domodossola 🏛 ¶ d.	0817	|	0917	|	1011	|	|	|	|	|	...	1317	|	|	1517	1617	|	|	|	2017	2117	|
Stresa d.	|	|	|	|	...	1050	|	|	|	|	...	|	|	|	|	|	|	|	|	2050	2150	|
Milano Lambrate a.	|	0955	|	|	...	|	|	|	|	|	...	|	|	|	|	|	|	|	|	|	|	|
Milano Rogoredo a.	|	1013	|	|	...	|	|	|	|	|	...	|	|	|	|	|	|	|	|	|	|	|
Milano Centrale a.	0950	|	1050	1050	...	1150	1150	1250	1350	1450	...	1455	1550	1650	1655	1750	1850	1950	2050	2150	2250	2250
Verona Porta Nuova a.	1128	|	...	...	...	...	1328	...	...	...	...	...	...	...	...	...	...	...	...	...	...	...
Venezia Mestre a.	1230	|	...	...	...	...	1430	...	...	...	...	...	...	...	...	...	...	...	...	...	...	...
Venezia Santa Lucia a.	1242	|	...	...	...	...	1442	...	...	...	...	...	...	...	...	...	...	...	...	...	...	...
Genova Piazza Principe a.	...	1304	...	...	...	...	...	...	...	...	...	...	...	...	...	...	...	...	...	...	...	...
Bologna Centrale a.	...	...	...	...	...	...	...	...	...	...	...	...	...	...	...	...	...	...	...	...	...	...

train type	EC	EC	EC	EC	EC	EC	EC	EC	EC	EC	EC	EC	EC	EC	EC	EC	EC	EC	EC	EC	EC	EC	EC	EC
train number	10	60	12	40	14	178	622	62	150	16	142	42	18	64	36	20	44	144	66	32	22	146	46	156
train number																120				112	122			
notes	🅁🍷	🅁🍷	🅁🍷	🅁🍷	🅁🍷	🅁🍷	🅁🍷	🅁🍷	🅁🍷	🅁🍷	🅁🍷	🅁🍷	🅁🍷	🅁🍷	🅁🍷	🅁🍷	🅁🍷	🅁🍷	🅁🍷	🅁🍷	🅁🍷	🅁🍷	🅁🍷	🅁🍷
notes							①–⑤	⑥⑦	F		①–⑤	⑥⑦			X		①–⑤	⑥⑦				⑤⑥	⑦–④	B
Bologna Centrale d.	...	...	...	...	...	...	...	...	...	...	...	...	...	...	...	...	...	...	...	...	...	...	...	...
Genova Piazza Principe d.	...	...	...	...	...	...	...	...	...	...	...	...	...	...	...	...	...	...	...	...	...	...	...	1656
Venezia Santa Lucia d.	...	...	...	...	...	...	...	...	...	...	...	...	...	...	...	...	...	...	...	1518	...	1618	1618	|
Venezia Mestre d.	...	...	...	...	...	...	...	...	...	...	...	...	...	...	...	...	...	...	...	1530	...	1630	1630	|
Verona Porta Nuova d.	...	...	...	...	...	...	...	...	...	...	...	...	...	...	...	...	...	...	...	1632	...	1732	1732	|
Milano Centrale d.	0710	0710	0810	0810	0910	1010	...	1105	1110	1310	...	1310	1510	1510	1610	1710	1710	1710	1805	1810	1910	1910	1910	|
Milano Rogoredo d.	|	|	|	|	|	|	...	|	|	|	...	|	|	|	|	|	|	|	|	|	|	|	|	1957
Milano Lambrate d.	|	|	|	|	|	|	...	|	|	|	...	|	|	|	|	|	|	|	|	|	|	|	|	2005
Stresa d.	|	0811	|	0911	|	|	...	|	|	|	...	1411	|	|	|	|	|	|	|	|	|	|	|	|
Domodossola 🏛 ¶ d.	|	0848	|	0948	|	|	...	1248	|	|	1448	1448	|	1648	|	|	1848	|	1948	|	|	2048	2048	|
Brig d.	|	0918	|	1020	|	|	1318	1318	|	|	1520	1520	|	1718	|	|	1920	1920	2019	|	|	2120	2126	|
Visp d.	|	0927	|	|	|	|	1327	1327	|	|	|	|	|	1727	|	|	|	|	2028	|	|	|	2136	|
Como San Giovanni d.	0754	|	0850	|	0950	1058	|	|	1150	1350	|	|	1550	|	1650	1750	|	|	|	1850	1950	|	|	2050
Chiasso 🏛 d.	0805	|	0905	|	1005	1124	|	|	1205	1405	|	|	1605	|	1705	1805	|	|	|	1905	2005	|	|	2105
Lugano d.	0830	|	0930	|	1030	1202	|	|	1230	1430	|	|	1630	|	1730	1830	|	|	|	1930	2030	|	|	2130
Bellinzona d.	0847	|	0947	|	1047	1217	|	|	1247	1447	|	|	1647	|	1747	1847	|	|	|	1947	2047	|	|	2147
Arth-Goldau d.	0945	|	1045	|	1145	1315	|	|	1345	1545	|	|	1745	|	1845	1945	|	|	|	2045	2145	|	|	2245
Luzern d.	|	|	|	|	|	1354	|	|	|	|	|	|	|	|	|	|	|	|	|	|	|	|	|	|
Spiez d.	|	0954	|	|	|	|	1354	1354	|	|	|	|	|	1754	|	|	|	|	2054	|	|	|	|	|
Bern a.	|	1025	|	|	|	|	1425	1425	|	|	|	|	|	1830	|	|	|	|	2125	|	|	|	|	|
Olten a.	|	1105	|	|	|	1428	1505	1505	|	|	|	|	|	1905	|	|	|	|	2204	|	|	|	|	|
Zürich HB a.	1027	|	1127	|	1227	|	|	|	1427	1627	|	|	1827	|	1927	2027	|	|	|	2127	2227	|	|	2327
Basel SBB a.	...	1132	...	|	...	1456	1532	1532	1528	...	|	|	...	1932	...	...	|	|	2235	...	...	|	|	...
Sion a.	...	...	...	1049	...	...	...	...	...	...	1549	1549	...	...	...	...	1949	1949	...	...	...	2149	2201	...
Montreux a.	...	...	...	1127	...	...	...	...	...	...	1627	1627	...	...	...	...	2027	2027	...	...	...	2228	2252	...
Lausanne a.	...	...	...	1150	...	...	...	...	...	...	1650	1650	...	...	...	...	2050	2050	...	...	...	2250	2316	...
Genève Cornavin a.	...	...	...	1231	...	...	...	...	...	...	1731	1731	...	...	...	...	2131	2131	...	...	...	2331	0005	...

A – To Pisa June 8 - Sept. 28, arrive 1600.
B – From Pisa June 8 - Sept. 28, depart 1320.
F – 12 Frankfurt - Basel - Zürich - Milano and v.v. (Table **73**).
X – June 1 - Sept. 28.
¶ – Ticketing point is **Iselle**.

WIEN - KLAGENFURT - VENEZIA 83

train type	NJ	RE	RE	RJ	RJ	RE	RE
train number	1237	1821	1821	131	133	1823	1823
train number				✕	✕		
notes		2	2			2	2
notes	B	Ⓒ	Ⓐ			Ⓐ	Ⓒ
Wien Hbf d.	2149	...	...	0624	1218	...	...
Wien Meidling d.	2156	...	...	0631	1225	...	...
Bruck an der Mur d.	|	...	...	0815	1415	...	...
Klagenfurt Hbf d.	0412	...	...	1021	1621	...	...
Villach Hbf d.	0500	0945	0945	1049	1649	1929	1929
Tarvisio 🏛 a.	0523	1012	1012	1111	1711	1959	1959
Udine a.	0623	1129	1151	1216x	1816	2113	2113
Trieste Centrale a.	|	1253	...	|	|	...	2239
Venezia Mestre a.	0822	...	...	1402x	1952	...	...
Venezia Santa Lucia a.	0834	...	...	1414x	2004	...	...

train type/number	NJ	RE	RE	RJ	RE	RE	RJ
train number	1236	1816	1820	132	1818	1822	130
notes		1820		✕	1822		✕
		2	2		2	2	
	B	Ⓒ	Ⓐ		Ⓒ	Ⓐ	
Venezia Santa Lucia d.	2105	...	...	0956	...	...	1552
Venezia Mestre d.	2117	...	...	1008	...	...	1604
Trieste Centrale d.	|	0543	...	|	1545	...	|
Udine d.	2247	0714	0714	1144	1715	1715	1744
Tarvisio 🏛 d.	0005	0825	0825	1249	1838	1838	1849
Villach Hbf a.	0027	0852	0852	1311	1905	1905	1911
Klagenfurt Hbf a.	0105	...	...	1337	...	...	1937
Bruck an der Mur a.	|	...	...	1543	...	...	2143
Wien Meidling a.	0810	...	...	1729	...	...	2329
Wien Hbf a.	0819	...	...	1736	...	...	2336

B – *ÖBB nightjet* – 🛏 1, 2 cl., 🛏 2 cl. (4, 6 berth), 2 Wien - Venezia and v.v. (Table **71**).
x – ①–⑥ June 28 - Aug. 8 arrive 54–60 minutes later.

86 ZÜRICH - INNSBRUCK - WIEN, BUDAPEST, GRAZ and ZAGREB

Services on this table are affected by the closure of the Tauern tunnel - for details see Table **970**.
For trains Villach - Ljubljana - Zagreb - Vinkovci and v.v. see Table **62**. For other trains Salzburg - Budapest and v.v. see Table **65**.

train type	*RJX*	*EC*	*RJX*	*RJX*	*RJX*	*RJX*	*RJX*	*NJ*	*EN*	*EN*	*NJ*
train number	**161**	**163**	**165**	**167**	**169**	**367**	**369**	**1465**	**40465**	**40467**	**467**
notes	✕	🍷	✕	✕	✕	✕	✕				
notes	**A**	**B**						**C**	**D**	**E**	**F**
Zürich HB d.	0640	0840	1040	1240	1440	1640	1840	2040	2040	2140	2140
Buchs 🛃 d.	0757	1000	1154	1354	1554	1800	1954	2204	2204	2305	2305
Feldkirch d.	0817	1017	1217	1417	1617	1817	2017	2245	2245	2324	2324
Bludenz d.	0830	1030	1230	1430	1630	1830	2030	2301	2301	2340	2340
St Anton am Arlberg d.	0903	1103	1303	1503	1703	1903	2103	2346	2346	|	|
Landeck - Zams d.	0927	1127	1327	1527	1727	1927	2127	0011	0011	0036	0036
Ötztal d.	0948	1148	1348	1548	1748	1948	2151	|	|	|	|
Innsbruck Hbf d.	1016	1221	1416	1616	1816	2016	2216	0059	0059	0128	0128
Jenbach d.	|	1243	|	|	|	|	|	|	|	|	|
Wörgl d.	1043	1258	1443	1643	1843	2043	2243	|	|	|	|
Salzburg Hbf d.	1207	|	1607	1807	2007	2207	0003	|	|	0353	0433
Linz Hbf d.	1317	|	1717	1917	2117	2320	...	|	|	0510	0558
St Pölten d.	1403	|	1803	2003	2203	0006	...	|	|	0600	0710
Wien Meidling a.	1425	|	1825	2025	2225	0028	...	|	|	0624	0751
Wien Hbf a.	1432	|	1832	2032	2232	0035	...	|	|	0632	0758
Wien Hbf d.	...	|	1842	2042	...	...	...	|	|	0640	...
Bratislava hl. st. a.	...	|	|	2151	...	...	...	|	|	|	...
Györ a.	...	|	1954	...	...	...	...	|	|	0754	...
Budapest Keleti a.	...	|	2119	...	...	...	...	|	|	0919	...
Kitzbühel d.	...	1329	...	...	...	...	...	|	|	...	...
St Johann in Tirol d.	...	1337	...	...	...	...	...	|	|	...	...
Saalfelden d.	...	1405	...	...	...	...	...	|	|	...	...
Zell am See d.	...	1416	...	...	...	...	...	|	|	...	...
Schwarzach St Veit d.	...	1456	...	...	...	...	...	0319	0319	...	...
Bischofshofen a.	...	|	...	...	...	...	...	|	|	...	...
Selzthal a.	...	1639	...	...	...	...	...	0449	|	...	...
Graz Hbf a.	...	1814	...	...	...	...	...	0658	0732	...	...
Villach Hbf a.	...	...	...	...	...	...	...	...	|	...	...
Klagenfurt a.	...	...	...	...	...	...	...	...	|	...	...
Jesenice 🛃 a.	...	...	...	...	...	...	...	...	|	...	...
Ljubljana ⊙ a.	...	...	...	...	...	...	...	...	|	...	...
Zagreb ⊙ a.	...	...	...	...	...	...	...	...	1133	...	...
Vinkovci ⊕ a.	...	...	...	...	...	...	...	...	...	...	...
Beograd Centar ⊕ a.	...	...	...	...	...	...	...	...	...	...	...

train type	*NJ*	*EN*	*NJ*	*EN*	*RJX*	*RJX*	*RJX*	*RJX*	*EC*	*RJX*	*RJX*
train number	**466**	**40462**	**1464**	**40414**	**366**	**368**	**160**	**162**	**164**	**166**	**168**
notes					✕	✕	✕	✕	🍷	✕	✕
notes	**F**	**E**	**C**	**D**					**B**		**A**
Beograd Centar ⊕ d.	...	...	...	...	...	...	...	...	...	...	...
Vinkovci ⊕ d.	...	...	...	...	...	...	...	...	...	...	...
Zagreb ⊙ d.	...	...	...	1840	...	...	...	...	...	...	...
Ljubljana ⊙ d.	...	...	...	|	...	...	...	...	...	...	...
Jesenice 🛃 d.	...	...	...	|	...	...	...	...	...	...	...
Klagenfurt d.	...	...	...	|	...	...	...	...	...	...	...
Villach Hbf d.	...	...	...	|	...	...	...	...	...	...	...
Graz Hbf d.	...	...	2226	2230	...	...	...	...	0945	...	...
Selzthal d.	...	...	0047	|	...	...	...	...	1119	...	...
Bischofshofen d.	...	...	0217	0217	...	...	...	...	1250	...	...
Schwarzach St Veit d.	...	...	0232	0232	...	...	...	...	1313	...	...
Zell am See d.	...	...	|	|	...	...	...	...	1344	...	...
Saalfelden d.	...	...	|	|	...	...	...	...	1354	...	...
St Johann in Tirol d.	...	...	|	|	...	...	...	...	1423	...	...
Kitzbühel d.	...	...	|	|	...	...	...	...	1431	...	...
Budapest Keleti d.	...	2040	|	|	...	...	...	0640	|	...	...
Györ d.	...	2202	|	|	...	...	...	0802	|	...	...
Bratislava hl. st. d.	...	|	|	|	...	...	0600	|	|	...	...
Wien Hbf a.	...	2320	|	|	...	...	0718	0918	|	...	...
Wien Hbf d.	2139	2328	|	|	...	0528	0728	0928	|	1328	1528
Wien Meidling d.	2147	2335	|	|	...	0535	0735	0935	|	1335	1535
St Pölten d.	2214	0001	|	|	...	0559	0759	0959	|	1359	1559
Linz Hbf d.	2310	0051	|	|	...	0645	0845	1045	|	1445	1645
Salzburg Hbf d.	0230	0230	|	|	0556	0756	0956	1156	|	1556	1756
Wörgl d.	|	|	|	|	0719	0919	1119	1319	1504	1719	1919
Jenbach d.	|	|	|	|	|	|	|	|	1518	|	|
Innsbruck Hbf d.	0431	0431	0453	0453	0747	0947	1147	1347	1547	1747	1947
Ötztal d.	|	|	|	|	0812	1012	1212	1412	1612	1812	2012
Landeck - Zams d.	0520	0520	0543	0543	0833	1033	1233	1433	1633	1833	2033
St Anton am Arlberg d.	|	|	0612	0612	0857	1057	1257	1457	1657	1857	2057
Bludenz d.	0625	0625	0706	0706	0931	1131	1331	1531	1731	1931	2131
Feldkirch d.	0640	0640	0739	0739	0944	1148	1348	1548	1744	1948	2148
Buchs 🛃 a.	0656	0656	0754	0754	0959	1206	1406	1606	1759	2006	2203
Zürich HB a.	0820	0820	0920	0920	1120	1320	1520	1720	1920	2120	2320

A – [12] 🍷 Zürich - Innsbruck - Wien and v.v. Conveys [12] 🍷 Bolzano (depart 0750; arrive 2215, *RJX* **184/185**) - Innsbruck - Wien and v.v.

B – TRANSALPIN – [1] (observation car), [12] 🍷 Zürich - Innsbruck - Graz and v.v.

C – *ÖBB nightjet* ZÜRICHSEE – 🛏 1, 2 cl., 🛌 2 cl. (4, 6 berth), [2] Zürich - Graz and v.v.

D – *ÖBB nightjet* – 🛏 1, 2 cl., 🛌 2 cl. (4, 6 berth), [2] Zürich - Zagreb and v.v.

E – 🛏 1, 2 cl., 🛌 2 cl., [2] Zürich - Wien - Budapest. Special fares payable.

F – *ÖBB nightjet* WIENER WALZER – 🛏 1, 2 cl., 🛌 2 cl. (4, 6 berth), [2] Zürich - Wien and v.v. Special fares payable.

⊙ – 🛃 between Ljubljana and Zagreb is Dobova.

⊕ – 🛃 between Vinkovci and Beograd is Šid.

RJX – ÖBB *Railjet* service. ✕, [1] (business class), [1] (first class), [2] (economy class).

WIEN and BUDAPEST - LJUBLJANA and ZAGREB 89

train type	EC	IC	IC	RJ	D	RJ	IC	IC	EN		EN
train number	**151**	**246**	**204**	**257**	**159**	**755**	**250**	**1204**	**1153**	**1246**	**1277**
train number	**134**										
notes	✕			✕		✕					
notes	**A**	**B**	**C**		**D**			**P**	**G**	**R**	**E**
Wien Hbf .... d.	0758	...	...	1458	...	1758	...	...	1905	...	2155
Wien Meidling .... d.	0805	...	...	1505	...	1805	...	...	1913	...	|
Wiener Neustadt Hbf.. d.	0832	...	...	1532	...	1832	...	...	1951	...	2355
Budapest Keleti ..... d.	|	...	...	|	...	|	1613	1845	|	2117	|
Budapest Déli .... d.	|	0900	1535	|	...	|	|	1901**k**	|	2136**k**	|
Székesfehérvár .... d.	|	0946	1621	|	...	|	|	1942	|	2216	|
Siófok .... d.	|	|	1657	|	...	|	|	2028	|	|	|
Fonyód .... d.	|	|	1737	|	...	|	|	2100	|	|	|
Szombathely .... d.	|	|	|	|	...	|	1906	|	|	|	|
Zalaegerszeg .... d.	|	1222	|	|	...	|	|	|	|	0149	|
Hodoš 🏛 .... d.	|	1320	|	|	...	|	|	|	|	0238	|
Graz Hbf .... d.	1038	|	|	1733	1838	2033	2138	|	2202	|	0230
Spielfeld-Straß 🏛 ...... d.	1125	|	|	...	1925	...	2225	|	2245	|	|
Maribor .... a.	1140	|	|	...	1940	...	2240	|	2301	|	0331
Pragersko .... a.	1159	1436	|	...	1959	...	2258	|	|	|	0352
Zidani Most .... a.	1303	1540	|	...	|	...	2400	|	|	|	0543
Nagykanizsa .... d.	|	|	1908	...	|	...	|	2201	|	|	|
Gyékényes 🏛 .... d.	|	|	1951	...	|	...	|	2247	|	|	|
Koprivnica 🏛 .... a.	|	|	2005	...	|	...	|	|	|	|	|
Dobova 🏛 .... a.	|	|	|	...	2145	...	|	|	0055	|	|
Zagreb .... a.	|	|	2200	...	2220	...	|	|	0131	|	|
Split .... a.	|	|	...	...	...	...	|	0939	1006	|	|
Ljubljana .... a.	1400	1642	...	...	...	...	0101	...	...	0645	0645
Koper .... a.	|	...	...	...	...	...	...	...	...	0931	|
Rijeka .... a.	|	...	...	...	...	...	...	...	...	1003	1003
Villa Opicina 🏛 ...... a.	1627	...	...	...	...	...	...	...	...	...	...
Trieste Centrale .... a.	...	...	...	...	...	...	...	...	...	...	...

train type	IC	RJ	D	RJ	IC	IC	EC	IC	EN	EN	
train number	**251**	**558**	**158**	**78**	**247**	**201**	**135**	**1205**	**1276**	**1152**	**1247**
train number							**150**				
notes		✕		✕			✕				
notes			**D**		**B**	**C**	**A**	**Q**	**F**	**H**	**S**
Trieste Centrale .... d.	...	...	...	...	...	...	...	...	...	...	...
Villa Opicina 🏛 .... d.	...	...	...	...	...	...	1338	...	...	...	...
Rijeka .... d.	...	...	...	...	...	...	|	...	1815	...	1815
Koper .... d.	...	...	...	...	...	...	|	...	|	...	1852
Ljubljana .... d.	0500	...	...	...	0915	...	1605	...	2220	...	2220
Split .... d.	|	...	...	...	|	...	|	1743	|	1722	|
Zagreb .... d.	|	...	0705	...	|	1630	|	|	|	0151	|
Dobova 🏛 .... d.	|	...	0810	...	|	|	|	|	|	0225	|
Koprivnica 🏛 .... d.	|	...	|	...	|	1801	|	|	|	|	|
Gyékényes 🏛 .... a.	|	...	|	...	|	1815	|	0447	|	|	|
Nagykanizsa .... a.	|	...	|	...	|	1848	|	0556	|	|	|
Zidani Most .... d.	0600	...	|	...	1016	|	1701	|	|	|	|
Pragersko .... d.	0702	...	0959	...	1123	|	1800	|	2343	|	|
Maribor .... d.	0719	...	1020	...	|	|	1821	|	0102	0447	|
Spielfeld-Straß 🏛 .... a.	0734	...	1035	...	|	|	1836	|	|	0502	|
Graz Hbf .... a.	0822	0926	1122	1226	|	|	1922	|	0158	0552	|
Hodoš 🏛 .... a.	|	|	...	|	1240	|	|	|	|	|	0252
Zalaegerszeg .... a.	|	|	...	|	1337	|	|	|	|	|	0336
Szombathely .... a.	1053	|	...	|	|	|	|	|	|	|	|
Fonyód .... a.	|	|	...	|	|	2022	|	0709	|	|	|
Siófok .... a.	|	|	...	|	|	2101	|	0739	|	|	|
Székesfehérvár .... a.	|	|	...	|	1611	2136	|	0827	|	|	0758
Budapest Déli .... a.	|	|	...	|	1659	2224	|	0916**k**	|	|	0845**k**
Budapest Keleti ..... a.	1344	|	...	|	...	...	|	0935	|	|	0906
Wiener Neustadt Hbf .. a.	...	1128	...	1428	...	...	2128	...	0400	0810	...
Wien Meidling .... a.	...	1155	...	1455	...	...	2155	...	|	0847	...
Wien Hbf .... a.	...	1202	...	1502	...	...	2202	...	0605	0854	...

A – EMONA – [12] ✕ Wien - Ljubljana and v.v. Conveys [12] Wien (**151/150**) - Ljubljana (**135/134**) - Villa Opicina and v.v.

B – CITADELLA – [2] Budapest - Ljubljana and v.v.

C – AGRAM-TÓPART – [12] Zagreb - Budapest and v.v.

D – CROATIA – [2] Graz - Zagreb and v.v.

E – ②④⑤⑦ June 27 - Aug. 29. ▬ 2 cl., [2] Warszawa - Wien - Rijeka (Table **99**).

F – ①③⑤⑦ June 29 - Aug. 31. ▬ 2 cl., [2] Rijeka - Wien - Warszawa (Table **99**).

G – ③⑤⑦ June 15 - Oct. 12. 🛏 1, 2 cl., ▬ 2 cl., [2] Bratislava - Wien - Split (Table **92**).

H – ①④⑥ June 16 - Oct. 13. 🛏 1, 2 cl., ▬ 2 cl., [2] Split - Wien - Bratislava (Table **92**).

P – June 19, 21, 26, 28, July **and** Aug. 2, 4, 6, 8, 10, 12, 14, 16, 18, 20, 22, 24, 26, 28, 30, Sept. 2, 4, 6, 11, 13. ADRIA – ✕ 🛏 1, 2 cl., ▬ 2 cl., [2] Budapest - Split.

Q – June 20, 22, 27, 29, July **and** Aug. 3, 5, 7, 9, 11, 13, 15, 17, 19, 21, 23, 25, 27, 29, 31, Sept. 3, 5, 7, 12, 14. ADRIA – ✕ 🛏 1, 2 cl., ▬ 2 cl., [2] Split - Budapest.

R – June 27 - Aug. 30. ISTRIA – ▬ 2 cl., [2] Budapest - Rijeka. Conveys ▬ 2 cl., [2] Budapest - Koper.

S – June 28 - Aug. 31. ISTRIA – ▬ 2 cl., [2] Rijeka - Budapest. Conveys ▬ 2 cl., [2] Koper - Budapest.

k – Budapest **Kelenföld**.

MARSEILLE - NICE - MILANO 90

train type		IC				IC				IC				IC				IC				
train number		**631**				**745**				**635**				**681**				**639**				
notes	2	R ⁄		2	2	R ⁄		2	2	R ⁄		2	2	R ⁄		2	2	R| ⁄				
notes																						
Marseille St Charles .... d.	...	...	...	0557	...	...	...	0955	...	...	...	1157	...	...	...	1457	...	...	...	...	...	...
Toulon .... d.	...	...	...	0642	...	...	...	1041	...	...	...	1242	...	...	...	1543	...	...	...	...	...	...
Cannes .... d.	0710	...	...	0805	0911	...	...	1205	1311	...	...	1404	1510	...	...	1707	1711	...	...	...	...	...
Nice .... d.	0750	...	...	0838	0950	...	...	1237	1350	...	...	1437	1550	...	...	1738	1750	...	...	...	...	...
Monaco - Monte Carlo .... d.	0816	...	...	...	1016	...	...	...	1416	...	...	...	1616	...	...	...	1817	...	...	...	...	...
Ventimiglia 🏛 .... a.	0843	...	...	...	1043	...	...	...	1444	...	...	...	1643	...	...	...	1843	...	...	...	...	...
Ventimiglia 🏛 .... d.	...	0910	...	...	...	1059	...	...	...	1510	...	...	...	1659	...	...	...	1910	...	...	...	...
San Remo .... d.	...	0923	...	...	...	1116	...	...	...	1523	...	...	...	1716	...	...	...	1923	...	...	...	...
Genova Piazza Principe .... a.	...	1105	...	...	...	1305	...	...	...	1705	...	...	...	1908	...	...	...	2108	...	...	...	...
Milano Centrale .... a.	...	1255	...	...	...	1455	...	...	...	1855	...	...	...	2100	...	...	...	2253	...	...	...	...

train type	IC				IC	IC				IC				IC				IC				
train number	**633**				**659**	**659**				**637**				**641**				**675**				
notes	R ⁄	2	2		R ⁄	R ⁄	2	2		R ⁄	2	2		R ⁄	2	2	2	R ⁄	2	2	2	2
notes					Ⓐ	Ⓒ									⑤–⑦	⑤⑥			①–④	⑥	⑤	⑦**k**
Milano Centrale .... d.	0700	...	...	...	0910	0910	...	...	...	1110	...	...	...	1510	...	...	...	1705	...	...	...	...
Genova Piazza Principe .... d.	0858	...	...	...	1058	1058	...	...	...	1258	...	...	...	1658	...	...	...	1858	...	...	...	...
San Remo .... d.	1042	...	...	...	1243	1301	...	...	...	1442	...	...	...	1842	...	...	...	2045	...	...	...	...
Ventimiglia 🏛 .... a.	1059	...	...	...	1307	1322	...	...	...	1459	...	...	...	1904	...	...	...	2107	...	...	...	...
Ventimiglia 🏛 .... d.	...	1117	...	...	...	...	1348	...	...	...	1518	...	...	...	1917	...	1948	...	2129	2129	2218	2218
Monaco - Monte Carlo .... d.	...	1150	...	...	...	...	1421	...	...	...	1551	...	...	...	1950	...	2022	...	2208	2208	2251	2251
Nice .... a.	...	1213	1324	...	...	...	1444	1525	...	...	1614	1725	...	...	2013	2022	2045	...	2231	2230	2314	2314
Cannes .... a.	...	1254	1400	...	...	...	1525	1602	...	...	1655	1802	...	...	2053	2102	2125	...	2322	...	2356	2356
Toulon .... a.	...	...	1520	...	...	...	...	1722	...	...	...	1921	...	...	...	2219	...	...	...	...	...	...
Marseille St Charles .... a.	...	...	1603	...	...	...	...	1803	...	...	...	2003	...	...	...	2303	...	...	...	...	...	...

k – From June 29.

⁄ – Supplement payable.

PRAHA - BRATISLAVA - ZAGREB - SPLIT 92

train type			EC		EN			
train number			**277**		**1153**			
notes			🍷	2	R			
notes					**B**			
Praha hl. n. .... d.	...	...	0942	...	...	...	...	...
Kolín .... d.	...	...	1018	...	...	...	...	...
Pardubice .... d.	...	...	1040	...	...	...	...	...
Brno hl. n. .... d.	...	...	1222	...	...	...	...	...
Břeclav .... d.	...	...	1255	...	...	...	...	...
Bratislava hl. st. .... d.	...	...	1402	1435	...	...	...	...
Bratislava Nové Mesto .... d.	...	...	...	1442	1600	...	...	...
Bratislava Petržalka .... d.	...	...	...	...	1701	...	...	...
Wien Hbf .... d.	...	...	...	...	1905	...	...	...
Wien Meidling .... d.	...	...	...	...	1913	...	...	...
Wiener Neustadt Hbf .... d.	...	...	...	...	1951	...	...	...
Graz Hbf .... d.	...	...	...	...	2202	...	...	...
Spielfeld-Straß 🏛 .... d.	...	...	...	...	2245	...	...	...
Maribor .... d.	...	...	...	...	2304	...	...	...
Dobova 🏛 .... d.	...	...	...	...	0110	...	...	...
Zagreb Zapadni Kolodvor .... a.	...	...	...	...	0131	...	...	...
Knin .... a.	...	...	...	...	0730	...	...	...
Perković .... a.	...	...	...	...	0824	...	...	...
Split .... a.	...	...	...	...	1006	...	...	...

train type			EN		EC			
train number			**1152**		**278**			
notes			R	2	🍷			
notes			**S**					
Split .... d.	...	...	1722	...	...	...	...	...
Perković .... d.	...	...	1835	...	...	...	...	...
Knin .... d.	...	...	1952	...	...	...	...	...
Zagreb Zapadni Kolodvor .... d.	...	...	0151	...	...	...	...	...
Dobova 🏛 .... a.	...	...	0212	...	...	...	...	...
Maribor .... a.	...	...	0427	...	...	...	...	...
Spielfeld-Straß 🏛 .... a.	...	...	0502	...	...	...	...	...
Graz Hbf .... a.	...	...	0552	...	...	...	...	...
Wiener Neustadt Hbf .... a.	...	...	0810	...	...	...	...	...
Wien Meidling .... a.	...	...	0847	...	...	...	...	...
Wien Hbf .... a.	...	...	0854	...	...	...	...	...
Bratislava Petržalka .... d.	...	...	1026	...	...	...	...	...
Bratislava Nové Mesto .... a.	...	...	1049	1118	...	...	...	...
Bratislava hl. st. .... a.	...	...	...	1125	1158	...	...	...
Břeclav .... a.	...	...	...	...	1304	...	...	...
Brno hl. n. .... a.	...	...	...	...	1336	...	...	...
Pardubice .... a.	...	...	...	...	1511	...	...	...
Kolín .... a.	...	...	...	...	1533	...	...	...
Praha hl. n. .... a.	...	...	...	...	1615	...	...	...

B – ③⑤⑦ June 15 - Oct. 12. 🛏 1, 2 cl., ▬ 2 cl., [2] Bratislava - Split.

S – ①④⑥ June 16 - Oct. 13. 🛏 1, 2 cl., ▬ 2 cl., [2] Bratislava - Split.

96 WIEN - BUDAPEST - LVIV - KYIV

train type		IC		EC		EC	RJX	
train number		**34**		**143**	**28**	**149**	**165**	**10**
notes	**642**	[R]				**749**		
notes		**A**		**B**		**C**		**D**
Wien Hbf d.	...	...	...	1042	...	1642	1842	...
Budapest Nyugati d.	...	0720	...	|	...	|	|	...
Budapest Keleti d.	...	|	...	1340	...	1940	2119	2240
Szolnok d.	...	0839	...	1502	...	2106	...	0018
Debrecen d.	...	0957	...	1634	...	2225	...	0159
Nyíregyháza d.	0432	1031	...	1715	...	2257	...	0240
Záhony 🏛 d.	0632	1240	...	1940	...	0108	...	0440
Chop 🏛 a.	0753	1358	...	2058	2238	0227	...	0558
Mukachevo a.	0932	1538	...	...	2330	0616	...	0900
Lviv a.	...	...	...	...	0308	0959	...	1228
Kyiv a.	...	...	...	...	1001	1641	...	1911

train type		RJX	EC		EC	IC		IC
train number	**9**	**162**	**749**		**146**	**33**		**31**
notes			**140**	**27**		[R]		[R]
notes	**D**		**E**		**B**	**A**		**A**
Kyiv d.	1016	...	1323	1957	...	...	...	...
Lviv d.	1701	...	2008	0317	...	...	...	...
Mukachevo d.	2028	...	2359	0701	...	1022	...	1630
Chop 🏛 d.	2332	...	0329	0750	0901	1202	...	1832
Záhony 🏛 a.	2250	...	0248	...	0820	1120	...	1750
Nyíregyháza a.	0110	...	0456	...	1025	1327	...	1927
Debrecen a.	0206	...	0529	...	1106	1402	...	2002
Szolnok a.	0347	...	0652	...	1257	1519	...	2119
Budapest Keleti a.	0600	0640	0820	...	1420	|	...	|
Budapest Nyugati a.	...	|	|	...	|	1639	...	2239
Wien Hbf a.	...	0918	1120	...	1720	...	...	...

A – LATORCA – [12] Budapest - Záhony - Chop - Mukachevo and v.v.
B – TISZA – [12] ✕ Wien - Budapest - Záhony - Chop and v.v.
C – HORTOBÁGY – 🛏 1, 2 cl. Wien (**149**) - Budapest - Záhony - Chop (**749**) - Lviv - Kyiv. [12] Wien - Záhony.
D – TRANSCARPATHIA – 🛏 2 cl. Budapest - Záhony - Chop - Lviv - Kyiv and v.v.
E – HORTOBÁGY – 🛏 1, 2 cl. Kyiv (**749**) - Lviv - Chop (**140**) - Záhony - Budapest - Wien. [12] Záhony - Wien.

99 WARSZAWA and KRAKÓW - PRAHA, WIEN, MÜNCHEN and BUDAPEST

train type	LE	IC	LE	EC	EC	IC¶	EC	IC¶	IC¶	IC¶	IC¶	IC¶	EC	TLK¶	IC¶	EC	IC	EN	EN	EN	♥	
train number	**410**	**101**	**412**	**103**	**203**	**116**	**105**	**114**	**114**	**131**	**131**	**114**	**107**	**212**	**112**	**109**	**110**	**407**	**407**	**407**	**1022**	
train number	🍸	✕	🍸	✕	✕	✕	✕	✕	**131**	✕	**114**	✕			✕	✕	✕	**409**	**457**	**442**		
notes	④–②	⊡	①⑥	⊡	⊡	⊡	⊡	⊡	⊡	⊡	⊡	⊡	⊡	⊡	⊡	⊡	⊡		**477**			
notes																**S**		**E**	**F**	**G**	**H**	
Gdynia Główny d.	...	...	...	...	...	...	...	...	...	...	...	...	...	...	...	...	...	...	...	...	...	...
Gdańsk Główny d.	...	...	...	...	...	...	...	...	...	...	...	...	...	...	...	...	...	...	...	...	...	...
Warszawa Wschodnia d.	...	...	...	...	...	0509	0559	...	...	0858	0858	...	...	...	1314	1344	1709	1944	1944	1944	...	...
Warszawa Centralna d.	...	...	...	...	...	0522	0609	...	...	0905	0905	...	...	...	1334	1405	1735	2000	2000	2000	...	...
Przemyśl d.	...	...	...	...	...	|	|	0815	0815	|	|	...	1116	...	|	|	|	|	|	|	2210	...
Rzeszów d.	...	...	...	...	...	|	|	0920	0920	|	|	...	1219	...	|	|	|	|	|	|	2304	...
Kraków Główny d.	0011	...	0409	0627	...	|	|	1110	1110	|	|	...	1359	1537	|	|	|	2243	2243	2243	0058	...
Katowice d.	|	0459	|	|	...	0818	0852	|	|	1146	1146	...	|	|	1624	1701	2022	|	|	|	|	...
Wrocław d.	|	|	|	|	0629	|	|	|	|	|	|	...	|	|	|	|	|	|	|	|	|	...
Chałupki 🏛 d.	|	0624	|	|	0816	0937	1023	|	|	|	|	...	1624	|	1742	1823	2143	|	|	|	|	...
Bohumín 🏛 a.	0233	0630	0624	0830	0822	0943	1030	1313	1313	1322	1322	←	1630	1740	1748	1830	2149	0102	0102	0102	|	...
Bohumín 🏛 d.	0349	0642	0649	0842	0842	1004	1042	→	1342	1342	1404	1404	1642	1804	1804	1842	2150	0145	0145	0327	|	...
Ostrava hl. n. a.	0356	0649	0658	0849	0849	1011	1049	...	1349	1349	1411	1411	1649	1811	1811	1849	2204	0152	0152	0334	0324	...
Přerov a.	0457	0746	0759	0946	0946	|	1146	...	1446	1446	|	|	1746	|	|	1946	...	|	|	|	|	...
Olomouc a.	0511	|	0813	|	|	1114	|	...	|	|	1514	1514	|	1914	1914	|	...	|	|	0438	0426	...
Pardubice a.	0627	|	0927	|	|	1235	|	...	|	|	1635	1635	|	2035	2035	|	...	|	|	0608	0541	...
Praha hl. n. a.	0727	|	1027	|	|	1336	|	...	|	|	1736	1736	|	2136	2136	|	...	|	|	0751	0639	...
Břeclav a.	...	0849	...	1049	1049	...	1249	...	1549	1549	...	...	1849	...	...	2049	...	0338	0338	...	...	...
Wien Hbf a.	...	0949	...	1149	1149	...	1349	...	|	|	...	...	1949	...	...	2149	...	0525	|	...	...	...
Graz a.	...	...	...	...	...	...	...	...	|	|	...	...	2233	...	...	0033x	...	|	|	...	...	...
Linz Hbf a.	...	...	...	...	...	...	...	...	|	|	...	...	...	...	...	...	...	0713	|	...	...	...
Salzburg Hbf 🏛 a.	...	...	...	...	...	...	...	...	|	|	...	...	...	...	...	...	...	0830	|	...	...	...
München Hbf a.	...	...	...	...	...	...	...	...	|	|	...	...	...	...	...	...	...	1024	|	...	...	...
Kúty 🏛 a.	...	...	...	...	...	...	...	...	1611	1611	...	...	...	...	...	...	...	...	0511	...	...	...
Bratislava hl. st. a.	...	...	...	...	...	...	...	...	1705	1705	...	...	...	...	...	...	...	...	0602	...	...	...
Štúrovo 🏛 △ a.	...	...	...	...	...	...	...	...	1834	1834	...	...	...	...	...	...	...	...	0724	...	...	...
Budapest Nyugati a.	...	...	...	...	...	...	...	...	1949	1949	...	...	...	...	...	...	...	...	0829	...	...	...

train type	IC	EC	IC	TLK	EC	IC¶	IC¶	EC	EC	EC		IC¶	EC	EC	LE	EC	LE	♥	EN	EN	EN	
train number	**111**	**108**	**113**	**113**	**106**	**115**	**115**	**130**	**130**	**104**		**117**	**102**	**202**	**411**	**100**	**413**	**1023**	**443**	**406**	**476**	
train number	✕	✕	✕	**213**	✕	**130**	✕	✕	**115**	✕		🍸	✕		🍸		🍸		**406**	**408**	**456**	
notes	⊡	⊡	⊡	⊡	⊡	⊡	⊡	⊡	⊡	⊡		⊡	⊡	⊡	③–⑦	⊡	⑤⑦		**408**		**406**	
notes		**T**																**H**	**J**	**E**	**K**	
Budapest Nyugati d.	...	...	...	...	...	...	...	0812	0812	...	...	...	...	...	...	...	...	...	...	...	1930	...
Štúrovo 🏛 △ d.	...	...	...	...	...	...	...	0923	0923	...	...	...	...	...	...	...	...	...	...	...	2036	...
Bratislava hl. st. d.	...	...	...	...	...	...	...	1057	1057	...	...	...	...	...	...	...	...	...	...	...	2158	...
Kúty 🏛 d.	...	...	...	...	...	...	...	1149	1149	...	...	...	...	...	...	...	...	...	...	...	2249	...
München Hbf d.	...	...	...	...	...	...	...	|	|	...	...	...	...	...	...	...	...	...	...	1835	|	...
Salzburg Hbf 🏛 d.	...	...	...	...	...	...	...	|	|	...	...	...	...	...	...	...	...	...	...	2030	|	...
Linz Hbf d.	...	...	...	...	...	...	...	|	|	...	...	...	...	...	...	...	...	...	...	2146	|	...
Graz d.	...	0326z	...	...	0526	...	...	|	|	...	...	...	...	...	...	...	...	...	...	|	|	...
Wien Hbf d.	...	0610	...	...	0810	...	...	|	|	1410	...	...	1610	1610	...	1810	...	...	...	2319	|	...
Břeclav d.	...	0709	...	...	0909	...	...	1209	1209	1509	...	...	1709	1709	...	1909	...	...	...	0100	0100	...
Praha hl. n. d.	...	|	0622	0622	|	1022	1022	|	|	|	...	1422	|	|	1658	|	2058	2147	2216	|	|	...
Pardubice d.	...	|	0722	0722	|	1122	1122	|	|	|	...	1522	|	|	1759	|	2201	2250	2327	|	|	...
Olomouc d.	...	|	0844	0844	|	1244	1244	|	|	|	...	1644	|	|	1917	|	2331	0008	0059	|	|	...
Přerov d.	...	0808	|	|	1009	|	|	1309	1309	1609	...	|	1809	1809	1934	2009	0039	|	|	|	|	...
Ostrava hl. n. d.	0542	0905	0950	0950	1105	1350	1350	1405	1405	1705	...	1750	1905	1905	2038	2105	0052	0113	0210	0242	0242	...
Bohumín 🏛 a.	0556	0912	0956	0956	1112	1356	1356	1412	1412	1712	...	1756	1912	1912	2041	2112	0143	|	0218	0248	0248	...
Bohumín 🏛 d.	0613	0927	1009	1017	1127	1438	1445	1438	1445	1727	...	1809	1927	1935	|	2127	|	|	0405	0405	0405	...
Chałupki 🏛 a.	0619	0933	1015	|	1133	|	|	|	|	1733	...	1815	|	1941	|	2133	|	|	|	|	|	...
Wrocław a.	|	|	|	|	|	|	|	|	|	|	...	|	|	2124	|	|	|	|	|	|	|	...
Katowice a.	0746	1108	1143	|	|	1629	|	1629	|	1904	...	1950	|	...	|	2302	|	|	|	|	|	...
Kraków Główny a.	|	|	|	1216	1417	|	1700	|	1700	|	...	|	2125	...	2256	...	0346	0443	0620	0620	0620	...
Rzeszów a.	|	|	|	...	1545	|	1849	|	1849	|	...	|	...	...	...	...	...	0636	|	|	|	...
Przemyśl a.	|	|	|	...	1650	|	1956	|	1956	|	...	|	...	...	...	...	...	0735	|	|	|	...
Warszawa Centralna a.	1038	1355	1426	...	...	1916	...	1916	...	2151	...	2250	...	...	...	...	...	...	0908	0908	0908	...
Warszawa Wschodnia a.	1046	1416	1446	...	...	1926	...	1926	...	2201	...	2256	...	...	...	...	...	...	0921	0921	0921	...
Gdańsk Główny a.	...	...	...	...	...	...	...	...	...	...	...	...	...	...	...	...	...	...	...	...	...	...
Gdynia Główny a.	...	...	...	...	...	...	...	...	...	...	...	...	...	...	...	...	...	...	...	...	...	...

E – CHOPIN – 🛏 1, 2 cl., ▬ 2 cl. [2] Warszawa - München and v.v.
F – CHOPIN – 🛏 1, 2 cl., ▬ 2 cl., [2] Warszawa (**407**) - Kraków - Bohumín (**457**) - Břeclav (**477**) - Budapest.
G – CHOPIN – 🛏 1, 2 cl., [2] Warszawa (**407**) - Bohumín (**442**) - Praha.
H – 🛏 (4 berth), [2] 🍸 Praha - Przemyśl and v.v.
J – CHOPIN – 🛏 1, 2 cl., [2] Praha (**443**) - Bohumín (**406**) - Warszawa.
K – CHOPIN – 🛏 1, 2 cl., ▬ 2 cl., [2] Budapest (**476**) - Břeclav (**456**) - Bohumín (**406**) - Kraków - Warszawa.
S – SOBIESKI [12] ✕ Warszawa - Wien. Conveys on ②④⑤⑦ June 27 - Aug. 29 ▬ 2 cl. [2] (*EN* **1277**) Warszawa - Wien - Rijeka (Table **89**).
T – SOBIESKI [12] ✕ Wien - Warszawa. Conveys on ①③⑤⑦ June 29 - Aug. 31 ▬ 2 cl. [2] (*EN* **1276**) Rijeka - Wien - Warszawa (Table **89**).

x – ①③⑤⑥ June 28 - Aug. 30.
z – ①②④⑥ June 30 - Sept. 1.

△ – Routeing point for international tickets: Szob.
⊡ – Compulsory reservation and supplement payable in Poland.
¶ – Classified *EC* in Czech Republic and Hungary.
♥ – Operated by REGIOJET. Separate fares apply.
LE – Operated by LEO EXPRESS. Separate fares apply.

GREAT BRITAIN

Operators: Passenger services are provided by a number of private passenger train operating companies or, in certain cases, by the government run "Operator of Last Resort". Together these operate the **National Rail** (www.nationalrail.co.uk) network on lines owned by the British national railway infrastructure company **Network Rail**. The following Network Rail codes are used in the table headings to indicate the operators of trains in each table:

AW	Transport for Wales	GW	Great Western Railway	ME	Merseyrail	SW	South Western Railway
CH	Chiltern Railways	HT	Hull Trains	NT	Northern Rail	TL	Thameslink Railway
CS	Caledonian Sleeper	IL	Island Line	NY	North Yorkshire Moors Railway	TP	TransPennine Express
EM	East Midlands Railway	LD	East Coast Trains (Lumo)	SE	Southeastern	VT	Avanti West Coast
GC	Grand Central Railway	LE	Greater Anglia	SN	Southern	WR	West Coast Railways
GN	Great Northern	LM	West Midlands Railway	SR	ScotRail	XC	Arriva Cross Country
GR	London North Eastern Railway	LM	London Northwestern Railway				

Timings: Except where indicated otherwise, timings are valid **May 18 - December 13, 2025.**
As service patterns at weekends (especially on ⑦) usually differ greatly from those applying on Mondays to Fridays, the timings in most tables are grouped by days of operation: Ⓐ = Mondays to Fridays; ⚒ = Mondays to Saturdays; ⑥ = Saturdays; ⑦ = Sundays. Track engineering work, affecting journey times, frequently takes place at weekends, so it is advisable to confirm your journey details locally if planning to travel in the period between the late evening of ⑤ and the late afternoon of ⑦. Confirm timings, too, if you intend travelling on public holidays (see page 4) as there may be alterations to services at these times. Suburban and commuter services are the most likely to be affected; the majority of long-distance and cross-country trains marked Ⓐ and ⚒ run as normal on these dates. No trains (except limited Gatwick and Heathrow Express services) run on **Dec. 25**, with only a limited service on certain routes on **Dec. 26**. In Scotland only trains between Edinburgh/Glasgow and England run on **Jan. 1**.

Services: Unless indicated otherwise (by '2' in the train column or '2nd class' in the table heading), trains convey both **first** (1st) and **standard** (2nd) classes of seated accommodation. Light refreshments (snacks, hot and cold drinks) are available from a **buffet car** or a **mobile trolley service** on board those trains marked 🍸 and ✕: the latter also convey a **restaurant car** or serve meals to passengers at their seats (this service is in some cases available to first-class ticket holders only). Note that catering facilities may not be available for the whole of a train's journey. **Sleeping-cars** (🛏) generally have one berth per compartment in first class and two in standard class.

Reservations: Seats on most long-distance trains and berths in sleeping-cars can be reserved in advance when purchasing travel tickets at railway stations or directly from train operating companies (quote the departure time of the train and your destination). Seat reservation is normally free of charge.

LONDON AIRPORT LINKS 100

Gatwick ✈

GATWICK EXPRESS: Daily non-stop rail service from/to **London Victoria**. Journey time: 30 minutes (30–40 minutes on ⑦).
From **London Victoria**: On ⚒ at 0513 Ⓐ, 0529 ⑥, 0559 and every 30 minutes until 2259; on ⑦ at 0500 and every 30 minutes until 0830, 0859 and every 30 minutes until 2159, 2229.
From **Gatwick Airport**: On ⚒ 0540, 0610 and every 30 minutes until 2310; on ⑦ at 0550, 0620, 0650, 0720, 0750, 0820, 0845, 0915 and every 30 minutes until 2315.
Other rail services via Gatwick Airport: London Victoria - Eastbourne Table **102**; Bedford - Brighton Table **103**; London Victoria - Brighton Table **103**; Reading - Gatwick Airport Table **114a**.

Heathrow ✈

HEATHROW EXPRESS: Daily non-stop rail service **London** Paddington - **Heathrow** Terminal 5 and v.v. Journey times: **Heathrow** Central ♣, 15 minutes, **Heathrow** Terminal 5, 21 minutes.
From **London** Paddington: 0510, 0525 and every 15 minutes until 2325.
From **Heathrow** Terminal 5 (5 minutes later from **Heathrow** Central): 0510 and every 15 minutes until 2240, 2255⚒, 2257⑦, 2310⚒, 2312⑦, 2325.

ELIZABETH LINE: Daily, frequent, rail services **London** Liverpool Street - Farringdon - **London** Paddington - **Heathrow** Terminals 4/5 and v.v.
Journey times from **London** Paddington: **Heathrow** Central ♣, 24 minutes, **Heathrow** Terminal 4/5, 30 minutes.

♣ – **Heathrow** Central serves Terminals 2 and 3. A free rail transfer service operates every 15 minutes **Heathrow** Central - **Heathrow** Terminal 5 and v.v.

PICCADILLY LINE: London Underground service between **Kings Cross St Pancras** and all **Heathrow** terminals via Central London. Journey time: 50–58 minutes.
Frequent trains (every 4–10 minutes) 0530⚒/0730⑦ - 2300⚒/2330⑦.

RAILAIR LINK 🚌 **Reading** railway station - **Heathrow Airport** (Service **RA1**).
From **Reading**: Services call at Heathrow Terminal 5 (± 51 minutes), Heathrow Terminal 2 (± 61 minutes), Heathrow Terminal 3 (± 70 minutes):
On Ⓐ at 0239, 0309, 0349, 0409, 0454, 0531, 0601, 0629, 0649, 0709, 0722, 0742, 0802, 0821, 0841, 0901, 0921, 0949 and every 20 minutes until 1509, 1525, 1545, 1605, 1625, 1642, 1702, 1722, 1745, 1810, 1835, 1909, 1939, 2011, 2041, 2109, 2209, 2309; on ⑥ at 0239, 0309, 0350, 0409, 0456, 0530, 0559, 0629, 0659, 0729, 0751, 0811, 0830 and every 20 minutes until 1150, 1201, 1228 and every 20 minutes until 1648, 1726, 1757, 1827, 1858, 1930, 2000, 2032, 2107, 2207, 2307; on ⑦ at 0239, 0309, 0352, 0409, 0452, 0527 and every 30 minutes until 2109, 2209, 2309.
From **Heathrow Airport** Terminal 3: Services call at Heathrow Terminal 2 (± 2 minutes), Heathrow Terminal 5 (± 18 minutes) and Reading Railway Station (± 60 minutes).
On ⚒ at 0017, 0407, 0437, 0507, 0537, 0607, 0637, 0707, 0737, 0807, 0837, 0900 and every 20 minutes until 1740Ⓐ, 1800Ⓐ, 1820Ⓐ, 1840Ⓐ, 1905, 1928Ⓐ, 1937⑥, 1947Ⓐ, 2007⑥, 2017Ⓐ, 2037⑥, 2047Ⓐ, 2107⑥, 2117Ⓐ, 2137⑥, 2147Ⓐ, 2217, 2317; on ⑦ at 0407 and every 30 minutes until 2317.

RAILAIR LINK 🚌 **Guildford** rail station - **Woking** rail station - **Heathrow Airport** (Service **RA2**).
From **Guildford**: Services call at Woking (± 29 minutes later), Heathrow Terminal 5 (± 59 minutes) and Heathrow Central Bus Station (± 80 minutes).
On Ⓐ at 0222, 0327, 0417, 0516, 0602, 0659, 0759, 0909, 1010 and hourly until 1410, 1459, 1559, 1659, 1808, 1922, 2054, 2214, 2254; on Ⓒ at 0227, 0322, 0422, 0515, 0604, 0704, 0804, 0910 and hourly until 1410, 1504, 1604, 1704, 1806, 1915, 2053, 2214, 2254. Additional 🚌 on Ⓐ at from Woking at 0320, 0415, 0515, 0607, 0703, 0803, 0903, 1012 and hourly until 1412, 1503, 1603, 1703, 1805, 1919, 2022, 2202; on Ⓒ at 0325, 0420, 0515, 0617, 0709, 0807, 0907, 1012 and hourly until 1412, 1507, 1607, 1707, 1809, 1910, 2021, 2202.

From **Heathrow** Central Bus Station: Services call at Heathrow Terminal 5 (± 17 minutes), Woking (± 53 minutes), and Guildford (± 81 minutes).
On Ⓐ at 0425, 0520, 0615, 0725, 0817, 0915 and hourly until 1815, 1917, 2017, 2122, 2222, 2303, 2343; on Ⓒ at 0420, 0515, 0615, 0716, 0815 and hourly until 1815, 1917, 2023, 2123, 2223, 2303, 2343. Additonal 🚌 terminating at Woking at 0350, 0455, 0545, 0646, 0746, 0845 and hourly until 1845, 1954, 2053.

Luton ✈

Thameslink Railway services Brighton - Gatwick Airport - London St Pancras - Luton Airport Parkway ◧ - Luton - Bedford: Table **103**.
East Midlands Trains services London St Pancras - Luton Airport Parkway ◧ - Luton - Leicester - Nottingham/Derby/Sheffield: Table **170**.
◧ – A frequent DART (Direct Air-Rail Transit) automated guided people mover is in operation between Luton Airport Parkway station and the airport terminal.

🚌 service **Milton Keynes** - **Luton Airport** and v.v. (Stagecoach route **MK1**. Journey ± 50 minutes); for connections from/to **Birmingham**, **Liverpool** and **Manchester** (Tables **151/2/4**).
From **Milton Keynes** railway station: Daily at 0530⚒, 0630, 0730, 0900 and hourly until 1500, 1610 and hourly until 2110, 2210⚒.
From **Luton Airport**: Daily at 0630⚒, 0730, 0830, 0940‡, 1040 and hourly until 1640, 1750, 1855, 1955, 2055⚒. ‡ – Runs Ⓒ and Ⓐ on school days.

Stansted ✈

STANSTED EXPRESS: Daily rail service from/to **London** Liverpool St. Journey time ± 45 minutes.
From **London** Liverpool Street: on Ⓐ at 0440, 0510, 0525, 0540, 0555, 0610, 0625, 0640, 0655, 0710, 0723, 0740, 0755, 0810 and every 15 minutes until 1640, 1654, 1710, 1724, 1740, 1754, 1810, 1824, 1840, 1854, 1910 and every 15 minutes until 2255, 2325; on Ⓒ at 0340⑥, 0410, 0440, 0510, 0525⑥, 0540, 0555⑥, 0610 and every 15 minutes until 2255, 2325.
From **Stansted Airport**: on Ⓐ at 0030, 0600, 0615, 0628, 0645, 0658, 0715, 0728, 0743, 0758, 0815 and every 15 minutes until 2300, 2314, 2330, 2345, 2359; on Ⓒ at 0030, 0530, 0600, 0615⑥, 0630, 0645⑥, 0700, 0715 and every 15 minutes until 2300, 2314, 2330, 2345, 2359.
Most trains call at **Tottenham Hale** for London Underground (Victoria Line) connections to/from Kings Cross, St Pancras, Euston, and Victoria stations.
For *Cross Country* and *Greater Anglia* services to/from Cambridge, Norwich, Peterborough, Leicester and Birmingham see Tables **207** and **208**.

City ✈

DOCKLANDS LIGHT RAILWAY from/to **Bank** (interchange with London Underground: Central, Circle, District, Northern, and Waterloo & City Lines).
Trains run every 7–10 minutes 0530 - 0030 on ⚒, 0700 - 2330 on ⑦. Journey time: ± 22 minutes.

Inter-Airport 🚌 links

Operator: National Express ✆ 08717 81 81 81. www.nationalexpress.com

Heathrow Central - **Gatwick** North Terminal. Journey time: 65–85 minutes
0040, 0250, 0305, 0310, 0400 then 2–3 services per hour until 2000, 2010, 2125, 2240.

Gatwick North Terminal - **Heathrow** Central.
0350, 0455Ⓐ, 0510Ⓒ, 0550Ⓐ, 0605Ⓒ, 0625 then 2–3 services per hour until 2305, 2345.

Heathrow Central - **Luton**. Journey time: 50–85 minutes
0030, 0640Ⓐ, 0655Ⓒ, 0730, 0820, 0830, 0930, 1005, 1050, 1150, 1220, 1340, 1400, 1500, 1615, 1630, 1730, 1830, 1845, 2000, 2045, 2130, 2230, 2300.

Luton - **Heathrow** Central.
0150, 0250, 0350, 0435Ⓐ, 0500Ⓒ, 0505, 0525, 0600Ⓐ, 0620, 0650Ⓒ, 0810, 0830Ⓐ, 0845Ⓒ, 0940, 1040, 1125, 1220, 1245, 1255, 1525, 1540Ⓒ, 1605Ⓐ, 1610Ⓒ, 1705, 1710Ⓒ, 1720Ⓐ, 1855Ⓒ, 1900, 1905Ⓐ.

Heathrow Central - **Stansted**. Journey time: 100 minutes
0735, 0915, 1105, 1305, 1430, 1715, 1920, 2120, 2330.

Stansted - **Heathrow** Central.
0230, 0445, 0640Ⓐ, 0700Ⓒ, 0900, 1020, 1315, 1455, 1715, 1915Ⓒ, 1925Ⓐ.

Stansted - **Luton**. Journey time: 1½ hours
0045, 0100, 0700, 0915, 1130, 1400, 1700, 1930, 2200.

Luton - **Stansted**.
0255, 0610, 0825Ⓐ, 0835Ⓒ, 1025Ⓐ, 1045Ⓒ, 1355, 1600Ⓐ, 1620Ⓒ, 1855, 2105, 2120.

Gatwick North Terminal - **Luton**. Journey time: 2½ hours
0650Ⓐ, 0705Ⓒ, 0910Ⓐ, 0925Ⓒ, 1055, 1335, 1605, 1655Ⓐ, 1705Ⓒ, 1955, 2135, 2305.

Luton - **Gatwick** North Terminal.
0150, 0435Ⓐ, 0500Ⓒ, 0600Ⓐ, 0620Ⓒ, 0810, 1125, 1220, 1255Ⓐ, 1525Ⓐ, 1540Ⓒ, 1710Ⓒ, 1720Ⓐ, 1900.

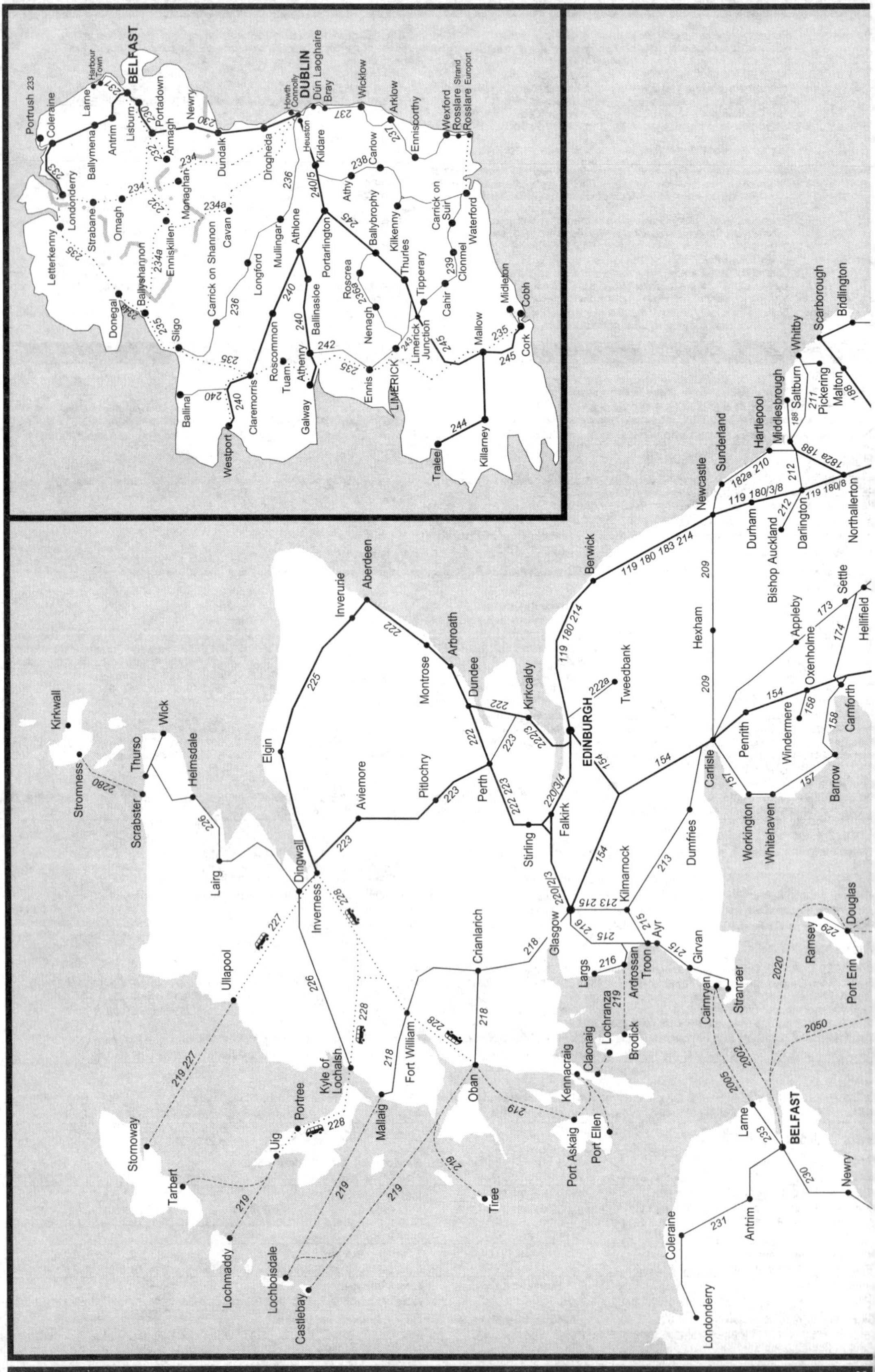
BELFAST
Portrush 233
Coleraine
Larne
Harbour Town
Ballymena
Antrim
Lisburn
Portadown
Newry
Armagh
Londonderry
Strabane
Omagh
Monaghan
Dundalk
Drogheda
Howth
Connolly
DUBLIN
Dún Laoghaire
Bray
Heuston
Wicklow
Arklow
Enniscorthy
Wexford
Rosslare Strand
Rosslare Europort
Kildare
Athy
Carlow
Letterkenny
Enniskillen
Cavan
Mullingar
Athlone
Portarlington
Ballybrophy
Kilkenny
Carrick on Suir
Waterford
Donegal
Ballyshannon
Carrick on Shannon
Longford
Roscrea
Thurles
Tipperary
Clonmel
Cahir
Sligo
Roscommon
Ballinasloe
Nenagh
Limerick Junction
Mallow
Midleton
Cobh
Cork
Ballina
Claremorris
Tuam
Athenry
Galway
Ennis
LIMERICK
Westport
Tralee
Killarney
Kirkwall
Stromness
Thurso
Wick
Scrabster
Helmsdale
Lairg
Elgin
Inverurie
Aberdeen
Arbroath
Montrose
Dundee
Kirkcaldy
Aviemore
Pitlochry
Perth
Stirling
Falkirk
EDINBURGH
Tweedbank
Berwick
Dingwall
Inverness
Ullapool
Stornoway
Kyle of Lochalsh
Portree
Uig
Tarbert
Lochmaddy
Lochboisdale
Castlebay
Mallaig
Fort William
Crianlarich
Oban
Tiree
Glasgow
Kilmarnock
Largs
Ardrossan
Troon
Ayr
Girvan
Lochranza
Brodick
Claonaig
Kennacraig
Port Askaig
Port Ellen
Cairnryan
Stranraer
Dumfries
Carlisle
Hexham
Newcastle
Sunderland
Hartlepool
Middlesbrough
Saltburn
Whitby
Scarborough
Pickering
Malton
Bridlington
Durham
Bishop Auckland
Darlington
Northallerton
Penrith
Appleby
Settle
Hellifield
Oxenholme
Windermere
Carnforth
Workington
Whitehaven
Barrow
Douglas
Ramsey
Port Erin
Larne
BELFAST
Newry
Antrim
Coleraine
Londonderry
119 180 183 214
119 180/214
119 180/3/8
182a 210
182a 188
212
209
154
157
158
173
174
211
222
222a
223
225
226
227
228
2280
219
219 227
218
216
215
213 215
220/2/3
220/3/4
222 223
2020
2050
2002
2005
229
230
231
233
234
234a
235
236
237
238
239
240
240/5
242
243
244
245

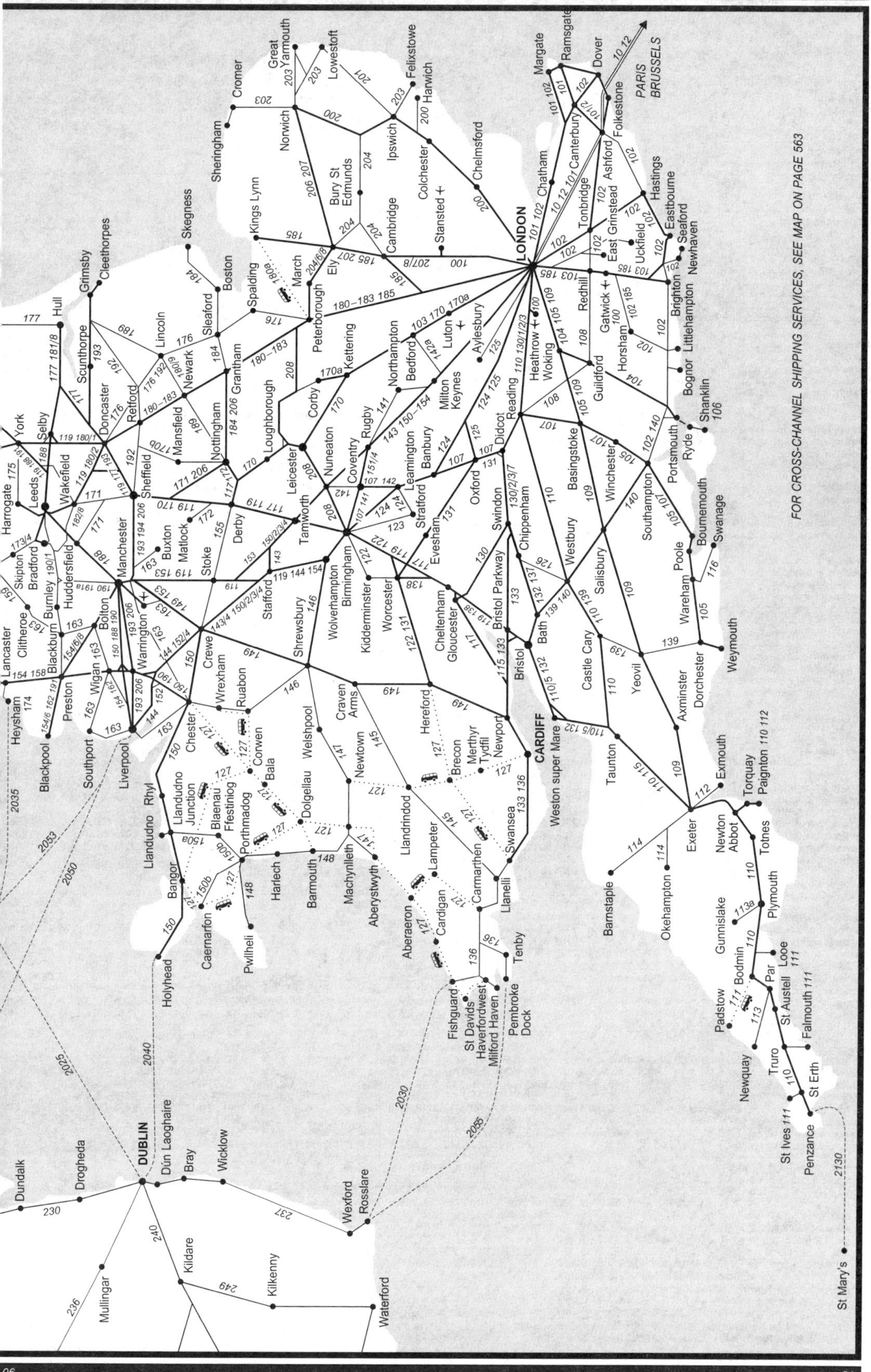
LONDON
CARDIFF
DUBLIN
PARIS
BRUSSELS
FOR CROSS-CHANNEL SHIPPING SERVICES, SEE MAP ON PAGE 563
Hull
York
Selby
Leeds
Harrogate
Skipton
Bradford
Wakefield
Huddersfield
Burnley
Clitheroe
Lancaster
Heysham
Blackpool
Preston
Blackburn
Bolton
Wigan
Southport
Liverpool
Warrington
Manchester
Buxton
Sheffield
Doncaster
Scunthorpe
Grimsby
Cleethorpes
Retford
Lincoln
Newark
Mansfield
Nottingham
Derby
Matlock
Stoke
Crewe
Chester
Wrexham
Ruabon
Shrewsbury
Stafford
Wolverhampton
Birmingham
Tamworth
Nuneaton
Leicester
Loughborough
Grantham
Sleaford
Boston
Skegness
Spalding
Peterborough
March
Ely
Kings Lynn
Sheringham
Cromer
Norwich
Great Yarmouth
Lowestoft
Bury St Edmunds
Ipswich
Felixstowe
Harwich
Colchester
Chelmsford
Cambridge
Stansted
Kettering
Corby
Northampton
Bedford
Luton
Milton Keynes
Aylesbury
Rugby
Coventry
Leamington
Banbury
Stratford
Evesham
Worcester
Kidderminster
Cheltenham
Gloucester
Hereford
Oxford
Didcot
Reading
Heathrow
Woking
Guildford
Swindon
Chippenham
Bath
Bristol
Bristol Parkway
Westbury
Salisbury
Basingstoke
Winchester
Southampton
Portsmouth
Ryde
Shanklin
Bournemouth
Poole
Swanage
Wareham
Weymouth
Dorchester
Yeovil
Castle Cary
Axminster
Taunton
Weston super Mare
Exeter
Exmouth
Barnstaple
Okehampton
Newton Abbot
Torquay
Paignton
Totnes
Plymouth
Gunnislake
Bodmin
Looe
Par
Padstow
Newquay
St Austell
Falmouth
Truro
St Erth
St Ives
Penzance
St Mary's
Chatham
Margate
Ramsgate
Canterbury
Dover
Folkestone
Ashford
Tonbridge
Hastings
Eastbourne
Seaford
Newhaven
Uckfield
East Grinstead
Redhill
Gatwick
Horsham
Brighton
Littlehampton
Bognor
Newport
Swansea
Llanelli
Carmarthen
Tenby
Pembroke Dock
Milford Haven
Haverfordwest
St Davids
Fishguard
Cardigan
Aberaeron
Lampeter
Llandrindod
Brecon
Merthyr Tydfil
Craven Arms
Newtown
Welshpool
Machynlleth
Aberystwyth
Barmouth
Dolgellau
Bala
Corwen
Harlech
Porthmadog
Pwllheli
Blaenau Ffestiniog
Llandudno Junction
Llandudno
Rhyl
Bangor
Caernarfon
Holyhead
Dundalk
Drogheda
Dún Laoghaire
Bray
Wicklow
Wexford
Rosslare
Kildare
Kilkenny
Waterford
Mullingar

High-speed supplement payable. For slower services see Table **102**

101 High-speed services LONDON - MARGATE, RAMSGATE and DOVER

2nd class SE

Via Faversham

km		Ⓐ	Ⓐ a	Ⓐ	Ⓐ	Ⓐ	Ⓐ	Ⓐ	Ⓐ	Ⓐ		Ⓐ	Ⓐ	Ⓐ	Ⓐ	Ⓐ	Ⓐ	Ⓐ n	Ⓐ	Ⓐ	Ⓐ	Ⓐ	Ⓐ	Ⓐ	Ⓐ
0	**London** St Pancras .... d.		...	0620	0720	0755	0820	0855	0920	0950		1350	1420	1450	1520	1550	1620	1650	1725	1755	1825	1855	1920	1950	2020
9	Stratford International ...... d.		...	0627	0727	0802	0827	0902	0927	0957		1357	1427	1457	1527	1557	1627	1657	1732	1802	1832	1902	1927	1957	2027
35	Ebbsfleet International .... d.		...	0639	0739	0817	0839	0916	0939	1009	and at	1409	1439	1509	1539	1609	1639	1709	1745	1815	1845	1915	1939	2009	2039
52	Rochester .... d.		...	0657	0757	0837	0857	0935	0957	1027	the same	1427	1457	1527	1557	1627	1657	1728	1806	1836	1906	1936	1957	2027	2057
54	Chatham .... d.		...	0701	0801	0841	0901	0939	1001	1031	minutes	1431	1501	1531	1601	1631	1701	1731	1810	1840	1910	1940	2001	2031	2101
70	Sittingbourne .... d.		*0607*	0718	0819	0858	0919	0956	1019	1048	past each	1448	1519	1548	1619	1648	1719	1750	1827	1857	1927	1958	2019	2048	2119
83	Faversham .... d.		0622	0727	0831	0907	0931	1005	1031	1057	hour until	1457	1531	1557	1630	1657	1730	1802	1836	1906	1936	2008	2031	2057	2131
100	Herne Bay .... d.		0638	...	0846	...	0946	...	1046	...		...	1546	...	*1651*	*1721*	*1751*	...	1851	1921	1951	...	2046	...	2146
118	**Margate** .... d.		0654	...	0900	...	1000	...	1100	...		...	1600	...	*1707*	*1737*	*1807*	...	1905	1936	2005	...	2100	...	2200
126	**Ramsgate** .... a.		0707	...	0911	...	1011	...	1111	...		...	1612	...	*1720*	*1753*	*1820*	...	1917	...	2017	...	2111	...	2211

	Ⓐ	Ⓐ A	Ⓐ	Ⓐ B	⑥	⑥	⑥	⑥	⑥	⑥		⑥	⑥	⑥	⑦	⑦	⑦	⑦	⑦	⑦		⑦	⑦	⑦
London St Pancras ....d.	2120	2220	2320	2350		...	...	...	0720	0820		2220	2320	2350		...	...	0820	0920	1020		2120	2220	2320
Stratford International......d.	2127	2227	2327	2357		...	...	...	0727	0827		2227	2327	2357		...	...	0827	0927	1027		2127	2227	2327
Ebbsfleet International ....d.	2139	2239	2339	0009		...	...	...	0739	0839	and at	2239	2339	0009		...	...	0839	0939	1039	and at	2139	2239	2339
Rochester.........................d.	2157	2257	2357	0027		...	*0640*	0720	0757	0857	the same	2257	2357	0027		...	0820	0857	0957	1057	the same	2157	2257	2357
Chatham...........................d.	2201	2301	0001	0031		...	*0644*	0723	0801	0901	minutes	2301	0001	0031		...	0823	0901	1001	1101	minutes	2201	2301	0001
Sittingbourne ....d.	2219	2319	0019	0048s		*0615*	*0715*	0741	0819	0919	past each	2319	0019	0049		0739	0842	0918	1018	1118	past each	2218	2318	0018
Faversham ....d.	2231	2330	0030	0059		0630	0730	0750	0831	0931	hour until	2330	0030	0058		0750	0852	0927	1027	1127	hour until	2227	2327	0027
Herne Bay ....d.	2246	*0006*	...	*0120*s		0647	0747	0806	0846	0946		2346	*0106*	*0139*s		0806	0909	0942	1042	1142		2242	*0009*	...
Margate ....d.	2300	*0022*	...	*0136*s		0703	0803	0822	0900	1000		2359	*0122*	*0155*s		0822	0925	0957	1057	1157		2257	*0025*	...
Ramsgate ....a.	2311	*0035*	...	*0149*		0716	0816	0835	0911	1011		0011	*0135*	*0209*		0835	0938	1009	1110	1210		2309	*0038*	...

	Ⓐ	Ⓐ	Ⓐ	Ⓐ	Ⓐ	Ⓐ	Ⓐ	Ⓐ	Ⓐ	Ⓐ	Ⓐ	Ⓐ	Ⓐ	Ⓐ		Ⓐ	Ⓐ	Ⓐ	Ⓐ	Ⓐ	Ⓐ	Ⓐ	Ⓐ	Ⓐ	①–④
Ramsgate ....d.		...	*0422*	...	*0522*	*0602*	*0620*	*0712*	*0740*	*0812*	*0843*	0921	...	1021		...	1621	...	*1712*	*1812*	1921	2021	2121	2205	2253
Margate ....d.		...	*0434*	0522	*0534*	0627	0700	*0724*	*0752*	*0824*	*0855*	0932	...	1032		...	1632	...	*1724*	*1824*	1932	2032	2132	2217	2305
Herne Bay ....d.		...	*0449*	0538	*0549*	0644	0714	*0740*	*0808*	*0840*	*0911*	0946	...	1046	and at	...	1646	...	*1739*	*1840*	1946	2046	2146	2232	2320
Faversham ....d.		0457	0525	0556	0628	0658	0728	0800	0829	0900	0932	1000	1032	1100	the same	1632	1700	1728	1759	1900	2000	2100	2200	2252	2337
Sittingbourne ....d.		0506	0534	0605	0636	0706	0736	0811	0840	0910	0940	1010	1040	1110	minutes	1640	1710	1740	1810	1910	2010	2110	2210	2303	2347
Chatham............................d.		0524	0554	0624	0654	0724	0754	0828	0858	0928	0958	1028	1058	1128	past each	1659	1728	1758	1828	1928	2028	2128	2228	2324	...
Rochester...........................d.		0528	0557	0627	0657	0727	0757	0832	0902	0932	1002	1032	1102	1132	hour until	1702	1732	1802	1832	1932	2032	2132	2232	2327	...
Ebbsfleet International ....a.		0546	0614	0644	0715	0744	0816	0849	0919	0949	1019	1049	1119	1149		1719	1749	1819	1849	1949	2049	2149	2249	...	...
Stratford International......a.		0557	0626	0656	0727	0757	0829	0900	0930	1000	1030	1100	1130	1200		1730	1800	1830	1900	2002	2100	2200	2300	...	...
London St Pancras ....a.		0606	0634	0704	0735	0805	0837	0910	0938	1008	1038	1110	1138	1208		1738	1810	1838	1908	2010	2108	2208	2308	...	...

	⑤	⑥	⑥	⑥	⑥		⑥	⑥	⑥	⑥	⑥	⑦	⑦	⑦	⑦	⑦		⑦	⑦		⑦	⑦	⑦
Ramsgate ....d.	2316		*0439*	...	0621		2021	2121	2153	2218	2316		...	*0650*	0818	0921		1421	1521		2121	*2153*	2253
Margate ....d.	2335c		*0451*	...	0632		2032	2132	2205	2230	2335c		...	*0702*	0829	0932		1432	1532		2132	*2205*	2305
Herne Bay ....d.	2350		*0507*	...	0646	and at	2046	2146	2220	2245	2350		...	*0717*	0843	0946	and at	1446	1546	and at	2146	*2220*	2320
Faversham ....d.	0007		0532	0600	0700	the same	2100	2200	2237	2302	0007		0700	0800	0858	1000	the same	1500	1600	the same	2200	2244	2344c
Sittingbourne ....d.	0018		0540	0610	0710	minutes	2110	2210	2245	2313	0018		0710	0810	0910	1010	minutes	1510	1610	minutes	2210	2255	2354
Chatham............................d.	0037		0558	0628	0728	past each	2128	2228	2302	2332	0037		0728	0828	0928	1028	past each	1528	1628	past each	2228	2315	...
Rochester...........................d.	0041		0602	0632	0732	hour until	2132	2232	2305	2335	0041		0732	0832	0932	1032	hour until	1532	1632	hour until	2232	2318	...
Ebbsfleet International ....a.	...		0619	0649	0749		2149	2249	...	...	...		0749	0849	0949	1049		1549	1649		2249	...	...
Stratford International......a.	...		0630	0700	0800		2200	2300	...	...	...		0800	0900	1000	1100		1600	1700		2300	...	...
London St Pancras ....a.	...		0638	0708	0810		2210	2308	...	...	...		0808	0908	1008	1108		1610	1708		2308	...	...

Via Ashford and Dover

km		Ⓐ	②–⑤	Ⓐ	Ⓐ	Ⓐ	Ⓐ	Ⓐ	Ⓐ	Ⓐ	Ⓐ	Ⓐ	Ⓐ	Ⓐ	Ⓐ	Ⓐ		Ⓐ	Ⓐ	Ⓐ	Ⓐ	Ⓐ	Ⓐ	Ⓐ	Ⓐ	Ⓐ
0	**London** St Pancras..... d.		0012	...	...	...	...	0637	0707	0739	0804	0840	0907	0936	1007	1040	✤	1407	1440	1507	1537	1604	1637	1707	1720	1734
9	Stratford International .. d.		0020	...	...	...	...	0645	0715	0748	0812	0848	0915	0943	1015	1048		1415	1448	1515	1545	1612	1645	1715	1728	1742
35	Ebbsfleet International . d.		0031	...	...	...	...	0656	0726	0759	0823	0859	0926	0956	1026	1059	and at	1426	1459	1526	1556	1623	1656	1726	|	1753
90	Ashford International..... d.		0050	0522	0555	0630	0700	0717	0747	0820	0847f	0920	0947	1020f	1047	1120	the same	1447	1520	1547	1620f	1647f	1720f	1749	1757	1816
112	Folkestone Central .... d.		...	0540	0614	|	0719	|	0802	|	0902	|	1002	|	1102	|	minutes	1502	|	1602	|	1703	|	1804	|	1831
124	**Dover** Priory .... a.		...	0551	0626	|	0729	|	0813	|	0913	|	1013	|	1113	|	past each	1513	|	1613	|	1714	|	1815	|	1842
112	Canterbury West .... d.		...	...	|	0653	|	0740	...	0835	|	0935	|	1035	|	1135	hour until	...	1535	...	1635	...	1735	|	1813	...
140	Ramsgate................... a.		...	...	0708	0718	0808	0805	...	0857	0951	0957	1051	1057	1151	1157		...	1557	...	1657	...	1757	1857	1834	...
149	**Margate** .... a.		...	...	...	0730	...	0817	...	0909	...	1009	...	1109	...	1209		...	1609	...	1709	...	1809	...	1846	...

	Ⓐ	Ⓐ	Ⓐ	Ⓐ		Ⓐ	Ⓐ	①	②	③–⑤	⑥	⑥	⑥	⑥	⑥	⑥	⑥	⑥	⑥		⑥	⑥	⑦	⑦	⑦
London St Pancras...... d.	1750	1807	1840	1907	✤	2240	2307	2340	2340	2340		0012	...	...	...	0640	...	0740	0807	✤	2304	2340		0012	...
Stratford International.... d.	1758	1814	1848	1914		2248	2315	2348	2348	2348		0020	...	...	...	0648	...	0748	0814		2312	2348		0020	...
Ebbsfleet International .. d.	|	1825	1859	1925	and at	2259	2326	2359	2359	2359		0031	...	...	...	0659	...	0759	0825	and at	2323	2359		0031	...
Ashford International..... d.	1827	1848	1920	1948	the same	2320	2347	0020	0020	0020		0050	0600	0635	0647	0720	0747	0820	0846	the same	2347f	0020		0050	0747
Folkestone Central ..... d.	|	1904	|	2003	minutes	|	0002	|	|	|		...	0615	|	0702	|	0802	|	0901	minutes	0002	|		...	0802
Dover Priory.............. a.	|	1914	|	2014	past each	|	0013	|	|	|		...	0626	|	0713	|	0813	|	0913	past each	0013	|		...	0813
Canterbury West........... d.	1842	|	1936	|	hour until	2335	|	*0103*r	0035	0035		...	|	0659	|	0735	|	0835	|	hour until	|	0035		...	|
Ramsgate.................... a.	1904	1951	1959	2051		2357	0051	0115	0057	0057		...	0704	0724	0751	0758	0851	0857	0950		0051	0057		...	0852
Margate .... a.	1916	...	2011	...		0009v	...	0128	*0124*j	0109		...	...	0736	...	0809	...	0909	...		...	0109		...	...

	⑦	⑦	⑦	⑦		⑦	⑦	⑦
London St Pancras...... d.	...	...	0840	0904	✤	2240	2307	2340
Stratford International.... d.	...	...	0848	0912		2248	2315	2348
Ebbsfleet International .. d.	...	...	0859	0923	and at	2259	2326	2359
Ashford International..... d.	0820	0846	0920	0947	the same	2320	2347	0018
Folkestone Central ..... d.	|	0902	|	1002	minutes	|	0002	...
Dover Priory.............. a.	|	0913	|	1013	past each	|	0013	...
Canterbury West........... d.	0835	|	0935	|	hour until	2335	...	...
Ramsgate.................... a.	0857	0951	0957	1051		2357	...	...
Margate .... a.	0909	...	1009	...		0009	...	...

	Ⓐ	Ⓐ	Ⓐ	Ⓐ	Ⓐ	Ⓐ	Ⓐ	Ⓐ	Ⓐ	Ⓐ	Ⓐ	Ⓐ b	Ⓐ
Margate.......................... d.		...	...	...	0537	...	0615	...	0645	...	0715	0654	0746
Ramsgate........................ d.		...	0452	...	0550	...	0628	0607	0658	...	0728	0710	0759
Canterbury West............. d.		...	0518	...	0612	...	0649	|	0719	...	0749	|	0823
Dover Priory................. d.		*0427*	|	0545	|	0618	|	0648	|	0718	|	0748	|
Folkestone Central........ d.		*0439*	|	0557	|	0628	|	0658	|	0728	|	0758	|
Ashford International...... d.		0510	0544	0613	0630	0646	0706	0716	0736	0746	0806	0816	0840
Ebbsfleet International.... a.		0528	0602	0632	0648	0704	|	0734	0754	0804	|	0834	0858
Stratford International..... a.		0540	0614	0643	0700	0716	0734	0746	0806	0816	0834	0846	0910
London St Pancras......... a.		0548	0623	0651	0708	0724	0742	0754	0814	0824	0843	0854	0918

	Ⓐ	Ⓐ	Ⓐ	Ⓐ	Ⓐ		Ⓐ	Ⓐ	Ⓐ	Ⓐ	Ⓐ	Ⓐ	Ⓐ	Ⓐ	Ⓐ		Ⓐ	Ⓐ	Ⓐ	①–④	⑤	①–④	⑤	⑥	⑥
Margate .... d.	...	0847	...	0947	...	✤	...	1544	...	1649	...	1749	...	1849	...	✤	2149	...	...	2249	2310	...	2330		...
Ramsgate....................... d.	...	0900	0908	1000	1008		...	1557	...	1702	...	1802	...	1902	1907		2202	2208	2242	2302	2323	2308	2343		0459
Canterbury West........... d.	...	0921	|	1021	|	and at	...	1620	...	1723	...	1823	...	1923	|	and at	2223	|	2307	2323	|	|	0004		0521
Dover Priory.............. d.	0848	|	0948	|	1045	the same	1540	|	1644	|	1748	|	1850	|	1945	the same	|	2248	|	|	0003	2348	|		*0455*
Folkestone Central ..... d.	0858	|	1000	|	1056	minutes	1550	|	1654	|	1758	|	1900	|	1955	minutes	|	2258	|	|	0013	2358	|		*0505*
Ashford International..... d.	0916	0941f	1019	1040	1116	past each	1612	1639	1716f	1740	1816	1840	1919	1940	2016	past each	2240	2316	2328	2338	0033	0019	0019		0540
Ebbsfleet International .. a.	0934	0959	1037	1058	1134	hour until	1631	1657	1734	1758	1834	1858	1937	1958	2034	hour until	2258	2335	...	...	...	...	...		0558
Stratford International.... a.	0946	1011	1049	1110	1146		1646	1709	1746	1810	1846	1910	1949	2010	2046		2310	2346	...	...	...	...	...		0610
London St Pancras .... a.	0954	1019	1057	1118	1154		1654	1719	1754	1819	1854	1918	1957	2018	2054		2318	2354	...	...	...	...	...		0618

	⑥	⑥	⑥	⑥	⑥	⑥	⑥		⑥	⑥	⑥	⑥	⑥	⑥	⑥	⑦	⑦	⑦	⑦	⑦		⑦	⑦	⑦	⑦
Margate .... d.	0546	...	0646	...	0749	...	0849	✤	...	2149	...	2222	...	2310	2330		...	...	0746	...	✤	...	2149	...	2249
Ramsgate....................... d.	0559	0605	0659	0705	0802	0808	0902		2108	2202	2208	2242	2302	2323	2343		0702	0707	0759	0805		2108	2202	2208	2302
Canterbury West........... d.	0621	|	0721	|	0823	|	0923	and at	|	2223	|	2307	2323	|	0004		0724	|	0821	|	and at	|	2223	|	2323
Dover Priory.............. d.	|	0646	|	0746	|	0845	|	the same	2145	|	2248	|	|	0003	|		|	0745	|	0843	the same	2148	|	2248	|
Folkestone Central ..... d.	|	0656	|	0756	|	0856	|	minutes	2156	|	2258	|	|	0013	|		|	0756	|	0854	minutes	2158	|	2258	|
Ashford International..... d.	0640	0716	0740	0816	0840	0917	0940	past each	2216	2240	2316	2328	2338	0030	0019		0743	0818	0841	0916	past each	2216	2240	2315	2338
Ebbsfleet International .. a.	0658	0734	0758	0834	0858	0935	0958	hour until	2234	2258	2334	...	...	...	...		0801	0836	0859	0934	hour until	2234	2258	...	...
Stratford International.... a.	0710	0746	0810	0846	0910	0946	1010		2246	2310	2346	...	...	...	...		0813	0847	0910	0946		2246	2310	...	...
London St Pancras .... a.	0718	0754	0818	0854	0918	0954	1018		2254	2318	2354	...	...	...	...		0821	0855	0918	0954		2254	2318	...	...

A – On ② service is operated by 🚌 from Faversham (Faversham d. 2356, Herne Bay a. 0033**s**, Margate a. 0041, Ramsgate a. 0102).
B – On ③ mornings service is operated by 🚌 from Faversham (Faversham d. 0106, Herne Bay a. 0143**s**, Margate a. 0151**s**, Ramsgate a. 0212).
a – Continues to London St Pancras via Ashford (see lower table).
b – From Faversham (see upper table).
c – Arrives 8 minutes earlier.
f – Arrives 5 minutes earlier.
j – Connection by 🚌.
n – Until Oct. 10.
r – Arrival time. Connection by 🚌 from Ashford.
s – Calls to set down only.
v – On ③ mornings connection by 🚌 arr. 0024.
✤ – Timings may vary ± 3 minutes.

SE, SN, SW

LONDON - THE SOUTH and SOUTH EAST 102

Typical off-peak journey time in hours and minutes
READ DOWN ↓ READ UP ↑

During peak hours on Ⓐ (0600 - 0900 and 1600 - 1900) services generally run more frequently (particularly to and from London) and journey times may vary.

LONDON VICTORIA - RAMSGATE SE

km					
0	0h00	↓	d. **London** Victoria....a.	↑	1h57
18	0h17		d. Bromley South.......d.		1h40
53	0h47	↓	d. Rochester.............d.	↑	1h12
72	1h09		d. Sittingbourne.........d.		0h50
84	1h21	↓	d. Faversham............d.	↑	0h42
101	1h36		d. Herne Bay.............d.		0h26
119	1h49	↓	d. Margate.................d.	↑	0h10
128	1h59		a. **Ramsgate**.............d.		0h00

Frequency: Hourly.
Usual off-peak departures:
From London Victoria at xx40.
From Ramsgate at xx53 (on Ⓐ: also 1546, 1612, 1650, 1712, 1750, 1812; not 1553, 1653, 1753).

LONDON VICTORIA - DOVER SE

km					
0	0h00	↓	d. **London** Victoria....a.	↑	2h02
18	0h17		d. Bromley South.......d.		1h43
53	0h47	↓	d. Rochester.............d.	↑	1h17
72	1h09		d. Sittingbourne.........d.		0h58
84	1h21	↓	d. Faversham............d.	↑	0h47
99	1h37		d. Canterbury East....d.		0h27
124	1h58	↓	a. **Dover** Priory.........d.	↑	0h00

Frequency: Hourly.
Usual off-peak departures:
From London Victoria at xx10 on ⚒; xx12 on ⑦.
From Dover Priory at xx18 on ⚒; xx50 on ⑦.

LONDON CHARING CROSS - CANTERBURY WEST SE

km					
0	0h00	↓	d. **London** Ch Cross.a.	↑	1h46
1	0h03		d. **London** W'loo (E)..a.		1h42
3	0h08	↓	d. **London** Bridge......a.	↑	1h36
36	0h32		d. Sevenoaks............d.		1h13
48	0h40	↓	d. Tonbridge..............d.	↑	1h04
90	1h20		a. Ashford Int'l...........d.		0h27
113	1h38	↓	a. **Canterbury** West..d.	↑	0h00

Frequency: Hourly.
Usual off-peak departures:
From London Charing Cross at xx34.
From Canterbury West at xx07 (on Ⓐ: also 1004, 1601 and every 30 minutes until 1901; not 1007, 1607, 1707, 1807, 1907).

LONDON CHARING CROSS - DOVER SE

km					
0	0h00	↓	d. **London** Ch Cross.a.	↑	1h58
1	0h03		d. **London** W'loo (E)..a.		1h53
3	0h08	↓	d. **London** Bridge......a.	↑	1h42
36	0h32		d. Sevenoaks............d.		1h18
48	0h40	↓	d. Tonbridge..............d.	↑	1h06
90	1h20		d. Ashford Int'l...........d.		0h29
113	1h40	↓	d. Folkstone Central..d.	↑	0h12
124	1h52		a. **Dover** Priory.........d.		0h00

Frequency: Hourly.
Usual off-peak departures:
From London Charing Cross at xx04.
From Dover at xx28 (on Ⓐ: also 0722, 0822, 0852, 0922, 1525; not 0728, 0828, 0928, 1528).

LONDON VICTORIA - ASHFORD INTERNATIONAL SE

km					
0	0h00	↓	d. **London** Victoria....a.	↑	1h29
18	0h17		d. Bromley South.......d.		1h14
28	0h28	↓	d. Swanley................d.	↑	1h03
56	0h52		d. West Malling..........d.		0h42
64	1h03	↓	d. Maidstone East.....d.	↑	0h30
68	1h09		d. Bearsted...............d.		0h25
95	1h31		a. **Ashford** Int'l..........d.		0h00

Frequency: Hourly.
Usual off-peak departures:
From London Victoria at xx55.
From Ashford International at xx56 (on Ⓐ: also 1527, 1627, 1652, 1727, 1827, 1855, 1926, 2024, 2126, 2243; not 1656, 1856, 1956, 2056, 2156, 2256).

LONDON CHARING CROSS - HASTINGS SE

km					
0	0h00	↓	d. **London** Ch Cross.a.	↑	1h43
1	0h03		d. **London** W'loo (E)..a.		1h39
3	0h08	↓	d. **London** Bridge....a.	↑	1h35
36	0h34		d. Sevenoaks............d.		1h09
48	0h43	↓	d. Tonbridge..............d.	↑	1h00
55	0h55		d. Tunbridge Wells △ d.		0h49
89	1h33	↓	d. Battle....................d.	↑	0h16
100	1h45		a. **Hastings**...............d.		0h00

Frequency: Twice an hour.
Usual off-peak departures:
From London Charing Cross at xx15, xx45.
From Hastings at xx30, xx50 (on Ⓐ: also 1520, 1546, 1620, 1720, 1747, 1820; not 1530, 1550, 1630, 1730, 1750, 1830.

LONDON VICTORIA - EASTBOURNE SN

km					
0	0h00	↓	d. **London** Victoria....a.	↑	1h26
17	0h16		d. East Croydon........d.		1h09
43	0h33	↓	d. Gatwick Airport......d.	↑	0h53
61	0h50		d. Haywards Heath.....d.		0h34
81	1h06	↓	d. Lewes...................d.	↑	0h19
106	1h27		a. **Eastbourne**..........d.		0h00

Frequency: Every 30 minutes on ⚒; hourly on ⑦.
Usual off-peak departures:
From London Victoria at xx24, xx54 on ⚒; xx46 on ⑦.
From Eastbourne at xx05, xx33 on ⚒; xx00 on ⑦.

ASHFORD - HASTINGS - EASTBOURNE - (BRIGHTON) SN

km					
0	0h00	↓	d. **Ashford** Int'l..........a.	↑	1h20
14	0h13		d. Appledore..............d.		1h07
25	0h24	↓	d. Rye.......................d.	↑	0h56
41	0h43		d. Ore.......................d.		0h40
42	0h47	↓	d. **Hastings**..............d.	↑	0h36
50	0h58		d. Bexhill...................d.		0h25
67	1h21	↓	a. **Eastbourne**...........d.	↑	0h00

Frequency: Hourly.
Usual off-peak departures:
From Ashford at xx24.
From Eastbourne at xx50.

☛ Local services are available Brighton / Lewes - Eastbourne - Hastings v.v.

LONDON BRIDGE - UCKFIELD SN

km					
0	0h00	↓	d. **London** Bridge......a.	↑	1h15
16	0h16		d. East Croydon........d.		0h59
32	0h29	↓	d. Oxted...................d.	↑	0h44
57	0h55		d. Eridge △...............d.		0h17
70	1h01	↓	d. Crowborough.........d.	↑	0h12
74	1h15		a. **Uckfield**...............d.		0h00

Frequency: Hourly.
Usual off-peak departures:
From London Bridge at xx07 on ⚒.
From Uckfield at xx33 on ⚒.
On ⑦ use East Grinstead services from / to London Victoria and change trains at Oxted (Uckfield d. xx34).

LONDON VICTORIA - EAST GRINSTEAD SN

km					
0	0h00	↓	d. **London** Victoria....a.	↑	0h56
17	0h17		d. East Croydon........d.		0h37
33	0h37	↓	d. Oxted...................d.	↑	0h16
42	0h43		d. Lingfield................d.		0h12
48	0h54	↓	a. **East Grinstead** ▽ d.	↑	0h00

Frequency: Every 30 minutes.
Usual off-peak departures:
From London Victoria at xx20, xx50 on ⚒⊠; xx21, xx51 on ⑦.
From East Grinstead at xx06, xx36 on ⚒⊠; xx12, xx42 on ⑦.

LONDON VICTORIA - LITTLEHAMPTON SN

km					
0	0h00	↓	d. **London** Victoria....a.	↑	1h42
17	0h16		d. East Croydon........a.		1h25
43	0h33	↓	d. Gatwick Airport......a.	↑	1h09
61	0h50		d. Haywards Heath.....a.		0h54
82	1h06	↓	d. Hove....................a.	↑	0h35
96	1h21		d. Worthing...............d.		0h21
114	1h41	↓	a. **Littlehampton**......d.	↑	0h00

Frequency: Every 30 minutes on ⚒; hourly on ⑦.
Usual off-peak departures:
From London Victoria at xx16, xx46 on ⚒; xx16 on ⑦.
From Littlehampton at xx12, xx42 on ⚒; xx13 on ⑦.

LONDON VICTORIA - BOGNOR REGIS SN

km					
0	0h00	↓	d. **London** Victoria....a.	↑	1h50
17	0h16		d. East Croydon........d.		1h30
43	0h37	↓	d. Gatwick Airport......d.	↑	1h08
61	1h03		d. Horsham...............d.		0h50
94	1h30	↓	d. Arundel.................d.	↑	0h16
110	1h40		d. Barnham...............d.		0h07
116	1h46	↓	a. **Bognor Regis**......d.	↑	0h00

Frequency: Every 30 minutes on ⚒; hourly on ⑦.
Usual off-peak departures:
From London Victoria at xx05, xx35 on ⚒; xx35 on ⑦.
From Bognor Regis at xx26, xx56 on ⚒; xx31 on ⑦.

BRIGHTON - PORTSMOUTH HARBOUR SN

km	◧				◧
0	0h00	↓	d. **Brighton**..............d.	↑	1h19
2	0h04		d. Hove.....................d.		1h15
16	0h22	↓	d. Worthing...............d.	↑	0h57
35	0h42		d. Barnham...............d.		0h39
45	0h49	↓	d. Chichester............d.	↑	0h31
59	1h04		d. Havant..................d.		0h17
71	1h16	↓	a. **Portsmouth** & SS.d.	↑	0h04
72	1h20		a. **Portsmouth** Hbr...d.		0h00

Frequency: Hourly.
Usual off-peak departures:
From Brighton at xx28 on ⚒; xx30 on ⑦.
From Portsmouth & Southsea at xx57 on ⚒; xx18 on ⑦.
See note ◧.

BRIGHTON - SOUTHAMPTON CENTRAL SN

km	◐				◐
0	0h00	↓	d. **Brighton**..............d.	↑	1h45
2	0h04		d. Hove.....................d.		1h41
16	0h23	↓	d. Worthing...............d.	↑	1h23
35	0h46		d. Barnham...............d.		1h00
45	0h54	↓	d. Chichester............d.	↑	0h52
59	1h06		d. Havant..................d.		0h38
75	1h22	↓	d. Fareham...............d.	↑	0h23
98	1h48		a. **Southampton** C...d.		0h00

Frequency: Every 30 minutes on ⚒; hourly on ⑦.
Usual off-peak departures:
From Brighton at xx13, xx43 on ⚒; xx00 on ⑦.
From Southampton at xx20, xx50 on ⚒; xx30 on ⑦.
See note ◐.

LONDON WATERLOO - READING SW

km					
0	0h00	↓	d. **London** Waterloo. a.	↑	1h22
16	0h16		d. Richmond............ d.		1h03
18	0h20	↓	d. Twickenham......... d.	↑	0h58
30	0h33		d. Staines................ d.		0h36
46	0h53	↓	d. Ascot.................. d.	↑	0h28
70	1h20		a. **Reading**............... d.		0h00

Frequency: Every 30 minutes.
Usual off-peak departures:
From London Waterloo at xx20, xx50 on ⚒; xx09, xx39 on ⑦.
From Reading at xx09, xx39 on ⚒; xx24, xx54 on ⑦.

LONDON WATERLOO - WINDSOR SW

km					
0	0h00	↓	d. **London** Waterloo. a.	↑	0h56
16	0h20		d. Richmond............ d.		0h34
18	0h24	↓	d. Twickenham......... d.	↑	0h30
30	0h39		d. Staines................ d.		0h15
41	0h53	↓	a. **Windsor** ▷......... d.	↑	0h00

Frequency: Every 30 minutes.
Usual off-peak departures:
From London Waterloo at xx03, xx33 on ⚒; xx25, xx44 on ⑦.
From Windsor at xx23, xx53 on ⚒; xx01, xx34 on ⑦.

SEAFORD - BRIGHTON SN

km					
0	0h00	↓	d. **Seaford**...............a.	↑	0h36
4	0h05		d. Newhaven Harbour.d.		0h30
5	0h07	↓	d. Newhaven Town....d.	↑	0h28
15	0h19		d. Lewes...................d.		0h18
22	0h26	↓	d. Falmer..................d.	↑	0h09
28	0h35		a. **Brighton**..............d.		0h00

Frequency: Every 30 minutes.
Usual off-peak departures:
From Seaford at xx24, xx53 on ⚒ (not 1253 on Ⓐ); xx29, xx59 on ⑦.
From Brighton at xx06, xx36 on ⚒ (not 1206 on Ⓐ); xx17, xx48 on ⑦.

TONBRIDGE - REDHILL SN

km					
0	0h00	↓	d. **Tonbridge**............a.	↑	0h31
7	0h08		d. Penshurst.............d.		0h22
15	0h15	↓	d. Edenbridge............d.	↑	0h16
22	0h21		d. Godstone..............d.		0h10
32	0h35	↓	a. **Redhill**.................d.	↑	0h00

Frequency: Hourly.
Usual off-peak departures:
From Tonbridge at xx01 on ⚒§; xx26 on ⑦.
From Redhill at xx00 on ⚒‡; xx21 on ⑦.

◧ – Journey time on ⑦ extended by up to 17 minutes. Most services on ⚒ run to / from Portsmouth & Southsea only.
◐ – Journey time on ⑦ extended by up to 10 minutes.
▷ – Windsor and Eton Riverside.

§ – Timings vary on Ⓐ before 1001 and 1401 - 2001.
‡ – Timings vary on Ⓐ before 1000 and 1500 - 2000.
⊠ – On Ⓐ runs hourly 0950 - 1350 from London Victoria; hourly 1106 - 1506 from East Grinstead.

△ – **Spa Valley Railway** (🚂 Eridge - Tunbridge Wells West: *8 km*). ✆ 01892 537715. www.spavalleyrailway.co.uk
▽ – **Bluebell Railway** (🚂 East Grinstead - Sheffield Park: *18 km*). ✆ 01825 720800. www.bluebell-railway.com

103 BEDFORD - LONDON - GATWICK ✈ - BRIGHTON

SN, TL

km		⚒	⚒	⚒	⚒	⚒	⚒	⚒	⚒	⚒	⚒	⚒		⚒	⚒	⚒	⚒	⚒	⑥	Ⓐ	⑦	⑦	⑦	⑦	⑦	⑦
0	**Bedford** 170a d.		0015	0115	0215	0315	0343	0413	0443	0515	0546	0616		2118	2148	2216	2243	2307	2337	2343		0558	0623	0653	0731	0803
31	Luton 170a d.		0040	0140	0240	0340	0408	0438	0508	0540	0613	0643		2143	2213	2241	2308	2332	0002	0010		0624	0649	0719	0757	0829
33	Luton Airport P ✈ ◇ 170a d.		0043	0143	0243	0343	0411	0441	0511	0543	0616	0646	and	2146	2216	2244	2311	2335	0005	0013		0627	0652	0722	0800	0832
48	St. Albans d.		0055	0155	0255	0355	0423	0453	0523	0555	0627	0657	at the	2157	2227	2255	2323	2347	0017	0025		0639	0704	0734	0812	0844
80	**London** St Pancras 170a d.		0132	0232	0332	0432	0452	0520	0550	0620	0650	0720	same	2220	2250	2323	2352	0024	0054	0054		0715	0741	0811	0841	0910
82	Farringdon 185 d.		|	|	|	|	0456	0524	0554	0624	0654	0724	minutes	2224	2254	2328	2356	0028	|	|		▬	▬	▬	▬	▬
83	**London** Blackfriars 185 d.		0140	0240	0340	0440	0501	0529	0559	0629	0659	0729	past	2229	2259	2331	0002	0032	0102	0102		⑦	⑦	⑦	⑦	⑦
84	**London** Bridge 185 d.		|	|	|	|	|	0535	0605	0635	0705	0735	each	2235	2305	2338	|	|	|	|		0709	0739	0809	0839	0909
99	East Croydon 185 d.		0207	0307	0407	0507	0528	0549	0619	0649	0719	0749	hour	2249	2319	2351	0028	0058	0128	0128		0723	0753	0823	0853	0923
124	Gatwick Airport ✈ 185 d.		0230	0330	0430	0532	0548	0605	0635	0705	0735	0805	until	2305	2335	0022	0049	0122	0158	0158		0743	0814	0843	0909	0939
142	Haywards Heath 185 d.		...	...	...	0550	0603	0622	0652	0722	0752	0822		2322	2352	0040	0104	...	0214	0214		0758	0831	0858	0925	0955
163	**Brighton** 185 a.		...	...	...	0610	0626	0643	0713	0743	0815	0845		2343	0013	0100	0124	...	0228	0228		0818	0851	0918	0946	1016

	⑦	⑦		⑦	⑦	⑦	⑦	⑦	⑦
Bedford 170a d.	0817	0847		2118	2148	2208	2243	2307	2343
Luton 170a d.	0842	0912		2143	2213	2233	2308	2332	0008
Luton Airport P ✈ ◇ 170a d.	0845	0915	and	2146	2216	2236	2311	2335	0011
St. Albans d.	0857	0927	at the	2157	2227	2248	2323	2347	0023
London St Pancras 170a d.	0924	0954	same	2224	2254	2324	2352	0024	0054
Farringdon 185 d.	0928	0958	minutes	2228	2258	2328	2356	0028	|
London Blackfriars 185 d.	0933	1003	past	2233	2303	2333	0002	0032	0102
London Bridge 185 d.	0939	1009	each	2239	2309	2339	|	|	|
East Croydon 185 d.	0953	1023	hour	2253	2323	2353	0028	0058	0128
Gatwick Airport ✈ 185 d.	1009	1039	until	2309	2339	0017	0049	0122	0158
Haywards Heath 185 d.	1025	1055		2326	2358	0034	0104	...	0214
Brighton 185 a.	1046	1116		2346	0018	0054	0124	...	0228

	⚒	⚒	⚒	⚒	⚒	⚒	⑥	Ⓐ	⚒	⚒	⚒	Ⓐ
Brighton 185 d.		0002	...	...	...	...	0412	0412	...	0526	0556	0626
Haywards Heath 185 d.		0023	...	...	...	...	0426	0426	...	0549	0619	0649
Gatwick Airport ✈ 185 d.		0042	0145	0245	0345	0425	0441	0441	0532	0606	0636	0706
East Croydon 185 d.		0110	0210	0310	0410	0440	0510	0510	0603	0621	0651	0721
London Bridge 185 d.		|	|	|	|	|	0527	0527	0621	0636	0706	0736
London Blackfriars 185 d.		0136	0236	0336	0436	0506	0533	0533	0627	0642	0712	0742
Farringdon 185 d.		|	|	|	|	0511	0538	0538	0631	0646	0716	0746
London St Pancras 170a d.		0144	0244	0344	0444	0516	0542	0542	0636	0651	0721	0751
St Albans City d.		0218	0318	0418	0518	0541	0603	0606	0655	0711	0739	|
Luton Airport P ◇ 170a d.		0230	0330	0430	0530	0553	0615	0619	0707	0723	0753	0815
Luton 170a d.		0234	0334	0434	0534	0557	0619	0622	0711	0727	0757	0819
Bedford 170a a.		0259	0359	0459	0559	0622	0644	0647	0738	0752	0822	0840

	⑥	Ⓐ	⑥	Ⓐ	⑥	⚒	⚒	⚒	⚒		⚒	⚒	Ⓐ	⑥	⚒	⚒	Ⓐ	⑥	⚒	⚒		⚒	⚒	⚒	⚒
Brighton 185 d.	0628	0656	0658	0726	0728	0756	0826	0858	0928		1528	1558	1628	1628	1658	1728	1758	1758	1828	1858		2058	2128	2158	2228
Haywards Heath 185 d.	0649	0719	0719	0749	0749	0819	0849	0919	0949		1549	1619	1649	1649	1719	1749	1819	1819	1849	1919		2119	2149	2219	2249
Gatwick Airport ✈ 185 d.	0706	0736	0736	0806	0806	0836	0906	0936	1006	and	1606	1636	1706	1706	1736	1806	1836	1836	1906	1936	and	2136	2206	2236	2306
East Croydon 185 d.	0721	0751	0751	0821	0821	0851	0921	0951	1021	at the	1621	1651	1721	1721	1751	1821	1851	1851	1921	1951	at the	2151	2221	2251	2321
London Bridge 185 d.	0736	0806	0806	0836	0836	0906	0936	1006	1036	same	1636	1706	1736	1736	1806	1836	1906	1906	1936	2006	same	2206	2236	2306	2336
London Blackfriars 185 d.	0742	0812	0812	0842	0842	0912	0942	1012	1042	minutes	1642	1712	1742	1742	1812	1842	1912	1912	1942	2012	minutes	2212	2242	2312	2342
Farringdon 185 d.	0746	0816	0816	0846	0846	0916	0946	1016	1046	past	1646	1716	1746	1746	1816	1846	1916	1916	1946	2016	past	2216	2246	2316	2346
London St Pancras 170a d.	0751	0821	0821	0851	0851	0921	0951	1021	1051	each	1651	1721	1751	1751	1821	1851	1921	1921	1951	2021	each	2221	2251	2321	2351
St Albans City d.	0811	|	0841	0909	0911	0941	1011	1041	1111	hour	1711	1741	1809	1811	1841	1911	1939	1941	2011	2041	hour	2241	2316	2346	0016
Luton Airport P ✈ ◇ 170a d.	0823	0845	0853	|	0923	0954	1023	1053	1123	until	1723	1753	|	1823	1853	1923	|	1953	2023	2053	until	2253	2328	2358	0028
Luton 170a d.	0827	0849	0857	0921	0927	0957	1027	1057	1127		1727	1757	1822	1827	1857	1927	1952	1957	2027	2057		2257	2332	0002	0032
Bedford 170a a.	0852	0910	0922	0944	0952	1022	1052	1122	1152		1752	1822	1844	1852	1922	1952	2014	2022	2052	2122		2325	2357	0027	0057

	⚒	⚒	⑦	⑦	⑦	⑦	⑦	⑦	⑦	⑦	⑦	⑦	⑦	⑦	⑦	⑦	⑦	⑦		⑦	⑦	⑦	⑦	⑦	⑦	⑦
Brighton 185 d.	2256	2323		0002	0542	0556	0626	0656	0726	0756	...	0828	0858	0928	0958	1028	1058	1128		2058	2128	2158	2228	2242	2318	2342
Haywards Heath 185 d.	2317	2344		0023	0604	0617	0647	0717	0747	0817	...	0849	0919	0949	1019	1049	1119	1149	and	2119	2149	2219	2249	2304	2334	0003
Gatwick Airport ✈ 185 d.	2334	0001		0042	0619	0634	0704	0734	0804	0834	0830	0906	0936	1006	1036	1106	1136	1206	at the	2136	2206	2236	2306	2321	2352	0021
East Croydon 185 d.	2353	0024		0110	0641	0654	0725	0754	0825	0852	0903	0921	0951	1021	1051	1121	1151	1221	same	2151	2221	2251	2321	2340	0012	0040
London Bridge 185 d.	|	|		|	0657	0712	0742	0815	0842	0907	0919	0936	1006	1036	1106	1136	1206	1236	minutes	2206	2236	2306	2336	|	|	|
London Blackfriars 185 d.	0022	0050		0136	▬	▬	▬	▬	▬	▬	0926	0942	1012	1042	1112	1142	1212	1242	past	2212	2242	2312	2347	0006	0038	0106
Farringdon 185 d.	0026	|		|	⑦	⑦	⑦	⑦	⑦	⑦	0930	0946	1016	1046	1116	1146	1216	1246	each	2216	2246	2316	2351	0011	|	|
London St Pancras 170a d.	0031	0058		0144	0633	0733	0803	0833	0851	0921	0935	0951	1021	1051	1121	1151	1221	1251	hour	2221	2251	2321	2356	0016	0046	0114
St Albans City d.	0058	0133		0218	0708	0808	0838	0908	0915	0945	0959	1016	1046	1116	1146	1216	1241	1311	until	2241	2313	2347	0024	0050	0120	0142
Luton Airport P ✈ ◇ 170a d.	0109	0144		0230	0719	0819	0849	0919	0928	0956	1011	1029	1059	1128	1159	1229	1252	1322		2252	2324	2359	0036	0101	0131	0153
Luton 170a d.	0114	0149		0234	0724	0824	0854	0924	0931	1001	1015	1032	1102	1132	1202	1232	1257	1327		2257	2329	0003	0040	0106	0136	0158
Bedford 170a a.	0139	0214		0259	0749	0849	0919	0949	0956	1026	1040	1057	1127	1157	1227	1257	1322	1352		2322	2354	0028	0105	0131	0201	0223

◇ – Luton Airport Parkway.

☛ Additional trains run Bedford - Gatwick Airport and v.v. Frequent services (operated by SN/GX) also run **London Victoria - Gatwick ✈ - Brighton** and v.v. (4 trains per hour on ⚒, 2 trains per hour on †). For other services London Victoria - Gatwick Airport and v.v. see Table **100**.

104 LONDON - GUILDFORD - PORTSMOUTH

Service valid until Sept. 20. SW

km		Ⓐ	Ⓐ	Ⓐ	Ⓐ	Ⓐ	Ⓐ	Ⓐ	Ⓐ	Ⓐ	Ⓐ	Ⓐ		Ⓐ	Ⓐ	Ⓐ	Ⓐ	Ⓐ	Ⓐ	Ⓐ	Ⓐ	Ⓐ	Ⓐ	Ⓐ	Ⓐ	Ⓐ
0	**London** Waterloo 105/9 d.		...	0508	0545	0615	0700	0730	0800	0830	0900	0930		1430	1500	1530	1600	1630	1700	1730	1800	1830	1900	1930	2000	2030
39	Woking 105/9 d.		...	0552	0617f	0644	0725	0755	0826	0855	0925	0955	and at	1455	1525	1555	1625	1655	1725	1755	1824	1855	1924	1955	2025	2055
49	Guildford d.		0509	0603	0630	0655	0734	0804	0835	0904	0933	1003	the same	1503	1533	1604	1634	1704	1734	1810	1834	1909	1933	2004	2033	2104
69	Haslemere d.		0524	0628	0655	0720	0753	0824	0854	0924	0955	1021	minutes	1521	1553	1628	1653	1725	1754	1828	1853	1926	1952	2024	2055	2122
88	Petersfield d.		0545	0645	0711	0737	0805	0836	0905	0935	1012	1032	past each	1532	1604	1645	1704	1736	1806	1840	1904	1938	2003	2036	2112	2133
107	Havant a.		0600	0700	0727	0752	0817	0851	0918	0951	1027	1045	hour until	1545	1617	1659	1717	1751	1818	1852	1917	1951	2016	2051	2127	2146
118	**Portsmouth** & Southsea a.		0616	0716	0746	0808	0830	0904	0931	1003	1043	1057		1557	1630	1716	1730	1804	1831	1905	1929	2003	2030	2104	2143	2158
120	**Portsmouth** Harbour a.		0620	0723	0750	0812	0836	0908	0936	1008	1048	1102		1602	1636	1720	1738	1810	1838	1911	1938	2009	2036	2108	2147	2202

	Ⓐ	Ⓐ	Ⓐ	Ⓐ	Ⓐ	Ⓐ	⑥	⑥	⑥	⑥	⑥	⑥		⑥	⑥	⑥	⑥	⑥	⑥	⑥	⑦	⑦	⑦	⑦	⑦	⑦
London Waterloo 105/9 d.	2100	2130	2200	2230	2300	2332		...	0545	0645	0730	0800		2100	2130	2200	2230	2300	2315	2345		...	0800	0830	0900	0930
Woking 105/9 d.	2125	2155	2225	2256	2328	0001		...	0618	0713	0755	0825	and at	2125	2155	2225	2255	2327	2344	0014		0732	0833	0857	0933	1002
Guildford d.	2134	2204	2234	2305	2340	0009		0515	0625	0724	0803	0833	the same	2133	2203	2233	2304	2336	2353	0026		0742	0842	0905	0942	1012
Haslemere d.	2155	2223	2255	2325	0005	0034		0530	0650	0749	0821	0853	minutes	2155	2221	2254	2324	2354	0013	0051		0807	0907	0923	1007	1030
Petersfield d.	2212	2234	2312	2336	0021	0050		0546	0706	0806	0832	0904	past each	2207	2232	2305	2335	0005	0024	0107		0823	0923	0934	1023	1041
Havant a.	2227	2246	2326	2350	0036	0105		0601	0722	0827	0845	0917	hour until	2220	2245	2318	2350	0018	0036	0122		0838	0938	0947	1040	1054
Portsmouth & Southsea a.	2244	2303	2343	0004	0052	0121		0617	0738	0848	0858	0930		2233	2257	2330	0004	0030	0049	0138		0853	0955	1000	1055	1107
Portsmouth Harbour a.	2248	2307	2348	0008	...	0125		0622	0743	0852	0902	0936		2237	2302	2335	0008	0035	0054	...		0857	1000	1004	1100	1112

	⑦	⑦	⑦	⑦	⑦	⑦	⑦		⑦	⑦	⑦	⑦	⑦
London Waterloo 105/9 d.	1000	1030	1100	1130	1200	1230	1300		2130	2200	2230	2300	2330
Woking 105/9 d.	1033	1102	1133	1202	1233	1257	1333	and at	2157	2232	2257	2332	0002
Guildford d.	1042	1112	1142	1212	1242	1305	1342	the same	2205	2242	2305	2342	0012
Haslemere d.	1107	1130	1207	1230	1307	1323	1407	minutes	2223	2307	2323	0007	0029
Petersfield d.	1123	1141	1223	1241	1323	1334	1423	past each	2234	2323	2334	0023	0040
Havant a.	1140	1154	1240	1254	1340	1346	1440	hour until	2247	2338	2348	0038	0053
Portsmouth & Southsea a.	1155	1207	1255	1308	1355	1359	1455		2300	2355	0001	0053	0105
Portsmouth Harbour a.	1200	1212	1300	1312	1400	1403	1500		2304	2359	0006	0058	0109

	Ⓐ	Ⓐ	Ⓐ	Ⓐ	Ⓐ	Ⓐ	Ⓐ	Ⓐ
Portsmouth Harbour d.		0425	0512	0523	0545	0610	0640	0713
Portsmouth & Southsea d.		0430	0517	0528	0550	0615	0644	0718
Havant d.		0446	0530	0544	0604	0627	0658	0732
Petersfield d.		0503	0544	0604	0618	0642	0714	0747
Haslemere d.		0521	0557	0623	0637	0658	0733	0800
Guildford d.		0550	0624	0643	0701	0715	0752	0819
Woking 105/9 a.		0600	0635	0651	0712	0726	0800	0827
London Waterloo 105/9 a.		0630	0709	0723	0743	0753	0827	0854

	Ⓐ	Ⓐ	Ⓐ	Ⓐ	Ⓐ	Ⓐ	Ⓐ	Ⓐ		Ⓐ	Ⓐ	Ⓐ	Ⓐ	Ⓐ	Ⓐ	Ⓐ	Ⓐ	Ⓐ	Ⓐ	Ⓐ	Ⓐ	Ⓐ	⑥	⑥	⑥	⑥
Portsmouth Harbour d.	0745	0815	0833	0915	0933	1015	1033	1115		1615	1633	1715	1733	1815	1833	1915	1933	2015	2033	2133	2233	2319		0441	0515	0533
Portsmouth & Southsea d.	0751	0820	0837	0919	0937	1019	1037	1119	and at	1620	1637	1720	1737	1820	1838	1920	1938	2020	2038	2138	2237	2324		0446	0520	0537
Havant d.	0804	0834	0854	0934	0954	1034	1054	1134	the same	1634	1654	1734	1754	1834	1855	1934	1954	2033	2054	2154	2253	2340		0502	0533	0553
Petersfield d.	0819	0849	0910	0948	1010	1048	1110	1148	minutes	1648	1710	1749	1810	1848	1911	1948	2011	2048	2111	2210	2309	2357		0519	0547	0609
Haslemere d.	0833	0902	0930	1002	1029	1102	1129	1202	past each	1701	1730	1803	1829	1901	1929	2000	2030	2101	2129	2228	2326	0015		0539	0600	0626
Guildford d.	0853	0919	0952	1019	1049	1119	1149	1219	hour until	1719	1748	1822	1849	1922	1948	2017	2049	2118	2150	2248	2353	0038		0604	0619	0650
Woking 105/9 a.	|	0927	0959	1026	1057	1126	1157	1227		1727	1756	1833	1856	|	1956	2026	2058	2126	2159	2255	0003	...		0611	0626	|
London Waterloo 105/9 a.	0930	0955	1032	1051	1124	1151	1223	1255		1752	1824	1859	1922	1959	2024	2051	2131	2151	2226	2320	0039	...		0641	0655	0734

	⑥	⑥	⑥	⑥		⑥	⑥	⑥	⑥	⑥	⑥	⑦	⑦	⑦	⑦	⑦	⑦	⑦	⑦	⑦	⑦		⑦	⑦	⑦
Portsmouth Harbour d.	0615	0645	0715	0745	✣	1945	2015	2033	2132	2233	2319		0643	0732	0743	0832	0848	0932	0948	1032	1048		2148	2232	2248
Portsmouth & Southsea d.	0619	0649	0721	0751		1951	2020	2038	2136	2238	2324		0648	0737	0747	0837	0852	0937	0952	1037	1052	and at	2152	2237	2252
Havant d.	0634	0705	0734	0804	and at	2004	2034	2054	2152	2254	2341		0702	0751	0802	0850	0907	0950	1007	1050	1107	the same	2207	2250	2307
Petersfield d.	0648	0719	0748	0818	the same	2018	2048	2110	2208	2310	2357		0719	0805	0819	0904	0924	1004	1024	1104	1124	minutes	2224	2304	2324
Haslemere d.	0700	0731	0800	0832	minutes	2032	2100	2128	2225	2328	0015		0739	0817	0839	0917	0942	1017	1042	1117	1142	past each	2242	2317	2342
Guildford d.	0719	0748	0819	0849	past each	2049	2119	2151	2249	2351	0037		0803	0835	0904	0935	1005	1035	1105	1135	1205	hour until	2305	2335	0008
Woking 105/9 a.	0728	0755	0827	0857	hour until	2057	2127	2159	2256	0002	...		0813	0842	0913	0942	1013	1042	1113	1142	1213		2314	2342	0017
London Waterloo 105/9 a.	0754	0820	0854	0924		2122	2152	2228	2325	0037	...		0849	0920	0949	1019	1048	1119	1148	1215	1244		2344	0015	...

f – Arrives 0611.

✣ – The 1045 from Portsmouth Harbour arrives London at 1228.

SW 🍸 on most trains. LONDON - SOUTHAMPTON - BOURNEMOUTH - WEYMOUTH 105

km			①	Ⓐ	Ⓐ	Ⓐ	Ⓐ	Ⓐ	Ⓐ	Ⓐ	Ⓐ	Ⓐ	Ⓐ	Ⓐ	Ⓐ		Ⓐ	Ⓐ	Ⓐ	Ⓐ	Ⓐ	Ⓐ	Ⓐ	Ⓐ	Ⓐ	Ⓐ
0	**London** Waterloo **104/9** d.	Ⓐ	0010	...	...	...	0530	...	...	0630	...	0703	0735	0805	0835	⊠	1505	1535	1605	1635	1705	1735	1805	1835	1905	1935
39	Woking **104/9** d.		0042	...	...	...	0601	...	...	0657	...	0730	0800	|	0900		|	1600	|	1659**u**	|	|	|	|	|	2000
77	Basingstoke **107 109** d.		0101	...	...	...	0621	...	...	0718	...	0750	0819	0849	|	and	1549	|	1648	1719	1746	1817	1846	1917	1948	|
107	Winchester **107** d.		0118	...	...	...	0638	...	...	0735	...	0807	0836	0906	0933	at	1605	1633	1705	1735	1803	1833	1903	1934	2005	2033
120	**Southampton** ✈ **107** d.		0132	...	...	...	0653	...	...	0750	...	0819	0850	0914	0942	the	1614	1642	1714	1744	1812	1842	1911	1943	2014	2042
128	**Southampton** Cen. **107** d.		0139	...	...	0617*	0702	...	0730	0759	...	0827	0859	0925	0952	same	1626**f**	1653	1725	1755	1822	1853	1922	1954	2025	2051
149	Brockenhurst **107** d.		...	...	0610*	0636*	0718	...	0757	0820	...	0844	0913	0940	1006	minutes	1640	1711	1739	1810	|	|	|	|	2040	2105
174	**Bournemouth** **107** d.		...	0606*	0640*	0707***f**	0746	0804	0818	0848	0904	0912	0932	1005	1025	past	1702	1728	1757	1826	1851	1923	1950	2022	2058	2124
183	Poole d.		...	0619*	0653*	0720*	0758	0817	0830	0900	0917	0923	0944	1016	1038	each	1717	1740	1810	1838	1903	1935	2003	2035	2110	2137
193	Wareham d.		...	0634*	0708	0735*	0812	0831	...	0912	0931	...	0956	1030	1050	hour	1730	1752	1824	1850	1917	1947	2017	2046	2122	2149
219	Dorchester South d.		...	0656	0735	0757	0833	0851	...	0933	0951	...	1013	1050	1106	until	1751	1809	1846	1908	1942•	2005	2038	2104	2149	2209
230	**Weymouth** a.		...	0709	0746	0810	0846	0905	...	0946	1005	...	1025	1107•	1118		1805	1818	1902	1918•	1956•	2019•	2054	2118	2201	2223

	Ⓐ	Ⓐ	Ⓐ	Ⓐ	Ⓐ	Ⓐ	Ⓐ		⑥	⑥	⑥	⑥	⑥	⑥	⑥	⑥	⑥	⑥	⑥	⑥		⑥	⑥	⑥	⑥	⑥
London Waterloo **104/9** d.	2005	2035	2105	2135	2205	2235	2335	⑥	0105	...	...	...	0530	...	0630	...	0735	0805	0835	0905	⊠	1905	1935	2005	2035	2105
Woking **104/9** d.	|	2100	|	2200	|	2300	0004		0142	...	...	...	0603	...	0657	...	0800	|	0900	|		|	2000	|	2100	|
Basingstoke **107 109** d.	2049	|	2149	|	2250	|	0035		0209**s**	...	...	...	0623	...	0718	...	0821	0849	|	0948	and	1948	|	2049	|	2148
Winchester **107** d.	2105	2133	2205	2234	2306	2333	0051		0226**s**	...	...	...	0642	...	0734	...	0838	0905	0933	1005	at	2005	2033	2105	2133	2205
Southampton ✈ **107** d.	2114	2142	2217	2243	2315	2342	0105		0239**s**	...	...	...	0655	...	0748	...	0851	0914	0942	1014	the	2014	2042	2114	2142	2214
Southampton Cen **107** d.	2125	2151	2227	2252	2324	2353	0113		0249	...	...	0615*	0705	0721	0800	0817	0900	0924	0951	1024	same	2024	2051	2124	2151	2229
Brockenhurst **107** d.	2142	2206	2247	2306	2343	0007	0130**s**		...	...	0610*	0634*	0721	0740	0817	0838	0914	0938	1006	1038	minutes	2038	2105	2143	2205	2248
Bournemouth **107** d.	2209	2224	2314	2324	0010	0024	0152		...	0606*	0640*	0706***f**	0749	0809	0844	0908	0930	1004	1024	1104	past	2104	2124	2212	2224	2317
Poole d.	...	2237	...	2337	...	0036	...		...	0619*	0652*	0719*	0801	0822	0857	0921	0943	1014	1037	1114	each	2115	2137	2227	2237	2331
Wareham d.	...	2249	...	2349	...	...	...		...	0634*	0707*	0734*	0813	0836	0909	0934	0955	1028	1049	1128	hour	2127	2149	...	2249	...
Dorchester South d.	...	2309	...	0010	...	...	...		...	0656	0730	0758	0833	0856	0929	0955	1011	1049	1105	1149	until	2151	2209	...	2309	...
Weymouth a.	...	2323	...	0024	...	...	...		...	0709	0743	0811	0846	0910	0943	1008	1023•	1105•	1116	1205•		2205	2223	...	2323	...

	⑥	⑥	⑥	⑥	⑥		⑦	⑦	⑦	⑦	⑦	⑦	⑦	⑦		⑦	⑦	⑦	⑦		⑦	⑦	⑦	⑦	⑦
London Waterloo **104/9** d.	2135	2205	2235	2305	2335	⑦	0010	0105	...	...	...	0753	0835	0853	⊠	1435	1454	1535	1605	⊠	2035	2105	2135	2205	2305
Woking **104/9** d.	2200	|	2300	2332	0003		0040	0149	...	...	...	0828	0907	0928		1507	1528	1607	1637		2107	2137	2207	2237	2337
Basingstoke **107 109** d.	|	2250	|	2352	0035		0100	0216**s**	...	0748	...	0848	0927	0948	and	1527	1547	1627	1657	and	2127	2157	2227	2257	2357
Winchester **107** d.	2233	2307	2333	0011	0051		0116	0233**s**	...	0807	...	0908	0944	1008	at	1544	1607	1644	1714	at	2144	2214	2244	2314	0014
Southampton ✈ **107** d.	2242	2315	2342	0026	0105		0129	0246**s**	...	0825	...	0927	0953	1027	the	1553	1625	1653	1727	the	2153	2227	2253	2327	0028
Southampton Cen **107** d.	2252	2324	2351	0037	0112		0138	0256	...	0834	0903	0935	1003	1035	same	1603	1634	1703	1736	same	2203	2236	2303	2336	0040
Brockenhurst **107** d.	2307	2343	0005	0053**s**	...		0154**s**	...	...	0855	0917	0957	1017	1057	minutes	1617	1655	1717	1757	minutes	2217	2257	2317	2355	0056**s**
Bournemouth **107** d.	2327	0011	0029	0117	...		0216	...	0839	0924	0939**f**	1024	1039**f**	1124	past	1639**f**	1723	1739**f**	1824	past	2239**f**	2324	2339**f**	0022	0120
Poole d.	2340	0024	0041	0129	...		...	...	0851	0933	0951	1034	1051	1134	each	1651	1733	1751	1834	each	2251	2334	2351	0035	0133
Wareham d.	2351	...	...	...	...		...	...	0903	...	1003	...	1103	...	hour	1703	...	1803	...	hour	2303	...	0003	...	...
Dorchester South d.	0012	...	...	...	...		...	...	0924	...	1024	...	1124	...	until	1724	...	1826	...	until	2324	...	0024	...	...
Weymouth a.	0026	...	...	...	...		...	...	0935	...	1037	...	1136	...		1736	...	1838	...		2336	...	0036	...	...

		Ⓐ	Ⓐ	Ⓐ	Ⓐ	Ⓐ	Ⓐ	Ⓐ	Ⓐ	Ⓐ	Ⓐ	Ⓐ	Ⓐ	Ⓐ	Ⓐ		Ⓐ	Ⓐ	Ⓐ	Ⓐ	Ⓐ	Ⓐ	Ⓐ	Ⓐ	Ⓐ	Ⓐ
Weymouth d.	Ⓐ	...	...	...	...	...	0550*	...	0620*	0650*	...	0721	0752	0817	0900	⊠	1517	1600	1617	1700	1717	1800	1819	1900	1915*	1957
Dorchester South d.		...	...	...	...	...	0602*	...	0632*	0702*	...	0733	0805	0830	0910		1530	1610	1630	1710	1730	1810	1831	1910	1927***f**	2008
Wareham d.		...	...	...	...	...	0625	...	0653*	0723*	...	0754	0825	0851	0927	and	1551	1627	1651	1727	1751	1827	1852	1927	1953*	2027
Poole d.		...	...	0457	0538	0553	0640	0648	0708	0738	0801	0808	0839	0907	0939	at	1605	1639	1705	1739	1807	1839	1906	1939	2008	2039
Bournemouth **107** d.		...	...	0512	0553	0609	0655	0702	0723	0753	0815	0822	0854	0922**f**	0957	the	1620	1657	1720	1757	1820	1857	1920	1957	2021	2057
Brockenhurst **107** d.		...	...	0535	0609	0638	|	0731	|	0809	0838	0850	0911	0944	1014	same	1644	1714	1744	1814	1844	1914	1944	2014	2044	2114
Southampton Cen **107** d.		0449	0515	0555	0630	0700	0730**f**	0800**j**	0800	0830	0900	0930**c**	0930	1000	1030	minutes	1700	1730	1800	1830	1900	1930	2000	2030	2100	2130
Southampton ✈ **107** d.		0500	0523	0603	0638	0708	0738	0809	0809	0838	0909	0938	0938	1008	1038	past	1708	1738	1808	1838	1908	1938	2008	2037	2107	2138
Winchester **107** d.		0517	0531	0618	0647	0718	0748	0818	0818	0848	0919	0948	0948	1018	1048	each	1718	1748	1818	1848	1918	1948	2018	2048	2118	2148
Basingstoke **107 109** a.		0538	0546	0635	0703	0734	|	0834	0834	|	0935	|	|	1034	|	hour	1734	|	1834	|	1934	|	2034	|	2135	|
Woking **104/9** a.		0605	...	0655	|	|	|	0854	0854	0922	0954	1020	1020	|	1120	until	|	1820	|	1924	|	2020	2053	2119	2155	2219
London Waterloo **104/9** a.		0634	...	0726	0747	0819	0848	0925	0925	0953	1026	1049	1049	1120	1147		1820	1849	1920	1951	2019	2049	2129	2148	2224	2244

	Ⓐ	Ⓐ	Ⓐ	Ⓐ		⑥	⑥	⑥	⑥	⑥	⑥	⑥	⑥	⑥	⑥		⑥	⑥	⑥	⑥	⑥	⑥	⑥	⑥	⑥	⑥
Weymouth d.	2005	2057	2207	2309	⑥	...	...	...	...	0537*	0612*	0652	0717	0800	0820	⊠	1800	1817	1900	1917	...	2007	2054	...	2210	2309
Dorchester South d.	2018	2109	2220	2321		...	...	...	...	0547*	0624*	0704	0729	0810	0833		1810	1830	1910	1930	...	2019	2107	...	2222	2321
Wareham d.	2040	2130	2241	2342		...	...	...	...	0606*	0645*	0725	0751	0827	0853	and	1827	1851	1927	1951	...	2040	2128	...	2242	2342
Poole d.	2052	2143	2253	2354		...	...	...	0525	0621	0700	0740	0805	0839	0907	at	1839	1905	1939	2005	2037	2053	2140	2152	2254	2354
Bournemouth **107** d.	2110	2210**c**	2310	0003		...	...	...	0540	0639	0719	0757	0820	0857	0922**f**	the	1857	1920	1957	2020	2056**f**	2110	2157	2210**f**	2311	0003
Brockenhurst **107** d.	2139	2239	2339	...		...	...	...	0609	0708	0742	0814	0844	0914	0944	same	1914	1944	2014	2044	2112	2139	2214	2238	2339	...
Southampton Cen **107** d.	2200	2300	2357	...		0508	0526*	0557	0630	0730	0800	0830	0900	0930	1000	minutes	1930	2000	2030	2100	2130	2200	2230	2300	2359	...
Southampton ✈ **107** d.	2208	2308	...	...		0516	0538	0605	0638	0738	0808	0838	0908	0938	1008	past	1938	2008	2038	2108	2138	2208	2238	2308	0010	...
Winchester **107** d.	2224	2324	...	...		0536	0557	0621	0648	0748	0818	0848	0918	0948	1018	each	1948	2018	2048	2118	2148	2223	2256	2325	...	...
Basingstoke **107 109** a.	2240	2343	...	...		0552	0618	0639	0704	|	0834	|	0934	|	1034	hour	|	2034	|	2134	|	2239	2313	2343	...	...
Woking **104/9** a.	2300	0020	...	...		0630	0658	0659	0723	0822	|	0920	|	1020	|	until	2020	|	2120	2154	2219	2300	2334	0018	...	...
London Waterloo **104/9** a.	2329	...	...	...		0659	0738	0729	0752	0848	0920	0947	1020	1047	1120		2046	2119	2146	2223	2244	2332	0012	0103	...	...

		⑦	⑦	⑦	⑦	⑦		⑦	⑦	⑦	⑦		⑦	⑦	⑦	⑦		⑦	⑦	⑦	⑦	⑦	⑦	⑦	⑦
Weymouth d.	⑦	...	...	...	...	0743*	...	...	0845	...	0945	⊠	...	1245	...	1346	⊠	1742	...	1845	...	1955	2055	2155	2256
Dorchester South d.		...	...	...	...	0755*	...	...	0857	...	0957		...	1257	...	1358		1757	...	1857	...	2007	2107	2207	2308
Wareham d.		...	...	...	...	0816*	...	...	0918	...	1018	and	...	1318	...	1419	and	1818	...	1918	...	2028	2128	2228	2329
Poole d.		...	...	0719	0747	0829	...	0852	0931	0953	1031	at	1253	1331	1353	1431	at	1831	1853	1931	1953	2047	2148**f**	2248**f**	2349**j**
Bournemouth **107** d.		...	...	0735	0803	0847	...	0903	0949	1004	1049	the	1304	1349	1404	1449	the	1849	1904	1949	2004	2104	2206	2306	0002
Brockenhurst **107** d.		...	...	0803	0831	0907	...	0931	1007	1032	1108	same	1332	1408	1432	1509	same	1908	1932	2008	2032	2133	2235	2335	...
Southampton Cen **107** d.		0652	0754	0826	0855	0925	...	0955	1025	1055	1125	minutes	1355	1425	1455	1525	minutes	1925	1955	2025	2055	2155	2255	2355	...
Southampton ✈ **107** d.		0700	0802	0834	0903	0933	...	1003	1033	1103	1132	past	1403	1433	1503	1533	past	1933	2003	2033	2103	2203	2303	...	...
Winchester **107** d.		0722	0823	0843	0923	0942	...	1023	1042	1123	1142	each	1423	1442	1517	1542	each	1942	2017	2042	2117	2217	2323	...	...
Basingstoke **107 109** a.		0742	0845	0901	0942	0958	...	1042	1058	1142	1158	hour	1443	1458	1533	1558	hour	1958	2033	2058	2133	2234	2342	...	...
Woking **104/9** a.		0802	0904	0928	1002	1019	...	1102	1118	1203	1218	until	1502	1518	1553	1618	until	2018	2053	2118	2153	2254	0002	...	...
London Waterloo **104/9** a.		0841	0940	1007	1040	1051	...	1139	1152	1237	1249		1537	1549	1624	1649		2049	2124	2149	2224	2324	0033	...	...

Brockenhurst - Lymington Pier (for ⛴ to Isle of Wight).
Journey 11 minutes. Trains call at Lymington Town 6 minutes later:
Ⓐ: 0559, 0629, 0659, 0729, 0759, 0835, 0910, 0942 and every 30 minutes until 1612, 1644, 1714, 1744, 1814, 1848 and every 30 minutes until 2218.
⑥: 0612, 0642 and every 30 minutes until 2112, 2148, 2218.
⑦: 0859, 0929 and every 30 minutes until 2059, 2129, 2159.

Lymington Pier - Brockenhurst.
Journey 11 minutes. Trains call at Lymington Town 2 minutes later:
Ⓐ: 0614 and every 30 minutes until 0814, 0855, 0927, 0957 and every 30 minutes until 1627, 1659, 1729, 1759, 1829, 1903 and every 30 minutes until 2203, 2236.
⑥: 0627, 0657 and every 30 minutes until 2127, 2203, 2236.
⑦: 0914, 0944 and every 30 minutes until 2114, 2144, 2214.

c – Arrives 13 minutes earlier.
f – Arrives 5–6 minutes earlier.
j – Arrives 2341.
s – Calls to set down only.
u – Calls to pick up only.
⊠ – Timings may vary ± 3 minutes.
* – 4–5 minutes later until Sept. 21.
• – 4–5 minutes earlier until Sept. 20.
☛ For ⛴ services Portsmouth / Poole – Jersey / Guernsey / St Malo and v.v., see Table **2100**.

IL 2nd class PORTSMOUTH - RYDE - SHANKLIN 106

Through fares including ferry are available. Allow 10 minutes for connections between trains and ferries. Operator: Wightlink ✆ 0333 999 7333. www.wightlink.co.uk

Portsmouth Harbour - Ryde Pier Head: ⛴
0515Ⓐ, 0615Ⓐ, 0715 and hourly until 1815, 1920, 2020, 2145, 2245.

Ryde Pier Head - Portsmouth Harbour: Journey: ± 22 minutes
0540Ⓐ, 0645Ⓐ, 0745 and hourly until 1845, 1945, 2052, 2215, 2310.

Additional services may operate on Ⓐ and on public holidays.

Island Line rail service *14 km.*

From Ryde Pier Head to Shanklin (Journey time approx. 27 minutes; calls at **Sandown** 21 minutes later): 0603⚒, 0647⚒, 0637⑦, 0726⚒, 0753⑦, 0803⚒, 0847, 0926, 1003*, 1047*, 1126* and at the same times every **two** hours until 1647*⚒, 1726, 1803, 1847, 1926, 2007⚒, 2052, 2157.

From Shanklin to Ryde Pier Head (Journey time approx. 27 minutes; calls at **Sandown** 7 minutes later): 0607⚒, 0651⚒, 0708⑦, 0730⚒, 0807, 0851, 0930, 1007*, 1051*, 1130* and at the same times every **two** hours until 1607*, 1651, 1730, 1807, 1851, 1930⚒, 2010, 2123, 2233.

* – Also calls at Smallbrook Junction (connection with **Isle of Wight Steam Railway** (🚂) 9 minutes from Ryde Pier Head / 16 minutes from Shanklin (only when steam railway is operating).

🚂 – **Isle of Wight Steam Railway** (🚂 Smallbrook Junction - Haven Street - Wootton: *9 km*). ✆ 01983 882204. www.iwsteamrailway.co.uk

107 BIRMINGHAM - READING - SOUTHAMPTON - BOURNEMOUTH

Most services convey 🍷 XC

km	⚒	Ⓐ	⑥	Ⓐ	⑥	⚒N	Ⓐ	⑥	⚒	Ⓐ	⑥	⚒	⚒	⚒	⚒	⚒	⑥	Ⓐ	⚒	⑥	Ⓐ	⚒	⑥	Ⓐ	Ⓐ	⑥
	Manchester Piccadilly **119** .. d.	...	...	0511	0511	...	...	...	0725	0825	0825	0925	...	1025	1125	...	1225	1225	1325	...	...	1425	1525	1525	...	...
	Newcastle **119** ... d.	...	...	|	|	...	...	...	|	|	|	|	0835	|	|	1035	|	|	|	1233	1236	|	|	|	1435	1433
	York **119** ... d.	...	...	|	|	...	0624	0624	|	|	|	|	0935	|	|	1136	|	|	|	1336	1336	|	|	|	1537	1538
0	**Birmingham** New St **141 150** d.	0603	0603	0703	0703	0803	0833	0838	0903	1003	1003	1103	1133	1203	1303	1333	1403	1403	1503	1533	1533	1603	1703	1703	1734	1733
13	Birmingham Int'l ✈ ... **141 150** d.	0613	0613	0713	0713	0813	|	|	0913	1013	1013	1113	|	1213	1313	|	1413	1413	1513	|	|	1613	1713	1713	|	|
30	**Coventry** ... **141 142 150** d.	0625	0626	0726	0726	0826	|	|	0926	1026	1026	1126	|	1226	1326	|	1426	1426	1526	|	|	1625	1726	1726	|	|
45	Leamington Spa. **124 141 142** d.	0638	0638	0739	0739	0838	0901	0905	0941	1038	1038	1138	1200	1238	1338	1400	1438	1438	1538	1600	1602	1638	1738	1739	1802	1801
77	Banbury ... **124** d.	0655	0655	0756	0756	0855	0923	0923	0958	1055	1056	1155	1217	1255	1355	1417	1456	1456	1555	1617	1619	1656	1755	1757	1819	1818
114	**Oxford** ... **131** d.	0716	0716	0816	0818	0916	0942	0943	1019	1116	1117	1215	1243	1316	1416	1442	1516	1516	1616	1643	1647v	1716	1817	1817	1841	1843
158	**Reading** ... **131** a.	0744	0742	0848	0841	0943	1007	1005	1045	1139	1142	1242a	1312	1342	1442	1508	1540	1542	1641	1707	1714	1741	1841	1841	1906	1909
158	**Reading** ... d.	0752	0752	0854	0852	0952	...	...	1052	1152	1152	1252	...	1352	1452	...	1552	1552	1652	...	...	1752	1852	1852	...	...
183	Basingstoke ... **105** a.	0809	0810	0910	0909	1009	...	...	1109	1209	1210	1309	...	1410	1509	...	1609	1611	1709	...	...	1809	1909	1910	...	...
213	Winchester ... **105** a.	0826	0830	0926	0926	1026	...	...	1126	1226	1226	1326	...	1426	1526	...	1626	1627	1726	...	...	1826	1926	1926	...	...
226	**Southampton** Airport ✈ . **105** a.	0834	0839	0935	0935	1035	...	...	1135	1236	1235	1335	...	1435	1535	...	1635	1636	1735	...	...	1834	1934	1935	...	...
234	**Southampton** Central .... **105** a.	0842	0847	0943	0943	1043	...	...	1143	1247	1243	1343	...	1443	1543	...	1643	1644	1743	...	...	1842	1942	1944	...	...
255	Brockenhurst ... **105** a.	|	|	0958	0958	|	...	...	|	|	|	|	...	|	|	...	|	|	|	...	...	1858y	1958	|	...	...
280	**Bournemouth** ... **105** a.	0913	0916	1013	1013	1112	...	...	1212	1315	1312	1412	...	1512	1612	...	1715	1721	1817h	...	...	1914	2013	2015	...	...

	⑥	Ⓐ	⑥	Ⓐ	Ⓐ	⑥	Ⓐ	⑥	Ⓐ
Manchester Piccadilly **119** ... d.	1625	1625	1725	1725	1825	1825	1925	1925	2025
Newcastle **119** ... d.	|	|	|	|	|	|	|	|	|
York **119** ... d.	|	|	|	|	|	|	|	|	|
Birmingham New St **141 150** d.	1803	1803	1903	1903	2003	2003	2103	2103	2203
Birmingham Int'l ✈ ... **141 150** d.	1813	1813	1913	1913	2013	2013	2114	2113	2213
Coventry ... **141 142 150** d.	1826	1826	1926	1926	2026	2026	2126	2126	2226
Leamington Spa.. **124 141 142** d.	1838	1839	1938	1939	2038	2038	2138	2138	2238
Banbury ... **124** d.	1855	1856	1955	1956	2055	2055	2155	2155	2255
Oxford ... **131** d.	1917	1916	2016	2019	2116	2116	2215	2216	2315
Reading ... **131** a.	1941	1941	2039	2043	2139	2140	2238	2239	2338
Reading ... d.	1952	1950	2052	2049	2152	2152	2249	2252	...
Basingstoke ... **105** a.	2009	2010	2109	2111	2209	2209	2307	2309	...
Winchester ... **105** a.	2026	2026	2126	2127	2226	2226	2327	2326	...
Southampton Airport ✈ .. **105** a.	2034	2035	2135	2136	2234	2235	2335	2334	...
Southampton Central ... **105** a.	2042	2043	2143	2144	2242	2243	2345	2342	...
Brockenhurst ... **105** a.	|	|	|	|	|	|	...	...	...
Bournemouth ... **105** a.	2112	2116	2215	2215	2316	2319	...	...	...

⑦	⑦	⑦	⑦	⑦	⑦	⑦	⑦	⑦	⑦	⑦S	⑦	⑦	⑦	⑦	⑦	⑦	⑦
Manchester Piccadilly **119** ... d.	...	0826	0927	1026	...	1124	...	1225	1325	...	1425	...	1525	1625	1725	1825	1925
Newcastle **119** ... d.	...	|	|	|	...	|	...	|	|	...	|	...	|	|	|	|	|
York **119** ... d.	...	|	|	|	...	|	...	|	|	...	|	1435	|	|	|	|	|
Birmingham New St **141 150** d.	0903	1003	1103	1203	1230	1303	1333	1403	1503	1533	1603	1630	1703	1803	1903	2003	2103
Birmingham Int'l ✈ ... **141 150** d.	0913	1013	1113	1213	1240	1313	|	1413	1513	|	1613	1641	1713	1813	1913	2013	2113
Coventry ... **141 142 150** d.	0926	1026	1126	1226	1252	1326	|	1426	1526	|	1626	1654	1726	1826	1926	2026	2126
Leamington Spa.. **124 141 142** d.	0938	1038	1138	1238	1308	1338	1400	1438	1540	1600	1638	1710	1738	1838	1938	2038	2138
Banbury ... **124** d.	0955	1055	1155	1255	1325	1355	1417	1455	1557	1617	1655	1727	1755	1855	1955	2055	2155
Oxford ... **131** d.	1016	1116	1216	1316	1345	1418c	1437	1516	1617	1637	1716	1747	1816	1916	2016	2116	2216
Reading ... **131** a.	1040	1139	1240	1339	1409	1442	1501	1539	1640	1701	1739	1812	1840	1939	2040	2139	2239
Reading ... d.	1052	1152	1252	1352	...	1452	...	1552	1652	...	1752	...	1852	1952	2052	2152	...
Basingstoke ... **105** a.	1110	1210	1311	1410	...	1510	...	1610	1710	...	1810	...	1910	2010	2110	2210	...
Winchester ... **105** a.	1126	1226	1327	1426	...	1526	...	1626	1726	...	1826	...	1926	2026	2126	2226	...
Southampton Airport ✈ .. **105** a.	1134	1234	1335	1434	...	1534	...	1634	1734	...	1834	...	1934	2034	2134	2234	...
Southampton Central ... **105** a.	1142	1244	1344	1442b	...	1544f	...	1642b	1744f	...	1842b	...	1942b	2045t	2142b	2242	...
Brockenhurst ... **105** a.	|	|	|	|	...	|	...	|	|	...	1903b	...	|	|	|	...	...
Bournemouth ... **105** a.	1227	1327	1427	1525	...	1625	...	1725	1827	...	1927	...	2027	2127	2227	...	...

⚒	⑥	Ⓐ	Ⓐ	⑥	Ⓐ	⑥	Ⓐ	⑥	Ⓐ	⑥	Ⓐ	⑥	Ⓐ	⑥	⚒	⚒	⚒	⚒	Ⓐ	⑥	⚒	Ⓐ	⑥	⚒	⚒	Ⓐ
Bournemouth ... **105** d.	...	...	...	...	...	...	0630	0635	0730	0745	0840	0845	...	...	0945	1045	1145	1245	...	...	1345	...	...	1445	1545	...
Brockenhurst ... **105** d.	...	...	...	...	...	...	|	|	|	|	|	|	...	...	1000	|	|	|	...	...	|	...	...	|	|	...
Southampton Central ... **105** d.	0515	0515	...	...	0615	0615	0715j	0715j	0815j	0815	0915	0915	...	...	1015	1115	1215	1315	...	...	1415	...	...	1515	1615	...
Southampton Airport ✈ .. **105** d.	0523	0523	...	...	0624	0624	0723	0723	0823	0823	0923	0923	...	...	1023	1123	1223	1323	...	...	1423	...	...	1523	1623	...
Winchester ... **105** d.	0531	0531	...	...	0633	0632	0731	0731	0831	0831	0933	0932	...	...	1031	1132	1231	1332	...	...	1431	...	...	1531	1631	...
Basingstoke ... **105** d.	0547	0549	...	...	0651	0649	0750	0747	0848	0849	0949	0949	...	...	1048	1149	1248	1349	...	...	1448	...	...	1548	1648	...
Reading ... a.	0609	0606	...	...	0708	0706	0809	0805	0911	0907	1010	1007	...	...	1108	1207	1306	1409	...	...	1506	...	...	1609	1706	...
Reading ... **131** d.	0615	0615	0645	0645	0715	0715	0815	0815	0915	0915	1015	1015	1046	1043	1114	1215	1315	1415	1445	1445	1514	1543	1545	1615	1715	1745
Oxford ... d.	0639	0639	0710	0712	0740	0739	0839	0840	0939	0939	1038	1039	1112	1112	1139	1239	1339	1439	1510	1511	1539	1610	1610	1639	1739	1811
Banbury ... **124** d.	0658	0658	0728	0730	0758	0757	0858	0858	0957	0958	1059	1058	1131	1131	1158	1258	1358	1458	1532	1529	1558	1628	1628	1658	1758	1830
Leamington Spa... **124 141** d.	0715	0716	0750	0749	0816	0815	0917	0916	1015	1016	1117	1116	1149	1149	1216	1316	1416	1515	1550	1549	1616	1649	1650c	1716	1816	1848
Coventry ... **141 142 150** d.	0730	0730	|	|	0830	0830	0930	0930	1030	1030	1130	1130	|	|	1230	1330	1430	1530	|	|	1630	|	|	1730	1830	|
Birmingham Int'l ✈ ... **141 150** d.	0741	0741	|	|	0841	0841	0941	0941	1041	1041	1141	1141	|	|	1241	1341	1441	1541	|	|	1641	|	|	1741	1841	|
Birmingham New St **141 150** a.	0751	0751	0815	0815	0851	0851	0951	0951	1051	1051	1151	1151	1216	1217	1251	1351	1451	1551	1618	1618	1651	1718	1718	1751	1851	1917
York **119** ... a.	|	|	1017	1017	|	|	|	|	|	|	|	|	1415	1415	|	|	|	|	1902	1901	|	1920	1915	|	|	2115
Newcastle **119** ... a.	|	|	1115	1117	|	|	|	|	|	|	|	|	1524	1524	|	|	|	|	2000	2004	|	...	...	|	|	...
Manchester Piccadilly **119** ... a.	0929	0929	...	...	1029	1029	1129	1129	1229	1229	1329	1329	...	...	1429	1529	1629	1729	...	...	1829	...	...	1929	2029	...

	⑥	⚒	⚒	Ⓐ	⑥	Ⓐ	Ⓐ	⑥
Bournemouth ... **105** d.	...	1645	1745	1845	1845	...	1945	1945
Brockenhurst ... **105** d.	...	|	|	1900	|	...	|	2000
Southampton Central ... **105** d.	...	1715	1815	1915	1915	...	2015	2015
Southampton Airport ✈ .. **105** d.	...	1723	1823	1923	1923	...	2023	2023
Winchester ... **105** d.	...	1731	1831	1931	1932	...	2032	2032
Basingstoke ... **105** d.	...	1749	1848	1949	1950	...	2049	2049
Reading ... a.	...	1808	1907	2009	2010	...	2108	2106
Reading ... **131** d.	1745	1815	1915	2015	2015	2042	2115	2115
Oxford ... d.	1810	1839	1939	2040	2040	2109	2139	2139
Banbury ... **124** d.	1828	1858	1958	2058	2058	2129	2157	2158
Leamington Spa... **124 141** d.	1850c	1916	2016	2116	2116	2149	2216	2216
Coventry ... **141 142 150** d.	|	1930	2030	2130	2130	|	2228	2230
Birmingham Int'l ✈ ... **141 150** d.	|	1941	2041	2141	2141	|	2238	2240
Birmingham New St **141 150** a.	1917	1951	2051	2151	2151	2221	2249	2250
York **119** ... a.	2126	|	|	|	|	|	...	...
Newcastle **119** ... a.	2228	|	|	|	|	|	...	...
Manchester Piccadilly **119** ... a.	...	2129	2230	2331	2329	0013	...	...

⑦	⑦	⑦	⑦	⑦	⑦	⑦	⑦	⑦	⑦	⑦	⑦	⑦	⑦	⑦	⑦	⑦	⑦	⑦
Bournemouth ... **105** d.	...	...	0940	1040	1140	...	1240	...	1340	...	1440	1540	...	1640	...	1740	1840	1940
Brockenhurst ... **105** d.	...	...	0955	|	|	...	|	...	|	...	|	|	...	|	...	1755	|	|
Southampton Central ... **105** d.	...	0915	1015r	1115r	1215r	...	1315r	...	1415r	...	1515c	1615c	...	1715r	...	1815c	1915r	2015r
Southampton Airport ✈ .. **105** d.	...	0923	1023	1123	1223	...	1323	...	1423	...	1523	1623	...	1723	...	1823	1923	2023
Winchester ... **105** d.	...	0931	1031	1131	1231	...	1331	...	1431	...	1531	1631	...	1731	...	1831	1931	2031
Basingstoke ... **105** d.	...	0949	1048	1147	1248	...	1349	...	1448	...	1549	1648	...	1749	...	1848	1949	2049
Reading ... a.	...	1006	1106	1205	1305	...	1406	...	1504	...	1606	1706	...	1806	...	1905	2006	2105
Reading ... **131** d.	0915	1015	1115	1215	1315	1344	1415	1444	1515	1544	1615	1715	1742	1815	1844	1915	2015	2111
Oxford ... d.	0940	1039	1139	1239	1339	1408	1439	1508	1540	1608	1639	1739	1806	1839	1908	1939	2039	2136
Banbury ... **124** d.	0958	1058	1158	1258	1358	1428	1458	1528	1558	1628	1658	1758	1824	1858	1926	1958	2058	2155
Leamington Spa... **124 141** d.	1016	1116	1216	1317	1416	1448	1516	1548	1616	1648	1716	1816	1844	1916	1944	2016	2116	2213
Coventry ... **141 142 150** d.	1030	1130	1230	1330	1430	1500	1530	1600	1630	1700	1730	1830	1858	1930	1956	2030	2130	2225
Birmingham Int'l ✈ ... **141 150** d.	1041	1141	1241	1341	1441	1510	1541	1610	1641	1710	1741	1841	1908	1941	2007	2041	2141	2235
Birmingham New St **141 150** a.	1051	1151	1251	1351	1451	1520	1551	1620	1651	1720	1751	1851	1918	1951	2017	2051	2151	2245
York **119** ... a.	|	|	|	|	|	1725	|	1822	|	1922	|	|	2119	|	...	|	|	...
Newcastle **119** ... a.	|	|	|	|	|	...	|	1928	|	2028	|	|	2245	|	...	|	|	...
Manchester Piccadilly **119** ... a.	1230	1329	1429	1529	1629	...	1729	...	1829	...	1929	2029	...	2129	...	2229	2328	...

N – From Nottingham (Table **120**).
S – From Sheffield (Table **119**).
a – Arrives 1237 on Ⓐ.
b – Departs 7 – 8 minutes later.
c – Arrives 5 – 6 minutes earlier.
f – Departs 6 minutes later.
h – Arrives 1812 on ⑥.
j – Arrives 11 – 12 minutes earlier.
r – Arrives 7 minutes earlier.
t – Departs 2050.
v – Arrives 1639.
y – ⑥ only.

108 GATWICK AIRPORT ✈ - READING

GW

km	Ⓐ	Ⓐ	Ⓐ	Ⓐ	Ⓐ	Ⓐ	Ⓐ	Ⓐ	Ⓐ	Ⓐ	Ⓐ	Ⓐ		Ⓐ	Ⓐ	Ⓐ	Ⓐ	Ⓐ	Ⓐ	Ⓐ	Ⓐ	Ⓐ	Ⓐ	Ⓐ	Ⓐ
0	**Gatwick Airport** ✈ ... **185** d.	0511	0559	...	0700	...	0759	...	0900	0930	0959	1029	and at the same	1459	1529	1559	1629	1659	1729	1759	1829	1859	1929	1959	2029
10	Redhill ... § **185** d.	0530	0614	0643	0712	0734	0812	0836	0914	0944	1010	1040	minutes	1510	1540	1610	1640	1710	1740	1810	1840	1910	1940	2010	2040
43	Guildford ... d.	0604	0647	0728t	0746	0814	0844	0920t	0944	1027t	1043	1120t	past each	1543	1616	1643	1715	1744	1818	1844	1920	1944	2020t	2044	2114
84	**Reading** ... a.	0653	0733	0815	0832	0901	0930	0957	1028	1104	1127	1157	hour until	1628	1702	1729	1800	1830	1903	1928	1957	2028	2057	2137	2149

	Ⓐ	Ⓐ	Ⓐ	Ⓐ	Ⓐ	⑥	⑥	⑥	⑥	⑥		⑥	⑥	⑥	⑥	⑥	⑥	⑥	⑥	⑦	⑦	⑦	⑦	⑦
Gatwick Airport ✈ .. **185** d.	2059	2130	2201	2230	2322	0524	0615	0659	0729	0759	and at the same	1859	1929	1959	2029	2059	2130	2216	2323	0612	0759	0855	0926	0955
Redhill ... § **185** d.	2110	2147	2212	2241	2334	0542	0628	0710	0740	0810	minutes	1910	1940	2010	2040	2110	2141	2231	2334	0623	0810	0906	0937	1006
Guildford ... d.	2148t	2228	2243	2324t	0004	0615	0713t	0739	0820t	0843	past each	1943	2020t	2043	2116	2143	2216	2312	0004	0656t	0852	0945t	1008	1045t
Reading ... a.	2233	2312	2321	0017	0045	0701	0750	0823	0857	0929	hour until	2027	2057	2133	2152	2227	2300	0001	0044	0740	0938	1022	1053	1123

		⑦	⑦	⑦	⑦	⑦	⑦	⑦	⑦	⑦	⑦
Gatwick Airport ✈ .. **185** d.	and at the same	1726	1755	1826	1852	1926	1955	2023	2055	2213	2305
Redhill ... § **185** d.	minutes	1737	1806	1837	1906	1937	2006	2037	2106	2226	2316
Guildford ... d.	past each	1808	1845t	1908	1945t	2008	2045t	2108	2145	2303t	2356
Reading ... a.	hour until	1853	1923	1954	2023	2053	2126	2152	2223	2340	0040

	Ⓐ	Ⓐ	Ⓐ	Ⓐ	Ⓐ	Ⓐ	Ⓐ	Ⓐ	Ⓐ
Reading ... d.	0432	0500	0531	0556	0628	0651	0720	0752	0825
Guildford ... d.	0512t	0549	0607	0642	0705	0748f	0808	0838	0911
Redhill ... ‡ **185** a.	0542	0629	0642	0722	0739	0828	0842	0908	0944
Gatwick Airport ✈ **185** a.	0555	...	0655	...	0754	...	0855	0926	0955

	Ⓐ	Ⓐ	Ⓐ	Ⓐ		Ⓐ	Ⓐ	Ⓐ	Ⓐ	Ⓐ	Ⓐ	Ⓐ	Ⓐ	Ⓐ	Ⓐ	Ⓐ	Ⓐ	Ⓐ	Ⓐ	Ⓐ	⑥	⑥	⑥	⑥	⑥
Reading ... d.	0854	0919	0954	1024	and at the same	1424	1454	1521	1554	1621	1650	1720	1750	1821	1854	1924	1954	2054	2136	2333	0432	0522	0554	0624	0654
Guildford ... d.	0936t	1008t	1036t	1108	minutes	1508	1536t	1607	1638	1707	1739	1806	1837	1905	1937t	2008	2037	2139	2220	0020	0510	0558	0636	0709	0736t
Redhill ... ‡ **185** a.	1014	1044	1114	1144	past each	1544	1614	1644	1715	1744	1814	1844	1914	1943	2014	2044	2114	2214	2300	0050	0540	0642	0714	0744	0814
Gatwick Airport ✈ .. **185** a.	1025	1055	1125	1155	hour until	1555	1625	1655	1725	1755	1825	1855	1925	1955	2025	2055	2125	2225	2312	0108	0555	0655	0725	0755	0825

	⑥	⑥	⑥	⑥	⑥		⑥	⑥	⑥	⑥	⑦	⑦	⑦	⑦	⑦	⑦	⑦	⑦		⑦	⑦	⑦	⑦	⑦
Reading ... d.	0724	0754	0819	0854	0924	and at the same	1954	2024	2135	2335	0610	0658	0749	0818	0849	0918	0948	1018	and at the same	1848	1918	1948	2114	2305
Guildford ... d.	0808	0836t	0908	0936t	1008	minutes	2036t	2108	2219	0019	0646	0734	0835	0857	0935	0957t	1035	1057t	minutes	1935	1957t	2035	2157	2349
Redhill ... ‡ **185** a.	0844	0914	0944	1014	1044	past each	2114	2148	2302	0049	0716	0804	0905	0936	1005	1036	1105	1136	past each	2005	2036	2117	2236	0028
Gatwick Airport ✈ .. **185** a.	0855	0925	0955	1025	1055	hour until	2125	2159	2314	0105	0727	0823	0917	0948	1017	1047	1117	1147	hour until	2017	2047	2131	2247	0039

f – Arrives 0737.
t – Arrives 4 – 5 minutes earlier.
§ – All trains reverse here and arrive 3 – 4 minutes earlier.
‡ – All trains reverse here and depart 3 – 5 minutes later.

SW LONDON - SALISBURY - EXETER 109

km		⚒	⚒	Ⓐ	⑥	Ⓐ	⑥	Ⓐ	⑥	⑥	Ⓐ	⑥	Ⓐ	⚒	⑥	Ⓐ	⚒E	⚒	Ⓐ	⚒	⚒	⚒	Ⓐ	⚒	⚒	⚒
0	**London** Waterloo **104/5** d.		...	...	...	...	...	...	...	0637	0635	0710	0710	0750	0820	0820	0850	0920	0950	1020	1050	1120	1120	1220	1250	1320
39	Woking **104 105** d.		...	...	...	...	...	...	...	0705	0702	0736	0736	0816	0846	0846	0916	0946	1016	1046	1116	1146	1146	1246	1316	1346
77	Basingstoke **105** d.		...	...	...	...	...	...	...	0725	0724	0759	0800	0837	0908	0908	0938	1008	1038	1108	1138	1208	1208	1308	1338	1408
107	Andover d.		...	...	...	...	...	...	...	0747	0746	0822	0823	0859	0926	0929t	1000	1026	1100	1126	1200	1226	1228	1326	1400	1426
134	**Salisbury** a.		...	...	...	...	...	...	...	0807	0806	0843	0843	0920	0942	0945	1021	1044	1119	1145	1220	1245	1245	1343	1420	1445
134	**Salisbury** d.		...	...	...	0610	0615	0738	0747	0813	0808	0847	0847	0923z	0947	0947	...	1047	1131	1147	▬	1247	1251	1347	▬	1447
169	Gillingham d.		...	0551	...	0642	0642	0811	0814	0900b	0837	0917	0917	|	1017	1018	...	1117	|	1217	...	1317	|	1417	...	1517
190	Sherborne d.		...	0606	...	0657	0657	0826	0829	0915	...	0932	0932	◧	1032	1033	...	1132	◧	1232	...	1332	◧	1432	...	1532
197	**Yeovil** Junction a.		...	0612	...	0703	0703	0832	0835	0920	...	0938	0938	|	1038	1039	...	1138	1301g	1238	Ⓐ	1338	1419g	1438	Ⓐ	1538
197	**Yeovil** Junction **139** d.		...	0615	0615	0707	0707	0839	0839	...	...	0939	0942	|	1039	1041	...	1139	|	1239	1338	1339	|	1439	1451	1539
200	**Yeovil** Pen Mill **139** a.		...	|	|	|	|	|	|	...	...	|	|	1052z	|	|	...	|	1256	|	1343	|	1412	|	1456	|
211	Crewkerne d.		...	0625	0624	0716	0716	0849	0849	...	...	0949	0951	...	1049	1051	...	1149	...	1249	...	1349	...	1449	...	1549
233	Axminster d.		0550	0657a	0657a	0737	0738	0903	0903	...	...	1003	1006	...	1103	1105	...	1203	...	1303	...	1403	...	1503	...	1603
249	Honiton d.		0604	0712	0712	0752	0754t	0916	0916	...	...	1016	1018	...	1116	1118	...	1216	...	1316	...	1416	...	1515	...	1616
277	**Exeter** St Davids △ a.		0632	0745	0743	0822	0823	0945	0943	...	...	1042	1043	...	1142	1143	...	1242	...	1342	...	1442	...	1543	...	1643

	⚒	⚒	⚒	Ⓐ	⑥	Ⓐ	⑥	Ⓐ	Ⓐ W	⑥	Ⓐ	Ⓐ	⑥	⑥	Ⓐ	Ⓐ	⑥	Ⓐ	⚒	⑥	Ⓐ	Ⓐ	⑥	Ⓐ	⑥	⑥
London Waterloo **104/5** d.	1350	1420	1450	1520	1520	1550	1620	1620	1650	1720	1723	1753	1750	1820	1823	1850	1920	1920	1950	2020	2020	2120	2120	2220	2220	2339
Woking **104 105** d.	1416	1446	1516	1546	1546	1616	1646	1646u	|	1746	|	|	1816	1846	|	|	1946	1946u	2016j	2046	2046	2146	2146	2246	2246	0008
Basingstoke **105** d.	1438	1508	1538	1608	1608	1638	1708	1707	1738t	1808	1807	1838	1838	1908	1908	1938c	2008	2007	2038	2108	2107	2207	2208	2307	2308	0029
Andover d.	1500	1526	1600	1626	1626	1700	1726	1730	1801	1826	1830	1901	1900	1926	1931	2001	2026	2030	2100	2126	2129	2229	2230	2329	2330	0052
Salisbury a.	1520	1546y	1620	1643	1642	1720	1742	1750	1821	1843	1850	1921	1920	1943	1951	2021	2044	2050	2120	2144	2149	2249	2249	2349	2349	0111
Salisbury d.	...	1547	...	1647	1647	1723	1747	1754	1824	1847	1854	1924	1926	1947	1954	2024	2047	2054	▬	2148	2151	...	2254	2351	...	...
Gillingham d.	...	1617	...	1717	1717	1752t	1817	1819	1852	1919	1920	1952	|	2017	2020	2052	2117	2119	...	2218	2218	...	2319s	0015s	...	...
Sherborne d.	...	1632	...	1732	1732	1807	1832	1834	1907	1934	1935	2007	◧	2032	2035	2107	2132	2134	...	2233	2233	...	2334s	0030s	...	...
Yeovil Junction a.	...	1638	...	1738	1738	1812	1838	1840	1912	1939	1940	2013	2045g	2038	2040	2113	2138	2139	Ⓐ	2238	2239	...	2340	0036	...	...
Yeovil Junction **139** d.	...	1639	...	1739	1739	...	1839	1841	1916	1941	1941	2017	|	2039	2041	2117	2139	2142	2145	2239	2240	...	...	...	...	...
Yeovil Pen Mill **139** a.	...	|	...	|	|	...	|	|	1921	|	|	2024	2037	|	|	2124	|	|	2150	|	|	...	...	...	...	...
Crewkerne d.	...	1649	...	1749	1749	...	1849	1850	...	1950	1951	...	...	2049	2051	...	2149	2152	...	2249	2250	...	...	...	...	...
Axminster d.	...	1703	...	1804	1803	...	1903	1905	...	2005	2005	...	...	2103	2105	...	2203	2206	...	2303	2305	...	...	...	...	...
Honiton d.	...	1716	...	1816	1816	...	1916	1917	...	2016	2017	...	...	2117	2117	...	2217	2218	...	2315	2338r	...	...	...	...	...
Exeter St Davids △ a.	...	1744	...	1849	1841	...	1942	1943	...	2042	2042	...	...	2142	2143	...	2245	2244	...	...	0005	...	...	...	...	...

	①–④	⑤	⑦	⑦	⑦	⑦	⑦	⑦	⑦	⑦	⑦	⑦	⑦	⑦	⑦	⑦	⑦	⑦	⑦	⑦	⑦	⑦	⑦	⑦ e	⑦	⑦
London Waterloo **104/5** d.	2340	2340		...	...	...	0815	0915	1015	1115	1215	...	1315	1415	...	1520	1620	1720	1745	1820	1845	1920	2020	2120	2220	2335
Woking **104 105** d.	0008	0008		...	...	...	0846	0946	1046	1146	1246	...	1345	1446	...	1546	1646	1746	1813	1846	1913	1946	2046	2146	2246	0008
Basingstoke **105** d.	0029	0029		...	0804	...	0907	1007	1107	1207	1307	1331	1407	1507	1531	1607	1707	1807	1834	1907	1934	2007	2107	2207	2307	0040
Andover d.	0051	0051		...	0826	...	0924	1026	1125	1224	1325	1353	1424	1524	1553	1625	1724	1825	1856	1925	1956	2025	2126	2224	2329	0103
Salisbury a.	0110	0110		...	0846	...	0941	1043	1142	1242	1343	1413	1442	1540	1613	1646	1742	1842	1917	1942	2017	2043	2143	2242	2348	0122
Salisbury d.	...	0114		0654	0847	...	0947	1047	1147	1247	1347	1419	1447	1547	1614	1647	1747	1847	...	1947	...	2047	2147	2247	...	...
Gillingham d.	...	0137s		0718	0917	...	1018	1117	1217	1317	1417	1451c	1517	1617	1643	1717	1817	1917	...	2017	...	2117	2218	2318	...	...
Sherborne d.	...	0153s		0733	0932	...	1033	1132	1232	1332	1432	1506	1532	1632	...	1732	1832	1932	...	2032	...	2132	2233	2333	...	...
Yeovil Junction a.	...	0159		0739	0938	...	1038	1138	1238	1338	1438	1511	1538	1638	...	1738	1838	1938	...	2038	...	2138	2238	2338	...	...
Yeovil Junction **139** d.	...	...		0740	0939	0946	1039	1139	1239	1339	1439	1516	1539	1639	...	1739	1839	1940	...	2039	...	2139	...	2339	...	...
Yeovil Pen Mill **139** a.	...	...		|	|	0951	|	|	|	|	|	1521	|	|	...	|	|	|	...	|	...	|	...	|	...	...
Crewkerne d.	...	...		0749	0949	...	1049	1149	1249	1349	1449	...	1549	1649	...	1749	1849	1950	...	2049	...	2149	...	2349	...	...
Axminster d.	...	...		0804	1003	...	1103	1203	1303	1403	1503	...	1603	1703	...	1803	1903	2004	...	2104	...	2204	...	0009	...	...
Honiton d.	...	...		0817	1016	...	1116	1216	1316	1416	1516	...	1616	1716	...	1816	1916	2017	...	2117	...	2217	...	0020s	...	...
Exeter St Davids △ a.	...	...		0847	1044	...	1143	1243	1343	1442	1542	...	1642	1747	...	1842	1942	2043	...	2143	...	2244	...	0047	...	...

	⚒	Ⓐ	Ⓐ	Ⓐ	⑥	⚒	Ⓐ	Ⓐ	⑥	Ⓐ	⑥ C	Ⓐ	⑥	Ⓐ	⚒	Ⓐ	⑥	⚒	⚒	Ⓐ	⚒E	⚒	⚒	Ⓐ	⚒	⚒
Exeter St Davids ▽ d.		...	...	0510	0510	...	...	...	...	0640	0640	0725	0725	...	0824	...	...	0925	...	...	1025	...	1125	...	1225	...
Honiton d.		...	...	0541	0541	0620	...	...	...	0711	0713	0752	0755	...	0855	...	...	0955	...	...	1055	...	1155	...	1255	...
Axminster d.		...	...	0553	0552	0631	...	...	...	0723	0724	0804	0806	...	0906	...	...	1006	...	...	1106	...	1206	...	1306	...
Crewkerne d.		...	...	0606	0605	0644	...	...	...	0736	0737	0817	0819	...	0919	...	...	1019	...	...	1119	...	1219	...	1319	...
Yeovil Pen Mill **139** d.		...	0541	|	|	|	0658	0711	...	|	|	|	|	...	|	...	...	|	...	1059	|	...	|	1256	|	...
Yeovil Junction **139** a.		..	0546	0615	0614	0653	|	0716	...	0744	0746	0825	0828	...	0929	...	...	1028	...	|	1128	...	1228	1301	1328	...
Yeovil Junction d.		0511	0550	0620	0620	0654	|	0720	...	0750	0753	0829	0829	...	0929	...	0953	1029	...	|	1129	...	1229	▬	1329	...
Sherborne d.		0517	0556	0626	0626	0700	◧	0726	...	0756	0759	0835	0835	...	0935	...	0959	1035	...	◧	1135	...	1235	...	1335	...
Gillingham d.		0534	0612	0642	0642	0716	|	0743	...	0812	0817	0851	0851	0918	0951	...	1017	1051	...	|	1151	...	1251	...	1351	...
Salisbury a.		0601	0639	0707	0707	0742	0811	0808	...	0837	0842	0917	0916	0943	1017	...	1042	1116	...	1212	1216	...	1319	⚒	1417	...
Salisbury d.		0605	0645	0715	0721	0745	0815	0815	0821	0846	0847	0921	0921	0947	1021	1047	1047	1121	1147	1221	1221	1247	1321	1347	1421	1447
Andover d.		0625	0705	0735	0738	0805	0835	0835	0838	0906	0906	0938	0938	1006	1038	1106	1106	1138	1206	1238	1238	1306	1338	1406	1438	1506
Basingstoke **105** d.		0651	0729	0759	0758	0829	0859	0859	0857	0930	0930	0957	0957	1030	1057	1130	1130	1157	1230	1257	1257	1330	1357	1429	1457	1530
Woking **104 105** d.		|	|	|	0818	0849	0919	0919	0917	0951	0950	1017	1017	1050	1116	1150	1150	1216	1250	1316	1316	1350	1416	1450	1516	1550
London Waterloo **104/5** a.		0736	0814	0843	0849	0918	0950	0950	0949	1020	1016	1049	1049	1116	1149	1216	1214	1249	1318	1349	1349	1417	1449	1516	1549	1616

	Ⓐ	Ⓐ	Ⓐ	⑥	Ⓐ	⚒	⚒	⚒	⚒	⑥	Ⓐ	⑥	Ⓐ	Ⓐ B	⑥	Ⓐ	Ⓐ	⑥	Ⓐ	⑥	Ⓐ	⑥	Ⓐ	⑥	Ⓐ	Ⓐ
Exeter St Davids ▽ d.	...	...	1325	1325	...	1425	...	1525	...	1625	1625	1725	1725	1748	1825	1825	...	...	1925	1925	...	...	2025	2025	...	...
Honiton d.	...	...	1355	1355	...	1455	...	1555	...	1655	1656	1756	1756	1818	1855	1856	...	...	1955	1955	...	...	2055	2056	...	...
Axminster d.	...	...	1406	1406	...	1506	...	1606	...	1706	1707	1808	1808	1828	1906	1908	...	...	2006	2006	...	...	2106	2108	...	...
Crewkerne d.	...	...	1419	1419	...	1519	...	1619	...	1719	1720	1821	1821	▬	1919	1921	...	...	2019	2019	...	...	2119	2121	...	...
Yeovil Pen Mill **139** d.	1345	1404	|	|	1459	|	...	|	...	|	|	|	|	...	|	|	...	...	|	|	2030	2039	|	|	2130	2152
Yeovil Junction **139** a.	|	1409	1428	1428	|	1528	...	1628	...	1728	1729	1829	1829	...	1928	1929	...	...	2028	2028	2035	2045	2128	2129	2135	|
Yeovil Junction d.	1338f	...	1429	1429	1451f	1529	...	1629	...	1729	1730	1830	1830	...	1929	1930	...	...	2029	2029	...	...	2129	2130	...	2145f
Sherborne d.	◧	...	1435	1435	◧	1535	...	1635	...	1735	1736	1837	1837	...	1935	1937	...	...	2035	2035	...	...	2135	2137	...	◧
Gillingham d.	|	...	1451	1451	|	1551	1618z	1651	...	1751	1752	1852	1852	...	1951	1952	...	...	2051	2051	...	...	2151	2152	...	|
Salisbury a.	1514	...	1518	1519	1613	1617	1643z	1717	...	1816	1822	1918	1922	Ⓐ	2016	2022	...	...	2121	2116	...	...	2221	2218	...	2342
Salisbury d.	1521	...	1521	1521	1621	1621	1647	1721	1747	1821	1826	1926	1925	1947	2026	2025	2052	2052	2125	2126	...	...	2225	2226	...	...
Andover d.	1538	...	1538	1538	1638	1638	1706	1738	1806	1838	1843	1945	1947	2004	2045	2044	2110	2112	2144	2145	...	...	2244	2245	...	...
Basingstoke **105** d.	1557	...	1557	1557	1657	1657	1730	1757	1830	1857	1901	2010	2011	2022	2110	2112t	2129	2130	2209	2209	...	...	2308	2309	...	...
Woking **104 105** d.	1617	...	1617	1616	1717	1716	1750	1816	1850	1916	1921	2036t	2031	...	2136t	2136t	2148	2150	2229	2228	...	...	2327	2329	...	...
London Waterloo **104/5** a.	1645	...	1645	1649	1751	1751	1819	1849	1919	1949	1949	2104	2101	...	2204	2205	2212	2216	2301	2258	...	...	2355	2359	...	...

	Ⓐ	⑥	Ⓐ	⑥	Ⓐ	⑦	⑦	⑦	⑦	⑦	⑦		⑦	⑦	⑦	⑦	⑦	⑦	⑦	⑦	⑦	⑦	⑦	⑦	⑦
Exeter St Davids ▽ d.	2126	2125	2225	2300	2306		...	...	0824	...	0925		1425	...	1525	...	1625	...	1725	1825	1925	2025	2125	2225	2313
Honiton d.	2156	2156	2257	2332	2337		...	...	0856	...	0955		1455	...	1555	...	1655	...	1755	1855	1955	2056	2156	2258	2340s
Axminster d.	2208	2208	2308	2343	2348		...	...	0907	...	1006	and	1506	...	1606	...	1706	...	1806	1906	2006	2108	2208	2309	2352s
Crewkerne d.	2221	2221	2321	2356	0001		...	...	0920	...	1019	at	1519	...	1619	...	1719	...	1819	1919	2019	2121	2221	2322	0008s
Yeovil Pen Mill **139** d.	|	|	|	|	|		...	...	|	0953	|	the	|	1543	|	...	|	...	|	|	|	|	|	|	|
Yeovil Junction **139** a.	2229	2229	2330	0005	0009		...	...	0929	|	1028	same	1528	1548	1628	...	1728	...	1828	1928	2028	2129	2229	2331	0017
Yeovil Junction d.	2230	2230	2331	0006	...		0729	0829	0930	0946f	1029	minutes	1529	1553	1629	...	1729	...	1829	1929	2029	2130	2230	2333	...
Sherborne d.	2236	2237	|	|	...		0735	0835	0936	◧	1035	past	1535	1559	1635	...	1735	...	1835	1935	2035	2137	2237	|	...
Gillingham d.	2252	2252	|	|	...		0751	0851	0952	|	1051	each	1551	1618	1651	1717	1751	...	1851	1951	2051	2152	2252	|	...
Salisbury a.	2320	2323	0017	0041	...		0816	0916	1016	1113	1116	hour	1616	1643	1719	1742	1816	...	1916	2016	2116	2217	2317	0009	...
Salisbury d.	...	...	...	...	...		0827	0927	1027	1127	1127	until	1627	1644	1727	1744	1827	1844	1927	2021	2121	2227	...	...	...
Andover d.	...	...	...	...	...		0845	0945	1045	1145	1145		1645	1704	1745	1803	1845	1903	1945	2040	2140	2246	...	...	...
Basingstoke **105** d.	...	...	...	...	...		0904	1004	1104	1204	1204		1704	1728	1804	1827	1904	1927	2004	2104	2204	2310	...	...	...
Woking **104 105** d.	...	...	...	...	...		0924	1025	1124	1224	1224		1724	|	1824	|	1924	|	2024	2124	2224	2330	...	...	...
London Waterloo **104/5** a.	...	...	...	...	...		0957	1055	1155	1254	1254		1754	1816	1854	1917	1954	2016	2054	2154	2254	2358	...	...	...

☛ Additional services **London** Waterloo - **Salisbury** and v.v.:
From **London** Waterloo: on Ⓐ at 1150, 2250; on ⑥ at 0950, 1150, 1550, 1650, 1850, 2050, 2250; on ⑦ at 1945, 2045.
From **Salisbury**: on Ⓐ at 0510, 0543, 1547; on ⑥ at 0515, 0547, 0621, 0646, 0947, 1547, 1847; on ⑦ at 0645, 0727.

B – From Barnstaple (Table **114**).
C – Conveys 🍴 Castle Cary - Salisbury - London (Tables **139** and **140**).
E – On ⑥ conveys 🍴 Frome - Salisbury - London and v.v. (Tables **139** and **140**).
W – To Westbury (Table **139**).

a – Arrives 0644.
b – Arrives 0842.
c – Arrives 7–8 minutes earlier.
e – Does not call at Exeter Central.
f – Calls at Yeovil Junction before Yeovil Pen Mill.
g – Calls at Yeovil Pen Mill before Yeovil Junction.
j – ⑥ only.
r – Arrives 2316.
s – Calls to set down only.

t – Arrives 5–6 minutes earlier.
u – Calls to pick up only.
y – Arrives 1542 on ⑥.
z – Ⓐ only.

◧ – Via Westbury (Tables **139** and **140**).
△ – Trains to Exeter St Davids also call at **Exeter Central** 5–6 minutes earlier.
▽ – Trains from Exeter St Davids also call at **Exeter Central** 4–5 minutes later.

110 LONDON and BRISTOL - EXETER - PLYMOUTH - PENZANCE

GW, XC

km			Ⓐ	Ⓐ	Ⓐ	Ⓐ	Ⓐ	Ⓐ	Ⓐ	Ⓐ	Ⓐ	Ⓐ	Ⓐ	Ⓐ	Ⓐ	Ⓐ	Ⓐ	Ⓐ	Ⓐ	Ⓐ	Ⓐ	Ⓐ	Ⓐ	Ⓐ	Ⓐ	Ⓐ	Ⓐ
			2	2	2	2	2			2	🍷	🍷	2	🍷	🍷D	🍷	2	🍷L	🍷	2	2	🍷Y	🍷	🍷	🍷M	2	🍷N
0	**London** Paddington . **130/1/2/3** d.	Ⓐ	...	...	...	...	...	...	...	...	0600	...	...	0702	...	0803	...	...	0903	...	...	...	0934	1003	...	...	...
58	**Reading** .... **130/1/2/3** d.		...	...	...	...	...	...	...	...	0627	...	...	0727	...	0829	...	...	0929	...	...	...	1002	1029t	...	...	...
85	Newbury .... d.		...	...	...	...	...	...	...	...	|	...	...	0742	...	|	...	...	|	...	...	...	|	|	...	...	...
154	Westbury .... **140** d.		...	...	...	...	...	...	...	...	|	...	...	0820	...	|	...	...	|	...	...	...	1048	|	...	...	...
186	Castle Cary .... **140** d.		...	...	...	...	...	...	...	...	|	...	...	0838	...	|	...	...	|	...	...	...	1105	|	...	...	...
	Birmingham New St **119** ... d.		...	...	...	...	...	...	...	...	|	0642	...	|	0712	|	...	0812	|	...	...	0912	|	|	0942	...	1012
	Cardiff Central **115** .... d.		...	...	...	...	...	...	...	...	|	|	...	|	|	|	...	|	|	...	...	|	|	|	|	...	|
	Bristol T M .... **115 132** d.		...	...	...	...	...	0555	0640	...	0738	0811	...	|	0845	|	...	0945	|	...	...	1045	|	|	1114	...	1145
230	Taunton .... **115 132** d.		...	...	...	...	...	0655	0711	...	0817	0842	...	0900	0917	0945	...	1017	1047	...	...	1117	1127	|	1159	...	1217
253	Tiverton Parkway .... **115** d.		...	...	...	...	...	0708	0723	...	0830	0854	...	0913	0930	|	...	1029	1100	...	...	1129	1140	|	1211	...	1230
279	**Exeter** St Davids .... **115** a.		...	...	...	...	...	0722	0737	...	0844	0908	...	0927	0946	1008	...	1044	1114	...	...	1144	1154	1203	1225	...	1244
279	**Exeter** St Davids .... **112** d.		...	...	0551	...	0655	0727	0743	0809	0846	0912	0926	0930	0947	1012	1027	1049	1115	...	1127	1148	1156	1206	1227	...	1249
297	Dawlish .... **112** d.		...	...	0604	....	0711	0739	|	|	|	|	0938	0945	|	|	1039	|	|	...	1139	|	1208	|	1239	...	|
302	Teignmouth .... **112** d.		...	...	0610	...	0716	0743	|	|	|	|	0943	0950	|	|	1044	|	|	...	1144	|	1213	|	1244	...	|
311	Newton Abbot .... **112** d.		...	...	0617	...	0723	0751	0802	0830	0907	0933	0951	0958	1009	1033	1052	1110	1136	...	1152	1210	1221	1226	1251	...	1309
321	Torquay .... **112** d.		...	...	|	...	|	|	|	|	|	0945	|	1011	|	|	|	|	|	...	|	|	1234	|	1301	...	|
324	**Paignton** .... 🚂 **112** a.		...	...	|	...	|	|	|	|	|	0951	|	1017	|	|	|	|	|	...	|	|	1239	|	1307	...	|
325	Totnes .... 🚂 d.		...	...	0630	...	0736	0802	0814	0842	|	▬	1004	...	1021	1044	1105	1122	1147	...	1204	1222	...	1238	...	...	1321
363	**Plymouth** .... a.		...	...	0702	...	0805	0831	0840	0912	0941	Ⓐ2	1034	...	1047	1110	1134	1148	1214	...	1233	1249	...	1303	...	...	1347
	Plymouth .... d.		0533	0640	0712	0742	0809	...	0847	0913	0946	1014	1042	...	...	1120	1142	...	...	1219	1240	...	...	1312	...	1340	...
368	Saltash .... d.		0543	0649	0726	0751	0826	...	|	0924	0955	1025	1054	...	...	1129v	1151	...	...	1228	1249	...	...	1321	...	1354	...
390	Liskeard .... d.		0602	0708	0747	0811	0845	...	0910	0945	1015	1043	1112	...	...	1143	1212	...	...	1246	1310	...	...	1339	...	1414	...
404	Bodmin Parkway .... 🚂 d.		0613	0719	0759	0822	0857	...	0922	0957	1027	1056	1125	...	...	1156	1224	...	...	1258	1322	...	...	1351	...	1426	...
410	Lostwithiel .... d.		0618	0724	0804	0827	0902	...	0928	1002	1032	1101	1130	...	...	|	1230	...	...	1303	1328	...	...	|	...	1431	...
417	Par .... ♡ d.		0625	0731	0812	0834	0910	...	0935	1010	|	1109	1137	...	...	1206	1237	...	...	1310	1335	...	...	1401	...	1438	...
	Newquay .... ♡ a.		|	|	|	|	|	...	|	|	|	|	|	...	...	|	|	...	...	|	|	...	...	|	...	|	...
424	St Austell .... d.		0632	0739	0819	0841	0917	...	0942	1017	1044	1116	1144	...	...	1213	1244	...	...	1317	1342	...	...	1408	...	1445	...
447	Truro .... d.		0649	0755	0836	0858	0934	...	0959	1034	1101	1132	1201	...	...	1230	1301	...	...	1334	1359	...	...	1425	...	1501	...
462	Redruth .... d.		0701	0807	0848	0910	0945	...	1010	1045	1112	1144	1213	...	...	1242	1313	...	...	1345	1411	...	...	1437	...	1513	...
467	Camborne .... d.		0707	0814	0855	0916	0951	...	1016	1051	1119	1150	1219	...	...	1248	1319	...	...	1351	1417	...	...	1444	...	1519	...
479	St Erth .... d.		0720	0826	0908	0927	1003	...	1029	1103	1131	1202	1231	...	...	1258	1331	...	...	1403	1429	...	...	1454	...	1531	...
488	**Penzance** .... a.		0729	0835	0919	0936	1012	...	1038	1112	1140	1211	1240	...	...	1309	1340	...	...	1412	1438	...	...	1503	...	1540	...

	Ⓐ	Ⓐ	Ⓐ	Ⓐ	Ⓐ	Ⓐ	Ⓐ	Ⓐ	Ⓐ	Ⓐ	Ⓐ	Ⓐ	Ⓐ	Ⓐ	Ⓐ	Ⓐ	Ⓐ	Ⓐ	Ⓐ	Ⓐ	Ⓐ	Ⓐ	Ⓐ	Ⓐ	Ⓐ	Ⓐ	Ⓐ
	🍷		🍷		🍷E	🍷y	🍷v	🍷y	🍷E	2	🍷	🍴		🍷G	2	🍷		2	🍷G	🍷	🍷	2	🍷E	🍷M	🍷	🍷C	🍷
London Paddington .. **130/1/2/3** d.	1036	...	1103	...	...	1203	1205	1205	...	...	1235	1303	...	...	...	1403	...	...	...	1436	1503	...	...	...	1603	...	1636
Reading .... **130/1/2/3** d.	1101	...	1129	...	...	|	1231u	1231u	...	...	1301	1329t	...	...	...	1429t	...	...	...	1501	1529t	...	...	...	1629t	...	1702
Newbury .... d.	1116	...	|	...	...	|	|	|	...	...	1316	|	...	...	...	|	...	...	...	1516	|	...	...	...	|	...	1717
Westbury .... **140** d.	1158	...	|	...	...	|	|	|	...	...	1357	|	...	...	...	|	...	...	...	1554	|	...	...	...	|	...	1758
Castle Cary .... **140** d.	1215	...	|	...	...	|	|	|	...	...	1415	|	...	...	...	|	...	...	...	1612	|	...	...	...	1725	...	1815
Birmingham New St **119** .... d.	|	...	|	...	1112	|	|	|	1212	...	|	|	...	1312	...	|	...	...	1412	|	|	...	1512	1542	|	1612	|
Cardiff Central **115** .... d.	|	...	|	...	|	|	|	|	|	...	|	|	...	|	...	|	1400	...	|	|	|	...	|	|	|	|	|
Bristol T M .... **115 132** d.	|	...	|	...	1245	|	|	|	1345	...	|	|	...	1445	...	|	1455	...	1545	|	|	...	1645	1712	|	1745	|
Taunton .... **115 132** d.	1238	...	1246	...	1317	|	1348	1348	1417	...	1438	1445	...	1517	...	1545	1555	...	1617	1635	1648	...	1717	1743	1749	1816	1837
Tiverton Parkway .... **115** d.	1251	...	1259	...	1329	|	|	|	1430	...	|	1458	...	1529	...	1558	1607	...	1630	|	1701	...	1729	1755	1802	1829	|
Exeter St Davids .... **115** a.	1307	...	1313	...	1344	|	1412	1412	1444	...	1508	1512	...	1544	...	1612	1621	...	1644	1659	1715	...	1746	1809	1815	1843	1904
Exeter St Davids .... **112** d.	...	1255	1315	...	1349	1403	1414	1414	1449	...	...	1513	1527	1549	...	1614	1625	...	1649	1701	1717	...	1749	1811	1820	1849	1912
Dawlish .... **112** d.	...	1308	|	...	|	|	|	|	|	...	...	|	1539	|	...	|	1637	...	|	1713	|	...	|	1824	|	|	|
Teignmouth .... **112** d.	...	1313	|	...	|	|	|	|	|	...	...	|	1544	|	...	|	1643	...	|	1718	|	...	|	1829	|	|	|
Newton Abbot .... **112** d.	...	1320	1335	...	1409	|	1435	1435	1509	...	...	1534	1552	1610	...	1635	1651	...	1709	1726	1738	...	1809	1836	1841	1909	1934
Torquay .... **112** d.	...	|	|	...	|	|	|	|	|	...	...	|	|	|	...	|	|	...	|	1739	|	...	|	1846	|	|	|
Paignton .... 🚂 **112** a.	...	|	|	...	|	|	|	|	|	...	...	|	|	|	...	|	|	...	|	1744	|	...	|	1853	|	|	|
Totnes .... 🚂 d.	...	1333	1347	...	1421	|	1446	1446	1521	...	...	1545	1604	1622	...	1647	1703	...	1721	...	1749	...	1821	...	1852	1921	1946
Plymouth .... a.	...	1402	1413r	...	1447	1455	1513	1513	1547	...	...	1613	1635	1648	...	1712	1732	...	1747	...	1817	...	1847	...	1920	1947	2015
Plymouth .... d.	...	1418	...	1442	...	1502	1516	...	1550	1556	...	...	1647	...	1700	1722	...	1746	...	...	1821	1830	...	...	1925	...	...
Saltash .... d.	...	1427	...	1451	...	1511	1525	...	|	1617	...	...	1656	...	1716	1732	...	1755	...	...	|	1847	...	...	1934	...	...
Liskeard .... d.	...	1446	...	1511	...	1528	1542	...	1614	1642	...	...	1714	...	1737	1751	...	1813	...	...	1845	1910	...	...	1954	...	...
Bodmin Parkway .... 🚂 d.	...	1457	...	1523	...	1541	1555	...	1626	1654	...	...	1726	...	...	1804	...	1825	...	...	1857	1922	...	...	2006	...	...
Lostwithiel .... d.	...	1502	...	1529	...	|	|	...	1632	1701	...	...	1731	...	...	1810	...	1831	...	...	|	1927	...	...	|	...	...
Par .... ♡ d.	...	1510	...	1536	...	1551	1605	...	1639	1709	...	...	1739	...	...	1817	...	1838	...	...	1908	1935	...	...	2016	...	...
Newquay .... ♡ a.	...	|	...	|	...	|	|	...	|	|	...	...	|	...	...	|	...	|	...	...	|	|	...	...	|	...	...
St Austell .... d.	...	1517	...	1543	...	1559	1612	...	1646	1717	...	...	1746	...	...	1824	...	1845	...	...	1915	1942	...	...	2023	...	...
Truro .... d.	...	1534	...	1600	...	1617	1629	...	1703	1734	...	...	1803	...	...	1841	...	1902	...	...	1932	1959	...	...	2040	...	...
Redruth .... d.	...	1545	...	1612	...	1629	1641	...	1714	1745	...	...	1814	...	...	1853	...	1913	...	...	1944	2011	...	...	2052	...	...
Camborne .... d.	...	1551	...	1618	...	1636	1648	...	1720	1751	...	...	1820	...	...	1900	...	1919	...	...	1951	2017	...	...	2059	...	...
St Erth .... d.	...	1603	...	1630	...	1650	1701	...	1733	1803	...	...	1832	...	...	1915	...	1931	...	...	2001	2029	...	...	2111	...	...
Penzance .... a.	...	1612	...	1639	...	1700	1710	...	1742	1812	...	...	1841	...	...	1925	...	1940	...	...	2010	2038	...	...	2120	...	...

	Ⓐ	Ⓐ	Ⓐ	Ⓐ	Ⓐ	Ⓐ	Ⓐ	Ⓐ	①–④	①–④	⑤	⑤	Ⓐ	Ⓐ	Ⓐ	Ⓐ	⑤	①–④		⑥	⑥	⑥	⑥	⑥	⑥	⑥	⑥
	🍷	🍷E	🍷	🍷	🍷		🍷E	🍷	🍴		🍴		🍷E	🍷	🍷E	🍷	A	A		2	2	2		2			
London Paddington .. **130/1/2/3** d.	1703	...	1736	1803	1808	...	...	1836	1904	...	1904	...	...	2003	...	2104	2345	2345	⑥	...	...	...	...	...	...	...	...
Reading .... **130/1/2/3** d.	1729t	...	1802	1829t	1837	...	...	1901	1931	...	1931u	...	...	2028t	...	2129	0049	0049		...	...	...	...	...	...	...	...
Newbury .... d.	|	...	1817	1844	1858	...	...	1916	|	...	|	...	...	2043	...	2144	|	|		...	...	...	...	...	...	...	...
Westbury .... **140** d.	|	...	1856	|	1945	...	...	1959	|	...	|	...	...	2122	...	2223	|	|		...	...	...	...	...	...	...	...
Castle Cary .... **140** d.	|	...	1913	|	▬	...	...	2017	|	...	|	...	...	2140	...	2242	|	|	♥	...	...	...	...	...	...	...	...
Birmingham New St **119** .... d.	|	1712	|	|	...	...	1812	|	|	...	|	...	1912	|	2012	|	|	|		...	...	...	...	...	...	...	...
Cardiff Central **115** .... d.	|	|	|	|	...	1759	|	|	|	...	|	...	|	|	|	|	|	|		...	...	...	...	...	...	...	...
Bristol T M .... **115 132** d.	|	1845	|	|	...	1857	1950	|	|	...	|	...	2045	|	2145	|	|	|		...	...	...	0535	...	0634	...	...
Taunton .... **115 132** d.	1848	1924	1936	1948	...	2002	2021	2040	2047	...	2047	...	2117	2202	2216	2304	0237j	0335j		...	...	...	0626	...	0714f	...	...
Tiverton Parkway .... **115** d.	1901	1936	1949	|	Ⓐ	2015	2033	2053	2100	...	2100	...	2130	2215	2228	2318	|	|		...	...	...	0640	...	0726	...	...
Exeter St Davids .... **115** a.	1915	1950	2003	2012	🍷	2029	2047	2108	2114	...	2114	...	2144	2229	2242	2332	0307	0414		...	...	...	0656	...	0740	...	...
Exeter St Davids .... **112** d.	1920	1952	2007	2014	←	2041	2050	2111	2118	2131	2118	2131	2151	2231	2243	2334	0410	0437		...	0628	...	0659	0723	0742	0752	...
Dawlish .... **112** d.	|	|	2030	|	2030	|	|	|	|	2143	|	2143	|	2243	|	|	|	|		...	0641	...	0722	0736	|	0805	...
Teignmouth .... **112** d.	|	|	→	|	2035	|	|	|	|	2148	|	2148	|	2248	|	|	|	|		...	0646	...	0727	0741	|	0810	...
Newton Abbot .... **112** d.	1942	2011	...	2034	2044	2102	2111	2131	2139	2156	2139	2156	2211	2256	2303	2354	0432	0459		...	0654	...	0736	0749	0802	0818	...
Torquay .... **112** d.	|	|	...	|	|	|	|	|	|	|	|	|	|	|	|	|	|	|		...	|	...	0747	|	|	|	...
Paignton .... 🚂 **112** a.	|	|	...	|	|	|	|	|	|	|	|	|	|	|	|	|	|	|		...	|	...	0755	|	|	|	...
Totnes .... 🚂 d.	1954	2023	...	2046	2056	2114	2125	2143	2151	2208	2151	2208	2223	2308	2315	0006	|	|		...	0707	...	...	0801	0814	0829	...
Plymouth .... a.	2020	2049	...	2112	2125	2143	2151	2210	2218	2237	2218	2237	2250	2337	2343	0032	0510	0538		...	0736	...	...	0832	0840	0858	...
Plymouth .... d.	2029	...	...	2117	...	2146	...	...	...	2240	2238	...	...	...	...	...	|	|		0515	0740	0807	...	...	0847	0900	0910
Saltash .... d.	2038	...	...	|	...	2155	...	...	...	2249	2247	...	...	...	...	...	|	|		0524	0749	0825	...	...	|	0910	0922
Liskeard .... d.	2058	...	...	2141	...	2215	...	...	...	2308	2306	...	...	...	...	...	0612	0612		0540	0809	0844	...	...	0910	0929	0944
Bodmin Parkway .... 🚂 d.	2110	...	...	2153	...	2227	...	...	...	2319	2317	...	...	...	...	...	0626	0626		0552	0821	0856	...	...	0922	0941	0956
Lostwithiel .... d.	2115	...	...	|	...	2232	...	...	...	2324	2322	...	...	...	...	...	0633	0633		0557	0826	0901	...	...	0928	|	1001
Par .... ♡ d.	2122	...	...	2205	...	2239	...	...	...	2332	2330	...	...	...	...	...	0641	0641		0604	0833	0909	...	...	0935	1000	1009
Newquay .... ♡ a.	|	...	...	|	...	|	...	...	...	|	|	...	...	...	...	...	|	|		|	|	|	...	...	|	1048	|
St Austell .... d.	2129	...	...	2212	...	2245	...	...	...	2338	2336	...	...	...	...	...	0649	0649		0611	0840	0916	...	...	0942	...	1016
Truro .... d.	2147	...	...	2229	...	2302	...	...	...	2355	2353	...	...	...	...	...	0706	0706		0627	0857	0933	...	...	0959	...	1033
Redruth .... d.	2159	...	...	2240	...	2313	...	...	...	0006	0004	...	...	...	...	...	0720	0720		0640	0909	0944	...	...	1010	...	1044
Camborne .... d.	2205	...	...	|	...	2319	...	...	...	0012	0010	...	...	...	...	...	0728	0728		0646	0914	0951	...	...	1016	...	1051
St Erth .... d.	2215	...	...	|	...	2331	...	...	...	0024	0022	...	...	...	...	...	0742	0742		0658	0926	1003	...	...	1029	...	1103
Penzance .... a.	2224	...	...	2300	...	2340	...	...	...	0033	0034	...	...	...	...	...	0754	0755		0707	0935	1012	...	...	1038	...	1112

A – THE NIGHT RIVIERA – Conveys 🛏 and (2). Calls to set down only after Newton Abbot. See also note ‡ on page 92.
B – From Gloucester (Table **138**).
C – From Aberdeen (Tables **119** and **222**).
D – From Derby (Table **119**).
E – From Edinburgh (Table **119**).
G – From Glasgow Central (Tables **119** / **220**).
L – From Leeds (Table **119**).
M – From Manchester Piccadilly (Table **119**).
N – From Newcastle (Table **119**).
Y – From York (Table **119**).
f – Arrives 0704.
j – Arrives 0230.
r – Connects with train in previous column.
t – Calls to pick up only on ⑤.
u – Calls to pick up only.
v – From Sept. 15.
y – Until Sept. 12.
♡ – See Table **113** for full local service Par - Newquay.
🚂 – See note 🚂 on page 92.
♥ – Service valid until Sept. 13.

GW, XC

LONDON and BRISTOL - EXETER - PLYMOUTH - PENZANCE

110

	⑥ 🍷	⑥ 🍷	⑥ 🍷	⑥	⑥ 🍷D	⑥ 🍷	⑥	⑥ 🍷L	⑥ 🍷	⑥ 🍷	⑥ 2	⑥ 🍷Y	⑥ 🍷	⑥ 2	⑥ 🍷M	⑥ 🍷N	⑥ 🍷	⑥ 🍷	⑥ 🍷	⑥ 2	⑥ 🍷E	⑥ 🍷	⑥ 🍷	⑥ 🍷E	⑥ 🍷	⑥ 🍷
London Paddington **130/1/2/3** d.	...	...	0703	...	...	0803	...	...	0835	0903	...	...	1002	...	...	...	1033	1028	1103	...	...	1135	1203	...	1235	1303
Reading **130/1/2/3** d.	...	...	0729**u**	...	...	0829**u**	...	...	0902**u**	0929**u**	...	...	1030**u**	...	...	...	1100**u**	1054**u**	1129**u**	...	...	1203**u**	1230**u**	...	1301**u**	1330
Newbury d.	...	...	|	...	...	|	...	...	0918	|	...	...	|	...	...	...	1116	|	|	...	...	|	|	...	1317	|
Westbury **140** d.	...	...	0815	...	...	|	...	...	0959	|	...	...	|	...	...	...	1154	|	|	...	...	1248	|	...	1358	|
Castle Cary **140** d.	...	...	|	...	...	|	...	...	1016	1025	...	...	|	...	...	...	1212	|	|	...	...	|	|	...	1415	|
Birmingham New St **119** d.	...	0641	|	...	0712	|	...	0812	|	|	...	0912	|	...	0942	1012	|	|	|	...	1112	|	|	1212	|	|
Cardiff Central **115** d.	...	|	|	...	|	|	...	|	|	|	...	|	|	...	|	|	|	|	|	...	|	|	|	|	|	|
Bristol T M **115 132** d.	0735	0811	|	...	0845	|	...	0945	|	|	...	1045	|	...	1115	1145	|	1207	|	...	1245	|	|	1345	|	|
Taunton **115 132** d.	0808	0842	0852	...	0917	0946	...	1017	1039	1048	...	1117	1145	...	1158	1217	1234	|	1244	...	1317	1325	1345	1417	1439	1445
Tiverton Parkway **115** d.	|	0854	|	...	0930	|	...	1029	1052	|	...	1130	1158	...	1210	1230	|	|	1257	...	1329	1338	|	1429	|	1458
Exeter St Davids **115** a.	0832	0908	0915	...	0945	1010	...	1044	1107	1111	...	1146	1212	...	1224	1244	1258	1306	1311	...	1346	1353	1409	1444	1504	1512
Exeter St Davids **112** d.	0834	0912	0919	0927	0949	1013	1028	1049	1112	1116	...	1149	1215	1219	1226	1249	1301	...	1314	...	1350	1358	1412	1449	1507	1515
Dawlish **112** d.	|	|	|	0940	|	|	1041	|	1132	|	...	|	|	1232	1238	|	1317	...	|	...	|	|	|	|	1521	|
Teignmouth **112** d.	|	|	|	0945	|	|	1046	|	1138	|	...	|	|	1237	1243	|	1323	...	|	...	|	|	|	|	1526	|
Newton Abbot **112** d.	0855	0934	0940	0952	1009	1033	1053	1110	1147	1136	...	1209	1236	1244	1250	1309	1331	...	1334	...	1410	1422	1433	1509	1535	1537
Torquay **112** d.	|	0946	|	|	|	|	|	|	1157	|	...	|	|	|	1300	|	1341	...	|	...	|	|	|	|	1546	|
Paignton 🚂 **112** a.	|	0952	|	|	|	|	|	|	1203	|	...	|	|	|	1306	|	1347	...	|	...	|	|	|	|	1552	|
Totnes 🚂 d.	0907	...	|	1005	1021	1046	1105	1122	...	1148	...	1221	1248	1257	...	1321	...	...	1346	...	1422	1434	1445	1521	...	1549
Plymouth a.	0934	...	1015	1034	1047	1112	1134	1148	...	1217	...	1247	1314	1326	...	1347	...	...	1412	...	1448	1500	1512	1547	...	1615
Plymouth d.	0945	...	1018	1041	...	1115	1139	...	...	1219	1241	...	1318	1343	...	...	...	...	1417	1443	...	1504	1516	1551	...	1618
Saltash d.	0955	...	1027	1054	...	|	1148	...	...	1229	1250	...	|	1352	...	...	...	...	1426	1454	...	|	|	|	...	1627
Liskeard d.	1012	...	1047	1113	...	1140	1209	...	...	1245	1310	...	1343	1413	...	...	...	...	1446	1517	...	1530	1541	1614	...	1647
Bodmin Parkway 🚂 d.	1024	...	1059	1125	...	1152	1221	...	...	1258	1323	...	1355	1425	...	...	...	...	1458	1529	...	1543	1553	1626	...	1659
Lostwithiel d.	|	...	1105	1130	...	|	1226	...	...	1304	1328	...	|	1430	...	...	...	...	1504	1534	...	|	|	|	...	|
Par ♡ d.	1035	...	1112	1137	...	1203	1233	...	...	1311	1336	...	1406	1437	...	...	...	...	1511	1541	...	1558	1605	1639	...	1710
Newquay ♡ a.	|	...	|	|	...	|	|	...	...	|	|	...	|	|	...	...	...	...	|	|	...	1646	|	|	...	|
St Austell d.	1043	...	1119	1144	...	1211	1240	...	...	1319	1343	...	1414	1444	...	...	...	...	1519	1548	...	...	1612	1646	...	1717
Truro d.	1100	...	1136	1201	...	1229	1257	...	...	1337	1359	...	1431	1501	...	...	...	...	1537	1605	...	...	1630	1703	...	1734
Redruth d.	1112	...	1147	1213	...	1241	1308	...	...	1349	1411	...	1443	1513	...	...	...	...	1549	1617	...	...	1642	1714	...	1745
Camborne d.	1119	...	1154	1219	...	1248	1314	...	...	1356	1418	...	1450	1519	...	...	...	...	1556	1623	...	...	1649	1720	...	1752
St Erth d.	1132	...	1207	1231	...	1259	1326	...	...	1409	1431	...	1500	1531	...	...	...	...	1609	1635	...	...	1659	1733	...	1805
Penzance a.	1141	...	1216	1240	...	1308	1335	...	...	1418	1440	...	1509	1540	...	...	...	...	1618	1644	...	...	1708	1742	...	1814

	⑥ 2	⑥ 🍷E	⑥ 🍷	⑥	⑥ 🍷G	⑥	⑥ 🍷	⑥ 🍷E	⑥ 🍷M	⑥ 🍷	⑥	⑥ 🍷C	⑥ 🍷	⑥ 🍷	⑥ 🍷E	⑥ 🍷	⑥	⑥ 🍷E	⑥ 🍷	⑥ 🍷E	⑥ 🍷	⑥ 🍷E	⑥ 🍷	⑦	⑦	⑦ 🍷
London Paddington **130/1/2/3** d.	...	...	1403	...	...	...	1503	...	...	1603	...	...	1635	1703	...	1803	...	...	1903	...	2003	...	2030		...	...
Reading **130/1/2/3** d.	...	...	1429**u**	...	...	...	1530**u**	...	...	1629**u**	...	...	1701**u**	1729**u**	...	1829**u**	...	...	1929	...	2028	...	2056		...	...
Newbury d.	...	...	|	...	...	...	1546	...	...	|	...	...	1716	|	...	|	...	...	1944	...	2043	...	|		...	...
Westbury **140** d.	...	...	|	...	...	...	1625	...	...	|	...	...	1754	|	...	|	...	...	2025	...	2121	...	|		...	...
Castle Cary **140** d.	...	...	|	...	...	...	1642	...	...	1726	...	...	1812	|	...	|	...	...	2043	...	2139	...	|		...	...
Birmingham New St **119** d.	...	1312	|	...	1412	...	|	1512	1542	|	...	1612	|	|	1712	|	...	1812	|	1912	|	2012	|		...	...
Cardiff Central **115** d.	...	|	|	...	|	...	|	|	|	|	...	|	|	|	|	|	1758	|	|	|	|	|	|		...	...
Bristol T M **115 132** d.	...	1445	|	...	1545	...	|	1645	1709	|	...	1745	|	|	1845	|	1851	1945	|	2045	|	2145	2209		...	...
Taunton **115 132** d.	...	1517	1545	...	1619	...	1705	1717	1740	1748	...	1817	1834	1844	1917	1944	1955	2017	2105	2117	2201	2217	2309		...	...
Tiverton Parkway **115** d.	...	1530	1558	...	1631	...	1718	1729	1752	1801	...	1830	1847	1857	1930	1957	2008	2030	2118	2129	2214	2230	2322		...	...
Exeter St Davids **115** a.	...	1547	1612	...	1647	...	1731	1745	1806	1815	...	1844	1900	1910	1944	2011	2022	2044	2133	2143	2228	2244	2337		...	...
Exeter St Davids **112** d.	...	1549	1615	1627	1649	1714	1734	1749	1810	1818	...	1847	1903	1917	1949	2014	2025	2049	2135	2150	2232	2249	...		...	...
Dawlish **112** d.	...	|	|	1640	|	|	1746	|	1825	|	...	|	1915	|	|	|	2037	|	2147	|	2244	|	...		...	...
Teignmouth **112** d.	...	|	|	1645	|	|	1751	|	1830	|	...	|	1920	|	|	|	2042	|	2152	|	2249	|	...		...	...
Newton Abbot **112** d.	...	1609	1635	1652	1709	1734	1759	1809	1837	1842	...	1909	1928	1938	2009	2034	2050	2109	2200	2210	2257	2309	...		...	...
Torquay **112** d.	...	|	|	|	|	|	|	|	1847	|	...	|	1941	|	|	|	|	|	|	|	|	|	...		...	...
Paignton 🚂 **112** a.	...	|	|	|	|	|	|	|	1853	|	...	|	1946	|	|	|	|	|	|	|	|	|	...		...	...
Totnes 🚂 d.	...	1621	1647	1705	1721	1746	1811	1821	...	1853	...	1921	...	1949	2021	2046	2102	2121	2212	2222	2309	2321	...		...	...
Plymouth a.	...	1648	1713	1734	1747	1812	1840	1847	...	1922	...	1947	...	2016	2047	2112	2132	2147	2238	2248	2338	2347	...		...	...
Plymouth d.	1638	...	1718	1743	...	1814	1844	...	...	...	1934	...	...	2023	...	2121	...	...	...	...	...	...	...		0845	0914
Saltash d.	1650	...	|	1753	...	1830	1853	...	...	...	1944	...	...	2032	...	2131	...	...	...	...	...	...	...		0901	|
Liskeard d.	1710	...	1743	1812	...	1847	1914	...	...	...	2002	...	...	2052	...	2147	...	...	...	...	...	...	...		0919	0937
Bodmin Parkway 🚂 d.	1722	...	1755	1824	...	1859	1926	...	...	...	2014	...	...	2104	...	2159	...	...	...	...	...	...	...		0931	0949
Lostwithiel d.	1727	...	|	1829	...	|	1932	...	...	...	2019	...	...	|	...	2205	...	...	...	...	...	...	...		0937	0955
Par ♡ d.	1735	...	1806	1837	...	1910	1939	...	...	...	2026	...	...	2115	...	2212	...	...	...	...	...	...	...		0944	1002
Newquay ♡ a.	|	...	|	|	...	|	|	...	...	...	|	...	...	|	...	|	...	...	...	...	...	...	...		|	|
St Austell d.	1742	...	1814	1844	...	1917	1946	...	...	...	2033	...	...	2122	...	2219	...	...	...	...	...	...	...		0951	1009
Truro d.	1758	...	1831	1900	...	1934	2003	...	...	...	2049	...	...	2139	...	2236	...	...	...	...	...	...	...		1008	1026
Redruth d.	1810	...	1843	1912	...	1945	2014	...	...	...	2101	...	...	2150	...	2247	...	...	...	...	...	...	...		1019	1037
Camborne d.	1817	...	1850	1919	...	1951	2021	...	...	...	2107	...	...	2157	...	2254	...	...	...	...	...	...	...		1026	1043
St Erth d.	1829	...	1900	1931	...	2001	2033	...	...	...	2119	...	...	2207	...	2306	...	...	...	...	...	...	...		1038	1056
Penzance a.	1838	...	1909	1940	...	2010	2042	...	...	...	2128	...	...	2216	...	2315	...	...	...	...	...	...	...		1047	1105

	⑦ 🍷	⑦ 2	⑦	⑦ 2	⑦ 🍷	⑦ 🍷a	⑦ 🍷	⑦ 🍷	⑦ 🍷	⑦ 🍷	⑦ 2	⑦ 🍷	⑦ 🍷	⑦ 2	⑦ 🍷L	⑦ 🍷	⑦ 🍷a	⑦ 🍷b	⑦	⑦ 🍷L	⑦ 🍷	⑦ 2	⑦ 🍷N	⑦ 🍷	⑦ 🍷	⑦
London Paddington **130/1/2/3** d.	...	...	...	...	...	...	0804	0759	...	0844	...	...	1003	...	...	1036	1103	1103	...	...	1203	...	...	1236	1303	...
Reading **130/1/2/3** d.	...	...	...	...	...	...	0829	0824	...	0909	...	...	1028	...	...	1101	1128	1128	...	...	1228	...	...	1301	1328	...
Newbury d.	...	...	...	...	...	...	0845	|	...	|	...	...	|	...	...	1116	|	|	...	...	|	...	...	1316	|	...
Westbury **140** d.	...	...	...	...	...	...	0923	|	...	0954	...	...	|	...	...	1155	|	|	...	...	|	...	...	1356	|	...
Castle Cary **140** d.	...	...	...	...	...	...	0941	|	...	1013	...	...	|	...	...	1213	|	|	...	...	|	...	...	1414	|	...
Birmingham New St **119** d.	...	...	...	...	...	...	|	|	...	|	...	0930	|	...	1030	|	|	|	...	1130	|	...	1212	|	|	...
Cardiff Central **115** d.	...	...	...	...	...	...	|	|	...	|	...	|	|	...	|	|	|	|	...	|	|	...	|	|	|	...
Bristol T M **115 132** d.	...	...	0754	...	0844	...	|	0935	0950	|	...	1055	|	...	1157	|	|	|	...	1251	|	...	1345	|	|	...
Taunton **115 132** d.	...	...	0849	...	0915	...	1003	1013	1021	1036	...	1126	1142	...	1228	1235	1242	1242	...	1323	1342	...	1417	1436	1442	...
Tiverton Parkway **115** d.	...	...	0902	...	0927	...	|	1028	1033	1049	...	1138	1156	...	1240	|	1256	1256	...	1335	1355	...	1429	|	1455	...
Exeter St Davids **115** a.	...	...	0914	...	0941	...	1026	1045	1050	1105	...	1152	1209	...	1254	1259	1309	1309	...	1349	1409	...	1444	1459	1509	...
Exeter St Davids **112** d.	...	0842	0920	...	0942	...	1029	...	1052	1107	1126	1153	1212	...	1256	1301	1312	1312	1320	1351	1412	...	1450	1501	1515	1527
Dawlish **112** d.	...	0854	0932	...	|	...	|	...	|	|	|	|	|	...	|	1314	|	|	1334	|	|	...	|	1517	|	1540
Teignmouth **112** d.	...	0858	0937	...	|	...	|	...	|	|	|	|	|	...	|	1319	|	|	1339	|	|	...	|	1522	|	1545
Newton Abbot **112** d.	...	0908	0945	...	1002	...	1049	...	1113	1127	1147	1213	1232	...	1316	1327	1332	1332	1346	1410	1432	...	1509	1530	1537	1553
Torquay **112** d.	...	|	|	...	|	...	|	...	|	|	|	|	|	...	|	1338	|	|	|	|	|	...	|	1543	|	|
Paignton 🚂 **112** a.	...	|	|	...	|	...	|	...	|	|	|	|	|	...	|	1344	|	|	|	|	|	...	|	1549	|	|
Totnes 🚂 d.	...	0920	0957	...	1014	...	1101	...	1125	1139	1159	1225	1244	...	1328	...	1344	1344	1359	1422	1444	...	1521	...	1549	1605
Plymouth a.	...	0950	1025	...	1040	...	1127	...	1151	1205	1230	1251	1311	...	1354	...	1411	1411	1428	1448	1510	...	1547	...	1615	1635
Plymouth d.	0930	0958	...	1032	...	1118	1135	...	...	1210	1238	1300	1315	1340	...	...	1415	...	1440	...	1515	1540	...	...	...	1640
Saltash d.	|	1007	...	1046	...	|	1144	...	...	|	1247	|	|	1349	...	...	|	...	1449	...	|	1549	...	...	...	1649
Liskeard d.	0954	1028	...	1104	...	1143	1203	...	...	1234	1305	1323	1339	1408	...	...	1440	...	1508	...	1539	1608	...	...	...	1707
Bodmin Parkway 🚂 d.	1006	1039	...	1116	...	1155	1215	...	...	1246	1317	1335	1351	1420	...	...	1452	...	1520	...	1552	1620	...	...	...	1720
Lostwithiel d.	|	1044	...	1121	...	|	1220	...	...	|	1322	|	|	1425	...	...	|	...	1525	...	|	1625	...	...	...	1725
Par ♡ d.	1016	1052	...	1128	...	1208	1227	...	...	1301	1329	|	1402	1432	...	...	1505	...	1532	...	1602	1632	...	...	...	1732
Newquay ♡ a.	|	|	...	|	...	1257	|	...	...	|	|	|	|	|	...	...	1555	...	|	...	|	|	...	...	...	|
St Austell d.	1023	1059	...	1134	...	...	1234	...	...	1308	1337	1350	1409	1439	...	...	...	...	1539	...	1610	1639	...	...	...	1739
Truro d.	1040	1115	...	1150	...	...	1251	...	...	1325	1353	1407	1426	1456	...	...	...	...	1555	...	1627	1655	...	...	...	1756
Redruth d.	1052	1127	...	1203	...	...	1301	...	...	1337	1406	1418	1438	1507	...	...	...	...	1607	...	1639	1707	...	...	...	1807
Camborne d.	1058	1133	...	1209	...	...	1309	...	...	1343	1412	|	1444	1513	...	...	...	...	1613	...	1646	1713	...	...	...	1813
St Erth d.	1108	1148**r**	...	1221	...	...	1320	...	...	1355	1423	1434	1456	1525	...	...	...	...	1625	...	1656	1725	...	...	...	1825
Penzance a.	1117	1158	...	1230	...	...	1330	...	...	1405	1432	1443	1506	1534	...	...	...	...	1634	...	1705	1734	...	...	...	1834

C – From Dundee (Tables **119** and **222**).
D – From Derby (Table **119**).
E – From Edinburgh (Table **119**).
G – From Glasgow Central (Tables **119** and **220**).
L – From Leeds (Table **119**).
M – From Manchester Piccadilly (Table **119**).
N – From Newcastle (Table **119**).
Y – From York (Table **119**).
a – Until Sept. 14.
b – From Sept. 21.
r – Arrives 1143.
♡ – See Table **113** for full local service Par - Newquay and v.v.
🚂 – See note 🚂 on page 92.

110 LONDON and BRISTOL - EXETER - PLYMOUTH - PENZANCE

GW, XC

	⑦ 🍷N	⑦ 🍷	⑦	⑦ 🍷E	⑦ 🍷	⑦ 🍷	⑦ 🍷M	⑦	⑦ 🍷E		⑦ 🍷	⑦ 2	⑦ 🍷E	⑦ 🍷	⑦ 🍷	⑦ 🍷	⑦ 🍷G	⑦ 🍷	⑦ 🍷	⑦ 🍷E	⑦ 🍷	⑦ 🍷	⑦ 🍷C	⑦ 🍷	⑦ 🍷E	⑦ 🍷	⑦ A
London Paddington. **130/1/2/3** d.	...	1403	...	...	1436	1503	...	...	...	...	1603	...	...	1636	1703	1630	...	1803	1800	...	1836	1903	...	2003	...	2103	2350
Reading **130/1/2/3** d.	...	1428	...	...	1501	1528	...	...	...	...	1628	...	...	1702	1728	1655	...	1828	1825	...	1901	1928	...	2028	...	2128	0049
Newbury d.	...	|	...	...	1516	|	...	...	...	...	|	...	...	1717	|	|	...	|	|	...	1916	|	...	2044	...	|	|
Westbury **140** d.	...	|	...	...	1555	|	...	...	...	...	|	...	...	1758	|	|	...	|	|	...	1956	|	...	2123	...	|	|
Castle Cary **140** d.	...	|	...	...	1614	|	...	...	...	...	|	...	...	1816	|	|	...	|	|	...	2014	|	...	2140	...	|	|
Birmingham New St **119** d.	1312	|	...	1412	|	|	1440	...	1512	...	|	...	1612	|	|	|	1712	|	|	1812	|	|	1912	|	2012	|	|
Cardiff Central **115** d.	|	|	...	|	|	|	|	...	|	...	|	...	|	|	|	|	|	|	|	|	|	|	|	|	|	|	|
Bristol Temple M.. **115 132** d.	1445	|	...	1545	|	|	1613	...	1645	...	|	...	1745	|	|	1810	1845	|	1935	1945	|	|	2045	|	2145	|	|
Taunton **115 132** d.	1517	1542	...	1617	1636	1642	1652	...	1717	...	1742	...	1817	1838	1843	1905	1917	1941	2007	2017	2036	2041	2124	2203	2217	2241s	|
Tiverton Parkway **115** d.	1530	1556	...	1629	|	1655	1704	...	1730	...	1755	...	1830	|	1857	|	1930	1954	|	2030	|	2054	2136	2216	2230	2254s	|
Exeter St Davids **115** a.	1546	1609	...	1645	1704	1711	1718	...	1747	...	1809	...	1845	1902	1912	1929	1945	2010	2030	2044	2100	2110	2150	2230	2244	2311	0321
Exeter St Davids **112** d.	1550	1612	1627	1650	...	1713	1720	1708	1752	...	1811	1827	1849	1904	1914	1931	1949	2012	2033	2049	2101	2112	2151	2232	2246	...	0437
Dawlish **112** d.	|	|	1643	|	...	|	1732	1737	|	...	|	1840	|	|	|	1943	|	|	|	|	2114	|	|	2244	|	...	|
Teignmouth **112** d.	|	|	1648	|	...	|	1737	1742	|	...	|	1845	|	|	|	1948	|	|	|	|	2119	|	|	2249	|	...	|
Newton Abbot **112** d.	1609	1633	1656	1710	...	1732	1744	1750	1811	...	1831	1852	1909	1924	1934	1956	2009	2032	2053	2109	2127	2132	2211	2257	2306	...	0459
Torquay **112** d.	|	|	|	|	...	|	1754	|	|	...	|	|	|	|	|	|	|	|	|	|	|	|	|	|	|	...	|
Paignton 🚂 **112** a.	|	|	|	|	...	|	1800	|	|	...	|	|	|	|	|	|	|	|	|	|	|	|	|	|	|	...	|
Totnes 🚂 d.	1621	1644	1708	1722	...	1745	...	1803	1823	...	1843	1905	1921	1936	1946	2008	2021	2044	2105	2121	2138	2144	2223	2309	2318	...	|
Plymouth a.	1647	1711	1738	1748	...	1813	...	1832	1849	...	1909	1935	1947	2005	2013	2034	2047	2110	2131	2147	2207	2213	2250	2335	2344	...	0538
Plymouth d.	...	1715	1740	...	...	...	...	1840	1905	...	1915	1940	...	...	2015	...	...	2115	...	...	...	...	...	...	...	...	|
Saltash d.	...	|	1779	...	...	...	...	1849	|	...	|	1949	...	...	|	...	...	2124	...	...	...	...	...	...	...	...	|
Liskeard d.	...	1739	1808	...	...	...	...	1908	1928	...	1939	2010	...	...	2040	...	...	2144	...	...	...	...	...	...	...	...	0612
Bodmin Parkway 🚂 d.	...	1751	1820	...	...	...	...	1920	1940	...	1951	2022	...	...	2052	...	...	2156	...	...	...	...	...	...	...	...	0626
Lostwithiel d.	...	|	1825	...	...	...	...	1925	|	...	|	2027	...	...	|	...	...	2202	...	...	...	...	...	...	...	...	0633
Par ♡ d.	...	1802	1832	...	...	...	...	1932	|	...	2002	2034	...	...	2103	...	...	2209	...	...	...	...	...	...	...	...	0641
Newquay ♡ a.	...	|	|	...	...	...	...	|	|	...	|	|	...	...	|	...	...	|	...	...	...	...	...	...	...	...	|
St Austell d.	...	1810	1839	...	...	...	...	1939	1959	...	2009	2041	...	...	2110	...	...	2216	...	...	...	...	...	...	...	...	0649
Truro d.	...	1827	1855	...	...	...	...	1955	2016	...	2026	2058	...	...	2127	...	...	2233	...	...	...	...	...	...	...	...	0706
Redruth d.	...	1839	1907	...	...	...	...	2007	2027	...	2038	2111	...	...	2139	...	...	2244	...	...	...	...	...	...	...	...	0720
Camborne d.	...	1846	1913	...	...	...	...	2013	|	...	2044	2117	...	...	2145	...	...	2251	...	...	...	...	...	...	...	...	0727
St Erth d.	...	1856	1925	...	...	...	...	2025	2041	...	2054	2128	...	...	2157	...	...	2303	...	...	...	...	...	...	...	...	0742
Penzance a.	...	1905	1934	...	...	...	...	2034	2050	...	2103	2137	...	...	2207	...	...	2312	...	...	...	...	...	...	...	...	0755

Ⓐ

	Ⓐ 🍷	Ⓐ 🍷	Ⓐ 🍷E	Ⓐ 🍷	Ⓐ 🍷	Ⓐ 🍷	Ⓐ 🍷E	Ⓐ 🍷	Ⓐ 🍷	Ⓐ 🍷	Ⓐ 2	Ⓐ 🍷E	Ⓐ	Ⓐ 🍷	Ⓐ 2	Ⓐ 🍷E	Ⓐ 🍷	Ⓐ 2	Ⓐ 🍷	Ⓐ 🍷B	Ⓐ 2	Ⓐ 🍷M	Ⓐ 🍷	Ⓐ 🍷E	Ⓐ 🍷	Ⓐ 2
Penzance d.	...	...	...	...	...	...	...	...	0503	...	0520	...	0540	0605	0628	...	...	...	0710	...	0745	...	0815	...	...	0850
St Erth d.	...	...	...	...	...	...	...	...	|	...	|	...	0548	|	0636	...	...	...	0719	...	0753	...	0824	...	...	0858
Camborne d.	...	...	...	...	...	...	...	...	|	...	0540	...	0601	0622	0649	...	...	...	0730	...	0806	...	0835	...	...	0911
Redruth d.	...	...	...	...	...	...	...	...	0524	...	|	...	0607	0628	0655	...	...	...	0737	...	0812	...	0842	...	...	0917
Truro d.	...	...	...	...	...	...	...	...	0536	...	0555	...	0619	0640	0707	...	...	...	0749	...	0825	...	0854	...	...	0929
St Austell d.	...	...	...	...	...	...	...	...	0553	...	▬	...	0635	0657	0724	...	...	...	0805	...	0841	...	0911	...	...	0946
Newquay ♡ d.	...	...	...	...	...	...	...	...	|	...	Ⓐ 2	...	|	|	|	...	...	...	|	...	|	...	|	...	...	|
Par ♡ d.	...	...	...	...	...	...	...	...	|	...	0618	...	0642	0705	0731	...	...	...	0813	...	0848	...	0919	...	...	0953
Lostwithiel d.	...	...	...	...	...	...	...	...	|	...	0625	...	0649	0712	0738	...	...	...	0820	...	0855	...	|	...	...	1000
Bodmin Parkway 🚂 d.	...	...	...	...	...	...	...	...	0609	...	0631	...	0655	0719	0743	...	...	...	0826	...	0900	...	0931	...	...	1006
Liskeard d.	...	...	...	...	...	...	...	...	0622	...	0644	...	0707	0732	0753	...	...	...	0839	...	0913	...	0946	...	...	1020
Saltash d.	...	...	...	...	...	...	...	...	0637	...	0704	...	0727	0753	0811b	...	...	...	0857	...	0931	...	1001	...	...	1039
Plymouth a.	...	...	...	...	...	...	...	...	0649	...	0720	...	0743	0806	0821	...	...	...	0908	...	0940	...	1011	...	...	1049
Plymouth d.	...	0454	0525	0532	0555	...	0620	0637	0655	...	...	0727	0745	0816	...	0827	0835	0849	0915	0927	0942	...	1015	1027	...	1052
Totnes 🚂 d.	...	|	0551	0601	|	...	0646	0706	|	...	...	0753	0814	0843	...	0853	0904	0915	0942	0953	1011	...	1042	1053	...	1120
Paignton 🚂 **112** d.	...	|	|	|	|	...	|	|	|	...	...	|	|	|	...	|	|	|	|	|	|	1014	|	|	1055	|
Torquay **112** d.	...	|	|	|	|	...	|	|	|	...	...	|	|	|	...	|	|	|	|	|	|	1020	|	|	1101	|
Newton Abbot **112** d.	...	0530	0604	0613	0631	...	0659	0718	0731	...	...	0806	0826	0855	...	0905	0916	0928	0954	1006	1023	1029	1054	1106	1113	1133
Teignmouth **112** d.	...	|	|	0620	|	...	|	0725	|	...	...	|	0833	|	...	|	0923	0935	|	|	|	1036	|	|	1120	|
Dawlish **112** d.	...	|	|	0625	|	...	|	0730	|	...	...	|	0838	|	...	|	0928	0940	|	|	|	1041	|	|	1125	|
Exeter St Davids **112** a.	...	0549	0623	0637	0650	...	0718	0742	0750	...	...	0825	0852	0914	...	0924	0940	0955	1013	1025	1050	1053	1113	1126	1136	1154
Exeter St Davids **115** d.	...	0552	0625	0639	0652	...	0720	0744	0752	...	...	0827	...	0916	...	0927	0943	...	1015	1027	...	1055	1115	1127	1143	...
Tiverton Parkway **115** d.	...	0606	0638	0653	|	...	0733	0758	|	←	...	0840	...	0930	...	0940	|	...	1030	1040	...	1108	1129	1140	|	...
Taunton **115 132** d.	...	0620	0651	0706	0715	...	0746	0810	0815	0824z	...	0853	...	0943	...	0953	1006	...	1042	1053	...	1121	1142	1153	1207	...
Bristol Temple M.. **115 132** a.	0510	|	0725	|	|	...	0827	→	|	|	...	0924	...	|	...	1026	|	...	|	1124	...	1154	|	1225	|	...
Cardiff Central **115** a.	|	|	|	|	|	...	|	...	|	|	...	|	...	|	...	|	|	...	|	|	...	|	|	|	|	...
Birmingham New St **119** a.	v	|	0855	|	|	←	0954	...	|	|	...	1055	...	|	...	1155	|	...	|	1255	...	1318	|	1355	|	...
Castle Cary **140** d.	|	0641	...	0726	|	0726	...	...	|	0844	...	...	...	|	...	...	1027	...	|	...	...	...	|	...	1228	...
Westbury **140** d.	0557y	0700	...	→	|	0757	...	...	|	0909	...	...	...	|	...	...	1046	...	|	...	...	...	|	...	1250	...
Newbury d.	0645	0745	...	...	0819	0840	...	...	|	|	...	...	...	|	...	...	1125	...	|	...	...	...	|	...	1333	...
Reading **130/1/2/3** a.	0704	0801	...	...	0835	0856	...	...	0930	1002	...	...	...	1058	...	...	1141	...	1159	...	...	...	1258	...	1349	...
London Paddington. **130/1/2/3** a.	0737	0835	...	...	0859	0921	...	...	0954	1029	...	...	...	1127	...	...	1205	...	1229	...	...	...	1329	...	1416	...

	Ⓐ 🍷	Ⓐ 🍷G	Ⓐ 2	Ⓐ 🍷	Ⓐ 🍷G	Ⓐ 🍷	Ⓐ 2	Ⓐ 🍷E	Ⓐ ✕	Ⓐ 🍷E	Ⓐ 2	Ⓐ 🍷	Ⓐ M🍷	Ⓐ 🍷E	Ⓐ M🍷	Ⓐ 🍷	Ⓐ 2	Ⓐ 2	Ⓐ 🍷	Ⓐ 🍷L	Ⓐ 2	Ⓐ 🍷a	Ⓐ 🍷	Ⓐ 🍷L	Ⓐ 2	Ⓐ 🍷	Ⓐ 2
Penzance d.	0910	...	0950	1020	...	...	1050	1115	...	...	1150	1215	...	...	...	...	1250	1315	...	...	1350	...	1415	...	1450	...	1515
St Erth d.	0920	...	0958	1029	...	...	1058	1124	...	...	1158	1224	...	...	...	...	1258	1323	...	...	1358	...	1424	...	1458	...	1523
Camborne d.	0934	...	1011	1040	...	...	1111	1136	...	...	1211	1235	...	...	...	...	1311	1336	...	...	1411	...	1435	...	1511	...	1536
Redruth d.	0941	...	1017	1046	...	...	1117	1143	...	...	1217	1242	...	...	...	...	1317	1342	...	...	1417	...	1442	...	1517	...	1542
Truro d.	0953	...	1029	1058	...	...	1129	1155	...	...	1229	1254	...	...	...	...	1329	1354	...	...	1429	...	1454	...	1529	...	1554
St Austell d.	1010	...	1046	1115	...	...	1146	1211	...	...	1246	1311	...	...	...	...	1346	1410	...	...	1446	...	1511	...	1546	...	1610
Newquay ♡ d.	|	...	|	|	...	...	|	|	...	...	|	|	...	...	...	...	|	|	...	...	|	...	|	...	|	...	|
Par ♡ d.	1019	...	1053	1124	...	...	1153	1218	...	...	1253	1319	...	...	...	...	1353	1417	...	...	1453	...	1519	...	1553	...	1617
Lostwithiel d.	|	...	1100	|	...	...	1200	1225	...	...	1259	|	...	...	...	...	1359	1424	...	...	1500	...	|	...	1600	...	1623
Bodmin Parkway 🚂 d.	1031	...	1106	1136	...	...	1206	1231	...	...	1306	1331	...	...	...	...	1406	1429	...	...	1506	...	1532	...	1606	...	1629
Liskeard d.	1044	...	1119	1149	...	...	1219	1244	...	...	1319	1344	...	...	...	...	1419	1442	...	...	1519	...	1545	...	1619	...	1642
Saltash d.	1059	...	1136	|	...	...	1236	|	...	...	1338	1359b	...	...	...	...	1436	1459	...	...	1536	...	1600b	...	1636	...	1701
Plymouth a.	1109	...	1146	1212	...	...	1246	1308	...	←	1352	1409	...	...	...	...	1447	1509	...	...	1546	...	1610	...	1645	...	1718
Plymouth d.	1115	1127	...	1215	1227	...	1252	→	1315	1327	▬	1415	...	1427	...	...	1449	...	1515	1527	...	1549	1615	1627	...	1650	...
Totnes 🚂 d.	1142	1153	...	1242	1253	...	1321	...	1342	1353	Ⓐ 🍷	1442	...	1453	...	...	1518	...	1542	1553	...	1615	1642	1653	...	1719	...
Paignton 🚂 **112** d.	|	|	...	|	|	...	|	...	|	|	1355	|	1438	|	...	...	|	...	|	|	...	|	|	|	...	|	...
Torquay **112** d.	|	|	...	|	|	...	|	...	|	|	1401	|	1444	|	...	...	|	...	|	|	...	|	|	|	...	|	...
Newton Abbot **112** d.	1154	1206	...	1255	1306	...	1333	...	1354	1406	1413	1454	1457r	1506	...	...	1530	...	1554	1606	...	1628	1654	1706	...	1731	...
Teignmouth **112** d.	|	|	...	|	|	...	|	...	|	|	1420	|	1504	|	...	...	1537	...	|	|	...	|	|	|	...	|	...
Dawlish **112** d.	|	|	...	|	|	...	|	...	|	|	1425	|	1509	|	...	...	1542	...	|	|	...	|	|	|	...	|	...
Exeter St Davids **112** a.	1212	1225	...	1313	1325	...	1354	...	1413	1425	1438	1512	1521	1526	...	...	1555	...	1612	1625	...	1649	1712	1725	...	1750	...
Exeter St Davids **115** d.	1215	1227	...	1315	1327	1342	...	...	1415	1427	1443	1515	1523	1527	...	1542	...	...	1615	1627	...	1651	1715	1727	...	1752	...
Tiverton Parkway **115** d.	1229	1239	...	1330	1340	1357	...	...	1430	1440	1457	1529	1536	1540	←	|	...	...	1629	1640	...	|	1729	1740	...	1806	...
Taunton **115 132** d.	1242	1253	...	1342	1353	1410	...	...	1443	1453	1510	1542	1548	1553	1600t	1605	...	...	1642	1653	...	1715	1742	1753	...	1819	...
Bristol Temple M.. **115 132** a.	|	1327	...	|	1424	|	...	...	|	1524	|	|	→	1625	1647	|	...	...	|	1726	...	|	|	1825	...	|	...
Cardiff Central **115** a.	|	|	...	|	|	|	...	...	|	|	|	|	...	|	|	|	...	...	|	|	...	|	|	|	...	|	...
Birmingham New St **119** a.	|	1455	...	|	1555	|	...	...	|	1655	|	|	...	1755	1825	|	...	...	|	1854	...	|	|	1954	...	|	...
Castle Cary **140** d.	|	...	...	|	...	1430	...	...	|	...	1531	|	...	...	...	1626	...	...	|	...	...	1736	|	...	...	1839	...
Westbury **140** d.	|	...	...	|	...	1452	...	...	|	...	1554	|	...	...	...	1646	...	...	|	...	...	1755	|	...	...	1858	...
Newbury d.	|	...	...	|	...	1533	...	...	|	...	|	|	...	...	...	1727	...	...	|	...	...	1840	|	...	...	1938	...
Reading **130/1/2/3** a.	1403	...	...	1504	...	1548	...	...	1558	...	1642	1702	...	...	...	1742	...	...	1757	...	...	1856	1900	...	...	1954	...
London Paddington. **130/1/2/3** a.	1427	...	...	1528	...	1617	...	...	1629	...	1707	1731	...	...	...	1807	...	...	1824	...	...	1924	1924	...	...	2023	...

A – THE NIGHT RIVIERA – Conveys 🛏 and 2. Calls to set down only after Newton Abbot. See also note ‡ on page 92.
B – To Dundee on ①–④; to Aberdeen on ⑤ (Tables **119** and **222**).
C – From Dundee (Tables **119** and **222**).
E – From / to Edinburgh (Table **119**).
G – From / to Glasgow Central (Tables **119** / **220**).
L – To Leeds (Table **119**).
M – From / to Manchester Piccadilly (Table **119**).
N – From Newcastle (Table **119**).
a – Until Sept. 12.
b – From Sept. 15.
r – Arrives 5 minutes earlier.
s – Calls to set down only.
t – Arrives 1548.
v – Via Trowbridge (Table **140**).
y – Arrives 0550.
z – Arrives 0810.
♡ – See Table **113** for full local service Par - Newquay and v.v.
🚂 – See note 🚂 on page 92.

GW, XC — PENZANCE - PLYMOUTH - EXETER - BRISTOL and LONDON — 110

	Ⓐ 🍷L	Ⓐ	Ⓐ F	Ⓐ ✕	Ⓐ 🍷	Ⓐ 2	Ⓐ 2	Ⓐ 2	Ⓐ 🍷	Ⓐ	Ⓐ 🍷	Ⓐ 2	Ⓐ 2	Ⓐ 2	Ⓐ 2	Ⓐ	Ⓐ 2	Ⓐ A		⑥ 🍷E	⑥ 🍷	⑥ 🍷E	⑥ 🍷	⑥ 🍷	⑥ 🍷	⑥ 🍷
Penzance d.	...	1552	...	1615	...	...	1650	1715	1750	...	1813	1850	1915	...	2015	...	2100	2145	⑥	...	...	...	...	...	...	...
St Erth d.	...	1600	...	1624	...	...	1658	1723	1759	...	1821	1859	1924	...	2024	...	2109	2155		...	...	...	...	...	...	...
Camborne d.	...	1613	...	1635	...	...	1711	1736	1812	...	1834	1912	1937	...	2036	...	2122	2208		...	...	...	...	...	...	...
Redruth d.	...	1619	...	1642	...	...	1717	1743	1818	...	1840	1918	1943	...	2043	...	2128	2216		...	...	...	...	...	...	...
Truro d.	...	1631	...	1655	...	...	1729	1755	1830	...	1852	1930	1955	2010	2055	...	2140	2229	♥	...	...	...	...	...	...	...
St Austell d.	...	1648	...	1711	...	...	1746	1811	1847	...	1908	1947	2011	2028	2111	...	2157	2247		...	...	...	...	...	...	...
Newquay ♡ d.	...	|	...	|	...	...	|	|	|	...	|	|	|	|	|	...	|	|		...	...	...	...	...	...	...
Par ♡ d.	...	1655	...	1719	...	...	1753	1818	1854	...	1915	1954	2019	2034	2119	...	2205	2256		...	...	...	...	...	...	...
Lostwithiel d.	...	1702	...	|	...	...	1800	1825	1901	...	|	2001	2025	...	2125	...	2212	|		...	...	...	...	...	...	...
Bodmin Parkway 🚂 d.	...	1707	...	1731	...	...	1806	1832	1908	...	1925	2007	2031	...	2132	...	2218	2308		...	...	...	...	...	...	...
Liskeard d.	...	1721	...	1744	*1756*	...	1817	1844	1921	...	1937	2021	2044	...	2144	...	2231	2326		...	...	...	...	...	...	...
Saltash d.	...	1738	...	|	*1811*	...	1836	1907	1936	...	|	2040	2104	...	2201	...	2251	|		...	...	...	...	...	...	...
Plymouth a.	...	1747	...	1807	*1822*	...	1846	1919	1946	...	2002	2050	2121	...	2213	...	2300	|		...	...	...	...	...	...	...
Plymouth d.	1727	...	1752	1816	1827	...	1848	▬	1949	...	2008	▬	2125	...	...	2223	2316	2355		0527	0558	0627	...	0641	0654	...
Totnes 🚂 d.	1753	...	1821	1843	1853	...	1917	Ⓐ 🍷	2018	...	|	Ⓐ 2	2155	...	...	2252	2345	0023		0553	0625	0653	...	0710	|	...
Paignton 🚂 112 d.	|	...	|	|	|	1851	|	1904	|	2011	|	2109	|	...	...	|	|	|		|	|	|	...	|	|	...
Torquay 112 d.	|	...	|	|	|	1856	|	1910	|	2017	|	2114	|	...	...	|	|	|		|	|	|	...	|	|	...
Newton Abbot 112 d.	1806	...	1834	1855	1906	1910	1929	1920	2030	2026	2044	2125	2208	...	...	2304	2358	0037		0606	0637	0706	...	0722	0731	...
Teignmouth 112 d.	|	...	1841	|	|	1917	|	1927	2037	|	|	2132	2215	...	...	2311	|	|		|	|	|	...	0729	|	←
Dawlish 112 d.	|	...	1846	|	|	1922	|	1932	2042	|	|	2137	2220	...	...	2316	|	|		|	|	|	...	0734	|	0734
Exeter St Davids 112 a.	1825	...	1901	1915	1925	1945	1949	1953	2054	2047	2107	2159	2237	...	...	2328	0021	0100		0625	0656	0725	...	→	0750	0755
Exeter St Davids 115 d.	1827	...	1903	1917	1927	1950	...	1955	2056	2051	2114	2200	...	...	...	...	...	0107		0627	0700	0727	0733	...	0751	0757
Tiverton Parkway 115 d.	1840	...	|	1931	1940	|	...	2009	2110	2104	2128	2217	...	...	...	...	...	|		0640	0714	0740	|	...	|	0811
Taunton 115 132 d.	1853	...	1927	1944	1953	2016	...	2022	2124	2117	2142	2233	...	...	...	...	...	0140		0653	0727	0753	0758	...	0815	0824
Bristol Temple M. 115 132 a.	1926	...	2003	|	2024	2119	...	|	2156	2148	2216	2315	...	...	...	...	...	|		0724	|	0824	0854	...	|	|
Cardiff Central 115 a.	|	...	...	|	|	2215	...	|	|	...	|	...	...	...	...	...	...	|		|	|	|	|	...	|	|
Birmingham New St 119 a.	2055	...	...	|	2200	...	...	|	|	...	2354	...	...	...	...	...	...	|		0855	|	0955	|	...	|	|
Castle Cary 140 d.	...	...	...	|	...	...	...	2041	|	...	...	...	...	...	...	...	...	|		...	0748	...	|	...	|	0844
Westbury 140 d.	...	...	...	|	...	...	...	2101	|	...	...	...	...	...	...	...	...	|		...	0809	...	|	...	|	0911
Newbury d.	...	...	...	|	...	...	...	2143	|	...	...	...	...	...	...	...	...	|		...	0848	...	|	...	0927	|
Reading 130/1/2/3 a.	...	...	...	2100	...	...	...	2200	2310	...	...	...	...	...	...	...	...	0359s		...	0903	...	1009	...	0943	1004
London Paddington 130/1/2/3 a.	...	...	...	2124	...	...	...	2229	2359	...	...	...	...	...	...	...	...	0508		...	0929	...	1037	...	1008	1029

	⑥ 🍷E	⑥ 2	⑥ 🍷	⑥ 🍷E	⑥ 🍷	⑥ 2	⑥ 🍷	⑥ 🍷B	⑥ 2	⑥ 🍷M	⑥ 🍷	⑥ 🍷E	⑥ 🍷	⑥	⑥ 🍷	⑥ 🍷G	⑥ 2	⑥ 🍷	⑥ 🍷G	⑥ 2	⑥ 🍷	⑥ 🍷	⑥ 🍷	⑥ 🍷	⑥ 🍷E	⑥ 2
Penzance d.	...	0540	0612	...	...	0640	0710	...	0740	...	0815	...	...	0851	0911	...	0950	1015	...	1039	1058	...	...	...	1115	1150
St Erth d.	...	0548	|	...	...	0648	0719	...	0748	...	0824	...	...	0859	0922	...	0958	1025	...	1047	1107	...	...	...	1124	1158
Camborne d.	...	0601	0629	...	...	0701	0733	...	0801	...	0835	...	...	0912	0935	...	1011	1036	...	1101	1121	...	...	...	1136	1211
Redruth d.	...	0607	0636	...	...	0707	0739	...	0807	...	0842	...	...	0918	0942	...	1017	1043	...	1108	1128	...	...	...	1143	1218
Truro d.	...	0619	0648	...	...	0719	0751	...	0820	...	0855	...	...	0930	0955	...	1030	1056	...	1120	1140	...	...	...	1155	1230
St Austell d.	...	0635	0705	...	...	0735	0808	...	0836	...	0912	...	...	0946	1012	...	1046	1113	...	1137	1156	...	...	...	1211	1246
Newquay ♡ d.	...	|	|	...	...	|	|	...	|	...	|	...	...	|	|	...	|	|	...	|	|	...	1120	...	|	|
Par ♡ d.	...	0642	0712	...	...	0742	0815	...	0844	...	0920	...	...	0953	1020	...	1053	1120	...	1145	|	...	1208	...	1218	1253
Lostwithiel d.	...	0649	|	...	...	0749	|	...	0851	...	|	...	...	1000	|	...	1059	|	...	1152	|	...	|	...	1225	1300
Bodmin Parkway 🚂 d.	...	0655	0724	...	...	0755	0827	...	0856	...	0932	...	...	1006	1032	...	1105	1132	...	1157	1213	...	1223	...	1231	1306
Liskeard d.	...	0708	0737	...	...	0808	0840	...	0909	...	0946	...	...	1019	1046	...	1118	1146	...	1211	1226	...	1236	...	1246	1319
Saltash d.	...	0727	0755	...	...	0828	0858	...	0927	...	|	...	...	1039	|	...	1135	|	...	1231	|	...	1254	...	|	1339
Plymouth a.	...	0745	0806	...	...	0846	0909	...	0937	...	1009	...	...	1049	1109	...	1145	1209	...	1242	1249	...	1305	...	1310	1353
Plymouth d.	0725	0747	0814	0827	...	0848	0914	0927	...	...	1014	1027	...	1050	1114	1127	...	1214	1227	1244	1255	...	1315	...	1328	...
Totnes 🚂 d.	0751	0816	0841	0853	...	0917	0941	0953	...	...	1041	1053	...	1119	1142	1153	...	1241	1253	1312	|	...	1342	...	1354	...
Paignton 🚂 112 d.	|	|	|	|	0855	|	|	|	...	1012	|	|	1055	|	|	|	...	|	|	|	|	...	|	1300	|	...
Torquay 112 d.	|	|	|	|	0901	|	|	|	...	1018	|	|	1102	|	|	|	...	|	|	|	|	...	|	1306	|	...
Newton Abbot 112 d.	0804	0828	0854	0906	0914	0929	0954	1006	...	1027	1054	1106	1113	1131	1155	1206	...	1254	1306	1324	1349	...	1354	1316f	1407	...
Teignmouth 112 d.	|	0835	|	|	0922	0936	|	|	...	1034	|	|	1120	1138	|	|	...	|	|	|	1352	...	|	1323	|	...
Dawlish 112 d.	|	0840	|	|	0927	0941	|	|	...	1039	|	|	1126	1143	|	|	...	|	|	|	|	...	|	1328	|	...
Exeter St Davids 112 a.	0823	0853	0913	0925	0943	0956	1013	1025	...	1051	1113	1125	1142	1156	1214	1225	...	1313	1325	1345	|	...	1413	1355	1426	...
Exeter St Davids 115 d.	0827	...	0916	0927	0946	...	1016	1027	...	1053	1116	1127	1145	...	1216	1227	...	1316	1327	...	|	1330	1416	1400	1428	...
Tiverton Parkway 115 d.	0840	...	0931	0940	|	...	1031	1040	...	1107	1131	1140	|	...	1231	1240	...	1331	1340	...	|	1346	1431	|	1441	...
Taunton 115 132 d.	0853	...	0945	0953	1009	...	1044	1053	...	1119	1144	1153	1208	...	1244	1253	...	1344	1353	...	|	1402	1444	1424	1454	...
Bristol Temple M. 115 132 a.	0924	...	|	1030	|	...	|	1124	...	1151	|	1228	|	...	|	1324	...	|	1424	...	|	|	|	1455	1528	...
Cardiff Central 115 a.	|	...	|	|	|	...	|	|	...	|	|	|	|	...	|	|	...	|	|	...	|	|	|	|	|	...
Birmingham New St 119 a.	1055	...	|	1155	|	...	|	1255	...	1319	|	1355	|	...	|	1455	...	|	1555	...	|	|	|	|	1655	...
Castle Cary 140 d.	...	...	|	...	1030	...	|	...	...	...	|	...	1228	...	|	...	...	|	...	...	|	1423	|	|	...	...
Westbury 140 d.	...	...	|	...	1049	...	|	...	...	...	|	...	1247	...	|	...	...	|	...	...	|	1449j	|	|	...	...
Newbury d.	...	...	|	...	1128	...	|	...	...	...	|	...	1329	...	|	...	...	|	...	...	|	1531	|	|	...	...
Reading 130/1/2/3 a.	...	...	1101	...	1143	...	1159	...	...	...	1259	...	1344	...	1359	...	...	1459	...	...	1530	1546	1559	1610	...	...
London Paddington 130/1/2/3 a.	...	...	1129	...	1208	...	1229	...	...	...	1329	...	1409	...	1429	...	...	1529	...	...	1557	1612	1629	1635	...	...

	⑥ 🍷M	⑥ 🍷	⑥ 🍷E	⑥ 🍷	⑥ 2	⑥ 🍷	⑥ 🍷Y	⑥ 2	⑥ 🍷	⑥ 🍷L	⑥ 🍷	⑥ 2	⑥ 🍷L	⑥ 2	⑥ 🍷	⑥ 🍷D	⑥ 2	⑥ 🍷	⑥ 🍷	⑥ 2	⑥ 🍷	⑥ 🍷	⑥ 2	⑥ 2	⑥ 2	⑥ 2
Penzance d.	...	1217	...	...	1250	1310	...	1350	1420	...	1445	1515	...	1550	1620	...	1645	...	...	1715	1745	1815	1930	...	2043	...
St Erth d.	...	1226	...	...	1258	1319	...	1358	1429	...	1454	1523	...	1558	1629	...	1654	...	...	1724	1754	1823	1939	...	2052	...
Camborne d.	...	1237	...	...	1311	1333	...	1411	1440	...	1508	1536	...	1611	1640	...	1707	...	...	1736	1807	1836	1952	...	2104	...
Redruth d.	...	1244	...	...	1318	1340	...	1418	1447	...	1515	1542	...	1618	1647	...	1713	...	...	1742	1814	1842	1957	...	2111	...
Truro d.	...	1257	...	...	1330	1353	...	1430	1500	...	1528	1555	...	1630	1700	...	1725	...	...	1754	1826	1854	2009	2017	2123	...
St Austell d.	...	1314	...	...	1346	1410	...	1446	1517	...	1545	1611	...	1646	1717	...	1742	...	...	1810	1842	1910	2025	2034	2139	...
Newquay ♡ d.	...	|	...	...	|	|	...	|	|	...	|	|	...	|	|	...	|	...	1716	|	|	|	|	|	|	2122
Par ♡ d.	...	1321	...	...	1354	1417	...	1453	1524	...	1552	1619	...	1653	1724	...	1749	...	1803	1817	1849	1917	2032	2042	2147	2212
Lostwithiel d.	...	|	...	...	1400	1424	...	1500	|	...	1559	1626	...	1700	|	...	1755	...	|	1824	1856	|	2039	▬	2153	2219
Bodmin Parkway 🚂 d.	...	1333	...	...	1407	1431	...	1506	1536	...	1606	1631	...	1706	1736	...	1802	...	1816	1830	1903	1927	2045		2200	2225
Liskeard d.	...	1346	...	...	1419	1444	...	1519	1549	...	1619	1644	...	1719	1749	...	1814	...	1826	1843	1915	1940	2101	...	2216r	2238
Saltash d.	...	|	...	...	1437	1502	...	1537	|	...	1637	1704	...	1737	|	...	1832	...	|	1900	1933	|	2120	⑥	2233	2258
Plymouth a.	...	1409	...	...	1447	1512	...	1547	1612	...	1647	1722	...	1747	1812	...	1842	...	1853	1910f	1943	2004	2138	2	2243	2314
Plymouth d.	...	1415	1427	...	1449	1515	1527	1548	1615	1627	1650	...	1727	...	1815	1827	1848	...	1916	...	1945	2011	...	2150	...	...
Totnes 🚂 d.	...	1442	1453	...	1518	1542	1553	1617	1642	1653	1719	...	1753	...	1844	1853	1917	...	1943	...	2014	|	...	2219	...	...
Paignton 🚂 112 d.	1412	|	|	1455	|	|	|	|	|	|	|	...	|	...	|	|	|	1928	|	...	|	|	...	|	...	...
Torquay 112 d.	1418	|	|	1502	|	|	|	|	|	|	|	...	|	...	|	|	|	1934	|	...	|	|	...	|	...	...
Newton Abbot 112 d.	1428	1454	1506	1512	1530	1554	1606	1629	1655	1706	1731	...	1806	...	1856	1906	1930	1944	1955	...	2026	2047	...	2232	...	...
Teignmouth 112 d.	1435	|	|	1519	1537	|	|	1636	|	|	1738	...	|	...	|	|	1937	|	|	...	2033	|	...	2239	...	...
Dawlish 112 d.	1440	|	|	1524	1542	|	|	1641	|	|	1743	...	|	...	|	|	1942	|	|	...	2038	|	...	2244	...	...
Exeter St Davids 112 a.	1450	1513	1525	1540	1555	1613	1625	1654	1715	1725	1755	...	1825	...	1916	1925	1954	2003	2015	...	2050	2107	...	2307	...	...
Exeter St Davids 115 d.	1452	1516	1527	1542	...	1616	1627	...	1717	1727	1757	...	1827	...	1918	1927	1955	2008	2018	...	2052	2109	...	...	...	...
Tiverton Parkway 115 d.	1505	1530	1540	1556	...	|	1640	...	1731	1740	1811	...	1840	...	1932	1940	2010	2021	|	...	2106	2122	...	...	...	...
Taunton 115 132 d.	1518	1544	1553	1609	...	1640	1653	...	1746	1753	1824	...	1853	...	1945	1953	2022	2034	2041	...	2119	2141a	...	...	...	...
Bristol Temple M. 115 132 a.	1557	|	1625	|	...	|	1726	...	|	1824	|	...	1927	...	|	2024	2125	2105	2131	...	2150	2214	...	...	...	...
Cardiff Central 115 a.	|	|	|	|	...	|	|	...	|	|	|	...	|	...	|	|	2214	...	...	...	|	...	...	...	...	...
Birmingham New St 119 a.	1719	|	1755	|	...	|	1855	...	|	1955	|	...	2055	...	|	2155	...	...	...	...	|	...	...	...	...	...
Castle Cary 140 d.	...	|	...	1629	...	|	...	...	|	...	1844	...	...	...	2006	...	...	...	...	...	|	...	...	...	...	...
Westbury 140 d.	...	|	...	1648	...	|	...	...	|	...	1905	...	...	...	2026	...	...	...	...	...	|	...	...	...	...	...
Newbury d.	...	|	...	1730	...	|	...	...	|	...	1944	...	...	...	|	...	...	...	...	...	|	...	...	...	...	...
Reading 130/1/2/3 a.	...	1659	...	1745	...	1756	...	...	1901	...	1959	...	...	...	2116	...	...	...	...	...	2310	...	...	...	...	...
London Paddington 130/1/2/3 a.	...	1729	...	1810	...	1825	...	...	1929	...	2025	...	...	...	2140	...	...	...	...	...	2340	...	...	...	...	...

A – THE NIGHT RIVIERA – Conveys 🛏 and (2). Calls to pick up only until Totnes. See also note ‡ on page 92.
B – To Aberdeen (Tables **119** and **222**).
D – To Derby (Table **119**).
E – To Edinburgh (Table **119**).
F – To Gloucester (Table **138**).
G – To Glasgow Central (Tables **119** and **220**).
L – To Leeds (Table **119**).
M – To Manchester Piccadilly (Table **119**).
Y – To York (Table **119**).
a – Arrives 2134.
f – Connects with train in previous column.
j – Arrives 1440.
r – Arrives 2211.
s – Calls to set down only.
♡ – See Table **113** for full local service Newquay - Par and v.v.
🚂 – See note 🚂 on page 92.
♥ – Service valid until Sept. 13.

110 PENZANCE - PLYMOUTH - EXETER - BRISTOL and LONDON GW, XC

⑦	⑦ 🍷	⑦ 🍷	⑦ 🍷	⑦ 🍷B	⑦	⑦ 🍷	⑦ 🍷	⑦ 🍷G	⑦ 🍷M	⑦ 2	⑦ 🍷	⑦ E	⑦	⑦ 🍷M	⑦ 🍷	⑦ 🍷	⑦ 🍷E	⑦ 2	⑦ 🍷M	⑦ 🍷	⑦ 🍷E	⑦ 2	⑦ 🍷	⑦ 🍷E	⑦ 🍷	⑦ 2
Penzance d.	...	...	...	...	...	0810	...	...	...	0846	0918	...	0945	...	1012	...	...	1050	...	...	1130	1149	1218	...	...	1249
St Erth d.	...	...	...	...	...	0818	...	...	...	0855	0927	...	0954	...	1021	...	...	1059	...	...	1138	1157	1227	...	...	1258
Camborne d.	...	...	...	...	...	0829	...	...	...	0908	0938	...	1006	...	1032	...	...	1111	...	...	1151	1210	1238	...	...	1311
Redruth d.	...	...	...	...	...	0825	...	...	...	0914	0945	...	1013	...	1039	...	...	1117	...	...	1157	1216	1245	...	...	1317
Truro d.	...	...	...	...	...	0847	...	...	...	0926	0957	...	1025	...	1051	...	...	1129	...	...	1209	1228	1257	...	...	1329
St Austell d.	...	...	...	...	...	0904	...	...	...	0942	1014	...	1041	...	1108	...	...	1145	...	...	1225	1244	1314	...	...	1345
Newquay ♡ d.	...	...	...	...	...	|	...	...	...	|	|	...	|	...	|	...	...	|	...	...	|	|	|	...	...	|
Par ♡ d.	...	...	...	...	...	0911	...	...	...	0948	1021	...	1048	...	1115	...	...	1152	...	...	1232	1251	1321	...	...	1352
Lostwithiel d.	...	...	...	...	...	|	...	...	...	0955	|	...	1054	...	|	...	...	1158	...	...	1238	1257	|	...	...	1358
Bodmin Parkway 🚂 d.	...	...	...	...	...	0922	...	...	...	1001	1033	...	1100	...	1127	...	...	1204	...	...	1244	1302	1333	...	...	1404
Liskeard d.	...	...	...	...	...	0935	...	...	...	1013	1048	...	1113	...	1140	...	...	1219	...	...	1256	1315	1346	...	...	1417
Saltash d.	...	...	...	...	...	0952	...	...	...	1033	|	...	1130	...	|	...	...	1236	...	...	|	1333	|	...	...	1437
Plymouth a.	...	...	...	...	...	1003	...	...	...	1043	1112	...	1140	...	1204	...	...	1246	...	...	1321	1344	1410	...	...	1446
Plymouth d.	...	0827	0914	0927	0943	1005	...	1027	...	1052	1115	1127	...	1200	1205	...	1227	1248	1300	1306	1327	1348	1415	1427	...	...
Totnes 🚂 d.	...	0854	0941	0953	1012	1032	...	1053	...	1121	1141	1153	...	1226	1233	...	1253	1317	1326	1333	1353	1417	1441	1453	...	...
Paignton 🚂 112 d.	...	|	|	|	|	|	1032	|	1049	|	|	|	...	|	|	...	|	|	|	|	|	|	|	|	1454	...
Torquay 112 d.	...	|	|	|	|	|	1038	|	1055	|	|	|	...	|	|	...	|	|	|	|	|	|	|	|	1500	...
Newton Abbot 112 d.	...	0907	0954	1006	1024	1044	1050	1106	1109r	1133	1154	1206	...	1239	1246	...	1306	1329	1339	1346	1406	1429	1454	1506	1510	...
Teignmouth 112 d.	...	0914	|	|	1031	|	1057	|	1116	1140	|	|	...	|	|	...	|	1336	|	|	|	1436	|	|	1517	...
Dawlish 112 d.	...	0919	|	|	1036	|	1102	|	1121	1145	|	|	...	|	|	...	|	1341	|	|	|	1441	|	|	1522	...
Exeter St Davids 112 a.	...	0931	1013	1025	1048	1103	1113	1125	1133	1201	1213	1225	...	1258	1305	...	1325	1355	1358	1403	1426	1454	1513	1525	1533	...
Exeter St Davids 115 d.	0830	0932	1014	1027	1050	1106	1116	1127	1134	...	1215	1227	...	1301	1306	1322	1327	...	1400	1406	1427	...	1516	1527	1535	...
Tiverton Parkway 115 d.	0845	0947	|	1040	1104	1121	|	1140	1148	...	1229	1240	...	1315	1321	|	1340	...	1414	1421	1441	...	1530	1540	|	...
Taunton 115 132 d.	0858	0959	1036	1053	1116	1133	1139	1153	1200	...	1243	1253	...	1328	1333	1346	1353	...	1426	1432	1453	...	1543	1553	1558	...
Bristol Temple M.. 115 132 a.	|	|	|	1124	1212	|	|	1224	1248	...	|	1324	...	1359	|	1419	1425	...	1458	|	1524	...	|	1624	|	...
Cardiff Central 115 a.	|	|	|	|	1257	|	|	|	|	...	|	|	...	|	|	|	|	...	|	|	|	...	|	|	|	...
Birmingham New St 119 .. a.	|	|	|	1249	...	|	|	1349	1418	...	|	1449	...	1518	|	|	1549	...	1618	|	1649	...	|	1749	|	...
Castle Cary 140 d.	0918	1020	|	...	...	|	1201	...	...	...	|	...	...	...	|	|	...	...	...	1454	...	...	|	...	1619	...
Westbury 140 d.	0937	1040	1113	...	...	|	1220	...	...	...	|	...	...	...	|	|	...	...	...	1513	...	...	|	...	1639	...
Newbury d.	1019	1119	|	...	...	|	1302	...	...	...	|	...	...	...	1442	|	...	...	...	|	...	...	|	...	1721	...
Reading 130/1/2/3 a.	1035	1135	1159	...	...	1248	1317	...	...	...	1358	...	...	...	1458	1534	...	...	...	1558	...	...	1658	...	1737	...
London Paddington 130/1/2/3 a.	1059	1159	1226	...	...	1314	1344	...	...	...	1424	...	...	...	1522	1559	...	...	...	1623	...	...	1724	...	1806	...

	⑦ 🍷	⑦ 🍷b	⑦ 🍷a	⑦ 🍷L	⑦ 2	⑦ 🍷	⑦ 🍷L	⑦ 🍷	⑦ 🍷	⑦ 2	⑦ 🍷	⑦ 🍷L	⑦ 2	⑦ 🍷	⑦ 🍷	⑦ 🍷	⑦ 🍷L	⑦	⑦ b	⑦ 🍷a	⑦ 🍷	⑦ 2	⑦ 🍷	⑦ 2	⑦ 2	⑦ A	⑦
Penzance d.	...	...	...	...	1349	1418	...	...	...	1449	1518	1537	1545	...	...	1618	...	1649	...	...	1755	1815	...	1915	2025	2115	2128
St Erth d.	...	...	...	...	1358	1426	...	...	...	1458	1527	1545	1554	...	...	1627	...	1658	...	...	1804	1824	...	1924	2034	2125	2136
Camborne d.	...	...	...	...	1411	1437	...	...	...	1511	1540	|	1607	...	...	1638	...	1717	...	...	1817	1837	...	1937	2047	2137	2149
Redruth d.	...	...	...	...	1417	1444	...	...	...	1517	1547	1559	1613	...	...	1645	...	1717	...	...	1823	1843	...	1943	2053	2146	2156
Truro d.	...	...	...	...	1429	1456	...	...	...	1529	1559	1612	1625	...	...	1657	...	1729	...	...	1835	1856	...	1956	2104	2201	2209
St Austell d.	...	...	...	...	1445	1513	...	...	...	1546	1616	1629	1641	...	...	1714	...	1745	...	...	1852	1912	...	2012	2121	2219	2227
Newquay ♡ d.	...	1335	...	...	|	|	...	...	...	|	|	|	|	...	...	|	...	|	1719	...	|	|	...	|	|	|	|
Par ♡ d.	...	1426f	...	...	1452	1521	...	...	...	1552	1623	|	1648	...	...	1721	...	1752	1810	...	1859	1919	...	2019	2128	|	2234
Lostwithiel d.	...	|	...	...	1458	|	...	...	...	1559	|	|	1655	...	...	|	...	1758	1819	...	|	1925	...	2025	2134	|	2240
Bodmin Parkway 🚂 d.	...	|	...	...	1504	1533	...	...	...	1605	1634	1644	1700	...	...	1733	...	1804	1826	...	1910	1931	...	2031	2140	2235	2246
Liskeard d.	...	|	...	...	1517	1546	...	...	...	1618	1647	1656	1713	...	...	1746	...	1817	1839	...	1924	1944	...	2044	2153	2250	2259
Saltash d.	...	|	...	...	1535	|	...	...	...	1635	|	|	1730	...	...	|	...	1836	|	...	|	2001	...	2104	2211	|	|
Plymouth a.	...	1510	...	...	1545	1609	...	...	...	1646	1711	1721	1740	...	...	1809	...	1850	1902	...	1947	2011	...	2122	2221	|	2323
Plymouth d.	1502	1515	1515	1527	1546	1615	1627	...	...	1649	1715	1727	...	1745	...	1815	1827	...	1915	1915	1950	...	2016	*2133*	2225	2320	...
Totnes 🚂 d.	|	1542	1541	1553	1615	1641	1653	...	...	1719	1741	1753	...	1814	...	1841	1853	...	1943	1943	2017	...	2043	*2201*	2255	2348	...
Paignton 🚂 112 d.	|	|	|	|	|	|	|	...	1655	|	|	|	...	|	1820	|	|	...	|	|	|	...	|	|	|	|	...
Torquay 112 d.	|	|	|	|	|	|	|	...	1700	|	|	|	...	|	1826	|	|	...	|	|	|	...	|	|	|	|	...
Newton Abbot 112 d.	1538	1555	1554	1606	1628	1654	1706	...	1712	1730	1754	1806	...	1826	1836	1854	1906	...	1956	1956	2029	...	2055	*2213*	2308	0001	...
Teignmouth 112 d.	|	|	|	|	1635	|	|	...	1719	1737	|	|	...	1833	|	|	|	...	2003	2003	|	...	|	*2220*	2315	|	...
Dawlish 112 d.	|	|	|	|	1641	|	|	...	1724	1742	|	|	...	1838	|	|	|	...	2008	2008	|	...	|	*2225*	2320	|	...
Exeter St Davids 112 a.	1557	1613	1613	1625	1656	1713	1725	...	1735	1805	1813	1825	...	1851	1855	1912	1925	...	2020	2020	2048	...	2114	*2243*	2333	0023	...
Exeter St Davids 115 d.	1559	1615	1615	1627	...	1717	1727	1732	1740	...	1815	1827	...	1852	1857	1915	1927	...	2021	2022	2050	...	2116	...	...	0107	...
Tiverton Parkway 115 d.	|	1630	1630	1640	...	1731	1740	|	|	...	1830	1840	...	|	1910	1929	1940	...	2036	2036	2104	...	2130	...	...	|	...
Taunton 115 132 d.	1622	1642	1642	1653	...	1744	1753	1757	1803	...	1842	1853	...	1916	1923	1942	1953	...	2048	2049	2117	...	2143	...	...	|	...
Bristol Temple M.. 115 132 a.	1659	|	|	1724	...	|	1824	1854	|	...	|	1924	...	|	1957	|	2028	...	|	|	|	...	2223	...	...	|	...
Cardiff Central 115 a.	|	|	|	|	...	|	|	|	|	...	|	|	...	|	|	|	|	...	|	|	|	...	|	...	...	|	...
Birmingham New St 119 .. a.	|	|	|	1849	...	|	1949	|	|	...	|	2049	...	|	2118	|	2149	...	|	|	|	...	|	...	...	|	...
Castle Cary 140 d.	|	|	|	...	...	|	...	|	1823	...	|	...	...	|	...	|	...	...	|	|	2137	...	|	...	...	|	...
Westbury 140 d.	|	|	|	...	...	|	...	|	1843	...	|	...	...	1953	...	|	...	...	|	|	2157	...	|	...	...	|	...
Newbury d.	|	|	|	...	...	|	...	|	1925	...	|	...	...	|	...	|	...	...	|	|	2236	...	|	...	...	|	...
Reading 130/1/2/3 a.	1809	1757	1757	...	...	1859	...	2009	1940	...	1957	...	...	2038	...	2057	...	...	2203	2204	2252	...	2340	...	...	0405s	...
London Paddington 130/1/2/3 a.	1835	1822	1822	...	...	1924	...	2035	2005	...	2023	...	...	2105	...	2125	...	...	2228	2228	2333	...	0014	...	...	0504	...

A – THE NIGHT RIVIERA – Conveys 🛏 and 2. Calls to pick up only until Totnes. See also note ‡.
B – To Dundee (Tables **119** and **222**).
E – To Edinburgh (Table **119**).
G – To Glasgow Central (Tables **119** and **220**).
L – To Leeds (Table **119**).
M – To Manchester Piccadilly (Table **119**).

a – From Sept. 21.
b – Until Sept. 14.
f – Arrives 1421.
r – Arrives 1103.

♡ – See Table **113** for full local service Newquay - Par and v.v.
‡ – Passengers may occupy cabins at London Paddington from 2230 and at Penzance from 2045⑦/2115Ⓐ.

🚂 – Dartmouth Steam Railway (Paignton - Kingswear *11km*). ✆ 01803 555 872. www.dartmouthrailriver.co.uk
Bodmin Railway (Bodmin Parkway - Bodmin General - Boscarne Junction *10 km*). ✆ 01208 73555. www.bodminrailway.co.uk
South Devon Railway (Totnes Riverside - Buckfastleigh *11km*). ✆ 01364 644 370. www.southdevonrailway.co.uk

111 BRANCH LINES and BUS CONNECTIONS IN CORNWALL 2nd class GW

Rail tickets are generally **not** valid on 🚌 services shown in this table.

LISKEARD - LOOE *'The Looe Valley Line'* *14 km*

From Liskeard:
on Ⓐ at 0655, 0816, 0937, 1048, 1154, 1257, 1358, 1515, 1618, 1719, 1824, 2005, 2116;
on ⑥ at 0655, 0815, 0936, 1051, 1150, 1254, 1355, 1510, 1623, 1724, 1825, 2007, 2110;
on ⑦ until Oct. 26 at 0931, 1034, 1211, 1351, 1512, 1625, 1755, 2015.

From Looe:
on Ⓐ at 0733, 0902, 1009, 1118, 1226, 1329, 1434, 1545, 1650, 1749, 1902, 2042, 2155;
on ⑥ at 0731, 0901, 1008, 1121, 1222, 1326, 1435, 1540, 1655, 1754, 1905, 2039, 2142;
on ⑦ until Oct. 26 at 1003, 1106, 1243, 1433, 1544, 1704, 1845, 2049.

Journey: 28–33 minutes.

TRURO - FALMOUTH DOCKS *'The Maritime Line'* *20 km*

From Truro:
on Ⓐ at 0600, 0630, 0713, 0743, 0815 and every 30 minutes until 1545, 1620, 1650, 1720, 1750, 1820, 1906, 1941, 2050, 2156, 2256; on ⑥ at 0604, 0631, 0715 and every 30 minutes until 1645, 1718, 1748, 1838, 1912, 1942, 2053, 2244; on ⑦ at 0850, 0950, 1050, 1155, 1255, 1400, 1500, 1600, 1700, 1800, 1900, 2000, 2102, 2204.

From Falmouth Docks:
on Ⓐ at 0630, 0713, 0743, 0815 and every 30 minutes until 1545, 1620, 1650, 1720, 1750, 1820, 1906, 1941, 2017, 2122, 2226, 2322; on ⑥ at 0631, 0715, 0745, 0815 and every 30 minutes until 1645, 1718, 1748, 1838, 1912, 1942, 2008, 2120, 2310; on ⑦ at 0921, 1021, 1121, 1221, 1321, 1426, 1526, 1626, 1726, 1826, 1926, 2026, 2128, 2233.

Trains call at ***Falmouth Town*** *22 minutes after Truro and 3 minutes after Falmouth Docks.*
Journey: 25 minutes.

f – School holidays (check locally for dates) and ⑥.
r – School days (check locally for dates).
t – Until Sept. 14.
v – From Sept. 21.

BODMIN PARKWAY - PADSTOW *Go Cornwall Bus 🚌 service 11*

From Bodmin Parkway station: on ⚒ at 0816, 0916 and hourly until 1516, 1616**f**, 1716, 1823, 1927, 2010, 2114; on ⑦ at 1000, 1200, 1400, 1600, 1800.

From Padstow Station Road: on ⚒ at 0637, 0728**r**, 0737**f**, 0807**f**, 0937, 1035 and hourly until 1435, 1535, 1640, 1740, 1840, 1930, 2030, 2115, 2220; on ⑦ at 0840, 1040, 1240, 1440, 1640.

Journey: 68 minutes. Buses also make calls in Bodmin town centre and at Bodmin General station, and call at ***Wadebridge*** *(35 minutes after Bodmin/25 minutes after Padstow).*

ST AUSTELL - EDEN PROJECT *Go Cornwall Bus 🚌 services 28, 31*

From St Austell bus station: on ⚒ at 0910, 1040, 1210, 1340, 1610; on ⑦ 1015, 1215, 1415, 1615.

From Eden Project: on ⚒ at 1016, 1316, 1533, 1728; on ⑦ 1110, 1310, 1510, 1710.

Journey: 21 minutes.

ST ERTH - ST IVES *'The St Ives Bay Line'* *7 km*

From St Erth: on Ⓐ at 0706, 0750, 0838, 0938, 1018 and every 30 minutes until 1848, 1920, 1950, 2020, 2050, 2120, 2230;
on ⑥ at 0702, 0747, 0849, 0923, 0952, 1021, 1051, 1122 and every 30 minutes until 1652, 1723, 1808, 1907, 2005, 2037, 2122, 2153;
on ⑦ at 0846**t**, 0915**v**, 0918**t**, 0951, 1048 and every 30 minutes until 1748, 1830, 1930.

From St Ives: on Ⓐ at 0732, 0807, 0902, 1003 and every 30 minutes until 1703, 1732, 1803, 1833, 1905, 1934, 2005, 2034, 2105, 2137, 2248;
on ⑥ at 0730, 0804, 0904, 0937, 1006, 1036, 1105, 1136 and every 30 minutes until 1706, 1737, 1828, 1922, 2020, 2052, 2137;
on ⑦ at 0903**t**, 0931, 1004, 1103 and every 30 minutes until 1333, 1401, 1433, 1503, 1602, 1633, 1703, 1733, 1803, 1903, 1948.

Journey: 10–13 minutes.

GW 2nd class — Local services EXMOUTH - EXETER - PAIGNTON — 112

km		Ⓐ	Ⓐ	Ⓐ	Ⓐ	Ⓐ	Ⓐ	Ⓐ	Ⓐ	Ⓐ	Ⓐ	Ⓐ	Ⓐ	Ⓐ	Ⓐ	Ⓐ	Ⓐ	Ⓐ	Ⓐ	Ⓐ	Ⓐ	Ⓐ	Ⓐ	Ⓐ	Ⓐ	Ⓐ
0	**Exmouth** d.	...	...	...	0551	0615	0655	0724	0754	0824	0854	0924	1000	1025	1057	1123	1157	1223	1257	1323	1357	1423	1457	1523	1555	1623
17	**Exeter** Central ⊙ d.	...	...	...	0616	0642	0724	0753	0826	0853	0923	0952	1024	1053	1121	1153	1221	1251	1321	1351	1421	1451	1522	1551	1623	1652
18	**Exeter** St Davids ⊙ a.	...	...	...	0618	0645	0727	0756	0829	0856	0926	0955	1027	1056	1124	1156	1224	1254	1324	1354	1424	1454	1525	1554	1626	1655
	Exeter St Davids 110 d.	0458	0534	0558	0628	0659	0730	0800	0833	0900	0933	0959	1031	1100	1130	1200	1230	1300	1329	1359	1429	1500	1530	1558	1631	1706
38	Dawlish 110 d.	0519	0550	0621	0651	0722	0759	0825	0901	0913	1003	1014	1054	1113	1153	1222	1253	1313	1352	1418	1452	1513	1553	1619	1704	1732
42	Teignmouth 110 d.	0524	0555	0626	0656	0727	0804	0830	0906	0918	1008	1019	1059	1118	1158	1227	1258	1318	1357	1423	1457	1518	1558	1624	1709	1737
50	Newton Abbot 110 d.	0533	0603	0635	0705	0737	0812	0838	0914	0926	1016	1035c	1106	1126	1206	1240t	1306	1326	1405	1431	1505	1526	1606	1632	1716	1745
60	Torquay 110 d.	0544	0614	0646	0717	0748	0824	0849	0926	0937	1027	1046	1118	1137	1218	1252	1317	1337	1417	1442	1517	1537	1617	1644	1728	1756
63	**Paignton** 🚂 110 a.	0550	0620	0652	0723	0754	0830	0855	0932	0943	1033	1052	1124	1143	1224	1259	1324	1343	1423	1448	1523	1543	1623	1650	1733	1802

	Ⓐ	Ⓐ	Ⓐ	Ⓐ	Ⓐ	Ⓐ	Ⓐ	Ⓐ C	Ⓐ B	Ⓐ B	Ⓐ	Ⓐ	Ⓐ	Ⓐ	⑥	⑥	⑥	⑥	⑥	⑥	⑥	⑥	⑥	⑥	⑥	⑥
Exmouth d.	1657	1726	1756	1826	1856	1925	1956	2024	...	2054	2126	2156	2225	2320	...	...	...	...	...	0655	0725	0755	0825	0855	0925	0955
Exeter Central ⊙ d.	1725	1754	1824	1855	1923	1953	2025	2052	...	2122	2154	2226	2255	2348	...	...	...	...	...	0724	0756	0826	0855	0923	0954	1022
Exeter St Davids ⊙ a.	1728	1757	1827	1858	1926	1956	2028	2055	...	2125	2157	2229	2258	2351	...	...	...	...	...	0727	0759	0828	0858	0926	0957	1025
Exeter St Davids 110 d.	1732	1800	1831	1902	1932	2000	2031	...	2059	...	2201	...	2302	...	0500	0530	0555	0635	0659	0730	0808	0837	0901	0930	1005	1031
Dawlish 110 d.	1803	1835	1851	1935	1952	2013	2105	...	2133	...	2224	...	2325	...	0521	0546	0618	0658	0722	0758	0829	0900	0914	0952	1028	1053
Teignmouth 110 d.	1808	1840	1856	1940	1957	2018	2110	...	2138	...	2229	...	2330	...	0526	0551	0623	0703	0727	0803	0834	0905	0919	0957	1034	1058
Newton Abbot 110 d.	1816	1849	1904	1948	2009t	2025	2117	...	2146	...	2237	...	2337	...	0534	0559	0632	0712	0736	0812	0842	0913	0927	1005	1042	1106
Torquay 110 d.	1827	1901	1916	1959	2021	2038	2128	...	2157	...	2248	...	2349	...	0545	0610	0643	0723	0747	0823	0853	0924	0938	1017	1054	1118
Paignton 🚂 110 a.	1833	1908	1924	2005	2027	2044	2134	...	2203	...	2254	...	2355	...	0552	0616	0649	0729	0755	0829	0900	0930	0944	1025	1100	1124

	⑥	⑥	⑥	⑥	⑥	⑥	⑥	⑥	⑥	⑥	⑥	⑥	⑥	⑥	⑥	⑥	⑥	⑥	⑥	⑥	⑥	⑥	⑥	⑥	⑥	⑥	⑥
Exmouth d.	1024	1057	1124	1157	1224	1257	1324	1357	1424	1457	1525	1555	1626	1656	1726	1758	1828	1857	1925	1956	2024	2054	2126	2156	2225	2255	2350
Exeter Central ⊙ d.	1053	1122	1153	1222	1258h	1323	1356	1422	1453	1522	1554	1623	1654	1725	1756	1828	1856	1923	1957	2026	2053	2126	2154	2226	2254	2323	0018
Exeter St Davids ⊙ a.	1056	1125	1156	1225	1301h	1326	1359	1425	1456	1525	1557	1626	1657	1728	1759	1831	1859	1926	2000	2029	2056	2129	2157	2229	2257	2326	0021
Exeter St Davids 110 d.	1100	1130	1200	1229	1305	1336	1406	1429	1459	1530	1605	1629	1703	1737	1802	1835	1906	1930	2006	2033	2100	...	2210	...	...	...	...
Dawlish 110 d.	1116	1153	1216	1252	1329	1404	1427	1452	1515	1553	1629	1652	1730	1804	1833	1902	1932	1953	2029	2103	2123	...	2233	...	...	...	...
Teignmouth 110 d.	1121	1158	1221	1257	1335	1409	1433	1457	1520	1558	1635	1657	1736	1809	1838	1907	1937	1958	2034	2108	2128	...	2238	...	...	...	...
Newton Abbot 110 d.	1130j	1206	1230	1305	1344	1418	1442	1506	1528j	1606	1645	1706	1744	1817	1849	1915	1946	2007	2043	2116	2136	...	2246	...	...	...	...
Torquay 110 d.	1142j	1218	1242	1318	1356	1429	1453	1517	1539j	1617	1656	1717	1755	1828	1900	1927	1957	2019	2054	2127	2147	...	2257	...	...	...	...
Paignton 🚂 110 a.	1148j	1224	1248	1325	1403	1435	1501	1523	1545j	1623	1702	1723	1801	1834	1906	1935	2003	2027	2100	2133	2153	...	2304	...	...	...	...

	⑦	⑦	⑦	⑦	⑦	⑦	⑦	⑦	⑦	⑦	⑦	⑦	⑦	⑦	⑦	⑦	⑦	⑦	⑦	⑦	⑦	⑦	⑦	⑦	⑦	⑦
Exmouth d.	...	0855	0955	1021	1055	1123	1157	1226	1257	1324	1357	1424	1457	1524	1557	1624	1658	1724	1758	1825	1859	1959	2059	2130	2230	2335
Exeter Central ⊙ d.	...	0924	1023	1050	1120	1152	1223	1255	1323	1352	1421	1454	1522	1551	1620	1653	1722	1752	1823	1852	1924	2028	2127	2158	2258	0002
Exeter St Davids ⊙ a.	...	0927	1026	1053	1123	1155	1227	1258	1326	1356	1424	1457	1525	1555	1624	1657	1725	1756	1827	1856	1927	2032	2131	2202	2302	0006
Exeter St Davids 110 d.	0820	0930	1032	...	1130	...	1229	1305	1329	...	1428	1505	1530	...	1630	1701	1730	...	1830	...	1935	2036	2138	*2232*	...	...
Dawlish 110 d.	0842	0958	1055	...	1153	...	1252	1328	1352	...	1451	1532	1553	...	1653	1716	1753	...	1853	...	2005	2103	2206	*2244*	...	...
Teignmouth 110 d.	0847	1003	1100	...	1158	...	1257	1333	1357	...	1456	1537	1558	...	1658	1721	1758	...	1858	...	2010	2108	2211	*2249*	...	...
Newton Abbot 110 d.	0854	1011	1107	...	1205	...	1304	1340	1405	...	1503	1544	1605	...	1705	1729	1805	...	1905	...	2018	2116	2219	*2256*	...	...
Torquay 110 d.	0905	1023	1119	...	1217	...	1316	1352	1417	...	1515	1556	1617	...	1717	1740	1817	...	1917	...	2029	2127	2230	...	...	...
Paignton 🚂 110 a.	0911	1029	1125	...	1223	...	1322	1359	1423	...	1521	1602	1623	...	1723	1746	1823	...	1923	...	2035	2133	2236	...	...	...

	②–⑤	Ⓐ	Ⓐ	Ⓐ	Ⓐ E	Ⓐ	Ⓐ	Ⓐ	Ⓐ	Ⓐ	Ⓐ	Ⓐ	Ⓐ	Ⓐ	Ⓐ	Ⓐ	Ⓐ	Ⓐ	Ⓐ	Ⓐ	Ⓐ	Ⓐ	Ⓐ	Ⓐ	Ⓐ	Ⓐ
Paignton 🚂 110 a.	0002	...	...	...	...	0557	0634	0719	0739	0815	0845	0916	0945	1024	1042	1120	1155	1220	1255	1320	1340	1420	1455	1522	1552	1616
Torquay 110 d.	0007	...	...	...	...	0602	0639	0724	0744	0820	0850	0921	0950	1029	1047	1125	1200	1225	1300	1325	1345	1425	1500	1527	1558	1621
Newton Abbot 110 d.	0018	...	...	...	...	0635a	0651	0736	0756	0832	0909b	0933	1009t	1041	1058	1138	1212	1237	1312	1338	1357	1437	1512	1539	1611	1633
Teignmouth 110 d.	0025	...	...	...	...	0642	0658	0743	0803	0839	0916	0940	1016	1048	1105	1145	1219	1244	1319	1345	1404	1444	1519	1546	1618	1640
Dawlish 110 d.	0030	...	...	...	...	0647	0703	0748	0808	0844	0921	0945	1021	1053	1110	1150	1224	1250	1324	1350	1409	1449	1524	1551	1623	1645
Exeter St Davids 110 a.	0047	...	...	...	...	0711	0739	0813	0842	0909	0951	1011	1047	1110	1147	1210	1246	1310	1347	1411	1447	1510	1547	1609	1646	1710
Exeter St Davids ⊙ d.	...	0520	0544	0607	0648	0716	0744	0817	0846	0916	0954	1015	1051	1115	1151	1215	1250	1313	1351	1415	1451	1515	1550	1616	1649	1715
Exeter Central ⊙ d.	...	0524	0548	0611	0652	0720	0748	0821	0851	0920	0958	1019	1055	1119	1155	1219	1254	1318	1355	1419	1455	1519	1554	1620	1653	1719
Exmouth a.	...	0547	0612	0639	0720	0749	0819	0849	0919	0949	1020	1049	1117	1147	1217	1247	1317	1347	1417	1447	1517	1547	1617	1648	1721	1751

	Ⓐ	Ⓐ	Ⓐ	Ⓐ	Ⓐ C	Ⓐ B	Ⓐ	Ⓐ	Ⓐ	Ⓐ	Ⓐ E	Ⓐ	Ⓐ	Ⓐ	⑥	⑥	⑥	⑥	⑥	⑥	⑥	⑥	⑥	⑥	⑥	⑥ k
Paignton 🚂 110 a.	1640	1719	1740	1819	1851	...	1915	1944	2031	2056	2109	2140	2221	2321	...	...	0610	0638	0710	0750	0816	0833	0916	0948	1020	1040
Torquay 110 d.	1645	1724	1745	1825	1856	...	1920	1949	2036	2101	2114	2145	2226	2326	...	...	0615	0643	0715	0755	0821	0838	0921	0956	1026	1045
Newton Abbot 110 d.	1657	1736	1757	1840	1910	...	1933	2001	2047	2112	2125	2156	2237	2337	...	...	0628	0655	0735r	0807	0833	0857z	0934	1012	1039	1057
Teignmouth 110 d.	1704	1743	1804	1847	1917	...	1940	2008	2054	2119	2132	2203	2244	2344	...	...	0635	0702	0742	0814	0840	0904	0942	1019	1046	1104
Dawlish 110 d.	1709	1748	1809	1852	1922	...	1945	2013	2059	2124	2137	2208	2249	2349	...	...	0640	0707	0747	0819	0845	0909	0947	1025	1051	1109
Exeter St Davids 110 a.	1735	1814	1843	1909	1945	...	2005	2038	2116	2149	2159	2234	2314	0014	...	...	0710	0738	0812	0842	0910	0934	1009	1047	1110	1139
Exeter St Davids ⊙ d.	1739	1818	1847	1913	...	1948	2015	2042	2120	2152	...	2240	*2340*	...	0608	0648	0717	0746	0817	0845	0915	0945	1017	1052	1117	1146
Exeter Central ⊙ d.	1746	1822	1851	1917	...	1951	2019	2047	2124	2156	...	2247g	*2344*	...	0612	0652	0721	0750	0821	0849	0920	0949	1021	1056	1121	1150
Exmouth a.	1821	1851	1920	1949	...	2019	2048	2118	2151	2220	...	2315	*0012*	...	0641	0721	0750	0820	0851	0920	0950	1019	1050	1120	1150	1220

	⑥ n	⑥	⑥	⑥	⑥ k	⑥ n	Ⓐ	Ⓐ	⑥	⑥	⑥	⑥	⑥	⑥	⑥	⑥	⑥	⑥	⑥	⑥	⑥	⑥	⑥	⑥	⑥	⑥	⑥
Paignton 🚂 110 a.	1055	1118	1153	1218	1239	1254	1320	1353	1422	1440	1518	1540	1617	1653	1717	1738	1819	1850	1918	1942	2022	2053	2115	2140	2158	2240	2317
Torquay 110 d.	1100	1124	1159	1224	1245	1300	1325	1358	1427	1445	1523	1545	1622	1659	1722	1743	1824	1855	1923	1947	2027	2058	2120	2145	2203	2245	2322
Newton Abbot 110 d.	1112	1137	1212	1236	1257	1312	1337	1411	1438	1458	1537	1557	1634	1712	1736	1755	1836	1909	1936	2000	2040	2110	2132	2157	2213	2257	2333
Teignmouth 110 d.	1119	1144	1219	1243	1304	1319	1344	1419	1445	1505	1544	1604	1642	1720	1743	1803	1844	1916	1943	2007	2047	2117	2139	2204	▬	2304	2340
Dawlish 110 d.	1125	1150	1225	1248	1309	1324	1349	1424	1450	1510	1550	1609	1647	1725	1749	1809	1849	1921	1948	2012	2052	2122	2144	2209	...	2309	2345
Exeter St Davids 110 a.	1147	1210	1247	1308	1339	1346	1409	1447	1510	1536	1609	1640	1711	1747	1814	1838	1909	1942	2012	2037	2115	2148	2206	2234	⑥	2334	0010
Exeter St Davids ⊙ d.	1152	1218	1252	1318	1346	1352	1417	1452	1518	1545	1618	1646	1718	1751	1818	1846	1916	1946	2017	2044	2118	2152	2217	...	2313	...	...
Exeter Central ⊙ d.	1156	1222	1256	1323	1350	1356	1421	1456	1522	1549	1622	1650	1723	1755	1822	1850	1921	1950	2021	2048	2122	2156	2221	...	2317	...	...
Exmouth a.	1220	1251	1320	1353	1420	1420	1450	1521	1551	1621	1652	1720	1754	1824	1852	1920	1950	2020	2050	2120	2152	2220	2251	...	2346	...	...

	⑦	⑦	⑦	⑦	⑦ B	⑦	⑦	⑦	⑦	⑦	⑦	⑦	⑦	⑦	⑦	⑦	⑦	⑦	⑦	⑦ D	⑦	⑦	⑦	⑦	⑦	⑦
Paignton 🚂 110 a.	...	...	...	0915	...	...	1057	...	1155	...	1255	...	1355	1416	1440	...	1555	1616	1640	1727	1755	1855	1945	2055	2201	2240
Torquay 110 d.	...	...	...	0920	...	...	1102	...	1200	...	1300	...	1400	1421	1445	...	1600	1621	1645	1732	1800	1900	1950	2100	2206	2245
Newton Abbot 110 d.	...	...	...	0932	...	...	1113	...	1211	...	1311	...	1411	1433	1457	...	1611	1633	1657	1742	1811	1911	2001	2111	2218	2256
Teignmouth 110 d.	...	...	...	0939	...	...	1120	...	1218	...	1318	...	1418	1440	1504	...	1618	1640	1704	▬	1818	1918	2008	2118	2225	2303
Dawlish 110 d.	...	...	...	0944	...	...	1125	...	1223	...	1323	...	1423	1445	1509	...	1623	1645	1709		1823	1923	2013	2123	2230	2308
Exeter St Davids 110 a.	...	...	...	1009	...	...	1150	...	1250	...	1348	...	1448	1510	1548	...	1648	1711	1750	⑦	1848	1948	2039	2147	2256	2322
Exeter St Davids ⊙ d.	0817	0915	0950	1013	1046	1115	1153	1216	1253	1313	1351	1415	1452	1515	1551	1616	1651	1716	1754	1816	1851	1951	2052	2153	2258	...
Exeter Central ⊙ d.	0821	0919	0954	1017	1050	1119	1157	1220	1257	1319	1355	1419	1456	1520	1555	1620	1655	1721	1758	1820	1855	1955	2056	2157	2302	...
Exmouth a.	0850	0950	1018	1047	1116	1150	1220	1251	1319	1350	1420	1450	1519	1550	1617	1650	1719	1750	1820	1850	1924	2024	2126	2226	2330	...

B – To/from Barnstaple (Table **114**).
C – To Cardiff Central (Table **115**).
D – Continues to Exeter St Davids arr. 1809.
E – To/from Bristol Temple Meads (Table **115**).

a – Arrives 0612.

b – Arrives 0901.
c – Arrives 1026.
g – Arrives 2243.
h – Arrives 1253. From Sept. 20 Exeter Central dep. 1254, Exeter St Davids arr. 1257.
j – Runs 8–11 minutes later from Sept. 20.

k – Until Sept. 13.
n – From Sept. 23.
r – Arrives 0725.
t – Arrives 5–6 minutes earlier.
z – Arrives 0848.

⊙ – See also Tables **109** and **114**.
🚂 – Dartmouth Steam Railway (Paignton - Kingswear). ✆ 01803 555 872. www.dartmouthrailriver.co.uk

GW 2nd class — 'The Atlantic Coast Line' — PAR - NEWQUAY — 113

Service until September 14

km		Ⓐ	Ⓐ	Ⓐ	Ⓐ	Ⓐ	Ⓐ	Ⓐ	Ⓐ	⑥	⑥	⑥ E	⑥	⑥	⑥ A	⑥	⑥	⑦	⑦	⑦ P	⑦	⑦ A	⑦	⑦
	Penzance 110 d.	...	*0710*	*0910*	*1050*	*1250*	*1450*	*1650*	*1915*	...	*0540*	0851	*1115*	*1250*	*1445*	*1645*	*1815*	...	*0918*	1050	*1218*	1349	*1618*	*1815*
	Plymouth 110 d.	...	*0712*	*0913*	*1120*	*1312*	*1502*	*1647*	*1925*	*0515*	|	0900	*1115*	*1318*	1504	*1718*	*1934*	...	*0958*	1118	*1238*	1415	*1640*	*1840*
0	**Par** d.	0625	0816	1016	1216	1416	1616	1816	2022	0625	0816	1000	1224	1416	1558	1816	2030	0855	1055	1208	1347	1505	1735	1935
33	**Newquay** a.	0713	0904	1104	1304	1504	1704	1904	2110	0713	0904	1048	1312	1504	1646	1904	2118	0945	1139	1257	1442	1555	1725	2019

	Ⓐ	Ⓐ	Ⓐ	Ⓐ	Ⓐ	Ⓐ		Ⓐ	Ⓐ	⑥	⑥	⑥ A	⑥	⑥	⑥ B	⑥	⑥	⑦	⑦	⑦ A	⑦	⑦	⑦ A	⑦
Newquay d.	0719	0920	1120	1320	1519	1720	...	1920	2113	0719	0945	1120	1320	1543	1716	1930	2122	0950	1151	1335	1450	1719	1830	2024
Par a.	0809	1008	1208	1408	1609	1808	...	2008	2200	0807	1034	1203	1408	1631	1802	2018	2210	1039	1242	1421	1542	1809	1914	2112
Plymouth 110 a.	*0908*	*1109*	*1308*	*1509*	*1718*	*1919*	...	*2121*	*2300*	*0909*	*1145*	1305	*1512*	*1747*	1853	*2138*	*2314*	*1140*	*1344*	1510	*1642*	*1902*	*2011*	*2221*
Penzance 110 a.	*0919*	*1112*	*1340*	*1540*	*1742*	*1925*	...	*2120*	*2300*	*0935*	*1216*	1335	*1540*	*1742*	1909	*2128*	*2315*f	*1158*	*1405*	1534	*1705*	*1934*	*2034*	*2312*

A – 🚃12 and 🍷 from/to London Paddington (Table **110**).
B – 🚃12 and 🍷 to Bristol Temple Meads (Table **110**).
E – 🚃12 from Exeter St Davids (Table **110**).
P – 🚃12 and 🍷 from Plymouth.
f – Change at Par.

113a PLYMOUTH - GUNNISLAKE

2nd class GW

km		Ⓐ	Ⓐ	Ⓐ	Ⓐ	Ⓐ	Ⓐ	Ⓐ	Ⓐ	Ⓐ	⑥	⑥	⑥	⑥	⑥	⑥	⑥	⑥	⑦	⑦	⑦	⑦	⑦	⑦a
0	**Plymouth** d.	0457	0631	0828	1028	1228	1427	1638	1838	2130	0627	0822	1024	1225	1424	1645	1830	2128	0903	1110	1320	1520	1744	2001
16	Bere Alston d.	0518	0657	0854	1054	1254	1453	1704	1904	2156	0653	0848	1050	1250	1450	1711	1856	2154	0929	1136	1346	1546	1810	2027
23	**Gunnislake** a.	0538	0717	0914	1114	1314	1513	1724	1924	2216	0713	0908	1110	1311	1510	1731	1916	2214	0949	1156	1406	1606	1830	2047

	Ⓐ	Ⓐ	Ⓐ	Ⓐ	Ⓐ	Ⓐ		Ⓐ	Ⓐ	Ⓐ	⑥	⑥	⑥	⑥	⑥	⑥	⑥	⑥	⑦	⑦	⑦	⑦	⑦	⑦a
Gunnislake d.	0541	0725	0920	1119	1320	1519	...	1733	1933	2222	0716	0914	1114	1314	1514	1734	1928	2220	1011	1210	1411	1611	1835	2052
Bere Alston d.	0602	0746	0941	1140	1341	1540	...	1754	1954	2243	0737	0935	1135	1335	1535	1755	1949	2241	1031	1230	1431	1631	1855	2112
Plymouth a.	0626	0816	1005	1204	1405	1604	...	1818	2018	2308	0803	1000	1200	1400	1600	1820	2014	2307	1056	1255	1457	1656	1920	2137

a – Until Sept. 14.

114 EXETER - BARNSTAPLE AND OKEHAMPTON

2nd class GW

km		Ⓐ	⑥	Ⓐ	⑥	⚒	Ⓐ	⑥	⚒	Ⓐ	⑥	⚒	⑥	Ⓐ	⚒	⚒	⚒	⚒	Ⓐ	⑥	⑥	Ⓐ	⚒	Ⓐ	⑥	⑥
0	**Exeter** Central .... **109 112** d.	...	...	...	...	w	...	...	...	0804	0813	0834	0915	0914	0934	1014	1032	1114	1132	1131	1214	1214	1232	1312	1313	1330
1	**Exeter** St Davids **109 112** d.	0522	0524	0612	0616	0630	0707	0710	0738	0810	0818	0839	0921	0919	0939	1019	1037	1119	1137	1136	1219	1219	1237	1319	1319	1335
12	Crediton d.	0532	0534	0624	0627	0641	0718	0724	0749	0828f	0831	0850	0931	0931	0950	1031	1051	1131	1151	1152r	1232	1231	1251	1331	1331	1351
48	**Okehampton** a.	|	|	|	|	0706	|	|	0815	|	|	0916	|	|	1017	|	1117	|	1217	1217	|	|	1316	|	|	1417
35	Eggsford d.	0554	0602	0653	0657	...	0755f	0759r	...	0902f	0904f	...	1002	1004r	...	1101	...	1201	...	...	1302	1304r	...	1401	1401	...
64	**Barnstaple** a.	0619	0628	0717	0723	...	0825	0830	...	0928	0931	...	1027	1028	...	1126	...	1226	...	...	1327	1328	...	1427	1429	...

	Ⓐ	⚒	⚒	⚒	⑥	Ⓐ	Ⓐ	⑥	⚒	Ⓐ	⑥	⑥	Ⓐ	Ⓐ	⑥	⚒	Ⓐ	⑥	⑥	Ⓐ	Ⓐ	⑥	⑥	Ⓐ	⑥	Ⓐ A	⑤
Exeter Central .... **109 112** d.	1332	1414	1432	1514	1531	1532	1613	1614	1632	1715	1714	1732	1735	1815	1818	...	1917	1917	...	...	2019	2019	...	...	2120	2122	2250
Exeter St Davids **109 112** d.	1338	1419	1437	1519	1538	1537	1618	1619	1637	1719	1720	1737	1740	1821	1824	1845	1922	1922	1933	1942	2023	2024	2112	2117	2124	2129	2255
Crediton d.	1352	1431	1450	1531	1549	1549	1631	1631	1649	1732	1733	1749	1751	1835	1838	1856	1937	1941f	1955t	1955	2035	2037	2127	2131	2139	2143	2307
Okehampton a.	1417	|	1515	|	1615	1615	|	|	1716	|	|	1815	1817	|	|	1922	|	|	2020	2020	|	|	2152	2157	|	|	|
Eggsford d.	...	1501	...	1601	...	...	1702	1705r	...	1803	1808r	...	...	1907r	1913t	...	2008r	2009	...	...	2109f	2108r	...	...	2208	2211	2337
Barnstaple a.	...	1526	...	1626	...	...	1728	1732	...	1833	1839	...	...	1931	1938	...	2032	2034	...	...	2133	2133	...	...	2235	2237	0004

	⑦	⑦	⑦	⑦	⑦	⑦	⑦	⑦	⑦	⑦	⑦	⑦	⑦	⑦	⑦	⑦	⑦	⑦	⑦	⑦	⑦	⑦	⑦	⑦	⑦	⑦
Exeter Central .... **109 112** d.	...	0838	0912	0932	1013	1031	1114	1133	1214	1231	1314	1332	1414	1432	1514	1532	1611	1632	1714	1732	1814	...	1914	...	2011	...
Exeter St Davids **109 112** d.	0825	0843	0920r	0937	1017	1038	1119	1138	1219	1239r	1319	1338	1419	1438	1522r	1538	1619	1638	1720	1743f	1819	1849	1919	1946	2018	2122
Crediton d.	0836	0855	0933	0951	1032	1051	1132	1150	1232	1253	1330	1350	1429	1451	1531	1550	1632	1651	1730	1754	1830	1859	1932	1958	2031	2133
Okehampton a.	|	0921	|	1017	|	1116	|	1216	|	1318	|	1415	|	1516	|	1615	|	1716	|	1819	|	1925	|	2023	|	2158
Eggsford d.	0906	...	1004	...	1104f	...	1205f	...	1302	...	1402r	...	1503f	...	1600	...	1702	...	1803f	...	1903f	...	2002	...	2102	...
Barnstaple a.	0930	...	1033	...	1128	...	1229	...	1331	...	1426	...	1527	...	1624	...	1732	...	1827	...	1927	...	2026	...	2131	...

	⑥	Ⓐ	⑥	⚒	Ⓐ	⑥	Ⓐ	⑥	Ⓐ	⑥	⚒	⚒	⚒	Ⓐ	⑥	Ⓐ	⑥	⚒	⚒	⚒	⑥	Ⓐ	⚒	⚒	Ⓐ	⑥
Barnstaple d.	0007	0625	0631	...	0722	0726	...	...	0835	0834	...	0935	...	1035	1035	...	...	1135	...	1232	...	...	1335	...	1435	1435
Eggsford d.	0029s	0652	0656	...	0754	0758	...	...	0901	0903	...	1003	...	1100	1100	...	...	1200	...	1303	...	...	1400	...	1500	1500
Okehampton d.	|	|	|	0725	|	|	0825	0825	|	|	0925	|	1025	|	|	1127	1127	|	1227	|	1326	1327	|	1426	|	|
Crediton d.	0049s	0718	0724	0749	0822	0829	0850	0852	0929	0930	0950	1029	1050	1129	1129	1151	1152	1228b	1252	1329	1350	1353	1428	1450	1529	1530r
Exeter St Davids **109 112** a.	0102	0730	0736	0801	0835	0844	0900	0903	0943	0942a	1004	1041	1103	1141	1143a	1201	1205	1241	1303	1341c	1402	1405	1441	1503	1541	1542a
Exeter Central .... **109 112** a.	...	0735	0740	0805	0839	0852	0905	0907	0947	0954	1008	1046	1108	1145	1155	1206	1209	1246	1307	1346c	1406	1409	1446	1508	1545	1554

	⑥	Ⓐ	Ⓐ	⑥	⚒	Ⓐ B	⑥	⚒	Ⓐ	⑥	⚒	Ⓐ A	⑥	⑥	Ⓐ	Ⓐ C	⑥	⚒	⑥	①–④	⑤	⑥	Ⓐ	Ⓐ	⑥	d	⑤
Barnstaple d.	...	...	1535	1535	...	1631	1639	...	1733	1736	...	1838	1843	...	...	1942	1942	...	2040	2041	2041	2140	2141	...	...	2240	2311
Eggsford d.	...	...	1600	1600	...	1703r	1704	...	1804	1807	...	1906	1912	...	...	2007	2010	...	2107	2108	2108	2209r	2212r	...	...	2305	2338
Okehampton d.	1525	1525	|	|	1625	|	|	1725	|	|	1830	|	|	1931	1931	|	|	2030	|	|	|	|	|	2219	2224	|	|
Crediton d.	1549	1551	1629	1629	1651	1731	1731	1749	1836r	1836	1855	1934	1946f	1955	1956	2038r	2038	2054	2139f	2142t	2142t	2235	2237	2249r	2248	2329	0002
Exeter St Davids **109 112** a.	1559	1603	1640	1644a	1704	1743v	1742	1801	1851	1850	1906	1946	1956	2006	2008	2053	2054	2104	2151	2155	2157	2249	2252	2300	2259	2344	0018
Exeter Central .... **109 112** a.	1604	1607	1645	1655	1708	1751	1746	1805	1856	1855	...	1951	2001	2011	2014	...	2101	...	...	...	2202	...	...	...	...	...	...

	⑦	⑦ A	⑦	⑦	⑦	⑦	⑦	⑦	⑦	⑦	⑦	⑦	⑦	⑦	⑦	⑦	⑦	⑦	⑦	⑦	⑦	⑦	⑦	⑦	⑦	⑦
Barnstaple d.	...	0936	...	1038	...	1133	...	1236	...	1336	...	1431	...	1532	...	1630	...	1737	...	1832	...	1936	...	2036	...	2136
Eggsford d.	...	1001	...	1103	...	1203	...	1303r	...	1401	...	1502	...	1559	...	1701	...	1802	...	1902f	...	2001	...	2103	...	2208
Okehampton d.	0926	|	1025	|	1125	|	1225	|	1325	|	1425	|	1523	|	1623	|	1725	|	1833	|	1930	|	2028	|	2203	|
Crediton d.	0950	1027	1049	1129	1149	1232	1252	1328	1349	1427	1453	1530r	1549	1631t	1649	1729r	1753	1829r	1858	1930f	1956	2029	2053	2132	2227	2237
Exeter St Davids **109 112** a.	1001	1041y	1059	1142	1200	1245	1304	1341	1401	1441	1504	1541	1559	1641	1700	1741	1805	1840	1909	1941	2007	2041	2104	2145	2239	2249
Exeter Central .... **109 112** a.	1005	1049	1105	1146	1206	1249	1309	1347	1406	1446	1508	1546	1604	1646	1705	1746	...	1845	...	1947	...	...	...	...	...	...

A – From/to Exmouth (Table **112**).
B – To Axminster (Table **109**).
C – To Paignton (Table **112**).
a – Departs 7–8 minutes later.
b – On ⑥ departs 1231**r**.
c – On ⑥ Exeter St Davids a. 1343, d. 1352, Exeter Central a. 1355.
d – ①–④ and ⑥.
f – Arrives 7–8 minutes earlier.
r – Arrives 5–6 minutes earlier.
s – Calls to set down only.
t – Arrives 9–11 minutes earlier.
v – Departs 1748.
w – Runs 3 minutes later on Ⓐ.
y – Departs 1046.

115 CARDIFF - BRISTOL - TAUNTON - EXETER (Local services)

GW

km		Ⓐ2	Ⓐ2	Ⓐ P	Ⓐ	Ⓐ	Ⓐ2	Ⓐ D	Ⓐ T	Ⓐ	Ⓐ2	Ⓐ	Ⓐ2	Ⓐ	Ⓐ2	Ⓐ	Ⓐ A	Ⓐ2	Ⓐ	Ⓐ2	Ⓐ	Ⓐ2	Ⓐ	Ⓐ2	Ⓐ P	Ⓐ2
0	**Cardiff** Central ‡ d.	...	...	...	...	...	0628	...	...	0657	0727	0800	0827	0900	0928	1000	...	1030	1100	1130	1200	1230	1300	1330	1400	1430
19	Newport ‡ d.	...	...	...	...	...	0642	...	...	0710	0742	0813	0841	0913	0942	1013	...	1044	1113	1146	1213	1244	1313	1344	1413	1444
61	**Bristol** Temple Meads a.	...	...	...	...	...	0718	...	...	0749	0816	0852	0919	0951	1017	1050	...	1118	1147	1217	1250	1317	1350	1417	1450	1517
	Bristol Temple M **110 132** d.	0502	0522	0555	0647	0703	0722	0738	0752	...	0821	0856	0923	0957	1021	1055	1114	1122	1155	1222	1256	1322	1358	1422	1455	1522
	Portsmouth Hbr **140** a.	|	|	|	|	|	0953	|	|	...	1052	|	1152	|	1252	|	|	1352	|	1452	|	1554	|	1654	|	1753
92	Weston-super-Mare ... **132** d.	0539	0544	0624	0708	0739	...	|	0826	...	...	0926	...	1027	...	1124	1139r	...	1224	...	1325	...	1426	...	1525	...
104	Highbridge and Burnham .. d.	0550	0555	0635	0719	0750	...	|	0837	...	...	0937	...	1038	...	1135	|	...	1235	...	1336	...	1437	...	1536	...
114	Bridgwater d.	0557	0602	0643	0727	0757	...	0805	0844	...	...	0944	...	1045	...	1143	|	...	1243	...	1343	...	1444	...	1543	...
134	**Taunton** **110 132** d.	0609	0614	0655	0740	0809	...	0817	0905j	...	...	1000n	...	1100	...	1204p	1159	...	1300k	...	1404p	...	1500r	...	1555	...
157	Tiverton Parkway **110** d.	|	0628	0708	0753	...	...	0830	0919	...	...	1013	...	1113	...	1217	1211	...	1313	...	1417	...	1513	...	1617	...
183	**Exeter** St Davids **110** a.	0636	0644	0722	0808	...	...	0844	0934	...	...	1031	...	1132	...	1232	1225	...	1331	...	1432	...	1532	...	1621	...

	Ⓐ	Ⓐ2	Ⓐ	Ⓐ2	Ⓐ	Ⓐ F	Ⓐ2	Ⓐ Q	Ⓐ F	Ⓐ2	Ⓐ	Ⓐ2	Ⓐ	Ⓐ2		Ⓐ	Ⓐ2	Ⓐ C	Ⓐ2	Ⓐ	⑤	①–④	Ⓐ2	⑤2	m2	⑥ R
Cardiff Central ‡ d.	1459	1530	1559	1627	1700	...	1727	1759	...	1830	1900	1928	2000	2030	...	2059	...	2130	...	2200	2230	2230	...	2330	2330	...
Newport ‡ d.	1512	1543	1613	1641	1713	...	1741	1813	...	1844	1913	1942	2013	2044	...	2112	...	2144	...	2216	2243	2248	...	2343	2348	...
Bristol Temple Meads a.	1549	1617	1651	1713	1750	...	1815	1855	...	1920	1951	2019	2054	2121	...	2148	...	2220	...	2306	2320	2333	...	0024	0038	...
Bristol Temple M **110 132** d.	1551	1622	1652	1722	1753	1815	1822	1857	1910	1925	1953	2025	2058	2126	...	...	2200	...	2305	...	...	...	2348	...	...	0535
Portsmouth Hbr **140** a.	|	1852	|	1952	|	|	2052	|	|	2151	|	2256	|	2353	...	...	|	...	|	...	...	...	|	...	...	|
Weston-super-Mare .... **132** d.	1625	...	1729	...	1828	1844	...	1932	1945r	...	2028	...	2135r	...	...	...	2239r	...	2340	...	...	...	0014s	...	...	0556
Highbridge and Burnham ... d.	1636	...	1740	...	1839	1855	...	1943	1957	...	2039	...	2146	...	...	...	2250	...	2351	...	...	...	0026s	...	...	0607
Bridgwater d.	1644	...	1748	...	1847	1902	...	1950	2005	...	2046	...	2154	...	...	...	2257	...	2358	...	...	...	0034s	...	...	0614
Taunton **110 132** d.	1655	...	1759	...	1858	1914	...	2002	2016	...	2057	...	2205	...	...	...	2314	...	0009s	...	...	...	0045s	...	...	0626
Tiverton Parkway **110** d.	...	...	...	...	...	...	...	2015	...	...	2110	...	...	...	...	...	2329	...	0024s	...	...	...	0100s	...	...	0640
Exeter St Davids **110** a.	...	...	...	...	...	...	...	2029	...	...	2125	...	...	...	...	...	2347	...	0040	...	...	...	0117	...	...	0656

	⑥	⑥	⑥	⑥2	⑥🍷	⑥	⑥2	⑥	⑥2	⑥		⑥ F	⑥2	⑥	⑥ A	⑥2	⑥	⑥2	⑥	⑥2	⑥	⑥2	⑥	⑥2	⑥	⑥2	⑥
Cardiff Central ‡ d.	...	...	...	0630	Q	...	0727	0800	0827	0900	...	...	0928	1000	...	1030	1100	1130	1200	1230	1300	1330	1400	1430	1500	1530	1558
Newport ‡ d.	...	...	...	0644	...	...	0741	0813	0841	0913	...	...	0943	1014	...	1044	1113	1144	1213	1244	1313	1344	1413	1446	1513	1544	1613
Bristol Temple Meads a.	...	...	...	0718	...	...	0816	0852	0917	0950	...	...	1016	1050	...	1117	1149	1217	1249	1317	1350	1417	1451	1519	1551	1617	1650
Bristol Temple M **110 132** d.	0608	0642	0718	0722	0735	0755	0821	0855	0922	0955	...	1009	1022	1055	1115	1122	1154	1222	1255	1323	1354	1422	1456	1523	1558	1622	1655
Portsmouth Hbr **140** a.	|	|	|	0951	|	|	1051	|	1151	|	...	|	1251	|	|	1351	|	1451	|	1551	|	1651	|	1751	|	1851	|
Weston-super-Mare .... **132** d.	0648f	0703	0754	...	|	0827r	...	0924	...	1024	...	1035	...	1124	1138r	...	1223	...	1325	...	1425	...	1524	...	1626	...	1724
Highbridge and Burnham ... d.	0659	0714	0805	...	|	0838	...	0935	...	1035	...	1046	...	1135	|	...	1234	...	1336	...	1436	...	1535	...	1637	...	1735
Bridgwater d.	0707	0722	0813	...	|	0846	...	0942	...	1042	...	1054	...	1142	|	...	1242	...	1343	...	1444	...	1543	...	1645	...	1743
Taunton **110 132** d.	0718	0735	0825	...	0808	0905p	...	0954	...	1054	...	1105	...	1154	1158	...	1300k	...	1355	...	1454	...	1600r	...	1655	...	1754
Tiverton Parkway **110** d.	...	0748	0838	...	|	|	...	1007	...	1107	...	...	...	...	1210	...	1313t	...	...	...	1510	...	1613	...	1710	...	...
Exeter St Davids **110** a.	...	0804	0852	...	0834	0931	...	1022	...	1122	...	...	...	...	1224	...	1331t	...	...	...	1524	...	1631	...	1724	...	...

A – [12] and 🍷 Manchester - Paignton (Tables **110** and **119**).
C – To Frome (Table **139**).
D – [12] and 🍷 London Paddington - Penzance (Table **110**).
E – To Exmouth (Table **112**).
F – [12] and 🍷 London Paddington - Taunton (Table **132**).
P – To Plymouth (Table **110**).
Q – To Penzance (Table **110**).
R – To Paignton (Table **110**).
T – From Gloucester (Table **138**).
f – Arrives 0635.
j – Arrives 0854.
k – Arrives 7–8 minutes earlier.
m – ①–④.
n – Arrives 0955.
p – Arrives 9–10 minutes earlier.
r – Arrives 5–7 minutes earlier.
s – Calls to set down only.
t – From Sept. 20.
‡ – For additional services see Tables **117**, **133** and **149**.

GW CARDIFF - BRISTOL - TAUNTON 115

	⑥2	⑥	⑥F	⑥2	⑥P	⑥2	⑥		⑥F	⑥2	⑥	⑥F	⑥2		⑥2	⑥J	⑥2	⑥	⑦	⑦P	⑦J	⑦	⑦2	⑦	⑦2	⑦	⑦2
Cardiff Central ‡ d.	1627	1658	...	1727	1758	1827	1900	...	...	1930	1954	...	2030	...	2100	...	2200	2247		...	...	...	0918	1000	1025	1057	1125
Newport ‡ d.	1641	1713	...	1741	1813	1841	1913	...	...	1943	2007	...	2043	...	2114	...	2214	2305		...	...	...	0936	1013	1039	1110	1139
Bristol Temple Meads a.	1717	1750	...	1817	1848	1917	1950	...	...	2017	2042	...	2115	...	2150	...	2249	2343		...	...	...	1015	1051	1112	1144	1210
Bristol Temple M **110 132** d.	1722	1755	1805	1822	1851	1922	1954	...	2010	2022	...	2105	2122	...	2155	2209	...	...		0754	0935	0955	1019	1100	1115	1147	1215
Portsmouth Hbr **140** a.	1951	|	|	2051	|	2151	|	...	|	2249	...	|	2350	...	|	|	...	...		|	|	|	1251	|	1351	|	1451
Weston-super-Mare ... **132** d.	...	1823	1833	...	1925	...	2025	...	2040	...	...	2136	...	...	2230	2236s	...	...		0820	|	1022	...	1128	...	1223	...
Highbridge and Burnham .. d.	...	1834	1844	...	1936	...	2036	...	2051	...	...	2147	...	...	2241	2248s	...	...		0830	|	1033	...	1139	...	1234	...
Bridgwater d.	...	1842	1852	...	1943	...	2043	...	2059	...	...	2155	...	...	2249	2256s	...	...		0837	1001	1040	...	1146	...	1242	...
Taunton **110 132** d.	...	1853	1903	...	1955	...	2054	...	2110	...	...	2206	...	...	2301	2309	...	...		0849	1013	1058b	...	1157	...	1253	...
Tiverton Parkway **110** d.	...	...	...	...	2008	...	...	...	...	...	...	...	...	...	2315	2322	...	...		0902	1028	1111	...	...	...	1306	...
Exeter St Davids **110** a.	...	...	...	...	2022	...	...	...	...	...	...	...	...	...	2331	2337	...	...		0914	1045	1129	...	...	...	1323	...

	⑦2	⑦2	⑦	⑦2	⑦	⑦2	⑦	⑦2	⑦	⑦F	⑦2	⑦	⑦B	⑦2	⑦2	⑦2	⑦	⑦2	⑦B	⑦	⑦2	⑦V	⑦	⑦2	⑦2	⑦W2	⑦2
Cardiff Central ‡ d.	1200	1225	1300	1325	1400	1425	1500	1525	1600	...	1625	1700	...	1725	...	1750	1800	1825	...	1900	1925	...	2000	2030	2130	2230	2311
Newport ‡ d.	1213	1239	1313	1340	1413	1439	1513	1541	1613	...	1640	1713	...	1739	...	1803	1814	1840	...	1913	1940	...	2013	2044	2144	2244	2325
Bristol Temple Meads a.	1251	1310	1348	1411	1451	1510	1548	1612	1651	...	1710	1749	...	1810	...	1838	1852	1913	...	1953	2011	...	2051	2120	2221	2322	2356
Bristol Temple M **110 132** d.	1255	1315	1355	1415	1455	1515	1553	1620	1655	1710	1715	1755	1810	1815	1825	1841	1855	1920	1935	1955	2015	2045	2053	2128	...	...	...
Portsmouth Hbr **140** a.	|	1552	|	1652	|	1751	|	1853	|	|	1952	|	|	2050	|	2123	|	2149	|	|	2249	|	|	2356	...	...	...
Weston-super-Mare ... **132** d.	1323	...	1423	...	1523	...	1629	...	1725	1738	...	1825	1839	...	1900	...	1928	...	|	2028	...	2103	2126	...	...	...	...
Highbridge and Burnham .. d.	1334	...	1434	...	1534	...	1640	...	1736	1749	...	1836	|	...	1912	...	1939	...	|	2039	...	|	2137	...	...	...	...
Bridgwater d.	1342	...	1442	...	1542	...	1648	...	1743	1756	...	1843	1854	...	1920	...	1946	...	|	2046	...	|	2144	...	...	...	...
Taunton **110 132** d.	1353	...	1453	...	1553	...	1703	...	1754	1808	...	1855	1905	...	1932	...	1957	...	2007	2058	...	2124	2155	...	...	...	...
Tiverton Parkway **110** d.	|	...	1506	...	|	...	1716	...	...	...	...	...	|	...	|	...	...	...	|	...	...	2136	...	...	...	...	...
Exeter St Davids **110** a.	1423	...	1520	...	1617	...	1730	...	...	...	...	...	1929	...	1958	...	...	...	2030	...	...	2150	...	...	...	...	...

	Ⓐ	Ⓐ	Ⓐ2	Ⓐ2	Ⓐ	Ⓐ2 W	ⒶS	Ⓐ	Ⓐ2	ⒶC 2	ⒶF	Ⓐ	ⒶF	Ⓐ2	Ⓐ	Ⓐ2	Ⓐ	Ⓐ2	Ⓐ	Ⓐ2	Ⓐ	Ⓐ2	Ⓐ	Ⓐ2	Ⓐ	Ⓐ2	Ⓐ2
Exeter St Davids **110** d.		...	...	...	...		...	0547	...		...	0644	...	...	...	...	0848	...	0950	...	1042	...	1150	...	1245	...	1350
Tiverton Parkway **110** d.		...	...	...	...	...	...	|	...	...	...	0659	...	...	...	...	0903	...	1005	...	1057	...	|	...	|	...	|
Taunton **110 132** d.		...	...	0510	...	...	...	0611	0637	...	0654	0711	0723	...	0819	...	0919r	...	1019	...	1109	...	1219b	...	1319b	...	1419b
Bridgwater d.		...	...	0521	...	...	...	0621	0648	...	0705	0721	0734	...	0829	...	0929	...	1029	...	1120	...	1229	...	1329	...	1429
Highbridge and Burnham .. d.		...	...	0528	...	...	...	0629	0655	...	0713	0728	0741	...	0836	...	0936	...	1036	...	1127	...	1236	...	1336	...	1436
Weston-super-Mare ... **132** d.		...	...	0546z	...	...	...	0642	0710r	...	0724	0739	0754	...	0848	...	0948	...	1048	...	1148f	...	1248	...	1348	...	1448
Portsmouth Hbr **140** d.		...	...	|	...	...	...	|	|	...	|	|	|	0601	|	0720	|	0823	|	0923	|	1023	|	1123	|	1223	|
Bristol Temple M **110 132** a.		...	...	0620	...	...	...	0717	0744	...	0752	0817	0823	0848	0920	0953	1020	1052	1117	1153	1217	1252	1316	1355	1416	1450	1516
Bristol Temple Meads d.		0520	0553	...	0628	0657	0707	0724	...	0757	...	0829	...	0858	0927	1002	1028	1057	1129	1158	1236	1257	1327	1401	1427	1457	1527
Newport ‡ a.		0605	0632	...	0705	0731	0749	0804	...	0832	...	0907	...	0931	1000	1038	1105	1132	1203	1235	1307	1330	1400	1434	1504	1532	1600
Cardiff Central ‡ a.		0621	0646	...	0719	0747	0805	0818	...	0848	...	0921	...	0945	1016	1052	1119	1146	1216	1249	1322	1344	1416	1449	1522	1546	1616

	Ⓐ 2	Ⓐ	Ⓐ A	Ⓐ 2	Ⓐ	Ⓐ 2	Ⓐ	Ⓐ 2	Ⓐ	Ⓐ 2	Ⓐ T	Ⓐ	Ⓐ 2	Ⓐ J	Ⓐ 2Q	Ⓐ E	⑤ 2	①–④	⑤ 2G	①–④ 2G	⑤ 2	①–④ 2	Ⓐ	Ⓐ	⑥	⑥ 2	⑥
Exeter St Davids **110** d.	...	1452	1523	...	1550	...	...	...	...	...	1903	...	...	1935	1950	2056	...	...	2100	2100	...	...	...	2243		...	...
Tiverton Parkway **110** d.	...	1507	1536	...	|	...	...	...	...	...	|	...	...	1950	|	2110	...	...	|	|	...	...	...	2258		...	...
Taunton **110 132** d.	...	1519	1600f	...	1618r	...	1710	...	1810	...	1927	1915	...	2003	2016	2124	...	...	2132r	2132r	...	...	2244	2310		0513	...
Bridgwater d.	...	1529	|	...	1628	...	1721	...	1821	...	1936	1926	...	2014	2026	|	...	...	2143	2143	...	...	2255	2320		0524	...
Highbridge and Burnham .. d.	...	1536	|	...	1635	...	1729	...	1829	...	|	1933	...	|	2034	|	...	...	2150	2150	...	...	2302	2327		0531	...
Weston-super-Mare ... **132** d.	...	1548	1630f	...	1646	...	1746b	...	1846b	...	|	1948r	...	2029	2048	|	...	...	2202	2202	...	...	2313	2341		0542	...
Portsmouth Hbr **140** d.	1323	|	|	1423	|	1523	|	1624	|	1724	|	|	1824	|	|	|	1923	1923	|	|	2024	2024	|	|		|	...
Bristol Temple M **110 132** a.	1552	1616	1647	1653	1719	1753	1820	1853	1920	1952	2003	2017	2051	2057	2119	2156	2150	2150	2232	2232	2250	2250	2348	0003		0618	...
Bristol Temple Meads d.	1557	1628	...	1657	1723	1757	1827	1858	1930	1957	...	2021	2057	...	2126	...	2156	2156	2236	2236	2258	2258	...	...		...	0628
Newport ‡ a.	1635	1706	...	1733	1756	1836	1909	1935	2008	2031	...	2055	2130	...	2202	...	2230	2236	2306	2312	2331	2337	...	...		...	0700
Cardiff Central ‡ a.	1650	1722	...	1749	1812	1849	1925	1951	2022	2046	...	2109	2144	...	2215	...	2244	2257	2319	2331	2345	2357	...	...		...	0714

	⑥2	⑥S	⑥	⑥2	⑥F	⑥	⑥2	⑥2	⑥J	⑥	⑥2	⑥	⑥2	⑥	⑥2	⑥	⑥F	⑥2	⑥	⑥2	⑥	⑥2	⑥c	⑥d	⑥2	⑥A	⑥
Exeter St Davids **110** d.	...	...	0542	...	...	...	...	...	0733	...	...	0848	...	0952	...	1043	...	...	1152	...	...	...	...	1350	...	1452	...
Tiverton Parkway **110** d.	...	...	0558	...	...	...	...	...	|	...	...	|	...	|	...	|	...	...	|	...	...	...	...	1405	...	1505	...
Taunton **110 132** d.	...	...	0611	...	0657	...	0738	...	0758	0818	...	0914	...	1018	...	1107	1125	...	1218	...	1318	...	1407	1418	...	1518	1522
Bridgwater d.	...	...	0621	...	0708	...	0749	...	0808	0829	...	0925	...	1028	...	1117	1136	...	1228	...	1329	...	1418	1428	...	|	1532
Highbridge and Burnham .. d.	...	...	0628	...	0715	...	0757	...	0815	0837	...	0933	...	1036	...	1125	1144	...	1236	...	1336	...	1425	1436	...	|	1539
Weston-super-Mare ... **132** d.	...	...	0640	...	0727	0738	0810	...	0827	0848	...	0945	...	1048	...	1145f	1158	...	1248	...	1348	...	1448f	1448	...	1540	1550
Portsmouth Hbr **140** d.	...	...	|	...	|	|	|	0608	|	|	0723	|	0823	|	0923	|	|	1023	|	1123	|	1223	|	|	1323	|	|
Bristol Temple M **110 132** a.	...	...	0713	...	0754	0815	0844	0851	0854	0916	0953	1014	1056	1116	1156	1216	1225	1252	1315	1353	1415	1452	1515	1515	1554	1557	1618
Bristol Temple Meads d.	0653	0704	0720	0757	...	0825	...	0857	...	0928	1000	1030	1100	1132	1200	1232	...	1258	1323	1359	1432	1500	1532	1532	1600	...	1622
Newport ‡ a.	0728	0744	0756	0829	...	0856	...	0929	...	0959	1033	1105	1132	1204	1233	1304	...	1331	1354	1434	1505	1532	1604	1604	1634	...	1653
Cardiff Central ‡ a.	0743	0800	0810	0845	...	0910	...	0943	...	1013	1050	1120	1146	1218	1250	1318	...	1346	1409	1449	1519	1546	1618	1618	1649	...	1707

	⑥2	⑥	⑥2	⑥	⑥2	⑥	⑥2	⑥R	⑥c	⑥2	⑥F	⑥	⑥2	⑥N	⑥	⑥F	⑥2	⑥2	⑦	⑦2	⑦2	⑦	⑦2 D	⑦	⑦2	⑦P	⑦2
Exeter St Davids **110** d.	...	1555	...	1652	...	...	...	...	1904	...	...	1955	...	2018	...	...	2117	...		...	0759	...		0946	...	1050	...
Tiverton Parkway **110** d.	...	|	...	|	...	...	...	...	1918	...	...	2010	...	|	...	...	2132	...		...	0814	...	...	1000	...	1104	...
Taunton **110 132** d.	...	1619	...	1718	...	1816	...	1910	1931	...	1956	2022	...	2041	2104	2130	2146	...		...	0827	...	...	1013	...	1116	...
Bridgwater d.	...	1630	...	1728	...	1827	...	1921	1942	...	2007	2033	...	2052	2115	2141	2157	...		...	0838	...	...	1023	...	1127	...
Highbridge and Burnham .. d.	...	1637	...	1736	...	1835	...	1928	|	...	2014	2040	...	2059	2122	2149	2204	...		...	0846	...	...	1030	...	1134	...
Weston-super-Mare ... **132** d.	...	1648	...	1748	...	1848	...	1940	1957	...	2026	2051	...	2111	2135	2200	2215	...		...	0857	...	...	1041	...	1145	...
Portsmouth Hbr **140** d.	1423	|	1523	|	1623	|	1723	|	|	1823	|	|	1923	|	|	|	|	2023		...	|	...	...	|	0909	|	1013t
Bristol Temple M **110 132** a.	1652	1720	1752	1816	1853	1916	1952	2007	2015	2052	2052	2125	2150	2131	2208	2228	2250	2252		...	0931	...	...	1108	1147	1212	1246
Bristol Temple Meads d.	1657	1732	1757	1832	1900	1930	1958	...	...	2057	...	2128	2200	...	...	...	...	2258		0905	0938	1005	1040	1111	1156	1215	1256
Newport ‡ a.	1732	1804	1833	1907	1933	2013	2030	...	...	2130	...	2201	2235	...	...	...	...	2337		0947	1010	1039	1108	1144	1227	1243	1326
Cardiff Central ‡ a.	1748	1818	1850	1921	1950	2027	2045	...	...	2145	...	2214	2255	...	...	...	...	2358		1007	1023	1054	1122	1158	1241	1257	1340

	⑦A	⑦	⑦2	⑦	⑦2	⑦	⑦2	⑦	⑦2	⑦B	⑦2	⑦2	⑦F	⑦	⑦2	⑦J	⑦	⑦2	⑦F	⑦	⑦2	⑦	⑦2	⑦2	⑦B	⑦2	⑦
Exeter St Davids **110** d.	1134	1147	...	...	...	1345	...	1450	...	1559	1548	...	...	1650	...	1732	...	...	...	...	...	...	...	2026	2116	...	...
Tiverton Parkway **110** d.	1148	1203	...	...	...	|	...	|	...	|	1602	...	...	1704	...	|	...	...	...	...	...	...	...	2041	2130	...	...
Taunton **110 132** d.	1200	1215	...	1316	...	1416a	...	1516	...	1622	1615	...	1657	1720	...	1757	1810	...	1857	1926	...	2016	...	2054	2143	...	2210
Bridgwater d.	|	1225	...	1327	...	1426	...	1527	...	1633	1625	...	1708	1730	...	1808	1821	...	1908	1937	...	2027	...	2105	|	...	2220
Highbridge and Burnham .. d.	|	1232	...	1334	...	1433	...	1534	...	|	1632	...	1715	1737	...	1815	1829	...	1915	1944	...	2034	...	2113	|	...	2227
Weston-super-Mare ... **132** d.	1225r	1243	...	1345	...	1444	...	1545	...	|	1645	...	1724	1748	...	1826	1840	...	1927	1954	...	2045	...	2125	2205	...	2239
Portsmouth Hbr **140** d.	|	|	1109	|	1209	|	1309	|	1409	|	|	1509	|	|	1609	|	|	1709	|	|	1809	|	1909	|	|	2009	|
Bristol Temple M **110 132** a.	1248	1311	1350	1413	1445	1512	1546	1612	1639	1659	1712	1750	1753	1815	1836	1854	1914	1940	1955	2027	2040	2118	2140	2159	2223	2241	2312
Bristol Temple Meads d.	...	1319	1356	1415	1456	1515	1556	1615	1643	...	1715	1756	...	1818	1844	...	...	1946	...	...	2045	...	2145	...	...	2245	...
Newport ‡ a.	...	1352	1426	1448	1530	1543	1626	1648	1715	...	1745	1827	...	1850	1917	...	...	2016	...	...	2114	...	2218	...	...	2316	...
Cardiff Central ‡ a.	...	1405	1440	1502	1545	1557	1640	1702	1729	...	1759	1841	...	1905	1931	...	...	2031	...	...	2129	...	2232	...	...	2330	...

A – (12) and 🍷 Paignton - Manchester Piccadilly (Tables **110** and **119**).
B – (12) and 🍷 London Paddington - Plymouth and v.v. (Table **110**).
C – From Frome (Table **139**).
D – From Weymouth (Table **139**).
E – (12) and 🍷 Penzance - London Paddington (Table **110**).
F – (12) and 🍷 London Paddington - Taunton and v.v. (Table **132**).
G – From Exmouth (Table **112**).
J – (12) and 🍷 London Paddington - Exeter St Davids and v.v. (Table **132**).
N – Until Sept. 13. From Newquay (Table **135**).
P – To/from Plymouth (Table **110**).
Q – From Paignton (Table **110**).
R – (12) Taunton - Gloucester (Table **138**).
S – (12) and 🍷 London Paddington - Swansea (Table **133**).
T – (12) Plymouth - Gloucester (Tables **110** and **138**).
V – (12) and 🍷 Dundee - Plymouth (Tables **110**, **119** and **222**).
W – To/from Westbury (Table **140**).
Y – (12) and 🍷 Paignton - London Paddington (Table **110**).

a – Arrives 1407.
b – Arrives 7 minutes earlier.
c – Until Sept. 13.
d – From Sept. 20.
f – Arrives 10–12 minutes earlier.
j – Arrives 0559 on ①.
r – Arrives 5–6 minutes earlier.
s – Calls to set down only.
t – Portsmouth and Southsea.
z – Arrives 0538.

‡ – For additional services see Tables **117**, **133** and **149**.

WR WAREHAM - SWANAGE 116

No through services will operate in 2025.

km													
0	**Wareham** **105** d.	...	...	...	...	...	**Swanage** ⊠ d.	...	...	...	...	...
9	Norden ⊠ a.	...	...	...	...	...	Corfe Castle ⊠ d.	...	...	...	...	...
10	Corfe Castle ⊠ a.	...	...	...	...	...	Norden ⊠ d.	...	...	...	...	...
18	**Swanage** ⊠ a.	...	...	...	...	...	**Wareham** **105** a.	...	...	...	...	...

⊠ – Additional steam trains run Norden - Corfe Castle - Swanage and v.v. Special fares apply. www.swanagerailway.co.uk ✆ 01929 425800.

117 NOTTINGHAM - DERBY - BIRMINGHAM - CARDIFF

2nd class only AW, XC

km			Ⓐ	⑥	⚒	Ⓐ	⑥	⚒	⑥🍷	Ⓐ🍷	Ⓐ	Ⓐ🍷	⑥🍷	ⒶF	⑥F	⚒	⚒	⚒🍷	⚒	Ⓐ🍷	⑥🍷	⚒	⑥	⑥🍷	Ⓐ🍷	⚒
0	**Nottingham** .... 155 172 d.		...	...	...	...	...	...	...	...	0600	...	0600	0639	0642	0704	0737	0807	0839	0907	0906	0941	...	1007	1006	1041
26	**Derby** .... 155 172 a.		...	...	...	...	...	...	...	...	0633	...	0631	0701	0703	0734	0802	0838	0907	0937	0935	1002	...	1034	1038	1102
	Derby .... 119 d.	⚒	...	...	...	...	...	...	0610	0610	0638	0649	0637	0705	0713	0736	0806	0842	0910	0941	0938	1007	...	1038	1041	1110
43	Burton-on-Trent .... 119 d.		...	...	...	...	...	...	0620	0621	0649	|	0649	0719	0723	0750	0818	0853	0921	0953	0950	1021	...	1050	1053	1121
64	Tamworth .... 119 d.		...	...	...	...	...	...	0630	0631	0700	0707	0702	0734c	0734	0803	0829	0904	0933	1005	1003	1033	...	1103	1105	1133
92	**Birmingham** New St...... 119 a.		...	...	...	...	...	...	0648	0652	0723	0726	0725	0756	0756	0826	0855	0926	0955	1027	1025	1055	...	1124	1123	1155
	Birmingham New St... 116/9 d.		...	...	0500	0536	0542	...	0712	0712	...	0730	0730	▬	▬	0830	▬	0930	▬	1030	1030	▬	...	1130	1130	▬
135	Worcestershire Parkway ....d.		...	...	|	|	|	...	|	|	...	0758	0758	⑥	Ⓐ	0858	⚒	0958	⚒	1058	1058	Ⓐ	...	1158	1158	⚒
174	Cheltenham Spa... 116/9 138 d.		0538	0540	0604	0641	0644	0743	0750	0759	...	0815	0815	0840	0843	0915	0940	1015	1040	1115	1115	1140	1140	1215	1215	1240
206	**Gloucester** .... 138 d.		0549	0549	0619	0653	0657	0753	...	...	...	0827	0827	0849	0853	0927	0949	1027	1049	1127	1127	1153	1149	1227	1227	1249
206	Lydney .... 🚂 d.		0608	0608	0638	0712	0716	0811	...	...	...	|	|	0908	0912	|	1008	1047	1108	|	|	1212	1208	|	|	1308
218	Chepstow ....d.		0617	0617	0647	0721	0725	0820	...	...	...	0853	0853	0917	0921	0953	1017	|	1117	1155	1155	1221	1217	1253	1253	1317
229	Caldicot ....d.		0625	0625	0656	0730	0734	0829	...	...	...	|	|	0925	0929	|	1025	|	1125	|	|	1229	1225	|	|	1325
246	Newport........... 115 133 149 a.		0639	0640	0709	0743	0749	0842	...	...	...	0911	0910	0939	0946	1010	1044j	1111	1139	1212	1212	1243	1239	1310	1311	1343j
265	**Cardiff** Central . 115 133 149 a.		0658	0655	0724	0757	0806	0859	...	...	...	0925	0926	0959	1001	1026	1100	1125	1159	1226	1226	1259	1259	1325	1325	1359

	⚒🍷	⚒	⚒🍷	⚒	⚒🍷	⚒🍷	⚒🍷	⚒	Ⓐ	⑥	⚒🍷	⚒	⚒🍷	ⒶB	Ⓐ	⑥	⚒🍷	Ⓐ	⑥	⑥	Ⓐ	⑥	Ⓐ	Ⓐ	⑥	⚒
Nottingham............. 155 172 d.	1107	1141	1207	1241	1307	1341	1407	1441	1507	1507	1541	1607	1641	...	1707	1707	1741	1805	1807	1845	1845	1907	1908	1935	1932	2039
Derby...................... 155 172 a.	1135	1203	1235	1304	1336	1402	1435	1504	1535	1534	1601	1635	1703	...	1735	1734	1806	1831	1834	1905	1909	1935	1938	2004	2003	2106
Derby............................119 d.	1138	1210	1238	1310	1338	1410	1438	1510	1538	1539	1610	1638	1709	1731	1738	1738	1810	1838	1838	1910	1912	1939	1943	2010	2010	2110
Burton-on-Trent ....119 d.	1150	1221	1250	1324	1350	1421	1450	1524	1550	1550	1621	1650	1723	1741	1750	1750	1824	1850	1850	1921	1923	1950	1954	2021	2021	2124
Tamworth ....119 d.	1202	1232	1303	1336	1403	1433	1502	1536	1602	1603	1632	1703	1735	|	1802	1802	1836	1902	1903	1933	1935	2003	2006	2033	2033	2136
Birmingham New St ....119 a.	1226	1256	1326	1356	1423	1456	1524	1600j	1623	1624	1657	1724	1756	1807	1823	1823	1855	1923	1923	1955	1956	2023	2026	2055	2059	2158
Birmingham New St .... 116/9 d.	1230	▬	1330	▬	1430	▬	1530	▬	1630	1630	▬	1730	▬	1812	1830	1830	▬	1930	...	...	▬	2030	2030	▬	▬	▬
Worcestershire Parkway .... d.	1258	⚒	1358	⚒	1458	⚒	1558	⚒	1658	1658	⚒	1758	⚒	|	1858	1858	⚒	1958	...	...	⚒	2058	2058	①–④	⑥	⑤
Cheltenham Spa .... 116/9 138 d.	1315	1340	1415	1437	1515	1540n	1615	1640	1719	1715	1745	1819	1840	1852	1915	1915	1940	2015	...	...	2041	2115	2115	2258	2258	2258
Gloucester.......................138 d.	1327	1349	1427	1449	1527	1549	1627	1649	1730	1727	1756	1830	1849	1912h	1924	1927	1949	2027	...	...	2055c	2127	2125	2310	2310	2310
Lydney.............................. 🚂 d.	1347	1408	|	1508	|	1608	1646	1708	1749	1747	1815	|	1908	|	...	|	2008	|	...	...	2113	2146	2144	2328	2328	2328
Chepstow .... d.	|	1417	1453	1517	1553	1617	1655	1717	|	|	1824	|	1917	|	...	|	2017	|	...	...	2122	2155	2154	2337	2337	2337
Caldicot .... d.	|	1425	|	1525	|	1625	|	1725	|	|	1832	|	1925	|	...	|	2025	|	...	...	2131	2204	2202	2346	2346	2346
Newport............. 115 133 149 a.	1411	1440	1510	1541	1611	1641	1712	1740	1814	1811	1845	1913	1942	1952	...	2008	2046	2108	...	...	2144	2218	2217	0014	0012	0005
Cardiff Central .. 115 133 149 a.	1425	1500	1525	1559	1625	1700	1726	1759	1828	1827	1901	1927	2000	2007	...	2022	2059	2126	...	...	2203j	2237	2236d	0039	0035	0019

	Ⓐ	Ⓐ	⑥		⑦	⑦	⑦🍷	⑦🍷	⑦	⑦🍷	⑦🍷	⑦	⑦🍷	⑦🍷	⑦	⑦🍷	⑦🍷	⑦	⑦🍷	⑦🍷	⑦	⑦🍷	⑦	⑦🍷	⑦	⑦
Nottingham............. 155 172 d.	*2054*	2136	2137		...	...	...	0955	...	1116	1216	...	1316	1416	...	1512	1616	...	1716	1816	...	*1825*	1915	*1923*	2015	*2122*
Derby...................... 155 172 a.	*2121*	2206	2208	⑦	...	...	...	1016	...	1136	1236	...	1337	1436	...	1533	1636	...	1739	1836	...	*1852*	1936	*1950*	2036	*2149*
Derby............................119 d.	2131	2210	2213		...	...	...	1021	...	1140	1240	...	1340	1440	...	1537	1640	...	1742	1840	...	1931	1940	2031	2040	2231
Burton-on-Trent ....119 d.	2141	2221	2224		...	...	...	1032	...	1151	1251	...	1351	1451	...	1548	1651	...	1753	1851	...	1941	1951	|	2051	2241
Tamworth ....119 d.	2151	2232	2235		...	...	...	1044	...	1203	1303	...	1403	1503	...	1600	1703	...	1805	1903	...	|	2003	2049	2103	2251
Birmingham New St ....119 a.	2208	2301	2304		...	...	...	1102	...	1221	1321	...	1421	1522	...	1621	1723	...	1823	1921	...	2004	2025	2106	2121	2309
Birmingham New St .... 116/9 d.	2212	...	...		...	*0930*	1012	1112	...	1230	1330	...	1430	1530	...	1630	1730	...	1830	1930	...	2012	...	2112	▬	...
Worcestershire Parkway .... d.	|	...	...		...	|	1040	1140	...	1258	1358	...	1458	1558	...	1658	1758	...	1858	1958	...	|	...	|	...	...
Cheltenham Spa .... 116/9 138 d.	2250	...	...		...	1038	1100	1200	1235	1315	1415	1408	1515	1615	1610	1715	1815	1835	1915	2015	2010	2050	...	2152	⑦	...
Gloucester.......................138 d.	...	...	...		0845	1049	1110	1210	1247	1327	1427	1432a	1527	1627	1630f	1727	1827	1848	1927	2027	2031e	...	...	2200	2241	...
Lydney.............................. 🚂 d.	...	...	...		0903	1108	|	|	1306	|	|	1451	|	|	1650	|	|	1907	|	|	2051	...	...	...	2300	...
Chepstow .... d.	...	...	...		0912	1117	|	|	1315	|	|	1500	|	|	1700	|	|	1916	|	|	2100	...	...	...	2309	...
Caldicot .... d.	...	...	...		0921	1126	|	|	1324	|	|	1509	|	|	1708	|	|	1925	|	|	2109	...	...	...	2318	...
Newport............. 115 133 149 a.	...	...	...		0941	1140	1151	1251	1336	1408	1510	1523	1608	1708	1722	1808	1908	1939	2008	2108	2126	...	...	...	2332	...
Cardiff Central .. 115 133 149 a.	...	...	...		1001	1153	1205	1305	1353	1422	1529	1537	1624	1723	1736	1822	1924	1953	2022	2122	2140	...	...	...	2345	...

		⚒	Ⓐ	⑥	⚒	⑥	Ⓐ	⑥🍷	Ⓐ🍷	⚒	⚒	⚒	⚒	⚒	⚒	⚒	⑥	Ⓐ	⑥🍷	ⒶB	⚒	⚒	⚒	Ⓐ🍷	⑥🍷	⑥
Cardiff Central .. 115 133 149 d.		...	...	...	...	...	...	...	...	...	0610	0640	0710	0745	0810	0845	0910	0910	0945	0945	1010	1045	1110	1145	1145	1210
Newport............. 115 133 149 d.	⚒	...	...	...	...	...	...	...	...	...	0623	0654	0723	0759	0824	0859	0924	0924	0959	0959	1024	1059	1124	1159	1159	1224
Caldicot .... d.		...	...	...	...	...	...	...	...	...	0636	0707	0737	|	0837	|	0937	0937	|	|	1037	|	1137	|	|	1237
Chepstow .... d.		...	...	...	...	...	...	...	...	...	0645	0715	0745	|	0845	0916	0945	0945	1016	1016	1045	|	1145	1216	1216	1245
Lydney.............................. 🚂 d.		...	...	...	...	...	...	...	...	...	0653	0724	0754	0823	0854	|	0954	0954	|	|	1054	1123	1154	|	|	1254
Gloucester.......................138 d.		...	...	...	...	...	...	0659	...	...	0716	0745	0815	0848c	0916	0948	1017	1017	1049c	1049	1116	1149	1216	1245	1245	1317
Cheltenham Spa .... 116/9 138 d.		...	...	...	...	...	...	0710	0714	...	0729	0755	0827	0858	0926	0959	1025	1027	1059	1059	1126	1159	1227	1255	1255	1325
Worcestershire Parkway .... d.		...	...	...	...	...	...	|	|	...	...	0814	▬	0914	▬	1014	▬	▬	1114	1114	▬	1214	▬	1314	1314	▬
Birmingham New St .... 116/9 a.		...	...	...	...	...	...	0755	0755	...	...	0845	⚒🍷	0945	⚒🍷	1045	⚒🍷	Ⓐ	1145	1149	⚒🍷	1245	⚒	1345	1345	⑥
Birmingham New St ....119 d.		0609	0649	0649	0708	0749	0749	0803	0803	0808	...	0849	0909	0949	1009	1049	1109	1149	1149	1203	1209	1249	1309	1349	1349	1409
Tamworth ....119 d.		0628	0706	0706	0728	0806	0806	0820	0822	0828	...	0906	0928	1006	1026	1106	1129	1208	1206	1219	1226	1306	1328	1407	1406	1428
Burton-on-Trent ....119 d.		0640	0717	0717	0741	0817	0823c	0831	0832	0839	...	0917	0940	1017	1037	1117	1141	1220	1218	1231	1237	1320	1340	1420	1417	1440
Derby............................119 a.		0657	0731	0729	0758	0830	0834	0841	0843	0854	...	0931	0952	1031	1053	1131	1155	1232	1229	1242	1253	1332	1353	1432	1429	1452
Derby...................... 155 172 d.		0709	0736	0742	0808	0838	0838	...	...	0900	...	0935	0958	1036	1059	1136	1159	1239	1236	...	1259	1336	1359	1438	1436	1501
Nottingham............. 155 172 a.		0739	0803	0806	0834	0903	0904	...	...	0924	...	1003r	1024	1103	1123	1201	1225	1302	1259	...	1324	1403	1424	1502	1503	1523

	Ⓐ	⚒🍷	⚒	⚒🍷	⑥	Ⓐ	⚒🍷	⑥	⚒	⚒🍷	⑥	Ⓐ	Ⓐ🍷	⑥🍷	⚒	⚒🍷	⚒	⚒	⚒	Ⓐ	⑥	⑥	Ⓐ	⚒	Ⓐ	⑥
Cardiff Central .. 115 133 149 d.	1210	1245	1310	1345	1410	1410	1445	...	1510	1545	1610	1610	1645	1645	1710	1745	1810	1845	1910	1950	2000	2048	2045	2109	2145	2210
Newport............. 115 133 149 d.	1224	1259	1324	1359	1424	1424	1459	...	1526	1559	1624	1624	1659	1659	1725	1759	1824	1859	1924	2003	2013	2102	2059	2124	2159	2224
Caldicot .... d.	1237	|	1337	|	1437	1437	|	...	1538	|	1637	1640	|	|	1738	|	1837	|	1937	2016	2027	|	|	2137	2212	2238
Chepstow .... d.	1245	1316	1345	|	1445	1445	1516	...	1546	1616	1645	1648	|	|	1746	1816	1845	1916	1945	2024	2036	|	|	2145	2220	2246
Lydney.............................. 🚂 d.	1254	|	1354	1423	1454	1454	|	...	1555	|	1654	1657	1725	1724	1755	|	1854	|	1954	2033	2044	|	|	2154	2229	2255
Gloucester.......................138 d.	1317	1349	1416	1449c	1517	1514	1549	...	1617	1645	1717	1718	1749	1749c	1817	1845	1917	1949c	2017	2056	2106	2149c	2142	2216	2251	2316
Cheltenham Spa .... 116/9 138 d.	1327	1359	1427	1459	1525	▬	1559	...	1627	1655	1725	1728	1759	1759	1827	1855	1927	1959	2027	2107	2117	2159	2152	2227	2302	2327
Worcestershire Parkway .... d.	▬	1414	▬	1514	▬	...	1614	...	▬	1714	▬	▬	1814	1814	▬	1914	...	2014	...	2121	|	2214	2209	▬	|	...
Birmingham New St .... 116/9 a.	Ⓐ	1445	⚒	1545	⑥	Ⓐ	1645	...	Ⓐ	1745	⑥	Ⓐ	1845	1845	⚒	1945	...	2046	...	2154	2206	2245	2246	Ⓐ	0002	...
Birmingham New St ....119 d.	1409	1449	1509	1549	1609	1609	1649	1709	1709	1749	1809	1809	1849	1849	1909	1949	...	2049	...	2203	2210	2249	...	2309	...	...
Tamworth ....119 d.	1429	1506	1528	1606	1628	1632	1706	1728	1732	1806	1828	1828	1908	1906	1926	2008	...	2108	...	2227	2229	2308	...	2328	...	...
Burton-on-Trent ....119 d.	1442	1517	1540	1617	1640	1643	1717	1740	1743	1817	1840	1840	1920	1917	1937	2020	...	2120	...	2239	2240	2320	...	2340	...	...
Derby............................119 a.	1453	1530	1555	1630	1652	1655	1731	1751	1755	1829	1854	1855	1932	1930	1952	2032	...	2138	...	2250	2255	2331	...	2354	...	...
Derby...................... 155 172 d.	1459	1536	1601	1636	1701	1701	1736	1759	1759	1836	1858	1913	1936	1940	1957	2036	...	2139t	...	2258	2259	*2347*	...	2358	...	...
Nottingham............. 155 172 a.	1522	1603r	1624	1703r	1724	1724	1803	1824	1824	1900	1921	1936	2001	2003	2020	2101	...	2208j	...	2326	2323	*0014*	...	0021	...	...

	⑥	①–④	⑤		⑦	⑦	⑦🍷	⑦	⑦🍷	⑦	⑦🍷	⑦🍷	⑦	⑦🍷	⑦🍷	⑦	⑦🍷	⑦🍷	⑦	⑦🍷	⑦🍷	⑦D	⑦🍷	⑦	⑦	⑦
Cardiff Central .. 115 133 149 d.	2318	2334	2347		0823	...	...	1030	1145	1229	1245	1345	1429	1445	1545	1629	1645	1745	1829	1845	...	1945	...	2024	2045	2235
Newport............. 115 133 149 d.	2337	2355	0003	⑦	0841	...	...	1043	1159	1242	1259	1359	1442	1459	1559	1643	1659	1759	1843	1859	...	1959	...	2037	2059	2248
Caldicot .... d.	2356	0014	0015		0905	...	...	1058	|	1256	|	|	1456	|	|	1657	|	|	1857	|	...	|	...	2050	|	2301
Chepstow .... d.	0005	0023	0024		0913	...	...	1107	|	1304	|	|	1505	|	|	1705	|	|	1905	|	...	|	...	2059	|	2310
Lydney.............................. 🚂 d.	0013	0031	0032		0922	...	...	1115	|	1313	|	|	1513	|	|	1714	|	|	1914	|	...	|	...	2107	|	2318
Gloucester.......................138 d.	0036	0054	0055		0943	1002	...	1137	1249	1334	1349f	1449f	1534	1549f	1649f	1735	1749f	1849f	1935	1949c	...	2049	...	2128	2149f	2338
Cheltenham Spa .... 116/9 138 d.	...	...	...		0954	1011	...	1146	1259	1345	1359	1459	1544	1559	1659	1745	1759	1859	1944	1959	2011	2059	2111	...	2159	*0010*
Worcestershire Parkway .... d.	...	...	...		...	|	...	▬	1314	...	1414	1514	...	1614	1714	...	1814	1914	...	2014	|	2114	|	...	2214	...
Birmingham New St .... 116/9 a.	...	...	...		...	1049	...	⑦	1345	...	1445	1545	...	1645	1745	...	1845	1945	...	2045	2049	2145	2149	...	2245	...
Birmingham New St ....119 d.	...	...	...		...	1103	1149	1249	1349	...	1449	1549	...	1649	1749	...	1849	1949	...	2049	2103	...	2203	...	...	...
Tamworth ....119 d.	...	...	...		...	1119	1206	1306	1406	...	1508	1606	...	1706	1806	...	1908	2006	...	2106	2119	...	2219	...	...	...
Burton-on-Trent ....119 d.	...	...	...		...	1130	1218	1318	1418	...	1520	1618	...	1718	1818	...	1920	2017	...	2117	2130	...	|	...	...	...
Derby............................119 a.	...	...	...		...	1140	1229	1330	1429	...	1531	1629	...	1729	1829	...	1931	2029	...	2129	2140	...	2237	...	...	...
Derby...................... 155 172 d.	...	...	...		...	...	1233	1334	1433	...	1535	1633	...	1733	1833	...	1937	2034	...	2134	*2219*	...	*2332*	...	...	...
Nottingham............. 155 172 a.	...	...	...		...	...	1253	1354	1453	...	1555	1653	...	1755	1855	...	1957	2054	...	2154	*2245*	...	*2359*	...	...	...

B – [12] and 🍷 Cardiff - Edinburgh and v.v. (Table **118**).
C – [12] and 🍷 Bristol Temple Meads - Stansted Airport (Tables **138** and **208**).
D – [12] Cardiff - Leicester (Table **208**).
E – [12] and 🍷 Gloucester - Stansted Airport (Table **208**).
F – [12] Nottingham - Bournemouth (Table **107**).
L – [12] Leicester - Gloucester (Table **208**).

a – Arrives 1418.
c – Arrives 5–6 minutes earlier.
d – Arrives 2229 on ⑤.
e – Arrives 2022.
f – Arrives 8–9 minutes earlier.
h – Arrives 1900.
j – Arrives 4–7 minutes earlier on ⑥.

n – ⑥ only.
r – Arrives 4 minutes earlier on Ⓐ.
t – Departs 2143 on Ⓐ.

🚂 – DEAN FOREST RAILWAY (Lydney Junction - Parkend. *7 km*). ✆ 01594 845840. www.deanforestrailway.co.uk
Lydney Junction station is 10 minutes walk from the National Rail station.

XC Most services convey 🍸 THE NORTH EAST and MANCHESTER - BIRMINGHAM - BRISTOL 119

km		⑥	Ⓐ	⑥	Ⓐ	Ⓐm	⑥m	Ⓐ	⑥	⚒q	Ⓐ	ⒶN	⑥N	Ⓐ	⑥	⑥	ⒶL	⑥	Ⓐd	⑥	Ⓐ	⑥	Ⓐ	Ⓐ	⑥
0	**Edinburgh** Waverley .... **180 214** d.	...	...	...	...	...	...	...	...	...	...	...	...	...	...	...	...	...	...	...	...	...	...	...	...
92	Berwick upon Tweed .... **214** d.	...	...	...	...	...	...	...	...	...	...	...	...	...	...	...	...	...	...	...	...	...	...	...	...
144	Alnmouth .... **214** d.	...	...	...	...	...	...	...	...	...	...	...	...	...	...	...	...	...	...	...	...	...	...	...	...
199	**Newcastle** .... **180 214** a.	...	...	...	...	...	...	...	...	...	...	...	...	...	...	...	...	...	...	...	...	...	...	...	...
	Newcastle .... **180 188** d.	...	...	...	...	...	...	...	...	...	...	...	...	...	...	...	...	...	...	...	...	...	...	0624	0624
223	Durham .... **180 188** d.	...	...	...	...	...	...	...	...	...	...	...	...	...	...	...	...	...	...	...	...	...	...	0637	0637
258	Darlington .... **180 188** d.	...	...	...	...	...	...	...	...	...	...	...	...	...	...	...	...	...	...	...	...	...	...	0655	0655
328	**York** .... **180 188** a.	...	...	...	...	...	...	...	...	...	...	...	...	...	...	...	...	...	...	...	...	...	...	0723	0723
	York .... **180 188 191** d.	...	...	...	...	...	...	...	...	...	...	...	...	...	...	0624	0624	...	...	...	...	0611	0645	0725	0726
370	**Leeds** .... **188 191** a.	...	...	...	...	...	...	...	...	...	...	...	...	...	...	|	|	...	...	...	...	0658	0709	|	|
	Leeds .... **180** d.	...	...	...	...	...	...	...	...	...	...	...	...	0611	0611	|	|	...	...	...	...	0711	0711	|	|
386	Wakefield Westgate .... **180** d.	...	...	...	...	...	...	...	...	...	...	...	...	0623	0623	|	|	...	...	...	...	0723	0723	|	|
	Doncaster .... **180** d.	...	...	...	...	...	...	...	...	...	...	...	...	|	|	0647	0647	...	...	...	...	|	|	0753	0752
432	**Sheffield** .... **170** d.	...	...	...	...	...	...	...	...	...	...	...	...	0656	0653	0718**b**	0718**b**	...	...	...	...	0756**r**	0753	0823	0821**r**
452	Chesterfield .... **170** d.	...	...	...	...	...	...	...	...	...	...	...	...	0708	0705	0731	0731	...	...	...	...	0808	0806	|	|
490	**Derby** .... **170** a.	...	...	...	...	...	...	...	...	...	...	...	...	0726	0723	0750	0749	...	...	...	...	0826	0824	0850	0849
	Derby .... **120** d.	...	...	0610	0610	...	...	...	...	...	...	0705	0713	0728	0728	0751	0751	...	...	...	...	0828	0828	0853	0853
508	Burton on Trent .... **120** d.	...	...	0620	0621	...	...	...	...	...	...	0719	0723	0738	0738	0803	0801	...	...	...	...	0838	0838	|	|
529	Tamworth .... **120** d.	...	...	0630	0631	...	...	...	...	...	...	0734**f**	0734	0749	0749	0813	0812	...	...	...	...	0848	0849	|	|
	Manchester Piccadilly ...... **152** d.	...	...	|	|	0511	0511	...	...	0603	0624	|	|	|	|	|	|	0703	0703	0725	0725	|	|	|	|
	Stockport .... **152** d.	...	...	|	|	|	|	...	...	|	0633	|	|	|	|	|	|	0711	0713	0733	0733	|	|	|	|
	Macclesfield .... **152** d.	...	...	|	|	|	|	...	...	|	0647	|	|	|	|	|	|	0724	0726	0746	0746	|	|	|	|
	Stoke on Trent .... **152** d.	...	...	|	|	0605	0605**r**	...	...	|	0704	|	|	|	|	|	|	0744	0744	0804	0804	|	|	|	|
	Stafford .... **144** d.	...	...	|	|	0622	0622	...	...	0659	0724	|	|	|	|	|	|	0801	0800	0821	0822	|	|	|	|
	Wolverhampton ...... **144 150/4** d.	...	...	|	|	0639	0640	...	...	0715	0741	|	|	|	|	|	|	0815	0815	0839	0839	|	|	|	|
556	**Birmingham** New St . **144 150/4** a.	...	...	0648	0652	0656**j**	0656**j**	...	...	0737	0804	0756	0756	0806	0806	0832	0828	0833	0833	0856	0856	0905	0907	0928	0927
	Birmingham New Street ..... **117** d.	0641	0642	0712	0712	0703	0703	0742	0742	...	...	0803	0803	0812	0812	0838	0833	0842	0842	0903	0903	0912	0912	...	...
	Reading **107** ....a.	|	|	|	|	0848	0841	|	|	...	...	0943	0941	|	|	1005	1007	|	|	1042	1045	|	|	...	...
	Bournemouth **107** ....a.	|	|	|	|	1013	1013	|	|	...	...	1112	1111	|	|	...	...	|	|	1211	1212	|	|	...	...
599	Worcestershire Parkway ...... **117** d.	|	|	|	|	...	...	|	|	...	...	...	...	|	|	...	...	0912	0916	...	...	|	|	...	...
629	Cheltenham Spa .... **117 138** d.	0726	0726	0752	0801	...	...	0826	0829	...	...	...	...	0852	0852	...	...	0929	0932	...	...	0952	0952	...	...
691	**Bristol** Parkway .... **138** d.	0756	0755	0825**r**	0830	...	...	0855	0858	...	...	...	...	0921	0922	...	...	0959	1002	...	...	1025**r**	1023	...	...
701	**Bristol** Temple Meads......... **138** a.	0805	0804	0834	0839	...	...	0906	0907	...	...	...	...	0930	0931	...	...	1008	1012	...	...	1036	1033	...	...
	Paignton **110** ....a.	0952	0951	|	|	...	...	...	...	...	...	...	...	|	|	...	...	...	...	...	...	|	|	...	...
	Plymouth **110** ....a.	...	...	1047	1047	...	...	...	...	...	...	...	...	1148	1148	...	...	...	...	...	...	1247	1249	...	...

	⑥	Ⓐ	⑥	Ⓐ	Ⓐ	⑥	⚒	Ⓐ	⑥	⑥	Ⓐ	⑥	Ⓐ	⑥	Ⓐ	⚒	⑥P	ⒶP	⚒	⑥	Ⓐ	ⒶG	⑥G	Ⓐ	⑥	⑥
Edinburgh Waverley ..... **180 214** d.	...	...	...	...	...	...	...	...	...	0606	0606	...	...	...	...	...	0704	0704	...	...	...	0807	0808	...	...	...
Berwick upon Tweed .... **214** d.	...	...	...	...	...	...	...	...	...	0647	0648	...	...	...	...	...	0749	0750	...	...	...	0848	0850	...	...	...
Alnmouth .... **214** d.	...	...	...	...	...	...	...	...	...	0708	0708	...	...	...	...	...	0809	0810	...	...	...	|	0910	...	...	...
Newcastle .... **180 214** a.	...	...	...	...	...	...	...	...	...	0734	0734	...	...	...	...	...	0839	0839	...	...	...	0937	0939	...	...	...
Newcastle .... **180 188** d.	...	...	...	...	0640	0640	...	...	...	0740	0739	0835	0835	...	...	...	0841	0841	...	...	...	0940	0941	1035	1035	...
Durham .... **180 188** d.	...	...	...	...	0653	0653	...	...	...	0753	0753	0848	0848	...	...	...	0854	0854	...	...	...	0953	0953	1048	1048	...
Darlington .... **180 188** d.	...	...	...	...	0711	0711	...	...	...	0811	0811	0906	0906	...	...	...	0912	0911	...	...	...	1010	1011	1106	1106	...
York .... **180 188** a.	...	...	...	...	0737	0739	...	...	...	0837	0837	0933	0934	...	...	...	0938	0937	...	...	...	1037	1037	1134	1134	...
York .... **180 188 191** d.	...	...	...	...	0744	0745	...	...	...	0844	0840	0935	0936	...	...	...	0944	0944	...	...	...	1043	1044	1136	1136	...
Leeds .... **188 191** a.	...	...	...	...	0808	0808	...	...	...	0907	0904	|	|	...	...	...	1008	1008	...	...	...	1108	1108	|	|	...
Leeds .... **180** d.	...	...	...	...	0811	0811	...	...	...	0911	0911	|	|	...	...	...	1011	1011	...	...	...	1111	1111	|	|	...
Wakefield Westgate .... **180** d.	...	...	...	...	0823	0823	...	...	...	0923	0923	|	|	...	...	...	1023	1023	...	...	...	1123	1123	|	|	...
Doncaster .... **180** d.	...	...	...	...	|	|	...	...	...	|	|	0958	0958	...	...	...	|	|	...	...	...	|	|	1159	1159	...
Sheffield .... **170** d.	...	...	...	...	0856	0856	...	...	...	0956	0956	1023	1026	...	...	...	1056	1056	...	...	...	1156	1156	1224	1224	...
Chesterfield .... **170** d.	...	...	...	...	0908	0908	...	...	...	1008	1008	|	|	...	...	...	1108	1108	...	...	...	1208	1208	|	|	...
Derby .... **170** a.	...	...	...	...	0926	0926	...	...	...	1026	1026	1050	1053	...	...	...	1126	1126	...	...	...	1226	1226	1251	1251	...
Derby .... **120** d.	...	...	...	...	0931	0933	...	...	...	1031	1031	1053	1055	...	...	...	1131	1131	...	...	...	1231	1231	1255	1253	...
Burton on Trent .... **120** d.	...	...	...	...	0941	0943	...	...	...	|	|	|	|	...	...	...	1141	|	...	...	...	|	|	|	|	...
Tamworth .... **120** d.	...	...	...	...	|	|	...	...	...	1049	1049	|	|	...	...	...	|	|	...	...	...	1249	1249	|	|	...
Manchester Piccadilly ...... **152** d.	0803	0803	0825	0825	|	|	0903	0925	0925	|	|	|	|	1003	1003	1025	|	|	1103	1125	1125	|	|	|	|	1203
Stockport .... **152** d.	0812	0813	0833	0833	|	|	0913	0933	0933	|	|	|	|	1013	1013	1033	|	|	1113	1133	1133	|	|	|	|	1212
Macclesfield .... **152** d.	0825	0826	0846	0846	|	|	0926	0946	0946	|	|	|	|	1027	1026	1046	|	|	1126	1146	1146	|	|	|	|	1225
Stoke on Trent .... **152** d.	0844	0844	0904	0904	|	|	0944	1004	1004	|	|	|	|	1044	1044	1104	|	|	1144	1204	1205	|	|	|	|	1244
Stafford .... **144** d.	0901	0900	0921	0921	|	|	1001	1022	1021	|	|	|	|	1101	1101	1121	|	|	1200	1221	1222	|	|	|	|	1301
Wolverhampton ...... **144 150/4** d.	0915	0915	0939**r**	0939**r**	|	|	1015	1039	1039**r**	|	|	|	|	1115	1115	1139	|	|	1215	1239**r**	1239	|	|	|	|	1315
Birmingham New St .. **144 150/4** a.	0933	0933	0956	0956	1004	1007	1033	1056	1056	1106	1106	1127	1126	1133	1133	1156	1206	1204	1233	1256	1256	1306	1306	1328	1327	1333
Birmingham New Street ..... **117** d.	0942	0942	1003	1003	1012	1012	1042	1103	1103	1112	1112	1133	1133	1142	1142	1203	1212	1212	1242	1303	1303	1312	1312	1333	1333	1342
Reading **107** ....a.	|	|	1142	1139	|	|	|	1237	1242	|	|	1311	1312	|	|	1342	|	|	|	1440	1442	|	|	1507	1508	|
Bournemouth **107** ....a.	|	|	1312	1315	|	|	|	1412	1412	|	|	...	...	|	|	1512	|	|	|	1612	1612	|	|	...	...	|
Worcestershire Parkway ...... **117** d.	1012	1013	...	...	|	|	1112	...	...	|	|	...	...	1212	1212	...	|	|	1312	...	...	|	|	...	...	1414
Cheltenham Spa .... **117 138** d.	1029	1029	...	...	1052	1052	1129	...	...	1152	1152	...	...	1229	1235	...	1252	1252	1329	...	...	1352	1352	...	...	1430
Bristol Parkway .... **138** d.	1058	1058	...	...	1122	1125	1158	...	...	1225**r**	1223	...	...	1259	1310	...	1322	1322	1358	...	...	1423	1425**r**	...	...	1500
Bristol Temple Meads......... **138** a.	1108	1107	...	...	1131	1134	1207	...	...	1235	1232	...	...	1308	1321	...	1332	1332	1408	...	...	1432	1435	...	...	1511
Paignton **110** ....a.	1306	1307	...	...	|	|	...	...	...	|	|	...	...	...	...	...	|	|	...	...	...	|	|	...	...	...
Plymouth **110** ....a.	...	...	...	...	1347	1347	...	...	...	1448	1447	...	...	...	...	...	1547	1547	...	...	...	1648	1648	...	...	...

	Ⓐ	Ⓐ	⑥	ⒶG	⑥G	⚒	⑥	Ⓐ	Ⓐ	⑥		⑥	Ⓐ	Ⓐ	⑥	⑥	Ⓐ	ⒶA	⑥D	⑥	Ⓐ	⚒	⑥	Ⓐ	Ⓐ	⑥
Edinburgh Waverley ..... **180 214** d.	...	...	...	0907	0907	...	...	...	1007	1005	...	...	...	...	...	...	...	1108	1108	...	...	...	1207	1207	...	...
Berwick upon Tweed .... **214** d.	...	...	...	0948	0949	...	...	...	1048	1048	...	...	...	...	...	...	...	1149	1149	...	...	...	1248	1248	...	...
Alnmouth .... **214** d.	...	...	...	1009	1010	...	...	...	|	|	...	...	...	...	...	...	...	1210	1210	...	...	...	|	|	...	...
Newcastle .... **180 214** a.	...	...	...	1038	1038	...	...	...	1134	1134	...	...	...	...	...	...	...	1238	1238	...	...	...	1334	1334	...	...
Newcastle .... **180 188** d.	...	...	...	1040	1041	...	...	...	1140	1140	...	1233	1236	...	...	...	...	1242	1242	...	...	...	1340	1340	1435	1433
Durham .... **180 188** d.	...	...	...	1052	1054	...	...	...	1153	1153	...	1248	1249	...	...	...	...	1254	1255	...	...	...	1353	1353	1448	1446
Darlington .... **180 188** d.	...	...	...	1111	1112	...	...	...	1211	1211	...	1306	1307	...	...	...	...	1312	1312	...	...	...	1411	1411	1506	1506
York .... **180 188** a.	...	...	...	1137	1138	...	...	...	1237	1237	...	1335	1334	...	...	...	...	1338	1340	...	...	...	1441	1437	1535	1536
York .... **180 188 191** d.	...	...	...	1144	1144	...	...	...	1243	1244	...	1336	1336	...	...	...	...	1344	1344	...	...	...	1444	1443	1537	1538
Leeds .... **188 191** a.	...	...	...	1207	1207	...	...	...	1306	1307	...	|	|	...	...	...	...	1407	1407	...	...	...	1507	1507	|	|
Leeds .... **180** d.	...	...	...	1211	1211	...	...	...	1311	1311	...	|	|	...	...	...	...	1411	1411	...	...	...	1511	1511	|	|
Wakefield Westgate .... **180** d.	...	...	...	1223	1223	...	...	...	1323	1323	...	|	|	...	...	...	...	1423	1423	...	...	...	1523	1523	|	|
Doncaster .... **180** d.	...	...	...	|	|	...	...	...	|	|	...	1359	1359	...	...	...	...	|	|	...	...	...	|	|	1559	1600
Sheffield .... **170** d.	...	...	...	1256	1256	...	...	...	1356	1356	...	1424	1424	...	...	...	...	1456	1456	...	...	...	1556	1556	1627	1624
Chesterfield .... **170** d.	...	...	...	1308	1308	...	...	...	1408	1408	...	|	|	...	...	...	...	1508	1508	...	...	...	1608	1608	|	|
Derby .... **170** a.	...	...	...	1326	1326	...	...	...	1426	1426	...	1451	1452	...	...	...	...	1526	1526	...	...	...	1626	1626	1651	1651
Derby .... **120** d.	...	...	...	1331	1331	...	...	...	1431	1431	...	1453	1453	...	...	...	...	1530	1531	...	...	...	1631	1631	1654	1653
Burton on Trent .... **120** d.	...	...	...	1341	1341	...	...	...	|	|	...	|	|	...	...	...	...	1540	1541	...	...	...	|	|	|	|
Tamworth .... **120** d.	...	...	...	|	|	...	...	...	1449	1449	...	|	|	...	...	...	...	|	|	...	...	...	1649	1649	|	|
Manchester Piccadilly ...... **152** d.	1203	1225	1225	|	|	1303	1325	1325	|	|	...	|	|	1403	1403	1425	1425	|	|	1503	1503	1525	|	|	|	|
Stockport .... **152** d.	1213	1233	1233	|	|	1313	1333	1333	|	|	...	|	|	1413	1412	1433	1433	|	|	1511	1513	1533	|	|	|	|
Macclesfield .... **152** d.	1226	1246	1246	|	|	1326	1346	1346	|	|	...	|	|	1426	1425	1446	1446	|	|	1526	1526	1546	|	|	|	|
Stoke on Trent .... **152** d.	1244	1304	1304	|	|	1344	1404	1404	|	|	...	|	|	1444	1444	1504	1504	|	|	1544	1544	1604	|	|	|	|
Stafford .... **144** d.	1300	1321	1321	|	|	1400	1421	1421	|	|	...	|	|	1500	1501	1521	1522	|	|	1601	1600	1621	|	|	|	|
Wolverhampton ...... **144 150/4** d.	1315	1339**r**	1338	|	|	1415	1439**r**	1439**r**	|	|	...	|	|	1515	1515	1539**r**	1539	|	|	1615	1615	1638	|	|	|	|
Birmingham New St .. **144 150/4** a.	1333	1356	1356	1404	1404	1433	1456	1456	1506	1505	...	1527	1528	1533	1533	1556	1556	1604	1604	1633	1633	1656	1706	1706	1727	1727
Birmingham New Street ..... **117** d.	1342	1403	1403	1412	1412	1442	1503	1503	1512	1512	...	1533	1533	1542	1542	1603	1603	1612	1612	1642	1642	1703	1712	1712	1734	1733
Reading **107** ....a.	|	1542	1540	|	|	|	1641	1640	|	|	...	1707	1714	|	|	1741	1740	|	|	|	|	1841	|	|	1906	1909
Bournemouth **107** ....a.	|	1721	1715	|	|	|	1812	1817	|	|	...	...	...	|	|	1912	1914	|	|	|	|	2015	|	|	...	...
Worcestershire Parkway ...... **117** d.	1413	...	...	|	|	1512	...	...	|	|	...	...	...	1615	1612	...	...	|	|	1715	1713	...	|	|	...	...
Cheltenham Spa .... **117 138** d.	1430	...	...	1452	1452	1529	...	...	1552	1552	...	...	...	1631	1629	...	...	1652	1652	1731	1731	...	1752	1752	...	...
Bristol Parkway .... **138** d.	1502	...	...	1521	1525**r**	1558	...	...	1622	1622	...	...	...	1700	1658	...	...	1722	1725**r**	1800	1800	...	1825**r**	1823	...	...
Bristol Temple Meads......... **138** a.	1513	...	...	1534	1536	1609	...	...	1631	1632	...	...	...	1709	1707	...	...	1731	1735	1809	1809	...	1834	1833	...	...
Paignton **110** ....a.	...	...	...	|	|	...	...	...	|	|	...	...	...	1853	1853	...	...	|	|	...	...	...	|	|	...	...
Plymouth **110** ....a.	...	...	...	1747	1747	...	...	...	1847	1847	...	...	...	...	...	...	...	1947	1947	...	...	...	2047	2049	...	...

FOR NOTES SEE TOP OF PAGE 101 ▶ ▶ ▶

119 THE NORTH EAST and MANCHESTER - BIRMINGHAM - BRISTOL

Most services convey 🍷 XC

	Ⓐ	⑥	⚒	⑥	ⒶC	⚒	⑥	Ⓐ	⑥	Ⓐ	⑥	Ⓐ	Ⓐ	⑥	Ⓐ	⑥	Ⓐ	⑥	⚒	⚒S	⑥c	Ⓐc	Ⓐ	Ⓐ	⑥
Edinburgh Waverley 180 214 d.	...	...	...	1308	1307	...	...	...	1404	1404	...	...	...	...	...	...	1507	1505	...	...	1607	1607	...	...	...
Berwick upon Tweed 214 d.	...	...	...	1350	1348	...	...	...	1446	1446	...	...	...	...	...	...	1552	1550	...	...	1648	1648	...	...	...
Alnmouth 214 d.	...	...	...	1410	1409	...	...	...	|	1506	...	...	...	...	...	...	|	1610	...	...	|	|	...	...	...
Newcastle 180 214 a.	...	...	...	1436	1435	...	...	...	1533	1538	...	...	...	...	...	...	1635	1639	...	...	1735	1734	...	...	...
Newcastle 180 188 d.	...	...	...	1441	1440	...	...	...	1540	1540	...	...	...	...	1633	1633	1640	1641	...	...	1740	1740	...	...	...
Durham 180 188 d.	...	...	...	1455	1453	...	...	...	1553	1553	...	...	...	...	1646	1646	1653	1653	...	...	1753	1753	...	...	...
Darlington 180 188 d.	...	...	...	1512	1511	...	...	...	1611	1611	...	...	...	...	1705	1704	1711	1711	...	...	1811	1811	...	...	...
York 180 188 a.	...	...	...	1539	1539	...	...	...	1637	1639	...	...	...	...	1734	1736	1737	1739	...	...	1839	1837	...	...	...
York 180 188 191 d.	...	...	...	1544	1542	...	...	...	1642	1644	...	...	...	...	1736	1738	1744	1743	...	...	1844	1844	...	...	...
Leeds 188 191 a.	...	...	...	1608	1606	...	...	...	1705	1707	...	...	...	...	|	|	1808	1807	...	...	1907	1907	...	...	...
Leeds 180 d.	...	...	...	1611	1611	...	...	...	1711	1711	...	...	...	...	|	|	1811	1811	...	...	1911	1911	...	...	...
Wakefield Westgate 180 d.	...	...	...	1623	1623	...	...	...	1723	1723	...	...	...	...	|	|	1823	1823	...	...	1923	1923	...	...	...
Doncaster 180 d.	...	...	...	|	|	...	...	...	|	|	...	...	...	...	1758	1800	|	|	...	...	|	|	...	...	...
Sheffield 170 d.	...	...	...	1656	1656	...	...	...	1756	1756	...	...	...	...	1824	1824	1856	1856	...	...	1956	1956	...	...	...
Chesterfield 170 d.	...	...	...	1708	1708	...	...	...	1808	1808	...	...	...	...	|	|	1908	1908	...	...	2008	2008	...	...	...
Derby 170 a.	...	...	...	1726	1726	...	...	...	1826	1826	...	...	...	...	1852	1851	1926	1926	...	...	2027	2026	...	...	...
Derby 120 d.	...	...	...	1731	1731	...	...	...	1831	1831	...	...	...	...	1853	1853	1931	1931	...	...	2031	2031	...	...	...
Burton on Trent 120 d.	...	...	...	1741	1741	...	...	...	|	|	...	...	...	...	|	|	1942	1941	...	...	|	|	...	...	...
Tamworth 120 d.	...	...	...	|	|	...	...	...	1849	1849	...	...	...	...	|	|	|	|	...	...	2049	2049	...	...	...
Manchester Piccadilly 152 d.	1603	1603	1625	|	|	1703	1725	1725	|	|	1803	1803	1825	1825	|	|	|	|	1903	1925	|	|	2003	2025	2025
Stockport 152 d.	1613	1613	1633	|	|	1713	1733	1733	|	|	1811	1813	1833	1833	|	|	|	|	1913	1933	|	|	2014	2033	2033
Macclesfield 152 d.	1626	1626	1646	|	|	1726	1746	|	|	|	1824	1826	1846	1846	|	|	|	|	1926	1946	|	|	2027	2046	2046
Stoke on Trent 152 d.	1644	1644	1704	|	|	1744	1804	|	|	|	1844	1844	1904	1904	|	|	|	|	1944	2004	|	|	2044	2104	2104
Stafford 144 d.	1700	1701	1721	|	|	1800	1821	1821	|	|	1901	1900	1922	1921	|	|	|	|	2001	2021	|	|	2101	2121	2123
Wolverhampton 144 150/4 d.	1715	1715	1739r	|	|	1815	1839r	1839r	|	|	1915	1915	1939	1939r	|	|	|	|	2015	2039r	|	|	2115	2139r	2141r
Birmingham New St 144 150/4 a.	1733	1733	1756	1804	1807	1833	1856	1856	1905	1907	1933	1933	1956	1956	1930	1926	2007	2005	2037d	2056	2106	2107	2131	2156	2200
Birmingham New Street 117 d.	1742	1742	1803	1812	1812	1842	1903	1903	1912	1912	...	...	2003	2003	...	...	2012	2012	...	2103	2112	2112	...	2203	...
Reading 107 a.	|	|	1941	|	|	|	2039	2043	|	|	...	...	2139	2140	...	...	|	|	...	2239	|	|	...	2338	...
Bournemouth 107 a.	|	|	2116a	|	|	|	2215	2215	|	|	...	...	2316	2319	...	...	|	|	...	...	|	|	...	...	...
Worcestershire Parkway 117 d.	1813	1814	...	|	|	1912	...	...	|	|	...	...	...	...	...	...	|	|	...	...	|	|	...	...	...
Cheltenham Spa 117 138 d.	1831	1831	...	1852	1852	1929	...	...	1952	1953	...	...	...	...	...	...	2052	2052	...	...	2152	2152	...	...	...
Bristol Parkway 138 d.	1904	1900	...	1925r	1936	1958	...	...	2021	2022	...	...	...	...	...	...	2127f	2125r	...	...	2231	2234	...	...	...
Bristol Temple Meads 138 a.	1913	1909	...	1936	1945	2008	...	...	2030	2032	...	...	...	...	...	...	2136	2134	...	...	2240	2243	...	...	...
Paignton 110 a.	...	...	...	|	|	...	...	...	|	|	...	...	...	...	...	...	|	|	...	...	...	...	...	...	...
Plymouth 110 a.	...	...	...	2147	2151	...	...	...	2248	2250	...	...	...	...	...	...	2343	2347	...	...	...	...	...	...	...

	Ⓐ	⑥	Ⓐ	⑥	⑥	Ⓐ	Ⓐ		⑦P	⑦m	⑦	⑦	⑦	⑦	⑦		⑦	⑦	⑦	⑦	⑦	⑦	⑦	⑦P	⑦
Edinburgh Waverley 180 214 d.	1707	1709	...	...	1807	1807	2007		...	...	...	...	...	...	...	...	...	...	...	...	0908	...	...	1008	...
Berwick upon Tweed 214 d.	1748	1750	...	...	1852	1852	2051	⑦	...	...	...	...	...	...	...	...	...	...	...	...	0950	...	...	1050	...
Alnmouth 214 d.	1809	1810	...	...	|	|	2112		...	...	...	...	...	...	...	...	...	...	...	...	|	...	...	|	...
Newcastle 180 214 a.	1838	1838	...	...	1938	1938	2139		...	...	...	...	...	...	...	...	...	...	...	...	1033	...	...	1136	...
Newcastle 180 188 d.	1840	1840	...	...	1941	1941	—		...	...	...	...	...	...	0834	...	...	0935	...	...	1040	...	...	1140	...
Durham 180 188 d.	1853	1853	...	...	1953	1953	...		...	...	...	...	...	...	0848	...	...	0948	...	...	1053	...	...	1153	...
Darlington 180 188 d.	1911	1911	...	...	2011	2011	...		...	...	...	...	...	...	1906	...	...	1006	...	...	1111	...	...	1211	...
York 180 188 a.	1938	1939	...	...	2038	2038	...		...	...	...	...	...	...	0932	...	...	1032	...	...	1137	...	...	1237	...
York 180 188 191 d.	1944	1944	...	...	2044	2040	...		...	...	...	...	...	...	0935	...	...	1035	...	...	1144	...	...	1244	...
Leeds 188 191 a.	2008	2008	...	...	2108	2103	...		...	...	...	...	...	...	0958	...	...	1059	...	...	1208	...	...	1307	...
Leeds 180 d.	2011	2011	...	...	2111	2111	...		...	...	0811	...	0900	...	1000	...	...	1100	...	...	1211	...	...	1311	...
Wakefield Westgate 180 d.	2023	2023	...	...	2123	2123	...		...	...	0824	...	0912	...	1012	...	...	1112	...	...	1223	...	...	1323	...
Doncaster 180 d.	|	|	...	...	|	|	...		...	...	|	...	0932	...	1032	...	...	1132	...	...	|	...	...	|	...
Sheffield 170 d.	2055	2056	...	...	2156	2202b	...		...	...	0856	...	0958	...	1056	...	...	1156	...	...	1256	...	...	1356	1421
Chesterfield 170 d.	2107	2108	...	...	2208	2225	...		...	...	0908	...	1010	...	1108	...	...	1208	...	...	1308	...	...	1408	|
Derby 170 a.	2125	2146	...	...	2226	2243	...		...	...	0926	...	1028	...	1127	...	...	1227	...	...	1327	...	...	1426	1448
Derby 120 d.	2131	2155	...	...	2229	2250	...		...	...	0931	...	1031	...	1131	...	...	1231	...	...	1331	...	...	1431	1453
Burton on Trent 120 d.	2141	2205	...	...	2239	2300	...		...	...	0941	...	|	...	1141	...	...	|	...	...	1341	...	...	|	|
Tamworth 120 d.	2151	2216	...	...	2249	2310	Ⓐ		...	...	|	...	1053r	...	|	...	...	1249	...	...	|	...	...	1449	|
Manchester Piccadilly 152 d.	|	|	2125	2125	|	|	2203		...	0826	|	0927	|	1026	|	...	1124	|	...	1225	|	1303	1325	|	|
Stockport 152 d.	|	|	2133	2133	|	|	2213		...	0836	|	0937	|	1036	|	...	1134	|	...	1233	|	1313	1333	|	|
Macclesfield 152 d.	|	|	2146	2146	|	|	2226		...	|	|	0950	|	1049	|	...	1147	|	...	1246	|	1326	1346	|	|
Stoke on Trent 152 d.	|	|	2204	2204	|	|	2244		...	|	|	1009	|	1106	|	...	1205	|	...	1304	|	1344	1404	|	|
Stafford 144 d.	|	|	2222	2221	|	|	2300		...	0925	|	1026	|	1124	|	...	1223	|	...	1321	|	1400	1421	|	|
Wolverhampton 144 150/4 d.	|	|	2238	2239	|	|	2316		...	0940	|	1040	|	1139	|	...	1239	|	...	1339r	|	1415	1439r	|	|
Birmingham New St 144 150/4 a.	2208	2232	2254	2257	2308	2328	2337		...	0956	1019	1056	1118	1156	1204	...	1256	1305	...	1356	1404	1433	1456	1506	1525
Birmingham New Street 117 d.	2212	...	...	...	...	...	...		0930	1003	1030	1103	1130	1203	1212	...	1303	1312	1342	1403	1412	1440	1503	1512	1533
Reading 107 a.	|	...	...	...	...	...	...		|	1139	|	1240	|	1339	|	...	1442	|	|	1539	|	|	1640	|	1701
Bournemouth 107 a.	|	...	...	...	...	...	...		|	1327	|	1427	|	1525	|	...	1625	|	|	1725	|	|	1827	|	...
Worcestershire Parkway 117 d.	|	...	...	...	...	...	...		|	...	|	...	|	...	|	...	...	|	|	...	|	|	...	|	...
Cheltenham Spa 117 138 d.	2252	...	...	...	...	...	...		1010	...	1110	...	1210	...	1252	...	...	1352	1429	...	1452	1526r	...	1552	...
Bristol Parkway 138 d.	2321	...	...	...	...	...	...		1040	...	1141	...	1239	...	1325r	...	...	1422	1458	...	1525	1555	...	1625r	...
Bristol Temple Meads 138 a.	2330	...	...	...	...	...	...		1049	...	1150	...	1248	...	1335	...	...	1432	1507	...	1535	1604	...	1635	...
Paignton 110 a.	...	...	...	...	...	...	...		|	...	|	...	|	...	|	...	...	|	...	...	|	1800	...	|	...
Plymouth 110 a.	...	...	...	...	...	...	...		1251	...	1354	...	1448	...	1547	...	...	1647	...	...	1748	...	...	1849	...

	⑦	⑦	⑦	⑦	⑦	⑦	⑦G	⑦	⑦	⑦	⑦	⑦	⑦D	⑦	⑦	⑦S	⑦	⑦	⑦c	⑦	⑦	⑦	⑦	⑦	⑦
Edinburgh Waverley 180 214 d.	...	...	1105	...	...	...	1207	...	...	1308	...	...	1408	...	...	...	1508	...	1608	...	...	1708	...	1805	2025
Berwick upon Tweed 214 d.	...	...	1150r	...	...	...	1252	...	...	1350	...	...	1449	...	...	...	1550	...	1650	...	...	1750	...	1850	2106
Alnmouth 214 d.	...	...	1210	...	...	...	|	...	...	1410	...	...	|	...	...	...	1610	...	|	...	...	1810	...	|	|
Newcastle 180 214 a.	...	...	1236	...	...	...	1338	...	...	1436	...	...	1535	...	...	...	1636	...	1736	...	...	1837	...	1936	2149
Newcastle 180 188 d.	...	...	1240	...	...	...	1340	...	...	1441	...	...	1540	1636	...	...	1640	...	1740	...	1824	1839	...	1939	...
Durham 180 188 d.	...	...	1252	...	...	...	1353	...	...	1454	...	...	1553	1648	...	...	1653	...	1753	...	1837	1851	...	1952	...
Darlington 180 188 d.	...	...	1310	...	...	...	1411	...	...	1512	...	...	1611	1706	...	...	1711	...	1811	...	1856	1909	...	2010	...
York 180 188 a.	...	...	1337	...	...	...	1439	...	...	1539	...	...	1639	1732	...	...	1738	...	1837	...	1923	1937	...	2036	...
York 180 188 191 d.	...	...	1340	1435	...	...	1444	...	...	1544	...	...	1645	1737	...	...	1742	...	1842	...	1925	1942	...	2043	...
Leeds 188 191 a.	...	...	1405	|	...	...	1507	...	...	1608	...	...	1709	|	...	...	1806	...	1907	...	|	2007	...	2106	...
Leeds 180 d.	...	...	1411	|	...	...	1511	...	...	1611	...	...	1711	|	...	...	1811	...	1911	...	|	2011	...	2110	...
Wakefield Westgate 180 d.	...	...	1423	|	...	...	1523	...	...	1623	...	...	1723	|	...	...	1823	...	1923	...	|	2023	...	2122	...
Doncaster 180 d.	...	...	|	1457	...	...	|	...	...	|	...	...	|	1759	...	...	|	...	|	...	1951	|	...	|	...
Sheffield 170 d.	...	...	1456	1521	...	...	1556	...	...	1656	...	...	1756	1824	...	...	1856	...	1957	...	2020r	2056	...	2156	...
Chesterfield 170 d.	...	...	1508	1550	...	...	1608	...	...	1708	...	...	1808	|	...	...	1908	...	2009	...	|	2108	...	2208	...
Derby 170 a.	...	...	1526	1553	...	...	1626	...	...	1726	...	...	1826	1851	...	...	1926	...	2027	...	2047	2126	...	2226	...
Derby 120 d.	...	...	1531	|	...	...	1631	...	...	1731	...	...	1828	1853	...	...	1931	...	2031	...	2049	2131	...	2231	...
Burton on Trent 120 d.	...	...	1541	|	...	...	|	...	...	1741	...	...	|	|	...	...	1941	...	|	...	|	2141	...	2241	...
Tamworth 120 d.	...	...	|	|	...	...	1649	...	...	|	...	...	1846	|	...	...	|	...	2049	...	|	2151	...	2251	...
Manchester Piccadilly 152 d.	1403	1425	|	|	1503	1525	|	1603	1625	|	1703	1725	|	|	1803	1825	|	1925	|	2108	|	|	2204	|	...
Stockport 152 d.	1413	1433	|	|	1513	1533	|	1613	1633	|	1713	1733	|	|	1813	1833	|	1933	|	2118	|	|	2212	|	...
Macclesfield 152 d.	1426	1446	|	|	1526	1546	|	1626	1646	|	1726	1746	|	|	1826	1846	|	1946	|	2131	|	|	2225	|	...
Stoke on Trent 152 d.	1444	1504	|	|	1544	1604	|	1644	1704	|	1744	1804	|	|	1844	1904	|	2004	|	2154	|	|	2246	|	...
Stafford 144 d.	1500	1521	|	|	1600	1621	|	1700	1721	|	1800	1821	|	|	1900	1921	|	2021	|	2210	|	|	2303	|	...
Wolverhampton 144 150/4 d.	1515	1539r	|	|	1615	1639r	|	1715	1739r	|	1815	1839r	|	|	1915	1939r	|	2039r	|	2228r	|	|	2318	|	...
Birmingham New St 144 150/4 a.	1533	1556	1604	1625	1633	1656	1706	1733	1756	1804	1832	1856	1903	1924	1933	1956	2004	2056	2106	2249	2124	2208	2334	2309	...
Birmingham New Street 117 d.	1540	1603	1612	1630	1640	1703	1712	1740	1803	1812	1840	1903	1912	...	...	2003	2012	2103	2112	...	...	2212	...	...	...
Reading 107 a.	|	1739	|	1812	|	1840	|	|	1939	|	|	2040	|	...	...	2139	|	2239	|	...	...	|	...	...	...
Bournemouth 107 a.	|	1927	|	...	|	2027	|	|	2127	|	|	2227	|	...	...	...	|	...	|	...	...	|	...	...	...
Worcestershire Parkway 117 d.	|	...	|	...	|	...	|	|	...	|	|	...	|	...	...	...	|	...	|	...	...	|	...	...	...
Cheltenham Spa 117 138 d.	1629	...	1652	...	1726r	...	1752	1829	...	1852	1926r	...	1954	...	...	...	2052	...	2152	...	...	2252	...	...	...
Bristol Parkway 138 d.	1658	...	1725r	...	1755	...	1825	1859	...	1925	1956	...	2024	...	...	...	2125r	...	2231	...	...	2321	...	...	...
Bristol Temple Meads 138 a.	1707	...	1735	...	1806	...	1835	1908	...	1935	2005	...	2034	...	...	...	2135	...	2240	...	...	2330	...	...	...
Paignton 110 a.	...	...	|	...	...	...	|	...	...	|	...	...	|	...	...	...	|	...	...	...	...	...	...	...	...
Plymouth 110 a.	...	...	1947	...	...	...	2047	...	...	2147	...	...	2250	...	...	...	2344	...	...	...	...	...	...	...	...

FOR NOTES SEE TOP OF PAGE 101 ▶ ▶ ▶

XC Most services convey 🍸 BRISTOL - BIRMINGHAM - MANCHESTER and THE NORTH EAST 119

km		⚒	⑥	⑥	Ⓐ	Ⓐ	⑥	⚒	⚒	⚒v	⚒S		⑥g	Ⓐ	Ⓐ	⑥	⚒	⑥S	ⒶS	Ⓐ	⑥	⚒	Ⓐ
	Plymouth **110** d.	...	...	...	...	...	...	...	...	...	...	...	...	...	...	...	...	...	...	0525	0527	...	...
	Paignton **110** d.	...	...	...	...	...	...	...	...	...	...	...	...	...	...	...	...	...	...	|	|	...	...
0	**Bristol** Temple Meads 138 d.	...	...	...	...	...	...	...	...	...	...	...	0615	0635	...	...	0700	...	...	0733	0733	0800	...
10	**Bristol** Parkway 138 d.	...	...	...	...	...	...	...	...	...	...	...	0624	0644	...	...	0709	...	...	0742	0742	0809	...
72	Cheltenham Spa 117 138 d.	...	...	...	...	...	...	...	...	...	...	...	0710	0714	...	...	0740	...	...	0812	0812	0840	...
102	Worcestershire Parkway 117 d.	...	...	...	...	...	...	...	...	...	...	...	|	|	...	...	|	...	...	0826	0826	|	...
	Bournemouth **107** d.	...	...	...	...	...	...	...	...	...	...	...	|	|	...	...	|	...	...	|	|	|	0630
	Reading **107** d.	...	...	...	...	...	...	...	...	...	0615	...	|	|	0645	0645	|	0715	0715	|	|	|	0815
145	**Birmingham** New Street 117 a.	...	...	...	...	...	...	...	...	...	0751	...	0755	0755	0815	0815	0819	0851	0851	0855	0855	0920	0951
	Birmingham New St 144 150/4 d.	0601	...	0603	0603	0630	0630	0701	0703	0726	0801	...	0803	0803	0827	0827	0830	0901	0901	0903	0903	0930	1001
166	Wolverhampton 144 150/4 d.	0619	...	|	|	0649	0649	0719	|	0745	0819	...	|	|	|	|	0849	0919	0919	|	|	0949	1019
190	Stafford 144 d.	0633	...	|	|	0703	0703	0733	|	0800	0833	...	|	|	|	|	0903	0933	0934	|	|	1003	1033
216	Stoke on Trent 144 152 d.	0649	...	|	|	0720	0721	0750	|	|	0849	...	|	|	|	|	0921	0949	0950	|	|	1021	1049
248	Macclesfield 152 d.	0706	...	|	|	0737	0737	0806	|	|	0906	...	|	|	|	|	0937	1006	1006	|	|	1037	1106
267	Stockport 152 d.	0720	...	|	|	0750	0751	0820	|	0851	0919	...	|	|	|	|	0951	1019	1020	|	|	1051	1119
277	**Manchester** Piccadilly 152 a.	0729	...	|	|	0759	0759	0829	|	0859	0929	...	|	|	|	|	0959	1029	1029	|	|	1059	1129
	Tamworth 120 d.	—	...	0619	0620	—	—	...	0719	...	...	...	0820	0822	|	|	...	...	...	|	|	...	...
	Burton on Trent 120 d.	...	...	0630	0630	...	...	...	0730	...	...	...	0831	0832	|	|	...	...	...	0927	0926	...	...
	Derby 120 a.	...	...	0640	0641	⑥	Ⓐ	...	0740	...	...	...	0841	0843	0858	0857	...	...	...	0937	0937	...	...
	Derby 170 d.	...	...	0645	0645	0658	0717	...	0745	...	...	...	0845	0845	0900	0900	...	...	...	0945	0945	...	...
	Chesterfield 170 d.	...	...	0703	0703	0735	0735	...	0805	...	...	...	0905	0905	|	|	...	...	...	1005	1005	...	...
	Sheffield 170 d.	...	...	0721r	0721f	0751	0751	...	0822	...	...	...	0921	0921	0932	0932r	...	...	...	1021	1021	...	...
	Doncaster 180 d.	...	...	|	|	0819r	0817	...	|	...	...	...	|	|	0956	0956	...	...	...	|	|	...	...
	Wakefield Westgate 180 d.	...	...	0747	0747	|	|	...	0849	...	...	...	0947	0947	|	|	...	...	...	1047	1047	...	...
	Leeds 180 a.	Ⓐ	...	0802	0802	|	|	...	0903	...	...	...	1001	1001	|	|	...	...	...	1102	1102	...	...
	Leeds 188 191 d.	0543	...	0808	0808	|	|	...	0908	...	...	...	1008	1008	|	|	...	...	...	1108	1108	...	...
	York 180 188 191 a.	0605	...	0830	0830	0839	0839	...	0930	...	...	...	1030	1030	1017	1017	...	...	...	1130	1130	...	...
	York 180 188 d.	0627	0632	0832	0832	0845	0845	...	0932	...	...	...	1032	1032	1019	1019	...	...	...	1132	1132	...	...
	Darlington 180 188 d.	0655	0700	0859	0900	0915	0915	...	1000	...	...	...	1100	1100	1046	1047	...	...	...	1200	1200	...	...
	Durham 180 188 d.	0714	0717	0916	0917	0933	0932	...	1017	...	...	...	1117	1118	1103	1104	...	...	...	1217	1217	...	...
	Newcastle 180 188 a.	0726	0729	0928	0929	0946	0945	...	1029	...	...	...	1129	1131	1115	1117	...	...	...	1229	1230	...	...
	Newcastle 180 214 d.	0735	0738	0935	0935	...	...	...	1035	...	...	...	1135	1135	...	...	...	...	...	1235	1234	...	...
	Alnmouth 214 a.	|	|	1000	1000	...	...	...	|	...	...	...	1159	1200	...	...	...	...	...	|	|	...	...
	Berwick upon Tweed 214 a.	0820	0823	1021	1021	...	...	...	1120	...	...	...	1221	1221	...	...	...	...	...	1320	1320	...	...
	Edinburgh Waverley 180 214 a.	0905	0912	1104	1108	...	...	...	1207	...	...	...	1305	1305	...	...	...	...	...	1409	1403	...	...

	⑥	Ⓐ	⑥	⑥	Ⓐ	⑥	Ⓐ		Ⓐ	⑥	⑥	Ⓐ	⚒	⚒	ⒶB	⑥	⚒		⚒	⑥	Ⓐ	⚒E	⑥	Ⓐ
Plymouth **110** d.	...	0620	0627	...	...	...	...	...	...	...	0725	0727	...	...	0827	0827	...	...	...	...	...	0927	...	...
Paignton **110** d.	...	|	|	...	...	...	...	...	...	...	|	|	...	...	|	|	...	...	...	...	...	|	1012	1014
Bristol Temple Meads 138 d.	...	0833	0833	...	...	0900	0900	...	...	...	0933	0933	1000	...	1033	1033	1100	...	...	...	...	1133	1200	1200
Bristol Parkway 138 d.	...	0842	0842	...	...	0909	0909	...	...	...	0942	0942	1009	...	1042	1042	1109	...	...	...	...	1142	1209	1209
Cheltenham Spa 117 138 d.	...	0912	0912	...	...	0940	0940	...	...	...	1012	1012	1040	...	1112	1112	1140	...	...	...	...	1212	1240	1240
Worcestershire Parkway 117 d.	...	0926	0926	...	...	|	|	...	...	...	1026	1026	|	...	1126	1126	|	...	...	...	...	1226	|	|
Bournemouth **107** d.	0635	|	|	...	...	|	|	...	0730	0745	|	|	|	0845	|	|	|	...	0945	...	...	|	|	|
Reading **107** d.	0815	|	|	...	...	|	|	...	0915	0915	|	|	|	1015	|	|	|	...	1114	1043	1046	|	|	|
Birmingham New Street 117 a.	0951	0954	0955	...	...	1019	1024	...	1051	1051	1055	1055	1119	1151	1155	1155	1219	...	1251	1217	1216	1255	1319	1318
Birmingham New St 144 150/4 d.	1001	1003	1003	1024	1027	1030	1030	...	1101	1101	1103	1103	1130	1201	1203	1203	1230	...	1301	1225	1224	1303	1330	1330
Wolverhampton 144 150/4 d.	1019	|	|	|	|	1049	1049	...	1119	1119	|	|	1149	1219	|	|	1249	...	1319	|	|	|	1349	1349
Stafford 144 d.	1033	|	|	|	|	1103	1103	...	1133	1133	|	|	1203	1233	|	|	1303	...	1333	|	|	|	1403	1403
Stoke on Trent 144 152 d.	1049	|	|	|	|	1121	1121	...	1149	1149	|	|	1221	1249	|	|	1321	...	1349	|	|	|	1421	1421
Macclesfield 152 d.	1106	|	|	|	|	1137	1137	...	1206	1206	|	|	1237	1306	|	|	1337	...	1406	|	|	|	1437	1437
Stockport 152 d.	1119	|	|	|	|	1151	1151	...	1219	1219	|	|	1251	1319	|	|	1351	...	1419	|	|	|	1451	1451
Manchester Piccadilly 152 a.	1129	|	|	|	|	1159	1159	...	1229	1229	|	|	1259	1329	|	|	1359	...	1429	|	|	|	1459	1459
Tamworth 120 d.	...	1019	1019	|	|	...	...	...	...	...	|	|	...	...	1219	1219	...	...	...	|	|	|	...	...
Burton on Trent 120 d.	...	|	|	|	|	...	...	...	...	...	1126	1126	...	...	1231	|	...	...	...	|	|	1326	...	...
Derby 120 a.	...	1038	1037	1056	1057	...	...	...	...	...	1136	1136	...	...	1242	1237	...	...	...	1257	1257	1338	...	...
Derby 170 d.	...	1045	1045	1100	1100	...	...	...	...	...	1145	1145	...	...	1245	1245	...	...	...	1300	1300	1345	...	...
Chesterfield 170 d.	...	1105	1105	|	|	...	...	...	...	...	1205	1204	...	...	1305	1305	...	...	...	|	|	1403	...	...
Sheffield 170 d.	...	1121	1121	1130	1132	...	...	...	...	...	1221	1221	...	...	1321	1321	...	...	...	1330	1330	1421	...	...
Doncaster 180 d.	...	|	|	1156	1155	...	...	...	...	...	|	|	...	...	|	|	...	...	...	1354	1355	|	...	...
Wakefield Westgate 180 d.	...	1147	1147	|	|	...	...	...	...	...	1247	1247	...	...	1347	1347	...	...	...	|	|	1447	...	...
Leeds 180 a.	...	1201	1201	|	|	...	...	...	...	...	1301	1301	...	...	1401	1401	...	...	...	|	|	1502	...	...
Leeds 188 191 d.	...	1208	1208	|	|	...	...	...	...	...	1308	1308	...	...	1408	1408	...	...	...	|	|	1508	...	...
York 180 188 191 a.	...	1230	1230	1217	1216	...	...	...	...	...	1330	1331	...	...	1430	1430	...	...	...	1415	1415	1530	...	...
York 180 188 d.	...	1232	1232	1225	1218	...	...	...	...	...	1332	1333	...	...	1432	1432	...	...	...	1423	1422	1532	...	...
Darlington 180 188 d.	...	1301	1301	1253	1246	...	...	...	...	...	1403	1403	...	...	1500	1503	...	...	...	1453	1453	1600	...	...
Durham 180 188 d.	...	1317	1317	1311	1303	...	...	...	...	...	1420	1420	...	...	1517	1519	...	...	...	1510	1509	1617	...	...
Newcastle 180 188 a.	...	1330	1330	1326	1316	...	...	...	...	...	1432	1432	...	...	1529	1532	...	...	...	1524	1524	1629	...	...
Newcastle 180 214 d.	...	1332	1335	...	...	...	...	...	...	...	1435	1435	...	...	1537	1534	...	...	...	...	...	1635	...	...
Alnmouth 214 a.	...	1356	1359	...	...	...	...	...	...	...	|	|	...	...	1602	1558	...	...	...	...	...	|	...	...
Berwick upon Tweed 214 a.	...	1418	1421	...	...	...	...	...	...	...	1520	1520	...	...	1623	1619	...	...	...	...	...	1720	...	...
Edinburgh Waverley 180 214 a.	...	1501	1504	...	...	...	...	...	...	...	1605	1606	...	...	1708	1704	...	...	...	...	...	1807	...	...

	⚒	⑥	Ⓐ	⑥	Ⓐ	⚒	ⒶG	⑥G		⑥	Ⓐ	⚒	⑥G	ⒶG	Ⓐ	⑥	⑥	Ⓐ	Ⓐ	⑥	⑥P	ⒶP	Ⓐ	⑥
Plymouth **110** d.	...	1027	1027	...	...	...	1127	1127	...	...	...	...	1227	1227	...	...	...	...	...	...	1328	1327	...	...
Paignton **110** d.	...	|	|	...	...	...	|	|	...	...	...	...	|	|	...	...	...	...	...	...	|	|	...	...
Bristol Temple Meads 138 d.	...	1233	1233	1300	1300	...	1333	1333	...	1400	1400	...	1433	1433	...	...	1500	1500	...	...	1533	1533	...	...
Bristol Parkway 138 d.	...	1242	1241	1309	1309	...	1342	1342	...	1409	1409	...	1442	1442	...	...	1509	1509	...	...	1542	1542	...	...
Cheltenham Spa 117 138 d.	...	1312	1312	1340	1340	...	1412	1412	...	1440	1440	...	1512	1512	...	...	1540	1540	...	...	1612	1612	...	...
Worcestershire Parkway 117 d.	...	1326	1326	|	|	...	1426	1426	...	|	|	...	1526	1526	...	...	|	|	...	...	1626	1626	...	...
Bournemouth **107** d.	1045	|	|	|	|	1145	|	|	...	|	|	1245	|	|	...	...	|	|	1345	1345	|	|	...	...
Reading **107** d.	1215	|	|	|	|	1315	|	|	...	|	|	1415	|	|	1445	1445	|	|	1514	1515	|	|	1543	1545
Birmingham New Street 117 a.	1351	1355	1355	1419	1425	1451	1455	1455	...	1519	1525	1551	1555	1555	1618	1618	1619j	1625	1651	1651	1655	1655	1718	1718
Birmingham New St 144 150/4 d.	1401	1403	1403	1430	1430	1501	1503	1503	...	1530	1530	1601	1603	1603	1630	1630	1630	1630	1701	1701	1703	1703	1728	1728
Wolverhampton 144 150/4 d.	1419	|	|	1449	1448	1519	|	|	...	1549	1548	1619	|	|	|	|	1649	1649	1719	1719	|	|	|	|
Stafford 144 d.	1433	|	|	1503	1503	1533	|	|	...	1603	1603	1633	|	|	|	|	1703	1703	1733	1733	|	|	|	|
Stoke on Trent 144 152 d.	1449	|	|	1521	1521	1549	|	|	...	1621	1621	1649	|	|	|	|	1721	1721	1749	1750	|	|	|	|
Macclesfield 152 d.	1506	|	|	1537	1537	1606	|	|	...	1637	1637	1706	|	|	|	|	1737	1737	1806	1806	|	|	|	|
Stockport 152 d.	1519	|	|	1551	1551	1619	|	|	...	1651	1651	1719	|	|	|	|	1751	1751	1819	1820	|	|	|	|
Manchester Piccadilly 152 a.	1529	|	|	1559	1559	1629	|	|	...	1659	1659	1729	|	|	|	|	1759	1759	1829	1829	|	|	|	|
Tamworth 120 d.	...	1419	1420	...	...	...	|	|	...	...	...	...	1619	1620	|	|	...	...	...	...	|	|	|	|
Burton on Trent 120 d.	...	|	|	...	...	...	1526	1526	...	...	...	...	|	|	|	1654	...	...	...	...	1726	1726	|	|
Derby 120 a.	...	1437	1438	...	...	...	1538	1538	...	...	...	...	1637	1640	1708	1708	...	...	...	...	1736	1737	1758	1758
Derby 170 d.	...	1445	1445	...	...	...	1545	1545	...	...	...	...	1645	1645	1717	1717	...	...	...	...	1745	1745	1800	1800
Chesterfield 170 d.	...	1505	1505	...	...	...	1605	1605	...	...	...	...	1705	1705	|	|	...	...	...	...	1805	1804	|	|
Sheffield 170 d.	...	1521	1521	...	...	...	1621	1621	...	...	...	...	1721	1721	1748	1748	...	...	...	...	1823r	1821	1829	1829
Doncaster 180 d.	...	|	|	...	...	...	|	|	...	...	...	...	|	|	|	|	...	...	...	...	|	|	1859	1854
Wakefield Westgate 180 d.	...	1547	1547	...	...	...	1647	1647	...	...	...	...	1747	1747	1817	1817	...	...	...	...	1850	1850	|	|
Leeds 180 a.	...	1601	1601	...	...	...	1701	1701	...	...	...	...	1801	1802	1834	1834	...	...	...	...	1904	1904	|	|
Leeds 188 191 d.	...	1608	1608	...	...	...	1708	1708	...	...	...	...	1808	1808	1836	1839	...	...	...	...	1908	1908	|	|
York 180 188 191 a.	...	1630	1630	...	...	...	1731	1730	...	...	...	...	1830	1830	1902	1901	...	...	...	...	1930	1931	1920	1915
York 180 188 d.	...	1632	1632	...	...	...	1732	1732	...	...	...	...	1832	1832	1904	1905	...	...	...	...	1935	1934	...	...
Darlington 180 188 d.	...	1700	1700	...	...	...	1800	1800	...	...	...	...	1901	1901	1931	1933	...	...	...	...	2008	2005	...	...
Durham 180 188 d.	...	1717	1717	...	...	...	1817	1817	...	...	...	...	1917	1918	1948	1950	...	...	...	...	2025	2023	...	...
Newcastle 180 188 a.	...	1730	1730	...	...	...	1830	1833	...	...	...	...	1930	1930	2000	2004	...	...	...	...	2037	2035	...	...
Newcastle 180 214 d.	...	1735	1734	...	...	...	1835	1837	...	...	...	...	1935	1935	...	...	...	...	...	...	2041	2041	...	...
Alnmouth 214 a.	...	1759	1759	...	...	...	|	|	...	...	...	...	1959	1959	...	...	...	...	...	...	|	|	...	...
Berwick upon Tweed 214 a.	...	|	|	...	...	...	1920	1920	...	...	...	...	2021	2021	...	...	...	...	...	...	2126	2126	...	...
Edinburgh Waverley 180 214 a.	...	1906	1904	...	...	...	2005	2006	...	...	...	...	2105	2104	...	...	...	...	...	...	2213	2215	...	...

FOR NOTES SEE TOP OF PAGE 101 ▶ ▶ ▶

119 BRISTOL - BIRMINGHAM - MANCHESTER and THE NORTH EAST

Most services convey 🍸 XC

	Ⓐ	⑥	⚒	Ⓐ	⑥	Ⓐ	⑥	⚒	⑥	Ⓐ	⚒	Ⓐ	⑥	⚒	⑥	Ⓐ	Ⓐ	⑥	⚒	⑥	Ⓐ	⑥	Ⓐ	⑥
Plymouth **110** d.	...	...	...	1427	1427	...	...	...	1527	1527	...	...	...	...	1627	1627	...	...	...	1727	1727	...	...	1827
Paignton **110** d.	...	1412	...	|	|	1438	...	...	|	|	...	...	...	...	|	|	...	...	...	|	|	...	...	|
Bristol Temple Meads **138** d.	1600	1600	...	1633	1633	1700	1700	...	1733	1733	1800	...	...	...	1833	1833	1855	1900	...	1930	1933	...	...	2033
Bristol Parkway **138** d.	1609	1609	...	1642	1642	1709	1709	...	1742	1742	1809	...	...	...	1842	1842	1905	1909	...	1938	1942	...	...	2042
Cheltenham Spa **117 138** d.	1640	1640	...	1712	1712	1740	1740	...	1812	1812	1840	...	...	...	1912	1912	1943	1940	...	2008	2012	...	...	2112
Worcestershire Parkway **117** d.	|	|	...	1726	1726	|	|	...	1826	1826	|	...	...	...	1926	1926	|	|	...	2023	2026	...	...	2127
Bournemouth **107** d.	|	|	1445	|	|	|	|	1545	|	|	|	...	...	1645	|	|	|	|	1745	|	|	1845	1845	|
Reading **107** d.	|	|	1615	|	|	|	|	1715	|	|	|	1745	1745	1815	|	|	|	|	1915	|	|	2015	2015	|
Birmingham New Street **117** a.	1724	1719	1751	1755	1755	1825	1819	1851	1855	1854	1918	1917	1917	1952	1955	1954	2040	2018	2051	2055	2055	2151	2151	2155
Birmingham New St **144 150/4** d.	1730	1730	1801	1803	1803	1830	1830	1901	1903	1903	...	1927	1927	2001	2003	2003	...	...	2101	2103	2103	2201	2201	2203
Wolverhampton **144 150/4** d.	1749	1749	1819	|	|	1849	1849	1919	|	|	...	|	|	2019	|	|	...	...	2119	|	|	2218	2219	|
Stafford **144** d.	1803	1803	1833	|	|	1904	1903	1933	|	|	...	|	|	2033	|	|	...	...	2133	|	|	2232	2234	|
Stoke on Trent **144 152** d.	1821	1821	1849	|	|	1921	1921	1949	|	|	...	|	|	2049	|	|	...	...	2149	|	|	2248	2250	|
Macclesfield **152** d.	1837	1837	1906	|	|	1937	1937	2006	|	|	...	|	|	2106	|	|	...	...	2206	|	|	2305	2307	|
Stockport **152** d.	1851	1851	1919	|	|	1951	1951	2019	|	|	...	|	|	2119	|	|	...	...	2219	|	|	2318	2321	|
Manchester Piccadilly **152** a.	1859	1859	1929	|	|	1959	1959	2029	|	|	...	|	|	2129	|	|	...	...	2230	|	|	2329	2331	|
Tamworth **120** d.	...	...	...	1819	1819	...	...	...	|	1919	...	|	|	...	2020	2019	...	...	...	2119	2126	...	...	2219
Burton on Trent **120** d.	...	...	...	|	|	...	...	...	1926	1930	...	|	|	...	|	|	...	...	...	2130	2137	...	...	2230
Derby **120** a.	...	...	...	1842	1839	...	...	...	1936	1942	...	1957	1957	...	2039	2037	...	...	...	2140	2147	...	...	2242
Derby **170** d.	...	...	...	1845	1845	...	...	...	1945	1945	...	2000	2000	...	2045	2045	...	...	...	2147	2154	...	...	...
Chesterfield **170** d.	...	...	...	1905	1905	...	...	...	2005	2005	...	|	|	...	2105	2105	...	...	...	2205	2212	...	...	...
Sheffield **170** d.	...	...	...	1921	1921	...	...	...	2021	2021	...	2030	2038**r**	...	2121	2121	...	...	...	2225	2226	...	...	...
Doncaster **180** d.	...	...	...	|	|	...	...	...	|	|	...	2055	2105	...	|	|	...	...	...	2255**b**	2300	...	...	...
Wakefield Westgate **180** d.	...	...	...	1947	1947	...	...	...	2047	2047	...	|	|	...	2147	2147	...	...	...	2313	2317	...	...	...
Leeds **180** a.	...	...	...	2002	2002	...	...	...	2101	2102	...	|	|	...	2203	2204	...	...	...	2327	2331	...	...	...
Leeds **188 191** d.	...	...	...	2008	2005	...	...	...	2108	2105	...	|	|	...	...	...	...	...	...	...	...	...	...	...
York **180 188 191** a.	...	...	...	2030	2027	...	...	...	2146	2135	...	2115	2126	...	...	...	...	...	...	...	...	...	...	...
York **180 188** d.	...	...	...	2032	2030	...	...	...	...	2146	...	...	2127	...	...	...	...	...	...	...	...	...	...	...
Darlington **180 188** d.	...	...	...	2100	2058	...	...	...	...	2216	...	...	2155	...	...	...	...	...	...	...	...	...	...	...
Durham **180 188** d.	...	...	...	2117	2115	...	...	...	...	2233	...	...	2212	...	...	...	...	...	...	...	...	...	...	...
Newcastle **180 188** a.	...	...	...	2130	2127	...	...	...	...	2245	...	...	2228	...	...	...	...	...	...	...	...	...	...	...
Newcastle **180 214** d.	...	...	...	2136	2136	...	...	...	...	...	...	...	...	...	...	...	...	...	...	...	...	...	...	...
Alnmouth **214** a.	...	...	...	2202	2200	...	...	...	...	...	...	...	...	...	...	...	...	...	...	...	...	...	...	...
Berwick upon Tweed **214** a.	...	...	...	|	|	...	...	...	...	...	...	...	...	...	...	...	...	...	...	...	...	...	...	...
Edinburgh Waverley **180 214** a.	...	...	...	2305	2302	...	...	...	...	...	...	...	...	...	...	...	...	...	...	...	...	...	...	...

	Ⓐ	Ⓐ	⑥	Ⓐ P		⑦	⑦	⑦	⑦	⑦	⑦	⑦ h	⑦ S	⑦	⑦	⑦	⑦ D	⑦	⑦	⑦ G	⑦	⑦	⑦	⑦
Plymouth **110** d.	1827	...	...	2008		...	...	...	...	...	...	...	...	...	...	...	0927	...	...	1027	...	...	1127	1200
Paignton **110** d.	|	...	...	|	⑦	...	...	...	...	...	...	...	...	...	...	...	|	...	...	|	1049	...	|	|
Bristol Temple Meads **138** d.	2033	...	...	2218		...	...	...	...	...	...	0915	...	1031	...	...	1131	...	...	1231	1300	...	1331	1400
Bristol Parkway **138** d.	2042	...	...	2227		...	...	...	...	...	...	0924	...	1040	...	...	1140	...	...	1240	1309	...	1340	1409
Cheltenham Spa **117 138** d.	2112	...	...	2257		...	...	...	...	...	...	1011	...	1111	...	...	1211	...	...	1311	1340	...	1411	1440
Worcestershire Parkway **117** d.	2126	...	...	|		...	...	...	...	...	...	|	...	|	...	...	|	...	...	|	|	...	|	|
Bournemouth **107** d.	|	...	...	|		...	...	...	...	...	...	|	...	|	...	0940	|	...	1040	|	|	1140	|	|
Reading **107** d.	|	2042	...	|		...	...	...	...	...	0915	|	1015	|	...	1115	|	...	1215	|	|	1315	|	|
Birmingham New Street **117** a.	2200	2221	...	2355		...	...	...	...	...	1051	1049**j**	1151	1149**j**	...	1251	1249**j**	...	1351	1349**j**	1418	1451	1449**j**	1518
Birmingham New St **144 150/4** d.	...	2230	2230	...		0901	...	0903	1001	1003	1101	1103	1201	1203	1245	1301	1303	1330	1401	1403	1430	1501	1503	1530
Wolverhampton **144 150/4** d.	...	2248	2250	...		0918	...	|	1018	|	1118	|	1219	|	|	1319	|	1349	1419	|	1449	1519	|	1549
Stafford **144** d.	...	2304	2304	...		0932	...	|	1033	|	1133	|	1233	|	|	1333	|	1403	1433	|	1503	1533	|	1603
Stoke on Trent **144 152** d.	...	2321	2321	...		0954	...	|	1052	|	1152	|	1249	|	|	1349	|	1421	1449	|	1521	1549	|	1621
Macclesfield **152** d.	...	|	2339	...		1011	...	|	1109	|	1208	|	1306	|	|	1406	|	1437	1506	|	1537	1606	|	1637
Stockport **152** d.	...	|	0001	...		1027	...	|	1124	|	1222	|	1319	|	|	1419	|	1451	1519	|	1551	1619	|	1651
Manchester Piccadilly **152** a.	...	0013	0009	...		1037	...	|	1133	|	1230	|	1329	|	|	1429	|	1500	1529	|	1600	1629	|	1700
Tamworth **120** d.	...	...	...	...		—	...	0919	...	1019	...	1119	...	1219	|	...	|	...	...	1419	...	...	|	...
Burton on Trent **120** d.	...	...	...	...		...	...	0930	...	1030	...	1130	...	|	|	...	1326	...	...	|	...	...	1526	...
Derby **120** a.	...	...	...	...		...	...	0940	...	1040	...	1140	...	1237	1315	...	1336	...	...	1437	...	...	1536	...
Derby **170** d.	...	...	...	...		...	...	0945	...	1045	...	1145	...	1245	1317	...	1345	...	...	1442	...	...	1542	...
Chesterfield **170** d.	...	...	...	...		...	...	1005	...	1105	...	1205	...	1305	|	...	1405	...	...	1500	...	...	1600	...
Sheffield **170** d.	...	...	...	...		...	0921	1021	...	1121	...	1221	...	1321	1352**t**	...	1421	...	...	1521**b**	...	...	1621**b**	...
Doncaster **180** d.	...	...	...	...		...	|	|	...	|	...	|	...	|	1415	...	|	...	...	|	...	...	|	...
Wakefield Westgate **180** d.	...	...	...	...		...	0947	1047	...	1147	...	1247	...	1347	|	...	1447	...	...	1547	...	...	1647	...
Leeds **180** a.	...	...	...	...		⑦	1002	1101	...	1202	...	1302	...	1401	|	...	1502	...	...	1602	...	...	1702	...
Leeds **188 191** d.	...	...	...	...		0917	1007	1107	...	1207	...	1307	...	1407	|	...	1507	...	...	1606	...	...	1707	...
York **180 188 191** a.	...	...	...	...		0940	1029	1129	...	1229	...	1329	...	1429	1436	...	1529	...	...	1628	...	...	1729	...
York **180 188** d.	...	...	...	...		0944	1031	1131	...	1231	...	1331	...	1431	1441	...	1531	...	...	1631	...	...	1731	...
Darlington **180 188** d.	...	...	...	...		1011	1059	1159	...	1259	...	1358	...	1459	1512	...	1559	...	...	1702	...	...	1759	...
Durham **180 188** d.	...	...	...	...		1028	1116	1216	...	1316	...	1415	...	1516	1531	...	1616	...	...	1718	...	...	1816	...
Newcastle **180 188** a.	...	...	...	...		1040	1128	1228	...	1328	...	1427	...	1528	1544	...	1628	...	...	1731	...	...	1828	...
Newcastle **180 214** d.	...	...	...	...		1042	1130	1230	...	1330	...	1430	...	1530	...	...	1630	...	...	1732	...	...	1835	...
Alnmouth **214** a.	...	...	...	...		|	1154	|	...	1354	...	|	...	1554	...	...	|	...	...	1757	...	...	|	...
Berwick upon Tweed **214** a.	...	...	...	...		1127	1216	1316	...	1416	...	1516	...	1616	...	...	1716	...	...	1818	...	...	1920	...
Edinburgh Waverley **180 214** a.	...	...	...	...		1215	1259	1359	...	1459	...	1602	...	1703	...	...	1759	...	...	1901	...	...	2007	...

	⑦	⑦	⑦	⑦	⑦	⑦	⑦ P	⑦	⑦	⑦	⑦	⑦	⑦	⑦	⑦	⑦	⑦	⑦	⑦	⑦ P	⑦	⑦	⑦	⑦
Plymouth **110** d.	...	...	1227	1300	...	...	1327	...	...	...	1427	...	1527	...	...	...	1627	...	...	1727	...	...	1827	...
Paignton **110** d.	...	...	|	|	...	...	|	...	...	...	|	...	|	...	...	...	|	...	...	|	1820	...	|	...
Bristol Temple Meads **138** d.	...	...	1431	1500	...	...	1531	...	1600	...	1631	...	1731	1800	...	...	1831	1900	...	1931	2000	...	2032	2210
Bristol Parkway **138** d.	...	...	1440	1509	...	...	1540	...	1609	...	1640	...	1740	1809	...	...	1840	1909	...	1940	2009	...	2041	2219
Cheltenham Spa **117 138** d.	...	...	1511	1540	...	...	1611	...	1639	...	1711	...	1811	1840	...	...	1911	1940	...	2011	2040	...	2111	2250
Worcestershire Parkway **117** d.	...	...	|	|	...	...	|	...	|	...	|	...	|	|	...	...	|	|	...	|	|	...	|	|
Bournemouth **107** d.	...	1240	|	|	...	1340	|	...	|	1440	|	1540	|	|	...	1640	|	|	1740	|	|	1840	|	|
Reading **107** d.	1344	1415	|	|	1444	1515	|	1544	|	1615	|	1715	|	|	1742	1815	|	|	1915	|	|	2015	|	|
Birmingham New Street **117** a.	1520	1551	1549**j**	1618	1620	1651	1650**j**	1720	1718	1751	1749**j**	1851	1849**j**	1918	1918	1951	1949**j**	2018	2051	2049**j**	2118	2151	2149**j**	2338
Birmingham New St **144 150/4** d.	1528	1601	1603	1630	1628	1701	1703	1728	1730	1801	1803	1901	1903	...	1928	2001	2003	...	2101	2103	...	2201	2203	...
Wolverhampton **144 150/4** d.	|	1619	|	1649	|	1719	|	|	1749	1819	|	1919	|	...	|	2019	|	...	2119	|	...	2219	|	...
Stafford **144** d.	|	1633	|	1703	|	1733	|	|	1803	1833	|	1933	|	...	|	2033	|	...	2133	|	...	2233	|	...
Stoke on Trent **144 152** d.	|	1649	|	1721	|	1749	|	|	1821	1849	|	1949	|	...	|	2049	|	...	2149	|	...	2249	|	...
Macclesfield **152** d.	|	1706	|	1737	|	1806	|	|	1837	1905	|	2006	|	...	|	2106	|	...	2206	|	...	2305	|	...
Stockport **152** d.	|	1719	|	1751	|	1819	|	|	1851	1919	|	2019	|	...	|	2120	|	...	2221	|	...	2320	|	...
Manchester Piccadilly **152** a.	|	1729	|	1800	|	1829	|	|	1859	1929	|	2029	|	...	|	2129	|	...	2229	|	...	2328	|	...
Tamworth **120** d.	|	...	1619	...	|	...	|	|	...	...	1819	...	|	...	|	...	2019	...	...	2119	...	...	2219	...
Burton on Trent **120** d.	|	...	|	...	|	...	1726	|	...	...	|	...	1925	...	|	...	|	...	...	2130	...	...	|	...
Derby **120** a.	1558	...	1637	...	1658	...	1736	1800	...	...	1837	...	1936	...	1958	...	2037	...	...	2140	...	...	2237	...
Derby **170** d.	1600	...	1641	...	1700	...	1745	1802	...	...	1845	...	1945	...	2000	...	2045	...	...	2145	...	...	2245	...
Chesterfield **170** d.	|	...	1659	...	|	...	1805	|	...	...	1905	...	2005	...	|	...	2105	...	...	2205	...	...	2305	...
Sheffield **170** d.	1629	...	1721	...	1729	...	1821	1836**b**	...	...	1921	...	2023	...	2030	...	2121	...	...	2221	...	...	2321	...
Doncaster **180** d.	1702	...	|	...	1758	...	|	1900	...	...	|	...	|	...	2058	...	|	...	...	|	...	...	|	...
Wakefield Westgate **180** d.	|	...	1747	...	|	...	1847	|	...	...	1947	...	2049	...	|	...	2147	...	...	2249	...	...	|	...
Leeds **180** a.	|	...	1801	...	|	...	1902	|	...	...	2002	...	2103	...	|	...	2202	...	...	2303	...	...	0012	...
Leeds **188 191** d.	|	...	1807	...	|	...	1907	|	...	...	2007	...	...	...	|	...	...	...	...	...	...	...	...	...
York **180 188 191** a.	1725	...	1830	...	1822	...	1929	1922	...	...	2029	...	...	...	2119	...	...	...	...	...	...	...	...	...
York **180 188** d.	...	...	1831	...	1827	...	1934	1928	...	...	2031	...	...	...	2121	...	...	...	...	...	...	...	...	...
Darlington **180 188** d.	...	...	1902	...	1858	...	2003	1958	...	...	2100	...	...	...	2159	...	...	...	...	...	...	...	...	...
Durham **180 188** d.	...	...	1919	...	1914	...	2020	2015	...	...	2117	...	...	...	2216	...	...	...	...	...	...	...	...	...
Newcastle **180 188** a.	...	...	1931	...	1928	...	2032	2028	...	...	2131	...	...	...	2245	...	...	...	...	...	...	...	...	...
Newcastle **180 214** d.	...	...	1935	...	...	...	2035	...	...	...	2136	...	...	...	...	...	...	...	...	...	...	...	...	...
Alnmouth **214** a.	...	...	1959	...	...	...	|	...	...	...	2200	...	...	...	...	...	...	...	...	...	...	...	...	...
Berwick upon Tweed **214** a.	...	...	2021	...	...	...	2120	...	...	...	2221	...	...	...	...	...	...	...	...	...	...	...	...	...
Edinburgh Waverley **180 214** a.	...	...	2105	...	...	...	2203	...	...	...	2304	...	...	...	...	...	...	...	...	...	...	...	...	...

FOR NOTES SEE TOP OF NEXT PAGE ▶ ▶ ▶

XC THE NORTH EAST and MANCHESTER - BIRMINGHAM - BRISTOL 119

NOTES FOR TABLE 119 (pages 97 – 100).

A – From / to Aberdeen (Table **222**).
B – Conveys [12] Cardiff Central (Table **117**) - Edinburgh.
C – Conveys [12] Edinburgh - Cardiff Central (Table **117**). Also calls at Gloucester (a. 1900 / d. 1907).
D – From Dundee (Table **222**).
E – On ①–④ to Dundee (Table **222**); on ⑤⑥ to Aberdeen (Table **222**).
G – From / to Glasgow Central (Table **220**).
L – From Leeds (d. 0543; arrives York 0605).
N – From Nottingham (Table **120**).
P – To / from Penzance (Table **110**).
S – To / from Southampton (Table **107**).

a – Arrives 2112 on ⑥.
b – Arrives 7 minutes earlier.
c – Also calls at Gloucester (a. 2200 / d. 2205).
d – Arrives 2033 on ⑥.
f – Arrives 6 minutes earlier.
g – Also calls at Gloucester (a. 0650 / d. 0659).
h – Also calls at Gloucester (a. 0950 / d. 1002).
j – Connects with train in previous column.
m – Also calls at Crewe (d. 0542 ⑥, 0544 Ⓐ, 0905 ⑦).
q – Also calls at Wilmslow (d. 0618) and Crewe (d. 0640).
r – Arrives 5 minutes earlier.
t – Arrives 1344.
v – Also calls at Crewe (a. 0820 / d. 0826).
z – ⑥ only.

LM 2nd class BIRMINGHAM - WORCESTER - HEREFORD 122

km																										
			Ⓐ	Ⓐ	Ⓐ	Ⓐ	Ⓐ	Ⓐ		Ⓐ	Ⓐ	Ⓐ	Ⓐ	Ⓐ	Ⓐ	Ⓐ	Ⓐ	Ⓐ	Ⓐ	Ⓐ	Ⓐ		⑥	⑥	⑥	⑥
0	**Birmingham** New Street ★ d.	Ⓐ	...	...	0700	0720	0800	0850		1450	1550	1650	1720	1750	1820	1850	1950	2100	2200	2230	2300	⑥	...	...	...	0650
21	Bromsgrove d.		...	...	0721	0744	0822	0912		1512	1611	1712	1742	1812	1842	1912	2012	2122	2220	|	2320		...	...	...	0712
32	Droitwich Spa ★ d.		...	...	0732	0754	0832	0925	and	1525	1620	1725	1753	1825	1851	1925	2025	2137f	2230	2311s	2330		...	...	...	0722
40	**Worcester** Shrub Hill ★ a.		...	...	|	|	0839	|		|	1627	|	1801	|	|	|	|	|	2238	|	2337		...	...	...	|
	Worcester Shrub Hill **131 138** d.		0556	0628	|	|	0850	|	hourly	|	1631	|	*1811*	|	|	|	|	|	*2258*	|	...		0534	0556	0629	|
41	**Worcester** Foregate St **131** ★ d.		0559	0631	0742	0804	0853	0934		1534	1634	1734	*1814*	1834	1902	1934	2034	2148	*2301*	2324	...		0541	0600	0631	0734
54	Great Malvern **131 138** d.		0610	0642	0801f	0816	0905	0946	until	1546	1646	1746	*1826*	1846	1915	*1953*	2046	2202	*2313*	...	...		0552	0611	0645	0746
65	Ledbury **131** d.		0622	0654	0812	...	0917	1000		1600	1700	1800	...	1900	1926	*2009*	2100	2218t	...	...	...		...	...	0659	0800
87	**Hereford** **131** a.		0639	0714	0830	...	0934	1018		1617	1717	1819	...	1917	1943	*2025*	2117	2234	...	...	...		...	...	0716	0817

	⑥		⑥	⑥	⑥	⑥	⑥	⑥	⑥	⑥		⑦	⑦	⑦	⑦	⑦	⑦	⑦	⑦	⑦	⑦	⑦	⑦	⑦	⑦	⑦
Birmingham New Street ★ d.	0750		1650	1720	1750	1850	1950	2050	2120	2221	⑦	...	1000	1100	1200	1300	1400	1500	1600	1700	1800	1900	2000	2100	2200	2230
Bromsgrove d.	0812		1712	1742	1812	1912	2012	2112	2142	2242		...	1020	1120	1220	1320	1420	1520	1620	1720	1820	1920	2020	2120	2220	2250
Droitwich Spa ★ d.	0825	and	1725	1751	1825	1925	2025	2125	2152	2251		...	1029	1129	1229	1329	1429	1529	1629	1729	1829	1929	2029	2129	2236	2259
Worcester Shrub Hill ★ a.	|		|	|	|	|	|	|	|	|		...	1037	|	1239	|	|	1538	1638	|	1840	1938	2041	2138	2245	2307
Worcester Shrub Hill **130 138** d.	|	hourly	|	|	|	|	|	|	|	|		0900	1042	|	1247	|	|	1551	1650	|	1848	1947	*2106*	2148	2250	...
Worcester Foregate St **130** ★ d.	0834		1734	1801	1834	1934	2034	2134	2201	2301		0903	1046	1138	1250	1339	1444t	1554	1653	1739	1851	1950	*2109*	2151	2253	...
Great Malvern **130 138** d.	0846	until	1746	1814	1846	1946	2047	2146	2214	2313		0914	1057	...	1301	...	1456	1606	1704	...	1902	2001	*2125*t	2202	2304	...
Ledbury **130** d.	0900		1800	...	1900	2000	2100	...	2226	...		0926	1109	...	1313	...	1508	1625f	1716	...	1914	2015	*2138*	2214	...	...
Hereford **130** a.	0918		1819	...	1917	2021	2117	...	2243	...		0943	1126	...	1331	...	1525	1642	1733	...	1931	2032	*2154*	2231	...	...

		Ⓐ	Ⓐ	Ⓐ	Ⓐ	Ⓐ	Ⓐ	Ⓐ	Ⓐ	Ⓐ		Ⓐ	Ⓐ	Ⓐ	Ⓐ	Ⓐ	Ⓐ	Ⓐ		⑥	⑥	⑥	⑥	⑥	⑥
Hereford **130** d.	Ⓐ	...	*0523*	...	...	0709	0734	...	0836	0940	♠	1740	1840	1950	2040	2125	2200	2259	⑥	...	...	0640	0740	0840	...
Ledbury **130** d.		...	*0540*	...	...	0726	0751	...	0855	1000		1800	1900	2011	2113c	2142	2218	2315		...	...	0659	0800t	0900	...
Great Malvern **130 138** d.		0543	0612	0644	...	0737	0812r	0842	0912f	1012	and	1812	1912	2027t	2126	2153	2232	2326		...	0617	0711	0812	0912	...
Worcester Foregate St **130** ★ d.		0559t	0624	0656	0723	0749	0824	0854	0924	1024		1824	1924	2040	2138	2206	2249	2338s		...	0629	0723	0824	0924	...
Worcester Shrub Hill **130 138** a.		|	|	0658	|	0752	|	|	|	|	hourly	|	|	|	|	|	2252	2346		...	|	0725	|	|	...
Worcester Shrub Hill ★ d.		|	|	0703	|	0757	|	|	|	|		|	|	|	|	|	...	...		0605	|	0731	|	|	0955
Droitwich Spa ★ d.		0609	0633	0713	0732	0805	0833	0903	0933	1033	until	1833	1933	2049	2147	2215	...	...		0614	0638	0739	0833	0933	1003
Bromsgrove d.		0618	0642	0723	0742	|	0843	0912	0943	1043		1843	1943	2058	|	2224	...	...		0623	0648	0748	0843	0943	1012
Birmingham New Street ★ a.		0645	0708	0746	0809	0836	0909	0936	1009	1109		1909	2009	2127	2218	2250	...	...		0646	0716	0816	0909	1009	1036

	⑥		⑥	⑥	⑥	⑥	⑥		⑦	⑦	⑦	⑦	⑦	⑦	⑦	⑦	⑦	⑦	⑦	⑦	⑦	⑦	⑦	⑦	⑦
Hereford **130** d.	0940		1840	1940	2040	2140	2250	⑦	...	...	1010	...	1202	...	1356	*1428*	1531	1600	1656	1730	1803	...	1956	2100	2242
Ledbury **130** d.	1000		1900	2000	2100	2200	2306		...	...	1027	...	1218	...	1419f	*1446*	1548	1621	1719j	1748	1819	...	2015	2116	2259
Great Malvern **130 138** d.	1012	and	1912	2012	2112	2212	2317		...	*0857*	1039	*1058*	1230	...	1431	*1458*	1600	1633	1731	1801	1831	*1857*	2027	2128	2311
Worcester Foregate St **130** ★ d.	1024		1924	2024	2124	2225	2329s		0855	*0911*	1052	1155	1242	1355	1445	*1511*	1613	1645	1743	1815	1843	*1911*	2045f	2140	2323
Worcester Shrub Hill **130 138** a.	|	hourly	|	|	|	2228	2332		0857	*0914*	1054	|	1244	|	1447	*1514*	1616	1647	1745	1818	1845	*1914*	2047	|	2325
Worcester Shrub Hill ★ d.	|		|	|	|	...	...		0905	1005	1059	|	1251	|	1455	1556	...	1655	1750	...	1855	1956	2055	|	...
Droitwich Spa ★ d.	1033	until	1933	2033	2133	...	...		0913	1013	1107	1204	1259	1404	1503	1604	...	1703	1800	...	1903	2004	2103	2149	...
Bromsgrove d.	1043		1943	2043	2146	...	...		0922	1023	1116	1214	1309	1413	1512	1613	...	1713	1812	...	1913	2013	2113	2158	...
Birmingham New Street ★ a.	1109		2009	2109	2215	...	...		0945	1046	1138	1237	1336	1437	1537	1636	...	1736	1836	...	1937	2037	2137	2221	...

c – Arrives 2056.
f – Arrives 6 – 7 minutes earlier.
j – Arrives 1711.
r – Arrives 0802.
s – Stops to set down only.
t – Arrives 5 minutes earlier.

♠ – The 1540 from Hereford arrives Birmingham New Street 1717.

★ – Regular trains also operate Birmingham **Moor Street** - Birmingham **Snow Hill** - Kidderminster 🚂 - Droitwich Spa - Worcester Shrub Hill / Worcester Foregate St (2 trains per hour on ⚒, hourly on ⑦). Journey times from Birmingham Moor Street: to Kidderminster ± 40 minutes, Droitwich Spa ± 50 minutes, Worcester Shrub Hill or Foregate St ± 65 minutes. Kidderminster is the station for the **Severn Valley Railway** (🚂 Kidderminster - Bridgnorth: *26 km*). ✆ 01299 403816. www.svr.co.uk

LM 2nd class STRATFORD UPON AVON - BIRMINGHAM 123

km																								
			Ⓐ	Ⓐ	and at	Ⓐ	Ⓐ	Ⓐ	Ⓐ	Ⓐ	Ⓐ	Ⓐ	Ⓐ	Ⓐ	and at	Ⓐ	Ⓐ	Ⓐ	Ⓐ	Ⓐ	Ⓐ	Ⓐ		⑥
0	**Stratford upon Avon** d.	Ⓐ	0607	0643	the same	1008	1043	1105	1143	1208	1243	1308	1343	1406	the same	1843	1908	2001	2101	2201	2243	2330	⑥	0643
13	Henley in Arden d.		|	0659	minutes	|	1059	|	1159	|	1259	|	1359	|	minutes	1859	|	2017	2117	2217	2257	|		0659
40	**Birmingham** Moor St d.		0657	0741	past each	1057	1141	1157	1241	1257	1341	1357	1441	1457	past each	1941	1957	2057	2157	2257	2332	0007		0741
41	**Birmingham** Snow Hill a.		0659	0745	hour until	1059	1143	1159	1243	1259	1343	1359	1443	1459	hour until	1943	1959	2059	2159	2259	2335	0010		0743

	⑥	⑥	and at	⑥	⑥	⑥	⑥	⑥	⑥	⑥	⑥	⑥	⑥	⑥	⑥	⑥	⑥		⑦	⑦		⑦	⑦	⑦	⑦
Stratford upon Avon d.	0743	0806	the same	1503	1543	1608	1643	1706	1743	1806	1843	1908	1943	2043	2143	2243	2330	⑦	0926	1026	and	1626	1726	1826	1926
Henley in Arden d.	0759	|	minutes	|	1559	|	1659	|	1759	|	1859	|	1959	2059	2159	2257	|		0942	1042	hourly	1642	1742	1842	1942
Birmingham Moor St d.	0841	0857	past each	1557	1641	1657	1741	1757	1841	1857	1941	1957	2041	2140	2241	2334	0004		1016	1117	until	1717	1817	1917	2017
Birmingham Snow Hill a.	0843	0859	hour until	1559	1643	1659	1744	1759	1843	1859	1943	1959	2043	2142	2243	...	0007		1019	1120		1719	1819	1919	2019

		Ⓐ	Ⓐ	Ⓐ	Ⓐ	Ⓐ	Ⓐ	Ⓐ	Ⓐ	Ⓐ	Ⓐ	Ⓐ	Ⓐ	Ⓐ	Ⓐ	Ⓐ	and at	Ⓐ	Ⓐ	Ⓐ	Ⓐ	Ⓐ	Ⓐ	Ⓐ	Ⓐ
Birmingham Snow Hill d.	Ⓐ	0551	...	0651	0735	0751	0835	0851	0935	0951	1035	1051	1135	1151	1235	1251	the same	1551	1635	1651	1735	1751	1835	1935	2021
Birmingham Moor St d.		0555	0639	0655	0739	0755	0839	0855	0939	0955	1039	1055	1139	1155	1239	1255	minutes	1555	1639	1655	1739	1755	1839	1939	2025
Henley in Arden d.		|	0718	|	0818	|	0918	|	1018	|	1118	|	1218	|	1318	|	past each	|	1718	|	1818	|	1918	2018	2104
Stratford upon Avon a.		0646	0734	0743	0834	0846	0934	0943	1034	1046	1134	1143	1234	1246	1334	1343	hour until	1647	1734	1747	1834	1847	1934	2034	2121

	Ⓐ	Ⓐ		⑥	⑥	⑥	⑥	⑥	⑥	and at	⑥	⑥	⑥	⑥		⑥	⑥		⑦	⑦	⑦	⑦		⑦	⑦
Birmingham Snow Hill d.	2130	2221	⑥	0625	0651	0735	0751	0835	0851	the same	1751	1835	1935	2035	...	2135	2221	⑦	0836	0926	1026	1126	and	1726	1826
Birmingham Moor St d.	2134	2225		0629	0655	0739	0755	0839	0855	minutes	1755	1839	1939	2039	...	2139	2225		0839	0929	1029	1129	hourly	1729	1829
Henley in Arden d.	2214	2304		0709	|	0818	|	0918	|	past each	|	1918	2018	2118	...	2218	2304		|	1003	1103	1203	until	1803	1903
Stratford upon Avon a.	2231	2321		0726	0741	0834	0842	0934	0947	hour until	1847	1934	2034	2134	...	2234	2320		0911	1018	1121	1218		1818	1918

🚂 – **THE SHAKESPEARE EXPRESS** – [12], ✕ (1st class only) and 🍷 Birmingham Snow Hill - Stratford upon Avon and v.v. on Aug. 3, 10, 31.
Also Stratford - Birmingham lunch time excursions on Apr. 6, 26, 27, June 8, July 27, Aug. 3, 10, 17, 24, 31, Oct. 26, Nov. 8, 9.
National Rail tickets NOT valid.
From Birmingham Snow Hill 1000 and 1356 (Birmingham Moor Street 5 minutes later); from Stratford upon Avon at 1236 and 1613. Journey time: 59 – 68 minutes.
To book and confirm timings contact **Vintage Trains Ltd.** ✆ 0121 708 4960. www.vintagetrains.co.uk/the-shakespeare-express

124 LONDON - BANBURY - BIRMINGHAM and STRATFORD UPON AVON

2nd class CH

km		Ⓐ	Ⓐ	Ⓐ	Ⓐ	Ⓐ	Ⓐ	Ⓐ	Ⓐ	Ⓐ	Ⓐ	Ⓐ	Ⓐ	Ⓐ	Ⓐ	Ⓐ	Ⓐ	Ⓐ	Ⓐ	Ⓐ	Ⓐ	Ⓐ	Ⓐ	Ⓐ	Ⓐ
0	**London** Marylebone 125 ◇ d.	0005	…	…	…	…	0604	…	0631	…	0707	0735	0807	…	0835	…	0902	0936	1002	…	1036	…	1102	1136	1202
45	High Wycombe 125 ◇ d.	0037	…	…	…	…	0628	…	0657	…	0732	|	0836	…	0905	…	0928	1005	1028	…	1105	…	1128	1205	1228
88	Bicester North d.	0106	…	…	0550	…	0655	…	0725	…	0757	0824	0858	…	0934	…	0956	1027	1056	…	1131	…	1156	1227	1256
111	Banbury 107 d.	0126	…	…	0606	…	0709	…	0742	…	0811	0842	0911	…	0951	…	1011	1041	1111	…	1148	…	1211	1241	1311
143	Leamington Spa 107 d.	…	0545	0555	0625	0658	0728	0739	0801	0806	0830	0901	0930	0939	…	1003	1030	1100	1130	1139	…	1203	1230	1300	1330
146	Warwick d.	…	0549	|	0629	0703	0732	0744	0805	0811	0835	0905	0935	0944	…	1008	1035	1104	1135	1144	…	1208	1235	1304	1335
147	Warwick Parkway d.	…	0552	|	0633	0706	0736	|	0809	|	0839	0910	0939	|	…	1011	1039	1109	1139	|	…	1211	1239	1308	1339
168	**Stratford-upon-Avon** a.	…	|	0618	|	|	|	0813	|	|	|	|	|	1013	…	|	|	|	|	1213	…	|	|	|	|
169	Solihull a.	…	0613	…	0652	0725	0755	…	0825	0833	0854	0925	0954	…	…	1033	1054	1124	1154	…	…	1233	1254	1323	1354
180	**Birmingham** Moor Street a.	…	0626	…	0703	0736	0805	…	0835	0844	0905	0934	1005	…	…	1044	1105	1133	1205	…	…	1244	1305	1333	1405
181	**Birmingham** Snow Hill a.	…	0629	…	…	…	0809	…	0839	…	…	0938	…	…	…	…	…	1137	…	…	…	…	…	1337	…

	Ⓐ	Ⓐ	Ⓐ	Ⓐ	Ⓐ	Ⓐ	Ⓐ	Ⓐ	Ⓐ	Ⓐ	Ⓐ	Ⓐ	Ⓐ	Ⓐ	Ⓐ	Ⓐ	Ⓐ	Ⓐ	Ⓐ	Ⓐ	Ⓐ	Ⓐ	Ⓐ	Ⓐ	Ⓐ	Ⓐ
London Marylebone 125 ◇ d.	…	1236	…	1302	1336	1402	…	1436	…	1502	1536	1607	…	1637	…	1707	1733	1807	…	1837	1906	1936	2002	2036	…	2102
High Wycombe 125 ◇ d.	…	1305	…	1327	1405	1428	…	1505	…	1527	|	|	…	|	…	|	|	|	…	|	|	|	2031	2105	…	2129
Bicester North d.	…	1331	…	1353	1427	1456	…	1527	…	1554	1627	1657	…	1724	…	1756	1827	1857	…	1927	1953	2027	2057	2127	…	2154
Banbury 107 d.	…	1346	…	1411	1441	1511	…	1541	…	1611	1641	1711	…	1743	…	1809	1841	1911	…	1941	2011	2041	2111	2141	…	2211
Leamington Spa 107 d.	1339	…	1402	1430	1500	1530	1540	1601	1606	1630	1700	1730	1739	1802	1809	1828	1900	1930	1939	2000	2030	2100	2130	2200	2226	2230
Warwick d.	1344	…	1407	1435	1504	1535	1545	1606	1611	1635	1704	1735	1744	1806	1814	1833	1905	1935	1944	2004	2035	2104	2135	2204	2231	2235
Warwick Parkway d.	|	…	1411	1439	1509	1539	|	1609	|	1639	1709	1739	|	1810	|	1837	1909	1939	|	2009	2039	2109	2139	2208	|	2239
Stratford-upon-Avon a.	1413	…	|	|	|	|	1614	|	|	|	|	|	1813	|	|	|	|	|	2013	|	|	|	|	|	2300	|
Solihull d.	…	…	1433	1454	1524	1554	…	1624	1633	1654	1724	1754	…	1825	1835	1853	1924	1954	…	2031	2054	2124	2154	2224	…	2300
Birmingham Moor Street a.	…	…	1444	1505	1533	1605	…	1634	1644	1705	1733	1804	…	1835	1846	1904	1935	2004	…	2041	2105	2133	2205	2233	…	2310
Birmingham Snow Hill a.	…	…	1448	…	1537	…	…	1637	…	…	1737	…	…	…	…	1908	1939	2009	…	2045	…	2137	…	2237	…	2313
Stourbridge Junction ▲ a.	…	…	…	…	…	…	…	…	…	…	…	…	…	…	…	1935	…	2037	…	…	…	…	…	…	…	2349

	Ⓐ	Ⓐ	Ⓐ	Ⓐ	⑥	⑥	⑥		⑥	⑥	⑥		⑥	⑥	⑥	⑥		⑥	⑥	⑥	⑥		⑥	⑥	⑥
London Marylebone 125 ◇ d.	2202	2230	2307	2311	0005	…	…	…	…	…	0702	…	…	0802	0902	…	…	0932	1002	1102	…	…	1202	1232	1302
High Wycombe 125 ◇ d.	|	2302	|	2346	0037	…	…	…	0613	…	0728	…	…	|	0928	…	…	|	1028	1127	…	…	1228	|	1328
Bicester North d.	2256	2329	2350	b	0106	…	…	…	0647	…	0755	…	…	0850	0955	…	…	1021	1055	1154	…	…	1255	1321	1355
Banbury 107 d.	2311	2343	0003	0107	0126	0600	…	…	0705	…	0810	…	…	0907	1010	…	…	1038	1110	1208	…	…	1310	1338	1410
Leamington Spa 107 d.	2330	0002	0022	…	…	0620	0644	…	0725	0800	0830	…	0839	0926	1030	1039	…	1056	1130	1228	1239	…	1330	1356	1430
Warwick d.	2334	0006	0026	…	…	0625	0648	…	0730	0804	0835	…	0844	0930	|	1044	…	1101	|	1233	1244	…	1335	1401	1435
Warwick Parkway d.	2339	0010	0030	…	…	0629	0650	…	0734	0807	0839	…	|	0934	1039	|	…	1104	1139	1238	|	…	1339	1404	1439
Stratford-upon-Avon a.	|	|	|	…	…	|	|	…	|	|	|	…	0913	|	|	1113	…	|	|	|	1313	…	|	|	|
Solihull a.	2354	0025	0045	…	…	0645	0711	…	0755	0825	0855	…	…	0955	1055	…	…	1126	1155	1255	…	…	1355	1426	1455
Birmingham Moor Street a.	0004	0036	0055	…	…	0657	0725	…	0806	0835	0906	…	…	1006	1105	…	…	1136	1205	1306	…	…	1405	1436	1505
Birmingham Snow Hill a.	…	…	…	…	…	…	0728	…	…	0839	…	…	…	…	…	…	…	…	…	…	…	…	…	…	…

	⑥	⑥	⑥	⑥		⑥	⑥	⑥	⑥	⑥	⑥	⑥		⑥	⑥	⑥	⑥	⑥	⑥	⑥	⑥	⑥	⑥	⑥	⑦
London Marylebone 125 ◇ d.	…	1402	1502	…	…	1532	1602	1632	1702	…	1732	1802	…	1832	1902	1932	…	2002	2032	2102	2202	2242	2312	2342	0800
High Wycombe 125 ◇ d.	…	1428	1528	…	…	|	1628	|	1728	…	|	1828	…	|	1928	|	…	2026	|	2128	2228	2319	2349	0020	0825
Bicester North d.	…	1455	1555	…	…	1621	1655	1725	1755	…	1823	1855	…	1921	1955	2025	…	2055	2121	2155	2254	2350	0020	0051	0853
Banbury 107 d.	…	1510	1610	…	…	1638	1710	1740	1810	…	1840	1910	…	1938	2010	2040	…	2110	2139	2210	2308	0004	0034	0108	0910
Leamington Spa 107 d.	1439	1530	1630	1639	…	1656	1730	1800	1830	1839	1859	1929	…	1956	2030	2100	2124	2130	2157	2230	2327	…	…	…	0928
Warwick d.	1444	1535	|	1644	…	1701	|	1805	|	1844	1904	1934	…	2001	2035	2105	2129	2135	2202	|	2332	…	…	…	0933
Warwick Parkway d.	|	1539	1639	|	…	1704	1739	1809	1839	|	1908	1938	…	2004	2039	2109	|	2139	2206	2239	2336	…	…	…	0938
Stratford-upon-Avon a.	1513	|	|	1713	…	|	|	|	|	1913	|	|	…	|	|	|	2158	|	|	|	|	…	…	…	|
Solihull a.	…	1555	1655	…	…	1726	1755	1825	1855	…	1925	1953	…	2026	2055	2125	…	2155	2224	2258	2351	…	…	…	1000
Birmingham Moor Street a.	…	1605	1705	…	…	1736	1805	1835	1905	…	1935	2003	…	2036	2105	2135	…	2205	2234	2308	0001	…	…	…	1010
Birmingham Snow Hill a.	…	…	…	…	…	…	…	…	…	…	…	2007	…	…	…	2138	…	…	…	…	…	…	…	…	…
Stourbridge Junction ▲ a.	…	…	…	…	…	…	…	…	…	…	…	2035	…	…	…	2205	…	…	…	…	…	…	…	…	…

	⑦	⑦	⑦	⑦	⑦	⑦		⑦	⑦	⑦	⑦	⑦	⑦	⑦		⑦	⑦	⑦	⑦	⑦	⑦	⑦	⑦	⑦	⑦	⑦
London Marylebone 125 ◇ d.	0900	…	1000	1100	1200	…	…	1238	1300	1400	…	1500	1600	…	…	1700	1738	1800	…	1838	1900	2000	2100	2208	2240	2315
High Wycombe 125 ◇ d.	0925	…	1025	1125	1225	…	…	|	1326	1425	…	1525	1625	…	…	1725	|	1825	…	|	1925	2025	2125	2232	2315	2350
Bicester North d.	0954	…	1052	1157t	1252	…	…	1326	1357	1452	…	1557t	1652	…	…	1754	1827	1852	…	1927	1954	2055	2153	2257	2346	0021
Banbury 107 d.	1012t	…	1109	1212	1309	…	…	1339	1412	1509	…	1612	1709	…	…	1808	1841	1909	…	1941	2009	2113	2207	2310	0001	0035
Leamington Spa 107 d.	1031	1044	1127	1231	1327	1337	…	1357	1431	1527	1537	1631	1727	1737	…	1827	1900	1927	1937	2000	2028	2132	2225	2329	…	…
Warwick d.	1037	1049	1131	1237	1331	1342	…	1401	1437	1531	1542	1637	1731	1742	…	|	1905	1931	1942	2005	|	2136	2231	2333	…	…
Warwick Parkway d.	1043	|	1135	1243	1335	|	…	1405	1443	1535	|	1643	1735	|	…	1838	1909	1935	|	2009	2040	2140	2237	2337	…	…
Stratford-upon-Avon a.	|	1113	|	|	|	1406	…	|	|	|	1606	|	|	1806	…	|	|	|	2006	|	|	|	|	|	…	…
Solihull a.	1100	…	1157	1300	1357	…	…	1420	1500	1557	…	1700	1757	…	…	1855	1925	1957	…	2025	2057	2202	2254	2352	…	…
Birmingham Moor Street a.	1110	…	1207	1310	1407	…	…	1430	1510	1607	…	1710	1807	…	…	1905	1934	2007	…	2034	2107	2212	2304	0002	…	…
Birmingham Snow Hill a.	…	…	…	…	…	…	…	…	…	…	…	…	…	…	…	…	1938	…	…	2038	…	…	…	…	…	…
Stourbridge Junction ▲ a.	…	…	…	…	…	…	…	…	…	…	…	…	…	…	…	…	2002	…	…	2102	…	…	…	…	…	…

	Ⓐ	Ⓐ	Ⓐ		Ⓐ	Ⓐ	Ⓐ	Ⓐ	Ⓐ	Ⓐ	Ⓐ		Ⓐ	Ⓐ	Ⓐ	Ⓐ		Ⓐ	Ⓐ		Ⓐ	Ⓐ		Ⓐ	Ⓐ
Stourbridge Junction ▲ d.	…	…	…	…	…	…	0614	…	…	…	…	…	…	…	…	…	…	…	…	…	…	…	…	…	…
Birmingham Snow Hill d.	…	…	…	…	…	…	0641	0700	…	…	…	…	…	…	…	0911	…	…	…	…	1011	…	…	…	…
Birmingham Moor Street d.	…	0515	0545	…	0615	…	0645	0704	0715	0720	0745	…	0815	…	0845	0915	…	0920	0945	…	1015	…	…	1045	1115
Solihull d.	…	0523	0553	…	0623	…	0654	0717	0724	0729	0754	…	0825	…	0855	0923	…	0929	0955	…	1024	…	…	1054	1124
Stratford upon Avon d.	…	|	|	…	|	0631	|	|	|	|	|	…	|	0831	|	|	…	|	|	…	|	1029	…	|	|
Warwick Parkway d.	…	0538	0608	…	0638	|	0710	0735	0741	|	0811	…	0843	|	0911	0938	…	|	1013	…	1039	|	…	1111	1144
Warwick d.	…	0541	0611	…	0641	0701	0714	0738	0745	0751	0815	…	0847	0902	0915	0941	…	0950	1017	…	1043	1059	…	1115	1148
Leamington Spa 107 d.	…	0547	0617	…	0647	0706	0720	0743	0751	0757	0821	…	0854	0908	0921	0947	…	0956	1023	…	1049	1103	…	1121	1154
Banbury 107 d.	0517	0605	0636	…	0705	…	0737	…	0808	…	0841	…	0917	…	0938	1006	…	…	1040	…	1108	…	…	1139	…
Bicester North d.	0533	0618	0653	…	0718	…	0751	…	0822	…	0855	…	0930	…	0951	1023	…	…	1053	…	1123	…	…	1153	…
High Wycombe 125 ◇ d.	0600	0644	|	…	|	…	|	…	0844	…	0920	…	|	…	|	1052	…	…	|	…	1152	…	…	|	…
London Marylebone 125 ◇ a.	0634	0710	0746	…	0810	…	0842	…	0913	…	0945	…	1022	…	1045	1120	…	…	1145	…	1219	…	…	1243	…

	Ⓐ	Ⓐ	Ⓐ	Ⓐ	Ⓐ	Ⓐ		Ⓐ	Ⓐ	Ⓐ	Ⓐ	Ⓐ	Ⓐ	Ⓐ		Ⓐ	Ⓐ	Ⓐ	Ⓐ	Ⓐ	Ⓐ		Ⓐ	Ⓐ		Ⓐ
Birmingham Snow Hill d.	…	…	1211	…	…	…	…	…	…	1411	…	…	1511	…	…	…	1611	…	…	1711	…	…	…	1811	…	…
Birmingham Moor Street d.	…	1145	1215	…	1245	1315	…	…	1345	1415	…	1445	1515	…	…	1545	1615	…	1645	1715	1721	…	1745	1815	…	…
Solihull d.	…	1154	1224	…	1254	1324	…	…	1354	1424	…	1454	1524	…	…	1554	1624	…	1654	1725	1730	…	1753	1823	…	…
Stratford upon Avon d.	…	|	|	1229	|	|	…	…	|	|	1431	|	|	…	…	|	|	1631	|	|	|	…	|	|	…	1831
Warwick Parkway d.	…	1211	1239	|	1311	1344	…	…	1411	1439	|	1511	1544	…	…	1611	1639	|	1712	1741	|	…	1811	1838	…	|
Warwick d.	…	1215	1243	1258	1315	1348	…	…	1414	1443	1502	1515	1548	…	…	1614	1643	1703	1715	1745	1751	…	1814	1841	…	1903
Leamington Spa 107 d.	…	1221	1249	1302	1321	1354	…	…	1420	1449	1507	1521	1554	…	…	1620	1649	1707	1721	1751	1757	…	1820	1847	…	1907
Banbury 107 d.	1205	1241	1308	…	1339	…	…	1405	1438	1507	…	1541	…	1604	…	1639	1709	…	1739	1809	…	…	1840	1905	…	…
Bicester North d.	1223	1255	1323	…	1353	…	…	1423	1451	1523	…	1554	…	1621	…	1653	1725	…	1753	1825	…	…	1853	1924	…	…
High Wycombe 125 ◇ d.	1252	|	1352	…	|	…	…	1452	|	1552	…	1617	…	1651	…	1717	1756	…	1817	1856	…	…	1917	1956	…	…
London Marylebone 125 ◇ a.	1323	1343	1419	…	1443	…	…	1524	1543	1619	…	1648	…	1726	…	1744	1826	…	1844	1928	…	…	1943	2026	…	…

	Ⓐ	Ⓐ	Ⓐ	Ⓐ	Ⓐ	Ⓐ	Ⓐ	Ⓐ	Ⓐ	Ⓐ	⑥	⑥	⑥	⑥	⑥	⑥	⑥	⑥	⑥	⑥	⑥	⑥	⑥	⑥	⑥
Stourbridge Junction ▲ d.	1820	…	…	…	…	…	…	…	2249	…	…	…	…	…	…	…	…	…	0819	…	…	…	…	…	…
Birmingham Snow Hill d.	1851	…	2011	2111	…	…	2216	…	2322	2341	…	…	…	…	…	…	…	…	0842	…	…	…	…	…	…
Birmingham Moor Street d.	1855	1915	2017	2115	2120	…	2220	…	2326	2345	…	…	0613	0643	0714	…	0743	0813	0846	0913	…	0943	1043	…	1143
Solihull d.	1909	1924	2026	2124	2129	…	2229	…	2342	2354	…	…	0622	0653	0724	…	0753	0823	0856	0922	…	0953	1053	…	1153
Stratford upon Avon d.	|	|	|	|	|	2133	|	2314	|	|	…	…	|	|	|	0731	|	|	|	|	0931	|	|	1131	|
Warwick Parkway d.	1930	1946	2041	2140	|	|	2251	|	0001	0009	…	…	0643	0710	0741	|	0810	0840	0912	0942	|	1010	1110	|	1210
Warwick d.	1935	1950	2044	2144	2150	2203	2254	2334	0004	0013	…	…	0646	0714	0745	0803	0814	0844	0916	0946	1002	1014	1114	1203	1214
Leamington Spa 107 d.	1943	1956	2050	2150	2156	2208	2300	2339	0007	0019	…	…	0652	0721	0751	0807	0820	0850	0922	0951	1006	1021	1121	1207	1221
Banbury 107 d.	…	2015	2109	2208	…	2232	2323	2359	…	0039	0538	0623	0710	0740	0810	…	0840	0910	0940	1009	…	1040	1140	…	1240
Bicester North d.	…	2029	2126	2221	…	2250	…	…	…	…	0557	0639	0726	0754	0823	…	0854	0924	|	|	…	1054	1154	…	1254
High Wycombe 125 ◇ d.	…	2101	2158	2247	…	2318	…	…	…	…	0628	0712	|	0820	|	…	0920	|	1014	|	…	1120	1220	…	1320
London Marylebone 125 ◇ a.	…	2130	2227	2315	…	2356	…	…	…	…	0700	0747	0815	0845	0917	…	0946	1017	1045	1113	…	1145	1245	…	1345

b – Via Oxford (Table **125**).
f – On ① and ⑤ departs 1737.
t – Arrives 5–6 minutes earlier.
◇ – Additional services operate between these stations.
▲ – Only through services are shown to Stourbridge Junction.

CH 2nd class BIRMINGHAM and STRATFORD UPON AVON - BANBURY - LONDON 124

	⑥	⑥	⑥	⑥	⑥	⑥	⑥	⑥	⑥		⑥	⑥	⑥	⑥	⑥	⑥	⑥	⑥	⑥	⑥	⑥	⑥	⑥	⑦	⑦	⑦
Birmingham Snow Hill .... d.	...	...	...	...	...	...	...	...	...	...	...	...	...	...	...	...	...	...	...	...	...	2255	...		...	...
Birmingham Moor Street ...... d.	1213	1243	...	1343	1443	1513	...	1543	1643	...	...	1743	1813	1843	1913	...	1943	2013	2113	...	2221	2259	2339		...	...
Solihull.............................. d.	1222	1253	...	1353	1453	1522	...	1553	1653	...	...	1753	1822	1853	1923	...	1953	2023	2122	...	2230	2316	2356		...	...
Stratford upon Avon .... d.	|	|	1331	|	|	|	1531	|	|	...	1731	|	|	|	|	1930	|	|	|	2215	|	|	|		...	...
Warwick Parkway .... d.	1243	1310	|	1410	1510	1543	|	1610	1710	...	|	1810	1843	1910	1940	|	2010	2040	2143	|	2253	2335	0015		...	...
Warwick.............................. d.	1246	1314	1402	1414	1514	1546	1602	1614	1714	...	1803	1814	1846	1914	1944	2000	2014	2044	2146	2236	2257	2338	0018		...	...
Leamington Spa.............. **107** d.	1252	1321	1407	1421	1520	1552	1607	1621	1721	...	1807	1821	1852	1921	1950	2004	2021	2050	2152	2242	2305	2343	0024		...	...
Banbury.......................... **107** d.	1310	1340	...	1440	1540	1610	...	1640	1740	...	...	1840	1910	1940	2010	...	2041	2110	2216**t**	2302	2324	...	...		0750	0834
Bicester North....................... d.	1326	1354	...	1454	1554	1626	...	1654	1754	...	...	1854	1926	1954	2024	...	2054	2124	2235	...	...	...	...		0804	0850
High Wycombe .... **125** ◇ d.	|	1420	...	1520	1620	|	...	1720	1820	...	...	1920	|	2020	|	...	2120	2150	2306	...	...	...	...		0835	0921
London Marylebone ... **125** ◇ a.	1415	1445	...	1545	1645	1715	...	1745	1845	...	...	1945	2015	2045	2115	...	2145	2215	2355	...	...	...	...		0909	0952
	⑦	⑦	⑦	⑦	⑦	⑦	⑦		⑦	⑦	⑦	⑦	⑦	⑦	⑦	⑦		⑦	⑦	⑦	⑦	⑦	⑦	⑦	⑦	⑦
Stourbridge Junction .... ▲ d.	...	...	...	...	...	0938	...	...	1042	...	...	...	...	...	...	...	...	...	...	...	...	...	...	...	...	...
Birmingham Snow Hill .... d.	...	...	...	...	...	1008	...	...	1108	...	...	...	...	...	...	...	...	...	...	...	...	...	...	...	...	...
Birmingham Moor Street ...... d.	0828	0846	0912	...	0942	1012	1035	...	1112	1137	...	1237	1341	...	1437	1512	...	1541	...	1637	1737	...	1837	2017	...	2118
Solihull.............................. d.	0837	0855	0922	...	0952	1022	1044	...	1122	1147	...	1247	1350	...	1447	1522	...	1550	...	1647	1747	...	1847	2026	...	2127
Stratford upon Avon .... d.	|	|	|	0936	|	|	|	...	|	|	1236	|	|	1436	|	|	...	|	1636	|	|	1836	|	|	2036	|
Warwick Parkway .... d.	0852	0916	0938	|	1010	1038	1105	...	1138	1204	|	1311	1406	|	1511	1538	...	1606	|	1711	1804	|	1911	2042	|	2148
Warwick.............................. d.	0855	0919	0942	1001	1014	1042	1108	...	1142	1208	1301	1315	1409	1501	1515	1542	...	1609	1701	1715	1808	1901	1915	2045	2101	2152
Leamington Spa.............. **107** d.	0901	0924	0948	1005	1021	1048	1115	...	1148	1215	1306	1321	1416	1505	1521	1549	...	1616	1706	1721	1815	1905	1921	2051	2106	2158
Banbury.......................... **107** d.	0918	0942	1007	...	1040	1107	1135	...	1207	1235	...	1338	1436	...	1538	1609	...	1636	...	1738	1835	...	1938	2110	2127	2218
Bicester North....................... d.	|	0958	1021	...	1054	1121	1151	...	1221	1249	...	1355	1450	...	1555	1623	...	1650	...	1755	1849	...	1955	2123	...	2235
High Wycombe .... **125** ◇ d.	|	1026	|	...	1122	|	1222	...	|	1322	...	1423	1523	...	1623	|	...	1723	...	1823	1922	...	2023	|	...	2304
London Marylebone ... **125** ◇ a.	1015	1052	1110	...	1148	1210	1248	...	1310	1348	...	1447	1547	...	1647	1715	...	1747	...	1848	1947	...	2047	2211	...	2352

t – Arrives 5–6 minutes earlier. ◇ – Additional services operate between these stations. ▲ – Only through services are shown to/from Stourbridge Junction.

CH 2nd class LONDON - HIGH WYCOMBE - OXFORD and LONDON - AYLESBURY 125

km																						
		Ⓐ	②–⑤	Ⓐ	Ⓐ	Ⓐ	Ⓐ	Ⓐ	Ⓐ	Ⓐ	Ⓐ	Ⓐ	Ⓐ	Ⓐ		Ⓐ	Ⓐ	Ⓐ	Ⓐ	Ⓐ	Ⓐ	Ⓐ	Ⓐ
0	**London** Marylebone .... **124** d.		0001	...	...	0608	0647	0711	0739	0811	0839	0906	0940	1006	and at	1440	1506	1540	1615	1645	1715	1745	1815
45	High Wycombe .... **124** d.		0030	...	...	0643	0720	0745	0805	0844	0911	0939	1013	1039	the same	1513	1539	1610	1646	1710	1746	1813**b**	1847
90	Bicester Village .... d.		0057	0603	0643	0718	0752	0819	0836	0919	0941	1012	1042	1112	minutes	1542	1612	1640	1720	1740	1820	1848	1919
103	**Oxford** Parkway .... d.		0106	0615	0652	0730	0804	0831	0846	0928	0950	1021	1052	1121	past each	1552	1621	1652	1729	1749	1829	1900	1928
108	**Oxford** .... a.		0116	0621	0658	0737	0810	0837	0853	0935	0957	1028	1100	1128	hour until	1558	1629	1658	1736	1757	1836	1906	1935

	Ⓐ	Ⓐ	Ⓐ	Ⓐ	Ⓐ	Ⓐ	Ⓐ	Ⓐ	Ⓐ	Ⓐ **A**	⑥	⑥	⑥	⑥	⑥	⑥	⑥	⑥		⑥	⑥	⑥	⑥
London Marylebone .... **124** d.	1845	1910	1940	2006	2040	2106	2135	2206	2234	2311		0001	0552	0637	0707	0737	0807	0837	and at	1837	1907	1937	2007
High Wycombe .... **124** d.	1913	1942	2017	2039	2112	2140	2207	2241	2317	2346		0030	0632	0712	0751	0812	0851	0912	the same	1912	1951	2012	2051
Bicester Village .... d.	1948	2019	2048	2112	2141	2212	2240	2314	2346	0018		0057	0704	0747	0819	0847	0919	0947	minutes	1947	2019	2046	2119
Oxford Parkway .... d.	1957	2028	2100	2121	2151	2221	2251	2324	2358	0027		0106	0713	0758	0828	0857	0928	0957	past each	1958	2028	2055	2128
Oxford .... a.	2004	2035	2108	2128	2157	2228	2257	2333	0005	0033		0116	0720	0805	0835	0904	0935	1005	hour until	2005	2035	2102	2135

	⑥	⑥	⑥	⑥	⑥	⑦	⑦	⑦	⑦	⑦	⑦	⑦	⑦	⑦	⑦	⑦		⑦	⑦	⑦	⑦	⑦	⑦
London Marylebone .... **124** d.	2037	2107	2137	2207	2307		...	0742	0812	0842	0912	0942	1012	1042	1112	1142	and at	2012	2042	2112	2142	2212	2310
High Wycombe .... **124** d.	2112	2151	2212	2251	2339		...	0816	0852	0916	0952	1016	1052	1116	1152	1216	the same	2052	2116	2152	2216	2252	2340
Bicester Village .... d.	2146	2219	2246	2319	0009		0749	0850	0923	0950	1023	1049	1123	1150	1223	1250	minutes	2123	2150	2223	2250	2323	0010
Oxford Parkway .... d.	2158	2228	2255	2328	0021		0758	0903	0933	1000	1033	1101	1133	1200	1233	1303	every **2**	2132	2200	2233	2303	2333	0020
Oxford .... a.	2205	2235	2302	2337	0027		0804	0909	0939	1006	1039	1107	1139	1206	1239	1309	hours until	2139	2206	2239	2309	2339	0026

	Ⓐ	Ⓐ	Ⓐ	Ⓐ	Ⓐ	Ⓐ	Ⓐ	Ⓐ	Ⓐ	Ⓐ	Ⓐ	Ⓐ	Ⓐ	Ⓐ	Ⓐ	Ⓐ		Ⓐ	Ⓐ	Ⓐ	Ⓐ	Ⓐ	Ⓐ
Oxford .... d.		0535	0605	0638	0705	0745	0803	0820	0845	0904	0949	1019	1049	1119	1149	1219	and at	1519	1549	1619	1649	1719	1749
Oxford Parkway .... d.		0541	0612	0645	0712	0752	0810	0826	0851	0911	0955	1026	1056	1125	1155	1225	the same	1525	1555	1625	1655	1725	1755
Bicester Village .... d.		0551	0623	0658	0723	0803	0823	0837	0900	0921	1008	1036	1108	1134	1208	1234	minutes	1535	1607	1635	1707	1738	1808
High Wycombe .... **124** d.		0625	0651	0726**r**	0752	0837	0855	0908	0929	|	1040	1107	1140	1203	1240	1303	past each	1604	1634	1710	1734	1807	1834
London Marylebone .... **124** a.		0702	0734	0803	0834	0909	0934	0940	0959	1018	1117	1142	1216	1239	1317	1339	hour until	1640	1714	1740	1814	1840	1913

	Ⓐ	Ⓐ	Ⓐ	Ⓐ	Ⓐ	Ⓐ	Ⓐ	Ⓐ		Ⓐ	Ⓐ	Ⓐ	⑥	⑥	⑥	⑥	⑥	⑥	⑥	⑥	⑥	⑥	⑥	⑥
Oxford .... d.	1821	1849	1919	1951	2019	2049	2119	2149	...	2219	2244	2324		0610	0645	0712	0745	0815	0845	0914	0945	1015	1045	1115
Oxford Parkway .... d.	1828	1855	1925	1957	2025	2056	2125	2156	...	2225	2250	2330		0617	0651	0719	0751	0821	0851	0920	0951	1021	1051	1121
Bicester Village .... d.	1838	1908	1937	2008	2037	2109	2136	2209	...	2234	2301	2343		0628	0703	0730	0803	0832	0903	0931	1004	1033	1103	1132
High Wycombe .... **124** d.	1907	1934	2009	2036	2109	2136	2208	2236	...	2306	2333	0016		0657	0735	0757	0835	0858	0935	0957	1036	1059	1135	1158
London Marylebone .... **124** a.	1939	2014	2043	2113	2147	2210	2245	2310	...	2339	0016	...		0736	0810	0840	0910	0940	1010	1040	1110	1135	1210	1240

		⑥	⑥	⑥	⑥	⑦	⑦	⑦	⑦	⑦		⑦	⑦	⑦		⑦	⑦	⑦	⑦	⑦	⑦	⑦
Oxford .... d.	and at	2045	2115	2210	2327		0741	0812	0841	0911	...	0941	1011	1041	and at	1941	2011	2041	2111	2141	2211	2327
Oxford Parkway .... d.	the same	2051	2121	2217	2333		0747	0818	0848	0919	...	0949	1017	1047	the same	1948	2017	2047	2117	2148	2217	2333
Bicester Village .... d.	minutes	2103	2132	2228	2344		0757	0829	0900	0932	...	1001	1028	1100	minutes	2000	2028	2100	2128	2200	2227	2344
High Wycombe .... **124** d.	past each	2135	2158	2300	...		|	0857	0933	0959	...	1033	1057	1133	past each	2033	2057	2133	2157	2233	2255	...
London Marylebone .... **124** a.	hour until	2210	2240	2340	...		0849	0937	1007	1040	...	1107	1137	1207	hour until	2107	2137	2207	2237	2307	2335	...

LONDON - AYLESBURY (60 km, journey ± 60 minutes)

From London Marylebone: on Ⓐ at 0010**a**, 0635*, 0652*, 0727*, 0757*, 0827, 0857*, 0927, 0956*, 1027, 1057*, 1157*, 1257*, 1327, 1357*, 1427, 1457*, 1527, 1557, 1611*, 1641*, 1711, 1730*, 1741, 1759*, 1811, 1830*, 1841, 1859*, 1932, 1956*, 2023, 2044, 2057*, 2127, 2144, 2157*, 2210, 2257*, 2316, 2357*; on ⑥ at 0010, 0652, 0727*, 0752 and at the same minutes past each hour until 1552, 1627, 1657*, 1727, 1757*, 1827, 1857*, 1957*, 2057*, 2157*, 2217, 2257*, 2317, 2357; on ⑦ at 0010, 0757* and hourly until 1557*, 1627, 1657* and at the same minutes past each hour until 1957*, 2057*, 2157*, 2227, 2257*, 2327, 2345.

From Aylesbury : on Ⓐ at 0520*, 0525, 0547*, 0605, 0624*, 0636, 0709*, 0729*, 0740, 0801*, 0817*, 0846*, 0921*, 0948, 1018*, 1048, 1118*, 1218*, 1318*, 1418*, 1448, 1518*, 1548, 1552, 1618*, 1645, 1712, 1748*, 1818, 1845*, 1918*, 2018, 2118*, 2148, 2248; on ⑥ at 0508, 0545, 0618*, 0648*, 0718, 0748*, 0818, 0848*, 0918, 0948*, 1018, 1048* and hourly until 1648*, 1748, 1818*, 1834, 1918*, 1934, 2018*, 2034, 2118*, 2134, 2218*; on ⑦ at 0718*, 0730, 0818*, 0848*, 0918, 0948*, 1018*, 1033 and at the same minutes past each hour until 1518*, 1548, 1618*, 1648, 1718*, 1748, 1818*, 1848, 1948*, 2048*, 2148*, 2248*.

A – To Banbury (departs Oxford 0041). See also Table **124**.

a – ②–⑤ only.

b – ①⑤ only.

f – Arrives 5 minutes earlier.

r – On ①⑤ departs 0733.

* – Continues to/starts from Aylesbury Vale Parkway (arrives 9–11 minutes after and departs 5 minutes before Aylesbury).

126 SWINDON - WESTBURY

2nd class GW

km			Ⓐ G	Ⓐ	Ⓐ		Ⓐ	Ⓐ	Ⓐ		Ⓐ H	Ⓐ	Ⓐ	⑥ F		⑥	⑥	⑥		⑥	⑥	⑥ d	⑥ c
0	**Swindon**	132 d.	0606	0844	1105	...	1314	1515	1735	...	1844	2012	2231	0844	...	1105	1313	1514	...	1735	1944	2110	2212
27	Chippenham	132 d.	0623	0859	1121	...	1330	1531	1750	...	1900	2028	2246	0859	...	1121	1329	1530	...	1751	1959	2125	2227
37	Melksham	d.	0632	0909	1131	...	1340	1540	1800	...	1909	2039	2256	0909	...	1131	1339	1539	...	1801	2009	2135	2237
46	Trowbridge	140 d.	0642	0918	1140	...	1349	1550	1809	...	1919	2048	2305	0918	...	1140	1348	1549	...	1810	2018	2144	2246
52	**Westbury**	140 a.	0649	0925	1147	...	1357	1559	1819	...	1926	2056	2312	0925	...	1148	1355	1558	...	1818	2029	2152	2255

		⑦	⑦ b	⑦ A a	A		⑦ C	⑦ E	⑦	⑦
Swindon	132 d.	0908	1141	1132	1332	...	1544	1744	1943	2134
Chippenham	132 d.	0923	1156	1147	1347	...	1559	1759	1959	2149
Melksham	d.	0932	1206	1157	1356	...	1609	1809	2009	2159
Trowbridge	140 d.	0942	1215	1206	1405	...	1618	1818	2018	2209
Westbury	140 a.	0949	1222	1213	1412	...	1625	1825	2025	2216

		Ⓐ T	Ⓐ	Ⓐ		Ⓐ	Ⓐ	Ⓐ	Ⓐ	Ⓐ B	Ⓐ	⑥	⑥		⑥	⑥		⑥	⑥	⑥ d	⑥ A c	⑦ W	⑦		⑦ A	⑦ C		⑦ C	⑦ D	⑦
Westbury	140 d.	0705	0745	0946	...	1217	1418	1623	1837	2006	2116	0745	0952	...	1217	1419	...	1623	1835	2008	2118	0816	1041	...	1213	1415	...	1652	1849	2038
Trowbridge	140 d.	0711	0752	0952	...	1223	1424	1629	1843	2012	2122	0752	0959	...	1223	1425	...	1629	1841	2015	2124	0823	1046	...	1219	1422	...	1658	1855	2044
Melksham	d.	0721	0802	1002	...	1233	1434	1639	1853	2022	2132	0802	1009	...	1233	1435	...	1639	1851	2025	2134	0832	1056	...	1231	1431	...	1708	1906	2054
Chippenham	132 d.	0731	0812	1012	...	1243	1444	1649	1904	2032	2142	0812	1019	...	1245	1445	...	1649	1901	2036	2144	0842	1106	...	1241	1441	...	1718	1917	2106
Swindon	132 a.	0747	0834	1029	...	1259	1500	1705	1921	2050	2158	0828	1036	...	1301	1501	...	1705	1917	2054	2200	0858	1123	...	1257	1458	...	1734	1934	2123

A – To/from Weymouth (Table **139**).
B – To Cheltenham Spa (Table **130**).
C – To/from Frome (Table **139**).
D – From Castle Cary (Table **139**).
E – To Salisbury (Table **140**).
F – Until Sept. 13 conveys 2 to Weymouth.
G – From Gloucester to Southampton Central (Tables **130** and **140**).
H – From Gloucester to Salisbury (Tables **130** and **140**).
T – From Salisbury to Worcester Foregate Street (Tables **140** and **130**).
W – From Warminster (Table **140**).
a – Until Oct. 26.
b – From Nov. 2.
c – Until Sept. 13.
d – From Sept. 20.

127 WELSH LONG DISTANCE BUS SERVICES

TrawsCymru operate several long distance bus services through Wales linking a number of main towns not served by rail services. The principal routes are shown below with the number of through journeys each way each day. For full timings and fares: ✆ +44 (0) 300 200 22 33; www.trawscymru.info

Service T1: Aberystwyth - Aberaeron - Lampeter/Llanbedr - Carmarthen and v.v.: on ⚒ 16 journeys; ⑦ 6 journeys.
Service T2: Aberystwyth - Machynlleth - Dolgellau - Minfford (for Portmeirion) - Porthmadog 🚂 - Caernarfon - Bangor and v.v.: on ⚒ 6 journeys; ⑦ 5 journeys.
Service T3: Wrexham - Ruabon - Llangollen 🚂 - Corwen 🚂 - Bala 🚂 - Dolgellau - Barmouth and v.v.: on ⚒ 6 journeys; ⑦ 5 journeys.
Service T4: Newtown - Llandrindod Wells - Builth Wells - Brecon - Merthyr Tydfil * (- Cardiff *) and v.v.: on ⚒ 8 journeys; ⑦ 4 journeys.
Service T5: Aberystwyth - Aberaeron - New Quay - Cardigan and v.v.: on Ⓐ 12 journeys; ⑥ 8 journeys; ⑦ no service.
Service T5: Cardigan - Fishguard - Haverfordwest and v.v.: on ⚒ 8 journeys; ⑦ no service.
Service T6: Brecon - Ystradgynlais - Neath - Swansea and v.v.: on ⚒ 11 journeys; ⑦ 5 journeys.
Service T8: Corwen 🚂 - Ruthin - Mold - Chester and v.v.: on ⚒ 9 journeys; ⑦ No service.
Service T10: Bangor - Betws y Coed - Corwen 🚂 and v.v.: on ⚒ 5 journeys; ⑦ 5 journeys.
Service T11: Haverfordwest - St Davids - Fishguard and v.v.: on ⚒ 7 journeys; ⑦ No service.
Service T12: Machynlleth - Newtown - Welshpool - Oswestry 🚂 (- Ruabon - Wrexham) and v.v.: on ⚒ 6 journeys; ⑦ No service.
Service T14: (Cardiff) - Brecon - Hay-on-Wye - Hereford and v.v.: on ⚒ 5 journeys; ⑦ No service.
Other short workings also operate on most services.

* – Frequent local trains also operate Merthyr Tydfil - Cardiff and v.v.
🚂 – Heritage and Tourist Railways:
Llangollen Railway: Llangollen - Corwen and v.v. (16km): ✆ +44 (0) 1978 860 979; www.llangollen-railway.co.uk
Bala Lake Railway: (narrow gauge) Bala - Llanuwchllyn and v.v. (7km): ✆ +44 (0) 1678 540 666; www.bala-lake-railway.co.uk
Cambrian Heritage Railways: Oswestry - Weston Wharf and v.v. (3km): ✆ +44 (0) 1691 728131; www.cambrianrailways.com
Ffestiniog Railway and Welsh Highland Railway. See table **150b**. ✆ 01766 516024. www.festrail.co.uk

130 LONDON - CHELTENHAM

Most London trains convey 🍸 GW

km			Ⓐ	Ⓐ	Ⓐ 2	Ⓐ	Ⓐ	Ⓐ	Ⓐ	Ⓐ	Ⓐ	Ⓐ	Ⓐ	Ⓐ	Ⓐ	Ⓐ	Ⓐ	Ⓐ	Ⓐ 2	Ⓐ	Ⓐ	Ⓐ 2	⑥	⑥	⑥	⑥
0	**London** Pad	131 132 133 d.	...	0630	A D	0731	0832	0932	1032	1132	1232	1332	1432	1532	1633	1732	1834	1936	C	2034	2131	...	...	0732	0832	0932
58	Reading	131 132 133 d.	...	0656	...	0757	0858	0958	1058	1158	1258	1358	1458	1558	1658u	1758u	1859	2001u	...	2100	2156	...	...	0758	0858	0958
85	Didcot Parkway	§ 131/2 133 d.	...	0710	...	0810	0912	1011	1111	1211	1311	1411	1511	1611	1712	1811	1912	|	...	2114	2209	...	...	0811	0911	1011
124	**Swindon**	131 132 133 a.	...	0725	...	0826	0928	1027	1127	1227	1327	1428	1528	1628	1728	1827	1928	2028	...	2129	2225	...	...	0828	0928	1028
	Swindon	d.	0632	0730	0754	0830	0930	1030	1130	1230	1330	1430	1530	1630	1730	1830	1930	2031	2054	2132	2227	2342	0730	0830	0930	1030
164	Stroud	d.	0700	0759	0822	0859	0959	1058	1159	1259	1359	1459	1559	1659	1759	1859	1959	2100	2122	2200	2256	0010	0758	0858	0958	1058
183	Gloucester	a.	0716	0818	0845	0915	1016	1115	1216	1316	1415	1516	1616	1715	1815	1917	2015	2116	2141	2217	2315	0029	0814	0915	1016	1116
	Gloucester	138 d.	0725	0824	0854	0922	1022	1122	1222	1322	1422	1522	1622	1722	1822	1925	2024	2125	2156	2226	2321	0034	0820	0922	1021	1121
194	**Cheltenham** Spa	138 a.	0733	0832	0903	0930	1031	1131	1232	1331	1431	1531	1631	1731	1831	1934	2033	2133	2206	2234	2331	0043	0830	0931	1031	1131
223	**Worcester** Shrub Hill	138 a.	0758	...	0927	...	...	...	...	...	...	...	...	...	...	...	...	2206	...	...	...	...	...	...	...	...

		⑥	⑥	⑥	⑥	⑥	⑥	⑥	⑥	⑥	⑥	⑥ 2	⑥ 2	⑦	⑦	⑦ 2	⑦	⑦	⑦ 2	⑦	⑦ 2	⑦ 2	⑦	⑦ 2	⑦ 2	⑦	⑦ 2
London Pad	131 132 133 d.	1030	1132	1232	1332	1432	...	1632	1732	1828	1932	...	...	...	...	...	...	...	...	...	...	...	1733	...	...	...	...
Reading	131 132 133 d.	1057u	1158	1258	1358	1458	...	1658	1758u	1853u	1958u	...	...	...	...	...	...	...	...	...	...	...	1758	...	...	...	...
Didcot Parkway	§ 131/2 133 d.	1112	1211	1311	1411	1511	...	1711	1811	|	2011	...	...	...	...	...	...	...	...	...	...	...	1811	...	...	...	...
Swindon	131 132 133 a.	1128	1228	1328	1428	1528	...	1728	1828	|	2028	...	...	...	...	...	...	...	...	...	...	...	1828	...	...	...	...
Swindon	d.	1130	1230	1330	1430	1530	1630	1730	1830	1925u	2030	2125	2239	0921	1017	1124	1230	1318	1417	1529	1632	1730	1828	1929	2032	2130	2313
Stroud	d.	1158	1258	1358	1458	1558	1658	1758	1858	1953	2058	2153	2307	0947	1044	1151	1257	1345	1444	1556	1659	1757	1855	1956	2059	2158	2340
Gloucester	a.	1216	1316	1416	1516	1616	1716	1816	1916	2016	2116	2211	2326	1007	1100	1212	1315	1403	1504	1614	1719	1819	1913	2018	2120	2218	2359
Gloucester	d.	1221	1321	1421	1521	1621	1721	1821	1921	2021	2121	2222	...	1014	1108	1215	1321	1411	1506	1620	1721	1821	1920	2019	2121	2225	0001
Cheltenham Spa	138 a.	1231	1331	1431	1531	1631	1731	1831	1931	2031	2131	2231	...	1023	1116	1224	1331	1421	1516	1630	1728	1830	1929	2028	2129	2233	0010
Worcester Shrub Hill	138 a.	...	...	...	...	...	...	...	...	...	...	...	...	...	...	...	...	...	...	...	...	...	...	...	...	...	...

		Ⓐ 2 B	Ⓐ	Ⓐ	Ⓐ	Ⓐ	Ⓐ	Ⓐ	Ⓐ	Ⓐ	Ⓐ	Ⓐ	Ⓐ	Ⓐ	Ⓐ 2 A	Ⓐ	Ⓐ	Ⓐ	Ⓐ	Ⓐ 2	⑥	⑥	⑥	⑥ E	⑥	⑥
Worcester Shrub Hill	138 d.	...	...	...	0725	...	...	...	...	...	...	...	...	...	...	...	...	...	...	...	...	...	...	...	...	...
Cheltenham Spa	138 d.	...	0553	0647	0755	0903	1003	1103	1203	1303	1403	1503	1603	1703	...	1803	1902	2002	2102	2216	0548	0649	0757	0845	0903	1003
Gloucester	138 a.	...	0603	0657	0804	0913	1011	1112	1212	1313	1413	1512	1613	1712	...	1813	1911	2014	2111	2225	0557	0659	0807	|	0912	1013
Gloucester	d.	0511	0610	0705	0814	0919	1019	1119	1219	1319	1419	1519	1619	1719	1750	1819	1919	2019	2119	2228	0604	0711	0817	|	0917	1018
Stroud	d.	0527	0627	0725	0831	0934	1035	1135	1235	1335	1434	1534	1634	1735	1807	1834	1936	2035	2135	2245	0621	0731	0834	0910	0935	1035
Swindon	a.	0555	0655	0754	0900	1003	1102	1202	1302	1403	1503	1602	1703	1803	1835	1903	2004	2103	2203	2313	0649	0759	0902	0940	1003	1103s
Swindon	131 132 133 d.	...	0657	0757	0902	1004	1104	1204	1304	1405	1504	1604	1704	1804	...	1904	2006	2104	2205	...	...	0802	0903	...	1005	|
Didcot Parkway	§ 131/2 133 d.	...	0714	0814	0919	1021	1120	1220	1320	1421	1521	1620	1721	1821	...	1921	2022	2121	2221	...	...	0819	0920	...	1021	|
Reading	131 132 133 a.	...	0726	0827	0932	1033	1133	1233	1333	1433	1533	1633	1733	1833	...	1933	2034	2133	2233	...	...	0832	0933	...	1034	1131
London Pad	131 132 133 a.	...	0757	0859	0959	1059	1159	1259	1359	1459	1559	1659	1759	1901	...	1959	2101	2207	2301	...	...	0859	0958	...	1059	1159

		⑥	⑥	⑥	⑥	⑥	⑥	⑥	⑥	⑥	⑥	⑥	⑥ 2	⑦ 2	⑦ 2	⑦	⑦	⑦ 2	⑦	⑦	⑦ 2	⑦	⑦ 2	⑦ 2	⑦	⑦ 2	⑦ 2
Worcester Shrub Hill	138 d.	...	...	...	...	...	...	...	...	...	...	...	...	...	...	...	...	...	...	...	...	...	...	...	...	...	...
Cheltenham Spa	138 d.	1103	1203	1303	1403	1503	1603	1703	1803	1903	2003	2105	2132	...	0928	1047	1155	1300	1400	1500	1600	1700	1800	1900	2000	2100	2200
Gloucester	138 a.	1112	1212	1313	1412	1512	1612	1712	1812	1912	2012	2114	2141	...	0938	1056	1205	1309	1409	1512	1609	1712	1810	1909	2009	2110	2210
Gloucester	d.	1118	1218	1318	1418	1518	1618	1718	1818	1918	2018	2119	2145	0905	0940	1103	1212	1314	1417	1514	1614	1714	1812	1911	2017	2113	2212
Stroud	d.	1134	1234	1334	1434	1534	1634	1734	1834	1934	2034	2136	2202	0922	0958	1119	1232	1332	1435	1530	1631	1730	1830	1928	2033	2130	2229
Swindon	a.	1203	1303	1403	1503	1603	1703	1803	1903	2003	2103	2204	2230	0950	1025	1147	1300	1359	1503	1558	1659	1759	1857	1955	2101	2157	2257
Swindon	131 132 133 d.	1204	1304	1404	1504	...	1704	1804	...	2004	2104	2210	...	...	...	1148	...	...	...	1559	...	1800	...	...	...	...	...
Didcot Parkway	§ 131/2 133 d.	1221	1321	1421	1521	...	1721	1821	...	2021	2121	2228	...	...	...	1205	...	...	...	1616	...	1817	...	...	...	...	...
Reading	131 132 133 a.	1234	1334	1434	1534	...	1734	1834	...	2034	2134	2241	...	...	...	1217	...	...	...	1628	...	1829	...	...	...	...	...
London Pad	131 132 133 a.	1259	1359	1459	1559	...	1759	1859	...	2058	2200	2306	...	...	...	1244	...	...	...	1654	...	1854	...	...	...	...	...

A – From/to Salisbury (Tables **126** and **140**).
B – To Southampton Central (Tables **126** and **140**).
C – From Westbury (Table **126**).
D – To Worcester Foregate Street (Table **138**).
E – To Bristol Temple Meads (Table **132**).
s – Calls to set down only.
u – Calls to pick up only.
§ – See Table **132** for connecting services to/from Oxford and Banbury.

GW Most trains convey 🍸 LONDON - OXFORD - WORCESTER - HEREFORD 131

km			Ⓐ2	Ⓐ	Ⓐ	Ⓐ	Ⓐ	Ⓐ	Ⓐ	Ⓐ	Ⓐ	Ⓐ	Ⓐ	Ⓐ	Ⓐ	Ⓐ	Ⓐ2	Ⓐ	Ⓐ	Ⓐ	Ⓐ	Ⓐ	Ⓐ	Ⓐ	Ⓐ
0	**London** Paddington ▷ d.	Ⓐ	...	0505	0553	0652	0750	0852	0952	1053	1152	1252	1350	1453	1523	1552	...	1658	1734	1757	1857	1953	2052	2153	2251
58	Reading ▷ d.		...	0540	0618	0718	0818	0919	1019	1119	1219	1318	1419	1518	1548	1618**u**	...	|	1801	1824	1923	2019	2118	2218	2332
85	Didcot Parkway § ▷ d.		...	0554	|	|	|	|	|	|	|	|	|	|	1603	|	1704	|	|	|	|	|	|	|	|
103	**Oxford** § ▷ d.		0510	0607	0652	0748**a**	0844	0945	1046	1145	1244	1344	1445	1545	1622**a**	1645	1723	1746	1825	1853	1947	2045	2144	2245**a**	2359
148	Moreton in Marsh d.		0535	...	0727	0822	0918	1019	1120	1223	1318	1418	1519	1619	1657	1719	1808	1825	1859	1929	2022	2119	2218	2322	0036
172	Evesham d.		0553	...	0756**f**	0841	0936	1038	1138	1241	1336	1436	1537	1638	1716	1748**f**	1823	1843	1914	1947	2040	2138	2236	2340	0054
187	Worcestershire Parkway d.		0607	...	0811	0856	0950	1052	1151	1254	1349	1450	1551	1652	1730	1803	...	1857	1925	2001	2054	2152	2250	2354	0106
194	**Worcester** Shrub Hill **122 138** a.		0615	...	0822	0904**c**	0958	1059	1200	1301	1357	1457	1559	1700	1737**j**	1810	...	1904	1932	2008	2102	2159	2257	0001	...
195	**Worcester** Foregate St **122** a.		...	...	0825	0917	1001	1102	1203	...	1400	1500	1603	1704	1747	1813	...	1908	1938	2011	2106	2202	2300	...	...
208	Great Malvern **122 138** a.		...	...	0838	0929	1014	1114	1215	...	1413	...	1615	...	...	1826	...	1925	1952	...	2118	2214**t**	2313	...	...
219	Ledbury **122** a.		...	...	...	...	...	...	1228	...	1427	...	...	...	...	...	...	...	2006	...	...	2240	...	...	...
241	**Hereford** **122** a.		...	...	...	...	...	...	1246	...	1444	...	...	...	...	...	...	...	2025	...	...	2257	...	...	...

		⑥	⑥	⑥	⑥	⑥	⑥	⑥	⑥	⑥	⑥	⑥	⑥	⑥	⑥	⑥	⑥	⑥		⑦	⑦	⑦	⑦	⑦	⑦
London Paddington ▷ d.	⑥	0522	0552	0652	0751	0852	0950	1052	1150	1252	1350	1452	1552	1650	1752	1852	1952	2152	⑦	0736	0847	0950	1050	1150	1250
Reading ▷ d.		0550	0619	0719	0819	0919	1018	1118	1219	1319	1419	1519	1619	1718	1819	1919	2019	2218		0814	0912	1014	1114	1214	1314
Didcot Parkway § ▷ d.		0604	0634	|	|	|	|	|	|	|	|	|	|	|	|	|	|	2234		0830	0930	1030	1130	1230	1330
Oxford § ▷ d.		0618	0648	0745	0845	0945	1045	1145	1245	1345	1448**a**	1545	1645	1745	1845	1945	2045	2250		0848	0947	1047	1147	1247	1347
Moreton in Marsh d.		...	0722	0819	0919	1019	1119	1219	1318	1421	1522	1619	1719	1819	1921	2019	2121	2326		0921	1021	1121	1221	1321	1421
Evesham d.		...	0741	0850**f**	0938	1038	1137	1238	1336	1440	1541	1638	1738	1837	1940	2037	2140	2345		0939	1039	1139	1239	1339	1439
Worcestershire Parkway d.		...	0755	0904	0952	1052	1150	1252	1350	1454	1555	1652	1752	1850	1955	2051	2154	2359		0953	1051	1151	1251	1351	1452
Worcester Shrub Hill **122 138** a.		...	0802	0911	1000	1059**c**	1157	1259**c**	1357	1501**j**	1602	1659	1759**c**	1857	2002**k**	2058	2201	0006		0958	1059	1159	1259	1359	1500
Worcester Foregate St **122** a.		...	0806	0914	1003	1112	1200	1312	1400	1511	1605	1702	1812	1900	2010	2101	2204	...		1002	1102	1202	1302	1403	1503
Great Malvern **122 138** a.		...	0818	0926	1016	1124	1212	1325	1412	...	1617	1714	1829	1912	...	2113	2223	...		1015	1114	1214**t**	1315	1415**t**	1515
Ledbury **122** a.		...	...	...	...	...	1226	...	1425	...	...	...	...	1926	...	...	...	...		...	...	1240	...	1440**k**	1532**d**
Hereford **122** a.		...	...	...	...	...	1243	...	1443	...	...	...	...	1943	...	...	...	...		...	...	1258	...	1504	1604

	⑦	⑦	⑦	⑦	⑦	⑦	⑦	⑦	⑦
London Paddington ▷ d.	1350	1450	1550	1650	1750	1850	1950	2050	2150
Reading ▷ d.	1414	1514	1614	1714	1814	1914	2014	2114	2214
Didcot Parkway § ▷ d.	1430	1530	1630	1730	1829	1930	2030	2130	2230
Oxford § ▷ d.	1447	1548	1647	1747	1847	1947	2047	2148	2247
Moreton in Marsh d.	1521	1622	1721	1821	1921	2021	2121	2222	2321
Evesham d.	1539	1640	1739	1839	1939	2041	2141	2240	2339
Worcestershire Parkway d.	1551	1652	1752	1851	1951	2056	2153	2252	2351
Worcester Shrub Hill **122 138** a.	1559	1700	1800	1859	1959	2105	2201	2300	2359
Worcester Foregate St **122** a.	1603	1703	1803	1902	2002	2108	2204	...	...
Great Malvern **122 138** a.	1616	1715	1815	1915	2014	2120**k**	2216	...	...
Ledbury **122** a.	...	...	...	...	...	2137	...	...	...
Hereford **122** a.	...	...	...	...	...	2154	...	...	...

		Ⓐ	Ⓐ	Ⓐ	Ⓐ	Ⓐ	Ⓐ2	Ⓐ	Ⓐ	Ⓐ
Hereford **122** d.	Ⓐ	...	...	...	0523	...	...	...	...	...
Ledbury **122** d.		...	...	...	0540	...	...	...	...	...
Great Malvern **122 138** d.		...	...	...	0553	...	...	0713	...	0856
Worcester Foregate St **122** d.		...	...	...	0606	...	...	0727	...	0909
Worcester Shrub Hill **122 138** d.		...	...	0516	0610	0643	0700	0731	0818	0915
Worcestershire Parkway d.		...	...	0522	0616	0649	|	0738	0825	0921
Evesham d.		...	...	0536	0635**a**	0700	0721	0751	0838	0935
Moreton in Marsh d.		...	...	0554	0654	0715	0740	0810	0856	0953
Oxford § ▷ d.		0520	0600	0631	0731	0753	0827	0847	0932	1029
Didcot Parkway § ▷ a.		0532	0612	|	|	|	0846	|	0944	1041
Reading ▷ a.		0546	0628	0653	0754	0814	...	0914	1000	1056
London Paddington ▷ a.		0612	0707	0724	0824	0844	...	0942	1025	1127

	Ⓐ	Ⓐ	Ⓐ	Ⓐ	Ⓐ	Ⓐ	Ⓐ	Ⓐ	Ⓐ	Ⓐ	Ⓐ2	Ⓐ	Ⓐ	Ⓐ	Ⓐ	Ⓐ		⑥	⑥	⑥	⑥	⑥	⑥	⑥	⑥
Hereford **122** d.	...	...	...	...	1318	...	1518	...	...	...	...	...	...	...	...	2200	⑥	...	0618	...	...	...	...	...	...
Ledbury **122** d.	...	...	...	...	1335	...	1535	...	...	...	...	...	...	...	...	2218		...	0635	...	...	...	...	...	...
Great Malvern **122 138** d.	0956	1059	1158	...	1355**b**	...	1555**b**	1632	...	...	...	1902	1945	...	...	2232		0554	0654	0743	...	0850	0959	1050	1155
Worcester Foregate St **122** d.	1010	1112	1212	...	1409	1518	1612	1646	1726	1802	...	1919	1959	2056	...	2249		0607	0708	0756	0828	0904	1013	1104	1209
Worcester Shrub Hill **122 138** d.	1016	1118	1217	1316	1417	1522	1617	1653	1730	1806	...	1925	2003	2104**a**	...	2253		0613	0712	0810	0832	0913**a**	1017	1115**b**	1215
Worcestershire Parkway d.	1022	1124	1223	1323	1423	1528	1623	1659	1737	1813	...	1932	2010	2111	...	2259		0619	0718	0818	0839	0919	1023	1121	1221
Evesham d.	1037	1137	1236	1336	1436	1538	1636	1714	1751	1826	1851	1944	2024	2125	...	2313		0635	0732	0833	0852	0933	1037	1135	1235
Moreton in Marsh d.	1055	1155	1254	1354	1454	1554	1655	1748**p**	1819**b**	1847	1910	2000	2045	2146	...	2331		0654	0751	0852	0910	0951	1056	1154	1254
Oxford § ▷ d.	1132	1232	1331	1431	1531	1631	1731	1832**e**	1902	1930	1950	2035	2132	2223	2307	0011		0731	0832	0932**a**	0948	1032	1132	1233	1332
Didcot Parkway § ▷ a.	1144	1245	1343	1443	1543	1643	1743	1846	|	1942	...	2047	|	|	2319	0023		0743	0844	0944	|	1044	1144	1245	1344
Reading ▷ a.	1157	1259	1357	1457	1558	1657	1757	1900	1923	1958	...	2101	2154	2246	2334	0036		0757	0858	0958	1013	1058	1158	1300	1358
London Paddington ▷ a.	1223	1325	1423	1522	1624	1729	1829	1929	1952	2029	...	2126	2224	2329	0012	0120**q**		0822	0923	1027	1040	1124	1223	1325	1424

	⑥	⑥	⑥	⑥	⑥	⑥	⑥	⑥	⑥	⑥		⑦	⑦	⑦	⑦	⑦	⑦	⑦	⑦	⑦	⑦	⑦	⑦	⑦	⑦
Hereford **122** d.	...	1320	...	1514	...	...	...	...	2020	...	⑦	...	...	...	...	...	...	...	1428	1531	...	1730	...	...	...
Ledbury **122** d.	...	1337	...	1531	...	...	...	...	2037	...		...	...	...	...	...	...	...	1446	1548	...	1748	...	...	...
Great Malvern **122 138** d.	...	1355**n**	1450	1543	1700	1748	1900	...	2055**n**	2244		...	0857	0958	1058	1157	...	1358	1458	1600	1658	1801	1857	1958	2046
Worcester Foregate St **122** d.	1305	1410	1504	1556	1715	1804	1915	2003	2109	2257		0815	0911	1011	1112	1211	1312	1411	1511	1613	1712	1815	1911	2011	2059
Worcester Shrub Hill **122 138** d.	1312	1415	1515**b**	1613**f**	1719	1815**b**	1919	2015**b**	2120**b**	2302		0819	0915	1015	1116	1215	1317	1415	1515	1617	1716	1819	1915	2016	2103
Worcestershire Parkway d.	1319	1421	1521	1619	1725	1821	1925	2021	2126	2308		0825	0921	1021	1122	1221	1323	1421	1521	1623	1722	1825	1921	2022	2109
Evesham d.	1333	1435	1535	1633	1738	1835	1938	2035	2142	2322		0838	0935	1034	1135	1234	1336	1434	1534	1636	1735	1838	1934	2035	2128**n**
Moreton in Marsh d.	1351	1454	1554	1651	1756	1855	1956	2054	2201	...		0856	0953	1052	1153	1252	1354	1452	1552	1654	1753	1856	1952	2054	2146
Oxford § ▷ d.	1431	1531	1630	1732	1832	1932	2032	2132	2237	...		0930	1028	1128	1228	1327	1428	1528	1628	1728	1828	1928	2028	2128	2224
Didcot Parkway § ▷ a.	1443	1543	1642	1744	1844	1944	2044	2144	2249	...		0945	1042	1142	1242	1342	1442	1542	1642	1744	1844	1944	2042	2140	2236
Reading ▷ a.	1457	1557	1656	1758	1858	1958	2058	2158	2303	...		1000	1058	1158	1258	1356	1456	1559	1656	1758	1859	1958	2056	2155	2250
London Paddington ▷ a.	1522	1622	1725	1824	1924	2023	2123	2223	2338	...		1026	1124	1224	1324	1421	1525	1625	1722	1825	1926	2025	2122	2223	2340

OTHER SERVICES LONDON - OXFORD

km			②–⑤	Ⓐ	Ⓐ	Ⓐ	Ⓐ		Ⓐ	Ⓐ	Ⓐ	Ⓐ	Ⓐ	Ⓐ	Ⓐ	Ⓐ
0	**London** Paddington d.	Ⓐ	0031	0505	0720	0823	0923	and at	1423	1623	1823	1923	2023	2123	2218	2314
30	Slough d.		0051	0522	|	|	|	the same	|	|	|	|	|	|	|	2331
58	Reading d.		0115	0540	0749	0848	0948	minutes	1448	1649	1850	1949	2048	2148	2243	0007**u**
85	Didcot Parkway § d.		0137	0554	0803	0905	1002	past each	1503	|	|	2005	2104	2204	|	0022**u**
103	**Oxford** § a.		0151	0607	0816	0921	1017	hour until	1516	1713	1912	2018	2117	2217	2309	0038

		⑥	⑥	⑥	⑥	♣	⑥	⑥	⑥	⑥	⑥	⑥
London Paddington d.	⑥	0031	0522	0622	0722	and at	1920	2022	2053	2122	2250	2333
Slough d.		0051	0536	|	|	the same	|	|	|	|	2306	2349
Reading d.		0115	0550	0649	0747	minutes	1948	2048	2119	2147	2326	0012
Didcot Parkway § d.		0137	0604	0703	0802	past each	2005	2103	2133	2202	2344	0029
Oxford § a.		0151	0618	0716	0815	hour until	2020	2116	2146	2215	2359	0045

		⑦	⑦	⑦	⑦		⑦	⑦	⑦	⑦	⑦
London Paddington d.	⑦	0920	1020	1120	1220	and at	2020	2119	2215	2233	2331
Slough d.		0935	1035	1135	1235	the same	2035	|	|	2250	2349
Reading d.		0948	1048	1148	1248	minutes	2048	2146	2240	2318**b**	0020**b**
Didcot Parkway § d.		1003	1103	1203	1303	past each	2103	2201	2252	2344	0045
Oxford § a.		1015	1115	1215	1317	hour until	2115	2214	*2340**	*0034**	*0125**

		①	Ⓐ	Ⓐ	Ⓐ	Ⓐ	Ⓐ	♣	Ⓐ	Ⓐ	Ⓐ	Ⓐ	Ⓐ	Ⓐ	Ⓐ	Ⓐ
Oxford § d.	Ⓐ	*0005**	0648	0700	0900	0959	1100	and at	1501	1600	1700	1800	2008	2102	2201	2307
Didcot Parkway § d.		0035	|	0712	|	|	|	the same	|	|	|	|	|	|	|	2319
Reading a.		0050	0710	0727	0924	1021	1122	minutes	1523	1625	1722	1823	2030	2124	2225	2334
Slough a.		0116	|	|	|	|	|	past each	|	|	|	|	|	|	|	|
London Padd'ton a.		0143	0739	0805	0952	1052	1152	hour until	1552	1657	1752	1854	2059	2154	2254	0012

		⑥	⑥	⑥	⑥	⑥	⑥	⑥	♣	⑥	⑥	⑥
Oxford § d.	⑥	0550	0630	0700	0800	0900	1000	1100	and at	2100	2200	2300
Didcot Parkway § d.		0602	0642	|	|	|	1012	|	the same	|	2212	2318
Reading a.		0617	0656	0724	0824	0923	1028	1124	minutes	2124	2229	2336
Slough a.		|	|	|	|	|	|	|	past each	|	2256	2357
London Paddington a.		0644	0721	0755	0854	0954	1056	1154	hour until	2152	2312	0020

		⑦	⑦	⑦	♥	⑦	⑦
Oxford § d.	⑦	0754	0902	1056	and at	1956	*2305**
Didcot Parkway § d.		0805	0913	1106	the same	2006	2350
Reading a.		0819	0926	1122	minutes	2022	0014
Slough a.		0833	0939	1135	past each	2035	0035
London Paddington a.		0851	0956	1152	hour until	2053	0105

a – Arrives 5–6 minutes earlier.
b – Arrives 8–10 minutes earlier.
c – Departs 11 minutes later.
d – Departs 1548.
e – Arrives 1825.
f – Arrives 12–14 minutes earlier.
j – Departs 8–10 minutes later.

k – Departs 5–6 minutes later.
n – Arrives 7 minutes earlier.
p – Arrives 1732.
q – Arrives 0115 on ②–⑤ mornings.
t – Departs 13–15 minutes later.
u – Calls to pick up only.

* – By 🚌.
▷ – See panel below main table for additional services London - Oxford and v.v.
See Tables **130**, **132** and **133** for other services London - Didcot and v.v.
§ See bottom of page 106 for the full service Didcot to Oxford and Banbury and v.v.
♣ – Timings may vary ± 2 minutes.
♥ – Arrivals into London Paddington may vary ± 2 minutes.

GW 2nd class Journey time: 6 minutes SLOUGH - WINDSOR 131a

From Slough:
Ⓐ: 0530, 0550, 0610, 0630 and every 20 minutes until 2230, 2259, 2319, 2345.
⑥: 0600, 0633, 0704, 0730 and every 20 minutes until 2030, 2058, 2128, 2158, 2228, 2310, 2353.
⑦: 0822, 0859, 0919 and every 20 minutes until 1859, 1928 and every 30 minutes until 2228, 2255, 2315.

From Windsor & Eton Central:
Ⓐ: 0540, 0600, 0620 and every 20 minutes until 2240, 2309, 2329, 2356.
⑥: 0620, 0650, 0720 and every 20 minutes until 2040, 2118, 2148, 2218, 2245, 2320.
⑦: 0003, 0832, 0909 and every 20 minutes until 1909, 1939 and every 30 minutes until 2209, 2238, 2305, 2325.

132 LONDON - BRISTOL - TAUNTON

Most trains convey 🍸 GW

km		Ⓐ	ⒶQ	ⒶD	Ⓐ	Ⓐ	Ⓐ	Ⓐ	Ⓐ	Ⓐ	Ⓐ	Ⓐ	Ⓐ	Ⓐ	Ⓐ	Ⓐ	Ⓐ	Ⓐ	Ⓐ	Ⓐ	Ⓐ	Ⓐ	Ⓐ	Ⓐ	Ⓐ	Ⓐ	Ⓐ
0	**London** Paddington ♥ d.		0523	0600	0628	0700	0729	0757	0830	0900	0930	1000	1030	1100	1130	1200	1230	1300	1330	1400	1430	1500	1530	1600	1630	1700	1730
58	Reading ♥ d.		0549	0627	0653	0725	0754	0825	0855	0925	0955	1025	1055	1125	1155	1225	1255	1326	1355	1425	1455	1525	1555	1625	1655	1726	1755
85	Didcot Parkway ♣ ✣ d.		0603	0640	|	0739	|	0839	|	0939	|	1038	|	1138	|	1238	|	1339	|	1438	|	1538	|	1639	|	1740	|
124	Swindon 126 130 133 137 d.		0621	0659	0722	0756	0820	0856	0924	0958r	1022	1056	1122	1155	1222	1302	1325	1356	1422	1458	1525	1555	1622	1656	1722	1757	1822
151	Chippenham 126 137 d.		0633	0711	0734	0809	0832	0908	0936	1010	1033	1108	1133	1207	1233	1313	1338	1409	1433	1511	1537	1607	1633	1708	1733	1809	1835
172	Bath Spa 137 140 d.		0647	0724	0747	0823	0845	0923r	0949	1023	1046	1122	1146	1220	1246	1326	1351	1423	1446	1525	1550	1622	1647	1722	1746	1823	1848
190	**Bristol** Temple Meads ★ a.		0658	0736	0803	0836	0857	0935	1001	1035	1058	1135	1158	1235	1258	1339	1403	1435	1458	1537	1608	1635	1659	1734	1757	1835	1900
221	Weston-super-Mare 115 a.		...	|	0842	...	...	...	1038	...	...	...	1248	...	...	...	1440	...	...	...	1641	...	1743	...	1842	...	1939
262	**Taunton** 110 115 a.		...	0816	...	...	...	...	...	...	...	...	...	...	...	...	...	...	...	...	...	...	...	...	1914	...	2016

	Ⓐ	Ⓐ	Ⓐ	Ⓐ	Ⓐ	Ⓐ	Ⓐ	Ⓐ	Ⓐ	Ⓐ	⑥	⑥	⑥	⑥	⑥	⑥	⑥2	⑥	⑥	⑥	⑥2	⑥B	⑥	⑥	⑥2	⑥	⑥
London Paddington ♥ d.	1801	1830	1900	1930	2000	2030	2102	2203	2228	2332		0600	0700	0730	0800	0830	C	0900	0930	1000	1013	1028	1045	1100	1115	1130	1200
Reading ♥ d.	1827	1855u	1927u	1955	2025	2055	2127	2228	2255	0004		0625	0725	0755	0825	0855	...	0925	0955u	1025u	1040	1054u	1110	1125u	1140	1155	1225
Didcot Parkway ♣ ✣ d.	1841	|	1941	2009	2038	2108	2140	2241	2311	0019		0638	0739	|	0839	|	...	0939	|	1039	1054	|	|	1139	1154	|	1239
Swindon 126 130 133 137 d.	1858	1922	1958	2026	2058r	2125	2159	2258	2328	0036		0703	0756	0821	0859	0923	0945	0956	1022	1056	1113	1122	|	1157	1217	1223	1258
Chippenham 126 137 d.	1910	1935	2010	2038	2110	2139	2211	2310	2340	0048	⊠	0717	0809	0833	0911	0936	1000	1008	1034	1108	...	1134	1146	1210	...	1235	1310
Bath Spa 137 140 d.	1923	1949	2023	2051	2123	2153	2225	2323	2353	0101		0730	0823	0846	0924	0950	1016	1023	1048	1123	...	1148	1200	1223	...	1248	1323
Bristol Temple Meads ★ a.	1935	2000	2037	2105	2136	2205	2239	2336	0008	0113		0744	0835	0858	0936	1002	1030	1035	1100	1135	...	1200	1212	1235	...	1300	1335
Weston-super-Mare 115 a.	...	2042	...	2144	...	2249	...	...	...	...		...	...	0929	...	1032	...	...	...	...	...	...	1235	...	...	1330	...
Taunton 110 115 a.	...	...	...	...	...	...	...	...	...	...		...	...	...	...	1105	...	...	...	...	...	...	...	...	...	...	...

	⑥	⑥	⑥2	⑥	⑥	⑥	⑥	⑥	⑥	⑥	⑥	⑥	⑥	⑥	⑥2	⑥	⑥	⑥	⑥2	⑥B	⑥	⑥	⑥	⑦	⑦B	⑦	⑦
London Paddington ♥ d.	1230	1300	1315	1330	1400	1430	1500	1530	1600	1630	1700	1730	1800	1830	1832	1900	1930	2000	2013	2030	2130	2230	2330		0759	0900	...
Reading ♥ d.	1255	1325	1342	1355	1425	1455	1525	1555	1625	1655	1725	1755	1825	1856	1900	1925	1955	2025	2040	2056	2155	2256	0005		0824	0929	...
Didcot Parkway ♣ ✣ d.	|	1339	1356	|	1439	|	1539	1608	1639	|	1739	|	1839	|	1915	1939	|	2038	2055	2111	2209	2309	0020		0840	0950	...
Swindon 126 130 133 137 d.	1325	1356	1415	1422	1458	1524	1557	1626	1658	1722	1756	1822	1857	1925	1934	1956	2022	2055	2114	2129	2226	2326	0038		0857	1006	1053
Chippenham 126 137 d.	1337	1408	...	1434	1510	1536	1609	1638	1710	1734	1808	1835	1909	1937	...	2008	2034	2107	...	2142	2238	2338	0050		0908	1017	1108
Bath Spa 137 140 d.	1351	1423	...	1448	1523	1552r	1623	1653	1723	1748	1825r	1848	1924	1950	...	2024r	2048	2120	...	2155	2251	2351	0103		0920	1030	1123
Bristol Temple Meads ★ a.	1403	1435	...	1500	1535	1605	1635	1705	1735	1800	1838	1900	1936	2002	...	2037	2102	2132	...	2206	2303	0003	0115		0931	1043	1136
Weston-super-Mare 115 a.	1432	...	...	1532	...	1631	...	1742	...	1831	...	1933	...	2038	...	...	2134	...	...	2236s	...	...	...		|	1109	...
Taunton 110 115 a.	...	...	...	...	...	...	...	...	...	1903	...	...	...	2110	...	...	2206	...	...	2307	...	...	...		1012	...	...

	⑦	⑦2	⑦	⑦	⑦2	⑦	⑦	⑦	⑦2	⑦	⑦	⑦2	⑦P	⑦	⑦2	⑦	⑦P	⑦2	⑦	⑦	⑦	⑦2	⑦	⑦	⑦	⑦	⑦
London Paddington ♥ d.	1030	1113	1130	1230	1312	1330	1430	1500	1513	1530	1600	1613	1630	1700	1713	1730	1800	1813	1830	1900	1930	2005	2030	2130	2215	2300	2333
Reading ♥ d.	1055	1140	1155	1255	1339	1355	1455	1525	1540	1555	1625	1640	1655	1725	1740	1755	1825	1840	1855	1925	1955	2032	2055	2155	2240	2337	0016
Didcot Parkway ♣ ✣ d.	1108	1154	1208	1308	1353	1408	|	1538	1554	|	1638	1654	|	1738	1754	|	1838	1854	|	1938	|	2046	|	2208	2253	2351s	0030s
Swindon 126 130 133 137 d.	1125	1213	1225	1325	1412	1425	1522	1554	1613	1622	1654	1713	1722	1754	1814	1822	1854	1914	1922	1954	2022	2106	2122	2225	2310	0010s	0048s
Chippenham 126 137 d.	1137	...	1237	1337	...	1437	1533	1607	...	1633	1707	...	1733	1807	...	1833	1907	...	1933	2007	2033	...	2133	2237	2322	0023s	0100s
Bath Spa 137 140 d.	1150	...	1250	1350	...	1450	1546	1620	...	1648	1720	...	1748	1820	...	1846	1920	...	1946	2020	2046	...	2146	2250	2335	0034s	0112s
Bristol Temple Meads ★ a.	1202	...	1305	1402	...	1505	1558	1632	...	1701	1732	...	1803	1832	...	1858	1932	...	1958	2032	2102	...	2158	2302	2347	0049	0126
Weston-super-Mare 115 a.	1236	...	...	...	...	...	|	...	...	1737	...	...	1837	...	...	1940	|	...	...	...	...	...	2235	...	...	...	...
Taunton 110 115 a.	...	...	...	...	...	...	1639	...	...	1808	...	...	1904	...	...	...	2006	...	...	...	...	...	...	...	...	...	...

	Ⓐ	Ⓐ	Ⓐ	Ⓐ	Ⓐ	Ⓐ	Ⓐ	Ⓐ		Ⓐ	Ⓐ	Ⓐ	Ⓐ	Ⓐ	Ⓐ	Ⓐ	Ⓐ	Ⓐ	Ⓐ	Ⓐ	Ⓐ	Ⓐ	Ⓐ	Ⓐ	Ⓐ	Ⓐ	Ⓐ
Taunton 110 115 d.		...	...	...	...	...	...	...	...	0654	0723	...	...	...	...	...	...	...	...	...	...	...	...	...	...	...	...
Weston-super-Mare 115 d.		...	...	...	...	...	0624	0652	...	0724	0754	...	...	0929	...	...	...	1123	...	...	...	1326	...	...	...	1528	...
Bristol Temple Meads ★ a.		0453	0510	0523	0547	0630	0700	0730	...	0800	0830	0900	0930	1000	1030	1100	1130	1200	1230	1300	1330	1400	1430	1500	1530	1600	1630
Bristol Parkway 133 d.		0503	|	|	|	|	|	|	...	|	|	|	|	|	|	|	|	|	|	|	|	|	|	|	|	|	|
Bath Spa 140 137 d.		|	|	0535	0602	0643	0713	0743	...	0813	0844	0913	0943	1013	1043	1113	1143	1213	1243	1313	1343	1413	1443	1513	1543	1613	1643
Chippenham 126 137 d.		|	a	0549	0615	0656	0726	0756	...	0826	0857	0928	0956	1026	1056	1126	1156	1226	1256	1326	1356	1426	1456	1526	1556	1626	1656
Swindon 126 130 133 137 d.		0528	|	0603	0629	0710	0740	0810	...	0840	0911	0945	1010	1041	1111	1140	1211	1240	1311	1341	1411	1441	1511	1541	1611	1641	1712
Didcot Parkway ♠ ✣ d.		0546	|	0619	0646	0727	|	0827	...	0857	0927	1002	1027	|	1128	|	1228	|	1328	1358	1428	1458	1528	1558	1627	1658	|
Reading ♥ a.		0558	0704	0631	0658	0740	|	0839	...	0910	0939	1014	1039	1107	1140	1207	1240	1305	1341	1411	1440	1511	1541	1611	1640	1711	1737
London Paddington ♥ a.		0629	0737	0657	0726	0809	0829	0905	...	0934	1006	1044	1107	1134	1209	1236	1307	1335	1405	1435	1507	1536	1607	1637	1705	1735	1805

	Ⓐ	Ⓐ	Ⓐ	Ⓐ	Ⓐ	Ⓐ	Ⓐ	ⒶB	ⒶD	Ⓐ	⑥	⑥	⑥	⑥2	⑥	⑥		⑥	⑥	⑥	⑥B	⑥	⑥	⑥2	⑥	⑥	⑥
Taunton 110 115 d.	...	...	...	...	...	...	...	2003	2124	...		...	...	...	...	...	...	...	0657	...	0758	...	...	...	...	...	...
Weston-super-Mare 115 d.	...	...	1728	...	1829	...	...	2029	|	...		...	...	...	...	0620	...	...	0727	...	0827	...	...	...	...	0958	...
Bristol Temple Meads ★ a.	1700	1729	1800	1830	1900	1930	2000	2100	2200	2242		0530	0600	...	0630	0700	...	0730	0800	0830	0900	0918	0930	...	1000	1030	1100
Bath Spa 140 137 d.	1713	1745	1813	1843	1913	1943	2013	2113	2213	2255		0543	0613	...	0643	0713	...	0743	0813	0843	0913	0931	0944	...	1013	1043	1113
Chippenham 126 137 d.	1726	1757	1826	1856	1926	1956	2026	2126	2227	2308		0556	0626	...	0656	0726	...	0756	0826	0856	0926	0944	0957	...	1026	1056	1126
Swindon 126 130 133 137 d.	1741	1811	1841	1911	1941	2011	2041	2141	2242	2322		0611	0641	0700	0711	0740	...	0811	0840	0911	0940	0958	1011	1025	1042	1111	1140
Didcot Parkway ♠ ✣ d.	1758	1828	1858	1928	1958	2028	2058	2158	2259	2339		0627	0657	0719	0728	0756	...	0828	0856	0927	0956	|	1026	1050	1059	1127	1157
Reading ♥ a.	1811	1841	1911	1941	2011	2041	2111	2211	2310	2352		0640	0710	0733	0741	0809	...	0841	0909	0940	1009	1023	1040	1104	1112	1140	1210
London Paddington ♥ a.	1838	1908	1937	2007	2035	2108	2135	2235	2359	0030		0705	0737	0758	0805	0835	...	0905	0936	1007	1037	1052	1105	1135	1137	1205	1235

	⑥2	⑥	⑥	⑥	⑥	⑥	⑥	⑥	⑥	⑥E	⑥f	⑥	⑥	⑥	⑥	⑥	⑥	⑥	⑥	⑥	⑥	⑥D	⑥	⑥	⑦	⑦	⑦2
Taunton 110 115 d.	...	...	...	...	1125	...	...	...	...	1424f	...	...	...	...	...	...	...	...	...	...	1956	2119	2130	...		...	...
Weston-super-Mare 115 d.	...	...	...	...	1158	...	1302	...	1402	|	...	1502	...	1602	...	1702	...	1802	...	...	2026	|	2200	...		...	...
Bristol Temple Meads ★ a.	...	1130	1200	...	1230	1300	1330	1400	1430	1500	1518	1530	1600	1630	1700	1730	1800	1830	1900	2000	2100	2200	2230	2330		0745	...
Bath Spa 140 137 d.	...	1143	1213	...	1243	1313	1343	1413	1443	1513	1531	1543	1613	1643	1713	1743	1813	1843	1913	2013	2115	2214	2245	2344		0758	...
Chippenham 126 137 d.	...	1156	1226	...	1256	1326	1356	1426	1456	1526	1545	1556	1626	1656	1726	1756	1826	1856	1926	2026	2128	2227	2300	2356s		0810	...
Swindon 126 130 133 137 d.	1146	1211	1240	1249	1311	1340	1411	1440	1511	1540	1600	1611	1640	1711	1740	1811	1840	1911	1941	2040	2142	2241	2315	0010		0824	0837
Didcot Parkway ♠ ✣ d.	1205	1228	1257	1306	1328	1357	1428	1457	1528	1557	1617	1627	1657	1728	1757	1826	1857	1928	1956	2056	2200	2257	2332	...		0841	0855
Reading ♥ a.	1219	1241	1310	1319	1341	1410	1441	1510	1541	1610	1631	1640	1710	1741	1810	1840	1910	1941	2010	2110	2213	2310	2345	...		0854	0909
London Paddington ♥ a.	1244	1305	1335	1344	1407	1435	1505	1535	1605	1635	1658	1707	1735	1805	1835	1907	1935	2005	2035	2135	2237	2340	0023	...		0922	0937

	⑦2	⑦	⑦	⑦2	⑦	⑦	⑦	⑦2	⑦	⑦2	⑦	⑦B	⑦	⑦	⑦2	⑦	⑦		⑦P	⑦	⑦	⑦2	⑦B	⑦2	⑦	⑦	⑦P
Taunton 110 115 d.	...	...	...	...	...	...	...	...	...	...	...	1346	...	...	...	...	...	...	1622	...	1657	...	1757	...	1857	...	2143
Weston-super-Mare 115 d.	...	0829	...	...	...	1131	...	...	...	...	1328	|	...	...	...	...	...	...	|	...	1724	...	1826	...	1927	2028	2205
Bristol Temple Meads ★ a.	...	0900	1000	...	1100	1200	1230	...	1300	...	1400	1430	1500	1530	...	1600	1630	...	1700	1730	1800	...	1900	...	2000	2100	2230
Bath Spa 140 137 d.	...	0913	1013	...	1113	1213	1243	...	1313	...	1413	1443	1513	1543	...	1613	1643	...	1713	1743	1813	...	1913	...	2013	2113	2243
Chippenham 126 137 d.	...	0926	1026	...	1126	1226	1255	...	1326	...	1426	1455	1526	1555	...	1626	1655	...	1726	1755	1826	...	1926	...	2026	2126	2256
Swindon 126 130 133 137 d.	0915	0940	1040	1130	1140	1240	1309	1330	1340	1430	1440	1509	1540	1609	1630	1640	1709	...	1740	1809	1840	1850	1940	1950	2040	2140	2310
Didcot Parkway ♠ ✣ d.	0932	0956	1056	1148	1156	1256	|	1348	1356	1449	1456	|	1556	|	1648	1656	|	...	1756	|	1856	1907	1956	2007	2056	2156	2327
Reading ♥ a.	0944	1009	1109	1202	1209	1309	1335	1402	1409	1502	1509	1534	1609	1635	1702	1709	1735	...	1809	1835	1909	1921	2009	2021	2109	2209	2340
London Paddington ♥ a.	1012	1036	1136	1229	1235	1335	1359	1429	1435	1529	1536	1559	1635	1659	1729	1735	1759	...	1835	1859	1936	1951	2035	2051	2136	2236	0014

B – To/from Exeter St Davids (Table **110**).
C – From Cheltenham Spa (Table **130**).
D – To/from Penzance (Tables **110**).
E – Until Sept.13 from Paignton (Table **110**).
P – To/from Plymouth (Table **110**).
Q – To Swansea via Bristol Parkway (Table **133**).

a – Via Westbury (Table **110**).
c – ① only. By 🚌. Arrives Oxford 0125.
d – ① only. By 🚌. Arrives Didcot Parkway 25 minutes later.
f – Until Sept. 13.
g – By 🚌. Arrives Oxford 2340.
h – By 🚌. Arrives Oxford 0034.
k – To Banbury (additional journey time ± 28 minutes).
n – From Banbury (departs ± 28 minutes earlier).
p – From Banbury (departs 0003).
r – Arrives 5 minutes earlier.
s – Calls to set down only.
t – By 🚌. Arrives Didcot Parkway 2345.

♥ – For additional services see Tables **110**, **130**, **131** and **133**.
✣ – For additional services see Tables **130**, **131** and **133**.
★ – For additional services see Tables **110**, **115**, **137** and **140**.

⊠ – An additional train runs on ⑥: London Paddington d. 0915, Reading d. 0942, Didcot Parkway d. 0956, Swindon a. 1015.

♣ – Connecting services **Didcot Parkway - Oxford (- Banbury)**. Journey time 13–20 minutes.

On Ⓐ at 0050 **c**, 0022 **b**, 0137 **b**, 0554, 0604, 0629 **k**, 0707, 0734 **k**, 0803, 0807, 0834 **k**, 0905, 0911, 0938, 1003, 1007, 1033 **k**, 1104, 1134, 1204, 1235 **k**, 1302, 1334, 1402, 1434 **k**, 1503, 1534, 1603, 1607, 1635 **k**, 1704, 1734 **k**, 1800, 1830 **k**, 1905, 1937, 2005, 2037 **k**, 2104, 2135, 2204, 2231 **k**, 2334.

On ⑥ at 0022, 0137, 0604, 0609 **k**, 0634, 0639, 0703, 0734, 0802, 0834 **k**, 0903, 0934, 1003, 1034 **k**, 1105, 1134, 1203, 1235 **k**, 1303, 1334, 1403, 1435 **k**, 1503, 1534, 1603, 1634 **k**, 1704, 1734, 1803, 1834, 1903, 1935 **k**, 2005, 2035, 2103, 2133, 2140, 2202, 2234, 2245, 2320, 2344.

On ⑦ at 0029, 0830, 0930, 1003, 1030 and at the same minutes past each hour until 1803, 1829, 1903, 1930, 2003, 2030, 2103, 2130, 2201, 2230, 2300 **g**, 2359 **h**.

♠ – Connecting services **(Banbury -) Oxford - Didcot Parkway**. Journey time 12–19 minutes.

On Ⓐ at 0005 **d**, 0011 **b**, 0335 **d**, 0355 **b**, 0520, 0534, 0600, 0604, 0634, 0700, 0704 **n**, 0734, 0758 **n**, 0827, 0904 **n**, 0932, 0934, 1009 **n**, 1029, 1104, 1132, 1204 **n**, 1232, 1304, 1331, 1409 **n**, 1431, 1507, 1531, 1534, 1604 **n**, 1631, 1635, 1705, 1731, 1734, 1804 **n**, 1832, 1834, 1907 **n**, 1930, 2011 **n**, 2035, 2106, 2205 **n**, 2256, 2307.

On ⑥ at 0011, 0520, 0550, 0605, 0630, 0704, 0731, 0805, 0832, 0904, 0932, 1000, 1005 **n**, 1032, 1104, 1132, 1205 **n**, 1233, 1304, 1332, 1405 **n**, 1431, 1504, 1531, 1604 **n**, 1630, 1703, 1732, 1804 **n**, 1832, 1904, 1932, 2005, 2032, 2105 **n**, 2132, 2200, 2205, 2237, 2243 **n**, 2300.

On ⑦ at 0754, 0902, 0930, 1028, 1056, 1128, 1156, 1228, 1256, 1327, 1356, 1428, 1456, 1528, 1556, 1628, 1656, 1728, 1756, 1828, 1856, 1928, 1956, 2028, 2128, 2224, 2305 **t**.

GW Most trains convey 🍷 LONDON - BRISTOL PARKWAY - CARDIFF - SWANSEA 133

km			Ⓐ	Ⓐ◇	Ⓐ	Ⓐ	Ⓐ	Ⓐ	Ⓐ	Ⓐ	Ⓐ	Ⓐ	Ⓐ	Ⓐ	Ⓐ	Ⓐ	Ⓐ	Ⓐ	Ⓐ	Ⓐ	Ⓐ	Ⓐ	Ⓐ	Ⓐ	Ⓐ2	Ⓐ	Ⓐ
0	**London** Padd. **130 131 132** d.		...	0523	0648	0712	0748	0818	0848	0918	0948	1015	1048	1116	1148	1213	1248	1315	1348	1415	1448	1516	1548	1618	1612	1648	1718
58	Reading .... **130 131 132** d.	Ⓐ	...	0549	0713	0739	0813	0843	0913	0943	1013	1041	1113	1141	1213	1240	1313	1341	1413	1440	1513	1541	1613	|	1643	1713	1743
85	Didcot Parkway. § **130/1 132** d.		...	0603	|	0754	|	|	|	|	|	1055	|	1157	|	1253	|	1355	|	1453	|	1555	|	|	1658	|	1756
124	Swindon .... **130 131 132** d.		...	0621	0740	0812	0840	0910	0941	1011	1042	1112	1140	1215	1240	1310	1340	1412	1440	1510	1540	1612	1640	|	1717	1742	1813
180	**Bristol** Parkway .... d.		0602	0728r	0804	0835	0904	0934	1005	1034	1105	1136	1204	1241	1304	1334	1405	1436	1503	1533	1604	1635	1704	1728	1739	1805	1837
215	Newport .... ‡ a.		0624	0749	0825	0854	0922	0952	1024	1052	1127	1154	1223	1301	1322	1354	1423	1455	1521	1551	1623	1653	1722	1747e	...	1824	1857
234	**Cardiff** Central .... ‡ a.		0637	0805	0839	0908	0935	1009	1037	1107	1140	1210	1236	1316	1335	1407	1436	1509	1534	1608	1636	1706	1736	1805	...	1837	1910
	Cardiff Central .... **136** d.		0639	0808	0842	...	0938	...	1039	...	1142	...	1239	...	1337	...	1439	...	1537	...	1639	...	1739	1809	...	1839	1918
266	Bridgend .... **136** a.		0658	0827	0901	...	0957	...	1058	...	1201	...	1258	...	1356	...	1458	...	1556	...	1658	...	1758	1828	...	1858	1942
286	Port Talbot .... **136** a.		0710	0839	0913	...	1009	...	1110	...	1213	...	1310	...	1408	...	1510	...	1608	...	1710	...	1811	1840	...	1910	1954
295	Neath .... **136** a.		0717	0846	0920	...	1017	...	1118	...	1220	...	1317	...	1416	...	1517	...	1615	...	1718	...	1819	1851	...	1918	2002
307	**Swansea** .... **136** a.		0729	0902	0932	...	1029	...	1130	...	1232	...	1330	...	1427	...	1530	...	1627	...	1730	...	1834	1903	...	1930	2014
	Carmarthen **136** .... a.		0824	...	1040	...	...	...	...	...	1328	...	...	...	1528	...	...	...	1721	...	...	...	...	1954	...	...	...

	Ⓐ✕	Ⓐ	Ⓐ	Ⓐ	Ⓐ	⑤	①–④	⑤	①–④	⑤	①–④		⑥F	⑥	⑥	⑥P	⑥	⑥	⑥	⑥	⑥	⑥	⑥	⑥	⑥	⑥	⑥
London Padd.. **130 131 132** d.	1748	1818	1848	1918	1948	2048	2048	2148	2148	2249	2246		...	0648	0748	0848	0948	1048	1148	1213	1248	1348	1448	1548	1616	1648	1718
Reading .... **130 131 132** d.	1813	1843	1913	|	2013	2113	2113	2213	2213	2327	2327	⑥	...	0713	0813	0913	1013	1113	1213	1240	1313	1413	1513	1613	1642	1713	1743
Didcot Parkway.. § **130/1 132** d.	|	1858	|	|	|	|	|	|	|	2342	2342		...	|	|	|	|	|	|	1256	|	|	|	|	1655	|	1757
Swindon .... **130 131 132** d.	1840	1915	1940	|	2040	2140	2140	2240	2240	0001	0001		...	0740	0840	0940	1040	1141	1240	1318	1340	1440	1540	1640	1712	1740	1814
Bristol Parkway .... d.	1904	1941	2004	2029	2103	2203	2203	2304	2304	0024	0024		0725r	0804	0904	1004	1104	1204	1304	1343	1404	1503	1604	1704	1737	1804	1837
Newport .... ‡ a.	1923	1958	2024	2048	2121	2223	2228	2322	2329	0042	0049		0744	0822	0922	1024	1127	1223	1322	1402	1422	1521	1623	1722	1756	1822	1855
Cardiff Central .... ‡ a.	1936	2014	2038	2101	2138	2237	2246	2335	2345	0054	0107		0800	0836	0936	1037	1141	1237	1336	1417	1436	1535	1637	1736	1810	1836	1909
Cardiff Central .... **136** d.	1939	2019	2040	2104	2144	2249	2249	2351	2351	0058	0111		0803	0840	0938	1039	1142	1240	1339	...	1440	1537	1640	1739	...	1839	1918
Bridgend .... **136** a.	1958	2044	2100	2123	2203	2308	2308	0012	0012	0117	0130		0822	0859	0957	1058	1201	1259	1358	...	1459	1556	1659	1758	...	1858	1937
Port Talbot .... **136** a.	2011	2056	2112	2139	2215	2320	2320	0024	0024	0141	0151		0835	0911	1010	1110	1213	1311	1410	...	1511	1608	1711	1810	...	1910	1949
Neath .... **136** a.	2019	2103	2119	2150	2223	2327	2327	0031	0031	0148	0158		0843	0918	1017	1117	1221	1318	1417	...	1519	1616	1718	1817	...	1918	1957
Swansea .... **136** a.	2034	2116	2132	2204	2235	2340	2340	0044	0044	0201	0211		0858	0931	1030	1130	1234	1331	1430	...	1534	1628	1732	1830	...	1933	2009
Carmarthen **136** .... a.	2140	...	...	...	...	...	...	...	...	...	...		...	1024	...	1224	...	1424	...	...	1626	...	1830	...	...	...	2102

	⑥	⑥	⑥	⑥	⑥	⑥	⑥		⑦	⑦	⑦	⑦	⑦	⑦	⑦	⑦	⑦	⑦	⑦	⑦	⑦	⑦	⑦	⑦	⑦	⑦	⑦
London Padd.. **130 131 132** d.	1748	1818	1848	1918	1948	2048	2202		...	0833	0931t	1013	1045	1145	1213	1245	1345	1413	1445	1545	1645	1745	1845	1945	2045	2145	2245
Reading .... **130 131 132** d.	1813	1843	1913	1943	2013	2113	2227	⑦	...	0859	0956t	1040	1110	1210	1240	1310	1410	1440	1510	1610	1710	1810	1910	2010	2110	2210	2315
Didcot Parkway.. § **130/1 132** d.	|	1857	|	1957	|	|	2240		...	0914	1009t	1055	|	|	1254	|	|	1454	|	|	|	|	|	|	2122	2222	2330s
Swindon .... **130 131 132** d.	1840	1914	1940	2015	2040	2140	2257		...	0932	1030	1115	1138	1238	1314	1338	1438	1514	1538	1638	1738	1838	1937	2037	2137	2237	2346s
Bristol Parkway .... d.	1904	1938	2004	2038	2104	2205	2319		0858	0956	1056	1141	1202	1301	1336	1401	1501	1539	1601	1701	1801	1901	2001	2101	2204	2304	0010
Newport .... ‡ a.	1922	1956	2022	2056	2123	2223	...		0923	1014	1114	...	1220	1320	...	1420	1525	1558	1620	1725	1820	1920	2020	2120	2222	2322	...
Cardiff Central .... ‡ a.	1937	2010	2036	2110	2136	2242	...		0942	1029	1128	...	1233	1334	...	1434	1539	1612	1634	1738	1834	1934	2035	2134	2236	2336	...
Cardiff Central .... **136** d.	1940	2012	2039	2114	2140	2250	...		0944	1031	1130	...	1235	1335	...	1435	1540	...	1635	1739	1835	1935	2036	2135	2236	2336	...
Bridgend .... **136** a.	1959	2031	2058	2133	2159	2309	...		1003	1050	1149	...	1255	1354	...	1454	1600	...	1654	1759	1854	1954	2055	2155	2255	2355	...
Port Talbot .... **136** a.	2011	2043	2110	2145	2211	2321	...		1015	1102	1201	...	1307	1408	...	1506	1612	...	1708	1811	1907	2007	2107	2206	2308	0008	...
Neath .... **136** a.	2018	2050	2117	2152	2218	2329	...		1023	1109	1209	...	1315	1415	...	1514	1620	...	1715	1819	1914	2014	2114	2214	2314	0017	...
Swansea .... **136** a.	2031	2104	2130	2205	2231	2343	...		1035	1122	1221	...	1329	1428	...	1529	1632	...	1730	1833	1929	2028	2127	2227	2326	0030	...
Carmarthen **136** .... a.	...	...	...	...	...	...	...		...	...	1316	...	...	1519	...	...	1724	...	...	...	...	...	...	...	...	...	...

		ⒶC	Ⓐ	Ⓐ	Ⓐ	Ⓐ	Ⓐ		Ⓐ	Ⓐ	Ⓐ	Ⓐ	Ⓐ	Ⓐ	Ⓐ	Ⓐ	Ⓐ	Ⓐ	Ⓐ	Ⓐ✕		Ⓐ	Ⓐ	Ⓐ	Ⓐ	Ⓐ	Ⓐ
Carmarthen **136** .... d.		...	...	...	...	...	...	...	...	...	...	0723	...	...	...	0921	...	...	...	1127	...	...	...	...	...	...	1420
Swansea .... **136** d.	Ⓐ	...	0346	0459	0529	0557	0626	...	0654	0718	0743	0821	...	0922	...	1022	...	1122	...	1222	...	...	1322	...	1422	...	1522
Neath .... **136** d.		...	0358	0511	0541	0609	0638	...	0706	0730	0755	0834	...	0934	...	1035	...	1134	...	1234	...	...	1334	...	1434	...	1534
Port Talbot .... **136** d.		...	0405	0518	0548	0616	0645	...	0713	0737	0802	0841	...	0941	...	1042	...	1143	...	1241	...	...	1341	...	1441	...	1541
Bridgend .... **136** d.		...	0425	0531	0601	0629	0658	...	0726	0750	0815	0854	...	0954	...	1055	...	1156	...	1254	...	...	1354	...	1454	...	1554
Cardiff Central .... **136** a.		...	0455	0551	0621	0649	0718	...	0746	0810	0835	0916	...	1014	...	1115	...	1217	...	1314	...	...	1414	...	1514	...	1614
Cardiff Central .... ‡ d.		...	0507	0554	0624	0651	0723	...	0749	0818	0837	0919	0949	1018	1050	1118	1150	1218	1250	1318	...	1350	1418	1454	1518	1554	1621
Newport .... ‡ d.		...	0525	0607	0637	0704	0737	...	0804	0831	0850	0933	1003	1034	1103	1131	1204	1232	1304	1331	...	1404	1431	1507	1531	1607	1635
Bristol Parkway .... d.		0503	0552	0628	0659	0729	0759	...	0826	0856	0915	0956	1024	1055	1125	1155	1225	1255	1327	1355	...	1427	1452	1527	1555	1628	1655
Swindon .... **130 131 132** d.		0528	0618	0653	0723	0753	0825	...	0850	0920	0941	1022	1048	1120	1151	1220	1249	1320	1352	1420	...	1451	1519	1551	1620	1652	1719
Didcot Parkway.. § **130/1 132** d.		0546	0636	|	|	0810	|	...	|	|	|	|	1105	|	1208	|	1305	|	|	|	...	|	|	|	|	|	1736
Reading .... **130 131 132** a.		0558	0648	0718	0748	0823	|	...	0917	0945	1008	1050	1118	1145	1220	1244	1317	1346	1416	1445	...	1516	1545	1616	1645	1718	1748
London Padd.. **130 131 132** a.		0629	0716	0744	0816	0849	0912	...	0944	1014	1036	1120	1146	1211	1249	1310	1345	1414	1444	1512	...	1543	1607	1641	1710	1742	1813

	Ⓐ	Ⓐ	Ⓐ	Ⓐ	Ⓐ	Ⓐ		Ⓐ	⑤	①–④		⑥	⑥	⑥	⑥	⑥	⑥		⑥	⑥	⑥2	⑥	⑥	⑥	⑥P	⑥	⑥
Carmarthen **136** .... d.	...	...	...	1619	...	1818	...	...	2020	2020		...	...	...	...	...	...	...	...	0724	...	...	0930	...	1130	...	...
Swansea .... **136** d.	...	1622	...	1722	1823	1919	...	2023	2123	2123	⑥	0356	0525	0552	0623	0654	0722	...	0747	0822	...	0923	1023	1121	1224	1320	...
Neath .... **136** d.	...	1634	...	1734	1835	1931	...	2035	2135	2135		0408	0537	0604	0635	0706	0734	...	0759	0834	...	0935	1035	1133	1236	1332	...
Port Talbot .... **136** d.	...	1641	...	1741	1842	1938	...	2042	2142	2142		0415	0544	0611	0642	0713	0742	...	0807	0842	...	0943	1043	1141	1243	1340	...
Bridgend .... **136** d.	...	1654	...	1754	1855	1953	...	2055	2155	2155		0428	0557	0624	0655	0726	0754	...	0819	0856	...	0956	1056	1154	1256	1353	...
Cardiff Central .... **136** a.	...	1714	...	1814	1915	2014	...	2116	2215	2215		0449	0618	0645	0716	0748	0815	...	0840	0917	...	1017	1117	1215	1317	1414	...
Cardiff Central .... ‡ d.	1650	1718	1750	1818	1918	2018	...	2120	2217	2217		0514	0620	0647	0718	0750	0823	...	0851	0919	...	1020	1120	1220	1320	1421	1441
Newport .... ‡ d.	1704	1731	1803	1831	1931	2032	...	2133	2232	2232		0527	0633	0700	0730	0803	0836	...	0904	0933	...	1033	1132	1234	1333	1434	1455
Bristol Parkway .... d.	1727	1755	1827	1853	1955	2055	...	2154	2254	2302		0554	0656	0721	0752	0825	0858	...	0928	0957	1024	1057	1157	1256	1357	1457	1517
Swindon .... **130 131 132** d.	1751	1819	1851	1917	2020	2119	...	2219	...	...		0618	0720	0747	0821f	0849	0923	...	0952	1021	1049	1121	1221	1320	1421	1523	1546
Didcot Parkway.. § **130/1 132** d.	|	|	|	1935	|	|	...	|	...	...		0635	|	0803	|	0905	|	...	|	|	1107	|	|	|	|	|	1604
Reading .... **130 131 132** a.	1816	1845	1916	1947	2044	2144	...	2243	...	...		0648	0745	0816	0846	0918	0948	...	1018	1046	1121	1146	1246	1346	1446	1548	1618
London Padd.. **130 131 132** a.	1841	1914	1944	2016	2110	2209	...	2311	...	...		0714	0811	0844	0914	0944	1013	...	1044	1114	1149	1214	1312	1411	1512	1614	1644

	⑥	⑥	⑥	⑥c	⑥Q	⑥	⑥	⑥		⑦	⑦	⑦	⑦a	⑦b	⑦	⑦	⑦	⑦	⑦	⑦	⑦	⑦	⑦	⑦	⑦	⑦	⑦
Carmarthen **136** .... d.	1330	...	1528	...	1628	1730	...	...		...	...	...	...	...	...	...	...	1125	...	...	1415	...	...	1630	...	...	1920
Swansea .... **136** d.	1423	1523	1622	1723	1723	1823	1922	2022	⑦	...	0755	...	0835	0835	0923	1022	1123	1223	1323	1422	1523	...	1625	1721	1823	1924	2020
Neath .... **136** d.	1435	1535	1634	1735	1735	1835	1934	2034		...	0807	...	0847	0847	0935	1035	1135	1235	1335	1434	1535	...	1635	1734	1835	1936	2032
Port Talbot .... **136** d.	1443	1543	1641	1742	1742	1843	1942	2042		...	0814	...	0854	0854	0942	1042	1142	1242	1342	1441	1542	...	1643	1742	1842	1942	2039
Bridgend .... **136** d.	1456	1556	1654	1755	1755	1856	1955	2054		...	0827	...	0907	0907	0955	1055	1155	1255	1357	1454	1554	...	1655	1754	1855	1956	2052
Cardiff Central .... **136** a.	1517	1617	1715	1816	1816	1917	2016	2115		...	0848	...	0928	0928	1016	1117	1216	1316	1416	1515	1615	...	1717	1816	1917	2017	2114
Cardiff Central .... ‡ d.	1520	1623	1718	1819	1819	1919	2022	2118		...	0850	...	0935	0935	1020	1120	1220	1320	1420	1515	1620	1650	1720	1820	1920	2020	2120
Newport .... ‡ d.	1533	1636	1731	1831	1831	1932	2035	2131		...	0908	...	0952	0953	1033	1133	1233	1332	1433	1529	1633	1704	1733	1832	1933	2033	2135
Bristol Parkway .... d.	1557	1658	1757	1858j	1858j	1956	2056	2150		0830	0934	0955	1013	1027f	1055	1155	1255	1355	1455	1555	1655	1726	1755	1855	1955	2055	2155
Swindon .... **130 131 132** d.	1621	1723	1821	1923	1923	2020	2120	...		0854	1000	1019	1037	1051	1119	1219	1319	1419	1519	1619	1719	1750	1819	1919	2019	2119	2220
Didcot Parkway.. § **130/1 132** d.	|	|	|	|	|	|	2136	...		0910	|	|	|	|	|	|	|	|	|	|	|	1807	|	|	2035	2135	2236
Reading .... **130 131 132** a.	1646	1748	1846	1948	1948	2046	2149	...		0925	1025	1044	1102	1116	1144	1244	1344	1444	1544	1644	1744	1821	1844	1943	2048	2148	2249
London Padd.. **130 131 132** a.	1714	1813	1912	2013	2013	2112	2214	...		0950	1050	1109	1127	1141	1210	1309	1409	1509	1609	1709	1809	1850	1909	2009	2114	2214	2327

C – From Bristol Temple Meads (d. 0453).
F – From Bristol Temple Meads (d. 0704).
P – Until Sept. 13 continues to / starts from Pembroke Dock (Table **136**).
Q – Until Sept. 13 from Pembroke Dock (Table **136**).

a – Until Oct. 26.
b – From Nov. 2.

c – From Sept. 20.
e – Departs 1752.
f – Arrives 7 – 8 minutes earlier.
j – Arrives 1853.
r – Arrives 0717.
s – Calls to set down only.

t – Departs 4 minutes later until Sept. 14.

◇ – Via Bristol Temple Meads (see Table **132**).
‡ – For additional services see Tables **115**, **117** and **149.**
§ – See Table **132** for connecting services to / from Oxford and Banbury.

136 CARDIFF - SWANSEA - SOUTH WEST WALES

2nd class AW

For service on ⑦ August 3 - September 14, see page 579.

km			Ⓐ	Ⓐ	Ⓐ	Ⓐ	Ⓐ	Ⓐ	Ⓐ	Ⓐ	Ⓐ	Ⓐ	Ⓐ	Ⓐ	Ⓐ	Ⓐ	Ⓐ	Ⓐ	Ⓐ	Ⓐ	Ⓐ	Ⓐ	Ⓐ	Ⓐ	Ⓐ	Ⓐ	Ⓐ
										B					A	K 🍷			🍷		A		a	🍷		A	
	Manchester Picc **149** d.	Ⓐ	...	...	...	...	...	...	...	...	...	...	...	...	...	...	...	...	0730	...	...	...	...	0930	...	...	...
0	**Cardiff** Central **133** d.		...	...	...	...	...	...	0535	0639	0643	...	0740	0747	0842	0847	0851	1006	1050	1054	1142	...	...	1247	1251	1337	...
32	Bridgend **133** d.		...	...	...	...	...	...	0608	0659	0710	...	0758	0814	0902	0907	0918	1026	1109	1121	1202	...	...	1306	1318	1357	...
52	Port Talbot **133** d.		...	...	...	...	...	...	0623	0711	0726	...	0810	0829	0914	0919	0933	1039	1120	1136	1214	...	...	1318	1333	1409	...
61	Neath **133** d.		...	...	...	...	...	...	0633	0718	0736	...	0817	0839	0921	0926	0944	1047	1127	1146	1221	...	...	1325	1343	1417	...
73	**Swansea** **133** a.		...	...	...	...	...	...	0651	0729	0754	...	0834	0857	0932	0941	1005	1103	1142	1204	1232	...	...	1340	1402	1427	...
73	**Swansea** **145** d.		...	...	...	...	...	0602	0657	0740	0800	0817	0849	▬	0956	0945	1009	1107	1146	1206	1244	...	...	1345	1407	1444	...
91	Llanelli **145** d.		...	...	...	...	...	0619	0714	0757	0817	0833	0906	...	1013	1002	1025	1124	1203	1224	1301	...	...	1402	1422	1501	...
124	**Carmarthen** **145** a.		...	...	...	...	...	0649	0744	0824	0847	0858	0936	Ⓐ a	1040	1032	1053	1149	1233	1250	1328	...	...	1432	1448	1528	...
124	**Carmarthen** d.		0455	0535	0550	0600	...	0654	0746	...	0853	0902	0942	0956	...	1033	1054	1154	1236	1254	...	1335	1355	1435	1454	...	1545
147	Whitland d.		0511	0551	0606	0616	...	0711	0802	...	0910	0918	0957	1012	...	1050	1111	1211	1251	1310	...	1350	1411	1450	1510	...	1600
172	Tenby d.		|	0622	|	|	...	0740	|	...	0938	|	|	1036	...	|	1138	|	|	1338	...	|	1435	|	1538	...	|
191	**Pembroke Dock** a.		|	0654	|	|	...	0811	|	...	1010	|	|	...	...	|	1211	|	|	1411	...	|	...	|	1611	...	|
166	Clarbeston Road ⊗ d.		0525	...	0622	0630	0718	...	0816	...	...	0932	1011	...	...	1105	...	1226	1306	...	...	1405	...	1505	...	...	1614
174	Haverfordwest d.		0534	...	|	0639	|	...	0825	...	...	|	1034h	...	...	1116	...	|	1315	...	...	1416	...	|	...	...	1623
189	**Milford Haven** a.		0552	...	|	0658	|	...	0843	...	...	|	1052	...	...	1135	...	|	1332	...	...	1434	...	|	...	...	1640
191	**Fishguard** Harbour a.		...	...	0646	...	0742	...	...	...	...	0957	...	...	...	...	...	1251	...	...	...	...	...	1530	...	...	...

	Ⓐ	Ⓐ	Ⓐ	Ⓐ	Ⓐ	Ⓐ	Ⓐ	Ⓐ	Ⓐ	Ⓐ	Ⓐ	Ⓐ	Ⓐ	Ⓐ	Ⓐ	⑤	Ⓐ	Ⓐ	⑤	①–④	Ⓐ	Ⓐ	Ⓐ	Ⓐ		⑥	⑥
	🍷		A				🍷				A	🍷		A	M	A			🍷	🍷							
Manchester Picc **149** d.	1130	...	...	...	...	...	1330	...	...	...	...	1530	...	...	1630	...	...	...	1730	1730	...	...	...	...	⑥	...	...
Cardiff Central **133** d.	1447	1451	1537	1543	1606	...	1647	1651	1745	1751	1809	1848	1851	1939	1947	...	...	1951	2058	2058	...	2227	...	2320		...	...
Bridgend **133** d.	1506	1518	1557	1611	1626	...	1706	1718	1806	1818	1829	1906	1918	1959	2007	...	...	2019	2117	2117	...	2246	...	2348		...	...
Port Talbot **133** d.	1518	1533	1609	1628	1640	...	1719	1733	1820	1833	1842	1918	1933	2012	2023	...	...	2033	2132	2132	...	2301	...	0003		...	...
Neath **133** d.	1525	1543	1616	1639	1649	...	1727	1743	1828	1843	1853	1926	1943	2020	2030	...	...	2043	2143	2143	...	|	...	0014		...	...
Swansea **133** a.	1540	1602	1627	1658	1705	...	1742	1800	1842	1901	1903	1941	2001	2034	2044	←	...	2103	2159	2159	...	|	...	0032		...	...
Swansea **145** d.	1545	1604	1637	...	1709	1736	1801	*1833*	1844	...	1910	1949	2004	→	...	2049	2055	...	2203	2209	2240	|	2345	0051		...	...
Llanelli **145** d.	1602	1621	1654	...	1726	1756	1818	*1854*	1904	...	1927	2006	2021	...	...	2106	2117t	...	2220	2227	2259	2335	0004	0108		...	...
Carmarthen **145** a.	1632	1651	1721	...	1757	1829	1849	...	1934	...	1954	2032	2051	...	...	2140	2152	...	2249	2259	2333	0010	0038	0138		...	...
Carmarthen d.	1634	1654	...	...	1759	1830	1854	...	1935	...	...	2035	2053	...	...	...	2155	...	2255	...	...	...	...	...		0454	0535
Whitland d.	1650	1710	...	...	1814	1846	1910	...	1951	...	...	2051	2109	...	...	...	2210	...	2311	...	...	...	...	...		0510	0551
Tenby a.	|	1739	...	...	|	|	1940	...	|	...	...	|	2142	...	...	...	|	...	|	...	...	...	...	...		|	0623
Pembroke Dock a.	|	1811	...	...	|	|	2012	...	|	...	...	|	2215	...	...	...	|	...	|	...	...	...	...	...		|	0655
Clarbeston Road ⊗ d.	1704	...	...	...	1828	1900	...	...	2005	...	...	2105	...	...	...	...	2224	...	2325	...	...	...	...	...		0524	...
Haverfordwest d.	1713	...	...	...	1837	|	...	...	2013	...	...	|	...	...	...	...	2233	...	2338t	...	...	...	...	...		0533	...
Milford Haven a.	1731	...	...	...	1854	|	...	...	2032	...	...	|	...	...	...	...	2249	...	2356	...	...	...	...	...		0551	...
Fishguard Harbour a.	...	...	...	...	...	1925	...	...	...	...	...	2128	...	...	...	...	...	...	...	...	...	...	...	...		...	...

	⑥	⑥	⑥	⑥	⑥	⑥ n	⑥ n	⑥ p	⑥	⑥	⑥	⑥	⑥	⑥	⑥	⑥	⑥	⑥	⑥	⑥	⑥	⑥	⑥	⑥	⑥	⑥	⑥
							🍷				🍷		A	K 🍷			A n	A p	🍷	n	p	n	🍷	A	🍷		
Manchester Picc **149** d.	...	...	...	...	...	...	...	...	...	...	...	...	...	...	...	...	...	...	0730	...	...	...	...	...	0930	...	...
Cardiff Central **133** d.	...	...	...	...	0542	...	0636	0636	...	...	0741	0744	0840	0847	0851	1007	1039	1039	1049	1053	1053	...	1209	1240	1247	1251	1406
Bridgend **133** d.	...	...	...	...	0609	...	0709	0709	...	...	0800	0811	0900	0906	0918	1027	1059	1059	1107	1120	1120	...	1229	1300	1306	1318	1426
Port Talbot **133** d.	...	...	...	...	0624	...	0725	0725	...	...	0813	0826	0912	0918	0933	1040	1111	1111	1119	1135	1135	...	1242	1312	1318	1333	1439
Neath **133** d.	...	...	...	...	0634	...	0736	0736	...	...	0821	0836	0919	0925	0943	1048	1118	1118	1126	1145	1145	...	1250	1319	1325	1343	1447
Swansea **133** a.	...	...	...	...	0652	...	0756	0756	...	...	0835	0854	0931	0939	0959	1103	1130	1130	1140	1204	1201	...	1305	1331	1340	1359	1503
Swansea **145** d.	...	...	...	0602	0657	0718	0800	0800	0818	0834	0844	▬	0940	0949	1007	1107	1140	1140	1149	1207	1207	1227	1308	1340	1348	1407	1507
Llanelli **145** d.	...	...	...	0619	0715	0735	0817	0817	0833	0851	0901	...	0957	1008	1024	1124	1157	1157	1206	1224	1224	1245	1325	1357	1408	1422	1524
Carmarthen **145** a.	...	...	...	0649	0745	0808	0846	0847	0858	0918	0931	⑥ n	1024	1040	1050c	1149	1224	1224	1237	1250	1250	1312	1350	1424	1438	1448	1549
Carmarthen d.	0550	0600	...	0654	0746	0814	...	0853	0900	...	0933	0953	...	1104	1056	1154	1231	...	1241	...	1253	*1336*	1356	...	1440	1454	1556
Whitland d.	0606	0616	...	0711	0802	0833	...	0910	0918	...	0948	1008	...	1121	1112	1209	1250	...	1256	...	1309	*1352*	1413	...	1455	1509	1612
Tenby a.	|	|	...	0740	|	0906	...	0939	|	...	|	1036	...	|	1140	|	1320	...	|	...	1338	*1419*	|	...	|	1537	|
Pembroke Dock a.	|	|	...	0812	|	0938	...	1011	|	...	|	1106	...	|	1213	|	1350	...	|	...	1411	...	|	...	|	1610	|
Clarbeston Road ⊗ d.	0622	0630	0718	...	0816	...	...	...	0932	...	1002	...	...	1136	...	1224	...	...	1310	...	...	...	1427	...	1510	...	1626
Haverfordwest d.	|	0639	|	...	0825	...	...	...	|	...	1016t	...	...	1144	...	|	...	...	1319	...	...	...	1436	...	|	...	1635
Milford Haven a.	|	0658	|	...	0843	...	...	...	|	...	1034	...	...	1203	...	|	...	...	1337	...	...	...	1454	...	|	...	1653
Fishguard Harbour a.	0646	...	0742	...	...	...	...	...	0957	...	...	...	...	...	...	1250	...	...	...	...	...	...	...	...	1535	...	...

	⑥	⑥	⑥	⑥	⑥	⑥	⑥	⑥	⑥	⑥	⑥	⑥	⑥	⑥	⑥	⑥	⑥	⑥	⑥	⑥	⑥	⑥		⑦	⑦	⑦	⑦
	A	🍷					A	🍷				🍷		A	M			🍷				A		b	b		b
Manchester Picc **149** d.	...	1130	...	...	...	...	...	1330	...	...	...	1530	...	...	1630	...	...	1730	...	...	...	...	⑦	...	...	...	...
Cardiff Central **133** d.	1440	1447	1451	1543	1606	...	1640	1647	1653	1745	1751	1850	1853	1918	1947	...	1951	2059	...	2157	2227	2250		...	...	0804	...
Bridgend **133** d.	1500	1506	1518	1612	1625	...	1700	1706	1720	1806	1819	1908	1920	1938	2007	...	2019	2118	...	2225	2255	2310		...	...	0826	...
Port Talbot **133** d.	1512	1519	1533	1628	1639	...	1712	1718	1735	1820	1834	1920	1935	1950	2023	...	2033	2133	...	2239	2310	2323		...	...	0838	...
Neath **133** d.	1520	1527	1543	1640	1648	...	1719	1725	1746	1828	1844	1928	1945	1958	2030	...	2043	2144	...	2246	2321	2331	♥	...	...	0846	...
Swansea **133** a.	1534	1542	1601	1658	1703	...	1732	1740	1804	1842	1903	1943	2001	2009	2046	...	2101	2200	...	2259	2340	2343		...	...	0902	...
Swansea **145** d.	1542	1549	1604	...	1705	1726	1740	1803	...	1845	...	1946	2006	2018	...	2052	...	2207	2242	2303	2344	*0012*		...	0814	▬	...
Llanelli **145** d.	1559	1608	1621	...	1722	1747	1800	1820	...	1902	...	2003	2023	2035	...	2109	...	2224	2301	2321	0002	*0029*		...	0832	...	...
Carmarthen **145** a.	1626	1639	1651	...	1752	1822	1830	1851	...	1932	...	2029	2053	2102	...	2138	...	2253	2335	2350	0032	*0100*		...	0903	⑦	...
Carmarthen d.	...	1640	1653	...	1756	1823	...	1854	...	1933	...	2034	2055	...	...	2140	...	...	...	...	...	...		0820	0906	0955	1010
Whitland d.	...	1656	1709	...	1812	1840	...	1910	...	1949	...	2050	2111	...	...	2155	...	...	...	...	...	...		0836	0922	1011	1026
Tenby d.	...	|	1738	...	|	|	...	1940	...	|	...	|	2142	...	...	|	...	...	...	...	...	...		|	0951	|	1058
Pembroke Dock a.	...	|	1810	...	|	|	...	2012	...	|	...	|	2215	...	...	|	...	...	...	...	...	...		|	1024	|	1130
Clarbeston Road ⊗ d.	...	1710	...	...	1826	1855	...	...	...	2003	...	2104	...	...	...	2209	...	...	...	...	...	...		0851	...	1026	...
Haverfordwest d.	...	1719	...	...	1834	|	...	...	...	2011	...	|	...	...	...	2218	...	...	...	...	...	...		0859	...	1035	...
Milford Haven a.	...	1737	...	...	1851	|	...	...	...	2030	...	|	...	...	...	2237	...	...	...	...	...	...		0918	...	1053	...
Fishguard Harbour a.	...	...	...	...	...	1920	...	...	...	...	...	2127	...	...	...	...	...	...	...	...	...	...		...	...	...	...

	⑦	⑦	⑦	⑦	⑦	⑦	⑦	⑦	⑦	⑦	⑦	⑦	⑦	⑦	⑦	⑦	⑦	⑦	⑦	⑦	⑦	⑦	⑦	⑦	⑦	⑦	⑦
	k				F	A	🍷		M	A	🍷	🍷	A	🍷	🍷	🍷			🍷	M	🍷			🍷			
Manchester Picc **149** d.	...	...	...	...	...	...	...	...	0930	...	1030	1129	...	...	1231	1330	...	1430	1430	1530	1630	...	...	1730	1830	...	1930
Cardiff Central **133** d.	...	...	...	0954	1114	1130	1206	...	1320	1335	1412	1452	1540	...	1603	1707	...	1809	1809	1855	1955	...	2019	2050	2149	2230	2300
Bridgend **133** d.	...	...	...	1021	1133	1150	1233	...	1340	1355	1431	1511	1601	...	1622	1726	...	1828	1828	1916	2014	...	2037	2109	2208	2248	2319
Port Talbot **133** d.	...	...	...	1036	1145	1202	1249	...	1356	1409	1448	1526	1613	...	1638	1742	...	1844	1844	1932	2029	...	2054	2123	2223	2301	2337
Neath **133** d.	...	...	...	1044	1153	1210	|	...	1403	1416	1456	1534	1621	...	1646	1749	...	1852	1852	1939	2037	...	2103	2131	2230	2309	2344
Swansea **133** a.	...	...	...	1059	1207	1221	|	...	1420	1428	1510	1548	1632	...	1700	1802	...	1907	1907	1955	2052	...	2117	2148	2245	2323	2359
Swansea **145** d.	...	1027	1043	1102	1217	1232	|	1403	...	1435	1513	...	1640	1649	1706	...	1844	1915	1915	...	...	2057	2120	...	2248	2334	...
Llanelli **145** d.	...	1043	1059	1121	1236	1249	1318	1421	...	1452	1532	...	1657	1707	1725	...	1902	1933	1933	...	...	2118	2139	...	2307	2352	...
Carmarthen **145** a.	...	1111	1125	1155	1307	1316	1345	1452	...	1519	1558	...	1724	1738	1754	...	1934	2001	2001	...	...	2152	2205	...	2339	0024	...
Carmarthen d.	1015	...	1128	1156	1309	...	1354	1455	...	...	1603	...	...	1744	1805	...	1935	2004	2004	...	...	2154	2207	...	...	...	...
Whitland d.	1031	...	1144	1212	1324	...	1410	1511	...	...	1619	...	...	1800	1821	...	1951	2025r	2029r	...	...	2209	2222	...	...	...	...
Tenby d.	1100	...	|	|	|	...	|	1540	...	...	|	...	...	1829	|	...	|	2055	|	...	...	|	|	...	...	...	...
Pembroke Dock a.	1131	...	|	|	|	...	|	1615	...	...	|	...	...	1901	|	...	|	2127	|	...	...	|	|	...	...	...	...
Clarbeston Road ⊗ d.	...	...	1157	1227	1337	...	1425	...	...	...	1634	...	...	...	1836	...	2006	...	2044	...	...	2223	2237	...	...	...	...
Haverfordwest d.	...	...	|	1236	|	...	1433	...	...	...	1642	...	...	...	1846	...	2016	...	2052	...	...	|	2246	...	...	...	...
Milford Haven a.	...	...	|	1254	|	...	1456	...	...	...	1659	...	...	...	1906	...	...	...	2115	...	...	|	2305	...	...	...	...
Fishguard Harbour a.	...	...	1223	...	1401	...	...	...	...	...	...	...	...	...	...	...	...	...	...	...	...	2246	...	...	...	...	...

A – To/from London Paddington (operated by GW, see Table **133**). Conveys (12) and 🍷.
B – From/to Bristol Parkway (operated by GW, see Table **133**). Conveys (12) and 🍷.
F – To/from Hereford (Table **149**).
H – To Shrewsbury (Table **149**).
K – From Crewe (Table **149**).
M – (12) and ✕ Manchester - Swansea and v.v.
S – From Shrewsbury (Table **145**).

a – Until Sept. 12.
b – Until July 27.
c – Connects with train in previous column.
e – Arrives 2136.
f – Arrives 1937.
h – Arrives 1019.
k – From Sept. 21.
n – Until Sept. 13.
p – From Sept. 20.

r – Arrives 2021.
s – Calls to set down only.
t – Arrives 5 minutes earlier.

⊗ – Trains call at Clarbeston Road on request (except trains starting or terminating there).
* – Connection by 🚌.
♥ – Service valid until July 27 and from Sept. 21. For service Aug. 3 - Sept. 14, see page 579.

AW 2nd class — SOUTH WEST WALES - SWANSEA - CARDIFF — 136

For service on ⑦ August 3 - September 14, see page 579.

		Ⓐ	Ⓐ	Ⓐ	Ⓐ	Ⓐ	Ⓐ	Ⓐ	Ⓐ	Ⓐ	Ⓐ	Ⓐ	Ⓐ	Ⓐ	Ⓐ	Ⓐ	Ⓐ	Ⓐ	Ⓐ	Ⓐ	Ⓐ	Ⓐ	Ⓐ	Ⓐ	Ⓐ
			M		♀				♀			A	♀	♀		a	A	♀			♀	A			a
Fishguard Harbour d.	Ⓐ	...	...	...	...	...	...	0650	...	...	0745	...	...	...	1001	...	✕	...	...	...	1300	...	...	...	...
Milford Haven d.		...	...	...	...	...	0554	|	0700	...	|	...	0900	...	|	...	...	1100	...	1200	|	...	...	1400	...
Haverfordwest d.		...	...	...	...	...	0609	|	0715	...	|	...	0915	...	|	...	...	1115	...	1216	|	...	...	1415	...
Clarbeston Road ⊗ d.		...	...	...	...	...	0617	0714	0723	...	0807	...	0923	...	1023	...	...	1123	...	1223	1323	...	...	1423	...
Pembroke Dock d.		...	...	...	...	...	|	▬	|	0707	|	...	|	0902	|	...	...	|	1102	|	|	...	1302	|	...
Tenby d.		...	...	...	...	...	|	...	|	0742	|	...	|	0937	|	1040	...	|	1138t	|	|	...	1338t	|	1439
Whitland d.		...	...	...	...	...	0631	Ⓐ	0737	0810	0821	...	0939	1005	1037	1105	...	1137	1206	1237	1337	...	1405	1437	1504
Carmarthen a.		...	...	...	...	...	0648	A	0755	0827	0839	...	0956	1021	1054	1121	...	1154	1222	1254	1354	...	1421	1454	1520
Carmarthen 145 d.		0438	...	0536	0604	...	0651	0723	0759	0831	...	0921	0957	1031	...	...	1127	1156	1234	1258	1356	1420	1432	1457	▬
Llanelli 145 d.		0503	...	0603	0632	0655	0720	0756	0827	0859	...	0949	1025	1054	...	...	1155	1223	1257	1322	1423	1448	1457	1521	...
Swansea 145 a.		0524	...	0621	|	0713	0740	0813	0847	0917	...	1007	1046	1116	...	...	1213	1244	1316	1343	1444	1505	1517c	1542	Ⓐ
Swansea 133 d.		...	0543	0631	|	0723	0752	0821	0852	0927	...	1022	1054	1128	...	...	1222	1254	1327	1352	1454	1522	1527	1552	1629
Neath 133 d.		...	0555	0645	|	0738	0804	0834	0905	0942	...	1035	1106	1143	...	...	1234	1306	1342	1403	1506	1534	1542	1604	1644
Port Talbot 133 d.		...	0602	0657	0707	0749	0811	0841	0913	0953	...	1042	1114	1154	...	...	1241	1314	1353	1410	1514	1541	1553	1611	1655
Bridgend 133 d.		...	0619	0711	0721	0804	0826	0854	0927	1008	...	1055	1127	1209	...	...	1254	1327	1408	1422	1528	1554	1608	1625	1710
Cardiff Central 133 a.		...	0641	0739	0744	0832	0846	0916	0950	1038	...	1115	1150	1238	...	...	1314	1350	1438	1443	1549	1614	1638	1646	1738
Manchester Picc 149 a.		...	1013	...	1113	...	...	...	1313	...	...	...	1513	...	...	...	...	1713	...	...	1915	...	...	...	...

	Ⓐ	Ⓐ	Ⓐ	Ⓐ	Ⓐ	Ⓐ	Ⓐ	Ⓐ	Ⓐ	Ⓐ	Ⓐ	Ⓐ	Ⓐ	Ⓐ	Ⓐ	Ⓐ	Ⓐ	Ⓐ	Ⓐ		⑥	⑥	⑥	⑥	⑥
	♀	A		♀			A					B											M		♀
Fishguard Harbour d.	...	...	...	1600	...	...	...	...	...	...	...	...	1929	...	...	...	2146	...	...		...	...	...	...	...
Milford Haven d.	1500	...	...	|	...	1655	...	...	1800	1904	...	...	|	...	2038	...	|	...	2320	⑥	0021	...	...	...	...
Haverfordwest d.	1515	...	...	|	...	1714	...	...	1815	1919	...	...	|	...	2053	...	|	...	2335		0036	...	...	...	...
Clarbeston Road ⊗ d.	1523	...	...	1623	...	1722	...	...	1823	1927	...	...	1950	...	2101	...	2208	...	2350		0044	...	...	...	...
Pembroke Dock d.	|	...	1502	|	...	|	...	1702	|	|	...	...	|	1907	|	2107	|	2226	|		|	...	...	...	...
Tenby d.	|	...	1537	|	...	|	...	1739t	|	|	...	...	|	1945f	|	2146e	|	2255	|		|	...	...	...	...
Whitland d.	1537	...	1605	1637	...	1737	...	1806	1837	1941	...	...	2005	2014	2115	2214	2222	2323	2357		0058	...	...	...	...
Carmarthen a.	1554	...	1621	1654	...	1753	...	1822	1854	1958	...	...	2023	2030	2132	2231	2239	2340	0014		0116	...	...	...	...
Carmarthen 145 d.	1556	1619	1632	1656	...	1758	1818	1832	1857	...	2002	2020	...	2032	2134	...	2242	...	...		...	0439	...	0536	0604
Llanelli 145 d.	1623	1647	1655	1723	...	1825	1846	1855	1928	...	2029	2048	...	2059	2201	...	2309	...	...		...	0503	...	0603	0632
Swansea 145 a.	1646	1708	1719	1746	...	1845	1909	1916	1948	...	2049	2107	...	2120	2221	...	2329	...	...		...	0520	...	0623	|
Swansea 133 d.	1652	1722	1727	1752	1828	1847	1919	1924	1952	...	2052	2123	...	2128	2228	...	2332	...	...		...	...	0539	0629	|
Neath 133 d.	1704	1734	1742	1803	1844	1858	1931	1939	2003	...	2107	2135	...	2143	2243	...	2346	...	...		...	...	0551	0643	|
Port Talbot 133 d.	1712	1741	1753	1810	1856	1905	1938	1950	2010	...	2118	2142	...	2155	2255	...	2358	...	...		...	...	0558	0655	0706
Bridgend 133 d.	1726	1754	1808	1823	1912	1921	1953	2005	2024	...	2133	2155	...	2210	2311	...	0017	...	...		...	...	0615	0709	0720
Cardiff Central 133 a.	1752	1814	1838	1843	1940	1947	2014	2035	2048	...	2155	2215	...	2235	2335	...	0038	...	...		...	...	0637	0737	0743
Manchester Picc 149 a.	2113	...	...	...	...	...	...	...	...	...	...	...	...	...	...	...	...	...	...		...	...	1013	...	1113

	⑥	⑥	⑥	⑥	⑥	⑥	⑥	⑥	⑥	⑥	⑥	⑥	⑥	⑥	⑥	⑥	⑥	⑥	⑥	⑥	⑥	⑥	⑥	⑥	⑥
				♀			A	♀n	♀	♀n	♀p		An	Ap	♀			A	♀	♀n	p		A		♀
Fishguard Harbour d.	...	...	0650	...	...	0800	...	...	...	...	...	1001	...	...	...	...	...	...	1300	...	...	...	...	...	...
Milford Haven d.	...	0556	|	0701	...	|	...	...	0859	...	...	|	...	...	1100	...	1208	...	|	...	...	1359	...	...	1502
Haverfordwest d.	...	0611	|	0716	...	|	...	...	0914	...	...	|	...	...	1115	...	1223	...	|	...	...	1415	...	...	1517
Clarbeston Road ⊗ d.	...	0619	0714	0724	...	0822	...	...	0922	...	...	1023	...	...	1123	...	1231	...	1322	...	...	1423	...	...	1525
Pembroke Dock d.	...	|	▬	|	0707	|	...	0832	|	...	0904	|	1002	...	|	1109	|	...	|	1244	1304	|	...	...	|
Tenby d.	...	|	...	|	0742	|	...	0904	|	...	0937	|	1038t	...	|	1146t	|	...	|	1318	1337	|	...	...	|
Whitland d.	...	0633	⑥	0738	0810	0836	...	0932	0936	1005	1005	1037	1107	...	1137	1214	1245	...	1337	1348	1405	1437	...	...	1539
Carmarthen a.	...	0651	A	0755	0827	0851	...	...	0953	1021	1021	1053	1123	...	1154	1231	1303	...	1354	1406	1422	1454	...	...	1556
Carmarthen 145 d.	...	0653	0724	0758	0832	0859	0930	...	0956	1031	1031	1056	1130	1130	1156	1236	1304	1330	1356	1428	1428	1456	1528	...	1558
Llanelli 145 d.	0655	0723	0757	0825	0900	0928	0958	...	1023	1054	1054	1120	1158	1158	1223	1258	1328	1358	1423	1455	1455	1520	1556	...	1625
Swansea 145 a.	0713	0743	0814	0845	0918	0949	1015	...	1044	1116	1116	1141	1216	1216	1244	1315	1349	1415	1444	1515	1518	1541	1613	...	1646
Swansea 133 d.	0727	0752	0822	0853	0929	0956	1023	...	1054	1125	1125	1152	1224	1224	1256	1325	1352	1423	1454	1528	1528	1552	1622	1629	1650
Neath 133 d.	0742	0804	0834	0905	0944	1007	1035	...	1105	1140	1140	1203	1236	1236	1308	1340	1403	1435	1505	1543	1543	1603	1634	1644	1701
Port Talbot 133 d.	0753	0811	0842	0912	0955	1014	1043	...	1112	1151	1151	1210	1243	1243	1315	1351	1410	1443	1512	1554	1554	1610	1641	1655	1708
Bridgend 133 d.	0808	0826	0856	0925	1010	1026	1056	...	1125	1206	1206	1222	1256	1256	1328	1406	1422	1456	1525	1609	1609	1622	1654	1710	1721
Cardiff Central 133 a.	0838	0846	0917	0950	1038	1046	1117	...	1150	1238	1238	1245	1317	1317	1350	1438	1446	1517	1549	1638	1638	1646	1715	1738	1743
Manchester Picc 149 a.	...	...	...	1313	...	...	...	...	1513	...	...	...	...	...	1713	...	...	...	1913	...	...	...	...	...	2113

	⑥	⑥	⑥	⑥	⑥	⑥	⑥	⑥	⑥	⑥	⑥	⑥	⑥	⑥	⑥	⑥	⑥		⑦	⑦	⑦	⑦	⑦	⑦	⑦
	An	p		A															♀	♀	♀	M	♀b	♀k	
Fishguard Harbour d.	...	...	1600	...	...	...	...	...	...	...	1929	...	...	...	2144	...	...		...	...	...	...	...	...	...
Milford Haven d.	...	...	|	...	...	1700	...	1800	...	1857	|	...	2038	...	|	...	2308	⑦	...	...	...	...	0935	...	...
Haverfordwest d.	...	...	|	...	...	1719	...	1815	...	1912	|	...	2053	...	|	...	2323		...	...	...	...	0950	...	...
Clarbeston Road ⊗ d.	...	...	1623	...	...	1727	...	1823	...	1920	1950	...	2101	...	2206	...	2331		...	...	...	...	0958	...	...
Pembroke Dock d.	1502	1504	|	...	...	|	1702	|	...	|	|	1907	|	2107	|	2218	|		...	...	...	...	|	...	...
Tenby d.	1538t	1537	|	...	...	|	1737	|	...	|	|	1951f	|	2142t	|	2247	|	♥	...	...	...	...	|	...	...
Whitland d.	1607	1605	1637	...	...	1741	1805	1837	...	1934	2005	2019	2115	2210	2220	2315	2345		...	...	...	...	1013	...	...
Carmarthen a.	1623	1622	1654	...	...	1757	1822	1854	...	1950	2023	2035	2132	2227	2237	2332	0003		...	...	...	...	1028	...	...
Carmarthen 145 d.	1628	1629	1656	1730	...	1800	1835	1856	1919	1956	...	2040	2137	...	2241	...	...		...	0837b	0934	...	1035	1035	1055
Llanelli 145 d.	1656	1652	1724	1758	...	1827	1858	1923	1947	2023	...	2108	2205	...	2309	...	...		...	0901b	0959	...	1059	1059	1124
Swansea 145 a.	1713	1715	1748	1815	...	1848	1917	1944	2004	2043	...	2130	2225	...	2327	...	...		...	0918b	1017	...	1118	1118	1144
Swansea 133 d.	1723	1729	1752	1823	1831	1850	1927	1952	...	2047	...	2131	2236	...	...	...	...		0841	0930	...	1032	1131	1131	...
Neath 133 d.	1735	1744	1803	1835	1846	1901	1942	2003	...	2102	...	2147	2252	...	...	...	...		0853	0942	...	1044	1143	1143	...
Port Talbot 133 d.	1742	1755	1810	1843	1857	1908	1953	2010	...	2113	...	2159	2304	...	...	...	...		0900	0949	...	1051	1150	1150	...
Bridgend 133 d.	1755	1810	1822	1856	1912	1922	2008	2022	...	2128	...	2214	2319	...	...	...	...		0916	1005	...	1108	1206	1206	...
Cardiff Central 133 a.	1816	1838	1846	1917	1941	1947	2038	2045	...	2152	...	2238	2342	...	...	...	...		0937	1025	...	1130	1226	1226	...
Manchester Picc 149 a.	...	...	...	...	...	...	...	...	...	...	...	...	...	...	...	...	...		1311	1415	...	1515	1615	1615	...

	⑦	⑦	⑦	⑦	⑦	⑦	⑦	⑦	⑦	⑦	⑦	⑦	⑦	⑦	⑦	⑦	⑦	⑦	⑦	⑦	⑦	⑦	⑦	⑦	⑦
	A	b	♀			M	A	♀			A	♀	H		k	b	A	S			F				
Fishguard Harbour d.	...	...	...	...	1239	...	...	...	1412	...	...	...	...	...	...	...	...	...	...	...	...	...	...	2301	...
Milford Haven d.	...	...	1124	...	|	...	...	1329	|	...	...	1530	...	...	1730	1741	...	...	...	1939	...	2135	...	|	2310
Haverfordwest d.	...	...	1139	...	|	...	...	1345	|	...	...	1546	...	...	1745	1756	...	...	...	1955	...	2151	...	|	2326
Clarbeston Road ⊗ d.	...	...	1147	...	1301	...	...	1353	1434	...	...	1554	...	...	1753	1804	...	...	...	2003	...	2159	...	2323	2334
Pembroke Dock d.	...	1027	|	1139	|	...	...	|	|	...	...	|	...	1622	|	|	...	...	1910	|	...	|	2200	|	|
Tenby d.	...	1059	|	1210	|	...	...	|	|	...	...	|	...	1653	|	|	...	...	1941	|	...	|	2232	|	|
Whitland d.	...	1129	1202	1239	1314	...	...	1408	1447	...	...	1609	...	1723	1809	1820	...	...	2010	2018	...	2214	2301	2336	2348
Carmarthen a.	...	1145	1217	1256	1331	...	...	1425	1504	...	...	1625c	...	1742	1826	1837	...	...	2026	2036c	...	2231	2319	2353	0007
Carmarthen 145 d.	1125	▬	1232	1258	1334	...	1415	1428	1506	...	1630	1641	...	1742	▬	...	1920	...	2042	...	2116	2234	...	...	...
Llanelli 145 d.	1153	⑦	1256	1327	1358	...	1446	1452	1535	...	1657	1710	...	1811	⑦	...	1954	2005	2111	...	2140	2303	...	...	...
Swansea 145 a.	1211	♀	1317	1346	|	...	1504	1513c	1557	...	1713	1732	...	1834	A	...	2012	2028	2136	...	2200	2323	...	...	...
Swansea 133 d.	1223	1251	1340	...	|	1455	1523	1532	...	1654	1721	1736	1834	...	1924	...	2020	2040	...	...	2205	2327	...	...	...
Neath 133 d.	1235	1303	1352	...	1421	1507	1535	1544	...	1706	1734	1747	1847	...	1936	...	2032	2051	...	...	2216	2339	...	...	...
Port Talbot 133 d.	1242	1311	1359	...	1429	1515	1542	1552	...	1713	1742	1755	1855	...	1942	...	2039	2100	...	...	2224	2346	...	...	...
Bridgend 133 d.	1255	1327	1415	...	1442	1532	1554	1607	...	1729	1754	1811	1911	...	1956	...	2052	2115	...	...	2240	0003	...	...	...
Cardiff Central 133 a.	1316	1347	1436	...	1504	1553	1615	1635	...	1749	1816	1833	1933	...	2017	...	2114	2139	...	...	2300	0029	...	...	...
Manchester Picc 149 a.	...	1715	1814	...	...	1914	...	2015	...	2115	...	2214	...	...	...	...	...	...	...	...	...	...	...	...	...

◄◄◄ FOR NOTES SEE PREVIOUS PAGE

GW All trains convey ♀ — BRISTOL - SWINDON - OXFORD — 137

km			⑥a		⑥a				⑥a		⑥a	
0	**Bristol** Temple Meads d.	...	1018	...	1518	...	**Oxford** d.	...	1202	...	1712	...
18	Bath Spa d.	...	1031	...	1531	...	Swindon d.	...	1233	...	1746	...
39	Chippenham d.	...	1044	...	1545	...	Chippenham d.	...	1245	...	1758	...
66	Swindon d.	...	1058	...	1600	...	Bath Spa d.	...	1300	...	1811	...
123	**Oxford** a.	...	1127	...	1629	...	**Bristol** Temple Meads a.	...	1312	...	1823	...

a – From Sept. 20.

138 WORCESTER - GLOUCESTER - BRISTOL

2nd class only GW

km		Ⓐ	Ⓐ	Ⓐ	Ⓐ A	Ⓐ p	Ⓐ	Ⓐ p		Ⓐ	Ⓐ	Ⓐ p	Ⓐ p	Ⓐ		Ⓐ	Ⓐ p	Ⓐ p	Ⓐ	Ⓐ	Ⓐ	Ⓐ p	Ⓐ p
0	**Great Malvern** 122 130 d.		...	...	...	...	...	...	...	...	...	...	...	...	...	...	...	...	...	...	...	...	...
13	**Worcester** Foregate Street 122 130 d.		...	...	...	...	0705	...	...	...	0953	1053	1149	1253	...	1352	1450	1549	1655	...	...	1853	...
14	**Worcester** Shrub Hill 122 130 d.		...	...	...	...	0708	*0725*	...	0900	0956	1057	1202j	1257	...	1357	1456	1557h	1658	1757	...	1857	...
39	Ashchurch for Tewkesbury d.		...	...	*0631*	...	0724	*0741*	...	0917	1013	1113	1219	1313	...	1413	1513	1613	1715	1815	...	1913	...
48	Cheltenham Spa ◧ 119 d.		...	0614	*0641*	...	0734	*0755*h	...	0926	1023	1123	1229	1323	...	1424	1523	1623	1725	1825	...	1923	...
61	**Gloucester** ◧ a.		...	0623	*0650*	...	0743	*0804*	...	0935	1032	1133	1239	1333	...	1433	1534	1633	1737	1834	...	1935	...
	Gloucester 139 d.		0604	0627	0658	0732	0748	0840	...	0940	1039	1140	1244	1338	...	1440	1540	1640	1740	1842	1912	1941	2009
115	**Bristol** Parkway 119 139 a.		0642	0702	0730	0810	0823	0914	...	1015	1114	1215	1317	1414	...	1515	1615	1713	1816	1917	1948	2014	2044
124	**Bristol** Temple Meads 119 139 a.		0656	0719	0749	0828	0835	0928	...	1027	1126	1228	1329	1427	...	1527	1628	1728	1828	1929	2002	2028	2057

	Ⓐ p	Ⓐ p	Ⓐ p	Ⓐ	Ⓐ p	⑥	⑥	⑥		⑥	⑥	⑥	⑥		⑥	⑥	⑥	⑥	⑥	⑥	⑥	⑥	⑥
Great Malvern 122 130 d.	...	...	...	2115	...		...	0635	...	...	...	...	...	...	...	...	...	...	...	...	...	...	...
Worcester Foregate Street 122 130 d.	1951	...	...	2128	...		...	0648	...	0740	0852	0952	1052	...	1152	1249	1351	1452	1549	1652	1752	...	1852
Worcester Shrub Hill 122 130 d.	1955	...	...	2134	2238		...	0652	...	0754j	0856	0956	1056	...	1156	1256	1356	1457	1554	1657	1757	...	1857
Ashchurch for Tewkesbury d.	2013	...	...	2150	2254		...	0708	...	0813	0913	1013	1113	...	1213	1313	1413	1513	1613	1713	1814	...	1913
Cheltenham Spa ◧ 119 d.	2023	...	2152	2200	2304		*0548*	0719	...	0823	0923	1023	1122	...	1223	1323	1423	1523	1623	1723	1824	...	1923
Gloucester ◧ a.	2032	...	2200	2209	2313		*0557*	0728	...	0832	0932	1032	1132	...	1232	1332	1432	1532	1632	1732	1833	...	1932
Gloucester 139 d.	2041	2112	2205	2213	2318		0612	0738	...	0841	0941	1041	1138	...	1241	1341	1441	1541	1641	1739	1841	1908	1938
Bristol Parkway 119 139 a.	2116	2148	2231	2250	2346		0649	0813	...	0916	1016	1116	1213	...	1316	1416	1516	1616	1716	1815	1916	1943	2013
Bristol Temple Meads 119 139 a.	2129	2202	2243	2303	2357		0709	0826	...	0928	1028	1128	1226	...	1328	1428	1528	1628	1728	1827	1928	2005r	2027

	⑥	⑥	⑥	⑥ p	⑥	⑦	⑦	⑦	⑦	⑦ p		⑦	⑦	⑦	⑦ p	⑦	⑦	⑦		⑦ p	⑦	⑦ p	⑦ p
Great Malvern 122 130 d.	...	...	...	...	2128		...	...	...	...	...	...	...	...	...	...	...	...	...	...	...	...	...
Worcester Foregate Street 122 130 d.	...	1950	...	...	2140		...	...	...	...	...	...	1346	...	1546	...	1752	...	...	1941	...	...	...
Worcester Shrub Hill 122 130 d.	...	1957	...	...	2145		...	0955	...	1154	...	...	1357f	...	1555h	...	1756	...	...	1955j	...	...	2154
Ashchurch for Tewkesbury d.	...	2013	...	...	2201		...	1012	...	1210	...	...	1413	...	1612	...	1813	...	...	2013	...	...	2210
Cheltenham Spa ◧ 119 d.	...	2024	...	2152	2211		0921	1021	...	1220	...	...	1423	...	1622	...	1823	...	...	2023	...	2152	2219
Gloucester ◧ a.	...	2033	...	2200	2220		0930	1031	...	1228	...	...	1435	...	1633	...	1833	...	...	2034	...	2200	2230
Gloucester 139 d.	2006	2040	2109	2205	2225		0931	1037	1140	1236	...	1340	1440	1539	1639	1741	1838	1940	...	2040	2141	2205	2235
Bristol Parkway 119 139 a.	2041	2115	2146	2230	2303		1010	1115	1217	1313	...	1416	1517	1617	1715	1816	1915	2017	...	2116	2219	2230	2315
Bristol Temple Meads 119 139 a.	2053	2128	2158	2240	2317		1024	1127	1229	1325	...	1428	1529	1629	1727	1828	1927	2029	...	2128	2231	2240	2327

	Ⓐ	Ⓐ	Ⓐ	Ⓐ	Ⓐ p	Ⓐ C	Ⓐ	Ⓐ p	Ⓐ p	Ⓐ	Ⓐ		Ⓐ p	Ⓐ p	Ⓐ	Ⓐ	Ⓐ p	Ⓐ p	Ⓐ	Ⓐ p	Ⓐ	Ⓐ B	Ⓐ p
Bristol Temple Meads 119 139 d.		...	0608	0710	0740	...	0808	0838	0938	1038	1137	...	1238	1339	1439	1538	1638	1738	1840	1908	1939	2009	...
Bristol Parkway 119 139 d.		...	0620	0724	0753	...	0822	0851	0950	1050	1148	...	1250	1351	1455	1551	1651	1750	1856	1920	1950	2021	...
Gloucester 139 a.		...	0701	0801	0830	...	0858	0929	1029	1130	1229	...	1330	1429	1532	1630	1729	1830	1933	1957	2028	2059	...
Gloucester ◧ d.		0604	0712	...	...	0854	...	0935	1035	1138	1235	...	1336	1436	1537	1637	1737	1837	1938	...	...	...	2125
Cheltenham Spa ◧ 119 d.		0615	0724	...	...	0903	...	0947	1045	1148	1245	...	1346	1447	1548	1650	1750	1848	1949	...	...	...	2133
Ashchurch for Tewkesbury d.		0623	0733	...	...	0911	...	0955	1053	1156	1254	...	1354	1455	1556	1658	1758	1855	1957	...	...	...	2143
Worcester Shrub Hill 122 130 a.		0640	0749	...	...	0927b	...	1016	1118	1218	1320	...	1415	1515t	1613g	1716	1817	1915a	2014g	...	...	...	2206
Worcester Foregate Street 122 130 a.		0643	...	...	...	0947	...	1019	1121	1221	1324	...	1418	1525	1620	...	1822	1927	2021	...	...	...	...
Great Malvern 122 130 a.		...	...	...	...	...	...	...	...	...	...	...	...	...	...	...	...	...	2033	...	...	...	...

	Ⓐ p	Ⓐ	Ⓐ	⑥	⑥	⑥	⑥		⑥	⑥	⑥	⑥	⑥	⑥		⑥	⑥	⑥ D	⑥	⑥	⑥	⑥	⑥
Bristol Temple Meads 119 139 d.	2100	2143	2246		...	...	0615	...	0634	0710	0742	0809	0838	0938	...	1038	1138	1238	1338	1438	1538	1638	1738
Bristol Parkway 119 139 d.	2111	2157	2259		...	...	0624	...	0651	0724	0755	0820	0851	0950	...	1050	1150	1250	1350	1450	1550	1650	1751
Gloucester 139 a.	2147	2236	2339		...	...	0650	...	0732	0800	0834	0857	0929	1029	...	1129	1229	1329	1429	1529	1629	1729	1830
Gloucester ◧ d.	2153	*2251*	*0034*		0520	0643	0659	...	0736	...	0838	...	0938	1038	...	1138	1238	1338	1438	1538	1638	1737	1838
Cheltenham Spa ◧ 119 d.	2203	*2300*	*0043*		0530	0654	0707	...	0748	...	0850	...	0948	1048	...	1150	1249	1348	1449	1549	1648	1748	1848
Ashchurch for Tewkesbury d.	2210	...	...		0538	0702	...	...	0756	...	0858	...	0956	1056	...	1158	1257	1356	1457	1557	1656	1756	1856
Worcester Shrub Hill 122 130 a.	2230	...	...		0555	0718a	...	...	0814	...	0917	...	1012g	1113	...	1215	1314	1413	1513t	1614	1712t	1813	1912t
Worcester Foregate Street 122 130 a.	...	...	...		0558	0730	...	...	...	...	0921	...	1021	1119	...	1219	1319	1418	1525	1618	1723	1819	1923
Great Malvern 122 130 a.	...	...	...		0611	...	...	...	...	...	...	...	...	...	...	...	...	...	...	...	...	...	...

	⑥	⑥	⑥ T	⑥ D	⑥	⑥	⑦	⑦ p	⑦ p	⑦	⑦	⑦		⑦ p	⑦	⑦	⑦	⑦ p	⑦	⑦ p	⑦	⑦	⑦
Bristol Temple Meads 119 139 d.	1838	1904c	2009	2037	2107	2218		0915	0939	1038	1139	1239	...	1339	1439	1538	1639	1739	1838	1938	2039	2139	2242
Bristol Parkway 119 139 d.	1850	1921	2022	2050	2120	2230		0924	0950	1050	1150	1250	...	1350	1450	1550	1650	1750	1850	1950	2050	2150	2254
Gloucester 139 a.	1929	1957	2059	2128	2157	2310		0950	1027	1129	1230	1329	...	1429	1529	1628	1730	1828	1930	2028	2129	2232	2333
Gloucester ◧ d.	1938	...	...	2136	*2216*	...		1002	1033	...	1234	...	...	1434	...	1634	...	1834	...	2036	...	...	*0001*
Cheltenham Spa ◧ 119 d.	1949	...	...	2146	*2225*	...		1010	1043	...	1245	...	...	1445	...	1645	...	1845	...	2046	...	...	*0010*
Ashchurch for Tewkesbury d.	1957	...	...	2154	...	...		...	1050	...	1253	...	...	1453	...	1653	...	1853	...	2054	...	...	...
Worcester Shrub Hill 122 130 a.	2013g	...	...	2210	...	...		...	1106	...	1308a	...	...	1508a	...	1708a	...	1907a	...	2111	...	...	...
Worcester Foregate Street 122 130 a.	2021	...	...	...	...	...		...	...	...	1320	...	...	1519	...	1720	...	1918	...	...	...	...	...
Great Malvern 122 130 a.	2033	...	...	...	...	...		...	...	...	...	...	...	...	...	...	...	...	...	...	...	...	...

A – 12 Gloucester - Exeter St Davids (Tables **115** and **110**).
B – 12 Plymouth - Gloucester (Tables **115** and **110**).
C – From Salisbury via Swindon (Tables **126, 130** and **140**).
D – From Salisbury (Table **140**).
E – To Southampton Central via Swindon (Tables **126, 130** and **140**).
K – To/from Frome (Table **139**).
T – 12 Taunton - Gloucester (Table **115**).

a – Departs 9–10 minutes later.
b – Departs 0945.
c – Departs 1910 from Sept. 20.
f – Arrives 1348.
g – Departs 5–6 minutes later.
h – Arrives 5 minutes earlier.

j – Arrives 10–12 minutes earlier.
p – Conveys 12.
r – Arrives 1957 from Sept. 20.
t – Departs 8 minutes later.

◧ – See also Tables **117** and **130**.

European Rail Timetable Subscription

Keep up to date with the latest changes to European rail schedules with a subscription.

See page 12 for details of our various subscription options

Order on-line at **www.europeanrailtimetable.eu**

✆ +44 (0) 1832 270198 (Monday to Friday 1000–1600)

GW, SW 2nd class — GLOUCESTER - BRISTOL - WESTBURY - WEYMOUTH — 139

km	Ⓐ	Ⓐ	Ⓐ	Ⓐ	Ⓐ	Ⓐ	Ⓐ	ⒶG	Ⓐ	Ⓐ	ⒶG	Ⓐ	ⒶG	Ⓐ	Ⓐ	Ⓐ	Ⓐ	Ⓐ	Ⓐ	Ⓐ	Ⓐ	Ⓐ	Ⓐ	Ⓐ	ⒶT	Ⓐ
0	**Gloucester** 138 d.	...	...	...	...	...	0811	...	0908	1012	...	1109	...	1209	1309	...	1409	1509	1609	1709	...	1809	...	...	...	...
48	**Bristol** Parkway 138 d.	...	...	0613	...	...	0846	...	0944	1047	...	1144	...	1244	1344	...	1447	1547	1644	1744	...	1845	...	...	...	...
58	**Bristol** Temple M. 138 a.	...	...	0631	...	...	0859	...	0956	1102	...	1156	...	1256	1357	...	1459	1559	1656	1759	...	1857	...	...	...	...
	Bristol Temple M. 140 d.	...	...	0640	0740	0803	0903	...	1004	1110	...	1203	...	1303	1403	1442	1503	1603	1706	1803	...	1904	1947	2050	2225	2345
76	Bath Spa 140 d.	...	...	0658	0759	0822	0921	...	1022	1128	...	1222	...	1322	1422	1501	1522	1622	1724	1822	...	1922	2006	2108	2241	0004
91	Bradford on Avon 140 d.	...	...	0715	0815	0834	0933	...	1034	1140	...	1234	...	1334	1434	1517	1534	1636	1740	1836	...	1934	2022	2124	2253	0020
96	Trowbridge 140 d.	...	...	0721	0822	0840	0940	...	1040	1146	...	1240	...	1340	1440	1523	1540	1642	1746	1842	...	1941	2028	2131	2259	0027
103	**Westbury** 140 a.	...	...	0728	0829	0847	0947	...	1051	1153	...	1248	...	1349	1447	1530	1547	1649	1754	1849	...	1949	2035	2138	2306	0034
	Westbury 110 d.	0625	0650	...	...	0850	1006	0956	1052	...	1206	1249	1323	...	1450	...	1548	1651	1806	1850	1945	...	2039	2140	2311	0035
112	Frome d.	0634	0659	...	...	0903	1016	1005	1103	...	1221t	1301	1347	...	1501	...	1559	1700	1823	1906	2000	...	2048	2149	2320	0044
134	Castle Cary 110 d.	...	0717	...	...	0921	...	1038a	1120	...	1242	1318	1359t	...	1518	...	...	1718	1841	1937d	...	...	...	2207	...	...
153	Yeovil Pen Mill 109 d.	...	0733	...	...	0935	...	1052	1134	...	1258	1332	1414	...	1532	...	...	1732	1855	1951	...	...	...	2221	...	...
	Yeovil Junction 109 a.	...	|	...	...	|	...	...	|	...	1303	|	1419	...	|	...	...	|	|	|	...	...	...	|	...	...
174	Maiden Newton d.	...	0757	...	...	0959	...	...	1158	...	...	1356	...	...	1556	...	...	1756	1914	2015	...	...	...	2244	...	...
186	Dorchester West d.	...	0810	...	...	1018f	...	...	1212	...	...	1412t	...	...	1612t	...	...	1814t	1925	2027	...	...	...	2255	...	...
200	**Weymouth** a.	...	0825	...	...	1034	...	...	1226	...	...	1426	...	...	1626	...	...	1827	1939	2041	...	...	...	2308	...	...

⑥	⑥	⑥	⑥	⑥C	⑥h	⑥k	⑥	⑥G	⑥	⑥	⑥	⑥	⑥	⑥	⑥	⑥	⑥	⑥	⑥	⑥G	⑥	⑥	⑥	⑥	⑦ ⑦
Gloucester 138 d.	...	...	...	0707	0809	0809	0908	...	1008	1108	1206	...	1309	...	1408	1508	1608	1708	1808	...	...	...	...	...	...
Bristol Parkway 138 d.	...	...	...	0745	0845	0845	0943	...	1044	1143	1241	...	1346	...	1443	1543	1643	1743	1843	...	...	...	...	...	...
Bristol Temple M 138 a.	...	...	...	0758	0859	0859	0956	...	1058	1159	1255	...	1359	...	1457	1556	1656	1756	1856	...	...	...	...	...	...
Bristol Temple M 140 d.	...	0640	0736	0805	0904	0908	1003	...	1103	1203	1303	...	1403	1444	1503	1603	1704	1803	1903	...	1947	2045	2215	2306	...
Bath Spa 140 d.	...	0658	0756	0823	0922	0926	1022	...	1122	1223	1322	...	1422	1502	1522	1622	1722	1822	1922	...	2006	2103	2233	2324	...
Bradford on Avon 140 d.	...	0715	0812	0835	0936	0938	1034	...	1134	1235	1334	...	1434	1517	1534	1636	1737	1836	1934	...	2022	2119	2249	2340	...
Trowbridge 140 d.	...	0721	0818	0842	0943	0944	1040	...	1145	1242	1340	...	1440	1524	1540	1644	1744	1842	1940	...	2028	2125	2255	2346	...
Westbury 140 a.	...	0728	0825	0849	0950	0951	1047	...	1152	1251	1347	...	1447	1531	1548	1652	1751	1849	1949	...	2035	2132	2302	2353	...
Westbury 110 d.	0650	...	...	0850	0952	0952	1049	1057	...	1252	...	1358	1451	...	1549	1654	1804	1850	...	1958	2039	2134	2303	2354	0900
Frome d.	0659	...	...	0904	1014j	1002	1103	1108	...	1302	...	|	1501	...	1559	1703	1816	1900	...	2007	2048	2143	2312	0003	0909
Castle Cary 110 d.	0717	...	...	0921	1038t	...	1120	...	...	1319	...	1414	1518	...	...	1721	1839e	1918	...	2024	...	2201	...	...	0927
Yeovil Pen Mill 108 d.	0733	...	...	0935	1053	...	1134	...	...	1333	...	...	1532	...	...	1736	1853	1935	...	2039	...	2217	...	...	0942
Yeovil Junction 108 a.	|	...	...	|	|	...	|	...	...	|	...	...	|	...	...	|	|	|	...	2045	...	|	...	...	|
Maiden Newton d.	0757	...	...	0958	1111	...	1157	...	...	1357	...	...	1557	...	...	1800	1912	2000	...	...	...	2240	...	...	1006
Dorchester West d.	0812e	...	...	1018f	1122	...	1212e	...	...	1412e	...	...	1612e	...	...	1812	1923	2010	...	...	...	2251	...	...	1016
Weymouth a.	0825	...	...	1032	1135	...	1226	...	...	1426	...	...	1626	...	...	1826	1936	2025	...	...	...	2305	...	...	1029

⑦	⑦	⑦	⑦	⑦H	⑦	⑦S	⑦S	⑦	⑦	⑦	⑦
Gloucester 138 d.	...	...	...	...	...	...	...	...	...	...	...
Bristol Parkway 138 d.	...	...	...	...	...	...	...	...	...	...	...
Bristol Temple M 138 a.	...	...	...	...	...	...	...	...	...	...	...
Bristol Temple M 140 d.	0908	...	1034	...	1330	...	...	1648	1748	2049	2235
Bath Spa 140 d.	0925	...	1051	...	1348	...	...	1706	1806	2107	2254
Bradford on Avon 140 d.	0941	...	1107	...	1404	...	...	1722	1822	2123	2310
Trowbridge 140 d.	0947	...	1113	1206	1410	1405	1618	1729	1829	2130	2316
Westbury 140 a.	0955	...	1120	1213	1418	1412	1625	1736	1836	2137	2323
Westbury 110 d.	0957	1110	...	1214	...	1413	1628	1737	1837	2138	...
Frome d.	1006	1119	...	1224	...	1423	1638	1746	1846	2148	...
Castle Cary 110 d.	1024	...	...	1241	...	1443	...	1802	1904	2205	...
Yeovil Pen Mill 109 d.	1038	...	...	1257	...	1458	...	...	1918	2221	...
Yeovil Junction 109 a.	|	...	...	|	...	|	...	...	|	|	...
Maiden Newton d.	1102	...	...	1321	...	1522	...	...	1941	2245	...
Dorchester West d.	1113	...	...	1331	...	1532	...	...	1952	2255	...
Weymouth a.	1126	...	...	1345	...	1545	...	...	2005	2308	...

Ⓐ	Ⓐ	ⒶT	ⒶK	Ⓐ	ⒶG	Ⓐ	Ⓐ	Ⓐ	Ⓐ	Ⓐ
Weymouth d.	...	...	...	...	...	0638	0733	...	...	0932
Dorchester West d.	...	...	...	...	...	0651	0746	...	...	0946
Maiden Newton d.	...	...	...	...	...	0704	0759	...	...	1000
Yeovil Junction 109 d.	...	...	...	...	...	|	|	...	...	|
Yeovil Pen Mill 109 d.	...	...	...	0618	0658	0735f	0823	...	...	1024
Castle Cary 110 d.	...	...	...	0649g	0712	0750	0837	...	...	1038
Frome d.	0612	0642	...	0707	0729	0808	0852	...	1026	1055
Westbury 110 a.	0620	0650	...	0717	0738	0817	0901	...	1035	1104
Westbury 140 d.	...	0659	0705	0718	...	0818	0902	1002	1040	1105
Trowbridge 140 d.	...	0705	|	0724	...	0824	0908	1009	1046	1112
Bradford on Avon 140 d.	...	0711	|	0730	...	0830	0914	1015	1052	1118
Bath Spa 140 d.	...	0730	|	0752	...	0850	0930	1028	1110	1131
Bristol Temple M. 140 a.	...	0748	|	0811	...	0909	0950	1046	1129	1149
Bristol Temple M. 138 d.	...	...	|	...	...	0913	1007	1108	...	1208
Bristol Parkway 138 d.	...	...	|	...	...	0926	1019	1119	...	1220
Gloucester 138 a.	...	...	0845	...	...	1002	1056	1156	...	1257

Ⓐ	ⒶG	Ⓐ	Ⓐ	Ⓐ	ⒶG	Ⓐ	ⒶG	Ⓐ	Ⓐ	Ⓐ	Ⓐ	ⒶD	Ⓐ	Ⓐ	Ⓐ	ⒶF	①–④
Weymouth d.	...	...	1130	...	...	1328	...	...	...	1528	1728	...	...	...	2014	...	2128
Dorchester West d.	...	...	1144	...	...	1342	...	...	...	1544	1742	...	...	...	2027	...	2141
Maiden Newton d.	...	...	1159	...	...	1357	...	...	...	1557	1757	...	...	...	2040	...	2154
Yeovil Junction 109 d.	...	...	|	...	1338	|	1451	...	...	|	|	1916	...	...	|	2145	|
Yeovil Pen Mill 109 d.	1059	...	1223	...	1345	1421	1459	...	...	1621	1821	1923	...	...	2104	2152	2221e
Castle Cary 110 d.	1114	...	1237	...	1410j	1435	1513	...	...	1635	1844f	1938	...	...	2118	2220r	2235
Frome d.	1132	...	1257	...	1432	1452	1530	...	1626	1652	1901	1956	2016	2058	2135	2245t	2252
Westbury 110 a.	1141	...	1306	...	1442	1501	1539	...	1635	1701	1910	2007	2025	2109	2144	2254	2301
Westbury 140 d.	...	1204	1307	1403	...	1502	...	1559	1640	1702	1918	...	...	...	2145	...	...
Trowbridge 140 d.	...	1211	1313	1409	...	1509	...	1609	1646	1709	1925	...	...	...	2152	...	...
Bradford on Avon 140 d.	...	1217	1319	1415	...	1515	...	1615	1652	1715	1931	...	...	...	2158	...	...
Bath Spa 140 d.	...	1230	1332	1428	...	1530	...	1628	1710	1728	1954	...	...	...	2216	...	...
Bristol Temple M 140 a.	...	1248	1351	1447	...	1549	...	1646	1728	1747	2013	...	...	...	2235	...	...
Bristol Temple M 138 d.	...	1308	1409	1508	...	1608	...	1708	...	1810	...	...	...	...	...	...	...
Bristol Parkway 138 d.	...	1319	1420	1522	...	1619	...	1720	...	1822	...	...	...	...	...	...	...
Gloucester 138 a.	...	1357	1457	1559	...	1656	...	1757	...	1904	...	...	...	...	...	...	...

⑥	⑥G	⑥	⑥	⑥	⑥	⑥	⑥G	⑥B	⑥
Weymouth d.	...	0638	0733	...	...	0930	...	...	...
Dorchester West d.	...	0651	0746	...	...	0944	...	...	...
Maiden Newton d.	...	0704	0759	...	...	1000t	...	...	...
Yeovil Junction 109 d.	...	|	|	...	...	|	...	...	...
Yeovil Pen Mill 109 d.	...	0730	0823	...	...	1024	...	...	...
Castle Cary 110 d.	0736	0752f	0837	...	...	1038	...	...	...
Frome d.	0754	0810	0852	...	1030	1057	1130	...	...
Westbury 110 a.	0803	0819	0901	...	1038	1107	1139	...	...
Westbury 140 d.	...	0820	0902	1004	1040	1108	...	1143	1202
Trowbridge 140 d.	...	0827	0909	1011	1046	1115	...	1150	1208
Bradford on Avon 140 d.	...	0833	0915	1017	1052	1121	...	1156	1214
Bath Spa 140 d.	...	0851	0930	1030	1110	1134	...	1213	1228
Bristol Temple M 140 a.	...	0909	0950	1048	1128	1152	...	1231	1247
Bristol Temple M 138 d.	...	0912	1008	1108	...	1208	...	1238	1308
Bristol Parkway 138 d.	...	0923	1020	1120	...	1220	...	1250	1320
Gloucester 138 a.	...	1000	1058	1156	...	1256	...	1329	1356

⑥	⑥	⑥	⑥	⑥	⑥	⑥	⑥A	⑥	⑥B	⑥h	⑥	⑥R	⑥	⑥
Weymouth d.	1130	...	1330	...	...	1530	...	1734	...	1845	...	1938	2040	...
Dorchester West d.	1144	...	1344	...	...	1544	...	1748	...	1859	...	1949	2053	...
Maiden Newton d.	1159e	...	1358	...	...	1557	...	1801	...	1915t	...	2002	2106	...
Yeovil Junction 109 d.	|	...	|	...	...	|	...	|	...	|	...	|	|	...
Yeovil Pen Mill 109 d.	1223	...	1422	...	...	1621	...	1825	...	1938t	...	2038p	2130	...
Castle Cary 110 d.	1237	...	1436	...	...	1635	...	1849n	...	1953	...	2052	2144	...
Frome d.	1254	...	1453	...	1630	1652	...	1908	...	2018	2058	2107	2201	2316
Westbury 110 a.	1303	...	1503	...	1638	1701	...	1917	...	2030	2107	2116	2210	2324
Westbury 140 d.	1305	1404	1505	1602	1640	1703	1844	1922	1945	2032	...	2118	2219	...
Trowbridge 140 d.	1311	1410	1511	1609	1646	1709	1850	1929	1951	2038	...	2124	2226	...
Bradford on Avon 140 d.	1317	1416	1517	1615	1652	1715	1856	1935	1957	2044	...	...	2233	...
Bath Spa 140 d.	1331	1430	1531	1628	1710	1729	1914	1956	2015	2057	...	...	2255	...
Bristol Temple M 140 a.	1349	1449	1549	1649	1728	1749	1932	2014	2033	2115	...	...	2314	...
Bristol Temple M 138 d.	1408	1506	1608	1708	...	1809	1937	...	2037	...	...	...	...	...
Bristol Parkway 138 d.	1420	1520	1620	1720	...	1821	1950	...	2050	...	...	...	...	...
Gloucester 138 a.	1458	1557	1656	1758	...	1858	2029	...	2128	...	...	...	...	...

⑦	⑦T	⑦Tc	⑦G	⑦	⑦S	⑦S	⑦	⑦S	⑦	⑦S	⑦	⑦
Weymouth d.	b	0801	...	...	1038	...	1405	...	1605	...	1753	2011
Dorchester West d.	...	0812	...	...	1051	...	1418	...	1618	...	1806	2024
Maiden Newton d.	...	0825	...	...	1104	...	1431	...	1631	...	1819	2037
Yeovil Junction 109 d.	...	|	0946	...	|	...	|	...	|	...	|	|
Yeovil Pen Mill 109 d.	...	0850	0953	...	1128	...	1457	...	1655	...	1847t	2101
Castle Cary 110 d.	...	0904	1007	...	1142	...	1511	...	1709	1810	1907t	2115
Frome d.	0922	0922	1024	1125	1202	1405	1529	1643	1727	1827	1924	2132
Westbury 110 a.	0931	0931	1033	1134	1212	1414	1537	1651	1736	1837	1934	2141
Westbury 140 d.	0932	0932	...	1136	1213	1415	1539	1652	1737	1849	1940	2143
Trowbridge 140 d.	0938	0938	...	1142	1219	1422	1545	1658	1743	1855	1946	2149
Bradford on Avon 140 d.	0944	0944	...	1148	...	...	1551	...	1749	...	1952	2155
Bath Spa 140 d.	1002	1002	...	1207	...	...	1608	...	1807	...	2010	2213
Bristol Temple M 140 a.	1020	1021	...	1225	...	...	1626	...	1825	...	2028	2231
Bristol Temple M 138 d.	...	...	...	...	...	...	...	...	...	...	...	...
Bristol Parkway 138 d.	...	...	...	...	...	...	...	...	...	...	...	...
Gloucester 138 a.	...	...	...	...	...	...	...	...	...	...	...	...

A – Salisbury - Cheltenham Spa (Tables **138** and **140**).
B – Salisbury - Worcester (Tables **138** and **140**).
C – From Cheltenham Spa (Table **138**).
D – From London Waterloo (Table **109**).
F – To / from Salisbury (Table **140**).
G – From / to London Waterloo (Tables **109** and **140**).
H – Until Oct. 26 from Swindon (Table **126**).
K – From Salisbury - Worcester Foregate Street via Swindon (Tables **126**, **138** and **140**).

R – Until Sept. 13 to Swindon (Table **126**).
S – From / to Swindon (Table **126**).
T – To / from Cardiff Central (Table **115**).

a – Arrives 1022.
b – From Nov. 2.
c – Until Oct. 26.
d – Arrives 1924.
e – Arrives 5 minutes earlier.

f – Arrives 9 – 10 minutes earlier.
g – Arrives 0631.
h – Until Sept. 13.
j – Arrives 12 minutes earlier.
k – From Sept. 20.
n – Arrives 1838.
p – Arrives 2024.
r – Arrives 2205.
t – Arrives 6 – 8 minutes earlier.

140 BRISTOL - WESTBURY - SOUTHAMPTON - PORTSMOUTH

2nd class GW, SW

km		⚒	⚒	Ⓐ	Ⓐ P	⑥	Ⓐ	⑥	Ⓐ A	⑥	Ⓐ G	⚒	⑥ F	⑥	Ⓐ	Ⓐ	⑥	⑥	Ⓐ	⚒	⚒	⑥	Ⓐ	⚒ D	⚒	⚒	⚒
	Cardiff Central **115** d.		...	...	...	...	...	...	...	...	...	0628	...	0727	0727	...	...	0827	0827	...	0928	...	...	...	1030	...	1130
0	**Bristol** Temple Meads **139** d.		...	0501	0510	...	0551	0546	...	...	...	0722	...	0821	0821	0843	0845	0922	0923	0945	1021	1043	1045	...	1122	1142	1222
19	Bath Spa **139** d.		...	0516	|	...	0609	0604	...	...	...	0735	...	0835	0838	0901	0903	0936	0937	1003	1035	1101	1103	...	1135	1159	1235
34	Bradford on Avon **139** d.		...	0528	0536	...	0626	0620	...	...	...	0747	...	0847	0851	0916	0919	0948	0949	1019	1047	1117	1119	...	1147	1215	1247
39	Trowbridge **126 139** d.		...	0534	0542	...	0632	0626	0642	...	...	0753	...	0853	0858	0923	0925	0954	0956	1025	1053	1123	1125	...	1154	1222	1254
45	**Westbury** **126 139** a.		...	0541	0550	...	0639	0634	0649	...	...	0801	...	0900	0905	0930	0932	1002	1003	1032	1101	1130	1132	...	1202	1229	1301
	Westbury d.		0523	0548	...	0601	0641	0646	0655	0705	0742	0801	0810	0903	0906	0933	0933	1003	1004	1035	1101	1132	1134	1143	1203	1230	1303
53	Warminster d.		0531	0556	...	0609	0649	0654	0704	0715	0750	0811	0818	0911	0914	0942	0942	1011	1012	1043	1111	1140	1142	1150	1211	1239	1311
85	**Salisbury** d.		0554	0618	...	0632	0711	0717	0737c	0737	0811	0833	0839	0933	0936	...	...	1033	1034	1105	1133	1201	1203	1212	1233	1301	1333
112	Romsey d.		...	0637	...	0650	0730	0736	0756	0756	...	0852	...	0951	0954	...	...	1051	1053	...	1152	...	...	...	1251	...	1351
123	**Southampton** Central a.		...	0647	...	0702	0740	0746g	0809	0808	...	0903	...	1003	1005	...	...	1103	1103	...	1204	...	...	...	1303	...	1404
147	Fareham a.		...	0710	...	0727	0803	0824	...	...	...	0927	...	1027	1028	...	...	1127	1127	...	1229	...	...	...	1328	...	1427
164	**Portsmouth** & Southsea a.		...	0731	...	0746	0822	0844	...	...	...	0948	...	1046	1048	...	...	1146	1147	...	1247	...	...	...	1347	...	1447
165	**Portsmouth** Harbour a.		...	0736	...	0751	0827	0848	...	...	...	0953	...	1051	1052	...	...	1151	1152	...	1252	...	...	...	1352	...	1452

	⚒	⚒	⑥	Ⓐ	Ⓐ H	⚒	Ⓐ H	⚒	⑥	Ⓐ	⚒	⑥	Ⓐ	⚒	⑥	Ⓐ	Ⓐ	⑥	Ⓐ	Ⓐ C	⑥	⑥	Ⓐ	⑥	Ⓐ	⑥	Ⓐ
Cardiff Central **115** d.	...	1230	...	...	...	1330	...	1430	...	...	1530	...	...	1627	...	...	1727	1727	...	...	...	1827	1830	1930	1928	2030	2030
Bristol Temple Meads **139** d.	1242	1322	1343	1346	...	1422	...	1522	1542	1545	1622	1645	1647	1722	1744	1748	1822	1822	1843	...	1845	1922	1925	2022	2025	2122	2126
Bath Spa **139** d.	1300	1335	1401	1403	...	1435	...	1535	1600	1602	1635	1703	1705	1735	1805v	1805	1837	1835	1901	...	1903	1935	1938	2035	2038	2136	2139
Bradford on Avon **139** d.	1316	1347	1417	1419	...	1447	...	1547	1615	1618	1647	1719	1721	1748	1821	1821	1850	1847	1916	...	1919	1947	1950	2047	2050	2148	2151
Trowbridge **126 139** d.	1322	1354	1423	1425	...	1454	...	1555	1622	1625	1654	1725	1727	1755	1827	1827	1857	1854	1923	1919	1925	1954	1957	2054	2056	2154	2158
Westbury **126 139** a.	1329	1402	1430	1432	...	1501	...	1602	1629	1632	1702	1732	1735	1803	1834	1834	1904	1901	1930	1926	1932	2001	2004	2101	2105	2201	2205
Westbury d.	1331	1403	1432	1434	1446	1502	1544	1603	1630	1634	1702	1734	1740	1803	1836	1835	1905	1903	...	1935	1935	2003	2005	2103	2106	2203	2206
Warminster d.	1340	1411	1441	1443	1454	1511	1553	1611	1639	1643	1711	1743	1749	1811	1846	1845	1913	1911	...	1945	1945	2011	2013	2111	2115	2213	2216
Salisbury d.	1402	1433	1502	...	1514	1533	1613	1633	1700	...	1733	1804	...	1833	1907	1906	1935	1933	...	2006	2006	2033	2035	2133	2137	2235	2238
Romsey d.	...	1452	...	...	...	1552	...	1651	...	...	1751	...	...	1852	...	...	1953	1952	...	...	...	2052	2053	2152	2155	2254	2256
Southampton Central a.	...	1504	...	...	...	1603	...	1703	...	...	1803	...	...	1903	...	...	2004	2003	...	...	...	2103	2104	2203	2206	2304	2307
Fareham a.	...	1527	...	...	...	1628	...	1727	...	...	1827	...	...	1927	...	...	2030	2028	...	...	...	2127	2127	2228	2229	2327	2330
Portsmouth & Southsea a.	...	1550j	...	...	...	1650j	...	1747	...	...	1848	...	...	1947	...	...	2048	2047	...	...	...	2146	2147	2245	2252	2346	2348
Portsmouth Harbour a.	...	1554j	...	...	...	1654j	...	1753	...	...	1852	...	...	1952	...	...	2052	2051	...	...	...	2151	2151	2249	2256	2350	2353

	⑥	Ⓐ	⚒ K	Ⓐ	⑦	⑦	⑦ H	⑦	⑦	⑦	⑦	⑦	⑦	⑦	⑦	⑦	⑦	⑦	⑦ R	⑦	⑦	⑦	⑦	⑦	⑦	⑦	⑦
Cardiff Central **115** d.	...	...	...	...		...	...	0918	1025	1125	1225	...	1325	...	1425	...	1525	1625	...	1725	1750	1825	...	1925	2030	...	2230
Bristol Temple Meads **139** d.	2142	2145	...	2306		0922	...	1019	1115	1215	1315	1330	1415	1440	1515	1541	1620	1715	...	1815	1841	1920	1934	2015	2128	2235	2330
Bath Spa **139** d.	2200	2203	...	2324		0936	...	1033	1135	1233	1333	1348	1433	1458	1533	1600	1638	1735	...	1830	1859	1933	1952	2035	2146	2254	2344
Bradford on Avon **139** d.	2216	2218	...	2340		0948	...	1045	1147	1249	1345	1404	1448	1514	1545	1616	1650	1747	...	1842	1915	1945	2008	2047	2158	2310	2356
Trowbridge **126 139** d.	2222	2225	...	2346		0954	...	1052	1153	1255	1352	1410	1455	1520	1552	1623	1656	1753	1818	1850	1922	1952	2014	2053	2204	2316	0002
Westbury **126 139** a.	2229	2232	...	2353		1000	...	1059	1200	1302	1359	1418	1502	1527	1559	1630	1703	1800	1825	1857	1929	2001	2021	2100	2211	2323	0009
Westbury d.	2233	2233	2312	...		1002	1043	1102	1201	1303	1400	...	1504	1529	1601	1643	1705	1802	1826	1901	1930	2002	2023	2103	2212	...	...
Warminster d.	2241	2241	2320	...		1012	1051	1110	1211	1311	1411	...	1512	1537	1611	1651	1714	1810	1834	1909	1938	2011	2031	2111	2220	...	...
Salisbury d.	2303	2303	2342	...		1034	1113	1133	1235	1334	1436	...	1536	1558	1634	1712	1737	1833	1855	1932	2000	2033	2053	2134	2243	...	...
Romsey d.	2323	2321	...	...		1052	...	1152	1254	1352	1454	...	1554	...	1653	...	1755	1851	...	1950	2019	2052	2111	2152	2301	...	...
Southampton Central a.	2334	2331	...	...		1103	...	1202	1304	1403	1505	...	1605	...	1703	...	1806	1902	...	2001	2029	2102	2122	2203	2312	...	...
Fareham a.	2357	0010	...	...		1126	...	1226	1327	1426	1528	...	1628	...	1727	...	1829	1927	...	2026	2058	2127	2202	2226	2335	...	...
Portsmouth & Southsea a.	0018	0028	...	...		1146	...	1246	1346	1446	1546	...	1647	...	1746	...	1848	1947	...	2044	2117	2144	2223	2244	2352	...	...
Portsmouth Harbour a.	...	...	...	...		1151	...	1251	1351	1451	1552	...	1652	...	1751	...	1853	1952	...	2050	2123	2149	2228	2249	2356	...	...

	⚒	Ⓐ	⑥	Ⓐ	Ⓐ E	Ⓐ	⑥	Ⓐ	⑥	⚒	Ⓐ	⑥	Ⓐ	⑥	Ⓐ G	⑥	Ⓐ	⑥ L	Ⓐ	⑥	⚒ V	Ⓐ H	⚒	⚒	⑥	Ⓐ	Ⓐ H
Portsmouth Harbour d.		...	...	...	...	...	...	0601	0608	...	0720	0723	...	...	...	0823	0823	...	0923	0923	...	...	1023	...	1123	1123	...
Portsmouth & Southsea d.		...	...	...	...	...	0540	0605	0612	...	0724	0727	...	...	...	0827	0827	...	0927	0927	...	...	1027	...	1127	1127	...
Fareham d.		...	...	0510	...	...	0601	0625	0632	...	0743	0747	...	...	...	0847	0847	...	0947	0947	...	...	1047	...	1147	1147	...
Southampton Central d.		...	...	0533	...	...	0629	0647	0657	...	0810	0809	0823	0830	...	0910	0911	...	1011	1010	...	...	1110	...	1210	1211	...
Romsey d.		...	...	0545	...	...	0640	0659	0711	...	0821	0821	0835	0841	...	0921	0922	...	1023	1022	...	...	1121	...	1221	1222	...
Salisbury d.		...	0605	0606	0635	0703	0704a	0719	0730	...	0840	0840	0857	0905	0923	0942	0942	1024	1042	1042	1112	1131	1142	1212	1242	1242	1251
Warminster d.		...	0626	0627	0656	0724	0725	0740	0751	...	0901	0901	0918	0926	0944	1003	1003	1045	1103	1103	1133	1152	1203	1233	1303	1303	1312
Westbury a.		...	0636	0638	0704	0733	0734	0751	0800	...	0909	0909	0927	0936	0952	1011	1011	1053	1111	1111	1142	1200	1211	1242	1311	1311	1320
Westbury **126 139** d.		0558	0638	0640	0705	0736	0736	0800	0803	0840	0914	0915	0940	0938	...	1012	1014	...	1112	1115	1143	...	1212	1243	1312	1312	...
Trowbridge **126 139** d.		0604	0644	0646	0711	0742	0742	0806	0809	0846	0921	0921	0946	0944	...	1019	1020	...	1118	1122	1150	...	1218	1250	1319	1318	...
Bradford on Avon **139** d.		0610	0650	0652	...	0748	0748	0812	0815	0852	0927	0927	0952	0950	...	1025	1026	...	1124	1128	1156	...	1224	1256	1325	1326	...
Bath Spa **139** d.		0628	0708	0710	...	0806	0807	0829	0832	0910	0940	0941	1010	1008	...	1042	1040	...	1138	1142	1213	...	1238	1313	1340	1340	...
Bristol Temple Meads **139** a.		0649	0727	0728	...	0824	0826	0848	0851	0930	0953	0953	1028	1027	...	1056	1052	...	1153	1156	1231	...	1252	1331	1353	1355	...
Cardiff Central **115** a.		0747	...	...	...	...	...	0945	0943	...	1052	1050	...	...	...	1146	1146	...	1249	1250	...	...	1346	...	1449	1449	...

	⚒	⑥	Ⓐ	⚒	⑥	Ⓐ	⑥	Ⓐ	⑥	Ⓐ	⑥	Ⓐ	⑥	Ⓐ	⑥	Ⓐ	⑥ B	Ⓐ	⑥	Ⓐ	⚒ T	⑥ H	⑥	Ⓐ	Ⓐ	⑥	Ⓐ
Portsmouth Harbour d.	...	1223	1223	...	1323	1323	...	...	1423	1423	1523	1523	...	...	1623	1624	...	...	1723	1724	...	...	1823	1824	...	...	1923
Portsmouth & Southsea d.	...	1227	1227	...	1327	1327	...	...	1427	1427	1528	1527	...	...	1627	1629	...	...	1727	1729	...	...	1827	1829	...	...	1929
Fareham d.	...	1247	1249	...	1347	1347	...	...	1447	1447	1547	1547	...	...	1647	1648	...	...	1747	1748	...	...	1847	1849	...	...	1949
Southampton Central d.	...	1310	1311	...	1410	1411	...	...	1510	1511	1610	1611	...	...	1710	1711	...	...	1810	1810	...	...	1910	1911	...	...	2011
Romsey d.	...	1321	1323	...	1421	1422	...	...	1521	1522	1621	1622	...	...	1721	1722	...	...	1821	1823	...	...	1921	1923	...	...	2023
Salisbury d.	1307	1342	1342	1406	1442	1443	1509	...	1542	1542	1642	1642	1706	...	1742	1742	1812	...	1842	1842	1913	1926	1942	1942	2011	2013	2042
Warminster d.	1328	1403	1403	1428	1503	1504	1530	1530	1603	1604	1703	1703	1730	1729	1803	1803	1833	1829	1903	1903	1934	1946	2003	2003	2032	2034	2103
Westbury a.	1338	1411	1411	1437	1511	1512	1539	1540	1611	1612	1711	1711	1739	1739	1811	1811	1842	1839	1911	1911	1944	1954	2011	2012	2042	2045	2111
Westbury **126 139** d.	1340	1412	1412	1440	1513	1513	1541	1541	1613	1613	1713	1713	1743	1741	1812	1812	1844	1841	1912	1912	1945	...	2014	2013	2045	2055	2112
Trowbridge **126 139** d.	1346	1418	1418	1446	1519	1520	1547	1548	1619	1619	1719	1719	1749	1747	1818	1818	1850	1848	1918	1918	1951	...	2020	2020	2051	2101	2118
Bradford on Avon **139** d.	1352	1424	1424	1452	1525	1526	1553	1554	1625	1625	1725	1727	1755	1753	1824	1824	1856	1855	1924	1924	1957	...	2026	2026	2057	2107	2124
Bath Spa **139** d.	1410	1438	1438	1510	1540	1539	1611	1611	1639	1639	1739	1740	1816	1811	1838	1838	1914	1913	1938	1938	2015	...	2040	2039	2114	2125	2138
Bristol Temple Meads **139** a.	1428	1452	1450	1530	1554	1552	1629	1629	1652	1653	1752	1753	1835	1829	1853	1853	1932	1931	1952	1952	2034	...	2052	2051	2132	2147	2150
Cardiff Central **115** a.	...	1546	1546	...	1649	1650	...	...	1748	1749	1850	1849	...	...	1950	1951	...	...	2045	2046	...	...	2145	2144	...	...	2257h

	⑥	⑥	Ⓐ	Ⓐ	⑥	Ⓐ	⑥	⑦	⑦ R	⑦	⑦	⑦	⑦	⑦	⑦	⑦		⑦	⑦	⑦	⑦	⑦	⑦	⑦	⑦	⑦	⑦
Portsmouth Harbour d.	1923	2023	2024	...	...	2123	2123		...	...	0909	...	1109	1209	1309	1409	...	1509	1609	...	1709	1809	...	1909	2009	2109	2206
Portsmouth & Southsea d.	1927	2027	2028	...	...	2127	2127		...	...	0914	1013	1114	1214	1314	1414	...	1514	1614	...	1714	1814	...	1914	2014	2114	2212
Fareham d.	1947	2047	2046	...	...	2147	2148		...	...	0934	1033	1134	1234	1334	1434	...	1534	1634	...	1734	1834	...	1934	2034	2134	2233
Southampton Central d.	2010	2112	2111	...	...	2222	2223		...	...	0957	1057	1157	1257	1357	1457	...	1557	1657	...	1757	1857	...	1957	2059	2156	2257
Romsey d.	2021	2123	2122	...	...	2235	2234		...	...	1008	1108	1208	1308	1408	1508	...	1608	1708	...	1808	1908	...	2008	2112	2207	2308
Salisbury d.	2041	2142	2142	2211	2213	2300t	2257		...	...	1027	1127	1227	1327	1427	1527	...	1630	1727	1759	1828	1927	1959	2027	2131	2227	2327
Warminster d.	2102	2203	2203	2234	2234	2321	2318		0806	...	1048	1148	1248	1349	1448	1548	...	1651	1748	1820	1849	1949	2020	2048	2152	2248	2348
Westbury a.	2110	2211	2211	2243	2245	2331	2330		0815	...	1058	1157	1258	1357	1458	1558	...	1700	1756	1829	1857	2001	2029	2057	2202	2256	2358
Westbury **126 139** d.	2112	2214	2212	2244	2250	2336	...		0816	0839	1102	1202	1300	1400	1502	1600	...	1702	1759	1830	1902	2002	2030	2102	2203	2257	...
Trowbridge **126 139** d.	2118	2220	2218	2251	2256	2342	...		0823	0845	1108	1208	1306	1407	1508	1607	...	1708	1805	1837	1908	2008	2037	2108	2209	2303	...
Bradford on Avon **139** d.	2124	2226	2224	2257	2302	2348	...		...	0851	1114	1214	1312	1413	1514	1613	...	1714	1811	1843	1914	2014	2043	2114	2215	2309	...
Bath Spa **139** d.	2138	2240	2238	2314	2320	0002	...		...	0910	1128	1228	1330	1426	1528	1626	...	1732	1825	1900	1928	2028	2100	2128	2229	2322	...
Bristol Temple Meads **139** a.	2150	2252	2250	2332	2340	0016	...		...	0928	1147	1246	1350	1445	1546	1639	...	1750	1836	1918	1940	2040	2118	2140	2241	2338	...
Cardiff Central **115** a.	2255	2358	2357r	...	...	...	...		...	...	1241	1340	1440	1545	1640	1729	...	1841	1931	...	2031	2129	...	2232	2330	...	...

A – From Gloucester via Swindon (Tables **126**, **130** and **138**).
B – To Cheltenham Spa (Table **138**).
C – From Gloucester (Tables **130** and **126**).
D – (Yeovil Pen Mill Ⓐ -) Frome - London Waterloo (Tables **109** and **139**).
E – To Worcester Foregate Street via Swindon (Tables **126**, **130** and **138**).
F – Castle Cary - London Waterloo (Tables **109** and **139**).
G – Yeovil Pen Mill - London Waterloo and v.v. (Tables **109** and **139**).
H – Yeovil Junction - London Waterloo and v.v. (Tables **109** and **139**).

K – From Yeovil Junction on Ⓐ (Table **139**).
L – London Waterloo - Frome (Tables **109** and **139**).
P – To London Paddington (Table **110**).
Q – Basingstoke - Yeovil Junction (Tables **109** and **139**).
R – To/from Swindon (Table **126**).
T – To Worcester Shrub Hill on ⑥ (Table **138**).
V – To Worcester Foregate Street on ⑥ (Table **138**).

a – Arrives 0658.
c – Arrives 0726.
f – Arrives 8–9 minutes earlier.
g – Departs 0802.
h – Arrives 2244 on ⑤.
j – Arrives 3–4 minutes earlier on ⑥.
r – Arrives 2345 on ⑤.
t – Arrives 2253.
v – Arrives 1800.

LM LONDON - NORTHAMPTON - BIRMINGHAM 141

Only selected services are shown. See Table **150** for faster services London - Watford / Milton Keynes / Rugby - Coventry - Birmingham and v.v.

km		Ⓐ	②–⑤	②–⑤	Ⓐ	Ⓐ	Ⓐ	Ⓐ	Ⓐ	Ⓐ	Ⓐ	Ⓐ	Ⓐ	Ⓐ	Ⓐ	Ⓐ	Ⓐ		Ⓐ	Ⓐ	Ⓐ	Ⓐ	Ⓐ	Ⓐ	Ⓐ
0	**London** Euston ... 143 d.		0009	0039	...	...	...	...	0535	0621	...	0723	0756	0823	0856	0923	0956		1556	1626	1656	1726	1756	1826	1856
28	Watford Junction ... d.		0030	0100	...	...	...	...	0555	0636	...	0738	|	0838	|	0938	|	and	|	|	|	|	|	|	|
64	Leighton Buzzard ... d.		0103	0133	...	...	...	...	0626	0654	...	0755	0825	0855	0925	0955	1025	at	1625	1655	1725	1755	1824	1855	1924
75	Bletchley ... d.		0110	0140	...	...	...	...	0633	0701	...	0802	0832	0902	0932	1002	1032	the	1632	1702	1732	1802	1832	1902	1932
80	Milton Keynes ... 143 d.		0116	0146	...	...	...	...	0638	0707	0738	0808	0838	0908	0938	1008	1038	same	1638	1708	1738	1808	1838	1908	1338
106	**Northampton** ... 143 a.		0132	0203	...	...	...	...	0655	0725	0754	0825	0855	0925	0955	1025	1056	minutes	1655	1724	1755	1825	1854	1924	1955
106	**Northampton** ... 143 d.		...	...	0515	0542	0606	0642	0711	0737	0810	0840	0910	0940	1010	1040	1110	past	1710	1740	1806	1840	1906	1940	2010
136	Rugby ... 143 d.		...	...	0537	0605	0634a	0705	0734	0801	0834	0904	0934	1004	1034	1104	1134	each	1734	1804	1834	1904	1934c	2004	2034
154	**Coventry** ... 107 d.		...	...	0547	0615	0645	0715	0745	0812	0845	0915	0945	1015	1045	1115	1145	hour	1745	1815	1845	1915	1945	2015	2045
171	**Birmingham** Int ✈ ... 107 d.		...	...	0606	0634	0704	0734	0803	0831	0904	0934	1004	1034	1104	1134	1204	until	1804	1834	1904	1934	2004	2034	2104
185	**Birmingham** New St ... 107 a.		...	...	0615	0645	0714	0744	0814	0844	0914	0945	1014	1044	1114	1144	1214		1814	1844	1915	1944	2014	2044	2114

	Ⓐ	Ⓐ	Ⓐ	Ⓐ	Ⓐ	Ⓐ	Ⓐ	Ⓐ	Ⓐ	Ⓐ	⑥	⑥	⑥	⑥	⑥	⑥	⑥	⑥	⑥	⑥	⑥		⑥	⑥	⑥
London Euston ... 143 d.	1923	1956	2023	2056	2123	2150	2209	2239	2309	2342		0009	0039	...	...	...	0539	0621	...	0723	0756		1823	1856	1920
Watford Junction ... d.	1938	|	2038	|	2138	2205	2229	2300	2329	0007		0030	0100	...	...	...	0558	0636	...	0738	|	and	1838	|	1935
Leighton Buzzard ... d.	1955	2025	2055	2125	2155	2223	2301	2334	0003	0035		0103	0133	...	...	...	0629	0652	...	0755	0825	at	1855	1925	1952
Bletchley ... d.	2002	2032	2102	2132	2202	2230	2308	2341	0010	0042		0110	0140	...	...	...	0636	0659	...	0802	0832	the	1902	1932	1959
Milton Keynes ... 143 d.	2008	2038	2108	2138	2208	2236	2317	2348	0019	0050		0116	0146	...	...	...	0641	0705	0738	0808	0838	same	1908	1938	2008
Northampton ... 143 a.	2025	2054	2125	2154	2225	2255	2334	0007	0037	0108		0136	0203	...	...	...	0658	0722	0755	0826	0855	minutes	1925	1955	2025
Northampton ... 143 d.	2040	2110	2134	2216	...	2312	...	...	...	...		...	*0510*	0543	0611	0642	0710	0740	0810	0840	0910	past	1940	2010	2040
Rugby ... 143 d.	2104	2134	2159	2242	...	2334	...	...	...	...		...	*0533*	0605	0634	0704	0734	0804	0834	0904	0934	each	2004	2034	2104
Coventry ... 107 d.	2115	2145	2215	2254	...	2345	...	...	...	...		...	*0543*	0616	0645	0715	0745	0815	0845	0915	0945	hour	2015	2045	2115
Birmingham Int ✈ ... 107 d.	2134	2204	2234	2313	...	0004	...	...	...	...		...	*0602*	0635	0704	0734	0803	0834	0904	0934	1004	until	2034	2104	2134
Birmingham New St ... 107 a.	2145	2216	2244	2324	...	0023	...	...	...	...		...	*0612*	0645	0714	0745	0815	0845	0914	0945	1014		2044	2114	2148

	⑥	⑥	⑥	⑥	⑥	⑥	⑥	⑥	⑥	⑥	⑥	⑥	⑦	⑦	⑦	⑦	⑦	⑦B	⑦	⑦B	⑦	⑦	⑦B	⑦	⑦	⑦B
London Euston ... 143 d.	1946	2003	2021	2039	2109	2127	2149	2210	2237	2309	2330	2353		0009	0655	...	0724	0751	0824	0853	...	0925	0956	...	1024	1052
Watford Junction ... d.	|	2018	2037	2054	2128	2144	2208	2229	2257	2328	2350	0012		0029	0715	...	0744	0807	0844	0911	...	0945	1012	...	1044	1114
Leighton Buzzard ... d.	2018	|	2058	2128	2158	2212	2242	2259	2331	2356	0025	0044		0103	0749	...	0814	0837	0914	0941	...	1015	1042	...	1114	1144
Bletchley ... d.	2025	2045	|	2135	2205	2219	2253	2306	2338	0003	0032	0055		0110	0756	...	0820	0843	0920	0948	...	1021	1049	...	1120	1151
Milton Keynes ... 143 d.	2032	2051	2108	2140	2213	2228	2257	2314	2347	0011	0040	0100		0119	0804	...	0829	0852	0929	0956	...	1030	1057	...	1129	1159
Northampton ... 143 a.	2052	2111	2126	2156	2230	2244	2314	2332	0005	0030	0058	0117		0137	0823	...	0847	0910	0947	1015	...	1047	1115	...	1146	1217
Northampton ... 143 d.	2103	...	2140	2205	2231	2254	...	...	...	...	...	...		...	...	...	0906	0927	0959	1028	1043	1100	1129	1140	1159	1219
Rugby ... 143 d.	2125	...	2204	2228	2253	2316	...	...	...	...	...	...		...	...	0857	0928	0949	1022	1050	1105	1123	1148	1203	1222	1241
Coventry ... 107 d.	2135	...	2215	2240	2303	2327	...	...	...	...	...	...		...	...	0908	0938	...	1033	...	1115	1134	...	1215	1233	...
Birmingham Int ✈ ... 107 d.	2154	...	2233	2258	2314	2345	...	...	...	...	...	...		...	...	0922	0957	...	1052	...	1134	1153	...	1234	1252	...
Birmingham New St ... 107 a.	2202	...	2243	2308	2325	0003	...	...	...	...	...	...		...	...	0939	1008	...	1103	...	1144	1204	...	1244	1304	...

	⑦	⑦	⑦	⑦		⑦	⑦	⑦	⑦	⑦	⑦	⑦	⑦	⑦	⑦	⑦
London Euston ... 143 d.	...	1124	1222	1256		1856	1922	1956	2020	...	2107	2131	2203	2242	2300	2340
Watford Junction ... d.	...	1144	1237	|	and	|	1937	|	2035	...	2123	2146	2222	2303	2320	0001
Leighton Buzzard ... d.	...	1214	1253	1324	at	1924	1953	2024	2052	...	2153	2218	2251	2333	2354	0034
Bletchley ... d.	...	1220	1300	1331	the	1931	2000	2031	2100	...	2200	2224	2258	2340	0001	0041
Milton Keynes ... 143 d.	...	1226	1306	1338	same	1938	2006	2038	2106	...	2208	2233	2307	2349	0009	0050
Northampton ... 143 a.	...	1244	1324	1354	minutes	1954	2024	2054	2123	...	2226	2248	2325	0004	0027	0107
Northampton ... 143 d.	1240	1309	1340	1409	past	2009	2040	2059	2131	2159	2239	2312	2333	...	...	...
Rugby ... 143 d.	1303	1331	1404	1432	each	2032	2103	2121	2153	2221	2301	2334	2355	...	...	...
Coventry ... 107 d.	1315	1343	1415	1442	hour	2042	2114	2135	2205	2235	2312	2345	0005	...	...	...
Birmingham Int ✈ ... 107 d.	1334	1402	1434	1501	until	2101	2133	2153	2223	2253	2321	0003	...	...	...	...
Birmingham New St ... 107 a.	1344	1413	1445	1513		2113	2142	2205	2234	2305	2340	0015	...	...	...	...

	Ⓐ	Ⓐ	Ⓐ	Ⓐ
Birmingham New St 107 d.		...	...	...
Birmingham Int ✈ .. 107 d.		...	...	...
Coventry ... 107 d.		...	...	0539
Rugby ... 143 d.		...	...	0552
Northampton ... 143 a.		...	...	0613
Northampton ... 143 d.		0414	0503	0617
Milton Keynes ... 143 d.		0432	0520	0632
Bletchley ... d.		0437	0524	|
Leighton Buzzard ... d.		0444	0531	|
Watford Junction ... d.		0514	0601	0654
London Euston ... 143 a.		0538	0622	0710

	Ⓐ	Ⓐ	Ⓐ	Ⓐ	Ⓐ	Ⓐ	Ⓐ	Ⓐ	Ⓐ	Ⓐ		Ⓐ	Ⓐ	Ⓐ	Ⓐ	Ⓐ	Ⓐ	Ⓐ	Ⓐ	Ⓐ	Ⓐ	⑥	⑥	⑥	⑥
Birmingham New St ... 107 d.	0535	...	0613	0636	0706	0736	0806	0836	0906	0936		1906	1936	2006	2036	...	2115	2136	2206	2250	2311		...	...	...
Birmingham Int ✈ ... 107 d.	0545	...	0625	0646	0716	0746	0816	0846	0916	0946	and	1916	1946	2016	2046	...	2125	2146	2216	2309	2322		...	...	...
Coventry ... 107 d.	0604	...	0644	0705	0735	0805	0835	0905	0935	1005	at	1935	2005	2035	2105	...	2144	2205	2235	2327	2334		...	...	...
Rugby ... 143 d.	0615	...	0656	0716	0746	0815	0846	0916	0946	1016	the	1946	2016	2046	2116	...	2155	2216	2246	2338	2345		...	...	...
Northampton ... 143 a.	0637	...	0719	0739	0807	0839	0907	0938	1007	1038	same	2008	2038	2107	2140	...	2217	2237	2309	0002	0008s		...	...	...
Northampton ... 143 d.	0639	0650	0730	0748	0818	0848	0918	0948	1018	1048	minutes	2016	2048	2116	2141	2214	...	2251	2328	...	|		0405	0448	0535
Milton Keynes ... 143 d.	0656	0707	0746	0805	0835	0905	0935	1005	1035	1105	past	2035	2105	2132	2158	2231	...	2308	2346	...	0027		0422	0504	0551
Bletchley ... d.	0701	0712	|	0810	0840	0910	0940	1010	1040	1110	each	2039	2110	|	2203	2237	...	2313	2351	...	|		0429	0509	0556
Leighton Buzzard ... d.	0708	0719	|	0817	0847	0917	0947	1017	1047	1117	hour	2046	2117	|	2210	2244	...	2320	2358	...	|		0436	0519	0603
Watford Junction ... d.	|	|	|	|	|	0933	|	1033	|	1133	until	|	2133	|	2232	2313	...	2351	0028	...	0056s		0511	0552	0629
London Euston ... 143 a.	0738	0750	0821	0848	0917	0949	1017	1049	1117	1150		2116	2149	*2224*	2252	2337	...	0012	0049	...	0117		0534	0614	0650

	⑥	⑥	⑥	⑥	⑥	⑥		⑥	⑥	⑥	⑥	⑥	⑥	⑥	⑥	⑥	⑥	⑥	⑥	⑦	⑦	⑦	⑦	⑦	⑦
Birmingham New St ... 107 d.	...	0535	0613	0636	0706	0736		1736	1806	1836	1906	1936	2006	2036	2106	...	2136	2206	2251		...	...	...	...	...
Birmingham Int ✈ ... 107 d.	...	0546	0624	0646	0716	0746	and	1746	1816	1846	1916	1946	2016	2046	2116	...	2146	2216	2303		...	...	...	...	...
Coventry ... 107 d.	0536	0605	0643	0705	0735	0805	at	1805	1835	1905	1935	2005	2035	2105	2135	...	2205	2235	2321		...	...	...	...	...
Rugby ... 143 d.	0546	0616	0654	0716	0746	0816	the	1816	1846	1916	1946	2016	2046	2116	2146	...	2216	2246	2332		...	...	...	...	...
Northampton ... 143 a.	0608	0638	0716	0740	0809	0839	same	1838	1909	1938	2008	2039	2108	2138	2207	...	2240	2308	2355		...	...	...	...	...
Northampton ... 143 d.	0617	0641	0718	0748	0818	0848	minutes	1848	1918	1946	2018	2048	2118	2148	2208	2231	2250	2324	...		*0615*t	0750	0824	0850	0926
Milton Keynes ... 143 d.	0632	0658	0735	0805	0835	0905	past	1905	1935	2003	2035	2105	2135	2208	2225	2248	2307	2341	...		0710	0806	0841	0906	0943
Bletchley ... d.	|	0703	0740	0810	0840	0910	each	1910	1940	2008	2040	2110	2140	...	2230	2253	2312	2346	...		0715	0811	0846	0911	0947
Leighton Buzzard ... d.	|	0710	0747	0817	0847	0917	hour	1917	1947	2015	2047	|	2147	2217	2237	2300	2319	2353	...		0722	0818	0853	0918	0954
Watford Junction ... d.	0654	|	|	0833	|	0933	until	1933	|	2035	2111	2143	2218	2244	2310	2330	2354	0016	...		0751	0847	0924	0948	1023
London Euston ... 143 a.	0709	0741	0817	0849	0917	0949		1949	2032	2054	2130	2203	2241	2304	2333	2357	0015	0034	...		0814	0910	0950	1010	1044

	⑦	⑦	⑦	⑦	⑦B	⑦	⑦	⑦	⑦	⑦		⑦	⑦	⑦	⑦	⑦	⑦	⑦B	⑦	⑦	⑦B	⑦	⑦	⑦	⑦
Birmingham New St ... 107 d.	0833	0907	0934	1006	...	1034	1106	1134	1206	1233		1706	1733	1806	1834	1906	1933	...	2006	2034	...	2106	2136	2210	2256
Birmingham Int ✈ ... 107 d.	0849	0925	0951	1023	...	1046	1116	1146	1216	1245	and	1716	1745	1816	1846	1916	1945	...	2016	2046	...	2125	2148	2228	2312
Coventry ... 107 d.	0908	0944	1010	1037	...	1108	1135	1204	1235	1304	at	1735	1804	1835	1905	1935	2004	...	2035	2105	...	2138	2208	2247	2324
Rugby ... 143 d.	0919	0955	1020	1047	1115	1121	1148	1216	1246	1316	the	1746	1816	1845	1915	1946	2015	2027	2046	2116	2129	2148	2220	2257	2336
Northampton ... 143 a.	0942	1018	1041	1108	1135	1145	1210	1237	1307	1338	same	1807	1839	1907	1937	2008	2036	2047	2108	2137	2152	2211	2241	2319	2356s
Northampton ... 143 d.	*1010*	1031	1042	1116	1141	1146	1215	1248	1315	1348	minutes	1815	1848	1915	1948	2016	...	2048	2126	...	2154	2218	*2302*	2327	|
Milton Keynes ... 143 d.	*1026*	1049	1059	1131	1157	1203	1232	1305	1332	1405	past	1832	1905	1932	2005	2033	...	2104	2142	...	2211	2235	*2318*	2343	0015s
Bletchley ... d.	*1031*	1054	1103	1135	1202	1209	1237	1310	1337	1410	each	1837	1910	1937	2010	2038	...	|	2147	...	2216	2240	*2323*	2348	|
Leighton Buzzard ... d.	*1038*	1101	1110	1142	1209	1216	1244	1317	1344	1417	hour	1844	1917	1944	2017	2045	...	|	2154	...	2223	2247	*2330*	2355	|
Watford Junction ... d.	*1107*	1125	1139	1209	1227	1235	|	1334	|	1434	until	|	1934	|	2034	|	...	|	2225	...	2254	2317	*0002*	0026	0045s
London Euston ... 143 a.	*1129*	1148	1203	1228	1242	1251	1315	1350	1415	1450		1915	1950	2015	2050	2124	...	2153	2246	...	2316	2338	*0025*	0046	0104

B – To / from Crewe via Nuneaton (Table **143**).
a – Arrives 0628.
c – Arrives 1929.
r – Arrives 6 minutes earlier.
s – Calls to set down only.
t – Connection by 🚌.

LM 2nd class only NUNEATON - COVENTRY - LEAMINGTON SPA 142

km		⚒	⚒	⚒	⚒	⑦				⚒	⑦								Ⓐ	⑥⑦	⑥	Ⓐ	⑦	Ⓐ
0	**Nuneaton** ... d.	0637	0737	0837	0937	...	1037	1137	1237	1337	1337	1437	1537	1637	1737	1837	1937	2037	2137	2137	2224	2237	2237	2327
16	**Coventry** ... 107 d.	0700	0800	0900	1000	1000	1100	1200	1300	1400	1400	1500	1600	1700	1800	1900	2000	2100	2200	2200	2246	2300	2305r	2349
24	Kenilworth ... d.	0707	0807	0907	1007	1007	1107	1207	1307	1407	1407	1507	1607	1707	1807	1907	2007	2107	2207	2207	2253	2307	2312	2356
32	**Leamington Spa** ... 107 a.	0715	0815	0916j	1015	1016	1116v	1216t	1316j	1416t	1418	1516	1617t	1716j	1816t	1916	2016	2114	2217	2214	2300	2314	2318	0003

	⚒	⚒	⚒		⚒					⑦		⚒	⚒		⑦				⑥		⑦		Ⓐ
Leamington Spa ... 107 d.	0540	0638	0739	...	0840	0940	1040	and	1740	1838	...	1840	1940	...	1949	2040	...	2140	2236	...	2240	...	2240
Kenilworth ... d.	0547	0644	0747	...	0847	0947	1047	hourly	1747	1845	...	1847	1947	...	1956	2047	...	2147	2243	...	2247	...	2247
Coventry ... 107 d.	0556	0656	0756	...	0856	0956	1056	until	1756	1856	...	1856	1956	...	2009f	2056	...	2156	2250	...	2254	...	2300f
Nuneaton ... a.	0618	0718	0818	...	0918	1018	1118		1818	1918	...	1918	2018	...	2031	2118	...	2218	...	...	...	...	2322

f – Arrives 6 minutes earlier.
j – Arrives 2 minutes earlier on ⑥.
r – Arrives 2258.
t – Arrives 2 minutes earlier on Ⓐ.
v – Arrives 1114 on ⚒.

142a BEDFORD - BLETCHLEY
2nd class only LM

km			Ⓐ	⑥	Ⓐ	⑥	Ⓐ	⑥	Ⓐ	⑥	⚒		⚒	⚒	⚒	⚒	⑥	Ⓐ	⑥	Ⓐ	⑥	Ⓐ
0	**Bedford**	d.	0610	0615	0710	0747	0808	0847	0924	0947	1047	and	1647	1747	1847	1947	2046	2047	2147	2147	2219	2238
20	Woburn Sands	d.	0641	0646	0741	0818	0839	0918	0955	1018	1118	hourly	1718	1818	1918	2018	2117	2118	2218	2218	2250	2309
27	**Bletchley**	a.	0651	0656	0751	0828	0849	0928	1005	1028	1128	until	1728	1828	1928	2028	2127	2130	2228	2228	2300	2319
	Milton Keynes 141	a.	*0706*	*0742*	*0807*	*0845*	*0907*	*0945*	*1016*	*1045*	*1145*		*1745*	*1846*	*1946*	*2045*	*2140*	*2146*	*2257*	*2300*	*2314*	*2348*

		Ⓐ	⑥		Ⓐ	⑥		Ⓐ	⑥		Ⓐ		⑥	⚒		⚒	⚒		⑥		Ⓐ
Milton Keynes 141	d.	*0432*	*0504*	...	*0550*	*0630*	...	*0707*	*0735*	...	*0735*	...	*0835*	*0935*	and	*1935*	*2035*	...	*2105*	...	*2127*
Bletchley	d.	0517	0517	...	0615	0642	...	0718	0752	...	0800	...	0852	0952	hourly	1952	2052	...	2132	...	2145
Woburn Sands	d.	0528	0528	...	0626	0653	...	0729	0803	...	0811	...	0906	1003	until	2003	2103	...	2143	...	2156
Bedford	a.	0559	0559	...	0657	0724	...	0800	0834	...	0842	...	0934	1034		2034	2134	...	2214	...	2227

143 LONDON - CREWE via Trent Valley
LM

See Tables **152**, **153** and **154** for other fast services London - Milton Keynes - Stafford - Crewe.

km			⚒	Ⓐ	⑥	Ⓐ	⑥	⑥‡	Ⓐ	⑥	⚒		⚒	⚒	⑥	Ⓐ	Ⓐ‡	⚒	⚒‡	⚒	⑥	Ⓐ	⑥‡	Ⓐ‡	⑥	⑥‡
0	**London** Euston	141 150/2 d.		...	...	...	...	0631	0643	0643	0746		1446	1546	1646	1646	1700	1746	1800	1846	1940	1946	2031	2030	2035	2031
28	Watford Junction	141 150 d.		...	...	...	...	│	│	│	│	and	│	│	│	│	│	│	│	│	│	│	2046u	│	2050	2046u
78	Milton Keynes	141 150 d.		...	...	...	...	0705	0716	0716	0819	at the	1519	1619	1719	1719	│	1819	│	1919	2024	2019	│	│	2122	│
104	Northampton	141 d.		0520	0514	0601	0602	│	│	│	│	same	│	│	│	│	│	│	│	│	│	│	│	│	│	│
132	Rugby	141 150/3 d.		0543	0542f	0624	0625	│	0739	0739	0842	minutes	1542	1642	1742	1742	│	1842	│	1942	2048	2042	│	│	2146	│
158	Nuneaton	153 d.		0555	0554	0637	0637	│	0754	0754	0854	past	1554	1654	1754	1757	│	1857	│	1954	2100	2054	│	│	2158	│
176	Tamworth (Low Level)	152 d.		0610	0608	0653	0653	0744	0808	0808	0908	each	1608	1708	1808	1813	1809	1913	1908	2008	2113	2108	2157	2135	2212	2157
186	Lichfield Trent Valley	152 d.		0616	0614	0659	0659	0750	0814	0814	0914	hour	1614	1714	1814	1820	1816	1919	1914	2014	2120	2114	2204	2143	2218	2204
214	Stafford	144 153 d.		0633	0634	0717	0720	0806	0832	0834	0934	until	1634	1734	1834	1837	1832	1936	1930	2034	2138	2134	│	2157	2241	│
253	**Crewe**	144 153 a.		0653	0654	0740	0740	0824	0851	0854	0954		1654	1754	1854	1859	1850	1957	1950	2057	2157	2154	2232	2216	2300	2232

		Ⓐ	Ⓐ‡	Ⓐ	Ⓐ‡	⑦	⑦	⑦	⑦	⑦	⑦	✣	⑦	⑦‡
London Euston	141 150/2 d.	2046	2110	2146	2200		0751	0853	0956	1052	1245		1945	2039
Watford Junction	141 150 d.	│	2125u	│	│		0807	0911	1012	1114	│	and	│	│
Milton Keynes	141 150 d.	2119	│	2219	2241		0852	0956	1057	1159	1319	at the	2019	2124
Northampton	141 d.	│	│	│	│		0927t	1028t	1129t	1219t	│	same	│	│
Rugby	141 150/3 d.	2142	2204	2242	│		0951	1051	1151	1242	1342	minutes	2042	│
Nuneaton	153 d.	2154	2216	2257	│		1004	1104	1204	1254	1354	past	2054	│
Tamworth (Low Level)	152 d.	2208	│	2311	2320s		1018	1118	1218	1308	1408	each	2108	2203
Lichfield Trent Valley	152 d.	2214	│	2318	2327s		1025	1124	1225	1314	1414	hour	2114	2210
Stafford	144 153 d.	2234	2240	2338	2341s		1041	1141	1241	1335	1435	until	2135	2225
Crewe	144 153 a.	2258	2259	0001	0009		1105	1205	1301	1358	1458		2154	2243

		⚒	Ⓐ	⑥	⚒‡	Ⓐ	⑥	⚒
Crewe	144 153 d.		0510	0525	...	0545	0606	0713
Stafford	144 153 d.		0533	0544	...	0609	0632	0732
Lichfield Trent Valley	152 d.		0549	0602	0641	0628	0649	0749
Tamworth (Low Level)	152 d.		0556	0608	0648	0635	0656	0756
Nuneaton	153 d.		0612	0624	│	0650	0711	0811
Rugby	141 150/3 d.		0627	0641	│	0708	0727	0827
Northampton	141 a.		│	│	│	│	│	│
Milton Keynes	141 150 a.		0648	0702	0725	0729	0749	0849
Watford Jn	141 150 a.		│	│	│	│	│	│
London Eus	141 150/2 a.		0724	0738	0800	0805	0827	0925

		⑥‡	⚒		⚒	Ⓐ	⑥	⑥	Ⓐ	Ⓐ	⑥	⑥‡	Ⓐ	Ⓐ‡	Ⓐ	⑦	⑦‡	⑦	⑦		⑦	⑦	⑦	⑦	⑦‡
Crewe	144 153 d.	...	0813		1713	1813	1813	1913	1913	2013	2013	...	2113	...	2213		...	0952	1113		1813	1913	2013	2113	2124
Stafford	144 153 d.	...	0832	and	1732	1832	1832	1932	1932	2032	2032	...	2132	...	2232		...	1017c	1132	and	1832	1932	2034	2131	2143
Lichfield Trent Valley	152 d.	0815	0849	at the	1749	1849	1849	1949	1949	2049	2049	2117	2149	2217	2249		0924	1035	1149	at the	1849	1949	2051	2148	2201
Tamworth (Low Level)	152 d.	0822	0856	same	1756	1856	1856	1956	1956	2056	2056	2124	2156	2224	2256		│	1042	1156	same	1856	1956	2058	2155	2207
Nuneaton	153 d.	│	0911	minutes	1811	1911	1911	2011	2011	2111	2111	│	2211	│	2311		│	1057	1211	minutes	1911	2011	2114	2210	2219
Rugby	141 150/3 d.	│	0927	past	1827	1927	1927	2027	2030	2127	2127	│	2226	│	2328		│	1115	1227	past	1927	2027	2129	2225	2234
Northampton	141 a.	│	│	each	│	│	│	2046	│	│	│	│	2249	│	...		│	1135	│	each	│	2047	2149	2247	│
Milton Keynes	141 150 a.	│	0948	hour	1848	1948	1948	...	2051	2148	2150	2203	...	2301	...		│	1155	1248	hour	1948	2103	2210	...	2305
Watford Junction	141 150 a.	│	│	until	│	│	2019	...	│	│	2224	2233s	...	2336s	...		│	1227	│	until	│	│	2253	...	2336s
London Euston	141 150/2 a.	0930	1024		1924	2024	2039	...	2127	2224	2244	2259	...	2359	...		1110	1242	1325		2025	2153	2316	...	2355

c – Arrives 1010.
f – Arrives 0537.
j – Departs 1607 from Sept. 15.
r – ⑥ only.
s – Calls to set down only.
t – See Table **141** for arrival times.
u – Calls to pick up only.
‡ – Fast service operated by VT (see Tables **152**/**154** for further details).
✣ – Arrivals into Crewe may be up to 4 minutes earlier.

144 BIRMINGHAM - CREWE - LIVERPOOL
2nd class only LM

km			⚒	Ⓐ	⑥	Ⓐ	Ⓐ	⚒	⚒	⚒	⚒	Ⓐ	⑥	⚒	Ⓐ	⑥	⚒	⚒	♠	⚒	⚒	⚒	⑥	Ⓐ	Ⓐ	⑥
0	**Birmingham** New Street	119 ▷ d.		...	...	...	0534	...	0634	0704	0734	0757	0804	0834	0857	0904	0934	1004		1804	1834	1934	2034	2034	2134	2134
19	Wolverhampton	119 ▷ d.		...	...	...	0553	...	0653	0723	0753	0823	0823	0853	0923	0923	0953	1023	and at	1823	1853	1953	2053	2053	2153	2153
43	Stafford	119 143 152 d.		...	...	...	0611	...	0711	0740	0811	0840	0840	0911	0940	0940	1011	1040	the same	1840	1911	2011	2111	2111	2211	2211
82	**Crewe**	143 152 d.		0534	0532	0611	0632	0702	0732	0802	0832	0902	0902	0932	1002	1002	1032	1102	minutes	1902	1932	2032	2132	2132	2232	2232
118	Runcorn	152 d.		0602	0558	0629	0658	0722	0758	0822	0858	0922	0922	0958	1022	1022	1058	1122	past each	1922	1958	2058	2153	2158	2258	...
131	**Liverpool** South Parkway ‡	a.		0611	0606	0637	0706	0730	0806	0830	0906	0934	0930	1006	1030	1030	1106	1130	hour until	1930	2006	2106	2201	2206	2306	...
140	**Liverpool** Lime Street	152 a.		0623	0624	0650	0717	0744	0817	0842	0917	0942	0942	1017	1042	1042	1117	1142		1950	2017	2117	2213	2217	2317	...

		⑥	Ⓐ	Ⓐ	⑦	⑦	⑦	⑦	⑦	⑦		⑦
Birmingham New Street	119 ▷ d.	2233	2233	2322		...	0932	1034	1134	1234		2134
Wolverhampton	119 ▷ d.	2253	2253	2343		...	0951	1053	1153	1253	and at	2153
Stafford	119 143 152 d.	2310	2311	2359		...	1009	1110	1210	1311	the same	2211
Crewe	143 152 d.	2330	2344	0022		0920	1031	1131	1231	1332	minutes	2232
Runcorn	152 d.	...	...	...		0946	1057	1157	1257	1359	past each	2258
Liverpool South Parkway ‡	a.	...	...	...		0955	1105	1205	1305	1407	hour until	2308
Liverpool Lime Street	152 a.	...	...	...		1005	1115	1215	1315	1418		2320

		⚒	Ⓐ	⑥	⚒	⚒	Ⓐ	⚒
Liverpool Lime Street	152 d.		...	...	0607	0633	0708	0733
Liverpool South Parkway ‡	d.		...	...	0619	0643	0720	0743
Runcorn	152 d.		...	...	0626	0651	0731	0751
Crewe	143 152 d.		0558	0617	0649	0719	0749	0819
Stafford	119 143 152 d.		0617	0639	0709	0739	0809	0839
Wolverhampton	119 ▷ a.		0634	0658	0728	0758	0828	0858
Birmingham New Street	119 ▷ a.		0653	0719	0748	0820	0848	0920

		Ⓐ	⑥	⚒	⚒	✣	⚒	⚒	⑥	⚒	Ⓐ	⑥	⚒	⚒	⑥	Ⓐ	Ⓐ	⑦	⑦	⑦		⑦	⑦	⑦	⑦
Liverpool Lime Street	152 d.	0808	0809	0833	0912		1812	1833	1912	1933	2008	2012	2033	2133	2217	2233	2333		...	1033		2033	2133	2233	2340
Liverpool South Parkway ‡	d.	0822	0821	0843	0924	and at	1824	1843	1924	1943	2020	2024	2043	2143	│	2243	2343		...	1043	and at	2043	2143	2243	2350
Runcorn	152 d.	0831	0831	0851	0931	the same	1831	1851	1931	1951	2027	2031	2051	2151	│	2251	2351		...	1051	the same	2051	2151	2251	0002
Crewe	143 152 d.	0849	0849	0919	0949	minutes	1849	1919	1955	2019	2050	2049	2119	2219	2252	2318	0020		0923	1119	minutes	2119	2219	2321	0031
Stafford	119 143 152 d.	0909	0909	0939	1009	past each	1909	1939	2013	2039	...	2109	2139	2239	...	...	...		0945	1139	past each	2139	2239	...	...
Wolverhampton	119 ▷ a.	0927	0928	0958	1028	hour until	1928	1958	2030	2058	...	2128	2158	2259	...	...	...		1002	1156	hour until	2156	2256	...	...
Birmingham New Street	119 ▷ a.	0948	0948	1020	1048		1948	2020	2048	2120	...	2148	2220	2320	...	...	...		1025	1218		2218	2318	...	...

‡ – 🚌 connections available to/from Liverpool John Lennon Airport ✈.
▷ – See also Tables **146** and **151**.
♠ – On Ⓐ the 1304 from Birmingham arrives Liverpool 1447.
✣ – On Ⓐ the 1612 from Liverpool arrives Birmingham 1752.

145 SHREWSBURY - SWANSEA
2nd class AW

km			Ⓐ	Ⓐ	⑥	⑦a	Ⓐ	⑥	⑦	⚒	⑦A	⚒
0	**Shrewsbury**	149 d.	0418	0527	0528	0943	1002	1006	1208	1354	1620	1835
20	Church Stretton	149 d.	0436	0545	0546	1001	1020	1024	1226	1412	1639	1853
32	Craven Arms	149 d.	0446	0555	0556	1011	1030	1034	1235	1423	1649	1904
52	Knighton	d.	0508	0631t	0625e	1035	1054	1058	1259	1447	1713	1928
84	**Llandrindod**	a.	0544	0712	0706	1114	1135	1139	1338	1529	1750	2009
84	**Llandrindod**	d.	▬	0730	0730	1132	1136	1142	1355	1535	1805	2027
110	Llanwrtyd	d.	Ⓐ	0801	0801	1203	1207	1213	1426	1606	1836	2058
128	Llandovery	d.	0644	0826	0826	1236	1232	1238	1451	1631	1902	2123
146	Llandeilo	d.	0705	0848	0848	1258	1254	1300	1513	1653	1923	2145
159	Pantyffynnon	d.	0723	0905	0905	1315	1311	1317	1530	1710	1941	2202
178	Llanelli	136 a.	0745	0928	0931	1337	1334r	1339	1551	1736	2003	2234v
196	**Swansea**	136 a.	0811	0951	0956	1400	1401	1402	1615	1801	2028	2258v
211	Carmarthen	136 a.	...	...	...	...	...	...	...	...	...	...

		Ⓐ	Ⓐ	⑥	Ⓐ	⑦a	Ⓐ	⑥	⑦	Ⓐ	⑥	⑦	⚒
Carmarthen	136 d.	...	0447	...	...	...	...	...	...	...	...	...	...
Swansea	136 d.	...	│	0451	0516	0854	0856	0859	1110	1251	1251	1518	1747
Llanelli	136 d.	...	0512	0513	0538	0916	0918	0921	1133	1315	1316	1542	1809
Pantyffynnon	d.	...	0534	0534	0600	0937	0940	0943	1154	1337	1340	1602	1831
Llandeilo	d.	...	0554	0554	0620	0957	1000	1003	1214	1357	1400	1622	1851
Llandovery	d.	...	0616	0616	0640	1019	1022	1025	1236	1419	1422	1644	1913
Llanwrtyd	d.	...	0641	0642	...	1044	1047	1050	1301	1444	1448	1709	1938
Llandrindod	a.	...	0713	0713	...	1114	1120	1123	1332	1517	1520	1741	2011
Llandrindod	d.	0553	0732	0732	...	1128	1140	1144	1344	1533	1534	1759	2024
Knighton	d.	0643p	0810	0810	...	1209	1218	1223	1422	1611	1612	1838	2102
Craven Arms	149 d.	0708	0835	0834	...	1235	1242	1246	1445	1635	1638	1901	2126
Church Stretton	149 d.	0721	0847	0846	...	1246	1254	1258	1458	1646	1649	1915	2138
Shrewsbury	149 a.	0738	0903	0902	...	1302	1312	1315	1514	1704	1706	1938	2159f

A – To Cardiff Central (Table **136**).
a – Aug. 3 - Sept. 14.
e – Arrives 0620.
f – Arrives 2155 on Ⓐ.
p – Arrives 0632.
r – Departs 1338.
t – Arrives 0619.
v – On ⑥ Llanelli a. 2230, Swansea a. 2255.

AW LM 2nd class

BIRMINGHAM - SHREWSBURY - CHESTER 146

km			⑥	Ⓐ	⚒ A	⚒	⚒	⚒ 🍷	⑥ 🍷	Ⓐ 🍷	⚒ c	⚒ F🍷	⚒ 🍷	⚒	⚒ 🍷	⚒ F🍷	⚒ 🍷	⚒ 🍷	⚒	⚒ F🍷	⚒ 🍷	⚒ 🍷	⚒ F🍷	⚒ 🍷	⚒ 🍷	⚒ F🍷
0	**Birmingham** Int ✈ d.	⚒	...	...	...	...	...	...	...	...	0708	0808	...	...	0908	1008	...	1108	...	1208	...	1308	1408	...	1508	1608
13	**Birmingham** New Street d.		...	...	0530	...	0549	0622	...	...	0722	0822	...	0852	0922	1022	...	1122	1152	1222	...	1322	1422	...	1522	1622
34	Wolverhampton d.		...	...	0549	...	0609	0642	...	...	0741	0841	...	0912	0941	1041	...	1141	1212	1241	...	1341	1441	...	1541	1641
59	Telford Central d.		...	...	|	...	0637	0659	...	...	0758	0858	...	0932	0958	1058	...	1158	1232	1259	...	1358	1459	...	1558	1659
65	Wellington d.		...	...	|	...	0646	0707	...	...	0806	0906	...	0940	1006	1106	...	1206	1240	1307	...	1406	1507	...	1606	1707
81	**Shrewsbury** a.		...	...	|	...	0700	0721	...	...	0824	0921	...	0953	1024	1121	...	1221	1259	1322	...	1421	1522	...	1620	1723
	Aberystwyth **147** a.		...	...	|	...	▬	0921	...	...	|	1122	...	...	|	1322	...	|	...	1521	...	|	1722	...	|	1923
	Cardiff Central **149** d.		...	...	|	...	...	...	0525	0519	|	...	0719r	...	|	...	0923	|	...	...	1123	|	...	1323	|	...
81	**Shrewsbury** d.		0536	0538	|	0615	...	...	0726	0726	0827	...	0926	...	1025	...	1127	1225	...	...	1327	1425	...	1527	1625	...
110	Gobowen d.		0553	0555	|	0632	⚒	...	0744	0743	0845	...	0943	...	1043	...	1145	1243	...	...	1344	1443	...	1544	1643	...
122	Ruabon d.		0605	0607	|	0644	B	...	0756	0755	0857	...	0955	...	1055	...	1157	1255	...	...	1356	1455	...	1556	1655	...
129	Wrexham General d.		0618	0615	|	0655	0703	...	0802	0802	0903	...	1002	...	1101	...	1204	1301	...	...	1403	1501	...	1603	1701	...
149	**Chester** a.		0634	0633	0645	0717	0720	...	0821	0821	0925	...	1021	...	1120	...	1225	1321	...	...	1421	1521	...	1623	1723	...
	Holyhead **150** a.		...	...	0823	...	...	...	1012	1012	1126e	...	1205	...	1322	...	1415	1521	...	...	1616	1711	...	1822	1916	...

	⚒ 🍷	Ⓐ 🍷L	⑥ 🍷L	⚒	⚒	Ⓐ C	⑥ 🍷	⚒	⚒ c	Ⓐ 🍷	⑥ 🍷	⚒	⚒	⑥ J	Ⓐ	⑥	Ⓐ M	⑥	Ⓐ	⑥ T	Ⓐ	⚒	⑥	Ⓐ		⑦
Birmingham Int ✈ d.	...	1708	1708	...	1808	...	...	...	1908	...	...	...	2008	...	...	2108	2109	...	...	...	...	...	...	2316	⑦	...
Birmingham New Street d.	...	1721	1722	1752	1822	...	...	1852	1922	...	...	1952	2022	...	...	2122	2122	...	...	2237	...	2256	2335	2340		0825
Wolverhampton d.	...	1741	1741	1812	1841	...	...	1912	1941	...	...	2011	2041	...	...	2141	2141	...	...	2256	...	2315	2355	0002		0844
Telford Central d.	...	1759	1758	1832	1859	...	...	1932	1959	...	...	2032	2059	...	...	2158	2159	...	...	2313	...	2342	0023	0031		0912
Wellington d.	...	1807	1806	1840	1907	...	...	1940	2007	...	...	2040	2107	...	...	2206	2207	...	...	2320	...	2351	0031	0040		0921
Shrewsbury a.	...	1821	1823	1853	1923	...	...	1956	2024	...	...	2056	2121	...	...	2220	2221	...	...	2335	...	0005	0047	0055		0934
Aberystwyth **147** a.	...	|	|	▬	2136f	...	...	▬	|	...	...	...	2341g	...	...	|	|	...	...	▬	...	...	...	...		▬
Cardiff Central **149** d.	1523	|	|	...	...	1722	1723	Ⓐ	|	1823	1823	...	...	1938	1938	|	|	2122	...	⑥	2135	...	...	...		⑦
Shrewsbury d.	1727	1827	1828	...	...	1928	1927	1940	2026	2027	2027	...	...	2144	2144	2225	2227	2326	2337	2338	2338	...	...	...		1019
Gobowen d.	1744	1845	1846	...	...	1946	1944	1959	2044	|	|	...	...	2202	2202	2243	2245	|	2354	2355	|	...	...	...		1037
Ruabon d.	1756	1857	1858	⚒	...	|	1956	2011	2056	⊕	⊕	...	...	2214	2214	2255	2257	⊕	0006	0007	⊕	...	...	...		1049
Wrexham General d.	1803	1903	1904	1916	...	2000	2005	2018	2102	|	|	...	...	2221	2221	2302	2304	|	0012	0014	|	...	...	...		1056
Chester a.	1822	1925	1926	1938	...	2018	2024	2037	2124	2123	2127	...	...	2240	2241	2318	2321	0020	0030	0034	0046	...	...	...		1114
Holyhead **150** a.	2016	...	...	...	...	2206	2228	...	...	...	2327	...	...	...	0106	...	...	...	*0235*	...	...	...	...	...		...

	⑦ F🍷	⑦ 🍷	⑦ F🍷	⑦ a🍷	⑦	⑦	⑦ F🍷	⑦ a🍷	⑦ b🍷	⑦ 🍷	⑦ F🍷	⑦ 🍷		⑦ 🍷	⑦ 🍷	⑦ a🍷	⑦	⑦	⑦	⑦	⑦	⑦ a	⑦ b	⑦	⑦	⑦
Birmingham Int ✈ d.	1006	1108	1208	...	1308	...	1407	...	...	1506	1607	...	...	1706	1806	...	...	1911	2010	2108	...	...	...	2211	2240	2307
Birmingham New Street d.	1022	1122	1222	...	1322	1356	1421	...	...	1522	1622	...	...	1722	1822	...	1856	1924	2024	2122	2207	...	...	2224	2255	2325
Wolverhampton d.	1041	1141	1241	...	1341	1414	1442	...	...	1543	1643	...	...	1743	1843	...	1914	1943	2043	2141	2228	...	...	2244	2316	2349
Telford Central d.	1059	1159	1300	...	1358	1442	1459	...	...	1600	1700	...	...	1800	1900	...	1942	2000	2101	2158	2256	...	...	2303	|	0017
Wellington d.	1106	1207	1309	...	1405	1451	1507	...	...	1608	1708	...	...	1808	1908	...	1951	2008	2108	2206	2304	...	...	2311	|	0025
Shrewsbury a.	1121	1222	1323	...	1419	1505	1521	...	...	1625	1723	...	...	1822	1922	...	2005	2022	2122	2220	2318	...	...	2327	2348	0040
Aberystwyth **147** a.	1321	|	1522	...	|	...	1724	...	...	|	1920	...	...	|	2122	...	...	|	2312	|	...	...	...	...	|	...
Cardiff Central **149** d.	▬	|	...	1114	|	...	...	1323	1330	|	...	1522	...	|	...	1716	...	|	▬	|	...	2108	2111	...	|	...
Shrewsbury d.	...	1222	...	1326	1422	...	...	1529	1531	1635	...	1731	...	1827	...	1926	...	2024	...	2231	...	2313	2317	...	2348	...
Gobowen d.	...	1240	...	1343	1440	...	...	1546	1549	1653	...	1748	...	1845	...	1944	...	2042	...	|	...	|	|	...	|	...
Ruabon d.	⑦B	1252	...	1355	1452	...	...	1558	1601	1705	...	1800	...	1857	...	1956	...	2054	⑦	⊕	...	⊕	⊕	...	⊕	...
Wrexham General d.	1206	1259	...	1402	1459	...	...	1616	1607	1712	...	1808	...	1906	...	2008t	...	2103	2238	|	...	|	|	...	|	...
Chester a.	1223	1319	...	1420	1519	...	...	1624	1625	1730	...	1826	...	1925	...	2026	...	2123	2256	2330	...	0024	0032	...	0044	...
Holyhead **150** a.	...	...	...	...	...	...	...	...	1836	...	...	2018	...	2128	...	2220	...	...	...	...	...	...	...	...	...	...

		Ⓐ	⑥	⚒	Ⓐ	⚒	⚒ 🍷	Ⓐ C	⑥ L	⑥ 🍷Q	Ⓐ Q	⚒	⚒ 🍷	⚒ 🍷	Ⓐ 🍷	⑥ 🍷	Ⓐ F🍷	⑥ F🍷	Ⓐ 🍷	⑥ 🍷	⑥ 🍷	Ⓐ 🍷	⚒ F🍷	⑥ 🍷	Ⓐ 🍷	⚒ 🍷
Holyhead **150** d.	⚒	...	...	...	...	0421	...	0527	...	...	...	0619	...	0722	0818	0813	...	...	0923	0923	1038	1038	...	1127	1130	1231
Chester d.		0422	0422	0526	...	0618	...	0716	0728	...	0730	0820	...	0924	1020	1020	...	...	1128	1128	1225	1225	...	1327	1327	1422
Wrexham General d.		|	|	0545	...	0632	...	0733	0744	...	0747	0834	...	0939	1034	1034	...	...	1143	1143	1239	1239	...	1345	1345	1436
Ruabon d.		⊕	⊕	0552	...	0639	...	|	0751	...	0754	0841	...	0946	1041	1041	...	...	1150	1150	1246	1246	...	1351	1351	1443
Gobowen d.		|	|	0604	...	0651	...	|	0803	...	0806	0853	...	0958	1053	1053	...	...	1202	1202	1258	1258	...	1403	1403	1455
Shrewsbury a.		0518	0518	0627	...	0712	...	0805	0825	...	0825	0912	...	1016	1113	1112	...	...	1222	1222	1318	1318	...	1423	1423	1514
Cardiff Central **149** a.		|	|	|	...	0918	...	0958	...	...	|	1116	...	|	1315	1315	...	...	|	|	1518	1519	...	|	|	1718
Aberystwyth **147** d.		|	|	|	...	...	0519	...	...	0619	|	...	0728	|	...	...	0929	0929	|	|	...	...	1128	|	|	...
Shrewsbury d.		0518	0522	0630	0657	...	0730	...	...	0830	0832	...	0930	1030	...	...	1130	1132	1230	1233	...	...	1330	1430	1430	...
Wellington d.		0532	0536	0644	0710	...	0744	...	...	0844	0846	...	0944	1044	...	...	1144	1146	1246	1247	...	...	1344	1444	1444	...
Telford Central d.		0538	0543	0651	0716	...	0751	...	...	0851	0853	...	0951	1051	...	...	1151	1153	1253	1254	...	...	1351	1452	1451	...
Wolverhampton a.		0555	0600	0710	0738	...	0810	...	...	0910	0911	...	1010	1110	...	...	1209	1211	1311	1312	...	...	1410	1509	1510	...
Birmingham New Street a.		0616	0622	0732	0801	...	0832	...	...	0931	0930	...	1032	1132	...	...	1232	1232	1331	1331	...	...	1432	1532	1532	...
Birmingham Int ✈ a.		0651	0651	0752	...	...	0851	...	...	0952	0952	...	1052	1151	...	...	1252	1253	1352	1353	...	...	1452	1552	1552	...

	⚒ F🍷	Ⓐ 🍷	⑥ 🍷	⑥ 🍷	Ⓐ 🍷	⚒ F🍷	⑥ 🍷	Ⓐ 🍷	⚒	⑥	Ⓐ 🍷	⚒	⚒	Ⓐ 🍷	⑥ 🍷	Ⓐ B	Ⓐ F	⑥ F	⑥	Ⓐ	⑥ B	Ⓐ	⑥	Ⓐ A	⑥	Ⓐ
Holyhead **150** d.	...	1327	1327	1428	1430	...	1530	1536	...	1629	1629	...	...	1719	1720	...	...	...	...	...	...	1920	1920	1948	...	...
Chester d.	...	1528	1527	1624	1624	...	1731	1736	...	1828	1829	1835	...	1917	1927	2020	...	...	2040	...	2108	2128	2124	2134	2224	2224
Wrexham General d.	...	1543	1542	1638	1638	...	1746	1752	...	1842	1843	1851	...	1932	1942	2034	...	...	2054	2100	2122	2143	2143	|	2239	2238
Ruabon d.	...	1550	1549	1645	1645	...	1753	1759	...	1849	1850	▬	...	1939	1948	▬	...	...	2101	2107	▬	2150	2150	|	2246	2245
Gobowen d.	...	1602	1601	1657	1657	...	1805	1811	...	1901	1902	...	...	1951	2000	...	...	...	2113	2119	...	2202	2202	|	2258	2257
Shrewsbury a.	...	1622	1621	1716	1716	...	1827	1831	...	1921	1922	⚒	...	2010	2019	...	...	...	2133	2139	...	2221	2221	|	2317	2315
Cardiff Central **149** a.	...	|	|	1921	1920	...	|	|	...	2122	2123	🍷	...	...	▬	...	...	...	...	...	...	|	|	|	▬	▬
Aberystwyth **147** d.	1329	|	|	...	...	1529	|	|	...	...	...	1727	...	...	⚒	⚒	1929	1929	...	...	Ⓐ	|	|	|	⚒	⑥
Shrewsbury d.	1531	1630	1634	...	...	1730	1831	1831	1905	...	...	1930	2005	...	2059	2105	2130	2130	...	...	2200	2230	2230	|	2240	2259
Wellington d.	1545	1644	1647	...	...	1744	1845	1845	1918	...	...	1944	2018	...	2112	2118	2144	2144	...	...	2213	2244	2244	|	2253	2312
Telford Central d.	1552	1651	1654	...	...	1751	1852	1852	1926	...	...	1951	2026	...	2118	2126	2151	2151	...	...	2221	2251	2251	|	2302	2318
Wolverhampton a.	1611	1711	1711	...	...	1811	1910	1910	1954	...	...	2009	2054	...	2138	2154	2210	2210	...	...	2249	2308	2309	2231	2332	2338
Birmingham New Street a.	1632	1732	1731	...	...	1832	1932	1932	2026	...	...	2032	2126	...	2200	2226	2235	2231	...	...	2321	2332	2330	2251	2351	2357
Birmingham Int ✈ a.	1652	1753	1752	...	...	1852	1952	1952	...	...	...	2052	...	...	...	...	2252	...	...	...	...	...	...	...	...	...

		⑦	⑦	⑦ 🍷	⑦ 🍷	⑦ 🍷	⑦ 🍷	⑦ b🍷	⑦ a🍷	⑦ F🍷	⑦	⑦ a🍷	⑦ F🍷	⑦ 🍷	⑦ a🍷	⑦ F🍷	⑦ 🍷	⑦ 🍷	⑦ B	⑦	⑦ 🍷	⑦ F	⑦	⑦	⑦	⑦
Holyhead **150** d.	⑦	...	...	...	...	...	...	1019	1019	...	...	...	...	...	...	...	...	1625	...	...	1825	...	...	...	...	...
Chester d.		...	...	...	0920	...	1132	1225	1229	...	1334	1430	...	1535	1630	...	1735	1825	1910	1938	2027	...	...	2127	2206	2302
Wrexham General d.		...	...	...	0935	...	1148	1240	1243	...	1349	1444	...	1551	1644	...	1750	1840	1925	1954	|	...	...	2142	2223	|
Ruabon d.		...	...	...	0942	...	1155	1247	1250	...	1356	1451	...	1558	1651	...	1757	1847	▬	2001	⊕	...	...	2149	...	⊕
Gobowen d.		...	...	...	0955	...	1207	1259	1302	...	1408	1503	...	1610	1703	...	1809	1859	...	2013	|	...	...	2201	...	|
Shrewsbury a.		...	...	...	1014	...	1226	1318	1321	...	1427	1522	...	1629	1722	...	1829	1920	⑦	2033	2120	...	...	2221	...	0020
Cardiff Central **149** a.		...	...	...	|	...	|	1527	1527	...	|	1722	...	|	1922	...	|	2129h	F	|	|	...	...	|	...	...
Aberystwyth **147** d.		...	...	...	|	0929	|	...	...	1129	|	...	1329	|	...	1527	|	...	1727	|	|	1928	...	|	...	...
Shrewsbury d.		0804	0840	0917	1030	1133	1232	...	...	1330	1430	...	1531	1631	...	1730	1831	...	1930	2033	2120	2133	2154	2223	...	...
Wellington d.		0820	0853	0931	1044	1147	1246	...	...	1344	1444	...	1545	1645	...	1744	1845	...	1944	2047	|	2147	2207	2237	...	...
Telford Central d.		0828	0902	0938	1051	1154	1254	...	...	1351	1451	...	1552	1652	...	1751	1852	...	1951	2054	|	2154	2215	2245	...	...
Wolverhampton a.		0846	0931	0957	1110	1212	1311	...	...	1409	1509	...	1610	1710	...	1810	1910	...	2010	2113	2153	2212	2244	2314	...	...
Birmingham New Street a.		0909	0951	1017	1132	1232	1332	...	...	1432	1532	...	1632	1731	...	1831	1932	...	2032	2133	2212	2232	2304	...	...	...
Birmingham Int ✈ a.		0930	...	1034	1151	1252	1351	...	...	1452	1551	...	1655	1752	...	1851	1952	...	2052	2151	2232	2249	...	...	...	...

A – [12] and 🍷 Birmingham New Street - Crewe - Holyhead and v.v. (Table **150**).
B – [12] and 🍷 Wrexham - London Euston and v.v. (Table **150**).
C – [12] and ✕ Cardiff - Holyhead and v.v.
F – Conveys [2] Birmingham - Pwllheli and v.v. (Table **148**).
J – To Llandudno Junction (Table **150**).
L – To/from Llandudno (Table **150**).
M – To Manchester Piccadilly (Table **150**).

P – [12] and 🍷 Chester - Crewe - Birmingham New Street (Table **150**).
Q – Also conveys [2] Crewe - Birmingham International (Table **149**).
T – To Crewe (Table **149**).

a – Aug. 3 - Sept. 14.
b – Until July 27 and from Sept. 21.
c – Conveys 🍷 on ⑥.
d – Conveys 🍷 on Ⓐ.

e – Arrives 1122 on ⑥.
f – Arrives 2124 on ①②③④⑥.
g – Arrives 2337 on ⑥.
h – Arrives 2123 Aug. 3 - Sept. 14.
r – Departs 0722 on ⑥.
t – Arrives 2003.

⊕ – Via Crewe (Table **149**).

147 SHREWSBURY - ABERYSTWYTH — 2nd class — AW

km		⚒	⚒	⚒	⚒🍷	⚒🍷	Ⓐ	⑥	⚒🍷	⚒🍷	⚒🍷	⚒🍷	⑥	Ⓐ🍷	k	⑤	kv	⑤	Ⓐ	⑥	⑦	⑦b	⑦a	⑦b
	Birmingham New Street **146** d.		...	...	0622	0822	*0922*	*0922*	1022	1222	1422	1622	*1722*	*1721*	1822	1822	*1922*	*1922*	2022	2022		...	...	🚌
0	**Shrewsbury** d.		...	...	0727	0930	1027	1033	1127	1327	1528	1730	1830	1830	1930	1930	2032	2032	2150	2147		...	0831	0830
32	Welshpool d.		...	0648	0749	0952	1051	1055	1149	1351	1552	1752	1853	1853	1952	1954	2054	2059t	2213	2209		...	0853	0915
54	Newtown d.		...	0703	0804	1007	1106	1110	1204	1406	1607	1807	1908	1908	2007	2009	2109	2114	2228	2224		...	0908	0940
63	Caersws d.		...	0710	0811	1014	1113	1117	1211	1413	1614	1814	1915	1915	2014	2017	2117	2122	2235	2231		...	0916	0955
98	**Machynlleth** a.		...	0742	0843	1046	1139	1143	1243	1445	1646	1845	1947	1945	2048	2048	2141	2153	2303	2259		...	0948	1035
98	**Machynlleth** **148** ▷ d.		0441	0747	0848	1050	1142	1144	1247	1449	1650	1849	1947	1950	2049	2057	2150	2157	2306	2306		0947	0949	1035
104	Dovey Junction **148** ▷ d.		0447	0755	0855	1056	1154	1154	1255	1455	1656	1857	2001n	1958	2057	2109	2158	2205	2312	2312		0956	0957	1045
118	Borth ▷ d.		0457	0805	0905	1106	1204	1204	1305	1505	1706	1907	2011	2008	2107	2119	2208	2215	2322	2322		1006	1007	1103
131	**Aberystwyth** 🚂 ▷ a.		0512	0822	0921	1122	1220	1220	1322	1521	1722	1923	2027	2024	2124	2136	2224	2231	2341	2337		1020	1020	1125

	⑦🍷	⑦🍷	⑦🍷	⑦	⑦🍷	⑦	⑦🍷	⑦🍷	⑦🍷	⑦
Birmingham New Street **146** d.	...	1022	1222	*1322*	1421	*1522*	1622	*1722*	1822	2024
Shrewsbury d.	1027	1128	1329	1429	1528	1629	1727	1828	1927	2128
Welshpool d.	1049	1150	1351	1451	1551	1651	1749	1850	1949	2150
Newtown d.	1104	1205	1406	1506	1606	1706	1804	1905	2004	2205
Caersws d.	1112	1212	1413	1514	1613	1713	1812	1912	2011	2212
Machynlleth a.	1143	1243	1445	1545	1644	1744	1843	1939	2042	2240
Machynlleth **148** ▷ d.	1143	1248	1449	1545	1649	1745	1847	1942	2047	2242
Dovey Junction **148** ▷ d.	1155	1256	1457	1555	1657	1755	1855	1955	2055	2248
Borth ▷ d.	1205	1306	1507	1605	1707	1805	1905	2005	2105	2258
Aberystwyth 🚂 ▷ a.	1221	1321	1522	1620	1724	1821	1920	2020	2122	2312

	⚒	⚒	⚒🍷	⚒🍷	⚒	⚒🍷	Ⓐ🍷
Aberystwyth 🚂 ▷ d.		0519	0619	0728	0829	0929	1128
Borth ▷ d.		0534	0634	0743	0844	0944	1143
Dovey Junction **148** ▷ d.		0544	0653j	0753	0858r	0954	1153
Machynlleth **148** ▷ a.		0554	0701	0802	0906	1003	1203
Machynlleth d.		0554	0705	0805	0906	1008	1205
Caersws d.		0619	0732	0832	0931	1035	1232
Newtown d.		0626	0739	0839	0940	1042	1239
Welshpool d.		0646t	0754	0854	0955	1056	1254
Shrewsbury a.		0709	0818	0918	1020	1119	1316
Birmingham New Street **146** a.		0832	*0930*	1032	*1132*	1232	1432

	⑥🍷	⚒🍷	⚒🍷	⚒🍷	⚒🍷	⚒	⑥	Ⓐ	⑦	⑦b	⑦a	⑦🍷	⑦	⑦🍷		⑦🍷	⑦🍷	⑦🍷	⑦🍷	⑦	⑦	⑦	⑦
Aberystwyth 🚂 ▷ d.	1128	1229	1329	1529	1727	1831	1929	1929		0829	0829	0929	1029	1129	...	1229	1329	1429	1527	1629	1727	1928	2315
Borth ▷ d.	1143	1244	1344	1544	1742	1846	1944	1944		0844	0844	0944	1044	1144	...	1244	1344	1444	1543	1644	1743	1943	2330
Dovey Junction **148** ▷ d.	1153	1257r	1354	1554	1753	1856	1959t	1959t		0856	0856	0954	1056	1154	...	1257	1356	1459r	1554	1659	1754	1953	2340
Machynlleth **148** ▷ a.	1203	1306	1403	1603	1801	1905	2008	2008		0904	0904	1003	1104	1203	...	1305	1404	1507	1602	1707	1803	2002	2349
Machynlleth d.	1205	1306	1407	1608	1806	1909	2011	2011		0905	0905	1007	1105	1206	...	1306	1407	1508	1607	1707	1806	2005	...
Caersws d.	1232	1331	1434	1635	1835	1936	2038	2038		0933	0938	1032	1132	1233	...	1333	1434	1535	1634	1734	1833	2032	...
Newtown d.	1239	1340	1441	1642	1842	1943	2045	2045		0940	0945	1039	1139	1240	...	1340	1441	1542	1641	1741	1840	2040	...
Welshpool d.	1254	1354	1455	1656	1857	1957	2100	2100		0954	0959	1054	1154	1254	...	1354	1456	1556	1655	1755	1854	2054	...
Shrewsbury a.	1318	1418	1518	1720	1919	2020	2125	2125		1016	1021	1118	1218	1318	...	1419	1519	1618	1719	1819	1918	2118	...
Birmingham New Street **146** a.	1432	*1532*	1632	1832	2032	...	2231	2235		*1132*	*1132*	1232	*1332*	1432	...	*1532*	1632	*1731*	1831	*1932*	2032	2232	...

a – Until Sept. 14.
b – From Sept. 21.
j – Arrives 0644.
k – ①②③④⑥.
n – Arrives 1955.
r – Arrives 3 minutes earlier.
t – Arrives 5 minutes earlier.
v – Conveys 🍷 on ⑥.
▷ – Additional journeys Machynlleth - Aberystwyth and v.v.:
From Machynlleth at 0537⚒, 0647⚒, 0750⑦, 0849⑦, 1049⑦, 1350⑦.
From Aberystwyth at 1829⑦, 2029⑦, 2031⑥, 2129Ⓒ, 2139Ⓐ, 2229Ⓒ, 2234Ⓐ, 2339⑥, 2344Ⓐ.
🚂 – Vale of Rheidol Railway (Aberystwyth - Devil's Bridge: *19 km*) ✆ 01970 625819. www.rheidolrailway.co.uk

148 MACHYNLLETH - PWLLHELI — 2nd class — AW

km		⚒	⚒	⚒	Ⓐ	⑥	⚒	⚒		⚒	⚒	⑥	①–④	⑤	⑦	⑦a	⑦b	⑦a	⑦		⑦	⑦	⑦
	Birmingham New Street **146** d.		...	*0622*	0822	0822	1022	1222	...	1422	1622	*1922**	*1922**	*1922**		...	...	...	1022	...	1222	1421	1622
	Shrewsbury **147** d.		...	*0727*	0930	0930	1127	1327	...	1528	1730	*2032*	*2032*	*2032*		...	...	...	1128	...	1329	1528	1727
0	**Machynlleth** **147** d.		0643	0852	1055	1055	1251	1456	...	1655	1904	2147	2147	2147		0845	1004	1045	1251	...	1453	1652	1855
6	Dovey Junction **147** d.		0649	0900	1101	1101	1259	1502	...	1701	1910	2153	2202t	2209t		0900f	1010	1100f	1300	...	1459	1702r	1901
16	Aberdovey d.		0702	0913	1114	1114	1312	1515	...	1714	1923	2206	2214	2221		0912	1023	1112	1313	...	1512	1715	1914
22	Tywyn 🚂 a.		0712	0923	1124	1124	1322	1525	...	1725	1933	2216	2224	2231		0918	1029	1118	1320	...	1519	1724	1921
22	Tywyn 🚂 d.		0714	0929	1130	1130	1325	1526	...	1729	1933	2217	2224	2231		0921	1030	1121	1324	...	1531	1729	1924
37	Fairbourne d.		0732	0948	1149	1149	1344	1545	...	1747	1951	2236	2243	2250		0940	1049	1140	1343	...	1549	1747	1943
41	**Barmouth** d.		0747	1001	1201	1201	1357	1558	...	1800	2004	2248	2255	2302		0949	1058	1149	1356	...	1559	1759	1953
58	Harlech a.		0813	1026	1226	1227	1422	1623	...	1825	2030	2314	2321	2328		1015	1124	1215	1422	...	1624	1825	2018
58	Harlech d.		0825	1026	1226	1227	1431	1628	...	1833	2030	2314	2321	2328		1024	1125	1217	1431	...	1624	1830	2022
67	Penrhyndeudraeth d.		0838	1039	1239	1240	1444	1640	...	1845	2043	2327	2334	2341		1037	1138	1230	1444	...	1637	1843	2035
69	Minffordd **150b** d.		0841	1042	1242	1243	1447	1644	...	1849	2047	2331	2338	2345		1041	1142	1234	1448	...	1641	1847	2038
72	**Porthmadog** **150b** d.		0850	1051	1251	1252	1456	1652	...	1857	2055	2339	2346	2353		1048	1154f	1246f	1456	...	1647	1855	2044
80	Criccieth d.		0857	1058	1258	1259	1503	1700	...	1904	2103	2347	2354	0001		1055	1201	1254	1503	...	1654	1902	2052
93	**Pwllheli** a.		0914	1115	1313	1316	1520	1717	...	1921	2118	0001	0006	0013		1111	1217	1308	1519	...	1710	1918	2107

	⚒	⚒	⚒	Ⓐ	⑥		⚒	⚒	⚒	Ⓐ	⑥		v	⑤	⑦	⑦a	⑦	⑦b		⑦a	⑦	⑦	⑦
Pwllheli d.		0629	0724	0934	0934	...	1137	1338	1537	1742	1742	...	2026	2026		0734	0934	1128	...	1131	1340	1533	1736
Criccieth d.		0643	0738	0948	0948	...	1151	1352	1551	1756	1756	...	2040	2040		0748	0948	1142	...	1145	1354	1547	1750
Porthmadog **150b** d.		0653	0747	0957	0957	...	1201	1402	1601	1806	1806	...	2056f	2056f		0758	0958	1157f	...	1155	1406	1557	1800
Minffordd **150b** d.		0657	0752	1001	1001	...	1205	1406	1605	1810	1810	...	2100	2100		0802	1002	1201	...	1159	1410	1601	1805
Penrhyndeudraeth d.		0701	0756	1005	1005	...	1209	1410	1609	1814	1814	...	2104	2104		0806	1006	1205	...	1203	1414	1605	1809
Harlech a.		0717	0811	1022	1022	...	1226	1427	1626	1830	1830	...	2119	2119		0823	1023	1219	...	1217	1428	1622	1823
Harlech d.		0717	0821	1029	1029	...	1228	1428	1629	1830	1830	...	2119	2119		0823	1028	1221	...	1217	1434	1629	1827
Barmouth d.		0749	0852f	1059	1059	...	1255	1455	1656	1857	1857	...	2146	2146		0850	1101f	1250	...	1245	1501	1656	1854
Fairbourne d.		0757	0900	1107	1107	...	1303	1503	1704	1905	1905	...	2154	2154		0858	1109	1258	...	1253	1509	1704	1903
Tywyn 🚂 a.		0817	0922	1129	1129	...	1325	1526	1726	1927	1927	...	2216	2216		0919	1130	1319	...	1314	1528	1726	1923
Tywyn 🚂 d.		0817	0927	1130	1130	...	1325	1526	1727	1934	1934	...	2225	2232		0919	1130	1320	...	1319	1528	1727	1924
Aberdovey d.		0823	0933	1136	1136	...	1331	1532	1733	1940	1940	...	2231	2238		0925	1136	1326	...	1325	1536	1733	1930
Dovey Junction **147** d.		0838	0948	1150	1150	...	1346	1547	1749	1956	1956	...	2246	2253		0940	1151	1341	...	1340	1551	1751	1948
Machynlleth **147** a.		0846	0955	1158	1158	...	1352	1555	1757	2004	2004	...	2253	2300		0947	1158	1349	...	1348	1559	1759	1955
Shrewsbury **147** a.		*1020*	1119	1316	1318	...	1518	1720	*1919*	*2125*	*2125*	...	...	...		*1118*	1318	1519	...	1519	1719	1918	2118
Birmingham New Street **145** a.		*1132**	1232	1432	1432	...	1632	1832	*2032*	*2235*	*2231*	...	...	...		*1232*	1432	1632	...	1632	1831	2032	2232

a – Aug. 3 - Sept. 14.
b – Not Aug. 3 - Sept. 14.
f – Arrives 5–9 minutes earlier.
r – Arrives 1658.
t – Arrives 2153.
v – ①②③④⑥.
* – Change at Shrewsbury and Machynlleth.
🚂 – Talyllyn Railway (Tywyn Wharf - Abergynolwyn - Nant Gwernol: *12 km*). ✆ 01654 710472.

149 CARDIFF - HEREFORD - CREWE - MANCHESTER — AW

km		Ⓐ	②–⑤ 2	Ⓐ 🍷	Ⓐ 2🍷	Ⓐ 2🍷	Ⓐ S🍴	Ⓐ 2🍷	Ⓐ2 C🍷	Ⓐ 🍴	Ⓐ 2🍷	Ⓐ2 M🍷	Ⓐ 🍴	Ⓐ 2🍷	Ⓐ2 M🍷	Ⓐ 🍴	Ⓐ 2🍷	Ⓐ2 M🍷	Ⓐ 🍴	Ⓐ 2🍷	Ⓐ F2	Ⓐ 2	Ⓐ 🍴	Ⓐ 🍷	Ⓐ2 M🍷	Ⓐ 2🍷	Ⓐ 🍷
0	**Cardiff** Central .. **133** § d.		0030	0432	0519	0549	0646	0719	0753	0853	0923	0953	1053	1123	1153	1253	1323	1353	1450	1523	1551	1616	1653	1722	1753	1823	1853
19	Newport **133** § d.		0055	0451	0538	0602	0659	0732	0807	0907	0938	1007	1107	1136	1207	1307	1336	1407	1503	1536	1604	1630	1707	1736	1807	1839	1907
30	Cwmbrân d.		0106	0503	0549	0612	0710	0743	0817	0919	0948	1017	1119	1147	1217	1319	1346	1417	1515	1547	1614	1640	1718	1748	1817	1850	1918
35	Pontypool & New Inn ..d.		0112	0509	0554	0618	|	0749	0822	|	0953	|	|	1154	|	|	1352	|	|	1553	1620	1645	1725	1754	1822	1856	|
50	Abergavenny d.		0121	0519	0604	0627	0724	0758	0831	0933	1003	1029	1133	1204	1230	1333	1401	1429	1529	1603	1629	1654	1735	1805	1831	1907	1932
89	**Hereford** d.		0147	0545	0629	0653	0750	0824	0857	0959	1028	1055	1159	1232	1256	1359	1427	1455	1555	1628	1655	1720	1801	1831	1857	1933	1958
109	Leominster d.		▬	0558	0642	0706	0804	0837	0910	1013	|	1108	1213	|	1309	1413	|	1508	1609	1641	1708	1732	1815	|	1909	|	2012
127	Ludlow d.		...	0610	0653	0716	0816	0847	0920	1025	1049	1119	1225	1254	1319	1425	1448	1519	1621	1652	1719	1743	1827	1853	1920	1953	2024
138	Craven Arms **145** d.		...	0619	0701	0725	0825	0856	0929	|	1057	1127	|	|	1328	|	1456	1527	|	1700	|	1752	|	|	1928	2002	|
150	Church Stretton **145** d.		Ⓐ	0629	0709	0733	0834	0904	0937	|	1106	1136	|	|	1336	|	1505	1536	|	1710	|	1801	|	|	1936	2010	|
170	**Shrewsbury** **145** a.		2	0645	0725	0749	0851	0924	0953	1054	1122	1152	1253	1322	1352	1453	1523	1552	1652	1725	1746	1817	1855	1925	1952	2026	2052
170	**Shrewsbury** ¶ d.		0531	0646	0726	0749	0851	0926	0954	1055	1127	1152	1255	1327	1353	1455	1527	1552	1655	1727	1749	1821	1856	1928	1953	2027	2101
200	Whitchurch ¶ d.		0557	0709	|	0809	0908	|	1010	|	|	1210	|	|	1410	|	|	1609	|	|	1809	1838	|	|	2009	|	|
223	**Crewe** ¶ a.		0622	0730	|	0829	0930	|	1029	1128	|	1230	1328	|	1429	1528	|	1629	1728	|	1829	1857	1928	|	2029	2102	2136
	Chester **146 150** a.		...	|	0821	|	|	1021	|	|	1225	|	|	1421	|	|	1623	|	|	1822	|	1925	|	2018	|	2123	|
	Holyhead **150** a.		...	|	1012	|	|	1203	|	|	1415	|	|	1616	|	|	1821	|	|	2015	|	...	|	2206	|	...	|
263	Stockport a.		...	0800	...	0900	1001	...	1101	1201	...	1301	1401	...	1501	1601	...	1701	1801	...	1901	...	2001	...	2101	...	2207
273	**Manchester** Piccadilly a.		...	0813	...	0913	1013	...	1113	1213	...	1313	1413	...	1513	1613	...	1713	1813	...	1915	...	2015	...	2113	...	2221

C – From/to Carmarthen (Table **136**).
D – From Milford Haven until July 27 (Table **136**); from Carmarthen from Sept. 21 (Table **136**).
F – From/to Fishguard Harbour (Table **136**).
J – To Llandudno Junction (Table **150**).
K – To/from Birmingham International (Table **146**).
M – To/from Milford Haven (Table **136**).
P – To Pembroke Dock (Table **136**).
S – From/to Swansea (Table **136**).
T – To Carmarthen on ①–④ (Table **136**); to Milford Haven on ⑤ (Table **136**).
V – From Birmingham New Street (Table **146**).
Z – From Carmarthen until July 27 (Table **136**); from Swansea from Sept. 21 (Table **136**).
a – Conveys 🍷 from Shrewsbury.
b – Arrives 1439.
c – Arrives 1208.
d – Arrives 1228.
e – Arrives 1637.
f – Arrives 2309.
j – Arrives 1600.
p – Arrives 7 minutes earlier.
r – Arrives 1238.
t – Change at Shrewsbury.

FOR OTHER NOTES SEE NEXT PAGE ►►►

AW

CARDIFF - HEREFORD - CREWE - MANCHESTER 149

For services on ⑦ August 3 - September 14 see page 579

	Ⓐ	Ⓐ	①–④	⑤		⑥	⑥	⑥	⑥	⑥2	⑥	⑥2	⑥		⑥	⑥2	⑥	⑥	⑥2	⑥	⑥	⑥2	⑥	⑥	⑥	⑥	⑥	⑥
	2	2	2	2		2	✕	2🍷	2🍷	S✕	🍷2	C🍷	✕		2🍷	M🍷	✕	2🍷	M🍷	✕	2🍷	M🍷	🍷	2🍷	2F	2	🍷	2🍷
Cardiff Central . **133** § d.	2010	2135	2221	2225	⑥	0035	0435	0525	0549	0643	0722	0753	0854	...	0923	0953	1053	1123	1153	1253	1325	1353	1453	1524	1553	1617	1653	1723
Newport **133** § d.	2029	2150	2241	2239		0057	0449	0538	0602	0657	0736	0806	0907	...	0938	1007	1107	1137	1207	1307	1338	1407	1508	1538	1606	1631	1707	1736
Cwmbrân d.	2039	2200	2252	2250		0108	0501	0549	0612	0709	0746	0816	0919	...	0948	1017	1119	1147	1217	1319	1348	1417	1519	1548	1616	1641	1718	1746
Pontypool & New Inn . d.	2044	2205	2257	2255		0114	0507	0554	0618	│	0752	0821	│	...	0954	│	│	1153	│	│	1354	│	│	1553	1622	1646	1725	1752
Abergavenny d.	2054	2215	2307	2305		0122	0517	0604	0627	0723	0801	0831	0933	...	1003	1029	1133	1202	1229	1333	1403	1429	1533	1603	1632	1656	1735	1801
Hereford d.	2119	2240	2333	2333		0149	0543	0629	0653	0749	0827	0856	0959	...	1029	1055	1159	1233d	1255	1359	1429	1455	1559	1628	1658	1722	1801	1827
Leominster d.	2132	2253	2346	2346		—	0556	0642	0706	0803	0840	0909	1013	...	│	1108	1213	│	1308	1413	│	1508	1613	1641	1711	1735	1815	│
Ludlow d.	2143	2304	2357	2357		...	0607	0653	0716	0814	0850	0920	1025	...	1049	1119	1225	1253	1319	1425	1449	1519	1625	1652	1722	1746	1827	1847
Craven Arms **145** d.	2151	2312	0006	0006		...	0616	0701	0725	0824	0859	0928	│	...	1058	1127	│	│	1327	│	1458	1527	│	1700	│	1755	│	1856
Church Stretton **145** d.	2200	2321	0015	0015		⑥	0625	0709	0733	0833	0907	0937	│	...	1106	1136	│	│	1336	│	1506	1536	│	1709	│	1803	│	1904
Shrewsbury **145** a.	2216	2337	0030	0031		2	0641	0725	0749	0848	0924	0953	1053	...	1122	1152	1253	1322	1352	1453	1522	1552	1653	1725	1749	1819	1855	1922
Shrewsbury ¶ d.	2216	2347	0034	0034		0531	0644	0726	0749	0850	0926	0953	1055	...	1127	1152	1255	1327	1352	1455	1527	1552	1655	1727	1750	1821	1856	1927
Whitchurch ¶ d.	2236	0004	0100	0100		0557	0706	│	0809	0907	│	1009	│	...	│	1209	│	│	1409	│	│	1609	│	│	1809	1837	│	│
Crewe ¶ a.	2255	0026	0123	0123		0622	0726	│	0829	0929	│	1029	1128	...	│	1229	1328	│	1428	1528	│	1629	1728	│	1829	1900	1928	│
Chester **146 150** a.	│	0046	...	...		...	│	0821	│	│	1021	│	│	...	1225	│	│	1421	│	│	1623	│	│	1822	│	1923	│	2024
Holyhead **150** a.	│	...	...	...		...	│	1012	│	│	1205	│	│	...	1415	│	│	1615	│	│	1822	│	│	2016	│	...	│	2228
Stockport a.	2324	...	...	...		...	0800	...	0900	1001	...	1101	1201	...	...	1301	1401	...	1501	1601	...	1701	1801	...	1901	...	2001	...
Manchester Piccadilly a.	2337	...	...	...		...	0814	...	0913	1013	...	1113	1213	...	...	1313	1413	...	1513	1613	...	1713	1813	...	1913	...	2013	...

	⑥2	⑥	⑥		⑥	⑥	⑥	⑥		⑦	⑦2	⑦2		⑦	⑦2	⑦	⑦2	⑦2		⑦	⑦	⑦2	⑦	⑦2		⑦	⑦	⑦
	M🍷	2🍷	🍷		J2	2	2	C2		2🍷	Sa	Z🍷		S🍷	D🍷	a2	S🍷	M🍷		2🍷	S🍷	M🍷	S2	M🍷		S2	2	C2
Cardiff Central . **133** § d.	1751	1823	1853	...	1938	2010	2122	2215	⑦	0842	0945	1043	...	1140	1240	1330	1351	1452	...	1522	1555	1641	1755	1842	...	1939	2111	2320
Newport **133** § d.	1805	1836	1907	...	1955	2027	2136	2229		0901	1004	1057	...	1154	1254	1344	1404	1507	...	1536	1609	1655	1809	1856	...	1953	2124	2337
Cwmbrân d.	1815	1846	1918	...	2005	2037	2146	2239		0912	1015	1107	...	1206	1304	1354	1415	1519	...	1546	1620	1705	1821	1907	...	2007	2134	2347
Pontypool & New Inn . d.	1820	1852	│	...	2010	2042	2151	2244	★	0917	1021	1113	...	1212	1310	1359	│	│	...	1551	│	1711	1826	│	...	2012	2140	2353
Abergavenny d.	1830	1901	1932	...	2020	2052	2200	2254		0927	1031	1123	...	1222	1320	1409	1429	1533	...	1600	1634	1721	1837	1920	...	2023	2149	0003
Hereford d.	1855	1927	1958	...	2046	2117	2226	2319		0953	1057	1151	...	1248	1347	1435	1454	1606j	...	1626	1701	1749	1905	1947	...	2050	2215	0030
Leominster d.	1908	│	2012	...	2059	2131	2239	—		1006	1110	1203	...	1302	1400	1449	1508	│	...	1639	│	1802	1918	2001	...	2104	2228	—
Ludlow d.	1919	1947	2024	...	2109	2142	2249	...		1017	1121	1214	...	1314	1412	1500	1519	1627	...	1650	1723	1813	1929	2012	...	2115	2239	...
Craven Arms **145** d.	1927	1956	│	...	2118	2150	2258	...		1025	│	1223	...	│	1421	1508	│	│	...	1659	│	1822	│	2021	...	2124	2248	...
Church Stretton **145** d.	1936	2004	│	...	2126	2159	2306	⑥		1034	│	1232	...	│	1430	│	│	│	...	1707	│	1831	│	2030	...	2133	2257	⑦
Shrewsbury **145** a.	1952	2026	2052	...	2142	2214	2322	**V**		1051	1151	1249	...	1343	1447	1531	1548	1655	...	1722	1750	1847	1959	2046	...	2150	2314	**K**2
Shrewsbury ¶ d.	1952	2027	2058	...	2144	2215	2326	2337		1054	1153	1257	...	1343	1457	1531	1556	1657	...	1732	1752	1857	2003	2053	...	...	2317	2348
Whitchurch ¶ d.	2009	│	│	...	│	2241	│	0001		│	│	│	...	│	│	│	│	│	...	│	│	│	│	│	...	...	2343	│
Crewe ¶ a.	2029	2101	2135	...	│	2305	2357	0021		1126	1225	1328	...	1421	1529	│	1627	1729	...	│	1828	1927	2035	2128	...	...	0006	0021
Chester **146 150** a.	│	2127	│	...	2240	│	0020	...		│	*1319*t	│	...	*1519*t	│	1625	*1730*t	│	...	1826	*1925*t	│	*2123*t	│	...	...	0032	0044
Holyhead **150** a.	│	2327	│	...	...	│	...	...		│	│	│	...	│	│	1836	│	│	...	2018	*2128*t	│	│	│	...	...	...	...
Stockport a.	2101	...	2208	...	...	2331	...	...		│	1259	1400	...	1502	1602	...	1702	1802	...	...	1902	2001	2102	2203	...	...	...	...
Manchester Piccadilly a.	2113	...	2220	...	...	2343	...	...		1214	1311	1415	...	1515	1615	...	1715	1814	...	...	1914	2015	2115	2214	...	...	...	...

		Ⓐ	Ⓐ	Ⓐ	Ⓐ	Ⓐ	Ⓐ2	Ⓐ	Ⓐ	Ⓐ	Ⓐ	Ⓐ	Ⓐ	Ⓐ2	Ⓐ	Ⓐ	Ⓐ2	Ⓐ	Ⓐ	Ⓐ2	Ⓐ	Ⓐ	Ⓐ2	Ⓐ	Ⓐ	Ⓐ2	Ⓐ	Ⓐ
		2	2	2K	🍷	2	M🍷	2	✕	✕	2M	2	✕	F🍷	2🍷	✕	M🍷	2🍷	✕	P🍷	2🍷	✕	F🍷	2🍷	S✕	T🍷	2🍷	✕
Manchester Piccadilly d.	Ⓐ	...	...	...	...	...	...	...	0627	...	0730	...	0830	0930	...	1030	1130	...	1230	1330	...	1430	1530	...	1630	1730	...	1830
Stockport d.		...	...	...	...	...	...	...	0637	...	0739	...	0839	0939	...	1040	1139	...	1240	1339	...	1440	1539	...	1640	1739	...	1840
Holyhead **150** d.		...	...	...	...	...	...	0421	│	0527	│	0619	│	│	0818	│	│	1038	│	│	1232	│	│	1430	│	│	1629	│
Chester **146 150** d.		...	...	0422	...	...	...	0618	│	0716	│	0820	│	│	1020	│	│	1225	│	│	1422	│	│	1624	│	│	1829	│
Crewe ¶ d.		...	...	0448	0513	...	0554	│	0709	│	0810	│	0910	1010	│	1110	1210	│	1310	1410	│	1510	1610	│	1710	1810	│	1910
Whitchurch ¶ d.		...	...	│	│	...	0611	│	│	│	0828	│	│	1028	│	│	1227	│	│	1427	│	│	1627	│	│	1828	│	│
Shrewsbury ¶ a.		...	...	0518	0543	...	0632	0712	0743	0805	0846	0912	0940	1046	1113	1141	1245	1318	1341	1445	1514	1541	1646	1716	1744	1849	1922	1944
Shrewsbury **145** d.		...	0514	...	0544	0610	0635	0713	0743	0809	0850	0913	0940	1047	1115	1143	1246	1318	1341	1448	1515	1542	1647	1717	1744	1850	1925	1944
Church Stretton **145** d.		...	│	...	0559	0624	0650	0727	0759	│	0904	0927	│	1101	1130	│	1300	1332	│	1502	1529	│	1701	1731	│	1904	1939	2000
Craven Arms **145** d.		...	│	...	0608	0632	0658	0735	0808	│	0912	0935	│	1109	1138	│	1308	1340	│	1510	1537	│	1709	1739	│	1912	1947	2009
Ludlow d.		...	0540	...	0617	0641	0706	0744	0817	0837	0921	0944	1007	1118	1147	1211	1317	1349	1408	1518	1546	1609	1717	1748	1811	1921	1956	2018
Leominster d.		...	0550	...	0629	0651	0717	0754	0828	│	0931	0954	1019	1128	│	1222	1327	│	1420	1529	1556	1620	1728	1758	1823	1931	│	2029
Hereford d.		0530	0606	...	0645	0710	0733	0810	0844	0900	0948	1010	1035	1144	1210	1245r	1343	1412	1438	1545	1612	1636	1744	1815	1839	1949	2019	2045
Abergavenny d.		0552	0632	...	0708	0734	0755	0832	0907	│	1010	1032	1059	1206	1232	1310	1405	1435	1501	1607	1634	1700	1805	1837	1903	2011	2041	2109
Pontypool & New Inn . d.		0601	0642	...	0718	0743	0805	0842	0917	│	│	1042	│	│	1242	│	│	1446	│	│	1644	1710	1815	1847	1913	2021	│	2119
Cwmbrân d.		0606	0648	...	0723	0748	0810	0847	0923	│	1022	1047	1112	1219	1247	1325	1418	1452	1515	1619	1649	1716	1820	1852	1919	2026	2054	2125
Newport **133** § a.		0619	0701	...	0732	0759	0822	0901	0937	0944	1034	1101	1123	1231	1259	1337	1430	1505	1527	1631	1701	1728	1832	1905	1930	2039	2106	2139
Cardiff Central . **133** § a.		0634	0716	...	0750	0816	0844	0918	0951	0958	1049	1116	1137	1245	1315	1352	1444	1519	1544	1646	1717	1744	1846	1920	1944	2054	2123	2154

	⑤	①–④	⑤	①–④	Ⓐ	Ⓐ		⑥	⑥	⑥	⑥	⑥	⑥2	⑥	⑥	⑥2	⑥	⑥	⑥2	⑥	⑥	⑥2	⑥	⑥	⑥2	⑥	⑥	⑥2
	2	2	2	2	2	2		2	2	2K	2🍷	2	M🍷	2	✕	M🍷	2	✕	F🍷	2🍷	✕	M🍷	2🍷	✕	P🍷	2🍷	🍷	F🍷
Manchester Piccadilly d.	1930	1930	2030	2030	...	2232	⑥	...	...	...	...	...	...	...	0627	0730	...	0830	0930	...	1030	1130	...	1230	1330	...	1430	1530
Stockport d.	1939	1939	2039	2039	...	2241		...	...	...	...	...	...	...	0637	0739	...	0839	0940	...	1040	1139	...	1240	1339	...	1440	1539
Holyhead **150** d.	│	│	*1831*	*1831*	...	│		...	...	...	...	...	...	0421	│	│	0620	│	│	0813	│	│	1038	│	│	1231	│	│
Chester **146 150** d.	│	│	*2023*	*2023*	2224	│		...	...	0422	...	...	...	0618	│	│	0820	│	│	1020	│	│	1225	│	│	1422	│	│
Crewe ¶ d.	2010	2010	2110	2110	│	2318f		...	...	0448	0512	...	0555	│	0709	0810	│	0910	1010	│	1110	1210	│	1310	1410	│	1510	1610
Whitchurch ¶ d.	2028	2028	2131	2131	│	2338		...	...	│	│	...	0612	│	│	0828	│	│	1028	│	│	1227	│	│	1427	│	│	1627
Shrewsbury ¶ a.	2049	2049	2158	2158	2315	0006		...	...	0518	0542	...	0633	0711	0743	0846	0912	0940	1046	1112	1141	1245	1318	1341	1445	1514	1541	1647
Shrewsbury **145** d.	2052	2052	2203	2203	2320	...		...	0515	...	0542	0610	0633	0713	0743	0850	0913	0940	1047	1116	1143	1246	1318	1343	1446	1515	1542	1647
Church Stretton **145** d.	2107	2107	2218	2218	2334	...		...	0530	...	0558	0624	0648	0727	0757	0904	0927	│	1101	1130	│	1300	1332	│	1500	1529	│	1701
Craven Arms **145** d.	2115	2115	2227	2227	2342	...		...	0538	...	0607	0632	0656	0735	0808	0912	0935	│	1109	1138	│	1308	1340	│	1508	1537	│	1709
Ludlow d.	2124	2124	2236	2236	2351	...		...	0546	...	0616	0641	0705	0744	0817	0920	0944	1007	1118	1147	1211	1317	1349	1410	1517	1546	1609	1717
Leominster d.	2135	2135	2248	2248	0002	...		...	0557	...	0628	0651	0715	0754	0828	0930	0954	1019	1128	│	1222	1327	│	1422	1527	1556	1621	1728
Hereford d.	2151	2151	2306	2306	0017	...		0526	0617	...	0645	0708	0731	0810	0844	0946	1010	1035	1144	1210	1240	1343	1412	1438	1543	1612	1637	1744
Abergavenny d.	2213	2213	2328	2328	0039	...		0548	0639	...	0708	0733	0753	0832	0908	1008	1032	1058	1206	1232	1304	1405	1434	1502	1605	1634	1700	1805
Pontypool & New Inn . d.	2223	2223	2338	2338	0050	...		0557	0649	...	0718	0743	0803	0842	0918	│	1042	│	│	1242	│	│	1444	│	│	1644	1710	1815
Cwmbrân d.	2229	2229	2343	2343	0055	...		0602	0654	...	0724	0748	0808	0847	0923	1021	1047	1112	1219	1247	1318	1418	1449	1515	1618	1649	1716	1820
Newport **133** § a.	2244	2242	2355	2356	0112	...		0615	0706	...	0735	0758	0821	0900	0936	1033	1101	1123	1231	1259	1330	1430	1501	1527	1630	1701	1728	1832
Cardiff Central . **133** § a.	2300	2304	0015	0021	0135	...		0630	0723	...	0750	0817	0842	0918	0950	1047	1116	1135	1245	1315	1345	1444	1518	1543	1644	1718	1744	1846

	⑥	⑥	⑥2	⑥	⑥	⑥	⑥	⑥	⑥		⑦	⑦	⑦	⑦2	⑦2	⑦		⑦2	⑦2	⑦2	⑦	⑦2	⑦2	⑦	⑦	⑦	⑦	⑦
	2🍷	S🍷	C🍷	2	🍷	2	2	2	2		🚌	F2	S🍷	M🍷	S🍷	2🍷		M🍷	S🍷	M🍷	S🍷	S🍷	S🍷	2🍷	C2	S2	2	2
Manchester Piccadilly d.	...	1630	1730	...	1830	1930	2030	2130	2233	⑦	...	...	0930	1030	1129	...	...	1231	1330	1430	1530	1630	1730	...	1830	1930	2030	...
Stockport d.	...	1640	1739	...	1840	1939	2039	2140	2242		...	...	0941	1040	1139	...	...	1241	1340	1440	1540	1640	1740	...	1840	1940	2040	...
Holyhead **150** d.	1428	│	│	1629	│	│	│	│	│		...	...	│	│	│	1017	...	│	│	│	│	│	│	1626	│	│	│	...
Chester **146 150** d.	1624	│	│	1828	│	│	│	│	│	★	...	...	*0920*t	│	*1132*t	1225	...	│	*1334*t	│	*1535*t	│	*1731*t	1821	│	*1938*t	│	2302
Crewe ¶ d.	│	1710	1810	│	1910	2010	2110	2210	2314		...	...	1012	1110	1216c	│	...	1310	1410	1510	1610	1710	1816p	│	1910	2016p	2110	2330
Whitchurch ¶ d.	│	│	1828	│	│	2028	2131	2230	2334		...	...	1031	│	│	│	...	│	│	│	│	│	│	│	│	│	2130	2352
Shrewsbury ¶ a.	1716	1744	1849	1921	1944	2049	2158	2259	0003		...	...	1055	1140	1246	1318	...	1343	1441	1541	1643	1741	1846	1919	1941	2047	2159	0020
Shrewsbury **145** d.	1717	1744	1850	1923	1944	2052	2159	...	...		0750	...	1101	1144	1248	1324	...	1346	1443	1543	1648	1743	1848	1923	1950	2047	2204	...
Church Stretton **145** d.	1731	│	1904	1937	2000	2107	2213	...	...		0820	...	1116	│	│	1339	...	│	1458	│	1703	│	1902	1937	│	2101	2219	...
Craven Arms **145** d.	1739	│	1912	1945	2009	2115	2222	...	...		0840	...	1125	│	│	1347	...	│	1506	│	1712	│	1910	1945	│	2109	2227	...
Ludlow d.	1748	1811	1922	1954	2018	2124	2232	...	...		0855	...	1134	1210	1314	1356	...	1412	1515	1608	1721	1808	1919	1954	2015	2118	2236	...
Leominster d.	1758	1823	1933	│	2029	2135	2243	...	...		0920	...	1146	1221	1325	1407	...	1423	1527	1620	1733	1819	│	2004	2026	2130	2247	...
Hereford d.	1815	1839	1952	2017	2046	2151	2300	...	...		0950	1007	1208	1241	1342	1423	...	1449b	1546	1650e	1749	1837	1944	2021	2042	2146	2304	...
Abergavenny d.	1837	1903	2014	2039	2110	2214	2323	...	...		...	1029	1231	1304	1404	1445	...	1511	1609	1713	1812	1859	2006	2044	2104	2209	2326	...
Pontypool & New Inn . d.	1847	1913	2024	│	2120	2224	2333	...	...		...	1039	1241	1314	1414	1456	...	│	1619	│	1822	1910	│	2054	│	2219	2336	...
Cwmbrân d.	1852	1919	2028	2052	2126	2230	2338	...	...		...	1045	1247	1320	1420	1500	...	1524	1624	1725	1828	1915	2019	2059	2118	2224	2342	...
Newport **133** § a.	1905	1930	2041	2104	2138	2243	2350	...	...		...	1057	1258	1332	1433	1513	...	1536	1639	1738	1840	1928	2031	2112	2132	2236	2356	...
Cardiff Central . **133** § a.	1921	1944	2056	2122	2150	2305	0012	...	...		...	1113	1316	1348	1449	1527	...	1555	1656	1754	1853	1943	2047	2129	2147	2252	0017	...

◄◄◄ **FOR OTHER NOTES SEE PREVIOUS PAGE.**

§ – See also Tables **115** and **117**.

★ – For services on ⑦ Aug. 3 - Sept. 14 see page 579.

¶ – Additional journeys Shrewsbury - Whitchurch - Crewe and v.v. (2nd class only):
From Shrewsbury at 0531✕, 0619⑥, 0622Ⓐ, 0819✕, 0825⑦, 1019, 1025⑦, 1219✕, 1220⑦, 1419✕, 1420⑦, 1616Ⓐ, 1619⑥, 1620⑦, 1820⑦, 1829✕, 2020⑦, 2035✕.
From Crewe at 0519✕, 0636⑥**K**, 0638Ⓐ**K**, 0734✕**K**, 0919✕, 0921⑦, 1119✕, 1125⑦, 1319✕ 1320⑦, 1519✕, 1520⑦, 1719✕, 1720⑦, 1920⑦, 1936✕, 2326Ⓐ,

150 HOLYHEAD - CHESTER - LONDON and MANCHESTER

AW, VT

⚒

km		②–⑥ 2	⚒ 2	⚒ 2	⚒ 2	⚒ 2	Ⓐ ✕	⑥ ✕	⑥ 2	Ⓐ 2	Ⓐ 2	⑥ 2	Ⓐ ✕	⚒ ✕W	⚒ 2🍷	⚒ 2	Ⓐ ✕	⑥ ✕	⚒ 2	⚒2 B	⑥ ✕	Ⓐ ✕	⚒ 2🍷	⑥ 2🍷	Ⓐ 2🍷	⑥ ✕
0	**Holyhead** ▽ d.	...	...	...	...	0421	0445	...	0454	0459	...	...	0527	0548	...	0619	0648	0652	...	0722	0746	...	...	0813	0818	0848
40	Bangor d.	...	...	...	...	0453	0512	...	0526	0531	...	...	0555	0615	...	0657	0715	0721	...	0801	0815	...	...	0853	0856	0915
	Llandudno ‡ d.	...	...	...	...	|	|	...	|	|	0554	0604	|	|	0642	|	|	|	0742	|	|	...	0842	|	|	|
64	Llandudno Junction ‡ d.	...	...	0437	...	0514	0532	...	0550	0555	0604	0616	0614	0633	0652	0721	0733	0739	0752	0825	0834	...	0852	0923f	0923	0933
71	Colwyn Bay d.	...	...	0443	...	0520	0539	...	5557	0602	0611	0622	0621	0640	0658	0728	0740	0746	0758	0831	0841	...	0858	0930	0930	0940
88	Rhyl d.	...	...	0455	...	0534	0550	...	0607	0612	0623	0634	0632	0651	0711	0738	0751	0757	0811	0842	0852	...	0911	0941	0941	0951
94	Prestatyn d.	...	...	0501	...	0539	0556	...	0613	0618	0629	0640	0639	0657	0717	0744	0757	0803	0817	0848	0858	...	0917	0947	0947	0957
136	**Chester** a.	...	...	0535	...	0609	0619	...	0647	0649	0702	0714	0708	0724	0748	0815	0824	0830	0849	0919	0925	...	0949	1016	1016	1024
136	**Chester** 190 ♥ d.	0351	0455t	0537	0552	0618	0624	0627	0652	0652	...	0728	0716	0732	0752	0820	0832	0832	0852	0924	0932	0932	0952	1020	1020	1032
170	**Crewe** ♥ § d.	|	|	0559	|	|	0654v	0654r	|	|	...	|	|	0754	|	|	0854	0854	|	|	0954	0954	|	|	|	1054
208	Stafford § a.	|	|	...	|	|	0713	0713	|	|	...	|	|	0813	|	|	0913	0913	|	|	1013	1013	|	|	|	1113
422	**London** Euston § a.	|	|	...	|	|	0835	0835	|	|	...	|	|	0937	|	|	1035	1035	|	|	1135	1135	|	|	|	1235
	Shrewsbury 146 149 a.	|	|	...	|	0712	...	...	|	|	...	0825	0805	...	|	0912	...	...	|	1016	...	...	|	1112	1113	...
	Cardiff Central 149 a.	|	|	...	|	0918	...	...	|	|	...	|	0958	...	|	1116	...	...	|	|	...	...	|	1315	1315	...
	Birmingham N St 146 a.	|	|	...	|	...	...	...	|	|	...	...	...	...	|	...	...	...	|	1132	...	...	|	...	...	...
165	Warrington Bank Quay 190 d.	|	|	...	0620	...	...	...	0720	0720	...	...	...	...	0820	...	...	...	0920	...	...	...	1020	...	...	...
201	**Manchester** Piccadilly a.	0452	0557	...	0654	...	...	...	0754	0754	...	...	...	...	0854	...	...	...	0954	...	...	...	1054	...	...	...
217	**Manchester** Airport a.	0511	0618	...	0715	...	...	...	0815	0815	...	...	...	...	0915	...	...	...	1015	...	...	...	1115	...	...	...

	Ⓐ ✕	⚒ 2🍷	⚒2 🍷B	Ⓐy ✕	⚒ 2🍷	⚒ 2	⚒ ✕	⚒ 2🍷	⚒2 🍷B	⚒ ✕	⚒ 2🍷	⚒ 2	⑥ ✕	Ⓐ ✕	⚒ 2🍷	⚒2 bB	⑥ 2	Ⓐ ✕	⑥ 2🍷	Ⓐ 2🍷	⚒ 2🍷	⚒ ✕	⚒ 2c	Ⓐ ✕	⑥2 🍷B	Ⓐ2 🍷B	⚒ 2c
Holyhead ▽ d.	0853	...	0923	...	...	1038	...	...	1127	...	...	1231	...	1248	1304	1327	1353	...	...	...	1428	1448	...	...	1530	1536	...
Bangor d.	0920	...	1003	...	...	1109	...	...	1208	...	...	1259	...	1315	1334	1406	1422	...	...	...	1457	1515	...	...	1609	1615	...
Llandudno ‡ d.	|	0942	|	...	1042	|	...	1142	|	...	...	|	...	|	|	|	|	...	1441	1441	|	|	1542	...	|	|	1642
Llandudno Junction ‡ d.	0938	0952	1028	...	1052	1127	...	1152	1233	...	1252	1317	...	1333	1353	1431	1440	...	1451	1451	1525	1533	1552	...	1634	1640	1652
Colwyn Bay d.	0945	0958	1034	...	1058	1134	...	1158	1239	...	1258	1324	...	1340	1359	1437	1445	...	1457	1457	1531	1540	1558	...	1640	1646	1658
Rhyl d.	0956	1011	1045	...	1111	1144	...	1211	1248	...	1311	1334	...	1351	1412	1446	1456	...	1510	1510	1541	1551	1611	...	1650	1657	1711
Prestatyn d.	1002	1017	1051	...	1117	1149	...	1217	1254	...	1317	1341	...	1356	1418	1452	1502	...	1516	1516	1548	1557	1617	...	1656	1703	1717
Chester a.	1028	1049	1125	...	1149	1218	...	1249	1324	...	1349	1412	...	1425	1451	1525	1525	...	1547	1547	1619	1625	1649	...	1728	1733	1749
Chester 190 ♥ d.	1032	1052	1128	1132	1152	1225	1232	1252	1327	1332	1352	1422	1432	1432	1452	1527	1532	1532	1552	1552	1624	1632	1652	1732	1731	1736	1752
Crewe ♥ § d.	1054	|	|	1154	|	|	1254	|	|	1354	|	|	1454	1454	|	|	1554	1554	|	|	|	1654	|	1754	|	|	|
Stafford § a.	1113	|	|	1213	|	|	1313	|	|	1413j	|	|	1513	1513	|	|	1613	1613	|	|	|	1713	|	1813	|	|	|
London Euston § a.	1235	|	|	1335	|	|	1437	|	|	1535	|	|	1635	1637	|	|	1735	1735	|	|	|	1836	|	1935	|	|	|
Shrewsbury 146 149 a.	...	|	1222	...	|	1318	...	|	1423	...	|	1514	...	...	|	1622	...	...	|	|	1716	...	|	...	1827	1831	|
Cardiff Central 149 a.	...	|	|	...	|	1519	...	|	|	...	|	1718	...	...	|	|	...	...	|	|	1921	...	|	...	|	|	|
Birmingham N St 146 a.	...	|	1331	...	|	...	...	|	1532	...	|	...	...	...	|	1732	...	...	|	|	...	...	|	...	1932	1932	|
Warrington Bank Quay 190 d.	...	1120	...	...	1220	...	...	1320	...	...	1420	...	...	...	1520	...	...	...	1620	1620	...	...	1720	...	...	...	1820
Manchester Piccadilly a.	...	1154	...	...	1254	...	...	1354	...	...	1454	...	...	...	1554	...	...	...	1654	1659	...	...	1754	...	...	...	1854
Manchester Airport a.	...	1215	...	...	1315	...	...	1415	...	...	1515	...	...	...	1615	...	...	...	1715	1718	...	...	1815	...	...	...	1915

	⚒ 2b	⚒ 2🍷	⚒ 2🍷	Ⓐ h✕	⚒ 2	⑥ 2	Ⓐ 2	⚒ 2	⚒ 2	Ⓐ ✕	⚒ 2	⑥ ...	Ⓐ ...	⚒ 2	⚒ 2	Ⓐ 2B	⑥ 2	⑦	⑦ 2	⑦ k	⑦k 2🍷	⑦n 2🍷	⑦ 🍷	⑦ 2	⑦ 2🍷	⑦ ✕	⑦ 2🍷
Holyhead ▽ d.	1629	...	1719	...	...	1827	1831	...	1920	1948	...	...	...	2031	...	...	...		...	0717	0740	0746	...	0849	...	0938	...
Bangor d.	1657	...	1758	...	...	1905	1909	...	1958	2018	...	...	...	2103	...	...	...		...	0746	0819	0824	...	0918	...	1005	...
Llandudno ‡ d.	|	1742	|	...	1842	|	|	1942	|	|	2043	...	...	|	2151	...	...		...	|	|	|	...	|	...	|	...
Llandudno Junction ‡ d.	1722	1752	1823	...	1852	1929	1933	1952	2023	2036	2053	...	...	2128	2205	...	...		...	0804	0844	0848	...	0937	...	1026	1035
Colwyn Bay d.	1728	1758	1829	...	1858	1935	1939	1958	2029	2043	2059	...	...	2134	2211	...	...		...	0810	0850	0855	...	0943	...	1032	1042
Rhyl d.	1742	1811	1838	...	1911	1945	1949	2011	2038	2054	2110	...	...	2147	2224	...	...		...	0822	0900	0905	...	0956	...	1043	1054
Prestatyn d.	1748	1817	1844	...	1917	1950	1954	2017	2044	2100	2116	...	...	2152	2229	...	...		...	|	0905	|	...	1002	...	1049	1100
Chester a.	1818	1851	1914	...	1949	2018	2022	2049	2115	2127	2145	...	...	2225	2301	...	...		...	0852	0935	0935	...	1033	...	1117	1133
Chester 190 ♥ d.	1828	1852	1917z	1932	1952	2023	2023	2052	2124	2134	2159	2151	2152	...	2303	2322	2323		0842	0858	0939	0939	1014	1039	1037	1128	1135
Crewe ♥ § d.	|	|	|	1955	|	2045	2049	|	|	2156	2219	|	|	...	2326	|	|		|	0920	|	|	1037	1102	|	1151	|
Stafford § a.	|	|	|	2013	|	...	...	|	|	2215	...	|	|	...	...	|	|		|	...	|	|	1055	...	|	1209	|
London Euston § a.	|	|	|	2140	|	...	...	|	|	|	...	|	|	...	...	|	|		|	...	|	|	1237	...	|	1336	|
Shrewsbury 146 149 a.	1922	|	2010z	...	|	...	...	|	2221	a	...	|	|	...	...	|	|		|	...	|	|	...	...	|	...	|
Cardiff Central 149 a.	2123	|	...	...	|	...	...	|	|	|	...	|	|	...	...	|	|		|	...	|	|	...	...	|	...	|
Birmingham N St 146 a.	...	|	...	...	|	...	...	|	2332	2251	...	|	|	...	...	|	|		|	...	|	|	...	...	|	...	|
Warrington Bank Quay 190 d.	...	1920	...	...	2020	...	...	2120	...	...	...	2220	2221	...	...	2350	2351		0909	...	1010	1010	...	...	1105	...	1203
Manchester Piccadilly a.	...	1954	...	...	2054	...	...	2154	...	...	...	2253	2255	...	...	0022	0026		0944	...	1045	1045	...	...	1139	...	1238
Manchester Airport a.	...	2015	...	...	2115	...	...	2215	...	...	...	...	2314	...	...	...	...		...	...	...	...	...	...	...	...	...

	⑦ 2🍷	⑦ 🍷W	⑦ 2	⑦ ✕	⑦ 2	⑦ ✕	⑦ 2	⑦ ✕	⑦ 2	⑦ ✕	⑦ 2🍷	⑦ 2🍷	⑦ ✕n	⑦ 2	⑦ 2🍷	⑦ 2	⑦ 2🍷	⑦ ✕	⑦ 2	⑦ 2B	⑦ 2	⑦ 2	⑦ 2	⑦ 2	⑦ 2	⑦ 2	⑦ 2
Holyhead ▽ d.	1017	...	...	1148	...	1248	...	1348	...	...	1430	1530	...	...	1625	...	1728	1753	...	1825	...	1930	...	2032	...	...	2140
Bangor d.	1057	...	...	1215	...	1315	...	1415	...	...	1510	1558	...	...	1704	...	1756	1820	...	1905	...	2010	...	2112	...	...	2209
Llandudno ‡ d.	|	...	1217	|	1312	|	1419	|	1519	...	|	|	...	1644	|	1802	|	|	1859	|	...	|	...	|	...	2139	|
Llandudno Junction ‡ d.	1122	...	1227	1233	1322	1333	1429	1433	1529	...	1534f	1623	...	1654	1723	1812	1820	1838	1909	1923	...	2034	...	2137	...	2150	2228
Colwyn Bay d.	1128	...	—	1240	—	1340	—	1440	—	...	1540	1629	...	—	1729	—	1826	1845	—	1929	...	2041	...	2143	...	—	2234
Rhyl d.	1142	...	...	1251	...	1351	...	1451	...	...	1553	1642	...	...	1744	...	1839	1856	...	1943	...	2053	...	2156	...	...	2244
Prestatyn d.	1148	...	⑦	1257	⑦	1357	⑦	1457	⑦	...	1559	1648	...	⑦	1750	⑦	1845	1902	⑦	1949	...	2059	...	2202	...	⑦	2250
Chester a.	1221	...	2🍷	1324	2	1424	2	1524	2	...	1632	1721	...	2	1822	2	1917	1927	2	2022	...	2130	...	2234	...	2	2319
Chester 190 ♥ d.	1225	1232	1236	1332	1336	1432	1436	1530	1536	1631	1636	1722	1732	1736	1825	1836	1922	1931	1936	2027	2036	2136	2143	2239	2242	2302	...
Crewe ♥ § d.	|	1255	|	1355	|	1455	|	1553	|	1655	|	1743	1755	|	|	|	1944	1955	|	2050	|	2158	|	2301	|	2330	...
Stafford § a.	|	1313	|	1413	|	1513	|	1613	|	1713	|	...	1813	|	|	|	...	2013	|	|	|	...	|	...	|	|	...
London Euston § a.	|	1436	|	1536	|	1636	|	1736	|	1836	|	...	1936	|	|	|	...	2158	|	|	|	...	|	...	|	|	...
Shrewsbury 146 149 a.	1321	...	|	...	|	...	|	...	|	...	|	...	...	|	1920	|	...	...	|	2120	|	...	|	...	|	0020	...
Cardiff Central 149 a.	1527	...	|	...	|	...	|	...	|	...	|	...	...	|	2129q	|	...	...	|	|	|	...	|	...	|	...	...
Birmingham N St 146 a.	...	...	|	...	|	...	|	...	|	...	|	...	...	|	...	|	...	...	|	2212	|	...	|	...	|	...	...
Warrington Bank Quay 190 d.	...	...	1303	...	1403	...	1503	...	1603	...	1703	...	...	1803	...	1903	...	...	2003	...	2103	...	2210	...	2310	...	...
Manchester Piccadilly a.	...	...	1337	...	1437	...	1536	...	1636	...	1737	...	...	1838	...	1936	...	...	2036	...	2137	...	2244	...	2343	...	...
Manchester Airport a.	...	...	1359	...	1457	...	1556	...	1656	...	1758	...	...	1857	...	1956	...	...	2056	...	2156	...	2259	...	2359	...	...

	②–⑥ 2	⚒ ✕	⚒ 2	⚒ 2🍷	⚒ 2🍷	⚒ 2🍷	⚒ 2	⚒ 2B	⚒ 2🍷	Ⓐ ✕	⑥ ✕	⚒ 2🍷	⚒ 2🍷	⚒ ✕	⚒2 🍷B	⚒ 2	Ⓐ ✕	⑥ ✕	⚒ 2🍷	⚒ 2🍷	⚒ ✕	⚒2 🍷B	⚒ 2🍷	⚒ ✕	⚒ 2🍷	⚒ 2🍷	Ⓐ ✕
Manchester Airport d.	...	...	0525	...	0625	...	0725	...	0825	...	...	...	0925	...	...	1025	...	...	...	1125	...	...	1225	...	...	1325	...
Manchester Piccadilly d.	0024	...	0542	...	0644	...	0744	...	0844	...	...	...	0944	...	...	1044	...	...	...	1144	...	...	1244	...	...	1344	...
Warrington Bank Quay 190 d.	|	...	0619	...	0717	...	0817	...	0917	...	...	...	1017	...	...	1117	...	...	...	1217	...	...	1317	...	...	1417	...
Birmingham N St 146 d.	|	0530	|	...	|	...	|	0722	|	...	...	...	|	...	0922	|	...	...	...	|	...	1122	|	...	...	|	...
Cardiff Central 149 d.	|	|	|	...	|	0519g	|	|	|	...	...	0719	|	...	|	|	...	...	0923	|	...	|	|	...	1123	|	...
Shrewsbury 146 149 d.	|	a	|	...	|	0726	|	0827	|	...	...	0926	|	...	1025	|	...	...	1127	|	...	1225	|	...	1327	|	...
London Euston § d.	|	|	|	...	|	|	|	|	|	0800	0800	|	|	0900	|	|	1000	1000	|	|	1100	|	|	1200	|	|	1300
Stafford § d.	|	0604	|	...	|	|	|	|	|	0926h	0924	|	|	1024	|	|	1124	1124	|	|	1224	|	|	1324	|	|	1424
Crewe ♥ § d.	|	0626	|	0659	|	|	|	|	|	0947	0945	|	|	1045	|	|	1145	1145	|	|	1245	|	|	1345	|	|	1445
Chester 190 ♥ a.	0124	0645	0651	0720	0750	0821	0851	0923	0950	1006	1005	1021	1050	1105	1120	1151	1206	1205	1225	1250	1305	1321	1350	1407	1421	1450	1505
Chester d.	...	0647	0652	0720	0751	0824	0855	0929	0959	1008	...	1024	1052	1113	1124	1152	...	1211	1229	1251	...	1322	1351	...	1425	1451	...
Prestatyn d.	...	0714	0720	0748	0819	0851	0923	0956	1026	1035	...	1053	1120	1141	1149	1220	...	1238	1254	1320	...	1350	1420	...	1452	1520	...
Rhyl d.	...	0720	0727	0754	0826	0857	0930	1002	1032	1041	...	1059	1127	1147	1156	1227	...	1244	1300	1326	...	1357	1426	...	1459	1526	...
Colwyn Bay d.	...	0731	0741	0808	0840	0910	0944	1011	1046	1053	...	1110	1142	1158	1210	1241	...	1255	1311	1341	...	1407	1441	...	1510	1541	...
Llandudno Junction ‡ d.	...	0738	0749	0816	0848	0918	0952	1018	1053	1100	...	1118	1150	1206	1218	1248	...	1303	1319	1349	...	1416	1448	...	1518	1548	...
Llandudno ‡ a.	...	|	0758	|	0858	|	1001	|	1102	|	...	|	|	|	|	...	...	|	|	1359	...	|	1458	...	|	1558	...
Bangor d.	...	0756	...	0839	...	0942	...	1042	...	1118	...	1135	1208	1223	1242	...	...	1320	1336	...	...	1441	...	...	1536	...	...
Holyhead ▽ a.	...	0823	...	0918	...	1012	...	1126	...	1144	...	1205	1236	1250	1322	...	...	1347	1415	...	...	1521	...	...	1616	...	...

B – To/from Birmingham International (Table **146**).
W – Conveys 🛏 and ✕ Wrexham - Chester - London Euston (Table **146**).

a – Via Wolverhampton (see Table **146**).
b – Conveys 🍷 on Ⓐ.
c – Conveys 🍷 on ⑥.

f – Arrives 5 minutes earlier.
g – Departs 0525 on ⑥.
h – From Sept. 15.
j – Calls on Ⓐ from Sept. 15.
k – Until Sept. 14.
n – From Sept. 21.

q – Arrives 2123 Aug. 3 - Sept. 14.
r – Arrives 0647.
t – Departs 0502 on ①.
v – Arrives 0644.
y – Also runs on ⑥ from Sept. 20.

z – On ⑥ Chester d. 1927, Shrewsbury a. 2019.
▽ – For ⛴ connections to/from **Dublin** see Table **2040**.
§ – See also Tables **143**, **151**, **152**, **154**.
‡ – For full service Llandudno - Llandudno Junction and v.v. see page 119.
♥ – For full service Chester - Crewe and v.v. see page 119.

AW, VT — HOLYHEAD - CHESTER - LONDON and MANCHESTER — 150

	⑥ ✕	⚒2 🍷B	⚒ 2🍷	Ⓐy ✕	⚒ 2🍷	⚒ 2🍷	⑥ ✕	Ⓐ ✕	⚒2 🍷B	⚒ 2🍷	⑥ ✕	Ⓐ h✕	⚒ 2🍷	⚒ 2	⑥ ✕	Ⓐ ✕	⚒2 🍷B	⚒ 2	Ⓐ ✕W	⑥ ✕	Ⓐ ✕	⑥ 🍷	⚒ 2	⑥ ✕W	Ⓐ ✕	Ⓐ 2	⑥ 2	⚒ 2
Manchester Airport d.	...	...	1425	...	...	1525	...	...	...	1625	...	...	...	1725	...	...	...	1825	...	...	...	...	1925	...	...	...	...	2025
Manchester Piccadilly d.	...	...	1444	...	...	1544	...	...	...	1644	...	...	...	1744	...	...	...	1844	...	...	...	...	1945	...	...	...	...	2044
Warrington Bank Quay **190** d.	...	...	1517	...	...	1617	...	...	...	1717	...	...	...	1818	...	...	...	1917	...	...	...	...	2017	...	...	...	...	2117
Birmingham N St **146** d.	...	1322	|	...	...	|	...	...	1522	|	...	...	...	|	...	...	1721	|	...	...	...	...	|	...	...	...	...	|
Cardiff Central **149** d.	...	|	|	...	1323	|	...	...	|	|	...	...	1523	|	...	...	|	|	...	...	1722	1723	|	...	...	1823	1823	|
Shrewsbury **146 149** d.	...	1425	|	...	1527	|	...	...	1625	|	...	...	1727	|	...	...	1827	|	...	...	1928	1927	|	...	...	2027	2027	|
London Euston § d.	1300	|	|	1400	|	|	1500	1500	|	|	1600	1602	|	|	1700	1700	|	|	1800	1800	|	|	|	1900	1900	|	|	|
Stafford § d.	1424	|	|	1523	|	|	1623	1624	|	|	1723	1723	|	|	1824	1832	|	|	1932	1930	|	|	|	2024	2024	|	|	|
Crewe ♥ § d.	1445	|	|	1544	|	|	1645	1645	|	|	1745	1744	|	|	1845	1853	|	|	1953	1953	|	|	|	2045	2053j	2102	2108f	|
Chester **190** ♥ a.	1504	1521	1550	1606	1623	1650	1705	1705	1723	1747	1805	1804	1822	1850	1905	1915	1926	1949	2013	2013	2018	2024	2049	2105	2113	2123	2127	2150
Chester d.	1512	1523	1551	...	1628	1651	...	1711	1727	1752	1810	...	1824	1851	...	1922	1931	...	...	2019	2025	2035	2050	...	2124	...	2128	...
Prestatyn d.	1539	1549	1620	...	1653	1720	...	1738	1754	1821	1838	...	1851	1919	...	1949	2001	...	...	2046	2052	2104	2117	...	2150	...	2156	...
Rhyl d.	1545	1556	1626	...	1659	1726	...	1744	1800	1827	1844	...	1857	1925	...	1955	2008	...	...	2052	2059	2110	2123	...	2156	...	2201	...
Colwyn Bay d.	1556	1606	1641	...	1710	1741	...	1755	1814	1842	1855	...	1910	1936	...	2006	2022	...	...	2103	2111	2122	2137	...	2207	...	2214	...
Llandudno Junction ‡ d.	1604	1613	1649	...	1718	1748	...	1803	1822	1849	1903	...	1918	1947	...	2013	2029	...	...	2111	2119	2131	2144	...	2215	...	2222	...
Llandudno ‡ a.	|	|	1659	...	|	1758	...	|	|	1859	|	...	|	|	...	|	2040	...	...	|	|	|	|	...	|	...	|	...
Bangor d.	1620	1637	...	...	1742	...	...	1820	1846	...	1920	...	1935	2011	...	2031	...	...	...	2128	2135	2148	2209	...	2232	...	2246	...
Holyhead ▽ a.	1652	1711	...	...	1822	...	...	1847	1916	...	1949	...	2016	2045	...	2057	...	...	...	2155	2206	2228	2252	...	2300	...	2327	...

	Ⓐ ✕	⑥ 2	⚒ 2	Ⓐ 2	⑥ 2	Ⓐ 2	⑥ 2	⑥ 2	Ⓐ 2	①–④ 2	⑤ 2	⑦	⑦ k2	⑦ 2	⑦ 🚌	⑦ 2	⑦ 2	⑦ ✕	⑦ 2🍷	⑦2 🍷	⑦ 2🍷	⑦ 2🍷	⑦ 2🍷	⑦ 2🍷	⑦ 2	⑦ 2🍷	⑦ ✕	⑦ 2🍷
Manchester Airport d.	...	...	2126	...	2225	2225	...	...	...	2325	2325		...	...	...	...	...	...	...	...	...	...	...	...	...	...	...	1441
Manchester Piccadilly d.	...	...	2144	...	2244	2244	2314	...	...	2342	2342		...	...	0718	...	0948	...	1052	...	1156	...	1257	...	1357	...	...	1457
Warrington Bank Quay **190** d.	...	...	2217	...	2317	2322	2348	...	...	|	|		...	...	0828	...	1019	...	1127	...	1230	...	1330	...	1429	...	...	1529
Birmingham N St **146** d.	...	...	|	...	|	|	|	...	...	|	|		...	...	|	...	|	...	|	...	|	...	|	...	|	...	...	|
Cardiff Central **149** d.	...	1938	|	1938	|	|	|	2122	2135	|	|		...	...	|	...	|	...	|	...	|	...	|	...	|	...	...	|
Shrewsbury **146 149** d.	...	2144	|	2144	|	|	|	2326	2338	|	|		...	...	|	...	|	...	|	...	|	...	|	...	|	...	...	|
London Euston § d.	2000	|	|	|	|	|	|	|	|	|	|		...	...	|	...	|	...	|	...	|	...	|	...	|	...	1300	|
Stafford § d.	2124	|	|	|	|	|	|	|	|	|	|		...	...	|	...	|	...	|	...	|	...	|	...	|	...	1424	|
Crewe ♥ § d.	2149	|	|	|	|	|	|	2358	0027	|	|		...	0835	|	0922	|	1036	|	1135	|	1235	|	1335	|	1429	1445	|
Chester **190** ♥ a.	2208	2240	2250	2241	2347	2353	0017	0020	0046	0046	0046		...	0856	0928	0941	1050	1155	1155	1157	1257	1256	1358	1355	1444	1449	1505	1557
Chester d.	2209	2243	...	2256	...	...	...	...	...	0051	0058		0621	0900	▬	0942	▬	1057	▬	1200	▬	1305	▬	1403	▬	1450	1518	...
Prestatyn d.	2236	2309	...	2325	...	...	...	...	...	0118	0125		0647	0926	...	1010	...	1124	...	1228	...	1333	...	1432	...	1518	1545	...
Rhyl d.	2242	2315	...	2331	...	...	...	...	...	0124	0131		0653	0933	⑦	1017	⑦	1130	⑦	1235	⑦	1340	⑦	1439	⑦	1524	1551	...
Colwyn Bay d.	2253	2328	...	2344	...	...	...	...	...	0134	0141		0703	0942	2	1031	2	1141	2	1244	2	1355	2	1454	2	1539	1602	...
Llandudno Junction ‡ d.	2303	2335	...	0001	...	...	...	...	...	0145	0149		0711	0949	1004	1039	1053	1148	1200	1252	1300	1408f	1407	1503	1506	1546	1609	...
Llandudno ‡ a.	|	...	...	|	...	...	...	...	...	|	|		|	|	1014	|	1103	|	1210	|	1310	|	1417	|	1516	|	|	...
Bangor d.	2322	...	...	0024	...	...	...	...	...	0202	0206		0728	1006	...	1103	...	1209g	...	1309	...	1433	...	1521	...	1611	1627	...
Holyhead ▽ a.	2350	...	...	0106	...	...	...	...	...	0235	0233		0755	1037	...	1144	...	1235	...	1340	...	1504	...	1602	...	1643	1653	...

	⑦ 2	⑦ ✕	⑦2 a🍷	⑦ 2🍷	⑦ 2	⑦ ✕	⑦ 2	⑦ 2	⑦ ✕	⑦ 2🍷	⑦ 2	⑦ 2	⑦ 🍷W	⑦2 🍷B	⑦ 2🍷	⑦ ✕	⑦2 b🍷	⑦ 2	⑦ ✕	⑦ 2	⑦ 2	⑦ n✕	⑦ 2	⑦ 2	⑦ 2B	⑦ 2	⑦ 2	⑦ 2
Manchester Airport d.	...	...	...	1541	...	...	1641	...	...	...	...	1741	...	...	1841	...	...	1941	...	2041	...	...	2141	...	...	2241	2307	...
Manchester Piccadilly d.	...	...	...	1557	...	...	1657	...	...	...	...	1757	...	...	1857	...	...	1957	...	2057	...	...	2157	...	...	2300	2325	...
Warrington Bank Quay **190** d.	...	...	...	1630	...	...	1730	...	...	...	...	1830	...	...	1931	...	...	2031	...	2129	...	...	2232	...	...	2330	2359	...
Birmingham N St **146** d.	...	...	...	|	...	...	|	...	...	...	...	|	...	1722	|	...	...	|	...	|	...	...	|	...	2122	|	|	2255
Cardiff Central **149** d.	...	...	1330	|	...	...	|	...	...	1522	...	|	...	|	|	...	1716	|	...	|	...	...	|	...	|	|	|	|
Shrewsbury **146 149** d.	...	...	1531	|	...	...	|	...	...	1731	...	|	...	1827	|	...	1926	|	...	|	...	...	|	...	2231	|	|	2348
London Euston § d.	...	1400	|	|	...	1500	|	...	1600	|	...	|	1700	|	|	1800	|	|	1900	|	...	2001	|	...	|	|	|	|
Stafford § d.	...	1524	|	|	...	1623	|	...	1724	|	...	|	1824	|	|	1924	|	|	2024	|	...	2124	|	...	|	|	|	|
Crewe ♥ § d.	1535	1545	|	|	1630	1648f	|	1735	1745	|	1829	|	1845	|	|	1945	|	|	2045	|	2135	2145	|	2229	2307g	|	|	0021
Chester **190** ♥ a.	1556	1605	1625	1659	1652	1708	1757	1755	1805	1826	1848	1859	1904	1925	2001	2005	2026	2100	2105	2157	2154	2205	2300	2251	2330	2358	0028	0044
Chester d.	1602	▬	1635	▬	1704	▬	...	1802	...	1830	1852	...	1917	1934	...	2011	2030	...	2111	...	2202	...	...	2302	...	...	0032	...
Prestatyn d.	1631	...	1703	...	1733	...	...	1831	...	1858	1920	...	1945	2003	...	2038	2058	...	2138	...	2231	...	...	2331	...	...	0057	...
Rhyl d.	1637	⑦	1710	⑦	1739	⑦	...	1837	...	1904	1927	...	1951	2009	...	2044	2104	...	2144	...	2237	...	...	2337	...	...	0103	...
Colwyn Bay d.	1652	2	1724	2	1754	2	...	1852	...	1918	1941	...	2002	2024	...	2055	2118	...	2155	...	2252	...	...	2347	...	...	0114	...
Llandudno Junction ‡ d.	1701	1704	1736	1740	1802	1833	...	1900	...	1926	1949	...	2010	2032	...	2103	2128	...	2203	...	2259	...	...	2354	...	...	0121	...
Llandudno ‡ a.	|	1714	|	1750	|	1844	...	|	...	|	|	...	|	|	...	|	|	...	|	...	|	...	...	|	...	...	|	...
Bangor d.	1719	...	1756	...	1827	...	...	1917	...	1950	2013	...	2029	2055	...	2120	2152	...	2220	...	2317	...	...	0018	...	...	0139	...
Holyhead ▽ a.	1800	...	1836	...	1857	...	...	1955	...	2018	2044	...	2056	2128	...	2147	2220	...	2247	...	2357	...	...	0051	...	...	0208	...

B – To / from Birmingham International (Table **146**).
W – Conveys 🛏 and ✕ London - Chester - Wrexham (Table **146**).
a – Until July 27 and from Sept. 21.
b – Aug. 3 - Sept. 14.
c – Conveys 🍷 on ⑥.
f – Arrives 6 minutes earlier.
g – Arrives 5 minutes earlier.
h – From Sept. 15.
j – Arrives 2042.
k – Until Sept. 14.
n – From Sept. 21.
y – Also runs on ⑥ from Sept. 20.
▽ – For ⛴ connections to/from **Dublin** see Table **2040**.
§ – See also Tables **143**, **152**, **153**, **154**.

♥ – Full service **Chester** - **Crewe**. Journey time ± 23 minutes.
On ⚒ at 0422, 0446 ⑥, 0448 Ⓐ, 0537, 0556, 0624 Ⓐ, 0627 ⑥, 0656, 0732, 0756, 0832, 0856, 0932, 0956, 1032, 1056, 1132 Ⓐ, 1156, 1232, 1256, 1332, 1356, 1432, 1456, 1532, 1556, 1632, 1656, 1732, 1755, 1856, 1932 Ⓐ **h**, 1956, 2023, 2032 ⑥, 2037 Ⓐ, 2055, 2134 Ⓐ, 2159, 2304.
On ⑦ at 0805, 0838, 0856, 0942, 0957, 1014, 1039, 1057, 1128, 1157, 1221, 1232, 1302, 1323, 1332, 1422, 1432, 1530, 1557, 1622, 1631, 1657, 1722, 1732 **n**, 1757, 1900, 1922, 1931, 1955, 2027, 2053, 2136, 2152, 2239, 2302.
Full service **Crewe** - **Chester**. Journey time ± 23 minutes.
On ⚒ at 0012 ①, 0021①, 0027 ②–⑥, 0617, 0626, 0659, 0721, 0820, 0921, 0945 ⑥, 0947 Ⓐ, 1021, 1045, 1121, 1145, 1221, 1245, 1321, 1345, 1421, 1445, 1521, 1545 Ⓐ, 1621, 1645, 1721, 1744Ⓐ **h**, 1745 ⑥, 1821, 1845 ⑥, 1853 Ⓐ, 1901, 1921 ⑥, 1929 Ⓐ, 1953, 2021, 2045 ⑥, 2053 Ⓐ, 2102 Ⓐ, 2108 ⑥, 2121 Ⓐ, 2149 Ⓐ, 2221, 2330, 2358 ⑥.
On ⑦ at 0835, 0922, 1007, 1036, 1104, 1135, 1155, 1235, 1255, 1335, 1355, 1429, 1445, 1500, 1535, 1545, 1557, 1630 **n**, 1648, 1735, 1745 **n**, 1829, 1845, 1929, 1945, 2027, 2045, 2135, 2203, 2229, 2307, 2339.

‡ – Full service **Llandudno** - **Llandudno Junction**. Journey time ± 10 minutes.
On ⚒ at 0554Ⓐ, 0604 ⑥, 0642, 0704, 0742, 0801, 0842, 0903 ⑥, 0942, 1004 ⑥, 1012, 1042, 1106 ⑥, 1142, 1251, 1315, 1413, 1441, 1504 ⑥, 1542, 1604⑥, 1612, 1642, 1704 ⑥, 1742, 1807, 1842, 1904, 1912 ⑥, 1942, 2008, 2043, 2137, 2151.
On ⑦ at 1018, 1107, 1139, 1217, 1312, 1326, 1353, 1419, 1519, 1547, 1617, 1644, 1718, 1802, 1859, 2139.
Full service **Llandudno Junction** - **Llandudno**. Journey time ± 10 minutes.
On ⚒ at 0540, 0620, 0651, 0729, 0749, 0824, 0848, 0925 ⑥, 0940, 0952, 1025 ⑥, 1053, 1125 ⑥, 1238, 1302 ⑥, 1303 Ⓐ, 1349, 1426, 1448, 1525 ⑥, 1542, 1548, 1625 ⑥, 1649, 1726 ⑥, 1748, 1826, 1837, 1849, 1927 ⑥, 1950, 2029, 2122, 2132 Ⓐ, 2134 ⑥.
On ⑦ at 1004, 1053, 1125, 1200, 1244, 1300, 1339, 1407, 1506, 1533, 1604, 1630, 1704, 1740, 1833, 2125.

AW 2nd class only — LLANDUDNO - BLAENAU FFESTINIOG — 150a

km		⚒	⚒	⑦	⚒	⚒	⑦	⚒	⑦	⑦	⚒
0	**Llandudno** d.	...	*0704*	1018	1012	1315	1312	1612	1547	1859	1904
5	**Llandudno** Junction a.	...	*0714*	1028	1021	1324	1322	1622	1557	1909	1914
5	**Llandudno** Junction d.	0521	0728	1029	1025	1326	1327	1623	1615	1915	1921
18	Llanrwst d.	0539	0752	1052	1048	1350	1350	1647	1638	1938	1945
24	Betws y Coed d.	0545	0758	1058	1054	1356	1356	1653	1644	1944	1951
44	**Blaenau Ffestiniog** a.	0614	0833	1131	1127	1429	1428	1726	1717	2016	2025

	⚒	⚒	⚒	⑦	⚒	⑦	⑦	⚒	⑦	⚒
Blaenau Ffestiniog d.	0618	0835	1137	1142	1439	1459	1728	1735	2020	2027
Betws y Coed d.	0644	0902	1204	1208	1506	1525	1755	1802	2047	2054
Llanrwst d.	0650	0908	1210	1214	1512	1531	1801	1808	2053	2100
Llandudno Junction a.	0716	0937	1237	1242	1541	1600	1830	1836	2122	2126
Llandudno Junction d.	*0729*	0940	1238	1244	1542	1604	1833	1837	2125	2132
Llandudno a.	*0740*	0951	1249	1255	1553	1614	1844	1847	2136	2146

Operators: See note △ — CAERNARVON - PORTHMADOG - BLAENAU FFESTINIOG — 150b

km	All services 🚂	D	F	C	F		A	E	D	B
0	**Blaenau Ffestiniog** d.	...	...	1140	...	...	1245	...	...	1625
19	Minffordd **148** d.	...	...	1235	...	...	1340	...	...	1720
22	**Porthmadog** Harbour **148** d.	1005	1020	1250	1340	...	1355	...	1405	1735
35	Beddgelert d.	1045	1100	...	1420	...	...	1430	1445	...
42	Rhyd Ddu d.	1115	...	...	...	...	...	1455	1515	...
50	Waunfawr d.	1140	...	...	...	...	...	1520	1540	...
61	**Caernarfon** a.	1225	...	...	...	...	...	1600	1620	...

All services 🚂	A	D	F	E	B		C	F	D
Caernarfon d.	...	1005	...	1130	...	...	...	...	1415
Waunfawr d.	...	1045	...	1200	...	...	...	...	1445
Rhyd Ddu d.	...	1115	...	1230	...	...	...	...	1515
Beddgelert d.	...	1140	1220	1300	...	...	...	1540	1540
Porthmadog Harbour **148** d.	1040	1225	1300	...	1420	...	1525	1620	1625
Minffordd **148** d.	1050	...	...	...	1430	...	1535	...	...
Blaenau Ffestiniog d.	1155	...	...	...	1535	...	1640	...	...

A – Mar. 29, 30, Apr. 1–25, 27–30, May 1 - Oct. 31 (not June 20–22, Oct. 3–6).
B – Daily Apr. 8–25, (not Apr. 11, 12); ②④ May 1 - July 17 (also May 4, 5, 24, 25, 26, 28, 30, July 2, 9, 16); daily July 19 - Aug. 30; ②④ Sept. 2–25 (also Sept. 3, Oct. 25, 28, 29, 30).
C – ②③④⑥ Apr. 12 - June 28 (also May 28, not June 21); ①②③④⑥ June 30 - Sept. 13; ②③④⑥ Sept. 16 - Oct. 25 (not Sept. 27, Oct. 4).
D – ②④⑥ Mar. 29 - Oct. 30 (not Apr. 5).
E – ①③⑤⑦ Apr. 6 - Apr. 30 (also Mar. 30, Apr. 2); ①③⑦ May 4 - June 30 (also May 30; not June 8); ①③⑤⑦ July 1 - Sept. 28; ③⑦ Oct. 1–29 (also Oct. 27, 31).
F – ③ Apr. 2 - July 16 (also Apr. 20, May 4, 25); ③⑦ July 20 - Sept. 3; ③ Sept. 10 - Oct. 29 (also Oct. 26).
△ – Operators: Ffestiniog Railway and Welsh Highland Railway. ✆ 01766 516024.

151 LONDON - BIRMINGHAM - WOLVERHAMPTON

Most trains convey ✕ VT

For slower trains via Northampton see Table **141**.

km			ⒶL	⑥E	ⒶE	⚒	ⒶG	⑥B	b	⚒	⚒	⚒E	⚒	⚒	ⒶG	⑥G	⚒	⚒	⚒E	a	⚒	ⒶG	⑥B	a	⚒	⚒E
0	**London** Euston 143 152/3 d.	⚒	0616	0616	0633	0710	0716	0716	0738	0810	0816	0838t	0910	0916	0934	0937	1010	1016	1038t	1110	1116	1138t	1138t	1210	1216	1238t
28	Watford Junction △ d.		0631	0631	|	|	0731	0731	|	|	0831	|	|	0931	|	|	|	1030	|	|	1131	|	|	|	1231	|
80	Milton Keynes 143 152/3 d.		0652	0652	0705	|	0752	0753	|	|	0852	|	|	0952	|	|	|	1052	|	|	1152	|	|	|	1252	|
133	Rugby d.		0715	0715	|	|	0814	0815	|	|	0915	|	|	1015	|	|	|	1115	|	|	1215	|	|	|	1315	|
151	**Coventry** 107 a.		0725	0725	0733	0804	0824	0825	0835	0904	0925	0934	1004	1025	1032	1031	1104	1125	1134	1205	1225	1234	1234	1305	1325	1334
168	Birmingham International ✈ 107 a.		0736	0736	0744	0815	0836	0836	0845	0915	0936	0945	1015	1036	1044	1044	1115	1137	1146	1216	1237	1245	1245	1316	1336	1345
182	**Birmingham** New Street 107 a.		0748	0748	0800	0827	0848	0848	0856	0927	0948	0956	1027	1048	1055	1055	1127	1154f	1158	1227	1254f	1258	1258	1327	1348	1356
	Birmingham New Street 119 d.		...	0807	0807	...	0907	0907	...	...	...	1007	...	...	1107	1107	...	...	1207	...	...	1307	1307	...	...	1407
190	Sandwell & Dudley a.		...	0815	0814	...	0915	0915	...	...	...	1015	...	...	1115	1115	...	...	1215	...	...	1315	1315	...	...	1415
202	**Wolverhampton** 119 a.		...	0829	0828	...	0929	0929	...	...	...	1029	...	...	1129	1129	...	...	1229	...	...	1329	1329	...	...	1429

	⚒	⚒	⚒G	Ⓐ	⚒	⚒E	b	Ⓐ	⑥	ⒶG	⑥G	⚒	⚒	⚒E	⚒	ⒶC	⑥	ⒶG	⑥P	Ⓐ	⑥	Ⓐ	⑥	ⒶC	⑥C	⚒
London Euston 143 152/3 d.	1310	1316	1338t	1410	1416	1438t	1510	1516	1516	1536	1538t	1610	1616	1638t	1710	1716	1716	1737	1738t	1810	1810	1816	1816	1836	1838t	1910
Watford Junction △ d.	|	1331	|	|	1431	|	|	|	1531	1551	|	|	1631	|	|	1731	1731	|	|	|	|	1831	1831	|	|	|
Milton Keynes 143 152/3 d.	|	1352	|	|	1452	|	|	1548	1552	|	|	|	1652	|	|	1752	1752	|	|	|	|	1852	1852	|	|	|
Rugby d.	|	1415	|	|	1515	|	|	1611	1615	|	|	|	1715	|	|	1815	1815	|	|	|	|	1915	1915	|	|	|
Coventry 107 a.	1404	1425	1434	1504	1525	1534	1604	1621	1625	1634	1634	1705	1725	1734	1804	1825	1825	1834	1834	1904	1904	1925	1925	1934	1934	2004
Birmingham International ✈ 107 a.	1415	1436	1445	1515	1536	1545	1615	1636	1636	1645	1645	1715	1736	1745	1815	1836	1836	1845	1845	1915	1915	1936	1936	1945	1945	2015
Birmingham New Street 107 a.	1427	1448c	1458	1527	1548c	1558	1627	1648	1648	1656	1656	1727	1748	1756	1827	1848	1848	1856	1856	1927	1926	1948	1948	2000	1956	2027
Birmingham New Street 119 d.	...	...	1507	...	...	1607	...	...	...	1707	1707	...	...	1807	...	1855	...	1907	1907	...	1937	1956	...	2007	2007	2038
Sandwell & Dudley a.	...	...	1515	...	...	1615	...	...	...	1715	1715	...	...	1815	...	|	...	1915	1915	...	1946	|	...	2014	2015	2047
Wolverhampton 119 a.	...	...	1529	...	...	1629	...	...	...	1729	1729	...	...	1829	...	1922	...	1929	1929	...	2000	2013	...	2029	2029	2100

	⚒	⑥C	ⒶC	Ⓐ	Ⓐ	⑥	Ⓐ	⑥		Ⓐ	⑥	Ⓐ	⑥	Ⓐ	①–④	⑤	①–④	⑤		⑦E	⑦G	⑦E	⑦G	⑦	⑦E	⑦
London Euston 143 152/3 d.	1916	1934	1938t	2010	2016	2025	2038t	2104	...	2106	2123	2130	2142	2230	2300	2300	2330	2330	⑦	0748	0850	0952	1049	1152	1239	1309
Watford Junction △ d.	1931	|	|	|	2031	2041	|	|	...	|	2140	2145	2158	2249	2317	2317	|	|		0803	0906	1007	1107	1208	|	|
Milton Keynes 143 152/3 d.	1952	|	|	|	2052	2114	|	2151	...	2137	2218	2205	2233	2329	2359	2359	0029	0029		0845	0939	1040	1139	1231	|	|
Rugby d.	2015	|	|	|	2115	2137	|	2215	...	|	2241	2228	2258	2359	0033	0053	0059	0109		0923	1015	1115	1215	1254	|	|
Coventry 107 a.	2025	2032	2034	2104	2125	2148	2134	2225	...	2204	2251	2239	2307	0009	0041	0101	0109	0119		0932	1024	1125	1225	1304	1334	1404
Birmingham International ✈ 107 a.	2036	2045	2045	2116	2136	2158	2145	2236	...	2215	2301	2250	2318	0020	0052	0112	0120	0129		0943	1036	1136	1236	1315	1345	1415
Birmingham New Street 107 a.	2048	2058	2056	2128	2148	2210	2156	2247	...	2227	2315	2302	2329	0033	0103	0123	0132	0142		0955	1048	1148	1248	1326	1356	1427
Birmingham New Street 119 d.	2055	2107	2107	2137	...	2219	2207	2250	...	2237	2320	2307	2344	0036	0106	0127	0135	0145		1007	1107	1207	1307	...	1407	...
Sandwell & Dudley a.	|	2115	2116	2146	...	2227	2215	2300	...	2246	2328	2315	2254	|	|	|	|	|		1015	1116	1215	1315	...	1415	...
Wolverhampton 119 a.	2114	2129	2129	2202	...	2240	2231	2311	...	2300	2342	2328	0008	0103	0131	0153	0202	0212		1029	1129	1229	1329	...	1429	...

	⑦	⑦G	⑦	⑦E	⑦	⑦	⑦G	⑦	⑦	⑦E	⑦	⑦	⑦P	⑦	⑦	⑦C	⑦	⑦	⑦C	⑦	⑦d	⑦	⑦	⑦	⑦	⑦
London Euston 143 152/3 d.	1315	1338	1415	1438	1509	1515	1538	1609	1615	1638	1709	1715	1738	1809	1815	1839	1909	1915	1939	2009	2015	2036	2056	2153	2225	2324
Watford Junction △ d.	1330	|	1430	|	|	1530	|	|	1630	|	|	1730	|	|	1830	|	|	1930	|	|	2030	|	2112	2212	2242	2339
Milton Keynes 143 152/3 d.	1352	|	1452	|	|	1552	|	|	1652	|	|	1752	|	|	1852	|	|	1952	|	|	2052	2114	2144	2247	2315	0014
Rugby d.	1415	|	1515	|	|	1615	|	|	1715	|	|	1815	|	|	1915	|	|	2015	|	|	2115	2138	|	2323	2348	0050s
Coventry 107 a.	1425	1434	1525	1534	1604	1625	1634	1704	1725	1734	1804	1825	1834	1904	1925	1934	2004	2025	2034	2104	2125	2147	2215	2333	2358	0100s
Birmingham International ✈ 107 a.	1436	1445	1536	1545	1615	1636	1645	1715	1736	1745	1815	1836	1845	1915	1936	1945	2015	2036	2045	2115	2136	2158	2227	2343	0008	0111s
Birmingham New Street 107 a.	1448	1456	1548	1556	1627	1648	1656	1727	1748	1756	1827	1848	1856	1927	1948	1956	2027	2048	2056	2127	2147	2209	2239	2355	0022	0123s
Birmingham New Street 119 d.	...	1507	...	1607	...	...	1707	...	...	1807	...	...	1907	...	...	2007	2037	2051	2107	2137	...	2217	2242	2359	0025	|
Sandwell & Dudley a.	...	1515	...	1615	...	...	1715	...	...	1815	...	...	1915	...	...	2015	2045	|	2115	2146	...	2226	2250	|	|	|
Wolverhampton 119 a.	...	1529	...	1629	...	...	1729	...	...	1829	...	...	1929	...	...	2029	2058	2109	2129	2159	...	2240	2303	0016	0042	0143

		Ⓐ	Ⓐ	⑥	Ⓐ	⑥	Ⓐ	⑥	⚒	⚒	Ⓐ	⑥	⚒M		⑥P	ⒶM	⚒	⚒	⚒H	⚒	⚒	⚒G	⚒	⚒	⚒E	⚒
Wolverhampton 119 d.	⚒	0457	0527	0527	0542	0542	0603	0605	0615	0645	...	...	0715	...	0741	0741	...	...	0845	...	...	0945	...	...	1045	...
Sandwell & Dudley d.		|	|	|	0553	0553	0614	0616	0626	0656	...	...	0726	...	0752	0754	...	...	0856	...	...	0956	...	...	1056	...
Birmingham New Street 119 a.		0524	0544	0544	0604	0604	0625	0625	0639	0708	...	...	0737	...	0804	0804	...	...	0906	...	...	1006	...	...	1107	...
Birmingham New Street 107 d.		0530	0550	0550	0606	0606	0628	0628	0647	0717	0721	0721	0747	...	0817	0817	0821	0847	0917	0921	0947	1017	1021	1047	1117	1121
Birmingham International ✈ 107 d.		0541	0600	0600	0617	0617	0639	0639	0658	0728	0733	0733	0758	...	0828	0828	0833	0858	0928	0933	0958	1028	1033	1058	1128	1133
Coventry 107 d.		0552	0612	0612	0629	0629	0650	0650	0710	0740	0745	0745	0810	...	0840	0840	0845	0910	0940	0945	1010	1040	1045	1110	1140	1145
Rugby d.		0604	|	0623	|	|	0701	0701	|	|	0756	0756	|	...	|	|	0856	|	|	0956	|	|	1056	|	|	1156
Milton Keynes 143 152/3 a.		0623	0641	0642	0656	0656	|	|	|	|	0816	0816	|	...	|	|	0916	|	|	1016	|	|	1116	|	|	1216
Watford Junction ▽ a.		0647	|	|	|	0718	0741	0740	|	|	|	0838	|	...	|	|	0938	|	|	1039	|	|	1138	|	|	1238
London Euston 143 152/3 a.		0703	0718	0718	0731	0735	0757	0756	0807	0838	0852	0854	0909	...	0938	0940	0954	1006	1038	1054	1106	1138	1154	1207	1238	1254

	⚒	aG	ⒶGn	a	⚒		aE	ⒶEn	a	⚒	ⒶG	⑥B	⚒		⚒	bE	⑥Ep	b	⚒	bG	⑥Gp	b	⚒	⚒E	⚒	⚒
Wolverhampton 119 d.	...	1145	1145	...	...	...	1245	1245	...	...	1345	1345	...	...	...	1445	1445	...	...	1545	1545	...	...	1645	...	...
Sandwell & Dudley d.	...	1156	1156	...	...	...	1256	1256	...	...	1356	1356	...	...	...	1456	1456	...	...	1556	1556	...	...	1656	...	...
Birmingham New Street 119 a.	...	1206	1206	...	...	...	1306	1306	...	...	1406	1406	...	...	...	1506	1506	...	...	1606	1606	...	...	1706	...	...
Birmingham New Street 107 d.	1147	1217	1221	1221	1247	...	1317	1321	1321	1347	1417	1417	1421	...	1447	1517	1521	1521	1547	1617	1621	1621	1647	1717	1721	1747
Birmingham International ✈ 107 d.	1158	1228	1233	1233	1258	...	1328	1333	1333	1358	1428	1428	1433	...	1458	1528	1533	1533	1558	1628	1633	1633	1658	1728	1733	1758
Coventry 107 d.	1210	1240	1245	1245	1310	...	1340	1345	1345	1410	1440	1440	1445	...	1510	1540	1545	1545	1610	1640	1645	1645	1710	1740	1745	1810
Rugby d.	|	|	1256	1256	|	...	|	1356	1356	|	|	|	1456	...	|	|	1556	1556	|	|	1656	1656	|	|	1755	|
Milton Keynes 143 152/3 a.	|	|	1315	1316	|	...	|	1415	1416	|	|	|	1516	...	|	|	1615	1616	|	|	1715	1716	|	|	1816	|
Watford Junction ▽ a.	|	|	1338	1338	|	...	|	1437	1438	|	|	|	1539	...	|	|	1637	1638	|	|	1738	1738	|	|	1839	|
London Euston 143 152/3 a.	1306	1338	1354	1354	1409	...	1438	1454	1454	1506	1538	1538	1554	...	1608	1640	1654	1654	1709	1738	1754	1754	1806	1839	1854	1906

	ⒶG	⑥B	⚒	⚒	ⒶE	⑥E	Ⓐ	ⒶG	⑥G		ⒶE	⑥E	⑥	ⒶC	ⒶE		⑦	⑦	⑦	⑦	⑦L		⑦	⑦	⑦	⑦
Wolverhampton 119 d.	1745	1745	...	...	1845	1845	...	1946	1945	...	2045	2045	2137	2145	2245	⑦	0801	0833	0901	1001	1101	...	1115	1145	...	1215
Sandwell & Dudley d.	1756	1756	...	...	1856	1856	...	1957	1956	...	2056	2056	2148	2156	2256		0812	0844	0912	1012	1112	...	1126	1156	...	1226
Birmingham New Street 119 a.	1806	1806	...	...	1907	1906	...	2006	2006	...	2106	2106	2157	2206	2307		0821	0853	0921	1021	1121	...	1140	1206	...	1240
Birmingham New Street 107 d.	1817	1817	1821	1847	1921	1921	1947	2021	2021	...	2111	2121	2203	2217	2311		0826	0856	0930	1030	1126	...	1147	1217	1221	1247
Birmingham International ✈ 107 d.	1828	1828	1833	1858	1933	1933	1958	2033	2033	...	2122	2133	2214	2228	2322		0837	0908	0941	1041	1137	...	1158	1228	1233	1258
Coventry 107 d.	1840	1840	1845	1910	1945	1945	2010	2045	2045	...	2134	2145	2226	2240	2334		0849	0919	0953	1053	1149	...	1210	1240	1245	1310
Rugby d.	|	|	1856	|	1956	1956	|	2056	2056	...	|	2156	2237	2251	2345		0900	|	1004	1104	1200	...	|	|	1256	|
Milton Keynes 143 152/3 a.	|	|	1916	|	2015	2017	|	2115	2117	...	2201	2218	2259	2323	0026		0937	1003	1038	1137	1221	...	|	|	1316	|
Watford Junction ▽ a.	|	|	1938	|	2038	2046	|	2137	2150	...	2227	2248	2335	2355	0056		1005	1032	1110	1206	|	...	|	|	1339	|
London Euston 143 152/3 a.	1938	1936	1954	2006	2055	2108	2106	2154	2214	...	2246	2310	0001	0019	0117		1028	1056	1134	1226	1256	...	1309	1339	1355	1407

	⑦P	⑦	⑦	⑦d	⑦G		⑦	⑦E	⑦	⑦	⑦G	⑦	⑦		⑦E	⑦	⑦	⑦G	⑦	⑦E	⑦	⑦	⑦G	⑦E	⑦	⑦G
Wolverhampton 119 d.	1245	1253	...	...	1345	...	...	1445	...	...	1545	...	...	...	1645	...	...	1745	...	1845	...	...	1945	2045	2205	2232
Sandwell & Dudley d.	1256	|	...	...	1356	...	...	1456	...	...	1556	...	...	...	1656	...	...	1756	...	1856	...	...	1956	2056	2216	2243
Birmingham New Street 119 a.	1306	1310	...	...	1406	...	...	1506	...	...	1606	...	...	...	1706	...	...	1806	...	1906	...	...	2006	2105	2225	2252
Birmingham New Street 107 d.	1317	1321	1347	1417	1421	...	1447	1517	1521	1547	1617	1621	1647	...	1717	1721	1747	1817	1847	1917	1922	1947	2021	2121	2230	2256
Birmingham International ✈ 107 d.	1328	1333	1358	1428	1433	...	1458	1528	1533	1558	1628	1633	1658	...	1728	1733	1758	1828	1858	1928	1933	1958	2033	2133	2241	2312
Coventry 107 d.	1340	1345	1410	1440	1445	...	1510	1540	1545	1610	1640	1645	1710	...	1740	1745	1810	1840	1910	1940	1945	2010	2045	2145	2253	2324
Rugby d.	|	1356	|	|	1457	...	|	|	1556	|	|	1656	|	...	|	1756	|	|	|	|	1956	|	2056	2156	2304	2336
Milton Keynes 143 152/3 a.	|	1416	|	|	1516	...	|	|	1616	|	|	1716	|	...	|	1816	|	|	|	|	2016	|	2119	2229	2337	0015s
Watford Junction ▽ a.	|	1439	|	|	1538	...	|	|	1639	|	|	1739	|	...	|	1839	|	|	|	|	2040	|	2149	2302	0008	0045
London Euston 143 152/3 a.	1439	1455	1507	1540	1554	...	1607	1639	1655	1707	1739	1755	1807	...	1839	1855	1907	1939	2007	2037	2057	2107	2209	2322	0028	0104

B – To/from Blackpool North (Table **154**).
C – To/from Crewe (Table **154**).
E – To/from Edinburgh (Table **154**).
G – To/from Glasgow Central (Table **154**).
H – From Lancaster (Table **154**).
L – To/from Liverpool Lime Street (Table **152**).
M – From Manchester Piccadilly (Table **152**).
P – To/from Preston (Table **154**).

a – Runs on ⑥ (also Ⓐ from Sept. 15).
b – Runs on Ⓐ (also ⑥ from Sept. 20).
c – On ⑥ until Sept. 13 arrives 7 minutes later.
d – From Sept. 21.
f – Arrives 6 minutes earlier on ⑥ (also Ⓐ from Sept. 15).
n – Until Sept. 12.
p – Until Sept. 13.
r – Departs 1940 on Ⓐ.

s – Calls to set down only.
t – Departs 2 minutes later from Sept. 15.

△ – Trains call here to pick up only.
▽ – Trains call here to set down only.

VT Most trains convey 🍸 LONDON - LIVERPOOL 152

km		Ⓐ	⑥	Ⓐ	⚒	⚒	⚒	⑥	Ⓐa	⚒	d	⚒	⚒	Ⓐ	⚒	⑥	⚒	⚒	Ⓐ	⑥	⚒	⑤c	⑥	⚒	⚒
0	**London** Euston 142/3 150/3/4 d.	0636	0633	0616	0741	0841	0941	1007	1007	1041	1107	1141	1241	1307	1341	1407	1441	1541	1600b	1607	1641	1707	1707	1741	1841
80	Milton Keynes 142/3 153/4 d.	0712	0705	0652	0815	0915	1015			1115		1215	1315		1415		1515	1615			1715			1815u	1915u
132	Rugby 142 143 153 d.			0715																					
176	Tamworth (Low Level) 143 d.		0744					1113	1113		1213			1413		1513			1712	1713			1813		
186	Lichfield Trent Valley 143 d.		0750					1120	1120		1220			1420		1520			1720	1720			1820		
214	Stafford 143 144 150 d.	0805	0806																						
253	Crewe 143 144 150 152 154 d.	0826	0826	0843	0926	1026	1126			1226		1326	1426		1526		1626	1726			1826			1926	2026
289	Runcorn 144 a.	0843	0843	0901	0943	1043	1144	1202	1213	1243	1304	1343	1443	1504	1543	1602	1643	1744	1814	1805e	1843	1901	1902	1943	2043
310	**Liverpool** Lime Street 144 a.	0904	0904	0923	1004	1104	1204	1223	1235	1304	1323	1404	1504	1523	1604	1623	1704	1804	1837	1837	1904	1923	1923	2005	2105

	⑥	Ⓐ	⑥	Ⓐ	⑥	Ⓐ	Ⓐ	⑦	⑦	⑦	⑦	⑦	⑦	⑦	⑦	⑦	⑦	⑦	⑦g	⑦	⑦	⑦	⑦	⑦	⑦
London Euston 142/3 150/3/4 d.	1907	1907	1937	1941	2012	2041	2200	0820	0919	1019	1119	1241	1341	1406	1441	1541	1606	1641	1706	1741	1841	1906	1941	2039	2121
Milton Keynes 142/3 153/4 d.			2015	2015		2115	2240	0908	1008	1109	1210	1315	1415		1515	1615		1715		1815	1915		2015	2124	
Rugby 142 143 153 d.					2120					1145	1233														
Tamworth (Low Level) 143 d.	2013	2013					2320s	1003	1103					1513			1713		1813			2013		2203	
Lichfield Trent Valley 143 d.	2020	2020					2327s	1009	1109					1521			1720		1820			2020		2210	
Stafford 143 144 150 d.					2152		2341s	1025	1126	1221	1306													2225	2325
Crewe 143 144 150 152 154 d.	2057		2126	2126	2211	2226	0009s	1044	1145	1243	1326	1426	1526		1626	1726		1826		1926	2026		2126	2245	2348
Runcorn 144 a.	2118	2103	2143	2143	2228	2244	0030s	1101	1202	1300	1343	1443	1543	1602	1643	1743	1802	1843	1902	1943	2043	2102	2143	2302	0006
Liverpool Lime Street 144 a.	2136	2122	2205	2204	2245	2305	0047	1118	1218	1318	1404	1504	1604	1621	1704	1804	1821	1904	1921	2004	2104	2129	2203	2328	0028

	⚒	⚒	Ⓐ	⑥	⑥	⚒	⑥h	Ⓐa	⚒	⑥	Ⓐ	⚒	Ⓐ	⚒	⚒	⚒	⚒	⚒	⚒a	⚒	⚒	Ⓐ	⚒	⑥	⚒
Liverpool Lime Street 144 d.	0525	0604	0643	0643	0709	0740	0804	0807	0843	0905	0908	0943	1008	1043	1143	1243	1308	1343	1408	1443	1543	1608	1643	1708	1743
Runcorn 144 d.	0542	0620	0702	0702	0730	0758	0820	0827	0900	0922	0928	1002	1028	1101	1201	1301	1327	1401	1428	1501	1601	1628	1700	1728	1801
Crewe 143 144 150 153 154 d.	0603			0723		0822			0922	0944		1022		1122	1222	1322		1422		1522	1622		1722		1822
Stafford 143 144 150 d.	0622	0654																							
Lichfield Trent Valley 143 d.		0710			0815		0915	0914		1015	1014		1114				1414		1514			1713		1816	
Tamworth (Low Level) 143 d.		0718			0822		0922	0922		1022	1020		1122				1421		1522			1720		1823	
Rugby 142 143 153 d.	0654	0738									1040u														
Milton Keynes 142/3 153/4 d.	0715			0829		0929			1029			1129		1228	1329	1429		1529		1629	1729		1829		1929
London Euston 142/3 150/3/4 a.	0753	0830	0856	0903	0930	1003	1030	1030	1103	1130	1130	1204	1230	1303	1403	1503	1532	1605	1631	1703	1803	1830	1903	1930	2003

	Ⓐa	Ⓐ	⑥	Ⓐ	⑥	Ⓐ	⑦	⑦	⑦	⑦	⑦	⑦	⑦	⑦	⑦	⑦g	⑦		⑦	⑦	⑦	⑦	⑦	⑦	⑦
Liverpool Lime Street 144 d.	1808	1843	1843	1943	1943	2051	0810	0834	0934	0943	1043	1143	1204	1243	1343	1412	1443	...	1543	1643	1712	1743	1843	1943	2043
Runcorn 144 d.	1828	1901	1902	2001	2001	2112	0827	0853	0953	1000	1102	1202	1220	1302	1402	1430	1502	...	1602	1702	1730	1802	1902	2002	2102
Crewe 143 144 150 153 154 d.		1922	1923	2022	2022	2133	0849	0915	1015	1021	1123	1223	1242	1323	1423		1523	...	1623	1723		1823	1923	2023	2124
Stafford 143 144 150 d.						2154		0934	1034	1040								...						2043	2143
Lichfield Trent Valley 143 d.	1914									❖			1315			1515		...			1815				2201
Tamworth (Low Level) 143 d.	1923												1322			1522		...			1822				2207
Rugby 142 143 153 d.						2234				1200								...							2234
Milton Keynes 142/3 153/4 d.		2029	2031	2130	2132	2257		1044	1147	1222	1231	1329		1429	1529		1629	...	1729	1829		1929	2029	2137	2307
London Euston 142/3 150/3/4 a.	2030	2103	2127	2205	2225	2356	1104	1140	1228	1256	1306	1404	1433	1504	1604	1631	1704	...	1804	1904	1931	2004	2104	2237	2355

a – From Sept. 15.
b – Departs 1607 from Sept. 15.
c – From Sept. 19.
d – Runs on ⑥ (also Ⓐ from Sept. 15).
e – Departs 1812.
g – From Sept. 21.
h – From Sept. 20.
s – Calls to set down only.
u – Calls to pick up only on Ⓐ.
❖ – Via Birmingham New Street (Table **151**).

VT Most trains convey 🍸 LONDON - MANCHESTER 153

km	km		Ⓐ	⚒	Ⓐ	⚒	⚒	⚒	⚒	⚒	⚒	⚒	⚒	⊠	⚒	⚒	⚒	⚒	⚒	⚒	⚒	⚒	⚒	⚒	⚒
0	0	**London** Euston. 150/1/2/4 d.	...	...	0610	0628	0646	0713	0733	0753	0813	0833	0853		1533	1553	1613	1633	1653	1713	1733	1753	1813	1833	1853
80	80	Milton Keynes 143 151/2/4 d.	...	...	0642	0700	0721			0824			0924	and at		1624			1724v			1824v			1924v
132	132	Rugby 142 143 152 d.	...	...			0744v			0847v			0947			1647			1745t			1845t			1947
155	155	Nuneaton 143 d.	...	...	0711			0810			0910			the same			1710			1810			1910		
235		Stoke on Trent 119 d.	...	...	0746		0827	0844		0927	0944		1027			1727	1744		1827	1844		1927	1944		2027
267		Macclesfield 119 d.	...	...	0802		0843			0943			1043	minutes		1743			1843			1943			2043
	214	Stafford 150 d.	...	...		0750			0850			0950			1650			1750t			1849t			1950	
	253	Crewe 150/2/4 d.	0610	0708		0810			0910			1010		past each	1710			1810			1910			2010	
	283	Wilmslow d.	0626	0724		0826			0926			1026			1726			1826			1926			2026	
287	293	Stockport 119 a.	0635	0735	0816	0835	0856	0909	0935	0956	1009	1035	1056	hour until	1735	1756	1809	1835	1856	1909	1935	1956	2009	2035	2056
296	302	**Manchester** Piccadilly 119 a.	0643	0743	0825	0845	0905	0919	0944	1005	1019	1044	1105		1744	1805	1819	1844	1905	1919	1944	2005	2019	2044	2105

	⚒	⚒	Ⓐ	Ⓐa	Ⓐ	⑥	Ⓐ	⑥	Ⓐ	Ⓐ	⑦	⑦	⑦	⑦	⑦	⑦	⑦	⑦	⑦		⑦	⑦	⑦	⑦	⑦
London Euston 150/1/2/4 d.	1913	1931	1953	2013	2033	2018	2053	2101	2139	2203	0807	0816	0916	1016	1116	1208	1232	1252	1312		1952	2012	2031	2125	2149
Milton Keynes 150/1/4 d.			2024			2104	2124	2146	2210	2246u	0857	0901	1002	1104	1203	1240		1324		and at	2024			2218	2242
Rugby 142 143 150/3 d.			2047				2147			2311								1347			2047				2318
Nuneaton 143 d.	2010			2110	2130	2136				2324		0946	1048	1149	1233	1310			1410	the same		2110			2329
Stoke on Trent 119 d.	2044		2127	2143		2210	2227		2310	2355s		1022	1125	1224	1311f	1344		1427	1444		2127	2144		2335	
Macclesfield 119 d.			2143	2200		2225	2244		2325	0011s		1038	1140	1240	1327			1443		minutes	2143			2352	
Stafford d.		2050						2237									1350						2150		2352s
Crewe 154 d.		2110			2210			2258			1020						1410			past each			2210		0015s
Wilmslow d.		2126			2226			2313			1035						1426						2226		
Stockport 119 a.	2109	2135	2156	2212	2235	2238	2258	2322	2338	0027s	1043	1050	1153	1253	1340	1409	1435	1456	1509	hour until	2156	2209	2235	0004	0039s
Manchester Piccadilly 119 a.	2119	2144	2205	2205	2245	2250	2307	2335	2348	0039	1056	1101	1205	1302	1349	1419	1444	1506	1519		2205	2220	2244	0014	0048

	⚒	⚒	⚒	⑥	Ⓐ	Ⓐ	⚒	⚒	⚒	⚒	⚒	⚒	⚒	⚒	⚒		⚒	⚒	⚒	⚒	Ⓐ	⑥	Ⓐ	⑥	Ⓐ
Manchester Piccadilly 119 d.	0505	0555	0603	0611	0615	0624	0630	0655	0715	0735	0755	0815	0835	0855	0915		1655	1715	1735	1755	1815	1815	1835	1835	1855
Stockport 119 d.	0514	0604		0620	0624	0633	0640	0704	0724	0744	0804	0824	0844	0904	0924	and at	1704	1724	1744	1804	1824	1824	1844	1844	1904
Wilmslow d.		0613	0620					0713			0813			0913			1713			1813					1913
Crewe 154 d.	0537	0632	0640					0732			0832			0932		the same	1732			1832					1932
Stafford d.	0556		0659			0724r		0752			0852			0952			1752			1852					1952
Macclesfield 119 d.				0633	0637	0647	0653		0737			0837			0937	minutes		1737			1837	1837			
Stoke on Trent 119 d.				0649	0653	0704	0710		0753	0810		0853	0910		0953			1753	1810		1853	1853	1910	1910	
Nuneaton 143 d.	0620	0711	❖				0743			0843			0943			past each			1843				1943	1943	
Rugby 142 143 150/3 d.	0633					❖			0834v			0934v			1034			1834			1934	1934			
Milton Keynes 150/1/4 d.	0654			0746	0746s				0855			0955			1055	hour until		1855			1955	1955			
London Euston 150/1/3/4 a.	0727	0813	0906	0820	0823	0940	0841	0912	0928	0943	1009	1027	1042	1110	1128		1909	1927	1941	2025h	2027	2043	2041	2058	2113

	⑥	Ⓐ	⑥	Ⓐ	Ⓐ	⑥	Ⓐ	Ⓐa	⑦	⑦	⑦	⑦	⑦	⑦	⑦	⑦	⑦	⑦		⑦	⑦	⑦	⑦	⑦	⑦
Manchester Piccadilly 119 d.	1855	1915	1915	1955	2015	2015	2115	2215	0805	0820	0920	1020	1035	1115	1135	1155	1215	1235		1835	1855	1915	1935	2023	2055
Stockport 119 d.	1904	1924	1924	2004	2024	2024	2124	2224	0815	0830	0930	1030	1047	1126	1146	1206	1224	1244	and at	1844	1904	1924	1944	2030	2104
Wilmslow d.	1913			2013					0823			1037				1213					1913				
Crewe 154 d.	1932			2032					0841			1056				1232			the same		1932				
Stafford d.	1952			2052					0900							1252					1952				
Macclesfield 119 d.		1937	1937		2037	2037	2137	2236		0843	0943		1059	1139	1159		1237		minutes			1937		2043	2117
Stoke on Trent 119 d.		1953	1953		2053	2053	2153	2253		0900	0959		1117	1155	1215		1253	1310		1910		1953	2010	2059	2132
Nuneaton 143 d.		2027	2028		2126			2326					1149					1343	past each	1943			2043		
Rugby 142 143 150/3 d.	2023	2040						2339					1204				1334					2039			2215
Milton Keynes 150/1/4 d.	2048	2101	2102		2158	2204	2303	0016	1009		1118	1217	1226	1254			1355		hour until					2200	2249
London Euston 150/1/3/4 a.	2133	2134	2152	2214	2231	2259	2359	0114	1059	1110	1212	1253	1301	1328	1342	1410	1428	1443		2042	2114	2147	2202	2257	2341

a – From Sept. 15.
f – Arrives 1306.
h – Arrives 2009 on Ⓐ.
r – Calls after Stoke-on-Trent.
s – Calls to set down only.
t – Calls to set down only on Ⓐ.
u – Calls to pick up only.
v – Calls to pick up only on Ⓐ.
❖ – Via Birmingham New Street (Table **150**).
⊠ – The 1513 from London Euston arrives Manchester Piccadilly at 1723.

154 LONDON, BIRMINGHAM and MANCHESTER - PRESTON - EDINBURGH and GLASGOW

TP, VT

km		⚒	Ⓐ	⑥	Ⓐ	⑥	⚒	⚒	Ⓐ	⑥	Ⓐ	⑥	⑥	Ⓐ	⚒	⚒	⚒	⑥	Ⓐ	Ⓐ	⑥	Ⓐ	⑥	⑥	Ⓐ
0	**London Euston** 143 150–3 d.		...	...	...	...	...	...	...	...	0531	0603	...	...	...	...	0730	0616	0633	...	...	0830	0830	0716	0716
78	Milton Keynes 143 151–3 d.		...	...	...	...	...	...	...	...	0617	0638	...	...	...	...	|	0652	0705	...	...	|	|	0752	0752
	Birmingham New St 144 151 d.		...	...	...	...	...	0604	...	...	|	|	0707	0707	...	...	|	0807	0807	...	...	|	|	0907	0907
	Wolverhampton 144 151 d.		...	...	0515	0515	...	0632	...	...	|	|	0732	0732	...	...	|	0832	0831	...	...	|	|	0932	0932
253	Crewe 143 144 150 152 153 d.		...	...	0559	0559	...	0709	...	...	0727	0754	0808	0809	...	...	|	0908	0909	...	...	|	|	1009	1009
291	Warrington Bank Quay d.		...	...	0617	0617	...	0727	...	...	0746	0812	0826	0827	...	...	0915	0927	0927	...	...	1015	1015	1027	1027
	Manchester Airport ✈ 156 158 d.		...	...	|	|	0603	|	0704	0704	|	|	|	|	...	0804	|	|	|	0904	0904	|	|	|	|
	Manchester Piccadilly 156 158 d.		0457	0457	|	|	0622	|	0721	0721	|	|	|	|	...	0821	|	|	|	0921	0921	|	|	|	|
	Liverpool Lime Street 162 d.		|	|	|	|	|	|	|	|	|	|	|	|	0813	|	|	|	|	|	|	|	|	|	|
310	Wigan North Western 162 d.		|	|	0628	0628	|	0738	|	|	0757	0823	0837	0838	0842	|	0926	0938	0938	|	|	1026	1026	1038	1038
334	**Preston** 156 158 162 d.		0536	0536	0644	0644	0704	0754	0801	0801	0814	0838	0853	0853	0858	0903	0941	0954	0954	1006t	1003	1042	1041	1054	1053
	Blackpool North 156 162 a.		|	|	|	|	|	|	|	|	|	|	|	|	|	|	|	|	|	|	|	|	|	1115	|
368	Lancaster 158 d.		0552	0552	0700	0700	0720	0809	0817	0817	0830	0853	0909	0909	0914	0919	0957	1009	1009	1022	1023	1057	1057	...	1110
398	Oxenholme 158 d.		0606	0606	0714	0714	0734	0823	0831	0831	0844	0907	|	|	0928	0933	|	1023	1023	1036	1037	1112	1112	...	|
450	Penrith d.		0631	0631	0739	0739	0759	|	0856	0856	|	0933	0944	0944	0953	0958	1032	|	|	1101	1102	|	1137	...	|
478	**Carlisle** 213 d.		0650	0648	0756	0756	0816	0902	0914	0915	0922	0949	1004	1002	1010	1016	1048	1102	1102	1119	1118	1150	1154	...	1158
519	Lockerbie d.		0709	0707	0814	0814	0835	|	0933	0935	|	|	|	|	1029	1035	|	|	|	1138	1138	|	|	...	|
641	**Edinburgh** Waverley △ a.		|	|	|	|	0941	1018	|	|	|	|	|	|	|	1137	|	1218	1220	|	|	|	|	...	|
643	**Glasgow** Central 213 a.		0822	0823	0916	0926	...	...	1035	1039	1042	1059	1116	1118	1131	...	1201	...	...	1239	1242	1304	1308	...	1315

	⚒	⚒	⚒	⚒	Ⓐ	⚒	⚒	⚒	⚒	⚒	⚒	⚒	Ⓐ	⑥		Ⓐ	⑥	⚒	⚒	⚒	⚒	Ⓐ	⑥	⑥	Ⓐ
London Euston 143 150–3 d.	...	0930	0838	...	0939	1030	0934d	...	...	1130	1038	...	1230	1230	...	1138	1138	...	1330	1238	...	1430	1430	1338	1338
Milton Keynes 143 151–3 d.	...	|	|	...	|	|	|	...	...	|	|	...	|	|	...	|	|	...	|	|	...	|	|	|	|
Birmingham New St 144 151 d.	...	|	1007	...	|	|	1107	...	...	|	1207	...	|	|	...	1307	1307	...	|	1407	...	|	|	1507	1507
Wolverhampton 144 151 d.	...	|	1032	...	|	|	1132	...	...	|	1232	...	|	|	...	1332	1331	...	|	1432	...	|	|	1532	1532
Crewe 143 144 150 152 153 d.	...	|	1109	...	1118	|	1209	...	...	|	1309	...	|	|	...	1410	1408	...	|	1509	...	|	|	1609	1609
Warrington Bank Quay d.	...	1115	1127	...	1138	1215	1227	...	...	1315	1327	...	1415	1415	...	1428	1426	...	1515	1527	...	1615	1615	1627	1627
Manchester Airport ✈ 156 158 d.	1004	|	|	1104	|	|	|	1204	...	|	|	1304	|	|	...	|	|	1404	|	|	1504	|	|	|	|
Manchester Piccadilly 156 158 d.	1021	|	|	1121	|	|	|	1222	...	|	|	1321	|	|	...	|	|	1421	|	|	1521	|	|	|	|
Liverpool Lime Street 162 d.	|	|	|	|	|	|	|	|	1212	|	|	|	|	|	...	|	|	|	|	|	|	|	|	|	|
Wigan North Western 162 d.	|	1126	1138	|	1151	1226	1238	|	1245j	1326	1338	|	1426	1426	...	1438	1437	|	1526	1538	|	1626	1626	1638	1638
Preston 156 158 162 d.	1059	1141	1153	1203	1211	1241	1254	1259	1309	1341	1354	1405r	1441	1441	...	1454	1454	1503	1541	1553	1601	1641	1642	1653	1653
Blackpool North 156 162 a.	|	|	|	|	1231	|	|	|	|	|	|	|	|	|	...	|	1515	|	|	|	|	|	|	|	|
Lancaster 158 d.	1115	1157	1209	1219	...	1257	1309	1315	1325	1357	1410	1421	1457	1457	...	1511	...	1519	1557	1609	1618	1657	1658	1709	1709
Oxenholme 158 d.	1128	|	1223	1233	...	|	1323	1329	1341	1411	|	1435	|	1511	...	|	...	1533	1611	1623	1633	1712	1712	1723	1723
Penrith d.	1153	1232	|	1258	...	1332	|	1355	1406	|	1446	1500	1533	|	...	|	...	1559	|	1648	1658	1738	1737	1748	1748
Carlisle 213 d.	1210	1249	1301	1315	...	1349	1402	1415r	1424	1449	1502	1517	1549	1549	...	1601	...	1616	1649	1705	1715	1755	1754	1806	1806
Lockerbie d.	1229	|	|	1334	...	|	|	1434	1443	|	|	1537	|	|	...	|	...	1635	|	|	1734	1814	|	|	|
Edinburgh Waverley △ a.	1333	|	1420	|	...	|	|	1539	|	|	1618	|	|	|	...	|	...	1740	|	1821	|	|	|	|	|
Glasgow Central 213 a.	...	1402	...	1439	...	1500	1517	...	1548	1603	...	1642a	1701	1700	...	1721	...	...	1801	...	1839	1918	1909	1917	1924

	⚒	⚒	Ⓐ	⑥	⚒	⚒	⚒	Ⓐ	⑥	Ⓐ	⑥	⚒	Ⓐ	⑥	⚒	Ⓐ	⚒	Ⓐ	⑥	Ⓐ	Ⓐ	Ⓐ	⑥	⑥	⑥
London Euston 143 150–3 d.	...	...	1530	1530	1438	...	1630	1536	1538	...	...	1730	1638	1638	...	1740	1830	1737	1738	1716	...	1930	1928	1840	...
Milton Keynes 143 151–3 d.	...	...	|	|	|	...	|	|	|	...	...	|	|	|	...	|	|	|	|	1752	...	|	|	|	...
Birmingham New St 144 151 d.	...	...	|	|	1607	...	|	1707	1707	...	...	|	1807	1807	...	|	|	1907	1907	1855	...	|	|	2007	...
Wolverhampton 144 151 d.	...	...	|	|	1632	...	|	1732	1732	...	...	|	1832	1832	...	|	|	1932	1932	1937b	...	|	|	2032	...
Crewe 143 144 150 152 153 d.	...	...	|	|	1709	...	|	1809	1809	...	...	|	1909	1909	...	1921	|	2009	2009	2040	...	|	2104	2108	...
Warrington Bank Quay d.	...	...	1715	1715	1727	...	1815	1827	1827	...	...	1914	1927	1927	...	1944	2015	2027	2027	...	...	2115	2126	...	...
Manchester Airport ✈ 156 158 d.	...	1604	|	|	|	1704	|	|	|	1804	1804	|	|	|	1904	|	|	|	|	...	2004	|	|	...	2104
Manchester Piccadilly 156 158 d.	...	1621	|	|	|	1721	|	|	|	1821	1821	|	|	|	1921	|	|	|	|	...	2022	|	|	...	2119
Liverpool Lime Street 162 d.	1612	|	|	|	|	|	|	|	|	|	|	|	|	|	|	|	|	|	|	...	|	|	|	...	|
Wigan North Western 162 d.	1643	|	1726	1726	1738	|	1826	1838	1838	|	|	1925	1938	1938	|	1958	2026	2038	2038	...	|	2126	2137	...	|
Preston 156 158 162 d.	1701	1704	1741	1741	1753	1803	1841	1853	1853	1905c	1905c	1941	1955	1955	2007	2015r	2041	2054	2052	...	2105	2143	2155	...	2206
Blackpool North 156 162 a.	|	|	|	|	|	|	|	|	|	|	|	|	|	|	|	2036	|	|	...	...	|	|	...	...	...
Lancaster 158 d.	1717	1722	1757	1758	1810	1819	1857	1909	1909	1921	1921	1957	2011	2011	2023	...	2057	2111	...	...	2121	2158	...	...	...
Oxenholme 158 d.	1731	1736	1812	1812	1824	1833	1911	|	1923	1935	1935	2012	2027	2025	2037	...	2111	2125	...	...	2135	2212	...	...	...
Penrith d.	1756	1801	|	|	1849	1859	1936	1945	1948	2001	2001	2037	|	2050	...	...	2136	|	...	...	2201	2238	...	...	...
Carlisle 213 d.	1813	1818	1850	1851	1907	1915	1953	2001	2005	2018	2018	2054	2105	2107	...	...	2153	2203	...	...	2218	2254	...	...	...
Lockerbie d.	1831	1837	|	|	|	1935	|	|	|	2037	2037	|	|	|	...	...	2211	|	...	...	2237	|	...	...	...
Edinburgh Waverley △ a.	|	1940	|	|	2024	|	|	|	|	2138	2141	|	2221	2222	...	...	|	|	...	...	2341	|	...	...	...
Glasgow Central 213 a.	1949	...	2001	2003	...	2039	2106	2112	2122	...	...	2208	...	...	...	...	2313	2317	...	...	...	0008	...	...	...

	Ⓐ	Ⓐ	⑥	Ⓐ	Ⓐ	⑦	⑦	⑦	⑦	⑦	⑦	⑦	⑦	⑦	⑦	⑦	⑦	⑦	⑦	⑦	⑦	⑦	⑦	⑦	⑦
London Euston 143 150–3 d.	...	2030	2031	1940	2110		...	...	...	...	...	0847	0748	...	0946	0850	...	1046	0952	...	1229	1049	...	...	1329
Milton Keynes 143 151–3 d.	...	|	|	|	|		...	...	...	...	...	0934	0845	...	1035	0939	...	1134	1040	...	|	1139	...	...	|
Birmingham New St 144 151 d.	...	|	|	2107	|		...	0845	0907	...	...	|	1007	...	|	1107	...	|	1207	...	|	1307	...	...	|
Wolverhampton 144 151 d.	...	|	|	2137	|		...	0904	0931	...	...	|	1032	...	|	1132	...	|	1232	...	|	1332	...	...	|
Crewe 143 144 150 152 153 d.	...	2219	2234	2233	2302		...	0939	1009	...	...	1058	1110	...	1158	1210	...	1257	1309	...	|	1409	...	...	|
Warrington Bank Quay d.	...	2237	2252	...	2320		...	0956	1027	...	...	1116	1128	...	1216	1228	...	1315	1327	...	1416	1427	...	...	1516
Manchester Airport ✈ 156 158 d.	2104	|	|	...	|		0905	|	|	...	1010	|	|	1110	|	|	1212	|	|	1313	|	|	...	1410	|
Manchester Piccadilly 156 158 d.	2119	|	|	...	|		0924	|	|	...	1026	|	|	1125	|	|	1226	|	|	1327	|	|	...	1426	|
Liverpool Lime Street 162 d.	|	|	|	...	|		|	|	|	1012	|	|	|	|	|	|	|	|	|	|	|	|	1412	|	|
Wigan North Western 162 d.	|	2248	2304	...	2332		|	1008	1038	1044	|	1127	1139	|	1227	1239	|	1326	1338	|	1427	1438	1443	|	1527
Preston 156 158 162 d.	2208	2301	2319	...	2346		1017k	1022	1054	1100	1108	1142	1156	1205	1242	1254	1305	1341	1354	1405	1442	1454	1459	1505	1542
Blackpool North 156 162 a.	|	...	...	...	...		|	...	|	|	|	|	|	|	|	|	|	|	|	|	|	|	|	|	|
Lancaster 158 d.	2224	...	...	...	...		1037r	...	1110	1116	1125	1158	1211	1221	1258	1310	1321	1357	1410	1422	1458	1510	1515	1521	1558
Oxenholme 158 d.	...	...	...	...	...		1051	...	1125	1130	1139	1212	1226	1235	1312	1324	1336	1411	|	1436	1512	1524	1529	1535	|
Penrith d.	...	...	...	...	...		1117	...	1151	1156	1204	1237	|	1301	1337	|	1401	1436	1445	1501	|	|	1555	1600	1635
Carlisle 213 d.	...	...	...	...	...		1134	...	1208	1215	1221	1254	1305	1318	1354	1403	1418	1453	1503	1517	1550	1603	1612	1617	1652
Lockerbie d.	...	...	...	...	...		1152	...	|	1234	1240	|	|	1337	|	|	1437	|	|	1537	|	|	1631	1637	|
Edinburgh Waverley △ a.	...	...	...	...	...		|	...	|	|	1343	|	1422	|	|	|	1539	|	1620	|	|	|	|	1743	|
Glasgow Central 213 a.	...	...	...	...	...		1254	...	1325	1336	...	1410	...	1444	1507	1518	...	1606	...	1643	1707	1717	1733	...	1806

	⑦	⑦	⑦	⑦	⑦	⑦	⑦	⑦	⑦	⑦	⑦	⑦	⑦	⑦	⑦	⑦	⑦	⑦	⑦	⑦	⑦	⑦	⑦	⑦	⑦
London Euston 143 150–3 d.	1238	...	1429	1338	...	...	1529	1438	...	1629	1538	...	...	1729	1638	...	1829	1738	...	1900	1929	1839	2028	1938	2053
Milton Keynes 143 151–3 d.	|	...	|	|	...	...	|	|	...	|	|	...	...	|	|	...	|	|	...	|	|	|	|	|	2139
Birmingham New St 144 151 d.	1407	...	|	1507	...	...	|	1607	...	|	1707	...	...	|	1807	...	|	1907	...	|	|	2007	|	2107	|
Wolverhampton 144 151 d.	1432	...	|	1532	...	...	|	1632	...	|	1732	...	...	|	1832	...	|	1932	...	|	|	2032	|	2132	|
Crewe 143 144 150 152 153 d.	1509	...	|	1609	...	1652	|	1709	...	|	1809	...	...	|	1909	...	|	2009	...	2042	|	2107	2203	2207	2250
Warrington Bank Quay d.	1527	...	1616	1627	...	1710	1716	1727	...	1815	1827	...	...	1915	1927	...	2015	2027	...	▬	2115	...	2221	...	2308
Manchester Airport ✈ 156 158 d.	|	1510	|	|	1610	|	|	|	1710	|	|	...	1810	|	|	1907	|	|	2010	...	|	...	|	...	|
Manchester Piccadilly 156 158 d.	|	1527	|	|	1626	|	|	|	1726	|	|	...	1826	|	|	1926	|	|	2026	...	|	...	|	...	|
Liverpool Lime Street 162 d.	|	|	|	|	|	|	|	|	|	|	|	1812	|	|	|	|	|	|	|	...	|	...	|	...	|
Wigan North Western 162 d.	1538	|	1627	1638	|	1721	1726	1738	|	1826	1838	1843	|	1926	1938	|	2026	2038	|	⑦	2126	...	2232	...	2319
Preston 156 158 162 d.	1554	1606	1642	1655	1705	1740	1742	1754	1807	1842	1854	1859	1904	1942	1956r	2008	2041	2052	2101	2109	2141	...	2245	...	2335
Blackpool North 156 162 a.	|	|	|	|	|	1800	|	|	|	|	|	|	|	|	|	|	|	...	...	|	|	...	...	...	...
Lancaster 158 d.	1610	1622	1658	1712	1721	...	1758	1810	1823	1857	1909	1915	1920	1958	2011	2025	2057	...	...	2125	2157	...	...	...	...
Oxenholme 158 d.	|	1636	1713	1727	1735	...	1813	1825	1837	1911	|	1929	1934	2012	2025	2040	2111	...	...	2139	2211	...	...	...	...
Penrith d.	1646	1702	1738	1752	1801	...	|	1850	1902	1937	1945	1954	1959	2037	2050	...	2136	...	...	2204	2236	...	...	...	...
Carlisle 213 d.	1703	1719	1755	1809	1818	...	1851	1907	1919	1953	2003	2011	2017	2053	2107	...	2153	...	...	2222	2253	...	...	...	...
Lockerbie d.	|	1738	|	1827	1837	...	|	|	1938	|	|	2030	2036	|	|	...	|	...	...	2241	|	...	...	...	...
Edinburgh Waverley △ a.	1820	|	|	|	1939	...	|	2024	|	|	|	|	2139	|	2226	...	|	...	...	2349	|	...	...	...	...
Glasgow Central 213 a.	...	1841	1911	1928	...	...	2005	...	2040	2105	2118	2133	...	2205	...	...	2308	...	...	...	0005	...	...	...	...

a – Arrives 3 minutes earlier on Ⓐ.
b – Arrives 1922.
c – Arrives 6 minutes earlier.
d – Departs 0937 on ⑥.
f – Arrives 2156.
j – Departs 1250 on Ⓐ.
k – Arrives 1004.
r – Arrives 5 minutes earlier.
t – Arrives 7 minutes earlier.

△ – All trains to **Edinburgh** Waverley call at Haymarket 5–9 minutes earlier.

TP, VT GLASGOW and EDINBURGH - PRESTON - MANCHESTER, BIRMINGHAM and LONDON 154

km		⚒	Ⓐ	⑥	⚒	⑥	Ⓐ	⚒	⑥	Ⓐ	①	②–⑤	⑥	⚒	⚒	⚒	⚒	⑥	Ⓐ	⚒	⚒	q	Ⓐp	Ⓐ
	Glasgow Central 213 d.	...	...	...	...	0426	0428	...	...	...	0422	0452	0452	0533	0548	...	0629	...	...	0709	0735	0800	0800	0744
	Edinburgh Waverley ▽ d.	...	...	...	...	|	|	...	...	...	|	|	|	|	|	0612	|	0652	0652	|	|	|	|	|
	Lockerbie d.	...	...	...	...	|	|	...	...	...	0550**d**	0608**k**	0554	|	|	0711	0726	|	|	0810	|	|	|	0900
	Carlisle 213 d.	...	...	...	...	0545	0543	...	...	...	0622**f**	0630	0623**f**	0647	0703	0734	0746	0804	0807	0835	0849	0910	0910	0925
	Penrith d.	...	...	...	...	0600	0559	...	...	...	0645**a**	0645	0644**f**	0702	0719	0748	0801	0819	0823	0850	|	|	|	0940
	Oxenholme 158 d.	...	...	...	...	0624	0623	0628	...	...	0709	0709	0708	0726	0743	0812	0825	0843	|	0914	0925	|	|	1004
	Lancaster 158 d.	0513	...	...	0628	0640	0638	0643	0658	0700	0724	0724	0723	0741	0758	0827	0841	0858	0858	0929	0940	0958	0958	1022
	Blackpool North 156 162 d.	|	0535	...	|	|	|	|	|	|	|	|	|	|	|	|	|	|	|	|	|	|	|	|
0	**Preston** 156 158 162 d.	0532	0600**r**	0618	0647	0700	0657	0704	0718	0718	0748**n**	0748**n**	0747**f**	0800	0817	0849	0900	0918	0918	0949	1000	1018	1018	1051**g**
24	Wigan North Western 162 d.	0546	0612	0631	|	0713	0711	0717	0731	0731	|	|	|	0813	0831	|	0913	0931	0931	|	1013	1031	1031	1104
	Liverpool Lime Street 162 a.	|	|	|	|	|	|	0757	|	|	|	|	|	|	|	|	|	|	|	|	|	|	|	1146
59	**Manchester** Piccadilly 156 158 a.	|	|	|	0729	|	|	...	|	|	0827	0827	0827	|	|	0926	|	|	|	1026	|	|	|	...
77	**Manchester** Airport ✈ 156 158 a.	|	|	|	0745	|	|	...	|	|	0844	0844	0844	|	|	0944	|	|	|	1044	|	|	|	...
—	Warrington Bank Quay d.	0557	0624	0642	...	0724	0722	...	0742	0742	...	...	...	0824	0842	...	0924	0942	0942	...	1024	1042	1042	...
0	Crewe 143 144 150 152 153 a.	|	0646	0700	...	|	|	...	0800	0800	...	...	...	|	0900	...	|	1000	1000	...	|	1100	1100	...
63	Wolverhampton 144 151 a.	|	...	0738	...	|	|	...	0838	0841	...	...	...	|	0941	...	|	1041	1041	...	|	1141	1141	...
82	**Birmingham** New St 144 151 a.	|	...	0804	...	|	|	...	0906	0906	...	...	...	|	1006	...	|	1106	1107	...	|	1206	1206	...
	Milton Keynes 143 151–3 a.	0725	...	|	...	|	|	...	|	|	...	...	...	|	|	...	|	|	|	...	|	|	1315	...
	London Euston 143 150–3 a.	0800	...	0938	...	0912	0915	...	1038	1038	...	...	...	1012	1138	...	1112	1238	1238	...	1213	1338	1354	...

	⚒	⑥	⚒	q	Ⓐp	Ⓐ	⑥	⚒	Ⓐ	⑥	⚒	Ⓐ	⑥	y	⑥w	⑥	Ⓐ	⚒	y	⑥w	⚒	⚒	⚒	⚒	⚒
Glasgow Central 213 d.	...	0810	0838	...	...	0909	0909	0936	0939	...	...	1038	1040	...	...	1107	1110	1136	1156	1156	1204**b**	...	1240	...	1309
Edinburgh Waverley ▽ d.	0811	|	|	0852	0852	|	|	|	|	...	1011	|	|	1052	1052	|	|	|	|	|	|	1211	|	1252	|
Lockerbie d.	0910	0915	|	|	|	1010	1010	|	|	...	1110	|	|	|	|	1210	1209	|	|	|	1305	1310	|	|	1409
Carlisle 213 d.	0932	0938	0948	1006	1006	1035	1033	1050	1058	...	1133	1148	1149	1205	1205	1233	1233	1249	1312	1312	1328	1334	1349	1406	1433
Penrith d.	0947	0953	1003	|	|	1050	1048	|	1114	...	1148	|	|	1221	1221	1248	1248	1305	|	|	1343	1349	|	1422	1448
Oxenholme 158 d.	1011	1017	|	1042	1042	1114	1112	1126	1139	...	1212	1224	1225	|	|	1312	1312	|	|	|	1407	1413	1425	|	1512
Lancaster 158 d.	1026	1032	1039	1057	1057	1130	1130	1141	|	...	1227	1239	1240	1256	1256	1327	1327	1340	1359	1359	1422	1428	1440	1458	1528
Blackpool North 156 162 d.	|	|	|	|	|	|	|	|	|	1151	|	|	|	|	|	|	|	|	|	|	|	|	|	|	|
Preston 156 158 162 d.	1047	1052	1100	1118	1118	1150	1150	1201	1218**r**	1218	1247	1259	1300	1317	1317	1349	1349	1400	1418	1418	1452**e**	1448	1500	1518	1549
Wigan North Western 162 d.	|	1105	1113	1131	1131	|	|	1214	1231	1231	|	1312	1313	1330	1330	|	|	1412	1431	1431	1505	|	1513	1531	|
Liverpool Lime Street 162 a.	|	1146	|	|	|	|	|	|	|	|	|	|	|	|	|	|	|	|	|	|	1546	|	|	|	|
Manchester Piccadilly 156 158 a.	1126	...	|	|	|	1226	1226	|	|	|	1326	|	|	|	|	1426	1426	|	|	|	...	1526	|	|	1626
Manchester Airport ✈ 156 158 a.	1144	...	|	|	|	1244	1244	|	|	|	1344	|	|	|	|	1444	1444	|	|	|	...	1544	|	|	1644
Warrington Bank Quay d.	...	...	1124	1142	1142	...	...	1225	1242	1242	...	1323	1324	1341	1341	...	...	1423	1442	1442	...	...	1524	1542	...
Crewe 143 144 150 152 153 a.	...	...	|	1200	1200	...	...	|	1300	1300	...	|	|	1400	1400	...	...	|	1500	1500	...	...	|	1600	...
Wolverhampton 144 151 a.	...	...	|	1241	1241	...	...	|	1342	1341	...	|	|	1441	1441	...	...	|	1541	1541	...	...	|	1642	...
Birmingham New St 144 151 a.	...	...	|	1306	1306	...	...	|	1406	1406	...	|	|	1506	1506	...	...	|	1606	1606	...	...	|	1706	...
Milton Keynes 143 151–3 a.	...	...	|	|	1415	...	...	|	|	|	...	|	|	|	1615	...	...	|	|	1715	...	...	|	|	...
London Euston 143 150–3 a.	...	...	1312	1438	1454	...	...	1415	1538	1538	...	1514	1512	1640	1654	...	...	1614	1738	1754	...	...	1715	1839	...

	Ⓐ	⑥	⑥	Ⓐ	⑥	Ⓐ	⚒	Ⓐ	⑥	Ⓐ	⑥	Ⓐ	⑥	Ⓐ	⑥	⚒	⚒	Ⓐ	⑥	Ⓐ	⑥	Ⓐ	⑥	Ⓐ	⑥
Glasgow Central 213 d.	1333	1335	...	1336	...	...	1434	...	...	1508	1508	1538	1538	1557	1557	...	1611	1640	1640	...	...	1707	1709	1730	1730
Edinburgh Waverley ▽ d.	|	|	...	|	1408	1412	|	1452	1452	|	|	|	|	|	|	1611	|	|	|	1652	1652	|	|	|	|
Lockerbie d.	|	|	...	|	1509	1511	|	|	|	1609	1610	|	|	|	|	1709	1716	|	|	|	|	1812	1810	1825	1825
Carlisle 213 d.	1448	1449	...	1454	1535**n**	1533	1547	1607	1604	1631	1633	1648	1648	1711	1710	1733	1741	1752	1752	1808	1807	1834	1833	1847	1846
Penrith d.	|	|	...	|	1550	1549	|	1623	1620	1646	1648	1703	1703	|	|	1748	1756	1808	1808	|	|	1849	1848	1902	1901
Oxenholme 158 d.	1524	1525	...	1536	1614	1613	1624	|	1644	1712	1712	|	|	1747	1746	1812	1821	1832	1832	1844	1843	1913	1912	1926	1925
Lancaster 158 d.	1539	1540	...	1558	1629	1628	1639	1659	1659	1727	1727	1739	1739	|	|	1827	1836	1847	1847	1859	1858	1929	1929	1941	1940
Blackpool North 156 162 d.	|	|	1551	|	|	|	|	|	|	|	|	|	|	|	|	|	|	|	|	|	|	|	|	|	|
Preston 156 158 162 d.	1559	1601	1618**r**	1618	1648	1648	1659	1718	1718	1748	1748	1758	1801**r**	1818	1818	1848	1857	1907	1906	1918	1918	1949	1949	2001	2000
Wigan North Western 162 d.	1612	1614	1631	1631	|	|	1712	1731	1731	|	|	1812	1814	1831	1831	|	1909	1920	1919	1931	1931	|	|	2014	2013
Liverpool Lime Street 162 a.	|	|	|	|	|	|	|	|	|	|	|	|	|	|	|	|	1946	|	|	|	|	|	|	|	|
Manchester Piccadilly 156 158 a.	|	|	|	|	1726	1726	|	|	|	1826	1826	|	|	|	|	1926	...	|	|	|	|	2028	2028	|	|
Manchester Airport ✈ 156 158 a.	|	|	|	|	1744	1744	|	|	|	1844	1844	|	|	|	|	1944	...	|	|	|	|	2045	2045	|	|
Warrington Bank Quay d.	1623	1625	1642	1642	...	...	1723	1742	1742	...	...	1824	1825	1842	1842	...	...	1931	1930	1942	1942	...	...	2025	2024
Crewe 143 144 150 152 153 a.	|	|	1700	1700	...	...	|	1800	1800	...	...	|	|	1900	1900	...	...	|	|	2000	2000	...	...	2044	2042
Wolverhampton 144 151 a.	|	|	1741	1741	...	...	|	1841	1842	...	...	|	|	1940	1941	...	...	|	|	2038	2041	...	...	|	|
Birmingham New St 144 151 a.	|	|	1806	1806	...	...	|	1907	1906	...	...	|	|	2006	2006	...	...	|	|	2106	2106	...	...	|	|
Milton Keynes 143 151–3 a.	|	|	|	|	...	...	|	2015	2017	...	...	|	1942	2115	2117	...	...	2046	2052	2201	2218	...	...	2152	2156
London Euston 143 150–3 a.	1813	1812	1936	1938	...	...	1912	2055	2108	...	...	2012	2029	2154	2214	...	...	2120	2140	2246	2310	...	...	2227	2254

	⚒	Ⓐ	⑥	Ⓐ	⑥	Ⓐ	Ⓐ	⑦	⑦	⑦	⑦	⑦	⑦	⑦	⑦	⑦	⑦	⑦	⑦	⑦	⑦	⑦	⑦	⑦
Glasgow Central 213 d.	...	1840	1840	...	...	2006	...	...	...	...	...	...	...	0916	0934	0946	...	1013	1034	...	1107	1135	1155	...
Edinburgh Waverley ▽ d.	1811	|	|	1852	1852	|	2012	...	...	...	...	...	...	|	|	|	1013	|	|	1051	|	|	|	1212
Lockerbie d.	1911	|	|	|	|	2103	2110	...	...	...	...	...	...	1022	|	|	1111	1117	|	|	1210	|	|	1310
Carlisle 213 d.	1934	1949	1949	2007	2004	2125	2132	...	...	...	...	...	...	1044	1050	1102	1134	1139	1147	1206	1233	1250	1306	1333
Penrith d.	1949	|	2004	|	2020	2141	2147	...	...	...	...	...	...	1059	1105	1118	1149	1154	1203	|	1248	1305	|	1348
Oxenholme 158 d.	2013	2025	2028	2043	2044	2205	2211	...	...	...	...	...	...	1123	1129	1142	1213	1218	1227	1242	1312	|	1342	1412
Lancaster 158 d.	2028	2040	2043	2058	2059	2220	2226	...	...	...	...	...	...	1138	1144	1157	1228	1235	1242	1257	1327	1341	1358	1427
Blackpool North 156 162 d.	|	|	|	|	|	|	|	...	...	...	...	...	...	|	|	|	|	|	|	|	|	|	|	|
Preston 156 158 162 d.	2047	2059	2105**r**	2118	2118	2239	2246	0854	0859	1001	1017	1057	1118	1157	1203	1218	1248	1255	1301	1318	1348	1401	1418	1448
Wigan North Western 162 d.	|	2112	2118	2131	2131	2252	|	0906	0912	1014	1030	1110	1131	|	1216	1231	|	1307	1314	1331	|	1414	1431	|
Liverpool Lime Street 162 a.	|	|	|	|	|	|	|	0943	|	|	|	|	|	|	|	|	|	1343	|	|	|	|	|	|
Manchester Piccadilly 156 158 a.	2126	|	|	|	|	|	2325	...	|	|	|	|	|	1242	|	|	1324	...	|	|	1424	|	|	1524
Manchester Airport ✈ 156 158 a.	2146	|	|	|	|	|	2343	...	|	|	|	|	|	1258	|	|	1342	...	|	|	1442	|	|	1542
Warrington Bank Quay d.	...	2123	2129	2142	2142	2304	...	...	0923	1025	1042	1121	1142	...	1227	1242	...	...	1325	1342	...	1425	1442	...
Crewe 143 144 150 152 153 a.	...	|	2147	2200	2200	2327	...	...	0941	1043	1100	1140	1200	...	|	1300	...	...	|	1400	...	|	1500	...
Wolverhampton 144 151 a.	...	|	2223	2241	2240	...	...	...	|	|	1134	|	1241	...	|	1338	...	...	|	1438	...	|	1538	...
Birmingham New St 144 151 a.	...	|	2248	2307	2305	...	...	...	|	|	1203	|	1306	...	|	1406	...	...	|	1506	...	|	1606	...
Milton Keynes 143 151–3 a.	...	2246**s**	...	0026	...	...	...	...	1105	1209	...	|	|	...	|	1516	...	...	|	|	...	|	|	...
London Euston 143 150–3 a.	...	2340	...	0117	...	...	...	...	1209	1246	...	1318	1439	...	1418	1554	...	...	1518	1639	...	1619	1739	...

	⑦	⑦	⑦	⑦	⑦	⑦	⑦	⑦	⑦	⑦	⑦	⑦	⑦	⑦	⑦	⑦	⑦	⑦	⑦	⑦	⑦	⑦	⑦	⑦	⑦
Glasgow Central 213 d.	1235	...	1312	1335	1355	1401	...	1434	...	1505	1535	1555	...	1638	...	1703	1734	...	1834	...	...	1856	...	2008	...
Edinburgh Waverley ▽ d.	|	1251	|	|	|	|	1412	|	1451	|	|	|	1614	|	1651	|	|	1813	|	1851	...	|	...	|	2014
Lockerbie d.	|	|	1412	|	|	1502	1510	|	|	1609	|	|	1712	|	|	1804	1831	1912	|	|	...	1955	...	2104	2112
Carlisle 213 d.	1350	1406	1435	1449	1507	1524	1533	1548	1603	1635**n**	1648	1710	1734	1751	1807	1828	1851	1935	1947	2007	...	2017	...	2125	2135
Penrith d.	|	1421	1450	|	1523	1539	1548	1603	1619	1650	|	1726	1749	1806	|	1843	1906	1950	|	2022	...	2032	...	2141	2150
Oxenholme 158 d.	1426	|	1514	1525	|	1603	1612	1627	1643	1714	1724	|	1813	1830	1843	1907	1930	2014	2023	|	...	2056	2135	2205	2214
Lancaster 158 d.	1441	1458	1529	1540	1558	1618	1627	1642	1658	1729	1739	|	1828	1845	1858	1923	1945	2029	2038	2058	...	2111	2153	2220	2229
Blackpool North 156 162 d.	|	|	|	|	|	|	|	|	|	|	|	|	|	|	|	|	|	|	|	|	...	|	|	|	|
Preston 156 158 162 d.	1501	1518	1548	1601	1618	1641**r**	1648	1702	1718	1748	1801**r**	1817	1848	1904	1918	1948**f**	2004	2046	2059	2118	2127	2132	2215	2241	2248
Wigan North Western 162 d.	1515	1531	|	1614	1631	1653	|	1715	1731	|	1814	1831	|	1917	1931	|	2017	...	2113	2131	|	2145	|	2254	|
Liverpool Lime Street 162 a.	|	|	|	|	|	1731	|	|	|	|	|	|	|	|	|	|	|	...	|	|	|	2219	|	|	|
Manchester Piccadilly 156 158 a.	|	|	1624	|	|	...	1724	|	|	1824	|	|	1924	|	|	2024	|	...	|	|	2207	...	2256	|	2323
Manchester Airport ✈ 156 158 a.	|	|	1642	|	|	...	1742	|	|	1842	|	|	1942	|	|	2042	|	...	|	|	2223	...	2315	|	2342
Warrington Bank Quay d.	1526	1542	...	1625	1642	...	...	1726	1742	...	1825	1842	...	1928	1942	...	2028	...	2124	2142	...	...	...	2305	...
Crewe 143 144 150 152 153 a.	|	1600	...	|	1700	...	...	|	1800	...	|	1900	...	|	2000	...	2047	...	2147**c**	2200	...	...	...	2325	...
Wolverhampton 144 151 a.	|	1638	...	|	1738	...	...	|	1838	...	|	1938	...	|	2038	...	|	...	2229	2236	...	...	...	...	...
Birmingham New St 144 151 a.	|	1706	...	|	1806	...	...	|	1906	...	|	2006	...	|	2105	...	|	...	2252	2257	...	...	...	...	...
Milton Keynes 143 151–3 a.	|	|	...	|	|	...	...	1842	|	...	|	2119	...	2043	2229	...	2152	...	0015**s**	...	...	...	...	...	...
London Euston 143 150–3 a.	1719	1839	...	1819	1939	...	...	1919	2037	...	2019	2209	...	2131	2322	...	2252	...	0104	...	...	...	...	...	...

– Arrives 0636.
– Departs 1208 on ⑥.
– Departs 2154.
– Arrives 0535.
– Arrives 1441.

f – Arrives 7–8 minutes earlier.
g – Arrives 1040.
j – Departs 0654.
k – Arrives 0552.
n – Arrives 6 minutes earlier.

p – Until Sept. 12.
q – Runs ⑥ (also Ⓐ from Sept. 15).
r – Arrives 5 minutes earlier.
s – Calls to set down only.
w – Until Sept. 13.

y – Runs on Ⓐ and also ⑥ from Sept. 20.

▽ – All trains from **Edinburgh** Waverley call at Haymarket 4–6 minutes later.

155 CREWE - STOKE - DERBY - NOTTINGHAM

2nd class only EM

km			⚒	Ⓐ	⑥	⑥	Ⓐ	⚒	⚒	⚒	♠	⑥	Ⓐ	⚒	⚒	⚒	⚒	Ⓐ	⑥		⑦	⑦	⑦	⑦	⑦	⑦	⑦	⑦
0	**Crewe** d.	⚒	0608	0705	0709	0809	0810	0910	1010	1110		1610	1610	1710	1810	1910	2010	2122	2127	⑦	1410	1510	1610	1710	1810	1910	2010	2122
24	**Stoke on Trent** d.		0633	0728	0734	0834	0833	0933	1033	1133		1632	1632	1733	1832	1934	2034	2147	2151		1432	1532	1634	1735	1836r	1935	2035	2144
33	Blythe Bridge d.		0645	0741	0746	0846	0846	0945	1046	1145	and	1644	1645	1746	1845	1946	2046	2159	2203		1445	1544	1646	1747	1848	1947	2047	2156
51	Uttoxeter d.		0658	0753	0759	0859	0858	0958	1058	1158		1657	1657	1758	1857	1959	2059	2212	2216		1457	1557	1659	1800	1901	2000	2100	2209
82	**Derby** a.		0722	0819	0822	0922	0921	1021	1121	1221	hourly	1720	1721	1821	1921	2022	2122	2234	2238		1520	1619	1722	1822	1923	2023	2122	2231
82	**Derby** 117 172 d.		0724	0823	0826	0926	0924	1023	1124	1223		1724	1728	1824	1925	2025	2126	2239	...		*1535*	*1633*	*1733*	*1833*	*1937*	*2034*	*2134*	*2332*
108	**Nottingham 117 172** a.		0756	0849	0858	0958	0949	1056	1155	1255	until	1755	1755	1848t	1953j	2054j	2155j	2302	...		*1555*	*1653*	*1755*	*1855*	*1957*	*2054*	*2154*	*2359*
	Nottingham **189** d.		0757	0852	0901	1001	0951	1058	1155	1255		1758	1800	1852t	...	...	...	...	...		...	...	...	...	...	...	...	...
	Newark Castle **189** a.		0834	0920	0929	1029	1019	1127	1233	1329		1826	1831	1928t	...	...	...	...	...		...	...	...	...	...	...	...	...

		⚒	⚒	⚒	⚒	⚒	⚒	⚒	⑥	Ⓐ	⚒	⚒	⚒	⚒	⚒	⑥	Ⓐ	Ⓐ	⑥	⚒		⑦	⑦	⑦	⑦	⑦	⑦	⑦
Newark Castle **189** d.	⚒	...	0625f	0736	0841	0936t	1036t	1135	1243	1246	1343	1438	1537	1637	1738	*1835*	1841	1944	1941	...	⑦	...	...	...	...	...	...	...
Nottingham **189** a.		...	0701f	0815	0915k	1015	1115	1212	1315	1315	1415	1515	1615	1715	1815	*1905*	1916	2012	2015	...		...	...	...	...	...	...	...
Nottingham 117 172 d.		0553f	0716	0817	0915	1017	1117	1216	1317	1317	1417	1517	1616	1716	1815	1916	1918	2015	2017	2117		*1416*	*1512*	*1616*	*1716*	*1816*	*1915*	*2015*
Derby 117 172 a.		0619f	0742	0844	0943	1043	1143	1243	1343	1344	1443	1543	1643	1743	1843	1943	1943	2041	2043	2143		*1436*	*1533*	*1636*	*1739*	*1836*	*1937*	*2036*
Derby d.		0642	0745	0847	0947	1046	1146	1246	1347	1348	1447	1547	1646	1746	1846	1947	1947	2046	2047	2146		1443	1542	1644	1746	1843	1944	2044
Uttoxeter d.		0707	0810	0910	1010	1110	1210	1310	1410	1411	1510	1610	1710	1811	1910	2010	2010	2110	2110	2210		1506	1605	1706	1808	1906	2007	2107
Blythe Bridge d.		0721	0823	0924	1024	1124	1224	1324	1424	1425	1524	1624	1724	1825	1924	2024	2024	2124	2124	2224		1519	1619	1720	1821	1919	2020	2121
Stoke on Trent d.		0734	0836	0937	1037	1137	1237	1337	1437	1437	1537	1637	1737	1837	1937	2037	2037	2137	2137	2237		1533	1634	1733	1834	1933	2034	2134
Crewe a.		0759	0900	0958	1058	1158	1258	1358	1458	1459	1558	1658	1759	1859	1958	2058	2058	2158	2158	2258		1554	1655	1754	1855	1954	2055	2155

f – Ⓐ only
j – Arrives 5–6 minutes earlier on Ⓐ.
k – Arrives 0911 on Ⓐ.
r – Arrives 1831.
t – Departs 3 minutes later on ⑥.
t – On ⑥ Nottingham a. 1853, d. 1855, Newark Castle a. 1931.
♠ – Arrivals into Newark Castle may be up to 3 minutes earlier.

156 MANCHESTER - PRESTON - BLACKPOOL

2nd Class only NT

For other trains Manchester - Preston and v.v. see Tables **154** and **158**.

km			⚒	⚒	⚒	⚒	⚒	⚒	⚒	⚒	⚒	♣	⚒	⚒	⚒	⚒	⚒	⚒	⚒	⚒	Ⓐ		⑦a	⑦b	⑦	⑦
0	**Manchester** Airport ✈ d.	⚒	0448	0548	0617	0648	0717	0748	0817	0848	0917	and at	1948	2017	2048	2117	2148	2217	2248	2317	2346	⑦	0737	...	0844	...
17	**Manchester** Piccadilly d.		0504	0602	0633	0702	0733	0802	0833	0902	0933	the same	2002	2033	2102	2133	2202	2235	2302	2332	0009		0800	...	0902	1004
35	Bolton d.		0523	0622	0653	0723	0753	0822	0853	0922	0953	minutes	2022	2053	2122	2153	2222	2254	2322	2351	0024		0819	0824	0923	1020
67	**Preston** a.		0551	0657	0728	0759	0828	0857	0926	0958	1026	past each	2057	2128	2152	2228	2250	2329	2353	0026	0056		0853	0858	0958	1057
67	**Preston** 191 d.		0553	0700	0729	0800	0829	0859	0930	0959	1028	hour until	2100	2130	2154	2230	2253	2330	2355	0027	0058		0855	0900	1000	1059
96	**Blackpool** North 191 a.		0618	0726	0753	0827	0854	0924	0954	1025	1051		2125	2153	2219	2253	2318	2354	0020	0051	0123		0920	0925	1025	1125

	⑦	⑦	⑦	⑦	⑦	⑦		⑦	⑦	⑦	⑦	⑦
Manchester Airport ✈ d.	1033	...	1110	...	1247	1345	and at	1845	1945	2045	2145	2245
Manchester Piccadilly d.	1055	1103t	1125	1203t	1303	1401	the same	1901	2001	2101	2201	2301
Bolton d.	1113	1118	1144u	1219	1322	1420	minutes	1920	2020	2120	2220	2320
Preston a.	1136	1153	1203	1254	1357	1457	past each	1957	2054	2157	2258	2357
Preston 191 d.	*1144*	1155	*1222*	1255	1359	1459	hour until	1959	2056	2159	2302	2359
Blackpool North 191 a.	*1206*	1220	*1246*	1321	1424	1524		2024	2121	2224	2328	0024

		⚒	⚒	⚒	⚒	⚒	⚒	⚒	⚒	⚒
Blackpool N . 191 d.	⚒	0459	0522	0555	0622	0654	0721	0753	0823	0854
Preston 191 a.		0523	0548	0619	0648	0720	0747	0819	0849	0919
Preston d.		0525	0551	0621	0649	0722	0749	0820	0851	0920
Bolton d.		0554	0621	0654	0722	0753	0822	0854	0921	0954
Manchester Picc a.		0615	0645	0716	0745	0816	0845	0915	0945	1015
Manchester Apt ✈ a.		0631	0700	0736	0800	0836	0900	0936	1000	1036

	♣	⚒	⚒	⚒	⚒	⚒	⚒	⚒	⑥	Ⓐ		⑦	⑦	⑦	⑦	⑦	⑦	⑦	⑦	⑦		⑦	⑦	⑦	⑦
Blackpool North 191 d.	and at	1922	1958	2022	2058	2121	2156	2223	2307	2322	⑦	0753	*0835*	0859	0957	1100	*1118*	1154	1254	1354	and at	1954	2053	2154	2224
Preston 191 a.	the same	1947	2023	2048	2122	2147	2221	2249	2333	2348		0814	*0900*	0924	1022	1125	*1140*	1220	1320	1420	the same	2020	2119	2220	2250
Preston d.	minutes	1949	2024	2050	2124	2148	2222	2250	2334	2349		0819	0912	0925	1024	1126	1157	1221	1321	1421	minutes	2021	2120	2222	2251
Bolton d.	past each	2021	2054	2121	2154	2222	│	2321	0008	0023		0847	│	0958	1057	1158	│	1256	1356	1456	past each	2056	2156	2256	2325
Manchester Piccadilly a.	hour until	2045	2115	2145	2215	2247	2310	2345	0026	0041		0906t	0958	1017t	1117t	1221	1242	1319	1419	1519	hour until	2119	2219	2318	2346
Manchester Airport ✈ a.		2100	2136	2201	2233	2302	...	0002	0044	0102		...	1025	...	...	1239	1258	1335	1435	1535		2135	2235	2334	...

a – Until Oct. 26.
b – From Nov. 2.
t – Manchester **Oxford Road**.
u – Calls to pick up only.
♣ – Timings at Preston and Blackpool may vary ± 3 minutes.

157 BARROW IN FURNESS - WHITEHAVEN - CARLISLE

2nd Class only NT

km			⚒	⚒	⚒	⚒	⚒	⚒	⚒	⚒	⚒	⚒	⚒	⚒	⚒	⑥	Ⓐ	Ⓐ	⚒	⚒	⑥	Ⓐ	⑥	Ⓐ
	Lancaster **158** d.		...	...	...	...	...	...	...	1014	...	...	1319	...	...	...	...	...	1601	...	...	...	1836	...
0	**Barrow in Furness** d.	⚒	...	...	0558	0651	0750	0928	1020	1119	1205	1313	1424	1449	1544	1611	1615	...	1716	1807	1857	1912	1944	1947
26	Millom d.		...	...	0627	0720	0818	0956	1048	1148	1233	1341	1452	1517	1612	1639	1643	...	1744	1835	1924	1940	2011	2015
47	Ravenglass for Eskdale 🚂 d.		...	...	0647	0739	0837	1016	1106	1206	1251	1400	1510	1535	1630	1657	1702	...	1803	1850	1942	1958	2030	...
56	Sellafield d.		...	...	0700	0753	0849	1032r	1118	1217	1303	1411	1522	1547	1642	1708	1714	...	1814	1901	1953	2011	2041	...
74	**Whitehaven** d.		...	0629	0724	0816	0909	1051	1145	1237	1338	1438	1541	1613	1701	1730	...	1750	1838	1922	2012	2037	2102	...
85	Workington d.		0549	0648	0746	0834	0928	1110	1203	1254	1356	1457	1600	1633	1720	1749	...	1808	1856	1943	2035r	2055	2121	...
92	Maryport d.		0558	0657	0755	0843	0937	1119	1213	1302	1406	1506	1609	1643	1729	1759	...	1818	1906	1953	2044	2105	2129	...
119	Wigton d.		0619	0718	0816	0904	0958	1140	1233	1323	1427	1527	1630	1705	1749	1820	...	1838	1926	2014	2105	2125	...	...
138	**Carlisle** a.		0639	0738	0836	0924	1018	1200	1253	1341	1450	1547	1651	1725	1810	1841	...	1858	1946	2034	2126	2145	...	...

	⑥	Ⓐ	⚒	Ⓐ	⚒		⑦	⑦		⑦	⑦	⑦C	⑦		⑦	⑦	⑦	⑦	⑦	⑦	⑦	⑦	⑦	⑦
Lancaster **158** d.	1913	1913	...	...	...	⑦	...	...	...	...	...	...	1011	...	...	...	1314	...	...	1603	...	...	...	...
Barrow in Furness d.	2018	2018	2110	...	2211		...	...	...	0905	...	0950	1116	...	1217	1310	1419	1454	1556	1716	...	1825	...	1909
Millom d.	2047	2046	2138	...	2239		...	...	...	0933	...	1017	1144	...	1245	1338	1444	1522	1624	1744	...	1853	...	1937
Ravenglass for Eskdale 🚂 d.	...	2104	▬	...	...		...	...	...	...	...	1035	1202	...	1303	1356	1459	1540	1643	1803	...	...	...	...
Sellafield d.	...	2115	⑥	...	...		...	...	...	...	...	1046	1213	...	1315	1407	1507	1552	1654	1814	...	...	...	...
Whitehaven d.	...	2134	2209	2209	...		...	...	...	...	1016	1111	1234	...	1338	1426	1530	1611	1716	1841	1938	...	2030	...
Workington d.	...	2153	2227	2227	...		0855	0940	...	...	1034	1130	1253	...	1359	1445	1549	1630	1735	1900	1956	...	2048	...
Maryport d.	...	2202	2236	2236	...		0904	0949	...	...	1044	1139	1302	...	1408	1454	1558	1639	1744	1909	2006	...	2058	...
Wigton d.	...	2222	...	2257	...		0925	1010	...	...	1104	1200	1322	...	1430	1515	1619	1700	1805	1930	2026	...	2118	...
Carlisle a.	...	2242	...	2317	...		0945	1030	...	...	1124	1220	1342	...	1450	1535	1639	1720	1825	1950	2046	...	2138	...

		⚒	⚒	⚒	⚒	⚒	⚒	⚒	⚒	⚒	⚒	⚒	⚒	⚒	⚒	Ⓐ	Ⓐ	⑥	⚒	⚒	Ⓐ	⑥	⑥	ⒶB
Carlisle d.	⚒	...	...	0553	0619	0710	0808	0902	1013	1108	1209	1308	1408	1440	1512	...	1559	1626	1707	1751	...	1846	1909	1909
Wigton d.		...	...	0611	0638	0729	0826	0920	1031	1125	1227	1326	1426	1458	1529	...	1617	1644	1725	1808	...	1904	1927	1926
Maryport d.		...	0548	0633	0701	0751	0848	0942	1053	1147	1249	1348	1448	1520	1551	...	1639	1706	1747	1830	...	1926	1948	1948
Workington d.		...	0558	0644	0712	0803	0858	0952	1103	1157	1259	1358	1458	1530	1602	...	1649	1716	1757	1841	...	1936	1959	1958
Whitehaven d.		...	0618	0703	0731	0823	0918	1012	1124	1216	1319	1418	1518	1550	1621	...	1709	1737	1818	1900	...	1956	2019	2018
Sellafield d.		...	0639	0723	0750	0843	0939	1031	1145	1239	1340	1440	1544	1611	1641	1724	...	1756	1840	1927	...	▬	2039	2041
Ravenglass for Eskdale 🚂 d.		...	0650	0735	0802	0855	0950	1043	1157	1250	1351	1452	1555	1623	1653	1735	...	1807	1849	1939	...	⑥	2051	2052
Millom d.		0610	0709	0754	0821	0914	1009	1102	1216	1308	1410	1511	1614	1642	1712	1754	...	1825	1905	2001	2029	2059	2109	2111
Barrow in Furness a.		0641	0741	0826	0853	0947	1041	1137	1248	1340	1442	1543	1646	1714	1745	1826	...	1857	1940	2036	2101	2129	2141	2143
Lancaster **158** a.		...	...	...	...	1105	...	...	1353	...	...	1653	...	1820	...	...	...	...	...	...	...	...	...	2246

	⚒	Ⓐ	⑥	⑥	Ⓐ		⑦	⑦	⑦		⑦		⑦	⑦	⑦	⑦	⑦	⑦	⑦	⑦	⑦	⑦	⑦	⑦
Carlisle d.	2000	2055	2106	2149	2201	⑦	...	...	0945	...	1023	...	1106	1207	1324	1400	1509	1616	1710	1810	...	1910	2010	2110
Wigton d.	2017	2112	2123	2206	2219		...	...	1002	...	1041	...	1124	1225	1342	1418	1527	1633	1728	1828	...	1928	2028	2128
Maryport d.	2039	2134	2145	2228	2241		...	0917	1024	...	1103	...	1146	1247	1403	1440	1549	1655	1750	1850	...	1950	2050	2150
Workington d.	2049	2144	2155	2238	2251		...	0927	1033	...	1114	...	1156	1258	1414	1450	1559	1706	1800	1900	...	2000	2100	2200
Whitehaven d.	2109	2204	2215	2258	2311		...	0947	1052	...	1133	...	1216	1318	1433	1510	1619	1725	1820	1920	...	2020	2120	2220
Sellafield d.	▬	...	...	...	...		...	1007	1110	...	1151	...	1239	1337	1452	1529	1641	1744	1841	...	...	...	...	...
Ravenglass for Eskdale 🚂 d.	⚒	...	...	...	...		...	1018	1121	...	1202	...	1250	1348	1501	1540	1652	1755	1852	...	...	...	...	...
Millom d.	2200	...	...	...	...		0950	1037	1139	...	1220	...	1309	1407	1517	1559	1711	1814	1911	...	1925	...	...	...
Barrow in Furness a.	2231	...	...	...	...		1021	1109	1211	...	1252	...	1341	1439	1548	1631	1743	1846	1943	...	1956	...	...	...
Lancaster **158** a.	...	...	...	...	...		...	...	...	...	1352	...	...	...	1652	...	1851	...	...	...	...	...	...	...

B – To Preston (Table **158**).
C – From Carnforth (Table **158**).
r – Arrives 5–6 minutes earlier.
🚂 – Ravenglass and Eskdale Railway. ✆ 01229 717171. www.ravenglass-railway.co.uk

NT 2nd Class only MANCHESTER - PRESTON - BARROW IN FURNESS and WINDERMERE 158

For other trains Manchester - Preston / Lancaster and v.v. see Tables **154** and **156**.

km			⚒	⚒	⚒	⚒	⚒	⚒	⚒	Ⓐ	⑥	⚒	Ⓐ	⑥	⚒A	⚒	⚒	⚒	⚒	Ⓐ	⑥	⚒A	Ⓐ	⑥	⚒	⚒
0	**Manchester** Airport ✈ d.	⚒	...	...	0529	...	...	...	...	0729	0729	...	0829	0829	...	0929	...	1029	...	1129	1129	...	1229	1229	...	1329
16	**Manchester** Piccadilly d.		...	...	0549	...	...	...	...	0750	0750	...	0850	0850	...	0950	...	1050	...	1150	1150	...	1250	1250	...	1350
34	Bolton d.		...	...	0608	...	...	...	...	0808	0808	...	0909	0909	...	1008	...	1108	...	|	1208	...	|	1309	...	1408
66	**Preston** a.		...	...	0632	...	...	...	...	0832	0832	...	0934	0934	...	1032	...	1132	...	1236	1235	...	1345	1335	...	1432
	Preston 154 d.		0518	...	0633	...	...	...	...	0834	0842	...	0945	0945	...	1033	...	1144	...	1246	1245	...	1346	1346	...	1445
99	Lancaster 154 174 d.		0539	0559	0653	*0700*	0733	*0809*	0821	0851	0900	*0914*	1003	1003	1014	1051	*1057*	1202	*1219*	1304	1303	1319	1404	1404	*1421*	1503
130	**Oxenholme** 154 d.		|	0617	|	0730	|	0829	|	|	|	0932	1021	1033	|	|	1121	|	1239	1334	1334	|	|	|	1439	|
132	Kendal d.		|	0621	|	0734	|	0833	|	|	|	0936	1025	1037	|	|	1125	|	1243	1338	1338	|	|	|	1443	|
146	**Windermere** a.		|	0636	|	0749	|	0848	|	|	|	0951	1041	1053	|	|	1140	|	1258	1354	1354	|	|	|	1456	|
109	Carnforth 174 d.		0550	...	0703	...	0744	...	0832	0901	0910	...	...	...	1024	1101	...	1212	...	...	...	1329	1414	1414	...	1513
118	Arnside d.		0600	...	0712	...	0754	...	0842	0910	0920	...	...	...	1034	1110	...	1221	...	...	...	1339	1423	1423	...	1523
124	Grange over Sands d.		0606	...	0718	...	0800	...	0848	0916	0925	...	...	...	1040	1116	...	1227	...	...	...	1345	1429	1429	...	1528
140	Ulverston d.		0622	...	0733	...	0816	...	0902	0931	0940	...	...	...	1056	1131	...	1242	...	...	...	1401	1444	1444	...	1544
155	**Barrow in Furness** a.		0643	...	0755	...	0838	...	0922	0953	1001	...	...	...	1118	1154	...	1302	...	...	...	1422	1505	1505	...	1605

	⚒	⚒	⚒	⚒A	⚒	⚒	⚒	⚒	⚒	⚒D	⚒	ⒶA	⑥B	Ⓐ	⑥	⚒	⚒	⑥	Ⓐ	⑥	Ⓐ	Ⓐ	⑥	⚒		⑦A
Manchester Airport ✈ d.	...	1429	...	...	1529	...	...	1629	...	...	1729	...	...	1829	1829	...	1929	...	...	...	...	...	...	2159	⑦	...
Manchester Piccadilly d.	...	1450	...	...	1550	...	...	1650	...	...	1750	...	...	1850	1850	...	1950	...	...	...	...	...	...	2217		...
Bolton d.	...	1508	...	...	1608	...	...	1708	...	...	1808	...	...	1909	1909	...	2008	...	...	...	...	...	...	2239		...
Preston a.	...	1532	...	...	1632	...	...	1732	...	...	1835	...	...	1932	1932	...	2032	...	...	...	...	...	...	2304		...
Preston 154 d.	...	1533	1553	...	1633	...	...	1734	...	...	1844	...	...	1934	1945	*1941*	2033	...	...	...	...	...	2211	2310		...
Lancaster 154 174 d.	*1519*	1551	1609	1601	1652	*1722*	1727	1751	*1810*	1836	1902	1913	1913	1951	2004	*1957*	2051	*2057*	*2057*	...	*2158*	2209	2231	2328		...
Oxenholme 154 d.	1537	1632	1621c	|	|	1742	|	|	1830	|	1921	|	|	|	|	2018	|	2117	2120	2205	2222	|	|	|		...
Kendal d.	1541	1636	...	|	|	1746	|	|	1834	|	1925	|	|	|	|	2022	|	2121	2124	2209	2226	|	|	|		...
Windermere a.	1556	1652	...	|	|	1801	|	|	1849	|	1941	|	|	|	|	2037	|	2136	2139	2224	2241	|	|	|		...
Carnforth 174 d.	...	...	...	1611	1701	...	1737	1801	...	1846	...	1923	1923	2001	2013	...	2100	...	...	...	...	2219	2242	2338		0855
Arnside d.	...	...	...	1622	1711	...	1747	1810	...	1856	...	1933	1933	2010	2023	...	2110	...	...	...	...	2229	2252	2348		0905
Grange over Sands d.	...	...	...	1628	1716	...	1753	1816	...	1902	...	1939	1939	2016	2028	...	2116	...	...	...	...	2235	2258	2353		0911
Ulverston d.	...	...	...	1645	1732	...	1808	1831	...	1918	...	1955	1955	2031	2043	...	2131	...	...	...	...	2251	2314	0009		0927
Barrow in Furness a.	...	...	...	1709	1753	...	1830	1852	...	1940	...	2017	2017	2053	2104	...	2153	...	...	...	...	2313	2336	0030		0948

	⑦	⑦A	⑦	⑦	⑦	⑦	⑦	⑦	⑦A	⑦	⑦	⑦	⑦	⑦A	⑦	⑦	⑦	⑦	⑦	⑦	⑦	⑦	⑦	⑦	⑦	⑦
Manchester Airport ✈ d.	...	...	...	0936	...	1033	...	...	...	1230	...	1330	...	...	1430	1530	...	1630	...	1730	...	1830	...	1930	...	...
Manchester Piccadilly d.	0856r	...	...	0955	...	1055	...	1154j	...	1248	...	1348	...	...	1448	1548	...	1648	...	1748	...	1848	...	1948	...	...
Bolton d.	0909	...	...	1011	...	1113	...	1208	...	1308	...	1408	...	...	1508	1608	...	1708	...	1808	...	1908	...	2008	...	...
Preston a.	0933	...	...	1035	...	1136	...	1233	...	1333	...	1433	...	...	1533	1633	...	1733	...	1832	...	1933	...	2033	...	...
Preston 154 d.	0948	...	...	1039	...	1146	...	1246	...	1345	*1341*	1446	...	...	1558	1647	*1655*	1746	...	1833	...	1946	*1942*	2046	*2041*	...
Lancaster 154 174 d.	1007	1011	*1037*	1059	*1125*	1204	*1221*	1304	1314	1403	*1357*	1504	*1510*	1603	1616	1707	*1712*	1804	*1810*	1852	1902	2004	*1958*	2105	*2057*	*2220*
Oxenholme 154 d.	1030b	|	1116	|	1202	|	1245	1333	|	|	1422	|	1529	|	1632	|	1730	|	1833	1928	|	|	2022	|	2121	|
Kendal d.	1034	|	1120	|	1206	|	1249	1337	|	|	1426	|	1533	|	1637	|	1734	|	1837	1933	|	|	2026	|	2125	|
Windermere a.	1049	|	1135	|	1219	|	1304	1353	|	|	1441	|	1548	|	1652	|	1749	|	1852	1948	|	|	2041	|	2140	|
Carnforth 174 d.	...	1021	...	1109	...	1215	...	...	1324	1413	...	1513	...	1613	...	1716	...	1814	...	...	1914	2014	...	2115	...	2230
Arnside d.	...	1031	...	1118	...	1224	...	...	1334	1422	...	1523	...	1623	...	1726	...	1823	...	...	1925	2023	...	2124	...	2240
Grange over Sands d.	...	1037	...	1123	...	1230	...	...	1340	1427	...	1528	...	1629	...	1731	...	1828	...	...	1931	2028	...	2129	...	2246
Ulverston d.	...	1053	...	1138	...	1245	...	...	1356	1442	...	1543	...	1645	...	1746	...	1843	...	...	1947	2043	...	2144	...	2301
Barrow in Furness a.	...	1115	...	1159	...	1305	...	...	1418	1503	...	1604	...	1707	...	1807	...	1904	...	...	2008	2105	...	2205	...	2323

		⚒	Ⓐ	⑥	⚒	⚒	⚒	⚒	⚒	⚒		⚒	⚒	Ⓐ	⑥	⚒A	⚒	⚒	⚒	⚒	⚒	⚒A	⚒	⚒	⚒	Ⓐ
Barrow in Furness d.	⚒	0458	0550	0550	0612	...	0650	0712	...	0748	...	...	0848	...	...	0958	...	1049	...	1151	...	1250	...	1352	...	1447
Ulverston d.		0516	0609	0609	0631	...	0709	0730	...	0807	...	...	0907	...	...	1017	...	1108	...	1210	...	1308	...	1411	...	1506
Grange over Sands d.		0528	0624	0624	0647	...	0724	0744	...	0822	...	...	0922	...	...	1032	...	1123	...	1225	...	1324	...	1426	...	1521
Arnside d.		0534	0630	0630	0653	...	0729	0750	...	0828	...	...	0928	...	...	1039	...	1129	...	1231	...	1330	...	1432	...	1527
Carnforth 174 d.		0543	0644	0642	0706	...	0743	0802	...	0839	...	...	0940	...	...	1055t	...	1140	...	1243	...	1343	...	1443	...	1539
Windermere d.		|	|	|	|	0642	|	|	0756	|	...	0852	|	0955	1008	|	1057	|	1147	|	1307	|	1400	|	1500	|
Kendal d.		|	|	|	|	0656	|	|	0810	|	...	0904	|	1009	1022	|	1111	|	1201	|	1321	|	1414	|	1514	|
Oxenholme 154 d.		|	|	|	|	0701	|	|	0815	|	...	0909	|	1016	1029	|	1116	|	1206	|	1329	|	1419	|	1519	|
Lancaster 154 174 d.		0550	0652	0649	0716	*0723*	0751	0812	*0839*	0848	...	*0928*	0950	1050d	1048	1105	*1139*	1149	*1226*	1251	1349t	1353	*1439*	1452	*1539*	1548
Preston 154 a.		0609	0711	0707	...	...	0809	...	...	0906	...	...	1008	1108	1106	...	...	1208	...	1309	1407	...	...	1510	...	1606
Preston d.		0611	0713	0711	...	...	0810	...	...	0910	...	...	1010	1110	1110	...	...	1210	...	1310	1410	...	...	1511	...	1607
Bolton d.		0634	0738	0737	...	...	0836	...	...	0934	...	...	1034	1134	1134	...	...	1234	...	1334	1434	...	...	1534	...	|
Manchester Piccadilly a.		0658	0758	0758	...	...	0858	...	...	0958	...	...	1058	1158	1158	...	...	1258	...	1358	1458	...	...	1558	...	1653
Manchester Airport ✈ a.		0715	0815	0815	...	...	0915	...	...	1015	...	...	1115	1215	1215	...	...	1315	...	1415	1515	...	...	1615	...	1711

	⑥	⚒	⚒A	⚒	⚒	⚒A	⚒	⚒	⚒	Ⓐ	⑥	⚒	⚒	⑥	Ⓐ	Ⓐ	⑥	⑥	Ⓐ	⚒C	⑥	Ⓐ		⑦	⑦	⑦
Barrow in Furness d.	1447	...	1550	1651	...	1719	...	1802	...	1856	1903	...	1945	...	...	2045	2042	...	...	2145	...	...	⑦	0753	0841	0905
Ulverston d.	1506	...	1608	1710	...	1737	...	1821	...	1915	1922	...	2004	...	...	2104	2101	...	...	2204	...	...		0812	0859	0922
Grange over Sands d.	1521	...	1624	1725	...	1752	...	1836	...	1931	1938	...	2019	...	...	2119	2116	...	...	2219	...	...		0827	0914	0934
Arnside d.	1527	...	1630	1731	...	1758	...	1842	...	1936	1943	...	2024	...	...	2125	2123	...	...	2226	...	...		0833	0920	0940
Carnforth 174 d.	1538	...	1643	1743	...	1810	...	1856	...	1952	1955	...	2042b	...	...	2138	2135	...	...	2238	...	...		0845	0931	0951
Windermere d.	|	1600	|	|	1707	|	1806	|	1855	|	|	1948	|	2041	2041	|	|	2141	2147	|	2229	2247		...	|	|
Kendal d.	|	1614	|	|	1721	|	1820	|	1909	|	|	2002	|	2055	2055	|	|	2155	2201	|	2243	2301		...	|	|
Oxenholme d.	|	1627b	|	|	1726	|	1825	|	1916	|	|	2007	|	2100	2100	|	|	2200	2206	|	2250	2308		...	|	|
Lancaster 174 d.	1550	1649t	1653	1751	|	1820	*1845*	1906	1934	2000	2004	*2027*	2050	*2119*	*2123*	2148	2143	...	*2225*	2246	2306	2326		...	0945b	1001
Preston a.	1608	1708	...	1809	*1815*	...	...	...	1954	2019	2023	...	2109	...	...	...	2205	...	...	2310	2324	2345		...	1004	...
Preston d.	1610	1710	...	1810	...	...	...	...	2010	...	...	...	2111	...	...	...	...	...	...	...	...	...		...	1009	...
Bolton d.	1634	1734	...	1834	...	...	...	...	2034	...	...	...	2134	...	...	...	...	...	...	...	...	...		...	1032	...
Manchester Piccadilly a.	1658	1758	...	1858	...	...	...	...	2058	...	...	...	2152r	...	...	...	...	...	...	...	...	...		...	1046j	...
Manchester Airport ✈ a.	1715	1815	...	1915	...	...	...	...	2115	...	...	...	...	...	...	...	...	...	...	...	...	...		...	...	...

	⑦	⑦	⑦	⑦	⑦	⑦	⑦	⑦A	⑦	⑦	⑦	⑦		⑦	⑦A	⑦	⑦	⑦	⑦A	⑦	⑦	⑦	⑦	⑦	⑦	⑦
Barrow in Furness d.	0952	...	1052	...	1147	...	...	1254	...	1349	...	1447	...	...	1550	...	1646	...	1746	...	1851	...	1952	...	2046	...
Ulverston d.	1010	...	1111	...	1206	...	...	1312	...	1407	...	1505	...	...	1608	...	1705	...	1805	...	1909	...	2011	...	2105	...
Grange over Sands d.	1025	...	1126	...	1221	...	...	1325	...	1422	...	1520	...	...	1624	...	1720	...	1820	...	1925	...	2026	...	2120	...
Arnside d.	1031	...	1131	...	1227	...	...	1331	...	1428	...	1526	...	...	1630	...	1725	...	1827	...	1931	...	2031	...	2126	...
Carnforth 174 d.	1043	...	1143	...	1239	...	...	1343	...	1439	...	1537	...	...	1642	...	1737	...	1842	...	1943	...	2043	...	2138	...
Windermere d.	|	1053	|	1139	|	1224	1308	|	1359	|	1448	|	...	1555	|	1659	|	1800	|	1901	|	1957	|	2047	|	2147
Kendal d.	|	1107	|	1153	|	1236	1322	|	1413	|	1502	|	...	1609	|	1713	|	1814	|	1916	|	2011	|	2101	|	2201
Oxenholme d.	|	1112	|	1158	|	1241	1329	|	1418	|	1507	|	...	1616	|	1718	|	1819	|	1922	|	2016	|	2106	|	2217f
Lancaster 174 d.	1051	*1137*	1151	*1227*	1247	*1326*	1349	1352	*1439*	1449	*1528*	1546	...	1648e	1652	*1738*	1748	*1843*	1851	1939	1952	*2037*	2051	...	2148	2233
Preston a.	1110	...	1209	...	1306	...	1407	...	...	1507	...	1605	...	1706	...	...	1807	...	...	1958	2015	...	2111	...	...	2252
Preston d.	1112	...	1211	...	1312	...	1411	...	...	1511	...	1612	...	1710	...	...	1810	...	...	2013	...	...	2112	...	...	...
Bolton d.	1135	...	1234	...	1335	...	1436	...	...	1534	...	1635	...	1734	...	...	1833	...	...	2036	...	...	2135	...	...	...
Manchester Piccadilly a.	1156	...	1256	...	1354	...	1456	...	...	1555	...	1655	...	1756	...	...	1855	...	...	2056	...	...	2154	...	...	...
Manchester Airport ✈ a.	1217	...	1317	...	1416	...	1514	...	...	1613	...	1714	...	1814	...	...	1914	...	...	2114	...	...	2213	...	...	...

A – From/to Carlisle (Table **157**).
B – To Millom (Table **157**).
C – From Carlisle on Ⓐ (Table **157**).
D – To Maryport on ⑥ (Table **157**).
a – ⑥ only.
b – Arrives 7–8 minutes earlier.
c – Connects with train in previous column.
d – Arrives 1033.
e – Arrives 1633.
f – Arrives 2206.
j – Manchester **Oxford Road**.
r – Manchester **Victoria**.
t – Arrives 5–6 minutes earlier.

NT 2nd Class only ROCHDALE - MANCHESTER - CLITHEROE - RIBBLEHEAD 159

km			⑥		⑥		
0	Rochdale 190 d.	...	0752	...	1452	...	...
17	**Manchester** Victoria 163 190 d.	...	0815	...	1515	...	...
34	Bolton 163 d.	...	0835	...	1535	...	...
56	Blackburn 163 d.	...	0908a	...	1615c	...	...
72	Clitheroe 163 d.	...	0931	...	1638	...	...
93	Hellifield 173 d.	...	0954	...	1701	...	...
118	**Ribblehead** 173 a.	...	1019	...	1726	...	...

		⑥		⑥		
Ribblehead 173 d.	...	1108	...	1805	...	...
Hellifield 173 d.	...	1130	...	1828	...	...
Clitheroe 163 d.	...	1154	...	1852	...	...
Blackburn 163 d.	...	1218	...	1918	...	...
Bolton 163 a.	...	1247	...	1947	...	...
Manchester Victoria 163 190 a.	...	1307	...	2008	...	...
Rochdale 190 a.	...	1329	...	2029	...	...

a – Arrives 0903.
c – Arrives 1604.

161 Caledonian Sleeper LONDON - SCOTLAND — CS

All trains in this table convey 🛏 (Classic, Club or Double) and 2nd class seats. Only available for overnight journeys. **Reservation compulsory**. Conveys ✕ and 🍷.
All-inclusive fares are available (www.sleeper.scot/tickets). Holders of regular tickets and rail passes may travel in seated accommodation free of charge (Ⓡ); travel in sleeping accommodation is also possible on payment of the appropriate supplement (a first-class ticket is required for Club or Double rooms). Early booking is recommended.

*See Table **154** for day trains*		⑦	⑦	⑦	Ⓐ	Ⓐ	Ⓐ	⑦	⑦	Ⓐ	Ⓐ
		◐	◐	◐	◐	◐	◐	⊕	⊕	⊕	⊕
London Euston	d.	2100**r**	2100**r**	2100**r**	2115	2115	2115	2330**t**	2330**t**	2345	2345
Watford Junction	d.	|	|	|	|	|	|	2344**f**	2344**f**	0010	0010
Crewe	d.	2330**f**	2330**f**	2330**f**	2345	2345	2345	|	|	|	|
Preston	d.	0020**f**	0020**f**	0020**f**	0030	0030	0030	|	|	|	|
Carlisle	a.	|	|	|	|	|	|	0440**f**	0440**f**	0507	0507
Motherwell	a.	|	|	|	|	|	|	|	0700	|	0700
Glasgow Central ⊠	a.	|	|	|	|	|	|	|	0730	|	0730
Edinburgh Waverley ⊠	a.	|	|	|	|	|	|	0730**z**	...	0730	...
Dundee **222**	a.	0611	|	|	0611**a**	|	|	...	...	...	...
Aberdeen **222**	a.	0750	|	|	0750**a**	|	|	...	...	...	...
Perth **223**	a.	...	0542	|	...	0542	|	...	...	...	...
Inverness **223**	a.	...	0845	|	...	0845	|	...	...	...	...
Fort William **218**	a.	...	...	1000	...	...	1000	...	...	...	...

*See Table **154** for day trains*		⑦	⑦	Ⓐ	Ⓐ	Ⓐ	Ⓐ	①–④	⑤	⑦	⑦	⑦
		⊕	⊕	◧	⊕							
Fort William **218**	d.	...	...	...	...	1950	...	...	...	1900	...	...
Inverness **223**	d.	...	...	...	...	|	2045	...	...	|	2025	...
Perth **223**	d.	...	...	...	...	|	2326	...	...	|	2306	...
Aberdeen **222**	d.	...	...	...	...	|	|	2026	2143	|	|	2036
Dundee **222**	d.	...	...	...	...	|	|	2154	2309	|	|	2157
Edinburgh Waverley	d.	2315**n**	...	2340	...	|	|	|	|	|	|	|
Glasgow Central	d.	|	2315**h**	|	2340	|	|	|	|	|	|	|
Motherwell	d.	|	2330**j**	|	2355	|	|	|	|	|	|	|
Carlisle	d.	0145**f**	0145**f**	0145	0145	|	|	|	|	|	|	|
Preston	a.	|	|	|	|	0435	0435	0435	0435	0435**f**	0435**f**	0435**f**
Crewe	a.	|	|	|	|	0530	0530	0530	0530	0529**f**	0529**f**	0529**f**
Watford Junction	a.	0640**f**	0640**f**	0640	0640	|	|	|	|	|	|	|
London Euston ⊡	a.	0715	0715	0715	0715	0800	0800	0800	0800	0800**g**	0800**g**	0800**g**

a – On ⑥ mornings Dundee a. 0605, Aberdeen a. 0740.
f – From June 22.
g – Until June 16 arrives 0845.
h – Until June 15 departs 2145.
j – Until June 15 departs 2203.
n – Until June 15 departs 2325.
r – Until June 15 departs 2020.
t – Until June 15 departs 2130.
z – Until morning of June 16 arrives 0524.

◐ – Sleeping-car passengers may occupy their cabins from 2030.
⊕ – Sleeping-car passengers may occupy their cabins from 2230.
◧ – Sleeping-car passengers may occupy their cabins from 2300.
⊡ – Sleeping-car passengers from Edinburgh and Glasgow may occupy their cabins until 0730.
⊠ – Sleeping-car passengers may occupy their cabins until 0800 following arrival at these stations

162 BLACKPOOL - PRESTON - LIVERPOOL — *See also Table 154* — 2nd class — NT

km			⚒	⚒	⚒	⚒	⚒		⚒	⚒	⚒	⚒	⚒	⚒		⑦	⑦	⑦	⑦	⑦	⑦		⑦	⑦	⑦
0	**Blackpool** North d.	⚒	0605	0705	0803	0905	1005		1705	1805	1905	2005	2109	2220	⑦	0757	0835	0937	1037	1137	1236		1937	2037	2203
28	**Preston** d.		0628	0728	0828	0928	1028	and	1728	1828	1928	2029	2132	2243		0824	0902	1004	1103	1204	1303	and	2003	2104	2228
52	Wigan North Western d.		0648	0748	0848	0948	1048	hourly	1750	1848	1949	2048	2152	2303		0842	0922	1023	1123	1224	1323	hourly	2023	2124	2248
70	St Helens Central d.		0701	0804	0907	1001	1101	until	1803	1901	2002	2101	2205	2318		0857	0938	1040	1140	1240	1339	until	2038	2140	2304
89	**Liverpool** Lime Street a.		0720	0828	0943	1020	1122		1824	1920	2021	2122	2230	2349**f**		0921	1008	1109	1209	1309	1409		2107	2209	2333

		⚒	⚒	⚒	⚒		⚒	⚒	⚒	⑥	Ⓐ		⑦	⑦	⑦	⑦		⑦	⑦	⑦	⑦	⑦	⑦
Liverpool Lime Street d.	⚒	0638	0739	0813	0839		2037	2115	2215	2315	2315	⑦	0829	0913	1017	1115		1815	1912	2012	2114	2215	2315
St Helens Central d.		0655	0756	0829	0856	and	2056	2143	2243	2344	2344		0855	0939	1043	1141	and	1842	1939	2039	2140	2241	2341
Wigan North Western d.		0709	0810	0842	0910	hourly	2110	2200	2300	0002	0005		0913	0956	1101	1159	hourly	1859	1956	2056	2157	2259	2359
Preston a.		0733	0834	0857	0933	until	2133	2220	2322	0023	0027		0934	1017	1122	1221	until	1921	2016	2118	2216	2321	0020
Blackpool North a.		0757	0858	...	0958		2157	2245	2347	...	*0123*		1000	1043	1148	1246		1946	2041	2143	2241	2346	0045

f – Arrives 2342 on Ⓐ.

☛ Hourly services also operate Preston - Lytham - St Annes-on-the-Sea - Blackpool South.

163 MANCHESTER and LIVERPOOL local services — 2nd class — ME, NT

MANCHESTER - CLITHEROE
Journey time: ± 76–80 minutes *57 km* NT

From Manchester Victoria:
Trains call at Bolton ± 19 and Blackburn ± 50 minutes later.
⚒: 0543, 0743, 0815⑥**R**, 0845, 0943 and hourly until 2043, 2143, 2215. Also 1515⑥**R**.
⑦: 0755, 0839, 0945, 1048, 1145 and hourly until 1645, 1756, 1845, 1945, 2112, 2207.

From Clitheroe:
Trains call at Blackburn ± 23 and Bolton ± 54 minutes later.
⚒: 0619, 0650, 0720, 0821 and hourly until 1521, 1625, 1720, 1821, 1852⑥**R**, 1921, 2020, 2121, 2237. Also 1154⑥**R**.
⑦: 0923, 1022 and hourly until 1623, 1719, 1823, 1947, 2023, 2123, 2243.

MANCHESTER - BUXTON
Journey time: ± 56–63 minutes *41 km* NT

From Manchester Piccadilly:
Trains call at Stockport ± 10, Hazel Grove ± 19 and New Mills Newtown ± 33 minutes later.
⚒: 0620, 0650, 0721, 0750, 0820, 0851, 0920, 0951 and hourly until 1551, 1620, 1651, 1721, 1751, 1820, 1851, 1920, 2020, 2120, 2219, 2310.
⑦: 0850, 0945, 1047, 1149, 1250, 1350, 1449 and hourly until 2049, 2150, 2248.

From Buxton: From Oct. 6 services will depart 2 minutes earlier.
Trains call at New Mills Newtown ± 21, Hazel Grove ± 34 and at Stockport ± 46 minutes later.
⚒: 0549, 0613, 0643, 0716, 0745, 0816, 0845, 0916, 0946 and hourly until 1546, 1615, 1646, 1716, 1745, 1816, 1846, 1916, 2013, 2114, 2159Ⓐ, 2213⑥, 2257.
⑦: 0813, 0855, 1001, 1058, 1157, 1300, 1356 and hourly until 1956, 2059, 2203, 2257.

CREWE - MANCHESTER AIRPORT ✈
Journey time: ± 42 minutes *37 km* NT

From Crewe:
Trains call at Wilmslow ± 26 minutes.
⚒: 0044②–⑥, 0616 and hourly until 1816, 1916.

From Manchester Airport:
Trains call at Wilmslow ± 15 minutes later.
⚒: 0551, 0701, 0801 and hourly until 1701, 1801, 1901.

MANCHESTER - WIGAN - SOUTHPORT
Journey time: ± 75 minutes *62 km* NT

From Manchester Victoria:
Trains call at Wigan Wallgate ± 35 minutes later.
⚒: 0608, 0632, 0709, 0727**p**, 0807, 0827**p**, 0909, 0927**p**, 1009, 1027**p** and at the same minutes past each hour until 1709, 1727**p**, 1808, 1827**p**, 1909, 1927**p**, 2027**p**, 2130**p**, 2240.
⑦: 0825, 0926, 1025, 1125 and hourly until 2025, 2125.

From Southport:
Trains call at Wigan Wallgate ± 30 minutes later.
⚒: 0603**p**, 0625, 0703**p**, 0725, 0803**p**, 0831, 0903**p**, 0924, 1003**p**, 1030, 1103**p**, 1124, 1203**p**, 1230, 1304**p**, 1324, 1403**p**, 1430, 1503**p**, 1524, 1603**p**, 1630, 1735**p**, 1724, 1803**p**, 1830, 1902**p**, 1930, 1956**p**, 2103**p**, 2225.
⑦: 0842, 0938 and hourly until 2038, 2138, 2254.

MANCHESTER - NORTHWICH - CHESTER
Journey time: ± 92 minutes *73 km* NT

From Manchester Piccadilly:
Trains call at Stockport ± 10, Altrincham ± 26 and Northwich ± 55 minutes later.
⚒: 0606⑥, 0610Ⓐ, 0709, 0810 and hourly until 1910, 2009, 2110, 2210, 2313Ⓐ, 2320⑥.
⑦: 0906, 1103, 1310, 1509, 1709, 1909, 2104.

From Chester:
Trains call at Northwich ± 32, Altrincham ± 62 and Stockport ± 75 minutes later.
⚒: 0556, 0648, 0756 and hourly until 2056, 2156, 2253.
⑦: 0903, 1056, 1259, 1503, 1703, 1906, 2059.

LIVERPOOL - BIRKENHEAD - CHESTER
Journey time: ± 42 minutes *29 km* ME

From Liverpool Lime Street (Low Level):
Trains call at Liverpool Central ± 2 minutes and Birkenhead Central ± 9 minutes later.
⚒: 0538, 0608, 0642, 0713, 0743Ⓐ, 0757, 0813, 0820Ⓐ, 0835Ⓐ, 0843⑥, 0850Ⓐ, 0858⑥, 0912 and every 14–16 minutes until 1913, 1943 and every 30 minutes until 2343.
⑦: 0813, 0843 and every 30 minutes until 2313, 2343.

From Chester:
Trains call at Birkenhead Central ± 33 minutes and Liverpool Central ± 44* minutes later.
⚒: 0554, 0630, 0659, 0722Ⓐ, 0730⑥, 0737Ⓐ, 0752Ⓐ, 0800⑥, 0807Ⓐ, 0815⑥, 0831 and every 14–16 minutes until 1830, 1848, 1900 and every 30 minutes until 2300.
⑦: 0800, 0830 and every 30 minutes until 2230, 2300.

LIVERPOOL - RUNCORN - CHESTER
Journey time: ± 50 minutes *43 km* AW

From Liverpool Lime Street:
Trains call at Liverpool South Parkway ± 9 minutes and Runcorn ± 19 minutes later.
⚒: 0646Ⓐ, 0652⑥, 0744, 0846 and hourly until 1747, 1946, 2047, 2147, 2206⑥, 2322Ⓐ.
⑦: 0946, 1049, 1156, 1257 and hourly until 2057, 2138, 2257, 2321.

From Chester:
Trains call at Runcorn ± 26 minutes and Liverpool South Parkway ± 35 minutes later.
⚒: 0542, 0637Ⓐ, 0643⑥, 0743 and hourly until 1642, 1843, 1943, 2043, 2102⑥, 2201Ⓐ
⑦: 0832, 0932, 1047 and hourly until 2047, 2155, 2227.

LIVERPOOL - SOUTHPORT
Journey time: ± 44 minutes *30 km* ME

From Liverpool Central:
⚒: 0608, 0624, 0638, 0653, 0708 and every 15 minutes until 2308, 2323, 2338
⑦: 0808, 0823, 0853, 0923, 0953, 1008**a**, 1023, 1038**a**, 1053 and at the same minutes past each hour until 1937**a**, 1953, 2023, 2053, 2123, 2153, 2223, 2253, 2323, 2338.

From Southport:
⚒: 0537, 0552, 0607, 0622, 0642, 0657 and every 15 minutes until 2242, 2257, 2318.
⑦: 0757, 0827, 0857, 0927, 0957, 1012**a**, 1027, 1042**a**, 1057 and at the same minutes past each hour until 1942**a**, 1957, 2027, 2127, 2157, 2227, 2257, 2318.

R – To/from Ribblehead (Table **159**).
a – Until Aug. 31.
p – Starts/terminates at Manchester **Oxford Road**, not Victoria.
* – Trains FROM Chester call at Liverpool Lime Street, then Liverpool Central.

EM Most trains convey 🍸 LONDON - LEICESTER - NOTTINGHAM, DERBY and SHEFFIELD 170

km		⚒	Ⓐ	⑥	Ⓐ	Ⓐ	⑥	⑥	Ⓐ	⑥	⚒	⑥	Ⓐ	⑥	Ⓐ	⑥	Ⓐ	⑥	Ⓐ	Ⓐ	⑥	⑥	Ⓐ	⑥	Ⓐ	⑥
0	**London** St Pancras . **170a** d.		...	...	...	0527	...	0530	0559	0600	0605	0630	...	0633	0635	0702	0702	0705	0705	0730	0732	0735	0735	0802	0803	0805
116	Kettering .... **170a** d.		...	...	0606	|	0609	|	|	|	0653	|	...	0721	0727	|	|	0757	0758	|	|	0822	0826	|	|	0854
133	Market Harborough............ d.		...	...	0618	|	0619	|	|	|	0704	|	...	0731	0737	|	|	0807	0808	|	|	0832	0836	|	|	0904
159	**Leicester** .... d.		0548	0550	0641a	0637y	0643a	0639y	0706	0707	0719	0734	0743	0745	0750	0807	0809	0821	0825	0840	0837	0846	0849	0906	0909	0917
180	Loughborough .... d.		0600	0600	0653	0647	0654	0649	|	0717	0729	0745	0753	0755	|	|	|	0831	0835	0850	0847	|	|	|	|	0927
191	East Midlands Parkway ..... d.		0607	0607	0700	0655	0701	0657	|	0725	0737	0753	0800	|	|	|	|	0839	0842	0857	0854	|	|	|	|	0935
204	**Nottingham**............... ‡ a.		|	|	0713	|	0717	|	|	|	0751	|	|	0814	0822	|	|	0853	0859	|	|	0911	0911	|	|	0950
207	**Derby** .... **119** a.		0622	0622	...	0708	...	0710	0729	0735	...	0806f	0814	...	...	0827	0830	...	...	0911	0908f	...	...	0927	0930	...
246	Chesterfield............. **119** ‡ a.		0643	0644	...	0727	...	0729	0747	0754	...	0828	0832	...	...	0846	0851	...	...	0929	0930	...	...	0945	0948	...
265	**Sheffield**................ **119** ‡ a.		0708	0708	...	0742	...	0743	0802	0807	...	0844	0845	...	...	0900	0906	...	...	0943	0945	...	...	0958	1001	...

	Ⓐ	⑥	Ⓐ	⑥	Ⓐ	⑥	Ⓐ	⑥	Ⓐ	⚒	⚒	⑥	Ⓐ	⚒	⚒	⚒	⚒	⚒	⚒	⚒	⑥	Ⓐ	⚒	⚒	⚒	⚒
ondon St Pancras... **170a** d.	0806	0832	0832	0835	0835	0902	0902	0905	0905	0932	0935	1002	1002	1005	1032	1035	1102	1105	1132	1135	1202	1202	1205	1232	1235	1302
ettering.................. **170a** d.	0856	|	|	0922	0926	|	|	0953	0956	|	1022	|	|	1054	|	1122	|	1153	|	1221	|	|	1253	|	1322	|
arket Harborough............d.	0906	|	|	0932	0936	|	|	1003	1006	|	1032	|	|	1104	|	1132	|	1203	|	1231	|	|	1304	|	1332	|
eicester...........................d.	0920	0937	0940	0946	0950	1006	1010	1018	1021	1037	1046	1106	1108	1117	1137	1147	1206	1218	1236	1247	1306	1307	1318	1337	1346	1406
ughborough......................d.	0930	0947	0950	|	|	|	|	1028	1031	1047	|	|	|	1127	1147	|	|	1228	1246	|	|	|	1328	1347	|	|
ast Midlands Parkway.......d.	0938	0954	0958	|	|	|	|	1035	1039	1054	|	|	|	1135	1154	|	|	1235	1253	|	|	|	1335	1354	|	|
Nottingham ....‡ a.	0954	|	|	1009	1012	|	|	1049	1051	|	1109	|	|	1150	|	1211r	|	1251	|	1309	|	|	1351	|	1409	|
erby........................**119** a.	...	1008	1011	...	...	1027	1030	...	...	1108	...	1127	1129	...	1208	...	1228	...	1308	...	1327	1329	...	1410	...	1428
hesterfield .... **119** ‡ a.	...	1028	1030	...	...	1045	1049	...	...	1128	...	1145	1147	...	1227	...	1248	...	1328	...	1346	1347	...	1429	...	1447
heffield .... **119** ‡ a.	...	1042	1043	...	...	1058	1105	...	...	1142	...	1159	1201	...	1244	...	1301	...	1343	...	1359	1405	...	1446r	...	1505n

	⚒	⚒	⚒	⚒	⚒	⚒	⚒	⚒	⚒	⚒	⚒	⑥	Ⓐ	⚒	⑥	Ⓐ	⑥	Ⓐ	⑥	Ⓐ	⑥	Ⓐ	⑥	Ⓐ	⑥	Ⓐ
ondon St Pancras... **170a** d.	1305	1332	1335	1402	1405	1432	1435	1502	1505	1531	1535	1602	1602	1605	1632	1632	1635	1635	1702	1702	1705	1705	1732	1732	1735	1735
ettering.................. **170a** d.	1353	|	1422	|	1453	|	1522	|	1552	|	1622	|	|	1652	|	|	1722	1726	|	|	1752	1758	|	|	1822	1826
arket Harborough............d.	1403	|	1432	|	1503	|	1532	|	1602	|	1632	|	|	1704	|	|	1732	1737	|	|	1803	1808	|	|	1832	1836
eicester...........................d.	1418	1436	1447	1506	1517	1537	1546	1606	1617	1636	1646	1706	1707	1718	1736	1741	1747	1751	1806	1811	1818	1823	1836	1841	1847	1850
ughborough......................d.	1428	1446	|	|	1528	1547	|	|	1627	1647	|	|	|	1728	1746	1751	|	|	|	|	1828	1834	1846	1851	|	|
ast Midlands Parkway.......d.	1435	1454	|	|	1535	1554	|	|	1634	1654	|	|	|	1737	1753	1758	|	1804	|	|	1835	1842	1854	1859	|	1903
Nottingham ....‡ a.	1450	|	1508	|	1551	|	1610	|	1650	|	1709	|	|	1751	|	|	1807	1821	|	|	1852	1855	|	|	1908	1913
erby........................**119** a.	...	1508	...	1528	...	1609	...	1628	...	1708	...	1726	1727	...	1808	1813f	...	...	1827	1834	...	...	1909	1912	...	...
hesterfield .... **119** ‡ a.	...	1527	...	1547	...	1629	...	1646	...	1729	...	1745	1747	...	1828	1836	...	...	1845	1853	...	...	1928	1931	...	...
heffield .... **119** ‡ a.	...	1542	...	1601	...	1642	...	1700	...	1744	...	1758	1805	...	1843	1851	...	...	1900	1917	...	...	1942	1948	...	...

	⑥	Ⓐ	⑥	Ⓐ	⑥	Ⓐ	⑥	Ⓐ	⑥	Ⓐ	⑥	Ⓐ	⑥	Ⓐ	⑥	Ⓐ	⑥	Ⓐ	⑥	Ⓐ	Ⓐ P	⚒	⚒	⚒	⚒	⑥
ondon St Pancras... **170a** d.	1802	1802	1805	1805	1832	1832	1835	1835	1902	1902	1905	1905	1932	1932	1935	1935	2002	2002	2005	2005	2	2031	2034	2102	2105	2132
ettering.................. **170a** d.	|	|	1852	1857	|	|	1922	1932j	|	|	1954	1956	|	|	2022	2026	|	|	2053	2057	...	|	2121	|	2153	|
arket Harborough............d.	|	|	1903	1907	|	|	1932	1943	|	|	2004	2006	|	|	2032	2036	|	|	2103	2107	...	|	2131	|	2203	|
eicester...........................d.	1906	1910	1918	1921	1936	1941	1946	1957	2006	2008	2018	2020	2037	2041	2047	2050	2106	2111	2117	2123	2130	2136	2146	2206	2218	2236
ughborough......................d.	|	|	1928	1931	1946	1951	|	2007	|	|	2028	2031	2047	2051	|	|	|	|	2128	2133	2152	2146	|	|	2228	2246
ast Midlands Parkway.......d.	|	|	1935	1938	1954	1959	|	|	|	|	2035	2038	2054	2058	2100	2104	|	|	2136	2141	2207z	2154	|	|	2235	2254
Nottingham ....‡ a.	|	|	1949	1956	|	|	2009	2024	|	|	2048	2053	|	|	2110	2114	|	|	2148	2155	2231	|	2214b	|	2249	|
erby........................**119** a.	1927	1931	...	...	2007	2012	...	...	2027	2031	...	...	2108	2112	...	...	2130	2131	...	...	...	2211	...	2228	...	2304
hesterfield .... **119** ‡ a.	1946	1949	...	...	2026	2031	...	...	2047	2051	...	...	2127	2131	...	...	2149	2150	...	...	...	2230	...	2246	...	2322
heffield .... **119** ‡ a.	1959	2002	...	...	2040	2050	...	...	2101	2116	...	...	2140	2146	...	...	2202	2203	...	...	...	2243	...	2300	...	2335

	Ⓐ	Ⓐ	⑥	⑥	Ⓐ	⑥	Ⓐ	Ⓐ	Ⓐ	⑦	⑦	⑦	⑦	⑦	⑦	⑦	⑦	⑦	⑦	⑦	⑦	⑦	⑦	⑦	⑦	⑦
ondon St Pancras... **170a** d.	2132	2135	2135	2215	2232	2232	2235	2304	2335		...	0900	0930	1005	1030	1100	1130	1202	1234	1302	1334	1402	1434	1502	1532	1535
ettering.................. **170a** d.	|	2222	2225	2304	|	2320	2322	0037j	0055		...	1001	1029	1104	1129	1201	1229	|	1330	|	1433	|	1521	|	1618	1624
arket Harborough............d.	|	2232	2235	2314	|	2330	2332	|	|		...	1011	1039	1114	1139	1211	1239	1257	1340	1355	1443	1455	1531	1555	|	1634
eicester...........................d.	2238	2246	2249	2328	2337	2345	2347	0131	0149j		1015	1025	1054	1129	1154	1226	1254	1313	1356	1411	1502	1511	1547	1611	1642	1653
ughborough......................d.	2248	|	2259	2338	2347	2355	2359	0141	0159		1025	1035	1104	1139	1204	1236	|	1323	1406	1421	1512	1521	1557	1621	1652	1703
ast Midlands Parkway.......d.	2256	2300	2306	2345	2354	0002	0010	0149	0207		1032	1043	1112	1147	1212	1244	|	1330	1414	1428	1519	1529	1605	1629	1659	1711
Nottingham ....‡ a.	|	2310	2316	|	|	0018	0025	|	0219		|	1056	|	1159	|	1258	1315	|	1427	|	1534	|	1623	|	|	1723
erby........................**119** a.	2309	...	...	2355	0008	0046	...	0204	...		1048	...	1125	...	1227	...	...	1344v	...	1442v	...	1542f	...	1642v	1713	...
hesterfield .... **119** ‡ a.	2328	...	...	...	0026	...	...	...	...		1111	...	1144	...	1246	...	...	1409	...	1504	...	1604	...	1702	1733	...
heffield .... **119** ‡ a.	2341	...	...	...	0039	...	...	...	...		1126	...	1157	...	1301	...	...	1428	...	1519	...	1619	...	1724	1750	...

	⑦	⑦	⑦	⑦	⑦	⑦	⑦	⑦	⑦	⑦	⑦	⑦	⑦	⑦	⑦	⑦	⑦	⑦	⑦	⑦	⑦	⑦	⑦	⑦	⑦	⑦
ondon St Pancras... **170a** d.	1602	1605	1632	1635	1702	1705	1732	1735	1802	1805	1832	1835	1902	1905	1932	1935	2002	2005	2032	2035	2102	...	2135	2202	2232	2300
ettering.................. **170a** d.	|	1651	|	1722	|	1751	|	1821	|	1851	|	1921	|	1951	|	2021	|	2051	|	2121	|	...	2230	|	2334	0018
arket Harborough............d.	1655	1701	|	1732	|	1801	|	1831	|	1901	|	1931	|	2001	|	2031	|	2101	|	2131	|	...	2240	2256	2344	0028
eicester...........................d.	1709	1719	1738	1748	1806	1819	1838	1849	1906	1918	1938	1947	2007	2019	2038	2048	2106	2117	2138	2147	2208	2230	2256	2312	2359	0044
ughborough......................d.	|	1729	1748	|	|	1829	1848	|	|	1928	1948	|	|	2029	2048	2058	2116	2127	2148	|	2218	2240	2306	|	0009	0054
ast Midlands Parkway.......d.	1723	1737	1755	1802	1820	1836	1855	1902	1920	1935	1955	2001	2020	2036	2055	2105	2124	2135	2155	|	2225	2247	2313	2325	0017	0101
Nottingham ....‡ a.	|	1750	|	1815	|	1851	|	1912	|	1950	|	2011	|	2050	|	2115	|	2148	|	2212	|	|	2326	|	0029	|
erby........................**119** a.	1733	...	1809f	...	1830	...	1909	...	1930	...	2009f	...	2030	...	2109	...	2134	...	2209	...	2239	2257	2350	2339	...	0112
hesterfield .... **119** ‡ a.	1751	...	1833	...	1848	...	1932	...	1950	...	2032	...	2049	...	2127	...	2153	...	2227	...	2257	...	...	2357	...	...
heffield .... **119** ‡ a.	1804	...	1848	...	1904	...	1946	...	2006	...	2047	...	2103	...	2141	...	2208	...	2242	...	2314	...	...	0013	...	...

	⚒	②–⑤	①	⑥	Ⓐ	⑥	Ⓐ	Ⓐ	⑥	Ⓐ	⚒	⚒	⚒	⑥	Ⓐ	⑥	Ⓐ L	⑥	Ⓐ	⑥	Ⓐ L	⑥	Ⓐ	⑥	Ⓐ	Ⓐ
heffield .... **119** ‡ d.		...	...	...	...	...	0458	...	0530	0530	...	0556	...	0633	0630	...	...	0700	0700	...	...	0731	0734	...	...	0757
hesterfield .... **119** ‡ d.		...	...	...	...	...	0510	...	0542	0543	...	0608	...	0645	0644	...	...	0712	0713	...	...	0743	0746	...	...	0811
erby........................**119** d.		0413	0440	0447	0447	0458	0530	...	0602	0602	...	0628	...	0705	0705	...	...	0732	0733	...	...	0804	0806	...	...	0832
Nottingham ....‡ d.		|	|	|	0514	0526	|	0549	|	|	0611	|	0649	|	|	0712	0712	|	|	0746	0748	|	|	0812	0811	|
ast Midlands Parkway.......d.		0424	0453	0500	0527	0536	0543	|	|	0615	0624	0641	0659	|	|	0724	0727	0745	|	|	0758	|	|	0824	0825	0845
ughborough......................d.		0431	0500	0508	0534	0543	0550	|	|	|	0632	0648	|	0719	0719	0732	|	0752	0750	|	|	|	0820	0832	|	0853
eicester...........................d.		0447j	0516j	0519	0547	0554	0602	0610	0623	0630	0643	0700	0713	0730	0731	0743	0743	0803	0801	0812	0813	0828	0831	0843	0842	0904
arket Harborough............d.		|	0529	0533	0600	0608	|	0624	0637	|	0656	|	0727	|	|	0757	0757	|	|	0826	0827	|	|	0857	0855	|
ettering.................. **170a** d.		0538	0539	|	0611	0618	|	0636	0647	|	0706	|	0737	|	|	0807	0808	|	|	0836	0837	|	|	0907	0913j	|
ondon St Pancras... **170a** a.		0636	0636	0627	0701	0704	0709	0735	0736	0739	0757c	0809	0827	0836	0838	0855	0856	0907	0909	0927	0927	0934	0939	0954	1006	1010

	⑥	⚒	⚒	⚒	⚒	⚒	⑥	Ⓐ	⚒	⚒	⚒	⑥	Ⓐ	⚒	⚒	⚒	⑥	Ⓐ	⚒	⚒	⚒	⑥	Ⓐ	⑥	Ⓐ	⚒
heffield .... **119** ‡ d.	0800	...	0835	...	0900	...	0929	0937	...	1000	...	1033	1037	...	1100	...	1130	1137	...	1200	...	1236	1237	...	...	1300
hesterfield .... **119** ‡ d.	0812	...	0849	...	0913	...	0941	0949	...	1013	...	1048	1049	...	1112	...	1142	1149	...	1212	...	1249	1249	...	...	1312
erby........................**119** d.	0832	...	0909	...	0932	...	1005j	1009	...	1032	...	1108	1110	...	1132	...	1208t	1209	...	1232	...	1309	1309	...	...	1332
Nottingham ....‡ d.	|	0850	|	0911	|	0950	|	|	1012	|	1050	|	|	1112	|	1150	|	|	1212	|	1250	|	|	1312	1312	|
ast Midlands Parkway.......d.	0845	|	|	0924	0945	|	|	|	1024	1045	|	|	|	1125	1145	|	|	|	1225	1245	|	|	|	1325	1325	1345
ughborough......................d.	0853	|	|	0932	0953	|	|	|	1032	1053	|	|	|	1132	1152	|	|	|	1232	1252	|	|	|	1332	1332	1352
eicester...........................d.	0904	0912	0930	0943	1004	1013	1027	1032	1043	1104	1112	1130	1133	1143	1204	1213	1231	1232	1243	1303	1313	1332	1332	1343	1345	1404
arket Harborough............d.	|	0926	|	0957	|	1026	|	|	1056	|	1125	|	|	1157	|	1226	|	|	1257	|	1326	|	|	1357	1358	|
ettering.................. **170a** d.	|	0936	|	1007	|	1036	|	|	1106	|	1136	|	|	1207	|	1236	|	|	1307	|	1336	|	|	1407	1408	|
ondon St Pancras... **170a** a.	1007	1027	1039	1055	1109	1127	1139	1136	1155	1209	1227	1239	1239	1255	1309	1327	1336	1339	1354	1409	1427	1436	1439	1454	1455	1509

	⑥	Ⓐ	⚒	⚒	⚒	⚒	⑥	Ⓐ	⑥	Ⓐ	Ⓐ	⑥	Ⓐ	⑥	⚒	⑥	Ⓐ	⚒	⚒	⑥	Ⓐ	⑥	Ⓐ	⑥	Ⓐ	Ⓐ
heffield .... **119** ‡ d.	...	...	1336	...	1400	...	1435	1437	...	...	1500	1501	...	...	1537	...	...	1600	...	1637	1637	...	...	1700	1701	...
hesterfield .... **119** ‡ d.	...	...	1349	...	1412	...	1449	1449	...	...	1512	1513	...	...	1549	...	...	1613	...	1649	1649	...	...	1712	1714	...
erby........................**119** d.	...	...	1409	...	1432	...	1510	1509	...	...	1532	1533	...	...	1609	...	...	1632	...	1710	1709	...	...	1732	1734	...
Nottingham ....‡ d.	1345	1350	|	1412	|	1449	|	|	1512	1512	|	|	1550	1550	|	1612	1611	|	1650	|	|	1711	1712	|	|	1750
ast Midlands Parkway.......d.	|	|	|	1424	1445	|	|	|	1524	1525	1545	1546	|	|	|	1624	1625	1645	|	|	|	1724	1725	1745	1748	|
ughborough......................d.	|	|	|	1432	1452	|	|	|	1532	1532	1552	1553	|	|	|	1632	1632	1653	|	|	|	1732	1732	1752	1755	|
eicester...........................d.	1413	1413	1431	1443	1504	1512	1532	1531	1543	1543	1603	1604	1612	1614	1630	1643	1643	1704	1713	1732	1730	1743	1745	1804	1806	1811
arket Harborough............d.	1426	1426	|	1456	|	1526	|	|	1556	1557	|	|	1625	1627	|	1656	1657	|	1726	|	|	1756	1758	|	|	1824
ettering.................. **170a** d.	1436	1437	|	1506	|	1536	|	|	1606	1607	|	|	1636	1637	|	1706	1707	|	1736	|	|	1806	1808	|	|	1834
ondon St Pancras... **170a** a.	1527	1526	1539c	1554	1609	1627	1636	1639	1654	1656	1709	1710	1728	1726	1740	1754	1806	1810	1827	1838	1841	1854	1905	1909	1910	1926

– From Lincoln (Table **184**).
– From Peterborough (Table **208**).
– Arrives 9 minutes earlier.
– Arrives 2208 on ⑥.

c – Arrives 3 minutes earlier on ⑥.
f – Departs 5–6 minutes later.
j – Arrives 5–6 minutes earlier.
n – Arrives 1459 on ⑥.

r – Arrives 3 minutes earlier on Ⓐ.
t – Arrives 1200.
v – Departs 7–9 minutes later.
y – Connects with train in previous column.

z – Arrives 2200.

‡ – For trains Nottingham - Sheffield and v.v. see Tables **171** and **206**.

170 SHEFFIELD, DERBY and NOTTINGHAM - LEICESTER - LONDON

Most trains convey 🍷 EM

	⑥	Ⓐ	⑥	Ⓐ	⑥	⚒	Ⓐ	⑥	Ⓐ	⑥	⑥	Ⓐ	⚒	⑥	Ⓐ	⑥	Ⓐ	⚒	⚒	⑥	Ⓐ	⑥	Ⓐ	⑥	⑥
Sheffield 119 ‡ d.	...	1732	1731	...	...	1800	...	...	1837	1837	...	...	1900	...	...	1934	1937	...	2000	...	...	2030	2037	...	2100
Chesterfield 119 ‡ d.	...	1745	1749	...	...	1812	...	...	1849	1849	...	...	1912	...	...	1946	1949	...	2012	...	...	2042	2050	...	2114
Derby 119 d.	...	1808	1810	...	...	1832	...	...	1909	1909	...	...	1932	...	...	2010	2010	...	2032	...	...	2102	2110	...	2135
Nottingham ‡ d.	1750	|	|	1810	1812	|	1850	1850	|	|	1912	1913	|	1950	1949	|	|	2011	|	2050	2048	|	...	2125	|
East Midlands Parkway d.	|	|	|	1823	1824	1845	|	|	|	|	1924	1926	1945	|	|	|	|	2023	2045	|	2102	2112	...	2137	2149
Loughborough d.	|	|	|	1830	1832	1852	|	|	|	|	1932	1933	1952	|	2004	|	|	2031	2052	|	2110	2119	...	2145	2157
Leicester d.	1813	1830	1833	1841	1843	1903	1911	1913	1930	1932	1943	1944	2003	2013	2015	2032	2033	2042	2104	2114	2123	2129	...	2156	2207
Market Harborough d.	1826	|	|	1855	1856	|	1925	1926	|	|	1956	1958	|	2026	2028	|	|	2056	|	2127	2137	...	...	2209	...
Kettering 170a d.	1836	|	|	1905	1906	|	1935	1936	|	|	2006	2008	|	2036	2038	|	|	2106	|	2137	2147	...	...	2219	...
London St Pancras 170a a.	1927	1938	1936	1955	1954	2007	2027	2027	2036	2039	2054	2054	2109	2126	2134	2138	2139	2156	2208	2234	2239	...	...	2316	...

	Ⓐ	Ⓐ	Ⓐ	Ⓐ	⑥2	⑥2	Ⓐ	⚒2	⑥	Ⓐ		⑦	⑦	⑦	⑦	⑦	⑦	⑦	⑦	⑦	⑦	⑦	⑦	⑦	⑦
Sheffield 119 ‡ d.	2101	...	2145	2156	2200	...	2229	...	2320	2330	⑦	...	...	0823	...	0926	...	...	1052	...	1152	...	1252	1331	...
Chesterfield 119 ‡ d.	2113	...	2201	2211	2214	...	2245	...	2332	2354		...	...	0835	...	0938	...	...	1105	...	1204	...	1304	1344	...
Derby 119 d.	2134	...	2220	2234	2236	...	2308	...	0006	0016		0757	...	0855	...	0959	...	...	1126	...	1225	...	1325	1406	...
Nottingham ‡ d.	|	2140	|	...	...	2233	...	2318	...	...		|	0821	|	0926	|	1016	1110	|	1209	|	1310	|	|	1410
East Midlands Parkway d.	2147	2156	2233	...	...	2250	...	2332	...	...		0810	0833	0908	0937	1013	1026	1122	1140	1221	1239	1323	1339	1416	1423
Loughborough d.	2154	|	2241	...	...	2259	...	2340	...	...		0817	0841	0915	0944	1021	1033	1130	1147	1229	1247	1330	1347	|	1430
Leicester d.	2206	2215j	2252	...	...	2322	...	2353	...	...		0829	0853	0927	0957	1033	1046	1144	1200	1242	1259	1343	1359	1432	1443
Market Harborough d.	|	2228	2305	...	...	...	...	...	...	...		0843	0907	0941	1011	1046	1059	1158	1213	1256	1312	1356	1412	|	1456
Kettering 170a d.	|	2240	2315	...	...	...	...	...	...	...		0853	0917	0951	1021	1056	1109	1208	|	1306	|	1406	|	|	1506
London St Pancras 170a a.	2316	2352	0023	...	...	...	...	...	...	...		0950	1015	1051	1121	1155	1210	1256	1308	1353	1408	1455	1508	1539	1556

	⑦	⑦	⑦	⑦	⑦	⑦	⑦	⑦	⑦	⑦	⑦	⑦	⑦	⑦	⑦	⑦	⑦	⑦	⑦	⑦	⑦	⑦	⑦	⑦	⑦
Sheffield 119 ‡ d.	1351	1432	...	1451	...	1531	...	1551	...	1628	...	1651	...	1728	...	1751	...	...	1851	...	1951	2028	...	...	2236
Chesterfield 119 ‡ d.	1404	1446	...	1504	...	1544	...	1604	...	1640	...	1703	...	1741	...	1803	...	...	1903	...	2003	2042	...	...	2248
Derby 119 d.	1425	1506	...	1528j	...	1606	...	1628j	...	1701	...	1725	...	1802	...	1826	...	...	1923	...	2025	2103	...	...	2322
Nottingham ‡ d.	|	|	1506	|	1547	|	1610	|	1647	|	1710	|	1745	|	1810	|	1845	1906	|	1959	|	|	2109	2150	...
East Midlands Parkway d.	1439	1516	1520	1542	1557	1616	1623	1642	1657	1712	1723	1739	1757	1813	1823	1839	1857	1919	1937	2012	2039	2117	2121	2202	...
Loughborough d.	1446	|	1528	1550	|	|	1630	1649	|	1719	1730	1746	|	|	1830	1847	|	1926	1944	2019	2046	2124	2129	2210	...
Leicester d.	1459	1532	1543	1602	1613	1632	1643	1702	1713	1732	1743	1802j	1813	1829	1843	1902	1913	1943t	1959	2032	2059	2136	2141	2221	...
Market Harborough d.	1512	|	1556	|	1626	|	1656	|	1726	|	1756	|	1826	1842	1856	|	1926	1956	|	2045	2112	2150	2154	...	...
Kettering 170a d.	|	|	1606	|	1636	|	1706	|	1736	|	1806	|	1836	|	1906	|	1936	2006	|	2055	|	2200	2205	...	...
London St Pancras 170a a.	1609	1639	1655	1709	1727	1739	1755	1809	1827	1839	1855	1909	1927	1939	1955	2009	2027	2055	2108	2155	2208	2303	2309	...	...

j – Arrives 5 minutes earlier. t – Arrives 1937. ‡ – For trains Sheffield - Nottingham see Tables **171** and **206**.

170a LONDON - KETTERING - CORBY

2nd class only EM

See Table **170** for other services London - Kettering and v.v.

km			Ⓐ	Ⓐ F	Ⓐ G	Ⓐ	Ⓐ G	Ⓐ	Ⓐ G	Ⓐ	Ⓐ	Ⓐ	Ⓐ	Ⓐ	Ⓐ	Ⓐ	Ⓐ	⊠	Ⓐ	Ⓐ	Ⓐ	Ⓐ	Ⓐ	Ⓐ
0	**London** St Pancras 170 d.	Ⓐ	0545	0559	0605	0617	0635	0647	0705	0718	0749	0818	0847	0915	0945	1015	1045		1545	1616	1647	1717	1747	1817
47	Luton ✈ Parkway d.		0607	|	|	0643	|	0709	|	0742	0811	0841	0912	0937	1007	1037	1107	and at	1608	1639	1709	1741	1812	1839
49	Luton d.		0610	|	|	0646	|	0712	|	0745	0814	0845	0915	0940	1010	1040	1110	the same	1611	1642	1712	1744	1815	1843
80	Bedford d.		0626	|	0639	0701	0711	0728	|	0800	0830	0901	0930	0956	1026	1056	1126	minutes	1627	1658	1728	1800	1830	1900
105	Wellingborough d.		0637	0642	|	0713	|	0739	0751	0811	0841	0912	0941	1007	1037	1107	1137	past each	1638	1709	1739	1811	1842	1911
116	Kettering 170 d.		0646	...	0653	0722	0726	0748	0757	0820	0849	0922	0951	1016	1046	1117	1146	hour until	1647	1718	1748	1820	1851	1920
128	**Corby** a.		0654	...	...	0730	...	0756	...	0828	0857	0930	0959	1024	1055	1125	1154		1655	1726	1756	1828	1859	1928

	Ⓐ A	Ⓐ	Ⓐ	Ⓐ		Ⓐ	Ⓐ	Ⓐ E	Ⓐ		⑥	⑥ F	⑥ G	⑥	⑥ G	⑥	⑥ G	⑥	⑥		⑥	⑥	⑥
London St Pancras 170 d.	1835	1847	1915	1945		2215	2247	2304	2354	⑥	0533	0600	0605	0608	0633	0646	0705	0715	0745		2115	2145	2218
Luton ✈ Parkway d.	|	1909	1937	2007	and at	2238	2316	2346	0033		0601	|	|	0630	|	0708	|	0737	0807	and at	2137	2207	2240
Luton d.	|	1912	1940	2010	the same	2241	2319	|	0036		0604	|	|	0633	|	0711	|	0740	0810	the same	2140	2210	2243
Bedford d.	|	1928	1956	2026	minutes	2256	2341	|	0101		0619	|	0638	0649	0706	0727	0739	0756	0826	minutes	2156	2228	2259
Wellingborough d.	|	1939	2007	2037	past each	2308	2354	0022	0112		0630	0642	|	0701	|	0738	0750	0807	0838	past each	2207	2240	2310
Kettering 170 d.	1938f	1949	2016	2047	hour until	2317	0003	0031	0122		0639	...	0652	0710	0720	0748	0756	0816	0846	hour until	2216	2248	2319
Corby a.	1947	1957	2026	2056		2325	0011	...	0131		0649	...	...	0720	...	0757	...	0824	0854		2224	2256	...

	⑥		⑦ G	⑦ F	⑦ G	⑦ F	⑦ G	⑦ G	⑦	⑦ G	⑦	⑦ G	⑦	⑦		⑦	⑦	⑦	⑦	⑦	⑦ E	⑦	⑦ G	⑦ E
London St Pancras 170 d.	2235	⑦	0900	0930	1005	1030	1100	1130	1214	1234	1314	1334	1414	1444		1914	1944	2014	2044	2114	2135	2212	2232	2300
Luton ✈ Parkway d.	|		0924	0953	1028	1053	1124	1154	1236	1257	1336	1357	1436	1506	and at	1936	2006	2036	2106	2136	2157	2236	2254	2330
Luton d.	|		0928	|	1031	|	1128	|	1239	|	1339	1400	1439	1509	the same	1939	2009	2039	2109	2139	|	2239	|	|
Bedford d.	2316	★	0942	1010	1045	1110	1142	1211	1255	1311	1355	1414	1455	1525	minutes	1955	2025	2055	2125	2155	2211	2255	2313	2359
Wellingborough d.	2335		0954	1022	1057	1122	1154	1222	1306	1323	1407	1426	1507	1537	past each	2006	2037	2107	2137	2207	2223	2307	2326	0011
Kettering 170 d.	...		1000	1028	1103	1128	1200	1228	1316	1329	1416	1432	1516	1547	hour until	2017	2045	2117	2145	2217	2229	2316	2332	0017
Corby a.	...		*1023*	*1108*	...	...	*1210*	*1238*	1324	*1356*	1424	*1454*	1525	1555		2025	...	2125	...	2225	...	2324	...	...

		Ⓐ	Ⓐ E	Ⓐ	Ⓐ	Ⓐ	Ⓐ	Ⓐ	Ⓐ	Ⓐ	Ⓐ A	Ⓐ	Ⓐ		Ⓐ	Ⓐ	Ⓐ	Ⓐ	Ⓐ	Ⓐ	Ⓐ	Ⓐ	Ⓐ	Ⓐ
Corby d.	Ⓐ	0432	...	0538	0610	0638	0709	0739	0808	0839	0848	0910	0938		1203	1239	1309	1339	1406	1440	1507	1540	1610	1640
Kettering 170 d.		0440	0538	0546	0618	0647	0717	0747	0816	0847	0913t	0919	0947	and at	1211	1247	1318	1347	1414	1448	1515	1548	1618	1648
Wellingborough d.		0448	|	0554	0626	0655	0725	0756	0825	0855	|	0927	0955	the same	1219	1255	1327	1355	1422	1456	1523	1556	1627	1656
Bedford d.		0507	|	0609	0640	0710	0740	0810	0839	0911	|	0940	1010	minutes	1238r	1310	1340	1410	1441	1510	1541	1610	1640	1712
Luton d.		0529	|	0625	0656	0726	0756	0825	0855	0927	|	0956	1025	past each	1255	1325	1356	1425	1456	1525	1556	1626	1656	1727
Luton ✈ Parkway d.		0532	0613	0628	0659	0729	0759	0828	0858	0930	|	0959	1028	hour until	1258	1328	1359	1428	1459	1528	1559	1629	1659	1730
London St Pancras 170 a.		0602	0636	0651	0724	0754	0824	0851	0921	0953	1006	1023	1052		1321	1351	1422	1451	1522	1551	1622	1653	1723	1753

	Ⓐ G	Ⓐ	Ⓐ F	Ⓐ	Ⓐ G	Ⓐ	Ⓐ G	Ⓐ	Ⓐ	Ⓐ	Ⓐ	Ⓐ	Ⓐ	Ⓐ G	Ⓐ		⑥	⑥	⊠	⑥	⑥	⑥ G	⑥	⑥ G
Corby d.	...	1703	...	1739	...	1806	...	1838	1909	1939	2010	2039	2142	...	2233	⑥	0510	0540		2040	2110	...	2140	*2201*
Kettering 170 d.	1707	1712	...	1748	1808	1815	1834	1846	1918	1948	2018	2048	2151	2240	2242		0519	0549	and at	2048	2119	2137	2148	2219
Wellingborough d.	|	1720	1754	1756	1815	1823	1841	1854	1927	1956	2027	2056	2159	|	2250		0527	0557	the same	2056	2128	|	2156	2227
Bedford d.	1726	1740v	|	1810	|	1840r	|	1909	1940	2010	2041	2110	2213	|	2304		0540	0610	minutes	2110	2141	2155	2210	|
Luton d.	|	1755	|	1826	|	1855	|	1924	1956	2025	2057	2126	2229	|	2322		0556	0626	past each	2125	2157	|	2225	|
Luton ✈ Parkway d.	|	1758	|	1829	|	1858	|	1927	1959	2028	2100	2129	2232	2316	2325		0559	0629	hour until	2128	2200	|	2228	|
London St Pancras 170 a.	1806	1823	1841	1852	1905	1921	1926	1950	2022	2051	2123	2152	2255	2352	2358		0623	0652		2151	2223	2234	2251	2316

	⑥		⑦ E	⑦ G	⑦ F	⑦ G	⑦ F	⑦ G	⑦	⑦	⑦	⑦	⑦	⑦		⑦	⑦	⑦ F	⑦	⑦ G		⑦	⑦ F	⑦ G
Corby d.	2240	⑦	...	...	...	*1000*	*1038*	...	1141	1227	1310	1341	1410	1440		1910	1940	...	2005	...	...	2110	*2140*	...
Kettering 170 d.	2248		0853	0917	0951	1021	1056	1109	1149	1235	1318	1349	1418	1448	and at	1918	1948	...	2018r	2055	...	2118	2200	2205
Wellingborough d.	...		0900	0924	0958	1029	1103	1116	1158	1244	1326	1357	1426	1456	the same	1926	1956	...	2026	2102	...	2126	2207	2213
Bedford d.	...		0913	0937	1011	1042	1116	1131	1210	1256	1339	1410	1439	1509	minutes	1940	2009	...	2039	2115	...	2139	2220	2227
Luton d.	...		|	0951	|	1057	|	|	1225	1312	1355	1425	1455	1525	past each	1956	2025	2044	2055	|	...	2155	2235	2242
Luton ✈ Parkway d.	...		0928	0955	1027	1100	1132	1147	1228	1315	1358	1428	1458	1528	hour until	1959	2028	|	2058	2131	...	2158	2238	2246
London St Pancras 170 a.	...		0950	1015	1051	1121	1155	1210	1252	1339	1422	1452	1522	1552		2023	2052	2108	2122	2155	...	2223	2303	2309

A – Conveys (12) London St Pancras - Melton Mowbray and v.v. (see panel).
E – To / from Derby (Table **170**).
F – To / from Sheffield (Table **170**).
G – To / from Nottingham (Table **170**).

d – ②–⑤ only.
f – Arrives 1927.

r – Arrives 4–5 minutes earlier.
t – Arrives 0857.
v – Arrives 1733.
★ – On ⑦ an additional train runs from Kettering to Corby at 0945.
⊠ – Timings may vary ± 2 minutes.
* – Connection by 🚌.

(LONDON -) CORBY - MELTON MOWBRAY

km		Ⓐ			Ⓐ	
	London St Pancras d.	1835	...	**Melton Mowbray** d.	0815	...
	Kettering d.	1938	...	Oakham d.	0827	...
0	**Corby** d.	1947	...	**Corby** d.	0848	...
23	Oakham a.	2006	...	Kettering a.	0857	...
43	**Melton Mowbray** a.	2017	...	**London** St Pancras a.	1006	...

170b NOTTINGHAM - WORKSOP

2nd class EM

The Robin Hood Line. *50km*. Journey: ± 69 minutes.

From Nottingham (trains call at Mansfield ± 31 minutes later): on ⚒ at 0516, 0625, 0725, 0800 **a** ⑥, 0825, 0859 **a** ⑥ and at the same times past each hour until 1559 **a** ⑥, 1625Ⓐ, 1627⑥, 1659 **a**, 1725, 1759 **a**, 1825, 1923 ⑥, 1925 Ⓐ, 2025, 2125, 2209 ⑥, 2222 **a** Ⓐ, 2258 **a** ⑥. On ⑦ at 0812 **a**, 0912 **a**, 1112 **a**, 1312 **a**, 1512 **a**, 1611 **a**, 1812 **a**, 1912 **a**, 2022 **a**.

From Worksop (trains call at Mansfield ± 33 minutes later): on ⚒ at 0536 ⑥, 0611 **b** Ⓐ, 0636, 0739, 0745 **b** Ⓐ, 0839, 0845 **b** ⑥ and at the same times past each hour until 1739, 1745 **b**, 1839, 1845 **b** ⑥, 1847 **b** Ⓐ, 1939, 2039, 2139, 2239, 0003 **b** Ⓐ. On ⑦ at 0900 **b**, 1002 **b**, 1200 **b**, 1400 **b**, 1559 **b**, 1701 **b**, 1900 **b**, 2108 **b**.

a – To Mansfield only. b – Starts from Mansfield.

NT 2nd class — NOTTINGHAM - SHEFFIELD - HUDDERSFIELD and LEEDS — 171

NOTTINGHAM - SHEFFIELD - LEEDS

km		⚒	⚒	⚒	⚒	⚒	⚒	⚒	⚒R	⚒	⚒L	⚒	⚒L	⚒	⚒L	♥⊡	⚒L	⚒	⑥L	ⒶL	⚒	⚒L	⚒	⚒L
0	**Nottingham** .170 206 d.	...	...	...	0521	...	...	0616	...	0718	...	0817	...	0917	...		...	1717	...	...	1817	...	1917	...
18	Langley Mill d.	...	...	...	|	...	...	0635	...	0737	...	0836	...	0936	...	and	...	1736	...	...	1836	...	1936	...
29	Alfreton 206 d.	...	...	...	|	...	...	0643	...	0745	...	0844	...	0944	...	at the	...	1744	...	...	1845	...	1945	...
45	Chesterfield .170 206 d.	...	...	...	0551	0626	...	0653	...	0758	...	0856	...	0955	...	same	...	1755	...	...	1856	...	1956	...
64	**Sheffield** .....170 206 a.	...	...	...	0616v	0643	...	0712	...	0816	...	0914	...	1013	...	minutes	...	1814	...	...	1914	...	2014	...
64	**Sheffield** .....192 193 d.	0528	0602	0619	...	0645	0704	0718	0745	0819	0848	0918	0947	1018	1045	past	1744	1818	1847	1849	1918	1945	2018	2046
70	Meadowhall ..192 193 d.	0534	0608	0625	...	0651	0710	0724	0753	0825	0855	0924	0954	1024	1052	each	1750	1824	1853	1855	1924	1951	2024	2052
90	Barnsley d.	0557	0630	0640	...	0705	0732	0740	0808	0840	0910	0940	1010	1039	1110	hour	1807	1840	1910	1910	1939	2010	2039	2109
107	Wakefield Kirkgate d.	0615	0650	0656	...	0723	0751	0757	0824	0857	0927	0956	1027	1055	1127	until	1825	1856	1927	1927	1955	2027	2055	2127
130	**Leeds** a.	0640	0725	0715	...	0744	0824	0815	0844	0915	0944	1015	1044	1114	1144		1844	1916	1945	1944	2014	2044	2114	2144

	⚒	⑥	Ⓐ	⚒	⑥	Ⓐ	⚒	⑦	⑦	⑦C	⑦	⑦	⑦	⑦	⑦	⑦	⑦	⑦	⑦	⑦	⑦	⑦	⑦	⑦	⑦
ottingham ..170 206 d.	2017	2112	2115	...	2226	2227	2308	...	...	...	...	1017	1118	1218	1318	1414	1517	1616	1719	1819	1919	...	2015	2133	2233
angley Mill d.	2036	2137	2140	...	2245	2246	2326	...	...	...	...	1036	1137	1237	1337	1433	1535	1634	1737	1837	1938	...	2034	2157	2257
lfreton 206 d.	2044	2145	2148	...	2253	2254	2334	...	...	...	...	1044	1145	1245	1345	1441	1543	1642	1745	1845	1946	...	2042	2205	2305
hesterfield ..170 206 d.	2055	2156	2158	...	2304	2304	2345	...	...	...	...	1055	1156	1256	1356	1453	1554	1653	1757	1856	1957	...	2055	2216	2316
heffield ......170 206 a.	2114	2215	2216	...	2319	2327	0004	...	...	...	...	1114	1214	1315	1414	1511	1611	1714	1815	1914	2015	...	2115	2234	2335
heffield ......192 193 d.	2118	2218	2218	2230	...	...	...	0839	0917	1017	1051	1117	1216	1317	1417	1516	1617	1717	1816	1917	2016	2047	2116	2244	...
leadowhall ..192 193 d.	2124	2224	2224	2236	...	...	...	0845	0923	1023	1057	1123	1223	1323	1423	1522	1623	1724	1822	1923	2023	2053	2122	2250	...
arnsley d.	2139	2239	2239	2258	...	...	...	0907	0938	1038	1112	1137	1237	1338	1437	1536	1637	1738	1836	1937	2037	2115	2136	2313	...
/akefield Kirkgate d.	2155	2255	2255	2319	...	...	...	0925	0958	1054	1133	1154	1257	1356	1455	1555	1654	1755	1853	1954	2054	2136	2153	2333	...
eeds a.	2215	2314	2317	2356	...	...	...	1000	1020	1114	1208	1214	1316	1415	1514	1614	1714	1815	1914	2016	2114	2210	2214	0007	...

	⚒	⚒	⚒	Ⓐ	⑥	⚒R	⚒L	⚒	⚒L	⚒	⚒L	⚒	♥	⚒	⚒L	⚒	⚒L	⚒	⚒L	⚒	⚒	⚒	⚒	⑥
eeds d.	...	...	...	...	...	...	0639	0708	0738	0804	0837	0909		1609	1638	1709	1738	1803	1838	1905	1932	2005	2032	2104
/akefield Kirkgate d.	...	...	...	...	...	...	0656	0727	0756	0823	0856	0925		1625	1656	1726	1756	1822	1858	1922	2003	2022	2103	2122
arnsley d.	...	*0526*	0551	...	...	...	0713	0743	0811	0839	0912	0941	and	1641	1712	1743	1813	1838	1914	1938	2022	2037	2122	2138
leadowhall ..192 193 d.	...	*0548*	0613	...	...	...	0727	0803f	0827	0854	0927	0957	at the	1657	1727	1757	1829	1856	1928	1957	2043	2051	2143	2155
heffield ......192 193 a.	...	*0557*	0622	...	...	...	0734	0810	0835	0904	0934	1004	same	1704	1734	1805	1838	1904	1937	2004	2052	2100	2152	2203
heffield ......170 206 d.	0514	0603	...	0642	0645	0703	...	0811	...	0906	...	1006	minutes	1706	...	1806	...	1906	...	2006	...	2104	...	2205
hesterfield ..170 206 d.	0530	0619	...	0659	0701	0718	...	0827	...	0922	...	1023	past	1722	...	1822	...	1922	...	2022	...	2120	...	2221
lfreton 206 d.	0543	0629	...	0710	0712	0729	...	0838	...	0933	...	1033	each	1733	...	1833	...	1933	...	2033	...	2130	...	2231
angley Mill d.	0551	0636	...	0718	|	0736	...	0845	...	0940	...	1040	hour	1740	...	1840	...	1940	...	2040	...	2137	...	2238
ottingham ..170 206 a.	0612	0700	...	0736	0740	0800c	...	0905	...	0959	...	1100	until	1759	...	1858	...	2000	...	2100	...	2159	...	2258

	Ⓐ	Ⓐ	⑥	⚒	⑥	Ⓐ	⑥	⚒	Ⓐ	⑦	⑦	⑦	⑦		⑦	⑦	⑦	⑦C	⑦	⑦	⑦	⑦	⑦	⑦
eeds d.	2104	...	...	2137	...	...	...	2232	2301	...	0832	0909	1009		1509	1609	1709	1809	1909	2009	2017	2106	2209	2219
/akefield Kirkgate d.	2126	...	...	2154	...	...	...	2303	2333	...	0903	0927	1026	and	1526	1626	1726	1826	1926	2026	2048	2128	2226	2252
arnsley d.	2142	...	...	2212	...	...	...	2321	2352	...	0921	0943	1042	at the	1542	1642	1742	1842	1942	2042	2106	2146	2241	2310
leadowhall ..192 193 d.	2156	...	...	2230	...	...	...	2342	0015	...	0942	0957	1056	same	1557	1657	1756	1857	1956	2055	2132f	2159	2257	2331
heffield ......192 193 a.	2203	...	...	2241	...	...	...	2351	0024	...	0949	1004	1104	minutes	1604	1706	1803	1904	2003	2103	2139	2206	2304	2338
heffield ......170 206 d.	2205	2238	2241	...	2256	2339	2342	...	...	0905	...	1008	1106	past	1605	1706	1805	1906	2006	2106	...	2208	*2330*	...
hesterfield ..170 206 d.	2221	2253	2255	...	2311	0003	2356	...	...	0921	...	1024	1122	each	1622	1722	1822	1922	2022	2122	...	2223	*2344*	...
lfreton 206 d.	2231	2304	2306	...	2322	|	|	...	...	0932	...	1035	1133	hour	1633	1733	1833	1933	2033	2133	...	2234	*2355*	...
angley Mill d.	2238	|	|	...	|	|	|	...	...	0940	...	1043	1140	until	1640	1740	1840	1940	2040	2141	...	2242	*0002*	...
ottingham ..170 206 a.	2257	2327	2331	...	2347	0038	0030	...	...	1001	...	1103	1201		1700	1800	1900	1959	2100	2201	...	2304	*0024*	...

SHEFFIELD - HUDDERSFIELD *'The Penistone Line'*

km		⚒	⚒	⚒		⚒	Ⓐ	⑥	⚒	⚒	⚒	⚒	⑦	⑦	⑦L	⑦L	⑦L	⑦L		⑦L	⑦	⑦	⑦	⑦
0	**Sheffield** ......192 193 d.	0537	0630	0735	and	1635	1735	1735	1835	1935	2035	2236	0937	1038	1138	1238	1338	1439	...	1537	1637	1740	1839	1939
6	Meadowhall ..192 193 d.	0543	0636	0741		1641	1741	1741	1841	1941	2041	2244	0944	1045	1144	1245	1344	1445	...	1544	1643	1746	1845	1945
26	Barnsley d.	0605	0701	0803	hourly	1703	1803	1803	1903	2003	2103	2306	1006	1107	1206	1307	1406	1502	...	1606	1703f	1808	1905f	2007
38	Penistone d.	0620	0717	0819		1719	1819	1820	1919	2019	2119	2326	1023	1124	1223	1324	1423	1519	...	1623	1720	1825	1922	2024
59	**Huddersfield** a.	0651t	0749t	0851t	until	1751t	1850t	1854t	1951t	2051t	2151t	2357t	1057	1158	1258	1357	1457	1552	...	1657	1754	1857	1955	2057

	⚒	⚒	⚒	⚒	⚒	⚒		⚒	⚒	⚒	⚒	⚒	⚒	⑦	⑦	⑦L	⑦L	⑦L	⑦L	⑦L	⑦L	⑦	⑦	⑦
uddersfield d.	0610	0712r	0812r	0912r	1012r	1112r	and	1712r	1812r	1912r	2012r	2112r	2249r	0910r	1015r	1119r	1216r	1319r	1415r	1515r	1615r	1715r	181r	1915r
enistone d.	0644	0743	0843	0943	1043	1143		1743	1843	1943	2043	2143	2323	0941	1047	1150	1247	1350	1446	1546	1647	1746	1848	1946
arnsley d.	0700	0800	0900	1000	1100	1200	hourly	1800	1900	2000	2100	2200	2339	0958	1103	1207	1304	1407	1503	1603	1704	1803	1905	2003
leadowhall . 192 193 d.	0721	0821	0921	1021	1121	1221		1821	1921	2021	2123	2221	0001	1022	1118	1228	1320	1428	1520	1626	1720	1826	1921	2024
heffield ..... 192 193 a.	0729	0829	0929	1029	1129	1228	until	1828	1930	2028	2131	2228	0009	1031	1126	1237	1328	1437	1529	1637	1729	1833	1930	2038

– To/from Carlisle (Table **173**).
– To/from Lincoln (Table **192**).
– From Retford (Table **192**).

c – Arrives 0756 on Ⓐ.
f – Arrives 5 minutes earlier.
r – Departs 3 minutes earlier from Oct. 6.

t – Arrives 3 minutes later from Oct. 6.
v – Arrives 0613 on Ⓐ.

♥ – Timings may vary ± 3 minutes
⊡ – Sheffield d. 1451 (not 1445), then Meadowhall d. 1457, Barnsley d. 1513, Wakefield d. 1528, Leeds a. 1548.

EM 2nd class — NOTTINGHAM - DERBY - MATLOCK — 172

km		⚒	⑥	Ⓐ	⑥	Ⓐ	Ⓐ	⑥	⚒	⑥	Ⓐ	⚒	⚒	⚒		⚒	⚒	Ⓐ	⑥	⑥	Ⓐ	Ⓐ	⑥	⚒	⚒	⑦
0	**Nottingham** .... ‡ d.	...	0542	...	0652	0653	0753	0754	0854	0954	0954	1054	1154	1254		1554	1654	1754	1754	1854	1856	1954	1954	2054	2154	...
26	**Derby** ‡ a.	...	0611	...	0723	0723	0823	0824	0924	1022	1023	1123	1224	1323	and	1624	1724	1823	1823	1921	1924	2021	2022	2126r	2223	...
26	**Derby** d.	0540	0630	0633	0724	0734	0836	0833	0933	1033	1036	1133	1233	1333		1633	1732	1824	1833	1933	1936	2022	2033	2136	2233	0756
34	Duffield ◧ d.	0547	0637	0640	0731	0741	0843	0840	0940	1040	1043	1140	1240	1340	hourly	1640	1739	1831	1840	1940	1943	2029	2041	2143	2240	0803
46	Whatstandwell . ◧ d.	0601	0651	0655	0746	0756	0857	0854	0954	1054	1058	1154	1255	1355		1655	1754	1846	1855	1955	1958	2044	2055	2157	2254c	0817
50	Cromford d.	0606	0657	0700	0751	0801	0903	0859	0959	1100	1103	1159	1300	1400	until	1700	1759	1851	1900	2000	2003	2049	2101	2202	2300c	0822
52	Matlock Bath ... ◧ d.	0609	0659	0703	0754	0804	0905	0902	1002	1103	1106	1202	1303	1403		1703	1802	1854	1903	2003	2006	2052	2104	2205	2303c	0825
53	**Matlock** ◧ a.	0614	0702	0706	0757	0807	0908	0905	1008	1106	1109	1207	1307	1407		1706	1807	1857	1906	2006	2009	2055	2107	2210	2306c	0828

	⑦	⑦	⑦	⑦		⑦	⑦	⑦	⑦	⑦
ottingham ...... ‡ d.	0930	1127	1330	1428		1729	1825	1923	2024	2122
erby ‡ a.	0957	1154	1358	1456	and	1757	1852	1950	2052	2149
erby d.	0959	1156	1359	1503		1806	1904	2004	2053	2153
uffield ◧ d.	1006	1203	1406	1510	hourly	1813	1911	2011	2100	2200
/hatstandwell . ◧ d.	1020	1217	1420	1524		1827	1925	2025	2114	2214
romford d.	1025	1222	1426	1530	until	1832	1930	2030	2120	2220
latlock Bath.... ◧ d.	1028	1225	1429	1533		1835	1933	2033	2123	2223
latlock ◧ a.	1031	1228	1432	1536		1838	1936	2036	2126	2226

	Ⓐ	⑥	⑥	⑥	Ⓐ	⚒	⚒	⑥	Ⓐ	⚒	⑥	Ⓐ	⚒
Matlock ◧ d.	0618	0619	0710	0810	0813	0913	1013	1113	1115	1213	1313	1315	1413
Matlock Bath..... ◧ d.	0620	0621	0712	0812	0815	0915	1015	1115	1118	1215	1315	1318	1415
Cromford d.	0623	0624	0715	0815	0818	0918	1018	1118	1121	1218	1318	1321	1418
Whatstandwell .. ◧ d.	0629	0630	0721	0821	0824	0924	1024	1124	1126	1224	1324	1326	1424
Duffield ◧ d.	0644	0645	0736	0836	0838	0939	1039	1139	1141	1239	1339	1341	1439
Derby a.	0651	0653	0745	0844	0846	0948	1048	1147	1149	1248	1347	1349	1448
Derby ‡ d.	0652	0654	0746	0847	0847	0950	1050	1150	1153	1250	1351	1351	1450
Nottingham ‡ a.	0722	0722	0824f	0916	0920	1024f	1125f	1216	1222	1317	1417	1419	1518

	⑥	Ⓐ	⑥	Ⓐ	⚒	⑥	Ⓐ	⚒	⑥	Ⓐ	⑥	Ⓐ	⑥	Ⓐ	⑥	Ⓐ	⑦	⑦	⑦	⑦	⑦	⑦	⑦		⑦	⑦	⑦
latlock ◧ d.	1513	1515	1613	1615	1713	1813	1814	1913	2013	2015	2115	2117	2213	2219	2313	2315	0839	1038	1237	1442	1541	1641	1741		2042	2144	2256
latlock Bath.... ◧ d.	1515	1517	1615	1617	1715	1815	1816	1915	2015	2017	2117	2119	2215	2221	2315	2317	0841	1040	1239	1444	1543	1643	1743	and	2044	2146	2258
romford d.	1518	1520	1618	1620	1718	1818	1819	1918	2018	2020	2120	2122	2218	2224	2318	2320	0844	1043	1242	1447	1546	1646	1746		2047	2149	2301
/hatstandwell . ◧ d.	1524	1526	1624	1626	1724	1824	1825	1924	2024	2026	2126	2128	2223	2230	2323	2326	0849	1048	1247	1452	1551	1651	1751	hourly	2052	2154	2306
uffield ◧ d.	1539	1541	1639	1640	1738	1839	1840	1938	2039	2041	2141	2143	2238	2245	2338	2340	0904	1103	1302	1508	1606	1706	1806		2107	2209	2323
erby a.	1546	1549	1646	1648	1746	1846	1848	1946	2046	2049	2148	2151	2246	2253	2346	2348	0911	1110	1309	1515	1613	1713	1815	until	2114	2216	2330
erby ‡ d.	1550	1551	1649	1650	1747	1850	1854	1948	2052	2100	2155	2152	*2259*	2254	2347	2349	0914	1112	1312	1516	1615	1715	1815		2116	2219	2332
ottingham ‡ a.	1626	1619	1717	1719	1817	1916	1925	2016	2122	2126	2225	2226	*2323*	2321	0014	0016	0941	1139	1339	1544	1641	1742	1843		2143	2245	2359

– Runs 4 minutes later on Ⓐ.
– Arrives 8 minutes earlier on Ⓐ.
– Arrives 2121 on Ⓐ.
– See Tables **117** and **155** for additional trains Nottingham - Derby and v.v.

◧ – Visitor attractions near these stations:
Duffield: Ecclesbourne Valley Railway (shares National Rail station). ✆ 01629 823076. www.e-v-r.com
Whatstandwell: Crich National Tramway Museum (1.6 km walk). ✆ 01773 854321. www.tramway.co.uk
Matlock Bath: Heights of Abraham (short walk to cable car). ✆ 01629 582365. www.heightsofabraham.com
Matlock: Peak Rail (shares National Rail station). ✆ 01629 580381. www.peakrail.co.uk

173 LEEDS - SETTLE - CARLISLE

All ⚒ trains convey 🍷 — 2nd class — NT

km		⚒ Ⓐ	⚒ ⑥	⚒	⚒ ⑥	⚒	⚒	⚒	⚒	⚒ ⑥	⚒	⚒	⚒	⚒ A	⑦	⑦ D	⑦	⑦	⑦	⑦	⑦ A
	London Kings Cross **180** d.	...	...	...	R	...	...	...	...	R	...	...	...	1803	...	🍷	...	...	...	...	1835
0	**Leeds** d.	0515	0620	0748	...	0920	1049	1318	1518	...	1648	1819	1949	2039	0909	1116	1232	1423	1622	1852	2101
27	**Keighley** 🚂 **174** ▷ d.	0542	0648	0812	...	0945	1113	1343	1543	...	1713	1842	2012	2101s	0939	1139	1255	1447	1647	1916	2119s
42	**Skipton** **174** ▷ d.	0600	0707	0826	...	0958	1127	1359	1558	...	1727	1856	2027	2119	0957	1152	1309	1503	1701	1933	2140
58	Hellifield **174** d.	0615	0721	0840	0954	1012	1141	1411	1612	1701	1741	1910	2042	...	1011	1204	1323	1517	1713	1945	...
66	**Settle** d.	0623	0729	0850	1003	1021	1151	1419	1620	1710	1749	1919	2051	...	1019	1213	1333	1526	1721	1953	...
76	Horton in Ribblesdale d.	0632	0738	0858	1012	1030	1159	1427	1629	1719	1758	1927	2059	...	1028	1221	1342	1535	1730	2002	...
84	Ribblehead d.	0640	0746	0906	1019	1038	1207	1435	1637	1726	1806	1935	2108	...	1036	1229	1351	1543	1738	2010	...
93	Dent d.	0649	0755	0916	...	1047	1217	1445	1646	...	1815	1945	...	...	1046	1239	1401	1553	1748	2020	...
99	Garsdale d.	0655	0801	0921	...	1053	1222	1450	1652	...	1821	1950	...	...	1052	1244	1407	1559	1753	2025	...
115	Kirkby Stephen d.	0707	0813	0934	...	1105	1235	1503	1704	...	1833	2003	...	...	1105	1256	1420	1612	1806	2038	...
132	Appleby d.	0720	0826	0947	...	1119	1248	1516	1717	...	1846	2015	...	...	1118	1309	1432	1624	1819	2051	...
149	Langwathby d.	0734	0840	1001	...	1133	1302	1530	1731	...	1900	2029	...	...	1132	1323	1446	1638	1833	2105	...
166	Armathwaite d.	0747	0853	1015	...	1146	1316	1543	1744	...	1913	2043	...	...	1146	1337	1500	1652	1847	2119	...
182	**Carlisle** a.	0802	0908	1030	...	1201	1331	1558	1759	...	1928	2058	...	...	1202	1352	1515	1708	1902	2139	...

	⚒ A	⚒ Ⓐ	⚒ ⑥	⚒ ⑥	⚒ Ⓐ	⚒ ⑥	⚒ ⑥	⚒	⚒	⚒	⚒	⚒ ⑥	⚒	⚒	⚒	⑦	⑦	⑦ E	⑦	⑦	⑦
Carlisle d.	...	0549	...	0753	0824	0927	R	1058	1336	1450	1618	R	1824	2013	...	0924	1223	1519	1607	1724	1911
Armathwaite d.	...	0603	...	0808	0838	0942	...	1112	|	1504	1632	...	1838	2027	...	0938	1237	1534	|	1738	1925
Langwathby d.	...	0617	...	0822	0852	0955	...	1126	|	1518	1646	...	1852	2041	...	0952	1251	1548	|	1752	1939
Appleby d.	...	0631	...	0836	0906	1010	...	1140	1412	1533	1701	...	1906	2055	...	1007	1306	1603	1644	1808	1954
Kirkby Stephen d.	...	0644	...	0849	0919	1024	...	1154	1426	1547	1715	...	1920	2108	...	1021	1319	1617	1658	1821	2007
Garsdale d.	...	0658	...	0903	0933	1037	...	1207	1440	1600	1728	...	1933	2122	...	1034	1333	1629	|	1835	2021
Dent d.	...	0703	...	0908	0938	1042	...	1212	|	1605	1733	...	1938	|	...	1040	1338	1635	|	1840	2026
Ribblehead d.	...	0712	0713	0918	0947	1052	1108	1222	1453	1615	1743	1805	1948	|	2145	1049	1348	1644	|	1850	2036
Horton in Ribblesdale d.	...	0719	0719	0925	0954	1058	1114	1228	|	1621	1749	1812	1954	|	2151	1056	1355	1651	|	1857	2043
Settle d.	...	0727	0727	0933	1002	1106	1122	1236	1506	1630	1758	1821	2002	2146	2159	1104	1403	1700	1735	1905	2051
Hellifield **174** d.	...	0736	0736	0941	1010	1114	1129	1244	1513	1639	1807	1828	2011	|	2208	1113	1412	1709	1742	1912	2100
Skipton **174** ▷ a.	0656	0752	0752	0958	1027	1129	...	1259	1530	1655	1823a	...	2027	2207	2225	1130	1428	1724	1757	1928	2116
Keighley 🚂 **174** ▷ a.	0709u	0805	0807	1009	1039	1139	...	1310	1541	1709	1839	...	2039	2222	2241	1140	1440	1738	1809	1940	2128
Leeds **174** ▷ a.	0733	0834	0835	1034	1108	1205	...	1335	1606	1736	1908	...	2106	2250	2311	1206	1507	1804	1835	2006	2155
London Kings Cross **180** a.	0959r	...	...	...	...	...	...	...	...	...	...	...	...	...	...	...	...	...	...	...	...

Local trains **Bradford Forster Square - Skipton** and v.v. *30 km.* Journey: ± 38 minutes. Trains call at **Keighley** (± 22 minutes later from Bradford, ± 14 minutes from Skipton).
From Bradford Forster Square: On ⚒ at 0603, 0641, 0711, 0741, 0810, 0836, 0908, 0941, 1011 and hourly until 1511, 1541 and half-hourly until 2011, 2048, 2120, 2211, 2311; on ⑦ at 0948 and hourly until 2248.
From Skipton: On ⚒ at 0604, 0634, 0709, 0737, 0820, 0834, 0904, 1004, 1104, 1204, 1310, 1405, 1434 and half-hourly until 1734, 1803, 1841, 1905, 1934, 2004, 2034, 2133, 2234; on ⑦ at 0844, 0942 and hourly until 2042, 2139.

Trains **Leeds - Bradford Forster Square** and v.v. *22km.* Journey: ± 25 minutes.
From Leeds: On ⚒ at 0630, 0711, 0742, 0812, 0842, 0912, 0931‡, 0942 and in the same pattern every **two** hours until 1612, 1641, 1709, 1731‡, 1736, 1812, 1843, 1859‡, 1912, 2107‡Ⓐ, 2153‡⑥; on ⑦ at 0836, 0941, 1041, 1139, 1241, 1341, 1441, 1541, 1633‡, 1641, 1744, 1841, 1942, 2041, 2142, 2200‡, 2241.
From Bradford Forster Square: On ⚒ at 0558, 0630‡, 0655, 0729, 0754, 0832, 0843‡, 0902, 0930, 1000, 1030, 1100, 1116‡, 1130 and in the same pattern every **two** hours until 1900, 1915‡, 1930; on ⑦ at 0913, 1013, 1025‡, 1113 and hourly until 1713, 1731‡, 1814, 1913, 2013, 2113, 2213, 2315.

Other local trains **Leeds - Skipton** and v.v. Journey: ± 45 minutes. Trains call at **Keighley** (± 25 minutes later from Leeds, ± 14 minutes from Skipton).
From Leeds: On ⚒ at 0515Ⓐ, 0626, 0656, 0723, 0752, 0825, 0856, 0926, 0956, 1026, 1056, 1126, 1155, 1226 and half-hourly until 1656, 1719, 1742, 1755, 1826 and half-hourly until 2256, 2320; on ⑦ at 1016, 1126, 1157, 1216, 1316, 1416, 1516, 1612, 1716 and hourly until 2116, 2220, 2323.
From Skipton: On ⚒ at 0544, 0618, 0640, 0701, 0716, 0730, 0744, 0809, 0845, 0917 and half-hourly until 1617, 1645, 1717, 1746, 1817 and half-hourly until 2117, 2149, 2247⑥, 2249Ⓐ; on ⑦ at 0834, 0912 and hourly until 1512, 1607, 1612, 1714, 1812, 1912, 2012, 2123, 2212, 2315.

A – Conveys (12) and 🍷.
D – From Sheffield (Table 171).
E – To Nottingham (Table 171).
R – To/from Rochdale (Table **159**).

a – Departs 1829.
r – Arrives 0950 on ⑥.
s – Calls to set down only.
u – Calls to pick up only.

‡ – From/to **London** Kings Cross (Table **180**) conveys (12) and 🍷.
▷ – See panels below main table for other local services, also for Skipton - Bradford and v.v. and Leeds - Bradford Forster Square and v.v.

🚂 – Keighley and Worth Valley Railway (Keighley - Haworth - Oakworth - Oxenhope, *8 km*). ✆ 01535 645214. www.kwvr.co.uk

174 LEEDS - LANCASTER - MORECAMBE - HEYSHAM

2nd class — NT

km	km		⚒ ⑥	⚒ Ⓐ	⚒ A	⚒	⚒	⚒	⚒ Ⓐ	⚒ ⑥	⚒ Ⓐ	⚒ ⑥	⚒	⚒	⚒	⑦	⑦	⑦	⑦	⑦	⑦	⑦
0	0	**Leeds** **173** d.	...	...	*0626*	0819	...	1018	...	...	1218	1218	1418	1726	1918	0831	1033	...	...	1329	1532	1731
27	27	Keighley 🚂 **173** d.	...	...	0704	0842	...	1043	...	...	1243	1243	1443	1753	1943	0859	1056	...	...	1352	1555	1754
42	42	Skipton **173** d.	0519	0522	0725	0856	...	1057	...	...	1257	1257	1458	1810	2000	0917	1110	...	...	1406	1609	1808
58	58	Hellifield **173** d.	0534	0537	0740	0910	...	1111	...	...	1311	1311	1513	1824	2014	0931	1124	...	...	1420	1623	1822
66	66	Giggleswick d.	0544	0547	0750	0920	...	1121	...	...	1321	1321	1523	1834	2025	0941	1134	...	...	1431	1634	1833
82	82	Bentham d.	0600	0602	0805	0935	...	1136	...	...	1336	1336	1537	1849	2040	0956	1149	...	...	1445	1648	1847
103	103	Carnforth **159** d.	0621	0622	0827	0956	...	1157	...	...	1357	1403g	1603g	1915g	2106g	1016	1210	...	...	1507	1710	1909
113		**Lancaster** ✣ **159** a.	0630	0631	0835	1005b	...	1206h	1241	1244	1408	1411	1611f	1924a	2115	1026	1220	1230	...	1518h	1721	1920
120	112	Morecambe ✣ a.	*0725*	*0725*	*0852*	1027	...	1222	1252	1255	1423	1425	1633	1952	*2145*	1040	...	1241	...	1534	1734	1933
127	119	**Heysham** Port a.	...	...	...	...	...	...	1310	1313	...	...	...	...	...	...	...	1300	...	...	...	...

	⚒	⚒	⚒	⚒ Ⓐ	⚒ ⑥	⚒	⚒	⚒ ⑥	⚒ Ⓐ	⚒	⚒ Ⓐ	⚒ ⑥	⚒ ⑥	⚒ Ⓐ	⑦	⑦	⑦	⑦	⑦	⑦	⑦
Heysham Port d.	...	...	...	...	...	1320	...	...	...	...	...	...	...	...	...	1304	...	...	...	...	...
Morecambe ✣ d.	*0557*	*0901*	1032	1232	1233	1338	1433	1732	1732	...	2005	2010	*2058*	*2056*	1049	1322	...	1539	...	1738	2003
Lancaster ✣ **159** d.	0648	0941	1046	1246	1248j	1349	1447	1746	1746	...	2030c	2030d	2131	2131	1103	1333	1344	1552	...	1751	2018
Carnforth **159** d.	0658	0951	1056	1256	1258	...	1457	1756	1756	...	2040	2040	2143	2143	1114	...	1354	1603	...	1801	2028
Bentham d.	0718	1011	1116	1316	1318	...	1517	1815	1815	...	2100	2100	2202	2202	1134	...	1414	1622	...	1821	2048
Giggleswick d.	0734	1027	1132	1331	1333	...	1533	1830	1831	...	2116	2116	2218	2218	1149	...	1429	1637	...	1837	2103
Hellifield **173** d.	0745	1039	1142	1342	1343	...	1543	1840	1842	...	2126	2126	2228	2228	1200	...	1440	1648	...	1848	2115
Skipton **173** a.	0802	1056	1158	1358	1359	...	1559	1857	1859	...	2142	2142	2244	2246	1217	...	1456	1704	...	1904	2132
Keighley 🚂 **173** a.	0817	1109	1209	1410	1410	...	1610	1909	1909	...	2155	2155	*2301*	*2303*	1232	...	1508	1718	...	1916	2143
Leeds **173** a.	0843	1133	1239	1438	1437	...	1638	1935	1935	...	2222	2222	*2332*	*2336*	1304	...	1535	1746	...	1945	2211

A – From Bradford Forster Square (d. 0641).

a – Departs 1940.
b – Departs 1016.
c – Arrives 2015.
d – Arrives 2020.
f – Departs 1622.
g – Arrives 5–6 minutes earlier.
h – Departs 5 minutes later.
j – Arrives 1243.

🚂 – Keighley and Worth Valley Railway (Keighley - Haworth - Oakworth - Oxenhope, *8 km*). ✆ 01535 645214. www.kwvr.co.uk

✣ – Full service **Lancaster - Morecambe** and v.v.: **From Lancaster**: On ⚒ at 0519, 0620, 0714, 0755, 0841, 0922, 1016, 1100, 1127, 1211, 1241Ⓐ, 1244⑥, 1359, 1412Ⓐ, 1414⑥, 1438⑥, 1450Ⓐ, 1523, 1622, 1644, 1712, 1804, 1827, 1916, 1940, 2034, 2134, 2204, 2237Ⓐ; on ⑦ at 1028, 1130, 1230, 1339, 1427, 1523, 1627, 1723, 1814, 1922, 2030, 2132.
From Morecambe: On ⚒ at 0557, 0659, 0735, 0821, 0901, 0941, 1032, 1115, 1142, 1232, 1338, 1421, 1433, 1505, 1540, 1638, 1659, 1732, 1821, 1842, 1934, 2005Ⓐ, 2010⑥, 2056Ⓐ, 2058⑥, 2148, 2220Ⓐ, 2221⑥, 2252Ⓐ; on ⑦ at 1049, 1203, 1322, 1402, 1442, 1539, 1651, 1738, 1829, 2003, 2056, 2200.

175 LEEDS - HARROGATE - YORK

2nd class — NT

See Table **180** for through services London - Harrogate and v.v. See Tables **119** and **188** for direct services Leeds - York and v.v.

km		⚒	⚒	Ⓐ	⑥	⚒	⚒	⚒	⚒	⚒	⚒	and at	⚒	⚒	⚒	⚒	Ⓐ	⑥	⚒	⚒	⚒	⚒	⚒	⚒	⚒
0	**Leeds** d.	0605	0623	0633	0633	0659	0715	0732	0801	0829	0858	the same	1629	1659	1730	1739	1749	1749	1809	1829	1859	1929	2006	2029	2129
29	**Harrogate** d.	0642	0652	0709	0709	0735	0752	0808	0837	0905	0934	minutes	1705	1735	1806	1816	1828f	1825	1846	1905	1935	2005	2042	2105	2205
36	Knaresborough d.	0652	...	0717	0718	0743	...	0817	0846	0914	0944	past each	1714	1744	1815	1826	1841	1841t	1855	1915	1944	2014	2051	2114	2213
62	**York** a.	0720	...	0746	0751	0811	...	0846	0914	0944	1013*	hour until	1744	1811	1845	...	1915r	1909	...	1945	2011	2044	2120	2145	2240

	⚒	⚒	⑦	⑦	⑦	⑦	and at	⑦	⑦	⑦	⑦	⑦	⑦
Leeds d.	2239	2339	0903	0937	1006	1036	the same	2006	2036	2105	2136	2227	2331
Harrogate d.	2316	0018	0941	1012	1042	1112	minutes	2042	2112	2142	2212	2303	0007
Knaresborough d.	...	...	0950	1021	1051	1121	past each	2051	2122	2152	2222	...	...
York a.	...	...	1020	1059	1123*	1153*	hour until	2122	...	2222	...	...	...

	⚒	⚒	⚒	⚒	⚒	⚒	⚒
York d.	...	...	...	...	0648	0707	...
Knaresborough d.	...	...	...	0654	0714	0736	...
Harrogate d.	0607	0633	0653	0704	0725	0745	0805
Leeds a.	0644	0710	0726	0741	0802	0823	084

	⚒	⚒	⚒	⚒	⚒	⚒	and at	⚒	⚒	Ⓐ	⑥	⚒	⚒	⑦	⑦	⑦	⑦	⑦	⑦	and at	⑦	⑦	⑦	⑦
York d.	0741	0812	...	0842	0910	0942	the same	1943	2012	2110	2110	2211	2243	...	...	0947	...	1047‡	1112‡	the same	2015	2046	2145	...
Knaresborough d.	0807	0837	0903	0912	0936	1007	minutes	2008	2037	2135	2137	2236	2309	...	...	1012	1041	1110	1141	minutes	2041	2112	2212	...
Harrogate d.	0817	0847	0913	0923	0946	1017	past each	2018	2046	2145	2148	2246	2319	0922	0952	1022	1052	1122	1151	past each	2052	2123	2222	231
Leeds a.	0853	0922	0949	0958	1024	1052*	hour until	2055	2122	2220	2224	2322	2355	0958	1029	1058	1128	1159	1228	hour until	2128	2159	2258	235

f – Arrives 1823. r – Arrives 1909 on ⑥. t – Arrives 1834. * – Arrivals may vary ± 4 minutes. ‡ – Departures from York may vary ± 4 minute

EM 2nd class PETERBOROUGH - LINCOLN - DONCASTER 176

km			Ⓐ	Ⓐ	ⒶR	Ⓐ		Ⓐ	Ⓐ	Ⓐ	Ⓐ	Ⓐ	Ⓐ	Ⓐ	Ⓐ		ⒶR	Ⓐ		⑥	⑥	⑥	⑥
0	**Peterborough** 180 d.	Ⓐ	0632	0731	0837	1028	...	1228	1320	1413	1511	1626	1710	1818	1926	...	2105	2311	⑥	0639	0737	0837	0936
27	Spalding d.		0652	0751	0856	1050	...	1247	1341	1440f	1532	1646	1729	1838	1946	...	2124	2333		0658	0756	0856	0956
57	Sleaford d.		0714	0813	0921	1117	...	1316	1406	1506f	1554	1709	1750	1906f	2008	...	2146	|		0720	0819	0918	1018
91	**Lincoln** 180 192 d.		0743	0846	0952	1148	...	1348	1435	1537	1623	1742	1820	1937	2037	...	2215	0018		0750	0851	0947	1049
117	Gainsborough Lea Road 192 d.		...	0908	...	1209	...	1414r	...	...	...	1803	...	1959	...	...	...	...		...	0912	...	1110
151	**Doncaster** a.		...	0934	...	1241	...	1442	...	...	...	1829	...	2025	...	...	...	...		...	0939	...	1135

	⑥	⑥	⑥		⑥	⑥	⑥	⑥	⑥
Peterborough 180 d.	1202	1400	1528	...	1642	1829	1926	2052	...
Spalding d.	1222	1420	1548	...	1701	1849	1946	2111	...
Sleaford d.	1244	1442	1610	...	1723	1911	2008	2133	2218
Lincoln 180 192 d.	1315	1514	1642	...	1755	1944r	2037	2203	2248
Gainsborough Lea Road 192 d.	1336	1535	...	...	...	2006	...	...	...
Doncaster a.	1404	1603	...	...	...	2033	...	...	...

		Ⓐ	ⒶR	Ⓐ		Ⓐ	Ⓐ	Ⓐ	Ⓐ
Doncaster d.	Ⓐ	...	...	...	...	0947	...	...	1248
Gainsborough Lea Road 192 d.		...	...	...	...	1012	...	...	1313
Lincoln 180 192 d.		0612	0709	0803	...	1036	1137	1234	1336
Sleaford d.		0643	0740	0835	...	1106	1207	1304	1407
Spalding d.		0704	0801	0856	...	1127	1228	1325	1430
Peterborough 180 a.		0724	0819	0921	...	1149	1248	1345	1453

	Ⓐ	Ⓐ	Ⓐ		Ⓐ	Ⓐ	Ⓐ		Ⓐ		⑥	⑥R	⑥	⑥	⑥		⑥	⑥	⑥	⑥	⑥	⑥	⑥
Doncaster d.	...	1455	...	...	...	...	1847	...	2049	⑥	...	...	...	0945	...	...	1145	...	1414	1615	...	...	2047
Gainsborough Lea Road 192 d.	...	1520	...	...	...	...	1912	...	2113		...	...	...	1009	...	...	1210	...	1439	1640	...	...	2112
Lincoln 180 192 d.	1436	1544	1633	...	1753	1835	1936	...	2137		0610	0719	0807	1031	1033	...	1235	1403	1502	1704	1800	1934	2135
Sleaford d.	1506	1615	1709	...	1824	1906	2009	...	2208		0640	0749	0838	...	1104	...	1305	1434	1533	1735	1833	2098f	2205
Spalding d.	1527	1636	1728	...	1845	1927	2030	...	2229		0701	0811	0859	...	1125	...	1326	1455	1554	1756	1854	2030	...
Peterborough 180 a.	1550	1657	1750	...	1905	1949	2049	...	2251		0720	0829	0918	...	1144	...	1347	1514	1613	1816	1914	2049	...

R – To/from Newark North Gate (Table **189**). **f** – Arrives 5–6 minutes earlier. **r** – Arrives 4 minutes earlier.

NT 2nd class SHEFFIELD - HULL - BRIDLINGTON - SCARBOROUGH and YORK - HULL 177

SHEFFIELD - HULL - SCARBOROUGH

km			⚒	⚒	⚒	⚒	⚒	⚒	Ⓐ	⑥	⚒	⚒	⚒	⚒	⚒Y	⚒	⚒Y	⚒		⚒	⚒Y	⚒Z	⚒Y	Ⓐ	⑥
0	**Sheffield** 193 d.	⚒	...	...	...	...	0542	...	0652	0655	...	0756	...	0856	...	0957	...	1056		1757	...	1857	...	1957	1957
6	Meadowhall 193 d.		...	...	...	...	0548	...	0658	0703	...	0802	...	0902	...	1003	...	1102	★	1803	...	1903	...	2003	2003
30	**Doncaster 181** 193 d.		...	...	...	...	0613	...	0728f	0726	...	0823	...	0924	...	1024v	...	1123		1826	...	1924	...	2024	2029j
58	Goole 181 d.		...	...	...	...	0638	...	0747	0746	...	0844	...	0943	...	1048	...	1142	and	1847	...	1942	...	|	|
	Selby 181 188 d.		...	...	...	...	|	...	|	|	...	|	...	|	1015	|	1113	|	at the	|	1915	|	2013	2041	2048
79	Brough 181 d.		...	...	...	...	0702	...	0802	0801	...	0900	...	0959	1041	1104	1139	1159	same	1903	1941	1959	2041	2101	2107
95	**Hull** 181 188 a.		...	...	...	...	0722	...	0818	0816	...	0917	...	1013	1054	1117	1153	1215	minutes	1917	1954	2013	2054	2117	2120
0	**Hull** △ 181 d.		0533	0558	0614	0638	0725	0745	0823	0823	0900	0921	1000	1020	1100	1121	1200	1222	past	1922	1958	2020	2100	...	...
13	Beverley △ 181 d.		|	0612	0628	0652	0739	0759	0837	0837	0914	0935	1014	1034	1114	1135	1214	1236	each	1936	2012	2034	2114	...	...
31	Driffield △ d.		|	0626	0645	0706	0753	0813	0849	0849	0928	0947	1028	1046	1128	1147	1230	1248	hour	1948	2028	2046	2128	...	...
50	**Bridlington** △ d.		0610	0645	0702	0730a	0812	0830	0905	0905	0945	1003	1045	1102	1145	1203	1247	1304	until	2004	2045	2103	2145	...	...
71	Filey d.		0630	...	...	0752	0834	...	0927	0927	...	1025	...	1124	...	1227	...	1326		2027	...	2125t	...	...	...
87	**Scarborough** a.		0647	...	...	0810	0851	...	0944	0944	...	1042	...	1141	...	1243	...	1343		2044	...	2141t	...	...	...

	Ⓐ	⑥	⑥	⚒	⚒		⑦	⑦b	⑦	⑦	⑦	⑦	⑦	⑦	⑦	⑦	⑦		⑦	⑦	⑦	⑦	⑦	⑦	⑦	⑦
Sheffield 193 d.	2056	2057	...	2157	2259	⑦	...	...	0804	0836	0925	1025	1134	1225	1324	1427	1524	...	1625	1724	1825	1925	2026	2126	...	2225
Meadowhall 193 d.	2102	2103	...	2203	2305		...	...	0810	0843	0931	1031	1141	1233	1330	1433	1530	...	1631	1730	1831	1931	2032	2132	...	2231
Doncaster. 181 193 d.	2123	2125	...	2225	2328		...	...	0842	0905	0952	1054	1202	1257	1353	1500j	1553	...	1655	1800j	1855	1953	2055	2158	2215	2252
Goole 181 d.	2145	2143	...	2244	2349		...	...	0908	0924	1016a	1114	1222	1316	1412	1519	1612	...	1719	1821	1914	2012	2116	2218	2241	2316a
Brough 181 d.	2200	2159	...	2302	0002		...	...	0926	0939	1031	1129	1239	1332	1427	1534	1627	...	1735	1837	1931	2028	2132	2233	2258	2336
Hull 181 a.	2213	2212	...	2316	0018		...	...	0946	0952	1044	1143	1254	1345	1441	1547	1640	...	1748	1850	1944	2041	2145	2246	2317	2354
Hull △ 181 d.	2216	...	2216	*2326*	...		0835	0934	...	1000	1048	1157	1305	1349	1446	1600	1650	1718	1759	1906	1949	2047	...	...	...	...
Beverley △ 181 d.	2230	...	2230	*2340*	...		0849	0946	...	1015	1102	1213	1320	1407	1503	1616	1707	1732	1815	1920	2004	2102	...	...	...	...
Driffield △ d.	2244	...	2244	...	...		0905	0958	...	1030	1117	1228	1334	1422	1518	1631	1722	1747	1830	1935	2018	2117	...	...	...	...
Bridlington △ d.	2301	...	2301	...	...		0922	1013	...	1052	1134	1253j	1351	1442	1540a	1653a	1744a	1805	1852a	1952	2036	2134	...	...	...	...
Filey d.	...	...	...	...	...		0944	1032	...	1116	1156	1317	1416	1516f	1620r	1718	1816j	...	1916	2016	...	...	...	...	...	...
Scarborough a.	...	...	...	...	...		1003	1047	...	1132	1214	1333	1432	1532	1636	1736	1832	...	1932	2032	...	...	...	...	...	...

		⚒	⚒	⚒	⚒	⚒	⚒	⚒Y	⚒	⚒Y	⚒	⚒Y		⚒	⚒Y	⚒	⚒Y	⚒	⚒Y	⑥	Ⓐ	⚒Y	⚒	⚒Y	⚒
Scarborough d.	⚒	...	...	...	...	...	0653	...	...	0815	0901	...		1601	...	1702	...	1800	...	1858	1858	...	2000	...	2100t
Filey d.		...	...	...	...	...	0708	...	...	0830	0916	...	★	1616	...	1717	...	1816	...	1914	1914	...	2017	...	2115t
Bridlington △ d.		...	...	0628	...	0706	0735a	0755	0839	0854	0940	0956		1640	1656	1740	1755	1839	1856	1938	1938	2000	2040	2058	2137
Driffield △ d.		...	...	0644	...	0721	0751	0810	0852	0910	0954	1011	and	1653	1711	1754	1811	1855	1911	1952	1952	2015	2054	2113	2153
Beverley △ 181 d.		...	...	0658	0715	0738	0806	0827	0905	0924	1006	1026	at the	1706	1728	1806	1827	1907	1926	2004	2004	2030	2106	2128	2208
Hull △ 181 a.		...	...	0714	0731	0753	0822	0842	0921	0940	1021	1041	same	1721	1743	1822	1842	1922	1941	2019	2019	2045	2121	2143	2225
Hull 181 188 d.		0518	0631	0721	...	...	0829	0846	0926	0947	1023	1047	minutes	1725	1750	1825	1847	1925	1945	2022	2023	2050	2125	2148	...
Brough 181 d.		0530	0643	0733	...	...	0841	0858	0938	0959	1035	1059	past	1737	1802	1837	1859	1937	1957	2034	2035	2102	2137	2205	...
Selby 181 188 d.		|	|	|	...	...	|	0925	|	1024	|	1126	each	|	1827	|	1927	|	2022	2054	2055	2127	|	2230	...
Goole 181 d.		0549	0658	0749	...	...	0856	...	0954	...	1050	...	hour	1754	...	1854	...	1953	...	|	|	...	2152	...	...
Doncaster. 181 193 d.		0615	0720	0822	...	...	0918	...	1020	...	1116	...	until	1821	...	1919	...	2020	...	2119	2118a	...	2215	...	...
Meadowhall 193 d.		0633	0739	0840	...	...	0940	...	1038	...	1137	...		1840	...	1940	...	2038	...	2137	2139	...	2234	...	...
Sheffield 193 a.		0642	0747	0848	...	...	0949	...	1048	...	1148	...		1848	...	1949	...	2046	...	2145	2150	...	2244	...	...

	⑤⑥	①–④	⚒	⚒	⚒		⑦	⑦	⑦	⑦	⑦	⑦	⑦	⑦	⑦	⑦	⑦	⑦	⑦	⑦	⑦	⑦	⑦	⑦	⑦	⑦
Scarborough d.	...	2118	...	2158t	...	⑦	...	...	...	1013	1056	...	1201	1301	1401	1501	1601	1701	...	1801	1901	2000	...	...	...	2126
Filey d.	...	2133	...	2213t	...		...	...	...	1028	1111	...	1216	1316	1416	1516	1616	1716	...	1816	1916	2015	...	...	...	2141
Bridlington △ d.	2156	2157	...	2237	2306		...	0943	...	1052	1134	...	1240	1340	1440	1540	1640	1740	1823	1840	1940	2039	...	...	2144	2203
Driffield △ d.	2211	2212	...	2248	2321		...	0959	...	1108	1149	...	1255	1355	1455	1555	1655	1755	1838	1856	1955	2054	...	...	2157	2219
Beverley △ 181 d.	2226	2227	...	2307	2336		...	1016	...	1123	1204	...	1310	1410	1510	1610	1710	1810	1855	1910	2010	2109	...	...	2210	2233
Hull △ 181 a.	2241	2242	...	2322	2351		...	1030	...	1139	1220	...	1325	1425	1525	1625	1725	1826	1911	1926	2025	2125	...	...	2226	2250
Hull 181 d.	...	...	2245	...	...		0927	1033	1125	...	...	1229	1329	1429	1530	1629	1730	1830	...	1929	2032	...	2128	2153	*2250*	...
Brough 181 d.	...	...	2257	...	...		0939	1045	1137	...	...	1241	1341	1441	1542	1641	1742	1842	...	1941	2044	...	2140	2210	*2307*	...
Goole 181 d.	...	...	2313	...	...		0954	1059	1155	...	...	1256	1356	1456	1557	1656	1756	1856	...	1956	2059	...	2155	2226	*2324*	...
Doncaster. 181 193 d.	...	...	2343	...	...		1021	1123	1219	...	...	1323	1421	1521	1622	1721	1822	1921	...	2021	2123	...	2221	2254	*2355*	...
Meadowhall 193 d.	...	...	0008	...	...		1039	1143	1237	...	...	1341	1439	1540	1640	1741	1840	1940	...	2039	2141	...	2243	...	...	...
Sheffield 193 a.	...	...	0017	...	...		1049	1151	1248	...	...	1350	1448	1549	1649	1750	1849	1948	...	2048	2149	...	2250	...	...	...

YORK - HULL

km			⚒	⚒d	⑥	Ⓐ	⚒	⚒B	⚒B	⚒B	⚒B	⚒B	⚒B	⚒B	⚒B	⚒B	⚒B	⚒B	⚒	⚒	⚒		⑦	⑦	⑦
0	**York** d.	⚒	0536	0604e	0730	0730	0845	0945	1044	1145	1243	1345	1443	1546	1643	1745	1845	1943	2042	2144	2247	⑦	0851	1001	1039
34	Selby 181 188 d.		0600	0651	0802	0803	0914	1015	1114	1214	1314f	1415	1510	1617	1715	1816	1915	2013	2112	2215	2318		0922	1021	1113
66	Brough 181 d.		|	0719	0833	0836	0940	1041	1140	1240	1340	1441	1536	1643	1742	1842	1941	2041	2136	2240	2343		0945	1042	1134
84	**Hull** 181 188 a.		0633	0740	0851	0854	0955	1054	1153	1254	1353	1454	1549	1656	1756	1855	1954	2054	2155	2255	2357		0959	1057	1149

	⑦	⑦	⑦	⑦	⑦	⑦	⑦	⑦	⑦	⑦	⑦
York d.	1153	1252	1356	1454	1554	1653	1756	1845	1955	2053	2155
Selby 181 188 d.	1213	1325	1425	1515	1626	1722	1828	1914	2017	2115	2230
Brough 181 d.	1234	1347	1447	1538	1647	1743	1849	1935	2038	2142	...
Hull 181 188 a.	1247	1400	1500	1551	1700	1757	1902	1949	2051	2201	...

		⚒	Ⓐ	⑥	⚒	⚒B	⚒S	⚒B	⚒B	⚒B	⚒B
Hull 181 188 d.	⚒	0545	0620	0622	0745	0846	0947	1047	1147	1247	1346
Brough 181 d.		0557	0632	0634	0757	0858	0959	1059	1159	1259	1358
Selby 181 188 d.		0627	0657	0659	0827	0926	1024	1126	1224	1327	1423
York a.		0658	0730	0733	0859	0957	1058	1158	1249	1359	1444

	⚒B	⚒B	⚒B	⚒B	⚒B	⚒B	⚒B	ⒶB	⑥B	⚒	⚒		⑦	⑦	⑦	⑦	⑦	⑦	⑦	⑦	⑦	⑦	⑦	⑦	⑦
Hull 181 188 d.	1447	1547	1647	1750	1847	1945	2050	2148	2148	2231	2303	⑦	0839	1040	1145	1234	1348	1421	1539	1634	1725	1841	1935	2023	2203
Brough 181 d.	1459	1559	1659	1802	1859	1957	2102	2205	2205	2243	2315		0851	1052	1157	1246	1400	1433	1551	1646	1737	1853	1947	2035	2215
Selby 181 188 d.	1524	1624	1727	1827	1927	2022	2127	2230	2230	2306	2335		0917	1115	1222	1311	1423	1456	1614	1709	1800	1916	2010	2101	2234
York a.	1558	1649	1759	1859	2000	2055	2201	2254	2301	...	*0011h*		0947	1146	1242	1345	1443	1525	1645	1747	1826	1946	2044	2125	*2314*

B – To/from Bridlington (see upper panel).
W – On ⑥ change at Hull.
Y – To/from York (see lower panel).
Z – On ①–④ change at Hull.

a – Arrives 5–6 minutes earlier.
b – Until Sept. 14.
d – On ②–⑤ change at Selby.
e – Departs 0615 on ①⑥.
f – Arrives 9–10 minutes earlier.

h – Ⓐ only.
j – Arrives 7–8 minutes earlier.
r – Arrives 1603.
t – ⑤⑥ only.
v – On ⑥ a. 1025, d. 1030.

★ – Timings may vary ± 4 minutes.
△ – Additional trains Hull - Bridlington and v.v.: **From Hull** on ⚒ at 0801, 1734. **From Bridlington** on ⚒ at 0911, 1827; on ⑦ at 2124.

180 LONDON - LEEDS, YORK, NEWCASTLE and EDINBURGH

Most services convey 🍸 GR

km		⚒	⑥	Ⓐ	ⒶA	⑥A	⚒	Ⓐ	⑥	⑥	Ⓐ	⚒	⚒	⚒	⚒	⚒	⚒	⚒	Ⓐ	⑥	⚒	⚒	⚒	⚒	Ⓐ	⑥
0	**London** Kings Cross 181/2/3/5 d.		...	...	...	...	0555	0615	0615	0633	0633	0700	0703	0706	0730	0733	0800	0803	0806	0806	0830	0833	0900	0903	0906	0906
44	Stevenage 183/5 d.		...	...	...	...	0617	0636	0639	0654	0655	|	|	0727	|	0755e	|	|	|	|	|	0855	|	|	0928	0928
123	**Peterborough** 185 176 d.		...	...	...	...	0648	0709	0710	0724	0726	0748	0752	0759	0818	|	|	0851	0855	0855	0918	|	0948	0952	0959	1001
170	Grantham 181 d.		...	...	...	...	0707	0728	0730	0743	0746	|	|	0819	|	0842	|	|	0914	0917	|	0942	|	|	1019	1022
193	Newark North Gate 189 d.		...	...	...	...	0719	0742	0742	|	|	|	|	0832	0847	|	|	|	0927	0931	0946	|	|	|	1033	1035
219	**Lincoln** 189 176 a.		...	...	...	...	|	|	|	|	|	|	|	|	|	|	|	|	0952	0956	|	|	|	|	|	|
223	Retford 181 d.		...	...	...	...	0734	0756	0757	|	|	|	|	0847	|	|	|	|	...	...	|	|	|	|	1047	1050
251	**Doncaster** 181 182 d.		0609	0609	...	...	0749	0813	0813	0818	0819	|	0842	0903	0911	0915	|	0943	...	...	1011	1014	|	1042	1105	1107
283	Wakefield Westgate 119 a.		|	|	...	...	0806	|	|	0835	0835	|	0859	|	|	0931	|	1000	...	...	|	1030	|	1059	|	|
299	**Leeds** 119 173/5 188 a.		|	|	0708	0708	0823	|	|	0852	0852	|	0916	|	|	0945	|	1017	...	...	|	1047	|	1114	|	|
319	Bradford Forster Square 173 a.		|	|	|	|	...	|	|	...	...	|	0952	|	|	|	|	...	...	...	|	...	|	1152	|	|
328	Harrogate 175 a.		|	|	|	|	...	|	|	...	...	|	▬	|	|	1024	|	...	...	...	|	...	|	▬	|	1130
303	**York** 182a a.		0629	0629	0731	0731	...	0833	0833	...	...	0853	Ⓐ	0929	0932	...	0950	...	...	...	1032	...	1053	Ⓐ	1130	...
	York 119 182a 188 d.		0637	0636	0735	0735	...	0836	0835	...	...	0856	0905	...	0935	...	0954	...	...	...	1035	...	1056	1107	...	...
351	Northallerton 182a 188 d.		0656	0656	|	|	...	0855	0856	...	...	|	0925	...	|	...	|	...	...	...	1054	...	|	1126	...	...
374	Darlington 119 188 d.		0711	0710	0803	0803	...	0910	0910	...	...	0924	0938	...	1006	...	1023	...	...	...	1108	...	1124	1139	...	...
409	Durham 119 188 d.		0729	0727	0822	0820	...	0927	0927	...	...	|	0955	...	1024	...	|	...	...	...	1126	...	|	1157	...	...
432	**Newcastle** 119 188 a.		0741	0740	0834	0833	...	0940	0940	...	...	0951	1011	...	1038	...	1050	...	...	...	1140	...	1151	1211	...	...
	Newcastle ‡ 119 d.		0745	0743	0847	0849	...	0946	0946	...	...	0954	...	...	1041	...	1053	...	...	...	1145	...	1154	...	...	...
632	**Edinburgh** Waverley ‡ 119 a.		0920	0924	1020	1021	...	1114	1109	...	...	1128c	...	...	1214	...	1224	...	...	...	1310	...	1326v	...	...	...

	⑥	Ⓐ	⚒	ⒶA	⑥A	⚒	⑥	Ⓐ	Ⓐ	⑥	⚒	Ⓐ	⑥	⚒	Ⓐ	⑥	⚒	⚒	⚒B	⚒	⚒	⚒	⚒	Ⓐ	⑥	⚒
London Kings Cross 181/2/3/5 d.	0930	0930	0933	1000	1000	1003	1006	1006	1030	1030	1033	1100	1100	1103	1106	1106	1130	1133	1200	1203	1206	1230	1233	1300	1300	1303
Stevenage 183/5 d.	|	|	0956	|	|	|	1028	1028	|	|	1056	|	|	|	1127	1127	|	1156	|	|	1227	|	1256	|	|	|
Peterborough 185 176 d.	1018	1018	|	|	|	1053	1058	1100	1118	1120	|	|	|	1153	1201	1200	1218	|	|	1252	1300	1318	|	1349	1349	1352
Grantham 181 d.	|	|	1042	|	|	|	1117	1121	|	|	1141	|	|	|	1220	1219	|	1242	|	|	1321	|	1342	|	|	|
Newark North Gate 189 d.	1046	1046	|	|	|	|	1131	1135	1146	1147	|	|	|	|	1232	1232	1247	|	|	|	1337	1346	|	|	|	|
Lincoln 189 176 a.	|	|	|	|	|	|	1156	1200	|	|	|	|	|	|	|	|	|	|	|	|	1402	|	|	|	|	|
Retford 181 d.	|	|	|	|	|	|	...	...	|	|	|	|	|	|	1250j	1246	|	|	|	|	...	|	|	|	|	|
Doncaster 181 182 d.	1111	1110	1115	|	|	1143	...	...	1211	1211	1214	|	|	1243	1305	1306j	1311	1315	|	1343	...	1410	1415	|	|	1442
Wakefield Westgate 119 a.	|	|	1131	|	|	1159	...	...	|	|	1230	|	|	1300	|	|	|	1330	|	1359	...	|	1431	|	|	1459
Leeds 119 173/5 188 a.	|	|	1145	|	|	1216	...	...	|	|	1247	|	|	1314	|	|	|	1345	|	1416	...	|	1449	|	|	1514
Bradford Forster Square 173 a.	|	|	|	|	|	...	...	...	|	|	...	|	|	1355	|	|	|	|	|	...	...	|	...	|	|	1552
Harrogate 175 a.	|	|	1225	|	|	...	...	...	|	|	...	|	|	▬	|	|	|	1425	|	...	...	|	...	|	|	▬
York 182a a.	1131	1132	...	1153	1149	...	...	...	1231	1231	...	1252	1252	Ⓐ	1330	1330	1332	...	1350	...	...	1432	...	1452	1452	Ⓐ
York 119 182a 188 d.	1135	1135	...	1156	1155	...	...	...	1235	1235	...	1255	1255	1307	...	...	1336	...	1355	...	...	1435	...	1455	1455	1507
Northallerton 182a 188 d.	|	|	...	|	|	...	...	...	1255	1255	...	|	|	1327	...	...	|	...	|	...	...	1455	...	|	|	1526
Darlington 119 188 d.	1206	1205	...	1225	1224	...	...	...	1309	1309	...	1324	1323	1341	...	...	1408	...	1424	...	...	1509	...	1523	1524j	1539
Durham 119 188 d.	1224	1222	...	|	|	...	...	...	1327	1327	...	|	|	1359	...	...	1427	...	|	...	...	1528	...	|	|	1557
Newcastle 119 188 a.	1237	1235	...	1252	1250	...	...	...	1340	1339	...	1352	1349	1413	...	...	1442	...	1452	...	...	1540	...	1550	1551	1611
Newcastle ‡ 119 d.	1240	1240	...	1255	1254	...	...	...	1343	1345	...	1355	1354	...	...	...	1445	...	1454	...	...	1544	...	1553	1559	...
Edinburgh Waverley ‡ 119 a.	1411	1415	...	1422	1427	...	...	...	1508	1512	...	1524	1526	...	...	...	1616	...	1626v	...	...	1714k	...	1723	1727	...

	⑥	Ⓐ	⚒	⚒	⚒A	⚒	⚒	Ⓐ	⑥	⚒	Ⓐ	⑥	⚒	Ⓐ	⑥	ⒶQ	⑥	Ⓐ	⚒	ⒶA	⑥	⚒	⚒	⚒	⚒	⑥
London Kings Cross 181/2/3/5 d.	1306	1306	1330	1333	1400	1403	1406	1430	1430	1433	1500	1500	1503	1506	1506	1527	1530	1530	1533	1600	1600	1603	1606	1630	1633	1700
Stevenage 183/5 d.	1328	1327	|	1355	|	|	1428	|	|	1456	|	|	|	1528	1528	|	|	|	1556	|	|	|	1627	|	1655	|
Peterborough 185 176 d.	1358	1402	1418	|	|	1452	1500	1518	1519	|	|	|	1551e	1559	1559	|	1618	1618	|	|	|	1653	1701	1718	|	|
Grantham 181 d.	1416	1422	|	1442	|	|	1520	|	|	1542	|	|	|	1618	1618	|	|	|	1642	|	|	|	1721	|	1742	|
Newark North Gate 189 d.	1428	1435	1446	|	|	|	1534	1546	1547	|	|	|	|	1630	1632	|	1647	1646	|	|	|	|	1737	1746	|	|
Lincoln 189 176 a.	|	|	|	|	|	|	1601	|	|	|	|	|	|	|	|	|	|	|	|	|	|	|	1803	|	|	|
Retford 181 d.	1447f	1450	|	|	|	|	...	|	|	|	|	|	|	1645	1650j	|	|	|	|	|	|	|	...	|	1805	|
Doncaster 181 182 d.	1505j	1507	1511	1515	|	1542	...	1610	1611	1616	|	|	1643	1705f	1707	|	1711	1710	1716	|	|	1741	...	1811	1821	|
Wakefield Westgate 119 a.	|	|	|	1531	|	1559	...	|	|	1632	|	|	1700	|	|	|	|	|	1734	|	|	1759	...	|	1836	|
Leeds 119 173/5 188 a.	|	|	|	1545	|	1616	...	|	|	1652	|	|	1714	|	|	|	|	|	1749	|	|	1816	...	|	1852	|
Bradford Forster Square 173 a.	|	|	|	|	|	...	...	|	|	...	|	|	1752	|	|	|	|	|	|	|	|	...	...	|	1930	|
Harrogate 175 a.	|	|	|	1625	|	...	...	|	|	...	|	|	▬	|	|	1721	|	|	1833	|	|	...	...	|	...	|
York 182a a.	1530	1530	1532	...	1552	...	...	1632	1632	...	1652	1651	Ⓐ	1728	1730	1726	1732	1732	...	1752	1751	...	...	1832	...	1852
York 119 182a 188 d.	...	...	1535	...	1555	...	...	1635	1635	...	1656	1654	1706	...	...	...	1735	1736	...	1756	1756	...	...	1835	...	1855
Northallerton 182a 188 d.	...	...	1555	...	|	...	...	1655	1655	...	|	|	1725	...	...	...	1755	1756	...	|	|	...	...	1855	...	|
Darlington 119 188 d.	...	...	1609	...	1624	...	...	1708	1709	...	1726	1724	1738	...	...	...	1808	1809	...	1824	1825	...	...	1908	...	1927
Durham 119 188 d.	...	...	1626	...	|	...	...	1725	1728	...	|	|	1756	...	...	...	1825	1827	...	|	|	...	...	1925e	...	|
Newcastle 119 188 a.	...	...	1639	...	1651	...	...	1738	1740	...	1752	1752	1810	...	...	...	1838	1841	...	1850	1854	...	...	1941t	...	1953
Newcastle ‡ 119 d.	...	...	1641	...	1700	...	...	1743	1745	...	1755	1755	...	...	...	...	1842	1844	...	1854	1858	...	...	1945	...	1956
Edinburgh Waverley ‡ 119 a.	...	...	1816	...	1830t	...	...	1909	1912	...	1924	1930	...	...	...	...	2011	2012	...	2020	2024	...	...	2114	...	2123

	Ⓐ	⚒	ⒶH	⑥H	Ⓐ	⑥	Ⓐ	⑥	Ⓐ	Ⓐ	⑥	⑥F	ⒶF	⑥	Ⓐ	Ⓐ	⑥	Ⓐ	⑥	Ⓐ	⑥	⚒	⑥	Ⓐ	①–④	⑤
London Kings Cross 181/2/3/5 d.	1700	1703	1718	1718	1730	1730	1733	1733	1748	1800	1800	1803	1803	1818	1818	1830	1830	1833	1833	1900	1900	1903	1906	1906	1930	1930
Stevenage 183/5 d.	|	|	|	|	|	|	1755	1756	|	|	|	|	|	|	|	|	|	1855	1856	|	|	|	1927	1928	|	|
Peterborough 185 176 d.	|	1752	1810	1811	1819	1818	|	|	1837	|	|	1851	1855f	1907	1910	1919	1918	|	|	|	|	1951	1957	2000	2019	2019
Grantham 181 d.	|	|	1829	1830	|	|	1844	1841	1907	|	|	|	|	1926	1929	|	|	1943	1943	|	|	|	2016	2021	|	|
Newark North Gate 189 d.	|	|	1841	1842	1847	1848	|	|	|	|	|	1922j	1925	|	|	1947	1948	|	|	|	|	|	2031	2037	2046	2046
Lincoln 189 176 a.	|	|	|	|	|	|	|	|	|	|	|	|	|	|	|	|	|	|	|	|	|	|	2056	2103	|	|
Retford 181 d.	|	|	|	|	|	|	|	|	1930	|	|	|	|	1949	|	|	|	2006	2006	|	|	|	...	...	|	|
Doncaster 181 182 d.	|	1843	1908	1905	|	|	1916	1917	1945	|	|	1950	1950	2007	|	2011	2012	2022	2022	|	|	2042	...	...	2110	2110
Wakefield Westgate 119 a.	|	1900	...	...	|	|	1935	1932	2000	|	|	2006	2006	2023	|	|	|	2038	2037	|	|	2059	...	...	|	|
Leeds 119 173/5 188 a.	|	1917	...	...	|	|	1951	1950	2017	|	|	2021	2021	2041	|	|	|	2053	2052	|	|	2116	...	...	|	|
Bradford Forster Square 173 a.	|	...	...	...	|	|	|	...	...	|	|	...	▬	...	|	|	|	2129	|	|	|	...	...	...	|	|
Harrogate 175 a.	|	...	...	...	|	|	2030	...	...	|	|	...	...	...	|	|	|	...	2130	|	|	...	...	...	|	|
York 182a a.	1849	...	...	...	1928	1928	...	...	...	1947	1952	...	Ⓐ	...	2016	2033	2033	...	...	2057	2049	...	...	...	2130	2130
York 119 182a 188 d.	1857	...	...	...	1931	1931	...	...	...	1954	1956	...	2007	...	2020	2036	2036	...	...	2059	2054	...	...	...	2133	2133
Northallerton 182a 188 d.	|	...	...	...	|	|	...	...	...	|	|	...	2026	...	2039	|	2055	...	...	|	|	...	...	...	2154	2154
Darlington 119 188 d.	1926	...	...	...	2000	2000	...	...	...	2022	2024	...	2039	...	2053	2106	2109	...	...	2127	2125	...	...	...	2208	2208
Durham 119 188 d.	|	...	...	...	2018	2018	...	...	...	|	|	...	2057	...	2111	2125	2127	...	...	|	|	...	...	...	2227	2227
Newcastle 119 188 a.	1952	...	...	...	2031	2030	...	...	...	2048	2050	...	2114	...	2125	2139	2141	...	...	2154	2153	...	...	...	2241	2241
Newcastle ‡ 119 d.	1958	...	...	...	2035	2034	...	...	...	2051	2055	...	...	...	...	2142	...	...	...	2156	...	...	...	...	...	2243
Edinburgh Waverley ‡ 119 a.	2125	...	...	...	2208	2159	...	...	...	2220	2238	...	...	...	...	2316	...	...	...	2324	...	...	...	...	...	0020

	⑥	Ⓐ	⑥	Ⓐ	⑥	Ⓐ	⑥	⑥	Ⓐ	⑥	Ⓐ	Ⓐ	⑥	Ⓐ	Ⓐ	Ⓐ	⑦	⑦	⑦	⑦	⑦	⑦	⑦	⑦	⑦	⑦A
London Kings Cross 181/2/3/5 d.	1930	1933	1933	2000	2000	2003	2003	2030	2033	2100	2100	2133	2200	2200	2300	2333		...	...	0848	0900	0903	0922	0930	0933	1000
Stevenage 183/5 d.	|	1955	1955	|	|	|	|	|	2055	|	2123	2155	|	|	|	|		...	...	|	|	0925	|	|	0956	|
Peterborough 185 176 d.	2018	|	|	|	2048	2052	2052	2120	2127	2150	2153	2228	2248	2248	2345s	0017s		...	...	|	|	0956	1011	1019	1027	|
Grantham 181 d.	|	2042	2042	|	|	|	2112	2139	2146	|	|	2248	2307	2308	0013s	0045s		...	...	|	|	1015	|	|	1047	|
Newark North Gate 189 d.	2046	|	|	|	2117	2120	|	2153	2200	|	2222	2301	2320	2322	0025s	0058s		...	...	|	|	1027	|	|	1104f	|
Lincoln 189 176 a.	|	|	|	|	|	|	|	|	|	|	|	|	|	|	|	|		...	...	|	|	|	|	|	1129	|
Retford 181 d.	|	|	|	|	|	|	|	2207	|	|	|	2316	2334	|	|	|		...	...	|	|	|	|	1057	...	|
Doncaster 181 182 d.	2112	2114	2114	|	2141	2145	2146	2223	2224	|	2249j	2337	2350	2354f	0054s	0125s		...	0936	|	|	1052	1058	1112	...	|
Wakefield Westgate 119 a.	|	2130	2130	|	|	2201	2204	2239	2239	|	|	2354	0006	|	|	|		...	|	|	|	1107	|	|	...	|
Leeds 119 173/5 188 a.	|	2148	2145	|	|	2221	2221	2257	2256	|	|	0011	0022	|	|	0217		0830	|	|	|	1122	|	|	...	|
Bradford Forster Square 173 a.	|	...	2217	|	|	...	...	...	...	|	|	...	...	|	|	...		|	|	|	|	|	|	|	...	|
Harrogate 175 a.	|	...	...	|	|	...	...	...	...	|	|	...	...	|	|	...		|	|	|	|	1159	|	|	...	|
York 182a a.	2132	...	...	2153	2202	...	...	...	...	2253	2309	...	...	0017	0130	...		0855	0956	1034	1047	...	1118	1133	...	1150
York 119 182a 188 d.	2135	...	...	2153	2204	...	...	...	...	2257	2312	...	...	0022	...	...		0900	1000	1037	1051	...	1122	1136	...	1155
Northallerton 182a 188 d.	2154	...	...	|	|	...	...	...	...	2316	2344	...	...	0043s	...	...		0919	|	|	|	...	|	|	...	|
Darlington 119 188 d.	2207	...	...	2222	2232	...	...	...	...	2329	2357	...	...	0100s	...	...		0932	1029	1105	1119	...	1150	1204	...	1224
Durham 119 188 d.	2225	...	...	2240	2250	...	...	...	...	2347	0015	...	...	0122s	...	...		0950	1047	1123	|	...	1208	1222	...	|
Newcastle 119 188 a.	2239	...	...	2254	2304	...	...	...	...	0001	0043	...	...	0154	...	...		1002	1059	1137	1147	...	1222	1234	...	1250
Newcastle ‡ 119 d.	...	...	...	...	...	...	...	...	...	...	...	...	...	...	...	...		1005	1102	1140	1152	...	...	1238	...	1253
Edinburgh Waverley ‡ 119 a.	...	...	...	...	...	...	...	...	...	...	...	...	...	...	...	...		1144	1230	1309	1318	...	...	1409	...	1418

FOR NOTES SEE PAGE 134 ▶ ▶ ▶ ▶

GR Most services convey 🍷

LONDON - LEEDS, YORK, NEWCASTLE and EDINBURGH — 180

	⑦	⑦	⑦	⑦	⑦	⑦	⑦	⑦	⑦B	⑦	⑦	⑦	⑦	⑦	⑦	⑦	⑦	⑦A	⑦	⑦	⑦	⑦	⑦	⑦	⑦	⑦	⑦
London Kings Cross **181/2/3/5** d.	1003	1007	1030	1100	1103	1122	1130	1135	1200	1203	1222	1230	1233	1300	1303	1330	1333	1400	1403	1430	1433	1436	1500	1503	1530	1533	1600
Stevenage **183/5** d.	│	│	│	│	1125	│	│	1156	│	│	│	│	1256	│	1325	│	1355	│	│	│	│	1458	│	1525	│	1556	│
Peterborough **185 176** d.	1052	1057	1118	│	1155	│	1218	1226	│	1252	1311	1318	│	│	1356	1418	1426	│	1453	1518	1521	│	│	1556	1619	1626	│
Grantham **181** d.	│	1117	│	│	1214	1225	│	1244	│	1312	│	│	1343	│	1415	│	1452f	│	1512	│	│	│	│	1615	1640	1652f	│
Newark North Gate **189** d.	│	1130	1147	│	1228	│	│	1258	│	1325	│	1347	│	│	1429	│	│	│	1526	│	1552j	1554	│	1628	│	1707	│
Lincoln **189 176** a.	│	│	│	│	│	│	│	1325	│	│	│	│	│	│	│	│	│	│	│	│	│	1623	│	│	│	1732	│
Retford **181** d.	│	│	│	│	│	│	1257	...	│	│	│	│	│	│	│	1457	1520f	│	│	│	│	...	│	1642	│	...	│
Doncaster **181 182** d.	1142	1156	1211	│	1251	│	1312	...	│	1350	1359	1411	1420	│	1454	1512	1536	│	1550	1611	1619j	...	│	1658	1712	...	│
Wakefield Westgate **119** a.	│	1211	│	│	1306	│	│	...	│	1406	│	│	1437	│	1510	│	1600	│	1606	│	1635	...	│	1714	│	...	│
Leeds **119 173/5 188** a.	│	1228	│	│	1321	│	│	...	│	1423	│	│	1454	│	1524	│	1619	│	1621	│	1652	...	│	1728	│	...	│
Bradford Forster Square **173** a.	│	...	│	│	│	│	│	...	│	...	│	│	...	│	│	│	...	│	1654	│	...	...	│	│	│	...	│
Harrogate **175** a.	│	...	│	│	1402	│	│	...	│	...	│	│	...	│	1559	│	...	│	...	│	...	...	│	1807	│	...	│
York **182a** a.	1203	...	1231	1249	...	1313	1332	...	1349	...	1419	1432	...	1454	...	1533	...	1549	...	1631	...	...	1651	...	1734	...	1750
York **119 182a 188** d.	1205	...	1235	1252	...	1317	1335	...	1353	...	1423	1435	...	1457	...	1535	...	1554	...	1635	...	...	1654	...	1737	...	1753
Northallerton **182a 188** d.	│	...	1255	│	...	1336	│	...	│	...	│	1455	...	│	...	│	...	│	...	1654	...	...	│	...	│	...	│
Darlington **119 188** d.	1233	...	1309	1320	...	1349	1403	...	1421	...	1451	1508	...	1525	...	1604	...	1622	...	1707	...	...	1722	...	1806	...	1821
Durham **119 188** d.	1251	...	1327	│	...	1407	1421	...	│	...	1509	1526	...	│	...	1622	...	│	...	1725	...	...	│	...	1824	...	│
Newcastle **119 188** a.	1303	...	1339	1346	...	1419	1433	...	1447	...	1523	1539	...	1553	...	1634	...	1648	...	1737	...	...	1748	...	1838	...	1847
Newcastle ‡ **119** d.	1311	...	1343	1349	...	1424	1440	...	1450	...	...	1546	...	1555	...	1638	...	1652	...	1745	...	...	1752	...	1842	...	1850
Edinburgh Waverley ‡ **119** a.	1435	...	1510	1518	...	1559	1609	...	1619	...	...	1709	...	1721	...	1807	...	1819	...	1909	...	...	1918	...	2012	...	2017

	⑦	⑦	⑦	⑦	⑦	⑦H	⑦	⑦	⑦	⑦	⑦	⑦	⑦F	⑦	⑦	⑦	⑦	⑦	⑦	⑦	⑦	⑦	⑦	⑦	⑦	⑦	⑦
London Kings Cross **181/2/3/5** d.	1605	1630	1635	1700	1705	1722	1730	1735	1800	1803	1827	1830	1835	1900	1903	1906	1930	1935	2000	2005	2035	2100	2105	2135	2200	2205	2235
Stevenage **183/5** d.	│	│	1657	│	│	│	│	1758	│	│	│	│	1857	│	│	1928	│	1958	│	│	2056	│	│	2156	│	│	│
Peterborough **185 176** d.	1654	1719	│	│	1753	│	1818	│	1849	1853	│	│	│	│	1951	1959	2019	2028	2048	2054	2127	2149	2153	2228	2249	2253	2328s
Grantham **181** d.	1713	│	1741	│	│	1827	1838	1843	│	│	│	│	1941	│	│	2018	│	2047	│	│	2147	│	│	2247	│	2313	2347s
Newark North Gate **189** d.	1726	1746	│	│	1821	1840	│	│	│	1922	│	1947	│	│	2018	2034	2048	│	│	│	2200	│	2222	2259	│	2326	2359s
Lincoln **189 176** a.	│	│	│	│	│	│	│	│	│	│	│	│	│	│	│	2059	│	│	│	│	│	│	│	│	│	│	│
Retford **181** d.	│	│	1804	│	│	│	│	│	│	│	│	│	2005	│	│	...	│	│	│	2134	│	│	│	2314	│	│	│
Doncaster **181 182** d.	1751	1811	1821j	│	1848	1904	1910	1918	│	1948	│	2011	2020	│	2044	...	2116j	2120	│	2149	2223	│	2250	2336j	2343	2356	0029s
Wakefield Westgate **119** a.	1807	│	1837	│	1903	...	│	1934	│	2005	│	│	2036	│	2102	...	│	2135	│	2205	2239	│	2307	2351	│	│	│
Leeds **119 173/5 188** a.	1823	│	1853	│	1918	...	│	1953	│	2020	│	│	2051	│	2119	...	│	2150	│	2222	2255	│	2323	0009	│	│	0111
Bradford Forster Square **173** a.	...	│	...	│	│	...	│	...	│	│	│	│	...	│	...	...	│	2222	│	...	...	│	...	...	│	│	...
Harrogate **175** a.	...	│	...	│	1953	...	│	...	│	2059	│	│	...	│	...	...	│	...	│	...	...	│	...	...	│	│	...
York **182a** a.	...	1831	...	1849	...	...	1933	...	1955	...	2019	2033	...	2050	...	...	2139	...	2152	...	...	2257	...	...	0008	0021	...
York **119 182a 188** d.	...	1836	...	1852	...	...	1939	...	2002	...	2027	2037	...	2053	...	...	2142	...	2156	...	...	2300	...	...	0012	...	...
Northallerton **182a 188** d.	...	1855	...	│	...	...	│	...	│	...	│	2056	...	│	...	...	│	...	2230	...	...	2335	...	...	0046s	...	...
Darlington **119 188** d.	...	1908	...	1921	...	...	2008	...	2030	...	2055	2111	...	2122	...	...	2224	...	2243	...	...	2350j	...	...	0059s	...	...
Durham **119 188** d.	...	1926	...	│	...	...	2026	...	│	...	2113	2129	...	│	...	...	2241	...	2302	...	...	0008	...	...	0117s	...	...
Newcastle **119 188** a.	...	1939	...	1948	...	...	2039	...	2057	...	2127	2141	...	2149	...	...	2310	...	2332	...	...	0038	...	...	0149	...	...
Newcastle ‡ **119** d.	...	1943	...	1951	...	...	2042	...	2100	...	...	2145	...	2152	...	...	...	...	...	...	...	...	...	...	...	...	...
Edinburgh Waverley ‡ **119** a.	...	2113	...	2118	...	...	2215	...	2227	...	...	2312	...	2328	...	...	...	...	...	...	...	...	...	...	...	...	...

⚒

	⚒	⚒	⚒	⚒	⚒	⚒	⚒	⚒	Ⓐ	⑥	⚒	⚒	Ⓐ	⑥	Ⓐ	⑥H	ⒶH	⑥F	ⒶF	⑥	Ⓐ	ⒶR	Ⓐ	⑥	⑥	Ⓐ
Edinburgh Waverley ‡ **119** d.	...	...	...	...	...	...	...	...	...	...	...	...	...	...	0540	...	...	...	...	...	...	...	...	...	0548	0548
Newcastle ‡ **119** a.	...	...	...	...	...	...	...	...	...	...	...	...	...	...	│	...	...	...	...	...	...	...	...	...	0723	0728
Newcastle **119 188** d.	...	...	...	0440	...	0528	...	...	0600	0600	...	...	0630	0630	│	...	...	...	...	0655	0655	...	...	...	0730	0730
Durham **119 188** d.	...	...	...	0455	...	0541	...	...	0613	0613	...	...	0644	0643	0702	...	...	...	...	0708	0709	...	...	...	0743	0743
Darlington **119 188** d.	...	...	...	0512	...	0600	...	...	0631	0632	...	...	0703	0702	0704	...	...	...	...	0727	0732f	...	...	...	0803	0803
Northallerton **182a 188** d.	...	...	...	0523	...	0611	...	...	│	│	...	...	0715	0714	│	...	...	...	...	│	│	...	...	...	│	│
York a.	...	...	...	0558	...	0630	...	...	0657	0658	...	...	0734	0736	│	...	...	...	...	0754	0758	0806	...	...	0830	0829
York **119 182a 185** d.	0440	...	...	0600	...	0634	...	...	0702	0702	...	...	0737	0738	│	...	...	...	...	0757	0802	0813	...	...	0832	0832
Harrogate **175** d.	│	...	...	│	...	│	...	...	│	│	...	...	│	│	│	...	...	...	...	│	│	│	0737	0737	│	│
Bradford Forster Square **173** d.	│	...	...	│	...	│	...	0630	│	│	...	...	│	│	│	...	...	...	...	│	│	│	│	│	│	│
Leeds **119 173/5 188** d.	│	0505	0530	│	0605	│	0640	0700	│	│	...	0715	│	│	│	...	...	0740	0741	│	│	│	0815	0816	│	│
Wakefield Westgate **119** d.	│	0518	0543	│	0618	│	0653	0714	│	│	...	0728	│	│	│	...	...	│	0754	│	│	│	0829	0829	│	│
Doncaster **181 182** d.	0506	0536	0602	0623	0637	0656	0714	│	│	│	...	0747	│	│	│	0758	0757	0809	0814	│	│	│	0848	0848	0856	0856
Retford **181** d.	│	0550	│	│	0651	│	│	│	│	│	...	│	│	│	│	│	│	│	│	0828	0836	│	│	│	│	│
Lincoln **189 176** d.	│	│	│	│	│	│	│	│	│	│	0730	│	│	│	│	│	│	│	│	│	│	│	│	│	│	│
Newark North Gate **189** d.	0536	0606	0627	0647	0706	│	0738	│	│	│	0758	│	│	│	│	0824	0822	0832	0839	│	│	│	│	│	0921	0921
Grantham **181** d.	0549	0617	0639	0658	0719	0727	│	│	│	│	│	0819	│	│	│	0835	0834	│	│	│	│	│	0923	0919	│	│
Peterborough **185 176** d.	0610	0640	0701	0720	0740	0749	│	│	0813j	0820	0829	│	0846	0850f	│	0858j	│	0901	0908	│	│	│	│	│	0950	0950
Stevenage **183/5** d.	│	│	│	│	│	│	│	│	│	│	0858	0904	│	│	│	│	│	│	│	│	│	│	1007	1005	│	│
London Kings Cross **181/2/3/5** a.	0700	0730	0752t	0810	0830	0838	0852t	0900	0908	0910	0923	0931	0937	0938	0940	0947	0951	0950	0959	0954	1002	1020	1031	1031	1038	1039

	Ⓐ	⑥	Ⓐ	⚒	⚒	⚒	⑥	Ⓐ	⑥	Ⓐ	Ⓐ	⑥	⚒	⑥	Ⓐ	Ⓐ	⚒	⚒	⑥	Ⓐ	⚒	⑥	Ⓐ	⑥	Ⓐ	⚒	⚒
Edinburgh Waverley ‡ **119** d.	...	0630	0630	...	...	0700	0730	0730	...	...	...	...	...	0800	0800	...	0830	...	...	...	...	0900	0900	0930	0930	...	...
Newcastle ‡ **119** a.	...	0755	0756	...	...	0824	0854	0855	...	...	...	...	...	0926	0927	...	0957	...	...	...	...	1024	1024	1056	1055	...	...
Newcastle **119 188** d.	0746	0759	0800	...	...	0828	0900	0858	...	...	...	...	...	0930	0934	0943	0959	...	...	...	...	1028	1027	1059	1058	...	...
Durham **119 188** d.	0759	│	│	...	...	0841	│	│	...	...	...	...	...	0944	0947	0958	│	...	...	...	...	1041	1040	│	│	...	...
Darlington **119 188** d.	0818	0827	0831	...	...	0900	0928	0926	...	...	...	...	...	1003	1005	1016	1028	...	...	...	...	1100	1100	1127	1128	...	...
Northallerton **182a 188** d.	0829	│	│	...	...	0911	│	│	...	...	...	...	...	│	│	1027	│	...	...	...	...	1111	1111	│	│	...	...
York **182a** a.	0851	0853	0857	...	...	0930	0954	0952	...	...	...	...	...	1030	1031	1049	1054	...	...	...	...	1130	1130	1154	1154	...	...
York **119 182a 185** d.	...	0858	0902	...	...	0932	0958	0958	...	...	1002	1002	...	1035	1034	...	1059	...	...	...	...	1133	1133	1158	1159	...	1202
Harrogate **175** d.	...	│	│	...	...	│	│	│	...	...	│	│	0936	│	│	...	│	...	...	...	...	│	│	│	│	...	│
Bradford Forster Square **173** d.	...	│	│	...	0843	│	│	│	...	...	│	│	│	│	│	...	│	...	...	...	...	│	│	│	│	1117	│
Leeds **119 173/5 188** d.	...	│	│	0846	0915	│	│	│	0946	0946	│	│	1016	│	│	...	│	1045	...	...	1115	│	│	│	│	1145	│
Wakefield Westgate **119** d.	...	│	│	0900	0928	│	│	│	0959	0959	│	│	1028	│	│	...	│	1058	...	...	1128	│	│	│	│	1158	│
Doncaster **181 182** d.	...	│	│	0922	0947	0956	│	│	1018	1019	1025	1029	1047	1058	1057	...	│	1120j	...	...	1147	1156	1155	│	│	1219	1225
Retford **181** d.	...	│	│	│	│	│	│	│	│	│	1040	1045	│	│	│	...	│	│	...	...	│	│	│	│	│	│	1240
Lincoln **189 176** d.	...	│	│	│	│	│	│	│	│	│	│	│	│	│	│	...	│	│	1127	1127	│	│	│	│	│	│	│
Newark North Gate **189** d.	...	│	│	│	│	1021	│	│	│	│	1055	1059	│	1121	1121	...	│	│	1159f	1156j	│	1220	1219	│	│	│	1256
Grantham **181** d.	...	│	│	│	1018	│	│	│	│	│	1107	1110	1119	│	│	...	│	│	1210	1209	1219	│	│	│	│	│	1308
Peterborough **185 176** d.	...	│	│	1010	│	1050	│	│	1107	1111j	1129	1131	│	1150	1150	...	│	1210	1231	1230	│	1248	1247	│	│	1311	1330
Stevenage **183/5** d.	...	│	│	│	1105	│	│	│	│	│	1158	1200	1204	│	│	...	│	│	1300	1259	1305	│	│	│	│	│	1359
London Kings Cross **181/2/3/5** a.	...	1048	1052	1100	1130	1138	1148	1148	1200	1159	1221	1223	1231	1238	1239	...	1249	1300	1323	1322	1331	1338	1338	1349	1352	1401	1423

	Ⓐ	⑥	Ⓐ	⑥	Ⓐ	⚒A	⚒	⚒	⚒	⚒	⚒B	⚒	Ⓐ	⑥	⚒	⚒	Ⓐ	⚒A	⚒	⚒	⚒	⑥	Ⓐ	⚒	⚒	Ⓐ	⑥
Edinburgh Waverley ‡ **119** d.	...	...	1000	1000	...	1030	...	...	...	1100	1130	...	...	...	...	1200	...	1230	...	...	...	1300	1300	1330	...	...	...
Newcastle ‡ **119** a.	...	...	1126	1125	...	1156	...	...	...	1224	1255	...	...	...	...	1327	...	1356	...	...	...	1423	1423	1456	...	...	...
Newcastle **119 188** d.	...	...	1131	1128	1149	1158	...	...	...	1226	1257	...	...	...	...	1330	1345	1359	...	...	...	1426	1426	1459	...	...	...
Durham **119 188** d.	...	...	1144	1142	1201	│	...	...	...	1240	│	...	...	...	...	1343	1358	│	...	...	...	1440	1440	│	...	...	...
Darlington **119 188** d.	...	...	1202	1203	1220	1228	...	...	...	1301	1327	...	...	...	...	1402	1417	1428	...	...	...	1501	1459	1527	...	...	...
Northallerton **182a 188** d.	...	...	│	│	1231	│	...	...	...	1312	│	...	...	...	...	│	1428	│	...	...	...	1512	1510	│	...	...	...
York a.	...	...	1229	1230	1252	1255	...	...	...	1331	1354	...	...	...	...	1429	1449	1455	...	...	...	1531	1529	1553	...	...	...
York **119 182a 185** d.	...	...	1232	1233	...	1258	...	...	...	1333	1359	...	1402	1405	...	1432	...	1458	...	...	...	1534	1532	1559	...	1602	1602
Harrogate **175** d.	1136	1136	│	│	...	│	...	...	...	│	│	...	│	│	1336	│	...	│	...	...	...	│	│	│	...	│	│
Bradford Forster Square **173** d.	│	│	│	│	...	│	...	...	...	│	│	1317	│	│	│	│	...	│	...	...	...	│	│	│	1516	│	│
Leeds **119 173/5 188** d.	1215	1215	│	│	...	│	1245	...	1315	│	│	1346	│	│	1415	│	...	│	1445	...	1515	│	│	│	1545	│	│
Wakefield Westgate **119** d.	1228	1228	│	│	...	│	1258	...	1328	│	│	1359	│	│	1428	│	...	│	1458	...	1528	│	│	│	1558	│	│
Doncaster **181 182** d.	1247	1249	1257	1255	...	│	1318	...	1347	1356	│	1419	1427j	1430	1447	1455	...	│	1519	...	1547	1556	1557j	│	1618	1627	1630
Retford **181** d.	│	│	│	│	...	│	│	...	│	│	│	│	1443	1445	│	│	...	│	│	...	│	│	│	│	│	1641	1644
Lincoln **189 176** d.	│	│	│	│	...	│	│	1324	│	│	│	│	│	│	│	│	...	│	│	1527	│	│	│	│	│	│	│
Newark North Gate **189** d.	│	│	1321	1319	...	│	│	1354f	│	1420	│	│	1458	1500	│	1519	...	│	│	1554	│	1620	1621	│	│	1656	1659
Grantham **181** d.	1318	1321	│	│	...	│	│	1407	1418	│	│	│	1509	1511	1518	│	...	│	│	1605	1618	│	│	│	│	1708	1710
Peterborough **185 176** d.	│	│	1350	1350j	...	│	1410	1430	│	1449	│	1511	1530	1532	│	1550	...	│	1611	1630j	│	1650	1650	│	1711	1730	1731
Stevenage **183/5** d.	1405	1406	│	│	...	│	│	1459	1505	│	│	│	1559	1600	1605	│	...	│	│	1659	1705	│	│	│	│	1759	1800
London Kings Cross **181/2/3/5** a.	1431	1431	1439	1438	...	1448	1500	1522	1530	1538	1549	1600	1622	1623	1631	1640	...	1648	1700	1722	1730	1738	1740	1750	1800	1822	1823

FOR NOTES SEE NEXT PAGE ▶ ▶ ▶ ▶

180 EDINBURGH - NEWCASTLE - YORK and LEEDS - LONDON

Most services convey 🍷 GR

	⚒	Ⓐ	⑥	Ⓐ	Ⓐ	⑥	⚒	Ⓐ	⑥	Ⓐ	⑥	Ⓐ	⑥	Ⓐ	⑥	⚒	Ⓐ	⑥	⚒	Ⓐ	⑥	Ⓐ	⑥	Ⓐ	Ⓐ	⑥	Ⓐ
Edinburgh Waverley ‡ **119** d.	...	1400	1400	...	1430	1430	...	...	...	...	...	1500	1500	1530	1530	...	...	...	...	1600	1600	...	1630	1630	...	...	...
Newcastle ‡ **119** a.	...	1528	1527	...	1557	1556	...	...	...	...	...	1624	1624	1657	1656	...	...	...	...	1722	1723	...	1756	1756	...	...	...
Newcastle **119 188** d.	...	1534	1530	1545	1600	1558	...	...	...	...	...	1629	1626	1659	1659	...	...	...	...	1727	1726	1745	1759	1759	...	...	...
Durham **119 188** d.	...	1547	1543	1558			...	...	...	...	...	1642	1640			...	...	...	...	1741	1740	1758			...	...	...
Darlington **119 188** d.	...	1605	1603	1616	1629	1627	...	...	...	...	...	1701	1700	1728	1728	...	...	...	...	1800	1800	1816	1828	1828	...	...	...
Northallerton **182a 188** d.	...			1627			...	...	...	...	...	1712	1711			...	...	...	...	1811	1811	1827			...	...	...
York **182a** a.	...	1631	1631	1649	1655	1654	...	...	...	...	...	1731	1730	1754	1754	...	...	...	...	1830	1830	1856	1854	1857	...	...	...
York **119 182a 185** d.	...	1634	1633	...	1658	1659	...	...	...	...	...	1733	1733	1758	1758	...	1802	1802	...	1832	1833	...	1859	1900	...	...	...
Harrogate **175** d.	1536			...			...	...	...	...	...					...			1736			...			...	...	...
Bradford Forster Square **173** d.				...			...	...	...	...	...					1716						...			...	...	...
Leeds **119 173/5 188** d.	1615			...			1645	...	...	1715	1715					1746			1815			...			1845	1845	1916
Wakefield Westgate **119** d.	1628			...			1658	...	...	1728	1728					1759			1828			...			1858	1858	1929
Doncaster **181 182** d.	1648	1658	1658j	...			1718	...	...	1746	1747	1756	1756			1818	1827j	1825	1848	1855	1856	...			1919	1923f	1949
Retford **181** d.				...				...	...	1800	1801						1841	1839				...					
Lincoln **189 176** d.				...				1727	1726													...					
Newark North Gate **189** d.		1721	1721	...				1754	1755j			1820	1821				1857	1856		1919	1920	...					
Grantham **181** d.	1719			...				1807	1808	1822	1824						1908	1908	1919			...					2019
Peterborough **185 176** d.		1750	1750	...			1810	1830	1830			1849	1851			1910	1930	1930		1947	1950	...			2011	2015	
Stevenage **183/5** d.	1805			...				1859	1859	1906	1909						1959	1959	2004	2015	2021	...	2028	2029			2106
London Kings Cross **181/2/3/5** a.	1831	1841	1838	...	1848	1852	1900	1922	1922	1930	1933	1938	1946	1949	1953	2001	2022	2023	2028	2038	2046	...	2052	2053	2059	2108	2129

	⑥	Ⓐ	⑥	Ⓐ	⑥	Ⓐ	Ⓐ A	⑥ A	⚒	⑥	⑥	Ⓐ	⑥	Ⓐ	Ⓐ A	⑦	⑦	⑦	⑦	⑦	⑦	⑦	⑦	⑦	⑦	⑦	⑦
Edinburgh Waverley ‡ **119** d.	...	1700	1700	...	...	...	1730	1730	...	...	1830	1830	1900	1937	2100		...	...	...	...	...	...	...	...	...	...	...
Newcastle ‡ **119** a.	...	1826	1826	...	...	...	1901	1900	...	...	1958	2014	2040	2109	2242		...	...	...	...	...	...	...	...	...	...	...
Newcastle **119 188** d.	...	1829	1829	1845	...	...	1904	1902	...	...	▬	2017	2044	2115	2245		...	...	...	0755	...	...	0825	0855	...	...	0925
Durham **119 188** d.	...	1842	1843	1858	...	...			...	...	...	2030	2057	2129	2300		...	...	...	0809	...	...	0838	0908	...	...	0938
Darlington **119 188** d.	...	1901	1901	1918	...	...	1933	1932	...	...	...	2049	2118	2148	2322		...	...	...	0827	...	...	0856	0928	...	...	0957
Northallerton **182a 188** d.	...			1929	...	...			...	...	...		2129	2200	2346s		...	...	...		...	...			...	...	1008
York **182a** a.	...	1927	1929	1951	...	...	1959	1959	...	...	...	2115	2148	2221	0009		...	...	...	0854	...	...	0922	0954	...	...	1027
York **119 182a 185** d.	...	1930	1932	...	...	...	2003	2002	...	...	...	2119	2150	2225	0013		0800	...	...	0858	...	...	0926	0958	...	...	1029
Harrogate **175** d.	...			...	...	...			...	...	...							...	...		...	...			...	0915	
Bradford Forster Square **173** d.	...			...	1915	1915			...	...	Ⓐ							...	...		...	...			...		
Leeds **119 173/5 188** d.	1916			...	1945	1945			...	2015	2045				0042			0805	...		0840	0905			0940	1006	
Wakefield Westgate **119** d.	1929			...	1958	1958			...	2028	2059				...			0819	...		0855	0918			0953	1019	
Doncaster **181 182** d.	1948	1953	1955	...	2018	2017	2027	2025	...	2048	2118	2142	2213	2248	...		0823	0838	0830		0921f	0938				1038	1055
Retford **181** d.				...					...	2102	2132		...	2304	...				0850q						1021	1052	
Lincoln **189 176** d.				...					2025				...		...												
Newark North Gate **189** d.		2017	2019	...					2051	2118		2205	...	2318	...				0905			1002	1009		1040j	1107	1119
Grantham **181** d.	2019			...					2104	2130	2155	2217	...	2330	...				0916			1015	1021			1118	
Peterborough **185 176** d.		2046	2051j	...	2105	2108	2116	2118j	2128	2150	2216	2237	...	2358	...		0911	0926	0938	1004	1008	1036	1041	1105	1109	1139	1151j
Stevenage **183/5** d.	2105	2115	2121	...			2145	2148	2158		2245	2305	...	0039s	...		0941					1107	1112				
London Kings Cross **181/2/3/5** a.	2131	2139	2146	...	2154	2200	2208	2216	2222	2240	2308	2330	...	0114	...		1005	1016	1026	1052	1057	1134	1137	1153	1158	1227	1239

	⑦	⑦	⑦	⑦	⑦	⑦	⑦	⑦	⑦	⑦	⑦	⑦	⑦	⑦	⑦	⑦	⑦	⑦	⑦	⑦	⑦	⑦ A	⑦	⑦	⑦	⑦	⑦ B
Edinburgh Waverley ‡ **119** d.	...	...	...	...	0900	0930	...	...	...	1000	1030	...	1100	1120	1130	...	...	...	...	1200	1220	1230	...	...	1300	1320	1330
Newcastle ‡ **119** a.	...	...	...	...	1023	1056	...	...	...	1127	1156	...	1223	1246	1256	...	...	...	...	1327	1347	1354	...	...	1427	1445	1456
Newcastle **119 188** d.	...	1000	...	...	1027	1100	...	...	...	1130	1158	...	1227	1252	1300	...	...	...	1315	1330	1350	1359	...	1416	1432	1451	1459
Durham **119 188** d.	...		...	...	1041		...	...	...	1144		...	1240	1306		...	...	...	1328	1344	1404		...	1429		1506	
Darlington **119 188** d.	...	1029	...	...	1100	1129	...	...	...	1203	1227	...	1259	1324	1330	...	...	...	1347	1402		1427	...	1447	1500	1524	1530
Northallerton **182a 188** d.	...		...	...	1112		...	...	...			...	1310			...	...	...	1400				...	1500			
York **182a** a.	...	1055	...	...	1131	1156	...	...	...	1229	1254	...	1329	1350	1357	...	...	...	1420	1428	1447	1456	...	1519	1527	1554	1557
York **119 182a 185** d.	...	1059	...	...	1133	1200	...	...	...	1232	1257	...	1331	1353	1402	...	...	...	1425	1431	1451j	1501	...	1526	1530	1558	1601
Harrogate **175** d.	...		...	...			...	...	1115			...				...	...	1315					...				
Bradford Forster Square **173** d.	...		...	1025			...	...				...				...	...						...				
Leeds **119 173/5 188** d.	...		1047	1105			1140	...	1205			1305				1340	...	1405					1505				
Wakefield Westgate **119** d.	...		1100	1118			1153	...	1218			1318				1353	...	1418					1518				
Doncaster **181 182** d.	...		1118	1138	1157		1212	...	1237	1255		1338	1356j			1420r	...	1437	1449	1456			1537	1549	1554		
Retford **181** d.	...		1136		1212			...					1411				...								1609		
Lincoln **189 176** d.	1055							1223									1420										
Newark North Gate **189** d.	1123j			1202				1249	1300	1319		1401					1446	1500		1519			1601	1612			
Grantham **181** d.	1134			1215				1302	1312			1413				1454	1459	1512			1540		1613				
Peterborough **185 176** d.	1158j	1206j		1239j	1253		1308r	1324	1333	1351j		1434	1451			1517	1523	1534	1542f	1551j			1635	1642	1650		
Stevenage **183/5** d.	1227			1309				1354				1503				1548	1554						1704				
London Kings Cross **181/2/3/5** a.	1250	1255	1258	1335	1341	1348	1357	1417	1421	1439	1445	1527	1540	1547	1556	1616	1619	1623	1635	1639	1645	1650	1728	1736	1739	1746	1749

	⑦	⑦	⑦ A	⑦	⑦	⑦	⑦	⑦	⑦	⑦	⑦	⑦	⑦	⑦	⑦	⑦ A	⑦	⑦	⑦	⑦	⑦	⑦	⑦	⑦	⑦	⑦	⑦
Edinburgh Waverley ‡ **119** d.	...	1400	1430	...	...	...	1450	...	1500	1530	...	...	...	1600	1620	1630	...	...	1700	1730	...	1800	...	1830	1900	2000	2100
Newcastle ‡ **119** a.	...	1528	1553	...	...	...	1616	...	1622	1656	...	...	...	1727	1747	1756	...	...	1823	1859	...	1928	...	1956	2030	2141	2237
Newcastle **119 188** d.	...	1531	1556	...	...	1606	1618	...	1626	1659	...	...	...	1730	1752	1759	...	...	1829	1903	...	1931	...	2001	2034	2144	...
Durham **119 188** d.	...	1545		...	...	1620	1631	...	1641		...	...	...	1743			...	...	1842		...	1944	...		2047	2157	...
Darlington **119 188** d.	...	1603	1627	...	...	1639	1650	...	1701	1729	...	...	...	1802	1822	1829	...	...	1901	1931	...	2003	...	2029	2106	2215	...
Northallerton **182a 188** d.	...			...	...	1651		...			...	...	...		1833		...	...	1913		...		...			2227	...
York **182a** a.	...	1629	1656	...	...	1710	1717	...	1728	1756	...	...	...	1828	1852	1859	...	...	1932	1957	...	2030	...	2055	2132	2258	...
York **119 182a 185** d.	...	1632	1659	...	...	1713	1720	...	1731	1759	...	...	...	1831	1854	1901	...	...	1937	2000	...	2032	...	2100	2135	2301	...
Harrogate **175** d.	...			...	...			...			...	1702	...				1800	...			...		...				...
Bradford Forster Square **173** d.	1536			...	...			...			...		1731					...			...		...				...
Leeds **119 173/5 188** d.	1616			...	1645			1716			...	1747	1815				1845	1916			1946		2045				...
Wakefield Westgate **119** d.	1629			...	1658			1729			...	1800	1828				1859	1929			1959		2058				...
Doncaster **181 182** d.	1648	1657		...	1721j	1736		1748	1758f		...	1818	1847	1855			1922j	1948	1959		2021j	2056	2117	2127	2159	2324	...
Retford **181** d.				...				1802			...							2003					2131			...	...
Lincoln **189 176** d.				1659							1800															...	...
Newark North Gate **189** d.		1720		1724	1746		1804				1826	1845		1919			1947		2023		2046	2120		2150	2222	...	...
Grantham **181** d.	1719			1736		1808		1825	1831		1839		1919		1944			2026		2049			2154	2202	2234	...	...
Peterborough **185 176** d.		1750		1805j	1814		1832		1852		1903j	1913		1954j			2016		2051	2109	2115	2151j	2216	2225j	2256	...	...
Stevenage **183/5** d.	1804			1834				1910			1932		2004					2111					2245	2254	2334s	...	...
London Kings Cross **181/2/3/5** a.	1827	1839	1849	1857	1905	1917	1921	1935	1942	1947	1959	2006	2028	2042	2048	2052	2106	2135	2139	2158	2205	2239	2310	2318	2359	...	...

NOTES for pages 132–134.

- **A** – To/from Aberdeen (Table **222**).
- **B** – To/from Inverness (Table **224**).
- **F** – To/from Skipton (Table **173**).
- **H** – To/from Hull (Table **181**).
- **Q** – To Middlesbrough (a. 1818).
- **R** – From Middlesbrough (d. 0708).
- **c** – Arrives 1120 on Ⓐ.
- **e** – Departs 3 minutes later on ⑥.
- **f** – Arrives 6–7 minutes earlier.
- **g** – Arrives 1924 on Ⓐ.
- **j** – Arrives 4–5 minutes earlier.
- **k** – Arrives 1710 on ⑥.
- **q** – Arrives 0842.
- **r** – Arrives 9 minutes earlier.
- **s** – Calls to set down only.
- **t** – Arrives 3 minutes earlier on Ⓐ.
- **v** – Arrives 1322 on Ⓐ.
- **‡** – For the full service Newcastle - Berwick upon Tweed - Edinburgh see Table **214**.

180a 🚌 PETERBOROUGH - KINGS LYNN 🚌

First Excel service **XL**

From **Peterborough** railway station to **Kings Lynn** bus station: Journey ± 81 minutes. Buses call at **Wisbech** bus station ± 43 minutes later.
On ⚒ at: 0704 Ⓐ, 0734, 0814, 0844 and every 30 minutes until 1844, 1944, 2044, 2248: On ⑦ at: 0904, 1004 and hourly until 1904.

From **Kings Lynn** railway station to **Peterborough** bus station: Journey ± 83 minutes. Buses call at **Wisbech** bus station ± 32 minutes later.
On ⚒ at: 0532 Ⓐ, 0602, 0632, 0702, 0732, 0802, 0832, 0902, 0927, 0957 and every 30 minutes until 1657, 1807, 1907, 2127: On ⑦ at: 0727, 0827 and hourly until 1727.

HT All trains convey 🍸 LONDON - HULL 181

km		Ⓐ	Ⓐ	Ⓐ	Ⓐ	Ⓐ	Ⓐ△	Ⓐ	Ⓐ	⑥	⑥	⑥	⑥	⑥△	⑥	⑥	⑦	⑦	⑦	⑦	⑦△	⑦	⑦
0	**London** Kings Cross 180 d.	0727	0948	1148	1348	1548	1718	1848	2030	0727	0948	1148	1448	1718	1748	1948	0838	1126	1250	1627	1722	1748	1952
44	Stevenage d.	|	|	|	|	|	|	|	|	|	|	|	|	|	|	|	|	|	|	|	|	1811**u**	|
170	Grantham 180 d.	0828	1050	1250	1449	1650	1829	1952	2131	0828	1049	1249	1550	1830	1850	2051	0937	1229	1350	1729	1827	1854	2052
223	Retford 180 d.	0852	1111	1311	1512	1712	|	2014	2153	0852	1111	1311	1611	|	1912	2114	0959	|	1412	1750	|	1915	2114
251	**Doncaster** 177 180 d.	0907	1126	1326	1528	1728	1911	2029	2208	0908	1126	1330	1628	1912**c**	1927	2129	1017**f**	1301	1428	1805	1906	1930	2129
280	Selby 177 a.	0923	1143	1341	1543	1744	1926	2046	2223	0923	1143	1345	1644	1927	1942	2144	1032	1318	1446	1821	1923	1946	2144
313	Brough 177 a.	0944	1205	1403	1608	1808	1947	2108	2245	0945	1205	1408	1706	1948	2004	2206	1053	1339	1507	1842	1945	2007	2207
330	**Hull** 177 a.	0958	1218	1417	1625	1825	2004	2123	2259	0958	1218	1425	1725	2005	2017	2220	1107	1353	1521	1856	2002	2021	2220
343	Beverley 177 a.	...	...	...	...	1843	...	2148	...	...	...	...	...	...	2041	...	...	...	...	...	...	2041	...

	Ⓐ	Ⓐ△	Ⓐ	Ⓐ	Ⓐ	Ⓐ	Ⓐ	Ⓐ	Ⓐ△	⑥	⑥△	⑥	⑥	⑥	⑥	⑥	⑦	⑦		⑦	⑦	⑦	⑦
Beverley 177 d.	0607	...	0753	...	...	...	...	...	...	0556	...	...	...	...	...	...	...	...	...	1228	...	...	...
Hull 177 d.	0627	0700	0824	1033	1233	1508	1708	1910	2029	0617	0700	0818	1033	1330	1531	1835	0809	0903	...	1248	1436	1621	1912
Brough 177 d.	0639	0713	0837	1045	1245	1521	1720	1922	2043	0629	0713	0835	1045	1343	1543	1847	0821	0916	...	1259	1448	1634	1924
Selby 177 d.	0703	0736	0902	1109	1308	1545	1743	1944	2105	0652	0736	0903	1108	1408	1606	1911	0843	0940	...	1322	1511	1704	1946
Doncaster 177 180 d.	0722**f**	0757	0926**f**	1126	1327	1605	1804	2004	2123	0710	0758	0926	1125	1426	1625	1928	0858	0959	...	1344	1528	1726	2008
Retford 180 d.	0741**f**	|	0940	1141	1341	1619	1818	2018	...	|	|	0940	1139	1440	1639	1942	0912	1013	...	1358	1543	1740	2022
Grantham 180 d.	0803	0834	1001	1202	1403	1641	1839	2040	...	0740	0835	1001	1200	1501	1701	2004	0934	1035	...	1419	1607	1802	2044
Stevenage a.	|	|	|	|	|	|	|	|	...	|	|	|	|	|	|	|	|	|		|	1652**s**	1845**s**	|
London Kings Cross 180 a.	0914	0951	1105	1305	1505	1744	1944	2147	...	0846	0947	1106	1307	1608	1807	2114	1041	1139	...	1535	1718	1908	2146

c – Arrives 1905. **f** – Arrives 5 minutes earlier. **s** – Stops to set down only. **u** – Stops to pick up only. △ – Operated by GR (Table **180**).

GC All trains convey 🍸 LONDON - BRADFORD 182

km		Ⓐ	Ⓐ	Ⓐ	Ⓐ	⑥	⑥	⑥	⑥	⑦	⑦	⑦	⑦
0	**London** Kings Cross 180 181 d.	1057	1456	1627	1948	1048	1525	1627	1957	1150	1550	1853	1927
123	Peterborough 180 d.	1146	|	|	|	|	|	|	2044	|	|	|	|
251	**Doncaster** 180 181 d.	1235	1631**a**	1802**f**	2119	1222**f**	1702	1802**a**	2134	1320	1721	2039**t**	2101
278	Pontefract Monkhill d.	1259	1655	|	|	|	|	|	2158	|	|	|	|
292	Wakefield Kirkgate d.	1315	1712	1836**r**	2143	1252	1724	1836**r**	2215	1343	1750	2103	2124
322	Halifax 190 d.	1349	1746	1909	2215	1324	1758	1910	2246	1413	1821	2133	2200
335	**Bradford** Interchange ‡ 190 a.	1402	1800	1923	2229	1338	1812	1924	2300	1427	1835	2147	2214

	Ⓐ	Ⓐ		Ⓐ	Ⓐ	⑥	⑥	⑥	⑥	⑦	⑦	⑦	⑦
Bradford Interchange ‡ 190 d.	0659	0757	...	1022	1449	0659	0846	1022	1528	0804	1210	1511	1559
Halifax 190 d.	0712	0811	...	1040	1502	0712	0900	1040**a**	1542	0817	1223	1525	1612
Wakefield Kirkgate d.	0747**a**	0854	...	1117	1537**a**	0745	0942	1120**a**	1620	0849	1259	1558	1647
Pontefract Monkhill d.	0802	0910	...	1134	1552	0800	0957	1134	1634	|	|	|	|
Doncaster 180 181 d.	0831	0935	...	1204	1623**f**	0829**a**	1024	1204	1705	0913	1322	1625	1711
Peterborough 180 d.	|	|	...	|	1719**f**	|	|	|	1753	|	|	|	|
London Kings Cross 180 181 a.	1007	1114	...	1344	1806	1007	1201	1344	1847	1042	1451	1756	1842

a – Arrives 5 minutes earlier.
f – Arrives 6 minutes earlier.
r – Arrives 11 minutes earlier.
t – Arrives 13 minutes earlier.

‡ – For additional services London - Leeds - **Bradford Forster Square**, see Table **180**.

GC All trains convey 🍸 LONDON - YORK - SUNDERLAND 182a

km		Ⓐ	Ⓐ	Ⓐ	Ⓐ	Ⓐ	Ⓐ	⑥	⑥	⑥		⑥	⑥	⑥	⑦	⑦		⑦	⑦	⑦
0	**London** Kings Cross 180 d.	0826	1127	1257	1427	1648	1927	0748	1127	1318	...	1427	1648	1927	0955	1350	...	1523	1653	1823
123	Peterborough 180 d.	0913	|	|	|	|	|	0836	|	|	...	|	|	|	|	|	...	|	|	|
303	**York** 180 188 d.	1025	1323	1451	1620**b**	1845**a**	2123	0945	1323	1515	...	1625**c**	1848**a**	2122**c**	1142	1538	...	1724**a**	1843	2012
339	Thirsk 188 d.	1043	1339	1508	1637	1902	2140	1003	1340	1532	...	1642	1905	2139	1159	1555	...	1742	1902	2031
351	Northallerton 180 188 d.	1059	1348	1517	1647	1911	2149	1014	1348	1543	...	1700	1913	2149	1207	1604	...	1758	1913	2039
375	Eaglescliffe d.	1117	1405	1533	1704	1929	2206	1031	1405	1603	...	1717	1930	2206	1225	1621	...	1815	1930	2056
399	Hartlepool d.	1136	1424	1556	1725	1951	2225	1050	1424	1623	...	1738	1952	2226	1245	1640	...	1836	1952	2116
428	**Sunderland** a.	1204	1449	1624	1753	2021	2252	1115	1449	1650	...	1806	2021	2253	1309	1707	...	1906	2021	2140

	Ⓐ	Ⓐ	Ⓐ		Ⓐ	Ⓐ	Ⓐ	⑥	⑥	⑥		⑥	⑥	⑥	⑦	⑦		⑦	⑦	⑦
Sunderland d.	0646	0853	1017	...	1230	1529	1730	0644	0829	0955	...	1219	1531	1731	0924	1028	...	1213	1414	1814
Hartlepool d.	0715	0920	1044	...	1254	1554	1800**a**	0714	0854	1022	...	1243	1600	1754	0949	1052	...	1238	1440	1840
Eaglescliffe d.	0735	0940	1104	...	1315	1615	1820	0735	0914	1046**a**	...	1304	1621	1814	1008	1113	...	1257	1459	1901
Northallerton 180 188 d.	0755	0959	1124	...	1340	1633	1841	0754	0932	1105	...	1325	1640	1833	1027	1133	...	1316	1517	1922
Thirsk 188 d.	0804	1008	1133	...	1349	1643	1854	0804	0946	1123**c**	...	1335	1651	1843	1036	1143	...	1325	1527	1931
York 180 188 d.	0823	1028	1154**a**	...	1408	1709	1913	0822	1010	1150	...	1352	1711	1902	1055	1203	...	1346	1548**a**	1949
Peterborough 180 d.	|	|	1304**a**	...	|	|	|	|	|	1301**a**	...	|	|	|	|	|	...	|	|	|
London Kings Cross 180 a.	1014	1231	1353	...	1606	1907	2106	1014	1214	1350	...	1544	1907	2058	1241	1349	...	1541	1741	2141

a – Arrives 5 minutes earlier. **b** – Arrives 1613. **c** – Arrives 8–11 minutes earlier. △ – Operated by GR (Table **180**).

LD All trains convey 🍸 2nd class only LONDON - NEWCASTLE - EDINBURGH 183

km		Ⓐ	Ⓐ	Ⓐ	Ⓐ	Ⓐ	⑥	⑥	⑥	⑥	⑥	⑦	⑦	⑦	⑦	⑦
0	**London** Kings Cross 180 d.	0548	1045	1218	1448	2027	0548	1025	1218	1548	1827	0852	1023	1213	1624	1924
44	Stevenage △ 180 d.	0610	|	1241	|	|	0611	|	1241	|	|	0913	1045	1235	|	|
432	**Newcastle** 180 214 d.	0841	1347	1516	1747	2308**c**	0841	1317	1518	1849	2124	1145**c**	1316	1510**c**	1921	2210
632	**Edinburgh** Waverley 180 214 a.	1007	1511	1641	1911	0043	1007	1442	1642	2013	2259	1313	1441	1636	2047	2335

	Ⓐ	Ⓐ	Ⓐ	Ⓐ	Ⓐ	⑥	⑥	⑥	⑥	⑥	⑥	⑦	⑦	⑦	⑦	⑦
Edinburgh Waverley 180 214 d.	0623	0924	1124	1613	1958	0536	0856	1256	1526	1756	2056	...	1054	1356	1550	1854
Newcastle 180 214 d.	0757	1055	1251	1752**c**	2135	0712**a**	1023	1422	1655	1934**b**	2220	0820	1221	1522	1718	2021
Stevenage ▽ 180 a.	|	|	1520	2018	0024	|	1248	1644	|	2202	...	1039	|	1739	1944	2258
London Kings Cross 180 a.	1046	1347	1544	2044	0105	0959	1314	1707	1948	2226	...	1107	1455	1806	2008	2320

a – Arrives 9 minutes earlier.
b – Arrives 1922.
c – Arrives 5–7 minutes earlier.
▽ – Trains call to set down only.
△ – Trains call to pick up only.

EM 2nd class SKEGNESS - NOTTINGHAM 184

km		⑥	Ⓐ	Ⓐ	⑥	⚒	⚒	⚒	⚒	Ⓐ	⑥	⚒	⚒	⑥	Ⓐ	⚒	⚒	⑥	Ⓐ	⑥	Ⓐ	Ⓐ	⑥	⑥	Ⓐ	⑥
0	**Skegness** d.	...	...	0706	0706	0818	0917**j**	1015	1114	1212	1215	1315	1416	1509	1512	1614	1722	1815	1815	1915	1920	2021	2022	2115	2120	...
8	Wainfleet d.	...	...	0716	0716	0827	0926**j**	1024	1123	1221	1224	1324	1425	1518	1521	1624	1731	1824	1824	1924	1929	2030	2031	2124	2129	...
38	Boston d.	0610	0613	0743	0743	0852	0951**j**	1049	1150**k**	1247	1249	1351	1450	1543	1546	1652	1758	1851	1855**t**	1949	1954	2055	2056	2151	2154	...
66	Sleaford d.	0633	0636	0811	0813	0916	1017	1113	1217	1313	1313	1415	1514	1614	1615	1715	1822	1915	1921	2016	2018	2124	2121	2214	2218	2247
89	Grantham a.	0700	0705	0840	0841	0941	1043	1139	1243	1339	1339	1441	1540	1641	1642	1741	1847	1942	1948	2043	2044	2149	2146	2240	|	|
89	Grantham 206 d.	0704	0711	0844	0844	0945	1046	1142	1246	1342	1342	1443	1543	1645	1650	1744	1850	1946	1951	2047	2047	2153	2150	2244	|	|
126	**Nottingham** 206 a.	0741	0756	0923	0920	1020	1121	1220	1322	1419	1419	1522	1621	1719	1724	1822	1922	2025	2031	2121	2121	2229	2227	2316	2305	2331

	⑦	⑦	⑦	⑦	⑦	⑦	⑦	⑦	⑦	⑦	⑦
Skegness d.	...	1015	1115	1215	1415	1515	1615	1715	1815	1907	2045
Wainfleet d.	...	1024	1124	1224	1424	1524	1624	1724	1824	1916	2054
Boston d.	0915	1052	1151	1252	1453	1550	1653	1754**f**	1853	1943	2120
Sleaford d.	0939	1116	1214	1316	1516	1613	1716	1817	1917	2008	2144
Grantham a.	1005	1142	1240	1342	1542	1639	1742	1843	1943	2034	2210
Grantham 206 d.	1010	1147	1245	1347	1547	1643	1747	1849	1947	2038	2215
Nottingham 206 a.	1045	1221	1321	1422	1624	1721	1821	1926	2021	2111	2252

	⚒	Ⓐ	⑥	⚒	⚒	⑥	Ⓐ	⑥	Ⓐ	⚒
Nottingham 206 d.	0509**v**	0547	0549	0642**n**	0746	0843	0847	0955	0955	1045
Grantham 206 a.	0552	|	|	0722	0825	0925	0929	|	|	1125
Grantham d.	▬	|	|	0725	0828	0931	0932	|	|	1128
Sleaford d.	⚒	0638	0645	0753	0857	0956	0958	1042	1043	1154
Boston d.	0620	0720**y**	0720**h**	0819	0921	1020	1022	1106	1111**f**	1218
Wainfleet d.	0644	0746	0747	0843	0945	1044	1046	1131	1142	1242
Skegness a.	0655	0758	0758	0853**j**	0957	1055	1057	1141	1152	1253

	⚒	⚒	⚒	⚒	⚒	⚒	⑥	Ⓐ	⚒	⑥	Ⓐ	⑥	Ⓐ	⑥
Nottingham 206 d.	1145	1245	1343**j**	1445	1545	1645	1745	1748	1846	1946	1948	2045	2048	2141
Grantham 206 a.	1221	1325	1423	1525	1627	1730	1825	1831	1924	2024	2030	2125	2129	2214
Grantham d.	1224	1327	1428	1527	1629	1732	1829	1834	1927	2028	2033	2129	2133	2217
Sleaford d.	1251	1354	1453	1553	1655	1800**j**	1854	1901	1956	2059**t**	2104**t**	2154	2158	2243
Boston d.	1314	1418	1517	1621	1718	1824**j**	1918	1930	2020	2123	2129	2218	2222	...
Wainfleet d.	1338	1442	1541	1646	1745	1849**j**	1942	1954	2044	...	...	...	...	...
Skegness a.	1350	1454	1553	1657	1758	1859**j**	1952	2005	2055	...	...	...	...	...

	⑦	⑦	⑦	⑦	⑦	⑦	⑦	⑦	⑦	⑦	⑦	⑦
Nottingham 206 d.	0830	0903	0950	1150	1250	1350	1449	1550	1650	1747	1830	1945
Grantham 206 a.	0916	0936	1027	1228	1327	1428	1525	1628	1729	1829	1907	2024
Grantham d.	▬	0940	1030	1231	1330	1432	1528	1631	1732	1832	1911	2028
Sleaford d.	⑦	1005	1057	1257	1356	1457	1554	1657	1758	1858	1936	2053
Boston d.	0920	1030	1120	1321	1420	1524	1618	1721	1822	1922	2000	2116
Wainfleet d.	0945	1055	1145	1346	1445	1548	1643	1746	1847	1947	2024	...
Skegness a.	0955	1105	1155	1356	1455	1559	1653	1756	1857	1957	2035	...

f – Arrives 5 minutes earlier. **j** – 3 minutes later on Ⓐ. **n** – Departs 0645 on ⑥. **v** – Departs 0513 on Ⓐ.
h – Arrives 0708. **k** – Departs 1154 on ⑥. **t** – Arrives 6 minutes earlier. **y** – Arrives 0701.

185 KINGS LYNN, CAMBRIDGE and PETERBOROUGH - LONDON - GATWICK ✈ - BRIGHTON GN, TL

KINGS LYNN - CAMBRIDGE - LONDON

km		✕	✕	Ⓐ	Ⓐ	⑥	Ⓐ	⑥	Ⓐ	⑥	Ⓐ	Ⓐ	⑥	Ⓐ	⑥	Ⓐ	Ⓐ	⑥	Ⓐ	⑥	Ⓐ	Ⓐ	⑥	Ⓐ
0	**Kings Lynn** d.		0444c	0514	...	...	0540	0542	0610	...	...	0640	0642	...	...	0710	...	0742	0742	...	0812	0842	0842	...
14	Downham Market d.		0458c	0528	...	...	0554	0556	0624	...	...	0654	0656	...	...	0724	...	0756	0756	...	0826	0856	0856	...
42	Ely **207 208** d.		0517	0548	0551	0553	0614	0618	0644	0653	0648	0714	0718	0728	0747	0744	0758	0818	0816	0853	0848	0916	0918	0947
66	**Cambridge** **207 208** a.		0537	0607	0611	0612	0633	0637	0703	0712	0708	0733	0737	0746	0806	0803	0818	0837	0835	0912	0907	0935	0937	1006
66	**Cambridge** d.		0537	0609	0615	0614	0639	0644	0709	0714	0715	0739	0744	0750	0814	0809	0820	0844	0837	0914	0909	0937	0944	1014
159	**London** Kings Cross a.		0632	0702	0725d	0702	0732	0732	0802	0802	0825d	0832	0832	0920d	0902	0902	0950d	0932	0932	1002	1004	1032	1032	1102

	⑥	✕	Ⓐ	⑥	✕	✕		✕	✕	Ⓐ	⑥	Ⓐ	⑥	Ⓐ	⑥	✕	Ⓐ	⑥	✕	Ⓐ	⑥	Ⓐ	✕
Kings Lynn d.	0912	0942	...	1012	1042	...	and at	...	1542	...	...	1640	1642	1710	...	1740	1810	...	1840	1910	...	...	1940
Downham Market d.	0927	0956	...	1029	1056	...	the same	...	1556	...	...	1654	1656	1724	...	1754	1824	...	1854	1924	...	...	1954
Ely **207 208** d.	0947	1018	1046	1053	1118	1153	minutes	1553	1618	1648	1653	1718	1718	1746	1752	1818	1846	1853	1918	1946	1953	2000	2018
Cambridge **207 208** a.	1006	1037	1105	1112	1137	1212	past each	1612	1637	1707	1712	1737	1737	1805	1811	1837	1905	1912	1937	2005	2012	2018	2037
Cambridge d.	1014	1044	1114	1114	1144	1214	hour until	1614	1644	1709	1714	1740	1744	1807	1814	1844	1907	1914	1944	2014	2014	2020	2044
London Kings Cross a.	1102	1132	1203	1205	1234	1302		1702	1732	1802	1802	1832	1832	1902	1902	1935	2002	2002	2032	2102	2102	2145d	2132

	Ⓐ	⑥	✕	⑥	Ⓐ	✕	Ⓐ	⑥	Ⓐ	⑥	⑦	⑦	⑦	⑦	⑦		⑦	⑦	⑦	⑦	⑦	⑦	⑦
Kings Lynn d.	2010	2012	2042	2112	...	2142	...	...	2244	2258		...	...	...	0825	and	1725	1754	1825	1925	2025	2125	2225
Downham Market d.	2024	2026	2056	2126	...	2156	...	...	2258	2313		...	...	...	0839		1739	1806	1839	1939	2039	2141	2239
Ely **207 208** d.	2046	2053y	2118	2147	2153	2218	2248	2253	2318	2331		...	...	...	0857	hourly	1757	1825	1857	1957	2057	2159	2257
Cambridge **207 208** a.	2105	2112	2137	2206	2212	2237	2307	2312	2337	2350		...	...	...	0917		1816	1842	1916	2016	2117	2218	2316
Cambridge d.	2114	2114	2144	2214	2214	2244	2310	2314	2353	2353		0640	0728	0822	0922	until	1822	1844	1922	2022	2122	2222	2322
London Kings Cross a.	2202	2202	2232	2302	2302	2332	0002	0007	0109	0104		0750	0832	0911	1011		1912	1936	2011	2111	2211	2312	0050

	✕	①	②–⑥	②–⑥	Ⓐ	Ⓐ	✕	⑥	Ⓐ	Ⓐ	⑥	Ⓐ	⑥		✕	⑥	Ⓐ	✕	✕	✕	✕	✕	
London Kings Cross d.		0002	0002	0032	...	...	0502	0539	0539	0602	0602	0639	0642	...	0712	0742	0739	0812	0842	0912	0942	1012	and at
Cambridge a.		0131	0112	0144	...	...	0618	0627	0627	0707	0711	0730	0730	...	0803	0830	0830	0902	0930	1003	1030	1100	the same
Cambridge **207 208** d.		...	...	...	0540	0610	0622z	0635	0635	0710	0713	0739	0735	...	0805	0835	0835	0905	0935	1005	1035	1103	minutes
Ely **207 208** d.		...	...	...	0559	0629	0642z	0655	0654	0729	0733	0758	0756	...	0825	0856	0856	0926	0956	1026	1056	1125	past each
Downham Market d.		...	...	...	0615	0645	...	0715	0713	0745	...	0815	0815	...	...	0915	0915	...	1015	...	1115	...	hour until
Kings Lynn a.		...	...	...	0630	0700	...	0730	0728	0800	...	0830	0830	...	...	0930	0930	...	1030	...	1130	...	

	✕	✕	⑥	Ⓐ	Ⓐ	⑥	⑥	Ⓐ	Ⓐ	Ⓐ	⑥	Ⓐ	⑥	Ⓐ	Ⓐ	⑥	Ⓐ	⑥	Ⓐ	Ⓐ	⑥	✕	Ⓐ	✕
London Kings Cross d.	1412	1442	1512	1512	1542	1542	1612	1612	1558d	1639	1642	1709	1712	1707d	1739	1742	1809	1812	1807d	1839	1842	1912	1907d	1939
Cambridge a.	1500	1530	1600	1600	1630	1630	1700	1703	1721	1730	1730	1803	1800	1814	1831	1830	1901	1900	1914	1930	1930	2003	2023	2032
Cambridge **207 208** d.	1505	1535	1605	1605	1635	1635	1705	1705	1722	1735	1735	1808	1805	1819	1835	1835	1905	1905	1919	1935	1935	2005	2025	2035
Ely **207 208** d.	1525	1554	1625	1627	1656	1656	1725	1726	1742	1756	1756	1827	1825	1838	1856	1856	1926	1926	1940	1956	1956	2024	2045	2055
Downham Market d.	...	1615	...	1645	1713	1715	...	1743	...	1813	1815	1843	...	...	1913	1915	1943	1944	...	2013	2015	2045	...	2115
Kings Lynn a.	...	1630	...	1700	1728	1730	...	1758	...	1828	1830	1858	...	...	1928	1930	1958	1959	...	2028	2030	2100	...	2130

	⑥	Ⓐ	✕	✕	⑥	Ⓐ	✕	⑥	Ⓐ	✕	✕	⑦	⑦	⑦	⑦	⑦	⑦		⑦	⑦	⑦	⑦	⑦
London Kings Cross d.	2009	2009	2039	2109	2139	2139	2209	2239	2239	2309	2327		0002	0032	0633	0754	0910	and	1910	2010	2110	2210	2310
Cambridge a.	2101	2100	2130	2201	2230	2231	2302	2330	2332	0002	0054		0112	0144	0746	0858	0958		2000	2059	2158	2259	0003
Cambridge **207 208** d.	2105	2103	2135	2205	2235	2235	2305	2335	2335	0005	...		...	...	...	0903	1003	hourly	2003	2103	2203	2303	0005
Ely **207 208** d.	2126	2124	2156	2226	2256	2256	2325	2355	2354	0024	...		...	...	...	0923	1022		2022	2124	2222	2322	0025
Downham Market d.	2145	...	2215	...	2312	2317	...	0011	0011	0041	...		...	...	...	0939	1038	until	2038	2140	2238	2338	0041
Kings Lynn a.	2200	...	2230	...	2327	2332	...	0026	0026	0056	...		...	...	...	0954	1053		2053	2155	2253	2353	0056

PETERBOROUGH and CAMBRIDGE - STEVENAGE - LONDON - GATWICK AIRPORT - HORSHAM and BRIGHTON ❖

km		✕	✕	✕	✕	✕	✕	✕	✕	✕	✕	✕	♥	✕	✕	✕	✕	✕	✕	✕	✕	✕	✕	✕	✕	✕
0	**Peterborough** d.		0323	0419	...	0453	...	0524	...	0554	...	0624		...	1824	...	1852	1924	...	1954	2024	...	2054	2124	...	2154
28	Huntingdon d.		0338	0433	...	0508	...	0540	...	0610	...	0640		...	1840	...	1910	1940	...	2010	2040	...	2110	2140	...	2210
	Cambridge d.		|	|	0453	|	0523	|	0553	|	0623	|		1823	|	1852	|	|	1953	|	|	2053	|	|	2153	|
79	Stevenage d.		0417	0513	0531	0547	0601	0617	0631	0647	0701	0717	and at	1901	1917	1931	1947	2017	2031	2047	2117	2131	2147	2217	2231	2247
119	Finsbury Park d.		0445	0537	0552	0607	0622	0637	0652	0707	0722	0737		1922	1937	1952	2007	2037	2052	2107	2137	2152	2207	2237	2252	2307
	London Kings Cross a.		0451	|	|	|	|	|	|	|	|	|	the same	|	|	|	|	|	|	|	|	|	|	|	|	|
122	**London** St Pancras **103** d.		...	0545	0600	0615	0630	0645	0700	0715	0730	0745		1930	1945	2000	2015	2045	2100	2115	2145	2200	2215	2245	2300	2315
124	Farringdon **103** d.		...	0549	0604	0619	0634	0649	0704	0719	0734	0749	times	1934	1949	2004	2019	2049	2104	2119	2149	2204	2219	2249	2304	2319
126	**London** Blackfriars **103** d.		...	0554	0609	0624	0639	0654	0709	0724	0739	0754		1939	1954	2009	2024	2054	2109	2124	2154	2209	2224	2254	2309	2324
128	**London** Bridge **102 103** d.		...	0600	0615	0630	0645	0700	0715	0730	0745	0800	past each	1945	2000	2015	2030	2100	2115	2130	2200	2215	2230	2300	2315	2330
143	East Croydon **102 103** d.		...	0617	0629	0647	0659	0717	0729	0747	0759	0817		1959	2017	2029	2047	2117	2129	2147	2217	2229	2247	2316	2329	2347
159	Redhill **102** d.		...	0637	|	0707	|	0737	|	0807	|	0837	hour until	|	2037	|	2107	2137	|	2207	2237	|	2308	2332	|	0002
169	Gatwick Airport ✈ **102 103** d.		...	0650	0645	0720	0715	0750	0745	0817	0815	0847		2015	2047	2045	2117	2147	2145	2217	2247	2245	2319	2345	2350	0017
187	**Horsham** **102** a.		...	0712	|	0744	|	0814	|	0842v	|	0913v		|	2110	|	2140	2212	|	2240	2310	|	2342	0008	|	0040
187	Haywards Heath **103** d.		...	...	0700	...	0730	...	0800	...	0830	...		2030	...	2100	...	...	2200	...	...	2300	...	...	0006	...
208	**Brighton** **103** a.		...	...	0718	...	0748	...	0818	...	0848	...		2048	...	2118	...	...	2218	...	...	2318	...	...	0023	...

	✕	✕	✕	✕	✕	⑦	⑦△	⑦△	⑦	⑦	⑦	and	⑦	⑦	⑦	⑦	⑦
Peterborough d.	2224	...	2254	2318	...		0545	0645	0745	...	0845		...	2045	...	2145	2245
Huntingdon d.	2240	...	2310	2334	...		0601	0659	0759	...	0859	at	...	2059	...	2159	2259
Cambridge d.	|	2253	|	|	2353		|	|	|	0828	|		2028	|	2128	|	|
Stevenage d.	2317	2331	2350	0013	0031		0640	0740	0836	0906	0936	the	2106	2136	2206	2236	2339
Finsbury Park d.	2337	2352	0010	0037	0056		0715	0802	0856	0926	0956		2126	2156	2226	2256	2359
London Kings Cross a.	2343	2359	0018	0047	0109		0723	0810	0902	|	1002	same	|	2202	|	2302	0007
London St Pancras **103** d.	...	...	...	...	...		▬	▬	▬	0934	▬		2135	▬	2235	▬	...
Farringdon **103** d.	...	...	...	...	...		...	...	...	0938	⑦	times	2139	⑦	2239	⑦	...
London Blackfriars **103** d.	...	...	...	...	...		⑦	⑦	⑦	0943	0948		2144	2148	2244	2248	...
London Bridge **102 103** d.	...	...	...	...	...		0719	0819	0855	0951	0955	past	2151	2155	2251	2255	...
East Croydon **102 103** d.	...	...	...	...	...		0735	0835	0912	1006	1012		2206	2212	2306	2312	...
Redhill **102** d.	...	...	...	...	...		0755	0855	0931	|	1031	each	|	2231	|	2331	...
Gatwick Airport ✈ **102 103** d.	...	...	...	...	...		0809	0909	0944	1022	1044		2222	2244	2322	2344	...
Horsham **102** a.	...	...	...	...	...		0831	0931	1006	|	1106	hour	|	2306	|	0006	...
Haywards Heath **103** d.	...	...	...	...	...		...	...	...	1037	...		2237	...	2337	...	...
Brighton **103** a.	...	...	...	...	...		...	...	...	1053	...	until	2253	...	2353	...	...

	✕	①	①	②–⑥	✕
Brighton **103** d.		...	...	...	...
Haywards Heath **103** d.		...	...	...	...
Horsham **102** d.		...	...	...	...
Gatwick ✈ **102 103** d.		...	...	...	...
Redhill **102** d.		...	...	...	...
East Croydon **102 103** d.		...	...	...	...
London Bridge **103** d.		...	...	...	...
London Blackfriars **103** d.		...	...	...	...
Farringdon **103** d.		...	...	...	...
London St Pancras **103** d.		...	...	...	...
London Kings Cross d.		0032	0132	0136	0512
Finsbury Park d.		0039	0139	0143	0518
Stevenage d.		0113	0219	0210	0537
Cambridge d.		|	|	|	|
Huntingdon d.		0151s	0253s	0248	0611
Peterborough a.		0210	0312	0306	0628

km		✕	✕	✕	✕	✕	✕	✕	✕	✕	✕	✕	✕	✕	✕	✕	✕	✕	★♣	✕	✕	✕	✕	✕	✕	✕
0	**Brighton** **103** d.	...	...	...	0506	...	0544c	...	0609a	...	0639a	...	0709a	...	0739a	...	0809a	...		...	1714	...	1744	...	1814	...
21	Haywards Heath **103** d.	...	...	...	0529	...	0601c	...	0631	...	0701	...	0731	...	0801	...	0831	...		...	1731	...	1801	...	1831	...
	Horsham **102** d.	...	...	...	|	0525	|	0552r	|	0625z	|	0654	|	0724	|	0755	|	0824		1654	|	1724	|	1754	|	1824
55	Gatwick Airport ✈ **102 103** d.	...	...	...	0546	0549	0616	0619	0646	0644a	0716	0719	0746	0749	0816	0818	0846	0849	and at	1719	1746	1749	1816	1819	1846	1849
	Redhill **102** d.	...	...	...	|	0559	|	0629	|	0659	|	0729	|	0759	|	0829	|	0859		1729	|	1759	|	1829	|	1859
65	East Cr'oydon **102 103** d.	...	...	...	0601	0615	0631	0645	0701	0715	0731	0745	0801	0815	0831	0845	0901	0915	the same	1745	1801	1815	1831	1845	1901	1915
81	**London** Bridge **102 103** d.	...	...	...	0616	0631	0646	0701	0716	0731	0746	0801	0816	0831	0846	0901	0916	0931		1801	1816	1831	1846	1901	1916	1931
82	**London** Blackfriars **103** d.	...	...	...	0622	0637	0652	0707	0722	0737	0752	0807	0822	0837	0852	0907	0922	0937	times	1807	1822	1837	1852	1907	1922	1937
84	Farringdon **103** d.	...	...	...	0626	0641	0656	0711	0726	0741	0756	0811	0826	0841	0856	0911	0926	0941		1811	1826	1841	1856	1911	1926	1941
86	**London** St Pancras **103** d.	...	...	...	0631	0646	0701	0716	0731	0746	0801	0816	0831	0846	0901	0916	0931	0946	past each	1816	1831	1846	1901	1916	1931	1946
	London Kings Cross d.	0532	0547	0617	|	|	|	|	|	|	|	|	|	|	|	|	|	|		|	|	|	|	|	|	|
90	Finsbury Park d.	0538	0553	0623	0638r	0653	0711j	0723	0738r	0753	0811j	0823	0841j	0853	0911j	0923	0941j	0953	hour until	1823	1838	1853	1910	1923	1938	1953
130	Stevenage d.	0559	0615	0645	0659r	0715	0732	0743	0759r	0815	0832	0845	0902	0915	0932	0945	1002	1015		1845	1900	1915	1932	1945	1959	2015
179	**Cambridge** d.	0638	|	|	0741	|	0811	|	0841	|	0911	|	0941	|	1011	|	1041	|		|	1941	|	2013	|	2039	|
	Huntingdon d.	...	0650	0720	...	0750	...	0818	...	0850	...	0920	...	0950	...	1020	...	1050		1920	...	1950	...	2020	...	2050
	Peterborough a.	...	0710t	0737	...	0808	...	0840k	...	0908	...	0939k	...	1007	...	1039	...	1106		1939	...	2006	...	2039	...	2106

a – Departs 5 minutes later on ⑥.
c – Ⓐ only.
d – London **Liverpool Street**.
j – Arrives 4 minutes earlier.
k – Arrives 4–6 minutes earlier on Ⓐ.
r – Departs 3 minutes later on ⑥.

s – Calls to set down only.
t – Arrives 0705 on ⑥.
v – On Ⓐ arrivals in Horsham may be up to 3 minutes earlier. On ⑥ all arrivals in Horsham are at xx10 and xx40.
z – ⑥ only.

★ – On ⑥ all trains from Brighton depart at xx14 and xx44 and on Ⓐ from 0914 onwards.
♣ – The 1514, 1544, 1614 and 1644 departures from Brighton depart Finsbury Park at 1638, 1708, 1738, and 1808, and Stevenage at 1700, 1730, 1800 and 1830 respectively.
❖ – See Table **180** for fast trains Peterborough - London Kings Cross (operated by GR). See upper panel for other fast trains Cambridge - London Kings Cross and v.v.

FOR OTHER NOTES SEE TOP OF NEXT PAGE → → →

GN, TL KINGS LYNN, CAMBRIDGE and PETERBOROUGH - LONDON - GATWICK - BRIGHTON 185

	⚒	⚒	⚒	⚒	⚒	⚒	⚒	⚒	⚒	⚒	⚒	⚒	⚒	⚒	⑦	⑦	⑦	⑦	⑦	⑦		⑦	⑦	⑦
Brighton 103 d.	1844	...	1914	...	...	2014	...	...	2114	...	...	2214	...	▽	...	...	...	*0757*	...	0922		...	2122	...
Haywards Heath 103 d.	1901	...	1931	...	...	2031	...	...	2131	...	...	2231	...	...	...	...	...	*0818*	...	0938		...	2138	...
Horsham 102 d.	|	1855	|	1925	1955	|	2025	2055	|	2125	2155	|	2225	2311	...	0645	0745	|	0837	|		2037	|	2137
Gatwick Airport ✈ 102 103 d.	1916	1919	1946	1949	2019	2046	2049	2119	2146	2149	2219	2246	2249	2335	...	0707	0807	0853	0900	0954	and at	2100	2153	2200
Redhill 102 d.	|	1929	|	1959	2029	|	2059	2129	|	2204	2234	|	2304	2349	...	0722	0822	|	0914	|		2115	|	2215
East Croydon 102 103 d.	1931	1945	2001	2015	2045	2101	2115	2145	2201	2216	2245	2301	2315	0010	...	0739	0839	0909	0933	1009	the same	2133	2209	2233
London Bridge 102 103 d.	1946	2001	2016	2031	2101	2116	2131	2201	2216	2231	2301	2316	2331	|	...	0757	0857	0926	0949	1026		2150	2226	2251
London Blackfriars 103 d.	1952	2007	2022	2037	2107	2122	2137	2207	2222	2237	2307	2322	2337	0037	...	▬	▬	0932	0954	1032	minutes	2156	2232	▬
Farringdon 103 d.	1956	2011	2026	2041	2111	2126	2141	2211	2226	2241	2311	2326	2341	0041	...	...	...	0936	▬	1036		▬	2236	...
London St Pancras 103 d.	2001	2016	2031	2046	2116	2131	2146	2216	2231	2246	2316	2331	2346	0046	...	⑦	⑦	0941	⑦	1041	past each	⑦	2241	⑦
London Kings Cross d.	|	|	|	|	|	|	|	|	|	|	|	|	|	|	0733	0813	0913	|	1013	|		2213	|	2322
Finsbury Park d.	2008	2023	2038	2053	2123	2138	2153	2223	2238	2253	2323	2338	2353	0053	0739	0819	0919	0948	1019	1048	hour until	2219	2248	2328
Stevenage d.	2029	2045	2059	2115	2145	2200	2215	2244	2259	2315	2345	2359	0014	0125	0804	0839	0939	1009	1040	1109		2240	2309	2348
Cambridge d.	2111f	|	2139	|	|	2239	|	|	2339	|	|	0039	|	|	|	|	|	1048	|	1148		|	2348	|
Huntingdon d.	...	2120	...	2150	2220	...	2250	2320	...	2350	0020	...	0050	0203	0842	0915	1015	...	1115	...		2315	...	0023
Peterborough a.	...	2139n	...	2206	2239n	...	2306	2339	...	0009	0039	...	0110	0221	0858	0931	1031	...	1131	...		2333	...	0042

f – Arrives 2108 on Ⓐ.
n – Arrives 4 minutes earlier on Ⓐ.

♥ – On Ⓐ the departures from Cambridge at 1453, 1523, 1553, 1623, 1653 and 1723 arrive Brighton 3 minutes later than shown.
△ – Subject to alteration from Sept. 21 with partial 🚌 replacement (earlier departures from Peterborough and Huntingdon).
▽ – Subject to alteration on ⑥ from Sept. 27 with partial 🚌 replacement (later arrivals at Huntingdon and Peterborough).

TP Most trains convey 🍷 THE NORTH EAST and YORKSHIRE - MANCHESTER and LIVERPOOL 188

km	km		①	②–⑤	⑥	②–⑤	⑥	①	⚒	⚒	⚒	⚒	⚒	②–⑥	⚒	①	⚒	⚒	⚒	⚒	⚒	⚒	⚒	Ⓐ	⑥	⚒
0		**Newcastle** 119 180 d.	...	...	...	...	...	...	...	...	...	...	...	0421	...	0448	...	...	0535	...	0600	...	...	0648	0659	...
23		Durham 119 180 d.	...	...	...	...	...	...	...	...	...	...	...	0437	...	0520	...	...	0551	...	0619	...	...	0703	0715	...
58		Darlington 119 180 d.	...	...	...	...	...	...	...	...	...	...	...	0455	...	0538	...	...	0610	...	0637	...	...	0721	0733	...
	0	**Saltburn** 212 d.	...	...	...	...	...	...	...	...	...	...	...	|	...	|	...	...	|	...	|	0554	...	|	|	...
	8	Redcar Central 212 d.	...	...	...	...	...	...	...	...	...	...	...	|	...	|	...	...	|	...	|	0603	...	|	|	...
	20	**Middlesbrough** 212 d.	...	...	...	...	...	...	...	...	...	...	...	|	...	|	...	...	|	...	|	0618	...	|	|	...
80	45	Northallerton 119 180 182a d.	...	...	...	...	...	...	...	...	...	...	...	|	...	|	...	...	0620	...	|	0650	...	0733	|	...
93	▬	Thirsk 182a d.	...	...	...	...	...	...	...	...	...	...	...	|	...	|	...	...	0630	...	|	0658	...	|	|	...
	0	**Scarborough** d.	...	...	...	...	...	...	...	...	...	...	...	|	...	|	...	0550	|	...	|	|	...	|	|	0648
	34	Malton d.	...	...	...	...	...	...	...	...	...	...	...	|	...	|	...	0615	|	...	|	|	...	|	|	0712
	67	**York** 119 180 182a a.	...	...	...	...	...	...	...	...	...	...	...	0538t	...	0604	...	0640	0647	...	0703	0717	...	0802	0800	0739
128	▬		...	...	...	...	...	...	...	...	...	...	...	|	...	|	...	▬	|	...	|	|	...	|	|	|
		York 119 177 191 d.	0134	0132	0152	0236	0253	0248	...	...	0503	...	0548	0540	0552a	0606	0617	⚒	0649	0658	0705	0719	...	0804	0803	0748
	0	**Hull** 177 181 d.	|	|	|	|	|	|	...	...	|	0459	|	|	|	|	|	0601	|	|	|	|	0653	|	|	|
	50	Selby 177 181 d.	|	|	|	|	|	|	...	...	|	0535	|	|	|	|	|	0633	|	|	|	|	0725	|	|	|
169	83	**Leeds** 119 191 a.	0200	0208	0218	0313	0319	0314	...	...	0543	0600	0612	0622	|	0628	0642	0658	0713	|	0727	0742	0754	0828	0827	0814
	0	**Leeds** d.	0201	0211	0220	0317	0320	0318	...	...	0545	0600	0615	0630	|	0630	0645	0700	0715	|	0730	0745	0800	0830	0830	0815
	41	Wakefield Kirkgate d.	|	|	|	|	|	|	...	0530	|	|	|	|	0631	|	|	|	|	0733	|	|	|	|	|	|
184	|	Dewsbury d.	|	|	|	|	|	|	...	|	0557	|	0626	|	|	|	0657	|	0726	|	|	0757	|	|	|	0826
195	67	Huddersfield d.	0242y	0249	0256	0354	0356	0354	...	0553	0608	0621	0637	0649	0655	0649t	0707	0720	0737	0755	0748t	0807	0820	0849	0849	0837
226	96	Stalybridge d.	|	|	|	|	|	|	...	0621	|	0640	0658	|	0722	|	|	0739	0758	0823	|	|	0840	|	|	|
237	|	**Manchester** Victoria a.	|	|	|	|	|	|	0553	|	0638	0652	0710	0718	|	0718	0737	0751	0809	|	0820	0838	0852	0919f	0919f	0909
241	108	**Manchester** Piccadilly a.	0336	0342	0329	0456	0428	0456	|	0636	0649	|	...	|	0737	|	0749	|	...	0839	|	0849	|	|	|	...
257	▬	**Manchester** Airport ✈ a.	0352	0359	0352	0514	0454	0514	|	...	0710	|	...	|	...	|	0810	|	...	...	|	0910	|	|	|	...
288		**Liverpool** Lime Street a.	...	...	...	...	...	...	0631	...	...	0732	...	0802	...	0802	...	0832	...	...	0859	...	0933	0959	0959	...

	⚒	⚒	⚒	⚒	⚒	⚒	⚒	⚒	⚒	⚒	⚒	⚒	⚒	⚒	⚒	⚒	⚒	⚒	⑥	Ⓐ	⚒	⚒	⚒	⚒	⚒	⚒	⚒
Newcastle 119 180 d.	...	...	...	...	...	0800	...	...	...	...	0902	...	...	...	...	1003	...	...	...	...	...	1101	...	...	...	...	1202
Durham 119 180 d.	...	...	...	...	...	0818	...	...	...	...	0918	...	...	...	...	1018	...	...	...	...	...	1117	...	...	...	...	1218
Darlington 119 180 d.	...	...	...	...	...	0836	...	...	...	...	0936	...	...	...	...	1036	...	...	...	...	...	1135	...	...	...	...	1236
Saltburn 212 d.	...	...	...	...	...	|	...	...	...	...	|	...	...	...	...	|	...	...	...	...	...	|	...	...	...	...	|
Redcar Central 212 d.	...	0656z	...	...	...	|	0759j	...	...	...	|	0858	...	...	...	|	0958	...	...	...	...	|	1058	...	...	...	|
Middlesbrough 212 d.	...	0714z	...	...	...	|	0820	...	...	...	|	0918	...	...	...	|	1020	...	...	...	...	|	1117	...	...	...	|
Northallerton 119 180 182a d.	...	0749	...	...	...	|	0851	...	...	...	|	0950	...	...	...	|	1051	...	...	...	...	|	1148	...	...	...	|
Thirsk 182a d.	...	0758	...	...	...	|	0859	...	...	...	|	0959	...	...	...	|	1059	...	...	...	...	|	1156	...	...	...	|
Scarborough d.	...	|	...	0748	...	|	|	...	0854	...	|	|	...	0954	...	|	|	...	1048	1054	...	|	|	...	1154	...	|
Malton d.	...	|	...	0812	...	|	|	...	0918	...	|	|	...	1018	...	|	|	...	1112	1118	...	|	|	...	1218	...	|
York 119 180 182a a.	...	0817	...	0838	...	0903	0917	...	0944	...	1003	1018	...	1044	...	1103	1118	...	1138	1144	...	1202	1217	...	1244	...	1302
York 119 177 191 d.	0756	0819	...	0849	0855	0905	0919	...	0949	0952k	1005	1020	...	1048	1052	1105	1120	...	1139	1148	1154c	1205	1219	...	1249	1253	1305
Hull 177 181 d.	|	|	0755	|	|	|	|	0903	|	|	|	|	1003	|	|	|	|	1103	|	|	|	|	|	1203	|	|	|
Selby 177 181 d.	|	|	0833	|	|	|	|	0935	|	|	|	|	1035	|	|	|	|	1135	|	|	|	|	|	1235	|	|	|
Leeds 119 191 a.	|	0843	0858	0913	|	0927	0943	0957	1013	|	1027	1043	1057	1111	|	1127	1143	1157	1203	1211	|	1227	1244	1257	1313	|	1327
Leeds d.	|	0845	0900	0915	|	0930	0945	1000	1015	|	1030	1045	1100	1115	|	1130	1145	1200	1215	1215	|	1230	1245	1300	1315	|	1330
Wakefield Kirkgate d.	0830	|	|	|	0933	|	|	|	|	1033	|	|	|	|	1133	|	|	|	|	|	1232	|	|	|	|	1333	|
Dewsbury d.	|	0857	|	0926	|	|	0957	|	1026	|	|	1057	|	1126	|	|	1157	|	1226	1226	|	|	1257	|	1326	|	|
Huddersfield d.	0855	0907	0921	0937	0955	0948t	1007	1020	1036	1055	1048t	1107	1121	1137	1155	1148t	1207	1220	1237	1237	1255	1249t	1307	1320	1337	1355	1348t
Stalybridge d.	0923	|	0940	|	1022	|	|	1040	|	1123	|	|	1140	|	1223	|	|	1240	|	|	1322	|	|	1339	|	1422	|
Manchester Victoria a.	|	0936	0952	1009	|	1019	1038	1052	1112	|	1120	1137	1152	1209	|	1219f	1237	1252	1309	1309	|	1321	1336	1351	1409	|	1422
Manchester Piccadilly a.	0938	0949	|	...	1037	|	1049	|	...	1138	|	1149	|	...	1238	|	1249	|	...	...	1337	|	1349	|	...	1437	|
Manchester Airport ✈ a.	...	1010	|	...	...	|	1109	|	...	...	|	1210	|	...	...	|	1309	|	...	...	...	|	1410	|	...	...	|
Liverpool Lime Street a.	...	...	1031	...	...	1059	...	1131	...	...	1159	...	1231	...	...	1259	...	1331	...	...	...	1359	...	1431	...	...	1459

	⚒	⚒	⚒	⚒	⚒	⚒	⚒	⚒	⚒	⚒	⚒	⚒	⚒	⚒	⚒	⚒	⚒	⚒	⚒	⚒	⚒	⚒	⑥	Ⓐ	⚒	⚒	⚒
Newcastle 119 180 d.	...	...	...	...	1301	...	...	...	...	1402	...	...	...	...	1502	...	...	...	...	1602	...	...	...	...	...	1702	...
Durham 119 180 d.	...	...	...	...	1316	...	...	...	...	1418	...	...	...	...	1518	...	...	...	...	1618	...	...	...	...	...	1718	...
Darlington 119 180 d.	...	...	...	...	1334	...	...	...	...	1436	...	...	...	...	1536	...	...	...	...	1636	...	...	...	...	...	1736	...
Saltburn 212 d.	...	...	...	...	|	...	...	...	...	|	...	...	...	...	|	...	...	...	...	|	...	...	...	...	...	|	...
Redcar Central 212 d.	1159	...	...	...	|	1258	...	...	...	|	1358	...	...	...	|	1457	...	...	...	|	1558	...	...	...	...	|	1658
Middlesbrough 212 d.	1220	...	...	...	|	1317	...	...	...	|	1420	...	...	...	|	1517	...	...	...	|	1620	...	...	...	...	|	1716
Northallerton 119 180 182a d.	1251	...	...	...	|	1350	...	...	...	|	1450	...	...	...	|	1550	...	...	...	|	1651	...	...	...	...	|	1750
Thirsk 182a d.	1259	...	...	...	|	1359	...	...	...	|	1459	...	...	...	|	1559	...	...	...	|	1659	...	...	...	...	|	1759
Scarborough d.	|	...	1254	...	|	|	...	1354	...	|	|	...	1454	...	|	|	...	1554	...	|	|	...	1650	1654	...	|	|
Malton d.	|	...	1318	...	|	|	...	1418	...	|	|	...	1518	...	|	|	...	1618	...	|	|	...	1714	1718	...	|	|
York 119 180 182a a.	1317	...	1347	...	1401	1417	...	1447n	...	1503	1518	...	1545	...	1602	1617	...	1644	...	1702	1717	...	1739	1744	...	1803	1817
York 119 177 191 d.	1320	...	1350	1354	1402	1420	...	1449n	1458	1504	1520	...	1547	1553	1605	1619	...	1649	1659	1704	1720	...	1742	1749	1754	1805	1818
Hull 177 181 d.	|	1303	|	|	|	|	1403	|	|	|	|	1503	|	|	|	|	1603	|	|	|	|	1703	|	|	|	|	|
Selby 177 181 d.	|	1335	|	|	|	|	1435	|	|	|	|	1535	|	|	|	|	1635	|	|	|	|	1735	|	|	|	|	|
Leeds 119 191 a.	1343	1357	1413	|	1427	1443	1457	1512	|	1527	1543	1557	1613	|	1627	1643	1658	1713	|	1727	1743	1757	1810	1812	|	1828	1842
Leeds d.	1345	1400	1415	|	1430	1445	1500	1515	|	1530	1545	1600	1615	|	1630	1645	1700	1715	|	1730	1745	1800	1815	1815	|	1830	1845
Wakefield Kirkgate d.	|	|	|	1432	|	|	|	|	1533	|	|	|	|	1633	|	|	|	|	1733	|	|	|	|	|	1833	|	|
Dewsbury d.	1357	|	1426	|	|	1457	|	1526	|	|	1557	|	1626	|	|	1657	|	1726	|	|	1756	|	1826	1826	|	|	1857
Huddersfield d.	1407	1420	1437	1455	1448t	1507	1520	1537	1555	1548t	1607	1621	1637	1655	1649t	1707	1720	1737	1756	1749t	1807	1820	1837	1837	1855	1848t	1907
Stalybridge d.	|	1440	|	1522	|	|	1539	|	1622	|	|	1640	|	1723	|	|	1740	|	1823	|	|	1840	|	|	1922	|	|
Manchester Victoria a.	1438	1452	1509	|	1520	1536	1551	1609	|	1619	1636	1652	1709	|	1719f	1737	1752	1809	|	1821	1837	1852	1909	1909	|	1919f	1936
Manchester Piccadilly a.	1449	|	...	1537	|	1549	|	...	1637	|	1649	|	...	1739	|	1749	|	...	1839	|	1849	|	...	...	1937	|	1949
Manchester Airport ✈ a.	1509	|	...	...	|	1610	|	...	...	|	1710	|	...	...	|	1810	|	...	...	|	1910	|	...	...	...	|	2010
Liverpool Lime Street a.	...	1531	...	...	1559	...	1634	...	...	1659	...	1731	...	...	1759	...	1833	...	...	1859	...	1931	...	...	...	2006	...

a – Departs 0559 on ⑥.
c – Departs 1158 on ⑥.
f – Departs 5 minutes later.

j – Departs 0805 on ⑥.
k – Departs 0958 on Ⓐ.
n – On ⑥ arrives 1444, departs 1446.

t – Connects with train in previous column.
y – Arrives 0235.
z – On ⑥ Redcar d. 0650, Middlesbrough d. 0719.

188 THE NORTH EAST and YORKSHIRE - MANCHESTER and LIVERPOOL

Most trains convey 🍷 TP

	⚒	⚒	⚒	⚒	⚒	⚒	⚒	⚒	⚒	⚒	⚒	⚒	⑥	Ⓐ	⚒	⑥	Ⓐ	⚒	⚒	⚒E	⚒	⑥	⚒	⑥	Ⓐ	⑥	⑤	①–④
Newcastle 119 180 d.	...	...	...	1803	...	...	...	...	1906	...	...	1944	...	...	...	...	...	...	...	2058	...	...	...	2149	2201	...	...	...
Durham 119 180 d.	...	...	...	1818	...	...	...	...	1922	...	...	1959	...	...	...	...	...	...	...	2114	...	...	...	2205	2214	...	...	...
Darlington 119 180 d.	...	...	...	1836	...	...	...	...	|	...	...	2017	...	...	...	...	...	...	...	2133	...	...	...	2223	2232	...	...	...
Saltburn 212 d.	...	...	...	|	...	...	...	...	|	...	...	|	...	...	...	...	...	2008	...	|	...	...	...	|	|	...	...	...
Redcar Central 212 d.	...	...	...	|	1758	...	...	...	|	1858	...	|	...	...	...	...	...	2019	...	|	2056	...	...	|	|	2156	2205	2205
Middlesbrough 212 d.	...	...	...	|	1820	...	...	...	|	1918	...	|	...	...	...	...	...	2035	...	|	2117	...	...	|	|	2211	2220	2220
Northallerton 119 180 182a d.	...	...	...	|	1851	...	...	...	|	1950	...	2028	...	...	...	...	...	2105	...	2143	2150	...	...	2234	2242	2241	2250	2250
Thirsk 182a d.	...	...	...	|	1859	...	...	...	|	1959	...	|	...	...	...	...	...	2113	...	|	2158	...	...	|	|	2249	2259	2259
Scarborough d.	...	1754	...	|	|	...	1854	...	|	|	...	|	1954	1954	...	2050	2054	|	...	|	|	...	2154	|	|	|	|	|
Malton d.	...	1818	...	|	|	...	1918	...	|	|	...	|	2018	2018	...	2114	2118	|	...	|	|	...	2218	|	|	|	|	|
York 119 180 182a a.	...	1847	...	1902	1918	...	1944	...	2003	2017	...	2048	2044	2044	...	2139	2143	2134t	...	2202	2220	...	2244	2253	2302	2318	2317	2317
	...	|	...	|	|	...	|	...	|	|	...	|	|	|	...	|	|	▬	...	|	...	...	▬	▬	▬	▬	|	2320
York 119 177 191 d.	...	1848	1854	1904	1919	...	1949	1952	2005	2020	...	2049	2046	2051	2052c	2142	2147	⚒	2159	2205	...	2244	①–④	⑤	⑥	...	2320	|
Hull 177 181 d.	1803	|	|	|	|	1903	|	|	|	|	2003	|	|	|	|	|	|	2103	|	|	...	|	2203	2203	2203	...	|	|
Selby 177 181 d.	1835	|	|	|	|	1935	|	|	|	|	2035	|	|	|	|	|	|	2135	|	|	...	|	2236	2236	2236	Ⓐ	|	0001
Leeds 119 191 a.	1858	1912	|	1927	1943	1957	2012	|	2027	2043	2100	2112	2131	2135	|	2204	2213	2212	|	2228	...	|	2310	2300	2258	🚌	2346	0004
Leeds d.	1900	1915	|	1930	1945	2000	2015	|	2030	2045	...	2115	2145	2144	|	2215	2215	...	|	2230	...	|	2315	...	2300	2325	2348	|
Wakefield Kirkgate d.	|	|	1933	|	|	|	|	2027k	|	|	...	|	|	|	2136	|	|	...	2231	|	...	2317	|	...	|	|	|	|
Dewsbury d.	|	1926	|	|	1957	|	2026	|	|	2057	...	|	2157	2156	|	2227	2226	...	|	2241	...	|	|	...	2311	2355	|	0046
Huddersfield d.	1921	1937	1955	1948t	2007	2020	2038	2055	2048t	2106	...	|	2207	2207	2158	2237	2237	...	2256	2251t	...	2337	0018j	...	2322	0030	0028	|
Stalybridge d.	1940	|	2022	|	|	2040	|	2123	|	2126	...	|	2230	2230	2226	2256	2256	...	2324	2311	...	0004	|	...	2341	...	|	0130
Manchester Victoria a.	1952	2010	|	2022	2037	2052	2110	|	2122	2138	...	2236	2242r	2242f	|	|	|	...	|	2323	...	|	0103	...	|	...	0057	...
Manchester Piccadilly a.	|	...	2037	|	2049	|	...	2140	|	2149	...	|	2300	2258	2241	2311	2314	...	2340	|	...	0019	...	...	2357	...	...	...
Manchester Airport ✈ a.	|	...	...	|	2110	|	...	...	|	2210	...	|	2314	2315	...	...	...	...	...	|	...	...	...	...	...	...	...	...
Liverpool Lime Street a.	2032	...	...	2056	...	2133	...	...	2205	...	...	2323	...	...	...	...	...	...	...	0005	...	...	...	...	...	...	...	...

	⑤	Ⓐ	①–④	⑥	Ⓐ		⑦	⑦	⑦	⑦	⑦a	⑦	⑦b	⑦	⑦	⑦	⑦	⑦	⑦	⑦	⑦	⑦	⑦	⑦	⑦	⑦	⑦	⑦
Newcastle 119 180 d.	...	...	⑥	...	...		...	...	...	0749	...	0759	...	...	...	0859	...	...	...	...	...	1003	...	...	...	...	1059	...
Durham 119 180 d.	...	...	...	...	...	⑦	...	...	...	0801	...	0815	...	...	...	0915	...	...	...	...	...	1019	...	...	...	...	1119	...
Darlington 119 180 d.	...	...	...	...	...		...	...	...	0820	...	0833	...	...	...	0933	...	...	...	...	...	1037	...	...	...	...	1137	...
Saltburn 212 d.	...	...	...	...	2310		...	...	...	|	...	|	...	...	...	|	...	...	0853	...	...	|	...	...	...	...	|	...
Redcar Central 212 d.	...	...	...	...	2318		...	...	...	|	...	|	...	...	...	|	...	...	0902	...	...	|	...	1002	...	...	|	...
Middlesbrough 212 d.	...	...	...	...	2331		...	...	...	|	...	|	...	...	...	|	...	...	0915	...	...	|	...	1017	...	...	|	...
Northallerton 119 180 182a d.	...	...	...	...	0002		...	...	...	0830	...	0844	...	...	...	|	...	...	0947	...	...	|	...	1050	...	...	|	...
Thirsk 182a d.	...	...	...	...	0010		...	...	...	|	...	|	...	...	...	|	...	...	0955	...	...	|	...	1058	...	...	|	...
Scarborough d.	...	2245	...	2245	|		...	...	...	|	...	|	...	...	...	|	0854	...	|	...	0954	|	...	|	...	1051	|	...
Malton d.	...	2311	...	2309	|		...	...	...	|	...	|	...	...	...	|	0918	...	|	...	1020	|	...	|	...	1118	|	...
York 119 180 182a a.	...	2335	...	2334	0040		...	...	...	0849	...	0903	...	...	...	0959	0944	...	1013	...	1045	1103	...	1116	...	1144	1203	...
York 119 177 191 d.	...	2339	...	2336	...		0817	...	0844	0852	...	0904	...	0916	...	1004	0950	1000	1020	...	1049	1104	1100	1120	...	1148	1204	1200
Hull 177 181 d.	2304	|	2303	|	...		|	0803	|	|	...	|	...	|	0855	|	|	|	|	1003	|	|	|	|	1103	|	|	|
Selby 177 181 d.	2336	|	2335	|	...		|	0836	|	|	...	|	...	|	0930	|	|	|	|	1035	|	|	|	|	1138	|	|	|
Leeds 119 191 a.	0003	0007n	0003*	0004	...		0841	0858	0906	0928	...	0928	...	0944	0955	1029	1013	|	1043	1056	1113	1127	|	1143	1200	1212	1227	|
Leeds d.	0013	0013n	...	...	...		0845	0900	0915	...	...	0930	...	0945	1000	1030	1015	|	1045	1100	1115	1130	|	1145	1203	1215	1230	|
Wakefield Kirkgate d.	|	|	...	...	...		|	|	|	...	0921	|	0935	|	|	|	|	1032	|	|	|	|	1132	|	|	|	|	1232
Dewsbury d.	|	|	...	...	...		0856	|	0926	...	|	|	|	0958	|	|	1027	|	1057	|	1127	|	|	1157	|	1227	|	|
Huddersfield d.	|	|	...	...	...		0906	0920	0936	...	0955v	0948t	0955	1008	1021	1049	1037	1055	1108	1120	1137	1148	1155	1208	1221	1237	1248	1255
Stalybridge d.	|	|	...	...	...		|	0941	|	...	1022	|	1022	|	1040	|	|	1123	|	1139	|	|	1223	|	1241	|	|	1323
Manchester Victoria a.	0115	0115	...	...	...		0939	0953	1006	...	|	1020	|	1040f	1052	1119f	1108	|	1138	1151f	1206	1220	|	1238	1253	1306	1319	|
Manchester Piccadilly a.	0125	0125	...	...	...		...	|	...	...	1038	|	1038	1056	|	|	...	1138	1149	|	...	|	1239	1250	|	...	|	1338
Manchester Airport ✈ a.	...	...	...	...	...		...	|	...	...	...	|	...	1118	|	|	...	...	1212	|	...	|	...	1312	|	...	|	...
Liverpool Lime Street a.	...	...	...	...	...		...	1034	...	...	...	1059	...	...	1129	1159	...	...	...	1234	...	1259	...	...	1334	...	1359	...

	⑦	⑦	⑦	⑦	⑦	⑦	⑦	⑦	⑦	⑦	⑦	⑦	⑦	⑦	⑦	⑦	⑦	⑦	⑦	⑦	⑦	⑦	⑦	⑦	⑦	⑦	⑦	⑦
Newcastle 119 180 d.	...	...	...	1201	...	...	...	...	1304	...	...	...	...	1402	...	...	...	...	1502	...	...	...	...	1559	...	...	...	...
Durham 119 180 d.	...	...	...	1217	...	...	...	...	1319	...	...	...	...	1418	...	...	...	...	1518	...	...	...	...	1615	...	...	...	...
Darlington 119 180 d.	...	...	...	1235	...	...	...	...	1337	...	...	...	...	|	...	...	...	...	1536	...	...	...	...	1633	...	...	...	...
Saltburn 212 d.	...	...	...	|	...	...	...	...	|	...	...	...	...	|	...	...	...	...	|	...	...	...	...	|	...	...	...	...
Redcar Central 212 d.	1102	...	...	|	...	1203	...	...	|	...	1302	...	...	|	...	1352	...	...	|	...	1502	...	...	|	...	1600	...	...
Middlesbrough 212 d.	1117	...	...	|	...	1218	...	...	|	...	1317	...	...	|	...	1414d	...	...	|	...	1517	...	...	|	...	1615	...	...
Northallerton 119 180 182a d.	1150	...	...	|	...	1249	...	...	|	...	1350	...	...	|	...	1447	...	...	|	...	1549	...	...	|	...	|	...	...
Thirsk 182a d.	1158	...	...	|	...	1258	...	...	|	...	1358	...	...	|	...	1455	...	...	|	...	1559	...	...	|	...	1653	...	...
Scarborough d.	|	...	1154	|	...	|	...	1254	|	...	|	...	1354	|	...	|	...	1454	|	...	|	...	1554	|	...	|	...	1654
Malton d.	|	...	1218	|	...	|	...	1318	|	...	|	...	1418	|	...	|	...	1518	|	...	|	...	1618	|	...	|	...	1718
York 119 180 182a a.	1216	...	1244	1302	...	1316	...	1345	1403	...	1416	...	1446	1501	...	1513	...	1544	1602	...	1617	...	1644	1701	...	1714	...	1744
York 119 177 191 d.	1220	...	1248	1304	1300	1320	...	1349	1405	1402	1420	...	1447	1504	1500	1520	...	1551	1604	1601	1620	...	1649	1705	1659	1720	...	1749
Hull 177 181 d.	|	1203	|	|	|	|	1303	|	|	|	|	1403	|	|	|	|	1503	|	|	|	|	1603	|	|	|	|	1703	|
Selby 177 181 d.	|	1235	|	|	|	|	1335	|	|	|	|	1437	|	|	|	|	1535	|	|	|	|	1637	|	|	|	|	1735	|
Leeds 119 191 a.	1243	1257	1312	1328	|	1343	1357	1412	1427	|	1443	1458	1513	1528	|	1543	1558	1614	1629	|	1643	1659	1713	1729	|	1743	1757	1813
Leeds d.	1245	1300	1315	1330	|	1345	1400	1415	1430	|	1445	1500	1515	1530	|	1545	1600	1615	1630	|	1645	1700	1715	1730	|	1745	1800	1815
Wakefield Kirkgate d.	|	|	|	|	1333	|	|	|	|	1434	|	|	|	|	1532	|	|	|	|	1634	|	|	|	|	1732	|	|	|
Dewsbury d.	1256	|	1327	|	|	1356	|	1427	|	|	1457	|	1527	|	|	1557	|	1627	|	|	1657	|	1727	|	|	1756	|	1827
Huddersfield d.	1308	1321	1337	1348	1355	1408	1420	1437	1448	1456	1508	1520	1537	1548	1555	1608	1621	1637	1648	1656	1708	1721	1737	1749	1755	1808	1820	1837
Stalybridge d.	|	1340	|	|	1423	|	1440	|	|	1523	|	1540	|	|	1623	|	1640	|	|	1724	|	1740	|	|	1823	|	1840	|
Manchester Victoria a.	1338	1352	1405	1420	|	1438	1452	1506	1519	|	1538	1552	1605	1620	|	1638	1652	1706	1719	|	1738	1752	1806	1819	|	1838	1852	1906
Manchester Piccadilly a.	1349	|	...	|	1438	1449	|	...	|	1539	1549	|	...	|	1638	1649	|	...	|	1739	1749	|	...	|	1838	1849	|	...
Manchester Airport ✈ a.	1412	|	...	|	...	1512	|	...	|	...	1612	|	...	|	...	1712	|	...	|	...	1812	|	...	|	...	1913	|	...
Liverpool Lime Street a.	...	1434	...	1459	...	...	1534	...	1558	...	...	1634	...	1658	...	...	1734	...	1758	...	...	1834	...	1858	...	...	1934	...

	⑦	⑦	⑦	⑦	⑦	⑦	⑦	⑦	⑦	⑦	⑦	⑦	⑦	⑦	⑦	⑦	⑦	⑦	⑦	⑦E	⑦	⑦	⑦b	⑦a	⑦	⑦	⑦	⑦
Newcastle 119 180 d.	1702	...	...	...	1803	...	...	...	...	1849	...	...	...	...	...	1942	...	...	...	2100	...	...	...	...	...	...	2153	...
Durham 119 180 d.	1718	...	...	...	1816	...	...	...	...	1905	...	...	...	...	...	1957	...	...	...	2116	...	...	...	...	...	...	2210	...
Darlington 119 180 d.	1736	...	...	...	1834	...	...	...	...	1923	...	...	...	...	...	2015	...	...	...	2135	...	...	...	...	...	...	2228	...
Saltburn 212 d.	|	...	...	...	|	...	...	...	...	|	...	...	...	...	...	|	2017	...	...	|	...	...	...	...	...	...	|	2311
Redcar Central 212 d.	|	1702	...	...	|	...	1801	...	...	|	...	1902	...	...	...	|	2027	...	...	|	2102	...	2157	2157	...	...	|	2319
Middlesbrough 212 d.	|	1717	...	...	|	...	1816	...	...	|	...	1917	...	...	...	|	2043	...	...	|	2117	...	2212	2212	...	...	|	2333
Northallerton 119 180 182a d.	|	1750	...	...	|	...	1848	...	...	|	...	1950	...	...	...	2026	2113	...	...	|	2148	...	2242	2242	...	...	|	|
Thirsk 182a d.	|	1759	...	...	|	...	1856	...	...	|	...	1958	...	...	...	|	2121	...	...	|	2157	...	2251	2251	...	...	|	|
Scarborough d.	|	|	...	1754	|	...	|	...	1854	|	...	|	...	...	1954	|	|	2054	...	|	|	2154	|	|	...	2245	|	|
Malton d.	|	|	...	1818	|	...	|	...	1918	|	...	|	...	...	2018	|	|	2118	...	|	|	2218	|	|	...	2311	|	|
York 119 180 182a a.	1802	1817	...	1844	1902	...	1914	...	1943	2001	...	2016	...	...	2044t	2045	2148	2144	...	2213	2227	2244	2317	2317	...	2335	2321	0034
	|	|	...	|	|	...	|	...	|	|	...	|	...	...	|	|	▬	|	...	|	▬	...	|	|	...	|	...	...
York 119 177 191 d.	1805	1820	...	1849	1905	1858	1920	...	1949	2005	2000	2020	...	2100	2050	2048	⑦	2147	2201	2216	⑦	...	2319	2319	...	2339	...	...
Hull 177 181 d.	|	|	1803	|	|	|	|	1903	|	|	|	|	2003	|	|	|	2103	|	|	|	2203	...	|	|	2303	|	...	...
Selby 177 181 d.	|	|	1835	|	|	|	|	1937	|	|	|	|	2037	|	|	|	2135	|	|	|	2235	...	|	|	2335	|	...	...
Leeds 119 191 a.	1828	1843	1858	1913	1926	|	1943	1959	2013	2028	|	2043	2100	|	2135	2112	2157	2211	|	2243	2257	...	2344	2344	2357	0006	...	...
Leeds d.	1830	1845	1900	1915	1930	|	1945	2000	2015	2030	|	2045	...	|	2145	2115	2200	2215	|	2245	2300	...	2345	2345	...	0008	...	...
Wakefield Kirkgate d.	|	|	|	|	|	1932	|	|	|	|	2032	|	...	2132	|	|	|	|	2234	|	|	...	|	|	...	|	...	...
Dewsbury d.	|	1858	|	1927	|	|	1957	|	2026	|	|	2057	...	|	2156	2126	|	2226	|	2256	2311	...	|	|	...	|	...	...
Huddersfield d.	1848	1908	1921	1937	1948	1955	2008	2020	2036	2048	2055	2107	...	2155	2207	|	2220	2236	2256	2306	2322	...	0026	0032e	...	|	...	...
Stalybridge d.	|	|	1940	|	|	2023	|	2040	|	|	2123	2126	...	2223	2226	|	2239	|	2323	|	2342	...	|	|	...	|	...	...
Manchester Victoria a.	1919	1938	1952	2005	2019	|	2038	2052	2105	2119f	|	2138	...	|	2238	2213h	2252	2304	|	2336	|	...	0112	0117	...	|	...	...
Manchester Piccadilly a.	|	1949	|	...	|	2038	2049	|	...	|	2139	2149	...	2238	2251	|	...	...	2339	|	2358	...	...	...	...	0128	...	...
Manchester Airport ✈ a.	|	2012	|	...	|	...	2108	|	...	|	...	2212	...	...	2312	|	...	...	...	|	...	...	...	...	...	...	...	...
Liverpool Lime Street a.	1958	...	2034	...	2055	...	...	2134	...	2202	...	...	...	...	...	2303	...	...	...	0017	...	...	...	...	...	...	...	...

E – From Edinburgh (Table **214**).
a – Until Aug. 24.
b – From Aug. 31.
c – Departs 2058 on ⑥.
d – Arrives 1406.
e – Arrives 0022.
f – Departs 5–6 minutes later.
h – Departs 2223.
j – Arrives 0006.
k – Departs 2033 on ⑥.
n – ⑥ mornings only.
p – On ②–⑤ mornings arrives 0110.
r – Departs 2250.
t – Connects with train in previous column.
v – Arrives 0943.
* – Connection by 🚌 on ②–⑤ mornings (arrives 0022).

TP Most trains convey 🍷 MANCHESTER and LIVERPOOL - THE NORTH EAST and YORKSHIRE 188

		①	⑥	②–⑤	①	⑥	②–⑤	⚒	⚒	①	②–⑤	⑥	Ⓐ	⑥	⚒	⚒	⚒	Ⓐ	⑥	⚒	⚒	⚒	⚒	⚒	⚒	⚒	⚒
Liverpool Lime Street d.		...	...	...	...	...	...	...	...	...	...	...	...	...	...	...	...	0520	0520	...	...	0554	...	...	0624	...	...
Manchester Airport ✈ d.	⚒	0038	0038	0038	...	...	...	...	...	0359	0407	0407	...	...	...	...	...	|	|	...	0540	|	...	...	|	0644	...
Manchester Piccadilly d.		0053	0103	0053	0244	0242	0244	...	...	0413	0422	0422	...	...	...	0535	...	|	|	0600	0558	|	0627	...	|	0658	0700
Manchester Victoria d.		|	|	|	|	|	|	...	...	|	|	|	0500	0500	0530	|	0545	0600	0600	|	0615r	0630	|	0645	0700	0715	|
Stalybridge d.		|	|	|	|	|	|	...	...	|	|	|	|	|	0541	0549	|	|	|	0612	|	0641	0644	|	|	|	0713
Huddersfield d.		|	0133	|	0347	0351c	0339	...	...	0513n	0516	0531	|	|	0602	0613	0617	0627	0627	0641	0646	0700	0712	0717	0730	0746	0740
Dewsbury d.		|	|	|	|	|	|	...	...	|	|	|	|	|	|	|	0626	|	|	|	0657	|	|	0726	|	0757	|
Wakefield Kirkgate d.		|	|	|	|	|	|	...	...	|	|	|	|	|	|	|	|	|	|	0702	|	|	|	|	|	|	0803
Leeds a.		0206	0207	0222	0407	0426	0412	...	...	0550	0550	0550	0612	0612	0624	0634f	0639	0646	0646	|	0709	0722	0734f	0740	0749	0810	|
Leeds 119 191 d.		0211	0214	0234	0420	0431	0417	0531	...	0552	0552	0552	0614	0615	0630	...	0641	0649	0651	|	0713	0727	...	0742	0751	0813	|
Selby 177 181 a.		|	|	|	|	|	|	0552	...	|	|	|	|	|	0700e	...	|	|	|	|	|	0753	...	|	|	|	|
Hull 177 181 a.		|	|	|	|	|	|	0626	...	|	|	|	|	|	0741	...	|	|	|	|	|	0829	...	|	|	|	|
York 119 177 191 a.		0239	0252	0312	0446	0457	0459	▬	...	0616	0616	0616	0637	0637	...	...	0707z	0711	0714	0736	0736	...	...	0807	0819	0836	0843
		...	...	...	...	...	...	⚒	...	|	|	|	|	|	...	...	|	|	|	...	|	...	...	|	|	|	...
York 119 180 182a d.		...	...	...	...	...	...	0530	0617	0618	0618	0618	0639	0642	...	...	0708	0713	0719	...	0738	...	...	0810	0821	0839	...
Malton d.		...	...	...	...	...	...	|	|	0642	0642	0642	|	|	...	...	0734	|	|	...	|	...	...	0835	|	|	...
Scarborough a.		...	...	...	...	...	...	|	|	0708	0708	0708	|	|	...	...	0759	|	|	...	|	...	...	0859	|	|	...
Thirsk 182a d.		...	...	...	...	...	...	0549	|	...	...	...	0657	0659	...	...	...	|	|	...	0755	...	...	...	|	0856	...
Northallerton 119 180 182a d.		...	...	...	...	...	...	0600	0636	...	...	...	0705	0707	...	...	...	0732	0738	...	0807	...	...	...	|	0906	...
Middlesbrough 212 a.		...	...	...	...	...	...	0634	|	...	...	...	0737	0739	...	...	...	|	|	...	0839	...	...	...	|	0938	...
Redcar Central 212 a.		...	...	...	...	...	...	0649g	|	...	...	...	0749	0753	...	...	...	|	|	...	0850	...	...	...	|	0950	...
Saltburn 212 a.		...	...	...	...	...	...	...	|	...	...	...	...	...	...	...	...	|	|	...	...	...	...	...	|	...	...
Darlington 119 180 d.		...	...	...	...	...	...	...	0649	...	...	...	...	...	...	...	...	0745	0751	...	...	...	...	...	0849	...	...
Durham 119 180 d.		...	...	...	...	...	...	...	0705	...	...	...	...	...	...	...	...	0802	0808	...	...	...	...	...	0905	...	...
Newcastle 119 180 a.		...	...	...	...	...	...	...	0725	...	...	...	...	...	...	...	...	0818	0826	...	...	...	...	...	0922	...	...

	⚒	⚒	⚒	⚒	⚒	⚒	⚒	⚒	⚒	Ⓐ	⑥	⚒	⚒	⚒	⚒	⚒	⚒	⚒	⚒	⚒	⚒	⚒	⚒	⚒	⚒	⚒	⚒
Liverpool Lime Street d.	0654	...	...	0724	...	...	0754	...	...	0823	0824	...	...	0854	...	0924	...	...	0954	...	1024	...	...	1054	...	1124	...
Manchester Airport ✈ d.	|	...	...	|	0744	...	|	...	...	|	|	0844	...	|	...	|	...	0944	|	...	|	1044	...	|	...	|	1144
Manchester Piccadilly d.	|	0730	...	|	0758	0800	|	0830	...	|	|	0858	0900	|	...	|	1000	0958	|	...	|	1058	1100	|	...	|	1158
Manchester Victoria d.	0730	|	0745	0800	0815	|	0830	|	0845	0900	0900	0915	|	0930	0945	1000	|	1015j	1030	1045	1100	1115j	|	1130	1145	1200	1215j
Stalybridge d.	0740	0744	|	|	|	0813	0841	0844	|	|	|	|	0913	0940	|	|	1013	|	1040	|	|	|	1113	1140	|	|	|
Huddersfield d.	0800	0813	0817	0830	0846	0840	0900	0912	0918	0931	0929	0946	0940	1000	1017	1030	1040	1045	1100	1117	1128	1145	1140	1200	1217	1230	1246
Dewsbury d.	|	|	0827	|	0857	|	|	|	0927	|	|	0957	|	|	1027	|	|	1057	|	1127	|	1157	|	|	1226	|	1257
Wakefield Kirkgate d.	|	|	|	|	|	0902	|	|	|	|	|	|	1002	|	|	|	1102	|	|	|	|	|	1202	|	|	|	|
Leeds a.	0822	0832f	0840	0851	0910	|	0923	0934f	0939	0949	0946	1010	|	1022	1040	1048	|	1110	1121	1140	1148	1210	|	1222	1241	1249	1310
Leeds 119 191 d.	0827	...	0842	0853	0913	|	0925	0935f	0942	0951	0949	1013	|	1027	1042	1051	|	1113	1127	1142	1150	1213	|	1227	1241	1251	1313
Selby 177 181 a.	0849	...	|	|	|	|	0948	|	|	|	|	|	|	1048	|	|	|	|	1152	|	|	|	|	1248	|	|	|
Hull 177 181 a.	0925	...	|	|	|	|	1025	|	|	|	|	|	|	1126	|	|	|	|	1226	|	|	|	|	1328	|	|	|
York 119 177 191 a.	...	...	0907	0915	0936	0942g	...	1000f	1008	1017	1014	1036	1036	...	1104	1114	1143p	1136	...	1207	1218g	1236	1236	...	1306	1318t	1336
York 119 180 182a d.	...	...	0910	0921	0939	...	...	...	1010	1022	1023	1039	...	...	1110	1121	...	1139	...	1210	1220	1239	...	..	1310	1320	1339
Malton d.	...	...	0935	|	|	...	...	...	1035	|	|	|	...	...	1135	|	...	|	...	1235	|	|	...	...	1335	|	|
Scarborough a.	...	...	0959	|	|	...	...	...	1059	|	|	|	...	...	1159	|	...	|	...	1259	|	|	...	...	1359	|	|
Thirsk 182a d.	...	...	...	|	0956	...	...	...	...	|	|	1056	...	...	...	|	...	1156	...	...	|	1256	...	...	...	|	1357
Northallerton 119 180 182a d.	...	...	...	|	1005	...	...	...	...	|	|	1104	...	...	...	|	...	1205	...	...	|	1305	...	...	...	|	1405
Middlesbrough 212 a.	...	...	...	|	1037	...	...	...	...	|	|	1137	...	...	...	|	...	1238	...	...	|	1337	...	...	...	|	1437
Redcar Central 212 a.	...	...	...	|	1049	...	...	...	...	|	|	1149	...	...	...	|	...	1249	...	...	|	1349	...	...	...	|	1449
Saltburn 212 a.	...	...	...	|	...	...	...	...	...	|	|	...	...	...	...	|	...	...	...	...	|	...	...	...	...	|	...
Darlington 119 180 d.	...	...	...	0949	...	...	...	...	...	1051	1052	...	...	...	...	1149	...	...	...	...	1248	...	...	...	...	1348	...
Durham 119 180 d.	...	...	...	1005	...	...	...	...	...	1108	1108	...	...	...	...	1205	...	...	...	...	1304	...	...	...	...	1404	...
Newcastle 119 180 a.	...	...	...	1024	...	...	...	...	...	1124	1125	...	...	...	...	1229t	...	...	...	...	1323	...	...	...	...	1422	...

	⚒	⚒	⚒	Ⓐ	⑥	⚒	⚒	⚒	⚒	⚒	⚒	⚒	⚒	Ⓐ	⑥	⚒	⚒	⚒	⚒	⚒	⚒	⚒	⚒	⚒	⚒	⚒	⚒
Liverpool Lime Street d.	...	1154	...	1224	1226	...	...	1254	...	1324	...	...	1354	...	...	1424	...	...	1454	...	...	1524	...	...	1554	...	...
Manchester Airport ✈ d.	...	|	...	|	|	1244	...	|	...	|	1344	...	|	...	...	|	...	1444	|	...	...	|	...	1544	|	...	...
Manchester Piccadilly d.	1200	|	...	|	|	1258	1300	|	...	|	1358	1400	|	...	...	|	1500	1458	|	1530	...	|	1600	1558	|	1630	...
Manchester Victoria d.	|	1230	1245	1300	1300	1315j	|	1330	1345	1400	1415j	|	1430	1445	1445	1500	|	1515j	1530	|	1545	1600	|	1615	1630	|	1645
Stalybridge d.	1213	1240	|	|	|	|	1313	1340	|	|	|	1413	1440	|	|	|	1513	|	1540	1544	|	|	1613	|	1640	1644	|
Huddersfield d.	1241	1300	1317	1329	1330	1346	1340	1400	1416	1430	1445	1440	1500	1518	1516	1528	1540	1545	1600	1612	1617	1630	1640	1646	1701	1713	1718
Dewsbury d.	|	|	1326	|	|	1357	|	|	1426	|	1457	|	|	1528	1526	|	|	1557	|	|	1626	|	|	1657	|	|	1727
Wakefield Kirkgate d.	1302	|	|	|	|	|	1402	|	|	|	|	1502	|	|	|	|	1602	|	|	|	|	|	1702	|	|	|	|
Leeds a.	|	1322	1340	1349	1349	1410	|	1422	1440	1448	1510	|	1522	1541	1538	1546	|	1610	1622	1630f	1641	1648	|	1711	1721	1732f	1739
Leeds 119 191 d.	|	1327	1341	1351	1351	1413	|	1427	1441	1451	1513	|	1527	1543	1540	1550	|	1613	1627	...	1642	1651	|	1713	1727	...	1742
Selby 177 181 a.	|	1353	|	|	|	|	|	1448	|	|	|	|	1556y	|	|	|	|	|	1653	...	|	|	|	|	1752	...	|
Hull 177 181 a.	|	1428	|	|	|	|	|	1525	|	|	|	|	1631	|	|	|	|	|	1728	...	|	|	|	|	1834y	...	|
York 119 177 191 a.	1342g	...	1407	1413	1413	1437	1436	...	1506	1513	1538	1540	...	1607	1607	1614	1636	1637	...	...	1706	1714	1739	1737	...	...	1807
York 119 180 182a d.	...	...	1410	1416	1420	1439	...	...	1510	1521	1538	...	...	1610	1610	1617	...	1639	...	...	1710	1717	...	1739	...	...	1810
Malton d.	...	...	1435	|	|	|	...	...	1535	|	|	...	...	1635	1635	|	...	|	...	...	1735	|	...	|	...	...	1835
Scarborough a.	...	...	1459	|	|	|	...	...	1559	|	|	...	...	1659	1659	|	...	|	...	...	1801	|	...	|	...	...	1859
Thirsk 182a d.	...	...	...	|	|	1456	...	...	...	|	1556	...	...	...	...	|	...	1656	...	...	...	|	...	1756	...	...	...
Northallerton 119 180 182a d.	...	...	...	|	|	1504	...	...	...	|	1605	...	...	...	...	|	...	1705	...	...	...	|	...	1805	...	...	...
Middlesbrough 212 a.	...	...	...	|	|	1537	...	...	...	|	1638	...	...	...	...	|	...	1737	...	...	...	|	...	1840	...	...	...
Redcar Central 212 a.	...	...	...	|	|	1549	...	...	...	|	1649	...	...	...	...	|	...	1749	...	...	...	|	...	1852	...	...	...
Saltburn 212 a.	...	...	...	|	|	...	...	...	...	|	...	...	...	...	...	|	...	...	...	...	...	|	...	...	...	...	...
Darlington 119 180 d.	...	...	...	1448r	1448	...	...	...	...	1549	...	...	...	...	...	1645	...	...	...	...	...	1748	...	...	...	...	...
Durham 119 180 d.	...	...	...	1504	1505	...	...	...	...	1605	...	...	...	...	...	1702	...	...	...	...	...	1805	...	...	...	...	...
Newcastle 119 180 a.	...	...	...	1521	1521	...	...	...	...	1622	...	...	...	...	...	1721	...	...	...	...	...	1822	...	...	...	...	...

	⚒	⚒	⚒	⚒	⚒	Ⓐ	⑥	⚒	⚒	⚒	⚒	⚒	⚒	⚒	⚒	⚒	⚒	⚒	⑥	Ⓐ	⚒	⚒	⚒	⑥	Ⓐ	Ⓐ	⑥
Liverpool Lime Street d.	1624	...	...	1654	...	...	...	1724	...	...	1754	...	...	1824	...	...	1854	...	1924	1924	...	...	1954	...	...	2024	2024
Manchester Airport ✈ d.	|	1644	...	|	...	...	...	|	1744	...	|	...	...	|	1844	...	|	...	|	|	1944	...	|	...	...	|	|
Manchester Piccadilly d.	|	1658	1700	|	1730	...	...	|	1758	1759	|	1830	...	|	1858	1900	|	...	|	|	1958	2000	|	...	...	|	|
Manchester Victoria d.	1700	1715	|	1730	|	1745	1745	1800	1815	|	1830	|	1845	1900	1915j	|	1930	1945	2000	2000	2015	|	2030	2045	2045	2100	2100
Stalybridge d.	|	|	1713	1740	1745	|	1757	|	|	1813	1840	1844	|	|	|	1913	1940	|	|	|	|	2013	2040	2056	2058	→	|
Huddersfield d.	1730	1745	1740	1800	1813	1817	1817	1830	1845	1840	1900	1913	1916	1930	1945	1940	2001	2017	2029	2028	2045	2040	2059	2116	2118	▬	→
Dewsbury d.	|	1757	|	|	|	1827	1827	|	1857	|	|	|	1925	|	1956	|	|	2026	|	|	2057	|	|	2126	2127	...	▬
Wakefield Kirkgate d.	|	|	1802	|	|	|	|	|	|	1902	|	|	|	|	|	2002	|	|	|	|	|	2102	|	|	|	...	...
Leeds a.	1748	1810	|	1822	1832f	1840	1840	1847	1910	|	1922	1932f	1939	1949	2010	|	2021	2040	2046	2046	2111	|	2121	2139	2140	Ⓐ	⑥
Leeds 119 191 d.	1751	1813	|	1827	...	1841	1842	1850	1912	|	1927	...	1941	1951	2013	|	2027	2042	2051	2049	2113	|	2125	2142	2143	2146	2147
Selby 177 181 a.	|	|	|	1848	...	|	|	|	|	|	1950	...	|	|	|	|	2052	|	|	|	|	|	2154	|	|	|	|
Hull 177 181 a.	|	|	|	1927	...	|	|	|	|	|	2025	...	|	|	|	|	2128	|	|	|	|	|	2228	|	|	|	|
York 119 177 191 a.	1819	1837	1840	...	...	1905	1910	1913	1937	1943d	...	...	2004	2013	2036	2041	...	2106	2113	2114	2136	2143t	...	2205	2205	2224	2224
York 119 180 182a d.	1820	1839	...	...	...	1910	1912	1916	1940	...	...	...	2010	2016	2039	...	...	2110	2119	2120	2139	...	...	2208	2220	2227	2227
Malton d.	|	|	...	...	...	1935	1938	|	|	...	...	...	2035	|	|	...	...	2135	|	|	|	...	...	|	|	2252	2251
Scarborough a.	|	|	...	...	...	2000	2002	|	|	...	...	...	2059	|	|	...	...	2159	|	|	|	...	...	|	|	2316	2315
Thirsk 182a d.	|	1856	...	...	...	...	...	|	1958	...	...	...	...	|	2057	...	...	...	|	|	2156	...	...	|	|	...	...
Northallerton 119 180 182a d.	|	1904	...	...	...	...	...	|	2007	...	...	...	...	|	2105	...	...	...	|	2139	2204	...	...	2230	2239	...	...
Middlesbrough 212 a.	|	1936	...	...	...	...	...	|	2040	...	...	...	...	|	2137	...	...	...	|	|	2236	...	...	|	|	...	...
Redcar Central 212 a.	|	1947	...	...	...	...	...	|	2051	...	...	...	...	|	2148	...	...	...	|	|	2248	...	...	|	|	...	...
Saltburn 212 a.	|	1956	...	...	...	...	...	|	...	...	...	...	...	|	...	...	...	...	|	|	2257	...	...	|	|	...	...
Darlington 119 180 d.	1849	...	...	...	...	...	...	1944	...	...	...	...	...	2044	...	...	...	...	2147	2154	...	...	...	2244	2252	...	...
Durham 119 180 d.	1905	...	...	...	...	...	...	2001	...	...	...	...	...	2100	...	...	...	...	2204	2210	...	...	...	2301	2309	...	...
Newcastle 119 180 a.	1925	...	...	...	...	...	...	2019	...	...	...	...	...	2117	...	...	...	...	2221	2228	...	...	...	2317	2324	...	...

c – Arrives 0322.
d – Arrives 1936 on ⑥.
e – Departs 0707.
f – From Aug. 30.
j – Arrives 7–8 minutes earlier.
n – Arrives 0505.
p – Arrives 1135 on Ⓐ.
r – Arrives 5–6 minutes earlier.
t – Arrives 5–7 minutes earlier on ⑥.
y – Arrives 4–5 minutes earlier on Ⓐ.
z – Arrives 0704 on ⑥.

188 MANCHESTER and LIVERPOOL - THE NORTH EAST and YORKSHIRE

Most trains convey 🍷 TP

	Ⓐ	⑥	⚒	⑥	Ⓐ	⚒	⑥	Ⓐ	⑤	①–④	⚒	⑥	⑤	①–④	⑥	Ⓐv	Ⓐ	Ⓐ	⑥	Ⓐ	Ⓐv	⚒	⑤	①–④		⑦
Liverpool Lime Street d.	...	...	...	...	...	...	2105	2105	...	...	...	...	...	...	2154	🚌	2147	🚌	...	...	🚌	2253	...	...		...
Manchester Airport ✈ d.	2044	2044	...	...	...	...	|	|	...	...	...	2140	2140	2140	|	...	|	...	2237	2244	...	|	2341	2341	⑦	...
Manchester Piccadilly d.	2058	2058	...	...	...	2100	|	|	...	...	2157	2158	2158	2158	|	...	|	...	2252	2258	...	|	2356	2356		...
Manchester Victoria d.	2115j	2115r	...	...	←	|	2145	2145	...	...	|	2215r	2215r	2215r	2230	...	2230r	...	2301	2315r	...	2330	0006	0015		...
Stalybridge d.	|	|	...	←	|	2113	2155	2155	...	...	2209	|	|	|	2241	...	2239	...	|	|	...	2341	|	|		...
Huddersfield d.	2146	2146	...	|	|	2140	2217	2215	...	...	2237	2242	2244	2244	2309	2255	2307	2325	2329	2352r	2355	0012t	0035	0102		...
Dewsbury d.	2156	2157	...	|	|	|	2226	2225	...	...	|	2257	|	|	|	2331	...	2359	2338	|	0031	...	|	|		...
Wakefield Kirkgate d.	|	|	...	|	|	2203	|	|	...	...	2259	|	|	|	|	|	...	|	|	|	|	...	|	|		...
Leeds a.	2210	2210	...	2219	2220	|	2239	2238	...	...	...	2311	2324	2324	2328	0024	...	0030s	2350	0033	0124	...	0110	0136		...
Leeds 119 191 d.	2214	2213	2221	2222	2224	|	2242	2245	2319	*2320**	...	2313	2327	2329	2330	...	...	|	2351	0035	...	...	0112	0139		...
Selby 177 181 a.	|	|	2257	|	|	|	|	|	2340	0010	...	|	|	|	2351	...	...	|	|	|	...	...	|	|		...
Hull 177 181 a.	|	|	2331	|	|	|	|	|	0014	0043	...	|	|	|	0024	...	...	|	|	|	...	...	|	|		...
York 119 177 191 a.	2237	2235	...	2244	2251	2241	2305	2324	...	...	...	2341	2355	0009	...	...	...	0130	0015	0113	...	...	0141	0216		...
York 119 180 182a d.	2240	...	...	2247	2309	*2305*	2307	2328	...	...	...	...	...	...	...	...	...	...	...	...	...	...	...	...		0845
Malton d.	|	...	...	|	|	*2329*	|	|	...	...	...	...	...	...	...	...	...	...	...	...	...	...	...	...		|
Scarborough a.	|	...	...	|	|	*2353*	|	|	...	...	...	...	...	...	...	...	...	...	...	...	...	...	...	...		|
Thirsk 182a d.	2259	...	...	2303	|	...	|	2350	...	...	...	...	...	...	...	...	...	...	...	...	...	...	...	...		0902
Northallerton 119 180 182a d.	2309	...	...	2311	2338	...	2326	2359	...	...	...	...	...	...	...	...	...	...	...	...	...	...	...	...		0910
Middlesbrough 212 a.	|	...	...	|	|	...	|	|	...	...	...	...	...	...	...	...	...	...	...	...	...	...	...	...		0942
Redcar Central 212 a.	|	...	...	|	|	...	|	|	...	...	...	...	...	...	...	...	...	...	...	...	...	...	...	...		0953
Saltburn 212 a.	|	...	...	|	|	...	|	|	...	...	...	...	...	...	...	...	...	...	...	...	...	...	...	...		...
Darlington 119 180 d.	2321	...	...	2324	2351	...	2339	0012	...	...	...	...	...	...	...	...	...	...	...	...	...	...	...	...		...
Durham 119 180 d.	...	...	...	2341	0007	...	2355	0029	...	...	...	...	...	...	...	...	...	...	...	...	...	...	...	...		...
Newcastle 119 180 a.	...	...	...	2358	0037	...	0010	0058	...	...	...	...	...	...	...	...	...	...	...	...	...	...	...	...		...

	⑦	⑦	⑦	⑦	⑦	⑦	⑦	⑦	⑦	⑦	⑦	⑦	⑦	⑦	⑦	⑦	⑦	⑦	⑦	⑦	⑦	⑦	⑦	⑦	⑦	⑦
Liverpool Lime Street d.	...	...	...	...	...	...	0811	...	...	*0836*	...	0922	...	...	0954	...	1025	...	...	1053	...	1125	...	...	1152	...
Manchester Airport ✈ d.	...	...	...	...	...	...	|	...	...	|	...	|	...	...	|	...	|	...	...	|	...	|	...	1135	|	...
Manchester Piccadilly d.	...	...	...	0814z	...	...	|	...	...	|	...	|	...	...	|	...	|	1100	...	|	...	|	1200	1201	|	...
Manchester Victoria d.	...	...	...	0825	...	...	0849	0900	0918	0930	0945	1000	1002	1015	1030	1045	1100	|	1115	1130	1145	1200	|	1215	1230	1245
Stalybridge d.	...	...	...	0835	...	...	|	0911	|	0941	|	|	1012	|	1041	|	|	1112	|	1140	|	|	1212	|	1241	|
Huddersfield d.	...	...	...	0854	...	...	|	0940	0946	0959	1014	1030	1040	1046	1100	1115	1130	1140	1146	1200	1215	1229	1240	1246	1259	1312
Dewsbury d.	...	...	...	|	...	...	0936	|	0957	|	1024	|	|	1056	|	1125	|	|	1157	|	1225	|	|	1257	|	1322
Wakefield Kirkgate d.	...	...	...	|	...	...	|	1007r	|	|	|	|	1102	|	|	|	|	1202	|	|	|	|	1302	|	|	|
Leeds a.	...	...	...	0912	...	...	0949	|	1011	1022	1037	1048	|	1108	1120	1138	1148	|	1210	1222	1238	1248	|	1310	1321	1335
Leeds 119 191 d.	0836	0842	...	0914	0930	0934	0950	|	1013	1027	1044	1051	|	1112	1127	1141	1151	|	1213	1227	1241	1249	|	1313	1326	1337
Selby 177 181 a.	0900	|	...	|	0954	|	|	|	|	1048	|	|	|	|	1147	|	|	|	|	1252	|	|	|	|	1353	|
Hull 177 181 a.	0933	|	...	|	1027	|	|	|	|	1121	|	|	|	|	1223	|	|	|	|	1328	|	|	|	|	1428	|
York 119 177 191 a.	...	0913	...	0936	...	1006	1016	1044	1038	...	1107	1113	1137	1137	...	1209	1213	1236	1235	...	1305	1311	1337	1337	...	1401
York 119 180 182a d.	...	0918	0918	0939	...	1010	1018	...	1041	...	1110	1116	...	1139	...	1210	1222	...	1238	...	1310	1314	...	1339	...	1410
Malton d.	...	0943	|	|	...	1035	|	...	|	...	1135	|	...	|	...	1235	|	...	|	...	1335	|	...	|	...	1435
Scarborough a.	...	1007	|	|	...	1059	|	...	|	...	1159	|	...	|	...	1259	|	...	|	...	1359	|	...	|	...	1459
Thirsk 182a d.	...	...	|	0959	...	...	|	...	1101	...	...	|	...	|	...	...	|	...	1255	...	...	|	...	1357	...	...
Northallerton 119 180 182a d.	...	...	|	1007	...	...	|	...	1111	...	...	|	...	1201	...	...	|	...	1303	...	...	|	...	1405	...	...
Middlesbrough 212 a.	...	...	|	1039	...	...	|	...	1143	...	...	|	...	1233	...	...	|	...	1334	...	...	|	...	1438	...	...
Redcar Central 212 a.	...	...	|	1050	...	...	|	...	1154	...	...	|	...	1245	...	...	|	...	1347	...	...	|	...	1449	...	...
Saltburn 212 a.	...	...	|	...	...	...	|	...	...	...	...	|	...	...	...	...	|	...	...	...	...	|	...	...	...	...
Darlington 119 180 d.	...	...	0946	...	...	...	1046	...	...	...	...	1144	...	...	...	...	1251	...	...	...	...	1342	...	...	...	...
Durham 119 180 d.	...	...	1003	...	...	...	1102	...	...	...	...	1201	...	...	...	...	1308	...	...	...	...	1359	...	...	...	...
Newcastle 119 180 a.	...	...	1021	...	...	...	1120	...	...	...	...	1217	...	...	...	...	1324	...	...	...	...	1414	...	...	...	...

	⑦	⑦	⑦	⑦	⑦	⑦	⑦	⑦	⑦	⑦	⑦	⑦	⑦	⑦	⑦	⑦	⑦	⑦	⑦	⑦	⑦	⑦	⑦	⑦	⑦	⑦
Liverpool Lime Street d.	1224	...	...	1252	...	1325	...	...	1352	...	1425	...	...	1452	...	1525	...	...	1552	...	1625	...	...	1652	...	1725
Manchester Airport ✈ d.	|	...	1235	|	...	|	...	1336	|	...	|	...	1436	|	...	|	...	1536	|	...	|	...	1636	|	...	|
Manchester Piccadilly d.	|	1300	1252	|	...	|	1400	1353	|	...	|	1500	1453	|	...	|	1600	1553	|	...	|	1700	1653	|	...	|
Manchester Victoria d.	1300	|	1315c	1330	1345	1400	|	1415c	1430	1445	1500	|	1515c	1530	1545	1600	|	1615c	1630	1645	1700	|	1715c	1730	1745	1800
Stalybridge d.	|	1312	|	1341	|	|	1412	|	1441	|	|	1512	|	1541	|	|	1613	|	1640	|	|	1712	|	1741	|	|
Huddersfield d.	1330	1340	1345	1400	1416	1430	1440	1445	1500	1515	1530	1540	1545	1559	1615	1631r	1640	1645	1659	1715	1730	1740	1745	1800	1815	1830
Dewsbury d.	|	|	1356	|	1425	|	|	1457	|	1525	|	|	1557	|	1625	|	|	1656	|	1725	|	|	1757	|	1825	|
Wakefield Kirkgate d.	|	1403	|	|	|	|	1503	|	|	|	|	1602	|	|	|	|	1703	|	|	|	|	1802	|	|	|	|
Leeds a.	1348	|	1410	1421	1438	1449	|	1510	1522	1538	1548	|	1610	1623	1639	1649	|	1710	1722	1738	1748	|	1810	1818	1838	1848
Leeds 119 191 d.	1351	|	1413	1426	1441	1452	|	1513	1527	1542	1551	|	1612	1627	1641	1652	|	1713	1727	1741	1751	|	1813	1826	1841	1851
Selby 177 181 a.	|	|	|	1450	|	|	|	|	1550	|	|	|	|	1654	|	|	|	|	1747	|	|	|	|	1848	|	|
Hull 177 181 a.	|	|	|	1528	|	|	|	|	1628	|	|	|	|	1728	|	|	|	|	1823	|	|	|	|	1922	|	|
York 119 177 191 a.	1414	1440	1435	...	1507	1514	1541	1541	...	1607	1613	1635	1635	...	1704	1714	1738	1738	...	1804	1813	1838	1836	...	1907	1913
York 119 180 182a d.	1418	...	1437	...	1510	1519	...	1542	...	1610	1618	...	1638	...	1710	1720	...	1741	...	1810	1821	...	1839	...	1910	1919
Malton d.	|	...	|	...	1535	|	...	|	...	1635	|	...	|	...	1735	|	...	|	...	1835	|	...	|	...	1935	|
Scarborough a.	|	...	|	...	1559	|	...	|	...	1659	|	...	|	...	1759	|	...	|	...	1859	|	...	|	...	1959	|
Thirsk 182a d.	|	...	1501	...	...	|	...	1605	...	...	|	...	1656	...	...	|	...	1758	...	...	|	...	1857	...	...	|
Northallerton 119 180 182a d.	|	...	1510	...	...	|	...	|	...	...	|	...	1705	...	...	|	...	1806	...	...	|	...	1906	...	...	|
Middlesbrough 212 a.	|	...	1541	...	...	|	...	1643	...	...	|	...	1737	...	...	|	...	1837	...	...	|	...	1936	...	...	|
Redcar Central 212 a.	|	...	1553	...	...	|	...	1655	...	...	|	...	1748	...	...	|	...	1849	...	...	|	...	1948	...	...	|
Saltburn 212 a.	|	...	...	...	...	|	...	...	...	...	|	...	...	...	...	|	...	...	...	...	|	...	1957	...	...	|
Darlington 119 180 d.	1446	...	...	...	...	1549	...	...	...	...	1646	...	...	...	...	1749	...	...	...	...	1851	...	...	...	...	1947
Durham 119 180 d.	1503	...	...	...	...	1605	...	...	...	...	1704	...	...	...	...	1805	...	...	...	...	1907	...	...	...	...	2003
Newcastle 119 180 a.	1518	...	...	...	...	1622	...	...	...	...	1721	...	...	...	...	1822	...	...	...	...	1924	...	...	...	...	2019

	⑦	⑦	⑦	⑦	⑦	⑦	⑦	⑦	⑦	⑦	⑦	⑦	⑦	⑦	⑦	⑦	⑦	⑦	⑦	⑦	⑦	⑦	⑦	⑦	⑦	⑦
Liverpool Lime Street d.	...	...	1752	...	1825	...	...	1852	...	1925	...	...	1952	...	2025	...	...	...	2051	2109	...	...	2152	...	2254	...
Manchester Airport ✈ d.	...	1736	|	...	|	...	1836	|	...	|	...	1936	|	...	|	...	2036	...	|	|	...	2136	|	2237	|	2336
Manchester Piccadilly d.	1800	1753	|	...	|	1900	1853	|	...	|	2000	1953	|	...	|	2058	2053	...	|	|	2158	2153	|	2251	|	2350
Manchester Victoria d.	|	1815c	1830	1845	1900	|	1915c	1930	1945	2000	|	2015c	2030	...	2100	|	2115c	...	2130	2145	|	2215p	2230	2315b	2330	0001
Stalybridge d.	1812	|	1841	|	|	1912	|	1940	|	|	2012	|	2041	...	|	2112	|	...	2141	2158	2211	|	2239	2325	2343	|
Huddersfield d.	1840	1845	1859	1915	1930	1940	1945	1959	2015	2030	2040	2046	2100	...	2129	2140	2145	...	2159	2218	2238	2243	2307	2346	0015	0028
Dewsbury d.	|	1857	|	1925	|	|	1957	|	2025	|	|	2057	|	...	|	|	2157	...	|	2227	|	2257	|	2357	...	|
Wakefield Kirkgate d.	1903	|	|	|	|	2002	|	|	|	|	2102	|	|	...	|	2202	|	...	|	|	2259	|	|	|	...	|
Leeds a.	|	1910	1922	1938	1948	|	2010	2023	2038	2047	|	2109	2122	...	2149	|	2211	...	2223	2240	...	2316	2325	0010	...	0106
Leeds 119 191 d.	|	1913	1927	1944	1951	|	2013	2027	2041	2051	|	2112	2127	2147	2151	|	2213	...	2225	2243	...	2319	2327	0014	...	0108
Selby 177 181 a.	|	|	1952	|	|	|	|	2048	|	|	|	|	2153	|	|	|	|	...	2251	|	...	|	2349	|	...	|
Hull 177 181 a.	|	|	2028	|	|	|	|	2121	|	|	|	|	2229	|	|	|	|	...	2324	|	...	|	0023	|	...	|
York 119 177 191 a.	1939	1936	...	2007	2013	2036	2036	...	2106	2113	2135	2135	...	2223	2214f	2241	2238	...	...	2307	...	2345	...	0044	...	0136
York 119 180 182a d.	...	1942	...	2010	2018	...	2040	...	2110	2118		2136	...	2224	2219	...	2247	2305	...	2309	...	...	...	...	...	...
Malton d.	...	|	...	2035	|	...	|	...	2135	|	...	|	...	2249	|	...	|	2329	...	|	...	...	...	...	...	...
Scarborough a.	...	|	...	2059	|	...	|	...	2159	|	...	|	...	2313	|	...	|	2353	...	|	...	...	...	...	...	...
Thirsk 182a d.	...	1959	...	...	|	...	2057	...	...	|	...	2159	...	...	|	...	2312	...	...	2331	...	...	...	...	...	...
Northallerton 119 180 182a d.	...	2007	...	...	|	...	2106	...	...	|	...	2207	...	...	2249	...	2320	...	...	2343	...	...	...	...	...	...
Middlesbrough 212 a.	...	2040	...	...	|	...	2137	...	...	|	...	2239	...	...	|	...	|	...	...	|	...	...	...	...	...	...
Redcar Central 212 a.	...	2052	...	...	|	...	2149	...	...	|	...	2251	...	...	|	...	|	...	...	|	...	...	...	...	...	...
Saltburn 212 a.	...	...	...	...	|	...	...	...	...	|	...	2304	...	...	|	...	|	...	...	|	...	...	...	...	...	...
Darlington 119 180 d.	...	...	...	...	2047	...	...	...	...	2154	...	...	...	...	2302	...	2334	...	...	2356	...	...	...	...	...	...
Durham 119 180 d.	...	...	...	...	2103	...	...	...	...	2210	...	...	...	...	2319	...	...	...	...	0012	...	...	...	...	...	...
Newcastle 119 180 a.	...	...	...	...	2119	...	...	...	...	2228	...	...	...	...	2348	...	...	...	...	0042	...	...	...	...	...	...

b – Arrives 2300.
c – Arrives 10–11 minutes earlier.
f – Connects with train in previous column.
j – Arrives 2235 on ⑥.
p – Arrives 2202.
r – Arrives 5–6 minutes earlier.
s – Stops to set down only.
t – Arrives 0008 on ⑦ mornings.
v – Until Aug. 29.
z – Until Oct. 26.
* – Connection by 🚌.

EM 2nd class — CLEETHORPES - GRIMSBY - LINCOLN - NEWARK - NOTTINGHAM — 189

km		Ⓐ	Ⓐ	Ⓐ L	Ⓐ L	Ⓐ	Ⓐ	Ⓐ	Ⓐ	Ⓐ	Ⓐ	Ⓐ	Ⓐ	Ⓐ	Ⓐ	Ⓐ	Ⓐ	Ⓐ	Ⓐ	Ⓐ	Ⓐ	Ⓐ	⑥	⑥	⑥	⑥	⑥	⑥
0	**Cleethorpes**... 192 193 d.		...	*0500*	...	0550	...	...	...	...	...	...	...	...	...	...	...	...	...	...	...	2158		...	*0500*	0634	...	...
5	**Grimsby** Town 192 193 d.		...	*0508*	...	0558	...	0741	0840	...	1040	...	1240	...	1438	...	1641	...	1838	...	...	2206		...	*0508*	0642	...	0838
27	Barnetby......... 192 193 d.		...	*0527*	...	0616	...	0801	0859	...	1059	...	1259	...	1457	...	1700	...	1857	...	...	2225		...	*0526*	0703	...	0858
51	Market Rasen ....d.		...	*0544*	...	0632	...	0819	0914	...	1114	...	1314	...	1512	...	1715	...	1913	...	...	2241		...	*0543*	0718	...	0913
75	**Lincoln** .... 180 a.		...	*0603*	...	0651	...	0837	0933	...	1133	...	1333	...	1531	...	1734	...	1931	...	...	2301		...	*0601*	0736	...	0931
	Lincoln ....d.		0516	0614	0640	0652	0747	0838	0935	1035	1135	1236	1335	1437	1533	1634	1736	1834	1932	2049	2132	2306		0518	0629	0739	0839	0933
101	Newark Castle .... ♧ d.		0558	0642	0714	0721**n**	0814	0906	1003	1105	1203	1304	1404	1504	1559	1705	1807	1903	2001	2115	2203	2332		0600	0658	0806	0907	1002
129	**Nottingham** .... ♧ a.		0634	0706	0741	...	0840	0927	1025	1126	1225	1326	1426	1526	1626	1728	1834	1926	2022	2143	2234	0003		0636	0724	0828	0928	1027

	⑥	⑥	⑥	⑥	⑥	⑥	⑥	⑥	⑥	⑥	⑥	⑥	⑦	⑦	⑦	⑦	⑦	⑦ D	⑦	⑦	⑦	⑦	⑦	⑦	⑦	⑦	⑦	⑦
Cleethorpes... 192 193 d.	...	1030	...	...	...	...	...	...	...	...	...	*1953*		...	...	...	...	...	1330	...	...	...	...	1823	...	...	2050	...
Grimsby Town 192 193 d.	...	1038	...	1240	...	1438	...	1638	...	1839	...	*2001*		...	...	...	...	...	1338	...	...	...	...	1831	...	...	2058	...
Barnetby......... 192 193 d.	...	1058	...	1259	...	1458	...	1657	...	1859	...	*2020*		...	...	...	...	...	1359	...	...	...	...	1850	...	...	2117	...
Market Rasen ....d.	...	1113	...	1314	...	1513	...	1712	...	1914	...	*2035*		...	...	...	...	...	1414	...	...	...	...	1906	...	...	2133	...
Lincoln .... 180 a.	...	1131	...	1333	...	1531	...	1730	...	1933	...	*2054*		...	...	...	...	...	1432	...	...	...	...	1925	...	...	2151	...
Lincoln ....d.	1035	1133	1235	1335	1437	1533	1636	1732	1830	1935	2042	2142		0900	1032	1124	1238	1338	1438	1524	1635	1738	1852	1932	2027	2103	...	2251
Newark Castle .... ♧ d.	1104	1202	1304	1403	1505	1605	1706	1800	1858	2003	2110	2210		0929	1059	1153	1307	1405	1507	1553	1705	1808	1921	2001	2056	2132	...	2320
Nottingham............ ♧ a.	1127	1226	1329	1425	1527	1629	1728	1826	1926	2029	2141	2240		1005	1124	1232	1332	1430	1544	1617	1740	1836	1958	2026	2121	2200	...	2356

	Ⓐ	Ⓐ	Ⓐ	Ⓐ	Ⓐ	Ⓐ	Ⓐ	Ⓐ		Ⓐ	Ⓐ	Ⓐ	Ⓐ	Ⓐ	Ⓐ	Ⓐ	Ⓐ	Ⓐ	Ⓐ	Ⓐ	Ⓐ	⑥	⑥	⑥	⑥	⑥	⑥	⑥
Nottingham............ ♧ d.		...	0539	0637	0737	0833	0935	1036	...	1134	1235	1334	1435	1534	1633	1735	1833	1934	2032	2133	2237		...	0513	0553	...	0736	...
Newark Castle .... ♧ d.		...	0606	0659	0803	0903	0957	1102	...	1157	1301	1356	1500	1557	1702	1804	1900	2004	2101	2206	2310		...	0536	0630	...	0801	0817**n**
Lincoln ....a.		...	0635	0731	0836	0933	1027	1131	...	1228	1330	1425	1530	1626	1731	1833	1929	2035	2129	2236	2339		...	0559	0659	...	0831	0839
Lincoln .... 180 d.		0458	0636	0734	...	0935	...	1133	...	...	1331	...	1532	...	1733	...	1930	...	2131	...	...		0523	...	...	0731	...	0841
Market Rasen ....d.		0514	0652	0750	...	0951	...	1149	...	...	1348	...	1548	...	1749	...	1948	...	2146	...	...		0539	...	...	0746	...	0857
Barnetby......... 192 193 a.		0530	0709	0806	...	1007	...	1205	...	...	1404	...	1604	...	1806	...	2006	...	2203	...	...		0555	...	...	0803	...	0913
Grimsby Town 192 193 a.		0550	0730	0828	...	1029	...	1227	...	...	1426	...	1626	...	1826	...	2027**t**	...	2224	...	...		0617	...	...	0824	...	0937
Cleethorpes... 192 193 a.		0602	...	...	...	...	...	...	...	...	...	...	...	...	...	...	2043	...	2232	...	...		0625	...	...	...	...	0947

	⑥	⑥	⑥	⑥	⑥	⑥	⑥	⑥	⑥	⑥	⑥	⑥	⑥	⑥	⑦	⑦	⑦	⑦	⑦	⑦	⑦	⑦	⑦	⑦	⑦	⑦	⑦	⑦
Nottingham............ ♧ d.	0847	0935	1039	1138	1239	1338	1440	1539	1635	1739	1834	1931	2031	2132		0933	1024	1125	1227	1337	1427	1536	1628	1727	1853	1930	2027	2230
Newark Castle .... ♧ d.	0913	0958	1101	1201	1301	1400	1503	1601	1702	1803	1902	1959	2059	2206		1009	1048	1201	1251	1401	1503	1601	1652	1803	1917	1955	2051	2306
Lincoln ....a.	0942	1027	1130	1230	1331	1430	1532	1631	1731	1832	1931	2024	2127	2232		1040	1114	1231	1317	1427	1533	1627	1723	1834	1947	2025	2121	2336
Lincoln .... 180 d.	...	...	1132	...	1332	...	1534	...	1732	1834	...	...	...	...		...	1115	...	...	...	...	1638	...	1836	...	...	...	...
Market Rasen ....d.	...	...	1148	...	1348	...	1549	...	1748	1850	...	...	...	...		...	1131	...	...	...	...	1654	...	1852	...	...	...	...
Barnetby......... 192 193 a.	...	...	1204	...	1404	...	1606	...	1805	1907	...	...	...	...		...	1147	...	...	...	...	1711	...	1908	...	...	...	...
Grimsby Town 192 193 a.	...	...	1228	...	1427	...	1629	...	1829	1930	...	...	...	...		...	1209	...	...	...	...	1734	...	1931	...	...	...	...
Cleethorpes... 192 193 a.	...	...	...	...	...	...	...	...	...	1941	...	...	...	...		...	1219	...	...	...	...	1743	...	1943	...	...	...	...

LINCOLN - NEWARK NORTHGATE Journey time 25 - 30 minutes.

From Lincoln: On Ⓐ at 0516 **N**, 0600, 0652 **G**, 0730 **K**, 0911, 1002 **P**, 1127 **K**, 1324 **K**, 1527 **K**, 1727 **K**, 2025 **K**, 2233 **P**; on ⑥ at 0518 **N**, 0608, 0730 **K**, 0745, 1004, 1127 **K**, 1204, 1324 **K**, 1411, 1527 **K**, 1605, 1655, 1726 **K**, 1801, 1912, 2025 **K**, 2135; on ⑦ at 0835, 1055 **K**, 1106, 1223 **K**, 1248, 1420 **K**, 1427, 1545, 1659 **K**, 1709, 1800 **K**, 1915, 1958, 2126, 2230.

From Newark Northgate: On Ⓐ at 0637 **P**, 0730, 0927 **K**, 0948, 1039, 1135 **K**, 1337 **K**, 1535 **K**, 1737 **K**, 2037 **K**, 2316; on ⑥ at 0646 **P**, 0817 **G**, 0931 **K**, 1040, 1131 **K**, 1235, 1337 **K**, 1452, 1534 **K**, 1646, 1727, 1737 **K**, 1839, 1944, 2031 **K**, 2211; on ⑦ at 0915, 1104 **K**, 1140, 1258 **K**, 1335, 1455, 1554 **K**, 1644, 1707 **K**, 1754, 1945, 2028, 2034 **K**, 2210, 2321.

C – From/to Crewe (Table **155**).
D – To Liverpool Lime Street (Table **206**).
G – From/to Cleethorpes (see table above).
K – From/to London Kings Cross (Table **180**).
L – To London St Pancras (Table **170**).
N – To Nottingham (see table above).

P – To/from Peterborough (Table **176**).
S – To Sleaford (Table **176**).

f – Arrives 5 minutes earlier.
n – Newark Northgate.
t – Departs 2036.

♧ – Additional journeys Newark Castle - Nottingham and v.v. Journey time: 28 – 36 minutes.
From Newark Castle on Ⓐ at: 0625**C**, 0736**C**, 0841**C**, 0936**C**, 1036**C**, 1136**C**, 1246**C**, 1343**C**, 1438**C**, 1537**C**, 1637**C**, 1738**C**, 1841**C**, 1944**C**. On ⑥ at: 0736**C**, 0843**C**, 0939**C**, 1039**C**, 1135**C**, 1243**C**, 1343**C**, 1438**C**, 1538**C**, 1638**C**, 1738**C**, 1835, 1941**C**.
From Nottingham on Ⓐ at: 0543, 0650, 0757**C**, 0852**C**, 0951**C**, 1058**C**, 1157**C**, 1255**C**, 1358**C**, 1456**C**, 1556**C**, 1656**C**, 1800**C**, 1852**C**. On ⑥ at: 0650, 0758**C**, 0901**C**, 1001**C**, 1059**C**, 1155**C**, 1256**C**, 1357**C**, 1457**C**, 1557**C**, 1657**C**, 1758**C**, 1855**C**.

NT 2nd class — LEEDS - BRADFORD - HALIFAX - MANCHESTER - CHESTER — 190

Additional trains run Leeds - Bradford - Manchester Victoria and v.v. on ⚒.

km		⚒	⚒	⚒	⚒		⚒	⚒	⚒	⚒	⚒	⚒	⚒	⚒	⚒	⚒	⑦	⑦	⑦	⑦		⑦	⑦	⑦	⑦	⑦
0	**Leeds** .... 191 d.		0542	0642	0743	♣	1343	1443	1543	1643	1741	1843	1941	2042	2142	2242		0819	0919	0943	♣♥	1944	2043	2144	2219	2319
15	**Bradford** Interchange..... 191 d.		0604	0704	0804		1405	1504	1604	1704	1804	1904	2004	2104	2205	2303		0839	0939	1004		2004	2104	2204	2239	2339
28	Halifax.......................... 191 d.		0616	0716	0816	and	1417	1516	1617	1716	1816	1916	2016	2116	2217	2316		0850	0950	1015	and	2015	2115	2215	2250	2350
42	Hebden Bridge .... 191 d.		0631	0731	0831		1432	1531	1631	1731	1831	1931	2031	2131	2232	2330		0905	1002	1030		2030	2129	2229	2303	0005
49	Todmorden.................. 191a d.		0637	0737	0838	hourly	1438	1537	1637	1737	1837	1937	2037	2137	2238	2336		0911	1008	1036	hourly	2036	2135	2235	2309	0011
63	Rochdale..................... 191a d.		0647	0747	0848		1448	1547	1648	1747	1847	1947	2047	2147	2248	2352		0923	1021	1046		2046	2145	2245	2321	0023
80	**Manchester** Victoria..... 191a a.		0702	0801	0902	until	1502	1601	1703	1802	1901	2001	2101	2204	2302	0006		0937	1035	1100	until	2100	2159	2300	2335	0037
113	Warrington Bank Quay ... 150 a.		0739	0839	0939		1538	1638	1739	1838	1939	2038	2138	...	...	...		...	...	1139		2139	...	...	...	...
142	**Chester**........................ 150 a.		0809	0901	1001		1601	1709	1809	1909	2002	2109	2202	...	...	...		...	...	1208		2207	...	...	...	...

	⚒	⚒	⚒	⚒	⚒	⚒	⚒	⚒		⚒	⚒	⚒	⚒	⚒	⚒	⚒	⚒	Ⓐ	⑦	⑦	⑦	⑦		⑦	⑦	⑦
Chester.........................150 d.		...	...	0621	0722	0821	0928	1026		1527	1628	1724	1824	1926	2027	...	...	2227		...	...	0925	♣	2025	...	...
Warrington Bank Quay.....150 d.		...	...	0649	0749	0849	0950	1049		1549	1650	1749	1849	1949	2049	...	...	2249		...	...	0946		2046	...	...
Manchester Victoria......191a d.		0551	0630	0721	0821	0921	1021	1121	and	1621	1721	1821	1922	2021	2121	2157	2257	2323		0829	0920	1020	and	2120	2154	2254
Rochdale.......................191a d.		0609	0645	0734	0835	0934	1034	1134		1634	1734	1834	1935	2034	2134	2210	2310	2336		0844	0933	1032		2132	2207	2307
Todmorden.....................191a d.		0624	0658	0744	0845	0943	1043	1143	hourly	1643	1743	1843	1944	2043	2143	2219	2319	2351		0853	0942	1042	hourly	2142	2218	2318
Hebden Bridge.................191 d.		0630	0704	0750	0851	0950	1050	1150		1650	1749	1850	1950	2050	2150	2225	2326	2357		0859	0948	1048		2148	2225	2324
Halifax............................191 d.		0644	0720	0805	0906	1005	1105	1205	until	1705	1804	1905	2005	2105	2205	2238	2337	0012		0914	1003	1103	until	2205	2238	2339
Bradford Interchange......191 d.		0702	0738	0821	0921	1021	1121	1221		1721	1820	1921	2021	2121	2221	2253	2353	0026		0928	1020	1118		2220	2254	2354
Leeds............................191 a.		0724	0759	0842	0942	1042	1143	1242		1742	1843	1942	2042	2142	2243	2314	0014	0043		0946	1040	1139		2239	2316	0014

♥ – The 1343 from Leeds runs 3 minutes later Halifax - Manchester Victoria.

♣ – Timings may vary ± 2 minutes.

NT 2nd class — YORK - LEEDS - BLACKBURN - BLACKPOOL — 191

km		⚒	⚒	⚒	⚒	⚒	⚒	⚒	⚒		⚒	⚒	⚒	⚒	⚒	⚒	⑦	⑦	⑦	⑦	⑦	⑦		⑦	⑦	⑦
0	**York**.......................... 119 188 d.		0518**j**	0612	0710	0822	0922	1023	1123	♣	1723	1822	1923	2023	2123	2219**g**		0923	1023	1123	1224	1323		1923	2023	2123
41	**Leeds**.................. 119 188 190 d.		0557	0658	0755	0857	0959	1058	1157		1757	1857	1957	2057	2157	2257		0957	1056	1157	1257	1357		1957	2058	2157
56	**Bradford** Interchange.........190 d.		0618	0717	0816	0917	1018	1119	1218	and	1819	1917	2017	2118	2216	2317		1016	1116	1217	1316	1416	and	2016	2119	2217
69	Halifax..............................190 d.		0629	0728	0827	0928	1029	1130	1229		1830	1928	2028	2129	2227	2328		1027	1127	1228	1327	1427		2027	2131	2228
83	Hebden Bridge....................190 d.		0639	0741	0838	0941	1041	1141	1243	hourly	1842	1941	2041	2142	2238	2340		1043	1143	1243	1343	1443	hourly	2042	2142	2243
103	Burnley Manchester Road. 191a d.		0703**f**	0802	0902	1002	1102	1202	1302		1902	2002	2102	2202	2302**f**	2359		1106	1206	1306	1406	1506		2106	2206	2308**f**
113	Accrington ....191a d.		0712	0812	0912	1012	1112	1212	1312	until	1912	2012	2112	2212	2311	0008		1115	1215	1315	1415	1515	until	2115	2215	2317
123	**Blackburn**.......................191a d.		0723	0821	0921	1021	1120	1221	1321		1921	2021	2121	2221	2321	0016		1124	1224	1325	1425	1524		2125	2225	2326
142	**Preston**...................... 156 162 a.		0745	0844	0938	1038	1138	1238	1338		1939	2038	2138	2238	2338	...		1142	1242	1343	1443	1543		2142	2242	2343
171	**Blackpool** North.......... 156 162 a.		0809	0909	1004	1104	1204	1304	1404		2004	2104	2206	2304	0004	...		1206	1306	1406	1506	1607		2206	2308	0007

	⚒	⚒	⚒	⚒	⚒	⚒		⚒	⚒	⚒	⚒	⚒	⚒	⑦	⑦	⑦	⑦	⑦	⑦	⑦		⑦	⑦	⑦	⑦	⑦
Blackpool North...........156 162 d.		0519	0619	0718	0819	0919	♣	1719	1819	1919	2019	2118	2202		...	...	0918	1022	1118	1218		1718	1818	1918	2018	2119
Preston.......................156 162 d.		0544	0644	0744	0844	0944		1744	1844	1944	2044	2143	2226		...	...	0942	1046	1142	1242		1742	1842	1942	2042	2143
Blackburn.........................191a d.		0604	0704	0804	0904	1004	and	1805	1904	2004	2104	2202	2242		...	0903	0958	1102	1159	1259	and	1759	1859	1959	2059	2200
Accrington ....191a d.		0613	0712	0813	0913	1013		1813	1912	2013	2112	2211	2250		...	0911	1006	1110	1207	1307		1807	1907	2007	2107	2208
Burnley Manchester Road..191a d.		0622	0721	0822	0922	1022	hourly	1822	1921	2022	2121	2220	2259		...	0920	1015	1119	1216	1316	hourly	1816	1916	2016	2116	2217
Hebden Bridge.................... 190 d.		0642	0742	0843	0943	1043		1843	1942	2043	2142	2241	2320		...	0941	1036	1140	1237	1337		1837	1937	2037	2137	2238
Halifax.............................. 190 d.		0653	0753	0854	0954	1054	until	1854	1953	2054	2153	2252	2331		0858	0955	1050	1155	1252	1351	until	1852	1952	2051	2152	2253
Bradford Interchange......... 190 d.		0707	0808	0908	1008	1108		1908	2007	2108	2207	2306	2348		0914	1010	1107**f**	1210	1307	1406		1906	2007	2106	2208	2308
Leeds...................119 188 190 a.		0729**z**	0827	0928	1027	1129		1927	2026	2129	2227	2326	0005		0934	1029	1126	1228	1327	1427		1926	2026	2125**a**	2227	2327
York...........................119 188 a.		0803	0900	0957	1057	1159		1958	2057	2157	2303**g**	0009**g**	...		1013	1058	1159	1258	1357	1459		2001	2100	2158	2258	2358

a – Departs 2130.
f – Arrives 5 – 6 minutes earlier.
g – ⑤⑥ only.
j – ①⑥ only.
t – Arrives 7 – 8 minutes earlier.
z – Departs 0736.
♣ – Timings may vary ± 2 minutes.

191a MANCHESTER - BURNLEY - BLACKBURN

2nd class NT

km		⚒	⚒	❖	⚒	⚒	⑦	⑦	⑦	❖	⑦
0	**Manchester** Vic **190** d.		0604		2204	2303		0833	0900		2201
17	Rochdale **190** d.		0618	and	2217	2317		0854	0921	and	2222
31	Todmorden **190** d.		0634	hourly	2233	2333		0909	0938	hourly	2239
45	Burnley ‡ **191** d.		0650		2248	2349		0925	0954		2255
54	Accrington **191** d.		0700	until	2259	2359		0936	1004	until	2305
63	**Blackburn** **191** a.		0711		2311	0012		0952	1019		2320

	⚒	⚒	❖	⚒	⚒	⑦	⑦	⑦		⑦	⑦	⑦	⑦	⑦
Blackburn **191** d.		0618		2220	2320		0748	0807		1907	2007	2113	2210	2300
Accrington **191** d.		0626	and	2228	2328		0758	0818	and	1918	2018	2123	2221	2310
Burnley ‡ **191** d.		0637	hourly	2239	2339		0809	0829	hourly	1929	2029	2135	2232	2321
Todmordon **190** d.		0654		2256	2355		0826	0846		1946	2046	2155	2249	2338
Rochdale **190** d.		0710	until	2310	0009		0840	0903	until	2003	2103	2212	2306	2355
Manchester V **190** a.		0725		2327	0025		0901	0924		2024	2124	2233	2327	0015

❖ – Timings may vary by up to 2 minutes.

‡ – Burnley Manchester Road.

192 LINCOLN and CLEETHORPES - SHEFFIELD

2nd class NT

km		⚒	ⒶN	⑥N	⚒L	⚒	⚒L	ⒶL	⑥L	⚒L	⚒L	⚒L	⚒L	⚒L	ⒶC	⚒L	⑥L	ⒶL	⚒L	⑥L	ⒶL	ⒶL	⑥L	ⒶL
0	**Lincoln** **176** d.		...	...	...	0644	0723	0825	0826	0915	1018	1122	1215	1328	...	1415	1521	1522	1617	1723	1723	1821	1823	1923
	Gainsborough Central d.		...	...	...	|	|	|	|	|	|	|	|	|	1418	|	|	|	|	|	|	|	|	|
26	Gainsborough Lea Road **176** d.		...	...	...	0705	0744	0846	0848	0937	1039	1143	1236	1349	|	1436	1542	1543	1638	1744	1745	1842	1844	1944
40	Retford d.		0613	0613	0656	0719	0758	0901	0901	0952	1054	1158	1251	1404	1435	1451	1556	1557	1653	1757	1800	1857	1857	2000
52	Worksop d.		0626	0625	0708	0730	0808	0912	0911	1003	1106	1209	1302	1415	1446	1502	1607	1608	1704	1808	1811	1908	1907	2011
78	**Sheffield** a.		0702	0658	0743	0804	0843	0945	0944	1042	1141	1241	1340	1446	1512	1543	1642	1642	1742	1844	1845	1942	1944	2043

	⑥L	⑥	Ⓐ	⚒	⚒	⚒	⑥	Ⓐ	⑦	⑦	⑦H	⑦H	⑦H	⑦H	⑦	⑦H	⑦	⑦	⑦	⑦	⑦	⑦	⑦	⑦
Lincoln **176** d.	1929	2019	2019	2128	...	...	2244	2244		...	1014	1114	1214	1314	...	1414	1511	1613	1715	1818	1919	2017	2120	2151
Gainsborough Lea Road **176** d.	1950	2040	2040	2149	...	...	2305	2305		...	1035	1135	1235	1335	...	1435	1532	1634	1736	1839	1940	2038	2141	2212
Retford d.	2002	2053	2055	2204	2251	...	2318	2320		0912	1050	1150	1250	1350	1416	1450	1547	1649	1751	1854	1955	2053	2156	2227
Worksop d.	2012	2104	2108	2215	2303	2320	2329	2332		0925	1102	1201	1301	1401	1428	1501	1557	1700	1802	1905	2006	2105	2207	2238
Sheffield a.	2043	2137	2146	2248	2337	2358r	0003	0006		0959	1133	1234	1334	1434	1500	1534	1630	1733	1836	1933	2040	2135	2241	2312

km		⚒	⚒	Ⓐ	⑥		⑥	Ⓐ	⚒L	⚒L	⚒L		ⒶC	⚒L	⚒L		⚒L	⚒L	⑥L	ⒶL	⚒L	⚒L	⚒L	⚒L
0	**Sheffield** d.		0545	0611	0613	...	0635	0635	0737	0838	0937	...	0954	1039	1137	...	1237	1339	1439	1440	1537	1638	1738	1841
25	Worksop d.		0616	0634	0636	...	0707	0707	0808	0911	1010	...	1018	1111	1211	...	1306	1408	1508	1509	1606	1709	1809	1914
38	Retford d.		0626	0647	0649	...	0717	0717	0818	0921	1020	...	1028	1121	1222	...	1316	1418	1518	1519	1616	1719	1819	1924
	Gainsborough Lea Road **176** d.		0641	...	...	...	0731	0732	0833	0937	1035	...	|	1137	1237	...	1330	1432	1532	1533	1631	1734	1834	1939
54	**Gainsborough** Central a.		|	...	...	...	|	|	|	|	|	...	1045	|	|	...	|	|	|	|	|	|	|	|
	Lincoln **176** a.		0704	...	...	...	0754	0755	0857	1001	1058	...	...	1202	1301	...	1355	1457	1555	1556	1655	1758	1857	2005

	ⒶL	⑥L	Ⓐ	⑥	⚒	⚒	⑦	⑦	⑦	⑦	⑦		⑦H	⑦	⑦H	⑦H	⑦H	⑦H		⑦H	⑦	⑦	⑦	⑦
Sheffield d.	1938	1940	2053	2053	2142	2243		0845	0941	1041	1141	...	1241	1315	1336	1441	1541	1640	...	1736	1842	1934	2020	2123
Worksop d.	2010	2011	2123	2125	2214	2314		0906	1012	1105	1212	...	1309	1346	1405	1507	1608	1711	...	1804	1914	2000	2051	2154
Retford d.	2020	2021	2133	2135	2227	...		0916	1022	1115	1222	...	1319	1357	1415	1517	1618	1721	...	1814	1924	2010	2100	2204
Gainsborough Lea Road **176** d.	2035	2035	2148	2150	...	...		0931	1037	1130	1237	...	1334	...	1430	1532	1633	1736	...	1829	1939	2025	2115	2219
Lincoln **176** a.	2058	2058	2211	2213	...	...		0954	1100	1154	1300	...	1357	...	1453	1555	1656	1759	...	1852	2003	2048	2138	2242

B – From Barnsley (Table **171**).
C – To / from Cleethorpes (See panel below main table).
H – To / from Huddersfield (Table **171**).
L – To / from Leeds (Table **171**).
N – To Nottingham (Table **171**).

r – Arrives 2353 on ⑥.

CLEETHORPES - GAINSBOROUGH - SHEFFIELD

km			Ⓐ	
0	**Cleethorpes** **193** d.	...	1320	...
5	Grimsby Town **189 193** d.	...	1327	...
28	Barnetby **189 193** d.	...	1343	...
61	**Gainsborough** Central a.	...	1418	...
114	*Sheffield* **192** a.	...	1512	...

		Ⓐ	
Sheffield **192** d.	...	0954	...
Gainsborough Central d.	...	1045	...
Barnetby **189 193** d.	...	1114	...
Grimsby Town **189 193** a.	...	1133	...
Cleethorpes **193** a.	...	1145	...

193 CLEETHORPES - DONCASTER - SHEFFIELD - MANCHESTER - LIVERPOOL

TP

km		⚒	Ⓐ	⑥	⚒	⚒	⚒	⚒	⚒	⚒		⚒	Ⓐ	⑥	⑥	Ⓐ	⚒
0	**Cleethorpes** **189 192** d.		...	...	...	...	0504	0626	0726	0826		1926	2026	2026	2122	2126	...
5	Grimsby Town **189 192** d.		...	...	...	...	0512	0634	0734	0834	❖	1934	2034	2034	2130	2134	...
29	Barnetby **189 192** d.		...	...	...	...	0532	0653	0753	0853		1953	2053	2053	2150	2153	...
48	Scunthorpe d.		...	...	...	...	0548	0708	0808	0908		2008	2108	2108	2205	2209	2248
85	**Doncaster** a.		...	...	...	...	0626	0738	0839	0938		2037	2136	2137	2234	2238	2328
85	**Doncaster** **177** d.		...	...	...	0536	0626	0741	0843	0942	and	2042	2142	2140	...	2244	*2335*
109	Meadowhall **177** d.		...	...	...	0558	0655	0759	0902	1002		2102	2202	2202	...	2313	*0004*
115	**Sheffield** **177** a.		...	...	...	0608	0705	0807	0909	1009	hourly	2109	2209	2208	...	2320	*0013*
115	**Sheffield** **206** d.		0320k	0319	0508	0609	0706	0808	0911	1011		2111	2211	2210	...	...	...
175	Stockport **206** a.		|	|	|	0653	0753	0853	0953	1053	until	2153	2255	2252	...	...	...
184	**Manchester** Piccadilly **206** a.		0453j	0451v	0605	0705	0805	0906	1005	1105		2205	2309	2305	...	...	...
	Manchester Airport ✈ a.		0525	0514	|	|	|	|	|	|		|	|	...	...	...	...
210	Warrington Central **206** a.		...	...	0635	0735	0830	0930	1035	1135‡		2235	2338	...	...	...	...
231	**Liverpool** South P'way **206** a.		...	...	0649	0749	0849	0948	1049	1150		2249	2353	...	...	...	...
240	**Liverpool** Lime Street **206** a.		...	...	0701	0800	0900	1000	1100	1200		2300	0007	...	...	...	...

	⑦	⑦	⑦	⑦	⑦	⑦		⑦	⑦	⑦	⑦
Cleethorpes **189 192** d.		...	...	...	0926	1026		1827	1926	2026	2126
Grimsby Town **189 192** d.		...	...	...	0934	1034	◧	1835	1934	2034	2134
Barnetby **189 192** d.		...	...	...	0953	1053		1855	1953	2053	2153
Scunthorpe d.		...	...	...	1010	1108		1911	2008	2108	2208
Doncaster a.		...	...	...	1039	1138		1941	2037	2141	2237
Doncaster **177** d.		...	...	0946	1044	1142	and	1944	2041	2144	2241
Meadowhall **177** d.		...	...	1005	1102	1201		2001	2103	2203	2315
Sheffield **177** a.		...	...	1012	1110	1209	hourly	2009	2109	2210	2322
Sheffield **206** d.		0811	0911	1014	1111	1211		2011	2111	2213	...
Stockport **206** a.		0852	0952	1055	1155	1254	until	2058	2158	2301	...
Manchester Piccadilly **206** a.		0904	1003	1106	1207	1306		2107	2207	2315	...
Manchester Airport ✈ a.		|	|	|	|	|		|	|	...	...
Warrington Central **206** a.		0930	1034	1132	1231	1331		2130	2231	...	...
Liverpool South P'way **206** a.		0949	1051	1150	1249	1349		2148	2248	...	...
Liverpool Lime Street **206** a.		1001	1102	1200	1301	1401		2159	2303	...	...

	⚒	⚒	Ⓐ	⑥	⚒	⚒	⚒		⚒	⚒	⚒	⑥	Ⓐ	⑥	Ⓐ	Ⓐ
Liverpool Lime Street **206** d.		...	...	...	0614	0719	0819		1819	1919	2019	2119	2118	...	2220	...
Liverpool South P'way **206** d.		...	...	...	0624	0729	0830	◧	1830	1930	2030	2130	2130	...	2230	...
Warrington Central **206** d.		...	...	...	0642	0746	0848‡		1844	1944	2044	2144	2144	...	2244	...
Manchester Airport ✈ d.		...	0543	0543	|	|	|		|	|	|	|	|	...	|	2331
Manchester Piccadilly **206** d.		...	0612y	0613y	0712	0813	0913		1913	2013	2113	2213	2213	2313	2320	2352
Stockport **206** d.		...	0624	0626	0724	0825	0925		1923	2023	2122	2223	2223	|	|	|
Sheffield **206** a.		...	0706	0707	0809	0909	1009	and	2008	2108	2209	2303	2307	0031	0017	0126
Sheffield **177** d.		0554	0709	0709	0811	0911	1011		2010	2110	2211	2304	2310	...	...	...
Meadowhall **177** d.		0600	0715	0715	0817	0917	1017	hourly	2016	2116	2217	|	|	...	...	...
Doncaster **177** a.		0632	0735	0733	0836	0937	1035		2036	2141	2235	2331	2354	...	...	...
Doncaster d.		0636	0736	0734	0838	0939	1036	until	2037	2147	2238	...	...	...	...	...
Scunthorpe d.		0702	0803	0801	0904	1005	1103		2103	2213	2312	...	...	...	...	...
Barnetby **189 192** d.		0717	0819	0815	0918	1019	1117		2117	2227	2326	...	...	...	...	...
Grimsby Town **189 192** a.		0739	0842	0838	0941	1042	1141		2140	2257c	2348	...	...	...	...	...
Cleethorpes **189 192** a.		0751	0854	0850	0953	1054	1153		2152	2307c	0001	...	...	...	...	...

	⑦	⑦	⑦	⑦	⑦		⑦	⑦	⑦	⑦	⑦
Liverpool Lime Street **206** d.		...	...	0920	1020		1920	2020	2120	2220	...
Liverpool South P'way **206** d.		...	...	0931	1031	◧	1931	2031	2131	2231	...
Warrington Central **206** d.		...	...	0948	1048		1948	2048	2149	2248	...
Manchester Airport ✈ d.		...	...	|	|		|	|	|	|	2330
Manchester Piccadilly **206** d.		0812	0909	1014	1120		2017	2117	2217	2315	2352
Stockport **206** d.		0822	0919	1023	1129		2026	2127	2226	2325	|
Sheffield **206** a.		0906	1006	1103	1209	and	2109	2210	2307	0007	0114
Sheffield **177** d.		0909	1010	1110	1210		2111	2212	2311	...	...
Meadowhall **177** d.		0915	1016	1116	1216	hourly	2117	2218	|	...	...
Doncaster **177** a.		0936	1036	1136	1234		2135	2236	2340	...	...
Doncaster d.		0938	1038	1139	1237	until	2137	2239	...	...	...
Scunthorpe d.		1004	1104	1205	1303		2204	2305	...	...	...
Barnetby **189 192** d.		1018	1118	1219	1317		2218	2319	...	...	...
Grimsby Town **189 192** a.		1040	1140	1241	1339		2240	2341	...	...	...
Cleethorpes **189 192** a.		1052	1152	1253	1351		2252	2353	...	...	...

c – Arrives 5 minutes earlier on ⑥.
j – Departs 0508; on ① arrives 0439.
k – On ① departs 0345.
t – Ⓐ only.
v – Departs 0458.
y – Arrives 0559.
◧ – Timings may vary ± 3 minutes.
‡ – Timings at Warrington may be up to 5 minutes earlier.
❖ – The 1526 from Cleethorpes arrives Liverpool at 1904.

194 SHEFFIELD - MANCHESTER (Hope Valley service)

2nd class only EM NT

km		⚒	Ⓐ	⑥	Ⓐ	⑥	Ⓐ	⑥	⚒	⚒	⚒		⚒	⚒	⑥	Ⓐ	Ⓐ	⑦	⑦	⑦	⑦	⑦	⑦		⑦	⑦
0	**Sheffield** **193** d.		...	...	0618	0620	0711	0713	0729j	0815	0914		2014	2114	2224	2245	2328		0914	1017	1115	1214	1314		2014	2216
16	Grindleford d.		...	...	0634	0636	0728	0728	|	0830	0929	and	2029	2129	2239	2300	2343		0929	1031	1131	1229	1329	and	2029	2231
18	Hathersage d.		...	...	0638	0640	0732	0731	|	0833	0932		2032	2132	2242	2303	2346		0932	1034	1134	1232	1332		2032	2234
24	Hope d.		...	...	0646	0648	0740	0739	|	0840	0939	hourly	2039	2139	2249	2311	2354		0939	1041	1142	1239	1339	hourly	2040	2241
32	Edale d.		...	...	0654	0656	0748	0747	|	0848	0947		2047	2147	2257	2319	0001		0947	1049	1150	1247	1347		2048	2249
41	Chinley d.		0625	0653	0702	0704	0756	0754	0804	0855	0954	until	2054	2154	2304	2327	0009		0954	1056	1159	1254	1354	until	2057	2256
67	**Manchester** Picc **193** a.		0709	0732	0736	0736	0834	0832	0835	0932	1032		2132	2233	2342	0012	0037		1032	1133	1237	1332	1434		2134	2337

	⚒	⚒	⚒	⚒		⚒	Ⓐ	⑥	⚒	Ⓐ	Ⓐ	⑥	⑦	⑦	⑦a	⑦b	⑦	⑦	⑦	⑦	⑦	⑦	⑦	⑦		⑦	⑦
Manchester Picc **193** d.		0546	0640	0748		1848	1946	1948	2048	2148	2230	2230		0745	0829	0845	0931	1045	1145	1245	1345	1445	1545	1645		2045	2213
Chinley d.		0615	0718	0823	and	1923	2021	2023	2123	2224	2254	2257		0822	0906	0922	1007	1122	1223	1322	1421	1521	1621	1720	and	2120	2245
Edale d.		0625	0727	0832		1933	2030	2032	2133	2233	2303	2306		0831	0915	0931	1017	1131	1232	1332	1430	1530	1630	1730		2129	2255
Hope d.		0631	0733	0838	hourly	1939	2036	2038	2139	2239	2309	2312		0837	0921	0937	1024	1137	1238	1338	1436	1536	1637	1736	hourly	2135	2301
Hathersage d.		0639	0739	0845		1946	2043	2046	2146	2246	2317	2320		0844	0928	0944	1031	1144	1245	1346	1443	1543	1644	1743		2142	2307
Grindleford d.		0644	0744	0850	until	1951	2048	2051	2151	2251	2322	2325		0849	0933	0949	1037	1149	1250	1351	1447	1547	1650	1747	until	2147	2313
Sheffield **193** a.		0658	0805	0906		2006	2100	2105	2206	2305	2336	2338		0904	0947	1003	1051	1203	1304	1404	1501	1601	1703	1802		2201	2326

a – Until Sept. 14.
b – From Sept. 21.
j – Departs 0735 on ⑥.

LE On ⚒ most Norwich trains convey 🍷 LONDON - HARWICH, IPSWICH and NORWICH 200

km		⚒	⚒	Ⓐ	Ⓐ	⑥	Ⓐ	⑥	⑥	Ⓐ	Ⓐ	⑥	Ⓐ	⑥	⑥	⑥	Ⓐ	⚒	⑥	Ⓐ	⚒	⚒	⚒	⚒	⑥	Ⓐ	⚒
			P	2	2	2			2		2		2C	2C	2							2		2			
0	**London** Liverpool Street d.		...	...	...	0534	0600	...	0602	0625	0630	0630	...	...	0636	0700	0700	0730	0800	0800	0830	0900	0930	1000	1030	1030	1100
6	Stratford d.		...	...	...	0541	|	...	0609	0632u	0637	0637u	...	...	0643	|	|	0737u	|	|	0837u	|	0937u	|	1037u	1037u	|
48	Chelmsford d.		...	...	...	0610	0628	...	0634	0656	0702	|	...	...	0710	0728	0728	|	0828	0830	|	0928	|	1028	|	|	1128
84	Colchester d.		0540	0615	...	0643	0648	...	0704	0720	0730	0717	...	...	0737	0747	0747	0817	0847	0849	0917	0947	1017	1047	1118	1121	1147
97	Manningtree ★ d.		0548	0623	...	0651	0656	...	0712	0728	0738	0725	...	...	0745	0755	0755	0825	0855	0857	0925	0955	1025	1055	1126	1129	1155
112	**Harwich** Int'l ★ d.		|	|	...	|	|	...	|	|	0752	|	0745	0750	0759	|	|	|	|	|	|	|	|	|	|	|	|
111	**Ipswich** 204 d.		0600	0633	0639	0702	0707	0710	0725	0739	...	0738	0819	0820	...	0806	0806	0838	0906	0908	0938	1006	1038	1106	1138	1140	1206
130	Stowmarket 204 d.		0611	...	0650	...	0718	0721	...	0750	...	0749	0832	0833	...	|	0817	0849	|	|	0949	|	1049	|	1149	1151	|
153	Diss d.		...	...	0702	...	0730	0733	...	0802	...	0800	...	...	...	0826	0829	0901	0927	0928	1000	1026	1100	1126	1200	1203	1226
185	**Norwich** a.		...	...	0724	...	0747	0750	...	0820	...	0818	...	...	...	0844	0847	0919	0944	0945	1019	1046	1118	1144	1218	1221	1244

	⚒	⚒	⚒	Ⓐ	⑥	⚒	⚒	⚒	⑥	Ⓐ	⚒	⑥	Ⓐ	⚒	Ⓐ	⑥	Ⓐ	⑥	Ⓐ	Ⓐ	⑥	⚒	⑥	Ⓐ	⑥	Ⓐ	⑥
							2		2	2				2			2					2			2	2	2
London Liverpool Street d.	1130	1200	1230	1300	1300	1330	1400	1430	1500	1500	1530	1600	1600	1630	1700	1700	1702	1730	1730	1800	1800	1802	1830	1830	1900	1900	1902
Stratford d.	1137u	|	1237u	|	|	1337u	|	1437u	|	|	1537u	|	|	1637a	1707u	|	1710	1737u	|	|	|	1809	1837u	1839u	|	|	|
Chelmsford d.	|	1228	|	1328	1328	|	1428	|	1528	1528	|	1628	|	|	|	1728	1733	|	|	|	1828	1834	|	|	|	|	1931
Colchester d.	1217	1247	1317	1347	1347	1417	1447	1517	1547	1547	1617	1647	1647	1717	|	1747	1759	1817	1820	1850	1847	1903	1917	1920	|	1947	1950
Manningtree ★ d.	1225	1255	1325	1355	1355	1425	1455	1525	1555	1555	1625	1655	1655	1725	|	1755	1807	1825	1828	1858	1855	1911	1925	1928	|	1955	1958
Harwich Int'l ★ d.	|	|	|	|	|	|	|	|	|	|	|	|	|	|	|	|	|	|	|	|	|	|	|	|	|	|	|
Ipswich 204 d.	1238	1306	1338	1406	1408	1438	1506	1538	1606	1608	1639	1706	1707	1737	1759	1806	1818	1838	1840	1910	1906	1924	1938	1940	1956	2007	2008
Stowmarket 204 d.	1249	|	1349	|	|	1449	|	1549	|	|	1651	1717	1718	1748	1810	|	...	1850	1851	1921	|	...	1950	1951	|	2018	...
Diss d.	1300	1326	1400	1427	1428	1500	1526	1600	1626	1628	1702	1729	1730	1800	1821	1826	...	1901	1903	1933	1926	...	2001	2003	2016	2030	...
Norwich a.	1318	1344	1421r	1444	1446	1518	1544	1619	1644	1646	1720	1746	1748	1819	1839	1844	...	1919	1921	1951	1944	...	2020	2021	2033	2048	...

	Ⓐ	⑥	⚒	Ⓐ	⑥	Ⓐ	⚒	⑥	Ⓐ	⚒	⚒	⚒	⚒	⑥	Ⓐ	⑥	Ⓐ	⑥	Ⓐ	⑦	⑦	⑦	⑦	⑦	⑦	⑦	⑦
	2	2		2	2	2		2L	2L	2	2		2			2	2				2	2	2		2C		2P
London Liverpool Street d.	1902	1904	1930	1936	2000	2000	2030	...	...	2036	2100	2130	2200	2230	2230	2302	2302	2330	2330		...	0645	...	...	...	0815	...
Stratford d.	1909	1911	1937u	1943	|	|	2037u	...	...	2043	|	2137u	|	2237u	2237u	2309	2309	2337u	2337u		...	0652	...	...	...	0822u	...
Chelmsford d.	1934	1936	|	2008	2028	2028	|	...	...	2108	2128	|	2228	2300	2300	2334	2334	2359	2359		...	0726	...	...	...	|	...
Colchester d.	2007	2004	2017	2038	2047	2049	2117	...	...	2137	2147	2217	2247	2319	2319	0002	0004	0019	0019		0730	0748	0813	...	...	0918	0925
Manningtree ★ d.	2015	2012	2025	2046	2055	2057	2125	...	...	2145	2155	2225	2255	2327	2327	0010	0012	0027	0027		0738	0756	0821	...	...	0926	0933
Harwich Int'l ★ d.	|	2026	|	2100	|	|	|	2138	2147	2159	|	|	|	|	|	|	|	|	|		|	0811	|	...	0850	|	|
Ipswich 204 d.	2027	...	2037	...	2106	2109	2138	2203	2213	...	2207	2238	2307	2338	2340	0022	0030	0039	0045t		0750	...	0831	0842	0920f	0937	0955v
Stowmarket 204 d.	...	...	2050	...	|	2120	2149	...	...	...	...	2249	...	2350	2351	...	...	0050	0057		...	...	...	0853	0932	0949	1006
Diss d.	...	...	2100	...	2126	2132	2200	...	...	...	...	2300	...	0002	0003	...	...	0101	0109		...	...	...	0905	...	1001	...
Norwich a.	...	...	2119	...	2144	2149	2218	...	...	...	...	2319	...	0019	0028	...	...	0119	0133		...	...	...	0924	...	1018	...

	⑦	⑦	⑦	⑦	⑦	⑦	⑦		⑦	⑦	⑦	⑦	⑦	⑦	⑦	⑦	⑦	⑦	⑦	⑦	⑦	⑦	⑦	⑦	⑦	⑦
	2		2		2	2			2		2	2			2		2	2		2	2		2		2	
London Liverpool Street d.	0908	0930	1008	1030	1100	1108	1130	and	1708	1730	1800	1808	1830	1900	1908	1930	2000	2008	2030	...	2108	2130	2208	2230	2308	2330
Stratford d.	0915	0937u	1015	1037u	|	1115	1137u	at	1715	1737u	|	1815	1837u	|	1915	1937u	2007	2015	2037u	...	2115	2137u	2215	2237u	2315	2337u
Chelmsford d.	0942	|	1042	|	|	1142	|	the	1742	|	|	1842	|	|	1942	|	2032	2042	|	...	2142	|	2242	|	2342	|
Colchester d.	1012	1017	1112	1117	1145	1212	1217	same	1812	1817	1845	1912	1917	1945	2012	2017	2054	2112	2117	...	2212	2217	2312	2317	0012	0017
Manningtree ★ d.	1020	1025	1120	1125	|	1220	1225	minutes	1820	1825	|	1920	1925	1953	2020	2025	2102	2120	2125	...	2220	2225	2320	2325	0020	0025
Harwich Int'l ★ d.	|	|	|	|	|	|	|	past	|	|	|	|	|	|	|	|	2116	|	|	2138	|	|	|	|	|	|
Ipswich 204 d.	1030	1036	1133	1137	1201	1230	1236	each	1830	1836	1901	1930	1936	2004	2030	2036	...	2130	2136	2204	2231	2236	2332	2337	0031	0037
Stowmarket 204 d.	...	1048	...	1148	1213	...	1248	hour	...	1848	1912	...	1948	2015	...	2048	...	...	2148	...	...	2248	...	2348	...	0048
Diss d.	...	1100	...	1200	1225	...	1300	until	...	1900	1924	...	2000	2027	...	2100	...	...	2200	...	...	2300	...	2359	...	0100
Norwich a.	...	1117	...	1218	1243	...	1318		...	1917	1941	...	2017	2044	...	2117	...	...	2217	...	...	2319	...	0017	...	0118

	⚒	Ⓐ	⑥	Ⓐ	⑥	Ⓐ	Ⓐ	⑥	Ⓐ	⑥	Ⓐ	⚒	⑥	Ⓐ	Ⓐ	⑥	⑥	Ⓐ	Ⓐ	⑥	⑥	Ⓐ	Ⓐ	⑥	Ⓐ	⑥	Ⓐ
							2			2	2	M	2	2	2	2			2	2		2	2				
Norwich d.		...	0500	0500	0532	0530	...	0600	0600	...	...	...	0632	0630	...	...	0700	0700	0730	0732	0800	0800	...	0830	0830	0857	0900
Diss d.		...	0517	0517	0549	0547	...	0617	0617	...	...	...	0649	0647	...	...	0717	0717	0747	0749	0817	0817	...	0847	0847	0914	0917
Stowmarket 204 d.		...	0528	0529	|	0559	...	0628	0629	...	...	...	|	0659	...	...	0728	0729	0759	|	0828	0828	...	0858	0858	|	0928
Ipswich 204 d.		0515	0541	0541	0610	0612	...	0641	0642	0653	0654	0658	0710	0712	...	...	0741	0743	0811	0810	0841	0839	...	0910	0910	0933	0941
Harwich Int'l ★ d.		|	|	|	|	|	0620	|	|	|	|	0727	|	|	0709	0720	|	|	|	|	|	|	0847	|	|	|	|
Manningtree ★ d.		0526	0551	0551	0620	0622	0633	0651	0652	0703	0705	...	0720	0722	0728	0734	0751	0752	0821	0820	0851	|	0904	0920	0920	|	0951
Colchester d.		0535	0600	0600	0630	0631	0642	0700	0701	0712	0714	...	0730	0731	0750v	0743	0800	0802	0831	0830	0900	|	0913	0930	0930	|	1000
Chelmsford d.		0556	|	0618	0648	|	0705	|	|	0741	0739	...	0748	|	0815	0811	|	|	|	0848	|	|	0942	|	0947	|	|
Stratford a.		0622s	0639s	0642s	|	0711s	0730s	0739s	0743s	0806	0804s	...	|	0813s	0844s	0836	0839s	0846s	0915s	|	0939s	0930s	1008	1009s	|	|	1039s
London Liverpool Street a.		0630	0647	0650	0717	0722	0741	0747	0754	0814	0814	...	0817	0824	0854	0844	0847	0857	0925	0917	0947	0939	1017	1017	1019	1031	1047l

	⑥	Ⓐ	⑥	Ⓐ	Ⓐ	⑥	⚒	⚒	⚒	⚒	⚒	⚒	⚒	⚒	⑥	Ⓐ	⚒	⑥	Ⓐ	Ⓐ	⑥	⑥	Ⓐ	⚒	⑥	Ⓐ	⚒
								2	2	2			2							2	2			2	2		
Norwich d.	0930	0932	1000	1000	1030	1032	1100	1132	1200	1232	1300	1330	1400	1430	1500	1500	1530	1600	1600	1630	1632	1700	1700	1730	1800	1800	1832
Diss d.	0947	0949	1017	1017	1048	1049	1117	1149	1217	1249	1317	1347	1417	1447	1517	1517	1547	1617	1617	1647	1649	1717	1717	1747	1817	1817	1849
Stowmarket 204 d.	0958	|	1028	1028	|	|	1128	|	1228	|	1328	|	1428	|	1528	1529	|	1628	1628	|	|	1728	1728	1758	1828	1828	|
Ipswich 204 d.	1010	1010	1041	1041	1109	1110	1141	1210	1241	1310	1341	1410	1441	1510	1541	1542	1610	1641	1642	1710	1710	1741	1741	1810	1841	1842	1910
Harwich Int'l ★ d.	|	|	|	|	|	|	|	|	|	|	|	|	|	|	|	|	|	|	|	|	|	|	|	|	|	|	|
Manningtree ★ d.	1020	1020	1051	1051	1120	1120	1151	1220	1251	1320	1351	1420	1451	1520	1551	1552	1620	1651	1652	1720	1720	1751	1751	1820	1851	1852	1920
Colchester d.	1030	1030	|	1100	1130	1130	1200c	1230	1300	1330	1400	1430	1500	1530	1600	1602	1630	1700	1702	1730	1730	1800	1802	1830	1900	1902	1930
Chelmsford d.	|	1048	|	|	1148	1148	|	1248	|	1348	|	1448	|	1548	|	1619	1648	|	1721	1748	1748	|	|	1848	|	|	1948
Stratford a.	1109s	|	1139s	1139s	|	|	1239s	|	1339s	|	1439s	|	1539s	|	1639s	1643s	|	1739s	1746s	1812s	|	1839s	1842s	|	1939s	1944s	|
London Liverpool Street a.	1117	1117	1147	1147	1217	1217	1247	1317	1347	1417	1447	1517	1547	1618	1647	1651	1719	1747	1754	1820	1817	1847	1850	1917	1947	1952	2018

	Ⓐ	⚒	⚒	⚒	⚒	⑥	Ⓐ	Ⓐ	⑥	Ⓐ	⑥	⚒	⚒	⑥	Ⓐ	⚒	⚒	⑥	Ⓐ	⑦	⑦	⑦	⑦	⑦	⑦	⑦	⑦
	2P		2		2	2C	2C	2	2	2P	2P		2			2P	2				2		2	2		2	2
Norwich d.	...	1900	...	2000	...	...	...	...	...	...	...	2100	...	2200	2202	...	...	2305	2305		...	0655	...	...	0800	0825	...
Diss d.	...	1917	...	2017	...	...	...	...	...	...	...	2117	...	2217	2219	...	...	2322	2323		...	0712	...	...	0817	0842	...
Stowmarket 204 d.	1915	1928	...	2028	...	2046	2046	...	...	2115	2116	2128	...	2228	2230	2310	...	2333	2335		...	0723	...	...	0829	0854	...
Ipswich 204 d.	1933f	1941	2010	2041	...	2101	2103	2110	2110	2130	2132f	2141	2223	2241	2243	2321	...	2345	2349		...	0735	0752	0811	0841	0906	0911
Harwich Int'l ★ d.	|	|	|	|	2045	2124	2129	|	|	|	|	|	|	|	|	|	2331	...	...		0720	|	0815	|	|	|	|
Manningtree ★ d.	1943	1951	2020	2051	2059	...	...	2119	2120	2139	2142	2151	2233	2251	2253	2331	2348	...	...		0733	0745	...	0821	0851	|	0921
Colchester d.	1953	2000	2030	2100	2112f	...	...	2128	2130	2151	2151	2200	2243	2300	2302	2341	2358	...	...		...	0754	...	0830	0900	0922	0930
Chelmsford d.	...	|	2048	|	2141	...	...	2146	2148	...	...	2221	2311	2321	2323	...	...	...	...		...	|	...	0859	|	|	0959
Stratford a.	...	2039s	|	2140s	2206	...	...	|	|	...	...	2247s	2336	2347s	2348s	...	...	...	...		...	0848s	...	0927	0939s	|	1027
London Liverpool Street a.	...	2047	2117	2149	2214	...	...	2216	2217	...	...	2255	2344	2355	2357	...	...	...	...		...	0857	...	0935	0947	1007	1035

	⑦	♠	⑦	⑦	⑦	⑦	⑦	⑦	⑦	⑦	⑦	⑦	⑦	⑦	⑦	⑦	⑦	⑦	⑦	⑦	⑦	⑦	⑦	⑦	⑦	⑦
			2		2	2			2		2		2	2P		2	2		2C	2	2P		2		2	
Norwich d.	0900	and	...	1500	1523	...	1600	1623	...	1700	...	1800	...	...	1900	...	...	2000	...	...	...	2100	...	2204	...	2305
Diss d.	0917	at	...	1517	1540	...	1617	1640	...	1717	...	1817	...	...	1917	...	...	2017	...	...	...	2117	...	2221	...	2322
Stowmarket 204 d.	0929	the	...	1529	1552	...	1629	1652	...	1729	...	1829	...	1911	1929	...	...	2029	2046	...	2111	2129	...	2232	...	2334
Ipswich 204 d.	0941	same	1511	1541	1604	1611	1641	1704	1711	1741	1811	1841	1911	1923	1941	2011	...	2041	2103	2111	2123	2141	2212	2244	...	2346
Harwich Int'l ★ d.	|	minutes	|	|	|	|	|	|	|	|	|	|	|	|	|	|	2030	|	2126	|	|	|	|	|	2300	...
Manningtree ★ d.	0951	past	1521	1551	|	1621	1651	|	1721	1751	1821	1851	1921	1933	1951	2021	2043	2051	...	2121	2132	2151	2221	2254	2316	...
Colchester d.	1000	each	1530	1600	1620	1630	1700	1720	1730	1800	1830	1900	1930	1941	2000	2030	2052	2100	...	2130	2142	2200	2230	2303	2326	...
Chelmsford d.	|	hour	1559	|	|	1659	|	|	1759	|	1859	|	1959	...	|	2059	2109	|	...	2159	...	|	2259	2324	...	...
Stratford a.	1039s	until	1627	1639s	1700s	1727	1739s	1800s	1827	1839s	1927	1939s	2027	...	2039s	2127	2134s	2139s	...	2227	...	2239s	2327	2349s	...	...
London Liverpool Street a.	1047		1635	1647	1708	1735	1747	1808	1835	1847	1935	1947	2035	...	2047	2135	2143	2147	...	2235	...	2247	2335	2359	...	...

C – To/from Cambridge (Table **204**).
L – To Lowestoft (Table **201**).
M – From Lowestoft on Ⓐ (Table **201**).
P – To/from Peterborough (Table **204**).

a – ⑥ only. Calls to pick up only.
c – Ⓐ only.
f – Arrives 5–6 minutes earlier.

r – Arrives 1418 on ⑥.
s – Calls to set down only.
t – Arrives 0037.
u – Calls to pick up only.
v – Arrives 10 minutes earlier.

♠ – The 0900 and 1400 from Norwich only convey (2).

★ – All trains Manningtree - Harwich International and v.v.

Manningtree - Harwich International: on Ⓐ at 0553, 0700, 0738, 0809, 0852, 1000 and hourly until 1700, 1756, 1837, 1907, 2000, 2045, 2101, 2200, 2300, 2335; on ⑥ at 0556, 0656, 0745, 0800 and hourly until 2001, 2012, 2100, 2145, 2200, 2300, 2335; on ⑦ at 0756, 0829 and hourly until 2029, 2102, 2129, 2229.

Harwich International - Manningtree on Ⓐ at 0529, 0620, 0629, 0709, 0733, 0808, 0847, 0927, 1031 and hourly until 1831, 1915, 1950, 2031, 2045, 2132, 2231, 2331; on ⑥ at 0631, 0720, 0731 and hourly until 2032, 2045, 2131, 2231, 2326; on ⑦ at 0720, 0900 and hourly until 2000, 2030, 2100, 2200, 2300.

201 IPSWICH - LOWESTOFT

2nd class only LE

km																								
			Ⓐ	Ⓐ	Ⓐ		Ⓐ	Ⓐ	Ⓐ	Ⓐ	Ⓐ		Ⓐ H		⑥		⑥ H		⑦	⑦	⑦	⑦		⑦	⑦	⑦
0	**Ipswich** d.	Ⓐ	0617	0731	0916		1516	1554	1717	1813	1917		2216	⑥	0716		2215	⑦	1008	1110	1208	1310	and in	2010	2108	2202
17	Woodbridge d.		0634	0749	0931	and	1531	1617f	1732	1830	1932	and	2231		0731	and	2230		1025	1125	1225	1325	the same	2025	2125	2219
36	Saxmundham d.		0744r	0811	0953	hourly	1553	1639	1754	1851	1954	hourly	2253		0753	hourly	2252		1047	1147	1247	1347	pattern	2047	2147	2240
65	Beccles d.		0815	0843	1024	until	1624	1718t	1825	1925	2025	until	2324		0824	until	2323		1118	1218	1318	1418	every **two** hours	2118	2218	2311
79	**Lowestoft** a.		0833	0902	1042		1642	1736	1843	1943	2043		2342		0844		2341		1136	1236	1336	1436	until	2136	2236	2330

		Ⓐ H	Ⓐ	Ⓐ	Ⓐ	Ⓐ	Ⓐ	Ⓐ		Ⓐ	Ⓐ	Ⓐ	Ⓐ	Ⓐ	Ⓐ	Ⓐ		⑥	♠	⑥		⑦	⑦	⑦	⑦		⑦
Lowestoft d.	Ⓐ	0524	0610	0638	0728	0906	1006	1106		1506	1606	1702	1807	1907	2007	2107	⑥	0606		2106	⑦	0805	0905	1005	1100		2000
Beccles d.		0540	0626	0654	0744	0924	1024	1124	and	1524	1624	1725t	1825	1925	2025	2125		0624	and	2124		0821	0921	1021	1121j	and	2021
Saxmundham d.		0611	0658	0725	0815	0955	1055	1155	hourly	1555	1704t	1756	1856	1956	2056	2156		0655	hourly	2155		0852	0952	1052	1152	hourly	2052
Woodbridge d.		0634	0721	0748	0838	1017	1117	1217	until	1617	1726	1818	1918	2018	2118	2218		0717	until	2217		0914	1014	1114	1214	until	2114
Ipswich a.		0654	0738	0805	0856	1033	1134	1235		1636	1745	1836	1935	2034	2134	2235		0734		2235		0931	1031	1131	1231		2131

H – To/from Harwich International (Table **200**).
f – Arrives 1610.
j – Arrives 6 minutes earlier.
r – Arrives 0655.
t – Arrives 8–9 minutes earlier.
♠ – The 0806 from Lowestoft arr. Ipswich 0936.

203 NORWICH and IPSWICH local services

2nd class LE

NORWICH - GREAT YARMOUTH

Journey time 32 - 37 minutes *30 km (33 km via Reedham*

From Norwich: Trains noted '**r**' call at **Reedham** 18–21 minutes later.

Ⓐ: 0508, 0623, 0654, 0736r, 0836, 0906**a**, 0936, 1025**a**, 1035, 1135r, 1234, 1318**a**, 1334, 1425**a**, 1440, 1536, 1640, 1706, 1736, 1840, 1940, 2040, 2140, 2300.

⑥: 0530r, 0636, 0706, 0736r, 0809, 0836, 0906**b**, 0936, 0955**b**, 1024**b**, 1034, 1120**b**, 1134r, 1216**b**, 1234, 1318**b**, 1334, 1418**b**, 1434, 1518**b**, 1534, 1640, 1706, 1734, 1806, 1840, 1940, 2040, 2140, 2300.

⑦: 0736r, 0845 and the service repeats at the same times **every 2 hours** until 2136r, 2236.

From Great Yarmouth: Trains noted '**r**' call at **Reedham** 12–14 minutes later.

Ⓐ: 0543, 0612, 0707, 0735, 0817, 0917, 0952**a**, 1017, 1113**a**, 1117, 1217, 1317, 1352**a**, 1417, 1517r, 1545**a**, 1617, 1717, 1747r, 1817, 1917, 2017, 2117, 2217, 2334r.

⑥: 0615, 0717, 0745, 0817, 0847, 0917, 0947**b**, 1017, 1041**b**, 1115**b**, 1117, 1157**b**, 1217, 1255**b**, 1317, 1355**b**, 1417, 1455**b**, 1512r, 1555**b**, 1617, 1717, 1747r, 1817, 1847r, 1917, 2017, 2117, 2217, 2334r.

⑦: 0817r, 0922 and the service repeats at the same times **every 2 hours** until 2217r, 2317r.

NORWICH - LOWESTOFT

Journey time 37 - 43 minutes *38 km*

From Norwich: Trains noted '**r**' call at **Reedham** 18–21 minutes later.

Ⓐ: 0536**r**, 0612**r**, 0645**r**, 0755**r**, 0855, 1005**r**, 1058, 1205**r**, 1258, 1405**r**, 1458**r**, 1550**r**, 1658**r**, 1750**r**, 1902**r**, 2005**r**, 2105**r**, 2205**r**, 2240**r**.

⑥: 0540**r**, 0650**r**, 0750**r**, 0855, 1005**r**, 1058, 1205**r**, 1258, 1405**r**, 1458**r**, 1555**r**, 1656**r**, 1750**r**, 1905**r**, 2005**r**, 2105**r**, 2205**r**, 2241**r**.

⑦: 0725, 0805**r**, 0907 and in the same pattern **every two hours** until 1907, 2005**r**, 2058**r**.

From Lowestoft: Trains noted '**r**' call at **Reedham** 20–23 minutes later.

Ⓐ: 0537**r**, 0634**r**, 0733**r**, 0750**r**, 0850**r**, 0948**r**, 1057, 1148**r**, 1257, 1348**r**, 1457, 1548**r**, 1648**r**, 1748**r**, 1848**r**, 1955**r**, 2057, 2148**r**, 2248**r**, 2330**r**.

⑥: 0639**r**, 0740**r**, 0848**r**, 0948**r**, 1057, 1148**r**, 1257, 1348**r**, 1457, 1548**r**, 1648**r**, 1748**r**, 1848**r**, 1955**r**, 2057, 2148**r**, 2248**r**, 2330**r**.

⑦: 0859, 0946**r**, 1105 and in the same pattern **every two hours** until 2105, 2146**r**, 2335**r**

NORWICH - SHERINGHAM (🚂)

Journey time 55 - 60 minutes *49 km*

From Norwich:

Trains call at **Hoveton and Wroxham** 🚂 ± 15 minutes, and **Cromer** ± 45 minutes later.

⚒: 0512 Ⓐ, 0520 ⑥, 0540 Ⓐ, 0545 ⑥, 0715, 0821, 0945, 1045 and hourly until 1745, 1855, 2000, 2115, 2245 ①–④, 2305 ⑤⑥.

⑦: 0839, 0945, 1039, 1145, 1239, 1345, 1439, 1545, 1639, 1745, 1839, 1945, 2039.

From Sheringham:

Trains call at **Cromer** ± 11 minutes, and **Hoveton and Wroxham** 🚂 ± 39 minutes later.

⚒: 0007 ⑥, 0622 ⑥, 0618 Ⓐ, 0714Ⓐ, 0717⑥, 0822Ⓐ, 0824⑥, 0943, 1046, 1143, 1246, 1343, 1446, 1545, 1648, 1748, 1851, 1954, 2109, 2217, 2347 ①–④ (also 0551 Ⓐ from Cromer).

⑦: 0007, 0942, 1043, 1142, 1243, 1342, 1443, 1542, 1643, 1742, 1843, 1942, 2043, 2143

IPSWICH - FELIXSTOWE

Journey time 26 minutes *25 km*

From Ipswich:

Ⓐ: 0504, 0604, 0714, 0815, 0857, 0958 and hourly until 2058, 2228.

⑥: 0558, 0658, 0758 and hourly until 2058, 2228.

⑦: 0955, 1055 and hourly until 1955.

From Felixstowe:

Ⓐ: 0534, 0636, 0747, 0854, 0928 and hourly until 2128, 2301.

⑥: 0628, 0728, 0828 and hourly until 2128, 2258.

⑦: 1025, 1125 and hourly until 2025.

a – ①⑤ July 21 - Sept. 5.
b – Until Sept. 13.
r – Via Reedham.

🚂 – Heritage and Tourist railways: **NORTH NORFOLK RAILWAY**: Sheringham - Holt and v.v. *8 km*. ✆ 01263 820800. www.nnrailway.co.uk
BURE VALLEY STEAM RAILWAY: Wroxham - Aylsham and v.v. *14 km*. ✆ 01263 733858. www.bvrw.co.uk
MID NORFOLK RAILWAY: Wymondham - Dereham and v.v. *18 km*. ✆ 01362 690633 www.mnr.org.uk (see Table **207**)

204 IPSWICH - CAMBRIDGE and PETERBOROUGH

2nd class only LE

km																										
			Ⓐ	⑥	⚒C	Ⓐ	⑥	Ⓐ	⑥	⚒	ⒶH	⑥H	⚒	⑥	Ⓐ	⚒	⚒	Ⓐ	⑥	⚒	⚒	Ⓐ	⑥	⚒	⚒	⑥	Ⓐ
0	**Ipswich** 200 d.	⚒	0510	0511	0600	0618	0619	0656	0720	0758	0819	0820	0920	0958	1001	1020	1120	1156	1158	1220	1320	1358	1401	1420	1520	1558	1600
19	Stowmarket 200 d.		0522	0525	0611	0631	0633	0710	0734	0809	0834	0834	0934	1009	1012	1034	1134	1207	1209	1234	1334	1410	1412	1434	1534	1609	1612
42	Bury St Edmunds d.		0543	0548	0628	0654	0654	0731	0759r	0829	0858	0857	0959r	1029r	1029	1059r	1159	1228	1229r	1259r	1359r	1429	1429	1459r	1559r	1629r	1629
65	Newmarket d.		0602	0607	|	0714	0718r	0750	0818	|	0918	0917	1018	|	|	1117	1218	|	|	1317	1418	|	|	1517	1618	|	|
88	**Cambridge** 208 a.		0628	0630	|	0737	0740	0817	0841	|	0941	0940	1040	|	|	1140	1240	|	|	1340	1440	|	|	1540	1640	|	|
73	Soham d.		...	...	0648	...	...	...	...	0849	...	...	...	1050	1049	...	...	1251	1249	...	...	1449	1449	...	...	1650	1650
82	Ely 206 208 a.		...	...	0657	...	...	...	...	0859	...	...	...	1059	1059	...	...	1259	1259	...	...	1459	1459	...	...	1659	1659
108	March 208 a.		...	...	0717	...	...	...	...	0919	...	...	...	1119	1119	...	...	1319	1319	...	...	1519	1519	...	...	1720	1719
132	**Peterborough** 206 208 a.		...	...	0739	...	...	...	...	0940	...	...	...	1140	1139	...	...	1340	1340	...	...	1540	1540	...	...	1740	1740

	⚒	⚒	Ⓐ	⑥	⑥	Ⓐ	⚒	⑥	Ⓐ	⚒	⚒	⚒		⑦	⑦a	⑦	⑦H	⑦C	⑦	⑦	⑦		⑦	⑦	⑦	⑦
Ipswich 200 d.	1620	1720	1750	1758	1820	1823	1920	2000	2001	2020	2120	2220		0736	0755	0820	0920	0955	1020	1120	1155		1755	1820	1920	2105
Stowmarket 200 d.	1634	1734	1803	1809	1834	1835	1934	2011	2013	2034	2134	2234	⑦	0750	0806	0834	0934	1006	1034	1134	1206	and in	1806	1834	1934	2119
Bury St Edmunds d.	1659r	1759r	1825	1829r	1859r	1859	1959r	2029	2030	2059r	2159r	2256		0811	0823	0857	0957	1023	1057	1157	1223	the same	1823	1857	1957	2140
Newmarket d.	1718	1818	|	|	1917	1917	2018	|	|	2117	2218	...		0830	|	0914	1018	|	1116	1218	|	pattern	|	1916	2018	2159
Cambridge 208 a.	1741	1840	|	|	1940	1941	2040	|	|	2140	2241	...		0854	|	0937	1039	|	1139	1239	|	every	|	1939	2039	2224
Soham d.	...	...	1847	1849	...	...	...	2049	2051	...	...	...		...	0842	...	...	1043	...	...	1243	**two** hours	1843	...	...	...
Ely 206 208 a.	...	...	1859	1859	...	...	...	2058	2059	...	...	...		...	0851	...	...	1052	...	...	1251	until	1851	...	...	...
March 208 a.	...	...	1920	1919	...	...	...	2118	2119	...	...	...		...	0912	...	...	1113	...	...	1312		1912	...	...	...
Peterborough 206 208 a.	...	...	1940	1940	...	...	...	2139	2140	...	...	...		...	0933	...	...	1133	...	...	1333		1933	...	...	...

		Ⓐ	⚒	Ⓐ	⑥	Ⓐ	⑥	⚒	⑥	Ⓐ	⚒	⑥	Ⓐ	⚒	⚒	⚒	⚒	⚒		⚒	⚒	⚒	Ⓐ	⑥	⑥	Ⓐ	⚒
Peterborough 206 208 d.	⚒	...	...	...	...	...	...	0750	...	...	...	0950	0950	...	...	1150	...	...	...	1350	...	...	1550	1551	...	...	...
March 208 d.		...	...	...	...	...	...	0809	...	...	...	1009	1009	...	...	1209	...	...	...	1409	...	...	1609	1610	...	...	...
Ely 206 208 d.		...	...	...	...	...	...	0830	...	...	...	1031	1032	...	...	1231	...	...	...	1431	...	...	1631	1631	...	...	...
Soham d.		...	...	...	...	...	...	0838	...	...	...	1039	1040	...	...	1239	...	...	...	1439	...	...	1639	1639	...	...	...
Cambridge 208 d.		...	...	0641	0642	0742	0746	|	0846	0844	0946	|	|	1046	1146	|	1246	1346	...	|	1446	1546	|	|	1646	1646	1746
Newmarket d.		...	...	0702	0703	0804	0807	|	0905	0906	1007	|	|	1105	1207	|	1305	1407	...	|	1505	1607	|	|	1707	1707	1807
Bury St Edmunds d.		0530	0625	0726r	0725	0826	0825	0859	0925	0926	1025	1100	1101	1125	1225	1300	1325	1425	...	1500	1525	1626	1659	1700	1726	1726	1826
Stowmarket 200 d.		0550	0645	0746	0746	0847	0846	0914	0946	0947	1046	1115	1116	1146	1246	1315	1346	1445	...	1515	1546	1646	1714	1715	1746	1748	1846
Ipswich 200 a.		0605	0701	0801	0802	0902	0902	0927	1002	1005	1102	1127	1128	1202	1302	1328	1402	1502	...	1527	1602	1702	1727	1727	1803	1804	1902

	⑥	ⒶC	⑥	Ⓐ	⚒H	ⒶC	⑥C	⚒	⚒	ⒶC	⑥C	⚒		⑦	⑦	⑦a	⑦	⑦	⑦		⑦C	⑦	⑦H	⑦C	⑦	⑦
Peterborough 206 208 d.	1751	1750	...	...	...	1950	1953	...	...	2146	2147	...		...	...	0950	...	...	1144	★	1741	...	...	1945	...	...
March 208 d.	1810	1809	...	...	...	2009	2012	...	...	2205	2206	...	⑦	...	...	1010	...	...	1203		1800	...	...	2004	...	...
Ely 206 208 d.	1831	1831	...	...	...	2032	2033	...	...	2226	2227	...		...	...	1031	...	...	1227	and in	1828	...	...	2027	...	...
Soham d.	1839	1839	...	...	...	2039	2041	...	...	2234	2235	...		...	...	1039	...	...	1235	the same	1836	...	...	2035	...	...
Cambridge 208 d.	|	|	1846	1846	1946	|	|	2046	2146	|	|	2246		0900	0946	|	1046	1146	|	pattern	|	1846	1946	|	2046	2250
Newmarket d.	|	|	1905	1905	2007	|	|	2105	2207	|	|	2307		0926	1007	|	1105	1207	|	every	|	1905	2007	|	2107	2311
Bury St Edmunds d.	1900	1900	1925	1925	2025	2100	2101	2125	2225	2255	2256	2326		0945	1024	1059	1124	1224	1256	**two** hours	1856	1924	2024	2056	2126	2330
Stowmarket 200 d.	1915	1915	1946	1946	2046	2115	2116	2146	2246	2310	2311	2346		1006	1045	1114	1145	1245	1311	until	1911	1945	2046	2111	2145	2349
Ipswich 200 a.	1927	1927	2002	2004	2102	2128	2127	2202	2302	2321	2322	0002		1023	1100	1126	1200	1300	1324		1923	2000	2102	2123	2200	0003

C – To/from Colchester (Table **200**).
H – To/from Harwich International (Table **200**).
a – Until Sept. 14.
r – Arrives 4–5 minutes earlier.
★ – Peterborough d. 1350 (not 1344), then March d. 1409, Ely d. 1431, Soham d. 1439, Bury St Edmunds d. 1459, Stowmarket d. 1514, Ipswich a. 1527.

EM 2nd class NORWICH - NOTTINGHAM - SHEFFIELD - MANCHESTER - LIVERPOOL 206

km		Ⓐ	Ⓐ	Ⓐ	Ⓐ	Ⓐ	Ⓐ	Ⓐ	Ⓐ		Ⓐ	Ⓐ	Ⓐ	Ⓐ	Ⓐ	Ⓐ	Ⓐ	Ⓐ	Ⓐ A	Ⓐ	⑥	⑥	⑥	⑥	⑥
0	**Norwich** 207 d.	...	...	...	0549	0651	0755	0856	0955	...	1056	1156	1256	1354	1456	1548	1656	1750	...	2008	...	...	...	0548	0650
49	Thetford 207 d.	...	...	...	0623	0723	0825	0924	1024	...	1124	1224	1324	1422	1524	1623	1727	1824	...	2036	...	...	...	0622	0718
86	Ely 204 207 208 d.	...	...	...	0649	0749	0853	0953	1051j	...	1151j	1250	1351j	1450j	1551j	1650j	1753	1852j	...	2103j	...	...	...	0651j	0749f
135	**Peterborough** 180 204/8 d.	...	...	...	0724	0829	0928	1027	1127	...	1226	1326	1427	1524	1627	1724	1829	1931	2006	2148	...	...	...	0727	0830
181	Grantham 180 184 d.	...	*0545*	*0647*	0755	0859	0959	1100	1159	...	1300	1359j	1459	1601j	1659	1759	1857	2005j	|	2218	...	*0542*	...	0757	0900
218	**Nottingham** 184 a.	...	*0625*	*0730*	0836	0938	1037	1137	1237	...	1337	1437	1537	1637	1739	1830	1931	2035	2231	2248	...	*0624*	...	0838	0936
218	**Nottingham** 171 d.	0521	0635	0743	0844	0945	1045	1145	1245	...	1345	1445	1545	1645	1745	1846	1947	2037	...	...	0521	0636	0746	0845	0945
247	Alfreton 171 d.	|	0658	0811	0909	1010	1109	1211	1312	...	1408	1508	1610	1709	1811	1911	2011	2102	...	...	|	0700	0811	0909	1009
264	Chesterfield 171 d.	0551	0708	0821	0921	1021	1122	1221	1322	...	1422	1522	1621	1721	1821	1921	2021	2113	...	...	0552	0712	0822	0921	1022
283	**Sheffield** 171 a.	0613	0725	0839	0939	1036	1138	1236	1337	...	1439	1537	1636	1737	1836	1937	2036	2137	...	...	0616	0730	0840	0938	1038
	Sheffield 193 d.	0618	0729	0845	0944	1043	1143	1243	1343	...	1443	1543	1643	1741	1841	1943	2040	...	...	...	0620	0735	0845	0943	1043
343	Stockport 193 d.	0726	0826	0925	1025	1125	1225	1325	1425	...	1525	1625	1726	1825	1925	2026	2125	...	...	...	0726	0826	0925	1025	1125
352	**Manchester** Picc 188 193 d.	0737	0837	0937	1037	1137	1237	1337	1437	...	1537	1637	1737	1837	1937	2037	2135	...	...	...	0737	0837	0937	1037	1137
378	Warrington Central d.	0758	0858	0958	1058	1158	1258	1358	1458	...	1558	1658	1800	1858	1958	2058	...	...	...	...	0758	0858	0958	1058	1158
388	Widnes d.	0806	0906	1006	1106	1206	1306	1406	1506	...	1606	1706	1808	1906	2006	2106	...	...	...	...	0806	0906	1006	1106	1206
399	**Liverpool** South Parkway d.	0818	0918	1018	1118	1218	1318	1418	1518	...	1618	1718	1818	1918	2018	2118	...	...	...	...	0818	0918	1018	1118	1218
408	**Liverpool** Lime Street 188 a.	0829	0929	1029	1129	1229	1329	1429	1529	...	1629	1729	1829	1929	2029	2130	...	...	...	...	0829	0929	1029	1129	1229

	⑥	⑥	⑥	⑥	⑥	⑥	⑥	⑥	⑥	⑥	⑥	⑥	⑦	⑦	⑦	⑦	⑦	⑦ L	⑦	⑦	⑦	⑦	⑦	⑦	⑦	⑦
Norwich 207 d.	0755	0853	0954	1056	1155	1255	1353	1455	1552	1654	1750	2013	...	...	...	0955	1056	...	...	1347	1453	1554	1654	1754	1855	2052
Thetford 207 d.	0823	0921	1022	1124	1223	1323	1422	1523	1622	1724	1823	2041	...	...	...	1023	1124	...	...	1415	1521	1622	1722	1822	1923	2120
Ely 204 207 208 d.	0850j	0947	1050	1150	1251j	1350j	1450j	1550j	1650	1751	1849	2109j	...	...	...	1049	1150	...	...	1442	1548	|	1749j	1848	1949	2146
Peterborough 180 204/8 d.	0928	1022	1124	1226	1328	1427	1525	1627	1725	1828	1928	2150j	...	...	...	1123	1226	...	1436	1523j	1624	1721j	1826	1922	2030j	2223
Grantham 180 184 d.	0958	1055	1156	1259	1358	1459	1557	1658	1759	1859	1957	2228j	...	...	...	1156	1258	...	1508	1603f	1657	1801	1900	2000j	2102	2255
Nottingham 184 a.	1037	1138	1237	1335	1434	1538	1640	1739	1840	1931	2036	2258	...	...	...	1227	1327	...	1539	1633	1733	1832	1936	2030	2132	2325
Nottingham 171 d.	1045	1144	1245	1344	1445	1545	1645	1745	1847	1935	2039	...	0942	1044	1142	1240	1340	1447	1543	1642	1746	1846	1947	...	...	...
Alfreton 171 d.	1109	1208	1312	1408	1509	1611	1714	1810	1912	2000	2104	...	1006	1107	1209	1306	1406	1509	1609	1711	1812	1912	2011	...	...	...
Chesterfield 171 d.	1123	1223	1322	1421	1522	1621	1725	1821	1923	2013	2115	...	1017	1118	1220	1317	1418	1521	1622	1722	1823	1923	2022	...	...	...
Sheffield 171 a.	1138	1241	1337	1440	1539	1636	1740	1839	1939	2029	2131	...	1035	1134	1235	1333	1433	1536	1637	1738	1838	1938	2037	...	...	...
Sheffield 193 d.	1144	1245	1344	1444	1543	1643	1744	1844	1943	2034	...	...	1041	1141	1241	1338	1437	1540	1641	1743	1842	1942	2042	...	...	...
Stockport 193 d.	1226	1325	1425	1525	1625	1726	1825	1926	2026	2124	...	...	1127	1227	1325	1427	1526	1626	1726	1826	1926	2029j	2124	...	...	...
Manchester Picc 188 193 d.	1237	1337	1437	1537	1637	1737	1837	1937	2037	2135	...	...	1138	1238	1337	1439	1537	1637	1737	1838	1938	2040	2133	...	...	...
Warrington Central d.	1258	1358	1458	1558	1658	1800	1858	1958	2058	...	...	...	1159	1259	1358	1500	1558	1658	1758	1858	1958	...	...	...	...	...
Widnes d.	1306	1406	1506	1606	1706	1808	1906	2006	2106	...	...	...	1207	1307	1406	1508	1606	1706	1806	1906	2006	...	...	...	...	...
Liverpool South Parkway d.	1318	1418	1518	1618	1718	1818	1918	2018	2118	...	...	...	1217	1317	1417	1517	1617	1717	1817	1917	2017	...	...	...	...	...
Liverpool Lime Street 188 a.	1329	1429	1529	1629	1729	1829	1929	2029	2129	...	...	...	1229	1329	1429	1529	1629	1729	1829	1929	2029	...	...	...	...	...

	Ⓐ	Ⓐ	Ⓐ	Ⓐ	Ⓐ	Ⓐ	Ⓐ	Ⓐ	Ⓐ	Ⓐ	Ⓐ	Ⓐ	Ⓐ	Ⓐ	Ⓐ	Ⓐ	Ⓐ	Ⓐ	⑥	⑥	⑥	⑥	⑥	⑥	⑥
Liverpool Lime Street 188 d.	A	...	...	0649	0748	0851	0951	1051	1151	1251	1351	1451	1551	1651	1751	1850	1951	2137	A	A	...	...	0649	0748	0951
Liverpool South Parkway d.	...	...	...	0659	0759	0902	1002	1102	1202	1302	1402	1502	1602	1702	1802	1901	2002	2148	...	...	...	...	0659	0759	1002
Widnes d.	...	...	...	0708	0808	0910	1010	1110	1210	1310	1410	1510	1610	1710	1810	1910	2010	2156	...	...	...	...	0708	0808	1010
Warrington Central d.	...	...	...	0717	0817	0919	1019	1119	1219	1319	1419	1519	1619	1719	1819	1919	2019	2205	...	...	...	...	0717	0817	1019
Manchester Picc 193 188 d. ★	...	...	...	0743	0843	0943	1043	1143	1243	1343	1443	1543	1643	1743	1843	1943	2043	2230	...	...	...	...	0743	0843	1043
Stockport 193 d.	...	...	...	0755	0854	0954	1055	1154	1254	1354	1454	1554	1654	1754	1854	1956	2054	2239	...	...	...	...	0755	0854	1054
Sheffield 193 a.	...	...	...	0834	0935	1034	1135	1234	1334	1436	1534	1632	1739	1840	1934	2039	2133	2336	...	...	...	...	0834	0932	1135
Sheffield 171 d.	...	0642	0743	0840	0940	1040	1140	1240	1340	1440	1540	1640	1745	1846	1940	2045	2140	2339	...	...	0645	0740	0839	0939	1140
Chesterfield 171 d.	...	0659	0757	0854	0954	1056	1155	1254	1354	1455	1555	1656	1801	1902	1954	2059	2156	0003	...	...	0701	0754	0855	0954	1155
Alfreton 171 d.	...	0710	0808	0905	1005	1108	1206	1306	1406	1506	1606	1707	1811	1913	2005	2110	2208	|	...	...	0712	0805	0906	1005	1206
Nottingham 171 a.	...	0736	0836	0932	1032	1134	1232	1334	1433	1529	1631	1730	1834	1937	2036	2131	2235	0038	...	...	0740	0833	0929	1029	1229
Nottingham 184 d.	0607	0741	0841	0941	1040	1139	1239	1339	1439	...	1640	1739	1840	...	2040	...	...	...	0500	0608	0742	0836	0939	1034	1234
Grantham 180 184 d.	|	0812	0913	1012	1111	1213	1311	1411	1512	...	1713	1815	1912	...	2113	...	...	...	|	|	0812	0909	1011	1107	1310
Peterborough 180 204/8 d.	0738	0843	0940	1045	1141	1244	1341	1441	1541	...	1744	1845	1941	...	2140	...	...	...	0627	0736	0842	0945	1040	1141	1339
Ely 204 207 208 d.	0816	0922j	1018j	1122	1218j	1327j	1416	1520j	1618	...	1821	1923	2019j	...	2217j	...	...	...	0707	0817	0925j	1022	1117	1217	1416
Thetford 207 d.	0838	0944	1039	1143	1241	1349	1438	1543	1639	...	1842	1944	2040	...	2238	...	...	...	0732	0839	0946	1043	1138	1239	1437
Norwich 207 a.	0915	1014	1110	1214	1314	1420	1509	1611	1711	...	1912	2018	2111	...	2315	...	...	...	0810	0916	1016	1114	1211	1310	1510

	⑥	⑥	⑥	⑥	⑥	⑥	⑥	⑥	⑥	⑥	⑥	⑥	⑦	⑦	⑦	⑦	⑦	⑦	⑦	⑦	⑦	⑦	⑦	⑦	⑦	⑦
Liverpool Lime Street 188 d.	1051	1151	1251	1351	1451	1551	1651	1751	1850	1951	2051	2137	...	...	...	...	...	1251	1351	1451	1551	1651	1751	1850	1951	2114
Liverpool South Parkway d.	1102	1202	1302	1402	1502	1602	1702	1802	1901	2002	2102	2148	...	...	...	...	...	1301	1401	1501	1601	1701	1801	1900	2001	2124
Widnes d.	1110	1210	1310	1410	1510	1610	1710	1810	1910	2010	2110	2156	...	...	...	...	...	1310	1410	1510	1610	1710	1810	1910	2010	2133
Warrington Central d.	1119	1219	1319	1419	1519	1619	1719	1819	1919	2019	2119	2205	...	...	...	...	...	1319	1419	1519	1619	1719	1819	1919	2019	2142
Manchester Picc . 193 188 d. ★	1143	1243	1343	1443	1543	1643	1743	1843	1943	2043	2143	2230	...	...	...	...	1244	1343	1443	1543	1643	1743	1843	1943	2043	2213
Stockport 193 d.	1155	1254	1354	1454	1554	1654	1754	1854	1954	2054	2153	2239	...	...	...	...	1255	1353	1454	1552	1653	1753	1853	1953	2053	2230
Sheffield 193 a.	1235	1334	1434	1534	1633	1737	1836	1935	2036	2135	2232	2338	...	...	...	...	1337	1436	1540	1634	1733	1835	1933	2033	2133	2326
Sheffield 171 d.	1239	1341	1440	1540	1640	1741	1840	1940	2042	2140	2241	2342	...	1045	1145	1245	1345	1440	1544	1638	1739	1839	1937	2037	2140	2330
Chesterfield 171 d.	1254	1355	1455	1554	1656	1757	1854	1955	2056	2156	2255	2356	...	1100	1200	1300	1359	1456	1559	1652	1753	1853	1952	2052	2156	2344
Alfreton 171 d.	1305	1406	1506	1605	1707	1808	1905	2006	2107	2207	2306	|	...	1111	1213	1311	1410	1508	1610	1703	1804	1904	2003	2103	2207	2355
Nottingham 171 a.	1329	1429	1537	1631	1730	1832	1928	2029	2129	2232	2331	0030	...	1132	1239	1332	1438	1531	1633	1730	1830	1927	2026	2126	2231	0024
Nottingham 184 d.	1334	1434	...	1639	1735	1838	...	2037	...	...	...	...	0918	1143	1243	1345	1443	1541	1644	1742	1847	...	2039	...	...	...
Grantham 180 184 d.	1410	1513	...	1712	1811	1911	...	2110	...	...	...	...	0950	1218	1315	1422j	1520	1616	1716	1817j	1924j	...	2113	...	...	...
Peterborough 180 204/8 d.	1441	1546j	...	1745j	1845j	1941	...	2140	...	...	...	...	1019	1252	1343	1452	1557j	1652	1756j	1850	1957	...	2141	...	...	...
Ely 204 207 208 d.	1519j	1622	...	1822	1923	2018	...	2217	...	...	...	...	1057	1334f	1419	1529j	1636	1729j	1835	1930j	2036	...	2219j	...	...	...
Thetford 207 d.	1540	1644	...	1843	1944	2040	...	2239	...	...	...	...	1122	1355	1446	1550	1657	1750	1856	1951	2057	...	2241	...	...	...
Norwich 207 a.	1611	1714	...	1917	2014	2109	...	2313	...	...	...	...	1158	1426	1524	1623	1727	1824	1927	2024	2133	...	2317	...	...	...

A – Via Melton Mowbray and Leicester (Table **208**).
L – From Lincoln (Table **189**).
f – Arrives 9–11 minutes earlier.
j – Arrives 5–8 minutes earlier.

★ – **Additional trains**: On Ⓐ **A** Nottingham d. 0456 – Peterborough d. 0627 **j** – Ely d. 0708 **j** – Thetford d. 0734 – Norwich a. 0811.
On Ⓐ Manchester Piccadilly d. 2141 – Sheffield a. 2234, d. 2238 – Chesterfield d. 2253 – Alfreton d. 2304 – Nottingham a. 2327.
On ⑥ Nottingham d. 1133 – Grantham d. 1212 **j** – Peterborough d. 1244 – Ely d. 1322 **j** – Thetford d. 1343 – Norwich a. 1414.
On ⑥ Manchester Piccadilly d. 2154 – Stockport d. 2204 – Sheffield a. 2249, d. 2256 – Chesterfield d. 2311 – Alfreton d. 2322 – Nottingham a. 2347.
On ⑦ Manchester Piccadilly d. 2144 – Stockport d. 2154 – Sheffield a. 2238, d. 2242 – Chesterfield d. 2258 – Alfreton d. 2309 – Nottingham a. 2338.

LE 2nd Class STANSTED AIRPORT - CAMBRIDGE - NORWICH 207

km		Ⓐ	Ⓐ	Ⓐ	Ⓐ	Ⓐ	Ⓐ	Ⓐ		Ⓐ	Ⓐ	Ⓐ	Ⓐ	Ⓐ	Ⓐ	Ⓐ	Ⓐ	⑥	⑥	⑥	⑥	⑥	
0	**Stansted Airport** ✈ 208 d.	...	...	...	...	...	...	1048	and at	1537	1648	1751	...	...	...	...	2210	...	0648	0748	0848	0948	and at
40	**Cambridge** 208 d.	0601	...	0700	0819	0913	1014	1120	the same	1616	1729	1830	1927	2018	2120	...	2257v	0605	0720	0820	0925j	1020	the same
63	Ely 206 208 d.	0619	0708	0717	0838	0929	1030	1137	minutes	1633	1748	1849	1944	2034	2136	2217	2314	0622	0738	0837	0944	1037	minutes
100	Thetford 206 d.	0643	0734	0744	0901	0953	1054	1200	past each	1700	1811	1912	2008	2058	2200	2238	2337	0646	0806	0901	1007	1100	past each
123	Attleborough d.	0702	0748	0803	0916	1008	1109	1216	hour until	1716	1826	1927	2023	2113	2215	2252	2352	0704	0824	0916	1022	1115	hour until
133	Wymondham 🚂 d.	0709	0755	0812	0926	1015	1116	1223		1723	1833	1934	2030	2120	2222	2259	2359	0711	0832	0926	1029	1125	
149	**Norwich** 206 a.	0725	0811	0826	0940	1029	1131	1239		1737	1847	1948	2044	2136	2235	2315	0013	0725	0847	0940	1043	1139	

	⑥	⑥	⑥	⑦	⑦		⑦	⑦	⑦	⑦
Stansted Airport ✈ 208 d.	2048	...	2210	0818	1009		1909	...	2009	2111
Cambridge 208 d.	2120	...	2255v	0851	1050j	and at	1950j	...	2049	2154
Ely 206 208 d.	2137	2217	2311	0908	1107	the same	2007	2036	2106	2211
Thetford 206 d.	2200	2239	2335	0934	1131	minutes	2031	2057	2129	2234
Attleborough d.	2215	2253	2350	0949	1146	past each	2046	2111	2144	2249
Wymondham 🚂 d.	2222	2300	2357	0956	1155	hour until	2053	2118	2151	2256
Norwich 206 a.	2236	2313	0010	1012	1213		2109	2133	2206	2313

	Ⓐ	Ⓐ	Ⓐ	Ⓐ	Ⓐ	Ⓐ	Ⓐ	Ⓐ	
Norwich 206 d.	0533	0549	0633	0726	0833	0927	1033	1127	
Wymondham 🚂 d.	0545	0601	0645	0738	0845	0939	1045	1139	and at
Attleborough d.	0552	0609	0652	0745	0852	0946	1052	1146	the same
Thetford 206 d.	0606	0623	0706	0759	0906	1000	1106	1200	minutes
Ely 206 208 d.	0632	0645	0734	0825	0931	1028	1131	1226	past each
Cambridge 208 a.	0650	...	0753	0847	0949	1045	1149	1244	hour until
Stansted ✈ 208 a.	...	...	...	...	1024	1124	1224	1324	

	Ⓐ	Ⓐ	Ⓐ	Ⓐ	Ⓐ	Ⓐ	Ⓐ	⑥	⑥	⑥		⑥	⑥	⑥	⑥	⑥	⑥	⑥	⑥	⑦		⑦	⑦
Norwich 206 d.	1627	1727	1750	1823	1928	2112	2240	0527	0548	0627		1521	1627	1721	1750	1827	1927	2110	2240	0903	and at	2003	2208
Wymondham 🚂 d.	1639	1739	1803	1835	1940	2124	2252	0539	0600	0639	and at	1533	1639	1733	1802	1839	1939	2122	2252	0915	the same	2015	2220
Attleborough d.	1648	1748	1810	1842	1947	2131	2259	0546	0608	0646	the same	1540	1646	1742	1809	1846	1946	2129	2259	0922	minutes	2022	2227
Thetford 206 d.	1702	1809	1824	1856	2001	2145	2313	0600	0622	0700	minutes	1558	1700	1800	1823	1900	2000	2143	2313	0936	past each	2036	2241
Ely 206 208 d.	1727	1838	1846	1926	2028	2210	2338	0627	0645	0727	past each	1627	1727	1827	1846	1927	2027	2208	2338	1003	hour until	2103	2306
Cambridge 208 a.	1744	1856	...	1946	2045	2227	2356	0647	...	0749	hour until	1644	1744	1844	...	1944	2044	2225	2356	1021		2120	2324
Stansted Airport ✈ 208 a.	...	...	...	...	2124	...	...	0724	...	0824		1724	1824	1924	...	2024	2124	...	...	1104		2204	...

j – Arrives 5 minutes earlier.
v – Arrives 2244.
🚂 – For Mid Norfolk Railway (1½ km to Wymondham Abbey). See note 🚂 in Table **203**.

208 STANSTED AIRPORT ✈ - CAMBRIDGE - PETERBOROUGH - LEICESTER - BIRMINGHAM XC

km			Ⓐ	⑥	⑥	Ⓐ	Ⓐ	⑥	Ⓐ	⑥		⚒	Ⓐ	⑥	⚒🍷		⚒🍷	⑥🍷	Ⓐ🍷	⚒🍷	⚒🍷	⚒	ⒶB	Ⓐ	⑥	Ⓐ
0	**Stansted Airport ✈ 207** d.	⚒	...	...	0527	0520	0612	0627	0721	0727	...	0826	0921	0927	1027		1427	1527	1522	1627	1727	1821f	...	1921	1927	2027
40	**Cambridge** 207 d.		0515	0515	0557j	0557	0657c	0658	0800	0800j	...	0900	1000j	1000j	1100j		1500j	1600j	1600j	1700j	1800j	1900j	...	2000j	2000j	2100
64	Ely **204 206 207** d.		0530	0530	0612	0612	0712	0713	0815	0815	...	0915	1015	1015	1115		1515	1615	1615	1715	1815	1915	...	2015	2015	2117
89	March **204** d.		0547	0547	0631	0631	0730	0730	0834	0832	...	0932	1032	1032	1132	and at	1532	1632	1634	1733	1834	1932	...	2032	2032	2134
113	**Peterborough** **204 206** a.		0607	0608	0652	0652	0750	0750	0851	0849	...	0949	1049	1049	1149	the same	1549	1649	1651	1751	1851	1949	...	2051	2049	2152
	Peterborough d.		0610	0610	0654	0654	0754	0754	0854	0854	...	0954	1054	1054	1154		1554	1654	1653	1754	1854	1954	2006	2053	2053	2200
131	Stamford d.		0623	0623	0707	0707	0807	0807	0907	0907	...	1007	1107	1107	1207	minutes	1607	1707	1707	1807	1907	2007	2022	2107	2107	2213
154	Oakham d.		0637	0637	0721	0721	0821	0821	0921	0921	...	1021	1121	1121	1221	past each	1621	1721	1721	1821	1921	2021	2038	2121	2121	2227
174	Melton Mowbray d.		0648	0648	0732	0732	0832	0832	0932	0932	...	1032	1132	1132	1232		1632	1732	1732	1832	1932	2032	2052	2132	2132	2238
197	**Leicester** d.		0707	0708	0750	0750	0850	0850	0950	0950	...	1050	1150	1150	1250	hour until	1650	1750	1750	1850	1950	2050	2117	2150	2150	2256
227	Nuneaton d.		0730	0730j	0809	0816	0909	0909	1009	1009	...	1109	1209	1209	1309		1709	1809	1816	1909	2009	2109	...	2209	2209	2316
244	Coleshill Parkway d.		0745	0747	0825	0831	0925	0925	1025	1025	...	1125	1225	1225	1325		1725	1825	1831	1925	2025	2125	...	2225	2225	2331
259	**Birmingham** New Street a.		0759	0802	0838	0845	0938	0938	1038	1038	...	1138	1238	1238	1338		1738	1838	1845	1938	2038	2138	...	2238	2238	2344

		⑦	⊖	⑦
Stansted Airport ✈ 207 d.	⑦	1027		1927
Cambridge 207 d.		1059j		1959j
Ely **204 206 207** d.		1115		2015
March **204** d.		1132	and at	2032
Peterborough **204 206** a.		1149	the same	2049
Peterborough d.		1154		2054
Stamford d.		1207	minutes	2107
Oakham d.		1221	past each	2121
Melton Mowbray d.		1232		2132
Leicester d.		1250	hour until	2150
Nuneaton d.		1309		2209
Coleshill Parkway d.		1325		2225
Birmingham New Street a.		1340		2238

		ⒶA	⑥A	Ⓐ	⑥	⚒A	Ⓐ🍷	⑥🍷	Ⓐ🍷	⑥🍷	Ⓐ	⑥	Ⓐ🍷	⑥🍷	Ⓐ🍷	⑥🍷	⚒🍷
Birmingham New Str d.	⚒	...	...	0519	0522	...	0622	0622	0722	0722	0752	0822	0922	0922	1022	1021	1122
Coleshill Parkway d.		...	...	0533	0536	...	0635	0636	0735	0736	0806	0836	0936	0935	1036	1035	1136
Nuneaton d.		...	...	0549	0551	...	0651	0651	0751	0751	0824	0851	0951	0951	1051	1051	1151
Leicester d.		...	...	0615	0615j	...	0714j	0714	0818	0813	0914a	0912	1015	1012	1113	1112	1212
Melton Mowbray d.		0537	0542	0631	0631	0654	0731	0731	0837	0829	0931	0928	1032	1028	1130	1128	1228
Oakham d.		0551	0554	0643	0643	0706	0742	0742	0849	0841	0942	0940	1044	1040	1141	1140	1240
Stamford d.		0605	0607	0657	0657	0719	0756	0756	0903	0855	0956	0954	1059	1054	1155	1154	1254
Peterborough a.		0621	0624	0710	0711	0735	0810	0810	0916	0909	1010	1007	1113	1107	1209	1207	1307
Peterborough **204 206** d.		0627	0627	0713	0713	0736	0819	0816	0919	0916	1013	1016	1115	1116	1214	1216	1316
March **204** a.		0643	0644	0732	0731	0755	0835	0832	0935	0932	1029	1032	1131	1132	1231	1232	1332
Ely **204 206 207** a.		0702	0704	0753	0753	0813	0852	0849	0952	0952	1051	1049	1149	1149	1249	1249	1349
Cambridge 207 a.		...	...	0808	0809	...	0910	0905t	1011	1009	1108	1105t	1205t	1205t	1305t	1305t	1406t
Stansted Airport ✈ .207 a.		...	...	0841	0841	...	0941	0941	1041	1041	1141	1141	1241	1241	1341	1341	1441

	⚒🍷	⚒🍷	Ⓐ🍷	⑥🍷	⚒	Ⓐ	⑥	Ⓐ	⑥	Ⓐ	⑥	Ⓐ	⑥	Ⓐ	⑥	Ⓐ		⑦🍷	⑦🍷	⑦🍷	⑦	⑦	⑦	⑦	⑦	⑦	⑦
Birmingham New Street d.	1220	1322	1422	1422	1522	1622	1622	1652	1722	1722	1822	1822	1922	1922	2022	2022	⑦	1122	1222	1322	1422	1522	1622	1722	1822	1922	2022
Coleshill Parkway d.	1234	1336	1436	1436	1536	1636	1636	1706	1736	1736	1836	1836	1936	1936	2036	2036		1136	1236	1336	1436	1536	1636	1736	1836	1936	2036
Nuneaton d.	1250	1351	1451	1451	1551	1651	1651	1728r	1751	1751	1851	1851	1951	1951	2051	2051		1151	1251	1351	1451	1551	1651	1751	1851	1951	2051
Leicester d.	1312	1412	1512	1512	1612	1713	1712	1756	1812	1817	1912	1916	2012	2015	2112	2119j		1212	1318	1416	1516	1616	1714	1812	1912	2012	2112
Melton Mowbray d.	1328	1428	1528	1528	1628	1730	1728	1813	1828	1834	1928	1933	2028	2032	2128	2135		1228	1334	1433	1533	1633	1730	1830	1928	2028	2128
Oakham d.	1340	1440	1540	1540	1640	1741	1740	1825	1840	1846	1940	1944	2040	2043	2140	2147		1240	1346	1444	1544	1644	1742	1842	1940	2040	2140
Stamford d.	1354	1454	1554	1554	1654	1755	1754	1839	1854	1900	1954	1958	2054	2057	2154	2201		1254	1400	1458	1558	1658	1756	1856	1954	2055	2154
Peterborough a.	1408	1509	1607	1607	1709	1809	1807	1853	1907	1913	2007	2012	2107	2112	2207	2216		1307	1413	1512	1613	1712	1810	1909	2007	2109	2207
Peterborough **204 206** d.	1416	1516	1620	1616	1716	1813	1816	1857	1916	1916	2016	2016	2116	2116	2216	2219		1319	1419	1519	1619	1719	1819	1919	2019	2119	2217
March **204** a.	1432	1532	1636	1632	1734	1829	1832	1916	1932	1932	2032	2032	2132	2132	2232	2235		1335	1435	1535	1635	1735	1835	1935	2035	2135	2233
Ely **204 206 207** a.	1449	1549	1653	1649	1756	1849	1849	1934	1949	1952	2049	2049	2149	2149	2249	2253		1352	1452	1552	1652	1752	1852	1952	2052	2152	2250
Cambridge 207 a.	1505t	1605	1710	1705t	1814	1908	1905t	1950	2005t	2008	2109	2108	2209	2205t	2305	2310		1408t	1508t	1608t	1708t	1808t	1908t	2008t	2108t	2208t	2306
Stansted Airport ✈ .207 a.	1554v	1641	1742	1741	1843	1941	1941	...	2041	2041	2141	2141	2241	2241	...	...		1445	1545	1645	1745	1845	1945	2045	2145	2245	...

A – (2) Nottingham - Norwich (Table **206**).
B – To Nottingham; Leicester dep. 2130 (Table **206**).
D – From Cardiff Central (Table **117**).

a – Arrives 0852.
c – Arrives 0644.
f – Departs 1827 on ⑥.

j – Arrives 4–5 minutes earlier.
r – Arrives 1722.
t – Departs 5–7 minutes later.
v – Arrives 1541 on ⑥.

⊖ – 🍷 conveyed on 1227, 1527, 1627 and 1727 from Stansted Airport.

☛ **Additional journeys Leicester - Birmingham New St and v.v.**
From Leicester:
On ⚒ at 0548⑥, 0618Ⓐ, 0722Ⓐ, 0816⑥, 0818Ⓐ, 0915Ⓐ, 0918⑥, 1016Ⓐ, 1018⑥, 1118 and hourly until 1918, 2018⑥, 2020Ⓐ, 2118, 2220⑥, 2225Ⓐ.
On ⑦ at 1020, 1117, 1220 and hourly until 2020, 2220.
From Birmingham New Street;
On ⚒ at 0552, 0652, 0752⑥, 0852 and hourly until 1552, 1652⑥, 1712Ⓐ, 1752, 1852, 1952, 2052, 2222.
On ⑦ at 0952, 1052 and hourly until 2152 **D**.

☛ **Full service Cambridge to Stansted Airport ✈** and v.v.
From Cambridge: On Ⓐ at 0444, 0517, 0634, 0734, 0811, 0911, 0950, 1011, 1048, 1111, 1150, 1211, 1248, 1311, 1348, 1411, 1448, 1511, 1547, 1607, 1647, 1711, 1816, 1911, 2011, 2048, 2111, 2211.
On ⑥ at 0451, 0540, 0610, 0640, 0648, 0736, 0748, 0811, 0848 and at the same times past each hour until 1711, 1748, 1817, 1848, 1911, 1948, 2011, 2048, 2111, 2211.
On ⑦ at 0739, 0825, 0915, 0925, 1015, 1025 and at the same times past each hour until 2115, 2125, 2215.
From Stansted Airport: On Ⓐ at 0520, 0612, 0721, 0826, 0921, 1027, 1048, 1127, 1148, 1227, 1248, 1327, 1348, 1427, 1448, 1522, 1537, 1627, 1648, 1727, 1751, 1821, 1921, 2027, 2127, 2210, 2227, 2257.
On ⑥ at 0527, 0627, 0648 and the same times past each hour until 2027, 2048, 2127, 2210, 2227, 2327.
On ⑦ at 0818, 0909, 1009, 1027 and the same times past each hour until 2027, 2104, 2111, 2209, 2227, 2304.

209 MORPETH - NEWCASTLE - CARLISLE 2nd class only NT

km			⚒	⚒	⚒	⚒	⚒H	⚒S	⚒	⚒	⚒	⚒	⚒	⚒	⑥	Ⓐ	⚒	⚒	⑥	Ⓐ	⚒	⚒	⚒	⚒	⚒	⚒	⚒	⚒
	Middlesbrough **210** d.	⚒	...	...	0548	...	...	0649	...	0731	...	...	0832	...	...	...	0931	...	...	...	1032	...	...	1132	...	...	1232	...
	Morpeth **214** d.		...	...	|	...	...	|	0759	|	0855	...	|	0955	...	...	|	1055	...	...	|	1155	...	|	1255	...	|	1355
0	**Newcastle** **214** d.		0542	0620	0702	0725	0740	0806	0823	0857	0923	0946	0957	1023	1031	1046	1057	1122	1147	1151	1158	1223	1239	1257	1323	1340	1355	1423
6	Metrocentre d.		0549	0629	0710	0734	0748	0814	0831	0906	0931	0954	1006	1031	1043	1054	1106	1131	1155	1201	1207	1231	1247	1306	1331	1348	1404	1431
19	Prudhoe d.		0604	0644	0725	0749	0759	0825	0846	0921	0942	1007	1021	1042	1054	1105	1121	1142	1206	1213	1222	1242	1259	1321	1342	1359	1419	1442
36	Hexham d.		0624	0659	0744	0801	0820	0838	0906	0941	0955	1022	1041	1055	1109	1118	1141	1155	1219	1232	1242	1255	1311	1341	1355	1412	1440	1455
62	Haltwhistle d.		0643	0722	0803	0824	...	0857	0929	...	1014	1042	...	1114	1132	1142	...	1214	1239	1253	...	1314	1334	...	1414	1435	...	1514
99	**Carlisle** a.		0714	0758	0836	0900	...	0932f	1002	...	1045	1116	...	1145	1205	1215	...	1245	1314	1327	...	1345	1407	...	1445	1510	...	1545

	Ⓐ	⑥	⚒K	⚒	⚒	⚒B	⚒	⚒	⚒	⚒	⚒	⚒	⚒K	⚒	Ⓐ	⑥	⚒	⑥	Ⓐ		⑦	⑦	⑦	✣W	⑦K	⑦	⑦
Middlesbrough **210** d.	...	...	1331	...	...	1432	...	...	...	...	1632	...	1730	...	...	...	...	...	2130	⑦	...	0832	0931		1730	1831	1931
Morpeth **214** d.	...	...	|	1455	...	|	1555	...	...	1655	|	1755	|	1855	1951	...	2102r	2215	|		...	|	|	and at	|	|	|
Newcastle **214** d.	1434	1440	1456	1523	1540	1556	1624	1640	1706	1723	1756	1823	1855	1923	2023	2033	2125	2239	2253		0845	0955	1055	the same	1855	1955	2100
Metrocentre d.	1443	1448	1505	1531	1548	1605	1632	1648	1714	1731	1805	1831	1904	1931	2031	2041	2133	2248	2302		0853	1003	1103	minutes	1903	2003	2109
Prudhoe d.	1454	1459	1520	1542	1559	1620	1643	1703	1729	1746	1821	1846	1919	1946	2046	2056	2148	2302	2317		0909	1018	1116	past each	1915	2018	2124
Hexham d.	1508	1512	1540	1555	1612	1640	1656	1722	1748	1805	1840	1905	1939	2006	2105	2115	2207	2321	2337		0928	1038	1136	hour until	1935	2037	2143
Haltwhistle d.	1531	1535	...	1614	1632	...	1715	1745	...	1828	...	1928	...	2029	2126	2136	2230	...	...		0951	1101	1159		1958	2100	2206
Carlisle a.	1603	1608	...	1645	1707	...	1747	1819	...	1903	...	2003	...	2103	2157	2211	2306	...	...		1025	1135	1233		2028	2134	2240

		⚒S	⚒	⑥	Ⓐ	⚒	⚒	⚒	⚒	⚒	⚒	⚒	⚒	⚒	⚒B	⚒	⚒	⚒K	⚒	⚒	⚒	⚒	⚒	⚒	⚒	⚒	⚒B	⚒
Carlisle d.	⚒	...	...	0557	0557	0632	0657	0724	0802	0820	0850	...	0922	0952	...	1023	1054	...	1125	1152	...	1225	1253	...	1332	1355	...	1435
Haltwhistle d.		...	...	0629	0629	0703	0729	0753	0832	0852	0920	...	0955	1020	...	1053	1122	...	1157	1220	...	1255	1321	...	1404	1423	...	1505
Hexham d.		0608	0635	0652	0652	0725	0752	0813	0856	0918	0942	0955	1018	1040	1055	1118	1142	1155	1218	1240	1255	1319	1341	1355	1425	1443	1455	1528
Prudhoe d.		0625	0653	0704	0710	0742	0810	0825	0913	0930	0954	1012	1030	1052	1112	1130	1154	1212	1230	1252	1312	1331	1353	1413	1437	1455	1512	1540
Metrocentre d.		0641	0709	0720	0725	0758	0826	0845	0930	0944	1006	1029	1044	1104	1129	1144	1207	1227	1244	1305	1329	1344	1405	1429	1449	1507	1529	1554
Newcastle **214** a.		0653	0720	0734	0737	0810	0838	0856	0946v	0955	1016	1040	1054	1115	1140	1156	1222	1239	1255	1314	1340	1353	1415	1440	1458	1518	1540	1605
Morpeth **214** a.		|	...	...	|	0833	...	0920	1018	...	...	|	1118	...	|	1218	...	|	1318	...	|	1418	...	|	1520	...	|	1626
Middlesbrough **210** a.		0818t	...	...	0900	...	...	...	...	...	...	1200	...	...	1259	...	...	1401	...	...	1500	...	...	1600	...	...	1700	...

	⚒	⚒K	⚒	⚒	⚒	⚒	⚒	⚒	⚒	⚒	⚒	Ⓐ	⑥	⚒	⚒	⚒T	⚒	⑥	Ⓐ		⑦	⑦	U Z	⑦	⑦	⑦	⑦
Carlisle d.	1454	...	1537	1552	...	1622	1652	...	1723	1753	...	1840	1849	...	2009	2107	2202	...	...	⑦	0844	0954		1754	1848	1948	2038
Haltwhistle d.	1522	...	1609	1622	...	1652	1720	...	1755	1821	...	1913	1921	...	2037	2139	2234	...	...		0916	1021	and at	1822	1920	2020	2110
Hexham d.	1542	1555	1630	1641	1655	1716	1740	1800	1819	1841	1855	1935	1943	2000	2101	2200	2258	2327	2341		0940	1046	the same	1846	1941	2043	2133
Prudhoe d.	1554	1612	1642	1653	1712	1728	1752	1817	1831	1853	1912	1947	1955	2018	2118	2217	2315	2345	2359		0957	1103	minutes	1903	1958	2101	2151
Metrocentre d.	1606	1629	1654	1705	1729	1740	1806	1833	1844	1905	1929	1959	2007	2033	2134	2233	2332	2357	0012		1013	1117	past each	1917	2014	2116	2206
Newcastle **214** a.	1617	1640	1704	1716	1739	1751	1816	1844	1854	1916	1940	2009	2018	2043	2144	2244	2343	0007	0027		1024	1127	hour until	1927	2024	2126	2217
Morpeth **214** a.	...	|	1729	...	|	1819	1839	|	...	...	|	...	2041	|	|	...	...	...	...		...	|		|	|	|	...
Middlesbrough **210** a.	...	1800	...	...	1859	...	...	2004	...	...	2104	...	...	2204	2305	...	...	...	...		...	1249		2049	2149	2249	...

B – From/to Battersby (Tables **210** and **211**).
H – From Hartlepool (Table **210**).
K – From/to Whitby (Tables **210** and **211**).
S – To/from Saltburn (Tables **210** and **212**).
T – To Sunderland (also Hartlepool on Ⓐ; Table **210**).

U – The 1054 and 1354 departures from Carlisle continue to Whitby (Tables **210** and **211**).
W – The 1430 departure from Middlesbrough starts from Whitby (Tables **210** and **211**).
Z – Timings at Haltwhistle may be up to 4 minutes later than shown.
Carlisle d. 1449 (not 1454), then Haltwhistle d. 1521, Hexham d. 1542, Prudhoe d. 1559, Metrocentre d. 1615, Newcastle a. 1625.

f – Arrives 0929 on Ⓐ.
r – Ⓐ only.
t – Arrives 0812 on Ⓐ.
v – Arrives 0942 on ⑥.

✣ – Timings may vary by ± 4 minutes.

NT 2nd class MIDDLESBROUGH - NEWCASTLE 210

km			⚒	Ⓐ	⑥	⚒S	⚒	⚒	⚒S	⚒	⚒	⚒	⚒	⚒	⚒	⚒	⚒	⚒A	⚒	⚒B	⚒	⚒	⚒	⚒A	⚒	⚒B	⚒	⚒	⚒
0	**Middlesbrough** .. d.	⚒	0548	...	...	0649	0656	0731	0749	0815	0832	0931	1015	1032	1132	1215	1232	1331	1415	1432	1532	1615	1632	1730	1815	1831	1931	2030	2130
9	Stockton .... d.		|	...	...	|	0708	0742	|	|	0843	0942	|	1043	1143	|	1243	1342	|	1442	1543	|	1643	1741	|	1842	1942	2041	2141
28	Hartlepool . **182a** d.		b	0639	0643	b	0727	0801	b	0840	0902	1001	1040	1102	1202	1240	1302	1401	1440	1501	1602	1642	1702	1800	1842	1901	2001	2100	2200
57	Sunderland **182a** d.		|	0708	0711	|	0756	0829	|	0909	0931	1030	1107	1130j	1231	1307	1330	1430	1509	1530	1630	1707	1730	1828	1908	1930	2029	2129	2228
76	**Newcastle** .... a.		0659	0733	0733	0800	0819	0855	0859	0931	0955	1055	1134	1154	1255	1334	1355	1454	1533	1554	1655	1729	1755	1852	1931	1950	2051	2153	2250
	Hexham **209** ... a.		0745	0820	0819	0839	...	0941	...	...	1041	1141	...	1242	1341	...	1441	1540	...	1640	...	...	1840	1939	...	...	...	...	2337r
	Carlisle **209** .... a.		0836	...	...	0932f	...	...	...	...	...	...	...	...	...	...	...	...	...	...	...	...	...	...	...	...	...	...	...

		⑦	⑦	⑦	⁂U	⑦A	⑦	⑦	⑦	⑦
Middlesbrough ... d.	⑦	0832	0931	1030		1730	1831	1931	2031	2132
Stockton .... d.		0844	0942	1041	and at	1742	1842	1942	2042	2143
Hartlepool .. **182a** d.		0903	1001	1100	the same	1801	1901	2002	2101	2201
Sunderland **182a** d.		0932	1029	1128	minutes	1829	1930	2031	2129	2229
Newcastle .... a.		0952	1050	1150	past each	1849	1950	2052	2150	2250
Hexham **209** .... a.		1037	1135	1238	hour until	1934	2037	2143	...	...
Carlisle **209** ..... a.		1135	1233	1331		2028	2134	2240	...	...

		⚒S	ⒶS	⑥S	⑥	Ⓐ	⚒	⑥	Ⓐ	⚒	⚒	⚒	⚒B	⚒
Carlisle **209** ...... d.	⚒	...	...	...	...	0557	...	...	...	...	...	...	...	...
Hexham **209** ..... d.		...	0609	0608	...	0652	...	...	...	...	...	0955	1055	...
Newcastle .... d.		0600	0653	0653	0734	0740	0817	0833	0840	0940	1017	1040	1140	1215
Sunderland . **182a** d.		0626	0714	0720	0756	0802	0838	0855	0901	1002	1037	1101	1201	1237
Hartlepool ... **182a** d.		0656	0741	0747	0828t	0829	0902	0924	0927	1028	1100	1128	1228	1301
Stockton .... d.		0714	0759	0805	0847	0848	|	0943	0945	1047	|	1146	1246	|
Middlesbrough ... a.		0729	0812	0818	0859	0900	0929	0958	1001	1101	1128	1200	1259	1328

	⚒A	⚒	⚒	⚒	⚒B	⚒	⚒A	⚒	⚒	⚒	⚒	⚒	⚒	⚒	⑥	Ⓐ	⑥
Carlisle **209** ..... d.	...	...	...	...	...	...	...	...	...	...	...	...	...	2009	...	2107	2107
Hexham **209** .... d.	1155	1255	...	1355	1455	...	1555	...	1655	...	1800	1855	2000	2101	...	2200	2200
Newcastle .... d.	1239	1340	1417	1440	1540	1616	1641	1723	1740	1821	1846	1945	2045	2146	2233	2248	2245
Sunderland **182a** d.	1302	1401	1437	1501	1601	1636	1702	1749	1801	1838	1906	2006	2106	2206	2252	2308	2305
Hartlepool .. **182a** d.	1328	1428	1459	1528	1628	1659	1728	1816	1827	1900	1932	2032	2132	2232	2319	2335	...
Stockton .... d.	1347	1446	|	1546	1646	|	1746	1834	1846	|	1951	2051	2151	2251	...	...	...
Middlesbrough .. a.	1401	1500	1529	1600	1700	1729	1800	...	1859	1928	2004	2104	2204	2305	...	...	...

		⑦	⑦A	⑦	⑦	⑦A	⑦	⁂W	⑦	⑦S	⑦
Carlisle **209** ..... d.	⑦	...	...	...	0954	1053	1153		1848	...	1948
Hexham **209** .... d.		...	...	...	1046	1145	1246	and at	1941	...	2043
Newcastle .... d.		0831	0932	1031	1131	1230	1330	the same	2031	2114	2131
Sunderland **182a** d.		0851	0952	1052	1151	1251	1350	minutes	2050	|	2151
Hartlepool .. **182a** d.		0917	1019	1118	1217	1318	1417	past each	2117	b	2217
Stockton .... d.		0936	1037	1137	1236	1336	1435	hour until	2135	|	2236
Middlesbrough .. a.		0948	1050	1149	1248	1349	1449		2149	2222	2249

A – To/from Whitby (Table **211**).
B – To/from Battersby (Table **211**).
S – To/from Saltburn (Table **212**).
U – The 1430 departure from Middlesbrough starts from Whitby (Table **211**).
W – The 1354 departure from Carlisle continues to Whitby (Table **211**).

b – Via Darlington (Table **212**).
f – 0929 on Ⓐ.
j – Departs 1134 on Ⓐ.
r – Ⓐ only.
t – Arrives 0822.

⁂ – Timings between Carlisle and Newcastle and v.v. may vary by ± 4 minutes. See Table **209**.

NT 2nd class MIDDLESBROUGH and PICKERING - WHITBY 211

km		⚒D	⑦D	⚒	⑦N	⚒H	⑦C	⚒H	⑦C	⚒H	⚒H	⚒
0	**Middlesbrough** ...... d.	0654	0841	1019	1050	1300	1350	1402	1653	1700	1800	2043
18	Battersby .... d.	0736r	0912	1050	1131r	1331	1425	1435	1726	1732	1831	2117
41	Glaisdale .... d.	0809	0945	1123	1204	...	1458	1509	1759	...	1904	2149
46	Grosmont .... d.	0818	0953	1131	1212	...	1506	1517	1807	...	1912	2157
56	**Whitby** .... a.	0838	1012	1151	1230	...	1525	1537	1826	...	1932	2216

	⚒	⑦D	⚒H	⑦C	⚒H	⑦C	⚒H	⚒N	⑦D	⚒	⚒
Whitby .... d.	0844	1022	1200	1249	...	1550	1557	...	1834	1942	2223
Grosmont .... d.	0901	1039	1217	1306	...	1608	1615	...	1851	1959	2239
Glaisdale .... d.	0912	1050	1228	1317	...	1618	1626	...	1902	2010	2249
Battersby .... d.	0947	1126	1303	1353	1351	1655t	1702t	1746	1938t	2046t	2324t
Middlesbrough ...... a.	1015	1152	1330	1428	1431	1728	1729	1830	2004	2112	2351

km		🚂		🚂		🚂		🚂		🚂		🚂
0	**Pickering** .... d.	...	...	0920	...	1055	...	1200	...	1510	...	1615
29	Grosmont .... a.	...	...	1025	...	1210	...	1305	...	1620	...	1720
29	Grosmont .... d.	0915	...	1040	...	...	...	1325	...	1630	...	...
39	**Whitby** .... a.	0945	...	1110	...	...	...	1350	...	1655	...	...

	🚂		🚂	🚂		🚂		🚂		🚂	
Whitby .... d.	1000	...	1235	...	...	1410	...	...	...	1710	...
Grosmont .... a.	1025	...	1300	...	...	1435	...	...	...	1735	...
Grosmont .... d.	1035	...	...	1330	...	1440	...	1640	...	1745	...
Pickering .... a.	1140	...	...	1450	...	1555	...	1750	...	1845	...

C – To/from Carlisle (Tables **209** and **210**).
D – To/from Darlington (Table **212**).
H – To/from Hexham (Table **210**).
N – To/from Newcastle (Table **210**).

r – Arrives 14–15 minutes earlier.
t – Arrives 5 minutes earlier.

🚂 – Daily services Mar. 23 - Nov. 3, 2024. 2025 timings to be announced. National Rail tickets **not** valid. An amended service operates on most ⑦ (also on ①–④ July 22 - Aug. 29 and on certain other dates); please confirm with operator. The North Yorkshire Moors Railway. ✆ 01751 472508. www.nymr.co.uk

NT 2nd class BISHOP AUCKLAND - DARLINGTON - MIDDLESBROUGH - SALTBURN 212

km			⑥D	ⒶD	⚒	⚒N	ⒶB	⑥B	⚒	⚒	♥	⚒
0	**Bishop Auckland** .... d.	⚒	...	...	...	...	...	...	0727	0827		2127
4	Shildon .... d.		...	...	...	...	...	...	0733	0833		2133
8	Newton Aycliffe .... d.		...	...	...	...	...	...	0737	0837	and at	2137
19	**Darlington** .... a.		...	...	...	...	...	...	0754	0853	the same	2153
19	**Darlington** .... ▶ d.		0614	0614	0628	...	...	...	0756	0855	minutes	2155
43	**Middlesbrough** ... **188** ▶ d.		0645	0650t	0711v	0728	0812	0817	0824	0924	past each	2224
55	Redcar Central..... **188** ▶ d.		0656	0701	0723	0741	0824	0829	0836	0936	hour until	2236
63	**Saltburn** .... **188** ▶ a.		0710	0715	0737	0757	0838	0844	0854	0951		2251

		⑦A	⑦	⑦	⑦	♥	⑦	⑦	⑦	⑦N	⑦
Bishop Auckland .... d.	⑦	...	...	0814	0924		1924	2024	...	...	...
Shildon .... d.		...	...	0820	0930		1930	2030	...	...	...
Newton Aycliffe .... d.		...	...	0824	0934	and at	1934	2034	...	...	...
Darlington .... a.		...	...	0840	0950	the same	1950	2050	...	...	...
Darlington .... ▶ d.		0809	0809	0842	0952	minutes	1953	2053	2127	2154	2252
Middlesbrough ... **188** ▶ d.		0837	0845r	0911	1021	past each	2021	2121	2157	2223	2322
Redcar Central..... **188** ▶ d.		...	0857	0923	1033	hour until	2033	2133	...	2235	...
Saltburn .... **188** ▶ a.		...	0911	0937	1047		2047	2147	...	2249	...

		⚒	⚒C	⚒	⚒N	⚒		⚒	⚒	⚒	⚒
Saltburn .... **188** ▷ d.	⚒	...	0622	0700	0722	0759		1957	2058	2159	2259
Redcar Central ..... **188** ▷ d.		...	0635	0713	0735	0812		2010	2111	2212	2312
Middlesbrough .... **188** ▷ d.		...	0649	0726	0749	0825	and at	2024	2124	2225	2326
Darlington .... ▷ a.		...	0717	0757	0818	0853	the same	2054	2155	2256	2354
Darlington .... d.		0644	...	0757	...	0855	minutes	2054	...	...	...
Newton Aycliffe .... d.		0658	...	0812	...	0909	past each	2108	...	...	...
Shildon .... d.		0703	...	0816	...	0914	hour until	2113	...	...	...
Bishop Auckland .... a.		0708	...	0822	...	0921		2120	...	...	...

		⑦	⑦	⑦	⑦	⑦	⑦A	⑦	♥	⑦	⑦A	⑦
Saltburn .... **188** ▷ d.	⑦	...	...	...	0957	1057	...	1157		1857	...	1957
Redcar Central ..... **188** ▷ d.		...	...	...	1010	1110	...	1210		1910	...	2010
Middlesbrough .... **188** ▷ d.		...	0823	0922	1024	1124	1153	1224	and at	1924	2006	2024
Darlington .... ▷ a.		...	0851	0951	1052	1152	1222	1253	the same	1952	2035	2053
Darlington .... d.		0741	0853	0953	1053	1154	...	1253	minutes	1954	...	...
Newton Aycliffe .... d.		0755	0907	1007	1107	1210	...	1309	past each	2008	...	...
Shildon .... d.		0800	0912	1012	1112	1214	...	1313	hour until	2013	...	...
Bishop Auckland .... a.		0805	0917	1017	1117	1220	...	1319		2018	...	...

A – To/from Whitby (Table **211**).
B – From Hexham (Table **210**).
C – To Carlisle (Table **210**).
D – Convey (2) to Whitby. (Table **211**).
N – To/from Newcastle (Table **210**).

r – Arrives 0837.
t – Arrives 0644.
v – Arrives 0659.
y – To Middlesbrough only.

♥ – Timings may vary by ± 3 minutes.
▶ – Additional trains Darlington - Middlesbrough - Saltburn. From Darlington on ⚒ at 0822 and hourly until 2022.
▷ – Additional trains Saltburn - Middlesbrough - Darlington. From Saltburn on ⚒ at 0822 and hourly until 2122; on ⑦ at 0920**y**, 2057, 2157, 2257.

SR 2nd class CARLISLE - DUMFRIES - GLASGOW 213

km			⚒	Ⓐ	⑥	⚒	Ⓐ	⑥	⚒	Ⓐ	⑥	Ⓐ	⑥	⑥	Ⓐ	⚒	⚒	⚒	⚒	⚒	⚒	⚒	⚒	⑥
0	**Carlisle** .... **154** d.	⚒	...	...	...	0608	0701	0702	0809	0854	0909	0954	0957	1109	1111	1215	1306	1408	1508	1609	1725	1758	1921	...
16	Gretna Green ....d.		...	...	...	0620	0713	0714	0821	0906	0921	1008	1009	1121	1123	1227	1318	1420	1521	1622	1741	1810	1936	...
28	Annan ....d.		...	...	...	0628	0722	0728b	0829	0914	0929	1021	1021	1129	1131	1235	1326	1429	1529	1631	1753	1820	1944	...
53	**Dumfries** ....d.		...	...	...	0647	0738	0744	0848	0931	0946	1040	1040	1146	1148	1253	1343	1453t	1546	1653b	1810	1838	2001	2049
124	Auchinleck.......................d.		...	0634	...	0735	...	...	0936	...	...	1130	1130	...	...	1342	...	1541	...	1741	...	1927	...	2139
146	**Kilmarnock**.................. ▽ d.		0620	0652	0653	0753	...	...	0958	...	...	1156	1157b	...	...	1359	...	1559	...	1759	...	1957r	...	2157
185	**Glasgow** Central .... **154** ▽ a.		0709	0731	0734	0836	...	...	1036	...	...	1234	1234	...	...	1439	...	1637	...	1839	...	2037	...	2237

	⚒	⚒	⑥	Ⓐ		⑦	⑦	⑦	⑦	⑦
Carlisle .... **154** d.	...	2111	2310	2310	⑦	1311	1511	1711	1911	2126
Gretna Green ....d.	...	2123	2322	2322		1323	1523	1723	1923	2138
Annan ....d.	...	2131	2330	2330		1331	1531	1731	1931	2146
Dumfries ....d.	2049	2148	2347	2350		1350	1548	1748	1950	2203
Auchinleck.......................d.	2139	...	...	...		1438	...	...	2038	...
Kilmarnock.................. ▽ d.	2157	...	...	...		1456	...	...	2057	...
Glasgow Central ... **154** ▽ a.	2239	...	...	...		1543	...	...	2134	...

		⚒	⚒	⚒	⚒	Ⓐ	⑥	⚒	Ⓐ	⑥
Glasgow Cent**154** ▽ d.	⚒	...	...	...	...	0707	0708	...	0913	0913
Kilmarnock......... ▽ d.		...	...	...	...	0753b	0755b	...	0958f	0957b
Auchinleck.................d.		...	...	...	...	0809	0811	...	1014	1013
Dumfries ....d.		0457	0604	0715	0758	0859	0901	1002	1104	1103
Annan ....d.		0512	0619	0730	0813	0914	0916	1017	1119	1118
Gretna Green ....d.		0521	0628	0739	0822	0923	0928	1026	1128	1127
Carlisle .... **154** a.		0534	0641	0755	0839	0941	0942	1040	1142	1140

	⚒	Ⓐ	⑥	⚒	⚒	⚒	Ⓐ	⑥	⚒	⚒	⚒	⚒	Ⓐ	Ⓐ	Ⓐ	Ⓐ	⑥	⚒		⑦	⑦	⑦	⑦	⑦
Glasgow Central .... **154** ▽ d.	...	1113	1114	...	1313	...	1513	1513	1612	...	1728	1913	2017	2114	...	2214	2213	2313	⑦	...	...	1503	...	2206
Kilmarnock .... ▽ d.	...	1154	1156	...	1356	...	1553	1556b	1655	...	1828v	1953	2054	2158	...	2253	2253	0001		...	...	1552	...	2243
Auchinleck ....d.	...	1210	1212	...	1412	...	1609	1612	1711	...	1844	2010	...	2215	...	2309	2309	...		...	...	1608	...	2300
Dumfries ....d.	1159	1300	1304	1358	1502	1602	1707c	1707t	1801	1903	1932	2100	...	2303	2308	2357	2357	...		1301	1501	1701	1902	2350
Annan ....d.	1214	1315	1320	1413	1517	1617	1722	1722	1816	1918	...	2116	...	...	2323	...	...	...		1316	1516	1716	1917	0005
Gretna Green ....d.	1223	1324	1328	1422	1526	1626	1731	1731	1825	1927	...	2124	...	...	2332	...	...	...		1326	1526	1727	1926	0014
Carlisle .... **154** a.	1239	1337	1342	1439	1540	1639	1744	1744	1839	1940	...	2139	...	...	2345	...	...	...		1339	1540	1740	1940	0027

b – Arrives 5–6 minutes earlier.
c – Arrives 1658.
f – Arrives 0951.
r – Arrives 1943 on Ⓐ; 1946 on ⑥.
t – Arrives 7 minutes earlier.
v – Arrives 1820.
▽ – Additional hourly services are available.

214 NEWCASTLE - EDINBURGH

Most services convey 🍸 — XC, TP, GR, LD, NT

km		⚒	⚒	⑥	Ⓐ	⚒	ⒶC	⑥C	⚒G	⚒F	ⒶAL	⑥AL	Ⓐ	⑥	Ⓐ	⚒C	⚒	Ⓐ	⑥	⚒C	⚒	⚒	⚒C	⚒	Ⓐ	⑥	⚒
	London Kings C 180 .d.		...	...	...	...	...	...	...	0548	...	...	...	...	...	...	0615	0700	0700	...	0730	0800	...	0830	0900	0900	...
0	**Newcastle** 209 d.		0557	0624	0628	0707	0735	0738	0743	0841	0847	0849	0856	0911	0922	0935	0946	0954	0954	1035	1041	1053	1135	1145	1154	1154	1206
26	Morpeth 209 d.		0619	0638	0642	0724	0749	0752	|	0855	0901	0904	|	0928	0936	|	|	|	|	1049	|	|	|	|	|	|	1224
56	Alnmouth d.		0635	0653	0657	0738	|	|	0809	|	|	|	|	0942	0950	1001	|	|	|	|	1108	|	1201	|	|	|	1238
107	Berwick-upon-Tweed d.		...	0714	0718	0759	0821	0826	0833	|	0934	0937	0941	1003	1011	1022	|	1037	1039	1121	|	1137	1222	|	1237	1238	1259
125	Reston d.		...	0725	0729	0810	|	|	|	|	|	|	|	1014	1022	|	|	|	|	|	|	|	|	|	|	|	1310
152	Dunbar d.		...	0741	0745	0826	|	|	0856	|	0957	0959	|	1030	1038	|	|	|	|	1144	|	|	|	|	|	|	1326
199	**Edinburgh** Waverley a.		...	0807	0809	0856	0905	0912	0924f	1007	1020	1021	1031	1059	1105	1108f	1114f	1120	1128	1207	1214	1224	1305	1310	1322	1326	1357t

	⑥C	ⒶC	⚒	⚒A	⑥	Ⓐ	⑥F	ⒶC	⑥C	⚒	ⒶF	⚒	⚒C	⚒	⚒H	⚒F	Ⓐ	⑥	⑥C	ⒶC	⚒	Ⓐ	⑥	⚒	⚒C	⚒	ⒶA
London Kings C 180 .d.	...	...	0930	1000	...	...	1025	...	...	1030	1045	1100	...	1130	1200	1218	...	...	...	...	1230	1300	1300	...	...	1330	1400
Newcastle 209 d.	1234	1235	1240	1254	...	...	1317	1332	1335	1343	1347	1354	1435	1445	1454	1516	...	...	1534	1537	1544	1553	1559	1614	1634	1641	1701
Morpeth 209 d.	1249	1249	1254	|	...	...	1331	|	|	|	1401	|	1449	|	|	1531	...	...	|	|	|	|	|	1631	1648	1655	|
Alnmouth d.	|	|	1308	|	...	...	|	1358	1401	|	|	|	|	1510	|	|	...	...	1559	1603	|	|	|	1645	|	1710	|
Berwick-upon-Tweed d.	1321	1321	|	1339	1345	1402	|	1419	1422	|	|	1438	1521	|	1540	|	1612	1614	1622	1624	|	1637	1644	1706	1721	|	1746
Reston d.	|	|	|	|	1356	1413	|	|	|	|	|	|	|	|	|	|	1623	1624	|	|	|	|	|	1718	|	|	|
Dunbar d.	|	|	|	|	1412	1429	|	|	|	|	|	|	|	|	|	|	1639	1652r	|	|	|	|	|	1734	|	|	|
Edinburgh Waverley a.	1403	1409	1415f	1427t	1439	1458	1442	1501	1504	1512t	1511	1526	1606	1616	1626t	1642	1703	1722	1704	1708	1714f	1723	1727	1803	1807	1816	1827

	⑥A	⚒C	⚒	ⒶF	Ⓐ	⑥	⚒E	⚒S	Ⓐ	⑥	⑥F	ⒶA	⑥	⚒S	⚒	⚒	⑥	Ⓐ	⚒C	Ⓐ	⑥	⑥	Ⓐ	⑥F	⚒C	Ⓐ	Ⓐ
London Kings C 180 .d.	1400	...	1430	1448	1500	1500	...	...	1530	1530	1548	1600	1600	...	1630	1700	1730	1730	...	1800	1800	...	...	1827	...	1830	1900
Newcastle 209 d.	1700	1734	1743	1747	1755	1755	1757	1835	1844	1842	1849	1854	1858	1935	1945	1956	2034	2035	2041	2051	2055	2059	2101	2124	2136	2142	2156
Morpeth 209 d.	|	|	|	1801	|	|	1819	|	|	|	1903	|	|	|	2000	|	|	|	2055	|	2110	2116	2116	2139	|	2157	|
Alnmouth d.	|	1800	|	|	|	|	1843	|	1911	1908	|	|	|	2001	|	|	|	2100	|	|	2125	2130	2130	|	2201	2213	|
Berwick-upon-Tweed d.	1743	|	|	|	1840	1839	|	1921	|	|	|	1939	1941	2022	|	2040	|	|	2127	2137	2148	2152	2151	|	|	|	2240
Reston d.	|	|	|	|	|	|	...	|	|	|	|	|	|	|	|	|	|	|	|	|	|	2203	2202	|	|	|	|
Dunbar d.	|	1841	|	|	|	|	...	|	|	|	|	|	|	|	|	|	|	2142	2150	|	2213	|	2220	|	|	|	|
Edinburgh Waverley a.	1830	1906	1912a	1911	1924	1930	...	2006	2012	2011	2013	2020	2024	2105	2114	2125	2159	2208	2215	2220	2238	2242	2253	2259	2305	2316	2324

	⑤	ⒶF	⑦	⑦	⑦	⑦	⑦L	⑦C	⑦G	⑦C	⑦	⑦F	⑦	⑦	⑦C	⑦	⑦A	⑦	⑦F	⑦	⑦C	⑦	⑦	⑦	⑦C	⑦	⑦H
London Kings C 180 .d.	1930	2027		...	...	...	...	...	...	...	0848	0852	0900	...	...	0930	1000	1003	1023	...	...	1030	1100	1122	...	1130	1200
Newcastle 209 d.	2243	2308		0845	0915	0919	1005	1042	1102	1130	1140	1145	1152	1158	1230	1238	1253	1311	1316	...	1330	1343	1349	1424	1430	1440	1450
Morpeth 209 d.	2258	2323		0900	|	0936	1019	1056	|	|	1154	1159	|	1213	1245	|	|	|	1330	...	|	|	|	1439	1445	|	|
Alnmouth d.	2313	|		0915	|	0950	1033	|	|	1156	|	|	|	1227	|	1303	|	|	|	...	1356	|	|	|	|	1506	|
Berwick-upon-Tweed d.	2336	|		0936	1000	1011	1055	1128	1147	1217	|	|	1235	1248	1317	|	1337	|	|	1406	1417	|	1433	|	1517	|	1537
Reston d.	|	|		0947	|	1022	|	|	|	|	|	|	|	1259	|	|	|	|	|	1417	|	|	|	|	|	|	|
Dunbar d.	|	|		1003	|	1038	1117	1151	|	|	|	|	|	1315	|	1344	|	|	|	1433	|	|	|	|	1540	|	|
Edinburgh Waverley a.	0020	0043		1027	1049	1106	1144	1215	1230	1259	1309	1313	1318	1346	1359	1409	1418	1435	1441	1456	1459	1510	1518	1559	1602	1609	1619

	⑦F	⑦	⑦C	⑦	⑦	⑦CJ	⑦	⑦A	⑦	⑦S	⑦	⑦	⑦C	⑦	⑦	⑦F	⑦C	⑦	⑦	⑦C	⑦	⑦	⑦	⑦C	⑦	⑦	⑦F
London Kings C 180 .d.	1213	...	...	1230	1300	...	1330	1400	...	...	1430	1500	...	1530	1600	1624	...	1630	1700	...	1730	1800	...	...	1830	1900	1924
Newcastle 209 d.	1510	...	1530	1546	1555	1630	1638	1652	1711	1732	1745	1752	1835	1842	1850	1921	1935	1943	1951	2035	2042	2100	2114	2136	2145	2152	2210
Morpeth 209 d.	1525	...	|	|	|	1645	|	|	1728	|	|	|	1849	|	|	1935	|	1957	|	2049	2057	|	2131	|	|	2206	2223
Alnmouth d.	|	...	1556	|	|	|	1704	|	1742	1758	|	|	|	1908	|	|	2001	|	|	|	2113	|	2145	2201	|	2220	|
Berwick-upon-Tweed d.	|	1610	1617	|	1638	1717	|	1738	1803	1819	|	1835	1921	|	1934	|	2022	|	2034	2121	|	2144	2206	2222	2229	2242	|
Reston d.	|	1620	|	|	|	|	|	|	1814	|	|	|	|	|	|	|	|	|	|	|	|	|	2217	|	|	|	|
Dunbar d.	|	1636	|	|	|	|	|	|	1830	|	|	|	1944	|	|	|	|	2050	|	|	|	|	2233	|	|	2304	|
Edinburgh Waverley a.	1636	1659	1703	1709	1721	1759	1807	1819	1857	1901	1909	1918	2007	2012	2017	2047	2105	2113	2118	2203	2215	2227	2300	2304	2312	2328	2335

	⚒	Ⓐ	Ⓐ	⑥	Ⓐ	⑥F	⑥	Ⓐ	⚒C	ⒶF	⑥	Ⓐ	⚒E	⚒	⚒C	⚒	⚒	ⒶS	⑥S	⚒	⑥F	⑥	Ⓐ	⚒S	ⒶF	⑥	Ⓐ
Edinburgh Waverley d.		...	0540	0526	0529	0536	0548	0548	0606	0623	0630	0630	...	0700	0704	0730	0800	0807	0808	0830	0856	0900	0900	0907	0924	0930	0930
Dunbar d.		...	|	0558c	0602c	|	0611	0611	|	|	|	|	...	|	0725	|	|	|	|	|	|	|	|	|	|	|	|
Reston d.		...	|	0613	0618	|	|	|	|	|	|	|	...	|	|	|	|	|	|	|	|	|	|	|	|	|	|
Berwick-upon-Tweed d.		0600	|	0625	0630	|	0634	0635	0647	|	0713	0713	...	|	0749	0812	|	0848	0850	0914	|	|	|	0948	|	1012	1013
Alnmouth d.		0622	|	0645	0650	|	0655	0657	0708	|	|	|	0719	|	0809	|	0900	|	0910	|	|	|	|	1009	|	|	|
Morpeth 209 d.		0638	|	0659	0704	0648	0710	0713	|	0738	|	|	0759	|	0824	|	|	0920	|	|	1006	|	|	|	1038	|	|
Newcastle 209 a.		0652	0702	0720	0722	0703	0723	0728	0734	0753	0755	0756	0822	0824	0839	0855	0927	0937	0939	0957	1020	1024	1024	1038	1052	1056	1055
London Kings C 180 .a.		1002	0940	...	...	0959	1038	1039	...	1046	1048	1052	...	1138	...	1148	1239	...	...	1249	1314	1338	1338	...	1347	1349	1352

	⚒	⚒	⚒C	⚒A	⚒	⚒CA	ⒶF	⚒H	⚒	⚒	⚒C	⚒A	⑥F	⚒	⚒C	⚒	⑥	Ⓐ	ⒶC	⑥C	⑥	Ⓐ	⑥	Ⓐ	Ⓐ	⑥	⑥C
Edinburgh Waverley d.	0933	1000	1005	1030	1100	1108	1124	1130	1133	1200	1207	1230	1256	1300	1307	1330	1400	1400	1404	1404	1408	1410	1430	1430	1500	1500	1505
Dunbar d.	0959	|	|	|	|	|	|	|	1200	|	|	|	|	|	|	|	|	|	|	|	1433	1435	|	|	|	|	1526
Reston d.	1015	|	|	|	|	|	|	|	1215	|	|	|	|	|	|	|	|	|	|	|	1449	1451	|	|	|	|	|
Berwick-upon-Tweed d.	1026	|	1048	1112	|	1149	|	|	1225	|	1248	1313	|	|	1348	1413	|	|	1446	1446	1500	1505	1512	1515	|	|	1550
Alnmouth d.	1047	1059	|	|	|	1210	|	|	...	1301	|	|	|	|	1409	|	1459	1500	1506	|	1521	1526	|	|	|	|	1610
Morpeth 209 d.	1101	|	1120	|	|	|	1234	|	...	|	1320	|	1406	|	|	|	1514	1515	1521	1518	1535	1540	|	|	|	|	|
Newcastle 209 a.	1121	1126	1134	1156	1224	1238	1248	1255	...	1327	1334	1356	1419	1423	1436	1456	1527	1528	1538	1533	1553	1554	1556	1557	1624	1624	1639
London Kings C 180 .a.	...	1439	...	1448	1538	...	1544	1549	...	1640	...	1648	1707	1740	...	1750	1838	1841	...	...	...	...	1852	1848	1938	1948	...

	ⒶC	⑥	Ⓐ	⑥F	⚒	Ⓐ	⑥	⚒C	ⒶF	⚒	⚒	ⒶC	⑥C	⚒A	⚒	⑥F	⚒C	⑥	Ⓐ2E	Ⓐ	⑥2	⑥G	⑥D	ⒶD	Ⓐ	ⒶF	⑥
Edinburgh Waverley d.	1507	1509	1514	1526	1530	1600	1600	1607	1613	1630	1700	1707	1709	1730	1734	1756	1807	1830	...	1830	...	1900	1903	1911	1937	1958	2000
Dunbar d.	1528	1535	1538	|	|	|	|	|	|	|	|	|	|	1753	1800	|	1828	|	...	1855	...	1922	1929	1938	|	|	2022
Reston d.	|	1550	1553	|	|	|	|	|	|	|	|	|	|	|	1815	|	|	|	...	|	...	|	1945	1954	|	|	2038
Berwick-upon-Tweed d.	1552	1604	1605	|	1614	|	|	1648	|	1712	|	1748	1750	1816	1827	|	1852	1913	...	1920	...	1947	1957	2005	2019	|	2052
Alnmouth d.	|	...	...	|	|	|	|	|	|	|	1800	1809	1810	|	1847	|	|	|	1926	1943	1946	2008	2018	2026	2040	|	2114
Morpeth 209 d.	|	...	...	1638	|	|	|	1720	1727	|	|	|	|	|	1901	1909	1924	|	1951	2000	2011	2025	2032	2041	2056	2114	2129
Newcastle 209 a.	1635	...	...	1652	1657	1722	1723	1735	1746	1756	1826	1838	1838	1901	1919	1922	1938	1958	2014	2014	2037	2040	2049	2056	2109	2132	2145
London Kings C 180 .a.	...	...	...	1948	1953t	2038	2046	...	2044	2053	2146j	...	...	2216v	...	2226	...	...	...	2330	...	...	...	...	0114	0105	...

	Ⓐ	⑥2	ⒶAL	⑤	⑦	⑦	⑦C	⑦	⑦	⑦	⑦C	⑦	⑦F	⑦	⑦C	⑦	⑦	⑦	⑦	⑦S	⑦	⑦A	⑦	⑦C	⑦	⑦H	⑦F
Edinburgh Waverley d.	2007	2056	2100	2200		0900	0908	0930	0933	1000	1008	1030	1054	1100	1105	1120	1130	1133	1200	1207	1220	1230	1300	1308	1320	1330	1356
Dunbar d.	|	|	2125	2222		|	|	|	1000	|	|	|	|	|	|	|	|	1159	|	1228	|	|	|	|	|	|	|
Reston d.	|	|	2141	|		|	|	|	1015	|	|	|	|	|	|	|	|	1215	|	|	|	|	|	|	|	|	|
Berwick-upon-Tweed d.	2051	|	2153	2247		|	0950	1013	1027	|	1050	1113	|	|	1150	|	1213	1225	|	1252	|	1312	1343	1350	|	1413	|
Alnmouth d.	2112	|	2214	2307		|	|	|	1047	1101	|	|	|	|	1210	|	|	...	1302	|	|	|	|	1410	|	|	|
Morpeth 209 d.	|	2207	2229	2325		|	|	|	1101	|	1122	|	1204	|	|	1233	|	...	|	1324	1333	|	|	|	|	|	1506
Newcastle 209 a.	2139	2220	2242	2356		1023	1033	1056	1119	1127	1136	1156	1218	1223	1236	1246	1256	...	1327	1338	1347	1354	1427	1436	1445	1456	1519
London Kings C 180 .a.	...	...	...	...		1341	...	1348	...	1439	...	1445	1455	1540	...	1547	1556	...	1639	...	1645	1650	1739	...	1746	1749	1806

	⑦	⑦CJ	⑦A	⑦	⑦	⑦	⑦C	⑦	⑦	⑦F	⑦	⑦C	⑦	⑦A	⑦	⑦C	⑦	⑦	⑦	⑦C	⑦	⑦F	⑦	⑦D	⑦G	⑦	⑦
Edinburgh Waverley d.	1400	1408	1430	1421	1450	1500	1508	1511	1530	1550	1600	1608	1620	1630	1700	1708	1730	1733	1800	1805	1830	1854	1900	1915	2000	2025	2100
Dunbar d.	|	|	|	1452c	|	|	|	1536	|	|	|	|	|	|	|	|	1752	1802	|	1826	|	|	1923	1940	2023	|	2122
Reston d.	|	|	|	1508	|	|	|	1551	|	|	|	|	|	|	|	|	|	1817	|	|	|	|	|	1956	|	|	2138
Berwick-upon-Tweed d.	|	1449	|	1519	1533	|	1550	1602	1612	|	|	1650	|	1713	|	1750	1817	1828	|	1850	1913	|	1947	2008	2048	2106	2149
Alnmouth d.	1501	|	|	1540	|	|	1610	...	|	|	1701	|	|	|	|	1810	|	1849	1901	|	|	|	|	2028	2110	|	2210
Morpeth 209 d.	|	1520	|	1554	|	|	|	...	|	1700	|	1722	1733	|	|	|	|	1903	|	1922	|	2004	|	2042	2127	|	|
Newcastle 209 a.	1528	1535	1553	1613	1616	1622	1636	...	1656	1714	1727	1736	1747	1756	1823	1837	1859	1920	1928	1936	1956	2018	2030	2056	2141	2149	2237
London Kings C 180 .a.	1839	...	1849	...	1921	1942	...	...	1947	2008	2042	...	2048	2052	2139	...	2158	...	2239	...	2318	2320	2359	...	...	...	...

A – To/from Aberdeen (Table **222**).
C – To/from destinations in Tables **119** and **110**.
D – To Liverpool Lime Street (Table **188**).
E – 2 Carlisle - Newcastle - Alnmouth and v.v. (Table **209**).
F – 2 London Kings Cross - Edinburgh and v.v. (Table **183**).

G – From/to Doncaster (Table **180**).
H – To/from Inverness (Tables **180** and **223**).
J – To/from Dundee (Table **222**).
L – To/from Leeds (Table **180**).
S – 12 Plymouth - Birmingham - Edinburgh - Glasgow Central and v.v. (Tables **119 110 and 220**).

a – Arrives 1909 on Ⓐ.
c – Arrives 7 minutes earlier.
f – Arrives 4–5 minutes earlier on ⑥.
j – Arrives 2139 on Ⓐ.
r – Arrives 1639.
t – Arrives 4–5 minutes earlier on Ⓐ.
v – Arrives 2208 on Ⓐ.

SR 2nd class GLASGOW and KILMARNOCK - STRANRAER 215

km		⚒	⚒	Ⓐ	⑥	⑥	Ⓐ	⚒	⑦	⚒	⚒	⑦	⚒	⚒	⑦	⚒	⚒	⑦	Ⓐ	⑥	⚒	⚒	⑦	⑥	Ⓐ	⑥	Ⓐ
0	**Glasgow** Central . **214/6** d.	...	...	...	...	0807	0809	...	...	...	...	...	...	...	...	...	...	...	1711	1713	...	...	...	...	...	...	...
39	**Kilmarnock** .... **214** a.	...	...	...	...	0846	0847	...	...	...	...	...	...	...	...	...	...	...	1752	1751	...	...	...	...	...	...	...
	Kilmarnock .... d.	...	...	0803	0803	0855	0854	1003	...	...	1204	...	1404	...	...	1604	1702	...	1803	1803	1903	...	...	2111	2111	...	...
56	Troon .... **216** d.	...	...	0815	0815	0907	0906	1017	...	...	1217	...	1417	...	...	1617	1714	...	1816	1816	1915	...	...	2123	2123	...	...
61	Prestwick Town .... d.	...	...	0820	0821	0912	0911	|	...	...	|	...	1422	...	...	1622	1720	...	1821	1821	|	...	...	|	|	...	...
66	**Ayr** 🚌 ⊠ .... **216** a.	...	...	0828	0829	0920	0919	1028	...	...	1226	...	1428	...	...	1628	1729	...	1829	1827	1927	...	...	2134	2136	...	...
	Ayr .... d.	0620	0729	0830	0831	...	...	1030	1106	1136	1228	1305	1430	1535	1506	1630	1732	1805	1831	1829	...	2026	1927	2136	2138	2232	2256
100	Girvan .... d.	0647	0800f	0856	0857	...	...	1057	1136f	1203	1254	1336f	1456	1602	1536f	1656	1803f	1835f	1857	1855	...	2053	1953	2204	2206	2258	2322
120	Barrhill .... d.	...	0819	...	...	...	...	...	1156	1222	...	1356	...	1621	1555	...	1823	1854	...	...	...	...	2017f	2223	2225	...	...
162	**Stranraer** .... a.	...	0855	...	...	...	...	...	1231	1257	...	1431	...	1656	1631	...	1857	1930	...	...	...	...	2053	2258	2300	...	...

	⑥	Ⓐ	⑥	Ⓐ		⚒	⚒	⚒	⑦	⑥	Ⓐ	⑦	⚒		⚒	⑦	⚒	⑥	Ⓐ	⑦	⚒	Ⓐ	⑥	⑦	⚒	⑥	Ⓐ
Stranraer .... d.	...	...	0704	0704	...	...	0900	...	1041	...	...	1241	1305	...	...	1441	...	1707	1707	1740	...	1908	1908	1940	...	...	...
Barrhill .... d.	...	...	0738	0738	...	...	0934	...	1116	...	...	1316	1339	...	...	1515	...	1742	1742	1814	...	1942	1942	2015	...	...	...
Girvan .... d.	0651	0652	0758	0759	...	0901	0952	1102	1134	1259	1259	1334	1357	...	1501	1534	1701	1800	1800	1833	1903	2000	2000	2033	2057	2303	2327
Ayr .... a.	0719	0719	0828	0827	...	0929	1020	1129	1202	1326	1326	1410	1426	...	1528	1601	1728	1828	1834	1901	1930	2032	2029	2101	2125	2330	2354
Ayr 🚌 ⊠ .... **216** d.	0720	0721	0830	0829	...	0930	...	...	...	1328	1328	...	...	...	...	...	1730	...	...	...	...	2034	2031	...	...	...	...
Prestwick Town .... d.	0725	0726	0835	0834	...	|	...	...	...	|	|	...	...	...	...	...	1735	...	...	...	...	2039	2036	...	...	...	...
Troon .... **216** d.	0730	0731	0840	0839	...	0939	...	...	...	1336	1337	...	...	...	...	...	1740	...	...	...	...	2044	2041	...	...	...	...
Kilmarnock .... a.	0745	0745	0854	0853	...	0954	...	...	...	1351	1352	...	...	...	...	...	1755	...	...	...	...	2058	2055	...	...	...	...
Kilmarnock .... **214** d.	...	...	0859	0858	...	...	...	...	...	...	...	...	...	...	...	...	...	...	...	...	...	...	...	...	...	...	...
Glasgow Central .. **214/6** a.	...	...	0936	0939	...	...	...	...	...	...	...	...	...	...	...	...	...	...	...	...	...	...	...	...	...	...	...

f – Arrives 4–5 minutes earlier.

⊠ – 🚌 connections operate between Ayr station and Cairnryan ferry port for pre-booked Rail & Sail ticket holders (see www.stenaline.co.uk/rail). For ⛴ Cairnryan - Belfast timings, see Table **2002**.

SR GLASGOW - AYR, ARDROSSAN and LARGS 216

Typical off-peak journey time in hours and minutes
READ DOWN ↓ READ UP ↑

Journey times may be extended during peak hours on Ⓐ (0600 - 0900 and 1600 - 1900) and also at weekends.
The longest journey time by any train is noted in the table heading.

GLASGOW CENTRAL - AYR — Longest journey: 1 hour 04 minutes SR

km	↓		↑
0	0h00	**Glasgow** Central ......d.	0h49
12	0h10	Paisley Gilmour St .....d.	0h40
43	0h25	Kilwinning ....d.	0h22
48	0h29	Irvine ....d.	0h18
56	0h37	Troon..........................d.	0h11
61	0h41	Prestwick Airport ✈ ..d.	0h07
67	0h52	**Ayr**.............................a.	0h00

From Glasgow Central:
On ⚒ at 0015 ②–⑥, 0600 and every 30 minutes until 2330.
On ⑦ at 0900 and every 30 minutes until 1900, 2000, 2100, 2200, 2300.
From Ayr:
On ⚒ at 0515, 0536, 0601⑥, 0603Ⓐ, 0635, 0705, 0727Ⓐ, 0737, 0756Ⓐ, 0805 and every 30 minutes until 1735, 1751, 1805, 1835⑥, 1839Ⓐ, 1905, 1935, 2003⑥, 2005Ⓐ, 2035⑥, 2038Ⓐ, 2105, 2133Ⓐ, 2135⑥, 2205Ⓐ, 2207⑥, 2233, 2305.
On ⑦ at 0845 and every 30 minutes until 1945, 2045, 2145, 2300.

GLASGOW CENTRAL - ARDROSSAN - LARGS — Longest journey: 1 hour 10 minutes SR

km	↓		↑
0	0h00	**Glasgow** Central ......d.	0h59
12	0h10	Paisley Gilmour St .....d.	0h46
43	0h29	Kilwinning ....d.	0h25
50	0h38	**Ardrossan** Sth Beach ..d.	0h17
64	0h49	Fairlie ....d.	0h05
69	0h56	**Largs** ....a.	0h00

From Glasgow Central:
On ⚒ at 0645 and hourly until 1945, 2045⑥, 2047Ⓐ, 2145, 2245, 2314 ①–④⑥, 2345 ⑤. Also 1717Ⓐ.
On ⑦ at 0940 and hourly until 2140, 2242.
From Largs:
On ⚒ at 0635, 0728 Ⓐ, 0807⑥, 0810Ⓐ, 0907 and hourly until 1707, 1809⑥, 1816Ⓐ, 1907, 2007, 2107Ⓐ, 2110⑥, 2207, 2253.
On ⑦ at 0854, 0954, 1054, 1154, 1253, 1354 and hourly until 2154, 2300.

SR 2nd class; most trains convey 🍸 GLASGOW - OBAN, FORT WILLIAM and MALLAIG 218

km		⚒	⚒	⚒A	Ba	⚒	Ⓐ	⑥	⑦g	⑦	⑦	Bc	⚒	⑦	⑦	⚒	⚒	Ⓐ	⚒		⑦	⑦	⚒	Ⓐ	⑥
	Edinburgh **220** .... d.	...	...	0450	...	...	...	...	...	...	...	...	...	...	...	...	...	...	...	...	...	...	...	...	...
0	**Glasgow** Queen Street... d.	...	0520	0548‡	...	0821	0821	0821	0903	...	0956	...	1036	1220	1220	1222	1222	...	1634	...	1821	1821	1823	1823	1823
16	Dalmuir .... d.	...	0538	0606	...	0841	0841	0841	0926	...	1016	...	1058	1235	1235	|	|	...	1658	...	1836	1836	1842	1842	1842
26	Dumbarton Central .... d.	...	0547	0617	...	0852	0852	0852	0935	...	1026	...	1108	1246	1246	1253	1253	...	1707	...	1845	1845	1852	1852	1852
40	Helensburgh Upper .... d.	...	0603	0633	...	0907	0907	0907	0950	...	1041	...	1127	1306	1306	1308	1308	...	1722	...	1905f	1905f	1907	1907	1907
51	Garelochhead .... d.	...	0614	0647	...	0918	0918	0918	1001	...	1052	...	1140	1318	1318	1320	1320	...	1733	...	1916	1916	1918	1918	1918
68	Arrochar & Tarbet .... d.	...	0634	0709	...	0938	0938	0938	1021	...	1112	...	1200	1338	1338	1340	1340	...	1757f	...	1936	1936	1938	1938	1938
81	Ardlui .... d.	...	0652f	0725x	...	0951	0951	0951	1034	...	1128	...	1214	1356h	1356h	1356	1356	...	1810	...	1951	1951	1953	1953	1953
95	**Crianlarich** .... a.	...	0708	0745	...	1007	1007	1007	1050	...	1145	...	1230	1412	1412	1412	1412	...	1826	...	2007	2007	2009	2009	2009
95	**Crianlarich** .... d.	...	0718	0748	...	1015	1021	1021	1054	...	1147	...	1233	1418	1424	1418	1424	...	1829	...	2014	2020	2014	2020	2020
	Dalmally .... d.	...	0751f	|	...	1042	|	|	1120	...	1215	...	1259	1444	|	1444	|	1705	1855	...	2040	|	2040	|	|
	Taynuilt .... d.	...	0811	|	...	1103	|	|	1141	...	1239	...	1320	1504	|	1505	|	1724	1919	...	2100	|	2103	|	|
162	**Oban** .... a.	...	0835	|	...	1127	|	|	1205	...	1304	...	1343	1527	|	1528	|	1747	1944	...	2124	|	2127	|	|
115	Bridge of Orchy .... d.	...	...	0818	...	...	1048	1048	...	...	...	...	...	...	1449	...	1449	...	...	...	...	2047	...	2045	2045
140	Rannoch .... d.	...	...	0845	...	...	1109	1109	...	...	...	...	...	...	1512	...	1512	...	...	...	...	2108	...	2108	2108
177	Roy Bridge .... d.	...	...	0931x	...	...	1148	1148	...	...	...	...	...	...	1550	...	1550	...	...	...	...	2146	...	2146	2146
183	Spean Bridge .... d.	...	...	0939	...	...	1159f	1154	...	...	...	...	...	...	1556	...	1556	...	...	...	...	2153	...	2154	2153
197	**Fort William** .... a.	...	...	1000	...	...	1212	1207	...	...	...	...	...	...	1609	...	1609	...	...	...	...	2206	...	2209	2206
197	**Fort William** .... d.	0815	...	...	1015	...	1218	1219	...	1212	...	1250	...	...	1619	...	1619	...	...	...	...	2214	...	2212	2212
223	Glenfinnan .... d.	0849	...	...	|	...	1251	1246	...	1246	...	|	...	...	1655	...	1655	...	...	...	...	2247	...	2247	2246
251	Arisaig .... d.	0922	...	...	|	...	1324	1319	...	1319	...	|	...	...	1728	...	1728	...	...	...	...	2320	...	2320	2319
259	Morar .... d.	0931	...	...	|	...	1333	1328	...	1327	...	|	...	...	1736	...	1736	...	...	...	...	2328	...	2328	2327
264	**Mallaig** .... a.	0938	...	...	1230	...	1340	1335	...	1338	...	1516	...	...	1743	...	1743	...	...	...	...	2339	...	2339	2338

	⚒	⚒	Ⓐ	⑥	⑦	⑦	⚒	⚒	Ⓐ	Ba	⑦	⑥	Ⓐ		⑦g	⑦	⑦	⚒	⚒	⑦A	Bc	⑦	⚒	⚒	ⒶA
Mallaig .... d.	...	0603	...	...	...	1006	1010	...	...	1410	...	...	...	...	...	1601	...	1605	...	...	1700	1815	1815	...	...
Morar .... d.	...	0614	...	...	...	1017	1017	...	...	|	...	...	...	...	...	1612	...	1612	...	...	|	1822	1822	...	...
Arisaig .... d.	...	0623	...	...	...	1027	1027	...	...	|	...	...	...	...	...	1622	...	1622	...	...	|	1832	1832	...	...
Glenfinnan .... d.	...	0655	...	...	...	1100	1101	...	...	|	...	...	...	...	...	1654	...	1654	...	...	|	1904	1904	...	...
Fort William .... a.	...	0727	...	...	...	1134	1135	...	...	1617	...	...	...	...	...	1728	...	1728	...	...	1908	1939	1939	...	...
Fort William .... d.	...	0744	...	...	...	1141	1141	...	...	...	...	...	...	...	...	1737	...	1737	...	1900	...	...	...	...	1950
Spean Bridge .... d.	...	0757	...	...	...	1157	1157	...	...	...	...	...	...	...	...	1751	...	1751	...	1918	...	...	...	...	2009
Roy Bridge .... d.	...	0804	...	...	...	1204	1204	...	...	...	...	...	...	...	...	1757	...	1757	...	1926x	...	...	...	...	2017x
Rannoch .... d.	...	0847f	...	...	...	1243	1243	...	...	...	...	...	...	...	...	1838	...	1838	...	2015	...	...	...	...	2108
Bridge of Orchy .... d.	...	0907	...	...	...	1304	1304	...	...	...	...	...	...	...	...	1858	...	1858t	...	2046	...	...	...	...	2136
Oban .... d.	0517	|	0856	0856	1211	|	|	1211	1441	...	1611	1611	1611	...	1704	|	1811	|	1811	|	...	...	...	2039	|
Taynuilt .... d.	0544	|	0919	0919	1238	|	|	1235	1506	...	1638	1634	1634	...	1732	|	1833	|	1833	|	...	...	...	2102	|
Dalmally .... d.	0603	|	0940	0940	1259	|	|	1300f	1526	...	1658	1654	1654	...	1755	|	1856	|	1856	|	...	...	...	2121	|
Crianlarich .... a.	0631	0931	1008	1008	1326	1334	1329	1332	1554	...	1726	1722	...	...	1823	1922	1927	1923t	1927t	2116	...	...	...	2149	2207
Crianlarich .... d.	0633	0933	1014	1014	1337	1337	1339	1339	1556	...	1727	1724	...	...	1824	1932	1932	1936	1936	2117	...	...	...	2149	2208
Ardlui .... d.	0651	0952	1029	1029	1355	1355	1355	1355	1611	...	1743	1742	...	...	1841	1952	1952	1954	1954	2138x	...	...	...	2205	2228x
Arrochar & Tarbet .... d.	0710f	1006	1043	1043	1409	1409	1409	1409	1627	...	1757	1756	...	...	1855	2006	2006	2008	2008	2156	...	...	...	2219	2244
Garelochhead .... d.	0730	1032f	1104	1104	1429	1429	1431	1431	1649	...	1819	1818	...	...	1917	2026	2026	2028	2028	2222	...	...	...	2239	2310
Helensburgh Upper .... d.	0742	1044	1117	1117	1440	1440	1444	1444	1700	...	1831	1830	...	...	1930	2040	2040	2039	2039	2238	...	...	...	2250	2323
Dumbarton Central .... d.	0759	1059	1130	1130	1456	1456	1502	1502	1713	...	1847	1844	...	...	1944	2054	2054	2053	2053	2254	...	...	...	2304	2338
Dalmuir .... d.	|	1109	1140	1140	1507	1507	1512	1512	1724	...	1858	1854	...	...	1956s	2104	2104	|	|	2306	...	...	...	2313	2351
Glasgow Queen Street... a.	0842	1133	1156	1200	1526	1526	1534	1534	1744	...	1920	1919	...	...	2014	2120	2120	2125	2125	2330¶	...	...	...	2332	0015¶
Edinburgh **220** .... a.	...	...	...	...	...	...	...	...	...	...	...	...	...	...	...	...	...	...	...	0024	...	...	...	...	0111

A – 🅁. 🛏2 (limited accommodation), 🛏 1, 2 cl. and ✕ London Euston - Fort William and v.v. (Table **161**).
B – THE JACOBITE – 🚂. 🅁. National Rail tickets **not** valid. To book ✆ 0333 996 6720 or visit www.westcoastrailways.co.uk

a – Apr. 7 - Oct. 24 §.
c – May 5 - Sept. 26 §.
f – Arrives 5–7 minutes earlier.
g – Until Oct. 19.
h – Arrives 1351.

t – 4 minutes later on ⑥.
x – Calls on request.
‡ – Low level platforms. Calls to pick up only.
¶ – Low-level platforms. Calls to set down only.
§ – No service Sept. 1– 5.

219 SCOTTISH ISLAND FERRIES

Caledonian MacBrayne Ltd operates numerous ferry services linking the Western Isles of Scotland to the mainland and to each other. Principal routes – some of which are seasonal – are listed below (see also the map on page **90**). Service frequencies, sailing-times and reservations: ✆ +44 (0)800 066 5000. www.calmac.co.uk

Ardrossan – Brodick (Arran)
Barra – Eriskay
Claonaig – Lochranza (Arran)
Colintraive – Rhubodach (Bute)
Fionnphort – Iona (Iona)
Gallanach - Kerrera (Kerrera)
Gourock - Kilcreggan
Gourock - Dunoon
Kennacraig – Port Ellen (Islay)
Largs – Cumbrae (Cumbrae)
Leverburgh (Harris) – Berneray (North Uist)
Lochaline – Fishnish (Mull)
Mallaig – Armadale (Skye)
Mallaig – Eigg, Muck, Rum and Canna
Mallaig – Lochboisdale (South Uist)
Oban – Castlebay (Barra)
Oban – Coll and Tiree
Oban – Colonsay, Port Askaig (Islay) and Kennacraig
Oban – Craignure (Mull)
Oban – Lismore
Portavadie (Cowal & Kintyre) – Tarbert (Loch Fyne)
Sconser (Skye) – Raasay
Tayinloan – Gigha
Troon – Brodick (Arran)
Tobermory (Mull) – Kilchoan
Uig (Skye) – Lochmaddy (North Uist)
Uig (Skye) – Tarbert (Harris)
Ullapool – Stornoway (Lewis)
Wemyss Bay – Rothesay (Bute)

220 EDINBURGH - GLASGOW

GR, SR, XC

EDINBURGH - FALKIRK - GLASGOW QUEEN STREET

km		⚒	⚒	⚒	⚒	Ⓐ	⚒	Ⓐ	⚒	Ⓐ	⑥	⚒	Ⓐ	⚒	Ⓐ	⑥	⚒	⑥	⚒	⑥	☆	⑥	⚒	⑥	⚒	⑥	Ⓐ
0	**Edinburgh** Waverley ... d.	⚒	0600	0645	0715	0730	0745	0800	0815	0830	0830	0845	0900	0915	0930	0930	0945	1000	1015	1030	and at	1530	1545	1600	1615	1630	1630
2	Haymarket ... d.		0604	0651	0719	0734	0750	0805	0821	0835	0835	0851	0906	0921	0935	0935	0950	1004	1021	1034	the same	1534	1549	1604	1621	1634	1634
28	Linlithgow ... d.		0618	0704	0732	|	0804	|	0834	|	0851	0906	|	0935	|	0949	1003	1017	1035	1047	minutes	1548	1604	1618	1634	1647	|
41	Falkirk High ... d.		0628	0714	0742	0756	0814	0829	0844	0854	0901	0916	0924	0945	0958	0959	1013	1027	1045	1057	past each	1558	1614	1627	1644	1658	1652
76	**Glasgow** Queen Street a.		0649	0737	0808	0822	0838	0853	0908	0916	0919	0938	0946	1007	1021	1018	1035	1045	1107	1118	hour until	1615	1638	1645	1707	1718	1714

	⚒	Ⓐ	⑥	⚒	Ⓐ	⚒	Ⓐ	⚒	Ⓐ	⚒	⚒	☆	⚒	⑤⑥	①–④		⑦	⑦	⑦	⑦	⑦	⑦	⑦	☆⊡	⑦	⑦
Edinburgh Waverley .... d.	1645	1700	1700	1715	1730	1745	1800	1815	1830	1845	1915	and at	2315	2345	2345	⑦	0800	0830	0900	0930	1000	1030	1100	and at	2300	2330
Haymarket ... d.	1650	1706	1706	1719	1735	1750	1806	1819	1838	1850	1920	the same	2320	2350	2350		0804	0834	0904	0936	1004	1034	1104	the same	2304	2334
Linlithgow ... d.	1706	|	1720	1733	|	1806	|	1833	|	1904	1933	minutes	2333	0004	0009		0824	0854	0924	0955	1022	1048	1117	minutes	2317	2347
Falkirk High ... d.	1716	1724	1730	1743	1755	1816	1825	1843	1856	1914	1943	past each	2345	0013	0020		0834	0902	0934	1004	1032	1055	1127	past each	2327	2357
Glasgow Queen Street. a.	1739	1748	1747	1808	1818	1838	1848	1906	1918	1936	2004	hour until	0012	0038	0043		0856	0924	0954	1024	1053	1115	1148	hour until	2348	0019

		⚒	⚒	⚒	Ⓐ	⑥	Ⓐ	Ⓐ	⚒	Ⓐ	⚒	Ⓐ	⑥	Ⓐ	⑥	⑥	Ⓐ	⚒	⑥	⚒	⑥	⚒	☆	⚒	⑥	⚒	⑥
Glasgow Queen Street. d.	⚒	0600	0645	0715	0730	0745	0745	0800	0815	0830	0845	0900	0900	0915	0915	0930	0930	0945	1000	1015	1030	1045	and at	1545	1600	1615	1630
Falkirk High ... d.		0619	0705	0735	0757	0804	0805	0823	0836	0854	0905	0922	0918	0936	0936	0951	0955	1007	1017	1035	1047	1105	the same	1604	1617	1634	1649
Linlithgow ... d.		0629	0715	0745	|	0814	0815	|	0845	|	0917	|	0927	0946	0945	1001	|	1017	1026	1045	1101	1115	minutes	1614	1627	1645	1658
Haymarket ... ▽ a.		0642	0733	0800	0817	0828	0832	0847	0859	0919	0930	0940	0940	0959	1004	1017	1021	1033	1042	1102	1114	1128	past each	1632	1641	1702v	1711
Edinburgh Waverley .... a.		0648	0738	0807	0822	0833	0837	0853	0905	0924	0935	0945	0945	1004	1009	1023	1026	1039	1048	1108	1119	1134	hour until	1637	1648	1707v	1716

	Ⓐ	⚒	⑥	Ⓐ	⚒	Ⓐ	⚒	Ⓐ	⚒	Ⓐ	⚒	⚒	☆	⚒	⚒		⑦	⑦	⑦	⑦	⑦	⑦	⑦	★⊙	⑦	⑦
Glasgow Queen Street. d.	1630	1645	1700	1700	1715	1730	1745	1800	1815	1830	1845	1915	and at	2315	2345	⑦	0756	0830	0900	0930	1000	1030	1100	and at	2300	2330
Falkirk High ... d.	1655	1706	1719	1725	1736	1752	1806	1822	1834	1854	1904	1934	the same	2334	0004		0816	0849	0919	0950	1020	1050	1120	the same	2320	2350
Linlithgow ... d.	|	1715	1729	|	1745	|	1816	|	1844	|	1916	1946	minutes	2344	0014		0826	0859	0927	0959	1030	1059	1127	minutes	2327	0001
Haymarket ... ▽ a.	1719	1730	1748	1754	1801	1818	1833	1850	1858	1917	1930	2001	past each	0002f	0028		0848	0919	0946	1017	1048	1112	1145	past each	2340	0016
Edinburgh Waverley .... a.	1724	1735	1753	1759	1806	1824	1839	1855	1903	1922	1935	2007	hour until	0007f	0036		0853	0924	0952	1022	1053	1117	1150	hour until	2345	0021

EDINBURGH - MOTHERWELL - GLASGOW CENTRAL

km			⑥	Ⓐ	Ⓐ 2	⑥ 2	⚒ 2	⑥ 2	Ⓐ 2	⑥ 2	Ⓐ 2	⑥ 2	Ⓐ 2	Ⓐ 2	⑥ 2	Ⓐ 2	⑥ 2	⑥ A	Ⓐ A	⚒ A	Ⓐ 2	⑥ 2		⑦ A
0	**Edinburgh** Waverley ... d.	⚒	0625	0625	0741	0742	1020	1150	1159	1349	1351	1550	1549	1749	1749	1829	1831	2013	2019	2113	2312	2321	⑦	1913
2	Haymarket ... d.		0629	|	0746	0746	1024	1154	1204	1353	1355	1554	1554	1753	1754	1834	1835	2017	2024	2117	2316	2326		1918
71	Motherwell ... a.		0704	0703	0833	0834	1103	1305	1303	1440	1440	1638	1639	1850	1906	1933	1935	2055	2101	2156	0022	0023		1953
92	**Glasgow** Central ... a.		0724	0725	0854	0857	1127	1324	1326	1502	1502	1657	1703	1914	1931	1956	1957	2113	2122	2213	...	...		2015

		Ⓐ 2	⑥ 2	⚒ A	⑥ 2	Ⓐ 2	⚒ A	⑥ 2		Ⓐ 2	Ⓐ 2	⑥ 2	⑥ 2	Ⓐ 2		⑥ 2	Ⓐ 2	Ⓐ 2	⑥ 2			⑦ A		⑦
Glasgow Central ... d.	⚒	...	...	0648	0704	0705	0748	0940	...	0943	1145	1146	1340	1342	...	1534	1531	1945	1947	...	⑦	1055	...	2100
Motherwell ... d.		0548	0559	0705	0721	0721	0804	1000	...	1005	1202	1202	1400	1403	...	1558	1556	2009	2009	...		1112	...	2119
Haymarket ... a.		0701	0707	0746	0821	0821	0851	1046	...	1055	1254	1254	1454	1502	...	1658	1702	2056	2056	...		1150	...	2156
Edinburgh Waverley ... a.		0707	0713	0752	0826	0826	0856	1051	...	1100	1301	1259	1500	1508	...	1704	1708	2101	2101	...		1155	...	2201

☛ Trains also run **Edinburgh Waverley - Bathgate - Airdrie - Glasgow Queen Street Low Level** (up to four trains per hour on Ⓐ; two per hour on ⑥⑦).
☛ Trains also run **Edinburgh Waverley - Shotts - Glasgow Central** (up to two trains per hour on ⚒ [one limited stop; one all stations]; every two hours on ⑦).

A – 12 and 🍷 Glasgow - Edinburgh - Plymouth and v.v. (Tables **110** and **119**).
f – Arrives 4 minutes earlier on ⑤⑥.
r – ⑥ only.
t – Departs 3 minutes later on Ⓐ.
v – Arrives 4 minutes earlier on Ⓐ.
☆ – Timings may vary by ± 4 minutes.
★ – Timings may vary by ± 5 minutes.
▽ – Trains call to set down only.
⊙ – The 1230, 1530 and 1730 from Glasgow arrive Haymarket 1318, 1618 and 1817 and Edinburgh 1323, 1623 and 1823 respectively. The 1230 from Glasgow departs Linlithgow 1305.
⊡ – The 1530 and 1728 from Edinburgh arrive Glasgow 1620 and 1820 respectively.

222 GLASGOW and EDINBURGH - DUNDEE - ABERDEEN

GR, SR, XC

🍷 conveyed on most trains with first class seating.

km		⚒ 2G	⑥ A	Ⓐ A	⚒ E	Ⓐ	⚒	⚒ 2	⚒	⚒ 2	⚒	⑥ 2	⚒ 2	⚒	⚒ 2	⚒	⚒ 2	Ⓐ 2	⑥ 2	⚒ 2	⚒	⚒	⚒ 2	⑦ ✗	⚒	⚒ 2	⑦	⑦
0	**Edinburgh** Waverley. **223/4** d.	...	...	...	...	...	0530	...	...	0559	0630	...	0655	0730	...	...	...	0758	0800	...	0829	...	0900	0910	0930	...	0935	...
2	Haymarket ... **223/4** d.	...	...	...	...	...	0535	...	...	0603	0635	...	0659	0735	...	...	...	0803	0804	...	0836	...	0904	0915	0935	...	0939	...
42	Kirkcaldy ... **223** d.	...	0517	...	...	...	0604	...	...	0640	0702	...	0736	|	...	...	...	0835	0837	...	|	...	0939	0950	|	...	1014	...
54	Markinch ... **223** d.	...	|	...	...	...	0613	...	...	0650	|	...	0745	|	...	...	...	0844	0846	...	|	...	0948	|	|	...	1023	...
82	Leuchars ... △ d.	...	0545	...	...	...	0634	...	...	0710	0727	...	0805	0826	...	...	...	0907	0917	...	0929	...	1009	1015	1024	...	1044	...
	Glasgow Queen St.. **223** d.	...	|	...	...	...	|	...	0551	|	|	0612	|	|	0710	0741	...	|	|	0810	|	0840	|	|	|	0908	|	0933
	Stirling ... **223/4** d.	...	|	...	...	...	|	...	0621	|	|	0642	|	|	0742	0809	...	|	|	0838	|	0909	|	|	|	0939	|	1010
	Perth ... **223** d.	...	|	...	0600	...	|	0638	0657	|	|	0726f	|	|	0823	0847f	...	|	|	0914	|	0950	|	|	|	1021	|	1049
95	**Dundee** ... d.	0545	0605	0611	0626	0642	0649	0706f	0723	0728	0742	0751	0820	0843	0847	0909	0929	0921	0932	0939	0948	1012	1026	1030	1041	1046	1100	1111
112	Carnoustie ... d.	0602	0623	0626	0638	|	0703	0722	|	...	0754	...	...	0901	...	|	0946	...	...	...	|	1030	...	|	|	...	|	1126
123	Arbroath ... d.	0609	0631	0633	0646	|	0712	0731	0743	...	0801	...	...	0909	...	0925	0955	...	...	...	1006	1037	...	1047	1059	...	1116	1134
145	Montrose ... d.	0624	0649	0650	0703	|	0728	...	0758	...	0817	...	...	0927	...	0939	...	...	...	...	1020	1051	...	1103	1114	...	1131	1149
184	Stonehaven ... d.	0650	0715	0715	0729	|	0752	...	0822	...	0838	...	...	0948	...	1003	...	...	...	...	1041	|	...	1127	1135	...	1153	1213
210	**Aberdeen** ... a.	0711	0740	0750	0751	0757	0812	...	0842	...	0856	...	...	1006	...	1023	...	...	...	...	1059	1127	...	1147	1152	...	1214	1234

	⚒	⚒ 2	⚒ 2	⚒ C	⚒ 2	⚒	⑦	⑦	⚒ 2	⚒	⚒ 2	⑦ 2	⚒	⑦	⚒ 2	⚒ 2	⚒ 2	⑦	⚒	⑦	⚒ 2	⚒	⚒ 2	⑦ 2	⚒	⑦	⑥ 2	Ⓐ 2
Edinburgh Waverley .. **223/4** d.	...	...	0957	1027	...	...	...	1050	1100	1130	...	1132	...	...	...	1158	...	1238	...	...	1257	1328	...	1336	...	...	1400	1359
Haymarket ... **223/4** d.	...	...	1003	1033	...	...	...	1054	1104	1135	...	1136	...	...	...	1202	...	1243	...	...	1301	1333	...	1340	...	...	1405	1403
Kirkcaldy ... **223** d.	...	...	1035	1105	...	...	...	1123	1136	|	...	1208	...	...	...	1238	...	1312	...	...	1339	|	...	1412	...	...	1437	1443
Markinch ... **223** d.	...	...	1046	|	...	...	...	|	1145	|	...	1217	...	...	...	1247	...	|	...	...	1347	|	...	1421	...	...	1446	1452
Leuchars ... △ d.	...	...	1106	1130	...	...	...	1148	1206	1224	...	1239	...	...	...	1307	...	1337	...	...	1408	1428	...	1443	...	...	1506	1513
Glasgow Queen St... **223** d.	0940	...	|	|	1010	1041	1045	|	|	|	1111	|	1141	1145	...	|	1211	|	1240	1243	|	|	1310	|	1340	1345	|	|
Stirling ... **223/4** d.	1009	...	|	|	1042	1108	1112	|	|	|	1141	|	1208	1212	...	|	1242	|	1307	1310	|	|	1341	|	1408	1412	|	|
Perth ... **223** d.	1046a	...	|	|	1122	1140	1145	|	|	|	1220	|	1241f	1247	...	|	1325	|	1337	1344	|	|	1422	|	1442f	1450	|	|
Dundee ... d.	1114f	1124	1123	1146	1149	1203	1214c	1214r	1222	1239	1245	1255	1303	1310	1324	1322	1349	1353	1402	1408	1423	1444	1447	1457	1514	1512	1522	1527
Carnoustie ... d.	|	1141	...	|	...	1221	|	|	...	|	...	...	|	|	1338	...	...	|	1420	|	...	|	...	...	|	1524	...	...
Arbroath ... d.	1130	1149	...	1203	...	1229	1230	1230	...	1256	...	...	1319	1327	1346	...	...	1409	1427	1425	...	1501	...	...	1536	1531	...	...
Montrose ... d.	1148	...	...	1219	...	1243	1245	1245	...	|	...	...	1333	1341	...	...	...	1423	1445	1439	...	|	...	...	1550	1545	...	...
Stonehaven ... d.	|	...	...	1243	...	1307	1307	1307	...	1330	...	...	|	1404	...	...	...	1447	|	1500	...	1539	...	...	|	1606	...	...
Aberdeen ... a.	1240t	...	...	1302	...	1328	1326	1326	...	1350	...	...	1409	1422	...	...	...	1505	1521	1517	...	1557	...	...	1626	1627	...	...

A – Ⓡ. 🛏 1,2 class and 2 London Euston - Aberdeen (departs London previous day). Train stops to set down only. See also Table **161**.
C – From stations in Table **180**.
E – To Inverurie (Table **225**).
G – To Inverness (Table **225**).
a – Arrives 1037.
c – Arrives 1207.
f – Arrives 5–6 minutes earlier.
r – Arrives 1202.
s – Calls to set down only.
t – Arrives 1225 on ⑥.
△ – Frequent 🚌 connections available to / from **St Andrews.** Journey 10 minutes. Operator: Stagecoach (routes 42A, 99).

GLASGOW and EDINBURGH - DUNDEE - ABERDEEN

🍷 conveyed on most trains with first class seating.

	⚒	⚒	⚒	⑦	⚒	⑦	⚒	Ⓐ	⑥	⚒	⑦	⚒	⑦	⚒	⚒	⑦	⚒	⚒	⑦	⚒	⑥	Ⓐ	⑦	Ⓐ	⑥	⑦	⚒	⚒
	2	C	2	C	G		2			2	2			2	2			2			2	2				2	2	
Edinburgh ‡ .. **223/4** d.	...	1430	...	1434	...	...	1500	1530	1530	...	1534	...	...	...	1559	1607	1629	...	...	...	1657	1657	1705	1730	1734	1735	...	...
Haymarket ..... **223/4** d.	...	1435	...	1439	...	...	1504	1535	1535	...	1538	...	...	...	1604	1611	1635**u**	...	...	...	1701	1701	1710	1738	1739	1739	...	...
Kirkcaldy .... **223** d.	...	1507	...	1511	...	...	1537**a**	|	|	...	1610	...	...	...	1636	1642	|	...	...	...	1734	1742	1740	|	|	1811	...	...
Markinch .... **223** d.	...	|	...	|	...	...	1545**a**	|	|	...	1623	...	...	...	1645	1651	|	...	...	...	1742	1751	|	|	|	1820	...	...
Leuchars .... △ d.	...	1531	...	1536	...	...	1609	1626	1629	...	1645	...	...	...	1705	1710	1725	...	...	...	1806	1816	1805	1835	1832	1842	...	...
Glasgow § .... **223** d.	...	|	1411	|	1439	1450	|	|	|	1511	|	1539	1545	...	|	|	|	1610	1645	1638	|	|	|	|	|	|	1710	1741
Stirling .... **223/4** d.	...	|	1442	|	1507	1519	|	|	|	1541	|	1609	1612	...	|	|	|	1639	1712	1706	|	|	|	|	|	|	1739**u**	1810
Perth .... **223** d.	...	|	1524	|	1541**f**	1555	|	|	|	1628**y**	|	1643	1648	...	|	|	|	1720	1742	1746**c**	|	|	|	|	|	|	1830**c**	1845
Dundee .... d.	1532	1550	1552	1552	1604	1617	1624	1641	1644	1656	1659	1705	1710	1726	1730**e**	1725	1742	1754**f**	1805	1809	1820	1830	1820	1852	1852	1856	1859	1911
Carnoustie .... d.	1549	|	...	|	1616	|	...	|	|	...	...	|	|	1743	...	1740	|	1816	|	|	...	...	|	1907	1907	...	...	1929
Arbroath .... d.	1557	1607	...	1609	1623	1634	...	1701	1704	...	...	1722	1726	1750	...	1747	1759	1824	1821	1835	...	...	1837	1914	1914	...	...	1937
Montrose .... d.	...	1623	...	1625	1637	1649	...	1715	1718	...	...	1736	1741	1805	...	1801	1815	...	1835	1849	...	...	1851	1928	1928	...	...	1951
Stonehaven .... d.	...	1646	...	1649	|	1712	...	1737	1739	...	...	1757	1806	1831	...	1824	1841	...	1856	|	...	...	1912	1951	1951	...	...	2012
Aberdeen .... a.	...	1706	...	1710	1715	1730	...	1754	1757	...	...	1815	1825	1852	...	1842	1859	...	1918	1928	...	...	1929	2009	2009	...	...	2032

	⑦	⚒	⑤⑥	①–④	⚒	⑦	⚒	⚒	⚒	⚒	⚒	⑦	⚒	⑦	⚒	Ⓐ	⚒	⑦	⚒	⚒	⚒	⑦	⚒	⑦	⚒	Ⓐ	⚒	⑦
		2	D	D	2	C	C		2		2	2			2	C			2				2	2	2	2	2	2
Edinburgh ‡ .. **223/4** d.	...	1746	1813	1813	...	1835	1835	...	1859	1930	...	1937	...	...	1959	2031	...	2100	2100	2129	...	...	2200	2228	2300	...	...	...
Haymarket ..... **223/4** d.	...	1751	1817	1817	...	1841	1840	...	1905	1935	...	1941	...	...	2004	2036	...	2105	2104	2134	...	...	2205	2232	2304	...	...	...
Kirkcaldy .... **223** d.	...	1831	1847	1847	...	1913	1914	...	1942	|	...	2013	...	...	2036	2110	...	2134	2136	2203	...	...	2238**b**	2315	2340	...	...	...
Markinch .... **223** d.	...	1840	1856	1856	...	|	|	...	1950	|	...	2022	...	...	2045	|	...	2143	2145	|	...	...	2247**b**	2324	2348	...	...	...
Leuchars .... △ d.	...	1902	1918	1918	...	1937	1941	...	2011	2024	...	2043	...	...	2105	2139	...	2206	2205	2228	...	...	2311**b**	2345	0009	...	...	...
Glasgow § .... **223** d.	1745	|	|	|	1810	|	|	1841	|	|	1909	|	1937	1944	|	|	2040	|	|	|	2140	2145	|	|	|	2310	2335	2340
Stirling .... **223/4** d.	1814	|	|	|	1839	|	|	1908	|	|	1943	|	2005	2011	|	|	2108	|	|	|	2209	2212	|	|	|	2339	0004	0019
Perth .... **223** d.	1847	|	|	|	1926**y**	|	|	1944	|	|	2025	|	2043**y**	2049	|	|	2145	|	|	|	2246	2249	|	|	|	0019	0042	0058
Dundee .... d.	1910	1918	1935	1931	1951	1953	1958	2008	2026	2046	2049	2057	2107	2112	2120	2154	2207	2224	2224	2248	2308	2312	2331**n**	2359	0025	0044	...	...
Carnoustie .... d.	1922	...	|	...	...	|	|	2026	...	|	...	...	2125	|	...	|	2225	|	...	|	2325	2323	...	...	...	...	...	...
Arbroath .... d.	1929	...	|	...	...	2010	2015	2034	...	2102	...	...	2132	2128	...	2211	2233	2244	...	2306	2332	2331	...	...	...	...	...	...
Montrose .... d.	1944	...	|	...	...	2026	2031	2048	...	2119	...	...	2150	2142	...	2226	2247	2258	...	2327**f**	2347	2345	...	...	...	...	...	...
Stonehaven .... d.	2010	...	|	...	...	2050	2054	2112	...	|	...	...	2214	2206	...	2250	|	2318	...	2349	0012	0006	...	...	...	...	...	...
Aberdeen .... a.	2029	...	2041	...	...	2110	2113	2132	...	2155	...	...	2233	2224	...	2309	2323	2336	...	0009	0032	0023	...	...	...	...	...	...

km		⚒	⚒	⚒	⚒	⚒	⚒	⚒	Ⓐ	⑥	⑦	⚒	⚒	⚒	⚒	Ⓐ	⑥	⑦	⚒	⚒	⚒	⑦	⚒	⑥	Ⓐ	⚒	⚒	⚒
		2	2	2	2	2		2			2	2		2	G	2	2			C	2	2	D	2	2			2
0	**Aberdeen** .... d.	...	...	...	...	...	0530	...	0557	0557	...	...	0639	...	0710	...	...	...	0724	0752	...	...	0820**t**	...	...	0835	0905	...
26	Stonehaven .... d.	...	...	...	...	...	0549	...	0613	0613	...	...	0655	...	0727	...	...	...	0744	0811	...	...	0837**t**	...	...	0855	0921	...
65	Montrose .... d.	...	...	...	...	...	0613	...	0635	0635	...	...	0716	...	0747	...	...	...	0807	0833	...	...	0858**t**	...	...	0918	0941	...
87	Arbroath .... d.	...	...	...	...	0606	0627	...	0649	0649	...	...	0730	0743	0801	...	...	...	0821	0850	...	...	0914**t**	...	...	0932	0956	...
97	Carnoustie .... d.	...	...	...	...	0613	|	...	0656	0656	...	...	|	0750	|	...	...	...	0828	|	...	...	|	...	...	0939	|	...
115	**Dundee** .... d.	...	0541	0548	0631	0638	0648	0712	0715	0715	0736	0736	0752	0815	0826	0840	0840	0845	0850	0908	0915	0925	0933	0944	0948	0959	1014	1018
149	**Perth** .... **223** d.	0516	|	0614	|	...	0711	0739	|	|	|	|	0814	0842	|	|	|	0907	0912	|	0941	|	|	|	|	1021	|	1043
202	Stirling .... **223/4** d.	0554	|	0652	|	...	0754	0817	|	|	|	|	0844	0920	|	|	|	0941	0947	|	1019	|	|	|	|	1051	|	1122
249	**Glasgow** § ... **223** a.	0632	|	0724	|	...	0828	0846	|	|	|	|	0921**q**	0956	|	|	|	1015	1015	|	1054	|	|	|	|	1121	|	1157
	Leuchars .... △ d.	...	0554	...	0644	...	...	...	0727	0727	0749	0749	...	...	0838	0853	0853	...	...	0922	...	0938	0946	0957	1001	...	1026	...
	Markinch .... **223** d.	...	0617	...	0709	...	...	...	|	|	0811	0811	...	...	|	0914	0915	...	...	|	...	1000	1008	1019	1022	...	|	...
	Kirkcaldy .... **223** d.	...	0628	...	0720	...	...	...	|	|	0822	0822	...	...	|	0925	0928	...	...	0947	...	1011	1018	1030	1033	...	|	...
	Haymarket .... **223/4** a.	...	0703	...	0758	...	...	...	0830	0822	0858	0903**j**	...	...	0933	0959	1008	...	...	1019	...	1055	1048	1109	1109	...	1118	...
	Edinburgh ‡ **223/4** a.	...	0709	...	0805	...	...	...	0835	0828	0903	0909	...	...	0938	1005	1014	...	...	1025	...	1100	1054	1114	1117	...	1125	...

	⚒	⚒	⑦	⚒	⑦	⚒	⑦	⑥	Ⓐ	⑦	⚒	⑦	⚒	⚒	⚒	⑦	⚒	⚒	⑦	⚒	⑦	⚒	⚒	⑦	⚒	⑦	⑦	⚒
	2	2			C	C	2	2	2	2	2				2	D	2	2	E		C	2		2	2			
Aberdeen .... d.	...	...	0930	0944	0947	0952	...	...	...	...	...	1033	1044	1101	...	...	...	...	1132	1137	1147	...	1207	...	...	1230	1244	1245
Stonehaven .... d.	...	...	0946	|	1006	1011	...	...	...	...	...	1049	|	1117	...	...	...	...	1149	1156	1206	...	1223	...	...	1247	1304	|
Montrose .... d.	...	...	1009	1020	1028	1033	...	...	...	...	...	1109	1116	1137	...	...	...	...	1211	1221	1228	...	1245	...	...	1308	1329	1318
Arbroath .... d.	1007	...	1024	1035	1045	1050	...	...	...	...	...	1124	1131	1152	...	...	1210	...	1225	1235	1245	...	1259	...	...	1323	1344	1332
Carnoustie .... d.	1014	...	1031	|	|	|	...	...	...	...	...	|	1138	|	...	...	1217	...	|	|	|	...	|	...	...	|	1350	1339
Dundee .... d.	1031	1040	1050	1055	1104	1109	...	1115	1115	1120	1142	1142	1158	1210	1215	1222	1234	1239	1243	1253	1304	1312	1317	1320	1342	1343	1406	1359
Perth .... **223** d.	...	|	1111	1120**f**	|	|	...	1141	1141	|	|	1215**r**	1219	|	1240	|	...	|	1309**f**	1315	|	1345**y**	|	|	|	1407	|	1421
Stirling .... **223/4** d.	...	|	1146	1152	|	|	1152	1219	1227	|	|	1248	1248	|	1317	|	...	|	1344	1345	|	1423	|	|	|	1442	|	1451
Glasgow § .... **223** a.	...	|	1214	1221	|	|	|	1250	1301	|	|	1315	1321	|	1353**g**	|	...	|	1413	1415	|	1454	|	|	|	1510	|	1521
Leuchars .... △ d.	...	1053	...	...	1118	1123	|	...	...	1133	1155	...	...	1222	...	1235	...	1252	...	...	1318	...	1329	1333	1355	...	1419	...
Markinch .... **223** d.	...	1115	...	...	|	|	|	...	...	1155	1217	...	...	|	...	1257	...	1313	...	...	|	...	|	1356	1415	...	|	...
Kirkcaldy .... **223** d.	...	1126	...	...	1143	1148	|	...	...	1206	1229	...	...	|	...	1307	...	1324	...	...	1344	...	|	1406	1427	...	1448	...
Haymarket ..... **223/4** a.	...	1206**j**	...	...	1216	1219	1235	...	...	1240	1304	...	...	1317	...	1336	...	1401	...	...	1420	...	1426	1440	1504	...	1518	...
Edinburgh ‡ .. **223/4** a.	...	1213**j**	...	...	1224	1225	1240	...	...	1245	1311	...	...	1323	...	1343	...	1408	...	...	1426	...	1431	1445	1509	...	1524	...

	⚒	⚒	⚒	⚒	⑦	⚒	⑦	⚒	⚒	⑦	⚒	⑦	⚒	⚒	⚒	⑦	⑦	⚒	⚒	⚒	⚒	⚒	⑦	⚒	⚒	⑦	⚒	⚒
	2		2	2			C		2	2	2			C	2					2	2		2	2			2	2
Aberdeen .... d.	...	1311	...	...	1334	1346	1347	1359	...	...	...	1433	1435	1452	...	1508	1531	...	1535	...	...	1604	...	...	1632	1631	...	1709
Stonehaven .... d.	...	|	...	...	1350	|	1406	1415	...	...	...	1450	|	1511	...	1528	1548	...	|	...	...	1624	...	...	|	1647	...	1728
Montrose .... d.	...	1344	...	...	1410	1423	1428	1435	...	...	...	1511	1509	1533	...	1549	1612	...	1612	...	...	1648	...	...	1705	1707	...	1755
Arbroath .... d.	...	1359	1409	...	1425	1437	1445	1450	...	...	...	1526	1525	1550	...	1603	1626	...	1627	1634	...	1703	...	...	1719	1722	...	1809
Carnoustie .... d.	...	|	1416	...	|	|	|	|	...	...	...	|	1532	|	...	1610	|	...	|	1641	...	1710	...	...	1726	|	...	1816
Dundee .... d.	1414	1419	1433	1440	1443	1456	1503	1510	1515	1515	1542	1545	1553	1609	1617	1624	1644	1638	1647	1659	1707	1725	1721	1740	1748	1740	1805	1835
Perth .... **223** d.	1440	|	...	|	1505	1519	|	|	1541	|	|	1609	1615	|	1646**f**	|	1706	|	1713**f**	...	1737**f**	|	|	|	1809	1801	1834**f**	...
Stirling .... **223/4** d.	1521	|	...	|	1544	1548	|	|	1622	|	|	1643	1644**s**	|	1726	|	1740	|	1748	...	1817	|	|	|	1844	1834	1919	...
Glasgow § .... **223** a.	1555	|	...	|	1612	1621	|	|	1656	|	|	1712	1718	|	1758	|	1809	|	1822	...	1852	|	|	|	1913	1909	1952	...
Leuchars .... △ d.	...	1431	...	1453	...	...	1517	1522	...	1528	1555	...	...	1624	...	1637	...	1654	...	...	...	1737	1734	1753	...	...	...	...
Markinch .... **223** d.	...	|	...	1514	...	...	|	|	...	1551	1617	...	...	|	...	|	...	1717	...	...	...	|	1757	1817	...	...	...	...
Kirkcaldy .... **223** d.	...	|	...	1525	...	...	1543	|	...	1601	1628	...	...	1649	...	1705	...	1730	...	...	...	|	1807	1828**v**	...	...	...	...
Haymarket ..... **223/4** a.	...	1524	...	1605	...	...	1618	1618	...	1635	1709	...	...	1720	...	1735	...	1804	...	...	...	1826	1841	1908	...	...	...	...
Edinburgh ‡ .. **223/4** a.	...	1529	...	1612	...	...	1624	1625	...	1640	1714	...	...	1726	...	1740	...	1810	...	...	...	1832	1846	1913	...	...	...	...

	⑦	⚒	⚒	⚒	⚒	⑦	⑦	Ⓐ	⚒	①–④	⑦	⚒	⚒	⑦	⚒	⑦	⚒	⚒	①–④	⑦	⚒	⚒	⑤⑥	①–④	⑤⑥	⑤	⚒	⑦
		2		2	2		2	C		⑥**h**			2					2	B	B			2	2		B		2
Aberdeen .... d.	1704	...	1745	...	...	1745	...	1818	1836	...	1904	1914	...	1946	1946	2008	2005	...	2026	2036	2037	2106	...	...	2135	2143	2224	2226
Stonehaven .... d.	1720	...	1801	...	...	1801	...	1837	|	...	1921	1930	...	2006	|	2024	2025	...	2043	2053	2056	|	...	...	2152	2201	2243	2246
Montrose .... d.	1742	...	1821	...	...	1824	...	1859	1912	...	1945	1954	...	2027	2019	2047	2048	...	2106	2117	2120	2139	...	...	2213	2226	2307	2310
Arbroath .... d.	1756	...	1836	...	1845	1839	...	1916	1926	...	1959	2008	...	2041	2033	2102	2103	...	2123	2133	2134	2154	...	...	2228	2244	2322	2324
Carnoustie .... d.	|	...	|	...	1852	|	...	|	1933	...	2007	2015	...	|	2041	|	|	...	2131	2141	2141	|	...	...	|	2253	2329	2331
Dundee .... d.	1814	1847	1854	1913	1910	1858	1916	1934	1947	1952	2023	2030	2044	2103	2102	2120	2121	2149	2154	2157	2201	2212	2231	2231	2249**f**	2309	2349	2348
Perth .... **223** d.	|	|	1918	1946**y**	...	1919	|	2014**f**	|	|	|	|	|	2127**f**	2123	|	|	|	|	|	2223	|	|	|	|	|	0012**t**	0011
Stirling .... **223/4** d.	|	|	1948	2027	...	1953	|	2047	|	|	|	|	|	2203	2153	|	|	|	|	|	2253	|	|	|	|	|	...	...
Glasgow § .... **223** a.	|	|	2022	2059	...	2021	|	2115	|	|	|	|	|	2238	2222	|	|	|	|	|	2321	|	|	|	|	|	...	...
Leuchars .... △ d.	1826	1900	...	...	...	...	1929	1948	...	|	2036	2045	2057	...	...	2132	2133	2201	2212	2216	...	2224	2244	2244	|	2328	...	...
Markinch .... **223** d.	|	1921	...	...	...	...	1951	|	...	2027**p**	|	|	2119	...	...	2154	2155	2223	|	|	...	|	2305	2305	|	|	...	...
Kirkcaldy .... **223** d.	1852	1933	...	...	...	...	2002	2013	...	2038**p**	2104	|	2130	...	...	2203	2208	2234	2252	2246	...	|	2316	2317	|	2359	...	...
Haymarket ..... **223/4** a.	1921	2006	...	...	...	...	2036	2043	...	2111	2133	2144	2207	...	...	2231	2241	2312**k**	...	...	...	2327	2350	0016	2354	...	...	...
Edinburgh ‡ .. **223/4** a.	1926	2012	...	...	...	...	2041	2049	...	2117	2138	2149	2212	...	...	2239	2246	2318**z**	...	...	...	2332	2356	0021	2359	...	...	...

B – [R]. 🛏 1, 2 class and [2] Aberdeen - London Euston. Train stops to pick up only. See also Table **161**.
C – From / to stations in Table **180**.
D – From / to stations in Tables **119** and **110**.
E – From Inverurie (Table **225**).
G – To / from Inverness (Table **225**).

a – Departs 4 – 6 minutes later on Ⓐ.
b – Departs 5 – 6 minutes later on ⑥.
c – Arrives 11 – 12 minutes earlier.
e – Arrives 1719 on ⑥.
f – Arrives 5 – 7 minutes earlier.
g – Arrives 1345 on ⑥.
h – On ⑥ conveys [2] only.
j – Arrives 4 minutes earlier on ⑥.
k – Arrives 2307 on ①–④.

n – Arrives 2328 on Ⓐ.
p – ⑥ only.
q – Arrives 0914 on ⑥.
r – Arrives 1201.
s – Calls to set down only.
t – Ⓐ only.
u – Calls to pick up only.
v – Departs 1832 on ⑥.

y – Arrives 8 – 9 minutes earlier.
z – Arrives 2313 on ①–④.

△ – Frequent 🚌 connections available to / from **St Andrews**. Journey 10 minutes. Operator: Stagecoach (routes 42A, 99).
§ – **Glasgow** Queen Street.
‡ – **Edinburgh** Waverley.

222a EDINBURGH - TWEEDBANK

2nd class SR

km		⚒	⚒	⚒	⚒	Ⓐ	⚒	Ⓐ	⑥	⚒	⚒	⚒	⚒	⑥	Ⓐ	⚒	⚒	⚒	⚒	⚒	⚒	⚒	⚒	⚒	⑥	Ⓐ
0	**Edinburgh** Waverley ..d.		0610	0642	0713	0740	0811	0843	0842	0913	0942	1011	1043	1113	1111	1144	1213	1243	1310	1344	1413	1442	1511	1542	1613	1619
13	Eskbank ....d.		0632	0703	0732	0802	0833	0904	0906	0935	1004	1035	1105	1133	1135	1205	1234	1305	1334	1404	1434	1503	1534	1603	1634	1639
15	Newtongrange ....d.		0636	0707	0736	0806	0836	0907	0909	0938	1008	1039	1108	1137	1139	1208	1237	1308	1338	1408	1438	1507	1537	1607	1638	1642
53	Galashiels ....d.		0707	0738	0808	0837	0908	0939	0941	1010	1039	1110	1140	1208	1210	1240	1309	1340	1409	1439	1509	1538	1609	1638	1709	1714
57	**Tweedbank** ....a.		0712	0743	0813	0842	0914	0943	0945	1015	1045	1114	1145	1212	1214	1244	1314	1344	1413	1444	1513	1542	1613	1643	1713	1718

	⑥	Ⓐ	⚒	Ⓐ	⑥	⚒	⚒	⑥	Ⓐ	⚒	⚒	⚒	⚒	⑦	⑦	⑦	⑦	⑦	⑦	⑦	⑦	⑦		⑦	⑦	⑦
Edinburgh Waverley ... d.	1643	1645	1715	1741	1744	1816	1842	1943	1943	2042	2143	2243	2343		0912	1011	1113	1212	1314	1411	1517	1611	and hourly until	2110	2210	2311
Eskbank ....d.	1704	1706	1737	1809	1805	1838	1906	2005	2009	2103	2203	2303	0004		0932	1031	1133	1232	1334	1433	1537	1631		2130	2230	2332
Newtongrange ....d.	1707	1710	1740	1812	1808	1841	1910	2009	2012	2107	2206	2307	0007		0935	1034	1136	1235	1337	1436	1540	1635		2134	2233	2336
Galashiels ....d.	1739	1741	1812	1844	1839	1913	1941	2040	2042	2139	2238	2338	0039		1007	1106	1208	1307	1409	1508	1612	1707		2206	2305	0008
Tweedbank ....a.	1743	1745	1816	1848	1844	1918	1946	2044	2047	2143	2245	2344	0045		1011	1110	1212	1311	1413	1512	1616	1712		2210	2309	0012

	⚒	⚒	Ⓐ	⚒	⚒	⚒	⚒	⚒	⚒	⚒	⚒	⚒	⚒	⚒	Ⓐ	⑥	⚒	⚒	⚒	⚒	⚒	⚒	⑥	Ⓐ	⑥	Ⓐ
Tweedbank ....d.		0548	0618	0649	0719	0749	0819	0849	0920	0950	1021	1050	1121	1150	1221	1219	1251	1320	1351	1420	1450	1520	1549	1549	1620	1622
Galashiels ....d.		0552	0622	0653	0723	0753	0823	0853	0924	0954	1025	1054	1125	1154	1225	1223	1255	1324	1355	1424	1454	1524	1553	1553	1624	1626
Newtongrange ....d.		0622	0652	0722	0752	0823	0853	0923	0954	1024	1055	1124	1155	1224	1255	1253	1325	1354	1425	1454	1524	1554	1623	1623	1654	1657
Eskbank ....d.		0625	0655	0725	0755	0826	0856	0926	0957	1027	1058	1127	1158	1227	1258	1256	1328	1357	1428	1457	1527	1557	1626	1626	1657	1700
Edinburgh Waverley ... a.		0649	0718	0747	0817	0848	0916	0948	1026f	1050	1122	1152	1219	1250r	1317	1320	1351	1419	1449	1519	1549	1618	1648	1652	1716	1724

	⚒	⑥	Ⓐ	⑥	Ⓐ	⚒	⑥	Ⓐ	⑥	Ⓐ	⚒	Ⓐ	⑥	⚒	⑥	Ⓐ	⑦	⑦	⑦	⑦	⑦	♠	⑦	⑦	⑦	⑦
Tweedbank ....d.	1650	1721	1725	1750	1752	1823	1850	1855	1922	1925	2019	2115	2119	2219	2319	2319		0846	0946	1046	1146	and hourly until	1947	2046	2142	2248
Galashiels ....d.	1654	1725	1729	1754	1756	1827	1854	1859	1926	1929	2023	2119	2123	2223	2323	2323		0850	0950	1050	1150		1951	2050	2146	2252
Newtongrange ....d.	1724	1755	1759	1824	1827	1857	1924	1929	1955	1959	2053	2149	2153	2253	2353	2353		0920	1020	1120	1220		2021	2120	2219	2322
Eskbank ....d.	1727	1758	1802	1827	1830	1900	1927	1932	1958	2002	2056	2152	2156	2256	2356	2356		0923	1023	1123	1223		2024	2123	2223	2325
Edinburgh Waverley ... a.	1752	1818	1823	1850	1851	1919	1949	1956	2019	2028	2118	2212	2219	2320	0019	0022		0943	1044	1145	1245		2044	2144	2243	2345

f – Arrives 1018 on ⑥. r – Arrives 1246 on Ⓐ. ♠ – The 1546 from Tweedbank arr. Edinburgh 1649.

223 EDINBURGH and GLASGOW - PERTH - INVERNESS

Most Inverness trains convey 🍷 SR

km		⚒	⚒A	⚒2	⚒	⚒2	⚒	Ⓐ2	⑥2	⑦	⑥2	Ⓐ2	⚒	⚒	⚒	⑦2	⑦	⚒2	Ⓐ2	⑥2	⚒	⚒2	⚒	⚒2	⑦	⑦P	⑥2	Ⓐ2
0	**Edinburgh** Wav'ley. **222/4** d.	...	...	0635	...	0734	0837	0836	0841	0925	0936	0939	...	...	1032	1035	...	1038	1135	1139	...	1235	1332	1335	1353	...	1435	1441
2	Haymarket .... **222/4** d.	...	...	0639	...	0738	0842	0842	0845	0930	0940	0943	...	...	1037	1039	...	1042	1139	1143	...	1239	1337	1339	1359	...	1440	1445
42	Kirkcaldy .... **222** d.	...	...	0720	...	0820	|	0923	0928	|	1021	1024	...	...	|	|	...	1123	1220	1223	...	1320	|	1422	|	...	1523	1526
54	Markinch .... **222** d.	...	...	0729	...	0829	|	0932	0937	|	1030	1033	...	...	|	|	...	1135	1229	1232	...	1330	|	1431	|	...	1532	1535
	Glasgow Queen St **222** d.	...	...	|	0707	|	*0840*	|	|	*0933*	|	|	1007	1041	|	|	1111	|	|	|	1207	|	|	|	*1345*	1438	|	|
	Stirling .... **222/4** d.	...	0459	|	0734	|	0931	|	|	1022	|	|	1036	1108	1117	1123	1141	|	|	|	1236	|	1417	|	1438	1508	|	|
91	**Perth** .... **222** d.	...	0542	0805	0811	0907k	1002	1011	1011	1053	1106	1107	1116f	1137	1153f	...	1221	1209	1303	1304	1311	1410	1450	1513	1512f	1546	1613	1613
116	Dunkeld & Birnam ....d.	...	0602	...	0834f	...	1019	...	...	1110	...	...	1141r	...	1210	...	1239	...	...	...	1327	...	1507	...	1530	|	...	...
137	Pitlochry ....d.	...	0616	...	0847	...	1033	...	...	1130r	...	...	1155	...	1226	...	1253	...	...	...	1340	...	1521	...	1544	1614	...	...
148	Blair Atholl ....d.	...	0628	...	0856	...	|	...	...	1140	...	...	|	...	1236	...	|	...	...	...	|	...	1531	...	1553	|	...	...
186	Dalwhinnie ....d.	...	0659	...	0921	...	|	...	...	1205	...	...	|	...	1303	...	|	...	...	...	|	...	1556	...	1622f	|	...	...
202	Newtonmore ....d.	...	0711	...	0931	...	|	...	...	1216	...	...	|	...	1314	...	|	...	...	...	|	...	1607	...	1632	|	...	...
207	Kingussie ....d.	0647	0717	...	0940	...	1115	...	...	1221	...	...	1237	...	1319	...	1337	...	...	...	1424	...	1615	...	1637	1656	...	...
226	Aviemore .... 🚂 d.	0700	0743	...	0952	...	1129	...	...	1233	...	...	1250	...	1333	...	1349	...	...	...	1438	...	1629	...	1649	1709	...	...
237	Carrbridge ....d.	0715f	0754	...	|	...	1138	...	...	1242	...	...	|	...	1342	...	1401	...	...	...	1452f	...	|	...	1658	|	...	...
282	**Inverness** ....a.	0748	0845	...	1029	...	1206	...	...	1319	...	...	1325	...	1416	...	1429	...	...	...	1529	...	1702	...	1725	1745	...	...

	⚒	⑥2	Ⓐ2	⑦	⚒	⑥K	ⒶK	⚒2	⑦K	⚒	⚒	⚒2	⑦2	⑦P	⑦2	⚒2	⚒	⑦2	⚒	⚒	⚒2	⚒2	Ⓐ2	⑥2	⑦2	Ⓐ2	⑥2	⚒2
Edinburgh Wav'ley **222/4** d.	...	1535	1538	1552	...	1633	1633	1635	1632	...	1731	1738	1750	...	1806	1840	...	1855	...	1934	1942	2039	2135	2143	2235	2233	2243	2314v
Haymarket .... **222/4** d.	...	1539	1542	1557	...	1638	1639	1639	1637	...	1737	1742	1754	...	1810	1845	...	1859	...	1939	1946	2043	2139	2148	2240	2238	2247	2318v
Kirkcaldy .... **222** d.	...	1620	1623	|	...	|	|	1720	|	...	|	1824	1826	...	|	1925	...	|	...	|	2027	2124	2220	2230	|	2319	2328	|
Markinch .... **222** d.	...	1629	1638f	|	...	|	|	1729	|	...	|	1833	1836	...	|	1934	...	2003	...	|	2036	2133	2229	2239	|	2328	2337	0024
Glasgow Queen St **222** d.	1507	|	|	*1545*	1638	|	|	|	*1645*	1741	|	|	|	1803	|	|	1906	|	1937	|	|	|	|	|	|	|	|	|
Stirling .... **222/4** d.	1535	|	|	1637	1706	1719	1719	|	1722	1810	1820	|	|	1834	1910r	|	1937	|	2005	2019	|	|	|	|	2333	|	|	|
Perth .... **222** d.	1619a	1710	1711	1711f	1734	1754	1757f	1808	1801f	1843	1903f	1906	1905	1912	1945	2014b	2028n	2034	2035	2059	2109	2207	2306	2310	0011	0003	0008	0055
Dunkeld & Birnam ....d.	1637	...	...	1727	...	|	|	...	|	...	1920	...	...	1929	...	...	2046	...	...	2116	...	...	...	...	...	...	...	...
Pitlochry ....d.	1652	...	...	1741	...	1824	1827	...	1831	...	1934	...	...	1942	...	...	2100	...	...	2130	...	...	...	...	...	...	...	...
Blair Atholl ....d.	1702	...	...	|	...	|	|	...	|	...	|	...	...	1952	...	...	|	...	...	2140	...	...	...	...	...	...	...	...
Dalwhinnie ....d.	|	...	...	|	...	|	|	...	|	...	|	...	...	2017	...	...	2137f	...	...	2210f	...	...	...	...	...	...	...	...
Newtonmore ....d.	|	...	...	|	...	|	|	...	|	...	|	...	...	2028	...	...	|	...	...	2221	...	...	...	...	...	...	...	...
Kingussie ....d.	1738	...	...	1824	...	1910	1914	...	1916	...	2017	...	...	2033	...	...	2153	...	...	2226	...	...	...	...	...	...	...	...
Aviemore .... 🚂 d.	1750	...	...	1837	...	1927f	1930	...	1932	...	2032	...	...	2046	...	...	2205	...	...	2239	...	...	...	...	...	...	...	...
Carrbridge ....d.	1758	...	...	|	...	|	|	...	|	...	|	...	...	2056	...	...	|	...	...	2248	...	...	...	...	...	...	...	...
Inverness ....a.	1826	...	...	1910	...	2004	2007	...	2009	...	2123c	...	...	2126	...	...	2243	...	...	2319	...	...	...	...	...	...	...	...

	⚒2	⚒2	⚒2	⚒	⚒2	⚒	⑦2	⚒	⑦2	⑦2	⚒K	⚒2	⑦2	⚒	⚒2	⚒	⑦K	⚒2	⑦	⑦	⚒	⚒	⚒2	⑦	⚒2	⚒	⚒	⚒2
Inverness ....d.	...	...	...	0536	...	0638z	...	...	...	...	0755	...	...	0841	...	0942	0940	...	...	1053	1050	...	...	1237	...	1248	...	...
Carrbridge ....d.	...	...	...	0603	...	|	...	...	...	...	|	...	...	0919	...	|	1011	...	...	|	|	...	...	1310	...	1325	...	...
Aviemore .... 🚂 d.	...	...	...	0612	...	0722	...	...	...	...	0832	...	...	0928	...	1031	1022	...	...	1128	1130	...	...	1319	...	1334	...	...
Kingussie ....d.	...	...	...	0624	...	0736	...	...	...	...	0846	...	...	0940	...	1043	1035	...	...	1139	1143	...	...	1338f	...	1346	...	...
Newtonmore ....d.	...	...	...	0629	...	|	...	...	...	...	|	...	...	0945	...	|	1040	...	...	|	|	...	...	1342	...	1351	...	...
Dalwhinnie ....d.	...	...	...	0640	...	|	...	...	...	...	|	...	...	0957	...	|	|	...	...	1152	|	...	...	|	...	1402	...	...
Blair Atholl ....d.	...	...	...	0704	...	0809	...	...	...	...	|	...	...	|	...	|	1117f	...	...	|	1216	...	...	1414	...	|	...	...
Pitlochry ....d.	...	...	...	0716	...	0819	...	...	...	...	0929	...	...	1033r	...	1127	1127	...	...	1223	1230	...	...	1425	...	1433	...	...
Dunkeld & Birnam ....d.	...	...	...	0733	...	0834	...	...	...	...	|	...	...	1046	...	|	|	...	...	1238	1242	...	...	1437	...	1446	...	...
Perth .... **222/4** d.	0600	0619	0716	0753	0806	0854	0901	0917	0917	0936	0959	1014	1010	1106	1115	1157	1201	1213	1215	1257	1305f	1315	1324	1456	1427	1507	1519	1525
Stirling .... **222** d.	|	|	|	0824	|	0934	|	|	0954	|	1033	|	1047	1145	|	1235	1238	|	1248	1326	1338	1345	|	1534	|	1541	1548	|
Glasgow Queen St **222** a.	|	|	|	0857	|	|	|	|	|	|	|	|	|	1214	|	*1321*	|	|	1315	*1413*	|	1415	|	1607	|	|	1621	|
Markinch .... **222** d.	0632	0647	0753	...	0837	|	0931	0946	|	1006	|	1053	|	...	1146	|	|	1251	...	|	|	...	1356	...	1456	|	...	1557
Kirkcaldy .... **222** d.	|	0657	0803	...	0847	|	0941	0957	|	|	|	1105	|	...	1157	|	|	1301	...	|	|	...	1407	...	1509	|	...	1608
Haymarket .... **222/4** a.	0733	0744	0851	...	0949	1009	1018	1044	1044	1114	1109	1148	1138	...	1238v	1309	1314	1346	...	1400	1422	...	1450	...	1553	1627	...	1652
Edinburgh Wav'ley **222/4** a.	0739	0749	0857	...	0956	1015	1023	1049	1049	1119	1115	1154	1143	...	1243v	1314	1320	1353	...	1406	1428	...	1457	...	1558	1633	...	1657

	⑦	Ⓐ2	⑥2	⚒	⚒2	⑦	⑦	⚒	⚒	⑦	⚒2	⚒	⚒2	Ⓐ	⑥	⚒2	⚒	⑦	⑦	⑤⑥	①–④	⑥	Ⓐ	⑦B	⑤2	①–④	⑥2	ⒶB
Inverness ....d.	1326	...	...	1450	...	1522	...	1544	...	1626	...	1726	...	1852	1853	...	...	1852	...	2	2	2021	2022	2025	...	2	...	2045
Carrbridge ....d.	|	...	...	|	...	|	...	1616	...	1658f	...	1759f	...	|	|	...	...	1925	...	...	...	2058	2058	|	...	...	...	|
Aviemore .... 🚂 d.	1407	...	...	1525	...	1557	...	1627	...	1708	...	1808	...	1933r	1933r	...	...	1934	...	...	...	2107	2107	2119	...	...	...	2132
Kingussie ....d.	1418	...	...	1536	...	1608	...	1639	...	1720	...	1820	...	1945	1945	...	...	1946	...	...	...	2119	2119	2133	...	...	...	2148
Newtonmore ....d.	|	...	...	|	...	|	...	1644	...	|	...	|	...	|	|	...	...	1951	...	...	...	2123	2123	2139	...	...	...	2154
Dalwhinnie ....d.	|	...	...	|	...	|	...	1656	...	|	...	|	...	|	|	...	...	2002	...	...	...	2135	2135	2154	...	...	...	2209
Blair Atholl ....d.	|	...	...	|	...	|	...	1722	...	1753	...	|	...	|	|	...	...	2025	...	...	...	2157	2201	2220	...	...	...	2235
Pitlochry ....d.	1459	...	...	1620	...	1650	...	1735	...	1803	...	1905	...	2030	2030	...	...	2035	...	...	...	2207	2215	2232	...	...	...	2247
Dunkeld & Birnam ....d.	|	...	...	1637	...	1704	...	1750	...	1820	...	1920	...	2047	2047	...	...	2049	...	...	...	2220	2227	2246	...	...	...	2303
Perth .... **222/4** d.	1529	1621	1622	1705j	1721	1722	1801	1820j	1814	1839	1913	1939	2019	2105	2105	2110	2123	2107	2127	2218	2218	2239	2246	2306	2311	2311	2317	2326
Stirling .... **222** d.	1558	|	|	1741	|	1752	1834	1853	|	1910	|	2015	|	2136	2136	|	2153	2137	2203	|	|	2311	2319	2351	|	|	|	0011
Glasgow Queen St **222** a.	*1712*	|	|	1814	|	|	1909	1922	|	1942	|	2045	|	|	|	|	2222	|	2238	|	|	2342	2357	...	|	|	|	...
Markinch .... **222** d.	|	1650	1654	...	1802	|	...	...	1843	...	1946	...	2048	|	|	2140	...	|	...	2249	2251	...	...	...	2339	2339	2345	...
Kirkcaldy .... **222** d.	|	1700	1707	...	1813	|	...	...	1855	...	1957	...	2058	|	|	2150	...	|	...	2259	2302	...	...	...	2350	2350	2358	...
Haymarket .... **222/4** a.	1638	1743	1751	...	1851	1831	...	...	1939	...	2039	...	2141	2210	2223	2233	...	2210	...	2344	0005	...	...	...	0031	0056	0037	...
Edinburgh Wav'ley **222/4** a.	1644	1748	1757	...	1858g	1837	...	...	1944	...	2044	...	2146	2215	2228	2239	...	2215	...	2349	0010	...	...	...	0036	0103	0043	...

A – Ⓡ. 🛏 1, 2 class and 🛋 2 London Euston - Inverness (departs London previous day). Station calls are to set down only until Newtonmore. See also Table **161**.
B – Ⓡ. 🛏 1, 2 class and 🛋 2 Inverness - London Euston. Station calls are to pick up only. See Table **161**.
K – From/to London Kings Cross (Table **180**).
P – To Elgin (Table **225**).

a – Arrives 1604.
b – Arrives 2010 on ⑥.
c – Arrives 2114 on ⑥.
e – Departs 1444 on Ⓐ.
f – Arrives 5–6 minutes earlier.
g – Arrives 1854 on ⑥.

j – Arrives 11–13 minutes earlier.
k – Arrives 0900 on ⑥.
n – Arrives 2007 on Ⓐ; 2018 on ⑥.
r – Arrives 7–9 minutes earlier.
t – Arrives 20 minutes earlier on Ⓐ.
v – 4 minutes later on ⑥.

y – Arrives 18–19 minutes earlier on Ⓐ.
z – Departs 0644 on ⑥.
🚂 – Strathspey Railway (Aviemore - Boat of Garten - Broomhill, *14 km*). ✆ 01479 810725. www.strathspeyrailway.co.uk

SR 2nd class only EDINBURGH - STIRLING 224

km			⚒	⚒	⚒	⚒	Ⓐ	⚒	⚒	⚒	⚒	⚒	⚒	⚒	⚒	Ⓐ	⑥	⚒	Ⓐ	⑥	⚒	⚒	⚒	Ⓐ	⑥	⚒	⚒
0	**Edinburgh** Waverley.d.	⚒	0518	0533	0604	0632	0703	0734	0804	0834	0906	0935	1003	1036	1104	1134	1136	1203	1232	1235	1305	1337	1403	1434	1436	1505	1533
2	Haymarket.....d.		0523	0537	0608	0636	0707	0738	0809	0838	0910	0939	1007	1041	1108	1138	1140	1208	1236	1240	1309	1341	1407	1438	1441	1509	1539
28	Linlithgow.....d.		0542	0556	0627	0656	0726	0757	0829	0857	0928	0958	1026	1100	1127	1156	1159	1226	1256	1258	1328	1359	1426	1453	1500	1527	1558
41	Falkirk Grahamston...d.		0553	0610	0638	0706	0738	0812	0841	0908	0940	1011	1041	1111	1140	1208	1213	1239	1312r	1312	1339	1412	1437	1510	1511	1540	1611
58	**Stirling**.....a.		0607	0625	0656	0720	0757	0828	0858	0922	0956	1028	1055	1126	1156	1222	1228	1257	1328	1328	1355	1426	1451	1526	1526	1557	1626

	⚒	⚒	⚒	⚒	⑥	Ⓐ	⚒	⚒	⚒	⚒	⚒	⚒	⑥	⑤	①-④		⑦	⑦	⑦	⑦	⑦	⑦	⑦	⑦	⑦	⑦	⑦
Edinburgh Waverley..d.	1604	1638	1705	1736	1803	1806	1836	1904	2003	2103	2203	2303	2332	2335	2335	⑦	0935	1035	1112	1134	1206	1234	1305	1336	1406	1437	1507
Haymarket.....d.	1608	1642	1710	1742	1808	1810	1840	1908	2007	2107	2208	2307	2336	2339	2339		0940	1039	1116	1138	1210	1238	1309	1341	1410	1441	1511
Linlithgow.....d.	1627	1700	1729	1801	1828	1829	1900	1927	2026	2125	2226	2325	2356	2359	0005		1003	1057	1135	1158	1231	1258	1328	1401	1430	1501	1530
Falkirk Grahamston.....d.	1637	1713	1742	1813	1841	1841	1914	1939	2036	2137	2241r	2336	0007	0009	0016		1014	1109	1146	1209	1244	1311	1339	1412	1440	1511	1542
Stirling.....a.	1651	1727	1800	1828	1859	1859	1930	1958	2051	2150	2256	2349	0022	0023	0032		1028	1123	1200	1223	1259	1325	1355	1426	1455	1527	1556

	⑦	⑦	⑦	⑦	⑦	⑦	⑦	⑦	⑦	⑦	⑦
Edinburgh Waverley..d.	1537	1606	1636	1705	1734	1806	1835	1936	2035	2130	2235
Haymarket.....d.	1541	1610	1641	1709	1738	1810	1839	1940	2039	2135	2240
Linlithgow.....d.	1600	1631	1700	1730	1756	1831	1900	2000	2057	2157	2300
Falkirk Grahamston.....d.	1610	1641	1711	1740	1807	1844	1911	2010	2108	2213r	2314
Stirling.....a.	1624	1656	1727	1757	1821	1901	1925	2024	2122	2227	2331

		⚒	Ⓐ	⚒	⚒	Ⓐ	⑥	⚒	⚒	⚒	⚒
Stirling.....d.	⚒	0521	0608	0635	0704	0721	0729	0809	0834	0908	0940
Falkirk Grahamston.....d.		0535	0622	0648	0718	0737	0743	0824	0848	0922	0955
Linlithgow.....d.		0545	0634	0659	0729	0749	0754	0835	0858	0933	1006
Haymarket.....a.		0604	0651	0720	0751	0806	0812	0855	0916	0953	1025
Edinburgh Waverley.....a.		0611	0656	0725	0757	0811	0818	0900	0921	0958	1031

	⚒	⚒	⚒	⚒	⚒	⚒	Ⓐ	⑥	⚒	⚒	⚒	Ⓐ	⑥	Ⓐ	⑥	Ⓐ	⑥	Ⓐ	⑥	⑥	Ⓐ	⚒	⚒	⚒	⚒	⚒	⚒
Stirling.....d.	1003	1039	1104	1135	1203	1240	1304	1304	1331	1403	1439	1504	1504	1534	1534	1603	1603	1633	1633	1700	1701	1735	1803	1830	1902	1939	2002
Falkirk Grahamston.....d.	1017	1053	1120	1148t	1221	1254	1319	1321	1347	1418t	1452	1518	1521	1548	1551	1617	1621	1647	1653r	1713	1715	1752	1817	1844	1917	1953	2015
Linlithgow.....d.	1028	1103	1131	1200	1231	1304	1329	1332	1359	1429t	1503	1529	1532	1559	1602	1628	1631	1657	1703	1724	1726	1804	1827	1855	1927	2004	2026
Haymarket.....a.	1049	1123	1151	1220	1251	1323	1348	1350	1418	1451	1523	1551	1550	1620	1620	1646	1650	1716	1722	1742	1746	1825	1846	1913	1950	2023	2045
Edinburgh Waverley..a.	1054	1128	1156	1227	1256	1328	1354	1356	1424	1456	1528	1556	1557	1627	1628	1652	1655	1721	1729	1748	1752	1830	1851	1923f	1955	2028	2050

	⚒	Ⓐ	⑥	⚒	⚒		⑦	⑦	⑦	⑦	⑦	⑦	⑦	⑦	⑦	⑦	⑦	⑦	⑦	⑦	⑦	⑦	⑦	⑦	⑦	⑦	⑦
Stirling.....d.	2038	2144	2144	2237	2326	⑦	0910	0954	1047	1108	1152	1208	1254	1308	1350	1418	1450	1518	1550	1618	1650	1718	1818	1919	2018	2108	2218
Falkirk Grahamston.....d.	2052	2157	2157	2250	2342		0924	1011	1104	1122	1206	1223	1311	1322	1404	1432	1507	1532	1604	1632	1704	1732	1832	1933	2032	2122	2233
Linlithgow.....d.	2103	2208	2208	2301	2352		0935	1022	1116	1133	1217	1233	1321	1333	1415	1443	1518	1543	1614	1643	1714	1742	1843	1944	2043	2132	2243
Haymarket.....a.	2123	2222	2227	2319	0012		1000	1044	1138	1154	1235	1251	1342	1353	1433	1501	1537	1601	1633	1701	1733	1801	1901	2002	2103	2152	2302
Edinburgh Waverley..a.	2128	2228	2232	2324	0017		1005	1049	1143	1159	1240	1256	1347	1358	1438	1506	1543	1606	1639	1706	1739	1806	1906	2007	2108	2158	2307

f – Arrives 1918 on Ⓐ. r – Arrives 5–6 minutes earlier. t – Departs 3 minutes later on ⑥.

SR 2nd class only ABERDEEN - ELGIN - INVERNESS 225

km			⚒	⚒H	⚒D	⚒H	⚒	⚒🍷	⚒	⚒🍷	⚒	⚒G	Ⓐ🍷	⑥🍷	⚒	⚒B	Ⓐ🍷	⑥🍷	⚒	⚒	⚒🍷	⚒H		⑦G	⑦G	⑦G	⑦G	⑦🍷
0	**Aberdeen**.....¶ d.	⚒	...	0614	0718	0823	0901	1008	1111	1157	1252	1341	1550	1550	1625	1725	1815	1818	1924	1957	2018	2200	⑦	1003	1300	1524	1800	2128
10	Dyce ✈.....¶ d.		...	0623	0727	0831	0910	1016	1120	1206	1301	1349	1559u	1559	1634	1734	1824	1827	1933	2006	2027	2208		1012	1309	1532	1809	2136
22	Kintore.....¶ d.		...	0632	0735	0840	0918	1026	1128	1214	1309	1359	1607u	1607	1642	│	1832	1835	1941	2014	2035	2218		1020	1317	1542	1817	2146
27	**Inverurie**.....¶ d.		...	0639	0742	0845	0925	1032	1135	1220	1316	1405	1618u	1618f	1649	1746	1840	1842	1948	2021	2041	2224		1026	1323	1547	1823	2151
44	Insch.....d.		...	0651	0755	0858	—	1046	—	1233	—	1419	1631	1631	—	1759	1852	1855	—	—	2054	2237		1039	1335	1600	1836	2204
65	Huntly.....d.		...	0708	0811	0915	...	1103	...	1250	...	1438	1656j	1656j	...	1815	1909	1911	...	...	2111	2254		1055	1352	1616	1852	2224
85	Keith.....d.		...	0723	0826	0930	⚒	1118	⚒	1304	⚒	1453	1718	1718	⚒	1830	1923	1926	Ⓐ	⑥	2126	2309		1110	1407	1637	1907	2239
114	**Elgin**.....d.		0656	0743	0849	0950	1051	1140	1236	1325	1425	1514	1738	1738	1802	1853	1946	1946	2018	2024	2149	2329		1130	1427	1659	1928	2259
137	Forres.....d.		0709	0756	0903	1003	1104	1153	1249	1338	1438	1527	1751	1751	1815	1906	1959	1959	2034	2040	2204	2342		1143	1440	1712	1941	2312
149	Nairn.....d.		0721	0806	0916	1015	1117	1204	1300	1351	1449	1538	1802	1802	1826	1918	2010	2010	2058t	2058j	2215	2352		1154	1451	1726f	1952	2322
160	Inverness Airport ✈ d.		0730	0815	0925	1024	1126	1213	1309	1400	1458	1547	1811	1811	1835	1927	2019	2019	2107	2107	2226	0001		1203	1500	1735	2001	2331
173	**Inverness**.....a.		0741	0826	0936	1035	1137	1224	1320	1412	1510	1558	1822	1822	1846	1939	2030	2030	2118	2118	2237	0013		1214	1511	1749	2014	2343

		⚒A	⚒G	⚒	⚒	⚒🍷	⚒	⚒G	⚒	⚒🍷	⚒	⚒🍷	⚒🍷	⚒	⚒G	⚒H	⚒	⚒	⚒	⚒		⑦G	⑦G	⑦G	⑦🍷	⑦C	⑦🍷	⑦C
Inverness.....d.	⚒	0454	0549	...	0659	0856	0946	1056	1144	1239	1330	1428	1535	1622	1720	1801	1856	2037	2130	2215	⑦	0959	1231	1529	1703	1800	2104	2142
Inverness Airport ✈ .d.		0504	0559	...	0709	0906	1001f	1106	1154	1249	1340	1438	1546	1632	1730	1813	1908	2047	2140	2226		1009	1241	1539	1713	1810	2114	2153
Nairn.....d.		0514	0609	...	0720	0917	1013	1116	1205	1301	1351	1449	1556	1642	1739	1826	1919	2057	2152	2235		1019	1251	1548	1723	1820	2123	2203
Forres.....d.		0524	0619	...	0731	0930	1024	1126	1216	1311	1402	1500	1607	1653	1750	1838	1930	2108	2203	2246		1030	1301	1558	1734	1830	2133	2214
Elgin.....d.		0537	0632	...	0753n	0952j	1038	1139	1230	1326	1415	1514	1620	1706	1803	1855f	1943	2122	2216	2259		1043	1314	1611	1747	1843	2146	2227
Keith.....d.		0556	0651	...	0818f	1013	—	1159	—	1346	—	1534	1640	—	1822	1915	—	—	2236	...		1103	1334	1632	1808	...	2207	...
Huntly.....d.		0611	0710f	0747	0842	1028	...	1216	...	1401	...	1549	1655	...	1844	1937	...	...	2253	...		1123	1352f	1647	1823	...	2222	...
Insch.....d.		0626	0726	0803	0859	1047	⚒	1234	⚒	1419	⚒	1605	1711	⚒	1900	1953	⚒	⚒	2309	...		1139	1408	1703	1839	...	2238	...
Inverurie.....¶ d.		0641	0738	0815	0911	1059	1156	1246	1328	1431	1515	1617	1723	1821	1912	2005	2048	2146	2321	...		1151	1420	1715	1851	...	2250	...
Kintore.....¶ d.		0647	0744	0820	0916	1104	1201	1251	1333	1437	1520	1623	1729	1826	1918	2010	2053	2151	2327	...		1157	1426	1721	1856	...	2256	...
Dyce ✈.....¶ d.		0656	0754	0831	0926	1114	1211	1300	1343	1447	1530	1632	1739	1836	1927	2020	2103	2201	2336	...		1205	1435	1729	1905	...	2304	...
Aberdeen.....¶ a.		0706	0803	0840	0935	1123	1220	1309	1352	1501r	1539	1641	1749	1845	1936	2032	2112	2210	2346	...		1215	1444	1739	1914	...	2314	...

A – [12] Inverness - Edinburgh (Table **222**).
B – [12] and 🍷 from Glasgow Queen St (Table **222**).
C – [12] and 🍷 Glasgow Queen Street - Inverness - Elgin (Table **223**).
D – From Dundee (Table **222**).
E – [12] to Glasgow Queen Street (Table **222**).
G – Conveys [12] and 🍷.
H – Conveys [12].

P – From Perth. Conveys [12] (Table **222**).
f – Arrives 5 minutes earlier.
j – Arrives 8 minutes earlier.
n – Arrives 0743.
r – Arrives 1456 on ⑥.
t – Arrives 2044.
u – Calls to pick up only.

¶ – Additional trains Aberdeen - Dyce - Kintore - Inverurie and v.v.:
From Aberdeen:
on ⚒ at 0752 **P**, 0925, 1042, 1226, 1400, 1436, 1504, 1602⑥, 1604Ⓐ, 1657, 1739, 1857, 2058, 2138, 2249;
on ⑦ at 1033, 1225, 1428, 1550, 1649, 2034.
From Inverurie:
on ⚒ at 0718, 0847, 0954, 1029, 1129, 1258, 1451, 1551, 1644, 1700, 1743, 1926, 2025, 2218;
on ⑦ at 1106 **E**, 1255, 1458, 1619, 1730, 2102.

SR 2nd class only INVERNESS - THURSO, WICK and KYLE OF LOCHALSH 226

km			⚒	⚒	⚒🍷	⚒	⚒		⚒	⚒🍷	⚒	⚒	⚒	⚒🍷	⚒	⑤⑥		⑦	⑦		⑦	⑦	⑦ a	⑦🍷	⑦
0	**Inverness**.....d.	⚒	0700	0855	1041	1056	1143	...	1335	1400	1450	1712	1754	1831	2129	2312	⑦	0938	1059	...	1220	1533	1754	1754	2106
16	Beauly.....d.		0715	0910	│	1113	1200	...	1350	1415	1505	1727	1809	1846	2144	2328		0953	1115	...	1235	1548	1809	1809	2121
21	Muir of Ord.....d.		0723	0916	1101	1119	1209	...	1356	1423	1511	1733	1815	1853	2150	2337f		0959	1121	...	1241	1556	1815	1815	2127
30	Dingwall.....d.		0737	0929	1112	1132	1221	...	1411	1437	1524	1747	1829	1906	2203	2351		1013	1134	...	1254	1609	1833t	1831t	2140
49	Garve.....d.		│	0952	│	1155	...	...	1434	│	│	│	1855f	│	│	│		│	1158	...	│	│	1856	│	│
75	Achnasheen.....d.		│	1019	│	1222	...	...	1504f	│	│	│	1922	│	│	│		│	1225	...	│	│	1922	│	│
104	Strathcarron.....d.		│	1048	│	1253	...	...	1533	│	│	│	1952	│	│	│		│	1255	...	│	│	1952	│	│
116	Stromeferry.....d.		│	1106	│	1310	...	...	1551	│	│	│	2009	│	│	│		│	1312	...	│	│	2009	│	│
124	Plockton.....d.		│	1118	│	1322	...	...	1603	│	│	│	2021	│	│	│		│	1324	...	│	│	2021	│	│
133	**Kyle of Lochalsh**.....a.		│	1131	│	1335	...	...	1616	│	│	│	2034	│	│	│		│	1347	...	│	│	2034	│	│
51	Invergordon.....d.		0757	...	1130	...	...	...	...	1454	1541	1805	...	1927	2221	0009		1032	...	...	1313	1626	...	1848	2159
71	Tain.....d.		0817	...	1149	...	...	...	...	1513	...	1825	...	1946	2240	0028		1050	...	...	1331	...	...	1907	2217
93	Ardgay.....d.		0833	...	1205	...	...	...	...	1529	...	1840	...	2002	...	...		...	...	...	...	...	...	1923	...
108	Lairg.....d.		0853	...	1221	...	...	...	...	1545	...	...	...	2018	...	...		...	...	...	...	...	...	1942	...
136	Golspie.....d.		0918	...	1246	...	...	...	...	1610	...	...	...	2043	...	...		...	...	...	...	...	...	2007	...
146	Brora.....d.		0929	...	1257	...	...	...	...	1621	...	...	...	2053	...	...		...	...	...	...	...	...	2018	...
163	Helmsdale.....d.		0947	...	1312	...	...	...	...	1636	...	...	...	2108	...	...		...	...	...	...	...	...	2033	...
201	Forsinard.....d.		1021	...	1346	...	...	...	...	1712	...	...	...	2142	...	...		...	...	...	...	...	...	2107	...
237	Georgemas Junction.....a.		1045	...	1410	...	...	...	...	1736	...	...	...	2206	...	...		...	...	...	...	...	...	2131	...
248	**Thurso**.....a.		1059	...	1424	...	...	...	...	1750	...	...	...	2220	...	...		...	...	...	...	...	...	2145	...
248	**Thurso**.....d.		1102	...	1427	...	...	...	...	1753	...	...	...	2223	...	...		...	...	...	...	...	...	2148	...
237	Georgemas Junction.....d.		1114	...	1439	...	...	...	...	1805	...	...	...	2235	...	...		...	...	...	...	...	...	2200	...
260	**Wick**.....a.		1131	...	1456	...	...	...	...	1822	...	...	...	2252	...	...		...	...	...	...	...	...	2217	...

a – Until Sept. 28. f – Arrives 4 minutes earlier. t – Arrives 1827.

226 THURSO, WICK and KYLE OF LOCHALSH - INVERNESS

2nd class only SR

	⚒	⚒	⚒	⚒		⚒	⚒🍷	⚒	⚒	⚒	⚒	⚒🍷		⚒	⚒🍷	⚒	⚒	⑦	⑦	⑦a	⑦	⑦🍷	⑦	⑦	⑦
Wick d.		...	...	...	...	0618	0802	...	...	...	...	1234	...	...	1600	...	...		...	...	...	1158	...	...	...
Georgemas Junction d.		...	...	...	...	0636	0820	...	...	...	...	1252	...	...	1618	...	...		...	...	...	1216	...	...	...
Thurso a.		...	...	...	...	0646	0830	...	...	...	...	1302	...	...	1628	...	...		...	...	...	1226	...	...	...
Thurso d.		...	...	...	...	0650	0834	...	...	...	...	1306	...	...	1632	...	...		...	...	...	1230	...	...	...
Georgemas Junction d.		...	...	...	...	0703	0847	...	...	...	...	1319	...	...	1645	...	...		...	...	...	1243	...	...	...
Forsinard d.		...	...	...	...	0727	0913	...	...	...	...	1347	...	...	1711	...	...		...	...	...	1309	...	...	...
Helmsdale d.		...	...	...	...	0801	0946	...	...	...	...	1421	...	...	1744	...	...		...	...	...	1342	...	...	...
Brora d.		...	...	...	...	0816	1002	...	...	...	...	1436	...	...	1800	...	...		...	...	...	1358	...	...	...
Golspie d.		...	...	...	...	0826	1012	...	...	...	...	1447	...	...	1810	...	...		...	...	...	1408	...	...	...
Lairg d.		...	...	0702	...	0852	1038	...	...	...	...	1512	...	...	1835	...	...		...	...	...	1433	...	...	...
Ardgay d.		0613	...	0719	...	0907	1054	...	...	...	...	1530	...	...	1851	1929	...		...	...	...	1449	...	...	...
Tain d.		0629	...	0735	...	0923	1110	...	...	...	...	1546	...	...	1907	1947	2245		1055	...	1358	1505	...	...	2222
Invergordon d.		0649	...	0758	...	0943	1131	...	...	...	1551	1610t	...	...	1925	2007	2305		1114	...	1418	1524	1631	...	2242
Kyle of Lochalsh d.		|	0545	|	...	|	|	...	1206	1346	|	|	...	1713	|	|	|		|	1020	|	|	|	1509	|
Plockton d.		|	0602	|	...	|	|	...	1219	1359	|	|	...	1726	|	|	|		|	1033	|	|	|	1525	|
Stromeferry d.		|	0614	|	...	|	|	...	1229x	1411	|	|	...	1738	|	|	|		|	1045	|	|	|	1537	|
Strathcarron d.		|	0633	|	...	|	|	...	1252	1434t	|	|	...	1757	|	|	|		|	1103	|	|	|	1556	|
Achnasheen d.		|	0702	|	...	|	|	...	1320	1503	|	|	...	1826	|	|	|		|	1131	|	|	|	1624	|
Garve d.		|	0729	|	...	|	|	...	1347	1529	|	|	...	1854	|	|	|		|	1157	|	|	|	1651	|
Dingwall d.		0708	0756	0816	...	1002	1153	1245	1410	1552	1611	1631	...	1924	1942	2026	2323		1135	1220	1436	1542	1649	1714	2300
Muir of Ord d.		0722	0809	0829	...	1015	1207	1258	1422	1604	1624	1645	...	1936	1953	2039	2335		1148	1242f	1448	1555	1702	1727	2313
Beauly d.		0727	0814	0835	...	1021	1212	1304	1427	1609	1629	1650	...	1941	|	2044	2340		1153	1247	1453	1600	1707	1732	2318
Inverness a.		0745	0829	0850	...	1039	1227	1321	1442	1627	1646	1708	...	1959	2014	2101	2355		1208	1302	1508	1615	1722	1753	2336

a – Until Sept. 28.
f – Arrives 1232.
t – Arrives 5 minutes earlier.
x – Calls on request.

227 🚌 INVERNESS - ULLAPOOL - STORNOWAY

Service valid until October 19, 2025

	①–⑥ 🚌	①–⑥ ⛴	⑦ 🚌	⑦ ⛴		①–⑤ 🚌	①–⑤ ⛴	⑦ 🚌	⑦ ⛴		⑥ 🚌	⑥ ⛴
Inverness d.	0810	...	0910	...	...	1510	...	1610	...	...	1640	...
Garve d.	0846	...	0946	...	...	1546	...	1646	...	...	1716	...
Ullapool a.	0930	...	1030	...	...	1630	...	1730	...	...	1800	...
Ullapool d.	...	1030	...	1130	...	...	1730	...	1830	...	...	1900
Stornoway a.	...	1310	...	1410	...	...	2010	...	2110	...	...	2140

	①–⑥ ⛴	①–⑥ 🚌	⑦ ⛴	⑦ 🚌		①–⑤ ⛴	①–⑤ 🚌		⑦ ⛴	⑦ 🚌	⑥ ⛴	⑥ 🚌
Stornoway d.	0700	...	0800	...	...	1400	...	...	1500	...	1530	...
Ullapool a.	0940	...	1040	...	...	1640	...	...	1740	...	1810	...
Ullapool d.	...	1000	...	1100	...	...	1700	...	...	1800	...	1830
Garve d.	...	1044	...	1144	...	...	1744	...	...	1844	...	1914
Inverness a.	...	1120	...	1220	...	...	1820	...	...	1920	...	1950

☛ Latest passenger check-in for ⛴ is 30 minutes before departure.

Operators: 🚌 Scottish Citylink (service **961**). www.citylink.co.uk ✆ +44 (0) 871 266 3333.
⛴ Caledonian MacBrayne. www.calmac.co.uk ✆ +44 (0) 800 066 5000.

228 🚌 INVERNESS - ISLE OF SKYE / FORT WILLIAM - OBAN

Service until Oct. 3, 2025

Service number	**919**	**916** ①–⑥	**919**	**915**	**917**	**919**	**918** ①–⑥	**919**	**919**	**915** ①–⑥	**915** ⑦	**919/8**	**919**	**917**	**919**	**919**	**919**	**918** ①–⑥	**915**	**917**	**919**	**917**	**916**	**919/8**
Inverness bus station d.	0710	...	0810	...	0830	0910	...	1010	1110	...	...	1210	1310	1315	1410	1510	1610	...	...	1625	1710	1745	...	1810
Invermoriston Public Hall d.	0805	...	0905	...	0925r	1005	...	1105	1205	...	...	1305	1405	1410r	1505	1605	1705	...	...	1720r	1805	1840r	...	1905
Kyle of Lochalsh Old Slipway d.	|	...	|	...	1042	|	...	|	|	...	...	|	|	1527	|	|	|	...	...	1837	|	1957	...	|
Portree Square a.	|	0830	|	...	1147	|	...	|	|	...	...	|	|	1629	|	|	|	...	...	1939	|	2056	...	|
Uig Pier a.	|	0900	|	...	*1340*	|	...	|	|	...	...	|	|	*1745*	|	|	|	...	...	...	|	...	...	|
Fort Augustus bus stance d.	0817	...	0917	...	...	1017	...	1117	1217	...	...	1317	1417	...	1517	1617	1717	...	...	...	1817	...	...	1917
Uig Pier d.	|	...	|	...	...	|	...	|	|	0930	...	|	|	...	|	|	|	...	1440	...	|	...	1840	|
Portree Square d.	|	...	|	0800	...	|	...	|	|	1035j	1035	|	|	...	|	|	|	...	1520p	...	|	...	1915	|
Kyle of Lochalsh Old Slipway d.	|	...	|	0910	...	|	...	|	|	1142t	1142t	|	|	...	|	|	|	...	1625	...	|	...	2018	|
Invergarry Jct. bus bay A82 d.	0832	...	0932	1025f	...	1032	...	1132	1232	1257f	1257f	1332	1432	...	1532	1632	1732	...	1740f	...	1832	...	2133	1932
Fort William bus station a.	0919	...	1019	1112	...	1119	...	1219	1319	1344	1344	1419	1519	...	1619	1719	1819	...	1821	...	1913	...	2214	2013
Fort William bus station d.	...	...	...	...	...	...	1130	...	...	...	...	1500	...	...	...	...	...	1830	...	...	...	...	...	2100
Ballachulish Tourist Office d.	...	...	...	...	...	...	1200	...	...	...	...	|	...	...	...	...	...	1900	...	...	...	...	...	|
Oban Station Road a.	...	...	...	...	...	...	1303	...	...	...	...	1625	...	...	...	...	...	2003	...	...	...	...	...	2225

Service number	**919**	**919**	**919/8**	**917**	**916**	**919**	**918** ①–⑥	**919**	**916** ①–⑥	**917**	**919/8**	**919**	**915**	**919**	**917**	**919**	**915**	**919**	**919**	**915**	**918** ①–⑥	**919**	**916**	**917**
Oban Station Road d.	...	...	0730	...	...	...	0930	...	...	...	1330	...	...	...	...	...	...	...	...	...	1645	...	...	...
Ballachulish Tourist Office d.	...	...	|	...	...	...	1034	...	...	...	|	...	...	...	...	...	...	...	...	...	1749	...	...	...
Fort William bus station a.	...	...	0858	...	...	...	1105	...	...	...	1458	...	...	...	...	...	...	...	...	...	1820	...	...	...
Fort William bus station d.	0735	0835	0935	...	1000	1035	...	1135	...	...	1235	1335	1355	1435	...	1535	1555	1635	1740	1750	...	1840	...	...
Invergarry Jct. bus bay A82 d.	0816	0916	1016	...	1041f	1116	...	1216	...	...	1316	1416	1436f	1516	...	1616	1636f	1716	1821	1831f	...	1921	...	...
Kyle of Lochalsh Old Slipway d.	|	|	|	...	1202t	|	...	|	...	...	|	|	1557t	|	...	|	1757t	|	|	1952t	...	|	...	...
Portree Square d.	|	|	|	...	1310	|	...	|	...	...	|	|	1715n	|	...	|	1859	|	|	2051	...	|	...	...
Uig Pier a.	|	|	|	...	1340	|	...	|	...	...	|	|	1745	|	...	|	...	|	|	...	...	|	...	...
Fort Augustus bus stance d.	0831	0931	1031	...	...	1131	...	1231	...	...	1331	1431	...	1531	...	1631	...	1731	1836	...	...	1936	...	...
Uig Pier d.	|	|	|	...	...	|	...	|	0930	...	|	|	...	|	...	|	...	|	|	...	...	|	1440	...
Portree Square d.	|	|	|	0900	...	|	...	|	1000	1030	|	|	...	|	1400	|	...	|	|	...	...	|	1510	1745
Kyle of Lochalsh Old Slipway d.	|	|	|	1008	...	|	...	|	...	1133	|	|	...	|	1133	|	...	|	|	...	...	|	...	1848
Invermoriston opposite Public Hall d.	0843	0943	1043	1123r	...	1143	...	1243	...	1248	1343	1443	...	1543	1248r	1643	...	1743	1848	...	...	1948	...	2003r
Inverness bus station a.	0944	1044	1144	1224	...	1244	...	1344	...	1349	1444	1544	...	1644	1719	1744	...	1844	1943	...	...	2043	...	2058

f – On A87 at Invergarry Hotel.
j – Arrives 1000.
n – Arrives 1659.
p – Arrives 1510.
r – At Glenmoriston Arms.
t – Arrives 6 minutes earlier.

Operators: Scottish Citylink. www.citylink.co.uk ✆ +44 (0) 871 266 3333.
West Coast Motors. www.westcoastmotors.co.uk ✆ +44 (0) 01586 552 319

229 ISLE OF MAN RAILWAYS

✆ +44 (0) 1624 662525

km	*Manx Electric Railway*	A	A	A	A	A	Af	A	A	Af
0	**Douglas** Derby Castle ‡ d.	0940	1010	1040	1140	1240	1340	1410	1510	1610
4	Groudle d.	0950	1020	1050	1150	1250	1350	1420	1520	1620
11	Laxey d.	1010	1040	1110	1210	1310	1410	1440	1540	1640
29	**Ramsey** a.	1055	1125f	1155	1255	1355	1455	1525	1625	...

	Ag	A	Ag	Af	A	A	Af	A	Af	A
Ramsey d.	...	1110	1140	1240	1340	1440	1510	1540	...	1640
Laxey d.	1025	1155	1225	1325	1425	1525	1555	1625	1655	1725
Groudle d.	1043	1213	1243	1343	1443	1543	1613	1643	1713	1743
Douglas Derby Castle ‡ a.	1055	1225	1255	1355	1455	1555	1625	1655	1725	1755

km	*Snaefell Mountain Railway*	B	Br	B		Br	B	B
0	**Laxey** d.	1015	1045	1115	and at the same minutes past each hour until	1445	1515	1545
8	**Summit** a.	1045	1115	1145		1515	1545	1615

	Bp	Br	Bq	Br		Br	B	B
Summit d.	1100	1120	1150	1220	and at the same minutes past each hour until	1520	1550	1630
Laxey a.	1130	1150	1220	1250		1540	1625	1700

km	*Isle of Man Steam Railway*	C	F	D	F	D	F	Ck	F	E✕
0	**Douglas** Railway Station ‡ d.	0950	1120	1150	1250	1350	1430	1550	1730	1900
9	Santon d.	1011x	1141x	1211x	1311x	1411x	1451	1611x	1751x	|
13	Ballasalla d.	1020	1150	1220	1320	1420	1500	1620	1800	1940
16	Castletown d.	1027	1157	1227	1327	1427	1507	1627	1807	1947
25	**Port Erin** a.	1050	1220	1250	1350	1450	1530	1650	1830	2015

	C	F	D	F	D	F	D	F	F	E✕
Port Erin d.	1000	1130	1200	1300	1400	1445	1600	1615	1745	2115
Castletown d.	1027	1157	1227	1327	1427	1507	1627	1637	1807	2142
Ballasalla d.	1035	1205	1235	1335	1435	1515	1635	1645	1815	2149
Santon d.	1047x	1217x	1247x	1347x	1447x	1527x	1647x	1657	1827x	|
Douglas Railway Station ‡ a.	1105	1235	1305	1405	1505	1545	1705	1715	1845	2230

A – Daily Mar. 18 - Sept. 14 (not Mar. 20, 21, 27, 28, Apr. 28, May 13, 20); ②–⑦ Sept. 1 - Nov. 2. An enhanced service runs on many dates May - Sept. (check locally for details).
B – Daily Mar. 29 - Sept. 14 (not Apr. 28); ②–⑦ Sept. 16 - Nov. 2 (not Oct. 17, 24, 31). An enhanced service operates May 26 - June 5.
C – ①④⑤⑥⑦ Mar. 20 – 30; daily Apr. 3 - Sept. 30 (not Apr. 22, 23, 29, 30, May 6, 13, 20); ①④⑤⑥⑦ Oct. 2 - Nov. 2.
D – ①④⑤⑥⑦ Mar. 20 - May 23 (also Apr. 8, 9, 15, 16, May 7, 14, 21); daily June 3 – 30 (not June 5, 10); ⑧ July 1 - Aug. 30 (not July 23 – 26, Aug. 6); daily Sept. 1 – 30 (not Sept. 3); ①④⑤⑥⑦ Oct. 2 - Nov. 2.
E – July 12, 19, 26, Aug. 2, 16, 30. Reservation essential.
F – May 18, 25 – 31, June 1, 2, July 6, 13, 20, 27, Aug. 1, 2, 10, 17, 24, 31.
G – June 3 – 6. Reservation essential.

f – Not Mar. 14, 15, 18, 21, 22, 25, Apr. 15, 22, 29, Oct. 29 - Nov. 3.
g – Runs 30 minutes later Mar. 14, 15, 18, 21, 22, 25, Apr. 15, 22, 29, Oct. 29 - Nov. 3.
h – Runs 30 minutes earlier on dates in note **F**.
k – Runs 10 minutes later on dates in note **F**.
p – Runs 10 minutes later Mar. 19 – 28.
q – Runs 20 minutes later Mar. 19 – 28.
r – Not Mar. 26, 27, 28, Oct. 29 - Nov. 3.
x – Calls on request.

‡ – 🚌 services **1**, **1H**, **2**, **2A**, **10**, **11**, **12**, **12A**, **13** connect Derby Castle and Lord Street Bus Station which is near the Steam Railway Station.

IRELAND

SEE MAP PAGE 80

Operators: Iarnród Éireann (**IÉ**), www.irishrail.ie Northern Ireland Railways (**NIR**), www.translink.co.uk Bus Éireann, www.buseireann.ie Ulsterbus, www.translink.co.uk and Dublin Area Rapid Transit (**DART**), www.irishrail.ie Most cross-border services are jointly operated.

Timings: **Rail**: **NIR** services are valid until December 7, 2025. **IÉ** services are valid from August 26, 2024 until further notice. **DART** services are valid until further notice.
Bus: **Ulsterbus** services are valid until further notice. **Bus Éireann** services are valid until further notice.

Rail services: Except for *Enterprise* cross-border expresses (for details, see Table **230** below), **all trains** convey *Standard* (2nd) class seating. Most express trains in the Republic of Ireland, as noted in the tables, also have first class accommodation.
On public holiday dates in the **Republic of Ireland**, DART trains run as on Sundays; outer-suburban services to or from Drogheda and Dundalk do not run. Other services may be amended, though most main-line trains run normally. All services are subject to alteration during the Christmas, New Year and Easter holiday periods.

Bus services: **Bus Éireann** and **Ulsterbus**: services are shown in detail where there is no comparable rail service; only basic information is given for other routes. Buses do not always call at the rail station, but usually stop nearby. Where possible the stop details are given in the station bank or as a footnote. On longer routes, a change of bus may be required – please check with the driver. At holiday times bus travellers should consult detailed leaflets or seek further information from the operator. **Bus Éireann**: ✆ +353 1 836 6111 (Dublin) or + 353 21 450 8188 (Cork); **Ulsterbus**: ✆ + 028 9033 3000 (Translink, Belfast). **Dublin Busáras** (bus station) is a 5 minute walk from Dublin Connolly station.

The Dublin Tram service (Luas) connects Dublin Connolly and Heuston stations at frequent intervals. Journey time is 14 minutes, depending on traffic conditions. See Dublin City Plan on page 31.

BELFAST - DUNDALK - DUBLIN — 230

NIR, IÉ

Enterprise express trains (*E*) convey Standard (2nd) class and Plus (1st) class seating. 🍸 (Café Bar and trolley service) and ✕ (at-seat meal service in Plus).

km		⚒	Ⓐ	Ⓐ	⑥	Ⓐ	Ⓐ (E)	⑥ (E)	Ⓐ	⚒ (E)	⑥	⚒	⚒ (E)	⚒	⚒ (E)	Ⓐ	⚒ (E)	⚒ S	⚒ (E)	⚒ S	⚒ (E)	⚒ S	⚒ (E)	⚒D	⚒ S	⚒ (E)	⚒D
0	**Belfast** GCS ♣ § d.		...	...	...	...	0600	0600	...	0700	...	...	0800	...	0900	...	1000	...	1100	...	1200	...	1300	...	...	1400	...
13	Lisburn § d.		...	...	...	...	│	│	0651	│	...	0759	│	0859	│	1001	│	1059	│	1159	│	1259	│	...	1359	│	...
42	Portadown § d.		...	...	...	...	0626	0630	0715	0730	...	0824	0830	0924	0930	1025	1030	1123	1130	1223	1230	1323	1330	...	1423	1430	...
71	Newry d.		...	...	...	...	0648	0653	▬	0753	...	▬	0853	▬	0953	▬	1053	▬	1153	▬	1253	▬	1353	...	...	1453	...
95	**Dundalk** d.		0530	0630	0640	0658	0708	0713	⚒D	0811	...	Ⓐ	0913	⚒D	1013	⚒D	1113	⚒D	1213	⚒D	1313	⚒D	1413	...	...	1513	...
131	Drogheda d.		0554	0655	0705	0719	0730	0737	0736	0835	0848	0900	0937	0943	1037	1043	1137	1143	1237	1243	1337	1343	1437	1443	...	1537	1543
148	Balbriggan d.		0609	0712	0721	0736	│	│	0754	│	0904	0916	│	0958	│	1059	│	1159	│	1259	│	1359	│	1459	...	│	1559
154	Skerries d.		0615	0718	0727	0743	│	│	0800	│	0910	0922	│	1004	│	1105	│	1205	│	1305	│	1405	│	1505	...	│	1605
168	Malahide d.		0631	0736	0743	0801	│	│	0819	│	0926	0937	│	1020	│	1121	│	1221	│	1321	│	1421	│	1521	...	│	1621
183	**Dublin** Connolly a.		0647	0759	0804	0819	0823	0815	0839	0920	0949	1001	1013	1047	1113	1142	1213	1243	1313	1342	1413	1442	1513	1543	...	1613	1643

	⚒ S	⚒ (E)	⚒ T	⚒ (E)	⚒ D	⚒ T	⚒ (E)	⚒ T	⚒ (E)	⚒	⚒	⚒ (E)	⑥	Ⓐ	⚒	⚒ (E)		⑦	⑦ (E)	⑦ (E)	⑦ (E)	⑦ (E)	⑦ (E)	⑦ (E)	⑦ (E)	⑦ (E)	
Belfast GCS ♣ § d.	...	1500	...	1600	...	...	1700	...	1800	...	...	1900	...	...	...	2100	...		0805	1005	1205	1405	1605	1705	1805	2005	...
Lisburn § d.	1459	│	1551	│	...	1652	│	1752	│	...	1852	│	...	...	2059	│	...		0818	*1000*	*1200*	*1400*	*1600*	*1700*	*1800*	*2000*	...
Portadown § d.	1523	1530	1614	1630	...	1715	1730	1815	1830	...	1915	1930	...	...	2122	2130	...		0845	1035	1235	1435	1635	1735	1835	2035	...
Newry d.	...	1553	▬	1653	...	...	1753	▬	1853	...	...	1953	...	...	...	2153	...		0906	1057	1257	1457	1657	1757	1857	2057	...
Dundalk d.	...	1613	⚒D	1713	...	...	1813	⚒T	1913	...	...	2013	...	...	...	2213	...		0924	1116	1316	1516	1716	1816	1916	2116	...
Drogheda d.	...	1637	1643	1737	1743	...	1837	1852	1937	1948	...	2037	2048	2105	...	2237	...		0945	1139	1339	1539	1739	1839	1939	2139	...
Balbriggan d.	...	│	1659	│	1759	...	│	1908	│	2004	...	│	2104	2121	...	│	...		│	│	│	│	│	│	│	│	...
Skerries d.	...	│	1705	│	1805	...	│	1914	│	2010	...	│	2110	2127	...	│	...		│	│	│	│	│	│	│	│	...
Malahide d.	...	│	1721	│	1821	...	│	1930	│	2026	...	│	2126	2143	...	│	...		│	│	│	│	│	│	│	│	...
Dublin Connolly a.	...	1713	1743	1813	1843	...	1913	1952	2013	2048	...	2113	2148	2203	...	2313	...		1020	1215	1415	1615	1815	1915	2015	2215	...

	⚒	⚒ (E)	⚒	Ⓐ (E)	⑥ (E)	⚒ A	Ⓐ (E)	⑥ (E)	⚒ B	⚒ (E)	⚒ C	⚒ (E)	⚒ C	⚒ (E)	⚒ U	Ⓐ	⚒ C	⚒ (E)	⚒ C	⚒ (E)	⚒ C	⚒ U	⚒ (E)	⚒ C	⚒ (E)	⚒ W	
Dublin Connolly d.		0550	...	0650	0650	0712	0740	0750	0801	0850	0927	0950	1027	1050	...	1107	1127	1150	1227	1250	1327	...	1350	1427	1450	...	...
Malahide d.		│	...	│	│	0727	│	│	0826	│	0948	│	1047	│	...	1127	1147	│	1247	│	1347	...	│	1447	│	...	...
Skerries d.		│	...	│	│	0742	│	│	0841	│	1002	│	1102	│	...	1142	1202	│	1302	│	1402	...	│	1501	│	...	...
Balbriggan d.		│	...	│	│	0748	│	│	0847	│	1007	│	1107	│	...	1147	1207	│	1307	│	1407	...	│	1507	│	...	...
Drogheda d.		0628	...	0720	0727	0803	0825	0827	0907	0927	1024	1027	1124	1127	...	1207	1224	1227	1326	1327	1424	...	1427	1524	1527	...	...
Dundalk d.		0650	...	0742	0749	▬	0850	0849	▬	0949	▬	1049	▬	1149	...	1230	...	1249	▬	1349	▬	...	1449	▬	1549	...	...
Newry d.		0708	...	0803	0808	⚒	0908	0908	⚒U	1008	⚒U	1108	⚒U	1208	...	...	...	1308	⚒U	1408	⚒U	...	1508	⚒W	1608	...	...
Portadown § d.		0729	0740	0829	0829	0840	0929	0929	0940	1029	1040	1129	1140	1229	1240	...	...	1329	1340	1429	1440	1440	1529	1541	1629	1644	...
Lisburn § a.		│	0806	│	│	0906	│	│	1004	│	1104	│	1204	│	1304	...	...	│	1404	│	1504	1504	│	1606	│	1710	...
Belfast GCS ♣ § a.		0758	...	0858	0858	...	0958	0958	...	1058	...	1158	...	1258	...	...	...	1358	...	1458	...	...	1558	...	1658	...	...

	⚒ C	⚒ (E)	⚒ C	⚒ (E)	⚒ U	Ⓐ	⚒ C	⚒ (E)	⚒	Ⓐ	⚒ C	⚒ (E)	⚒	⚒ (E)	⚒	⚒	⚒	⚒	⑦	⑦ (E)	⑦ (E)	⑦ (E)	⑦ (E)	⑦ (E)	⑦ (E)	⑦ (E)	⑦ (E)
Dublin Connolly d.	1527	1550	1627	1650	...	1707	1727	1750	...	1807	1827	1850	2017	2050	...	2148	2255	2348		0850	1050	1250	1350	1450	1650	1850	2050
Malahide d.	1547	│	1647	│	...	1728	1747	│	...	1831	1847	│	2042	│	...	2215	2320	0012		│	│	│	│	│	│	│	│
Skerries d.	1601	│	1701	│	...	1744	1802	│	...	1847	1901	│	2057	│	...	2231	2335	0027		│	│	│	│	│	│	│	│
Balbriggan d.	1607	│	1707	│	...	1750	1807	│	...	1853	1907	│	2103	│	...	2237	2340	0033		│	│	│	│	│	│	│	│
Drogheda d.	1624	1627	1724	1727	...	1810	1824	1828	...	1913	1924	1928	2124	2128	...	2258	0001	0052		0928	1128	1328	1428	1528	1728	1928	2128
Dundalk d.	...	1649	▬	1749	...	1834	...	1850	...	1938	...	1950	▬	2150	...	2320t	0026	0119		0950	1150	1350	1450	1550	1750	1950	2150
Newry d.	...	1708	⚒W	1808	...	...	...	1908	...	...	...	2008	⚒	2208	...	...	...	...		1008	1208	1408	1508	1608	1808	2008	2208
Portadown § d.	...	1729	1744	1829	1839	...	...	1929	1940	...	...	2029	2040	2229	2240	...	...	...		1030	1230	1430	1530	1630	1830	2030	2229
Lisburn § a.	...	│	1809	│	1902	...	...	│	2004	...	...	│	2104	│	2304	...	...	...		*1104*	*1304*	*1504*	*1604*	*1704*	*1904*	*2104*	2256
Belfast GCS ♣ § a.	...	1758	...	1858	...	...	...	1958	...	...	...	2058	...	2258	...	...	...	...		1100	1300	1500	1600	1700	1900	2100	2308

A – On ⑥ runs 13 – 19 minutes later.
B – On ⑥ runs 20 minutes later.
C – On ⑥ runs 4 – 9 minutes earlier.
D – On ⑥ runs 2 – 5 minutes later.
S – On ⑥ runs 11 – 12 minutes earlier.
T – On ⑥ runs 3 – 4 minutes earlier.
U – On ⑥ runs 10 minutes later.
W – On ⑥ runs 6 – 9 minutes later.
t – Ⓐ only
§ – Other local trains run Belfast - Lisburn - Portadown and v.v.
♣ – Belfast Grand Central Station (formerly Great Victoria Street).

BELFAST - LARNE and BANGOR — 231

NIR

From Belfast GCS ♣ – Ⓐ: 0615 **H**, 0740 **H**, 0845 **H** and hourly until 1345 **H**, 1445, 1515, 1545, 1630 **H**, 1705 **H**, 1730, 1815 **H**, 1915 **H**, 2015 **H**, 2115 **H**, 2215 **H**, 2315 **H**, 2345 **H**.
⑥: 0715 **H**, and hourly until 2215 **H**, 2345 **H**. ⑦: 0945 **H**, and every **two** hours until 2145 **H**.

From Larne Town – Ⓐ: 0608 **S**, 0648 **S**, 0736 **S** 0758 **S** and hourly until 1458 **S**, 1551, 1627, 1737 **S**, 1828, 1928 **S**, 2028 **S**, 2128 **S**, 2228 **S**.
⑥: 0628 **S**, and hourly until 2228 **S**. ⑦: 0858 **S**, and every **two** hours until 2058 **S**.

Trains call at: Carrickfergus 35 - 36 minutes from Belfast and 26 - 31 minutes from Larne and Whitehead 47 - 49 minutes from Belfast, 17 - 21 minutes from Larne.

Trains marked **H** arrive Larne **Harbour** 4 minutes after Larne **Town**. Trains marked **S** depart Larne **Harbour** 3 minutes before Larne **Town**. Journey time Belfast GCS - Larne Harbour 65 - 70 mins.

From Belfast GCS ♣ – Ⓐ: 0620, 0640, 0735, 0800, 0835, 0905 and every 30 mins. until 1605, 1640, 1700, 1720, 1740, 1800, 1840, 1905 and every 30 mins. until 2135, 2235, 2340.
⑥: 0735, 0805 and every 30 mins. until 2105, 2135, 2235, 2355. ⑦: 0935 and hourly until 2135, 2235.

From Bangor – Ⓐ: 0610, 0651, 0711, 0731, 0811, 0831, 0911, 0941 and every 30 mins. until 1611, 1637, 1657, 1717, 1757, 1817, 1841, 1911, 1941, 2011, 2041, 2111, 2141, 2241.
⑥: 0641, 0741, 0811 and every 30 mins. until 2011, 2041, 2111, 2141, 2241. ⑦: 0841 and hourly until 2041, 2141.

♣ – Belfast Grand Central Station (formerly Great Victoria Street).

🚌 BELFAST - ENNISKILLEN and ARMAGH — 232

Ulsterbus **251, 261**

From Belfast ★ to Enniskillen (Bus Stn) (journey time 2 hours 15 mins)
Ⓐ: 0805, 0905 and hourly until 1905, 2005.
⑥: 1005, 1205, 1405, 1505, 1605, 1805, 2005.
⑦: 1605, 2005.

From Enniskillen (Bus Stn) to Belfast ★
Ⓐ: 0725, 0825, and hourly until 1625, 1725, 1825 ◧.
⑥: 0725, 0925, 1125, 1225, 1325, 1525, 1725.
⑦: 1225, 1525, 1725.

From Belfast ★ to Armagh (Bus Stn) (journey time 1 hour 25 mins)
Ⓐ: 0800, 0945, 1045, 1145, 1245, 1345, 1445, 1645, 1715, 1745, 1845, 1945, 2115.
⑥: 1045, 1245, 1445, 1745, 1845, 2005.
⑦: 1335, 1735, 2015, 2200.

From Armagh (Bus Stn) to Belfast ★
Ⓐ: 0630, 0715, 0805, 0905, 1005, 1105, 1205, 1305, 1505, 1605, 1705, 1805.
⑥: 0730, 0905, 1105, 1305, 1605, 1705.
⑦: 1210, 1410, 1610, 1830, 2015.

Buses call at Portadown (Market Street) 40 - 75 minutes from Belfast and Portadown (Northern Bank) 20–30 minutes from Armagh (Bus Stn).

◧ – Change at Dungannon; arrive Europa Buscentre 2140.
★ – Europa Buscentre.

233 BELFAST - LONDONDERRY and PORTRUSH — NIR

km		Ⓐ	⚒	⚒	⚒	⚒	⚒		⚒	⚒	Ⓐ	⑥		⑦	⑦	⑦	⑦	⑦		⑦	⑦	⑦	⑦	
	Belfast GCS ★ d.	0605	...	0710	...	0810	...	and at	2110	...	2240	2310	...	...	...	0910	...	1010	and at	1910	...	2010	2140	...
0	**Belfast** LP ♣ d.	0615	...	0720	...	0820	...	the same	2120	...	2250	2320	...	...	...	0920	...	1020	the same	1920	...	2020	2150	...
33	Antrim d.	0642	...	0747	...	0847	...	minutes	2147	...	2317	2347	...	...	...	0947	...	1047	minutes	1947	...	2047	2217	...
52	Ballymena d.	0658	...	0803	...	0903	...	past every	2203	...	2330	0001	...	...	...	1003	...	1103	past every	2003	...	2103	2231	...
97	**Coleraine** d.	0743	0745	0843	0845	0943	0945	hour	2243	2245	0005	0037	...	0848	0945	1043	1045	1143	**two** hours	2043	2045	2143	2307	...
107	Portrush a.	|	0757	|	0857	|	0957	until	|	2257	...	...	...	0900	0957	|	1057	1157	until	|	2057	2157	...	...
151	**Londonderry** a.	0822	...	0922	...	1022	...		2322	...	...	...	...	...	...	1122	...	...		2122	...	...	...	...

	Ⓐ	⚒	Ⓐ	Ⓐ	⑥	⑥	⚒	⚒		⚒	⚒	Ⓐ	Ⓐ	⑥	⚒	⑦	⑦	⑦		⑦	⑦	⑦	⑦	⑦
Londonderry d.	...	...	0612	...	...	0640	...	0738	and at	...	2038	...	2138	2138	...	...	...	0938	and at	...	...	1938	...	...
Portrush d.	...	0605	|	0705	0702	|	0802	|	the same	2102	|	2202	|	|	2302	0902	1002	|	the same	1902	2002	|	2102	2202
Coleraine d.	0550	0620	0651	0719	0714	0720	0814	0819	minutes	2114	2119	2214	2219	2216	2314	0920	1014	1019	minutes	1919	2014	2019	2119	2214
Ballymena d.	0626	0700	0730	0800	...	0800	...	0900	past every	...	2200	...	2300	...	...	1000	...	1100	past every	2000	...	2100	2200	...
Antrim d.	0642	0714	0747	0814	...	0814	...	0914	hour	...	2214	...	2316	...	...	1014	...	1114	**two** hours	2014	...	2114	2217	...
Belfast LP ♣ a.	0710	0741	0818	0842	...	0841	...	0941	until	...	2241	...	2342	...	...	1041	...	1141	until	2041	...	2141	2244	...
Belfast GCS ★ a.	0720	0750	0827	0850	...	0850	...	0950		...	2250	...	...	...	...	1050	...	1150		2050	...	2150	2253	...

★ – Belfast Grand Central Station (formerly Great Victoria Street).

♣ – Belfast Lanyon Place (formerly Central Station).

Ulsterbus 212 express 🚌 service, Belfast - Londonderry. Journey time: 1 hour 40 minutes.
Ⓐ: 0630, 0700 and every 30 minutes until 1900, 1930 then 2030, 2130, 2300.
⑥: 0645, 0900, 1000, 1030 and every 30 minutes until 1900, 1930 then 2030, 2130, 2300.
⑦: 0830, 1030, 1100 and every 30 minutes until 1930 then 2030, 2130, 2215, 2300.

Ulsterbus 212 express 🚌 service, Londonderry - Belfast. Journey time: 1 hour 45 minutes.
Ⓐ: 0415, 0530, 0600, and every 30 minutes until 1700 then 1800, 1930, 2100, 2200, 2300.
⑥: 0645, 0730, 0800 and every 30 minutes until 1630, 1700 then 1800, 1930, 2100, 2200, 2300.

234 🚌 DUBLIN - LONDONDERRY — Ulsterbus **X3, X4**

	X4	X3	X4	X3	X4	X4	X3	X4	
Dublin Busáras d.	0630	1000	1100	1215	1515	1800	2015	2230	...
Dublin Airport ✈ △ d.	0650	1020	1120	1235	1535	1820	2035	2250	...
Monaghan d.	|	1205	|	1420	|	|	2220	|	...
Omagh ▽ a.	|	1300	|	1515	|	|	2315	|	...
Strabane ▽ a.	|	1330	|	1545	|	|	2345	|	...
Londonderry a.	1035	1400	1505	1615	1920	2155	0015	0155	...

	X4	X4	X4	X3	X4	X3	X3	X4	
Londonderry d.	0130	0415	0550	0700	0950	1200	1500	1730	...
Strabane △ d.	|	|	|	0730	|	1230	1530	|	...
Omagh △ d.	|	|	|	0800	|	1300	1600	|	...
Monaghan d.	|	|	|	0905	|	1405	1705	|	...
Dublin Airport ✈ ▽ a.	0500	0800	0935	1040	1335	1540	1840	2115	...
Dublin Busáras a.	0520	0820	0955	1100	1355	1600	1900	2135	...

△ – Buses call here to pick up only. ▽ – Buses call here to set down only. ☛ The calling point in each town is the bus station unless otherwise indicated.

234a 🚌 DUBLIN - DONEGAL — Bus Éireann **30**

Dublin Busáras d.	0630	0800	0930	1100	1230	1400	1530	1700	1830	2000	2130	2300	0030
Dublin Airport ✈ △ d.	0650	0820	0950	1120	1250	1420	1550	1720	1850	2020	2150	2320	0050
Virginia d.	0755	0925	1057	1227	1357	1527	1657	1827	1957	2125	2255	0025	0155
Cavan d.	0830	1000	1135	1305	1435	1605	1735	1905	2035	2200	2330	0100	0230
Enniskillen d.	0921	1051	1226	1356	1526	1656	1826	1956	2126	2251	0020	0150	0320
Ballyshannon d.	1000	1130	1307	1437	1607	1737	1907	2037	2207	2330	0059	0229	0359
Donegal ⊡ a.	1022	1152	1327	1457	1627	1757	1927	2057	2227	2350	0119	0249	0419

Donegal ⊡ d.	0100	0230	0400	0530	0700	0830	1000	1130	1300	1430	1600	1730	1900
Ballyshannon d.	0118	0248	0418	0548	0720	0850	1020	1150	1320	1450	1620	1750	1920
Enniskillen d.	0158	0328	0500	0630	0802	0932	1102	1232	1402	1532	1702	1832	2002
Cavan d.	0255	0425	0555	0730	0900	1030	1200	1330	1500	1630	1800	1930	2100
Virginia d.	0322	0452	0622	0759	0929	1059	1229	1359	1529	1659	1829	1957	2127
Dublin Airport ✈ ▽ a.	0431	0601	0732	0910	1042	1212	1342	1514	1644	1814	1944	2111	2240
Dublin Busáras a.	0456	0626	0757	0935	1107	1237	1407	1539	1709	1839	2009	2136	2305

△ – Buses call here to pick up only. ▽ – Buses call here to set down only. ⊡ – Donegal **Abbey Hotel**.

235 🚌 LONDONDERRY - GALWAY and GALWAY - CORK — Bus Éireann **51, 64, 480**

	⚒									⑤⑦
Londonderry d.	...	...	...	0715	0915	1110	...	1530	1830	...
Letterkenny d.	...	...	...	0755	0957	1150	...	1610	1910	...
Donegal (Abbey Hotel) d.	...	0635	...	0840	1040	1240	...	1655	1955	...
Ballyshannon d.	...	0655	...	0900	1100	1300	...	1715	2015	...
Sligo d.	0600	0740	0800	1000	1200	1400	1600	1815	2105	2115
Ireland West Airport Knock d.	0652	...	0905	1105	1305	1500	1705	|	...	|
Knock d.	0710	...	0924	1125	1324	1520	1725	1920	...	2230
Claremorris (Dalton St.) d.	|	...	|	1135	|	1530	1735	|	...	2240
Galway (Bus Station) ✣ a.	0842	...	1045	1240	1445	1635	1840	2040	...	2345

Galway (Bus Station) ✣ d.	...	...	0705	0805		1705	1805	1905	2005
Ennis d.	...	...	0820	0920		1820	1925	2025	2125
Shannon Airport ✈ d.	...	...	0850	0950	and	1850	1955	2055	2155
Limerick (Colbert Rail Station) a.	...	...	0920	1020	hourly	1920	2025	2125	2225
Limerick (Colbert Rail Station) d.	0725	0835	0935	1035	until	1935	2035	...	...
Mallow (Town Park) d.	0830	0940	1040	1140		2040	2140	...	...
Cork a.	0915	1025	1125	1225		2125	2225	...	...

Cork d.	...	...	0725	0825		1725	1825	1925	2055
Mallow (Town Park) d.	...	...	0800	0900		1800	1900	2000	2130
Limerick (Colbert Rail Station) a.	...	...	0910	1010	and	1910	2010	2110	2240
Limerick (Colbert Rail Station) d.	0725	0825	0925	1025	hourly	1925	2025	...	...
Shannon Airport ✈ d.	0755	0855	0955	1055	until	1955	2055	...	...
Ennis d.	0825	0925	1025	1125		2025	2125	...	...
Galway (Bus Station) ✣ a.	0945	1045	1145	1245		2145	2245	...	...

	⚒	⚒		⚒						⑤
Galway (Bus Station) ✣ d.	0600	...	0845	1030	...	1200	*1410*	1600	1810	...
Claremorris (Dalton St.) d.	0700	...	|	1135	...	1305	|	|	1911	...
Knock d.	0710	...	1005	1145	...	1315	*1530*	1725	1921	...
Ireland West Airport Knock d.	0730	...	1025	1205	...	1335	*1550*	1745	|	...
Sligo d.	0845	0855	1145	1310	1330	1500	1710	1905	2040	2100
Ballyshannon d.	...	0945	1232	...	1417	1547	1757	1952	...	2147
Donegal (Abbey Hotel) d.	...	1015	1252	...	1437	1607	1817	2012	...	2207
Letterkenny d.	...	1110	1340	...	1525	1655	1905	2100	...	2250
Londonderry a.	...	1145	1420	...	1605	1735	1945	2140	...	2330

✣ – Change buses at Galway. Minimum connection time 45 minutes.

☛ The calling point in each town is the bus station unless otherwise indicated.

236 DUBLIN - SLIGO — IÉ

km		⚒	Ⓐ 🍷	⚒ 🍷	⚒ 🍷	⚒ 🍷	⚒ 🍷	⚒ 🍷	⚒ 🍷	Ⓐ	Ⓐ	⚒ 🍷	Ⓐ		⑦	⑦ 🍷		⑦ 🍷		⑦ 🍷	⑦ 🍷	⑦ 🍷	⑦ 🍷
0	**Dublin** Connolly d.		0655	0905	1105	1305	1505	1600	1705	1718	1816	1930	2055	...		0905	...	1305	...	1505	1605	1705	1930
26	Maynooth d.		0735	0938	1138	1338	1538	1637	1744	1801	1851	2005	2137	...		0938	...	1338	...	1538	1638	1745	2007
83	Mullingar d.		0817	1019	1219	1419	1619	1719	1825	1850	1931	2046	2216	...		1019	...	1419	...	1619	1719	1826	2048
125	**Longford** d.		0854	1050	1249	1449	1649	1750	1856	1936	1929	2120	...	...		1050	...	1449	...	1650	1750	1857	2122
143	Dromod d.		0909	1104	1304	1504	1704	1807	1911	...	...	2133	...	...		1104	...	1504	...	1705	1807	1911	2135
159	Carrick on Shannon d.		0921	1117	1317	1517	1717	1820	1923	...	...	2145	...	...		1117	...	1517	...	1718	1820	1924	2147
173	Boyle d.		0939	1141	1341	1541	1741	1834	1944	...	...	2158	...	...		1141	...	1541	...	1741	1834	1945	2200
219	**Sligo** a.		1017	1218	1418	1618	1818	1913	2022	...	...	2235	...	...		1218	...	1618	...	1819	1911	2022	2237

	⚒	Ⓐ	Ⓐ	Ⓐ 🍷	⚒ 🍷	⚒ 🍷	⚒ 🍷	⚒ 🍷	⚒ 🍷	⑥ 🍷	Ⓐ 🍷	⚒ 🍷		⑦	⑦ 🍷	⑦ 🍷		⑦ 🍷		⑦ 🍷	⑦ 🍷		⑦ 🍷
Sligo d.		...	...	0540	0640	0905	1105	1305	1505	1705	1705	1905	...		0905	1105	...	1305	...	1505	1705	...	1905
Boyle d.		...	...	0614	0713	0938	1138	1338	1538	1738	1738	1943	...		0938	1141	...	1338	...	1538	1738	...	1943
Carrick on Shannon d.		...	...	0625	0726	0951	1151	1351	1551	1751	1751	1955	...		0951	1155	...	1351	...	1551	1751	...	1956
Dromod d.		...	...	0637	0739	1004	1204	1404	1604	1807	1807	2007	...		1004	1207	...	1404	...	1604	1807	...	2007
Longford d.		0538	0614	0651	0752	1017	1217	1417	1617	1823	1823	2020	...		1017	1220	...	1417	...	1617	1823	...	2020
Mullingar d.		0610	0644	0723	0824	1058	1258	1458	1658	1906	1908	2052	...		1058	1251	...	1458	...	1658	1906	...	2053
Maynooth d.		0657	0727	0808	0905	1140	1340	1539	1746	1949	1958	2134	...		1140	1333	...	1539	...	1746	1949	...	2135
Dublin Connolly a.		0737	0806	0843	0943	1211	1411	1617	1818	2024	2032	2207	...		1211	1405	...	1613	...	1820	2024	...	2208

236a BALLYBROPHY - ROSCREA - LIMERICK — IÉ

km		Ⓐ	⚒ 🍷	⚒		⚒h ◇✕	⚒		⑦	⑦	
0	**Dublin** Heuston d.	...	0800	...	...	1800	...	...	1825	...	...
107	Ballybrophy d.	...	0851	0900	...	1855	1905	...	1932	1940	...
123	Roscrea d.	...	...	0917	...	...	1922	...	|	1957	...
154	Nenagh d.	0749	...	0950	...	...	1955	...	|	2030	...
199	**Limerick** Colbert a.	0842	...	1043	...	...	2047	...	2041	2123	...

	Ⓐ	⑥	⚒		⚒	⚒ ◇🍷		⑦	⑦	
Limerick Colbert d.	0645	0700	0745	...	1710	...	...	1735	1820	...
Nenagh d.	0753	0753	|	...	1803	...	...	1828	|	...
Roscrea d.	0826	0826	|	...	1836	...	...	1901	|	...
Ballybrophy d.	0846	0846	0851	...	1855	1858	...	1921	1925	...
Dublin Heuston a.	...	...	0957	...	...	2001	...	...	2036	...

h – ✕ on Ⓐ, 🍷 on ⑥. ◇ – Also conveys 1st class.

IÉ DUBLIN - ROSSLARE 237

km		⚒		⑥	Ⓐ		Ⓐ	⑥		Ⓐ	Ⓐ	Ⓐ	⑥		Ⓐ		⑦	⑦		⑦		⑦	
0	**Dublin Connolly** ▲ d.		...	0755	0928	...	1328	1355	...	1628	1728	1828	1840	...	2008	...		1025	...	1345	...	1845	...
11	Dún Laoghaire ▲ d.		...	0821	0954	...	1354	1421	...	1654	1754	1854	1906	...	2034	...		1047	...	1407	...	1907	...
21	Bray ▲ d.		...	0842	1018	...	1418	1442	...	1718	1818	1918	1925	...	2057	...		1110	...	1431	...	1930	...
47	Wicklow d.		...	0911	1045	...	1445	1508	...	1743	1845	1946	1956	...	2121	...		1138	...	1457	...	1958	...
80	Arklow d.		...	0936	1110	...	1510	1533	...	1809	1911	2012	2022	...	2147	...		1204	...	1524	...	2024	...
97	Gorey d.		...	0950	1123	...	1523	1547	...	1822	1928	2025	2036	...	2201	...		1217	...	1543	...	2037	...
126	Enniscorthy d.		...	1011	1144	...	1543	1608	...	1842	1948	2045	2056	...	...	...		1238	...	1603	...	2058	...
150	**Wexford** d.		...	1031	1205	...	1605	1629	...	1904	2010	2107	2117	...	...	...		1301	...	1626	...	2121	...
160	Rosslare Strand d.		...	1050	1223	...	1623	1647	...	1922	2028	...	2135	...	...	...		1319	...	1644	...	2139	...
166	**Rosslare** Europort a.		...	1057	1229	...	1629	1654	...	1927	2033	...	2142	...	...	...		1325	...	1650	...	2145	...

	⚒	Ⓐ	Ⓐ	⑥	Ⓐ	⑥		Ⓐ	⑥		Ⓐ	⑥		Ⓐ	Ⓐ	⑦		⑦		⑦		⑦	
Rosslare Europort d.		...	0535	...	0715	0720	...	1250	1315	...	1755	1805	...	...	...		...	0945	...	1410	...	1805	...
Rosslare Strand d.		...	0540	...	0721	0725	...	1255	1320	...	1800	1810	...	...	...		...	0951	...	1416	...	1811	...
Wexford d.		...	0559	...	0740	0744	...	1314	1339	...	1818	1829	...	2125	...		...	1010	...	1436	...	1831	...
Enniscorthy d.		...	0623	...	0800	0805	...	1338	1403	...	1843	1853	...	2150	...		...	1032	...	1457	...	1852	...
Gorey d.		0545	0643	0645	0820	0825	...	1358	1423	...	1902	1913	...	2209	2215		...	1052	...	1517	...	1912	...
Arklow d.		0558	0657	0700	0833	0838	...	1410	1436	...	1915	1926	...	...	2227		...	1105	...	1531	...	1925	...
Wicklow d.		0628	0729	0731	0901	0909	...	1443	1509	...	1945	1957	...	...	2255		...	1137	...	1557	...	1957	...
Bray ▲ d.		0656	0758	0802	0927	0936	...	1510	1535	...	2010	2025	...	...	2324		...	1204	...	1624	...	2025	...
Dún Laoghaire ▲ d.		0717	0819	0824	0950	0958	...	1530	1557	...	2028	2043	...	...	2340		...	1222	...	1642	...	2043	...
Dublin Connolly ▲ a.		0744	0847	0850	1019	1020	...	1555	1619	...	2050	2106	...	...	0005		...	1244	...	1704	...	2105	...

▲ – Additional surburban trains (*DART*) run Howth - Dublin Connolly - Dún Laoghaire - Bray. Trains run every 10 - 15 mins. on ⚒, every 20 - 30 mins. on ⑦.

IÉ DUBLIN - KILKENNY - WATERFORD 238

km		⚒	⚒ 🍷	Ⓐ	⚒ 🍷	Ⓐ	⚒ 🍷	⚒ 🍷	⑤ 🍷	⚒ 🍷	⚒ 🍷	⚒ 🍷	Ⓐ	⑦	⑦ 🍷		⑦ 🍷		⑦ 🍷		⑦ 🍷		⑦ 🍷
0	**Dublin Heuston** △ d.		0720	0826	1015	1225	1315	1510	1610	1640	1735	1835	2020		0910	...	1315	...	1515	...	1735	...	1850
48	Kildare △ d.		0747	0853	1039	1252	|	1538	|	1720	1805	1903	2107		0938	...	1340	...	1540	...	1800	...	1914
72	Athy d.		0809	0912	1056	1316	1353	1555	1648	1738	1822	1920	2123		0955	...	1357	...	1556	...	1818	...	1931
90	Carlow d.		0822	0927	1109	1331	1412	1610	1659	1751	1835	1942	2141		1012	...	1410	...	1610	...	1832	...	1944
106	Muine Bheag d.		0847	...	1124	...	1426	1622	|	1804	1848	1955	2152		1025	...	1423	...	1623	...	1846	...	1957
130	**Kilkenny** a.		0904	...	1142	...	1443	1640	|	1822	1905	2012	2209		1042	...	1442	...	1642	...	1906	...	2014
130	**Kilkenny** d.		0908	...	1147	...	1447	1644	|	1826	1911	2016	2213		1046	...	1446	...	1649	...	1912	...	2018
147	Thomastown d.		0920	...	1159	...	1459	1656	|	1838	1923	2028	2225		1058	...	1458	...	1701	...	1924	...	2030
179	**Waterford** a.		0945	...	1224	...	1532	1720	1752	1904	1948	2056	2250		1123	...	1523	...	1726	...	1949	...	2055

	⚒	Ⓐ	⚒ 🍷	⚒ 🍷	⚒ 🍷	Ⓐ	⚒ 🍷	⚒ 🍷	Ⓐ	⚒ 🍷	⑤⑥	⚒ 🍷	Ⓐ	⑦	⑦ 🍷		⑦ 🍷		⑦ 🍷		⑦ 🍷		⑦ 🍷
Waterford d.		...	0555	0650	0750	...	1100	1305	...	1450	1605	1825	2020		0905	...	1200	...	1400	...	1600	...	1825
Thomastown d.		...	0616	|	0811	...	1121	1326	...	1513	|	1855	2048		0925	...	1220	...	1420	...	1620	...	1845
Kilkenny a.		...	0631	0724	0826	...	1137	1341	...	1528	|	1910	2103		0941	...	1236	...	1436	...	1637	...	1901
Kilkenny d.		...	0635	0728	0830	...	1143	1345	...	1532	|	1914	2107		0945	...	1240	...	1444	...	1644	...	1908
Muine Bheag d.		...	0651	0744	0846	...	1159	1401	...	1548	|	1930	2123		1000	...	1255	...	1459	...	1659	...	1923
Carlow d.		0630	0703	0756	0857	1010	1211	1413	1515	1607	1700	1942	2141		1013	...	1308	...	1512	...	1712	...	1944
Athy d.		0641	0715	0810	0912	1021	1224	1426	1526	1619	1712	1955	2152		1026	...	1321	...	1526	...	1726	...	1957
Kildare △ d.		0701	0734	|	0934	1040	1244	1446	1545	1639	1735	2015	2211		1046	...	1341	...	1550	...	1747	...	2017
Dublin Heuston △ a.		0742	0806	0901	1002	1113	1315	1517	1616	1707	1802	2042	2257		1114	...	1413	...	1623	...	1820	...	2049

△ – For additional trains Dublin - Kildare and v.v, see Tables **240**, **245**.

IÉ LIMERICK - WATERFORD 239

km			⚒ 🍷	⚒			⚒	⚒		
0	**Limerick Colbert** d.	...	0855	...	...	...	1745	...	...	...
35	**Limerick Junction** d.	...	0924	0945	...	...	1819	1840	...	...
40	Tipperary d.	...	...	0958	...	...	...	1853	...	...
62	Cahir d.	...	...	1021	...	...	...	1916	...	...
79	Clonmel d.	...	...	1039	...	...	...	1934	...	...
101	Carrick on Suir d.	...	...	1102	...	...	...	1957	...	...
124	**Waterford** a.	...	...	1130	...	...	...	2028	...	...

		⚒	⚒			⚒	⚒		
Waterford d.	...	0720	...	...	...	1625	...	...	...
Carrick on Suir d.	...	0746	...	...	...	1651	...	...	...
Clonmel d.	...	0808	...	...	...	1713	...	...	...
Cahir d.	...	0827	...	...	...	1732	...	...	...
Tipperary d.	...	0849	...	...	...	1754	...	...	...
Limerick Junction a.	...	0903	0941	...	...	1808	1811	...	...
Limerick Colbert a.	...	...	1008	...	...	...	1839	...	...

IÉ LIMERICK JUNCTION - LIMERICK - GALWAY 239a

km		⚒	⚒	⚒	⚒	⚒	⚒		⑦	⑦	⑦	⑦
0	**Limerick Jct** .... **239b** d.	...	...	...	1542	...	...	...	...	...	...	...
35	**Limerick** ¶ ..... **245** d.	0555	0920	1420	1630	1805	1950	...	0900	1228	1555	1815
74	Ennis ..... **245** d.	0649x	1000	1502	1709	1912z	2030	...	0943	1310	1635	1855
103	Gort d.	0711	1021	1524	...	1941	2051	...	1005	1332	1700	1923
132	Athenry ..... **240** d.	0749	1053	1556	...	2014	2119	...	1037	1404	1732	1955
152	**Galway** ..... **240** a.	0809	1113	1615	...	2033	2142	...	1055	1423	1751	2014

	⚒	⚒	⚒	⚒	⚒	⚒	⚒	⑦	⑦	⑦	⑦
Galway ..... **240** d.	...	0615	...	1025	1345	1750	1845	0825	1155	1610	1830
Athenry ..... **240** d.	...	0637	...	1051	1408	1821	1912	0846	1218	1632	1855
Gort d.	...	0711	...	1118	1434	1847	1941	0913	1244	1701	1923
Ennis ..... **245** d.	0650	0740	1000	1142	1501	1911	2005	0941	1308	1725	1947
Limerick ¶ ..... **245** a.	0730	0820	1040	1222	1542	1952	...	1020	1348	1805	2027
Limerick Jct 239b a.	...	...	1124	...	...	...	...	...	...	...	...

x – Arrive 0634. **z** – Arrive 1844. ¶ – Limerick Colbert.

IÉ LIMERICK JUNCTION - LIMERICK 239b

Shuttle service connecting with main-line trains. *35 km.* Journey time : 25 - 40 minutes. For through services to or from Dublin Heuston see Table **245**.

From Limerick Junction ⚒: 0811, 0838, 0941, 1041, 1138, 1241, 1337, 1437, 1542, 1632, 1732, 1832, 1942, 2048, 2240. Also 0731 Ⓐ.
⑦: 1006, 1137, 1337, 1447, 1537, 1647, 1737, 1847, 1935, 2040.

From Limerick Colbert ⚒: 0525, 0610, 0725, 0903, 0955, 1055, 1150, 1255, 1350, 1455, 1555, 1650, 1745, 1850, 1955, 2100. Also 0655 Ⓐ.
⑦: 0925, 1050, 1245, 1352, 1445, 1550, 1645, 1750, 1845, 1950.

240 DUBLIN - GALWAY, BALLINA and WESTPORT IÉ

km		Ⓐ	⑥	Ⓐ	Ⓐ 🍷	⑥	Ⓐ	A 🍷	A	⑤	⑤	⚒ 🍷	⚒ 🍷	⚒ 🍷	⚒ 🍷	⚒ 🍷	⚒ 🍷	⚒ 🍷	①–④	⑤	⚒ 🍷	⚒ 🍷	⚒ 🍷	⚒ 🍷	⚒	⚒ 🍷
0	**Dublin Heuston 245** d.	...	...	...	0545	...	...	0735	...	0735	...	0925	1130	1245	1330	1445	1535	1630	1710	1710	1730	1815	1830	1935	...	2030
48	Kildare **245** d.	...	...	...	0614	...	...	0800	...	0800	...	│	│	│	│	│	│	1700	1739	1739	│	│	│	│	...	│
67	Portarlington **245** d.	...	...	...	0628	...	...	0816	...	0816	...	0958	1206	1319	1405	1519	1614	│	1755	1755	1813	│	1915	2013	...	2111
93	Tullamore d.	...	...	...	0650	0650	0727	0832	...	0832	...	1015	1222	1336	1421	1544	1637	1726	1811	1811	1830	1914	│	2028	...	2134
129	**Athlone** d.	...	...	0708	0730	0730	0758	0908	0910	0910**x**	0908	1044	1248	1409	1447	1612	1704	1751	1851	1852	1905	1940	1956	2101	2108	2205
152	Ballinasloe d.	...	...	│	0744	0744	0813	0922	│	│	0922	1100	1304	│	1503	│	1720	1808	...	│	1921	│	2013	2116	│	2221
187	Athenry **239a** d.	...	...	│	0816	0816	0838	0947	│	│	0951	1129	1327	│	1526	│	1742	1837	...	│	1945	│	2034	2143	│	2245
208	**Galway 239a** a.	...	...	│	0836	0836	0858	1012	│	│	1013	1153	1353	│	1548	│	1759	1854	...	│	2007	│	2056	2204	│	2307
160	Roscommon d.	...	...	0729	▬	...	...	...	0930	0930	▬	...	...	1435	▬	1636	▬	▬	...	1947	...	2011	▬	...	2129	▬
186	Castlerea d.	...	...	0747	...	...	...	...	0948	0948	...	...	...	1453	...	1654	...	...	...	2005	...	2029	...	...	2147	...
204	Ballyhaunis d.	...	...	0803	...	...	...	...	1002	1002	...	...	...	1507	...	1708	...	...	...	2019	...	2043	...	...	2201	...
222	Claremorris d.	...	...	0817	Ⓐ	...	...	...	1018	1018	⚒	...	...	1522	⚒	1724	⚒	⚒	...	2034	...	2058	⚒	...	2216	⚒
240	Manulla Junction § d.	0538	0737	0831	0840	...	...	...	1032	1032	1039	...	...	1536	1538	1738	1742	1848	...	│	...	2113	2116	...	2229	2233
273	**Ballina** a.	0605	0804	│	0907	...	...	...	│	│	1106	...	...	│	1605	│	1809	1915	...	│	...	│	2143	...	│	2300
246	Castlebar d.	...	...	0838	...	...	...	...	1038	1038	...	...	...	1542	...	1744	...	...	...	2052	...	2119	...	...	2236	...
264	**Westport** a.	...	...	0855	...	...	...	...	1057	1057	...	...	...	1600	...	1802	...	...	...	2110	...	2137	...	...	2253	...

⑦	⑦ 🍷	⑦	⑦ 🍷	⑦ 🍷	⑦ 🍷	⑦	⑦ 🍷	⑦ 🍷	⑦ 🍷	⑦ 🍷	⑦ 🍷	⑦
Dublin Heuston 245 d.	0800	...	1030	1140	1340	...	1440	1540	1635	1830	1845	2030
Kildare **245** d.	0824	...	1058	1204	1408	...	│	│	│	1859	1909	│
Portarlington **245** d.	0837	...	1110	1217	1421	...	1513	│	1708	1913	1922	2107
Tullamore d.	0854	...	1126	1245	1438	...	1537	1631	1726	1931	1949	2123
Athlone d.	0925	0942	1200	1324	1510	...	1604	1659	1809	2000	2025	2149
Ballinasloe d.	0941	│	1216	1339	│	...	1620	│	1821	│	2040	2205
Athenry **239a** d.	1005	│	1242	1400	│	...	1643	│	1850	│	2104	2225
Galway 239a a.	1027	│	1302	1420	│	...	1707	│	1912	│	2125	2247
Roscommon d.	▬	1003	▬	▬	1533	...	...	1730	▬	2024	▬	...
Castlerea d.	...	1022	...	...	1552	...	...	1748	...	2042	...	...
Ballyhaunis d.	...	1036	...	...	1606	...	...	1802	...	2056	...	...
Claremorris d.	⑦	1051	⑦	⑦	1623	...	...	1825	⑦	2111	⑦	...
Manulla Junction § d.	0813	1105	1109	1342	1637	1640	...	1839	1842	2126	2128	...
Ballina a.	0840	│	1136	1409	│	1707	...	│	1909	│	2155	...
Castlebar d.	...	1112	...	...	1644	...	...	1845	...	2132	...	...
Westport a.	...	1129	...	...	1701	...	...	1903	...	2149	...	...

	Ⓐ	Ⓐ	Ⓐ	⑥	⚒ 🍷	⚒	⚒ 🍷	Ⓐ
Westport d.	...	...	0515	...	...	...	0715	...
Castlebar d.	...	...	0528	...	...	...	0728	...
Ballina d.	...	0505	│	...	...	0705	│	...
Manulla Junction § d.	...	0532	0534	...	...	0732	0735	...
Claremorris d.	...	▬	0547	...	...	▬	0748	...
Ballyhaunis d.	...	...	0600	...	...	...	0802	...
Castlerea d.	...	...	0613	...	...	⚒	0816	...
Roscommon d.	...	Ⓐ	0632	...	...	🍷	0836	...
Galway 239a d.	...	0525	│	...	0625	0730	│	0905
Athenry **239a** d.	...	0543	│	...	0642	0748	│	0922
Ballinasloe d.	...	0605	│	...	0704	0813	│	0943
Athlone d.	0520	0624	0700	0700	0723	0830	0909	1003
Tullamore d.	0545	0648	0725	0725	0747	0854	0933	1034
Portarlington **245** d.	0602	0708	0742	0742	│	0914	0951	1053
Kildare **245** d.	0617	0721	0757	0757	0816	│	│	│
Dublin Heuston 245 a.	0655	0756	0831	0827	0845	0952	1027	1129

	⑥	⚒	⚒ 🍷	⚒ 🍷	⚒	⚒ 🍷	⚒ 🍷	⚒	⚒ 🍷	⚒ 🍷	⚒	⚒ 🍷	⚒ 🍷	⚒	⚒
Westport d.	...	...	0945	...	...	1310	...	...	1620	...	...	1825	...	...	...
Castlebar d.	...	...	0958	...	...	1323	...	...	1633	...	...	1838	...	...	...
Ballina d.	...	0935	│	...	1300	│	...	1505	│	...	1816	│	...	2043	2200
Manulla Junction § d.	...	1002	1004	...	1327	1329	...	1532	│	...	1843	1845	...	2110	2227
Claremorris d.	...	▬	1020	...	▬	1343	...	...	1650	...	▬	1858	...	▬	▬
Ballyhaunis d.	...	...	1033	...	...	1357	...	...	1710	...	...	1912	...	...	...
Castlerea d.	...	Ⓐ	1048	...	Ⓐ	1411	...	...	1723	...	...	1926	...	⚒	Ⓐ
Roscommon d.	...		1107	...	🍷	1436	...	...	1743	...	...	1946	...		
Galway 239a d.	0925	1005	│	1105	1305	│	1505	...	│	1720	1818	│	1925	2050	2225
Athenry **239a** d.	0948	1028	│	1131	1328	│	1527	...	│	1744	1839	│	1945	2113	2247
Ballinasloe d.	1010	1101	│	1154	1351	│	1548	...	│	1810	1922	│	2013	2140	2312
Athlone d.	1028	1118	1138	1212	1409	1500	1612	...	1809	1829	1939	2019	2035	2207	2329
Tullamore d.	1053	1145	1203	1241	1440	1526	1637	...	...	1853	...	2052	2115	2233	...
Portarlington **245** d.	1112	1204	1228	1300	1506	1544	1655	...	...	1915	...	2110	2133	2252	...
Kildare **245** d.	│	│	│	│	│	│	1707	...	...	1927	...	│	│	2304	...
Dublin Heuston 245 a.	1150	1241	1305	1337	1543	1624	1740	...	...	1958	...	2145	2209	2336	...

⑦	⑦	⑦ 🍷	⑦	⑦	⑦	⑦ 🍷	⑦	⑦ 🍷	⑦ 🍷	⑦	⑦ 🍷
Westport d.	...	0750	...	...	...	1320	...	1545	...	...	1750
Castlebar d.	...	0803	...	...	...	1333	...	1558	...	...	1803
Ballina d.	0740	│	1035	...	1310	│	1535	│	...	1740	│
Manulla Junction § d.	0807	0810	1102	...	1337	1339	1602	1605	...	1807	1809
Claremorris d.	▬	0823	▬	...	▬	1352	▬	1622	...	▬	1825
Ballyhaunis d.	...	0837	...	...	...	1406	...	1635	...	...	1838
Castlerea d.	⑦	0851	⑦	...	⑦	1420	⑦	1649	...	⑦	1851
Roscommon d.	🍷	0912	🍷	...	🍷	1440	🍷	1710	...	🍷	1910
Galway 239a d.	0800	│	1100	1220	1340	│	1500	│	1700	1800	│
Athenry **239a** d.	0818	│	1118	1241	1401	│	1518	│	1722	1818	│
Ballinasloe d.	0844	│	1141	1303	1426	│	1542	│	1745	1845	│
Athlone d.	0903	0939	1200	1324	1446	1509	1605	1742	1807	1914	1937
Tullamore d.	0935	1006	1226	1350	1518	1538	1633	1806	1832	1931	2008
Portarlington **245** d.	0953	1026	1245	1409	1537	1555	1651	1826	1851	1949	2031
Kildare **245** d.	1006	│	1258	│	│	│	1703	1839	│	│	│
Dublin Heuston 245 a.	1037	1102	1328	1445	1614	1631	1734	1908	1929	2025	2106

A – ①②③④⑥.

x – Arrive 0906.

§ – Passenger transfer point only.

244 (DUBLIN -) CORK - MALLOW - TRALEE IÉ

km		⚒	⚒	⚒	⚒	⚒	⚒	⚒ ◇✕	⚒		⑦	⑦ ◇🍷	⑦	⑦	⑦	⑦	⑦		
0	**Cork 245** d.	0625	0900	*1025*	*1225*	*1425*	*1655*	*1855*	2055	...	0855	*1010*	1215	1450	*1625*	1850	*2045*	...	...
	Dublin **245** d.	│	*0700*	*0900*	*1100*	*1300*	*1500*	1705	*1900*	...	│	0830	*1000*	*1300*	*1500*	*1700*	1905	...	...
34	**Mallow 245** d.	0650	0926	1125	1325	1525	1725	1921	2125	...	0920	1037	1250	1530	1725	1930	2112	...	...
66	Millstreet d.	0716	0948	1148	1348	1548	1748	1948	2148	...	0943	1103	1316	1553	1749	1953	2137	...	...
100	Killarney d.	0749	1021	1221	1421	1621	1821	2022	2218	...	1013	1135	1346	1626	1827	2031	2209	...	...
134	**Tralee** a.	0826	1058	1258	1458	1658	1858	2100	2258	...	1050	1223	1424	1704	1904	2109	2247	...	...

	①	②–⑤	⚒ ◇✕	⚒	⚒	⚒	⚒	⚒	⚒		⑦		⑦ 🍷	⑦ 🍷	⑦	⑦	⑦ 🍷	⑦	
Tralee d.	0430	0545	0705	0905	1105	1305	1505	1705	1905	...	0710	...	1150	1350	1510	1710	1750	1915	...
Killarney d.	0505	0622	0745	0941	1141	1341	1541	1741	1941	...	0746	...	1226	1432	1546	1744	1829	1951	...
Millstreet d.	0532	0650	0815	1010	1210	1410	1610	1810	2010	...	0814	...	1255	1501	1615	1812	1859	2019	...
Mallow 245 d.	0558	0729	0843	1037	1237	1437	1637	1842	2041	...	0849	...	1321	1528	1642	1842	1926	2051	...
Dublin **245** a.	*0819*	*0928*	1045	*1256*	*1457*	*1655*	*1904*	*2105*	*2301*	...	*1056*	...	1526	1738	*1855*	*2059*	2129	│	...
Cork 245 a.	*0715*	0754	*0915*	*1141*	*1341*	*1533*	*1732*	1904	2104	...	0915	...	*1350*	*1633*	*1723*	1908	*2029*	2115	...

◇ – Also conveys 🛏1.

CORK - COBH Journey time: 26 minutes *19 km.*

Ⓐ 0530, 0630, 0700, 0730, then half hourly until 1900, 1930, 2000, 2100, 2200, 2300.
⑥ 0600, 0700, 0730, 0800, then half hourly until 1900, 1930, 2000, 2100, 2200, 2300.
† 0800, 0900, 1000, then hourly until 2200, 2300.

COBH - CORK

Ⓐ 0600, 0700, 0730, 0800, then half hourly until 1930, 2000, 2030, 2130, 2230, 2330.
⑥ 0630, 0730, 0800, 0830, then half hourly until 1930, 2000, 2030, 2130, 2230, 2330.
† 0830, 0930, 1030, then hourly until 2230, 2330.

CORK - MIDLETON Journey time: 23 mins. *19 km.*

Ⓐ 0545, 0615, 0645, 0715, then half hourly until 1845, 1915, 2015, 2115, 2245.
⑥ 0545, 0615, 0715, 0815, then hourly until 2015, 2115, 2245.
† 0815, 0915, 1015 then hourly until 2015, 2115, 2245.

MIDLETON - CORK

Ⓐ 0615, 0645, 0715, 0745, then half hourly until 1915, 1945, 2045, 2145, 2315.
⑥ 0615, 0645, 0745, 0845, then hourly until 2045, 2145, 2315.
† 0845, 0945, 1045, then hourly until 2045, 2145, 2315.

IÉ DUBLIN - LIMERICK, TRALEE and CORK 245

km			Ⓐ ◇🍷	⚒ ◇🍷	⚒	⚒ ◇🍷	⚒	⚒ ◇🍷	⚒	⚒ ◇🍷	⚒	⚒ ◇🍷	⚒	⚒ ◇🍷	⚒	⚒ ◇🍷	⚒	⚒ ◇🍷	⚒	⚒ ◇🍷	⚒ 🍷	⚒ 🍷	⚒ ◇🍷	⚒
0	**Dublin Heuston** **240** d.		0600	0700	...	0800	...	0900	...	1000	...	1100	...	1200	...	1300	...	1400	...	1500	1525	1530	1600	...
48	Kildare **240** d.		|	|	...	|	...	|	...	|	...	|	...	|	...	|	...	|	...	|	1612	1556	|	...
67	Portarlington **240** d.		|	|	...	|	...	|	...	|	...	|	...	|	...	|	...	|	...	|	1626	1608	|	...
82	Portlaoise d.	⚒	|	0740	...	|	...	0940	...	1043	...	1140	...	1240	...	1340	...	1442	...	|	1637	1619	|	...
107	Ballybrophy d.		|	|	...	0852	...	0955	...	|	...	|	...	|	...	|	...	1457	...	|	▬	1634	|	...
127	Templemore d.		|	|	...	0904	...	|	...	|	...	1203	...	|	...	|	...	|	...	|	...	1646	|	...
139	Thurles d.		0707	0813	...	0917	...	1017	...	1114	...	1217	...	1312	...	1412	...	1519	...	1607	⚒	1659	1708	...
172	**Limerick Junction** § d.		0726	0832	0838	0935	0941	1035	1041	1132	1138	1235	1241	1331	1337	1431	1437	1537	1542	1626	1632	|	1727	1732
208	**Limerick Colbert** § **239a** a.		*0758*	|	0905	|	1008	|	1108	|	1205	|	1308	|	1404	|	1504	|	1609	|	1659	1743	|	1759
**	Ennis **239a** a.		|	|	*0959*	|	...	|	▬	|	1309	|	▬	|	*1459*	|	▬	|	1709	|	▬	...	|	*1844*
208	Charleville d.		0745	|	...	|	...	1055	⚒	|	...	1255	⚒	|	...	|	⚒	|	...	1645	⚒	...	|	...
232	**Mallow** **244** d.		0805	0908	...	1010	...	1115	1125	1207	...	1314	1325	1406	...	1506	1525	1612	...	1705	1725	...	1802	...
	Tralee **244** a.		|	*1058*	...	|	...	|	1258	|	...	|	1458	|	...	|	1658	|	...	|	1858	...	|	...
266	**Cork** **244** a.		0832	0935	...	1038	...	1141	...	1232	...	1341	...	1433	...	1533	...	1639	...	1732	...	...	1828	...

	⚒ 🍷	⚒ ◇✕	⚒	⚒ ◇✕	⚒ 🍷	⚒ ◇✕	⚒	⚒ ◇🍷	⚒	⚒	Ⓐ	⑥	⚒		⑦ ◇🍷	⑦	⑦	⑦ ◇🍷	⑦	⑦	⑦ 🍷	⑦ ◇🍷	⑦	⑦
Dublin Heuston **240** d.	1625	1700	...	1705	1725	1800	...	1900	...	...	2100	2100	...		0830	...	...	1000	...	...	1135	1200	...	...
Kildare **240** d.	|	|	...	|	1755	|	...	|	...	...	|	|	...		|	...	...	|	...	...	|	|	...	...
Portarlington **240** d.	1700	|	...	|	1807	|	...	|	...	...	|	|	...		|	...	...	|	...	...	|	|	...	...
Portlaoise d.	1711	|	...	|	1818	|	...	1944	...	...	2140	2140	...	⑦	0909	...	...	1040	...	...	1214	1240	...	...
Ballybrophy d.	1725	|	...	1800	1832	1855	...	1959	...	...	2155	|	...		|	...	...	|	...	...	1228	|	...	...
Templemore d.	1735	|	...	1811	1843	|	...	2011	...	...	|	|	...		|	...	...	|	...	...	1241	|	...	...
Thurles d.	1747	|	...	1824	1856	1917	...	2024	...	...	2216	2216	...		0941	...	...	1112	...	...	1255	1312	...	...
Limerick Junction § d.	1811	1827	1832	|	|	1936	1942	2043	2048	...	2235	2235	2240		0958	1006	...	1131	...	1137	|	1331	1337	...
Limerick Colbert § **239a** a.	1839	|	1858	|	1942	|	2009	|	2115	...	|	|	2307		|	1033	...	|	...	1204	1338	|	1404	1410
Ennis **239a** a.	...	|	...	|	*2029*	|	2109	|	...	...	|	|	...		|	1124	...	|	...	*1307*	...	|	...	1449
Charleville d.	...	|	...	1858	...	|	...	2102	...	...	|	|	...		1017	...	...	|	...	...	...	|	...	...
Mallow **244** d.	...	1902	...	1921	...	2011	...	2122	...	2125	2311	2311	...		1037	...	1048	1206	1250	...	...	1406	...	...
Tralee **244** a.	...	|	...	2100	...	|	...	|	...	2258	|	|	...		1223	...	|	|	1424	...	...	|	...	...
Cork **244** a.	...	1929	...	...	...	2037	...	2148	...	...	2339	2339	...		...	...	1110	1233	...	...	...	1433	...	...

	⑦ ◇🍷	⑦	⑦ 🍷	⑦ ◇🍷	⑦	⑦ ◇🍷	⑦	⑦ 🍷	⑦ ◇🍷	⑦	⑦	⑦ ◇🍷	⑦	⑦ 🍷	⑦ 🍷	⑦	⑦ ◇🍷	⑦	⑦	⑦ 🍷	⑦	⑦		
Dublin Heuston **240** d.	1300	...	1335	1400	...	1500	...	1535	1600	...	...	1700	...	1800	1825	...	1900	1905	...	1925	2100	2110	...	...
Kildare **240** d.	|	...	|	|	...	|	...	|	|	...	...	|	...	|	1853	...	|	|	...	1958	|	2138	...	...
Portarlington **240** d.	|	...	|	|	...	|	...	|	|	...	...	|	...	|	1907	...	|	1937	...	2012	|	2150	...	...
Portlaoise d.	|	...	1415	1440	...	|	...	1615	1640	...	...	|	...	1839	1918	...	|	|	...	2023	2140	2201	...	...
Ballybrophy d.	|	...	1430	|	...	|	...	1631	|	...	...	|	...	|	1932	...	|	|	...	2037	|	|	...	...
Templemore d.	|	...	1443	|	...	|	...	1643	|	...	...	|	...	|	1942	...	|	|	...	2048	|	|	...	...
Thurles d.	1407	...	1457	1512	...	1607	...	1657	1712	...	...	1807	...	1911	1954	...	2007	2016	...	2101	2212	2232	...	...
Limerick Junction § d.	|	...	|	1531	1537	|	...	|	1731	1737	...	|	...	1928	|	...	|	2033	2040	|	2230	|	...	...
Limerick Colbert § **239a** a.	|	...	1541	|	1604	|	...	1741	|	1804	1815	|	...	*2002*	2041	2050	|	|	2107	2145	|	2316	...	...
Ennis **239a** a.	|	...	*1634*	|	...	|	...	...	|	...	1854	|	...	|	...	2129	|	|	...	...	|	...	...	...
Charleville d.	1441	...	...	|	...	|	...	...	1750	...	...	|	...	|	...	...	|	2052	...	...	|	...	...	...
Mallow **244** d.	1501	1530	...	1606	...	1656	1725	...	1810	...	...	1856	1930	2003	...	...	2056	2112	...	...	2306	...	...	...
Tralee **244** a.	|	1704	...	|	...	|	1904	...	|	...	...	|	2109	|	...	...	|	2247	...	...	|	...	...	...
Cork **244** a.	1528	...	...	1633	...	1723	...	...	1837	...	...	1923	...	2029	...	...	2126	...	...	...	2331	...	...	...

		⚒	①	⚒ 🍷	Ⓐ 🍷	⚒ 🍷	②–⑤	⚒	⚒ ◇✕	⚒	⚒ 🍷	⚒ ✕	⚒	⚒	⚒	⚒ ◇🍷	⚒	⚒ ◇🍷	⚒	⚒ ◇🍷	⚒	⚒ ◇🍷	⚒	⚒ ◇🍷
Cork **244** d.		...	...	0540	0615	...	...	...	0700	...	...	...	...	...	...	0925	...	1025	...	1125	...	1225	...	1325
Tralee **244** d.		...	0430	|	|	...	0545	...	|	...	...	0705	...	...	...	|	...	*0905*	...	|	...	*1105*	...	|
Mallow **244** d.	⚒	...	0558	0604	|	...	0719	...	0721	...	...	0843	...	...	...	0946	...	1046	...	1146	...	1246	...	1345
Charleville d.		...	...	0618	|	...	...	...	|	...	...	0858	...	...	...	|	...	1102	...	|	...	|	...	|
Ennis **239a** d.		...	...	|	|	...	...	...	|	0650	...	|	0740	...	...	|	1000	|	...	|	*1142*	|	...	|
Limerick Colbert § **239a** d.		0525	...	*0610*	|	0640	...	0725	|	0730	0745	|	0820	0855	0955	|	1055	|	1150	|	1255	|	1350	|
Limerick Junction § d.		0558	...	0643	|	|	...	0759	0801	...	|	0920	...	0927	1023	1025	1124	1127	1220	1222	1323	1325	1419	1421
Thurles d.		0614	...	0700	|	0723	...	...	0818	...	0828	|	...	0946	...	1042	...	|	...	1241	...	|	...	1437
Templemore d.		0623	...	|	|	0732	...	...	|	...	0837	|	...	|	...	|	...	1151	...	|	...	1348	...	|
Ballybrophy d.		0634	...	|	|	0743	...	...	|	...	0851	|	...	|	...	|	...	|	...	1258	...	|	...	|
Portlaoise d.		0654	...	|	|	0801	...	...	|	...	0909	|	...	|	...	1114	...	|	...	1318	...	1415	...	1510
Portarlington **240** d.		|	...	|	|	0811	...	...	|	...	|	|	...	|	...	|	...	|	...	|	...	|	...	|
Kildare **240** d.		0717	...	|	|	0824	...	...	|	...	|	|	...	|	...	|	...	|	...	|	...	|	...	|
Dublin Heuston **240** a.		0750	...	0819	0829	0855	...	...	0928	...	0957	1045	...	1056	...	1156	...	1256	...	1400	...	1457	...	1555

	⚒	⚒	⚒ ◇🍷	⚒	⚒ ◇🍷	⚒	⚒ ◇🍷	⚒	⚒ ◇🍷	⚒	⚒	⚒ ◇🍷	⚒	Ⓐ ◇🍷	⚒	⚒ ◇🍷			⑦	⑦ 🍷	⑦ 🍷	⑦	⑦ 🍷	⑦ ◇🍷
Cork **244** d.	...	...	1425	...	1525	...	1625	...	1725	...	...	1825	...	1925	...	2025	...		...	...	0825	...	...	1025
Tralee **244** d.	...	...	*1305*	...	|	...	*1505*	...	|	...	...	*1705*	...	|	...	*1905*	...		...	...	*0710*	...	...	|
Mallow **244** d.	...	...	1446	...	1546	...	1646	...	1746	...	...	1846	...	1946	...	2047	...	⑦	...	...	0846	...	...	1046
Charleville d.	...	...	1502	...	|	...	1702	...	|	...	...	1902	...	|	...	2104	...		...	...	0902	...	...	1102
Ennis **239a** d.	1325	...	|	*1501*	|	...	|	...	|	1725	...	|	*1911*	|	...	|	...		0740	...	|	0941	...	|
Limerick Colbert § **239a** d.	1405	1455	|	1555	|	1650	|	1745	|	1805	1850	|	1955	|	2100	|	...		0820	0825	|	1020	1025	*1050*
Limerick Junction § d.	...	1523	1526	1623	1624	1718	1726	1819	1823	...	1918	1926	2023	2025	2129	2130	...		...	|	0925	...	|	1125
Thurles d.	...	...	1545	...	1641	...	1745	...	1841	...	...	1945	...	2042	...	2147	...		...	0908	|	...	1108	1144
Templemore d.	...	...	|	...	|	...	1755	...	|	...	...	1955	...	|	...	|	...		...	0917	|	...	1117	|
Ballybrophy d.	...	...	|	...	|	...	|	...	1858	...	...	|	...	|	...	|	...		...	0928	|	...	1128	|
Portlaoise d.	...	...	|	...	1713	...	1822	...	1918	...	...	2022	...	2114	...	2220	...		...	0946	1013	...	1146	1216
Portarlington **240** d.	...	...	|	...	|	...	|	...	|	...	...	|	...	|	...	|	...		...	0958	|	...	1156	|
Kildare **240** d.	...	...	|	...	|	...	|	...	|	...	...	|	...	|	...	|	...		...	1014	|	...	1209	|
Dublin Heuston **240** a.	...	...	1655	...	1759	...	1904	...	2001	...	...	2105	...	2156	...	2301	...		...	1044	1056	...	1237	1258

	⑦ 🍷	⑦ ◇🍷	⑦ 🍷	⑦	⑦ ◇🍷	⑦ 🍷	⑦ ◇🍷	⑦ 🍷	⑦	⑦ ◇🍷	⑦	⑦ 🍷	⑦ ◇🍷	⑦	⑦ ◇🍷	⑦ 🍷	⑦	⑦ ◇🍷	⑦ 🍷	⑦	⑦ ◇🍷			
Cork **244** d.	...	1225	...	...	1325	...	1425	...	...	1525	...	...	1625	...	1725	...	...	1825	...	...	1925	...	...	...
Tralee **244** d.	...	|	1150	...	|	...	|	1350	...	|	...	...	*1510*	...	|	...	...	*1710*	1750	...	|	...	...	...
Mallow **244** d.	...	1246	1321	...	1346	...	1445	1528	...	1546	...	...	1646	...	1746	...	...	1846	1926	...	1946	...	...	...
Charleville d.	...	1302	1336	...	|	...	1500	1543	...	|	...	...	1702	...	|	...	...	1902	|	...	|	...	...	...
Ennis **239a** d.	*1135*	|	|	*1308*	|	...	|	|	...	|	1515	...	|	...	|	*1725*	...	|	|	1900	|	...	...	...
Limerick Colbert § **239a** d.	1225	*1245*	|	1352	|	1420	|	|	1550	|	1556	1620	|	1750	|	1820	1845	|	|	1950	|	...	...	...
Limerick Junction § d.	|	1325	1357	1420	1423	|	|	|	1619	1622	...	|	|	1819	1823	|	1916	1925	2000	2018	2023	...	...	...
Thurles d.	1308	1344	1416	...	1441	1503	1537	1619	...	1641	...	1703	1741	...	1841	1903	...	1944	2018	...	2041	...	...	...
Templemore d.	1317	|	|	...	|	1512	|	|	...	|	...	1712	|	...	|	1912	...	|	|	...	|	...	...	...
Ballybrophy d.	1328	|	|	...	|	1524	|	|	...	|	...	1724	|	...	|	1925	...	|	|	...	|	...	...	...
Portlaoise d.	1346	1416	|	...	|	1545	1609	|	...	|	...	1743	1813	...	|	1943	...	2016	|	...	2113	...	...	...
Portarlington **240** d.	1356	|	|	...	|	1600	|	1657	...	|	...	1753	|	...	|	1955	...	|	|	...	|	...	...	...
Kildare **240** d.	1409	|	|	...	|	1614	|	1710	...	|	...	1806	|	...	|	2008	...	|	|	...	|	...	...	...
Dublin Heuston **240** a.	1437	1500	1526	...	1552	1642	1651	1738	...	1751	...	1834	1855	...	1951	2036	...	2059	2129	...	2155	...	...	...

◇ – Also conveys [1].

§ – Also Table **239b**.

** – Limerick - Ennis: *39 km*.

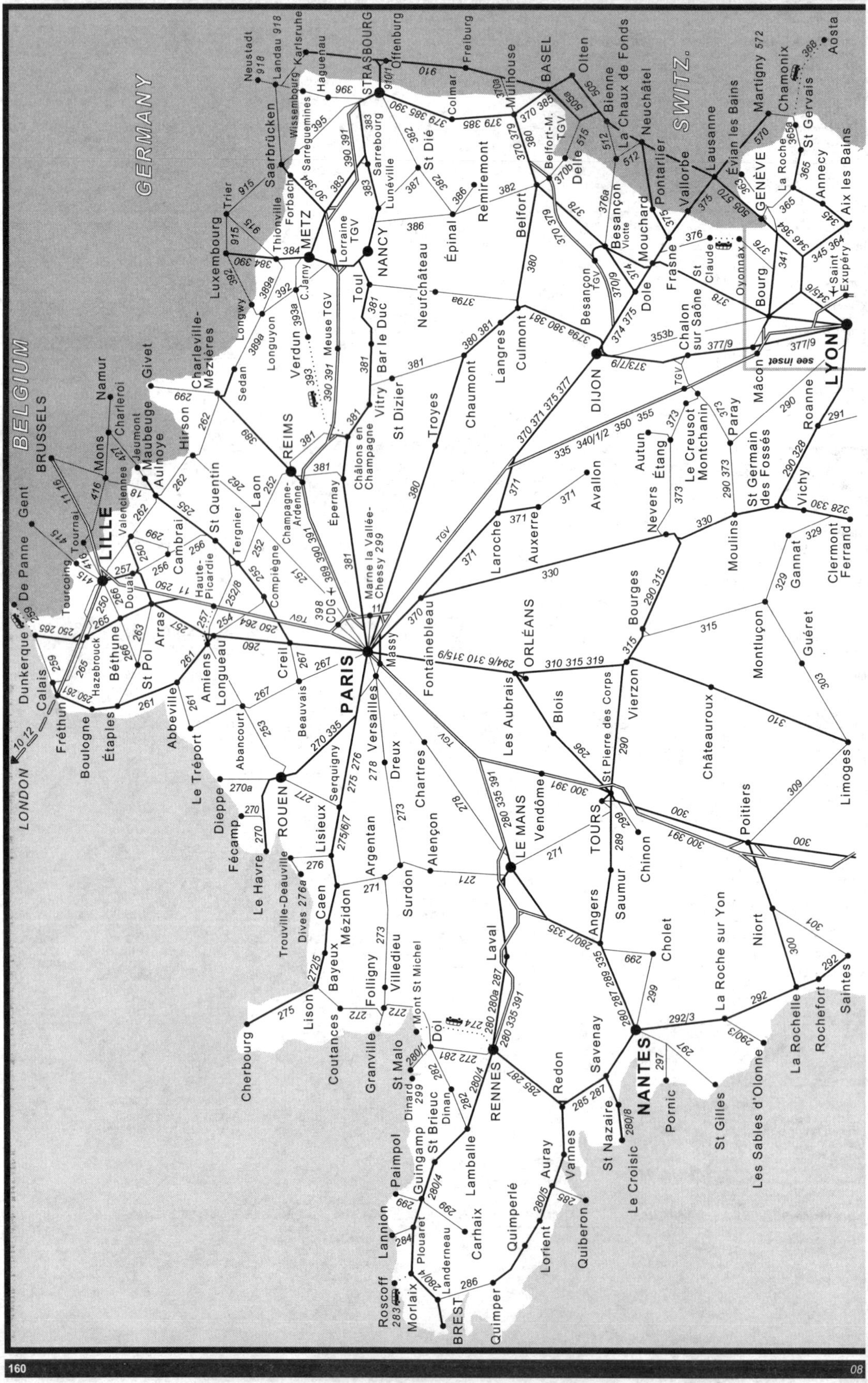
BELGIUM
GERMANY
SWITZ.
LONDON
BRUSSELS
Gent
Mons
Namur
Charleroi
De Panne
Tournai
Tourcoing
LILLE
Dunkerque
Calais
Fréthun
Boulogne
Étaples
Hazebrouck
Béthune
St Pol
Arras
Douai
Valenciennes
Jeumont
Maubeuge
Aulnoye
Cambrai
St Quentin
Hirson
Givet
Charleville-Mézières
Sedan
Longwy
Longuyon
Luxembourg
Trier
Saarbrücken
Thionville
Forbach
Sarreguemines
Wissembourg
Neustadt
Landau
Karlsruhe
Haguenau
STRASBOURG
Offenburg
Freiburg
Colmar
Mulhouse
BASEL
Olten
Bienne
La Chaux de Fonds
Neuchâtel
Pontarlier
Vallorbe
Lausanne
Évian les Bains
Martigny
Chamonix
Aosta
St Gervais
La Roche
Annecy
Aix les Bains
GENÈVE
Bourg
Oyonnax
St Claude
Saint Exupéry
LYON
see inset
Mâcon
Roanne
Vichy
Clermont Ferrand
St Germain des Fossés
Paray
Le Creusot Montchanin
Chalon sur Saône
Dijon
Dole
Besançon TGV
Besançon Viotte
Mouchard
Frasne
Belfort
Belfort-M. TGV
Delle
Remiremont
Épinal
St Dié
Lunéville
Sarrebourg
NANCY
METZ
Lorraine TGV
Toul
Neufchâteau
Bar le Duc
C.Jarny
Verdun
Meuse TGV
REIMS
Laon
Tergnier
Haute-Picardie
Compiègne
Champagne-Ardenne
Épernay
Châlons en Champagne
Vitry
St Dizier
Troyes
Chaumont
Langres
Culmont
Laroche
Auxerre
Avallon
Autun
Étang
Nevers
Moulins
Gannat
Montluçon
Guéret
Limoges
Bourges
Vierzon
Châteauroux
Poitiers
Niort
La Rochelle
Rochefort
Saintes
ORLÉANS
Les Aubrais
Blois
St Pierre des Corps
TOURS
Chinon
Saumur
Angers
Cholet
LE MANS
Vendôme
Fontainebleau
Marne la Vallée-Chessy
CDG
Massy
PARIS
Versailles
Dreux
Chartres
Creil
Beauvais
Amiens
Longueau
Abbeville
Le Tréport
Abancourt
ROUEN
Serquigny
Dieppe
Fécamp
Le Havre
Lisieux
Trouville-Deauville
Dives
Caen
Mézidon
Argentan
Surdon
Alençon
Bayeux
Lison
Cherbourg
Coutances
Granville
Folligny
Villedieu
Mont St Michel
Dol
St Malo
Dinard
Dinan
St Brieuc
Lamballe
Guingamp
Paimpol
Lannion
Plouaret
Morlaix
Roscoff
Landerneau
BREST
Carhaix
Quimper
Quimperlé
Lorient
Auray
Quiberon
Vannes
RENNES
Laval
Redon
Savenay
St Nazaire
Le Croisic
NANTES
Pornic
St Gilles
Les Sables d'Olonne
La Roche sur Yon
TGV

08

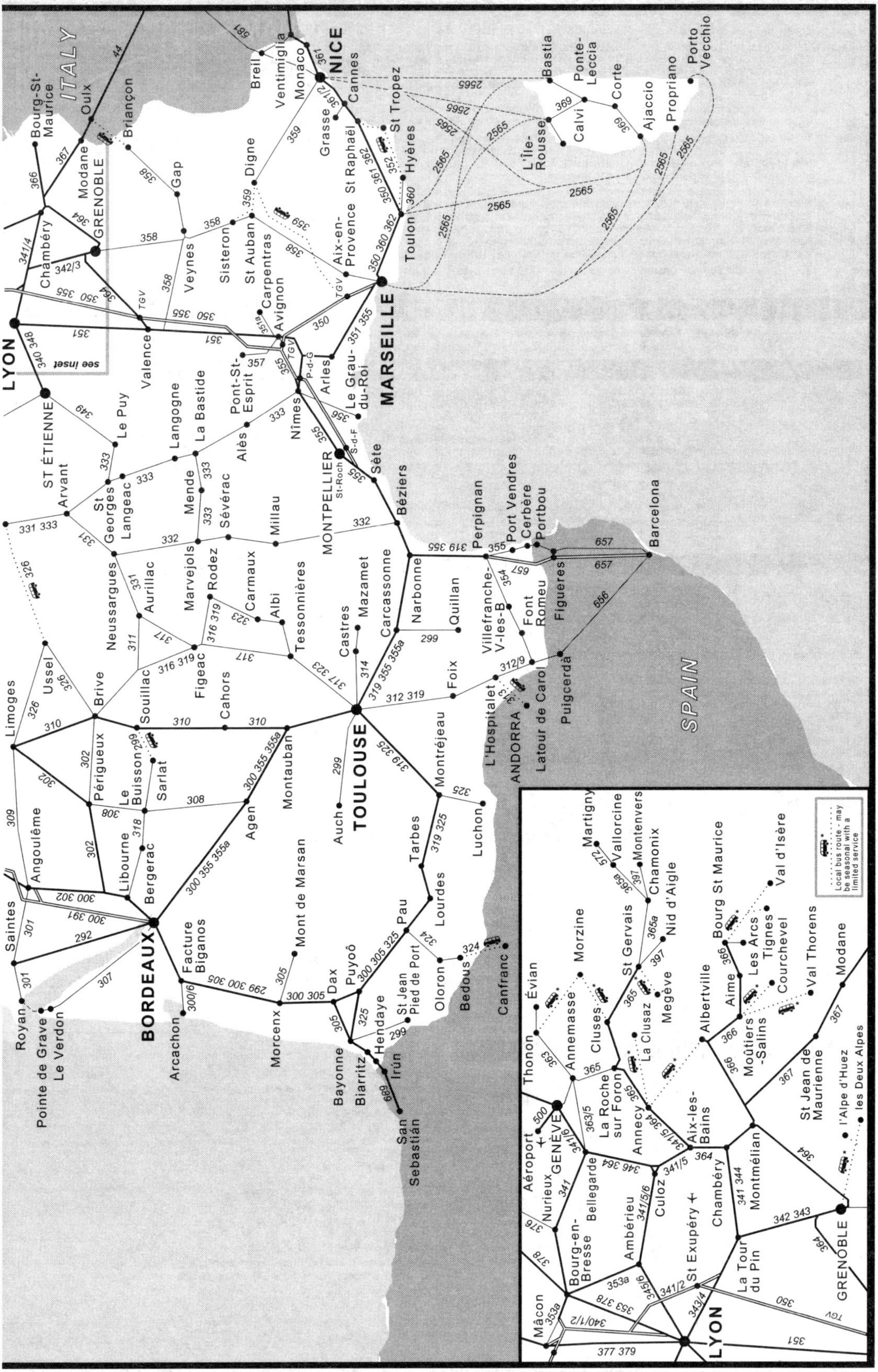
ITALY
SPAIN
LYON
ST ÉTIENNE
GRENOBLE
MARSEILLE
NICE
MONTPELLIER
TOULOUSE
BORDEAUX
see inset
Bourg-St-Maurice
Oulx
Briançon
Modane
Chambéry
Gap
Veynes
Sisteron
Digne
St Auban
Carpentras
Avignon
Valence
Le Puy
Breil
Ventimiglia
Monaco
Cannes
Grasse
St Tropez
St Raphaël
Hyères
Toulon
Aix-en-Provence
Arles
Le Grau-du-Roi
Nîmes
Pont-St-Esprit
Alès
Langogne
La Bastide
Mende
Sévérac
Millau
Arvant
St Georges
Langeac
Neussargues
Aurillac
Marvejols
Rodez
Carmaux
Albi
Tessonnières
Castres
Mazamet
Carcassonne
Narbonne
Béziers
Sète
Perpignan
Port Vendres
Cerbère
Portbou
Barcelona
Figueres
Villefranche-V-les-B
Font Romeu
Quillan
Foix
L'Hospitalet
ANDORRA
Latour de Carol
Puigcerdà
Montréjeau
Luchon
Tarbes
Lourdes
Pau
Oloron
Bedous
Canfranc
Auch
Montauban
Agen
Cahors
Figeac
Souillac
Brive
Ussel
Limoges
Périgueux
Le Buisson
Sarlat
Bergerac
Libourne
Angoulême
Saintes
Royan
Pointe de Grave
Le Verdon
Arcachon
Facture Biganos
Mont de Marsan
Morcenx
Dax
Puyoô
Bayonne
Biarritz
Hendaye
Irún
San Sebastián
St Jean Pied de Port
Bastia
Ponte-Leccia
Calvi
L'Île-Rousse
Corte
Ajaccio
Propriano
Porto Vecchio
Mâcon
Bourg-en-Bresse
Nurieux
Bellegarde
Aéroport
GENÈVE
Thonon
Évian
Annemasse
Morzine
Cluses
La Roche sur Foron
Annecy
La Clusaz
St Gervais
Megève
Nid d'Aigle
Chamonix
Montenvers
Vallorcine
Martigny
Ambérieu
Culoz
Aix-les-Bains
St Exupéry
La Tour du Pin
Montmélian
Albertville
Moûtiers-Salins
Aime
Bourg St Maurice
Les Arcs
Tignes
Val d'Isère
Courchevel
Val Thorens
St Jean de Maurienne
l'Alpe d'Huez
les Deux Alpes
Local bus route - may be seasonal with a limited service

FRANCE

SEE MAP PAGES 160 and 161

Operator: Société Nationale des Chemins de Fer Français (SNCF), unless otherwise shown.

Services: Most long distance trains convey first and second class accommodation; many regional services are now second class only (travel classes are not usually indicated in our tables). *TGV* (*Train à Grande Vitesse*) high-speed trains have a bar car selling drinks, light meals and refreshments (some short-distance services have only vending machines). Selected international *TGV* trains have an at-seat meal service in first class. Certain other long-distance trains, branded *Intercités*, also offer a refreshment service, often from a trolley wheeled through the train. Regional and local trains (outside Paris) are classified *TER* (*Transport Express Régional*). Domestic overnight trains convey modern couchettes (four-berth in first class, six-berth in second class) and reclining seats (second class only). Couchette compartments for the exclusive use of women are available on request. Note that all luggage placed on luggage racks must be labelled. The regular *TGV* network is branded ***inOui***. SNCF subsidiary ***Ouigo*** operate an extensive network of low-cost high-speed services, together with some traditional loco-hauled services (branded ***Ouigo Classique***). Tickets for Ouigo services are only available via its website.

Timings: **Tables 250 to 329 are valid July 5 - August 31, 2025** (except where shown - for services until July 4 please see previous editions). **Tables 330 to 397 are valid June 15 - December 13, 2025** (except where shown). Amended services operate on and around public holidays; whilst we try to show holiday variations, passengers are advised to confirm train times locally before travelling during these periods. For Public holiday dates see page 4. Engineering work can often affect schedules; major changes are shown in the tables where possible but other changes may occur at short notice.

Tickets: Special fares (which include a seat reservation) are payable for travel by *TGV*, overnight trains and those *Intercités* which require compulsory reservation (🅁 in our tables); Interrail and Eurail pass holders must pay a reservation fee to use these services. Optional seat reservations are also available on other long-distance trains. Seat reservation is also compulsory for journeys from / to Paris on long-distance TER services radiating from Paris St Lazare and Paris Est (a €1,70 fee is payable by Interrail and Eurail pass holders). In north-eastern France, regional tickets are valid on *TGV* services for many local journeys (without prior reservation) on payment of a €2 TER-GV supplement per journey (this is indicated in the relevant tables where available). Traditional tickets for regional journeys may need to be date-stamped before boarding the train using a self-service validating machine (composteur) - please check if in doubt. Note that where two *TGV* units are coupled together, they will often carry different train numbers for reservation purposes.

Note: *TGV* services **Lille Europe - Charles de Gaulle ✈ - Marne-la-Vallée - Lyon / Bordeaux / Rennes / Nantes** are shown in the International section (Table **11**).

250 TGV NORD

HIGH-SPEED TRAINS. For Paris Charles de Gaulle ✈ - Lille services see Table **11**. Journeys to / from Paris are 🅁 with supplement.
For other journeys, *TGV* and ♣ trains are classified *TER-GV* and require payment of a €2 *Grande Vitesse* supplement per journey (🅁 not required).

PARIS - LILLE FLANDRES

km		TGV	TGV	TGV	TGV	TGV		TGV	TGV	TGV	TGV	TGV		TGV	TGV	TGV	TGV	TGV		TGV	TGV	TGV	TGV	TGV
		7007	**7015**	**7023**	**7025**	**7031**		**7035**	**7037**	**7043**	**7045**	**7047**		**7053**	**7057**	**7061**	**7065**	**7069**		**7073**	**7077**	**7081**	**7297**	**7297**
		Ⓐ		⑥	Ⓑ	Ⓒ		⑥	Ⓐ	⑥⑦	⑦	Ⓐ		⑤⑦	Ⓐ	Ⓒ	Ⓐ	①–⑥		⑦	⑤	⑦	①–④	⑥
				d	**e**					**d**	**f**			**g**				**h**		**f**	**j**	**f**	**A**	**B**
0	**Paris** Nord d.	0741	0841	0942	1012	1145	...	1245	1314	1445	1515	1545	...	1645	1713	1744	1813	1845	...	1921	1945	2015	2149	2203
227	**Lille** Flandres a.	0848	0948	1044	1119	1248	...	1348	1418	1548	1618	1648	...	1748	1818	1849	1918	1948	...	2023	2048	2118	2311	2318
		TGV	TGV	TGV	TGV		TGV	TGV	TGV	TGV		TGV	TGV	TGV		TGV	TGV	TGV	TGV		TGV	TGV	TGV	TGV
		7200	**7002**	**7006**	**7014**		**7016**	**7026**	**7028**	**7030**		**7032**	**7038**	**7044**		**7046**	**7052**	**7060**	**7068**		**7072**	**7076**	**7078**	**7082**
		Ⓐ	①–④	①–⑥	Ⓒ		Ⓐ	①–⑥	⑦	⑥		Ⓐ	⑥	Ⓐ		⑦	Ⓑ		⑤⑦		④⑤	⑥	⑤	⑦–④
		C	**k**	**h**			**m**	**h**	**f**	**d**			**d**			**f**	**e**		**g**		**e**	**d**	**j**	**n**
	Lille Flandres d.	0552	0639	0711	0812	...	0842	1012	1042	1112	...	1142	1312	1442	...	1512	1612	1712	1811	...	1842	1912	1942	2012
	Paris Nord a.	0709	0749	0819	0916	...	0949	1117	1147	1217	...	1247	1417	1547	...	1617	1719	1821	1920	...	1949	2017	2047	2117

PARIS - LILLE EUROPE, DUNKERQUE, BOULOGNE and RANG DU FLIERS

Subject to alteration July 5, 6, 26, 27. For return service see next page. For other trains Calais - Rang du Fliers and v.v. see Table **261**.

km		TGV	TGV	TGV	TGV		TGV	TGV	TGV	TGV		TGV	TGV	TGV		TGV	TGV	TGV	TGV		TGV	TGV	TGV	TGV
		7551	**7359**	**7159**	**7155**		**7163**	**7363**	**7365**	**7565**		**7165**	**7265**	**7569**		**7369**	**7171**	**7571**	**7571**		**7371**	**7173**	**7273**	**7575**
		Ⓐ	⑥	⑥	Ⓐ		⑦	⑦	⑥	⑥		Ⓐ	Ⓐ	Ⓐ		Ⓐ	⑥	Ⓒ	⑦		⑦	⑤	⑤	⑥
				d			**f**	**f**	**d**	**d**							**d**		**f**		**f**	**j**	**j**	**d**
0	**Paris** Nord d.	0652	0751	0751	0752	...	0951	0951	1050	1050	...	1052	1052	1222	...	1225	1351	1351	1351	...	1351	1428	1428	1551
179	Arras a.	0741	0840	0840	0840	...	1040	1040	1140	1140	...	1141	1141	1313	...	1313	1440	1440	1440	...	1440	1517	1517	1640
199	Lens a.	|	0902	|	|	...	|	1102	1202	|	...	|	|	|	...	1329	|	|	|	...	1502	1532	|	|
204	Douai a.	|	|	0858	0858	...	1058	|	|	|	...	1159	|	|	...	|	1458	|	|	...	|	1603	|	|
240	**Valenciennes** a.	|	|	0934	0934	...	1134	|	|	|	...	1235	|	|	...	|	1534	|	|	...	|	1631	|	|
218	Béthune a.	|	0916	...	...	...	...	1116	1216	|	...	...	|	|	...	1342	...	|	|	...	1516	...	|	|
	Lille Europe a.	0808	|	...	...	...	...	|	|	1204	...	...	1207	1340	...	|	...	1504	1504	...	|	...	1558	1707
252	Hazebrouck a.	|	0939	...	...	...	...	1139	1239	|	...	...	|	|	...	1405	...	|	|	...	1539	...	...	|
292	**Dunkerque** a.	|	1004	...	...	...	...	1204	1304	|	...	...	1251	|	...	1430	...	|	|	...	1604	...	...	|
326	**Calais** Fréthun a.	0843	...	...	...	...	...	...	...	1243	...	...	...	1413	...	...	...	1543	1543	...	...	...	...	1743
360	**Boulogne** Ville a.	0918	...	...	...	...	...	...	...	1316	...	...	...	1446	...	...	...	1616	1616	...	...	...	...	1814
387	Étaples-Le Touquet a.	...	...	...	...	...	...	...	...	1334	...	...	...	1504	...	...	...	...	1634	...	...	...	...	...
398	**Rang du Fliers** ⊕ a.	...	...	...	...	...	...	...	...	1344	...	...	...	1514	...	...	...	...	1644	...	...	...	...	...
		TGV	TGV	TGV		TGV	TGV	TGV		TGV	TGV	TGV		TGV	TGV	TGV		TGV	TGV	TGV		TGV	TGV	TGV
		7575	**7577**	**7277**		**7377**	**7177**	**7281**		**7581**	**7181**	**7585**		**7385**	**7185**	**7289**		**7389**	**7189**	**7391**		**7591**	**7591**	**7195**
		⑥	Ⓐ	⑦		①–④	⑦	⑥		Ⓐ	①–⑥	⑦		Ⓑ	Ⓐ	⑥		Ⓒ	⑦	Ⓐ		Ⓐ	Ⓐ	
		r		**f**		**k**	**f**				**h**					**d**			**f**				**s**	**t**
	Paris Nord d.	1551	1651	1651	...	1651	1651	1752	...	1752	1752	1851	...	1851	1851	1951	...	1951	1951	2024	...	2024	2024	2151
	Arras a.	1640	1740	1740	...	1740	1740	1841	...	1841	1841	1940	...	1940	1940	2040	...	2040	2040	2114	...	2114	2114	2240
	Lens a.	|	|	|	...	1802	|	|	...	|	|	|	...	2002	|	|	...	2102	|	2137	...	|	|	|
	Douai a.	|	|	|	...	|	1758	|	...	|	1859	|	...	|	1957	|	...	|	2058	|	...	|	|	2302
	Valenciennes a.	|	|	|	...	|	1834	|	...	|	1934	|	...	|	2034	|	...	|	2134	|	...	|	|	2338
	Béthune a.	|	|	|	...	1816	...	|	...	|	...	|	...	2016	...	|	...	2116	...	2151	...	|	|	...
	Lille Europe a.	1707	1806	1807	...	|	...	1908	...	1909	...	2004	...	|	...	2105	...	|	...	|	...	2140	2140	...
	Hazebrouck a.	|	|	|	...	1839	...	|	...	|	...	|	...	2039	...	...	...	2139	...	2214	...	|	|	...
	Dunkerque a.	|	|	1851	...	1904	...	1951	...	|	...	|	...	2104	...	...	...	2204	...	2242	...	|	|	...
	Calais Fréthun a.	1743	1843	...	...	...	...	...	...	1944	...	2042	...	...	...	...	...	...	...	...	...	2213	2213	...
	Boulogne Ville a.	1814	1918	...	...	...	...	...	...	2017	...	2115	...	...	...	...	...	...	...	...	...	...	2247	...
	Étaples-Le Touquet a.	1831	...	...	...	...	...	...	...	2035	...	2133	...	...	...	...	...	...	...	...	...	...	...	...
	Rang du Fliers ⊕ a.	1841	...	...	...	...	...	...	...	2045	...	2143	...	...	...	...	...	...	...	...	...	...	...	...

TER-GV TRAINS LILLE - DUNKERQUE

Subject to alteration July 5, 6, 25 – 27, Aug. 23, 24.

	♣	♣	♣	♣	♣	♣	♣	♣	♣	♣	♣
	Ⓐ	Ⓐ	Ⓐ	⑦	⑥	Ⓐ	Ⓐ	Ⓐ	Ⓐ	Ⓐ	⑦
				f	**d**						**f**
Lille Europe d.	0659	0850	1050	1120	1221	1321	1550	1650	1750	1850	1920
Dunkerque a.	0732	0921	1121	1151	1252	1352	1621	1721	1821	1921	1951
	♣	♣	♣	♣	♣	♣	♣	♣	♣	♣	♣
	Ⓐ	Ⓐ	Ⓐ	Ⓐ	⑥	Ⓐ	Ⓐ	Ⓐ	Ⓐ	⑦	⑦
									D	**f**	**f**
Dunkerque d.	0800	0904	1000	1300	1307	1446	1600	1700	1835	1930	2030
Lille Europe a.	0831	0935	1031	1331	1338	1517	1631	1731	1906	2001	2101

A – Also July 25, Aug. 8, 15. To Roubaix (a. 2335), Tourcoing (a. 2342). Via Arras (a. 2246).
B – Also July 7 – 10. To Roubaix (a. 2342), Tourcoing (a. 2348). Via Arras (a. 2253).
C – From Tourcoing (d. 0521 **p**), Roubaix (d. 0526 **p**). Via Arras (d. 0618).
D – To Arras (a. 1942) and Amiens (a. 2018).
E – Ⓐ until July 25; ① from July 28.
F – ⑤⑥ (also July 22 – 24, 28, Aug. 14; not July 25).

d – Also Aug. 15.
e – Not Aug. 15.
f – Also July 14.
g – Also July 14, Aug. 14; not Aug. 15.
h – Not July 14.
j – Also Aug. 14; not Aug. 15.
k – Not July 14, Aug. 14.
m – Until Aug. 22.
n – Not Aug. 14.
p – Not July 8 – 11, 14, Aug. 15.
q – Not July 26, Aug. 16.
r – From July 26 (also Aug. 15).
s – July 7 – 25.
t – July 6, 13, 14, Aug. 31.
u – Also July 14, Aug. 15; not July 5, 12, 19.
v – Also July 6, 13, 14, Aug. 15, 31.

⊕ – Full name is Rang du Fliers - Verton - Berck.
♣ – TER à Grande Vitesse (*TER-GV*) service via high-speed line.

TGV – High-speed train. 🅁. 🍸.

TGV NORD 250

HIGH-SPEED TRAINS. For Paris Charles de Gaulle ✈ - Lille services see Table **11**. Journeys to/from Paris are 🅁 with supplement.
For other journeys, *TGV* and ♣ trains are classified *TER-GV* and require payment of a €2 *Grande Vitesse* supplement per journey (🅁 not required).

RANG DU FLIERS, BOULOGNE, DUNKERQUE and LILLE EUROPE - PARIS

Subject to alteration July 5, 6, 26, 27. For return service and footnotes see previous page. For other trains Rang du Fliers - Calais and v.v. see Table **261**.

	TGV **7104**	*TGV* **7304**	*TGV* **7208**		*TGV* **7508**	*TGV* **7112**	*TGV* **7312**		*TGV* **7212**	*TGV* **7116**	*TGV* **7516**		*TGV* **7218**	*TGV* **7518**	*TGV* **7320**		*TGV* **7520**	*TGV* **7322**	*TGV* **7522**		*TGV* **7124**	*TGV* **7324**	
	Ⓐ	Ⓐ	Ⓐ			Ⓒ	⑥		⑦	⑤⑥	①–⑥		⑦	⑦	Ⓐ		Ⓐ	⑥	⑥		⑦	⑦	
					E		**d**		**f**	**F**	**h**		**f**	**f**				**d**	**d**		**f**	**f**	
Rang du Fliers ⊕ d.	...	...	...	...	...	...	...	...	...	...	...	...	...	...	...	...	...	...	1209	...	...	...	...
Étaples-Le Touquet d.	...	...	...	...	...	...	...	...	...	...	...	...	...	...	...	...	...	...	1219	...	...	...	...
Boulogne Ville d.	...	...	...	...	0625	...	...	...	...	...	0929	...	...	1035	...	...	1148	...	1239	...	...	...	...
Calais Fréthun d.	...	...	...	...	0705	...	...	...	...	...	1007	...	...	1115	...	...	1230	...	1318	...	...	...	...
Dunkerque d.	...	0556	0655	...	|	...	0756	...	...	...	|	...	1125	|	1211	...	|	1256	|	...	...	1347	...
Hazebrouck d.	...	0620	|	...	|	...	0820	...	...	...	|	...	|	|	1234	...	|	1320	|	...	...	1414	...
Lille Europe d.	...	|	0740	...	0740	...	|	...	0851	...	1051	...	1205	1205	|	...	1303	|	1351	...	...	|	...
Béthune d.	...	0643	|	...	|	...	0843	...	|	...	|	...	|	|	1257	...	|	1343	|	...	...	1440	...
Valenciennes d.	0616	|	|	...	|	0816	|	...	|	1016	|	...	|	|	|	...	|	|	|	...	1416	|	...
Douai d.	0652	|	|	...	|	0851	|	...	|	1051	|	...	|	|	|	...	1323	|	|	...	1451	|	...
Lens d.	|	0657	|	...	|	|	0857	...	|	|	|	...	|	|	1313	...	|	1357	|	...	|	1455	...
Arras d.	0715	0715	0808	...	0808	0918	0918	...	0918	1118	1118	...	1232	1232	1341	...	1341	1418	1418	...	1518	1518	...
Paris Nord a.	0809	0809	0902	...	0902	1009	1009	...	1009	1215	1215	...	1324	1324	1432	...	1432	1509	1509	...	1609	1609	...

	TGV **7226**	*TGV* **7130**		*TGV* **7330**	*TGV* **7334**	*TGV* **7134**		*TGV* **7534**	*TGV* **7434**		*TGV* **7238**	*TGV* **7142**	*TGV* **7342**		*TGV* **7242**	*TGV* **7344**		*TGV* **7544**	*TGV* **8144**	*TGV* **7546**		*TGV* **7546**	
	⑥	Ⓑ		Ⓐ	⑦	⑤		Ⓑ	⑥		Ⓐ	⑥	⑦		⑥	⑥		⑥⑦	⑦	Ⓐ		⑦	
	d	**e**			**f**	**j**		**e**	**q**			**v**	**f**		**d**	**d**		**u**	**f**			**f**	
Rang du Fliers ⊕ d.	...	...	...	...	...	...	...	1603	...	...	...	...	...	...	...	...	...	1855	...	...	...	...	...
Étaples-Le Touquet d.	...	...	...	...	...	...	...	1613	...	...	...	...	...	...	...	...	...	1905	...	...	...	...	...
Boulogne Ville d.	...	...	...	...	...	...	...	1634	1636	...	...	...	...	...	...	...	...	1925	...	1954	...	2032	...
Calais Fréthun d.	...	...	...	...	...	...	...	1713	1716	...	...	...	...	...	...	...	...	2003	...	2032	...	2111	...
Dunkerque d.	...	...	...	1556	1656	...	...	|	|	...	1808	...	1856	...	1913	1954	...	|	...	|	...	|	...
Hazebrouck d.	...	...	...	1620	1720	...	...	|	|	...	|	...	1920	...	|	|	...	|	...	|	...	|	...
Lille Europe d.	1600	...	...	|	|	...	...	1748	1751	...	1851	...	|	...	1952	2050	...	2050	...	2102	...	2151	...
Béthune d.	|	...	...	1644	1743	...	...	|	|	...	|	...	1943	...	|	|	...	|	...	|	...	|	...
Valenciennes d.	|	1616	...	|	|	1716	...	|	|	...	|	1916	|	...	|	|	...	|	2016	|	...	|	...
Douai d.	|	1651	...	|	|	1751	...	|	|	...	|	1952	|	...	|	|	...	|	2051	2134	...	|	...
Lens d.	|	|	...	1658	1757	|	...	|	|	...	|	|	1957	...	|	|	...	|	|	|	...	|	...
Arras d.	1626	1718	...	1718	1818	1818	...	1818	1818	...	1918	2018	2018	...	2018	2118	...	2118	2118	2154	...	2218	...
Paris Nord a.	1716	1808	...	1808	1910	1910	...	1910	1910	...	2009	2110	2110	...	2110	2208	...	2208	2208	2248	...	2308	...

FOR RETURN SERVICE AND FOOTNOTES SEE PREVIOUS PAGE.

PARIS - SOISSONS - LAON 251

km		Ⓐ	⑥	Ⓐ	Ⓒ	Ⓐ	Ⓒ	Ⓐ		†	⚒	Ⓐ	Ⓒ	⑥	Ⓐ			Ⓒ	Ⓐ	⑥	Ⓐ	Ⓐ	Ⓒ	⑥
0	**Paris** Nord d.	0635	0731	0734	0831	0834	0930	0933	...	1031	1131	1223	1331	1431	1531	1634	...	1732	1734	1831	1834	1934	2031	2131
61	Crépy-en-Valois d.	0717	0812	0816	0915	0916	1015	1014	...	1121	1213	1305	1414	1518	1615	1715	...	1815	1816	1917	1916	2017	2114	2217
105	Soissons d.	0750	0842	0845	0949	0947	1044	1043	...	1150	1242	1334	1443	1550	1644	1744	...	1844	1851	1949	1945	2050	2143	2247
140	**Laon** a.	0815	0906	0908	1013	1010	1107	1108	...	1214	1308	1401	1507	1615	1708	1809	...	1908	1916	2013	2009	2115	2207	2311
		①	Ⓐ	Ⓐ	⑥	Ⓐ	Ⓒ	†			⑥	Ⓒ		Ⓐ	Ⓐ	Ⓒ		Ⓐ	Ⓐ	Ⓒ	Ⓐ	Ⓐ	Ⓒ	⑥
	Laon d.	0505	0535	0630	0635	0737	0740	0839	...	0934	1044	1137	1237	1331	1536	1538	...	1631	1730	1732	1830	1940	2038	2136
	Soissons d.	0529	0559	0657	0700	0802	0805	0904	...	0958	1108	1202	1302	1359	1601	1603	...	1655	1754	1757	1900	2005	2103	2203
	Crépy-en-Valois d.	0600	0629	0727	0730	0833	0835	0934	...	1029	1139	1232	1332	1431	1631	1633	...	1727	1825	1832	1933	2036	2134	2231
	Paris Nord a.	0638	0708	0809	0812	0911	0912	1015	...	1112	1220	1313	1413	1513	1710	1712	...	1809	1910	1913	2014	2117	2214	2313

AMIENS - LAON - REIMS 252

Timings of Laon - Reims and v.v. trains will vary by a few minutes from August 11.

km		Ⓐ	⑥	Ⓐ	Ⓐ		Ⓒ	Ⓐ	Ⓑ	⑥		Ⓐ	†	⚒		Ⓐ	Ⓐ	⑥	Ⓑ		⑥	⑥⑦	Ⓐ	†
0	**Amiens** 258 d.	0558	0625	0625	0825	...	0858	1025	1225	1325	...	...	1558	1625	...	1658	1725	1758	1825	...	1858	1923	1925	1958
59	Ham (Somme) 258 d.	0643	0712	0713	0913	...	0943	1113	1313	1413	...	...	1643	1713	...	1747	1813	1843	1913	...	1943	1959	2013	2043
80	Tergnier d.	0704	0726	0731	0931	...	1004	1131	1331	1431	...	1654	1704	1731	...	1804	1831	1905	1931	...	2003	2013	2031	2106
108	**Laon** a.	0730	0748	0757	0957	...	1025	1158	1358	1457	...	1718	1725	1757	...	1825	1857	1928	1957	...	2025	2033	2057	2128
		⚒	⚒	⑥		⑦	†		⑥	Ⓐ		Ⓐ	†	⚒		Ⓐ	Ⓒ		Ⓐ	Ⓐ		Ⓐ	Ⓒ	Ⓐ
	Laon d.	0559	0659	0734	...	0824	0834	...	0841	0959	...	1201	1234	1334	...	1559	1659	...	1734	1759	...	1859	1933	1959
	Tergnier d.	0626	0727	0803	...	0845	0903	...	0902	1025	...	1229	1303	1403	...	1627	1727	...	1803	1827	...	1927	2003	2027
	Ham (Somme) 258 d.	0646	0746	0817	...	0859	0917	...	0916	...	...	1248	1317	1417	...	1646	1746	...	1817	1846	...	1946	2017	2046
	Amiens 258 a.	0733	0833	0902	...	0935	1002	...	0951	...	...	1335	1402	1502	...	1735	1835	...	1902	1933	...	2033	2102	2134

km		Ⓐ	Ⓐ		Ⓐ	Ⓐ		†	⑥		Ⓒ	⚒		†	Ⓐ		⑥	Ⓐ		†	Ⓐ		Ⓒ	Ⓐ
			w								**x**													**y**
0	**Laon** d.	0629	0705	...	0734	0811	...	0829	0838	...	1035	1339	...	1429	1635	...	1635	1729	...	1730	1841	...	1934	2041
52	**Reims** a.	0721	0749	...	0826	0856	...	0922	0930	...	1121	1437	...	1521	1719	...	1726	1821	...	1821	1933	...	2027	2119
		Ⓐ	Ⓐ	⑥		⑥	†		†	Ⓐ		⑥	Ⓐ	Ⓒ		Ⓐ	Ⓐ		Ⓐ	⑥		†	Ⓐ	Ⓐ
																	w							
	Reims d.	0634	0719	0738	...	0935	0938	...	1141	1238	...	1242	1441	1534	...	1626	1711	...	1740	1833	...	1835	1841	1938
	Laon a.	0726	0803	0830	...	1027	1025	...	1233	1331	...	1333	1525	1627	...	1721	1757	...	1833	1926	...	1926	1933	2030

w – July 7 – 11 and from Aug. 18. **x** – From Aug. 10. **y** – From Aug. 11.

AMIENS - ROUEN 253

km		Ⓐ	Ⓐ	Ⓐ		⑥	†	Ⓐ		Ⓐ	⑥	†		†	Ⓐ	Ⓐ		⑥	†	Ⓐ		Ⓐ		
0	**Amiens** d.	0556	0702	0813	...	0833	0927	1028	...	1216	1258	1422	...	1628	1728	1828	...	1829	1830	1930	...	2028	...	...
31	Poix de Picardie d.	0616	0722	0835	...	0853	0947	1048	...	1236	1319	1446	...	1648	1748	1849	...	1851	1851	1951	...	2048	...	...
52	Abancourt d.	0628	0734	0847	...	0905	0959	1100	...	1248	1331	1458	...	1700	1800	1901	...	1903	1903	2003	...	2100	...	...
73	Serqueux d.	0643	0749	0900	...	0918	1014	1115	...	1301	1345	1513	...	1716	1815	1917	...	1916	1915	2016	...	2114	...	...
121	**Rouen** Rive-Droite a.	0726	0829	0938	...	0959	1055	1157	...	1341	1427	1556	...	1755	1855	1958	...	1952	1952	2053	...	2157	...	...
		Ⓐ	⑥		Ⓐ	†		Ⓐ	Ⓐ		Ⓐ	⑥		Ⓐ	Ⓒ		Ⓐ	Ⓐ		Ⓐ	Ⓒ			
	Rouen Rive-Droite d.	0622	0708	...	0717	0903	...	1025	1118	...	1209	1306	...	1613	1708	...	1719	1821	...	1909	1910	...	...	...
	Serqueux d.	0659	0742	...	0754	0940	...	1102	1154	...	1248	1336	...	1650	1742	...	1756	1857	...	1949	1947	...	...	...
	Abancourt d.	0713	0754	...	0807	0954	...	1116	1207	...	1257	1343	...	1704	1754	...	1810	1910	...	2003	2001	...	...	...
	Poix de Picardie d.	0725	0806	...	0819	1006	...	1128	1219	...	1302	1357	...	1716	1807	...	1822	1922	...	2015	2013	...	...	...
	Amiens a.	0746	0827	...	0840	1027	...	1153	1240	...	1336	1430	...	1737	1828	...	1843	1943	...	2036	2034	...	...	...

254 AMIENS - COMPIÈGNE

km																									
		Ⓐ	⑥	†	Ⓐ	Ⓐ	⑥	†	†	⑥	Ⓐ	⑥	†		Ⓐ	Ⓒ	Ⓐ	Ⓐ	Ⓒ	Ⓐ	†	⑥	Ⓐ	†	⑥
0	**Amiens** 260 d.	0618	0700	0734	0734	0855	0914	0930	1118	1127	1229	1247	1329	...	1610	1618	1640	1702	1733	1818	1910	1928	1929	2019	2037
5	Longueau 260 d.	|	|	|	0740	|	0920	0936	|	|	1235	1253	1335	...	|	|	|	1708	1739	1824	|	|	|	2025	2043
36	Montdidier d.	0652	0730	0805	0814	0927	0954	1008	1148	1157	1307	1323	1407	...	1639	1648	1710	1742	1811	1903	1941	1957	2003	2057	2115
76	**Compiègne** a.	0728	0759	0834	0851	0953	1030	1042	1217	1226	1342	1358	1441	...	1708	1717	1737	1820	1845	1938	2010	2025	2029	2131	2149

	Ⓐ	Ⓐ	Ⓐ	⑥	†	Ⓐ	Ⓐ	⑥	†	Ⓐ	⑥	†	⑥	†	Ⓐ	Ⓒ	Ⓐ	Ⓒ	Ⓐ	Ⓐ	⑥	†	†	⑥
Compiègne d.	0544	0622	0700	0704	0739	0744	0901	0918	0933	1059	1106	1120	1247	1333	1447	1621	1644	1736	1752	1831	1906	1914	2021	2041
Montdidier d.	0619	0652	0740	0731	0806	0814	0927	0953	1009	1126	1131	1147	1323	1408	1513	1648	1711	1811	1827	1904	1932	1940	2056	2116
Longueau 260 d.	0652	|	0823	|	0829	|	|	1022	1039	|	|	|	1353	1438	|	|	|	1841	1859	|	|	|	2126	2146
Amiens 260 a.	0658	0726	0829	0759	0834	0845	0955	1028	1045	1155	1159	1213	1358	1443	1542	1716	1745	1847	1905	1934	1959	2007	2131	2151

255 PARIS - COMPIÈGNE - ST QUENTIN - CAMBRIAI and MAUBEUGE

Frequent additional services are available Paris - Compiègne and v.v.

km																									
		⑥	⚒	Ⓐ	Ⓐ	Ⓐ	⑥	Ⓑ		⑥		†	⑥	Ⓐ	⑥	Ⓐ	†	⑥	⑥	Ⓑ	Ⓐ	†	⑥	⑥	Ⓐ
0	**Paris** Nord d.	...	...	...	0634	0716	...	0729	0833	...	0915	1009	1016	1032	...	...	...	1215	...	1233	1309	1317	...	1417	1433
51	Creil d.	...	...	...	0706	|	...	0804	0904	...	|	|	|	1105	...	...	...	|	...	1304	|	|	...	|	1505
84	**Compiègne** d.	...	0627	...	0728	0800	0805	0827	0928	...	1000	1053	1101	1127	...	...	1235	1259	1318	1327	1401	1401	1407	1500	1527
108	Noyon d.	...	0648	...	0741	|	0829	0841	0942	...	|	|	|	1140	...	...	1257	|	1342	1340	|	|	1430	|	1540
124	Chauny d.	...	0701	...	0752	|	0839	0852	0953	...	|	|	|	1150	...	...	1309	|	1355	1350	|	|	1442	|	1550
131	Tergnier d.	...	0710	0744	0800	|	0847	0858	1001	...	|	|	|	1158	...	...	1315	|	1401	1358	|	|	1448	|	1558
154	**St Quentin** 256 d.	0628	0729	0800	0813	0835	0906	0911	1014	1024	1033	1126	1134	1213	1224	1225	1332	1333	1419	1411	1435	1434	1506	1534	1611
181	Busigny 256 d.	0649	...	0821	...	|	...	...	...	1045	...	|	|	|	1245	1246	...	...	...	...	|	...	...	|	...
	Caudry 256 d.	|	...	|	...	|	...	...	...	|	...	|	|	|	|	|	...	...	...	...	|	...	...	|	...
207	**Cambrai** Ville 256 a.	|	...	|	...	|	...	...	...	|	...	|	|	|	|	|	...	...	...	...	|	...	...	|	...
217	Aulnoye Aymeries 262 d.	0712	...	0846	...	0906	...	...	...	1109	...	1200	1208	1245	1309	1316	...	...	...	...	1506	...	...	1605	...
229	**Maubeuge** 262 a.	...	...	...	...	0918	...	...	...	...	...	1209	1217	1255	...	...	...	...	...	...	1518	...	...	1614	...

	Ⓒ	Ⓐ	Ⓐ	Ⓐ	⑥	Ⓑ		Ⓒ	⚒	Ⓐ	Ⓐ	Ⓐ		Ⓒ	Ⓐ	†	Ⓐ	Ⓒ		Ⓐ	†	Ⓐ	Ⓑ	Ⓒ
Paris Nord d.	...	...	...	...	1632	1633	1716	...	...	1733	...	1816	...	...	1833	1835	...	1918	...	1932	2018	2033	2131	2234
Creil d.	...	...	...	...	1704	1704	|	...	...	1804	...	|	...	...	1904	1907	...	|	...	2005	|	2106	2207	2305
Compiègne d.	...	...	1632	1705	1728	1728	1800	...	1807	1827	...	1901	...	1904	1927	1930	...	2002	2008	2028	2101	2129	2230	2326
Noyon d.	...	...	1656	1729	1741	1740	|	...	1830	1840	...	|	...	1928	1940	1944	...	|	2032	2041	|	2142	2243	2339
Chauny d.	...	...	1709	1742	1750	1750	|	...	1842	1851	...	|	...	1941	1951	1954	...	|	2044	2051	|	2152	2253	2349
Tergnier d.	...	...	1715	1748	1758	1758	|	...	1848	1858	1902	|	...	1947	1958	2002	2005	|	2050	2059	|	2159	2300	2356
St Quentin 256 d.	1624	1732	1733	1806	1811	1811	1835	1849	1906	1911	1916	1936	...	2006	2011	2017	2019	2036	2109	2113	2135	2212	2313	0009
Busigny 256 d.	1645	1754	...	...	1827	...	|	1910	...	...	1937	1952	...	...	...	2039	2039	|	...	...	|	...	...	...
Caudry 256 d.	|	|	...	...	1835	...	|	|	...	...	|	2001	...	...	...	2047	|	|	...	...	|	...	...	...
Cambrai Ville 256 a.	|	|	...	...	1847	...	|	|	...	...	|	2013	...	...	...	2058	|	|	...	...	|	...	...	...
Aulnoye Aymeries 262 d.	1709	1824	...	...	...	...	1906	1934	...	...	2001	...	...	...	...	...	2100	2109	...	...	2206	...	...	...
Maubeuge 262 a.	...	...	...	...	...	...	1918	...	...	...	...	...	...	...	...	...	...	2118	...	...	2216	...	...	...

	⚒	Ⓐ	Ⓐ	Ⓐ	⑥	Ⓐ	Ⓐ	Ⓐ	Ⓑ	⚒	⑥	Ⓐ	⚒	†	Ⓐ	⑥	Ⓐ	⑥	Ⓐ	⑥	Ⓐ	⚒	†	Ⓐ
Maubeuge 262 d.	...	...	...	...	...	...	...	0642	...	...	...	...	0742	0842	...	...	...	1040	...	...	1142	...	...	...
Aulnoye Aymeries 262 d.	...	...	...	...	...	0613	...	0654	...	...	0729	0729	0754	0853	...	...	...	1050	...	1129	1154	...	...	1219
Cambrai Ville 256 d.	...	...	0547	...	0608	|	0637	|	...	...	|	|	|	|	...	...	...	|	...	|	|	...	1213	|
Caudry 256 d.	...	...	0601	...	0620	|	0649	|	...	...	|	|	|	|	...	...	...	|	...	|	|	...	1226	|
Busigny 256 d.	...	...	0611	...	0629	0643	0657	|	...	...	0754	0758	|	|	...	...	...	|	...	1153	|	...	1238	1249
St Quentin 256 d.	0548	0553	0626	0648	0651	0703	0717	0725	0748	0753	0814	0818	0825	0924	0948	1006	1048	1122	1153	1214	1225	1248	1251	1309
Tergnier d.	0603	0612	|	0703	0704	0716	...	|	0802	0812	...	...	|	|	1003	1021	1103	|	1212	...	|	1303	1304	...
Chauny d.	0609	0618	|	0710	0710	...	...	|	0809	0818	...	...	|	|	1009	1028	1109	|	1218	...	|	1310	1310	...
Noyon d.	0619	0631	|	0720	0720	...	...	|	0820	0831	...	...	|	|	1018	1038	1118	|	1231	...	|	1321	1320	...
Compiègne d.	0633	0655	0700	0734	0734	...	...	0801	0834	0855	...	...	0901	0958	1032	1053	1132	1157	1255	...	1301	1335	1334	...
Creil d.	0659	...	|	0757	0758	...	...	|	0858	...	...	...	|	|	1058	1115	1157	|	...	...	|	1358	1359	...
Paris Nord a.	0729	...	0745	0827	0827	...	...	0842	0927	...	...	...	0943	1045	1127	1144	1227	1249	...	...	1409	1427	1428	...

	⑥	⑥	⑥	†	Ⓐ	†	Ⓐ		Ⓐ	†	Ⓐ	†		Ⓐ	Ⓒ	†	⑥	Ⓐ		Ⓐ	⚒	†	†	†
Maubeuge 262 d.	...	...	...	1400	...	...	1542	...	...	1642	...	...	...	...	...	1740	1741	1742	...	...	...	...	1955	...
Aulnoye Aymeries 262 d.	...	1329	...	1410	...	...	1554	...	...	1652	...	...	...	1721	1729	1750	1751	1754	...	1845	...	1944	2006	...
Cambrai Ville 256 d.	...	|	...	|	...	...	|	...	...	|	...	...	...	|	|	|	|	|	...	|	...	|	|	...
Caudry 256 d.	...	|	...	|	...	...	|	...	...	|	...	...	...	|	|	|	|	|	...	|	...	|	|	...
Busigny 256 d.	...	1353	...	|	...	...	|	...	...	|	...	...	...	1745	1753	|	|	|	...	1915	...	2009	|	...
St Quentin 256 d.	1358	1414	1425	1441	1448	1449	1625	1648	1653	1727	1748	1753	...	1805	1814	1824	1825	1825	1853	1936	1948	2029	2036	2049
Tergnier d.	1416	...	|	|	1503	1509	|	1702	1712	|	1803	1812	...	1818	...	|	|	|	1912	1949	2003	...	|	2106
Chauny d.	1421	...	|	|	1510	1515	|	1710	1721	|	1810	1818	...	...	...	|	|	|	1921	...	2010	...	|	2112
Noyon d.	1433	...	|	|	1520	1528	|	1721	1734	|	1821	1831	...	...	...	|	|	|	1934	...	2020	...	|	2121
Compiègne d.	1455	...	1500	1515	1534	1551	1659	1735	1755	1801	1835	1855	...	...	...	1858	1859	1859	1955	...	2034	...	2109	2135
Creil d.	...	...	|	|	1558	...	|	1759	...	|	1858	...	...	...	...	|	|	|	...	...	2058	...	|	2159
Paris Nord a.	...	...	1544	1559	1627	...	1742	1828	...	1844	1927	...	...	...	...	1942	1943	1942	...	...	2129	...	2154	2231

256 LILLE - DOUAI - CAMBRAI - ST QUENTIN

For Paris - St Quentin - Cambrai and v.v. see Table **255**. Additional trains run Douai - Cambrai Ville and v.v. approximately every two hours.

km																								
		Ⓐ	⑥	Ⓐ		Ⓐ	Ⓒ	Ⓒ		Ⓐ	Ⓐ	Ⓒ		Ⓒ	Ⓐ	Ⓐ		Ⓒ	Ⓐ	Ⓐ		Ⓒ	Ⓐ	
0	**Lille** Flandres 257 d.	0723	0808	0823	...	0923	1005	1205	...	1223	1323	1405	...	1605	1623	1723	...	1805	1823	1923	...	2005	2023	...
34	Douai 257 d.	0747	0828	0847	...	0947	1026	1226	...	1247	1347	1426	...	1626	1647	1747	...	1826	1847	1946	...	2026	2047	...
66	**Cambrai** Ville 255 d.	0832	0906	0932	...	1032	1106	1306	...	1332	1432	1506	...	1706	1732	1832	...	1906	1932	2031	...	2106	2132	...
82	Caudry 255 d.	0844	0919	0945	...	1045	1119	1319	...	1345	1445	1519	...	1719	1745	1845	...	1919	1945	2043	...	2119	2145	...
92	Busigny 255 d.	0852	0927	0953	...	1053	1127	1327	...	1353	1453	1527	...	1727	1753	1853	...	1927	1954	2052	...	2127	2153	...
119	**St Quentin** 255 a.	0912	0948	1009	...	1108	1148	1351	...	1408	1508	1548	...	1748	1809	1908	...	1948	2009	2107	...	2148	2209	...

	Ⓐ	Ⓐ	Ⓒ		Ⓐ	Ⓒ	Ⓐ		Ⓒ	Ⓐ	Ⓒ		Ⓐ	Ⓒ	Ⓐ		Ⓒ	Ⓐ	Ⓐ		Ⓒ	Ⓐ	
St Quentin 255 d.	0552	0651	0712	...	0750	0912	0951	...	1112	1151	1312	...	1451	1512	1651	...	1712	1746	1851	...	1912	1950	...
Busigny 255 d.	0608	0707	0733	...	0807	0933	1007	...	1133	1207	1333	...	1507	1533	1707	...	1733	1807	1909	...	1933	2007	...
Caudry 255 d.	0617	0716	0741	...	0816	0941	1016	...	1141	1216	1341	...	1516	1541	1716	...	1741	1816	1917	...	1941	2016	...
Cambrai Ville 255 d.	0639	0738	0802	...	0838	1003	1038	...	1203	1238	1403	...	1538	1603	1738	...	1803	1838	1939	...	2003	2038	...
Douai 257 a.	0716	0816	0835	...	0917	1035	1116	...	1235	1316	1435	...	1616	1635	1815	...	1835	1916	2016	...	2035	2116	...
Lille Flandres 257 a.	0738	0838	0855	...	0938	1055	1138	...	1255	1338	1455	...	1638	1655	1838	...	1855	1938	2038	...	2055	2138	...

LILLE - DOUAI - ARRAS - AMIENS and PARIS 257

For *TGV* and *TER-GV* trains Lille Europe / Douai - Arras and v.v. via the high-speed line see Table **250**.

km		Ⓐ	Ⓐ	⑥	Ⓐ	Ⓒ	Ⓐ	Ⓐ		Ⓒ	Ⓐ	Ⓐ	Ⓒ	Ⓐ	Ⓒ	Ⓐ		Ⓐ	Ⓒ	Ⓐ	Ⓐ	Ⓒ	Ⓐ	Ⓒ
0	**Lille** Flandres **256** d.	0553	0653	0705	0753	0905	0953	1053	...	1105	1153	1253	1305	1353	1505	1553	...	1653	1705	1753	1853	1905	1953	2105
34	Douai **256** d.	0616	0716	0726	0815	0926	1015	1114	...	1126	1215	1314	1326	1416	1526	1614	...	1715	1726	1816	1913	1926	2015	2126
59	Arras d.	0631	0732	0742	0831	0942	1030	1129	...	1142	1229	1330	1342	1431	1541	1629	...	1730	1741	1832	1928	1942	2030	2142
96	Albert d.	0652	0750	0803	0851	1003	1051	1148	...	1203	1251	1352	1403	1452	1603	1651	...	1750	1802	1850	1951	2003	2052	2203
127	**Amiens** a.	0711	0811	0827	0911	1023	1110	1210	...	1225	1311	1412	1423	1510	1623	1710	...	1812	1823	1910	2010	2023	2110	2223

	Ⓐ	⑥	Ⓐ	Ⓐ	⑥	†	Ⓐ	Ⓒ	Ⓐ	Ⓐ	Ⓒ	Ⓐ	Ⓒ	Ⓐ	Ⓐ	Ⓒ	Ⓐ	Ⓐ	Ⓒ	Ⓐ	Ⓐ	Ⓒ	Ⓐ
Amiens d.	0549	0636	0650	0750	0834	0835	0850	1037	1050	1150	1237	1250	1434	1450	1550	1637	1650	1750	1837	1849	1950	2043	2101
Albert d.	0608	0701	0709	0811	0854	0855	0910	1057	1110	1209	1257	1310	1454	1510	1610	1657	1710	1810	1857	1909	2010	2103	2122
Arras d.	0630	0724	0731	0831	0916	0917	0930	1119	1131	1231	1319	1330	1516	1531	1631	1719	1731	1829	1919	1929	2030	2126	2142
Douai **256** d.	0646	0739	0746	0846	0931	0931	0945	1134	1146	1246	1334	1345	1532	1546	1646	1734	1747	1846	1934	1945	2045	2141	2157
Lille Flandres **256** a.	0707	0758	0807	0907	0955	0953	1007	1155	1207	1307	1355	1407	1553	1607	1707	1755	1808	1907	1955	2007	2107	2202	2217

WEEKEND TER SERVICE LILLE - ARRAS - PARIS

	Ⓒ	†	⑥		Ⓒ	Ⓒ	
Lille Flandres **256** d.	0914	1900	1914	**Paris** Nord d.	1019	1828	...
Douai **256** d.	0935	1920	1935	Creil d.	1048	1858	...
Arras d.	0951	1936	1951	Longueau d.	1124	1936	...
Longueau d.	1025	2014	2026	**Arras** d.	1157	2010	...
Creil d.	1102	2057	2114	Douai **256** d.	1211	2029	...
Paris Nord a.	1130	2131	2143	**Lille** Flandres **256** a.	1232	2051	...

🚌 AMIENS - TGV HAUTE-PICARDIE 🚌

SNCF 🚌 service Ⓡ. Journey 45 minutes.

From **Amiens** at 0940, 1710.

From **TGV Haute-Picardie** at 1354, 1805, 1958.

For *TGV* services calling at TGV Haute-Picardie see Table **11**.

AMIENS - ST QUENTIN 258

km		Ⓐ	⚒	Ⓐ	Ⓒ	⚒	Ⓐ	Ⓒ	Ⓐ	Ⓐ	Ⓒ	Ⓐ
0	**Amiens** **252** d.	0646	0745	0945	1045	1245	1345	1545	1645	1746	1845	1944
59	Ham (Somme) **252** d.	0723	0822	1023	1123	1323	1423	1623	1723	1824	1923	2023
76	**St Quentin** a.	0742	0842	1042	1143	1342	1442	1642	1742	1846	1942	2042

	Ⓐ	⚒	Ⓐ	Ⓒ	Ⓐ	⚒	Ⓐ	Ⓒ	⚒	Ⓐ	†
St Quentin d.	0616	0716	0816	0918	1124	1216	1516	1716	1816	1916	2015
Ham (Somme) **252** d.	0637	0737	0838	0937	1145	1237	1537	1737	1837	1936	2035
Amiens **252** a.	0715	0815	0915	1015	1225	1315	1615	1816	1917	2014	2113

CALAIS - DUNKERQUE - DE PANNE 259

km		Ⓐ	⚒		Ⓐ	⑥		Ⓐ	Ⓐ		Ⓐ	
0	**Calais** Ville d.	0602	0702	...	0802	1202	...	1302	1549	...	1835	...
23	Gravelines d.	0623	0724	...	0824	1224	...	1323	1607	...	1856	...
46	**Dunkerque** a.	0647	0747	...	0847	1247	...	1347	1627	...	1919	...

	Ⓐ	⑥		Ⓐ	⑥		Ⓐ	Ⓐ		Ⓐ	
Dunkerque d.	0600	0700	...	0703	1300	...	1730	1830	...	1930	...
Gravelines d.	0624	0724	...	0725	1323	...	1754	1854	...	1954	...
Calais Ville a.	0645	0744	...	0750	1343	...	1816	1914	...	2013	...

🚌 **DUNKERQUE - LEFFRINCKOUCKE - ADINKERKE (DE PANNE STATION)** Operator: DK'BUS (www.dkbus.com).

Route C1: Dunkerque Gare - Leffrinckoucke (Fort Des Dunes). Every 10 mins. Ⓐ / 12 mins. ⑥ / 20 mins. †. Journey 20 mins.

Route 20: Leffrinckoucke (Fort Des Dunes) - Bray Dunes - Gare d'Adinkerke - De Panne. Every 25 – 40 mins. (hourly on ⑦). Journey 33 mins. Connects at De Panne with coastal tram (Table **406**).

PARIS - AMIENS 260

For other trains Paris - Creil and v.v. see Table **255**. For other trains Longeau - Amiens and v.v. see Table **254**.

km		Ⓐ	⚒	Ⓑ	Ⓐ	⑥	Ⓐ	Ⓒ	Ⓒ	⚒	†	Ⓐ		⑥	†	†	⑥	Ⓑ	⑥	②③	①④⑤	⑥	⑤	†
0	**Paris** Nord d.	0601	0702	0802	0725	0829	0903	0903	0928	1029	1107	1130	...	1132	1202	1219	1306	1322	1328	1357	1408	1429	1502	1528
51	Creil d.	0631	0733	0832	0758	|	0943	0943	|	|	1143	|	...	|	1232	1255	1343	|	|	1439	1439	|	1532	|
66	Clermont-de-l'Oise d.	0641	0742	0842	|	|	0959	0957	|	|	1156	|	...	|	1241	1310	1407	|	|	1449	1449	|	1542	|
81	St Just en Chaussée d.	0651	0751	0850	|	|	1008	1012	|	|	1205	|	...	|	1250	1322	1421	|	|	1458	1458	|	1551	|
126	Longueau d.	0715	0814	0915	0834	0931	1037	1044	1030	1131	1232	1233	...	1235	1314	1352	1450	1431	1432	1522	1522	1531	1615	1630
131	**Amiens** a.	0721	0820	0920	0837	0935	1042	1049	1034	1135	1237	1238	...	1241	1320	1357	1455	1435	1437	1528	1528	1535	1620	1636
	Boulogne Ville **261** a.	...	...	...	0958	1055	...	...	1155	1255	...	...	...	...	...	...	...	1556	...	...	...	1701	...	1757
	Calais Ville **261** a.	...	...	...	...	...	...	...	1231	1333	...	...	...	...	...	...	...	...	...	...	...	1743	...	1844

	⚒	Ⓐ	Ⓐ	Ⓒ	Ⓐ	⑥	†		⚒	†	Ⓐ	Ⓐ	Ⓒ	Ⓐ	Ⓐ d		Ⓒ	Ⓐ	⑥	†	Ⓐ e	Ⓒ	Ⓒ
Paris Nord d.	1602	1628	1700	1705	1729	1730	1749	...	1800	1803	1829	1900	1903	1929	1929	...	1929	2000	2001	2029	2106	2106	2226
Creil d.	1632	1657	1730	1742	|	|	|	...	1832	1833	|	1932	1942	|	|	...	|	2030	2031	|	2142	2142	2302
Clermont-de-l'Oise d.	1642	|	1740	1757	|	|	|	...	1842	1842	|	1942	1958	|	|	...	|	2039	2042	|	2158	2158	2312
St Just en Chaussée d.	1651	|	1750	1813	|	|	|	...	1852	1851	|	1952	2013	|	|	...	|	2048	2052	|	2207	2207	2322
Longueau d.	1715	1733	1814	1846	1832	1830	1852	...	1916	1915	1932	2017	2045	2031	2031	...	2031	2113	2116	2132	2234	2234	2346
Amiens a.	1720	1737	1821	1851	1838	1837	1856	...	1921	1920	1938	2022	2051	2035	2035	...	2035	2118	2121	2137	2239	2239	2351
Boulogne Ville **261** a.	...	1857	...	...	...	1957	2015	...	...	...	...	...	...	2158	2158	...	2158	...	...	...	...	...	...
Calais Ville **261** a.	...	1932	...	...	...	2032	2051	...	...	...	...	...	...	...	2235	...	2235	...	...	...	...	...	...

	⑥	Ⓐ	Ⓐ		Ⓒ	Ⓐ	⚒		Ⓐ	Ⓐ			⚒	Ⓑ	†		⑥	Ⓐ	⑥		Ⓒ	f	†
Calais Ville **261** d.	...	...	...	...	...	...	...	...	...	...	...	...	0634	...	...	...	...	...	...	...	0934	...	...
Boulogne Ville **261** d.	...	...	...	...	...	...	...	...	...	...	...	...	0705	...	...	...	...	...	...	...	1004	1104	...
Amiens d.	0535	0538	0604	...	0621	0622	0638	...	0704	0722	0738	...	0824	0837	0917	...	0919	1008	1038	...	1123	1223	1322
Longueau d.	0540	0544	0611	...	0627	0629	0644	...	0710	0728	0744	...	0829	0843	0923	...	0925	1013	1044	...	1128	1229	1328
St Just en Chaussée d.	0608	0607	0643	...	0656	|	0708	...	0742	|	0807	...	|	0908	0952	...	0954	1038	1107	...	|	|	|
Clermont-de-l'Oise d.	0617	0616	0659	...	0705	|	0718	...	0759	|	0816	...	|	0917	1001	...	1003	1047	1117	...	|	|	|
Creil d.	0636	0628	0718	...	0720	|	0729	...	0817	|	0829	...	|	0929	1020	...	1020	1101	1129	...	|	|	|
Paris Nord a.	0711	0657	0755	...	0755	0732	0758	...	0855	0831	0858	...	0932	0959	1055	...	1055	1132	1158	...	1230	1337	1439

	⑥	⚒	†				⑦ g		Ⓐ	Ⓐ	†			Ⓐ	Ⓑ		Ⓒ	Ⓒ	Ⓐ		Ⓑ	†	
Calais Ville **261** d.	...	...	...	...	...	1434	...	...	...	...	1537	...	...	...	...	...	...	1735	1736	...	...	1929	...
Boulogne Ville **261** d.	1204	...	...	...	...	1505	...	...	...	...	1606	...	...	...	1705	...	...	1806	1806	...	...	1958	...
Amiens d.	1323	1436	1543	...	1606	1623	1652	...	1706	1722	1723	...	1738	1806	1824	...	1904	1923	1941	...	2038	2117	...
Longueau d.	1330	1442	1549	...	1612	1628	1659	...	1711	1729	1729	...	1744	1811	1829	...	1910	1928	1946	...	2043	2123	...
St Just en Chaussée d.	|	1507	1611	...	1642	|	|	...	1741	|	|	...	1809	1841	|	...	1942	|	2010	...	2107	|	...
Clermont-de-l'Oise d.	|	1516	1620	...	1659	|	|	...	1800	|	|	...	1819	1900	|	...	2001	|	2018	...	2116	|	...
Creil d.	|	1527	1630	...	1718	|	|	...	1818	|	|	...	1830	1919	|	...	2020	|	2028	...	2127	|	...
Paris Nord a.	1431	1558	1658	...	1754	1731	1802	...	1855	1831	1831	...	1859	1954	1931	...	2056	2031	2057	...	2157	2228	...

d – Until Aug. 1.
e – From Aug. 11.
f – Ⓐ until Aug. 8; ② from Aug. 12.
g – From July 27.

261 AMIENS - BOULOGNE - CALAIS

Additional trains are available Amiens - Abbeville and v.v. Other connections Paris - Calais are available by changing at Lille or Hazebrouck (Tables **250**/**265**).

km		⑥	Ⓐ	Ⓐ		Ⓐ	Ⓒ	Ⓐ		Ⓐ	⑥	Ⓐ		⑥	⑦	⑥		Ⓒ	Ⓐ	⚒		Ⓐ	⑥	Ⓑ
	Paris Nord **260** d.	...	...	...	...	...	...	...	...	0725	...	...	...	0829	...	...	...	0928	...	1029	...	...	...	1322
0	**Amiens** d.	0529	0548	...	...	0648	0738	0748	...	0840	0848	...	...	0938	0955	1010	...	1037	1048	1138	...	1243	1337	1438
45	Abbeville d.	0556	0614	...	...	0715	0805	0815	...	0905	0917	...	...	1002	1031	1034	...	1102	1115	1203	...	1310	1403	1503
58	Noyelles sur Mer 🚂 d.	0605	0623	...	...	0724	0814	0824	...	0914	0927	...	...	1011	1043	1044	...	1111	1124	1212	...	1319	1413	1512
85	Rang du Fliers-Verton-Berck d.	0624	0642	0647	...	0743	0833	0842	...	0933	0946	1018	...	1030	1102	1102	...	1129	1142	1230	...	1338	1431	1530
96	Étaples-Le Touquet d.	0632	0649	0655	...	0750	0840	0850	...	0940	0955	1026	...	1038	1111	1111	...	1137	1150	1238	...	1346	1439	1538
123	**Boulogne** Ville d.	0654	0708	0722	...	0809	0904	0909	...	0958	1017	1050	...	1055	1133	1130	...	1156	1209	1257	...	1405	1502	1556
130	Wimille-Wimereux d.	0704	|	0731	...	|	0913	|	...	...	1027	1059	...	...	|	|	...	|	|	|	...	|	1511	...
140	Marquise-Rinxent d.	0712	0724	0738	...	0824	0921	0924	...	...	1034	1108	...	...	|	|	...	1208	1225	|	...	1420	1519	...
157	**Calais** Fréthun d.	0729	|	0802	...	|	0938	|	...	...	1052	1125	...	...	|	|	...	|	|	|	...	|	1537	...
165	**Calais** Ville a.	0738	0746	0811	...	0852	0947	0946	...	...	1102	1134	...	...	1207	1210	...	1231	1247	1333	...	1443	1545	...

	Ⓐ d	†	⑥		Ⓐ	Ⓐ f	†		Ⓐ	Ⓒ	Ⓐ		Ⓐ	⑥	†		Ⓐ	Ⓐ e	Ⓐ		Ⓐ d	Ⓒ	
Paris Nord **260** d.	...	...	1429	...	...	...	1528	...	...	...	1628	...	...	1730	1749	...	...	...	1929	...	1929	1929	...
Amiens d.	...	1534	1537	...	1546	...	1639	...	...	1737	1740	...	...	1840	1858	...	1948	1948	2038	...	2038	2038	...
Abbeville d.	...	1601	1605	...	1613	...	1704	...	...	1804	1804	...	...	1906	1922	...	2015	2015	2105	...	2105	2105	...
Noyelles sur Mer 🚂 d.	...	1610	1614	...	1622	...	1713	...	...	1813	1813	...	...	1915	1931	...	2024	2024	2114	...	2114	2114	...
Rang du Fliers-Verton-Berck d.	1620	1629	1632	...	1640	1647	1731	...	1748	1832	1832	...	1847	1933	1950	...	2042	2042	2132	...	2132	2132	...
Étaples-Le Touquet d.	1628	1637	1640	...	1648	1655	1739	...	1756	1840	1840	...	1855	1940	1958	...	2050	2050	2140	...	2140	2140	...
Boulogne Ville d.	1719	1700	1703	...	1707	1723	1803	...	1821	1903	1858	...	1920	1959	2017	...	2109	2109	2200	...	2200	2200	...
Wimille-Wimereux d.	1729	1709	|	...	|	1732	|	...	1831	1912	|	...	1929	|	|	...	...	|	...	...	|	|	...
Marquise-Rinxent d.	1738	1718	|	...	1722	1740	|	...	1839	1921	|	...	1938	|	|	...	...	2124	...	...	|	|	...
Calais Fréthun d.	1802	1735	|	...	|	1804	|	...	1857	1938	|	...	1956	|	|	...	...	|	...	...	|	|	...
Calais Ville a.	1811	1744	1743	...	1744	1813	1844	...	1902	1947	1932	...	2004	2032	2051	...	...	2146	...	...	2235	2235	...

	Ⓐ	⚒		⑥	Ⓐ		Ⓐ f	Ⓐ d		Ⓒ	Ⓐ		Ⓒ	Ⓒ		g	⑥		Ⓐ	⑥		†	
Calais Ville d.	0518	0634	...	0708	0720	...	0759	0805	...	0810	0920	...	0934	1009	...	...	...	...	1144	1208	...	1317	...
Calais Fréthun d.	|	|	...	0717	|	...	0811	0814	...	0819	|	...	|	1018	...	...	...	...	1153	1217	...	1326	...
Marquise-Rinxent d.	0536	|	...	0729	0739	...	0828	0833	...	0831	0940	...	|	1031	...	...	...	...	1205	1229	...	1339	...
Wimille-Wimereux d.	|	|	...	0737	|	...	0835	0841	...	0839	|	...	|	1039	...	...	...	...	1214	1238	...	1347	...
Boulogne Ville d.	0552	0705	...	0748	0756	...	0846	0851	...	0850	0956	...	1004	1049	...	1104	1204	...	1223	1248	...	1357	...
Étaples-Le Touquet d.	0608	0720	...	0808	0812	...	0910	0916	...	0909	1012	...	1020	1109	...	1120	1220	...	1245	1308	...	1417	...
Rang du Fliers-Verton-Berck d.	0617	0729	...	0816	0821	...	0917	0922	...	0918	1020	...	1028	1118	...	1129	1229	...	...	1317	...	1426	...
Noyelles sur Mer 🚂 d.	0635	0746	...	0834	0838	...	...	...	...	0936	1038	...	1046	1136	...	1146	1247	...	...	1335	...	1444	...
Abbeville d.	0644	0755	...	0844	0847	...	...	...	...	0945	1048	...	1055	1145	...	1155	1256	...	...	1344	...	1453	...
Amiens a.	0712	0820	...	0910	0914	...	...	...	...	1011	1114	...	1120	1211	...	1220	1320	...	...	1410	...	1519	...
Paris Nord **260** a.	...	0932	...	...	...	...	...	...	...	...	...	...	1230	...	...	1337	1431	...	...	...	...	...	...

		Ⓐ		†	Ⓐ		⑥	Ⓑ		Ⓐ	⑥⑦		Ⓒ	Ⓐ		Ⓐ	Ⓐ		⑥	Ⓐ		†	
Calais Ville d.	1434	1518	...	1537	1603	...	1613	...	...	1705	1720	...	1735	1736	...	1820	1904	...	1909	1918	...	1929	...
Calais Fréthun d.	|	|	...	|	1612	...	1622	...	...	1714	|	...	|	|	...	|	1914	...	1917	|	...	|	...
Marquise-Rinxent d.	|	1536	...	|	1625	...	1634	...	...	1734	|	...	|	|	...	1836	1925	...	1929	1934	...	|	...
Wimille-Wimereux d.	|	|	...	|	1633	...	1642	...	...	1742	|	...	|	|	...	|	1932	...	1938	|	...	|	...
Boulogne Ville d.	1505	1552	...	1606	1642	...	1653	1705	...	1751	1752	...	1806	1806	...	1852	1953	...	1948	1950	...	1958	...
Étaples-Le Touquet d.	1520	1608	...	1621	1705	...	1713	1720	...	1816	1807	...	1821	1822	...	1908	2019	...	2008	2008	...	2014	...
Rang du Fliers-Verton-Berck d.	1529	1617	...	1630	1712	...	1721	1729	...	1823	1816	...	1830	1830	...	1917	2026	...	2017	2017	...	2022	...
Noyelles sur Mer 🚂 d.	1546	1634	...	1647	...	...	1739	1746	...	...	1835	...	1847	1848	...	1935	...	...	2035	2035	...	2040	...
Abbeville d.	1555	1644	...	1656	...	...	1748	1755	...	...	1846	...	1856	1857	...	1944	...	...	2044	2044	...	2049	...
Amiens a.	1620	1713	...	1720	...	...	1814	1820	...	...	1913	...	1921	1921	...	2012	...	...	2110	2112	...	2114	...
Paris Nord **260** a.	1731	...	...	1831	...	...	...	1931	...	...	...	...	2031	2057	...	...	...	...	...	...	...	2228	...

🚌 ABBEVILLE - LE TRÉPORT 🚌

🚌 number **732**. Service until July 7 - August 22, 2025. *37 km*. Journey 70 minutes (* – 50 minutes):

From **Abbeville** at 0641 Ⓐ, 0820 ⑥, 0830 Ⓐ, 0920 Ⓐ, 1100 Ⓐ, 1120 Ⓒ, 1130 Ⓐ, 1220 ⚒, 1411 ⚒, 1520 Ⓑ, 1620 ⑥, 1735 Ⓐ, 1820 ⑥, 1825 Ⓐ, 1915 Ⓐ, 1920 ⑥, 1937 †, 2040 ⑤.

From **Le Tréport** at 0608 Ⓐ, 0624 ⑥, 0714 Ⓐ, 0819 ⑥, 0914 Ⓐ, 0929 Ⓒ, 1219 ⚒, 1500 Ⓐ, 1544 Ⓐ, 1619 ⑥, 1624 Ⓐ, 1629 †, 1655 †, 1729, 1919 ⑥.

d – Until Aug. 1.
e – Until July 25.
f – From Aug. 4.
g – Ⓐ until Aug. 8; ② from Aug. 12.
🚂 – *Chemin de fer de la Baie de Somme*. Noyelles sur Mer station is adjacent to the SNCF station. www.chemindefer-baiedesomme.fr.

262 LILLE - MAUBEUGE, JEUMONT, LAON and CHARLEVILLE MÉZIÈRES

Laon 🚌 timings are at the POMA gare routière (bus station).

km		Ⓐ	Ⓐ	Ⓐ		Ⓐ 🚌	Ⓐ	Ⓐ		Ⓐ	⑥	⑥		⑥ 🚌	Ⓐ f	Ⓐ		⑥	Ⓐ f	Ⓐ f		Ⓐ 🚌	†	Ⓒ
0	**Lille** Flandres d.	...	0535	0605	...	...	...	0705	...	...	0705	...	...	...	0735	...	...	0835	0837	0905	...	...	0905	1035
48	Valenciennes d.	0542	0612	0642	...	...	...	0742	...	0751	0753	...	...	...	0812	0851	...	0914	0912	0941	...	...	0951	1114
82	Aulnoye Aymeries **255** d.	0612	0637	0717	...	...	0745	0817	...	0821	0822	0830	...	...	0837	0921	...	0939	0937	1017	...	...	1021	1139
94	**Maubeuge** **255** a.	0622	0647	|	...	...	|	|	...	0831	0833	|	...	...	0847	0931	...	0949	0947	|	...	...	1031	1150
104	**Jeumont** a.	0630	...	|	...	...	|	|	...	0839	0842	|	...	...	...	0939	...	0958	...	|	...	...	1039	1158
94	Avesnes d.	...	...	0728	...	...	0801	0827	...	...	...	0839	...	...	...	...	...	...	...	1028	...	...	...	...
123	Hirson d.	...	...	0751	...	0801	0830	0851	...	...	...	0904	...	0914	...	...	...	...	...	1051	...	1101	...	...
184	**Charleville-Mézières** a.	...	...	...	...	0901	...	...	...	...	...	...	...	1014	...	...	...	...	...	...	...	1201	...	...

	Ⓒ	Ⓐ f	Ⓒ		Ⓐ f	Ⓒ	Ⓐ f		Ⓐ 🚌	Ⓐ f	Ⓐ h		Ⓒ	Ⓒ	Ⓐ f		Ⓐ	Ⓐ	Ⓒ		Ⓒ	Ⓐ	⑥ 🚌
Lille Flandres d.	...	1205	1205	...	1235	1235	1305	...	...	1335	...	...	1438	...	1605	...	...	1635	1635	...	...	...	...
Valenciennes d.	...	1242	1253	...	1312	1314	1342	...	...	1412	1418	...	1519	...	1642	...	1651	1713	1714	...	...	...	...
Aulnoye Aymeries **255** d.	1146	1317	1322	...	1337	1348	1417	...	...	1437	1447	...	1544	1602	1717	...	1721	1738	1739	...	1746	1747	...
Maubeuge **255** a.	|	|	1332	...	1347	|	|	...	...	1447	1458	...	1554	|	|	...	1731	1748	1749	...	|	|	...
Jeumont a.	|	|	1341	...	...	|	|	...	...	...	1506	...	1603	|	|	...	1739	...	1758	...	|	|	...
Avesnes d.	1155	1328	...	...	...	1359	1427	...	...	...	...	...	...	1611	1727	...	...	...	...	...	1755	1802	...
Hirson d.	1219	1351	...	...	...	1422	1451	...	1501	...	...	...	...	1636	1751	...	...	...	...	...	1819	1830	1829
Charleville-Mézières a.	...	...	...	...	...	1500	...	...	1601	...	...	...	...	...	...	...	...	...	...	...	...	...	1929

	Ⓐ	Ⓒ	Ⓐ		Ⓐ 🚌	Ⓐ	Ⓒ		† 🚌	Ⓒ	Ⓐ		Ⓐ	Ⓐ	†		Ⓐ	Ⓐ	Ⓐ		Ⓒ	Ⓐ	Ⓐ
Lille Flandres d.	1705	1705	1805	...	...	...	...	...	...	1832	1835	...	1905	...	1905	...	1935	2005	2035	...	2035	2105	2135
Valenciennes d.	1742	1753	1842	...	...	1851	...	...	...	1911	1911	...	1942	1951	1951	...	2012	2042	2112	...	2114	2142	2211
Aulnoye Aymeries **255** d.	1818	1823	|	...	...	1921	1942	...	...	1943	1937	...	2018	2021	2021	...	2037	2117	2137	...	2139	2217	2235
Maubeuge **255** a.	|	1833	|	...	...	1931	|	...	...	1953	1945	...	|	2032	2031	...	2045	|	2147	...	2150	|	2245
Jeumont a.	|	1842	|	...	...	1939	|	...	...	2002	1957	...	|	2040	2040	...	2057	|	...	...	2158	|	2253
Avesnes d.	1828	...	1910	...	...	...	1953	...	...	...	...	...	2027	...	...	...	...	2127	...	...	...	2228	...
Hirson d.	1853	...	1929	...	1939	...	2017	...	2029	...	...	...	2051	...	...	...	...	2151	...	...	...	2251	...
Charleville-Mézières a.	1935	...	...	...	2039	...	...	...	2129	...	...	...	...	...	...	...	...	...	...	...	...	...	...

d – Until Aug. 1.
f – From Aug. 4.
h – Aug. 4–22.

FOR RETURN SERVICE AND HIRSON - LOAN 🚌 SERVICE SEE NEXT PAGE →

CHARLEVILLE MÉZIÈRES, LAON, JEUMONT and MAUBEUGE - LILLE 262

Laon 🚌 timings are at the POMA gare routière (bus station).

	Ⓐ	Ⓐ	Ⓐ		⑥	Ⓐ	Ⓐ		⑥	Ⓐ	Ⓐ		⑥	Ⓐ 🚌	Ⓐ		⑥ 🚌	Ⓒ	Ⓒ		Ⓐ f	Ⓐ f	Ⓐ f
Charleville-Mézières d.	...	...	...	...	...	...	...	...	...	...	0630	...	...	0658	...	...	0731	...	...	...	...	...	...
Hirson d.	...	...	0633	...	...	...	0616	...	0642	...	0708	...	...	0758	0808	...	0831	0841	...	...	...	0908	...
Avesnes d.	...	...	0653	...	...	...	0644	...	0708	...	0732	...	...	...	0833	...	...	0906	...	...	...	0932	...
Jeumont d.	0521	0606	|	...	0620	0640	|	...	|	...	|	...	0720	...	|	...	...	|	0903	...	...	|	1021
Maubeuge 255 d.	0528	0614	|	...	0630	0652	|	...	|	0714	|	...	0727	...	|	...	...	|	0911	...	0913	|	1028
Aulnoye Aymeries 255 d.	0542	0625	|	...	0648	0709	0714	...	0717	0725	0752	...	0740	...	0852	...	...	0915	0924	...	0925	0952	1042
Valenciennes d.	0609	0650	0720	...	0716	0739	0742	...	...	0750	0820	...	0810	...	0920	...	...	...	0948	...	0950	1020	1109
Lille Flandres a.	...	0725	0755	...	0800	...	...	...	...	0823	0855	...	0855	...	0955	...	...	...	1025	...	1025	1055	...
	Ⓒ	†	⑥		Ⓐ 🚌	Ⓐ f	Ⓐ f		⑥ 🚌	Ⓒ	Ⓒ		Ⓐ f	Ⓐ f	Ⓒ		Ⓒ	Ⓐ 🚌	Ⓐ f		Ⓐ f	Ⓐ f	Ⓐ d
Charleville-Mézières d.	...	...	...	...	0958	...	...	...	1131	...	...	...	...	...	...	...	...	1358	...	...	...	...	...
Hirson d.	1041	...	...	...	1058	1108	...	...	1231	1241	...	...	1339	...	1443	...	...	1458	1508	...	...	...	...
Avesnes d.	1105	...	...	...	...	1133	...	...	...	1305	...	...	1406	...	1508	...	...	...	1532	...	...	...	...
Jeumont d.	|	1104	1120	...	...	|	...	...	...	|	1304	...	|	...	|	...	1504	...	|	...	...	1621	1621
Maubeuge 255 d.	|	1111	1128	...	...	|	1214	...	...	|	1311	...	|	1414	|	...	1511	...	|	...	1614	1628	1628
Aulnoye Aymeries 255 d.	1115	1124	1141	...	...	1153	1225	...	...	1315	1324	...	1415	1426	1517	...	1524	...	1552	...	1625	1642	1652
Valenciennes d.	...	1148	1210	...	...	1220	1250	...	...	...	1348	...	...	1450	...	...	1548	...	1620	...	1650	1709	1725
Lille Flandres a.	...	1225	1255	...	...	1255	1325	...	...	...	1425	...	...	1525	...	...	1625	...	1655	...	1725	...	...
	Ⓐ f	† 🚌	Ⓒ		⑥	†	Ⓐ		Ⓐ	Ⓐ	Ⓒ		Ⓐ f	Ⓐ 🚌	Ⓒ		Ⓐ	Ⓐ	†		Ⓐ	Ⓐ	
Charleville-Mézières d.	...	1536	...	...	...	...	...	...	...	...	...	...	...	1758	1803	...	...	...	...	...	...	...	...
Hirson d.	1620	1636	1646	...	...	...	1708	...	...	...	...	...	1808	1858	1842	...	1908	...	...	...	2008	2108	...
Avesnes d.	1648	...	1711	...	...	...	1732	...	...	...	...	...	1832	...	1906	...	1932	...	...	...	2032	2133	...
Jeumont d.	|	...	|	...	1700	1720	|	...	...	1821	1824	...	|	...	|	...	|	2006	2020	...	|	|	...
Maubeuge 255 d.	|	...	|	...	1707	1728	|	...	1814	1828	1832	...	|	...	|	...	|	2014	2028	...	|	|	...
Aulnoye Aymeries 255 d.	1703	...	1720	...	1721	1741	1752	...	1825	1842	1844	...	1852	...	1926	...	1955	2025	2041	...	2054	2153	...
Valenciennes d.	...	...	...	...	1745	1810	1820	...	1850	1909	1913	...	1920	...	1950	...	2021	2050	2110	...	2120	2220	...
Lille Flandres a.	...	...	...	...	1822	1855	1855	...	1925	...	1958	...	1955	...	2025	...	2055	2125	2155	...	2155	2255	...

🚌 HIRSON - LAON 🚌

56 km. Journey 90 minutes:

From **Hirson** at 0551 ⚒, 0745 Ⓐ, 0755 ⑥, 0848 †, 0956 ⑥, 1113 Ⓐ, 1151 ⑥, 1220 ③, 1520 †, 1555 ⚒, 1730 Ⓐ, 1748 ⑥, 1750 †, 1830 Ⓐ, 1908 Ⓐ.

From **Laon** at 0623 Ⓐ, 0745 ⑥, 0825 Ⓐ, 1015 ⑥, 1045 †, 1235 ⚒, 1444 †, 1521 ⑥, 1558 Ⓐ, 1725 Ⓐ, 1738 †, 1825 Ⓐ, 1842 ⑥, 1942 ⑥, 2015 †, 2033 Ⓐ.

FOR RETURN SERVICE AND FOOTNOTES SEE PREVIOUS PAGE.

ÉTAPLES - ARRAS 263

km																								
		Ⓐ	⑥ j	⑥ k	Ⓐ	⑥	Ⓐ	⑥	†	⑥	Ⓐ	†	Ⓐ	⑥	†	Ⓐ	Ⓐ	†	⑥	Ⓐ	Ⓒ	†	⑥	Ⓐ
0	**Étaples Le Touquet** d.	0515	0539	0610	0626	0738	0830	0831	0831	1107	...	1152	1330	1349	1454	1526	1626	1637	1647	1737	1754	...	...	1900
12	Montreuil sur Mer d.	0525	0549	0620	0635	0747	0840	0840	0840	1116	...	1201	1339	1359	1504	1535	1636	1647	1657	1746	1803	...	...	1910
33	Hesdin d.	0549	0615	0646	0706	0814	0900	0911	0911	1147	...	1232	1410	1425	1530	1556	1700	1711	1717	1817	1830	...	...	1940
61	St Pol sur Ternoise a.	0614	0642	0713	0732	0840	0924	0938	0938	1214	...	1259	1436	1452	1557	1620	1724	1735	1742	1844	1856	...	...	2007
61	St Pol sur Ternoise ▲ d.	0629	0644	0715	0734	0842	0926	0947	0954	1216	1217	1301	1438	1454	1600	1624	1731	1737	1744	1849	...	1922	1938	...
101	**Arras** ▲ a.	0707	0721	0752	0811	0919	1003	1024	1035	1253	1254	1338	1515	1531	1637	1701	1808	1815	1821	1926	...	2003	2019	...
		Ⓐ	Ⓐ 🚌	Ⓐ	⑥ 🚌	Ⓒ	Ⓐ	†	⑥	†	Ⓐ	⑥	Ⓐ	†	Ⓐ	⑥	Ⓐ	†	Ⓐ	Ⓐ	†	⑥	Ⓐ	†
	Arras ▲ d.	...	0531	...	0746	...	0941	0955	1040	1124	1258	1450	1543	1556	1639	1700	1746	1753	...	1845	1922	1938	1939	...
	St Pol sur Ternoise ▲ a.	...	0626	...	0834	...	1022	1031	1116	1201	1339	1531	1620	1637	1720	1737	1827	1834	...	1926	1959	2015	2015	...
	St Pol sur Ternoise d.	0522	...	0636	...	0844	1025	1033	1118	1203	1341	1533	1632	1642	1747	...	...	...	1912	...	...	2017	...	2023
	Hesdin d.	0547	...	0704	...	0909	1050	1100	1145	1230	1408	1600	1658	1709	1815	...	...	...	1938	...	...	2044	...	2051
	Montreuil sur Mer d.	0606	...	0730	...	0932	1109	1125	1210	1255	1433	1625	1717	1734	1840	...	...	...	1957	...	...	2109	...	2116
	Étaples Le Touquet a.	0615	...	0739	...	0941	1118	1134	1219	1304	1442	1634	1726	1743	1849	...	...	...	2006	...	...	2118	...	2125

j – Until July 26.
k – From Aug. 2.

▲ – Also from St Pol sur Ternoise at 0558 Ⓐ, 0635 Ⓐ 🚌, 1935 Ⓐ 🚌;
Also from Arras at 0645 Ⓐ, 0857 ⑥, 1225 ⑥, 1759 ⑥.

ARRAS and LILLE - HAZEBROUCK - DUNKERQUE and CALAIS 265

See Table **250** for *TGV* and *TER-GV* services.

km																								
			Ⓐ	Ⓐ	Ⓐ	Ⓐ	Ⓐ	Ⓐ	Ⓐ	Ⓐ	Ⓐ	Ⓐ		Ⓐ	Ⓐ	Ⓐ	Ⓐ	Ⓐ	Ⓐ	Ⓐ	Ⓐ	Ⓐ	Ⓐ	Ⓐ
	Arras d.	Ⓐ	...	...	0550	0618	...	...	0718	...	...	0818	...	...	...	...	...	...	1214	1255	...	...	...	...
	Lens d.		...	...	0608	0636	...	...	0736	...	...	0835	...	...	...	...	...	...	1232	1309	...	...	...	...
	Béthune d.		...	...	0626	0655	...	...	0755	...	...	0855	...	...	...	...	...	...	1252	1326	...	...	...	...
	Lillers d.		...	...	0635	0704	...	...	0804	...	...	0904	...	...	...	...	...	...	1301	1335	...	...	...	...
0	**Lille** Flandres d.		...	0613	|	|	0713	0740	|	0813	0840	|	...	0913	0940	1013	1213	1240	|	|	1413	1540	...	1613
22	Armentières d.		...	0628	|	|	0728	0754	|	0828	0854	|	...	0928	0954	1029	1228	1254	|	|	1428	1554	...	1628
47	Hazebrouck d.		0623	0648	0654	0723	0748	0816	0823	0848	0916	0923	...	0948	1016	1048	1248	1314	1320	1352	1448	1616	1623	1648
87	**Dunkerque** a.		|	|	0728	|	|	0848	|	|	0948	|	...	|	1048	|	|	1348	|	1426	|	1648	|	|
68	St Omer d.		0641	0701	...	0740	0801	...	0842	0901	...	0940	...	1001	...	1101	1301	...	1339	...	1501	...	1642	1701
109	**Calais** Ville a.		0718	0729	...	0818	0829	...	0923	0929	...	1015	...	1029	...	1129	1329	...	1426	...	1529	...	1719	1729
		Ⓐ	Ⓐ	Ⓐ	Ⓐ	Ⓐ	Ⓐ		Ⓐ	Ⓐ	Ⓐ	Ⓐ	Ⓐ	⑤	Ⓐ	Ⓐ	Ⓐ			⑥	⑥	⑥	Ⓒ	Ⓒ
	Arras d.	...	1618	...	1655	...	1712	...	...	1755	...	...	1918	...	1959	...	...	...	Ⓒ	...	...	0713	...	0802
	Lens d.	...	1636	...	1710	...	1735	...	...	1812	...	...	1936	...	2015	...	...	...		...	...	0731	...	0820
	Béthune d.	...	1655	...	1727	...	1759	...	...	1829	...	...	1955	...	2032	...	...	...		...	...	0748	...	0837
	Lillers d.	...	1704	...	1735	...	1812	...	...	1838	...	...	2004	...	2041	...	...	...		...	...	0757	...	0846
	Lille Flandres d.	1640	|	1713	|	1740	|	...	1813	|	1840	1913	|	2013	|	2040	2113	...		0639	0705	|	0805	|
	Armentières d.	1654	|	1728	|	1754	|	...	1828	|	1854	1927	|	2028	|	2054	2128	...		0653	0721	|	0822	|
	Hazebrouck d.	1716	1723	1748	1759	1816	1835	...	1848	1859	1916	1948	2023	2048	2059	2115	2148	...		0712	0747	0813	0849	0902
	Dunkerque a.	1748	|	|	1837	1848	...	...	|	1937	1948	|	|	|	2137	2149	|	...		|	0819	...	0921	...
	St Omer d.	...	1741	1801	...	...	...	...	1901	...	...	2001	2040	2101	...	...	2201	...		0724	...	...	...	...
	Calais Ville a.	...	1821	1829	...	...	...	...	1929	...	...	2029	2117	2129	...	...	2229	...		0754	...	...	...	...

FOR ADDITIONAL TRAINS SEE NEXT PAGE →

265 ARRAS and LILLE - HAZEBROUCK - DUNKERQUE and CALAIS

See Table **250** for *TGV* and *TER-GV* services.

	©	©	©	©	©	©		©	©	⑥	©	©		©	©	©	⑥		©	©	©	©	©	©
Arras d.	...	...	1006	...	...	...	...	...	1308	...	...	1506	...	...	...	1706	...	...	...	...	1906	...	...	...
Lens d.	...	...	1024	...	...	...	...	...	1326	...	...	1523	...	...	...	1724	...	...	...	...	1924	...	...	...
Béthune d.	...	...	1041	...	...	...	...	...	1343	...	...	1540	...	...	...	1741	...	...	...	...	1941	...	...	...
Lillers d.	...	...	1050	...	...	...	...	...	1352	...	...	1549	...	...	...	1750	...	...	...	...	1950	...	...	...
Lille Flandres d.	0839	0939	|	1039	1139	1239	...	1313	|	1339	1439	|	...	1539	1639	|	1739	...	1813	1839	|	1939	2039	2139
Armentières d.	0853	0953	|	1053	1153	1253	...	1329	|	1353	1453	|	...	1553	1653	|	1753	...	1829	1853	|	1953	2053	2152
Hazebrouck d.	0912	1012	1106	1112	1211	1312	...	1354	1408	1412	1512	1606	...	1612	1712	1806	1812	...	1854	1912	2006	2012	2112	2211
Dunkerque a.	|	1043	...	|	1243	|	...	1426	...	1443	|	...	...	1645	|	...	1843	...	1926	|	...	2043	|	2242
St Omer d.	0924	...	...	1125	...	1324	...	...	...	...	1524	...	...	...	1724	...	...	...	...	1926	...	...	2124	...
Calais Ville a.	0954	...	...	1155	...	1355	...	...	...	...	1554	...	...	...	1754	...	...	...	...	1956	...	...	2154	...

		Ⓐ	Ⓐ	Ⓐ	Ⓐ	Ⓐ	Ⓐ	Ⓐ	Ⓐ	Ⓐ	Ⓐ	Ⓐ	Ⓐ	Ⓐ	Ⓐ	Ⓐ	Ⓐ	Ⓐ	Ⓐ	Ⓐ	Ⓐ	Ⓐ	Ⓐ	Ⓐ
Calais Ville d.	Ⓐ	...	0531	...	...	...	0630	0644	...	0733	...	0833	0840	...	...	1033	...	1133	...	...	1245	...	1431	...
St Omer d.		...	0559	...	...	...	0701	0721	...	0801	...	0901	0916	...	...	1102	...	1201	...	...	1321	...	1501	...
Dunkerque d.		...	|	...	0612	0627	|	|	0712	|	0812	|	|	0912	...	|	1112	|	...	1232	|	1431	|	1512
Hazebrouck d.		0538	0614	0624	0646	0702	0715	0739	0746	0815	0846	0915	0936	0945	1108	1116	1146	1215	1238	1306	1339	1507	1515	1546
Armentières d.		|	0633	|	0706	|	0733	|	0806	0833	0906	0933	|	1006	|	1133	1206	1233	|	...	...	|	1533	1606
Lille Flandres a.		|	0647	|	0720	|	0747	|	0820	0847	0920	0947	|	1020	|	1147	1220	1247	|	...	...	|	1547	1620
Lillers d.		0556	...	0646	...	0718	...	0756	...	...	...	...	0953	...	1124	...	...	...	1256	...	...	1523	...	...
Béthune d.		0606	...	0701	...	0728	...	0806	...	...	...	...	1003	...	1134	...	...	...	1306	...	...	1533	...	...
Lens d.		0626	...	0725	...	0745	...	0826	...	...	...	...	1022	...	1151	...	...	...	1326	...	...	1551	...	...
Arras a.		0643	...	0747	...	0759	...	0843	...	...	...	...	1039	...	1204	...	...	...	1343	...	...	1607	...	...

	Ⓐ	Ⓐ	Ⓐ	Ⓐ	Ⓐ	Ⓐ	Ⓐ	Ⓐ	Ⓐ	Ⓐ	Ⓐ	Ⓐ	Ⓐ	Ⓐ	Ⓐ			⑥	⑥	⑥	⑥	⑥	†	†
Calais Ville d.	...	1633	1645	...	...	1730	1743	1831	1842	...	...	1933	1942	...	2031	...	Ⓒ	...	0606	...	...	...	...	...
St Omer d.	...	1701	1721	...	...	1801	1819	1901	1919	...	...	2001	2019	...	2101	...		...	0636	...	...	...	...	...
Dunkerque d.	1612	|	|	1712	1732	|	|	|	|	1912	1932	|	|	2012	|	...		0533	|	...	0633	0710	...	0733
Hazebrouck d.	1646	1715	1739	1747	1808	1815	1837	1915	1936	1946	2007	2015	2037	2046	2115	...		0607	0650	0652	0707	0743	0755	0807
Armentières d.	1706	1733	|	1805	|	1833	|	1933	...	2006	|	2033	...	2106	2133	...		0631	0707	|	0731	0807	|	0831
Lille Flandres a.	1720	1747	|	1820	|	1847	|	1947	...	2020	|	2047	...	2120	2147	...		0647	0721	|	0747	0823	|	0847
Lillers d.	...	...	1757	...	1823	...	1855	...	...	...	2023	...	...	...	...	...		...	...	0708	...	...	0811	...
Béthune d.	...	...	1807	...	1833	...	1905	...	...	...	2033	...	...	...	...	...		...	...	0718	...	...	0822	...
Lens d.	...	...	1827	...	1851	...	1924	...	...	...	2051	...	...	...	...	...		...	...	0735	...	...	0839	...
Arras a.	...	...	1843	...	1903	...	1940	...	...	...	2103	...	...	...	...	...		...	...	0752	...	...	0856	...

	⑥	©	©	©	©	©	©		©	©	⑥	©	©	©	©	⑥		⑥	©	©	⑥	©	†	©
Calais Ville d.	...	0806	...	...	1006	...	...	...	1213	...	...	1406	...	...	1606	...	...	...	...	1806	...	...	...	2006
St Omer d.	...	0836	...	...	1036	...	...	...	1242	...	...	1436	...	...	1636	...	...	...	...	1835	...	...	...	2036
Dunkerque d.	...	|	0917	...	|	1112	...	...	|	1233	1317	|	1516	...	|	1717	...	...	1733	|	...	1917	...	|
Hazebrouck d.	0824	0850	0950	1000	1050	1146	1154	...	1256	1306	1350	1450	1548	1552	1650	1750	...	1754	1807	1850	1932	1950	1954	2050
Armentières d.	|	0907	1007	|	1107	1206	|	...	1313	1330	1407	1507	1606	|	1707	1807	...	|	1831	1907	|	2007	|	2107
Lille Flandres a.	|	0921	1021	|	1121	1220	|	...	1327	1347	1421	1521	1620	|	1721	1821	...	|	1847	1921	|	2021	|	2121
Lillers d.	0840	...	...	1017	...	...	1210	...	...	...	...	...	...	1608	...	...	...	1811	...	...	1948	...	2011	...
Béthune d.	0850	...	...	1026	...	...	1221	...	...	...	...	...	...	1618	...	...	...	1821	...	...	1958	...	2021	...
Lens d.	0907	...	...	1044	...	...	1238	...	...	...	...	...	...	1635	...	...	...	1838	...	...	2015	...	2038	...
Arras a.	0924	...	...	1101	...	...	1255	...	...	...	...	...	...	1651	...	...	...	1854	...	...	2032	...	2058	...

FOR ADDITIONAL SERVICES SEE PREVIOUS PAGE.

266 ST POL SUR TERNOISE - BÉTHUNE - LILLE

Frequent additional services are available Béthune - Lille and v.v.

km		Ⓐ	Ⓐ	⑥	Ⓐ	Ⓐ 🚌		⑥	⑥	†	Ⓐ 🚌	⑥		Ⓐ	Ⓐ	⑥	†	Ⓐ 🚌		Ⓐ	⑥	†	Ⓐ 🚌	©
0	**St Pol sur Ternoise** d.	0544	0639	0702	0739	0749	...	0904	0959	1005	1001	1202	...	1215	1444	1505	1602	1623	...	1744	1802	1808	1828	1858
32	Béthune d.	0618	0711	0736	0811	0852	...	0938	1033	1039	1104	1236	...	1249	1519	1538	1636	1726	...	1819	1836	1841	1931	1931
74	**Lille** Flandres a.	0654	*0754*	0829	*0854*	...	...	1018	1116	1117	*1154*	1329	...	1344	1554	1617	1717	*1824*	...	1854	1929	1933	*2024*	*2018*

		Ⓐ 🚌	Ⓐ 🚌	©	Ⓐ	⑥		†	Ⓐ 🚌	⑥	Ⓐ	⑥		Ⓐ	†	Ⓐ 🚌	Ⓐ	⑥		Ⓐ	⑥		†	⑥
	Lille Flandres d.	*0615*	*0706*	...	*0815*	0954	...	1042	*1115*	1231	1306	1542	...	1606	1642	*1615*	*1736*	1831	...	1906	1831	...	*1831*	1942
	Béthune d.	0730	0757	0809	0922	1035	...	1124	1226	1325	1349	1626	...	1644	1724	1730	1833	1935	...	1944	1935	...	1950	2028
	St Pol sur Ternoise a.	0833	0900	0841	0954	1106	...	1156	1329	1356	1421	1658	...	1715	1756	1833	1905	2007	...	2016	2007	...	2021	2059

267 PARIS - BEAUVAIS - LE TRÉPORT and BEAUVAIS - CREIL

km		Ⓐ	⑥	Ⓐ	Ⓐ	©	Ⓐ	©	Ⓐ				©	Ⓐ		Ⓐ	⑥	Ⓐ	Ⓐ	†	⑥	Ⓐ	⚒	Ⓑ	©
0	**Paris** Nord d.	0607	0631	0638	0737	0801	0850	0933	1001	1101	1201	1401	1601	1607	1701	1737	1801	1807	1837	1844	1901	1907	2001	2101	2201
	Persan-Beaumont d.	0638	0700	0709	0809	0834	0924	1000	1036	1136	1236	1436	1634	1638	1738	|	1835	1838	|	1927	1935	1938	2035	2136	2236
80	**Beauvais** a.	0720	0741	0751	0851	0918	1005	1041	1118	1218	1318	1518	1718	1719	1820	1847	1920	1920	1940	2009	2020	2020	2118	2218	2317
					Ⓐ	©	|	|					|	|								Ⓐ			
80	**Beauvais** d.	...	...	...	0859	0926	1014	1043	...	...	1329	1527	1720	1721	...	...	...	...	...	...	...	2117	...	...	...
129	Abancourt d.	...	...	...	0944	1013	1048	1117	...	...	1415	1613	1800	1800	...	...	...	...	...	...	...	2202	...	...	...
183	Eu d.	...	...	...	1029	1058	|	|	...	...	1500	1658	|	|	...	...	...	...	...	...	...	2246	...	...	...
186	**Le Tréport** a.	...	...	...	1033	1102	1129	1159	...	...	1504	1702	1842	1842	...	...	...	...	...	...	...	2251	...	...	...

	⚒	©	Ⓐ	Ⓐ	©	⑥	†	Ⓐ	⑥	Ⓑ			©	Ⓐ			⚒	⑥	†	Ⓐ	©	Ⓐ	⑥	†
Le Tréport d.	...	...	...	0556	...	0659	0800	0851	0919	...	1221	...	1322	1520	...	1706	...	...	...	1856	1921	1957	2007	2020
Eu d.	...	...	...	0601	...	0704	0804	0855	0924	...	|	...	1326	1525	...	1711	...	...	...	|	|	2002	2012	2025
Abancourt d.	...	...	...	0646	...	0748	0849	0946	1015	...	1303	...	1417	1615	...	1758	...	...	...	1938	2003	2047	2056	2110
Beauvais a.	...	...	...	0731	...	0834	0934	1031	1100	...	1337	...	1503	1701	...	1844	...	...	...	2012	2037	2132	2141	2155
				Ⓐ		⚒	†	©	⚒		|		⚒	Ⓐ		†				|	|		|	|
Beauvais d.	0540	0627	0640	0740	0744	0840	0940	1040	1140	1240	1339	1440	1640	1710	1740	1852	1901	1940	1951	2014	2039	...	2143	2157
Persan-Beaumont d.	0623	0709	0723	0823	0828	0923	1016	1123	1223	1321	1423	1523	1723	1754	1823	1932	1944	2022	2032	2055	2124	...	2227	2237
Paris Nord a.	0657	0742	0755	0856	0857	0957	1056	1156	1257	1357	1457	1557	1757	1825	1857	2000	2028	2057	2109	2128	2159	...	2257	2310

BEAUVAIS - CREIL *37 km.* Journey 45–50 minutes (85 minutes by 🚌).

From **Beauvais** at 0529 Ⓐ, 0608 Ⓐ, 0641 ⑥, 0646 Ⓐ, 0657 Ⓐ, 0753 Ⓐ, 0822 Ⓐ, 0920 ⑥, 0930 †, 1047 ⑥, 1145 Ⓐ, 1255 †, 1300 Ⓐ, 1305 ⑥, 1609 ⚒, 1649 Ⓐ, 1736, 1852 Ⓐ, 2025 †, 2044 ⑥.

From **Creil** at 0642 Ⓐ, 0721 Ⓐ, 0731 ⑥, 0755 Ⓐ, 0830 †, 0900 Ⓐ, 0928 ⑥, 1134 Ⓐ, 1200 †, 1212 ⑥, 1310 Ⓐ, 1402 ⚒, 1646 ©, 1659 Ⓐ, 1745 ⚒, 1829 Ⓐ, 1915 ©, 1948 Ⓐ, 2044 Ⓐ 🚌.

PARIS - ROUEN - LE HAVRE 270

km			Ⓐ	Ⓐ	Ⓐ	Ⓐ	Ⓐ ◧	Ⓐ	Ⓐ ◧	Ⓐ	Ⓐ ◧	Ⓐ	Ⓐ ◧	Ⓐ	Ⓐ ◧	Ⓐ	Ⓐ	Ⓐ ◧	Ⓐ ◧	Ⓐ	Ⓐ ◧	Ⓐ	Ⓐ ◧	Ⓐ	Ⓐ	Ⓐ ◧	Ⓐ
0	**Paris** St Lazare d.	Ⓐ	...	0546	...	0609	0640	0712	0740	0814	0840	1011	1040	1112	1140	...	1212	1240	1340	1412	1440	1512	1540	...	1611	1640	1650
57	Mantes la Jolie d.		...	│	...	0649	│	│	│	0846	│	1044	│	│	│	...	1245	│	│	1445	│	│	│	...	1650	│	1730
79	Vernon-Giverny d.		...	0637	...	0704	│	0803	│	0902	│	1100	│	1205	│	...	1301	│	│	1500	│	1605	│	...	1705	│	1751
111	Val de Reuil d.		...	0656	...	0723	│	0822	│	0921	│	1119	│	1224	│	...	1320	│	│	1520	│	1624	│	...	1725	│	1810
126	Oissel d.		...	0709	...	0735	│	0834	│	0933	│	1130	│	1236	│	...	1335	│	│	1534	│	1636	│	...	1737	│	1819
140	**Rouen** Rive-Droite a.		0642	0718	0729	0746	0754	0844	0859	0943	0955	1140	1201	1246	1257	1307	1345	1359	1454	1544	1559	1646	1701	1735	1747	1759	1829
178	Yvetot a.		0706	...	0753	...	0817	...	0921	...	1019	...	1223	...	│	1333	...	1422	1516	...	1622	...	1723	1759	...	1822	...
203	Bréauté-Beuzeville a.		0720	...	0808	...	0830	...	0935	...	1033	...	1237	...	│	1347	...	1435	1530	...	1635	...	1736	1814	...	1835	...
228	**Le Havre** a.		0737	...	0825	...	0845	...	0949	...	1048	...	1252	...	1345	1407	...	1451	1545	...	1652	...	1751	1832	...	1852	...

	Ⓐ	Ⓐ	Ⓐ ◧	Ⓐ	Ⓐ	Ⓐ ◧	Ⓐ	Ⓐ	Ⓐ ◧	Ⓐ	Ⓐ B ◧	Ⓐ	⑤ ◧			⑥	⑥	⑥	⑥	Ⓒ ◧	Ⓒ	Ⓒ ◧	⑥ A ◧	Ⓒ ◧	Ⓒ	Ⓒ
Paris St Lazare d.	...	1712	1740	1749	1811	1840	1850	1911	1940	2012	2040	2112	2140	...	Ⓒ	...	0609	...	0712	0740	0812	0840	0912	0940	...	1012
Mantes la Jolie d.	...	│	│	│	1852	│	│	│	│	2051	│	2150	│	...		...	0642	...	│	│	0852	│	│	│	...	1052
Vernon-Giverny d.	...	1803	│	1843	1909	│	1942	2005	│	2106	│	2205	│	...		...	0702	...	0804	│	0913	│	│	│	...	1112
Val de Reuil d.	...	1822	│	1903	1930	│	2001	2024	│	2125	│	2224	│	...		...	0721	...	0823	│	0932	│	│	│	...	1130
Oissel d.	...	1833	│	1914	1942	│	2013	2033	│	2135	│	2236	│	...		...	0735	...	0834	│	0944	│	│	│	...	1142
Rouen Rive-Droite a.	1837	1843	1902	1926	1954	2004	2023	2043	2106	2145	2201	2246	2302	...		0607	0745	0801	0844	0900	0954	1003	1029	1109	1118	1152
Yvetot a.	1901	...	1926	...	...	2026	...	...	│	...	2223	...	│	...		0631	...	0825	...	0922	...	1025	...	1132	1142	...
Bréauté-Beuzeville a.	1914	...	1941	...	...	2040	...	...	│	...	2237	...	│	...		0644	...	0838	...	0936	...	1038	...	1145	1155	...
Le Havre a.	1931	...	1956	...	...	2055	...	...	2152	...	2251	...	2348	...		0701	...	0856	...	0952	...	1053	...	1202	1212	...

	Ⓒ ◧	Ⓒ	⑥ ◧	⑥	Ⓒ	Ⓒ ◧	Ⓒ ◧	Ⓒ	Ⓒ ◧	⑥ ◧	⑥	Ⓒ	Ⓒ ◧	†	⑥	Ⓒ ◧	Ⓒ	Ⓒ	Ⓒ ◧	Ⓒ	Ⓒ ◧	Ⓒ	Ⓒ ◧	†	Ⓒ ◧	Ⓒ
Paris St Lazare d.	1040	1112	1140	...	1212	1240	1340	1412	1440	1540	...	1612	1640	1712	1712	1740	...	1812	1840	1911	1940	2012	2040	2112	2140	2212
Mantes la Jolie d.	│	│	│	...	1252	│	│	1450	│	│	...	1651	│	│	1751	│	...	1852	│	│	│	2051	│	│	│	2252
Vernon-Giverny d.	│	1204	│	...	1312	│	│	1510	│	│	...	1711	│	1803	1807	│	...	1913	│	2005	│	2112	│	2204	│	2307
Val de Reuil d.	│	1224	│	...	1331	│	│	1530	│	│	...	1730	│	1822	1826	│	...	1932	│	2024	│	2131	│	2223	│	2326
Oissel d.	│	1236	│	...	1343	│	│	1542	│	│	...	1742	│	1833	1837	│	...	1944	│	2035	│	2143	│	2234	│	2337
Rouen Rive-Droite a.	1205	1246	1257	1307	1352	1405	1504	1552	1604	1702	1720	1751	1805	1843	1847	1901	1908	1956	2004	2045	2101	2153	2204	2244	2302	2347
Yvetot a.	1228	...	│	1331	...	1428	1526	...	1626	│	1744	...	1828	...	...	│	1933	...	2026	...	│	...	2226	...	│	...
Bréauté-Beuzeville a.	1242	...	│	1344	...	1441	1540	...	1640	│	1757	...	1841	...	...	│	1946	...	2040	...	│	...	2241	...	│	...
Le Havre a.	1257	...	1343	1401	...	1457	1600	...	1655	1748	1814	...	1857	...	...	1947	2003	...	2055	...	2148	...	2255	...	2348	...

		Ⓐ	Ⓐ	Ⓐ ◧	Ⓐ	Ⓐ	Ⓐ	Ⓐ ◧	Ⓐ	Ⓐ ◧	Ⓐ	Ⓐ	Ⓐ ◧	Ⓐ	Ⓐ ◧	Ⓐ	Ⓐ ◧	Ⓐ	Ⓐ	Ⓐ ◧	Ⓐ	Ⓐ	Ⓐ ◧	Ⓐ ◧	Ⓐ	Ⓐ
Le Havre d.	Ⓐ	...	...	0522	...	0601	...	0628	...	0709	...	0732	0805	...	0912	...	1007	1026	...	1210	...	1232	1310	1406	...	1433
Bréauté-Beuzeville d.		...	...	0537	...	0618	...	0643	...	0724	...	0748	0821	...	0927	...	1022	1046	...	1225	...	1249	│	1421	...	1450
Yvetot d.		...	...	0551	...	0634	...	0657	...	0737	...	0804	0835	...	0941	...	1036	1100	...	1238	...	1302	│	1434	...	1503
Rouen Rive-Droite d.		0518	0545	0615	0636	0659	0701	0722	0741	0801	0817	0829	0859	0915	1005	1013	1100	1127	1213	1302	1312	1327	1357	1459	1511	1529
Oissel d.		0528	0554	│	0646	...	0711	│	0751	│	0828	...	│	0925	│	1024	│	...	1223	│	1322	...	│	│	1521	...
Val de Reuil d.		0537	0605	│	0657	...	0721	│	0800	│	0837	...	│	0936	│	1034	│	...	1235	│	1334	...	│	│	1535	...
Vernon-Giverny d.		0557	0626	│	0717	...	0741	│	0820	│	0857	...	│	0956	│	1054	│	...	1255	│	1354	...	│	│	1555	...
Mantes la Jolie a.		0612	0642	│	│	...	0757	│	│	│	0913	...	│	1011	│	1110	│	...	│	│	1410	...	│	│	1612	...
Paris St Lazare a.		0654	0718	0739	0816	...	0836	0839	0917	0920	0949	...	1023	1048	1123	1148	1223	...	1348	1423	1448	...	1518	1623	1648	...

	Ⓐ ◧	Ⓐ	Ⓐ	Ⓐ	Ⓐ ◧	Ⓐ	Ⓐ ◧	Ⓐ	Ⓐ ◧	Ⓐ	Ⓐ	Ⓐ ◧			⑥	†	⑥	⑥	Ⓒ ◧	Ⓒ	Ⓒ ◧	⑥	Ⓒ	Ⓒ ◧	Ⓒ	Ⓒ ◧
Le Havre d.	1508	...	1603	...	1707	...	1802	...	1905	...	1927	2007	...	Ⓒ	...	...	...	0631	0702	...	0802	...	0847	0902	...	1003
Bréauté-Beuzeville d.	1523	...	1618	...	1722	...	1818	...	1921	...	1944	2023	...		...	...	...	0648	0718	...	0818	...	0904	0916	...	1019
Yvetot d.	1537	...	1631	...	1736	...	1832	...	1935	...	2000	2036	...		...	...	...	0701	0732	...	0832	...	0917	0930	...	1033
Rouen Rive-Droite d.	1601	1609	1652	1715	1800	1817	1857	1914	2000	2010	2025	2101	...		0604	0714	0716	0726	0757	0809	0857	0912	0942	0955	1011	1057
Oissel d.	│	1619	...	1726	│	1827	│	1924	│	2020	...	│	...		0614	0724	0726	...	│	0819	│	0922	...	│	1021	│
Val de Reuil d.	│	1634	...	1738	│	1841	│	1938	│	2034	...	│	...		0625	0735	0737	...	│	0832	│	0935	...	│	1033	│
Vernon-Giverny d.	│	1655	...	1758	│	1902	│	1958	│	2054	...	│	...		0646	0755	0758	...	│	0853	│	0955	...	│	1053	│
Mantes la Jolie d.	│	│	...	│	│	1917	│	2014	│	│	...	│	...		0706	0810	│	...	│	0914	│	1011	...	│	1114	│
Paris St Lazare a.	1720	1748	...	1849	1920	1949	2023	2048	2120	2150	...	2223	...		0751	0848	0848	...	0923	0948	1023	1048	...	1122	1148	1223

	⑥	† ◧	Ⓒ	Ⓒ ◧	⑥	†	⑥	⑥ ◧	Ⓒ	Ⓒ ◧	Ⓒ ◧	Ⓒ		Ⓒ ◧	Ⓒ	Ⓒ ◧	⑥	†	Ⓒ ◧	† A ◧	Ⓒ ◧	Ⓒ	Ⓒ	Ⓒ ◧	Ⓒ	Ⓒ ◧
Le Havre d.	...	1107	...	1204	...	...	1232	1310	...	1406	1505	...	...	1603	...	1702	...	...	1802	...	1902	...	1932	2010	...	2104
Bréauté-Beuzeville d.	...	│	...	1220	...	...	1249	│	...	1421	1520	...	...	1619	...	1718	...	...	1818	...	1918	...	1949	│	...	2120
Yvetot d.	...	│	...	1234	...	...	1302	│	...	1435	1534	...	...	1633	...	1732	...	...	1832	...	1932	...	2002	│	...	2134
Rouen Rive-Droite d.	1113	1154	1212	1258	1311	1313	1327	1357	1409	1459	1558	1612	...	1658	1714	1757	1808	1809	1857	1920	1957	2011	2027	2057	2113	2159
Oissel d.	1123	│	1222	│	1321	1323	...	│	1419	│	│	1622	...	│	1724	│	1818	1820	│	│	│	2021	...	│	2123	│
Val de Reuil d.	1134	│	1233	│	1336	1336	...	│	1432	│	│	1633	...	│	1735	│	1833	1832	│	│	│	2032	...	│	2135	│
Vernon-Giverny d.	1155	│	1253	│	1356	1356	...	│	1453	│	│	1654	...	│	1756	│	1853	1853	│	│	│	2052	...	│	2155	│
Mantes la Jolie d.	1210	│	1314	│	│	│	...	│	1513	│	│	1714	...	│	│	│	1914	1914	│	│	│	2113	...	│	2210	│
Paris St Lazare a.	1248	1323	1348	1423	1448	1448	...	1523	1548	1623	1723	1748	...	1823	1849	1923	1948	1948	2025	2048	2123	2148	...	2223	2248	2312

FÉCAMP - LE HAVRE

km		Ⓐ 🚌	Ⓐ	Ⓐ 🚌	†	⑥	Ⓐ	⚒	†	†	⑥	Ⓐ 🚌	†	⚒	†	⑥	†	Ⓐ 🚌	Ⓐ	⑥	†	Ⓐ	Ⓒ	Ⓐ 🚌	⑥ 🚌	†	Ⓐ
0	**Fécamp** d.	0558	0644	0708	0730	0747	0753	0928	0930	1130	1145	1158	1330	1345	1530	1542	1635	1638	1728	1733	1735	1828	1832	1905	1908	1930	1937
20	Bréauté-Beuzeville a.	0628	0704	0738	0750	0807	0813	0949	0950	1150	1205	1228	1350	1405	1550	1602	1655	1708	1748	1753	1755	1848	1852	1935	1938	1950	1957
45	**Le Havre** a.	...	0727	...	...	0832	0836	1012	...	...	1229	...	...	1429	...	1626	1719	...	1812	...	1819	1912	1916	...	...	...	...

	Ⓐ 🚌	Ⓐ 🚌	Ⓐ 🚌	⑥	Ⓐ	⑥ 🚌	†	⑥	Ⓐ 🚌	†		Ⓒ	Ⓐ 🚌	Ⓐ	Ⓒ	Ⓐ 🚌		Ⓐ 🚌	† 🚌	⚒	⑥ 🚌	†	Ⓐ	⑥ 🚌	Ⓑ	⑤ 🚌
Le Havre d.	...	...	...	0827	0832	...	...	1033	...	...	1237	1437	...	1632	...	...	1734	...	...	1844	...	...	1936	...	...	...
Bréauté-Beuzeville d.	0728	0758	0818	0851	0857	0928	1000	1057	1058	1100	1301	1501	1458	1656	1700	1728	1800	1825	1900	1908	1958	2000	2001	2048	2101	2248
Fécamp a.	0758	0828	0848	0911	0917	0958	1020	1117	1128	1120	1321	1521	1528	1716	1720	1758	1820	1855	1920	1927	2028	2020	2021	2118	2121	2318

A – To/from Dieppe (Table **270a**). B – Ⓐ until Aug. 13; ⑤ from Aug. 22. ◧ – [R] for journeys to/from Paris.

ROUEN - DIEPPE 270a

km			Ⓐ	Ⓐ	Ⓐ	Ⓐ	Ⓐ	Ⓐ	Ⓐ	Ⓐ	Ⓐ	Ⓐ	Ⓐ	Ⓐ	Ⓐ	Ⓐ	Ⓐ	Ⓐ	Ⓐ			⑥	⑥	⑥ C	†	Ⓒ	⑥
0	**Rouen** Rive-Droite d.	Ⓐ	0646	0715	0746	0908	1010	1211	1332	1410	1608	1646	1710	1746	1810	1846	1918	2014	2117	...	Ⓒ	0644	0908	1032	1046	1214	1248
63	**Dieppe** a.		0745	0802	0846	0955	1057	1259	1432	1501	1657	1746	1757	1846	1857	1946	2004	2101	2204	...		0741	0955	1116	1146	1301	1348

	Ⓒ	⑥	†	⑥	Ⓒ	†	⑥	Ⓒ		
Rouen Rive-Droite d.	1414	1615	1710	1745	1814	1842	1915	2114	...	...
Dieppe a.	1503	1702	1756	1846	1902	1947	2002	2201	...	...

		Ⓐ	Ⓐ	Ⓐ	Ⓐ	Ⓐ		Ⓐ	Ⓐ	Ⓐ	Ⓐ
Dieppe d.	Ⓐ	0521	0617	0704	0716	0805	...	0817	1004	1204	1316
Rouen Rive-Droite a.		0605	0712	0751	0820	0849	...	0916	1049	1249	1414

	Ⓐ	Ⓐ	Ⓐ	Ⓐ	Ⓐ	Ⓐ	Ⓐ			⑥	⑥	†	⑥	⑥	†		Ⓒ	⑥	Ⓒ	†	⑥	† C		†	⑥	†
Dieppe d.	1404	1518	1601	1716	1816	1904	2007	...	Ⓒ	0618	0702	0755	0802	1004	1016	...	1204	1317	1550	1703	1804	1826	...	1916	1921	2004
Rouen Rive-Droite a.	1450	1616	1645	1816	1916	1949	2049	...		0718	0747	0840	0847	1047	1116	...	1246	1420	1634	1747	1847	1917	...	2015	2022	2047

C – To/from Paris (Table **270**).

271 CAEN - LE MANS - TOURS

At Le Mans 🚌 services use the Gare Routière (bus station) adjacent to the railway station.

km			Ⓐ	Ⓐ	Ⓐ 🚌	Ⓐ	Ⓐ		①–④	⑤	Ⓐ	Ⓐ	Ⓐ			⑥	Ⓒ	⑥	Ⓒ	†	⑥	†	†	†		
0	**Caen** 277 d.	Ⓐ	0708	0744	0924	1248	1441	...	1648	1648	1748	1848	2009	...	Ⓒ	0705	0858	1042	1249	1645	1747	1753	1814	2014	...	...
23	Mézidon 277 d.		0722	0758	|	1303	1455	...	1702	1702	1803	1902	2023	...		0719	0912	1056	1303	1659	1801	1808	1828	2028	...	...
67	Argentan 273 d.		0751	0826	1024	1331	1523	...	1729	1729	1830	1929	2051	...		0746	0940	1124	1330	1727	1827	1835	1856	2102	...	...
82	Surdon 273 d.		0800	0835	|	1342	1533	...	1738	1738	1839	1938	2100	...		0755	|	1133	1339	|	1836	1844	1905	|	...	...
91	Sées d.		0809	0844	|	1352	1542	...	1747	1746	1848	1946	2108	...		0804	|	1142	1347	1743	1845	1853	1913	2117	...	...
111	Alençon ◧ d.		0824	0901	1109	1408	1558	...	1802	1802	1903	2000	2122	...		0818	1010	1158	1403	1758	1859	1910	1927	2132	...	...
166	**Le Mans** ◧ a.		0916	0938	1224	1444	1634	...	1834	1834	1936	...	...	...		0904	1042	1234	1439	1834	1934	1943	*2116*	2208	...	...
	Tours (below) a.		...	1049	...	1555	...	...	...	...	...	...	...	...		...	1157	...	1550	...	...	2052	...	...	...	...

		Ⓐ	①	②–⑤	Ⓐ	Ⓐ	Ⓐ 🚌	Ⓐ	⑤ 🚌	Ⓐ	Ⓐ	Ⓐ			⑥	†	⑥	⑥	⑥	†	⑥	†	†		
Tours (below) d.	Ⓐ	...	...	...	...	...	...	1112	...	...	1628	...	...	Ⓒ	...	0915	0900	...	1633	1633	...	...	1914	...	...
Le Mans ◧ d.		...	0613	...	0726	0826	0929	1225	1336	1636	1733	1834	...		0725	1018	1024	1325	1742	1743	1835	1926	2015	...	...
Alençon ◧ d.		0550	0650	0651	0757	0902	1044	1302	1451	1722	1814	1914	...		0815	1059	1059	1418	1821	1823	1911	2003	2052	...	...
Sées d.		0603	0703	0704	0810	0916	|	1315	|	1735	1827	1928	...		0828	1115	1112	1431	1834	1836	1924	2016	2105	...	...
Surdon 273 d.		0611	0712	0713	0819	0926	|	1324	|	1744	1836	1937	...		0836	1125	1122	1440	1843	1845	1933	2025	|	...	...
Argentan 273 d.		0621	0722	0723	0829	0936	1129	1334	1536	1753	1846	1947	...		0845	1137	1134	1449	1855	1855	1942	2035	2123	...	...
Mézidon 277 d.		0647	0748	0742	0855	1002	|	1359	|	1819	1911	2015	...		0913	1202	1159	1516	1927	1921	2010	2101	2150	...	...
Caen 277 a.		0700	0802	0802	0909	1015	1229	1415	1636	1832	1925	2029	...		0927	1216	1213	1529	1942	1935	2023	2115	2204	...	...

km			②–⑤	Ⓐ	Ⓐ		Ⓐ	Ⓐ	Ⓐ		Ⓐ	①–③	④⑤			⑥	Ⓒ ⊖	†	⑥	Ⓒ		Ⓒ	†	†	†	
	Caen (above) d.	Ⓐ	...	...	0744	...	...	1248	...	...	...	...	...	...	Ⓒ	...	0858	...	...	1249	...	...	...	...	1753	...
0	**Le Mans** ◧ d.		0624	0743	0947	...	1244	1453	1644	...	1844	1950	2001	...		0624	1044	1237	1244	1445	...	1644	1753	1844	1950	...
49	Château du Loir ◧ d.		0654	0813	1018	...	1315	1524	1714	...	1915	2019	2031	...		0654	1111	1325	1315	1519	...	1714	1835	1915	2023	...
99	**Tours** a.		0736	0847	1049	...	1346	1555	1745	...	1946	2057	2109	...		0736	1157	1355	1346	1550	...	1745	1913	1946	2052	...

		①	Ⓐ	Ⓐ	Ⓐ	Ⓐ	⑤	Ⓐ	Ⓐ	Ⓐ	Ⓐ	⑤			⑥	⑥ ⊖	†	†	⑥	†	⑥	Ⓒ	†	†	
Tours d.	Ⓐ	0600	0609	0805	1112	1215	1417	1515	1628	1726	1812	2115	...	Ⓒ	0740	0900	0915	1015	1229	1633	1633	1812	1914	2115	...
Château du Loir ◧ d.		0630	0646	0836	1145	1245	1446	1545	1658	1808	1845	2145	...		0809	0947	0944	1044	1311	1703	1704	1845	1943	2145	...
Le Mans ◧ a.		0716	0732	0909	1216	1316	1518	1616	1728	1853	1916	2216	...		0856	1018	1014	1130	1359	1737	1736	1916	2011	2216	...
Caen (above) a.		...	...	...	1415	...	...	...	1925	...	...	...	...		...	1213	1216	...	...	1935	1942	...	2204	...	...

⊖ – Also calls at St Pierre des Corps 14 minutes before / after Tours.

◧ – Additional trains are available Alençon - Le Mans - Château du Loir and v.v.

272 CAEN - COUTANCES - GRANVILLE - RENNES

At Caen and Rennes 🚌 services use the bus station (gare routière) adjacent to the railway station.

km			Ⓐ	Ⓐ 🚌	Ⓐ	Ⓐ	Ⓐ	Ⓐ 🚌	Ⓐ	Ⓐ 🚌	⑤	①–④			⑥	†	Ⓒ	Ⓒ	Ⓒ	Ⓒ		⑥ 🚌	⑥	†	Ⓒ	
0	**Caen** ● 275 d.	Ⓐ	0601	0730	0910	1105	1304	1615	1706	...	1803	1804	...	Ⓒ	0810	0907	1010	1205	...	1509	...	...	1712	1712	1910	...
30	Bayeux ● 275 d.		0623	|	0927	1122	1328	|	1728	...	1825	1826	...		0827	0925	1027	1222	...	1533	...	...	1734	1734	1932	...
57	Lison ● 275 d.		0640	|	0941	1136	1346	|	1745	...	1842	1842	...		0841	0941	1042	1235	...	1552	...	...	1752	1752	1949	...
75	Saint Lô ● d.		0655	|	0954	1150	1400	|	1801	...	1858	1858	...		0856	0956	1056	1249	...	1605	...	...	1804	1804	2004	...
105	Coutances ● d.		0722	|	1015	1212	1422	|	1822	...	1919	1919	...		0918	1022	1117	1309	...	1627	...	...	1826	1826	2025	...
143	**Granville** a.		0749	|	1041	1238	1448	|	1848	...	1946	1945	...		0945	1048	1143	1335	...	1653	...	...	1852	1852	2050	...
143	**Granville** 273 d.		0800	|	...	1258	...	|	...	1858	2001	...	...		0958	1058	...	...	1416	...	...	1703	...	1903	...	...
157	Folligny 273 d.		0811	|	...	1309	...	|	...	|	2012	...	...		1009	1109	...	...	1427	...	...	|	...	1914	...	...
176	Avranches d.		0825	0900	...	1323	...	1750	...	1928	2026	...	...		1023	1123	...	...	1440	...	...	1733	...	1928	...	...
198	Pontorson ⊡ d.		0843	|	...	1341	...	|	...	|	2044	...	...		1041	1141	...	...	1459	...	...	|	...	1945	...	...
219	Dol de Bretagne 281 d.		0900	|	...	1358	...	|	...	|	2101	...	...		1058	1158	...	...	1516	...	...	|	...	2003	...	...
277	**Rennes** 281 a.		0933	1020	...	1431	...	1905	...	2048	2134	...	...		1133	1233	...	...	1549	...	...	1853	...	2036	...	...

		Ⓐ	Ⓐ	Ⓐ 🚌	Ⓐ	Ⓐ		Ⓐ 🚌	Ⓐ	Ⓐ 🚌	Ⓐ			⑥	†	†	⑥	† 🚌	Ⓒ	Ⓒ	Ⓒ	Ⓒ	Ⓒ	†	
Rennes 281 d.	Ⓐ	...	...	0730	1117	...	...	1510	...	1615	1757	...	Ⓒ	...	...	...	0805	1021	...	1406	...	...	1728	2100	...
Dol de Bretagne 281 d.		...	...	|	1153	...	...	|	...	|	1830	...		...	...	...	0839	|	...	1440	...	...	1801	2133	...
Pontorson ⊡ d.		...	...	|	1211	...	...	|	...	|	1848	...		...	...	...	0856	|	...	1459	...	...	1819	2149	...
Avranches d.		...	...	0851	1231	...	...	1620	...	1735	1905	...		...	...	...	0913	1135	...	1517	...	...	1834	2206	...
Folligny 273 d.		...	...	|	1246	...	...	|	...	|	1924	...		...	...	...	0928	|	...	1532	...	...	1850	2221	...
Granville 273 a.		...	...	|	1256	...	...	1700	...	|	1936	...		...	...	...	0938	1205	...	1542	...	...	1901	2231	...
Granville d.		0605	0655	|	1307	1505	...	...	1711	|	1952	...		0807	0907	0955	1005	...	1409	...	1600	1800	1910	...	...
Coutances ● d.		0632	0732	|	1335	1532	...	...	1738	|	2027	...		0834	0934	1026	1034	...	1436	...	1628	1828	1937	...	...
Saint Lô ● d.		0654	0757	|	1359	1554	...	...	1802	|	2049	...		0858	1002	1058	1057	...	1457	...	1650	1850	2005	...	...
Lison ● 275 d.		0707	0810	|	1412	1608	...	...	1817	|	2102	...		0911	1015	1111	1109	...	1510	...	1703	1903	2019	...	...
Bayeux ● 275 d.		0724	0827	|	1426	1624	...	...	1832	|	2116	...		0930	1032	1128	1126	...	1526	...	1720	1920	2034	...	...
Caen ● 275 a.		0745	0849	1020	1442	1646	...	...	1848	1905	2133	...		0952	1054	1152	1147	...	1549	...	1742	1943	2051	...	...

● – Also Caen - Coutances at 0701 Ⓐ, 0809 Ⓐ, 1014 Ⓐ, 1214 Ⓐ, 1611 Ⓐ, 1911 Ⓐ, 2006 †; Coutances - Caen at 0601 Ⓐ, 0643 ⑥, 0840 Ⓐ, 1036 Ⓐ, 1236 Ⓐ, 1642 Ⓐ, 1836 Ⓐ. Additional connections may be available by changing to / from 🚌 services at Lison - please check locally.

⊡ – Full name is Pontorson - Mont St Michel (*10 km* from Mont St Michel).

273 PARIS - DREUX - MONT ST MICHEL and GRANVILLE

🅁 required for journeys from Paris. Suburban trains run Paris - Dreux approximately hourly (RER Line N). For connections Surdon - Alençon see Table **271**.

km		①	Ⓐ	Ⓐ	Ⓐ 🚌	Ⓒ	Ⓒ	Ⓒ 🚌		†	Ⓐ		Ⓒ	Ⓐ	⑥	⑤		⑤	Ⓒ	Ⓐ	①–④	⑤	Ⓐ	Ⓒ
0	**Paris** Montparnasse 278 d.	0602	0732	0732	...	0854	0854	...	...	0927	0945	1054	1354	1354	1527	1528	...	1613	1654	1713v	1813	1813	1943	1953
17	Versailles Chantiers 278 d.	|	|	|	...	0907	0907	...	...	|	|	|	|	|	|	|	...	|	|	|	1827	1826	|	2006
82	**Dreux** d.	0707	0820	0820	...	0942	0942	...	...	1014	1033	|	1441	1442	1614	|	...	|	|	|	1914	1915	2043	2043
118	Verneuil sur Avre d.	0727	0840	0840	...	1001	1001	...	...	1037	1056	1159	1501	1502	1637	|	...	1731	1759	1831	1936	1937	2102	2103
142	L'Aigle d.	0742	0855	0855	...	1015	1015	...	...	1051	1110	1213	1516	1517	1651	1645	...	1746	1813	1846	1951	1952	2117	2117
183	Surdon 271 d.	0805	0918	0918	...	1036	1036	...	...	1115	1132	|	1537	1538	1716	|	...	1807	1834	1907	2012	2017	2138	2138
198	Argentan 271 d.	0815	0929	0929	...	1046	1046	...	...	1125	1144	1243	1547	1550	1725	1714	...	1817	1844	1918	2021	2039	2148	2148
226	Briouze d.	0833	0946	0946	...	1102	1102	...	...	1142	...	|	1603	1606	...	|	...	|	|	1935	...	2056	2204	2205
243	Flers d.	0844	0957	0957	...	1113	1113	...	...	1152	...	1307	1613	1616	...	1737	...	1840	1908	1947	...	2106	2214	2215
272	Vire d.	0901	1013	1013	...	1129	1129	...	...	1208	...	1323	1629	1632	...	1753	...	1856	1924	2003	...	2122	2230	2232
298	Villedieu les Poêles d.	0917	1029	1029	...	1145	1145	...	...	1224	...	1338	1645	1648	...	1810	...	1912	1939	2019	...	2138	2246	2247
313	Folligny 272 d.	|	1046	1053	...	1202	1210	...	...	1234	...	|	|	|	...	|	...	|	|	2029	...	|	|	|
332	Avranches d.	|	|	1107	...	|	1224	...	...	|	...	|	|	|	...	|	...	|	|	|	...	|	|	|
354	Pontorson - Mont St Michel a.	|	|	1125	1155	|	1242	1305	...	|	...	|	|	|	...	|	...	|	|	|	...	|	|	|
364	**Mont St Michel** Le Verger a.	|	|	...	1222	|	...	1332	...	|	...	|	|	|	...	|	...	|	|	|	...	|	|	|
328	**Granville** 272 a.	0936	1056	...	...	1213	...	...	...	1244	...	1356	1702	1706	...	1829	...	1930	1956	2039	...	2155	2303	2305

FOR RETURN SERVICE AND FOOTNOTES SEE NEXT PAGE →

GRANVILLE and MONT ST MICHEL - DREUX - PARIS 273

🅁 required for journeys to Paris. Suburban trains run Dreux - Paris approximately hourly (RER Line N). For connections Alençon - Surdon see Table **271**.

	①	②–⑤	⑥	†	Ⓐ	⑥	†			⑥	Ⓐ	⚒	⑤	†		†	†		Ⓒ 🚌	Ⓒ	Ⓒ	Ⓐ 🚌	Ⓐ	Ⓐ	†
Granville **272** d.	0450	...	...	...	0556	0623	0655	...	0858	1050	...	1156	1247	1400	1553	1705	...	...	...	...	1829	...	...	1838	2004
Mont St Michel Le Verger d.	|	...	...	...	|	|	|	...	|	|	...	|	|	|	|	|	...	...	1715	...	|	1722	...	|	|
Pontorson - Mont St Michel d.	|	...	...	...	|	|	|	...	|	|	...	|	|	|	|	|	...	...	1742	1806	|	1749	1814	|	|
Avranches d.	|	...	...	...	|	|	|	...	|	|	...	|	|	|	|	|	...	...	...	1823	|	...	1831	|	|
Folligny **272** d.	|	...	...	...	|	|	|	...	|	|	...	|	|	|	|	|	...	...	...	1856	1856	...	1901	1901	2015
Villedieu les Poêles d.	0508	...	...	...	0614	0641	0713	...	0917	1108	...	1214	1306	1418	1611	1723	...	...	...	1906	1907	...	1911	1911	2025
Vire d.	0523	...	...	...	0629	0656	0728	...	0933	1123	...	1229	1323	1434	1627	1738	...	...	...	1923	1923	...	1927	1927	2040
Flers d.	0540	...	...	...	0646	0713	0745	...	0950	1140	...	1246	1342	1450	1645	1755	...	...	...	1941	1941	...	1944	1944	2057
Briouze d.	0551	...	...	...	0656	0723	0756	...	|	1151	...	1257	|	1501	|	1806	...	...	...	1951	1951	...	1955	1955	2108
Argentan **271** d.	0608	0611	0613	0638	0714	0741	0814	...	1015	1208	1212	1314	1410	1518	1713	1823	1934	...	...	2009	2009	...	2013	2013	2126
Surdon **271** d.	0617	0620	0622	0647	0724	0751	0824	...	1025	1218	1221	1323	|	1528	|	|	1944	...	...	2019	2019	...	2022	2022	|
L'Aigle d.	0642	0642	0647	0713	0745	0814	0845	...	1047	1243	1243	1345	1440	1549	1743	1851	2008	...	...	2041	2041	...	2044	2044	2157
Verneuil sur Avre d.	0656	0656	0701	0726	0759	0828	0859	...	1101	1256	1257	1358	1454	1603	1758	|	2021	...	...	2054	2054	...	2058	2058	2209
Dreux d.	0718	0718	0723	0748	0818	0848	0918	...	|	1318	1319	1418	|	|	|	|	2043	...	...	2115	2115	...	2118	2118	2229
Versailles Chantiers **278** d.	0804	0804	|	|	|	|	|	...	|	|	|	|	|	|	|	|	2120	...	...	|	|	...	|	|	2307
Paris Montparnasse **278** a.	0816	0816v	0816	0835	0917	0940	1006	...	1206	1406	1415v	1506	1605v	1715	1915	2006	2132	...	...	2206	2206	...	2206	2206	2318

v – Paris Montparnasse **Vaugirard** (5 – 10 minute walk from Montparnasse main concourse).

FOR RETURN SERVICE SEE PREVIOUS PAGE.

Keolis Armor 🚌 RENNES - MONT ST MICHEL 🚌 274

km																			
0	**Rennes** gare routière d.	0845	1045	1300	...	...	...	...	...	...	**Mont St Michel** Le Verger d.	1135	1700	1800	...	...	...	...	...	...
68	**Mont St Michel** Le Verger a.	1000	1200	1415	...	...	...	...	...	...	**Rennes** gare routière a.	1250	1815	1915	...	...	...	...	...	...

Service until November 2, 2025. Operator: Keolis Armor (www.keolis-armor.com). Rail tickets and passes not valid. The gare routière at Rennes is adjacent to the railway station. At Mont St Michel the coach terminates at Le Verger close to the tourist information office. A free *Passeur* motorised shuttle service operates along the causeway to Mont St Michel itself taking 25 minutes (or 45 minutes walk, *2.4 km*). Horse-drawn shuttles (*Maringotes*) taking 35 minutes are also available, fee payable.

PARIS - CAEN - CHERBOURG 275

🅁 required for journeys to/from Paris. Other services: Paris - Lisieux Table **276**; Lisieux - Mézidon - Caen Table **277**; Mézidon - Caen Table **271**, Caen - Lison Table **272**.

km			Ⓐ	Ⓐ	Ⓐ	①–④	⑤	Ⓐ		Ⓐ	Ⓐ	Ⓐ	Ⓐ	Ⓐ		Ⓐ	Ⓐ	Ⓐ	Ⓐ		Ⓐ	Ⓐ	①–④	Ⓐ	⑤	①–④	⑤
0	**Paris** St Lazare d.	Ⓐ	...	...	0612	0829	0859	0959	...	...	1059	1159	1259	1356	...	...	1459	1558	1659	...	1709	1759	1808	1859	1959	1959	2059
108	Evreux d.		...	...	0723	0934	|	1101	...	...	|	|	|	1459	...	...	|	|	|	...	1815	|	1918	|	|	2101	|
160	Bernay d.		...	...	0748	0959	|	1127	...	...	|	|	|	1525	...	...	|	|	|	...	1841	|	1943	|	|	2126	|
191	Lisieux d.		...	...	0803	1014	|	1142	...	...	|	|	|	1540	...	...	|	|	|	...	1856	|	1958	|	|	2142	|
239	**Caen** d.		0553	0651	0829	1040	1058	1206	...	1222	1257	1406	1457	1602	...	1626	1659	1757	1906	...	1920	2009	2022	2110	2157	2205	2257
269	Bayeux d.		0609	0707	0845	1057	1114	...	...	1238	1313	...	1513	...	...	1642	1715	1813	1922	...	...	2026	...	2126	2213	...	2313
296	Lison d.		0623	0721	0859	1111	1129	...	...	1252	1327	...	1527	...	...	1656	1729	1827	1936	...	...	2040	...	2140	2227	...	2327
314	Carentan d.		0634	0732	0911	1122	1140	...	...	1303	1339	...	1539	...	...	1707	1741	1839	1947	...	...	2051	...	2152	2238	...	2339
343	Valognes d.		0650	0748	0924	1136	1153	...	...	1319	1352	...	1552	...	...	1723	1754	1852	2001	...	...	2105	...	2205	2252	...	2352
371	**Cherbourg** a.		0706	0804	0940	1151	1209	...	...	1335	1408	...	1608	...	...	1739	1810	1908	2017	...	...	2121	...	2221	2307	...	0008

		⑥	†	†	⑥	Ⓒ	Ⓒ	Ⓒ		Ⓒ	Ⓒ	Ⓒ	Ⓒ	†	Ⓒ	⑥	†	⑥		†	Ⓒ	†	⑥	†	Ⓒ	Ⓒ
Paris St Lazare d.	Ⓒ	...	...	0759	0759	0859	0959	1059	...	1159	1259	1428	1459	1558	1658	1728	1728	1759	...	1759	1859	1928	1958	1959	2059	2230
Evreux d.		...	...	|	|	|	|	|	...	|	|	1531	|	|	|	1831	1836	|	...	|	|	2031	2101	|	|	2332
Bernay d.		...	...	|	|	|	|	|	...	|	|	1556	|	|	|	1856	1902	|	...	|	|	2056	2126	|	|	2358
Lisieux d.		...	...	|	|	|	|	|	...	|	|	1611	|	|	|	1911	1917	|	...	|	|	2110	2141	|	|	0013
Caen d.		0824	0917	0957	0959	1059	1156	1259	...	1408	1459	1636	1659	1756	1900	1935	1942	1957	...	1959	2100	2135	2205	2156	2259	0035
Bayeux d.		0840	0933	...	1015	1117	...	1316	...	...	1515	...	1716	...	1916	...	...	...	...	2016	2116	...	...	...	2316	...
Lison d.		0853	0947	...	1029	1131	...	1330	...	...	1529	...	1730	...	1930	...	...	...	...	2030	2130	...	...	...	2330	...
Carentan d.		0904	0958	...	1041	1142	...	1341	...	...	1541	...	1741	...	1942	...	...	...	...	2041	2142	...	...	...	2340	...
Valognes d.		0920	1013	...	1055	1155	...	1355	...	...	1554	...	1755	...	1955	...	...	...	...	2054	2155	...	...	...	2354	...
Cherbourg a.		0936	1028	...	1110	1211	...	1411	...	...	1610	...	1811	...	2011	...	...	...	...	2110	2211	...	...	...	0009	...

		Ⓐ	Ⓐ	Ⓐ	Ⓐ	Ⓐ		Ⓐ	Ⓐ	Ⓐ	Ⓐ	Ⓐ	Ⓐ		Ⓐ	Ⓐ	Ⓐ	Ⓐ	Ⓐ	Ⓐ		①–④	⑤	⑤	Ⓐ	Ⓐ
Cherbourg d.	Ⓐ	...	...	0546	0614	0644	...	...	0719	...	0850	1046	1140	...	1246	...	1441	1519	...	1645	...	1743	1751	...	1820	1917
Valognes d.		...	...	0602	0630	0700	...	...	0735	...	0907	1103	1158	...	1303	...	1459	1535	...	1702	...	1800	1808	...	1835	1933
Carentan d.		...	...	0616	0645	0714	...	...	0750	...	0920	1117	1211	...	1317	...	1512	1550	...	1716	...	1814	1822	...	1850	1947
Lison d.		...	...	0628	0656	0726	...	...	0801	...	0931	1128	1222	...	1328	...	1523	1601	...	1727	...	1825	1833	...	1901	1958
Bayeux d.		...	...	0642	0710	0740	...	...	0815	...	0945	1142	1236	...	1342	...	1537	1615	...	1741	...	1839	1847	...	1915	2012
Caen d.		0458	0608	0700	0726	0758	...	0824	0831	0903	1004	1200	1255	...	1400	1424	1556	1631	1657	1759	...	1857	1905	1926	1931	2031
Lisieux d.		0522	0631	|	...	|	...	0847	...	|	|	|	1320	...	|	1447	|	...	|	|	...	1920	|	1950	...	2053
Bernay d.		0537	0646	|	...	|	...	0902	...	|	|	|	1335	...	|	1502	|	...	|	|	...	1935	|	2005	...	2108
Evreux d.		0603	0713	|	...	|	...	0929	...	|	|	|	1402	...	|	1529	|	...	|	|	...	2001	|	2032	...	2135
Paris St Lazare a.		0715	0819	0858	...	0957	...	1031	...	1104	1203	1402	1504	...	1556	1631	1801	...	1901	1956	...	2103	2103	2136	...	2251

		⑥	Ⓒ	⑥	†	Ⓒ	Ⓒ	⑥		†	Ⓒ	Ⓒ	Ⓒ	⑥	Ⓒ	Ⓒ	†	⑥		†	†	⑥	⑥	†	⑥	†
Cherbourg d.	Ⓒ	...	0652	...	...	...	0849	1046	...	1052	...	1251	...	1348	1442	...	1647	1647	...	...	1843	1848	...	1916	...	2048
Valognes d.		...	0709	...	...	...	0907	1103	...	1109	...	1308	...	1405	1500	...	1704	1704	...	...	1901	1905	...	1935	...	2105
Carentan d.		...	0723	...	...	...	0920	1117	...	1123	...	1322	...	1419	1513	...	1717	1717	...	...	1918	1918	...	1951	...	2118
Lison d.		...	0734	...	...	...	0931	1128	...	1134	...	1333	...	1430	1524	...	1728	1728	...	...	1929	1929	...	2004	...	2129
Bayeux d.		...	0748	...	...	...	0945	1142	...	1148	...	1347	...	1444	1538	...	1742	1742	...	...	1943	1943	...	2021	...	2143
Caen d.		0654	0806	0822	0825	0906	1004	1200	...	1206	1305	1405	1423	1502	1557	1706	1801	1801	...	1906	2002	2002	2022	2043	2103	2202
Lisieux d.		0718	|	0846	0848	|	|	|	...	|	|	|	1446	|	|	|	|	|	...	|	|	|	2046	2111	|	|
Bernay d.		0733	|	0901	0903	|	|	|	...	|	|	|	1501	|	|	|	|	|	...	|	|	|	2101	|	|	|
Evreux d.		0800	|	0928	0930	|	|	|	...	|	|	|	1528	|	|	|	|	|	...	|	|	|	2128	|	|	|
Paris St Lazare a.		0903	1002	1030	1036	1104	1202	1402	...	1402	1502	1602	1630	1703	1801	1904	2002	2003	...	2106	2202	2202	2229	2302	2301	2358

PARIS - LISIEUX - TROUVILLE DEAUVILLE 276

🅁 required for journeys from Paris. For other services Paris - Lisieux see Table **275**.

km		Ⓐ	⑥	Ⓐ	†	Ⓐ	Ⓒ	Ⓐ	†	⑥	⑤	⑥		Ⓐ	Ⓐ	Ⓒ	Ⓐ	⑥	⑤	⑥	①–④	†	Ⓐ	†	⑤	†	⑤
0	**Paris** St Lazare d.	...	...	...	...	0727	0828	...	0928	1029	1030	...	1228	...	1608	1628	...	...	1808	1828	...	1828	1908	...	2008	2028	2108
108	Evreux d.	...	...	...	...	0837	0933	...	1031	1133	1134	...	1331	...	1715	1736	...	...	1918	1931	...	1934	2019	...	2113	2131	2213
160	Bernay d.	...	...	...	...	0902	0959	...	1056	1159	1159	...	1356	...	1740	1804	...	...	1943	1956	...	2002	2046	...	2138	2156	2238
191	**Lisieux** d.	0719	0735	0833	0850	0918	1014	1049	1112	1214	1215	1302	1412	1713	1756	1819	1844	1855	1959	2012	2013	2018	2103	2147	2154	2212	2254
209	Pont l'Évêque d.	0737	0750	0848	0905	0931	1028	1105	1125	1227	1228	1316	1425	1731	1809	1832	1857	1910	2012	2025	2026	2031	2116	2202	2207	2225	2307
221	**Trouville-Deauville** a.	0746	0759	0857	0914	0939	1037	1114	1134	1236	1237	1325	1436	1740	1819	1841	1906	1919	2021	2034	2035	2040	2125	2211	2216	2234	2316

FOR RETURN SERVICE SEE NEXT PAGE →

276 TROUVILLE DEAUVILLE - LISIEUX - PARIS

🄡 required for journeys from Paris. For other services Lisieux - Paris see Table **275**.

	Ⓐ	Ⓐ	Ⓐ	Ⓐ	Ⓒ	Ⓒ	Ⓐ	Ⓒ	⑤		†	Ⓐ	⑥	Ⓐ	Ⓐ	Ⓒ	Ⓐ	Ⓒ	Ⓐ	†	⑥	①–④	†	⑤	†	†
Trouville-Deauville ... d.	0556	0641	0727	0800	0814	1016	1021	1216	1217	1342	1616	1620	1623	1643	1722	1723	1758	1821	1917	1923	2014	2017	2020	2024	2044	2120
Pont l'Évêque .... d.	0605	0649	0737	0809	0822	1028	1032	1227	1228	1351	1625	1629	1632	1652	1731	1732	1809	1832	1926	1932	2025	2026	2031	2033	2053	2131
Lisieux.................... d.	0619	0706	0751	0825	0838	1042	1046	1241	1242	1408	1638	1643	1646	1707	1745	1746	1824	1846	1939	1946	2041	2039	2045	2047	2106	2145
Bernay....................... d.	...	...	0806	...	...	1059	1102	1256	1258	...	1654	1658	1701	...	1800	1801	...	1902	...	2001	...	...	2100	2102	...	2201
Evreux....................... d.	...	...	0833	...	...	1127	1128	1325	1326	...	1720	1725	1728	...	1827	1828	...	1928	...	2028	...	...	2128	2129	...	2227
Paris St Lazare .... a.	...	...	0938	...	...	1230	1231	1429	1431	...	1829	1829	1829	...	1930	1930	...	2029	...	2129	...	...	2232	2232	...	2330

FOR RETURN SERVICE SEE PREVIOUS PAGE.

276a TROUVILLE DEAUVILLE - DIVES - CABOURG

Rail tickets may not be valid on 🚌 services.

TROUVILLE-DEAUVILLE - DIVES-SUR-MER. Journey 30 minutes. From **Trouville-Deauville** at 0904 Ⓐ, 1053 ⚒, 1145 †, 1252 ⚒, 1447, 1605 †, 1642 ⑥, 1734 †, 1829 Ⓐ, 1853 Ⓒ, 2034 ⑤, 2043 ⑥, 2044 ①–④, 2053 †; from **Dives-sur-Mer** Gare SNCF at 0516 Ⓐ, 0936 Ⓒ, 0942 Ⓐ, 1137 ⚒, 1241 †, 1338 ⚒, 1525 †, 1543 ⑥, 1638 Ⓐ, 1645 †, 1738 ⑥, 1817 †, 1926 Ⓐ, 1932 Ⓒ.

🚌 **DEAUVILLE - DIVES-SUR-MER**. *NOMAD Calvados* route **111**. Journey 34 – 46 minutes. From **Deauville** Gare Routière at 0605 Ⓐ, 0700 ⚒, 0810 ⚒, 0910, 1010 ⚒, 1110, 1210 ⚒, 1410, 1500 Ⓐ, 1515 †, 1610 ⚒, 1710, 1810 ⚒, 1847 ⚒, 2010 †, 2045 ⚒; from **Dives-sur-Mer** Gare SNCF at 0612 Ⓐ, 0807 ⚒, 0826 †, 0958 ⚒, 1007 †, 1107 ⚒, 1202 ⚒, 1207 †, 1313 ⚒, 1413 ⚒, 1507 Ⓑ, 1603 ⚒, 1612 †, 1735 ⑥, 1745 Ⓐ, 1853 Ⓐ, 1906 †, 1917 ⚒, 2005 Ⓐ, 2101 †. 🚌 continue to / from **Cabourg** Hôtel de ville (journey Dives - Cabourg 2 minutes).

277 ROUEN - LISIEUX - CAEN

For other trains Mézidon - Caen see Table **271**.

km			Ⓐ	Ⓐ	Ⓐ	Ⓐ	Ⓐ		Ⓐ	Ⓐ	Ⓐ	Ⓐ	Ⓐ			⑥	†	⑥	Ⓒ	Ⓒ	Ⓒ	†	†	⑥
0	**Rouen** Rive Droite...............d.	Ⓐ	0558	0706	0809	1003	1204	...	1401	1605	1702	1804	1905	...	Ⓒ	0703	0948	1006	1216	1507	1702	1803	1902	1906
23	Elbeuf-St Aubin....................d.		0614	0722	0825	1018	1218	...	1415	1619	1718	1819	1922	...		0719	1003	1021	1232	1522	1717	1823	1917	1922
73	Serquigny ....d.		0647	0756	0901	1050	1251	...	1449	1653	1752	1852	1954	...		0752	1037	1053	1305	1556	1750	1901	1949	1955
83	Bernay.................................d.		0655	0804	0908	1057	1258	...	1456	1701	1800	1859	2001	...		0800	1045	1100	1312	1603	1758	1908	1956	2002
114	Lisieux................................d.		0712	0820	0925	1114	1316	...	1514	1717	1816	1917	2019	...		0817	1102	1117	1329	1621	1814	1925	2013	2019
139	Mézidon...............................d.		0728	0834	0939	1129	1332	...	1530	1733	1831	1933	2035	...		0833	1116	1131	1344	1636	1830	1939	2029	2035
162	**Caen** ....a.		0742	0846	0953	1142	1346	...	1544	1746	1844	1948	2049	...		0847	1129	1145	1400	1651	1843	1952	2043	2049

		Ⓐ	Ⓐ	Ⓐ	Ⓐ	Ⓐ	⑤	①–④	Ⓐ	Ⓐ	Ⓐ	Ⓐ			⑥	Ⓒ	Ⓒ	⑥	†	Ⓒ	†	⑥	†
Caen ....d.	Ⓐ	0555	0714	0808	1009	1209	1406	1410	1605	1706	1806	1916	...	Ⓒ	0709	1008	1219	1513	1603	1710	1806	1900	2009
Mézidon...d.		0609	0728	0822	1024	1222	1420	1424	1620	1720	1820	1929	...		0723	1022	1233	1527	1617	1724	1820	1914	2022
Lisieux..d.		0623	0743	0837	1038	1236	1434	1438	1634	1734	1834	1943	...		0737	1036	1247	1541	1631	1738	1834	1928	2036
Bernay...d.		0640	0800	0854	1056	1252	1450	1455	1652	1750	1851	1959	...		0754	1053	1303	1558	1648	1755	1851	1944	2052
Serquigny ....d.		0648	0807	0901	1103	1300	1506	1502	1659	1758	1858	2007	...		0802	1100	1311	1605	1655	1803	1858	1952	2100
Elbeuf-St Aubin..............................d.		0721	0839	0934	1135	1335	1532	1538	1734	1832	1930	2040	...		0833	1137	1343	1637	1727	1834	1930	2024	2132
Rouen Rive Droite..........................a.		0736	0855	0950	1152	1355	1548	1554	1752	1848	1947	2057	...		0851	1159	1401	1652	1746	1854	1946	2041	2147

278 PARIS - CHARTRES - LE MANS

For *TGV* trains see Table **280**. For *Ouigo Classique* trains see Table **295**. Additional trains are available Nogent le Rotrou - Le Mans and v.v.

km		Ⓐ	Ⓐ	⚒	⚒		Ⓐ	Ⓐ								①–④	⑤⑥	†				⑤	①–④	Ⓐ
0	**Paris** Montparnasse ....d.	...	...	0609	0636	...	0709	0739	0809	0906	...	1009	1106	1209	...	1306	1306	1306	1409	...	1506	...	...	1609
17	Versailles Chantiers..............d.	...	...	0625	0649	...	0725	0753	0825	0921	...	1025	1120	1225	...	1322	1320	1322	1425	...	1521	...	...	1624
48	Rambouillet..........................d.	...	...	0645	0709	...	0745	0815	0846	0939	...	1044	1139	1245	...	1342	1339	1342	1445	...	1539	...	...	1645
88	**Chartres** ....d.	0619	0645	0724	0737	...	0829	0858	0922	1008	...	1124	1208	1325	...	1411	1409	1411	1524	...	1608	1614	1629	1724
149	Nogent le Rotrou ....d.	0659	0733	...	0813	...	0922	...	...	1046	...	...	1246	...	...	1448	1447	1448	...	...	1645	1705	1805	...
211	**Le Mans**..............................a.	0747	0822	...	0854	...	...	...	...	1126	...	...	1325	...	...	1528	1527	...	...	...	1725	1755	1854	...

	Ⓒ	Ⓐ	Ⓐ		Ⓑ	⑥	Ⓑ		Ⓐ	Ⓐ	Ⓑ			Ⓐ	Ⓐ			Ⓐ			Ⓑ		Ⓐ
Paris Montparnasse ....d.	1609	1624	1639	...	1705	1706	1709	...	1724	1739	1805	...	1809	1824	1839	...	1906	1939	2009	...	2106	2209	2302
Versailles Chantiers ....d.	1626	1640	1654	...	1722	1722	1725	...	1739	1753	1822	...	1825	1839	1853	...	1921	1953	2025	...	2121	2225	2321
Rambouillet......................................d.	1645	1700	1714	...	|	1741	1745	...	1801	1814	|	...	1845	1900	1915	...	1939	2015	2045	...	2142	2245	2344
Chartres..d.	1730	1729	1754	...	1806	1810	1824	...	1830	1857	1905	...	1925	1929	1955	...	2008	2057	2124	...	2209	2324	0020
Nogent le Rotrou ....d.	1826	1825	...	...	1844	1847	...	...	1923	...	1943	...	...	2021	...	...	2045	...	...	...	2244	...	...
Le Mans...a.	1918	1915	...	...	1925	1925	...	...	...	...	2022	...	...	...	...	...	2127	...	...	...	2322	...	...

	Ⓐ	⚒	Ⓐ		Ⓐ		⚒	Ⓐ		Ⓐ	⚒		Ⓐ	Ⓐ	⑥	†			Ⓒ	Ⓐ			
Le Mans...d.	...	...	...	...	0537	...	...	...	...	0630	...	...	0638	0725	0734	...	...	...	0938	0939	...	1138	...
Nogent le Rotrou ....d.	...	...	0536	...	0615	...	...	0636	...	0708	...	...	0730	0812	0812	0816	...	...	1014	1014	...	1215	...
Chartres..d.	0536	0605	0631	0636	0657	...	0705	0732	0736	0751	0805	...	0834	0851	0851	0852	0936	...	1052	1052	1136	1252	1336
Rambouillet......................................d.	0617	0646	0701	0717	|	...	0746	0801	0817	0820	0846	...	0903	0920	0920	0919	1017	...	1119	1119	1217	1319	1417
Versailles Chantiers ....a.	0634	0706	0721	0736	0739	...	0806	0821	0836	0839	0906	...	0923	0939	0939	0935	1034	...	1140	1140	1234	1339	1434
Paris Montparnasse ....a.	0650	0720	0735	0750	0753	...	0820	0835	0850	0853	0920	...	0936	0953	0953	0950	1050	...	1153	1153	1250	1353	1450

		⚒	†			Ⓐ		†	⑥		Ⓐ	†	Ⓐ		Ⓐ	Ⓐ					†	Ⓐ	†
Le Mans...d.	1238	1338	...	...	...	...	1534	...	...	...	...	1633	...	...	1638	...	1738	...	...	1938	...	...	2138
Nogent le Rotrou ....d.	1330	1414	1416	...	...	...	1613	...	...	...	1637	1711	...	...	1732	...	1814	1843	...	2014	...	...	2215
Chartres..d.	1420	1452	1452	1536	...	1639	1652	1719	1733	...	1735	1750	1805	...	1822	1836	1851	1938	...	2051	2131	2133	2251
Rambouillet......................................d.	...	1519	1519	1618	...	|	1719	1800	1814	...	1816	1819	1846	...	...	|	1919	2019	...	2119	2209	2209	2319
Versailles Chantiers ....a.	...	1539	1539	1634	...	|	1739	1822	1836	...	1836	1841	1906	...	...	|	1939	2039	...	2139	2227	2227	2339
Paris Montparnasse ....a.	...	1553	1553	1650	...	1737	1753	1836	1850	...	1850	1853	1920	...	...	1945	1953	2053	...	2153	2241	2245	2353

SUBURBAN TRAINS PARIS - VERSAILLES

- **RER Line C**: Paris Austerlitz - Versailles Château Rive Gauche. Journey 40 minutes.
- **RER Line L**: Paris St Lazare - Versailles Rive Droite. Journey 35 – 40 minutes.
- **RER Line N**: Paris Montparnasse - Versailles Chantiers. Journey 13 – 27 minutes.

Trains run every 15 – 30 mins. 0600 - 2400 (2100 Line **C**). Line **C** serves St Michel Notre Dame. Detailed schedules can be found at www.transilien.com.

The Château is approximately 600 metres from Château Rive Gauche station, approximately 1400 metres from Rive Droite station and approximately 1600 metres from Chantiers station.

TGV BRETAGNE - PAYS DE LA LOIRE 280

PARIS - RENNES

Most trains continue to St Malo (Tables **281**), Lorient or Brest (Table **284**), or Quimper (Table **285**). For additional trains Paris - Le Mans see Paris - Nantes sub-table.

km																										
		Ouigo	*TGV*	*TGV*	*TGV*	*TGV*	*TGV*	*TGV*	*TGV*	*TGV*	*TGV*	*TGV*	*TGV*	*TGV*	*TGV*	*TGV*	*Ouigo*	*TGV*	*TGV*	*TGV*	*TGV*	*TGV*	*TGV*	*TGV*	*TGV*	*TGV*
		7611	**8081**	**8603 8703**	**8089**	**8711**	**8605**	**8707**	**8083**	**8691**	**8691**	**8615 8715**	**8717**	**8085**	**8619**	**8085**	**7615**	**8619**	**8719**	**8051**	**8087**	**8099**	**8623**	**8623**	**8693**	**8623**
			①–⑥		⑦	①–⑥		⑦		①–④	⑥		⑥		⑦	①–④		①–⑥	⑦	⑤	⑦	⑤	⑤	⑦	⑦	⑥
		⊠		**A**			**B**		**F**		**e**	**C**	**e**	**E**			⊠					**f**	**f**			**e**
0	**Paris** Montparnasse d.	0643	0707	0734	0822	0822	0843	0843	0956	0956	1000	1057	1157	1215	1222	1223	1247	1257	1257	1335	1347	1348	1420	1447	1447	1447
	Le Mans d.	|	|	0837	|	|	|	|	|	|	|	|	|	|	|	|	1346	|	|	|	|	|	|	|	|	|
	Laval d.	|	0822	|	|	|	0958	0958	|	|	|	|	|	|	|	|	1417	|	|	|	1501	1501	|	|	|	|
	Vitré d.	|	0842	|	|	|	|	|	|	|	|	|	|	|	|	|	|	|	|	|	|	|	|	|	|	|
364	**Rennes** a.	0815	0903	0925	0950	0956	1025	1025	1125	1125	1130	1225	1325	1348	1401	1350	1441	1425	1425	1507	1526	1525	1548	1619	1619	1622

	TGV	*TGV*	*TGV*	*TGV*	*TGV*	*TGV*	*TGV*	*TGV*	*TGV*	*TGV*	*TGV*	*TGV*	*TGV*	*TGV*	*TGV*	*TGV*	*TGV*	*TGV*	*TGV*	*TGV*	*TGV*	*TGV*	*TGV*	*TGV*	*TGV*
	8623	**8723**	**8631**	**8629**	**8729**	**8067**	**8091**	**8639**	**8731**	**8639**	**8731**	**8735**	**8095**	**8093**	**8075**	**8641**	**8739**	**8649**	**8751**	**8097**	**8655**	**8755**	**8063**	**8069**	**8791**
	①–④	①–④	⑤	⑥–④		①–⑥	⑦	⑦	⑦	①–④	①–④	⑤	⑤	⑦–④	⑤	⑥–④	⑥–④	⑤	Ⓑ	⑤	⑤	⑤	⑥–④	⑦	⑤
					D																				
Paris Montparnasse d.	1448	1448	1650	1657	1657	1715	1715	1755	1755	1800	1800	1800	1815	1815	1843	1859	1859	1957	1957	2015	2057	2057	2115	2215	2215
Le Mans d.	|	|	|	|	|	1813	1813	|	|	|	|	|	|	|	1942	|	|	|	|	2113	|	|	2213	2313	2313
Laval d.	|	|	|	|	|	1844	1844	|	|	|	|	|	|	1929	2017	|	|	|	|	2144	|	|	2244	2344	2344
Vitré d.	|	|	|	|	|	|	|	|	|	|	|	|	|	1950	2041	|	|	|	|	|	|	|	|	|	0004
Rennes a.	1622	1622	1822	1825	1825	1909	1909	1925	1925	1925	1925	1925	1943	2010	2101	2025	2025	2125	2125	2209	2225	2225	2309	0009	0025

	TGV	*TGV*	*TGV*	*TGV*	*TGV*		*TGV*	*TGV*	*TGV*	*TGV*	*TGV*	*TGV*		*TGV*	*TGV*	*TGV*	*TGV*	*TGV*	*TGV*		*Ouigo*	*TGV*	*TGV*	*TGV*	*TGV*
	8072	**8082**	**8080**	**8602**	**8702**		**8052**	**8604**	**8606**	**8706**	**8608**	**8708**		**8610**	**8710**	**8710**	**8796**	**8090**	**8090**		**7612**	**8720**	**8622**	**8722**	**8626**
	Ⓐ	②–⑥	①	①–⑥	①–⑥		Ⓑ	①	①–⑥	①–⑥	⑦	⑦		①–⑥	Ⓐ	⑥	⑥	⑥	Ⓑ				⑤⑦		①–④
																					⊠			⊡	
Rennes d.	0533	0648	0700	0735	0735	...	0748	0835	0935	0935	0954	1014	...	1135	1135	1135	1217	1227	1252	...	1330	1335	1535	1535	1552
Vitré d.	0555	|	|	|	|	...	|	|	|	|	|	|	...	|	|	|	|	|	|	...	|	|	|	|	|
Laval d.	0616	0716	|	|	|	...	0816	|	|	|	|	|	...	1203	1203	1203	|	|	|	...	|	|	|	|	|
Le Mans d.	0648	0748	0748	|	|	...	0848	|	|	|	|	|	...	|	|	|	|	|	|	...	|	|	|	|	|
Paris Montparnasse a.	0745	0845	0845	0909	0909	...	0945	1009	1107	1107	1129	1144	...	1315	1315	1315	1349	1400	1421	...	1502	1505	1703	1703	1731

	TGV	*TGV*	*TGV*	*TGV*		*TGV*	*TGV*	*TGV*	*TGV*		*TGV*	*TGV*	*TGV*	*TGV*	*Ouigo*		*TGV*	*TGV*	*TGV*	*TGV*		*TGV*	*TGV*	*TGV*	*TGV*
	8626	**8630**	**8074**	**8086**		**8086**	**8086**	**8690**	**8634**		**8730**	**8636**	**8088**	**8642**	**7616**		**8092**	**8692**	**8646**	**8746**		**8646**	**8098**	**8652**	**8752**
	⑥	⑤	Ⓐ	⑤		Ⓒ	①–④		⑦				①–⑥	Ⓑ			⑦	⑦	⑦–④	①–⑥		⑤⑥	⑦	⑦	⑦
								⊡							⊠										
Rennes d.	1552	1609	1631	1635	...	1635	1643	1735	1735	...	1735	1835	1906	1935	1948	...	2035	2035	2135	2135	...	2147	2148	2235	2235
Vitré d.	|	|	1657	|	...	|	|	|	|	...	|	|	|	|	|	...	|	|	|	|	...	|	|	|	|
Laval d.	|	|	1717	|	...	|	|	|	|	...	|	1903	|	|	2015	...	|	|	|	|	...	|	2218	|	|
Le Mans d.	|	|	1749	|	...	|	|	|	|	...	|	|	|	|	2048	...	|	|	|	|	...	|	2249	|	|
Paris Montparnasse a.	1731	1738	1848	1802	...	1805	1811	1904	1904	...	1904	2015	2034	2104	2149	...	2210	2210	2304	2304	...	2323	2345	0004	0004

PARIS - NANTES

Certain trains continue to Les Sables d'Olonne (Tables **293**), St Nazaire (Table **288**) or Le Croisic (Table **288**).

km																										
		TGV	*Ouigo*		*TGV*	*TGV*		*TGV*	*TGV*		*TGV*	*TGV*		*TGV*	*TGV*		*TGV*	*TGV*		*Ouigo*	*TGV*					
		8911	**7621**		**8883**	**8803**		**8913**	**8973**		**8871**	**8917**		**8921**	**8921**		**8977**	**8923**		**7623**	**8813**					
		①–⑥			Ⓐ	⑥					Ⓑ	⑥		①–④	⑤–⑦		⑤–⑦				⑤					
			⊠																	⊠						
0	**Paris** Montparnasse d.	0626	0744	...	0748	0748	...	0939	0939	...	1039	1039	...	1215	1252	...	1330	1452	...	1548	1619	...	...	...	...	...
	Le Mans d.	0736	0841	...	|	|	...	1036	1036	...	1136	1136	...	|	|	...	1428	|	...	|	|	...	...	...	...	...
254	Sablé d.	|	|	...	0854	0854	...	|	|	...	|	|	...	|	|	...	1450	|	...	|	|	...	...	...	...	...
302	Angers St Laud d.	0817	0922	...	0917	0917	...	1118	1118	...	1217	1217	...	1342	1417	...	1514	1617	...	1712	|	...	...	...	...	...
390	**Nantes** a.	0854	1000	...	0954	0956	...	1154	1154	...	1254	1254	...	1420	1454	...	1551	1654	...	1750	1823	...	...	...	...	...

	TGV	*TGV*		*TGV*	*TGV*		*TGV*	*TGV*		*TGV*	*TGV*		*TGV*	*TGV*		*TGV*	*TGV*		*TGV*	*TGV*					
	8881	**8895**		**8905**	**8927**		**8821**	**8897**		**8931**	**8985**		**8887**	**8935**		**8937**	**8827**		**8939**	**8829**					
		Ⓐ		⑦–④	⑤		⑤	①–③					⑥–④	⑤		⑤	⑦–④		⑤	⑥					
		g																							
Paris Montparnasse d.	1637	1739	...	1751	1751	...	1823	1843	...	1852	1852	...	1939	1939	...	2052	2152	...	2152	2152	...	...	...	...	...
Le Mans d.	1737	1833	...	|	|	...	|	1940	...	|	|	...	2036	2037	...	|	|	...	|	|	...	...	...	...	...
Sablé d.	|	...	...	|	|	...	|	...	...	1958	1958	...	|	|	...	|	|	...	|	|	...	...	...	...	...
Angers St Laud d.	1818	...	...	1917	1917	...	|	...	...	2022	2022	...	2117	2117	...	2217	2317	...	2317	2324	...	...	...	...	...
Nantes a.	1900	...	...	1954	1954	...	2020	...	...	2059	2059	...	2154	2154	...	2254	2354	...	2354	0001	...	...	...	...	...

	TGV	*TGV*		*TGV*	*TGV*		*TGV*	*TGV*		*TGV*	*Ouigo*		*Ouigo*	*TGV*		*TGV*	*TGV*		*TGV*	*TGV*					
	8860	**8900**		**8804**	**8910**		**8808**	**8872**		**8912**	**7622**		**7622**	**8972**		**8916**	**8916**		**8874**	**8814**					
	Ⓐ	Ⓐ		②–⑦	①		⑥	Ⓐ		②–⑥	Ⓒ		Ⓐ			⑥	①⑤		①–⑥	Ⓐ					
											⊠		⊠												
Nantes d.	0508	0604	...	0704	0705	...	0808	0904	...	0904	1040	...	1050	1104	...	1209	1209	...	1304	1404	...	...	...	...	...
Angers St Laud d.	0548	|	...	0744	0745	...	0849	0944	...	0944	1120	...	1130	1145	...	|	|	...	1345	1444	...	...	...	...	...
Sablé d.	0611	|	...	|	|	...	|	|	...	|	|	...	|	|	...	|	|	...	|	|	...	...	...	...	...
Le Mans d.	0634	|	...	|	|	...	|	1026	...	1026	|	...	|	1227	...	|	|	...	1427	|	...	...	...	...	...
Paris Montparnasse a.	0733	0808	...	0914	0913	...	1013	1122	...	1122	1241	...	1254	1322	...	1410	1410	...	1522	1608	...	...	...	...	...

	TGV	*TGV*		*TGV*	*TGV*		*TGV*	*Ouigo*		*TGV*	*TGV*		*TGV*	*TGV*		*TGV*	*TGV*		*TGV*	*TGV*					
	8922	**8922**		**8880**	**8984**		**8926**	**7624**		**8928**	**8986**		**8930**	**8932**		**8988**	**8826**		**8934**	**8936**					
	⑦	⑥		⑦	①–⑥		⑥⑦			⑦	⑥		⑦	①–⑥		⑦	⑤		⑦	⑦					
								⊠									**h**								
Nantes d.	1504	1504	...	1604	1708	...	1804	1840	...	1857	1907	...	2004	2004	...	2104	2108	...	2207	2252	...	...	...	...	...
Angers St Laud d.	1545	1545	...	1644	1749	...	1845	|	...	1944	1947	...	2044	2044	...	2144	2149	...	2247	|	...	...	...	...	...
Sablé d.	|	|	...	|	|	...	1907	|	...	|	|	...	|	|	...	|	|	...	|	|	...	...	...	...	...
Le Mans d.	1626	1627	...	1726	|	...	1932	|	...	|	|	...	2126	2126	...	|	|	...	|	|	...	...	...	...	...
Paris Montparnasse a.	1722	1722	...	1822	1912	...	2027	2038	...	2108	2110	...	2222	2222	...	2313	2313	...	0008	0049	...	...	...	...	...

A – ①②③④⑥ until Aug. 2; ①–④ from Aug. 4.
B – ⑤–⑦ until Aug. 3 (also July 14); ⑦ from Aug. 10 (also Aug. 14).
C – Daily until Aug. 8; Ⓑ from Aug. 10.
D – ①②③④⑥⑦ until Aug. 7; ①②③④⑦ from Aug. 10.
E – ⑤⑥ until Aug. 2; ⑥ from Aug. 9 (also Aug. 14).
F – Ⓒ until Aug. 3; ⑦ from Aug. 10.

e – Until Aug. 2.
f – Until Aug. 1 (also Aug. 14).
g – Until July 25.
h – Until Aug. 8.

⊡ – ①②③④⑥.

⊠ – OUIGO low-cost TGV service. Internet booking only (www.ouigo.com).

TGV – High-speed train. Ⓡ. 🍷.

SUMMARY OF TGV EXCEPTION AND ADDITIONAL RUNNING DATES:

① also July 15; not July 14.
⑤ also Aug. 14; not Aug. 15.
⑦ also July 14.
Ⓑ not Aug. 15.
⑤⑥ also Aug. 14.
⑤⑦ also July 14, Aug. 14; not Aug. 15.
①–③ not July 14.
①–④ not July 14, Aug. 14.
①–⑥ not July 14.
②–⑥ not July 15.
⑥–④ also Aug. 15; not Aug. 14.
①②③④⑥ also Aug. 15; not July 14, Aug. 14.

280a LE MANS - NANTES, LAVAL and RENNES

TER services. For *TGV* services see Table **280**. For other services Sablé sur Sarthe - Nantes and Laval - Rennes see Table **287**.

km		Ⓐ	Ⓐ	⑥	†	Ⓐ	Ⓐ	Ⓐ	Ⓐ	⑥		Ⓐ	Ⓐ	⑤	Ⓒ	⚒	Ⓐ	Ⓐ	Ⓒ	Ⓐ	Ⓐ	†	Ⓐ	Ⓐ	†	†
0	**Le Mans** ◧ d.	0543	0641	0700	0725	0706	0741	0752	1043	1057	1227	1309	1506	1541	1557	1644	1656	1741	1747	1759	1839	1857	1910	1943	1943	2043
49	Sablé sur Sarthe ◧ d.	0606	0711	0726	0747	0732	0811	0828	1106	1128	1259	1332	1532	1612	1628	1706	1728	1811	1820	1831	1900	1920	1936	2014	2026	2105
97	Angers St Laud d.	0633	0733	0803	0809	0808	0836	0905	1131	1207	1336	1356	1606	1638	1705	1730	1803	1836	1858	1905	1933	1944	2008	2036	2104	2128
185	**Nantes** a.	0715	0815	0846	0850	...	0917	...	1215	...	...	1438	...	1720	...	1818	...	1916	...	...	2015	2027	...	2117	...	2211

		Ⓐ	Ⓐ	Ⓐ	⚒	Ⓐ	Ⓐ	⑥		⚒	†	Ⓐ	⑥	Ⓐ	Ⓒ	Ⓐ	Ⓑ	Ⓐ	Ⓐ	Ⓑ	⑥	Ⓐ	†	Ⓐ	†	⑥
	Nantes d.	...	0609	0644	...	0744	...	...	1144	...	...	...	1542	1544	...	...	1643	...	1744	...	...	1848	...	...	2112	2112
	Angers St Laud d.	0552	0704	0728	0751	0832	0853	1052	1228	1252	1349	1352	1628	1628	1654	1703	1728	1753	1828	1851	1852	1933	1935	2000	2155	2201
	Sablé sur Sarthe ◧ d.	0628	0727	0754	0826	0854	0927	1130	1254	1330	1427	1426	1656	1654	1731	1738	1754	1829	1854	1927	1930	1956	1956	2037	2217	2223
	Le Mans ◧ a.	0656	0753	0820	0901	0916	0954	1203	1316	1408	1501	1454	1720	1716	1804	1810	1816	1900	1919	1954	2002	2021	2019	2103	2238	2244

km		Ⓐ	Ⓐ	⑥	Ⓐ	Ⓐ	⑥	Ⓐ	⑥	†	⚒	⑥	†	Ⓐ	⑥	†	⑤	Ⓑ	Ⓐ	⑥	Ⓐ	†	Ⓐ		Ⓑ	Ⓑ
0	**Le Mans** d.	0630	0651	0703	0718	0821	0920	0949	1049	1120	1220	1352	1441	1448	1520	1522	1531	1618	1640	1649	1721	1725	1749	1826	1921	2021
90	Laval d.	0724	0754	0754	0811	0913	1013	1054	1154	1212	1327	1454	1532	1553	1612	1626	1619	1713	1730	1754	1815	1830	1854	1915	2027	2113
125	Vitré a.	0747	...	...	...	...	...	...	...	...	...	...	...	...	...	...	1638	...	1757	...	...	...	...	...	...	...
163	**Rennes** a.	0819	...	...	...	...	...	...	...	...	...	...	...	...	...	...	1711	...	1829	...	...	...	...	...	...	...

		Ⓐ	Ⓐ	Ⓐ	⑥	Ⓐ	⑥	†	⑥	Ⓐ	Ⓐ	Ⓒ	Ⓐ	Ⓒ	†	⑤	Ⓐ	⑥	Ⓑ	Ⓒ	Ⓐ	Ⓐ	Ⓒ	Ⓐ	Ⓐ	†
	Rennes d.	...	...	0629	...	...	...	...	...	...	...	...	...	...	...	...	...	...	...	...	...	1742	...	...	...	...
	Vitré d.	...	...	0653	...	...	...	...	...	...	...	...	...	...	...	...	...	...	...	...	...	1813	...	...	...	...
	Laval d.	0605	0647	0721	0804	0804	0905	0925	0942	0952	1105	1146	1245	1305	1407	1546	1605	1622	1647	1727	1744	1831	1847	1908	1947	2008
	Le Mans a.	0708	0738	0811	0853	0858	1008	1015	1034	1045	1208	1238	1350	1408	1510	1642	1709	1712	1738	1830	1850	1922	1938	2011	2038	2058

◧ – Additional trains Le Mans - Sablé sur Sarthe at 0621 Ⓐ, 0820 Ⓐ, 0914 ⑥, 1121 Ⓒ, 1614 Ⓐ, 1621 †, 1814 ⑥, 1848 Ⓐ, 1949 ①–④, 2006 ⑤.
Additional trains Sablé sur Sarthe - Le Mans at 0640 Ⓐ, 0716 ⚒, 0937 †, 0954 ⑥, 1054 Ⓐ, 1154 Ⓒ, 1536 †, 1654 †, 1715 Ⓐ, 1813 †, 2054 Ⓐ.

281 (PARIS -) RENNES - ST MALO

TGV timings may vary by a few minutes - please check your reservation. For *TGV* exception and additional running dates see Table **280**.

km		Ⓐ	⚒	*TGV* **8081** ①–⑥	Ⓐ	*TGV* **8089** ⑦	Ⓒ	*TGV* **8083** **d**		†	⚒	Ⓐ	*TGV* **8085** ⑤ **f**		*TGV* **8085** ⑥ **e**	*TGV* **8085** ①–④	⑥	*TGV* **8087** ⑦	*TGV* **8099** ⑤ **f**	Ⓐ	Ⓑ	⑥	†	Ⓐ	⑥	Ⓐ
0	**Paris** Montparnasse d.	...	...	0707	...	0822	...	0956	...	...	...	...	1215	...	1215	1223	...	1347	1348	...	...	...	...	...	...	...
364	**Rennes** a.	...	...	0903	...	0950	...	1125	...	...	...	...	1348	...	1348	1350	...	1526	1525	...	...	...	...	...	...	...
364	**Rennes** 272 d.	0639	0735	0907	0935	0954	1040	1130	1135	1235	1235	1335	1353	...	1354	1354	1457	1530	1530	1605	1635	1636	1735	1735	1735	1804
422	Dol 272 d.	0717	0813	0941	1013	|	1116	1203	1214	1311	1319	1413	1426	...	1432	1426	1543	|	|	1646	1713	1714	1812	1813	1816	1846
445	**St Malo** a.	0733	0829	0954	1029	1036	1130	1216	1231	1325	1335	1429	1440	...	1445	1440	1557	1613	1612	1702	1729	1730	1825	1829	1832	1904

	†	Ⓐ	⑥	*TGV* **8091** ⑦	Ⓐ		*TGV* **8095** ⑤	*TGV* **8093** ⑦–④	Ⓒ	*TGV* **8097** ⑤
Paris Montparnasse d.	...	...	...	1715	...	...	1815	1815	...	2015
Rennes a.	...	...	...	1909	...	...	1943	2010	...	2209
Rennes 272 d.	1835	1835	1835	1913	1935	...	1956	2014	2040	2213
Dol 272 d.	1914	1917	1921	|	2013	...	2030	2048	2119	2246
St Malo a.	1928	1933	1934	1954	2029	...	2043	2101	2135	2300

	TGV **8082** ②–⑥	*TGV* **8080** ①	⑥	Ⓐ	Ⓐ		Ⓐ	⑥	†	Ⓐ
St Malo d.	0556	0607	0623	0627	0658	...	0758	0827	0834	0837
Dol 272 d.	0612	0623	0639	0643	0716	...	0817	0843	0848	0851
Rennes 272 a.	0644	0654	0725	0725	0756	...	0856	0925	0925	0925
Rennes d.	0648	0700	...	...	...	...	...	...	...	...
Paris Montparnasse a.	0845	0845	...	...	...	...	...	...	...	...

		TGV **8090** ⑥	*TGV* **8090** Ⓑ	⚒		Ⓑ	⑥	Ⓐ		*TGV* **8086** ⑤	*TGV* **8086** Ⓒ	*TGV* **8086** ①–④		Ⓐ	Ⓒ			*TGV* **8088** ①–⑥	Ⓐ	Ⓒ		*TGV* **8092** ⑦	Ⓒ	Ⓐ	*TGV* **8098** ⑦
St Malo d.	1031	1139	1204	1217	...	1331	1423	1431	...	1538	1538	1547	...	1625	1628	1731	...	1814	1831	1832	...	1937	2028	2031	2100
Dol 272 d.	1047	|	|	1234	...	1347	1439	1447	...	1554	1554	1603	...	1641	1641	1747	...	1830	1847	1846	...	1952	2042	2047	|
Rennes 272 a.	1125	1221	1246	1316	...	1425	1525	1525	...	1625	1625	1634	...	1720	1720	1825	...	1901	1925	1925	...	2025	2121	2125	2142
Rennes d.	...	1227	1252	...	...	...	...	...	...	1635	1635	1643	...	...	...	...	...	1906	...	...	...	2035	...	...	2148
Paris Montparnasse a.	...	1400	1421	...	...	...	...	...	...	1802	1805	1811	...	...	...	...	...	2034	...	...	...	2110	...	...	2345

d – Ⓒ until Aug. 3; ⑦ from Aug. 10. **e** – Until Aug. 2. **f** – Until Aug. 1 (also Aug. 14). *TGV* – High-speed train. 🅁. 🍷.

282 DOL - DINAN - ST BRIEUC

km		⑥	Ⓐ		Ⓐ	⑥		⚒	†			⚒		Ⓐ	Ⓒ			Ⓐ		⑥	⑤		⑦–④	⑤		
0	**Dol** d.	...	...	...	0822	0847	...	0943	1120	...	...	1323	...	...	...	...	1724	1921	...	1925	2032	...	2051	2248	...	...
32	**Dinan** d.	0741	0745	...	0845	0906	...	1002	1140	...	1220	1342	...	1705	1745	...	1752	1943	...	1944	2051	...	2110	2307	...	...
73	Lamballe 284 d.	0815	0819	...	...	...	...	...	...	...	1254	...	...	1739	1819	...	...	...	...	...	...	...	...	...	...	...
94	**St Brieuc** 284 a.	0831	0835	...	...	...	...	...	...	...	1310	...	...	1755	1835	...	...	...	...	...	...	...	...	...	...	...

	Ⓐ	Ⓐ		⑥	Ⓐ		⚒	Ⓒ		⚒	Ⓐ			Ⓒ		Ⓐ	Ⓒ		Ⓐ	Ⓒ		⑤	①–④		
St Brieuc 284 d.	...	...	...	...	...	...	0844	...	...	...	1320	...	...	1647	...	...	...	...	1806	1852	...	...	...	...	...
Lamballe 284 d.	...	...	...	...	...	...	0900	...	...	...	1336	...	...	1703	...	...	...	...	1822	1908	...	...	...	...	...
Dinan d.	0559	0739	...	0806	0904	...	0932	1014	...	1210	1408	...	1530	1735	...	1838	1847	...	1854	1940	...	1957	2023	...	...
Dol a.	0618	0807	...	0934	0932	...	...	1042	...	1229	...	...	1549	...	...	1900	1906	...	...	...	...	2016	2042	...	...

283 MORLAIX - ROSCOFF

Service July 5 - August 31.

	⚒						⚒								Ⓐ				Ⓐ		Ⓒ		⑤†		Ⓐ
Morlaix, Gare SNCF d.	0655	...	0745	...	0855	...	1130	...	1200	...	1240	...	1535	...	1610	...	1700	...	1815	...	1820	...	2020	...	2120
St Pol de Léon, Ti Kastelliz ⊡ d.	0720	...	0815	...	0915	...	1150	...	1230	...	1300	...	1605	...	1630	...	1725	...	1845	...	1850	...	2040	...	2140
Roscoff, Ferry d.	0735	...	0830	...	0930	...	1205	...	1245	...	1315	...	1620	...	|	...	1740	...	1900	...	1905	...	2055	...	2155
Roscoff, Quai d'Auxerre ⊙ a.	0740	...	0835	...	0935	...	1210	...	1250	...	1320	...	1625	...	1645	...	1745	...	1905	...	1910	...	2100	...	2200

	⚒	Ⓑ		⑥ ●			Ⓐ							Ⓐ			Ⓐ		†	⑥		Ⓐ	Ⓑ		⑥
Roscoff, Quai d'Auxerre ⊙ d.	0650	0745	...	0745	0845	...	1015	1045	...	1145	1240	...	1350	1455	...	1545	1655	...	1700	1700	...	1730	1900	...	1915
Roscoff, Ferry d.	|	|	...	0735	0850	...	|	1050	...	1150	1245	...	|	|	...	1550	|	...	|	1705	...	1735	|	...	|
St Pol de Léon, Ti Kastelliz ⊡ d.	0705	0800	...	0800	0905	...	1030	1105	...	1205	1300	...	1405	1510	...	1605	1705	...	1715	1720	...	1750	1915	...	1930
Morlaix, Gare SNCF a.	0730	0825	...	0825	0925	...	1050	1130	...	1230	1325	...	1425	1530	...	1625	1730	...	1735	1750	...	1820	1935	...	1950

⊡ – 300 metres from railway station. ⊙ – 400 metres from railway station. ● – Calls at Roscoff Ferry then Quai d'Auxerre.

(PARIS -) RENNES - LANNION and BREST

TGV timings may vary by a few minutes - please check your reservation. For *TGV* exception and additional running dates see Table **280**.

km		Ⓐ ⊖	⑥	Ⓐ	Ⓐ	Ⓐ	Ⓐ	Ⓐ	*Ouigo* **7611** ⊠	*TGV* **8603** **A**	⚒	⑥	*TGV* **8605** **B**		†	Ⓐ	*TGV* **8691** ①–④	*TGV* **8691** ⑥ **e**	⑥ ⊖	Ⓐ	† ⊖	⑥	*TGV* **8615** **C**		⚒	
	Paris Montparnasse d.	...	...	...	...	...	...	...	0643	0734	...	...	0843	...	...	...	0956	1000	...	...	...	...	1057	...	...	...
	Rennes a.	...	...	...	...	...	...	...	0815	0925	...	...	1025	...	...	...	1125	1130	...	...	...	...	1225	...	...	...
0	**Rennes** d.	...	...	...	...	0635	0700	0737	0822	0933	...	0937	1033	...	1040	1041	1134	1134	...	...	...	1141	1233	...	1237	1335
80	Lamballe 282 d.	...	...	...	...	0731	0738	0833	|	1012	...	1030	1112	...	1129	1120	|	|	...	...	...	1219	1312	...	1335	1412
101	St Brieuc 282 d.	...	...	...	0728	0746	0750	0847	0909	1025	...	1045	1125	...	1140	1133	1223	1222	...	...	...	1231	1325	...	1350	1425
132	Guingamp d.	...	...	...	0747	...	0808	...	0927	1042	1052	...	1141	...	...	1150	1240	1240	...	...	...	1248	1341	...	...	1442
158	Plouaret-Trégor d.	0627	...	...	0801	...	0822	...	|	|	1107	...	|	...	...	|	|	|	1249	...	1254	1302	1356	1408	...	1456
175	**Lannion** a.	|	...	...	0818	...	|	...	|	|	1123	...	|	...	...	|	1310	1309	|	...	|	|	|	1425	...	|
189	Morlaix d.	0651	0710	0754	...	...	0841	...	0957	1112	...	...	1211	...	...	1219	...	...	1306	1309	1311	1321	1416	...	...	1514
	Landivisiau d.	0708	0725	0816	...	...	0856	...	|	|	...	...	|	...	...	1235	...	...	1320	1324	1326	1337	|	...	...	1529
230	Landerneau 286 d.	0720	0737	0828	...	...	0907	...	|	|	...	...	|	...	...	1245	...	...	1332	1336	1336	1347	|	...	...	1540
248	**Brest** 286 a.	0736	0751	0844	...	...	0919	...	1035	1145	...	...	1244	...	...	1258	...	...	1346	1352	1348	1359	1449	...	...	1552

	Ⓐ	*TGV* **8619** ⑦	*TGV* **8619** ①–⑥	Ⓐ	Ⓒ	Ⓒ	⑤	⑤†	⑤	⊡	*TGV* **8623** ⑤ **f**	*TGV* **8623** ⑦		*TGV* **8693** ⑦	*TGV* **8623** ⑥ **e**	*TGV* **8623** ①–④	Ⓐ	⚒	† ⊖	Ⓐ ⊖	Ⓒ		†	⑥ ⊖	Ⓐ
Paris Montparnasse d.	...	1222	1257	...	...	...	...	...	...	...	1420	1447	...	1447	1447	1448	...	...	...	...	...	...	...	...	...
Rennes a.	...	1401	1425	...	...	...	...	...	...	...	1548	1619	...	1619	1622	1622	...	...	...	...	...	...	...	...	...
Rennes d.	...	1406	1429	...	1435	...	...	1437	1535	...	1553	1625	...	1625	1631	1631	...	...	...	...	1637	1735	...	...	1739
Lamballe 282 d.	...	|	|	...	1512	...	...	1526	1612	...	|	|	...	|	|	|	...	...	...	...	1726	1812	...	...	1837
St Brieuc 282 d.	...	1455	1516	...	1525	...	...	1539	1625	...	1642	1714	...	1720	1722	1721	...	1730	...	...	1740	1825	...	...	1849
Guingamp d.	...	|	|	...	1542	...	...	...	1641	...	1700	|	...	1738	1739	1737	...	1750	...	...	...	1842	1856	...	...
Plouaret-Trégor d.	1506	|	|	...	1556	1617	...	...	|	...	|	|	...	1754	|	|	...	1805	1830	1846	...	1856	1911	1912	...
Lannion a.	1523	|	|	...	|	1634	...	...	|	...	|	|	...	1810	|	|	...	1826	1848	1903	...	|	1927	1929	...
Morlaix d.	...	|	|	1606	1614	...	1657	...	1711	1713	1730	1757	...	...	1809	1806	1813	...	...	...	...	1915	...	...	...
Landivisiau d.	...	|	|	1620	1630	...	1712	...	1727	1727	|	|	...	...	|	|	1827	...	...	...	...	1931	...	..	...
Landerneau 286 d.	...	|	|	1633	1641	...	1724	...	1738	1739	|	|	...	...	|	|	1838	...	...	...	...	1941	...	...	...
Brest 286 a.	...	1607	1625	1649	1653	...	1740	...	1751	1756	1803	1830	...	...	1842	1839	1851	...	...	...	...	1953	...	...	...

	TGV **8631** ⑤	*TGV* **8629** ⑥–④	Ⓐ		⚒	*TGV* **8639** ⑦	*TGV* **8639** ①–④		*TGV* **8635** ⑤	*TGV* **8695** ⑤	①–④	†	†	⑤⑥	⑤	*TGV* **8641** ⑥–④	*TGV* **8645** ⑤		⑤	⑥–④	*TGV* **8649** ⑤	†	⑤	*TGV* **8655** ⑤	*TGV* **8657** ⑦
Paris Montparnasse d.	1650	1657	...	...	...	1755	1800	...	1804	1804	...	...	...	...	...	1859	1900	...	...	...	1957	...	...	2057	2353
Rennes a.	1822	1825	...	...	...	1925	1925	...	|	|	...	...	...	...	...	2025	|	...	...	...	2125	...	...	2225	|
Rennes d.	1826	1833	...	...	1837	1933	1933	...	|	|	...	...	1937	1944	...	2033	|	...	2040	...	2133	2139	...	2233	|
Lamballe 282 d.	1905	|	...	...	1930	|	|	...	|	|	...	...	2026	2022	...	2112	|	...	2118	...	2212	2216	...	|	|
St Brieuc 282 d.	1919	1921	...	...	1944	2020	2020	...	2021	2026	2026	...	2037	2034	...	2125	2111	...	2131	...	2225	2229	...	2320	0423
Guingamp d.	1935	1937	...	1947	...	2036	2036	...	|	2043	2042	2044	...	2051	2102	2142	|	...	2147	...	2241	2246	...	2337	0440
Plouaret-Trégor d.	|	|	...	2003	...	|	|	...	|	|	2056	2059	...	2105	2117	2157	|	...	2201	2203	2257	2300	2302	|	|
Lannion a.	|	|	...	2021	...	|	|	...	|	2112	2112	2115	...	|	2133	|	|	...	|	2220	|	|	2319	|	|
Morlaix d.	2004	2006	2013	...	...	2106	2106	...	2102	...	...	...	...	2124	...	2216	|	...	2220	...	2315	2319	...	0006	0511
Landivisiau d.	|	|	2027	...	...	|	|	...	|	...	...	...	...	2140	...	|	|	...	2236	...	|	2335	...	|	|
Landerneau 286 d.	|	|	2040	...	...	|	|	...	|	...	...	...	...	2150	...	2241	|	...	2246	...	2340	2345	...	|	0537
Brest 286 a.	2037	2039	2051	...	...	2139	2139	...	2135	...	...	...	...	2202	...	2253	2218	...	2258	...	2352	2357	...	0039	0552

	Ⓐ	*TGV* **8602** ①–⑥	Ⓐ ⊖	Ⓐ	Ⓐ	Ⓐ	*TGV* **8604** ①	⑥	Ⓐ	Ⓐ	⑥	*TGV* **8606** ①–⑥		*TGV* **8608** ⑦	†	⑥	Ⓐ		*TGV* **8610** ①–⑥	⑥	⑥	Ⓑ	Ⓐ	⑥	Ⓐ
Brest 286 d.	...	0522	...	0539	...	...	0631	...	0701	...	...	0722	...	0744	...	0801	0805	...	0905	0931	...	1034	...	...	...
Landerneau 286 d.	...	|	...	0550	...	...	|	...	0717	...	...	|	...	|	...	0815	0821	...	0919	0942	...	1045	...	...	...
Landivisiau d.	...	|	...	0600	...	...	|	...	0729	...	...	|	...	|	...	0827	0833	...	|	0952	...	1055	...	...	...
Morlaix d.	...	0554	...	0616	...	...	|	...	0744	...	...	0754	...	|	...	0842	0848	...	0943	1008	...	1111	...	...	...
Lannion d.	...	|	0604	|	...	0624	|	...	...	0726	0740	|	...	|	...	...	...	0937	|	|	...	|	...	1131	1140
Plouaret-Trégor d.	...	|	0620	0632	...	0640	|	...	...	0742	0756	|	...	|	...	...	...	0953	1001	1025	...	1128	...	1147	1155
Guingamp d.	...	0623	...	0647	...	0657	|	...	...	0757	0810	0822	...	0842	...	...	...	...	1017	1039	...	1143	...	...	1209
St Brieuc 282 d.	0616	0641	...	0704	0713	0719	0741	0815	...	...	0828	0840	...	0901	0917	...	...	...	1036	1056	1159	1200	1204	...	1226
Lamballe 282 d.	0627	|	...	0715	0724	...	|	0826	...	...	...	|	...	|	0928	...	...	...	1048	1108	1214	1211	1218	...	...
Rennes a.	0721	0729	...	0757	0817	...	0829	0921	...	...	...	0929	...	0950	1021	...	...	...	1129	1150	1316	1252	1316	...	...
Rennes d.	...	0735	...	...	...	...	0835	...	...	...	...	0935	...	0954	...	...	...	...	1135	...	...	...	...	...	...
Paris Montparnasse a.	...	0909	...	...	...	...	1009	...	...	...	...	1107	...	1129	...	...	...	...	1315	...	...	...	...	...	...

	Ouigo **7612** ⊠	†	⑥ ⊖	† ⊖	⑥	Ⓐ	*TGV* **8622** ⑤⑦			*TGV* **8626** ①–④	*TGV* **8626** ⑥	*TGV* **8630** ⑤		⑥	Ⓐ	*TGV* **8630** ⊡	†	Ⓐ	Ⓒ	⑥	⑤	*TGV* **8634** ⑦	*TGV* **8690** ⊡	Ⓐ	†
Brest 286 d.	1115	...	...	...	...	1250	1330	...	1306	1338	1338	1344	...	1355	...	1409	1434	...	...	1504	1509	1514	...	...	...
Landerneau 286 d.	|	...	...	...	...	1306	|	...	1318	|	|	|	...	1408	...	|	1445	...	...	1515	1520	|	...	...	...
Landivisiau d.	|	...	...	...	...	1318	|	...	1328	|	|	|	...	1420	...	|	1455	...	...	1525	1530	|	...	...	...
Morlaix d.	1148	...	...	...	...	1333	|	...	1343	|	|	1418	...	1434	...	1443	1510	...	...	1540	1546	1545	...	...	...
Lannion d.	|	...	1225	1230	...	...	|	1333	|	|	|	|	...	...	1433	|	|	...	1533	|	|	|	1559	...	...
Plouaret-Trégor d.	|	...	1241	1246	...	...	|	1349	1400	|	|	1436	...	...	1449	1501	1527	...	1549	1557	|	1604	|	...	...
Guingamp d.	1218	...	...	...	...	...	|	...	1414	|	1437	1452	...	...	...	1517	1542	...	...	1612	1615	1619	|	...	...
St Brieuc 282 d.	1236	1317	...	...	1407	...	1441	...	1431	1455	1455	1511	...	...	...	1536	1559	1612	...	1628	1632	1637	1643	1712	1717
Lamballe 282 d.	|	1329	...	...	1421	...	|	...	1442	|	|	1523	...	...	...	1548	1610	1626	...	1640	1643	1649	|	1726	1728
Rennes a.	1325	1421	...	...	1521	...	1529	...	1525	1544	1544	1603	...	...	...	1629	1651	1720	...	1720	1725	1729	1729	1821	1821
Rennes d.	1330	...	...	...	...	...	1535	...	...	1552	1552	1609	...	...	...	1635	...	...	...	...	...	1735	1735	...	...
Paris Montparnasse a.	1502	...	...	...	...	...	1703	...	...	1731	1731	1738	...	...	...	1805	...	...	...	...	...	1904	1904	...	...

	Ⓐ	*TGV* **8636**	†	Ⓐ	⑥	Ⓐ	Ⓐ	Ⓒ	⑤⑥	*TGV* **8642** Ⓑ	† ⊖	Ⓐ ⊖		*TGV* **8644** ⑦	Ⓑ	*TGV* **8692** ⑦	⑥	Ⓐ	†	①–④	⑤–⑦	*TGV* **8646** ⑦–④	*TGV* **8646** ⑤⑥	†	*TGV* **8652** ⑦
Brest 286 d.	1557	1614	1633	...	...	1651	...	...	1706	1722	1731	1740	...	1800	1808	...	1809	1900	...	...	...	1922	1936	...	2019
Landerneau 286 d.	1613	|	1644	...	...	1706	...	...	1717	|	1742	1753	...	|	1820	...	1822	1914	...	...	...	|	|	...	|
Landivisiau d.	1625	|	1653	...	...	1719	...	...	1727	|	1752	1803	...	|	1830	...	1834	1926	...	...	...	|	|	...	|
Morlaix d.	1640	1647	1709	...	...	1735	...	...	1742	1754	1806	1818	...	|	1845	...	1848	1947	...	...	...	1954	2008	...	2050
Lannion d.	...	|	|	...	...	...	1734	1734	|	|	|	|	...	|	|	1855	|	...	...	1933	1935	|	|	2037	|
Plouaret-Trégor d.	...	|	1726	...	...	...	1749	1750	1759	|	1823	1839	...	|	1901	|	1905	...	...	1949	1951	|	|	2053	|
Guingamp d.	...	1715	1740	...	...	...	1803	1805	1813	1823	...	...	...	|	1916	1925	...	...	...	2003	2005	2023	2037	2107	2119
St Brieuc 282 d.	...	1733	1757	1812	1815	...	1821	...	1830	1841	...	...	...	1909	1932	1943	...	...	2017	2018	...	2041	2054	...	2136
Lamballe 282 d.	...	1745	1808	1826	1827	...	...	...	1842	|	...	...	...	|	1943	|	...	...	2030	...	...	|	|	...	2149
Rennes a.	...	1825	1850	1921	1921	...	...	...	1925	1929	...	...	...	|	2025	2029	...	...	2121	...	...	2129	2143	...	2229
Rennes d.	...	1835	...	...	...	...	...	...	...	1935	...	...	...	|	...	2035	...	...	...	...	...	2135	2147	...	2235
Paris Montparnasse a.	...	2015	...	...	...	...	...	...	...	2104	...	...	...	2121	...	2210	...	...	...	...	...	2304	2323	...	0004

A – ①②③④⑥ until Aug. 2; ①–④ from Aug. 4.
B – ⑤–⑦ until Aug. 3 (also July 14); ⑦ from Aug. 10 (also Aug. 14).
C – Daily until Aug. 8; Ⓑ from Aug. 10.
e – Until Aug. 2.
f – Until Aug. 1 (also Aug. 14).

⊡ – ①②③④⑥.
⊖ – 2 Lannion - Brest and v.v. (see both sides of table).
⊠ – OUIGO low-cost TGV service. Internet booking only (www.ouigo.com).
TGV – High-speed train. 🅁. 🍷.

285 (PARIS -) RENNES - QUIMPER and NANTES - QUIMPER

TGV timings may vary by a few minutes - please check your reservation. For *TGV* exception and additional running dates see Table **280**.

km		Ⓐ	Ⓐ	Ⓐ	Ⓐ	Ⓐ	⑥	*TGV* **8703** ①–④	*TGV* **8703** ⑥ e	Ⓐ	†	⑥	⑥	† Q	*TGV* **8711** ①–⑥	*TGV* **8707** ⑦	†	Ⓐ	Ⓐ	⑥	*TGV* **8715** C	†	⑥	†	Ⓐ	Ⓒ
	Paris Montparnasse d.	...	...	...	...	...	...	0734	0734	...	...	...	...	...	0822	0843	...	...	...	...	1057	...	...	...	...	...
	Rennes a.	...	...	...	...	...	...	0925	0925	...	...	...	...	...	0956	1025	...	...	...	...	1225	...	...	...	...	...
0	**Rennes** d.	0621	...	...	0704	...	0840	0929	0929	0938	...	...	0941	0956	1001	1029	1135	...	1135	...	1229	...	...	...	1239	1239
	Nantes 288 d.	|	0614	0642	|	0714	|	|	|	|	0919	0924	|	|	|	|	|	1118	|	1119	|	1215	1226	1242	|	|
	Savenay 288 d.	|	0638	0704	|	0747	|	|	|	|	0952	0946	|	|	|	|	|	1140	|	1142	|	1246	1249	|	|	|
72	Redon d.	0706	0712	0746	0746	0812	0924	|	|	1015	1023	1023	1023	1035	|	1106	1212	1217	1217	1215	|	1316	1320	1326	1323	1331
127	Vannes d.	0737	...	0815	0815	...	0957	1028	1028	1041	...	1052	1052	1104	1104	1132	1241	1246	1246	...	1328	...	...	1352	1354	1401
146	Auray d.	...	...	0827	0827	...	1009	1041	1041	1053	...	1104	1104	1114	1118	1145	1253	1258	1258	...	1342	...	...	|	...	...
180	Lorient d.	...	...	0850	0850	...	1029	1100	1100	1113	...	1125	1125	...	1137	1203	1315	1319	1319	...	1401	...	...	1420	...	...
200	Quimperlé d.	...	...	0902	0902	...	1041	|	1112	1125	...	1137	1137	...	|	|	1327	1331	1331	...	|	...	...	|	...	...
247	**Quimper** a.	...	...	0929	0929	...	1107	1134	1141	1152	...	1205	1205	...	1212	1239	1353	1359	1359	...	1434	...	...	1455	...	...

	Ⓐ	*TGV* **8717** ⑥ e	†	Ⓐ	⑥	⑥	⑤	⑤	⑥	*TGV* **8719** ⑦	*Ouigo* **7615** ⊠	†	Ⓐ	*TGV* **8723** ①–④	*TGV* **8725** ⑦	*TGV* **8725** ⑤⑥	Ⓐ	†	⚒	Ⓐ	Ⓐ	Ⓒ R		Ⓐ	Ⓐ
Paris Montparnasse d.	...	1157	...	...	...	...	...	...	...	1257	1247	...	...	1448	1503	1505	...	...	...	...	...	...	...	...	...
Rennes a.	...	1325	...	...	...	...	...	...	...	1425	1441	...	...	1622	|	|	...	...	...	...	...	...	...	...	...
Rennes d.	...	1329	1335	...	...	1335	1339	1435	...	1431	1445	1457	1604	1627	|	|	...	1635	1639	...	1705	...	1735	...	1739
Nantes 288 d.	1259	|	|	1314	1315	|	|	|	1419	|	|	|	|	|	|	|	1614	|	|	1648	|	1656	|	1714	|
Savenay 288 d.	|	|	|	1337	1339	|	|	|	1441	|	|	|	|	|	|	|	1637	|	|	1710	|	|	|	1739	|
Redon d.	1342	|	1412	1412	1418	1418	1424	1511	1514	|	|	1546	1640	|	|	|	1712	1712	1723	1747	1747	1741	1812	1814	1823
Vannes d.	1411	1428	1441	...	1447	1447	1454	1539	...	1532	1548	1621	1709	1728	1729	1729	...	1741	1800	1815	1815	1809	1838	...	1900
Auray d.	1423	1441	1453	...	1459	1457	...	1552	...	1545	1601	...	1721	1742	1744	1744	...	1754	...	1828	1828	|	1850	...	...
Lorient d.	1444	1500	1515	...	1520	...	...	1612	...	1605	1620	...	1742	1801	1804	1804	...	1815	...	1850	1850	1838	1909	...	...
Quimperlé d.	1456	|	1527	...	1532	...	...	1624	...	|	|	...	1754	1814	|	|	...	1827	...	1902	1902	|	1922	...	...
Quimper a.	1524	1534	1553	...	1559	...	...	1650	...	1638	1700	...	1822	1843	1841	1841	...	1853	...	1929	1929	1913	1950	...	...

	†	Ⓐ R	*TGV* **8729** ①–④ D	*TGV* **8727** ⑤	⚒	†	⑤	⑥–④	Ⓐ	*TGV* **8731** ⑦	*TGV* **8731** ①–④	*TGV* **8735** ⑤	Ⓐ	⑥	⑥	†	*TGV* **8739** ⑥–④	Ⓐ	†	*TGV* **8747** ⑤	⑤	*TGV* **8751** Ⓑ	*TGV* **8753** ⑤	*TGV* **8755** ⑤	*TGV* **8791** ⑤
Paris Montparnasse d.	...	...	1657	1657	...	...	...	...	...	1755	1800	1800	...	...	...	...	1859	...	...	1915	...	1957	2019	2057	2215
Rennes a.	...	...	1825	|	...	...	...	...	...	1925	1925	1925	...	...	...	...	2025	...	...	|	...	2125	|	2225	0025
Rennes d.	...	...	1829	|	...	...	1839	1839	...	1929	1929	1929	1939	...	1941	1939	2029	...	...	|	2043	2129	|	2229	0029
Nantes 288 d.	1719	1757	|	|	1814	1827	|	|	1914	|	|	|	|	1926	|	|	|	2014	2016	|	|	|	|	|	|
Savenay 288 d.	1753	|	|	|	1838	1848	|	|	1937	|	|	|	|	1948	|	|	|	2037	2050	|	|	|	|	|	|
Redon d.	1827	1842	|	1904	1912	1915	1918	1923	2011	|	|	|	2023	2024	2024	2028	2106	2110	2123	|	2128	2206	2224	|	|
Vannes d.	...	1909	1928	1930	...	1945	1944	2002	...	2028	2028	2028	2054	2053	2053	2105	2131	...	...	2135	2159	2231	2250	2328	0128
Auray d.	...	1921	1941	1944	...	1957	1957	...	...	|	|	2042	...	2106	2106	...	2144	...	...	|	...	2244	2304	2341	0141
Lorient d.	...	1940	2000	2004	...	2017	2016	...	...	2055	2054	2101	...	2127	2127	...	2203	...	...	2201	...	2304	2324	0000	0158
Quimperlé d.	...	|	|	2017	...	2030	2028	...	...	|	|	|	...	2139	2139	...	2216	...	...	|	...	2317	2337	|	...
Quimper a.	...	2015	2037	2046	...	2057	2055	...	...	2127	2127	2134	...	2206	2206	...	2245	...	...	2232	...	2344	0007	0033	...

	Ⓐ	Ⓐ	*TGV* **8702** ①–⑥	Ⓐ	Ⓐ	Ⓐ	⚒		Ⓐ	⑥	*TGV* **8706** ①–⑥	Ⓐ	†	*TGV* **8708** ⑦	②–⑦ R	① R	*TGV* **8710** Ⓐ		*TGV* **8710** ⑥	Ⓐ	*TGV* **8796** ⑥	⑥	Ⓑ	*TGV* **8720**	⚒
Quimper d.	...	...	0508	0535	0535	...	...	...	0638	...	0718	...	...	0807	0853	0857	0902	...	0902	0949	...	1038	...	1122	...
Quimperlé d.	...	...	0537	0601	0601	...	...	...	0705	...	|	...	...	|	|	|	0933	...	0933	1016	...	1105	...	|	...
Lorient d.	...	...	0552	0614	0614	...	...	...	0718	...	0754	...	...	0843	0927	0931	0948	...	0948	1029	1041	1118	...	1200	...
Auray d.	...	...	0609	0634	0634	...	...	...	0739	...	0813	...	...	|	|	|	1008	...	1008	1050	1059	1139	...	|	...
Vannes d.	0604	...	0623	0646	0646	0703	...	...	0751	0757	0827	...	...	0910	0955	0957	1022	...	1023	1103	1113	1152	1158	1228	...
Redon d.	0634	0647	0651	0721	0727	0733	0747	...	0821	0827	|	0847	0932	|	1023	1025	1049	...	1051	1133	|	1221	1228	|	1247
Savenay 288 d.	|	0719	|	|	0752	|	0821	...	|	|	|	0921	1005	|	|	|	|	...	|	|	|	|	|	|	1321
Nantes 288 a.	|	0744	|	|	0816	|	0844	...	|	|	|	0944	1039	|	1105	1108	|	...	|	1216	|	|	|	|	1344
Rennes a.	0721	...	0725	0756	...	0817	...	...	0856	0917	0925	...	...	1008	...	...	1125	...	1125	...	1211	1256	1316	1325	...
Rennes d.	...	...	0735	...	...	...	...	...	...	...	0935	...	...	1014	...	...	1135	...	1135	...	1217	...	...	1335	...
Paris Montparnasse a.	...	...	0909	...	...	...	...	...	...	...	1107	...	...	1144	...	...	1315	...	1315	...	1349	...	...	1505	...

	Ⓐ	Ⓐ	†	⑤	⑥	⑥	*TGV* **8722** ⊡		†	⑤	⑥	†	*TGV* **8724** ①–④	*TGV* **8724** ⑥	†	⑥	†		Ⓐ	*TGV* **8730**	†	Ⓐ	Ⓐ	Ⓐ	Ⓒ
Quimper d.	1202	1202	1205	...	1236	...	1312	...	1336	1352	...	...	1407	1411	...	...	1504	...	...	1512	...	...	1557	...	1611
Quimperlé d.	1229	1229	1232	...	1303	...	|	...	1403	1419	...	...	|	|	...	...	1531	...	...	1541	...	...	1624	...	1638
Lorient d.	1243	1243	1246	...	1316	...	1348	...	1416	1432	...	...	1444	1447	...	...	1544	...	...	1555	...	...	1637	...	1652
Auray d.	1304	1304	1306	...	1337	...	1408	...	1437	1454	...	...	1504	1505	...	...	1605	...	...	1615	...	...	1658	...	1711
Vannes d.	1316	1316	1319	1340	1349	1401	1424	...	1449	1506	...	...	1518	1518	1556	1603	1617	...	...	1629	1657	1658	1710	...	1723
Redon d.	1349	1357	1350	1405	1420	1432	1451	...	1523	1536	1547	1550	|	|	1627	1634	1646	...	1647	|	1727	1728	1741	1747	1750
Savenay 288 d.	|	1423	|	|	|	|	|	...	|	|	1621	1619	|	|	|	|	1711	...	1721	|	|	|	|	1821	|
Nantes 288 a.	|	1446	|	|	1504	|	|	...	1605	|	1644	1644	|	|	|	|	1733	...	1744	|	|	|	|	1844	|
Rennes a.	1425	...	1425	1439	...	1521	1525	...	...	1610	...	...	|	|	1717	1717	...	...	...	1725	1817	1813	1817	...	1825
Rennes d.	...	...	...	...	...	...	1535	...	...	...	...	...	|	|	...	...	...	...	...	1735	...	...	...	...	...
Paris Montparnasse a.	...	...	...	...	...	...	1703	...	...	...	...	...	1744	1744	...	...	...	...	...	1904	...	...	...	...	...

	Ⓒ	*TGV* **8732** ⑦	Ⓑ	⑥		Ⓑ	⑤	*Ouigo* **7616** ⊠	† Q		⑥	⑥	*TGV* **8742** ⑦	Ⓐ	Ⓐ		Ⓐ	†	†	*TGV* **8744** ⑦		*TGV* **8746** ①–⑥	*TGV* **8794** ⑦	⑤	*TGV* **8752** ⑦
Quimper d.	...	1656	...	...	...	...	1716	1739	...	...	1755	1755	1802	...	1835	...	1835	1839	1839	1906	...	1916	...	2005	2019
Quimperlé d.	...	|	...	...	...	...	1743	|	...	...	1822	1822	1832	...	1901	...	1901	1906	1906	|	...	|	...	2033	|
Lorient d.	...	1731	...	...	...	...	1757	1815	...	...	1835	1835	1847	...	1914	...	1914	1919	1919	1943	...	1953	2029	2046	2055
Auray d.	...	|	...	...	...	...	1815	1834	1842	...	1856	1856	1906	...	1934	...	1934	1940	1940	2001	...	2011	2047	2107	2113
Vannes d.	...	1757	1803	1810	...	...	1827	1847	1854	...	1908	1908	1919	...	1946	...	1946	1952	1952	2014	...	2024	2101	2119	2126
Redon d.	1800	|	1833	1843	...	1847	1853	|	1923	...	1941	1947	1946	1949	2021	...	2027	2025	2032	|	...	2051	|	2149	|
Savenay 288 d.	1833	|	|	|	...	1919	|	|	|	...	|	2012	|	2021	|	...	2053	|	2107	|	...	|	|	|	|
Nantes 288 a.	1855	|	|	|	...	1946	|	|	|	...	|	2040	|	2044	|	...	2116	|	2141	|	...	|	|	|	|
Rennes a.	...	|	1917	1925	...	...	1927	1944	2001	...	2017	...	|	...	2056	...	...	2101	...	|	...	2125	|	2223	2225
Rennes d.	...	|	...	...	...	...	...	1948	...	...	...	...	|	...	...	...	...	...	...	|	...	2135	|	...	2235
Paris Montparnasse a.	...	2020	...	...	...	...	...	2149	...	...	...	...	2205	...	...	...	...	...	...	2242	...	2304	2328	...	0004

C – Daily until Aug. 8; Ⓑ from Aug. 10.
D – ⑥–④ until Aug. 7; ⑦–④ from Aug. 10.
Q – 2 Rennes - Quiberon and v.v.
R – 2 Nantes - Brest and v.v.
e – Until Aug. 2.
⊡ – ①②③④⑥.
⊠ – OUIGO low-cost TGV service. Internet booking only (www.ouigo.com).
TGV – High-speed train. R. 🍸.

AURAY - QUIBERON. *28 km.* Journey 50–55 minutes.

From Auray at 0830, 1017, 1115⚒, 1116†**Q**, 1205, 1407, 1504, 1614, 1736Ⓐ, 1802Ⓒ, 1835Ⓐ, 1857Ⓒ, 1949Ⓐ, 2003Ⓒ.

From Quiberon at 0920, 1112, 1309, 1357, 1500, 1604, 1726Ⓐ, 1752⑥, 1752†**Q**, 1831Ⓐ, 1853Ⓒ, 1939Ⓐ, 1959Ⓒ, 2122.

BREST - QUIMPER 286

km		Ⓐ	A	Ⓐ		Ⓐ	⑥	†		Ⓐ	†	⑥		⑥		†	Ⓐ	⑥		Ⓐ	†	⑥		Ⓐ	Ⓐ	†
0	**Brest** 284 d.	0636	0750	0838	...	1000	1056	1153	...	1237	1336	1344	...	1432	...	1535	1626	1629	...	1735	1751	1757	...	1841	1944	2002
18	Landerneau 284 d.	0647	|	0850	...	1012	1108	1250	...	1249	1348	1356	...	1444	...	1547	1640	1642	...	1748	1803	1809	...	1853	1956	2014
72	Châteaulin d.	0732	|	0933	...	1050	1146	1243	...	1333	1431	1434	...	1528	...	1629	1726	1726	...	1833	1841	1847	...	1938	2045	2052
102	**Quimper** a.	0752	0853	0954	...	1111	1207	1304	...	1354	1452	1454	...	1549	...	1650	1747	1747	...	1853	1901	1908	...	1958	2106	2113

	Ⓐ	Ⓐ	⑥	Ⓐ		⑥	†	Ⓐ	⑥		Ⓐ	†	⑥	†	†		⑥	Ⓐ	Ⓐ	Ⓐ		⑥ A	† A	Ⓐ A	†
Quimper d.	0608	0709	0805	0910	...	1000	1031	1209	1220	...	1310	1408	1505	1606	1702	...	1703	1703	1810	1915	...	1915	1917	2022	2135
Châteaulin d.	0629	0734	0835	0931	...	1021	1052	1230	1240	...	1335	1429	1526	1627	1722	...	1724	1724	1831	1936	...	|	|	|	2156
Landerneau 284 d.	0710	0823	0913	1005	...	1100	1130	1311	1319	...	1415	1508	1605	1705	1800	...	1802	1811	1916	2018	...	|	|	|	2234
Brest 284 a.	0723	0835	0925	1017	...	1112	1142	1324	1331	...	1427	1520	1617	1717	1813	...	1814	1823	1928	2031	...	2018	2020	2124	2246

A – To/from Nantes (Table **285**).

RENNES - NANTES 287

Other journeys Rennes - Nantes and v.v. are possible by changing trains at Redon (see both directions of Table **285**).

km		Ⓐ	Ⓐ	Ⓐ	Ⓐ	Ⓐ		⑥	⑥	Ⓐ	Ⓒ	Ⓐ			Ⓐ	①–④	⑤	†	†	Ⓐ		Ⓐ	Ⓒ	Ⓐ	Ⓐ	†
0	**Rennes** 280a d.	0556	0629	0652	0656	0744	...	0800	0856	0905	1056	1056	1156	...	1256	1456	1456	1555	1648	1656	...	1700	1756	1800	1856	1920
38	Vitré 280a d.	0617	0653	0717	0726	0814	...	0830	0917	0927	1117	1117	1226	...	1317	1517	1517	1617	1717	1717	...	1730	1817	1830	1917	1941
73	Laval 280a d.	0636	0720	0736	0751	0839	...	0855	0937	0947	1137	1137	1251	...	1337	1537	1537	1637	1741	1736	...	1755	1837	1855	1936	2001
126	Sablé sur Sarthe a.	0700	...	0800	...	...	...	...	1000	1010	1200	1200	...	...	1400	1600	1559	1704	...	1800	...	...	1900	...	2002	2021
126	Sablé sur Sarthe 280a d.	0711	...	0811	...	...	...	...	1006	1011	1206	1210	...	...	1406	1608	1612	1706	...	1811	...	...	1906	...	2014	2023
174	Angers St Laud 280a d.	0733	...	0836	...	...	...	...	1033	1035	1232	1233	...	...	1430	1634	1638	1730	...	1835	...	...	1933	...	2036	2049
262	**Nantes** 280a a.	0815	...	0917	...	...	...	...	1115	1115	1315	1315	...	...	1515	1715	1720	1815	...	1916	...	...	2015	...	2117	2132

	Ⓐ	Ⓐ	Ⓐ	Ⓐ	Ⓐ		⑥	Ⓐ	⑥	Ⓐ	Ⓒ			Ⓐ	Ⓐ	⑤	Ⓐ	†	Ⓐ		Ⓒ	Ⓐ	Ⓒ	Ⓐ	Ⓑ
Nantes 280a d.	...	0544	...	...	0644	...	...	0744	0844	0944	1044	...	...	1144	1344	...	1544	1544	...	...	...	...	1744	1744	1944
Angers St Laud 280a d.	...	0628	...	...	0728	...	...	0832	0927	1028	1127	...	...	1228	1428	...	1628	1627	...	...	...	...	1829	1828	2028
Sablé sur Sarthe 280a a.	...	0649	...	...	0749	...	...	0853	0949	1049	1149	...	...	1249	1449	...	1649	1649	...	...	...	...	1850	1849	2049
Sablé sur Sarthe d.	...	0655	...	...	0809	...	...	...	0957	1057	1157	...	...	1257	1457	...	1657	1657	...	...	...	...	1857	1901	2057
Laval 280a d.	0636	0719	0724	0802	0832	...	0906	...	1020	1120	1222	1302	...	1320	1520	1619	1720	1720	1730	...	1804	1906	1920	1924	2120
Vitré 280a d.	0701	0740	0747	0827	0852	...	0931	...	1040	1140	1242	1327	...	1339	1540	1638	1740	1740	1757	...	1830	1931	1940	1943	2140
Rennes 280a a.	0731	0801	0819	0857	0912	...	1001	...	1101	1201	1301	1357	...	1401	1601	1711	1801	1801	1829	...	1859	2001	2001	2005	2201

NON-STOP TRAINS VIA SAVENAY

km		Ⓐ		⚒		Ⓒ		⚒		Ⓐ		†		⑥		Ⓐ		†								
0	**Rennes** d.	0735	...	0835	...	1035	...	1235	...	1335	...	1435	...	1635	...	1731	...	1745	...	1835	...	1935	...	...	...	...
145	**Nantes** a.	0852	...	0952	...	1152	...	1352	...	1452	...	1552	...	1752	...	1852	...	1900	...	1954	...	2052	...	...	...	...

	Ⓐ		⑥		Ⓒ		⚒		†		Ⓐ		⑥		Ⓐ				Ⓑ		⚒		†		
Nantes d.	0705	...	0805	...	1005	...	1205	...	1305	...	1405	...	1509	...	1605	...	1705	...	1802	...	1905	...	2005	...	...
Rennes a.	0821	...	0821	...	1121	...	1321	...	1421	...	1521	...	1625	...	1721	...	1821	...	1921	...	2023	...	2121	...	...

NANTES - ST NAZAIRE - LE CROISIC 288

TGV timings may vary by a few minutes - please check your reservation. For *TGV* exception and additional running dates see Table **280**.

km		Ⓐ	Ⓐ	Ⓐ	⑥	Ⓐ		Ⓐ	*TGV* **8911** ①–⑥	†	⑥	Ⓒ	Ⓐ		Ⓒ	*TGV* **8913**	Ⓐ	*TGV* **8917** ⑥	Ⓐ	†		Ⓒ	*TGV* **8921** ①–④	*TGV* **8921** ⑤–⑦	Ⓐ	Ⓐ
	Paris Montparnasse d.	...	...	...	...	...	...	...	0626	...	...	...	...	...	...	0939	...	1039	...	...	...	...	1215	1252	...	...
	Nantes a.	...	...	...	...	...	...	...	0854	...	...	...	...	...	...	1154	...	1254	...	...	...	...	1420	1454	...	...
0	**Nantes** 285 d.	0631	0709	0734	0746	0809	...	0834	0900	0900	0908	1010	1015	...	1109	1200	1234	1300	1309	1310	...	1412	1426	1500	1504	1636
39	Savenay 285 d.	0657	0731	0800	0820	0830	...	0900	|	0922	0930	1037	1038	...	1130	|	1300	|	1330	1332	...	1434	|	|	1526	1702
64	**St Nazaire** d.	0720	0747	0823	0844	0847	...	0923	0937	0937	0952	1055	1056	...	1146	1236	1323	1337	1346	1348	...	1449	1506	1536	1548	1725
79	Pornichet d.	...	0759	...	0856	0859	...	...	0949	0949	1006	1110	1113	...	1159	|	...	1350	1359	1400	...	1501	|	|	1600	...
83	La Baule Escoublac d.	...	0808	...	0906	0908	...	...	0957	0958	1014	1121	1121	...	1208	1253	...	1400	1408	1407	...	1510	1525	1554	1607	...
90	**Le Croisic** a.	...	0821	...	0919	0921	...	...	1009	1011	1026	1138	1133	...	1221	1303	...	1412	1421	1421	...	1523	1534	1603	1620	...

	TGV **8923**	Ⓐ	Ⓐ	†		⑥	Ⓐ	Ⓐ	⑥		⑦–④	⑤	⑤	①–④	*TGV* **8905** ⑦–④		*TGV* **8927** ⑤	⑤⑥	*TGV* **8931**	⑤		*TGV* **8935** ⑤	⑥–④	*TGV* **8937** ⑤	*TGV* **8939** ⑤
Paris Montparnasse d.	1452	...	...	...	...	...	...	...	...	...	...	...	...	...	1751	...	1751	...	1852	...	...	1939	...	2052	2152
Nantes a.	1654	...	...	...	...	...	...	...	...	...	...	...	...	...	1954	...	1954	...	2059	...	...	2154	...	2254	2354
Nantes 285 d.	1700	1709	1734	1756	...	1806	1806	1838	1846	...	1909	1918	1923	1940	2000	...	2000	2009	2105	2134	...	2205	2213	2300	2359
Savenay 285 d.	|	1730	1800	1821	...	1828	1830	1904	1920	...	1930	1945	1957	2006	|	...	|	2031	|	2203	...	|	2239	|	|
St Nazaire d.	1736	1746	1823	1843	...	1844	1846	1927	1945	...	1946	2010	2018	2029	2034	...	2037	2047	2141	2219	...	2242	2255	2341	0037
Pornichet d.	1748	1759	...	1855	...	1856	1859	...	1958	...	1959	2021	...	...	...	...	2050	2101	|	2230	...	2254	2306	|	0054
La Baule Escoublac d.	1757	1808	...	1915	...	1906	1908	...	2006	...	2008	2028	...	...	...	...	2058	2109	2159	2237	...	2302	2312	2358	|
Le Croisic a.	1809	1821	...	1928	...	1918	1921	...	2019	...	2021	2041	...	...	...	...	2110	2122	2209	2249	...	2315	2325	0006	0103

	TGV **8900** Ⓐ	⚒	*TGV* **8910** ①	Ⓐ	Ⓐ	Ⓐ	Ⓒ		Ⓐ	*TGV* **8912** ②–⑥	Ⓐ	Ⓐ	†	⑥	*TGV* **8916** ⑥	*TGV* **8916** ①⑤	Ⓒ		Ⓐ	Ⓐ	Ⓐ	*TGV* **8922** ⑥	*TGV* **8922** ⑦	①–④	⑤
Le Croisic d.	...	0536	0555	...	0638	...	0726	...	0738	0754	...	0838	0928	0943	1046	1050	1154	...	...	1238	...	1348	1353	1434	1438
La Baule Escoublac d.	...	0549	0606	...	0651	...	0746	...	0751	0807	...	0851	0941	0956	1103	1107	1209	...	...	1251	...	1402	1407	1447	1451
Pornichet d.	...	0556	|	...	0658	...	0758	...	0758	|	...	0858	0949	1004	1110	1114	1216	...	...	1258	...	|	|	1454	1458
St Nazaire d.	0524	0608	0623	0634	0710	0734	0811	...	0810	0824	0836	0909	1000	1015	1124	1126	1230	...	1236	1310	1334	1419	1424	1510	1510
Savenay 285 d.	|	0622	|	0658	0724	0758	0828	...	0824	|	0900	0924	1016	1030	|	|	1254	...	1300	1324	1358	|	|	1524	1524
Nantes 285 a.	0558	0646	0659	0724	0748	0824	0851	...	0848	0858	0926	0948	1043	1052	1159	1201	1328	...	1326	1348	1424	1453	1458	1548	1548
Nantes d.	0604	...	0705	...	...	...	...	...	...	0904	...	...	...	...	1209	1209	...	...	...	...	...	1504	1504	...	...
Paris Montparnasse a.	0808	...	0913	...	...	...	...	...	...	1122	...	...	...	...	1410	1410	...	...	...	...	...	1722	1722	...	...

	Ⓑ	Ⓐ	Ⓐ	*TGV* **8926** ⑥⑦	Ⓐ	⑥	†		*TGV* **8928** ⑦	Ⓐ	†	⑥	Ⓐ	*TGV* **8930** ⑦	*TGV* **8932** ①–⑥	†	Ⓐ		Ⓒ	†	⑤	⑥	*TGV* **8934** ⑦	⑥	*TGV* **8936** ⑦
Le Croisic d.	1538	...	1638	1653	...	1705	1725	...	1746	...	1812	1823	1838	1849	1855	1859	1938	...	1951	2037	...	2037	2049	2132	2144
La Baule Escoublac d.	1551	...	1651	1707	...	1718	1738	...	1800	...	1824	1835	1851	1904	1907	1917	1951	...	2007	2050	...	2050	2106	2144	2156
Pornichet d.	1559	...	1658	|	...	1725	1747	...	|	...	1831	1855	1858	1911	|	1929	1958	...	2015	2057	...	2100	2113	2153	|
St Nazaire d.	1611	1634	1710	1724	1737	1737	1800	...	1816	1836	1842	1909	1912	1924	1924	1945	2010	...	2027	2109	2109	2112	2126	2205	2212
Savenay 285 d.	1626	1658	1724	|	1801	1800	1814	...	|	1900	1902	1925	1926	|	|	2002	2024	...	2042	2124	2124	2126	|	2219	|
Nantes 285 a.	1648	1724	1748	1758	1828	1833	1836	...	1851	1930	1936	1948	1950	1958	1958	2025	2048	...	2106	2147	2158	2148	2201	2240	2246
Nantes d.	...	...	...	1804	...	...	...	...	1857	...	...	...	...	2004	2004	...	...	...	...	...	...	...	2207	...	2252
Paris Montparnasse a.	...	...	...	2027	...	...	...	...	2108	...	...	...	...	2222	2222	...	...	...	...	...	...	...	0008	...	0049

TGV – High-speed train. 🅁. 🍷.

289 NANTES - ANGERS - TOURS

For additional trains Nantes - Angers St Laud and v.v. see Tables **280a, 287** and **290**.

km																									
			Ⓐ	Ⓐ	Ⓐ	Ⓐ	Ⓐ	Ⓐ	Ⓐ	Ⓐ	Ⓐ	Ⓐ	Ⓐ	Ⓐ	Ⓐ	Ⓐ	Ⓐ	⑤	Ⓐ	Ⓐ	Ⓐ	Ⓐ	Ⓐ	Ⓐ	Ⓐ
								A						**A**											**A**
0	**Nantes** d.	Ⓐ	...	...	0544	...	...	0712	0744	...	0912	0944	...	1112	1144	...	1417	...	...	1612	1643	...	...	1712	1812
88	Angers St Laud d.		...	...	0626	0635	...	0757	0828	0836	0957	1026	1035	1156	1226	1239	1519	1536	1536	1656	1725	1635	...	1756	1857
132	Saumur Rive Droit d.		0605	0640	...	0711	0800	0818	...	0915	1021	...	1109	1217	...	1313	...	1611	1611	1721	...	1711	1803	1820	1918
199	**Tours** a.		0658	0732	...	0753	0841	0851	...	...	1054	...	1202	1249	...	1403	...	1700	...	1801	...	...	1845	1901	1951
			⑥	†	⑥	⑥	⑥	Ⓒ	Ⓒ	Ⓒ	Ⓒ	†	†	⑥	†	†	†	⑥	†	Ⓒ	†	†	⑥	†	†
									B														**B**	**B**	
	Nantes d.	Ⓒ	...	...	...	...	0844	...	0908	1144	...	...	...	...	1544	...	...	1603	1643	...	...	1912	2019	2035	2213
	Angers St Laud d.		...	...	...	0736	0925	0935	0957	1226	1239	1358	...	...	1625	1635	...	1710	1725	1735	...	1959	2108	2126	2258
	Saumur Rive Droit d.		0642	0800	0801	0811	...	1011	1020	...	1313	1434	1630	1643	...	1711	1803	...	...	1811	1911	2021	2131	2149	2319
	Tours a.		0732	0841	0842	...	...	...	1052	...	1403	...	1723	1727	...	...	1901	...	...	1855	1953	2100	2204	2223	2352
			Ⓐ	Ⓐ	Ⓐ	Ⓐ	Ⓐ	Ⓐ	Ⓐ	Ⓐ	Ⓐ	Ⓐ	Ⓐ	Ⓐ	⑤	Ⓐ	Ⓐ	Ⓐ	Ⓐ	Ⓐ	Ⓐ	Ⓐ	Ⓐ	Ⓐ	⑤
								A			**A**									**C**					
	Tours d.	Ⓐ	...	0615	0652	...	...	0808	0900	...	1237	1242	...	1400	1440	1559	...	...	1738	1807	1832	...	2004	2110	2110
	Saumur Rive Droit d.		0620	0654	0732	0749	...	0840	0941	...	1309	1347	...	1442	1537	1639	1648	...	1846	1839	1921	...	2045	2149	2150
	Angers St Laud d.		0703	...	0801	0824	0836	0904	1016	1035	1334	1424	1430	...	1603	1702	1724	1743	1923	1903	1956	2036	...	...	2224
	Nantes a.		0746	...	0843	...	0917	0950	...	1115	1415	...	1515	...	1646	1746	...	1838	...	1946	...	2117	...	...	...
			Ⓒ	Ⓒ	Ⓒ		†	†	⑥		⑥	†	†		⑥	Ⓒ	⑥		⑥	†	†		†	⑥	†
			B													**D**	**B**				**A**				
	Tours d.	Ⓒ	0809	...	...	...	...	...	1242	...	1400	1400	1455	...	1459	1554	1807	...	1832	1845	1908	...	2001	2110	2230
	Saumur Rive Droit d.		0844	1043	...	...	1148	...	1347	...	1442	1447	1539	...	1540	1636	1839	...	1921	1946	1941	...	2045	2149	2309
	Angers St Laud d.		0909	1119	1135	...	1224	1232	1424	...	...	...	1603	...	1604	1701	1903	...	1956	2024	2004	...	...	...	...
	Nantes a.		0952	...	1241	...	...	1315	...	...	...	...	1649	...	1649	1745	1946	...	...	...	2046	...	...	...	...

A – Nantes - Orléans and v.v. **B** – Le Croisic - Orléans and v.v. **C** – Orléans - Nantes (- Le Croisic ⑤). **D** – Tours - Le Croisic.

290 NANTES and TOURS - BOURGES - NEVERS - MOULINS - LYON

Trains with numbers are classified *INTERCITÉS* - timings may vary by a few minutes. See Table **335** for *TGV* trains Nantes / Tours - Le Mans / St Pierre des Corps - Lyon and v.v.

km																								
								4402				**4404**			**4406**									
		⚒	Ⓐ	Ⓐ		⚒				†						Ⓑ	†	⑥		⑦–④	⑤		⚒	†
0	**Nantes** 280 289 d.	...	...	...	...	...	...	0626	...	...	...	1148	...	...	1447	...	...	...	...	...	...	...	...	...
88	Angers St Laud 280 289 d.	...	...	...	...	...	...	0711	...	...	...	1233	...	...	1531	...	...	...	...	...	...	...	...	...
132	Saumur Rive Droit 289 d.	...	...	...	...	...	...	0735	...	...	...	1255	...	...	1554	...	...	...	...	...	...	...	...	...
**	**Tours** 289 d.	...	...	0628	...	0654	...	|	0929	...	1205	|	...	1414	|	1729	...	1754	...	1829	1829	1929	2053	2053
202	St Pierre des Corps d.	...	...	0636	...	0701	...	0813	0936	...	1212	1334	...	1421	1635	1736	...	1801	...	1836	1836	1936	2100	2100
231	Chenonceaux d.	...	...	0656	...	0722	...	|	0956	...	1232	|	...	1441	|	1756	...	1821	...	1855	1855	1956	2127	2127
257	St Aignan Noyers d.	...	...	0714	...	0740	...	|	1013	...	1250	|	...	1458	|	1813	...	1838	...	1912	1912	2014	2145	2145
312	Vierzon Ville 315 d.	...	...	0752	...	0823	...	0917	1053	...	1331	1437	...	1538	1740	1852	...	1919	...	1954	1954	2058	2223	2225
344	**Bourges** 315 a.	...	...	...	...	0841	...	0934	1110	...	1349	1454	...	1554	1757	...	...	1938	...	2013	2013	2116	...	2245
344	**Bourges** 315 d.	...	...	...	...	0843	...	0936	...	...	1351	1456	...	1556	1759	...	...	1940	...	2015	2023	2118	...	...
413	**Nevers** 315 a.	...	...	...	...	0925	...	1013	...	...	1430	1534	...	1635	1836	...	...	2019	...	2104	2112	2159	...	...
413	**Nevers** 330 d.	...	0529	...	0831	...	...	1028	...	1232	1440	1549	...	...	1851	...	...	...	...	...	...	...	...	...
473	**Moulins-sur-Allier** 330 373 d.	...	0604	...	0906	...	...	1057	...	1310	1508	1618	...	...	1920	...	...	...	...	...	...	...	...	...
	Digoin 373 d.	...	0647	...	0950	...	...	|	...	1353	1552	|	...	...	|	...	...	...	...	...	...	...	...	...
	Paray le Monial 373 d.	0535	0702	...	1009	...	...	|	...	1406	1606	|	...	...	|	...	2009	...	...	...	...	...	...	...
514	St Germain des Fossés d.	|	|	...	|	...	...	1119	...	...	|	1640	...	...	1942	...	|	...	...	...	...	...	...	...
580	Roanne 328 d.	|	|	...	|	...	...	1200	...	...	|	1722	...	...	2022	...	|	...	...	...	...	...	...	...
673	**Lyon** Part Dieu 328 a.	0722	|	...	1152	...	...	1304	...	...	1752	1826	...	...	2126	...	2152	...	...	...	...	...	...	...
678	**Lyon** Perrache 328 a.	0733	0850	...	1203	...	...	1316	...	...	1803	1838	...	...	2140	...	2206	...	...	...	...	...	...	...

km																								
											4502		**4504**				**4506**	**4506**						
		②–⑤	①	Ⓐ	Ⓐ	†	⑥	Ⓒ	⚒	Ⓒ		⑤		Ⓐ	Ⓒ	Ⓐ			Ⓐ	Ⓐ	†	Ⓒ	Ⓐ	Ⓐ
																	d	**e**						
0	**Lyon** Perrache 328 d.	...	...	...	...	...	...	...	...	0805	0920	...	1151	...	...	1325	1453	1453	...	1658	...	1808	1808	1941
5	**Lyon** Part Dieu 328 d.	...	...	...	...	...	...	...	...	0815	0934	...	1204	...	...	1338	1504	1504	...	|	...	1822	1822	2000
	Roanne 328 d.	...	...	...	...	...	...	...	...	|	1041	...	1312	...	...	|	1613	1613	...	|	...	|	|	|
	St Germain des Fossés d.	...	...	...	...	...	...	...	...	|	1121	...	1352	...	...	|	1656	1653	...	|	...	|	|	|
129	Paray le Monial 373 d.	...	...	...	...	...	...	...	...	0957	|	...	|	...	...	1518	|	|	...	1849	...	2006	2014	2144
140	Digoin 373 d.	...	...	...	...	...	...	...	...	1011	|	...	|	...	...	1531	|	|	...	...	...	2019	2027	2157
196	**Moulins-sur-Allier** 330 373 d.	...	...	...	...	...	...	...	...	1104	1142	...	1414	...	...	1629	1717	1714	...	...	...	2113	2121	2249
256	**Nevers** 330 a.	...	...	...	...	...	...	...	...	1134	1211	...	1443	...	...	1700	1746	1744	...	...	...	2152	2207	2325
256	**Nevers** 315 d.	...	...	0511	0553	0649	0700	0954	...	1144	1221	...	1453	1553	1653	1715	1812	1754	...	...	1904	...	...	...
325	**Bourges** 315 a.	...	...	0603	0646	0743	0751	1046	...	1236	1309	...	1544	1646	1746	1809	1903	1903	...	...	1957	...	...	...
325	**Bourges** 315 d.	...	0514	0605	0648	0745	0753	1048	1148	1238	1311	1425	1546	1647	1748	1811	1905	1905	...	...	1959	...	...	...
357	Vierzon Ville 315 d.	0531	0533	0624	0708	0805	0811	1108	1208	1258	1330	1450	1605	1706	1808	1831	1924	1924	2008	...	2018	...	...	...
412	St Aignan Noyers d.	0609	0611	0704	0748	0847	0851	1149	1249	1338	|	1531	|	1747	1848	1923	|	|	2049	...	2058	...	...	...
438	Chenonceaux d.	0631	0632	0723	0805	0905	0908	1208	1306	1357	|	1552	|	1805	1905	1946	|	|	2106	...	2116	...	...	...
467	St Pierre des Corps d.	0701	0701	0744	0826	0927	0929	1231	1327	1419	1434	1615	1713	1829	1926	2008	2029	2029	2127	...	2137	...	...	...
**	**Tours** 289 a.	0707	0707	0749	0831	0932	0934	1236	1332	1424	|	1620	|	1835	1931	2013	|	|	2132	...	2142	...	...	...
537	Saumur Rive Droit 289 d.	...	...	...	...	...	...	...	...	...	1507	...	1747	...	...	...	2101	2101	...	...	...	...	...	...
581	Angers St Laud 280 289 d.	...	...	...	...	...	...	...	...	...	1530	...	1810	...	...	...	2124	2124	...	...	...	...	...	...
669	**Nantes** 280 289 a.	...	...	...	...	...	...	...	...	...	1612	...	1852	...	...	...	2205	2205	...	...	...	...	...	...

ADDITIONAL TRAINS TOURS - CHENONCEAUX - ST AIGNAN NOYERS

km		†	⑥	Ⓐ	⑥	Ⓐ	†			
0	**Tours** d.	1453	1454	1754	1854	1854	1854	...	...	...
3	St Pierre des Corps d.	1500	1501	1801	1901	1901	1901	...	...	...
32	Chenonceaux d.	1529	1527	1829	1927	1930	1930	...	...	...
58	**St Aignan Noyers** a.	1552	1549	1852	1949	1953	1954	...	...	...

	⑥	⑥	†	Ⓐ	⑥	Ⓐ	†		
St Aignan Noyers d.	0636	1607	1607	1907	2007	2007	2007	...	...
Chenonceaux d.	0658	1629	1631	1930	2029	2030	2031	...	...
St Pierre des Corps d.	0725	1657	1701	2001	2057	2100	2101	...	...
Tours a.	0730	1702	1706	2007	2102	2106	2106	...	...

d – Until July 18 **e** – From July 19. ** – Tours - St Pierre des Corps is *3 km*.

291 ROANNE - ST ÉTIENNE

km																								
		Ⓐ	⚒		⚒	Ⓐ		Ⓒ	Ⓐ		⚒	Ⓐ			Ⓑ		⑤	Ⓐ			†			
0	**Roanne** d.	0523	0617	...	0726	0826	...	0856	0956	...	1053	1226	...	1356	1556	...	1656	1726	...	1824	1924	...	...	...
80	**St Étienne** Châteaucreux a.	0633	0728	...	0836	0936	...	1006	1106	...	1203	1336	...	1506	1706	...	1806	1836	...	1936	2036	...	...	...
		⚒	⚒		†	Ⓐ		⑥	Ⓐ					Ⓐ			Ⓐ	Ⓐ		Ⓐ			†	
	St Étienne Châteaucreux d.	0625	0724	...	0824	0854	...	0954	1124	...	1224	1454	...	1556	1654	...	1724	1754	...	1854	1956	...	2054	...
	Roanne a.	0735	0834	...	0934	1004	...	1104	1234	...	1334	1604	...	1706	1804	...	1834	1904	...	2004	2106	...	2204	...

NANTES - LA ROCHELLE - BORDEAUX 292

Trains with numbers are classified *INTERCITÉS*.

km		Ⓐ	⑥	Ⓐ		Ⓐ	Ⓐ	†		⑥	Ⓐ	Ⓐ	Ⓐ		⚒	**3831**				Ⓐ	**3833**		⑤	Ⓒ	Ⓐ	
0	**Nantes** 293 d.	...	...	...	...	...	...	...	...	...	...	...	...	...	...	0738	...	...	0955	...	1147	...	...	...	...	...
77	La Roche sur Yon 293 d.	...	...	...	...	...	...	...	...	...	...	...	...	...	...	0819	...	...	1036	...	1228	...	...	...	...	...
113	Luçon d.	...	...	...	...	...	...	...	...	...	...	...	...	...	...	0843	...	...	1100	...	1252	...	...	...	...	...
	La Rochelle P Dauphine d.	...	...	...	...	0603	...	...	...	...	0706	...	0758	...	0837	|	...	...	|	1230	|	...	...	...	...	...
180	**La Rochelle** Ville a.	...	...	...	...	0608	...	...	...	...	0711	...	0803	...	0842	0928	...	...	1139	1236	1331	...	...	...	...	...
180	**La Rochelle** Ville d.	...	0527	0528	...	0610	...	0713	...	0713	0715	0739	0805	...	0844	0932	1126	...	...	1238	1335	...	...	1526	...	...
209	Rochefort d.	...	0549	0551	...	0638	...	0736	...	0737	0743	0802	0834	...	0913	0953	1148	...	...	1306	1356	...	...	1548	...	...
253	Saintes d.	0540	0619	0621	...	0715	0723	0807	...	0813	...	0832	0908	...	0948	1025	1218	...	...	1340	1427	...	1523	1618	1619	...
	Angoulême **301** a.	|	|	|	...	0812	|	|	...	|	...	|	...	...	...	|	|	...	...	...	|	...	|	|	|	...
	Jonzac d.	0619	0658	0659	...	...	0802	0845	...	0852	...	0910	...	...	...	1102	1257	...	...	...	1504	...	1602	1657	1658	...
376	**Bordeaux** St Jean a.	0722	0800	0805	...	...	0905	0948	...	0954	...	1012	...	...	...	1156	1400	...	...	...	1558	...	1704	1800	1759	...

	Ⓐ	†	Ⓐ		⑥	Ⓐ	Ⓐ		**3835**	Ⓐ	†	⚒		†	Ⓐ	**3837**		Ⓐ	†	⑥		†	Ⓐ	Ⓐ	
Nantes 293 d.	...	...	...	...	...	...	...	...	1559	...	...	...	...	...	...	1755	...	...	...	...	...	...	1935	...	...
La Roche sur Yon 293 d.	...	...	...	...	...	...	...	...	1642	...	...	...	...	...	...	1836	...	...	...	...	...	...	2028	...	...
Luçon d.	...	...	...	...	...	...	...	...	1707	...	...	...	...	...	...	1900	...	...	...	...	...	...	2109	...	...
La Rochelle Porte Dauphine d.	1526	1559	...	...	1628	1648	1710	...	|	1808	...	1848	...	1859	1909	|	...	...	2014	2019	...	2131	|	2156	...
La Rochelle Ville a.	1531	1604	...	...	1633	1653	1715	...	1746	1813	...	1853	...	1904	1915	1939	...	...	2019	2024	...	2136	2150	2201	...
La Rochelle Ville d.	1533	1606	1626	...	1635	1655	1717	...	1750	1818	1828	1857	...	1906	1917	1943	...	2018	2021	2026	...	2138	...	2203	...
Rochefort d.	1602	1635	1648	...	1704	1724	1746	...	1811	1846	1850	1926	...	1935	1945	2005	...	2047	2050	2055	...	2207	...	2232	...
Saintes d.	...	1724	1721	...	...	1801	...	...	1843	1921	1920	2000	...	...	...	2034	...	2121	2123	...	...	...	...	2306	...
Angoulême **301** a.	...	|	|	...	...	1902	...	...	|	...	|	...	...	...	...	|	...	...	...	...	...	...	...	...	...
Jonzac d.	...	1803	1800	...	...	...	...	...	1920	...	1958	...	...	...	...	2111	...	...	...	...	...	...	...	...	...
Bordeaux St Jean a.	...	1905	1903	...	...	...	...	...	2014	...	2101	...	...	...	...	2206	...	...	...	...	...	...	...	...	...

	Ⓐ	Ⓐ	Ⓐ		Ⓐ	⑥	Ⓐ		Ⓐ	Ⓐ	**3852**	⑥		Ⓐ	†	⑥		**3854**					**3856**	Ⓐ	
Bordeaux St Jean d.	...	...	...	...	...	...	0555	...	...	0655	0754	...	...	...	...	0856	...	0947	...	...	...	1255	1403	...	...
Jonzac d.	...	...	...	...	...	...	0652	...	...	0753	0841	...	...	...	...	0952	...	1033	...	...	...	1352	1449	...	...
Angoulême **301** a.	...	...	...	...	0611	...	|	...	...	|	|	...	...	...	...	|	...	|	...	...	...	|	|	...	...
Saintes d.	...	0547	0633	...	0712	0716	0737	...	...	0839	0925	...	...	1006	1006	1038	...	1117	1227	...	...	1439	1533	...	...
Rochefort d.	...	0621	0708	...	0746	0751	...	...	0815	0907	0956	1029	...	1041	1041	1106	...	1148	1302	...	...	1507	1604	1624	...
La Rochelle Ville a.	...	0648	0737	...	0814	0819	...	...	0843	0930	1015	1057	...	1108	1111	1129	...	1207	1329	...	...	1530	1623	1652	...
La Rochelle Ville d.	0619	0650	0739	...	0816	0821	...	...	0845	...	1019	1059	...	1110	...	...	...	1211	1331	1419	...	...	1627	1654	...
La Rochelle Porte Dauphine a.	|	0656	0745	...	0822	0826	...	...	0851	...	|	1105	...	1116	...	...	...	|	1337	|	...	...	|	1700	...
Luçon d.	0659	...	...	...	...	...	...	...	...	...	1059	...	...	...	...	...	...	1251	...	1500	...	...	1708	...	...
La Roche sur Yon 293 d.	0724	...	...	...	...	...	...	...	...	...	1124	...	...	...	...	...	...	1316	...	1524	...	...	1747	...	...
Nantes 293 a.	0805	...	...	...	...	...	...	...	...	...	1206	...	...	...	...	...	...	1400	...	1606	...	...	1832	...	...

	†	⑥	Ⓐ		Ⓐ	Ⓐ	Ⓐ		⑥	†	Ⓐ	Ⓒ		①–④	⑤	**3858**		†	Ⓐ	Ⓒ		Ⓐ	⑥	Ⓑ	
Bordeaux St Jean d.	...	...	1455	...	...	...	1554	...	1559	1559	...	...	...	1655	1655	1806	...	...	...	1855	...	1855	...	1956	...
Jonzac d.	...	...	1552	...	...	...	1651	...	1655	1655	...	...	...	1752	1751	1852	...	...	...	1951	...	1955	...	2053	...
Angoulême **301** a.	...	...	|	...	...	...	|	...	|	|	1644	...	...	|	|	|	...	...	...	|	...	|	...	|	...
Saintes d.	1631	...	1637	...	1648	...	1735	...	1741	1741	1751	1812	...	1839	1840	1936	...	...	2008	2038	...	2047	...	2140	...
Rochefort d.	1706	1714	...	...	1722	1758	...	...	1810	1810	1826	1848	...	1907	1908	2005	...	2030	2043	2106	...	2115	2133	2208	...
La Rochelle Ville a.	1735	1742	...	...	1749	1826	...	...	1830	1831	1854	1916	...	1929	1930	2024	...	2058	2110	2128	...	2137	2201	2230	...
La Rochelle Ville d.	1737	1744	...	...	1751	1828	...	...	1832	...	1856	1918	...	...	...	2028	...	2100	2112	...	...	...	2203	...	...
La Rochelle Porte Dauphine a.	1742	1750	...	...	1757	1834	...	...	1838	...	1901	1924	...	...	...	|	...	2106	2118	...	...	...	2209	...	...
Luçon d.	...	...	...	...	...	...	...	...	...	...	...	...	...	...	...	2109	...	...	...	...	...	...	...	...	...
La Roche sur Yon 293 d.	...	...	...	...	...	...	...	...	...	...	...	...	...	...	...	2133	...	...	...	...	...	...	...	...	...
Nantes 293 a.	...	...	...	...	...	...	...	...	...	...	...	...	...	...	...	2216	...	...	...	...	...	...	...	...	...

NANTES - LES SABLES D'OLONNE 293

TGV timings may vary by a few minutes - please check your reservation. For *TGV* exception and additional running dates see Table **280**.

km		Ⓐ	Ⓐ			Ⓒ	A		*TGV* **8973**	Ⓐ		Ⓒ	⑤		*TGV* **8977** ⑤–⑦	①–④		Ⓐ	†		⚒	⑤–⑦	*TGV* **8985** Ⓑ		*TGV* **8985** ⑥	⑤†
	Paris Montparnasse d.	...	...	...	...	...	...	...	0939	...	...	...	...	...	1330	...	...	...	...	...	...	...	1852	...	1852	...
	Nantes a.	...	...	...	...	...	...	...	1154	...	...	...	...	...	1551	...	...	...	...	...	...	...	2059	...	2059	...
0	**Nantes** 292 d.	0634	0743	...	0935	1035	1108	...	1205	1305	...	1308	1428	...	1606	1635	...	1735	1808	...	1908	2008	2110	...	2110	2213
77	La Roche sur Yon 292 d.	0728	0839	...	1028	1127	1202	...	1249	1358	...	1401	1515	...	1653	1734	...	1828	1902	...	2002	2101	2153	...	2203	2306
114	**Les Sables d'Olonne** a.	0800	0909	...	1101	1153	1233	...	1314	1430	...	1431	1540	...	1718	1811	...	1903	1934	...	2032	2129	2219	...	2228	2335

	①	Ⓐ	Ⓐ	Ⓒ	Ⓐ	*TGV* **8972**	⑥		Ⓐ		Ⓐ	Ⓒ	*TGV* **8984** ①–⑥	Ⓐ	①–④	†	⑤		*TGV* **8986** ⑥	†	Ⓐ	⚒	*TGV* **8988** ⑦	†	⑥
Les Sables d'Olonne d.	0526	0621	0728	0730	0809	0944	1030	...	1033	1201	1359	1402	1544	1601	1701	1724	1724	...	1744	1828	1831	1928	1944	2028	2136
La Roche sur Yon 292 d.	0554	0700	0759	0801	0838	1011	1102	...	1104	1235	1433	1433	1610	1633	1732	1755	1755	...	1811	1859	1901	1959	2011	2059	2202
Nantes 292 a.	0649	0758	0854	0854	0930	1054	1154	...	1157	1326	1525	1525	1657	1725	1828	1847	1850	...	1856	1954	1954	2054	2053	2154	2247
Nantes d.	...	...	...	...	...	1104	...	...	...	...	...	...	1708	...	...	...	...	...	1907	...	...	...	2104	...	...
Paris Montparnasse a.	...	...	...	...	...	1322	...	...	...	...	...	...	1912	...	...	...	...	...	2110	...	...	...	2313	...	...

A – ①②③④⑥.

TGV – High-speed train. 🅁. 🍷.

PARIS - LES AUBRAIS - ORLÉANS 294

WARNING! Subject to alteration from July 21.

km		Ⓐ	⑥	Ⓐ	⚒	†	Ⓐ	⑥	†	†	⑥	Ⓑ		⚒	⑤	Ⓐ		Ⓐ		†	Ⓐ			Ⓑ	Ⓒ	①–④
0	**Paris** Austerlitz 296 315 d.	0622	0642	0642	0822	0922	0922	1022	1037	1122	1223	1322	1522	1622	1639	1722	1742	1751	1821	1843	1843	1922	1950	2022	2122	2252
119	Les Aubrais-Orléans 296 315 a.	0719	0815	0815	0919	1021	1025	1121	1208	1223	1357	1421	1619	1719	1749	1819	1909	1848	1919	1942	2015	2019	2126	2121	2219	2355
121	**Orléans** a.	0726	0820	0821	0926	1028	1032	1129	1216	1230	1403	1429	1626	1726	1757	1826	1915	1855	1926	1950	2021	2026	2132	2128	2226	0002

	⚒	Ⓐ	Ⓐ	Ⓐ	Ⓐ	⑥	⚒	Ⓒ	Ⓐ	†	Ⓐ	⑥	⑥		⑤	†	Ⓐ	Ⓐ	Ⓒ	†	Ⓐ	Ⓒ	Ⓐ	†	⚒
Orléans d.	0504	0603	0634	0702	0732	0742	0844	0933	1001	1034	1129	1228	1334	1531	1634	1637	1703	1728	1734	1811	1828	1917	1933	2041	2134
Les Aubrais-Orléans 296 315 d.	0511	0610	0641	0709	0739	0749	0851	0940	1008	1040	1136	1235	1341	1538	1641	1644	1710	1734	1741	1818	1836	1924	1940	2047	2141
Paris Austerlitz 296 315 a.	0608	0708	0738	0808	0838	0917	0948	1036	1108	1218	1240	1406	1439	1646	1740	1746	1808	1906	1839	1916	2015	2021	2038	2147	2238

295 OUIGO CLASSIQUE SERVICES PARIS - RENNES, NANTES and BORDEAUX

Ouigo Classique low-cost trains. Internet booking only (www.ouigo.com). For services to Lyon see Table **377**.
WARNING! Outline service shown. For confirmed timings and running days please consult the Ouigo website.

	4091	**4089**	**4089**	**4093**	**4093**	**4095**	**4097**	**4097**	
		⑤	①–④	①–⑥	⑦	⑥⑦	①–⑤	⑤	
							e	f	
Paris Austerlitz d.	0758	1257	1258	1315	1325	1858	1858	1957	...
Juvisy d.	|	1314	|	1338	1341	|	|	|	...
Massy-Palaiseau d.	0826	1337	1339	1355	1355	1926	1925	2026	...
Versailles Chantiers d.	0840	1358	1358	1411	1411	1954	1941	2048	...
Chartres d.	0928	1439	1439	1451	1450	2036	2034	2133	...
Le Mans d.	1028	1545	1541	1553	1553	2137	2136	2237	...
Laval d.	1113	|	|	1639	1639	2221	2221	2321	...
Rennes d.	1151	|	|	1718	1717	2302	2305	2357	...
Angers St-Laud d.	...	1632	1628	...	...	...	...	...	...
Nantes a.	...	1715	1711	...	...	...	...	...	...

	4080	**4080**	**4096**	**4092**	**4082**	**4094**	**4094**	**4096**	**4096**
	①–⑤	①–⑤	⑥⑦	①–⑤	①–⑤	Ⓑ	⑥		⑥⑦
	h	g						j	k
Nantes d.	0738	0738	...	...	1248	...	...	...	...
Angers St-Laud d.	0826	0826	...	...	1334	...	...	...	...
Rennes d.	|	|	0756	0802	|	1320	1400	1900	1900
Laval d.	|	|	0845	0845	|	1402	1438	1942	1942
Le Mans d.	0913	0913	0933	0934	1422	1448	1522	2027	2027
Chartres d.	1014	1014	1045	1045	1524	1548	1630	2127	2127
Versailles Chantiers a.	1053	1101	1133	1133	1600	1623	1708	2210	|
Massy-Palaiseau a.	1110	1117	1149	1150	1628	1641	1730	2229	2229
Juvisy a.	1129	|	|	|	|	1703	1752	|	|
Paris Austerlitz a.	1146	1147	1221	1218	1706	1721	1809	2257	2257

	4071	**4089**	**4085**	**4085**					
		⑥⑦	①–④	⑤					
			d						
Paris Austerlitz d.	0710	1257	1812	1812	...	...	...	...	...
Juvisy d.	0725	1314	1827	1827	...	...	...	...	...
Les Aubrais-Orléans d.	0822	1413	1925	1929	...	...	...	...	...
Blois d.	0855	1455	1955	2005	...	...	...	...	...
St Pierre des Corps d.	0924	1524	2036	2050	...	...	...	...	...
Saumur d.	1000	1602	2111	2127	...	...	...	...	...
Angers St-Laud d.	1027	1627	2137	2150	...	...	...	...	...
Nantes a.	1111	1711	2219	2237	...	...	...	...	...
Futuroscope d.	...	...	...	...	...	...	...	...	...
Poitiers d.	...	...	...	...	...	...	...	...	...
Angoulême d.	...	...	...	...	...	...	...	...	...
Bordeaux St Jean a.	...	...	...	...	...	...	...	...	...

	4080	**4082**	**4076**	**4076**					
	⑥⑦	⑥⑦	①–⑤	⑥⑦					
Bordeaux St Jean d.	...	...	...	...	...	...	...	...	...
Angoulême d.	...	...	...	...	...	...	...	...	...
Poitiers d.	...	...	...	...	...	...	...	...	...
Futuroscope d.	...	...	...	...	...	...	...	...	...
Nantes d.	0738	1248	1844	1844	...	...	...	...	...
Angers St-Laud d.	0824	1334	1930	1931	...	...	...	...	...
Saumur d.	0851	1405	1954	1955	...	...	...	...	...
St Pierre des Corps d.	0928	1449	2032	2032	...	...	...	...	...
Blois d.	0959	1526	2102	2102	...	...	...	...	...
Les Aubrais-Orléans d.	1033	1602	2135	2135	...	...	...	...	...
Juvisy a.	1131	1649	2231	2231	...	...	...	...	...
Paris Austerlitz a.	1146	1706	2247	2247	...	...	...	...	...

d – From Aug. 18.
e – Not ⑤ July 18 - Aug. 8.
f – July 18 - Aug. 8.
g – From Aug. 18 (also July 28 - Aug. 1).
h – Until Aug. 14 (not July 28 - Aug. 1).
j – ①–⑤ until Aug. 15 (also July 5, 6); daily from Aug. 18.
k – July 26 - Aug. 17.

296 PARIS and ORLÉANS - BLOIS - TOURS and NANTES

WARNING! Paris trains are subject to alteration from August 4. For *TGV* services Paris - Tours see Table **300**. For *Ouigo Classique* trains Paris - Nantes see Table **295**.

km																								
		②–⑤ 🚌	Ⓐ	A	Ⓐ	Ⓐ	⚒	Ⓐ	Ⓒ	Ⓐ	†	⑥		Ⓐ	†	⑥	Ⓐ B	⑥	⑥	⑥	†	Ⓐ	⑥	⑥
	Paris Austerlitz ◧ d.	...	...	...	...	...	...	0737	0737	...	...	...	...	...	...	0952	...	...	1058	...	...	...	...	1237
	Les Aubrais-Orléans ◧ d.	0005	...	...	...	...	...	0837	0837	...	...	...	...	...	...	1050	...	...	1158	...	...	...	...	1339
0	**Orléans** d.	|	0558	0637	0706	0710	0736	|	|	0839	0911	0938	...	1039	1045	|	1111	1138	|	1210	1238	1302	1308	|
27	Beaugency d.	|	0616	0656	|	0728	0756	|	0855	0858	0929	0957	...	1057	1103	1106	1129	1157	1214	1241	1257	1323	1327	1355
59	Blois d.	0105	0635	0716	0734	0747	0815	0901	0915	0917	0948	1017	...	1116	1121	1126	1152	1217	1233	1302	1316	1341	1346	1415
91	Amboise d.	|	0657	0735	|	0806	0833	0920	0934	0935	1010	1036	...	1139	1140	1145	1210	1237	1252	1325	1334	1400	1405	1434
112	St Pierre des Corps a.	|	0714	0754	0759	0820	0849	0934	0948	0951	1026	1051	...	1157	1154	1156	1222	1252	1308	1344	1350	1421	1423	1447
115	**Tours** a.	0205	0721	0759	0806	0827	0856	0941	0955	0958	1033	1058	...	1204	1201	1203	1228	1300	1316	1352	1357	1428	1430	1455
		Ⓐ		Ⓐ	†	⚒ C	Ⓐ	†	⚒	† B	Ⓑ	Ⓐ		⑤	①–④	Ⓒ	Ⓐ	Ⓒ	Ⓐ			Ⓑ	⑤	⑥
	Paris Austerlitz ◧ d.	...	...	...	...	...	...	1636	...	...	...	...	...	1735	1737	1735	...	...	1837	...	...	...	2306	2309
	Les Aubrais-Orléans ◧ d.	...	...	...	...	...	...	1734	...	...	...	...	...	1838	1838	1837	...	...	1936	...	...	...	0024	0011
	Orléans d.	1347	1438	1538	1633	1638	1709	|	1738	1740	1743	1802	...	|	|	|	1840	1903	|	1939	2041	2138	|	|
	Beaugency d.	|	1457	1557	1651	1657	1728	1751	1757	1759	1812	|	...	|	|	1854	1859	1922	|	1958	2100	2157	|	|
	Blois d.	1413	1517	1616	1710	1717	1747	1812	1816	1819	1837	1834	...	1907	1902	1914	1918	1941	2001	2017	2119	2217	0057	0037
	Amboise d.	1432	1536	1636	1729	1736	1806	1831	1836	1838	1901	|	...	1928	1921	1934	1937	2000	2021	2036	2139	2237	0116	0056
	St Pierre des Corps a.	1451	1552	1650	1743	1750	1820	1846	1851	1851	1916	1859	...	1943	1934	1947	1952	2015	2034	2052	2154	2251	0128	0109
	Tours a.	1458	1559	1658	1750	1757	1827	1853	1859	1858	1923	1906	...	1954	1941	1955	1959	2022	2041	2059	2202	2259	0136	0116

	Ⓐ	Ⓐ	⑥	Ⓐ	Ⓐ	⚒	Ⓐ	Ⓐ	Ⓒ	Ⓒ	Ⓐ B			Ⓒ D	Ⓐ m	Ⓐ n	Ⓒ	⑥	Ⓐ	Ⓐ B	Ⓒ	Ⓐ	⑤⑦
Tours d.	0501	0601	0604	0612	0636	0701	0733	0737	0801	0826	0901	...	0938	1102	1109	1109	1109	1201	1224	1259	1401	1435	1503
St Pierre des Corps d.	0509	0608	0612	0620	0643	0709	0741	0745	0808	0834	0909	...	0945	1109	1117	1117	1117	1208	1231	1307	1408	1441	1510
Amboise d.	0523	0622	0624	0634	0658	0721	|	0800	0823	0846	0921	...	0959	1121	1129	1129	1132	1223	1245	1320	1423	1456	1524
Blois d.	0543	0643	0645	0656	0725	0743	0807	0820	0843	0907	0941	...	1020	1144	1153	1153	1154	1243	1306	1343	1443	1517	1545
Beaugency d.	0602	0702	0704	|	0743	0802	|	0838	0901	0927	0959	...	1040	1202	|	1212	1217	1302	1324	1402	1502	1537	1603
Orléans a.	0622	0721	|	|	0812	0826	0836	0857	0922	|	1024	...	1102	1221	1225	1231	|	1322	1345	1424	1522	1557	1622
Les Aubrais-Orléans ◧ d.	...	...	0725	0726	...	...	...	...	...	0949	...	...	...	...	...	...	1242	...	...	...	...	...	...
Paris Austerlitz ◧ a.	...	...	0823	0823	...	...	...	...	...	1047	...	...	...	...	...	...	1346	...	...	...	...	...	...
	Ⓐ	Ⓐ	†	⚒	⚒	†	Ⓐ		†	Ⓐ	Ⓐ	Ⓒ	Ⓐ	Ⓒ	Ⓐ			Ⓐ B	†	Ⓐ	Ⓐ	⑥ D	† D
Tours d.	1516	1516	1600	1601	1630	1639	1700	...	1700	1712	1732	1739	1801	1815	1826	...	1910	2001	2040	2100	2202	2214	2233
St Pierre des Corps d.	1524	1524	1607	1608	1638	1646	1708	...	1708	1720	1740	1747	1809	1822	1833	...	1917	2009	2047	2107	2209	2223	2242
Amboise d.	1536	1536	1620	1623	1656	1700	1722	...	1724	1734	|	1801	1823	1834	|	...	1931	2021	2102	2122	2223	2235	2254
Blois d.	1557	1557	1641	1643	1718	1721	1743	...	1745	1756	1808	1821	1843	1854	1905	...	1952	2043	2125	2142	2243	2258	2316
Beaugency d.	|	|	1700	1702	1745	1740	1802	...	1805	|	|	1839	1902	1913	|	...	2011	2102	2145	2201	2302	2317	2335
Orléans a.	1627	|	|	1722	1817	1800	1822	...	|	|	1834	1858	1922	|	1931	...	2031	2124	2205	2221	2322	2337	2356
Les Aubrais-Orléans ◧ d.	...	1626	1719	...	...	...	...	...	1825	1825	...	...	...	1937	...	...	...	...	...	...	...	...	...
Paris Austerlitz ◧ a.	...	1724	1819	...	...	...	...	...	1923	1923	...	...	...	2037	...	...	...	...	...	...	...	...	...

A – Orléans - Nantes (- Le Croisic Ⓒ).
B – Orléans - Nantes and v.v.
C – Orléans - Nantes (- Le Croisic ⑤⑥).
D – Orléans - Le Croisic and v.v.
m – Until Aug. 1.
n – From Aug. 4.
◧ – See also Tables **294** and **315**.

NANTES - PORNIC and ST GILLES CROIX DE VIE 297

km																											
			Ⓐ	Ⓐ	Ⓒ	Ⓒ	Ⓐ	⑥	⑥	†	Ⓒ	Ⓐ	Ⓐ		⑥	Ⓐ	⚒	Ⓒ	Ⓐ	Ⓐ	⚒	†	Ⓐ	†	⑥	Ⓐ	Ⓐ
0	**Nantes**	d.	0707	0707	0909	0909	1010	1010	1109	1109	1209	1113	1229	1309	1409	1429	1509	1609	1612	1612	1707	1709	1738	1804	1809	1814	1846
24	Ste Pazanne ◧	d.	0747	0750	0945	0948	1043	1043	1142	1142	1240	1147	1302	1342	1442	1459	1541	1642	1650	1653	1738	1743	1811	1838	1842	1850	1923
54	**Pornic**	a.	0815	|	1013	|	1111	|	1210	|	1308	|	1330	|	1510	|	1610	|	|	1721	|	1810	1839	|	1910	|	1950
63	Challans	d.	...	0815	...	1011	...	1107	...	1206	...	1210	...	1404	...	1522	...	1705	1712	...	1804	...	...	1901	...	1917	...
84	**St Gilles Croix de Vie**	a.	...	0832	...	1028	...	1123	...	1222	...	1227	...	1422	...	1538	...	1722	1729	...	1822	...	...	1918	...	1934	...

		Ⓐ	⑤	⑤⑥	†	①–④	①–④ 🚌	⑤	Ⓑ	⑤
Nantes	d.	1913	1934	2009	2009	2015	2015	2035	2113	2220
Ste Pazanne ◧	d.	1947	2007	2040	2042	2046	2100	2106	2146	2250
Pornic	a.	|	2035	|	2110	2114	|	2134	|	|
Challans	d.	2009	...	2103	...	...	2140	...	2209	2328
St Gilles Croix de Vie	a.	2026	...	2122	...	...	2212	...	2225	2359

		Ⓐ	Ⓐ	Ⓐ	Ⓐ	Ⓐ	⑥	⑥	Ⓐ	†
St Gilles Croix de Vie	d.	0539	...	0639	...	0733	...	0733	...	...
Challans	d.	0556	...	0656	...	0749	...	0750	...	...
Pornic	d.	|	0628	|	0716	|	0740	|	0825	0909
Ste Pazanne ◧	d.	0618	0656	0717	0745	0812	0818	0818	0853	0949
Nantes	a.	0650	0729	0750	0816	0844	0850	0850	0924	1020

		Ⓒ	Ⓐ	Ⓒ	Ⓐ	Ⓐ		⚒	† 🚌	⑥	†	Ⓒ	Ⓐ	Ⓐ	Ⓒ	Ⓐ	†	⑥	Ⓐ	Ⓐ	Ⓐ	⑥	Ⓒ	Ⓒ	†	Ⓒ
St Gilles Croix de Vie	d.	0903	0939	...	1042	...	1239	...	1350	1439	...	1539	1544	...	...	...	1735	...	1744	...	1833	1839	...	1933	2043	...
Challans	d.	0919	0955	...	1059	...	1255	...	1422	1456	...	1556	1601	...	...	...	1752	...	1803	...	1850	1856	...	1950	2100	...
Pornic	d.	|	|	1050	|	1150	|	1348	|	|	1450	|	|	1620	1650	1741	|	1750	|	1849	|	|	1940	|	|	2125
Ste Pazanne ◧	d.	0948	1018	1118	1121	1218	1317	1416	1502	1518	1518	1618	1622	1651	1718	1809	1813	1818	1824	1922	1922	1918	2018	2018	2122	2153
Nantes	a.	1021	1051	1150	1153	1250	1350	1450	1542	1550	1550	1650	1653	1728	1750	1836	1844	1850	1859	1954	1954	1950	2050	2050	2154	2225

◧ – 🚌 call at Ste Pazanne **Rue du Vigneau**.

OTHER LOCAL SERVICES 299

BAYONNE - ST JEAN PIED DE PORT

km																									
				Ⓐ	Ⓐ		Ⓐ	Ⓐ		Ⓐ	Ⓐ		Ⓐ			Ⓒ	Ⓒ		Ⓒ	Ⓒ		Ⓒ			
0	**Bayonne**	d.	Ⓐ	0638	0742	...	0849	1235	...	1424	1713	...	1837	...	Ⓒ	0814	1120	...	1420	1820	...	2103	...	...	...
	Cambo les Bains	d.		0705	0806	...	0921	1304	...	1448	1742	...	1905	...		0838	1144	...	1444	1844	...	2127	...	...	...
50	**St Jean Pied de Port**	a.		0741	...	...	0957	1340	...	1525	1818	...	1943	...		0915	1221	...	1521	1921	...	2204	...	...	...

			Ⓐ	Ⓐ		Ⓐ	Ⓐ		Ⓐ	Ⓐ		Ⓐ			Ⓒ	Ⓒ		Ⓒ	Ⓒ		Ⓒ			
St Jean Pied de Port	d.	Ⓐ	0624	...	...	0840	1223	...	1543	1701	...	1825	...	Ⓒ	0628	0938	...	1234	1640	...	1923	...	...	...
Cambo les Bains	d.		0706	0813	...	0920	1303	...	1621	1741	...	1904	...		0706	1015	...	1311	1717	...	2010	...	...	...
Bayonne	a.		0731	0838	...	0947	1329	...	1646	1806	...	1931	...		0731	1040	...	1336	1743	...	2035	...	...	...

CARCASSONNE - LIMOUX - QUILLAN

km																									
			Ⓐ 🚌	⚒	Ⓐ 🚌	⚒ 🚌	⑥ 🚌	† 🚌	⚒	⚒ 🚌	⚒	⚒ 🚌	† 🚌		⚒ 🚌	† 🚌	⚒	⚒ 🚌	Ⓐ 🚌	⚒	⚒ 🚌	Ⓐ 🚌	⚒	⑥–④ 🚌	† 🚌
0	**Carcassonne**	d.	0635	0712	...	0800	0915	0935	1027	...	1225	...	1240	...	1425	1440	1604	...	1640	1742	...	1830	1907	...	1905
26	Limoux	d.	0720	0740	0800	0845	1000	1020	1056	1115	1253	1303	1325	...	1510	1525	1633	1638	1725	1811	1815	1915	1935	1945	1950
54	**Quillan**	a.	0806	...	0844	0934	1049	1109	...	1159	...	1347	1414	...	1559	1614	...	1722	1814	...	1904	2004	...	2029	2039

		⚒ 🚌	⚒	Ⓐ 🚌	Ⓐ 🚌	⚒		Ⓒ 🚌	Ⓐ 🚌	⚒ 🚌	⚒	† 🚌		🚌	⚒ 🚌	⚒	⚒ 🚌	⚒		Ⓐ	† 🚌	⚒ 🚌	⚒	⚒ 🚌
Quillan	d.	0535	...	0609	0700	...	...	0745	0815	1030	...	1050	...	1245	1356	...	1555	...	...	1620	1710	1727	...	1820
Limoux	d.	0615	0627	0654	0740	0800	...	0825	0855	1110	1139	1135	...	1330	1440	1445	1635	1643	...	1705	1755	1811	1822	1905
Carcassonne	a.	...	0656	0740	...	0829	...	0911	0941	...	1211	1221	...	1416	...	1514	...	1717	...	1751	1841	...	1853	1951

ANGERS ST LAUD - CHOLET — Journey 41 – 50 minutes *60 km*

From Angers St Laud at 0619 Ⓐ, 0723 Ⓐ, 0823 Ⓐ, 0930 ⑥, 1023 Ⓐ, 1123, 1256 ⚒, 1623 Ⓐ, 1723 Ⓐ, 1759 Ⓐ, 1823 ⚒, 1927 Ⓐ, 1954 †, 2028, 2128 ⑤, 2238 †.

From Cholet at 0550 Ⓐ, 0610 Ⓐ, 0645 ⚒, 0711 Ⓐ, 0749 Ⓐ, 0849, 1049 Ⓐ, 1149 ⑥, 1230 Ⓐ, 1355, 1649 Ⓐ, 1750 Ⓐ, 1755 Ⓒ, 1842 †, 1850 Ⓐ, 1920 Ⓐ, 1924 Ⓒ, 2154 †.

CHARLEVILLE MÉZIÈRES - GIVET — Journey 60 – 65 minutes *64 km*

Service July 14 - Aug. 22.

From Charleville Mézières at 0705 ⚒, 0735, 0835, 0935, 1035, 1135, 1235, 1335, 1435, 1535, 1635, 1735, 1835, 1935, 2035.

From Givet at 0620 Ⓐ, 0650 †, 0715 ⑥, 0720 Ⓐ, 0820, 0920, 1020, 1120, 1220, 1320, 1418 ⑥, 1420 Ⓑ, 1520, 1620, 1720, 1820, 1920.

DINARD - ST MALO

🚌 : Approximately hourly on Ⓐ (fewer on Ⓒ). Journey 21 – 26 minutes. *11 km.* Operator: Breizgo en Ille-et-Vilaine route **16**.

⛴ : *Le Bus de Mer* passenger ferry operates a frequent daily service. Journey 10 minutes. Operator: Compagnie Corsaire (compagniecorsaire.com).

GUINGAMP - CARHAIX — Journey 65 – 70 minutes *56 km*

From Guingamp at 0751 Ⓐ, 1047 ⚒, 1347, 1543 ①–④, 1745 ⚒, 1942 Ⓒ, 2048 Ⓐ, 2220 ⑤.

From Carhaix at 0627 Ⓐ, 0905 ⚒, 1057 †, 1203 Ⓐ, 1227 ⑥, 1359 Ⓐ, 1601, 1800 †, 1909 Ⓐ.

GUINGAMP - PAIMPOL — Journey: 47 – 53 minutes *47 km*

From Guingamp at 0825 Ⓐ, 1154, 1406, 1739 †, 1741 ⚒, 1952 †, 2007 Ⓐ, 2202 ⑤.

From Paimpol at 0715 Ⓐ, 0918, 1308, 1612, 1833 †, 1908 ⚒.

LILLE - LENS — Journey 42 – 46 minutes *39 km*

From Lille Flandres: on Ⓐ at 0640, 0647, 0740, 0747, 0810, 0847, 0910, 1047, 1110, 1147, 1210, 1247, 1347, 1510, 1547, 1610, 1626, 1710, 1740, 1840, 1847, 1940, 1947, 2047; on ⑥ at 0645, 0806, 0857, 0948, 1206, 1219, 1319, 1357, 1546, 1604, 1719, 1819, 1948, 2006, 2057; on † at 0857, 0948, 1151, 1206, 1319, 1448, 1604, 1648, 1819, 1948, 2006, 2057.

From Lens: on Ⓐ at 0614, 0641, 0710, 0714, 0741, 0814, 0841, 0910, 0952, 1110, 1114, 1210, 1214, 1310, 1314, 1441, 1510, 1610, 1614, 1714, 1741, 1814, 1841, 1941, 2014; on ⑥ at 0556, 0706, 0737, 0802, 1036, 1110, 1202, 1301, 1436, 1510, 1702, 1835, 1910, 2036; on † at 0802, 1036, 1110, 1202, 1436, 1510, 1636, 1802, 1910, 1936.

NANTES - CHOLET — Journey 52 – 70 minutes *65 km*

From Nantes at 0629 Ⓐ, 0729 ⚒, 0829 †, 0835 Ⓐ 🚌, 0910 Ⓒ 🚌, 1100 ⑥ 🚌, 1133 Ⓐ, 1259 ⚒, 1330 ⑤ † 🚌, 1545 ⑥ 🚌, 1548 Ⓐ, 1620 Ⓐ 🚌, 1728 Ⓐ, 1730 Ⓒ 🚌, 1829 Ⓑ, 1929 ⚒, 2035 †.

From Cholet at 0605 Ⓐ, 0640 Ⓐ, 0744 ⚒, 1010 †, 1040 🚌, 1240 ⚒, 1420 ⑥ 🚌, 1444 Ⓐ, 1553 ⑤ 🚌, 1608 † 🚌, 1610 Ⓐ, 1710 Ⓑ, 1710 ⑥ 🚌, 1745 Ⓐ 🚌. 1855 ⚒, 1935 †, 1943 ①–④ 🚌, 2033 ⑤Ⓒ 🚌.

PARIS - DISNEYLAND (Marne la Vallée - Chessy) *32 km*

Châtelet les Halles - Gare de Lyon - Marne la Vallée Chessy (for Disneyland).

Approximately every 15 – 30 minutes 0500 - 2400 on RER Line A. Journey: 45 minutes.

Operator: RATP. For *TGV* services serving Marne la Vallée see Tables **11** and **391**.

🚌 SOUILLAC - SARLAT 🚌 *30 km*

🚌 (Nouvelle Aquitaine Cars Régionaux Ligne **335**). Journey 50 minutes.

From Souillac Gare at 0650 Ⓐ, 0850 †, 0940 ⑥, 1340, 1945 Ⓐ.

From Sarlat Gare at 0612 Ⓐ, 1222 Ⓐ, 1232 Ⓒ, 1315 ③, 1638 ①②④⑤, 1732 Ⓒ, 1815 Ⓐ.

Warning! *Service is amended during school holiday periods.*

TOULOUSE - AUCH — Journey 85 – 95 minutes *88 km*

From Toulouse Matabiau at 0624 ⚒, 0724 Ⓐ, 0824, 1024, 1223, 1424, 1523 Ⓐ, 1624, 1723 Ⓐ, 1824, 2024.

From Auch at 0603 ⚒, 0705 Ⓐ, 0806, 0905 Ⓐ, 1005, 1205, 1406, 1605, 1705 Ⓐ, 1807, 2007.

TOURS - CHINON — Journey 50 minutes (🚌 80 minutes) *49 km*

From Tours at 0632 Ⓐ, 0740 Ⓐ, 0903 Ⓐ, 0928 Ⓒ, 1101 Ⓐ, 1232, 1410 Ⓐ, 1624, 1732 Ⓐ, 1850 Ⓐ, 2004 Ⓑ, 2019 ⑥.

From Chinon at 0639 Ⓐ, 0701 ⑥, 0748 Ⓐ, 0757 †, 0840 Ⓐ, 1109, 1239 Ⓐ, 1417, 1601 Ⓐ, 1740 Ⓐ, 1747 Ⓒ, 1857 Ⓐ, 2011 Ⓐ.

VALENCIENNES - CAMBRAI — Journey 50 minutes *40 km*

From Valenciennes at 0650 ⑥, 0653 Ⓐ, 0827 ⑥, 1152 ⑥, 1253 Ⓐ, 1730 Ⓒ, 1753 Ⓐ, 1853 Ⓐ, 1934 Ⓒ.

From Cambrai Ville at 0557 Ⓐ, 0653 ⚒, 0750 ⑥, 0753 Ⓐ, 1245 ⑥, 1253 Ⓐ, 1630 Ⓒ, 1653 Ⓐ, 1839 Ⓒ.

300 TGV SUD EUROPE ATLANTIQUE

TGV timings may vary by a few minutes - please check your reservation. For *TGV* exception and additional running dates see Table **280**.

PARIS - BORDEAUX NON-STOP TRAINS

For stopping trains see Paris - La Rochelle and Bordeaux sub-table. Many trains continue to/from Toulouse (sub-table below) or to destinations on Tables **305** and **306**.

km		TGV	TGV	Ouigo	TGV	TGV	TGV	TGV		TGV	TGV	TGV	Ouigo	TGV	TGV	TGV	TGV	TGV		TGV	TGV	TGV	TGV	TGV	TGV	TGV
		8503 8571	**8531**	**7671**	**8537**	**8572**	**8473**	**8505**		**8473 8507**	**8479**	**8541**	**7673**	**8547**	**8509**	**8575**	**8511**	**8475 8547**		**8549**	**8590**	**8477**	**8517**	**8519**	**8551**	**8593**
		①-⑥	①-⑥				⑥⑦			①-④	⑤			⑤⑥	⑦		①-⑥	⑦		Ⓑ	⑤	⑦		⑦	⑥	
				⊠		A		B			d		⊠			C										D
0	**Paris** Montparnasse d.	0632	0703	0825	1005	1005	1035	1035	...	1106	1206	1206	1237	1400	1400	1400	1501	1518	...	1606	1606	1709	1709	1806	1806	1806
540	**Bordeaux** St Jean a.	0849	0914	1034	1214	1214	1247	1247	...	1314	1423	1423	1446	1614	1614	1614	1711	1727	...	1814	1814	1917	1917	2014	2014	2014

	TGV	TGV	TGV	TGV		TGV	TGV	TGV	TGV
	8593	**8519 8593**	**8477**	**8551**		**8419**	**8521**	**8523**	**8553**
	⑤	①-④	①-⑤	Ⓑ			⑤⑥	⑤	⑤
						E			
Paris Montparnasse d.	1808	1809	1839	1839	...	1907	1907	1948	1948
Bordeaux St Jean a.	2016	2017	2050	2050	...	2114	2114	2212	2212

	TGV	TGV		TGV	TGV	TGV		TGV	TGV
	8478	**8402**		**8404**	**8502**	**8530**		**8560**	**8504**
	①-⑥				①-⑥			①-⑥	
		G							
Bordeaux St Jean d.	0646	0712	...	0744	0846	0946	...	0946	1046
Paris Montparnasse a.	0900	0922	...	1001	1056	1200	...	1200	1258

	TGV	TGV	TGV	TGV		TGV	TGV	TGV	TGV		Ouigo	TGV	TGV	TGV	TGV		TGV	TGV	TGV	TGV		TGV	TGV	TGV	TGV
	8534	**8534**	**8562**	**8508**		**8536**	**8580**	**8540**	**8582**		**7672**	**8472**	**8542**	**8542**	**8514**		**8544**	**8516**	**8584**	**8550**		**8586**	**8550**	**8522**	**8588**
	①-⑥	⑦	⑦	Ⓑ			①-⑥						①-⑤	⑥⑦	⑤-⑦			Ⓑ	⑥⑦	①-⑤		①-⑤	⑥⑦	⑦	⑦
											⊠														
Bordeaux St Jean d.	1212	1212	1212	1246	...	1346	1346	1546	1546	...	1653	1708	1740	1746	1846	...	1846	1946	1946	2049	...	2049	2050	2212	2212
Paris Montparnasse a.	1426	1430	1430	1456	...	1601	1601	1759	1759	...	1908	1927	1950	2005	2100	...	2100	2156	2156	2300	...	2300	2300	0025	0025

PARIS - BORDEAUX - TOULOUSE

km		TGV		Ouigo		TGV		TGV		Ouigo		TGV		TGV		TGV		TGV		TGV		TGV		TGV		
		8503		**7671**		**8505**		**8507**		**7673**		**8509**		**8511**		**8517**		**8519**		**8519**		**8521**		**8523**		
		①-⑥						①-④				⑦		①-⑥				⑦		①-④		⑤⑥		⑤		
				⊠		B				⊠																
0	**Paris** Montparnasse d.	0632	...	0825	...	1035	...	1106	...	1237	...	1400	...	1501	...	1709	...	1806	...	1809	...	1907	...	1948	...	...
540	**Bordeaux** St Jean a.	0849	...	1034	...	1247	...	1314	...	1446	...	1614	...	1711	...	1917	...	2014	...	2017	...	2114	...	2212	...	...
540	**Bordeaux** St Jean d.	0858	...	1040	...	1252	...	1320	...	1452	...	1624	...	1717	...	1923	...	2024	...	2023	...	2120	...	2222	...	...
676	Agen d.	1013	...	1156	...	1407	...	1434	...	1607	...	|	...	|	...	2037	...	2137	...	2137	...	2238	...	2336	...	...
746	Montauban a.	|	...	1235	...	1445	...	1512	...	1646	...	|	...	|	...	2114	...	2214	...	2214	...	2316	...	|	...	...
797	**Toulouse** Matabiau a.	1128	...	1313	...	1522	...	1548	...	1728	...	1849	...	1941	...	2150	...	2250	...	2250	...	2352	...	0046	...	...

	TGV		TGV		TGV		TGV		Ouigo		TGV		TGV		TGV		Ouigo		TGV						
	8502		**8504**		**8508**		**8512**		**7672**		**8514**		**8514**		**8516**		**7674**		**8522**						
	①-⑥				Ⓑ						⑤		⑥⑦		Ⓑ				⑦						
							F		⊠								⊠								
Toulouse Matabiau d.	0610	...	0812	...	1020	...	1215	...	1417	...	1608	...	1615	...	1709	...	1810	...	1935	...	...	...	...	...	...
Montauban d.	0649	...	0850	...	|	...	|	...	1456	...	|	...	|	...	1747	...	1849	...	|	...	...	...	...	...	...
Agen d.	0726	...	0928	...	|	...	1326	...	1534	...	1726	...	1726	...	1825	...	1927	...	|	...	...	...	...	...	...
Bordeaux St Jean a.	0840	...	1040	...	1240	...	1440	...	1648	...	1840	...	1840	...	1940	...	2040	...	2206	...	...	...	...	...	...
Bordeaux St Jean d.	0846	...	1046	...	1246	...	1446	...	1653	...	1846	...	1846	...	1946	...	2045	...	2212	...	...	...	...	...	...
Paris Montparnasse a.	1056	...	1258	...	1456	...	1716	...	1908	...	2100	...	2100	...	2156	...	2324	...	0025	...	...	...	...	...	...

PARIS - TOURS, POITIERS, LA ROCHELLE and BORDEAUX

Subject to alteration on ①-⑤ July 21 - August 14. Some trains continue to/from destinations on Tables **305** and **306**.

km		TGV	TGV	TGV	TGV	TGV	TGV	TGV	TGV	TGV	TGV	TGV	TGV		TGV	TGV	TGV	TGV	TGV	TGV	TGV	TGV	TGV	Ouigo	TGV	Ouigo
		8441	**8371**	**8483**	**8531**	**8371**	**8331**	**8331**	**8533**	**8471**	**8373**	**8375**	**8445**		**8445**	**8377**	**8379**	**8379**	**8333**	**8303**	**8333**	**8335**	**8361**	**7653**	**8485**	**7641**
		①-⑤	①-⑥	①-⑥	⑦	⑦	Ⓑ	⑥	Ⓑ	⑥	⑥		⑥⑦		①-⑤		⑦	⑤	⑦	⑤⑥	⑤⑥	①-④	⑤-⑦		⑤⑥	
										e						G								⊠	e	⊠
0	**Paris** Montparnasse d.	0600	0644	0644	0647	0651	0727	0730	0752	0752	0818	0911	0953	...	1000	1211	1218	1219	1226	1227	1227	1227	1335	1344	1414	1527
	Vendôme-Villiers TGV d.	|	|	|	|	|	0811	0814	|	|	|	|	|	...	|	|	|	|	1310	1311	1311	1311	|	|	|	|
	St Pierre des Corps a.	0703	|	|	|	|	0835	0837	|	|	|	1012	1101	...	1101	1317	1317	|	1335	1335	1335	1335	|	|	1513	|
	St Pierre des Corps d.	0707	|	|	|	|	0839	0841	|	|	|	1016	1105	...	1105	1321	1321	|	1343	1340	1343	1339	|	|	1517	|
	Tours a.	|	|	|	|	|	|	|	|	|	|	|	|	...	|	|	|	|	|	1345	|	1345	|	|	|	|
	Châtellerault d.	|	|	|	|	|	0908	0909	|	|	|	|	|	...	|	|	|	|	1414	...	1413	1425	|	|	|	|
	Futuroscope d.	|	|	|	|	|	0925	0925	|	|	|	|	|	...	|	|	|	|	1429	...	1429	1441	|	|	|	|
318	**Poitiers** a.	0739	0811	0811	|	0815	0935	0935	0917	0917	0946	1050	1137	...	1137	1352	1352	1341	1438	...	1443	1452	|	|	1549	1645
318	**Poitiers** d.	0742	0815	0823	|	0823	...	...	0920	0920	0950	1053	1140	...	1140	1355	1355	1344	...	...	...	...	|	|	1553	1649
398	Niort d.	|	0905	|	|	0908	...	...	|	|	1037	1143	|	...	|	1440	1440	1429	...	...	...	...	1558	|	|	1734
465	**La Rochelle** Ville a.	|	0945	|	|	0949	...	...	|	|	1114	1225	|	...	|	1522	1517	1506	...	...	...	...	1619	|	|	1816
	Angoulême d.	0825	...	0906	0837	...	...	...	|	|	...	...	1223	...	1223	...	...	...	...	...	...	...	...	1532	1636	...
	Libourne d.	|	...	0951	|	...	...	...	|	|	...	...	|	...	|	...	...	...	...	...	...	...	...	|	1721	...
	Bordeaux St Jean a.	0902	...	1011	0915	...	...	...	1018	1018	...	...	1302	...	1302	...	...	...	...	...	...	...	...	1607	1743	...

	TGV	TGV	TGV	TGV	TGV	TGV	TGV	TGV	TGV	TGV	TGV	TGV		TGV	TGV	TGV	TGV	Ouigo	TGV	TGV	TGV	TGV	TGV	TGV	TGV
	8311	**8447**	**8313**	**8449**	**8313**	**8389**	**8367**	**8315**	**8317**	**8397**	**8391**	**8491**		**8319**	**8345**	**8393**	**8321**	**7659**	**8395**	**8495**	**8439**	**8347**	**8347**	**8323**	**8461**
	⑤		⑦	①-⑤	①-⑤	⑦	①-⑥	⑥		⑤	⑦-④				①-⑥					⑤⑦	①-④	①-⑤	⑦	⑦	⑤⑦
									H					J			K	⊠	L						
Paris Montparnasse d.	1529	1601	1629	1642	1642	1653	1727	1727	1756	1819	1819	1819	...	1828	1828	1919	1928	1944	2023	2023	2034	2042	2058	2058	2145
Vendôme-Villiers TGV d.	1613	|	1714	1727	1727	|	1811	1811	1840	|	|	|	...	1913	1913	|	2012	|	|	|	|	2127	2142	2142	|
St Pierre des Corps a.	1635	|	1736	1749	1749	|	1834	1834	1910	|	|	|	...	1938	1938	2019	2035	2042	|	|	|	2149	2205	2205	2245
St Pierre des Corps d.	1638	|	1740	1753	1756	|	1838	1842	1913	|	|	|	...	1939	1944	2023	2039	2045	|	|	|	2153	2209	2213	2249
Tours a.	1643	|	1745	|	1801	|	|	1848	1918	|	|	|	...	1944	|	|	2044	|	|	|	|	|	|	2219	|
Châtellerault d.	...	|	...	1822	...	1815	|	...	...	|	|	|	...	...	2013	|	...	|	|	|	|	2220	2236	...	|
Futuroscope d.	...	|	...	|	...	|	|	...	...	|	|	|	...	...	|	|	...	|	|	|	|	|	|	...	|
Poitiers a.	...	1724	...	1839	...	1834	|	...	...	1945	1945	1945	...	...	2033	2054	...	2115	2145	2146	|	2241	2258	...	2321
Poitiers d.	...	1727	...	1842	...	1838	|	...	...	1949	1949	1954	...	...	...	2058	...	2118	2149	2153	|	...	...	...	2323
Niort d.	...	|	...	|	...	1932	1946	...	...	2040	2040	|	...	...	...	2143	...	|	2249	|	|	...	...	...	|
La Rochelle Ville a.	...	|	...	|	...	2009	2028	...	...	2117	2121	|	...	...	...	2225	...	|	2331	|	|	...	...	...	|
Angoulême d.	...	1808	...	1923	...	...	...	...	...	...	...	2034	...	...	...	...	...	2158	...	2236	2229	...	...	...	0008
Libourne d.	...	|	...	|	...	...	...	...	...	...	...	2118	...	...	...	...	...	|	...	2322	|	...	...	...	|
Bordeaux St Jean a.	...	1744	...	2001	...	...	...	...	...	...	...	2144	...	...	...	...	...	2236	...	2345	2311	...	...	...	0047

A – Daily until Aug. 3; ①-⑤ from Aug. 4.
B – ⑤⑥⑦ until Aug. 3; ⑥⑦ from Aug. 9.
C – ⑤⑥⑦ until July 27; ⑤⑥ from Aug. 2.
D – ⑥⑦ until Aug. 3; ⑦ from Aug. 10.
E – ①-④ until July 24; ④ from July 31 (also Aug. 25-27).
F – Daily until July 20; ⑥⑦ from July 26.
G – ①②③④⑥.
H – ①-⑤ until July 31; ①-④ from Aug. 4 (also Aug. 29).
J – Ⓑ until July 27; ⑤⑦ from Aug. 1 (also Aug. 25-28).
K – ①-⑥ until July 26; ⑤⑥ from Aug. 1 (also Aug. 25-28).
L – ⑤⑦ until July 27; ⑦ from Aug. 3 (also Aug. 29).

M – July 7-11, 15-18, 21-25, Aug. 25-29.
N – ①-⑤ until July 25 (also Aug. 25-29).
P – Daily until July 27; ①⑥⑦ July 28 - Aug. 16 (also Aug. 18, 25-29).

d – Until Aug. 1.
e – Until Aug. 2.
f – From Aug. 4.

⊠ – OUIGO low-cost TGV service. Internet booking only (www.ouigo.com).

TGV – High-speed train. Ⓡ. 🍸.

*For TGV exception and additional running dates see Table **280**.*

TGV SUD EUROPE ATLANTIQUE 300

TGV timings may vary by a few minutes - please check your reservation. For *TGV* exception and additional running dates see Table **280**.

PARIS - TOURS, POITIERS, LA ROCHELLE and BORDEAUX

Subject to alteration on ①–⑤ July 21 - August 14. Some trains continue to/from destinations on Tables **305** and **306**.

	TGV	*TGV*	*TGV*	*TGV*		*TGV*	*TGV*	*TGV*	*TGV*		*TGV*	*TGV*	*TGV*	*Ouigo*	*Ouigo*		*TGV*	*TGV*	*TGV*	*TGV*		*TGV*	*TGV*	*TGV*	*TGV*
	8300	**8306**	**8330**	**8480**		**8422**	**8370**	**8308**	**8310**		**8332**	**8310**	**8440**	**7652**	**7652**		**8362**	**8340**	**8338**	**8314**		**8340**	**8338**	**8486**	**8374**
	①–⑤			①–⑤		①	①–⑥		⑥		①–⑤	①–⑤	⑦	①–⑤	⑥⑦			⑥	①–⑤	⑦		⑦	①–⑤		
		M						**N**						⊠	⊠				**d**				**f**		
Bordeaux St Jean d.	...	...	...	0515	...	0539	...	...	...	...	...	...	0655	0838	0841	...	...	...	...	...	...	...	...	1015	...
Libourne d.	...	...	...	0538	...	│	...	...	...	...	...	...	│	│	│	...	...	...	...	...	...	...	...	1042	...
Angoulême d.	...	...	...	0623	...	0617	...	...	...	...	...	...	0735	0920	0920	...	...	...	...	...	...	...	...	1127	...
La Rochelle Ville d.	...	...	...	│	...	│	0539	...	...	...	...	...	│	│	│	...	0848	...	...	...	...	...	...	│	1049
Niort d.	...	...	...	│	...	│	0621	...	...	...	...	...	│	│	│	...	0930	...	...	...	...	...	...	│	1131
Poitiers a.	...	...	...	0704	...	│	0708	...	...	...	...	...	0816	1003	1003	...	│	...	...	...	...	...	...	1208	1213
Poitiers d.	...	...	0632	0714	...	│	0714	...	...	...	0727	...	0819	1007	1007	...	│	1116	1116	...	...	1119	1140	1219	1219
Futuroscope d.	...	...	│	│	...	│	│	...	...	...	│	...	│	│	│	...	│	1127	1127	...	...	1130	│	│	│
Châtellerault d.	...	...	0651	│	...	│	│	...	...	...	0747	...	│	│	│	...	│	1144	1144	...	...	1145	│	│	│
Tours d.	0605	0642	│	│	...	│	│	0754	0813	...	│	0813	│	│	│	...	│	│	│	1213	...	│	│	│	│
St Pierre-des-Corps a.	0611	0648	0722	│	...	│	│	0800	0819	...	0815	0819	0852	│	│	...	1035	1213	1215	1219	...	1214	1215	│	│
St Pierre des Corps d.	0615	0654	0725	│	...	│	│	0803	0825	...	0825	0825	0856	│	│	...	1039	1217	1224	1224	...	1225	1224	│	│
Vendôme-Villiers TGV d.	0637	0716	0747	│	...	│	│	│	0848	...	0852	0852	│	│	│	...	│	1241	1247	1247	...	1248	1246	│	│
Paris Montparnasse a.	0723	0801	0832	0841	...	0813	0841	0905	0932	...	0937	0937	1005	1134	1134	...	1139	1332	1332	1332	...	1332	1330	1345	1345

	Ouigo	*TGV*	*TGV*	*TGV*		*TGV*	*TGV*	*TGV*	*TGV*		*TGV*	*TGV*	*TGV*	*TGV*	*TGV*		*TGV*	*Ouigo*	*TGV*	*TGV*		*Ouigo*	*TGV*	*TGV*	*TGV*
	7656	**8378**	**8470**	**8512**		**8316**	**8342**	**8318**	**8318**		**8380**	**8488**	**8364**	**8320**	**8442**		**8388**	**7642**	**8324**	**8476**		**7674**	**8454**	**8392**	**8396**
			⑥			⑤		⑥	⑤⑦					Ⓑ	⑦		⑦		⑦	⑦			⑤⑦	⑦	⑦
	⊠			**F**							**P**							⊠				⊠			
Bordeaux St Jean d.	1158	...	1446	1446	...	...	...	...	...	...	...	1618	...	...	1758	...	...	...	...	1938	...	2045	2107	...	...
Libourne d.	│	...	│	│	...	...	...	...	...	...	...	1641	...	...	│	...	...	...	...	│	...	│	│	...	...
Angoulême d.	1236	...	1523	1523	...	...	...	...	...	...	...	1726	...	...	1837	...	...	...	...	2023	...	2123	2149	...	...
La Rochelle Ville d.	│	1347	│	│	...	...	...	...	...	...	1545	│	1700	...	│	...	1833	1925	...	│	...	│	│	2109	2152
Niort d.	│	1429	│	│	...	...	...	...	...	...	1623	│	1742	...	│	...	1911	2007	...	│	...	│	│	2151	2230
Poitiers a.	│	1516	│	│	...	...	...	...	...	...	1712	1806	│	...	│	...	1954	2050	...	│	...	│	2230	2235	2312
Poitiers d.	│	1519	│	│	...	...	1619	...	...	...	1714	1809	│	...	│	...	2000	2053	...	│	...	│	2241	2241	2315
Futuroscope d.	│	│	│	│	...	...	1629	...	...	...	│	│	│	...	│	...	2010	│	...	│	...	│	│	│	│
Châtellerault d.	│	│	│	│	...	...	1644	...	...	...	│	│	│	...	│	...	2024	│	...	│	...	│	│	│	│
Tours d.	│	│	│	│	...	1617	│	1715	1717	...	│	│	│	1857	│	...	│	│	2117	│	...	│	│	│	│
St Pierre-des-Corps a.	1339	1551	│	│	...	1622	1715	1722	1722	...	│	│	│	1902	1938	...	2053	│	2122	2130	...	│	2312	2312	│
St Pierre des Corps d.	1343	1556	│	│	...	1625	1728	1728	1728	...	│	│	│	1905	1942	...	2056	│	2125	2134	...	│	2316	2316	│
Vendôme-Villiers TGV d.	│	│	│	│	...	1647	1751	1751	1751	...	│	│	│	1927	│	...	│	│	2147	│	...	│	│	│	│
Paris Montparnasse a.	1441	1655	1716	1716	...	1731	1836	1836	1836	...	1842	1935	1944	2011	2048	...	2201	2213	2231	2235	...	2324	0018	0018	0040

FOR RETURN SERVICE AND FOOTNOTES SEE PREVIOUS PAGE.

TOURS - POITIERS - ANGOULÊME and POITIERS - LA ROCHELLE 300a

TER regional trains. For *TGV* trains see Table **300**.

km		Ⓐ	Ⓐ	⚒	Ⓐ	Ⓒ	Ⓐ	Ⓐ		⚒	Ⓒ	Ⓐ	Ⓒ		Ⓐ	Ⓒ		Ⓐ		Ⓐ	Ⓐ	Ⓐ		Ⓐ	⑥	†
0	**Tours** d.	...	...	0600	...	...	0735	...	...	...	...	...	...	1216	...	...	...	1637	...	...	1742	...	1842	...	...	2040
68	Châtellerault d.	...	0634	0651	0733	0824	0827	0843	...	0934	1134	1142	...	1311	1534	1534	1634	1723	...	1735	1831	1835	1928	1934	2037	2127
90	Futuroscope d.	...	0658	0716	0757	0848	0839	0859	...	1001	1158	1206	...	1337	1558	1558	1659	1736	...	1800	1844	1859	1941	1959	2101	2140
101	**Poitiers** a.	...	0707	0726	0807	0857	0847	0909	...	1011	1207	1215	...	1348	1607	1610	1708	1744	...	1808	1853	1908	1950	2008	2110	2149
101	**Poitiers** d.	0610	0710	...	0810	0900	...	...	...	...	...	1218	1300	...	1612	...	1711	...	...	1813	...	1913	...	...	...	...
166	Ruffec d.	0648	0750	...	0848	0942	...	...	...	...	...	1304	1343	...	1655	...	1754	...	...	1858	...	1957	...	...	...	...
213	**Angoulême** a.	0715	0818	...	0915	1009	...	...	...	...	...	1331	1411	...	1722	...	1822	...	...	1930	...	2024	...	...	...	...

	Ⓐ	Ⓐ	Ⓐ	⚒	Ⓒ	Ⓐ	Ⓐ	Ⓐ	†			Ⓒ		Ⓐ	Ⓐ	Ⓒ		Ⓐ	Ⓒ	Ⓐ	†	⑥	Ⓐ	Ⓑ	Ⓐ
Angoulême d.	...	...	...	...	...	0629	0729	0836	0927	...	...	1246	...	...	1428	...	...	1634	1649	1740	1830	1832	1834	...	1932
Ruffec d.	...	...	...	...	...	0657	0756	0903	0955	...	...	1314	...	...	1458	...	...	1703	1716	1808	1857	1900	1902	...	1959
Poitiers d.	...	...	...	...	...	0743	0839	0948	1039	...	...	1357	...	...	1544	...	...	1739	1758	1846	1941	1943	1941	...	2038
Poitiers d.	0550	0608	0650	0734	0739	0746	0844	...	...	1052	1231	...	1442	1504	1547	1550	1728	1744	...	1849	...	1946	...	2008	...
Futuroscope d.	0600	0616	0700	0742	0749	0755	0854	...	...	1102	1244	...	1452	1512	1557	1600	1736	1754	...	1858	...	1955	...	2018	...
Châtellerault d.	0624	0629	0724	0754	0813	0820	0918	...	...	1126	1311	...	1524	1525	1621	1624	1747	1818	...	1923	...	2020	...	2041	...
Tours a.	...	0718	...	0848	...	...	...	...	...	...	1410	...	...	1614	...	...	1841	...	...	...	...	...	...	2123	...

km		Ⓐ	Ⓐ	⑥		Ⓐ	Ⓐ	Ⓒ			Ⓐ	†		⑥	Ⓐ	Ⓐ		Ⓐ	⑥	†		Ⓐ	†			
0	**Poitiers** d.	0551	0624	0652	...	0754	0950	1005	...	1226	1530	1559	...	1615	1620	1716	...	1755	1812	1815	...	1906	1924	...	...	...
80	Niort d.	0640	0731	0751	...	0853	1037	1105	...	1323	1620	1647	...	1710	1721	1825	...	1855	1912	1914	...	2005	2021	...	...	...
147	**La Rochelle** Ville a.	0728	0819	0838	...	0940	1118	1152	...	1410	1706	1728	...	1751	1806	1913	...	1940	1959	2001	...	2046	2106	...	...	...

	①	⑥	Ⓐ		Ⓐ	†	Ⓐ		⑥	Ⓐ			Ⓐ	Ⓒ	Ⓐ		Ⓑ	⚒	⑤		†	⑥			
La Rochelle Ville d.	0557	0616	0622	...	0711	0754	0755	...	0919	1027	1225	...	1619	1627	1711	...	1739	1829	1930	...	2011	2030	...	...	...
Niort d.	0641	0703	0709	...	0756	0841	0840	...	1006	1114	1313	...	1704	1707	1756	...	1827	1917	2017	...	2056	2115	...	...	...
Poitiers a.	0738	0804	0804	...	0856	0935	0935	...	1101	1202	1408	...	1800	1752	1853	...	1928	2014	2105	...	2156	2204	...	...	...

ANGOULÊME and NIORT - SAINTES - ROYAN 301

km		Ⓐ	Ⓐ	Ⓐ	Ⓐ		⑥	†	⚒						Ⓐ	Ⓒ	Ⓐ		Ⓐ	Ⓐ	⑥	†	Ⓐ	†	⑤	
0	**Angoulême** d.	0611	...	0719	...	0916	...	...	1038	...	1251	...	1509	...	1644	1713	1747	...	1825	...	1914	1928	1949	...	...	2210
49	Cognac d.	0648	...	0757	...	0954	...	...	1119	...	1330	...	1545	...	1727	1749	1824	...	1905	...	1950	2006	2027	...	...	2246
	Niort d.	│	0643	│	0738	│	0940	1031	│	1237	│	1447	│	...	│	│	│	1752	│	1847	│	│	│	1948	2056	│
75	**Saintes** a.	0709	0751	0817	0848	1013	1047	1139	1139	1345	1349	1549	1605	...	1748	1808	1843	1902	1925	1957	2010	2026	2051	2056	2205	2306
75	**Saintes** ◇ d.	0712	...	0823	...	1019	1050	1142	1145	...	1401	...	1610	...	1751	1816	...	1904	...	...	...	2032	2053	2103	2208	2312
	La Rochelle Ville **292** a.	0814	...	│	...	│	│	│	│	...	│	...	│	...	1854	│	...	│	...	...	...	│	│	│	│	│
111	**Royan** ◇ a.	...	...	0852	...	1045	1117	1208	1212	...	1427	...	1639	...	...	1844	...	1933	...	...	...	2059	2124	2130	2234	2339

km		Ⓐ	Ⓐ	⑥	Ⓐ	Ⓐ	⚒		Ⓒ	Ⓐ	Ⓐ			Ⓒ	Ⓐ	Ⓒ	Ⓐ	Ⓐ	Ⓐ	Ⓒ		†	⚒	†	†	⑤
0	**Royan** ◇ d.	0535	...	...	...	...	0736	0928	...	...	...	1232	1329	1535	1536	...	...	...	...	1729	...	1827	1935	1940	...	...
	La Rochelle Ville **292** d.	│	...	...	...	0610	│	│	...	...	...	│	│	│	│	...	...	...	1655	│	...	│	│	│	...	...
36	**Saintes** ◇ a.	0601	...	...	...	0712	0806	0958	...	...	...	1258	1357	1600	1602	...	...	...	1758	1754	...	1955	2003	2005	...	...
36	**Saintes** d.	0607	0611	0626	0705	0715	0808	1006	1001	1016	1230	1301	1400	1606	1610	1623	1706	1720	1801	1800	1818	1903	2006	2017	2014	2033
116	**Niort** a.	│	0723	│	0821	│	│	│	1116	1116	│	1412	│	│	│	1726	│	1832	│	│	1931	│	│	│	2115	2135
	Cognac d.	0627	...	0645	...	0736	0828	1025	...	...	1250	...	1420	1626	1630	...	1726	...	1825	1820	...	1924	2026	2037	...	...
	Angoulême a.	0705	...	0723	...	0812	0908	1103	...	...	1328	...	1500	1702	1711	...	1810	...	1902	1902	...	2005	2106	2113	...	...

◇ – Additional trains Saintes - Royan and v.v.: from Saintes at 0728 Ⓐ, 1450 †, 1759 Ⓐ, 1846 ⑤, 2158 ①–④; from Royan at 0634 Ⓐ, 0834 Ⓐ, 1720 Ⓐ, 1959 ⑤, 2126 Ⓐ, 2145 Ⓒ.

302 BORDEAUX - ANGOULÊME, PÉRIGUEUX, BRIVE LA GAILLARD, TULLE and LIMOGES

TER services. For *TGV* services Bordeaux - Angoulême see Table **300**.

km		Ⓐ	Ⓐ	⑥	Ⓐ	Ⓐ	Ⓐ	Ⓐ	Ⓐ	†	Ⓐ	⑥	⑥	Ⓐ	⑥	†	Ⓐ	Ⓒ	Ⓒ	Ⓐ	Ⓐ	Ⓐ	Ⓒ	Ⓐ	Ⓒ
0	**Bordeaux** St Jean .... **306** d.	...	...	...	...	0548	0606	0627	0650	0716	0720	0724	0752	0823	0826	0927	1027	1027	...	1127	...	1227	1227	1252	1325
37	Libourne .... **306** d.	...	...	...	...	0612	0629	0652	0714	0741	0743	0750	0815	0849	0851	0950	1052	1054	...	1153	...	1253	1252	1316	1348
53	Coutras .... **306** d.	...	...	...	...	0624	0639	0702	0726	|	0752	0800	0828	0859	0900	1002	|	1103	...	1202	...	1303	1301	1329	1400
135	**Angoulême** .... a.	...	...	...	...	0715	|	|	0817	|	|	|	0922	|	|	1053	|	|	...	|	...	|	|	1423	1451
93	Mussidan .... d.	...	...	...	...	...	0707	0730	...	|	0819	0820	...	0927	0929	...	|	1131	...	1231	...	1332	1330	...	...
129	**Périgueux** .... a.	...	...	...	...	...	0731	0759	...	0826	0837	0837	...	0948	0950	...	1137	1152	...	1252	...	1354	1351	...	...
129	**Périgueux** .... **326** d.	0431	0603	0631	0700	...	0738	0802	...	0833	0844	0844	...	...	0954	...	1144	...	1234	...	1329	1357	1358	...	...
203	**Brive la Gaillarde** .... **326** a.	|	|	|	|	...	|	0859	...	|	|	|	...	...	1049	...	|	...	|	...	|	1452	|	...	...
	Tulle .... **326** a.	|	|	|	|	...	|	0931	...	|	|	|	...	...	1117	...	|	...	|	...	|	1520	|	...	...
166	Thiviers .... d.	0459	0634	0703	0738	...	0804	...	...	0856	0910	0910	...	...	...	...	1207	...	1304	...	1403	...	1422	...	...
228	**Limoges** Benedictins .... a.	0546	0725	0750	0825	...	0845	...	...	0937	0952	0951	...	...	...	...	1248	...	1353	...	1449	...	1506	...	...

		Ⓐ	Ⓐ		Ⓒ	Ⓐ	Ⓐ		Ⓐ	Ⓐ	Ⓒ	Ⓐ	†		Ⓐ	Ⓒ	Ⓐ		Ⓐ	Ⓐ	†	†	Ⓑ	⑥	
	Bordeaux St Jean .... **306** d.	1327	...	1426	...	1527	...	1617	...	1648	...	1727	1727	...	1758	1826	1827	1850	1900	1925	1927	...	2027	2027	2127
	Libourne .... **306** d.	1354	...	1452	...	1552	...	1647	...	1715	...	1756	1754	...	1824	1851	1853	1912	1925	1954	1952	...	2053	2052	2153
	Coutras .... **306** d.	|	...	1502	...	1603	...	1656	...	1727	...	1805	1803	...	1834	|	1903	1924	|	2003	2001	...	2103	2101	2203
	Angoulême .... a.	|	...	|	...	|	...	|	...	1818	...	|	|	...	|	|	|	2015	|	|	|	...	|	|	|
	Mussidan .... d.	|	...	1531	...	1631	...	1726	...	...	...	1833	1832	...	1902	|	1931	...	|	2032	2030	...	2131	2130	2231
	Périgueux .... a.	1437	...	1553	...	1652	...	1748	...	...	...	1854	1852	...	1922	1936	1955	...	2010	2052	2050	...	2152	2150	2252
	Périgueux .... **326** d.	1444	1530	...	1635	...	1709	...	1813	...	1825	1907	...	...	1925	1943	...	...	2023	...	2053	2126	...	2153	...
	Brive la Gaillarde .... **326** a.	|	|	...	|	...	|	...	|	...	|	|	...	...	2023	|	...	...	|	...	2147	|	...	2247	...
	Tulle .... **326** a.	|	|	...	|	...	|	...	|	...	|	|	...	...	...	|	...	...	|	...	...	|	...	...	...
	Thiviers .... d.	1507	1558	...	1706	...	1740	...	1851	...	1855	1933	...	...	...	2005	...	...	2049	...	...	2157	...	...	...
	Limoges Benedictins .... a.	1548	1645	...	1753	...	1827	...	1944	...	1944	2016	...	...	...	2047	...	...	2131	...	...	2244	...	...	...

		Ⓐ	Ⓐ	⑥	Ⓐ	Ⓐ	Ⓐ	Ⓐ	Ⓐ	⑥	⚒	Ⓑ	Ⓐ		⑥	⚒	†	⚒	†	Ⓐ	Ⓐ	Ⓒ		Ⓐ	Ⓐ
	Limoges Benedictins .... d.	...	...	...	...	...	0550	...	0609	0615	...	...	0713	...	...	0828	...	...	0926	1011	...	1105	...	1135	...
	Thiviers .... d.	...	...	...	...	...	0635	...	0701	0701	...	...	0802	...	...	0908	...	...	1005	1051	...	1143	...	1230	...
	Tulle .... **326** d.	...	...	...	...	...	|	...	|	|	...	...	|	...	0709	|	...	...	|	|	1045	|	...	|	...
	Brive la Gaillarde .... **326** d.	...	...	...	0532	...	|	...	|	|	...	...	|	...	0737	|	...	...	|	|	1113	|	...	|	...
	Périgueux .... **326** a.	...	...	...	0626	...	0657	...	0735	0730	...	...	0830	...	0831	0928	...	...	1026	1111	1206	1204	...	1258	...
	Périgueux .... d.	0532	0600	0603	0627	...	0704	0731	...	...	...	0807	...	...	0834	0935	...	1005	1033	1118	1209	1211	...	...	1320
	Mussidan .... d.	0554	0624	0624	0653	...	0726	0752	...	...	...	0829	...	...	0856	|	...	1026	|	1137	1231	1233	...	...	1341
	Angoulême .... d.	|	|	|	|	0644	|	|	...	...	0742	|	...	...	|	|	0944	|	|	|	|	|	1239	...	|
	Coutras .... **306** d.	0623	0653	0653	0722	0735	0754	0821	...	...	0834	0858	...	...	0924	|	1035	1054	|	|	1259	1302	1330	...	1409
	Libourne .... **306** d.	0634	0705	0703	0733	0747	0807	0832	...	...	0847	0908	...	...	0935	1021	1047	1105	1118	1207	1310	1313	1343	...	1420
	Bordeaux St Jean .... **306** a.	0700	0732	0732	0804	0810	0834	0900	...	...	0910	0935	...	...	1001	1047	1110	1131	1144	1232	1336	1338	1409	...	1442

		Ⓒ	Ⓒ	Ⓐ		Ⓐ	Ⓐ	Ⓐ		Ⓒ	Ⓐ		Ⓐ	Ⓒ		Ⓒ	Ⓐ		†	Ⓐ	Ⓐ	⑥	†	Ⓐ	†
	Limoges Benedictins .... d.	1214	...	1305	...	...	1549	...	...	1617	1634	...	1730	1815	...	...	1839	...	1916	...	2023	2028	2109	2215	2310
	Thiviers .... d.	1305	...	1345	...	...	1636	...	...	1704	1720	...	1817	1854	...	...	1931	...	2006	...	2112	2113	2155	2300	2357
	Tulle .... **326** d.	|	...	|	...	...	|	...	...	|	|	...	|	|	...	...	|	...	|	...	|	|	|	|	|
	Brive la Gaillarde .... **326** d.	|	...	|	...	...	|	...	...	|	|	1709	|	|	...	...	|	...	|	...	|	|	|	|	|
	Périgueux .... **326** a.	1334	...	1408	...	...	1656	...	...	1732	1756	1804	1841	1916	...	...	2000	...	2031	...	2138	2138	2222	2326	0023
	Périgueux .... d.	...	1407	1415	1605	...	1704	...	...	...	...	1807	1848	1930	...	2007	...	...	...	2036	...	...	...	...	...
	Mussidan .... d.	...	1429	1437	1627	...	1728	...	...	...	...	1835	|	|	...	2028	...	...	...	2057	...	...	...	...	...
	Angoulême .... d.	...	|	|	|	1643	|	1743	...	...	...	|	|	|	1842	|	...	...	...	|	...	...	...	...	...
	Coutras .... **306** d.	...	1458	1506	1656	1734	1759	1834	...	...	...	1904	|	|	1933	2057	...	...	...	2126	...	...	...	...	...
	Libourne .... **306** d.	...	1508	1516	1707	1746	1810	1846	...	...	...	1914	1933	2016	1945	2110	...	...	...	2136	...	...	...	...	...
	Bordeaux St Jean .... **306** a.	...	1534	1541	1732	1810	1835	1910	...	...	...	1941	1958	2042	2010	2136	...	...	...	2202	...	...	...	...	...

303 LIMOGES - MONTLUÇON

km		Ⓐ	⚒	⑥ 🚌		†	† 🚌	Ⓐ		†	⑥	Ⓐ		Ⓐ 🚌	Ⓒ	Ⓐ		Ⓑ	Ⓐ	Ⓒ		Ⓐ			
0	**Limoges** Benedictins .... d.	0651	0732	...	...	0915	...	1000	...	1223	1224	1301	...	...	1513	1551	...	1710	1810	1911	...	2033	...	...	...
78	Guéret .... d.	0758	0838	0855	...	1025	1035	1109	...	1329	1332	1409	...	1425	1619	1658	...	1817	1920	2017	...	2140	...	...	...
156	**Montluçon** Ville .... a.	...	...	1003	...	...	1143	1210	...	...	...	...	...	1533	1720	...	...	...	2021	...	...	...	...	...	...

		Ⓐ	Ⓐ 🚌	⚒		Ⓐ	Ⓒ	Ⓐ		⑥	Ⓐ	†		Ⓐ	† 🚌	†		⑥ 🚌	⚒	†		Ⓐ			
	Montluçon Ville .... d.	...	0554	...	...	0736	0841	...	...	...	...	...	...	1514	1528	...	...	1605	...	...	...	...	...	...	...
	Guéret .... d.	0620	0700	0716	...	0839	0943	1143	...	1203	1327	1343	...	1616	1628	1639	...	1711	1735	1819	...	1838	...	...	...
	Limoges Benedictins .... a.	0727	...	0825	...	0946	1051	1250	...	1311	1435	1450	...	1723	...	1746	...	...	1844	1925	...	1945	...	...	...

305 BORDEAUX - MONT DE MARSAN

km		Ⓐ	⚒	Ⓐ	Ⓒ		†	⚒		Ⓐ		Ⓒ	Ⓐ	Ⓐ		Ⓒ	Ⓐ	†	⑥		Ⓐ	†	⑤	①–④	
0	**Bordeaux** St Jean .... **306** d.	0546	...	0743	0838	...	...	1044	1246	1444	...	1544	1652	1744	...	1744	...	...	1944	...	1946	2028	2031	2031	...
40	Facture Biganos .... **306** d.	0613	...	0808	0901	...	...	1108	1308	1508	...	1608	1715	1809	...	1808	...	...	2008	...	2008	2051	|	|	...
109	Morcenx .... d.	0652	0746	0845	0939	...	1118	1145	1346	1546	...	1651	1756	1847	...	1849	2005	2017	2046	...	2046	2128	2125	2126	...
147	**Mont de Marsan** .... a.	0724	0816	0909	1002	...	1147	1209	1416	1616	...	1716	1829	1911	...	1918	2034	2043	2114	...	2114	2152	2145	2146	...

		Ⓐ	⚒	Ⓐ		⑥	†				Ⓐ			†	Ⓐ	⑥		†	Ⓐ	Ⓐ		Ⓒ	Ⓐ		
	Mont de Marsan .... d.	0523	0650	0742	...	0854	0902	1049	...	1245	1446	1547	...	1747	1754	1754	...	1815	1839	1924	...	1950	2044	...	...
	Morcenx .... d.	0544	0724	0815	...	0919	0933	1115	...	1316	1512	1614	...	1810	1827	1827	...	1846	1914	1954	...	2015	2113	...	...
	Facture Biganos .... **306** d.	|	...	0853	...	0959	...	1153	...	1354	1550	1652	...	1850	1906	1906	...	...	1952	...	...	2055	2153	...	...
	Bordeaux St Jean .... **306** a.	0646	...	0916	...	1024	...	1217	...	1417	1616	1716	...	1917	1931	1932	...	...	2015	...	...	2118	2216	...	...

BORDEAUX - TARBES and HENDAYE 305

For additional trains Puyoô - Tarbes see Table **325**. For overnight trains Paris - Lourdes - Hendaye see Table **319**. For connections Hendaye - Irún see Table **689**.

BORDEAUX - PAU - TARBES

km						*TGV* 8571				*TGV* 8572	*TGV* 8572					*TGV* 8575			*TGV* 8590				*TGV* 8593	*TGV* 8593	*TGV* 8593	*TGV* 8593
		Ⓐ	Ⓐ	⑥	Ⓐ	①–⑥	†	⑥	Ⓐ	①–⑤	⑥⑦	Ⓐ	†	⑤	⑥		Ⓒ	Ⓐ	⑤	Ⓒ	⑤	①–④	⑦	⑥	⑤	①–④
											d					A								e		
	Paris Montparnasse d.	...	...	...	...	0632	...	...	...	1005	1005	...	...	...	...	1400	...	...	1606	...	...	...	1806	1806	1808	1809
	Bordeaux St Jean a.	...	...	...	...	0849	...	...	...	1214	1214	...	...	...	...	1614	...	...	1814	...	...	...	2014	2014	2016	2017
0	**Bordeaux** St Jean **306** d.	...	0616	0744	0818	0854	0916	1019	...	1220	1220	1324	...	1519	1519	1620	1717	1719	1820	1845	1919	1924	2020	2020	2024	2027
40	Facture Biganos **306** d.	...	0639	0809	0841	|	0938	1042	...	|	|	1346	...	1542	1542	|	1740	1742	|	1909	1941	1946	|	|	|	|
109	Morcenx d.	...	0716	0845	0919	|	1010	1114	...	|	|	1418	...	1614	1613	|	1818	1820	|	1947	2018	2023	|	|	|	|
148	**Dax** a.	...	0736	0904	0938	1003	1029	1133	...	1328	1333	1437	...	1633	1632	1732	1837	1839	1928	2007	2037	2041	2127	2132	2135	2133
148	**Dax** ◇ d.	0642	0747	0915	0949	1006	1032	1144	1242	1336	1341	1448	1542	1644	1643	1736	1848	1850	1936	2018	2040	2044	2131	2140	2139	2137
179	Puyoô ◇ d.	0700	0805	0933	1007	|	1050	1202	1300	|	|	1506	1600	1702	1701	|	1906	1908	|	2036	2058	2103	|	|	|	|
193	Orthez ◇ d.	0712	0817	0946	1020	|	1103	1215	1312	1407	1414	1519	1612	1714	1714	1810	1918	1920	|	2047	2111	2115	2203	2213	2212	2208
233	**Pau** ◇ d.	0738	0841	1009	1044	1057	1127	1238	1336	1432	1441	1542	1636	1738	1738	1836	1942	1944	2028	2111	2135	2139	2228	2239	2239	2232
272	Lourdes a.	0806	...	...	...	1121	1156	...	1404	1457	1508	...	1705	...	1807	1907	...	2016	2053	2140	2203	...	2252	2305	2304	2257
293	**Tarbes** a.	0822	...	...	...	1147	1212	...	1420	1523	1537	...	1721	...	1822	1933	...	2032	2119	2156	2219	...	2319	2333	2332	2323

					TGV 8560			*TGV* 8562				*TGV* 8580		*TGV* 8582				*TGV* 8584			*TGV* 8586				*TGV* 8588
	Ⓐ	①	②–⑤	Ⓐ	①–⑥	Ⓐ	Ⓒ	⑦	Ⓐ	⑥	†	①–⑥	Ⓐ		†	⑤	†	⑥⑦	Ⓐ	†	①–⑤	①–④	⑤†	⑥	⑦
Tarbes d.	...	0513	...	...	0637	...	0750	0901	...	...	...	1039	1200	1236	1340	1432	...	1626	1636	...	1736	...	...	1830	1919
Lourdes d.	...	0527	...	...	0658	...	0805	0925	...	...	...	1103	1214	1300	1355	1447	...	1652	1651	...	1800	...	...	1845	1936
Pau ◇ d.	0504	0557	0559	0655	0728	0822	0835	0953	1022	1055	1123	1132	1245	1329	1425	1517	1541	1722	1723	1804	1828	1908	1914	1915	2004
Orthez ◇ d.	0529	0621	0623	0720	0752	0847	0859	|	1047	1119	1148	|	1309	1353	1449	1541	1605	1747	1747	1828	1852	1933	1939	1939	|
Puyoô ◇ d.	0540	0632	0634	0731	|	0858	0910	|	1058	1130	1159	|	1320	|	1500	1552	1616	|	1758	1839	|	1944	1950	1950	|
Dax ◇ a.	0558	0650	0652	0749	0820	0916	0927	1040	1115	1149	1217	1219	1338	1420	1517	1610	1634	1816	1816	1857	1920	2002	2007	2008	2051
Dax d.	0610	0653	0655	...	0829	0928	0930	1049	1127	...	...	1229	1350	1429	1529	...	1646	1821	1828	1909	1929	...	2019	2020	2054
Morcenx d.	0629	0712	0715	...	|	0947	0950	|	1147	...	...	|	1409	|	1548	...	1705	|	1847	1929	|	...	2041	2040	|
Facture Biganos **306** d.	0706	0749	0752	...	|	1019	1022	|	1219	...	...	|	1441	|	1620	...	1743	|	1919	2001	|	...	2113	2112	|
Bordeaux St Jean **306** a.	0733	0815	0815	...	0940	1042	1044	1206	1242	...	...	1340	1504	1540	1643	...	1805	1936	1942	2023	2043	...	2138	2138	2202
Bordeaux St Jean d.	...	...	...	...	0946	...	...	1212	...	...	...	1346	...	1546	...	...	...	1946	...	...	2049	...	...	...	2212
Paris Montparnasse a.	...	...	...	...	1200	...	...	1430	...	...	...	1601	...	1759	...	...	...	2156	...	...	2300	...	...	...	0025

BORDEAUX - BAYONNE - HENDAYE

km																*TGV* 8531	*TGV* 8531			*TGV* 8533				*TGV* 8535	*TGV* 8537	*TGV* 8537
		Ⓐ	①	②–⑤	Ⓐ	⑥		Ⓐ	Ⓐ	Ⓐ	⑥	Ⓐ	†		Ⓐ	⑦	①–⑥		⑥	Ⓑ		Ⓐ	†	⑥	①–⑤	⑥⑦
															B											
	Paris Montparnasse d.	...	...	...	...	...	...	...	...	...	...	...	...	...	...	0647	0703	...	...	0752	...	...	...	0922	1005	1005
	Bordeaux St Jean a.	...	...	...	...	...	...	...	...	...	...	...	...	...	...	0915	0914	...	...	1018	...	...	...	|	1214	1214
0	**Bordeaux** St Jean **306** d.	...	0507	...	...	...	...	0616	...	...	0744	0818	0819	...	...	0921	0920	...	1019	1024	...	1049	1119	|	1220	1220
40	Facture Biganos **306** d.	...	0529	...	...	...	...	0639	...	...	0809	0841	0841	...	...	|	|	...	1042	|	...	1114	1141	|	|	|
109	Morcenx d.	...	0606	...	...	...	...	0716	...	...	0845	0919	0918	...	...	|	|	...	1114	|	...	1148	1213	|	|	|
148	**Dax** a.	...	0624	...	...	...	...	0736	...	...	0904	0938	0937	...	...	1032	1028	...	1133	1136	...	1207	1232	1242	1328	1333
148	**Dax** d.	0544	0627	0628	0703	0717	...	0743	0810	0844	0911	0945	0940	...	...	1035	1032	1044	1140	1140	...	1210	1235	1246	1332	1337
199	**Bayonne** d.	0628	0714	0714	0747	0802	...	0828	0854	0928	0948	1017	1012	...	1044	1107	1106	1128	1212	1212	...	1243	1308	1319	1406	1413
209	Biarritz d.	0637	0723	0723	0757	0811	...	0837	0904	0937	0957	1026	1021	...	1053	1118	1119	1137	1221	1223	...	1252	1317	1330	1419	1424
222	St Jean de Luz d.	0653	0739	0738	0812	0826	...	0852	0919	0953	1012	1041	1037	...	1109	1134	1134	1153	1236	1239	...	1307	1332	1346	1434	1440
235	**Hendaye** a.	0707	0753	0753	0826	0840	...	0906	0933	1007	1025	1055	1051	...	1123	1147	1147	1207	1250	1252	...	1321	1346	1359	1447	1453

				TGV 8541					*TGV* 8547					*TGV* 8547		*TGV* 8549	★ 14155				★ 14157	★ 14155	*TGV* 8551	*TGV* 8551	*TGV* 8553
		Ⓒ	Ⓐ		⑦–④		⑤⑥	Ⓐ	⑤⑥		Ⓒ	Ⓐ		⑦	⑥	Ⓑ	Ⓐ	Ⓒ	Ⓐ		⑥	†	⑥	Ⓑ	⑤
																	C				C	C			
Paris Montparnasse d.	...	...	...	1206	...	...	...	...	1400	...	...	...	...	1518	...	1606	...	...	...	...	...	...	1806	1839	1948
Bordeaux St Jean a.	...	...	...	1423	...	...	...	...	1614	...	...	...	...	1727	...	1814	...	...	...	...	...	...	2014	2050	2212
Bordeaux St Jean **306** d.	...	1324	1324	1429	1519	...	1519	...	1620	...	1717	1719	...	1733	...	1820	...	1845	1846	...	...	...	2020	2056	2218
Facture Biganos **306** d.	...	1346	1346	|	1541	...	1542	...	|	...	1740	1742	...	|	...	|	...	1909	1911	...	...	...	|	|	|
Morcenx d.	...	1417	1418	|	1612	...	1613	...	|	...	1818	1820	...	|	...	|	...	1947	1947	...	...	...	|	|	|
Dax a.	...	1436	1437	1528	1631	...	1633	...	1732	...	1837	1839	...	1847	...	1928	...	2007	2006	...	...	...	2132	2206	2328
Dax d.	1344	1439	1444	1532	1634	...	1639	1710	1736	1744	1844	1846	...	1851	1910	1932	...	2014	2009	...	...	...	2136	2210	2332
Bayonne d.	1428	1512	1516	1606	1719	...	1724	1754	1808	1828	1917	1920	...	1925	1954	2006	2013	2047	2043	...	2114	2151	2208	2242	0006
Biarritz d.	1438	1521	1525	1619	1728	...	1733	1803	1820	1837	1926	1929	...	1937	2003	2019	2027	2056	2052	...	2127	2204	2219	2254	0018
St Jean de Luz d.	1453	1536	1540	1634	1743	...	1749	1819	1836	1853	1941	1944	...	1953	2019	2035	2044	2111	2108	...	2144	2219	2235	2310	0034
Hendaye a.	1507	1550	1554	1647	1757	...	1804	1833	1849	1907	1955	1958	...	2006	2033	2047	2056	2125	2122	...	2156	2231	2248	2324	0047

				TGV 8530					*TGV* 8534		*TGV* 8534		★ 14142				*TGV* 8536						*TGV* 8540		
	Ⓐ	⚒	Ⓐ			⚒	Ⓐ	⚒	①–⑥		⑦	Ⓐ		†	⑥			Ⓒ	Ⓐ	Ⓐ		†			†
													C							B				E	
Hendaye d.	0451	0554	0639	0712	...	0728	0810	0852	0928	...	0934	1010	1020	1052	1056	...	1110	1210	1232	1246	...	1252	1312	1352	1410
St Jean de Luz d.	0503	0606	0651	0726	...	0740	0822	0904	0940	...	0946	1022	1031	1104	1108	...	1123	1222	1245	1259	...	1304	1325	1404	1422
Biarritz d.	0515	0618	0703	0739	...	0752	0834	0916	0953	...	0959	1034	1042	1116	1121	...	1135	1234	1257	1311	...	1316	1338	1416	1435
Bayonne d.	0529	0632	0716	0754	...	0805	0848	0929	1011	...	1014	1047	1053	1129	1135	...	1150	1248	1310	1322	...	1329	1353	1429	1448
Dax a.	0602	0715	0800	0824	...	0849	0920	1013	1043	...	1044	1119	...	1213	1205	...	1223	1320	1342	...	...	1413	1424	1513	1521
Dax d.	0610	0718	...	0829	...	...	0928	...	1048	...	1049	1127	...	...	1208	...	1226	1323	1350	...	...	...	1429	...	1529
Morcenx d.	0629	0737	...	|	...	...	0947	...	|	...	|	1147	...	...	1228	...	|	1347	1409	...	...	...	|	...	1548
Facture Biganos **306** d.	0706	0814	...	|	...	...	1019	...	|	...	|	1219	...	...	1300	...	|	1420	1441	...	...	...	|	...	1620
Bordeaux St Jean **306** a.	0733	0838	...	0940	...	...	1042	...	1206	...	1206	1242	...	...	1322	...	1340	1442	1504	...	...	...	1540	...	1643
Bordeaux St Jean d.	...	...	...	0946	...	...	...	...	1212	...	1212	...	...	...	...	...	1346	...	...	...	...	...	1546	...	...
Paris Montparnasse a.	...	...	...	1200	...	...	...	...	1426	...	1430	...	...	...	...	...	1601	...	...	...	...	...	1759	...	...

		TGV 8542	*TGV* 8542				*TGV* 8544								*TGV* 8550		*TGV* 8550								
	Ⓑ	①–⑤	⑥⑦	†		⚒		Ⓐ	Ⓒ		Ⓐ	†	Ⓐ	⑥	⑥⑦		①–⑤	†	⑥	⑤†		⑥	①–④		
																		D	B						
Hendaye d.	1452	1501	1507	1529	...	1602	1612	1629	1652	...	1657	1752	1754	1759	1806	...	1812	1828	1844	1900	...	1902	1902	2006	...
St Jean de Luz d.	1504	1514	1520	1541	...	1615	1625	1941	1704	...	1709	1804	1806	1811	1819	...	1825	1840	1857	1912	...	1914	1914	2018	...
Biarritz d.	1516	1528	1534	1553	...	1627	1638	1953	1716	...	1722	1816	1818	1824	1832	...	1837	1853	1910	1924	...	1927	1926	2030	...
Bayonne d.	1529	1544	1550	1606	...	1641	1653	1706	1729	...	1735	1829	1831	1837	1849	...	1853	1904	1922	1938	...	1940	1939	2043	...
Dax a.	1613	1616	1621	1638	...	1711	1722	1750	1813	...	1820	1901	1915	1907	1919	...	1924	...	...	2011	...	2012	2017	2127	...
Dax d.	...	1621	1626	1646	...	1714	1727	...	...	...	1828	1909	...	1910	1925	...	1929	...	...	2019	...	2020	2020	...	...
Morcenx d.	...	|	|	1705	...	1733	|	...	...	...	1847	1929	...	1929	|	...	|	...	...	2041	...	2040	2041	...	...
Facture Biganos **306** d.	...	|	|	1743	...	1810	|	...	...	...	1919	2001	...	2001	|	...	|	...	...	2113	...	2112	2113	...	...
Bordeaux St Jean **306** a.	...	1734	1740	1805	...	1832	1836	...	...	...	1942	2023	...	2023	2040	...	2043	...	...	2138	...	2138	2139	...	...
Bordeaux St Jean d.	...	1740	1746	...	...	...	1846	...	...	...	...	...	...	...	2050	...	2049	...	...	...	...	...	...	...	...
Paris Montparnasse a.	...	1950	2005	...	...	...	2100	...	...	...	...	...	...	...	2300	...	2300	...	...	...	...	...	...	...	...

A – ⑤⑥⑦ until July 27; ⑤⑥ from Aug. 2.
B – 2 Pau - Hendaye and v.v.
C – 12 Toulouse - Hendaye and v.v.
D – 2 Hendaye - Tarbes.
E – ①②③④⑥.

d – Until Aug. 3.
e – Until Aug. 2.

◇ – Additional trains Dax - Pau and v.v.: from Dax at 0948 †, 1242 †, 1642 ①–④, 1804 Ⓐ, 1942 ①–④, 2016 Ⓐ; from Pau at 1514 ①②③④⑥, 1625 Ⓐ, 1812 Ⓐ.

★ – *INTERCITÉS.*

TGV – High-speed train. Ⓡ. 🍷.

306 COUTRAS - BORDEAUX - ARCACHON

km		TGV 8471 ⑥ e⊡	TGV 8473 ⑥⑦	TGV 8473 ①-④	TGV 8479 ⑤ d⊡	TGV 8475 ⑦	TGV 8477 ⑦	TGV 8477 ①-④	TGV 8477 ⑤ ⊡	
0	**Paris** Montparnasse d.	0752	1035	1106	1206	1518	1709	1839	1839	...
537	**Bordeaux** St Jean a.	1018	1247	1314	1423	1727	1917	2050	2050	...
537	**Bordeaux** St Jean **305** d.	1024	1257	1328	1426	1737	1927	2100	2100	...
577	Facture Biganos **305** d.	1048	1320	1353	1449	1800	1949	2122	2122	...
614	**Arcachon** a.	1109	1337	1410	1510	1815	2003	2137	2140	...

	TGV 8478 ①-⑥	TGV 8470 ⑥ ⊡	TGV 8472	TGV 8476 ⑦ ⊡					
Arcachon d.	0600	1350	1623	1850	...	...	...	...	...
Facture Biganos d.	0617	1411	1641	1911	...	...	...	...	...
Bordeaux St Jean a.	0640	1436	1702	1932	...	...	...	...	...
Bordeaux St Jean d.	0646	1446	1708	1938	...	...	...	...	...
Paris Montparnasse a.	0900	1715	1927	2235	...	...	...	...	...

km		Ⓐ	⚒	Ⓐ	⚒	Ⓐ	†	Ⓑ		⑥	Ⓐ		Ⓐ		Ⓒ	Ⓐ			Ⓐ	Ⓐ	Ⓒ	Ⓐ	Ⓐ	⚒
0	**Coutras** **302** d.	...	0644	...	...	...	0910	...	...	1015	...	...	1312	...	1511	...	...	...	...	1910	...	...	...	...
16	Libourne **302** d.	0622	0656	0724	0823	0922	0922	1024	...	1026	1124	1223	1324	1423	1523	1624	...	1724	1824	1922	1923	2023	2124	2156
53	**Bordeaux** St Jean **302** a.	0658	0729	0759	0858	0958	0958	1059	...	1059	1159	1258	1358	1458	1558	1659	...	1759	1859	1957	1958	2058	2159	2231
53	**Bordeaux** St Jean **305** d.	0703	0733	0803	0903	1003	1003	1103	...	1103	1203	1303	1403	1503	1603	1703	...	1803	1903	2003	2003	2103	2203	2235
93	Facture Biganos **305** d.	0734	0804	0834	0934	1034	1034	1134	...	1134	1234	1334	1434	1534	1634	1734	...	1834	1934	2034	2034	2134	2234	2304
109	La Teste d.	0751	0821	0851	0951	1051	1051	1151	...	1151	1251	1351	1451	1551	1651	1751	...	1851	1951	2051	2051	2151	2251	2321
112	**Arcachon** a.	0755	0825	0855	0955	1055	1055	1155	...	1155	1255	1355	1455	1555	1655	1755	...	1855	1955	2055	2055	2155	2255	2325

	⚒	⚒	Ⓐ	⑥		Ⓐ	Ⓐ		Ⓒ	Ⓐ	Ⓐ	Ⓒ			Ⓐ		Ⓐ	Ⓒ	Ⓒ	Ⓐ			
Arcachon d.	0605	0703	0736	0805	0905	1005	1105	...	1105	1205	1305	1305	1405	1505	1605	...	1705	1705	1735	1805	1905	2005	2105
La Teste d.	0609	0707	0740	0809	0909	1009	1109	...	1109	1209	1309	1309	1409	1509	1609	...	1709	1709	1739	1809	1909	2009	2109
Facture Biganos **305** d.	0626	0724	0757	0826	0926	1026	1126	...	1126	1226	1326	1326	1426	1526	1626	...	1726	1726	1756	1826	1926	2026	2126
Bordeaux St Jean **305** a.	0658	0756	0826	0858	0958	1058	1158	...	1158	1258	1358	1358	1458	1558	1658	...	1800	1758	1827	1858	2000	2058	2158
Bordeaux St Jean **302** d.	0702	0800	0830	0902	1002	1102	1202	...	1202	1302	1402	1402	1502	1602	1702	...	1805	1802	1831	1902	2004	2102	2202
Libourne **302** a.	0736	0836	0903	0936	1036	1136	1236	...	1236	1336	1436	1436	1536	1636	1736	...	1838	1836	1905	1936	2037	2136	2236
Coutras **302** a.	...	...	...	0948	...	...	1248	...	...	...	...	1448	...	...	...	...	1851	...	...	...	2049	...	...

Full service Bordeaux - Arcachon and v.v.: From **Bordeaux St Jean** at 0603 Ⓐ, 0703 Ⓑ, 0733 ⚒, 0803, 0903, 1003, 1032 Ⓑ, 1103, 1132 Ⓒ, 1203, 1303, 1403, 1503, 1603, 1703, 1732 Ⓐ, 1803, 1832 Ⓐ, 1903, 1935 Ⓐ, 2003, 2032 †, 2103, 2203, 2235 ⚒; from **Arcachon** at 0605 ⚒, 0636, 0650 Ⓐ, 0703 ⚒, 0720 Ⓐ, 0736 ⚒, 0805, 0838, 0905, 0935 Ⓐ, 1005, 1105, 1205, 1305, 1405, 1505, 1605, 1705, 1735, 1805, 1829 Ⓐ, 1836 Ⓒ, 1905, 2005, 2036 Ⓐ, 2105, 2212.

d – Until Aug. 1. **e** – Until Aug. 2. ⊡ – Via La Teste. Calls 5 minutes before / 7 minutes after Arcachon.

307 BORDEAUX - LE VERDON - POINTE DE GRAVE

km			⚒	Ⓐ		Ⓒ	†	⚒		†	Ⓐ			⑥	†			Ⓐ		Ⓐ		†		
0	**Bordeaux** St Jean d.	0758	0858	0956	...	1012	1100	1158	...	1159	1254	1359	...	1456	1559	1658	...	1756	1854	1958	...	2025	...	...
19	Blanquefort d.	0823	0922	1022	...	1033	1123	1222	...	1222	1323	1423	...	1519	1624	1723	...	1819	1923	2020	...	2048	...	...
35	Margaux d.	0843	0943	1043	...	1047	1141	1241	...	1241	1342	1442	...	1538	1643	1742	...	1838	1942	2039	...	2106	...	...
57	Pauillac d.	0907	1002	1105	...	1105	1201	1304	...	1304	1405	1504	...	1557	1704	1805	...	1857	2001	2058	...	2126	...	...
76	Lesparre d.	0922	1017	1120	...	1120	1216	1319	...	1319	1419	1519	...	1612	1719	1820	...	1912	2016	2114	...	2140	...	...
102	Soulac sur Mer d.	0945	...	1143	...	1143	...	1342	...	1342	...	1542	...	...	...	1843	...	...	2039	2137	...	...	...	...
109	**Le Verdon** a.	0952	...	1150	...	1150	...	1349	...	1349	...	1550	...	...	...	1850	...	...	2047	2144	...	...	...	...
112	**Pointe de Grave** a.	0956	...	1154	...	1154	...	1353	...	1353	...	1554	...	...	...	1855	...	...	...	...	...	...	...	...

	⑥	Ⓐ	Ⓐ		†	⚒			⚒				Ⓐ	Ⓒ	Ⓒ		Ⓐ	Ⓒ	Ⓒ		Ⓐ		
Pointe de Grave d.	...	...	...	...	...	...	1014	...	...	1213	1413	...	...	...	1714	...	1714	...	1911	...	1911	...	...
Le Verdon d.	...	...	0651	...	0818	0819	1018	...	...	1217	1417	...	...	...	1718	...	1718	...	1915	...	1915	...	...
Soulac sur Mer d.	...	...	0658	...	0825	0826	1025	...	...	1224	1424	...	...	...	1725	...	1725	...	1922	...	1922	...	...
Lesparre d.	0624	0629	0721	...	0849	0850	1048	...	1153	1247	1448	...	1628	1648	1748	...	1748	1854	1945	...	1945	...	...
Pauillac d.	0639	0644	0738	...	0906	0906	1106	...	1208	1303	1503	...	1643	1703	1806	...	1806	1909	2002	...	2002	...	...
Margaux d.	0659	0704	0800	...	0928	0928	1127	...	1228	1326	1524	...	1703	1727	1823	...	1825	1929	2027	...	2025	...	...
Blanquefort d.	0718	0723	0822	...	0947	0948	1149	...	1251	1349	1546	...	1722	1749	1838	...	1849	1949	2049	...	2048	...	...
Bordeaux St Jean a.	0742	0747	0846	...	1010	1012	1212	...	1314	1412	1610	...	1745	1813	1859	...	1912	2014	2112	...	2117	...	...

⛴ **POINTE DE GRAVE - ROYAN**. Journey 25 minutes. At least 8 sailings daily, more in Summer. For schedules see www.gironde.fr/deplacements/les-bacs-girondins-ferries.

308 PÉRIGUEUX - LE BUISSON - AGEN

km		Ⓐ	⚒	†	Ⓐ	Ⓒ	Ⓐ	Ⓐ	Ⓒ		Ⓐ	†	A	⑥	Ⓐ	†	Ⓐ	①-④ g	⑥	①-④	⑤	†	⑥	①-④	†	⑤
0	**Périgueux** d.	...	...	...	...	0824	0838	0941	1214	...	1252	1434	1516	1640	1651	...	...	1734	...	...	1820	1830	1840	2000	2005	2028
40	Les Eyzies d.	...	...	...	...	0853	0913	1010	1249	...	1327	1509	1546	1715	1726	...	...	1809	...	...	1857	1859	1915	2035	2040	2103
57	Le Buisson d.	...	...	...	...	0910	0929	1027	1306	...	1343	1526	1602	1732	1743	...	...	1826	...	...	1915	1916	1932	2051	2057	2120
108	Monsempron Libos d.	0633	0758	0817	0955	1004	...	1121	...	1317	...	...	1655	...	...	1801	1805	...	1846	1926	2007	2009	...	...	...	...
152	**Agen** a.	0718	0846	0902	1040	1047	...	1204	..	1402.	...	...	1740	...	...	1846	1859	...	1931	2013	2052	2052	...	...	...	...

	①	②-⑤ h		Ⓐ	Ⓐ	Ⓒ	Ⓐ		Ⓒ	Ⓐ	A	†		†	⑥	Ⓐ	Ⓐ	†	⚒	⑤	Ⓑ	⑥	①-④	†	⑤
Agen d.	...	...	...	0741	0900	0915	...	1223	...	...	1424	...	...	1553	...	...	1637	1706	1748	1748	1909	1945	2049	2108	2117
Monsempron Libos d.	...	...	...	0826	0943	1005	...	1307	...	...	1512	...	...	1636	...	...	1724	1751	1833	1833	1954	2030	2134	2153	2202
Le Buisson d.	0617	0617	0720	...	1037	1058	1139	...	1332	1441	1608	1627	...	1732	1740	1838	...	...	...	1926	...	...	...	...	...
Les Eyzies d.	0634	0635	0737	...	1054	1116	1156	...	1349	1458	1625	1644	...	1750	1757	1856	...	...	...	1944	...	...	...	...	...
Périgueux a.	0709	0709	0812	...	1123	1144	1231	...	1424	1533	1659	1719	...	1819	1832	1933	...	...	...	2019	...	...	...	...	...

A – ⑥ until Aug. 2; ⚒ from Aug. 4. **g** – To Sarlat (a. 1859). **h** – From Sarlat (d. 0547).

309 LIMOGES - ANGOULÊME and POITIERS

km		Ⓐ 🚌	Ⓐ 🚌	Ⓐ	Ⓐ		⚒ 🚌	⑥	†		⑥ 🚌		† 🚌	Ⓐ 🚌	†		⚒	Ⓐ 🚌	Ⓐ		⑤Ⓒ 🚌		Ⓐ	†
0	**Limoges** Benedictins d.	0505	0640	0700	0756	...	0850	0900	1005	...	1140	1213	1240	1400	1510	...	1604	1655	1712	...	1805	1810	1920	2011
42	St Junien ◧ d.	0535	0720	0742	0839	...	0930	0941	1046	...	1220	1253	1320	1440	1551	...	1645	1735	1754	...	1845	1853	2003	2052
50	Saillat Chassenon a.	|	|	...	0845	...	|	0947	1052	...	|	1259	|	|	1557	...	1651	|	...	...	|	1858	2009	2058
122	**Angoulême** a.	0720	0855	...	...	...	1115	...	...	...	1405	...	1505	1625	...	...	...	1910	...	...	2030	...	...	...

	Ⓐ	Ⓐ 🚌	⑥	Ⓐ 🚌		Ⓐ	⑥	†		⑥ 🚌		Ⓐ 🚌		Ⓐ		⑥ 🚌	Ⓐ 🚌			† 🚌	Ⓐ 🚌	† 🚌	⑤⑥ 🚌
Angoulême d.	...	0545	...	0740	...	...	...	...	...	1205	...	1240	...	...	...	1655	1730	...	...	1900	2000	2120	2120
Saillat Chassenon d.	0649	|	0743	|	...	0857	1000	1101	...	|	1403	|	1701	...	...	|	|	1908	...	|	|	|	|
St Junien ◧ d.	0656	0715	0750	|	...	0904	1007	1108	...	1345	1410	1420	1708	1804	...	1835	1910	1915	...	2040	2130	2300	2305
Limoges Benedictins a.	0736	0800	0830	0940	...	0944	1047	1148	...	1430	1449	1505	1749	1845	...	1920	1955	1957	...	2125	2215	2345	2355

km		Ⓐ	Ⓐ	⑥ 🚌	⑥	Ⓐ	†		†	Ⓐ	⑥	Ⓑ	Ⓐ	⑤	†		
0	**Limoges** Benedictins d.	0502	0553	0600	0748	0840	0950	1242	1457	1534	1644	1738	1843	1949	2016	...	...
139	**Poitiers** a.	0748	0848	0903	1033	1133	1238	1533	1738	1828	1933	2028	2133	2238	2303	...	...

	Ⓐ	Ⓐ	⑥	†			Ⓑ	⑥	Ⓑ		Ⓐ	⑥ 🚌	†	Ⓐ		
Poitiers d.	0450	0750	0750	0845	...	1150	1430	1535	1630	...	1735	1820	1905	1920	...	...
Limoges Benedictins a.	0746	1044	1049	1143	...	1446	1726	1836	1935	...	2041	2123	2204	2220	...	...

WARNING!

Due to engineering work all services Limoges - Poitiers and v.v. are operated by 🚌 between Le Dorat and Poitiers (except where noted).

◧ – 🚌 call at St Junien **champ de foire**.

PARIS - LIMOGES - TOULOUSE 310

Intercités services are valid **July 6 - August 3**. For *Intercités* service August 4 – 31 see page 604.
Timings of *Intercités* services may vary by a few minutes - please check your reservation. For *TGV* services Paris - Toulouse see Table **300**.

km		★ 3605	★ 3615	★ 3615		★ 3619	★ 3625	★ 3629		★ 3635	★ 3635	★ 3645		★ 3655	★ 3655	★ 3655		★ 3665	★ 3675	★ 3685		■ 3751	
		⚒	†	Ⓐ				†		A	B			⑥	Ⓐ	⑦		C	Ⓐ			Ⓡ	
0	**Paris** Austerlitz 294 315 d.	0622	0728	0728	...	0828	1028	1128	...	1216	1228	1428	...	1613	1628	1628	...	1728	1828	1928	...	2213	...
119	Les Aubrais-Orléans 294 315 d.	0731	|	|	...	0931	|	1240	...	|	|	1535	...	|	|	|	...	|	|	|	...	2322	...
200	Vierzon Ville 315 d.	0813	0908	0908	...	1011	1207	1315	...	1408	1408	1611	...	1755	|	1809	...	1908	2006	2108	...	|	...
236	Issoudun d.	|	|	|	...	|	1228	|	...	|	|	|	...	1815	1826	1830	...	|	2028	|	...	|	...
263	Châteauroux d.	0843	0940	0942	...	1042	1245	1348	...	1440	1440	1643	...	1831	1843	1846	...	1940	2044	2140	...	|	...
294	Argenton sur Creuse d.	|	0957	|	...	1059	|	|	...	1457	1457	|	...	|	|	|	...	1957	|	2157	...	|	...
341	La Souterraine d.	0921	1023	1023	...	1124	1323	1427	...	1523	1523	1722	...	1908	|	1924	...	2023	2123	|	...	|	...
400	**Limoges** Benedictins a.	0953	1055	1055	...	1155	1355	1457	...	1555	1555	1755	...	1940	1955	1957	...	2055	2155	2221	...	|	...
400	**Limoges** Benedictins d.	0956	1058	1058	...	1158	1358	1500	...	1558	1558	1758	...	1943	1958	2000	...	2058	2158	2223	...	|	...
459	Uzerche d.	|	1137	1138	...	|	1437	|	...	|	|	|	...	2021	2037	2038	...	|	2238	2258	...	|	...
499	**Brive la Gaillarde** a.	1100	1203	1203	...	1259	1504	1601	...	1701	1701	1901	...	2047	2103	2104	...	2200	2303	0001	...	|	...
499	**Brive la Gaillarde** d.	1103	...	...	...	1302	...	...	...	1704	1704	1904	...	...	...	...	...	2203	...	...	...	|	...
536	Souillac d.	1128	...	...	...	1329	...	...	...	1730	1730	1930	...	...	...	...	...	2230	...	...	...	0440	...
559	Gourdon d.	1145	...	...	...	1346	...	...	...	1748	1748	1946	...	...	...	...	...	2247	...	...	...	0457	...
600	**Cahors** d.	1213	...	...	...	1413	...	...	...	1815	1815	2014	...	...	...	...	...	2314	...	...	...	0527	...
639	Caussade d.	1240	...	...	...	1440	...	...	...	...	...	2041	...	...	...	...	...	...	...	...	...	0557	...
662	Montauban 355 355a d.	1255	...	...	...	1455	...	...	...	...	...	2056	...	...	...	...	...	...	...	...	...	0615	...
713	**Toulouse** Matabiau 355 355a a.	1332	...	...	...	1532	...	...	...	...	...	2132	...	...	...	...	...	...	...	...	...	0700	...

	■ 3750	★ 3604	★ 3614	★ 3624	★ 3628	★ 3634	★ 3634	★ 3638	★ 3644	★ 3644		★ 3648	★ 3650	★ 3654	★ 3654	★ 3664	★ 3674	★ 3684	★ 3684	★ 3694	★ 3694	
	Ⓡ	Ⓐ		⚒	†	Ⓐ D	⑥	†	Ⓐ	⑥		†		Ⓒ	Ⓐ	†		⑥	Ⓑ	①–⑤	⑥⑦	
Toulouse Matabiau 355 355a d.	2216	...	...	...	...	...	...	...	0635	0718	...	...	1027	...	...	...	...	...	...	1600	1607	...
Montauban 355 355a d.	2255	...	...	...	...	...	...	...	0720	0800	...	...	1105	...	...	...	...	...	...	1638	1644	...
Caussade d.	2312	...	...	...	...	...	...	...	0738	0816	...	...	1120	...	...	...	...	...	...	1654	1659	...
Cahors d.	2342	...	...	...	...	0644	0644	0754	0811	0843	...	...	1146	1242	1244	...	...	...	...	1726	1726	...
Gourdon d.	0013	...	...	...	...	0711	0711	0821	0844	0911	...	...	1214	1309	1312	...	...	...	...	1753	1753	...
Souillac d.	0031	...	...	...	...	0728	0728	0838	0903	0928	...	...	1231	1326	1328	...	...	...	...	1810	1810	...
Brive la Gaillarde a.	|	...	...	...	...	0754	0754	0903	0934	0954	...	...	1256	1352	1354	...	...	...	...	1835	1835	...
Brive la Gaillarde d.	|	0358	0455	0558	0702	0756	0756	0906	0937	0957	...	1102	1258	1354	1357	1557	1657	1754	1755	1838	1838	...
Uzerche d.	|	|	0522	|	|	0824	0824	0933	|	|	...	1128	|	1421	1425	|	|	1821	1822	|	|	...
Limoges Benedictins a.	|	0459	0559	0659	0803	0901	0901	1011	1051	1100	...	1206	1400	1459	1501	1659	1759	1900	1901	1940	1939	...
Limoges Benedictins d.	|	0502	0602	0702	0806	0903	0904	1013	1103	1103	...	1209	1403	1501	1504	1701	1801	1902	1903	1942	1942	...
La Souterraine d.	|	0534	0636	0735	0839	|	0937	1044	1136	1136	...	|	1435	1536	1538	1734	1834	1935	1936	2016	2016	...
Argenton sur Creuse d.	|	|	0700	|	0903	0957	1002	|	|	|	...	1301	1459	|	|	1759	1859	1959	|	|	|	...
Châteauroux d.	|	0611	0718	0815	0921	1015	1020	1124	1214	1214	...	1321	1516	1615	1618	1817	1918	2017	2013	2057	2057	...
Issoudun d.	|	0628	|	0831	|	|	|	1141	|	|	...	1337	|	1631	|	|	|	|	2030	|	|	...
Vierzon Ville 315 d.	|	0650	0751	0854	|	|	1055	1202	1248	1248	...	1359	1550	1653	1653	1855	1955	2050	2052	2131	2131	...
Les Aubrais-Orléans 294 315 a.	0555	|	|	|	1032	|	|	|	1328	1329	...	|	1629	|	|	|	|	|	|	2207	2207	...
Paris Austerlitz 294 315 a.	0703	0831	0931	1031	1134	1231	1231	1332	1431	1431	...	1531	1734	1831	1831	2030	2131	2231	2231	2310	2310	...

TER REGIONAL SERVICES

	⚒	⚒	Ⓐ		⚒	†	⚒		Ⓒ	Ⓒ	Ⓐ		Ⓐ	⑥		⑥	Ⓐ	†		Ⓐ	⑥	Ⓐ
Orléans 315 d.	...	...	0644	...	0741	...	...	...	1044	...	...	...	...	1615	...	...	...	1709	...	1743	1746	1842
Salbris 315 d.	...	...	0723	...	0820	...	...	...	1123	...	...	...	...	1654	...	...	...	1748	...	1822	1825	1921
Vierzon Ville 315 d.	...	0630	0741	...	0838	...	1030	...	1140	...	...	...	1708	1713	...	...	1736	1815	...	1840	1843	1939
Issoudun d.	...	0653	0806	...	0900	...	1052	...	1203	...	...	...	1729	1734	...	...	1757	1836	...	1903	1904	2001
Châteauroux d.	0626	0711	0824	...	0918	0959	1107	...	1221	1519	1702	...	1747	1752	...	1758	1812	1853	...	1919	1919	2019
Argenton sur Creuse d.	0643	0727	0841	...	0935	1015	1123	...	1238	1537	1719	...	1812	...	...	1817	1827	1916	...	1936	1944	2036
La Souterraine d.	0713	0756	...	...	...	1044	1151	...	...	1606	1750	...	...	...	...	1845	1856	1945	...	...	...	2105
Limoges Benedictins a.	0754	0839	...	...	...	1128	1238	...	...	1650	1837	...	...	...	...	1929	1835	2025	...	...	...	2150

	Ⓐ	Ⓐ	①	⑥		⚒	†	⚒	Ⓐ	Ⓐ	Ⓒ		Ⓐ	Ⓑ	⑥	†	⑥		Ⓐ	⚒	Ⓐ	Ⓐ
Limoges Benedictins d.	...	...	0532	...	...	0721	0723	...	0823	...	1321	...	1321	...	1557	1559	...	...	1620	1718	...	1823
La Souterraine d.	...	...	0614	...	...	0804	0811	...	0911	...	1405	...	1405	...	1642	1643	...	...	1705	1903	...	1911
Argenton sur Creuse d.	...	0645	0645	0646	...	0833	0840	0919	0940	1204	1434	...	1434	1619	1710	1711	...	...	1733	1833	1919	1940
Châteauroux d.	0638	0724	0724	0724	...	0851	0856	0939	0956	1222	1449	...	1451	1638	1727	1730	1738	...	1751	1851	1938	1956
Issoudun d.	0656	0741	0741	0741	...	0907	...	0956	...	1238	...	...	1507	1654	...	1747	1755	...	1809	1907	1954	...
Vierzon Ville 315 d.	0721	0809	0809	0809	...	0930	...	1020	...	1301	...	...	1530	1720	...	1811	1820	...	1835	1930	2020	...
Salbris 315 d.	0736	0825	0825	0826	...	...	...	1036	...	1318	...	...	...	1737	...	...	1836	...	1852	...	2036	...
Orléans 315 a.	0816	0905	0905	0905	...	...	...	1116	...	1357	...	...	...	1820	...	...	1916	...	1931	...	2116	...

	Ⓐ		Ⓐ		⚒		Ⓐ		†		⚒		Ⓑ		Ⓐ		Ⓒ		Ⓐ		Ⓐ	
Limoges Benedictins d.	0555	...	0615	...	0707	...	0815	...	1015	...	1230	...	1645	...	1745	...	1820	...	1845	...	2027	...
Uzerche d.	0633	...	0705	...	0758	...	0905	...	1106	...	1320	...	1736	...	1817	...	1910	...	1935	...	2117	...
Brive la Gaillarde a.	0700	...	0734	...	0827	...	0935	...	1135	...	1349	...	1805	...	1846	...	1940	...	2004	...	2146	...

	Ⓐ		⚒		Ⓐ		Ⓐ				⑥		Ⓐ				Ⓐ		Ⓑ			
Brive la Gaillarde d.	0610	...	0710	...	0810	...	1031	...	1228	...	1450	...	1715	...	1815	...	1915	...	2014	...	...	...
Uzerche d.	0640	...	0740	...	0840	...	1101	...	1258	...	1521	...	1745	...	1845	...	1944	...	2041	...	...	...
Limoges Benedictins a.	0730	...	0830	...	0930	...	1151	...	1347	...	1614	...	1835	...	1935	...	2034	...	2120	...	...	...

	Ⓐ	Ⓐ	⑥	†		Ⓐ	Ⓒ	Ⓐ	Ⓐ	⚒	†			⚒	†	⚒	†		Ⓐ	⚒	†	⑥
Brive la Gaillarde d.	...	0613	0625	...	...	0718	0825	...	0934	...	1018	...	...	1422	...	...	1625	...	1718	...	1825	2028
Souillac d.	...	0639	0650	...	...	0742	0850	...	0959	...	1043	...	...	1447	...	...	1650	...	1744	...	1850	2053
Gourdon d.	...	0655	0705	...	...	0757	0905	...	1014	...	1058	...	...	1502	...	...	1705	...	1800	...	1905	2108
Cahors d.	0613	0723	0731	0731	...	0823	0931	0931	1040	1124	1124	...	1324	1528	1530	1727	1731	...	1828	1925	1931	2134
Caussade d.	0641	0750	0758	0758	...	0851	0958	0958	...	1151	1151	...	1352	1556	1557	1755	1758	...	1855	1953	1958	2201
Montauban 355 355a d.	0658	0807	0815	0815	...	0907	1015	1015	...	1208	1208	...	1408	1612	1614	1811	1815	...	1912	2010	2015	2218
Toulouse Matabiau 355 355a a.	0735	0847	0905	0905	...	0945	1105	1106	...	1257	1257	...	1458	1659	1703	1902	1905	...	2001	2059	2105	2308

	Ⓐ	Ⓐ E		Ⓒ				Ⓒ		Ⓐ	Ⓒ		Ⓒ	Ⓐ		Ⓐ	Ⓒ		Ⓐ	Ⓐ		Ⓒ
Toulouse Matabiau 355 355a d.	0544	0626	...	0701	0859	...	1100	1258	...	1259	1502	...	1652	1718	...	1819	1855	...	1912	1952	...	2100
Montauban 355 355a d.	0635	0734	...	0752	0949	...	1150	1349	...	1349	1553	...	1742	1756	...	1858	1946	...	1951	2031	...	2150
Caussade d.	0651	0750	...	0808	1006	...	1206	1405	...	1406	1609	...	1759	1813	...	1914	2002	...	2007	2047	...	2207
Cahors d.	0719	0819	...	0835	1035	...	1233	1433	...	1434	1637	...	1826	1840	...	1941	2030	...	2034	2114	...	2234
Gourdon d.	0747	...	...	...	1101	...	...	1500	...	1503	1705	...	...	1908	...	2008	2056	...	...	...	...	...
Souillac d.	0802	...	...	...	1116	...	...	1515	...	1518	1720	...	...	1924	...	2023	2111	...	...	...	...	...
Brive la Gaillarde a.	0828	...	...	...	1140	...	...	1539	...	1545	1748	...	...	1950	...	2047	2135	...	...	...	...	...

A – July 7 – 11, 15 – 18.
B – Not July 7 – 11, 15 – 18.
C – Until July 19 (also July 25, 26).
D – Until July 19.
E – Until Aug. 1.

★ – *INTERCITÉS*. Ⓡ.
■ – *INTERCITÉS DE NUIT*. Conveys 🛏 1, 2 cl. and (2).
Overnight journeys only. **Timings and running days may vary**. For confirmed days of running and timings please consult the SNCF journey planner: www.sncf-connect.com.

311 BRIVE - AURILLAC

km		Ⓐ	⑥	Ⓐ	Ⓐ 🚌	Ⓒ	Ⓒ	Ⓐ 🚌	Ⓐ	Ⓒ
0	**Brive la Gaillarde** .... **316** d.	1129	1135	1410	1515	1531	1719	*1935*	2218	2218
27	St Denis-près-Martel ...... **316** d.	1151	1202	1434	|	1556	1745	2010	2242	2242
102	**Aurillac** .... a.	1318	1321	1556	1710	1726	1910	2201	0004	0007

	Ⓐ	⚒	Ⓒ	Ⓐ	†	Ⓒ	Ⓐ		
Aurillac .... d.	0518	0740	1041	1150	1435	1514	1559	1704	...
St Denis-près-Martel ... **316** d.	0643	0900	1201	1311	1557	1636	1718	1824	...
Brive la Gaillarde ...... **316** a.	0708	0923	1227	1337	1621	1702	1743	1844	...

312 TOULOUSE - LATOUR DE CAROL

For overnight trains see Table **319**. For *Le Petit Train Jaune* Latour de Carol - Villefranche and v.v. see Table **354**. For Latour de Carol - Barcelona and v.v. see Table **656.**

km		Ⓐ		Ⓐ	Ⓒ	Ⓐ	⑤	Ⓒ	Ⓐ	Ⓐ	Ⓒ	Ⓐ	Ⓒ	Ⓐ	Ⓒ	Ⓐ	Ⓐ	Ⓒ	Ⓐ	Ⓒ	Ⓐ	Ⓐ	⑥–④ 🚌	⑤
0	**Toulouse** Matabiau .... ⊡ d.	0646	0747	0847	0847	0947	1047	1047	1216	1247	1247	1347	1347	1547	1547	1647	1747	1747	1849	1947	1949	2047	2145	2147
65	Pamiers .... ⊡ d.	0741	0842	0946	0944	1045	1146	1144	1315	1346	1346	1442	1443	1644	1644	1746	1845	1846	1945	2050	2049	2144	2311	2242
83	Foix .... ⊡ d.	0757	0901	1001	1000	1101	1200	1201	1334	1400	1403	1459	1505	1659	1659	1804	1859	1900	2003	2106	2106	2159	2337	2258
123	Ax-les-Thermes .... d.	0839	0941	...	1041	1142	...	1243	1413	...	1442	1541	1546	1739	1744	1845	1939	1947	2043	2148	...	...	0024	*0001**
144	L'Hospitalet-près-l'Andorre .... d.	...	1006	...	...	1209	...	1308	...	...	...	1607	1617	1806	1817	...	...	2014	2111	...	...	...	...	...
163	**Latour de Carol** .... a.	...	1028	...	...	1230	...	1329	...	...	...	1627	1638	1827	1838	...	...	2034	2133	...	...	...	...	...

	⚒	Ⓐ	⚒	Ⓐ	Ⓒ		Ⓐ	①⑤	Ⓒ		Ⓐ	Ⓒ	Ⓐ	Ⓒ	Ⓑ	Ⓐ	Ⓒ	Ⓐ	Ⓐ	Ⓒ	Ⓒ	Ⓐ	†
Latour de Carol .... d.	...	...	...	...	...	0727	...	...	...	1031	...	...	1330	1333	...	...	1524	...	1630	...	1724	1831	2037
L'Hospitalet-près-l'Andorre .... d.	...	...	...	...	...	0750	...	...	...	1054	...	...	1353	1356	...	...	1547	...	1653	...	1747	1854	2100
Ax-les-Thermes .... d.	...	...	0613	...	...	0817	0920	...	1018	1121	1213	1222	1420	1422	...	1615	1615	...	1720	1721	1815	1921	2128
Foix .... ⊡ d.	0556	0628	0654	0723	0756	0902	1003	1100	1104	1202	1257	1307	1500	1504	1602	1658	1700	1731	1805	1802	1901	2002	2211
Pamiers .... ⊡ d.	0613	0646	0712	0743	0814	0919	1020	1117	1118	1220	1316	1322	1518	1520	1618	1715	1716	1747	1819	1818	1917	2018	2224
Toulouse Matabiau .... ⊡ a.	0712	0747	0814	0845	0914	1014	1115	1214	1214	1315	1414	1414	1614	1614	1714	1814	1814	1847	1916	1916	2014	2114	2317

⊡ – Other trains Toulouse - Foix at 0716 Ⓐ, 1447 Ⓑ, 1616 Ⓐ, 1647 Ⓒ, 1716 Ⓐ, 1816 Ⓐ, 1847 Ⓒ, 1916 Ⓐ; other trains Foix - Toulouse at 1900 Ⓐ, 2001 Ⓒ.

* – Connection by 🚌.

313 🚌 ANDORRA 🚌

Toulouse Matabiau ...... d.	0945	1345	1745
Toulouse Airport ✈ ...... d.	1015	1415	1815
Andorra bus station ...... a.	1345	1745	2145

Andorra bus station .. d.	0800	1200	1600
Toulouse Airport ✈ .. d.	1130	1530	1930
Toulouse Matabiau ... a.	1145	1545	1945

☛ Also from Toulouse Matabiau at 2145 and from Andorra bus station at 0400.
Operated by ANDBUS. www.andorrabybus.com.

Andorra bus station ...... d.	0515	1700	...
Soldeu .... d.	0555	1740	...
Pas de la Casa .... d.	0610	1755	...
L'Hospitalet ● .... a.	0635	1820	...
Ax-les-Thermes .... a.	0700	1845	...

Ax-les-Thermes .... d.	0930	2100	...
L'Hospitalet ● .... d.	1015	2125	...
Pas de la Casa .... d.	1040	2150	...
Soldeu .... d.	1055	2205	...
Andorra bus station .. a.	1130	2245	...

● – L'Hospitalet-près-l'Andorre.

Operated by Hife. www.hife.es.

314 TOULOUSE - CASTRES - MAZAMET

km		Ⓐ	⚒	†			Ⓑ	Ⓐ			
0	**Toulouse** Matabiau ...... ▲ d.	0541	0750	0840	1143	1344	1543	1643	1740	1847	2043
86	Castres .... ▲ a.	0654	0905	0957	1251	1451	1656	1749	1854	2000	2158
86	Castres .... d.	0704	0913	1002	1301	1501	1702	1759	1909	2009	2203
105	**Mazamet** .... a.	0723	0934	1022	1320	1520	1721	1818	1928	2029	2223

	Ⓐ	Ⓐ	Ⓐ							Ⓒ
Mazamet .... d.	0525	0549	0634	0737	1027	1231	1431	1729	1822	1939
Castres .... a.	0544	0608	0652	0756	1045	1249	1449	1747	1840	1957
Castres .... ▲ d.	0551	0614	0658	0802	1051	1255	1455	1753	1858	200
Toulouse Matabiau .... ▲ a.	0701	0730	0806	0911	1201	1402	1602	1909	2011	

▲ – Additional train Toulouse - Castre at 0901 Ⓐ; additional train Castre - Toulouse at 1615 Ⓐ.

315 PARIS and ORLÉANS - VIERZON - BOURGES - NEVERS and MONTLUÇON

Warning! Paris services are subject to alteration from August 2.

km ●		Ⓐ	Ⓐ	⚒	⚒ 🚌	⚒	⑥	⚒ 🚌	Ⓑ	⑥	A	Ⓐ d	⑤		Ⓒ	Ⓐ	† 🚌	Ⓐ	†	Ⓐ	Ⓐ	Ⓐ	Ⓑ	Ⓑ
0	**Paris** Austerlitz .... **310** d.	...	...	...	...	0707	...	...	...	...	...	...	...	1207	...	...	...	...	...	...	...	...	1705	...
	Orléans .... **310** d.	...	0607	0710	...	|	...	...	0907	0912	...	...	1207	|	...	...	...	1407	1605	...	1630	1707	|	1810
119	Les Aubrais-Orléans ...... **310** d.	...	|	|	...	0807	....	...	|	|	...	...	|	1307	...	...	...	|	|	...	|	|	1806	|
178	Salbris .... d.	...	0643	0746	...	0835	...	...	0944	0949	...	...	1243	1335	...	...	...	1444	1641	...	1709	1744	1831	1846
200	Vierzon Ville .... **290 310** d.	...	0658	0801	0823	0850	0905	0925	1000	1005	1021	...	1300	1350	...	...	...	1500	1657	...	1727	1800	1847	1900
232	**Bourges** .... **290** a.	...	0726	0821	|	0908	|	|	1020	1025	|	...	1320	1407	...	...	...	1528	1717	...	1754	1820	1905	1921
	Bourges .... **290** d.	...	0729	...	|	...	|	|	...	...	|	1207	...	...	1417	1434	...	...	1720	1735	...	1823	1908	...
	Nevers .... **290** a.	...	0816	...	|	...	|	|	...	...	|	|	...	...	|	|	...	...	1807	|	...	1910	1947	...
291	St Amand-Montrond-Orval .... d.	0644	...	...	|	...	1002	|	...	...	1120	1257	...	...	1502	1524	1720	...	...	1833	...	...	...	...
341	**Montluçon** .... a.	0727	...	...	0958	...	1037	1100	...	...	1154	1331	...	...	1536	1601	1820	...	...	1916	...	...	...	...

	①–④	†	Ⓐ	⑤ e			⑤†	⑤†
Paris Austerlitz .... **310** d.	...	...	...	...	1907	...	2107	...
Orléans .... **310** d.	...	...	1909	...	|	...	|	...
Les Aubrais-Orléans .... **310** d.	...	...	|	...	2008	...	2207	...
Salbris .... d.	...	...	1945	...	2035	...	2232	...
Vierzon Ville .... **290 310** d.	1921	...	2000	...	2050	...	2247	2257
Bourges .... **290** a.	|	...	2020	...	2107	...	2304	|
Bourges .... **290** d.	|	1935	...	2038	2110	2118	2306	|
Nevers .... **290** a.	|	|	...	|	2147	|	2344	|
St Amand-Montrond-Orval .... d.	2020	2026	...	2126	...	2206	...	2352
Montluçon .... a.	2055	2111	...	2201	...	2242	...	0027

	Ⓐ	⚒	⚒	Ⓐ 🚌		⑥	⑥	Ⓐ g
Montluçon .... d.	...	0534	...	0603	...	0611	...	...
St Amand-Montrond-Orval .... d.	...	0608	...	|	...	0645	...	...
Nevers .... **290** d.	...	|	0600	|	...	|	...	0639
Bourges .... **290** a.	...	|	0651	|	...	|	...	0738
Bourges .... **290** d.	0635	|	0654	|	...	|	0740	0741
Vierzon Ville .... **290 310** d.	0657	0703	0714	0738	...	0742	0801	0802
Salbris .... d.	0712	...	0728	...	...	...	|	0817
Les Aubrais-Orléans .... **310** d.	|	...	0756	...	...	...	|	|
Orléans .... **310** a.	0749	...	|	...	...	...	0841	0854
Paris Austerlitz .... **310** a.	...	...	0854	...	...	...	...	...

	Ⓐ 🚌	Ⓐ			A	Ⓐ h	†		🚌 f	Ⓐ d		Ⓐ	Ⓐ	Ⓐ	Ⓒ				Ⓐ	⑤ 🚌	†	†	Ⓐ
Montluçon .... d.	0630	...	0818	...	1043	...	...	...	1300	1406	...	...	...	...	...	...	1713	...	1748	1847	1908	...	1936
St Amand-Montrond-Orval .... d.	|	...	0853	...	1118	...	...	...	1405	1440	...	...	...	...	...	...	1748	...	1832	2007	1942	...	2009
Nevers .... **290** d.	|	0732	|	0853	|	1235	1300	...	|	|	...	...	1644	1737	...	...	|	...	|	|	|	2007	...
Bourges .... **290** a.	|	0837	0939	0947	|	1335	1352	...	1535	1535	...	...	1744	1837	...	...	1837	...	1921	|	2030	2059	...
Bourges .... **290** d.	|	0840	...	0947	|	1338	1354	...	...	...	1552	1641	1747	1840	1840	...	...	1852	...	|	...	2102	...
Vierzon Ville .... **290 310** d.	0835	0902	...	1006	1213	1401	1413	...	...	...	1611	1702	1808	1902	1902	...	...	1912	...	2104	...	2121	...
Salbris .... d.	...	0916	...	1020	...	1417	1427	...	...	...	1627	1715	1822	1916	1916	...	...	1927	...	...	...	2135	...
Les Aubrais-Orléans .... **310** d.	...	|	...	1048	...	|	1454	...	...	...	1655	|	|	|	|	...	...	1956	...	...	...	2203	...
Orléans .... **310** a.	...	0953	...	|	...	1457	|	...	...	...	|	1752	1859	1952	1953	...	...	|	...	...	...	|	...
Paris Austerlitz .... **310** a.	...	...	...	1152	...	...	1551	...	...	...	1753	...	...	...	...	...	...	2054	...	...	...	2301	...

A – ⚒ until Aug. 9; ⑥ from Aug. 16.
d – Until Aug. 8.
e – From Aug. 8.
f – Aug. 14, 22, 29.
g – Until Aug. 14.
h – Until Aug. 1.
● – *km* via Bourges (Montluçon is *327 km* for trains not calling at Bourges).

BRIVE - RODEZ 316

For overnight trains Paris - Rodez - Albi see Table **319**.

km		⑥	Ⓐ	Ⓑ	Ⓐ	Ⓒ	Ⓐ	Ⓐ		Ⓑ	
0	**Brive la Gaillarde** 311 d.	0541	0550	0744	1116	1327	1435	1707	1935	2226	...
27	St Denis-près-Martel 311 d.	0605	0613	0808	1140	1350	1501	1741	2003	2248	...
45	Rocamadour-Padirac d.	0623	0631	0829	1158	1408	1521	1800	2021	2306	...
53	Gramat d.	0629	0638	0836	1204	1415	1528	1807	2027	2312	...
88	Figeac 317 d.	0655	0706	0903	1233	1441	1555	1834	2054	2339	...
94	Capdenac 317 d.	0705	0716	0913	1243	1451	1607	1845	2103	2349	...
109	Viviez-Decazeville d.	0720	0731	0930	1257	1506	1622	1900	2118	0004	...
161	**Rodez** a.	0809	0819	1018	1349	1553	1709	1947	2205	0051	...

	Ⓐ	⑥	†	Ⓐ		Ⓐ	Ⓒ	Ⓐ	Ⓒ	
Rodez d.	0609	0714	0807	0841	1047	1250	1416	1502	1602	1737
Viviez-Decazeville d.	0657	0802	0855	0929	1135	1340	1507	1550	1650	1825
Capdenac 317 d.	0715	0819	0912	0946	1152	1357	1524	1608	1707	1843
Figeac 317 d.	0722	0826	0919	0953	1159	1406	1531	1615	1715	1850
Gramat d.	0748	0851	0944	1020	1225	1433	1556	1642	1740	1915
Rocamadour-Padirac d.	0754	0858	0951	1026	1232	1440	1603	1650	1746	1922
St Denis-près-Martel 311 d.	0813	0917	1010	1045	1251	1500	1622	1710	1805	1941
Brive la Gaillarde 311 a.	0837	0940	1033	1109	1315	1524	1645	1736	1830	2007

AURILLAC - TOULOUSE 317

km		Ⓐ	⚒	†	⚒	†	Ⓐ	A	†		B
0	**Aurillac** ◧ d.	...	0649	...	0849	...	...	1256	...	1649	1830
65	Figeac 316 ◧ d.	0600	0805	0805	1004	1004	1202	1405	1602	1805	1947
71	Capdenac 316 d.	0610	0815	0815	1014	1014	1211	1415	1611	1815	...
100	Villefranche de Rouergue d.	0638	0845	0845	1044	1044	1239	1445	1639	1845	...
117	Najac d.	0653	0900	0900	1058	1058	1254	1459	1653	1859	...
170	Gaillac 323 d.	0742	0949	0949	1145	1145	1341	1546	1742	1949	...
224	**Toulouse** Matabiau 323 a.	0831	1034	1031	1229	1223	1423	1629	1825	2033	...

	Ⓐ	⚒	†	†	A	⑥–④	⑤	Ⓐ	Ⓐ	Ⓒ
Toulouse Matabiau 323 d.	0653	0857	0857	1105	1303	1701	1701	1811	1909	1909
Gaillac 323 d.	0742	0937	0937	1145	1341	1741	1742	1850	1949	1949
Najac d.	0828	1028	1028	1231	1428	1828	1828	1937	2035	2035
Villefranche de Rouergue d.	0844	1043	1043	1247	1444	1844	1844	1953	2051	2051
Capdenac 316 ⊡ d.	0914	1112	1112	1317	1514	1914	1914	2023	2121	2121
Figeac 316 ⊡ d.	0924	1119	1118	1324	1521	1921	1921	2031	2130	2129
Aurillac ⊡ a.	...	1231	...	...	1632	...	2032	2141	...	2238

A – To/from Clermont Ferrand (Table **331**).
B – By 🚌 on ⑤.
◧ – Also Aurillac - Figeac at 2117⑤.
⊡ – Also Capdenac - Aurillac at 0550⚒, 0815⑥ 🚌, 0822Ⓐ.

BORDEAUX - BERGERAC - SARLAT 318

km		⚒	⚒	Ⓐ	⚒	†	Ⓐ	Ⓐ	Ⓒ	Ⓐ	Ⓐ	Ⓒ	Ⓐ	Ⓐ	Ⓒ	Ⓒ	Ⓐ	Ⓐ		Ⓐ	①–④	⑤	Ⓒ	Ⓐ	⑤
0	**Bordeaux** St Jean 300 302 d.	...	0550	0700	0739	0800	0840	0940	0942	1040	1139	1139	1240	1339	1341	1539	1600	1637	1739	1839	1941	1941	1941	2134	2227
37	Libourne 300 302 d.	...	0620	0725	0805	0825	0906	1006	1008	1106	1205	1205	1306	1405	1407	1605	1625	1703	1805	1908	2006	2007	2007	2204	2253
45	St Émilion d.	...	0628	0732	0813	0832	0913	1013	1015	1113	1213	1212	1313	1412	1414	1612	1632	1710	1813	1916	2014	2014	2015	2211	2300
77	Ste Foy la Grande d.	...	0701	0805	0839	0856	0937	1038	1043	1139	1239	1241	1339	1441	1441	1641	1659	1740	1838	1944	2040	2039	2044	2235	2323
99	**Bergerac** d.	0615	0720	0827	0859	0919	0952	1058	1101	1156	1253	1300	1359	1459	1500	1700	1718	1802	1859	2003	2054	2057	2058	2252	2340
135	Le Buisson 308 d.	0647	...	...	0934	0954	...	1131	1134	...	...	...	1434	...	1534	...	1753	...	1934	...	...	2128	...	...	...
168	**Sarlat** 308 a.	0717	...	...	1004	1024	...	1200	1203	...	...	...	1503	...	1603	...	1822	...	2005	...	...	2157	...	...	...

	Ⓐ	⑥	Ⓐ	Ⓐ	⑥	Ⓐ	Ⓐ	†	⑥	Ⓑ	⑥	Ⓐ	Ⓒ	Ⓐ	Ⓐ	Ⓐ	Ⓒ	Ⓒ	Ⓐ	Ⓐ		Ⓐ	Ⓐ	Ⓒ
Sarlat 308 d.	...	...	...	0620	0623	...	0730	0749	...	...	0914	...	...	1104	...	1251	1257	...	...	...	1725	...	1906	1907
Le Buisson 308 d.	...	...	...	0651	0653	...	0800	0820	...	...	0944	...	...	1134	...	1322	1328	...	...	...	1756	...	1937	1938
Bergerac d.	0532	0603	0621	0727	0730	0804	0836	0855	0909	1008	1022	1106	1201	1207	1301	1359	1407	1600	1621	1737	1833	1908	2008	2012
Ste Foy la Grande d.	0548	0619	0640	0745	0748	0821	0857	0912	0927	1022	1044	1122	1220	1222	1320	1420	1424	1619	1640	1756	1856	1925	2023	2027
St Émilion d.	0612	0646	0708	0814	0814	0846	0929	0936	0957	1046	1107	1146	1250	1246	1348	1448	1448	1651	1711	1830	1932	1952	2047	2051
Libourne 300 302 d.	0620	0653	0716	0821	0821	0854	0937	0944	1005	1054	1115	1154	1258	1254	1356	1455	1456	1658	1718	1838	1939	1959	2055	2059
Bordeaux St Jean 300 302 a.	0645	0717	0739	0847	0846	0919	1003	1009	1030	1123	1140	1219	1323	1319	1419	1520	1521	1724	1744	1904	2005	2025	2120	2124

OVERNIGHT TRAINS PARIS - AURILLAC, RODEZ, ALBI, TARBES and LATOUR DE CAROL 319

INTERCITÉS DE NUIT – 🛏 1, 2 cl. and (2). Overnight journeys only. Other trains: Toulouse Table **310**; Cerbère Table **355**; Briançon Table **358**; Nice Table **361**.
Timings and running days may vary. For confirmed days of running and timings please consult the SNCF journey planner: www.sncf-connect.com.

	3755 ⑥C	3755 ⑦D	3789 E	3755 ⑤F	3755 G	3789 H		
Paris Austerlitz d.	1921	1921	1921	1928	1928	1928	...	...
St Denis-près-Martel a.	0438	0438	0557	0438	0438	0557	...	...
Aurillac a.	|	|	0730	|	|	0730	...	...
Rocamadour-Padirac a.	0458	0459	...	0458	0459	...	...	...
Gramat a.	0505	0507	...	0505	0507	...	...	...
Figeac a.	0536	0538	...	0536	0538	...	...	...
Capdenac a.	0545	0547	...	0545	0547	...	...	...
Viviez-Decazeville a.	0601	0606	...	0601	0606	...	...	...
Rodez a.	0657	0708	...	0657	0708	...	...	...
Carmaux a.	...	...	...	0840	...	...	...	...
Albi Ville a.	...	...	...	0905	...	...	...	...

	3790 J	3754 M	3754 L	3754 K	3790 L			
Albi Ville d.	...	...	...	2050	...	...	...	...
Carmaux d.	...	...	...	2115	...	...	...	...
Rodez d.	...	2219	2219	2237	...	...	...	...
Viviez-Decazeville d.	...	2312	2312	2330	...	...	...	...
Capdenac d.	...	2330	2330	2348	...	...	...	...
Figeac d.	...	2340	2340	2357	...	...	...	...
Gramat d.	...	0012	0012	0028	...	...	...	...
Rocamadour-Padirac d.	...	0019	0019	0035	...	...	...	...
Aurillac d.	2238	|	|	|	2238	...	...	...
St Denis-près-Martel d.	0007	0039	0039	0056	0007	...	...	...
Paris Austerlitz a.	0838	0831	0931	0838	0931	...	...	...

	3731 ①–⑤	3971						
Paris Austerlitz d.	2141	2207	...	...	...	...	...	...
Les Aubrais-Orléans d.	2256	2322	...	...	...	...	...	...
Dax a.	0643	|	...	...	...	...	...	...
Bayonne a.	0719	|	...	...	...	...	...	...
Orthez a.	0824	|	...	...	...	...	...	...
Pau a.	0850	|	...	...	...	...	...	...
Lourdes a.	0918	|	...	...	...	...	...	...
Tarbes a.	0937	|	...	...	...	...	...	...
Biarritz a.	...	|	...	...	...	...	...	...
St Jean de Luz a.	...	|	...	...	...	...	...	...
Hendaye a.	...	|	...	...	...	...	...	...
Pamiers a.	...	0813	...	...	...	...	...	...
Foix a.	...	0828	...	...	...	...	...	...
Ax-les-Thermes a.	...	0915	...	...	...	...	...	...
L'Hospitalet-près-l'Andorre a.	...	0943	...	...	...	...	...	...
Latour de Carol a.	...	1010	...	...	...	...	...	...

	3970	3740 ①–⑤						
Latour de Carol d.	1848	...	...	...	...	...	...	...
L'Hospitalet-près-l'Andorre d.	1915	...	...	...	...	...	...	...
Ax-les-Thermes d.	1948	...	...	...	...	...	...	...
Foix d.	2034	...	...	...	...	...	...	...
Pamiers d.	2049	...	...	...	...	...	...	...
Hendaye d.	|	...	...	...	...	...	...	...
St Jean de Luz d.	|	...	...	...	...	...	...	...
Biarritz d.	|	...	...	...	...	...	...	...
Tarbes d.	|	1900	...	...	...	...	...	...
Lourdes d.	|	1918	...	...	...	...	...	...
Pau d.	|	1947	...	...	...	...	...	...
Orthez d.	|	2012	...	...	...	...	...	...
Bayonne d.	|	2101	...	...	...	...	...	...
Dax d.	|	2135	...	...	...	...	...	...
Les Aubrais-Orléans a.	0555	0610	...	...	...	...	...	...
Paris Austerlitz a.	0703	0732	...	...	...	...	...	...

C – ⑥ Aug. 9–30.
D – ⑦ Aug. 10–31.
E – ⑥⑦ Aug. 9–31 (also Aug. 15).
F – ⑤ Also Aug. 14; not Aug. 15.
G – ①②③④⑦ July 6 - Aug. 1; ①–④ Aug. 4–28 (not Aug. 14).
H – ⑤⑥ July 11 - Aug. 2 (also July 13); ⑤ Aug. 8–29 (also Aug. 14; not Aug. 15).
J – ①②③④⑦ (not July 13, 14, Aug. 14).
K – Also July 14; not July 13.
L – ⑤⑥ (also July 13, Aug. 14).
M – ①–④ (not July 14, Aug. 14).

323 TOULOUSE - ALBI - RODEZ

Timings may vary by up to 10 minutes from July 21. For overnight trains see Table **319**.

km																								
		Ⓐ			①⑤		Ⓒ		Ⓐ					Ⓐ			Ⓐ	Ⓐ			†	⚒	Ⓐ	
0	**Toulouse** Matabiau .... 317 d.	0605	0712	0917	1005	...	1005	1116	1231	1307	...	1411	1635	1710	...	1736	1752	1815	1837	...	1914	1928	2025	2126
54	Gaillac .... 317 d.	0648	0811	1004	1051	...	1051	1200	1320	1358	...	1457	1725	1757	...	1822	1841	1905	1922	...	2005	2020	2114	2211
75	**Albi** Ville .... d.	0703	0825	1025	1105	...	1105	1217	1341	1418	...	1512	1745	1819	...	1836	1902	1924	1937	...	2029	2040	2134	2231
92	Carmaux .... d.	0720	0842	1042	1122	...	1121	1234	1358	1434	...	1529	1802	...	...	1853	1919	...	1954	...	2045	2056	2150	2248
158	**Rodez** .... a.	0824	0946	...	1220	...	...	1336	...	...	...	1631	...	...	...	1957	...	...	2054	...	2146	2157	...	...

	Ⓐ	⚒	Ⓐ	Ⓒ	Ⓐ	⑥	Ⓐ	†				Ⓐ	Ⓒ	Ⓐ				Ⓐ		† 🚌	Ⓐ	†	⚒
Rodez .... d.	...	...	...	...	0620	0634	0739	...	0834	1022	...	1224	...	...	1430	...	1636	1727	1844	...	...	2102	2113
Carmaux .... d.	0522	0556	0617	0644	0721	0736	0843	0843	0934	1123	1144	1323	1323	1454	1530	1649	1735	1825	1955	...	...	2210	2213
Albi Ville .... d.	0539	0613	0634	0704	0740	0756	0902	0902	0951	1141	1201	1342	1342	1513	1547	1706	1754	1845	2012	2023	2054	2232	2232
Gaillac .... 317 d.	0558	0633	0657	0725	0756	0811	0918	0918	1004	1200	1223	1358	1358	1533	1602	1725	1808	1906	2032	2047	2114	2246	2246
Toulouse Matabiau .... 317 a.	0648	0720	0744	0820	0836	0851	1000	1000	1044	1240	1312	1439	1439	1619	1641	1820	1852	1954	2119	2153	2200	2325	2325

324 PAU - OLORON - CANFRANC

🚌 services are subject to confirmation. For connections to Zaragoza (Spain) see Table **670**.

km																								
		🚌	Ⓒ		Ⓐ	🚌			🚌			🚌			🚌					🚌				
0	**Pau** .... d.	...	0706	...	0715	...	...	0848	...	...	1203	...	...	1433	...	...	1557	1738	...	...	1906	...	2030	...
36	Oloron-Ste-Marie .... d.	0700	0742	...	0751	...	...	0924	...	...	1239	...	...	1509	...	...	1633	1814	...	...	1942	...	2106	...
61	Bedous (Gare) .... d.	0733	0812	...	0821	0850	...	0953	1035	...	1309	1510	...	1539	1640	...	...	1844	...	1856	2011	...	...	...
77	Urdos (Douane) 🛃 .... d.	0758	...	...	...	0913	...	...	1100	...	...	1535	...	...	1710	...	...	...	...	1921	...	...	...	...
96	**Canfranc** (Gare) .... a.	0829	...	...	...	0941	...	...	1131	...	...	1553	...	...	1723	...	...	...	...	1939	...	...	...	...

	⚒	Ⓒ		Ⓐ			🚌						🚌	🚌			🚌			🚌			
Canfranc (Gare) .... d.	...	...	...	...	...	...	0830	...	...	...	...	...	1420	1600	...	...	1725	...	...	1950	...	...	...
Urdos (Douane) 🛃 .... d.	...	...	...	...	...	...	0847	...	...	...	...	...	1450	1630	...	...	1755	...	...	2020	...	...	...
Bedous (Gare) .... d.	...	0712	...	0721	0854	...	0913	1209	...	1439	...	...	1516	1656	...	1744	1821	...	1912	2046	...	...	...
Oloron-Ste-Marie .... d.	0622	0746	...	0755	0928	...	...	1243	...	1513	1641	...	...	...	...	1818	...	...	1946	2122	...	...	...
Pau .... a.	0659	0822	...	0832	1004	...	...	1319	...	1549	1717	...	...	...	...	1854	...	...	2022	...	...	...	...

325 TOULOUSE - TARBES - PAU - BAYONNE

Trains with numbers are classified *Intercités*.

km																								
														14141			14143	14143				14151		
		Ⓐ	Ⓐ	⑥	Ⓐ	◧		⑥	Ⓐ	†	†	⚒			Ⓐ	Ⓒ	Ⓒ	Ⓐ			†		Ⓐ	Ⓒ
0	**Toulouse** Matabiau .... d.	...	...	...	0634	...	...	0736	0736	0736	0832	0832	...	0933	1016	1031	1133	1133	...	1232	...	1333	1431	1431
91	St Gaudens .... d.	...	...	...	0734	...	...	0831	0836	0831	0934	0936	...	|	1116	1131	1222	1222	...	1331	...	1422	1526	1530
104	Montréjeau .... d.	...	...	...	0744	...	...	0841	0846	0841	0945	0946	...	1031	1126	1142	|	|	...	1342	...	|	1537	1541
121	Lannemezan .... d.	...	...	...	0757	...	...	0854	0859	0854	0957	0959	...	|	1139	1154	|	|	...	1355	...	|	1549	1554
158	**Tarbes** .... 305 d.	...	0612	0714	0825	...	...	0922	0825	0922	1023	1025	...	1107	1205	1220	1307	1307	...	1421	...	1507	1617	1619
179	Lourdes .... 305 d.	...	0628	0729	0841	...	...	0938	0941	0943	...	...	...	1124	...	...	1324	1324	...	...	...	1524	...	...
218	**Pau** .... 305 d.	0611	0704	0802	0909	0921	...	1007	1010	1012	...	...	...	1152	...	...	1352	1352	...	...	1504	1552	...	...
258	Orthez .... 305 d.	0634	0729	0826	...	0945	...	...	...	...	...	...	...	1215	...	...	1415	1415	...	...	1529	1615	...	...
272	Puyoô .... 305 d.	0647	0742	0837	...	0957	...	...	...	...	...	...	...	|	...	...	|	|	...	...	1540	|	...	...
323	**Bayonne** .... a.	0726	0821	0915	...	1034	...	...	...	...	...	...	...	1300	...	...	1459	1516	...	...	1618	1659	...	...

				14155								14157				14157							
	Ⓐ	Ⓐ		Ⓐ ◧		†	Ⓒ	Ⓐ	⑥ A		Ⓐ	⑥ ◧	Ⓐ		Ⓐ	† ◧	Ⓐ	Ⓒ		Ⓐ	Ⓒ	Ⓐ	
Toulouse Matabiau .... d.	1442	...	1531	1631	...	...	1631	1642	1701	...	...	1731	1736	...	1742	1805	1831	1831	...	1841	1931	1931	2031
St Gaudens .... d.	1555	...	1627	|	...	...	1731	1755	1803	...	...	|	1831	...	1855	|	1926	1931	...	1954	2026	2031	2131
Montréjeau .... d.	1606	...	1638	|	...	...	1741	1806	1814	...	...	|	1842	...	1906	1904	1937	1942	...	2005	2037	2042	2142
Lannemezan .... d.	...	...	1651	1742	...	...	1754	...	...	...	...	1842	1855	...	...	1918	1950	1954	...	...	2049	2054	2155
Tarbes .... 305 d.	...	...	1719	1807	...	1810	1820	...	...	...	...	1907	1923	...	...	1943	2017	2020	...	...	2118	2121	2221
Lourdes .... 305 d.	...	...	1735	1824	...	1824	...	...	...	...	...	1924	1939	...	...	2000	...	...	...	...	2133	2136	...
Pau .... 305 d.	...	1709	1803	1852	...	1859	...	...	...	...	1924	1952	2007	...	...	2028	...	...	...	...	2202	2205	...
Orthez .... 305 d.	...	1733	...	1915	...	1923	...	...	...	...	1949	2015	...	...	...	2051	...	...	...	...	...	...	...
Puyoô .... 305 d.	...	1745	...	|	...	1934	...	...	...	...	2000	|	...	...	...	|	...	...	...	...	...	...	...
Bayonne .... a.	...	1826	...	1959	...	2017	...	...	...	...	2038	2059	...	...	...	2137	...	...	...	...	...	...	...

									14140		14140	14140										14142	
	Ⓐ	Ⓐ	⑥	Ⓐ		Ⓒ	Ⓐ	Ⓐ	Ⓐ		†	⑥	Ⓐ		Ⓒ	⑤–①	②–④	⑤–①		②–④		◧	
Bayonne .... d.	...	...	...	...	...	...	0634	...	0657	...	0659	0701	0752	...	0755	...	...	...	...	...	...	1103	...
Puyoô .... 305 d.	...	...	...	...	...	...	0715	...	|	...	|	|	0832	...	0833	...	...	...	...	...	...	|	...
Orthez .... 305 d.	...	...	...	...	...	...	0727	...	0748	...	0745	0748	0845	...	0845	...	...	...	...	...	...	1149	...
Pau .... 305 d.	...	...	...	0559	...	0655	0751	...	0812	...	0809	0812	0909	...	0909	...	...	0959	...	1005	...	1212	1256
Lourdes .... 305 d.	...	...	...	0628	...	0724	...	...	0839	...	0839	0839	...	...	...	...	...	1028	...	1035	...	1240	1325
Tarbes .... 305 d.	...	0545	0644	0645	...	0740	...	0743	0856	...	0856	0856	...	...	...	0945	0948	1045	...	1052	1144	1257	1342
Lannemezan .... d.	...	0612	0710	0713	...	0807	...	0809	|	...	|	|	...	...	...	1010	1014	1113	...	1120	1210	|	1408
Montréjeau .... d.	0602	0625	0722	0725	...	0820	...	0822	|	...	|	|	...	...	...	1023	1026	1125	...	1132	1222	1332	1421
St Gaudens .... d.	0610	0633	0730	0733	...	0828	...	0830	0937	...	0937	0937	...	...	...	1031	1034	1134	...	1141	1231	|	1429
Toulouse Matabiau .... a.	0721	0729	0829	0829	...	0923	...	0930	1025	...	1025	1025	...	...	...	1130	1133	1229	...	1244	1330	1426	1529

						14148	14148				14150												
		Ⓐ ◧			Ⓐ	Ⓐ	Ⓒ		Ⓒ	Ⓐ			Ⓐ	Ⓐ	Ⓒ		Ⓐ	†	†	Ⓐ		† ◧	⑥ ◧
Bayonne .... d.	...	1333	...	...	...	1445	1503	...	...	...	1703	...	1732	...	...	...	...	1745	...	1842	...	1921	1932
Puyoô .... 305 d.	...	1410	...	...	...	|	|	...	...	...	|	...	1812	...	...	...	...	1822	...	1920	...	2001	2010
Orthez .... 305 d.	...	1423	...	...	...	1548	1549	...	...	...	1749	...	1824	...	...	...	...	1834	...	1932	...	2013	2023
Pau .... 305 d.	...	1447	...	...	...	1611	1612	...	...	1659	1813	...	1848	1856	...	...	...	1858	1958	1956	...	2037	2046
Lourdes .... 305 d.	...	...	...	...	...	1639	1640	...	...	1728	1840	...	...	1926	...	...	...	...	2027	...	...	2110	...
Tarbes .... 305 d.	1446	...	1542	...	...	1655	1657	...	1744	1745	1857	...	...	1942	1944	...	...	...	2044	...	...	2124	...
Lannemezan .... d.	1513	...	1608	...	...	1720	1721	...	1810	1813	|	...	...	2010	2009	...	...	...	2112	...	...	...	...
Montréjeau .... d.	1526	...	1620	...	1701	|	|	...	1822	1825	|	...	...	2022	2022	...	2041	...	2124	...	...	...	...
St Gaudens .... d.	1534	...	1629	...	1710	|	|	...	1830	1834	1939	...	...	2031	2030	...	2049	...	2133	...	...	...	...
Toulouse Matabiau .... a.	1629	...	1729	...	1821	1825	1825	...	1929	1929	2026	...	...	2129	2129	...	2201	...	2228	...	...	...	...

MONTRÉJEAU - LUCHON

km										
		Ⓐ 🚌	🚌	🚌	Ⓒ 🚌	Ⓐ 🚌	Ⓒ 🚌	⑥ A	Ⓐ 🚌	🚌
0	Montréjeau .... d.	0754	0859	1144	1359	1600	1800	1824	1853	2059
	Luchon Gare .... a.	0848	0953	1238	1453	1654	1852	1859	1947	2153

	Ⓐ 🚌	⚒ 🚌	† 🚌	⚒ 🚌	† 🚌	Ⓐ 🚌	Ⓒ 🚌	Ⓒ 🚌	Ⓐ 🚌
Luchon Gare .... ⊡ d.	0615	0901	1015	1111	1246	1451	1512	1656	1957
Montréjeau .... ⊡ d.	0710	0956	1110	1206	1341	1546	1607	1751	2052

A – 2 Toulouse - Luchon.

◧ – To/from Hendaye (Table **305**).

⊡ – Also from Luchon at 1714 Ⓐ 🚌, 1910 Ⓒ 🚌.

PÉRIGUEUX, BRIVE LA GAILLARD and LIMOGES - USSEL and CLERMONT FERRAND 326

km		Ⓐ	⑥	Ⓐ	Ⓐ	⑥	Ⓑ	Ⓐ	Ⓐ	Ⓐ	Ⓒ	⑥	†	Ⓐ	Ⓐ 🚌	⑤	Ⓐ	†	⑥	①–④		⑤	Ⓒ	Ⓐ
	Bordeaux St Jean **302** d.	...	...	...	...	...	...	...	...	0627	...	0826	...	...	...	...	...	...	...	...	...	...	...	1227
0	**Périgueux** **302** d.	...	...	...	0624	0624	...	...	0731	0802	...	0954	0955	...	...	...	...	...	...	...	1233	...	...	1357
74	**Brive la Gaillarde** **302** a.	...	...	...	0726	0729	...	...	0835	0859	...	1049	1056	...	...	...	...	...	...	...	1336	...	...	1452
74	**Brive la Gaillarde** **302** d.	0626	0630	0701	▬	0739	0741	0824	...	0906	0921	1052	1059	1123	...	1208	1241	1312	1329	1331	...	1417	1453	1455
100	Tulle **302** a.	0651	0655	0728	① 🚌	0804	0809	0851	...	0931	0948	1117	1126	1148	...	1235	1306	1339	1355	1357	...	1444	1518	1520
100	Tulle d.	0700	...	...	0735	...	...	...	...	...	0958	...	...	...	1200	1242	...	1349	1404	1404	...	1452	...	...
153	Meymac d.	0754	...	...	0835	...	...	...	...	...	1053	...	...	...	1308	1343	...	1443	1459	1459	...	1547	...	...
166	**Ussel** a.	0806	...	...	0857	...	...	...	...	...	1105	...	...	...	1330	1354	...	1455	1510	1511	...	1559	...	...

	⚒	⑥	†	①–④	⑤	①–④	†	⑤⑥	Ⓐ	⑤	①–④	⑤Ⓒ	①–④	⑥	⑤	†	Ⓐ	⑤	†	†	Ⓐ	†	⑥
Bordeaux St Jean **302** d.	...	...	...	...	...	...	...	...	...	...	...	...	...	...	...	...	1758	...	...	1927	...	...	2027
Périgueux **302** d.	...	1558	1603	...	...	...	...	...	1635	...	...	1756	1756	...	...	...	1925	...	...	2053	2106	...	2153
Brive la Gaillarde **302** a.	...	1700	1705	...	...	...	...	...	1752	...	...	1859	1900	...	...	...	2023	...	...	2147	2209	...	2247
Brive la Gaillarde **302** d.	1621	...	1708	1709	1709	1746	1751	1751	...	1828	1853	...	1911	1912	1913	1930	...	2035	2112	...	...	2224	...
Tulle **302** a.	1647	...	1733	1734	1734	1811	1817	1817	...	1855	1918	...	1936	1937	1940	1956	...	2101	2137	...	...	2249	...
Tulle d.	...	...	1741	1743	...	...	...	1826	...	...	1926	...	...	...	1949	2004	...	2115	...	...	...	...	...
Meymac d.	...	...	1835	1837	...	...	...	1921	...	...	2022	...	...	...	2050	2059	...	2210	...	...	...	...	...
Ussel a.	...	...	1846	1849	...	...	...	1933	...	...	2033	...	...	...	2103	2111	...	2222	...	...	...	...	...

	Ⓐ	Ⓐ	⚒	Ⓐ	⑥	Ⓐ	Ⓐ	Ⓒ	Ⓐ	Ⓐ	⑥	†	Ⓐ	†	Ⓑ	⑥	Ⓐ	Ⓐ	†	†	⚒	Ⓐ	Ⓒ
Ussel d.	...	...	...	0542	...	...	...	...	...	...	0758	0846	...	...	...	...	...	...	1236	...	1251	...	...
Meymac d.	...	...	...	0555	...	...	...	...	...	...	0811	0859	...	...	...	...	...	...	1248	...	1304	...	...
Tulle a.	...	...	...	0649	...	...	...	...	...	...	0905	0952	...	...	...	...	...	...	1343	...	1359	...	...
Tulle **302** d.	...	0523	...	0655	0709	...	0736	0817	0817	0859	0914	1001	1045	...	1201	1223	...	1324	1353	...	1409	1526	1534
Brive la Gaillarde **302** a.	...	0549	...	0721	0734	...	0802	0842	0843	0926	0940	1027	1110	...	1227	1248	...	1349	1418	...	1435	1552	1600
Brive la Gaillarde **302** d.	0532	...	0620	...	0737	0749	...	0845	...	...	...	...	1113	1124	...	1251	1251	...	...	1430	...	...	...
Périgueux **302** a.	0626	...	0723	...	0831	0855	...	0947	...	...	...	...	1206	1224	...	1356	1357	...	...	1530	...	...	...
Bordeaux St Jean **302** a.	0804	...	...	...	1001	...	...	...	...	...	...	...	1336	...	...	...	...	...	...	...	...	...	...

	Ⓐ	⑤	†		Ⓐ	⑥		①–④	⑤	†	①–④	⑤⑥	†	①–④ 🚌	†	⑤	⑤⑥ 🚌	①–④	⚒	†	①–④	⑤	†
Ussel d.	...	1454	1507	...	...	...	...	1625	1628	1631	...	1702	...	1725	...	...	1800	...	...	1854	1931	1951	...
Meymac d.	...	1507	1520	...	...	...	...	1637	1641	1644	...	1719	...	1749	...	...	1824	...	...	1907	1944	2009	...
Tulle a.	...	1605	1613	...	...	...	...	1730	1734	1737	...	1813	...	1858	...	...	1933	...	...	2000	2040	2103	...
Tulle **302** d.	...	1614	1622	...	1702	1714	...	1738	1744	1744	1818	1821	1827	...	...	1908	...	...	1948	2009	2047	2110	2147
Brive la Gaillarde **302** a.	...	1640	1648	...	1730	1741	...	1806	1811	1811	1845	1847	1852	...	...	1935	...	...	2014	2035	2114	2135	2212
Brive la Gaillarde **302** d.	1640	...	...	1709	...	...	1814	...	1814	1814	...	...	...	...	1936	1938	...	1940	...	...	...	...	...
Périgueux **302** a.	1744	...	...	1804	...	...	1919	...	1919	1919	...	...	...	...	2038	2042	...	2042	...	...	...	...	...
Bordeaux St Jean **302** a.	...	...	...	1941	...	...	...	...	...	...	...	...	...	...	...	...	...	...	...	...	...	...	...

LIMOGES - USSEL

km			†	Ⓐ	⑥	⑤	†		A	B
0	**Limoges** Bénédictins ◧ d.	1005	1218	1245	1426	1540	1554	1828	2038	2116
99	Meymac ◧ d.	1145	1358	1424	1604	1717	1734	2007	2215	2253
111	**Ussel** ◧ a.	1157	1410	1436	1616	1729	1746	2019	2227	2305

	⑥	Ⓐ	Ⓒ	Ⓐ	⚒	†	⑤	†	Ⓑ
Ussel ◧ d.	0644	0812	0955	1041	1234	1254	1510	1543	1759
Meymac ◧ d.	0657	0825	1008	1054	1247	1307	1523	1556	1812
Limoges Bénédictins ◧ a.	0835	1002	1147	1232	1424	1445	1702	1735	1949

🚌 USSEL - CLERMONT FERRAND 🚌

km		🚌	🚌	🚌 Ⓒ	🚌 ⚒	🚌 †	🚌 ⑤	🚌		
0	**Ussel** d.	0825	1125	1230	1530	1625	1945	2110	...	...
	Clermont Ferrand a.	1010	1310	1410	1715	1810	2130	2250	...	...

	🚌	🚌	🚌	🚌 Ⓐ	🚌				
Clermont Ferrand d.	0745	1045	1245	1645	1745	...	...	...	...
Ussel a.	0930	1230	1430	1830	1930	...	...	...	...

A – ①–④ until July 31.

B – ⑤† until Aug. 3; Ⓑ from Aug. 4.

◧ – Also from Limoges at 0537 Ⓐ, 0749 ⑥; also from Ussel at 0612 Ⓐ, 1724 ⑥, 2031 ⑤.

CLERMONT FERRAND - LYON 328

For rail journeys Clermont Ferrand - St Étienne and v.v., travel via Roanne (see Table **291** for connecting services).

km			Ⓐ	⚒	⚒	†	⚒	Ⓐ	⚒				C		Ⓐ C		Ⓑ	†	Ⓑ C		C	Ⓑ	🚌	†
0	**Clermont Ferrand** ... **329 330** d.	...	...	...	0604	...	...	0702	...	...	0902	...	...	1202	...	1402	1501	1552	...	1702	...	1801	...	2002
14	Riom-Châtel-Guyon **329 330** d.	...	...	...	0613	...	...	|	...	...	0911	...	...	1211	...	1411	1510	1601	...	1711	...	1810	...	2011
55	Vichy **330** d.	...	...	...	0636	...	...	|	...	...	0934	...	...	1234	...	1434	1534	1624	...	1734	...	1834	...	2035
129	Roanne **290** d.	0608	0634	0708	0722	0725	0734	|	0834	0934	1020	1134	1250	1320	1450	1520	1620	1710	1750	1820	1850	1919	1945	2120
171	Tarare d.	0644	0710	0744	0757	0803	0810	|	0910	1010	1051	1210	1330	1351	1530	1551	1651	1741	1830	1851	1930	1950	2050	2150
222	**Lyon** Part Dieu **290** a.	0726	0752	0826	0834	0853	0852	0918	0952	1052	1126	1252	|	1426	|	1626	1726	1818	|	1926	|	2026	2200	2226
227	**Lyon** Perrache **290** a.	0738	0803	0840	0848	0903	0903	0930	1003	1103	1140	1303	1424	1440	1624	1640	1740	1832	1924	1940	2024	2040	...	2239

	⚒		⚒				D	Ⓐ		⚒			⚒				Ⓐ	Ⓐ	†	Ⓑ		⚒	†
Lyon Perrache **290** d.	0620	0657	0757	0957	1120	1157	1236	1338	1420	1457	1557	1620	1657	1720	1757	1820	1857	1920	1920	1957	2020	2041	2057
Lyon Part Dieu **290** d.	0634	0708	0808	1008	1134	1208	|	1350	1434	1508	1608	1634	1708	1734	1808	1834	1908	1934	1934	2008	2034	2052	2108
Tarare d.	0709	0802	0850	1050	1209	1250	1329	1441	1509	1550	1650	1709	1750	1809	1850	1909	1950	|	2009	2050	2109	2134	2150
Roanne **290** d.	0744	0843	0927	1127	1244	1327	1410	1521	1545	1627	1731	1744	1828	1844	1928	1945	2027	|	2044	2127	2145	2211	2227
Vichy **330** d.	0828	...	...	...	1328	...	...	...	1630	...	...	1828	...	1928	...	2029	...	|	2129	...	2229	...	...
Riom-Châtel-Guyon **329 330** d.	0851	...	...	...	1351	...	...	...	1652	...	...	1851	...	1951	...	2051	...	|	2151	...	2251	...	...
Clermont Ferrand **329 330** a.	0900	...	...	...	1400	...	...	...	1701	...	...	1900	...	2000	...	2100	...	2148	2200	...	2300	...	...

C – Also at 0650 ⚒, 1650 ⚒.

D – Also at 1636 Ⓐ, 1736, 1836 Ⓐ, 1936.

MONTLUÇON - VICHY and CLERMONT FERRAND 329

km		Ⓐ	Ⓐ	⑥	Ⓐ	Ⓐ 🚌		⑥ 🚌	①Ⓒ	②–⑤ 🚌	⚒ 🚌	Ⓐ			† 🚌		Ⓑ	Ⓐ 🚌		Ⓐ	Ⓐ	† 🚌		†
0	**Montluçon** Ville d.	...	0555	...	0658	0710	...	0726	0828	0844	0937	1038	...	1220	1321	...	1654	1707	...	...	...	1830	1841	1936
13	Commentry d.	...	0606	...	0710	|	...	0751	0839	0909	|	1050	...	1233	1346	...	1707	|	...	...	...	|	1854	1947
67	Gannat d.	0646	0705	0705	0807	0820	...	0846	0931	1012	|	1139	...	1334	1444	1617	1804	1827	...	1840	1907	|	1952	2045
	Vichy a.	|	|	|	|	0850	...	0915	|	|	1125	|	...	|	1511	|	|	1857	...	|	|	2000	|	|
94	Riom-Châtel-Guyon **328 330** d.	0714	0730	0729	0830	...	...	...	0947	1045	...	1158	...	1354	...	1643	1829	...	...	1908	1927	...	2011	2105
108	**Clermont Ferrand** ... **328 330** a.	0726	0742	0742	0840	...	...	...	0956	1110	...	1208	...	1404	...	1655	1839	...	...	1920	1939	...	2020	2114

	Ⓐ	①			Ⓐ 🚌	⚒	🚌			Ⓑ	Ⓐ		⚒	⑤† 🚌	Ⓐ		†	Ⓐ	⑤		†	🚌	⑤† 🚌
Clermont Ferrand **328 330** d.	0600	0635	0734	...	...	1218	...	...	1348	1649	1717	...	1745	...	1821	...	1914	1915	2007	...	2015	...	...
Riom-Châtel-Guyon **328 330** d.	0609	0645	0747	...	...	1231	...	...	1401	1702	1730	...	1757	...	1833	...	1926	1927	2016	...	2025	...	...
Vichy d.	|	|	|	...	0912	|	1345	...	|	|	|	...	|	1845	|	...	|	|	|	...	|	2010	2245
Gannat d.	0626	0707	0808	...	|	1253	1415	...	1425	1727	1754	...	1823	|	1900	...	1951	1953	2036	...	2046	2040	2315
Commentry d.	0718	0814	0857	...	|	1346	1510	...	...	1820	...	...	1914	|	...	...	2041	2042	2127	...	2136	2135	0010
Montluçon Ville a.	0731	0827	0908	...	1103	1357	1533	...	...	1832	...	...	1926	2012	...	...	2054	2054	2138	...	2147	2158	0034

330 PARIS - NEVERS - CLERMONT FERRAND

Timings of *INTERCITÉS* services are subject to frequent variations – please check your reservation for confirmed timings. Regional services are also subject to minor timing variations. Services from/to Paris are subject to alteration on Oct. 18, 19, 25, 26, Nov. 1, 2. On ⑥⑦ Sept. 6 - Oct. 5 (also on Nov. 8, 9) services may run from/to Paris Gare de Lyon (instead of Bercy)

km									5951	5955				5959	5963			5967		5971	5973		5977	5979	5983	5983
									🅁★	🅁★				🅁★	🅁★			🅁★		🅁★	🅁★		🅁★	🅁★	🅁★	🅁★
		①–⑥	①–⑥	Ⓐ	①–⑥	Ⓐ	①–⑥	Ⓑ	①–⑥		①–⑥	①–⑥	Ⓐ				Ⓐ	⑤	Ⓑ		Ⓐ	⑦	Ⓐ			⑤
		b	b		b		b	◐	b		b	b M		⊗				f	h		n	z	n	A	B	v
0	**Paris** Bercy ▶ d.	...	...	...	...	...	...	...	0700	0900	...	...	...	1300	1401	...	...	1459	...	1601	1657	...	1757	1758	1857	1857
254	**Nevers** ‡ ▶ d.	...	...	*0529*	...	...	0707	...	0900	1100	...	...	...	1500	1600	...	...	1700	...	1800	1900	...	|	2001	2100	2100
314	Moulins sur Allier ‡ d.	0506**g**	0559	0627	0643	0719	0745	0812	0930	1130	1219	1312	1418	1531	1630	1647	1715	1730	1805	1830	1930	1937	|	2031	2130	2130
355	St Germain des Fossés ‡ d.	0535	0622	0655	0710	0745	0810	0837	|	|	1243	1340	1443	|	|	1713	1742	|	1833	|	|	2001	|	|	|	2151
365	Vichy ▷ d.	0544	0631	0703	0719	0754	0819	0846	0958	1157	1252	1349	1452	1559	1659	1722	1750	1758	1842	1858	1958	2010	|	2059	2157	2201
406	Riom - Châtel-Guyon ▷ d.	0605	0652	0725	0741	0815	0840	0908	1022	1220	1314	1412	1515	1622	1723	1743	1812	1822	1904	1921	2020	2033	|	2122	2220	2224
420	**Clermont Ferrand** ▷ a.	0614	0701	0735	0750	0824	0850	0917	1030	1229	1322	1424	1524	1631	1732	1752	1821	1830	1913	1930	2029	2042	2116	2131	2229	2233

	5950	5950	5954		5958					5962		5966			5970	5974		5978			5982		5986		5990	
	🅁★	🅁★	🅁★		🅁★					🅁★		🅁★			🅁★	🅁★		🅁★			🅁★		🅁★		🅁★	
	①	②–⑤	Ⓐ	Ⓐ	⑥	Ⓐ	Ⓐ	①–⑥	Ⓐ		⑥	①–⑥	①–⑥	①–⑥		⑦	Ⓐ		Ⓐ	Ⓐ	Ⓑ		⑦			
	g	c	n		k			b			k	b ⊗	b	b		e					h	M	e ¶		△	
Clermont Ferrand ▷ d.	0524	0525	0551	0616	0627	0643	0717	0745	0808	0825	0842	1027	1034	1241	1328	1430	1540	1624	1644	1713	1725	1741	1830	1841	1926	2021
Riom - Châtel-Guyon ▷ d.	0535	0536	|	0625	0638	0652	0726	0754	0820	0835	0851	1038	1043	1250	1339	1441	1549	1634	1653	1722	1736	1750	1840	1850	1937	2030
Vichy ▷ d.	0558	0559	|	0646	0700	0714	0747	0816	0842	0858	0913	1100	1105	1311	1402	1503	1611	1657	1715	1743	1759	1813	1903	1911	2000	2051
St Germain des Fossés ‡ d.	0608	|	|	0655	|	0723	0756	0824	0850	|	0921	|	1124**j**	1320	|	|	1620	|	1724	1752	|	1822	|	1920	|	2100
Moulins sur Allier ‡ d.	0628	0625	|	0720	0726	0751	0822	0847	...	0923	0950	1126	1152	1345	1429	1529	1646	1723	1750	1814	1824	1849	1928	1945	2026	2123
Nevers ‡ ▶ d.	0657	0654	|	0754	0755	...	...	0918	...	0956	...	1155	...	...	1459	1558	...	1753	...	...	1854	...	1958	...	2055	...
Paris Bercy ▶ a.	0858	0857	0905	...	0957	...	...	...	...	1159	...	1359	...	...	1657	1759	...	1958	...	...	2057	...	2216	...	2257	...

ADDITIONAL TER TRAINS PARIS - NEVERS
Warning! Timing variations are possible – please check before travelling.

km			Ⓐ			①–⑥	①–⑥		Ⓐ	Ⓐ	Ⓒ	Ⓐ	⑦
					d ⊗	b n ⊗	b						e
0	**Paris** Bercy d.	...	0711	0911	...	...	1410	...	1702	1802	1804	1902	2009
119	Montargis d.	...	0814	1010	...	...	1510	...	1810	1910	1912	2010	2110
155	Gien d.	...	0836	1031	...	...	1532	...	1832	1932	1934	2032	2132
196	Cosne d.	0734	0859	1054	1234	1334	1555	1746	1855	1955	1957	2055	2155
228	La Charité d.	0800	0918	1114	1300	1400	1614	1811	1912	2012	2016	2114	2211
254	**Nevers** a.	0825	0938	1133	1325	1425	1633	1836	1932	2033	2036	2133	2231

	Ⓐ	Ⓐ	⑥	Ⓐ	Ⓐ			Ⓐ	⑦	①–⑥		
			k				⊗		e	b		◧
Nevers d.	0502	0602	0622	0727	0835	1026	1235	1428	1620	1635	1826	1935
La Charité d.	0522	0622	0644	0747	0900	1046	1301	1448	1640	1701	1846	2002
Cosne d.	0539	0639	0702	0806	0925	1105	1326	1505	1700	1726	1905	2027
Gien d.	0602	0702	0727	0829	...	1128	...	1528	1725	...	1928	...
Montargis d.	0624	0724	0749	0851	...	1150	...	1549	1748	...	1950	...
Paris Bercy a.	0729	0828	0848	0956	...	1250	...	1651	1850	...	2049	...

A – ⑦ to June 29; Ⓑ July 6 - Aug. 31 (not Aug. 15); ⑦ from Sept. 7 (also Nov. 11).
B – ①②③④⑥⑦ (not Aug. 14).
M – From/to Montchanin (Table **373**).

b – Not July 14, Nov. 11.
c – Not July 15, Aug. 15, Nov. 11, 12.
d – Not July 12, 19, 26, Aug. 2, 9, 16, 23, 30.
e – Also July 14, Nov. 11.
f – Also Aug. 14; not Aug. 15.
g – ① (also July 15, Nov. 12; not July 14).
h – Not Aug. 15.
j – Arrives 1114.
k – Also Aug. 15.
n – Not July 7 - Aug. 30.
v – Also Aug. 14.
z – Also July 14, Nov. 11; not July 13.

◧ – Runs 7–8 minutes **earlier** on ⑦.
◐ – Runs 4–5 minutes earlier on Aug. 15.

⊗ – Subject to alteration/cancellation Sept. 29 - Oct. 3 and Nov. 17–21.
△ – Not Nov. 15. On ①–⑤ Sept. 1 - Oct. 17 departures Clermont Ferrand - Moulins are up to 16 minutes earlier, does not call at Nevers and arrives Paris up to 20 minutes later.
¶ – On July 14, Nov. 11 does not call at Nevers and arrives Paris Bercy 2247 From Nov. 16 arrives Paris **Gare de Lyon** (not Bercy).
★ – *INTERCITÉS*. 🍸.
▶ – For additional trains see panel below main table.
▷ – See also Tables **328** and **329**.
‡ – See also Table **290**.

331 CLERMONT FERRAND - NEUSSARGUES - AURILLAC

km		Ⓐ	Ⓐ	⑥u	⑥u				⑤		Ⓐ	⑦	Ⓐ	⑥	⑦	Ⓐ	⑤	
			🚌		🚌	T	B		f			z		k	z		d	A
0	**Clermont Ferrand** ‡ d.	0543	...	0735	...	1038	1251	...	...	1648	1748	1757	1842	1850	1958	2012	2123	2138
36	Issoire ‡ d.	0611	...	0803	...	1103	1316	...	...	1716	1815	1825	1910	1919	2026	2040	2150	2206
61	Arvant ‡ d.	0629	0636	0821	0826	1121	1336	...	...	1736	1837	1844	1929	1938	2046	2059	2210	2226
85	Massiac-Blesle d.	...	0652	...	0842	1141	1356	...	...	1756	1901	1904	1949	1958	2106	2118	2230	2245
111	**Neussargues** a.	...	0723	...	0913	1202	1418	...	...	1817	1922	1925	2010	2019	2127	2139	2251	2306
111	**Neussargues** d.	...	0723	...	0913	1203	...	1438	1608	1818	1925	1926	2013	2020	2128	2140	2252	2307
120	Murat (Cantal) d.	...	0738	...	0928	1213	...	1447	1617	1827	1934	1935	2022	2029	2137	2149	2301	2315
131	Le Lioran d.	...	0750	...	0940	1226	...	1459	1629	1838	1952	1947	2034	2041	2148	2201	2313	2327
168	**Aurillac** a.	...	0837	...	1027	1255	...	1528	1701	1907	2021	2020	2104	2110	2218	2230	2342	2357

	①–⑥		Ⓐ	①–⑥								Ⓐ		Ⓐ	⑦		
	b		🚌	b					B		T				z		
Aurillac d.	0552	...	0713	...	...	1027	...	1330	...	...	1633	1742	...	1919	1951	...	...
Le Lioran d.	0623	...	0800	...	...	1059	...	1402	...	...	1709	1814	...	1951	2024	...	...
Murat (Cantal) d.	0634	...	0812	...	...	1110	...	1413	...	...	1721	1829	...	2002	2035	...	...
Neussargues a.	0642	...	0827	...	...	1118	...	1422	...	...	1729	1837	...	2011	2043	...	...
Neussargues d.	0643	...	0827	...	...	1119	...	...	1446	...	1732	1838	...	2012	2044	...	...
Massiac-Blesle d.	0705	...	0858	...	...	1143	...	...	1507	...	1757	1900	...	2033	2107	...	...
Arvant ‡ d.	0724	...	0914	0929	...	1202	...	...	1527	...	1817	1920	...	2053	2128	...	...
Issoire ‡ d.	0746	...	...	0950	...	1221	...	...	1546	...	1836	1939	...	2112	2147	...	...
Clermont Ferrand ‡ a.	0819	...	...	1019	...	1249	...	...	1611	...	1904	2007	...	2140	2215	...	...

A – ⑦ to July 6; ⑤⑦ July 11 - Aug. 31 (also July 14; not July 13); ⑦ from Sept. 7 (also Nov. 11).
B – To/from Béziers (Table **332**).
T – To/from Toulouse (Table **317**).

b – Not July 14, Nov. 11.
d – Not July 11 - Aug. 29.
f – Also Aug. 14; not Aug. 15.
k – Also Aug. 15.
u – Not Nov. 1.
z – Also July 14, Nov. 11; not July 13.

‡ – See also Table **333**.

332 (CLERMONT FERRAND -) NEUSSARGUES - BÉZIERS

SERVICE FROM JULY 5

km						🚌			🚌	🚌	🚌
		⚒	⚒	Ⓐ	⚒	⚒		⑤		⑥	Ⓑ
								F			w
0	**Clermont Ferrand 331** d.	...	...	...	...	1050	1251	...	1650	1950	2130
111	**Neussargues 331** d.	...	...	...	...	|	1437	...	|	|	|
130	St Flour ⊖ d.	...	...	...	*1051**	|	1458	*1536**	|	|	|
168	St Chély d'Apcher d.	...	...	...	1130	1225	1538	1627	1830	2125	2300
201	Marvejols ♥ d.	...	...	...	1207	1300**h**	1615	1705	1905**h**	2200**h**	2335**h**
	Mende ♥ a.	...	...	...	|	1340	|	|	1945	2240	0015
243	Sévérac le Château d.	...	...	...	1257	▬	1703	1754	▬	...	...
273	Millau a.	...	...	...	1329	...	1735	1826	†	...	...
273	Millau d.	0550	...	...	1330	...	1738	1828	2105	...	...
352	Bédarieux d.	0712	0842	1243	1450	1727	1858	1946	2232	...	...
394	**Béziers** a.	0745	0915	1317	1522	1801	1932	2019	2305	...	...

	🚌									
	⚒	⚒	⚒		⑤	Ⓐ			⑦	⑤
					F			P	G	F
Béziers d.	...	0637	0757	0933	...	1200	1643	1821	1900	1901
Bédarieux d.	...	0713	0830	1008	...	1233	1716	1859	1944	1947
Millau a.	...	0832	▬	1125	...	▬	▬	2016	2056	2104
Millau d.	...	0836	🚌	1127	1341	🚌	🚌	...	2101	...
Sévérac le Château d.	...	0906		1158	1411	Ⓐ	Ⓒ	...	2137	...
Mende ♥ d.	0700	|	0945	|	|	1535	1600	...	|	...
Marvejols ♥ d.	0735**h**	0954	1025	1250	1459	1610**h**	1635**h**	...	2231	...
St Chély d'Apcher d.	0820	1030	1115	1328	1535	1655	1720	...	2307	...
St Flour ⊖ d.	|	...	|	1407	...	|	|	...	...	...
Neussargues 331 a.	|	...	|	1428	...	|	|	...	...	...
Clermont Ferrand 331 a.	1000	...	1300	1611	...	1835	1900	...	...	...

OTHER 🚌 LINKS. See Tables **331** and **333** for connecting rail services Clermont Ferrand - Arvant/Massiac and v.v.

	🚌	🚌	🚌	🚌	🚌	🚌	🚌	🚌	🚌	🚌
	Ⓐ	Ⓐ	⑥		⚒		Ⓑ		⑤r	†
Clermont Ferrand 331 333 d.	...	...	...	...	1050	...	...	1830	...	2148
Arvant **331 333** d.	...	0741	0826	...	|	...	...	|	...	|
Massiac-Blesle **331** d.	0710	0800	0845	1150	|	1810	1910	|	2125	|
St Flour ⊖ a.	0735	0825	0910	1210	1220**t**	1830	1930	2010	2145	2313

	🚌	🚌	🚌		🚌	🚌	🚌	🚌	🚌
	⚒	⚒				Q	⑤r	Ⓐ	†
St Flour ⊖ d.	0627	0845	1110	...	1552	1712	1727	1822	1925
Massiac-Blesle **331** a.	0647	|	1135	...	|	1737	|	1847	|
Arvant **331 333** a.	...	|	...	...	|	...	1805	...	|
Clermont Ferrand 331 333 a.	...	1010	...	...	1717	...	...	...	2050

F – ⑤ from Sept. 5 (not Oct. 24, 31).
G – ⑦ from Sept. 7 (not Oct. 5–26).
P – Daily July 5 - Sept. 4; ①②③④⑥⑦ from Sept. 6 (also Oct. 31).
Q – ①②③④⑥⑦ (also Aug. 15).

h – Bus stop Henri IV (near Tourist Office).
r – Not Aug. 15.
t – 1230 on ⑤.

w – Runs 20 minutes later on †.

* – By 🚌 to St Chély d'Apcher.
⊖ – St Flour - Chaudes Aigues.
♥ – See Table **333** for connecting rail services Marvejols - Mende and v.v.

☛ 🚌 services in this table are operated on behalf of SNCF. Rail tickets valid. **🚌 timings are valid until Aug. 31.**

CLERMONT FERRAND - NÎMES and LE PUY EN VELAY 333

km		① a	②–⑤ u	⑥ t	②–⑤ u	Ⓐ 🚌	B	Ⓒ N	Ⓐ	⑦ 🚌	†	⑥	① c	Ⓒ J	🚌	L	Ⓒ J	Ⓒ J	🚌	Ⓒ	Ⓐ	F	Ⓒ	Ⓐ		
0	**Clermont Ferrand** .. 331 ¶ d.	...	...	...	...	...	...	...	0645	...	...	0735	...	...	...	...	0919	...	...	1257	1257	...	1430	1448	1640	1938
36	Issoire 331 ¶ d.	...	...	...	...	...	...	...	0713	...	...	0803	...	...	...	...	0949	...	...	1325	1325	...	1509	1519	1708	2016
61	Arvant 331 ¶ d.	...	...	...	...	...	...	...	0735	...	...	0822	...	...	...	...	1009	...	...	1345	1345	...	1532	1541	1727	2038
71	Brioude ¶ d.	...	...	...	...	...	...	...	0744	...	...	0831	...	...	...	...	1018	...	...	1355	1355	...	1540	1549	1736	2046
95	St Georges d'Aurac ¶ d.	...	...	...	...	...	...	...	0803	...	...	0849	...	...	...	...	1042	...	...	|	|	...	▬	▬	1804r	▬
03	Langeac d.	...	...	...	...	...	...	...	0811	...	...	0857	...	...	...	...	1056	...	...	1421	1421	...	⑤	...	1813	⑦
70	Langogne d.	...	...	...	...	...	...	...	0942r	0924	...	1031r	1052	...	1230	...	1239y	1244	...	1547	1547	...	h	...	1946j	d
	Marvejols d.	...	...	...	0700	0734	...	0750	|	|	...	|	|	...	|	...	...	|	*1332**	|	|	...	1720	🚌	|	2233
	Mende d.	0450	0547	...	0752	0838j	0840	0840	|	|	...	|	|	1127	|	1149	...	|	1454	|	|	1652	1832v	1834	|	2316
88	La Bastide-St Laurent d.	0605r	0706j	0707	...	0949n	0949	0949	1010r	0949	1012	1051	1111	1236	1255	1307r	...	1307	1602	1611	1612r	1808r	1940	1942	2016j	...
41	Grand Combe la Pise d.	0710	0810	0811	...	...	...	...	1110	...	1112	1151	1211	...	...	1410	...	1413	...	1711	1714	1913	...	...	2116	...
54	Alès d.	0727	0830	0831	...	...	...	...	1128	...	1132	1213r	1229	...	...	1432	...	1430	...	1728	1731	1931	...	...	2132	...
03	**Nîmes** Centre a.	0806	0902	0903	...	...	...	...	1200	...	1204	1246	1305	...	...	1504	...	1504	...	1800	1804	2003	...	...	2204	...

km		Ⓐ	⑥ k		①–⑥ b	① c		⚒ N	D 🚌	⑥ J	† J	Ⓒ J	N	n	🚌	⑤ h	⚒ 🚌		🚌	H	Ⓑ	M	† d	🚌	⑤ h	⑤ h
	Nîmes Centre d.	...	...	...	...	0718	0816	...	...	0951z	1019	...	1210	1214	...	...	...	1420	...	...	1656	1820	1821	...	2121	...
	Alès d.	...	...	...	...	0758r	0851	...	...	1030z	1054	...	1253	1253	...	...	...	1453	...	...	1750j	1857	1857	...	2158	...
	Grand Combe la Pise d.	...	...	...	...	0816	0907	...	...	1051z	1114	...	1310	1310	...	...	...	1509	...	...	1815r	1914	1914	...	2214	...
0	La Bastide-St Laurent d.	...	...	...	...	0920	1008	1010	1012	1159	1215	...	1422r	1422r	1420	...	...	1610	1615	...	1917	2023r	2023r	2020	2316	2321
47	Mende d.	...	...	...	...	|	|	1119	1121	|	|	...	1531	1532	|	1612	1618	|	1723	1730	|	2132	2135	|	...	0028●
82	**Marvejols** a.	...	...	...	...	|	|	1205	1206	|	|	...	...	...	|	1659	1655	|	*1820*h	1818	|	...	2217	|	...	|
	Langogne d.	...	...	...	...	0940	1032	...	...	1219	1235	1252	...	...	1444	▬	▬	1630	...	...	1939	...	...	2045	...	2346
	Langeac d.	...	...	...	...	...	1154	...	...	...	...	1422r	...	...	...	Ⓐ	Ⓒ	1754	...	...	2103	...	...	...	...	...
	St Georges d'Aurac ¶ d.	...	...	...	...	...	1202	...	...	...	...	1430	...	...	...			1803	...	...	2111	...	...	...	...	...
	Brioude ¶ d.	0555	0630	0706	1104	...	1221	...	...	...	...	1449	...	...	...	1604	1604	1822	...	...	2131	...	...	...	...	...
	Arvant 331 ¶ d.	0603	0638	0714	1112	...	1229	...	...	...	...	1457	...	...	...	1612	1612	1831	...	...	2139	...	...	...	...	...
	Issoire 331 ¶ d.	0624	0659	0735	1133	...	1250	...	...	...	...	1516	...	...	...	1633	1633	1849	...	...	2158	...	...	...	...	...
	Clermont Ferrand .. 331 ¶ a.	0655	0738	0814	1211	...	1317	...	...	...	...	1546	...	...	...	1707	1712	1917	...	...	2225	...	...	...	...	...

CLERMONT FERRAND - LE PUY EN VELAY

km		Ⓐ	🚌 ①–⑥ b◧⊡		🚌 ⊡	🚌 ⊡	①–⑥ b	🚌 ⑦ e△	⑤ f	🚌 Ⓐ ⊡	🚌 ⑤ f	⑦ §
0	**Clermont Ferrand** d.	0543	...	0949	...	...	1758	*1757*‡	1858	...	*2012*‡	2050
36	Issoire d.	0611	...	1017	...	...	1826	*1825*‡	1926	...	*2040*‡	2119
61	Arvant d.	0630	...	1036	...	...	1845	1900	1945	...	2103	2140
71	Brioude d.	0640	...	1045	1358	...	1854	1913	1954	2052	2118	2149
95	St Georges d'Aurac d.	0707	...	1110	|	...	1918	|	2019	|	|	2214
03	Langeac d.	|	0817	|	|	1818	|	|	|	|	2156	|
47	**Le Puy en Velay** a.	0758	0903	1201	1506	1908	2010	2021	2110	2200	2242	2306

	① g	E	①–⑥ b	🚌 ①–⑥ b◐⊡	🚌 ⑦ e⊡	🚌 Ⓐ	⑥ k		🚌 ⊡	🚌 Ⓐ	⑦ w
Le Puy en Velay d.	0523	0610	0807	0945	1059	1205	1210	1601	1654	1918	1953
Langeac d.	|	|	|	|	|	|	|	|	1744	|	|
St Georges d'Aurac d.	0616	0703	0859	|	|	|	1303	1654	...	|	2046
Brioude d.	0641	0725	0921	1049	1203	1311	1324	1715	...	2026	2107
Arvant d.	0650	0734	0929	...	...	1326	1333	1724	...	2043	2116
Issoire d.	0712	0754	0950	...	...	1408	1354	1745	...	*2112*‡	2137
Clermont Ferrand a.	0745	0824	1019	...	...	1448	1422	1813	...	*2140*‡	2204

– ⑦ to June 29; Ⓐ July 7 - Aug. 29; † from Sept. 7.
– Daily to July 4; † July 6 - Aug. 24; daily from Aug. 31.
– ②–⑤ to July 18; Ⓐ July 21 - Aug. 22; ②–⑤ from Aug. 26 (not Nov. 12).
– ⑤⑦ to June 29; † July 6 - Aug. 31; ⑤† from Sept. 5 (not Oct. 24, 31).
– ①–④ to June 26; ⚒ June 30 - Aug. 30; ①–④ from Sept. 1 (also Oct. 24, 31; not Nov. 11).
– Until Sept. 14.
– Ⓐ to Sept. 12; daily from Sept. 15.
– ⚒ (daily June 30 - Sept. 6 and Oct. 13–31).
– July 5 - Aug. 31.
– ②–⑥ (⚒ July 7 - Aug. 30); not Nov. 1, 11, 12.
– Also July 15, Nov. 12; not July 14.
– Not July 14, Nov. 11.
– Also Nov. 12; not July 7 - Sept. 1, Oct. 20, 27.

d – Not July 6 - Aug. 31, Oct. 19, 26.
e – Also July 14, Nov. 11.
f – Also Aug. 14; not Aug. 15.
g – Also Nov. 12; not July 14 - Aug. 18.
h – ⑤ (not July 4 - Aug. 29, Oct. 24, 31).
j – Arrives 10–15 minutes earlier.
k – Also Aug. 15.
n – Not July 5 - Aug. 31.
p – 3–4 minutes later on Ⓐ.
r – Arrives 6–9 minutes earlier.
t – Not July 5 - Aug. 30, Oct. 25, Nov. 1.
u – Not July 15, Aug. 15, Nov. 11, 12.
v – Arrives 1807.
w – Also July 14, Nov. 11; not July 13.
y – 1228 on ⑥ (also July 14, Aug. 15).
z – 4–8 minutes later from July 5.

* – On ⚒ July 5 - Aug. 30 connection is by train (departs Marvejols 1351).
§ – Also July 14, Nov. 11; not July 13. Runs 16–18 minutes **earlier** until July 6.
● – Via Langogne.
△ – Connecting train Clermont Ferrand - Arvant does not run on July 13.
◧ – On ⑥ (also Aug. 15) Langeac d. 0902, Le Puy en Velay a. 0948.
◐ – On ⑥ (also Aug. 15) Le Puy en Velay d. 0952, Brioude a. 1054.
◇ – Departs 0931 on ⑥ July 5 - Aug. 30.
⊙ – Departs 2118 on ⑤ July 4 - Aug. 29 (also Aug. 15; not Aug. 15).
⊡ – See main panel for connecting rail service from / to Clermont Ferrand.
¶ – See panel below main table for services to / from Le Puy en Velay.
‡ – Connecting service is by train.
▶ – Other trains Alès - Nîmes (journey 31–43 minutes). **From Alès** at 0558 Ⓐ **n**, 0626 Ⓐ, 0658, 0759 ⚒, 0831 Ⓒ, 0832 ① **a**, 0922 Ⓒ◇, 0930 Ⓐ, 1031 Ⓐ, 1229 Ⓐ, 1324, 1527 Ⓒ, 1530 Ⓐ, 1636 Ⓐ, 1834 Ⓐ, 1926 ⑥, 1931 Ⓑ, 2027. **From Nîmes** at 0614 Ⓐ, 0656 Ⓐ **n**, 0714 **R**, 0748 Ⓐ, 0921 Ⓐ, 1021 **L**, 1121 Ⓐ, 1257 Ⓐ, 1321 Ⓐ, 1521 Ⓐ, 1618, 1722 ⚒, 1937 Ⓐ, 2021, 2121⊙.

TGV services LYON - MASSY - LE MANS - RENNES and NANTES 335

See Table **290** for slower services via Bourges. Subject to alteration / cancellation on June 15, 21, 28, 29, July 19, 20. Timings may vary by a few minutes (please check your reservation).

	TGV **5380**	*TGV* **5350** ①–⑤ M	*TGV* **5350** N	*TGV* **5376** L	*TGV* **5376** v	*TGV* **5354**	*TGV* **5366** A	*TGV* **5382** Ⓑ h	*TGV* **5382** ⑥ k		*TGV* **5386**	*TGV* **5358**	
Marseille St Charles **350** d.	...	...	...	0715	0734	...	0832t	...	1036	...	1436	...	...
Avignon TGV **350** d.	...	...	...	0747	0806	...	0907t	...	1115	...	1515	...	...
Montpellier Sud de France **355** d.	...	...	...	|	|	...	|	...	|	...	|	1641	...
yon Perrache d.	0612	0612	0612	|	|	1016e	|	1136	|	...	|	|	...
yon Part Dieu d.	0630	0630	0630	0909	0930	1030	1030	1151	1230	...	1630	1830	...
lassy TGV a.	0834	0834	0834	1134p	1138p	1234	1234	1353	1437	...	1834	2033	...
lassy TGV d.	0842	0842	0846	1137p	1141p	1242	1242	1359	1442	...	1841	2038r	...
Versailles Chantiers a.	|	|	|	1155	1155	|	|	|	|	...	|	|	...
Mantes la Jolie a.	|	|	|	1229	1229	|	|	|	|	...	|	|	...
Rouen Rive Droite a.	|	|	|	1317	1317	|	|	|	|	...	|	|	...
Le Havre a.	|	|	|	1405	1412	|	|	|	|	...	|	|	...
St Pierre des Corps a.	|	|	0943	...	...	|	|	|	|	...	|	2131	...
Saumur Rive Droit a.	|	|	|	...	...	|	|	|	|	...	|	2205	...
e Mans 280 a.	0929	0929	|	...	...	1329	1329	1451	1531	...	1929	|	...
Laval 280 a.	1002	|	|	...	...	|	|	|	|	...	2002	|	...
Rennes 280 a.	1030	|	|	...	...	|	|	1540	1626	...	2030	|	...
ngers St Laud 280 a.	...	1028	1039	...	...	1409	1409	...	...	...	...	2230	...
antes 280 a.	...	1119	1119	...	...	1450	1450	...	...	...	...	2311	...

	TGV **5300** ① g	*TGV* **5300** ②–⑦ s	*TGV* **5332** D	*TGV* **5332** E	*TGV* **5336**	*TGV* **5336** ⑦ w	*TGV* **5306** ⑤ f	*TGV* **5306** B	*TGV* **5326** A¶	*TGV* **5316** ⑥⑦ H	*TGV* **5316** J	*TGV* **5320**	*TGV* **5338**
antes 280 d.	0451	0455j	...	...	...	...	1244	1244	1537	...	...	1704	...
ngers St Laud 280 d.	0530	0534	...	...	...	...	1326	1326	1621	...	...	1744	...
Rennes 280 d.	|	|	0731	0740	1231	1231	|	|	|	...	...	|	1730
Laval 280 d.	|	|	|	|	1259	1259	|	|	|	...	...	|	|
e Mans 280 d.	|	|	0828	0830	1330	1330	|	|	1710	...	...	1830	1830
Saumur Rive Droit d.	0553	|	|	|	|	|	1350	1350	|	...	...	|	|
St Pierre des Corps d.	0628	0628	|	|	|	|	1428	1428	|	...	...	|	|
Le Havre d.	|	|	|	|	|	|	|	|	|	1515	1556	|	|
Rouen Rive Droite d.	|	|	|	|	|	|	|	|	|	1604	1644	|	|
Mantes la Jolie d.	|	|	|	|	|	|	|	|	|	1650	1732	|	|
Versailles Chantiers d.	|	|	|	|	|	|	|	|	|	1740	1810	|	|
lassy TGV a.	0718	0718	0917	0921	1418	1418	1518	1518	1809	1802p	1823p	1918	1918
lassy TGV d.	0726	0726	0924	0924	1426	1426	1526	1526	1821	1805p	1826p	1925	1925
yon Part Dieu a.	0930	0930	1130	1130	1630	1630	1730	1730	2030	2030	2030	2130	2130
yon Perrache a.	|	|	|	|	...	|	|	1749	|	|	|	2147	2147
Montpellier Sud de France **355** a.	1120	1120	|	|	...	1835z	|	...	|	|	|	...	...
Avignon TGV **350** a.	...	...	1244	1244	...	...	1852	...	2152	2152	2152	...	...
Marseille St Charles **350** a.	...	...	1324	1324	...	...	1924	...	2224	2224	2224	...	...

A – Runs on July 12, 13 and ⑥⑦ Sept. 6 - Oct. 5.
B – ①②③④⑥⑦ (also Aug. 15; not Aug. 14).
D – ⑥ to Sept. 6 (also Aug. 15); ①–⑥ from Sept. 8 (not Nov. 11).
E – Ⓑ to Sept. 7 (not Aug. 15); ⑦ from Sept. 14 (also Nov. 11).
H – ⑥⑦ July 19 - Aug. 17.
J – ①–⑤ (also June 21, 22, July 5, 6, Aug. 23, 24, 30, 31, Oct. 11, 12, 18, 19, 25, 26, Nov. 1, 2, Dec. 6, 7, 13; not Nov. 10, 11). On July 14 Mantes la Jolie d. 1731, Versailles Chantiers d. 1801, Massy Palaiseau a. 1814, d. 1817. On ①–⑤ July 15 - Aug. 15 Mantes la Jolie d. 1727, Versailles Chantiers d. 1758, Massy Palaiseau a. 1811, d. 1814.
L – Runs on July 20, Aug. 4–10, 15 only.
M – ①–⑤ Sept. 15 - Oct. 10.
N – Daily to Sept. 14; ⑥⑦ Sept. 20 - Oct. 5; daily from Oct. 11.

e – 4–6 minutes earlier on July 12, 13, ⑥⑦ Sept. 6 - Oct. 5.
f – Also Aug. 14; not Aug. 15.
g – Also July 15, Nov. 12; not July 14.
h – Not Aug. 15.
j – 0451 Oct. 14–16, 21–24, 28–31, Oct. 4–7, 13, 14.
k – Also Aug. 15.
p – Massy **Palaiseau**.
r – 2041 from Sept. 1.
s – Also July 14; not July 15, Nov. 12.
t – On Sept. 6, 7, Oct. 4, 5 Marseille d. 0842, Avignon d. 0912.
v – Not June 15, 28, 29, July 12, 13, 20, Aug. 4–10, 15, ⑥⑦ Sept. 6 - Oct. 5, Nov. 8–11, 15, 16, 22, 23, 29, 30.
w – Also Nov. 11; not Nov. 9.
z – Montpellier **Saint-Roch**.

TGV – High-speed train. 🅁. 🍷.

¶ – On Sept. 13, 20, 27 Nantes d. 1559, Angers d. 1644, Le Mans d. 1730, Massy a. 1820, d. 1825 and then as shown.

340 PARIS - LYON and ST ÉTIENNE

TGV trains

For Charles de Gaulle ✈ - Marne la Vallée - Lyon see Table **11**. For Paris - Lyon St Exupéry ✈ see Table **342**.
Timings may vary by a few minutes – please check your reservation for confirmed timings.
Warning! Services to / from St Étienne are subject to alteration Oct. 11, 12.

km		TGV 6641	FR 9281	TGV 6603	TGV 6643	FR 9281	TGV 6605	TGV 6681	TGV 6607	FR 6647	TGV 6609	TGV 6611	TGV 6613	Ouigo 7803	TGV 6685	TGV 6615		TGV 6617	FR 6651	TGV 6619	FR 9287	TGV 6621	TGV 6687	TGV 6623	FR 665
		Ⓐ	A	①–⑥	Ⓐ	B	Ⓒ	①–⑥																	
			M ♠	d	n	M ♠	s	b		♠				⊠		D			♠		M ♠			k	♠
0	**Paris** Gare de Lyon ..... **341** d.	0620	0641	0700	0725	0729	0751	0751	0859	0955	0959	1059	1151	1226	1251	1251	...	1353	1413	1459	1518	1552	1659	1659	170
303	Le Creusot TGV .... d.	0643	|	|	|	|	0915	0915	|	|	|	|	1315	|	|	|	...	1517	|	|	|	1715	|	|	|
363	Mâcon Loché TGV .... **341** a.	|	|	|	|	|	|	|	|	|	|	|	|	|	|	|	...	|	|	|	|	1733	|	|	|
427	**Lyon** Part-Dieu .... a.	0822	0838	0856	0922	0926	0956	0956	1056	1152	1156	1256	1356	1422	1455	1455	...	1556	1609	1656	1714	1800	1856	1856	190
	St Étienne Châteaucreux a.	|	...	|	|	...	|	1048	|	|	|	|	|	|	1548	|	...	|	|	|	...	|	1948	|	...
432	**Lyon** Perrache .... a.	0835	...	0910	0936	...	1010	...	1110	1207	1211	1311	1410	1436	...	1510	...	1610	1637	1710	...	1814	...	1910	...

	TGV 6663	TGV 6627	TGV 6669	TGV 6665	TGV 6689	Ouigo 7805	FR 6655		TGV 6633	
	Ⓐ		Ⓐ	Ⓑ					Ⓑ	
	k		n	t		⊠	♠		t	
Paris Gare de Lyon ...... **341** d.	1725	1752	1825	1841	1859	1925	1959	...	2059	...
Le Creusot TGV .... d.	|	1915	|	|	|	|	|	...	2223	...
Mâcon Loché TGV .... **341** a.	|	|	|	|	|	|	|	...	2241	...
Lyon Part-Dieu .... a.	1922	1956	2022	2035	2056	2122	2156	...	2308	...
St Étienne Châteaucreux . a.	|	|	|	|	2148	|	|	...	|	...
Lyon Perrache .... a.	1936	2010	2036	2049	...	2136	2210	...	2324	...

	TGV 6602	TGV 6642	TGV 6644	FR 6650	TGV 6690	TGV 6692	TGV 6608		Ouigo 780
	Ⓐ	Ⓐ	Ⓐ		①–⑥				
		n	n	♠	d				⊠
Lyon Perrache .... d.	0550	0624	0638	0646	...	...	0750	...	082
St Étienne Châteaucreux .... d.	|	|	|	|	0612	0642r	|	...	|
Lyon Part-Dieu .... d.	0604	0638	0652	0700	0704	0734	0804	...	083
Mâcon Loché TGV .... **341** d.	0631	|	|	|	|	|	|	...	|
Le Creusot TGV .... d.	0653	|	|	|	|	|	0846	...	|
Paris Gare de Lyon .... **341** a.	0816	0835	0851	0858	0903	0931	1008	...	103

	TGV 6612	TGV 6614	FR 9292	TGV 6616	TGV 6616		TGV 6694	TGV 6618	FR 6654		TGV 6620	TGV 6622	Ouigo 7804	TGV 6624		TGV 6626	FR 6656	TGV 6696	TGV 6628		TGV 6630	FR 6658	TGV 6632	FR 9296	TGV 663
				①–⑤	⑥⑦																		Ⓑ		
		G	M ♠						♠				⊠				♠					♠	t	M ♠	
Lyon Perrache .... d.	0950	1049	...	1124	1146	...	...	1249	1254	...	1350	1450	1524	1550	...	1650	1708	...	1750	...	1850	...	1950	...	205
St Étienne Châteaucreux . d.	|	|	...	|	|	...	1212	|	|	...	|	|	|	|	...	|	|	1644	|	...	|	...	|	...	|
Lyon Part-Dieu .... d.	1004	1103	1128	1138	1200	...	1304	1304	1308	...	1404	1504	1538	1604	...	1704	1722	1738	1804	...	1904	1938	2004	2038	210
Mâcon Loché TGV .... **341** d.	|	|	|	|	|	...	|	|	|	...	|	|	|	|	...	|	|	|	|	...	|	|	|	|	|
Le Creusot TGV .... d.	1046	|	|	|	|	...	|	|	|	...	1446	|	|	1646	...	|	|	|	1846	...	|	|	|	|	214
Paris Gare de Lyon ...... **341** a.	1209	1301	1323	1335	1357	...	1501	1501	1505	...	1609	1700	1734	1808	...	1900	1919	1934	2008	...	2100	2136	2200z	2234	2308

- **A** – ①–⑤ to July 4; ①–⑤ Sept. 22 - Oct. 17.
- **B** – ⑥⑦ to June 29; daily July 5 - Sept. 21; ⑥⑦ Sept. 27 - Oct. 12; daily from Oct. 18.
- **D** – Daily to July 4; ⑤ July 11 - Aug. 29 (also Aug. 14; not Aug. 15); daily from Sept. 1.
- **E** – Ⓑ to July 6; ③④⑤⑦ July 9 - Aug. 24 (also July 14; not Aug. 15); Ⓑ from Aug. 27.
- **G** – Daily to July 20; Ⓒ July 26 - Aug. 24; daily from Aug. 30.
- **M** – To / from Milano (Table **44**).

- **b** – Not July 14, Nov. 11.
- **d** – Not July 14, Nov. 10, 11.
- **k** – Not July 5 - Aug. 31.
- **n** – Not July 21 - Aug. 29.

- **r** – 0646 on ② (not Nov. 11).
- **s** – Not Nov. 11.
- **t** – Not Aug. 15.
- **z** – Arrival time may be up to 21 minutes later on certain dates.

TGV – High-speed train. Ⓡ. 🍷.
FR – Italian high-speed train. Ⓡ. 🍷.

♠ – *Frecciarossa* high-speed train. Operated by Trenitalia. Ⓡ. 🍷.
⊠ – OUIGO low-cost TGV service. Internet bookings only at www.ouigo.com

341 PARIS - GENÈVE and ANNECY

Other *TGV* services: Paris - Chambéry, see Tables **44** and **366**; Paris - Mâcon Loché, see Table **340**; Paris - Lyon St Exupéry ✈, see Table **342**.

Warning! Timings may vary by a few minutes – please check your reservation for confirmed timings.

PARIS - GENÈVE - LAUSANNE (see Table 375 for Paris - Lausanne via Dijon)

km		TGV 9761	TGV 9763	TGV 9765	TGV 9773	TGV 9775	TGV 9777	TGV 9781		TGV 9789	
		①–⑥								H	
0	**Paris** Gare de Lyon ... d.	0615	0818	1017	1218	1417	1617	1817	...	2016	...
406	Bourg-en-Bresse .. **376** d.	0812	1012	1212	1412	1612	1812	2010	...	2212	...
439	Nurieux-Brion .... **376** a.	|	|	|	|	|	|	2035	...	|	...
470	Bellegarde .... **346** a.	0859	1059	1259	1459	1659	1859	2100	...	2259	...
503	**Genève** . **346 505 570** a.	0929	1129	1329	1529	1729	1929	2129	...	2329	...
563	**Lausanne** ..... **505 570** a.	1012k	...	...	...	1812j	2012r	...	...	...	...

	TGV 9760		TGV 9764	TGV 9768	TGV 9770	TGV 9774	TGV 9776	TGV 9780		TGV 978
										Ⓑ
	J									w
Lausanne .... **505 570** d.	...	...	...	0946j	...	1346j	...	...	...	194
Genève **346 505 570** d.	0629	...	0829	1030v	1229	1430v	1629	1829	...	203
Bellegarde .... **346** d.	0702	...	0900	1102	1301	1502	1702	1902	...	210
Nurieux-Brion ... **376** d.	|	...	0926	|	|	|	|	|	...	|
Bourg-en-Bresse . **376** d.	0751	...	0953	1152	1352	1552	1751	1952	...	2151
Paris Gare de Lyon .. a.	0943	...	1145	1343	1542	1742	1942	2142	...	2342

PARIS - CHAMBÉRY - ANNECY

km		TGV 6931		TGV 6937		TGV 6941		TGV 6949	TGV 6951	TGV 6953	
		①–⑥								⑤	
		d								f	
0	**Paris** Gare de Lyon ... d.	0645	...	0945	...	1245t	...	1745	1845	2037	...
363	Mâcon Loché TGV ..... d.	0823	...	1123	...	1423	...	1923	2023	2216	...
441	Lyon St Exupéry ✈ .... d.	|	...	|	...	|	...	|	|	|	...
532	**Chambéry** .... **345 364** a.	0936	...	1234	...	1535	...	2041	2136	2333	...
546	Aix les Bains . **345 364** a.	0959	...	1258	...	1558	...	2105	2201	2354	...
585	**Annecy** .... **345 364** a.	1030	...	1329	...	1632x	...	2135p	2231q	0026	...

	TGV 6960		TGV 6964		TGV 6972		TGV 6978	TGV 6980	TGV 6986	TGV 6986
								⑦	Ⓐ	⑥⑦
	L							e		s
Annecy .... **345 364** d.	0527	...	0922y	...	1227c	...	1529b	1729	1919n	1929
Aix les Bains **345 364** d.	0558	...	0953	...	1259	...	1559	1758	1959	1959
Chambéry ... **345 364** d.	0623	...	1022	...	1324	...	1623	1822	2022	2022
Lyon St Exupéry ✈ ... d.	|	...	|	...	|	...	|	|	|	|
Mâcon Loché TGV .... d.	0738	...	1138	...	1441	...	1738	1939	2138	2138
Paris Gare de Lyon .. a.	0917	...	1315	...	1618	...	1914	2115	2314z	2314

- **H** – ①④⑤⑦ to July 6; ⑤⑦ July 11 - Aug. 17; Ⓑ from Aug. 22 (also Oct. 18, 25, Nov. 1).
- **J** – ①–⑥ to July 7; ①⑥ July 12 - Aug. 18; ①–⑥ from Aug. 23 (also Oct. 19, 26, Nov. 2).
- **L** – ①–⑥ to July 4; ① July 7 - Aug. 25 (also July 15; not July 14); ①–⑥ from Sept. 1 (not Nov. 11).

- **b** – Not July 18. Departs 1527 on Ⓐ July 21 - Aug. 29.
- **c** – Not July 13.
- **d** – Not July 5 - Aug. 30, Nov. 11.
- **e** – Also July 14, Nov. 11.
- **f** – Also Aug. 14; not Aug. 15. Departs Paris 4–5 minutes later on July 4, 18, 18, 25, Aug. 1, 8, 14, 22, 29, Sept. 5, Dec. 12.
- **j** – Not June 28 - Aug. 24, Nov. 1, 2, 22, 23.
- **k** – Not June 28 - Aug. 23, Nov. 1, 22.
- **n** – Not July 16, 17.
- **p** – Not July 15. Arrives 2139 on † (also July 7 – 10 and on ①–④ July 21 - Aug. 28).
- **q** – Daily to June 28; ⑤⑥ July 4 - Aug. 23 (also July 13, 14, Aug. 10; not July 12, Aug. 15); daily from Aug. 29.
- **r** – Daily to June 27; ①–⑤ June 30 - Aug. 22; daily from Aug. 25 (not Nov. 1, 2, 22, 23).
- **s** – Not Oct. 25, Nov. 1.
- **t** – 1242 on Sept. 23, 24, 30, Oct. 1.
- **v** – 8 minutes earlier on June 28, 29, July 5, 6, 19, 20, Aug. 9, 10, Nov. 1, 2, 22, 23.
- **w** – Does not run on ②③ June 3 - July 2. On June 29, July 6, 20, Aug. 10, Nov. 2, 23 does not run Lausanne - Genève and departs Genève 2022.
- **x** – Not July 12, 16, 17, Aug. 15, 16.
- **y** – Not July 13, 16, 17, 18, Aug. 16.
- **z** – Arrival time may be up to 17 minutes later on certain dates.

TGV – High-speed train. Ⓡ. 🍷.

PARIS - GRENOBLE 342

Timings may vary by a few minutes – please check your reservation for confirmed timings. **Warning!** Subject to alteration on Aug. 2, 3, 9, 10.

km		TGV 6905	TGV 6905	TGV 6911	TGV 6917	TGV 6919	TGV 6921	TGV 6923	TGV 6925	TGV 6927	TGV 6929	TGV 6929
		①–⑥	⑦	①–⑥			⑤					⑤⑦
		r	c	A			n	B	n	D	E	t
0	**Paris** Gare de Lyon .... **350/1** d.	0713	0803	1013	1214	1513	1613	1712	1813	1913	1914	2012
441	Lyon St Exupéry ✈ ..... **350/1** a.	0906	0955	1205	1406	1704	1805	1906	2005	2105	2106	2205
441	Lyon St Exupéry ✈ .... d.	0910	0959	1210	1410	1708	1810	1910	2010	2110	2110	2209
553	**Grenoble** .... a.	1013	1109	1314	1513	1813	1913	2013	2113	2213	2214	2313v

	TGV 6902	TGV 6906	TGV 6906	TGV 6908		TGV 6910	TGV 6920	TGV 6922	TGV 6924	TGV 6928	TGV 6928
		①–④	⑤⑥					Ⓑ		⑦	
	G	m	w			H		z		e	F
Grenoble .... d.	0546	0646	0747	0946	...	1247	1445	1645	1845	2044	2101
Lyon St Exupéry ✈ .... a.	0649	0749	0849	1049	...	1349	1548	1748	1949	2148	2202
Lyon St Exupéry ✈ .... **350/1** d.	0654	0754	0855	1054	...	1354	1554	1753	1954	2152	2206
Paris Gare de Lyon .... **350/1** a.	0847	0947	1047	1246	...	1546	1746	1946	2146	2345	0008

A – ①–⑥ to July 4; ①–⑥ from Sept. 1 (not Nov. 11).
B – Ⓑ (daily June 29 - Sept. 5).
D – ①–④ to July 3; Ⓑ July 6 - Sept. 4 (not Aug. 15); ①–④ from Sept. 8 (not Nov. 11).
E – Runs on Oct. 5, 26 only.
F – Runs on July 14 only.
G – ①–⑤ to July 4; ① July 7 - Aug. 25 (also July 15; not July 14); Ⓐ from Sept. 1.
H – Daily to July 4 (also July 6, 14); ⑦ July 20 - Aug. 24; daily from Aug. 31.

c – Also July 14.
e – Also Nov. 11.
m – Not July 14, Aug. 14, Nov. 11.
n – Not July 5 - Aug. 31.
r – Not July 14.
t – Also Aug. 14, Nov. 11; not Aug. 15, Oct. 5, 26.
v – 48 – 53 minutes later on July 27, Aug. 1, 3, 8, 10, 17, 24, 31, Sept. 7, 14.
w – Also Aug. 14.
z – Not Aug. 15.

TGV – High-speed train. 🅁. 🍷.

LYON - GRENOBLE 343

Timings are subject to minor variations. **Warning!** Subject to alteration on Aug. 2, 3, 9, 10.

km																									
		①–⑥ b	Ⓐ		Ⓐ		Ⓐ		Ⓐ ⊗	⊗	⊗	⊗	⊗	Ⓐ			Ⓐ		Ⓐ		w	Ⓑ r	⑥k 🚌	⑤⑦ f🚌	🚌
0	**Lyon** Part-Dieu .. **344** d.	0616	0645	0716	0745	0816	0845	0916	0945	1016	1116	1216	1316	1345	1416	and at	1845	1916	1945	2016	2116	2216	2216	2320	2320
41	Bourgoin-Jallieu . **344** d.	0644	0711	0743	0811	0843	0911	0943	1011	1043	1144	1243	1343	1411	1443	the same	1911	1943	2011	2043	2143	2243	2307	|	0011
56	La Tour du Pin ... **344** d.	0654	0721	0753	0822	0853	0921	0953	1022	1053	1154	1253	1354	1422	1453	minutes	1922	1954	2022	2053	2153	2253	|	|	0031
104	Voiron .... d.	0724	0754	0824	0855	0924	0954	1024	1055	1124	1224	1324	1425	1454	1524	past each	1955	2025	2054	2124	2223	2324	|	|	0121
129	**Grenoble** .... a.	0739	0809	0839	0909	0939	1009	1039	1109	1139	1239	1339	1439	1509	1540	hour until	2009	2040	2109	2140	2239	2339	0015	0050	0156

	①–⑥ b	Ⓐ				Ⓐ	⊗	⊗	⊗	⊗		Ⓐ		Ⓐ		Ⓐ		Ⓐ		Ⓐ		🚌		Ⓑ z	⑥k 🚌
Grenoble .... d.	0521	0551	0621	and at	0921	0951	1021	1121	1221	1321	1421	1451	1521	1551	1621	1651	1721	1751	1821	1851	1921	1947	2021	2121	2123
Voiron .... d.	0538	0608	0638	the same	0938	1008	1038	1138	1238	1338	1437	1508	1538	1608	1638	1708	1738	1808	1838	1908	1938	|	2038	2138	2153
La Tour du Pin ..... **344** d.	0607	0638	0707	minutes	1007	1038	1107	1207	1307	1407	1506	1537	1607	1637	1707	1737	1807	1837	1907	1937	2007	|	2107	2207	2238
Bourgoin-Jallieu ... **344** d.	0618	0649	0718	past each	1018	1048	1118	1218	1318	1418	1517	1548	1618	1648	1718	1748	1818	1848	1917	1948	2018	|	2118	2218	2300
Lyon Part-Dieu .... **344** a.	0644	0715	0744	hour until	1044	1115	1144	1244	1344	1444	1544	1615	1644	1715	1744	1815	1844	1915	1944	2016	2044	2116	2144	2244	2400

b – Not July 14, Nov. 11.
f – Also July 14, Aug. 14, Nov. 11; not Aug. 15.
k – Also Aug. 15.
r – Ⓑ to July 14 (also July 20, Aug. 14, Sept. 12); Ⓑ Sept. 19 - Oct. 3; ⑤ Oct. 10 – 24 (also Oct. 19); Ⓑ from Oct. 31.

w – Not July 27 – 29, Aug. 1 – 13, Oct. 5 – 9, 13 – 16, 20 – 23, 26 – 30.
z – Not Aug. 15.

⊗ – Subject to alteration / cancellation Sept. 15 – 19, 22 – 26.

LYON - CHAMBÉRY 344

km																								
		Ⓐ 🚌	①–⑥ b	①–⑥ b				Ⓐ ⊙	Ⓒ				①–⑥ b		Ⓐ						Ⓐ			
0	**Lyon** Part Dieu .... **343 345** d.	0620	0650	0750	0850	0950	...	1034	1050	...	1150	1250	1350	1450	1550	1650	1750	1850	1950	2050	2150	...	...	...
41	Bourgoin-Jallieu .... **343** d.	|	0717	0817	0917	1018	...	|	1117	...	1217	1314	1417	1517	1616	1717	1817	1917	2017	2117	2217	...	...	...
56	La Tour du Pin .... **343** d.	|	0727	0827	0927	1029	...	|	1128	...	1227	1325	1427	1527	1626	1727	1827	1927	2027	2127	2227	...	...	...
106	**Chambéry** .... **345** a.	0750	0816	0916	1016	1119	...	1158	1215	...	1316	1416	1516	1616	1715	1816	1916	2016	2116	2216	2316	...	...	...

	①–⑥ b	①–⑥ b			Ⓐ	Ⓒ		Ⓐ d⊙	⑥ k	h⊙							Ⓑ z	Ⓑ z					
Chambéry .... **345** d.	0544	0644	0744	0844	0944	1044	...	1137	1144	1150	...	1244	1344	1444	1544	1644	1744	1844	1944	2044	...	...	...
La Tour du Pin .... **343** d.	0632	0732	0833	0932	1032	1135	...	|	1233	|	...	1334	1432	1532	1632	1732	1832	1932	2031	2134	...	...	...
Bourgoin-Jallieu .... **343** d.	0643	0743	0844	0943	1043	1146	...	|	1244	|	...	1346	1443	1543	1643	1743	1843	1943	2042	2145	...	...	...
Lyon Part Dieu .... **343 345** a.	0710	0811	0910	1010	1110	1214	...	1303	1310	1322	...	1410	1510	1610	1710	1810	1910	2011	2110	2210	...	...	...

b – Not July 14, Nov. 11.
d – Not Aug. 25 – 29, Oct. 6 – 17.
h – Aug. 25 – 29 only.
k – Not Aug. 15.

z – Not Aug. 15.

⊙ – Via Aix les Bains (Table **345**).

LYON - AIX LES BAINS - ANNECY 345

Timings are subject to minor variations. **Warning!** Rail services are subject to alteration on July 12, 13, 16, 17, 18, 26, 27, Aug. 16.

km																										
		🚌 Ⓐ	Ⓐ	①–⑥ b	①–⑥ b⊠	①–⑥ b	🚌 ⑦ e	Ⓐ	🚌 Ⓐ	Ⓒ	Ⓐ	Ⓐ ⊙	🚌 ⑦ e	①–⑥ b⊗	🚌 Ⓐ	⊗	🚌 Ⓐ	Ⓐ	⊠	Ⓐ	⊠	Ⓑ z		①–⑥ b	⑦ e	A
0	**Lyon** Part Dieu **344/6** d.	0608	...	...	0708	0808	0808	0908	1008	1008	1034	...	1208	1208	1308	1408j	1508	...	1608	...	1708	1808	...	1907	1907	2108
46	Ambérieu .... **346** d.	|	0614	0714	0732	0834	|	0933	|	1033	|	1214	|	1233	|	1433	|	1614	1633	...	1733	1833	1914	1933	1933	2133
96	Culoz .... **346** d.	|	0652	0752	0804	|	|	|	|	|	|	1252	|	|	|	|	|	1652	|	1751	|	|	1952	|	|	2204
118	Aix les Bains .... a.	|	0711	0811	0819	0918	0935	1018	|	1118	1146	1311	|	1318	|	1518	|	1711	1718	1811	1818	1919	2011	2019	2019	2220
118	Aix les Bains ...... **364** d.	|	0713	0813	*0834*	0925	0935	1025	|	1125	1148	1313	|	1325	|	1525	|	1713	*1732*	1813	*1835*	*1934*	2013	2025	2025	2227
132	**Chambéry 344 364** a.	|	0725	0825	|	|	|	|	|	|	1158	1325	|	|	|	|	|	1725	|	1825	|	|	2025	|	|	|
157	**Annecy** .... **364** a.	0759	...	...	*0915*	1007	1010	1107	1159	1207	...	...	1359	1407	1459	1607	1659	...	*1813*	...	*1915*	*2015*	...	2100	2107	2258

	Ⓐ	Ⓐ	⚒	Ⓐ	⚒ ⊠	🚌 ⑦ e	🚌 Ⓐ	Ⓒ	Ⓐ ⊠⊗	Ⓐ ⊡⊗	⑥ p	🚌 Ⓑ z	🚌 Ⓐ	①–⑥ b⊖	⊗	①–⑥ b	⑦ e	Ⓐ	⊠	🚌 ⑥ k		Ⓑ z⊠	Ⓐ	⊠	🚌 Ⓐ	⑦ e
Annecy .... **364** d.	...	0559	0653	...	*0743*	0800	0900	0943	1053	...	1153	1200	1300	...	1353	1553	1553	...	*1643*z	1700	...	*1743*	...	*1843*	2000	2053
Chambéry 344 364 d.	0534	|	|	0734	|	|	|	|	|	1137	|	|	|	1234	|	|	|	1634	|	|	1734	|	1834	|	|	|
Aix les Bains .... **364** a.	0546	0632	0734	0745	*0823*	|	|	1025	1134	1147	1232	|	|	1246	1433	1633	1634	1646	*1723*z	|	1746	*1823*	1846	*1923*	|	2133
Aix les Bains .... d.	0548	0641	0741	0747	0841	|	|	1032	1141	1150	1241	|	|	1248	1440	1639	1641	1648	1740	|	1748	1841	1848	1941	|	2140
Culoz .... **346** d.	0608	|	|	0807	|	|	|	|	|	1206	|	|	|	1308	|	|	1656	1708	1756	|	1808	|	1908	|	|	|
Ambérieu .... **346** d.	0646	0728	0827	0846	0928	|	|	1119	1228	1238	1328	|	|	1346	1527	1726	1726	...	1828	|	1846	1928	1946	2028	|	2227
Lyon Part Dieu. **344/6** a.	...	0752	0853	...	0952	0952	1052	1147	1252	1303	1352	1352	1452	...	1553	1752	1752	...	1852	1852	...	1952	...	2052	2152	2252

A – Runs Lyon - Aix les Bains daily to July 14 (also July 18, 19; not July 12), ⑦ July 20 - Sept. 14, ⑤–⑦ Sept. 19 - Oct. 5 and daily from Oct. 10. Runs Aix les Bains - Annecy on ⑤⑥ to July 19 (also July 13, 14, Aug. 10; not July 12), ⑤⑥ Sept. 19 - Oct. 4 and daily from Oct. 10. **Subject to alteration**.

b – Not July 14, Nov. 11.
e – Also July 14, Nov. 11.
j – 1406 on Ⓒ July 26 - Sept. 13.

k – Also Aug. 15.
p – Not Aug. 2 - Sept. 13.
z – Ⓑ (not Aug. 15).

⊠ – Subject to alteration July 21 - Sept. 13 (please check before travelling).
⊙ – Runs 35 – 44 minutes later Aug. 25 – 29.
⊡ – Runs 11 – 19 minutes later Aug. 25 – 29.
⊗ – Not Oct. 6 – 10, 13 – 17.

346 LYON - BELLEGARDE - GENÈVE

Subject to alteration on Aug. 2, 3.

km																								
															TGV 9752									
		①–⑤	①–⑤	⑥	①–⑤	①–⑥			①–⑥		①–⑤					①–⑤		①–⑤	Ⓑ	①–⑤		①–⑤	①–⑤	
									b	n					A				z					
	Marseille St Charles **350** d.	...	...	...	...	...	...	...	...	...	...	...	...	...	1347	...	...	...	...	...	...	...	...	...
0	**Lyon** Part Dieu **345** d.	...	...	...	...	0638	...	0838	0938	1038	...	1238	...	1438	1540	...	1638	...	1738	...	1838	...	...	2038
50	Ambérieu **345** d.	...	...	...	...	0703	...	0902	1003	1103	...	1303	...	1503	|	...	1703	...	|	...	|	...	...	2104
102	Culoz **345 364** d.	...	...	...	...	0740	...	0940	1040	1140	...	1340	...	1540	|	...	1740	...	1840	...	1940	...	...	2140
135	Bellegarde **364** a.	...	...	...	...	0804	...	1004	1104	1204	...	1404	...	1604	1658	...	1804	...	1904	...	2004	...	...	2204
135	Bellegarde **364** d.	0553	0623	0653	0723	0807	...	1007	1107	1207	1246	1407	...	1607	1711	1725	1807	1825	1907	1925	2007	2025	2125	2207
168	**Genève** **364 500 570** a.	0627	0657	0727	0757	0835	...	1035	1135	1235	1318	1435	...	1635	1745	1757	1835	1857	1935	1957	2035	2057	2157	2238
	Lausanne **500 570** a.	...	...	...	...	...	...	...	...	...	...	...	...	...	1840	...	...	...	...	...	...	...	...	...

						TGV 9756																	
	①–⑤	①–⑥	①–⑥	①–⑥				Ⓒ	Ⓐ	①–⑤	①–⑥			①–⑤	⑦	①–⑤	⑦	①–⑥	①–⑤	①–⑤	⑦	①–⑥	①–⑤	①–⑤
		b		b		A					b				e		e	b			e	b		
Lausanne **500 570** d.	...	...	...	...	...	0746	...	...	...	...	...	...	...	...	...	...	...	...	...	...	...	...	...	...
Genève **364 500 570** d.	0503	0514	0503	0614	0714	0842	0930	1130	1130	1203	1225	1330	1530	1603	1625	1703	1714	1730	1803	1903	1914	1930	2018	2118
Bellegarde **364** a.	0538	0544	0637	0646	0746	0910	0957	1157	1200	1237	1253	1357	1557	1637	1654	1737	1746	1757	1837	1937	1946	1957	2053	2153
Bellegarde **364** d.	...	0555	...	0650	0752	0913	1000	1200	1205	...	1256	1400	1600	...	1657	...	1756	1800	...	...	1952	2000	...	...
Culoz **345 364** d.	...	0620	...	0715	0818	|	1024	1222	1227	...	1321	1424	1624	...	|	...	1818	1824	...	...	2018	2024	...	...
Ambérieu **345** d.	...	0657	...	0755	0857	|	|	1257	1302	...	1357	1457	1658	...	|	...	1857	1857	...	...	2057	2058	...	...
Lyon Part Dieu **345** a.	...	0722	...	0822	0922	1026	1122	1320	1326	...	1422	1522	1722	...	1810	...	1922	1922	...	...	2122	2122	...	...
Marseille St Charles **350** a.	...	...	...	...	...	1210	...	...	...	...	...	...	...	...	...	...	...	...	...	...	...	...	...	...

A – *TGV Lyria*. June 28 - Aug. 24 only.

b – Not July 14, Nov. 11.

e – Also July 14, Nov. 11.

n – Not Aug. 25 – 29.

z – Not Aug. 15.

TGV – High-speed train. 🅁. 🍷.

348 LYON - ST ÉTIENNE

TER services

For *TGV* trains Paris - St Étienne, see Table **340**. Subject to alteration on Oct. 11, 12.

km																								
		①–⑥	Ⓐ	①–⑥	①–⑥	Ⓐ	Ⓐ			Ⓐ	Ⓐ	①–⑥		Ⓐ			Ⓐ	①–⑥		Ⓐ			Ⓐ	①–⑥
		b		b	b						n	b		n		q		b						b
0	**Lyon** Part-Dieu d.	...	0624	...	0654	...	0724	...	0754	...	0824	...	0854	0924	...	0954	1024	...	1054	1124	...	1154	1224	...
	Lyon Perrache d.	0531	|	0631	|	0701	|	0731	|	0801	|	0831	|	|	0931	|	|	1031	|	|	1131	|	|	1231
22	Givors Ville d.	0558	0641	0658	0711	0728	0741	0758	0811	0828	0841	0858	0911	0941	0958	1011	1041	1058	1111	1141	1158	1212	1241	1258
47	St Chamond d.	0617	0700	0717	0730	0747	0800	0817	0830	0847	0900	0917	0930	1000	1017	1030	1100	1117	1130	1200	1217	1230	1300	1317
59	**St Étienne** Châteaucreux a.	0626	0710	0726	0740	0756	0810	0826	0840	0856	0910	0926	0940	1010	1026	1040	1110	1126	1140	1210	1226	1240	1310	1326

		Ⓐ			Ⓐ	①–⑥		Ⓐ			Ⓐ	Ⓐ	①–⑥		Ⓐ	Ⓐ			Ⓐ	Ⓐ	①–⑥		Ⓐ	Ⓐ
						b							b					p			b	r		
Lyon Part-Dieu d.	1254	1324	...	1354	1424	...	1454	1524	...	1554	...	1624	...	1654	...	1724	...	1754	...	1824	...	1854	...	1924
Lyon Perrache d.	|	|	1331	|	|	1431	|	|	1531	|	1601	|	1631	|	1701	|	1731	|	1801	|	1831	|	1901	|
Givors Ville d.	1311	1341	1358	1411	1441	1458	1511	1541	1558	1611	1628	1641	1658	1711	1728	1741	1758	1811	1828	1841	1858	1911	1928	1941
St Chamond d.	1330	1400	1417	1430	1500	1517	1530	1600	1617	1630	1647	1700	1717	1730	1747	1800	1817	1830	1847	1900	1917	1930	1947	2000
St Étienne Châteaucreux a.	1340	1410	1426	1440	1510	1526	1540	1610	1626	1640	1656	1710	1726	1740	1756	1810	1826	1840	1856	1910	1926	1940	1956	2010

				①–⑥	Ⓑ	①–⑤		⑥⑦	①–④	
		s		b	z	A	C	△	m 🚌	🚌
Lyon Part-Dieu d.	...	1954	2024	...	2124	2202	2224	2324	2324	0024
Lyon Perrache d.	1931	|	|	2031	|	|	|	|	|	|
Givors Ville d.	1958	2011	2041	2058	2141	2225	2241	2341	0000	0100
St Chamond d.	2017	2030	2100	2117	2200	2243	2300	0000	0028	0128
St Étienne Châteaucreux a.	2026	2040	2110	2126	2210	2253	2310	0010	0045	0145

	Ⓐ	Ⓐ	Ⓐ	Ⓐ	①–⑥	Ⓐ	Ⓐ	①–⑥
			q		b			b
St Étienne Châteaucreux d.	0520	0534	0550	0604	0620	0634	0650	0704
St Chamond d.	0530	0543	0600	0613	0630	0643	0700	0713
Givors Ville d.	0548	0602	0618	0632	0648	0702	0718	0732
Lyon Perrache a.	|	0629	|	0659	|	0729	|	0759
Lyon Part-Dieu a.	0606	...	0636	...	0706	...	0736	...

		Ⓐ	Ⓐ			Ⓐ	Ⓐ	①–⑥		Ⓐ			Ⓐ	①–⑥		Ⓐ			Ⓐ	①–⑥		Ⓐ		
	q							b	q					b						b				
St Étienne Châteaucreux d.	0720	0734	0750	0804	0820	0834	0850	0904	0920	0950	1004	1020	1050	1104	1120	1150	1204	1220	1250	1304	1320	1350	1404	1420
St Chamond d.	0730	0743	0800	0813	0830	0843	0900	0913	0930	1000	1013	1030	1100	1113	1130	1200	1213	1230	1300	1313	1330	1400	1413	1430
Givors Ville d.	0748	0802	0818	0832	0848	0902	0918	0932	0948	1018	1032	1048	1118	1132	1148	1218	1232	1248	1318	1332	1348	1418	1432	1448
Lyon Perrache a.	|	0829	|	0859	|	0929	|	0959	|	|	1059	|	|	1159	|	|	1259	|	|	1359	|	|	1459	|
Lyon Part-Dieu a.	0806	...	0836	...	0906	...	0936	...	1006	1036	...	1105	1136	...	1206	1236	...	1306	1336	...	1406	1436	...	1506

	Ⓐ	①–⑥		Ⓐ			Ⓐ	Ⓐ	①–⑥		Ⓐ	Ⓐ			Ⓐ	Ⓐ	①–⑥				Ⓑ		①–⑤	
		b	q	q		t		q	b	q		q		q		q	b	u		q	z		B	D
St Étienne Châteaucreux d.	1450	1504	1520	1550	1604	1620	1634	1650	1704	1720	1734	1750	1804	1820	1834	1850	1904	1920	2004	2020	2120	...	2216	2220
St Chamond d.	1500	1513	1530	1600	1613	1630	1643	1700	1713	1730	1743	1800	1813	1830	1843	1900	1913	1930	2013	2030	2130	...	2226	2230
Givors Ville d.	1518	1532	1548	1618	1632	1648	1702	1718	1732	1748	1802	1818	1832	1848	1902	1918	1932	1948	2032	2048	2148	...	2245	2248
Lyon Perrache a.	|	1559	|	|	1659	|	1729	|	1759	|	1829	|	1859	|	1929	|	1959	|	2059	|	|	...	2306	|
Lyon Part-Dieu a.	1536	...	1606	1636	...	1706	...	1736	...	1806	...	1836	...	1906	...	1936	...	2006	...	2106	2206	...	...	2306

A – ①–⑤ until Sept. 19.
B – July 21 - Oct. 3.
C – ⑥⑦ to Sept. 14; daily from Sept. 20.
D – Daily to July 20; ⑥⑦ July 26 - Sept. 28; daily from Oct. 4. On June 22, July 6, Aug. 17, 24, 31, Oct. 11, 12, 26, Nov. 9, 23 service is diverted to run to Lyon **Perrache** (not Part-Dieu).

b – Not July 14, Nov. 11.
m – Not July 14, Aug. 14, Nov. 11.
n – Not July 28 - Aug. 14, Aug. 22 - Sept. 12.

p – Not ①–⑥ July 28 - Aug. 16, ①–⑥ Aug. 22 - Sept. 13.
q – Not July 21 - Aug. 16, Aug. 22 - Sept. 13.
r – Not July 28 - Aug. 16, Aug. 22 - Sept. 13.
s – Not Ⓑ July 28 - Aug. 14, Ⓑ Aug. 22 - Sept. 12.
t – Not ①–⑥ July 21 - Aug. 16, ①–⑥ Aug. 22 - Sept. 13.
u – Not Ⓑ July 21 - Aug. 14, Ⓑ Aug. 22 - Sept. 12.
z – Not Aug. 15.

△ – Runs 10 – 12 minutes earlier on Oct. 4. On June 22, July 6, Aug. 17, 24, 31, Oct. 11, 12, 26, Nov. 9, 23 service is diverted to run from Lyon **Perrache** (not Part-Dieu).

349 ST ÉTIENNE - LE PUY

Warning! Subject to alteration from Sept. 29.

km																								
		Ⓐ	①–⑥				⑦	①–⑥			⑥ k	Ⓐ		Ⓐ	Ⓒ	Ⓐ	Ⓐ		⑥	⑦		Ⓐ		
			b				e	b			🚌	🚌							B k	B e	A	B		
0	**St Étienne** Châteaucreux d.	0531	0648	...	0854	...	1054	1101	...	1252	1400	1425	1558	1717	1755	1805	1854	...	2005	2010	2014	2020	...	2200
15	Firminy d.	0553	0710	...	0911	...	1110	1117	...	1309	|	|	1614	1734	1811	1827	1912	...	2028	2033	2037	2037	...	2223
88	**Le Puy en Velay** a.	0725	0825	...	1025	...	1220	1227	...	1421	1520	1545	1720	1848	1922	1934	2020	...	2134	2139	2143	2143	...	2327

	Ⓐ		Ⓐ	①–⑥	Ⓐ	Ⓒ	Ⓐ		①–⑥	⑦				⑦	⑥ k	Ⓐ	Ⓒ		Ⓑ	Ⓒ		⑦	
				b					b	e				e	🚌				z			B e	D
Le Puy en Velay d.	0433	...	0543	0643	0739	0839	0846	...	1033	1043	...	1235	...	1445	1545	1613	1639	...	1735	1838	...	1939	1939
Firminy d.	0538	...	0649	0754	0853	0953	0953	...	1143	1150	...	1349	...	1556	|	1726	1753	...	1853	1950	...	2055	2057
St Étienne Châteaucreux a.	0557	...	0706	0810	0910	1009	1009	...	1205	1206	...	1405	...	1612	1705	1743	1810	...	1910	2007	...	2112	2113

A – Until July 12.
B – From July 13.
D – Ⓑ to July 11; Ⓐ from July 15.

b – Not July 14, Nov. 11.
e – Also July 14, Nov. 11.

k – Also Aug. 15.
z – Not Aug. 15.

PARIS / LYON - AVIGNON - MARSEILLE - TOULON - NICE 350

***TGV* SERVICES FROM / TO PARIS** (see next page for services from / to / via Lyon). For other *TGV* trains Paris - Valence TGV and v.v., see Table **355**.
For *TGV* trains Paris - Valence Ville - Avignon Centre, see Table **351**. For regional TER services Marseille - Nice, also overnight service Paris - Nice, see Table **361**.
Timings may vary by a few minutes – please check your reservation for confirmed timing.

WARNING! On certain dates when there is high demand for services to / from Nice, public stops at Avignon, Aix-en-Provence, Marseille and Toulon may not be available.

km		*FR* **6147** ♠	*Ouigo* **7829** ⊠	*TGV* **6101** Ⓐ		*TGV* **6169** ⑤ F	*TGV* **6169** ①–④ T	*TGV* **6103**	*TGV* **6161** ①–④ T	*Ouigo* **7851** ⊠	*TGV* **6173** n	*TGV* **6155** n	*TGV* **6173** A	*TGV* **6155** A	*TGV* **6107**	*TGV* **6175**	*TGV* **6109**	*FR* **6105** ⑥A ♠	*TGV* **6183** ⑤ F	*TGV* **6165** L	*TGV* **6167** ⑤ F	*FR* **6105** C ♠	*TGV* **6111**
0	**Paris** Gare de Lyon .... **342 351 355** d.	0555	0603	0629r	...	0646	0654	0736	0748	0821	0909	0909	0916	0916	0937	1009	1037	1028	1104	1121	1126	1113	1137
441	Lyon St Exupéry ✈ .... **342 351** d.	0748	|	|	...	|	|	|	|	|	|	|	|	|	|	|	|	1249	|	|	|	1317j	|
527	Valence TGV .... **355** d.	|	|	|	...	|	|	|	|	|	|	|	|	|	|	|	|	|	|	|	|	|	|
657	**Avignon** TGV .... d.	0840	0849	0920	...	0939	0936	1020	|	|	|	|	1204	1204	1221	|	1320	1355j	1345	1405	1413	1413	1421
731	Aix-en-Provence TGV .... d.	0903	0912	0944	...	|	|	1044	|	1120	|	|	|	|	1244	|	1344	1431j	|	|	|	1435	1444
750	**Marseille** St Charles .... a.	0915	0924	0956	...	|	|	1058	|	|	1214	1214	|	|	1256	1315	1357	1443	|	|	|	1446	1456
750	**Marseille** St Charles .... **360 361** d.	...	...	...	...	|	|	...	|	|	1228	1228	|	|	...	1328	...	...	|	|	|	...	...
817	**Toulon** .... **360 361** a.	...	...	...	...	1047	1047	...	1136	1210	1311	1311	1311	1311	...	1410	...	...	1449	1511	1519	...	...
	Toulon .... **361** d.	...	...	...	...	1050	1052	...	1140	1214	1316	1324	1316	1325	...	1414	...	...	1453	1515	1523	...	...
	Hyères .... **360** a.	...	...	...	...	|	|	...	|	|	|	1340	|	1340	...	|	...	...	|	|	|	...	...
885	Les Arcs-Draguignan .... **361** a.	...	...	...	...	1133	1143	...	|	|	|	...	|	...	...	1449	...	...	|	|	|	...	...
911	St Raphaël-Valescure .... **361** a.	...	...	...	...	1157	1210	...	1230	1304	1403	...	1403	...	...	|	...	...	1540	1602	1610	...	...
943	**Cannes** .... **361** a.	...	...	...	...	1255	1244	...	1255	1331	1427	...	1427	...	...	1527	...	...	1613	1627	1635	...	...
954	Antibes .... **361** a.	...	...	...	...	1308	1257	...	1309	1343	1440	...	1442	...	...	1540	...	...	1627	1640	1648	...	...
974	**Nice** .... **361** a.	...	...	...	...	1334	1324	...	1333	1411	1503	...	1503	...	...	1608	...	...	1651	1702	1716	...	...

	FR **6105** X ♠	*FR* **6105** B ♠	*Ouigo* **7825** ⊠	*TGV* **6177**	*FR* **6140** ♠	*TGV* **6115**	*TGV* **6185** ⑥ S	*TGV* **6163** D	*TGV* **6117**	*Ouigo* **7853** ⊠	*TGV* **6171** ⑥ S	*TGV* **6121** G	*TGV* **6181** Y	*TGV* **6123** d	*TGV* **6153** Ⓑ h◇	*TGV* **6127**	*TGV* **6187** ⑤ f	*FR* **6157** J ♠	*FR* **6157** ⑥A ♠	*TGV* **6129**	*Ouigo* **7827** ⊠		*TGV* **6137** N
Paris Gare de Lyon .... **342 351 355** d.	1115	1130	1236	1409	1425	1437	1456	1521	1538	1609	1614	1638	1721	1737	1809	1837	1918z	1904	1907	1937	2008	...	2136
Lyon St Exupéry ✈ .... **342 351** d.	1338j	1338j	|	|	|	|	|	|	|	|	|	|	|	|	|	|	|	2100	2104	|	|	...	|
Valence TGV .... **355** d.	|	|	|	|	|	|	|	|	|	1829	|	|	|	|	|	|	|	|	|	|	|	...	|
Avignon TGV .... d.	1439	1439	1520	|	|	1720	1736	1804	1821	|	1902	1920	|	2020	|	2120	2203	2211	2203	2220	2249	...	0018
Aix-en-Provence TGV .... d.	1510j	1509j	1544	|	1733	1746	|	|	1845	|	|	1944	2020	2044	|	2144	|	2236	2225	2244	2312	...	0040
Marseille St Charles .... a.	1521	1521	1558	1714	1746	1800	|	|	1857	|	|	1956	|	2057	2114	2157	|	2248	2237	2257	2324	...	0052
Marseille St Charles .... **360 361** d.	...	...	...	1728	...	...	|	|	...	|	|	...	|	...	2128	...	|	...	...	...	...	...	...
Toulon .... **360 361** a.	...	...	...	1810	...	...	1843	1911	...	2011	2019	...	2109	...	2209	...	2308	...	...	...	...	...	...
Toulon .... **361** d.	...	...	...	1814	...	...	1847	1915	...	2015	2023	...	2113	...	...	...	2312	...	...	...	...	...	...
Hyères .... **360** a.	...	...	...	|	...	...	|	|	...	|	|	...	|	...	...	...	|	...	...	...	...	...	...
Les Arcs-Draguignan .... **361** a.	...	...	...	|	...	...	|	|	...	2050	|	...	|	...	...	...	|	...	...	...	...	...	...
St Raphaël-Valescure .... **361** a.	...	...	...	1902	...	...	1938	2002	...	|	2111	...	2201	...	...	...	2400	...	...	...	...	...	...
Cannes .... **361** a.	...	...	...	1927	...	...	2013	2027	...	2128	2136	...	2226	...	...	...	0025	...	...	...	...	...	...
Antibes .... **361** a.	...	...	...	1940	...	...	2026	2040	...	2140	2149	...	2238	...	...	...	0038	...	...	...	...	...	...
Nice .... **361** a.	...	...	...	2003	...	...	2051	2103	...	2203	2207	...	2257	...	...	...	0056	...	...	...	...	...	...

	TGV **6102** Ⓐ a	*TGV* **6136** ⑦ R	*TGV* **6136** ①–④ m	*FR* **6104** ⑥A ¶♠	*TGV* **6150** Ⓐ	*FR* **6104** M ♠	*TGV* **6106**	*Ouigo* **7822** ⊠	*Ouigo* **7858** ⊠	*TGV* **6112**		*FR* **6146** ♠	*TGV* **6188** W	*TGV* **6172** ⑥ S	*TGV* **6184** ⑥ S	*Ouigo* **7820** U⊠	*TGV* **6116**	*TGV* **6174**	*TGV* **6170** H	*TGV* **6120** J h	*TGV* **6176**	*TGV* **6122**	*FR* **6166** ⑥A ♠
Nice .... **361** d.	...	...	...	...	...	...	...	...	0558	...	...	...	0759	0858	0910	...	...	0959	1057	...	1159	...	...
Antibes .... **361** d.	...	...	...	...	...	...	...	...	0620	...	...	...	0818	0919	0933	...	...	1020	1117	...	1220	...	...
Cannes .... **361** d.	...	...	...	...	...	...	...	...	0633	...	...	...	0831	0931	0945	...	...	1033	1129	...	1233	...	...
St Raphaël-Valescure .... **361** d.	...	...	...	...	...	...	...	...	|	...	...	...	0855	0957	1009	...	...	1058	1155	...	1258	...	...
Les Arcs-Draguignan .... **361** d.	...	...	...	...	...	...	...	...	0710	...	...	...	0911	|	|	...	...	|	|	...	|	...	...
Hyères .... **360** d.	...	...	...	...	...	...	...	...	|	...	...	...	|	|	|	...	...	|	|	...	|	...	...
Toulon .... **361** a.	...	...	...	...	...	...	...	...	0746	...	...	...	0946	1044	1057	...	...	1145	1245	...	1346	...	...
Toulon .... **360 361** d.	...	...	...	...	0549	...	...	...	0750	...	...	...	0950	1048	1101	...	...	1149	1249	...	1351	...	...
Marseille St Charles .... **360 361** a.	...	...	...	...	|	...	...	...	|	...	...	...	1032	|	|	...	...	1232	|	...	1432	...	...
Marseille St Charles .... d.	0518	0603	0604	0604	|	0652	0701	0800	|	0904	...	0953	1046	|	|	1154	1203	1246	|	1403	1446	1500	1521
Aix-en-Provence TGV .... d.	0532	0617	0618	0618	0642	0707	0718	|	0841	0918	...	1007	|	|	|	1208	1218	|	|	1418	|	1518	1535
Avignon TGV .... d.	0555	0640	0641	0641	0705	0730	0740	0830	|	0941	...	1030	|	1157	1207	1231	1241	|	1356	1441	|	1541	1557
Valence TGV .... **355** d.	|	|	|	|	|	|	|	|	|	|	...	|	|	|	|	|	|	|	|	|	|	|	|
Lyon St Exupéry ✈ .... **342 351** d.	|	|	|	0758j	|	0824	|	|	0954	|	...	1125	|	|	|	1325	|	|	|	|	|	|	1650
Paris Gare de Lyon .... **342 351 355** a.	0839	0922	0923	0954	0951	1018	1023	1117	1152	1223	...	1318	1351	1435	1445	1518	1523	1551	1634	1722	1750	1822	1841

	TGV **6166** ⑦ R		*FR* **6108** J ♠	*TGV* **6124**	*FR* **6108** J ♠	*TGV* **6162** ①–④ T	*TGV* **6128** b	*Ouigo* **7856** ⊠	*Ouigo* **7824** ⊠		*TGV* **6168**	*TGV* **6182** P	*TGV* **6182** ⑦ A	*FR* **6148** K ♠	*TGV* **6132**	*FR* **6148** ⑦A ♠	*TGV* **6180** t		*TGV* **6134** ⑦	*TGV* **6186** ⑦ e		*TGV* **6144** Q	*TGV* **6144** ⑦
Nice .... **361** d.	1255	...	...	...	...	1402	...	1458	...	...	1553	1602	1623	...	...	...	1658	...	...	1753	...	...	...
Antibes .... **361** d.	1320	...	...	...	...	1418	...	1519	...	...	1619	1632	1649	...	...	...	1720	...	...	1820	...	...	...
Cannes .... **361** d.	1334	...	...	...	...	1432	...	1533	...	...	1632	1646	1702	...	...	...	1733	...	...	1833	...	...	...
St Raphaël-Valescure .... **361** d.	1359	...	...	...	...	1457	...	1557	...	...	1658	1714	1727	...	...	...	|	...	...	1858	...	...	...
Les Arcs-Draguignan .... **361** d.	|	...	...	...	...	|	...	|	...	...	|	|	|	...	...	...	1810	...	...	|	...	...	...
Hyères .... **360** d.	|	...	...	1449	...	|	...	|	...	...	|	|	|	...	...	...	|	...	...	|	...	...	...
Toulon .... **361** a.	|	...	...	1505	...	1546	...	1645	...	...	1745	|	1814	...	...	...	1845	...	...	1945	...	...	...
Toulon .... **360 361** d.	|	...	...	1510	...	1550	...	1649	...	...	1749	|	1818	...	...	...	1849	...	...	1949	...	...	...
Marseille St Charles .... **360 361** a.	|	...	...	1550	...	|	...	|	...	...	1832	|	|	...	...	...	|	...	...	|	...	...	...
Marseille St Charles .... d.	|	...	1547	1604	...	|	1703	|	1734	...	1845	|	|	1849	1904	1912	|	...	2004	|	...	2046	2104
Aix-en-Provence TGV .... d.	|	...	1601	1618	...	|	1718	1742	1750	...	|	|	|	1905	1918	1926	|	...	2018	|	...	2100	2118
Avignon TGV .... d.	|	...	1625	1641	...	1711	1741	|	1812	...	|	|	1926	1927	1941	1949	1958	...	2041	2104	...	2123	2141
Valence TGV .... **355** d.	|	...	|	|	←	|	|	|	|	...	|	|	|	|	|	|	|	...	|	|	...	|	|
Lyon St Exupéry ✈ .... **342 351** d.	|	...	1725	|	1735	|	|	|	|	...	|	|	|	2021	|	|	|	...	|	|	...	|	|
Paris Gare de Lyon .... **342 351 355** a.	1847	...	→	1922	1931	1951	2022	2042	2052	...	2150	2222	2203	2214	2222‡	2228	2238‡	...	2323‡	2349‡	...	0021‡	0022‡

A – July 5 - Aug. 31.
B – ①–⑤ July 1 - Aug. 29 (also Sept. 16, 17, 30, Oct. 15, 28, 29, Nov. 4, 5, 11, 12, 18, 19, 26, 28, Dec. 3).
C – ⑥⑦ to June 29; ⑦ July 6 - Aug. 31; ⑥⑦ from Sept. 6.
D – Daily to Sept. 4; ⑦–④ Sept. 7 - Nov. 17 (not Nov. 4); ①③④⑦ from Nov. 19.
F – ⑤ July 11 - Aug. 29 (also Aug. 14; not Aug. 15).
G – Ⓑ to June 27; daily June 29 - Sept. 5; Ⓑ Sept. 7 - Nov. 16; ③④⑤⑦ from Nov. 19.
H – ⑥⑦ to June 29; daily July 5 - Aug. 31.
J – Daily to July 4; Ⓑ July 6 - Aug. 29; daily from Aug. 31.
K – Daily to July 5; ①–⑥ July 7 - Aug. 30; daily from Sept. 1.
L – Daily to Nov. 2; ⑤⑥ from Nov. 7.
M – Ⓑ to Aug. 29 (also June 28); daily from Aug. 31. Departure times are 5 – 8 minutes earlier on June 25, July 9, 30, Aug. 13, 27. Timings at Lyon St Exupéry and Paris are 20 – 32 minutes later on July 29, Sept. 17, 30, Oct. 15, Nov. 4, 5, 18, 19, Dec. 3.
N – ⑤⑦ to June 29; ⑤ July 4 - Aug. 8 (also Aug. 14); ⑤⑦ from Sept. 5 (also Nov. 11). On June 15, 22, 29 Paris d. 2114, Avignon d. 0002, Aix-en-Provence d. 0025, Marseille a. 0036. On June 27, July 4 Paris d. 2127, Avignon d. 0007, Aix-en-Provence d. 0030, Marseille a. 0041.
P – Runs on July 14 only.
Q – Runs on July 14 and Nov. 11 only.
R – ⑦ July 6 - Aug. 31 (also July 14).
S – ⑥ July 5 - Aug. 30 (also Aug. 15).
T – ①–④ July 7 - Aug. 28 (not July 14, Aug. 14).
U – Daily to Sept. 19 (also Sept. 21); ①–⑥ from Sept. 22. July 7 - Aug. 31 departs Marseille 1203, Aix-en-Provence 1218, Avignon 1241, arrives Paris 1522 (not calling at Lyon St Exupéry).
W – Daily to Nov. 2; Ⓒ from Nov. 8.
X – ①–⑤ to June 30; ①–⑤ from Sept. 1 (not Sept. 16, 17, 30, Oct. 15, 28, 29, Nov. 4, 5, 11, 12, 18, 19, 26, 28, Dec. 3).
Y – ⑤⑥ (daily July 4 - Aug. 31).

a – Not Nov. 13, 20, 27, Dec. 4, 11.
b – Not Oct. 4, 11, Nov. 15, 22, 29, Dec. 6, 13.
d – Not Nov. 15, 22, 29, Dec. 6, 13.
e – Also July 14, Nov. 11.
f – Also Aug. 14; not Aug. 15.
h – Not Aug. 15.
j – Arrives 7 – 15 minutes earlier.
m – Not July 14, Aug. 14, Nov. 11.
n – Not July 5 - Aug. 31.
r – 4 – 5 minutes later until Aug. 29 and on ① from Sept. 1.
t – Not Oct. 25, Nov. 1, 15, 19, 22, 26, 29, Dec. 3, 6, 10, 13.
z – Departs 2 – 3 minutes later to July 4 / from Sept. 5.

TGV – High-speed train. 🅁. 🍷. *FR* – Italian high-speed train. 🅁. 🍷.

¶ – Also runs on June 21. On July 5 Lyon St Exupéry d. 0734, Paris a. 0928.
‡ – Arrival may be up to 30 minutes later on certain dates.
◇ – Subject to alteration / cancellation on certain dates from Sept. 5.
♠ – *Frecciarossa* high-speed train. Operated by Trenitalia. 🅁. 🍷.
⊠ – OUIGO low-cost TGV service. Internet bookings only at www.ouigo.com.

350 PARIS / LYON - AVIGNON - MARSEILLE - TOULON - NICE

TGV **SERVICES FROM / TO / VIA LYON** (see previous page for services from / to Paris Gare de Lyon). Timings may vary by a few minutes – please check your reservation for confirmed timings.

Warning! Subject to alteration on Nov. 1. Services via Massy are subject to alteration / cancellation on June 15, 21, 28, 29, July 19, 20.
Services via Strasbourg are subject to alteration / cancellation on June 28, 29, Oct. 18, 19.

	TGV 6801	*TGV* 6805	*Ouigo* 7831	*TGV* 5102	*TGV* 9756	*TGV* 9810	*TGV* 5332	*TGV* 5113	*Ouigo* 7897	*TGV* 9877	*TGV* 6813	*Ouigo* 7841	*Ouigo* 7835	*TGV* 9830	*TGV* 5306	*TGV* 5537	*TGV* 5537	*Ouigo* 7845	*TGV* 9580	*TGV* 9835	*TGV* 5135	*TGV* 5326	*TGV* 5316	*TGV* 5124
				①–⑥				⑥					R		⑤					⑥	⑤			⑧
			U⊠	a	Y△			k	⊠	L		⊠	⊠		f		E	⊠	F	k	f	A	w♧	h
Brussels Midi **11** d.	...	...	...	...	...	0637**t**	...	0817**v**	...	...	...	...	...	1317**y**	...	...	...	...	...	1617**p**	...	...	...	...
Lille Europe **11** d.	...	...	...	0550**r**	...	0722	...	0901	...	...	...	...	...	1401	...	...	...	...	...	1702	1702	...	...	1822**d**
Lille Flandres **11** d.	...	...	...	|	...	|	...	|	...	...	...	1130	1300	|	...	...	...	1520	...	|	|	...	...	1822**g**
Charles de Gaulle + **11** d.	...	...	0700**x**	0657	...	0827	...	0959	1102	...	...	1233	1358	1459	...	...	...	1632	...	1800	1800	...	...	2000
Marne la Vallée-Chessy **11** d.	...	...	0717	0713	...	0843	...	1013	1116	...	...	1249	1413	1515	...	...	...	1649	...	1813	1813	...	...	2013
Nantes **335** d.	...	...	|	|	...	|	...	|	|	...	...	|	|	|	1244	...	...	|	...	|	|	1537◊	...	|
Rennes **335** d.	...	...	|	|	...	|	0731•	|	|	...	...	|	|	|	|	...	...	|	...	|	|	|	...	|
Le Havre **335** d.	...	...	|	|	...	|	|	|	|	...	...	|	|	|	|	...	...	|	...	|	|	|	1556	|
Massy TGV **335** d.	...	...	|	|	...	|	0924	|	|	...	...	|	|	|	1526	...	...	|	...	|	|	1821◊	1826**z**	|
Nancy **379** d.	...	...	|	|	...	|	|	|	|	...	...	|	|	|	|	1224	1224	|	...	|	|	|	|	|
Metz **379** d.	...	...	|	|	...	|	|	|	|	0809	...	|	|	|	|	|	|	|	...	|	|	|	|	|
Strasbourg **379** d.	...	...	|	|	...	|	|	|	|	0904	...	|	|	|	|	1337	1337	|	1616	|	|	|	|	|
Dijon Ville **379** d.	...	...	|	|	...	|	|	|	|	1121	...	|	|	|	|	1617	1617	|	|	|	|	|	|	|
Genève **346** d.	...	...	|	|	0842	|	|	|	|	|	...	|	|	|	|	|	|	|	|	|	|	|	|	|
Lyon Part Dieu ▶ d.	0628	0806	|	0907	1031	1040	1140	1206	|	1310	1355	|	1606	1706	1737	1806	1806	|	2006	2010	2010	2040	2040	2206
Lyon St Exupéry + d.	|	|	|	|	|	|	|	|	1304	|	|	1437	|	|	|	|	|	1835	|	|	|	|	|	|
Valence TGV ▶ d.	0705	0848	|	|	|	1120	|	|	|	1351	|	|	|	|	1819	|	|	1901	|	2055	2055	2120	2120	|
Avignon TGV d.	0740	0928	0953	1012	1136	1155	1249	1311	|	1429	1500	1530	1712	1812	1855	1911	1911	1937	2112	2129	2129	2155	2155	2312
Aix en Provence TGV d.	0802	0952	1016	1034	1158	|	1312	1333	1411	1452	1522	1552	|	1834	|	1933	1933	2003	2134	2152	2152	|	|	2336
Marseille St Charles a.	0814	1004	1028	1050	1210	1224	1324	1346	|	1506	1534	1608	1742	1849	1924	1945	1945	2016	2146	2204	2204	2224	2224	2348
Marseille St Charles **360 361** d.	...	1020	...	...	...	...	...	...	|	...	1549	...	...	...	...	2001	2001	...	...	...	...	...	...	...
Toulon **360 361** a.	...	1106	...	...	...	...	...	...	1507	...	1636	...	...	...	...	2044	2044	...	...	...	...	...	...	...
Les Arcs-Draguignan **361** a.	...	|	...	...	...	...	...	...	...	...	...	...	...	...	...	...	2126	...	...	...	...	...	...	...
St Raphaël-Valescure **361** a.	...	1201	...	...	...	...	...	...	...	...	...	...	...	...	...	...	2143	...	...	...	...	...	...	...
Cannes **361** a.	...	1227	...	...	...	...	...	...	...	...	...	...	...	...	...	...	2210	...	...	...	...	...	...	...
Antibes **361** a.	...	1240	...	...	...	...	...	...	...	...	...	...	...	...	...	...	2222	...	...	...	...	...	...	...
Nice **361** a.	...	1302	...	...	...	...	...	...	...	...	...	...	...	...	...	...	2240	...	...	...	...	...	...	...

	Ouigo 7838	*TGV* 9854	*TGV* 5376	*TGV* 9583	*TGV* 5366	*TGV* 5516	*TGV* 5516	*Ouigo* 7842	*TGV* 6850	*TGV* 5382	*TGV* 9866	*TGV* 5192	*TGV* 9752	*TGV* 5386	*TGV* 9868	*TGV* 9896	*Ouigo* 7898	*Ouigo* 7832	*TGV* 9882	*TGV* 6866	*Ouigo* 7836	*TGV* 6852	*TGV* 6852	*TGV* 6852
									⑧	⑥		⑥									R	①–⑥	⑦	⑦
	⊠		w♡	F	Q		D	⊠	h	k		k	Y			L⊗	⊠	⊠			T⊠	b	M	N
Nice **361** d.	...	...	...	...	...	...	0657	...	...	...	...	...	...	...	...	...	...	...	...	1512	...	...	...	...
Antibes **361** d.	...	...	...	...	...	...	0717	...	...	...	...	...	...	...	...	...	...	...	...	1534	...	...	...	...
Cannes **361** d.	...	...	...	...	...	...	0731	...	...	...	...	...	...	...	...	...	...	...	...	1547	...	...	...	...
St Raphaël-Valescure **361** d.	...	...	...	...	...	...	0755	...	...	...	...	...	...	...	...	...	...	...	...	1613	...	...	...	...
Les Arcs-Draguignan **361** d.	...	...	...	...	...	...	0811	...	...	...	...	...	...	...	...	...	...	...	...	1630	...	...	...	...
Toulon **360 361** d.	...	...	...	...	...	0850	0850	...	...	...	...	...	...	...	...	...	1550**c**	...	...	1712	...	1915	1915	1927
Marseille St Charles **360 361** a.	...	...	...	...	...	0931	0931	...	...	...	...	...	...	...	...	...	|	...	...	1759	...	1959	1959	2007
Marseille St Charles d.	0612	0634	0734	0812	0832‡	0945	0945	1002	1020	1036	1212	1334	1346	1436	1512	1554	|	1646	1712	1815	1827	2012	2012	2020
Aix en Provence TGV d.	0626	0650	|	0826	|	0959	0959	1017	1036	1050	1227	1348	1400	1450	1526	1610	1643	|	1726	1829	1842	2027	2027	2034
Avignon TGV d.	0648	0715	0806	0848	0907‡	1022	1022	1039	1059	1115	1250	1410	1422	1515	1549	1633	|	1719	1749	1851	1905	2049	2051	2056
Valence TGV ▶ d.	|	|	0844	|	0944‡	|	|	|	1134	|	|	|	|	|	|	1714	|	|	|	1926	|	2124	2127	2130
Lyon St Exupéry + a.	0741	|	|	|	|	|	|	1130	|	|	|	|	|	|	|	|	1758	1811	|	|	1957	|	|	|
Lyon Part Dieu ▶ a.	|	0820	0920	0954	1023	1126	1126	|	1210	1220	1353	1514	1532	1620	1654	1750	|	|	1854	2002	|	2158	2204	2206
Genève **346** a.	|	|	|	|	|	|	|	|	...	|	|	|	1745	|	|	|	|	|	|	...	|	...	...	...
Dijon Ville **379** a.	|	|	|	|	|	1326	1326	|	...	|	|	|	...	|	|	1940	|	|	|	...	|	...	...	...
Strasbourg **379** a.	|	|	|	1343	|	1554	1554	|	...	|	|	|	...	|	|	2207	|	|	|	...	|	...	...	...
Metz **379** a.	|	|	|	...	|	|	|	|	...	|	|	|	...	|	|	2302	|	|	|	...	|	...	...	...
Nancy **379** a.	|	|	|	...	|	1702	1702	|	...	|	|	|	...	|	|	...	|	|	|	...	|	...	...	...
Massy TGV **335** a.	|	|	1138**z**	...	1234	...	...	|	...	1437	|	|	...	1834	|	...	|	|	|	...	|	...	...	...
Le Havre **335** a.	|	|	1412	...	|	...	...	|	...	|	|	|	...	|	|	...	|	|	|	...	|	...	...	...
Rennes **335** a.	|	|	...	...	|	...	...	|	...	1626	|	|	...	2030	|	...	|	|	|	...	|	...	...	...
Nantes **335** a.	|	|	...	...	1450	...	...	|	...	...	|	|	...	...	|	...	|	|	|	...	|	...	...	...
Marne la Vallée-Chessy **11** a.	0933	1016	...	...	...	...	...	1317	...	...	1546	1707	...	...	1846	...	1947	2006	2046	...	2146	...	...	...
Charles de Gaulle + **11** a.	0949	1030	...	...	...	...	...	1331	...	...	1600	1722	...	...	1900	...	...	2022	2100**e**	...	2201	...	...	...
Lille Flandres **11** a.	1048	|	...	...	...	...	...	1434	...	...	|	1902	...	...	|	...	...	...	|	...	...	...	...	...
Lille Europe **11** a.	...	1127	...	...	...	...	...	...	...	...	1658	...	...	...	1958	...	...	...	2158**e**	...	...	...	...	...
Brussels Midi **11** a.	...	1211**q**	...	...	...	...	...	...	...	...	1743**q**	...	...	...	2043**q**	...	...	...	2243**n**	...	...	...	...	...

D – ⑥⑦ to June 22 daily June 28 - Sept. 8; ⑥⑦ from Sept. 13 (also Nov. 12; not Oct. 11, 12).
E – ⑤⑥ to June 21; daily June 27 - Sept. 7; ⑤⑥ from Sept. 12 (also Nov. 11; not Oct. 10, 11).
F – From / to Frankfurt (Table **47**).
L – From / to Luxembourg (Table **379**).
M – ⑦ to June 29 (also July 14); ⑦ from Sept. 7 (also Nov. 11).
N – ⑦ July 6 - Aug. 31.
Q – Runs on July 12, 13 and ⑥⑦ Sept. 6 - Oct. 5.
R – ⑥⑦ June 21 - July 6; daily July 12 - Sept. 28; ⑥⑦ Oct. 4 - Nov. 23; daily from Nov. 29.
T – To Tourcoing, a. 2309 (2323 on ①–⑤ from Aug. 18).
U – Daily to Sept. 19 (also Sept. 21); ①–⑥ from Sept. 22.
Y – June 28 - Aug. 24. From / to Lausanne (Table **346**).

a – Not July 14, Nov. 10, 11.
b – Not July 14, Nov. 11.
c – 1546 on ①–④ July 7 - Aug. 28.
d – ①–⑤ (not July 14, Aug. 15).
e – On ①–⑤ from Sept. 1 arrives Charles de Gaulle + 2103, Lille Europe 2205.
f – Also Aug. 14; not Aug. 15.
g – ⑦ (also July 14).
h – Not Aug. 15.
k – Also Aug. 15.
n – 2259 on ①–⑤ Aug. 18 – 29; 2302 on ⑥⑦ Aug. 16 – 31.
p – 1559 on Aug. 16, 23, 30; 1609 on June 21, July 26.

q – 32 – 40 minutes later Aug. 16 – 31.
r – Departure time varies from 0550 to 0559. On ②–⑥ Oct. 21 - Nov. 1 departs Lille **Flandres** 0532 (not Lille Europe).
t – 0627 on June 21, 22, July 12, 13, 19 – 21, Aug. 2, 3, 9, 10, 15, Sept. 20; 0603 on ⑥⑦ Aug. 16 – 31; 0619 on ①–⑤ Aug. 18 – 29.
v – ⑥ July 5 - Aug. 30 (also Aug. 15). Departs 0759 Aug. 16 – 30.
w – Does not run June 15, 28, 29, July 12, 13, ⑥⑦ Sept. 6 - Oct. 5, Nov. 8 – 11, 15, 16, 22, 23, 29, 30.
x – Not June 15, 16.
y – Not Aug. 16, 18, 23, 25, 30. Departs 1300 on ②③④⑤⑦ Aug. 17 – 31.
z – Massy **Palaiseau**.

TGV – High-speed train. 🅡. 🍸.

• – 0740 on ⑧ to Sept. 7 (not Aug. 15) and on ⑦ from Sept. 14 (also Nov. 11).
‡ – On Sept. 6, 7, Oct. 4, 5 departs Marseille 0842, Avignon 0912, Valence 0949.
◊ – On Sept. 13, 20, 27 departs Nantes 1559, Massy 1825.
△ – Subject to alteration on Aug. 3.
⊗ – Subject to alteration on on ①–⑤ from Nov. 10 (also on Sept. 28, Oct. 11, 26, Nov. 23, Dec. 7).
♧ – On July 14 Massy Palaiseau d. 1817. On ①–⑤ July 15 - Aug. 15 Massy Palaiseau d. 1814. On ⑥⑦ July 19 - Aug. 17 Le Havre d. 1515, Massy Palaiseau d. 1805.
♡ – On July 20, Aug. 4 – 10, 15 Marseille d. 0715, Avignon d. 0747, Valence d. 0824, Lyon Part Dieu a. 0859, Massy Palaiseau a. 1134, Le Havre a. 1405.
⊠ – OUIGO low-cost TGV service. Internet bookings only at www.ouigo.com.
▶ – For other trains Valence TGV - Lyon and Paris see Table **355**. For Valence Ville - Lyon see Table **351**.

LYON - VALENCE - AVIGNON - MARSEILLE via 'classic' line 351

All TER trains are 2nd class only except through services between Lyon and Marseille. Minor timing variations are possible.
Warning! Subject to alteration on July 12–14, Oct. 4, 5, 11, 12, Nov. 8, 9.

km			◇	Ⓒ	Ⓐ	Ⓐ	①–⑥ b	Ⓒ	Ⓐ	⑥	Ⓐ	Ⓐ		Ⓐ				①–⑥ b⊗	⊗	⊗	Ⓒ S	⊗	⊗		⑤ z
	Lyon Perrache d.	...	...	...	...	...	0539	...	...	...	...	0639	...	0739	...	...	...	...	...	...	1142	...	...	...	...
0	**Lyon** Part-Dieu d.	...	...	...	...	...	|	...	...	0620	0620	|	0720	|	*0820*	0920	...	1020	...	1120	|	1220	1320	...	...
32	Vienne d.	...	...	...	...	...	0602	...	...	0639	0640	0701	0740	0801	*0839*	0939	...	1039	...	1140	1202	1240	1339	...	...
87	Tain-l'Hermitage-Tournon d.	...	...	...	...	...	0640	...	...	0720	0720	0739	0824	0840	*0917*	1019	...	1119	...	1219	|	1324	1417	...	...
105	**Valence** Ville a.	...	...	...	...	...	0652	...	...	0732	0733	0752	0836	0852	*0929*	1031	...	1131	...	1231	1242	1336	1430	...	...
105	**Valence** Ville d.	...	...	0559	0604	0625	...	0703	0704	▬	0736	...	0838	...	0937	1034	...	1133	1222	...	1244	1338	1432	...	1454
150	Montélimar d.	...	...	0626	0631	0653	...	0731	0731	...	0807	...	0901	...	1004	1057	...	1200	1256	...	1307	1401	1459	...	1524
202	Orange d.	...	...	0702	0707	0729	...	0808	0807	...	0844	...	0935	...	1048	1128	...	1234	1332	...	1342	1434	1533	...	1601
230	**Avignon** Centre a.	...	...	0727	0734	0751	...	0832	0832	Ⓐ	0859	...	0949	...	1113	1144	...	1251	1355	...	1400	1449	1551	...	1624
230	**Avignon** Centre d.	0555	0655	0748	...	0754	...	0852	...	0853	...	...	0952	...	1116	*1152*	1253	...	1358	...	...	1452	...	1606	1653
265	Arles 355 d.	0612	0712	0807	...	0812	...	0911	...	0910	...	...	1011	...	1133	*1211*	1312	...	1417	...	...	1511	...	1623	1712
299	Miramas 355 d.	0635	0735	0834	...	0835	...	0937	...	0935	...	...	1035	...	1156	*1235*	1335	...	1442	...	...	1534	...	1647	1738
328	Vitrolles (for ✈) ⊖ 355 d.	0656	0756	0858	...	0855	...	1000	...	0958	...	...	1054	...	1215	*1259*	1358	...	1505	...	...	1554	...	1709	1800
351	**Marseille** St Charles 355 a.	0710	0810	0919	...	0909	...	1020	...	1019	...	...	1110	...	1229	*1319*	1418	...	1529	...	...	1616	...	1728	1819

	①–⑥ b⊗		Ⓒ	①–④ b	①–④ b	⑤–⑦ e	⑤	Ⓒ	Ⓐ	⑦ e	①–⑥ b		Ⓐ		⑤t A	Ⓒ	Ⓐ	Ⓒ	Ⓐ	Ⓑ z	⊖			C	⑥⑦
Lyon Perrache d.	1339	...	...	...	...	...	...	...	1539	...	...	1639	...	...	...	1738	1738	...	...	1839	...	1939	...	...	...
Lyon Part-Dieu d.	|	1420	...	...	1520	1520	...	...	|	...	1620	|	...	1720	...	|	|	1820	1820	|	1920	|	2020	2120	2220
Vienne d.	1401	1440	...	...	1540	1540	...	...	1601	...	1640	1701	...	1740	...	1800	1800	1840	1840	1901	1940	2001	2040	2140	2240
Tain-l'Hermitage-Tournon d.	1439	1511	...	...	1618	1619	...	...	1639	...	1719	1739	...	1823	...	1838	1838	1918	1918	1939	2019	2041	2118	2218	2319
Valence Ville a.	1451	1525	...	...	1630	1632	...	...	1652	...	1731	1752	...	1835	...	1851	1851	1930	1932	1952	2032	2052	2132	2230	2330
Valence Ville d.	▬	...	1542	1628	...	1633	...	...	1655	1708	1734	▬	1805	1837	1855	1854	1903	1932	1934	▬	2033	▬	...	...	...
Montélimar d.	...	...	1610	1655	...	1656	...	...	1723	1738	1801	...	1833	1900	1919	1921	1930	2001	2003	...	2055	...	...	...	...
Orange d.	①–④	...	1647	1731	...	1726	...	...	1800	1818	1836	...	1908	1934	1950	1956	2005	2036	2038	Ⓐ	2129	...	...	...	...
Avignon Centre a.	b	...	1713	1751	...	1749	...	...	1822	1842	1851	...	1932	1949	2006	2020	2029	2055	2055		2149	T	...	...	...
Avignon Centre d.	1653	...	1716	1754	...	...	1754	1755	...	...	...	1916	...	1952	...	...	...	...	...	2115	...	2157	...	...	...
Arles 355 d.	1711	...	1733	1812	...	...	1812	1814	...	...	...	1933	...	2011	...	...	...	...	...	2133	...	2214x	...	...	...
Miramas 355 d.	1737	...	1754	1835	...	...	1835	1839	...	...	...	1956	...	2035	...	...	...	...	...	2157	...	2238	...	...	...
Vitrolles (for ✈) ⊖ 355 d.	1800	...	1814	1855	...	...	1856	1903	...	...	...	2019	...	2054	...	...	...	...	...	2220	...	2301	...	...	...
Marseille St Charles 355 a.	1819	...	1831	1909	...	...	1912	1922	...	...	...	2037	...	2109	...	...	...	...	...	2239	...	2320	...	...	...

	Ⓐ	Ⓐ	①–⑥ b	①–⑥ b	①–⑥ b		①–⑥ b	①–⑥ b	Ⓐ	①–⑥ b	Ⓐ		Ⓐ	Ⓐ ⊗	⊗	⊗	⊗	Ⓒ		⊗	⚒		Ⓑ z		⚒
Marseille St Charles 355 d.	...	...	...	...	...	...	...	...	...	...	...	0647	0738	...	...	0838	...	0935	1042	...	...	1142	...	1250	...
Vitrolles (for ✈) ⊖ 355 d.	...	...	...	...	...	...	...	...	...	...	...	0706	0759	...	...	0857	...	0957	1102	...	...	1201	...	1306	...
Miramas 355 d.	...	...	...	...	...	...	...	...	...	...	*0626*	0726	0824	...	...	0923	...	1021	1125	...	...	1225	...	1325	...
Arles 355 d.	...	...	...	...	...	...	...	...	...	...	*0651*	0750	0846	...	...	0947	...	1042	1147	...	...	1247	...	1350	...
Avignon Centre a.	...	...	...	...	...	...	...	...	...	...	*0709*	0807	0903	...	...	1006	...	1059	1204	...	...	1304	...	1407	...
Avignon Centre d.	...	...	...	...	0540	...	0613	...	0642	0706	0728	0810	...	0911	...	1015	...	...	...	1214	...	1307	...	1410	...
Orange d.	...	...	...	...	0600	...	0630	...	0702	0728	0752	0827	...	0926	...	1041	...	...	...	1229	...	1331	...	1427	...
Montélimar d.	...	0537	...	...	0634	...	0703	...	0737	0802	0829	0901	...	1003	...	1118	...	...	...	1304	...	1408	...	1501	...
Valence Ville a.	...	0603	...	...	0700	...	0726	...	0803	0828	0856	0922	...	1033	...	1145	...	...	...	1325	...	1436	...	1522	...
Valence Ville d.	0536	0606	0628	0636	0704	0704	0729	0736	0806	0830	...	0924	...	1036	1128	...	1228	...	...	1328	1436	...	1506	1524	1605
Tain-l'Hermitage-Tournon d.	0547	0617	0639	0647	0716	0716	0740	0747	0817	0841	...	0936	...	1047	1139	...	1239	...	...	1339	1447	...	1517	1536	1616
Vienne d.	0628	0658	0721	0728	0757	0757	0821	0828	0858	0922	...	1021	...	1121	1221	...	1321	...	...	1421	1522	...	1558	1621	1657
Lyon Part-Dieu a.	|	|	0740	|	|	|	0840	|	|	0940	...	1040	...	1140	1240	...	1340	...	...	1440	1540	...	|	1640	|
Lyon Perrache a.	0649	0719	...	0749	0819	0819	...	0849	0919	...	...	...	...	...	...	...	...	...	...	...	...	...	1619	...	1719

		Ⓑ z				⑦ e			Ⓒ S	Ⓐ	Ⓑ z		Ⓒ	Ⓐ	⑦ eA			Ⓐ	Ⓐ R	①–⑤ L🚌	Ⓒ	Ⓑ u		Ⓐ T	Ⓒ T⊡
Marseille St Charles 355 d.	1338	...	1440	...	...	...	1538	...	...	...	...	1650	...	1730	...	1748	...	1832	...	...	1832	1937	2033	2138	2238
Vitrolles (for ✈) ⊖ 355 d.	1357	...	1459	...	...	...	1557	...	...	...	...	1706	...	1745	...	1805	...	1846	...	...	1851	1957	2057	2157	2256
Miramas 355 d.	1421	...	1525	...	...	...	1622	...	...	...	...	1726	...	1807	...	1825	...	1908	...	...	1919	2022	2121	2221	2325
Arles 355 d.	1447	...	1547	...	...	...	1647	...	...	...	...	1750	...	1833	...	1846	...	1930	...	...	1943	2046	2245	2242x	2346
Avignon Centre a.	1504	...	1604	...	...	...	1704	...	...	...	...	1807	...	1852	...	1904	...	1948	...	...	2004	2103	2204	2259	0004
Avignon Centre d.	1528	...	...	1612	...	...	...	1712	1725	1727	...	1810	1827	1856	1901	...	1927	1951	...	...	2028	▬	...	...	...
Orange d.	1552	...	...	1627	...	...	...	1732	1747	1752	...	1827	1851	1920	1917	...	1949	2015	...	...	2054	...	...	...	...
Montélimar d.	1629	...	...	1702	...	1736	...	1807	1829	1829	...	1901	1928	1957	1952	...	2023	2052	...	...	2130	⑥	...	...	...
Valence Ville a.	1656	...	...	1728	...	1803	...	1833	1850	1856	...	1922	1956	2024	2013	...	2049	2119	...	...	2156		...	...	...
Valence Ville d.	...	1706	...	1730	1806	1806	...	1836	1853	...	1906	1924	...	...	...	...	2052	...	2126	2145	...	2206	...	...	...
Tain-l'Hermitage-Tournon d.	...	1717	...	1741	1817	1817	...	1847	|	...	1917	1936	...	...	...	...	2103	...	2137	|	...	2217	...	...	...
Vienne d.	...	1758	...	1821	1858	1858	...	1921	1940	...	1958	2021	...	...	...	...	2144	...	2217	2240	...	2259	...	...	...
Lyon Part-Dieu a.	...	|	...	1840	|	|	...	1940	1958	...	|	2040	...	...	...	...	2202	...	2237	2325	...	2319	...	...	...
Lyon Perrache a.	...	1819	...	...	1919	1919	...	...	...	...	2019	...	...	...	...	...	...	...	...	...	...	...	...	...	...

TGV services from/to Paris. Timings may vary by a few minutes – please check your reservation for confirmed timings.
See Table **350** for *TGV* services Paris/Lyon - Valence TGV - Avignon TGV - Marseille, Table **355** for *TGV* services Paris/Lyon - Valence TGV - Montpellier.

	TGV **6191** ②–④ a	*TGV* **6191** G		*TGV* **6193** E		*TGV* **6195** Ⓑ z			
Paris Gare de Lyon § d.	0713	0713	...	1214	...	1712	...	...	...
Lyon St Exupéry TGV ✈ § d.	0914	0914	...	1414	...	1921	...	...	...
Valence Ville a.	0942	0943	...	1442	...	1949	...	...	...
Montélimar a.	1008	1008	...	1507	...	2013	...	...	...
Orange a.	1035	1036	...	1535	...	2041	...	...	...
Avignon Centre a.	1053	1054	...	1555	...	2059	...	...	...
Arles a.	1117	...	...	1616	...	2119	...	...	...
Miramas a.	1142	...	...	1639	...	2143	...	...	...

	TGV **6194** ①–④ m	*TGV* **6194** H	*TGV* **6194** ⑤⑥		*TGV* **6196** D		*TGV* **6198**			
Miramas d.	0515	0604	0617	...	...	...	1719	...	...	...
Arles d.	0539	0641	0641	...	...	...	1742	...	...	...
Avignon Centre d.	0559	0701	0702	...	1403	...	1803	...	...	...
Orange d.	0616	0719	0721	...	1420	...	1820	...	...	...
Montélimar d.	0644	0747	0748	...	1449	...	1848	...	...	...
Valence Ville d.	0708	0811	0812	...	1513	...	1912	...	...	...
Lyon St Exupéry TGV ✈ § a.	0737	0840	0842	...	1543	...	1943	...	...	...
Paris Gare de Lyon § a.	0947	1049	1047	...	1746	...	2146	...	...	...

A – To/from Annecy (Table **364**).
C – ⑥⑦ to Oct. 5; daily from Oct. 12.
D – ①⑤⑥⑦ (also July 15, Aug. 14, Nov. 11, 12).
E – ①⑤⑥⑦ (also July 15, Aug. 14, Nov. 11, 12; not Sept. 29, Oct. 3, 6, 10).
G – ①⑤⑥ (also July 15, Aug. 14, Nov. 12; not July 14).
H – Runs on Aug. 14 only.
L – ①–⑤ to Oct. 10 (also Nov. 7, 10; not July 14).
R – Ⓐ from Oct. 13 (not Nov. 7, 10).
S – Ⓒ until Sept. 28.
T – June 30 - Aug. 31.

a – Not July 15, Aug. 14, Nov. 11, 12.
b – Not July 14, Nov. 11.
e – Also July 14, Nov. 11.
m – Not July 14, Aug. 14, Nov. 11.

t – Also Aug. 14; not Aug. 15.
u – Also Nov. 1.
x – Not Aug. 25–29.
z – Not Aug. 15.

TGV – High-speed train. Ⓡ. 🍷.

⊗ – Subject to alteration on ①–⑤ Sept. 29 - Oct. 24.
⊖ – Subject to alteration Sept. 1–5, 8–12, 29, 30, Oct. 1–3, 6–10, 27–31, Nov. 3–7.
◇ – On Ⓒ Avignon d. 0653. Arles d. 0714, Miramas d. 0739, Vitrolles d. 0801, Marseille a. 0820.
⊡ – Runs 3–4 minutes later on ⑥.
⊖ – Vitrolles Aéroport Marseille-Provence ✈. A shuttle bus runs to the airport terminal (journey: 5 minutes).
§ – See Table **342** for full service Paris - Lyon St Exupéry and v.v.

351a AVIGNON TGV - AVIGNON CENTRE - CARPENTRAS

km		Ⓐ	⚒			Ⓐ			Ⓒ		Ⓒ						Ⓐ				Ⓐ		Ⓐ			†
0	**Avignon** TGV ◇ d.	...	0612	0643	0712	0743	0812	0912	0943	1012	1112	1143	1212	1312	1412	1512	1543	1612	1643	1712	1743	1812	1843	1912	2012	2212
4	**Avignon** Centre ◇ a.	...	0617	0648	0717	0748	0817	0917	0948	1018	1117	1148	1217	1317	1417	1517	1548	1616	1648	1717	1748	1817	1848	1917	2017	2217
	Avignon Centre d.	0552	0621	0652	0721	0752	0821	0921	0952	1022	1121	1152	1221	1321	1421	1521	1552	1620	1652	1721	1752	1821	1852	1921	2021	2221
31	**Carpentras** a.	0623	0653	0723	0753	0823	0853	0953	1023	1053	1153	1223	1253	1353	1453	1553	1623	1653	1723	1753	1823	1853	1923	1953	2053	2253

	⚒	Ⓐ				Ⓐ				Ⓒ		Ⓒ	Ⓐ					Ⓐ		Ⓐ			Ⓑz		
Carpentras d.	0609	0639	0709	0739	0809	0839	0909	1009	1039	1103	1209	1239	1239	1309	1439	1509	1609	1639	1709	1739	1809	1909	1939	2009	2109h
Avignon Centre a.	0639	0709	0739	0809	0840	0909	0939	1039	1109	1133	1239	1308e	1314	1339	1509	1539	1639	1709	1739	1809	1839	1939	2010	2039	2139h
Avignon Centre ◇ d.	0644	0713	0744	0813	0845	0913	0944	1045	1112	1144	1244	1313e	...	1345	1513	1544	1644	1713	1744	1813	1844	1944	2013	2044	2144
Avignon TGV ◇ a.	0650	0718	0750	0818	0850	0918	0950	1050	1118	1150	1250	1318e	...	1350	1518	1550	1650	1718	1750	1818	1850	1950	2018	2050	2150

e – 4 minutes later on ⑥ (also Aug. 15; not Aug. 2, 9). **h** – Oct. 27–31, Nov. 3–7 departs Carpentras 2102, arrives Avignon Centre 2127. **k** – Not Nov. 1. **z** – Also Nov. 1.

◇ – **Additional trains** Avignon TGV - Avignon Centre and v.v.: **From Avignon TGV** at 0612 †, 0843, 1043, 1112 Ⓐ, 1243, 1343, 1443, 1543 Ⓒ, 1842 ⑥ **k**, 1843 †, 1939, 2043 Ⓒ, 2112, 2143 Ⓑ **z** and 2212 ⚒. **From Avignon Centre** at 0538, 0613, 0644 †, 0913 Ⓒ, 1013, 1144 Ⓐ, 1219 Ⓒ, 1311 Ⓐ, 1413, 1445, 1612, 1713 Ⓒ, 1912, 2013 ⑥ **k** and 2113 †.

352 🚌 TOULON - ST TROPEZ - ST RAPHAËL

🚌 route **879**: **Toulon** Gare Routière (adjacent to railway station) → **St Tropez** Gare Routière. *84 km.* Journey 1 hr 40 m - 1 hr 45 m.
From Toulon at 0620 ⚒, 0900 ⚒, 1130, 1530 ⚒ and 1815. **From St Tropez** at 0600 ⚒, 1230 ⚒, 1630, 1730 ⚒ and 1830 ⚒.

🚌 route **876**: **St Tropez** Gare Routière → **St Raphaël** Gare Routière (adjacent to railway station). *35 km* Journey 1 hr 20 m - 1 hr 30 m.
From St Tropez at 0630, 0730, 0830, 0930, 1130 and hourly until 1930; then 2045.
From St Raphaël at 0615, 0715, 0815, 0915, 1115, 1315, 1515 and hourly until 2015.

Operator: ZOU! ✆ 0 809 400 013
https://zou.maregionsud.fr

☛ **Note**: Route **876** is subject to confirmation from July 5.

353 LYON - BOURG EN BRESSE

Local stopping trains via Villars-les-Dombes. See Table **378** for services via Ambérieu.

km		Ⓐ	Ⓐ	①–⑥ b	Ⓐ	⑦e 🚌	Ⓐ 🚌	①–⑥ b	Ⓐ		Ⓐ	①–⑥ b	Ⓐ		Ⓐ	①–⑥ b	Ⓐ		Ⓐ	①–⑥ b	①–⑥ b		A	⑤⑦ f	Ⓐ 🚌
0	**Lyon** Perrache d.	0601	0631	0701	0801	...	...	1001	1101	1201	1301	1401	1501	1601	1642	1701	1731	1801	1842	1901	2001	...	2101	2117	...
5	**Lyon** Part Dieu d.	0612	0642	0712	0812	0812	0912	1012	1112	1212	1312	1412	1512	1612	1656	1712	1742	1812	1856	1912	2012	...	2112	2134	2220
65	**Bourg en Bresse** a.	0712	0738	0812	0912	0933	1033	1112	1212	1312	1412	1512	1612	1712	1747	1812	1844	1912	1947	2012	2112	...	2212	2232	2341

	Ⓐ	①–⑥ b	⑦e 🚌	Ⓐ	①–⑥ b	Ⓐ		Ⓐ	①–⑥ b	Ⓐ 🚌			Ⓐ	①–⑥ b	Ⓐ	Ⓐ 🚌			①–⑥ b		Ⓐ			Ⓑ z
Bourg en Bresse d.	0517	0548	0600	0617	0648	0714	0748	0814	0848	0927	...	1048	1148	1248	1348	1427	...	1548	1648	1748	1848	1948	...	2048
Lyon Part Dieu a.	0618	0648	0718	0718	0748	0804	0848	0904	0948	1048	...	1148	1248	1348	1448	1548	...	1648	1748	1848	1948	2048	...	2148
Lyon Perrache a.	0629	0659	...	0729	0759	0817	0859	0917	0959	...	...	1159	1259	1359	1459	...	...	1659	1759	1859	1959	2100	...	2159

A – ①②③④⑥ (also Aug. 15; not July 14, Aug. 14, Nov. 11). **b** – Not July 14, Nov. 11. **e** – Also July 14, Nov. 11. **f** – Also July 14, Aug. 14, Nov. 11; not Aug. 15. **z** – Not Aug. 15.

353a MÂCON - BOURG EN BRESSE - AMBÉRIEU

km		🚌 Ⓒd	Ⓐn	🚌 Ⓒd	Ⓐn		🚌		🚌 Ⓐ	🚌 A	Ⓐm	🚌		Ⓐn	🚌 A	🚌	🚌 A	Ⓐn	Ⓐn	🚌 Ⓒd	🚌 A	Ⓐn	🚌 Ⓒd	Ⓐn	🚌 A	🚌 Ⓐ	🚌 Ⓒ
0	**Mâcon** Ville d.	...	0704	0727	0807	...	0904	...	1104	...	...	...	1304	1304	1504	...	...	1704	1704	...	1804	1804	1904	1904	2004	2104
37	Bourg en Bresse a.	...	0731	0829	0836	...	1006	...	1206	...	...	...	1333	1406	1606	...	...	1731	1806	...	1831	1906	1931	2006	2106	2137
37	Bourg en Bresse **378** d.	0716	0733	...	...	0841	*1016*r	1043	...	1216	1232	1316	...	...	...	1616	1632	1733	...	1816	1833	*1916*	1933	...	...	...
68	**Ambérieu** **378** a.	0755	0756	...	...	0901	*1055*r	1101	...	1255	1256	1355	...	...	...	1655	1656	1756	...	1855	1856	*1955*	1956	...	...	...

	🚌 A	Ⓐn	🚌 A	🚌	🚌 B	🚌	🚌 Ⓐ	🚌 A	Ⓐn	🚌	Ⓐm	🚌 Ⓒd	🚌	🚌	Ⓐn	🚌 Ⓒd	Ⓐn	🚌 A	🚌 Ⓐr	Ⓐn	🚌 Ⓒd	🚌 A		Ⓐn	🚌 Ⓒd	🚌
Ambérieu **378** d.	...	0655	0705	...	0905	...	...	...	...	1205	1304	1305	...	1505	...	...	1704	1705	...	1804	1805	...	1859	1904	...	2115
Bourg en Bresse **378** a.	...	0717	0745	...	0945	...	...	...	...	1245	1328	1345	...	1545	...	...	1726	1745	...	1826	1845	...	1917	1926	...	2155
Bourg en Bresse d.	0650	0719	...	0750	...	0950	1050	1215	1227	...	...	...	1350	...	1627	1650	1728	...	1755	1828	...	1850	...	1928	1950	...
Mâcon Ville a.	0753	0747	...	0853	...	1053	1153	1318	1256	...	...	...	1453	...	1656	1753	1756	...	1838	1856	...	1953	...	1956	2053	...

A – Ⓐ July 15 - Aug. 22; ①–⑤ Oct. 20–31.
B – ①–⑥ (not July 14, Nov. 11).
d – Ⓒ (runs daily July 12 - Aug. 24 and Oct. 18 - Nov. 2).
m – Ⓐ until July 11 (also Oct. 6–10, 13–17); Ⓐ from Nov. 3.
n – Not July 15 - Aug. 22, Oct. 20–31.
r – Does not run on Ⓐ July 15 - Aug. 22.

353b DIJON - BOURG EN BRESSE

km		Ⓐ		Ⓒ		C		Ⓐ		
0	**Dijon** Ville d.	0644	...	0844r	...	1244	...	1744	1843	...
30	St Jean de Losne d.	0716	...	0917	...	1313	...	1816	1916	...
86	Louhans d.	0754	...	0955	...	1352	...	1854	1953	...
140	**Bourg en Bresse** a.	0826	...	1026	...	1426	...	1926	2025	...

	Ⓐ			D	E	F			⑦e
Bourg en Bresse d.	0534	0634	...	1117	1126	1134	...	1734	1834
Louhans d.	0606	0706	...	1150	1159	1207	...	1806	1906
St Jean de Losne d.	0645	0745	...	1228	1237	1245	...	1845	1945
Dijon Ville a.	0716	0816	...	1258	1307	1316	...	1916	2016

C – Daily until July 20; Ⓒ July 26 - Nov. 2; daily from Nov. 8.
D – ①–⑤ until July 8 (also July 17, 18).
E – Runs on July 12, Aug. 16 only.
F – ⑥ to Oct. 4 (also July 9–11, 15, 16, Aug. 15; not July 12, Aug. 16); ①–⑥ from Oct. 6 (not Nov. 11).
e – Also July 14, Nov. 11.
r – 0842 on July 12, 13, 14, Aug. 16, 17.

354 PERPIGNAN - VILLEFRANCHE - LATOUR DE CAROL

Warning! Services Perpignan - Villefranche and v.v. are subject to alteration until Sept. 28 with partial 🚌 replacement (journey times extended by up to 45 minutes); please check before travelling.

km			Ⓐ	Ⓐ	Ⓐ	Ⓐ	Ⓐ	Ⓐ	Ⓐ	Ⓐ			Ⓒ	Ⓒ	Ⓒ	Ⓒ	Ⓒ	Ⓒ	†	†					
0	**Perpignan** d.	Ⓐ	0710	0910	1110	1310	1510	1720	1819	1916	...	Ⓒ	0810	1010	1210	1410	1610	1807	1910	2010	...	...	...	...	...
40	Prades-Molitg les Bains d.		0748	0948	1148	1348	1548	1759	1858	1955	...		0850	1049	1249	1448	1649	1845	1953	2049	...	...	...	...	...
46	**Villefranche-Vernet les Bains** a.		0756	0956	1156	1356	1556	1806	1906	2002	...		0900	1056	1256	1456	1656	1852	2000	2056	...	...	...	...	...

		Ⓐ	Ⓐ	Ⓐ	Ⓐ	Ⓐ	Ⓐ	Ⓐ	Ⓐ			⑥k	⑥k	Ⓒ	Ⓒ	Ⓒ	Ⓒ	Ⓒ	Ⓒ					
Villefranche-Vernet les Bains d.	Ⓐ	0606	0706	0806	1006	1206	1406	1606	1816	...	Ⓒ	0706	0806	0906	1106	1306	1506	1706	1908	...	...	...	...	...
Prades-Molitg les Bains d.		0614	0714	0814	1014	1214	1414	1614	1824	...		0714	0814	0914	1114	1314	1514	1714	1916	...	...	...	...	...
Perpignan a.		0655	0756	0855	1057	1256	1456	1657	1906	...		0756	0855	0955	1155	1355	1557	1755	1955	...	...	...	...	...

VILLEFRANCHE - LATOUR DE CAROL *Petit Train Jaune* Narrow gauge, 2nd class. In summer most trains include open sightseeing carriages.

SERVICE UNTIL JULY 4 AND SEPTEMBER 1–28

km									n	
0	**Villefranche-Vernet les Bains** d.	0857	1004	...	1349	...	1546	...	1749	...
28	Mont Louis la Cabanasse d.	1025r	1132r	...	1508	...	1709r	...	1909	...
35	Font Romeu-Odeillo-Via d.	1044	1158r	...	1526	...	1728	...	1934	...
56	Bourg Madame d.	...	1257	...	...	...	...	...	2032	...
63	**Latour de Carol** a.	...	1313	...	...	...	...	...	2048	...

Latour de Carol d.	0826	...	...	...	...	...	1511	...	...
Bourg Madame d.	0846	...	...	...	...	...	1532	...	...
Font Romeu-Odeillo-Via d.	0958r	...	1104	...	1545	...	1643r	...	1748
Mont Louis la Cabanasse d.	1030r	...	1135r	...	1614r	...	1715r	...	1818r
Villefranche-Vernet les Bains a.	1140	...	1251	...	1727	...	1829	...	1928

SERVICE JULY 5 - AUGUST 31

km										
0	**Villefranche-Vernet les Bains** d.	0902	1006	...	1327	...	1525	...	1735	...
28	Mont Louis la Cabanasse d.	1039r	1146r	...	1456	...	1706r	...	1908	...
35	Font Romeu-Odeillo-Via d.	1058	1210	...	1515	...	1725	...	1930	...
56	Bourg Madame d.	...	1305	...	...	...	...	...	2025	...
63	**Latour de Carol** a.	...	1323	...	...	...	...	...	2043	...

Latour de Carol d.	0839	...	...	...	...	...	1508	...	...
Bourg Madame d.	0900	...	...	...	...	...	1528	...	...
Font Romeu-Odeillo-Via d.	1008r	...	1115	...	1531	...	1636r	...	1744
Mont Louis la Cabanasse d.	1041t	...	1143r	...	1559r	...	1709t	...	1812r
Villefranche-Vernet les Bains a.	1203	...	1254	...	1715	...	1823	...	1929

k – Not Nov. 1. **n** – Not Sept. 28. **r** – Arrives 8–10 minutes earlier. **t** – Arrives 15 minutes earlier.

PARIS, LYON and MARSEILLE - MONTPELLIER - BORDEAUX and PERPIGNAN 355

TGV services from / to Paris. Timings may vary by a few minutes – please check your reservation for confirmed timings. Subject to alteration Nov. 8 – 10.

WARNING! On certain dates when there is high demand for services to / from Perpignan, public stops at Valence, Nîmes and Montpellier may not be available.

km	All services 🅁	TGV 6221 Ⓐ n	TGV 9711 M		TGV 9713	TGV 6231 ⑥ N	TGV 6211 H	Ouigo 7885 ⊠	TGV 6229 n	TGV 6229 H	TGV 6275	Ouigo 7875 ⊠		TGV 9715		TGV 6277	TGV 6223 n	TGV 6225		TGV 6279 ①–④ D	TGV 6279 ⑤ s	TGV 6279 G	TGV 6227 E	TGV 6227 ⑤⑦ t
0	**Paris** Gare de Lyon **342 351** d.	0636	0638	...	0741	0842	0909	0941	1041	1042	1055	1146	...	1441	...	1655	1655	1741	...	1854	1855	1855	1941	1951
441	Lyon St Exupéry ✈. **342 351** d.	|	|	...	|	|	|	1136	|	|	|	|	...	|	...	|	|	|	...	|	|	|	|	|
527	Valence TGV d.	0856	0856	...	0958	1057	1131	|	1258	1258	1308	1359	...	1656	...	1910**r**	1916**r**	1956	...	2108	2108	2108	2156	2208
676	**Nîmes** Pont-du-Gard d.	|	|	...	1038	|	|	|	|	|	1349	1440	...	|	...	1952	|	|	...	|	2149	2149	|	|
	Nîmes Centre d.	0946	0945	...	|	1145	1221	1246	1348	1348	|	|	...	1746	...	|	2004	2046	...	2158	|	|	2246	2258
	Montpellier Saint-Roch a.	1011	1011	...	|	1211	1250	1311	1413	1413	|	|	...	1811	...	|	2029	2111	...	2224	|	|	2311	2323
	Montpellier Saint-Roch d.	1016	1016	...	|	1217	...	1317	...	1419	|	|	...	1817	...	|	...	2117	...	...	|	|	...	...
730	**Montpellier** Sud-de-France a.	|	|	...	1059	|	...	|	...	|	1408	1500	...	|	...	2011	...	|	...	...	2208	2208	...	...
	Montpellier Sud-de-France d.	|	|	...	1116	|	...	|	...	|	...	...	...	|	...	2017	...	|	...	...	2217	...	...	...
759	Sète a.	1033	|	...	|	1233	...	1333	...	1435	...	...	...	|	...	2033	...	2133	...	...	2233	...	...	...
782	Agde a.	1049	|	...	|	1249	...	1349	...	1451	...	...	...	|	...	2049	...	2149	...	...	2249	...	...	...
803	Béziers a.	1104	1104	...	1204	1304	...	1404	...	1505	...	...	...	1905	...	2104	...	2204	...	...	2304	...	...	...
829	**Narbonne** a.	1121	1120	...	1221	1321	...	1421	...	1522	...	...	...	1921	...	2121	...	2221	...	...	2321	...	...	...
892	**Perpignan** a.	1156	1156	...	1257	1357	...	1457	...	1557	...	...	...	1957	...	2157	...	2257	...	...	2359	...	...	...
	Barcelona Sants **13 657** a.	...	1328	...	1429	...	...	...	...	...	...	...	...	2129	...	...	...	...	...	...	...	...	...	...

All services 🅁	TGV 6200 R		TGV 6250 Ⓐ	TGV 6250 ⑥ k	TGV 6202 P	TGV 6254 © H		TGV 9708	TGV 6204 © n	TGV 6204 U	TGV 6258 B	TGV 6220 ①–⑥ H	TGV 6220 ⑦ H	Ouigo 7872 ⊠		TGV 6206 Y	TGV 6206 Q		Ouigo 7882 ⊠		TGV 9704 M v	TGV 6224 A	TGV 6262 ⑤–⑦ J	TGV 9706
Barcelona Sants **13 657** d.	...	...	...	...	...	...	...	0928	...	...	...	...	...	...	...	...	...	...	...	...	1520	...	...	1625
Perpignan d.	...	...	0602	...	0700	0747	...	1102	1202	...	1302	...	...	...	...	...	1502	...	1602	...	1702	1702	...	1758
Narbonne d.	...	...	0639	...	0738	0826	...	1140	1239	...	1340	...	...	...	...	...	1540	...	1640	...	1740	1740	...	1837
Béziers d.	...	...	0655	...	0755	0843	...	1157	1256	...	1357	...	...	...	...	...	1557	...	1657	...	1757	1757	...	1853
Agde d.	...	...	0708	...	0809	0857	...	|	1310	...	1411	...	...	...	...	...	1611	...	1711	...	|	1811	...	|
Sète d.	...	...	0726	...	0827	0915	...	|	1328	...	1429	...	...	...	...	...	1629	...	1729	...	|	1830	...	|
Montpellier Sud-de-France a.	...	...	0745	...	|	0932	...	1247	|	...	1447	...	...	...	...	...	|	...	1744	...	|	|	...	|
Montpellier Sud-de-France d.	...	...	0752	0752	|	0938	...	1254	|	...	1452	...	...	1552	...	...	|	...	1751	...	|	|	1943	|
Montpellier Saint-Roch a.	...	...	|	|	0844	|	...	|	1344	...	|	...	...	|	...	...	1645	...	|	...	1845	1845	|	1945
Montpellier Saint-Roch d.	0550	...	|	|	0849	|	...	|	1349	1350	|	1517	1521	|	...	1650	1650	...	|	...	1850	1850	|	1950
Nîmes Centre d.	0619	...	|	|	0918	|	...	|	1418	1419	|	1549	1550	|	...	1719	1719	...	|	...	1919	1919	|	2020
Nîmes Pont-du-Gard d.	|	...	0813	0813	|	1000	...	1317	|	|	1514	|	|	1613	...	|	|	...	1813	...	|	|	2005	|
Valence TGV d.	0705	...	0853	0853	1005	1039	...	1358	1505	1505	1555	1635	1638	1653	...	1805	1805	...	|	...	2005	2006	2045	2108
Lyon St Exupéry ✈.. **342 351** d.	|	...	|	|	|	|	...	|	|	|	|	|	|	|	...	|	|	...	1912	...	|	|	|	|
Paris Gare de Lyon . **342 351** a.	0919	...	1105	1105	1219	1251	...	1613	1718	1718	1811	1847	1851	1904	...	2018	2018	...	2104	...	2218‡	2218‡	2256	2318‡

TGV services from / to / via Lyon and Montpellier. Timings may vary by a few minutes – please check your reservation for confirmed timings. Subject to alteration on Nov. 1, 8, 9, 10.
Services via Massy are subject to alteration / cancellation on June 15, 21, 28, 29, July 19, 20. Services via Strasbourg are subject to alteration / cancellation on June 28, 29, Oct. 18, 19.

km	All services 🅁	TGV 6821 ⊗		AVE 9730 ■		TGV 5300	TGV 6823 ©	TGV 5521	Ouigo 7867 ⊠T		TGV 9812	TGV 6823 Ⓐ		TGV 9826	AVE 9742		TGV 5336 ⑦ w	TGV 9879 L	TGV 6825	TGV 5120 F		TGV 9836	TGV 9836 ⑤ f	TGV 9836 ⑥ k
	Brussels Midi **11** d.	...	...	...	...	...	...	...	...	...	0817**z**	...	...	1017**z**	...	...	...	...	...	...	...	1617**y**	1617**y**	1617**y**
	Lille Europe **11** d.	...	...	...	...	...	...	...	...	...	0901	...	...	1101	...	...	...	...	...	1526	...	1702	1702	1702
	Charles de Gaulle ✈ **11** d.	...	...	...	...	...	...	...	0855	...	0959	...	...	1159	...	...	...	...	...	1625	...	1800	1800	1800
	Marne la Vallée - Chessy **11** d.	...	...	...	...	...	...	...	0913	...	1013	...	...	1213	...	...	...	...	...	1642	...	1813	1813	1813
	Metz **379** d.	...	...	...	...	...	...	0546**e**	|	...	|	...	...	|	...	...	...	1210	...	|	...	|	|	|
	Strasbourg **379** d.	...	...	...	...	...	...	0647	|	...	|	...	...	|	...	...	...	1305	...	|	...	|	|	|
	Dijon Ville **379** d.	...	...	...	...	...	...	0921	|	...	|	...	...	|	...	...	...	1521	...	|	...	|	|	|
	Nantes **335** d.	...	...	...	...	0455**j**	...	|	|	...	|	...	...	|	...	...	...	|	...	|	...	|	|	|
	Rennes **335** d.	...	...	...	...	|	...	|	|	...	|	...	...	|	...	...	1231	|	...	|	...	|	|	|
	Massy TGV d.	...	...	...	...	0726	...	|	|	...	|	...	...	|	...	...	1426	|	...	|	...	|	|	|
0	**Lyon** Part Dieu **350** d.	0640	...	...	...	0940	1010	1107	1110	...	1210	1210	...	1410	1435	...	1640	1710	1810	1840	...	2010	2010	2010
	Lyon St Exupéry ✈ d.	|	...	...	...	|	|	|	|	...	|	|	...	|	|	...	|	|	|	|	...	|	|	|
104	Valence TGV **350** d.	0716	...	...	...	1020	1048	|	1151	...	1249	1249	...	1450	1511	...	1718	1751	1849	1924	...	2050	2050	2050
	Marseille St Charles .. **350** d.	|	...	0804	...	|	|	|	|	...	|	|	...	|	|	...	|	|	|	|	...	|	|	|
	Aix en Provence TGV. **350** d.	|	...	0818	...	|	|	|	|	...	|	|	...	|	|	...	|	|	|	|	...	|	|	|
	Avignon TGV **350** d.	|	...	0840	...	|	|	|	|	...	|	|	...	|	|	...	|	|	|	|	...	|	|	|
	Nîmes Pont-du-Gard d.	|	...	|	...	1100	|	|	1231	...	|	|	...	1530	|	...	|	|	|	|	...	|	|	|
263	**Nîmes** Centre d.	0806	...	0902	...	|	1137	1225	|	...	1337	1337	...	|	1559	...	1807	1840	1937	2018	...	2139	2139	2139
313	**Montpellier** Saint-Roch a.	0836	...	0928	...	|	1202	1254	|	...	1403	1403	...	|	1624	...	1835	1905	2001	2050	...	2204	2204	2204
	Montpellier Saint-Roch d.	0844	...	0933	...	|	1207	...	|	...	...	1409	...	|	1628	...	...	...	2006	...	...	...	2209	2209
	Montpellier Sud-de-France a.	|	...	|	...	1120	|	...	1250	...	...	|	...	1550	|	...	...	...	|	...	...	...	|	|
	Montpellier Sud-de-France d.	|	...	|	...	...	|	...	...	...	...	|	...	...	|	...	...	...	|	...	...	...	|	|
340	Sète d.	|	...	|	...	...	|	...	...	...	...	|	...	...	|	...	...	...	2025	...	...	...	2228	2228
363	Agde d.	|	...	|	...	...	|	...	...	...	...	|	...	...	|	...	...	...	|	...	...	...	2244	2245
384	Béziers d.	0924	...	|	...	...	1245	...	...	...	...	1449	...	...	|	...	...	...	2050	...	...	...	2258	2300
410	**Narbonne** a.	0937	...	1031	...	...	1259	...	...	...	...	1502	...	...	1718	...	...	...	2102	...	...	...	2311	2314
	Carcassone a.	1007	...	|	...	...	1330	...	...	...	...	1533	...	...	|	...	...	...	2134	...	...	...	|	|
	Toulouse Matabiau a.	1055	...	|	...	...	1415	...	...	...	...	1621	...	...	|	...	...	...	2219	...	...	...	|	|
473	**Perpignan** a.	...	...	1108	...	...	...	...	...	...	...	...	...	...	1753	...	...	...	...	...	...	...	2350	2352
	Barcelona Sants **13 657** a.	...	...	1238	...	...	...	...	...	...	...	...	...	...	1934	...	...	...	...	...	...	...	...	...

A – ①–⑤ to July 4; ①–⑤ Aug. 1 - Oct. 31 (also Oct. 11); daily from Nov. 3.
B – Ⓑ (daily June 29 - Sept. 5).
D – ①–④ until Aug. 7.
E – ①–④ to July 3; ①–③ July 7 - Aug. 27 (not July 14); ①–④ from Sept. 1 (not Nov. 11).
F – ④⑤⑦ (also July 14, Nov. 10, 11; not July 13, Aug. 15, Nov. 9).
G – ⑤–⑦ to Aug. 3; daily from Aug. 8.
H – July 5 - Aug. 31.
J – ⑤–⑦ July 5 - Aug. 31 (also July 14, Aug. 14). Runs 25 – 26 minutes **earlier** on Aug. 14.
L – From Luxembourg (Table **379**).
M – ⑥⑦ to June 29; daily July 5 - Aug. 31; ⑥⑦ Sept. 6 - Nov. 2.
N – ⑥ July 5 - Aug. 30 (also Aug. 15).
P – Daily to July 6; ⑤–⑦ July 11 - Aug. 24 (also Aug. 14); daily from Aug. 29.
Q – ⑦ to June 29; ⑤–⑦ July 5 - Aug. 31 (also July 14, Aug. 14); ⑦ from Sept. 7 (also Nov. 11).
R – ①–⑤ to July 4; ①–④ July 7 - Aug. 28 (not July 14, Aug. 14); Ⓐ from Sept. 1.
T – From Tourcoing (d. 0744; see Table **11**). On June 16 does not run Tourcoing - Lyon. On July 13 starts from Lille Flandres (d. 0750; not serving Tourcoing).
U – Ⓐ (daily June 30 - Sept. 5).
Y – ①–⑥ to July 4; ①–④ July 7 - Aug. 28 (not July 14, Aug. 14); ①–⑥ from Sept. 1 (not Nov. 11).

e – Not June 22, Sept. 1. Departs 0543 from Nov. 17.
f – Also Aug. 14; not Aug. 15.
j – 0451 on ① (also July 15, Oct. 14 – 16, 21 – 24, 28 – 31, Nov. 4 – 7, 12 – 14; not July 14, Nov. 11).
k – Also Aug. 15.
n – Not July 5 - Aug. 31.
r – Arrives 1906.
s – Also July 6, 20, 27, Aug. 3, 10, 14, 17, 24, 31; not Aug. 15.
t – Also July 14, Aug. 14, Nov. 11; not Aug. 15.
v – Not Oct. 11.
w – Also Nov. 11; not Nov. 9.
y – 8 – 13 minutes earlier June 16 – 21, 23 – 27, July 22 – 28. 17 – 18 minutes **earlier** Aug. 16 – 31.
z – 17 – 34 minutes **earlier** Aug. 16 – 31.

TGV – High-speed train. 🅁. 🍸.
AVE – Spanish high-speed train. 🅁. 🍸.

‡ – Later arrival on many dates.
■ – To Madrid (Table **13**).
⊗ – Subject to alteration / cancellation on ①–⑤ Mar. 17 – 28.
⊠ – OUIGO low-cost TGV service. Internet bookings only at www.ouigo.com.

355 PARIS, LYON and MARSEILLE - MONTPELLIER - BORDEAUX and PERPIGNAN

TGV services from / to / via Montpellier and Lyon. Timings may vary by a few minutes – please check your reservation for confirmed timings. Subject to alteration on Nov. 1, 8, 9, 10. Services via Massy are subject to alteration / cancellation on June 15, 21, 28, 29, July 19, 20. Services via Strasbourg are subject to alteration / cancellation on June 28, 29, Oct. 18, 19.

km	All services 🄡	*TGV* 5156 ①⑤ q	*TGV* 9898 L		*TGV* 9862 ①–⑤ a	*TGV* 9862 ⑥⑦ w	*TGV* 6871		*AVE* 9737	*TGV* 5158 ⑥ s		*TGV* 5500	*Ouigo* 7860 ⊠		*TGV* 9864		*TGV* 5358	*TGV* 5182	*TGV* 6873		*AVE* 9725 H ■	*AVE* 9725 n ■	*TGV* 6875 ①–⑥ b	*TGV* 6875 ⑦ e
	Barcelona Sants **13 657** d.	...	...	...	...	...	...	...	0819	...	...	...	...	...	...	...	...	...	...	...	1634	1634	...	...
	Perpignan d.	...	...	...	...	0704	...	...	0952	...	...	...	...	...	...	...	...	...	...	...	1805	1806	...	...
	Toulouse Matabiau d.	...	...	...	...	|	0739	...	|	...	...	...	...	...	...	...	...	...	1543	...	|	|	1722v	1739
	Carcassone d.	...	...	...	...	|	0823	...	|	...	...	...	...	...	...	...	...	...	1629	...	|	|	1829	1828
	Narbonne d.	...	...	...	...	0745	0855	...	1029	...	...	...	...	...	...	...	...	...	1659	...	1842	1847	1900	1859
	Béziers d.	...	...	...	...	0804	0911	...	|	...	...	...	...	...	...	...	...	...	1715	...	|	|	1915	1914
	Agde d.	...	...	...	...	0818	|	...	|	...	...	...	...	...	...	...	...	...	|	...	|	|	|	|
	Sète d.	...	...	...	...	0835	0940	...	|	...	...	...	...	...	...	...	...	...	1742	...	|	|	1942	1941
	Montpellier Sud-de-France a.	...	...	...	...	|	0956	...	|	...	...	...	...	...	...	...	...	...	|	...	|	|	1956	|
	Montpellier Sud-de-France d.	...	...	...	0912	|	1005	...	|	...	...	...	1359	...	...	...	1641	1710	|	...	|	|	2000	|
	Montpellier Saint-Roch a.	...	...	...	|	0852	|	...	1120	...	...	...	|	...	...	...	|	|	1757	...	1952	1952	|	1957
	Montpellier Saint-Roch d.	0525	0631	...	|	0857	|	...	1129	1158	...	1357	|	...	1451	...	|	|	1801	...	1957	2002	|	2003
0	**Nîmes** Centre d.	0553	0658	...	|	0925	|	...	1200	1225	...	1427	|	...	1519	...	|	|	1828	...	2026	2032	|	2032
	Nîmes Pont-du-Gard d.	|	|	...	0933	|	1029	...	|	|	...	|	1421	...	|	...	1702	1732	|	...	|	|	2021	|
82	**Avignon** TGV **350** a.	|	|	...	|	|	|	...	|	|	...	|	|	...	|	...	|	|	|	...	2049	2054	|	|
116	Aix en Provence TGV **350** a.	|	|	...	|	|	|	...	|	|	...	|	|	...	|	...	|	|	|	...	2111	2117	|	|
135	**Marseille** St Charles **350** a.	|	|	...	|	|	|	...	|	|	...	|	|	...	|	...	|	|	|	...	2129	2132	|	|
	Valence TGV **350** d.	0644	0748	...	1015	1015	1112	...	1246	1314	...	1514	|	...	1615	...	1744	1815	1914	...	...	...	2100	2119
	Lyon St Exupéry ✈ a.	|	|	...	|	|	|	...	|	|	...	|	1520	...	|	...	|	|	|	...	...	...	|	|
	Lyon Part Dieu **350** a.	0720	0824	...	1050	1050	1148	...	1320	1349	...	1550	|	...	1650	...	1820	1850	1950	...	...	...	2136	2154
	Massy TGV a.	|	|	...	|	|	...	...	...	|	...	|	|	...	|	...	2033	|	...	...	...	...	...	...
	Rennes **335** a.	|	|	...	|	|	...	...	...	|	...	|	|	...	|	...	|	|	...	...	...	...	...	...
	Nantes **335** a.	|	|	...	|	|	...	...	...	|	...	|	|	...	|	...	2311	|	...	...	...	...	...	...
	Dijon Ville **379** a.	|	0959	...	|	|	...	...	...	|	...	1740	|	...	|	...	...	|	...	...	...	...	...	...
	Strasbourg **379** a.	|	1224	...	|	|	...	...	...	|	...	2013	|	...	|	...	...	|	...	...	...	...	...	...
	Metz **379** a.	|	1324	...	|	|	...	...	...	|	...	2109	|	...	|	...	...	|	...	...	...	...	...	...
	Marne la Vallée - Chessy **11** a.	0917	...	...	1246	1246	...	...	...	1546	...	...	1719	...	1846	...	...	2046	...	...	...	...	...	...
	Charles de Gaulle ✈ **11** a.	0933	...	...	1301	1301	...	...	...	1600	...	...	1735	...	1900	...	...	2100	...	...	...	...	...	...
	Lille Europe **11** a.	1040•	...	...	1424	1424	...	...	...	1658	...	...	1844•	...	1958	...	...	2158	...	...	...	...	...	...
	Brussels Midi **11** a.	...	...	...	1525y	1525x	...	...	...	...	...	...	...	...	2043p	...	...	...	...	...	...	...	...	...

INTERCITÉS and *TER* services. See above and page 205 for *TGV* and *AVE* services. See Table **300** for *TGV* services Toulouse - Bordeaux - Paris. **Minor timing variations are possible**. Subject to alteration on Oct. 4, 5, 11, 12, Nov. 8 – 10. Journeys to Bordeaux are subject to alteration on June 28, 29.

km		⑥ k	Ⓐ	Ⓐ	Ⓐ n	5737 5741 ♣🄡	⑥ k	Ⓐ	4752 ①–⑥ r ★🄡	Ⓐ	Ⓐ	⑥ k	†	Ⓐ	Ⓒ n	Ⓒ H	Ⓐ	Ⓐ	D	Ⓐ	4756 ⊕ ★🄡	Ⓐ	Ⓑ d	Ⓐ	Ⓒ
0	**Marseille** St Charles **351** d.	...	...	...	...	...	...	...	...	...	...	...	...	...	...	...	...	0623	...	...	0719	...	...	...	...
23	Aéroport Marseille ✈ ‡ **351** d.	...	...	...	...	...	...	...	...	...	...	...	...	...	...	...	...	0637	...	...	|	...	...	...	...
52	Miramas **351** d.	...	...	...	...	...	...	...	...	...	...	...	...	...	...	...	...	0656	...	...	|	...	...	...	...
86	Arles **351** d.	...	...	...	...	...	...	...	...	...	...	...	...	...	...	...	...	0717	...	...	0808	...	...	...	...
	Avignon Centre **357** d.	...	...	...	...	...	...	...	...	...	0618	...	...	0634	...	...	...	|	0735	0736	|	...	0833	...	...
100	Tarascon-sur-Rhône d.	...	...	...	...	...	...	...	...	...	0632	...	...	0647	...	...	...	0725	0748	0749	|	...	0846	...	...
118	**Nîmes** Pont-du-Gard d.	...	...	...	...	...	...	...	...	...	0644	...	...	0659	...	...	...	0734	0800	0801	|	...	0858	...	...
	Paris Austerlitz d.	...	...	...	...	2057	...	...	...	...	|	...	...	|	...	...	...	|	|	|	|	...	|	...	...
128	**Nîmes** Centre **357** d.	...	0511	0532	...	0557	0609	0611	0634t	0649	0655	0659	0711	0711	...	...	...	0747	0813	0813	0836	0850	0911	...	...
154	Lunel d.	...	0529	0549	...	|	0627	0628	|	0708	0715	0719	0729	0729	...	...	...	0806	0830	0831	|	0908	0929	...	...
178	**Montpellier** Saint-Roch a.	...	0546	0604	...	0625	0643	0644	0658t	0725	0738	0742	0746	0746	...	...	...	0823	0846	0848	0901	0923	0946	...	...
	Montpellier Saint-Roch d.	...	0550	0607	...	|	0646	0648	0703t	0729	0741	0746	0750	0750	...	...	...	0827	0850	0852	0905	0927	0950	...	...
198	Frontignan d.	...	0602	0627	...	|	0659	0659	|	0746	0758	0803	0803	0803	...	...	...	0839	0903	0903	|	0938	1001	...	...
205	Sète d.	...	0611	0635	...	0645	0707	0708	|	0755	0805	0812	0812	0812	...	...	...	0848	0913	0913	0923	0947	1010	...	...
228	Agde d.	...	0625	0651	...	0702	0726	0724	|	0811	...	0828	0826	0826	...	...	...	0902	0927	0927	|	1000	1024	...	...
249	Béziers d.	...	0638	0706	...	0715	0741	0738	0745	0826	...	0841	0840	0840	...	...	...	0915	0940	0940	|	1013	1038	...	...
	Toulouse Matabiau **355a** d.	...	|	|	...	|	|	|	|	|	...	|	|	|	0713	0713	0716	|	|	|	|	|	|	0925j	0922
275	**Narbonne** a.	...	0652	0723	...	0735	0757	0752	0759c	0842	...	0859	0852	0853	0849	0849	0849	0929	0954	0954	0958c	1026	1052	1056	1057
	Narbonne **355a** d.	0706	0707	0726	0737	|	...	0807	0802	...	...	0907	...	...	0903	0903	0859	...	1007	1007	1002	▬	...	1108	1110
334	Carcassonne **355a** d.	|	|	0800	|	|	...	|	0834	...	...	0940	...	...	|	|	|	...	|	|	1033	...	...	|	|
425	**Toulouse** Matabiau **355a** a.	|	|	0913	|	|	...	|	0918	...	...	1040	...	...	|	|	|	...	|	|	1115	...	...	|	|
	Toulouse Matabiau **355a** d.	|	|	...	|	|	...	|	0924	...	...	...	...	...	|	|	|	...	|	|	1120	...	...	|	|
476	Montauban **355a** d.	|	|	...	|	|	...	|	1000	...	...	...	...	...	|	|	|	...	|	|	1157	...	...	|	|
546	Agen **355a** d.	|	|	...	|	|	...	|	1038	...	...	...	...	...	|	|	|	...	|	|	1235	...	...	|	|
603	Marmande **355a** d.	|	|	...	|	|	...	|	|	...	...	...	...	...	|	|	|	...	|	|	|	...	...	|	|
682	**Bordeaux** St Jean **355a** a.	|	|	...	|	|	...	|	1154	...	...	...	...	...	|	|	|	...	|	|	1349	...	...	|	|
296	Port la Nouvelle d.	0719	0720	...	0750	0755z	...	0820	...	...	...	...	...	...	0916	0916	0913	...	1020	1020	...	...	...	1121	1123
330	Rivesaltes d.	0742	0743	...	0814	0819z	...	0843	...	...	...	...	...	...	0938	0939	0937	...	1043	1043	...	**A**	...	1144	1146
338	**Perpignan** a.	0748	0750	...	0820	0828	...	0849	...	...	...	...	...	...	0944	0945	0943	...	1050	1050	...	⊖	...	1150	1152
	Perpignan d.	0751	0755	...	...	|	...	0854	...	...	...	...	...	...	0949	0950	...	...	...	...	...	1055	...	...	1157
360	Argelès sur Mer d.	0808	0811	...	...	0848	...	0909	...	...	...	...	...	...	1004	1006	...	...	...	...	...	1111	...	...	1214
365	Collioure d.	0813	0816	...	...	0855	...	0914	...	...	...	...	...	...	1009	1011	...	...	...	...	...	1116	...	...	1218
368	Port Vendres d.	0817	0819	...	...	0900	...	0918	...	...	...	...	...	...	1013	1014	...	...	...	...	...	1119	...	...	1222
373	Banyuls sur Mer d.	0822	0824	...	...	0907	...	0923	...	...	...	...	...	...	1018	1019	...	...	...	...	...	1124	...	...	1227
380	Cerbère **657** a.	0827	0830	...	...	0916	...	0929	...	...	...	...	...	...	1023	1026	...	...	...	...	...	1130	...	...	1233
382	**Portbou** **657** a.	0841	0844	...	...	...	...	0944	...	...	...	...	...	...	1037	...	...	...	...	...	...	1144	...	...	...

A – Ⓐ (daily June 30 - Sept. 5).
D – Avignon - Narbonne on ⑥ (not Nov. 1); Narbonne - Perpignan on Ⓒ.
H – July 5 - Aug. 31.
L – To Luxembourg (Table **379**).

a – Not Aug. 15.
b – Not July 14, Nov. 11.
c – Connects with train in preceding column.
d – Also Nov. 1.
e – Also July 14, Nov. 11.
j – 0922 July 7 - Aug. 29.
k – Not Nov. 1.
n – Not July 5 - Aug. 31.
p – 33 – 40 minutes later Aug. 16 – 31.
q – Also July 15, Nov. 12; not June 16, July 14, Aug. 15, Nov. 10.
r – Not July 14, Aug. 16, Nov. 11.
s – Also Aug. 15; not Aug. 16.
t – ① to Aug. 4 (also July 15; not July 14); ①–⑥ from Aug. 11 (not Aug. 16, Nov. 11).
v – 1739 from Sept. 20.
w – Also Aug. 15.

x – Not Aug. 16 – 31.
y – Not Aug. 19 – 22, 25 – 29. Arrives 1601 on Aug. 18, 25.
z – Mornings July 6 - Sept. 1.

TGV – High-speed train. 🄡. 🍸.
AVE – Spanish high-speed train. 🄡. 🍸. Special fares.

• – Lille **Flandres**.
■ – From Madrid (Table **13**).
⊕ – Subject to alteration Nov. 17 – 21, 24 – 28.
⊖ – Subject to alteration / cancellation on certain ①–⑤ dates.
‡ – Vitrolles Aéroport Marseille-Provence ✈. A shuttle bus runs to / from the airport terminal (journey time: 5 minutes).
★ – *INTERCITÉS*. 🄡. 🍸. Minor timing variations are possible.
♣ – ⑤⑦ to June 29; daily July 4 - Aug. 31; ⑤⑦ Sept. 5 - Oct. 12; daily Oct. 17 - Nov. 2; ⑤⑦ from Nov. 7. Conveys 🛏 1, 2 cl. and 2 (reclining). 🄡. For overnight journeys only. **Sample timings shown – subject to frequent variations**. For confirmed timings, please consult the SNCF journey planner: www.sncf-connect.com.
⊠ – OUIGO low-cost TGV service. Internet bookings only at www.ouigo.com.

PARIS, LYON and MARSEILLE - MONTPELLIER - BORDEAUX and PERPIGNAN 355

INTERCITÉS and *TER* services. See pages 205 and 206 for *TGV* and *AVE* services. See Table **300** for *TGV* services Toulouse - Bordeaux - Paris.
Minor timing variations are possible. Subject to alteration on Oct. 4, 5, 11, 12, Nov. 8 – 10. Journeys to Bordeaux are subject to alteration on June 28.

km						4758					4760								4762						
			Ⓐ	Ⓒ	Ⓐ		Ⓐ	Ⓐ	Ⓒ			Ⓐ	Ⓐ	Ⓒ	Ⓐ		⑥			Ⓑ	Ⓐ	Ⓒ	Ⓐ	Ⓐ	
																	kn	B							E
						★🅁					★🅁								★🅁						
	Marseille St Charles .... **351** d.	0824	...	...	...	0923	...	...	...	...	1122	...	...	...	...	1223	...	...	1325j	...	...	...	...	...	...
	Aéroport Marseille ✈ ‡ . **351** d.	0838	...	...	...	|	...	...	...	...	|	...	...	...	...	1238	...	...	|	...	...	...	...	...	...
	Miramas .... **351** d.	0857	...	...	...	|	...	...	...	...	|	...	...	...	...	1256	...	...	|	...	...	...	...	...	...
	Arles .... **351** d.	0919	...	...	...	|	...	...	...	...	1210	...	...	...	...	1318	...	...	|	...	...	...	...	...	...
0	**Avignon** Centre .... **357** d.	|	...	0933	0934	|	...	...	...	1134	|	1219	...	...	...	|	1334	1335	|	...	...	...	...	...	1534
21	Tarascon-sur-Rhône .... d.	0928	...	0946	0947	|	...	...	...	1147	|	1233	...	...	...	1327	1347	1348	|	...	...	...	...	...	1547
39	**Nîmes** Pont-du-Gard .... d.	0937	...	0958	0959	|	...	...	...	1159	|	1245	...	...	...	1338	1400	1400	|	...	...	...	...	...	1600
49	**Nîmes** Centre .... **357** d.	0950	...	1009	1010	1033	...	...	...	1212	1238	1256	...	...	...	1353	1412	1412	1435	1511	...	...	1536	...	1612
	Lunel .... d.	1008	1013	1027	1028	|	...	...	...	1230	|	1317	...	...	...	1410	1430	1430	|	1529	...	...	1553	...	1630
	Montpellier Saint-Roch .... a.	1024	1036	1044	1044	1057	...	...	...	1246	1301	1340	...	...	...	1426	1446	1446	1459	1545	...	...	1609	...	1647
	Montpellier Saint-Roch .... d.	...	1039	1048	1048	1101	1150	...	...	1249	1305	...	1351	...	...	1430	1450	1450	1504	1549	...	...	1612	...	1651
	Frontignan .... d.	...	1050	1059	1059	|	1201	...	...	1301	|	...	1403	...	...	1447	1501	1502	|	1604	...	...	1625	...	1702
	Sète .... d.	...	1057	1108	1108	|	1210	...	...	1310	1323	...	1412	...	...	1456	1510	1511	|	1613	...	...	1635	...	1711
	Agde .... d.	...	...	1122	1123	|	1224	...	...	1324	|	...	1426	...	...	1512	1525	1525	|	1627	...	...	1651	...	1726
	Béziers .... d.	...	...	1135	1136	1142	1238	...	...	1338	|	...	1440	...	...	1527	1537	1538	1545	1640	...	...	1710t	...	1739
	Toulouse Matabiau **355a** .. d.	...	...	|	|	|	|	1118	1118	|	|	...	|	1323	1312	|	|	|	|	|	1519	1520	|	...	|
	Narbonne .... a.	...	...	1148	1150	1156c	1251	1251	1251	1352	1358c	...	1453	1458	1447	1544	1553	1554	1558c	1655	1652	1652	1723	...	1753
	Narbonne .... **355a** d.	...	...	...	1207	1200	...	1304	1304	1407	1402	...	...	1508	1513	...	1608	1607	1602	...	1705	1705	1727	1740	1807
	Carcassonne .... **355a** d.	...	...	...	|	1231	...	|	|	|	1433	...	...	|	|	...	|	|	1632	...	|	|	1758	|	|
	Toulouse Matabiau **355a** a.	...	...	...	|	1313	...	|	|	|	1515	...	...	|	|	...	|	|	1718	...	|	|	1906	|	|
	Toulouse Matabiau **355a** d.	...	...	...	|	1318	...	|	|	|	1522	...	...	|	|	...	|	|	1726	...	|	|	▬	|	|
	Montauban .... **355a** d.	...	...	...	|	1354	...	|	|	|	1558	...	...	|	|	...	|	|	1803	...	|	|	...	|	|
	Agen .... **355a** d.	...	...	...	|	|	...	|	|	|	1635	...	...	|	|	...	|	|	1840	...	|	|	...	|	|
	Marmande .... **355a** d.	...	...	...	|	1459	...	|	|	|	|	...	...	|	|	...	|	|	|	...	|	|	...	|	|
	Bordeaux St Jean .. **355a** a.	...	...	...	|	1547	...	|	|	|	1749	...	...	|	|	...	|	|	1954	...	|	|	...	|	|
	Port la Nouvelle .... d.	...	...	...	1220	...	...	1317	1317	1420	...	...	...	1521	1526	...	1621	1622	▬	...	1718	1719	...	1753	1821
	Rivesaltes .... d.	...	...	...	1244	...	...	1340	1340	1443	...	...	...	1544	1548	...	1644	1644	Ⓐ	...	1741	1742	Ⓐ	1815	1845
	Perpignan .... a.	...	...	...	1250	...	...	1346	1348	1449	...	...	...	1551	1554	...	1650	1650		...	1748	1748		1821	1852
	Perpignan .... d.	...	...	...	1255	...	...	...	1353	1454	...	...	...	1556	...	...	...	1655	1725	...	...	1754	1754	1826	1856r
	Argelès sur Mer .... d.	...	...	...	1310	...	...	...	1408	1510	...	...	...	1611	...	...	...	1710	1741	...	...	1810	1810	1840	1913r
	Collioure .... d.	...	...	...	1315	...	...	...	1413	1515	...	...	...	1616	...	...	...	1715	1745	...	...	1815	1815	1845	1918r
	Port Vendres .... d.	...	...	...	1319	...	...	...	1417	1519	...	...	...	1620	...	...	...	1719	1749	...	...	1818	1818	1849	1922r
	Banyuls sur Mer .... d.	...	...	...	1324	...	...	...	1422	1524	...	...	...	1625	...	...	...	1724	1754	...	...	1823	1824	1854	1927r
	Cerbère .... **657** a.	...	...	...	1330	...	...	...	1428	1530	...	...	...	1632	...	...	...	1730	1800	...	...	1829	1830	1900	1934r
	Portbou .... **657** a.	...	...	...	1344	...	...	...	1443n	1544	...	...	...	...	...	...	...	1744	...	...	...	1843	1844	...	...

		4764															4766						4770		
			Ⓐ	†	Ⓐ	①–④	⑤	Ⓒ	Ⓐ	Ⓒ	Ⓐ	Ⓐ	Ⓐ	†	⑥	Ⓐ					⑥	Ⓑ	Ⓐ	⑥	Ⓑ
	P					m	f		n		H	n			k		L				k	d		k	d
		★🅁															★🅁						★🅁		△
Marseille St Charles ..... **351** d.	...	1525	...	...	...	...	...	...	1624	1624	1624	...	...	...	...	...	1722	...	...	1823	...	...	1923	...	...
Aéroport Marseille ✈ ‡ .. **351** d.	...	|	...	...	...	...	...	...	1638	1638	1638	...	...	...	...	...	|	...	...	1837	...	...	|	...	...
Miramas .... **351** d.	...	|	...	...	...	...	...	...	1656	1657	1657	...	...	...	...	...	|	...	...	1856	...	...	|	...	...
Arles .... **351** d.	...	|	...	...	...	...	...	...	1718	1718	1718	...	...	...	...	...	|	...	...	1918	...	...	|	...	...
Avignon Centre .... **357** d.	1535	|	...	...	1635	...	...	...	|	|	|	...	1722	1730	1734	1735	|	1834	...	|	1934	1933	|	...	2133
Tarascon-sur-Rhône .... d.	1548	|	...	...	1648	...	...	...	1727	1727	1727	...	|	1747	1747	1748	|	1847	...	1927	1947	1946	|	...	|
Nîmes Pont-du-Gard .... d.	1600	|	...	...	1700	...	...	...	1736	1739	1739	...	|	1759	1759	1800	|	1859	...	1937	1959	1958	|	...	2159
Nîmes Centre .... **357** d.	1613	1635	1649	1710	1713	...	...	...	1750	1751	1751	...	1755	1812	1812	1813	1834	1912	...	1951	2008	2011	2034	2211	2212
Lunel .... d.	1630	|	1706	1728	1731	...	...	...	1807	1809	1812	1811	1819	1829	1829	1830	|	1930	...	2008	...	2029	|	2229	2229
Montpellier Saint-Roch .... a.	1646	1659	1723	1745	1746	...	...	...	1824	1826	1831	1832	1837	1845	1845	1846	1859	1948	...	2024	...	2046	2059	2246	2246
Montpellier Saint-Roch .... d.	1650	1704	1727	1749	1750	...	...	...	1828	1830	1835	1835	...	1849	1849	1850	1904	1952	...	2028	...	2050	2104	2250	2250
Frontignan .... d.	1701	|	1740	1801	1801	...	...	...	1840	1847	1852	1852	...	1902	1902	1902	|	2003	...	2040	...	2101	|	2302	2302
Sète .... d.	1710	|	1749	1810	1811	...	...	...	1849	1856	1901	1901	...	1911	1911	1911	|	2012	...	2049	...	2110	|	2311	2311
Agde .... d.	1724	|	1803	1826	1826	...	...	...	1904	1912	1918	1917	...	1925	1926	1925	|	2027	...	2103	...	2125	|	2325	2325
Béziers .... d.	1738	1744	1816	1839	1839	...	...	...	1917	1927	1933	1932	...	1938	1938	1938	1945	2041	...	2116	...	2138	2145	2338	2338
Toulouse Matabiau **355a** .. d.	|	|	|	|	|	1710	1710	1710	|	|	|	|	...	|	|	|	|	|	1921	|	...	|	|	|	|
Narbonne .... a.	1752	1759c	1829	1852	1852	1852	1852	1852	1930	1943	1949	1948	...	1951	1952	1952	1958c	2054	2052	2130	...	2152	2158c	2352	2352
Narbonne .... **355a** d.	1807	1802	1837	...	...	1902	1902	1902	...	...	...	...	...	2006	...	2007	2002	▬	2108	▬	...	2207	2202	...	...
Carcassonne .... **355a** d.	|	1833	|	...	...	|	|	|	...	...	...	...	...	|	...	|	2033	...	|	...	...	|	2233	...	...
Toulouse Matabiau. **355a** a.	|	1916	|	...	...	|	|	|	...	...	...	...	...	|	...	|	2119	...	|	...	...	|	2316	...	...
Toulouse Matabiau. **355a** d.	|	1922	|	...	...	|	|	|	...	...	...	...	...	|	...	|	2124z	...	|	...	...	|	...	...	...
Montauban .... **355a** d.	|	1958	|	...	...	|	|	|	...	...	...	...	...	|	...	|	2200z	...	|	...	...	|	...	...	...
Agen .... **355a** d.	|	|	|	...	...	|	|	|	...	...	...	...	...	|	...	|	2240z	...	|	...	...	|	...	...	...
Marmande .... **355a** d.	|	2103	|	...	...	|	|	|	...	...	...	...	...	|	...	|	|	...	|	...	...	|	...	...	...
Bordeaux St Jean .. **355a** a.	|	2150	|	...	...	|	|	|	...	...	...	...	...	|	...	|	2334z	...	|	...	...	|	...	...	...
Port la Nouvelle .... d.	1820	...	1850	...	...	1916	1916	1916	...	...	...	...	...	2019	...	2020	...	...	2121	...	...	2220	...	...	...
Rivesaltes .... d.	1844	...	1914	...	...	1940	1940	1940	...	...	...	...	...	2043	...	2043	...	†	2144	⑥	...	2244	...	...	...
Perpignan .... a.	1850	...	1920	...	...	1947	1947	1947	...	...	...	...	...	2049	...	2050	...	H	2150	H	...	2250	...	...	...
Perpignan .... d.	1855	...	...	...	...	...	1952	1952	...	...	...	...	...	...	...	2055	...	2128	...	2209	...	...	...	...	...
Argelès sur Mer .... d.	1910	...	...	...	...	...	2007	2007	...	...	...	...	...	...	...	2110	...	2144	...	2225	...	...	...	...	...
Collioure .... d.	1915	...	...	...	...	...	2011	2012	...	...	...	...	...	...	...	2115	...	2149	...	2230	...	...	...	...	...
Port Vendres .... d.	1919	...	...	...	...	...	2015	2016	...	...	...	...	...	...	...	2119	...	2153	...	2234	...	...	...	...	...
Banyuls sur Mer .... d.	1924	...	...	...	...	...	2020	2021	...	...	...	...	...	...	...	2124	...	2159	...	2239	...	...	...	...	...
Cerbère .... **657** a.	1930	...	...	...	...	...	2026	2027	...	...	...	...	...	...	...	2130	...	2205	...	2246	...	...	...	...	...
Portbou .... **657** a.	1944	...	...	...	...	...	...	...	...	...	...	...	...	...	...	...	...	...	...	...	...	...	...	...	...

B – Ⓑ to June 27; daily June 29 - Sept. 5; Ⓑ from Sept. 7 (also Nov. 1).
E – ⑥⑦ to June 29; ⑥ July 5 - Aug. 30; Ⓒ from Sept. 6.
H – July 5 - Aug. 31.
L – ⑤⑥ to Sept. 20; daily from Sept. 22.
P – ①–⑤ to June 27; Ⓑ June 30 - Sept. 5; Ⓐ from Sept. 8.

c – Connects with train in preceding column.
d – Also Nov. 1.
f – Also Aug. 14; not Aug. 15.
j – 1321 on ⑥⑦ to June 29 and daily July 5 - Aug. 31.
k – Not Nov. 1.

m – Not July 14, Aug. 14, Nov. 11.
n – Not July 5 - Aug. 31.
r – ⑥ July 5 - Aug. 30.
t – Arrives 1702.
z – ⑤⑥ (not Nov. 22).

△ – Does not run Montpellier - Narbonne on ①–④ to July 10 and ①–④ July 15 - Aug. 7. This service may be subject to alteration on certain other dates - please check before travelling.
‡ – Vitrolles Aéroport Marseille-Provence ✈. A shuttle bus runs to / from the airport terminal (journey time: 5 minutes).
★ – *INTERCITÉS*. 🅁. 🍸. Minor timing variations are possible.

355 PERPIGNAN and BORDEAUX - MONTPELLIER - MARSEILLE, LYON and PARIS

INTERCITÉS and *TER* services. See pages 205 and 206 for *TGV* and *AVE* services. See Table **300** for *TGV* services Paris - Bordeaux - Toulouse.
Minor timing variations are possible. Subject to alteration on Oct. 4, 5, 11, 12, Nov. 8–10. Journeys from Bordeaux are subject to alteration on June 28, 29.

																	4651								
	Ⓐ	Ⓐ		Ⓐ	Ⓐ	Ⓐ H	Ⓐ n	⑥ k	Ⓐ n	Ⓐ H	Ⓐ	⚒	Ⓐ n	Ⓐ n	Ⓐ	Ⓐ n	Ⓐ ★🅁	Ⓐ	Ⓒ	⑥ k	† ◇	Ⓐ	Ⓐ	Ⓐ	Ⓒ
Portbou 657 d.	...	...	...	...	...	...	...	...	...	...	...	...	...	...	...	...	...	...	...	...	...	...	...	...	...
Cerbère 657 d.	...	...	...	...	...	...	...	...	...	...	0527	...	...	...	...	...	...	0627	...	...	...	0657	0725	...	0723
Banyuls sur Mer d.	...	...	...	...	...	...	...	...	...	...	0533	...	...	...	...	...	...	0633	...	...	...	0703	0731	...	0730
Port Vendres d.	...	...	...	...	...	...	...	...	...	...	0539	...	...	...	...	...	...	0639	...	...	...	0709	0737	...	0735
Collioure d.	...	...	...	...	...	...	...	...	...	...	0542	...	...	...	...	...	...	0642	...	...	...	0712	0740	...	0739
Argelès sur Mer d.	...	...	...	...	...	...	...	...	...	...	0547	...	...	...	...	...	...	0647	...	...	...	0717	0745	...	0744
Perpignan a.	...	...	...	...	...	...	...	...	...	...	0603	...	...	...	...	...	...	0703	...	...	...	0733	0801	...	0800
Perpignan d.	...	...	...	...	...	*0532*	*0537*	...	...	...	▬	0615	...	...	...	0638	...	0710	0709	...	...	0738	0808	...	0807
Rivesaltes d.	...	...	...	...	...	*0539*	*0544*	...	...	...	...	0622	...	...	...	0644	...	0717	0716	...	...	0745	0814	...	0814
Port la Nouvelle d.	...	...	...	...	...	*0603*	*0609*	...	...	...	...	0646	...	...	...	0708	...	0740	0739	...	...	0808	0837	...	0839
Bordeaux St Jean 355a d.	...	...	...	...	...	|	|	...	...	...	...	|	...	...	...	|	...	|	|	...	...	|	|	...	|
Marmande 355a d.	...	...	...	...	...	|	|	...	...	...	...	|	...	...	...	|	...	|	|	...	...	|	|	...	|
Agen 355a d.	...	...	...	...	...	|	|	...	...	...	...	|	...	...	...	|	...	|	|	...	...	|	|	...	|
Montauban 355a d.	...	...	...	...	...	|	|	...	...	...	...	|	...	...	...	|	...	|	|	...	...	|	|	...	|
Toulouse Matabiau 355a a.	...	...	...	...	...	|	|	...	...	...	...	|	...	...	...	|	...	|	|	...	...	|	|	...	|
Toulouse Matabiau 355a d.	...	...	...	...	...	|	|	...	...	...	...	|	...	...	0546	|	0645	|	|	...	...	|	|	...	|
Carcassonne 355a d.	...	...	...	...	...	|	|	...	...	...	Ⓒ	|	...	...	0654	|	0729	|	|	...	...	|	|	...	|
Narbonne 355a a.	...	...	...	...	...	*0617*	*0623*	...	...	...		0701	...	...	0724	0721	0758	0755**c**	0754	...	...	0823	0850	...	0900
Narbonne d.	...	...	0531**t**	...	0557	0622	0628	0631	...	0646	0651**r**	0711	0709	...	0726	...	0801	0806	...	0806	0806	0831	0905	0902	0915
Toulouse Matabiau 355a a.	...	...	|	...	|	|	|	|	...	|	|	0847	|	...	|	...	|	|	...	|	|	|	1037	|	|
Béziers d.	0444**v**	...	0546**t**	...	0612	0639	0643	0645	...	0701	0709	...	0724	...	0745	...	0818	0823	...	0823	0823	0846	...	0917	0930
Agde d.	0457**v**	...	0559**t**	...	0627	0652	0656	0657	...	0713	0725	...	0736	...	0759	...	|	0836	...	0836	0836	0858	...	0929	0943
Sète d.	0514**v**	...	0615**t**	...	0646	0711	0713	0713	0730	0730	0746	...	0753	...	0816	...	|	0853	...	0856	0853	0915	...	0946	1002
Frontignan d.	0519**v**	...	0621**t**	...	0652	0716	0719	0718	0736	0736	0752	...	0758	...	0822	...	|	0859	...	0902	0858	0921	...	0952	1008
Montpellier Saint-Roch a.	0531**v**	...	0633**t**	...	0709	0733	0731	0730	0755	0755	0809	...	0810	...	0837	...	0856	0913	...	0915	0915	0933	...	1003	1019
Montpellier Saint-Roch d.	0534	...	0637	0644	0713	0737	0735	0732	0758	0758	0813	...	0814	...	0839	...	0900	0917	...	0919	0919	...	...	1011	1023
Lunel d.	0551	...	0654	0659	0730	0754	0752	0747	0813	0813	0829	...	0831	...	0854	...	|	0933	...	0935	0937	...	...	1028	1039
Nîmes Centre 357 d.	0611	0649	0714	0729	0751	0816	0814	0815	0839	0849**j**	0849	...	0850	0902	0910	...	0928	0949	...	0954	0958	...	...	1049	1058
Nîmes Pont-du-Gard d.	0622	0700	0726	0739	0800	0825	0825	0826	...	0859	0859	...	0859	|	...	...	|	...	...	1006	1009	...	...	1100	1109
Tarascon-sur-Rhône d.	0630	0711	0736	0750	0813	0836	0836	0840	...	0911	0911	...	0911	|	...	...	|	...	...	1017	1023	...	...	1115	1120
Avignon Centre 357 a.	|	0722	|	0802	0826	|	|	0856	...	0923	0923	...	0923	0940	...	...	|	...	...	|	|	...	...	1127	1132
Arles 351 d.	0641	...	0745	...	...	0845	0845	...	...	...	...	...	...	...	...	...	|	...	...	1028	1032	...	...	...	...
Miramas 351 d.	0703	...	0807	...	...	0907	0907	...	...	...	...	...	...	...	...	...	|	...	...	1053	1056	...	...	...	...
Aéroport Marseille ✈ ‡ 351 d.	0723	...	0825	...	...	0924	0924	...	...	...	...	...	...	...	...	...	|	...	...	1111	1114	...	...	...	...
Marseille St Charles 351 a.	0742	...	0842	...	...	0939	0938	...	...	...	...	...	...	...	...	...	1036	...	...	1130	1129	...	...	...	...

		4655					**4657**								**4659**						**4661**				
	Ⓐ	★🅁		⑥ k	†	Ⓐ	★🅁	Ⓐ ⊖	Ⓐ	Ⓐ	Ⓒ	Ⓐ	Ⓐ	⚒ ●	⊕ ★🅁	A	Ⓐ	Ⓒ n		Ⓐ	★🅁	B	⑥ kn		Ⓐ
Portbou 657 d.	...	...	...	0916	...	...	...	1004	...	...	1105**n**	...	...	1206	...	...	...	...	...	...	...	1359	...	...	...
Cerbère 657 d.	0827	...	...	0939	0939	...	...	1025	...	...	1127	...	...	1227	...	...	...	1329	...	...	...	1420	...	...	...
Banyuls sur Mer d.	0833	...	...	0945	0946	...	...	1031	...	...	1133	...	...	1233	...	...	...	1335	...	...	...	1427	...	...	...
Port Vendres d.	0839	...	...	0951	0952	...	...	1037	...	...	1138	...	...	1239	...	...	...	1341	...	...	...	1433	...	...	...
Collioure d.	0842	...	...	0955	0955	...	...	1040	...	...	1142	...	...	1242	...	...	...	1345	...	...	...	1437	...	...	...
Argelès sur Mer d.	0847	...	...	1000	1000	...	...	1045	...	...	1147	...	...	1247	...	...	...	1350	...	...	...	1443	...	...	...
Perpignan a.	0903	...	...	1015	1015	...	...	1101	...	...	1204	...	...	1303	...	...	...	1405	...	...	...	1502	...	...	...
Perpignan d.	0910	...	...	1024	1022	1022	...	▬	1113	...	1211	1213	...	1310	...	...	1415	1412	...	...	...	1507	1510	...	1607
Rivesaltes d.	0917	...	...	1033	1029	1028	...	...	1119	...	1218	1219	...	1317	...	...	1421	1419	...	...	...	1514	1517	...	1613
Port la Nouvelle d.	0940	...	...	1055	1052	1052	...	...	1143	...	1241	1242	...	1340	...	...	1445	1442	...	...	...	1539	1540	...	1636
Bordeaux St Jean 355a d.	|	0610	...	|	|	|	0807	...	|	...	|	|	...	|	1009	...	|	|	...	...	1210	|	|	...	|
Marmande 355a d.	|	|	...	|	|	|	0855	...	|	...	|	|	...	|	|	...	|	|	...	...	|	|	|	...	|
Agen 355a d.	|	0723	...	|	|	|	|	...	|	...	|	|	...	|	1123	...	|	|	...	...	1324	|	|	...	|
Montauban 355a d.	|	0801	...	|	|	|	0959	...	|	...	|	|	...	|	1200	...	|	|	...	...	1401	|	|	...	|
Toulouse Matabiau 355a a.	|	0837	...	|	|	|	1036	...	|	...	|	|	...	|	1237	...	|	|	...	...	1438	|	|	...	|
Toulouse Matabiau 355a d.	|	0842	...	|	|	|	1042	...	|	...	|	|	...	|	1242	...	|	|	...	...	1445	|	|	...	|
Carcassonne 355a d.	|	0927	...	|	|	|	1129	...	|	...	|	|	...	|	1328	...	|	|	...	...	1529	|	|	...	|
Narbonne 355a a.	0955	0958	...	1110	1105	1105	1158	...	1156**c**	...	1254	1255	...	1354	1358	...	1457	1455	...	...	1558	1552**c**	1554**c**	...	1649
Narbonne d.	...	1002	1009	1118	1118	1118	1202	...	1209	1217	1308	1309**e**	1309	...	1402	1431	1510	1510	1509	...	1602	1607	1609	1631	1702
Toulouse Matabiau 355a a.	...	|	|	1252	1253	1253	|	...	|	|	|	1441**e**	|	...	|	|	1642	1642	|	...	|	|	|	|	1833
Béziers d.	...	1018	1024	...	...	▬	|	...	1224	1234	1324	...	1324	...	1418	1446	▬	...	1524	...	1618	1623	1624	1646	▬
Agde d.	...	|	1036	...	...	...	|	...	1236	1250	1336	...	1336	...	|	1459	...	...	1536	...	|	1636	1636	1659	...
Sète d.	...	|	1053	...	...	...	1239	...	1253	1308	1353	...	1353	...	|	1515	...	...	1554	...	|	1653	1653	1715	...
Frontignan d.	...	|	1058	...	...	Ⓐ	|	Ⓒ	1258	1314	1358	...	1358	...	|	1521	Ⓒ	...	1559	...	|	1658	1658	1720	⚒
Montpellier Saint-Roch a.	...	1055	1110	...	...		1254		1310	1331	1410	...	1410	...	1456	1533	n	...	1611	...	1655	1710	1710	1733	
Montpellier Saint-Roch d.	...	1100	1114	...	...	1228	1258	1314	1314	...	...	...	1414	...	1501	1537	1537	...	1615	...	1659	1714	1714	1736	1744
Lunel d.	...	|	1131	...	...	1251	|	1331	1331	...	...	...	1431	...	|	1554	1554	...	1632	1637	|	1731	1731	1751	1816
Nîmes Centre 357 d.	...	1128	1151	...	...	1315	1327	1350	1351	...	...	...	1451	...	1529	1614	1614	...	1651	1705	1728	1750	1750	1814	1839
Nîmes Pont-du-Gard d.	...	|	1201	...	...	|	|	1359	1400	...	...	...	1500	...	|	1624	1624	...	1701	1715	|	1759	1759	1824	1847
Tarascon-sur-Rhône d.	...	|	1212	...	...	|	|	1410	1412	...	...	...	1511	...	|	1635	1636	...	1712	1728	|	1810	1810	1836	1858
Avignon Centre 357 a.	...	|	1226	...	...	1344	|	1427	1427	...	...	...	1523	...	|	|	|	...	1726	1740	|	1824	1822	|	1909
Arles 351 d.	...	|	...	...	...	...	1350	...	...	...	...	...	...	...	|	1644	1645	...	...	...	1752	...	...	1844	...
Miramas 351 d.	...	|	...	...	...	...	|	...	...	...	...	...	...	...	|	1706	1707	...	...	...	|	...	...	1907	...
Aéroport Marseille ✈ ‡ 351 d.	...	|	...	...	...	...	|	...	...	...	...	...	...	...	|	1724	1724	...	...	...	|	...	...	1924	...
Marseille St Charles 351 a.	...	1237	...	...	...	...	1438	...	...	...	...	...	...	...	1637	1738	1738	...	...	...	1839	...	...	1941	...

A – Ⓐ (daily June 30 - Sept. 5).
B – Ⓑ to June 27; daily June 29 - Sept. 5; Ⓑ from Sept. 7 (also Nov. 1).
H – July 5 - Aug. 31.
R – ⑦ to Aug. 3 (not July 13); Ⓑ from Aug. 10 (not Aug. 15).
S – ①–⑤ June 16 - Aug. 8.

c – Connects with train in preceding column.
d – Also Nov. 1.
e – Until July 4 departs Narbonne 1308, arrives Toulouse 1450.
f – 3 minutes earlier until June 29.
j – Arrives 0840.
k – Not Nov. 1.
n – Not July 5 - Aug. 31.
r – Not July 14.
t – Ⓑ (daily from Aug. 10).
v – ① to Aug. 4 (also July 15; not July 14); Ⓐ Aug. 11 - Sept. 12; ① from Sept. 15.

◇ – Runs 4–13 minutes later on Aug. 15.
⊕ – Subject to alteration Nov. 17–21, 24–28.
● – Runs daily Portbou - Perpignan June 30 - Sept. 6.
⊖ – Subject to alteration / cancellation on certain ①–⑤ dates.
◧ – Also runs on † July 6 - Aug. 31..
★ – *INTERCITÉS*. 🅁. 🍷. Minor timing variations are possible.
♣ – ⑤⑦ to June 29; daily July 4 - Aug. 31; ⑤⑦ Sept. 5 - Oct. 12; daily Oct. 17 - Nov. 2; ⑤⑦ from Nov. 7. Conveys 🛏 1, 2 cl. and (2) (reclining). 🅁. For overnight journeys only. **Sample timings shown – subject to frequent variations**. For confirmed timings, please consult the SNCF journey planner: www.sncf-connect.com.
‡ – Vitrolles Aéroport Marseille-Provence ✈. A shuttle bus runs to the airport terminal (journey time: 5 minutes).

PORTBOU - PERPIGNAN - MONTPELLIER - MARSEILLE, LYON and PARIS 355

INTERCITÉS and *TER* services. See pages 205 and 206 for *TGV* and *AVE* services. See Table **300** for *TGV* services Paris - Bordeaux - Toulouse.
Minor timing variations are possible. Subject to alteration on Oct. 4, 5, 11, 12, Nov. 8 – 10. Journeys from Bordeaux are subject to alteration on June 28, 29.

	Ⓒ H	Ⓒ n		Ⓐ	4663 ★🅁		†	⑥ k	Ⓐ	Ⓐ	Ⓒ	†	Ⓑ d	4665 ★🅁	A	Ⓒ n	5738 5744 ♣🅁	Ⓐ	Ⓒ	4669 R ★🅁	4669 ①–⑤ S ★🅁	Ⓐ ◧	⑥ H	† H	⑥ H
Portbou 657 d.	...	1501	...	...	...	1604	...	...	...	...	...	...	...	...	1806	...	...	...	1906	...	...	2005	...	...	...
Cerbère 657 d.	1522	1522	...	...	...	1625	...	...	...	...	1727	...	...	...	1827	...	1900	...	1927	...	...	2027	2113	2217	2313
Banyuls sur Mer d.	1528	1528	...	...	...	1632	...	...	...	...	1733	...	...	...	1833	...	1908	...	1933	...	...	2034	2119	2224	2319
Port Vendres d.	1534	1534	...	...	...	1637	...	...	...	...	1739	...	...	...	1839	...	1914	...	1939	...	...	2040	2125	2229	2325
Collioure d.	1538	1538	...	...	...	1641	...	...	...	...	1743	...	...	...	1842	...	1919	...	1942	...	...	2044	2129	2233	2328
Argelès sur Mer d.	1543	1543	...	...	...	1646	...	...	...	...	1748	...	...	...	1847	...	1925	...	1947	...	...	2049	2134	2238	2334
Perpignan a.	1604	1603	...	...	...	1704	...	...	...	...	1803	...	...	...	1906	...	|	...	2004	...	...	2107	2150	2254	2349
Perpignan d.	1609	1608	...	...	...	1708	...	...	...	1813	1813**f**	...	...	...	1911	1909	1945	2010	2011	...	...	...	...	...	...
Rivesaltes d.	1615	1615	...	...	...	1715	...	...	...	1819	1820**f**	...	...	...	1918	1916	1959**H**	2016	2017	...	...	...	...	...	...
Port la Nouvelle d.	1638	1638	...	...	...	1739	...	...	...	1842	1843**f**	...	...	...	1941	1940	2024**H**	2041	2041	...	...	...	...	...	...
Bordeaux St Jean 355a d.	|	|	...	...	1410	|	...	...	...	|	|	...	...	1609	|	|	|	|	|	1809	1809	...	...	...	...
Marmande 355a d.	|	|	...	...	|	|	...	...	...	|	|	...	...	|	|	|	|	|	|	1858	1858	...	...	...	...
Agen 355a d.	|	|	...	...	1523	|	...	...	...	|	|	...	...	1723	|	|	|	|	|	|	|	...	...	...	...
Montauban 355a d.	|	|	...	...	1601	|	...	...	...	|	|	...	...	1802	|	|	|	|	|	2002	2002	...	...	...	...
Toulouse Matabiau 355a a.	|	|	...	...	1638	|	...	...	...	|	|	...	...	1839	|	|	|	|	|	2039	2038	...	...	...	...
Toulouse Matabiau 355a d.	|	|	...	...	1642	|	1648	1648	1648	|	|	...	...	1845	|	|	|	|	|	2044	2044	...	...	...	...
Carcassonne 355a d.	|	|	...	...	1729	|	1756	1752	1757	|	|	...	...	1929	|	|	|	|	|	2129	2129	...	...	...	...
Narbonne 355a a.	1649	1650	...	...	1758	1753**c**	1827	1823	1827	1856	1856**f**	...	...	1958	1955**c**	1955**c**	|	2054	2054	2158	2158	...	...	...	...
Narbonne d.	1701	1701	1709	1724	1802	1808	1830	1826	1830	1909	1911**f**	1915	1919	2002	2009	2009	2041	2109	2109	2202	2202	...	...	...	...
Toulouse Matabiau **355a** a.	1833	1834	|	|	|	|	|	|	|	2041	2042	|	|	|	|	|	|	|	|	|	|	...	...	...	...
Béziers d.	...	...	1724	1742	1818	1824	1846	1844	1846	...	...	1934	1934	2018	2024	2024	2058	2124	2124	|	2216	...	...	...	...
Agde d.	...	...	1736	1757	|	1836	1900	1858	1859	...	...	1948	1948	|	2036	2037	2111	2136	2136	|	...	...	...	...	...
Sète d.	...	...	1753	1816	|	1853	1917	1918	1917	...	...	2007	2005	|	2052	2054	2128	2153	2153	2239	...	...	...	...	...
Frontignan d.	...	...	1758	1821	|	1858	1922	1923	1923	...	...	2012	2010	|	2058	2100	|	2159	2159	|	...	...	...	...	...
Montpellier Saint-Roch a.	...	...	1810	1833	1856	1910	1932	1934	1934	...	...	2024	2022	2055	2110	2112	|	2210	2210	2255	...	...	...	...	...
Montpellier Saint-Roch d.	...	...	1814	1837	1901	1914	1935	1937	1937	...	...	2031	2026	2100	2114	2116	2145	2214	2214	2259	...	...	...	...	...
Lunel d.	...	...	1831	1854	|	1930	1951	1953	2006	...	...	2048	2043	|	2131	2133	|	2231	2231	|	...	...	...	...	...
Nîmes Centre 357 d.	...	...	1851	1911	1929	1949	2006	2009	2023	...	...	2105	2102	2129	2148	2150	2212	2248	2248	2324	...	...	...	...	...
Paris Austerlitz a.	...	...	|	...	|	|	...	...	...	...	...	...	|	|	...	...	0753	...	...	...	...	...	...	...	...
Nîmes Pont-du-Gard d.	...	...	1900	...	|	2000	...	...	...	...	...	...	2113	|	...	...	...	...	...	...	...	...	...	...	...
Tarascon-sur-Rhône d.	...	...	1911	...	|	2011	...	...	...	...	...	...	2125	|	...	...	...	...	...	...	...	...	...	...	...
Avignon Centre 357 a.	...	...	1925	...	|	2022	...	...	...	...	...	...	2137	|	...	...	...	...	...	...	...	...	...	...	...
Arles 351 d.	...	...	...	...	|	...	...	...	...	...	...	...	...	|	...	...	...	...	...	...	...	...	...	...	...
Miramas 351 d.	...	...	...	...	|	...	...	...	...	...	...	...	...	|	...	...	...	...	...	...	...	...	...	...	...
Aéroport Marseille ✈ ‡ 351 d.	...	...	...	...	|	...	...	...	...	...	...	...	...	|	...	...	...	...	...	...	...	...	...	...	...
Marseille St Charles 351 a.	...	...	...	...	2041	...	...	...	...	...	...	...	...	2243	...	...	...	...	...	...	...	...	...	...	...

← **FOR NOTES SEE PREVIOUS PAGE**

TER services

Local services BORDEAUX - AGEN - TOULOUSE - NARBONNE 355a

See Table **355** for *TGV* and *INTERCITÉS* services Bordeaux - Toulouse - Narbonne and v.v. See Table **300** for *TGV* services (Paris -) Bordeaux - Toulouse and v.v.

BORDEAUX - AGEN. ***Note:*** *On Aug. 15, Nov. 1 services in the Bordeaux - Agen panel run as on ⑥. Subject to alteration on June 28, 29.*

km		A	① g	⚒	Ⓐ	N	Ⓐ n	Ⓐ	Ⓒ	Ⓐ	⑥	⚒	†	Ⓐ	†	⚒	Ⓑ	Ⓐ n		Ⓐ	Ⓑ	⑥	†	E	Ⓑ
0	**Bordeaux** St Jean d.	...	0616	0654	0724	0827	0833	1018	1105	1127	1226	1333	1346	1518	1629	1634	1728	1801	1833	1858**v**	1929	1933	2033	2053	2139
79	Marmande d.	0700	0714	0757	0820	0923	0929	1115	1203	1253	1400	1430	1443	1616	1755	1733	1824	1913	1931	2002	2032	2059	2159	2150	2235
136	**Agen** a.	0735	0748	0832	0855	0958	1004	1149	1237	...	...	1504	1517	1652	...	1808	1857	...	2005	...	2107	...	...	2225	2310

	Ⓐ n	Ⓐ	⚒	Ⓐ	⑥	Ⓐ	Ⓐ		Ⓒ	†	Ⓐ	Ⓐ	Ⓒ	Ⓐ	⑥	Ⓐ		Ⓑ	Ⓐ	†	⚒	B	⑤⑥ r	D	†
Agen d.	...	0525	0604	...	...	0657	0802	0901	1057	...	1157	...	1255	1307	...	1358	1543	1702	...	...	1758	1907	2038	2039	2051
Marmande d.	0527	0600	0639	0650	0711	0732	0837	0936	1132	1209	1232	1308	1330	1342	1409	1434	1618	1736	1755	1805	1833	1942	2113	2114	2124
Bordeaux St Jean a.	0643	0657	0735	0802	0833	0831	0933	1032	1228	1336	1328	1433	1427	...	1536	1531	1717	1834	1915	1932	1930	2036	2209	...	2220

AGEN - TOULOUSE. *Minor timing variations are also possible.*

km		Ⓐ	⚒	Ⓐ	Ⓐ	⑥	Ⓐ n	Ⓐ H	Ⓐ	Ⓒ	Ⓐ								Ⓐ	Ⓒ	Ⓐ		Ⓒ	Ⓐ
0	**Agen** d.	...	...	0540	...	0620	0644	0644	0749	0817	0840	...	1018	1138	...	1414	...	1615	1743	1840	1843	...	2014	2044
70	Montauban 310 d.	0532	0604	0626	0636	0708	0732	0732	0837	0905	0928	...	1106	1226	...	1502	...	1703	1831	1928	1931	...	2103	2132
121	**Toulouse** Matabiau 310 a.	0621	0654	...	0726	0745	0810	0821	0914	0942	1006	...	1143	1306	...	1540	...	1740	1909	2005	2009	...	2140	2211

	Ⓐ	⑥	Ⓐ	Ⓐ	Ⓒ								Ⓒ	Ⓐ	Ⓐ	Ⓐ	Ⓒ	Ⓐ		†	Ⓐ	Ⓐ	⑥	Ⓐ
Toulouse Matabiau 310 d.	0544	0548	0643**b**	0748	0755	...	0952	...	1153	...	1425	...	1550	1551	1642**c**	1745	1749	1853	...	1951	1952	...	2015	2028
Montauban 310 d.	0631	0628	0727	0826	0834	...	1031	...	1232	...	1505	...	1629	1630	1721	1828	1829	1932	...	2034	2029	2036	2055	2115
Agen a.	0715	0715	0815	0914	0921	...	1118	...	1320	...	1552	...	1717	1717	1809	1915	1917	2019	...	2121	...	2122	2142	...

TOULOUSE - CARCASSONNE - NARBONNE (- PERPIGNAN). *Minor timing variations are possible. Subject to alteration June 16 – 20, 23 – 27, 30, July 1 – 4.*

km		Ⓐ p	Ⓐ ⊡	Ⓐ	Ⓐ	Ⓒ ⊖	Ⓐ	⑥	Ⓐ		Ⓒ ⊖	Ⓐ H	Ⓐ n	Ⓒ	Ⓐ	Ⓐ	Ⓒ ⊖	Ⓐ	Ⓐ H	Ⓐ n	Ⓒ ⊖	Ⓐ	Ⓐ	Ⓒ ⊖	
0	**Toulouse** Matabiau d.	0521	0546	0614	0653	0713	0716	0806	0806	...	0922	0922	0925	1012	1012	1118	1118	1211	1312	1312	1323	1418	1519	1520	1613**j**
55	Castelnaudary d.	0602	0632	0657	0740	0754	0756	0849	0852	...	1004	1003	1005	1056	1058	1159	1159	1256	1354	1356	1404	1503	1600	1600	1700
91	**Carcassonne** d.	0623	0654	0720	0802	0817	0818	0911	0914	...	1026	1025	1026	1119	1122	1221	1221	1317	1416	1417	1426	1524	1622	1622	1723
128	Lézignan d.	0642	0712	0738	0821	0836	0836	0929	0933	...	1045	1044	1044	1139	1142	1239	1239	1335	1435	1435	1445	1542	1640	1640	1742
150	**Narbonne** a.	0654	0724	0750	0833	0849	0849	0942	0945	...	1057	1056	1056	1152	1154	1251	1251	1347	1447	1447	1458	1554	1652	1652	1754
	Perpignan **355** a.	...	...	...	...	0945	0943	...	...	...	1152	1150	1150	...	...	1346	1348	...	1554	1554	1551	...	1748	1748	...

	⑥ k ⊡	† ⊡	Ⓐ ⊡	①–④ e	⑤ f ⊖	Ⓒ ⊖	Ⓐ	Ⓐ n		Ⓒ	Ⓐ	
Toulouse Matabiau d.	1648	1648	1648	1710	1710	1710	1749	1849	1921	2009	2017	...
Castelnaudary d.	1730	1733	1735	1756	1756	1756	1837	1939	2001	2055	2102	...
Carcassonne d.	1752	1756	1757	1821	1821	1820	1858	2001	2022	2118	2122	...
Lézignan d.	1811	1815	1815	1839	1840	1840	1917	2019	2040	2137	2140	...
Narbonne a.	1823	1827	1827	1852	1852	1852	1929	2032	2052	2150	2152	...
Perpignan **355** a.	...	...	...	1947	1947	1947	...	...	2150	...	...	...

	Ⓐ	Ⓐ	⚒	Ⓐ ⊡		Ⓐ ⊖	⑥ ⊡	⑥	Ⓐ
Perpignan **355** d.	...	...	0615	...	...	0808	...	...	...
Narbonne d.	0524	0603	0711	0726	0808	0905	0907	1008	1007
Lézignan d.	0537	0616	0724	0740	0821	0917	0920	1021	1020
Carcassonne d.	0556	0636	0744	0800	0841	0937	0940	1041	1039
Castelnaudary d.	0618	0657	0806	0822	0902	0958	1001	1102	1100
Toulouse Matabiau a.	0709	0737	0847	0913	0949	1037	1040	1144	1147

	Ⓐ	† ⊖	⑥ k ⊖		Ⓒ	Ⓐ M	Ⓐ L	①–④ m	⑤ w	Ⓒ ⊖	Ⓐ	Ⓐ	Ⓐ	Ⓐ	Ⓒ n ⊖	Ⓒ H ⊖	Ⓐ ⊡	Ⓐ	†	Ⓐ n	Ⓐ	Ⓒ t ⊖	E	R	Ⓒ H
Perpignan **355** d.	1022	1022	1024	...	...	1213	1213	...	...	1412	1415	...	...	1607	1608	1609	...	...	...	...	1813	1813	...	...	...
Narbonne d.	1118	1118	1118	1209	1309	1309	1308	1412	1412	1510	1510	1608	1628	1702	1701	1701	1727	1807	1824	1837	1909	1911	2012	2022	2117
Lézignan d.	1131	1131	1131	1222	1321	1321	1321	1425	1426	1522	1522	1621	1641	1714	1715	1714	1739	1820	1837	1850	1922	1924	2025	2035	2130
Carcassonne d.	1151	1151	1150	1241	1341	1341	1341	1444	1446	1542	1542	1640	1700	1734	1734	1733	1758	1840	1856	1909	1941	1943	2045	2054	2149
Castelnaudary d.	1212	1213	1212	1302	1402	1402	1406	1505	1508	1603	1603	1700	1722	1754	1756	1753	1820	1901	1918	1931	2002	2004	2106	2116	2210
Toulouse Matabiau a.	1253	1253	1252	1352**q**	1441	1441	1450	1549	1555	1642	1642	1743	1808	1833	1834	1833	1906	1947	1959	2013	2041	2042	2147	2155	2249

A – ②–⑤ (not July 15, Aug. 15, Nov. 11, 12)
B – Ⓑ to July 6; ⑤† July 11 - Aug. 24 (also Aug. 14; not Aug. 15); Ⓑ from Aug. 29.
D – ①–④ to July 3; ⑤ July 11 - Aug. 29 (also Aug. 14; not Aug. 15); ①–④ from Sept. 1 (not Nov. 11).
E – ①–⑥ to July 5; ⑥ July 12 - Aug. 30; ⚒ from Sept. 1.
H – July 5 - Aug. 31.
L – Until July 4.
M – From July 7.
N – ⑥ (⚒ July 5 - Aug. 30).

R – † (Ⓑ July 6 - Aug. 31).

b – 12 – 17 minutes earlier July 7 - Aug. 29, Oct. 20 – 31.
c – 1640 on ②–⑤ June 17 - July 4.
e – ①–④ (not July 14, Aug. 14, Nov. 11).
f – Also Aug. 14; not Aug. 15.
g – Also July 15, Nov. 12; not July 14.
j – 1609 on ⑤ June 20 - Aug. 8 (also Aug. 22, 29).
k – Not Nov. 1.
m – Not July 14, Nov. 11.

n – Not July 5 - Aug. 31.
p – Not July 7 - Aug. 29, Oct. 20 – 31.
q – 1345 on Ⓒ.
r – Not July 11, 18, 25, Aug. 1, 8, 22, 29.
t – Departure times are 2 – 3 minutes earlier until June 29.
v – 1847 July 7 - Aug. 29.
w – Not Aug. 15.

⊖ – To / from Portbou and / or Cerbère (Table **355**).
⊡ – To / from Nîmes (Table **355**).

356 NÎMES - LE GRAU-DU-ROI

SERVICE UNTIL JUNE 27

km		Ⓒ	Ⓐ		Ⓒ	Ⓐ					
0	**Nîmes** Centre d.	1038	1038	...	1255	1301	...	1736	...	...	...
39	Aigues-Mortes a.	1115	1124	...	1336	1346	...	1825	...	...	...
45	**Le Grau-du-Roi** a.	1123	1132	...	1344	1354	...	1833	...	...	...

	Ⓐ		Ⓒ	Ⓐ				Ⓐ	Ⓒ	
Le Grau-du-Roi d.	0640	...	1149	1153	...	1603	...	1843	1844	...
Aigues-Mortes d.	0648	...	1158	1202	...	1614	...	1852	1852	...
Nîmes Centre a.	0736	...	1239	1251	...	1706	...	1941	1937	...

SERVICE JUNE 28 - AUGUST 31 *Subject to confirmation*

km		Ⓒ							Ⓒ	Ⓐ	
0	**Nîmes** Centre d.	0905	1030	...	1315	1418	...	1732	1854	1901	...
39	Aigues-Mortes a.	0954	1114	...	1359	1457	...	1826	1942	1950	...
45	**Le Grau-du-Roi** a.	1001	1121	...	1406	1504	...	1833	1949	1957	...

	Ⓒ								Ⓒ	Ⓐ
Le Grau-du-Roi d.	1020	...	1305	...	1614	1731	1844	...	2006	2010
Aigues-Mortes d.	1029	...	1314	...	1623	1739	1854	...	2015	2019
Nîmes Centre a.	1119	...	1403	...	1706	1830	1941	...	2100	2101

357 AVIGNON - PONT-SAINT-ESPRIT

km		⚒		†	G	J 🚌	H	J	†	⚒	†
	Nîmes Centre ... **355** d.	...	...	...	...	...	1341	1510	...	...	...
	Avignon Centre **355** a.	...	...	...	...	...	1411	1540	...	...	...
0	**Avignon** Centre d.	0623	0822	1023	1221	1230	1423**t**	1553	1623	1822	1908
35	Bagnols-sur-Cèze d.	0645	0844	1045	1245	1312	1445**t**	1615	1645	1844	1930
47	**Pont-Saint-Esprit** a.	0652	0851	1053	1252	1329	1452**t**	1622	1653	1851	1938

	⚒	†	J	G	J 🚌	H	†	⚒v			†
Pont-Saint-Esprit d.	0703	0806	0859	1003	1100	1200	1406	1605	1724	...	2003
Bagnols-sur-Cèze d.	0711	0815	0907	1011	1117	1209	1415	1613	1734	...	2012
Avignon Centre a.	0732	0839	0929	1037	1159	1230	1437	1641	1803	...	2035
Avignon Centre **355** d.	...	...	...	...	...	1242	...	...	...	...	...
Nîmes Centre ... **355** a.	...	...	...	...	...	1318	...	...	...	...	...

G – ⑥ to June 21; ⚒ from June 23.
H – Ⓒ to June 15; daily from June 21.
J – Ⓐ until June 20.
t – 12–13 minutes later on July 9, Aug. 20.
v – On July 9, Aug. 20 Pont-Saint-Esprit d. 1611, Bagnols d. 1620, Avignon a. 1642.

358 MARSEILLE, VALENCE and GRENOBLE - GAP - BRIANÇON

SERVICE UNTIL SEPTEMBER 7

km		5787/9 N				Ⓐ	⑥	⑥ D						G	⑤†	①–④ m	⑥	Ⓑ d	A	Ⓑ h	Ⓑ	⑤†			
0	**Marseille** St Charles ▷ d.	...	0653	0741	0853	...	...	...	1153	1311	...	1452	1641	...	...	...	1741	1741	1841	1841	...	...	1953	2153	2253
37	Aix en Provence ▷ d.	...	0739	0825	0939	...	...	...	1240	1354	...	1539	1724	...	...	...	1827	1826	1922	1922	...	...	2039	2238	2338
106	Manosque-Gréoux d.	...	▬	0910	...	...	...	...	▬	1435	...	...	1807	...	...	...	1909	1908	2004	2004	...	...	...	...	...
139	Château Arnoux - St Auban d.	...	...	0937	...	...	...	...	...	1501	...	...	1834	...	...	...	1934	1934	2032	2032	...	...	...	...	...
156	Sisteron d.	...	...	0951	...	...	...	...	...	1517	...	...	1848	...	...	...	1948	1947	2046	2045	...	...	...	...	...
	Paris Austerlitz d.	2055	...	|	...	...	...	...	...	|	...	...	|	...	...	...	|	▬	|	|	...	...	...	...	...
	Valence TGV d.	|	...	|	...	0955	0955	1227	...	|	1426	...	|	1747	1747	...	|	...	|	|	1957	1957	...	...	...
	Valence Ville **364** d.	|	...	|	...	1004	1004	1238	...	|	1438	...	|	1800	1800	...	|	...	|	|	2007	2007	...	...	...
	Crest d.	0433	...	|	...	1036	1036	1310	...	|	1513	...	|	1834	1834	...	|	...	|	|	2039	2039	...	...	...
	Die d.	0510	...	|	...	1113	1119	1347	...	|	1552	...	|	1911	1911	...	|	...	|	|	2116	2116	...	...	...
206	Veynes-Dévoluy a.	0620	...	1034	...	1209	1215	1443	...	1600	1650	...	1935	2006	2006	...	2036	...	2127	2127	2211	2211	...	...	...
206	Veynes-Dévoluy d.	|	Ⓐ	1037	...	1233	1218	1446	Ⓒ	1603	1700	...	1938	2009	2009	...	2043	⑤⑥	2129	2129	2214	2214	...	...	...
233	**Gap** a.	0647		1057	...	1253	1239	1506		1625	1721	...	1958	2029	2030	...	2103	z	2149	2157	2235	2235	...	...	...
233	**Gap** d.	|	0831	1059	...	1256	1256	1511	1550	1631	1726	...	2001	...	2050	2052	2104	2143	2152	2200**p**	...	2238	...	...	...
270	Embrun d.	0733	0908	1134	...	1331	1331	1552	1633	1708	1808	...	2048**t**	...	2131	2132	2142	2217	2227	2235**p**	...	2311	...	...	...
287	Montdauphin-Guillestre d.	0750	0923	1150	...	1347	1347	1607	1647	1725	1823	...	2104	...	2146	2147	2156	2232	2242	2250**p**	...	2326	...	...	...
302	L'Argentière les Écrins d.	0804	0934	1201	...	1358	1358	1618	1659	1742	1837	...	2116	...	2158	2159	2208	2243	2253	2302**p**	...	2338	...	...	...
315	**Briançon** a.	0824	0949	1216	...	1411	1411	1631	1714	1756	1849	...	2129	...	2210	2213	2221	2258	2306	2315**p**	...	2350	...	...	...

	Ⓐ	⑥	Ⓐ a	Ⓐ	Ⓐ	① g	⑥	⑥	†	Ⓑ	Ⓐ			Ⓒ	Ⓐ	B		Ⓒ	⑤†	⑥ C		⑥	Ⓑ		5790/2 N
Briançon d.	...	...	...	...	...	0441	0507	...	...	0606	0653	0829	...	0843	1051	1053	1248	1319	1343	1343	1510	1726	1726	1821	1957
L'Argentière les Écrins d.	...	...	...	...	...	0454	0520	...	...	0619	0706	0841	...	0856	1104	1107	1301	1332	1400	1401	1523	1740	1740	1839	2014
Montdauphin-Guillestre d.	...	...	...	...	...	0505	0531	...	...	0630	0717	0852	...	0907	1115	1118	1312	1349	1415	1412	1534	1751	1751	1850	2027
Embrun d.	...	...	...	...	...	0520	0546	...	...	0645	0738	0906	...	0922	1133	1136	1329	1406	1445**t**	1427	1549	1805	1805	1905	2045
Gap a.	...	...	...	...	...	0553	0619	...	...	0725	0812	0939	...	0955	1205	1211	1403	1441	1519	1502	1623	1838	1838	1938	|
Gap d.	...	...	0506	0538	0556	0556	0622	...	0621	0728	▬	0940	...	0958	1208	1214	1406	▬	1522	1508	1627	1839	1841	▬	2130
Veynes-Dévoluy a.	...	...	0528	0559	0616	0616	0651	...	0652	0750	...	1001	...	1018	1228	1243	1427	...	1543	1528	1648	1900	1902	...	|
Veynes-Dévoluy d.	...	...	0531	0602	0619	0619	0653	0658	0658	0755	...	1004	...	1021	1231	1246	1430	...	1553	1531	1653	1903	1904	...	2202
Die d.	...	...	|	|	0715	0715	0750	|	|	0853	...	|	...	1122	1326	1350	|	...	|	1633	1751	|	|	...	2314
Crest d.	...	...	|	|	0751	0751	0827	|	|	0932	...	|	...	1201	1401	1424	|	...	|	1708	1832	|	|	...	2354
Valence Ville **364** a.	...	...	|	|	0820	0820	0857	|	|	1003	...	|	...	1231	1430	1454	|	...	|	1738	1901	|	|	...	|
Valence TGV a.	...	...	|	|	0831	0831	0907	|	|	1016	...	|	...	1243	1440	1507	|	...	|	1801	1911	|	|	...	|
Paris Austerlitz a.	...	...	|	|	▬	...	▬	|	|	▬	...	|	...	▬	▬	...	|	...	|	▬	▬	|	|	...	0753
Sisteron d.	0545	0600	0615	0646	...	...	...	0742	0742	...	...	1049	...	...	...	...	1516	...	1637	...	...	1949	1949	...	...
Château Arnoux - St Auban d.	0558	0614	0628	0659	Ⓑ	...	...	0756	0756	...	Ⓒ	1102	...	...	...	...	1529	...	1650	...	...	2003	2002	...	...
Manosque-Gréoux d.	0625	0640	0655	0725		...	...	0823	0823	...		1128	...	...	...	...	1554	...	1718	...	...	2030	2030	...	...
Aix en Provence ▷ d.	0710	0725	0740	0811	0824	...	0853	0910	0910	0953	1053	1212	1353	1453	1553	...	1640	1754**j**	1810	1923	2023	2113	2113	2223	...
Marseille St Charles ▷ a.	0749	0807	0819	0849	0908	...	0937	0949	0949	1037	1137	1250	1437	1537	1637	...	1719	1837	1849	2007	2107	2149	2149	2307	...

GRENOBLE - GAP *Service from June 28*

km			⑦ e	①–⑥ b	⑥ k	Ⓑ z	⑥ k	Ⓑ s	⑥ k	Ⓐ	⑦ e	⑤f 🚌
0	**Grenoble** d.	0809	1020	1020	1303	1338	1554	1607	1809	1809	1814	2030
109	Veynes-Dévoluy a.	1022	1230	1238	1525	1548	1803	1817	2030	2030	2030	2247
109	Veynes-Dévoluy d.	1023	1231	1247	1533**v**	1549	1807	1818	2031	...	...	2247
136	**Gap** a.	1044	1252	1308	1553**v**	1610	1827	1839	2052	...	...	2314

	⑤⑥ w	①–④ r		Ⓑ z	⑥ k	⑥ k	⑤⑦ u 🚌	⑥ k	Ⓑ z	
Gap d.	...	...	0709	1152	1153	1351	1425	1740	1747	1857
Veynes-Dévoluy a.	...	...	0729	1212	1213	1411	1450	1800	1807	1917
Veynes-Dévoluy d.	0525	0537	0730	1216	1216	1412	1450	1805	1808	1918
Grenoble a.	0734	0745	0939	1432	1432	1623	1632	2017	2017	2132

OTHER LOCAL TRAINS MARSEILLE - AIX EN PROVENCE (2nd class).

From Marseille St Charles at 0537, 0623 Ⓐ, 0723 Ⓐ, 0753, 0811 Ⓐ, 0823 Ⓐ, 0923 Ⓐ, 0953 Ⓒ, 1053 Ⓒ, 1123 Ⓐ, 1254, 1323 Ⓐ, 1353, 1423 Ⓐ, 1522, 1554 Ⓐ, 1612 Ⓐ, 1623 Ⓐ, 1653, 1711 Ⓐ, 1723, 1753, 1811 Ⓐ, 1823 Ⓐ, 1853, 1923 Ⓐ, 2023 Ⓐ, 2053 **E** and 2113 ⑤ **z**.

From Aix en Provence at 0553, 0623 Ⓐ, 0640 Ⓐ, 0653, 0723 Ⓐ, 0753, 0840 Ⓐ, 1123 Ⓐ, 1152, 1223 Ⓐ, 1253, 1323 Ⓐ, 1423 Ⓐ, 1523 Ⓐ, 1623 Ⓐ, 1653, 1710 Ⓐ, 1723 Ⓐ, 1823, 1853 Ⓐ, 1953 ①–④ **m**, 2010 ⑤ **z** and 2123.

A – Runs on July 13 only.
B – Runs on Aug. 2, 16, 30 only.
C – ⑥ July 5 - Aug. 23 (not Aug. 2, 16).
D – ⑥ July 5 - Aug. 30.
E – ①②③④⑥⑦ (also Aug. 15).
G – ①②③④⑥ (not June 9, July 14).
N – Conveys 🛏 1, 2 cl. and (2) (reclining). 🅁.
For overnight journeys only. **Timings may vary**. Please consult the SNCF journey planner for confirmed timings: www.sncf-connect.com.

a – Not Aug. 14.
b – Not July 14, Nov. 11.
d – Not July 13, Aug. 14.
e – Also July 14, Nov. 11.
f – Also Aug. 14; not Aug. 15.
g – ① (also July 15; not July 14).
h – Not July 13.
k – Also Aug. 15.
j – 1753 on ⑥.
m – Not July 14.
p – Aug. 14, 15 only.
r – Not July 14, Aug. 14, Nov. 11.
t – Arrives 10–11 minutes earlier.
u – Also July 14, Aug. 14, Nov. 11; not Aug. 15.
v – On Aug. 15 Veynes d. 1548, Gap a. 1608.
w – Also Aug. 14.
z – Not Aug. 15.

▷ – For other local trains see panel below main table.

🚌 BRIANÇON - OULX 🚌
Route 76

	🅁			⑥⑦
Briançon rail station d.	0705	1250	1555	1655
Oulx rail station a.	0805	1350	1655	1755

	🅁			⑥⑦
Oulx rail station d.	1145	1255	1445	1945
Briançon rail station a.	1240	1350	1540	2040

On-line bookings only at https://zou.maregionsud.fr at least 48 hours before departure.

NICE - ANNOT - DIGNE — 359

2nd class only

km	CP ▲		⑦◇			Ⓑ	Ⓑ
0	**Nice** (Gare CP) d.	0800	0840	1220	1720	1800	1930
24	Plan du Var d.	0843	0929	1303	1803	1848	2018
41	Villars sur Var d.	0903	0949	1323	1823	1908	2038
58	Puget Théniers d.	0923	1014	1343	1843	1932	2057
64	Entrevaux d.	0931	1022	1351	1851	1940	...
78	Annot d.	0954	1044	1414	1914	1955	...
96	Thorame Haute d.	1014	1104	1434	1934	...	...
106	St André les Alpes d.	1030	1115	1450	1950	...	...
150	**Digne** ● 🚌 a.	1118	...	1538	2038	...	...

CP ▲	⚒	⚒			⑦◇	
Digne ● 🚌 d.	...	...	0819	1239	...	1739
St. André les Alpes. d.	...	...	0910	1330	1552	1830
Thorame Haute d.	...	...	0922	1342	1604	1842
Annot d.	0545	...	0950	1410	1624	1908
Entrevaux d.	0601	...	1006	1426	1640	1924
Puget Théniers d.	0609	0651	1014	1434	1652	1934
Villars sur Var d.	0629	0711	1034	1454	1712	1954
Plan du Var d.	0655	0733	1055	1515	1732	2015
Nice (Gare CP) a.	0737	0817	1137	1557	1817	2057

TRAIN DES PIGNES steam train, **2025**

⑦ May 4 - Oct. 26 ⊠

Puget Théniers 1100 → Annot 1205
Annot 1535 → Puget Théniers 1615

Also calls at Entrevaux

www.traindespignes.fr

🚌 LER route 66, operated by Autocars Payan.

	🚌 ⚒	🚌		🚌		🚌		🚌	
Digne △ d.	0455	0730	...	1145	...	1340	...	1630	...
Digne (Gare) ★ d.	0458	0733	...	1148	...	1343	...	1633	...
Manosque-Gréoux (Gare) d.	0607	0846	...	1301	...	1456	...	1746	...
Aix en Provence TGV a.	0707	0946	...	1401	...	1556	...	1846	...
Aéroport Marseille ✈ a.	0720	1000	...	1415	...	1610	...	1900	...

	🚌 ⚒		🚌		🚌		🚌		🚌
Aéroport Marseille ✈ d.	0955	...	1255	...	1540	...	1830	...	2105
Aix en Provence TGV d.	1025	...	1325	...	1610	...	1900	...	2130
Manosque-Gréoux (Gare) a.	1125	...	1425	...	1710	...	2000	...	2220
Digne (Gare) ★ a.	1238	...	1538	...	1823	...	2113	...	2323
Digne △ a.	1240	...	1540	...	1825	...	2115	...	2325

△ – Gare Routière (bus station).
▲ – Narrow gauge railway, operated by Chemins de Fer de Provence. **All services are operated by 🚌 between St André les Alpes and Digne until further notice**.
● – 🚌 Digne - Sisteron and v.v. LER route 400. Journey time: 51 – 64 minutes.
From Digne (Gare Routière) at 0510 Ⓐ, 0630 Ⓐ, 0750 Ⓐ, 0810 Ⓒ, 0820 Ⓐ, 0850 Ⓐ, 1010 Ⓐ, 1215 Ⓐ, 1510 Ⓐ, 1550 ⑥, 1600 †, 1610 Ⓐ, 1710, 1810 ⚒ and 1910.
From Sisteron (Gare SNCF) at 0650 Ⓐ, 0720 Ⓐ, 0751 Ⓐ, 0902 Ⓐ, 0950 ⚒, 1207, 1250 Ⓐ, 1356 Ⓐ, 1627 Ⓐ, 1750 Ⓐ, 1850 and 2001.

⊠ – ⑦ May 4 - Oct. 26 (also ⑥ June 7 – 28, ④⑤ July 17 - Aug. 29, ⑥ Sept. 6 – 27). Also runs on Nov. 8 as follows: Puget - Annot - Le Fugeret (a. 1255) and v.v. (return train departs Le Fugeret 1525, Annot 1655, arrives Puget 1735).
◇ – ⑦ May 4 - Oct. 26. Connects with *Train des Pignes* steam train (see panel). Also runs on ①–⑤ July 1 - Aug. 29.
★ – Nearest bus stop: Rond-Point du 4 Sept 1870 (approximately 300m from Digne Gare CP).

🚌 information: ✆ 0 809 400 013 https://zou.maregionsud.fr

MARSEILLE - TOULON - HYÈRES — 360

Local *TER* services. For *TGV* service Paris - Hyères, see Table **350**.

km		Ⓐ	Ⓐ		Ⓐ		Ⓐ		Ⓒ	Ⓒ	Ⓐ	Ⓒ	Ⓒ	Ⓐ	Ⓒ	Ⓐ	Ⓒ	Ⓐ	Ⓐ	Ⓒ		Ⓐ	Ⓒ	Ⓒ	Ⓐ
0	**Marseille** St Charles **361** d.	0535	0607	0635	0707	0735	0807	0835	0907	0935	1007	1007	1036	1036	1103	1103	1132	1135	1205	1207	1236	1305	1307	1323	1336
17	Aubagne d.	0550	0622	0650	0722	0750	0822	0850	0922	0949	1021	1022	1050	1051	1121	1122	1147	1150	1220	1221	1251	1320	1321	1343	1351
27	Cassis • d.	0558	0630	0658	0730	0758	0830	0858	0930	0957	1029	1030	1058	1059	1129	1130	1155	1158	1228	1229	1259	1328	1329	1351	1359
37	La Ciotat d.	0605	0637	0705	0738	0805	0837	0905	0937	1004	1036	1037	1105	1106	1136	1137	1203	1205	1235	1236	1306	1335	1336	1358	1406
51	Bandol d.	0617	0649	0717	0749	0817	0849	0917	0949	1016	1047	1048	1117	1118	1148	1149	1215	1216	1247	1248	1318	1347	1348	1410	1417
67	**Toulon** **361** a.	0630	0702	0730	0803	0830	0903	0930	1003	1030	1101	1102	1131	1134	1202	1202	1230	1231	1301	1302	1333	1400	1402	1423	1432
67	**Toulon** d.	0633	0705	0733	...	0833	...	0933	...	1033	1104	...	1134	...	...	1205	1232	...	1304	...	...	1403	...	1425	...
87	**Hyères** a.	0657	0728	0757	...	0857	...	0957	...	1056	1127	...	1157	...	...	1227	1257	...	1327	...	...	1427	...	1447	...

	◧	◧	Ⓒ	Ⓐ		Ⓐ	Ⓒ		Ⓐ	Ⓐ	Ⓐ		Ⓐ	Ⓐ	Ⓒ	Ⓐ		Ⓐ		Ⓐ				F	G
Marseille St Charles **361** d.	1407	1434	1504	1505	1535	1605	1607	1635	1645	1707	1715	1735	1745	1805	1807	1811	1836	1907	1936	2007	2035	...	2136	2236	2336
Aubagne d.	1422	1449	1519	1520	1550	1620	1622	1650	1702	1722	1731	1750	1802	1820	1822	1826	1854	1922	1951	2022	2050	...	2151	2255	2356
Cassis • d.	1430	1457	1527	1528	1558	1628	1630	1658	|	1729	|	1757	|	1828	1830	1834	|	1930	1959	2030	2058	...	2159	2303	0005
La Ciotat d.	1437	1504	1534	1535	1605	1635	1637	1705	1716	1736	1745	1805	1816	1835	1837	1842	1908	1938	2006	2038	2105	...	2206	2310	0012
Bandol d.	1449	1516	1546	1547	1617	1647	1648	1717	|	1748	|	1816	|	1847	1848	1853	1920	1949	2018	2049	2117	...	2218	2322	0025
Toulon **361** a.	1504	1530	1600	1600	1630	1700	1702	1731	1736	1801	1805	1830	1836	1901	1902	1907	1931	2003	2031	2103	2130	...	2232	2336	0040
Toulon d.	...	1533	*1605*h	1603	1633	1703	*1705*h	1734	...	1804	...	1833	...	1904	...	...	1934	...	2033	...	2133	...	...	...	...
Hyères a.	...	1557	*1627*h	1627	1657	1726	*1727*h	1757	...	1827	...	1857	...	1927	...	...	1957	...	2057	...	2157	...	...	...	...

	Ⓐ			Ⓐ	Ⓐ	Ⓐ		Ⓐ	Ⓐ	Ⓐ◇		Ⓐ				Ⓒ	Ⓒ	Ⓒ	Ⓐ	Ⓐ	Ⓒ	Ⓒ	Ⓐ	Ⓐ	Ⓒ
Hyères d.	...	...	...	...	0602	...	0632	...	0705	...	0732	0802	0832	...	0932	...	1031	...	1104	...	1132	...	1202	...	1232
Toulon a.	...	...	...	...	0624	...	0653	...	0727	...	0755	0824	0855	...	0954	...	1053	...	1126	...	1153	...	1224	...	1255
Toulon **361** d.	0530	...	0556	0624	0627	0651	0656	0725	0730	0754	0758	0827	0857	0927	0957	1027	1056	1127	1129	1156	1156	1226	1227	1256	1258
Bandol d.	0545	...	0611	|	0643	|	0712	|	0746	|	0814	0843	0913	0942	1013	1042	1112	1142	1144	1211	1212	1243	1243	1311	1314
La Ciotat d.	0556	...	0623	0645	0655	0713	0723	0746	0757	0815	0825	0855	0925	0954	1025	1054	1124	1154	1156	1223	1224	1254	1255	1323	1325
Cassis • d.	0604	...	0631	|	0702	|	0731	|	0805	|	0833	0903	0933	1002	1032	1101	1131	1201	1203	1231	1231	1302	1302	1331	1333
Aubagne d.	0611	...	0638	0658	0710	0726	0738	0759	0812	0828	0840	0911	0941	1009	1040	1109	1139	1209	1211	1238	1239	1310	1310	1338	1340
Marseille St Charles **361** a.	0626	...	0653	0715	0724	0741	0753	0814	0827	0843	0855	0925	0955	1024	1054	1124	1154	1224	1226	1253	1255	1324	1324	1353	1355

	Ⓒ	Ⓐ			Ⓐ		D	Ⓐ E	Ⓐ		Ⓒ	Ⓐ	Ⓒ h		Ⓐ	Ⓒ h		Ⓐ						F	G
Hyères d.	...	1302	...	1402	...	...	1528	1532	...	1631	...	1704	1704	1732	1758	1804	1831	...	1932	...	2032	...	2127	...	...
Toulon a.	...	1324	...	1424	...	...	1553	1554	...	1653	...	1727	1727	1754	1819	1826	1853	...	1954	...	2054	...	2149	...	...
Toulon **361** d.	1327	1327	1356	1427	1450	1526	1556	1557	1626	1656	1727	1730	...	1757	1821	...	1856	1927	1957	...	2057	...	2152	2227	2327
Bandol d.	1342	1343	1411	1443	1505	1541	1612	1612	1642	1712	1742	1745	...	1813	1836	...	1912	1942	2013	...	2112	...	2208	2242	2342
La Ciotat d.	1354	1354	1423	1454	1517	1553	1623	1624	1654	1723	1754	1757	...	1824	1847	...	1923	1954	2024	...	2123	...	2219	2254	2354
Cassis • d.	1401	1402	1431	1502	1524	1600	1631	1632	1702	1731	1802	1804	...	1831	1900	...	1931	2002	2031	...	2131	...	2227	2301	0001
Aubagne d.	1409	1409	1438	1509	1532	1608	1639	1639	1709	1738	1809	1812	...	1839	1908	...	1938	2009	2039	...	2138	...	2234	2309	0009
Marseille St Charles **361** a.	1424	1424	1453	1524	1554	1624	1653	1654	1724	1753	1824	1826	...	1853	1924	...	1953	2024	2053	...	2153	...	2253	2324	0024

D – Daily to July 6; Ⓒ July 12 - Aug. 24; daily from Aug. 29.
E – July 7 - Aug. 28.
F – ⑤⑥ (daily June 20 - Sept. 6).
G – ⑥ (Ⓒ July 5 - Aug. 31).
h – July 5 - Aug. 31.
◧ – Timings may vary by up to 3 minutes on Ⓐ July 7 - Aug. 29.
• – Cassis station is located 4 km from Cassis town.
◇ – From Les Arcs Draguignan (Table **361**).

European Rail Timetable Subscription

Keep up to date with the latest changes to European rail schedules with a subscription.

See page 12 for details of our various subscription options

Order on-line at **www.europeanrailtimetable.eu**

✆ +44 (0) 1832 270198 (Monday to Friday 1000 – 1600)

361 LES ARCS-DRAGUIGNAN and GRASSE - CANNES - NICE - MONACO - VENTIMIGLIA

See Table **362** for fast *TER* services Marseille - Toulon - Nice and *Intercités de Nuit* overnight service from Paris. See Table **350** for long-distance *TGV* services.

km		⑦			①–⑤ m					①–⑤ m														
0	**Les Arcs-Draguignan** d.	...	...	...	...	...	...	...	...	0559	...	...	...	0655	...	...	...	0759	...	0827	...	...	...	0927
23	Fréjus d.	...	...	...	...	...	...	...	...	0612	...	...	...	0708	...	...	...	0812	...	0841	...	...	...	0940
26	St Raphaël-Valescure d.	...	...	...	...	...	...	...	...	0616	...	...	...	0712	...	...	...	0817	...	0845	...	...	...	0944
30	Boulouris sur Mer d.	...	...	...	...	...	...	...	...	0620	...	...	...	0716	...	...	...	0821	...	0849	...	...	...	0948
50	Mandelieu-la-Napoule d.	...	...	...	...	...	...	...	...	0643	...	...	...	0742	...	...	...	0846	...	0914	...	...	...	1013
	Grasse d.	0009	...	...	...	...	...	...	...	|	0639	...	0709	|	0739	...	0809	|	0839	|	0909	...	0939	|
58	**Cannes** d.	0037	...	...	0537	0610	0623	0640	0653	0653	0710	0722	0740	0751	0811	0824	0839	0854	0911	0923	0939	0952	1011	1023
67	Juan les Pins d.	0049	...	...	0549	0622	0633	0652	0703	0703	0721	0732	0749	0802	0821	0832	0850	0902	0920	0934	0951	1004	1020	1033
69	Antibes d.	0053	...	...	0552	0625	0636	0655	0706	0706	0724	0736	0753	0805	0824	0835	0853	0905	0924	0937	0954	1007	1024	1036
78	Cagnes sur Mer d.	0104	...	...	0603	0634	0645	0704	0715	0715	0733	0744	0802	0814	0833	0844	0902	0914	0933	0945	1003	1015	1033	1045
84	Nice St Augustin ✈ ⊡ d.	0115	...	...	0613	0642	0655	0712	0725	0725	0741	0754	0810	0824	0841	0854	0910	0924	0941	0956	1011	1025	1041	1055
89	**Nice** Ville a.	0120	...	...	0619	0648	0700	0718	0731	0731	0747	0800	0816	0831	0847	0900	0916	0931	0947	1001	1017	1030	1047	1100
	Nice Ville d.	0123	...	0550	0622	0651	0703	0721	0734	0734	0750	0803	0819	0834	0850	0903	0919	0934	0950	1004	1020	1033	1050	1103
94	Villefranche sur Mer d.	0131	...	0557	0630	0659	0711	0728	0741	0741	0758	0810	0827	0842	0858	0911	0927	0941	0958	1012	1028	1041	1058	1111
96	Beaulieu sur Mer d.	0135	...	0601	0633	0702	0714	0732	0745	0745	0801	0814	0830	0845	0901	0914	0930	0945	1001	1015	1031	1044	1101	1114
99	Eze d.	0139	...	0604	0637	0706	0718	0735	0748	0748	0805	0817	0834	0848	0905	0918	0934	0949	1005	1019	1035	1048	1105	1118
105	**Monaco-Monte Carlo** d.	0150	...	0616	0648	0717	0730	0747	0800	0800	0816	0829	0846	0900	0916	0929	0946	1000	1016	1029	1046	1100	1116	1130
109	Cap Martin-Roquebrune d.	0155	...	0621	0653	0722	0735	0752	0805	0805	0821	0834	0851	0905	0921	0934	0951	1005	1021	1034	1051	1105	1121	1134
114	Menton d.	0202	...	0629	0700	0729	0741	0759	0811	0811	0828	0840	0859	0911	0929	0941	0959	1011	1029	1040	1059	1111	1129	1141
124	**Ventimiglia** a.	0217	...	0643	...	0743	...	0813	...	...	0843	...	0913	...	0943	...	1013	...	1043	...	1113	...	1143	...

		①–⑤	⑥⑦	⑥⑦	⑥⑦	⑥⑦	①–⑤	⑥⑦	⑥⑦	①–⑤												⑥⑦	
Les Arcs-Draguignan d.	...	...	...	...	1027	...	...	...	...	...	1127	...	...	...	1229	...	...	...	1326	...	...	...	...	1426
Fréjus d.	...	...	...	...	1040	...	...	...	...	...	1140	...	...	...	1242	...	...	...	1339	...	...	...	...	1439
St Raphaël-Valescure d.	...	...	...	...	1043	...	...	...	...	...	1143	...	...	...	1246	...	...	...	1342	...	...	...	...	1442
Boulouris sur Mer d.	...	...	...	...	1047	...	...	...	...	...	1147	...	...	...	1250	...	...	...	1346	...	...	...	...	1446
Mandelieu-la-Napoule d.	...	...	...	...	1112	...	...	...	...	...	1212	...	...	...	1315	...	...	...	1412	...	...	...	...	1511
Grasse d.	1009	...	...	1039	|	1109	...	...	1139	...	|	1209	...	1239	|	1309	...	1339	|	1409	...	...	1439	|
Cannes d.	1041	1051	1051	1111	1122	1139	...	1152	1211	1212	1222	1241	1251	1311	1324	1341	1354	1410	1422	1439	1454	1510	1510	1521
Juan les Pins d.	1050	1101	1101	1120	1132	1151	...	1202	1221	1222	1229	1251	1301	1321	1335	1350	1404	1421	1429	1451	1501	1521	1521	1530
Antibes d.	1054	1105	1105	1124	1135	1154	...	1205	1224	1225	1233	1254	1304	1324	1338	1354	1407	1424	1432	1454	1508	1524	1524	1534
Cagnes sur Mer d.	1102	1113	1113	1133	1144	1203	...	1214	1233	1234	1241	1303	1313	1333	1346	1402	1416	1433	1441	1503	1513	1533	1533	1542
Nice St Augustin ✈ ⊡ d.	1110	1123	1123	1141	1154	1211	...	1224	1241	1242	1252	1311	1323	1341	1357	1411	1426	1441	1451	1511	1524	1541	1541	1553
Nice Ville a.	1116	1129	1129	1147	1159	1217	...	1229	1247	1247	1257	1317	1329	1347	1402	1416	1432	1446	1457	1517	1531	1547	1547	1559
Nice Ville d.	1119	...	1132	1150	1202	1220	1225	1232	1250	1250	1300	1320	1332	1350	1405	1419	1435	1449	1500	1520	1534	1550	1550	1602
Villefranche sur Mer d.	1127	...	1140	1158	1209	1228	1232	1240	1258	1258	1308	1328	1340	1358	1413	1427	1443	1458	1509	1528	1541	1558	1558	1610
Beaulieu sur Mer d.	1130	...	1143	1201	1213	1231	1236	1243	1301	1301	1311	1331	1343	1401	1416	1430	1446	1501	1513	1532	1545	1601	1601	1613
Eze d.	1134	...	1146	1205	1216	1235	1239	1247	1305	1305	1315	1335	1347	1405	1420	1434	1450	1505	1516	1535	1548	1605	1605	1616
Monaco-Monte Carlo d.	1145	...	1158	1216	1228	1246	1251	1259	1317	1317	1326	1346	1359	1416	1431	1446	1501	1516	1528	1547	1600	1616	1616	1628
Cap Martin-Roquebrune d.	1150	...	1203	1221	1233	1251	1256	1304	1322	1322	1331	1351	1404	1421	1436	1451	1506	1521	1533	1552	1605	1621	1621	1633
Menton d.	1159	...	1208	1229	1238	1258	1304	1310	1330	1330	1337	1400	1410	1429	1442	1459	1512	1528	1539	1600	1611	1628	1628	1639
Ventimiglia a.	1213	...	...	1243	...	1313	1321	...	1344	1344	...	1414	...	1444	...	1513	...	1543	...	1614	...	1643	1643	...

																				B	A	A	D
Les Arcs-Draguignan d.	...	...	...	1527e	...	...	...	1627	...	...	...	1727	...	...	...	1825	...	...	...	1926	...	...	...	...
Fréjus d.	...	...	...	1540e	...	...	...	1640	...	...	...	1740	...	...	...	1838	...	...	...	1939	...	...	...	...
St Raphaël-Valescure d.	...	...	...	1544e	...	...	...	1644	...	...	...	1743	...	...	...	1842	...	...	...	1942	...	...	...	...
Boulouris sur Mer d.	...	...	...	1548e	...	...	...	1648	...	...	...	1747	...	...	...	1846	...	...	...	1947	...	...	...	...
Mandelieu-la-Napoule d.	...	...	...	1613	...	...	...	1713	...	...	...	1812	...	...	...	1911	...	...	...	2012	...	...	...	...
Grasse d.	1509	...	1539	|	1609	...	1639	|	1709	...	1739	|	1809	...	1839	|	1909	...	1939	|	2009	2009	...	...
Cannes d.	1539	1551	1609	1623	1641	1652	1711	1723	1739	1754	1811	1822	1838	1852	1910	1921	1939	1952	2010	2021	2038	2038	...	2048
Juan les Pins d.	1551	1601	1620	1630	1651	1703	1722	1733	1751	1801	1820	1832	1850	1902	1922	1931	1950	2002	2020	2032	2047	2050	...	2058
Antibes d.	1554	1605	1623	1634	1654	1706	1726	1737	1754	1804	1824	1836	1854	1905	1925	1934	1954	2006	2023	2035	2051	2054	...	2101
Cagnes sur Mer d.	1603	1613	1631	1642	1703	1715	1734	1745	1803	1813	1833	1844	1902	1914	1934	1943	2002	2015	2032	2044	2059	2102	...	2110
Nice St Augustin ✈ ⊡ d.	1612	1624	1640	1653	1711	1725	1742	1755	1811	1823	1841	1854	1911	1925	1942	1953	2011	2025	2040	2054	2108	2109	...	2119
Nice Ville a.	1618	1629	1645	1658	1717	1730	1747	1801	1817	1831	1847	1900	1916	1931	1948	1959	2016	2031	2046	2059	2113	2114	...	2125
Nice Ville d.	1621	1632	1648	1701	1720	1733	1750	1804	1820	1834	1850	1903	1919	1934	1951	2002	2019	2034f	2049	2102f	...	2116	...	2133
Villefranche sur Mer d.	1630	1640	1656	1709	1728	1741	1758	1811	1828	1842	1858	1910	1927	1943	1958	2009	2027	2043f	2056	2110f	...	2124	...	2141
Beaulieu sur Mer d.	1633	1643	1700	1713	1731	1744	1801	1815	1831	1845	1901	1914	1930	1947	2002	2013	2031	2047f	2100	2113f	...	2127	...	2144
Eze d.	1636	1647	1703	1716	1735	1748	1805	1818	1835	1848	1905	1917	1934	1950	2005	2016	2034	2050f	2103	2117f	...	2130	...	2148
Monaco-Monte Carlo d.	1648	1659	1715	1728	1746	1759	1817	1830	1846	1900	1917	1929	1945	2002	2017	2028	2046	2102f	2115	2129f	...	2139	2150	2200
Cap Martin-Roquebrune d.	1653	1704	1721	1733	1751	1804	1822	1835	1851	1905	1922	1934	1950	2007	2022	2033	2051	2107f	2120f	2134f	...	...	2154	2205
Menton d.	1700	1710	1729	1740	1800	1810	1829	1841	1859	1911	1929	1940	1957	2013	2029	2039	2058	2119f	2127f	2140f	...	...	2201	2212
Ventimiglia a.	1714	...	1743	...	1814	...	1843	...	1913	...	1943	...	2013	...	2043	...	2113	...	2144f	...	...	...	2222	...

	⑦–④ E	B 🚌	⑤–⑦	①–④ n	①–④	⑤–⑦	⑦ Ct	①–④ Cr	⑤⑥	⑦–④ p 🚌	⑦–④ 🚌	⑤–⑦ u	①–④ E	⑥	G	F	⑥ z	①–④ H	⑤	⑥ w	⑥	⑤	⑥	L
Les Arcs-Draguignan d.	...	...	...	...	2032	2032	...	...	...	...	...	...	2125	...	...	2152	2152	2230	2230	2230	...	...	2327	2328
Fréjus d.	...	...	...	...	2045	2045	...	...	...	...	...	...	2138	...	...	2205	2205	2243	2243	2243	...	...	2340	2340
St Raphaël-Valescure d.	...	...	...	...	2049	2049	...	...	...	...	...	...	2142	...	...	2209	2209	2248	2248	2248	...	...	2343	2344
Boulouris sur Mer d.	...	...	...	...	2053	2053	...	...	...	...	...	...	2146	...	...	2213	2213	2252	2252	2252	...	...	2347	2348
Mandelieu-la-Napoule d.	...	...	...	...	|	|	...	...	...	...	...	...	2211	...	...	2238	2238	2317	2317	2317	...	...	0012	0013
Grasse d.	...	...	2035	2051	|	|	2109	2109	2109	...	...	2139	|	2209	2209	|	|	|	|	|	2309	2309	|	|
Cannes d.	...	...	2115	2114	2122	2123	2141	2143	2141	...	...	2206	2219	2239	2239	2248	2248	2325	2327	2327	2339	2341	0022	0021
Juan les Pins d.	...	...	2124	...	2130	2134	2151	2152	2151	...	...	...	...	2249	2251	2301v	2301	...	2339	2339	2351	2353	0035	...
Antibes d.	...	...	2128	...	2134	2137	2154	2156	2154	...	...	...	...	2252	2254	2304v	2304	...	2343	2342	2355	2357	0038	...
Cagnes sur Mer d.	...	...	2136	...	2142	2145	2203	2204	2203	...	...	...	...	2303	2305	2315v	2315	...	2353	2353	0006	0007	0049	...
Nice St Augustin ✈ ⊡ d.	...	...	2144	...	2153	2156	2211	2212	2211	...	...	...	...	2313	2315	2325v	2325	...	0004	0003	0016	0018	0058	...
Nice Ville a.	...	...	2150	...	2158	2201	2217	2218	2217	...	...	...	...	2318	2321	2331v	2331	...	0009	0008	0021	0023	0104	...
Nice Ville d.	2133	...	2153g	...	...	2204k	2220	2221	2220	...	...	...	...	2321	...	...	2334	...	...	0011	0024	...	0107	...
Villefranche sur Mer d.	2142	...	2201g	...	...	2212k	2228	2229	2228	...	...	...	...	2329	...	...	2342	...	...	0019	0032	...	0115	...
Beaulieu sur Mer d.	2145	...	2204g	...	...	2216k	2231	2232	2231	...	...	...	...	2333	...	...	2345	...	...	0022	0035	...	0118	...
Eze d.	|	...	2207g	...	...	2219k	2235	2236	2234	...	...	...	...	2336	...	...	2349	...	...	0026	0039	...	0122	...
Monaco-Monte Carlo d.	2156	2200	2219g	...	...	2229k	2246	2246	2245	2245	2315	...	...	2348	...	...	0000	...	...	0037	0050	...	0133	...
Cap Martin-Roquebrune d.	2201	|	2224g	...	...	2234k	2251	2252	2250	2300	2330	...	...	2352	...	...	0005	...	...	0042	0055	...	0138	...
Menton d.	2207	|	2231g	...	...	2240k	2257	2257	2257	2315	2345	...	...	2359	...	...	0011	...	...	0048	0102	...	0145	...
Ventimiglia a.	...	2250	2245g	...	...	...	...	...	2311	...	...	...	...	0013	...	...	...	...	...	...	0116	...	...	...

A – ⑤⑥ to June 28; daily June 30 - Sept. 14; ⑤–⑦ from Sept. 9.
B – ⑦–④ to June 29; ①–④ from Sept. 15.
C – June 30 - Sept. 7.
D – Daily to Sept. 6; ⑤⑥ from Sept. 12. Does not run Nice - Menton on ⑦–④ until June 26.
E – Until June 26.
F – ⑤ to June 27; ①–⑤ June 30 - Sept. 5; ⑧ from Sept. 8.
G – ⑧ June 27 - Aug. 17 (also June 20); ⑤⑦ Aug. 22 - Sept. 7; ⑤ from Sept. 12.
H – ①–④ from June 30 (also ⑦ from Sept. 14).
L – ⑤ to June 27; ⑤⑦ from July 4.

e – 5 minutes later on ⑤ July 11 - Aug. 29.
f – ⑤⑥ to June 21; daily from June 27.
g – ⑤⑥ to June 28; ⑤–⑦ from July 4.

k – ⑤⑥ to July 4; ⑥⑦ July 5 - Sept. 14; ⑤–⑦ from Sept. 19.
m – Not Aug. 15.
n – Not June 30 - Sept. 11.
p – Not June 30 - Sept. 7.
r – Not July 14.
t – Also July 14.
u – Not July 4.
v – Cannes - Nice on ⑤ (also ①–④ June 30 - Aug. 14).
w – Also ⑦ July 6 - Sept. 7.
z – Also ⑦ June 29 - Sept. 7.

⊡ – Situated approximately 800 metres from Nice ✈ terminal building.

VENTIMIGLIA - MONACO - NICE - CANNES - GRASSE and LES ARCS-DRAGUIGNAN 361

See Table **362** for fast *TER* services Nice - Toulon - Marseille and *Intercités de Nuit* overnight service to Paris. See Table **350** for long-distance *TGV* services.

km			⑦	⑦	⑦			①–⑤		⑥	⑧											⑥⑦			
	Ventimiglia	d.	...	0017	...	...	...	0515j	...	...	0547b	...	0617	...	0647	...	0717	...	0747	...	0817	0817	...	0847	...
	Menton	d.	0006	0036	0106	...	...	0535j	0552c	0606	0606	0622	0636	0652	0706	0721	0736	0751	0806	0820	0836	0836	0851	0907	0921
	Cap Martin-Roquebrune	d.	0012	0042	0112	...	...	0541j	0558c	0612	0613	0628	0642	0658	0712	0728	0743	0758	0813	0829	0843	0843	0858	0914	0928
	Monaco-Monte Carlo	d.	0020	0049	0120	...	...	0549j	0605c	0619	0620	0636	0650	0705	0720	0736	0750	0805	0820	0836	0850	0850	0906	0922	0936
	Eze	d.	0029	0058	0129	...	...	0558j	0614c	0628	0629	0645	0659	0715	0729	0745	0759	0815	0829	0845	0859	0859	0915	0931	0945
	Beaulieu sur Mer	d.	0032	0102	0133	...	...	0602j	0618c	0632	0633	0649	0702	0718	0732	0749	0803	0818	0833	0849	0903	0903	0919	0936	0949
	Villefranche sur Mer	d.	0035	0105	0136	...	...	0605j	0621c	0635	0636	0652	0706	0721	0735	0752	0806	0821	0836	0853	0906	0906	0922	0939	0952
	Nice Ville	a.	0043	0113	0144	...	...	0614j	0628c	0643	0643	0659	0713	0729	0742	0800	0813	0829	0844	0900	0913	0913	0929	0947	1000
	Nice Ville	d.	0046	0116	0147	...	0602	0617	0631	0646	0646	0702	0716	0732	0745	0803	0816	0832	0847	0903	0916	0916	0932	0950	1003
	Nice St Augustin ✈ ⊡	d.	0053	0122	0154	...	0608	0623	0638	0653	0653	0709	0722	0739	0752	0810	0822	0839	0853	0909	0923	0923	0939	0957	1009
	Cagnes sur Mer	d.	0102	0132	0204	...	0618	0632	0648	0700	0700	0718	0729	0748	0759	0819	0830	0848	0901	0919	0930	0930	0949	1004	1019
	Antibes	d.	0113	0142	0214	...	0626	0643	0656	0709	0709	0727	0738	0757	0808	0827	0838	0857	0910	0927	0939	0939	0957	1012	1027
	Juan les Pins	d.	0116	0146	0218	...	0629	0646	0659	0712	0712	0730	0741	0800	0811	0831	0841	0900	0913	0930	0942	0942	1001	1015	1030
0	**Cannes**	d.	0128	0157	0228	...	0637	0657	0709	0723	0724	0738	0753	0810	0823	0838	0853	0910	0925	0938	0952	0953	1010	1027	1038
17	Grasse	a.	|	0222	...	...	...	0724	|	0753	0753	...	0823	|	0853	...	0923	|	0953	...	...	1023	|	1053	...
	Mandelieu-la-Napoule	d.	0137	...	...	...	...	...	0718	...	...	...	...	0818	...	...	...	0919	...	...	...	...	1019	...	...
	Boulouris sur Mer	d.	0202	...	...	...	...	...	0743	...	...	...	...	0844	...	...	...	0944	...	...	...	...	1044	...	...
	St Raphaël-Valescure	d.	0206	...	...	...	...	...	0747	...	...	...	...	0848	...	...	...	0948	...	...	...	...	1048	...	...
	Fréjus	d.	0210	...	...	...	...	...	0751	...	...	...	...	0852	...	...	...	0952	...	...	...	...	1052	...	...
	Les Arcs-Draguignan	a.	0223	...	...	...	...	...	0803	...	...	...	...	0904	...	...	...	1005	...	...	...	...	1105	...	...

		①–⑤	⑥⑦		①–⑤	⑥⑦							⑥⑦	⑥⑦ ¶	⑥⑦		⑥⑦	⑥⑦	①–⑤						
Ventimiglia	d.	0909	0917	...	0947	0947	...	1017	...	1048	...	1117	...	1151	...	1218	1218	...	...	1248	...	1317	...	1348	...
Menton	d.	0929	0936	0951	1007	1006	1021	1036	1051	1107	1121	1136	1152	1210	1222	1237	1237	1251	1255	1307	1322	1337	1352	1407	1422
Cap Martin-Roquebrune	d.	0936	0943	0958	1013	1013	1029	1043	1057	1114	1128	1143	1158	1216	1229	1243	1243	1257	1301	1314	1330	1343	1358	1414	1428
Monaco-Monte Carlo	d.	0943	0950	1005	1020	1020	1036	1050	1105	1121	1136	1150	1205	1223	1236	1251	1251	1304	1308	1321	1337	1350	1405	1421	1436
Eze	d.	0952	0959	1015	1029	1029	1045	1059	1114	1130	1145	1159	1215	1232	1246	1300	1300	1313	1317	1330	1347	1359	1415	1430	1445
Beaulieu sur Mer	d.	0956	1003	1018	1033	1033	1049	1103	1117	1134	1149	1203	1218	1236	1250	1303	1303	1317	1321	1334	1352	1403	1418	1434	1449
Villefranche sur Mer	d.	0959	1006	1021	1036	1036	1052	1106	1120	1137	1152	1206	1222	1239	1253	1306	1306	1320	1324	1337	1355	1406	1421	1437	1452
Nice Ville	a.	1006	1013	1029	1043	1043	1100	1113	1128	1144	1159	1213	1228	1246	1301	1313	1313	1328	1332	1344	1403	1413	1429	1444	1500
Nice Ville	d.	1009	1016	1032	1046	1046	1103	1116	1131	1147	1202	1216	1231	1249	1304	...	1316	1331	1335	1347	1406	1416	1432	1447	1503
Nice St Augustin ✈ ⊡	d.	1016	1023	1039	1053	1053	1110	1122	1139	1154	1210	1223	1238	1256	1311	...	1323	1339	1341	1354	1413	1423	1439	1454	1509
Cagnes sur Mer	d.	1023	1030	1048	1100	1100	1119	1130	1148	1201	1219	1230	1247	1303	1321	...	1330	1348	1351	1401	1422	1430	1448	1501	1519
Antibes	d.	1032	1039	1057	1109	1109	1127	1138	1157	1209	1228	1239	1256	1312	1330	...	1339	1357	1359	1410	1431	1438	1457	1510	1527
Juan les Pins	d.	1035	1042	1100	1112	1112	1131	1141	1200	1213	1231	1242	1259	1315	1334	...	1342	1400	1402	1413	1434	1442	1500	1513	1530
Cannes	d.	1045	1053	1110	1122	1124	1138	1153	1210	1224	1239	1254	1308	1327	1342	...	1353	1410	1412	1425	1442	1453	1510	1525	1538
Grasse	a.	...	1123	|	...	1153	...	1223	|	1253	...	1323	|	1353	...	...	1423	|	|	1453	...	1523	|	1553	...
Mandelieu-la-Napoule	d.	...	...	1119	...	...	...	...	1219	...	...	...	1317	...	...	...	...	1418	1421	...	...	...	1519	...	...
Boulouris sur Mer	d.	...	...	1144	...	...	...	...	1244	...	...	...	1342	...	...	...	...	1444	1446	...	...	...	1544	...	...
St Raphaël-Valescure	d.	...	...	1148	...	...	...	...	1248	...	...	...	1346	...	...	...	...	1448	1450	...	...	...	1548	...	...
Fréjus	d.	...	...	1152	...	...	...	...	1252	...	...	...	1350	...	...	...	...	1452	1454	...	...	...	1552	...	...
Les Arcs-Draguignan	a.	...	...	1205	...	...	...	...	1305	...	...	...	1402	...	...	...	...	1505	1507	...	...	...	1605	...	...

					⊖																	①–④	⑤–⑦	♡	♡
Ventimiglia	d.	1419	...	1448	...	1518	...	1547	...	1618	...	1648	...	1718	...	1748	...	1818	...	1848	...	1909	1917	...	1948
Menton	d.	1437	1451	1507	1520	1537	1552	1606	1621	1637	1651	1707	1722	1737	1752	1807	1822	1837	1851	1907	1921	1930	1936	1949	2008
Cap Martin-Roquebrune	d.	1443	1457	1514	1528	1544	1558	1613	1628	1643	1658	1713	1729	1744	1758	1813	1829	1843	1857	1914	1927	1936	1943	1956	2014
Monaco-Monte Carlo	d.	1450	1504	1521	1536	1551	1605	1620	1636	1651	1705	1721	1736	1751	1805	1821	1836	1851	1904	1921	1934	1943	1950	2003	2022
Eze	d.	1459	1513	1530	1545	1600	1614	1629	1645	1700	1714	1730	1745	1800	1814	1830	1846	1900	1913	1930	1943	1952	1959	2013	2031
Beaulieu sur Mer	d.	1503	1517	1534	1549	1604	1618	1633	1649	1703	1718	1733	1749	1804	1818	1833	1850	1903	1917	1934	1947	1956	2003	2017	2035
Villefranche sur Mer	d.	1506	1520	1537	1552	1607	1621	1636	1652	1706	1721	1736	1752	1807	1821	1836	1853	1906	1920	1937	1950	1959	2006	2020	2038
Nice Ville	a.	1513	1528	1545	1559	1614	1628	1643	1659	1713	1729	1744	1800	1814	1829	1844	1901	1913	1927	1944	1957	2007	2013	2027	2045
Nice Ville	d.	1516	1531	1548	1602	1617	1631	1646	1702	1716	1732	1747	1803	1817	1832	1847	1904	1916	1930	1947	2000	2010	2016	2030	2048
Nice St Augustin ✈ ⊡	d.	1523	1539	1555	1610	1625	1639	1652	1709	1723	1739	1753	1810	1823	1839	1854	1910	1923	1937	1954	2007	2016	2022	2038	2055
Cagnes sur Mer	d.	1530	1548	1602	1620	1633	1648	1700	1718	1730	1748	1801	1819	1831	1848	1901	1919	1930	1947	2001	2016	2024	2030	2047	2103
Antibes	d.	1539	1557	1611	1629	1641	1657	1708	1727	1739	1757	1809	1827	1839	1857	1909	1928	1939	1955	2010	2025	2033	2038	2056	2112
Juan les Pins	d.	1542	1600	1614	1632	1644	1700	1711	1730	1742	1800	1812	1831	1842	1900	1913	1931	1942	1958	2013	2028	2036	2041	2059	2115
Cannes	d.	1553	1610	1626	1640	1655	1710	1723	1738	1754	1810	1824	1838	1853	1909	1924	1939	1954	2008	2025	2036	2046	2053	2109	2125
Grasse	a.	1623	|	1653	...	1723	|	1753	...	1823	|	1853	...	1923	|	1953	...	2023	|	2049y	...	...	2123	|	2154
Mandelieu-la-Napoule	d.	...	1619	...	...	...	1719	...	...	...	1818	...	...	...	1918	...	...	...	2017	...	...	...	...	2118	...
Boulouris sur Mer	d.	...	1644	...	...	...	1744	...	...	...	1844	...	...	...	1942	...	...	...	2042	...	...	...	...	2143	...
St Raphaël-Valescure	d.	...	1648	...	...	...	1748	...	...	...	1848	...	...	...	1947	...	...	...	2046	...	...	...	...	2148	...
Fréjus	d.	...	1652	...	...	...	1752	...	...	...	1852	...	...	...	1952	...	...	...	2050	...	...	...	...	2152	...
Les Arcs-Draguignan	a.	...	1705	...	...	...	1805	...	...	...	1905	...	...	...	2005	...	...	...	2103	...	...	...	...	2205	...

			⑤–⑦	①–④			①–④ J	K	M	N		⑤⑥	⑦–④	①–④ Q	⑥	①–④ P	⑧	⑤⑥	⑥	⑤	⑤⑥	⑤	⑥	⑦–④ 🚌	⑥
Ventimiglia	d.	...	2017	2018	...	2047	2047	2047	...	...	2109	...	...	...	2129	2129	2137	...	2216	2218	2235	...	...	...	2317
Menton	d.	2021	2036	2037	2045	2107	2107	2107	2112	2112	2129	...	...	2148	2154	2155	2201	2206	2235	2237	2254	2306	2306	...	2337
Cap Martin-Roquebrune	d.	2029	2043	2043	2051	2113	2113	2113	2120	2120	2135	...	...	2154	2200	2201	...	2212	2242	2243	2301	2312	2312	...	2343
Monaco-Monte Carlo	d.	2036	2050	2051	2058	2120	2120	2120	2127	2127	2140	2149	2150	2201	2208	2208	...	2220	2249	2251	2308	2319	2319	2330	2350
Eze	d.	2045	2059	2100	2107	2129	2129	2129	2140	2140	...	2158	2159	2210	2217	2217	...	2229	2258	2300	2318	2328	2328	2351	2359
Beaulieu sur Mer	d.	2049	2103	2103	2111	2138	2138	2138	2144	2144	...	2202	2203	2214	2220	2221	...	2232	2302	2303	2322	2332	2332	2359	0003
Villefranche sur Mer	d.	2052	2106	2106	2114	2142	2142	2142	2147	2147	...	2205	2206	2217	2223	2224	...	2236	2305	2307	2325	2335	2335	0009	0006
Nice Ville	a.	2100	2113	2114	2122	2149	2149	2149	2154	2154	...	2212	2213	2224	2230	2231	...	2243	2312	2314	2332	2342	2343	0043	0013
Nice Ville	d.	2103	2116	2117	2125	...	2152	2151	...	2157	...	2215	...	...	...	2234	...	2246	2315	2317	...	2345	2346	...	0016
Nice St Augustin ✈ ⊡	d.	2109	2123	2124	2132	...	2159	2157	...	2204	...	2222	...	...	...	2241	...	2253	2322	2324	...	2352	2352	...	0023
Cagnes sur Mer	d.	2119	2131	2131	2141	...	2206	2205	...	2214	...	2229	...	...	...	2248	...	2302	2331	2333	...	0001	0002	...	0032
Antibes	d.	2127	2139	2139	2150	...	2215	2213	...	2223	...	2238	...	...	...	2257	...	2313	2342	2344	...	0012	0012	...	0043
Juan les Pins	d.	2130	2142	2143	2153	...	2218	2216	...	2226	...	2241	...	...	...	2300	...	2316	2345	2347	...	0015	0016	...	0046
Cannes	d.	2138	2154	2152	2202	...	2227	2227	...	2234	...	2253	...	...	...	2322	...	2328	2357	2356	...	0025	0027	...	0058
Grasse	a.	...	2223h	...	|	...	...	2253	...	...	...	2323	...	...	...	...	...	|	0023	...	...	...	|	...	0123
Mandelieu-la-Napoule	d.	...	...	...	|	...	...	...	...	...	...	...	...	...	...	...	...	2336	...	...	...	...	0035	...	...
Boulouris sur Mer	d.	...	...	...	2238	...	...	...	...	...	...	...	...	...	...	...	...	2358	...	...	...	...	0101	...	...
St Raphaël-Valescure	d.	...	...	...	2242	...	...	...	...	...	...	...	...	...	...	...	...	0002	...	...	...	...	0105	...	...
Fréjus	d.	...	...	...	2246	...	...	...	...	...	...	...	...	...	...	...	...	0006	...	...	...	...	0109	...	...
Les Arcs-Draguignan	a.	...	...	...	2300	...	...	...	...	...	...	...	...	...	...	...	...	0018	...	...	...	...	0121	...	...

J – ①–④ June 30 - Sept. 4 (also Nov. 11).
K – ⑤–⑦ to Sept. 7; ⑤⑥ from Sept. 12. Terminates at Cannes on ⑦ until June 22.
M – ⑤⑥ to June 28; daily June 30 - Sept. 28; ⑤–⑦ from Oct. 3.
N – ⑤⑥ (daily June 30 - Sept. 6).
P – ①–④ June 30 - Sept. 11. Terminates at Nice Ville Sept. 8 – 11.
Q – From Sept. 29.

b – ⑦ to June 22; ⑧ from June 29.
c – ⑥⑦ to June 22; daily from June 28.
h – ⑤⑥ to June 21; ⑤–⑦ from June 27.
j – From June 30.
y – ①–⑥ (daily June 30 - Sept. 13).

♡ – Terminates at Cannes on ⑦–④ until June 26.
⊖ – Runs 2 – 5 minutes earlier on ⑦ July 6 - Aug. 31 (also July 14).
¶ – Runs daily Cannes - Grasse.
⊡ – Situated approximately 800 metres from Nice ✈ terminal building.

362 MARSEILLE - NICE

TER and Intercités de Nuit

SERVICE FROM JUNE 29. See Table **350** for long-distance *TGV* services. See Table **361** for *TER* local services Les Arcs-Draguignan - Cannes - Nice - Monaco - Ventimiglia and v.v.
Minor timing variations are possible on certain dates.

km			5781 ★												⑥D	B		E	A	⑤⑥				
	Paris Austerlitz	d.	...	2056n	...	...	...	...	...	...	...	...	...	...	...	...	...	...	...	...	...	...	...	...	...
0	**Marseille** St Charles ... 360	d.	0557	0633b	0657	0757	0855	0955	1058	1157	1257	1355	1457	1557	1657	1755	1755	1857	1955	2057	2157	...	...	...	...
67	**Toulon** ... 360	d.	0643	0712	0743	0843	0943	1042	1143	1242	1342	1441	1543	1643	1743	1842	1843	1944	2043	2143	2243	...	...	...	...
135	Les Arcs-Draguignan	d.	0724	0752	0821	0922	1021	1123	1222	1320	1421	1520	1623	1721	1821	1921	1921	2026	2121	2224	2319	...	...	...	...
161	St Raphaël-Valescure	d.	0741	0808	0837	0939	1038	1139	1238	1337	1438	1536	1640	1738	1838	1936	1938	2043	2138	2241	2335	...	...	...	...
193	**Cannes**	d.	0807	0832	0905	1005	1105	1205	1307	1405	1505	1605	1708	1806	1905	2007	2007	2109	2205	2306	0000	...	...	...	...
204	Antibes	d.	0818	0843	0917	1017	1117	1216	1317	1417	1517	1617	1719	1817	1917	2017	2017	2121	2216	2318	0012	...	...	...	...
219	Nice St Augustin ✈ ⊡	d.	0830	|	0931	1030	1130	1230	1330	1430	1530	1630	1731	1830	1931	2031	2031	2133	2228	2331	0028	...	...	...	...
224	**Nice** Ville	a.	0838	0909	0938	1038	1137	1237	1341	1437	1537	1637	1738	1838	1937	2037	2037	2139	2234	2337	0034	...	...	...	...

		Ⓐ	⑥	①–⑤																5772 ★				⑥k	G
Nice Ville	d.	...	...	0531t	...	...	0625	0725	0825	0925	1025	1125	1224	1324	1422	1525	1613	1725	1824	1900	1922	2022	...	2110	2130
Nice St Augustin ✈ ⊡	d.	...	...	0538t	...	...	0632	0733	0833	0933	1033	1133	1233	1333	1432	1533	1620	1733	1833	|	1931	2032	...	2117	2140
Antibes	d.	...	...	0550	...	...	0649	0748	0848	0947	1049	1147	1249	1347	1449	1549	1636	1747	1849	1918	1947	2049	...	2135	2157
Cannes	d.	...	...	0602	...	...	0701	0800	0901	1001	1102	1159	1302	1359	1501	1601	1648	1800	1901	1930	2001	2101	...	2146	2210
St Raphaël-Valescure	d.	...	...	0626	...	...	0724	0824	0925	1024	1125	1223	1325	1423	1524	1625	1713	1823	1925	1954	2024	2125	...	2209	2249
Les Arcs-Draguignan	d.	0604	0604	0643	0657	...	0740	0841	0940	1040	1140	1240	1340	1439	1539	1642	1731	1839	1942	2011	2041	2142	...	2225	2306
Toulon	a.	0705	0705	0718	0805	...	0817	0916	1015	1119	1215	1315	1415	1518	1615	1717	1809	1918	2017	2049	2119	2218	...	2258	2342
Marseille St Charles	a.	0814	...	0803	...	...	0903	1003	1107	1203	1303	1401	1503	1603	1703	1803	1903	2003	2103	2132b	2204	2303	...	2341	0028
Paris Austerlitz	a.	...	...	...	...	...	...	...	...	...	...	...	...	...	...	...	...	...	...	0753p	...	...	...	...	...

A – Daily until Aug. 17; ⑤–⑦ Aug. 22 - Sept. 7; ⑤⑥ from Sept. 12 (also Nov. 11).
B – Ⓑ to Aug. 29 (not Aug. 15); daily from Aug. 31.
D – ⑥ July 5 - Aug. 30 (also Aug. 15).
E – Daily to Sept. 13; ⑤⑥ Sept. 19 - Nov. 15 (also Nov. 11); daily from Nov. 21.
G – Runs on Oct. 11 only.

b – Marseille **Blancarde**.
k – Also Aug. 15; not Oct. 11, Nov. 8, 15, 22, Dec. 13.

n – Departure time varies (from 2056 to 2125).
p – Arrival time varies (from 0655 to 0905).
t – 3 minutes earlier Oct. 20 - Nov. 14.

★ – Conveys 🛏 1, 2 cl. and (2) (reclining). Ⓡ. For overnight journeys only. **Sample timings shown – subject to frequent variations.** For confirmed timings, please consult the SNCF journey planner: www.sncf-connect.com.
⊡ – Situated approximately 800 metres from Nice ✈ terminal building.

363 BELLEGARDE and GENÈVE - ANNEMASSE - ÉVIAN LES BAINS

See Table **346** for connecting trains Lyon Part Dieu - Bellegarde and v.v. French holiday dates apply.
Services from mid-morning to mid-afternoon may be subject to alteration on Nov. 3–7, 10, 12–14.

km				🚌 ⑥⑦				①–⑤	①–⑤			①–⑤			Ⓑ	⑥⑦	①–⑤	🚌 ①–⑤		Ⓒ	🚌 Ⓐ	Ⓑ				
	Paris Gare de Lyon **341**	d.	...	...	...	...	...	...	...	...	...	...	...	...	...	...	...	...	...	...	...	...	...	...	...	...
	Bellegarde ... **365**	d.	...	...	...	...	0615	...	0715	...	...	...	...	0815	0915	...	...	...	...	1015	1015	1115	...	...	1215	...
0	**Genève** ... **365** ‡	d.	0001	...	...	0631	|	0701	|	0731	0801	...	0831	|	|	0931	0931	...	1031	|	|	|	1131	1231	|	1331
9	Genève Eaux Vives **365** ‡	d.	0017	...	...	0647	|	0717	|	0747	0817	...	0847	|	|	0947	0947	...	1047	|	|	|	1147	1247	|	1347
17	Annemasse ... **365** ‡	a.	0025	...	...	0655	0655	0725	0755	0755	0825	...	0855	0855	0955	0955	0955	...	1055	1055	1105	1155	1155	1255	1255	1355
17	Annemasse	d.	...	0035	...	...	0701	0731	...	0801	...	0831	...	0901	...	1001	1001	...	...	1101	1105	...	1201	...	1301	1401
47	Thonon les Bains	d.	...	0120	...	...	0730	0800	...	0830	...	0906	...	0930	...	1030	1029	1039	...	1130	1150	...	1230	...	1330	1430
56	**Évian les Bains**	a.	...	0140	...	...	0739	0809	...	0839	...	0914	...	0939	...	1039	...	1059	...	1139	1210	...	1239	...	1339	1439

		TGV 6503 ⑦ A	*TGV* 6503 ⑥ k	*TGV* 6503 C						①–⑤			①–⑤			①–⑤										🚌 ⑤ f
Paris Gare de Lyon **341**	d.	1034	1045	1104	...	...	...	...	...	...	...	...	...	...	...	...	...	...	...	...	...	...	...	...	...	...
Bellegarde ... **365** ‡	d.	1338a	1330a	1348a	...	1415	...	...	1615	...	1715	...	...	...	1815	...	1915	...	...	2015	2115	...	...	2215	...	2315
Genève ... **365** ‡	d.	|	|	|	1431	|	1531	1631	|	1701	|	1731	1801	1831	|	1901	|	1931	2031	|	|	2131	2231	|	2331	|
Genève Eaux Vives **365** ‡	d.	|	|	|	1447	|	1547	1647	|	1717	|	1747	1817	1847	|	1917	|	1947	2047	|	|	2147	2247	|	2347	|
Annemasse ... **365**	a.	1418	1421	1422	1455	1455	1555	1655	1655	1725	1755	1755	1825	1855	1855	1925	1955	1955	2055	2055	2155	2155	2255	2255	2355	0003
Annemasse	d.	|	|	|	...	1500	1601	...	1701	1731	...	1801	1831	...	1901	1931	...	2001	...	2101	...	2201	...	2301	...	0003
Thonon les Bains	d.	1504a	1507a	1507a	...	1530	1630	...	1730	1800	...	1830	1900	...	1930	2000	...	2030	...	2130	...	2230	...	2330	...	0048
Évian les Bains	a.	1515	1518	1518	...	1539	1639	...	1739	1809	...	1839	1909	...	1939	2009	...	2039	...	2139	...	2239	...	2339	...	0108

		①–⑥		①–⑤			①–⑤			①–⑤					Ⓒ	Ⓐ		🚌 ①–⑤	⑥⑦			①–⑤				⑥⑦
Évian-les-Bains	d.	0521	...	0551	0621	...	0648	0721	...	0751	0821	...	...	0921	1021	1021	...	1044	1121	...	...	...	...	1221	...	1251
Thonon-les-Bains	d.	0530	...	0600	0630	...	0700	0730	...	0800	0830	...	...	0930	1030	1030	...	1104	1130	...	...	1141	...	1230	...	1300
Annemasse	a.	0559	...	0629	0659	...	0729	0759	...	0829	0859	...	...	0959	1059	1059	...	1150	1159	...	...	1214	...	1259	...	1329
Annemasse ... **365** ‡	d.	0605	0605	0635	0705	0705	0735	0805	0805	0835	0905	0905	...	1005	1105	1112	1105	1150	1205	1205	1205	...	1220	1305	1305	1335
Genève Eaux Vives **365** ‡	d.	0613	|	0643	|	0713	0743	0813	|	0843	|	0913	...	1013	|	|	1113	|	1213	1213	|	...	1228	|	1313	1343
Genève ... **365** ‡	a.	0628	|	0658	|	0728	0758	0828	|	0858	|	0928	...	1028	|	|	1128	|	1228	1228	|	...	1243	|	1328	1358
Bellegarde ... **365**	a.	...	0642	...	0742	...	...	...	0842	...	0942	...	...	...	1142	1157	...	1240	...	...	1244	...	...	1342	...	...
Paris Gare de Lyon **341**	a.	...	...	...	...	...	...	...	...	...	...	...	...	...	...	...	...	...	...	...	...	...	...	...	...	...

		①–⑤	Ⓑ	*TGV* 6504 ⑦ e	Ⓐ	Ⓒ			Ⓑ			*TGV* 6506 ⑦ e	*TGV* 6506 ⑥ A	①–⑤	①–⑤	①–⑤	①–⑥								Ⓑ	
Évian-les-Bains	d.	1321	...	1341	1421	1421	...	1521	...	1621	...	1644	1701	1651	1721	...	1751	1821	...	1921	...	2021	...	...	2151	...
Thonon-les-Bains	d.	1330	...	1352	1430	1430	...	1530	...	1630	...	1655	1712	1700	1730	...	1800	1830	...	1930	...	2030	...	...	2200	...
Annemasse	a.	1359	...	|	1459	1459	...	1559	...	1659	...	|	|	1729	1759	...	1829	1859	...	1959	...	2059	...	...	2229	...
Annemasse ... **365** ‡	d.	1405	1405	1427	...	1505	1505	1605	1605	1705	1705	1724	1758	1735	1805	1805	1835	1905	1905	2005	2005	2105	2105	...	...	2235
Genève Eaux Vives **365** ‡	d.	1413	|	|	...	|	1513	1613	|	|	1713	|	|	1743	1813	|	1843	|	1913	2013	|	|	2113	...	...	2243
Genève ... **365** ‡	a.	1428	|	|	...	|	1528	1628	|	|	1728	|	|	1758	1828	|	1858	|	1928	2028	|	|	2128	...	...	2258
Bellegarde ... **365**	a.	...	1442	1511d	...	1542r	...	...	1642	1742	...	1811d	1843d	...	...	1842	...	1942	...	...	2043	2142	...	...	...	...
Paris Gare de Lyon **341**	a.	...	...	1815	...	...	...	...	...	...	...	2119	2128	...	...	...	...	...	...	...	...	...	...	...	...	...

A – July 5 - Aug. 31.
C – Runs on Aug. 16, 23, 30 only.

a – Arrival time.
d – Departure time.
e – Also July 14, Nov. 11.
f – Also Aug. 14; not Aug. 15.

k – Also July 14, Aug. 15; not Aug. 16, 23, 30.
r – 1547 on public holidays.

TGV – High-speed train. Ⓡ. 🍷. Only for journeys from/to Paris. Timings may vary - please check your reservation.

‡ – Frequent additional services (every 15 minutes during the day) operate Genève - Annemasse and v.v.

GENÈVE and ANNECY - CHAMBÉRY - GRENOBLE - VALENCE 364

Subject to alteration on July 12, 13, 26, 27, Aug. 2, 3, 9, 10, 15, 16, Oct. 4, 5, Nov. 8, 9. Journeys from / to Annecy are subject to alteration July 16 – 18.

km		Ⓐ	①–⑥ b	Ⓐ	①–⑥ b		①–⑥ b	Ⓐ	①–⑥ b			Ⓒ	Ⓒ			Ⓒ						Ⓐ	a	Ⓑ c	Ⓐ
0	**Genève** ... **341 346** d.	...	...	...	...	...	...	...	0659	...	...	...	...	0959	...	...	...	1159	...	...	...	1459	...	...	...
33	Bellegarde ... **341 346** d.	...	...	...	...	...	...	...	0728	...	...	...	...	1028	...	...	...	1228	...	...	...	1528	...	...	...
66	Culoz ... **346** d.	...	...	...	...	...	...	...	|	...	...	...	...	|	...	...	...	|	...	...	...	|	...	...	...
	Annecy ... **341 345** d.	...	...	...	0543	...	0643	0725	|	0743	0843	0843	0943	|	1043	1143	...	|	1243	1343	1443	|	1543	1643	1718
88	Aix les Bains ... **341 345** d.	...	...	...	0626	...	0726	0803	0808	0826	0926	0926	1025	1106	1126	1226	...	1306	1326	1426	1526	1606	1626	1726	1759
102	**Chambéry** ... **341 345** a.	...	...	...	0637	...	0737	0814	0818	0837	0937	0937	...	1116	1137	1237	...	1317	1337	1437	1537	1617	1637	1737	1810
102	**Chambéry** ... d.	...	0540	*0557*n	0640	...	0740	...	0821	0840	...	0940	...	1119	1140	1240	1240	1320	1340	1440	1540	1620	1640	1740	...
116	Montmélian ... d.	...	0550	*0606*n	0650	...	0750	...	|	0850	...	0950	...	|	1150	1250	1250	|	1350	1450	1550	|	1650	1750	...
165	**Grenoble** ... a.	...	0627	*0651*n	0727	...	0827	...	0902	0927	...	1028	...	1202	1227	1327	1327	1402	1427	1527	1627	1702	1727	1827	...
165	**Grenoble** ... d.	0601	0630	0709	0730	0730	0830	...	...	0930	...	1031	...	1205	1230	1330	1330	...	1430	1530	1630	1705	1730	1830	...
242	Romans-Bourg de Péage ... d.	0658	0727	0758	0827	0827	0928	...	...	1027	...	1127	...	1258	1327	1427	1427	...	1530	1628	1727	1758	1827	1927	...
249	Valence TGV ... a.	0704	0733	0804	0833	0833	0934	...	...	1033	...	1133	...	1304	1333	1433	1433	...	1536	1634	1733	1804	1833	1933	...
259	**Valence** Ville ... a.	0715	0743	0814	0843	0843	0948	...	...	1043	...	1143	...	1314	1343	1447	1447	...	1545	1644	1743	1814	1843	1943	...

		⑤–⑦ s		①–⑥ b			Ⓐ		🚌
Genève ... **341 346** d.	1642	1642	...	...	...	1842	...	...	...
Bellegarde ... **341 346** d.	1712	1712	...	...	...	1911	...	...	...
Culoz ... **346** d.	1747**k**	1747**k**	...	...	...	1944**k**	...	...	...
Annecy ... **341 345** d.	|	|	1743	...	1843	|	1930	1943	2038
Aix les Bains ... **341 345** d.	1806	1806	1826	...	1926	2003	2007	2026	2136
Chambéry ... **341 345** a.	1817	1817	1837	...	1938	2013	2019	2037	2208
Chambéry ... d.	1821	1821	1840	...	1941	2021	...	2040	...
Montmélian ... d.	|	|	1850	...	1951	|	...	2050	...
Grenoble ... a.	1902	1902	1927	...	2027	2102	...	2127	...
Grenoble ... d.	...	1905	1930	1941	2030	...	...	...	...
Romans-Bourg de Péage ... d.	...	1958	2027	2059	2127	...	...	...	...
Valence TGV ... a.	...	2004	2033	2105	2133	...	...	...	...
Valence Ville ... a.	...	2014	2043	2114	2143	...	...	...	...

	①–⑤	①–⑥ b	①–⑥ b n	Ⓐ	Ⓐ	①–⑥ b	①–⑥	Ⓐ		Ⓐ	
Valence Ville ... d.	...	...	...	...	...	0524	...	...	...	0617	0644
Valence TGV ... d.	...	...	...	...	...	0532	...	...	...	0626	0655
Romans-Bourg de Péage . d.	...	...	...	...	...	0540	...	...	...	0635	0703
Grenoble ... a.	...	...	...	...	...	0648	...	...	...	0729	0755
Grenoble ... d.	0507	...	0539	...	0632	...	0658	...	0732	0732	0758
Montmélian ... d.	0544	...	0626	...	0710	...	|	...	0811	0811	|
Chambéry ... a.	0554	...	0635	...	0719	...	0740	...	0820	0820	0839
Chambéry ... **341 345** d.	0557	0623	...	0645	0722	...	0743	0800	0823	0823	0842
Aix les Bains ... **341 345** d.	0609	0635	...	0658	0735	...	0754	0813	0834	0834	0855
Annecy ... **341 345** a.	|	0714	...	0738	0815	...	|	0855	0915	0915	|
Culoz ... **346** d.	0632**k**	...	...	...	...	...	|	...	...	...	|
Bellegarde ... **341 346** a.	0658	...	...	...	...	...	0832	...	...	...	0931
Genève ... **341 346** a.	0730	...	...	...	...	...	0900	...	...	...	1000

	①–⑥ b	Ⓐ		Ⓐ								Ⓐ		Ⓐ						⊡△	⑤⑦r a△	⊙△	♡△	🚌	⊖△
Valence Ville ... d.	...	0717	0817	0917	1017	...	...	1217	1317	1345	1417	...	1515	...	1617	1645	1716	1745	1817	1917	2016	2117	2117	...	2217
Valence TGV ... d.	...	0726	0826	0926	1026	...	...	1226	1326	1355	1426	...	1524	...	1626	1655	1726	1755	1826	1926	2025	2126	2126	...	2226
Romans-Bourg de Péage ... d.	...	0735	0835	0935	1035	...	...	1235	1335	1403	1435	...	1533	...	1635	1703	1734	1803	1835	1935	2034	2135	2135	...	2235
Grenoble ... a.	...	0829	0929	1029	1129	...	...	1329	1429	1455	1529	...	1628	...	1729	1755	1829	1851	1929	2029	2129	2229	2229	...	2329
Grenoble ... d.	...	...	0932	...	1132	1158	1232	1332	1432	1458	1532	...	1631	...	1732	1758	1832	*1909*	1932	2032	2132	...	2232	...	...
Montmélian ... d.	...	...	1011	...	1211	|	1310	1411	1511	|	1611	...	1709	...	1811	|	1911	*1954*	2011	2111	2211	...	2311	...	...
Chambéry ... a.	...	...	1020	...	1220	1239	1319	1420	1520	1540	1620	...	1718	...	1820	1843	1920	*2003*	2020	2120	2220	...	2320	...	...
Chambéry ... **341 345** d.	...	...	1023	...	1223	1242	1322	1423	1523	1543	1623	1700	1721	1800	1823	1846	1923	...	2023	2123	2223	...	...	2330	...
Aix les Bains ... **341 345** d.	0925	...	1036	...	1234	1255	1334	1436	1534	1556	1636	1712	1732	1811	1835	1857	1934	...	2036	2134	2234	...	...	2350	...
Annecy ... **341 345** a.	1007	...	1117	...	1315	|	1417	1515	1616	|	1715	1759	1813	1859	1915	|	2015	...	2115	2212	2312**v**	...	...	0022	...
Culoz ... **346** d.	...	...	...	...	...	|	...	...	...	|	...	...	...	...	...	|	...	...	...	...	...	...	...	...	...
Bellegarde ... **341 346** d.	...	...	...	...	...	1331	...	...	...	1631	...	...	...	...	...	1932	...	...	...	...	...	...	...	...	...
Genève ... **341 346** a.	...	...	...	...	...	1400	...	...	...	1700	...	...	...	...	...	2000	...	...	...	...	...	...	...	...	...

a – To / from Avignon on dates in Table **351**.
b – Not July 14, Nov. 11.
c – Not Aug. 15.
k – Arrives 7 minutes earlier.
n – Not July 15 - Aug. 23.
r – ⑤⑦ (also July 14, Nov. 5, 6, 11; not Aug. 15). Terminates at Grenoble on July 13, 14, Nov. 9, 11.
s – Also July 14, Aug. 14, Nov. 11.
v – ⑤ to Oct. 3 (not Aug. 15); ⑤⑦ from Oct. 10 (also Nov. 5, 6; not Nov. 9).
♡ – ⑥ to July 26 (also July 20; not July 12); Ⓒ Aug. 15 - Sept. 28; ⑥ from Nov. 1.
⊡ – Daily to July 19; ⑤⑥ July 25 - Aug. 23; daily from Aug. 29.
⊙ – Daily to Oct. 3 (also Oct. 10, 11; not July 12 – 14, 27 – 29, Aug. 1 – 13); ①–⑥ from Oct. 17 (not Oct. 27 – 30, Nov. 11).
⊖ – Ⓑ to July 25 (also July 30, 31, Aug. 14; not July 15 – 17); ⑤ Aug. 22 - Sept. 12 (also Oct. 2); Ⓑ from Aug. 31.
△ – This service is subject to alteration – please check before travelling.

Products for sale from European Rail Timetable Limited

3rd Edition 3rd Revision of the
Rail Map Europe.
£12.99 + p&p

European Rail Timetable
Two seasonal editions.
£49.98 + p&p

18th Edition of the
Europe by Rail guidebook.
£20.99 + p&p

Autumn 2024 digital edition of the
Beyond Europe Timetable.
£4.99

Order on-line at **www.europeanrailtimetable.eu**
Telephone **01832 270198**

365 BELLEGARDE / GENÈVE / ANNECY - LA ROCHE SUR FORON - ST GERVAIS

See panel below main table for *TGV* services from / to Paris.
Services from mid-morning to mid-afternoon may be subject to alteration on ①–⑤ Sept. 15 - Oct. 10 and Nov. 3 – 7.

km		①–⑤	Ⓐ			Ⓑ	①–⑤		◇		Ⓑ	①–⑤ 🚌	Ⓒ		⑥ 🚌		Ⓑ	①–⑤ 🚌		⑥⑦	①–⑤		①–⑤ 🚌		⊕
	Lyon Part-Dieu **346** d.	...	...	...	...	...	...	...	...	...	...	...	...	...	...	...	...	...	...	...	...	...	...	...	...
0	**Bellegarde** **363** d.	...	...	...	...	...	0715	0815	...	...	0915	1015	1015	...	1115	...	1115	1215	1215	...	...	...	...	1415	...
	Genève **363** ▷ d.	...	...	0631	0731	...	|	|	0831	0931	|	|	|	1031	|	1131	|	|	|	1231	1231	1331	...	|	1431
	Genève Eaux Vives **363** ▷ d.	...	...	0647	0747	...	|	|	0847	0947	|	|	|	1047	|	1147	|	|	|	1247	1247	1347	...	|	1447
38	Annemasse **363** ▷ a.	...	...	0655	0755	...	0755	0855	0855	0955	0955	|	1055	1055	|	1155	1155	|	1255	1255	1255	1355	...	1455	1455
38	Annemasse ▷ d.	...	...	0702	...	0802	0802	...	0902	...	1002	|	...	1102	|	...	1202	|	...	1302	1302	...	1405	...	1502
•	**Annecy** ▷ d.	...	...	|	...	|	|	...	|	...	|	|	...	|	|	...	|	|	...	|	|	...	|	...	|
55	La Roche sur Foron ▷ a.	...	...	0719	...	0818	0818	...	0919	...	1019	1106	...	1119	1206	...	1219	1306	...	1319	1319	...	1432	...	1519
55	La Roche sur Foron d.	0624	0655	0723	...	0823	0823	...	0924	...	1024	1106	...	1124	1206	...	1224	1306	...	1324	1324	...	1432	...	1524
77	Cluses (Haute-Savoie) d.	0653	0724	0753	...	0854	0854	...	0953	...	1053	1150	...	1153	1250	...	1253	1350	...	1353	1349	...	1516	...	1553
96	Sallanches Megève d.	0710	0740	0810	...	0910	0910	...	1010	...	1110	1214	...	1210	1314	...	1310	1414	...	1410	1412	...	1540	...	1610
102	**St Gervais-les-Bains** a.	0714	0745	0815	...	0915	0915	...	1016	...	1116	1230	...	1216	1330	...	1316	1430	...	1416	1417	...	1556	...	1616

			①–⑤			①–⑤	①–⑤				①–⑤							⑥	Ⓑh 🚌			⑤	⑦–④ 🚌		⑤f 🚌
Lyon Part-Dieu **346** d.	...	...	...	...	...	...	...	...	...	...	...	...	...	...	...	...	...	...	...	...	...	...	...	...	...
Bellegarde **363** d.	...	...	...	1615	...	...	...	...	1715	...	...	1815	...	...	1915	2015	...	...	2015	...	...	2115	2115	...	2215
Genève **363** ▷ d.	*1531*	1546	...	|	1631	1646	...	1731	|	1746	...	|	1831	1931	|	|	2031	2031	|	...	2131	|	|	...	|
Genève Eaux Vives **363** ▷ d.	*1547*	1602	...	|	1647	1702	...	1747	|	1802	...	|	1847	1947	|	|	2047	2047	|	...	2147	|	|	...	|
Annemasse **363** ▷ a.	*1555*	1610	...	1655	1655	1710	...	1755	1755	1810	...	1855	1855	1955	1955	2055	2055	2055	2105	...	2155	2155	|	...	|
Annemasse ▷ d.	1602	1619	...	...	1702	1719	...	...	1802	1819	...	...	1902	...	2002	...	...	2102	2105	...	...	2202	|	...	|
Annecy ▷ d.	|	|	1552	...	|	|	1652	...	|	|	1752	...	|	...	|	...	...	|	|	...	...	|	|	...	|
La Roche sur Foron ▷ a.	1619	1638	1636	...	1719	1738	1736	...	1819	1838	1836	...	1919	...	2019	...	...	2119	2132	...	...	2219	2206	...	2306
La Roche sur Foron d.	1624	...	1646	...	1724	...	1746	...	1824	...	1846	...	1924	...	2024	...	...	2124	2132	...	...	2224	2206	...	2306
Cluses (Haute-Savoie) d.	1653	...	1710	...	1753	...	1810	...	1853	...	1910	...	1953	...	2053	...	...	2153	2216	...	...	2253	2250	...	2350
Sallanches Megève d.	1710	...	1725	...	1810	...	1823	...	1910	...	1923	...	2010	...	2108	...	...	2210	2240	...	...	2310	2314	...	0014
St Gervais-les-Bains a.	1716	...	1731	...	1816	...	1829	...	1916	...	1929	...	2016	...	2114	...	...	2216	2256	...	...	2316	2330	...	0030

			①–⑤				①–⑤				①–⑤				①–⑤ 🚌	⑥⑦			⑥ 🚌	Ⓑ	Ⓒ	Ⓐ			
St Gervais-les-Bains d.	0450	...	0520	...	0549	...	0633	...	0649	...	0733	...	0749	...	0819	0849	...	...	0930	0949	...	...	...	1049	...
Sallanches Megève d.	0455	...	0525	...	0555	...	0638	...	0654	...	0739	...	0755	...	0835	0854	...	...	0946	0955	...	...	...	1054	...
Cluses (Haute-Savoie) d.	0511	...	0541	...	0611	...	0653	...	0711	...	0754	...	0811	...	0854	0911	...	...	1010	1011	...	...	...	1111	...
La Roche sur Foron a.	0537	...	0603	...	0637	...	0715	...	0738	...	0815	...	0837	...	0934	0937	...	...	1054	1037	...	...	...	1137	...
La Roche sur Foron ▷ d.	0541	...	...	0623	0641	...	0725	0723	0742	...	0825	0823	0841	...	0934	0941	...	...	1054	1041	...	...	...	1141	...
Annecy ▷ a.	|	...	...	|	|	...	0806	|	|	...	0906	|	|	...	|	|	...	...	|	|	...	...	...	|	...
Annemasse ▷ a.	0558	...	...	0640	0658	...	...	0740	0758	...	...	0840	0858	...	1001	0958	...	...	|	1058	...	...	...	1158	...
Annemasse **363** ▷ d.	0605	0605	...	0650	0705	0705	...	0750	0805	0805	...	0850	0905	0905	...	...	1005	...	|	1105	1105	1112	...	1205	1205
Genève Eaux Vives **363** ▷ d.	|	0613	...	0658	0713	|	...	0758	|	0813	...	0858	0913	|	...	...	1013	...	|	1113	|	|	...	|	1213
Genève **363** ▷ a.	|	0628	...	0713	0728	|	...	0813	|	0828	...	0913	0928	|	...	...	1028	...	|	1128	|	|	...	|	1228
Bellegarde **363** a.	0642	...	...	...	...	0742	...	...	0842	...	...	...	...	0942	...	...	...	...	1145	...	1142	1157	...	1244	...
Lyon Part-Dieu **346** a.	...	...	...	...	...	...	...	...	...	...	...	...	...	...	...	...	...	...	...	...	...	...	...	...	...

	⑥ 🚌	Ⓑ			Ⓑ		①–⑤ 🚌		⑥⑦	Ⓒ		Ⓑ				①–⑤							Ⓑ		
St Gervais-les-Bains d.	1125	1149	...	...	1249	...	1259	...	1349	...	...	1449	...	1549	...	1649	...	1749	...	1849	...	...	1949	...	...
Sallanches Megève d.	1141	1155	...	...	1254	...	1315	...	1355	...	...	1454	...	1555	...	1655	...	1755	...	1854	...	...	1954	...	...
Cluses (Haute-Savoie) d.	1205	1211	...	...	1311	...	1339	...	1411	...	...	1511	...	1611	...	1711	...	1811	...	1911	...	...	2011	...	...
La Roche sur Foron a.	1249	1237	...	...	1337	...	1423	...	1437	...	...	1537	...	1638	...	1738	...	1838	...	1937	...	...	2037	...	...
La Roche sur Foron ▷ d.	1249	1241	...	...	1341	...	1423	...	1441	...	...	1541	...	1642	...	1742	...	1842	...	1941	...	...	2041	...	...
Annecy ▷ a.	|	|	...	...	|	...	|	...	|	...	...	|	...	|	...	|	...	|	...	|	...	...	|	...	...
Annemasse ▷ a.	|	1258	...	...	1358	...	1450	...	1458	...	...	1558	...	1658	...	1758	...	1858	...	1958	...	...	2058	...	...
Annemasse **363** ▷ d.	|	1305	1305	...	1405	1405	1450	1505	1505	1505	...	1605	1605	1705	1705	1805	1805	1905	1905	2005	2005	...	...	2105	2105
Genève Eaux Vives **363** ▷ d.	|	1313	|	...	|	1413	|	1513	1513	|	...	|	1613	1713	|	|	1813	1913	|	|	2013	...	...	|	2113
Genève **363** ▷ a.	|	1328	|	...	|	1428	|	1528	1528	|	...	|	1628	1728	|	|	1828	1928	|	|	2028	...	...	|	2128
Bellegarde **363** a.	1340	...	1342	...	1442	...	1540	...	...	1542r	...	1642	...	...	1742	1842	...	...	1942	2043	...	...	...	2142	...
Lyon Part-Dieu **346** a.	...	...	...	...	...	...	...	...	...	...	...	...	...	...	...	...	...	...	...	...	...	...	...	...	...

ANNECY - ANNEMASSE - GENÈVE

	①–⑤		①–⑤		①–⑤			Ⓑ		Ⓑ		①–⑤	⑦	①–⑤	⑥⑦	Ⓑ								⑥	⑤
Annecy d.	*0510**	0544	*0610**	0644	*0710**	0744	0844	0944	1044	1144	1244	*1340**	1344	*1440**	1444	1544	*1552*t	1644	1744	*1752*t	1844	1944	2044	2137	*2140**
La Roche sur Foron a.	|	0619	|	0719	|	0819	0919	1019	1119	1219	1319	|	1419	|	1519	1619	*1636*t	1719	1818	*1836*t	1919	2019	2119	2209	|
La Roche sur Foron d.	|	0623	|	0723	|	0823	0923	1023	1123	1223	1323	|	1423	|	1523	1623	1642	1723	1823	1842	1923	2023	2123	2210	|
Annemasse a.	*0610**	0640	*0710**	0740	*0810**	0840	0940	1040	1140	1240	1340	*1440**	1440	*1540**	1540	1640	1658	1740	1840	1858	1940	2040	2140	2225	*2240**
Annemasse ◧ d.	0620	0650	0720	0750	0820	0850	0950	1050	1150	1250	1350	1450	1450	1550	1550	1650	1705	1750	1850	1905	1950	2050	2150	*2235*	2250
Genève Eaux Vives ◧ d.	0628	0658	0728	0758	0828	0858	0958	1058	1158	1258	1358	1458	1458	1558	1558	1658	1713	1758	1858	1913	1958	2058	2158	*2243*	2258
Genève ◧ a.	0643	0713	0743	0813	0843	0913	1013	1113	1213	1313	1413	1513	1513	1613	1613	1713	1728	1813	1913	1928	2013	2113	2213	*2258*	2313

	Ⓑ		①–⑤		Ⓑ				⑥⑦	①–⑤		⑦	①–⑤			①–⑤	⑥⑦	①–⑤		①–⑤			Ⓑ	①–⑥	⑤⑥
Genève ◧ d.	0546	0631	...	0646	0746	0846	0946	1046	1146	1146	1246	1346	1346	1446	1546	1646	1646	1716	1746	1816	1846	1946	2046	2146	2246
Genève Eaux Vives ◧ d.	0602	0647	...	0702	0802	0902	1002	1102	1202	1202	1302	1402	1402	1502	1602	1702	1702	1732	1802	1832	1902	2002	2102	2202	2302
Annemasse ◧ a.	0610	0655	...	0710	0810	0910	1010	1110	1210	1210	1310	1410	1410	1510	1610	1710	1710	1740	1810	1840	1910	2010	2110	2210	2310
Annemasse d.	0619	0702	...	0719	0819	0919	1019	1119	1219	*1220**	1319	1419	*1420**	1519	1619	1719	*1720**	*1750**	1819	*1850**	1919	2019	2119	*2220**	*2320**
La Roche sur Foron a.	0638	0719	...	0738	0838	0938	1038	1138	1238	|	1338	1438	|	1538	1638	1738	|	|	1838	|	1938	2038	2138	|	|
La Roche sur Foron d.	0642	...	0725	0742	0842	0942	1042	1142	1242	|	1342	1442	|	1542	1643	1743	|	|	1843	|	1942	2042	2142	|	|
Annecy a.	0716	...	0806	0816	0916	1016	1116	1216	1316	*1320**	1416	1516	*1520**	1616	1716	1816	*1820**	*1850**	1916	*1950**	2016	2116	2216	*2320**	*0020**

TGV services. For other services Paris - Bellegarde, see Table **341**.

	TGV **6467** ⑥ **A**		*TGV* **6473** ⑥ **B**	*TGV* **6473** **C**						
Paris Gare de Lyon d.	0634	...	1045	1104	...	...	...	...	...	...
Bellegarde a.	0928	...	1330	1348	...	...	...	...	...	...
Annemasse a.	1018	...	1421	1422	...	...	...	...	...	...
Cluses (Haute-Savoie) a.	1110	...	1509	1509	...	...	...	...	...	...
Sallanches Megève a.	1126	...	1528	1528	...	...	...	...	...	...
St Gervais-les-Bains a.	1136	...	1536	1536	...	...	...	...	...	...

	TGV **6482** ⑥ **D**		*TGV* **6484** ⑥ **D**							
St Gervais-les-Bains d.	1251	...	1625	...	...	...	...	...	...	...
Sallanches Megève d.	1302	...	1633	...	...	...	...	...	...	...
Cluses (Haute-Savoie) d.	1317	...	1658	...	...	...	...	...	...	...
Annemasse d.	1707	...	1758	...	...	...	...	...	...	...
Bellegarde d.	1444	...	1843	...	...	...	...	...	...	...
Paris Gare de Lyon a.	1759	...	2128	...	...	...	...	...	...	...

A – ⑥ July 5 - Aug. 30 (not Aug. 16).
B – ⑥ July 5 - Aug. 9 (also Aug. 15).
C – Runs on Aug. 16, 23, 30 only.
D – ⑥ July 5 - Aug. 30.

f – Also Aug. 14; not Aug. 15.
h – Not Aug. 15.
r – 1547 on public holidays.
t – ①–⑤ only.

TGV – High-speed train. [R]. 🍷. Minor timing variations are possible.

* – By 🚌.
◇ – Change trains at Annemasse on ⑥.
⊕ – Change trains at Annemasse on ①–⑤.
▷ – For other trains Genève - Annemasse - La Roche sur Foron - Annecy, see panel below main table.
◧ – Frequent services (every 15 minutes during the day) operate Genève - Annemasse and v.v.
• – Annecy to La Roche sur Foron is 39 km.

ST GERVAIS - CHAMONIX - VALLORCINE (- MARTIGNY) 365a

Mont-Blanc Express. For full details of journeys Vallorcine - Martigny and v.v., see Table **572**. **SERVICE UNTIL SEPTEMBER 14.**

km																									
																						Ⓐ **n**			
0	**St Gervais** d.	0628	0705	0808	...	0928	1028	...	1128	...	1228	...	1328	...	1428	...	1528	...	1628	...	1728	1810	1828	1928	2028
9	Les Houches d.	0654	0733	0836	...	0954	1054	1124	1154	1224	1254	1324	1354	1424	1454	1524	1554	1624	1654	1724	1754	1835	1854	1954	2054
20	**Chamonix** Mont-Blanc a.	0713	0750	0852	...	1013	1113	1141	1213	1241	1313	1341	1413	1441	1513	1541	1613	1641	1713	1741	1813	1850	1913	2013	2113
20	**Chamonix** Mont-Blanc d.	0728	0828	0928	...	1028	1128	1157	1228	1257	1328	1357	1428	1457	1528	1557	1628	1657	1728	1757	1828	1857	1928	2028	...
24	Les Tines d.	0737	0837	0937	...	1037	1137	1205	1237	1305	1337	1405	1437	1505	1537	1605	1637	1705	1737	1805	1837	1905	1937	2037	...
28	Argentière Haute Savoie d.	0746	0846	0946	...	1046	1146	1216	1246	1316	1346	1416	1446	1516	1546	1616	1646	1716	1746	1816	1846	1916	1946	2046	...
35	**Vallorcine** a.	0801	0901	1001	...	1101	1201	1231	1301	1331	1401	1431	1501	1531	1601	1631	1701	1731	1801	1831	1901	1931	2001	2101	...
	Change trains																								
35	**Vallorcine** ★ **572** d.	0813	0913	1013	...	1113	1213	...	1313	...	1413	...	1513	...	1613	...	1713	...	1813	...	1913	...	2013	2113	...
56	**Martigny** **572** a.	0909	1009	1109	...	1209	1309	...	1409	...	1509	...	1609	...	1709	...	1809	...	1909	...	2009	...	2109	2209	...

Martigny **572** d.	...	...	0656	...	0814	0914	1014	...	1114	...	1214	...	1314	...	1414	...	1514	...	1614	...	1714	...	1814	1914
Vallorcine ★ **572** a.	...	...	0747	...	0905	1005	1105	...	1205	...	1305	...	1405	...	1505	...	1605	...	1705	...	1805	...	1905	2005
Change trains																								
Vallorcine d.	0640	0710	0810	...	0910	1010	1110	1140	1210	1240	1310	1340	1410	1440	1510	1540	1610	1640	1710	1740	1810	1840	1910	2010
Argentière Haute Savoie d.	0654	0727	0827	...	0927	1027	1127	1157	1227	1257	1327	1357	1427	1457	1527	1557	1627	1657	1727	1757	1827	1857	1927	2027
Les Tines d.	0703	0737	0837	...	0937	1037	1137	1206	1237	1306	1337	1406	1437	1506	1537	1606	1637	1706	1737	1806	1837	1906	1937	2037
Chamonix Mont-Blanc a.	0710	0745	0845	...	0945	1045	1145	1217	1245	1317	1345	1417	1445	1517	1545	1617	1645	1717	1745	1814	1845	1917	1945	2045
Chamonix Mont-Blanc d.	0715	0755	0855	...	0955	1055	1155	1223	1255	1323	1355	1423	1455	1523	1555	1623	1655	1723	1755	1833	1855	1923	1955	...
Les Houches d.	0732	0814	0914	...	1014	1114	1214	1240	1314	1340	1414	1440	1514	1540	1614	1640	1714	1740	1814	1850	1914	1940	2014	...
St Gervais a.	0757	0840	0940	...	1040	1140	1240	...	1340	...	1440	...	1540	...	1640	...	1740	...	1840	...	1940	...	2040	...

n – Not June 30 - Aug. 29.

★ – 🛃 is at Le Châtelard Frontière (see Table **572**).

(PARIS -) CHAMBÉRY - ALBERTVILLE - BOURG ST MAURICE 366

km																							
		🚌		🚌	🚌				*TGV*			🚌									🚌		🚌
		Ⓐ	Ⓐ	Ⓐ	Ⓐ				**6419**		①–⑥	Ⓐ			Ⓐ	①–⑥		Ⓐ	①–⑥		①–④		①–⑥
							⊗		⑥ **B**		**b** ⊗		⊗			**b**			**b**		**D**		**b**
	Paris Gare de Lyon **341** d.	...	...	...	...	...	...	...	0746	...	...	...	...	...	...	...	...	...	...	...	...	...	...
	Lyon Part Dieu **344** d.	...	...	...	...	...	...	...	|	...	...	...	...	...	...	...	...	...	...	...	...	...	...
	Aix les Bains **345 364** d.	...	...	...	...	...	0939	...	|	...	...	...	1339	...	1539	1640	1739	1839	1939	2039	...	...	...
0	**Chambéry** **341 345 364 367** d.	0551	0653	...	0807	...	0953	...	1055**a**	...	1153	1251	1353	...	1553	1653	1753	1853	1953	2053	...	...	2200
13	Montmélian **367** d.	0621	0703	...	0837	...	1003	...	|	...	1203	|	1403	...	1603	1703	1803	1903	2003	2103	...	...	2230
25	St Pierre d'Albigny **367** d.	0639	0712	...	0852	...	1012	...	|	...	1213	|	1413	...	1612	1713	1814	1913	2012	2112	...	...	2245
48	Albertville a.	0717	0738	...	0918	...	1038	...	1137	...	1238	1349	1438	...	1638	1738	1838	1938	2036	2138	...	...	2311
48	Albertville d.	0717	0745	...	0918	...	1044	...	|	...	1245	1349	1445	...	1645	1745	1845	1945	2045	2145**f**	2155	...	2311
76	**Moûtiers-Salins** d.	0747	0810	0845	0948	...	1113	...	1209**a**	...	1313	1419	1513	...	1713	1813	1913	2013	2113	2213**f**	2228	...	2346
91	Aime la Plagne d.	0802	...	0900	1003	...	1129	...	1229**a**	...	1329	|	1529	...	1729	1829	1929	2029	2129	2229**f**	2246	...	0001
98	Landry d.	0812	...	0910	1013	...	1138	...	1240**a**	...	1338	|	1538	...	1738	1838	1938	2038	2138	2238**f**	2258	...	0012
105	**Bourg St Maurice** ♥ a.	0824	...	0922	1025	...	1145	...	1250	...	1345	1449	1545	...	1745	1845	1945	2045	2145	2245**f**	2311	...	0026

	🚌					🚌	🚌			🚌							*TGV*			🚌		
	Ⓐ		①–⑥			⑦	Ⓐ	Ⓐ		Ⓐ				①–⑥			**6434**	Ⓐ		Ⓐ		
			h			**e**						⊗		**b** ⊗		⊗	⑥ **C**	⊗				
Bourg St Maurice ♥ d.	0417	...	0513	0613	...	0717	0759	...	...	0841	...	1013	...	1213	...	1413	1447	1513	1613	1639	...	1813
Landry d.	|	...	0521	0621	...	0728	0810	...	...	0852	...	1021	...	1221	...	1421	1457	1521	1621	1651	...	1821
Aime la Plagne d.	|	...	0532	0632	...	0740	0822	...	...	0904	...	1032	...	1232	...	1432	1507	1531	1632	1703	...	1832
Moûtiers-Salins d.	0447	...	0549	0649	...	0802	0839	0849	...	0921	...	1049	...	1249	...	1449	1528	1549	1649	1720	...	1849
Albertville a.	0522	...	0615	0715	...	0847	...	0915	...	0956	...	1115	...	1315	...	1515	|	1615	1715	1755	...	1915
Albertville d.	0522	...	0622	0722	...	0847	...	0922	...	0956	...	1122	...	1322	...	1522	1600	1622	1722	1755	...	1922
St Pierre d'Albigny **367** d.	0544	...	0647	0748	...	0915	...	0948	...	1028	...	1148	...	1348	...	1548	|	1648	1748	1822	...	1948
Montmélian **367** d.	0559	...	0658	0758	...	0930	...	0958	...	1043	...	1158	...	1358	...	1558	|	1658	1758	1837	...	1958
Chambéry **341 345 364 367** a.	0629	...	0707	0807	...	1000	...	1007	...	1113	...	1207	...	1407	...	1607	1637**d**	1707	1807	1907	...	2007
Aix les Bains **345 364** a.	...	...	...	0821	...	...	...	...	...	...	...	...	...	1421	...	1621	|	1721	1821	...	...	2021
Lyon Part Dieu **344** a.	...	...	...	...	...	...	...	...	...	...	...	...	...	...	...	...	|	...	...	...	...	...
Paris Gare de Lyon **341** a.	...	...	...	...	...	...	...	...	...	...	...	...	...	...	...	...	1946	...	...	...	...	...

B – ⑥ July 5 - Aug. 30 (also Aug. 15).
C – ⑥ July 5 - Aug. 30.
D – ①–④ until Sept. 18 (not Aug. 14).

a – Arrival time.
b – Not July 14, Nov. 11.
d – Departure time.
e – Also July 14, Nov. 11.
f – ⑤–⑦ to Sept. 14 (also Aug. 14); daily from Sept. 19.
h – Not July 14, 15, Nov. 11.

TGV – High-speed train. 🅁. 🍷. Only for journeys from / to Paris.

⊗ – Subject to alteration / cancellation on ①–⑤ Sept. 22 - Oct. 10.
♥ – A funicular railway operates between Bourg St Maurice and the Les Arcs resort area during the winter and summer seasons. Frequent departures. Journey time: 7 minutes. Summer 2025 season: ⑥⑦ June 14 – 22; daily June 28 - Aug. 31; ⑥⑦ Sept. 6 – 14.

European Rail Timetable Subscription

Keep up to date with the latest changes to European rail schedules with a subscription.

See page 12 for details of our various subscription options

Order on-line at **www.europeanrailtimetable.eu**

✆ +44 (0) 1832 270198 (Monday to Friday 1000 – 1600)

367 CHAMBÉRY - MODANE

See Table **44** for international *TGV* and *FR* services Paris - Chambéry - Modane - Milano and v.v.

km																								
					🚌		*TGV* **6401**													🚌			🚌	🚌
		①–⑥	Ⓐ		Ⓐ		⑥							Ⓐ	①–⑥				⑤⑦	①–④	Ⓑ		⑥	⑤
		b					**A**								**b**				**f**	**m**	**r**		**t**	**v**
	Paris Gare de Lyon **341** d.	...	...	...	...	...	0746	...	...	...	...	...	...	...	...	...	...	...	...	...	...	...	...	...
	Lyon Part Dieu **344** d.	...	...	...	...	...	|	...	...	...	...	...	...	...	...	...	...	...	...	...	...	...	...	...
0	**Chambéry** **364 366** d.	0629	0729	...	0833	...	1104	1129	...	1248	...	1446	...	1646	1748	1829	1929	...	2048	2057	2148	...	2154	2231
14	Montmélian **364 366** d.	0640	0740	...	|	...	|	1140	...	1259	...	1457	...	1656	1758	1839	1940	...	2058	|	2159	...	2224	2301
26	St Pierre d'Albigny **366** d.	0649	0749	...	|	...	|	1149	...	1309	...	1505	...	1706	1809	1848	1949	...	2106	|	2209	...	2240	2317
61	St Avre la Chambre d.	0721	0821	...	0956	...	1138	1220	...	1340	...	1535	...	1736	1839	1918	2021	...	2140	2220	2240	...	2315	2352
71	St Jean de Maurienne d.	0731	0831	...	1011	...	1149	1230	...	1349	...	1554	...	1745	1848	1927	2031	...	2149	2235	2249	...	2330	0011
83	St Michel-Valloire d.	0742	0842	...	1027	...	1201	1241	...	1404	...	1607	...	1756	1902	1938	2042	...	2202	2251	2300	...	2346	0023
99	**Modane** a.	0756	0856	...	1047	...	1219	1255	...	1418	...	1621	...	1810	1916	1954	2056	...	2216	2311	2316	...	0006	0043

	🚌			🚌		🚌							🚌		*TGV* **6406**								
	Ⓐ		①–⑥	⑦	①–⑥	Ⓐ		Ⓒ	Ⓐ	Ⓐ			Ⓐ		⑥	Ⓒ	Ⓐ		Ⓐ				Ⓑ
			w	**e**	**b**				**n**	**E**					**A**								**z**
Modane d.	0436	...	0550	0601	0701	0752	...	0939	0939	0939	...	1131	1205	1346	1443	1601	1601	...	1708	...	1821	...	2009
St Michel-Valloire d.	0456	...	0606	0621	0718	0812	...	0954	0954	0954	...	1149	1225	1403	1500	1618	1618	...	1730	...	1837	...	2026
St Jean de Maurienne d.	0512	...	0619	0637	0730	0828	...	1010	1010	1009	...	1212	1241	1416	1521	1630	1635	...	1743	...	1849	...	2038
St Avre la Chambre d.	0527	...	0628	0652	0739	0843	...	1035**j**	1026	1035**j**	...	1227	1256	1426	1533	1639	1643	...	1752	...	1857	...	2047
St Pierre d'Albigny **366** d.	|	...	0658	0743	0809	|	...	1105	1105	1106	...	1257	1347	1457	|	1709	1714	...	1821	...	1928	...	2117
Montmélian **364 366** d.	|	...	0707	0759	0819	|	...	1114	1114	1116	...	1305	1403	1506	|	1719	1722	...	1830	...	1938	...	2126
Chambéry **364 366** a.	0629	...	0716	0829	0828	1006	...	1122	1122	1124	...	1314	1423	1515	1626	1728	1731	...	1839	...	1947	...	2134
Lyon Part Dieu **344** a.	...	...	...	...	...	...	...	...	...	...	...	...	...	...	|	...	...	...	...	...	...	...	...
Paris Gare de Lyon **341** a.	...	...	...	...	...	...	...	...	...	...	...	...	...	...	1946	...	...	...	...	...	...	...	...

A – ⑥ July 5 - Aug. 30.
E – Ⓐ July 7 - Aug. 29.

b – Not July 14, Nov. 11.
e – Also July 14, Nov. 11.
f – Also July 14, Aug. 14, Nov. 11; not Aug. 15.
j – Arrives 11–12 minutes earlier.
m – Not July 14, Aug. 14, Nov. 11.
n – Not July 7 - Aug. 29.
r – Not June 15, 22, 29, July 6, Aug. 15.
t – Also Aug. 15.
v – Also Aug. 14; not Aug. 15.
w – Not June 16, 23, 30, July 7, 14, Nov. 11.
z – Not Aug. 15.

TGV – High-speed train. 🅁. 🍸. Only for journeys from/to Paris.

368 🚌 CHAMONIX - MONT BLANC TUNNEL - COURMAYEUR

SAT / Arriva Italia

By 🚌. Journey 45 minutes. **Service is confirmed until June 27.**
Dec. 17 - Apr. 14: From Chamonix (Avenue de Courmayeur) at 0830, 0930, 1615, 1730. From Courmayeur (Piazzale Monte Bianco) at 0815, 0945, 1615, 1730.
Apr. 15 - June 27 (see note ⊗): From Chamonix (Avenue de Courmayeur) at 0900, 1815. From Courmayeur (Piazzale Monte Bianco) at 1015, 1700.
June 28 - Aug. 31: From Chamonix (Avenue de Courmayeur) at 0900, 1245, 1530, 1800. From Courmayeur (Piazzale Monte Bianco) at 1015, 1145, 1545, 1800.

Arriva Italia — 🚌 **COURMAYEUR - PRÉ ST DIDER - AOSTA**

Courmayeur △ d.	0645	0745	0835	and	1635	1745	1845	1935	2035	2135
Pré St Didier d.	0653	0753	0843	hourly	1643	1753	1853	1943	2043	2143
Aosta ⊡ a.	0745	0845	0935	until	1735	1845	1945	2035	2135	2235

Aosta ⊡ d.	0645	0745	0845	0945	1045	1145	1245	1335	1445	and	2145
Pré St Didier d.	0737	0837	0937	1037	1137	1237	1337	1427	1537	hourly	2237
Courmayeur △ a.	0745	0845	0945	1045	1145	1245	1345	1435	1545	until	2245

△ – P. le Monte Bianco.
⊡ – Autostazione (bus station).
⊗ – Services are suspended on ⑦ May 25 - June 22 (also the morning service in each direction on June 23).

Operators: SAT Mont-Blanc ✆ + 33 (0)450 780 533 sat-montblanc.com
Arriva Italia Aosta ✆ + 39 02 841 21000 aosta.arriva.it

369 CORSICAN RAILWAYS

Narrow gauge. 2nd class.

SERVICE UNTIL JUNE 29

km																											
		Ⓐ	⚒	⚒	Ⓐ	⚒	Ⓐ					⚒		Ⓐ	⚒		⚒					Ⓐ				Ⓑ**d**	⚒
0	**Bastia** d.	...	...	...	0600	0612	0628	0712	0757	0825	0913	0947	1022	1058	1132	1215	1320	1406	1500	1539	1615	1708	1722	...	1805	1841	1936
10	Biguglia d.	...	...	...	0613	0627	0644	0730	0811	0841	0930	1003	1038	1114	1147	1231	1336	1422	1516	1552	1633	1726	1736	...	1823	1859	1951
22	Casamozza d.	...	...	...	0629	0642	0658	0744	0827	0855	0946	1017	1052	1130	1202	1245	1350	1437	1530	1610	1649	1743	1751	...	1839	1915	2005
47	Ponte Leccia d.	...	...	...	0712	...	...	...	0906	▬	1025	...	...	...	1237	...	▬	▬	▬	1645	...	▬	1831	1840	...	1952	...
98	Ile Rousse ▽ d.	...	...	...	|	...	...	...	|	...	1140	...	...	...	|	...	...	...	...	|	...	...	|	2005	...	|	...
120	**Calvi** ▽ a.	...	...	...	|	...	...	...	|	...	1215	...	...	...	|	...	...	...	...	|	...	...	|	2040	...	|	...
74	Corté d.	...	...	...	0801**e**	...	...	...	0947	...	...	...	...	...	1316	...	...	...	...	1724	...	...	1911	...	...	2026	...
90	Vivario d.	...	...	...	0832	...	...	...	1018	...	...	...	...	...	1347	...	...	...	...	1755	...	...	1942	...	...	...	...
107	Vizzavona d.	...	...	...	0853	...	...	...	1037	⚒	...	...	...	...	1406	...	⚒	⚒	⚒	1817	...	Ⓐ	2001	...	...	...	...
145	Mezzana d.	0715	0828	0916	0941	...	...	...	1129	1320	...	...	...	...	1454	...	1640	1755	1845	1907	...	2000	2049	...	...	...	...
158	**Ajaccio** a.	0735	0848	0936	1001	...	...	...	1149	1340	...	...	...	...	1514	...	1700	1815	1905	1927	...	2020	2106	...	...	...	...

	Ⓐ	⚒	⚒		⚒	①	Ⓐ	**B**	Ⓐ		⚒	⚒	Ⓐ		⚒	⚒	⚒			Ⓐ			⚒		⚒	⚒	Ⓐ
Ajaccio d.	...	...	...	...	...	...	0555	...	0645	0743	0804	0852	...	...	...	1105	1210	...	...	...	...	1523	1615	1707	1730	1820	1935
Mezzana d.	...	...	...	...	...	...	0613	...	0705	0801	0824	0912	...	...	...	1128	1230	...	...	...	...	1544	1635	1728	1750	1840	1955
Vizzavona d.	...	...	...	...	...	...	0701	...	▬	0852	▬	▬	...	...	...	1216	▬	...	...	...	...	1632	▬	1818	...	...	...
Vivario d.	...	...	...	...	...	...	0720	...	...	0911	...	...	...	...	...	1235	...	...	...	...	...	1651	...	1837	...	...	...
Corté d.	...	...	0633	...	...	...	0802	...	...	0946	...	...	...	...	...	1315	...	...	...	...	...	1725	...	1913	...	...	...
Calvi ▽ d.	...	...	|	...	...	0630	|	0705	...	|	...	...	...	...	...	|	...	...	...	...	1600	|	...	|	...	...	...
Ile Rousse ▽ d.	...	...	|	...	...	0712	|	0747	...	|	...	...	...	...	...	|	...	...	...	...	1636	|	...	|	...	...	...
Ponte Leccia d.	...	...	0711	...	...	0826	0838	0907**f**	⚒	1023	Ⓐ	Ⓒ	...	...	...	1349	...	...	...	...	1750	1802	⚒	1951	...	...	...
Casamozza d.	0629	0659	0746	0813	0903	...	0915	0947	1023	1058	1117	1132	1205	1311	1357	1424	1500	1618	1711	1757	...	1843	2010	2026	...	...	...
Biguglia d.	0645	0717	0801	0829	0917	...	0930	1003	1038	1114	1133	1147	1220	1325	1411	1439	1516	1633	1726	1811	...	1859	2024	2040	...	...	...
Bastia a.	0700	0734	0818	0846	0933	...	0943	1018	1053	1128	1152	1202	1236	1341	1427	1452	1531	1648	1742	1827	...	1915	2039	2053	...	...	...

B – ②–⑦ (runs daily Casamozza - Bastia).
d – Not June 8.
e – Arrives 0746.
f – Arrives 0901.

▽ – **Additional journeys** Ile Rousse - Calvi and v.v. (journey 40 minutes):
From Ile Rousse at 0900, 1050, 1320, 1505, 1735 and 1920.
From Calvi at 0800, 0950, 1230, 1410, 1640 and 1830.

TGV Rhin-Rhône — PARIS - DIJON - BESANÇON - MULHOUSE - BASEL — 370

Regional TER services: Table **371** Paris - Dijon; Table **374** Dijon - Besançon; Table **378** Besançon - Belfort; Table **378a** Belfort - Mulhouse; Table **385** Mulhouse - Basel.
Timings may vary by a few minutes – please check your reservation for confirmed timings. **Warning!** Subject to alteration on June 28, 29.
Zürich timings may vary on Sept. 6, 7, 20, 21 (earlier departures / later arrivals).

km		*TGV* 6741 Ⓐ M	*TGV* 6701 Ⓐ N	*TGV* 9203	*TGV* 9261 L	*TGV* 6703 ⑥⑦ d△	*TGV* 6703 R	*TGV* 9211 H	*TGV* 6705 S	*TGV* 9269 EL	*TGV* 9213 ⊗	*TGV* 9215 J	*TGV* 6743 Q	*TGV* 9219	*TGV* 6745 Ⓑ h	*TGV* 6709	*TGV* 9277 L	*TGV* 9223	*TGV* 6711	*TGV* 6715 T	*TGV* 6715 V	*TGV* 6753 Y	*TGV* 6753 ⑤ h	*TGV* 6753 ⑦ e
0	**Paris** Gare de Lyon ... **375** d.	0649	0650	0721	0755	0919	0920	1021	1117	1155	1222	1421	1451	1621	1651	1716	1756	1821	1851t	2020	2022	2105	2115	2121
212	Montbard ... d.	0755	0757	|	|	1024	|	|	|	|	|	|	1556	|	1757	|	|	|	1956	|	|	2210	2220	2225
287	**Dijon** Ville ... **375** a.	0831	0831	|	0931	1101	1056	1157	1253	1330	1357	|	1631	|	1831	1853	1929	1957	2032	2157	2157	2246	2255	2301
287	**Dijon** Ville ... **375 377 379** d.	0835	0835	|	0935	1104	1104	1201	1256	1333	1401	|	1635	|	1835	1856	1932	2001	2037	2201	2201	2250	2257	2303
333	Dole ... **375** a.	|	|	|	0958	|	|	|	|	1357	|	|	1658	|	1858	|	1955	|	|	|	|	|	2322	|
364	**Besançon** Franche-Comté TGV **379** d.	0908	0905**a**	|	...	1134	1133	|	1325	...	|	|	|	|	|	1925	...	|	2106	2231	2228**a**	2317**a**	|	2333**a**
377	Besançon Viotte ... a.	|	0919	|	...	|	|	|	|	...	|	|	1726	|	1926	|	...	|	|	|	2242	2331	2347	2347
446	Belfort Montbéliard TGV ... **379** d.	0932	...	0941	...	1158	1157	|	1349	...	|	1641	...	1841	...	1949	...	|	2130	2256	...	...	...	...
491	**Mulhouse** ... **379** a.	0954	...	1003	...	1220	1220	1303	1412	...	1503	1703	...	1903	...	2013	...	2103	2152	2320	...	...	...	...
525	**Basel** SBB ... a.	...	...	1026	...	...	...	1326	...	...	1526	1726	...	1926	...	...	...	2126	...	...	...	...	...	...
	Zürich HB **510** ... a.	...	...	1126**q**	...	...	...	1426**x**	...	...	1626**x**	1826**r**	...	2026	...	...	...	2226	...	...	...	...	...	...

	TGV 6760 Ⓐ	*TGV* 6700 U	*TGV* 6700 ⑦ e	*TGV* 6762 ①–⑥ b	*TGV* 9262 ①–⑤ AL	*TGV* 6702	*TGV* 9264 BL	*TGV* 9206 ⊡	*TGV* 9210 G	*TGV* 6704 Z	*TGV* 6704 D	*TGV* 9218 ⊖	*TGV* 9268 EL	*TGV* 9222 C	*TGV* 6706 Ⓑ h	*TGV* 9226	*TGV* 9270 L	*TGV* 6764 ⑤ P	*TGV* 6708	*TGV* 6766 ①–④ m	*TGV* 6766 ⑦ e	*TGV* 9234 w	*TGV* 6730 ⑦ e	*TGV* 6768 ⑤ f
Zürich HB **510** ... d.	...	...	...	...	...	...	...	0734	0934	...	...	1134**x**	...	1334**x**	...	1534**x**	...	...	...	...	...	1834**y**	...	...
Basel SBB ... d.	...	...	...	...	...	...	...	0834	1034	...	...	1234	...	1434	...	1634	...	...	...	...	...	1934	...	...
Mulhouse ... **379** d.	...	0546	0605	...	...	0747	...	0856	1056	1155	1205	1256	...	1456	1540	1656	...	...	1746	...	...	1956	...	...
Belfort Montbéliard TGV ... **379** d.	...	0611	0630	...	...	0812	...	0921	|	1220	1231	1321	...	|	1605	|	...	...	1810	...	...	2021	...	...
Besançon Viotte ... d.	0532	|	|	0636	...	|	...	|	|	|	|	|	...	|	|	|	...	1809	|	1932	1933	|	...	2022
Besançon Franche-Comté TGV **379** d.	|	0635	0655	0651	...	0835	...	|	|	1244	1254	|	...	|	1628	|	...	|	1833	|	1952	|	...	|
Dole ... **375** d.	0557	|	|	|	0804	|	0904	|	|	|	|	|	1401	|	|	|	1800	1834	|	1958	|	|	...	2047
Dijon Ville ... **375 377 379** a.	0622	0702	0723	0723	0828	0902	0928	|	1158	1311	1322	|	1425	1559	1656	1800	1825	1857	1902	2023	2023	|	...	2111
Dijon Ville ... **375** d.	0626	0706	0727	0727	0832	0906	0932	|	1202	1315	1326	|	1429	1602	1700	1803	1828	1906	1906	2027	2027	|	2110	2115
Montbard ... d.	0704	|	0805	0806	|	|	|	|	|	1408	1408	|	|	|	1738	|	|	|	|	|	2104	|	|	|
Paris Gare de Lyon ... **375** a.	0809	0843	0911	0911	1013	1043	1109	1139	1339	1515	1515	1538	1605	1738	1842	1938	2004	2044	2043	2204	2208	2242‡	2246	2252

LOCAL CONNECTING TRAINS BESANÇON FRANCHE-COMTÉ TGV - BESANÇON VIOTTE

km		①–⑥ b	⑦ e												ⓑ h						①–⑥ b			Ⓑ
0	Besançon Viotte ... d.	0608	0628	...	0808	...	0938	...	1138	1233	...	1338	1415	1508	1606	...	1735	1808	...	1902	1957	2038	...	2208
13	Besançon Franche-Comté TGV ... a.	0623	0643	...	0823	...	0953	...	1153	1245	...	1353	1431	1523	1618	...	1748	1823	...	1915	2010	2053	...	2223

	①–⑥ b	⑦ e		K	Ⓐ M									Ⓑ h						①–⑥ b	⑤–⑦	①–④		Ⓑ
Besançon Franche-Comté TGV ... d.	0655	0702	...	0850	0915	...	1103	1211	...	1337	1416	1451	1537	1637	...	1807	1842	1937	...	2037	2113	2123	...	2238
Besançon Viotte ... a.	0709	0721	...	0905	0928	...	1118	1226	...	1352	1430	1504	1552	1652	...	1822	1857	1952	...	2052	2128	2137	...	2252

A – Sept. 1 - Dec. 5.
B – Daily to Aug. 31; ⑥⑦ from Sept. 6 (also Dec. 8 – 12).
C – Daily to Aug. 31; ⑥⑦ from Sept. 6.
D – ⑥⑦ (also Aug. 15; runs daily July 5 – 27).
E – Daily to Aug. 17; ⑥⑦ from Aug. 23.
G – Daily to July 27; ⑥⑦ from Aug. 30.
H – Daily to Aug. 24; ⑥⑦ from Aug. 30. On ①–④ July 28 - Aug. 21 (also Aug. 22) departs Paris 0950 and does not call at Dijon.
J – Daily to July 27; daily Aug. 24 – 31; ⑥⑦ from Sept. 6.
K – Daily to July 27; Ⓒ from Aug. 2.
L – *TGV Lyria*. To / from Lausanne (Table **375**).
M – From July 28.
N – Until July 25.
P – ⑤ to Aug. 29 (also Aug. 14; not Aug. 15).
Q – Ⓑ to Aug. 31 (not Aug. 15); ⑦ from Sept. 7 (also Dec. 8 – 12).
R – ①–⑤ to July 25 (also Aug. 1, 8, Oct. 11; not July 14).
S – Daily to July 27; ⑤–⑦ Aug. 1 – 17; ⑥⑦ from Aug. 23 (also Dec. 8 – 12). On ①–⑤ June 16 – 30 departs Paris 1103, then runs 5 minutes later Dijon - Mulhouse.
T – Ⓑ to July 6; ⑤⑦ July 11 - Aug. 10 (also July 14, Aug. 14, 17, 24); Ⓑ from Aug. 29.
U – ①–⑥ to July 5; ①⑥ July 7 - Aug. 30 (also July 15, Aug. 15; not July 14); ①–⑥ from Sept. 1 (not Nov. 11).
V – Runs on Aug. 22 only.
Y – Runs on Aug. 14 only.
Z – ①–⑤ until July 4; ①–⑤ July 28 - Aug. 14 (also Dec. 8 – 12). Timings at Montbard and Paris are 7 – 19 minutes later on ①–⑤ July 28 - Aug. 14.

a – Arrival time.
b – Not July 14, Nov. 11.
d – Also July 14, Aug. 15; not Oct. 11.
e – Also July 14, Nov. 11.
f – ⑤ (also Aug. 14; not Aug. 15). Departure times may be 2 – 3 minutes earlier until July 25. On Aug. 14 departs Besançon 2012, Dole 2045.
h – Not Aug. 15.
m – ①–④ (not July 14, Aug. 14, Nov. 11). Arrives Paris 13 – 20 minutes later until July 3, Sept. 1 – 18, Oct. 6 – 30, Dec. 1 – 4.
q – Not June 21, 22, July 2 – 6, 12, 13, 19, 20, Sept. 6, 7, 20, 21.
r – ⑥⑦ (not June 21, 22, July 5, 6, 12, 13, 19, 20, Sept. 6, 7, 20, 21).
t – 1848 until July 6.
w – Not Oct. 25, Nov. 1.
x – Not June 21, 22, July 5, 6, 12, 13, 19, 20, Sept. 6, 7, 20, 21.
y – Not June 21, July 5, 6, 12, 13, 19, 20, Sept. 6, 7, 20, 21.

TGV – High-speed train. 🅁. 🍸.

△ – Runs 46 – 52 minutes earlier on June 21.
⊗ – On ①–⑤ from Aug. 18 departs Paris 1052, does not call at Dijon, arrives Mulhouse 1427 and then as shown.
⊖ – On ①–⑤ from Aug. 18 departs Mulhouse 1304, does not call at Belfort Montbéliard and arrives Paris 1555.
⊡ – On ①–⑤ from July 28 (not Aug. 15) does not call at Belfort Montbéliard and arrives Paris 1159.
‡ – 18 – 24 minutes later on ①–④ Sept. 1 – 11, ①–④ Oct. 6 – 30 and ①–④ from Dec. 1.

MULHOUSE - FREIBURG — 370a

km		①–⑤	①–⑥	⑦						🚌
0	**Mulhouse** ... d.	0633**f**	0830**k**	0831**k**	1031	1231	1431**r**	1630	1829**v**	2015
19	Neuenburg 🛃 ... d.	0653	0851	0851	1051	1251	1451	1651	1851	2047
22	Müllheim (Baden) ... a.	0657	0855	0855	1055	1255	1455	1657	1855	2053
51	Müllheim (Baden) ... **912** d.	*0705*	*0904*	0908	*1104*n	*1306*	*1501*	*1707*	*1907*	*2104*t
51	**Freiburg** (Brsg) Hbf ... **912** a.	*0724*	*0927*	0929	*1124*n	*1325*	*1523*	*1726*	*1926*	*2124*t

	①–⑤	①–⑥	⑦							🚌
Freiburg (Brsg) Hbf ... **912** d.	*0627*	*0918*	0936	*1034*	*1232*	*1432*	*1632*	*1832*	2033	...
Müllheim (Baden) ... **912** a.	*0648*	*0936*	0955	*1052*	*1251*	*1451*	*1651*	*1851*	2052	...
Müllheim (Baden) ... d.	0703	0945	0956	1103	1308	1503	1703	1903	...	2103
Neuenburg 🛃 ... d.	0707	0950	1000	1108	1313	1508	1708	1908	...	2109
Mulhouse ... a.	0727	1012**z**	1019	1129	1332	1527	1727	1928	...	2138

f – 0629 June 30 - Aug. 29.
k – 0829 until Aug. 31.
n – On ⑦ (also June 19, Oct. 3, Nov. 1) Müllheim d. *1102*, Freiburg a. *1121*.
r – 1426 on ①–⑤ to June 27 and daily July 1 - Aug. 31.
t – Connection is by train.
v – 1828 July 31 - Aug. 31 (not Aug. 3); 1831 on ⑦ (also Nov. 1; not July 13, Aug. 10, 17, 24, 31).
z – 1016 June 30 - Aug. 30.

BELFORT - MEROUX - DELLE — 370b

See Table **515** for full service Meroux - Delle - Biel/Bienne and v.v. French holiday dates apply.

km		Ⓐ	H	①–⑥ r	Ⓐ n	Ⓐ n	E		Ⓐ n	Ⓐ n	G		Ⓐ n		Ⓐ n	⑦ e	⑥ k	⑦ e	Ⓐ	Ⓑ z			Ⓐ	⑦ e	D	Ⓐ
0	**Belfort** Ville ... d.	0448	0548	...	0704	0748	*0748*	*0848*	1002	...	*1148*	*1248*r	1348	...	1548	1548	1602	1624	1648	1728	*1848*	*1948*z	2048	2112	*2148*	2220
7	Meroux TGV ⊡ ... a.	0456	0556	...	0712	0756	*0756*	*0856*	1010	...	*1156*	*1256*r	1356	...	1556	1556	1611	1631	1656	1735	*1856*	*1956*z	2056	2120	*2156*	2228
7	Meroux TGV ⊡ .. **515** d.	0457	...	0603	0714	0803	0803	0903	...	1103	1203	1303	...	1403	1603	...	1612	1634	1702	1736	1903	2003	...	2122	2203	2229
21	**Delle** 🛃 ... **515** a.	0513	...	0619	0731	0820	0819	0919	...	1119	1219	1319	...	1419	1619	...	1631	1653	1719	1757	1919	2019	...	2138	2219	2245
	Biel/Bienne **515** ... a.	...	...	0741	...	...	0941	1041	...	1241	1341	1441	...	1541	...	...	...	...	...	...	2041	2142	...	...	...	...

	①–⑥ rD	Ⓐ n	①–⑥ r	Ⓐ	E			Ⓐ n		H		Ⓐ n		Ⓐ n	⑦ e	H	Ⓑ z	Ⓑ z			Ⓑ z	Ⓐ			Ⓑ z
Biel/Bienne **515** ... d.	...	...	...	...	0619	0719	...	0919	1019	...	1119	...	1219	...	1519	...	...	...	1719	1819	...	...	2019	...	...
Delle 🛃 ... **515** d.	0541	...	0655	0745	0741	0841	...	1041	1141	...	1241	...	1341	1441	1641	1641	1741	1803	1841	1941	...	...	2141	...	2252
Meroux TGV ⊡ ... **515** a.	0556	...	0711	0801	0756	0856	...	1056	1156	...	1256	...	1356	1457	1656	1657	1758	1818	1856	1956	...	...	2156	...	2308
Meroux TGV ⊡ ... d.	...	0603	0713	0806	*0805*	...	0943	*1103*	...	1229	...	1303	*1403*	1503	*1703*	1703	1802	1819	*1903*	...	2006	2103	...	2203	2309
Belfort Ville ... a.	...	0612	0722	0815	*0815*	...	0952	*1112*	...	1238	...	1312	*1412*	1512	*1712*	1712	1812	1828	*1914*	...	2015	2112	...	2212	2318

D – To / from Delémont (Table **515**).
E – ⑥ to July 5; ①–⑥ July 7 - Aug. 30 (not July 14); ⑥ from Sept. 6.
G – Daily to July 6; Ⓒ July 12 - Aug. 24; daily from Aug. 30.
H – ①–⑥ to July 5; ⑥ July 12 - Aug. 30 (also Aug. 15); ①–⑥ from Sept. 1 (not Nov. 11).
e – Also July 14, Nov. 11.
k – Also Aug. 15.
n – Not July 7 - Aug. 29.
r – ①–⑥ (not July 14, Nov. 11).
z – Ⓑ (not Aug. 15).

⊡ – Meroux station platforms are located directly above Belfort-Montbéliard TGV station.

371 PARIS - LAROCHE MIGENNES - AUXERRE and DIJON

TER services

For *TGV* services Paris - Dijon, see Table **370**. **Warning!** Subject to minor timing variations. Other short-term alterations are possible, particularly affecting trains departing mid-morning to mid-afternoon on Ⓐ. On June 14, 15, 21, 22 services run from to Paris Gare de Lyon (not Bercy). **Readers are advised to confirm timings before travelling.**

km		Ⓐ	①–⑥ b	①–⑥ b	①–⑥ b	Ⓐ	Ⓐ		Ⓐ ▲	Ⓒ		①–⑥ b	Ⓒ	Ⓐ	Ⓐ	Ⓒ		Ⓐ 🚌	Ⓑ	⑥	Ⓒ	Ⓐ	Ⓒ	Ⓐ ⊡	Ⓒ	Ⓒ
0	**Paris** Bercy ▽ d.	...	...	...	...	0612	...	...	0732●	0735	...	0835	...	...	0921	0921	...	...	1035	1035	...	1135‡	1135	...	...	1235
79	Montereau ▽ d.	...	...	0558	...	0655	...	...	|	|	0755	|	...	...	|	|	0955	...	|	|	...	|	|	1155	1155	|
113	Sens d.	...	...	0624	...	0720	...	...	0831	0832	0836r	0932	...	...	1032	1032	1036r	...	1132	1132	...	1233	1233	1221	1236r	1332
147	Joigny d.	...	...	0649	...	0744	...	...	0848	0849	0900	0948	...	...	1049	1049	1100	...	1148	1149	...	1249	1249	1243	1300	1349
	Auxerre d.	0529	0633	|	...	|	*0734*	0834j	|	|	|	|	1031c	1033	|	|	|	...	|	|	1230	|	|	|	|	|
156	Laroche Migennes a.	0550	0654	0657	...	0750	*0751*	0854	0854	0857	0907	0956	1052	1053	1055	1057	1107	...	1155	1156	1253	1256	1257	1251	1306	1356
156	Laroche Migennes d.	0557	...	0658	0707	0758	0800	...	0858	0901	0909	0958	...	...	...	1101	1109	1112	1158	1205	...	...	1301	...	1307	1359
175	**Auxerre** a.	|	...	|	0724	0811	|	...	|	|	0926	1011	...	...	...	|	1126	|	1211	1218	...	...	|	...	1324	1412
230	Avallon a.	|	...	|	...	0905	|	...	|	|	...	1105k	...	...	...	|	...	|	...	...	...	...	|	...	...	1506
197	Tonnerre d.	0623	...	0721	...	...	0822	...	0924	0924	...	...	...	...	...	1124	...	1221	...	...	...	...	1324	...	...	...
243	Montbard d.	0649	...	0747	...	...	0848	...	0950	0949	...	...	...	...	...	1149	...	1319	...	...	...	...	1349	...	...	...
315	**Dijon** Ville a.	0728	...	0825	...	...	0927	...	1027	1027	...	...	...	...	...	1227	...	1448	...	...	...	...	1427	...	...	...
	Lyon Part Dieu **377** a.	...	...	...	...	...	...	...	1244	1244	...	...	...	...	...	1444	...	...	...	...	...	...	1644	...	...	...

	Ⓐ	Ⓐ ■	①–⑥ b			Ⓐ	Ⓑ z⊙				Ⓐ n	A	⑥ k	Ⓑ z	⑦ e	⑥ k	Ⓐ	Ⓐ		Ⓐ	⑥ k	⑦ e	⑦ e	Ⓐ	⑥ k	Ⓐ
Paris Bercy ▽ d.	1235	...	...	1333	...	1435	...	...	1535	...	1627	1627	1635	...	...	...	...	...	1728	...	...	...	1827	1827	1835	...
Montereau ▽ d.	|	...	...	|	1355	|	...	...	|	1555	|	|	|	...	...	...	...	1753	|	...	1755	1755	|	|	|	...
Sens d.	1332	...	...	1432	1436r	1532	...	...	1632	1636r	1732	1732	1732	...	...	...	...	1820	1832	...	1836r	1836r	1932	1933	1932	...
Joigny d.	1349	...	...	1449	1500	1549	...	...	1649	1701	1748	1749	1749	...	...	...	...	1843	1849	...	1900	1900	1949	1950	1949	...
Auxerre d.	|	*1334*	1434	|	|	|	1532	1633	|	|	|	|	|	1731	1826	1829	1830y	|	|	←	|	|	|	|	|	...
Laroche Migennes a.	1356	*1351*	1453	1455	1507	1556	1553	1653	1657	1707	1755	1756	1756	1752	1851	1850	1852	1849	1857	1849	1907	1907	1956	1957	1956	...
Laroche Migennes d.	1405	1416	...	1459	1509	1605	1609	...	1701	1708	1805	1805	1758	1809	...	...	...	→	1901	1909	1909	1916	1958	...	1958	2002
Auxerre a.	1418	|	...	|	1526	1618	|	...	|	1724	1818	1820	1811	|	...	...	...	...	|	1926	1926	1933	2011	...	2011	|
Avallon a.	1512	|	...	|	...	...	|	...	|	...	...	1922	...	|	...	...	...	...	|	2017n	...	...	...	...	...	|
Tonnerre d.	...	1443	...	1522	...	...	1636	...	1724	...	...	...	...	1836	...	...	...	...	1924	...	...	...	...	...	...	2028
Montbard d.	...	1509	...	1548	...	...	1701	...	1749	...	...	...	...	1902	...	...	...	...	1949	...	...	...	...	...	...	2054
Dijon Ville a.	...	1550	...	1626	...	...	1740	...	1827	...	...	...	...	1940	...	...	...	...	2027	...	...	...	...	...	...	2133
Lyon Part Dieu **377** a.	...	...	...	1844	...	...	...	...	2044	...	...	...	...	...	...	...	...	...	2244z	...	...	...	...	...	...	...

	Ⓐ	⑦ e		Ⓐ		Ⓐ	Ⓒ ◐		Ⓒ	Ⓑ	⑥
Paris Bercy ▽ d.	...	...	...	...	1927	...	...	2035v	...	2235t	2331
Montereau ▽ d.	...	...	...	1955	|	...	1955	|	2155	|	|
Sens d.	...	...	...	2020	2032	...	2036r	2132	2220	2340	0031
Joigny d.	...	...	...	2043	2049	...	2100	2149	2243	0005	0048
Auxerre d.	...	*1940*	2033	|	|	←	|	|	|	|	|
Laroche Migennes a.	...	*1958*	2053	2050	2057	2050	2107	2156	2250	0012	0055
Laroche Migennes d.	2009	2009	...	→	2101	2109	2109	2158	...	...	...
Auxerre a.	2026	|	...	...	|	2126	2126	2211	...	...	...
Avallon a.	...	|	...	...	|	2219f	2219	...	...	...	...
Tonnerre d.	...	2034	...	...	2124	...	...	...	...	...	...
Montbard d.	...	2100	...	...	2149	...	...	...	...	...	...
Dijon Ville a.	...	2139	...	...	2227	...	...	...	...	...	...
Lyon Part Dieu **377** a.	...	...	...	...	...	...	...	...	...	...	...

	Ⓐ	⑥ k	Ⓐ	⑥ k	Ⓐ	⑥ k	Ⓐ	①–⑥ b	Ⓑ z	Ⓐ
Lyon Part Dieu **377** d.	...	...	...	...	...	...	...	...	...	...
Dijon Ville d.	...	...	...	...	...	0535	0535	...	...	0621
Montbard d.	...	...	...	...	...	0611	0611	...	...	0658
Tonnerre d.	...	...	...	...	...	0637	0637	...	...	0723
Avallon d.	...	...	...	...	0542	|	|	...	...	|
Auxerre d.	0445	0545	*0529*	0633	0634	|	|	...	...	|
Laroche Migennes a.	0502	0602	*0550*	0652	0654	0659	0659	...	←	0756
Laroche Migennes d.	0504	0605	0604	0655	0710	0703	0703	0707	0710	0809
Auxerre a.	|	|	|	|	→	|	|	0724	|	0826
Joigny d.	0512	0613	0612	0703	...	0711	0712	...	0718	...
Sens d.	0530	0630	0630	0742r	...	0729	0730	...	0742	...
Montereau ▽ d.	|	|	|	0805	...	|	|	...	0805	...
Paris Bercy ▽ a.	0635	0725	0735	...	...	0826	0832	...	...	...

	⑦ e	①–⑥ b	⑥ k	①–⑥ b		Ⓐ	⑦ e	①–⑥ b	①–⑥ b	⑦ e	Ⓐ ⊡	⑥ k	Ⓐ	Ⓒ			Ⓐ ⊡	Ⓒ	Ⓒ	Ⓐ	Ⓒ	Ⓐ	⑦ e	⑥ k	⑦ e	①–⑥ b
Lyon Part Dieu **377** d.	...	...	...	0516g	...	...	...	...	...	...	...	...	...	0716	...	...	...	...	0916	...	...	...	...	...	...	...
Dijon Ville d.	...	...	...	0735	...	...	...	0824	...	...	...	...	...	0935	...	...	...	...	1135	...	...	...	...	...	...	...
Montbard d.	...	...	...	0811	...	...	...	0901	...	...	...	...	...	1011	...	...	...	...	1211	...	...	...	...	...	...	...
Tonnerre d.	...	...	...	0837	...	...	...	0926	...	...	...	...	...	1037	...	...	...	...	1237	...	...	...	...	...	...	...
Avallon d.	...	...	0739	|	...	...	...	|	...	0939	0940	...	...	|	...	...	...	...	|	...	...	...	...	1250	...	...
Auxerre d.	0745	0734	0832	|	...	0834	0834	|	0944	1031	1033	1034	...	|	...	1146	...	1230	|	...	...	1334	1340	1343	...	1434
Laroche Migennes a.	0802	0751	0853	0859	...	0854	0856	0954	1001	1052	1053	1051	...	1059	...	1202	...	1253	1259	...	...	1351	1359	1401	...	1453
Laroche Migennes d.	0804	0804	0855	0903	0909	0909	0911	1009k	1004	1055	1056	1053	1103	1103	1109	1205	1253	1256	1303	1305	1307	1404	1404	1404	1453	1456
Auxerre a.	|	|	|	|	0926	|	|	1026k	|	|	|	|	|	|	1126	|	|	|	|	|	1324	|	|	|	|	|
Joigny d.	0812	0812	0903	0912	...	0917	0919	...	1012	1103	1104	1101	1111	1110	...	1213	1301	1304	1312	1313	...	1412	1412	1413	1501	1504
Sens d.	0830	0829	0942r	0929	...	0942	0942	...	1029	1142r	1142r	1142r	1129	1128	...	1230	1341r	1341r	1330	1329	...	1430	1430	1430	1542r	1542r
Montereau ▽ d.	|	|	1005	|	...	1005	1005	...	|	1205	1205	1205	|	|	...	|	1405	1405	|	|	...	|	|	|	1605	1605
Paris Bercy ▽ a.	0925	0935	...	1027	...	...	...	...	1133	...	...	...	1225	1225	...	1325	...	...	1426	1431	...	1525	1525	1525	...	...

	⊠■		Ⓐ	Ⓒ		■		Ⓑ z	Ⓑ z	Ⓒ	Ⓐ	⑦ e	⑥ k	Ⓐ		①–⑥ b	⑦ e	Ⓑ z	Ⓐ	⑦ e	Ⓐ	A			◐	Ⓑ z
Lyon Part Dieu **377** d.	1116	...	...	...	...	1316	...	...	...	...	...	...	...	...	1516	...	...	...	...	...	...	...	...	1716	...	...
Dijon Ville d.	1335x	...	...	...	...	1535	...	1633	...	...	...	...	...	...	1735	...	...	1833	...	...	...	...	...	1935	...	2037
Montbard d.	1411	...	...	...	...	1611	...	1710	...	...	...	...	...	...	1811	...	...	1910	...	...	...	...	...	2011	...	2129
Tonnerre d.	1437	...	...	...	...	1636	...	1735	...	...	...	...	...	...	1836	...	...	1935	...	...	...	...	...	2036	...	2154
Avallon d.	|	...	...	...	...	|	...	|	...	1653	1653	...	...	...	|	...	...	|	...	...	...	1931	...	|	...	|
Auxerre d.	|	...	*1532*	1534	1633	|	...	|	...	1747	1747	1826	1829	1830y	|	...	...	|	...	1940	1945	2033	2033	|	...	|
Laroche Migennes a.	1459	...	*1553*	1551	1653	1659	...	1758	...	1804	1803	1851	1850	1852	1859	...	...	1958	...	1958	2002	2053	2053	2059	...	2221
Laroche Migennes d.	1503	1509	1604	1604	1656	1703	1708	...	1805	1807	1806	1854	1853	...	1903	1909	1916	...	2009	2004	2005	...	...	2103	2109	2228
Auxerre a.	|	1526	|	|	|	|	1724	...	1820	|	|	|	|	...	|	1926	1933	...	2026	|	|	...	...	|	2126	2245
Joigny d.	1512	...	1613	1612	1703	1709	...	...	...	1815	1815	1902	1901	...	1910	...	...	...	...	2012	2013	...	...	2112	...	...
Sens d.	1530	...	1630	1630	1742r	1727	...	...	...	1831	1841	1942r	1942r	...	1928	...	...	...	...	2040	2040	...	...	2130	...	...
Montereau ▽ d.	|	...	|	|	1805	|	...	...	...	|	|	2005	2005	...	|	...	...	...	...	|	|	...	...	|	...	...
Paris Bercy ▽ a.	1626	...	1725	1725	...	1824	...	...	...	1925	1949	...	...	...	2025	...	...	...	...	2149	2150	...	...	2226	...	...

LOCAL TRAINS PARIS - MONTEREAU - LAROCHE MIGENNES. For faster trains see the main part of Table **371** above.

km								Ⓐ		Ⓐ	Ⓐ		Ⓐ	Ⓐ		Ⓐ	Ⓐ	Ⓐ								
0	**Paris** Gare de Lyon d.	0646	0746	0846	1046		1546	1621	1646	1713	1721	1746	1813	1821	1846	1913	1921	1945	2046	2146	2243	...	...	...	...	...
45	Melun d.	0713	0813	0913	1113	and	1613	1649	1713	|	1747	1813	|	1847	1913	|	1948	2013	2113	2213	2314	...	...	...	...	...
60	Fontainebleau-Avon d.	0726	0826	0926	1126	hourly	1626	1701	1726	|	1801	1826	|	1901	1926	|	2001	2026	2126	2226	2326	...	...	...	...	...
79	Montereau d.	0744	0844	0944	1144	until	1644	1719	1744	1807	1823	1844	1909	1923	1944	2009	2019	2049	2144	2244	2344	...	...	...	...	...
113	Sens d.	...	...	...	...		...	...	...	1836	1852	...	1935	1952	...	2036	...	2136p	...	...	...	...	...	...	...	...
147	Joigny d.	...	...	...	...		...	...	...	1900	1918	...	2000	2018	...	2100	...	2200	...	...	...	...	...	...	...	...
156	**Laroche Migennes** a.	...	...	...	...		...	...	...	1907	1925	...	2007	2025	...	2107	...	2207	...	...	...	...	...	...	...	...

	⑥ k	Ⓒ	Ⓐ	Ⓐ	Ⓐ	Ⓒ		Ⓐ	Ⓐ		Ⓐ	Ⓐ	⑦ e	Ⓒ	Ⓐ										
Laroche Migennes d.	0410	...	0410	...	0453	0510	...	0539	0553	...	0639	0653	0710	...	...	...	...		...	...	...	...	...	...	...
Joigny d.	0418	...	0419	...	0501	0518	...	0547	0602	...	0647	0701	0718	...	...	...	...		...	...	...	...	...	...	...
Sens d.	0442	...	0444	...	0527	0542	...	0614	0627	...	0713	0726	0742	...	...	...	...		...	...	...	...	...	...	...
Montereau d.	0505	0515	0515	0544	0556	0605	0615	0645	0656	0715	0745	0755	0805	0815	0822	0915	1115	and	2115	2215	...	...	...	...	...
Fontainebleau-Avon d.	...	0533	0532	0602	|	...	0632	0702	|	0732	0802	|	...	0832	0840	0932	1132	hourly	2132	2231	...	...	...	...	...
Melun d.	...	0546	0545	0615	|	...	0645	0714	|	0745	0815	|	...	0845	0853	0945	1145	until	2145	2243	...	...	...	...	...
Paris Gare de Lyon a.	...	0614	0615	0643	0647	...	0713	0744	0747	0813	0843	0847	...	0913	0921	1013	1213		2213	2313	...	...	...	...	...

A – ⑦ to June 29; Ⓑ July 6 - Aug. 31 (not Aug. 15); ⑦ from Sept. 7 (also Nov. 11).
b – Not July 14, Nov. 11.
c – 1034 on ⑥ (also Aug. 15).
e – Also July 14, Nov. 11.
f – ⑤ (not Aug. 15).
g – ① (also July 15, Nov. 12; not July 14).
j – 0832 on ⑥ (also Aug. 15).
k – ⑥ (also Aug. 15).

n – Not July 7 - Aug. 29.
p – Arrives 2115.
r – Arrives 14–18 minutes earlier.
t – 2213 on ①–⑤ July 7–25.

v – 2027 on †.
x – 1331 on certain dates.
y – 1826 July 7 - Aug. 29.
z – Ⓑ (not Aug. 15).

▲ – On Ⓐ from July 28 runs Paris - Laroche Migennes only.
⊠ – Runs 44–53 minutes later Dijon - Paris on ①–④ July 28 - Aug. 14.
■ – Subject to alteration / cancellation on Ⓐ from Aug. 18.
◐ – Subject to alteration / cancellation on July 14, Aug. 17, 31.

● – Paris **Gare de Lyon** (not Bercy).
‡ – Departs from Paris **Gare de Lyon** on certain dates.
◇ – Change trains at Laroche Migennes on Ⓐ.
⊙ – On ⑦ (also July 14, Nov. 11) depart Auxerre 1534 and change trains at Laroche Migennes.
⊡ – Runs 13–18 minutes later Sens - Laroche and v.v. on certain dates.
▽ – See panel below main table for other local services Paris - Montereau and v.v.

DIJON and CHALON SUR SAÔNE - MONTCHANIN - NEVERS 373

km																									
		Ⓐ	①–⑥	Ⓐ	Ⓐ	①–⑥	①–⑥	Ⓐ	Ⓑ	①–⑥	Ⓐ	Ⓐ		①–⑥	①–⑥	Ⓐ	Ⓑ	Ⓑ	①–⑥	①–⑥	Ⓑ	Ⓑ	⑦		
			b	n		b	b		z	b				b	b		z	z	b	b	z	z	e		
0	**Dijon** Ville ... 377 d.	...	...	...	0612	...	0712	...	0812	0947	...	...	1212	...	1412	...	1546	...	...	1712	...	1812	1812	...	1912
37	Beaune ... 377 d.	...	...	...	0632	...	0731	...	0831	1008	...	...	1231	...	1431	...	1607	...	...	1731	...	1831	1831	...	1931
	Chalon sur Saône ... 377 d.	...	...	*0549*	|	0707	|	0807	|	|	1007	...	|	1407	|	...	|	1607	1711	|	1801	|	|	1902	|
	Chagny ... 377 d.	...	...	0622	|	0719	|	0822	|	|	1022	...	|	1422	|	...	|	1622	1723	|	1822	|	|	1922	|
81	**Montchanin** ... d.	...	...	0648	0659	0748	0800	0848	0858	1036	1048	...	1258	1448	1458	...	1635	1648	1748	1758	1848	1858	1858	1948	1958
89	Le Creusot Ville ... d.	...	...	...	0706	...	0807	...	0905	1043	...	...	1305	...	1505	...	1642	...	...	1805	...	1905	1905	...	2005
111	Étang ... ★ d.	0605	...	...	0722	...	0822	...	0921	1059	...	...	1321	...	1521	...	1657	...	...	1821	...	1920	1921	...	2021
	Autun ... ★ a.	|	...	...	|	...	|	...	|	|	...	...	|	...	|	...	|	...	...	|	...	...	|	...	|
179	Decize ... d.	0647	0718	...	0804	...	0904	...	1003	1142	...	1318	1403	...	1603	1648	1740	...	...	1903	...	...	2003	...	2103
216	**Nevers** ... a.	0719	0750	...	0829	...	0929	...	1029	1208	...	1350	1429	...	1629	1720	1806	...	...	1929	...	...	2029	...	2129

km																									
		Ⓐ	①	①–⑥	⑥	Ⓐ	①–⑥	Ⓑ	Ⓐ				Ⓐ	Ⓐ	Ⓐ		Ⓐ	Ⓐ	Ⓑ	Ⓑ	Ⓐ	⑥	⑥	Ⓐ	Ⓑ
			g	b	k		b	z											z	z		k‡	k		z
	Nevers ... d.	...	0531	...	0629	0629	...	0731	...	0931	...	1058	1229	1330	...	1531	1610	1709	1730	...	1810	1841	...	1848	1931
	Decize ... d.	...	0557	...	0654	0657	...	0757	...	0957	...	1123	1302	1356	...	1557	1642	1741	1757	...	1842	1906	...	1920	1957
0	Autun ... ★ d.	...	|	...	|	|	...	|	...	|	...	|	...	|	...	|	▬	▬	|	...	...	|	...	|	|
15	Étang ... ★ d.	0640	0640	...	0737	0741	...	0840	...	1040	...	1206	...	1440	...	1640	Ⓑ	①–⑥	1840	...	...	1950	...	2003	2040
▬	Le Creusot Ville ... d.	0655	0655	...	0752	0757	...	0855	...	1055	...	1222	...	1456	...	1655	z	b	1855	...	...	2006	...	...	2056
0	**Montchanin** ... d.	0703	0703	0712	0804	0804	0812	0903	0912	1103	1112	1229	...	1503	1512	1703	1712	1812	1903	1912	...	2013	2019	...	2103
29	Chagny ... 377 d.	|	|	0742	|	|	0842	|	0942	|	1138	|	...	|	1538	|	1742	1838	|	1942	...	|	2047	...	|
44	**Chalon sur Saône** ... 377 a.	|	|	0753	|	|	0853	|	0953	|	1149	|	...	|	1549	|	1753	1849	|	1953	...	|	2058	...	|
	Beaune ... 377 d.	0729	0729	...	0831	0831	...	0929	...	1129	...	1258	...	1529	...	1729	...	...	1930	...	...	2039	...	...	2129
	Dijon Ville ... 377 a.	0749	0749	...	0852	0852	...	0948	...	1148	...	1317	...	1548	...	1748	...	...	1950	...	...	2058	...	...	2153

MONTCHANIN - PARAY LE MONIAL - MOULINS SUR ALLIER

km											
		Ⓐ	①–⑥	Ⓑ	①–⑥		①–⑥	Ⓑ		Ⓑ	
			b	z	b		b	z		z	
0	**Montchanin** ... ▷ d.	0708	0808	0908	1108	1308	1508	1708	1808	1908	2008
15	Montceau les Mines ... ▷ d.	0722	0822	0922	1122	1322	1522	1722	1822	1922	2022
50	Paray le Monial ... 290 ▷ d.	0752	0852	0952	1156	1352	1552	1752	1852	1952	2052
61	Digoin ... 290 d.	...	...	...	1209	...	...	...	...	...	...
117	**Moulins sur Allier** ... 290 a.	...	...	...	1302	...	...	...	...	...	...
	Clermont Ferrand 330 ... a.	...	...	...	1424	...	...	...	...	...	...

	Ⓐ	①–⑥			①–⑥		Ⓑ		Ⓑ
		b			b		z		z
Clermont Ferrand 330 ... d.	...	...	...	...	...	...	...	...	1741
Moulins sur Allier ... 290 d.	...	...	...	...	...	...	...	...	1906
Digoin ... 290 d.	...	...	...	...	...	...	...	...	1951
Paray le Monial ... 290 ▷ d.	0608	0708	1008	1211	1408	1608	1808	1908	2008
Montceau les Mines ... ▷ d.	0638	0738	1038	1239	1438	1638	1838	1938	2039
Montchanin ... ▷ a.	0652	0752	1052	1252	1452	1652	1852	1952	2052

b – Not July 14, Nov. 11.
e – Also July 14, Nov. 11.
g – Also July 15, Nov. 12; not July 14.
k – Also Aug. 15.
m – Not Nov. 12.
n – Not July 7 - Aug. 29.

w – ①②④⑤⑥ (also Nov. 12; not July 14, Nov. 11).
z – Not Aug. 15.

‡ – Runs up to 5 minutes **earlier** on Aug. 15.

▷ – Additional journeys Montchanin - Paray and v.v. on Ⓐ:
From Montchanin at 1608. **From Paray le Monial** at 0808, 1708.

★ – 🚌 **ÉTANG - AUTUN** and v.v. Journey time 19–21 minutes:
From Étang at 0645 ① **g**, 0726 Ⓐ, 0828 ⑥ **k**, 0925 Ⓑ **z**, 1045 Ⓐ, 1210 Ⓒ, 1326, 1526 Ⓐ, 1605 ①–⑥ **b**, 1702 Ⓑ **z**, 1825 ①–⑥ **b**, 1845 Ⓐ, 1925 Ⓑ **z** and 2045 Ⓑ **z**.
From Autun at 0534 Ⓐ, 0609 Ⓐ, 0650 Ⓐ, 0706 ① **g**, 0809 Ⓐ, 0850 ⑦ **e**, 1007, 1133 **w**, 1230 ③ **m**, 1449 Ⓐ, 1626, 1749 ①–⑥ **b**, 1809 Ⓑ **z**, 1849 ⑦ **e**, 1918 ⑥ **k** and 1950 ⑦ **e**.

DIJON - DOLE - BESANÇON 374

km																											
		Ⓐ		Ⓐ		Ⓐ						Ⓐ		Ⓐ	Ⓐ		Ⓐ		Ⓐ		Ⓐ			Ⓑz			
0	**Dijon** Ville ... 375 d.	0509	0609	0640	0709	0740	0809	0909	1012	1109	1209	1309	1342	1409	1509	1540	1609	1640	1709	1740	1809	1840	1909	1940	2009	2109	2209
32	Auxonne ... d.	0529	0630	0659	0730	0759	0829	0929	1032	1129	1230	1329	1404	1429	1529	1602	1629	1702	1729	1802	1829	1902	1929	2002	2029	2129	2230
46	Dole Ville ... 375 d.	0539	0641	0709	0742	0808	0839	0939	1042	1139	1242	1339	1414	1439	1539	1612	1639	1712	1739	1812	1839	1912	1939	2012	2039	2139	2241
91	**Besançon** Viotte ... a.	0604	0717	0734	0814	0836	0904	1004	1107	1204	1314	1404	1446	1504	1604	1644	1704	1744	1804	1844	1904	1944	2004	2044	2104	2204	2315

	Ⓐ		Ⓐ	Ⓐ				Ⓐ				Ⓐ		Ⓐ					Ⓑz		Ⓐ		Ⓐ		Ⓐ		
Besançon Viotte ... d.	0455	0556	0625	0656	0716	0756	0856	0916	0956	1056	...	1206	1225	1256	1356	1456	1556	1616	1656	1716	1756	1816	1856	1916	1956	2056	2156
Dole Ville ... 375 d.	0529	0622	0659	0722	0749	0822	0922	0949	1022	1122	...	1233	1259	1322	1422	1522	1622	1649	1722	1749	1822	1849	1922	1949	2022	2122	2221
Auxonne ... d.	0538	0631	0708	0731	0758	0831	0931	0958	1031	1131	...	1242	1308	1331	1431	1531	1631	1658	1731	1758	1831	1858	1931	1957	2031	2131	2231
Dijon Ville ... 375 a.	0600	0651	0730	0751	0820	0852	0951	1020	1051	1151	...	1302	1330	1351	1451	1551	1651	1720	1753	1820	1851	1920	1951	2020	2051	2151	2251

z – Not Aug. 15.

PARIS - DIJON - LAUSANNE and NEUCHÂTEL 375

TGV timings may vary by a few minutes on certain dates – please check your reservation.

km																									
								TGV	*TGV*						*TGV*			*TGV*					*TGV*	*TGV*	
								9761	**9261**						**9269**			**9775**					**9777**	**9277**	
		①–⑤		Ⓐ	⑥	Ⓐ	Ⓐ	①–⑥												①–⑤	⑤				
		a			k		C	y			C				E	E		z		a¶	f¶		D		
0	**Paris** Gare de Lyon ... 370 d.	...	...	...	...	...	...	0615	0755	...	...	...	...	...	1155	...	...	1417	...	...	...	...	1617	1756	...
287	**Dijon** Ville ... 370 374 d.	...	...	...	...	0509	...	|	0935	...	...	1012	...	...	1333	...	...	|	...	...	...	1730	|	1932	...
333	Dole Ville ... 374 376 d.	...	...	...	0616	0537	0616	|	1000	...	1014	1040	1114	...	1358	...	...	|	...	...	...	1806	|	1957	...
359	Arc-et-Senans ... d.	...	...	...	0638	...	0639	|	|	...	1034	...	1133	...	|	...	...	|	...	...	...	1826	|	|	...
365	Mouchard ... 376 d.	...	...	...	0647	...	0653j	|	|	...	1040	...	1142	...	|	...	...	|	...	...	...	1842j	|	2014	...
389	Andelot ... 376 d.	...	...	...	0706	...	0713	◐	|	...	1059	...	1205	...	|	...	...	◐	...	...	...	1905	◐	|	...
410	Frasne ... d.	0623	...	0717	0722	...	...	|	1044	1053	...	...	1220	...	1444	1453	...	|	...	1755	1847	1918	|	2044	2053
426	Pontarlier ... d.	|	...	0732	0737	...	...	|	|	1106	...	...	1235	...	|	1506	...	|	...	1810	1858	1931	|	|	2106
490	**Neuchâtel** ... a.	|	...	...	...	...	...	|	|	1153	...	...	...	...	|	1553	...	|	...	...	...	...	|	|	2153
434	Vallorbe ... ▷ a.	0642	0647	...	...	...	...	|	1057	...	...	...	...	...	1457	...	...	|	...	...	...	...	|	2057	...
480	**Lausanne** ... ▷ a.	...	0733	...	...	...	...	1012	1140	...	...	...	...	...	1540	...	...	1812	...	...	...	...	2012	2140	...

							TGV		*TGV*	*TGV*			*TGV*	*TGV*					*TGV*						*TGV*
							9262		**9264**	**9768**			**9268**	**9774**					**9270**						**9784**
	①–⑤	Ⓐ	①–⑥	①–⑤	①–⑤	①–⑤	①–⑤								①–⑤		①–⑤				①–⑤	Ⓐ	①–④	⑤–⑦	Ⓑ
	a		sC	a	a	A	A	B	B	z		E	E	z	a		a¶				a¶				w
Lausanne ... ▷ d.	...	...	...	*0457*	*0557*	...	0619	...	0719	0946	...	...	1219	1346	...	1627	...	...	1619	1727	...	...	...	...	1946
Vallorbe ... ▷ d.	...	...	...	0548	0648	...	0700	...	0800	|	...	...	1258	|	...	1712	1720	...	1658	1812	1820	...	...	...	|
Neuchâtel ... d.	...	...	...	|	|	0606	|	0706	|	|	...	1206	|	|	...	...	|	1606	|	...	|	...	...	...	|
Pontarlier ... d.	0509	0557	...	|	|	0656	|	0756	|	|	1128r	1256	|	|	1628	...	|	1656	|	...	|	1736	1819	1831	|
Frasne ... d.	0519	0621j	...	0604	0704	0706	0717	0806	0816	|	1145r	1306	1316	|	1639	...	1738	1706	1715	...	1839	1752	1847p	1847	|
Andelot ... 376 d.	...	0634	0759	...	...	...	|	...	|	◐	1202	▬	|	◐	...	...	...	...	|	...	...	...	1905	1905	◐
Mouchard ... 376 d.	...	0707h	0818	...	...	...	0746	...	0846	|	1220	...	|	|	...	...	...	...	|	...	...	...	1922	1922	|
Arc-et-Senans ... d.	...	0712	0823	...	...	...	|	...	|	|	1226	...	|	|	...	...	...	...	|	...	...	...	1928	1928	|
Dole Ville ... 374 376 d.	...	0730	0841	...	...	...	0804	...	0904	|	1245	1259	1401	|	...	...	...	...	1800	...	...	...	1944	1944	|
Dijon Ville ... 370 374 a.	...	0756	...	...	...	...	0828	...	0928	|	...	1330	1425	|	...	...	...	...	1825	...	...	...	*2020*	*2020*	|
Paris Gare de Lyon ... 370 a.	...	...	...	...	...	...	1013	...	1109	1343	...	...	1605	1742	...	...	...	...	2004	...	...	...	...	...	2342v

A – Sept. 1 - Dec. 5.
B – Daily to Aug. 31; ⑥⑦ from Sept. 6 (also Dec. 8–12).
C – To/from St Claude (Table **376**).
D – Daily to June 27; ①–⑤ June 30 - Aug. 22; daily from Aug. 25 (not Nov. 1, 2, 22, 23).
E – Daily to Aug. 17; ⑥⑦ from Aug. 23.

a – Not Aug. 1.
f – Also Aug. 14; not Aug. 1.
h – Arrives 0651.
j – Arrives 7–9 minutes earlier.
k – Also Aug. 15.
p – Arrives 1834.
r – ①–⑥ (not July 14, Nov. 11).

s – Not July 14, Oct. 20–31, Nov. 1, 11.
v – Arrival time may be up to 17 minutes later on certain dates.
w – Not June 17, 18, 24, 25, 29, July 1, 2, 6, 20, Aug. 10, Nov. 2, 23.
y – Not June 28 - Aug. 23, Nov. 1, 22.
z – Not June 28 - Aug. 24, Nov. 1, 2, 22, 23.

TGV – *TGV Lyria*. High-speed train. Ⓡ. 🍸.

¶ – 🚌 12 Pontarlier - Frasne - Vallorbe and v.v.
◐ – Via Genève (Table **341**).
▷ – Additional local services Vallorbe - Lausanne and v.v. (journey time ±45 minutes):
From Vallorbe at 0516 and hourly until 0016.
From Lausanne at 0457 and hourly until 2257.

376 DOLE / BESANÇON - MOREZ - ST CLAUDE - BOURG EN BRESSE

km												
		⑥	Ⓒ	Ⓐ			🚌 ⑤ f	⑤ f●	D	⑤⑦ d	🚌 ⊖	🚌 ⑤⑦ d
0	**Dole** Ville ....**375** d.	0616	...	0616	1014	*1114*	1612	...	1806	...	...	...
	Besançon ◇ .**378** d.	|	...	|	|	|	|	1639	|	...	...	...
26	Arc-et-Senans **375/8** d.	0638	...	0639	1034	*1133*	|	1701	1826	...	...	...
32	Mouchard....... **375/8** d.	0647	...	0653**h**	1040	*1142*	1659	1709	1842**h**	...	...	2045
56	Andelot............. **375** d.	0705	0717	0717	1104	1209	...	1734**h**	1900	1914	1910	|
70	Champagnole ....d.	...	0742**j**	0742**j**	1120	1220	...	1746	...	1925	1930	2127
105	Morez.......................d.	...	0834	0834	1213	1313**h**	...	1844	...	2016	2017	2209
128	**St Claude** ....a.	...	0905	0905	1245	1346	...	1916	...	2047	2057	2249

	① g	①–⑥ s		⑤ f	🚌 ⑤ f	E	🚌 Ⓐ		Ⓑ z	
St Claude .... d.	0443	0615	0953	1507	...	1551	...	1719	1719	...
Morez.............................. d.	0520	0652	1030	1544	...	1628	...	1758**h**	1758**h**	...
Champagnole .... d.	0608	0740	1144**t**	1632	...	1715	1735	1848	1848	...
Andelot .... **375** a.	0618	0753	1157	1643	...	...	1755	1900	1900**r**	1905
Mouchard ....**375/8** a.	0641	0817	*1219*	1705	1715	...	1825	...	1928	1921
Arc-et-Senans ....**375/8** a.	*0711*	0822	*1225*	1712	|	...	|	...	1934	1927
Besançon-Viotte . **378** a.	|	|	|	1738	|	...	|	...	1959	|
Dole Ville .... **375** a.	*0729*	0841	*1245*	...	1802	...	1912	...	...	1944

ST CLAUDE - OYONNAX - BOURG EN BRESSE

km												
		🚌 Ⓐ	⚒	⚒	🚌	🚌 ⚒	Ⓐ	🚌	🚌 ⚒	🚌	🚌	†
0	**St Claude** ..... 🚌 ⊠ d.	...	*0550*a	*0645*	*0840*	*0940*	*1140*	*1235*c	*1440*a	*1630*a	*1725*	...
32	Oyonnax .... 🚌 ⊠ d.	...	*0626*a	*0721*	*0916*	*1016*	*1216*	*1311*c	*1516*a	*1706*a	*1801*	...
32	Oyonnax ....d.	0530	0638	0733	0925	1025	1238	1320	1525	1725	1810	1838
45	Brion Montréal ⊡ .....d.	0547	0653	0749	0942	1042	1254	1343	1542	1742	1827	1854
48	Nurieux Brion ....d.	|	0657	0753	|	|	1258	|	|	|	|	1857
81	**Bourg en Bresse** ▷ a.	0627	0731	0832	1022	1122	1332	1423	1622	1822	1907	1932
	Lyon Part Dieu ....▷ a.	...	0830	...	...	...	...	...	...	...	...	...

	🚌 Ⓐ	Ⓐ	🚌 ⑥	🚌	🚌 ⚒	🚌 ⚒	Ⓑ		🚌	🚌 Ⓑ
Lyon Part Dieu .... ▷ d.	...	...	...	...	...	...	...	...	...	...
Bourg en Bresse ...... ▷ d.	0645	0845	0850	1030	1235	1430	1730	1838	1930	2025
Nurieux Brion .... d.	|	0925	|	|	|	|	1808	1915	|	|
Brion Montréal ⊡ .... d.	0725	0929	0930	1110	1315	1510	1812	1918	2010	2105
Oyonnax .... a.	0742	0944	0947	1134	1332	1527	1827	1934	2027	2129
Oyonnax .... 🚌 ⊠ d.	*0750*	*0955*	*0955*	*1143*	*1340*	*1535*	*1838*a	*1948*a	*2038*	...
St Claude .... 🚌 ⊠ a.	*0826*	*1031*	*1031*	*1219*	*1416*	*1611*	*1914*a	*2024*a	*2114*	...

D – From Dijon Ville (d. 1730).
E – ①–④ (not July 7 - Aug. 28, Oct. 20–30, Nov. 11). Runs 18 minutes **earlier** on ③.

a – Ⓐ only.
c – Ⓒ only.
d – Also July 14, Aug. 14, Nov. 11; not Aug. 15.
f – Also Aug. 14; not Aug. 15.
g – Also July 15, Nov. 12; not July 14.
h – Arrives 6–9 minutes earlier.
j – Arrives 0730.
r – Departs 1908.

s – Not July 14, Oct. 20–31, Nov. 1, 11.
t – Arrives 1117.
z – Not Aug. 15.

⊖ – ①②③④⑥ (also Aug. 15; not July 14, Aug. 14, Nov. 11).
● – Retimed July 11 - Aug. 29 (also on Oct. 24, 31): Besançon d. 1606, Arc-et-Senans d. 1628, Mouchard d. 1633, Andelot d. 1657, Champagnole d. 1709, Morez d. 1800, St Claude a. 1832.
⊠ – All services St Claude - Oyonnax and v.v. are by 🚌.
⊡ – Brion Montréal la Cluse.
◇ – Besançon-Viotte.
▷ – See Tables **353** and **378** for full service Bourg en Bresse - Lyon and v.v.

376a BESANÇON - LE LOCLE - LA CHAUX DE FONDS

km											
		①–⑤ a	①–⑤ a		Ⓐ				Ⓐ		
0	**Besançon** Viotte........... d.	...	0452	...	0704	0931	1409	...	1737	1934	...
32	La Valdahon.................. d.	0449	0543	...	0752	1016	1450	1543	1830	2019	...
66	Morteau .... d.	0528	0627	0728	*0846**	1055	1528	1628	1906	2058	...
79	Le Locle.................**511** d.	0544	0645	0744	...	1114	1544	1644	...	2114	...
87	**La Chaux de Fonds 511** a.	0554	0654	0754	...	1124	1554	1654	...	2124	...

	①–⑤ a	①–⑤ a					Ⓐ	Ⓐ		⑦–④
La Chaux de Fonds.. **511** d.	0600	0700	0800	1200	1600	1700	...	...	2130	2130
Le Locle .... **511** d.	0607	0708	0809	1208	1609	1708	...	...	2139	2139
Morteau...........................d.	0621	0722	0826	1225	1626	1725	*1817**	1913	2154	2156
La Valdahon ....d.	0659	...	0903	1303	1704	1803	1907	1952	...	2232
Besançon Viotte ....a.	0737	...	0943	1343	1750	1853	1950	2037	...	...

a – Not Aug. 1.

* – Connecting service is by 🚌.

377 DIJON - CHALON SUR SAÔNE - MÂCON - LYON

TER services

For *TGV* services Dijon - Lyon, see Table **379**.
Warning! Timing variations and other short term alterations are possible, particularly affecting services from / to Paris – readers are advised to confirm timings before travelling.

km																									
		Ⓐ	①–⑥ b	Ⓐ	⑥ k	Ⓐ		①–⑥ b	Ⓐ		Ⓐ	★			Ⓐ	⚒		Ⓐ			⑦ e	Ⓐ	Ⓐ		
	Paris Bercy **371**........... d.	...	...	...	...	...	...	...	...	...	...	...	0735**h**	...	...	...	0921**c**	...	...	1135**c**	...	...	...	...	1333
0	**Dijon** Ville .... **373** d.	...	...	0549	...	...	0643	0722	0743	0849	0943	1026	1049	...	1143	1153	1243	1343	1353	1443	...	1543	...	1553	1648
37	Beaune.................... **373** d.	...	...	0608	...	...	0703	0750	0803	0908	1003	|	1108	...	1203	1223	1303	1403	1423	1503	...	1603	...	1623	1708
52	Chagny.............................d.	...	...	0617	...	...	0714	0759	0814	0917	1014	|	1117	...	1214	1234	1314	1414	1434	1514	...	1614	...	1634	1717
67	**Chalon sur Saône** ....d.	...	...	0628	...	...	0725	0812	0825	0927	1025	1100	1127	...	1225	1245	1325	1425	1449	1525	...	1625	...	1649	1727
125	Mâcon Ville........................d.	0602	0636	0658	0658	0728	0758	...	0858	0958	1058	1129	1158	1236	1258	1324	1358	1458	...	1558	1656	1658	1736	...	1758
163	Villefranche sur Saône ....d.	0632	0707	0721	0721	0751	0821	...	0921	1021	1121	|	1221	1307	1321	...	1421	1521	...	1621	1719	1721	1807	...	1821
197	**Lyon** Part Dieu ....a.	0656	|	0744	0744	0814	0844	...	0944	1044	1144	1204	1244	|	1344	...	1444	1544	...	1644	1742	1744	|	...	1844
	Lyon Perrache ....a.	...	0734	...	...	0825	...	...	...	...	...	1216	...	1334	...	...	...	...	...	...	...	...	1834	...	...

		Ⓐ			Ⓐ	⑥ k	⑦ e	Ⓑ z	⚒	
Paris Bercy **371**............d.	...	...	...	1535	...	...	...	1728	...	...
Dijon Ville .... **373** d.	...	1743	1749	1849	1943	1953	2012	2047	2053	2212
Beaune..................... **373** d.	...	1803	1819	1908	2003	2023	2041	2106	2123	2241
Chagny............................d.	...	1814	1831	1917	2014	2035	2054	2115	2135	2254
Chalon sur Saône ....d.	...	1825	1845	1927	2025	2049	2107	2126	2144	2307
Mâcon Ville.......................d.	1836	1858	...	1958	2058	...	...	2158	...	...
Villefranche sur Saône.....d.	1907	1921	...	2021	2121	...	...	2221	...	...
Lyon Part Dieu................a.	|	1944	...	2044	2144	...	...	2244	...	...
Lyon Perrache ....a.	1934	...	...	...	...	...	...	2300**e**	...	...

	①–⑥ b	Ⓑ z	①–⑥ b	① g	⚒	Ⓐ			Ⓐ	Ⓐ
Lyon Perrache .... d.	...	...	...	0500	...	0604	...	...	0726	...
Lyon Part Dieu .... d.	...	...	...	0516	...	0617	0716	...	|	0816
Villefranche sur Saône...... d.	...	...	...	0539	...	0639	0739	...	0754	0839
Mâcon Ville .... d.	...	...	0604	0604	...	0704	0804	...	0824	0904
Chalon sur Saône........... d.	0556	0614	0634	0634	0716	0737	0834	0913	...	0936
Chagny .... d.	0606	0624	0643	0643	0726	0747	0843	0923	...	0947
Beaune ....**373** d.	0615	0635	0652	0652	0737	0758	0852	0942	...	0957
Dijon Ville ....**373** a.	0639	0707	0711	0711	0807	0817	0911	1011	...	1017
Paris Bercy **371** .... a.	...	...	1025	1025	...	...	1225**c**	...	...	...

		Ⓒ	Ⓐ		Ⓐ		Ⓐ		Ⓐ	Ⓐ		★		Ⓐ		Ⓒ	⚒	Ⓐ	Ⓐ	⑦ e	Ⓐ		Ⓐ		Ⓒ
Lyon Perrache ....d.	0826	...	...	...	...	...	...	...	1326	...	...	1538	...	...	...	...	1725	1735	...	...	1835	...	...	2105	2205
Lyon Part Dieu.................d.	|	0916	0916	...	1016	1116	1216	1316	|	1416	1516	1552	...	1616	1716	...	|	1746	1816	...	1846	1916	2016	2116	2216
Villefranche sur Saône.....d.	0853	0939	0939	...	1039	1139	1239	1339	1354	1439	1539	|	...	1639	1739	...	1755	1810	1839	...	1910	1939	2039	2140	2239
Mâcon Ville.......................d.	0924	1004	1004	...	1104	1204	1304	1404	1424	1504	1604	1634	...	1704	1804	1823	1824	1832	1904	1920	1932	2004	2104	2202	2302
Chalon sur Saône ....d.	...	1034	1036	1116	1137	1234	1337	1434	...	1537	1634	1703	1715	1737	1834	1914	...	...	1937	1958	...	2034	2137	...	...
Chagny............................d.	...	1043	1043	1125	1147	1243	1347	1443	...	1547	1643	|	1726	1747	1843	1929	...	...	1947	2008	...	2044	2147	...	...
Beaune..................... **373** d.	...	1052	1057	1137	1158	1252	1358	1452	...	1558	1652	|	1737	1758	1852	1941	...	...	1958	2019	...	2053	2158	...	...
Dijon Ville .... **373** a.	...	1111	1117	1207	1217	1311	1417	1511	...	1617	1711	1736	1807	1817	1911	2010	...	...	2017	2052	...	2112	2217	...	...
Paris Bercy **371**...........a.	...	1426	...	...	...	1626**r**	...	1824**t**	...	...	2025	...	...	...	2226	...	...	...	...	...	...	...	...	...	...

b – Not July 14, Nov. 11.
c – Ⓒ only.
e – ⑦ (also July 14, Nov. 11).
g – Also July 15, Nov. 12; not July 14.
h – On Ⓐ departs Paris **Gare de Lyon** (d. 0732; not Bercy). Does not run Paris - Dijon on Ⓐ from July 28.
k – Also Aug. 15.

r – 1719 on ①–④ July 28 - Aug. 14. Subject to alteration / cancellation Dijon - Paris on Ⓐ from Aug. 18.
t – Subject to alteration / cancellation Dijon - Paris on Ⓐ from Aug. 18.
z – Not Aug. 15.

★ – *INTERCITÉS* service from / to Nancy (Tables **379** and **379a**).

LYON - LONS-LE-SAUNIER - BESANÇON - BELFORT 378

Minor timing variations are possible. See Table **379** for *TGV* services Lyon - Besançon Franche-Comté TGV - Belfort Montbéliard TGV.

km		①–⑥	①–⑥	Ⓐ	Ⓐ	Ⓐ			Ⓐ			Ⓐ	①–⑥	①–⑥			Ⓐ			Ⓐ	Ⓑ		Ⓒ	①–⑥	Ⓐ	⑤⑦
		b	**b**	**n**									**b**	**b**										**b**		**f**
0	**Lyon** Perrache... **353** d.	...	...	...	0601	...	0716	...	...	...	...	1301	...	1401	...	...	...	...	1616	1616	1716	1816	1816	1901	...	2117
5	**Lyon** Part-Dieu .. **353** d.	...	...	...	0612	...	0730	0942	0942	...	...	1312	...	1412	...	...	...	...	1630	1630	1730	1830	1830	1912	...	2134
	Ambérieu .... ‡ d.	...	...	...	|	...	|	|	|	...	...	|	...	|	...	...	...	...	|	|	1801	1859	1859	|	...	|
65	Bourg-en-Bresse **353** ‡ d.	...	...	...	0712	0719	0819	1021	1021	...	...	1412	1419**v**	1512	1518	...	...	...	1719	1719	1820	1919	1919	2012	2038	2234
129	**Lons-le-Saunier** .... d.	0543	0615	0645	▬	0801	0901	1101	1102	...	1215	▬	1501	▬	1601	...	1701	1715	1801	1801	1859	2001	2001	...	2122	2317
178	Mouchard.................. d.	0627	0703	0722	...	0840	0938	1137	1137	...	1302	...	1538	...	1638	...	1738	1802	1838	1838	...	2038	2038	...	...	...
184	Arc-et-Senans .... d.	0634	0708	0729	Ⓐ	0846	0943	1145	1145	...	1307	①–⑥	1543	...	1643	...	1743	1807	1843	1843	...	2043	2043	...	...	...
218	**Besançon** Viotte....... a.	0710	0740	0755		0909	1009	1209	1209	...	1340	**b**	1609	...	1711	...	1809	1840	1909	1909	...	2109	2109	...	...	...
218	**Besançon** Viotte.. ▷ d.	0714	...	...	0814	...	1014	...	1214	1232	...	1514	...	1614	...	1732	1814**n**	...	...	1914	...	...	2114	...	...	...
297	Montbéliard .... ▷ d.	0810	...	...	0910	...	1110	...	1310	1341	...	1610	...	1710	...	1841	1910**n**	...	...	2010	...	...	2210	...	...	...
315	**Belfort** Ville .... ▷ a.	0824	...	...	0924	...	1124	...	1324	1356	...	1624	...	1724	...	1856	1924**n**	...	...	2024	...	...	2224	...	...	...

	①–⑥	Ⓐ	Ⓐ		Ⓐ			①–⑥			①–⑥	①–⑥	Ⓐ				Ⓐ		Ⓑ	Ⓐ	Ⓐ		Ⓐ	Ⓐ		
	b							**b**			**b**	**b v**							**z**		**n**					
Belfort Ville .... ▷ d.	...	...	0535	...	0604	0604	...	0736	...	0936	...	...	...	...	1204	1336	...	1536	1536	1636	...	...	1736	...	1836	2036
Montbéliard........... ▷ d.	...	...	0549	...	0620	0620	...	0750	...	0950	...	...	...	...	1220	1350	...	1550	1550	1650	...	...	1750	...	1850	2051
Besançon Viotte ... ▷ a.	...	...	0646	...	0728	0728	...	0846	...	1046	...	...	...	...	1328	1446	...	1646	1646	1746	...	...	1849	...	1946	2146
Besançon Viotte .... d.	...	0601	...	0651	0731	...	0851	0851	1004	...	1051	...	...	1220	...	1451	1520	1651	1651	▬	1751	1820	...	1900	1951	...
Arc-et-Senans........... d.	...	0633	...	0716	0755	...	0913	0913	1028	...	1116	...	...	1252	...	1516	1552	1716	1716	...	1816	1852	...	1932	2016	...
Mouchard .... d.	...	0640	...	0722	0801	...	0920	0920	1034	...	1122	...	...	1300	...	1522	1600	1722	1722	Ⓐ	1822	1900	...	1938	2022	...
Lons-le-Saunier........ d.	0601	0730	...	0801	0844	...	1001	1001	...	...	1159	1301	...	1347	...	1601	1645	1759	1801		1859	1945	...	2022	2101	...
Bourg-en-Bresse **353** ‡ d.	0643	...	...	0843	...	...	1043	1043	...	...	...	1341	1348	1427	...	1643	...	...	1843	1848	...	...	...	...	2143	...
Ambérieu.................‡ d.	|	...	...	0902	...	...	1102	1102	...	...	...	...	|	...	...	|	...	...	|	|	...	...	...	...	2202	...
Lyon Part-Dieu....**353** a.	0730	...	...	0930	...	...	1130	1130	...	...	...	...	1448	...	...	1730	...	...	1930**e**	1948	...	...	...	...	2230	...
Lyon Perrache .. **353** a.	0744	...	...	...	...	...	1144	1144	...	...	...	...	1459	...	...	1744	...	...	...	1959	...	...	...	...	2244	...

OTHER SERVICES **BESANÇON** - **BELFORT**

	Ⓐ	Ⓐ	Ⓑ**z**	⑦**e**		Ⓐ	Ⓐ	Ⓒ		Ⓐ		Ⓐ
Besançon Viotte ...... d.	0532	0614	0632	0714	0732	1114	1314	1332	1632	1714	1832	2014
Montbéliard................ d.	0641	0714	0741	0810	0841	1210	1410	1441	1742	1810	1941	2110
Belfort Ville .... a.	0656	0728	0756	0824	0856	1224	1424	1456	1757	1824	1956	2124

	Ⓐ**n**	Ⓐ	Ⓐ	Ⓐ	Ⓐ				
Belfort Ville .... d.	0636	0704	0836	1136	1236	1304	1704	1819	1936
Montbéliard .... d.	0651	0720	0851	1150	1251	1320	1720	1833	1951
Besançon Viotte............. a.	0746	0828	0946	1246	1347	1428	1828	1942	2046

b – Not July 14, Nov. 11.
e – ⑦ (also July 14, Nov. 11).
f – Also July 14, Aug. 14, Nov. 11; not Aug. 15.
n – Not July 7 - Aug. 29.
v – Does not run on Ⓐ July 21 - Oct. 3.
z – Not Aug. 15.
‡ – See also Table **353a**.
▷ – See also panel below main table.

LUXEMBOURG - METZ - STRASBOURG - DIJON - LYON 379

TGV timings may vary by a few minutes – please check your reservation.
Warning! Certain services are subject to alteration on June 28, 29, Oct. 18, 19, Nov. 1, 8, 9, 10.

km		*TGV* **5521**	**4200**	*TGV* **9877**	*TGV* **9879**	*TGV* **5537**		*TGV* **9580**	*TGV* **5535**
			★				⊡	♣	⑦ **w**
0	**Luxembourg** .... **384** d.	...	...	0715**x**	1115**x**	...	...	...	...
34	Thionville .... **384** d.	...	...	0740**x**	1143**x**	...	...	...	...
64	**Metz** .... **383 384** d.	0546**j**	...	0809	1210	...	...	...	...
	Nancy .... ▷ d.	|	0746	|	|	1224	...	...	...
209	**Strasbourg**........................ **383** a.	0640**j**	|	0857	1259	1329	...	...	...
209	**Strasbourg**........................ **385** d.	0647	|	0904	1305	1337	...	1616	1903
274	Colmar..................................... **385** d.	0716	|	|	|	1407	...	|	1933
315	**Mulhouse** .... **370 385** d.	0752	◐	0957	1357	1440	...	1709	2002
360	Belfort Montbéliard TGV.......... **370** d.	0818	|	1021	1421	1506	...	1734	2029
442	**Besançon** Franche-Comté TGV **370** d.	0843	|	1044	1444	1536	...	1758	2052
519	**Dijon** Ville......................... **370** ▷ a.	0911	1014	1111	1511	1604	...	|	2119
519	**Dijon** Ville............................. **377** d.	0921	1026	1121	1521	1617	1749	|	2129
556	Beaune .... **377** d.	|	|	|	|	1640	1819	|	|
586	**Chalon sur Saône** .... **377** d.	0958	1100	|	|	|	1845	1856	|
644	Mâcon Ville .... **377** d.	|	1129	1223	1621	|	...	|	2230
716	**Lyon** Part Dieu .... **377** a.	1059	1204	1258	1656	1756	...	1956	2304
	Lyon Perrache..............................a.	|	1216	|	|	|	...	|	2318
	Valence TGV **350**.....................a.	|	...	1346	1746	|	...	|	...
	Avignon TGV **350**.....................a.	|	...	1426	|	1908	...	2109	...
	Aix en Provence TGV **350**.........a.	|	...	1449	|	1930	...	2131	...
	Marseille St Charles **350** ....a.	|	...	1506	|	1945	...	2146	...
	Nice Ville **350**..............................a.	|	...	...	|	2240**p**	...	...	...
	Nîmes Centre **355** ....a.	1222	...	...	1838	...	...	...	...
	Montpellier Saint-Roch **355** ....a.	1254	...	...	1905	...	...	...	...

	TGV **5512**	*TGV* **9898**	*TGV* **9583**		*TGV* **5516**		**4302**	*TGV* **5500**	*TGV* **9896**
	① **g**		♣	⊡			★		⊗
Montpellier Saint-Roch **355** .....d.	...	0631	...	...	...	...	...	1357	...
Nîmes Centre **355** ....d.	...	0658	...	...	...	...	...	1427	...
Nice Ville **350**.........................d.	...	|	...	...	0657**v**	...	...	|	...
Marseille St Charles **350** .....d.	...	|	0812	...	0945	...	...	|	1554
Aix en Provence TGV **350**...d.	...	|	0826	...	0959	...	...	|	1610
Avignon TGV **350**...................d.	...	|	0848	...	1022	...	...	|	1633
Valence TGV **350**...................d.	...	0748	|	...	|	...	...	1514	1714
Lyon Perrache..............................d.	0542	|	|	...	|	...	1538	|	|
Lyon Part Dieu .... **377** d.	0556	0833	1004	...	1138	...	1552	1604	1802
Mâcon Ville .... **377** d.	|	|	|	...	1216	...	1634	1641	|
Chalon sur Saône .... **377** d.	|	|	1106	1116	|	...	1703	|	1906
Beaune .... **377** d.	|	|	|	1137	1305	...	|	|	|
Dijon Ville.......................... **377** a.	0729	0959	|	1207	1326	...	1736	1740	1940
Dijon Ville.......................**370** ▷ d.	0738	1008	|	...	1338	...	1746	1750	1950
Besançon F-C TGV ⊠ .... **370** d.	0811	1036	1204	...	1408	...	|	1822	2020
Belfort Montbéliard TGV...... **370** d.	0834	1059	1228	...	1431	...	|	1847	2046
Mulhouse.................. **370 385** d.	0904	1124	1254	...	1458	...	◐	1912	2112
Colmar.................................. **385** d.	|	1152	|	...	1527	...	|	1944	|
Strasbourg .... **385** a.	0955	1224	1343	...	1554	...	|	2013	2207
Strasbourg .... **383** d.	...	1231	...	...	1600	...	|	2021	2214
Nancy .... ▷ a.	...	|	...	...	1702	...	2016	|	|
Metz .... **383 384** a.	...	1324	...	...	...	...	...	2109	2302
Thionville .... **384** a.	...	1348**y**	...	...	...	...	...	...	2323**z**
Luxembourg .... **384** a.	...	1415**y**	...	...	...	...	...	...	2349**z**

g – Not July 7 - Aug. 25, Nov. 10.
j – Not June 22, Sept. 1. Departs Metz 0543 from Nov. 17.
p – ⑤⑥ to June 21; daily June 27 - Sept. 7; ⑤⑥ from Sept. 12 (also Nov. 11; not Oct. 10, 11).
v – ⑥⑦ to June 22 daily June 28 - Sept. 8; ⑥⑦ from Sept. 13 (also Nov. 12, not Oct. 11, 12).
w – Not July 6 - Aug. 24, Nov. 9.
x – Luxembourg - Metz is subject to alteration / cancellation July 12 - Sept. 14.
y – Metz - Luxembourg is subject to alteration / cancellation July 12 - Sept. 14 (also on July 5, 6).
z – Metz - Luxembourg is subject to alteration / cancellation July 11 - Sept. 14 (also on June 22, July 5, 6).

TGV – High-speed train. 🅁. 🍷.
⊗ – Subject to alteration on on ①–⑤ from Nov. 10 (also on Sept. 28, Oct. 11, 26, Nov. 23, Dec. 7).
★ – *INTERCITÉS*.
◐ – Via Neufchâteau (Table **379a**).
⊡ – *TER* local service.
♣ – From / to Frankfurt (Tables **48** and **912**).
⊠ – Besançon Franche-Comté TGV.
▷ – See Table **379a** for other TER services Nancy - Dijon and v.v.

NANCY - NEUFCHÂTEAU - DIJON 379a

Warning! Subject to alteration July 11 – 14.

km				L	⚒	†	⚒¶	†	⑥**k**	Ⓐ**n**¶		Ⓒ	Ⓐ		⑥**k**	⑦	Ⓐ		Ⓒ					
0	**Nancy** .... **381** d.	0646	...	0746	0858	0955	1054	1154	1259	1305	...	1520	1607	1654	1722	1754	1807	...	1959	...	...	...	...	...
33	Toul.................................. **381** d.	0707	...	0807	0919	1017	1117	1217	1321	1328	...	1541	1629	1714	1744	1817	1832	...	2022	...	...	...	...	...
76	Neufchâteau ....d.	0740**r**	...	0834	0943	1041	1141	1241	1345	1353	...	1605	1653	1738	1808	1841	1856	...	2055	...	...	...	...	...
151	Culmont Chalindrey ....a.	0827	...	0920	...	...	...	...	...	...	...	...	...	1824	...	...	...	...	...	...	...	...	...	...
151	Culmont Chalindrey **380 381** d.	0836	...	0930	...	...	...	...	...	...	...	...	...	1831	...	...	...	...	...	...	...	...	...	...
228	**Dijon** Ville .... **380 381** a.	0920	...	1014	...	...	...	...	...	...	...	...	...	1924	...	...	...	...	...	...	...	...	...	...

	⚒		Ⓐ**n**	†	⑥**k**	Ⓐ	†	⑥**k**	Ⓐ¶		🚌⊠	¶		Ⓐ**n**¶	Ⓒ		Ⓒ	Ⓐ		⑥**k**	⑦	L		
Dijon Ville .... **380 381** d.	...	...	...	...	...	...	...	...	...	...	1015	1100	...	...	...	...	...	...	...	...	...	1746	...	2005
Culmont Chalindrey . **380 381** a.	...	...	...	...	...	...	...	...	...	...	1130	1147	...	...	...	...	...	...	...	...	...	1833	...	2053
Culmont Chalindrey ....d.	...	...	...	...	...	...	...	...	...	...	1145	1157	...	...	...	...	...	...	...	...	...	1845	...	2059
Neufchâteau ....d.	0655	...	0800	0852	0952	0958	1052	1151	1155	...	1300	1248	...	1407	1412	...	1612	1706	...	1825	1850	1932	...	2147
Toul................................... **381** d.	0721	...	0825	0919	1018	1024	1119	1217	1221	...	|	1315	...	1432	1438	...	1637	1733	...	1851	1920	1957	...	2211
Nancy .... **381** a.	0745	...	0848	0940	1040	1045	1141	1240	1244	...	1410	1336	...	1455	1500	...	1659	1754	...	1915	1940	2016	...	2230

L – *INTERCITÉS*. To / from Lyon (Table **379**).
k – Not Nov. 1.
n – Not July 15 - Aug. 14.
r – Arrives 0731
¶ – Subject to alteration / cancellation from Sept. 22 (please check before travelling).
⊠ – Rail replacement 🚌 which operates when the 1100 from Dijon Ville does not run.

380 PARIS - TROYES - BELFORT - MULHOUSE

SERVICE UNTIL JUNE 29 AND FROM SEPTEMBER 1. See page 602 for amended services June 30 - August 31.
Warning! Subject to alteration on Sept. 13, 14, 27, 28, Oct. 4, 5, 11, 12, 18, 19, Oct. 25, 26, Nov. 1, 2, 8, 9.
Timetable amendments are possible on other dates, particularly affecting trains departing mid-morning to mid-afternoon on Ⓐ.
Readers are strongly advised to confirm timings before travelling on services in this table.

km	🅁 for journeys from Paris	Ⓐ	①–⑥ b	Ⓐ	Ⓐ	①	②–⑤ b	⑥ k	N ⊗	Ⓐ	⑥ k	Ⓐ	Ⓒ	Ⓐ	Ⓐ ⊗	†	⑥ k	Ⓐ ⊗	⊗	⚒	⑥ k	Ⓐ ⊗	⑥ k	⑦
0	**Paris** Est d.	...	...	...	...	...	...	...	...	0542	0642	0642	0742	0742	0842	0842	0842	...	...	0942	1042	1142	1142	1142
110	Nogent sur Seine d.	...	...	...	...	...	...	...	...	0644	0739	0739	0839	0840	0939	0939	0939	...	...	1040	1139	1239	1239	1239
129	Romilly sur Seine d.	...	...	...	...	...	...	...	...	0656	0750	0750	0850	0851	0950	0950	0950	...	...	1051	1150	1250	1250	1250
166	**Troyes** a.	...	...	...	...	...	...	...	...	0718	0811	0811	0911	0914	1011	1011	1012	...	...	1114	1214	1311	1311	1311
	Troyes d.	...	...	...	...	0507	0515	0639	...	0720	0813	0813	0913	...	1013	1013	1019	...	...	...	...	1313	1316	1316
221	Bar sur Aube d.	...	...	...	...	0538	0545	0709	...	0750	0843	0843	0943	...	1043	1043	1050	...	...	...	...	1343	1346	1346
262	Chaumont **381** d.	...	...	...	...	0600	0607	0731	...	0811	0904	0904	1004	...	1104	1104	1111	...	...	...	...	1404	1407	1408
296	Langres **381** d.	...	...	...	...	0623	0629	0752	...	0833	0925	0926	1025	...	1126	1124	1132	...	...	...	...	1426	1427	1428
307	Culmont Chalindrey **379a 381** d.	...	...	...	...	0637v	0641	0800	0836	0841	0933	0935	1033	...	1135	1134	1141	...	...	...	...	1435	1436	1436
	Dijon Ville **379a 381** a.	...	...	...	...	0741	0741	...	0920	...	...	|	...	...	|	|	|	...	...	...	...	1521	1522	...
380	Vesoul d.	0638	0738	0808	0838	...	...	...	...	...	...	1013	...	...	1213	1212	1219	1238	1338	...	...	...	...	...
410	Lure **382** d.	0656	0756	0826	0856	...	...	...	...	...	...	1030	...	...	1230	1229	1236	1256	1356	...	...	...	...	...
442	**Belfort** Ville **382** ▷ d.	0724	0824	0854	0924	...	...	...	...	...	...	1050	...	...	1248	1249	1256	1324	1424	...	...	...	...	...
474	Altkirch ▷ d.	...	...	...	...	...	...	...	...	...	...	1106	...	...	...	1306	1313	...	...	...	...	...	...	...
490	**Mulhouse** ▷ a.	...	...	...	...	...	...	...	...	...	...	1116	...	...	...	1316	1323	...	...	...	...	...	...	...

🅁 for journeys from Paris	⚒	Ⓐ	⚒	†		Ⓑ z	Ⓒ	①–④ b	⑤	N	⑥ k	①–④ b	†	⑤	Ⓐ	⚒	⑦	Ⓐ	A	⑤†	Ⓑ	①–⑤ w	⑥⑦	⑥⑦
Paris Est d.	1242	...	1342	1342	...	...	1512	1512	1513	...	1642	1642	1642	1642	1712	1742	1812	1812	1842	1842	1942	2041	2042	2212
Nogent sur Seine d.	1340	...	1439	1437	...	...	1610	1610	1610	...	1740	1738	1739	1738	1814	1840	1910	1914	1939	1939	2040	2138	2139	2310
Romilly sur Seine d.	1351	...	1450	1448	...	...	1621	1621	1621	...	1751	1749	1750	1749	1825	1851	1921	1925	1950	1950	2051	2149	2150	2321
Troyes a.	1414	...	1511	1511	...	...	1643	1643	1644	...	1812	1810	1811	1811	1848	1914	1944	1948	2011	2012	2114	2210	2211	2344
Troyes d.	...	...	1513	1518	...	...	1645	1653	1654	...	1816	1812	1813	1818	...	...	...	...	2013	2017	...	2212	2213	...
Bar sur Aube d.	...	...	1543	1548	...	...	1715	1724	1725	...	1846	1842	1843	1849	...	...	...	...	2043	2047	...	2242	2242	...
Chaumont **381** d.	...	...	1604	1610	...	...	1736	1745	1746	...	1907	1903	1904	1910	...	...	...	...	2104	2108	...	2303	2304	...
Langres **381** d.	...	...	1625	1630	...	...	1756	1807	1805	...	1928	1924	1924	1930	...	...	...	...	2125	2128	...	2325	2326	...
Culmont Chalindrey **379a 381** d.	...	...	1634	1639	...	...	1805	1815	1813	1831	1938	1938v	1939v	1939	...	...	...	...	2133	2135	...	2333	2334	...
Dijon Ville **379a 381** a.	...	...	|	|	...	...	...	...	...	1924	|	|	|	|	...	...	...	...	|	|	...	...	...	...
Vesoul d.	...	1638	1713	1717	1738	1838	...	...	...	...	2016	2017	2017	2017	...	...	...	...	2211	2213	...	...	...	...
Lure **382** d.	...	1656	1730	1734	1756	1856	...	...	...	...	2033	2034	2034	2034	...	...	...	...	2228	2230	...	...	...	...
Belfort Ville **382** ▷ d.	...	1724	1748	1753	1824	1924	...	...	...	...	2053	2054	2054	2054	...	...	...	...	2249	2249	...	...	...	...
Altkirch ▷ d.	...	...	...	...	...	...	...	...	...	...	2109	2111	2110	2111	...	...	...	...	2305	2305	...	...	...	...
Mulhouse ▷ a.	...	...	...	...	...	...	...	...	...	...	2120	2121	2121	2121	...	...	...	...	2315	2316	...	...	...	...

🅁 for journeys to Paris	Ⓐ	⚒	Ⓐ	⚒	Ⓐ	Ⓐ	⑥ k	Ⓑ	⑥ k	Ⓐ	Ⓐ	①–⑥ b	⚒	Ⓐ		Ⓐ	⚒	⑥⑦	N ⊗	Ⓐ ⊗		Ⓐ	⑥⑦	Ⓑ z ⊗
Mulhouse ▷ d.	...	...	...	...	...	...	...	0520	...	...	...	...	...	...	0742	...	...	...	...	...	...	...	...	...
Altkirch ▷ d.	...	...	...	...	...	...	...	0530	...	...	...	...	...	...	0752	...	...	...	...	...	...	...	...	...
Belfort Ville **382** ▷ d.	...	...	...	...	...	...	...	0548	...	0636	0706	0736	...	...	0811	0936	...	...	...	...	...	...	...	1236
Lure **382** d.	...	...	...	...	...	...	...	0606	...	0705	0734	0805	...	...	0829	1005	...	...	...	...	...	...	...	1305
Vesoul d.	...	...	...	...	...	...	...	0623	...	0722	0751	0822	...	...	0846	1022	...	...	...	...	...	...	...	1322
Dijon Ville **379a 381** d.	...	...	...	...	...	...	...	|	...	...	...	...	...	0819	|	...	...	...	1100	...	...	...	...	...
Culmont Chalindrey **379a 381** d.	...	...	...	...	0545	...	0610	0701	0725	...	...	...	...	0905	0925	...	...	1125	1147	1225	...	...	1326	...
Langres **381** d.	...	...	...	...	0555	...	0619	0709	0734	...	...	...	...	...	0934	...	...	1134	...	1234	...	...	1335	...
Chaumont **381** d.	...	...	...	...	0616	...	0640	0729	0755	...	...	...	...	...	0955	...	...	1155	...	1255	...	...	1355	...
Bar sur Aube d.	...	...	...	...	0637	...	0701	0749	0816	...	...	...	...	...	1016	...	...	1216	...	1316	...	...	1416	...
Troyes a.	...	...	...	...	0705	...	0732	0818	0845	...	...	...	...	...	1045	...	...	1245	...	1345	...	...	1445	...
Troyes d.	0517	0547	0613	0647	0712	0747	0747	0820	0847	...	...	...	0947	...	1047	...	1147	1247	...	1347	...	1447	1447	...
Romilly sur Seine d.	0537	0607	0633	0707	0732	0807	0807	0839	0907	...	...	...	1007	...	1107	...	1207	1307	...	1407	...	1507	1506	...
Nogent sur Seine d.	0550	0620	0646	0720	0745	0820	0820	0852	0920	...	...	...	1020	...	1120	...	1220	1320	...	1420	...	1520	1519	...
Paris Est a.	0646	0716	0746	0816	0846	0916	0916	0946	1016	...	...	...	1116	...	1216	...	1316	1416	...	1516	...	1615	1616	...

🅁 for journeys to Paris	⑦	Ⓐ ⊗	⑥ k	①–⑥ b ⊗	⑥ k	Ⓐ			⑥ k	Ⓒ	Ⓐ		Ⓐ	Ⓑ	Ⓐ		Ⓐ		Ⓑ z		N	⑦		†
Mulhouse ▷ d.	1231	...	...	...	...	...	...	...	...	1531	1535	...	...	...	...	...	...	...	...	...	...	...	...	...
Altkirch ▷ d.	1242	...	...	...	...	...	...	...	...	1542	1545	...	...	...	...	...	...	...	...	...	...	...	...	...
Belfort Ville **382** ▷ d.	1304	1311	...	1336	...	...	...	...	...	1602	1604	...	...	...	1636	1736	...	1806	1836	...	...	...	...	...
Lure **382** d.	1325	1329	...	1405	...	...	...	...	...	1621	1622	...	...	...	1705	1805	...	1824	1905	...	...	...	...	...
Vesoul d.	1343	1346	...	1422	...	...	...	...	...	1638	1639	...	...	...	1722	1822	...	1841	1922	...	...	...	...	...
Dijon Ville **379a 381** d.	|	|	...	...	...	...	...	...	1613	|	|	...	1705	...	...	...	1805	|	...	...	2005	...	...	2125
Culmont Chalindrey **379a 381** d.	1428v	1425	1426	...	...	1551	...	...	1719	1726v	1720	...	1807	...	...	...	1904	1920	...	...	2053	2108	...	2223
Langres **381** d.	1438	1434	1435	...	...	1600	...	...	...	1736	1728	...	1816	...	...	...	1913	1929	...	...	...	2117	...	...
Chaumont **381** d.	1457	1455	1455	...	...	1621	...	...	...	1757	1750	...	1836	...	...	...	1934	1950	...	...	...	2138	...	...
Bar sur Aube d.	1518	1516	1516	...	...	1641	...	...	...	1819	1811	...	1857	...	...	...	...	2011	...	...	...	2158	...	...
Troyes a.	1547	1545	1545	...	...	1710	...	...	...	1846	1841	...	1926	...	...	...	...	2041	...	...	...	2228	...	...
Troyes d.	1549	1547	1547	...	1647	1717	1747	...	...	1848	1848	...	...	1948	...	...	...	2048	...	...	...	...	...	...
Romilly sur Seine d.	1608	1607	1607	...	1707	1737	1807	...	...	1907	1907	...	...	2007	...	...	...	2107	...	...	...	...	...	...
Nogent sur Seine d.	1620	1620	1620	...	1720	1750	1820	...	...	1920	1920	...	...	2020	...	...	...	2120	...	...	...	...	...	...
Paris Est a.	1716	1716	1716	...	1816	1846	1916	...	...	2020	2017	...	...	2116	...	...	...	2218	...	...	...	...	...	...

Other trains **BELFORT - MULHOUSE**

	⚒	Ⓐ	⚒	Ⓐ	Ⓒ	Ⓐ	Ⓐ	Ⓒ	Ⓐ	Ⓐ	Ⓒ	Ⓐ	Ⓒ	Ⓐ	Ⓐ		Ⓐ	†	Ⓐ	⚒	†	Ⓐ	Ⓐ	⑥ k	†	Ⓐ 🚌
Belfort Ville d.	0555	0631	0701	0734	0736	0806	0906	1005	1006	1202	1210	1304	1404	1506	1606	1706	1736	1800	1806	1848	1900	1907	2006	2016	2057	2102
Altkirch d.	0619	0653	0723	0755	0758	0826	0926	1025	1026	1222	1231	1326	1426	1525	1626	1726	1758	1822	1828	1910	1922	1928	2026	2036	2119	2148
Mulhouse a.	0637	0710	0740	0811	0815	0839	0939	1040	1039	1234	1245	1339	1439	1539	1639	1740	1810	1839	1840	1922	1939	1940	2040	2050	2134	2213

	Ⓐ	⚒	Ⓐ	Ⓐ		Ⓐ	Ⓐ	Ⓒ	Ⓐ	Ⓐ	Ⓒ		Ⓐ		†	⚒	Ⓐ	Ⓐ		Ⓐ	Ⓐ		Ⓐ			Ⓐ 🚌
Mulhouse d.	0620	0650	0723	0802	0823	0923	1023	1122	1220	1310	1315	...	1423	...	1559	1619	1650	1719	1751	1823	1901	1929	2020	2056	...	2230
Altkirch d.	0632	0704	0735	0816	0835	0935	1035	1136	1235	1322	1332	...	1435	...	1616	1636	1707	1736	1808	1838	1915	1946	2037	2110	...	2254
Belfort Ville a.	0654	0727	0758	0840	0857	0956	1056	1159	1256	1343	1355	...	1456	...	1640	1659	1730	1800	1831	1901	1939	2010	2100	2132	...	2345

A – ①②③④⑥ (not Nov. 1, 11).
N – From / to Nancy (Table **379a**).

⊗ – Subject to alteration / cancellation on certain ①–⑤ dates.
▷ – See panel below main table for other trains Belfort - Mulhouse and v.v.

b – Not Nov. 11.
k – Not Nov. 1.
v – Arrives 6–9 minutes earlier.
w – Not Sept. 15 – 19, 22 – 24, Nov. 17 – 21.
z – Not Aug. 15.

PARIS and REIMS - CHÂLONS EN CHAMPAGNE - NANCY (also CHÂLONS - ST DIZIER - DIJON) 381

TER services. [R] for all journeys from/to Paris. See Table **390** for faster *TGV* services Paris - Nancy and Strasbourg. **Warning!** Services from/to Paris are subject to alteration on Sept. 6, 20, 21, Oct. 18, Nov. 1, 11, 15, 16, 22, 23, 29, 30. Services via Nancy are subject to alteration on July 12–14 (also from late evening on July 11). Timetable amendments are possible on other dates, particularly affecting trains departing mid-morning to mid-afternoon on Ⓐ. **Timings are subject to minor variations - please check before travelling**.

km	[R] for journeys from Paris	Ⓐ	Ⓐ	Ⓐ	⑥ k	Ⓐ	Ⓐ	Ⓐ	Ⓐ	Ⓐ n	Ⓐ	Ⓒ	⑥ k	†	Ⓐ	Ⓐ	Ⓐ ⊗	Ⓐ	†	⑥ k		Ⓐ ⊗	Ⓐ n⊗	Ⓐ ⊗	†
0	**Paris** Est d.	...	...	...	...	...	...	...	...	...	0636	...	...	...	...	0736	...	...	0836	0836	...	0836	...	...	...
95	Château Thierry d.	...	...	...	...	...	...	...	...	...	0731	...	...	...	...	0827	...	...	0931	0925	...	0929	...	...	...
	Reims ♠ d.	...	...	...	...	...	0620	...	0705	0740	|	0731	...	...	0809	|	0835**n**	...	|	|	0935	|	...	...	...
142	Épernay ♠ d.	...	...	...	...	...	|	0654	|	|	0758	|	0819	...	|	0854	|	...	0958	0957	|	0957	...	...	...
*172**	**Châlons en Champagne** a.	...	...	...	...	...	0654	0709	0748	0815	0813	0809	0833	...	0851	0909	0909**n**	...	1013	1012	1018	1013	...	...	...
172	**Châlons en Champagne** d.	...	...	...	...	...	0657	0711	...	...	0823	0823	0834	...	...	0912	0918	...	1015	1014	...	1023	...	...	...
205	Vitry le François d.	...	...	...	...	...	0716	0728	...	...	0841	0842	0851	...	...	0930	0936	...	1033	1034	...	1041	...	...	...
	St Dizier d.	...	...	...	...	0622	0736	|	...	...	0859	0902	|	...	...	|	0955	...	|	|	...	1059	...	...	...
	Chaumont **380** d.	...	...	...	...	0719	0824	|	...	...	...	0956	|	...	...	|	1049	...	|	|	...	...	...	...	...
	Langres **380** d.	...	...	...	...	0742	0846	|	...	...	...	...	|	...	...	|	...	...	|	|	...	...	...	...	...
	Culmont Chalindrey **380** d.	...	...	...	...	0750	0854	|	...	...	...	...	|	...	...	|	...	...	|	|	...	...	...	...	...
	Dijon Ville **380** a.	...	...	...	...	...	...	|	...	...	...	...	|	...	...	|	...	...	|	|	...	...	...	...	...
255	**Bar le Duc** d.	0554	0615	0723	0726	...	...	0754	...	...	...	...	0917	0921	...	0955	...	1005	1058	1100	...	...	1126	1213	1228
	Metz Ville a.	|	|	|	|	...	...	|	...	...	...	...	|	|	...	|	...	|	...	|	...	...	|	|	|
295	Commercy d.	0615	0641	0744	0746	...	...	0815	...	...	...	...	0942	0942	...	1017	...	1026	...	1121	...	...	1147	1239	1249
321	Toul d.	0630	0659	0759	0801	...	...	0830	...	...	...	...	1001	0957	...	1034	...	1041	...	1136	...	...	1201	1258	1304
354	**Nancy** a.	0654	0725	0825	0825	...	...	0854	...	...	...	...	1026	1021	...	1055	...	1105	...	1155	...	...	1225	1325	1328
	Strasbourg **383** a.	...	...	...	...	...	...	...	...	...	...	...	...	...	...	1240	...	...	...	1335	...	...	...	...	...

[R] for journeys from Paris	Ⓐ	⑥ k	⊗	†	⑥ k	Ⓐ ⊗	⊗	Ⓐ n⊗	⑥ k	⑥ k	Ⓐ ⊗	Ⓑn z⊗	Ⓐ	⚒	Ⓒ	Ⓒ	Ⓐ ⊗	Ⓐ ⊗		Ⓐ	Ⓒ	Ⓐ	Ⓐ ⊗	⑥ k	Ⓐ
Paris Est d.	...	0936	...	1036	1036	1036	...	...	1136	...	...	...	...	...	...	1236	1236	...	...	...	...	...	1436	1436	...
Château Thierry d.	...	1031	...	1131	1131	1131	...	...	1231	...	...	...	...	...	...	1331	1331	...	...	...	...	...	1531	1531	...
Reims ♠ d.	1035	|	1135	|	|	|	...	...	|	...	...	...	...	1235	1335**c**	|	|	1335	...	1437	1505	1535	|	|	...
Épernay ♠ d.	|	1058	|	1158	1158	1158	...	...	1258	...	...	...	...	|	|	1358	1358	|	...	|	|	|	1558	1558	...
Châlons en Champagne a.	1109	1113	1209**e**	1213	1213	1213	←	...	1313	...	...	...	...	1318	1409	1413	1413	1409	...	1520	1539	1609	1613	1613	←
Châlons en Champagne d.	...	...	1223	...	1215	1215	1223	...	1315	...	...	...	...	...	...	1415	...	1423	...	...	1553	1620	1615	...	1620
Vitry le François d.	...	...	→	...	1233	1233	1242	...	1333	...	...	...	...	...	...	1433	...	1442	...	...	1612	→	1633	...	1639
St Dizier d.	...	...	...	...	1252	|	1302	...	|	...	...	...	...	...	...	1452	...	1502	...	...	1632	...	1652	...	1658
Chaumont **380** d.	...	...	...	...	...	|	1356**r**	...	|	...	...	...	...	...	...	...	...	1549	...	...	1718	...	...	...	1748
Langres **380** d.	...	...	...	...	...	|	...	...	|	...	...	...	...	...	...	...	...	1612	...	...	...	...	...	...	...
Culmont Chalindrey **380** d.	...	...	...	...	...	|	...	...	|	...	...	...	...	...	...	...	...	1623	...	...	...	...	...	...	...
Dijon Ville **380** a.	...	...	...	...	...	|	...	...	|	...	...	...	...	...	...	...	...	1710	...	...	...	...	...	...	...
Bar le Duc d.	...	...	...	...	...	1258	...	1306	1358	1426	1425	1526	1626	...	...	...	...	...	...	...	...	...	...	...	...
Metz Ville a.	...	...	...	...	...	...	...	|	...	|	|	|	|	...	...	...	...	...	...	...	...	...	...	...	...
Commercy d.	...	...	...	...	...	...	...	1327	...	1447	1446	1547	1647	...	...	...	...	...	...	...	...	...	...	...	...
Toul d.	...	...	...	...	...	...	...	1341	...	1501	1501	1601	1701	...	...	...	...	...	...	...	...	...	...	...	...
Nancy a.	...	...	...	...	...	...	...	1405	...	1525	1525	1625	1724	...	...	...	...	...	...	...	...	...	...	...	...
Strasbourg **383** a.	...	...	...	...	...	...	...	...	...	...	...	...	...	...	...	...	...	...	...	...	...	...	...	...	...

[R] for journeys from Paris	A	Ⓐ n⊗	Ⓐ	⑥ k	†	Ⓐ n	Ⓐ	Ⓐ n	Ⓐ	† ⊠	⑥ k	Ⓐ	⑥ k	†	⑥ k	Ⓐ n	Ⓐ	Ⓐ	†	Ⓒ		Ⓐ	2785 ⑦ j♥	2785 Ⓐ p♥	Ⓐ n
Paris Est d.	...	...	...	...	...	...	...	...	1636	1636	1636	...	...	...	...	...	1736	...	...	...	1836	...	1920	1928	...
Château Thierry d.	...	...	...	...	...	...	...	...	1723	1731	1731	...	...	...	...	...	1831	...	...	...	1931	...	|	|	...
Reims ♠ d.	...	...	...	...	...	1605	1635	1705	|	|	|	1734	1735	1735	1749	1805	|	1835	1831	1935	|	1935	⊙	◐	...
Épernay ♠ d.	1614	1617	...	...	...	|	|	|	1750	1759	1758	|	|	|	1816	|	1858	|	1912	|	1958	|	|	|	...
Châlons en Champagne a.	1630	1632	...	...	...	1639	1709	1739	1805	1815	1813	1817	1818	1818	1832	1839	1913	1918	1929	2009	2013	2018	2027	2032	...
Châlons en Champagne d.	1632	1634	...	...	...	...	1723	...	1807	1817	1815	1822	1823	1823	1833	...	1915	1923	1930	...	2015	2023	2030	2035	...
Vitry le François d.	1649	1651	...	...	...	...	1741	...	1823	1835	1833	1841	1842	1842	1851	...	1933	1941	1947	...	2033	2042	2049	2055	...
St Dizier d.	|	|	...	...	...	...	1801	...	|	|	|	1900	1902	1902	|	...	1952	2001	|	...	2052	2101	|	|	...
Chaumont **380** d.	|	|	...	...	...	...	1855	...	|	|	|	...	1958	1958	|	...	...	2048	|	...	...	...	|	|	...
Langres **380** d.	|	|	...	...	...	...	...	...	|	|	|	...	2019	2018	|	...	...	2111	|	...	...	...	|	|	...
Culmont Chalindrey **380** d.	|	|	...	...	...	...	...	...	|	|	|	...	2027	2028	|	...	...	2120	|	...	...	...	|	|	...
Dijon Ville **380** a.	|	|	...	...	...	...	...	...	|	|	|	...	...	2115	|	...	...	...	|	...	...	...	|	|	...
Bar le Duc d.	1716	1716	1725	1721	1826	...	...	...	1847	1905	1858	...	...	...	1919	...	...	...	2014	...	...	...	2113	2119	2125
Metz Ville a.	1814	1811	|	|	|	...	...	...	|	|	...	...	...	...	|	...	...	...	|	...	...	...	...	...	|
Commercy d.	...	...	1745	1746	1847	...	...	...	1909	1929	...	...	...	...	1942	...	...	...	2040	...	...	...	...	...	2146
Toul d.	...	...	1800	1804	1901	...	...	...	1926	1945	...	...	...	...	2002	...	...	...	2059	...	...	...	...	...	2200
Nancy a.	...	...	1824	1829	1925	...	...	...	1948	2006	...	...	...	...	2026	...	...	...	2126	...	...	...	...	...	2224
Strasbourg **383** a.	...	...	...	...	...	...	...	...	2119	2141**y**	...	...	...	...	...	...	...	...	...	...	...	...	...	...	...

[R] for journeys from Paris	Ⓐ	⑤ f	Ⓐ	Ⓒ	†	⑤ f▽	Ⓐ ▲	†	
Paris Est d.	...	1936	1936	2035	...	2136	2136	2236	...
Château Thierry d.	...	2031	2031	2134	...	2231	2231	2331	...
Reims ♠ d.	2035	|	|	|	2225	|	|	|	...
Épernay ♠ d.	|	2058	2058	2200	|	2258	2258	2358	...
Châlons en Champagne a.	2109	2113	2113	2216	2300	2313	2313	0013	...
Châlons en Champagne d.	...	2115	...	...	...	2315	...	...	...
Vitry le François d.	...	2133	...	...	...	2333	...	...	...
St Dizier d.	...	2152	...	...	...	|	...	...	...
Chaumont **380** d.	...	...	...	...	...	|	...	...	...
Langres **380** d.	...	...	...	...	...	|	...	...	...
Culmont Chalindrey **380** d.	...	...	...	...	...	|	...	...	...
Dijon Ville **380** a.	...	...	...	...	...	|	...	...	...
Bar le Duc d.	...	...	...	...	...	2358	...	...	...
Metz Ville a.	...	...	...	...	...	...	...	...	...
Commercy d.	...	...	...	...	...	...	...	...	...
Toul d.	...	...	...	...	...	...	...	...	...
Nancy a.	...	...	...	...	...	...	...	...	...
Strasbourg **383** a.	...	...	...	...	...	...	...	...	...

km	[R] for journeys to Paris	Ⓐ		⚒	Ⓐ	⑥ k	Ⓐ	2778 ①–⑥ t♥	Ⓐ	Ⓐ n	Ⓐ
	Strasbourg **383** d.	...	...	...	...	...	...	...	...	...	...
	Nancy d.	...	...	...	...	...	...	...	...	...	...
	Toul d.	...	...	...	...	...	...	...	...	...	...
	Commercy d.	...	...	...	...	...	...	...	...	...	...
	Metz Ville d.	...	...	...	...	...	...	...	...	...	...
	Bar le Duc d.	...	...	...	...	...	...	0610	...	...	...
0	**Dijon** Ville **380** d.	...	...	...	...	...	...	|	...	...	...
77	Culmont Chalindrey **380** d.	...	...	...	...	...	...	|	...	...	0538
88	Langres **380** d.	...	...	...	...	...	...	|	...	...	0548
122	Chaumont **380** d.	...	...	...	...	...	...	|	...	...	0609
195	**St Dizier** d.	...	...	0533	...	...	0557	|	0633	...	0658
224	Vitry le François d.	...	...	0554	...	...	0617	0636	0654	...	0718
257	**Châlons en Champagne** a.	...	...	0610	...	...	0637	0652	0710	...	0737
257	**Châlons en Champagne** d.	0512	...	0612	0612	0644	0646	0655	0712	0720	0739
	Épernay ♠ d.	0529	...	0629	|	|	|	|	0729	|	|
315	**Reims** ♠ a.	|	...	|	0655	0728	0730	◧	|	0755	0825
	Château Thierry d.	0559	...	0659	...	...	...	|	0759	...	...
	Paris Est a.	0653	...	0753	...	...	...	0801	0853	...	...

A – ①–⑤ July 15 - Aug. 14 (not July 21–24).

b – 1241 on † from July 6.
c – 1327 on † from July 6.
d – On ⑥ from July 5 (not Nov. 1) Châlons a. 1341, d. 1343.
e – 1216 on ⑥ from July 5 (not Nov. 1).
f – Not Aug. 15.
g – 4–5 minutes earlier until July 11.
j – Also July 14, Nov. 11; not July 13, Nov. 9. Departs Paris 7–10 minutes earlier July 6 - Aug. 31.
k – Not Nov. 1.
n – Not ①–⑤ July 15 - Aug. 14.
p – Not Nov. 10.
q – Not July 4, 18.
r – 1348 on Ⓒ.
t – Not July 14, Aug. 16, Nov. 10, 11.
v – Arrives 1637.
w – Also Aug. 15, Nov. 1.

x – Not June 16, 30, July 7, 21.
y – Not June 15, 22, 29, July 6, 20.
z – Also Nov. 1.

❖ – Subject to alteration on July 12 (diverted between Saverne and Bar le Duc).
◇ – Subject to alteration on July 13, Nov. 30 (diverted between Saverne and Bar le Duc).
⊠ – Subject to alteration on July 13 (diverted between Bar le Duc and Saverne). On Aug. 15 departs Bar le Duc 1904, Commercy 1926, Toul 1941. On Sept. 14 timings Château Thierry - Nancy are 2–8 minutes **earlier**.
▽ – Runs up to 90 minutes **earlier** on July 18.
▲ – Runs 43–60 minutes **earlier** July 15–17.
● – Subject to alteration on June 23, Oct. 6, 13.
⊗ – Subject to alteration on certain ①–⑤ dates.

⊙ – Via Champagne-Ardenne TGV (a. 2000, d. 2006).
◐ – Via Champagne-Ardenne TGV (a. 2008, d. 2011).
◧ – Via Champagne-Ardenne TGV (a. 0715, d. 0718).
♥ – *TGV* train. [R]. 🍷.
* – *188 km* via high-speed line.

♠ – **ÉPERNAY - REIMS**. *31 km*. Journey: 34–35 minutes.
From Épernay: On Ⓐ at 0632 **n**, 0649, 0732, 0802, 0832, 0902 **n**, 1002, 1102, 1202, 1302, 1402, 1432 **n**, 1602, 1632 **n**, 1702, 1732 **n**, 1802, 1832, 1902, 2012 and 2102 ⑤ **f**.
On Ⓒ at 0642 ⑥ **k**, 0802 ⑥ **k**, 1002, 1202, 1402, 1602, 1802 and 2012.
From Reims: On Ⓐ at 0549, 0649, 0719 **n**, 0749, 0819 **n**, 0849, 0949, 1049, 1149, 1249, 1349, 1419, 1549 **n**, 1619, 1649, 1719 **n**, 1749, 1819 **n**, 1849, 1949 and 2049 ⑤ **f**.
On Ⓒ at 0719 ⑥ **k**, 0919, 1119, 1249 ⑥ **k**, 1319 †, 1519, 1719 and 1919.

381 NANCY - CHÂLONS EN CHAMPAGNE - REIMS and PARIS (also DIJON - ST DIZIER - CHÂLONS)

TER services. 🅁 for all journeys to Paris. See Table **390** for faster *TGV* services Paris - Nancy and Strasbourg. **Warning!** Services to Paris are subject to alteration on Sept. 6, 20, 21, Oct. 18, Nov. 1, 11, 15, 16, 22, 23, 29, 30. Services via Nancy are subject to alteration on July 12 – 14 (also from late evening on July 11). Timetable amendments are possible on other dates, particularly affecting trains departing mid-morning to mid-afternoon on Ⓐ. **Timings are subject to minor variations - please check before travelling**.

km	🅁 for journeys to Paris	Ⓒ	Ⓒ	Ⓐ	Ⓐ	⑥	Ⓐ		Ⓐ	Ⓒ	†	⑥	Ⓐ	Ⓐ	Ⓐ	Ⓐ	⑥	Ⓐ	Ⓐ	⑥	†	†	Ⓒ	Ⓐ	Ⓐ
				●	n	k						k	⊗		⊗		k	n	n	k✣				⊗	
	Strasbourg **383** d.	...	...	0444x	...	...	...	...	...	...	...	...	...	...	...	...	...	...	...	0819	...	...	...	...	...
	Nancy d.	...	...	0616	...	0635	...	...	...	...	...	...	...	...	...	0735	0801	0835	0935	1002	1001	...	...	...	...
	Toul d.	...	...	0640	...	0658	...	...	...	...	...	...	...	...	...	0758	0827	0858	0958	1024	1025	...	...	...	...
	Commercy d.	...	...	0658	...	0714	...	...	...	...	...	...	...	...	...	0813	0843	0913	1013	1039	1041	...	...	...	...
	Metz Ville d.	...	...	│	...	│	...	...	...	...	...	...	...	...	...	│	│	│	│	│	│	...	...	...	...
	Bar le Duc d.	...	...	0722	...	0736	...	...	...	...	...	0900	...	...	...	0835	0908	0935	1035	1102	1103	1109	...	...	...
0	**Dijon** Ville **380** d.	...	...	│	...	...	...	...	...	...	...	│	...	...	...	...	...	...	...	│	...	│	...	...	...
77	Culmont Chalindrey **380** d.	...	...	│	...	...	0629	...	...	0732	...	│	...	...	0952	...	...	...	...	│	...	│	...	...	...
88	Langres **380** d.	...	...	│	...	...	0638	...	...	0741	...	│	...	...	1002	...	...	...	...	│	...	│	...	...	...
122	Chaumont **380** d.	...	...	│	...	...	0701	...	...	0802	...	│	...	...	1023	...	...	...	...	│	...	│	...	...	...
195	**St Dizier** d.	0709	...	│	...	...	0800	...	...	0900	...	│	0933	...	1110	...	...	...	...	│	...	│	...	1133	...
224	Vitry le François d.	0730	...	0750	...	...	0820	...	...	0919	...	0924	0954	...	1130	...	...	...	...	1127	...	1133	...	1154	...
257	**Châlons en Champagne** a.	0746	...	0807	...	...	0837	...	...	0937	...	0940	1010	...	1148	...	...	...	...	1144	...	1149	...	1210	...
257	**Châlons en Champagne** d.	0748	0752	0812	0820**g**	...	0850	...	0941	0950	0941	0942	1012	1050	1150	...	...	...	...	1149	...	1151	1200	1212	1242
	Épernay ♠ d.	0805	│	0830	│	...	│	...	│	│	0957	0959	1029	│	│	...	...	...	...	1207	...	1209	│	1229	│
315	**Reims** ♠ a.	│	0835	│	0855	...	0925	...	1024	1025	│	│	│	1125	1225	...	...	...	...	│	...	│	1235**b**	│	1325
	Château Thierry d.	0835	...	0859	...	...	...	...	...	...	1025	1024	1059	...	...	...	...	...	...	1235	...	1236	...	1259	...
	Paris Est a.	0923	...	0953	...	...	...	...	...	...	1123	1123	1153	...	...	...	...	...	...	1323	...	1323	...	1353	...

🅁 for journeys to Paris	⑥	Ⓐ	Ⓒ	Ⓐ	Ⓐ	Ⓐ	Ⓐ	Ⓐ	Ⓒ	⑥	⑥		Ⓒ	Ⓐ	Ⓐ	Ⓐ	Ⓐ	Ⓐ	Ⓒ	†	Ⓐ	Ⓐ	Ⓐ	Ⓐ	Ⓒ
	k	⊗		⊗	n⊗	⊗		⊗		k	k	⊗		⊗	⊗	⊗		n⊗			n		⊗		
Strasbourg **383** d.	...	...	...	...	...	...	...	...	...	...	...	...	...	...	...	...	...	...	...	...	...	...	...	...	...
Nancy d.	...	...	...	1035	1132	...	...	1235	1234	...	...	...	...	1334	...	...	...	1435	1441	...	...	...	...	...	...
Toul d.	...	...	...	1058	1155	...	...	1258	1259	...	...	...	...	1359	...	...	...	1458	1503	...	...	...	...	...	...
Commercy d.	...	...	...	1113	1210	...	...	1313	1318	...	...	...	...	1418	...	...	...	1513	1518	...	...	...	...	...	...
Metz Ville d.	...	...	...	│	│	...	...	│	│	...	...	...	...	│	1406	...	...	│	│	...	...	...	...	...	...
Bar le Duc d.	...	...	...	1135	1232	1329	...	1333	1345	...	1409	...	...	1445	1505	...	...	1535	1538	...	...	...	...	...	...
Dijon Ville **380** d.	...	...	...	...	...	│	...	...	...	...	│	...	...	...	│	...	...	...	│	...	...	...	...	...	...
Culmont Chalindrey **380** d.	...	...	...	...	...	│	...	...	...	...	│	...	...	...	│	...	...	...	│	...	...	...	1458	...	...
Langres **380** d.	...	...	...	...	...	│	...	...	...	...	│	...	...	...	│	...	...	...	│	...	...	...	1507	...	...
Chaumont **380** d.	...	1204	1213	...	...	│	...	...	...	...	│	1413	...	...	│	...	...	...	│	...	...	...	1529	...	...
St Dizier d.	...	1300	1300	...	...	│	...	...	...	...	│	1500	1509	...	│	...	...	...	│	...	...	...	1616	1633	...
Vitry le François d.	...	1320	1320	...	...	1354	...	...	...	...	1433	1520	1530	...	1532	...	...	...	1604	...	...	...	...	1654	...
Châlons en Champagne a.	...	1338	1337**d**	...	...	1410	...	...	...	...	1449	1537	1546	...	1548	...	...	...	1620	...	...	...	...	1710	...
Châlons en Champagne d.	1248	1350	1350**d**	...	...	1412	1442	...	...	1450	1451	1550**n**	1548	...	1550	1609	1612	...	1621	1647	1650	1712	...	1712	1742
Épernay ♠ d.	1305	│	│	...	...	1431	│	...	...	│	1509	│	1605	...	1607	1632	│	...	1646**v**	1704	│	│	...	1729	│
Reims ♠ a.	│	1425	1425	...	...	│	1525	...	...	1525	│	1625**n**	│	...	...	│	1655	...	1707	│	1725	1755	...	│	1825
Château Thierry d.	1332	...	...	...	...	1500	...	...	...	...	1536	...	1635	...	...	1659	...	...	...	1731	...	...	...	1759	...
Paris Est a.	1423	...	...	...	...	1553	...	...	...	...	1623	...	1723	...	...	1753	...	...	...	1823	...	...	...	1853	...

🅁 for journeys to Paris	⑥	Ⓐ	Ⓐ	Ⓐ	Ⓐ	⑥	†	†	Ⓐ	Ⓐ	Ⓐ	†	Ⓐ		⑥	Ⓐ	Ⓐ	⑥	Ⓑ		Ⓐ	⑥		⑤	⑦–④
	k	n			n	k						◇			k			k	z			k		f	w
Strasbourg **383** d.	...	...	...	...	...	...	...	...	...	...	...	1617	1617	...	...	...	...	...	...	...	...	...	...	...	...
Nancy d.	...	...	...	...	1536	1609	1620	...	...	1636	1707	1746	1746	...	...	...	...	1801	1835	...	1935	1934	...	2035	2035
Toul d.	...	...	...	...	1559	1633	1650	...	...	1659	1733	1806	1807	...	...	...	...	1824	1858	...	2001	2001	...	2058	2058
Commercy d.	...	...	...	...	1613	1647	1711	...	...	1713	1751	1822	1822	...	...	...	...	1840	1913	...	2020	2019	...	2113	2113
Metz Ville d.	...	...	...	...	│	│	│	...	...	│	│	│	│	...	...	1831	...	│	│	...	│	│	...	│	│
Bar le Duc d.	...	...	...	...	1633	1711	1739	...	...	1735	1818	1844	1844	...	1905	1927	...	1903	1935	...	2046	2046	...	2133	2135
Dijon Ville **380** d.	...	...	...	...	...	...	│	...	...	...	...	│	│	...	│	│	1805	...	...	...	...	...	...	│	...
Culmont Chalindrey **380** d.	...	...	...	...	...	...	│	...	1639	...	...	│	│	...	│	│	1904	...	...	...	...	...	...	│	...
Langres **380** d.	...	...	...	...	...	...	│	...	1648	...	...	│	│	...	│	│	1913	...	...	...	...	...	...	│	...
Chaumont **380** d.	...	...	...	...	...	...	│	...	1712	...	...	│	│	1802	│	│	1935	...	...	...	...	...	...	│	...
St Dizier d.	...	...	...	1733	...	...	│	1759	1800	...	...	│	│	1859	│	│	2024	...	...	...	...	...	...	│	...
Vitry le François d.	...	...	...	1754	...	...	1807	1819	1820	...	...	1910	1911	1919	1928	1954	2044	...	...	...	...	...	...	2201	...
Châlons en Champagne a.	...	...	...	1810	...	...	1823	1834	1837	...	...	1928	1930	1937	1944	2009	2104	...	...	...	...	...	...	2217	...
Châlons en Champagne d.	1750	1750	1812	1812	...	...	1824	1836	1850	...	...	1930	1932	1950	1946	2011	2106	...	...	...	...	...	...	2218**q**	...
Épernay ♠ d.	1807	│	│	1829	...	...	1842	1853	│	...	...	1952	1949	│	2002	2027	│	...	...	...	...	...	...	2235**q**	...
Reims ♠ a.	│	1825	1855	│	...	...	...	│	1925	...	...	│	│	2025	│	...	2146	...	...	...	...	...	...	...	...
Château Thierry d.	1835	...	...	1859	...	...	...	1923	...	...	...	2024	2020	...	2028	...	...	...	...	...	...	...	...	...	...
Paris Est a.	1923	...	...	1951	...	...	...	2016	...	...	...	2123	2123	...	2123	...	...	...	...	...	...	...	...	...	...

← FOR NOTES, SEE PREVIOUS PAGE

382 STRASBOURG - ST DIÉ - ÉPINAL - BELFORT

STRASBOURG - ST DIÉ - ÉPINAL *Service until July 13 and from August 16*

km	Ⓐ	Ⓐ	Ⓐ	Ⓐ¶	Ⓐ¶	Ⓐ¶	Ⓐ¶	Ⓐ¶	Ⓐ‡	Ⓐ	Ⓐ	Ⓐ	Ⓐ	Ⓐ
0	**Strasbourg** ▷ d.	...	0523	0655	0858	...	1207	1305	1434	1625	1701	1804	1834	2004
9	Entzheim Aéroport ✈ ▷ d.	...	│	0704	0906	...	1215	1313	1443	│	1710	1812	1842	2013
19	Molsheim ▷ d.	...	0537	0713	0914	...	1224	1321	1452	1641	1719	1820	1849	2021
87	**St Dié** a.	...	0728	0832	1026	...	1346	1433	1617	1757	1850	1938	2002	2146
	St Dié d.	0632	0736	0839	1035	1200	...	1441	*1701*	1807	*1914*	...	2012	...
147	**Épinal** a.	0726	0829	0932	1130	1252	...	1532	*1755*	1904	*2005*	...	2106	...

	⑥	⑥k	⑥k	⑥k	⑥k	⑥k	⑥k	⑥k	⑥k	⑥
Strasbourg ▷ d.		...	0706	0906	1206	...	1506	1714	1806	2014
Entzheim Aéroport ✈ ▷ d.		...	0715	0915	1215	...	1515	1722	1816	2022
Molsheim ▷ d.		...	0725	0925	1225	...	1525	1731	1825	2029
St Dié a.		...	0830	1029	1330	...	1629	1857	1930	2136
St Dié d.		0605	0837	1036	1337	1502	1636	...	1937	2144
Épinal a.		0656	0930	1129	1430	1556	1731	...	2031	2237

	†	†	†		†	†	†	†	†	
Strasbourg ▷ d.		...	0806	...	1130	1333	1414	1606	1814	...
Entzheim Aéroport ✈ ▷ d.		...	0814	...	1138	1341	1422	1615	1822	...
Molsheim ▷ d.		...	0822	...	1146	1349	1429	1625	1830	...
St Dié a.		...	0930	...	1300	1457	1550	1729	1938	...
St Dié d.		0732	0937	...	1307	1504	...	1737	1946	...
Épinal a.		0825	1030	...	1359	1557	...	1829	2036	...

	Ⓐ	Ⓐ	Ⓐ	Ⓐ	Ⓐ¶	Ⓐ¶	Ⓐ¶	Ⓐ¶	Ⓐ‡	Ⓐ	Ⓐ	Ⓐ	Ⓐ
Épinal d.		...	0630	0733	0836	1033	1156	1338	...	1658	1810	1911	2052
St Dié a.		...	0724	0827	0930	1127	1250	1430	...	1753	1903	2005	2143
St Dié d.		0611	0731	...	0941	1135	1300	1438	1634	1802	...	2015	...
Molsheim ▷ d.		0745	0841	...	1059	1245	1415	1556	1748	1919	...	2122	...
Entzheim Aéroport ✈ ▷ d.		│	0848	...	1106	1253	1422	1604	1757	1927	...	2129	...
Strasbourg ▷ a.		0802	0856	...	1114	1301	1430	1613	1806	1935	...	2137	...

	⑥	⑥k	⑥k	⑥k	⑥k	⑥k	⑥k	⑥k	⑥k	⑥k
Épinal d.		...	0640	0734	1033	1234	1502	1633	1834	2050
St Dié a.		...	0731	0825	1126	1325	1555	1727	1925	2141
St Dié d.		0611	...	0833	1133	1333	...	1734	1933	2149
Molsheim ▷ d.		0735	...	0939	1239	1439	...	1839	2039	2257
Entzheim Aéroport ✈ ▷ d.		0743	...	0946	1247	1446	...	1846	2046	2305
Strasbourg ▷ a.		0751	...	0954	1254	1454	...	1854	2054	2313

	†	†	†	†		†	†	†	†	†
Épinal d.		...	0834	1037	...	1409	1633	...	1843	2052
St Dié a.		...	0925	1127	...	1500	1724	...	1934	2145
St Dié d.		0757	0933	1134	...	1507	1732	1816	1941	...
Molsheim ▷ d.		0909	1039	1239	...	1614	1839	1931	2046	...
Entzheim Aéroport ✈ ▷ d.		0916	1046	1246	...	1622	1846	1938	2053	...
Strasbourg ▷ a.		0924	1054	1254	...	1630	1854	1946	2101	...

ÉPINAL - BELFORT

km		Ⓐ	Ⓐ	Ⓐ	Ⓐ		Ⓐ			Ⓑ	
		H🚌		t	n	H🚌		n	H🚌	w	r
0	**Épinal** d.	0500	...	0624	0951	1100	...	1528	1700	...	1855
58	Luxeuil les Bains d.	0619	...	0713	1036	1219	...	1611	1819	...	1939
76	Lure **380** d.	0644	0656	0727	1049	1244	1256	1625	1844	1856	1953
108	**Belfort** Ville **380** a.	...	0724	0754	1118	...	1324	1654	...	1924	2022

	Ⓐ	Ⓐ	Ⓐ		Ⓑ		Ⓑ	Ⓑ		
	n		H🚌	n	w	H🚌	rz	w	H🚌	r
Belfort Ville **380** d.	0606	0636	...	1106	1236	...	1706	1836	...	2006
Lure **380** d.	0634	0704	0710	1134	1304	1310	1734	1904	1910	2034
Luxeuil les Bains d.	0647	...	0738	1147	...	1338	1747	...	1938	2048
Épinal a.	0733	...	0902	1234	...	1502	1833	...	2102	2133

H – June 30 - Aug. 29.
k – Not Nov. 1.
n – Not June 30 - Aug. 29.
r – Not June 30 - Aug. 28.
t – Not July 1 - Aug. 29.
w – Not Aug. 15.
z – Also Nov. 1.
¶ – Subject to alteration / cancellation July 7 – 11, Aug. 18 – 22, 25 – 29, Oct. 20 – 24, 27 – 31.
‡ – Subject to alteration / cancellation Oct. 20 – 24.
▷ – Additional trains run Strasbourg - Entzheim Aéroport (300 metres from terminal) - Molsheim and v.v.: 3 – 4 per hour on Ⓐ, 1 – 2 per hour on ⑥, hourly on †.

METZ and NANCY - STRASBOURG — 383

See Table **390** for faster *TGV* services Paris - Strasbourg. **Services are subject to timing variations – SEE NOTES ❦ AND ❖.**
TER services from / to Paris are subject to alteration on Sept. 6, 20, 21, Oct. 18, Nov. 11, 15, 16, 22, 23, 29, 30.

km	*km*	SEE NOTE ❦	A	*TGV* **5521** ◧ 🅁	⑥ k	Ⓐ	Ⓐ	Ⓐ	⚒	Ⓐ	⑥ k		⚒	*TGV* **9877** 🅁	Ⓐ	⑥ k	†	Ⓐ	Ⓐ	Ⓐ	Ⓒ	⑥ k	Ⓐ	Ⓐ	*TGV* **2587** ⑦e 🅁
0	*0*	**Metz** d.	...	0546	...	...	...	0617	0641	...	...	...	0747	0809	...	...	...	0842	...	0917	0942	...	1017	1034	...
45	*45*	Morhange d.	...	│	...	...	...	0650	0706	...	...	...	0820	│	...	...	...	0907	...	0950	1008	...	1050	1101	...
		Paris Est **381** d.	...	│	...	...	...	│	│	...	...	...	│	│	...	...	...	│	...	│	│	...	│	│	0913f
		Nancy **387** d.	...	│	...	...	0611	│	│	0712	0713	...	│	│	0813	0813	0813	│	0913	│	│	1009	│	│	1058
		Lunéville **387** d.	...	│	...	...	0629	│	│	0731	0731	...	│	│	0831	0831	0831	│	0931	│	│	1027	│	│	│
	87	Sarrebourg d.	0528	│	0558	0617	0653	0718	│	0754	0755	...	0848	│	0856	0857	0854	│	0955	1018	│	1050	1118	│	1140
87		Réding d.	0533	│	0602	0622	0658	...	0729	0757	│	...	...	│	│	│	│	0930	│	...	1031	│	...	1125	│
110		Saverne d.	0549	│	0620	0639	0716	...	0743	0813	0815	...	...	│	0913	0914	0914	0945	1014	...	1046	1110	...	1143	1158
137		Brumath d.	0617	│	0647	0654	0730	...	0758	0828	0829	...	...	│	0928	0928	0928	0959	1028	...	1100	1126	...	1158	│
154		**Strasbourg** a.	0633	0640	0703	0708	0742	...	0810	0840	0840	...	...	0857	0940	0940	0940	1010	1040	...	1112	1138	...	1210	1221

SEE NOTE ❦	Ⓐ ◇	Ⓒ	†	*TGV* **9879** 🅁	⑥ k ◇	Ⓐ	*TGV* **5537** 🅁	Ⓐ	⑥ k	†	Ⓐ	⑥ k	Ⓐ	⑥ k	Ⓑ z	⑥ k	Ⓐ	Ⓐ n	⑥ k	Ⓐ	⑥ k	†	†	Ⓐ	Ⓑ z
Metz d.	...	1050	...	1210	...	...	...	...	1243	1243	...	...	1342	1344	...	...	1403	1442	...	1517	1542	1547	...	...	1642
Morhange d.	...	1123	...	│	...	...	...	...	1307	1308	...	...	1407	1416	...	...	1435	1507	...	1550	1607	1620	...	...	1707
Paris Est **381** d.	0736	│	...	│	0836	...	...	...	│	│	...	...	│	│	...	...	│	│	...	│	│	│	...	...	│
Nancy **387** d.	1059	│	1113	│	1159	1213	1224	...	│	│	1310	1313	│	│	1414	1414	│	│	1513	│	│	│	1611	1613	│
Lunéville **387** d.	1119	│	1131	│	1219	1231	│	←	│	│	1328	1331	│	│	1432	1432	│	│	1531	│	│	│	1629	1631	│
Sarrebourg d.	1143	1151	1155	│	1242	1253	│	1255	│	│	1355	1355	│	1444	1455	1458	1503	│	1554	1618	│	1648	1655	1654	│
Réding d.	│	...	│	│	│	→	│	│	1330	1331	│	│	1430	...	│	│	...	1530	│	...	1630	...	│	│	1730
Saverne d.	1203	...	1215	│	1259	...	│	1314	1345	1347	1411	1415	1444	...	1515	1515	...	1544	1614	...	1644	...	1712	1714	1745
Brumath d.	│	...	1229	│	│	...	│	1328	1359	1401	1425	1429	1458	...	1529	1529	...	1558	1628	...	1658	...	1726	1728	1759
Strasbourg a.	1240	...	1240	1259	1335	...	1329	1340	1410	1413	1436	1441	1510	...	1540	1540	...	1610	1641	...	1710	...	1738	1740	1810

SEE NOTE ❦	⑥ k	⚒	Ⓐ	⚒	*Ouigo* **7693** ⊠ 🅁	⚒	†	†	Ⓐ	Ⓐ	Ⓐ	†		⑥ k	⚒	Ⓐ ◇	†	† ◇⊡	⑥ k	Ⓐ	Ⓐ	†		*TGV* **2583** ⑦ B 🅁	*TGV* **2583** Ⓐ d 🅁
Metz d.	1652	...	1717	1740	1804	...	1747	...	...	1817	1843	1842	...	1919	1944	...	1951	...	...	2017	2042	2042	...	...	...
Morhange d.	1725	...	1750	1805	│	...	1820	...	...	1850	1907	1907	...	1952	2009	...	2024	...	...	2050	2108	2107	...	...	...
Paris Est **381** d.	│	...	│	│	│	...	│	...	...	│	│	│	...	│	│	1636	│	1636	...	│	│	│	...	1924	1943
Nancy **387** d.	│	1713	│	│	│	...	│	1810	1813	│	│	│	1913	│	│	1954	│	2016	2015	│	│	│	...	2114	2120
Lunéville **387** d.	│	1731	│	│	│	...	│	1828	1831	│	│	│	1931	│	│	2012	│	2035	2033	│	│	│	...	2134	│
Sarrebourg d.	1753	1757	1818	│	│	...	1848	1852	1857	1918	│	│	1954	2020	│	2036	2052	2057	2056	2118	│	│	...	2158	2200
Réding d.	...	│	...	1828	│	←	...	│	│	...	1930	1930	│	...	2032	│	...	│	│	...	2130	2130	...	│	│
Saverne d.	...	1814	...	1844	│	1846	...	1912	1914	...	1945	1948	2014	...	2047	2053	...	2115y	2114	...	2145	2145	...	2216	2218
Brumath d.	...	1828	...	→	│	1900	...	1927	1928	...	1959	2002	2028	...	2101	│	...	│	2128	...	2159	2159	...	│	│
Strasbourg a.	...	1840	...	...	1900	1911	...	1939	1940	...	2010	2014	2040	...	2112	2119	...	2141y	2140	...	2211	2211	...	2240	2242

km	SEE NOTE ❖	Ⓐ ● ◇	*TGV* **2654** Ⓐ E P 🅁	*TGV* **2654** ⑥ u P 🅁	*TGV* **2584** G 🅁	⚒	Ⓐ	Ⓐ	Ⓐ	⚒	⑥ k	Ⓐ	⑥ k ⊖ ◇	†	Ⓐ	Ⓐ	Ⓒ	Ⓐ	⑥ k	⑥ k	†	Ⓐ	Ⓒ	Ⓐ	Ⓐ
0	**Strasbourg** d.	0444r	0520	0533	0539	...	0614	0646	...	0719	0749	0752	0819	0821	0822	...	...	0849	0923	0949	0949	...	1019	1019	1049
17	Brumath d.	│	│	│	│	...	0627	0658	...	0730	0801	0803	│	0832	0833	...	...	0900	0935	1000	1000	...	1031	1030	1100
44	Saverne d.	0507r	0543	0558	0606	...	0644	0712	...	0746	0815	0818	0844	0848	0848	...	...	0915	0950	1014	1015	...	1046	1046	1115
67	Réding d.	│	│	│	│	...	│	0728	...	│	0830	0832	│	│	│	...	...	0929	│	1030	1031	...	│	│	1129
70	Sarrebourg d.	0524	0614	0624	0624	0636	0700	│	0736	0803	│	│	0903	0906	0907	0906	0909	│	1009	│	│	1036	1103	1105	│
117	Lunéville **387** d.	0550	│	│	0649	│	0726	│	│	0829	│	│	0928	0930	0930	│	│	│	1032	│	│	│	1129	1128	│
150	**Nancy** **387** a.	0612	│	│	0710	│	0744	│	│	0848	│	│	0952	0949	0948	│	│	│	1050	│	│	│	1147	1147	│
	Paris Est **381** a.	0953	│	│	0846	│	...	│	│	...	│	│	1323	...	...	│	│	│	...	│	│	│	...	...	│
	Morhange d.	...	│	│	...	0704	...	0752	0804	...	0853	0856	...	...	...	0935	0937	0952	...	1053	1055	1104	...	...	1152
	Metz a.	...	0702	0711	...	0736	...	0816	0836	...	0917	0920	...	...	...	1007	1009	1016	...	1118	1119	1136	...	...	1216

SEE NOTE ❖	Ⓐ	⑥ k	Ⓐ	⑥ k		*TGV* **9898** 🅁	*Ouigo* **7692** ⊠ 🅁	†	*TGV* **2588** ⑦e 🅁	Ⓐ n	Ⓒ	⑥ k	⑥ k	Ⓐ	Ⓐ	⑥ k	Ⓐ	Ⓐ	†	Ⓐ	*TGV* **5516** 🅁	Ⓑ z ⊕ ◇	†	⑥ k	Ⓐ
Strasbourg d.	...	...	1119	1146	1219	1231	1250	...	1242	1249	1349	1422	...	1422	1449	1519	1519	...	1550	...	1600	1617	...	1648	1649
Brumath d.	...	...	1130	1157	1230	│	│	...	│	1300	1400	1433	...	1434	1500	1531	1530	...	1603	...	│	│	...	1659	1700
Saverne d.	...	...	1146	1212	1246	│	│	...	1305	1315	1415	1448	...	1450	1515	1546	1546	...	1619	...	│	1641	...	1714	1715
Réding d.	...	...	│	1226	│	│	│	...	│	1329	1429	│	...	│	1529	│	│	...	1634	...	│	│	...	1729	1732
Sarrebourg d.	1136	1211	1202	│	1305	│	│	1311	1323	│	│	1507	1511	1509	│	1603	1605	1606	│	1636	│	1700	1708	│	1744j
Lunéville **387** d.	│	│	1229	│	1328	│	│	│	│	│	│	1529	│	1532	│	1626	1628	│	│	│	│	1723	│	│	│
Nancy **387** a.	│	│	1247	│	1347	│	│	│	1405	│	│	1547	│	1550	│	1644	1647	│	│	│	1702	1745	│	│	│
Paris Est **381** a.	│	│	...	│	...	│	│	│	1606	│	│	...	│	...	│	...	...	│	│	│	...	2123	│	│	│
Morhange d.	1204	1238	...	1249	...	│	│	1339	...	1352	1452	...	1539	...	1552	...	...	1636	1658	1704	...	...	1736	1753	1809
Metz a.	1236	1311	...	1316	...	1324	1337	1411	...	1416	1516	...	1611	...	1618	...	...	1710	1725	1736	...	...	1808	1816	1835

SEE NOTE ❖	⚒	†	⑥ k	†	Ⓐ	Ⓐ	†	⑥ k	Ⓑ z	Ⓐ	†	⑥ k	Ⓐ	Ⓐ	†	⑥ k	Ⓐ	*Ouigo* **7694** ⊠ a 🅁	*TGV* **5500** 🅁		Ⓐ	† △		Ⓐ	*TGV* **9896** 🅁
Strasbourg d.	1719	1719	...	1747	1749	...	...	1819	1819	1848	1848	1849	1919	...	1949	1949	1949	1958	2021	...	2051	2054	...	2154	2214
Brumath d.	│	1730	...	1759	1800	...	...	1830	1830	1859	1859	1900	1930	...	2001	2001	2001	│	│	...	2102	2110	...	2210	│
Saverne d.	1743	1746	...	1813	1814	...	...	1846	1846	1913	1914	1915	1945	...	2016	2016	2016	│	│	...	2117	2138	...	2237	│
Réding d.	│	│	...	1828	1830	...	...	│	│	1930	1928	1929	1959	...	│	│	2034	│	│	...	2131	2153	...	2253	│
Sarrebourg d.	1801	1803	1808	│	│	1836	1904	1903	1904	│	│	│	2004	2008	2033	2036	2039	│	│	...	│	2157	...	2258	│
Lunéville **387** d.	1826	1826	│	│	│	│	│	1926	1930	│	│	│	2026	│	2059	2059	...	│	│	...	│	...	...	...	│
Nancy **387** a.	1844	1844	│	│	│	│	│	1944	1948	│	│	│	2044	│	2117	2117	...	│	│	...	│	...	...	...	│
Paris Est **381** a.	...	...	│	│	│	│	│	...	...	│	│	│	...	│	...	...	...	│	│	...	│	...	...	...	│
Morhange d.	...	...	1836	1851	1853	1904	1932	...	...	1953	1951	1952	...	2032	...	...	...	│	│	...	2154	...	...	...	│
Metz a.	...	...	1908	1915	1917	1936	2004	...	...	2018	2015	2016	...	2058	...	...	...	2046	2109	...	2218	...	...	...	2302

A – ②–⑤ to July 25; Ⓐ from July 28.
B – ⑦ from Sept. 7 (also Nov. 11). Sept. 21 - Oct. 26 does not call at Saverne and arrives Strasbourg 2230.
E – Ⓐ July 7 - Aug. 29. On July 7, 21 Strasbourg d. 0541, Sarrebourg d. 0624, Metz a. 0712 (not calling at Saverne). Departs Strasbourg and Saverne 5–7 minutes later from July 28.
G – ②–⑤ to July 4 (not June 19); Ⓐ from Sept. 1 (not Oct. 6, 13, Nov. 10).
P – To Paris (Table **390**).

a – Not June 23–27, 30, July 1–4, 7–11, 21–25, Aug. 14–16, 18–22, 25–29.
d – Not Nov. 10.
e – Also July 14, Nov. 11.
f – 0909 July 6 - Aug. 31.
j – Arrives 1736.
k – Not Nov. 1.
n – Not July 15 - Aug. 14.
r – Not June 16, 30, July 7, 21.
u – Also Aug. 15; not Aug. 16. Departs Strasbourg 4–5 minutes earlier Sept. 27 - Nov. 1.
y – Not June 15, 22, 29, July 6, 20.
z – Also Nov. 1.

TGV – High-speed train. 🅁. 🍷. Minor timing variations may apply on certain dates.

❦ – Timings of eastbound services Nancy - Strasbourg may vary by up to 11 minutes July 7 - Sept. 7.
❖ – Timings of westbound TER services from Strasbourg to Metz, Sarrebourg and Nancy may vary by up to 12 minutes June 16 - July 25.
△ – On ⑦ until July 20 operated by 🚌 Saverne - Réding (a. 2220) - Sarrebourg (a. 2230).
◧ – Not June 22, Sept. 1. Departs Metz 0543 from Nov. 17.
⊡ – Subject to alteration on July 13 (diverted between Bar le Duc and Saverne).
⊖ – Subject to alteration on July 12 (diverted between Saverne and Bar le Duc).
⊕ – Subject to alteration on July 13, Nov. 30 (diverted between Saverne and Bar le Duc).
● – Subject to alteration on June 23, Oct. 6, 13.
◇ – 🅁 for journeys from / to Paris.
⊠ – OUIGO low-cost TGV. Internet bookings only: www.ouigo.com

384 Regional trains NANCY - METZ - LUXEMBOURG

French holiday dates apply (but with variations on June 23, July 14, Nov. 11; see shaded box below). See Table **390** for *TGV* trains Paris - Metz - Luxembourg.
Timings may vary by up to 5 minutes on certain dates (earlier departures possible). **WARNING!** Journeys to / from Luxembourg are subject to alteration **July 12 - Sept. 14** with all trains replaced by 🚌 Thionville / Bettembourg - Luxembourg and v.v. in amended timings. Certain services to / from Luxembourg are also subject to alteration on June 28, 29, July 5, 6.

km		Ⓐ	Ⓐ	Ⓐ r	⚒	Ⓐ	⑥ k	Ⓐ	Ⓐ n	⚒	Ⓐ		Ⓐ nE	Ⓐ n	Ⓐ		⑥ k	Ⓐ	Ⓐ	Ⓐ	⚒ n	†	Ⓐ	⑥ k	Ⓐ
0	**Nancy** 392 d.	...	...	0528	...	0620	0650	0651	0703	...	0720	0750	0806	...	0820	0828	0850	0851	...	0920	0950	0950	...	...	1020
28	Pont-à-Mousson .. 392 d.	...	...	0554	...	0637	0707	0708	0721	...	0737	0807	0823	...	0837	0853	0907	0908	...	0937	1007	1007	...	...	1037
37	Pagny sur Moselle d.	...	...	0603	...	0645	0715	0715	0728	...	0745	0815	0830	...	0845	0903	0915	0915	...	0945	1015	1015	...	...	1044
57	**Metz** a.	...	...	0621	...	0658	0728	0728	0743	...	0758	0828	0843	...	0901	0921	0928	0928	...	0958	1028	1028	...	...	1058
57	**Metz** 393a d.	0533	0603	...	0633	0703	0733	0733	...	0748	0803	0833	...	0903	...	...	0933	...	0933	...	...	1030	1030	1036	...
75	Hagondange 393a d.	0545	0615	...	0645	0715	0745	0745	...	0804	0815	0845	...	0918	...	...	0945	...	0944	...	...	1045	1045	1054	...
87	Thionville d.	0557	0627	...	0657	0728	0758	0758	...	0818	0827	0858	...	0936	...	...	0957	...	0958	...	...	1057	1057	1118	...
110	Bettembourg 🏛 ... 449 d.	0611	0641	...	0711	0741	0811	0811	...	0835	0841	0911	...	0952	...	...	1011	...	1011	...	...	1111	1111	1135	...
121	**Luxembourg** 449 a.	0622	0652	...	0722	0752	0822	0822	...	0845	0852	0922	...	1003	...	...	1022	...	1022	...	...	1122	1122	1145	...

	†	⑥ k	Ⓐ n	Ⓑ n	Ⓐ n		Ⓐ n	Ⓐ n		Ⓐ n	⑥ k	Ⓑ z	Ⓐ n	Ⓐ	Ⓒ	n	Ⓐ n	Ⓐ		Ⓐ	Ⓐ n		Ⓐ	Ⓐ	Ⓒ
Nancy 392 d.	1028	1050	...	...	1120	1150	1220	...	1250	1320	1350	1350	1420	1450	1450	...	1520	...	1550	1620	...	1650	1720	1750	1750
Pont-à-Mousson 392 d.	1053	1107	...	...	1137	1207	1237	...	1307	1337	1407	1407	1437	1507	1507	...	1537	...	1607	1637	...	1707	1737	1807	1807
Pagny sur Moselle d.	1103	1115	...	...	1145	1215	1245	...	1314	1345	1415	1415	1445	1515	1515	...	1545	...	1615	1645	...	1715	1745	1815	1815
Metz a.	1121	1128	...	...	1158	1228	1258	...	1328	1359	1428	1428	1458	1528	1528	...	1558	...	1628	1658	...	1728	1758	1828	1828
Metz 393a d.	...	1133	1133	1144	...	1233	...	1303	1333	...	1432	1433	...	1533	...	1546	...	1603	1633	...	1703	1730	1803	...	1833
Hagondange 393a d.	...	1145	1145	1201	...	1245	...	1316	1344	...	1444	1445	...	1545	...	1602	...	1617	1645	...	1715	1745	1815	...	1845
Thionville d.	...	1157	1158	1218	...	1258	...	1328	1357	...	1458	1458	...	1558	...	1618	...	1635	1658	...	1727	1757	1828	...	1857
Bettembourg 🏛 449 d.	...	1211	1211	1235	...	1311	...	1341	1411	...	1511	1511	...	1611	...	1635	...	1652	1711	...	1741	1811	1841	...	1911
Luxembourg 449 a.	...	1222	1222	1245	...	1322	...	1352	1422	...	1522	1522	...	1622	...	1645	...	1703	1722	...	1752	1822	1852	...	1922

	Ⓐ n	Ⓑ z	Ⓐ	Ⓐ	Ⓒ	Ⓐ n	⚒	Ⓐ n	Ⓐ R	Ⓒ	Ⓐ	Ⓐ n	Ⓑ z	⑥ k	Ⓐ n	†	Ⓐ s	Ⓒ	Ⓐ	†	⑤⑥ t	Ⓐ V	Ⓐ X🚌	⑥ k	Ⓒ 🚌
Nancy 392 d.	...	...	1822	1850	1850	...	...	1920	1950	1950	...	2020	2050	2050	...	...	2150	2150	...	...	...	2237	2237	2250	2328
Pont-à-Mousson 392 d.	...	...	1839	1907	1907	...	...	1937	2007	2007	...	2037	2107	2107	...	...	2207	2207	...	...	...	2303	2331	2307	0019
Pagny sur Moselle d.	...	...	1846	1915	1915	...	...	1945	2014	2015	...	2045	2115	2115	...	...	2215	2215	...	...	...	2310	2350	2315	|
Metz a.	...	...	1900	1928	1928	...	...	1958	2029	2028	...	2058	2128	2128	...	...	2228	2228	...	...	...	2328	0024	2328	0113
Metz 393a d.	1833	1842	1903	...	1933	1933	1946	...	...	2033	2033	...	...	2133	2133	2146	...	2233	2246	2316	2324	...	...	...	...
Hagondange 393a d.	1845	1904	1918	...	1945	1945	2004	...	...	2044	2044	...	...	2145	2145	2203	...	2245	2303	2332	2341	...	...	...	...
Thionville d.	1858	1918	1935	...	1957	1958	2019	...	...	2056	2057	...	...	2157	2157	2218	...	2257	2318	2344	2355	...	...	...	...
Bettembourg 🏛 449 d.	1911	1935	1952	...	2011	2011	2035	...	...	2111	2111	...	...	2211	2211	2235	...	2311	2335	...	0011	...	...	...	...
Luxembourg 449 a.	1922	1945	2003	...	2022	2022	2045	...	...	2122	2122	...	...	2222	2222	2245	...	2322	2345	...	0021	...	...	...	...

	Ⓐ	Ⓐ	Ⓐ	⑥ k	Ⓐ	Ⓐ	Ⓐ nE	Ⓐ	Ⓐ	⑥ k	†	Ⓐ	Ⓐ	Ⓒ	Ⓐ	Ⓐ	Ⓐ n		⑥ k	Ⓐ	Ⓐ	Ⓑ n	Ⓐ n		Ⓐ n
Luxembourg 449 d.	...	0516	...	0539	0546	...	...	0616	0628	0628	...	0709	0739	0739	...	0809	...	0816	0839	0839	...	...	...	0939	...
Bettembourg 🏛 449 d.	...	0526	...	0551	0556	...	...	0626	0640	0640	...	0721	0751	0751	...	0821	...	0826	0851	0851	...	...	...	0951	...
Thionville d.	...	0545	0604	0604	0613	0634	...	0645	0657	0659	...	0734	0804	0804	...	0834	...	0845	0904	0904	...	...	0924	1004	...
Hagondange 393a d.	...	0556	0616	0616	0624	0646	...	0656	0713	0711	...	0745	0815	0816	...	0845	...	0856	0915	0915	...	...	0934	1015	...
Metz 393a a.	...	0614	0627	0628	0641	0657	...	0714	0729	0730	...	0757	0827	0827	...	0857	...	0914	0927	0927	...	...	0952	1031	...
Metz d.	0602	...	0632	0632	...	0702	0713	...	0732	0732	0732	0802	...	0832	0832	...	0902	...	0932	...	0932	0939	1002	1032	1102
Pagny sur Moselle d.	0615	...	0645	0645	...	0715	0726	...	0745	0745	0745	0815	...	0845	0845	...	0915	...	0945	...	0945	0959	1016	1045	1115
Pont-à-Mousson 392 d.	0623	...	0653	0652	...	0723	0733	...	0753	0753	0752	0823	...	0853	0853	...	0923	...	0952	...	0953	1006	1023	1053	1123
Nancy 392 a.	0640	...	0710	0709	...	0740	0750	...	0810	0811	0809	0840	...	0910	0910	...	0940	...	1009	...	1010	1032	1041	1110	1140

	Ⓒ	⑥ k	Ⓐ	†	Ⓐ n		Ⓐ n	Ⓐ		Ⓐ n	Ⓐ n	Ⓒ	Ⓐ	Ⓐ n	Ⓑ nz	Ⓐ	⑥ k	Ⓑ z	Ⓐ n	Ⓒ	Ⓐ	Ⓐ n	Ⓐ		Ⓐ
Luxembourg 449 d.	1016	...	1039	...	...	1139	1209	1216	1239n	...	1258	1339	1339	...	1416	1439	1439	...	...	1539	1539	1558	...	1639	1658
Bettembourg 🏛 449 d.	1026	...	1051	...	...	1151	1221	1226	1251n	...	1310	1351	1351	...	1426	1451	1451	...	...	1551	1551	1610	...	1651	1710
Thionville d.	1044	...	1105	...	...	1204	1234	1245	1304n	...	1332	1404	1404	...	1445	1504	1504	...	...	1604	1604	1626	...	1704	1729
Hagondange 393a d.	1056	...	1116	...	...	1216	1245	1256	1316n	...	1344	1416	1416	...	1457	1516	1515	...	...	1615	1616	1638	...	1716	1741
Metz 393a a.	1118	...	1127	...	...	1230	1258	1314	1327n	...	1402	1427	1428	...	1514	1527	1527	...	...	1627	1627	1659	...	1727	1759
Metz d.	...	1132	1132	1138	1202	1232	*1302*	...	1332	1402	...	1432	...	1502	...	...	1532	1532	1602	1632	*1632*	...	1702	1732	*1802*
Pagny sur Moselle d.	...	1145	1145	1157	1215	1245	*1315*	...	1345	1415	...	1445	...	1515	...	...	1545	1545	1615	1645	*1645*	...	1715	1745	*1815*
Pont-à-Mousson 392 d.	...	1153	1153	1206	1223	1253	*1323*	...	1353	1422	...	1453	...	1523	...	...	1552	1553	1622	1652	*1653*	...	1723	1753	*1823*
Nancy 392 a.	...	1210	1210	1232	1240	1310	*1340*	...	1410	1440	...	1510	...	1540	...	...	1609	1610	1639	1709	*1710*	...	1740	1810	*1840*

	Ⓐ nE		Ⓐ	Ⓑ z	⑥ k	Ⓐ n	Ⓐ n	⚒	Ⓐ	Ⓒ	Ⓐ		Ⓐ n	Ⓑ z	†	Ⓐ n	Ⓐ	Ⓐ V	Ⓐ X🚌	Ⓒ	Ⓐ n	Ⓐ	Ⓐ n	Ⓒ 🚌	Ⓒ
Luxembourg 449 d.	...	1739	1809	1839	1839	...	1909	1916	1939	1939	...	...	2009	2016	...	2039	2116	...	...	2139	2139	2216	2239	...	2256
Bettembourg 🏛 449 d.	...	1751	1821	1851	1851	...	1921	1926	1951	1951	...	...	2021	2026	...	2051	2126	...	...	2151	2151	2226	2251	...	2306
Thionville d.	...	1807	1834	1904	1907	...	1935	1945	2006	2004	...	...	2034	2045	...	2104	2145	...	...	2204	2204	2245	2304	...	2321
Hagondange 393a d.	...	1817	1846	1916	1919	...	1948	1956	2017	2016	...	...	2046	2056	...	2116	2156	...	...	2216	2216	2256	2316	...	2332
Metz 393a a.	...	1829	1857	1927	1931	...	2001	2014	2028	2027	...	...	2057	2114	...	2127	2214	...	...	2228	2228	2314	2327	...	2349
Metz d.	1813	1832	*1902*	1932	1934	2002	...	...	...	2032	2032	2039	...	...	2132	2132	...	2225	2225	2232	...	...	...	2339	...
Pagny sur Moselle d.	1827	1845	*1915*	1945	1947	2015	...	...	...	2045	2045	2057	...	...	2145	2145	...	2244	2259	2245	...	...	...	0024	...
Pont-à-Mousson 392 d.	1835	1853	*1923*	1953	1954	2023	...	...	...	2052	2053	2106	...	...	2152	2153	...	2251	2318	2252	...	...	...	|	...
Nancy 392 a.	1854	1911	*1940*	2010	2011	2040	...	...	...	2109	2110	2132	...	...	2209	2210	...	2319	0012	2309	...	...	...	0116	...

E – From / to Épinal (Table **386**).
R – From Remiremont (Table **386**).
V – From Aug. 25.
X – Until Aug. 22.

k – Not Nov. 1.
n – Not ①–⑤ July 15 - Aug. 14.
r – Not July 16 – 18.
s – Not July 15 – 18.
t – Not Aug. 15, Nov. 1.
z – Also Nov. 1.

PUBLIC HOLIDAY ALTERATIONS

On June 23 (a public holiday in Luxembourg) many services to / from Luxembourg operate as on ⑦. On July 14, Nov. 11 (public holidays in France) many services to / from Luxembourg operate as on Ⓐ.
Please check locally if travelling on these dates.

STRASBOURG - MULHOUSE - BASEL — 385

French holiday dates apply

For *TGV* trains Paris - Strasbourg - Colmar see Table **390**. For *TGV* trains Luxembourg - Metz - Strasbourg - Mulhouse - Lyon - Marseille / Montpellier see Table **379**.
Subject to alteration on June 28, 29. Certain services to / from Basel are subject to alteration July 7 – 11.

km		Ⓐ	Ⓐ	⚒	Ⓐ ⊙	⑥ k2	Ⓐ	Ⓒ	Ⓐ	Ⓒ 2		Ⓐ	⑥ k2		Ⓐ	⑥ k2	⚒	† 2	Ⓐ	⑥ k2		Ⓐ	Ⓒ 2		⚒ 2		Ⓐ
0	**Strasbourg** d.	...	0519	0551	0621	0621	0651	0651	0721	0721	0751	0821	0821	0851	0921	0921	0951	0951	1021	1021	1051	1121	1121	1151	1221	1251	1321
43	Sélestat d.	...	0539	0611	0641	0645	0711	0713	0741	0744	0811	0841	0844	0911	0941	0944	1011	1016	1041	1044	1111	1141	1144	1211	1242f	1311	1341
65	Colmar d.	...	0551	0623	0653	0659	0723	0725	0753	0758	0823	0853	0858	0923	0953	0958	1023	1028	1053	1058	1123	1153	1158	1223	1253f	1323	1353
106	**Mulhouse** ‡ d.	0546	0616	0646	0716	0728	0746	0749	0816	0825	0846	0916	0925	0946	1016	1025	1046	1055	1116	1125	1146	1216	1225	1246	1314f	1346	1416
133	St Louis (Haut Rhin) ‡ d.	0601	0631	0701	0731	...	0801	0812	0831	...	0901	0931	...	1001	1031	...	1101	...	1131	...	1201	1231	...	1301	...	1401	1431
140	**Basel** SBB ‡ a.	0608	0638	0708	0738	...	0808	0820	0840	...	0908	0938	...	1008	1040	...	1108	...	1138	...	1208	1240	...	1308	...	1408	1440

	⚒	† 2	⑥ k2		Ⓐ	⑥ k2		Ⓑ z	⑥ k2		Ⓐ	⑥ k2		Ⓑ z	⑥ k2		Ⓑ z	⑥ k2		Ⓑ z	⑥ k2	Ⓐ 2	⚒ ⊗	† 2	⊗ 2	⑦ e2	B2
Strasbourg d.	1351	1351	1421	1451	1521	1521	1551	1621	1621	1651	1721	1721	1751	1821	1821	1851	1921	1921	1951	2021	2021	2051	2121	2121	2221	2251	2320
Sélestat d.	1411	1416	1443	1512	1541	1544	1610	1641	1644	1711	1741	1744	1811	1841	1844	1911	1941	1942	2011	2041	2044	2114	2141	2144	2242j	2311	2346
Colmar d.	1423	1428	1456	1524	1553	1558	1622	1653	1658	1723	1753	1758	1823	1853	1858	1923	1953	1954	2023	2053	2058	2128	2153	2158	2254j	2323	0000
Mulhouse ‡ d.	1446	1455	1525	1546	1616	1625	1646	1716	1725	1746	1816	1825	1846	1916	1925	1946	2016	2021	2046	2116	2125	2157	2216	2225	2320j	2344	0025
St Louis (Haut Rhin) ‡ d.	1501	...	...	1601	1631	...	1701	1731	...	1801	1831	...	1901	1931	...	2001	2031	...	2101	2131v	...	...	2231r	...	...	...	...
Basel SBB ‡ a.	1508	...	...	1608	1640	...	1708	1738	...	1808	1838	...	1908	1940	...	2008	2038	...	2108	2138v	...	...	2238r	...	...	...	...

SEE NOTE ✣	A2	⑥ k2	Ⓐ	Ⓐ		† 2	⑥ k2	Ⓐ		⑥ k2	Ⓐ		Ⓒ 2	Ⓐ		⑥ k2		Ⓐ	† 2	⚒	Ⓐ		Ⓐ		Ⓐ	† 2	⚒
Basel SBB ‡ d.	...	...	0521	0536	0621	...	...	0651	0721	...	0751	0821	...	0851	0921	...	1021	1051	...	1121	1151	1221	1251	1321	...	...	1421
St Louis (Haut Rhin) ‡ d.	...	...	0529	0544	0629	...	...	0659	0729	...	0759	0829	...	0859	0929	...	1029	1100	...	1129	1159	1230	1300	1329	...	...	1430
Mulhouse ‡ d.	0457	0535	0546	0601	0646	0700	0704	0716	0746	0803	0816	0846	0904	0916	0946	1005	1046	1116	1135	1146	1216	1246	1316	1346	1414	1435	1446
Colmar d.	0518	0603	0606	0629	0706	0727	0732	0736	0806	0832	0836	0906	0931	0936	1006	1033	1106	1136	1203	1206	1236	1306	1336	1406	1435	1503	1506
Sélestat d.	0530	0616	0619	0642	0719	0738	0743	0749	0819	0844	0849	0919	0943	0949	1019	1046	1119	1149	1216	1219	1249	1319	1349	1419	1447	1516	1519
Strasbourg a.	0556	0639	0639	0709	0739	0804	0809	0809	0839	0909	0909	0939	1009	1009	1039	1109	1139	1209	1239	1239	1309	1339	1409	1439	1509	1539	1539

SEE NOTE ✣	⑥ k2	Ⓐ	† 2	⚒	⑥ k2	Ⓐ		†	⑥ k2	Ⓐ		⑥ k2	Ⓑ z		⑥ k2	Ⓐ		⑥ k2	Ⓑ z	† 2	⚒ d	⑥ k2	Ⓐ ⊗	†	Ⓐ c⊗	⑥ k2	Ⓑ ⊗◇
Basel SBB ‡ d.	...	1451	...	1521	...	1551	1621	1639	...	1651	1721	...	1751	1821	...	1851	1921	...	1951	...	2021	...	2037	2121	2151	...	...
St Louis (Haut Rhin) ‡ d.	...	1500	...	1529	...	1559	1629	1646	...	1659	1729	...	1759	1830	...	1900	1929	...	1959	...	2029	...	2044	2130	2200	...	...
Mulhouse ‡ d.	1514	1516	1535	1546	1605	1616	1646	1703	1705	1716	1746	1805	1816	1846	1904	1917	1946	2004	2016	2035	2046	2103	2113	2146	2216	2234	2330
Colmar d.	1535	1536	1603	1606	1633	1636	1706	1731	1733	1736	1806	1833	1836	1906	1932	1936	2006	2032	2036	2105	2106	2130	2139	2206	2236	2302	2359
Sélestat d.	1547	1549	1616	1619	1646	1649	1719	1742	1746	1749	1819	1846	1849	1919	1943	1949	2019	2043	2049	2117	2119	2142	2152	2219	2249	2313	0012
Strasbourg a.	1609	1609	1639	1639	1709	1709	1739	1810	1809	1809	1839	1909	1909	1939	2009	2009	2039	2109	2109	2139	2139	2211	2214	2239	2309	2339	0040

A – ①–⑤ to June 23 (also July 7, 21); Ⓐ from July 28.
B – ①–⑥ to June 21; ⑥ from July 5 (not Aug. 2, 9, Oct. 11, 18, Nov. 1, 8).
c – July 28 - Aug. 1 departs Mulhouse 2225, Colmar 2255, Sélestat 2310, arrives Strasbourg 2330.
d – Runs daily Basel - Mulhouse.
e – Also July 14, Nov. 11.
f – On ⑥ Sélestat d. 1244, Colmar d. 1258, Mulhouse a. 1325.
j – On ⑥ Sélestat d. 2243, Colmar d. 2256, Mulhouse a. 2325.
k – Not Nov. 1.
r – Not Aug. 2, 9, 16.
v – Not Aug. 3, 10, 17.
w – Not June 30 - Aug. 15.
z – Also Nov. 1.

⊙ – Also runs on † Mulhouse - Basel.
◇ – Also Nov. 1; not Aug. 15. On † Mulhouse d. 2338, Colmar d. 0003, Sélestat d. 0015, Strasbourg a. 0040 (with variations of up to 4 minutes on certain dates).
⊗ – Does not run on Ⓐ June 23 - July 25.
✣ – Timings in the Basel - Mulhouse - Strasbourg direction may vary by up to 3 minutes.
‡ – **Other local trains Mulhouse - Basel** (journey 30 – 32 minutes).
From Mulhouse on ①–⑤: 0449 **w**, 0549, 0619, 0649 **w**, 0719, 0749, 0819 **w**, 0919, 1119, 1219 **w**, 1319, 1419 **w**, 1549, 1619, 1649 **w**, 1719, 1749, 1819 **w**, 1849, 1919, 1949 **w** and 2019.
From Mulhouse on ⑥: 0619, 0719, 0749, 0919, 1119, 1319, 1419 and hourly until 1919.
From Mulhouse on ⑦: 0749, 0919, 1119, 1319, 1519, 1819 and 1949.
From Basel SBB on ①–⑤: 0608 **w**, 0638, 0708, 0738 **w**, 0808, 0839, 1039, 1138 **w**, 1239, 1338 **w**, 1538, 1608 **w**, 1639, 1708, 1738 **w**, 1808, 1838, 1908 **w**, 1939, 2138 **w** and 2238.
From Basel SBB on ⑥: 0708, 0808, 0839, 1039, 1239, 1439, 1538, 1639, 1738, 1838 and 2038.
From Basel SBB on ⑦: 0839, 1039, 1239, 1439, 1738, 1908 and 2038.

NANCY - ÉPINAL - REMIREMONT — 386

TER services

For through *TGV* services from / to Paris, see Table **390**.

km		Ⓐ	Ⓐ	⚒ n	⚒	Ⓐ nm	Ⓒ	Ⓐ ⊗	Ⓑ ⊗	Ⓐ ⊗	⑥ k	⑥ k	†	Ⓐ ⊗	†	⚒ ⊗	Ⓑ z⊗	⑥ k	⚒ ⊖	†	Ⓒ	Ⓐ ◇	n	Ⓐ	Ⓒ	Ⓐ	Ⓐ n
0	**Nancy** d.	0555	0620	0655	0720	0755	0824	0821	0855	0930	0930	1020	1020	1103	1120	1120	1220t	1220t	1320	1320	1420	1420	1520	1555	1620	1620	1655
74	Épinal a.	0651	0719	0751	0818	0851	0913	0918	0951	1021	1024	1106	1113	1159	1204	1218	1318	1321	1418	1418	1512f	1518	1618	1651	1715	1718	1751
74	Épinal d.	...	0722	...	0820	...	0915	0920	...	1023	...	...	1115	...	...	1220	1320	1323	1420	...	...	1520	1620	...	...	1720	...
100	**Remiremont** a.	...	0751	...	0850	...	0938	0951	...	1053	...	...	1143	...	...	1251	1351	1356	1451	...	...	1552	1651	...	...	1751	...

			⚒	Ⓐ nm		Ⓑ z	⑥ k		⑥	Ⓐ ▲	†
Nancy d.	1720	1755	1820	1857	1920	2020	2025	2124	2205	2220	2255
Épinal a.	1818	1850	1919	1953	2018	2118	2109	2218	2301	2318	2358
Épinal d.	1820	...	1920	...	2020n	...	...	2220	...	...	...
Remiremont a.	1851	...	1951	...	2050n	...	...	2251	...	...	...

	Ⓐ	Ⓐ n	⑥ k	Ⓐ	⚒	†	⚒ vm	Ⓐ	⑥ k	Ⓐ		Ⓐ ⊗
Remiremont d.	...	0512e	...	...	0615	...	...	0712	...	...	0812	0912
Épinal a.	...	0541e	...	...	0641	...	...	0741	...	...	0841	0941
Épinal d.	0500	0543	0547	0551	0645	0647	0705	0743	0746	0805	0843	0943
Nancy a.	0559	0641	0640	0648	0738	0740	0802	0840	0841	0902	0940	1040

	Ⓒ	Ⓐ ⊗	Ⓒ	Ⓐ ⊗	⚒ ⊗	⚒ ⊗	†	Ⓐ ⊗	Ⓐ ⊗	⑥ k	⊗	Ⓐ ⊖	†	⑥ k		Ⓐ	⚒	†	Ⓑ zm		⑥ k	Ⓐ	†	Ⓐ n	⑥ k	Ⓐ n	†
Remiremont d.	...	1012	1033	...	...	1212	1212	...	1312	...	1412	1513	...	...	1612	...	1712	...	1812	...	1902	1912	1930	...	2012	2012	...
Épinal a.	...	1041	1102	...	...	1241	1241	...	1340	...	1441	1541	...	...	1641	...	1741	...	1841	...	1923	1941	1951	...	2043	2041	...
Épinal d.	0946r	1043	1104	1106	1143j	1243	1242	1326	1342	1356	1446	1543	1543	1553	1643	1706	1743	1756	1843	1906	1925	1943	1953	2006	2045	2043	2148
Nancy a.	1040	1140	1201	1202	1240	1340	1341	1410	1436	1440	1541	1640	1640	1637	1739	1802	1840	1840	1940	2002	2017	2040	2040	2102	2140	2145	2240

e – ① to July 7; ① Aug. 18 - Sept. 8; Ⓐ from Sept. 15.
f – 1504 on †.
j – 1142 on ⑥.
k – Not Nov. 1.
m – From / to Metz (Table **384**).
n – Not ①–⑤ July 15 - Aug. 14.
r – 0955 on †.
t – 1218 July 7 - Sept. 7.
v – On ⑥ Épinal d. 0706, Nancy a. 0803.
z – Also Nov. 1.
⊗ – Subject to alteration / cancellation on Ⓐ July 7 - Aug. 29.
⊖ – Subject to alteration / cancellation on Ⓐ July 7 - Aug. 22.
◇ – Subject to alteration / cancellation July 7 – 11, Aug. 18 – 22.
▲ – Operated by 🚌 June 30 - Sept. 5 (Épinal a. 0009).

NANCY - LUNÉVILLE - ST DIÉ — 387

TER services

For through *TGV* services from / to Paris, see Table **390**. **Warning!** Subject to alteration on Aug. 15 – 17. Certain timings vary July 7 - Sept. 7 (see note ⌧).

km		Ⓐ n	Ⓐ		⑥ k	Ⓐ	Ⓐ n	⑥ k	†	Ⓐ	⑥ k	⑥ k		Ⓒ	Ⓐ			Ⓐ n	⑥ k	Ⓐ	⑥ k	Ⓐ n	†	⑥ k	Ⓐ	⚒
0	**Nancy** 383 d.	0542	0650	0750	0854	0859	0926	0950	0955	1028	1051	1136	...	1250	1305	...	1410	1450	1453	1550	1551	1650	1652	1653	1708	1750
33	Lunéville 383 d.	0604	0711	0811	0912	0921	0952	1009	1016	1058	1112	1155	...	1311	1331	...	1429	1511	1512	1611	1612	1711	1710	1711	1730	1811
84	**St Dié** a.	0703	0755	0854	0951	1002	1030	1055	1055	1141	1154	1237	...	1355	1413	...	1511	1552	1551	1653	1652	1753	1758	1752	1829	1853

	†	Ⓐ	⑥ k	Ⓐ n	⑥ k	†	Ⓐ n	①–⑤ D		Ⓐ 🚌	
Nancy 383 d.	1759	1850	1850	1909	2002	2002	2002	2002	...	2159	...
Lunéville 383 d.	1822	1911	1910	1931	2021	2021	2031	2034	...	2239	...
St Dié a.	1902	1951	1952	2026	2059	2106	2117	2124	...	2343	...

	E		⑥ k	Ⓐ	Ⓐ	†	Ⓐ	⑥ k	Ⓐ	Ⓒ	Ⓐ n
St Dié d.	0506	...	0557	0606	0630	0700	0732	0808	0809	0906	0907
Lunéville 383 d.	0544	...	0638	0653	0729	0741	0832	0855	0851	0952	0952
Nancy 383 a.	0603	...	0658	0714	0749	0802	0851	0913	0914	1010	1012

	⑥ k	Ⓐ	Ⓒ		⑥ k	Ⓐ	Ⓒ	⑥ k	Ⓐ	⑥ k	†	Ⓐ n	⑥ k	Ⓐ	Ⓐ n	⑥ k	†	Ⓐ	⑥ k		⑥ k	†	Ⓐ	⑥ k	†	Ⓐ n
St Dié d.	1000	1046	1108	...	1208	1226	1252	1403	1442	1520	1555	1557	1608	1632	1708	1708	1730	1807	1808	...	1910	1922	1930	1958	2004	2005
Lunéville 383 d.	1037	1132	1149	...	1249	1310	1349	1446	1535j	1601	1641	1640	1651	1729	1749	1749	1815	1850	1849	...	1952	2009	2032	2040	2052	2052
Nancy 383 a.	1056	1151	1210	...	1310	1333	1410	1504	1554j	1619	1658	1658	1710	1747	1807	1810	1833	1908	1910	...	2010	2034	2050	2100	2113	2110

D – July 15 - Aug. 14.
E – ① to June 30; Ⓐ from July 7.
j – 3 – 4 minutes earlier until July 25.
k – Not Nov. 1.
n – Not ①–⑤ July 15 - Aug. 14.
⌧ – Timings of services from Nancy to St Dié may vary July 7 - Sept. 7: Nancy timings may vary by up to 10 minutes (earlier departures possible); timings at Lunéville and St Dié may vary by up to 4 minutes. Services in the opposite direction are generally unaffected.

389 PARIS - REIMS - CHARLEVILLE MÉZIÈRES - SEDAN

TGV timings are subject to minor variations – please check your reservation for confirmed timings. *TGV* services are subject to alteration on Oct. 10–12, 17–19, Nov. 22, 23.

km		Ⓐ	⑥ t	Ⓐ v	⚒	Ⓐ v	*TGV* 2707 Ⓐ an	Ⓐ ⊖	⑥ t	✝	*TGV* 2709 ①–⑥ b⊗	Ⓐ ⊖	⑥ t	✝	⚒ v⊖	*TGV* 2719 H	*TGV* 2721 ⑦ e	⑥	Ⓐ ⊖	Ⓐ v⊖	✝	Ⓐ ⊖	⑥ t
0	**Paris** Est ... 390 d.	...	...	...	...	...	0739	...	...	...	0828	...	...	...	...	1028	1028	...	...	...	...	...	...
136	Champagne Ardenne TGV **390 391a** d.	...	...	...	...	0740	|	0810	0810	...	|	...	0910	1010	1010	|	|	1110	1110	1140	1210	1210	1210
147	**Reims** ... **391a** a.	...	...	...	...	0752	0825	0822	0822	...	0914	...	0922	1022	1022	1114	1114	1122	1122	1152	1222	1222	1222
147	**Reims** ... d.	0630	0630	0700	0735	0800	...	0830	0830	0830	0919	0930	0930	1030	1030	...	1120	1130	1130	1200	1230	1230	1230
186	Rethel ... d.	0653	0653	0723	0758	0823	...	0853	0853	0853	0942	0953	0953	1053	1053	...	1143	1153	1153	1223	1253	1253	1253
235	**Charleville-Mézières** ... a.	0725	0725	0751	0830	0851	...	0925	0925	0925	1010	1025	1025	1125	1125	...	1211	1225	1225	1251	1325	1325	1325
235	**Charleville-Mézières** ... **389a** d.	0730	0730	...	0835r	...	...	0930r	0930	0930	1019r	1030r	1030	...	1130r	...	...	1230	1230r	...	...	1330r	1330
255	**Sedan** ... **389a** a.	0750	0755	...	0855r	...	...	0950r	0955	0955	1035r	1050r	1050	...	1150r	...	...	1250	1255r	...	...	1350r	1355

	Ⓐ ⊖	✝	⑥ t	Ⓐ ⊖	*TGV* 2733 ⑤ n	*TGV* 2735 ⑥ k	⊖	Ⓐ v	Ⓒ	Ⓐ	*TGV* 2743 L		*TGV* 2743 ①–④ M	Ⓐ v		Ⓐ v	*TGV* 2747 N	⑥ t	Ⓑ z	Ⓐ v	*TGV* 2751	⚒	✝
Paris Est ... 390 d.	...	...	...	...	1258	1328	...	...	...	...	1538	...	1558	...	...	...	1728	...	...	...	1828	...	...
Champagne Ardenne TGV **390 391a** d.	1240	...	1310	1310	|	|	1410	...	1510	1518	|	1610	|	1640	1710	1740	|	1810	1810	1840	|	1910	2010
Reims ... **391a** a.	1252	...	1322	1322	1344	1414	1422	...	1522	1526	1625	1622	1644	1652	1722	1752	1814	1822	1822	1852	1914	1922	2022
Reims ... d.	1300	...	1330	1330	...	...	1430	...	1530	1530	...	1630	...	1700	1730	1800	...	1830	1830	1900	1920	1930	2030
Rethel ... d.	1323	...	1353	1353	...	...	1453	...	1553	1553	...	1653	...	1723	1753	1823	...	1853	1853	1923	1943	1953	2053
Charleville-Mézières ... a.	1351	...	1425	1425	...	...	1525	...	1625	1625	...	1725	...	1751	1825	1855	...	1925	1925	1951	2011	2026	2125
Charleville-Mézières ... **389a** d.	...	1430	1430	1430r	...	...	1530r	1600	1630t	1630	...	1730	...	1800	1830	...	...	...	1930	...	2020	2031	2130
Sedan ... **389a** a.	...	1450	1450	1457r	...	...	1550r	1625	1650t	1650	...	1755	...	1825	1855	...	...	...	1955	...	2035	2050	2155

	⚒	*TGV* 2757 ⑤⑦ u	*TGV* 2759 B	*TGV* 2765 ⑦ P	*TGV* 2759 ⑤ n	Ⓐ	🚌 ⑥	*TGV* 2765 ⑦ n
Paris Est ... 390 d.	...	2028	2058	2058	2104	...	...	2128
Champagne Ardenne TGV **390 391a** d.	2016	|	|	|	|	...	...	|
Reims ... **391a** a.	2028	2114	2144	2144	2150	...	...	2214
Reims ... d.	2030	...	...	2149	...	2200	2200	2219
Rethel ... d.	2053	...	...	2212	...	2223	|	2242
Charleville-Mézières ... a.	2125	...	...	2240	...	2255	2320	2310
Charleville-Mézières ... **389a** d.	...	...	...	2249	...	...	...	2319
Sedan ... **389a** a.	...	...	...	2305	...	...	...	2335

	Ⓐ	*TGV* 2706 Ⓐ a	Ⓐ v	Ⓐ	⑥ t	*TGV* 2712 Ⓐ	Ⓐ	*TGV* 2714 ①–⑥ b¶	Ⓐ
Sedan ... **389a** d.	...	...	0535	0605	0605	...	0638	0652	0705
Charleville-Mézières ... **389a** a.	...	...	0600	0624	0630	...	0657	0707	0729
Charleville-Mézières ... d.	0534	...	0608	0629	0635	...	0704	0716	0734
Rethel ... d.	0606	...	0636	0701	0707	...	0736	0747	0806
Reims ... a.	0630	...	0700	0725	0731	...	0800	0809	0830
Reims ... **391a** d.	0636	0645	0706	0736	0736	0745	0805	0815	0836
Champagne Ardenne TGV **390 391a** d.	0648	|	0718	0748	0748	|	0817	|	0848
Paris Est ... **390** a.	...	0731	...	...	...	0831	...	0901	...

	⑥ t	*TGV* 2716 Ⓐ an	*TGV* 2720 ⑦ e	Ⓐ v	Ⓐ v	⑥ t	✝	⚒ ⊖	⚒ ⊖	*TGV* 2722 Ⓐ an	*TGV* 2726 ⑥ k‡	⊖	Ⓐ v⊖	*TGV* 2738 ⑦ e	*TGV* 2730 Ⓐ D	⚒ ⊖	Ⓐ v⊖	*TGV* 2730 Ⓐ E	✝	Ⓐ ⊖	⑥ t	⑥ t	Ⓐ ⊖
Sedan ... **389a** d.	0710	...	0723	0735	0800	*0800*	0905	0910r	1010r	...	1053	1110r	...	...	1151	1205r	...	1252r	1305	1309r	1310	1405	1410r
Charleville-Mézières ... **389a** a.	0729	...	0737	0800	0825	*0824*	0929	0929r	1029r	...	1107	1129r	...	...	1207	1229r	...	1307r	1329	1329r	1329	1429	1429r
Charleville-Mézières ... d.	0734	...	0747	0808	0830	0830	0934	0934	1034	...	1117	1134	1208	...	1217	1234	1305	1316	1334	1334	1334	1434	1434
Rethel ... d.	0806	...	0818	0836	0905	0903	1006	1006	1106	...	1148	1206	1236	...	1248	1306	1337	1347	1406	1406	1406	1506	1506
Reims ... a.	0830	...	0839	0900	0930	0930	1030	1030	1130	...	1209	1230	1300	...	1309	1330	1400	1409	1430	1430	1430	1530	1530
Reims ... **391a** d.	0836	0845	0845	0906	0936	0936	1036	1036	1136	1156	1215	1236	1306	1315	1315	1336	1406	1415	1436	1436	1436	1536	1536
Champagne Ardenne TGV **390 391a** d.	0848	|	|	0918	0948	0948	1048	1048	1148	|	|	1248	1318	|	|	1348	1418	|	1448	1448	1448	1548	1548
Paris Est ... **390** a.	...	0931	0931	...	...	...	...	...	...	1242	1301	...	...	1401	1402	...	...	1501	...	...	...	...	...

	TGV 2750 ⑥ k	⊖	*TGV* 2752 A	*TGV* 2754 ⑦ e△	*TGV* 2752 ①–④ M	Ⓒ	Ⓐ ⊖	Ⓐ v	✝	⚒	*TGV* 2756 R	Ⓐ	*TGV* 2760 C	⑥ t	Ⓑ z	*TGV* 2762 T	Ⓐ	⑥ t	Ⓐ	⑥ t	✝	Ⓐ v	*TGV* 2766 ⑦ s
Sedan ... **389a** d.	...	1510r	...	...	...	1605t	1610	1635	1705	1710	...	1735	...	1805	1810	...	*1835*v	...	*1905*	2005	2010	*2019*	2052
Charleville-Mézières ... **389a** a.	...	1529r	...	...	...	1629t	1629	1700	1729	1729	...	1800	...	1829	1829	...	*1900*v	...	*1929*	2030	2029	*2034*	2107
Charleville-Mézières ... d.	...	1534	...	1602	...	1634	1634	1708	1734	1734	...	1808	...	1834	1834	...	1908	1934	2005	2035	2034	2105	2117
Rethel ... d.	...	1606	...	1632	...	1706	1706	1736	1806	1806	...	1836	...	1906	1906	...	1936	2006	2037	2107	2106	2137	2148
Reims ... a.	...	1630	...	1654	...	1730	1730	1800	1830	1830	...	1900	...	1930	1930	...	2000	2030	2101	2131	2130	2200	2209
Reims ... **391a** d.	1615	1636	1700	1700	1730	1736	1736	1806	1836	1836	1845	1906	1915	1936	1936	1945	...	...	...	...	...	...	2215
Champagne Ardenne TGV **390 391a** d.	|	1648	|	|	|	1748	1748	1818	1848	1848	|	1918	|	1948	1948	|	...	...	...	...	...	...	|
Paris Est ... **390** a.	1701	...	1746	1746	1816	...	...	...	...	...	1931	...	2001	...	...	2031	...	...	...	...	...	...	2301

A – Ⓐ to July 4; ⑤ July 11 - Aug. 29 (also Aug. 14; not Aug. 15); Ⓐ from Sept. 1 (not Nov. 10).
B – ①②③④⑥ to July 3; ①–⑥ July 5 - Aug. 30 (not July 14); ①②③④⑥ from Sept. 1 (not Nov. 11).
C – ①②③④⑥ to July 5; ⑥ July 12 - Aug. 30 (also Aug. 15); ①②③④⑥ from Sept. 1 (bot Nov. 11).
D – Ⓐ July 7 - Aug. 29. Does not run Sedan - Reims July 7–11.
E – Ⓐ (not July 7 - Aug. 29, Nov. 10). Does **not** run Sedan - Charleville - Reims Sept. 1–5, 29, 30, Oct. 1–3, 6–10.
H – ①–⑥ to July 5; ⑥ July 12 - Aug. 30 (also Aug. 15); ①–⑥ from Sept. 1 (not Nov. 11).
L – Ⓑ to July 6; ⑤⑦ July 11 - Aug. 24 (also July 14, Aug. 14; not July 13, Aug. 15); Ⓑ from Aug. 29 (not Nov. 10).
M – ①–④ July 7 - Aug. 28 (not July 14, Aug. 14).
N – Daily to July 5; ①–⑥ July 7 - Aug. 30 (not July 14); daily from Sept. 1.

P – ⑦ July 6 - Aug. 31 (also July 14; not July 13).
R – ⑤⑦ to July 4; Ⓐ July 7 - Aug. 29; ⑤⑦ from Sept. 5 (also Nov. 11). Arrives Paris 1936 on ①–④ (not Aug. 14).
T – ⑤ to July 11 (also July 6); ⑦ July 13 - Aug. 31 (also July 14); ⑤ from Sept. 5.

a – Not Nov. 10.
b – Not July 14, Nov. 11.
e – Also July 14, Nov. 11.
k – Also Aug. 15, Nov. 10.
n – Not July 5 - Aug. 31.
r – Not June 16–20, 23–27, 30, July 1–4, 7–11, Sept. 1–5, 29, 30, Oct. 1–3, 6–10, 13–17, 20–24, 27–31.
s – Also July 14; not July 13.
t – ⑥ (not Nov. 1).
u – Also Nov. 11; not July 6, 13, 18, 20, 25, 27, Aug. 1–31.

v – Does not run on ①–⑤ July 15 - Aug. 14.
z – Also Nov. 1.

TGV – High-speed train. 🅁. 🍷.

⊖ – Subject to alteration / cancellation Sept. 1–5, 29, 30, Oct. 1–3, 6–10.
⊗ – Terminates at Reims July 7–11, Sept. 1–5, 29, 30, Oct. 1–3, 6–10.
¶ – Does not run Sedan - Reims on July 15.
‡ – Runs 12–15 minutes earlier on Nov. 10.
△ – Runs 15–16 minutes later July 6 - Aug. 31.

389a CHARLEVILLE MÉZIÈRES - LONGUYON - LONGWY and THIONVILLE

km		Ⓐ	Ⓐ v	Ⓐ B	Ⓐ v	Ⓐ A🚌	Ⓐ B	⑥ t	Ⓐ C▲	✝	Ⓐ	✝	
0	**Charleville-Mézières** ... **389** d.	0520	...	0620	...	0620	...	0920	1120	1330	1720	1820	...
20	**Sedan** ... **389** d.	0536	...	0636	...	0646	...	0935	1136	1345	1736	1835	...
69	Montmédy ... d.	0607	...	0707	...	0739	...	1006	1207	1416	1807	1908	...
	Longwy ... **392** d.	|	0615	|	*0654*	|	0818	|	|	|	|	|	...
91	Longuyon ... **392** a.	0621	0628	0721	*0706*	0807	0830	1020	1221	1430	1821	1922	...
91	Longuyon ... **392** d.	0630	0629	0730	0730	0807	0831	1025	1230	1435	1830	1923	2000
	Longwy ... **392** a.	0642	|	0742	|	0842	|	1037	1242	1447	1842	|	2012
132	Hayange ... d.	...	0701	...	0801	...	0902	...	...	...	...	1954	...
140	**Thionville** ... a.	...	0709	...	0810	...	0910	...	...	...	...	2002	...

	Ⓐ	Ⓐ v	Ⓐ B	Ⓐ C▲	⑥ t	✝	Ⓐ B	Ⓐ B	Ⓐ A🚌	Ⓐ v	Ⓐ	✝ ◇
Thionville ... d.	...	0636	...	...	...	1621	1710	...	...	1841	...	...
Hayange ... d.	...	0644	...	...	...	1629	1718	...	...	1849	...	...
Longwy ... **392** d.	0654	|	...	1320	1426	|	|	1816	1816	|	1916	2017
Longuyon ... **392** a.	0706	0716	...	1332	1438	1659	1749	1828	1843	1920	1928	2029
Longuyon ... **392** d.	0711	...	0730	1337	1443	1700	1750	1833	1843	1921	1933	2034
Longwy ... **392** a.	|	...	0742	|	|	|	1803	|	|	1934	|	|
Montmédy ... d.	0725	...	...	1351	1458	1713	...	1847	1911	...	1947	2049
Sedan ... **389** d.	0757	...	...	1423	1529	1745	...	1919	2004	...	2019	2120
Charleville-Mézières ... **389** a.	0812	...	...	1438	1544	1800	...	1934	2040	...	2034	2137

A – Until July 4.
B – From July 7.
C – From July 21.

t – Not Nov. 1.
v – Not July 15 - Aug. 14.

◇ – On Aug. 15 departs Longuyon 2040, Montmédy 2058, Sedan 2136, arrives Charleville-Mézières 2154.
▲ – **Subject to alteration/cancellation**. Please check before travelling on this service.

PARIS - STRASBOURG, NANCY, METZ and LUXEMBOURG 390

SERVICE TO JULY 4 AND FROM SEPTEMBER 1. See pages 603 and 604 for service July 5 - August 31.
See Tables **30** and **32** for full details of international *TGV/ICE* services between Paris and Germany (including services via Forbach and Saarbrücken).
See Table **391** for *TGV* services from/to Marne la Vallée and Paris Charles de Gaulle ✈. Timings may vary by a few minutes – please check your reservation for confirmed timings.
Subject to alteration on Oct. 17 – 19, Nov. 22, 23. **Warning! Journeys to/from Luxembourg are subject to alteration on June 28, 29, Sept. 1 – 14.**

km		*ICE*	*TGV*	*TGV*	*TGV*	*TGV*	*TGV*	*TGV*	*TGV*	*TGV*	*TGV*	*TGV*		*TGV*	*TGV*	*TGV*	*TGV*	*TGV*	*TGV*	*ICE*	*Ouigo*	*TGV*	*TGV*	*ICE*	*TGV*
		9571	**2501**	**9561**	**2363**	**2801**	**2801**	**2503**	**2407**	**2407**	**2807**	**2807**		**2571**	**2571**	**2587**	**2571**	**2365**	**2429**	**9591**	**7691**	**2409**	**2815**	**9573**	**9593**
			Ⓐ	①–⑥	①–⑥	①	②–⑤	⑥	Ⓑ	⑥	②–⑥	①		Ⓐ	⑦	⑦	⑥	①–④	⑤			⑥		Ⓑ	⑥
		♧	h	⊡	b	g	q	t	h	t	s	g		h	e	e	t	m		♡	⊠	t		♧	♧
0	**Paris** Est d.	0654	0707	0718r	0718r	0719	0728	0746	0758	0805	0814	0821	...	0911	0913	0913	0917	0925	0925	0955	1008	1025	1039	1054	1054
136	Champagne-Ardenne TGV ★ a.	|	0746	|	|	0802	|	0827	0838	0845	0853	|	...	0951	|	|	|	|	|	|	|	|	|	|	|
136	Champagne-Ardenne TGV ★ d.	|	0749	|	|	0805	|	0830	0841	0848	0856	|	...	0954	|	|	|	|	|	|	|	|	|	|	|
236	Meuse TGV d.	|	|	|	|	|	|	0858	0908	|	|	|	...	|	1016	1016	|	|	|	|	|	|	|	|	|
330	**Nancy** 386 387 a.	|	0844	|	|	|	|	0936	|	|	|	|	...	1049	1051	1051	1049	|	|	|	|	|	|	|	|
	St Dié 387 a.	|	...	|	|	|	|	...	|	|	|	|	...	|	|	|	|	|	|	|	|	|	|	|	|
	Épinal 386 a.	|	...	|	|	|	|	...	|	|	|	|	...	1140	1143	|	1142	|	|	|	|	|	|	|	|
	Remiremont 386 a.	|	...	|	|	|	|	...	|	|	|	|	...	1208	1208	|	1208	|	|	|	|	|	|	|	|
315	**Metz** 384 a.	|	...	|	|	0851	0851	...	|	|	0944	0944	...	...	...	▽	...	|	|	|	|	|	1203	|	|
345	Thionville 384 a.	|	...	|	|	0916	0916	...	|	|	1008	1008	...	...	...	|	...	|	|	|	|	|	1227	|	|
379	**Luxembourg** 384 a.	|	...	|	|	0945	0945	...	|	|	1032	1032	...	...	...	|	...	|	|	|	|	|	1251	|	|
304	Lorraine TGV d.	|	...	|	|	...	...	...	|	|	...	...	...	...	...	|	...	|	|	|	|	|	...	|	|
439	**Strasbourg** 385 a.	0839	...	0902	0902	...	...	...	0959	0959	...	...	...	...	...	1221	...	1111	1111	1140	1154	1211	...	1239	1239
482	Sélestat 385 a.	...	...	...	|	...	...	...	...	...	...	...	...	...	...	...	...	|	...	...	...	...	...	...	...
504	**Colmar** 385 a.	...	...	...	0943	...	...	...	...	...	...	...	...	...	...	...	...	1145	...	...	...	...	...	...	...

	TGV	*TGV*	*TGV*	*TGV*	*TGV*	*TGV*	*TGV*	*TGV*		*TGV*	*TGV*	*TGV*	*TGV*	*TGV*	*TGV*	*TGV*	*TGV*	*TGV*	*ICE*	*TGV*	*TGV*	*TGV*	*Ouigo*		*TGV*
	2411	**2507**	**2507**	**2505**	**2421**	**2421**	**2421**	**2421**		**2817**	**9575**	**2369**	**2591**	**2509**	**2509**	**2431**	**2431**	**2511**	**9563**	**2613**	**9577**	**2513**	**7693**		**2515**
	⑤	Ⓑ	⑥	⑤			⑤	① E				Ⓑ	⑦	①–④	⑤	⑤	⑦	⑥		Ⓐ	Ⓑ	Ⓑ			Ⓐ
		h	t		♠	■					♧	h	e	m			e	t	⊡	h	⊙	h	⊠		h
Paris Est d.	1057	1104	1123	1221	1246	1246	1255	1255	...	1339	1354	1354	1358	1358	1406	1425	1455	1458	1521	1524	1554	1607	1616	...	1713
Champagne-Ardenne TGV ★ a.	|	|	|	1302	1327	1326	|	1337	...	|	|	|	1438	1438	|	|	|	1538	|	|	|	1646	|	...	|
Champagne-Ardenne TGV ★ d.	|	|	|	1305	1330	1329	|	1340	...	|	|	|	1441	1441	|	|	|	1541	|	|	|	1649	|	...	|
Meuse TGV d.	|	|	|	|	|	|	|	|	...	|	|	|	1509	1509	1509	|	|	1609	|	|	|	|	|	...	|
Nancy 386 387 a.	|	1236	1255	1400	|	|	|	|	...	|	|	|	1544	1544	1544	|	|	1644	|	|	|	1744	|	...	1844
St Dié 387 a.	|	...	...	...	|	|	|	|	...	|	|	|	1645	...	...	|	|	...	|	|	|	...	|	...	...
Épinal 386 a.	|	...	...	...	|	|	|	|	...	|	|	|	...	...	...	|	|	...	|	|	|	...	|	...	...
Remiremont 386 a.	|	...	...	...	|	|	|	|	...	|	|	|	...	...	...	|	|	...	|	|	|	...	|	...	...
Metz 384 a.	|	...	...	...	|	|	|	|	...	1503	|	|	...	...	...	|	|	...	|	1648	|	...	1741	...	...
Thionville 384 a.	|	...	...	...	|	|	|	|	...	1527	|	|	...	...	...	|	|	...	|	...	|	...	|	...	...
Luxembourg 384 a.	|	...	...	...	|	|	|	|	...	1551	|	|	...	...	...	|	|	...	|	...	|	...	|	...	...
Lorraine TGV d.	|	...	...	...	|	1410	|	|	...	...	|	|	...	...	...	|	|	...	|	...	|	...	|	...	...
Strasbourg 385 a.	1243	...	...	...	1440	1447	1440	1459	...	...	1539	1539	...	...	...	1611	1641	...	1707	...	1741	...	1900	...	...
Sélestat 385 a.	...	...	...	...	...	...	...	...	...	...	...	|	...	...	...	...	...	...	...	...	...	...	...	...	...
Colmar 385 a.	...	...	...	...	...	...	...	...	...	...	...	1627	...	...	...	...	...	...	...	...	...	...	...	...	...

	TGV	*TGV*	*TGV*	*TGV*	*TGV*	*TGV*	*TGV*	*TGV*	*TGV*	*TGV*	*TGV*	*TGV*	*TGV*	*TGV*	*TGV*	*TGV*	*TGV*	*TGV*	*TGV*		*TGV*	*TGV*		*TGV*	*TGV*
	9531	**2833**	**9579**	**2573**	**2593**	**2425**	**2625**	**2625**	**2377**	**2785**	**2595**	**2583**	**2785**	**2839**	**2583**	**2519**	**2465**	**2465**	**2843**		**2527**	**2647**		**2471**	**2471**
					Ⓐ	②–④	⑤	①–④		⑦	⑦	⑦	Ⓐ		Ⓐ	⑥	Ⓒ	Ⓐ	⑥⑦		⑤⑦	⑤⑦		⑤	⑦
	⊖		⊕			q		m		v B	e	e	h B		h	t	t	h ❖	e		e	e			e
Paris Est d.	1725	1740	1754	1807	1807	1823	1840	1840	1854	1920	1924	1924	1928	1940	1943	2007	2025	2025	2040	...	2113	2140	...	2155	2205
Champagne-Ardenne TGV ★ a.	|	|	|	|	|	|	|	1919	|	2000	|	|	2008	|	|	|	|	|	|	...	|	|	...	|	|
Champagne-Ardenne TGV ★ d.	|	|	|	|	|	|	|	1922	|	...	|	|	...	|	|	|	|	|	|	...	|	|	...	|	|
Meuse TGV d.	|	|	|	1909	1909	|	|	|	|	...	2028	2028	...	|	|	2109	|	2127	|	...	|	|	...	|	|
Nancy 386 387 a.	|	|	|	1944	1944	|	|	|	|	...	2104	2104	...	|	2114	2144	|	|	|	...	2244	|	...	|	|
St Dié 387 a.	|	|	|	|	2047	|	|	|	|	...	2158	|	...	|	|	...	|	|	|	...	...	|	...	|	|
Épinal 386 a.	|	|	|	2039	...	|	|	|	|	...	...	|	...	|	|	...	|	|	|	...	...	|	...	|	|
Remiremont 386 a.	|	|	|	2104	...	|	|	|	|	...	...	|	...	|	|	...	|	|	|	...	...	|	...	|	|
Metz 384 a.	|	1904	|	...	...	|	2004	2010	|	...	...	▽	...	2104	▽	...	|	|	2204	...	...	2303	...	|	|
Thionville 384 a.	|	1927	|	...	...	|	...	...	|	...	...	|	...	2127	|	...	|	|	2227	...	...	...	...	|	|
Luxembourg 384 a.	|	1953	|	...	...	|	...	...	|	...	...	|	...	2153	|	...	|	|	2253	...	...	...	...	|	|
Lorraine TGV d.	|	...	|	...	...	|	...	...	|	...	...	|	...	...	|	...	|	2148	...	...	...	...	...	|	|
Strasbourg 385 a.	1911	...	1939	...	...	2008	...	...	2040	...	...	2240z	...	...	2242	...	2211	2225	...	...	...	...	...	2340	2351
Sélestat 385 a.	...	...	...	...	...	...	...	...	2106	...	...	...	...	...	...	...	...	...	...	...	...	...	...	...	...
Colmar 385 a.	...	...	...	...	...	...	...	...	2120	...	...	...	...	...	...	...	...	...	...	...	...	...	...	...	...

	TGV	*TGV*	*TGV*	*TGV*	*TGV*	*TGV*	*TGV*	*TGV*	*TGV*	*TGV*	*TGV*	*TGV*	*TGV*	*TGV*	*TGV*	*TGV*	*TGV*	*TGV*	*TGV*	*TGV*	*TGV*	*ICE*	*TGV*	*TGV*	*TGV*
	2530	**2650**	**2778**	**2400**	**2404**	**2404**	**2584**	**2574**	**2654**	**2854**	**2350**	**9530**	**2534**	**2596**	**9534**	**2352**	**9578**	**9532**	**2860**	**2860**	**2656**	**9568**	**2536**	**2578**	**2406**
	Ⓐ	Ⓐ	①–⑥		Ⓐ	Ⓐ		⚒	⑥	①–⑤	①–⑥	Ⓐ	⑦	①–⑥	⑦	⑦	①–⑥	⑥	⑦	⑥	①–⑤	Ⓑ	⚒	†	Ⓐ
	h	h	m B	Y	H	G	J				b	h ⊖			⊖		♧	k ⊖				⊡			h
Colmar 385 d.	...	...	...	...	...	...	...	...	...	...	0638	...	...	...	...	0735	...	...	...	...	...	...	...	...	...
Sélestat 385 d.	...	...	...	...	...	...	...	...	...	...	0652	...	...	...	...	0749	...	...	...	...	...	...	...	...	...
Strasbourg 385 d.	...	...	...	0623	0631	0642	0539	...	0533f	...	0719	0749	...	...	0820	0820	0821	0821	...	...	...	0852	...	...	1031
Lorraine TGV d.	...	...	...	|	|	|	|	...	|	...	0759	|	...	...	|	|	|	|	...	...	...	|	...	...	|
Luxembourg 384 d.	...	...	...	|	|	|	|	...	▽	0640	|	|	...	...	|	|	|	|	0757	0757	...	|	...	...	|
Thionville 384 d.	...	...	...	|	|	|	|	...	|	0702	|	|	...	...	|	|	|	|	0823	0823	...	|	...	...	|
Metz 384 d.	...	0623	...	|	|	|	▽	...	0726	0726	|	|	...	...	|	|	|	|	0849	0850	0854	|	...	...	|
Remiremont 386 d.	...	|	...	|	|	|	|	0559	|	|	|	|	...	...	|	|	|	|	|	|	|	|	...	0859	|
Épinal 386 d.	...	|	...	|	|	|	|	0624	|	|	|	|	...	...	|	|	|	|	|	|	|	|	...	0923	|
St Dié 387 d.	...	|	...	|	|	|	|	|	|	|	|	|	...	0714	|	|	|	|	|	|	|	|	...	|	|
Nancy 386 387 d.	0612	|	...	|	|	|	0716	0716	|	|	|	|	0811	0815	|	|	|	|	|	|	|	|	1011	1011	|
Meuse TGV d.	|	|	...	|	0721	0734	|	|	|	|	|	|	0848	|	|	|	|	|	|	0920	0924	|	|	|	|
Champagne-Ardenne TGV ★ a.	|	|	...	|	|	|	|	|	|	|	|	|	|	|	|	|	|	|	|	|	|	|	1104	1104	|
Champagne-Ardenne TGV ★ d.	|	|	0718	|	|	|	|	|	|	|	|	|	|	|	|	|	|	|	|	|	|	|	1107	1107	|
Paris Est a.	0746	0750	0801	0816	0820	0835	0846	0846	0850	0854	0916	0935	0948	0946	1005	1005	1006	1006	1013	1021	1025	1038	1148	1148	1216

B – To/from Bar le Duc (Table **381**).
D – Sept. 20, 27, Oct. 4, 11, Nov. 8, 10, 15.
E – ① from Sept. 1 (also Nov. 12; not Nov. 10).
G – Until July 4.
H – From Sept. 1.
J – ②–⑤ to July 4 (not June 19); Ⓐ from Sept. 1 (not Oct. 6, 13, Nov. 10).
L – Nov. 10 only.
P – June 22, Sept. 21, 28, Oct. 5, 19, Nov. 23.
Q – June 15, 29, Sept. 7, 14, Oct. 12, 26, Nov. 2, 9, 11, 16, 30, Dec. 7.
Y – June 16, 23, 30, Sept. 8, 15, 22, 29, Oct. 6, 13, Nov. 12, 17.

b – Not Nov. 11.
c – 1506 on Sept. 19 - Nov. 7.
e – Also Nov. 11.
f – 4–5 minutes earlier Sept. 27 - Nov. 1.
g – Also Nov. 12; not Nov. 10.
h – Not Nov. 10.
k – Also Nov. 10, 11.
m – Not Nov. 10, 11.
q – Not Nov. 11, 12.
r – 0715 on ① (also Nov. 12; not Nov. 10).
s – Also Nov. 10; not Nov. 11, 12.

t – Also Nov. 10.
v – Also Nov. 11; not Nov. 9.
z – Not June 15, 22, 29. Arrives 2230 Sept. 21 - Oct. 26.

TGV – High-speed train. 🅁. 🍸.
ICE – German high-speed train. 🅁. ✕.

▲ – Does not call at Metz June 23 – 27, 30, July 1 – 4.
Does not call at Metz and arrives Paris 2143 July 7 – 11, 21 – 25.
♠ – ⑦ to June 29; ②③④⑦ from Sept. 2 (not Nov. 12).
■ – ①–④ to July 3. Runs 9 – 14 minutes later on ①.
❖ – Runs 10 minutes later Sept. 1 – 12.
¶ – On Nov. 10 Nancy d. 1910, Meuse d. 1954, Champagne-Ardenne a. 2018, d. 2021, Paris a. 2102.
▽ – Via Saverne (Table **383**).
⊕ – (12) Paris - Stuttgart (- München ⑥). See Table **32**.
⊙ – To/from München via Stuttgart (Table **32**).
⊡ – To/from Frankfurt (Table **30**).
♧ – To/from Stuttgart (Table **32**).
♡ – To/from Berlin via Frankfurt (Table **30**).
⊖ – From/to Freiburg (Brsg) Hbf (Table **32**).
★ – See Table **391a** for rail connections from/to Reims.
⊠ – OUIGO low-cost TGV. Internet bookings only: www.ouigo.com

390 PARIS - STRASBOURG, NANCY, METZ and LUXEMBOURG

SERVICE TO JULY 4 AND FROM SEPTEMBER 1. See pages 603 and 604 for service July 5 - August 31.
See Tables **30** and **32** for full details of international *TGV*/*ICE* services between Germany and Paris (including services via Forbach and Saarbrücken).
See Table **391** for *TGV* services to Marne la Vallée and Paris Charles de Gaulle ✈. Timings may vary by a few minutes – please check your reservation for confirmed timings.
Subject to alteration on Oct. 17–19, Nov. 22, 23. **Warning! Journeys from Luxembourg are subject to alteration on June 28, 29, Sept. 1–14.**

	TGV **2864** Ⓑ	*TGV* **2864** ⑥	*TGV* **2356** ①–⑥ b	*TGV* **9576** ⊙	*ICE* **9566** ⑥ ⊡	*TGV* **2416** D	*ICE* **9574** ♧	*TGV* **2540** ⑦ e	*TGV* **2540** Ⓐ h	*Ouigo* **7692** ⊠	*TGV* **2580** ⑥ t	*TGV* **2580** Ⓐ h	*TGV* **2580** ⑦ e	*TGV* **2588** ⑦ e	*TGV* **2870** ⑥	*TGV* **2870** Ⓑ	*TGV* **2430** ⑤⑥ t	*TGV* **2358** ①–④ m	*TGV* **2546** ⑤	*TGV* **2440** ⑦ e	*TGV* **2440** ⑤	*TGV* **2440** ①–④ m	*TGV* **2542** ⑦ e	*TGV* **2542** Ⓐ h	*ICE* **9572** Ⓑ ♧
Colmar 385 d.	...	...	1001	...	...	...	...	...	...	...	...	...	...	...	...	...	...	1415	...	...	...	...	...	...	...
Sélestat 385 d.	...	...	|	...	...	...	...	...	...	...	...	...	...	...	...	...	...	|	...	...	...	...	...	...	...
Strasbourg 385 d.	...	...	1046	1046	1052	1147	1222	...	...	1250	...	...	...	1242	...	...	1449	1450	...	1519	1531	1544	...	...	1620
Lorraine TGV d.	...	...	|	|	|	|	|	...	...	|	...	...	...	|	...	...	|	|	...	|	|	|	...	...	|
Luxembourg 384 d.	1010	1010	|	|	|	|	|	...	...	|	...	...	...	|	1410	1410	|	|	...	|	|	|	...	...	|
Thionville 384 d.	1034	1034	|	|	|	|	|	...	...	|	...	...	...	|	1434	1434	|	|	...	|	|	|	...	...	|
Metz 384 d.	1057	1059	|	|	|	|	|	...	...	1352	...	...	...	▽	1459	1505	|	|	...	|	|	|	...	...	|
Remiremont 386 d.	|	|	|	|	|	|	|	...	...	|	1255	1255	1254	|	|	|	|	|	...	|	|	|	...	...	|
Épinal 386 d.	|	|	|	|	|	|	|	...	...	|	1319	1319	1319	|	|	|	|	|	...	|	|	|	...	...	|
St Dié 387 d.	|	|	|	|	|	|	|	...	...	|	|	|	|	|	|	|	|	|	...	|	|	|	...	...	|
Nancy 386 387 d.	|	|	|	|	|	|	|	1311	1311	|	1411	1411	1414	1414	|	|	|	|	1510c	|	|	|	1624	1624	|
Meuse TGV d.	|	|	|	|	|	|	|	|	1348	|	|	|	1451	1451	1530	|	|	|	|	|	|	|	|	|	|
Champagne-Ardenne TGV ★ a.	|	|	|	|	|	|	|	|	|	|	|	1503	1515	1515	|	|	|	|	|	|	|	|	|	1717	|
Champagne-Ardenne TGV ★ d.	|	|	|	|	|	|	|	|	|	|	|	1507	1518	1518	|	|	|	|	|	|	|	|	|	1720	|
Paris Est a.	1220	1222	1231	1231	1238	1335	1406	1441	1448	1517	1542	1548	1606	1606	1630	1630	1635	1635	1638	1705	1717	1735	1754	1801	1805

	TGV **9592** ⑥ ♧	*TGV* **2872** Ⓑ h	*TGV* **2872** ⑥ t	*TGV* **2442** ⑦ e	*TGV* **2442** ⑤	*TGV* **2544** ⑥ t	*TGV* **2680** Ⓑ h	*TGV* **2450** L	*TGV* **2362** Ⓑ h	*TGV* **2548** Ⓐ h	*TGV* **2598** ⑦ e	*ICE* **9590** ♡	*TGV* **2454** ⑦ e	*TGV* **2454** Ⓐ h	*TGV* **9560** ⊡	*TGV* **2550** ⑥ t¶	*TGV* **2886**	*TGV* **2552** Ⓑ h	*TGV* **9570** ♧	*Ouigo* **7694** ▲⊠	*TGV* **2892** ⑦ e	*TGV* **2470** ⑤	*TGV* **2554** ⑦ e	*TGV* **2474** P	*TGV* **2474** Q
Colmar 385 d.	...	...	...	...	...	...	...	...	1645	...	...	...	...	...	...	...	...	...	...	...	...	...	...	...	...
Sélestat 385 d.	...	...	...	...	...	...	...	...	|	...	...	...	...	...	...	...	...	...	...	...	...	...	...	...	...
Strasbourg 385 d.	1620	...	...	1649	1652	...	...	1719	1719	...	...	1801	1812	1819	1857	...	...	...	2025	1958	...	2047	...	2119	2152
Lorraine TGV d.	|	...	...	|	|	...	...	|	|	...	...	|	|	|	|	...	...	...	|	|	...	|	...	|	|
Luxembourg 384 d.	|	1610	1610	|	|	...	...	|	|	...	...	|	|	|	|	...	1846	...	|	|	2011	|	...	|	|
Thionville 384 d.	|	1634	1634	|	|	...	...	|	|	...	...	|	|	|	|	...	1912	...	|	|	2035	|	...	|	|
Metz 384 d.	|	1657	1657	|	|	...	1728	|	|	...	...	|	|	|	|	...	1942	...	|	2101	2108	|	...	|	|
Remiremont 386 d.	|	|	|	|	|	...	|	|	|	...	...	|	|	|	|	...	|	...	|	|	|	|	...	|	|
Épinal 386 d.	|	|	|	|	|	...	|	|	|	...	...	|	|	|	|	...	|	...	|	|	|	|	...	|	|
St Dié 387 d.	|	|	|	|	|	...	|	|	|	...	1710	|	|	|	|	...	|	...	|	|	|	|	...	|	|
Nancy 386 387 d.	|	|	|	|	|	1718	|	|	|	1811	1811	|	|	|	|	1920	|	1943	|	|	|	|	2116	|	|
Meuse TGV d.	|	|	|	|	|	|	|	|	|	1847	1848	|	|	|	|	1957	|	|	|	|	|	|	|	|	|
Champagne-Ardenne TGV ★ a.	|	|	1746	|	|	|	1816	|	|	|	|	|	1921	1928	|	2020	2029	2037	|	|	|	|	|	|	|
Champagne-Ardenne TGV ★ d.	|	|	1749	|	|	|	1819	|	|	|	|	|	1924	1931	|	2023	2032	2040	|	|	|	|	|	|	|
Paris Est a.	1805	1820	1830	1835	1839	1848	1901	1905	1905	1948	1948	1955	2005	2012	2041	2105	2113	2120	2213	2224	2232	2235	2246	2305	2338

← **FOR NOTES, SEE PREVIOUS PAGE.**

391 STRASBOURG - BRUSSELS, NANTES, RENNES and BORDEAUX

Timings may vary by a few minutes on certain dates – please check your reservation. **WARNING!** Services via Massy are subject to alteration on June 15, 28, 29, July 19, 20.

	TGV **9890**	*TGV* **5450** B	*TGV* **5486** ⊖	*TGV* **9594** ⑥ F	*TGV* **5470**	*TGV* **5477** ⑥ Q		*TGV* **5454** ⑥ k	*TGV* **5454** Ⓑ h	*TGV* **5454** ⑥ G	*TGV* **5472** ⑤⑦ H	*TGV* **9894**	*TGV* **5488** Ⓑ d	
Strasbourg d.	0559	0619	0731	0854	1001	1001	...	1351	1401	1500	1648	1701	1701	...
Lorraine TGV ♠ d.	0638	0656	0809	0943	1038	1038	...	1434	1439	1541	1726	1742	1742	...
Meuse TGV ♠ d.	0659	|	|	1003	1059	1059	...	1454	1500	1603	|	1809	1809	...
Champagne-Ardenne TGV ★ a.	0723	0738	0847	1027	1123	1123	...	1518	1523	1627	1804	1833	1833	...
Champagne-Ardenne TGV ★ d.	0726	0745	0858	1030	1129	1129	...	1521	1526	1630	1811	1836	1836	...
Marne la Vallée - Chessy § d.	|	|	|	|	|	|	...	|	|	|	|	|	|	...
Paris Charles de Gaulle ✈ a.	0756	|	0928	|	1159	1159	...	1552	1556	1700	|	1906	1906	...
Paris Charles de Gaulle ✈ d.	0807	|	0943	|	1217	1217	...	1607	1613	1715	|	1912	1921	...
Haute Picardie TGV a.	|	|	|	|	|	|	...	|	|	|	|	1944j	|	...
Lille Europe a.	0858	|	|	|	|	|	...	|	|	|	|	2016j	|	...
Brussels Midi/Zuid a.	0943t	|	|	|	|	|	...	|	|	|	|	2101j	|	...
Marne la Vallée - Chessy § a.	...	0816	0953	1059	1227	1227	...	1616	1623	1724	1841	...	1930	...
Marne la Vallée - Chessy § d.	...	0830	1002	1104	1232	1232	...	1621	1631	1732	1903	...	1935	...
Massy TGV a.	...	0904	1034	1139	1304	1304	...	1652	1704	1804	1934	...	2005	...
St Pierre des Corps a.	...	1003	1132	1237	|	|	...	1750	1803	1903	|	...	|	...
Le Mans a.	...	|	|	|	1359	1359	...	|	|	|	2029	...	2100	...
Angers a.	...	|	1236	|	|	|	...	|	|	|	|	...	2140	...
Nantes a.	...	|	1319	|	|	|	...	|	|	|	|	...	2223	...
Laval a.	...	|	...	|	|	|	...	|	|	|	2103	...	...	...
Rennes a.	...	|	...	|	1447	1447	...	|	|	|	2129	...	...	...
Quimper a.	...	|	...	|	...	1706	...	|	|	|	...	...	...	...
Poitiers a.	...	1039	...	1317	...	...	...	1825	1839	1937	...	...	...	...
Angoulême a.	...	1122	...	1357	...	...	...	1906	1920	2023e	...	...	...	...
Bordeaux St Jean a.	...	1202	...	1435	...	...	...	1948	2001	2101e	...	...	...	...

	TGV **9870**	*TGV* **5482** ①–⑥ b	*TGV* **5464** ①⑥ J	*TGV* **5440** †	*TGV* **5440** ⚒	*TGV* **5466** ⑦ R	*TGV* **9874** p	*TGV* **5444** D	*TGV* **9874** A	*TGV* **5480** L	*TGV* **5480** ⑦ M	*TGV* **5480** ⑥ N	*TGV* **5460**	*TGV* **9599** ⑥ F
Bordeaux St Jean d.	...	...	...	0854	0854	...	...	1257	...	...	...	...	...	1556
Angoulême d.	...	...	...	0935	0935	...	...	1336	...	...	...	...	...	1635
Poitiers d.	...	...	...	1020	1019	...	...	1420	...	...	...	...	...	1719
Quimper d.	...	...	...	|	|	0823	...	|	...	...	...	...	...	|
Rennes d.	...	...	0827	|	|	1031	...	|	...	...	...	...	1603	|
Laval d.	...	...	0855	|	|	|	...	|	...	...	...	...	|	|
Nantes d.	...	0808z	|	|	|	|	...	|	...	1408	1428	1437	|	|
Angers d.	...	0848z	|	|	|	|	...	|	...	1448	1509	1517	|	|
Le Mans d.	...	0930	0930	|	|	1120	...	|	...	1530	|	|	1658	|
St Pierre des Corps d.	...	|	|	1055	1054	|	...	1456	...	|	1614	1621	|	1756
Massy TGV d.	...	1024	1024	1156	1156	1222	...	1555	...	1626	1726	1720	1755	1855
Marne la Vallée - Chessy § a.	...	1055	1055	1226	1230	1256	...	1626	...	1657	1758	1756	1825	1926
Marne la Vallée - Chessy § d.	...	1100	1100	1230	1237	1300	...	1636	...	1701	1804	1802	1830	1931
Brussels Midi/Zuid d.	0717v	|	|	|	|	|	1317q	|	1503	|	|	|	|	|
Lille Europe d.	0802	|	|	|	|	|	1401	|	1552	|	|	|	|	|
Haute Picardie TGV d.	|	|	|	|	|	|	|	|	|	|	|	|	|	|
Paris Charles de Gaulle ✈ a.	0857	1109	1109	|	|	1310	1453	|	1643	1711	1813	1811	1839	|
Paris Charles de Gaulle ✈ d.	0902	1122	1122	|	|	1325	1459	|	1654	1729	1829	1827	1853	|
Marne la Vallée - Chessy § d.	|	|	|	|	|	|	1527r	|	|	|	|	|	|	|
Champagne-Ardenne TGV ★ a.	0934	1152	1152	1258	1309	1354	1555	1704	1723	1759	1859	1859	1929	1959
Champagne-Ardenne TGV ★ d.	0937	1155	1155	1301	1312	1357	1604	1707	1726	1809	1902	1902	1935	2002
Meuse TGV ♠ a.	1002	|	|	1325	1335	1422	|	1731	|	|	|	|	2000	2026
Lorraine TGV ♠ a.	1025	1232	1232	1349	1356	1443	1648	1752	1803	1848	1941	1943	2025	2048
Strasbourg a.	1105	1312	1312	1429	1437	1525	1737	1838	1842	1933	2024	2024	2106	2129

A – July 5, 12, 18, 25, 26, Aug. 1, 2, 8, 9, 14, 15, Oct. 18, 25, Nov. 1.
B – ①⑤⑦ July 6 - Aug. 31 (also July 15, Aug. 14; not July 18).
D – ①⑤⑦ July 6 - Aug. 31 (also July 15, Aug. 14). Does not call at Angoulême on Aug. 25, 29.
F – ⑥ July 5 - Aug. 30. From/to Frankfurt (Table **910**).
G – ⑥ July 5 - Aug. 30 (also Aug. 15).
H – ⑤⑦ July 6 - Aug. 29 (also July 14, Aug. 14; not Aug. 15).
J – ①⑥ July 7 - Aug. 30 (also July 15, Aug. 15; not Aug. 16).
L – Daily to June 27; Ⓐ June 30 - Aug. 29; daily from Sept. 1.
M – ⑦ July 6 - Aug. 31 (also July 14).
N – ⑥ July 5 - Aug. 30 (also Aug. 15).
Q – ⑥ July 5 - Aug. 30. Also calls at Vannes (a. 1554), Auray (a. 1607) and Lorient (a. 1627).
R – ⑦ July 6 - Aug. 31. Also calls at Lorient (d. 0858), Auray (d. 0917) and Vannes (d. 0930).

b – Not Aug. 16.
d – Not Aug. 15.
e – On July 5 Angoulême a. 2028, Bordeaux a. 2119.
h – Not Aug. 15, Nov. 10.
j – Aug. 16–31 arrives Haute Picardies 1954, Lille Europe 2036, Brussels 2207 (2201 on ⑤⑦).
k – Also Nov. 10; not July 5 - Aug. 30.
p – Not July 5, 12, 18, 25, 26, Aug. 1, 2, 8, 9, 14, 15, Oct. 18, 25, Nov. 1.
q – Not Aug. 16, 18–21, 23, 25–28, 30. Departs 1300 on Aug. 17, 22, 24, 29, 31.
r – Arrives 1509.
t – 18–19 minutes later Aug. 16–31.
v – 0659 Aug. 16–31.
z – 5 minutes earlier July 5 - Aug. 30.

TGV – High-speed train. Ⓡ. 🍷.

⊖ – Subject to alteration/cancellation on Sept. 1, 2, 15–19, 22–26, 29, 30, Oct. 1–3, 6–10, 13–17, Nov. 3–7, 12–14, Dec. 7.
§ – Station for Disneyland Paris.
★ – See Table **391a** for rail connections from/to Reims.
♠ – Connecting 🚌 services operate on the following routes:
Nancy - Lorraine TGV (journey 35 minutes);
Metz - Lorraine TGV (journey 25 minutes);
Verdun - Meuse TGV (journey 25 minutes).

REIMS - CHAMPAGNE ARDENNE TGV 391a

	⚒	Ⓐ	⚒		Ⓐ	†		⚒	Ⓐ	⚒w	Ⓐ		Ⓐ	⚒	Ⓐ		Ⓐ		Ⓐ			⚒	Ⓐ		Ⓐ
Reims d.	0636	0706	0736	...	0805	0806	...	0836	0906	0936	1006	1036	1106	1136	1206	1236	1306	1336	1406	1436	...	1536	1606	1636	1706
Champagne-Ardenne TGV a.	0648	0718	0748	...	0817	0818	...	0848	0918	0948	1018	1048	1118	1148	1218	1248	1318	1348	1418	1448	...	1548	1618	1648	1718

		Ⓐ		Ⓐ			Ⓐ	†		
Reims d.	1736	1806	1836	1906	1936	...	2036	2106	...	...
Champagne-Ardenne TGV a.	1748	1818	1848	1918	1948	...	2048	2118	...	...

	⚒	Ⓐ	⚒	Ⓑz	⚒	Ⓐ	w	Ⓐ	⚒
Champagne-Ardenne TGV d.	0710	0740	0810	0840	0910	0940	1010	1040	1110
Reims a.	0722	0752	0822	0852	0922	0952	1022	1052	1122

	Ⓐ		Ⓐ		Ⓐ		Ⓐ	Ⓒ	Ⓐ			Ⓐ		Ⓐ		Ⓐ		Ⓐ		†	⚒		Ⓐ		†
Champagne-Ardenne TGV d.	1140	1210	1240	1310	1340	1410	1440	1510	1518	...	1610	1640	1710	1740	1810	1840	1910	1940	...	2010	2016	...	2110	...	2147
Reims a.	1152	1222	1252	1322	1352	1422	1452	1522	1526	...	1622	1652	1722	1752	1822	1852	1922	1952	...	2022	2028	...	2122	...	2159

w – Does not run on ①–⑤ July 15 - Aug. 14.

z – Also Nov. 1.

LONGWY - NANCY / LUXEMBOURG 392

LONGWY - NANCY (see note ⊖).

km											
		Ⓐ w	⚒		Ⓒ	Ⓐ w⊗	Ⓐ ⊗	Ⓒ		⑦s v	†
0	**Longwy** 389a d.	0547	0647	...	1047	1247	1447	1642	...	...	1921	...
16	Longuyon 389a d.	0601	0701	...	1100	1301	1501	1654	...	...	1935	...
57	Conflans-Jarny d.	0631	0731	...	1130	1331	1531	1731	...	1932	2005	...
100	Pont-à-Mousson 384 d.	0700	0800	...	1200	1402	1602	1800	...	2003	2034	...
128	**Nancy** 384 a.	0720	0820	...	1220	1420	1620	1820	...	2020	2054	...

	⚒ w⊗		⊗		†	Ⓐ			⑤f v
Nancy 384 d.	0839	...	1239	...	1639	1739	1839	...	1954
Pont-à-Mousson 384 d.	0859	...	1259	...	1659	1759	1900	...	2012
Conflans-Jarny d.	0930	...	1330	...	1730	1830	1930	...	2041
Longuyon 389a d.	1000	...	1400	...	1759	1900	2000	...	...
Longwy 389a a.	1012	...	1412	...	1812	1912	2012	...	...

LONGWY - LUXEMBOURG

km																	
		①–⑤ a	①–⑥ b	①–⑤ a	①–⑥ b	①–⑤ a	①–⑤ a	①–⑤ a⊗	①–⑤ a⊗	①–⑤ a	①–⑤ a	①–⑤ a	①–⑤ a	①–⑥ b	①–⑤ a	①–⑥ b	①–⑤ a
0	**Longwy** d.	0620	0650	0720	0750	0820	0850	1320	1350	1650	1720	1750	1820	1850	1920	1950	2020
8	Rodange 🏛 ⊡ d.	0630	0700	0730	0800	0830	0900	1330	1400	1700	1730	1800	1830	1900	1930	2000	2029
10	Pétange ⊡ d.	0634	0704	0734	0804	0834	0904	1334	1404	1704	1734	1804	1834	1904	1934	2004	2034
27	**Luxembourg** ⊡ a.	0657	0727	0757	0827	0857	0927	1357	1427	1727	1757	1827	1857	1927	1957	2027	2056

	①–⑤ a	①–⑤ a	①–⑥ b	①–⑤ a	①–⑥ b	①–⑤ a	①–⑤ a	①–⑤ a⊗	①–⑤ a⊗	①–⑤ a	①–⑤ a	①–⑤ a	①–⑤ a	①–⑥ b	①–⑤ a	①–⑥ b	①–⑤ a
Luxembourg ⊡ d.	0504	0534	0604	0634	0704	0734	0804	1204	1234	1604	1634	1704	1734	1804	1834	1904	1934
Pétange ⊡ d.	0527	0557	0627	0657	0727	0757	0827	1227	1257	1627	1657	1727	1757	1827	1857	1927	1957
Rodange 🏛 ⊡ d.	0532	0602	0632	0702	0732	0802	0832	1232	1302	1632	1702	1732	1802	1832	1902	1932	2002
Longwy a.	0539	0609	0639	0709	0739	0809	0839	1239	1309	1639	1709	1739	1809	1839	1909	1939	2009

LONGWY - METZ 🚌 service (journey 55 minutes):

From Longwy at 0505 Ⓐ, 0630 Ⓐ, 0740, 0945 ⚒, 1235 ⑥ **t**, 1242 Ⓐ, 1335 †, 1445 ⚒, 1545 Ⓐ, 1615 ⑥ **t**, 1620 Ⓑ **z**, 1745 ⑥ **t**, 1823 Ⓐ, 1925 Ⓐ and 1930 Ⓒ.

From Metz at 0635 Ⓐ, 0838 Ⓐ, 0920 ⚒, 1020 †, 1220 ⚒, 1430 ⑥ **t**, 1520 Ⓑ **z**, 1620 ⚒, 1720 Ⓐ, 1820 Ⓐ, 1830 Ⓒ, 2026 Ⓐ, 2030 ⑥ **t**, 2120 †, 2218 ⑥ **t** and 2237 Ⓐ.

a – Not June 23, Aug. 15.
b – Not June 23, Aug. 15, Nov. 1.
f – Not July 11 - Aug. 29, Oct. 24, 31.
s – Also Nov. 11; not July 6 - Aug. 24, Oct. 19, 26.
t – Not Nov. 1.
v – From/to Verdun (Table **393a**).

w – Does not run on ①–⑤ July 15 - Aug. 14.
z – Also Nov. 1.

⊖ – Journeys between Longwy and Nancy are also possible via Metz (see Longwy - Metz 🚌 panel together with Table **384**).
⊗ – Subject to alteration / cancellation on certain ①–⑤ dates. Please check before travelling on this service.
⊡ – Additional trains run Rodange - Luxembourg and v.v. (see Table **449**).

Journey time: 1 hour 48 minutes — 🚌 CHÂLONS EN CHAMPAGNE - VERDUN 🚌 393

From Châlons en Champagne at 0823 Ⓐ, 1025 Ⓒ, 1230 Ⓐ, 1425 Ⓒ, 1430 Ⓐ, 1830 Ⓐ, 1840 †, 2025 Ⓒ and 2030 Ⓐ.

From Verdun at 0512 Ⓐ, 0742 Ⓒ, 1012 Ⓐ, 1209 Ⓐ, 1222 Ⓒ, 1509 Ⓐ, 1622 †, 1732 Ⓑ (also Nov. 1) and 1742 ⑥ (not Nov. 1).

VERDUN - METZ 393a

km																									
		Ⓐ w	Ⓐ	⑥ t	Ⓐ	Ⓐ	Ⓐ	⑥t 🚌	Ⓐ 🚌	⊗	†	Ⓐ 🚌	Ⓐ w⊗	⑥ t	Ⓐ w⊗	Ⓐ w⊗	⑥ t	Ⓐ	†	† 🚌	Ⓐ	Ⓐ	⑦ s	Ⓐ 🚌	†
0	**Verdun** d.	...	...	...	0638	...	0738	0800	0905	1038	...	1205	1238	...	1438	1638	1638	...	...	1745	1813	...	1853	1859	1940
40	Conflans-Jarny d.	0530	0625	0628	0720	0742	0815	0850	0955	1114	1233	1255	1314	1423	1515	1715	1715	1734	1740	1835	1850	1904	1932	1949	2016
	Nancy 392 a.	|	|	|	|	|	|	|	|	|	|	|	|	|	|	|	|	|	|	|	|	|	2020	|	|
66	Hagondange 384 d.	0609	0703	0706	|	0811	0847	|	|	1147	1310	|	1347	1503	1547	1742	1747	1808	1819	|	|	1938	...	|	|
84	**Metz** 384 a.	*0627*	*0729*	0718	0754	*0827*	0901	0930	1035	1201	1323	1335	*1414*	1518	1601	*1818*	1801	*1830*	1835	1915	1924	...	...	2029	2051

	Ⓐ	Ⓐ 🚌	Ⓐ w	Ⓐ ⊗	⑥ t	Ⓐ w⊗	Ⓐ w⊗	Ⓒ	Ⓐ 🚌	Ⓐ w⊗	⑥t 🚌	Ⓐ	†	†	Ⓐ 🚌	Ⓐ	⑥ t	Ⓐ	⑥ t	Ⓐ 🚌	Ⓐ w	†	† 🚌	⑤ f	⑥ t
Metz 384 d.	0606	0708	*0733*	*0833*	0855	1038	1238	1255	1345	*1446*	1630	1637	1637	...	1710	*1730*	1734	1821	1855	1900	*1933*	1937	...	...	2029
Hagondange 384 d.	|	|	0750	0904	0908	1051	1251	1310	|	1511	|	1652	1651	...	|	1750	1750	|	1908	|	1953	1952	...	...	2042
Nancy 392 d.	|	|	|	|	|	|	|	|	|	|	|	|	|	...	|	|	|	|	|	|	|	|	...	1954	|
Conflans-Jarny d.	0643	0758	0825	0943	0939	1123	1323	1343	1430	1543	1715	1724	1729	1743	1805	1820	1827	1853	1940	1945	2031	2029	2033	2042	2120
Verdun a.	0718	0845	...	1018	1015	1158	1358	1417	1517	1618	1802	1759	...	1817	1852	...	...	1927	2015	2032	...	...	2120	2117	...

f – Not July 11 - Aug. 29, Oct. 24, 31.
s – Also Nov. 11; not July 6 - Aug. 24, Oct. 19, 26.
t – Not Nov. 1.

w – Does not run on ①–⑤ July 15 - Aug. 14.

⊗ – Subject to alteration / cancellation on certain ①–⑤ dates. Please check before travelling on this service.

French holiday dates apply — METZ - FORBACH - SAARBRÜCKEN 394

WARNING! Timings may vary by a few minutes – readers are advised to confirm timings before travelling.

km																											
		Ⓐ	Ⓐ w	⑥ t	Ⓐ	Ⓐ	⑥ t	Ⓐ	⚒	†	Ⓐ w	⑥ t	Ⓐ ⊗	Ⓒ	Ⓐ w⊗	Ⓐ ⊗	Ⓒ	⚒ ⊗	Ⓐ w	Ⓐ	†	⑥ t	⚒ w		Ⓐ	Ⓐ	Ⓒ
0	**Metz** d.	...	0538	0608	0637	0704	0738	0738	0838	0838	0938	0938	1038	1038	1138	1238	1238	1338	1438	1538	1538	1538	1638	...	1713	1735	1735
50	St Avold d.	...	0609	0641	0708	0738	0811	0809	0911	0910	1009	1011	1111	1112	1209	1311	1312	1408	1509	1608	1610	1612	1708	...	1746	1808	1810
70	Forbach a.	...	0626	0658	0725	0752	0825	0825	0926	0926	1024	1025	1126	1125	1225	1325	1325	1425	1524	1625	1625	1625	1725	...	1800	1825	1825
70	Forbach d.	0531	*0631*	0659	*0731*	...	...	*0831*	0932	*0931*	*1031*	...	1130	*1131*	*1231*	*1331*	1330	*1431*	*1531*	*1631*	*1631*	1631	...	1731	...	*1831*	*1831*
81	**Saarbrücken** a.	0542	*0645*	0709	*0742*	...	...	*0842*	0940	*0942*	*1042*	...	1140	*1142*	*1242*	*1342*	1340	*1442*	*1542*	*1642*	*1642*	1642	...	1742	...	*1842*	*1842*

	Ⓐ		Ⓑ	Ⓐ w	Ⓐ	Ⓒ	Ⓐ	Ⓐ r	Ⓒ	Ⓐ	†	
Metz d.	1813	1838	...	1910	1935	1938	2038	...	2138	2238	2238	...
St Avold d.	1849	1908	...	1945	2008	2010	2109	...	2209	2309	2310	...
Forbach a.	1904	1925	...	2000	2025	2025	2125	...	2225	2325	2326	...
Forbach d.	...	...	1931	...	*2031*	*2031*	*2131*r	2245	...	*2344*r	2330	...
Saarbrücken a.	...	...	1942	...	*2042*	*2042*	*2142*r	2255	...	*2355*r	2340	...

	Ⓐ k	Ⓐ	⑥ t	Ⓐ	Ⓐ	⚒	Ⓐ	Ⓑ z	⑥ t	Ⓐ	Ⓐ	⚒ w
Saarbrücken d.	0446	...	0450	...	0616	...	...	*0716*	0721	...	0816	...
Forbach a.	0456	...	0500	...	0629	...	...	*0726*	0731	...	0826	...
Forbach d.	...	0503	0503	0607	...	0633	0707	0733	0733	0800	...	0834
St Avold d.	...	0519	0520	0621	...	0648	0723	0749	0750	0814	...	0850
Metz a.	...	0550	0552	0656	...	0721	0756	0820	0822	0846	...	0924

	Ⓐ	Ⓐ w	Ⓒ	Ⓐ ⊗	Ⓐ ⊗	Ⓒ	Ⓐ w⊗	⑥ t	⑥ t	Ⓐ ⊗	†	⑥ t	Ⓐ	†	Ⓐ		Ⓐ w	Ⓒ	Ⓐ			⚒ w	†	Ⓑ r	Ⓐ	Ⓐ r	Ⓐ r
Saarbrücken d.	0921	*1016*	*1016*	*1116*	1221	...	*1316*	1321	*1416*	*1416*	1421	1521	*1516*	*1616*	*1616*	*1716*	...	*1816*	*1816*	*1916*	2016	...	...	2116	...	2225	2325
Forbach a.	0931	*1026*	*1026*	*1126*	1230	...	*1326*	1331	*1426*	*1426*	1431	1531	*1526*	*1626*	*1626*	*1726*	...	*1826*	*1826*	*1926*	2026	...	...	2126	...	2236	2339
Forbach d.	0933	1033	1036	1133	1233	1233	1333	1333	1433	1433	1433	1533	1536	1633	1633	1733	1809	1833	1836	1933	...	2033	2034	...	2134	...	...
St Avold d.	0949	1049	1050	1149	1247	1247	1349	1350	1447	1449	1447	1547	1551	1647	1649	1750	1824	1847	1852	1948	...	2047	2050	...	2148	...	...
Metz a.	1021	1120	1123	1221	1320	1320	1420	1422	1520	1520	1520	1621	1622	1721	1721	1821	1857	1921	1925	2022	...	2120	2120	...	2222	...	...

k – Not June 20.
r – Not June 19.
t – Not Nov. 1

w – Does not run on ①–⑤ July 15 - Aug. 14.
z – Also Nov. 1.

⊗ – Subject to alteration / cancellation on June 23–27, ①–⑤ Sept. 1 - Oct. 10, Nov. 10, 12, 13, 14, 17–21.

395 STRASBOURG - SAARBRÜCKEN

French holiday dates apply

km																									
		Ⓐ n	Ⓐ ⊗		⚒ ⊗		†	⚒ ⊖		Ⓐ n◇		⊖		Ⓐ n◇	†	Ⓐ	⑥ k	Ⓑ b	Ⓐ n	⑥ k	Ⓐ		Ⓑ b	⑥	Ⓑ b
0	**Strasbourg** d.	0529	0634	...	0734	...	0849	0934	...	1135	...	1234	...	1430	1434	1534	1534	1634	1704	1734	1734	...	1834	1934	2004
71	Diemeringen d.	0621	0726	...	0827	...	0942	1026	...	1227	...	1326	...	1524	1526	1626	1627	1726	1756	1826	1827	...	1926	2027	2056
97	Sarreguemines a.	0644	0750	...	0850	...	1005	1050	...	1250	...	1350	...	1545	1550	1650	1651	1750	1820	1850	1850	...	1950	2050	2120
	Sarreguemines 🚋 ▲ d.	...	...	...	0911z	...	1011z	...	...	1252z	...	...	...	...	...	...	1711z	...	...	...	...	...	...	2111z	...
115	**Saarbrücken** Hbf ▲ a.	...	...	...	0927z	...	1027z	...	...	1311z	...	...	...	...	...	...	1727z	...	...	...	...	...	...	2127z	...

	Ⓐ	Ⓐ n	⚒	Ⓐ n	⑥ k	Ⓐ	†	⚒ ⊖		†	⚒ ⊖		⚒ ⊖	†		⑥ k	Ⓐ n◇	Ⓐ ⊗	Ⓑ bn	Ⓑ b	⑥ k	Ⓑ b		Ⓒ 🚌
Saarbrücken Hbf ▲ d.	...	...	...	...	...	...	0654z	...	...	...	0939z	...	...	1139z	...	...	1339z	...	...	...	1739z	...	...	...
Sarreguemines 🚋 ▲ a.	...	...	...	...	...	...	0713z	...	...	...	1000z	...	...	1200z	...	...	1401z	...	...	...	1800z	...	...	...
Sarreguemines d.	0500	0537	0607	0637	0707	0707	0719	0807	...	1007	1007	...	1207	1207	...	1407	1407	1507	1607	1707	1807	1837	...	1907
Diemeringen d.	0523	0600	0630	0701	0730	0731	0742	0831	...	1030	1030	...	1230	1230	...	1430	1430	1530	1630	1730	1830	1900	...	1937
Strasbourg a.	0616	0654	0725	0755	0825	0825	0837	0925	...	1125	1125	...	1325	1325	...	1525	1525	1625	1725	1825	1925	1955	...	2115

SAARBAHN LIGHT RAIL SERVICE **S1 SARREGUEMINES - SAARBRÜCKEN** ⊡

	⚒	Ⓐ	⚒	Ⓐ				
Sarreguimes (Bahnhof) d.	0516	0546	0616	0646	0716	hourly ◐ until	2316	0016
Saarbrücken Hbf a.	0545	0615	0645	0715	0745		2345	0045

	⚒	Ⓐ	⚒	Ⓐ	⚒	Ⓐ			
Saarbrücken Hbf d.	0440	0510	0540	0610	0640	0710	0740	hourly ◧ until	2340
Sarreguimes (Bahnhof) a.	0510	0540	0610	0640	0710	0740	0810		0010

b – Also Nov. 1.
k – Not Nov. 1.
n – Not ①–⑤ July 15 - Aug. 14.
z – Not July 7 - Aug. 17.

⊗ – Subject to alteration July 28–31, Aug. 1, 4–8.
⊖ – Subject to alteration July 28–31, Aug. 1, 4–8, Oct. 20–24, 27–31.
◇ – Subject to alteration Oct. 20–24, 27–31.

▲ – For additional light rail service Sarreguemines - Saarbrücken see below main table.
⊡ – Operated by Saarbahn (www.saarbahn.de). In Saarbrücken also serves city centre.
◐ – Every 30 minutes 0716 - 0916 and 1216 - 2116 on Ⓐ, 0816 - 1816 on ⑥, 1216 - 1816 on †.
◧ – Every 30 minutes 0740 - 0840 and 1140 - 2040 on Ⓐ, 0740 - 1740 on ⑥, 1140 - 1740 on †.

396 STRASBOURG - WISSEMBOURG

Additional trains run Strasbourg - Haguenau and v.v. See Table **918** for connecting trains Wissembourg - Neustadt (Weinstr) and v.v.

km		Ⓐ	Ⓐ	Ⓐ	Ⓐ	Ⓐ	Ⓐ	Ⓐ	Ⓐ	Ⓐ	Ⓐ	Ⓐ	Ⓐ	Ⓐ	Ⓐ	Ⓐ	Ⓐ	Ⓐ
											n							
0	**Strasbourg** d.		0635	0727	0927	1127	1235	1327	1431	1604	1705	1727	1805	1835	1905	1927	2057	2110
34	Haguenau a.		0657	0751	0952	1152	1257	1353	1504	1625	1726	1749	1827	1856	1927	2000	2119	2147
	Haguenau d.		0702	0801*	0954r	1154v	1306r	1355r	1514*	1626	1727	1752	1830	1903	1930	2010*	2120	2157*
66	**Wissembourg** a.		0731	0838*	1020r	1221v	1340r	1421r	1551*	1655	1753	1830	1906	1930	2006	2047*	2146	2234*

	⑥	⑥ k	⑥ k	⑥ k	⑥ k	⑥ k	⑥ k	⑥ k
Strasbourg d.		0705	0757	0927	1128	1235	1327	1528
Haguenau a.		0727	0819	0949	1150	1256	1349	1550
Haguenau d.		0730	0822	0950	1153	1258	1350	1551
Wissembourg a.		0757	0849	1023	1220	1331	1423	1631

	⑥ k	⑥ k	⑥ k	†	†	†	†	†	†	†	†	
Strasbourg d.	1727	1827	2005		0827	1127	1327	1627	1727	1808	2012	...
Haguenau a.	1749	1850	2026		0848	1148	1348	1648	1748	1829	2033	...
Haguenau d.	1757	1851	2028		0849	1149	1349	1649	1749	1835	2035	...
Wissembourg a.	1830	1922	2101		0922	1222	1422	1720	1822	1911	2110	...

	Ⓐ	Ⓐ	Ⓐ	Ⓐ n	Ⓐ	Ⓐ	Ⓐ	Ⓐ	Ⓐ	Ⓐ
Wissembourg d.		0600	0629	0702	0738	0856*	1037t	1229z	1430t	1559t
Haguenau a.		0631	0700	0731	0808	0933*	1106t	1300z	1455t	1624t
Haguenau d.		0633	0702	0733	0809	0943	1109	1302	1459	1630
Strasbourg a.		0655	0725	0755	0833	1020	1133	1325	1525	1655

	Ⓐ	Ⓐ n	Ⓐ	Ⓐ		⑥	⑥ k	⑥ k	⑥ k	⑥ k	⑥ k	⑥ k	⑥ k	⑥ k	⑥ k	⑥ k	
Wissembourg d.	1701	1800	1836	1936	...		0601	0658	0725	0857	1037	1258	1436	1550	1729	1937	...
Haguenau a.	1725	1827	1901	2001	...		0631	0728	0801	0922	1108	1332	1507	1626	1754	2009	...
Haguenau d.	1729	1831	1903	2002	...		0633	0731	0803	0923	1110	1341	1509	1631	1757	2010	...
Strasbourg a.	1755	1855	1925	2027	...		0655	0753	0825	0945	1133	1420	1533	1655	1821	2033	...

	†	†	†	†	†	†	†	†	†
Wissembourg d.		0739	0937	1044	1244	1437	1649	1837	2037
Haguenau a.		0809	1008	1108	1315	1508	1723	1910	2109
Haguenau d.		0811	1010	1110	1317	1510	1724	1911	2110
Strasbourg a.		0833	1033	1133	1340	1533	1745	1933	2133

k – Not Nov. 1.
n – Not July 15 - Aug. 14.
r – By 🚌 Sept. 29 - Oct. 3 (arrives Wissembourg 16–27 minutes later).
t – By 🚌 Sept. 29 - Oct. 3 (departs Wissembourg 15–18 minutes **earlier**).
v – By 🚌 on Sept. 29, 30, Oct. 2, 3 (arrives Wissembourg 1237).
z – By 🚌 on Sept. 29, 30, Oct. 2, 3 (departs Wissembourg 1147).
* – By 🚌.

397 PRIVATE TOURIST RAILWAYS

MER DE GLACE - TRAIN DE MONTENVERS

✆ 04.50.53.22.75. www.montblancnaturalresort.com

From Chamonix (200 metres from SNCF station) to Montenvers 'Mer de Glace' (altitude 1913 metres). Journey time: 20 minutes. Services generally run every 30 minutes (except where shown). A more frequent service (every 20 minutes) is provided during periods of high demand. **Closed for maintenance May 12–23 and Nov. 3 - Dec. 12.**

A cable car takes visitors to the ice grotto inside the glacier (please check for opening dates).

Nov. 30 - Mar. 14: from Chamonix hourly 1000 - 1600; returning until 1630.
Mar. 15 - May 4: from Chamonix 1000 - 1630; returning until 1700. See note ⊡.
May 5–11: from Chamonix 1000 - 1630; returning until 1700. See note ◇.
May 24 - July 4: from Chamonix 0830 - 1630; returning until 1700.
July 5 - Aug. 31: from Chamonix 0830 - 1700; returning until 1730.
Sept. 1–14: from Chamonix 0830 - 1630; returning until 1700.
Sept. 16 - Nov. 2: from Chamonix 0930 - 1600; returning until 1630. See note ◇.

⊡ – Hourly until 1400, then every 30 minutes.
◇ – Hourly (every 20–30 minutes during periods of high demand).

PANORAMIQUE DES DÔMES

Electric rack railway from the foot to the summit of Le puy de Dôme. Journey: 15 minutes. **2025 service**. No service Mar. 17–21, Nov. 17–21. www.panoramiquedesdomes.fr

Until Mar. 16 ☆: Hourly departures 1000 - 1700, returning 1030 - 1730.
Mar. 22 - June 30: Departures every 40 minutes 0900 - 1900, returning 0920 - 1920.
July 1 - Aug. 31: Departures every 20 minutes 0900 - 2000, returning 0920 - 2020.
Sept. 1 - Nov. 2: Departures every 40 minutes 0900 - 1900, returning 0920 - 1920.
From Nov. 5 ◇: Hourly departures 1000 - 1700, returning 1030 - 1730.

☆ – ③–⑦ until Mar. 17 (also Feb. 24, 25, Mar. 3, 4).
◇ – ③–⑦ from Nov. 5 (also Nov. 10, 11, Dec. 22, 23, 29, 30; not Dec. 25).

TRAMWAY DU MONT BLANC

The highest rack railway in France. www.montblancnaturalresort.com
✆ 04.50.53.22.75.

Winter: December 14, 2024 - March 30, 2025

Runs from St Gervais Le Fayet (opposite SNCF station) to Bellevue (altitude 1794 metres). 9 km. Journey ±60 minutes.

From St Gervais at 1000 ⊖, 1100, 1200 ⊖, 1300, 1400 ⊖, 1500 and 1600.
From Bellevue at 1000 ⊖, 1100 ⊖, 1200, 1300 ⊖, 1400, 1500 ⊖, 1600 and 1700 ⊖.

⊖ – ⑥⑦ (daily during school holidays).

Summer: June 14 - September 28, 2025

From St Gervais Le Fayet (opposite SNCF station) to Bellevue (9 km; altitude 1794 metres), Mont Lachat (11 km; altitude 2073 metres) and Nid d'Aigle (12.5km; altitude 2372 metres). Journey times: To / from Bellevue 49 minutes uphill, 53 minutes downhill; to / from Mont Lachat 56 minutes uphill, 67 minutes downhill.
Note: No regular service Mont Lachat - Nid d'Aigle this year.

June 14 - July 5 and August 30 - September 28:
St Gervais Le Fayet → Bellevue → Mont Lachat at 0700, 0900, 1000 ¶, 1100, 1200, 1300 ¶, 1400 and 1500.
Mont Lachat → Bellevue → St Gervais Le Fayet at 0820, 1020, 1120 ¶, 1220, 1320, 1420 ¶, 1520 and 1620.

July 6 - August 29:
St Gervais Le Fayet → Bellevue → Mont Lachat at 0700, 0900 and hourly until 1600 (also 0800 ¶, 1030 ¶, 1330 ¶ and 1530 ¶).
Mont Lachat → Bellevue → St Gervais Le Fayet at 0820, 1020 and hourly until 1720 (also 0920 ¶, 1150 ¶, 1450 ¶ and 1650 ¶).

¶ – Runs only at weekends when there is sufficient demand.

398 PARIS AÉROPORTS ✈ - CENTRAL PARIS

See page 33 for plan of central Paris

CHARLES DE GAULLE ✈ - PARIS

VAL shuttle train: air terminals - RER / TGV station.

Roissyrail (RER line B): Aéroport Charles de Gaulle TGV - central Paris. Frequent service approx. 0500 - 2400.

Journey time from Charles de Gaulle ✈:

Gare du Nord	35 minutes
Châtelet les Halles ★	38 minutes
St Michel Notre Dame	40 minutes
Antony (for Orly ✈, see right panel)	58 minutes

★ Cross - platform interchange with RER for Gare de Lyon.

ORLY ✈ - PARIS (Metro line 14)

Metro line 14 direct to central Paris.
Frequent service (every 6–15 minutes) 0530 - 0030.

Journey time from Orly ✈:

Bercy	21 minutes
Gare de Lyon	22 minutes
Châtelet	26 minutes
Gare St Lazare	31 minutes

ORLY ✈ - PARIS (*VAL* + RER line B)

VAL light rail: Orly 4 - Orly 1-2-3 - Antony (8 minutes). Frequent service daily 0600 - 2330.
Cross platform interchange with RER line B (below).

RER line B: Antony - Paris. Frequent service 0500 - 2400.

Journey time from Antony:

Denfert Rochereau	18 minutes
St Michel Notre Dame	24 minutes
Châtelet les Halles	26 minutes
Gare du Nord	30 minutes

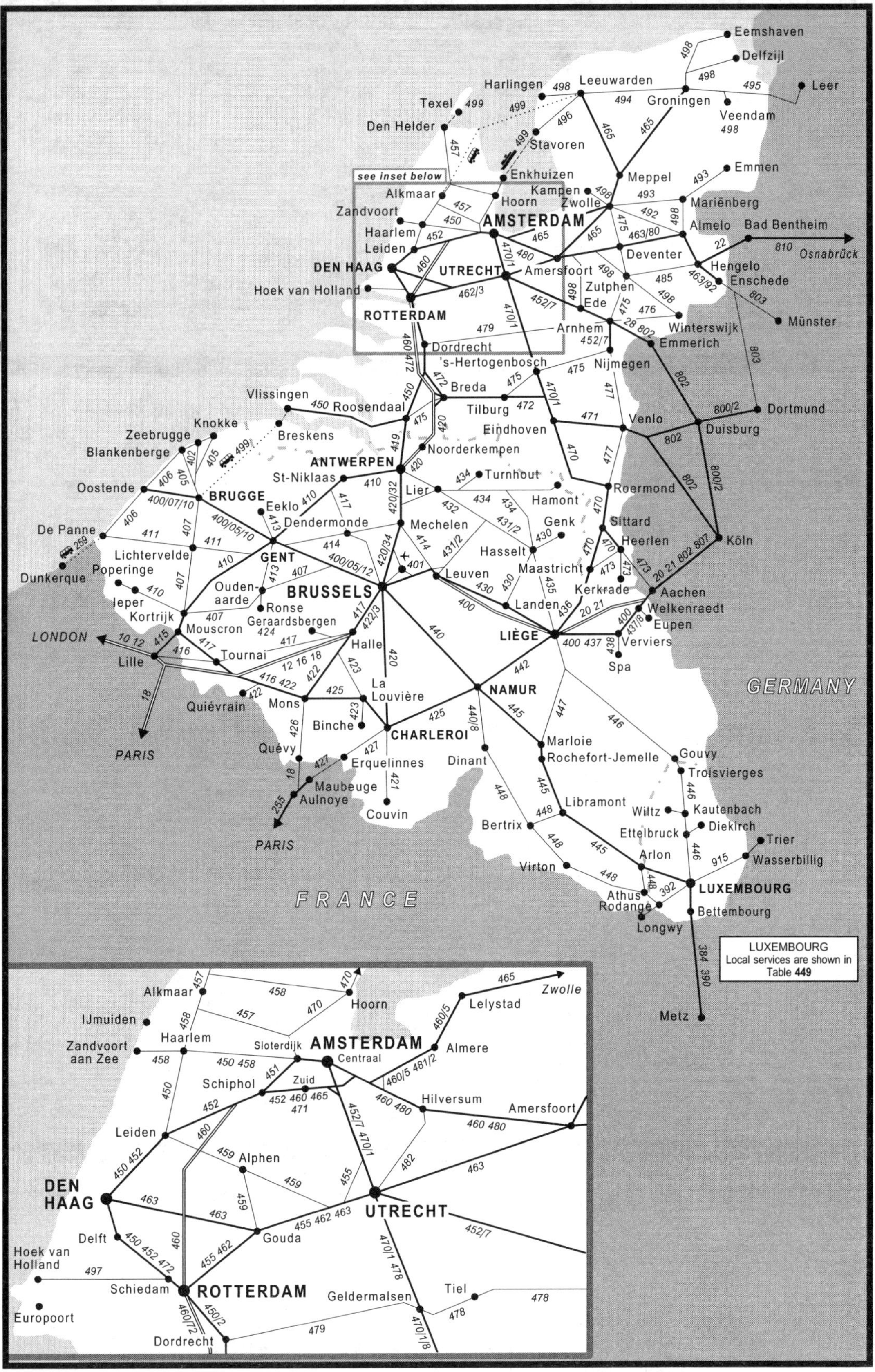
Eemshaven
Delfzijl
Leer
Harlingen
Leeuwarden
Groningen
Veendam
Texel
Den Helder
Stavoren
Enkhuizen
see inset below
Alkmaar
Hoorn
Kampen
Zwolle
Meppel
Emmen
Mariënberg
Zandvoort
Haarlem
Leiden
AMSTERDAM
Almelo
Bad Bentheim
Osnabrück
DEN HAAG
UTRECHT
Amersfoort
Deventer
Hengelo
Enschede
Hoek van Holland
Zutphen
Ede
Münster
ROTTERDAM
Arnhem
Winterswijk
Emmerich
Dordrecht
's-Hertogenbosch
Nijmegen
Vlissingen
Roosendaal
Breda
Tilburg
Dortmund
Knokke
Breskens
Eindhoven
Venlo
Duisburg
Zeebrugge
Blankenberge
Noorderkempen
ANTWERPEN
St-Niklaas
Turnhout
Oostende
BRUGGE
Lier
Roermond
Hamont
Eeklo
Dendermonde
Mechelen
Genk
Sittard
De Panne
Heerlen
Köln
Lichtervelde
GENT
Hasselt
Dunkerque
Poperinge
Leuven
Maastricht
Oudenaarde
BRUSSELS
Kerkrade
Aachen
Ieper
Ronse
Landen
Welkenraedt
Kortrijk
Geraardsbergen
Eupen
LONDON
Mouscron
LIÈGE
Verviers
Lille
Tournai
Halle
Spa
GERMANY
La Louvière
NAMUR
Quiévrain
Mons
PARIS
Binche
CHARLEROI
Marloie
Quévy
Rochefort-Jemelle
Gouvy
Erquelinnes
Dinant
Troisvierges
Maubeuge
Aulnoye
Couvin
Libramont
Wiltz
Kautenbach
Bertrix
Diekirch
Ettelbruck
PARIS
Trier
Arlon
Wasserbillig
Virton
FRANCE
LUXEMBOURG
Athus
Rodange
Bettembourg
Longwy
LUXEMBOURG
Local services are shown in
Table 449
Metz
Alkmaar
Hoorn
Lelystad
Zwolle
IJmuiden
Haarlem
Zandvoort aan Zee
Sloterdijk
AMSTERDAM
Centraal
Almere
Schiphol
Zuid
Hilversum
Amersfoort
Leiden
Alphen
DEN HAAG
UTRECHT
Delft
Gouda
Hoek van Holland
Schiedam
ROTTERDAM
Geldermalsen
Tiel
Europoort
Dordrecht

BELGIUM and LUXEMBOURG

Operators: **Belgium**: Nationale Maatschappij der Belgische Spoorwegen / Société Nationale des Chemins de fer Belges (NMBS / SNCB). www.belgianrail.be
Luxembourg: Société Nationale des Chemins de fer Luxembourgeois (CFL). www.cfl.lu

Services: All trains convey first and second classes of seating accommodation unless otherwise indicated. Most trains shown in our Belgian tables are classified *IC* (InterCity). Trains for two or more different destinations are sometimes linked together for part of their journey and passengers should be careful to board the correct portion of the train. The line numbers used by Belgian Railways in their public timetables are shown as small numbers in the table headings. Second class travel within Luxembourg is free of charge (no tickets required).

Timings: Valid **December 15, 2024 - December 13, 2025**. Local train services may be amended on and around the dates of public holidays (see page 4).

Reservations: Seat reservations are not available for journeys wholly within Belgium or Luxembourg. Reservations are compulsory for international journeys on *Thalys* and *Eurostar* trains (for timings see International section). Supplements are not payable for journeys in Belgium or Luxembourg. However, a higher level of fares is payable on *Thalys* trains.

Dutch-language forms of some **French-language** Belgian names

Aarlen = **Arlon**
Aat = **Ath**
Bergen = **Mons**
Doornik = **Tournai**
Duinkerke = **Dunkerque** (France)
Hoei = **Huy**
Luik = **Liège**
Moeskroen = **Mouscron**
Namen = **Namur**
Nijvel = **Nivelles**
Rijsel = **Lille** (France)
's Gravenbrakel = **Braine le Comte**
Wezet = **Visé**

French-language forms of some **Dutch-language** Belgian names

Anvers = **Antwerpen**
Audenarde = **Oudenaarde**
Bruges = **Brugge**
Courtrai = **Kortrijk**
Dixmude = **Diksmuide**
Furnes = **Veurne**
Gand = **Gent**
Hal = **Halle**
La Panne = **De Panne**
Lierre = **Lier**
Louvain = **Leuven**
Malines = **Mechelen**
Menin = **Menen**
Ostende = **Oostende**
Renaix = **Ronse**
Roulers = **Roeselare**
Saint Nicolas = **Sint Niklaas**
Saint Trond = **Sint Truiden**
Termonde = **Dendermonde**
Tirlemont = **Tienen**
Tongres = **Tongeren**
Ypres = **Ieper**

Some other places outside Belgium

Aken / Aix la Chapelle = **Aachen**
Keulen / Cologne = **Köln**
Londen / Londres = **London**

400 OOSTENDE - BRUSSELS - LIÈGE - VERVIERS - EUPEN

Lines 50a, 36, 37

For *Eurostar* trains Paris - Brussels - Liège - Köln and *ICE* trains Brussels - Köln - Frankfurt see Table **21**.

km																								
			Ⓐ	Ⓐ	Ⓐ	Ⓐ	Ⓐ	Ⓐ	Ⓐ	Ⓐ ⊡	Ⓐ		Ⓐ	Ⓐ	Ⓐ	Ⓐ	Ⓐ	Ⓐ	Ⓐ	Ⓐ	Ⓐ	Ⓐ △	Ⓐ	Ⓐ △
0	**Oostende** ▶ d.	Ⓐ	...	...	0442	...	0535	...	0643	...	0742		...	1742	...	1842	...	1942	...	2042	...	2142	...	2307
22	Brugge ▷ d.		...	...	0458	...	0552	...	0659	...	0758		...	1758	...	1858	...	1958	...	2058	...	2158	...	2322
	Kortrijk **410** d.		...	0416	|	0517	|	0617	|	0717	|	and	1716	|	1816	|	1917	|	2017	|	2117	|	2217	|
62	Gent Sint-Pieters ▷ d.		...	0455	0524	0555	0624	0655	0724	0755	0824	at	1755	1824	1855	1924	1955	2024	2051	2124	2151	2224	2251	2348
114	**Brussels** Midi / Zuid ▷ a.		...	0524	0552	0624	0652	0724	0752	0824	0852	the	1824	1852	1924	1952	2024	2052	...	2152	...	2252	...	0017
114	**Brussels** Midi / Zuid d.		...	0528	0556	0628	0656	0728	0756	0828	0856	same	1828	1856	1928	1956	2028	2056	...	2156	...	2256	...	0020
116	Brussels Central d.		...	0533	0601	0633	0701	0733	0801	0833	0901	minutes	1833	1901	1933	2001	2033	2101	...	2201	...	2301	...	0025
118	Brussels Nord d.		...	0539	0608	0640	0708	0740	0808	0840	0908	past	1841	1908	1939	2008	2039	2108	...	2208	...	2308	...	0031
148	Leuven d.		...	0556	0625	0658	0727	0758	0827	0858	0927	each	1858	1927	1955	2027	2056	2127	...	2226	...	2326	...	0051
221	**Liège** Guillemins a.		...	...	0700	0732	0759	0831	0859	0931	0959	hour	1931	1959	...	2059	...	2159	...	2259	...	2359	...	0144
221	**Liège** Guillemins **437** d.		...	...	0703	0735	0803	0836	0901	0934	1001	until	1934	2003	...	2103	...	2203	...	2303	...	0023	...	...
241	Pepinster **437** d.		...	...	|	0752	|	0854	|	0953	|		1953	|	...	|	...	|	...	|	...	|	...	...
245	**Verviers** Central **437** d.		...	...	0722	0800	0822	0901	0922	1000	1022		2000	2022	...	2122	...	2222	...	2322	...	0043	...	...
258	Welkenraedt **437** d.		0636	...	0735	0811	0835	0912	0935	1011	1035		2011	2035	...	2135	...	2233	...	2333	...	0053	...	...
264	**Eupen** a.		0643	...	0742	...	0842	...	0942	...	1042		...	2042	...	2142	...	...	...	...	...	...	...	...

		Ⓐ	Ⓐ △	Ⓐ	Ⓐ	Ⓐ	Ⓐ	Ⓐ	Ⓐ	Ⓐ	Ⓐ	Ⓐ ⊙	Ⓐ		Ⓐ	Ⓐ	Ⓐ	Ⓐ	Ⓐ	Ⓐ	Ⓐ	Ⓐ	Ⓐ	Ⓐ △
Eupen d.	Ⓐ	...	...	...	...	...	0617	...	0717	...	0811	...	0917		1717	...	1817	...	1917	...	2017	...	2117	2221
Welkenraedt **437** d.		...	...	...	0525	0549	0625	0649	0725	0748	0823	0848	0925		1725	1748	1825	...	1925	...	2025	...	2125	2229
Verviers Central **437** d.		...	...	...	0538	0602	0638	0702	0738	0801	0836	0902	0940	and	1738	1801	1838	...	1938	...	2038	...	2138	2241
Pepinster **437** d.		...	...	...	|	0608	|	0708	|	0807	|	0908	|	at	|	1807	|	...	|	...	|	...	|	|
Liège Guillemins a.		...	...	...	0556	0625	0656	0725	0757	0824	0854	0925	0958	the	1756	1824	1856	...	1956	...	2056	...	2156	2300
Liège Guillemins **437** d.		...	0437	...	0600	0629	0702	0730	0802	0827	0902	0930	1002	same	1802	1828	1902	...	2002	...	2102	...	2202	2304
Leuven d.		...	0536	0604	0636	0704	0736	0804	0836	0906	0936	1006	1036	minutes	1836	1906	1936	2005	2036	2104	2136	...	2236	2344
Brussels Nord d.		...	0554	0623	0654	0723	0756	0823	0856	0923	0954	1023	1054	past	1854	1923	1954	2023	2054	2123	2154	...	2254	0018
Brussels Central d.		...	0559	0628	0659	0728	0801	0828	0901	0928	0959	1028	1059	each	1859	1928	1959	2028	2059	2128	2159	...	2259	0023
Brussels Midi / Zuid a.		...	0603	0632	0703	0732	0805	0832	0905	0932	1003	1032	1103	hour	1903	1932	2003	2032	2103	2132	2203	...	2303	0027
Brussels Midi / Zuid ▷ d.		...	0607	0636	0707	0737	0808	0837	0908	0937	1007	1037	1107	until	1907	1937	2007	2037	2107	2137	2207	...	2307	0030
Gent Sint-Pieters ▷ d.		0609	0639	0707	0739	0809	0839	0909	0939	1009	1039	1109	1139		1939	2009	2039	2109	2139	2209	2239	2309	2339	0102
Kortrijk **410** a.		0641	|	0741	|	0841	|	0941	|	1041	|	1141	|		|	2041	|	2141	|	2241	|	2341	|	|
Brugge ▷ d.		...	0704	...	0804	...	0904	...	1004	...	1104	...	1204		2004	...	2104	...	2204	...	2304	...	0006	0127
Oostende ▶ a.		...	0717	...	0817	...	0917	...	1017	...	1117	...	1217		2017	...	2117	...	2217	...	2317	...	0019	0140

		Ⓒ	Ⓒ	Ⓒ		Ⓒ	Ⓒ	Ⓒ	Ⓒ △	Ⓒ △
Oostende ▶ d.	Ⓒ	...	0443	0542		1843	1943	2043	2143	2308
Brugge ▷ d.		...	0459	0558		1859	1959	2059	2159	2323
Gent Sint-Pieters ▷ d.		...	0524	0625		1925	2025	2125	2225	2348
Brussels Midi / Zuid ▷ a.		...	0553	0653		1953	2053	2153	2253	0017
Brussels Midi / Zuid d.		...	0556	0656	and	1956	2056	2156	2256	0020
Brussels Central d.		...	0601	0701		2001	2101	2201	2301	0025
Brussels Nord d.		...	0607	0707	hourly	2007	2107	2207	2307	0031
Leuven d.		...	0625	0727		2027	2127	2227	2327	0051
Liège Guillemins a.		...	0702	0800	until	2100	2200	2300	0021	0144
Liège Guillemins **437** d.		...	0703	0803		2103	2203	2303	0023	...
Pepinster **437** d.		...	|	|		|	|	|	|	...
Verviers Central **437** d.		...	0722	0822		2122	2222	2322	0043	...
Welkenraedt **437** d.		0636	0735	0835		2135	2233	2333	0053	...
Eupen a.		0643	0742	0842		2142	...	...	...	...

	Ⓒ △	Ⓒ	Ⓒ	Ⓒ	Ⓒ		Ⓒ	Ⓒ	Ⓒ △
Eupen d.	...	...	...	0717	0817		2017	2117	2221
Welkenraedt **437** d.	...	0522	0625	0725	0825		2025	2125	2229
Verviers Central **437** d.	...	0535	0638	0738	0838		2038	2138	2241
Pepinster **437** d.	...	|	|	|	|		|	|	|
Liège Guillemins a.	...	0553	0656	0756	0856	and	2056	2156	2300
Liège Guillemins **437** d.	0437	0557	0700	0800	0900		2100	2200	2304
Leuven d.	0534	0634	0734	0833	0933	hourly	2134	2234	2400
Brussels Nord d.	0551	0651	0751	0851	0951		2151	2251	0018
Brussels Central d.	0556	0656	0756	0856	0956	until	2156	2256	0023
Brussels Midi / Zuid a.	0600	0700	0800	0900	1000		2200	2300	0027
Brussels Midi / Zuid ▷ d.	0603	0703	0803	0903	1003		2203	2303	0030
Gent Sint-Pieters ▷ d.	0637	0737	0837	0937	1037		2237	2337	0101
Brugge ▷ d.	0702	0802	0902	1002	1102		2302	0002	0126
Oostende ▶ a.	0715	0815	0915	1015	1115		2315	0015	0139

▶ – Oostende - Brugge: see also Tables **407**, **410**; Oostende - Gent see also Table **410**.
△ – Via Landen (Table **430**) between Leuven and Liège (not high-speed line).
▷ – For Brugge - Gent - Brussels see also Table **405**.
⊡ – Trains from Kortrijk at 0815 and 1017 terminate at Leuven.
⊙ – No trains from Welkenraedt at 1048 or 1348 (they start from Leuven at 1205 and 1505).

☛ *For slower trains Brussels - Liège via Landen see Table **430**.*
*For Aachen change at Verviers or Welkenraedt (Table **437**).*

401 BRUSSELS - BRUSSELS AIRPORT ✈

Line 36c

FROM BRUSSELS MIDI / ZUID TO AIRPORT ✈

Ⓐ: 0409, 0440, 0451, 0509, 0513, 0540, 0544, 0551 then at 09 13 23 40 44 51 minutes past each hour until 2123 then 2140, 2151, 2209, 2213, 2223, 2240, 2251, 2309, 2313, 2323.

Ⓒ: 0451, 0509, 0523, 0540, 0544, 0551, 0609, 0623, 0640, 0644, 0651 then at 09 13 23 40 44 51 minutes past each hour until 2209, 2213, 2223, 2240, 2251, 2309, 2351.

☛ All services call at Brussels Central 4 minutes later and Brussels Nord 10 minutes later. Journey time to airport: from Brussels Midi / Zuid 20 – 33 minutes, from Brussels Centraal 16 – 28 minutes, from Brussels Nord 10 – 20 minutes.

FROM AIRPORT ✈ TO BRUSSELS MIDI / ZUID

Ⓐ: 0442, 0513, 0524, 0530, 0542, 0557, 0613, 0624, 0630, 0642, 0657, 0713, 0724, 0729, 0742, 0757, 0813, 0824, 0829, 0842, 0854, 0857 then at 13 24 30 42 54 57 mins past each hour until 2324, 2330, 2342, 2354, 2357.

Ⓒ: 0530, 0542, 0557, 0613, 0630, 0642, 0657, 0713, 0724, 0730, 0742, 0757 then at 13 24 30 42 54 57 minutes past each hour until 2257, 2313, 2330, 2342, 2354, 0030.

☛ All services call at Brussels Nord (11 – 18 minutes from airport), Brussels Centraal (16 – 23 minutes from airport) and Brussels Midi / Zuid (21 – 28 minutes from airport). Full name of airport is Brussels Airport - Zaventem.

EUROPEAN QUARTER: Brussels Luxembourg - Brussels Schumann - Brussels Airport. Journey 18 – 21 minutes. Hourly journeys on Ⓐ run from / to Charleroi (Table **420**).
Brussels Luxembourg to Airport: on Ⓐ every 30 minutes 0654 – 2254, on Ⓒ hourly 0436 – 2336. Airport to Brussels Luxembourg: on Ⓐ every 30 minutes 0547 – 2147, on Ⓒ hourly 0505 – 0005.

FOR DIRECT SERVICES TO AND FROM BRUSSELS AIRPORT SEE THE FOLLOWING TABLES:
Aalst **412**, Antwerpen **420** / **432**, Brugge **405**, Charleroi **420**, Denderleeuw **412**, Gent **405**, Hasselt **432**, Kortrijk **407**, Leuven **430** / **432**, Mechelen **432**, Mons **422**, Namur **440**, Tournai **417**.

Line 50a — ZEEBRUGGE - BRUGGE — 402

km			Ⓐ	Ⓐ	Ⓐ	Ⓐ	Ⓐ		Ⓐ	Ⓐ	Ⓐ	Ⓐ	Ⓐ	Ⓐ		Ⓒ	Ⓒ	Ⓒ	Ⓒ		Ⓒ	Ⓒ	Ⓒ
0	Zeebrugge Strand § d.	Ⓐ	...	...	...	...	...	and	...	...	...	...	...	...	Ⓒ	0707	0807	0907	1007	and	1807	1907	2007
0	Zeebrugge Dorp § d.		0708	0739	0808	0908	1008	hourly	1608	1644	1708	1808	1908	2008		|	|	|	|	hourly	|	|	|
15	Brugge a.		0722	0754	0822	0922	1022	until	1622	1659	1722	1822	1922	2022		0722	0822	0922	1022	until	1822	1922	2022

		Ⓐ	Ⓐ	Ⓐ	Ⓐ	Ⓐ		Ⓐ	Ⓐ	Ⓐ	Ⓐ	Ⓐ	Ⓐ		Ⓒ	Ⓒ	Ⓒ	Ⓒ		Ⓒ	Ⓒ	Ⓒ	
Brugge d.	Ⓐ	0634	0708	0734	0834	0934	and	1534	1634	1716	1734	1834	1934	Ⓒ	0634	0734	0834	0934	and	1734	1834	1934	...
Zeebrugge Dorp § a.		0649	0724	0749	0849	0949	hourly	1549	1649	1731	1749	1849	1949		|	|	|	|	hourly	|	|	|	...
Zeebrugge Strand § a.		...	...	...	...	...	until	...	...	...	...	...	...		0650	0750	0850	0950	until	1750	1850	1950	...

§ – During high summer (June 30 to August 29) trains on Ⓐ serve Zeebrugge Strand (not Zeebrugge Dorp).

☛ Most trains continue beyond Brugge as stopping services to Gent (not shown). Change at Brugge for Brussels and faster service to Gent (Tables **400**/**405**).

Line 50a — KNOKKE and BLANKENBERGE - BRUGGE - GENT - BRUSSELS — 405

For additional trains Brugge - Gent - Brussels see Table **400**. For Brugge - Gent (- Antwerpen) see Table **410**.

km			Ⓐ	Ⓐ	Ⓐ	Ⓐ	Ⓐ		Ⓐ	Ⓐ	Ⓐ n	Ⓐ		Ⓒ	Ⓒ	Ⓒ	Ⓒ	Ⓒ	Ⓒ		Ⓒ	Ⓒ	Ⓒ n
0	**Knokke** d.	Ⓐ	...	0446	...	0546	...	and	...	2046	...	2146	Ⓒ	...	...	0646	...	0746	...	and	...	2046	2146
•	Blankenberge d.		...	|	0515	|	0615	at	2015	|	2115	|		...	...	|	0719	|	0819	at	2019	|	|
22	Brugge a.		...	0507	0526	0607	0626	the	2026	2107	2126	2207		...	...	0707	0730	0807	0830	the	2030	2107	2207
22	Brugge d.		0409	0511	0530	0611	0630	same	2030	2111	2130	2211		0534	0634	0711	0734	0811	0834	same	2034	2111	...
62	**Gent** Sint-Pieters d.		0440	0541	0600	0641	0700	minutes	2100	2141	2200	2241		0603	0703	0741	0803	0841	0903	minutes	2103	2141	...
119	**Brussels** Midi / Zuid d.		0513	0613	0636	0714	0736	past	2136	2213	2236	2313		0636	0736	0813	0836	0913	0936	past	2136	2213	...
121	Brussels Central d.		0518	0618	0641	0719	0741	each	2141	2218	2241	2318		0641	0741	0818	0841	0918	0941	each	2141	2218	...
123	Brussels Nord d.		0525	0625	0648	0725	0748	hour	2148	2225	2245	2325		0648	0748	0825	0848	0925	0948	hour	2148	2225	...
135	**Brussels Airport** ✈ a.		0536	0636	▽	0736	▽	until	▽	2236	...	2336		▽	▽	0836	▽	0936	▽	until	▽	2236	...

		Ⓐ	Ⓐ	Ⓐ	Ⓐ	Ⓐ	Ⓐ		Ⓐ	Ⓐ	Ⓐ	Ⓐ	Ⓐ		Ⓒ n	Ⓒ	Ⓒ	Ⓒ		Ⓒ	Ⓒ	Ⓒ	Ⓒ n
Brussels Airport ✈ d.	Ⓐ	▽	0524	▽	0624	▽	0724	and	▽	2124	▽	2224	2324	Ⓒ	...	...	▽	0724	and		2124	▽	▽
Brussels Nord d.		0516	0538	0616	0638	0715	0738	at	2117	2138	2217	2238	2337		...	...	0715	0738	at	2116	2138	2215	2315
Brussels Central d.		0521	0543	0621	0643	0720	0743	the	2122	2143	2222	2243	2342		...	...	0720	0743	the	2121	2143	2220	2320
Brussels Midi / Zuid d.		0529	0551	0630	0651	0729	0750	same	2129	2151	2229	2251	2349		...	...	0728	0751	same	2128	2151	2228	2328
Gent Sint-Pieters d.		0600	0622	0701	0726	0800	0822	minutes	2200	2222	2300	2322	0032		...	...	0800	0822	minutes	2200	2222	2300	2400
Brugge a.		0626	0650	0727	0753	0826	0850	past	2226	2250	2326	2350	0100		...	...	0826	0850	past	2226	2250	2329	0026
Brugge d.		0630	0654	0730	0756	0830	0854	each	2230	2254	...	...	...		0654	0730	0830	0854	each	2230	2254	2332	...
Blankenberge a.		0641	|	0741	|	0841	|	hour	2241	|	...	...	...		|	0741	0841	|	hour	2241	|	2343	...
Knokke a.		...	0715	...	0817	...	0915	until	...	2315	...	...	...		0715	...	...	0915	until	...	2315	...	...

n – An additional journey runs one hour later.

▽ – To / from Leuven, Hasselt / Genk (Table **430**).

• – Blankenburg - Brugge: *15 km*.

De Lijn 'Kusttram' — KNOKKE - OOSTENDE - DE PANNE (Coastal Tramway) — 406

KNOKKE railway station - **OOSTENDE** railway station *Journey 66 - 70 minutes*

Ⓐ: 0416, 0446, 0516, 0546, 0616, 0636, 0716, 0736, 0816, 0836, 0856, 0916 and every 20 minutes until 1717, 1737, 1757, 1817, 1837, 1857, 1917, 1947, 2021, 2051, 2121, 2151, 2221, 2321.

Ⓒ: 0021⑦, 0516⑥, 0546, 0616⑥, 0636, 0656, 0716, 0736, 0751, 0806, 0821, 0836, 0851 and every 15 minutes until 1736, 1747, 1802, 1817, 1832, 1847, 1917, 1947, 2021, 2051, 2121, 2151, 2221, 2251, 2321, 2351⑥.

Calls at Heist (+ 6 minutes), Zeebrugge (+ 13 minutes), Blankenberge (+ 25 minutes).

OOSTENDE railway station - **DE PANNE** railway station *Journey 73 - 81 minutes*

Ⓐ: 0525, 0555, 0625, 0655, 0725, 0745, 0805, 0825, 0845, 0905, 0925, 0945 and every 15 minutes until 1805, 1826, 1856, 1926, 1956, 2026, 2056, 2126, 2156, 2226, 2326, 2356.

Ⓒ: 0026, 0425⑥, 0525⑥, 0555⑥, 0625⑥, 0655, 0725⑥, 0735⑥, 0745, 0805, 0825, 0845, 0900, 0915, 0930, 0945,1000 and every 15 minutes until 1830, 1856, 1926, 1956, 2026, 2056, 2126, 2156, 2226, 2256, 2326, 2356.

Calls at Middelkerke (+ 23 minutes), Nieuwpoort (+ 41 minutes), Koksijde (+ 60 minutes).

DE PANNE railway station - **OOSTENDE** railway station *Journey 73 - 81 minutes*

Ⓐ: 0413, 0513, 0613, 0643, 0711, 0728, 0748, 0805, 0825, 0845, 0900 and every 15 minutes until 1745, 1802, 1818, 1835, 1851 1906, 1921, 1951, 2021, 2051, 2121, 2151, 2221, 2321, 2351.

Ⓒ: 0021, 0513⑥, 0613, 0643⑥, 0711, 0728⑥, 0748⑥, 0805, 0825⑥, 0835⑦, 0845⑥, 0900 and every 15 minutes until 1745, 1802, 1818, 1835, 1851, 1921, 1951, 2021, 2051, 2121, 2151, 2221, 2251, 2321, 2351.

Calls at Koksijde (+ 19 minutes), Nieuwpoort (+ 38 minutes), Middelkerke (+ 56 minutes).

OOSTENDE railway station - **KNOKKE** railway station *Journey 66 - 71 minutes*

Ⓐ: 0425, 0455, 0525, 0555, 0625, 0645, 0705, 0725, 0745, 0805, 0825, 0845, 0905, 0925, 0945, and every 20 minutes until 1845, 1905, 1935, 2003, 2033, 2103, 2133, 2203, 2233, 2333.

Ⓒ: 0003, 0033, 0555, 0640, 0655, 0710, 0725, 0745, 0805, 0825, 0845, 0905, 0925, 0935, 0945, 1005, and every 15 minutes until 1905, 1935, 2003, 2033, 2103, 2133, 2203, 2233, 2333.

Calls at Blankenberge (+ 37 minutes), Zeebrugge (+ 47 minutes), Heist (+ 58 minutes).

A change of tram may be necessary at Oostende. In July and August trams run every 10 minutes during the day.
Connections with rail services are available at Knokke (Table **405**), Zeebrugge (Table **402**), Blankenberge (Table **405**), Oostende (Tables **400/07/10**) and De Panne (Table **411**).

Lines 66, 89 — OOSTENDE - BRUGGE - KORTRIJK - BRUSSELS — 407

For direct trains Oostende - Brugge - Brussels via Gent (also Kortrijk - Gent - Brussels) see Table **400**. For direct trains Brugge - Brussels - Brussels Nationaal ✈ see Table **405**.

km			Ⓐ	Ⓐ	Ⓐ	Ⓐ	Ⓐ	Ⓐ	Ⓐ	Ⓐ	Ⓐ		Ⓐ	Ⓐ	Ⓐ		Ⓒ	Ⓒ	Ⓒ	Ⓒ		Ⓒ	Ⓒ	Ⓒ
0	**Oostende** ▷ d.	Ⓐ	...	...	...	...	0558	...	...	0758	0858		1958	2058	2158	Ⓒ	...	...	...	0648		1948	2048	2148
22	Brugge ▷ d.		...	...	...	...	0616	...	...	0816	0916		2016	2116	2216		...	...	...	0705		2005	2105	2205
39	Torhout d.		...	...	...	...	0632	...	...	0832	0932		2032	2132	2232		...	...	...	0721		2021	2121	2221
44	Lichtervelde § d.		...	...	...	...	0637	...	...	0837	0937		2037	2137	2237		...	...	...	0735		2035	2135	2235
52	Roeselare d.		...	...	...	...	0644	...	...	0844	0944	and	2044	2144	2244		...	...	...	0743	and	2043	2143	2243
73	**Kortrijk** a.		...	...	...	...	0705	...	...	0905	1005		2105	2205	2305		...	...	...	0804		2104	2204	2304
73	**Kortrijk** d.		0512	0542	0611	0642	0711	0742	0811	0911	1011	hourly	2111	2211	...		0509	0609	0709	0809	hourly	2109	...	...
98	Oudenaarde d.		0532	0602	0632	0702	0732	0802	0832	0932	1032		2132	2232	...		0529	0629	0729	0829		2129	...	...
115	Zottegem d.		0545	0617	0645	0717	0745	0818	0845	0945	1045	until	2145	2245	...		0545	0645	0745	0845	until	2145	...	...
136	Denderleeuw d.		0601	0636	0701	0740	0802	0840	0901	1001	1106		2201	2305	...		0601	0701	0801	0901		2201	...	...
158	**Brussels** Midi / Zuid d.		0623	0655	0723	0759	0823	0859	0923	1023	1123		2223	2323	...		0623	0723	0823	0923		2223	...	...
160	Brussels Central d.		0628	0700	0728	0804	0828	0905	0928	1028	1128		2228	2328	...		0628	0728	0828	0928		2228	...	...
162	Brussels Nord d.		0634	0704	0734	0808	0834	0908	0934	1034	1134		2234	2334	...		0634	0734	0834	0934		2234	...	...
174	**Brussels Airport** ✈ a.		0647	...	0747	...	0847	...	0947	1047	1147		2247	2347	...		0647	0747	0847	0947		2247	...	...

		Ⓐ	Ⓐ	Ⓐ	Ⓐ		Ⓐ	Ⓐ	Ⓐ	Ⓐ	Ⓐ	Ⓐ	Ⓐ	Ⓐ			Ⓒ	Ⓒ		Ⓒ	Ⓒ	Ⓒ	Ⓒ	
Brussels Airport ✈ d.	Ⓐ	...	...	0513	0613		1613	1713	1813	...	1913	2013	2113	2213	...	Ⓒ	...	0613		1913	2013	2113	2213	...
Brussels Nord d.		...	...	0527	0627		1627	1727	1827	...	1927	2027	2127	2227	...		...	0627		1927	2027	2127	2227	...
Brussels Central d.		...	...	0532	0632		1632	1732	1832	...	1932	2032	2132	2232	...		...	0632		1932	2032	2132	2232	...
Brussels Midi / Zuid d.		...	...	0539	0639		1639	1739	1839	...	1939	2039	2139	2242	...		...	0639		1939	2039	2139	2239	...
Denderleeuw d.		...	...	0601	0701		1701	1801	1901	...	2001	2101	2201	2302	...		...	0700		2000	2100	2200	2300	...
Zottegem d.		...	...	0618	0718	and	1718	1818	1918	...	2018	2118	2218	2318	...		...	0716	and	2016	2116	2216	2316	...
Oudenaarde d.		...	...	0631	0731		1732	1832	1932	...	2032	2132	2232	2332	...		...	0732		2032	2132	2232	2332	...
Kortrijk a.		...	...	0648	0748	hourly	1749	1849	1949	...	2049	2151	2249	2350	...		...	0749	hourly	2049	2149	2249	2349	...
Kortrijk d.		0455	0555	0655	0755		1755	1855	1955	2055	...	2155	...	...	...		0657	0757		2057	2157	...	...	...
Roeselare d.		0517	0617	0717	0817	until	1817	1917	2017	2117	...	2217	...	...	...		0718	0818	until	2118	2218	...	...	...
Lichtervelde § d.		0524	0624	0724	0824		1824	1924	2024	2124	...	2224	...	...	...		0735	0835		2135	2235	...	...	...
Torhout d.		0529	0629	0729	0829		1829	1929	2029	2129	...	2229	...	...	...		0740	0840		2140	2240	...	...	...
Brugge ▷ d.		0549	0649	0749	0849		1851	1949	2049	2149	...	2249	...	...	...		0758	0858		2158	2258	...	...	...
Oostende ▷ a.		0603	0703	0803	0903		1905	2003	2103	2203	...	2303	...	...	...		0812	0912		2212	2312	...	...	...

▷ – See also Tables **400** and **410**.
§ – On Ⓒ trains arrive 10 minutes earlier.

ADDITIONAL TRAINS *Journey 47 - 49 minutes*
Brugge - Kortrijk: Ⓐ hourly 0557 - 2257; Ⓒ every 2 hours 0737 - 1937.
Kortrijk - Brugge: Ⓐ hourly 0516 - 2116; Ⓒ every 2 hours 0637 - 2037.

410 POPERINGE - KORTRIJK - GENT - ANTWERPEN

Lines 69, 75, 59

km																							
		Ⓐ	Ⓐ	Ⓐ	Ⓐ				Ⓐ										Ⓐ	Ⓐ			
0	**Poperinge** d.	...	0407	...	...	0507	...		...	1907	...	2007	...	2107	...	2207	...		0547	0649	...	...	...
10	Ieper d.	...	0415	...	...	0515	...		...	1915	...	2015	...	2115	...	2215	...		0556	0658	...	...	...
23	Comines / Komen d.	...	0425	...	...	0525	...	and	...	1925	...	2025	...	2125	...	2225	...		0606	0708	...	...	...
32	Menen d.	...	0435	...	...	0535	...	at	...	1935	...	2035	...	2135	...	2235	...		0617	0719	...	...	...
43	**Kortrijk** a.	...	0450	...	...	0550	...	the	...	1950	...	2050	...	2150	...	2250	...	A	0633	0735	...	...	...
43	**Kortrijk** d.	...	0459	...	...	0559	...	same	...	1959	...	2059	...	2159	...	2259	...	L	0639	0739	...	...	...
	Oostende ▷ d.	...	|	...	...	|	0609	minutes	...	|	2009	|	2109	|	2209	|	...	S	|	|	...	...	...
	Brugge ▷ d.	...	|	...	△	|	0625	past	△	|	2025	|	2125	|	2225	|	...	O	|	|	...	...	...
85	**Gent** Sint-Pieters ▷ a.	...	0524	...	0607	0624	0649	each	2007	2024	2049	2124	2149	2224	2249	2324	...		0717	0816	...	...	...
85	**Gent** Sint-Pieters d.	0427	0527	0553	0610	0627	0652	hour	2010	2027	2053	2127	2153	2227	2253	2327	...		...	...	...	...	...
112	Lokeren d.	0449	0549	0615	0633	0649	0715	until	2033	2049	2115	2149	2215	2249	2315	2349	...		...	...	...	...	...
125	Sint-Niklaas d.	0500	0600	0626	0645	0700	0726		2045	2100	2126	2200	2226	2300	2326	2400	...		...	...	...	...	...
148	Antwerpen Berchem d.	0519	0619	0650	0705	0719	0750		2105	2119	2150	2219	2250	2319	2350	0019	...		...	...	...	...	...
151	**Antwerpen** Centraal a.	0523	0623	0654	0709	0723	0754		2109	2123	2154	2223	2254	2323	2354	0023	...		...	...	...	...	...

	Ⓐ						Ⓐ			Ⓐ				Ⓐ				Ⓐ	Ⓒ		Ⓐ	Ⓐ		
Antwerpen Centraal d.	0436	0506	0536	...	0606	0636	0649	0706	0736	0751		2006	2036	2051	2106	2136	2236	2336	2336		...	...	...	...
Antwerpen Berchem d.	0441	0512	0542	...	0612	0642	0654	0712	0742	0756		2012	2042	2056	2112	2142	2242	2342	2342		...	...	...	...
Sint-Niklaas d.	0500	0536	0600	...	0636	0700	0715	0736	0800	0817	and	2036	2100	2117	2136	2200	2300	2400	2400		...	...	...	...
Lokeren d.	0510	0546	0610	...	0646	0710	0725	0746	0810	0828	at	2046	2110	2128	2146	2210	2310	0010	0010		...	...	...	...
Gent Sint-Pieters a.	0532	0608	0633	...	0708	0733	0750	0808	0833	0850	the	2107	2133	2149	2208	2233	2340	0033	0033	A	...	...	...	...
Gent Sint-Pieters ▷ d.	0536	0612	0636	0653	0711	0736	0753	0811	0836	0853	same	2111	2136	2153	2211	2236	2343	...	0039	L	1718	1821	...	...
Brugge ▷ d.	|	0638	|	△	0738	|	△	0838	|	△	minutes	2138	|	△	2238	|	|	...	|	S	|	|	...	...
Oostende ▷ a.	|	0651	|	...	0751	|	...	0851	|	...	past	2151	|	...	2253	|	|	...	|	O	|	|	...	...
Kortrijk a.	0601	...	0701	...	...	0801	...	...	0901	...	each	...	2201	...	...	2301	0018	...	0113		1755	1855	...	...
Kortrijk d.	0604	...	0708	...	...	0810	...	...	0910	...	hour	...	2210	...	...	2310	...	...	...		1759	1859	...	...
Menen d.	0619	...	0723	...	...	0825	...	...	0925	...	until	...	2225	...	...	2327	...	...	...		1815	1915	...	...
Comines / Komen d.	0629	...	0733	...	...	0835	...	...	0935	...		...	2235	...	...	2337	...	...	...		1826	1926	...	...
Ieper d.	0639	...	0743	...	...	0845	...	...	0945	...		...	2245	...	...	2347	...	...	...		1836	1936	...	...
Poperinge a.	0647	...	0751	...	...	0853	...	...	0953	...		...	2253	...	...	2354	...	...	...		1844	1944	...	...

ADDITIONAL TRAINS KORTRIJK - GENT

		Ⓐ§		Ⓐ§		Ⓒ		Ⓒ
Kortrijk d.	Ⓐ	0416	hourly	2215	Ⓒ	0520	hourly	2220
Gent Sint-Pieters a.		0452	until	2247		0552	until	2252

		Ⓐ§		Ⓐ§		Ⓒ		Ⓒ
Gent Sint-Pieters d.	Ⓐ	0609	hourly	2309	Ⓒ	0608	hourly	2308
Kortrijk a.		0641	until	2343		0639	until	2339

△ – From / to De Panne (Table **411**).
▷ – See also Table **400** (also **407** Oostende - Brugge).
§ – Most journeys continue to / from Brussels (Table **400**).

☛ *Between Kortrijk and Antwerpen most trains are attached to Lille - Kortrijk - Antwerpen trains (Table **415**).*

411 DE PANNE - LICHTERVELDE - GENT

Line 73

km									
			Ⓐ		Ⓐ ◧		Ⓒ △		Ⓒ △
0	**De Panne** § d.	Ⓐ	0452		1852	Ⓒ	0552		2052
5	Veurne d.		0501	and	1901		0601	and	2101
20	Diksmuide d.		0513		1913		0613		2113
39	Lichtervelde d.		0530	hourly	1930		0630	hourly	2130
56	Tielt d.		0542		1942		0642		2143
86	**Gent** Sint-Pieters a.		0606	until	2007		0706	until	2208
	Antwerpen **410** a.		0709		2109		|		|
	Brussels Midi / Zuid a.		...		...		0807		2308
	Brussels Nord a.		...		...		0824		2320

		Ⓐ ◐		Ⓐ		Ⓒ △		Ⓒ △
Brussels Nord d.	Ⓐ	...		...	Ⓒ	0540		2040
Brussels Midi / Zuid d.		...		...		0552		2052
Antwerpen **410** d.		0649	and	2051		|	and	|
Gent Sint-Pieters d.		0753		2153		0653		2153
Tielt d.		0819	hourly	2220		0719	hourly	2219
Lichtervelde d.		0832		2232		0732		2232
Diksmuide d.		0849	until	2249		0749	until	2249
Veurne d.		0901		2301		0801		2301
De Panne § a.		0908		2308		0808		2308

△ – Runs Gent - Brussels and v.v. via Aalst (Table **412**).
◧ – Also De Panne - Gent at 1952Ⓐ, 2052Ⓐ.
◐ – Also Gent - De Panne at 0553Ⓐ, 0653Ⓐ.
§ – De Panne railway station is situated in Adinkerke. Connection available with the coastal tramway (Table **406**).

412 GENT - AALST - DENDERLEEUW - BRUSSELS

Line 50

For direct trains Gent - Brussels see Tables **400** and **405**

km										
		Ⓐ								
0	**Gent** Sint-Pieters d.	0439	0539	and at	1639**d**	1739	1839	1939	2039	2139
28	Aalst d.	0512	0612	the same	1712	1812	1912	2012	2112	2212
35	Denderleeuw d.	0520	0620	minutes	1720	1820	1920	2020	2120	2220
58	**Brussels** Midi / Zuid d.	0540	0640	past	1741	1840	1940	2040	2140	2240
60	Brussels Central d.	0545	0645	each	1746	1845	1945	2045	2145	2245
62	Brussels Nord d.	0552	0652	hour	1752	1852	1952	2052	2152	2252
74	**Brussels Airport** ✈ a.	0603	0703	until	1803	1903	2003	2103	2203	2303

Brussels Airport ✈ d.	0557	0657	and at	1857	1957	2057	2157	2257	...
Brussels Nord d.	0611	0711	the same	1911	2011	2111	2211	2311	...
Brussels Central d.	0616	0716	minutes	1916	2016	2116	2216	2316	...
Brussels Midi / Zuid d.	0626	0724	past	1924	2024	2124	2224	2324	...
Denderleeuw d.	0644	0742	each	1942	2042	2142	2242	2342	...
Aalst d.	0652	0750	hour	1950	2050	2150	2250	2350	...
Gent Sint-Pieters a.	0720**f**	0820	until	2020	2121	2220	2320	0020	...

d – Departs 1636 on Ⓐ.
f – Arrives 0723 on Ⓐ.

413 EEKLO - GENT - OUDENAARDE - RONSE

Line 86

km										
			Ⓐ		Ⓐ‡		Ⓒ		Ⓒ	⑥
0	**Eeklo** d.	Ⓐ	0509		2011	Ⓒ	0711	and hourly	1911	2011
27	**Gent** St-Pieters a.		0546	and	2046		0746	on ⑥,	1946	2046
27	**Gent** St-Pieters d.		0557	hourly	2057		0757	every two	1957	2057
52	Oudenaarde a.		0627	until	2127		0827	hours on †	2027	2127
52	Oudenaarde d.		0634	△	2136		0835	until	2035	2135
66	**Ronse** a.		0645		2147		0846		2046	2146

		Ⓐ		Ⓐ		Ⓒ		Ⓒ	⑥◐
Ronse d.	Ⓐ	0514		2014	Ⓒ	0714	and hourly	1914	2014
Oudenaarde a.		0525	and	2025		0725	on ⑥,	1925	2025
Oudenaarde d.		0533	hourly	2033		0733	every two	1933	2033
Gent St-Pieters a.		0603	until	2103		0803	hours on †	2003	2103
Gent St-Pieters d.		0614	▽	2114		0815	until	2015	2115
Eeklo a.		0649		2149		0849		2049	2149

△ – Also Gent - Ronse at 0622Ⓐ, 1223Ⓐ, 1622Ⓐ, 1722Ⓐ, 1825Ⓐ.
▽ – Also Ronse - Gent at 0546Ⓐ, 0646Ⓐ, 0746Ⓐ, 2114Ⓐ, 2214Ⓐ.
‡ – Also Eeklo - Gent - Oudenaarde at 2111, 2211Ⓐ.
◐ – Also Ronse - Gent at 2113⑦.

414 GENT - MECHELEN - LEUVEN

Line 53

For Mechelen - Leuven via Brussels Nationaal ✈ see Table **432**

km																								
			Ⓐ	Ⓐ	Ⓐ	Ⓐ	Ⓐ	Ⓐ	Ⓐ		Ⓐ	Ⓐ	Ⓐ	Ⓐ	Ⓐ		Ⓒ	Ⓒ	Ⓒ	Ⓒ		Ⓒ	Ⓒ	Ⓒ
0	**Gent** St-Pieters d.	Ⓐ	0421	...	...	0521	0557	...	0621	and at the same	2057	...	2121	2157	2257	Ⓒ	0621	...	0721	...	and at the same	2121	...	...
30	Dendermonde d.		0500	0524	...	0600	0624	...	0700	minutes	2124	...	2200	2224	2320		0659	...	0759	...	minutes	2159	...	...
57	Mechelen d.		0528	0548	0622	0628	0648	0722	0728	past each	2148	2222	2228	2253	...		0725	0736	0825	0836	past each	2225	2236	2336
82	**Leuven** a.		...	0614	0653	...	0714	0753	...	hour until	2214	2253	...	2317	...		...	0805	...	0905	hour until	...	2305	0005

		Ⓐ	Ⓐ	Ⓐ	Ⓐ	Ⓐ	Ⓐ	Ⓐ		Ⓐ	Ⓐ	Ⓐ	Ⓐ		Ⓒ	Ⓒ	Ⓒ	Ⓒ	Ⓒ		Ⓒ	Ⓒ	Ⓒ	Ⓒ
Leuven d.	Ⓐ	0506	0546	...	0606	0646	...	0706	and at the same	2146	...	2206	2246	Ⓒ	...	0654	...	0754	...	and at the same	...	2154	...	2254
Mechelen d.		0538	0615	0632	0638	0715	0732	0738	minutes	2215	2232	2238	2315		0636	0723	0736	0824	0836	minutes	2136	2223	2236	2323
Dendermonde d.		...	0640	0703	...	0740	0803	...	past each	2240	2303	...	2336		0704	...	0804	...	0904	past each	2204	...	2304	...
Gent St-Pieters a.		...	0703	0740	...	0803	0839	...	hour until	2303	2339	...	...		0739	...	0839	...	0939	hour until	2239	...	2339	...

LILLE - MOUSCRON - KORTRIJK 415

Line 75

A change at Kortrijk may be necessary on certain journeys. Lille - Mouscron is subject to alteration on French and Belgian public holidays.

km																								
		Ⓐ	⚒	⚒	Ⓐ					Ⓐ		Ⓒ	Ⓐ	Ⓒ	⑥	Ⓑ		Ⓐ	†	⚒				
0	**Lille** Flandres ▷ d.	0627	0709	0809	0830	0909	1009	1109	1209	1227	1309	1403	1409	1509	1603	1609	1709	1727	1803	1809	1909	2009	2109	2209
10	Roubaix ▷ d.	0637	0723	0823	0840	0919	1019	1119	1219	1240	1319	1417	1419	1519	1617	1619	1723	1737	1817	1822	1919	2019	2119	2219
12	Tourcoing 🏛 ▷ d.	0641	0727	0827	0844	0924	1024	1124	1224	1244	1324	1422	1424	1524	1622	1624	1727	1741	1822	1827	1924	2024	2124	2224
18	Mouscron 417 d.	...	0736	0836	...	0936	1036	1136	1236	...	1336	1436	1436	1536	1636	1636	1736	...	1836	1836	1936	2036	2136	2236
30	**Kortrijk** 417 d.	...	0759	0859	...	0959	1059	1159	1259	...	1359	1459	1458	1559	1659	1657	1759	...	1859	1859	1959	2059	2159	2258
	Gent St Peters **410** d.	...	0827	0927	...	1027	1127	1227	1327	...	1427	1527	1527	1627	1727	1726	1827	...	1927	1927	2027	2127	2227	2327
	Antwerpen **410** a.	...	0923	1023	...	1123	1223	1323	1423	...	1523	1623	1623	1723	1823	1823	1923	...	2023	2023	2123	2223	2323	0023

	Ⓐ	Ⓐ	⚒	⚒	†	Ⓐ	⚒	†	Ⓒ			Ⓐ						Ⓐ					
Antwerpen **410** d.	0436	...	0536	0636	0636	...	0736	0736	0836	0936	1036	...	1136	1236	1336	1436	1536	...	1636	1736	1836	1936	...
Gent St Peters **410** d.	0536	...	0636	0736	0737	...	0836	0837	0937	1036	1136	...	1236	1336	1436	1536	1636	...	1736	1836	1936	2036	...
Kortrijk 417 d.	0614	...	0714	0814	0814	...	0914	0914	1014	1114	1214	...	1314	1414	1514	1614	1714	...	1814	1914	2014	2114	...
Mouscron 417 d.	0630	...	0727	0827	0830	...	0930	0930	1030	1130	1230	...	1327	1430	1530	1630	1727	...	1827	1930	2030	2130	...
Tourcoing 🏛 ▷ d.	0637	0720	0733	0833	0837	0916	0937	0937	1037	1137	1237	1320	1333	1437	1537	1637	1733	1816	1833	1937	2037	2137	...
Roubaix ▷ d.	0641	0724	0737	0837	0841	0920	0941	0941	1041	1141	1241	1324	1337	1441	1541	1641	1737	1821	1837	1941	2041	2141	...
Lille Flandres ▷ a.	0651	0733	0751	0851	0851	0929	0951	0951	1051	1151	1251	1333	1351	1451	1551	1651	1751	1830	1851	1951	2051	2151	...

▷ – Frequent services Lille Flandres - Lille Europe - Roubaix / Tourcoing are operated by the Lille *VAL* métro (Line 2) or by tram.

☛ *Between Kortrijk and Antwerpen these trains are attached to Poperinge - Kortrijk - Gent - Antwerpen trains (Table* **410***).*

LILLE - TOURNAI - MONS 416

Lines 78, 118

km																									
			Ⓐ	Ⓐ	Ⓐ	Ⓐ	Ⓐ	Ⓐ	Ⓐ	Ⓐ	Ⓐ	Ⓐ	Ⓐ	Ⓐ	Ⓐ	Ⓐ	Ⓐ	Ⓐ	Ⓐ	Ⓐ	Ⓐ	Ⓐ	Ⓐ	Ⓐ	
						d		d																	
0	**Lille** Flandres § d.	Ⓐ	...	...	0601	...	0708	...	0732	0808	0908	1008	...	1208	1308	...	1508	1608	1708	1808	1908	2008	...	2208	...
	Mouscron 417 d.		...	0522	|	0622	|	0717	|	|	|	|	...	|	|	...	|	|	|	|	|	|	...	|	...
25	**Tournai** 417 a.		...	0539	0630	0639	0738	0733	0758	0837	0935	1035	...	1237	1335	...	1535	1636	1735	1835	1935	2035	...	2235	...
25	**Tournai** d.		...	0544	...	0644	...	0744	...	0844	0944	1044	1144	1244	1344	1444	1544	1644	1744	1844	1944	2044	2144	...	...
64	Saint-Ghislain d.		...	0606	...	0706	...	0806	...	0906	1006	1106	1206	1306	1406	1506	1606	1706	1806	1906	2006	2106	2206	...	...
73	**Mons** d.		...	0616	...	0716	...	0816	...	0916	1016	1116	1216	1316	1416	1516	1616	1716	1816	1916	2016	2116	2216	...	...
	Charleroi Central **425** d.		0550	0650	...	0750	...	0850	...	0950	1050	1150	1250	1350	1450	1550	1650	1750	1850	1950	2050	2150	2250	...	...
	Namur **425** a.		0622	0722	...	0822	...	0922	...	1022	1122	1222	1322	1422	1522	1622	1722	1822	1922	2022	2122	2222	2322	...	...

		Ⓐ	Ⓐ	Ⓐ	Ⓐ	Ⓐ	Ⓐ	Ⓐ	Ⓐ	Ⓐ	Ⓐ	Ⓐ	Ⓐ	Ⓐ	Ⓐ	Ⓐ	Ⓐ	Ⓐ	Ⓐ	Ⓐ	Ⓐ	Ⓐ	Ⓐ	Ⓐ	
																k		k							
Namur **425** d.	Ⓐ	...	...	...	0538	0638	0738	0838	0938	1038	1138	1238	1338	1438	...	1538	...	1638	...	1738	1838	1938	2038	2138	...
Charleroi Central **425** d.		...	...	...	0613	0713	0813	0913	1013	1113	1213	1313	1413	1513	...	1613	...	1713	...	1813	1913	2013	2113	2213	...
Mons d.		0451	...	0551	0646	0746	0846	0946	1046	1146	1246	1346	1446	1546	...	1647	...	1747	...	1847	1946	2046	2146	2246	...
Saint-Ghislain d.		0505	...	0605	0654	0754	0854	0954	1054	1154	1254	1354	1454	1554	...	1655	...	1755	...	1855	1954	2054	2154	2254	...
Tournai a.		0534	...	0634	0714	0814	0914	1014	1114	1214	1314	1414	1514	1614	...	1715	...	1815	...	1915	2014	2114	2214	2314	...
Tournai 417 d.		...	0622	0647	0722	0824	0924	1024	1124	1224	1322	...	1522	1621	1649	1719	1725	1820	1824	1925	2024	2124	...	...	...
Mouscron 417 a.		...	|	|	|	|	|	|	|	|	|	...	|	|	|	1736	|	1836	|	|	|	|	...	...	...
Lille Flandres § a.		...	0652	0722	0752	0852	0952	1052	1152	1254	1352	...	1552	1652	1722	...	1752	...	1852	1952	2052	2152	...	...	...

		Ⓒ	Ⓒ	Ⓒ		Ⓒ	Ⓒ	Ⓒ	
Mouscron 417 d.	Ⓒ	0607	0707	0807		2007	2107	2213	...
Tournai 417 d.		0622	0722	0822	and	2022	2122	2229	...
Saint-Ghislain d.		0651	0751	0851	hourly	2051	2151	2258	...
Mons d.		0707	0807	0907	until	2107	2207	2312	...
Charleroi Central **425** d.		0755	0855	0955		2155	2255	...	...
Namur **425** d.		0828	0928	1028		2228	2326	...	...
Liège Guillemins **442** a.		0914	1014	1114		2314	...	...	...

		Ⓒ	Ⓒ	Ⓒ	Ⓒ		Ⓒ	Ⓒ	Ⓒ
Liège Guillemins **442** d.	Ⓒ	...	...	0645	0745		1945	2045	2145
Namur **425** d.		...	0633	0733	0833	and	2033	2133	2234
Charleroi Central **425** d.		0607	0707	0807	0907	hourly	2107	2207	2307
Mons d.		0658	0758	0858	0958	until	2158	2258	...
Saint-Ghislain d.		0712	0812	0912	1012		2212	2312	...
Tournai 417 d.		0743	0843	0943	1043		2243	2343	...
Mouscron 417 a.		0757	0857	0957	1057		2257	2357	...

		⑥	⑥	Ⓒ	Ⓒ		Ⓒ	Ⓒ	Ⓒ	Ⓒ	Ⓒ	Ⓒ
Lille Flandres § d.	Ⓒ	0647	0742	0842	0947	hourly	1647	1742	1847	1946	2047	2147
Tournai a.		0714	0814	0914	1014	until	1714	1814	1914	2014	2114	2214

		⑥	⑥	Ⓒ		Ⓒ	Ⓒ
Tournai d.	Ⓒ	0646	0746	0846	hourly	2046	2146
Lille Flandres § a.		0714	0819	0914	until	2114	2214

d – From Kortrijk (depart 0608 and 0705).
k – To Kortrijk (arrive 1749 and 1849).
§ – 🏛 between Lille and Tournai = Blandain.

KORTRIJK - MOUSCRON - TOURNAI - BRUSSELS - SINT NIKLAAS 417

Lines 94, 60

For direct trains Kortrijk - Brussels see Table **400** (via Gent) and Table **407** (via Oudenaarde)

km																							
			Ⓐ	Ⓐ	Ⓐ	Ⓐ	Ⓐ	Ⓐ	Ⓐ		Ⓐ	Ⓐ	Ⓐ	Ⓐ	Ⓐ		Ⓐ	Ⓐ	Ⓐ		Ⓒ		Ⓒ
0	**Kortrijk** 415 d.	Ⓐ	...	...	...	...	...	...	...	...	0638	...	...	0739	...		2038	...	2138	Ⓒ	...		...
13	Mouscron 415/6 d.		...	...	...	...	0549	0606	...	...	0649	0706	...	0751	...		2049	...	2149		...		...
32	**Tournai** 416 d.		0445	0509	0545	0557	0609	0628	0645	0657	0709	0728	0745	0810	0845	and	2109	2145	2209		0545		2245
50	Leuze d.		0458	0522	0558	0610	0622	0640	0658	0710	0722	0740	0758	0822	0858	at	2122	2158	2222		0558		2258
62	Ath d.		0508	0533	0608	0620	0633	0650	0708	0720	0733	0750	0808	0833	0908	the	2133	2208	2233		0608	and	2307
100	Halle d.		0537	0602	0637	|	0702	|	0737	|	0802	|	0837	0902	0937	same	2202	2237	2302		0637		2337
116	**Brussels** Midi / Zuid a.		0548	0612	0648	0700	0714	0728	0748	0800	0815	0828	0849	0914	0948	minutes	2215	2248	2315		0648	hourly	2348
116	**Brussels** Midi / Zuid d.		0551	0617	0651	0703	0717	0730	0751	0803	0818	0830	0851	0917	0951	past	2217	2251	2317		0651		2351
118	Brussels Central d.		0556	0622	0656	0708	0721	0735	0756	0808	0823	0835	0856	0922	0956	each	2222	2256	2322		0656	until	2356
120	Brussels Nord d.		0604	0630	0704	0712	0729	0739	0803	0812	0830	0839	0904	0930	1004	hour	2230	2304	2330		0704		0004
132	**Brussels Airport** ✈ a.		0624	|	0724	...	|	...	0824	...	|	...	0924	|	1024	until	|	2324	|		0724		0024
154	Dendermonde a.		...	0656	...	...	0756	...	...	...	0856	...	...	0956	...		2256	...	0014		...		...
168	Lokeren 410 a.		...	0720	...	...	0820	...	...	...	0920	...	...	1020	...		2320	...	...		...		...
181	**Sint-Niklaas** 410 a.		...	0732	...	...	0832	...	...	...	0932	...	...	1032	...		2332	...	...		...		...

		Ⓐ		Ⓐ	Ⓐ	Ⓐ	Ⓐ		Ⓐ	Ⓐ	Ⓐ	Ⓐ	Ⓐ	Ⓐ	Ⓐ	Ⓐ		Ⓐ	Ⓐ		Ⓒ		Ⓒ
Sint-Niklaas 410 d.	Ⓐ	...	...	...	0527	...	0628		...	1928	...	2028	...	2128	...	2228		...	...	Ⓒ	...		...
Lokeren 410 d.		...	...	...	0541	...	0641		...	1941	...	2041	...	2141	...	2241		...	...		...		...
Dendermonde d.		...	...	...	0604	...	0704	and	...	2004	...	2104	...	2204	...	2304		...	...		...		...
Brussels Airport ✈ d.		0442	...	0542	|	0642	|	at	1942	|	2042	|	2142	|	2242	|		...	...		0542		2242
Brussels Nord d.		0501	...	0601	0634	0701	0734	the	2001	2034	2101	2134	2201	2234	2301	2334	A	1616	1717		0601	and	2301
Brussels Central d.		0506	...	0606	0639	0706	0739	same	2006	2039	2106	2139	2206	2239	2306	2339	L	1621	1722		0606		2306
Brussels Midi / Zuid a.		0510	...	0610	0643	0710	0743	minutes	2010	2043	2110	2143	2210	2243	2310	2343	S	1625	1726		0610	hourly	2310
Brussels Midi / Zuid d.		0514	...	0614	0647	0714	0747	past	2014	2047	2114	2147	2214	2247	...	2349	O	1627	1728		0614		2314
Halle d.		0525	...	0625	0658	0725	0758	each	2025	2058	2125	2158	2225	2258	...	0001		|	|		0625	until	2325
Ath d.		0555	...	0655	0729	0755	0829	hour	2055	2129	2155	2226	2255	2329	...	0031		1706	1806		0655		2355
Leuze d.		0604	...	0704	0738	0804	0838	until	2104	2138	2204	...	2304	2338	...	...		1716	1815		0704		0004
Tournai 416 d.		0616	...	0716	0753	0816	0853		2116	2153	2216	...	2316	2350	...	...		1730	1830		0716		0016
Mouscron 415/6 d.		...	...	...	0812	...	0912		...	2212	...	...	...	...	...	...		1750	1850		...		...
Kortrijk 415 a.		...	...	...	0822	...	0922		...	2221	...	...	...	...	...	...		...	...		...		...

419 ROOSENDAAL - ESSEN - ANTWERPEN — Line 12

km		Ⓐ	Ⓐ ♡	Ⓐ	Ⓐ ♡	Ⓐ	Ⓐ ♡		Ⓐ	Ⓐ ♡	Ⓐ	Ⓐ ♡	Ⓐ	Ⓒ	Ⓒ	Ⓒ		Ⓒ	Ⓒ
0	**Roosendaal** d.	...	...	0622	...	0722	...	and at the same minutes past each hour until	2122	...	2222	...	2322	...	0709	0809	and hourly until	2109	2209
8	Essen 🏛 d.	0505	0547	0632	0647	0732	0747		2132	2147	2232	2247	2332	0621	0721	0821		2121	2221
26	Kapellen d.	0522	0605	0652	0705	0752	0805		2152	2205	2252	2305	2352	0641	0741	0841		2141	2241
41	**Antwerpen** Centraal a.	0535	0622	0710	0722	0810	0822		2210	2222	2310	2322	0010	0703	0803	0903		2203	2303

	① c	②–⑤ b	Ⓐ ♡	Ⓐ	Ⓐ ♡	Ⓐ		Ⓐ	Ⓐ ♡		⑦ c	⑥ b	Ⓒ	Ⓒ	Ⓒ		Ⓒ	Ⓒ
Antwerpen Centraal d.	0005	0010	0539	0550	0639	0650	and at the same minutes past each hour until	2150	2239	...	0005	0010	0557	0657	0757	and hourly until	2157	2305
Kapellen d.	0028	0028	0557	0608	0657	0708		2208	2257	...	0028	0028	0618	0718	0818		2218	2328
Essen 🏛 d.	0048	0048	0613	0631	0713	0731		2231	2313	...	0048	0048	0644	0744	0844		2244	2348
Roosendaal a.	...	...	...	0638	...	0738		2238	...	...	...	...	0652	0752	0852		2252	...

b – Not days following public holidays. **c** – Also days following public holidays. ♡ – To/from Brussels (Table **420**); most continue to/from Charleroi Central.

420 ROTTERDAM - ANTWERPEN - BRUSSELS - CHARLEROI — Lines 25, 124

For *Eurostar* services Paris - Brussels - Antwerpen - Amsterdam and *ECD services Brussels - Antwerpen - Amsterdam see Table* **18**.

km		Ⓐ	Ⓐ	Ⓐ ♡	Ⓐ	Ⓐ	Ⓐ ♡	Ⓐ	Ⓐ	Ⓐ ♥	Ⓐ ♡	Ⓐ		Ⓐ	Ⓐ ♥	Ⓐ	Ⓐ	Ⓐ ⊡	Ⓐ ♡	Ⓐ ♥	Ⓐ	Ⓐ ♥	Ⓐ ⊡
0	**Rotterdam** Centraal d.				...	...	...	...	...	0709	...	...	and at the same minutes past each hour until	...	2009	...	...	...	...	2109	...	2209	...
47	Breda 🏛 d.	...	...	...	...	...	...	...	...	0742	...	...		...	2042	...	...	...	...	2142	...	2242	...
80	Noorderkempen (Brecht) d.	...	...	...	...	...	...	...	...	0801	...	...		...	2101	...	...	...	...	2201	...	2301	...
104	**Antwerpen** Centraal 432 d.	0454	0553	0625	0654	0705	0725	0754	0805	0819	0825	0856		2105	2119	2125	2154	2205	2225	2219	2254	2319	2305
106	Antwerpen Berchem d.	0459	0558	0630	0659	0711	0730	0759	0811	0825	0830	0901		2111	2125	2130	2159	2210	2230	2225	2259	2325	2310
128	Mechelen 432 d.	0514	0614	0645	0714	0732	0745	0814	0832	0839	0845	0916		2132	2139	2145	2214	2247	2245	2239	2314	2339	2347
	Brussels Airport ✈ 432 a.	|	|	|	|	|	|	|	|	0849	|	|		|	2149	|	|	|	|	2249	|	2349	|
148	Brussels Nord d.	0532	0632	0702	0732	0756	0802	0832	0856	0908	0902	0932		2154	2208	2202	2232	2316	2302	2308	2332	0008	0016
150	Brussels Central d.	0537	0637	0707	0737	0801	0807	0837	0901	0913	0907	0937		2159	2213	2207	2237	2321	2307	2313	2337	0013	0021
152	**Brussels** Midi/Zuid a.	0541	0641	0711	0741	0805	0811	0841	0905	0917	0911	0941		2203	2217	2211	2241	2325	2311c	2317	2341	0017	0025
152	**Brussels** Midi/Zuid d.	0544	0645	0715	0745	...	0815	0845	...	...	0915	0945		...	...	2215	2245	2332	...	...	...	...	0027
181	Nivelles d.	0612	0712	0743	0812	...	0843	0912	...	...	0943	1012		...	...	2243	2312	|	...	...	...	...	|
207	**Charleroi** Central a.	0635	0735	0806	0835	...	0906	0935	...	...	1006	1035		...	...	2306	2335	0029	...	...	...	...	0123

	Ⓐ ♡	Ⓐ ⊡				Ⓒ	Ⓒ	Ⓒ	Ⓒ	Ⓒ	Ⓒ	Ⓒ	Ⓒ ♥	Ⓒ		Ⓒ	Ⓒ	Ⓒ	Ⓒ ♥	Ⓒ	Ⓒ ♥	Ⓒ ⊡	
Rotterdam Centraal d.	...	...	...	...	...	...	...	...	...	...	...	...	0709	...	and at the same minutes past each hour until	...	...	...	2109	...	2209	...	...
Breda 🏛 d.	...	...	...	...	...	...	...	...	...	...	...	...	0742	...		...	...	...	2142	...	2242	...	...
Noorderkempen (Brecht) d.	...	...	...	...	...	...	...	...	...	...	...	...	0801	...		...	...	...	2201	...	2301	...	...
Antwerpen Centraal 432 d.	2325	0005	...	...	...	...	...	0603	...	0703	...	0803	0819	...		...	2103	2203	2219	2303	2319	2358	...
Antwerpen Berchem d.	2330	0010	...	...	...	...	0541	0608	0641	0708	0741	0808	0825	0841		2041	2108	2208	2225	2308	2325	0003	...
Mechelen 432 d.	2345	0047	...	...	...	...	0602	0633	0702	0733	0802	0833	0839	0902		2102	2133	2233	2239	2333	2339	0037	...
Brussels Airport ✈ 432 a.	|	|	...	...	...	...	|	|	|	|	|	|	0849	|		|	|	|	2249	|	2349	|	...
Brussels Nord d.	0009	|	...	...	...	0554	0624	0654	0724	0754	0824	0854	0908	0924		2124	2154	2253	2308	2354	0008	0103	...
Brussels Central d.	0014	|	...	...	...	0559	0629	0659	0729	0759	0829	0859	0913	0929		2129	2159	2258	2313	2359	0013	0107	...
Brussels Midi/Zuid a.	0017c	0125	...	...	...	0604	0634	0704	0734	0804	0834	0904	0917	0934		2134	2204	2302	2317	0003	0017	0111	...
Brussels Midi/Zuid d.	...	...	...	...	...	0607	0637	0707	0737	0807	0737	0907	...	0937		2137	2207	2305	...	...	...	...	...
Nivelles d.	...	...	...	...	...	0634	0704	0734	0804	0834	0904	0934	...	1004		2204	2234	2334	...	...	...	...	...
Charleroi Central a.	...	...	...	...	...	0657	0728	0757	0828	0857	0928	0957	...	1028		2228	2257	2357	...	...	...	...	...

	Ⓐ ♡	Ⓐ	Ⓐ ⊡	Ⓐ ♥	Ⓐ ♡	Ⓐ	Ⓐ	Ⓐ ♥	Ⓐ ♡	Ⓐ	Ⓐ	Ⓐ ♥	Ⓐ ♡		Ⓐ ♥	Ⓐ ♡	Ⓐ	Ⓐ	Ⓐ ♥	Ⓐ ♡	Ⓐ	Ⓐ ♡	Ⓐ
Charleroi Central d.	...	...	0426	...	...	...	0525	...	0554	...	0625	...	0654	and at the same minutes past each hour until	...	1854	...	1925	...	1954	2025	2054	2125
Nivelles d.	...	...	0454	...	...	...	0550	...	0619	...	0650	...	0719		...	1919	...	1950	...	2019	2050	2119	2150
Brussels Midi/Zuid a.	...	...	0535	...	...	...	0616	...	0645	...	0716	...	0745		...	1945	...	2016	...	2045	2116	2145	2216
Brussels Midi/Zuid d.	0450	0520	0538	0544	0550	0556	0620	0644	0650	0659	0720	0744	0750		1944	1950	1956	2020	2044	2050	2120	2150	2220
Brussels Central d.	0455	0525	0542	0549	0555	0601	0625	0649	0655	0704	0725	0749	0755		1949	1955	2001	2025	2049	2055	2125	2155	2225
Brussels Nord d.	0503	0533	0549	0556	0603	0609	0633	0656	0703	0710	0733	0756	0803		1956	2003	2008	2033	2056	2103	2133	2203	2233
Brussels Airport ✈ 432 d.	|	|	|	0611	|	|	|	0711	|	|	|	0811	|		2011	|	|	|	2111	|	|	|	|
Mechelen 432 d.	0519	0549	0616	0624	0619	0629	0649	0724	0719	0729	0749	0824	0819		2024	2019	2029	2049	2124	2119	2149	2219	2249
Antwerpen Berchem d.	0532	0602	0651	0638	0632	0649	0702	0738	0732	0749	0802	0838	0832		2038	2032	2049	2102	2138	2132	2202	2232	2302
Antwerpen Centraal 432 d.	0536	0606	0655	0645	0636	0653	0706	0745	0736	0753	0806	0845	0836		2045	2036	2053	2106	2145	2133	2206	2236	2306
Noorderkempen (Brecht) d.	...	...	...	0701	...	...	...	0801	...	...	...	0901	...		2101	...	...	...	2201	...	...	...	...
Breda 🏛 a.	...	...	...	0718	...	...	...	0818	...	...	...	0918	...		2118	...	...	...	2218	...	...	...	...
Rotterdam Centraal a.	...	...	...	0750	...	...	...	0850	...	...	...	0950	...		2150	...	...	...	2250	...	...	...	...

	Ⓐ	Ⓐ	Ⓐ	Ⓐ ⊡	Ⓐ	Ⓒ ♥	Ⓒ	Ⓒ ♥	Ⓒ	Ⓒ ♥	Ⓒ	Ⓒ ♥	Ⓒ	Ⓒ		Ⓒ ♥	Ⓒ	Ⓒ	Ⓒ	Ⓒ	Ⓒ	Ⓒ	⑥ ⊡
Charleroi Central d.	2154	...	2225	...	...	...	0505	...	0605	...	0705	...	0805	0832	and at the same minutes past each hour until	...	2005	2032	2105	2132	2205	2232	...
Nivelles d.	2219	...	2250	...	...	...	0529	...	0629	...	0729	...	0829	0857		...	2029	2057	2130	2157	2229	2257	2304
Brussels Midi/Zuid a.	2245	...	2317	...	...	...	0556	...	0656	...	0756	...	0856	0824		...	2056	2124	2156	2223	2257	2323	2346
Brussels Midi/Zuid d.	2250	2256	2320	2338	2356	0544	0559	0644	0659	0744	0759	0844	0859	0927		2044	2059	2127	2159	2227	2259	2327	2349
Brussels Central d.	2255	2301	2325	2342	0001	0549	0604	0649	0704	0749	0804	0849	0904	0932		2049	2104	2132	2204	2232	2304	2332	2353
Brussels Nord d.	2303	2308	2329	2349	0008	0556	0610	0656	0710	0756	0810	0856	0910	0940		2056	2110	2140	2210	2240	2310	2340	2359
Brussels Airport ✈ 432 d.	|	|	...	|	|	0611	|	0711	|	0811	|	|	|	|		2111	|	|	|	|	|	|	|
Mechelen 432 d.	2319	2329	...	0016	0029	0624	0636	0724	0736	0824	0836	0924	0936	1002		2124	2136	2202	2236	2302	2336	0002	0025
Antwerpen Berchem d.	2332	2349	...	0051	0054	0638	0655	0738	0755	0838	0855	0938	0955	1019		2138	2155	2219	2255	2319	2355	0019	0058
Antwerpen Centraal 432 d.	2336	2353	...	0055	0058	0645	0659	0745	0759	0845	0859	0945	0959	...		2145	2159	...	2259	...	2359	...	0102
Noorderkempen (Brecht) d.	...	...	...	...	...	0701	...	0801	...	0901	...	1001	...	...		2201	...	...	...	...	...	...	...
Breda 🏛 a.	...	...	...	...	...	0726	...	0826	...	0926	...	1026	...	...		2226	...	...	...	...	...	...	...
Rotterdam Centraal a.	...	...	...	...	...	0750	...	0850	...	0950	...	1050	...	...		2250	...	...	...	...	...	...	...

c – Connects with train to Charleroi in preceding column.

♥ – EuroCity service (see also Table **18**).
♡ – From/to Essen (Belgium), Table **419**.
⊡ – Local train.

BRUSSELS AIRPORT ✈ - CHARLEROI

Runs Ⓐ only

	Ⓐ		Ⓐ	
Brussels Airport ✈ d.	0547	and hourly until	2147	...
Brussels Schuman d.	0603		2203	...
Brussels Luxembourg d.	0608		2208	...
Nivelles d.	0655		2255	...
Charleroi Central a.	0722		2322	...

	Ⓐ		Ⓐ	
Charleroi Central d.	0536	and hourly until	2136	...
Nivelles d.	0604		2204	...
Brussels Luxembourg d.	0654		2254	...
Brussels Schuman d.	0657		2257	...
Brussels Airport ✈ a.	0713		2313	...

421 CHARLEROI - MARIEMBOURG - COUVIN — Line 132

km		Ⓐ	Ⓐ	Ⓐ		Ⓐ	Ⓐ	Ⓒ		Ⓒ
0	**Charleroi** Central d.	0542	0653	0821	⊡	2121	2221	0815		2215
18	Berzée d.	0608	0718	0842	every	2142	2242	0839	every	2239
22	Walcourt d.	0615	0726	0849	hour	2148	2248	0846	**two**	2247
35	Philippeville d.	0630	0741	0904	until	2203	2303	0902	hours	2303
48	Mariembourg ▲ d.	0643	0751	0916	△	2215	2315	0915	until	2315
53	**Couvin** a.	0649	0757	0921		2221	2321	0921		2321

	Ⓐ	Ⓐ	Ⓐ		Ⓐ	Ⓐ	Ⓒ		Ⓒ
Couvin d.	0427	0522	1005		1505	2105	0640		2040
Mariembourg ▲ d.	0438	0531	1014	every	1514	2114	0649	every	2049
Philippeville d.	0449	0543	1026	hour	1526	2126	0702	**two**	2103
Walcourt d.	0503	0604	1042	until	1542	2142	0717	hours	2117
Berzée d.	0509	0612	1048	▽	1648	2148	0724	until	2124
Charleroi Central a.	0535	0633	1108		1608	2208	0746		2146

△ – Also from Charleroi Central at 1653, 1744, 1838.
▽ – Also from Couvin at 0607, 0633, 0719, 0811, 0906, 1604, 1639, 1807, 1906, 2005.
⊡ – Journey at 1721 from Charleroi Central leaves up to 3 minutes earlier.

▲ – For MARIEMBOURG - TREIGNES heritage railway operated by *Chemin de Fer à Vapeur des 3 Vallées* (CFV3V). For days of running and timings see www.cfv3v.eu

BRUSSELS - MONS - QUIÉVRAIN 422

Lines 96, 97

km			Ⓐ	Ⓐ ◇	Ⓐ	Ⓐ ◇	Ⓐ		Ⓐ ◇	Ⓐ	Ⓐ ◇	Ⓐ	Ⓐ ◇	Ⓐ	Ⓐ ◇	Ⓐ	Ⓐ ◇	Ⓐ			Ⓒ		Ⓒ
0	**Brussels Airport** ✈ d.	Ⓐ	0530	...	0630	...	0729		...	1930	...	2030	...	2130	...	2230	...	2330	...	Ⓒ	0530		2230
12	Brussels Nord **423** d.		0543	0613	0643	0713	0743	and	1913	1943	2013	2043	2113	2143	2213	2243	2313	2343	...		0543		2243
14	Brussels Central **423** d.		0548	0618	0648	0718	0748	at	1918	1948	2018	2048	2118	2148	2218	2248	2318	2348	...		0548		2248
16	**Brussels** Midi / Zuid **423** d.		0556	0626	0656	0726	0756	the	1926	1955	2026	2055	2126	2156	2226	2256	2326	2356	...		0556	and	2256
32	Halle **423** d.		|	0636	|	0736	|	same	1936	|	2036	|	2136	|	2236	|	2336	|	...		|	hourly	|
45	Braine-le-Comte **423** d.		0617	0648	0717	0748	0818	minutes	1947	2017	2048	2117	2148	2217	2248	2317	2348	0018	...		0617	until	2317
51	Soignies d.		0624	0654	0724	0754	0824	past	1954	2024	2054	2124	2154	2224	2254	2324	2354	0024	...		0623		2323
76	**Mons** a.		0643	0712	0743	0812	0843	each	2012	2043	2112	2143	2212	2243	2312	2343	0012	0043	...		0642		2342
76	**Mons** d.		...	0716	...	0816	...	hour	2016	...	2116	...	2216	...	2316	...	...	...	...		⊡		⊡
86	Saint-Ghislain d.		...	0734	...	0834	...	until	2034	...	2130	...	2230	...	2330	...	...	...	...		⊡		⊡
96	**Quiévrain** a.		...	0750	...	0850	...		2050	...	...	...	...	...	...	...	...	...	...		⊡		⊡

		Ⓐ	Ⓐ ◇	Ⓐ	Ⓐ ◇	Ⓐ	Ⓐ ◇	Ⓐ	Ⓐ ◇	Ⓐ		Ⓐ ◇	Ⓐ	Ⓐ ◇	Ⓐ	Ⓐ ◇	Ⓐ				Ⓒ		Ⓒ
Quiévrain d.	Ⓐ	...	...	...	0511	...	0611	...	0711	...		1911	...	2011	...	2111	...	...	...	Ⓒ	⊡		⊡
Saint-Ghislain d.		...	...	...	0531	...	0631	...	0731	...	and	1931	...	2031	...	2131	...	...	...		⊡		⊡
Mons a.		...	...	...	0545	...	0645	...	0745	...	at	1945	...	2045	...	2145	...	...	...		⊡		⊡
Mons d.		0420	0450	0520	0550	0618	0650	0718	0750	0820	the	1950	2018	2050	2120	2150	2220	...	...		0520	and	2220
Soignies d.		0440	0509	0540	0609	0637	0709	0738	0809	0840	same	2009	2040	2109	2140	2209	2240	...	...		0540	hourly	2240
Braine-le-Comte **423** d.		0447	0516	0547	0616	0644	0716	0745	0816	0847	minutes	2016	2047	2116	2147	2216	2247	...	...		0547	until	2247
Halle **423** d.		|	0526	|	0626	|	0726	|	0826	|	past	2026	|	2126	|	2226	|	...	...		|		|
Brussels Midi / Zuid **423** d.		0509	0540	0609	0640	0709	0740	0809	0840	0909	each	2040	2109	2140	2209	2240	2309	...	...		0609		2309
Brussels Central **423** d.		0514	0545	0614	0645	0714	0745	0814	0845	0914	hour	2045	2114	2145	2214	2245	2314	...	...		0614		2314
Brussels Nord **423** d.		0520	0549	0620	0649	0721	0749	0821	0849	0920	until	2049	2120	2149	2220	2249	2320	...	...		0620		2320
Brussels Airport ✈ a.		0531	...	0631	...	0732	...	0832	...	0931		...	2131	...	2231	...	2331	...	...		0631		2331

◇ – From / to Hasselt / Tongeren (Table **431**). ⊡ – MONS - QUIÉVRAIN LOCAL TRAINS ON Ⓒ: from Mons hourly 0703 - 2103, from Quiévrain hourly 0738 - 2138.

BRUSSELS - LA LOUVIÈRE - BINCHE 423

Lines 96, 108

For additional trains Brussels - Halle - Braine-le-Comte see Table **422**

km			Ⓐ		Ⓐ	Ⓐ	Ⓐ		Ⓒ		Ⓒ
0	**Brussels** Nord d.	Ⓐ	0618		2018	2118	2218	Ⓒ	0618		2218
2	Brussels Central d.		0623		2023	2123	2223		0623		2223
4	**Brussels** Midi / Zuid d.		0630	and	2030	2130	2230		0630	and	2230
20	Halle d.		0641	hourly	2041	2141	2241		0643	hourly	2243
33	Braine-le-Comte d.		0658	until	2058	2158	2258		0700	until	2300
52	**La Louvière** Centre d.		0718		2118	2218	2318		0721		2321
55	La Louvière Sud a.		0722		2122	2222	2322		0725		2325
64	**Binche** a.		0741		2141	...	...		0748		2348

		Ⓐ		Ⓐ		Ⓒ	Ⓒ		Ⓒ
Binche d.	Ⓐ	0520		2120	Ⓒ	0511	0611		2211
La Louvière Sud d.		0538		2138		0535	0635		2235
La Louvière Centre d.		0544	and	2144		0542	0642	and	2242
Braine-le-Comte d.		0605	hourly	2205		0606	0703	hourly	2303
Halle d.		0620	until	2220		0620	0720	until	2320
Brussels Midi / Zuid d.		0633		2233		0633	0733		2333
Brussels Central d.		0638		2238		0638	0738		2338
Brussels Nord a.		0642		2242		0642	0742		2342

☛ On Ⓐ trains run beyond Brussels to / from Turnhout (Table **434**).

BRUSSELS - GERAARDSBERGEN 424

Lines 94, 123 (S6)

km			Ⓐ		Ⓐ		Ⓒ		Ⓒ
0	**Brussels** Nord d.	Ⓐ	0508		2108	Ⓒ	0608		2208
2	Brussels Centraal d.		0512	and	2112		0612	and	2212
4	**Brussels** Midi / Zuid d.		0519	hourly	2119		0619	hourly	2219
18	Halle d.		0532	until	2132		0632	until	2232
33	Edingen d.		0544		2144		0644		2244
49	**Geraardsbergen** a.		0604		2204		0704		2304

		Ⓐ		Ⓐ		Ⓒ		Ⓒ
Geraardsbergen d.	Ⓐ	0455		2055	Ⓒ	0655		2255
Edingen d.		0517	and	2117		0717	and	2316
Halle d.		0529	hourly	2129		0729	hourly	2329
Brussels Midi / Zuid d.		0544	until	2144		0744	until	2344
Brussels Centraal d.		0548		2148		0748		2348
Brussels Nord a.		0552		2152		0752		2352

MONS - CHARLEROI - NAMUR 425

Lines 118, 130

km			Ⓐ	Ⓐ	Ⓐ	Ⓐ ♡	Ⓐ	Ⓐ ♡	Ⓐ		Ⓐ	Ⓐ	Ⓐ	Ⓐ	Ⓐ	Ⓐ		Ⓒ	Ⓒ ♡	Ⓒ ♡		Ⓒ ♡	Ⓒ ♡
	Tournai **416** d.	Ⓐ	...	...	...	0544	...	0644	...	and at	1943	...	2044	...	2144	...	Ⓒ	...	0622	0722		2022	2122
0	**Mons** d.		0437	...	0538	0616	0638	0716	0738	the same	2016	2038	2116	2138	2216	2238		0607	0707	0807		2107	2207
20	La Louvière Centre d.		0452	...	0556	0632	0656	0732	0756	minutes	2032	2056	2132	2156	2232	2256		0624	0724	0824	and	2124	2224
41	**Charleroi** Central d.		0513	0550	0619	0650	0719	0750	0819	past	2050	2119	2150	2219	2250	2315		0655	0755	0855	hourly	2155	2255
56	Tamines d.		0527	0603	0631	0703	0731	0803	0831	each	2103	2131	2203	2233	2303	...		0708	0808	0908	until	2208	2308
78	**Namur** d.		0553	0622	0653	0722	0753	0822	0853	hour	2122	2153	2222	2256	2322	...		0728	0828	0928		2228	2326
	Liège Guillemins **442** a.		0635	...	0735	...	0835	...	0935	until	...	2235	...	...	...	...		0814	0914	1014		2314	...

		Ⓐ	Ⓐ	Ⓐ	Ⓐ	Ⓐ	Ⓐ	Ⓐ		Ⓐ	Ⓐ	Ⓐ	Ⓐ	Ⓐ	Ⓐ	Ⓐ		Ⓒ ♡	Ⓒ ♡	Ⓒ ♡		Ⓒ ♡	Ⓒ
Liège Guillemins **442** d.	Ⓐ	...	...	...	0524	...	0624	...	and at	1924	...	2024	...	2124	...	2224	Ⓒ	...	...	0645		2045	2145
Namur d.		...	0503	0538	0611	0638	0711	0738	the same	2011	2038	2111	2138	2210	2238	2310		...	0633	0733		2133	2234
Tamines d.		...	0526	0557	0630	0657	0730	0757	minutes	2030	2057	2130	2157	2232	2257	2332		...	0653	0753	and	2153	2254
Charleroi Central d.		0446	0546	0613	0646	0713	0746	0813	past	2046	2113	2146	2213	2250	2311	2347		0607	0707	0807	hourly	2207	2307
La Louvière Centre d.		0506	0606	0630	0706	0730	0806	0830	each	2106	2130	2206	2230	2309	...	...		0640	0740	0840	until	2240	...
Mons d.		0522	0622	0646	0722	0746	0822	0846	hour	2122	2146	2222	2246	2327	...	...		0658	0758	0858		2258	...
Tournai **416** a.		...	...	0714	...	0814	...	0914	until	...	2214	...	2314	...	...	...		0741	0841	0941		2341	...

♡ – From / to Mouscron (Table **416**).

MONS - QUÉVY 426

Line 96

km		Ⓐ	Ⓐ	Ⓐ	and	Ⓐ	Ⓐ	Ⓐ	Ⓐ	Ⓐ	Ⓐ	Ⓐ
0	Mons d.	0715	0836	0922	hourly	1622	1650	1721	1829	1932	2022	2122
18	Quévy d.	0730	0851	0937	until	1637	1705	1735	1844	1947	2035	2137

	Ⓐ	Ⓐ	Ⓐ	Ⓐ	Ⓐ	Ⓐ	Ⓐ	and	Ⓐ	Ⓐ
Quévy d.	0523	0557	0623	0712	0723	0756	0823	hourly	1923	2023
Mons a.	0538	0615	0638	0730	0738	0811	0838	until	1938	2038

No service on Ⓒ.

CHARLEROI - MAUBEUGE 427

km		Ⓐ	Ⓐ	Ⓒ							Ⓐ	Ⓒ
0	**Charleroi** Central d.	0524	0618	0624	0824	1024	1224	1424	1624	1824	1925	2024
14	Thuin d.	0545	0637	0643	0845	1045	1245	1445	1645	1845	1946	2043
29	Erquellinnes d.	0608	0707	0708	0908	1108	1308	1508	1708	1909	2008	2108
40	**Maubeuge** 🏛 a.	0617	0717	0717	0917	1117	1317	1517	1717	1919	2017	2117

	Ⓐ								Ⓐ	Ⓒ	
Maubeuge 🏛 d.	0645	0745	0945	1145	1345	1545	1745	1945	2045	2145	...
Erquelinnes d.	0658	0755	0955	1155	1355	1555	1806	1955	2055	2156	...
Thuin d.	0722	0818	1018	1218	1418	1618	1828	2018	2118	2219	...
Charleroi Central a.	0741	0838	1038	1238	1438	1638	1848	2038	2138	2236	...

☛ For connections Maubeuge - Paris see Table **255**.

430 BRUSSELS - LANDEN - HASSELT, GENK and LIÈGE

Lines 36, 21

For direct services Brussels - Liège via high-speed line see Table **400**. For other services Brussels - Hasselt on Ⓐ (via Aarshot) see Table **431**.

km			Ⓐ	Ⓐ	Ⓐ	Ⓐ	Ⓐ	Ⓐ	Ⓐ	Ⓐ	Ⓐ	Ⓐ	Ⓐ		Ⓐ	Ⓐ	Ⓐ	Ⓐ	Ⓐ	Ⓐ	Ⓐ	
					△	•		△	•	△	•	△	•		△	•	♡	•			b	
0	**Brussels** Midi / Zuid d.	Ⓐ	0511	0513	0611	0613	0636	0711	0714	0811	0814	0911	0913		2111	2113	2211	2213	2256	2313	0020	...
2	Brussels Central d.		0516	0518	0616	0618	0641	0716	0719	0816	0819	0916	0918	and	2116	2118	2216	2218	2301	2319	0025	...
4	Brussels Nord d.		0522	0525	0622	0625	0648	0722	0725	0822	0825	0922	0925	at	2122	2125	2222	2225	2308	2325	0031	...
16	**Brussels Airport** ✈ d.		|	0538	|	0638	|	|	0738	|	0838	|	0938	the	|	2138	|	2238	|	2338	|	...
33	Leuven d.		0542	0556	0642	0656	0707	0742	0756	0842	0856	0942	0956	same	2142	2156	2242	2256	2326	2356	0051	...
64	Tienen d.		0555	0610	0655	0710	0721	0755	0810	0855	0910	0955	1010	minutes	2155	2210	2255	2310	2340	0010	0105	...
64	Landen d.		0606	0620	0706	0721	0732	0806	0821	0906	0921	1006	1021	past	2206	2221	2306	2321	2351	0020	0116	...
75	Sint-Truiden d.		0617	|	0717	|	0744	0817	|	0917	|	1017	|	each	2217	|	2317	|	|	...	|	...
92	**Hasselt** d.		0635	|	0735	|	0802	0835	|	0935	|	1035	|	hour	2235	|	2332	|	|	...	|	...
108	Genk a.		0653	|	0753	|	0820	0853	|	0953	|	1053	|	until	2253	|	...	|	|	...	|	...
103	**Liège** Guillemins a.		...	0649	...	0753	...	...	0853	...	0953	...	1053		...	2253	...	2353	0020	...	0144	...

		Ⓒ	Ⓒ	Ⓒ	Ⓒ	Ⓒ	Ⓒ	Ⓒ	Ⓒ	Ⓒ	Ⓒ	Ⓒ		Ⓒ	Ⓒ	Ⓒ	Ⓒ	Ⓒ	Ⓒ	Ⓒ	Ⓒ	Ⓒ	Ⓒ
				♡			♡			♡				♡			♡		♡		b		b
Brussels Midi / Zuid d.	Ⓒ	...	...	0636	...	...	0736	...	...	0836	...	...		2036	...	...	2136	...	2236	...	2256	...	0020
Brussels Central d.		...	...	0641	...	...	0741	...	...	0841	...	...	and	2041	...	...	2141	...	2241	...	2301	...	0025
Brussels Nord d.		...	...	0648	...	...	0748	...	...	0848	...	...	at	2048	...	...	2148	...	2248	...	2307	...	0031
Brussels Airport ✈ d.		...	0559	|	...	0659	|	...	0759	|	...	0859	the	|	...	2059	|	2159	|	2259	|	2359	|
Leuven d.		...	0615	0707	...	0715	0807	...	0815	0907	...	0915	same	2107	...	2115	2207	2215	2307	2315	2327	0012	0051
Tienen d.		...	0630	0721	...	0730	0821	...	0830	0921	...	0930	minutes	2121	...	2130	2221	2230	2321	2330	2341	...	0105
Landen d.		0638	0643	0732	0738	0743	0832	0838	0843	0932	0938	0943	past	2132	2138	2143	2232	2243	2332	2343	2351	...	0115
Sint-Truiden d.		|	...	0741	|	...	0841	|	...	0941	|	...	each	2141	|	...	2241	...	2341	...	|	...	|
Hasselt d.		|	...	0800	|	...	0900	|	...	1000	|	...	hour	2200	|	...	2300	...	2400	...	|	...	|
Genk a.		|	...	0818	|	...	0918	|	...	1018	|	...	until	2218	|	...	2318	...	0018	...	|	...	|
Liège Guillemins a.		0722	...	...	0822	...	...	0922	...	...	1022	...			2222	...	...	...	...	...	0020	...	0144

		Ⓐ	Ⓐ	Ⓐ	Ⓐ	Ⓐ	Ⓐ	Ⓐ	Ⓐ	Ⓐ	Ⓐ	Ⓐ	Ⓐ		Ⓐ	Ⓐ	Ⓐ	Ⓐ	Ⓐ		Ⓐ	Ⓐ	Ⓐ
		•	♡	b	♡	•	△	♡	•	△	♡	•	△		♡	•	△	•	△		•	△	•
Liège Guillemins d.	Ⓐ	0408	...	0437	...	0508	...	...	0607	...	...	0708	...		...	1708	...	1808	...		2108	...	2208
Genk d.		|	...	|	...	|	0506	0539	|	0606	0639	|	0706	and	1639	|	1706	|	1806	and	|	2106	|
Hasselt d.		|	0427	|	...	|	0527	0600	|	0628	0700	|	0727	at	1700	|	1727	|	1827	at	|	2127	|
Sint-Truiden d.		|	0444	|	...	|	0544	0620	|	0644	0720	|	0743	the	1720	|	1744	|	1844	the	|	2144	|
Landen d.		0439	0454	0508	0530	0539	0554	0630	0638	0653	0730	0738	0753	same	1730	1739	1754	1839	1854	same	2139	2154	2239
Tienen d.		0451	0505	0519	0541	0551	0605	0641	0650	0704	0741	0750	0804	minutes	1741	1751	1805	1851	1905	minutes	2151	2205	2251
Leuven d.		0507	0521	0536	0558	0607	0621	0657	0707	0719	0757	0807	0819	past	1758	1807	1821	1907	1921	past	2207	2221	2307
Brussels Airport ✈ d.		0524	|	|	|	0624	|	|	0724	|	|	0824	|	each	|	1824	|	1924	|	each	2224	|	2324
Brussels Nord d.		0538	0540	0554	0616	0638	0640	0715	0738	0738	0815	0838	0838	hour	1816	1838	1840	1938	1940	hour	2238	2240	2338
Brussels Central d.		0543	0545	0559	0621	0643	0645	0720	0743	0743	0820	0843	0843	until	1821	1843	1845	1943	1945	until	2243	2245	2343
Brussels Midi / Zuid a.		0547	0549	0600	0625	0647	0649	0724	0747	0747	0824	0847	0847		1825	1847	1849	1947	1949		2247	2252	2347

		Ⓒ	Ⓒ	Ⓒ	Ⓒ	Ⓒ	Ⓒ	Ⓒ	Ⓒ	Ⓒ	Ⓒ	Ⓒ		Ⓒ	Ⓒ	Ⓒ	Ⓒ	Ⓒ	Ⓒ			
		b			♡			♡			♡				♡			♡	b			
Liège Guillemins d.	Ⓒ	0437	...	...	...	...	0637	...	...	0737	...	...		2037	...	...	2137	...	2304	...	...	...
Genk d.		|	...	...	...	...	|	0640	...	|	0740	...	and	|	2040	...	|	2140	|	...	...	...
Hasselt d.		|	...	...	0602	...	|	0702	...	|	0802	...	at	|	2102	...	|	2202	|	...	...	...
Sint-Truiden d.		|	...	...	0618	...	|	0718	...	|	0818	...	the	|	2118	...	|	2218	|	...	...	...
Landen d.		0506	0517	0617	0628	0717	0720	0728	0817	0820	0828	0917	same	2120	2128	2217	2220	2228	2333	...	...	...
Tienen d.		0516	0532	0632	0639	0732	...	0739	0832	...	0839	0932	minutes	...	2139	2232	...	2239	2344	...	...	...
Leuven d.		0534	0548	0648	0655	0748	...	0755	0848	...	0855	0948	past	...	2155	2248	...	2255	2400	...	...	...
Brussels Airport ✈ d.		|	0601	0701	|	0801	...	|	0901	...	|	1001	each	...	|	2301	...	|	|	...	...	...
Brussels Nord d.		0551	...	...	0715	...	...	0815	...	...	0915	...	hour	...	2215	...	...	2315	0018	...	...	...
Brussels Central d.		0556	...	...	0720	...	...	0820	...	...	0920	...	until	...	2220	...	...	2320	0023	...	...	...
Brussels Midi / Zuid a.		0600	...	...	0724	...	...	0824	...	...	0924	...		...	2224	...	...	2324	0027	...	...	...

b – From / to Brugge and Oostende (Table **400**).

♡ – From / to Brugge and Gent, (most trains also from / to Blankenberge) Table **405**.

△ – From / to Gent via Aalst (Table **412**).

• – From / to Brugge, (most trains also from / to Knokke) Table **422**.

431 BRUSSELS - AARSCHOT - HASSELT - TONGEREN

Line 35

No service on Ⓒ via this route. For other trains Brussels - Hasselt (via Landen) see Table **430**.

km			Ⓐ	Ⓐ	Ⓐ	Ⓐ		Ⓐ	Ⓐ	Ⓐ
0	**Brussels** Midi / Zuid d.	Ⓐ	0540	0640	0740	0840		2040	2140	2240
2	Brussels Central d.		0545	0645	0745	0845		2045	2145	2245
4	Brussels Nord d.		0552	0652	0752	0852	and	2052	2152	2252
46	Aarschot 432 d.		0622	0722	0822	0922	hourly	2122	2222	2322
63	Diest 432 d.		0635	0735	0835	0935	until	2135	2235	2335
84	**Hasselt** 432 d.		0653	0753	0853	0953		2153	2249	2349
110	Tongeren 435 a.		0719	0819	0919	1019		2219	...	...

		Ⓐ	Ⓐ	Ⓐ		Ⓐ	Ⓐ	Ⓐ	Ⓐ
Tongeren 435 d.	Ⓐ	...	0542	0642		1841	1941	2041	2141
Hasselt 432 d.		0511	0611	0711		1915	2015	2115	2215
Diest 432 d.		0528	0628	0728	and	1931	2031	2131	2231
Aarschot 432 d.		0544	0644	0744	hourly	1944	2044	2144	2244
Brussels Nord d.		0613	0713	0813	until	2013	2113	2213	2313
Brussels Central d.		0618	0718	0818		2018	2118	2218	2318
Brussels Midi / Zuid a.		0622	0722	0822		2022	2122	2222	2322

432 ANTWERPEN - BRUSSELS NATIONAAL ✈ - AARSCHOT - HASSELT

Lines 35, 36c, 16

For Antwerpen - Hasselt via Mol see Table **434**. For additional trains Brussels Nationaal ✈ - Leuven see Table **430**.

km	*Via Airport*		Ⓐ		Ⓐ		Ⓒ		Ⓒ	Ⓒ
0	**Antwerpen** Centraal 420 d.	Ⓐ	0449		2249	Ⓒ	0549		2149	2249
24	Mechelen 420 d.		0508		2308		0608		2208	2308
40	**Brussels Airport** ✈ 420 d.		0521	and	2321		0621	and	2221	2321
59	Leuven d.		0542	hourly	2342		0642	hourly	2242	2342
75	Aarschot d.		0557	until	2357		0656	until	2256	2356
92	Diest d.		0610		0010		0715		2315	0015
113	**Hasselt** a.		0624		0024		0731		2331	0031

		Ⓐ		Ⓐ		Ⓒ		Ⓒ	Ⓒ
Hasselt d.	Ⓐ	0436		2236	Ⓒ	0627		2127	2237
Diest d.		0450		2250		0644		2144	2244
Aarschot d.		0502	and	2302		0703	and	2203	2303
Leuven d.		0524	hourly	2324		0724	hourly	2224	2324
Brussels Airport ✈ 420 d.		0541	until	2341		0741	until	2241	2341
Mechelen 420 d.		0554		2354		0754		2254	0234
Antwerpen Centraal 420 a.		0611		0011		0811		2311	0011

km	*Via Lier*		Ⓐ		Ⓐ		Ⓒ		Ⓒ	Ⓒ
					n					
0	**Antwerpen** Centraal d.	Ⓐ	0617		2217	Ⓒ	0616		2216	2316
14	Lier d.		0635	and	2235		0633	and	2233	2333
41	Aarschot d.		|	hourly	|		|	hourly	|	|
59	Diest d.		0705	until	2305		0702	until	2302	0002
80	**Hasselt** a.		0719		2319		0715		2315	0015

		Ⓐ		Ⓐ		Ⓒ	Ⓒ		Ⓒ
Hasselt d.	Ⓐ	0441		1941	Ⓒ	0543	0643		2243
Diest d.		0455	and	1955		0557	0657	and	2257
Aarschot d.		|	hourly	|		|	|	hourly	|
Lier d.		0626	until	2026		0628	0728	until	2328
Antwerpen Centraal a.		0541		2042		0643	0743		2343

km	*Via Lier*		Ⓐ		Ⓐ		Ⓒ		Ⓒ	Ⓒ
0	**Antwerpen** Centraal d.	Ⓐ	0630	and	2230	Ⓒ	0647	and	2147	2247
14	Lier d.		0649	hourly	2249		0706	hourly	2206	2306
41	Aarschot d.		0712	until	2312		0735	until	2235	2335
57	**Leuven** a.		0724		2324		0748		2248	2348

		Ⓐ		Ⓐ		Ⓒ		Ⓒ	Ⓒ
Leuven d.	Ⓐ	0636	and	2036	Ⓒ	0611	and	2111	2211
Aarschot d.		0650	hourly	2050		0625	hourly	2125	2225
Lier d.		0713	until	2113		0656	until	2156	2256
Antwerpen Centraal a.		0728		2128		0713		2213	2313

n – No journey at 2117 from Antwerpen Centraal.

Line 15 BRUSSELS and ANTWERPEN - LIER - TURNHOUT / HASSELT / HAMONT 434

km			Ⓐ	Ⓐ	Ⓐ	Ⓐ	Ⓐ	Ⓐ	Ⓐ		Ⓐ	Ⓐ	Ⓐ	Ⓐ	Ⓐ	Ⓐ	Ⓐ	Ⓐ	Ⓐ	Ⓐ	Ⓐ	Ⓐ	Ⓐ
	Brussels Midi / Zuid ▷ d.	Ⓐ	...	...	...	...	0633	...	...		1833	...	...	1933	...	...	2033	...	...	2133	...	2233	...
	Brussels Central ▷ d.		...	...	...	...	0638	...	...		1838	...	...	1938	...	...	2038	...	...	2138	...	2238	...
	Brussels Nord ▷ d.		...	...	...	...	0644	...	...	and	1844	...	...	1944	...	...	2044	...	...	2144	...	2244	...
	Mechelen ▷ d.		...	...	...	...	0705	...	...	at	1904	...	...	2004	...	...	2104	...	...	2204	...	2304	...
0	**Antwerpen** Centraal d.		...	0545	0609	0646	|	0709	0747	the	|	1909	1947	|	2009	2047	|	2109	2147	|	2224	|	2324
2	Antwerpen Berchem d.		...	0552	0615	0652	|	0715	0752	same	|	1915	1952	|	2015	2052	|	2115	2152	|	2229	|	2329
15	Lier d.		...	0603	0627	0703	0723	0727	0803	minutes	1922	1927	2003	2022	2027	2103	2122	2127	2203	2222	2245	2322	2345
34	Herentals d.		...	0622	0643	0722	0739	0742	0822	past	1938	1942	2022	2038	2042	2122	2138	2142	2222	2238	2307	2338	0008
	Turnhout a.		...	0638	|	0738	0754	|	0838	each	1953	|	2038	2053	|	2138	2153	|	2238	2253	|	2353	|
46	Geel d.		...	...	0656	...	...	0755	...	hour	...	1955	...	...	2055	...	...	2155	...	...	2320	...	0021
56	Mol d.		0607	...	0705	...	...	0810	...	until	...	2010	...	...	2110	...	...	2210	...	...	2332	...	0028
99	**Hasselt** a.		0653	...	0754**r**	...	...	0853**r**	...		...	2053**r**	...	...	2153**r**	...	...	2253**r**	...	...	|	...	...
77	Overpelt d.		...	...	0721	...	...	0827	...		...	2027	...	...	2127	...	...	2227	...	...	2342	...	...
79	Neerpelt d.		...	...	0730	...	...	0832	...		...	2032	...	...	2132	...	...	2232	...	...	2350	...	...
87	**Hamont** a.		...	...	0738	...	...	0840	...		...	2040	...	...	2140	...	...	2240	...	...	...	...	...

km			Ⓐ	Ⓐ	Ⓐ	Ⓐ	Ⓐ	Ⓐ	Ⓐ	Ⓐ	Ⓐ	Ⓐ	Ⓐ		Ⓐ	Ⓐ	Ⓐ	Ⓐ	Ⓐ	Ⓐ	Ⓐ	Ⓐ	
	Hamont d.	Ⓐ	...	...	...	0526	...	...	0619	...	...	0719	...		...	1919	...	...	2019	...	2119	...	...
	Neerpelt d.		...	...	...	0536	...	...	0631	...	...	0730	...		...	1930	...	...	2030	...	2130	...	...
	Overpelt d.		...	...	...	0540	...	...	0634	...	...	0733	...	and	...	1933	...	...	2033	...	2133	...	...
	Hasselt d.		...	...	...	|	...	...	0607**s**	...	...	0707**s**	...	at	...	1907**s**	...	...	2007**s**	...	2107**s**	2207	...
	Mol d.		0458	...	...	0558	...	...	0658	...	...	0757	...	the	...	1958	...	...	2058	...	2158	2253	...
	Geel d.		0506	...	...	0606	...	...	0706	...	...	0805	...	same	...	2006	...	...	2106	...	2206	...	...
0	**Turnhout** d.		|	0504	0521	|	0604	0621	|	0704	0721	|	0804	minutes	1921	|	2004	2021	|	2104	|	...	...
18	Herentals d.		0519	0523	0543	0619	0623	0643	0719	0723	0743	0818	0823	past	1944	2019	2023	2044	2119	2123	2219	...	...
38	Lier d.		0535	0539	0558	0635	0639	0658	0735	0739	0758	0835	0839	each	1958	2035	2039	2058	2135	2139	2235	...	...
	Antwerpen Berchem d.		0547	|	0609	0647	|	0709	0747	|	0809	0847	|	hour	2009	2047	|	2109	2147	|	2247	...	...
	Antwerpen Centraal a.		0551	|	0613	0651	|	0713	0751	|	0813	0851	|	until	2013	2051	|	2113	2151	|	2251	...	...
55	Mechelen ▷ d.		...	0558	...	...	0658	...	...	0758	...	...	0858		...	...	2058	...	...	2158	...	...	...
75	Brussels Nord ▷ d.		...	0618	...	...	0718	...	...	0818	...	...	0918		...	...	2118	...	...	2218	...	...	...
77	Brussels Central ▷ d.		...	0623	...	...	0723	...	...	0823	...	...	0923		...	...	2123	...	...	2223	...	...	...
79	**Brussels** Midi / Zuid ▷ a.		...	0627	...	...	0727	...	...	0827	...	...	0927		...	...	2127	...	...	2227	...	...	...

		Ⓒ	Ⓒ	Ⓒ	Ⓒ		Ⓒ	Ⓒ △	Ⓒ ▽	Ⓒ
Antwerpen C. d.	Ⓒ	0609	0709	0753	0809		2009	2053	2109	2309
Ant. Berchem d.		0615	0715	0759	0815	and	2015	2059	2115	2315
Lier d.		0627	0727	0810	0827	at	2027	2110	2127	2327
Herentals d.		0642	0742	0832	0842	the	2042	2132	2142	2342
Turnhout a.		|	|	0847	|	same	|	2147	|	|
Geel d.		0655	0755	...	0855	minutes	2055	...	2155	2355
Mol d.		0710	0810	...	0910	past	2110	...	2210	0010
Hasselt a.		0753**x**	0853**x**	...	0953**x**	each	2153**x**	...	|	|
Overpelt d.		0727	0827	...	0927	hour	2127	...	2227	0027
Neerpelt d.		0732	0832	...	0932	until	2132	...	2232	0032
Hamont a.		0740	0840	...	0940		2140	...	2240	0040

		Ⓒ	Ⓒ	Ⓒ	Ⓒ	Ⓒ	Ⓒ		Ⓒ	Ⓒ	Ⓒ	Ⓒ
Hamont d.	Ⓒ	...	0619	...	0719	...	0819		2019	...	2119	...
Neerpelt d.		...	0630	...	0730	...	0830	and	2030	...	2130	...
Overpelt d.		...	0643	...	0733	...	0833	at	2033	...	2133	...
Hasselt d.		...	|	...	|	...	0807**z**	the	2007**z**	...	2107**z**	...
Mol d.		...	0658	...	0758	...	0858	same	2058	...	2158	...
Geel d.		...	0706	...	0806	...	0906	minutes	2106	...	2206	...
Turnhout d.		0616	|	0716	|	0816	|	past	|	2116	|	2216
Herentals d.		0632	0719	0732	0819	0832	0919	each	2119	2132	2219	2232
Lier d.		0652	0735	0752	0835	0852	0935	hour	2135	2152	2235	2252
Ant. Berchem d.		0704	0747	0804	0847	0904	0947	until	2147	2204	2247	2304
Antwerpen C. a.		0708	0751	0808	0851	0908	0951		2151	2208	2251	2308

r – Portion for Hasselt is detached from the main train at Mol (departs Mol xx07 or xx08).
s – Portion from Hasselt attaches to the main train at Mol (arrives Mol xx53; Hamont portion arrives xx49).
x – Hourly on ⑥. On ⑦ Hasselt is served every **two** hours (from Antwerpen even hours 0609 - 2009). Note **r** applies.
z – Hourly on ⑥. On ⑦ Hasselt is served every **two** hours (departing on even hours 0807 - 2008). Note **s** applies.

▷ – See also Table **420**.
△ – Also at 2153, 2253, 2353.
▽ – Also at 2209.

☛ *On Ⓐ Turnhout trains run beyond Brussels to / from Binche (Table* ***423****).*

Line 34 LIÈGE - HASSELT 435

km			Ⓐ	Ⓐ		Ⓐ		Ⓒ		Ⓒ
0	**Liège** Guillemins d.	Ⓐ	0619	0719	and	2119	Ⓒ	0637	and	2137
27	Tongeren **431** d.		0659	0800	hourly	2200		0716	hourly	2216
53	**Hasselt** **431** a.		0722	0823	until	2223		0738	until	2238

		Ⓐ	Ⓐ		Ⓐ		Ⓒ		Ⓒ
Hasselt **431** d.	Ⓐ	0537	0637	and	2037	Ⓒ	0620	and	2120
Tongeren **431** d.		0600	0700	hourly	2100		0643	hourly	2143
Liège Guillemins a.		0639	0739	until	2139		0723	until	2223

Line 40 LIÈGE - MAASTRICHT 436

km		Ⓐ	⚒					
0	**Liège** Guillemins d.	0508	0608	0708		2108	2208	2308
19	Visé 🏛 d.	0527	0627	0727	and	2127	2225	2327
32	**Maastricht** a.	0542	0642	0742	hourly	2142	2242	2342
	Heerlen **473** a.	0618	0718	0818	until	2218	2316	0018
	Aachen Hbf **473** a.	0642	0742	0842		2242	2342	0042

	Ⓐ	⚒			⊠				
Aachen Hbf **473** d.	...	0617	0717	0817		2017	2117	2215	2317
Heerlen **473** d.	...	0644	0744	0844	and	2044	2144	2244	2344
Maastricht d.	0616	0716	0816	0916	hourly	2116	2216	2316	0016
Visé 🏛 d.	0633	0736	0835	0933	until	2133	2233	2333	0033
Liège Guillemins a.	0650	0753	0852	0950		2150	2250	2350	0050

☛ **Note**: Belgian holiday dates apply.

Line 37 LIÈGE - VERVIERS - AACHEN 437

For international trains Brussels - Liège - Aachen and beyond see Tables **20** / **21**.

km								
0	**Liège** Guillemins **400** d.	0518		1918	2022	2120	2218	2318
20	Pepinster **400 438** d.	0546	and	1946	2049	2147	2246	2346
24	**Verviers** C **400 438** d.	0551	hourly	1951	2054	2152	2251	2351
37	Welkenraedt 🏛 **400** d.	0607	until	2007	2108	2206	2306	0006
58	**Aachen** Hbf a.	0622		2022	2122	2222	...	...

Aachen Hbf d.	...	...	0637	0737	0837	0937		2137	2237
Welkenraedt 🏛 **400** d.	0453	0553	0654	0753	0854	0953	and	2153	2254
Verviers C **400 438** d.	0509	0609	0709	0808	0909	1008	hourly	2208	2309
Pepinster **400 438** d.	0514	0614	0714	0813	0914	1013	until	2213	2314
Liège Guillemins **400** a.	0541	0639	0741	0838	0941	1038		2238	2341

Line 44 SPA - PEPINSTER - VERVIERS 438

km		Ⓐ	Ⓐ					Ⓒ	
0	Spa Géronstère d.	0538	0638	0738	and	1938	2038	2138	...
1	**Spa** d.	0541	0641	0741	hourly	1941	2041	2141	...
13	Pepinster **400 437** d.	0601	0701	0801	until	2001	2101	2201	...
17	**Verviers** Central **400 437** a.	0606	0706	0806		2006	2106	2206	...

							Ⓒ	
Verviers Central **400 437** d.	0654	0754	0854	and	1954	2054	2154	...
Pepinster **400 437** d.	0701	0801	0901	hourly	2001	2101	2201	...
Spa d.	0721	0821	0921	until	2021	2121	2221	...
Spa Géronstère a.	0723	0823	0923		2023	2123	2223	...

440 BRUSSELS - NAMUR - DINANT

Lines 161, 154

km			Ⓐ	Ⓐ	Ⓐ	Ⓐ	Ⓐ	Ⓐ	Ⓐ	Ⓐ	Ⓐ	Ⓐ	Ⓐ		Ⓐ	Ⓐ	Ⓐ	Ⓐ	Ⓐ		Ⓐ	Ⓐ	Ⓐ	
	Brussels Airport ✈ d.	Ⓐ	...	...	...	0617	...	...	0717	...	...	0817	...	and	...	2117	...	...	...		...	...	...	...
0	**Brussels** Midi / Zuid d.		...	0532	0603	|	0632	0703	|	0733	0803	|	0832	at	2103	|	2132	2203	2232	A	1607	1636	1807	...
2	Brussels Central d.		...	0537	0608	|	0637	0708	|	0738	0808	|	0837	the	2108	|	2137	2208	2237	L	1612	1641	1812	...
4	**Brussels** Nord d.		...	0543	0614	|	0643	0714	|	0744	0814	|	0843	same	2114	|	2143	2214	2243	S	1622	1652	1822	...
9	Brussels Schuman d.		...	0552	0623	0633	0652	0723	0733	0752	0823	0833	0852	minutes	2123	2133	2152	2223	2252	O	1630	1700	1830	...
10	Brussels Luxembourg d.		...	0556	0627	0638	0656	0727	0738	0756	0827	0838	0856	past	2127	2138	2156	2227	2256		1634	1705	1834	...
33	Ottignies d.		...	0617	0649	0702	0717	0749	0802	0817	0849	0902	0917	each	2149	2202	2217	2249	2320		1656	1727	1854	...
48	Gembloux d.		...	0630	0703	0715	0730	0803	0815	0830	0903	0915	0930	hour	2203	2215	2230	2303	2334		1710	1740	1907	...
65	**Namur** ▷ d.		0631	0643	0720	0731	0743	0820	0831	0843	0920	0931	0943	until	2220	2231	2243	2320	2346		1723	1754	1921	...
	Liège Guillemins **442** a.		|	◇	0808	|	◇	0908	|	◇	1008		◇		2308	|	◇	0008	◇		◇	...	◇	...
93	**Dinant** ▷ a.		0703	...	...	0803	...	...	0903	...	...	1003	...		...	2303	...	...	...		...	...	...	...

		Ⓐ	Ⓐ	Ⓐ	Ⓐ	Ⓐ	Ⓐ	Ⓐ	Ⓐ	Ⓐ	Ⓐ		Ⓐ	Ⓐ	Ⓐ	Ⓐ	Ⓐ	Ⓐ		Ⓐ	Ⓐ	Ⓐ	Ⓐ
Dinant ▷ d.	Ⓐ	...	...	0457	...	...	0557	...	...	0657	...		...	2057	...	2138	...	...		...	...	...	...
Liège Guillemins **442** d.		...	◇	|	0451	◇	|	0551	◇	|	0651	and	◇	|	2051	|	◇	2151		◇	◇	...	...
Namur d.		0420	0519	0529	0544	0616	0632	0644	0716	0732	0744	at	2116	2132	2144	2208	2216	2241	A	0637	0737	0837	0941
Gembloux d.		0434	0532	...	0559	0630	0646	0659	0730	0746	0759	the	2130	2146	2159	...	2230	...	L	0651	0752	0852	|
Ottignies d.		0449	0545	...	0613	0644	0659	0713	0744	0759	0813	same	2144	2159	2213	...	2244	...	S	0705	0806	0906	|
Brussels Luxembourg d.		0519	0606	...	0634	0705	0722	0734	0805	0822	0834	minutes	2205	2222	2234	...	2305	...	O	0727	0827	0927	1027
Brussels Schuman d.		0522	0609	...	0638	0709	0726	0738	0809	0826	0838	past	2209	2226	2238	...	2309	...		0731	0831	0931	1031
Brussels Nord d.		0531	0619	...	0648	0719	|	0748	0819	|	0848	each	2219	|	2248	...	2319	...		0742	0842	0944	1044
Brussels Central d.		0535	0624	...	0653	0724	|	0753	0824	|	0853	hour	2224	|	2253	...	2324	...		0747	0847	0949	1049
Brussels Midi / Zuid a.		0539	0628	...	0657	0728	|	0757	0828	|	0857	until	2228	|	2257	...	2328	...		0751	0851	0953	1053
Brussels Airport ✈ a.		...	...	...	...	...	0743	...	...	0843	...		...	2243	...	...	...	...		...	...	...	...

		Ⓒ	Ⓒ	Ⓒ	Ⓒ		Ⓒ	Ⓒ	Ⓒ	Ⓒ	Ⓒ
Brussels Midi / Zuid d.	Ⓒ	0603	0632	0703	0732	and	2103	2132	2203	2232	2332
Brussels Central d.		0607	0637	0707	0737	at	2107	2137	2207	2237	2337
Brussels Nord d.		0614	0643	0714	0743	the	2114	2143	2214	2243	2343
Brussels Schuman d.		0623	0652	0723	0752	same	2123	2152	2223	2252	2352
Brussels Luxembourg d.		0628	0656	0728	0756	minutes	2128	2156	2228	2256	2356
Ottignies d.		0649	0717	0749	0817	past	2149	2217	2249	2317	0017
Gembloux d.		0702	0730	0802	0831	each	2202	2230	2303	2330	0030
Namur ▷ d.		0717	0743	0817	0844	hour	2217	2243	2316	2343	0043
Dinant ▷ a.		0749	◇	0849	◇	until	2249	◇	...	...	...

		Ⓒ	Ⓒ	Ⓒ	Ⓒ	Ⓒ		Ⓒ	Ⓒ
Dinant ▷ d.	Ⓒ	...	...	...	0613	◇	and	2113	◇
Namur d.		0515	0547	0616	0647	0716	at	2147	2216
Gembloux d.		0530	0600	0630	0700	0730	the	2200	2230
Ottignies d.		0544	0613	0644	0713	0744	same	2213	2244
Brussels Luxembourg d.		0605	0635	0705	0735	0805	minutes	2235	2305
Brussels Schuman d.		0609	0639	0709	0739	0809	past	2239	2309
Brussels Nord d.		0619	0649	0719	0749	0819	each	2249	2319
Brussels Central d.		0624	0653	0724	0753	0824	hour	2253	2324
Brussels Midi / Zuid a.		0628	0657	0728	0757	0828	until	2257	2328

◇ – To / from Arlon, Luxembourg or other destinations in Table **445**.

▷ – See also Table **448**.

442 NAMUR - LIÈGE

Line 125

km			Ⓐ	Ⓐ	Ⓐ	Ⓐ	Ⓐ	Ⓐ		Ⓐ	Ⓐ	Ⓐ	Ⓐ	Ⓐ		Ⓒ	Ⓒ	Ⓒ ▽	Ⓒ ▽		Ⓒ ▽	Ⓒ ▽	Ⓒ ▽
	Mons **425** d.	Ⓐ	0437	...	0538	...	0638	...	and at	1938	...	2038	...	...	Ⓒ	...	0607	0707	0807		1907	2007	2107
	Charleroi Central **425** d.		0513	...	0619	...	0719	...	the	2019	...	2119	...	...		...	0655	0755	0855		1955	2055	2155
	Brussels Midi / Zuid **440** . § d.		|	...	|	0603	|	0703	same	|	2003	|	2103	2203		...	|	|	|	and	|	|	|
0	**Namur** d.		0553	0620	0653	0720	0753	0820	minutes	2053	2120	2153	2220	2320		0628	0728	0828	0928	hourly	2028	2128	2228
20	Andenne d.		0606	0634	0706	0734	0806	0834	past	2106	2134	2206	2234	2334		0642	0742	0842	0942	until	2042	2142	2242
31	Huy d.		0615	0645	0715	0745	0815	0845	each	2115	2145	2215	2245	2345		0653	0753	0853	0953		2053	2153	2253
60	**Liège** Guillemins d.		0638	0711	0738	0811	0838	0911	hour	2138	2211	2238	2311	0011		0717	0817	0917	1017		2117	2217	2317
63	**Liège** St Lambert a.		0646	0719	0746	0819	0846	0919	until	2146	2219	2246	2319	0019		0726	0826	0926	1026		2126	2226	2326

		Ⓐ	Ⓐ	Ⓐ	Ⓐ	Ⓐ	Ⓐ	Ⓐ		Ⓐ	Ⓐ	Ⓐ	Ⓐ	Ⓐ		Ⓒ ▽	Ⓒ ▽	Ⓒ ▽	Ⓒ ▽		Ⓒ ▽	Ⓒ	Ⓒ
Liège St Lambert d.	Ⓐ	0441	0513	0541	0613	0641	0713	0741	and at	2013	2041	2113	2141	2213	Ⓒ	0633	0733	0833	0933		2033	2133	...
Liège Guillemins d.		0451	0524	0551	0624	0651	0724	0751	the	2024	2051	2124	2151	2224		0645	0745	0845	0945		2045	2145	2245
Huy d.		0514	0545	0614	0645	0714	0745	0814	same	2045	2114	2145	2214	2245		0707	0807	0907	1007	and	2107	2207	2307
Andenne d.		0525	0554	0625	0654	0725	0754	0825	minutes	2054	2125	2154	2225	2254		0718	0818	0918	1018	hourly	2118	2218	2318
Namur d.		0544	0611	0644	0711	0744	0811	0844	past	2111	2144	2210	2241	2310		0733	0833	0933	1033	until	2133	2234	2333
Brussels Midi / Zuid **440** .. § a.		0657	|	0757	|	0857	|	0957	each	|	2257	|	...	|		|	|	|	|		|	|	...
Charleroi Central **425** d.		...	0646	...	0746	...	0846	...	hour	2146	...	2250	...	2347		0807	0907	1007	1107		2207	2307	...
Mons **425** a.		...	0722	...	0822	...	0922	...	until	2222	...	2327	...	...		0856	0956	1056	1156		2256	...	...

§ – For direct trains Brussels - Liège see Table **400**.

▽ – From / to Mouscron via Tournai (Table **416**).

☛ On Ⓒ trains continue beyond Liège to / from Liers.

445 (BRUSSELS -) NAMUR - LUXEMBOURG

Line 162

km			Ⓐ	Ⓐ	Ⓐ	Ⓐ	Ⓐ		Ⓐ	Ⓐ	Ⓐ	Ⓐ		Ⓐ	Ⓐ		Ⓒ	Ⓒ		Ⓒ	Ⓒ	Ⓒ	Ⓒ
	Brussels Midi / Zuid **440** d.	Ⓐ	...	...	0532	0632	0733		1932	2032	2132	2232		1607	1807	Ⓒ	0632	0732		1832	1932	2032	2132
	Brussels Nord **440** d.		...	...	0543	0643	0744		1943	2043	2143	2243		1622	1822		0643	0743		1843	1943	2043	2143
	Brussels Luxembourg **440** d.		...	...	0556	0656	0756		1956	2056	2156	2256		1634	1834		0656	0756		1856	1956	2056	2156
0	**Namur** d.		0536	0603	0647	0747	0847	and	2047	2147	2247	2348	A	1725	1923		0746	0846	and	1946	2046	2146	2246
29	Ciney d.		0558	0621	0703	0804	0903	hourly	2103	2203	2304	0004	L	1801	1939		0802	0902	hourly	2002	2102	2202	2302
52	Marloie d.		0617	0646	0722	0823	0922	until	2122	2222	2323	...	S	1820	2001		0821	0921	until	2021	2121	2221	2321
58	Rochefort-Jemelle d.		0623	0651	0728	0829	0928	⊡	2128	2228	2328	...	O	1825	2007		0828	0928	⊡	2028	2128	2228	2326
90	Libramont d.		0656	0719	0756	0856	0956		2155	2256	...	...		...	...		0856	0956		2056	2156	2256	...
137	Arlon a.		0722	0753	0822	0922	1022		2222	2322	...	...		...	...		0922	1022		2122	2222	2322	...
137	Arlon ▷ d.		0729	0801	0829	0929	1029		2229	2329	...	...		...	...		0929	1029		2129	2229	2329	...
165	**Luxembourg** ▷ a.		0749	0825	0849	0949	1049		2249	2349	...	...		...	...		0949	1049		2149	2249	2349	...

		Ⓐ	Ⓐ	Ⓐ	Ⓐ	Ⓐ	Ⓐ	Ⓐ	Ⓐ	Ⓐ		Ⓐ	Ⓐ	Ⓐ	Ⓐ	Ⓐ		Ⓒ	Ⓒ	Ⓒ		Ⓒ	Ⓒ
Luxembourg ▷ d.	Ⓐ	...	...	...	0511	...	0611	0711	0741	0811		2011	2111	2211	2311	2400	Ⓒ	...	0611	0711		2011	*2111*
Arlon ▷ a.		...	...	...	0531	...	0631	0731	0801	0831		2031	2131	2231	2331	0029		...	0631	0731		2031	*2131*
Arlon d.		...	0436	...	0536	...	0636	0736	0815	0836		2036	2136	...	...	...		...	0636	0736		2036	2136
Libramont d.		...	0507	...	0607	...	0708	0807	0843	0907	and	2107	2207	...	...	...		...	0707	0807	and	2107	2207
Rochefort-Jemelle d.		0436	0531	0553	0631	0635	0732	0831	|	0931	hourly	2131	2231	...	...	...		0631	0731	0831	hourly	2131	2230
Marloie d.		0444	0539	0602	0639	0644	0740	0839	|	0939	until	2139	2239	...	...	...		0639	0739	0839	until	2139	...
Ciney d.		0502	0557	0619	0656	0716	0757	0856	|	0956	♡	2156	2256	...	...	...		0656	0756	0856	♡	2156	...
Namur d.		0519	0616	0637	0716	0737	0816	0916	0941	1016		2216	2312	...	...	...		0716	0815	0915		2216	...
Brussels Luxembourg **440** .. d.		0606	0705	0727	0805	0827	0905	1005	1027	1105		2305	...	...	...	...		0805	0905	1005		2305	...
Brussels Nord **440** d.		0619	0719	0742	0819	0842	0919	1019	1044	1119		2319	...	...	...	...		0819	0919	1019		2319	...
Brussels Midi / Zuid **440** a.		0628	0728	0751	0828	0851	0928	1028	1053	1128		2328	...	...	...	...		0828	0928	1028		2328	...

⊡ – A change of train at Arlon is required for the following departures from Brussels: Ⓐ – 0832, 1532, 1632, 1733; ⑥ – 1132; ⑦ – 1032, 1432, 1832, 1932, 2032.

♡ – A change of train at Arlon is required for the departures from Luxembourg: Ⓐ 0511, 0611, 1211; ⑦ – 0611, 1411.

▷ – Additional local trains run Arlon - Kleinbettingen 🚍 - Luxembourg (journey time: 20 – 30 minutes).

LIÈGE - GOUVY - CLERVAUX - LUXEMBOURG — 446

Line 43 / L10

km		Ⓐ	Ⓐ					A		A		A		A		A		A		A		A		
0	**Liège** Guillemins **447** d.	...	...	...	...	...	0607	0707	0807	0907	1007	1107	1207	1307	1407	1507	1607	1707	1807	1907	2007	2107	2207	...
23	Rivage **447** d.	...	...	...	...	...	0632	0732	0832	0932	1032	1132	1232	1332	1432	1532	1632	1732	1832	1932	2032	2132	2232	...
31	Aywaille d.	...	...	...	...	...	0640	0740	0840	0940	1040	1140	1240	1340	1440	1540	1640	1740	1840	1940	2040	2140	2240	...
58	Trois-Ponts d.	...	...	...	...	...	0702	0802	0902	1002	1102	1202	1302	1402	1502	1602	1702	1802	1902	2002	2102	2202	2302	...
70	Vielsalm d.	...	...	...	...	...	0712	0812	0912	1012	1112	1212	1312	1412	1512	1612	1712	1812	1912	2014	2114	2214	2312	...
81	Gouvy 🏨 d.	...	...	...	0523a	0623a	0724	0824	0924	1024	1124	1224	1324	1424	1524	1624	1724	1824	1924	2024	2124	2224	2322	...
91	Troisvierges d.	0405	0435	0505	0535	0635	0735	0835	0935	1035	1135	1235	1335	1435	1535	1635	1735	1835	1935	2035	2135	2235	...	...
99	**Clervaux** d.	0414	0444	0514	0544	0644	0744	0844	0944	1044	1144	1244	1344	1444	1544	1644	1744	1844	1944	2044	2144	2244	...	...
114	Kautenbach d.	0431	0501	0531	0601	0701	0801	0901	1001	1101	1201	1301	1401	1501	1601	1701	1801	1901	2001	2101	2201	2301	...	...
129	Ettelbruck d.	0446	0516	0546	0616	0716	0816	0916	1016	1116	1216	1316	1416	1516	1616	1716	1816	1916	2016	2116	2216	2316	...	...
141	Mersch d.	0456	0528	0556	0628	0728	0828	0928	1028	1128	1228	1328	1428	1528	1628	1728	1828	1928	2028	2128	2228	2328	...	...
160	**Luxembourg** a.	0515	0546	0615	0646	0746	0846	0946	1046	1146	1246	1346	1446	1546	1646	1746	1846	1946	2046	2146	2246	2346	...	...

	Ⓐ	Ⓐ	B	Ⓐ	B		B		B		B		B		B		B		B				
Luxembourg d.	...	...	0516	...	0616	0716	0816	0916	1016	1116	1216	1316	1416	1516	1616	1716	1816	1916	2016	2116	2216	2316	...
Mersch d.	...	...	0533	...	0633	0733	0833	0933	1033	1133	1233	1333	1433	1533	1633	1733	1833	1933	2033	2133	2233	2333	...
Ettelbruck d.	...	...	0545	...	0645	0745	0845	0945	1045	1145	1245	1345	1445	1545	1645	1745	1845	1945	2045	2145	2245	2345	...
Kautenbach d.	...	...	0600	...	0700	0800	0900	1000	1100	1200	1300	1400	1500	1600	1700	1800	1900	2000	2100	2200	2300	2400	...
Clervaux d.	...	...	0616	...	0716	0816	0916	1016	1116	1216	1316	1416	1516	1616	1716	1816	1916	2016	2116	2216	2316	0016	...
Troisvierges d.	...	...	0633	...	0733	0833	0933	1033	1133	1233	1333	1433	1533	1633	1733	1833	1933	2033	2133	2233	2324	0024	...
Gouvy 🏨 d.	0506	0542	0643	0712	0743	0843	0943	1043	1143	1243	1343	1443	1543	1643	1743	1843	1943	2043	2143	2243	...	...	...
Vielsalm d.	0516	0552	0652	0722	0752	0852	0952	1052	1152	1252	1352	1452	1552	1652	1752	1852	1952	2052	2152	2252	...	...	...
Trois-Ponts d.	0527	0602	0702	0733	0802	0902	1002	1102	1202	1302	1402	1502	1602	1702	1802	1902	2002	2102	2202	2302	...	...	...
Aywaille d.	0549	0623	0723	0802	0823	0923	1023	1123	1223	1323	1423	1523	1623	1723	1823	1923	2023	2123	2223	2323	...	...	...
Rivage **447** d.	0557	0631	0731	0810	0831	0931	1031	1131	1231	1331	1431	1531	1631	1731	1831	1931	2031	2131	2231	2331	...	...	...
Liège Guillemins **447** a.	0622	0655	0755	0835	0855	0955	1055	1155	1255	1355	1455	1555	1655	1755	1855	1955	2055	2155	2255	2355	...	...	...

A – Runs ①–⑤ (not Belgian holidays) Liège - Troisvierges; daily Troisvierges - Luxembourg.
B – Runs daily Luxemourg - Troisvierges; ①–⑤ (not Belgian holidays) Troisvierges - Liège.

a – ①–⑤ (not Belgian holidays).

ADDITIONAL TRAINS TROISVIERGES - CLERVAUX - LUXEMBOURG:
From Troisvierges hourly 0605Ⓐ - 2205Ⓐ. From Luxembourg hourly 0544Ⓐ - 2344Ⓐ.

CONNECTING TRAINS KAUTENBACH - WILTZ (journey 12–14 minutes):
From Kautenbach: On Ⓐ every 30 minutes 0533 - 2303 then 0003; on Ⓒ hourly 0603, 0703, 0804 - 2304.
From Wiltz: On Ⓐ every 30 minutes 0416 - 2246 then 2346; on Ⓒ hourly 0546 - 0746, and 0842 - 2342.

LIÈGE - MARLOIE - ROCHEFORT JEMELLE — 447

Line 43

km			Ⓐ	Ⓐ		Ⓐ	Ⓐ	Ⓐ	Ⓐ	Ⓐ	Ⓐ	Ⓐ	Ⓐ		Ⓒ	Ⓒ	Ⓒ	Ⓒ	Ⓒ	Ⓒ	Ⓒ	Ⓒ
0	**Liège** St Lambert d.	Ⓐ	0600	0700		1600	...	1700	1800	1900	2000	2100	2200	Ⓒ	0802	1002	1202	1402	1602	1802	2002	2202
3	**Liège** Guillemins **446** d.		0612	0712	and	1612	1644	1712	1812	1912	2012	2112	2212		0813	1013	1213	1413	1613	1813	2013	2213
26	Rivage **446** d.		0642	0742	hourly	1642	1714	1742	1842	1942	2042	2142	2242		0843	1043	1243	1443	1643	1843	2043	2243
46	Barvaux d.		0706	0806	until	1706	1739	1806	1906	2006	2106	2206	2306		0906	1106	1306	1506	1706	1906	2106	2306
68	Marloie **445** d.		0724	0824		1724	1803	1824	1924	2024	2132	2226	2326		0924	1124	1324	1524	1724	1924	2124	2326
74	**Rochefort-Jemelle** **445** a.		...	...		...	1808	...	...	...	2138	2232	2332		...	...	...	...	...	...	...	2332

		Ⓐ	Ⓐ	Ⓐ	Ⓐ	Ⓐ	Ⓐ		Ⓐ	Ⓐ			Ⓒ	Ⓒ	Ⓒ	Ⓒ	Ⓒ	Ⓒ	Ⓒ	Ⓒ		
Rochefort-Jemelle **445** d.	Ⓐ	0426	0526	0603	...	...	...		...	...	...	Ⓒ	0728	...	...	...	...	...	...	...	...	...
Marloie **445** d.		0436	0536	0609	0636	0736	0836	and	1936	2036	...		0736	0936	1136	1336	1536	1736	1936	2136	...	...
Barvaux d.		0454	0554	0628	0654	0754	0854	hourly	1954	2054	...		0754	0954	1154	1354	1554	1754	1954	2154	...	...
Rivage **446** d.		0518	0618	0653	0718	0818	0918	until	2018	2118	...		0823	1023	1223	1423	1618	1818	2018	2218	...	...
Liège Guillemins **446** d.		0551	0651	0726	0751	0851	0951		2051	2151	...		0851	1051	1251	1451	1651	1851	2051	2251	...	...
Liège St Lambert a.		0558	0658	0734	0758	0858	0958		2058	2158	...		0858	1058	1258	1458	1658	1858	2058	2258	...	...

ARDENNES LOCAL SERVICES — 448

Lines 154, 166, 165

km			Ⓐ		Ⓐ	Ⓐ	Ⓐ	Ⓐ		Ⓒ		Ⓒ
0	**Namur** ... **440** d.	Ⓐ	0846	and	1346	1452	1552	1652	Ⓒ	0552	and	1952
28	Dinant.... **440** d.		0917	hourly	1417	1523	1623	1723		0623	every	2023
43	Houyet d.		0941	until	1441	1541	1641	1741		0641	**two**	2041
52	Beauraing d.		0950	•	1450	1550	1650	1750		0650	hours	2050
100	Bertrix d.		1037		1537	1637	1737	1837		0737	until	2137
108	**Libramont** a.		1046		1546	1646	1746	1846		0746		2146

		Ⓐ	Ⓐ	Ⓐ		Ⓐ		Ⓒ		Ⓒ
Libramont d.	Ⓐ	0614	0714	0814	and	1314	Ⓒ	0714	and	1914
Bertrix d.		0632	0732	0832	hourly	1332		0732	every	1932
Beauraing d.		0711	0811	0911	until	1411		0811	**two**	2011
Houyet d.		0719	0819	0919	▲	1419		0819	hours	2019
Dinant **440** d.		0738	0838	0944		1444		0838	until	2038
Namur **440** a.		0808	0908	1015		1515		0909		2109

km			Ⓐ		Ⓐ	Ⓐ‡		Ⓒ		Ⓒ
0	**Libramont** d.	Ⓐ	0657		2057	2157	Ⓒ	0757	and	2157
8	Bertrix d.		0707	and	2107	2206		0807	every	2207
33	Florenville d.		0720	hourly	2120	...		0820	**two**	2220
57	Virton d.		0739	until	2139	...		0839	hours	2239
85	Athus ▷ d.		0802		2202	...		0902	until	2302
98	**Arlon** a.		0818		2218	...		0918		2318

		Ⓐ	Ⓐ		Ⓐ		Ⓒ		Ⓒ
Arlon d.	Ⓐ	0540	0640		2140	Ⓒ	0540		1940
Athus ▷ d.		0601	0701	and	2201		0601	and	2001
Virton d.		0622	0722	hourly	2222		0622	every	2022
Florenville d.		0639	0738	until	2239		0639	**two**	2039
Bertrix d.		0654	0753		2254		0654	hours	2054
Libramont a.		0703	0802		2303		0703	until	2103

• – Additional journeys on Ⓐ from **Namur** at 0551, 0652, 0752, 1752, 1852 and 1952.
▲ – Additional journeys on Ⓐ from **Libramont** at 1414, 1514, 1614, 1714, 1814 and 1914.
▷ – Athus - Luxembourg: see Table **449**.
‡ – Also 2257 Ⓐ to Bertrix.

LUXEMBOURG – local services — 449

Operator: CFL

		⚒		⚒		†		†		†
Luxembourg **446** d.	⚒	0453	every	2353	†	0453	and	1153	every	2353
Ettelbruck **446** d.		0535	30	0035		0535	hourly	1235	30	0035
Diekirch a.		0540	minutes until	0040		0540	until	1240	mins until	0040

		⚒		⚒		†		†		†
Diekirch d.	⚒	0421	every	2321	†	0551	and	1051	every	2321
Ettelbruck **446** d.		0428	30	2328		0558	hourly	1058	30	2328
Luxembourg **446** a.		0508	minutes	0008		0638	until	1138	minutes	0008

		⚒		⚒	†	†		†		†
Luxembourg d.	⚒	0520	every	2350		0550	and	1150	every	2350
Pétange d.		0544	30	0014		0614	hourly	1214	30	0014
Rodange d.		0550	minutes	0020		0620	until	1220	minutes	0020
Athus (Belgium) ▷ a.		0555		0025		0625		1225		0025

		⚒		⚒		†		†		†
Athus (Belgium) ▷ d.	⚒	0435	every	2335	†	0635	and	1135	every	2335
Rodange d.		0441	30	2341		0641	hourly	1141	30	2341
Pétange d.		0446	mins	2346		0646	until	1146	minutes	2346
Luxembourg a.		0510		0010		0710		1210		0010

Luxembourg → Bettembourg → Esch-sur-Alzette → Pétange → Rodange
(journey 10–13 mins to Bettembourg, 23–25 mins to Esch, 46–51 mins to Pétange, 48–57 mins to Rodange):
⚒: 0521 and approx. every 30 minutes to 1921, 1932 and every 30 minutes until 2332, 0002.
†: 0502 and hourly to 2302, 0002.

Rodange → Pétange → Esch-sur-Alzette → Bettembourg → Luxembourg
(journey 4–5 mins to Pétange, 23–29 mins to Esch, 35–41 mins to Bettembourg, 48–56 mins to Luxembourg):
⚒: 0451, 0551, 0621, 0651 and every 30 minutes to 1921, 2032 and every 30 minutes to 2332.
†: 0432, 0532 and hourly to 1232 and every 30 minutes to 2302, 2332.

Luxembourg → Wasserbillig (journey 31–42 minutes):
0510 Ⓐ, 0542 Ⓒ and approx. every 30 minutes to 2342 (some continue to Trier, Table **915**).

Wasserbillig → Luxembourg (journey 35–42 minutes):
0435, and approx. every 30 minutes to 2335, 0006 (some from Trier, Table **915**).

Luxembourg → Kleinbettingen (journey 19–21 minutes) ⊠:
Ⓐ: 0439, 0525 and approx. every 30 minutes to 2055, 2120, 2220, 2320, 2400.
Ⓒ: 0439, 0545 and hourly to 2245.

Kleinbettingen → Luxembourg (journey 19–21 minutes) ⊠:
Ⓐ: 0440, 0515, 0546, 0615, 0636 and approx. every 30 mins to 2115, 2150, 2250, 2350.
Ⓒ: 0515⑥ 0615 and hourly to 2315.

Bettembourg → Dudelange → **Volmerange-les-Mines** (journey 17 minutes):
0440, 0510 and approx. every 30 mins to 1940, 2018, 2048 and every 30 mins to 0018.
† runs only to Dudelange Usines, hourly from 0518–1218, then every 30 mins to 0018.

Volmerange-les-Mines → Dudelange → **Bettembourg** (journey 19 minutes):
0444, 0514, 0544, 0614, 0644, 0704, 0734 and every 30 mins to 1204 then 1244, 1314 then xx14 and xx44 until 1944, then 2022, 2052 and xx22 and xx52 until 2352, 0022.
† runs only from Dudelange Usines, hourly from 0600–1400, then every 30 mins to 0030.

▷ – For connections to / from Arlon see Table **448**.
⊠ – Certain trains continue to / from Arlon (Belgium).

NETHERLANDS

SEE MAP PAGE 231

Operator: **NS** – Nederlandse Spoorwegen (unless otherwise indicated) www.ns.nl

Services: Trains convey first- and second-class seated accommodation unless otherwise indicated in the tables. Domestic trains using the Amsterdam Zuid - Schiphol ✈ - Rotterdam - Breda high-speed line (Table **460**) are designated *Intercity direct*, whilst the fast Brussels trains are designated *Eurocity Direct* (see under Supplements below). Other domestic fast trains are designated *Intercity (IC)*, whilst local stopping trains are known as *Sprinter* trains (shown as *RE* on station departure boards). Some trains consist of portions for two or more destinations - be careful to join the correct part of the train.

Timings: Valid **until December 13**, 2025.

Holidays: Unless otherwise indicated, a **Sunday** service operates on Dec. 25, 26, Jan. 1, Apr. 21, June 9. A **Saturday** service operates on May 29 (Ascension Day).
No trains, other than international services, will run between ± 2000 hours on Dec. 31 and ± 0200 on Jan. 1.

Tickets: A nationwide smartcard system called *OV-chipkaart* is used for all public transport in the Netherlands. Personalised and anonymous cards can be loaded and topped up with travel credit, or disposable single use cards can be purchased from ticket machines (a €1 supplement is payable for single use cards). Alternatively, e-tickets may be purchased on-line and printed yourself. You must always check-in and check-out your OV-chipkaart for each journey. *Eurocity Direct* trains require specific tickets south of Rotterdam.

Supplements: A supplement of €3.00 is payable for journeys on the section of high-speed line between Schiphol ✈ and Rotterdam (Table **460**), also for internal journeys on *ICE* trains between Amsterdam and Arnhem. Supplements may be purchased from special Supplement Pillars (using your OV-chipkaart), from ticket machines, or online.

450 AMSTERDAM - DEN HAAG - ROTTERDAM - ROOSENDAAL - VLISSINGEN *IC trains*

For high-speed services Amsterdam Zuid - Schiphol ✈ - Rotterdam see Table **460**. For Amsterdam Centraal - Rotterdam via Gouda see Table **455**.

km																							
		Ⓐ	Ⓐ	①–③	④⑤	⑥	⚒	Ⓐ	Ⓒ		Ⓐ	Ⓒ			Ⓐ	Ⓒ							
0	**Amsterdam** Centraal ..... **458** d.	...	...	0506	...	...	0536	0605	...	0636	0706	0706	0736		1806	1806	1836	1906	1936	2006	2036	2106	2136
5	Amsterdam Sloterdijk ..... **458** d.	...	...	0511	...	...	0541	0610	...	0641	0711	0711	0741	and at	1811	1811	1841	1911	1941	2011	2041	2111	2141
19	**Haarlem** ..... **458** d.	...	...	0523	0525	...	0553	0623	...	0653	0723	0723	0753		1823	1823	1853	1923	1953	2023	2053	2123	2153
47	Leiden Centraal ..... **452** d.	...	...	0545	0545	...	0615	0645	...	0715	0745	0745	0815	the	1845	1845	1915	1945	2015	2045	2115	2145	2215
63	**Den Haag** HS ..... **452 472** d.	...	...	0559	0559	...	0629	0659	...	0729	0759	0759	0829	same	1859	1859	1929	1959	2029	2059	2129	2159	2229
71	Delft ..... **452 472** d.	...	...	0606	0606	...	0636	0706	...	0735	0806	0805	0835		1906	1905	1935	2005	2036	2105	2136	2205	2236
81	Schiedam Centrum ..... **452** d.	...	...	0614	0614	...	0644	0714	...	0743	0814	0813	0843	minutes	1914	1913	1943	2013	2044	2113	2144	2213	2244
85	**Rotterdam** Centraal **452 472** a.	...	...	0619	0619	...	0649	0719	...	0749	0819	0818	0849	past	1919	1918	1949	2018	2049	2118	2149	2218	2249
85	**Rotterdam** Centraal **452 472** d.	...	...	0621	0621	...	0651	0721	...	0751	0821	0821	0851		1921	1921	1951	2021	2051	2121	2151	2221	2251
105	Dordrecht ..... **452 472** d.	...	...	0637	0637	...	0707	0737	...	0807	0837	0837	0907	each	1937	1937	2007	2037	2107	2137	2207	2237	2307
143	**Roosendaal** ..... a.	...	...	0700	0700	...	0730	0800	...	0830	0900	0900	0930		2000	2000	2030	2100	2130	2200	2230	2300	2330
143	**Roosendaal** ..... d.	0606	0638	0703	0703	0706	0736	0803	0806	0836	0903	0906	0936	hour	2003	2006	2036	2106	2136	2206	2236	2306	2336
156	Bergen op Zoom ..... d.	0615	0647	0712	0712	0715	0745	0812	0815	0845	0912	0915	0945	until	2012	2015	2045	2115	2145	2215	2245	2315	2345
193	Goes ..... d.	0646	0715	0732	0732	0746	0816	0832	0846	0916	0932	0946	1016		2032	2046	2116	2146	2216	2246	2316	2346	0016
212	Middelburg ..... d.	0701	0729	0744	0744	0801	0831	0844	0901	0931	0944	1001	1031		2044	2101	2131	2201	2231	2301	2331	0001	0031
218	**Vlissingen** ..... a.	0709	0737	0751	0751	0809	0839	0851	0909	0939	0951	1009	1039		2051	2109	2139	2209	2239	2309	2340	0010	0039

					⑤⑥		b	⑦
Amsterdam Centraal ..... **458** d.	2206	2236	2306	2336	2336	0006	0035	0106
Amsterdam Sloterdijk ..... **458** d.	2211	2241	2311	2341	2341	0011	0040	0111
Haarlem ..... **458** d.	2223	2253	2323	2353	2353	0023	0051	0123
Leiden Centraal ..... **452** d.	2245	2315	2345	0015	0015	0045	0114	0145
Den Haag HS ..... **452 472** d.	2259	2329	2359	0029	0029	0059	0129	0200
Delft ..... **452 472** d.	2305	2336	0005	0036	0036	0105	0136	0206
Schiedam Centrum ..... **452** d.	2313	2344	0013	0044	0044	0113	0144	0214
Rotterdam Centraal **452 472** a.	2318	2349	0018	0049	0049	0118	0152	0219
Rotterdam Centraal **452 472** d.	2321	2351	0021	...	0051	...	...	...
Dordrecht ..... **452 472** d.	2337	0007	0037	...	0107	...	...	...
Roosendaal ..... a.	2400	0030	0059**a**	...	0139	...	...	...
Roosendaal ..... d.	0006	...	...	...	...	...	...	...
Bergen op Zoom ..... d.	0015	...	...	...	...	...	...	...
Goes ..... d.	0046	...	...	...	...	...	...	...
Middelburg ..... d.	0101	...	...	...	...	...	...	...
Vlissingen ..... a.	0109	...	...	...	...	...	...	...

	Ⓐ	⚒	†	Ⓐ	⚒	Ⓐ	⚒	†	Ⓐ	⚒
Vlissingen ..... d.	...	...	...	...	...	...	...	...	0540	...
Middelburg ..... d.	...	...	...	...	...	...	...	...	0546	...
Goes ..... d.	...	...	...	...	...	...	...	...	0558	...
Bergen op Zoom ..... d.	...	...	...	...	...	0544	...	...	0617	...
Roosendaal ..... a.	...	...	...	...	...	0554	...	...	0627	...
Roosendaal ..... d.	...	...	...	0531	...	0601	0601	...	0631	0631
Dordrecht ..... **452 472** d.	...	...	...	0554	...	0624	0624	...	0654	0654
Rotterdam Centraal ..... **452 472** a.	...	...	...	0608	...	0638	0638	...	0708	0708
Rotterdam Centraal ..... **452 472** d.	0512	0542	0602	0612	0612	0642	0642	0642	0711	0712
Schiedam Centrum ..... **452** d.	0516	0546	|	0616	0616	0646	0646	0646	0716	0716
Delft ..... **452 472** d.	0524	0554	0612	0624	0624	0654	0654	0654	0724	0724
Den Haag HS ..... **452 472** d.	0533	0603	0621	0633	0633	0703	0703	0703	0733	0733
Leiden Centraal ..... **452** d.	0547	0617	0640	0647	0647	0717	0717	0717	0747	0747
Haarlem ..... **458** d.	0609	0639	0702	0709	0709	0739	0739	0739	0809	0809
Amsterdam Sloterdijk ..... **458** d.	0618	0648	0711	0718	0718	0748	0748	0748	0818	0818
Amsterdam Centraal ..... **458** a.	0624	0654	0717	0724	0724	0754	0754	0754	0824	0824

	†	⑥	Ⓐ	†	⚒	†	Ⓒ	Ⓐ			Ⓒ	Ⓐ								⑤⑥			
Vlissingen ..... d.	...	0551	0610	...	0621	...	0651	0710	0721		1851	1910	1921	1951	2021	2051	2121	2151	2221	2251	2251	2321	...
Middelburg ..... d.	...	0559	0616	...	0629	...	0659	0716	0729		1859	1916	1929	1959	2029	2059	2129	2159	2229	2259	2259	2329	...
Goes ..... d.	...	0614	0628	...	0644	...	0714	0728	0744	and at	1914	1928	1944	2014	2044	2114	2144	2214	2244	2314	2314	2344	...
Bergen op Zoom ..... d.	...	0644	0647	...	0714	...	0744	0747	0814	the	1944	1947	2014	2044	2114	2144	2214	2244	2314	2344	2344	0014	...
Roosendaal ..... a.	...	0654	0657	...	0724	...	0754	0757	0824		1954	1957	2024	2054	2124	2154	2224	2254	2324	2354	2354	0024	...
Roosendaal ..... d.	...	0701	0701	0701	0731	0731	0801	0801	0831	same	2001	2001	2031	2101	2131	2201	2231	2301	2331	0001	0001	...	...
Dordrecht ..... **452 472** d.	...	0724	0724	0724	0754	0754	0824	0824	0854	minutes	2024	2024	2054	2124	2154	2224	2254	2324	2354	0024	0024	...	...
Rotterdam Centraal **452 472** a.	...	0738	0738	0738	0808	0808	0838	0838	0908		2038	2038	2108	2138	2208	2238	2308	2338	0008	0038	0038	...	...
Rotterdam Centraal **452 472** d.	0712	0742	0741	0742	0811	0812	0842	0841	0912	past	2042	2041	2112	2142	2212	2242	2312	2342	0012	0042	...	...	...
Schiedam Centrum ..... **452** d.	0716	0746	0746	0746	0816	0816	0846	0846	0916		2046	2046	2116	2146	2216	2246	2316	2346	0016	0046	...	...	...
Delft ..... **452 472** d.	0724	0754	0754	0754	0824	0824	0854	0854	0924	each	2054	2054	2124	2154	2224	2254	2324	2354	0024	0054	...	...	...
Den Haag HS ..... **452 472** d.	0733	0803	0803	0803	0833	0833	0903	0903	0933	hour	2103	2103	2133	2203	2233	2303	2333	0003	0033	0103	...	...	...
Leiden Centraal ..... **452** d.	0747	0817	0817	0817	0847	0847	0917	0917	0947	until	2117	2117	2147	2217	2247	2317	2347	0017	0047	0117	...	...	...
Haarlem ..... **458** d.	0809	0839	0839	0839	0909	0909	0939	0939	1009		2139	2139	2209	2239	2309	2339	0009	0049	0109	0139	...	...	...
Amsterdam Sloterdijk ..... **458** d.	0818	0848	0848	0848	0918	0918	0948	0948	1018		2148	2148	2218	2248	2318	2348	0018	0048	0118	0148	...	...	...
Amsterdam Centraal ..... **458** a.	0824	0854	0854	0854	0924	0924	0954	0954	1024		2154	2154	2224	2254	2324	2354	0024	0054	0124	0154	...	...	...

AMSTERDAM - DEN HAAG CENTRAAL *See note* ❖

km		Ⓐ	Ⓐ	Ⓐ	Ⓐ	Ⓐ	Ⓐ	Ⓐ	⚒										⑤⑥	⑤⑥	⑤⑥	⑤⑥	⑤⑥	⑥⑦
0	**Amsterdam** Centraal ..... **458** d.	0620	0650	0720	0750	0820	0850	0920	0950	1020	1050		1750	1820	1850	1920		2120	2150	2220	2250	2320	2350	0020
5	Amsterdam Sloterdijk ..... **458** d.	0625	0655	0725	0755	0825	0855	0925	0955	1025	1055	every	1755	1825	1855	1925	every	2125	2155	2225	2255	2325	2355	0025
19	**Haarlem** ..... **458** d.	0636	0706	0736	0806	0836	0906	0936	1006	1036	1106	30	1806	1836	1907	1937	30	2137	2207	2237	2307	2337	0007	0037
47	Leiden Centraal ⊙ ..... **452** d.	0658	0728	0758	0828	0858	0928	0958	1028	1058	1128	mins	1828	1859	1932	2002	mins	2202	2232	2302	2332	0002	0032	0102
62	**Den Haag** Centraal ⊡ ... **452** a.	0712	0742	0812	0842	0912	0942	1012	1042	1112	1142		1842	1912	1942	2012		2212	2242	2312	2342	0012	0042	0112

	Ⓐ§	Ⓐ§	Ⓐ§	Ⓐ§	Ⓐ§	Ⓐ§	Ⓐ§	⚒§	§	§	§	§	§						⑤⑥	⑤⑥	⑤⑥	⑤⑥	⑤⑥	⑥⑦
Den Haag Centraal ..... **452** d.	0617	0647	0717	0747	0817	0847	0917	0947	1017	1047		1817	1847	1917	1947	2017	2047	2117	2147	2217	2247	2317	2347	0017
Leiden Centraal ..... **452** d.	0633	0703	0733	0803	0833	0903	0933	1003	1033	1103	every	1833	1903	1933	2003	2033	2103	2133	2203	2233	2303	2333	0003	0033
Haarlem ..... **458** d.	0655	0725	0755	0825	0855	0925	0955	1025	1055	1125	30	1855	1925	1955	2025	2055	2125	2155	2225	2255	2325	2355	0025	0055
Amsterdam Sloterdijk ..... **458** d.	0704	0734	0804	0834	0904	0934	1004	1034	1104	1134	mins	1904	1934	2004	2034	2104	2134	2204	2234	2304	2334	0004	0034	0104
Amsterdam Centraal ..... **458** a.	0710	0740	0810	0840	0910	0940	1010	1040	1110	1140		1910	1940	2010	2040	2110	2140	2210	2240	2310	2340	0010	0040	0110

a – Morning of ①–⑤ only.
b – Terminates at Den Haag on ④.

⊙ – Departures 0658 to 1828 are 4 minutes later on ⑤–⑦.
⊡ – Arrivals 0712 to 1842 are 3 minutes earlier on ①–④.

§ – On ①–④ departs 3 minutes later from Den Haag Centraal, 1 minute later from Leiden.
❖ – See main table for Amsterdam Centraal - Den Haag HS.

☛ In addition to the *IC* trains shown, local *Sprinter* services run every 10 minutes Den Haag Centraal - Den Haag HS - Rotterdam Centraal - Dordrecht and v.v.

451 AMSTERDAM CENTRAAL - SCHIPHOL ✈ *Airport Sprinter*

From Amsterdam Centraal: 0514Ⓐ, 0519Ⓒ, 0534, 0549⚒, 0605, 0619, 0635, 0641Ⓐ, 0649, 0656Ⓐ, 0705, 0713Ⓐ, 0719, 0726Ⓐ, 0735, 0741Ⓐ, 0749, 0756Ⓐ, 0805, 0813Ⓐ, 0819, 0826Ⓐ, 0835, 0841Ⓐ, 0849, 0856Ⓐ, 0905, 0913Ⓐ, 0919, 0926, 0935, 0941, 0949, 0956 and at 05, 13, 19, 26, 35, 41, 49, 56 minutes past each hour until 2105 then at 05, 19, 35, 49 minutes past each hour until 0035, also 0105⑥⑦.

From Schiphol ✈: 0608, 0623, 0629Ⓐ, 0638, 0648Ⓐ, 0655, 0703Ⓐ, 0708, 0718Ⓐ, 0723, 0729Ⓐ, 0738, 0748Ⓐ, 0755, 0803Ⓐ, 0808, 0818Ⓐ, 0823, 0829Ⓐ, 0838, 0848Ⓐ, 0855 and at 03, 08, 18, 23, 29, 38, 48, 55 minutes past each hour until 2108 then at 08, 23, 38, 55 minutes past each hour until 0008, also 0023⑥⑦, 0038, 0108⑥⑦.

Journey 15-16 minutes. Trains continue beyond Schiphol ✈ to / from Hoofddorp. Additional trains run approx hourly at night.

☛ For **Amsterdam Zuid** - Schiphol ✈ see Tables **452**, **460**, **465**, **471**.

IC trains ROTTERDAM - DEN HAAG - AMSTERDAM ZUID - UTRECHT - NIJMEGEN 452

For faster trains Rotterdam - Schiphol ✈ - Amsterdam Zuid via high-speed line see Table **460**. For services to/from Amsterdam Centraal see Tables **450** and **457**.

km		Ⓐ	Ⓐ d	Ⓐ ⊡	Ⓐ ◧b	Ⓐ ⊡	Ⓐ ◧b	Ⓐ ⊡f	①–④	⚒ ◧d	Ⓐ ⊡f	①–④	⚒ ◧d	⚒ ⊡	①–④	⚒ ◧d	⚒ ⊡	①–④	◧	⚒ ⊡h	①–④	◧	⚒ ⊡h	①–④	◧
0	Dordrecht 450 d.	...	...	...	...	...	...	0634	...	...	0704	...	...	0734a	...	...	0804	...	...	0834	...	...	0904	...	...
20	**Rotterdam** Cent. 450 d.	...	...	0552	...	0622	...	0652	0703	...	0722	0733	...	0752	0803	...	0822	0833	...	0852	0903	...	0922	0933	...
24	Schiedam Cent. 450 d.	...	...	0556	...	0626	...	0656	|	...	0726	|	...	0756	|	...	0826	|	...	0856	|	...	0926	|	...
34	Delft 450 d.	...	...	0604	...	0634	...	0704	0713	...	0734	0743	...	0804	0813	...	0834	0843	...	0904	0913	...	0934	0943	...
42	**Den Haag** HS 450 d.	...	...	0613	...	0643	...	0713	0723	...	0743	0753	...	0813	0823	...	0843	0853	...	0913	0923	...	0943	0953	...
	Den Haag Cent. d.	0530	0600	|	0630	|	0700	|	|	0730	|	|	0800	|	|	0830	|	|	0900	|	|	0930	|	|	1000
58	Leiden Cent. 450 a.	0542	0612	0625	0642	0655	0712	0725	0735	0742	0755	0805	0812	0825	0835	0842	0855	0905	0912	0925	0935	0942	0955	1005	1012
58	Leiden Cent. d.	0547	0617	0627	0647	0657	0717	0727	0738	0747	0757	0808	0817	0827	0838	0847	0857	0908	0917	0927	0938	0947	0957	1008	1017
85	Schiphol ✈ 471 d.	0605	0635	0645	0705	0715	0735	0745	0756	0805	0815	0825	0835	0845	0856	0905	0915	0925	0935	0945	0956	1005	1015	1025	1035
94	**Amsterdam** Zuid 471 a.	0611	0641	0652	0711	0722	0741	0752	0803	0811	0822	0832	0841	0852	0903	0911	0922	0932	0941	0952	1003	1011	1022	1032	1041
94	**Amsterdam** Zuid 471 d.	0612	0642	0656	0712	0726	0742	0756	0806	0812	0826	0836	0842	0856	0906	0912	0926	0936	0942	0956	1006	1012	1026	1036	1042
130	**Utrecht** Cent. 471 a.	0634	0705	0718	0734	0748	0804	0818	0828	0834	0848	0858	0904	0918	0928	0934	0948	0958	1004	1018	1028	1034	1048	1058	1105
130	**Utrecht** Cent. 457 d.	0640	0709	0724	0739	0754	0809	0824	0834	0839	0854	0904	0909	0924	0934	0939	0954	1004	1009	1024	1034	1039	1054	1107	1109
170	Ede-Wageningen 457 d.	0702	0732	v	0803	v	0833	v	0858	0903	v	0928	0933	v	0958	1003	v	1028	1033	v	1058	1103	v	1130	1133
187	**Arnhem** Cent. 457 a.	0712	0744	...	0815	...	0845	...	0908	0915	...	0938	0945	...	1008	1015	...	1038	1045	...	1108	1115	...	1141	1145
187	**Arnhem** Cent. ‡ 457 d.	0720	0750	...	0820	...	0850	...	...	0920	...	...	0950	...	...	1020	...	...	1050	...	...	1120	...	...	1150
205	**Nijmegen** ‡ 457 a.	0732	0802	...	0832	...	0902	...	...	0932	...	...	1002	...	...	1032	...	...	1102	...	...	1132	...	...	1202

	⊡	①–④	◧	⊡	①–④	◧	⊡		①–④		⊡	①–④		△		△								
Dordrecht 450 d.	0934r	...	...	1004	...	...	1034		...	...	1804	...	...	1834	...	1904	...	1939	...	2009	...	2039	...	2109
Rotterdam Cent. 450 d.	0952	1003	...	1022	1033	...	1052		1803	...	1822	1833	...	1852	...	1922	...	1956	...	2026	...	2056	...	2126
Schiedam Cent. 450 d.	0956	|	...	1026	|	...	1056	and	|	...	1826	|	...	1856	...	1926	...	2000	...	2030	...	2100	...	2130
Delft 450 d.	1004	1013	...	1034	1043	...	1104	at	1813	...	1834	1843	...	1904	...	1934	...	2008	...	2038	...	2108	...	2138
Den Haag HS 450 d.	1013	1023	...	1043	1053	...	1113	the	1823	...	1843	1853	...	1917	...	1947	...	2017	...	2047	...	2117	...	2147
Den Haag Cent. d.	|	|	1030	|	|	1100	|	same	|	1830	|	|	1900	|	1930	|	2000	|	2030	|	2100	|	2130	|
Leiden Cent. 450 a.	1025	1035	1042	1055	1105	1112	1125	minutes	1835	1842	1855	1905	1912	1929	1942	1959	2012	2029	2042	2059	2112	2129	2142	2159
Leiden Cent. d.	1027	1038	1047	1057	1108	1117	1127	past	1838	1847	1857	1908	1917	1930	1947	2000	2017	2030	2047	2100	2117	2130	2147	2200
Schiphol ✈ 471 d.	1045	1056	1105	1115	1125	1135	1145	each	1856	1905	1915	1925	1935	1946	2005	2016	2035	2046	2105	2116	2135	2146	2205	2216
Amsterdam Zuid 471 a.	1052	1103	1111	1122	1132	1141	1152	hour	1903	1911	1922	1932	1941	1953	2011	2023	2041	2053	2111	2123	2141	2153	2211	2223
Amsterdam Zuid 471 d.	1056	1106	1112	1126	1136	1142	1156	until	1906	1912	1926	1936	1942	1956	2012	2026	2042	2056	2112	2126	2142	2156	2212	2226
Utrecht Cent. 471 a.	1118	1128	1134	1148	1158	1204	1218		1928	1934	1948	1958	2004	2018	2034	2048	2104	2118	2134	2148	2204	2218	2234	2248
Utrecht Cent. 457 d.	1124	1134	1139	1154	1204	1209	1224		...	1940	1954	...	2010	2024	2040	2054	2110	2124	2140	2154	2210	2224	2240	2254
Ede-Wageningen 457 d.	v	1158	1203	v	1228	1233	v		...	2002	v	...	2032	v	2102	v	2132	v	2202	v	2232	v	2302	e
Arnhem Cent. 457 a.	...	1208	1215	...	1238	1245	...		...	2012	...	...	2042	...	2112	...	2142	...	2212	...	2242	...	2312	...
Arnhem Cent. ‡ 457 d.	...	...	1220	...	...	1250	...		...	2020	...	...	2050	...	2120	...	2150	...	...	...	...	...	...	...
Nijmegen ‡ 457 a.	...	...	1232	...	...	1302	...		...	2032	...	...	2102	...	2132	...	2202	...	...	...	...	...	...	...

									⑥⑦
Dordrecht 450 d.	...	2139	...	2209	...	2239	...	...	...
Rotterdam Cent. 450 d.	...	2156	...	2226	...	2256	...	...	...
Schiedam Cent. 450 d.	...	2200	...	2230	...	2300	...	...	...
Delft 450 d.	...	2208	...	2238	...	2308	...	...	...
Den Haag HS 450 d.	...	2217	...	2247	...	2317	...	...	...
Den Haag Cent. d.	2200	|	2230	|	2300	|	2330	0000	0030
Leiden Cent. 450 a.	2212	2229	2242	2259	2312	2329	2342	0012	0042
Leiden Cent. d.	2217	2230	2247	2300	2317	2330	2347	0017	0047
Schiphol ✈ 471 d.	2235	2246	2305	2315	2335	2345	0005	0035	0105
Amsterdam Zuid 471 a.	2241	2253	2311	...	2341	...	0011	0041	0111
Amsterdam Zuid 471 d.	2242	2256	2312	...	2342	...	0012	0042	...
Utrecht Cent. 471 a.	2304	2318	2334	...	0004	...	0034	0104	...
Utrecht Cent. 457 d.	...	2324	...	...	...	...	...	...	...
Ede-Wageningen 457 d.	...	v	...	...	...	...	...	...	...
Arnhem Cent. 457 a.	...	...	...	...	...	...	...	...	...
Arnhem Cent. ‡ 457 d.	...	...	...	...	...	...	...	...	...
Nijmegen ‡ 457 a.	...	...	...	...	...	...	...	...	...

	Ⓐ ▽	Ⓐ u	①–④	Ⓐ ▽	Ⓐ k	Ⓐ ▽	Ⓐ ◐n	①–④	⚒ ▽	Ⓐ ⊙n	①–④
Nijmegen ‡ 457 d.	...	...	...	...	...	...	0628	...	...	0658	...
Arnhem Cent. ‡ 457 a.	...	...	...	...	...	...	0640	...	...	0710	...
Arnhem Cent. 457 d.	...	...	...	...	0617	...	0645	0651	...	0715	0721
Ede-Wageningen 457 d.	...	...	...	e	0627	v	0655	0701	v	0725	0731
Utrecht Cent. 457 a.	...	...	...	0635	0649	0705	0717	0726	0735	0747	0756
Utrecht Cent. 471 d.	...	0625	0632	0642	0655	0712	0722	0732	0742	0752	0802
Amsterdam Zuid 471 a.	...	0647	0654	0704	0717	0734	0744	0754	0804	0817	0824
Amsterdam Zuid 471 d.	0637	0648	0656	0707	0720	0737	0747	0756	0807	0820	0827
Schiphol ✈ 471 d.	0644	0655	0705	0714	0729	0744	0755	0805	0814	0829	0835
Leiden Cent. a.	0700	0713	0722	0730	0745	0800	0813	0822	0830	0845	0852
Leiden Cent. 450 d.	0701	0718	0725	0731	0748	0801	0818	0825	0831	0848	0855
Den Haag Cent. a.	|	0729	|	|	0759	|	0829	|	|	0859	|
Den Haag HS 450 d.	0714	...	0739	0744	...	0814	...	0839	0844	...	0909
Delft 450 d.	0720	...	0745	0750	...	0820	...	0845	0850	...	0915
Schiedam Cent. 450 d.	0728	...	|	0758	...	0828	...	|	0858	...	|
Rotterdam Cent. 450 a.	0733	...	0756	0803	...	0833	...	0856	0903	...	0926
Dordrecht 450 a.	0752	...	...	0822	...	0852	...	...	0922	...	...

	⚒ ▽	Ⓐ ◐s	①–④	⚒ ▽	Ⓐ ⊙s	①–④	⚒ ▽	Ⓐ ◐s	①–④	▽	⚒ ⊙s	①–④	▽	⚒ ◐s	①–④	▽	⊙	①–④	▽	◐	①–④	▽	⊙	
Nijmegen ‡ 457 d.	...	0728	...	...	0758	...	...	0828	...	...	0858a	...	...	0928	...	...	0958r	...	...	1028	...	...	1058	
Arnhem Cent. ‡ 457 a.	...	0740	...	...	0810	...	...	0840	...	...	0910a	...	...	0940	...	...	1010r	...	...	1040	...	...	1110	
Arnhem Cent. 457 d.	...	0745	0751	...	0815	0821	...	0845	0851	...	0915	0921	...	0945	0951	...	1015	1021	...	1045	1051	...	1115	
Ede-Wageningen 457 d.	v	0755	0801	v	0825	0831	v	0855	0901	v	0925	0931	v	0955	1001	v	1025	1031	v	1055	1101	v	1125	and
Utrecht Cent. 457 a.	0805	0817	0826	0835	0847	0856	0905	0917	0926	0935	0947	0956	1005	1017	1026	1035	1047	1056	1105	1117	1126	1135	1147	at
Utrecht Cent. 471 d.	0812	0822	0832	0842	0852	0902	0912	0922	0932	0942	0952	1002	1012	1022	1032	1042	1052	1102	1112	1122	1132	1142	1152	the
Amsterdam Zuid 471 a.	0834	0844	0854	0904	0917	0924	0934	0944	0954	1004	1017	1024	1034	1044	1054	1104	1117	1124	1134	1144	1154	1204	1214	same
Amsterdam Zuid 471 d.	0837	0847	0856	0907	0920	0927	0937	0947	0956	1007	1020	1027	1037	1047	1056	1107	1120	1127	1137	1147	1156	1207	1219	minutes
Schiphol ✈ 471 d.	0844	0855	0905	0914	0929	0935	0944	0955	1005	1014	1029	1035	1044	1055	1105	1114	1129	1135	1144	1155	1205	1214	1227	past
Leiden Cent. a.	0900	0913	0922	0930	0945	0952	1000	1013	1022	1030	1045	1052	1100	1113	1122	1130	1145	1152	1200	1213	1222	1230	1244	each
Leiden Cent. 450 d.	0901	0918	0925	0931	0948	0955	1001	1018	1025	1031	1048	1055	1101	1118	1125	1131	1148	1155	1201	1218	1225	1231	1247	hour
Den Haag Cent. a.	|	0929	|	|	0959	|	|	1029	|	|	1059	|	|	1129	|	|	1159	|	|	1229	|	|	1259	until
Den Haag HS 450 d.	0914	...	0939	0944	...	1009	1014	...	1039	1044	...	1109	1114	...	1139	1144	...	1209	1214	...	1239	1244	...	
Delft 450 d.	0920	...	0945	0950	...	1015	1020	...	1045	1050	...	1115	1120	...	1145	1150	...	1215	1220	...	1245	1250	...	
Schiedam Cent. 450 d.	0928	...	|	0958	...	|	1028	...	|	1058	...	|	1128	...	|	1158	...	|	1228	...	|	1258	...	
Rotterdam Cent. 450 a.	0933	...	0956	1003	...	1026	1033	...	1056	1103	...	1126	1133	...	1156	1203	...	1226	1233	...	1256	1303	...	
Dordrecht 450 a.	0952	...	...	1022	...	...	1052	...	...	1122	...	...	1152	...	...	1222	...	...	1252	...	...	1322	...	

	①–④ z		◐		⊙																				⑥⑦
Nijmegen ‡ 457 d.	...	...	1728	...	1758	...	1828	...	1858	...	1928	...	1958	...	2028	...	2058	...	2128	...	...	...	...	...	0117
Arnhem Cent. ‡ 457 a.	...	...	1740	...	1810	...	1840	...	1910	...	1940	...	2010	...	2040	...	2110	...	2140	...	...	...	...	...	0133
Arnhem Cent. 457 d.	1721	...	1745	...	1815	...	1847	...	1917	...	1947	...	2017	...	2047	...	2117	...	2147	...	...	...	...	...	0139
Ede-Wageningen 457 d.	1731	v	1755	v	1825	v	1857	v	1927	v	1957	v	2027	v	2057	v	2127	v	2157	v	...	v	v	...	0150
Utrecht Cent. 457 a.	1756	1805	1817	1835	1847	1905	1919	1935	1949	2005	2019	2035	2049	2105	2119	2135	2149	2205	2219	2235	...	2305	2335	...	0211
Utrecht Cent. 471 d.	1802	1812	1822	1842	1852	1912	1925	1942	1955	2012	2025	2042	2055	2112	2125	2142	2155	2212	2225	2242	2255	2325	2355	0025	...
Amsterdam Zuid 471 a.	1824	1834	1844	1904	1917	1934	1947	2004	2017	2034	2047	2104	2117	2134	2147	2204	2217	2234	2247	2304	2317	2347	0017	0047	...
Amsterdam Zuid 471 d.	1827	1837	1847	1907	1920	1937	1948	2007	2020	2037	2048	2107	2120	2137	2148	2207	2219	2237	2248	2307	2319	2348	0019	0049	...
Schiphol ✈ 471 d.	1835	1844	1855	1914	1929	1944	1955	2014	2029	2044	2055	2114	2129	2144	2155	2214	2227	2244	2255	2313	2327	2355	0027	0057	...
Leiden Cent. a.	1852	1900	1913	1930	1945	2000	2013	2030	2045	2100	2113	2130	2145	2200	2213	2230	2243	2300	2313	...	2343	0013	0043	0113	...
Leiden Cent. 450 d.	1855	1901	1918	1931	1948	2001	2018	2031	2048	2101	2118	2131	2148	2201	2218	2231	2248	2301	2318	...	2348	0018	0048	0117x	...
Den Haag Cent. a.	|	|	1929	|	1959	|	2029	|	2059	|	2129	|	2159	|	2229	|	2259	|	2329	...	2359	0029	0059	0130x	...
Den Haag HS 450 d.	1909	1914	...	1944	...	2014	...	2044	...	2114	...	2144	...	2214	...	2244	...	2314	...	...	...	...	...	...	...
Delft 450 d.	1915	1920	...	1950	...	2020	...	2050	...	2120	...	2150	...	2220	...	2250	...	2320	...	...	...	...	...	...	...
Schiedam Cent. 450 d.	|	1928	...	1958	...	2028	...	2058	...	2128	...	2158	...	2228	...	2258	...	2328	...	...	...	...	...	...	...
Rotterdam Cent. 450 a.	1926	1933	...	2003	...	2033	...	2103	...	2133	...	2203	...	2233	...	2303	...	2333	...	...	...	...	...	...	...
Dordrecht 450 a.	...	1952	...	2022	...	2052	...	2122	...	2152	...	2222	...	...	...	...	...	...	...	...	...	...	...	...	...

a – Ⓐ only.
b – Runs on ⚒ Den Haag Centraal - Utrecht.
d – Runs daily Den Haag Centraal - Utrecht.
e – To/from Eindhoven (Table **471**).
f – ⚒ from Schiphol.
h – Daily from Schiphol.
k – Daily from Amsterdam Zuid.
n – ⚒ from Utrecht; daily from Amsterdam Zuid.
r – ⚒ only.

s – Daily from Utrecht.
u – Daily from Amsterdam Zuid. Earlier trains run at 0548⚒ Amsterdam Zuid - Den Haag Cent and 0552Ⓐ Utrecht - Den Haag Cent.
v – To/from Venlo (Table **471**).
x – ①⑥⑦ only.
z – Additional journeys run at 1751 and 1821 on ①–④ Arnhem - Schiphol.
‡ – See also Table **475**.

◧ – On ①–④ arrives Amsterdam Zuid 1 minute later, departs 3 minutes later, arrives/departs Utrecht 4 minutes later.
◐ – Except on ①–④, arrives/departs Utrecht 3 minutes later, Amsterdam Zuid arrives 3 minutes later, departs 1 minute later.
⊡ – Runs 3–5 minutes later to Leiden except on ①–④.
⊙ – Arrives/departs Utrecht 3 minutes later except on ①–④.
△ – On ⑤–⑦ runs 4–5 minutes later Dordrecht - Delft.
▽ – On ①–④ (until 1831 departure from Leiden) runs 3–4 minutes later Leiden - Dordrecht.

455 AMSTERDAM - GOUDA - ROTTERDAM *Sprinter trains*

For Amsterdam - Rotterdam via high-speed line see Table **460** (via Den Haag see Table **450**). For other trains Gouda - Rotterdam see Table **462**.

km		Ⓐ	⚒z	⚒	b					
0	**Amsterdam** Centraal d.	...	0549	0619	0649	0719	0749		2319	2349
6	Amsterdam Amstel d.	...	0558	0628	0658	0728	0758	and every	2327	2357
9	Duivendrecht d.	...	0601	0631	0701	0731	0801	30 minutes	2330	0000
27	Breukelen d.	0549	0618	0648	0718	0748	0818		2348	0018
40	Woerden d.	0558	0628	0658	0728	0758	0828	until	2358	0028
56	**Gouda** d.	0611	0641	0711	0741	0811	0841		0011	0041
70	Rotterdam Alexander d.	0624	0654	0724	0754	0824	0854		0024	0054
80	**Rotterdam** Centraal a.	0634	0704	0734	0804	0834	0904		0034	0104

	Ⓐ	Ⓐ	⚒	⚒					
Rotterdam Centraal d.	0524	0554	0624	0654	0724	0754		2324	2354
Rotterdam Alexander d.	0534	0604	0634	0704	0734	0804	and every	2334	0004
Gouda d.	0549	0619	0649	0719	0749	0819	30 minutes	2349	0019
Woerden d.	0603	0633	0703	0733	0803	0833		0003	0033
Breukelen d.	0611	0641	0711	0741	0811	0841	until	0011	0041
Duivendrecht d.	0628	0658	0728	0758	0828	0858		0029	0059
Amsterdam Amstel d.	0632	0702	0732	0802	0832	0902		0033	0103
Amsterdam Cent. a.	0641	0711	0741	0811	0841	0911		0042	0112

b – From Alkmaar on † (Table **457**).
z – From Alkmaar (Table **457**).
☛ Most trains continue beyond Amsterdam to / from Sloterdijk, Zaandam and Uitgeest.

457 DEN HELDER - ALKMAAR - AMSTERDAM - ARNHEM - NIJMEGEN *IC trains*

km		Ⓐ	⚒§	Ⓐ	Ⓐb	†§	Ⓐh	Ⓑd	⚒d	Ⓐm										⑥⑦		⑥⑦	⑥⑦
0	**Den Helder** d.	...	...	...	0504	...	0534	0604	0634	0646	0704	0734	0804	0834		2104	2134	2204	2304	...	0004	0004	0034
35	Heerhugowaard 458 d.	...	...	...	0531	...	0601	0631	0701	0715	0731	0801	0831	0901		2131	2201	2231	2331	...	0031	0031	0101
42	**Alkmaar** 458 a.	...	...	...	0541	...	0611	0641	0711	0724	0741	0811	0841	0911		2141	2211	2241	2341	...	0041	0041	0111
42	**Alkmaar** 458 470 d.	...	0502	0516	0544	0603	0614	0644	0714	0727	0744	0814	0844	0914		2144	2214	2244	2344	...	...	0044	...
54	Castricum 458 470 d.	...	0512	0527	0555	0613	0625	0655	0725	0735	0755	0825	0855	0925		2155	2225	2255	2355	...	...	0055	...
71	Zaandam 470 d.	...	0536	0540	0608	0635	0638	0708	0738	0749	0808	0838	0908	0938	and every	2208	2238	2308	0008	...	...	0118	...
78	Amsterdam Sloterdijk 470 d.	...	0542	0547	0615	0641	0645	0715	0745	0756	0815	0845	0915	0945	30 minutes	2215	2245	2315	0015	...	...	0125	...
83	**Amsterdam** Centraal 470 a.	...	0547	0553	0621	0647	0651	0721	0751	0802	0821	0851	0921	0951		2221	2251	2321	0021	...	...	0131	...
83	**Amsterdam** Centraal 470 d.	...	...	0554	0624	...	0654	0724	0754	...	0824	0854	0924	0954	until	2224	2254	2323	0023	0119	...	...	...
89	Amsterdam Amstel 470 d.	...	...	0602	0632	...	0702	0732	0802	...	0832	0902	0932	1002		2232	2302	2331	0031	|	...	...	...
122	**Utrecht** Centraal 470 a.	...	...	0621	0651	...	0721	0751	0821	...	0851	0921	0951	1021		2251	2321	2351	0051	0148	...	...	...
122	**Utrecht** Centraal 452 d.	0553	...	0623	0653	...	0723	0753	0823	...	0853	0923	0953	1023		2253	2323	2353	0053	0154	...	...	...
162	Ede-Wageningen 452 d.	0620	...	0650	0720	...	0750	0818	0848	...	0918	0948	1018	1048		2320	2350	0020	0119	0220	...	...	...
179	**Arnhem** Cent. 452 a.	0630	...	0700	0730	...	0800	0828	0858	...	0928	0958	1028	1058		2330	2400	0030	0130	0232	...	...	...
179	**Arnhem** Cent. 452 475 d.	0635	...	0705	0735	...	0805	0835	0905	...	0935	1005	1035	1105		2335	0005	0035	0135	0239	...	...	...
197	**Nijmegen** 452 475 a.	0647	...	0717	0747	...	0817	0847	0917	...	0947	1017	1047	1117		2347	0017	0047	0151	0253	...	...	...

	Ⓐ	Ⓐ	Ⓐ	Ⓐk	⚒	†	⚒	†									①②	③–⑦		①②	③–⑥	⑦	⑥⑦
Nijmegen 452 475 d.	...	...	...	0536	0613	...	0643	...	0713	0743x	0813	0843		2113	2143	2213	2243	2243	2313	2343	2343	2343	...
Arnhem Cent. 452 475 a.	...	...	...	0556	0626	...	0656	...	0726	0756	0826	0856		2126	2156	2226	2256	2256	2326	2356	2356	2356	...
Arnhem Cent. 452 d.	...	...	0531	0601	0631	...	0701	...	0731	0801	0831	0901		2131	2201	2231	2301	2301	2331	0001	0001	0001	...
Ede-Wageningen 452 d.	...	...	0541	0611	0641	...	0711	...	0741	0811	0841	0911		2141	2211	2241	2311	2311	2341	0011	0011	0011	...
Utrecht Centraal 452 a.	...	...	0608	0638	0708	...	0738	...	0808	0838	0908	0938		2208	2238	2308	2338	2338	0008	0038	0038	0038	...
Utrecht Centraal 470 d.	...	...	0609	0639	0709	0708	0739	0738	0809	0839	0909	0939		2209	2239	2309	2339	2339	0009	0039	0039	...	...
Amsterdam Amstel 470 d.	...	...	0627	0657	0727	0729	0757	0759	0827	0857	0927	0957	and every	2227	2257	2329	2359	2359	0029	0059	0059	...	...
Amsterdam Centraal 470 d.	...	...	0635	0705	0735	0737	0805	0807	0835	0905	0935	1005		2235	2305	2337	0007	0007	0037	0107	0107	...	...
Amsterdam Centraal 470 d.	0529	0609	0639	0709	0739	0739	0809	0809	0839	0909	0939	1009	30 minutes	2239	2309	2339	0009	0009	...	...	0109	...	0149
Amsterdam Sloterdijk 470 d.	0535	0615	0645	0715	0745	0745	0815	0815	0845	0915	0945	1015		2245	2315	2345	0015	0015	...	...	0115	...	0154
Zaandam 470 d.	0541	0622	0652	0722	0752	0752	0822	0822	0852	0922	0952	1022	until	2252	2322	2352	0021	0021	...	...	0122	...	0201
Castricum 458 470 d.	0606	0634	0704	0734	0804	0804	0834	0834	0904	0934	1004	1034		2304	2334	0004	0035	0035	...	...	0146	...	0226
Alkmaar 458 470 a.	0618	0646	0716	0746	0816	0816	0846	0846	0916	0946	1016	1046		2316	2346	0016	0046	0046	...	...	0158	...	0237
Alkmaar 458 d.	0619	0649	0719	0749	0819	0819	0849	0849	0919	0949	1019	1049		2319	2349	0019	...	0049	...	...	0202z	...	0238
Heerhugowaard 458 d.	0627	0657	0727	0757	0827	0827	0857	0857	0927	0957	1027	1057		2327	2357	0027	...	0057	...	...	0210z	...	0246
Den Helder a.	0656	0726	0756	0826	0856	0856	0926	0926	0956	1026	1056	1126		2356	0026	0056	...	0126	...	...	0237z	...	...

b – ⚒ from Utrecht.
d – Daily from Amsterdam Centraal.
h – ⚒ from Amsterdam Centraal.
k – ⚒ from Utrecht, daily from Amsterdam Centraal.
m – To Maastricht on ①–④ (Table **470**). On ⑤ arrives Amsterdam Centraal at 0811.
x – Departs 0736 on †.
z – Morning of ⑥⑦ only.
§ – Local *Sprinter* train. To Rotterdam (Table **455**).

458 AMSTERDAM - HAARLEM - ALKMAAR - HOORN *Sprinter trains*

Local *Sprinter* trains. For faster *Intercity* trains Amsterdam - Alkmaar and Hoorn via Zaandam see Tables **457** and **470**.

km		Ⓐ	Ⓐu	K																J	①–⑤	⑥⑦
0	**Amsterdam** Centraal 450 d.	0526	0556	0626	0656	0726		1756	1826	1856	1926	1956	2026	2056	2126	2156	2226	2256	2326	2356	0026	0056	0126
5	Amsterdam Sloterdijk 450 d.	0531	0601	0631	0701	0731		1801	1831	1901	1931	2001	2031	2101	2131	2201	2231	2301	2331	0001	0031	0101	0131
19	**Haarlem** 450 d.	0545	0615	0645	0715	0745	and	1815	1845	1915	1945	2015	2045	2115	2145	2215	2245	2315	2345	0015	0045	0114	0144
30	Beverwijk d.	0602	0632	0702	0732	0802	every	1832	1902	1932	2002	2032	2102	2132	2202	2232	2302	2332	0002	0032	0102	...	...
41	Castricum 457 d.	0619	0645	0715	0745	0815	30	1845	1915	1949	2019	2049	2119	2149	2219	2249	2319	2349	0019	0049	0115	...	...
53	**Alkmaar** 457 a.	0630	0656	0726	0756	0826	minutes	1856	1930	2000	2030	2100	2130	2200	2230	2300	2330	0000	0030	0100	0126	...	...
53	**Alkmaar** 457 d.	0631	0701	0731	0801	0831	until	1901	1931	...	2031	...	2131	...	2231	...	2331	0001	0031x	...	...	...	...
59	Heerhugowaard 457 d.	0639	0709	0739	0809	0839		1909	1939	...	2039	...	2139	...	2239	...	2339	0009	0039x	...	...	...	...
76	**Hoorn** a.	0654	0724	0754	0824	0854		1924	1954	...	2054	...	2154	...	2254	...	2354	0024	0054x	...	...	...	...

	Ⓐ	Ⓐ	Ⓐ	⚒	L	L		M		M												
Hoorn d.	...	...	...	...	0606	0636	0706	0736	0806	0836	0906	0936		1906	1936	2006	...	2106	...	2206	...	2306	...
Heerhugowaard 457 d.	...	...	...	...	0621	0651	0721	0751	0821	0851	0921	0951		1921	1951	2021	...	2121	...	2221	...	2321	...
Alkmaar 457 a.	...	...	...	...	0629	0659	0729	0759	0829	0859	0929	0959	and	1929	1959	2029	...	2129	...	2229	...	2329	...
Alkmaar ⊡ 457 d.	...	0506	0530	0600	0630	0700	0730	0800	0830	0900	0930	1000	every	1930	2000	2030	2100	2130	2200	2230	2300	2330	0000
Castricum ⊡ 457 d.	...	0516	0540	0610	0640	0710	0740	0810	0840	0910	0940	1010	30	1940	2010	2040	2110	2140	2210	2240	2310	2340	0010
Beverwijk d.	...	0529	0559	0628	0658	0728	0758	0828	0858	0928	0958	1028	minutes	1958	2028	2058	2128	2158	2228	2258	2328	2358	0028
Haarlem 450 d.	0531	0547	0617	0647	0717	0747	0817	0847	0917	0947	1017	1047	until	2017	2047	2117	2147	2217	2247	2317	2347	0017	0047
Amsterdam Sloterdijk 450 a.	0544	0600	0630	0700	0730	0800	0830	0900	0930	1000	1030	1100		2030	2100	2130	2200	2230	2300	2330	2400	0030	0100
Amsterdam Centraal 450 a.	0549	0605	0635	0705	0735	0805	0835	0905	0935	1005	1035	1105		2035	2105	2135	2205	2235	2305	2335	0005	0035	0105

AMSTERDAM - HAARLEM - ZANDVOORT AAN ZEE

km	△	Ⓐ	Ⓐ	⚒					N	⑥⑦
0	**Amsterdam** Centraal d.	0611	0641	0711	0741	0811	every	2311	2341	0011
5	Amsterdam Sloterdijk d.	0616	0646	0716	0746	0816	30	2316	2346	0016
19	**Haarlem** d.	0630	0700	0730	0800	0830	minutes	2330	0003	0030
27	**Zandvoort** aan Zee a.	0640	0710	0740	0810	0840	until	2340	0010	0040

	Ⓐ	Ⓐ	⚒		⚒				b
Zandvoort aan Zee d.	0549	0619	0649	0719	0749	0819	every	2349	0019
Haarlem d.	0601	0631	0701	0731	0801	0831	30	0001	0030
A'dam Sloterdijk d.	0614	0644	0714	0744	0814	0844	minutes	0014	...
Amsterdam Cent. a.	0619	0649	0719	0749	0819	0849	until	0019	...

J – ④⑤⑥⑦ (daily to Haarlem).
K – ⚒ from Amsterdam, daily from Haarlem.
L – Ⓐ from Hoorn, daily from Alkmaar.
M – ⚒ from Hoorn, daily from Alkmaar.
N – ①②③④⑦ (daily to Haarlem).
b – Runs 30 minutes later on ⑥⑦.
u – Also runs on ⑥ Alkmaar - Hoorn.
x – Morning of ⑥⑦ only.
⊡ – Certain departures are 4 minutes later on ①–⑤.
△ – Additional trains run Haarlem - Zandvoort at 0530Ⓐ, 0600Ⓐ, 0630⚒, 0700.

459 LEIDEN - ALPHEN - UTRECHT and GOUDA *Sprinter trains*

km		Ⓐ	⚒	⚒						
0	**Leiden** Centraal d.	0553	0623	0653	0723	0753	and every	2323	2353	0023
15	Alphen a/d Rijn d.	0609	0639	0709	0739	0809	30 minutes	2339	0009	0039
34	Woerden d.	0625	0654	0724	0754	0824	until	2354	0024	0054
50	**Utrecht** Centraal a.	0634	0704	0734	0804	0834		0004	0034	0104

	Ⓐ	⚒	Ⓐ						
Utrecht Centraal d.	0555	0625	0655	0725	0755	and every	2326	2356	0026
Woerden d.	0607	0637	0707	0737	0807	30 minutes	2337	0007	0037
Alphen a/d Rijn d.	0624	0654	0724	0754	0824	until	2354	0024	0054
Leiden Centraal a.	0637	0707	0737	0807	0837		0007	0037	0107

ALPHEN A/D RIJN - GOUDA and v.v. *17 km*. Journey: 22 – 29 minutes.

From Alphen a/d Rijn Ⓐ: 0610 and every 15 minutes until 1910, then every 30 minutes until 0040. Ⓒ: 0710⑥, 0740⑥, 0810 and every 30 minutes until 0040.

From Gouda Ⓐ: 0530, 0551, 0613 and every 15 minutes until 1858, then every 30 minutes until 0028 (❦). Ⓒ: 0628⑥, 0658⑥, 0728, 0758 and every 30 minutes until 0028 (❦).

❦ – Departures from Gouda at xx28 run 7 minutes earlier every **two** hours 0821 to 2221.

High-Speed Line LELYSTAD and AMERSFOORT - AMSTERDAM - ROTTERDAM - BREDA 460

Services via the Schiphol ✈ - Rotterdam - Breda **high-speed line**. Supplement payable Schiphol ✈ - Rotterdam and v.v. See Table **18** for Eurostar services.

km			Ⓐ		Ⓐ	Ⓐ	Ⓒ		⚒	⑦		Ⓐ		Ⓐ	Ⓒ			Ⓐ		Ⓐ	Ⓒ			Ⓐ
0	**Lelystad** Centrum 465 d.	...	...	...	...	...	...	...	...	...	...	0653	...	0721	...	...	...	0753	...	0821	...	...	...	0853
18	Almere Buiten d.	...	...	...	...	...	...	...	...	...	...	0705	...	0735	...	...	...	0805	...	0835	...	...	...	0905
24	Almere Centrum 465 d.	...	...	...	...	...	...	...	...	...	...	0712	...	0742	...	...	...	0812	...	0842	...	...	...	0912
*39	**Amersfoort** Centraal ◇ d.	...	...	...	...	0611	...	...	0641	...	...	|	0711	|	...	0741	...	|	0811	|	...	0841	...	|
*23	Hilversum ◇ d.	...	...	...	...	0623	...	...	0653	...	...	|	0723	|	...	0753	...	|	0823	|	...	0853	...	|
48	Duivendrecht d.	...	...	...	...	0638	...	...	0708	...	...	0728	0738	|	...	0808	...	0828	0838	|	...	0908	...	0928
53	**Amsterdam** Zuid 465 a.	...	...	...	...	0643	...	...	0713	...	...	0733	0743	0801	...	0813	...	0833	0843	0901	...	0913	...	0933
53	**Amsterdam** Zuid d.	0603	0612	...	0634	0644	0644	0703	0714	0714	...	0734	0744	0803	0803	0814	...	0834	0844	0903	0903	0914	...	0934
62	**Schiphol** d.	0611	0622	...	0641	0652	0652	0711	0722	0722	...	0741	0752	0811	0811	0822	...	0841	0852	0911	0911	0922	...	0941
115	**Rotterdam** Centraal a.	0639	0648	...	0708	0718	0718	0739	0748	0748	...	0808	0818	0839	0839	0848	...	0908	0918	0939	0939	0948	...	1008
115	**Rotterdam** Centraal 472 d.	0641	0653	0709	...	0723	...	0741	0753**a**	...	0809	...	0823**a**	0841	0841	0853**r**	0909	...	0923**r**	0941	0941	0953	1009	...
162	**Breda** 472 a.	|	0715	0734	...	0745	...	|	0815**a**	...	0834	...	0845**a**	|	|	0915**r**	0934	...	0945**r**	|	|	1015	1034	...
	Antwerpen Cent. **420** ☆ a.	0726	...	0816	...	...	...	0826	...	...	0916	...	...	0926	0925	...	1016	...	...	1026	1025	...	1116	...
	Brussels Midi/Zuid **420** ☆ a.	0811**v**	...	0917	...	...	...	0911**v**	...	...	1017	...	...	1011	1003	...	1117	...	...	1111	1103	...	1217	...

	⑤⑥		Ⓐ	Ⓒ			⚒	⑦		⚒	⑦			⚒	⑦			⚒	⑦			⚒	⑦
Lelystad Centrum 465 d.	...	...	0921	...	...	...	0953	...	...	1021	...	...	...	1053	...		...	1821	...	...	...	1853	...
Almere Buiten d.	...	...	0935	...	...	...	1005	...	...	1035	...	...	...	1105	...		...	1835	...	...	...	1905	...
Almere Centrum 465 d.	...	...	0942	...	...	...	1012	...	...	1042	...	...	...	1112	...	and	...	1842	...	...	...	1912	...
Amersfoort Centraal ◇ d.	...	0911	|	...	0941	...	|	...	1011	|	...	1041	...	|	...	at	1811	|	...	1841	...	|	...
Hilversum ◇ d.	...	0923	|	...	0953	...	|	...	1023	|	...	1053	...	|	...	the	1823	|	...	1853	...	|	...
Duivendrecht d.	...	0938	|	...	1008	...	1028	...	1038	|	...	1108	...	1128	...	same	1838	|	...	1908	...	1928	...
Amsterdam Zuid 465 a.	...	0943	1001	...	1013	...	1033	...	1043	1101	...	1113	...	1133	...	minutes	1843	1901	...	1913	...	1933	...
Amsterdam Zuid d.	0934	0944	1003	1003	1014	...	1034	1034	1044	1103	1103	1114	...	1134	1134	past	1844	1903	1903	1914	...	1934	1934
Schiphol d.	0942	0952	1011	1011	1022	...	1041	1041	1052	1111	1111	1122	...	1141	1141	each	1852	1911	1911	1922	...	1941	1941
Rotterdam Centraal a.	1008	1018	1039	1039	1048	...	1108	1108	1118	1139	1139	1148	...	1208	1208	hour	1918	1939	1939	1948	...	2008	2008
Rotterdam Centraal 472 d.	...	1023	1041	1041	1053	1109	...	...	1123	1141	1141	1153	1209	...	...	until	1923	1941	1941	1953	2009	...	...
Breda 472 a.	...	1045	|	|	1115	1134	...	...	1145	|	|	1215	1234	...	...		1945	|	|	2015	2034	...	...
Antwerpen Cent. **420** ☆ a.	...	...	1126	1125	...	1216	...	...	...	1226	1225	...	1316	...	...		...	2026	2025	...	2116	...	...
Brussels Midi/Zuid **420** ☆ a.	...	...	1211	1203	...	1317	...	...	...	1311**x**	1303	...	1417	...	...		...	2111**x**	2103	...	2217	...	...

Lelystad Centrum 465 d.	...	...	...	...	...	...	...	...	...	...	...	...	...	...	...	...	...	...	...	...	...	...	...	...
Almere Buiten d.	...	...	...	...	...	...	...	...	...	...	...	...	...	...	...	...	...	...	...	...	...	...	...	...
Almere Centrum 465 d.	...	...	...	...	...	...	...	...	...	...	...	...	...	...	...	...	...	...	...	...	...	...	...	...
Amersfoort Centraal ◇ d.	1911	...	1941	...	...	2011	...	2041	...	...	2111	...	2141	...	2211	...	2241	...	...	...	...	...	...	...
Hilversum ◇ d.	1923	...	1953	...	...	2023	...	2053	...	...	2123	...	2153	...	2223	...	2253	...	...	...	...	...	...	...
Duivendrecht d.	1938	...	2008	...	...	2038	...	2108	...	...	2138	...	2208	...	2238	...	2308	...	...	...	...	...	...	...
Amsterdam Zuid 465 a.	1943	...	2013	...	...	2043	...	2113	...	...	2143	...	2213	...	2243	...	2313	...	...	...	...	...	...	...
Amsterdam Zuid d.	1944	2003	2014	...	2034	2044	2103	2114	...	2134	2144	2203	2214	2234	2244	2303	2314	...	...	...	...	...	...	...
Schiphol d.	1952	2011	2022	...	2041	2052	2111	2122	...	2141	2152	2211	2222	2241	2252	2311	2322	...	...	...	...	...	...	...
Rotterdam Centraal a.	2018	2039	2048	...	2108	2118	2139	2148	...	2208	2218	2238	2248	2308	2318	2338	2348	...	...	...	...	...	...	...
Rotterdam Centraal 472 d.	...	2041	...	2109	...	...	2141	...	2209	...	...	...	...	...	...	...	...	...	...	...	...	...	...	...
Breda 472 a.	...	|	...	2134	...	...	|	...	2234	...	...	...	...	...	...	...	...	...	...	...	...	...	...	...
Antwerpen Cent. **420** ☆ a.	...	2126	...	2216	...	...	2226	...	2316	...	...	...	...	...	...	...	...	...	...	...	...	...	...	...
Brussels Midi/Zuid **420** ☆ a.	...	2211**v**	...	2317	...	...	2311**v**	...	0017	...	...	...	...	...	...	...	...	...	...	...	...	...	...	...

	⚒	Ⓐ	⚒	Ⓐ u		Ⓐ		Ⓐ u			Ⓐ	Ⓒ		Ⓐ u	⑥			Ⓐ	Ⓒ	⚒	⚒ t	⑦		
Brussels Midi/Zuid **420** ☆ d.	...	...	...	...	...	...	...	...	0544	...	0649	0657	...	...	...	0644	...	0749	0757	...	...	...	0744	...
Antwerpen Cent. **420** ☆ d.	...	...	...	...	...	...	...	...	0645	...	0735	0735	...	...	...	0745	...	0835	0835	...	...	...	0845	...
Breda 472 d.	...	...	...	...	0645**a**	...	0715**a**	...	0726	0745**a**	|	|	0815**a**	...	...	0826	0845**a**	|	|	0915	...	...	0926	0945
Rotterdam Centraal 472 a.	...	...	...	...	0707**a**	...	0737**a**	...	0750	0807**a**	0819	0819	0837**a**	...	...	0850	0907**a**	0919	0919	0937	...	...	0950	1007
Rotterdam Centraal d.	0611	0621	0641	0651	0711	0721	0741	0751	...	0811	0821	0821	0841	0851	0852	...	0911	0921	0921	0941	0951	0952	...	1011
Schiphol d.	0638	0650	0708	0718	0738	0750	0808	0818	...	0838	0850	0850	0908	0918	0919	...	0938	0950	0950	1008	1018	1019	...	1038
Amsterdam Zuid a.	0644	0656	0714	0724	0744	0756	0814	0824	...	0844	0856	0856	0914	0924	0926	...	0944	0956	0956	1014	1024	1025	...	1044
Amsterdam Zuid 465 d.	0646	0657	0716	0726	0746	0757	0816	0826	...	0846	0857	...	0916	0926	...	...	0946	0957	...	1016	1026	...	...	1046
Duivendrecht d.	0650	|	0720	0731	0750	|	0820	0831	...	0850	|	...	0920	0931	...	...	0950	|	...	1021	1031	...	...	1051
Hilversum ◇ d.	0707	|	0737	|	0807	|	0837	|	...	0907	|	...	0937	|	...	...	1007	|	...	1037	|	...	...	1107
Amersfoort Centraal ◇ a.	0718	|	0748	|	0818	|	0848	|	...	0918	|	...	0948	|	...	...	1018	|	...	1048	|	...	...	1118
Almere Centrum 465 d.	...	0720	...	0749	...	0820	...	0849	...	...	0920	...	...	0949	...	...	...	1020	...	...	1049	...	...	...
Almere Buiten d.	...	0727	...	0754	...	0827	...	0854	...	...	0927	...	...	0954	...	...	...	1027	...	...	1054	...	...	...
Lelystad Centrum 465 a.	...	0738	...	0806	...	0838	...	0906	...	...	0938	...	...	1006	...	...	...	1038	...	...	1106	...	...	...

	⚒	⑦		⚒ t	⑦			⚒	⑦			⚒ t	⑦			Ⓐ	Ⓒ					Ⓐ	Ⓒ
Brussels Midi/Zuid **420** ☆ d.	0849**z**	0857	...	...	...	0844	...	0949**z**	0957		...	...	...	1644	...	1749	1757	...	...	1744	...	1849	1857
Antwerpen Cent. **420** ☆ d.	0935	0935	...	...	...	0945	...	1035	1035		...	...	...	1745	...	1835	1835	...	...	1845	...	1935	1935
Breda 472 d.	|	|	1015	...	...	1026	1045	|	|	and	1815	...	...	1826	1845	|	|	1915	...	1926	1945	|	|
Rotterdam Centraal 472 a.	1019	1019	1037	...	...	1050	1107	1119	1119	at	1837	...	...	1850	1907	1919	1919	1937	...	1950	2007	2019	2019
Rotterdam Centraal d.	1021	1021	1041	1051	1052	...	1111	1121	1121	the	1841	1851	1852	...	1911	1921	1921	1941	1952	...	2011	2021	2021
Schiphol d.	1050	1050	1108	1118	1119	...	1138	1150	1150	same	1908	1918	1919	...	1938	1950	1950	2008	2019	...	2038	2050	2050
Amsterdam Zuid a.	1056	1056	1114	1124	1125	...	1144	1156	1156	minutes	1914	1924	1925	...	1944	1956	1956	2014	2025	...	2044	2056	2056
Amsterdam Zuid 465 d.	1057	...	1116	1126	...	...	1146	1157	...	past	1916	1926	...	...	1946	...	...	2016	...	...	2046	...	...
Duivendrecht d.	|	...	1121	1131	...	...	1151	|	...	each	1921	1931	...	...	1951	...	...	2021	...	...	2051	...	...
Hilversum ◇ d.	|	...	1137	|	...	...	1207	|	...	hour	1937	|	...	...	2007	...	...	2037	...	...	2107	...	...
Amersfoort Centraal ◇ a.	|	...	1148	|	...	...	1218	|	...	until	1948	|	...	...	2018	...	...	2048	...	...	2118	...	...
Almere Centrum 465 d.	1120	...	...	1149	...	...	...	1220	...		...	1949	...	...	...	...	...	...	...	...	...	...	...
Almere Buiten d.	1127	...	...	1154	...	...	...	1227	...		...	1954	...	...	...	...	...	...	...	...	...	...	...
Lelystad Centrum 465 a.	1138	...	...	1206	...	...	...	1238	...		...	2006	...	...	...	...	...	...	...	...	...	...	...

					Ⓐ	Ⓒ					Ⓐ	Ⓒ					Ⓐ	Ⓒ		⑤⑥				
Brussels Midi/Zuid **420** ☆ d.	...	...	1844	...	1949	1957	...	...	1944	...	2049	2057	...	...	2044	...	2149	2157	...	...	...	...	...	...
Antwerpen Cent. **420** ☆ d.	...	...	1945	...	2035	2035	...	...	2045	...	2135	2135	...	...	2145	...	2235	2235	...	...	...	...	...	...
Breda 472 d.	2015	...	2026	2045	|	|	...	...	2126	...	|	|	...	...	2226	...	|	|	...	...	...	...	...	...
Rotterdam Centraal 472 a.	2037	...	2050	2107	2119	2119	...	...	2150	...	2219	2219	...	...	2250	...	2319	2319	...	...	...	...	...	...
Rotterdam Centraal d.	2041	2052	...	2111	2121	2121	2141	2152	...	2211	2221	2221	2241	2251	...	2311	2321	2321	2341	2341	...	...	...	...
Schiphol d.	2108	2119	...	2138	2150	2150	2208	2219	...	2238	2250	2250	2308	2320	...	2338	2350	2350	0008	0008	...	...	...	...
Amsterdam Zuid a.	2114	2125	...	2144	2156	2156	2214	2225	...	2244	2256	2256	2314	2326	...	2344	2356	2356	0014	0014	...	...	...	...
Amsterdam Zuid 465 d.	2116	...	...	2146	...	...	2216	...	...	2246	...	...	2316	...	...	2346	...	...	...	0016	...	...	...	...
Duivendrecht d.	2121	...	...	2151	...	...	2220	...	...	2250	...	...	2320	...	...	2350	...	...	...	0020	...	...	...	...
Hilversum ◇ d.	2137	...	...	2207	...	...	2237	...	...	2307	...	...	2337	...	...	0007	...	...	...	0037	...	...	...	...
Amersfoort Centraal ◇ a.	2148	...	...	2218	...	...	2248	...	...	2318	...	...	2348	...	...	0018	...	...	...	0048	...	...	...	...
Almere Centrum 465 d.	...	...	...	...	...	...	...	...	...	...	...	...	...	...	...	...	...	...	...	...	...	...	...	...
Almere Buiten d.	...	...	...	...	...	...	...	...	...	...	...	...	...	...	...	...	...	...	...	...	...	...	...	...
Lelystad Centrum 465 a.	...	...	...	...	...	...	...	...	...	...	...	...	...	...	...	...	...	...	...	...	...	...	...	...

a – Ⓐ only.
r – ⚒ only.
t – Departs Rotterdam one minute later on ⑤⑥.
u – Departs Rotterdam one minute later on ⑤.
v – Arrives 8 minutes earlier on ⑥⑦.
x – Arrives 8 minutes earlier on ⑥.
z – Departs 8 minutes later on ⑥.

☆ – For Eurostar trains Amsterdam - Rotterdam - Antwerpen - Brussels - Paris see Table **18**.
◇ – Most trains continue to / from Amersfoort Schothorst. For Amsterdam Centraal - Hilversum - Amersfoort see Table **480**.
* – Distance from Duivendrecht.
§ – Special tickets required south of Rotterdam.

☛ Domestic trains via the high-speed line are classified *Intercity direct*, fast Brussels trains are *Eurocity Direct* §, Rotterdam - Brussels via Breda trains are *Eurocity*. Supplement payable Schiphol - Rotterdam or v.v.
For Amsterdam Centraal - Rotterdam via Den Haag see Table **450**.
For Amsterdam Centraal - Rotterdam via Gouda see Table **455**.
For Amsterdam Centraal - Schiphol ✈ see Table **451**.
For Amsterdam Centraal - Almere Centrum see Table **481**.

462 ROTTERDAM - GOUDA - UTRECHT *IC trains*

Certain journeys continue to/from Amersfoort and Enschede (Table **463**). For additional trains Rotterdam - Gouda see Table **455**.

km		⑥⑦	Ⓐ	⚒	Ⓐ	⚒	Ⓐ		Ⓐ		Ⓐ		Ⓐ		Ⓐ		Ⓐ		⚒		⚒				
0	**Rotterdam** Centraal ... d.	0410	0550	0620	0635	0650	0705	0720	0735	0750	0805	0820	0835	0850	0905	0920	0935	0950	1005	1020	1035	1050	1105	1120	1135
10	Rotterdam Alexander .. d.	0418	0558	0628	0643	0658	0713	0728	0743	0758	0813	0828	0843	0858	0913	0928	0943	0958	1013	1028	1043	1058	1113	1128	1143
24	Gouda .... **463** d.	0428	0609	0639	0654	0709	0724	0739	0754	0809	0824	0839	0854	0909	0924	0939	0954	1009	1024	1039	1054	1109	1124	1139	1154
56	**Utrecht** Centraal.. **463** a.	0447	0627	0657	0712	0727	0742	0757	0812	0827	0842	0857	0912	0927	0942	0957	1012	1027	1042	1027	1112	1127	1142	1157	1212

									⑥⑦
Rotterdam Centraal .... d.	1150	and every 15 minutes until	2050	2120	and every 30 minutes until	2350	0020	0050
Rotterdam Alexander ... d.	1158		2058	2128		2358	0028	0058
Gouda .... **463** d.	1209		2109	2139		0009	0039	0109
Utrecht Centraal... **463** a.	1227		2127	2157		0027	0057	0127

	⑥⑦ u	Ⓐ	Ⓐ	Ⓐ	Ⓐ	⚒	Ⓐ	⚒	Ⓐ	
Utrecht Centraal .... **463** d.	0458	0603	0618	0633	0648	0703	0718	0733	0748	0803
Gouda .... **463** d.	0518	0622	0636	0652	0706	0722	0736	0752	0806	0822
Rotterdam Alexander .... d.	0527	0631	0646	0701	0716	0731	0746	0801	0816	0831
Rotterdam Centraal .... a.	0535	0640	0655	0710	0725	0740	0755	0810	0825	0840

	Ⓐ		Ⓐ		Ⓐ		⚒		⚒														⑥⑦
Utrecht Centraal... **463** d.	0818	0833	0848	0903	0918	0933	0948	1003	1018	1033	1048	1103	and every 15 minutes until	2018	2033	2103	2133	2203	2233	2303	2333	0003	0033	0118
Gouda .... **463** d.	0836	0852	0906	0922	0936	0952	1006	1022	1036	1052	1106	1122		2036	2052	2122	2152	2222	2252	2322	2352	0022	0052	0137
Rotterdam Alexander ... d.	0846	0901	0916	0931	0946	1001	1016	1031	1046	1101	1116	1131		2046	2101	2131	2201	2231	2301	2331	0001	0031	0101	0146
Rotterdam Centraal .... a.	0855	0910	0925	0940	0955	1010	1025	1040	1055	1110	1125	1140		2055	2110	2140	2210	2240	2310	2340	0010	0040	0110	0155

u – An additional journey runs at 0258⑥⑦.

463 DEN HAAG - UTRECHT - AMERSFOORT - ENSCHEDE *IC trains*

For Rotterdam - Amersfoort via high-speed line and Amsterdam Zuid see Table **460**.

km		Ⓐ	Ⓐ	⚒	E	⑥	Ⓐ	⚒	⑥	G	⚒	⑥	G		Ⓒ	Ⓐ		Ⓒ	Ⓐ		†	⚒		†	⚒
	Rotterdam C. **462** .... d.	...	...	...	...	0620	...	...	0650	...	...	0720	...	...	0750	...	...	0820	...	...	0850	...	...	0920	...
0	**Den Haag** Cent. .... d.	...	0540	...	0610	|	0625	0640	|	0655	0710	|	0725	0740	|	0755	0810	|	0825	0840	|	0855	0910	|	0925
28	Gouda .... **462** d.	...	0559	...	0629	0639	0644	0659	0709	0714	0729	0739	0744	0759	0809	0814	0829	0839	0844	0859	0909	0914	0929	0939	0944
60	**Utrecht** Cent. ...... **462** a.	...	0617	...	0647	0657	0702	0717	0727	0732	0747	0757	0802	0817	0827	0832	0847	0857	0902	0917	0927	0932	0947	0957	1002
60	**Utrecht** Cent. .... d.	...	0621	...	0651	0707	0707	0721	0737	0737	0751	0807	0807	0821	0837	0837	0851	0907	0907	0921	0937	0937	0951	1007	1007
81	**Amersfoort** Cent. .... a.	...	0633	...	0703	0720	0720	0733	0750	0750	0803	0820	0820	0833	0850	0850	0903	0920	0920	0933	0950	0950	1003	1020	1020
81	**Amersfoort** Cent. **480** d.	0622	0635	0652	0705	0722	0722	0735	0752	0752	0805	0822	0822	0835	0852	0852	0905	0922	0922	0935	0952	0952	1005	1022	1022
124	Apeldoorn .... **480** d.	0647	△	0717	▽	0747	0747	△	0817	0817	▽	0847	0847	△	0917	0917	▽	0947	0947	△	1017	1017	▽	1047	1047
139	Deventer .... **480** d.	0701	...	0731	...	0801	0801	...	0831	0831	...	0901	0901	...	0931	0931	...	1001	1001	...	1031	1031	...	1101	1101
177	Almelo .... **492** d.	0725	...	0755	...	0825	0825	...	0855	0855	...	0925	0925	...	0955	0955	...	1025	1025	...	1055	1055	...	1125	1125
192	**Hengelo** .... **480 492** d.	0737	...	0807	...	0837	0837	...	0907	0907	...	0937	0937	...	1007	1007	...	1037	1037	...	1107	1107	...	1137	1137
200	**Enschede** .... **492** a.	0744	...	0814	...	0844	0844	...	0914	0914	...	0944	0944	...	1014	1014	...	1044	1044	...	1114	1114	...	1144	1144

		†	⚒		†	⚒																		
Rotterdam C. **462** ..... d.	...	0950	...	...	1020	...	...	...	...	...	...	...	and at the same minutes past each hour until	...	...	...	...	...	...	...	2050	...	2120	...
Den Haag Cent. .... d.	0940	|	0955	1010	|	1025	1040	1055	1110	1125	1140	1155		1910	1925	1940	1955	2010	2025	2040	|	2110	|	2140
Gouda .... **462** d.	0959	1009	1014	1029	1039	1044	1059	1114	1129	1144	1159	1214		1929	1944	1959	2014	2029	2044	2059	2109	2129	2139	2159
Utrecht Cent. .... **462** a.	1017	1027	1032	1047	1057	1102	1117	1132	1147	1202	1217	1232		1947	2002	2017	2032	2047	2102	2117	2127	2147	2157	2217
Utrecht Cent. .... d.	1021	1037	1037	1051	1107	1107	1121	1137	1151	1207	1221	1237		1951	2007	2021	2037	2051	2107	2121	2137	2151	2207	2221
Amersfoort Cent. .... a.	1033	1050	1050	1103	1120	1120	1133	1150	1203	1220	1233	1250		2003	2020	2033	2050	2103	2120	2133	2150	2203	2220	2233
Amersfoort Cent. . **480** d.	1035	1052	1052	1105	1122	1122	1135	1152	1205	1222	1235	1252		2005	2022	2035	2052	2105	2122	2135	2152	2205	2222	2235
Apeldoorn .... **480** d.	△	1117	1117	▽	1147	1147	△	1217	▽	1247	△	1317		▽	2047	△	2117	▽	2147	△	2217	▽	2247	△
Deventer .... **480** d.	...	1131	1131	...	1201	1201	...	1231	...	1301	...	1331		...	2101	...	2131	...	2201	...	2231	...	2301	...
Almelo .... **492** d.	...	1155	1155	...	1225	1225	...	1255	...	1325	...	1355		...	2125	...	2155	...	2225	...	2255	...	2325	...
Hengelo .... **480 492** d.	...	1207	1207	...	1237	1237	...	1307	...	1337	...	1407		...	2137	...	2207	...	2237	...	2307	...	2337	...
Enschede .... **492** a.	...	1214	1214	...	1244	1244	...	1314	...	1344	...	1414		...	2144	...	2214	...	2244	...	2314	...	2344	...

						⚒	⑤⑥			⑥	Ⓒ
Rotterdam C. **462** ..... d.	2150	...	2220	...	2250	...	2320	...	2350	...	...
Den Haag Cent. .... d.	|	2210	|	2240	|	2310	|	2340	|	0010	0110
Gouda .... **462** d.	2209	2229	2239	2259	2309	2329	2339	2359	0009	0029	0129
Utrecht Cent. .... **462** a.	2227	2247	2257	2317	2327	2347	2357	0017	0027	0047	0147
Utrecht Cent. .... d.	2237	2251	2307	2321	2337	2351	0007	0021	0037	0051	...
Amersfoort Cent. .... a.	2250	2303	2320	2333	2350	0003	0020	0033	0050	0103	...
Amersfoort Cent. . **480** d.	2252	2305	2322	2335	2352	0005	0022	...	...	0105	...
Apeldoorn .... **480** d.	2317	▽	2347	z	0017	▽	0047	...	...	▽	...
Deventer .... **480** d.	2331	...	0001	...	0031	...	0101	...	...	...	...
Almelo .... **492** d.	2355	...	0025	...	0055	...	0125	...	...	...	...
Hengelo .... **480 492** d.	0007	...	0037	...	0107	...	0137	...	...	...	...
Enschede .... **492** a.	0014	...	0044	...	0114	...	0144	...	...	...	...

	Ⓐ	Ⓐ	Ⓐ	Ⓐ	Ⓐ	Ⓐ	Ⓐ	⑥	J
Enschede .... **492** d.	...	...	0446	...	0516	...	0546	0546	...
Hengelo .... **480 492** d.	...	...	0454	...	0524	...	0554	0554	...
Almelo .... **492** d.	...	...	0506	...	0536	...	0606	0606	...
Deventer .... **480** d.	...	...	0533	...	0603	...	0633	0633	...
Apeldoorn .... **480** d.	z	z	0544	z	0614	▽	0644	0644	△
Amersfoort Cent. .... **480** a.	0524	0554	0608	0624	0638	0654	0708	0708	0724
Amersfoort Cent. .... d.	0526	0556	0610	0626	0640	0656	0710	0710	0726
Utrecht Cent. .... a.	0539	0609	0623	0639	0653	0709	0723	0723	0739
Utrecht Cent. .... **462** d.	0543	0613	0628	0643	0658	0713	0728	0733	0743
Gouda .... **462** d.	0602	0632	0647	0702	0717	0732	0747	0752	0802
Den Haag Cent. .... a.	0621	0651	0706	0721	0736	0751	0806	|	0821
Rotterdam Cent. **462** ...... a.	...	...	...	...	...	...	...	0810	...

	Ⓐ	⑥	⚒	Ⓐ	⑥		Ⓐ	Ⓒ		⚒	†			⚒	†		⚒	†						
Enschede .... **492** d.	0616	0616	...	0646	0646	...	0716	0716	...	0745	0745	...	...	0816	0816	...	0846	0846	...	0916	...	0945	...	and at the same minutes past each hour until
Hengelo .... **480 492** d.	0624	0624	...	0654	0654	...	0724	0724	...	0754	0754	...	...	0824	0824	...	0854	0854	...	0924	...	0954	...	
Almelo .... **492** d.	0636	0636	...	0706	0706	...	0736	0736	...	0806	0806	...	...	0836	0836	...	0906	0906	...	0936	...	1006	...	
Deventer .... **480** d.	0703	0703	...	0733	0733	...	0803	0803	...	0833	0833	...	...	0903	0903	...	0933	0933	...	1003	...	1033	...	
Apeldoorn .... **480** d.	0714	0714	▽	0744	0744	△	0814	0814	▽	0844	0844	...	△	0914	0914	▽	0944	0944	△	1014	▽	1044	△	
Amersfoort Cent. . **480** a.	0738	0738	0754	0808	0808	0824	0838	0838	0854	0908	0908	...	0924	0938	0938	0954	1008	1008	1024	1038	1054	1108	1124	
Amersfoort Cent. .... d.	0740	0740	0756	0810	0810	0826	0840	0840	0856	0910	0910	...	0926	0940	0940	0956	1010	1010	1026	1040	1056	1110	1126	
Utrecht Cent. .... a.	0753	0753	0809	0823	0823	0839	0853	0853	0909	0923	0923	...	0939	0953	0953	1009	1023	1023	1039	1053	1109	1123	1139	
Utrecht Cent. .... **462** d.	0758	0803	0813	0828	0833	0843	0858	0903	0913	0928	0933	...	0943	0958	1003	1013	1028	1033	1043	1058	1113	1128	1143	
Gouda .... **462** d.	0817	0822	0834	0847	0852	0902	0917	0922	0932	0947	0952	...	1002	1017	1022	1032	1047	1052	1102	1117	1132	1147	1202	
Den Haag Cent. .... a.	0836	|	0852	0908	|	0921	0936	|	0951	1006	|	...	1021	1036	|	1051	1106	|	1121	1136	1151	1206	1221	
Rotterdam C. **462** ..... a.	...	0840	...	...	0910	...	...	0940	...	...	1010	...	...	...	1040	...	...	1110	...	...	...	...	...	

																					⑤⑥ u		⑤⑥		
Enschede .... **492** d.	1816	...	1846	...	1916	...	1945	...	2016	...	2046	...	2116	...	2146	...	2216	...	2246	...	...	...	2316	...	...
Hengelo .... **480 492** d.	1824	...	1854	...	1924	...	1954	...	2024	...	2054	...	2124	...	2154	...	2224	...	2254	...	...	...	2324	...	...
Almelo .... **492** d.	1836	...	1906	...	1936	...	2006	...	2036	...	2106	...	2136	...	2206	...	2236	...	2306	...	...	...	2336	...	...
Deventer .... **480** d.	1903	...	1933	...	2003	...	2033	...	2103	...	2133	...	2203	...	2233	...	2303	...	2333	...	...	...	0003	...	...
Apeldoorn .... **480** d.	1914	▽	1944	△	2014	▽	2044	△	2114	▽	2144	△	2214	▽	2244	△	2314	▽	2344	...	△	...	0014	...	...
Amersfoort Cent. . **480** a.	1938	1954	2008	2024	2038	2054	2108	2124	2138	2154	2208	2224	2238	2254	2308	2324	2338	2354	0008	...	0024	...	0038	...	...
Amersfoort Cent. .... d.	1940	1956	2010	2026	2040	2056	2110	2126	2140	2156	2210	2226	2240	2256	2310	2326	2340	2356	0010	...	0026	...	...	...	...
Utrecht Cent. .... a.	1953	2009	2023	2039	2053	2109	2123	2139	2153	2209	2223	2239	2253	2309	2323	2339	2353	0009	0023	...	0039	...	...	...	...
Utrecht Cent. .... **462** d.	1958	2013	2028	2043	2058	2113	2133	2143	2203	2213	2233	2243	2303	2313	2333	2343	0003	0013	0033	...	0043	...	...	...	...
Gouda .... **462** d.	2017	2032	2047	2102	2117	2132	2152	2202	2222	2232	2252	2302	2322	2332	2352	0002	0022	0032	0052	...	0102	...	...	...	...
Den Haag Cent. .... a.	2036	2051	2106	2121	2136	2151	|	2221	|	2251	|	2321	|	2351	|	0021	|	0051	|	...	0121	...	...	...	...
Rotterdam C. **462** ..... a.	...	...	...	...	...	...	2210	...	2240	...	2310	...	2340	...	0010		0040	...	0110	...	...	...	...	...	...

E – Ⓐ from Den Haag, ⚒ from Utrecht.
G – Ⓐ from Den Haag, daily from Amersfoort.
J – From Leeuwarden on Ⓐ, Zwolle on ⑥, Amersfoort on †.

u – Next day from Amersfoort.
z – To/from Zwolle (Table **465**).

△ – To/from Zwolle and Leeuwarden (Table **465**).
▽ – To/from Zwolle and Groningen (Table **465**).

☛ For Enschede to Amsterdam and v.v. change at Utrecht for trains in Table **470** or at Deventer for trains in Table **480**.

IC trains AMSTERDAM - LELYSTAD - ZWOLLE - GRONINGEN and LEEUWARDEN 465

Intercity trains - for local *Sprinter* services see below main table

km		Ⓐ	Ⓐ	⑥t A	Ⓐ	Ⓐ	Ⓐ	⚒	Ⓐ ◁		⚒	⚒ ◁		⚒	⚒ ◁		◁		◁		◁		◁	
	Den Haag Cent. **463** d.	...	...	...	...	...	0540	...	...	...	0610**a**	...	...	0640	...	0710**r**	...	0740	...	0810	...	0840	...	...
	Utrecht Cent. **463** d.	...	...	...	...	...	0621	...	...	...	0651	...	...	0721	...	0751**r**	...	0821	...	0851	...	0921	...	...
	Amersfoort Cent. d.	...	...	...	0605	...	0635	...	...	...	0705	...	...	0735	...	0805	...	0835	...	0905	...	0935	...	...
0	Schiphol ✈ **460** d.	...	...	0449	|	...	|	...	0602	...	|	0630	...	|	0702	|	0730	|	0802	|	0830	|	0902	...
9	**Amsterdam Zuid** **460** d.	...	...	0511**c**	|	...	|	...	0611	...	|	0641	...	|	0711	|	0741	|	0811	|	0841	|	0911	...
38	Almere Centrum **460** d.	...	...	0535	|	...	|	...	0633	...	|	0703	...	|	0733	|	0803	|	0833	|	0903	|	0933	...
62	Lelystad Centrum **460** d.	0547	...	0550	|	...	|	...	0647	...	|	0717	...	|	0747	|	0817	|	0847	|	0917	|	0947	...
112	**Zwolle** a.	0613	...	0615	0640	...	0710	...	0713	...	0740	0743	...	0810	0813	0840	0843	0910	0913	0940	0943	1010	1013	...
112	**Zwolle** d.	0615	0618	0617	0645	0648	0718	0718	0715	...	0745	0748	0818	0818	0815	0845	0848	0918	0915	0945	0948	1018	1015	...
139	Meppel d.	|	0634	|	|	0704	0734	0734	|	...	|	0804	0834	0834	|	|	0904	0934	|	|	1004	1034	|	...
153	Steenwijk d.	|	0643	|	|	0713	0743	0743	|	...	|	0813	0843	0843	|	|	0913	0943	|	|	1013	1043	|	...
177	Heerenveen d.	|	0656	|	|	0726	0756	0756	|	...	|	0826	0856	0856	|	|	0926	0956	|	|	1026	1056	|	...
206	**Leeuwarden** a.	|	0713	|	|	0743	0813	0813	|	...	|	0843	0913	0913	|	|	0943	1013	|	|	1043	1113	|	...
189	Assen d.	0655	...	0656	0725	...	...	...	0755	...	0825	...	...	...	0855	0925	...	...	0955	1025	...	...	1055	...
216	**Groningen** a.	0711	...	0712	0741	...	...	...	0811	...	0841	...	...	...	0911	0941	...	...	1011	1041	...	...	1111	...

			◁		◁			◁		◁		◁		◁		◁			⚒	⑤⑥ ◁	⑥⑦	⑥	⑥⑦ A	
	Den Haag Cent. **463** d.	0910	...	0940	...		2010	...	2040	...	2110	...	2140	...	2210	...	2240	...	2310	...	...	0010	...	...
	Utrecht Cent. **463** d.	0951	...	1021	...	and at	2051	...	2121	...	2151	...	2221	...	2251	...	2321	...	2351	...	...	0051	...	...
	Amersfoort Cent. d.	1005	...	1035	...		2105	...	2135	...	2205	...	2235	...	2305	...	2335	...	0005	...	...	0105	...	...
	Schiphol ✈ **460** d.	|	0930	|	1002	the	|	2030	|	2102	|	2130	|	2202	|	2230	|	2302	|	2330	0002	|	0242	...
	Amsterdam Zuid **460** d.	|	0941	|	1011		|	2041	|	2111	|	2141	|	2211	|	2241	|	2311	|	2341	0011	|	0259**c**	...
	Almere Centrum **460** d.	|	1003	|	1033	same	|	2103	|	2133	|	2203	|	2233	|	2303	|	2333	|	0003	0033	|	0320	...
	Lelystad Centrum **460** d.	|	1017	|	1047	minutes	|	2117	|	2147	|	2217	|	2247	|	2317	|	2347	|	0017	0047	|	0334	...
	Zwolle a.	1040	1043	1110	1113		2140	2143	2210	2213	2240	2243	2310	2313	2340	2343	0010	0013	0044	0042	0113	0140	0359	...
	Zwolle d.	1045	1048	1118	1115	past	2145	2148	2218	2215	2245	2248	2318	2315	2345	2348	...	0015	0046	0048	0115	0145	...	...
	Meppel d.	|	1104	1134	|	each	|	2204	2234	|	|	2304	2334	|	|	0004	...	|	|	0104	|	0201	...	...
	Steenwijk d.	|	1113	1143	|		|	2213	2243	|	|	2313	2343	|	|	0013	...	|	|	0113	|	|	...	...
	Heerenveen d.	|	1126	1156	|	hour	|	2226	2256	|	|	2326	2356	|	|	0029	...	|	|	0129	|	|	...	...
	Leeuwarden a.	|	1143	1213	|	until	|	2243	2313	|	|	2343	0013	|	|	0052	...	|	|	0152	|	|	...	...
	Assen d.	1125	...	...	1155		2225	...	...	2255	2325	...	...	2355	0025	...	...	0055	0125	...	0155	0232	...	...
	Groningen a.	1141	...	...	1211		2241	...	...	2311	2341	...	...	0011	0041	...	...	0111	0142	...	0211	0253	...	...

	⑥⑦ A		⑥t A	Ⓐ	Ⓐ	⚒	Ⓐ	Ⓐ	Ⓐ ◁	⑥ u	Ⓐ	Ⓐ ◁	⑥	Ⓐ	⚒ ◁	⑦ u	⚒	◁		◁		◁		◁
Groningen d.	...	...	0142	...	...	...	...	...	0518	0536	0549	...	...	...	0619	0636	0649	...	...	0719	0749	...	...	0819
Assen d.	...	...	0159	...	...	...	...	...	0535	0558	0605	...	...	...	0635	0658	0705	...	...	0735	0805	...	...	0835
Leeuwarden d.	...	...	|	...	...	...	...	0507	|	|	|	0547	...	0617	|	|	|	0637**z**	0717	|	|	0737**x**	0817	|
Heerenveen d.	...	...	|	...	...	...	...	0530	|	|	|	0604	...	0634	|	|	|	0659**z**	0734	|	|	0759**x**	0834	|
Steenwijk d.	...	...	|	...	...	...	...	0546	|	|	|	0617	...	0647	|	|	|	0716	0747	|	|	0816	0847	|
Meppel d.	...	...	|	...	...	...	...	0556	|	0629	|	0626	...	0656	|	0729	|	0726	0756	|	|	0826	0856	|
Zwolle a.	...	...	0237	...	...	...	...	0611	0615	0644	0644	0641	...	0711	0714	0744	0744	0741	0811	0814	0844	0841	0911	0914
Zwolle d.	0121	...	0240	0449	0519	0546	0549	0617	0619	0646	0646	0649	0649	0716	0719	0746	0746	0749	0816	0819	0846	0849	0916	0919
Lelystad Centrum **460** d.	0146	...	0307	|	|	0613	|	0643	|	0713	0713	|	|	0743	|	0813	0813	|	0843	|	0913	|	0943	|
Almere Centrum **460** d.	0201	...	0321	|	|	0628	|	0658	|	0728	0728	|	|	0758	|	0828	0828	|	0858	|	0928	|	0958	|
Amsterdam Zuid **460** a.	0220**c**	...	0341**c**	|	|	0647	|	0717	|	0747	0747	|	|	0817	|	0847	0847	|	0917	|	0947	|	1017	|
Schiphol ✈ **460** a.	0236	...	0355	|	|	0656	|	0730	|	0756	0756	|	|	0830	|	0856	0856	|	0930	|	0956	|	1030	|
Amersfoort Cent. a.	...	...	...	0524	0554	...	0624	...	0654	...	...	0724	0724	...	0754	...	...	0824	...	0854	...	0924	...	0954
Utrecht Cent. **463** a.	...	...	...	0539	0609	...	0639	...	0709	...	...	0739	0739	...	0809	...	...	0839	...	0909	...	0939	...	1009
Den Haag Cent. **463** a.	...	...	...	0621	0651	...	0721	...	0751	...	...	0821	0821	...	0852	...	...	0921	...	0951	...	1021	...	1051

		◁		◁		◁		◁		◁			◁		◁		◁		⑤⑥ ◁			⑤⑥	
Groningen d.	0849	...	...	0919	0949	...	...	1019	1049	...		...	2119	2149	...	...	2219	2249	...	...	2319	2349	...
Assen d.	0905	...	...	0935	1005	...	...	1035	1105	...		...	2135	2205	...	...	2235	2305	...	...	2335	0005	...
Leeuwarden d.	|	0847	0917	|	|	0947	1017	|	|	1047	and at	2117	|	|	2147	2217	|	|	2247	2317	|	|	...
Heerenveen d.	|	0904	0934	|	|	1004	1034	|	|	1104	the	2134	|	|	2204	2234	|	|	2304	2334	|	|	...
Steenwijk d.	|	0917	0947	|	|	1017	1047	|	|	1117	same	2147	|	|	2217	2247	|	|	2317	2347	|	|	...
Meppel d.	|	0926	0956	|	|	1026	1056	|	|	1126		2156	|	|	2226	2256	|	|	2326	2356	|	|	...
Zwolle a.	0944	0941	1011	1014	1044	1041	1111	1114	1144	1141	minutes	2211	2214	2244	2241	2311	2314	2344	2341	0011	0014	0044	...
Zwolle d.	0946	0949	1016	1019	1046	1049	1116	1119	1146	1149		2216	2219	2246	2249	2316	2319	2346	2349	...	...	0046	...
Lelystad Centrum **460** d.	1013	|	1043	|	1113	|	1143	|	1213	|	past	2243	|	2313	|	2343	|	0013	|	...	...	0112	...
Almere Centrum **460** d.	1028	|	1058	|	1128	|	1158	|	1228	|	each	2258	|	2328	|	2358	|	0028	|	...	...	0127	...
Amsterdam Zuid **460** a.	1047	|	1117	|	1147	|	1217	|	1247	|		2317	|	2347	|	0017	|	0047	|	...	...	0147**c**	...
Schiphol ✈ **460** a.	1056	|	1130	|	1156	|	1230	|	1256	|	hour	2330	|	2356	|	0030	|	0058	|	...	...	0206	...
Amersfoort Cent. a.	...	1024	...	1054	...	1124	...	1154	...	1224	until	...	2254	...	2324	...	2354	...	0024	...	...	...	...
Utrecht Cent. **463** a.	...	1039	...	1109	...	1139	...	1209	...	1239		...	2309	...	2339	...	0009	...	0039	...	...	...	...
Den Haag Cent. **463** a.	...	1121	...	1151	...	1221	...	1251	...	1321		...	2351	...	0021	...	0051	...	0121	...	...	...	...

LOCAL *SPRINTER* TRAINS LELYSTAD - ZWOLLE

Certain trains continue to Leeuwarden (below)

km		Ⓐ	⚒	Ⓐ		Ⓐ		◧			
0	**Lelystad** Cent. d.	0553	0623	0653	0723	0753	0823	every	2223	2323	0023
21	Dronten d.	0606	0636	0706	0736	0806	0836	30	2236	2336	0036
34	Kampen Zuid d.	0614	0644	0714	0744	0814	0844	minutes	2244	2344	0044
50	**Zwolle** a.	0624	0654	0724	0754	0824	0854	until	2254	2354	0054

⊡	⚒	Ⓐ		⚒		◐			d	b
Zwolle d.	0637	0707	0737	0807	0837	every	2137	2237	2337	0007
Kampen Zuid d.	0646	0716	0746	0816	0846	30	2146	2246	2346	0016
Dronten d.	0655	0725	0755	0825	0855	minutes	2154	2255	2355	0025
Lelystad C. a.	0707	0737	0807	0837	0907	until	2207	2307	0007	0037

LOCAL *SPRINTER* TRAINS ZWOLLE - LEEUWARDEN

Certain trains start from Lelystad (above)

km		Ⓐ	⚒	Ⓐ						
0	**Zwolle** d.	0556	0626	0656	0726	every 30	2026	2126	2226	2256
27	Meppel d.	0612	0642	0712	0742	minutes on Ⓐ	2042	2142	2242	2312
41	Steenwijk d.	0621	0651	0721	0751	and	2051	2151	2251	2321
65	Heerenveen d.	0635	0705	0735	0805	hourly on Ⓒ	2105	2205	2305	2335
94	**Leeuwarden** a.	0656	0726	0756	0826		2126	2226	2326	2356

	Ⓐ	⚒	Ⓐ					⑤⑥	
Leeuwarden d.	0603	0633	0703	0733	every 30	2133	2233	2333	...
Heerenveen d.	0623	0653	0723	0753	minutes on Ⓐ	2153	2253	2353	...
Steenwijk d.	0639	0709	0739	0809	and	2209	2309	0009	...
Meppel d.	0648	0718	0748	0818	hourly on Ⓒ	2218	2318	0018	...
Zwolle a.	0703	0733	0803	0833		2233	2333	0033	...

LOCAL *SPRINTER* TRAINS ZWOLLE - GRONINGEN

km		Ⓐ	⚒	⚒		⚒		⚒				◇
0	**Zwolle** d.	0552	0652	0722	0752	0822	0852	0922	0952	and	2252	2352
27	Meppel d.	0608	0708	0738	0808	0838	0908	0938	1008	every	2308	0008
47	Hoogeveen d.	0619	0719	0749	0819	0849	0919	0949	1019	30	2319	0019
77	Assen d.	0637	0737	0807	0837	0907	0937	1007	1037	mins	2337	0037
104	**Groningen** a.	0657	0757	0827	0857	0927	0957	1027	1057	until	2357	0057

	Ⓐ	⚒	⚒	⚒		⚒		❦			
Groningen d.	0533	0603	0633	0703	0733	0803	0833	and	2233	2333	...
Assen d.	0554	0623	0653	0723	0753	0823	0853	every	2253	2353	...
Hoogeveen d.	0610	0640	0710	0740	0810	0840	0910	30	2310	0010	...
Meppel d.	0622	0652	0722	0752	0822	0852	0922	mins	2322	0022	...
Zwolle a.	0638	0708	0738	0808	0838	0908	0938	until	2338	0038	...

A – Operated by Arriva. 🅁 special fares payable.

a – Ⓐ only.
b – Runs 30 minutes later on ⑥⑦.
c – Amsterdam **Centraal**.
d – ①③④⑥⑦ only.
r – ⚒ only.
t – ⑥ to May 10 (not Feb. 15, 22, Mar. 29, Apr. 19).
u – Also calls at Hoogeveen (0617 and 0717).

x – On ①–⑥ departs Leeuwarden 0747, Heerenveen 0804.
z – On ①–⑤ departs Leeuwarden 0647, Heerenveen 0704.

❦ – Journeys at 0903 and 1003 run on ⚒ only.
◧ – Journeys at 0853 and 0953 run on ⚒ only.
◐ – The journey at 0907 runs on ⚒ only.
◁ – Connects at Zwolle with train in previous column.
◇ – An additional journey runs at 0018 on ①, 0052 on ②–⑦.
⊡ – Additional journeys run at 0537Ⓐ, 0607Ⓐ.

Timings may vary by up to 3 minutes

470 ENKHUIZEN - AMSTERDAM - EINDHOVEN - MAASTRICHT and HEERLEN

IC trains

km		Ⓐ	Ⓐ	⑥ ¶	Ⓐ	Ⓐ	Ⓐ	⚒	Ⓐ	Ⓐ	⑥	⑥	Ⓐ	①–④	⑤⑥ ◇	①–④	⑤–⑦		①–④	⑤–⑦	①–④		①–④ h	⑤⑥ e
0	**Enkhuizen** d.	...	...	...	...	...	0509	...	...	0539	...	0539	...	...	0609	0609	...	...	...	0639	0639	...	...	0709
18	Hoorn d.	...	...	...	...	...	0537	...	...	0607	...	0607	...	...	0637	0640	...	...	...	0707	0710	...	...	0737
	Alkmaar 457 d.	...	...	...	...	...	|	...	...	|	...	|	...	0627	|	|	...	...	0657	|	|	...	0727	|
	Castricum 457 d.	...	...	...	...	...	|	...	...	|	...	|	...	0635	|	|	...	...	0705	|	|	...	0735	|
	Zaandam 457 d.	...	...	...	...	...	|	...	...	|	...	|	...	0649	|	|	...	...	0719	|	|	...	0749	|
57	Amsterdam Sloterdijk 457 d.	...	...	p	...	...	0602	...	...	0632	...	0632	...	0656	0702	0705	...	...	0725	0732	0735	...	0756	0802
62	**Amsterdam** Centraal 457 a.	...	...	0500	...	...	0608	...	...	0638	...	0638	...	0702	0708	0711	...	...	0731	0738	0741	...	0802	0808
62	**Amsterdam** Centraal ▷ d.	...	...	0509	0541	...	0611	...	...	0641	...	...	...	0705	0711	0715	...	...	0734	0741	0745	...	0805	0811
68	Amsterdam Amstel d.	...	...	|	0548	...	0619	...	...	0648	...	...	...	0713	0719	0723	...	...	0742	0748	0753	...	0813	0819
101	**Utrecht** Centraal ▷ 471 d.	...	...	0543	0609	...	0639	...	...	0709	...	...	...	0733	0739	0744	...	...	0803	0809	0814	...	0833	0839
149	's-Hertogenbosch 471 d.	...	...	0613	0638	...	0708	...	...	0738	...	...	...	0806	0808	0815	...	...	0836	0838	0845	...	0906	0908
181	**Eindhoven** Centraal 471 a.	...	...	0631	0657	...	0727	...	...	0757	...	...	...	0824	0827	0833	...	...	0854	0857	0903	...	0924	0927
181	**Eindhoven** Centraal d.	0559	0629	0632	0659	0708	0729	0729	0738	0759	0759	...	0808	0827	0829	0838	0829	0838	0857	0859	0908	0908	0927	0929
210	Weert d.	0616	0646	0650	0716	0726	0746	0745	0756	0816	0815	...	0826	0845	0846	0856	0846	0856	0915	0916	0926	0926	0945	0946
234	Roermond d.	0630	0700	0703	0730	0740	0800	0800	0810	0830	0830	...	0840	0900	0900	0910	0900	0910	0930	0930	0940	0940	1000	1000
258	Sittard ★ d.	0646	0716	0717	0746	0756	0816	0816	0826	0846	0846	...	0856	0916	0916	0926	0916	0926	0946	0946	0956	0956	1016	1016
277	**Heerlen** ★ a.	|	|	|	|	0811	|	|	0841	|	|	...	0911	|	|	0941	|	0941	|	|	1011	1011	|	|
280	**Maastricht** a.	0700	0730	0730	0800	...	0830	0830	...	0900	0900	...	...	0930	0930	...	0930	...	1000	1000	...	...	1030	1030

	①–④		①–④	⑤–⑦	①–④		①–④	⑤–⑦ ◇	①–④			①–④	⑤–⑦	①–④					†		†		
Enkhuizen d.	0709	...	...	0739	0739	...	...	0809	0809	...	and at	...	1739	1739	...	1809	...	1839	...	1909	...	1939	...
Hoorn d.	0740	...	...	0807	0810	...	...	0837	0840	...	the	...	1807	1810	...	1837	...	1907	...	1937	...	2007	...
Alkmaar 457 d.	|	...	0757	|	|	...	0827	|	|	...	same	1757	|	|	...	|	...	|	...	|	...	|	...
Castricum 457 d.	|	...	0805	|	|	...	0835	|	|	...	minutes	1805	|	|	...	|	...	|	...	|	...	|	...
Zaandam 457 d.	|	...	0819	|	|	...	0849	|	|	...	past	1819	|	|	...	|	...	|	...	|	...	|	...
Amsterdam Sloterdijk 457 d.	0805	...	0826	0832	0835	...	0856	0902	0905	...	each	1825	1832	1835	...	1902	...	1932	...	2002	...	2032	...
Amsterdam Centraal 457 a.	0811	...	0832	0838	0841	...	0902	0908	0911	...	hour	1831	1838	1841	...	1908	...	1938	...	2008	...	2038	...
Amsterdam Centraal ▷ d.	0815	...	0835	0841	0845	...	0905	0911	0915	...	until	1834	1841	1846	...	1911	...	1941	...	2011	...	2041	...
Amsterdam Amstel d.	0823	...	0843	0848	0853	...	0913	0919	0923	...	◇	1842	1848	1854	...	1919	...	1948	...	2019	...	2048	...
Utrecht Centraal ▷ 471 d.	0844	...	0903	0909	0914	...	0933	0939	0944	...		1903	1909	1914	...	1939	...	2009	...	2039	...	2109	...
's-Hertogenbosch 471 d.	0915	...	0936	0938	0945	...	1006	1008	1015	...		1935	1938	1944	...	2008	...	2038	...	2108	...	2138	...
Eindhoven Centraal 471 a.	0933	...	0954	0957	1003	...	1024	1027	1033	...		1954	1957	2003	...	2027	...	2057	...	2127	...	2157	...
Eindhoven Centraal d.	0938	0938	0957	0959	1008	1008	1027	1029	1038	1038		1957	1959	2008	2008	2029	2038	2059	2108	2129	2138	2159	...
Weert d.	0956	0956	1015	1016	1026	1026	1045	1046	1056	1056		2015	2016	2026	2026	2046	2056	2116	2126	2146	2156	2216	...
Roermond d.	1010	1010	1030	1030	1040	1040	1100	1100	1110	1110		2030	2030	2040	2040	2100	2110	2130	2140	2200	2210	2230	...
Sittard ★ d.	1026	1026	1046	1046	1056	1056	1116	1116	1126	1126		2046	2046	2056	2056	2116	2126	2146	2156	2216	2226	2246	...
Heerlen ★ a.	1041	1041	|	|	1111	1111	|	|	1141	1141		|	|	2111	2111	|	2141	|	2211	|	2241	|	...
Maastricht a.	...	...	1100	1100	...	...	1130	1130	...	...		2100	2100	...	...	2130	...	2200	...	2230	...	2300	...

Enkhuizen d.	2009	2039	2109	2139	2209	2239	2339	...
Hoorn d.	2037	2107	2137	2207	2237	2307	0005	...
Alkmaar 457 d.	|	|	|	|	|	|	|	...
Castricum 457 d.	|	|	|	|	|	|	|	...
Zaandam 457 d.	|	|	|	|	|	|	0034	...
Amsterdam Sloterdijk 457 d.	2102	2132	2202	2232	2302	2332	0040	...
Amsterdam Centraal 457 a.	2108	2138	2208	2238	2308	2338	0046	...
Amsterdam Centraal ▷ d.	2111	2141	2211	2241	2311	2341	...	...
Amsterdam Amstel d.	2119	2148	2219	2248	2319	2348	...	...
Utrecht Centraal ▷ 471 d.	2139	2209	2239	2309	2339	0009	...	...
's-Hertogenbosch 471 d.	2208	2238	2308	2338	0008	0038	...	...
Eindhoven Centraal 471 a.	2227	2257	2327	2357	0027	0057	...	...
Eindhoven Centraal d.	2229	2259	2329	2359	...	...	...	...
Weert d.	2246	2316	2346	0016	...	...	...	...
Roermond d.	2300	2330	0000	0030	...	...	...	...
Sittard ★ d.	2316	2346	0016	0046	...	...	...	...
Heerlen ★ a.	|	|	|	|	...	...	...	...
Maastricht a.	2330	2400	0030	0100	...	...	...	...

	Ⓐ	Ⓐ	Ⓐ f	①–④	⑤	⑥	①–④	①–④ u	⑤	⑥ b	①–④
Maastricht d.	...	...	...	...	0531	...	0531	...	0601	...	0601
Heerlen ★ d.	...	...	...	...	|	...	|	0549	|	...	|
Sittard ★ d.	...	...	...	...	0547	...	0547	0605	0617	...	0617
Roermond d.	...	...	...	...	0602	...	0602	0620	0632	...	0632
Weert d.	...	...	...	...	0616	...	0616	0634	0646	...	0646
Eindhoven Centraal a.	...	...	...	...	0632	...	0632	0651	0702	...	0702
Eindhoven Centraal 471 d.	...	0534	0604	0627	0634	...	0636	0657	0704	0704	0706
's-Hertogenbosch 471 d.	...	0553	0623	0648	0653	...	0658	0718	0723	0723	0728
Utrecht Centraal ▷ 471 d.	...	0622	0652	0719	0722	...	0729	0749	0752	0752	0759
Amsterdam Amstel d.	...	0641	0711	0737	0741	...	0747	0807	0811	0811	0817
Amsterdam Centraal ▷ a.	...	0648	0718	0745	0748	...	0755	0815	0818	0818	0825
Amsterdam Centraal 457 d.	0622	0651	0721	0749	0751	0752	0758	0819	0821	0822	0828
Amsterdam Sloterdijk 457 d.	0628	0658	0728	0754	0758	0758	0805	0824	0828	0828	0835
Zaandam 457 d.	|	|	|	|	|	|	0812	|	|	|	0842
Castricum 457 d.	|	|	|	|	|	|	0824	|	|	|	0854
Alkmaar 457 a.	|	|	|	|	|	|	0833	|	|	|	0903
Hoorn d.	0659	0729	0759	0829	0829	0829	...	0859	0859	0859	...
Enkhuizen a.	0723	0753	0823	0853	0853	0853	...	0923	0923	0923	...

	①–④	Ⓐ	⑤⑥ d	①–④	①–④	Ⓐ	⑤⑥ d	①–④	①–④	⚒ ⊗	⑤–⑦	①–④	①–④	L	⑤–⑦	①–④	①–④	L ⊗	⑤–⑦	①–④		①–④	
Maastricht d.	...	...	0631	0631	...	...	0701	0701	...	...	0731	0731	...	...	0801	0801	...	...	0831	0831	and at	...	...
Heerlen ★ d.	0619	0619	|	|	0649	0649	|	|	0719	0719	|	|	0749	0749	|	|	0819	0819	|	|	the	1649	1649
Sittard ★ d.	0635	0635	0647	0647	0705	0705	0717	0717	0735	0735	0747	0747	0805	0805	0817	0817	0835	0835	0847	0847	same	1705	1705
Roermond d.	0650	0650	0702	0702	0720	0720	0732	0732	0750	0750	0802	0802	0820	0820	0832	0832	0850	0850	0902	0902	minutes	1720	1720
Weert d.	0704	0704	0715	0716	0734	0734	0746	0746	0804	0804	0815	0816	0834	0834	0846	0846	0904	0904	0916	0916	past	1734	1734
Eindhoven Centraal a.	0721	0721	0732	0732	0751	0751	0802	0802	0821	0821	0832	0832	0851	0851	0902	0902	0921	0921	0932	0932	each	1751	1751
Eindhoven Centraal 471 d.	0727	...	0734	0736	0757	...	0804	0806	0827	...	0834	0836	0857	...	0904	0906	0927	...	0934	0936	hour	1757	...
's-Hertogenbosch 471 d.	0748	...	0753	0758	0818	...	0823	0828	0848	...	0853	0858	0918	...	0923	0928	0948	...	0953	0958	until	1818	...
Utrecht Centraal ▷ 471 d.	0819	...	0822	0829	0849	...	0852	0859	0919	...	0922	0929	0949	...	0952	0959	1019	...	1022	1029		1849	...
Amsterdam Amstel d.	0837	...	0841	0847	0907	...	0911	0917	0937	...	0941	0947	1007	...	1011	1017	1037	...	1041	1047		1907	...
Amsterdam Centraal ▷ a.	0845	...	0848	0855	0915	...	0918	0925	0945	...	0948	0955	1015	...	1018	1025	1045	...	1048	1055		1915	...
Amsterdam Centraal 457 d.	0849	...	0851	0858	0919	...	0921	0928	0949	...	0951	0958	1019	...	1021	1028	1049	...	1051	1058		1919	...
Amsterdam Sloterdijk 457 d.	0854	...	0858	0905	0924	...	0928	0935	0954	...	0958	1005	1024	...	1028	1035	1054	...	1058	1105		1924	...
Zaandam 457 d.	|	...	|	0912	|	...	|	0942	|	...	|	1012	|	...	|	1042	|	...	|	1112		|	...
Castricum 457 d.	|	...	|	0924	|	...	|	0954	|	...	|	1024	|	...	|	1054	|	...	|	1124		|	...
Alkmaar 457 a.	|	...	|	0933	|	...	|	1003	|	...	|	1033	|	...	|	1103	|	...	|	1133		|	...
Hoorn d.	0929	...	0929	...	0959	...	0959	...	1029	...	1029	...	1059	...	1059	...	1129	...	1129	...		1959	...
Enkhuizen a.	0953	...	0953	...	1023	...	1023	...	1053	...	1053	...	1123	...	1123	...	1153	...	1153	...		2023	...

	⑤–⑦	①–④	①–④	⑤–⑦								†									⑤⑥			⑥ ¶
Maastricht d.	1701	1701	...	...	1731	...	1801	...	1831	...	1901	...	1931	...	2001	2031	2101	2131	2201	2231	2231	2301	0001	0055
Heerlen ★ d.	|	|	1719	1719	|	1749	|	1819	|	1849	|	1919	|	1949	|	|	|	|	|	|	|	|	|	|
Sittard ★ d.	1717	1717	1735	1735	1747	1805	1817	1835	1847	1905	1917	1935	1947	2005	2017	2047	2117	2147	2217	2247	2247	2317	0017	0111
Roermond d.	1732	1732	1750	1750	1802	1820	1832	1850	1902	1920	1932	1950	2002	2020	2032	2102	2132	2202	2232	2302	2302	2332	0036	0125
Weert d.	1746	1746	1804	1804	1815	1834	1846	1904	1916	1934	1946	2004	2016	2034	2046	2116	2146	2216	2246	2316	2316	2346	0050	0139
Eindhoven Centraal a.	1802	1802	1821	1821	1832	1851	1902	1921	1932	1951	2002	2021	2032	2051	2102	2132	2202	2232	2302	2332	2332	0002	0106	0154
Eindhoven Centraal 471 d.	1804	1806	...	1834	1834	...	1904	...	1934	...	2004	...	2034	...	2104	2134	2204	2234	2304	2334	2334	...	...	0158
's-Hertogenbosch 471 d.	1823	1828	...	1853	1853	...	1923	...	1953	...	2023	...	2053	...	2123	2153	2223	2253	2323	2353	2353	...	...	0218
Utrecht Centraal ▷ 471 d.	1852	1859	...	1922	1922	...	1952	...	2022	...	2052	...	2122	...	2152	2222	2252	2322	2352	0022	0022	...	...	0250
Amsterdam Amstel d.	1911	1917	...	1941	1941	...	2011	...	2041	...	2111	...	2141	...	2211	2241	2311	2341	0011	0041	0041	...	...	|
Amsterdam Centraal ▷ a.	1918	1925	...	1948	1948	...	2018	...	2048	...	2118	...	2148	...	2218	2248	2318	2348	0018	0048	0048	...	...	0319
Amsterdam Centraal 457 d.	1921	1928	...	1951	1951	...	2022	...	2052	...	2122	...	2152	...	2222	2252	2322	2352	0022	...	0052	...	...	0326
Amsterdam Sloterdijk 457 d.	1928	1935	...	1958	1958	...	2028	...	2058	...	2128	...	2158	...	2228	2258	2328	2358	0028	...	0057	...	...	p
Zaandam 457 d.	|	1942	...	|	|	...	|	...	|	...	|	...	|	...	|	|	|	|	0034	...	0104	...	...	...
Castricum 457 d.	|	1954	...	|	|	...	|	...	|	...	|	...	|	...	|	|	|	|	|	...	|	...	...	...
Alkmaar 457 a.	|	2003	...	|	|	...	|	...	|	...	|	...	|	...	|	|	|	|	|	...	|	...	...	...
Hoorn d.	1959	...	...	2029	2029	...	2059	...	2129	...	2159	...	2229	...	2259	2329	2359	0029	0059	...	0138	...	...	...
Enkhuizen a.	2023	...	...	2053	2053	...	2123	...	2153	...	2223	...	2253	...	2323	2353	0023	0053z	0123c	...	0202	...	...	...

L – 0749 and 0819 run on ⚒; daily from 0849.
b – © from Amsterdam Centraal.
c – Mornings of ⑥⑦ only.
d – ⑤–⑦ from Eindhoven.
e – ⑤–⑦ from Amsterdam Centraal.
f – Daily from Amsterdam Centraal.
h – From Den Helder (Table **457**).

p – To / from Schiphol ✈ (a. 0340 / d. 0446).
u – Also ⑤ Heerlen - Eindhoven.
z – Not morning of ③④.
◇ – Trains departing 0609 on ⑤⑥ and 0809, 1009, 1209, 1409, 1609 on ⑤–⑦ conveys through portions for the Eindhoven - Heerlen train.
¶ – Operated by Arriva.

⊗ – Trains departing 0719 on ⑤⑥ and 0919, 1119, 1319, 1519 on ⑤–⑦ convey through portions for the Enkhuizen train in next column.
▷ – For Amsterdam **Zuid** - Utrecht see Tables **452** and **471**. For Amsterdam **Zuid** - Eindhoven see Table **471**.

NOTES ARE CONTINUED AT FOOT OF NEXT PAGE

IC trains

SCHIPHOL - AMSTERDAM - UTRECHT - EINDHOVEN - VENLO 471

km		Ⓐ	Ⓐ	⚒	Ⓐ	Ⓐ	Ⓒ	†	Ⓐb	†	⚒	†	⚒	†	⚒	†	⚒							
0	**Schiphol** ✈ .... **452** d.	...	...	...	0615	0645	...	0705	0715	0735	0745	0805	0815	0835	0845	0905	0915	0945	1015	and	2116	2146	2216	2246
9	**Amsterdam** Zuid ..... **452** d.	...	...	...	0626	0656	...	0712	0726	0742	0756	0812	0826	0842	0856	0912	0926	0956	1026	every	2126	2156	2226	2256
45	**Utrecht** Centraal ..... **452** a.	...	...	...	0648	0718	...	0734	0748	0804	0818	0834	0848	0904	0918	0934	0948	1018	1048	30	2148	2218	2248	2318
45	**Utrecht** Centraal ..... **470** d.	...	...	*0609*a	0654	0724	...	0754	0754	0824	0824	0854	0854	0924	0924	0954	0954	1024	1054	minutes	2154	2224	2254	2324
93	's-Hertogenbosch ..... **470** d.	...	...	*0635*a	0725	0755	...	0824	0825	0854	0855	0924	0925	0954	0955	1024	1025	1054	1124	until	2224	2254	2324	2354
125	**Eindhoven** Centraal **470** a.	...	...	*0657*a	0743	0813	...	0843	0843	0913	0913	0943	0943	1013	1013	1043	1043	1113	1143		2243	2313	2343	0013
125	**Eindhoven** Centraal .... d.	0619	0649	0719	0749	0819	0819	0849	0849	0919	0919	0949	0949	1019	1019	1049	1049	1119	1149		2249	2319	...	0019
138	Helmond .... d.	0628	0658	0728	0758	0828	0828	0858	0858	0928	0928	0958	0958	1028	1028	1058	1058	1128	1158		2258	2328	...	0028
176	**Venlo** .... a.	0658	0728	0758	0828	0858	0858	0928	0928	0958	0958	1028	1028	1058	1058	1128	1128	1158	1228		2328	2358	...	0058

	Ⓐ	Ⓐ	Ⓐ	⚒	⚒	†	⚒	†															
Venlo .... d.	...	0533	0603	0633	0703	0703	0733	0733	0803	0833	0903	0933	and	1903	1933	2003	2033	2103	2133	2203	2303	...	...	...
Helmond .... d.	...	0601	0631	0701	0731	0731	0801	0801	0831	0901	0931	1001	every	1931	2001	2031	2101	2131	2201	2231	2331	...	...	...
Eindhoven Centraal .... a.	...	0611	0641	0711	0741	0741	0811	0811	0841	0911	0941	1011	30	1941	2011	2041	2111	2141	2211	2241	2341	...	...	...
Eindhoven Centraal . **470** d.	0547	0617	0647	0717	0747	0747	0817	0817	0847	0917	0947	1017	minutes	1947	2017	2047	2117	2147	2217	2247	...	...	...	...
's-Hertogenbosch .... **470** d.	0608	0638	0708	0738	0808	0808	0838	0838	0908	0938	1008	1038	until	2008	2038	2108	2138	2208	2238	2308	...	...	...	...
Utrecht Centraal .... **470** a.	0635	0705	0735	0805	0835	0835	0905	0905	0935	1005	1035	1105		2035	2105	2135	2205	2235	2305	2335	...	...	...	...
Utrecht Centraal .... **452** d.	0642	0712	0742	0812	0842	0855	0912	0925	0942	1012	1042	1112		2042	2112	2142	2212	2242	2325	2355	...	...	...	...
Amsterdam Zuid .... **452** a.	0704	0734	0804	0834	0904	0917	0934	0947	1004	1034	1104	1134		2104	2134	2204	2234	2304	2347	0017	...	...	...	...
Schiphol ✈ .... **452** a.	0713	0743	0813	0843	0913	0926	0943	0954	1013	1043	1113	1143		2113	2143	2213	2243	2313	2354	0025	...	...	...	...

a – Ⓐ only.
b – Daily from Utrecht.

☛ Most journeys from Schiphol start from Dordrecht via Rotterdam and Den Haag HS and v.v. (see Table **452**).

DEN HAAG - ROTTERDAM - TILBURG - EINDHOVEN 472

km		Ⓐ	Ⓐv	Ⓐ	⚒z	⚒					⑤⑥
0	**Den Haag** Centraal ⊖ ..d.	...	0548	0619	0648	0718	0748	0818	and	2319	2349
2	**Den Haag** HS .... ▽ d.	...	0553	0623	0653	0723	0753	0823	every	2323	2353
10	Delft .... ▽ d.	...	0600	0630	0700	0730	0800	0830	30	2330	0000
24	**Rotterdam** Cent. .... ▽ a.	...	0611	0642	0712	0742	0812	0842	mins	2342	0012
24	**Rotterdam** Cent. ... **460** d.	0544	0614	0644	0714	0744	0814	0844	until	2344	0014
71	Breda .... **460** d.	0608	0638	0708	0738	0808	0838	0908		0008	0038
92	Tilburg .... △ d.	0624	0654	0724	0754	0824	0854	0924		0024	0054
129	**Eindhoven** Cent. .... a.	0646	0716	0746	0816	0846	0916	0946		0046	0116

	Ⓐ	Ⓐ	⚒		⚒					
Eindhoven Cent. .... d.	0514	0544	0614	0644	0714	0744	0814	and	2244	2314
Tilburg .... △ d.	0537	0607	0637	0707	0737	0807	0837	every	2307	2337
Breda .... **460** d.	0553	0623	0653	0723	0753	0823	0853	30	2323	2353
Rotterdam Cent. ... **460** a.	0615	0645	0715	0745	0815	0845	0915	mins	2345	0015
Rotterdam Cent. ...... ▽ d.	0618	0648	0718	0748	0818	0848	0918	until	2348	0018
Delft .... ▽ d.	0629	0659	0729	0759	0829	0859	0929		2359	0029
Den Haag HS .... ▽ a.	0636	0706	0736	0806	0836	0906	0936		0006	0036
Den Haag Cent. .... a.	0641	0711	0741	0811	0841	0911	0941		0011	0041

DORDRECHT - BREDA *30 km* Journey time 23 minutes. Local *Sprinter* trains (continuing to / from Tilburg, Nijmegen and Arnhem; not shown in ERT).
From Dordrecht: 0028Ⓐ, 0558⚒, 0628Ⓐ, 0658, 0728Ⓐ, 0758, 0828⚒, 0858 and every 30 minutes until 2228, 2328.
From Breda: 0539Ⓐ, 0609Ⓐ, 0639, 0709Ⓐ, 0739, 0809⚒, 0839, 0909 and every 30 minutes until 2239, 2339.

v – ⚒ from Rotterdam.
z – Daily from Rotterdam.

⊖ – Departures from Den Haag Centraal 0648 to 2248 are 1 minute later on ⑤-⑦ (daily 1919 - 2249).
△ – For Breda - Tilburg see also Table **475**.
▽ – For additional trains see Tables **450** and **452**.

☛ Additional journeys: Rotterdam - Eindhoven 0103⑥⑦; Eindhoven - Rotterdam 2344, 0042⑥⑦, 0142⑥⑦.

Operated by **Arriva** (NS tickets valid)

MAASTRICHT - HEERLEN - AACHEN 473

km		⚒	Ⓐ	Ⓐ		⚒		⚒		⚒		n											
	Liège Guillemins **436** ....d.	...	0508	...	0608r	...	0708	...	0808	...	0908	...	and at	1608	...	1708	...	1808	1908	2008	2108	2208	2308
0	**Maastricht** ....d.	...	0554	...	0654	0724	0754	0824	0854	0924	0954	1024	the same	1654	1724	1754	1824	1854	1954	2054	2154	2254	2354
11	Valkenburg ....d.	...	0605	...	0705	0735	0805	0835	0905	0935	1005	1035	minutes	1705	1735	1805	1835	1905	2005	2105	2205	2305	0005
24	**Heerlen** ....d.	0618	0618	0648	0718	0748	0818	0848	0918	0948	1018	1048	past each	1718	1748	1818	1848	1918	2018	2118	2218	2318	0018
34	Herzogenrath 🏛 ⊖ .... **802** d.	0630	0630	0700	0730	0800	0830	0900	0930	1000	1030	1100	hour	1730	1800	1830	1900	1930	2030	2130	2230	2330	0030
48	**Aachen** Hbf................. **802** a.	0942	0642	0712	0742	0812	0842	0912	0942	1012	1042	1112	until	1742	1812	1842	1912	1942	2042	2142	2242	2342	0042

	⚒	Ⓐ		⚒		⚒		⚒		⚒		⚒											
Aachen Hbf.................. **802** d.	0617	0647	0717	0747	0817	0847	0917	0947	1017	1047	1117	1147	1217	1247	and at	1817	1847	1917	2017	2117	2217	2317	0017
Herzogenrath 🏛 ⊖ .... **802** d.	0630	0700	0730	0800	0830	0900	0930	1000	1030	1100	1130	1200	1230	1300	the same	1830	1900	1930	2030	2130	2230	2330	0030
Heerlen ....d.	0643	0713	0743	0813	0843	0913	0943	1013	1043	1113	1143	1213	1243	1313	minutes	1843	1913	1943	2043	2143	2243	2343	0042
Valkenburg ....d.	0655	0725	0755	0825	0855	0925	0955	1025	1055	1125	1155	1225	1255	1325	past each	1855	1925	1955	2055	2155	2255	2355	...
Maastricht .... a.	0705	0736	0805	0836	0905	0936	1005	1036	1105	1136	1205	1236	1305	1336	hour	1905	1936	2005	2105	2205	2305	0005	...
Liège Guillemins **436** ....a.	0753	...	0852	...	0950	...	1050	...	1150	...	1250	...	1350	...	until	1950	...	2050	2150	2250	2350	0050	...

MAASTRICHT - HEERLEN - KERKRADE

km		Ⓐ	Ⓐ	⚒						
0	**Maastricht** ....d.	0542	0612	0642	0712	0742	and every	2242	2312	2342
11	Valkenburg ....d.	0556	0626	0656	0726	0756	30 minutes	2256	2326	2356
24	**Heerlen** ....d.	0615	0645	0715	0745	0815	until	2315	2345	0015
33	**Kerkrade** Centrum ....d.	0627	0657	0727	0757	0827		2327	2357	0027

	Ⓐ	⚒	⚒					
Kerkrade Centrum ....d.	0605	0635	0705	0735	0805	and every	2335	0005
Heerlen ....d.	0619	0649	0719	0749	0819	30 minutes	2349	0019
Valkenburg ....d.	0636	0706	0736	0806	0836	until	0006	0036
Maastricht ....a.	0649	0719	0749	0819	0849		0019	0049

n – Departures at 1024, 1124, 1224 run on ⚒ only.
r – ⚒ only.
⊖ – Connections are available at Herzogenrath for Düsseldorf and Dortmund (Table **802**).

IC trains

ROOSENDAAL - 's-HERTOGENBOSCH - NIJMEGEN - ARNHEM - ZWOLLE 475

km		Ⓐ	Ⓐ	Ⓐ	Ⓒ	⑥	Ⓐ	Ⓒ	Ⓐ	†	⚒												
0	**Roosendaal** ....d.	...	...	...	...	...	0527	...	0557	...	0627	0657	0727	0757		2127	2157	2227	2257	2327	2357	...	...
23	Breda .... **472** d.	...	...	...	...	...	0550	...	0620	...	0650	0720	0750	0820		2150	2220	2250	2320	2350	0020	...	...
44	Tilburg .... **472** d.	...	...	...	...	...	0603	...	0633	...	0703	0733	0803	0833		2203	2233	2303	2333	0003	0033	...	...
67	**'s-Hertogenbosch** ....a.	...	...	...	...	...	0618	...	0649	...	0719	0749	0819	0849	and	2218	2248	2318	2348	0018	0048	...	...
67	**'s-Hertogenbosch** ....d.	...	...	...	...	...	0624	...	0654	...	0724	0754	0824	0854	every	2224	2254	2324	2354	...	...	...	...
86	Oss ....d.	...	...	...	...	...	0635	...	0705	...	0735	0805	0835	0905	30	2235	2305	2335	0005	...	...	...	...
110	**Nijmegen** ....a.	...	...	...	...	...	0652	...	0722	...	0752	0822	0852	0922	minutes	2252	2322	2352	0022	...	...	...	...
110	**Nijmegen** .... **452 457** d.	...	...	0624	...	0655	0654	*0713*	0724	0755	0754	0824	0854	0924	until	2255	2325	2355	0025	...	...	...	...
129	**Arnhem** Centraal.... **452 457** a.	...	...	0637	...	0707	0707	*0726*	0737	0807	0807	0837	0907	0937		2307	2337	0007	0037	...	...	...	...
129	**Arnhem** Centraal.................d.	...	0611	0641	...	0711	0711	0741	0741	0811	0811	0841	0911	0941		2311	2341	0011	...	...	...	...	...
145	Dieren ....d.	...	0623	0653	...	0723	0723	0753	0753	0823	0823	0853	0923	0953		2323	2353	0023	...	...	...	...	...
159	Zutphen ....d.	0603	0633	0703	0703	0733	0733	0803	0803	0833	0833	0903	0933	1003		2333	0003	0032	...	...	...	...	...
174	Deventer...................................d.	0616	0646	0716	0716	0746	0746	0816	0816	0846	0846	0916	0946	1016		2346	0016	...	...	...	...	...	...
204	**Zwolle** ....a.	0640	0710	0740	0740	0810	0810	0840	0840	0910	0910	0940	1010	1040		0010	0040	...	...	...	...	...	...

	Ⓐ	Ⓐ	Ⓐ	†	⑥	Ⓐ	Ⓐ	⑥	†	Ⓐ	⑥	†	⚒	†									
Zwolle ....d.	...	...	...	...	...	...	0550	...	...	0620	...	...	0650	...	0720	0750		2120	2150	2220	2250	2320	2350
Deventer....................................d.	...	...	...	...	...	...	0615	...	...	0645	...	...	0715	...	0745	0815		2145	2215	2245	2315	2345	0015
Zutphen ....d.	...	...	...	...	...	0558	0628	...	...	0658	0658	...	0728	0728	0758	0828		2158	2228	2258	2328	2356	0028
Dieren.......................................d.	...	...	...	...	...	0607	0637	...	...	0707	0707	...	0737	0737	0807	0837	and	2207	2237	2307	2337	...	0037
Arnhem Centraal..................a.	...	...	...	...	...	0619	0649	...	...	0719	0719	...	0749	0749	0819	0849	every	2219	2249	2319	2349	...	0049
Arnhem Centraal..... **452 457** d.	...	...	0553	...	...	0623	0653	0653	...	0723	0723	0723	0753	0753	0823	0853	30	2223	2253	2323	2353	...	...
Nijmegen .... **452 457** a.	...	...	0607	...	...	0637	0706	0707	...	0736	0737	0737	0806	0807	0837	0907	minutes	2237	2307	2337	0007	...	...
Nijmegen ....d.	...	...	0608	...	...	0638	0708	0708	...	0738	0738	0738	0808	0808	0838	0908	until	2238	2308	2338	...	...	...
Oss ....d.	...	...	0624	...	...	0654	0724	0724	...	0754	0754	0754	0824	0824	0854	0924		2254	2324	2354	...	...	...
's-Hertogenbosch ....a.	...	...	0636	...	...	0706	0736	0736	...	0807	0806	0806	0837	0836	0907	0937		2306	2336	0006	...	...	...
's-Hertogenbosch ....d.	0542	0612	0642	...	0712	0712	0742	0742	0742	0812	0812	0812	0842	0842	0912	0942		2312	2342	0012	...	...	...
Tilburg .... **472** d.	0558	0628	0658	...	0728	0728	0758	0758	0758	0828	0828	0828	0858	0858	0928	0958		2328	2358	0028	...	...	...
Breda .... **472** d.	0615	0645	0715	0745	0745	0745	0815	0815	0815	0845	0845	0845	0915	0915	0945	1015		2345	0015	0045	...	...	...
Roosendaal ....a.	0633	0703	0733	0803	0803	0803	0833	0833	0833	0903	0903	0903	0933	0933	1003	1033		0003	0033	0103	...	...	...

NOTES FOR TABLE 470 (CONTINUED FROM PREVIOUS PAGE):

★ – Local trains (journey 20 mins ¶): **From Sittard** 0618Ⓐ, 0648⚒, 0718⚒, 0748 and every 30 minutes until 0048. **From Heerlen** 0552Ⓐ, 0622⚒, 0652⚒, 0722 and every 30 minutes until 0022.

476 ARNHEM - WINTERSWIJK

Operated by **Arriva** (NS tickets valid) 2nd class only

km		Ⓐ	Ⓐ	⚒	⚒		◧			Ⓒ	⑦
0	**Arnhem** Cent. ..d.	0605	0635	0705	0731	0805	every	2305	0005	0035	0105
14	Zevenaar..........d.	0620	0650	0720	0750	0820	30	2320	0020	0050	0120
30	Doetinchem......d.	0638	0708	0738	0808	0838	minutes	2338	0038	0108	0137
64	**Winterswijk**.....a.	0710	0740	0810	0840	0910	until	0010	0110	0140	0212

	Ⓐ	Ⓐ	⚒	Ⓐ		❦		⑤⑥	⑦	⑦
Winterswijk...d.	0520	0550	0620	0650	0720	every	2320	2350	0020	0050
Doetinchem.....d.	0553	0623	0653	0723	0753	30	2353	0023	0053	0123
Zevenaar.......d.	0610	0640	0710	0740	0810	minutes	0010	0040	0110	0140
Arnhem Cent.a.	0625	0654	0725	0755	0825	until	0025	0055	0125	0155

◧ – Journeys at 0835, 0935, 1035, 1135, 2135, 2235 run on ⚒ only. Journeys shown as 1135, 1335, 1535, 1735, 1935 depart Arnhem 4 minutes earlier.

❦ – Journeys at 0750, 0850, 0950, 1050, 1150, 2050, 2150, 2250 run on ⚒ only.

477 NIJMEGEN - VENLO - ROERMOND

Operated by **Arriva** (NS tickets valid)

km		Ⓐh	Ⓐh	⚒d	⚒d						
0	**Nijmegen**.........d.	0538	0608	0638	0708	0738	0808	every	2308	2338	0008
24	Boxmeer...........d.	0602	0632	0702	0732	0802	0832	30	2332	0002	0032
39	Venray.............d.	0615	0645	0715	0745	0815	0845	minutes	2345	0015	0045
61	**Venlo**..............d.	0633	0703	0733	0803	0833	0903	until	0003	0030	0100
84	**Roermond**.......a.	0656	0726	0756	0826	0856	0926		0026	...	...

	Ⓐ	Ⓐ	⚒	Ⓐk	Ⓐd	⚒d	⚒d			
Roermond.....d.	...	...	...	0604	0634	0704	0734	0804	every	2304
Venlo............d.	0459	0529	0559	0629	0659	0729	0759	0829	30	2329
Venray............d.	0515	0545	0615	0645	0715	0745	0815	0845	minutes	2345
Boxmeer.........d.	0530	0600	0630	0700	0730	0800	0830	0900	until	0000
Nijmegen......a.	0552	0622	0652	0722	0752	0822	0852	0922		0022

d – Daily from Venlo.

h – ⚒ from Venlo. Additional journeys run Venlo - Roermond at 0533Ⓐ, 0603Ⓐ.

k – ⚒ from Venlo.

478 TIEL - GELDERMALSEN - UTRECHT and 's-HERTOGENBOSCH

km			①–④	①–④	①–④		①–④	①–④	①–④		①–④		⑤	⑤	⑤⑥	⑤⑥	⑤–⑦	⑤–⑦		⑤–⑦
0	**Tiel** .... d.	①–④	0553	0623	0653	every	1923	1948	2018	every	2348	⑤–⑦	0548	0618	0648	0718	0748	0818	every	2348
12	Geldermalsen.... a.		0604	0634	0704	30	1934	1959	2029	30	2359		0559	0629	0659	0729	0759	0829	30	2359
12	Geldermalsen.... d.		0608	0642	0712	minutes	1942	2000	2030	minutes	0000		0600	0630	0700	0730	0800	0830	minutes	0000
38	**Utrecht** Cent..... a.		0632	0708	0738	until	2008	2024	2054	until	0024		0624	0654	0724	0754	0824	0854	until	0024

		①–④	①–④		①–④	①–④	①–④	①–④		①–④	①–④		⑤	⑤	⑤–⑦	⑤–⑦		⑤–⑦	⑤–⑦	⑤–⑦
Utrecht Cent. .....d.	①–④	0552	0622	every	1822	1901	1936	2006	every	2336	0006	⑤–⑦	0606	0636	0706	0736	every	2306	2336	0006
Geldermalsen .....a.		0616	0646	30	1846	1925	2000	2030	30	2400	0030		0630	0700	0730	0800	30	2330	2400	0030
Geldermalsen .....d.		0624	0654	minutes	1854	1927	2001	2031	minutes	0001	0031		0631	0701	0731	0801	minutes	2331	0001	0031
Tiel.....................a.		0635	0705	until	1905	1938	2012	2042	until	0012	0042		0642	0712	0742	0812	until	2342	0012	0042

GELDERMALSEN - 's-HERTOGENBOSCH *22 km.* Journey time 16 minutes

From Geldermalsen ①–④: 0608, 0641, 0711 and every 30 minutes until 1911, then 1932, 1947, 2017 and every 30 minutes until 2347, 0017, 0017.
⑤: 0608, 0647, 0717 and every 30 minutes until 0017. ⑥: 0717 and every 30 minutes until 0017. †: 0747, 0847, 0917 and every 30 minutes until 0017.

From 's-Hertogenbosch ①–④: 0529, 0603, 0633 and every 30 minutes until 1933, then 1959, 2029 and every 30 minutes until 2359.
⑤: 0529, 0559, 0629 and every 30 minutes until 2359. ⑥: 0629 and every 30 minutes until 2359. †: 0729 and every 30 minutes until 2359.

ARNHEM - TIEL Operated by **Arriva** (NS tickets valid). 2nd class only. *44 km.* Journey time 35 – 36 minutes.

From Arnhem Ⓐ: 0607, 0638 and every 30 minutes until 2038, then 2138, 2238, 2338. ⑥: 0838 and hourly until 2338. †: 0938 and hourly until 2338, also 0038.

From Tiel Ⓐ: 0547 and every 30 minutes until 2047, then 2147, 2247. ⑥: 0747 and hourly until 2347. †: 0847 and hourly until 2247.

479 DORDRECHT - GELDERMALSEN

Operated by **R-net** (NS tickets valid); 2nd class only

km		Ⓐ	⑥	Ⓐ	⑥	Ⓐ	⑥	Ⓐ	Ⓒ	Ⓐ	⑥	Ⓐ		Ⓒ	Ⓐ	⑥	Ⓐ	Ⓐ	Ⓒ				
0	**Dordrecht**..................d.	0512	0541	0546	0611	0616	0641	0646	0711	0716	0741	0746	and at same	1911	1916	1941	1946	2005	2011	2111	2211	2311	0011
10	Sliedrecht...................d.	0524	0553	0558	0623	0628	0653	0658	0723	0728	0753	0758	minutes past	1923	1928	1953	1958	2018	2023	2123	2223	2323	0023
24	Gorinchem..................d.	0541	0611	0614	0641	0644	0711	0714	0741	0744	0811	0814	each hour	1941	1944	2011	2014	2044	2041	2141	2241	2341	0038
49	**Geldermalsen**...........a.	0603	0635	0637	0705	0707	0735	0737	0805	0807	0835	0837	until	2005	2007	2035	2037	2108	2105	2205	2305	0005	0100

	Ⓐ	⑥	Ⓐ	⑥	Ⓐ	⑥	Ⓐ	Ⓒ	Ⓐ		⑥	Ⓐ	Ⓒ	Ⓐ	⑥	Ⓐ	Ⓒ	Ⓐ					
Geldermalsen............d.	0614	0641	0644	0711	0714	0741	0744	0811	0814	and at same	1941	1944	2011	2014	2041	2044	2111	2113	2211	2311	0011	0106	...
Gorinchem..................d.	0643	0709	0713	0739	0743	0809	0813	0839	0843	minutes past	2009	2013	2039	2039	2109	2108	2139	2139	2239	2339	0039	0130	...
Sliedrecht...................d.	0658	0723	0728	0753	0758	0823	0828	0853	0858	each hour	2023	2028	2053	2054	2123	2123	2153	2153	2253	2353	0053	0144	...
Dordrecht...................a.	0709	0734	0739	0804	0809	0834	0839	0904	0909	until	2034	2041	2104	2105	2134	2134	2204	2204	2304	0004	0104	0155	...

480 AMSTERDAM - AMERSFOORT - HENGELO

IC trains

For *IC* trains Rotterdam - Schiphol ✈ - Amsterdam Zuid - Hilversum - Amersfoort see Table **460**.

km		*IC*141 ♥	Ⓐ	Ⓐ	⚒	*IC*143 ♥	⚒			*IC*145 ♥				*IC*147 ♥				*IC*149 ♥				*IC*241 ♥	Ⓐ		
0	**Amsterdam** Cent. ......d.	0600	0630	0700	0730	0800	0830	0900	0930	1000	1030	1100	1130	1200	1230	1300	1330	1400	1430	1500	1530	1600	1604	1630	1700
29	Hilversum ....d.	0622	0652	0722	0752	0822	0852	0922	0952	1022	1052	1122	1152	1222	1252	1322	1352	1422	1452	1522	1552	1622	1626	1652	1722
45	**Amersfoort** Cent........a.	0634	0703	0733	0803	0834	0903	0933	1003	1034	1103	1133	1203	1234	1303	1333	1403	1434	1503	1533	1603	1634	1637	1703	1733
45	**Amersfoort** Cent. **463** d.	0636	0706	0736	0806a	0836	0906a	0936a	...	1036	...	1136a	...	1236	...	1336a	...	1436	...	1536a	1606a	1636	1644	1706a	1736a
88	Apeldoorn............ **463** d.	0702	0732	0802	0832a	0902	0932a	1002a	...	1102	...	1202a	...	1302	...	1402a	...	1502	...	1602a	1632a	1702	1710	1732a	1802a
103	Deventer.............. **463** d.	0718	0742	0812	0842a	0918	0942a	1012a	...	1118	...	1212a	...	1318	...	1412a	...	1518	...	1612a	1642a	1718	1720	1742a	1812a
156	**Hengelo**.............. **463** a.	0751	...	...	...	0951	...	...	...	1151	...	...	...	1351	...	...	...	1551	...	...	...	1751	...	...	...

		*IC*243 ♥						⑥⑦	⑥⑦
Amsterdam Cent.........d.	1730	1800	1830	1900	1930		2330	0030	0100
Hilversum ....d.	1752	1822	1852	1922	1952	every	2352	0052	0122
Amersfoort Cent.........a.	1803	1834	1903	1933	2003	30	0003	0103	0133
Amersfoort Cent.. **463** d.	1806a	1836	1906a	...	...	mins	...	0106	...
Apeldoorn............. **463** d.	1832a	1902	1932a	...	...	until	...	0132	...
Deventer............... **463** d.	1842a	1918	1942a	...	...		...	0142	...
Hengelo.............. **463** a.	...	1951	...	...	...		...	...	...

	Ⓐ	Ⓐ	⚒	Ⓐ	⚒			*IC*242 ♥				*IC*240 ♥
Hengelo .... **463** d.	...	...	...	...	...	...	...	0809	...	...	...	1009
Deventer........... **463** d.	...	...	...	0648	0720a	0748a	0818a	0847	0920a	0948a	...	1047
Apeldoorn .... **463** d.	...	...	...	0700	0730a	0800a	0830a	0859	0930a	1000a	...	1059
Amersfoort C.... **463** a.	...	...	...	0724	0754a	0824a	0854a	0924	0954a	1024a	...	1124
Amersfoort C..........d.	0554	0624	0654	0726	0754	0824	0854	0926	0954	1026	1054	1126
Hilversum..................d.	0609	0639	0709	0739	0809	0839	0909	0939	1009	1039	1109	1139
Amsterdam Cent.....a.	0629	0659	0729	0759	0829	0859	0929	0959	1029	1059	1129	1159

				*IC*148 ♥				*IC*146 ♥				*IC*144 ♥				*IC*142 ♥				*IC*140 ♥			⊡	⊡	
Hengelo.............. **463** d.	...	...	...	1209	...	...	...	1409	...	...	...	1609	...	...	...	1809	...	...	...	2009	...	...	...	...	...
Deventer.............. **463** d.	...	1148a	...	1247	...	1348a	...	1447	...	1548a	1618a	1647	1720a	1748a	1818a	1847	...	...	...	2047	...	...	...	...	...
Apeldoorn............. **463** d.	...	1200a	...	1259	...	1400a	...	1459	...	1600a	1630a	1659	1730a	1800a	1830a	1859	...	...	...	2059	...	...	...	...	...
Amersfoort Cent.. **463** a.	...	1224a	...	1324	...	1424a	...	1524	...	1624a	1654a	1724	1754a	1824a	1854a	1924	...	...	...	2124	...	...	...	...	...
Amersfoort Cent.........d.	1154	1224	1254	1326	1354	1424	1454	1526	1554	1624	1654	1726	1754	1824	1854	1926	1954	2024	2054	2126	2154	2224	2254	2324	2354
Hilversum ....d.	1209	1239	1309	1339	1409	1439	1509	1539	1609	1639	1709	1739	1809	1839	1909	1939	2009	2039	2109	2139	2209	2239	2309	2339	0009
Amsterdam Cent.........a.	1229	1259	1329	1359	1429	1459	1529	1559	1629	1659	1729	1759	1829	1859	1929	1959	2029	2059	2129	2159	2229	2259	2329	2359	0029

LOCAL *SPRINTER* SERVICES AMSTERDAM - AMERSFOORT

km		Ⓐ	Ⓐ	⚒	⚒				④–①	④–①	⑥⑦
0	**Amsterdam** Cent. ......d.	0541	0611	0641	0711	0741	and	2341	0011	0041	0111
14	Weesp........................d.	0559	0629	0659	0729	0759	every	2359	0029	0059	0129
23	Naarden-Bussum..... ‡ d.	0605	0635	0705	0735	0805	30	0005	0035	0105	0135
29	Hilversum .... ‡ d.	0615	0645	0715	0745	0815	mins	0014	0044	0114	0144
36	Baarn ....d.	0620	0650	0720	0750	0820	until	0020	0050	0120	0150
45	**Amersfoort** Cent.........a.	0628	0658	0728	0758	0828		0027	0057	0127	0157

	Ⓐ		⚒						⑥⑦	⑥⑦
Amersfoort Cent. ....d.	0449	0530	0601	0631	0701	and	2301	2331	0001	0031
Baarn.........................d.	0456	0537	0608	0638	0708	every	2308	2338	0008	0038
Hilversum.............. ‡ d.	0503	0544	0615	0645	0715	30	2315	2345	0015	0045
Naarden-Bussum .. ‡ d.	0512	0553	0624	0654	0724	mins	2324	2354	0024	0054
Weesp ....d.	0521	0602	0632	0702	0732	until	2332	0002	0032	0102
Amsterdam Cent.....a.	0537	0618	0648	0718	0748		2348	0018	0048	0118

a – Ⓐ only.

‡ – See also Table **482**.

⊡ – Departs Amersfoort 4 minutes later on ⑦–④.

♥ – *IC* service to / from Germany via Bad Bentheim (see Table **22**).

AMSTERDAM CENTRAAL - ALMERE 481

NON-STOP Intercity trains from Amsterdam Centraal. For *IC* trains Amsterdam Zuid - Almere - Lelystad see Tables **460** and **465**.

km		Ⓐ	⚒	⚒		⚒		every		F	⑥⑦
0	**Amsterdam** Cent. ......d.	0638	0708	0738	0808	0838	0908	30	2338	0008	0038
30	**Almere** Centrum.........a.	0657	0727	0757	0827	0857	0927	mins	2357	0027	0057

	Ⓐ	⚒	⚒		⚒		every		⑥⑦	G
Almere Centrum......d.	0601	0631	0701	0731	0801	0831	30	2301	0001	0202
Amsterdam Cent.....a.	0622	0652	0722	0752	0822	0852	mins	2322	0022	0222

– Daily to Almere; extends to Lelystad Centrum on ④⑤ (arrive 0044).

G – Runs on ⑥⑦. Starts from Lelystad (d. 0147).

ALMERE - HILVERSUM - UTRECHT 482

Sprinter trains

km	▽	⚒	Ⓐ		⚒		⚒			
0	**Almere** Centrum.........d.	0621	0651	0721	0751	0821	0851	0921	and	2351
20	Naarden-Bussum.. ⊗ d.	0641	0712	0741	0811	0841	0912	0941	every 30	0011
26	Hilversum .... ⊗ d.	0647	0718	0747	0817	0847	0918	0947	minutes	0017
43	**Utrecht** Centraal.........a.	0706	0735	0806	0836	0906	0935	1006	until	0036

▽	⚒	Ⓐ		⚒		⚒			
Utrecht Centraal......d.	0624	0655	0724	0754	0824	0855	0924	and	2354
Hilversum............ ⊗ d.	0642	0712	0742	0812	0842	0912	0942	every 30	0012
Naarden-Bussum ⊗ d.	0650	0720	0750	0820	0850	0920	0950	minutes	0020
Almere Cent. ....a.	0708	0738	0808	0838	0908	0938	1008	until	0038

▽ – Aditional journeys run from Almere at 0051⑥⑦, 0551Ⓐ and from Utrecht at 0054⑥⑦, 0555Ⓐ.

⊗ – See also Table **480**.

OLDENZAAL - HENGELO - ZUTPHEN 485

Operated by **Blauwnet** (NS tickets valid) 2nd class only

km		Ⓐ	Ⓐ	Ⓐ	⚒		◧		Ⓑd	⚒	†d	⚒
0	**Oldenzaal** ... ★ d.	...	0603	0633	0703	0733		2103	2133	2203	2233	2303
11	**Hengelo** ...... ★ a.	...	0613	0643	0713	0743	every	2113	2143	2213	2243	2313
11	**Hengelo** ....d.	0546	0616	0646	0716	0746	30	2116	2146	2216	2246	2316
26	Goor.................d.	0602	0632	0702	0732	0801	mins	2131	2201	2231	2301	2331
39	Lochem ....d.	0610	0640	0710	0740	0810		2140	2210	2240	2310	2340
56	**Zutphen**...........a.	0623	0653	0723	0753	0823		2156	2223	2256	2323	2356

	Ⓐ	Ⓐ	Ⓐd	⚒		◐§		Ⓐ			
Zutphen ....d.	0539	0606	0636	0706	0736		2036	2106	2139	2239	2340
Lochem..........d.	0551	0621	0651	0721	0751	every	2051	2121	2151	2251	2351
Goor ....d.	0600	0630	0700	0730	0800	30	2100	2130	2200	2300	0000
Hengelo ....a.	0614	0644	0714	0744	0814	mins	2114	2144	2214	2314	0014
Hengelo ... ★ d.	0617	0647	0717	0747	0817		2117	2147	2217	2317	0017
Oldenzaal. ★ a.	0627	0657	0727	0757	0827		2127	2157	2227	2327	0027

– Daily Oldenzaal - Hengelo and v.v.
– On † runs hourly 0733 to 1433 then every 30 minutes.
– On † runs hourly 0736 to 1336 then every 30 minutes.

★ – Additional journeys: Oldenzaal - Hengelo 2333, 0003②–⑦, 0033; Hengelo - Oldenzaal: 0547Ⓐ, 0647⚒. See Table **811** for other journeys Bad Bentheim - Oldenzaal - Hengelo and v.v.

§ – Hourly departures from Zutphen shown as xx36 between 0736 and 2036 depart 3 minutes later on Ⓒ (also daily at 2039).

ZWOLLE - ENSCHEDE 492

Operated by **Blauwnet** (NS tickets valid)

km		Ⓐ§	⚒	⚒	Ⓐ				Ⓐ		△
0	**Zwolle**.............d.	0639	0652	0721	0739	0752	0821		1939	1951	2021
18	Raalte................d.	0652	0709	0736	0752	0809	0836	and at	1952	2008	2036
32	Nijverdal ....d.	0700	0718	0747	0800	0818	0847	the same	2000	2018	2047
44	Almelo .... **463** d.	0710	0730	0800	0810	0830	0900	minutes	2010	2030	2100
59	Hengelo..... **463** a.	0720	0743	0813	0820	0843	0913	past each	2020	2043	2113
59	Hengelo..... **463** d.	0722	0747	0817	0822	0847	0917	hour until	2022	2048	2118
67	**Enschede** . **463** a.	0729	0756	0827	0829	0856	0927		2029	2057	2127

	Ⓐ‡	⚒	⚒	Ⓐ				Ⓐ		▽
Enschede 463 d.	0631	0634	0704	0731	0734	0804		1931	1934	2004
Hengelo ... **463** a.	0638	0643	0713	0738	0743	0813	and at	1938	1943	2013
Hengelo ... **463** d.	0639	0646	0716	0739	0746	0816	the same	1939	1947	2017
Almelo ..... **463** d.	0650	0700	0730	0750	0800	0830	minutes	1950	2001	2031
Nijverdal ....d.	0700	0716	0743	0800	0816	0843	past each	2000	2016	2043
Raalte..............d.	0709	0724	0754	0809	0824	0854	hour until	2009	2024	2054
Zwolle ....a.	0721	0739	0809	0821	0839	0909		2021	2039	2109

– Earlier journeys run at 0522Ⓐ, 0552Ⓐ.
– Earlier journeys run at 0504Ⓐ, 0534Ⓐ, 0604Ⓐ.

△ – Later journeys run every 30 minutes until 2351.
▽ – Later journeys run every 30 minutes until 2334 (also 0003 on ⑥⑦).

ZWOLLE - EMMEN 493

Operated by **Blauwnet** (NS tickets valid)

km		Ⓐ	Ⓐ	⚒	Ⓐ				⊕		△
0	**Zwolle**.............d.	0552	0622	0652	0722	0752	0822	0852	and at	2222	2252
23	Ommen ....d.	0607	0637	0707	0737	0807	0837	0907	the same	2237	2307
34	Mariënberg ....d.	0614	0644	0714	0744	0814	0844	0914	minutes	2244	2314
55	Coevorden........d.	0630	0700	0730	0800	0830	0900	0930	past each	2300	2330
75	**Emmen** ....a.	0650	0720	0750	0815	0850	0915	0950	hour until	2315	2350

	Ⓐ§	Ⓐ		⚒		◇				▽
Emmen ....d.	0541	0610	0641	0711**z**	0741	0815	0841	and at	2115	2141
Coevorden .... d.	0600	0630	0700	0730	0800	0832	0900	the same	2132	2200
Mariënberg ... d.	0616	0646	0716	0746	0816	0846	0916	minutes	2146	2216
Ommen..........d.	0623	0653	0723	0753	0823	0853	0923	past each	2153	2223
Zwolle ....a.	0638	0708	0738	0808	0838	0908	0938	hour until	2208	2238

– 0715 on ⑥.
– An earlier journey runs at 0512Ⓐ.
– Later journeys run at 2322⚒, 2355⚒, 0023②–⑦, 0057⑦.
– Later journeys run at 2215⚒, 2241, 2315⚒, 2341⑥, 0019②–⑦.

⊕ – 1622 and 1722 journeys arrive Emmen 5 minutes later on Ⓐ.
◇ – 1715 and 1815 journeys depart Emmen 4 minutes earlier on Ⓐ (and Coevorden 2 minutes earlier).

LEEUWARDEN - GRONINGEN 494

Operated by **Arriva** (NS tickets valid)

km		Ⓐ	Ⓐ	⚒	Ⓐ		Ⓐ	⚒	Ⓐ		⚒	†	⚒	⚒			⚒	†	⚒	⚒		⚒	†	⚒
0	**Leeuwarden**.....d.	0550	0616	0620	0646	0650	0716	0720	0746	0750	0816	0819	0820	0846	0850	and at the	1916	1919	1920	1946	1950	2016	2019	2020
25	Buitenpost ....d.	0613	|	0643	0703	0713	|	0743	0803	0813	|	0835	0843	0903	0913	same minutes	|	1935	1943	2003	2013	2032	2035	2043
42	Zuidhorn ....d.	0626	0641	0656	|	0726	0741	0756	|	0826	0841	0845	0856	|	0926	past each	1941	1945	1956	|	2026	2042	2045	2056
54	**Groningen** ....a.	0636	0651	0706	0721	0736	0751	0806	0821	0836	0851	0856	0906	0921	0936	hour until	1951	1956	2006	2021	2036	2051	2056	2106

								†	⚒
eeuwarden......d.	2050	2119	2150	2219	2250	2319	2350	0055	0056
uitenpost ....d.	2113	2135	2213	2235	2313	2335	0013	0117	0119
uidhorn ....d.	2126	2145	2226	2245	2326	2345	0026	0130	0131
roningen ....a.	2136	2156	2236	2256	2336	2356	0036	0140	0140

	Ⓐ	⚒	Ⓐ	⚒	Ⓐ		Ⓐ	⚒	†	⚒		⚒	⚒
Groningen...............d.	0554	0624	0639	0654	0709	0724	0739	0754	0802	0809	0824	0839	0854
Zuidhorn ....d.	0602	0632	0647	0702	|	0732	0747	0802	0810	|	0832	0847	0902
Buitenpost..................d.	0615	0645	|	0715	0726	0745	|	0815	0821	0826	0845	|	0915
Leeuwarden ....a.	0640	0710	0714	0740	0744	0810	0814	0840	0839	0844	0910	0914	0940

	†	⚒		⚒	⚒		†	⚒		⚒	⚒	†	⚒		⚒	†	⚒							
roningen ....d.	0902	0909	0924	0939	0954	and at the	1902	1909	1924	1939	1954	2002	2009	2024	2039	2102	2109	2124	2202	2224	2302	2324	0002	0056
uidhorn ....d.	0910	|	0932	0947	1002	same minutes	1910	|	1932	1947	2002	2010	|	2032	2047	2110	2126	2132	2210	2232	2310	2332	0010	0104
uitenpost ....d.	0921	0926	0945	|	1015	past each	1921	1926	1945	|	2015	2021	2026	2045	|	2121	|	2145	2221	2245	2321	2345	0021	0117
eeuwarden......a.	0939	0944	1010	1014	1040	hour until	1939	1944	2010	2014	2040	2039	2044	2110	2114	2139	2144	2210	2239	2310	2339	0010	0040	0140

GRONINGEN - BAD NIEUWESCHANS - LEER 495

🚐 **GRONINGEN - LEER** Non-stop rail replacement 🚐. Operated by Arriva (NS rail tickets valid). See note ☆

km	🚐	⚒									
0	**Groningen** ⊖...........d.	0610	0810	1010	1210	1410	1610	1810	2010	...	...
72	**Leer** ....a.	0725	0925	1125	1325	1525	1725	1925	2125	...	...

🚐	⚒									
Leer ....d.	0730	0930	1130	1330	1530	1730	1930	2130	...	...
Groningen ⊖ ....a.	0825	1025	1225	1425	1625	1825	2025	2225	...	...

GRONINGEN - BAD NIEUWESCHANS Operated by **Arriva** (NS tickets valid); 2nd class only

km		⚒v	⚒	⚒	⚒	⚒	⚒	⚒	†	†	†	†
0	**Groningen** ....d.	0532	0617	every	1917	1957	and	2257	0657	0757	and	2257
34	Winschoten.................d.	0610	0650	30	1950	2032	hourly	2330	0741	0830	hourly	2330
46	**Bad Nieuweschans** ...a.	0620	0700	mins	2000	2042	until	2340	0751	0840	until	2340

	⚒u	⚒	⚒	⚒	⚒	⚒u	†	†	†u
Bad Nieuweschans d.	0730	every	1930	2020	and	2320	0820	and	2320
Winschoten..............d.	0740	30	1940	2032	hourly	2335	0835	hourly	2335
Groningen ....a.	0813	mins	2013	2042	until	0009	0909	until	0009

🚐 **BAD NIEUWESCHANS - LEER** DB Weser-Ems-Bus line 620, rail tickets valid

km	🚐	⚒	†		⚒	†			
0	Bad Nieuweschans §...d.	0636	0646	and at the	1936	1946	2046	2146	2246
10	Weener.......................d.	0658	0706	same minutes	1958	2006	2106	2206	2306
26	Leer △ ....a.	0723	0725	past each hour	2023	2025	2125	2225	2325

🚐									
Leer △ ....d.	0530	0630	and	1730	1830	1930	2030	2130	2230
Weener.......................d.	0548	0648	hourly	1748	1854	1948	2048	2148	2248
Bad Nieuweschans § a.	0609	0717t	until	1817t	1917	2009	2109	2209	2309

– Arrives 8 minutes earlier on †.
– Additional journeys run at 0630⚒, 2350, 0110.
– On ⑥ Groningen d. 0541, Bad Nieuweschans a. 0625.
△ – Leer bus station (adjacent to railway station), bay 8.

⊖ – Groningen bus station (adjacent to rail station), bay Q.
◇ – On ⚒ departs Bad Nieuweschans 1 minute later.
§ – Bus stop is adjacent to railway station.
☆ – Through rail services may recommence in late 2025 on the reopening of the Friesenbrücke.

496 LEEUWARDEN - STAVOREN

Operated by **Arriva** (NS tickets valid); 2nd class only

km		Ⓐ	Ⓐ	⚒	Ⓐ	⚒	†		◧			⑤⑥
0	**Leeuwarden**.....d.	0527	0553	0622	0653	0723	0723	0823	and	2223	2323	2323
22	Sneek..............d.	0546	0616	0646	0716	0746	0742	0846	hourly	2246	2342	2346
51	**Stavoren**..........a.	0613	0643	0713	0743	0813	...	0913	until	2313	...	0013

	Ⓐ	Ⓐ	⚒d	Ⓐ	⚒d		◐		⑥⑦
Stavoren.......d.	0618	0647	0717	0747	0818	0918	and	2318	0018
Sneek.............d.	0648	0718	0748	0818	0848	0948	hourly	2348	0045
Leeuwarden..a.	0707	0738	0808	0838	0908	1007	until	0007	0103

d – ⚒ from Stavoren; daily from Sneek.

◧ – Additional journeys run at 1553Ⓐ, 1653Ⓐ, 1753Ⓐ.

◐ – Certain journeys depart Stavoren 1 minute earlier. Additional journeys run at 1647Ⓐ, 1747Ⓐ, 1847Ⓐ.

☛ Additional trains run Leeuwarden - Sneek and v.v. on ⚒.

497 SCHIEDAM - HOEK VAN HOLLAND

Services are operated by *Rotterdamse Elektrische Tram N.V.* (RET). Local RET fares apply.

Metro line **B**: (Nesselande -) Schiedam Centrum - Hoek van Holland Haven - Hoek van Holland Strand. Journey time: 27 minutes. All services call at Vlaardingen Centrum and Maassluis Centrum.

Departures from Schiedam Centrum: * terminates at Hoek van Holland Haven

On Ⓐ at 0603, 0617, 0632, 0647, 0717, 0739, 0759, 0819 and every 20 minutes until 1859; 1917, 1931, 2002, 2033 and every 30 minutes until 2333, also 0003.

On ⑥ at 0718*, 0733, 0803 and every 30 minutes until 1103; 1118, 1139, 1159 and every 20 minutes until 1839; 1903 and every 30 minutes until 2333, also 0003.

On ⑦ at 0803 and every 30 minutes until 1003; 1029 and every 30 minutes until 1929; 2003 and every 30 minutes until 2333, also 0003.

Departures from Hoek van Holland Strand (3 minutes later from Haven):

On Ⓐ at 0634, 0653, 0714 and every 20 minutes until 1915; 1944, 1953, 2014 and every 30 minutes until 2344, also 0014, 0044 (also from Haven 0547, 0617).

On ⑥ at 0814 and every 30 minutes until 1044; 1115 and every 20 minutes until 1815; 1834, 1855, 1914 and every 30 minutes until 2344, 0014, 0044 (also from Haven 0647, 0717, 0747).

On ⑦ at 0843 and approx every 30 minutes until 2344, 0014, 0044 (also from Haven 0747, 0817).

498 OTHER BRANCH LINES

ALMELO – MARIËNBERG

Operated by **Blauwnet** (NS tickets valid) *19 km.* Journey time 17 – 19 minutes.

From Almelo: 0618 Ⓐ, 0648 Ⓐ, 0718 Ⓐ, 0748 ⚒, 0817 Ⓐ, 0848, 0948, 1048, 1148, 1248, 1318 ⚒, 1348, 1417 ⚒, 1448, 1518 ⚒, 1548, 1617 ⚒, 1648, 1718 ⚒, 1748, 1817 ⚒, 1848, 1918 ⚒, 1948, 2048, 2148, 2248, 2352.

From Mariënberg: 0555 Ⓐ, 0625 Ⓐ, 0655 Ⓐ, 0725, 0755 Ⓐ, 0825, 0855 Ⓐ, 0925, 1025, 1125, 1225, 1325, 1355 ⚒, 1425, 1455 ⚒, 1525, 1555 ⚒, 1625, 1655 ⚒, 1725, 1755 ⚒, 1825, 1855 Ⓐ, 1925, 2025, 2125, 2225, 2325.

AMERSFOORT – EDE-WAGENINGEN

Operated by **RRReis** (NS tickets valid) *34 km.* Journey time 37 – 38 minutes.

From Amersfoort Centraal: 0509 Ⓐ, 0539 ⚒, 0609 ⚒, 0639 ⚒, 0709, 0739 and every 30 minutes until 2339, 0009④–⑦.

From Ede-Wageningen: 0553 Ⓐ, 0623 ⚒, 0653 ⚒, 0723 ⚒, 0753, 0823, 0853 and every 30 minutes until 0023.

Trains call at Barneveld Centrum (16 mins from Amersfoort, 20 mins from Ede-Wageningen)

APELDOORN – ZUTPHEN

Operated by **Arriva** (NS tickets valid) *18 km.* Journey time 13 – 19 minutes.

From Apeldoorn: 0636 Ⓐ, 0706 Ⓐ, 0712 ⑥, 0736 Ⓐ, 0806 Ⓐ, 0808 Ⓒ, 0822 Ⓒ, 0836 Ⓐ, 0906 Ⓐ, 0908 Ⓒ, 0922 Ⓒ, 0936 Ⓐ and at 06 Ⓐ, 08 Ⓒ, 22 Ⓒ, 36 Ⓐ minutes past each hour until 1906 Ⓐ, 1908 Ⓒ, 1923 Ⓒ, 1936 Ⓐ; then 2001, 2022, 2101, 2122, 2201, 2222, 2301, 2322, 0000.

From Zutphen: 0612 Ⓐ, 0636 Ⓐ, 0654⑥, 0706 Ⓐ, 0736 Ⓐ, 0738 Ⓒ, 0754 Ⓒ, 0806 Ⓐ, 0836 Ⓐ, 0838 Ⓒ, 0854 Ⓒ and at 06 Ⓐ, 36 Ⓐ, 38 Ⓒ, 54 Ⓒ minutes past each hour until 1806 Ⓐ, 1836 Ⓐ, 1838 Ⓒ, 1854 Ⓒ, 1906 Ⓐ, 1936 Ⓐ, 1938 Ⓒ, 2005, 2038, 2105, 2138, 2205, 2238, 2305, 2338.

GRONINGEN – DELFZIJL

Operated by **Arriva** (NS tickets valid) *38 km.* Journey time 37 – 39 minutes. 2nd class.

From **Groningen**: 0518 Ⓐ, 0548 ⚒, 0618, 0648 ⚒, 0718, 0748 ⚒ and at 18 and 48 ⚒ minutes past each hour until 2018, 2048 ⚒; then 2118, 2218, 2318, 0018.

From **Delfzijl**: 0600 Ⓐ, 0630 ⚒, 0700, 0730 ⚒, 0800, 0830 ⚒ and at 00 and 30 ⚒ minutes past each hour until 2100, 2130 ⚒; then 2200, 2300, 0000, 0100.

GRONINGEN – EEMSHAVEN

Operated by **Arriva** (NS tickets valid) *45 km.* Journey time: 51 – 55 minutes. 2nd class.

From Groningen: 0552Ⓐ, 0622, 0652Ⓐ, 0722Ⓐ, 0852⚒, 0922†, 1052⑥, 1122⑥, 1222, 1422Ⓒ, 1522, 1552Ⓐ, 1622Ⓐ, 1652⚒.

From Eemshaven: 0648Ⓐ, 0718, 0748Ⓐ, 0818Ⓐ, 0948⚒, 1018†, 1148⑥, 1218⑥, 1318, 1518Ⓒ, 1618, 1648Ⓐ, 1718Ⓐ, 1748⚒.

GRONINGEN – VEENDAM 🚂

Operated by **Arriva** (NS tickets valid) *29 km.* Journey time 29 minutes. 2nd class.

From Groningen: ⚒: 0458 Ⓐ, 0528 Ⓐ, 0558, 0628 and every 30 minutes until 1928, then 2027, 2127, 2227, 2327, 0046.

†: 0727 and hourly until 2327, also 0046.

From Veendam: ⚒: 0533Ⓐ, 0603Ⓐ and every 30 minutes until 2003, then 2110, 2210, 2310, 0010, 0119.

†: 0810 and hourly until 2310, also 0010, 0119.

Trains call at Hoogezand-Sappemeer (16 mins from Groningen, 11 mins from Veendam).

LEEUWARDEN – HARLINGEN Haven ★

Operated by **Arriva** (NS tickets valid) *26 km* Journey time 28 – 29 minutes. 2nd class

From Leeuwarden: 0540 Ⓐ, 0550 Ⓐ, 0620 Ⓐ, 0640 ⑥, 0650 ⚒, 0720 ⚒, 0740 †, 0750, 0820, 0850, 0920, 0950 and every 30 minutes until 2020; then 2120, 2220, 2320.

From Harlingen Haven: 0611 Ⓐ, 0641 Ⓐ, 0711 ⚒, 0741 ⚒, 0811, 0841 and every 30 minutes until 2111; then 2148, 2248, 2348.

UTRECHT – MALIEBAAN for Utrecht Railway Museum

Special service for visitors to the Railway Museum. Journey time 18 minutes.

Days of operation: ②–⑦ (also Dec. 23, 30, Feb. 17, 24, Apr. 21 - May 5, June 9, July 7 - Aug. 25, Oct. 13, 20).

From Utrecht Centraal: 0931 and hourly until 1631.

From Utrecht Maliebaan: 0955 and hourly until 1555, also 1710.

ZUTPHEN – WINTERWIJK

Operated by **Arriva** (NS tickets valid) *43 km.* Journey time 34 – 35 minutes.

From Zutphen: 0632Ⓐ, 0702Ⓐ, 0732Ⓐ, 0737⑥, 0802Ⓐ, 0837, 0907Ⓐ, 0937, 1007Ⓐ, 1037, 1107Ⓐ, 1137, 1207Ⓐ, 1237, 1307 and every 30 minutes until 2037, 2107Ⓐ, 2137, 2207Ⓐ, 2237, 2307Ⓐ, 2337, 0019.

From Winterswijk: 0550Ⓐ, 0617Ⓐ, 0621⑥, 0647Ⓐ, 0717Ⓐ, 0721Ⓒ, 0747Ⓐ, 0820, 0851Ⓐ, 0921, 0951Ⓐ, 1021, 1051Ⓐ, 1121, 1151Ⓐ, 1221 and every 30 minutes until 2021, 2051Ⓐ, 2121, 2151Ⓐ, 2221, 2321, 0021⑦.

ZWOLLE – KAMPEN

Operated by **Blauwnet** (NS tickets valid) *13 km.* Journey time 11 minutes.

From Zwolle: 0547 Ⓐ, 0617 Ⓐ, 0647 ⚒, 0717, 0747 and every 30 minutes until 2347, 0017.

From Kampen: 0602 Ⓐ, 0632 Ⓐ, 0702 ⚒, 0732, 0802, 0832 and every 30 minutes until 2332, 0002, 0032.

★ – For ⛴ to / from Terschelling and Vlieland (see www.rederij-doeksen.nl). Trains also call at Harlingen (station for the town centre), 3 minutes from Harlingen Haven.

🚂 – Station for *Museumspoorlijn STAR*. Steam trains operate Veendam - Stadskanaal. For days of running see www.stadskanaalrail.nl.

499 OTHER 🚌 and ⛴ LINES

ALKMAAR – LEEUWARDEN

🚌 *Qbuzz* route **350.** Journey 1 hr 40 m – 1 hr 50 m

From Alkmaar bus station (bay F), adjacent to rail station:

Ⓐ: 0528, 0556, 0623, 0653, 0723, 0753, 0826, 0857, 0927, 0958 and every 30 mins until 1358, 1427, 1455, 1525, 1554, 1620, 1650, 1720, 1750, 1827, 1930, 2030, 2130, 2230.

⑥: 0631, 0731, 0831, 0930, 1030, 1128, hourly until 1728, 1829, 1929, 2029, 2129.

†: 0831, 0931, 1031, 1131, 1229, 1329, 1429, hourly until 2229.

From Leeuwarden bus station (bay N), adjacent to rail station:

Ⓐ: 0511, 0541, 0611, 0641, 0711, 0741, 0813, 0843, 0915, 0945 and every 30 mins until 1515, 1544, 1614, 1644, 1714, 1747, 1818, 1919, 2019, 2119, 2219, 2319.

⑥: 0717, 0817, 0917 and hourly until 2017, 2119, 2219.

†: 0818, 0918, 1018, 1115 and hourly until 1715, 1818, 1919, 2019, 2119, 2219.

DEN HELDER – TEXEL

⛴ *TESO* www.teso.nl Sailing time 20 minutes

From Den Helder Havenhoofd: 0630 ⚒, 0730 ⚒, 0830 and hourly until 2130.

From Texel ('t Horntje ferryport): 0600 ⚒, 0700 ⚒, 0800 and hourly until 2100.

Sailings are increased to every 30 minutes at holiday times.

Connecting 🚌 route **33** departs Den Helder rail station 18 minutes before sailing time. On Texel 🚌 route **28** connects 't Horntje ferryport with Den Burg and De Koog.

ENKHUIZEN – STAVOREN

⛴ *Rederij V & O* www.veerboot.info Sailing time ± 1 hr 25 m

Conveys foot passengers, cycles and mopeds only.

From Enkhuizen Spoorhaven: 0845 **A**, 1245 **A**, 1645**A**.

From Stavoren: 1025 **A**, 1425 **A**, 1825 **A**.

A – ②–⑦ Apr. 27 - Sept. 28 (daily July 1 - August 30), also Apr. 19 - 21. No winter service.

VLISSINGEN – BRESKENS

⛴ *Westerschelde Ferry* www.westerscheldeferry.nl Sailing time 23 minutes

Conveys foot passengers, cycles and mopeds only. Adjacent to railway station at Vlissingen.

WINTER (early September to mid-April):

From Vlissingen: 0548 Ⓐ, 0648 Ⓐ, 0748, 0848 and hourly until 2048, 2148Ⓐ.

From Breskens: 0618 Ⓐ, 0718 Ⓐ, 0818, 0918 and hourly until 2118, 2218Ⓐ.

SUMMER (mid-April to early September):

From Vlissingen: 0548 Ⓐ, 0648 Ⓐ, 0748, hourly to 2148 (every 30 mins 0948 to 1748).

From Breskens: 0618 Ⓐ, 0718 Ⓐ, 0818, hourly until 2218 (every 30 mins 1018 to 1818).

BRESKENS ferryport – BRUGGE rail station

🚌 *Connexxion* route **42** Journey time 85 minutes

Connects with the Vlissingen - Breskens ferry (see above).

From Breskens: 0615 Ⓐ, 0715 ⚒, 0815 ⚒, 0915, 1015 and hourly until 2015.

From Brugge: 0648 ⚒, 0748 ⚒, 0848, 0948 and hourly until 1948; then 2048 ⚒.

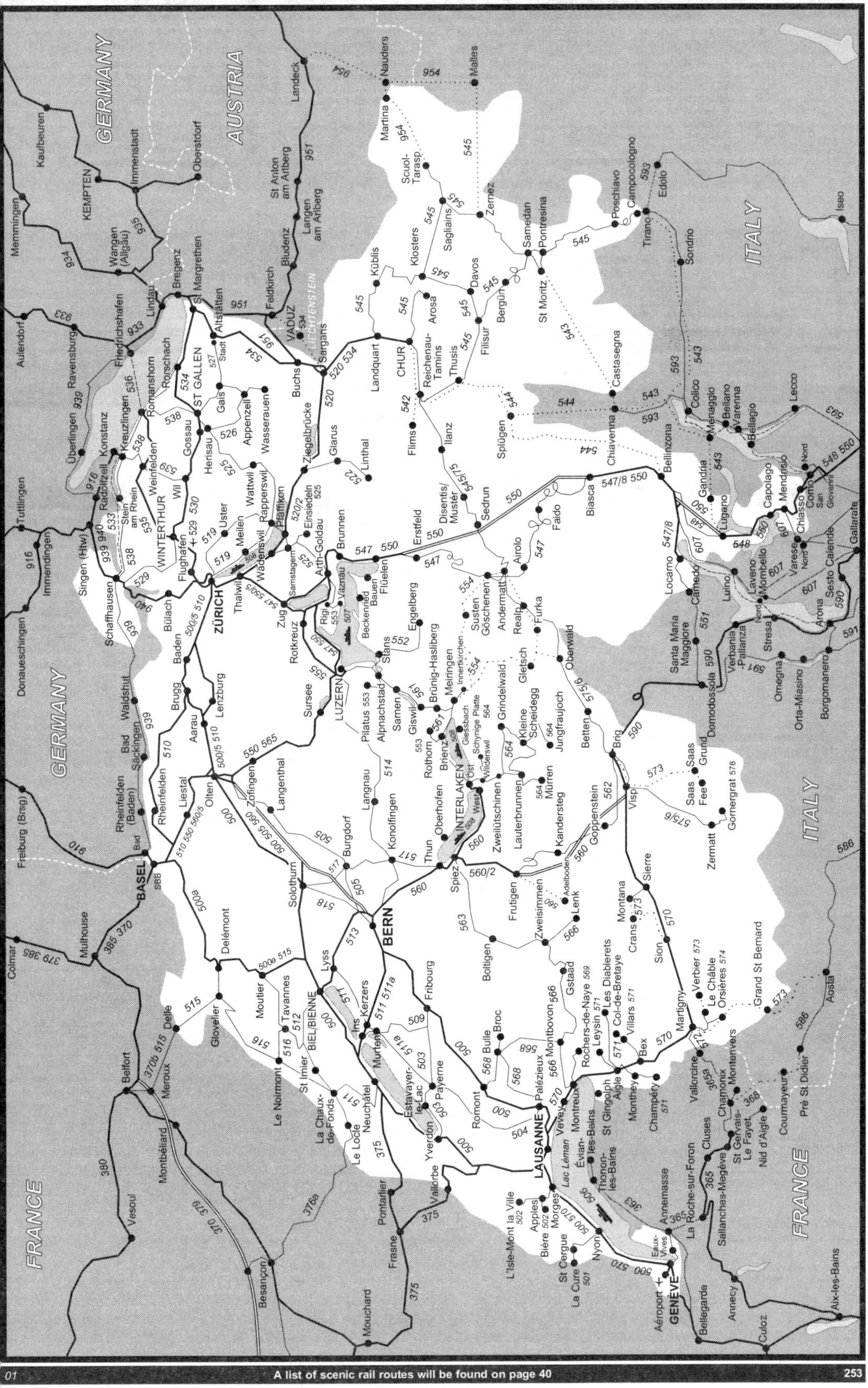
FRANCE
GERMANY
AUSTRIA
ITALY
LIECHTENSTEIN
BASEL
ZÜRICH
BERN
LUZERN
LAUSANNE
GENÈVE
INTERLAKEN
ST GALLEN
WINTERTHUR
CHUR
BIEL/BIENNE
VADUZ
KEMPTEN
Lac Léman
Brig
Visp
Zermatt
Sion
Sierre
Martigny
Montreux
Vevey
Neuchâtel
Fribourg
Thun
Spiez
Olten
Aarau
Schaffhausen
Konstanz
Bellinzona
Lugano
Locarno
Chiasso
Domodossola
St Moritz
Davos
Andermatt
Göschenen
Arth-Goldau
Zug
Brienz
Meiringen
Grindelwald
Lauterbrunnen
Kleine Scheidegg
Jungfraujoch
Gstaad
Zweisimmen
Yverdon
Vallorbe
Delémont
Solothurn
Biasca
Tirano
Chamonix

SWITZERLAND

Operators: There are numerous operators of which Schweizerische Bundesbahnen (SBB)/Chemins de fer Fédéraux (CFF)/Ferrovie Federali Svizzere (FFS) is the principal: www.sbb.ch Bus services are provided by PostAuto/Autopostale (PA): www.postauto.ch. Table headings show the operators' initials; abbreviations used in the European Rail Timetable are

AB	Appenzeller Bahnen	MGB	Matterhorn Gotthard Bahn	SBS	Schweizerische Bodensee-Schifffahrtsgesellschaft
BLM	Bergbahn Lauterbrunnen - Mürren	MOB	Montreux - Oberland Bernois	SGV	Schifffahrtsgesellschaft des Vierwaldstättersees
BLS	BLS Lötschbergbahn	MThB	Mittelthurgau Bahn	SMC	Sierre - Montana - Crans
BOB	Berner Oberland Bahnen	MVR	Montreux - Vevey Riviera	SNCF	Société Nationale des Chemins de Fer Francais
BRB	Brienz - Rothorn Bahn	NStCM	Nyon-St Cergue-Morez	SOB	Schweizerische Südostbahn
BSB	Bodensee-Schiffsbetriebe	PA	PostAuto / Autopostale / AutoDaPosta	THURBO	an alliance of MThB and SBB
CGN	Compagnie Générale de Navigation	PB	Pilatus Bahn	TMR	Transports de Martigny et Régions
CJ	Chemins de fer du Jura	RA	RegionAlps	TPC	Transports Publics du Chablais
FART	Ferrovie Autolinee Regionali Ticinesi	RB	Rigi Bahnen	TPF	Transports Publics Fribourgeois
FS	Ferrovie dello Stato	RBS	Regionalverkehr Bern - Solothurn	URh	Untersee und Rhein
GGB	Gornergrat Bahn	RhB	Rhätische Bahn	WAB	Wengernalpbahn
JB	Jungfraubahn	RM	Regionalverkehr Mittelland	ZB	Zentralbahn
MBC	Morges - Bière - Cossonay	SBB	Schweizerische Bundesbahnen	ZSG	Zürich Schifffahrtsgesellschaft

Services: All trains convey first and second class seating except where indicated in the table header. For most local services you must be in possession of a valid ticket before boarding

Train Categories:
- *TGV* French high-speed **Train à Grande Vitesse**.
- *ICE* German high-speed **InterCity Express** train.
- *RJ* Austrian high-speed **Railjet** train.
- *EC* **EuroCity** quality international express train.
- *IC* **InterCity** quality internal express train.
- *IR* **InterRegio** fast inter-regional train.
- *RE* **RegioExpress** semi-fast regional train.

Catering: ✕ – Restaurant / Bistro car; (🍸) – Vending machine with drinks and snacks; 🍸 – Minibar (trolley service).
Please note that catering facilities may not be open for the whole journey and may vary from those shown in our tables.

Timings: Valid **until December 13**, 2025. National public holidays are on Dec. 25, 26, Jan. 1, 2, Apr. 18, 21, May 29, June 9 and Aug. 1.

Supplements: Most internal Swiss journeys can be made without supplement (including domestic journeys on international services). A supplement is payable on a small number of trains (mainly tourist services) and these are indicated in the relevant tables. Special 'global' fares are payable for international *TGV* journeys between Switzerland and France with compulsory reservation. A supplement is payable and compulsory reservation required for international journeys on *EC* trains between Switzerland and Italy.

Reservations: As well as compulsory reservations for international journeys mentioned above, optional seat reservations are also available on other *ICE*, *RJ*, *EC* and *IC* trains. Reservation is recommended for travel in first class panorama cars. Standard fares in Switzerland are generally calculated according to distance, although artificially inflated tariff-kilometres are used on certain routes. However, distances shown in our tables are always actual kilometres.

500 GENÈVE and LAUSANNE - ZÜRICH via Bern or Biel / Bienne SBB

SERVICES VIA BERN. See pages 256 – 258 for services via Biel / Bienne.

For other semi-fast *IR* services Bern - Olten - Zürich via Burgdorf and Brugg, see Table **505**.

km ⊕		*IR* 2155		*IC* 703		*IR* 2505	*IR* 2505 ①	*IC* 805	24509	*IC* 705	*RE* 18401	*IR* 2507	*IC* 807	*IR* 1707	*IC* 707 Ⓐ	*IC* 901 Ⓒ	*IR* 2509	*IC* 809	*IR* 1709	*IC* 709	*IR* 2511	*IC* 811	*IR* 1711	*IC* 711
				✕			g	✕		✕			✕		✕	H✕		✕		✕		✕		✕
0	Genève Aéroport ✈ 570 d.	...	...	...	...	...	...	...	...	...	...	...	...	0511	0525	0525	0544	...	0614	0625	0645	...	0711	0725
6	**Genève** 570 d.	...	...	...	...	...	...	...	...	...	0408	...	...	0522	0533	0535	0553	...	0624	0635	0654	...	0723	0735
27	Nyon 570 d.	...	...	...	...	...	...	...	...	...	0425	...	...	0539	|	|	0609	...	0639	|	0709	...	0739	|
53	Morges 504 570 d.	...	...	...	...	...	...	...	...	...	0447	...	...	0601**p**	|	|	0626	...	0655	|	0726	...	0801**p**	|
61	Renens 504 570 d.	...	...	...	...	...	...	...	...	...	0454	...	...	|	0608	0608	|	...	|	0708	|	...	|	0808
66	**Lausanne** 504 570 a.	...	...	...	...	...	...	...	...	...	0459	...	...	0612	0614	0614	0637	...	0707	0714	0737	...	0812	0814
66	**Lausanne** 504 d.	...	...	...	...	...	0440	...	0449	...	...	0540	...	...	0617	0617	0640	...	...	0717	0740	...	...	0817
87	Palézieux 504 d.	...	...	...	...	...	0457	...	0511	...	...	0557	...	...	|	|	0657	...	...	|	0757	...	...	|
106	Romont 568 d.	...	...	...	...	...	0513	...	0526	*0538*	...	0613	...	...	|	|	0713	...	...	|	0813	...	...	|
132	Fribourg 568 d.	...	...	...	...	0533	0533	...	0552	0603	...	0633	...	...	0703	0703	0733	...	...	0803	0833	...	...	0903
	Brig 560 d.	...	...	...	...	|	|	...	...	|	...	|	0542	...	|	|	|	...	...	|	|	0745	...	|
	Interlaken Ost 560 d.	...	...	...	...	|	|	...	...	|	...	|	|	...	|	|	|	0659	...	|	|	|	...	|
163	**Bern** 568 a.	...	...	...	...	0556	0556	...	...	0626	...	0656	0653	...	0726	0726	0756	0756	...	0826	0856	0853	...	0926
163	**Bern** 505 560 d.	0418**e**	...	0529**f**	...	0600	0600	0602	...	0631	...	0700	0702	...	0731	0731	0800	0802	...	0831	0900	0902	...	0931
	Luzern 565 a.	|	...	|	...	0701	0701	|	...	|	...	0801	|	...	|	|	0901	|	...	|	1001	|	...	|
225	**Olten** 505 560 d.	0446	...	0557	...	...	...	0631	...	|	...	...	|	...	|	|	...	|	...	|	...	|	...	|
238	Aarau 505 510 d.	0456	...	|	...	...	...	|	...	|	...	...	|	...	|	|	...	|	...	|	...	|	...	|
280	**Zürich** HB 505 510 a.	0528	...	0628	...	...	...	0701	...	0728	...	...	0758	...	0828	0828	...	0858	...	0928	...	0958	...	1028
	Zürich Flughafen ✈ 530/5 a.	0541	...	0651	...	...	...	0714	...	0751	...	...	0814	...	0851	...	...	0914	...	0951	...	1014	...	1051
	St Gallen 530 a.	...	...	0752	...	...	...	|	...	0852	...	...	|	...	0952	...	...	|	...	1052	...	|	...	1152
	Romanshorn 535 a.	...	...	...	...	...	...	0812	...	...	...	...	0912	...	...	...	...	1012	...	...	...	1112	...	...

	IR 2513	*IC* 813	*IR* 1713	*IC* 713 Ⓐ	*IC* 903 Ⓒ	*IR* 2515	*IC* 815	*IR* 1715	*IC* 715	*IR* 2517	*IC* 817	*IR* 1717	*IC* 717	*IR* 2519	*IC* 819	*IR* 1719	*IC* 719 Ⓐ	*IC* 907 Ⓒ	*IR* 2521	*IC* 821	*IR* 1721	*IC* 721	*IR* 2523	*IC* 823
		✕		✕	H✕		✕		✕		✕		✕		✕		✕	H✕		✕		✕		✕
Genève Aéroport ✈ 570 d.	0745	...	0814	0825	0825	0845	...	0914	0922	0945	...	1014	1025	1045	...	1114	1125	1125	1145	...	1214	1225	1245	...
Genève 570 d.	0754	...	0824	0835	0835	0854	...	0924	0931	0954	...	1024	1035	1054	...	1124	1135	1135	1154	...	1224	1235	1254	...
Nyon 570 d.	0809	...	0839	|	|	0909	...	0939	|	1009	...	1039	|	1109	...	1139	|	|	1209	...	1239	|	1309	...
Morges 504 570 d.	0826	...	0855	|	|	0926	...	0955	|	1026	...	1055	|	1126	...	1155	|	|	1226	...	1255	|	1326	...
Renens 504 570 d.	|	...	|	0908	0908	|	...	|	1008	|	...	|	1108	|	...	|	1208	1208	|	...	|	1308	|	...
Lausanne 504 570 a.	0837	...	0907	0914	0914	0937	...	1007	1014	1037	...	1107	1114	1137	...	1207	1214	1214	1237	...	1307	1314	1337	...
Lausanne 504 d.	0840	...	...	0917	0917	0940	...	...	1017	1040	...	...	1117	1140	...	...	1217	1217	1240	...	...	1317	1340	...
Palézieux 504 d.	0857	...	...	|	|	0957	...	...	|	1057	...	...	|	1157	...	...	|	|	1257	...	...	|	1357	...
Romont 568 d.	0913	...	...	|	|	1013	...	...	|	1113	...	...	|	1213	...	...	|	|	1313	...	...	|	1413	...
Fribourg 568 d.	0933	...	...	1003	1003	1033	...	...	1103	1133	...	...	1203	1233	...	...	1303	1303	1333	...	...	1403	1433	...
Brig 560 d.	|	...	...	|	|	|	0945	...	|	|	...	...	|	|	1145	...	|	|	|	1245	...	|	|	...
Interlaken Ost 560 d.	|	0859	...	|	|	|	|	...	|	|	1059	...	|	|	|	...	|	|	|	|	...	|	|	1359
Bern 568 a.	0956	0956	...	1026	1026	1056	1053	...	1126	1156	1156	...	1226	1256	1253	...	1326	1326	1356	1353	...	1426	1456	1456
Bern 505 560 d.	1000	1002	...	1031	1031	1100	1102	...	1131	1200	1202	...	1231	1300	1302	...	1331	1331	1400	1402	...	1431	1500	1502
Luzern 565 a.	1101	|	...	|	|	1201	|	...	|	1301	|	...	|	1401	|	...	|	|	1501	|	...	|	1601	|
Olten 505 560 d.	...	|	...	|	|	...	|	...	|	...	|	...	|	...	|	...	|	|	...	|	...	|	...	|
Aarau 505 510 d.	...	|	...	|	|	...	|	...	|	...	|	...	|	...	|	...	|	|	...	|	...	|	...	|
Zürich HB 505 510 a.	...	1058	...	1128	1128	...	1158	...	1228	...	1258	...	1328	...	1358	...	1428	1428	...	1458	...	1528	...	1558
Zürich Flughafen ✈ 530/5 a.	...	1114	...	1151	...	...	1214	...	1251	...	1314	...	1351	...	1414	...	1451	...	...	1514	...	1551	...	1614
St Gallen 530 a.	...	|	...	1252	...	...	|	...	1352	...	|	...	1452	...	|	...	1552	...	...	|	...	1652	...	|
Romanshorn 535 a.	...	1212	...	...	...	...	1312	...	...	...	1412	...	...	...	1512	...	...	...	...	1612	...	...	...	1712

H – To / from Chur (Table **520**).

c – Ⓒ only.
e – 0404 on June 16 – 20, 23 – 27, July 28, Sept. 8, 13 – 15, 22 – 26, 29, 30, Oct. 1 – 3, 25 – 27, Nov. 17, Dec. 1, 8.
f – 0513 on June 16 – 20, 23 – 27, July 28, Sept. 8, 13 – 15, 22 – 26, 29, 30, Oct. 1 – 3, 25 – 27, Dec. 8.
g – Not June 9.
j – 2 – 3 minutes later on Ⓐ.
n – 4 – 5 minutes later on ⑤⑥.

p – Arrives 5 – 6 minutes earlier.
q – 4 – 5 minutes later June 28 - Aug. 24.
r – Also June 8, July 31.
s – Not June 8, July 31.
t – Also June 9, Aug. 1.

◧ – Conveys ✕ until Bern.
⊕ – Distance via the Bern - Olten high-speed line.

SBB GENÈVE and LAUSANNE - ZÜRICH via Bern or Biel / Bienne 500

SERVICES VIA BERN. See pages 256 – 258 for services via Biel / Bienne.

For other semi-fast *IR* services Bern - Olten - Zürich and v.v. via Burgdorf and Brugg, see Table **505**.

	IR 1723	*IC* 723 Ⓐ ✕	*IC* 909 Ⓒ H✕	*IR* 2525	*IC* 825 ✕	*IR* 1725	*IC* 725 ✕	*IR* 2527	*IC* 827 ✕	*IR* 1727	*IC* 727 ✕	*IR* 2529	*IC* 829 ✕	*IR* 1729	*IC* 729 ✕	*IR* 2531	*IC* 831 ✕	*IR* 1731	*IC* 731 ✕	*IR* 2533	*IC* 833 ✕		*IR* 1733	*IC* 733 ✕
Genève Aéroport + 570 d.	1311	1325	1325	1345	...	1414	1425	1445	...	1514	1525	1545	...	1614	1625	1645	...	1714	1721	1745	...	...	1811	1825
Genève 570 d.	1323	1335	1335	1354	...	1424	1435	1454	...	1524	1535	1554	...	1624	1635	1654	...	1724	1731	1754	...	...	1823	1835
Nyon 570 d.	1339	|	|	1409	...	1439	|	1509	...	1539	|	1609	...	1639	|	1709	...	1739	|	1809	...	...	1839	|
Morges 504 570 d.	1401**p**	|	|	1426	...	1455	|	1526	...	1555	|	1626	...	1655	|	1726	...	1755	|	1826	...	...	1901**p**	|
Renens 504 570 d.	|	1408	1408	|	...	|	1508	|	...	|	1608	|	...	|	1708	|	...	|	1808	|	...	...	|	1908
Lausanne 504 570 a.	1412	1414	1414	1437	...	1507	1514	1537	...	1607	1614	1637	...	1707	1714	1737	...	1807	1814	1837	...	...	1912	1914
Lausanne 504 d.	...	1417	1417	1440	...	...	1517	1540	...	...	1617	1640	...	...	1717	1740	...	...	1817	1840	...	...	...	1917
Palézieux 504 d.	...	|	|	1457	...	...	|	1557	...	...	|	1657	...	...	|	1757	...	...	|	1857	...	...	...	|
Romont 568 d.	...	|	|	1513	...	...	|	1613	...	...	|	1713	...	...	|	1813	...	...	|	1913	...	...	...	|
Fribourg 568 d.	...	1503	1503	1533	...	...	1603	1633	...	...	1703	1733	...	...	1803	1833	...	...	1903	1933	...	...	...	2003
Brig 560 d.	...	|	|	|	1445	...	|	|	...	...	|	|	1645	...	|	|	...	...	|	|	1845	...	...	|
Interlaken Ost 560 d.	...	|	|	|	|	...	|	|	1559	...	|	|	|	...	|	|	1759	...	|	|	|	...	...	|
Bern 568 a.	...	1526	1526	1556	1553	...	1626	1656	1656	...	1726	1756	1753	...	1826	1856	1856	...	1926	1956	1953	...	...	2026
Bern 505 560 d.	...	1531	1531	1600	1602	...	1631	1700	1702	...	1731	1800	1802	...	1831	1900	1902	...	1931	2000	2002	...	...	2031
Luzern 565 a.	...	|	|	1701	|	...	|	1801	|	...	|	1901	|	...	|	2001	|	...	|	2101	|	...	...	|
Olten 505 560 d.	...	|	|	...	|	...	|	...	|	...	|	...	|	...	|	...	|	...	|	...	|	...	...	|
Aarau 505 510 d.	...	|	|	...	|	...	|	...	|	...	|	...	|	...	|	...	|	...	|	...	|	...	...	|
Zürich HB 505 510 a.	...	1628	1628	...	1658	...	1728	...	1758	...	1828	...	1858	...	1928	...	1958	...	2028	...	2058	...	...	2128
Zürich Flughafen + 530/5 a.	...	1651	...	...	1714	...	1751	...	1814	...	1851	...	1914	...	1951	...	2014	...	2051	...	...	...	...	2151
St Gallen 530 a.	...	1752	...	...	|	...	1852	...	|	...	1952	...	|	...	2052	...	|	...	2152	...	...	...	...	2252
Romanshorn 535 a.	...	...	...	...	1812	...	...	...	1912	...	...	...	2012	...	...	...	2112	...	...	...	...	...	...	...

	IR 2535	*IC* 835 ✕	*IR* 1735	*IC* 735 ⑤⑥ r✕	*IC* 735 ⑦–④ s✕	*IR* 2537	*IC* 837	*IR* 1737	*IC* 737 ✕	*RE* 18487 Ⓐ	*RE* 18487 Ⓒ	*IR* 2539	*IR* 2539 ⑤⑥	*IC* 839	*IR* 1739	*IC* 739 ◧	*RE* 18489	*IR* 2541	*IC* 841	*RE* 18491	*IR* 2543	*IC* 843 ⑥⑦ t	*RE* 18439	*RE* 18441
Genève Aéroport + 570 d.	1845	...	1914	1921	1921	1945	...	2014	2025	...	2030	...	2045	...	2111	...	...	...	...	2230	...	...	2300**n**	0000**k**
Genève 570 d.	1854	...	1924	1935	1935	1954	...	2024	2035	2038	2039	...	2054	...	2121	...	2138	...	...	2238	...	...	2308**n**	0008**k**
Nyon 570 d.	1909	...	1939	|	|	2009	...	2039	|	2055	2055	...	2109	...	2136	...	2155	...	...	2255	...	...	2325**n**	0025**k**
Morges 504 570 d.	1926	...	1955	|	|	2026	...	2055	|	2116	2116	...	2126	...	2152	...	2217	...	...	2317	...	...	2346	0046
Renens 504 570 d.	|	...	|	2008	2008	|	...	|	2108	2124	2124	...	|	...	2201	...	2224	...	...	2324	...	...	2354	0054
Lausanne 504 570 a.	1937	...	2007	2014	2014	2037	...	2107	2114	2129	2129	...	2137	...	2208	...	2229	...	...	2329	...	...	2359	0059
Lausanne 504 d.	1940	...	...	2017	2017	2040	...	...	2117	...	...	2140	2140	...	...	2217	...	2240	...	...	2344	...	...	...
Palézieux 504 d.	1957	...	...	|	|	2057	...	...	|	...	...	2157	2157	...	...	|	...	2257	...	...	0000	...	...	...
Romont 568 d.	2013	...	...	|	|	2113	...	...	|	...	...	2213	2213	...	...	|	...	2313	...	...	0016	...	...	...
Fribourg 568 d.	2033	...	...	2103	2103	2133	...	...	2203	...	...	2233	2233	...	...	2303	...	2333	...	...	0034	...	...	...
Brig 560 d.	|	...	...	|	|	|	...	...	|	...	...	|	|	...	...	|	...	|	...	...	|	...	...	...
Interlaken Ost 560 d.	|	1959	...	|	|	|	...	...	|	...	...	|	|	...	...	|	...	|	...	...	|	...	...	...
Bern 568 a.	2056	2056	...	2126	2126	2156	...	...	2226	...	...	2256	2256	...	...	2326	...	2356	...	...	0100	...	...	...
Bern 505 560 d.	2100	2102	...	2131	2131	2200	2202	...	2231	...	...	2300	2300	2302	...	2331	...	...	0002	...	...	0106	...	...
Luzern 565 a.	2201	|	...	|	|	2301	|	...	|	...	...	0001	0001	|	...	|	...	...	|	...	...	|	...	...
Olten 505 560 d.	...	|	...	|	2200	...	2230	...	2300	...	...	...	...	2330	...	0002	...	...	0035	...	...	0134	...	...
Aarau 505 510 d.	...	|	...	|	|	...	|	...	|	...	...	...	...	|	...	0012	...	...	|	...	...	0145	...	...
Zürich HB 505 510 a.	...	2158	...	2228	2231	...	2302	...	2331	...	...	...	...	0001	...	0040	...	...	0106	...	...	0210	...	...
Zürich Flughafen + 530/5 a.	...	2214	...	2251	2251	...	2314	...	...	...	...	...	...	...	...	...	...	...	...	...	...	...	...	...
St Gallen 530 a.	...	|	...	2352	2352	...	|	...	...	...	...	...	...	...	...	...	...	...	...	...	...	...	...	...
Romanshorn 535 a.	...	2312	...	...	...	...	0012	...	...	...	...	...	...	...	...	...	...	...	...	...	...	...	...	...

	IC 842	*IC* 844 ⑥⑦ t		*RE* 18402	*RE* 18404	*RE* 18450	*IR* 2504	*IC* 702 ✕	*IR* 1704	*IR* 2506	*IC* 704 ✕	*IR* 1706	*IC* 804 ✕	*IR* 2508	*IC* 706 ✕	*IR* 1708	*IC* 806 ✕	*IR* 2510	*IC* 708 ✕	*IR* 1710	*IC* 808 ✕	*IR* 2512	*IC* 710 ✕	*IR* 1712
Romanshorn 535 d.	...	...	...	...	...	...	...	...	...	...	...	...	...	...	...	...	0547	...	...	...	0647	...	...	...
St Gallen 530 d.	...	...	...	...	...	...	...	...	...	...	...	...	...	...	0507	...	|	...	0607	...	|	...	0707	...
Zürich Flughafen + 530/5 d.	...	...	...	...	...	...	...	...	...	...	...	...	...	...	0608	...	0645	...	0708	...	0745	...	0808	...
Zürich HB 505 510 d.	0002	0102	...	...	...	...	...	...	...	...	0519	...	0602	...	0632	...	0702	...	0732	...	0802	...	0832	...
Aarau 505 510 d.	|	|	...	...	...	...	...	...	...	...	0548	...	|	...	|	...	|	...	|	...	|	...	|	...
Olten 505 560 d.	0035	0135	...	...	...	...	...	...	...	...	0602**p**	...	|	...	|	...	|	...	|	...	|	...	|	...
Luzern 565 d.	|	|	...	...	...	...	...	...	...	...	|	...	|	0600	|	...	|	0700	|	...	|	0800	|	...
Bern 505 560 a.	0104	0204	...	...	...	...	...	...	...	...	0628	...	0658	0700	0728	...	0758	0800	0828	...	0858	0900	0928	...
Bern 568 d.	...	...	...	...	...	...	0504	0534	...	0604	0634	...	0704	0704	0734	...	0807	0804	0834	...	0904	0904	0934	...
Interlaken Ost 560 a.	...	...	...	...	...	...	|	|	...	|	|	...	0759	|	|	...	|	|	|	...	0959	|	|	...
Brig 560 a.	...	...	...	...	...	...	|	|	...	|	|	...	...	|	|	...	0911	|	|	...	...	|	|	...
Fribourg 568 d.	...	...	...	...	...	...	0527	0557	...	0627	0657	...	...	0727	0757	...	...	0827	0857	...	...	0927	0957	...
Romont 568 d.	...	...	...	...	...	...	0546	|	...	0646	|	...	...	0746	|	...	...	0846	|	...	...	0946	|	...
Palézieux 504 d.	...	...	...	...	...	...	0603	|	...	0703	|	...	...	0803	|	...	...	0903	|	...	...	1003	|	...
Lausanne 504 a.	...	...	...	...	...	...	0620	0643	...	0720	0743	...	...	0820	0843	...	...	0920	0943	...	...	1020	1043	...
Lausanne 504 570 d.	...	...	...	0350	0450	0530	0623	0646	0652	0723	0746	0752	...	0823	0846	0852	...	0923	0946	0952	...	1023	1046	1052
Renens 504 570 d.	...	...	...	0355	0455	0535	|	0653	|	|	0753	|	...	|	0853	|	...	|	0954	|	...	|	1053	|
Morges 504 570 d.	...	...	...	0401	0501	0543	0634	|	0704	0734	|	0804	...	0834	|	0904	...	0934	|	1004	...	1034	|	1104
Nyon 570 d.	...	...	...	0424	0524	0605	0650	|	0720	0750**j**	|	0820	...	0850	|	0920	...	0950	|	1020	...	1050	|	1120
Genève 570 a.	...	...	...	0444	0541	0621	0705	0725	0735	0805**j**	0825**q**	0835	...	0905	0925	0935	...	1005	1029	1035	...	1105	1125	1135
Genève Aéroport + 570 a.	...	...	...	0452	0549	0630**c**	0715	0735	0744	0815**j**	0836**q**	0844	...	0915	0935	0944	...	1015	1041	1044	...	1115	1136	1144

	IC 810 ✕	*IR* 2514	*IC* 712 ✕	*RE* 18418	*IC* 812 ✕	*IR* 2516	*IC* 714 ✕	*IR* 1716	*IC* 814 ✕	*IR* 2518	*IC* 716 Ⓐ ✕	*IC* 900 Ⓒ H✕	*IR* 1718	*IC* 816 ✕	*IR* 2520	*IC* 718 ✕	*IR* 1720	*IC* 818 ✕	*IR* 2522	*IC* 720 ✕	*IR* 1722		*IC* 820 ✕	*IR* 2524
Romanshorn 535 d.	0747	...	...	...	0847	...	...	...	0947	...	...	...	...	1047	...	...	...	1147	...	...	...	...	1247	...
St Gallen 530 d.	|	...	0807	...	|	...	0907	...	|	...	1007	...	...	|	...	1107	...	|	...	1207	...	...	|	...
Zürich Flughafen + 530/5 d.	0845	...	0908	...	0945	...	1008	...	1045	...	1108	...	...	1145	...	1208	...	1245	...	1308	...	...	1345	...
Zürich HB 505 510 d.	0902	...	0932	...	1002	...	1032	...	1102	...	1132	1132	...	1202	...	1232	...	1302	...	1332	...	...	1402	...
Aarau 505 510 d.	|	...	|	...	|	...	|	...	|	...	|	|	...	|	...	|	...	|	...	|	...	...	|	...
Olten 505 560 d.	|	...	|	...	|	...	|	...	|	...	|	|	...	|	...	|	...	|	...	|	...	...	|	...
Luzern 565 d.	|	0900	|	...	|	1000	|	...	|	1100	|	|	...	|	1200	|	...	|	1300	|	...	...	|	1400
Bern 505 560 a.	0958	1000	1028	...	1058	1100	1128	...	1158	1200	1228	1228	...	1258	1300	1328	...	1358	1400	1428	...	...	1458	1500
Bern 568 d.	1007	1004	1034	...	1107	1104	1134	...	1204	1204	1234	1234	...	1307	1304	1334	...	1404	1404	1434	...	...	1507	1504
Interlaken Ost 560 a.	|	|	|	...	|	|	|	...	1259	|	|	|	...	|	|	|	...	1459	|	|	...	...	|	|
Brig 560 a.	1113	|	|	...	1213	|	|	...	...	|	|	|	...	1413	|	|	...	...	|	|	...	...	1613	|
Fribourg 568 d.	...	1027	1057	...	...	1127	1157	...	...	1227	1257	1257	...	...	1327	1357	...	...	1427	1457	...	...	...	1527
Romont 568 d.	...	1046	|	...	...	1146	|	...	...	1246	|	|	...	...	1346	|	...	...	1446	|	...	...	...	1546
Palézieux 504 d.	...	1103	|	...	...	1203	|	...	...	1303	|	|	...	...	1403	|	...	...	1503	|	...	...	...	1603
Lausanne 504 a.	...	1120	1143	...	...	1220	1243	...	...	1320	1343	1343	...	...	1420	1443	...	...	1520	1543	...	...	...	1620
Lausanne 504 570 d.	...	1123	1146	1200	...	1223	1246	1252	...	1323	1346	1346	1352	...	1423	1446	1452	...	1523	1546	1552	...	...	1623
Renens 504 570 d.	...	|	1153	1205	...	|	1253	|	...	|	1354	1354	|	...	|	1453	|	...	|	1553	|	...	...	|
Morges 504 570 d.	...	1134	|	1213	...	1234	|	1304	...	1334	|	|	1404	...	1434	|	1504	...	1534	|	1604	...	...	1634
Nyon 570 d.	...	1150	|	1235	...	1250	|	1320	...	1350	|	|	1420	...	1450	|	1520	...	1550	|	1620	...	...	1650
Genève 570 a.	...	1205	1225	1251	...	1305	1325	1335	...	1405	1429	1429	1435	...	1505	1525	1535	...	1605	1625	1635	...	...	1705
Genève Aéroport + 570 a.	...	1215	1236	...	...	1315	1335	1344	...	1415	1441	1441	1444	...	1515	1535	1544	...	1615	1636	1644	...	...	1715

← FOR NOTES, SEE PREVIOUS PAGE.

500 ZÜRICH - LAUSANNE and GENÈVE via Bern or Biel / Bienne SBB

SERVICES VIA BERN. See below and pages 257 / 258 for services via Biel / Bienne.
For other semi-fast *IR* services Zürich - Olten - Bern via Brugg and Burgdorf, see Table **505**.

	IC 722	*IC* 902	*RE* 18428	*IC* 822	*IR* 2526	*IC* 724	*IR* 1726	*IC* 824	*IR* 2528	*IC* 726	*IR* 1728	*IC* 826	*IR* 2530	*IC* 728	*IC* 906	*IR* 1730	*IC* 828	*IR* 2532	*IC* 730	*RE* 18436	*IC* 830	*IR* 2534	*IR* 2534	*RE* 1848
	Ⓐ	Ⓒ												Ⓐ	Ⓒ								⑤⑥	⑤⑥
	✕	H✕		✕		✕		✕		✕		✕		✕	H✕		✕		✕		✕			
Romanshorn **535** d.	...	...	...	1347	...	...	...	1447	...	...	...	1547	...	...	...	...	1647	...	...	...	1747	...	...	...
St Gallen **530** d.	1307	...	...	|	...	1407	...	|	...	1507	...	|	...	1607	...	...	|	...	1707	...	|	...	...	...
Zürich Flughafen ✈ **530/5** d.	1408	...	...	1445	...	1508	...	1545	...	1608	...	1645	...	1708	...	...	1745	...	1808	...	1845	...	...	...
Zürich HB **505 510** d.	1432	1432	...	1502	...	1532	...	1602	...	1632	...	1702	...	1732	1732	...	1802	...	1832	...	1902	...	...	...
Aarau **505 510** d.	|	|	...	|	...	|	...	|	...	|	...	|	...	|	|	...	|	...	|	...	|	...	...	...
Olten **505 560** d.	|	|	...	|	...	|	...	|	...	|	...	|	...	|	|	...	|	...	|	...	|	...	...	...
Luzern **565** d.	|	|	...	|	1500	|	...	|	1600	|	...	|	1700	|	|	...	|	1800	|	...	|	1900	1900	...
Bern **505 560** a.	1528	1528	...	1558	1600	1628	...	1658	1700	1728	...	1758	1800	1828	1828	...	1858	1900	1928	...	1958	2000	2000	...
Bern **568** d.	1534	1534	...	1604	1604	1634	...	1707	1704	1734	...	1804	1804	1834	1834	...	1907	1904	1934	...	2004	2004	2004	...
Interlaken Ost **560** a.	|	|	...	1659	|	|	...	|	|	|	...	1859	|	|	|	...	|	|	|	...	2059	|	|	...
Brig **560** a.	|	|	...	...	|	|	...	1813	|	|	...	...	|	|	|	...	2013	|	|	...	...	|	|	...
Fribourg **568** d.	1557	1557	...	...	1627	1657	...	...	1727	1757	...	...	1827	1857	1857	...	...	1927	1957	...	...	2027	2027	...
Romont **568** d.	|	|	...	...	1646	|	...	...	1746	|	...	...	1846	|	|	...	...	1946	|	...	...	2046	2046	...
Palézieux **504** d.	|	|	...	...	1703	|	...	...	1803	|	...	...	1903	|	|	...	...	2003	|	...	...	2103	2103	...
Lausanne **504** a.	1643	1643	...	...	1720	1743	...	...	1820	1843	...	...	1920	1943	1943	...	...	2020	2043	...	...	2120	2120	...
Lausanne **504 570** d.	1646	1646	1700	...	1723	1746	1752	...	1823	1846	1852	...	1923	1946	1946	1952	...	2023	2046	2100	...	...	2123	2130
Renens **504 570** d.	1653	1653	1705	...	|	1753	|	...	|	1853	|	...	|	1954	1954	|	...	|	2053	2105	...	...	|	2135
Morges **504 570** d.	|	|	1713	...	1734	|	1804	...	1834	|	1904	...	1934	|	|	2004	...	2034	|	2113	...	...	2134	2143
Nyon **570** d.	|	|	1735	...	1750	|	1820	...	1850	|	1920	...	1950	|	|	2020	...	2050	|	2134	...	...	2150	2204
Genève **570** a.	1725	1725	1751	...	1805	1825	1835	...	1905	1925	1935	...	2005	2029	2029	2035	...	2105	2125	2151	...	...	2205	2221
Genève Aéroport ✈ **570** a.	1735	1735	...	...	1815	1835	1844	...	1915	1935	1944	...	2015	2041	2041	2047	...	2115	2135	2200	...	...	2216	2229

	RE 18482	*IC* 732	*IC* 908	*IR* 1734	*IC* 832	*IR* 2536	*RE* 18484	*IC* 734	*IC* 734	*IR* 1736	*RE* 18440	*IC* 834	*IR* 2538	*RE* 18486	*IC* 736	*IC* 836	*IR* 2540	*RE* 18488	*IC* 738	*IC* 838	*IR* 2502	*IR* 2502	*RE* 18446	*IC* 740
	⑦–④	Ⓐ	Ⓒ						⑤⑥	⑦–④	⑤⑥										②–⑤	⑥–①	⑥⑦	
		✕	H✕		✕			✕	✕			✕	¶						✕		d	h	w	
Romanshorn **535** d.	...	...	...	...	1847	...	...	...	...	...	...	1947	...	...	...	2047	...	...	...	2147	...	...	...	...
St Gallen **530** d.	...	1807	...	...	|	...	...	1907	1907	...	...	|	...	...	2007	|	...	...	2107	|	...	...	...	...
Zürich Flughafen ✈ **530/5** d.	...	1908	...	...	1945	...	...	2008	2008	...	...	2045	...	...	2108	2145	...	...	2208	2245	...	...	...	...
Zürich HB **505 510** d.	...	1932	1932	...	2002	...	...	2032	2032	...	...	2102	...	...	2132	2202	...	...	2232	2302	...	...	...	2332
Aarau **505 510** d.	...	|	|	...	|	...	...	|	|	...	...	|	...	...	|	|	...	...	|	|	...	...	...	|
Olten **505 560** d.	...	|	|	...	|	...	...	|	|	...	...	|	...	...	|	2235	...	...	2304	2335	...	...	...	0004
Luzern **565** d.	...	|	|	...	|	2000	...	|	|	...	...	|	2100	...	|	|	2200	...	|	|	...	...	...	|
Bern **505 560** a.	...	2028	2028	...	2058	2100	...	2128	2128	...	...	2158	2200	...	2228	2302	2300	...	2331	0002	...	...	...	0031
Bern **568** d.	...	2034	2034	...	...	2104	...	2134	2134	...	...	...	2204	...	2234	...	2308	...	...	...	0008	0008	...	...
Interlaken Ost **560** a.	...	|	|	...	...	|	...	|	|	...	...	...	|	...	|	...	|	...	...	...	|	|	...	...
Brig **560** a.	...	|	|	...	...	|	...	|	|	...	...	...	|	...	|	...	|	...	...	...	|	|	...	...
Fribourg **568** d.	...	2057	2057	...	...	2127	...	2157	2157	...	...	...	2227	...	2256	...	2331	...	...	...	0033	0034	...	...
Romont **568** d.	...	|	|	...	...	2146	...	|	|	...	...	...	2246	...	...	...	2349	...	...	...	...	0052	...	...
Palézieux **504** d.	...	|	|	...	...	2203	...	|	|	...	...	...	2303	...	...	...	0007	...	...	...	...	0108t	...	...
Lausanne **504** a.	...	2143	2143	...	...	2220	...	2243	2243	...	...	...	2320	...	...	...	0023	...	...	...	...	0125t	...	...
Lausanne **504 570** d.	2130	...	...	2151	...	...	2230	...	2246	2252	2300	...	...	2330	...	...	...	0030	...	...	...	...	0150	...
Renens **504 570** d.	2135	...	...	2157	...	...	2235	...	2253	2258	2305	...	...	2335	...	...	...	0035	...	...	...	...	0157	...
Morges **504 570** d.	2153j	...	...	2204	...	...	2242	...	|	2305	2313	...	...	2343	...	...	...	0042	...	...	...	...	0204	...
Nyon **570** d.	2216	...	...	2222	...	...	2305	...	|	2323	2334	...	...	0005	...	...	...	0105	...	...	...	...	0225	...
Genève **570** a.	2233	...	...	2238	...	...	2321	...	2325	2338	2351	...	...	0022	...	...	...	0122	...	...	...	...	0241	...
Genève Aéroport ✈ **570** a.	2241	...	...	2248	...	...	2330	...	2335	2348	2359	...	...	0030	...	...	...	...	...	...	...	...	...	...

SERVICES VIA NEUCHÂTEL AND BIEL / BIENNE. See above and pages 254 / 255 for services via Bern.

km ⊕		*IC* 1507	*IC* 507	*IC* 1509	*IR* 1805	*IC* 509	*RE* 18403	*IC* 707 901	*IC* 1511	*IC* 1807	*IC* 511	*RE* 18405	*IR* 1651	*IC* 709	*IC* 1513	*IR* 1809	*IC* 513	*RE* 18407	*IR* 1653	*IC* 711	*IC* 1515	*IR* 1811	*IC* 515	*RE* 18409	*IC* 713 903
													Ⓐ						Ⓐ						
		✕	R✕	✕		R✕		✕	✕		R✕			✕	✕		R✕			✕	✕		R✕		✕
0	**Lausanne** d.	...	...	...	...	0534	...	...	0604	...	0634	...	...	...	0704	...	0734	...	...	...	0804	...	0834	...	...
	Genève Aéroport ✈ **570** d.	...	...	...	...	|	...	0525	|	...	|	0600	0606	0625	|	0655	|	...	0706	0725	|	0755	|	...	0825
	Genève **570** d.	...	...	...	0446	|	0508	0533	|	0605	|	0608	0615	0635	|	0705	|	0708	0715	0735	|	0805	|	0808	0835
	Nyon **570** d.	...	...	...	0503	|	0525	|	|	|	◇	0625	0631	|	|	|	◇	0725	0731	|	|	|	◇	0825	|
	Morges **570** d.	...	...	...	0524	|	0546	|	|	|	◇	0646	0652	|	|	|	◇	0746	0752	|	|	|	◇	0846	|
5	Renens d.	...	...	...	0531	0541	0553	0608	0611	0637	0641	0653	|	0708	0711	0737	0741	0753	|	0808	0811	0837	0841	0853	0908
39	Yverdon d.	...	...	...	...	0601	...	|	0631	...	0701	...	0720	|	0731	...	0801	...	0820	|	0831	...	0901	...	|
75	Neuchâtel d.	...	...	...	...	0622	...	|	0653	...	0722	...	0742	|	0753	...	0822	...	0842	|	0853	...	0922	...	|
105	**Biel / Bienne** a.	...	...	...	...	0642	...	|	0713	...	0742	...	...	|	0813	...	0842	...	...	|	0913	...	0942	...	|
	Biel / Bienne d.	0516	0542	0616	...	0644	...	◧	0716	...	0745	...	...	◧	0816	...	0845	...	...	◧	0916	...	0945	...	◧
119	Grenchen Süd d.	0525	0552	0625	...	0653	...	|	0725	...	|	...	...	|	0825	...	|	...	...	|	0925	...	|	...	|
130	Solothurn d.	0534	0601	0634	...	0701	...	|	0734	...	0801	...	...	|	0834	...	0901	...	...	|	0934	...	1001	...	|
166	**Olten** **505** d.	0559	0620	0659	...	0720	...	|	0759	...	0820	...	...	|	0859	...	0920	...	...	|	0959	...	1020	...	|
179	Aarau **505 510** d.	|	0631	|	...	0731	...	|	|	...	0831	...	...	|	|	...	0931	...	...	|	|	...	1031	...	|
221	**Zürich** HB **505 510** a.	0630	0656	0730	...	0756	...	0828	0830	...	0856	...	...	0928	0930	...	0956	...	...	1028	1030	...	1056	...	1128
	Zürich Flughafen ✈ **530/5** a.	0642e	0712z	...	...	0812z	...	0851a	0842e	...	0912z	...	...	0951	...	...	1012z	...	...	1051	1042e	...	1112z	...	1151a
	St Gallen **530** a.	0732a	0802	...	...	0902	...	0952a	0932a	...	1002	...	...	1052	...	...	1102	...	...	1152	1132a	...	1202	...	1252a

	IC 1517	*IR* 1813	*IC* 517	*RE* 18411	*IC* 715	*IC* 1519	*IR* 1815	*IC* 519	*RE* 18413	*IC* 717	*IC* 1521	*IR* 1817	*IC* 521	*RE* 18415	*IC* 719 907	*IC* 1523	*IR* 1819	*IC* 523	*RE* 18417	*IC* 721	*IC* 1525	*IR* 1821	*IC* 525	*RE* 18419	*IC* 723 909
	✕		R✕		✕	✕		R✕		✕	✕		R✕		✕	✕		R✕		✕	✕		R✕		✕
Lausanne d.	0904	...	0934	...	...	1004	...	1034	...	...	1104	...	1134	...	...	1204	...	1234	...	...	1304	...	1334	...	...
Genève Aéroport ✈ **570** d.	|	0855	|	...	0922	|	0955	|	...	1025	|	1055	|	...	1125	|	1155	|	...	1225	|	1255	|	...	1325
Genève **570** d.	|	0905	|	0908	0931	|	1005	|	1008	1035	|	1105	|	1108	1135	|	1205	|	1208	1235	|	1305	|	1308	1335
Nyon **570** d.	|	|	◇	0925	|	|	|	◇	1025	|	|	|	◇	1125	|	|	|	◇	1225	|	|	|	◇	1325	|
Morges **570** d.	|	|	◇	0946	|	|	|	◇	1046	|	|	|	◇	1146	|	|	|	◇	1246	|	|	|	◇	1346	|
Renens d.	0911	0937	0941	0953	1008	1011	1037	1041	1053	1108	1111	1137	1141	1153	1208	1211	1237	1241	1253	1308	1311	1337	1341	1353	1408
Yverdon d.	0931	...	1001	...	|	1031	...	1101	...	|	1131	...	1201	...	|	1231	...	1301	...	|	1331	...	1401	...	|
Neuchâtel d.	0953	...	1022	...	|	1053	...	1122	...	|	1153	...	1222	...	|	1253	...	1322	...	|	1353	...	1422	...	|
Biel / Bienne a.	1013	...	1042	...	|	1113	...	1142	...	|	1213	...	1242	...	|	1313	...	1342	...	|	1413	...	1442	...	|
Biel / Bienne d.	1016	...	1045	...	◧	1116	...	1145	...	◧	1216	...	1245	...	◧	1316	...	1345	...	◧	1416	...	1445	...	◧
Grenchen Süd d.	1025	...	|	...	|	1125	...	|	...	|	1225	...	|	...	|	1325	...	|	...	|	1425	...	|	...	|
Solothurn d.	1034	...	1101	...	|	1134	...	1201	...	|	1234	...	1301	...	|	1334	...	1401	...	|	1434	...	1501	...	|
Olten **505** d.	1059	...	1120	...	|	1159	...	1220	...	|	1259	...	1320	...	|	1359	...	1420	...	|	1459	...	1520	...	|
Aarau **505 510** d.	|	...	1131	...	|	|	...	1231	...	|	|	...	1331	...	|	|	...	1431	...	|	|	...	1531	...	|
Zürich HB **505 510** a.	1130	...	1156	...	1228	1230	...	1256	...	1328	1330	...	1356	...	1428	1430	...	1456	...	1528	1530	...	1556	...	1628
Zürich Flughafen ✈ **530/5** a.	...	...	1212z	...	1251	1242v	...	1312z	...	1351	...	...	1412z	...	1451a	1442v	...	1512z	...	1551	...	...	1612z	...	1651a
St Gallen **530** a.	...	...	1302	...	1352	1332b	...	1402	...	1452	...	...	1502	...	1552a	1532b	...	1602	...	1652	...	...	1702	...	1752a

H – From Chur (Table **520**).
R – To Rorschach (Table **530**).

a – Ⓐ only.
b – Ⓑ only.
d – Not Aug. 1.
e – Ⓐ (not Aug. 11 - Oct. 3).

h – Also Aug. 1.
j – Arrives 2143.
t – 7 minutes later on ① from June 16.
v – Ⓑ (not Aug. 11 - Oct. 3).
w – Also June 9, Aug. 1.
z – Not Aug. 11 - Oct. 3.

◧ – Via Bern.
¶ – Runs as *IC* **1490** on ⑦ (also June 9; not June 8).
◇ – See Table **570** for connecting service from Nyon and Morges (via Renens).
⊕ – Distance via the Solothurn - Olten high-speed line.
Note: Genève - Yverdon direct is *86 km* (for trains not calling at Renens).

SBB ZÜRICH - LAUSANNE and GENÈVE via Bern or Biel / Bienne 500

SERVICES VIA NEUCHÂTEL AND BIEL/BIENNE. See pages 254 – 256 for services via Bern.

	IC 1527	IR 1823	IC 527	RE 18421	IC 725	IC 1529	IR 1825	IC 529	RE 18423	IC 727	IC 1531	IR 1827	IC 531	RE 18425	IR 1671	IC 729	IC 1533	IR 1829	IC 533	IR 1673	IC 731	IC 1535	IR 1831	IC 535	RE 18429
															Ⓐ										
	✕		R✕		✕	✕		R✕		✕	✕		R✕			✕	✕		✕		✕	✕		✕	
Lausanne d.	1404	...	1434	...	...	1504	...	1534	...	...	1604	...	1634	...	...	...	1704	...	1734	...	...	1804	...	1834	...
Genève Aéroport ✈ .. 570 d.	|	1355	|	...	1425	|	1455	|	...	1525	|	1555	|	...	1606	1625	|	1655	|	1706	1721	|	1755	|	...
Genève 570 d.	|	1405	|	1408	1435	|	1505	|	1508	1535	|	1605	|	1608	1615	1635	|	1705	|	1715	1731	|	1805	|	1808
Nyon 570 d.	|	|	◇	1425	|	|	|	◇	1525	|	|	|	◇	1625	1631	|	|	|	◇	1731	|	|	|	◇	1825
Morges 570 d.	|	|	◇	1446	|	|	|	◇	1546	|	|	|	◇	1646	1652	|	|	|	◇	1752	|	|	|	◇	1846
Renens d.	1411	1437	1441	1453	1508	1511	1537	1541	1553	1808	1611	1637	1641	1653	|	1708	1711	1737	1741	|	1808	1811	1837	1841	1853
Yverdon d.	1431	...	1501	...	|	1531	...	1601	...	|	1631	...	1701	...	1720	|	1731	...	1801	1820	|	1831	...	1901	...
Neuchâtel d.	1453	...	1522	...	|	1553	...	1622	...	|	1653	...	1722	...	1742	|	1753	...	1822	1842	|	1853	...	1922	...
Biel / Bienne a.	1513	...	1542	...	|	1613	...	1642	...	|	1713	...	1742	...	...	|	1813	...	1842	...	|	1913	...	1942	...
Biel / Bienne d.	1516	...	1545	...	◧	1616	...	1645	...	◧	1716	...	1745	...	...	◧	1816	...	1845	...	◧	1916	...	1945	...
Grenchen Süd d.	1525	...	|	...	|	1625	...	|	...	|	1725	...	|	...	...	|	1825	...	|	...	|	1925	...	|	...
Solothurn d.	1534	...	1601	...	|	1634	...	1701	...	|	1734	...	1801	...	...	|	1834	...	1901	...	|	1934	...	2001	...
Olten 505 d.	1559	...	1620	...	|	1659	...	1720	...	|	1759	...	1820	...	...	|	1859	...	1920	...	|	1959	...	2020	...
Aarau 505 510 d.	|	...	1631	...	|	|	...	1731	...	|	|	...	1831	...	...	|	|	...	1931	...	|	|	...	2031	...
Zürich HB 505 510 a.	1630	...	1656	...	1728	1730	...	1756	...	1828	1830	...	1856	...	...	1928	1930	...	1956	...	2028	2030	...	2056	...
Zürich Flughafen ✈ 530/5 a.	1642**v**	...	1712**z**	...	1751	...	...	1812**z**	...	1851	1842**e**	...	1912**z**	...	...	1951	...	...	2012**z**	...	2051	...	...	...	...
St Gallen 530 a.	1732**b**	...	1802	...	1852	...	...	1902	...	1952	1932**a**	...	2002	...	...	2052	...	...	2102	...	2152	...	...	...	...

	IR 1675	IC 733	IC 1537	IR 1833	IC 537	IR 1677	IC 735	IC 1539	IR 1835	IC 539	RE 18433	IC 737	IC 1541	RE 18487	IR 1837	IC 541	IR 1739	IC 1543	RE 18489	IC 1839	IC 543	IR 1741	IC 1545	IR 1743	IC 1547
	Ⓐ														⑤⑥					⑤⑥					
		✕	✕		✕		✕	✕		✕		✕	⊖			◐							D		
Lausanne d.	...	...	1904	...	1934	...	...	2004	...	2034	...	...	2104	...	...	2134	...	2204	...	...	2234	...	2304	...	0004
Genève Aéroport ✈ .. 570 d.	1806	1825	|	1855	|	1906	1921	|	1955	|	...	2025	|	2030**c**	2055	|	2111	|	...	2155	|	2211	|	2311	|
Genève 570 d.	1815	1835	|	1905	|	1915	1931	|	2005	|	2008	2035	|	2038	2105	|	2121	|	2138	2205	|	2220	|	2321	|
Nyon 570 d.	1831	|	|	|	◇	1931	|	|	|	◇	2025	|	|	2055	|	|	2136	|	2155	|	|	2236	|	2336	|
Morges 570 d.	1852	|	|	|	◇	1952	|	|	|	◇	2046	|	|	2116	|	|	2152	|	2217	|	|	2252	|	2352	|
Renens d.	|	1908	1911	1937	1941	|	2008	2011	2037	2041	2053	2108	2111	2123	2137	2141	2200	2211	2223	2237	2241	2302	2311	0003	0011
Yverdon d.	1920	|	1931	...	2001	2020**r**	|	2031	▬	2101	...	|	2131	...	...	2201	...	2231	...	...	2301	▬	2331	▬	0031**j**
Neuchâtel d.	1942	|	1953	...	2022	2042**r**	|	2053	...	2122	...	|	2153	...	...	2222	...	2253	...	...	2322	...	2353	...	0053**j**
Biel / Bienne a.	...	|	2013	...	2042	...	|	2113	*IR*	2142	...	|	2213	...	...	2242	...	2313	...	...	2342	*IC*	0013	...	0113**j**
Biel / Bienne d.	...	◧	2016	...	2045	...	◧	2116	**2191**	2145	...	◧	2216	...	...	2245	...	2316	...	...	2346	**841**	...	0021**k**	...
Grenchen Süd d.	...	|	2025	...	|	...	|	2125		|	...	|	2225	...	...	2256	...	2325	...	...	2356		...	0035**k**	...
Solothurn d.	...	|	2034	...	2101	...	|	2134		2201	...	|	2234	...	...	2305	...	2334	...	...	0005		...	0054	...
Olten 505 d.	...	|	2059	...	2120	...	|	2159	2202	2220	...	|	2302**p**	...	...	2333	...	2357	...	...	0037**n**	0035	...	0128	...
Aarau 505 510 d.	...	|	|	...	2131	...	|	|	2214	2231	...	|	2314	...	...	2344	...	...	...	...	0047	|	...	...	...
Zürich HB 505 510 a.	...	2128	2130	...	2156	...	2228*	2230**q**	2254	2256	...	2331	2354	...	...	0010	...	...	...	...	0113	0106	...	...	...
Zürich Flughafen ✈ 530/5 a.	...	2151	...	...	...	...	2251	...	...	...	...	...	...	...	...	...	...	...	...	...	...	...	...	...	...
St Gallen 530 a.	...	2252	...	...	...	...	2352	...	...	...	...	...	...	...	...	...	...	...	...	...	...	...	...	...	...

	IR 1652	IC 504	IR 1804	IC 1504	IC 702	IR 1654	RE 18408	IC 1606	IR 1806	IC 1506	IC 704	IR 1656	RE 18410	IC 508	IR 1808	IC 1508	IC 706	IR 1658	RE 18412	IC 510	IR 1810	IC 1510	IC 708	RE 18414	IC 512
	Ⓐ					Ⓐ						Ⓐ						Ⓐ							
				✕				D✕		✕	✕			✕		✕	✕			R✕		✕	✕		R✕
St Gallen 530 d.	...	...	...	...	...	...	...	...	...	...	...	...	...	...	...	...	0507	...	...	0558	...	0628**a**	0607	...	0658
Zürich Flughafen ✈ 530/5 d.	...	...	...	...	...	...	...	...	...	...	...	...	...	...	...	...	0608	...	...	0648**y**	...	0718**g**	0708	...	0748**y**
Zürich HB 505 510 d.	...	...	...	...	...	...	...	...	...	...	0519	...	...	0604	...	0630	0632	...	...	0704	...	0730	0732	...	0804
Aarau 505 510 d.	...	...	...	...	...	...	...	...	...	...	|	...	...	0630	...	|	|	...	...	0730	...	|	|	...	0830
Olten 505 d.	...	...	...	...	...	...	...	...	...	0602	|	...	...	0641	...	0702	|	...	...	0741	...	0802	|	...	0841
Solothurn d.	...	...	...	...	...	...	...	*0539*	...	0626	|	...	...	0659	...	0726	|	...	...	0759	...	0826	|	...	0859
Grenchen Süd d.	...	...	...	...	...	...	...	*0552*	...	0634	|	...	...	|	...	0734	|	...	...	|	...	0834	|	...	|
Biel / Bienne a.	...	...	...	...	...	...	...	*0608*	...	0643	◧	...	...	0715	...	0743	◧	...	...	0815	...	0843	◧	...	0915
Biel / Bienne d.	...	0518	...	0548	...	...	...	0618	...	0648	|	...	...	0718	...	0748	|	...	...	0818	...	0848	|	...	0918
Neuchâtel d.	0518	0539	...	0609	...	0618	...	0639	...	0709	|	0718	...	0739	...	0809	|	0818	...	0839	...	0909	|	...	0939
Yverdon d.	0542	0559	...	0629	...	0642	...	0659	...	0729	|	0742	...	0759	...	0829	|	0842	...	0859	...	0929	|	...	0959
Renens d.	|	0620	0623	0650	0653	|	0705	0720	0723	0750	0753	|	0805	0820	0823	0850	0853	|	0905	0920	0923	0950	0954	1005	1020
Morges 570 d.	0608	◇	|	|	|	0708	0713	◇	|	|	|	0808	0813	◇	|	|	|	0908	0913	◇	|	|	|	1013	◇
Nyon 570 d.	0627	◇	|	|	|	0727	0735	◇	|	|	|	0827	0835	◇	|	|	|	0927	0935	◇	|	|	|	1035	◇
Genève 570 a.	0643	|	0655	|	0725	0743	0751	|	0755	|	0825**t**	0843	0851	|	0855	|	0925	0943	0951	|	0955	|	1029	1051	|
Genève Aéroport ✈ .. 570 a.	0656	|	0705	|	0735	0756	...	|	0805	|	0836**t**	0856	...	|	0905	|	0935	0956	...	|	1005	|	1041	...	|
Lausanne a.	...	0626	...	0656	...	...	...	0726	...	0756	...	...	...	0826	...	0856	...	...	...	0926	...	0956	...	...	1026

	IR 1812	IC 1512	IC 710	IR 1662	RE 18416	IC 514	IR 1814	IC 1514	IC 712	RE 18418	IC 516	IR 1816	IC 1516	IC 714	RE 18420	IC 518	IR 1818	IC 1518	IC 716 900	RE 18422	IC 520	IR 1820	IC 1520	IC 718	RE 18424
				Ⓒ																					
		✕	✕			R✕		✕	✕		R✕		✕	✕		R✕		✕	✕		R✕		✕	✕	
St Gallen 530 d.	...	...	0707	...	...	0758	...	0828**a**	0807	...	0858	...	...	0907	...	0958	...	1028**a**	1007**a**	...	1058	...	...	1107	...
Zürich Flughafen ✈ 530/5 d.	...	...	0808	...	...	0848**y**	...	0918**g**	0908	...	0948**y**	...	...	1008	...	1048**y**	...	1118**g**	1108**a**	...	1148**y**	...	...	1208	...
Zürich HB 505 510 d.	...	0830	0832	...	...	0904	...	0930	0932	...	1004	...	1030	1032	...	1104	...	1130	1132	...	1204	...	1230	1232	...
Aarau 505 510 d.	...	|	|	...	...	0930	...	|	|	...	1030	...	|	|	...	1130	...	|	|	...	1230	...	|	|	...
Olten 505 d.	...	0902	|	...	...	0941	...	1002	|	...	1041	...	1102	|	...	1141	...	1202	|	...	1241	...	1302	|	...
Solothurn d.	...	0926	|	...	...	0959	...	1026	|	...	1059	...	1126	|	...	1159	...	1226	|	...	1259	...	1326	|	...
Grenchen Süd d.	...	0934	|	...	...	|	...	1034	|	...	|	...	1134	|	...	|	...	1234	|	...	|	...	1334	|	...
Biel / Bienne a.	...	0943	◧	...	...	1015	...	1043	◧	...	1115	...	1143	◧	...	1215	...	1243	◧	...	1315	...	1343	◧	...
Biel / Bienne d.	...	0948	|	...	...	1018	...	1048	|	...	1118	...	1148	|	...	1218	...	1248	|	...	1318	...	1348	|	...
Neuchâtel d.	...	1009	|	1018	...	1039	...	1109	|	...	1139	...	1209	|	...	1239	...	1309	|	...	1339	...	1409	|	...
Yverdon d.	...	1029	|	1042	...	1059	...	1129	|	...	1159	...	1229	|	...	1259	...	1329	|	...	1359	...	1429	|	...
Renens d.	1023	1050	1053	|	1105	1120	1123	1150	1153	1205	1220	1223	1250	1253	1305	1320	1323	1350	1354	1405	1420	1423	1450	1453	1505
Morges 570 d.	|	|	|	1108	1113	◇	|	|	|	1213	◇	|	|	|	1313	◇	|	|	|	1413	◇	|	|	|	1513
Nyon 570 d.	|	|	|	1127	1135	◇	|	|	|	1235	◇	|	|	|	1335	◇	|	|	|	1435	◇	|	|	|	1535
Genève 570 a.	1055	|	1125	1143	1151	|	1155	|	1225	1251	|	1255	|	1325	1351	|	1355	|	1429	1451	|	1455	|	1525	1551
Genève Aéroport ✈ .. 570 a.	1105	|	1136	1156	...	|	1205	|	1236	...	|	1305	|	1335	...	|	1405	|	1441	...	|	1505	|	1535	...
Lausanne a.	...	1056	...	...	...	1126	...	1156	...	...	1226	...	1256	...	...	1326	...	1356	...	...	1426	...	1456	...	...

D – From / to Delémont (Table **505a**).
R – To / from Rorschach (Table **530**).

a – Ⓐ only.
b – Ⓑ only.
c – Ⓒ only.
e – Ⓐ (not Aug. 11 - Oct. 3).
f – 10 – 12 minutes later on ⑦–④.
g – Ⓐ from July 7.
h – Ⓑ from July 7.
j – 4 – 5 minutes later on ①–⑤.
k – 3 minutes later on ①⑥⑦ (also June 10).
n – Arrives 0030 (connects with train in next column).
p – Arrives 2257.
q – ⑤⑥ (also June 8, July 31).

r – On Ⓐ departs Yverdon 2023, arrives Neuchâtel 2044.
t – 4 – 5 minutes later June 28 - Aug. 24.
u – ⑤⑥ (also June 8, July 31). Runs daily Zürich - Biel/Bienne.
v – Ⓑ (not Aug. 11 - Oct. 3).
x – 3 – 5 minutes later on ①–⑤.
y – From July 7.
z – Not Aug. 11 - Oct. 3.

* – 2231 on ⑦–④ (not June 8, July 31).
◧ – Via Bern.
◐ – Conveys ✕ until Biel/Bienne.
⊖ – Runs as *IR* **2193** Olten - Zürich (via Brugg – see Table **505**).
◇ – See Table **570** for connecting service from / to Nyon and Morges (via Renens).
⊙ – See Table **570** for faster connecting service on ⑤⑥.

500 ZÜRICH - LAUSANNE and GENÈVE via Bern or Biel / Bienne SBB

SERVICES VIA NEUCHÂTEL AND BIEL/BIENNE. See pages 254–256 for services via Bern.

	IC 522	*IR* 1822	*IC* 1522	*IC* 720	*RE* 18426	*IC* 524	*IR* 1824	*IC* 1524	*IC* 722 902	*IR* 1674 Ⓐ	*RE* 18428	*IC* 526	*IR* 1826	*IC* 1526	*IC* 724	*IR* 1676 Ⓒ	*RE* 18430	*IC* 528	*IR* 1828	*IC* 1528	*IC* 726	*IR* 1678 Ⓐ	*RE* 18432	*IC* 530	*IR* 1830
	R✕		✕	✕		R✕		✕	✕			R✕		✕	✕			R✕		✕	✕			R✕	
St Gallen **530** d.	1158	...	1228**a**	1207	...	1258	...	...	1307**a**	...	...	1358	...	1428**b**	1407	...	...	1458	...	...	1507	...	...	1558	...
Zürich Flughafen ✈ **530/5** d.	1248**y**	...	1318**g**	1308	...	1348**y**	...	...	1408**a**	...	...	1448**y**	...	1518**h**	1508	...	...	1548**y**	...	...	1608	...	...	1648**y**	...
Zürich HB **505 510** d.	1304	...	1330	1332	...	1404	...	1430	1432	...	...	1504	...	1530	1532	...	...	1604	...	1630	1632	...	...	1704	...
Aarau **505 510** d.	1330	...	|	|	...	1430	...	|	|	...	...	1530	...	|	|	...	...	1630	...	|	|	...	...	1730	...
Olten **505** d.	1340	...	1402	|	...	1441	...	1502	|	...	...	1541	...	1602	|	...	...	1641	...	1702	|	...	...	1741	...
Solothurn d.	1359	...	1426	|	...	1459	...	1526	|	...	...	1559	...	1626	|	...	...	1659	...	1726	|	...	...	1759	...
Grenchen Süd d.	|	...	1434	|	...	|	...	1534	|	...	...	|	...	1634	|	...	...	|	...	1734	|	...	...	|	...
Biel / Bienne a.	1415	...	1443	◧	...	1515	...	1543	◧	...	...	1615	...	1643	◧	...	...	1715	...	1743	◧	...	...	1815	...
Biel / Bienne d.	1418	...	1448	|	...	1518	...	1548	|	...	...	1618	...	1648	|	...	...	1718	...	1748	|	...	...	1818	...
Neuchâtel d.	1439	...	1509	|	...	1539	...	1609	|	1618	...	1639	...	1709	|	1718	...	1739	...	1809	|	1818	...	1839	...
Yverdon d.	1459	...	1529	|	...	1559	...	1629	|	1642	...	1659	...	1729	|	1742	...	1759	...	1829	|	1842	...	1859	...
Renens d.	1520	1523	1550	1553	1605	1620	1623	1650	1653	|	1705	1720	1723	1750	1753	|	1805	1820	1823	1850	1853	|	1905	1920	1923
Morges **570** d.	◇	|	|	|	1613	◇	|	|	|	1708	1713	◇	|	|	|	1808	1813	◇	|	|	|	1908	1913	◇	|
Nyon **570** d.	◇	|	|	|	1635	◇	|	|	|	1727	1735	◇	|	|	|	1827	1835	◇	|	|	|	1927	1935	◇	|
Genève **570** a.	|	1555	|	1625	1651	|	1655	|	1725	1743	1751	|	1755	|	1825	1843	1851	|	1855	|	1925	1943	1951	|	1955
Genève Aéroport ✈ **570** a.	|	1605	|	1636	...	|	1705	|	1735	1756	...	|	1805	|	1835	1856	...	|	1905	|	1935	1956	...	|	2005
Lausanne a.	1526	...	1556	...	...	1626	...	1656	...	...	...	1726	...	1756	...	...	...	1826	...	1856	...	...	...	1926	...

	IC 1530	*IC* 728 906	*RE* 18434	*IC* 532	*IR* 1832	*IC* 1532	*IC* 730	*RE* 18436	*IC* 534	*RE* 18482	*IC* 1534	*IR* 1734	*IC* 536	*RE* 18484	*IC* 1536	*IC* 734 ⑤⑥	*IR* 1736 ⑦–④	*IC* 538	*IR* 1838 ⑤⑥	*EC* 46 ⑦–④	*IC* 1538	*RE* 18442	*IC* 540	*RE* 18488	*IC* 542 ⑤⑥
	✕	✕		R✕		✕	✕		R✕		✕		R		✕	✕		R			◐		◐		u
St Gallen **530** d.	1628**b**	1607**a**	...	1658	...	...	1707	...	1758	...	1828**b**	...	1858	...	...	1907	...	1958	...	...	...	...	...	...	...
Zürich Flughafen ✈ **530/5** d.	1718**h**	1708**a**	...	1748**y**	...	...	1808	...	1848**y**	...	1918**h**	...	1948**y**	...	...	2008	...	2048**y**	...	...	...	...	...	...	...
Zürich HB **505 510** d.	1730	1732	...	1804	...	1830	1832	...	1904	...	1930	...	2004	...	2030	2032	...	2104	...	...	2130	...	2204	...	2304
Aarau **505 510** d.	|	|	...	1830	...	|	|	...	1930	...	|	...	2030	...	|	|	...	2130	...	...	|	...	2230	...	2330
Olten **505** d.	1802	|	...	1841	...	1902	|	...	1941	...	2002	...	2041	...	2102	|	...	2141	...	...	2202	...	2240	...	2340
Solothurn d.	1826	|	...	1859	...	1926	|	...	1959	...	2026	...	2059	...	2126	|	...	2159	...	...	2226	...	2258	...	0005
Grenchen Süd d.	1834	|	...	|	...	1934	|	...	|	...	2034	...	|	...	2134	|	...	|	...	...	2234	...	2306	...	0013
Biel / Bienne a.	1843	◧	...	1915	...	1943	◧	...	2015	...	2043	...	2115	...	2143	◧	...	2215	...	...	2243	...	2315	...	0022
Biel / Bienne d.	1848	|	...	1918	...	1948	|	...	2018	...	2048	...	2118	...	2148	|	...	2218	...	...	2248	...	2318	...	0024
Neuchâtel d.	1909	|	...	1939	...	2009	|	...	2039	...	2109	...	2139	...	2209	|	...	2239	...	...	2309	...	2339	...	0044
Yverdon d.	1929	|	...	1959	...	2029	|	...	2059	...	2129	...	2159	...	2229	|	...	2259	...	...	2329	...	2359	...	0103
Renens d.	1950	1954	2005	2020	2023	2050	2053	2105	2120	2135	2150	2157	2220	2235	2250	2253	2258	2320	2323	2325	2350	0005	0020	0035	0122
Morges **570** d.	|	|	2013	◇	|	|	|	2113	|	2143**f**	|	2204	|	2242	|	|	2305	|	2330	2332	⊙	0013**x**	|	0042	|
Nyon **570** d.	|	|	2035	◇	|	|	|	2134	|	2204**f**	|	2222	|	2305	|	|	2323	|	2346	2350	⊙	0034**x**	|	0105	|
Genève **570** a.	|	2029	2051	|	2055	|	2125	2151	⊙	2221**f**	|	2238	⊙	2321	|	2325	2338	|	0004	0005	⊙	0051**x**	|	0122	|
Genève Aéroport ✈ **570** a.	|	2041	...	|	2105	|	2135	2200	⊙	2229**f**	|	2248	⊙	2330	|	2335	2348	|	0011	...	|	...	|	...	|
Lausanne a.	1956	...	...	2026	...	2056	...	...	2126	...	2156	...	2226	...	2356	...	...	2326	...	...	2356	...	0029	...	0129

← FOR NOTES, SEE PAGE 257

500a BIEL/BIENNE and PORRENTRUY - BASEL SBB

SERVICE FROM SEPTEMBER 29. See page 605 for service until September 28.

km		*IC* 1545 L		*IC* 1607 ✕		*IC* 1609 ✕		*IC* 1611 ✕	✣		*IC* 1637		*IC* 1639		*IC* 1641		
0	**Biel / Bienne** **515** d.	0019	...	0548	...	0649	...	0749	and at	...	2048	...	2148	...	2248	...	2319
13	Grenchen Nord **515** d.	0029	...	0559	...	0659	...	0759	the same	...	2059	...	2159	...	2259	...	2329
24	Moutier **515** d.	0038	...	0608	...	0708	...	0808	minutes	...	2108	...	2208	...	2308	...	2338
	Porrentruy **515** d.	|	0508	|	0610	|	0710	|	past each	2010	|	2110	|	2210	|	2310	|
	Glovelier **515** d.	|	0525	|	0625	|	0725	|	hour until	2025	|	2125	|	2225	|	2325	|
35	Delémont **515** a.	0048	0539	0618	0639	0718	0739	0818		2039	2118	2139	2218	2239	2318	2339	2348
	Delémont d.	...	0543	0623	0643	0723	0743	0823		2043	2123	2143	2223	2243	2323	2343	...
74	**Basel** SBB a.	...	0623	0655	0723	0755	0823	0855		2123	2155	2223	2255	2323	2358	0028	...

			IC 1606 L		*IC* 1608 ✕		*IC* 1610 ✕			*IC* 1636 ✕		*IC* 1638		*IC* 1640		*IC* 1642	
Basel SBB d.	...	*0457*	...	0534	0603	0634	0703	0734	and at	2003	2034	2103	2134	2203	2234	2303	2342
Delémont a.	...	*0537*	...	0617	0637	0717	0737	0817	the same	2037	2117	2137	2217	2237	2317	2337	0022
Delémont **515** d.	0510	0551	0542	0621	0642	0721	0742	0821	minutes	2042	2121	2142	2221	2242	2321	...	0023
Glovelier **515** d.	|	0603	|	0633	|	0733	|	0833	past each	|	2133	|	2233	|	2333	...	0035
Porrentruy **515** a.	|	0620	|	0650	|	0750	|	0850	hour until	|	2150	|	2250	|	2350	...	0052
Moutier **515** d.	0520	...	0552	...	0652	...	0752	...		2052	...	2152	...	2252	...	...	...
Grenchen Nord **515** d.	0530	...	0601	...	0701	...	0801	...		2101	...	2201	...	2301	...	...	...
Biel / Bienne **515** d.	0541	...	0611	...	0711	...	0811	...		2111	...	2211	...	2311	...	...	...

L – From / to Lausanne (Table **500**).

✣ – *IC* services may depart Biel/Bienne at xx48 (not xx49).

☛ See Table **515** for other services Biel/Bienne - Delémont - Porrentruy and v.v.

501 NYON - ST CERGUE - LA CURE

Narrow gauge 2nd class only NStCM

km		⚒⊗	⚒⊗	⊗		⚒							⚒		⚒		Ⓐe		Ⓐe						
0	**Nyon** d.	0547	0629	0659	0729	0759	0829	0859	and at the same	1529	1559	1629	1659	1729	1759	1829	1859	1929	1959	2029	2059	2129	2229	2329	0029
19	St Cergue d.	0625	0704	0736	0758	0833	0905	0933	minutes past	1605	1633	1705	1733	1805	1833	1905	1933	2005	2033	2103	2135	2203	2303	0003	0103
27	**La Cure** a.	0638	0717	0749	0812	...	0918	...	each hour until	1618	...	1718	...	1818	...	1918	...	2018	...	...	2148	...	...	...	...

	Ⓐe		Ⓐe	Ⓐe	⑥d	⚒⊗		⚒							⚒		⚒		Ⓐe					
La Cure d.	...	*0550***e**	...	*0646*	0650	0720	0752	...	0850	...	and at the same	1550	...	1650	...	1750	...	1850	...	1950	2050	2152	...	...
St Cergue d.	0537	0607	0637	0707	0707	0737	0807	0837	0907	0937	minutes past	1607	1637	1707	1737	1807	1837	1907	1937	2007	2107	2207	2337	0037
Nyon a.	0612	0642	0712	0742	0742	0812	0842	0912	0942	1012	each hour until	1642	1712	1742	1812	1842	1912	1942	2012	2042	2142	2242	0012	0112

d – Also Sept. 22.

e – Ⓐ (not Sept. 22).

⊗ – Change trains at St Cergue on Ⓐ (except on Sept. 22).

502 MORGES - BIÈRE and L'ISLE MONT LA VILLE

Narrow gauge 2nd class only MBC

km		⑥⑦k			⚒	Ⓐ		⚒		⚒		⚒		Ⓐ			Ⓐ						
0	**Morges** d.	0054	...	...	0554	0624	0654	0724	0754	0824	0854	0924	0954	1024	1054	and at the same	2024	2054	...	2154	...	2254	...	2354
12	Apples a.	0113	...	...	0613	0643	0713	0743	0813	0843	0913	0943	1013	1043	1113	minutes past	2043	2113	...	2213	...	2313	...	0013
19	**Bière** a.	0125	...	...	0625	0655	0725	0755	0825	0855	0925	0955	1025	1055	1125	each hour until	2055	2125	...	2225	...	2325	...	0025

	⑥⑦k			⚒	Ⓐ		⚒		⚒		⚒		Ⓐ			Ⓐ							
Bière d.	0003	...	...	0503	0533	0603	0633	0703	0733	0803	0833	0903	0933	and at the same	1903	1933	2003	...	2103	...	2203	...	2303
Apples d.	0014	...	...	0514	0544	0614	0644	0714	0744	0814	0844	0914	0944	minutes past	1914	1944	2014	...	2114	...	2214	...	2314
Morges a.	0035	...	...	0535	0605	0635	0705	0735	0805	0835	0905	0935	1005	each hour until	1935	2005	2035	...	2135	...	2235	...	2335

km		⑥⑦k	⑥⑦k				Ⓐ		Ⓐ	Ⓒ	Ⓐ		Ⓒ	Ⓐ											
0	Apples d.	0014	0114	...	0540	0614	0644	0714	0744	0814	0914	1014	1114	1144	1214	...	1414	1514	1614	1714	1814	1914	2014	2214	2314
11	L'Isle Mont la Ville a.	0028	0128	...	0554	0628	0657	0728	0757	0828	0928	1028	1128	1157	1228	...	1428	1528	1628	1728	1828	1928	2028	2228	2328

	⑥⑦k			Ⓐ	Ⓒ	Ⓐ	Ⓐ	Ⓒ	Ⓐ	Ⓒ	Ⓐ		Ⓒ	Ⓐ										
L'Isle Mont la Ville d.	0056	...	0558	0629	0656	0659	0729	0756	0759	0856	0956	1056	1156	1159	1256	...	1456	1556	1656	1756	1856	1956	2056	2256	2356
Apples a.	0110	...	0612	0642	0710	0712	0742	0810	0812	0910	1010	1110	1210	1212	1310	...	1510	1610	1710	1810	1910	2010	2110	2310	0010

k – Also June 9, Aug. 1.

SBB — YVERDON - FRIBOURG — 503

km			⑥⑦c		⑥⑦c																	
0	**Yverdon** d.	0004	0004	...	0106	...	0504	0534	and at the	1304	1334	1404	...	1504	1534	and at the	2204	2234	2304	2334	...	...
18	Estavayer-le-Lac d.	0019	0019	...	0120	...	0519	0549	same minutes	1319	1349	1419	...	1519	1549	same minutes	2219	2249	2319	2349	...	...
28	Payerne d.	0029	0031	...	0130	...	0531	0601	past each	1331	1401	1431	...	1531	1601	past each	2231	2301	2331	2359	...	...
50	**Fribourg** a.	...	0058	...	...	...	0558	0628	hour until	1358	1428	1458	...	1558	1628	hour until	2258	2328	2358	...	...	...

		⑥⑦c		⑥⑦c																			
Fribourg d.	0002	0002	...	0102	...	...	...	0532	0602	and at the	1332	1402	...	1502	1532	1602	and at the	2232	2302	2332	...	...
Payerne d.	0029	0031	...	0131	...	0501	0531	0601	0631	same minutes	1401	1431	...	1531	1601	1631	same minutes	2301	2331	0001	...	...
Estavayer-le-Lac d.	...	0040	...	0140	...	0510	0540	0610	0640	past each	1410	1440	...	1540	1610	1640	past each	2310	2340	0010	...	...
Yverdon a.	...	0056	...	0156	...	0526	0556	0626	0656	hour until	1426	1426	...	1556	1626	1656	hour until	2326	2356	0026	...	...

c – Mornings of ⑥⑦ (also June 9, Aug. 1).

SBB — MORGES - LAUSANNE - PALÉZIEUX - PAYERNE — 504

SERVICE FROM JUNE 9

km															
	Morges 500 d.	...	0511	0541		2011	2041	...	2141e	...	2241e	...	2341e	...	...
	Renens 500 d.	...	0521	0550		2021	2050	...	2150	...	2250	...	2350	...	...
0	**Lausanne** 500 d.	0458	0528	0558	and at the	2028	2058	...	2158	...	2258	...	2358	...	...
21	Palézieux 500 a.	0516	0545	0616	same minutes	2045	2116	...	2216	...	2316	...	0016	...	...
	Palézieux d.	0516	0547	0616	past each	2047	2116	...	2216	...	2316	...	0016	...	...
38	Moudon d.	0536	0608	0636	hour until	2108	2136	...	2236	...	2336	...	0036	...	...
58	**Payerne** a.	0558	0627	0658		2127	2158	...	2258	...	2358	...	0058	...	...
	Murten 511a a.	0623	...	0723		...	2223	...	2323	...	0023	...	...	...	...

Murten 511a d.	...	0438	...		1838	...	1938	...	2038	...	2138	...	2238	...	2338
Payerne d.	0432	0502	0532		1902	1932	2002	2032	2102	...	2202	...	2302	...	0002
Moudon d.	0451	0520	0551	and at the	1920	1951	2020	2051	2120	...	2220	...	2320	...	0020
Palézieux a.	0509	0542	0612	same minutes	1942	2012	2042	2112	2142	...	2242	...	2342	...	0042
Palézieux 500 d.	0515	0544	0615	past each	1944	2015	2044	2115	2144	...	2244	...	2344	...	0044
Lausanne 500 a.	0532	0602	0632	hour until	2002	2032	2102	2131	2202	...	2302	...	0002	...	0102
Renens 500 a.	0539	0609	0639		2009	2039	2109	2140	2209	...	2309	...	0009	...	...
Morges 500 a.	0548	0618	0648		2018	2048	2118f	2149	2218f	...	2318f	...	0018h	...	...

e – 3 minutes earlier on ⑦–④.
f – 4 minutes later on ⑦–④.
h – 0022 on ①–⑤.

SBB, BLS, SOB — Semi-fast services BERN - ZÜRICH (via Burgdorf and Brugg) — 505

SERVICE FROM JUNE 15. See Table **500** for fast services Bern - Zürich and v.v. Services are operated by SBB except where otherwise indicated.
Note: Non-stop services between Bern and Olten operate via the high-speed line.

km		*IR* 2847	*IR* 2849		*IR* 2155	*IR* 2353	*IR* 2353	*IR* 2159	*IR* 2357	*IR* 2809	*IR* 2161	*IR* 2359	★	*IR* 2831	*IR* 2183	*IR* 2381	*IR* 2833	*IR* 2185	*IR* 2383	*IR* 2835	*IR* 2187	*IR* 2385	*IR* 2837	*IR* 2189	*IR* 2387
			⑥⑦			Ⓒ	Ⓐ		Ⓐ																
		⊙	c⊙		F	⊡	◇		§	⊙		⊡		⊙		⊡	⊙		⊡	⊙		⊡	⊙		⊡
0	**Bern** 500 517 d.	0006	0109	...	0418j	0436	0438	...	0538	0607	0633	0638	and at	1707	1733	1738	1807	1833	1838	1907	1933	1938	2007	2033	2038
23	Burgdorf 517 d.	0022	0125	...	|	0451	0453	...	0553	0621	|	0653		1721	|	1753	1821	|	1853	1921	|	1953	2021	|	2053
40	Herzogenbuchsee d.	0035	0138	...	|	0505	0505	...	0605	0634	|	0705	the same	1734	|	1805	1834	|	1905	1934	|	2005	2034	|	2105
47	Langenthal d.	0041	0144	...	|	0512	0512	...	0612	0641	|	0712		1741	|	1812	1841	|	1912	1941	|	2012	2041	|	2112
67	**Olten** 500 a.	0055	0158	...	0444	0524	0524	...	0624	0654	0700	0724	minutes	1754	1800	1824	1854	1900	1924	1954	2000	2024	2054	2100	2124
67	**Olten** 500 d.	...	...	...	0446	0526	0526	0602	0626	...	0702	0730		...	1802	1830	...	1902	1930	...	2002	2030	...	2102	...
80	Aarau 500 510 d.	...	...	...	0456	0536	0536	0614	0640	...	0714	|	past each	...	1814	|	...	1914	|	...	2014	|	...	2114	...
	Lenzburg 510 d.	...	...	...	0503	0542	0542	|	0649	...	|	|		...	|	|	...	|	|	...	|	|	...	|	...
98	Brugg 510 d.	...	...	...	|	|	|	0630	|	...	0730	|	hour until	...	1830	|	...	1930	|	...	2030	|	...	2130	...
107	Baden 510 a.	...	...	...	|	|	|	0638	|	...	0738	|		...	1838	|	...	1938	|	...	2038	|	...	2138	...
129	**Zürich** HB 500 510 a.	...	...	...	0528	0606	0606	0654	0713	...	0754	0806		...	1854	1906	...	1954	2006	...	2054	2106	...	2154	...
	Chur 520 a.	...	...	...	...	0748	0748	...	...	...	...	0948		...	...	2048	...	...	2149	...	...	2249	...	...	...

	IR 2839	*IR* 2191	*IR* 2191	*IR* 2389	*IR* 2841	*IR* 2193	*IR* 2599	*RE* 4793	*IR* 2845	*IC* 739	*IR* 2399	*IC* 543
			⑤⑥									
	⊙		k	⊡	⊙	L			⊙	L	⊡	L
Bern 500 517 d.	2107	...	2133	2138	2206	...	2233	...	2306	2331	2338	...
Burgdorf 517 d.	2121	...	|	2153	2222	...	2251	...	2322	|	2354	...
Herzogenbuchsee d.	2134	...	|	2205	2235	...	2303	...	2335	|	0006	...
Langenthal d.	2141	...	|	2212	2241	...	2310	...	2341	|	0012	...
Olten 500 a.	2154	...	2200	2225	2255	...	2325	...	2356	2357	0026	...
Olten 500 d.	...	2202	2202	...	...	2302	...	2335	...	0002	...	0037
Aarau 500 510 d.	...	2214	2214	...	...	2314	...	2345	...	0012	...	0047
Lenzburg 510 d.	...	|	|	...	...	|	...	|	...	0019	...	0054
Brugg 510 d.	...	2230	2230	...	...	2330	...	0003	...	|	...	|
Baden 510 a.	...	2238	2238	...	...	2338	...	0013	...	|	...	|
Zürich HB 500 510 a.	...	2254	2254	...	...	2354	...	0042	...	0040	...	0113
Chur 520 a.	...	...	...	...	...	...	...	...	...	...	...	...

	IR 2846		*IR* 2806	*IR* 2352	*IC* 704	*IR* 2808	*IR* 2354	*IR* 2158	*IR* 2810
	⑥⑦		Ⓐ						
	c⊙		⊙	⊡	G✕	⊙	⊡		⊙
Chur 520 d.	...	...	...	...	...	...	0411t	...	...
Zürich HB 500 510 d.	...	...	...	...	0519	...	0553	0606	...
Baden 510 d.	...	...	...	...	|	...	|	0622	...
Brugg 510 d.	...	...	...	...	|	...	|	0632	...
Lenzburg 510 d.	...	...	...	...	0540	...	|	|	...
Aarau 500 510 d.	...	...	...	...	0548	...	|	0646	...
Olten 500 a.	...	...	...	...	0557	...	0628	0655	...
Olten 500 d.	0039	...	0506	0536	0602	0606	0636	0656	0706
Langenthal d.	0052	...	0518	0548	|	0618	0648	|	0718
Herzogenbuchsee d.	0057	...	0524	0554	|	0624	0654	|	0724
Burgdorf 517 d.	0111	...	0538	0606	|	0638	0706	|	0738
Bern 500 517 a.	0126	...	0553	0621	0628	0653	0721	0724	0753

	IR 2356	★	*IR* 2180	*IR* 2832	*IR* 2378	*IR* 2182	*IR* 2834	*IR* 2380	*IR* 2382	*IR* 2184	*IR* 2836	*IR* 2384	*IR* 2386	*IR* 2186	*IR* 2838	*IR* 2388	*IR* 2390	*IR* 2188	*IR* 2840	*IR* 2594	*IR* 2190	*IR* 2842	*IR* 2596	*IR* 2192	*IC* 740
								⚒	†			R	⑤v			†	⚒								
	⊡			⊙	⊡		⊙	⊡			⊙	⊡			⊙	◇			⊙	⊡		⊙	⊡		
Chur 520 d.	0511	and at	...	...	1611	...	...	1711	...	...	...	1811	...	...	...	1911	...	...	...	...	...	...	...	...	...
Zürich HB 500 510 d.	0653		1706	...	1753	1806	...	1853	1855	1906	...	1953	1955	2006	...	2053	2055	2106	...	...	2206	...	...	2306	2332
Baden 510 d.	|	the same	1722	...	|	1822	...	|	|	1922	...	|	|	2022	...	|	|	2122	...	...	2222	...	...	2322	|
Brugg 510 d.	|		1732	...	|	1832	...	|	|	1932	...	|	|	2032	...	|	|	2132	...	...	2232	...	...	2332	|
Lenzburg 510 d.	|	minutes	|	...	|	|	...	|	|	|	...	|	|	|	...	|	|	|	...	...	|	...	...	|	|
Aarau 500 510 d.	|		1746	...	|	1846	...	|	|	1946	...	|	|	2046	...	|	|	2146	...	...	2246	...	...	2346	|
Olten 500 a.	0728	past each	1755	...	1828	1855	...	1928	1928	1955	...	2028	2028	2055	...	2128	2128	2155	...	...	2256	...	...	2356	0002
Olten 500 d.	0736		1756	1806	1836	1856	1906	1936	1936	1956	2006	2036	2036	2056	2106	2136	2136	2156	2206	2237	...	2302	2337	...	0004
Langenthal d.	0748	hour until	|	1818	1848	|	1918	1948	1948	|	2018	2048	2048	|	2118	2148	2148	|	2218	2249	...	2313	2349	...	|
Herzogenbuchsee d.	0754		|	1824	1854	|	1924	1954	1954	|	2024	2054	2054	|	2124	2154	2154	|	2224	2255	...	2319	2355	...	|
Burgdorf 517 d.	0806		|	1838	1906	|	1938	2006	2006	|	2038	2106	2106	|	2138	2209	2209	|	2236	2309	...	2331	0009	...	|
Bern 500 517 a.	0821		1824	1853	1921	1924	1953	2021	2021	2024	2053	2121	2121	2124	2153	2226	2226	2224	2253	2326	...	2345	0026	...	0031

F – Continues to Zürich Flughafen (a. 0541).
G – To Genève Aéroport (Table **500**).
L – From Lausanne (Table **500**).
R – ①②③④⑥⑦ (also Aug. 1).

c – Also June 9, Aug. 1.
j – 0404 on June 16 – 20, 23 – 27, July 28, Sept. 8, 13 – 15, 22 – 26, 29, 30, Oct. 1 – 3, 25 – 27, Nov. 17, Dec. 1, 8.
k – ⑤⑥ (also June 8, July 31).

t – † only.
v – Not Aug. 1.

⊙ – Operated by BLS.
◇ – Operated by SOB.
⊡ – Operated by either SBB or SOB.
§ – Runs as *RE* **4509** Olten - Zürich.
★ – Train numbers increase by 2 each hour.

506 LAC LÉMAN — CGN

GENÈVE - YVOIRE - LAUSANNE

	D◇	G◇	W	C	S◇	D◇	G	J	S◇	S◇
Genève Mont-Blanc.....d.	1045	1045	1235	...	...	1445	1445	...	...	...
Genève Jardin-Anglais.d.	|	|	|	1235	1235	|	|	1900	1900	...
Nyon.....d.	1205	1205	1345	|	|	|	|	|	|	...
Yvoire (France).....d.	1225	1235	...	1405	1405	1612	1620	2030	2030	2035
Morges.....d.	...	1350	...	...	...	...	1735	...	...	2152
Lausanne-Ouchy.....a.	...	1428	...	...	...	...	1810	...	...	2230

	G◇	D◇	W	C	S◇	G◇	D◇	S◇	S◇	J
Lausanne-Ouchy.....d.	1055	...	...	...	...	1440	...	1850	...	...
Morges.....d.	1133	...	...	...	...	1518	...	1930	...	...
Yvoire (France).....d.	1255	1255	...	1410	1410	1640	1640	2029	2035	2035
Nyon.....d.	1320	1320	1350	|	|	1705	1705	...	2055	2055
Genève Jardin-Anglais.....a.	|	|	|	1530	1530	|	|	...	2220	2220
Genève Mont-Blanc.....a.	1435	1435	1505	...	...	1830	1830	...	...	...

LAUSANNE - ST GUINGOLPH

	WINTER	W	W	W		SUMMER		◇	S	S		◇		S	S	S	◇			T	
Lausanne-Ouchy.....d.		...	1230	1600	...		...	0905	0910	...	1020	1155	...	1235	...	1435	1530	...	...	1820	...
Vevey-Marché.....d.		...	|	1648	...		...	|	1015	...	1130	|	1330	1342	...	1520	|	1530	1730	1910	...
Vevey-La Tour.....d.	December 15	...	|	|	...		...	|	|	...	1135	|	1335	...	...	...	|	1535	|	|	...
Montreux.....d.	to	...	|	1710	...		...	1008	1040	...	1205	|	1405	...	...	...	|	1605	1755	1932	...
Territet.....d.	April 17	...	|	|	...	April 18	...	|	|	...	1212	|	1412	...	...	...	|	1612	|	|	...
Château-de-Chillon.....d.		...	|	1720	...		...	|	1050	...	1220	|	1420	...	...	...	|	1620	|	|	...
Villeneuve.....d.	and	...	|	1730	...	to	...	|	1058	...	1228	|	1428	...	...	...	|	1628	|	|	...
Bouveret.....d.		1035	|	1753	...		0840	|	1120	...	1250	|	1450	...	...	...	|	1650	1820	|	...
St Gingolph.....d.	October 13	|	1325	...	...	October 12	|	|	1133	...	1303	1250	1503	...	...	...	1625	1703	...	|	...
Bouveret.....d.	to	|	1340	...	...		|	|	|	...	|	1303	|	...	...	...	1638	|	...	|	...
Villeneuve.....d.	December 13	|	1405	...	...	→	|	|	|	...	|	1325	|	...	...	...	1700	|	...	|	...
Château-de-Chillon.....d.		|	1415	...	...		|	|	|	...	|	1335	|	...	...	...	1710	|	...	|	...
Montreux.....d.	→	1100	1430	...	...		0905	1010	|	...	|	1348	|	...	...	...	1723	|	...	|	...
Vevey-Marché.....d.		1123	1453	...	...		0927	1032	|	1345	1325	1410	1525	...	1545	...	1745	1725	...	|	...
Lausanne-Ouchy.....a.		1220	1550	...	...		1012	1140	1228	1430	...	1515	...	...	1650	...	1830	...	...	2035	...

LAUSANNE - ÉVIAN-LES-BAINS (France) Journey 35 minutes
From Lausanne-Ouchy: 0450⚒, 0540Ⓐ **z**, 0610⚒, 0707Ⓐ **z**, 0737 **K**, 0920, 1100, 1230, 1400, 1530, 1715, 1840, 2000, 2130 **M**, 2245 **N**.
From Évian les Bains: 0530⚒, 0625Ⓐ **z**, 0655, 0750Ⓐ **z**, 0820 **K**, 1005, 1145, 1315, 1445, 1615, 1800, 1920, 2040, 2208 **M**, 2325 **N**.

C – Ⓒ May 3 - June 22; Ⓒ Sept. 6 - Oct. 12 (also Sept. 15).
D – Ⓐ Apr. 22 - May 30; Ⓐ Sept. 16 - Oct. 10.
G – Ⓒ Apr. 18 - Oct. 12 (daily June 2 - Sept. 15).
J – May 31 - June 27 and Sept. 1 – 13.
K – ⚒ (daily June 28 - Aug. 31).
M – Ⓐ (⚒ Apr. 18 - June 27; daily June 28 - Aug. 31; ⚒ Sept. 1 - Oct. 12).
N – Ⓐ (daily June 28 - Aug. 31).
S – June 28 - Aug. 31.
T – Ⓒ Apr. 18 - Oct. 12 (daily June 2 - 27, Sept. 1 - 15).
W – ⑦ Dec. 15 - Jan. 5 (also Dec. 25, Jan. 1, 2), † Feb. 9 - Mar. 2, Ⓒ Mar. 8 - Apr. 13, † Oct. 19 - Dec. 7.
z – Not Dec. 23 - Jan. 3.
◇ – Normally operated by historic steamship.

Operator: CGN – Compagnie Générale de Navigation www.cgn.ch
Additional sailings operate Lausanne-Ouchy - Thonon-les-Bains and Nyon - Yvoire.

507 VIERWALDSTÄTTERSEE — SGV

	SUMMER		Ⓐ	S	T	⊙	⛴ ⑦R		G	⛴	△		R	N	⛴ G	R	N		R	N	⊡ R	N⑥	
Luzern (Bahnhofquai).....d.		...	0620	...	0812	0912	0940	1012	1040	1112	1212	1312	1412	1412	1435	1512	1512	1612	1712	1712	1912	1912	...
Verkehrshaus Lido.....d.		...	|	...	0822	0922	|	1022	|	1122	1222	1322	1422	1422	|	1522	1522	1622	1722	|	1922	|	...
Weggis.....d.		...	0659	...	0853	0953	1024	1053	1124	1153	1253	1353	1453	1453	|	1553	1553	1653	1753	1747	1953	1953	...
Vitznau.....d.	April 18	...	...	...	0910	1010	1040	1110	1140	1210	1310	1410	1510	1510	1519	1610	1610	1710	1810	...	2010	2009	...
Beckenried.....d.		...	...	...	0926	1027	1123	1127	...	1227	1327	1427	1527	1527	...	1627	1627	1800	1835	...	2031	...	...
Gersau.....d.	to	...	...	...	...	1045	...	1145	...	1245	1345	1445	1545	1545	...	1645	1645	1817	|	...	...	...	...
Treib.....d.		0828	...	1002	...	1102	...	1202	...	1302	1402	1502	1602	1602	...	1702	1702	1834	1902	...	...	...	...
Brunnen.....d.	October 19	0836	...	1011	...	1111	...	1211	...	1311	1411	1511	1611	1611	...	1711	1709	1841	1909	...	...	...	...
Rütli.....d.		0846	...	1021	...	1121	...	1221	...	1321	1421	1521	1621	1621	...	1721	...	...	...	...	...	...	...
Sisikon.....d.	→	...	...	|	...	|	...	|	...	1332	|	|	1632	1632	...	1732	...	...	...	...	...	...	...
Tellsplatte.....d.		...	...	1045	...	|	...	|	...	1339	|	|	1639	1639	...	1739	...	...	...	...	...	...	...
Bauen.....d.		...	...	1035*	...	1135	...	1235	...	|	1435	1535	|	1649	...	1749	...	...	...	...	...	...	...
Flüelen.....a.		...	...	1057	...	1155	...	1255	...	1355	1455	1555	1655	1708	...	1808	...	...	...	...	...	...	...

	SUMMER	Ⓐ		T		S	G		⛴ ⑦R	S	L	⊙		⛴ G	⛴	△	N		R		⊡ R	N⑥	
Flüelen.....d.		...	...	...	...	...	...	0948	...	1100	...	1200	1300	...	1400	1500	...	1600	1700	...	...	...	...
Bauen.....d.		...	...	...	...	...	...	1008	...	1121	...	|	1321	...	1421	|	...	1621	1721	...	...	...	...
Tellsplatte.....d.		...	...	...	...	...	...	1018	...	|	...	1216	|	...	|	1516	...	|	|	...	...	...	...
Sisikon.....d.	April 18	...	...	...	...	...	...	1025	...	|	...	1224	|	...	|	1524	...	|	|	...	...	...	...
Rütli.....d.		...	...	...	...	...	...	1036	...	1136	...	1236	1336	...	1436	1536	...	1636	1736	...	...	...	...
Brunnen.....d.	to	...	0819	...	0919	0949	...	1049	...	1149	1149	1249	1349	...	1449	1549	...	1649	1749	1849	...	...	...
Treib.....d.		...	0827	...	0927	0957	...	1057	...	1157	1157	1257	1357	...	1457	1557	...	1657	1757	1857	...	...	...
Gersau.....d.	October 19	...	...	...	0942	...	...	1114	...	1214	1214	1314	1414	...	1514	1614	...	1714	1814	...	...	...	...
Beckenried.....d.		...	...	0932	1000	...	...	1132	1135	1232	1232	1332	1432	...	1532	1632	...	1732	1832	...	2032	...	...
Vitznau.....d.	→	...	...	0949	1049	...	1142	1149	|	1249	1249	1349	1449	1521	1549	1649	...	1749	1849	...	|	2010	...
Weggis.....d.		0707	...	1005	1105	...	|	1205	|	1305	1305	1405	1505	1538	1605	1705	1749	1805	1905	...	2057	|	...
Verkehrshaus Lido.....d.		|	...	1035	|	...	|	1235	|	1335	1335	1435	1535	|	1635	1735	|	1835	1935	...	2135	|	...
Luzern (Bahnhofquai).....a.		0742	...	1047	1147	...	1230	1247	1235	1347	1347	1447	1547	1623	1647	1747	1825	1847	1947	...	2147	2147	...

WINTER ★	n							n		Ⓐ
Luzern (Bahnhofquai).....d.	0912	1012	1112	1200	...	1300	1412	1512	1612	1712
Verkehrshaus Lido.....d.	0922	1022	1122	1210	...	|	1422	1522	1622	|
Weggis.....d.	0953	1053	1153	1240	...	|	1453	1553	1653	1747
Vitznau.....d.	1009	1109	1209	1254	1309	1348	1509	1609	1709	...
Beckenried.....d.	1027	1127	...	...	1327	...	1526	1627	1726	...
Gersau.....d.	1045	1145	...	...	1345	...	...	1645	...	...
Treib.....d.	1102	1202	...	...	1402	...	...	1702	...	...
Brunnen.....d.	1111	1211	...	...	1411	...	...	1709	...	...
Rütli.....d.	1121	1221	...	...	1421r	...	...	...	...	...
Bauen.....d.	...	1235	...	...	1435r	...	...	...	...	...
Flüelen.....a.	...	1255	...	...	1457r	...	...	...	...	...

WINTER ★	n					w		n	Ⓐ	
Flüelen.....d.	...	...	...	...	...	1300	...	1500r	...	...
Bauen.....d.	...	...	...	...	...	|	...	1521r	...	...
Rütli.....d.	...	...	...	...	...	1336	...	1536	...	...
Brunnen.....d.	0949	...	1149	...	...	1349	...	1549	...	...
Treib.....d.	0957	...	1157	...	...	1357	...	1557	...	...
Gersau.....d.	1014	...	1214	...	...	1414	...	1614	...	...
Beckenried.....d.	1032	...	1232	...	...	1432	1532	1632	...	1732
Vitznau.....d.	1049	1210	1249	1256	1349	1449	1549	1649	...	1749
Weggis.....d.	1105	|	...	1312	1405	1505	1605	1705	1749	1805
Verkehrshaus Lido.....d.	|	|	...	1335	1435	1535	1635	1735	|	|
Luzern (Bahnhofquai).....a.	1141	1255	...	1347	1447	1547	1647	1747	1825	1841

	Q	B	F	A	P	E‡	F	A	A	S
Luzern (Bahnhofquai).....d.	0838	0900	0938	1038	1150	1200	1238	1338	1438	1638
Verkehrshaus Lido.....d.	|	0910	0948	1048	1200	1210	1248	1348	1448	1648
Küssnacht am Rigi.....a.	|	0953	|	|	|	1253	|	|	|	|
Kehrsiten Dorf ◧.....d.	|	...	|	1131	|	...	|	1409	1527	|
Hergiswil.....d.	|	...	1016	|	1231	...	1314	1424	1542	|
Stansstad.....d.	|	...	1026	1143	1241	...	1323	1434	1551	1713
Alpnachstad.....a.	0925	...	1049	1205	1304	...	1345	1457	1610	1735

	Q	B	F	A	E§	P	F	A	A	S
Alpnachstad.....d.	0930	...	1055	1222	...	1308	1407	1517	1627	1738
Stansstad.....d.	0951	...	1118	|	...	|	1429	1540	1649	1800
Hergiswil.....d.	|	...	1128	1247	...	|	1439	|	1659	1810
Kehrsiten Dorf ◧.....d.	|	...	1143	|	...	|	1454	1552	|	|
Küssnacht am Rigi.....d.	|	0956	|	|	1256	|	|	|	|	|
Verkehrshaus Lido.....d.	1016	|	1204	1316	1333	|	1515	1613	|	|
Luzern (Bahnhofquai).....a.	1028	1053	1216	1328	1347	1355	1527	1625	1736	1845

A – May 12 - Oct. 19.
B – † Apr. 18 - May 18; Ⓒ May 24 - July 4; daily July 5 - Aug. 17; † Aug. 24 - Oct. 19.
E – Apr. 18 - Oct. 19.
F – May 24 - Oct. 19 (also May 17, 18).
G – † May 24 - Sept. 7 (daily July 5 - Aug. 17).
L – Apr. 18 - May 23.
N – Apr. 18 - May 23 and Sept. 8 - Oct. 19.
P – Ⓒ May 24 - Sept. 7 (daily July 5 - Aug. 17).
Q – Ⓒ May 24 - Oct. 19 (daily July 5 - Aug. 17).
R – May 24 - Sept. 7.
S – May 24 - Oct. 19.
T – May 24 - Sept. 7, also Ⓒ Sept. 13 - Oct. 19.
n – Change vessels at Beckenried.
r – Ⓒ (daily Dec. 23 – 31, Mar. 10 - Apr. 17).
w – Also calls at Tellsplatte (1316) and Sisikon (1324).
★ – Timings apply Dec. 15 - Apr. 17 and Oct 20 - Dec. 13. Additional sailings: Luzern 0620Ⓐ - Weggis 0659Ⓐ and Weggis 0707Ⓐ - Luzern 0742Ⓐ.
◧ – Hourly sailings link Luzern with Kehrsiten-Bürgenstock.
⊙ – ⛴ May 24 - Sept. 7 (also † Sept. 14 - Oct. 19).
⊡ – ⛴ on ⑤⑥.
△ – ⛴ May 24 - Sept. 7 (also ⚒ Sept. 8 - 27).
‡ – There is an additional sailing at 1400 **P**.
§ – There is an additional sailing at 1456 **P**.
* – Calls at Bauen before Tellsplatte.
⛴ – Normally operated by historic steamship.

Operator: SGV – Schifffahrtsgesellschaft Vierwaldstättersee www.lakelucerne.ch

OTHER SWISS LAKES 508

ZÜRICHSEE (operator: ZSG)

	A	A		B		B	B	A	A	
Zürich (Bürkliplatz) d.	0920	1020	1120	1220	1320	...	1420	1520	1720	...
Erlenbach d.	0958	|	|	1258	1358	...	|	|	|	...
Thalwil d.	|	1055	1155	|	|	...	1455	1555	1755	...
Wädenswil d.	1045	1145	1245	1345	1445	1455	1545	1645	1853	...
Rapperswil a.	1130	1237	1337	1430	1530	1605	1637	1737	1944	...

	A	A		B	B		B	A	A	
Rapperswil d.	1140	1245	1345	1400	1440	1540	1645	1745	1950	...
Wädenswil d.	1227	1339	1439	1453	1527	1627	1739	1839	2038	...
Thalwil d.	|	1431	1531	...	|	|	1831	1931	2124	...
Erlenbach d.	1313	|	|	...	1613	1713	|	|	|	...
Zürich (Bürkliplatz) a.	1350	1505	1605	...	1650	1750	1905	2005	2200	...

BRIENZERSEE (operator: BLS)

	E	E	E	E	F	F ⛴	F	F ⛴	F	G ⛴	H
Interlaken Ost d.	1007	1207	1307	1507	0907	1107	1207	1407	1607	1907	1140
Iseltwald d.	1046	1252	1352	1552	0952	1152	1252	1452	1652	1952	1236
Brienz a.	1120	1320	1420	1620	1020	1220	1320	1520	1720	2020	1310

	E	E	E	E	F	F ⛴	F	F ⛴	F	G ⛴	H
Brienz d.	1140	1340	1440	1640	1040	1240	1440	1540	1740	2040	1320
Iseltwald d.	1208	1408	1517	1708	1117	1308	1508	1608	1817	2108	1407
Interlaken Ost a.	1253	1453	1553	1753	1153	1353	1553	1653	1853	2153	1450

THUNERSEE (operator: BLS)

	R	N	P		R ⛴	K	R	R	M	L ⛴	
Thun d.	0840	0940	0940	1140	1240	1440	1440	1540	1810	1840	...
Oberhofen d.	|	|	1003	1203	1303	1503	1503	1603	|	1903	...
Spiez d.	0928	1014	1028	1228	1328	1528	1528	1628	1914	1928	...
Beatenbucht d.	0954	...	1102	1302	1402	1602	1602	1702	...	2002	...
Interlaken West a.	1049	...	1149	1349	1449	...	1649	1749	...	...	...

	N	R	P		K	R ⛴	R	M	R	L ⛴	
Interlaken West d.	...	1110	1210	1410	...	1510	1710	...	1810	...	...
Beatenbucht d.	...	1158	1258	1458	1603	1558	1758	...	|	2005	...
Spiez d.	1016	1234	1334	1534	1634	1634	1834	1916	1934	2034	...
Oberhofen d.	|	1257	1357	1557	1657	1657	|	|	1957	2057	...
Thun a.	1050	1320	1420	1620	1720	1720	1920	2020	2015	2120	...

A – May 1 - Sept. 30.
B – Ⓒ Apr. 6 - Oct. 19 (daily May 1 - Sept. 30).
E – Apr. 12 - May 9.
F – May 10 - Oct. 19.
G – ⑥ May 31 - Aug. 23.
H – Oct. 20 - Dec. 7.
K – ⑤–⑦ Dec. 15 - Jan. 5 and Mar. 1–23; daily Mar. 24 - May 16 and Oct. 13 - Dec. 13.

L ②–⑥ May 17 - Sept. 13 (not Aug. 1).
M – ⑤⑥ Apr. 4 - May 17; ⑤⑥ July 4 - Aug. 30.
N – ⑦ Jan. 12 - Feb. 23.
P – ⑤–⑦ Dec. 15 - Jan. 5 and Mar. 1–23; daily Mar. 24 - Dec. 13.
R – May 17 - Oct. 12.
⛴ – Operated by historic steamship.

Operators:
BLS – BLS Schifffahrt ✆ +41 (0) 58 327 48 11 (www.bls.ch).
ZSG – Zürichsee Schifffahrtsgesellschaft ✆ +41 (0) 44 487 13 33 (www.zsg.ch).

TPF FRIBOURG - MURTEN - INS - NEUCHÂTEL 509

km		Ⓐ						Ⓒ			Ⓒ						
0	**Fribourg** d.	0428	0517	0547	0617	0647	0717	0717	0747	0817	0817	0847	0917	0947	and at the	2317	2347
22	Murten d.	0518e	0547	0618	0647	0718	0747	0747	0818	0847	0847	0918	0947	1018	same minutes	2347	0018
32	Ins 511 d.	0527	0600	0627	0700	0727	...	0800	0827	...	0900	0927	1000	1027	past each	0000	0027
45	**Neuchâtel** 511 a.	0542	0613	0642	0713	0742	...	0813	0847	...	0913	0942	1013	1042	hour until	0013	0042

	Ⓐ							Ⓒ			Ⓒ					
Neuchâtel 511 d.	0446	0517	0546	0617	0646	0717	...	0746	0817	...	0846	0917	0946	and at the	2317	2346
Ins 511 d.	0459	0530	0559	0630	0659	0730	...	0759	0830	...	0859	0930	0959	same minutes	2330	2359
Murten d.	0510	0540	0610	0640	0710	0740	0810	0810	0840	0910	0910	0940	1010	past each	2340	0010
Fribourg a.	0543	0613	0643	0713	0743	0813	0843	0843	0913	0943	0943	1013	1043	hour until	0013	0043

e – Arrives 0458.

SBB BASEL - ZÜRICH 510

Non-stop *IC*, *ICE* and *TGV* services.

km		*IC* 551	*IC* 1251	*IC* 559	*IC* 1253	*IC* 561	*ICE* 3	*IC* 1255	*IC* 563	*ICE* 271	*IC* 565	*IC* 767	*TGV* 9203	*EC* 151	*IC* 569	*IC* 771	*IC* 591	*IC* 571	*IC* 773	*TGV* 9211	*IC* 775	*IC* 575	*ICE* 73	*TGV* 9213	*EC* 9	*IC* 579	*ICE* 75
							①–⑤	⑥⑦									Ⓐ	Ⓒ									
			✗	✗	✗	✗	L✗	c✗	✗	G✗	✗		P	M✗	✗			✗	✗	P	✗	✗	G✗	P	G✗	✗	G✗
0	**Basel** SBB d.	0533	0606	0633	0706	0733	0806	0806	0833	0906	0933	1006	1033	1106	1133	1206	1233	1233	1306	1333	1406	1433	1506	1533	1606	1633	1706
91	**Zürich** HB a.	0626	0700	0726	0800	0826	0900	0900	0926	1000	1026	1100	1126	1200	1226	1300	1326	1326	1400	1426	1500	1526	1600	1626	1700	1726	1800
	Chur 520 a.	...	...	0852	0922t	0952t	...	1022x	1052	1122	1152	...	...	...	1352	...	...	1452	1522	...	...	1652	...	...	...	1852	...

	IC 581	*TGV* 9215	*IC* 595	*IC* 783	*IC* 583	*ICE* 77	*TGV* 9219	*IC* 787	*IC* 587	*ICE* 79	*TGV* 9223	*IC* 791	*IC* 793	
	Ⓐ	Ⓒ	Ⓒ									⑤⑥	⑤⑥	
	✗	zP	Q		✗	G✗	P	¶	✗	G	P			
Basel SBB d.	1733	1733	1733	1806	1833	1906	1933	2006	2033	2106	2133	2206	2306	...
Zürich HB a.	1826	1826	1826	1900	1926	2000	2026	2100	2126	2200	2226	2300	2400	...
Chur 520 a.	1952	...	...	...	2052	...	...	...	2252r	...	...	...	...	...

	ICE 78		*IC* 556	*IC* 556	*IC* 760	*TGV* 9206	*ICE* 76	*IC* 560	*IC* 764
				⚒					
	G		✗	✗	✗	P	G	✗	✗
Chur 520 d.	...	...	...	0508	...	...	...	0708	...
Zürich HB d.	0559	...	0634	0634	0659	0734	0759	0834	0859
Basel SBB a.	0653	...	0728	0728	0753	0828	0853	0928	0953

	TGV 9210	*IC* 552	*ICE* 74	*IC* 564	*EC* 8	*TGV* 9218	*IC* 770	*IC* 568	*IC* 772	*TGV* 9222	*ICE* 70	*EC* 150	*IC* 776	*TGV* 9226	*IC* 778	*IC* 576	*ICE* 272 292	*IC* 578	*IC* 782	*TGV* 9234	*ICE* 4	*IC* 582	*IC* 584	*IC* 788	*IC* 1258	*IC* 790	*IC* 792
	v	R																				S		⑦	Ⓒ	Ⓑ	⑤⑥
	P		G	✗	G✗	P	✗	✗	✗	P	G✗	M✗	✗	P	✗	✗	G	✗	¶	P	G✗	✗	✗	w		n	
Chur 520 d.	...	...	...	0908	...	...	1038	1108	...	...	1238	...	...	...	...	1508	...	1608t	...	...	...	1808t	1908	...	...	...	...
Zürich HB d.	0934	0934	0959	1034	1059	1134	1159	1234	1259	1334	1359	1434	1459	1534	1559	1634	1659	1734	1759	1834	1859	1934	2034	2059	2134	2159	2259
Basel SBB a.	1028	1028	1053	1128	1153	1228	1253	1328	1353	1428	1453	1528	1553	1628	1653	1728	1753	1828	1853	1928	1953	2028	2128	2153	2228	2253	2353

IR and *RE* services

km																								
0	**Basel** SBB d.	0437	...	0511	0537	0543	...	and at	1911	1937	1943	...	2011	2043	...	2111	2143	...	2211	2243	...	2311	...	0011
17	Rheinfelden d.	0450	...	0525	0550	|	...		1925	1950	|	...	2025	|	...	2125	|	...	2225	|	...	2325	...	0025
57	Brugg 505 d.	0520	...	0600	0620	|	...	the same	2000	2020	|	...	2100	|	...	2200	|	...	2300	|	...	0000	...	0100
66	Baden 505 d.	0529	...	0608	0629	|	...		2008	2029	|	...	2108	|	...	2208	|	...	2308	|	...	0008	...	0108
	Liestal d.	|	...	|	|	0554	...	minutes	|	|	1954	...	|	2054	...	|	2154	...	|	2254	...	|	...	|
	Aarau 500 505 d.	|	...	|	|	0623	0653	past each	|	|	2023	2053	|	2123	2153	|	2223	2253	|	2323	...	|	...	|
	Lenzburg 505 d.	|	...	|	|	0631	0702	hour until	|	|	2031	2102	|	2131	2202	|	2231	2302	|	2331	...	|	...	|
88	**Zürich** HB ...500/5 530 535 a.	0549	...	0624	0649	0652	0722		2024	2049	2052	2122	2124	2152	2222	2224	2252	2322	2324	2352	...	0024	...	0124
	Zürich Flughafen ✈ 530 535 a.	0604f	...	...	0704f	...	...		...	2104f	...	...	...	...	...	...	...	...	...	...	...	...	...	...

km		⑥⑦j																						
	Zürich Flughafen ✈ 530 535 d.	...	...	...	...	0556f	...	...	...	0656f	...	...	and at	...	2056f	...	...	...	...	...	...	...	...	...
0	**Zürich** HB ...500/5 530 535 d.	0108	0508	0535	0608	0610	0636	0638	0708	0710	0736	0738		2108	2110	2136	2138	2208	2236	2238	2308	2336	2338	0008
32	Lenzburg 505 d.	0129	0529	|	0629	|	|	0658	0729	|	|	0758	the same	2129	|	|	2158	2229	|	2258	2329	|	2358	0029
41	**Aarau** 500 505 d.	0136	0536	|	0636	|	|	0705	0736	|	|	0805		2136	|	|	2205	2236	|	2305	2336	|	0005	0036
77	Liestal d.	0202	0602	|	0702	|	|	...	0802	|	|	...	minutes	2202	|	|	...	2302	|	...	0002	|	...	0102
	Baden 505 d.	|	|	0551	|	0632	0652	...	|	0732	0752	...	past each	|	2132	2152	...	|	2252	...	|	2352	...	|
	Brugg 505 d.	|	|	0600	|	0641	0702	...	|	0741	0802	...		|	2141	2202	...	|	2302	...	|	0002	...	|
	Rheinfelden d.	|	|	0634	|	0713	0734	...	|	0810	0834	...	hour until	|	2210	2234	...	|	2334	...	|	0034	...	|
91	**Basel** SBB a.	0214	0614	0650	0714	0732	0748	...	0814	0824	0850	...		2214	2224	2248	...	2314	2348	...	0014	0048	...	0114

G – International service from/to Germany (Table **910**).
L – ①–⑤ (not June 9, Oct. 3). From Karlsruhe (Table **910**).
M – [12] ✗ Frankfurt - Basel - Zürich - Milano and v.v.
P – From/to Paris (Table **370**). [R] for international journeys.
Q – Ⓒ Aug. 1–23.
R – July 29 - Aug. 24.
S – ①–⑥ (daily until June 28).

c – ⑥⑦ (also June 9, Oct. 3).
f – July 7 - Aug. 10 and from Oct. 4.
j – Also June 9, Aug. 1.
n – Not June 1, 8, 9, 15, 22, Aug. 1.
r – ①–④ (not June 9).
t – Ⓐ only.
v – Not July 29 - Aug. 24.

w – From June 29.
x – Not Oct. 3.
z – Not Aug. 1–23.
¶ – ✗ on Ⓐ.

511 BERN - NEUCHÂTEL - LA CHAUX DE FONDS - LE LOCLE SBB, BLS

km			Ⓐ															⊠							
0	**Bern** d.	...	0504	...	0553	0608	...	0653	0708	...	0753j	0808	...	0853j	0908	...	0953		1808	...	1853	1908	...	1953	2008
22	Kerzers d.	...	0531	...	0611	0631	...	0711	0731	...	0811	0831	...	0911	0931	...	1011	and at	1831	...	1911	1931	...	2011	2031
30	Ins 508 d.	...	0538	...	0618	0638	...	0718	0738	...	0818	0838	...	0918	0938	...	1018	the same	1838	...	1918	1938	...	2018	2038
43	**Neuchâtel** 508 d.	0529	0556	0600	0629	0656	0700	0729	0756	0800	0829	0856	0900	0929	0956	1000	1029	minutes	1856	1900	1929	1956	2000	2029	2056
72	**La Chaux de Fonds** a.	0557	...	0627	0657	...	0727	0757	...	0827	0857	...	0927	0957	...	1027	1057	past each	...	1927	1957	...	2027	2057	...
	La Chaux de Fonds d.	*0605*	...	0631	*0705*	...	0731	*0805*	...	0831	*0903*	...	0931	*1003*	...	1031	*1103*	hour until	...	1931	*2003*	...	2037	*2103*	...
80	**Le Locle** a.	*0614*	...	0640	*0714*	...	0740	*0814*	...	0840	*0912*	...	0940	*1012*	...	1040	*1112*		...	1940	*2012*	...	2046	*2112*	...

Bern d.	...	2053	2108	...	2153	2208	...	2253	2308	...	2337	0008
Kerzers d.	...	2111	2131	...	2211	2231	...	2311	2331	...	0003	0034
Ins 508 d.	...	2118	2138	...	2218	2238	...	2318	2338	...	0010	0041
Neuchâtel 508 d.	2100	2129	2156	2200	2229	2256	2300	2329	2356	0000	0026	0056
La Chaux de Fonds a.	2127	2157	...	2227	2257	...	2327	2357	...	0027	...	...
La Chaux de Fonds d.	2137	*2203*	...	2237	*2303*	...	2337	...	...	0037	...	...
Le Locle a.	2146	*2212*	...	2246	*2312*	...	2346	...	...	0046	...	...

		Ⓐ					Ⓐ		
Le Locle d.	...	*0450*	...	0520	...	*0550*	...	0620	...
La Chaux de Fonds a.	...	*0459*	...	0529	...	*0559*	...	0629	...
La Chaux de Fonds d.	...	0501	...	0532	...	0602	...	0632	...
Neuchâtel 508 d.	0502	0532	...	0600	0604	0632	0656	0700	0704
Ins 508 d.	0517	0542	...	...	0618	0642	0709	...	0718
Kerzers d.	0528	0549	...	...	0630	0649	0719	...	0730
Bern a.	0552	0608	...	...	0652	0708	0738	...	0752

Le Locle d.	*0650*	0720	...		*2050*	2120	...	*2150*	2220	...	*2250*	...	2320	...
La Chaux de Fonds a.	*0659*	0729	...	and at	*2059*	2129	...	*2159*	2229	...	*2259*	...	2329	...
La Chaux de Fonds d.	0702	0732	...	the same	2102	2132	...	2202	2232	...	2302	...	2332	...
Neuchâtel 508 d.	0732	0800	0804	minutes	2132	2200	2204	2232	2300	2304	2332	...	2400	0004
Ins 508 d.	0742	...	0818	past each	2142	...	2218	2242	...	2318	2342	...	...	0018
Kerzers d.	0749	...	0830	hour until	2149	...	2230	2249	...	2330	2349	...	...	0038r
Bern a.	0808	...	0852		2208	...	2252	2306	...	2352	0006	...	...	0103

j – 5 minutes **earlier** on Ⓐ until July 4.
r – Arrives 0027.
⊠ – Variations to connecting train departures from La Chaux de Fonds (to Le Locle): *1200* (not 1203), *1600* (not 1603) and *1700* (not 1703).

511a BERN - MURTEN - PAYERNE (- LAUSANNE) SBB, BLS

SERVICE FROM JUNE 9

km					Ⓐ												⊡										
0	**Bern** 511 d.	...	...	...	*0504*	0534	...	0608	0634	...	0708	0734	...	0808	0834	...		1308	1334	...	1408	1434	...	1508	1534	...
22	Kerzers ▲ 511 d.	...	...	...	0535	0606	...	0635	0706	...	0735	0806	...	0835	0906	...	and at	1335	1406	...	1435	1506	...	1535	1606	...
30	Murten a.	...	...	...	0543	0614	...	0643	0714	...	0743	0814	...	0843	0914	...	the same	1343	1414	...	1443	1514	...	1543	1614	...
	Murten d.	0438	...	0538	0545	0623t	0638	0645	0723t	0738	0745	0823t	0838	0845	...	0938	minutes	1345	...	1738	1445	1523t	1538	1545	1623t	1638
37	Avenches d.	0445	...	0545	0553	0630t	0645	0653	0730t	0745	0753	0830t	0845	0853	...	0945	past each	1353	...	1445	1453	1530t	1545	1553	1630t	1645
48	**Payerne** a.	0457	...	0557	...	0644t	0657	...	0744t	0757	...	0844t	0857	...	...	0957	hour until	...	...	1457	...	1544t	1557	...	1644t	1657
	Lausanne 504 a.	0602	...	0702	...	...	0802	...	...	0902	...	...	1002	...	...	1102		...	...	1602	...	...	1702	...	...	1802

Bern 511 d.	1608	1634	...	1708	1734	...	1808	1834	...	1908	*1934*	...	2008	2034	...	2108	2134	...	2208	2234	...	2308	2337	...	0008	...	...
Kerzers ▲ 511 d.	1635	1706	...	1735	1806	...	1835	1906	...	1935	2006	...	2035	2106	...	2135	2206	...	2235	2306	...	2335	0006	...	0035	...	...
Murten a.	1643	1714	...	1745	1814	...	1843	1914	...	1943	2014	...	2043	2114	...	2143	2214	...	2243	2314	...	2343	0014	...	0043	...	...
Murten d.	1645	...	1738	1745	1823t	1838	1845	1923t	1938	1945	...	2038	2045	...	2138	2145	...	2238	2245	...	2338	2345	...	...	0045	...	...
Avenches d.	1653	...	1745	1753	1830t	1845	1853	1930t	1945	1953	...	2045	2053	...	2145	2153	...	2245	2253	...	2345	2353	...	...	0053	...	...
Payerne a.	...	...	1757	...	1844t	1857	...	1944t	1957	...	...	2057	...	...	2157	...	...	2257	...	...	2357	...	...	...	...	...	...
Lausanne 504 a.	...	...	1902	...	...	2002	...	...	2102	...	...	2202	...	...	2302	...	...	0002	...	...	0102	...	...	...	...	...	...

Lausanne 504 d.	...	...	...	0458	...	...	0558	...	...	0658	...		...	0958	...	...	1058	...	...	1158	...	...	1258	...	...	1358
Payerne d.	0504	...	...	0604	0618t	...	0704	0718t	...	0804	...	and at	...	1104	...	...	1204	1218t	...	1304	...	...	1404	...	...	1504
Avenches d.	0515	...	0605	0615	0631t	0705	0715	0731t	0805	0815	...	the same	1105	1115	...	1205	1215	1231t	1305	1315	...	1405	1415	...	1505	1515
Murten a.	0523	...	0613	0623	0638t	0713	0723	0738t	0813	0823	...	minutes	1113	1123	...	1213	1223	1238t	1313	1323	...	1413	1423	...	1513	1523
Murten d.	...	0543	0614	...	0643	0714	...	0743	0814	...	0843	past each	1314	...	1143	1214	...	1243	1314	...	1343	1414	...	1443	1514	...
Kerzers ▲ 511 a.	...	0553	0624	...	0653	0724	...	0753	0824	...	0853	hour until	1124	...	1153	1224	...	1253	1324	...	1353	1424	...	1453	1524	...
Bern 511 a.	...	0626	0652	...	0726	0752	...	0826	0852	...	0926		1152	...	1226	1252	...	1326	1352	...	1426	1452	...	1526	1552	...

Lausanne 504 d.	...	...	1458	...	...	1558	...	...	1658	...	...	1758	...	...	1858	...	...	1958	...	...	2058	...	...	2158	...	...	2258
Payerne d.	1518t	...	1604	1618t	...	1704	1718t	...	1804	1818t	...	1904	1918t	...	2004	...	...	2104	...	...	2204	...	...	2304	...	...	0004
Avenches d.	1531t	1605	1615	1631t	1705	1715	1731t	1805	1815	1831t	1905	1915	1931t	2005	2015	...	2105	2115	...	2205	2215	...	2305	2315	...	0005	0015
Murten a.	1538t	1613	1623	1638t	1713	1723	1738t	1813	1823	1838t	1913	1823	1938t	2013	2023	...	2113	2123	...	2213	2223	...	2313	2323	...	0013	0023
Murten d.	1543	1614	...	1643	1714	...	1743	1814	...	1843	1914	...	1943	2014	...	2043	2114	...	2143	2214	...	2243	2314	...	2343	0014	*0043*
Kerzers ▲ 511 a.	1553	1624	...	1653	1724	...	1753	1824	...	1853	1924	...	1953	2024	...	2053	2124	...	2153	2224	...	2253	2324	...	2353	0024	*0053*
Bern 511 a.	1626	1652	...	1726	1752	...	1826	1852	...	1926	1952	...	2026	2052	...	2126	2152	...	2226	2252	...	2326	2352	...	0030	0103	...

t – Ⓐ only.

⊡ – The 1134 from Bern to Murten extends to Avenches (d. 1230), Payerne (a. 1244) on Ⓐ.

▲ – Connecting trains **KERZERS - LYSS**. *17 km*. Journey 19–20 minutes. From **Kerzers**: 0606 and hourly until 2306. From **Lyss**: 0535 and hourly until 2235; then 2336.

512 BIEL / BIENNE - LA CHAUX DE FONDS and MOUTIER SBB

km		⑥⑦r		Ⓐ									
0	**Biel / Bienne** d.	0026	...	0518	0547	0620	and at	1847	1920	1947	2047		2347
14	Sonceboz-Sombeval a.	0043	...	0535	0559	0637	the same	1859	1937	1959	2059	and	2359
14	Sonceboz-Sombeval d.	0047	...	0541	0600	0641	minutes	1900	1941	2000	2100	hourly	0000
28	St Imier d.	0104	...	0600	0613	0700	past each	1913	2000	2018	2118	until	0018
44	**La Chaux de Fonds** a.	0119	...	0617	0628	0717	hour until	1928	2017	2034	2134		0034

	Ⓐ											A	⑤⑥v
La Chaux de Fonds d.	0441	...	0532	0542	and at	1932	1942	2042	2142	2242	...	2342	2342
St Imier d.	0457	...	0545	0559	the same	1945	1959	2059	2159	2259	...	2359	2359
Sonceboz-Sombeval a.	0518	...	0558	0619	minutes	1958	2019	2119	2219	2319	...	0019	0019
Sonceboz-Sombeval d.	0520	...	0559	0621	past each	1959	2021	2121	2221	2321	...	0021	0021
Biel / Bienne a.	0538	...	0612	0640	hour until	2012	2041	2141	2241	2341	...	0041	0046

A – ⑦–④ (also Aug. 1).
B – Mornings of ①–⑤ until June 30.
D – Daily until June 29; ⑤⑥ from July 4 (not Aug. 1).
c – Ⓒ only.
j – Not July 7–11, 14–18, 21–25, 28–31, Aug. 4–8, 11–15, Oct. 6–10, 13–17.
r – Not Aug. 2.
v – Not Aug. 1.
△ – The 1521 from Moutier departs 1516 until Sept. 19 (no change to other timings).

(BIEL/BIENNE -) SONCEBOZ-SOMBEVAL - MOUTIER

km		Ⓐ		Ⓒ	Ⓐ	Ⓐ		Ⓐ					Ⓐ		Ⓐ			Ⓐ			D	D	D	B
	Biel / Bienne d.	...	0547c	0620	...	...	0720	...	0820	and	1120	1220	...	1320	...	and at the same	1820	...	1920	2020	2120	2220	2320	...
0	Sonceboz-Sombeval d.	0539	0603	0639	0639	0703	0739	0803	0839	hourly	1139	1239	1303	1339	1403	minutes past	1839	1903	1939	2043	2143	2243	2339	0003
7	Tavannes d.	0546	0610	0646	0646	0710	0746	0810	0846	until	1146	1246	1310	1346	1410	each hour until	1846	1910	1946	2050	2150	2250	2346	0010
25	**Moutier** a.	0611	0635	0711	0711j	0735	0811c	0835	0911		1211	1311c	1335	1411c	1435		1911c	1935	2011	2113	2213	2313	0011	0035

	Ⓐ		Ⓐ							Ⓐ		Ⓐ		△	Ⓐ					D	D		D	⑤⑥v
Moutier d.	0521	0545	0621	0645j	0721	0745c	0845	and	1145	1221	1245c	1321	1345c	and at the same	1821	1845c	1921	2025	...	2125	2225	...	2321	2321
Tavannes d.	0545	0609	0645	0709	0745	0809	0909	hourly	1209	1245	1309	1345	1409	minutes past	1845	1909	1945	2049	...	2149	2249	...	2345	2345
Sonceboz-Sombeval a.	0553	0616	0653	0716	0753	0816	0916	until	1216	1253	1316	1353	1416	each hour until	1853	1916	1953	2056	...	2156	2256	...	2353	2353
Biel / Bienne a.	...	0640	...	0741	...	0841	0941		1241	...	1341	...	1441		...	1941	...	2112	...	2212	2312	...	...	0015

513 BERN - BIEL SBB

km			⑥⑦n		Ⓐ												
0	**Bern** d.	0012	0112	...	0500	0530	0612	0642	and at the same	2012	2042	2112	2132	2212	2232	2312	2332
23	Lyss d.	0030	0135	...	0522	0552	0630	0700	minutes past	2030	2100	2130	2154	2230	2254	2330	2354
34	**Biel / Bienne** a.	0039	0144	...	0535	0605	0639	0709	each hour until	2039	2109	2139	2207	2239	2307	2339	0007

	⑥⑦n															
Biel / Bienne d.	0026	...	0518	0552	0622	0652	and at the same	2022	2052	2122	2154	2222	2254	2322	2354	...
Lyss d.	0035	...	0531	0601	0631	0701	minutes past	2031	2101	2131	2207	2231	2307	2331	0007	...
Bern a.	0052	...	0554	0618	0648	0718	each hour until	2048	2118	2148	2230	2248	2330	2348	0030	...

n – Also June 9, Aug. 1.

☛ Additional stopping services operate.

BLS — BERN - LUZERN — 514

SERVICE FROM AUGUST 1. See page 605 for service until July 31.

km		Ⓐ			Ⓐ	★				★					★				★					
0	**Bern** d.	...	...	...	0536	0600	...	0612	0636	0700	and at	...	2112	2136	2200	...	2212	2236	2300	2312	2342	0012	...	...
21	Konolfingen d.	...	...	...	0552	|	...	0634	0652	|	the same	...	2134	2152	|	...	2234	2252	|	2334	0005	0034	...	...
38	Langnau d.	0508	0536	0606	0606	|	0636	0652	0706	|	minutes	2136	2152	2206	|	2236	2252	2306	|	2352	0023	0052	...	...
75	Wolhusen d.	0545	0620	0645	0645	|	0720	...	0745	|	past each	2220	...	2245	|	2320	...	2345	|	...	...	...	...	...
96	**Luzern** a.	0603	0643	0703	0703	0701	0743	...	0803	0801	hour until	2243	...	2303	2301	2343	...	0010	0001	...	...	...	...	...

		Ⓐ		★				★					★					★					
Luzern d.	...	0450	...	0600	0557	...	0616	0700	0657	and at	...	2116	2200	2157	...	2216	2257	2300	...	2316	...	0016	...	...
Wolhusen d.	...	0514	...	|	0615	...	0644	|	0715	the same	...	2144	|	2215	...	2244	2315	|	...	2344	...	0041	...	...
Langnau d.	0507	0554	0607	|	0654	0707	0721	|	0754	minutes	2207	2221	|	2254	2307	2321	2351	|	0007	0021	...	0118	...	...
Konolfingen d.	0526	0607	0626	|	0707	0726	...	|	0807	past each	2226	...	|	2307	2326	...	...	|	0026	...	...	...	...	...
Bern a.	0548	0627	0648	0700	0727	0748	...	0800	0827	hour until	2248	...	2300	2327	2348	...	...	2400	0048	...	...	...	...	...

★ – Fast *IR* service via Zofingen (see Table **565**).

SBB — BIEL/BIENNE - DELÉMONT - DELLE - MEROUX — 515

km																								
0	**Biel / Bienne** 500a d.	...	...	...	...	0619	0719	0819	0919	1019	1119	1219	1319	1419	1519**c**	1619	1719	1819	1919	2019	2119	2219	...	2319
13	Grenchen Nord 500a d.	...	...	...	...	0629	0729	0829	0929	1029	1129	1229	1329	1429	1529**c**	1629	1729	1829	1929	2029	2129	2229	...	2329
24	Moutier 500a d.	...	...	...	...	0638	0738	0838	0938	1038	1138	1238	1338	1438	1538**c**	1638	1738	1838	1938	2038	2138	2238	...	2338
35	Delémont 500a d.	0417	0449	...	0551	0651	0751	0851	0951	1051	1151	1251	1351	1451	1551	1651	1751	1851	1951	2051	2151	2251	...	2351
47	Glovelier 500a d.	0429	0501	...	0603	0703	0803	0903	1003	1103	1203	1303	1403	1503	1603	1703	1803	1903	2003	2103	2203	2303	...	0003
63	Porrentruy 500a d.	0448	0520	...	0622	0722	0822	0922	1022	1122	1222	1322	1422	1522	1622	1722	1822	1922	2022	2122	2222	2322	...	0020
75	**Delle** 🏛 a.	0504	0536	...	0638	0738	0838	0938	1038	1138	1238	1338	1438	1538	1638	1738	1838	1938	2038	2138	2238	2338	...	...
75	**Delle** 🏛 370b d.	...	0541**r**	...	...	0741**k**	0841	0941	1041**e**	1141	1241	1341	...	...	1641**v**	1741**t**	1841	1941	...	2141	...	...	...	...
89	Meroux TGV ⊡ 370b a.	...	0556**r**	...	...	0756**k**	0856	0956	1056**e**	1156	1256	1356	...	...	1656**v**	1756**t**	1856	1956	...	2156	...	...	...	...

Meroux TGV ⊡ 370b d.	...	...	...	0603**r**	...	0803**k**	0903	1003	1103**e**	1203	1303	1403	...	...	1703**v**	1803**t**	1903	2003	...	...	2203	...	...	...
Delle 🏛 370b a.	...	...	...	0619**r**	...	0819**k**	0919	1019	1119**e**	1219	1319	1419	...	...	1719**v**	1819**t**	1919	2019	...	...	2219	...	...	...
Delle 🏛 d.	...	...	0518	0621	0721	0821	0921	1021	1121	1221	1321	1421	1521	1621	1721	1821	1921	2021	2121	...	2221	2321	...	0022
Porrentruy 500a d.	0436	...	0540	0640	0740	0840	0940	1040	1140	1240	1340	1440	1540	1640	1740	1840	1940	2040	2140	...	2240	2340	...	0042
Glovelier 500a d.	0451	...	0555	0655	0755	0855	0955	1055	1155	1255	1355	1455	1555	1655	1755	1855	1955	2055	2155	...	2255	2355	...	0057
Delémont 500a d.	0510	...	0612	0712	0812	0912	1012	1112	1212	1312	1412	1512	1612	1712	1812	1912	2012	2112	2212	...	2309	0009	...	0110
Moutier 500a d.	0520	...	0622	0722	0822	0922	1022	1122	1222	1322	1422	1522	1622	1722	1822	1922	2022	2122	2222	...	...	...	...	...
Grenchen Nord 500a d.	0530	...	0630	0730	0830	0930	1030	1130	1230	1330	1430	1530	1630	1730	1830	1930	2030	2130	2230	...	...	...	...	...
Biel / Bienne 500a a.	0541	...	0641	0741	0841	0941	1041	1141	1241	1341	1441	1541	1641	1741	1841	1941	2041	2142	2241	...	...	...	...	...

c – Ⓒ to Sept. 14; daily from Sept. 20.
e – ①–⑤ to July 4 (not June 9); ①–⑤ from Sept. 1 (not Nov. 11).
k – ⑥ to July 5; ①–⑥ July 7 - Aug. 30 (not July 14); ⑥ from Sept. 6.
r – ①–⑥ (not June 9, July 14, Aug. 1, Nov. 11).
t – ⑥ (also Aug. 15).
v – ⑦ (also June 9, July 14, Nov. 11).
⊡ – Meroux station platforms are located directly above the Belfort-Montbéliard TGV platforms.

CJ (narrow guage) — LA CHAUX DE FONDS - LE NOIRMONT - GLOVELIER and TAVANNES — 516

km		Ⓐ	Ⓐ	⚒	⚒							Ⓐ	Ⓐ										Y	Z
0	**La Chaux de Fonds** d.	...	0602	...	0702	...	0802	...	and at	1802	...	1832	...	1902	...	...	2002	...	...	2102	...	...	2237	2337
21	Le Noirmont a.	...	0627	...	0727	...	0827	...		1827	...	1856	...	1927	...	...	2027	...	...	2127	...	...	2302	0002
	Le Noirmont d.	0559	0634	0630	0729	0730	0829	0830	the same	1829	1830	1859	1908	1929	2011	...	2029	2111	...	2129	2211	...	2302	0002
	Tavannes a.	0642	|	0707	|	0807	|	0907	minutes	|	1907	|	1943	|	2045	...	|	2145	...	|	2245	...	|	|
26	Saignelégier a.	...	0641	...	0736	...	0836	...		1836	...	1906	...	1936	...	...	2036	...	...	2136	...	...	2309	0009
	Saignelégier d.	...	0650	...	0746	...	0846	...	past each	1846	...	...	...	1946	...	...	...	...	...	...	...	...	...	...
46	Combe-Tabeillon d.	...	0711	...	0808	...	0908	...	hour until	1908	...	...	...	2008	...	...	...	...	...	...	...	...	...	...
51	**Glovelier** a.	...	0721	...	0818	...	0918	...		1918	...	...	...	2018	...	...	...	...	...	...	...	...	...	...

km		Ⓐ	Ⓐ	⚒												Ⓐ								
	Glovelier d.	...	...	...	...	...	...	0741**a**	...	0841	and at	...	1541	...	1638	1705	...	1741	...	1841	...	1941	...	2041
	Combe-Tabeillon d.	...	...	...	...	...	...	0750**a**	...	0850		...	1550	...	1646	1714	...	1750	...	1850	...	1950	...	2050
	Saignelégier a.	...	...	...	...	...	...	0814**a**	...	0914	the same	...	1614	...	1714	1738	...	1814	...	1914	...	2014	...	2114
	Saignelégier d.	0518	...	0620	...	0720	...	0820	...	0920	minutes	...	1620	...	1720	1752	...	1820	...	1920	...	2020	...	2120
0	**Tavannes** d.	|	0547	|	0647	|	0747	|	0847	|		1547	|	1647	|	|	1747	|	1847	|	1947	|	2051	|
23	Le Noirmont a.	0524	0622	0625	0724	0727	0824	0827	0924	0927	past each	1624	1627	1724**b**	1727	1759	1824**b**	1827	1924	1927	2025	2027	2124	2127
	Le Noirmont d.	0524	...	0627	...	0727	...	0827	...	0927	hour until	...	1627	...	1727	1801	...	1827	...	1927	...	2027	...	2127
	La Chaux de Fonds a.	0552	...	0656	...	0756	...	0856	...	0956		...	1656	...	1756	1824	...	1856	...	1956	...	2056	...	2156

Y – ⑦–④ (also Aug. 1).
Z – ⑤⑥ (not Aug. 1).
a – Ⓐ only.
b – 2 minutes later on Ⓐ.

BLS — SOLOTHURN - BURGDORF - THUN — 517

km		⚒	⚒	⚒**d**			⚒**d**			⚒**d**			⚒**d**			⚒**d**									
0	**Solothurn** ▷ d.	...	0514	...	0542	0611**t**	...	0646	0717	...	0746	0817	...	0846	0917	...	0946	1017	...		2146	2217	...	2246	2317	...
5	Biberist Ost ▷ d.	...	0520	...	0547	0616**t**	...	0650	0722	...	0750	0822	...	0850	0922	...	0950	1022	...	and at	2150	2222	...	2250	2322	...
21	**Burgdorf** ▷ a.	...	0544	...	0610	0645	...	0712	0745	...	0812	0845	...	0912	0945	...	1012	1045	...		2212	2245	...	2312	2345	...
21	**Burgdorf** 505 d.	0448	0551	*0549*	0625	0651	*0649*	0725	0751	*0749*	0825	0851	*0849*	0925	0951	*0949*	1025	1051	*1049*	the same	2225	2251	*2249*	2325	2351	*2349*
28	Hasle-Rüegsau d.	0501	|	0601	0638	|	0702	0738	|	0802	0838	|	0902	0938	|	1002	1038	|	1102	minutes	2238	|	2302	2338	|	0001
46	Konolfingen a.	0523	|	0623	0659	|	0723	0759	|	0823	0859	|	0923	0959	|	1023	1059	|	1123		2259	|	2323	2359	|	0023
46	Konolfingen d.	0536	|	0636	0700	|	0736	0800	|	0836	0900	|	0936	1000	|	1036	1100	|	1136	past each	2300	|	2336	0000	|	0036
	Bern ... 505 560 d.	|	0612	|	|	0712	|	|	0812	|	|	0912	|	|	1012	|	|	1112	|	hour until	|	2312	|	|	0012	|
	Belp d.	|	0624	|	|	0724	|	|	0824	|	|	0924	|	|	1024	|	|	1124	|		|	2324	|	|	0032	|
61	**Thun** 560 a.	0557	0651	0657	0719	0751	0757	0819	0851	0857	0919	0951	0957	1019	1051	1057	1119	1151	1157		2319	2351	2357	0019	0059	0057

km			Ⓐ	⚒**d**			⚒**d**			⚒**d**			⚒**d**			⚒**d**										
0	**Thun** 560 d.	0502	0540	0603	0608	0640	0703	0708	0740	0803	0808	0840	0903	0908	0940	1003	1008	1040	1103	1108		2240	2303	2308	2340	0003
22	Belp d.	0528	|	|	0635	|	|	0735	|	|	0835	|	|	0935	|	|	1035	|	|	1135	and at	|	|	2335	|	|
34	**Bern** ... 505 560 d.	0550	|	|	0650	|	|	0750	|	|	0850	|	|	0950	|	|	1050	|	|	1150		|	|	2350	|	|
	Konolfingen a.	|	0559	0624	|	0659	0724	|	0759	0824	|	0859	0924	|	0959	1024	|	1059	1124	|	the same	2259	2324	|	2359	0024
	Konolfingen d.	|	0559	0635	|	0659	0735	|	0759	0835	|	0859	0935	|	0959	1035	|	1059	1135	|	minutes	2259	2335	|	2359	0035
	Hasle-Rüegsau d.	|	0622	0656	|	0722	0756	|	0822	0856	|	0922	0956	|	1022	1056	|	1122	1156	|		2322	2356	|	0022	0058
57	**Burgdorf** 505 a.	0608	0632	*0711*	0708	0732	*0811*	0808	0832	*0911*	0908	0932	*1011*	1008	1032	*1111*	1108	1132	*1211*	1208	past each	2332	*0011*	0008	0032	0107
57	**Burgdorf** ▷ d.	0615	0647	...	0715	0747	...	0815	0847	...	0915	0947	...	1015	1047	...	1115	1147	...	1215	hour until	2347	...	0015	...	...
73	Biberist Ost ▷ d.	0635	0705	...	0735	0805	...	0835	0905	...	0935	1005	...	1035	1105	...	1135	1205	...	1235		0005	...	0035	...	...
78	**Solothurn** ▷ a.	0642	0712	...	0742	0812	...	0842	0912	...	0942	1012	...	1042	1112	...	1142	1212	...	1242		0012	...	0042	...	...

d – Runs daily Konolfingen - Thun and v.v.
t – 6 minutes later on Ⓒ.
▷ – Additional trains Solothurn - Burgdorf and v.v.: **From Solothurn** at 2346 and 0017. **From Burgdorf** at 0502 ⚒, 0527 and 0647 Ⓒ.

Narrow gauge. RBS — BERN - SOLOTHURN — 518

km		⚒	⚒		Ⓐ		Ⓐ			Ⓐ		Ⓐ		Ⓐ								
0	**Bern** RBS d.	0511	0550	0605	0620	0635	0650	and at the same	1705	1720	1735	1750	1805	1820	1835	1905	and every	2235	2305	2335	...	0011
14	Jegenstorf d.	0530	0603	0618	0633	0648	0703	minutes past	1718	1733	1748	1803	1818	1833	1848	1918	30 minutes	2248	2318	2348	...	0030
34	**Solothurn** a.	0555	0625	0640	0655	0710	0725	each hour until	1740	1755	1810	1825	1840	1855	1910	1940	until	2310	2340	0013	...	0055

			Ⓐ		Ⓐ			Ⓐ		Ⓐ												
Solothurn d.	0515	0547	0602	0617	0632	0647	and at the same	1802	1817	1832	1847	1917	1947	2017	2047	2117	2147	2217	2247	2317	...	2350
Jegenstorf d.	0539	0609	0624	0639	0654	0709	minutes past	1824	1839	1854	1909	1939	2009	2039	2109	2139	2209	2239	2309	2339	...	0013
Bern RBS a.	0552	0622	0637	0652	0707	0722	each hour until	1837	1852	1907	1922	1952	2022	2052	2122	2152	2222	2252	2322	2352	...	0031

519 ZÜRICH - RAPPERSWIL - PFÄFFIKON

SBB (S-Bahn **5** and **7**)

km																										
0	**Zürich** HB .... **520** d.	0541	0554	0611	0624	0641	0654		2011	2024	2041	2054	2111	2124	2141	2154	2211	2224	2241	2254	2311	2324	2341	2354
	Meilen .... d.	0558	│	0628	│	0658	│	and at	2028	│	2058	│	2128	│	2158	│	2228	│	2258	│	2328	│	2358	│
	Stäfa .... d.	0608	│	0638	│	0708	│	the same	2038	│	2108	│	2138	│	2208	│	2238	│	2308	│	2338	│	0008	│
19	Uster .... d.	│	0609	│	0639	│	0709	minutes	│	2039	│	2109	│	2139	│	2209	│	2239	│	2309	│	2339	│	0009
26	Wetzikon .... d.	│	0615	│	0645	│	0715	past each	│	2045	│	2115	│	2145	│	2215	│	2245	│	2315	│	2345	│	0015
41	**Rapperswil** .... a.	0622	0631	0652	0701	0722	0731	hour until	2052	2101	2122	2131	2152	2201	2222	2231	2252	2301	2322	2331	2352	0001	0022	0031
	Rapperswil .... **525** d.	...	0632	...	0710	...	0732		...	2110	...	2132	...	...	...	...	...	...	...	...	...	...	...	...
45	Pfäffikon ...... **520 525** a.	...	0638	...	0715	...	0738		...	2115	...	2138	...	...	...	...	...	...	...	...	...	...	...	...

km																								
	Pfäffikon ...... **520 525** d.	...	...	...	0622r	...	0651	...	0722	...		2051	...	2122	...	2151	...	...	...	...	...	...	...	...
	Rapperswil .... **525** d.	...	...	...	0627r	...	0656	...	0727	...	and at	2056	...	2127	...	2156	...	...	...	...	...	...	...	...
0	**Rapperswil** .... d.	0539	0559	0609	0629	0639	0659	0709	0729	0739	the same	2059	2109	2129	2139	2159	2209	2229	2239	2259	2309	2329	2339	2359
	Wetzikon .... d.	│	0615	│	0645	│	0715	│	0745	│	minutes	2115	│	2145	│	2215	│	2245	│	2315	│	2345	│	0015
	Uster .... d.	│	0621	│	0651	│	0721	│	0751	│	past each	2121	│	2151	│	2221	│	2251	│	2321	│	2351	│	0021
9	Stäfa .... d.	0553	│	0623	│	0653	│	0723	│	0753	hour until	│	2123	│	2153	│	2223	│	2253	│	2323	│	2353	│
16	Meilen .... d.	0603	│	0633	│	0703	│	0733	│	0803		│	2133	│	2203	│	2233	│	2303	│	2333	│	0003	│
32	**Zürich** HB .... **520** a.	0617	0635	0647	0705	0717	0735	0747	0805	0817		2135	2147	2205	2217	2235	2247	2305	2317	2335	2347	0005	0017	0035

r – ⚒ only.

☛ Additional trains run Zürich - Rapperswil via Uster.

520 ZÜRICH - SARGANS - CHUR

SBB

See Table **534** for other connecting trains Sargans - Buchs and v.v. Trains operated by SOB convey (🍷).

km		*IR* 2395		*IR* 2353	*IC* 557	*RJX* 161	*IC* 911	*IR* 2355	*IC* 559	*IC* 1253	*IC* 913	*IR* 2359	*IC* 561	*IC* 901	*EC* 163	*IC* 1255	*IR* 2361	*IC* 563	*ICE* 271	*IR* 2363	*IC* 565	*RJX* 165	*IC* 919	*IR* 2365	*IC* 567	*IC* 903
										Ⓐ	Ⓒ		Ⓐ	Ⓒ		Ⓒ							Ⓒ		Ⓐ	Ⓒ
		◇		B⊡	✕	E✕	✕	⊡	✕	✕	✕	B⊡	✕	A✕	E✕	✕	B⊡	✕	G✕	B⊡	✕	H✕	✕	B⊡	✕	A✕
	Basel SBB **510** ...... d.	...	...	...	...	...	...	...	0633	0706	...	...	0733	...	...	0806v	...	0833	0906	...	0933	...	...	...	...	...
0	**Zürich** HB **522 555** ¶ d.	0023	...	0612	0638	0640	0707	0712	0738	0807	0807	0812	0838	0838	0840	0907	0912	0938	1007	1012	1038	1040	1107	1112	1138	1138
12	Thalwil .... **555** d.	0031	...	0621	│	│	│	0721	│	│	│	0821	│	│	│	│	0921	│	│	1021	│	│	│	1121	│	│
24	Wädenswil .... **522** d.	0040	...	0631	│	│	│	0731	│	│	│	0831	│	│	│	│	0931	│	│	1031	│	│	│	1131	│	│
33	Pfäffikon .... **522** ¶ d.	0048	...	0641	│	│	│	0741	│	│	│	0841	│	│	│	│	0941	│	│	1041	│	│	│	1141	│	│
57	Ziegelbrücke ...... **522** d.	0103	...	0700	│	│	│	0800	│	│	│	0900	│	│	│	│	1000	│	│	1100	│	│	│	1200	│	│
90	**Sargans** .... **534** d.	0125	...	0726	0733	0736	0803	0826	0833	0903	0903	0926	0933	0933	0936	1003	1026	1033	1103	1126	1133	1136	1203	1226	1233	1233
106	Buchs .... **534** a.	│	...	│	│	0748	│	│	│	│	│	│	│	│	0948	│	│	│	│	│	│	1148	│	│	│	│
103	Landquart .... **534 545** d.	0137	...	0738	0742	...	0812	0838	0842	0912	0912	0938	0942	0942	...	1012	1038	1042	1112	1138	1142	...	1212	1238	1242	1242
116	**Chur** .... **534 545** a.	0147	...	0748	0752	...	0822	0848	0852	0922	0922	0948	0952	0922	...	1022	1048	1052	1122	1148	1152	...	1222	1248	1252	1252

	IC 921	*IR* 2367	*IC* 569	*RJX* 167	*IC* 923	*IR* 2369	*IC* 571	*IC* 773	*IR* 2371	*IC* 573	*IC* 907	*RJX* 169	*IC* 927	*IR* 2373	*IC* 575	*IC* 929	*IR* 2375	*IC* 577	*IC* 909	*RJX* 367	*IC* 931	*IR* 2377	*IC* 579	*IC* 933	*IR* 2379	*IC* 581
					Ⓒ					Ⓐ	Ⓒ		Ⓒ					Ⓐ	Ⓒ							
	✕	B◇	✕	J✕		B⊡	✕	✕	B⊡	✕	A✕	E✕	✕	B⊡	✕	✕	B⊡	✕	A✕	E✕	✕	B⊡	✕	✕	B⊡	✕
Basel SBB **510** ...... d.	...	...	1133	...	...	...	1233c	1306	...	...	...	...	...	...	1433	...	...	...	...	...	...	...	1633	...	...	1733j
Zürich HB. **522 555** ¶ d.	1207	1212	1238	1240	1307	1312	1338	1407	1412	1438	1438	1440	1507	1512	1538	1607	1612	1638	1638	1640	1707	1712	1738	1807	1812	1838
Thalwil .... **555** d.	│	1221	│	│	│	1321	│	│	1421	│	│	│	│	1521	│	│	1621	│	│	│	│	1721	│	│	1821	│
Wädenswil .... **522** d.	│	1231	│	│	│	1331	│	│	1431	│	│	│	│	1531	│	│	1631	│	│	│	│	1731	│	│	1831	│
Pfäffikon .... **522** ¶ d.	│	1241	│	│	│	1341	│	│	1441	│	│	│	│	1541	│	│	1641	│	│	│	│	1741	│	│	1841	│
Ziegelbrücke ...... **522** d.	│	1300	│	│	│	1400	│	│	1500	│	│	│	│	1600	│	│	1700	│	│	│	│	1800	│	│	1900	│
Sargans .... **534** d.	1303	1326	1333	1336	1403	1426	1433	1503	1526	1533	1533	1536	1603	1626	1633	1703	1726	1733	1733	1736	1803	1826	1833	1903	1926	1933
Buchs .... **534** a.	│	│	│	1348	│	│	│	│	│	│	│	1548	│	│	│	│	│	│	│	1748	│	│	│	│	│	│
Landquart .... **534 545** d.	1312	1338	1342	...	1412	1438	1442	1512	1538	1542	1542	...	1612	1638	1642	1712	1738	1742	1742	...	1812	1838	1842	1912	1938	1942
Chur .... **534 545** a.	1322	1348	1352	...	1422	1448	1452	1522	1548	1552	1552	...	1622	1648	1652	1722	1748	1752	1752	...	1822	1848	1852	1922	1948	1952

	RJX 369	*IR* 2381	*IC* 583	*IR* 2383	*IC* 585	*IR* 2385	*IC* 597	*IC* 587	*IR* 2391	*IC* 589	*IR* 2393
							⑤–⑦	①–④			
	E✕	B⊡	✕	B⊡	✕	B⊡	e	d	⊡		⊡
Basel SBB **510** ...... d.	...	...	1833	...	...	...	...	2033	...	...	...
Zürich HB. **522 555** ¶ d.	1840	1912	1938	2012	2038	2112	2138	2138	2212	2238	2312
Thalwil .... **555** d.	│	1921	│	2021	│	2121	│	│	2221	│	2321
Wädenswil .... **522** d.	│	1931	│	2031	│	2131	│	│	2231	│	2331
Pfäffikon .... **522** ¶ d.	│	1941	│	2041	│	2141	│	│	2241	│	2341
Ziegelbrücke ...... **522** d.	│	2000	│	2100	│	2200	│	│	2300	│	0000
Sargans .... **534** d.	1936	2026	2033	2128	2133	2228	2233	2233	2328	2336	0031
Buchs .... **534** a.	1948	│	│	│	│	│	│	│	│	│	│
Landquart .... **534 545** d.	...	2038	2042	2140	2142	2240	2242	2242	2340	2349	0042
Chur .... **534 545** a.	...	2048	2052	2149	2152	2249	2252	2252	2348	2400	0051

	IR 2350	*IR* 2354	*IC* 556	*IR* 2356	*IC* 558	*IR* 2358	*IC* 912	*IC* 560	*IR* 2360	*IC* 562
	⚒	†	⚒				Ⓐ			
	◇	B◇	✕	B⊡	✕	B⊡	✕	✕	B◇	✕
Chur .... **534 545** d.	0411	0411	0508	0511	0608	0611	0638	0708	0711	0808
Landquart .... **534 545** d.	0420	0420	0518	0520	0618	0620	0648	0718	0720	0818
Buchs .... **534** d.	│	│	│	│	│	│	│	│	│	│
Sargans .... **534** d.	0433	0433	0527	0533	0627	0633	0657	0727	0733	0827
Ziegelbrücke .... **522** d.	0500	0500	│	0600	│	0700	│	│	0800	│
Pfäffikon .... **522** ¶ d.	0519	0519	│	0619	│	0719	│	│	0819	│
Wädenswil .... **522** d.	0529	0529	│	0629	│	0729	│	│	0829	│
Thalwil .... **555** d.	0539	0539	│	0639	│	0739	│	│	0839	│
Zürich HB ...... **522 555** ¶ a.	0548	0548	0622	0648	0722	0748	0753	0822	0848	0922
Basel SBB **510** .... a.	...	...	0728	...	...	...	...	0928	...	...

	IR 2362	*IC* 916	*IC* 564	*IR* 2364	*IC* 918	*RJX* 366	*IC* 566	*IC* 900	*IR* 2366	*IC* 770	*IC* 568	*IR* 2368	*IC* 922	*RJX* 368	*IC* 570	*IR* 2370	*ICE* 70	*IC* 572	*IC* 902	*IR* 2372	*IC* 926	*RJX* 160	*IC* 574	*IR* 2374	*IC* 928	*IC* 576
					Ⓒ		Ⓐ	Ⓒ					Ⓒ					Ⓐ	Ⓒ		Ⓒ					
	B⊡	✕	✕	B⊡	✕	E✕	✕	A✕	B◧	✕	✕	B⊡		E✕	✕	B⊡	G✕	✕	A✕	B⊡	✕	J✕	✕	B⊡	✕	✕
Chur .... **534 545** d.	0811	0838	0908	0911	0938	...	1008	1008	1011	1038	1108	1111	1138	...	1208	1211	1238	1308	1308	1311	1338	...	1408	1411	1438	1508
Landquart .... **534 545** d.	0820	0848	0918	0920	0948	...	1018	1018	1020	1048	1118	1120	1148	...	1218	1220	1248	1318	1318	1320	1348	...	1418	1420	1448	1518
Buchs .... **534** d.	│	│	│	│	│	1011	│	│	│	│	│	│	│	1211	│	│	│	│	│	│	│	1411	│	│	│	│
Sargans .... **534** d.	0833	0857	0927	0933	0957	1023	1027	1027	1033	1057	1127	1133	1157	1223	1227	1233	1257	1327	1327	1333	1357	1423	1427	1433	1457	1527
Ziegelbrücke ...... **522** d.	0900	│	│	1000	│	│	│	│	1100	│	│	1200	│	│	│	1300	│	│	│	1400	│	│	│	1500	│	│
Pfäffikon .... **522** ¶ d.	0919	│	│	1019	│	│	│	│	1119	│	│	1219	│	│	│	1319	│	│	│	1419	│	│	│	1519	│	│
Wädenswil .... **522** d.	0929	│	│	1029	│	│	│	│	1129	│	│	1229	│	│	│	1329	│	│	│	1429	│	│	│	1529	│	│
Thalwil .... **555** d.	0939	│	│	1039	│	│	│	│	1139	│	│	1239	│	│	│	1339	│	│	│	1439	│	│	│	1539	│	│
Zürich HB. **522 555** ¶ a.	0948	0953	1022	1048	1053	1120	1122	1122	1148	1153	1222	1248	1253	1320	1322	1348	1353	1422	1422	1448	1453	1520	1522	1548	1553	1622
Basel SBB **510** ...... a.	...	...	1128	...	...	...	...	...	...	1253	1328	...	...	...	...	...	1453	...	...	...	...	...	...	...	...	1728

	IR 2376	*IC* 930	*RJX* 162	*IC* 578	*IC* 906	*IR* 2378	*IC* 932	*IC* 580	*IR* 2380	*IC* 934	*EC* 164	*IC* 582	*IC* 908	*IR* 2384	*IC* 936	*IC* 584	*IR* 2388	*IC* 938	*RJX* 166	*IC* 586	*IR* 2392	*IC* 588	*IR* 2394	*RJX* 168	*IR* 2396	*IR* 2398
		Ⓒ		Ⓐ	Ⓒ							Ⓐ	Ⓒ			‡		†								P
	B⊡	✕	H✕	✕	A✕	B⊡	✕	✕	B⊡	✕	E✕	✕	L✕	B⊡	✕	✕	B⊡		E✕	✕	⊡	✕	⊡	E✕	◇	⊡
Chur .... **534 545** d.	1511	1538	...	1608	1608	1611	1638	1708	1711	1738	...	1808	1808	1811	1838	1908	1911	1938	...	2008	2011	2108	2111	...	2211	2311
Landquart .... **534 545** d.	1520	1548	...	1618	1618	1620	1648	1718	1720	1748	...	1818	1818	1820	1848	1918	1920	1948	...	2018	2020	2118	2120	...	2220	2320
Buchs .... **534** d.	│	│	1611	│	│	│	│	│	│	│	1811	│	│	│	│	│	│	│	2011	│	│	│	│	2211	│	│
Sargans .... **534** d.	1533	1557	1623	1627	1627	1633	1657	1727	1733	1757	1823	1827	1827	1833	1857	1927	1933	1957	2023	2027	2033	2127	2133	2223	2233	2333
Ziegelbrücke ...... **522** d.	1600	│	│	│	│	1700	│	│	1800	│	│	│	│	1900	│	│	2000	│	│	│	2100	│	2200	│	2300	0000
Pfäffikon .... **522** ¶ d.	1619	│	│	│	│	1719	│	│	1819	│	│	│	│	1919	│	│	2019	│	│	│	2119	│	2219	│	2319	0019
Wädenswil .... **522** d.	1629	│	│	│	│	1729	│	│	1829	│	│	│	│	1929	│	│	2029	│	│	│	2129	│	2229	│	2329	0029
Thalwil .... **555** d.	1639	│	│	│	│	1739	│	│	1839	│	│	│	│	1939	│	│	2039	│	│	│	2139	│	2239	│	2339	0039
Zürich HB. **522 555** ¶ a.	1648	1653	1720	1722	1722	1748	1753	1822	1848	1853	1920	1922	1922	1948	1953	2022	2048	2053	2120	2122	2148	2222	2248	2323	2348	0048
Basel SBB **510** ...... a.	...	...	...	1828	...	...	...	...	...	...	...	2028	...	...	...	2128	...	...	...	...	...	...	...	...	...	...

A – From / to Genève (Table **500**).
B – From / to Bern (Table **505**).
E – International service to / from stations in Austria (Tables **86** and **951**).
G – International service from / to stations in Germany (Tables **73** and **910**).
H – 🅁 ✕ Budapest - Wien - Zürich and v.v. (Table **86**).
J – 🅁 ✕ Bratislava - Wien - Zürich and v.v. (Table **86**).
L – To Lausanne (Table **500**).
P – ①②③④⑥⑦ (also Aug. 1).

c – Ⓒ only.
d – Not June 9.
e – Also June 9.
j – Ⓐ only.
v – Not Aug. 1.

◇ – Operated by SOB.
⊡ – Operated by either SBB or SOB.
‡ – Train number **590** on ⑥.
¶ – See Table **519** for other trains Zürich - Pfäffikon via Uster.

SBB, SOB (ZÜRICH -) ZIEGELBRÜCKE - LINTHAL 522

km												
	Zürich HB 520 d.	...	...	...	0643		1743	...	1843	...		...
	Wädenswil 520 d.	...	...	...	0700	and	1800	...	1900	...	and	...
	Pfäffikon 520 d.	...	...	...	0707		1807	...	1907	...		...
0	**Ziegelbrücke** 520 d.	0434	0534	0634	0734	hourly	1834	1902	1934	2002	hourly	2302
11	Glarus d.	0446	0546	0646	0746		1846	1916	1946	2016		2316
16	Schwanden d.	0459	0559	0659	0759	until	1859	1929	1954	2029	until	2329
27	**Linthal** a.	0516	0616	0716	0816		1916	1946	...	2046		2346

	Ⓐ								
Linthal d.	0442	0542		1842	...	1946	2012		0012
Schwanden d.	0504	0604	and	1904	1934	2004	2034	and	0034
Glarus d.	0514	0614		1914	1944	2014	2044		0044
Ziegelbrücke 520 a.	0525	0625	hourly	1925	1957	2025	2057	hourly	0057
Pfäffikon 520 a.	0552	0652		1952	...	...	...		...
Wädenswil 520 a.	0600	0700	until	2000	...	...	...	until	...
Zürich HB 520 a.	0617	0717		2017	...	...	...		...

SOB LUZERN - ARTH GOLDAU - ST GALLEN 525

km			IR 2009 V			Ⓐ	IR 2011 V	Ⓒ				IR 2013 V			IR 2015 V	⊠			IR 2039 V		IR 2041 V		IR 2043 V	IR 16891	IR 2045 ⑥⑦c
0	**Luzern** 547 550 d.	...	...	...	...	*0539*	...	*0539*	...	...	*0639*	...	...	...	0739		...	...	1939	...	*2039*	...	*2139*	*2218*	...
16	Küssnacht am Rigi d.	...	...	...	...	*0558*	...	*0558*	...	...	*0658*	...	...	...	0800	and at	...	...	2000	...	*2059*	...	*2159*	|	...
28	**Arth Goldau** 547 550 a.	...	...	...	...	*0610*	...	*0610*	...	...	*0710*	...	...	...	0811		...	...	2011	...	*2111*	...	*2211*	*2245*	...
28	**Arth Goldau** d.	...	*0510*a	...	...	0615	...	0615	...	...	0715	...	...	...	0816	the same	...	...	2016	...	2116	...	2216	2315	...
	Einsiedeln ● d.	0516	|	0543r	0616	|	...	|	0645	0711	|	...	0745	0811	|		1945	2011	|	2111	|	2211	|	|	...
48	Biberbrugg ● d.	0523	0538a	0550r	0625	0637	0638	0640	0651	0725f	0737	0738	0751	0825f	0838	minutes	1951	2025f	2038	2125f	2138	2225f	2238	2339	...
54	Samstagern ● d.	0533	|	0600	0633	...	|	...	0700	0733	...	|	0800	0833	|		2000	2033	|	2133	2145	2233	2245	2348	...
62	Pfäffikon d.	0546	0554a	0616	0646	...	0654	...	0716	0746	...	0754	0816	0846	0854	past each	2016	2046	2054	2146	2154	2246	2254	0001	...
66	**Rapperswil** a.	0553	0603a	0623	0653	...	0703	...	0723	0753	...	0803	0823	0853	0903		2023	2053	2103	2153	2203	2253	2303	0006	...
66	**Rapperswil** d.	...	0607	...	...	...	0707	...	...	...	...	0807	...	...	0907	hour until	...	...	2107	...	2207	...	2307	...	0007
94	Wattwil d.	...	0627	...	...	...	0727	...	...	...	...	0827	...	...	0927		...	...	2127	...	2227	...	2327	...	0028
117	Herisau d.	...	0647	...	...	...	0747	...	...	...	...	0847	...	...	0947		...	...	2147	...	2247	...	2347	...	0048
125	**St Gallen** a.	...	0655	...	...	...	0755	...	...	...	...	0855	...	...	0955		...	...	2155	...	2255	...	2355	...	0056

			IR 2006 V				IR 2008 V				IR 2010 V		⊠		IR 2034 V			IR 2036 V		IR 2038 V			IR 2040 V	IR 2042 V	IR 2044 V
St Gallen d.	...	...	0505	...	...	...	0605	...	...	...	0705	...		...	1905	...	...	2005	...	2105	...	...	2205	2305	0005
Herisau d.	...	...	0513	...	...	...	0613	...	...	...	0713	...	and at	...	1913	...	...	2013	...	2113	...	...	2213	2313	0013
Wattwil d.	...	...	0532	...	...	...	0632	...	...	...	0732	...		...	1932	...	...	2032	...	2132	...	...	2232	2332	0032
Rapperswil a.	...	...	0553	...	...	...	0653	...	...	...	0753	...	the same	...	1953	...	...	2053	...	2153	...	...	2253	2353	0056
Rapperswil d.	...	*0536*	0556	0606	...	...	0656	0706	...	0736	0756	0806		1936	1956	2006	2036	2056	2106	2156	...	2206	*2256*	*0006*	...
Pfäffikon d.	...	*0542*	0602	0612	...	...	0702	0712	...	0742	0802	0812	minutes	1942	2002	2012	2042	2102	2112	2202	...	2212	*2301*	*0011*	...
Samstagern ● d.	...	*0555*	|	0625	...	...	|	0725	...	0755	|	0825		1955	|	2025	2055	2111	2125	2211	...	2225	*2313*	*0024*	...
Biberbrugg ● d.	*0540*a	0606	0618	0639j	0640	...	0718	0739j	0738	0805	0820	0839j	past each	2005	2020	2039j	2105	2120	2139j	2219	2222	2239j	*2322*	...	...
Einsiedeln ● a.	|	|	[redacted]	0646	|	...	|	0746	|	0812	|	0846		2012	|	2046	2112	|	2146	...	|	2246	|	...	...
Arth Goldau a.	*0605*a	0635	...	...	0705	...	*0745*	...	0804	...	0845	...	hour until	...	2045	...	...	2145	...	...	2248	...	*2348*	...	...
Arth Goldau 547 550 d.	0620	...	0646	...	*0715*	0747	...	...	*0815*	...	0849	...		...	2049	...	...	*2149*	...	...	*2315*	...	...	...	...
Küssnacht am Rigi d.	0632	...	0700	...	|	0800	...	...	|	...	0901	...		...	2101	...	...	*2201*	...	...	|	...	...	...	...
Luzern 547 550 a.	0653	...	0721	...	*0741*	0821	...	...	*0841*	...	0921	...		...	2121	...	...	*2221*	...	...	*2341*	...	...	...	...

EINSIEDELN - BIBERBRUGG - WÄDENSWIL

km		Ⓐ							and at			
0	**Einsiedeln** d.	0454	0524	0557	0624	0657	0724	0759	the same	2224	2259	2324
6	Biberbrugg d.	0501	0532	0607	0632	0707	0732	0807	minutes	2232	2307	2332
11	Samstagern d.	0509	0541	0617	0641	0717	0741	0817	past each	2241	2317	2341
17	**Wädenswil** a.	0518	0550	0626	0650	0726	0750	0826	hour until	2250	2326	2350

	Ⓐ					and at			
Wädenswil d.	0541	0610	0634	0710	0734	the same	2310	2334	0015
Samstagern d.	0550	0617	0641	0717	0741	minutes	2317	2341	0026
Biberbrugg d.	0558	0626	0651	0726	0751	past each	2326	2351	0033
Einsiedeln a.	0605	0633	0658	0733	0758	hour until	2333	2358	0040

V – VORALPEN EXPRESS – Most convey (🍷).
a – Ⓐ only.
c – Also June 9, Aug. 1.
f – Arrives 7 minutes earlier.
j – Arrives 5 minutes earlier.
r – On Ⓒ Einsiedeln d. 0545, Biberbrugg d. 0551.
⊠ – Train numbers increase by 2 each hour.
● – See panel below main table for services Einsiedeln - Samstagern - Wädenswil and v.v.

AB (narrow gauge) GOSSAU - APPENZELL - WASSERAUEN 526

km		Ⓐ	e																						
0	**Gossau** ▷ d.	0551	0621	0651	0721	0751	and at	1021	1051	1121	1151	1221	1251	1321	1351	1421	1451	1521	1551	1621	1651	1721	1751	1851	1951	2051
5	Herisau ▷ d.	0558	0628	0658	0728	0758	the same	1028	1058	1128	1158	1228	1258	1328	1358	1428	1458	1528	1558	1628	1658	1728	1758	1858	1958	2058
15	Urnäsch ▷ d.	0613	0643	0713	0743	0813	minutes	1043	1113	1143	1213	1243	1313	1343	1413	1443	1513	1543	1613	1643	1713	1743	1813	1913	2013	2113
26	**Appenzell** ▷ a.	0630	0700	0730	0800	0830	past each	1100	1130	1200	1230	1300	1330	1400	1430	1500	1530	1600	1630	1700	1730	1800	1830	1930	2030	2130
32	**Wasserauen** a.	0642	0712	0742	0812t	0842	hour until	1112t	1142	1212	1242	1312	1342t	1412	1442t	1512	1542t	1612	1642	1712	1742	1812	1842	*1945**	*2045**	*2145*‡

Wasserauen d.	...	0648a	0718e	0748	0818t	and at	1118t	1148	1218	1248	1318	1348t	1418	1448t	1518	1548t	1618	1648	1718	1748	1818	1848	...	*1947**	*2047**	*2147*‡
Appenzell ▷ d.	0630	0700	0730	0800	0830	the same	1130	1200	1230	1300	1330	1400	1430	1500	1530	1600	1630	1700	1730	1800	1830	1900	1930	2000	2100	2200
Urnäsch ▷ d.	0645	0715	0745	0815	0845	minutes	1145	1215	1245	1315	1345	1415	1445	1515	1545	1615	1645	1715	1745	1815	1845	1915	1945	2015	2115	2215
Herisau ▷ d.	0702	0732	0802	0832	0902	past each	1202	1232	1302	1332	1402	1432	1502	1532	1602	1632	1702	1732	1802	1832	1902	1932	2002	2032	2132	2232
Gossau ▷ a.	0708	0738	0808	0838	0908	hour until	1208	1238	1308	1338	1408	1438	1508	1538	1608	1638	1708	1738	1808	1838	1908	1938	2008	2038	2138	2238

a – Ⓐ only.
e – Ⓐ (daily Apr. 22 - Nov. 7).
t – Apr. 26 - Nov. 2.
* – By 🚌 from / to Appenzell.
‡ – Apr. 26 - Nov. 2. By 🚌 from / to Appenzell.
▷ – **Additional journeys** Gossau - Appenzell:
From Gossau at 1821, 1921, 2021, 2151, 2251 and 2351.
From Appenzell at 0500 ⚒, 0530 Ⓑ, 0600 **e** and 2300.

AB (narrow gauge rack railway) ST GALLEN - APPENZELL 527

km		⑥⑦ c		⚒			⚒														A	Ⓐ	Ⓐ
0	**St Gallen** d.	0000	...	0522	0552	0622	0652	0722	0752	0822	0852	0922	0952	1022	1052	1122	1156	1226	and every	2256	2326	A	1652	1752
7	Teufen d.	0014	...	0536	0606	0636	0706	0736	0806	0836	0906	0936	1006	1036	1106	1136	1210	1240	30 minutes	2310	2340	L	1703	1803
14	Gais ▲ d.	0027	...	0549	0619	0649	0719	0749	0819	0849	0919	0949	1019	1049	1119	1149	1223	1253	until	2323	2353	S	1714	1814
20	**Appenzell** a.	0037	...	0558	0628	0658	0728	0758	0828	0858	0928	0958	1028	1058	1128	1158	1233	1303		2333	0003	O	1724	1824

	Ⓐ	⚒		Ⓐ	⚒	Ⓐ			Ⓐ	Ⓒ											♠			⑤⑥ d
Appenzell d.	0458	0513	0540	0546	0610	0636	0640	0710	0736	0740	0810	0840	0910	0940	1010	1040	1110	1146	1214	1244	and every	2244	2314	2344
Gais ▲ d.	0508	0523	0553	0605	0623	0645	0653	0723	0745	0753	0823	0853	0923	0953	1023	1053	1123	1157	1227	1257	30 minutes	2257	2327	2353
Teufen d.	0521	0536	0606	0621	0636	0656	0706	0736	0756	0806	0836	0906	0936	1006	1036	1106	1136	1210	1240	1310	until	2310	2340	0004
St Gallen a.	0537	0552	0622	0637	0652	0710	0722	0752	0810	0822	0852	0922	0952	1022	1052	1122	1152	1226	1256	1326		2326	2356	0020

▲ – Rail service **Gais - Altstätten Stadt** and v.v. *8 km*. Journey time: 20 – 23 minutes. **Operator**: AB.
A connecting 🚌 service operates Altstätten Stadt - Altstätten SBB station (in Table **534**). Journey time: 6 minutes.
From **Gais**: 0622 Ⓐ, 0722, 0822 and hourly until 1122; 1224 and hourly until 1824; then 1924 🚌 and 2024 🚌.
From **Altstätten Stadt**: 0655 Ⓐ, 0748 Ⓐ, 0755 Ⓒ, 0855 and hourly until 1155; 1259 and hourly until 1859; then 1959 🚌, 2059 🚌.

c – Also June 9, Aug. 1.
d – Also June 8, July 31.
♠ – On Ⓐ the 1714, 1814 from Appenzell departs 2 minutes **earlier**; the 1844, 1914, 1944 departs 4 minutes **earlier**; other timings follow the regular pattern.

SBB WINTERTHUR - SCHAFFHAUSEN 529

km																						
0	**Winterthur** d.	0542	0606	0619	0642	and at the same	2106	2119	2142	2206	2242	2306	2342	0012	...	...	...	...	...	...	...	...
26	Schloss Laufen am Rheinfall d.	0606	0630	|	0706	minutes past	2130	|	2206	2230	2306	2330	0006	0036	...	...	...	...	...	...	...	...
30	**Schaffhausen** a.	0613	0638	0646	0713	each hour until	2138	2146	2213	2238	2313	2338	0013	0043	...	...	...	...	...	...	...	...

Schaffhausen d.	0515	0521	0546	and at the same	2015	2021	2046	2121	2146	2221	2246	2321	2347	...	...	...	...	...	...	...
Schloss Laufen am Rheinfall d.	|	0526	0551	minutes past	|	2026	2051	2126	2151	2226	2251	2326	2352	...	...	...	...	...	...	...
Winterthur a.	0542	0554	0619	each hour until	2042	2054	2119	2154	2219	2254	2319	2354	0023	...	...	...	...	...	...	...

530 ZÜRICH - ST GALLEN SBB

km		IR 3251			IR 3253	EC 297 D M✕	IC 701 ✕	IC 505 ✕	IR 3255	IC 1507 Ⓐ ✕	IC 703 ✕	IC 507 ✕	IR 3257	EC 97 M✕	IC 705 F✕	IC 509 ✕	IR 3259	IC 1511 Ⓐ	IC 707 ✕	IC 707 Ⓐ ✕	IC 511 ✕	IR 3261	EC 99 M✕	IC 709 ✕	IC 513 ✕	IR 3263
	Genève 500 ▷ d.	...	...	...	...	...	...	...	...	...	...	...	...	...	...	...	...	...	...	0533	...	...	...	0635	...	...
	Lausanne 500 d.	...	...	...	...	...	...	...	...	...	...	...	...	...	...	0534	...	0604	...	0617	0634	...	...	0717	0734	...
	Biel/Bienne 500 d.	...	...	...	...	...	...	...	...	0516	...	0542	...	...	...	0644	...	0716	...	|	0745	...	...	|	0845	...
	Bern 500 d.	...	...	...	...	...	...	...	...	|	0529j	|	...	...	0631	|	...	|	...	0731	|	...	...	0831	|	...
0	**Zürich** HB ● 535 d.	...	...	...	...	0535	0539	0603	0609	0633	0639	0703	0709	0733	0739	0803	0809	0833	0839	0839	0903	0909	0933	0939	1003	1009
10	**Zürich** Flug ✈ ● 535 d.	...	...	...	...	|	0553	0613z	0623	0643z	0653	0713z	0723	0743z	0753	0813z	0823	0843z	0853	0853	0913z	0923	0943z	0953	1013z	1023
30	Winterthur 535 d.	...	...	0511	...	0558	0608	0629	0638	0659	0708	0729	0738	0758	0808	0829	0838	0859	0908	0908	0929	0938	0958	1008	1029	1038
57	Wil d.	0456	...	0542	0556	|	0626	|	0656	|	0726	|	0756	|	0826	|	0856	|	0926	0926	|	0956	|	1026	|	1056
78	Gossau d.	0514	...	...	0614	|	0644	|	0714	|	0744	|	0814	|	0844	|	0914	|	0944	0944	|	1014	|	1044	|	1114
87	**St Gallen** 534 a.	0522	...	...	0622	0630	0652	0702	0722	0732	0752	0802	0822	0830	0852	0902	0922	0932	0952	0952	1002	1022	1030	1052	1102	1122
103	Rorschach 534 a.	0538	...	...	0638	...	...	0721	0738	...	...	0821	0838	...	...	0921	0938	...	...	...	1021	1038	...	...	1121	1138
	Sargans 534 a.	0624	...	...	0724	...	...	...	0824	...	...	...	0924	...	...	...	1024	...	...	...	...	1124	...	...	...	1224

	IC 1515 Ⓐ	IC 711 ✕	IC 515 ✕	IR 3265	EC 191 M✕	IC 713 ✕	IC 713 Ⓐ ✕	IC 517 ✕	IR 3267	IC 1519 Ⓑ	IC 715 ✕	IC 519 ✕	IR 3269	EC 193 M✕	IC 717 ✕	IC 521 ✕	IR 3271	IC 1523 Ⓑ	IC 719 ✕	IC 719 Ⓐ ✕	IC 523 ✕	IR 3273	EC 195 M✕	IC 721 ✕	IC 525 ✕	IR 3275
Genève 500 ▷ d.	...	0735	...	...	...	...	0835	...	...	...	0931	...	...	...	1035	...	...	...	...	1135	...	...	...	1235	...	...
Lausanne 500 d.	0804	0817	0834	...	...	...	0917	0934	...	1004	1017	1034	...	...	1117	1134	...	1204	...	1217	1234	...	...	1317	1334	...
Biel/Bienne 500 d.	0916	|	0945	...	...	...	|	1045	...	1116	|	1145	...	...	|	1245	...	1316	...	|	1345	...	...	|	1445	...
Bern 500 d.	|	0931	|	...	...	...	1031	|	...	|	1131	|	...	...	1231	|	...	|	...	1331	|	...	...	1431	|	...
Zürich HB ● 535 d.	1033	1039	1103	1109	1133	1139	1139	1203	1209	1233	1239	1303	1309	1333	1339	1403	1409	1433	1439	1439	1503	1509	1533	1539	1603	1609
Zürich Flug ✈ ● 535 d.	1043z	1053	1113z	1123	1143z	1153	1153	1213z	1223	1243z	1253	1313z	1323	1343z	1353	1413z	1423	1443z	1453	1453	1513z	1523	1543z	1553	1613z	1623
Winterthur 535 d.	1059	1108	1129	1138	1158	1208	1208	1229	1238	1259	1308	1329	1338	1358	1408	1429	1438	1459	1508	1508	1529	1538	1558	1608	1629	1638
Wil d.	|	1126	|	1156	|	1226	1226	|	1256	|	1326	|	1356	|	1426	|	1456	|	1526	1526	|	1556	|	1626	|	1656
Gossau d.	|	1144	|	1214	|	1244	1244	|	1314	|	1344	|	1414	|	1444	|	1514	|	1544	1544	|	1614	|	1644	|	1714
St Gallen 534 a.	1132	1152	1202	1222	1230	1252	1252	1302	1322	1332	1352	1402	1422	1430	1452	1502	1522	1532	1552	1552	1602	1622	1630	1652	1702	1722
Rorschach 534 a.	...	...	1221	1238	...	...	...	1321	1338	...	...	1421	1438	...	...	1521	1538	...	...	...	1621	1638	...	...	1721	1738
Sargans 534 a.	...	...	...	1324	...	...	...	...	1424	...	...	...	1524	...	...	...	1624	...	...	...	...	1724	...	...	...	1824

	IC 1527 Ⓑ	IC 723 ✕	IC 723 Ⓐ ✕	IC 527 ✕	IR 3277	EC 197 M✕	IC 725 ✕	IC 529 ✕	IR 3279	IC 1531 Ⓐ ✕	IC 727 ✕	IC 531 ✕	IR 3281	EC 199 M✕	IC 729 ✕	IC 533 ✕	IR 3283	IC 731 ✕	IR 3285	IC 733 ✕	IR 3287	IC 735	IR 3289	◇		IR 3293
Genève 500 ▷ d.	...	...	1335	...	...	...	1435	...	...	...	1535	...	...	...	1635	...	...	1731	...	1835	...	1935	...	...	...	...
Lausanne 500 d.	1404	...	1417	1434	...	...	1517	1534	...	1604	1617	1634	...	...	1717	1734	...	1817	...	1917	...	2017	...	...	...	...
Biel/Bienne 500 d.	1516	...	|	1545	...	...	|	1645	...	1716	|	1745	...	...	|	1845	...	|	...	|	...	|	...	...	...	...
Bern 500 d.	|	...	1531	|	...	...	1631	|	...	|	1731	|	...	...	1831	|	...	1931	...	2031	...	2131	...	...	...	...
Zürich HB ● 535 d.	1633	1639	1639	1703	1709	1733	1739	1803	1809	1833	1839	1903	1909	1933	1939	2003	2009	2039	2109	2139	2209	2239	2309	2339	...	0017
Zürich Flug ✈ ● 535 d.	1643z	1653	1653	1713z	1723	1743z	1753	1813z	1823	1843z	1853	1913z	1923	1943z	1953	2013z	2023	2053	2123	2153	2223	2253	2323	2350	...	0030
Winterthur 535 d.	1659	1708	1708	1729	1738	1758	1808	1829	1838	1859	1908	1929	1938	1958	2008	2029	2038	2108	2138	2208	2238	2308	2338	0008	...	0045
Wil d.	|	1726	1726	|	1756	|	1826	|	1856	|	1926	|	1956	|	2026	|	2056	2126	2156	2226	2256	2326	2356	0031	...	0103
Gossau d.	|	1744	1744	|	1814	|	1844	|	1914	|	1944	|	2014	|	2044	|	2114	2144	2214	2244	2314	2344	0014	0048	...	0121
St Gallen 534 a.	1732	1752	1752	1802	1822	1830	1852	1902	1922	1932	1952	2002	2022	2030	2052	2102	2122	2152	2222	2252	2322	2352	0022	0055	...	0128
Rorschach 534 a.	...	...	...	1821	1838	...	...	1921	1938	...	...	2021	2038	...	...	...	...	...	...	...	...	...	...	...	...	...
Sargans 534 a.	...	...	...	...	1924	...	...	...	2024	...	...	...	2124	...	...	...	...	...	...	...	...	...	...	...	...	...

	IR 3292	⑥⑦ d ◇	⑥⑦ d		IR 3252	IC 706 ✕	IR 3254	IC 510 ✕	IC 708 ✕	IC 1510 Ⓐ	IR 3256	IC 512 ✕	IC 710 ✕	EC 290 ⚒n L✕	IR 3258	IC 514 ✕	IC 712 ✕	IC 1514 Ⓐ	IR 3260	IC 516 ✕	IC 714 ✕	EC 198 M✕	IR 3262	IC 518 ✕	IC 716 Ⓐ ✕	IC 716 ✕
Sargans 534 d.	...	...	...	...	...	...	...	...	...	...	0535	...	...	...	0635	...	...	...	0735	...	...	...	0835	...	...	...
Rorschach 534 d.	...	...	...	...	...	...	...	0539	...	...	0621	0639	...	...	0721	0739	...	...	0821	0839	...	...	0921	0939	...	...
St Gallen 534 d.	0037	...	...	...	0437	0507	0537	0558	0607	0628	0637	0658	0707	0729	0737	0758	0807	0828	0837	0858	0907	0929	0937	0958	1007	1007
Gossau d.	0044	...	...	...	0444	0514	0544	|	0614	|	0644	|	0714	|	0744	|	0814	|	0844	|	0914	|	0944	|	1014	1014
Wil d.	0102	0105	...	...	0504	0534	0604	|	0634	|	0704	|	0734	|	0804	|	0834	|	0904	|	0934	|	1004	|	1034	1034
Winterthur 535 d.	...	0128	0135	...	0524	0554	0624	0633	0654	0703	0724	0733	0754	0803	0824	0833	0854	0903	0924	0933	0954	1003	1024	1033	1054	1054
Zürich Flug ✈ ● 535 a.	...	...	|	...	0536	0606	0636	0646t	0706	0716t	0736	0746t	0806	0816t	0836	0846t	0906	0916t	0936	0946t	1006	1016t	1036	1046t	1106	1106
Zürich HB ● 535 a.	...	...	0158	...	0551	0621	0651	0657	0721	0727	0751	0757	0821	0827	0851	0857	0921	0927	0951	0957	1021	1027	1051	1057	1121	1121
Bern 500 a.	...	...	...	...	...	0728	...	|	0828	|	...	|	0928	...	...	|	1028	|	...	|	1128	...	...	|	1228	...
Biel/Bienne 500 a.	...	...	...	...	...	|	...	0815	|	0843	...	0915	|	...	...	1015	|	1043	...	1115	|	...	...	1215	|	...
Lausanne 500 a.	...	...	...	...	...	0843	...	0926	0943	0956	...	1026	1043	...	...	1126	1143	1156	...	1226	1243	...	...	1326	1343	...
Genève 500 ▷ a.	...	...	...	...	...	0925	...	...	1029	...	...	...	1125	...	...	...	1225	...	...	...	1325	...	...	...	1429	...

	IC 1518 Ⓐ	IR 3264	IC 520 ✕	IC 718 ✕	EC 196 M✕	IR 3266	IC 522 ✕	IC 720 ✕	IC 1522 Ⓐ	IR 3268	IC 524 ✕	IC 722 Ⓐ ✕	IC 722 ✕	EC 194 M✕	IR 3270	IC 526 ✕	IC 724 ✕	IC 1526 Ⓑ	IR 3272	IC 528 ✕	IC 726 ✕	EC 192 M✕	IR 3274	IC 530 ✕	IC 728 Ⓐ ✕	IC 728 ✕
Sargans 534 d.	...	0935	...	...	...	1035	...	...	...	1135	...	...	...	...	1235	...	...	...	1335	...	...	...	1435	...	...	...
Rorschach 534 d.	...	1021	1039	...	...	1121	1139	...	...	1221	1239	...	...	...	1321	1339	...	...	1421	1439	...	...	1521	1539	...	...
St Gallen 534 d.	1028	1037	1058	1107	1129	1137	1158	1207	1228	1237	1258	1307	1307	1329	1337	1358	1407	1428	1437	1458	1507	1529	1537	1558	1607	1607
Gossau d.	|	1044	|	1114	|	1144	|	1214	|	1244	|	1314	1314	|	1344	|	1414	|	1444	|	1514	|	1544	|	1614	1614
Wil d.	|	1104	|	1134	|	1204	|	1234	|	1304	|	1334	1334	|	1404	|	1434	|	1504	|	1534	|	1604	|	1634	1634
Winterthur 535 d.	1103	1124	1133	1154	1203	1224	1233	1254	1303	1324	1333	1354	1354	1403	1424	1433	1454	1503	1524	1533	1554	1603	1624	1633	1654	1654
Zürich Flug ✈ ● 535 a.	1116t	1136	1146t	1206	1216t	1236	1246t	1306	1316t	1336	1346t	1406	1406	1416t	1436	1446t	1506	1516t	1536	1546t	1606	1616t	1636	1646t	1706	1706
Zürich HB ● 535 a.	1127	1151	1157	1221	1227	1251	1257	1321	1327	1351	1357	1421	1421	1427	1451	1457	1521	1527	1551	1557	1621	1627	1651	1657	1721	1721
Bern 500 a.	|	...	|	1328	...	...	|	1428	|	...	|	1528	...	...	...	|	1628	|	...	|	1728	...	...	|	1828	...
Biel/Bienne 500 a.	1243	...	1315	|	...	...	1415	|	1443	...	1515	|	...	...	...	1615	|	1643	...	1715	|	...	...	1815	|	...
Lausanne 500 a.	1356	...	1426	1443	...	...	1526	1543	1556	...	1626	1643	...	...	...	1726	1743	1756	...	1826	1843	...	...	1926	1943	...
Genève 500 ▷ a.	...	...	...	1525	...	...	...	1625	...	...	...	1725	...	...	...	...	1825	...	...	...	1925	...	...	...	2029	...

	IC 1530 Ⓑ	IR 3276	IC 532 ✕	IC 730 ✕	EC 190 M✕	IR 3278	IC 534 ✕	IC 732 Ⓐ ✕	IC 732 ✕	IC 1534 Ⓑ	IR 3280	IC 536 ✕	IC 734 ✕	EC 98 M✕	IR 3282	IC 538 ✕	IC 736 F	IR 3284	IC 738 ✕	EC 96 M✕	IR 3286	◇	IR 3288		EC 296 Ⓑc M✕	IR 3290
Sargans 534 d.	...	1535	...	...	...	1635	...	...	...	...	1735	...	...	...	1835	...	...	1935	...	...	2035	...	2135	...	...	...
Rorschach 534 d.	...	1621	1639	...	...	1721	1739	...	...	...	1821	1839	...	...	1921	1939	...	2021	...	...	2121	...	2221	...	...	...
St Gallen 534 d.	1628	1637	1658	1707	1729	1737	1758	1807	1807	1828	1837	1858	1907	1929	1937	1958	2007	2037	2107	2129	2137	2213	2237	...	2329	2337
Gossau d.	|	1644	|	1714	|	1744	|	1814	1814	|	1844	|	1914	|	1944	|	2014	2044	2114	|	2144	2222	2244	...	|	2344
Wil d.	|	1704	|	1734	|	1804	|	1834	1834	|	1904	|	1934	|	2004	|	2034	2104	2134	|	2204	2239	2304	...	|	0004
Winterthur 535 d.	1703	1724	1733	1754	1803	1824	1833	1854	1854	1903	1924	1933	1954	2003	2024	2033	2054	2124	2154	2203	2224	2301	2324	...	0003	0028
Zürich Flug ✈ ● 535 a.	1716t	1736	1746t	1806	1816t	1836	1846t	1906	1906	1916t	1936	1946t	2006	2016t	2036	2046t	2106	2136	2206	2216t	2236	2314	2336	...	0016f	0040
Zürich HB ● 535 a.	1727	1751	1757	1821	1827	1851	1857	1921	1921	1927	1951	1957	2021	2027	2051	2057	2121	2151	2221	2227	2251	2325	2351	...	0027	0053
Bern 500 a.	|	...	|	1928	...	...	|	2028	...	|	...	|	2128	...	...	|	2228	...	2331	...	...	...	...	...	...	...
Biel/Bienne 500 a.	1843	...	1915	|	...	...	2015	|	...	2043	...	2115	|	...	...	2215	...	...	...	...	...	...	...	...	...	...
Lausanne 500 a.	1956	...	2026	2043	...	...	2126	2143	...	2156	...	2226	2243	...	...	2326	...	...	...	...	...	...	...	...	...	...
Genève 500 ▷ a.	...	...	...	2125	...	...	...	...	...	...	...	...	2325k	...	...	...	...	...	...	...	...	...	...	...	...	...

D – ①–⑥ (not June 9).
F – From/to Fribourg (Table **500**).
L – From/to Lindau (Table **75**).
M – From/to München (Table **75**).

c – Not June 8.
d – Also June 9, Aug. 1.

f – From July 8.
j – 0513 on June 16–20, 23–27, July 28, Sept. 8, 13–15, 22–26, 29, 30, Oct. 1–3, 25–27, Nov. 17, Dec. 1, 8.
k – ⑤⑥ only.
n – ①–⑥ (not Aug. 1).
t – From July 7.
z – Not Aug. 11 - Oct. 3.

◇ – Operated by THURBO.
▷ – Most Genève services start from/continue to Genève Aéroport (see Table **500**).
● – Frequent services operate **Zürich - Zürich Flughafen** and v.v. (up to 12 trains per hour 0600 - 2400).

URh — SCHAFFHAUSEN - KREUZLINGEN — 533

	✕A		✕B		✕A		✕A	✕F	
Schaffhausen d.	0910	...	1110	...	1318	...	1518	1650	...
Stein am Rhein d.	1115	...	1315	...	1523	...	1723	1850	...
Kreuzlingen Hafen a.	1355	...	1555	...	1805	...	2005	...	...

	✕A		✕G	✕F		✕A		✕E	
Kreuzlingen Hafen d.	0900	...	1100	1200	...	1427	...	1627	...
Stein am Rhein d.	1130	...	1330	1530r	...	1657	...	1857	...
Schaffhausen a.	1245	...	1445	1645	...	1815	...	2015	...

A – ④–① Apr. 18 - May 5 (not Apr. 28); daily May 6 - Oct. 5.
B – ⑦ Apr. 18 - June 22; daily June 28 - Sept. 14; ⑦ Sept. 21 - Oct. 5; daily Oct. 6 - 19.
E – ⑦ Apr. 18 - June 22; daily June 29 - Sept. 14; ⑦ Sept. 21 - Oct. 5. Terminates Stein am Rhein on Aug. 9.
F – ④ July 3 - Sept. 11.
G – ④–① Apr. 18 - May 5 (not Apr. 28); daily May 6 - Oct. 19.
r – Arrives 1425.

SBB — ST GALLEN - BUCHS - CHUR — 534

km		IR 3251 W	IR 2201 ⊙	IR 3253 W	IR 2203 ⊙	IR 3255	IR 2205 ⊙	⊡	IR 3279	IR 2229 ⊙	IR 3281	IR 2231 ⊙	◇	⊙	◇	⊙	◇		EC 297 Mb	EC 97 M	EC 99 M	EC 191 M	EC 193 M	EC 195 M	EC 197 M	EC 199 M
	Zürich HB 530 d.	...	...	...	...	0609	...	and at	1809	...	1909	...	...	...	...	...	...		0535	0733	0933	1133	1333	1533	1733	1933
0	**St Gallen** 530 d.	0525	0555	0625	0655	0725	0755		1925	1955	2025	2055	2125	2138	2225	2238	2325	A	0632	0832	1032	1232	1432	1632	1832	2032
16	Rorschach 530 d.	0539	0609	0639	0709	0739	0809	the same	1939	2009	2039	2109	2139	2156	2239	2256	2339	L	|	|	|	|	|	|	|	|
27	**St Margrethen** 952 d.	0546	0616	0646	0716	0746	0816		1946	2016	2046	2116	2146	2207	2246	2307	2346	S	0651	0851	1051	1251	1451	1651	|	2051
	Bregenz 952 a.	|	|	|	|	|	|	minutes	|	|	|	|	|	|	|	|	|	O	0700	0900	1100	1300	1500	1700	1858	2100
39	Altstätten d.	0559	0629	0659	0729	0759	0829		1959	2029	2059	2129	2159	2220	2259	2320	0003		...	...	...	...	...	...	...	...
65	**Buchs** 520 d.	0615	0645	0715	0745	0815	0845	past each	2015	2045	2115	2145	2215	2247	2315	2347	0018		...	...	...	...	...	...	...	...
81	Sargans ⊖ 520 a.	0624	0654	0724	0754	0824	0854		2024	2054	2124	2154	2224	2300	2324	0000	0028		...	...	...	...	...	...	...	...
81	Sargans ⊖ 520 d.	0628	0656	0733	0756	0833	0856	hour until	2033	2056	2128	2156	2228	2306	2328	0006	0031		...	...	...	...	...	...	...	...
93	Landquart 520 a.	0639	0708	0741	0808	0841	0908		2041	2108	2139	2208	2239	2318	2339	0018	0042		...	...	...	...	...	...	...	...
107	**Chur** 520 a.	0648	0718	0752	0818	0852	0918		2052	2118	2149	2218	2249	2326	2348	0026	0051		...	...	...	...	...	...	...	...

	IR 3256	IR 2206 ⊙	IR 3258	IR 2208	IR 3260	IR 2210 ⊙	IR 3262	⊡	IR 2234 ⊙	IR 3286	IR 2236	IR 3288	⊙	◇	⊙	◇		EC 290 L	EC 198 M	EC 196 M	EC 194 M	EC 192 M	EC 190 M	EC 98 M	EC 96 M	EC 296 Md
Chur 520 d.	0508t	0542	0608	0642	0708	0742	0808	and at	1942	2008	2042	2108	2131	2211	2231	2301		...	...	...	...	...	...	...	...	...
Landquart 520 d.	0518t	0551	0618	0651	0718	0751	0818		1951	2018	2051	2118	2139	2220	2239	2309		...	...	...	...	...	...	...	...	...
Sargans ⊖ 520 a.	0527t	0603	0627	0703	0727	0803	0827	the same	2003	2027	2103	2127	2151	2232	2251	2321	A	...	...	...	...	...	...	...	...	...
Sargans ⊖ 520 d.	0535	0605	0635	0705	0735	0805	0835		2005	2035	2105	2135	2205	2235	2305	2340	L	...	...	...	...	...	...	...	...	...
Buchs 520 d.	0545	0615	0645	0715	0745	0815	0845	minutes	2015	2045	2115	2145	2219	2245	2319	2349	S	...	...	...	...	...	...	...	...	...
Altstätten d.	0600	0630	0700	0730	0800	0830	0900		2030	2100	2130	2200	2238	2300	2338	0004	O	...	...	...	...	...	...	...	...	...
Bregenz 952 d.	|	|	|	|	|	|	|	past each	|	|	|	|	|	|	|	|		0700	0900	1100	1300	1500	1700	1900	2100	2300
St Margrethen 952 d.	0613	0643	0713	0743	0813	0843	0913		2043	2113	2143	2213	2253	2313	2353	0014		0710	0910	1110	1310	1510	1710	1910	2110	2310
Rorschach 530 d.	0621	0651	0721	0751	0821	0851	0921	hour until	2051	2121	2151	2221	2303	2321	0003	0021		|	|	|	|	|	|	|	|	|
St Gallen 530 a.	0635	0704	0735	0804	0835	0904	0935		2104	2135	2204	2235	2320	2334	0020	0034		0728	0928	1128	1328	1528	1728	1928	2128	2328
Zürich HB 530 a.	0751	...	0851	...	0951	...	1051		...	2251	...	2351	...	...	...	...		0827	1027	1227	1427	1627	1827	2027	2227	0027

FELDKIRCH (AUSTRIA) - VADUZ (LIECHTENSTEIN) - SARGANS (bus). Line number **11**.

	Ⓐ	⚒	⚒																				
Feldkirch (Bahnhof) d.	...	...	...	...	0624	0654	and at the	1724	1754	1824	1854	1924	1954	2024	2054	2124	2154	2224	2254	...	...	...	...	...
Schaan (Bahnhof) d.	0515	0530	0600	0630	0700	0730	same minutes	1800	1830	1900	1930	2000	2030	2100	2130	2200	2230	2300	2330	...	...	...	...	...
Vaduz Post d.	0526	0541	0611	0641	0711	0741	past each	1811	1841	1909	1941	2009	2041	2109	2141	2209	2239	2309	2339	...	...	...	...	...
Sargans (Bahnhof) a.	0557	0612	0642	0712	0742	0812	hour until	1842	1912	...	2012	...	2112	...	2212	...	...	...	...	...	...	...	...	...

	⚒	⚒		Ⓐ		Ⓐ			Ⓐ															
Sargans (Bahnhof) d.	...	...	...	0544	...	0614	0644	...	0714	0744	0814	and at the	1844	1914	1944	...	2044	...	2144	...	2244	...	...	...
Vaduz Post d.	...	0548	0618	0618	0648	0648	0718	0748	0748	0818	0848	same minutes	1918	1948	2018	2048	2118	2148	2218	2248	2318	...	...	...
Schaan (Bahnhof) d.	0530	0600	0630	0630	0700	0700	0730	0800	0800	0830	0900	past each	1930	2000	2030	2100	2130	2200	2230	2300	2330	...	...	...
Feldkirch (Bahnhof) a.	0606	0636	0706	0706	0736	0736	0806	0836	0836	0906	0936	hour until	2006	2036	2106	2136	2206	2236	2306	2336	...	...	...	...

A – ①–⑥ (not Aug. 1). From Lindau (Table **75**).
M – (12) ✕ Zürich - Lindau - München and v.v.
W – From Wil (Table **530**).
b – ①–⑥ (not June 9).
d – Ⓑ (not June 8).
t – Runs 2–5 minutes later on †.
⊖ – See panel below main table for bus links to/from Vaduz.

SBB, THURBO — ZÜRICH - KONSTANZ and ROMANSHORN — 535

km		◇	◇ Ⓐt	◇	IC 803 ✕	◇	IR 2107	◇	IC 805 ✕	◇	IR 2109	◇	IC 807 A✕	◇	IR 2111	◇	IC 809 A✕	◇u	IR 2113	◇	⊡	IC 831 A✕	◇u	IR 2135	◇	IC 845
	Bern 500 d.	...	...	...	...	...	...	...	0602	...	...	...	0702	...	...	...	0802	...	...	...		1902	...	...	...	...
0	**Zürich** HB ‡530 d.	...	0535	...	0605	...	0635	...	0705	...	0735	...	0805	...	0835	...	0905	...	0935	...	and at	2005	...	2035	...	2105
10	**Zürich** Flug ✈ ‡530 d.	...	|	...	0616	...	0646	...	0716	...	0746	...	0816	...	0846	...	0916	...	0946	...		2016	...	2046	...	2116
30	Winterthur 530 d.	...	0601	...	0631	...	0701	...	0731	...	0801	...	0831	...	0901	...	0931	...	1001	...	the same	2031	...	2101	...	2131
46	Frauenfeld d.	...	0612	...	0642	...	0712	...	0742	...	0812	...	0842	...	0912	...	0942	...	1012	...	minutes	2042	...	2112	...	2142
64	Weinfelden 538/9 d.	0606	0625	0627	0655	0706	0725	0727	0755	0759	0825	0827	0855	0906	0925	0927	0955	1006	1025	1027	past each	2055	2106	2125	2127	2155
87	Kreuzlingen a.	0631	0643	|	|	0731	0743	|	|	0819	0843	|	|	0931	0943	|	|	1031	1043	|		|	2131	2143	|	|
88	**Konstanz** a.	0634	0650	|	|	0742	0750	|	|	0823	0850	|	|	0934	0950	|	|	1034	1050	|	hour until	|	2134	2150	|	|
86	**Romanshorn** 538/9 a.	...	...	0642	0712	...	...	0742	0812	...	...	0842	0912	...	...	0942	1012	...	...	1042		2112	...	...	2142	2212
	Rorschach 538 a.	...	...	0706	...	...	...	0806	...	...	...	0906	...	...	...	1006	...	...	...	1106		...	...	...	2206	...

	◇	IR 2137	◇	IC 835 A	◇	IR 2139 ◐	◇	IC 837	◇	◇	◇	◇
Bern 500 d.	...	...	...	2102	...	...	...	2202	...	...	...	...
Zürich HB ‡530 d.	...	2135	...	2205	...	2235	...	2305	...	2339	0008	...
Zürich Flug ✈ ‡530 d.	...	2146	...	2216	...	2246	...	2316	...	2350	0019	...
Winterthur 530 d.	...	2201	...	2231	...	2301	...	2331	...	0006	0034	...
Frauenfeld d.	...	2212	...	2242	...	2312	...	2342	...	0016	0045	...
Weinfelden 538/9 d.	2159	2225	2227	2255	2306	2325	2327	2355	2359	0027	0100	0106
Kreuzlingen a.	2219	2243	|	|	2331	2343	|	|	0019	0048	|	0130
Konstanz a.	2223	2250	|	|	2334	2350	|	|	0023	0051	|	0135
Romanshorn 538/9 a.	...	...	2242	2312	...	...	2342	0012	...	...	0117	...
Rorschach 538 a.	...	...	2306	...	...	...	0006	...	...	...	...	...

	◇	IR 2106	◇	IC 806 A✕	◇	IR 2108	◇z	IC 808 A✕	⊡
Rorschach 538 d.	0454	...	...	...	0554	...	...	...	
Romanshorn 538/9 d.	0517	...	...	0547	0617	...	...	0647	and at
Konstanz d.	|	0509	0524	|	|	0609	0624	|	
Kreuzlingen d.	|	0516	0527	|	|	0616	0627	|	the same
Weinfelden 538/9 d.	0533	0536	0554	0606	0633	0636	0654	0706	minutes
Frauenfeld d.	...	0548	...	0618	...	0648	...	0718	
Winterthur 530 d.	...	0601	...	0631	...	0701	...	0731	past each
Zürich Flughafen ✈ ‡530 a.	...	0614	...	0644	...	0714	...	0744	hour until
Zürich HB ‡530 a.	...	0625	...	0655	...	0725	...	0755	
Bern 500 a.	...	...	...	0758	...	...	...	0858	

	◇	IR 2130	◇z	IC 830 A✕	◇	IR 2132	◇	IC 832 ✕	◇	IR 2134	◇	IC 834 ✕	◇	IR 2136	◇	IC 836 ✕	◇	IR 2138 ◐	◇	IC 838	◇	◇	◇	IC 840	◇	◇	◇
Rorschach 538 d.	1654	...	...	...	1754	...	...	...	1854	...	...	...	1954	...	...	...	2054	...	...	...	2154	...	...	...	2254	...	...
Romanshorn 538/9 d.	1717	...	...	1747	1817	...	...	1847	1917	...	...	1947	2017	...	...	2047	2117	...	...	2147	2217	...	...	2247	2317	...	...
Konstanz d.	|	1709	1724	|	|	1809	1835	|	|	1909	1924	|	|	2009	2035	|	|	2109	2124	|	|	2209	2235	|	|	2309	0009
Kreuzlingen d.	|	1716	1727	|	|	1816	1838	|	|	1916	1927	|	|	2016	2038	|	|	2116	2127	|	|	2216	2238	|	|	2316	0020
Weinfelden 538/9 d.	1733	1736	1754	1806	1833	1836	1859	1906	1933	1936	1954	2006	2033	2036	2059	2106	2133	2136	2154	2206	2233	2236	2259	2306	2333	2336	0047
Frauenfeld d.	...	1748	...	1818	...	1848	...	1918	...	1948	...	2018	...	2048	...	2118	...	2148	...	2218	...	2248	...	2318	...	2348	...
Winterthur 530 d.	...	1801	...	1831	...	1901	...	1931	...	2001	...	2031	...	2101	...	2131	...	2201	...	2231	...	2301	...	2331	...	2359	...
Zürich Flug ✈ ‡530 a.	...	1814	...	1844	...	1914	...	1944	...	2014	...	2044	...	2114	...	2144	...	2214	...	2244	...	2314	...	2344	...	|	...
Zürich HB ‡530 a.	...	1825	...	1855	...	1925	...	1955	...	2025	...	2055	...	2125	...	2155	...	2225	...	2255	...	2325	...	2355	...	0035	...
Bern 500 a.	...	...	...	1958	...	...	...	2058	...	...	...	2158	...	...	...	2302	...	...	...	0002	...	...	...	...	...	...	...

A – From/to stations in Table **560**.
– Not May 1.
– Additional fast trains run every **two** hours 0959 to 1959 (Kreuzlingen a. xx19, Konstanz a. xx23).
z – Additional fast trains run every **two** hours 0635 to 1635 (Kreuzlingen d. xx38, Konstanz a. xx59).
◇ – Operated by THURBO.
◐ – Operated by THURBO on ⑦–④.
⊡ – Train numbers increase by 2 each hour.
‡ – Frequent services operate **Zürich - Zürich Flughafen** and v.v. (up to 13 trains per hour 0600 - 2400).

536 ⛴ ROMANSHORN - FRIEDRICHSHAFEN ferry service — BSB / SBS

	h	s	e	k	k		k	e	f
Romanshorn Autoquai ..... d.	0522	0622	0722	0822	0922	and hourly	1822	1922	2022
Friedrichshafen Fähre ..... a.	0608	0708	0808	0908	1008	until	1908	2008	2108

	h	s	e	k		k	e	f
Friedrichshafen Fähre .... d.	0520	0620	0720	0820	and hourly	1720	1820	1920	2020
Romanshorn Autoquai ...... a.	0606	0706	0806	0906	until	1806	1906	2006	2106

e – Daily Mar. 15 - Nov. 14; ①–⑤ Nov. 17 - Dec. 12.
f – Daily Mar. 15 - Nov. 15.
h – ①–⑤ Mar. 17 - Nov. 14.
k – Daily Mar. 15 - Dec. 13.
s – ①–⑤ Mar. 15 - Dec. 13.
Operator: BSB / SBS. www.bodensee-schiffe.ch ✆ 071 466 78 88

538 SCHAFFHAUSEN - ROMANSHORN - RORSCHACH and ST GALLEN — THURBO

km								⚒																	
0	**Schaffhausen** .... d.	...	...	...	...	...	...	...	...	0519	...	0549	...	...	0619	...	and at	1949	...	...	2019	...	2049	...
20	Stein am Rhein .... d.	...	...	...	...	0513	...	...	...	0543	...	0613	...	...	0643	...	the same	2013	...	...	2043	...	2113	...
46	**Kreuzlingen** .... d.	0445	...	0515	...	0545	...	...	...	0615	...	0645	...	...	0715	...	minutes	2045	...	...	2115	...	2145	...
	Konstanz .... d.	|	...	|	...	|	...	...	0609	|	...	|	...	0709	|	...	past each	|	...	2109	|	...	|	...
47	Kreuzlingen Hafen .... d.	0447	...	0517	...	0547	...	...	0612	0617	...	0647	...	0712	0717	...	hour until	2047	...	2112	2117	...	2147	...
	Weinfelden .... **535 539** d.	|	...	|	...	|	...	0557	|	|	0627	|	*0655*	|	|	0727		|	*2055*	|	|	2127	|	*2155*
65	**Romanshorn**.... **535 539** a.	0512	...	0542	...	0612	...	0612	0625	0642	0642	0712	*0712*	0725	0742	0742		2112	*2112*	2125	2142	2142	2212	*2212*
65	**Romanshorn** .... d.	0514	0516	0544	0546	0614	0616	0616	0626	0644	0646	0714	0716	0726	0744	0746		2114	2116	2126	2144	2146	2214	2216
	St Gallen .... a.	0541	|	0611	|	0641	|	|	0644	0711	|	0741	|	0744	0811	|		2141	|	2144	2211	|	2241	|
73	Arbon .... a.	...	0525	...	0555	...	0625	0625	...	...	0655	...	0725	...	...	0755		...	2125	...	...	2155	...	2225
80	**Rorschach** .... a.	...	0536	...	0606	...	0636	0636	...	...	0706	...	0736	...	...	0806		...	2136	...	...	2206	...	2236

											⑥⑦j
Schaffhausen .... d.	2119	...	2149	...	2219	...	2249	...	2319	2349	...
Stein am Rhein .... d.	2143	...	2213	...	2243	...	2313	...	2343	0013	...
Kreuzlingen .... d.	2215	...	2245	...	2315	...	2345	...	0015	0044	0105
Konstanz .... d.	|	...	|	...	|	...	|	...	|	...	|
Kreuzlingen Hafen .... d.	2217	...	2247	...	2317	...	2347	...	0017	...	0107
Weinfelden..... **535 539** d.	|	2227	|	*2255*	|	2327	|	*2355*	|	...	|
Romanshorn.... **535 539** a.	2242	2242	2312	*2312*	2342	2342	0012	*0012*	0042	...	0128
Romanshorn .... d.	2244	2246	2314	2316	2344	2346	0014	0017	...	...	*0133*
St Gallen .... a.	2311	|	2341	|	0011	|	0041	|	...	...	*0158*
Arbon .... a.	...	2255	...	2325	...	2355	...	0025	...	...	...
Rorschach .... a.	...	2306	...	2336	...	0006	...	0036	...	...	...

				Ⓐ					
Rorschach .... d.	...	...	...	...	...	0454	...	0524	...
Arbon .... d.	...	...	...	...	...	0504	...	0534	...
St Gallen .... d.	...	...	...	...	...	|	...	|	0519
Romanshorn .... a.	...	...	...	...	...	0513	...	0542	0546
Romanshorn ...... **535 539** d.	...	...	...	0448	...	0517	0518	*0547*	0548
Weinfelden .... **535 539** a.	...	...	...	|	...	0533	|	*0605*	|
Kreuzlingen Hafen .... d.	...	...	...	0511	...	...	0541	...	0611
Konstanz .... a.	...	...	...	|	...	...	|	...	|
Kreuzlingen .... d.	0446	...	0515	0515	...	...	0546	...	0615
Stein am Rhein .... d.	0516	...	0546	0546	...	...	0616	...	0646
Schaffhausen .... a.	0541	...	0613	0613	...	...	0643	...	0713

Rorschach .... d.	0554	...	...	0624	...	0654	...	and at	...	2124	...	2154	...	2224	...	2254	...	...	2324	...	2354	...	0024	...
Arbon .... d.	0604	...	...	0634	...	0704	...	the same	...	2134	...	2204	...	2234	...	2304	...	...	2334	...	0004	...	0034	...
St Gallen .... d.	|	0549	0615	|	0619	|	0649	minutes	2115	|	2119	|	2149	|	2219	|	2249	...	|	2319	|	2349	|	0019
Romanshorn .... a.	0613	0616	0633	0643	0646	0713	0716	past each	2133	2143	2146	2213	2216	2243	2246	2313	2316	...	2343	2346	0013	0016	0043	0046
Romanshorn .... **535 539** d.	0617	0618	0633	*0647*	0648	0717	0718	hour until	2133	*2147*	2148	2217	2218	*2247*	2248	2317	2318	...	...	2348	...	0018	...	0048
Weinfelden..... **535 539** a.	0633	|	|	*0705*	|	0733	|		|	*2205*	|	2233	|	*2305*	|	2333	|	...	...	|	...	|	...	|
Kreuzlingen Hafen .... d.	...	0641	0647	...	0711	...	0741		2147	...	2211	...	2241	...	2311	...	2341	...	...	0011	...	0041	...	0107
Konstanz .... a.	...	|	0650	...	|	...	|		2150	...	|	...	|	...	|	...	|	...	...	|	...	|	...	|
Kreuzlingen .... d.	...	0646	...	...	0715	...	0746		...	...	2215	...	2246	...	2315	...	2346	...	...	0015	...	0044	...	0110
Stein am Rhein .... d.	...	0716	...	...	0746	...	0816		...	...	2246	...	2316	...	2346	...	0016	...	...	0046	...	...	...	...
Schaffhausen .... a.	...	0743	...	...	0813	...	0843		...	...	2313	...	2343	...	0013	...	0043	...	...	0111	...	...	...	...

j – Mornings of ⑥⑦ (also June 9, Aug. 1).

539 ROMANSHORN - WEINFELDEN - WIL — THURBO

km			Ⓐ			Ⓐ					
0	**Romanshorn** ‡ d.	...	0507	0537	and at the same	1907	1937	2037	2137	2237	2337
22	Weinfelden ... ‡ d.	0502	0532	0602	minutes past	1932	2002	2102	2202	2302	0002
41	**Wil** .... a.	0527	0557	0627	each hour until	1957	2027	2127	2227	2327	0027

	Ⓐ			Ⓐ					
Wil .... d.	0502	0532	and at the same	1902	1932	2032	2132	2232	2332
Weinfelden..... ‡ a.	0530	0559	minutes past	1930	1959	2059	2159	2259	2359
Romanshorn ‡ a.	0553	0623	each hour until	1953	2023	2123	2223	2323	0023

‡ – See also Tables **535** and **538**.

542 🚌 CHUR - FLIMS — PostAuto

🚌 **Chur** (Postautostation) - **Flims** Dorf (Post). Journey time: 26–41 minutes. Additional journeys operate until Apr. 21 and June 7 - Oct. 19.

From **Chur**: 0600, 0630, 0658, 0728, 0758, 0828, 0858 and at 28 and 58 minutes past each hour until 1958, then 2058, 2158, 2258.

From **Flims** Dorf: 0526, 0556 ⚒, 0628, 0658, 0713 Ⓐ, 0728, 0758, 0828, 0858, 0928, 095 and at 28 and 58 minutes past each hour until 1958, then 2028, 2125, 2225, 2325.

543 🚌 ST MORITZ and TIRANO - CHIAVENNA - LUGANO — PostAuto, RhB

			P🅁		B🅁					
St Moritz, Bahnhof .... d.	0817	0917	1000	1017	...	1117		1917	2017	2115
Silvaplana .... d.	0826	0926	1008**u**	1026	...	1126		1926	2026	2134
Sils / Segl Maria, Posta .. d.	0835	0935	1015**u**	1035	...	1135	and	1935	2035	2140
Maloja, Posta .... d.	0850	0950	1026**u**	1050	...	1150		1950	2050	2150
Castasegna 🏛 .... d.	0932	1032	|	1132	...	1232	hourly	2032	2132	2224
Chiavenna, Stazione .... d.	0955	1055	1130**u**	1155	...	1255		2055	2155	*2245*
Tirano, Stazione .... d.	...	...	|	...	1420	...	until	...	...	...
Menaggio .... d.	...	...	1235	...	|	...		...	...	...
Lugano, Stazione ◐ ..... a.	...	...	1340	...	1730	...		...	...	...

						B🅁	P🅁				
Lugano, Stazione ◐ .... d.	...	...	...		...	1000	1440	...	...	...	...
Menaggio .... d.	...	...	...		...	|	1527	...	...	...	...
Tirano, Stazione .... a.	...	...	...	and	...	1300	|	...	...	...	...
Chiavenna, Stazione ...... d.	0705	0805	0905		1605	...	1625**s**	1705	1805	1905	2005
Castasegna 🏛 .... d.	0722	0822	0922	hourly	1622	...	|	1722	1822	1922	2022
Maloja, Posta .... d.	0810	0910	1010		1710	...	1727**s**	1810	1910	2014	2114
Sils / Segl Maria, Posta .... d.	0824	0924	1024	until	1724	...	1738**s**	1824	1924	2026	2126
Silvaplana. .... d.	0832	0932	1032		1732	...	1745**s**	1832	1932	2038	2138
St Moritz, Bahnhof.......... a.	0843	0943	1043		1743	...	1800	1843	1943	2059	2159

B – *Bernina Express*: ④–⑦ Feb. 13 - Mar. 30; daily Mar. 31 - Oct. 26; ④–⑦ Oct. 30 - Nov. 23. 🅁 www.berninaexpress.ch or ✆ 081 288 6565.
P – *Palm Express*. 🅁 www.postauto.ch/90.631 or ✆ +41 848 818 818.
s – Stops to set down only.
u – Stops to pick up only.
◐ – 🏛 is at Gandria.

☛ **Additional journeys** St Moritz - Chiavenna and v.v.
From St Moritz at 0617, 0717.
From Chiavenna at 0615.

544 🚌 CHUR - BELLINZONA and CHIAVENNA — PostAuto

km				S A	B				S A	⑥ C											S A					
0	**Chur** Postautostation .... d.	0658	...	...	0758	0808	0858	...	...	0958	1008	1058	...	1208	1258	...	1408	1458	...	1608	...	1658	...	1808	...	2008
40	Thusis Bahnhof .... ⊡ d.	0725	0735	...	0825	0835	0925	0935	...	1025	1035	1125	1135	1235	1325	1335	1435	1525	1535	1635	...	1725	1735	1835	1935	2035
64	Splügen Dorf .... d.	0754	0816	0820	|	0906	0954	1016	1020	|	1106	1154	1216	1306	1354	1416	1506	1554	1616	1706	1715	1754	1816	1906	2016	2106
	San Bernardino Villaggio ..... a.	0810	0836	|	0910	0924	1010	1036	|	1110	1124	1210	1236	1324	1410	1436	1524	1610	1636	1724	|	1810	1836	1924	2036	2124
	Chiavenna Stazione ◐ .... a.	|	...	1020	|	|	|	...	1220	|	|	|	...	|	|	...	|	|	...	|	1915	|	...	|	...	|
179	**Bellinzona** Stazione .... a.	0904	...	...	1000	1020	1104	...	...	1200	1220	1304	...	1420	1504	...	1620	1704	...	1820	...	1904	...	2020	...	2220

				S A												S A				S A		B			⑥ C	
Bellinzona Stazione .... d.	...	...	0740	...	...	0856	0940	...	1056	1140	...	1256	1340	...	1456	...	1540	...	1656	...	1740	1756	...	1856	1956	2056
Chiavenna Stazione ◐.. d.	...	...	|	0745	...	|	|	...	|	|	...	|	|	...	|	1445	|	...	|	1645	|	|	...	|	|	|
San Bernardino Villaggio ... d.	0635	0722	0835	|	0922	0951	1035	1122	1151	1235	1322	1351	1435	1522	1551	|	1635	1722	1751	|	1835	1851	1922	1951	2051	2144
Splügen Dorf .... d.	0653	0743	0853	0940	0943	1009	1053	1143	1209	1253	1343	1409	1453	1543	1609	1640	1653	1743	1809	1840	1853	1909	1943	2009	2109	2201
Thusis Bahnhof .... ⊙ a.	0725	0823	0925	...	1023	1035	1125	1223	1235	1325	1423	1435	1525	1623	1635	...	1725	1823	1835	...	1925	1935	2023	2035	2141	2228
Chur Postautostation .... a.	0752	...	0952	...	...	1102	1152	...	1302	1352	...	1502	1552	...	1702	...	1752	...	1902	...	1952	2002	...	2102	2208	...

A – June 14 - Oct. 26.
B – June 7 - Oct. 19.
C – June 7 - Oct. 18.
S – Splügen Pass service.

⊡ – Stops to pick up only.
⊙ – Stops to set down only.
◐ – 🏛 is at Splügen Pass.

Operator: PostAuto AG. www.postauto.ch ✆ +41 848 818 818.

Narrow gauge

RHÄTISCHE BAHN (RhB) services 545

DISENTIS / MUSTÉR - CHUR

km		Ⓐ		⚒							
0	**Disentis / Mustér** d.	*0439**	0544	0615	0644	0744	and	1944	2044	*2146**	*2257**
12	Trun d.	*0453**	0602	0631	0702	0802	hourly	2002	2102	*2201**	*2312**
30	Ilanz d.	0524	0624	0654	0724	0824	until	2024	2124	2229	2340
49	Reichenau-Tamins d.	0549	0649	0719	0749	0849		2049	2149	2251	0001
59	**Chur** a.	0602	0702	0733	0802	0902		2102	2202	2305	0011

	⚒								ALSO		
Chur d.	0612	0653	0755	and	1955	2102	2202	2302	A	1725	1825
Reichenau-Tamins d.	0625	0705	0805	hourly	2005	2112	2212	2312	L	|	|
Ilanz d.	0653	0733	0833	until	2033	2140	2236	2336	S	1802	1902
Trun d.	0715	0754	0854		2054	*2204**	*2300**	*0000**	O	1825	1925
Disentis / Mustér a.	0731	0811	0911		2111	*2223**	*2319**	*0019**		1841	1941

CHUR - LANDQUART - KLOSTERS - SCUOL TARASP / DAVOS

km		Ⓐ M	⚒			Ⓐ			M			M				M			M			M			M
0	**Chur** 520 534 d.	...	*0453*	0521r	...	*0550*	*0621*	...	*0653*	*0721*	...	*0753*	*0821*	...		*1453*	*1521*	...	*1553*	*1621*	...	*1653*	*1721*	...	*1753*
14	**Landquart** 520 534 a.	...	*0514*	0550r	...	*0611*	*0641*	...	*0711*	*0741*	...	*0811*	*0841*	...	and at	*1511*	*1541*	...	*1611*	*1641*	...	*1711*	*1741*	...	*1811*
14	**Landquart** d.	0454	0520	0550	...	0617	0647	...	0720	0749	0749	0820	0849	0849		1520	1549	1549	1620	1649	1649	1720	1749	1749	1820
35	Küblis d.	0514	0541	0614	...	0645	0714	...	0741	0811	0811	0841	0911	0911	the same	1541	1611	1611	1641	1711	1711	1741	1811	1811	1841
44	Klosters Dorf d.	|	0554	0627	...	0658	0727	...	|	0824	0824	|	0924	0924		|	1624	1624	|	1724	1724	|	1824	1824	|
46	**Klosters** Platz a.	0528	0557	0630	...	0701	0730	...	0758	0828	0828	0858	0928	0928	minutes	1558	1628	1628	1658	1728	1728	1758	1828	1828	1858
46	**Klosters** Platz 🚗 d.	...	0600	0631	0632	0702	0732	0732	0801	0831	0832	0901	0931	0932		1601	1631	1632	1701	1731	1732	1801	1831	1832	1901
61	**Davos** Dorf d.	...	0624	0655	|	0726	|	0759	0824	0859	|	0924	0959	|	past each	1624	1659	|	1724	1759	|	1824	1859	|	1924
64	**Davos** Platz a.	...	0628	0659	|	0730	|	0803	0827	0903	|	0927	1003	|		1627	1703	|	1727	1803	|	1827	1903	|	1927
68	Sagliains ¶ 🚗 a.	...	...	...	0658	...	0754	...	...	...	0854	...	...	0954	hour until	...	...	1654	...	...	1754	...	...	1854	...
77	Ardez ⊗ a.	...	...	...	0708	...	0806	...	...	...	0906	...	...	1006		...	...	1706	...	...	1806	...	...	1906	...
85	**Scuol-Tarasp** a.	...	...	...	0718	...	0815	...	...	...	0915	...	...	1015		...	...	1715	...	...	1815	...	...	1915	...

			M				f		j	f		⑤⑥ e	
Chur 520 534 d.	*1821*	...	*1853*	*1921*	...	*2014**	...	*2114**	...	...	*2214**	...	*2314**
Landquart 520 534 a.	*1841*	...	*1911*	*1941*	...	*2043**	...	*2143**	...	...	*2243**	...	*2343**
Landquart d.	1849	1849	1920	1949	1949	2047	...	2147	...	...	2247	...	0001
Küblis d.	1911	1911	1941	2013	2013	2114	...	2214	...	...	2314	...	0027
Klosters Dorf d.	1924	1924	|	2026	2026	2127	...	2227	...	...	2327	...	0040
Klosters Platz a.	1928	1928	1958	2029	2029	2130	...	2230	...	...	2330	...	0044
Klosters Platz 🚗 d.	1931	1932	2001	2031	2032f	2131	2134	2231	2234	...	2331	2334	0044
Davos Dorf d.	1955	|	2026	2056	|	2156	|	2256	|	...	2356	|	0108
Davos Platz a.	1959	|	2030	2059	|	2159	|	2259	|	...	2359	|	0112
Sagliains ¶ 🚗 a.	...	1954	...	...	2054f	...	2158	...	2258	2258	...	2358	...
Ardez ⊗ a.	...	2006	...	...	2106f	...	2208	...	2308	2308	...	0008	...
Scuol-Tarasp a.	...	2015	...	..	2115f	...	2218	...	2318	2318	...	0018	...

	⚒	Ⓐ E	Ⓐ	Ⓒ		Ⓐ			
Scuol-Tarasp d.	...	...	0541	0541	...	...	0641	...	...
Ardez ⊗ d.	...	...	0550	0550	...	...	0650	...	...
Sagliains ¶ 🚗 d.	...	...	0605	0605	...	...	0705	...	...
Davos Platz d.	0501	...	|	|	0559	0629	|	0701	...
Davos Dorf d.	0505	...	|	|	0603	0633	|	0705	...
Klosters Platz 🚗 a.	0528	...	0626	0626	0627	0656	0726	0728	...
Klosters Platz d.	0529	0557	0629	...	0629	0658	...	0730	...
Klosters Dorf d.	0532	0600	0632	...	0632	0701	...	0733	...
Küblis d.	0546	0614	0646	...	0646	0715	...	0748	...
Landquart a.	0613	0641	0713	...	0713	0739	...	0810	...
Landquart 520 534 d.	*0618*	*0648*	*0718*	...	*0718*	*0748*	...	*0818*	...
Chur 520 534 a.	*0637*	*0706*	*0737*	...	*0737*	*0806*	...	*0837*	...

	M			M			M				M			M					z	f		j		⑤⑥ e	
Scuol-Tarasp d.	...	0741	...	...	0841	...	...		1641	...	...	1741	...	...	1841	...	1941	...	2033	2041	...	2141	...	2241	...
Ardez ⊗ d.	...	0749	...	...	0849	...	...	and at	1649	...	...	1749	...	...	1849	...	1949	...	2042	2049	...	2150	...	2250	...
Sagliains ¶ 🚗 d.	...	0805	...	...	0905	...	...		1705	...	...	1805	...	...	1905	...	2005	...	|	2105	...	2203	...	2303	...
Davos Platz d.	0732	|	0756	0832	|	0856	0932	the same	|	1656	1732	|	1756	1832	|	1856	|	2000	|	|	2100	|	2200	|	2252
Davos Dorf d.	0737	|	0801	0837	|	0901	0937		|	1701	1737	|	1801	1837	|	1901	|	2004	|	|	2105	|	2205	|	2257
Klosters Platz 🚗 a.	0758	0826	0828	0858	0926	0928	0958	minutes	1726	1728	1758	1826	1828	1858	1926	1928	2026	2027	2126	2126	2128	2226	2228	2322	2320
Klosters Platz d.	0800	0830	0830	0900	0930	0930	1000		1730	1730	1800	1830	1830	1900	1930	1930	2029	2029	...	...	2129	...	2229	...	2324
Klosters Dorf d.	|	0833	0833	|	0933	0933	|	past each	1733	1733	|	1833	1833	|	1933	1933	2032	2032	...	...	2132	...	2232	...	2327
Küblis d.	0818	0848	0848	0918	0948	0948	1018		1748	1748	1818	1848	1848	1918	1948	1948	2046	2046	...	...	2146	...	2246	...	2340
Landquart a.	0839	0910	0910	0939	1010	1010	1039	hour until	1810	1810	1839	1910	1910	1939	2010	2010	2113	2113	...	...	2213	...	2313	...	0007
Landquart 520 534 d.	*0848*	...	*0918*	*0948*	...	*1018*	*1048*		...	*1818*	*1848*	...	*1918*	*1948*	...	*2018*	...	*2117**	...	...	*2217**	...	*2317**	...	*0017**
Chur 520 534 a.	*0906*	...	*0937*	*1006*	...	*1037*	*1106*		...	*1837*	*1906*	...	*1937*	*2006*	...	*2037*	...	*2144**	...	...	*2244**	...	*2344**	...	*0044**

SCUOL TARASP and KLOSTERS - ST MORITZ and PONTRESINA

km		Ⓐ				⚒																				
0	**Scuol-Tarasp** d.	...	...	0558	*0641*	...	0733	...	0833	...	0933	...	1033	...	1133	...	1233	...	1333	...	1433	...	1533	...	1633	...
8	Ardez ⊗ d.	...	...	0609	*0650*	...	0742	...	0842	...	0942	...	1042	...	1142	...	1242	...	1342	...	1442	...	1542	...	1642	...
	Landquart ◐ d.	0454	...	|	|	...	|	0720	|	0820	|	0920	|	1020	|	1120	|	1220	|	1320	|	1420	|	1520	|	1620
	Klosters Platz d.	0530	...	|	|	...	|	0802	|	0902	|	1002	|	1102	|	1202	|	1302	|	1402	|	1502	|	1602	|	1702
17	Sagliains ¶ a.	|	...	|	*0701*	...	0753	|	0853	|	0953	|	1053	|	1153	|	1253	|	1353	|	1453	|	1553	|	1653	|
	Sagliains ¶ d.	|	...	|	0703	...	0754	|	0854	|	0954	|	1054	|	1154	|	1254	|	1354	|	1454	|	1554	|	1654	|
19	Susch ⊗ d.	0553	...	0622	0705	...	0759	0819	0859	|	0959	|	1059	|	1159	|	1259	|	1359	|	1459	|	1559	|	1659	|
25	Zernez ⊖ d.	0602	...	0630	0713	...	0807	0830	0907	0930	1007	1030	1107	1130	1207	1230	1307	1330	1407	1430	1507	1530	1607	1630	1707	1730
42	Zuoz d.	0622	0633r	0651	0733	0757	0829	0849	0929	0949	1029	1049	1129	1149	1229	1249	1329	1349	1429	1449	1529	1549	1629	1649	1729	1749
52	Samedan a.	0633	0646r	0708	0748	0813	0843	0902	0943	0958	1043	1058	1143	1158	1243	1258	1343	1358	1443	1458	1543	1558	1643	1658	1743	1758
52	Samedan ▲ d.	0636	0650	0714	0750	0814	0847	0905	0947	1000	1047	1100	1147	1200	1247	1300	1347	1400	1447	1500	1547	1600	1647	1700	1747	1800
	St Moritz ▲ a.	0643	|	0722	|	0822	|	0914	|	1007	|	1107	|	1207	|	1307	|	1407	|	1507	|	1607	|	1707	|	1807
57	**Pontresina** a.	...	0658	...	0758	...	0855	...	0955	...	1055	...	1155	...	1255	...	1355	...	1455	...	1555	...	1655	...	1755	...

							f		⑤⑥ e	f	⑤⑥ e
Scuol-Tarasp d.	1733	...	1833	...	1933	...	2033	*2141*f	2241	...	...
Ardez ⊗ d.	1742	...	1842	...	1942	...	2042	*2150*f	2250	...	...
Landquart ◐ d.	|	1720	|	1820	|	1920	|	|	|	...	...
Klosters Platz d.	|	1802	|	1902	|	2002	|	|	|	...	...
Sagliains ¶ a.	1753	|	1853	|	1953	|	2053	*2200*f	2300	...	...
Sagliains ¶ d.	1754	|	1854	|	1954	|	2054	2203f	...	2303	2359
Susch ⊗ d.	1759	|	1859	|	1959	2019	2059	2205f	...	2305	0003
Zernez ⊖ d.	1807	1830	1907	1930	2007	2030	2107	2213f	...	2313	0010
Zuoz d.	1829	1849	1929	1949	2029	2049	2129	2234	...	2334	0029
Samedan a.	1843	1858	1943	2002	2043	2102	2143	2248	...	2348	0041
Samedan ▲ d.	1847	1900	1947	2005	2047	2103	2147	2250	...	2350	0042
St Moritz ▲ a.	|	1907	|	2014	|	2110	|	|	...	2358	0049
Pontresina a.	1855	...	1955	...	2055	...	2155	2258	...	...	...

	Ⓐ		⚒								
Pontresina d.	...	...	0537	0558b	...	0705	...	0805	...	0905	...
St Moritz ▲ d.	0445	0502c	|	|	0645	|	0748	|	0853	|	0953
Samedan ▲ a.	0452	0509c	0544	0605b	0652	0712	0757	0812	0900	0912	1000
Samedan d.	0453	0513	0549	0609	0653	0716	0758	0816	0901	0916	1001
Zuoz d.	0506	0526	0603	0623	0706	0733	0811	0829	0911	0929	1011
Zernez ⊖ d.	0526	0546	...	0646	0730	0752	0831	0852	0931	0952	1031
Susch ⊗ d.	0533	0553	...	0653	0736	0800	|	0900	|	1000	|
Sagliains ¶ a.	|	0556	...	0656	|	0803	|	0903	|	1003	|
Sagliains ¶ d.	|	0558	...	*0658*	|	0804	|	0904	|	1004	|
Klosters Platz a.	0551	|	...	|	0756	|	0856	|	0956	|	1056
Landquart ◐ a.	0641	|	...	|	0839	|	0939	|	1039	|	1139
Ardez ⊗ d.	...	0610	...	*0708*	...	0814	...	0914	...	1014	...
Scuol-Tarasp a.	...	0619	...	*0718*	...	0825	...	0925	...	1025	...

																				f		f		f		⑤⑥ e
Pontresina d.	1005	...	1105	...	1205	...	1305	...	1405	...	1505	...	1605	...	1705	...	1805	1905	2005	2005	2103	2103	2202	2202	2302	2302
St Moritz ▲ d.	|	1053	|	1153	|	1253	|	1353	|	1453	|	1553	|	1653	|	1753	|	|	|	|	|	|	|	|	|	|
Samedan ▲ a.	1012	1100	1112	1200	1212	1300	1312	1400	1412	1500	1512	1600	1612	1700	1712	1800	1812	1912	2012	2012	2110	2110	2209	2209	2309	2309
Samedan d.	1016	1101	1116	1201	1216	1301	1316	1401	1416	1501	1516	1601	1616	1701	1716	1801	1816	1916	2016	2016	2113	2113	2213	2213	...	2313
Zuoz d.	1029	1111	1129	1211	1229	1311	1329	1411	1429	1511	1529	1611	1629	1711	1729	1811	1829	1929	2029	2029	2126	2127	2226	2227	...	2327
Zernez ⊖ d.	1052	1131	1152	1231	1252	1331	1352	1431	1452	1531	1552	1631	1652	1731	1752	1831	1852	1952	...	2052	...	2146	...	2246	...	2346
Susch ⊗ d.	1100	|	1200	|	1300	|	1400	|	1500	|	1600	|	1700	|	1800	|	1900	2000	...	2100	...	2153	...	2253	...	2353
Sagliains ¶ a.	1103	|	1203	|	1303	|	1403	|	1503	|	1603	|	1703	|	1803	|	1903	2003	...	2103	...	2156	...	2256	...	2356
Sagliains ¶ d.	1104	|	1204	|	1304	|	1404	|	1504	|	1604	|	1704	|	1804	|	1904	2004	...	2104	...	*2158*	...	*2258*	...	*2358*
Klosters Platz a.	|	1156	|	1256	|	1356	|	1456	|	1556	|	1656	|	1756	|	1856	|	|	...	|	...	|	...	|	...	|
Landquart ◐ a.	|	1239	|	1339	|	1439	|	1539	|	1639	|	1739	|	1839	|	1939	|	|	...	|	...	|	...	|	...	|
Ardez ⊗ d.	1114	...	1214	...	1314	...	1414	...	1514	...	1614	...	1714	...	1814	...	1914	2014	...	2114	...	*2208*	...	*2308*	...	*0008*
Scuol-Tarasp a.	1125	...	1225	...	1325	...	1425	...	1525	...	1625	...	1725	...	1825	...	1925	2025	...	2125	...	*2218*	...	*2318*	...	*0018*

FOR NOTES SEE NEXT PAGE →

545 RHÄTISCHE BAHN (RhB) services

Narrow gauge

CHUR - ST MORITZ

km																											
							951						955														
													Z										D		⑤⑥		
			⚒	⚒ v	⚒	🍷	🍷	B🍷	🍷				🍷	B🍷	🍷	🍷									e		
0	**Chur**	d.	0428	0508	0600	0658	0758	0817	0858	0958	1058	1158	1258	1328	1358	1458	1558	1658	1758	1858	1958	2055	2055	2155	2155	2256	0003
10	Reichenau-Tamins	d.	0440	0518	0613	0708	0808	|	0908	1008	1108	1208	1308	|	1408	1508	1608	1708	1808	1908	2008	2108	2108	2208	2208	2309	0013
27	Thusis	d.	0503	0540	0636	0728	0828	0852	0928	1028	1128	1228	1328	1400	1428	1528	1628	1728	1828	1928	2028	2130	2132	2231	2232	2331	0036
41	Tiefencastel	d.	▬	0556	▬	0744	0844	0914	0944	1044	1144	1244	1344	|	1444	1544	1644	1744	1844	1944	2044	...	2147	...	2247	▬	...
51	**Filisur**	d.	...	0614	...	0800	0900	0932	1000	1100	1200	1300	1400	1432	1500	1600	1700	1800	1900	2000	2100	...	2205	...	2305	...	...
59	Bergün / Bravuogn	d.	...	0627	...	0813	0913	09476	1013	1113	1213	1313	1413	1446	1513	1613	1713	1813	1913	2013	2113	...	2217	...	2317	...	...
72	Preda	d.	...	0644	...	0831	0931	|	1031	1131	1231	1331	1431	|	1531	1631	1731	1831	1931	2031	2131	...	2234	...	2334	...	...
84	**Samedan**	a.	...	0658	...	0843	0943	|	1043	1143	1243	1343	1443	|	1543	1643	1743	1843	1943	2043	2144	...	2248	...	2348	f	...
84	**Samedan**	d.	0550	0659	0750	0845	0945	|	1045	1145	1245	1345	1445	|	1545	1645	1745	1845	1945	2045	2150	...	2250	...	...	2350	...
	Pontresina	a.	|	|	|	|	|	1020	|	|	|	|	|	1520	|	|	|	|	|	|	|	...	|	...	...	|	...
87	Celerina	d.	0553	0702	0753	0849	0949	...	1049	1149	1249	1349	1449	...	1549	1649	1749	1849	1949	2049	2153	...	2253	...	...	2353	...
89	**St Moritz**	a.	0558	0707	0758	0853	0953	...	1053	1153	1353	1353	1453	...	1553	1653	1753	1853	1953	2053	2158	...	2258	...	...	2358	...

											950							952								
											Z													⑤⑥		
		⚒	⚒	Ⓐ d	⚒	⚒	†					B🍷	🍷	🍷			🍷	🍷	B🍷	🍷	🍷			e		
St Moritz	d.	...	...	*0445*	0537	...	0558	0707	0807	0907	1007	...	1107	1207	1307	1407	1507	1607	...	1707	1807	1907	2007	2102	2102	2202	...
Celerina	d.	...	...	*0448*	0541	...	0601	0710	0810	0910	1010	...	1110	1210	1310	1410	1510	1610	...	1710	1810	1910	2010	2106	2106	2205	...
Pontresina	d.	...	...	|	|	...	|	|	|	|	|	1030	|	|	|	|	|	|	1630	|	|	|	|	|	|	|	...
Samedan	a.	...	...	*0453*	0544	...	0605	0714	0814	0914	1014	|	1114	1214	1314	1414	1514	1614	|	1714	1814	1914	2014	2110	2110	2209	...
Samedan	d.	...	...	0511	0546	...	0607	0716	0816	0916	1016	|	1116	1216	1316	1416	1516	1616	|	1716	1816	1916	2016	2116	▬	▬	...
Preda	d.	...	...	|	0600	...	0621	0729	0829	0929	1029	|	1129	1229	1329	1429	1529	1629	|	1729	1829	1929	2029	2129	...	...	...
Bergün / Bravuogn	d.	...	...	0540	0617	...	0638	0747	0847	0947	1047	1112	1147	1247	1347	1447	1547	1647	1713	1747	1847	1947	2047	2147	...	...	...
Filisur	d.	...	...	0553	0632	...	0651	0800	0900	1000	1100	1126	1200	1300	1400	1500	1600	1700	1728	1800	1900	2000	2100	2202	...	...	...
Tiefencastel	d.	...	...	0611	0650	...	0708	0815	0915	1015	1115	|	1215	1315	1415	1515	1615	1715	1743	1815	1915	2015	2117	2218	...	...	...
Thusis	d.	0509	0614	0628	0708	0728	0728	0833	0933	1033	1133	1202	1233	1333	1433	1533	1633	1733	1802	1833	1933	2033	2133	2233	2233	2335	0040
Reichenau-Tamins	d.	0535	0639	0652	|	0753	0753	0852s	0952s	1052s	1152s	|	1252s	1352s	1452s	1552s	1652s	1752s	|	1852s	1952s	2052s	2156	2256	2256	2356x	0102x
Chur	a.	0548	0652	0705	0740	0805	0805	0904	1004	1104	1204	1231	1304	1404	1504	1604	1704	1804	1831	1904	2004	2104	2208	2308	2308	0010	0112

ST MORITZ - TIRANO

km																											
									971		951				973			955		975			🚌		🚌		
									Z						Z			Z		L							
						⚒			A🍷	▷	B🍷				A🍷		▷	B🍷		A🍷	▷					Ⓐ	
0	**St Moritz**	d.	...	...	...	0629	0748	0848	0917	0948	...	1048	1148	1248	1317	1348	1448	...	1548	1614	1648	1748	...	1848	...	1948	2020
6	**Pontresina**	a.	...	...	...	0638	0757	0857	0925	0957	...	1057	1157	1257	1325	1357	1457	...	1557	1622	1657	1757	...	1857	...	1957	2029
6	**Pontresina**	d.	...	...	...	0702	0808	0904	0928	1008	1025	1104	1208	1304	1328	1408	1504	1525	1605	1623	1704	1808	...	1904	...	2004	▬
12	Morteratsch	⊗ d.	...	...	...	0711	0818	0913	|	1018	|	1113	1218	1313	|	1418	1513	|	1618	|	1713	1818	...	1913	...	2013	...
17	Bernina Diavolezza	⊗ d.	...	...	...	0720	0828	0923	|	1028	1042	1123	1228	1323	|	1428	1523	1549	1628	1639	1723	1828	...	1922	...	2022	...
22	Ospizio Bernina	d.	...	...	...	0731	0838	0933	|	1038	|	1133	1238	1333	|	1438	1533	1619	1638	1652	1733	1838	...	1932	...	2032	...
27	Alp Grüm	a.	...	...	...	0740	0849	0942	1006	1049	1101	1142	1249	1342	1407	1449	1542	1628	1649	1700	1742	1849	...	1942	...	2042	...
27	Alp Grüm	d.	...	...	...	0744	0853	0944	1018	1053	1115	1144	1253	1344	1418	1453	1544	1640	1653	1716	1744	1853	...	1946	...	2046	...
44	**Poschiavo**	a.	...	...	...	0830	0941	1022	1054	1141	1201	1222	1341	1422	1453	1541	1622	1715	1741	1800	1822	1932	...	2023	...	2123	🚌
44	**Poschiavo**	d.	0620	0742	0834	0834	0942	1023	1056	1142	1210	1223	1342	1423	1455	1542	1623	1724	1742	1801	1823	...	1934	...	2034	...	2134
48	Le Prese	d.	0627	0749	0841	0841	0949	1030	1103	1149	1221	1230	1349	1430	1502	1549	1630	1732	1749	|	1830	...	1940	...	2040	...	2140
51	Miralago	⊗ d.	0633	0754	0847	0847	0954	1035	|	1154	|	1235	1354	1435	|	1554	1635	|	1754	|	1835	...	1944	...	2044	...	2144
54	Brusio	⊗ d.	0642	0803	0857	0857	1002	1043	|	1202	|	1243	1402	1443	|	1602	1643	|	1802	|	1843	...	1948	...	2048	...	2148
58	Campocologno 🏛	d.	0654	0814	0908	0908	1014	1052	|	1214	|	1252	1414	1452	|	1614	1652	|	1814	|	1852	...	1952	...	2052	...	2152
61	**Tirano**	a.	0703	0823	0917	0917	1023	1100	1132	1223	1249	1300	1423	1500	1531	1623	1700	1759	1823	1839	1900	...	2000	...	2100	...	2200

				🚌			950			972			974		952			976				🚌		🚌	🚌	🚌
							Z			L			Z					Z								
		⚒					B🍷		▷	A🍷		▷	▷	A🍷		B🍷			A🍷			S				
Tirano	d.	...	...	0653	...	0741	0806	0900	0941	1006	1100	1141	1300	1317	1341	1424	1500	1541	1606	1700	1741	1900	...	1939	2002	2102	2202
Campocologno 🏛	d.	...	...	0659	...	0752	|	0908	0952	|	1108	1152	1308	|	1352	|	1508	1552	|	1708	1752	1910	...	1947	2008	2108	2208
Brusio	⊗ d.	...	...	0706	...	0802	|	0916	1002	|	1116	1202	1316	|	1402	|	1516	1602	|	1716	1802	1920	...	1956	2012	2112	2212
Miralago	⊗ d.	...	...	0710	...	0810	|	0923	1010	|	1123	1210	1323	|	1410	|	1523	1610	|	1723	1810	1927	...	2003	2015	2115	2215
Le Prese	d.	...	...	0712	...	0815	0835	0928	1015	1041	1128	1215	1328	1344	1415	1455	1528	1615	1640	1728	1815	1932	...	2007	2018	2118	2218
Poschiavo	a.	...	...	0728	...	0825	0845	0936	1025	1048	1136	1225	1336	1353	1425	1506	1536	1625	1647	1736	1825	1940	...	2016	2028	2135	2235
Poschiavo	d.	0628	...	...	0732	0828	0847	0937	1028	1050	1137	1228	1337	1357	1428	1510	1537	1628	1648	1737	1828	...	2005	...	...	...	...
Alp Grüm	a.	0706	...	...	0811	0906	0923	1010	1106	1126	1210	1306	1410	1442	1506	1545	1610	1706	1727	1810	1906	...	|	...	...	...	...
Alp Grüm	d.	0708	...	...	0813	0908	0948	1013	1108	1142	1213	1308	1413	1459	1508	1545	1613	1708	1742	1813	1908	...	|	...	...	...	...
Ospizio Bernina	d.	0715	...	...	0820	0915	0958	1020	1115	|	1220	1315	1420	|	1515	|	1620	1715	|	1820	1915	...	2036	...	...	...	...
Bernina Diavolezza	⊗ d.	0726	...	...	0833	0927	|	1034	1127	1200	1234	1327	1434	|	1527	|	1634	1727	|	1834	1927	...	2041	...	...	...	...
Morteratsch	⊗ d.	0738	...	...	0844	0940	|	1047	1140	|	1244	1340	1444	|	1540	|	1644	1740	|	|	1940	...	2047	...	...	...	...
Pontresina	a.	0748	...	...	0856	0951	1025	1056	1151	1225	1253	1351	1453	1534	1551	1623	1653	1751	1815	1853	1951	...	2101	...	...	...	...
Pontresina	d.	0801	0801	...	0901	1001	...	1101	1201	1227	1301	1401	1501	1536	1601	...	1701	1801	1817	1901	2001	...	...	...	...	...	...
St Moritz	a.	0811	0811	...	0911	1011	...	1111	1211	1235	1311	1411	1511	1545	1611	...	1711	1811	1825	1911	2011	...	...	...	...	...	...

DAVOS - FILISUR

km			⚒			♣					
0	Davos Platz	d.	0605	...	0731	and hourly	2031	...	...	...	...
16	**Filisur**	a.	0630	...	0756	until	2056	...	...	...	...

		⚒			♣					
Filisur	d.	0634	...	0804	and hourly	2104	...	...	...	...
Davos Platz	a.	0659	...	0829	until	2129	...	...	...	...

CHUR - AROSA

km			⚒								●
0	**Chur**	d.	0459	0600	0708	and	1908	2006	2100	...	2300
18	Langwies	d.	0540	0641	0750	hourly	1950	2044	2140	...	2341
26	**Arosa**	a.	0557	0700	0809	until	2009	2102	2157	...	2358

		⚒	Ⓐ	Ⓒ							
Arosa	d.	0602	0637	0649	0749	and	1749	1849	1949	2107	2203
Langwies	d.	0618	0653	0705	0805	hourly	1805	1905	2004	2123	2219
Chur	a.	0700	0735	0751	0851	until	1851	1948	2045	2205	2300

A – BERNINA EXPRESS – [12] [panorama car]. Ⓡ for travel in panorama car.
B – BERNINA EXPRESS – [12] [panorama car] Chur - Pontresina - Tirano and v.v. Ⓡ for travel in panorama car.
D – ⑤⑥ until Nov. 15 (also June 8, July 31); daily from Nov. 18.
E – From St. Moritz (see lower panel on page 269).
L – Daily until Oct. 26; ①⑤⑥⑦ Oct. 31 - Nov. 3 and from Dec. 5.
M – Conveys [12] Landquart - Klosters - St Moritz and v.v. (see lower panel on page 269).
S – To Samedan (a. 2104).
Y – Until Oct. 19.
Z – Until Oct. 26.

b – † only.
c – Ⓒ only.
d – From Nov. 18.
e – Also July 31; not Aug. 1.
f – ⑤⑥ until Oct. 25 (also June 8, July 31); daily from Oct. 31.
j – ⑤⑥ until Nov. 22 (also June 8, July 31); daily from Nov. 28.
r – ⚒ only.
s – Calls to set down only.
v – Runs daily Samedan - St Moritz.
x – Calls on request.
z – ⑦–④ until Oct. 30 (not June 8, July 31).

▷ – Conveys open sightseeing car June 23 - Aug. 31 (subject to fine weather).
* – By 🚌.
⊗ – Request stop.
◐ – See upper panel.
▲ – See Chur - St Moritz panel on page 270 for connecting trains Samedan - St Moritz and v.v
♣ – Variations May 17 - Oct. 26: the 1031 and 1531 from Davos are retimed to depart at 1018 and 1518 (Filisur a. 1053, 1553); the 1104 and 1604 from Filisur are retimed to depart at 1106, 1606 (Davos a. 1150, 1650). These retimed services are operated with historic rolling stock (including open sightseeing cars).
● – By 🚌 in similar timings on ①–④ until Nov. 27 (not June 9, July 31).
¶ – Sagliains station can only be used for changing trains.

⊖ – 🚌 **ZERNEZ - MALLES**. Operator PostAuto ✆ +41 (0) 848 818 818. Journey ± 1 h 30 m
From Zernez: 0715, 0809, 0933, 1033 and hourly until 1933, then 2115.
From Malles / Mals: 0553, 0653, 0747, 0847 and hourly until 1647, then 1715Ⓒ, 1815, 1905 **Y**, 2005.

🚗 – Car-carrying trains operate Klosters Selfranga - Sagliains and v.v. ✆ +41 (0) 81 288 37 24 (www.rhb.ch/en/car-transporter).

SBB, SOB LUZERN and ZÜRICH - BELLINZONA - LOCARNO (via Gotthard pass) 547

See Table **550** for faster services via the Gotthard and Ceneri Base tunnels.

km		C	IR ⊙	IC ◇¶	IR ⊙	IC ◇	IR ⊙		EC ◇	IR ⊙	IC ◇	IR ⊙	IC ◇	IR ⊙	IC ◇	IR ⊙	IC ◇	IR ⊙	IC/IR ◇	IR ⊙	IC ◇	IR ⊙	IC/IR ◇	IR ◇	
	Basel SBB **565** ...... d.	...	...	0503	...	...	0603		1503	...	...	1603	1703	...	...	1803	1903	...	...	2003	2103	...	...	2203**t**	...
	Luzern......... **525 550** d.	...	...	0618	...	...	0718		1618	...	...	1718	1818	...	...	1918	2018	...	...	2118	2218	...	...	2318	...
0	**Zürich** HB .... **550** d.	...	...	|	0605	0705	|		|	1605	1705	|	|	1805	1905	|	|	2005	2105	|	|	2205	2305	|	...
29	Zug .... **550** d.	...	...	|	0630	0730	|		|	1630	1730	|	|	1830	1930	|	|	2030	2130	|	|	2230	2330	|	...
45	**Arth-Goldau 525 550** a.	...	...	0645	0645	0745	0745	and in	1645	1645	1745	1745	1845	1845	1945	1945	2045	2045	2145	2145	2245	2245	2345	2345	...
45	**Arth-Goldau** .... **550** d.	...	...	—	0654	—	0754	the same	—	1654	—	1754	—	1854	—	1954	—	2054	—	2154	...	2254	...	...	2355
53	Schwyz .... d.	...	...	...	0702	...	0802		...	1702	...	1802	...	1902	...	2002	...	2102	...	2202	...	2302	...	...	0002
56	Brunnen .... d.	...	...	...	0706	...	0806	pattern	...	1706	...	1806	...	1906	...	2006	...	2106	...	2206	...	2306	...	...	0005
68	Flüelen..................... d.	...	...	...	0715	...	0815	every **two**	...	1715	...	1815	...	1915	...	2015	...	2115	...	2215	...	2315	...	...	0015
71	Altdorf............... **550** d.	...	...	...	0718	...	0818		...	1718	...	1818	...	1918	...	2018	...	2118	...	2218	...	2318	...	...	0017
77	**Erstfeld** .... d.	...	0625	...	0725	...	0825	hours until	...	1725	...	1825	...	1925	...	2025	...	2125	...	2224	...	2324	...	...	0024
106	Göschenen .... d.	...	0651	...	0751	...	0851		...	1751	...	1851	...	1951	...	2051	...	2151	...	...	...	...	...	...	...
122	Airolo .... d.	0612	0702	...	0802	...	0902		...	1802	...	1902	...	2002	...	2102	...	2202	...	...	...	...	...	...	...
142	Faido .... d.	0630	0721	...	0821	...	0921		...	1821	...	1921	...	2021	...	2121	...	2221	...	...	...	...	...	...	...
168	Biasca................ **548** d.	0655	0745	...	0845	...	0945		...	1845	...	1945	...	2045	...	2145	...	2245	...	...	...	...	...	...	...
187	**Bellinzona**... **548 550** a.	0709	0800	...	0900	...	1000		...	1900	...	2000	...	2100	...	2200	...	2300	**E**	...	...	...	...	...	...
187	**Bellinzona**............ ▷ d.	*0719*	0804	0819	0904	0919	1004		1819	1904	1919	2004	2019	...	2119	...	2219	...	2319	...	...	...	...	...	...
208	**Locarno** .... ▷ a.	*0745*	0827	0845	0927	0945	1027		1845	1927	1945	2027	2045	...	2145	...	2244	...	2345	...	...	...	...	...	...

km		IR ⊙	IR ⊙	IC ◇		IR ⊙		IR ⊙		IR ⊙		IR ⊙			IR ⊙		IR ⊙		IR ⊙		IR ⊙				
	Locarno .... ▷ d.	...	...	...	0515	...	0615	...	0715	0733	0815	0833	0915		1733	1815	1833	1915	1933	2015	2033	2115	...	...	...
	Bellinzona............ ▷ a.	...	...	...	0541	...	0641	...	0741	0755	0841	0855	0941		1755	1841	1855	1941	1955	2041	2055	2141	...	...	...
	Bellinzona... **548 550** d.	...	...	...	...	0559	—	0659	—	0759	—	0859	—		1759	—	1859	—	1959	—	2059	—	...	...	...
	Biasca................ **548** d.	...	...	...	...	0614	...	0714	...	0814	...	0914	...		1814	...	1914	...	2014	...	2114	...	...	...	...
	Faido .... d.	...	...	...	...	0639	...	0739	...	0839	...	0939	...	and in	1839	...	1939	...	2039	...	2139	...	...	...	...
	Airolo .... d.	...	...	...	...	0657	...	0757	...	0857	...	0957	...	the same	1857	...	1957	...	2057	...	2157	...	...	...	...
	Göschenen .... d.	...	...	...	...	0709	...	0809	...	0909	...	1009	...		1909	...	2009	...	2109	...	2209	...	...	...	...
	Erstfeld .... d.	0531	0631	...	...	0734	...	0834	...	0934	...	1034	...	pattern	1934	...	2034	...	2134	...	2234	...	...	2301	...
	Altdorf............... **550** d.	0537	0637	...	...	0739	...	0839	...	0939	...	1039	...	every **two**	1939	...	2039	...	2139	...	2239	...	...	2306	...
	Flüelen..................... d.	0541	0641	...	...	0744	...	0844	...	0944	...	1044	...		1944	...	2044	...	2144	...	2244	...	...	2309	...
	Brunnen .... d.	0554	0654	...	...	0755	...	0855	...	0955	...	1055	...	hours until	1955	...	2055	...	2155	...	2255	...	2307	2320	...
	Schwyz .... d.	0558	0658	...	...	0759	IC	0859	IC	0959	IC	1059	IC		1959	IC	2059	IC	2159	IC	2259	IC	2310	2323	...
	Arth-Goldau .... **550** a.	0607	0707	...	...	0807	◇	0907	◇	1007	◇	1107	◇		2007	◇	2107	◇	2207	◇	2307	◇	2319	2331	...
0	**Arth-Goldau 525 550** d.	0615	0715	0715	...	0815	0815	0915	0915	1015	1015	1115	1115		2015	2015	2115	2115	2215	2215	2315	2315	2320	2332	...
	Zug .... **550** a.	|	0730	|	...	|	0830	0930	|	|	1030	1130	|		|	2030	2130	|	|	2230	2330	|	|	2353	2358
	Zürich HB .... **550** a.	|	0755	|	...	|	0855	0955	|	|	1055	1155	|		|	2055	2155	|	|	2255	2355	|	|	...	0025
28	**Luzern**......... **525 550** a.	0641	...	0741	...	0841	...	...	0941	1041	...	...	1141		2041	...	...	2141	2241	...	...	2341	2353	...	...
	Basel SBB **565** ...... a.	0756	...	0856	...	0956	...	...	1056	1156	...	...	1256		2156‡	...	...	2301	0001	...	...	0103	...	...	...

– To Chiasso (Table **548**).
– ⑤⑥ until June 7; daily June 9 - Aug. 30; ⑤⑥ from Sept. 5 (also Dec. 7).
– ⑥⑦ until June 8; daily June 10 - Aug. 31; ⑥⑦ from Sept. 6 (also Dec. 8).
- On ⑦–④ departs *2156* (change trains at Olten).
– Service shown here for connecting purposes only. Most run to/from Bellinzona via the Gotthard Base Tunnel (see Table **550** for full details).
– The 0503 from Basel departs 2 minutes earlier on ①–⑤ (subsequent services in the regular pattern depart Basel at xx03 on a daily basis).
– On ⑦–④ the 1733 from Locarno requires a change trains at Olten (arrives Basel *2201*). All other earlier trains in this pattern are through services to Basel on a daily basis (arriving xx56).
– Local trains Bellinzona - Locarno and v.v.:
From Bellinzona: 0449 and every 30 minutes until 2219; then 2249 **E**, 2319 **E**, 2349 **E** and 0021 **F**.
From Locarno: 0435, 0515, 0545 and every 30 minutes until 2245; then 2315 **E**, 2345 **E** and 0015 **F**.

GOTTHARD PANORAMA EXPRESS

	3093 ♣🍷		**3092** ♣🍷
Arth-Goldau .... d.	1335	**Lugano** .... d.	0918
Flüelen .... d.	1409	**Bellinzona**.............. d.	0953
Göschenen.................. d.	1453	Airolo .... d.	1048
Airolo......................... d.	1510	Göschenen .... d.	1105
Bellinzona .... a.	1606	Flüelen...................... d.	1141
Lugano...................... a.	1641	**Arth-Goldau**............ a.	1200

♣ – ②–⑦ Apr. 18 - Oct. 19 (also June 9).
Conveys [1st class coach symbol] [panorama cars] only; supplement payable.
All-inclusive train/ferry tour packages Luzern - Lugano and v.v. are available (see Table **507** ferry services).
⊙ – *TRENO GOTTARDO*. Operated by SOB. Conveys 🍷.

SBB Local services BIASCA and LOCARNO - LUGANO - MILANO 548

km										A															
0	Biasca................ **547** d.	...	...	0515	...	0555	...	0625	...	0655	...	0721**d**	...	0755	...	0825		...	1855	...	1925	...	1955	...	2025
19	**Bellinzona**......... **547** a.	...	...	0529	...	0609	...	0639	...	0709	...	0735**d**	...	0809	...	0839		...	1909	...	1939	...	2009	...	2039
19	**Bellinzona**......... **607** d.	0433	0517	0533	...	0616	...	0641	...	0716	...	0746	...	0816	...	0846	and at	...	1916	...	1946	...	2016	...	2046
2‡	**Locarno** .... d.	|	|	|	0552	|	0622	|	0652	|	0722	|	0752	|	0822	|	the same	1852	|	1922	|	1952	|	2022	|
0‡	Cadenazzo ..... **607** d.	|	|	|	0609	|	0639	|	0709	|	0739	|	0809	|	0839	|		1909	|	1939	|	2009	|	2039	|
48	**Lugano** .... **607** a.	0505	0551	0605	0624	0635	0654	0658	0724	0735	0754	0805	0824	0835	0854	0905	minutes	1924	1935	1954	2005	2024	2035	2054	2105
48	**Lugano** .... **607** d.	0506	0602	0606	...	0636	0702	0706	0725	0736	0802**r**	0806	0825	0836	0902**r**	0906	past each	1925	1936	2002**r**	2006	2025	2036	2102**r**	2106
67	Mendrisio .... **607** d.	0532	0618	0632	...	0657	0718	0732	0742	0757	0818	0832	0841	0857	0918	0932		1941	1957	2018	2032	2041	2057	2118	2132
74	**Chiasso** .... **607** a.	0540	0626	0640	...	0706	0726	0740	0750	0806	0826	0840	0849	0906	0926	0940	hour until	1949	2006	2026	2040	2049	2106	2126	2140
74	**Chiasso** 🏛 .... **607** d.	0543	0631	0647**c**	...	...	0731	0743	...	...	0831	0843	...	...	0931	0943		...	...	2031	2043	...	...	2131	...
78	Como S. Giovanni **607** d.	0554	0636	0654**c**	...	...	0736	0750	...	...	0836	0850	...	...	0936	0950		...	...	2036	2050	...	...	2136	...
25	**Milano** Centrale .... a.	...	0717	...	...	...	0817	...	...	...	0917	...	...	...	1017	...		...	...	2117	...	...	...	2217	...

asca .... **547** d.	...	2055	...	2125	...	2155	...	2225	...	2255	...	2325
ellinzona .... **547** a.	...	2109	...	2139	...	2209	...	2239	...	2309	...	2339
ellinzona .... **607** d.	...	2116	...	2146	...	2216	...	2246	...	2316	...	2346
Locarno .... d.	2052	|	2122	|	2152	|	2222	|	2252	|	2322**z**	|
Cadenazzo ..... **607** d.	2109	|	2139	|	2209	|	2239	|	2309	|	2339	|
ugano............ **607** a.	2124	2135	2154	2206	2224	2235	2254	2305	2324	2335	2354	0005
ugano............ **607** d.	...	2136	2155	2206	...	2236	2255	2306	...	2336	2355	0006
endrisio .... **607** d.	...	2157	2216	2232	...	2257	2316	2332	...	2357	0016	0032
hiasso............ **607** a.	...	2206	2226	2240	...	2306	2326	2340	...	0006	0026	0040
hiasso 🏛 .... **607** d.	...	...	2235**a**	...	...	...	...	...	...	...	...	...
omo S. Giovanni **607** d.	...	...	2241**a**	...	...	...	...	...	...	...	...	...
ilano Centrale .... a.	...	...	...	...	...	...	...	...	...	...	...	...

Milano Centrale .... d.	...	...	...	...	...	...	...	...	...
Como S. Giovanni...... **607** d.	...	0511	...	...	...	0611	...	...	...
Chiasso 🏛 .... **607** a.	...	0517	...	...	...	0617	...	...	...
Chiasso.................... **607** d.	0452	0520	0534	0554	...	0620	0634	0654	0711
Mendrisio .... **607** d.	0501	0534	0543	0604	...	0634	0641	0704	0718
Lugano.................... **607** a.	0521	0554	0604	0624	...	0654	0658**t**	0724	0734
Lugano.................... **607** d.	0522	0603	0605	0625	0635	0655	0705**t**	0725	0735
Cadenazzo .... **607** d.	|	|	0620	|	0650	|	0720	|	0750
Locarno .... a.	|	|	0638	|	0708	|	0738	|	0808
Bellinzona............... **607** a.	0553	0619	...	0643	...	0713	...	0743	...
Bellinzona............... **547** d.	0556	0620	...	0650	...	0720	...	0750	...
Biasca...................... **547** a.	0610	0637	...	0707	...	0737	...	0807	...

	m																				**z**		**z**		
ilano Centrale .... d.	...	0643	...	...	...		1843	...	...	...	1943	...	...	...	2043	...	...	...	2143	...	...	...	2243	2243	...
omo S. Giovanni **607** d.	0710	0723	...	...	0810		1923	...	...	2010	2023	...	...	2110	2123	...	...	...	2223	...	...	...	2323	2323	...
hiasso 🏛 .... **607** a.	0717	0729	...	...	0817	and at	1929	...	...	2017	2029	...	...	2117	2129	...	...	...	2229	...	...	...	2329	2329	...
hiasso............ **607** d.	0720	0734	0754	0811	0820	the same	1934	1954	2011	2020	2034	2054	...	2120	2134	2154	...	2220	2234	2254	...	2320	2334	2334	2354
endrisio .... **607** d.	0734	0741	0804	0818	0834		1941	2004	2018	2034	2041	2104	...	2134	2141	2204	...	2234	2243	2304	...	2334	2343	2343	0004
ugano............ **607** a.	0754	0758**t**	0824	0834	0854	minutes	1958**t**	2024	2034	2054	2058**t**	2124	...	2154	2158	2224	...	2254	2304	2324	...	2354	0004	0004	0024
ugano............ **607** d.	0755	0805**t**	0825	0835	0855	past each	2005**t**	2025	2035	2055	2105**t**	2125	2135	2155	2205	2225	2235	2255	2305	2325	2335	2355	0005	0005	0025
Cadenazzo ..... **607** d.	|	0820	|	0850	|		2020	|	2050	|	2120	|	2150	|	2220	|	2250	|	2320	|	2350	|	0020	0020	|
Locarno .... a.	|	0838	|	0908	|	hour until	2038	|	2107	|	2138	|	2207	|	2238	|	2307**z**	|	2338**z**	|	0008	|	0038	...	|
ellinzona .... **607** a.	0813	...	0843	...	0913		...	2043	...	2113	...	2143	...	2213	...	2243	...	2313	...	2343	...	0026	...	...	0056
ellinzona .... **547** d.	0820	...	0850	...	0920		...	2050	...	2120	...	2150	...	2220	...	2250	...	2320	...	2350	...	...	...	...	...
asca .... **547** a.	0837	...	0907	...	0937		...	2107	...	2137	...	2207	...	2237	...	2307	...	2337	...	0007	...	...	...	...	...

– From Airolo (Table **547**).
- ①–⑤.
- ⑥⑦ (also June 2, Aug. 15, Dec. 8).

d – 4 minutes later on ⑥⑦ (also June 9, 19, Aug. 1, 15, Dec. 8).
m – Change trains at Mendrisio on dates in note **c**.
r – 2 minutes earlier June 21 - Aug. 31.
t – June 21 - Aug. 31 arrives 2 minutes later, departs 1 minute earlier.

z – ⑤⑥ until June 7; daily June 9 - Aug. 30; ⑤⑥ from Sept. 5 (also Dec. 7).
‡ – Distance from Lugano.

550 ZÜRICH and LUZERN - LUGANO - MILANO (via Gotthard and Ceneri Base Tunnels) SBB, FS

See Table 547 for slower regional services via the classic Gotthard route. See Table 525 for other connecting trains Luzern - Arth-Goldau and v.v.

km		IR 2409	IC 659	EC 31	IR 2311	IC 861	EC 11	IR 2413	IC 663	EC 33	IR 2315	IC 865	EC 13	IR 2417	IC 667	EC 35	IR 2319	IC 869	EC 15	IR 2421	IC 671	EC 151	IR 2323	IC 873	EC 17	IR 2425
				⊙ ◧			◧			◧			◧			◧			◧						¶ ◧	
		★	✕	✕	★	✕	✕	★	✕	V✕	★	✕	✕	★	✕	H✕	★	✕	✕	★	✕	F✕	★	✕	✕	★
0	**Zürich** HB 547 555 d.	0605	...	0633	...	0705	0733	0805	...	0833	...	0905	0933	1005	...	1033	...	1105	1133	1205	...	1233	...	1305	1333	1405
29	Zug 547 555 d.	0630	...	0700	...	0730	0800	0830	...	0900	...	0930	1000	1030	...	1100	...	1130	1200	1230	...	1300	...	1330	1400	1430
	Basel SBB 565 d.	|	0503j	|	0603	|	|	|	0703	|	0803	|	|	|	0903	|	1003	|	|	|	1103	1106z	1203	|	|	|
	Luzern 525 547 d.	|	0618	|	0718	|	|	|	0818	|	0918	|	|	|	1018	|	1118	|	|	|	1218	|	1318	|	|	|
45	**Arth-Goldau** 525 547 a.	0645	0645	0716	0745	0745	0816	0845	0845	0916	0945	0945	1016	1045	1045	1116	1145	1145	1216	1245	1245	1316	1345	1345	1416	1445
45	**Arth-Goldau** 547 d.	...	0649	0718	...	0749	0818	...	0849	0918	...	0949	1018	...	1049	1118	...	1149	1218	...	1249	1318	...	1349	1418	...
51	Altdorf 547 d.	...	|	|	...	0808	|	...	|	|	...	1008	|	...	|	|	...	1208	|	...	|	|	...	1408	|	...
165	Bellinzona ▲ 547 a.	...	0742	0812	...	0842	0912	...	0942	1012	...	1042	1112	...	1142	1212	...	1242	1312	...	1342	1412	...	1442	1512	...
165	Bellinzona 548 607 d.	...	0744	0814	...	0844	0914	...	0944	1014	...	1044	1114	...	1144	1214	...	1244	1314	...	1344	1414	...	1444	1514	...
186	**Lugano** 548 607 a.	...	0758t	0828	...	0858t	0928	...	0958t	1028	...	1058t	1128	...	1158t	1228	...	1258t	1328	...	1358t	1428	...	1458t	1528	...
186	**Lugano** 548 607 d.	...	...	0830	...	...	0930	...	...	1030	...	...	1130	...	...	1230	...	...	1330	...	...	1430	...	...	1530	...
212	**Chiasso** 🏛 548 607 d.	...	...	0902	...	...	1002	...	...	1102	...	...	1202	...	...	1302	...	...	1402	...	...	1502	...	...	1602	...
216	Como S. Giovanni 548 607 d.	...	...	0910	...	...	1010	...	...	1110	...	...	1210	...	...	1310	...	...	1410	...	...	1510	...	...	1610	...
263	**Milano** Centrale 548 a.	...	...	|	...	...	1050	...	...	1150	...	...	1250	...	...	1350k	...	...	1450	...	...	1550	...	...	1650	...
	Milano Lambrate a.	...	...	0955	...	...	...	...	...	...	...	...	...	...	...	1355p	...	...	...	...	...	...	...	...	...	...

	IC 675	IC 1475	IR 2327	IC 877	EC 19	IR 2429	EC 173	IC 1479	IR 2331	IC 881	EC 21	IR 2433	IC 683	IC 1483	IR 2335	IC 885	EC 23	IR 2437	IC 687	IC 1487	IR 2339	IC 889	IR 2441	IC 691	IC 893	IC 895
					⊠ ◧						◧						◧			⑦		①–⑥			①–⑤	⑥
	✕		★	✕	✕	★	✕		★	✕	✕	★	✕		★	✕	✕	★	✕	✕	★	✕	★	✕		
Zürich HB 547 555 d.	...	1433	...	1505	1533	1605	...	1633	...	1705	1733	1805	...	1833	...	1905	1933	2005	...	2033	...	2105	2205	...	2305	2305
Zug 547 555 d.	...	1500	...	1530	1600	1630	...	1700	...	1730	1800	1830	...	1900	...	1930	2000	2030	...	2100	...	2130	2230	...	2330	2330
Basel SBB 565 d.	1303	|	1403	|	|	|	1503	|	1603	|	|	|	1703	|	1803	|	|	|	1903	|	2003	|	|	2103	|	|
Luzern 525 547 d.	1418	|	1518	|	|	|	1618	|	1718	|	|	|	1818	|	1918	|	|	|	2018	|	2118	|	|	2218	|	|
Arth-Goldau 525 547 a.	1445	1516	1545	1545	1616	1645	1645	1716	1745	1745	1816	1845	1845	1916	1945	1945	2016	2045	2045	2116	2145	2145	2245	2245	2345	2345
Arth-Goldau 547 d.	1449	1518	...	1549	1618	...	1649	1718	...	1749	1818	...	1849	1918	...	1949	2018	...	2049	2118	...	2149	...	2249	2349	2349
Altdorf 547 d.	|	|	...	1608	|	...	|	|	...	1808	|	...	|	|	...	2008	|	...	|	2138	...	2208	...	|	0008	0008
Bellinzona ▲ 547 a.	1542	1612	...	1642	1712	...	1742	1812	...	1842	1912	...	1942	2012	...	2042	2112	...	2142	2212	...	2242	...	2342	0047	0055
Bellinzona 548 607 d.	1544	1614	...	1644	1714	...	1744	1814	...	1844	1914	...	1944	2014	...	2044	2114	...	2144	2214	...	2244	...	2344	...	0057
Lugano 548 607 a.	1558t	1628	...	1658t	1728	...	1758t	1828	...	1858t	1928	...	1958t	2028	...	2058t	2128	...	2158	2228	...	2258	...	2358	...	0111
Lugano 548 607 d.	...	...	...	...	1730	...	1810	...	...	...	1930	...	...	...	...	...	2130	...	2200	...	...	2300	...	...	...	...
Chiasso 🏛 548 607 d.	...	...	...	...	1802	...	1855	...	...	...	2002	...	...	...	...	...	2202	...	2230	...	...	2330	...	...	...	...
Como S. Giovanni 548 607 d.	...	...	...	...	1810	...	1903	...	...	...	2010	...	...	...	...	...	2210	...	...	...	...	...	...	...	...	...
Milano Centrale 548 a.	...	...	...	...	1850	...	1950	...	...	...	2050	...	...	...	...	...	2250	...	...	...	...	...	...	...	...	...
Milano Lambrate a.	...	...	...	...	...	...	...	...	...	...	...	...	...	...	...	...	...	...	...	...	...	...	...	...	...	...

	IC 862	IC 664	IR 2410	IC 1462	IC 866	IR 2312	IC 1466	IC 668	IR 2414	EC 10	IR 2316	IC 870	EC 12	IC 672	IR 2418	EC 14	IC 874	IR 2320	IC 1474	EC 178	IR 2422	EC 150	IC 878	IR 2324	IC 1478	IC 680
	①–⑥			Ⓐ						◧			◧			◧						◧				
			★			★		✕	★	✕	★	✕	✕	✕	★	✕	✕	★		✕	★	F✕	✕	★		✕
Milano Lambrate d.	...	...	...	...	...	...	...	...	...	...	...	...	...	...	...	...	...	...	...	...	...	...	...	...	...	...
Milano Centrale 548 d.	...	...	...	...	...	...	...	...	...	0710	...	...	0810	...	...	0910	...	...	...	1010	...	1110	...	...	...	...
Como S. Giovanni 548 607 d.	...	...	...	...	...	...	...	...	...	0754	...	...	0850	...	...	0950	...	...	...	1059	...	1150	...	...	...	...
Chiasso 🏛 548 607 d.	...	0530	...	0604	...	...	0704	...	...	0805	...	...	0905	...	...	1005	...	...	...	1124	...	1205	...	...	...	...
Lugano 548 607 a.	...	0558	...	0628	...	...	0728	...	...	0828	...	...	0928	...	...	1028	...	...	...	1150	...	1228	...	...	...	...
Lugano 548 607 d.	...	0600	...	0630	0702r	...	0730	0802r	...	0830	...	0902r	0930	1002r	...	1030	1102r	...	1130	1202r	...	1230	1302r	...	1330	1402
Bellinzona 548 607 a.	...	0616	...	0646	0716	...	0746	0816	...	0846	...	0916	0946	1016	...	1046	1116	...	1146	1216	...	1246	1316	...	1346	1416
Bellinzona ▲ 547 d.	0507	0617	...	0647	0717	...	0747	0817	...	0847	...	0917	0947	1017	...	1047	1117	...	1147	1217	...	1247	1317	...	1347	1417
Altdorf 547 d.	0550	|	...	|	0750	...	|	|	...	|	...	0950	|	|	...	|	1150	...	|	|	...	|	1350	...	|	|
Arth-Goldau 547 a.	0611	0711	...	0742	0811	...	0842	0911	...	0942	...	1011	1042	1111	...	1142	1211	...	1242	1311	...	1342	1411	...	1442	1511
Arth-Goldau 525 547 d.	0615	0715	0715	0745	0815	0815	0845	0915	0915	0945	1015	1015	1045	1115	1115	1145	1215	1215	1245	1315	1315	1345	1415	1415	1445	1515
Luzern 525 547 a.	|	0741	|	|	|	0841	|	0941	|	|	1041	|	|	1141	|	|	|	1241	|	1341	|	|	|	1441	|	1541
Basel SBB 565 a.	|	0856	|	|	|	0956	|	1056	|	|	1156	|	|	1256	|	|	|	1356	|	1456	|	1528z	|	1556	|	1656
Zug 547 555 a.	0630	...	0730	0800	0830	...	0900	...	0930	1000	...	1030	1100	...	1130	1200	1230	...	1300	...	1330	1400	1430	...	1500	...
Zürich HB 547 555 a.	0655	...	0755	0827	0855	...	0927	...	0955	1027	...	1055	1127	...	1155	1227	1255	...	1327	...	1355	1427	1455	...	1527	...

	IR 2426	EC 16	IC 882	IR 2328	IC 1482	IC 684	IR 2430	EC 18	IC 886	IR 2332	EC 30	IC 688	IR 2434	EC 20	IC 890	IR 2336	IC 1490	EC 32	IC 692	IR 2438	EC 22	IC 894	IR 2340	EC 34	IC 696	IR 2442
		◧						◧			◧			◇			⑦	◧			‡ ◧			◧		
	★	✕	✕	★	✕	✕	★	✕	✕	★	✕	✕	★	◧✕	✕	★	L	V✕	✕	★	✕	✕	★	G✕		★
Milano Lambrate d.	...	...	...	...	...	...	...	...	...	...	...	...	...	...	...	...	...	...	...	...	...	...	...	2005	...	...
Milano Centrale 548 d.	...	1310	...	...	...	...	...	1510	...	...	...	...	...	1710	...	...	...	1810	...	...	1910	..	...	|	...	...
Como S. Giovanni 548 607 d.	...	1350	...	...	...	...	...	1550	...	...	...	...	...	1750	...	...	...	1850	...	...	1950	...	...	2050	...	...
Chiasso 🏛 548 607 d.	...	1405	...	...	...	...	...	1605	...	...	1705	...	...	1805	...	...	...	1905	...	...	2005	...	...	2105	...	...
Lugano 548 607 a.	...	1428	...	...	...	...	...	1628	...	...	1728	...	...	1828	...	...	...	1928	...	...	2028	...	...	2128	...	...
Lugano 548 607 d.	...	1430	1502r	...	1530	1602r	...	1630	1702r	...	1730	1802r	...	1830	1902r	...	...	1930	2002r	...	2030	2102r	...	2130	2202	...
Bellinzona 548 607 a.	...	1446	1516	...	1546	1616	...	1646	1716	...	1746	1816	...	1846	1916	...	...	1946	2016	...	2046	2116	...	2146	2216	...
Bellinzona ▲ 547 d.	...	1447	1517	...	1547	1617	...	1647	1717	...	1747	1817	...	1847	1917	...	1921	1947	2017	...	2047	2117	...	2147	2217	...
Altdorf 547 d.	...	|	1550	...	|	|	...	|	1750	...	|	|	...	|	1950	...	|	|	|	...	|	2150	...	|	|	...
Arth-Goldau 547 a.	...	1542	1611	...	1642	1711	...	1742	1811	...	1842	1911	...	1942	2011	...	|	2042	2111	...	2142	2211	...	2242	2311	...
Arth-Goldau 525 547 d.	1515	1545	1615	1615	1645	1715	1715	1745	1815	1815	1845	1915	1915	1945	2015	2015	|	2045	2115	2115	2145	2215	2215	2245	2315	2315
Luzern 525 547 a.	|	|	|	1641	|	1741	|	|	|	1841	|	1941	|	|	|	2041	2039	|	2141	|	|	|	2241	|	2341	|
Basel SBB 565 a.	|	|	|	1756	|	1856	|	|	|	1956	|	2056	|	|	|	2156e	...	|	2301	|	|	|	0001	|	0103	|
Zug 547 555 a.	1530	1600	1630	...	1700	...	1730	1800	1830	...	1900	...	1930	2000	2030	...	...	2100	...	2130	2200	2230	...	2300	...	2330
Zürich HB 547 555 a.	1555	1627	1655	...	1727	...	1755	1827	1855	...	1927	...	1955	2027	2055	...	...	2127	...	2155	2227	2255	...	2327	...	2355

B – To/from Bologna (Table **600**).
F – To/from Frankfurt via Basel (Table **910**).
G – Until Sept. 28 runs as *EC* **156** and operates from Pisa via Genova. From Sept. 29 operates from Genova (also Sestri Levante on ⑥⑦). See also Table **610**.
H – To Genova (Table **610**) from Sept. 29 (extended to Sestri Levante on ⑥⑦). Train number **37** until Sept. 28.
L – ⑦ (also June 9; not June 8). From Locarno (d. 1900).
V – To/from Venezia (Table **605**).

e – On ⑦–④ change trains at Olten (arrives Basel *2201*).
j – 0501 on ①–⑤.
k – Until Sept. 28.
p – From Sept. 29.
r – 4 minutes **earlier** June 21 - Aug. 31.
t – 4 minutes later June 21 - Aug. 31.
z – Via Zürich.

¶ – Train number *EC* **117** on ⑤–⑦ (also June 9).
⊠ – Train number *EC* **119** on ⑤–⑦ (also June 9).
◇ – Train number *EC* **120** on ⑤–⑦ (also June 9).
‡ – Train number *EC* **122** on ⑤–⑦ (also June 9).
⊙ – Until Sept. 28 runs as *EC* **155** and continues to Pisa via Genova (Table **610**). From Sept. 29 continues to Bologna (Table **600**).
◧ – Supplement payable in Italy and for international journeys.
★ – Operated by SOB. See Table **547** for full details.
▲ – For connecting services Bellinzona - Locarno and v.v. see Table 547

551 LOCARNO - DOMODOSSOLA FART

km																									
																					⑤⑦				
0	**Locarno** d.	0538	0649	0750	0804	0851	0951	1051	1121	...	1251	1350	1451	1514	1551	1623	1651	1750	1825	1851	1921	...	...	...	...
20	Camedo 🏛 d.	0617	0732	0826	0844	0926	1026	1126	1206	...	1326	1431	1526	1555	1626	1706	1726	1826	1905	1925	2001	...	...	...	...
26	Re d.	...	...	0842	...	0942	1042	1142	...	...	1342	...	1542	...	1642	...	1742	1842	...	1940	...	...	...	...	...
34	S. Maria Maggiore d.	...	...	0855	...	0955	1055	1155	...	...	1355	...	1555	...	1655	...	1755	1855	...	1953	...	...	...	...	...
53	**Domodossola** a.	...	...	0940	...	1040	1140	1240	...	...	1442	...	1640	...	1740	...	1840	1940	...	2040	...	...	...	...	...

																				A		B	⑤⑦		
Domodossola d.	...	...	...	...	0826	0926	1026	1126	...	1226	1326	...	...	...	1526	...	...	1726	...	1900	...	1941	2026	...	...
S. Maria Maggiore d.	...	...	...	...	0912	1012	1112	1212	...	1312	1412	...	...	...	1612	...	...	1812	...	1952	...	2027	2112	...	...
Re d.	...	...	...	...	0924	1024	1124	1224	...	1324	1424	...	...	...	1624	...	...	1824	...	2004	...	2039	2124	...	...
Camedo 🏛 d.	0623	0655	0748	0850	0940	1040	1140	1240	1248	1340	1440	1448	...	1610	1640	1725	...	1840	1925	2021	2025	2055	2140	...	...
Locarno a.	0710	0740	0835	0935	1020	1120	1220	1320	1336	1421	1520	1536	...	1657	1720	1810	...	1920	2010	2102	2110	2135	2220	...	...

A – ⑥⑦ until July 20 (also June 9, 19); daily from July 26.
B – ①–⑤ until July 25 (not June 9, 19).

Reservations are possible through www.vigezzinacentovalli.com.

ZB (narrow gauge rack railway)

LUZERN - STANS - ENGELBERG 552

km		E			E				E			E		🚌				🚌					ⒸT	ⒸT
0	**Luzern** .... **561** d.	0504	0527	0557	0610	0627		2057	2110	2127	2157	2210	2227	...	2257	2310	2327	...	2357	0032	0102		0836	0936
9	Hergiswil .... **561** d.	0515	0540	0610	|	0640	and at	2110	|	2140	2210	|	2240	...	2310	2318	2340	...	0010	0045	0114	EXTRA	0847	0947
11	Stansstad.................. d.	0518	0544	0614	|	0644	the same	2114	|	2144	2214	|	2244	...	2314	2322	2344	...	0014	0050	0118	SERVICES	0850	0950
14	Stans .... d.	0522	0548	0618	0624	0648	minutes	2118	2124	2148	2218	2224	2248	...	2318	2326	2348	...	0018	0054	0122	▶▶▶	0854	0954
18	Dallenwil .... d.	0529	0552	...	0629	0652	past each	...	2129	2152	...	2229	2252	...	2322	...	2352	...	0022	0059	...		|	|
21	Wolfenschiessen .... d.	0533	0557	...	0634	0657	hour until	...	2134	2157	...	2233	2257	2259	...	...	2357	2359	0027	0103	...		|	|
33	**Engelberg** .... ⊡ a.	0553	...	...	0653	...		...	2153	...	...	2253	...	2317	...	...	...	0017	...	...	...		0921	1021

		🚌			E				E			E			E		🚌		🚌			ⒸT	ⒸT
ngelberg .... ⊡ d.	...	0502	...	...	0602	...		...	2102	...	...	2202	...	...	2302	...	2339	...	0018	...		1624	1724
Volfenschiessen .... d.	0453	0520	0522	0601	0622	...	and at	2101	2122	...	2201	2222	...	2301	2322	...	2357	0001	0036	0038	EXTRA	|	|
)allenwil.............................. d.	0456	...	0527	0604	0629	...	the same	2104	2129	...	2204	2229	...	2304	2329	2334	...	0004	...	0041	SERVICES	|	|
tans...................................... d.	0501	...	0532	0610	0634	0640	minutes	2110	2134	2140	2210	2234	2240	2310	2334	2340	...	0010	...	0047	▶▶▶	1701	1801
tansstad .... d.	0505	...	0535	0614	|	0644	past each	2114	|	2144	2214	|	2244	2314	|	2344	...	0014	...	0051		1705	1805
lergiswil .... **561** d.	0509	...	0540	0618	|	0648	hour until	2118	|	2148	2218	|	2248	2318	|	2348	...	0018	...	0055		1709	1809
uzern .... **561** a.	0522	...	0549	0631	0649	0701		2131	2149	2201	2231	2249	2301	2331	2349	0001	...	0031	...	0108		1719	1819

– LUZERN - ENGELBERG EXPRESS. Conveys panorama cars.
T – Until Oct. 26.
⊡ – Station for Titlis, accessible by cable-car.

RB (2nd class only)

MOUNTAIN RAILWAYS IN CENTRAL SWITZERLAND 553

ARTH-GOLDAU - RIGI KULM Dec. 15 - Mar. 9

km						b					b	⑤	
0	Arth-Goldau.... d.	0755	0908	1008	1108	1208	1308	1423	1523	1623	1723	1823	...
9	Rigi Kulm .... a.	0840	0947	1047	1147	1247	1347	1502	1602	1702	1802	1902	...

				b						b	⑤	
Rigi Kulm .... d.	0858	1001	1101	1201	1301	1416	1516	1616	1716	1816	1916	...
Arth-Goldau. a.	0948	1048	1148	1248	1348	1503	1603	1703	1803	1903	2003	...

Mar. 10 - Dec. 13

km											C	F	
0	Arth-Goldau.... d.	0755	0855	0955	1055	1155	1255	1355	1455	1555	1655	1755	...
9	Rigi Kulm .... a.	0834	0934	1034	1134	1234	1334	1434	1534	1634	1734	1834	...

										C	F	
Rigi Kulm .... d.	0848	0948	1048	1148	1248	1348	1448	1548	1648	1748	1848	...
Arth-Goldau. a.	0935	1035	1135	1235	1335	1435	1535	1635	1735	1835	1935	...

RIGI KULM - VITZNAU

km												A				k	h	k								
0	Rigi Kulm .... d.	...	...	0900	1000	1100	1200	...	1300	1400	...	1430	1500	1600	1700	1800	...	1900	2000**k**	...	2240**k**	...	...	...	...	...
2	Rigi Staffelhöhe......... d.	0715	...	0910	1010	1110	1210	...	1310	1410	...	1446	1510	1610	1710	1810	1830	1910	2010	...	2250	...	...	...	...	...
7	Vitznau .... a.	0749	...	0940	1040	1140	1240	...	1340	1440	...|	1513	1540	1640	1740	1840	1900	1940	2040	...	2320	...	...	...	...	...

							⑦D		A						k	h	k		k			k			
'itznau................................ d.	0635	...	0815	0915	...	1015	1050	1115	1150	1215	1315	1415	1515	1615	1715	1740	1815	1915	1915	...	2205	2205	...	...	...
ligi Staffelhöhe..................... d.	0659	...	0837	0937	...	1037	1115	1137	1215	1237	1337	1437	1537	1637	1737	1801	1837	1937	1937	...	2227	2227	...	...	...
ligi Kulm .... a.	...	...	0847	0947	...	1047	1125	1147	1225	1247	1347	1447	1547	1647	1747	1811**g**	1847	1947**g**	1947	...	...	2237	...	...	...

LPNACHSTAD - PILATUS KULM. Narrow gauge rack railway. *5 km*. Journey time: 30 minutes uphill, 40 minutes downhill. **Operator**: PB ✆ 041 329 11 11.
ervices run daily **May 12 - November 16** (weather permitting). **No winter service**.
rom **Alpnachstad**: 0810**r**, 0845, 0920, 0955, 1030, 1105, 1140, 1215, 1250, 1325, 1400, 435, 1510, 1545, 1620, 1655**r**, 1730**r**.
From **Pilatus Kulm**: 0809**r**, 0844**r**, 0919, 0954, 1029, 1104, 1139, 1214, 1249, 1324, 1359, 1434, 1509, 1544, 1619, 1654, 1729**r**, 1804**r**.

RIENZ - BRIENZER ROTHORN. Narrow gauge rack railway. *8 km*. Most services operated by steam train. Journey time: 55–65 minutes. Reservation recommended.
perator: BRB, ✆ 033 952 22 22. Services run **June 7 - October 26** (subject to demand and weather conditions on the mountain). Extra trains may run at busy times. **No winter service**.
rom **Brienz**: 0736**B**, 0836, 0940, 1045, 1145, 1258, 1358, 1458, 1636.
From **Brienzer Rothorn**: 0906**B**, 0938, 1115, 1220, 1328, 1428, 1528, 1628, 1740.

– † May 25 - July 6; daily July 7 - Aug. 17; † Aug. 24 - Sept. 7 (also July 5).
– ⑥⑦ July 5 - Sept. 28.
– Ⓒ Mar. 15 - Apr. 27; daily Apr. 28 - Oct. 19; Ⓒ from Oct. 25 (also Dec. 8).
– ⑦ May 25 - Sept. 7.
– ⑤ Mar. 14 - Apr. 18; ⑤–⑦ Apr. 25 - Oct. 24; ⑤ from Oct. 31 (also May 29, June 9, 19).
b – Not Dec. 9 – 13, 16 – 20.
g – ⑤⑥ until May 23; ⑤⑥ from Sept. 12.
h – Not May 24 - Sept. 7.
k – May 24 - Sept. 7.
r – May 12 - Oct. 25.

PA

🚌 MEIRINGEN - ANDERMATT 554

Summer only. Operated by Postauto AG ✆ +41 (0) 848 818 818.

	A	E	A	D	E	A	AⒸ	D	A	A	E
leiringen Bahnhof.......... d.	...	...	*0850*	0925	...	1050	1055	1325	1322	1520	...
Steingletscher, Susten .. a.	...	...	*0941*	|	...	|	1146	|	1413	|	...
Steingletscher, Susten .. d.	...	...	1000	|	...	|	...	|	1419	|	...
Susten Passhöhe.......... d.	...	...	1010	|	...	|	...	|	1429	|	...
Göschenen Bahnhof.... d.	...	...	1049	|	...	|	...	|	1508	|	...
irimsel Passhöhe............ d.	0912	...	|	1030**t**	...	1205	...	1440	|	1635	...
iletsch Post..................... d.	0922	...	|	1040**t**	...	1215	...	1450	|	1645	...
berwald Bahnhof .... a.	0937	...	|	1055**t**	...	1230	...	1505	|	1700	...
berwald Bahnhof .... d.	...	0942	|	...	1220	...	...	...	|	...	*1704*
iletsch Post..................... a.	...	0954	|	...	1232	...	...	...	|	...	*1716*
iletsch Post..................... d.	...	0954	|	...	1232	...	...	...	|	...	1720
urka Passhöhe................ d.	...	1010	|	...	1252	...	...	...	|	...	1740
lealp Post .... d.	...	...	|	...	1316	...	...	...	|	...	1804
ndermatt Bahnhof......... a.	...	...	1104**r**	...	1335	...	...	...	1523**r**	...	1823

	A	A	E	A	B	AⒸ	A	D	E	A	A
Andermatt Bahnhof...... d.	0858**r**	...	0830	...	...	...	...	...	1534	1551**r**	...
Realp Post..................... d.	|	...	0842	...	...	...	...	...	1546	|	...
Furka Passhöhe............ d.	|	...	0907	...	...	...	...	...	1611	|	...
Gletsch Post .... a.	|	...	0935	...	...	...	...	...	1639	|	...
Gletsch Post .... d.	|	...	1005	...	...	...	...	...	*1645*	|	...
Oberwald Bahnhof .... a.	|	...	1020	...	...	...	...	...	*1700*	|	...
Oberwald Bahnhof .... d.	|	*0845*	...	1030	1104	...	1250	1530	...	|	1704
Gletsch Post .... d.	|	*0857*	...	1042	1116	...	1302	1542	...	|	1716
Grimsel Passhöhe......... d.	|	0912	...	1111	1133	...	1333	1611	...	|	1733
Göschenen Bahnhof. d.	0911	|	...	|	|	...	|	|	...	1611	|
Susten Passhöhe ...... d.	0946	|	...	|	|	...	|	|	...	1646	|
Steingletscher, Susten a.	0956	|	...	|	|	...	|	|	...	1656	|
Steingletscher, Susten d.	*1000*	|	...	|	|	1150	|	|	...	1720	|
Meiringen Bahnhof....... a.	*1051*	1012	...	1212	1234	1241	1434	1712	...	1811	1834

– June 28 - Oct. 5.
– June 7 – 27 and Oct. 6 – 12 (not June 21, 22).
D – June 7 - Oct. 12 (not June 21, 22).
E – June 28 - Oct. 5 (not Sept. 6).
r – Not Sept. 6
t – 25 minutes later June 28 - Oct. 5.

SBB (train category *IR*)

ZÜRICH FLUGHAFEN ✈ - ZÜRICH - LUZERN 555

km		①–⑤ a	⑥⑦ b	⑥⑦ d		⑥⑦ d		⑥⑦ d		⑥⑦ d												Ⓐ n	Ⓐ n		
0	**Zürich** HB .... **520** d.	0008	0010	0035	...	0135	...	0235	...	0335	...	0535	0610	0635	and at	2210	2235	2310	2335	...	A	1639	1739	...	...
12	Thalwil .... **520** d.	0017	|	0045	...	|	...	|	...	|	...	0545	|	0645	the same	|	2245	|	2345	...	L	|	|	...	...
29	Zug........................... d.	0035	0032	0102	...	0157	...	0257	...	0357	...	0603	0632	0703	minutes	2232	2303	2332	0003	...	S	1712	1812	...	...
39	Rotkreuz .... d.	0046	|	0109	...	0206	...	0306	...	0406	...	0611	|	0711	past each	|	2311	|	0011	...	O	1723	1823	...	...
57	**Luzern**...................... a.	0107	0051	0123	...	0223	...	0323	...	0423	...	0625	0651	0725	hour until	2251	2325	2351	0025	...		1739	1839	...	...

		⑥⑦ d		⑥⑦ d		⑥⑦ d	⑥⑦ d					Ⓐ n			Ⓐ n										
uzern .... d.	0021	0035	0051	0135	...	0235	0335	...	0452	0535	0609	0620	0635	0709	0720	0735	0809	0835	and at	2209	2235	2309	2335	...	...
otkreuz.......................... d.	0039	0048	0110	0151	...	0251	0351	...	0513	0548	|	0635	0648	|	0735	0748	|	0848	the same	|	2248	|	2348	...	...
ug .... d.	0051	0057	0122	0200	...	0300	0400	...	0526	0558	0629	0647	0658	0729	0747	0758	0829	0858	minutes	2229	2258	2329	2358	...	...
halwil................ **520** d.	...	0114	...	0216	...	0316	0416	...	0543	0614	|	|	0714	|	|	0814	|	0914	past each	|	2314	|	0014	...	...
ürich HB.......... **520** a.	...	0123	...	0225	...	0325	0425	...	0555	0625	0651	0720	0725	0751	0820	0825	0851	0925	hour until	2251	2325	2351	0025	...	...

– Also Aug. 2.
– Not Aug. 2.
d – Also June 9, Aug. 1.
n – Not July 28 - Aug. 8.

SWITZERLAND

560 BASEL - BERN - INTERLAKEN and BRIG

SBB

See Table **562** for services via Kandersteg

km		IC	IC	IC	IC	IC	EC	IC	IC	IC	IC	IC	IC	IC	IC	IC	IC	IC	IC	IC	EC	IC	IC	IC	ICE	IC
		955	**802**	**607**	**957**	**804**	**61**	**959**	**806**	**1304**	**333**	**961**	**808**	**613**	**963**	**810**	**615**	**965**	**812**	**617**	**63**	**967**	**814**	**619**	**275**	**816**
										⑥											⑥⑦r					
			✕	✕		✕	✕§	✕	✕	d⊖	✕		✕		✕	✕	✕	✕	✕	D✕	§✕	✕	✕		G✕	✕
	Romanshorn **535** d.	...	...	...	...	...	...	...	0547	...	...	...	0647	...	...	0747	...	...	0847	...	...	...	0947	...	...	1047
	Zürich Flughafen ✈ **535** d.	...	...	...	...	...	...	...	0645	...	...	...	0745	...	...	0845	...	...	0945	...	...	...	1045	...	...	1145
	Zürich HB **505** d.	...	...	...	...	0602	...	...	0702	0738	...	...	0802	...	...	0902	...	...	1002	...	...	...	1102	...	...	1202
0	**Basel** SBB **565** d.	...	...	0522	0556	|	0628	0656	|	|	0728	0756	|	0828	0856	|	0928	0956	|	1028	1028	1056	|	1128	1156	|
39	Olten **505 565** d.	...	...	0558	0629	|	0658	0729	|	|	0758	0829	|	0858	0929	|	0958	1029	|	1058	1058	1129	|	1158	1229	|
101	**Bern** **505** a.	...	...	0626	0656	0658c	0726	0756	0758c	|	0826	0856	0858c	0926	0956	0958c	1026	1056	1058c	1126	1126	1156	1158c	1226	1256	1258c
101	**Bern** d.	0604	0607	0634	0707	0704	0734	0804	0807	|	0834	0907	0904	0934	1004	1007	1034	1104	1107	1134	1134	1207	1204	1234	1304	1307
132	Thun d.	0624	0627	0654	0727	0724	0754	0824	0827	0850	0854	0927	0924	0954	1024	1027	1054	1124	1127	1154	1154	1227	1224	1254	1324	1327
142	**Spiez** ▷ d.	0635	0638	0705	0738	0735	0805	0835	0838	0900	0905	0938	0935	1005	1035	1038	1105	1135	1138	1205	1205	1238	1235	1305	1335	1338
158	Interlaken West ▷ a.	0653	|	0722	|	0753	|	0853	|	|	0922	|	0953	|	1053	|	1122	1153	|	|	|	|	1253	1322	1353	|
160	**Interlaken** Ost ▷ a.	0659	|	0728	|	0759	|	0859	|	|	0928	|	0959	|	1059	|	1128	1159	|	|	|	|	1259	1328	1359	|
197	Visp **570** a.	...	0704	...	0804	...	0831	...	0904	0929	...	1004	...	1031	...	1104	...	...	1204	1231	1231	1304	...	...	...	1404
206	**Brig** **570 590** a.	...	0713	...	0813	...	0841	...	0913	0938	...	1013	...	1040	...	1113	...	...	1213	1241	1241	1313	...	...	...	1413
	Domodossola 🏛 **590** a.	...	...	...	...	...	0912	...	...	1007	...	...	...	...	...	...	...	...	...	...	1312	...	...	...	...	...
	Milano Centrale **590** a.	...	...	...	...	...	1043r	...	...	...	...	...	...	...	...	...	...	...	...	...	1443	...	...	...	...	...

	EC	IC	IC	IC	EC	IC	IC	IC	IC	IC	IC	IC	IC	IC	IC	EC	ICE	IC	IC	IC	IC	IC	ICE	IC	IC	IC
	65	**971**	**818**	**623**	**7**	**820**	**625**	**975**	**822**	**627**	**977**	**824**	**629**	**979**	**826**	**67**	**371**	**828**	**633**	**983**	**830**	**635**	**373**	**637**	**639**	**987**
																								①–⑥	⑦	
	✕§	✕	✕		G✕	✕		✕	✕	✕		✕	✕		✕	✕§	G✕			✕	✕	✕	G			
Romanshorn **535** d.	...	...	1147	...	...	1247	...	...	1347	...	...	1447	...	...	1547	...	...	1647	...	...	1747	...	...	...	...	...
Zürich Flughafen ✈ **535** d.	...	...	1245	...	...	1345	...	...	1445	...	...	1545	...	...	1645	...	...	1745	...	...	1845	...	...	...	...	...
Zürich HB **505** d.	...	...	1302	...	...	1402	...	...	1502	...	...	1602	...	...	1702	...	...	1802	...	...	1902	...	...	...	...	...
Basel SBB **565** d.	1228	1256	|	1328	1356	|	1428	1456	|	1528	1556	|	1628	1656	|	1728	1756	|	1828	1856	|	1928	1956	2028	2028	2056
Olten **505 565** d.	1258	1329	|	1358	1429	|	1458	1529	|	1558	1629	|	1658	1729	|	1758	1829	|	1858	1929	|	1958	2029	2058	2058	2129
Bern **505** a.	1326	1356	1358c	1426	1456	1458c	1526	1556	1558c	1626	1656	1658c	1726	1756	1758c	1826	1856	1858c	1926	1956	1958c	2026	2056	2126	2126	2156
Bern d.	1334	1407	1404	1434	1504	1507	1534	1607	1604	1634	1704	1707	1734	1807	1804	1834	1904	1907	1934	2007	2004	2034	2107	2134	2134	2207
Thun d.	1354	1427	1424	1454	1524	1527	1554	1627	1624	1654	1724	1727	1754	1827	1824	1854	1924	1927	1954	2027	2024	2054	2127	2154	2154	2227
Spiez ▷ d.	1405	1438	1435	1505	1535	1538	1605	1638	1635	1705	1735	1738	1805	1838	1835	1905	1935	1938	2005	2038	2035	2105	2138	2205	2205	2238
Interlaken West ▷ a.	|	|	1453	1522	1553	|	|	|	1653	1722	1753	|	|	|	1853	|	1953	|	2022	|	2053	|	2154	|	|	2254
Interlaken Ost ▷ a.	|	|	1459	1528	1559	|	|	|	1659	1728	1759	|	|	|	1859	|	1959	|	2028	|	2059	|	2200	|	|	2259
Visp **570** a.	1431	1504	...	...	...	1604	1631	1704	...	...	...	1804	1831	1904	...	1931	...	2004	...	2104	...	2131	...	2231	|	...
Brig **570 590** a.	1441	1513	...	...	...	1613	1640	1713	...	...	...	1813	1841	1913	...	1941	...	2013	...	2113	...	2141	...	2241	2303	...
Domodossola 🏛 **590** a.	1512	...	...	...	...	...	...	...	...	...	...	...	...	...	...	2012	...	...	...	...	...	...	...	...	...	...
Milano Centrale **590** a.	1643r	...	...	...	...	...	...	...	...	...	...	...	...	...	...	2143r	...	...	...	...	...	...	...	...	...	...

	IC	IC	IC	IC	IC	IC	IC	IC	IC
	641	**643**	**645**	**989**	**647**	**649**	**838**	**991**	**993**
		①–⑥	⑦		①–⑥	⑦			⑥⑦
		⊖							w
Romanshorn **535** d.	...	...	...	...	...	...	...	...	...
Zürich Flughafen ✈ **535** d.	...	...	...	...	...	...	...	...	...
Zürich HB **505** d.	...	...	...	...	...	...	...	...	...
Basel SBB **565** d.	2128	...	...	2156	2228	2228	*2258*n	...	...
Olten **505 565** d.	2158	...	...	2229	2258	2258	2335	...	...
Bern **505** a.	2226	...	...	2256	2326	2326	0002	...	...
Bern d.	...	2234	2234	2308	2337	2339	...	0008	0109
Thun d.	...	2254	2254	2328	2357	2359	...	0032	0139
Spiez ▷ d.	...	2305	2305	2339	0008	0010	...	0042	0149
Interlaken West ▷ a.	...	|	|	2356	|	0026	...	0058	0205
Interlaken Ost ▷ a.	...	|	⊙	0001	|	0031	...	0103	0210
Visp **570** d.	...	2334	|	...	0033	...	...	...	...
Brig **570 590** a.	...	2344	0012	...	0043	...	...	...	...
Domodossola 🏛 **590** a.	...	...	...	...	...	...	...	...	...
Milano Centrale **590** a.	...	...	...	...	...	...	...	...	...

	IC		IC	IC	ICE	IC	IC	IC	IC	IC	IC	IC
	956		**604**	**606**	**372**	**807**	**608**	**960**	**809**	**610**	**962**	**811**
		②–⑦	①	②–⑦								
					G✕	⊖✕	✕	✕	✕	✕	✕	✕
Milano Centrale **590** d.	...	...	...	...	...	...	...	...	...	...	...	...
Domodossola 🏛 **590** d.	...	...	...	...	...	...	...	...	...	...	...	...
Brig **570 590** d.	...	...	...	0516	...	0542	...	0645	...	0718	...	0745
Visp **570** d.	...	...	...	0525	...	0551	...	0654	...	0727	...	0754
Interlaken Ost ▷ d.	0457	0530	0531	|	0559	|	0629	|	0659	|	0759	|
Interlaken West ▷ d.	0502	0534	0536	|	0604	|	0634	|	0704	|	0804	|
Spiez ▷ d.	0519	0549	0554	0554	0623	0622	0654	0722	0723	0754	0823	0822
Thun d.	0529	...	0604	0604	0634	0633	0704	0733	0734	0804	0834	0833
Bern a.	0553	...	0625	0625	0656	0653c	0725	0753	0756c	0825	0856	0853c
Bern **505** d.	0604	...	0636t	0636t	0704	0702	0736t	0804	0802	0836t	0904	0902
Olten **505 565** a.	0630	...	0703t	0703t	0730	|	0803t	0830	|	0903t	0930	|
Basel SBB **565** a.	0701	...	0732	0732	0801	|	0832	0901	|	0932	1001	|
Zürich HB **505** a.	...	...	...	...	...	0758	...	...	0858	...	...	0958
Zürich Flug ✈ **535** a.	...	...	...	...	...	0814	...	...	0914	...	...	1014
Romanshorn **535** a.	...	...	...	...	...	0912	...	...	1012	...	...	1112

	IC	IC	IC	EC	ICE	IC	IC	IC	IC	IC	EC	IC	IC	IC	IC	IC	EC	IC	IC	IC	ICE	IC	IC	IC	IC	IC
	612	**964**	**813**	**60**	**278**	**815**	**616**	**968**	**817**	**618**	**6**	**819**	**620**	**972**	**821**	**622**	**52**	**974**	**823**	**624**	**376**	**825**	**626**	**978**	**827**	**628**
																	⑥⑦r									
			✕	✕§	G✕	✕	✕		✕		G✕	✕	✕	✕	✕	D✕	✕§	✕	✕		G✕	✕		✕	✕	✕
Milano Centrale **590** d.	...	...	...	0705r	...	...	...	...	...	...	...	...	...	...	...	...	1105	...	...	...	...	...	...	...	...	...
Domodossola 🏛 **590** d.	...	...	...	0848	...	...	...	...	...	...	...	...	...	...	...	...	1248	...	...	...	...	...	...	...	...	...
Brig **570 590** d.	...	0845	...	0918	...	0945	...	1045	...	1118	...	1145	...	...	1245	1318	1318	1345	...	...	...	1445	1518	1545	...	...
Visp **570** d.	...	0854	...	0927	...	0954	...	1054	...	1127	...	1154	...	...	1254	1327	1327	1354	...	...	...	1454	1527	1554	...	...
Interlaken Ost ▷ d.	0829	|	0859	|	0959	|	1029	|	1059	|	1159	|	1229	1259	|	|	|	|	1359	1429	1459	|	|	|	1559	1629
Interlaken West ▷ d.	0834	|	0904	|	1004	|	1034	|	1104	|	1204	|	1234	1304	|	|	|	|	1404	1434	1504	|	|	|	1604	1634
Spiez ▷ d.	0854	0922	0923	0954	1023	1022	1054	1122	1123	1154	1223	1222	1254	1323	1322	1354	1354	1422	1423	1454	1523	1522	1554	1622	1623	1654
Thun d.	0904	0933	0934	1004	1034	1033	1104	1133	1134	1204	1234	1233	1304	1334	1333	1404	1404	1433	1434	1504	1534	1533	1604	1633	1634	1704
Bern a.	0925	0953	0956c	1025	1056	1053c	1125	1153	1156c	1225	1256	1253c	1325	1356	1353c	1425	1425	1453	1456c	1525	1556	1553c	1624	1653	1656c	1725
Bern **505** d.	0936t	1004	1002	1036t	1104	1102	1136t	1204	1202	1236t	1304	1302	1336t	1404	1402	1436t	1436t	1504	1502	1536t	1604	1602	1636t	1704	1702	1736
Olten **505 565** a.	1003t	1030	|	1103t	1130	|	1203t	1230	|	1303t	1330	|	1403t	1430	|	1503t	1503t	1530	|	1603t	1630	|	1703t	1730	|	1803
Basel SBB **565** a.	1032	1101	|	1132	1201	|	1232	1301	|	1332	1401	|	1432	1501	|	1532	1532	1601	|	1632	1701	|	1732	1801	|	1832
Zürich HB **505** a.	...	...	1058	...	...	1158	...	...	1258	...	...	1358	...	...	1458	...	...	...	1558	...	...	1658	...	...	1758	...
Zürich Flughafen ✈ **535** a.	...	...	1114	...	...	1214	...	...	1314	...	...	1414	...	...	1514	...	...	...	1614	...	...	1714	...	...	1814	...
Romanshorn **535** a.	...	...	1212	...	...	1312	...	...	1412	...	...	1512	...	...	1612	...	...	...	1712	...	...	1812	...	...	1912	...

	IC	IC	IC	EC	EC	IC	IC	IC	IC	IC	IC	IC	IC	EC	IC	IC	IC	IC	IC	IC	IC	IC	IC	IC	IC	IC
	1302	**980**	**829**	**64**	**64**	**982**	**831**	**632**	**984**	**833**	**634**	**986**	**835**	**66**	**336**	**837**	**638**	**338**	**990**	**839**	**640**	**646**	**992**	**642**	**841**	**1094**
	⑦			Ⓐ	Ⓒ																①–⑥			⑦		⑤⑥
	e⊖		✕	✕§	✕§		✕		✕	✕	✕		✕	✕§												k
Milano Centrale **590** d.	...	...	...	1505r	1505r	...	...	...	...	...	...	...	...	1805r	...	...	...	...	...	...	...	...	...	...	...	...
Domodossola 🏛 **590** d.	...	...	...	1648	1648	...	...	...	...	...	...	...	...	1948	...	...	...	...	...	...	...	...	...	...	...	...
Brig **570 590** d.	1618	...	1645	1718	1720	1745	...	...	...	1845	1918	1945	...	2019	...	...	2118	...	...	...	2218	...	...	2225	...	...
Visp **570** d.	1627	...	1654	1727	1729	1754	...	...	...	1854	1927	1954	...	2028	...	...	2127	...	...	...	2227	...	...	|	...	...
Interlaken Ost ▷ d.	|	1659	|	|	|	|	1759	1829	1859	|	|	|	1959	|	2059	...	|	...	2200	...	|	...	2300	|	...	2329
Interlaken West ▷ d.	|	1704	|	|	|	|	1804	1834	1904	|	|	|	2004	|	2104	...	|	...	2205	...	|	...	2305	|	...	2334
Spiez ▷ d.	1658	1723	1722	1754	1756	1822	1823	1854	1923	1922	1954	2022	2023	2054	2122	...	2154	...	2222	...	2254	...	2322	2324	...	2354
Thun d.	1709	1734	1733	1804	1807	1833	1834	1904	1934	1933	2004	2033	2034	2104	2133	...	2204	...	2233	...	2304	...	2333	2335	...	0004
Bern a.	|	1756	1753c	1825	1830	1853	1856c	1925	1956	1953c	2025	2053	2056c	2125	2153	...	2225	...	2253	...	2325	...	2353	2356	...	0025
Bern **505** d.	|	1804	1802	1836t	1836t	1904	1902	1936t	2004	2002	2036t	2104	2102	2136t	...	2202	...	2236	...	2302	...	2336	...	...	0002	...
Olten **505 565** a.	1749	1830	|	1903t	1903t	1930	|	2003t	2030	|	2103t	2130	|	2203t	...	2228	...	2303	...	2328	...	0003	...	...	0028	...
Basel SBB **565** a.	|	1901	|	1932	1932	2001	|	2032	2101	|	2132	2201	|	2235f	...	*2301*	...	2337v	...	*0001*	...	0037z	...	...	*0103*	...
Zürich HB **505** a.	1832	...	1858	...	...	...	1958	...	...	2058	...	...	2158	...	...	...	...	...	...	...	...	...	...	...	...	...
Zürich Flughafen ✈ **535** a.	...	...	1914	...	...	...	2014	...	...	...	...	...	2214	...	...	...	...	...	...	...	...	...	...	...	...	...
Romanshorn **535** a.	...	...	2012	...	...	...	2112	...	...	...	...	...	2312	...	...	...	...	...	...	...	...	...	...	...	...	...

D – ①–⑤ (also Aug. 31, Sept. 6, 7); runs daily June 8 - Aug. 1.
G – From/to stations in Germany (Table **910**).

c – Connects with train in previous column.
d – Also Aug. 1; not Aug. 2.
e – Also June 9; not June 8.
f – 2239 on ⑦–④ until June 12; 2237 on ⑦–④ from June 15.
k – Also June 8, July 31.

n – *2256* on ⑦–④.
r – Not June 8 - July 27, Aug. 31 - Sept. 12.
s – Departs 0606 on © June 15 - Oct. 5.
t – 2 minutes later until June 14.
v – 2341 on ⑦–④.
w – Mornings of ⑥⑦ (also June 9, Aug. 1).
z – 0041 on mornings of ①–⑤.

⊙ – Via Kandersteg (Table **562**).
⊖ – Also calls at Frutigen (Table **562**).
§ – 🅁 and supplement payable for journeys to/from Milano.
▷ – Other trains Spiez - Interlaken West - Interlaken Ost and v.v. (operated by BLS):
From Spiez at 0556**s**, 0806, 0823, 1006, 1023, 1206, 1223, 1406, 1523, 1606, 1723, 1806, 1906 and 2106.
From Interlaken Ost: 0729, 0907, 0929, 1107, 1129, 1329, 1407, 1529, 1607, 1729, 1807, 1929 and 2029.

ZB (narrow gauge rack railway) — LUZERN - INTERLAKEN — 561

km		Ⓐ	Ⓐ			L			L				L			L			L			L		
0	**Luzern** 552 d.	...	...	...	0542	0606	0612	0642	0706	0712	0742		1706	1712	1742	1806	1812	1842	1906	1912	1942	2006	2012	2042
9	Hergiswil 552 d.	...	...	...	0554	|	0624	0654	|	0724	0754		|	1724	1754	|	1824	1854	|	1924	1954	|	2024	2054
13	Alpnachstad ⊙ d.	...	...	...	0559	|	0629	0659	|	0729	0759	and at	|	1729	1759	|	1829	1859	|	1929	1959	|	2029	2059
15	Alpnach Dorf d.	...	...	...	0601	|	0631	0701	|	0731	0801		|	1731	1801	|	1831	1901	|	1931	2001	|	2031	2101
21	Sarnen d.	...	...	...	0609	0624	0639	0709	0724	0739	0809	the same	1724	1739	1809	1824	1839	1909	1924	1939	2009	2024	2039	2109
23	Sachseln d.	...	...	...	0613	0628	0643	0713	0728	0743	0813		1728	1743	1813	1828	1843	1913	1928	1943	2013	2028	2043	2113
29	Giswil d.	...	...	...	0621	0637	0651	0721	0737	0751	0821	minutes	1737	1751	1821	1837	1851	1921	1937	1951	2021	2037	2051	2121
36	Lungern d.	...	...	...	▬	0651	...	▬	0751	...	▬		1751	...	▬	1851	...	...	1951	▬	...	2051	▬	...
40	Brünig Hasliberg d.	...	...	...	...	0703	...	...	0803	...	...	past each	1803	...	...	1903	...	...	2003	...	...	2103	...	...
45	**Meiringen** ● a.	...	...	...	...	0716	...	...	0816	...	...		1816	...	...	1916	...	...	2016	...	...	2116	...	...
45	**Meiringen** ● d.	0515	0545	0615	0651	0722	...	0751	0822	...	0851	hour until	1822	...	1851	1922	...	...	...	2021	...	...	2121	...
58	**Brienz** ⊡ d.	0528	0556	0628	0702	0733	...	0802	0837	...	0902		1837	...	1902	1935	...	...	...	2032	...	...	2132	...
65	Oberried d.	0538	0608	0638	0712	0744	...	0812	|	...	0912	◧	|	...	1912	1944	...	...	...	2042	...	...	2142	...
74	**Interlaken** Ost a.	0550	0620	0650	0724	0754	...	0824	0854	...	0924		1854	...	1924	1954	...	...	...	2054	...	...	2154	...

	L			L				▽		S	S
Luzern 552 d.	2106	2112	2142	2206	2212	2242	2312	2342		0855	0955
Hergiswil 552 d.	|	2124	2154	|	2224	2254	2324	2354		|	|
Alpnachstad ⊙ d.	|	2129	2159	|	2229	2259	2329	2359		|	|
Alpnach Dorf d.	|	2131	2201	|	2231	2301	2331	0001		|	|
Sarnen d.	2124	2139	2209	2224	2239	2309	2339	0009	A	0917	1017
Sachseln d.	2128	2143	2213	2228	2243	2313	2343	0013	L	|	|
Giswil d.	2137	2151	2221	2237	2251	2321	2351	0021	S	0927	1027
Lungern d.	2151	▬	...	2251	▬	...	...	...	O	|	|
Brünig Hasliberg d.	2203	...	...	2303	⑤⑥	...	...	...		0951	1051
Meiringen ● a.	2216	...	...	2316	k	...	...	...		1005	1105
Meiringen ● d.	...	2221	...	...	2321	...	...	...		1011	1111
Brienz ⊡ d.	...	2232	...	...	2332	...	...	...		1023	1123
Oberried d.	...	2242	...	...	2342	...	...	...		|	|
Interlaken Ost a.	...	2254	...	...	2354	...	...	...		1041	1141

	⑥⑦ z					L		Ⓐ	L	
Interlaken Ost d.	0006	...	...	...	...	...	...	0557	...	...
Oberried d.	0017	...	...	...	...	...	...	0608	...	...
Brienz ⊡ d.	0027	...	...	...	...	...	...	0619	...	...
Meiringen ● a.	0039	...	...	...	...	...	...	0630	...	...
Meiringen ● d.	...	...	...	...	...	0541	...	▬	0641	...
Brünig Hasliberg d.	...	...	...	...	...	0551	...	...	0651	...
Lungern d.	...	...	...	...	...	0604	...	...	0704	...
Giswil d.	...	...	0505	0535	0605	0621	0635	0705	0721	0735
Sachseln d.	...	...	0513	0543	0613	0629	0643	0713	0729	0743
Sarnen d.	...	...	0519	0549	0619	0635	0649	0719	0735	0749
Alpnach Dorf d.	...	...	0524	0554	0624	|	0654	0724	|	0754
Alpnachstad ⊙ d.	...	...	0529	0559	0629	|	0659	0729	|	0759
Hergiswil 552 d.	...	...	0533	0603	0633	|	0703	0733	|	0803
Luzern 552 a.	...	...	0546	0616	0646	0655	0716	0746	0755	0816

	Ⓐ		L			L				L			L △				L						S	S
Interlaken Ost d.	0627	...	0704	...	0733	0804	...	0833		1904	...	1933	2004	...	...	2104	...	...	...	2204	2304		1615	1715
Oberried d.	0638	...	0715	...	0744	|	...	0844		|	...	1946	2015	...	...	2115	...	...	...	2215	2315		|	|
Brienz ⊡ d.	0650	...	0725	...	0754	0825	...	0854	and at	1925	...	1955	2025	...	...	2127	...	...	...	2225	2325		1634	1734
Meiringen ● a.	0704	...	0735	...	0806	0835	...	0906		1935	...	2007	2036	...	...	2137	...	...	...	2237	2337		1645	1745
Meiringen ● d.	...	...	0741	...	▬	0841	...	▬	the same	1941	...	▬	2041	...	...	...	2141	...	...	▬	▬	A	1650	1750
Brünig Hasliberg d.	...	...	0751	...	...	0851	...	...		1951	...	...	2051	...	...	...	2151	...	...	...	...	L	1703	1803
Lungern d.	...	...	0804	...	...	0904	...	...	minutes	2004	...	...	2104	...	...	...	2204	...	...	...	...	S	|	|
Giswil d.	...	0805	0821	0835	0905	0921	0935	1005		2021	2035	2105	2121	2135	2205	...	2221	2235	2305	2335	0005	O	1730	1830
Sachseln d.	...	0813	0829	0843	0913	0929	0943	1013	past each	2029	2043	2113	2129	2143	2213	...	2229	2243	2313	2343	0013		|	|
Sarnen d.	...	0819	0835	0849	0919	0935	0949	1019		2035	2049	2119	2135	2149	2219	...	2235	2249	2319	2349	0019		1741	1841
Alpnach Dorf d.	...	0824	|	0854	0924	|	0954	1024	hour until	|	2054	2124	|	2154	2224	...	|	2254	2324	2354	0024		|	|
Alpnachstad ⊙ d.	...	0829	|	0859	0929	|	0959	1029		|	2059	2129	|	2159	2229	...	|	2259	2329	2359	0029		|	|
Hergiswil 552 d.	...	0833	|	0903	0933	|	1003	1033	◧	|	2103	2133	|	2203	2233	...	|	2303	2333	0003	0033		|	|
Luzern 552 a.	...	0846	0855	0916	0946	0955	1016	1046		2055	2116	2146	2155	2216	2246	...	2255	2316	2346	0016	0046		1804	1904

L – LUZERN - INTERLAKEN EXPRESS. (12) [panorama cars]. The following services convey ✗: From Luzern 0806 - 1506; from Interlaken 1004 - 1704.
S – May 3 - Oct. 5.

k – ⑤⑥ (not Aug. 1).
z – ⑥⑦ (not Aug. 2).

◧ – For additional summer relief journeys see the last two columns in each direction.
△ – Change trains at Meiringen on ④.
▽ – Additional journeys run from Luzern at 0012 and 0042.

⊙ – Station for Pilatusbahn (Table **553**).
⊡ – Station for Brienz Rothorn Bahn (Table **553**).

● – Rail service **Meiringen - Innertkirchen** and v.v. Narrow gauge. 2nd class only. *5 km*. Journey time: 11 minutes. **Operator**: ZB.
From Meiringen: 0612 Ⓐ, 0634 Ⓐ, 0656, 0718 Ⓐ, 0745, 0818 Ⓐ, 0845, 0945, 1045, 1118 Ⓐ, 1145, 1218 Ⓐ, 1245, 1318 Ⓐ, 1345, 1445, 1545, 1618 Ⓐ, 1645, 1718 Ⓐ, 1745, 1818 Ⓐ, 1845, 1918 Ⓐ, 1945, 2045, 2145 and 2245 ⑤⑥ **k**.
From Innertkirchen Kraftwerk: 0558 Ⓐ, 0623 Ⓐ, 0629 ©, 0645 Ⓐ, 0707, 0729 Ⓐ, 0802, 0829 Ⓐ, 0902, 1002, 1102, 1129 Ⓐ, 1202, 1229 Ⓐ, 1302, 1329 Ⓐ, 1402, 1502, 1602, 1629 Ⓐ, 1702, 1729 Ⓐ, 1802, 1829 Ⓐ, 1902, 1929 Ⓐ, 2002, 2102 and 2202 ⑤⑥ **k**.

BLS — BERN - SPIEZ - BRIG (via Lötschberg pass) — 562

Most services from / to Bern (except *IC* / *EC* trains) also convey (12) Bern - Spiez - Zweisimmen (Table **563**).
Passengers from Bern and Thun should ensure they join the correct portion for their destination. See Table **560** for faster services via the Lötschberg Base Tunnel.

km						*IC* **1304** ⑥**E**		© **c**	Ⓐ **a**							Ⓐ	©						*IC* **643** ①–⑥	*IC* **645** ⑦	
		Ⓐ																							
0	**Bern** 560 d.	...	...	0639	0739	...	0839	0939	0939	1039	1139	1239	1339	1439	1539	1639	1639	1739	1839	1939	*2034*	*2134*	2234	2234	*2337**
31	Thun 560 d.	...	...	0701	0801	0850	0901	1001	1001	1101	1201	1301	1401	1501	1601	1701	1701	1801	1901	2001	*2054*	*2154*	2254	2254	*2357**
41	**Spiez** 560 a.	...	...	0710	0810	0859	0910	1010	1010	1110	1210	1310	1410	1510	1610	1710	1710	1810	1910	2010	*2103*	*2203*	2303	2303	*0007**
41	**Spiez** d.	...	0612	0712	0812	0900	0912	1012	1012	1112	1212	1312	1412	1512	1612	1712	1712	1812	1912	2012	2112	2212	2305	2305	0015
55	Frutigen ● d.	...	0625	0725	0825	0913	0925	1025	1025	1125	1225	1325	1425	1525	1625	1725	1725	1825	1925	2025	2125	2225	2318	2317	0028
72	Kandersteg 🚗 d.	...	0641	0741	0841	|	0941	1041	1041	1141	1241	1341	1441	1541	1641	1741	1741	1841	1941	2041	2141	2241	|	2335	0044
89	Goppenstein 🚗 d.	0542	0652	0752	0852	|	0952	1052	1052	1152	1252	1352	1452	1552	1652	1752	1752	1852	1952	2052	2152	2252	|	2348	0055
115	**Brig** 560 a.	0607	0718	0822	0918	0938	1022	1118	1122	1222	1318	1422	1518	1622	1718	1818	1822	1918	2022	2122	2218	2322	2344	0012	0123
	Domodossola 589 a.	0653v	0753	...	0953	...	...	1153	...	...	1353	...	1553	...	1753	1854z	...	1953	...	...	2253	...	...	...	...

		IC **807** **R** ✗												*IC* **1302** ⑦**F**				*IC* **634**		*EC* **66**		*IC* **638**		*IC* **992**
Domodossola 589 d.	0435	...	...	0558	0658v	0758	...	0958	...	1158c	...	1358	...	...	1558	...	1758	...	...	1948	1958	...	...	...
Brig 560 d.	0511	0542	...	0636	0736	0836	0936	1036	1136	1236	1336	1436	1536	1618	1636	1736	1836	1918	1936	2019	2036	2118	2207	...
Goppenstein 🚗 d.	0536	|	...	0702	0802	0902	1002	1102	1202	1302	1402	1502	1602	|	1702	1802	1902	|	2002	|	2102	|	2233	...
Kandersteg 🚗 d.	0548	|	←	0714	0814	0914	1014	1114	1214	1314	1414	1514	1614	|	1714	1814	1914	|	2014	|	2114	|	2245	...
Frutigen ● d.	0604	0608	0630	0730	0830	0930	1030	1130	1230	1330	1430	1530	1630	1645	1730	1830	1930	|	2030	|	2130	|	2301	...
Spiez a.	→	0621	0644	0744	0844	0944	1044	1144	1244	1344	1444	1544	1644	1656	1744	1844	1944	1953	2044	2053	2144	2153	2315	...
Spiez 560 d.	...	0622	0650	0750	0850	0950	1050	1150	1250	1350	1450	1550	1650	1658	1750	1850	...	1954	...	2054	...	2154	...	2322
Thun 560 a.	...	0631	0658	0758	0858	0958	1058	1158	1258	1358	1458	1558	1658	1707	1758	1858	...	2003	...	2103	...	2203	...	2331
Bern 560 a.	...	0653	0722	0822	0922	1022	1122	1222	1322	1422	1522	1622	1722	...	1822	1922	...	2025	...	2125	...	2225	...	2353

E – ⑥ (also Aug. 1; not Aug. 2). From Zürich HB (Table **560**).
F – ⑦ (also June 9; not June 8). To Zürich HB (Table **560**).
R – (12) Brig - Zürich - Romanshorn.

a – Not June 2, Aug. 15, Dec. 8.
c – Also June 2, Aug. 15, Dec. 8.
v – Ⓐ from July 28.
z – 1924 until July 25.

***** – 2 minutes later on ⑦.

🚗 – Car-carrying shuttle available. ✆ +41 (0) 58 327 31 32. www.bls.ch/en/fahren/autoverlad/kandersteg-goppenstein

● – 🚌 **SERVICE FRUTIGEN - ADELBODEN**. 20 km. Journey ±30 minutes. Operator: Autoverkehr Frutigen-Adelboden (AFA). ✆ +41 (0) 33 673 74 74.
From Frutigen: 0615 Ⓐ, 0632, 0700 Ⓐ, 0732, 0800, 0832, 0900 ©, 0932, 1000 ©, 1032, 1132 and hourly until 1532; then 1603 ©, 1632, 1700, 1732, 1800, 1832, 1900 Ⓐ, 1932, 2032, 2132, 2232 and 2325.
From Adelboden (Post): 0533 Ⓐ, 0551, 0622 Ⓐ, 0651, 0725, 0751, 0825 ©, 0851, 0925 ©, 0951, 1051 and hourly until 1451; then 1525 ©, 1551, 1625, 1651, 1725, 1751, 1825 Ⓐ, 1851, 1951, 2051, 2151 and 2225.

563 INTERLAKEN - SPIEZ - ZWEISIMMEN BLS

km			Ⓐ		Ⓐ		Ⓒ		★			★						★			★		Ⓐ	
	Interlaken Ost ◇ .... **560** d.	...	...	...	...	...	...	...	0907	...	...	1107	...	...	...	...	...	1407	...	...	1607	...	...	...
	Bern **560 562** △............d.	...	...	0639	...	0739	...	0839	|	0939	1039	|	1139	...	1239	...	1339	|	1439	1539	|	1639	...	1739
0	**Spiez**............................ **560** d.	0612	0638	0712	0738	0812	0838	0912	0938	1012	1112	1138	1212	...	1312	1338	1412	1438	1512	1612	1638	1712	1738	1812
11	Erlenbach im Simmental ....d.	0629	0653	0729	0753	0829	0853	0929	0953	1029	1129	1153	1229	...	1329	1353	1429	1453	1529	1629	1653	1729	1753	1829
26	Boltigen ....d.	0649	0711	0749	0811	0849	0911	0949	1011	1049	1149	1211	1249	...	1349	1411	1449	1511	1549	1649	1711	1749	1811	1849
35	**Zweisimmen**.......................a.	0659	0720	0759	0820	0859	0920	0959	1020	1059	1159	1220	1259	...	1359	1420	1459	1520	1559	1659	1720	1759	1820	1859
	Montreux **566** .... a.	...	...	...	...	...	...	...	1227	...	...	1427	...	...	...	...	...	1727	...	...	1927	...	...	...

	①–⑥	⑦							
Interlaken Ost ◇.......... **560** d.	1807	...	...	...	...	...	...	...	...
Bern **560 562** △...............d.	|	...	1839	1939	...	...	...	...	...
Spiez .... **560** d.	1838	1838	1912	2012	2107	2207	2307	0016	...
Erlenbach im Simmental ....d.	1853	1853	1929	2029	2121	2221	2321	0032	...
Boltigen ....d.	1911	1911	1949	2049	2140	2240	2340	0051	...
Zweisimmen.......................a.	1920	1920	1959	2059	2152	2252	2352	0102	...
Montreux **566**.................. a.	...	...	...	...	...	...	...	...	...

	Ⓐ	Ⓐ	Ⓒ	Ⓐ				Ⓐ		★
Montreux **566** .... d.	...	...	...	...	...	...	...	...	...	0733
Zweisimmen ....d.	0539	0554	0602	0639	0702	0739	0802	0839	0902	0939
Boltigen ....d.	0548	0602	0610	0648	0710	0748	0810	0848	0910	0948
Erlenbach im Simmental ....d.	0605	0622	0630	0705	0730	0805	0830	0905	0930	1005
Spiez........................ **560** a.	0621	0639	0647	0721	0747	0821	0847	0921	0947	1021
Bern **560 562**..................a.	...	0722	0722	...	0822	|	0922	...	1022	|
Interlaken Ost ◇........ **560** a.	...	...	...	...	...	0848	...	...	...	1048

			★		Ⓒ			★				★												
Montreux **566**.................. d.	...	...	0933	...	...	...	...	1233	...	...	...	1433	...	...	...	...	...	...	...	...	...	...	...	...
Zweisimmen.......................d.	1002	1102	1139	1202	1239	1302	1402	1439	1502	1539	1602	1639	1702	1802	1902	2002	2104	2204	2304	...	0013	...	...	...
Boltigen ....d.	1010	1110	1148	1210	1248	1310	1410	1448	1510	1548	1610	1648	1710	1810	1910	2012	2114	2214	2314	...	0023	...	...	...
Erlenbach im Simmental ....d.	1030	1130	1205	1230	1305	1330	1430	1505	1530	1605	1630	1705	1730	1830	1930	2031	2134	2234	2334	...	0044	...	...	...
Spiez .... **560** a.	1047	1147	1221	1247	1321	1347	1447	1521	1547	1621	1647	1721	1747	1847	1947	2047	2150	2250	2350	...	0101	...	...	...
Bern **560 562**...................a.	1122	1222	...	1322	...	1422	1522	|	1622	...	1722	|	1822	1922	...	...	...	...	...	...	...	...	...	...
Interlaken Ost ◇.......... **560** a.	...	...	1248	...	...	...	...	1548	...	...	...	1748	...	...	...	...	...	...	...	...	...	...	...	...

★ – GOLDEN PASS EXPRESS – Conveys panorama cars. Reservation recommended. Also conveys Prestige class (🄿 and supplement payable). www.gpx.swiss.

◇ – Trains also call at Interlaken West.

△ – Trains from Bern convey portions for Zweisimmen and Brig; please ensure you join the correct portion.

564 INTERLAKEN - KLEINE SCHEIDEGG - JUNGFRAUJOCH BOB, WAB, JB (narrow gauge rack railway)

INTERLAKEN - LAUTERBRUNNEN / GRINDELWALD

km																	🚌	🚌 f					
0	**Interlaken** Ost.....................d.	0604	0604	0634	0634	and every	2004	2004	2034	2034	2104	2104	...	2204	2204	...	2304	2304	...	...	...	...	...
3	Wilderswil ⊡.........................d.	0610	0610	0640	0640	30 minutes	2010	2010	2040	2040	2110	2110	...	2210	2210	...	2311	2311	...	...	...	...	...
8	Zweilütschinen.......................d.	0617	0618	0647	0648	until	2017	2018	2047	2048	2117	2118	...	2217	2218	...	2318	2318	...	...	...	...	...
	Grindelwald Terminal..... 🚡 a.	|	0635	|	0705		|	2035	|	2105	|	2135	...	|	2235	...	|	|	...	...	...	...	...
19	**Grindelwald** ....a.	|	0640	|	0710		|	2040	|	2110	|	2140	...	|	2240	...	|	2335	...	...	...	...	...
	Lauterbrunnen ....a.	0626	...	0656	...		2026	...	2056	...	2126	...	...	2226	...	...	2325	...	...	...	...	...	...

km																		🚌		🚌			
0	**Lauterbrunnen** ....d.	...	0532	...	0602	...	0632	and every	...	2002	...	2032	...	...	2132	...	...	2230	...	2330	...	...	...
	Grindelwald ....d.	0517	|	0547	|	0617	|	30 minutes	1947	|	2017	|	...	2117	|	...	2217	|	...	|	...	...	...
	Grindelwald Terminal..... 🚡 d.	0521	|	0551	|	0621	|	until	1951	|	2021	|	...	2121	|	...	|	|	...	|	...	...	...
4	Zweilütschinen.......................d.	0541	0541	0612	0612	0642	0642		2012	2012	2042	2042	...	2142	2142	...	2234	2236	...	2336	...	...	...
9	Wilderswil ⊡..........................d.	0547	0547	0618	0618	0648	0648		2018	2018	2048	2048	...	2148	2148	...	2241	2245	...	2345	...	...	...
12	**Interlaken** Ost.....................a.	0552	0552	0624	0624	0654	0654		2024	2024	2054	2054	...	2154	2154	...	2251	2254	...	2354	...	...	...

GRINDELWALD - KLEINE SCHEIDEGG *No service May 5 – 16 or Oct. 27 - Nov. 7*

km			L			L		L	L			L	L										
0	**Grindelwald**..............d.	0745	0815	0845	and at the same	1615	1645	1715	1745	1745	1815	1845	1915	...	...	...	...	...	...	...	...	...	...
1	Grindelwald Grund......d.	0753	0823	0853	minutes past	1623	1653	1723	1753	1750	1820	1850	1920	...	...	...	...	...	...	...	...	...	...
9	**Kleine Scheidegg**......a.	0817	0847	0917	each hour until	1647	1717	1747	1817	...	...	...	...	...	...	...	...	...	...	...	...	...	...

		L		L		L			L			L	L									
Kleine Scheidegg ....d.	...	...	...	0831	0901	0931	and at the same	1601	1631	1701	1731	1801	1831	...	...	...	...	...	...	...	...	...
Grindelwald Grund ....d.	0736	0806	0836	0906	0936	1006	minutes past	1636	1706	1736	1806	1836	1906	...	...	...	...	...	...	...	...	...
Grindelwald ....a.	0740	0810	0840	0910	0940	1010	each hour until	1640	1710	1740	1810	1840	1910	...	...	...	...	...	...	...	...	...

LAUTERBRUNNEN - WENGEN - KLEINE SCHEIDEGG **Not Nov. 10 - Dec. 5 (see note ◨)**

km											N	N	s											
0	**Lauterbrunnen** ....d.	0600	0630	0700	0730	0800	0830	and every	1600	1630	1700	1730	1800	1800	1830	1900	1930	2000	2030	2100	2130	2230	2332	0032
4	Wengen.......................a.	0611	0641	0711	0742	0812	0842	30 minutes	1612	1642	1712	1742	1812	1812	1842	1912	1941	2011	2041	2111	2141	2241	2343	0044
4	Wengen.......................d.	...	...	...	0746	0816	0846		1616	1646	1716	1746	1816	...	...	...	...	...	...	...	...	...	...	...
11	**Kleine Scheidegg**......a.	...	...	...	0808	0838	0908	until	1638	1708	1738	1808	1838	...	...	...	...	...	...	...	...	...	...	...

														N	N	s								
Kleine Scheidegg ......d.	...	...	...	...	...	...	...	0814	0844	and every	1614	1644	1714	1744	1814	1844	...	...	...	...	...	...	...	...
Wengen.......................a.	...	...	...	...	...	...	...	0839	0909	30 minutes	1639	1709	1739	1809	1839	1909	...	...	...	...	...	...	...	...
Wengen.......................d.	0504	0540	0613	0643	0713	0742	0812	0842	0912		1642	1712	1742	1812	1842	1912	1912	1943	2013	2043	2113	2213	2313	0013
Lauterbrunnen...........a.	0517	0553	0626	0656	0726	0755	0825	0855	0925	until	1655	1725	1755	1825	1855	1925	1925	1956	2026	2056	2126	2226	2326	0026

KLEINE SCHEIDEGG - JUNGFRAUJOCH *Reservation recommended*

km				v	s					s	e	s									
0	**Kleine Scheidegg**......d.	**Dec. 21 - Jan. 5**	...	*0827*	0830	0900	0930	and	1630	1700	...	...	**Jan. 6 - Apr. 17**	*0827*	*0857*r	*0927*	*0957*r	and at the same	*1527*	*1557*r	1627
2	Eigergletscher......... 🚡 a.	**and**	...	*0832*	0835	0905	0935	every 30	1635	1705	...	...	**and**	*0832*	*0902*r	*0932*	*1002*r	minutes	*1532*	*1602*r	1632
2	Eigergletscher.............d.	**Apr. 18 - Nov. 9**	0815	0845	0845	0915	0945	minutes	1645	1715	1715	1745	**Nov. 10 - Dec. 13**	0845	0915	0945	1015	past each	1545	1615	...
9	**Jungfraujoch**.............a.		0841	0911	0911	0941	1011	until	1711	1741	1741	1811		0911	0941	1011	1041	hour until	1611	1641	...

			e						e	s	e	s									
Jungfraujoch ....d.	**Dec. 21 - Jan. 5**	*0817*s	0847	0917	0947	and	1617	1647	1717	1747	1747	1817	**Jan. 6 - Apr. 17**	...	0917	0947	and at the same	1517	1547	1617	1647
Eigergletscher ....a.	**and**	*0841*s	0911	0941	1011	every 30	1641	1711	1741	1811	1811	1841	**and**	...	0941	1011	minutes	1541	1611	1641	1711
Eigergletscher .... 🚡 d.	**Apr. 18 - Nov. 9**	0846	...	0946**s**	1016	minutes	1646	1716**e**	1746	1816	...	...	**Nov. 10 - Dec. 13**	0916r	*0946*	*1016*r	past each	*1546*	*1616*r	*1646*	...
Kleine Scheidegg ......a.		0854	...	0954**s**	1024	until	1654	1724**e**	1754	1824	...	...		0924r	*0954*	*1024*r	hour until	*1554*	*1624*r	*1654*	...

GRINDELWALD TERMINAL - EIGERGLETSCHER *Eiger Express* gondola service. Journey time 20 minutes. Frequent departures between the following times:
From Grindlewald: 0800 - 1545 (0745 - 1745 Apr. 18 - May 16 and Aug. 25 - Nov. 11; 0715 - 1815 May 17 - Aug. 24).
From Eigergletscher: 0800 - 1720 (0745 - 1820 Apr. 18 - May 16 and Aug. 25 - Nov. 11; 0715 - 1850 May 17 - Aug. 24).

WILDERSWIL - SCHYNIGE PLATTE Operates June 14 - Oct 26 Narrow gauge rack railway. Journey time 52 minutes. *7 km.* Operator: BOB. *Service may be suspended in bad weather.*
From Wilderswil: 0725, 0805**h**, 0845, 0925, 1005, 1045, 1125, 1205, 1245, 1325, 1405, 1445, 1525, 1605, 1645.
From Schynige Platte: 0821, 0901**h**, 0941, 1021, 1101, 1141, 1221, 1301, 1341, 1421, 1501, 1541, 1621, 1701, 1753.

LAUTERBRUNNEN - MÜRREN Cableway **Lauterbrunnen - Grütschalp** and narrow gauge railway **Grütschalp - Mürren**. Total journey time 20 minutes; distance *5 km*. Operator: BLM.
No service Apr. 22 - May 2 or Oct. 27 - Nov. 9.
From Lauterbrunnen: 0613, 0631, 0701, 0731, 0801, 0835, 0905 and every 30 minutes until 1935. **Extra departures** Dec. 21 - Apr. 21, May 3 - Oct 26: every 30 mins 0921 - 1653, also 2035.
From Mürren: 0558, 0628, 0658, 0728 and every 30 minutes until 1858. **Extra departures** Dec. 21 - Apr. 21, May 3 - Oct. 26: every 30 minutes 0943 - 1713, also 1958.

MÜRREN - SCHILTHORN Cable car. **Operates Mar. 15 - Dec. 13.** Journey 17 minutes (two sections). Operator: Schilthornbahn.
From Mürren: 0740**z**, 0810, 0830 and every 30 minutes until 1600, 1630**z**. **From Schilthorn**: 0850, 0920 and every 30 minutes until 1720, 1750**u**.

L – Dec. 21 - May 4, May 17 - Oct. 26.
N – Dec. 21 - Nov. 9 (daily Lauterbrunnen - Wengen and v.v.).
e – Apr. 18 - Nov. 9.
f – Not June 8, July 31.
h – June 28 - Oct. 12.
r – Jan. 6 - Apr. 17.
s – May 17 - Aug. 24.
u – Mar. 15 - Oct. 12.
v – Not May 17 - Aug. 24.
z – May 3 - Oct. 12.
⊡ – For rack railway to Schynige Platte - see below main table.
◨ – No service Wengen - Kleine Scheidegg or v.v. Nov. 10 - Dec. 5. A normal service runs Lauterbrunnen - Wengen and v.v. in the times shown.
🚡 – For *Eiger Express* cable car (see below main table).

SBB, SOB

BASEL and BERN - LUZERN

km		*IR* 2349 ⑥⑦	*IC* 659	*IR* 2457 Ⓐ	*RE* 4709	*IR* 2505	*IR* 2311 ★ L	*IR* 2459	*RE* 4711	*IR* 2507	*IC* 663 ✕	*IR* 2461	*RE* 4713	*IR* 2509	*IR* 2315 ★ L	*IR* 2463	*RE* 4715	*IR* 2511	*IC* 667 ✕	*IR* 2465	*RE* 4717	*IR* 2513	*IR* 2319 ★ L	*IR* 2467	*RE* 4719	*IR* 2515
0	**Basel** SBB **560** d.	0100	0501**r**	...	...	...	0603	0616	...	...	0703	0716	...	...	0803	0816	...	...	0903	0916	...	...	1003	1016	...	...
14	Liestal d.	0110	|	...	...	...	|	0627	...	...	|	0727	...	...	|	0827	...	...	|	0927	...	...	|	1027	...	...
21	Sissach d.	0117	|	...	...	...	|	0633	...	...	|	0733	...	...	|	0833	...	...	|	0933	...	...	|	1033	...	...
39	**Olten** **560** d.	0137	0530	0549	0606	...	0630	0649	0706	...	0730	0749	0806	...	0830	0849	0906	...	0930	0949	1006	...	1030	1049	1106	...
	Genève Aéroport ✈ **500** d.	|	|	|	|	...	|	|	|	...	|	|	|	0544	|	|	|	0645	|	|	|	0745	|	|	|	0845
	Genève **500** d.	|	|	|	|	...	|	|	|	...	|	|	|	0553	|	|	|	0654	|	|	|	0754	|	|	|	0854
	Lausanne **500** d.	|	|	|	|	0440**g**	|	|	|	0540	|	|	|	0640	|	|	|	0740	|	|	|	0840	|	|	|	0940
	Bern d.	|	|	|	|	0600	|	|	|	0700	|	|	|	0800	|	|	|	0900	|	|	|	1000	|	|	|	1100
47	Zofingen d.	0144	|	0558	0613	0629	|	0658	0713	0729	|	0758	0813	0829	|	0858	0913	0929	|	0958	1013	1029	|	1058	1113	1129
69	Sursee d.	0158	|	0612	0631	0642	|	0712	0731	0742	|	0812	0831	0842	|	0912	0931	0942	|	1012	1031	1042	|	1112	1131	1142
95	**Luzern** a.	0217	0605	0630	0655	0701	0705	0730	0755	0801	0805	0830	0855	0901	0905	0930	0955	1001	1005	1030	1055	1101	1105	1130	1155	1201
	Lugano **550** a.	...	0758	...	...	...	...	...	...	...	0958	...	...	...	...	...	...	...	1158	...	...	...	...	...	...	...

	IC 671 ✕	*IR* 2469	*RE* 4721	*IR* 2517	*IR* 2323 ★ L	*IR* 2471	*RE* 4723	*IR* 2519	*IC* 675 ✕	*IR* 2473	*RE* 4725	*IR* 2521	*IR* 2327 ★ L	*IR* 2475	*RE* 4727	*IR* 2523	*EC* 173 M ✕	*IR* 2477	*RE* 4729	*IR* 2525	*IR* 2331 ★ L	*IR* 2479	*RE* 4731	*IR* 2527	*IC* 683 ✕	*IR* 2481
Basel SBB **560** d.	1103	1116	...	...	1203	1216	...	...	1303	1316	...	...	1403	1416	...	...	1503	1516	...	...	1603	1616	...	...	1703	1716
Liestal d.	|	1127	...	...	|	1227	...	...	|	1327	...	...	|	1427	...	...	|	1527	...	...	|	1627	...	...	|	1727
Sissach d.	|	1133	...	...	|	1233	...	...	|	1333	...	...	|	1433	...	...	|	1533	...	...	|	1633	...	...	|	1733
Olten **560** d.	1130	1149	1206	...	1230	1249	1306	...	1330	1349	1406	...	1430	1449	1506	...	1530	1549	1606	...	1630	1649	1706	...	1730	1749
Genève Aéroport ✈ **500** d.	|	|	|	0945	|	|	|	1045	|	|	|	1145	|	|	|	1245	|	|	|	1345	|	|	|	1445	|	|
Genève **500** d.	|	|	|	0954	|	|	|	1054	|	|	|	1154	|	|	|	1254	|	|	|	1354	|	|	|	1454	|	|
Lausanne **500** d.	|	|	|	1040	|	|	|	1140	|	|	|	1240	|	|	|	1340	|	|	|	1440	|	|	|	1540	|	|
Bern d.	|	|	|	1200	|	|	|	1300	|	|	|	1400	|	|	|	1500	|	|	|	1600	|	|	|	1700	|	|
Zofingen d.	|	1158	1213	1229	|	1258	1313	1329	|	1358	1413	1429	|	1458	1513	1529	|	1558	1613	1629	|	1658	1713	1729	|	1758
Sursee d.	|	1212	1231	1242	|	1312	1331	1342	|	1412	1431	1442	|	1512	1531	1542	|	1612	1631	1642	|	1712	1731	1742	|	1812
Luzern a.	1205	1230	1255	1301	1305	1330	1355	1401	1405	1430	1455	1501	1505	1530	1555	1601	1605	1630	1655	1701	1705	1730	1755	1801	1805	1830
Lugano **550** a.	1358	...	...	...	...	...	...	...	1558	...	...	...	...	...	...	...	1758	...	...	...	...	...	...	...	1958	...

	RE 4733	*IR* 2529	*IR* 2335 ★ B	*IR* 2483	*RE* 4735	*IR* 2531	*IC* 687 C	*IR* 2485	*RE* 4737	*IR* 2533	*IR* 2339 ★ E	*IR* 2487	*RE* 4739	*IR* 2535	*IC* 691 C	*IR* 2489	*RE* 4741	*IR* 2537	*IR* 2343 ★ A	*IR* 2491 ⑤⑥	*RE* 4743	*IR* 2539	*IR* 2345	*IR* 2493 ⑤⑥	*RE* 4745	*IR* 2347 ★
Basel SBB **560** d.	...	...	1803	1816	...	...	1903	1916	...	...	2003	2016	...	...	2103	2116	...	...	2203**z**	2216	...	...	2256**e**	2316	...	0004
Liestal d.	...	...	|	1827	...	...	|	1927	...	...	|	2027	...	...	|	2127	...	...	|	2227	...	...	2306**e**	2327	...	0014
Sissach d.	...	...	|	1833	...	...	|	1933	...	...	|	2033	...	...	|	2133	...	...	|	2233	...	...	|	2333	...	|
Olten **560** d.	1806	...	1830	1849	1906	...	1930	1949	2006	...	2030	2049	2106	...	2130	2149	2206	...	2230	2249	2307	...	2330	2348	0007	0035
Genève Aéroport ✈ **500** d.	|	1545	|	|	|	1645	|	|	|	1745	|	|	|	1845	|	|	|	1945	|	|	|	2045**k**	|	...	|	|
Genève **500** d.	|	1554	|	|	|	1654	|	|	|	1754	|	|	|	1854	|	|	|	1954	|	|	|	2054**k**	|	...	|	|
Lausanne **500** d.	|	1640	|	|	|	1740	|	|	|	1840	|	|	|	1940	|	|	|	2040	|	|	|	2140	|	...	|	|
Bern d.	|	1800	|	|	|	1900	|	|	|	2000	|	|	|	2100	|	|	|	2200	|	|	|	2300	|	...	|	|
Zofingen d.	1813	1829	|	1858	1913	1929	|	1958	2013	2029	|	2058	2113	2129	|	2158	2213	2229	|	2256	2314	2329	|	...	0014	0042
Sursee d.	1831	1842	|	1912	1931	1942	|	2012	2031	2042	|	2112	2131	2142	|	2212	2231	2242	|	...	2332	2342	|	...	0033	0056
Luzern a.	1855	1901	1905	1930	1955	2001	2005	2030	2055	2101	2105	2130	2155	2201	2205	2230	2255	2301	2305	...	2355	0001	0005	...	0055	0116
Lugano **550** a.	...	...	...	...	...	...	2158	...	...	...	...	...	...	...	2358	...	...	...	...	...	...	...	...	...	...	...

km		*IR* 2344 ⑥⑦	*IR* 2304 ★	*RE* 4706	*IR* 2456	*IR* 2456 Ⓐ	*IR* 2306	*IR* 2508	*RE* 4708	*IR* 2458	*IR* 2308 ★ E	*IR* 2510	*RE* 4710	*IR* 2460	*IC* 664 C	*IR* 2512	*RE* 4712	*IR* 2462	*IR* 2312 ★ B	*IR* 2514	*RE* 4714	*IR* 2464	*IC* 668 ✕	*IR* 2516	*RE* 4716	*IR* 2466
	Lugano **550** d.	...	...	...	...	...	...	...	...	...	...	...	...	...	0600	...	...	...	...	...	...	...	0802	...	...	...
0	**Luzern** d.	0047	0454	0458	...	0530	0554	0600	0605	0630	0654	0700	0705	0730	0754	0800	0805	0830	0854	0900	0905	0930	0954	1000	1005	1030
26	Sursee d.	0107	|	0524	...	0548	|	0618	0627	0648	|	0718	0727	0748	|	0818	0827	0848	|	0918	0927	0948	|	1018	1027	1048
48	Zofingen d.	0120	|	0545	...	0603	|	0632	0645	0703	|	0732	0745	0803	|	0832	0845	0903	|	0932	0945	1003	|	1032	1045	1103
111	**Bern** a.	|	|	|	...	|	|	0700	|	|	|	0800	|	|	|	0900	|	|	|	1000	|	|	|	1100	|	|
	Lausanne **500** a.	|	|	|	...	|	|	0820	|	|	|	0920	|	|	|	1020	|	|	|	1120	|	|	|	1220	|	|
	Genève **500** a.	|	|	|	...	|	|	0905	|	|	|	1005	|	|	|	1105	|	|	|	1205	|	|	|	1305	|	|
	Genève Aéroport ✈ **500** a.	|	|	|	...	|	|	0915	|	|	|	1015	|	|	|	1115	|	|	|	1215	|	|	|	1315	|	|
	Olten **560** d.	0137	0530	0552	0612	0612	0630	...	0652	0712	0730	...	0752	0812	0830	...	0852	0912	0930	...	0952	1012	1030	...	1052	1112
	Sissach d.	|	|	...	0627	0627	|	...	...	0727	|	...	...	0827	|	...	...	0927	|	...	...	1027	|	...	...	1127
	Liestal d.	0154	|	...	0634	0634	|	...	...	0734	|	...	...	0834	|	...	...	0934	|	...	...	1034	|	...	...	1134
	Basel SBB **560** a.	0205	0556	...	0645	0645	0656	...	...	0745	0756	...	...	0847	0856	...	...	0947	0956	...	...	1045	1056	...	...	1145

	IR 2316 ★ L	*IR* 2518	*RE* 4718	*IR* 2468	*IC* 672 ✕	*IR* 2520	*RE* 4720	*IR* 2470	*IR* 2320 ★ L	*IR* 2522	*RE* 4722	*IR* 2472	*EC* 178 M ✕	*IR* 2524	*RE* 4724	*IR* 2474	*IR* 2324 ★ L	*IR* 2526	*RE* 4726	*IR* 2476	*IC* 680 ✕	*IR* 2528	*RE* 4728	*IR* 2478	*IR* 2328 ★ L	*IR* 2530
Lugano **550** d.	...	...	...	...	1002	...	...	...	...	...	...	...	1202	...	...	...	...	...	...	...	1402	...	...	...	...	...
Luzern d.	1054	1100	1105	1130	1154	1200	1205	1230	1254	1300	1305	1330	1354	1400	1405	1430	1454	1500	1505	1530	1554	1600	1605	1630	1654	1700
Sursee d.	|	1118	1127	1148	|	1218	1227	1248	|	1318	1327	1348	|	1418	1427	1448	|	1518	1527	1548	|	1618	1627	1648	|	1718
Zofingen d.	|	1132	1145	1203	|	1232	1245	1303	|	1332	1345	1403	|	1432	1445	1503	|	1532	1545	1603	|	1632	1645	1703	|	1732
Bern a.	|	1200	|	|	|	1300	|	|	|	1400	|	|	|	1500	|	|	|	1600	|	|	|	1700	|	|	|	1800
Lausanne **500** a.	|	1320	|	|	|	1420	|	|	|	1520	|	|	|	1620	|	|	|	1720	|	|	|	1820	|	|	|	1920
Genève **500** a.	|	1405	|	|	|	1505	|	|	|	1605	|	|	|	1705	|	|	|	1805	|	|	|	1905	|	|	|	2005
Genève Aéroport ✈ **500** a.	|	1415	|	|	|	1515	|	|	|	1615	|	|	|	1715	|	|	|	1815	|	|	|	1915	|	|	|	2015
Olten **560** d.	1130	...	1152	1212	1230	...	1252	1312	1330	...	1352	1412	1430	...	1452	1512	1530	...	1552	1612	1630	...	1652	1712	1730	...
Sissach d.	|	...	...	1227	|	...	...	1327	|	...	...	1427	|	...	...	1527	|	...	...	1627	|	...	...	1727	|	...
Liestal d.	|	...	...	1234	|	...	...	1334	|	...	...	1434	|	...	...	1534	|	...	...	1634	|	...	...	1734	|	...
Basel SBB **560** a.	1156	...	...	1245	1256	...	...	1345	1356	...	...	1445	1456	...	...	1545	1556	...	...	1645	1656	...	...	1745	1756	...

	RE 4730	*IR* 2480	*IC* 684 ✕	*IR* 2532	*RE* 4732	*IR* 2482	*IR* 2332 ★ L	*IR* 2534	*RE* 4734	*IR* 2484	*IC* 688 ✕	*IR* 2536	*RE* 4736	*IR* 2486	*IR* 2336 ★ L	*IR* 2538 ¶	*RE* 4738	*IR* 2488 ⑤⑥	*IC* 692 ✕	*IR* 2540	*RE* 4740	*IR* 2490 ⑤⑥	*IR* 2340 ★ L	*IR* 2542	*RE* 4742	*IC* 696
Lugano **550** d.	...	...	1602	...	...	...	...	...	...	...	1802	...	...	...	...	...	...	...	2002	...	...	...	...	...	...	2202
Luzern d.	1705	1730	1754	1800	1805	1830	1854	1900	1905	1930	1954	2000	2005	2030	2054	2100	2105	2130	2154	2200	2205	...	2254	2300	2305	2354
Sursee d.	1727	1748	|	1818	1827	1848	|	1918	1927	1948	|	2018	2027	2048	|	2118	2127	2148	|	2218	2227	...	|	2318	2327	|
Zofingen d.	1745	1803	|	1832	1845	1903	|	1932	1945	2003	|	2032	2045	2103	|	2132	2145	2203	|	2232	2245	2303	|	2332	2345	|
Bern a.	|	|	|	1900	|	|	|	2000	|	|	|	2100	|	|	|	2200	|	|	|	2300	|	|	|	2400	|	|
Lausanne **500** a.	|	|	|	2020	|	|	|	2120	|	|	|	2220	|	|	|	2320	|	|	|	0023	|	|	|	...	|	|
Genève **500** a.	|	|	|	2105	|	|	|	2205**k**	|	|	|	...	|	|	|	...	|	|	|	...	|	|	|	...	|	|
Genève Aéroport ✈ **500** a.	|	|	|	2115	|	|	|	2216**k**	|	|	|	...	|	|	|	...	|	|	|	...	|	|	|	...	|	|
Olten **560** d.	1752	1812	1830	...	1852	1912	1930	...	1952	2012	2030	...	2052	2112	2130	...	2152	2212	2233	...	2253	2312	2333	...	2353	0035
Sissach d.	...	1827	|	...	...	1927	|	...	...	2027	|	...	...	2127	|	...	...	2227	|	...	...	2327	|	...	...	|
Liestal d.	...	1834	|	...	...	1934	|	...	...	2034	|	...	...	2134	|	...	...	2234	2250	...	...	2334	2349	...	...	0052
Basel SBB **560** a.	...	1845	1856	...	...	1945	1956	...	...	2045	2056	...	...	2145	2156**y**	...	...	2245	2301	...	...	2345	0001	...	...	0103

A – To Arth-Goldau (Table **547**).
B – To/from Bellinzona via Göschenen (Table **547**).
C – To/from Chiasso (Table **550**).
E – To/from Erstfeld (Table **547**).
L – To/from Locarno via Göschenen (Table **547**).
M – To/from Milano (Table **550**).

e – 2 minutes later on ⑤⑥.
g – ① (not June 9).
k – ⑤⑥ only.
r – 0503 on ⑥⑦.
y – On ⑦–④ change trains at Olten (Basel a. *2201*).
z – On ⑦–④ d. *2156* and change trains at Olten.

¶ – Runs as *IC* **1490** on ⑦.
★ – Operated by SOB. Conveys (🍸).

566 LENK - ZWEISIMMEN - MONTREUX
MOB (narrow gauge)

km		2203	2205	2207	2207	2209	2211	2213	2215	4065	2217	2219	4069	2221	2223	2225	4075	2227	2229	4079	2231	2233	2435	2437	2439	2241
				Ⓐ	Ⓒ																		2235	2237	2239	
							P	P	P	E🍷	P	B	E🍷	P	P	P	E🍷	P	B	E🍷			c	c	c	
	Interlaken Ost **563** d.	...	...	...	...	...	...	...	...	0907	...	...	1107	...	...	...	1407	...	...	1607	...	...	...	...	...	...
	Spiez **563** d.	...	...	...	...	...	...	...	...	0938	...	...	1138	...	...	...	1438	...	...	1638	...	...	...	...	...	...
0	**Zweisimmen** ‡ d.	...	0502**a**	0602	0602	0702	0802	0902	1002	1030	1102	1202	1230	1302	1402	1502	1530	1602	1702	1730	1802	1902	2002	2102	2202	2302
9	Saanenmöser ‡ d.	...	0518**a**	0618	0618	0718	0818	0918	1018	1044	1118	1218	1244	1318	1418	1518	1544	1617	1718	1744	1817	1918	2018	2118	2218	2318
11	Schönried ‡ d.	...	0522**a**	0622	0622	0722	0822	0922	1022	1047	1122	1222	1247	1322	1422	1522	1547	1622	1722	1747	1822	1922	2022	2122	2222	2322
16	**Gstaad** ‡ d.	0456	0535	0635	0637	0737	0837	0937	1037	1100	1137	1237	1300	1337	1437	1537	1600	1637	1737	1800	1837	1937	2037	2137	2237	2337
19	Saanen d.	0459	0539	0638	0641	0741	0841	0941	1041	|	1141	1241	|	1341	1441	1541	|	1641	1741	|	1841	1941	2041	2141	2241	2341
23	Rougemont d.	0505	0544	0643	0646	0746	0846	0946	1046	|	1146	1246	|	1346	1446	1546	|	1646	1746	|	1846	1946	2046	2146	2246	2346
29	Château d'Oex d.	0518	0557	0656	0704	0804	0904	1004	1104	1117	1204	1304	1317	1404	1504	1604	1617	1704	1804	1817	1904	2004	2104	2204	2304	2357
40	**Montbovon** d.	0535	0623	0714	0723	0823	0923	1023	1123	1135	1223	1323	1335	1423	1523	1623	1637	1724	1823	1837	1924	2023	2123	2223	2323	...
51	Les Avants § d.	0600	0648	0736	0748	0848	0948	1048	1148	|	1248	1348	|	1448	1548	1648	|	1748	1848	|	1948	2048	2148	2248	2348	...
55	Chamby ⊗ § d.	0607	0659	0746	0759	0859	0959	1059	1159	|	1259	1359	|	1459	1559	1659	|	1759	1859	|	1959	2100	2200	2300	0000	...
58	Chernex § d.	0605	0705	0754	0805	0905	1005	1105	1205	|	1305	1405	|	1505	1605	1705	|	1805	1905	|	2005	2105	2205	2305	0005	...
62	**Montreux** § a.	0628	0717	0804	0817	0917	1017	1117	1217	1227	1317	1417	1427	1517	1617	1717	1727	1817	1917	1927	2017	2118	2218	2318	0018	...

	2202	2204	2206	2208	4064	2210	2212	4068	2214	2216	2218	4074	2220	2222	4078	2224	2226	2326	2228	2230	2232	2234	2236	2238	2240	2242
	Ⓐ																	Ⓐ**d**				2434	2436	2438		
					E🍷	P	P	E🍷	B	P	P	E🍷	P	P	E🍷	B	P		P	P		c	c	c		
Montreux § d.	...	0443	0543	0643	0733	0743	0843	0933	0943	1043	1143	1233	1243	1343	1433	1443	1543	1617	1643	1743	1843	1943	2043	2143	2243	2343
Chernex § d.	...	0453	0552	0652	|	0752	0852	|	0952	1052	1152	|	1252	1352	|	1452	1552	1631	1652	1752	1852	1952	2053	2153	2253	2353
Chamby ⊗ § d.	...	0500	0600	0700	|	0800	0900	|	1000	1100	1202	|	1300	1402	|	1500	1600	1636	1700	1800	1900	2000	2100	2200	2300	0000
Les Avants § d.	...	0510	0610	0710	|	0810	0910	|	1010	1110	1211	|	1310	1411	|	1510	1610	1647	1710	1810	1910	2010	2110	2210	2310	0010
Montbovon d.	...	0537	0633**r**	0737	0822	0837	0937	1022	1037	1137	1237	1322	1337	1437	1522	1537	1637	1714	1737	1837	1937	2037	2137	2237	2337	0037
Château d'Oex d.	0500	0600	0700	0800	0840	0900	1000	1040	1100	1200	1300	1340	1400	1500	1540	1600	1700	1729	1800	1900	2002	2102	2202	2302	0005	0055
Rougemont d.	0512	0612	0712	0812	|	0912	1012	|	1112	1212	1312	|	1412	1512	|	1612	1712	...	1812	1912	2014	2114	2214	2314	0017	...
Saanen d.	0518	0618	0718	0818	|	0918	1018	|	1118	1218	1318	|	1418	1518	|	1618	1718	...	1818	1918	2020	2120	2220	2320	0023	...
Gstaad ‡ d.	0523	0625	0725	0825	0900	0925	1025	1100	1125	1225	1325	1400	1425	1525	1600	1625	1725	...	1825	1925	2025	2125	2225	2325	0027	...
Schönried ‡ d.	0530	0633	0733	0833	0907	0933	1033	1107	1133	1233	1333	1407	1433	1533	1607	1633	1733	...	1833	1933	2033	2133	2233	2333	...	...
Saanenmöser ‡ d.	0536	0638	0738	0838	0912	0938	1038	1112	1138	1238	1338	1412	1438	1538	1612	1638	1738	...	1838	1938	2038	2138	2238	2338	...	...
Zweisimmen ‡ a.	0550	0657	0757	0857	0929	0957	1057	1129	1157	1257	1357	1429	1457	1557	1629	1657	1757	...	1857	1955	2055	2155	2255	2355	...	...
Spiez **563** a.	...	...	...	...	1021	...	...	1221	...	...	...	1521	...	...	1721	...	...	...	...	...	...	...	...	...	...	...
Interlarken Ost **563** a.	...	...	...	...	1048	...	...	1248	...	...	...	1548	...	...	1748	...	...	...	...	...	...	...	...	...	...	...

ZWEISIMMEN - LENK *13 km* Journey time 18 minutes

From Zweisimmen: 0505 Ⓐ, 0541 Ⓐ, 0607 and hourly until 2207, 2307 ⑤⑥. **Additional trains**: 0635 Ⓐ, 0935 Ⓒ, 1035 Ⓒ, 1135 Ⓐ, 1235, 1535, 1735 Ⓐ, 1835 Ⓐ.

From Lenk: 0529 Ⓐ, 0607 Ⓐ, 0635, 0707 Ⓐ, 0735 and hourly until 2235, 2335 ⑤⑥. **Additional trains**: 1007 Ⓒ, 1107 Ⓒ, 1207 Ⓐ, 1307 Ⓐ, 1407 Ⓒ, 1607, 1807 Ⓐ, 1907 Ⓐ.

B – GOLDEN PASS BELLE ÉPOQUE – Conveys Belle Époque carriages. ◧
E – GOLDEN PASS EXPRESS – Conveys panorama cars. ◧ Also conveys Prestige class (Ⓡ and supplement payable).
P – GOLDEN PASS PANORAMIC – Conveys panorama cars. ◧

a – Ⓐ only.
c – Change trains at Château d'Oex.
d – Runs daily Montreux - Les Avants. Similar trains run at 1717Ⓐ and 1817Ⓐ.
r – 0637 on Ⓒ.

◧ – Reservation recommended. Reservations: www.gpx.swiss.
⊗ – Chamby is a request stop.
‡ – Additional local trains Zweisimmen - Gstaad:
From Zweisimmen: 0630 Ⓐ, 0730 Ⓐ, 0830 Ⓐ, 1130 Ⓒ, 1430 Ⓒ, 1630, 1830 Ⓐ.
From Gstaad: 0503 Ⓐ, 0603 Ⓐ, 0703 Ⓐ, 0803 Ⓐ, 1203 Ⓒ, 1503, 1703.
§ – Additional local trains Les Avants - Montreux:
From Les Avants: 0513, 0713, 0813 and hourly until 2013.
From Montreux: 0520 and hourly until 2020, also 0049 ⑥⑦.
Certain trains extend to/from Château d'Oex.

568 MONTBOVON - BULLE - PALÉZIEUX and ROMONT
TPF

MONTBOVON - BULLE - PALÉZIEUX *Narrow gauge*

km		Ⓐ	⑥	Ⓐ	Ⓐ	Ⓒ	Ⓐ	Ⓐ	⑥	Ⓒ	Ⓐ	Ⓐ	Ⓒ	Ⓐ	△	Ⓐ	Ⓒ	Ⓐ	Ⓐ	⑥			
0	**Montbovon** d.	...	...	...	...	...	0538	...	0638	...	0647	...	0738	0738		...	2138	2138	...	2238	2238	2338	...
13	Gruyères d.	...	...	...	...	...	0558	0632	0658	...	0707	0732	0758	0758	and at the	2132	2158	2158	2232	2258	2258	2358	...
17	**Bulle** a.	...	...	...	...	...	0606	0640	0706	...	0714	0740	0806	0806	same minutes	2140	2206	2206	2240	2306	2306	0006	...
17	**Bulle** d.	0502	0516	0532	0602	0616	0632	0702	0716	0716	0732	0802	0816	0832	past each	2202	2216	2232	2302	2316	...	...	...
37	Châtel-St Denis a.	0526	0539	0556	0626	0639	0656	0726	0739	0739	0756	0826	0839	0856	hour until	2226	2239	2256	2326	2339	...	...	...
37	Châtel-St Denis d.	0529	0542	0559	0629	0642	0659	0729	0742	0742	0759	0829	0842	0859		2229	2242	2259	2329	2342	...	...	...
41	**Palézieux** a.	0539	0552	0609	0639	0652	0709	0739	0752	0752	0809	0839	0852	0909		2239	2252	2309	2339	2352	...	...	...

	⚒	Ⓐ	Ⓐ	⑥	Ⓒ	Ⓐ	Ⓐ	Ⓒ	Ⓐ	Ⓐ	Ⓒ		Ⓐ	Ⓐ	Ⓒ	Ⓐ	Ⓐ	Ⓒ	Ⓐ	Ⓒ	⑥	Ⓐ	Ⓐ
Palézieux d.	...	...	0549	0609	...	0619	0649	0709	0719	0749	0809		2119	2149	2209	2219	2249	2209	2249	2309	2309	2319	2349
Châtel-St Denis a.	...	...	0558	0618	...	0628	0658	0718	0728	0758	0818	and at the	2128	2158	2218	2228	2258	2218	2258	2318	2318	2328	2358
Châtel-St Denis d.	...	...	0605	0619	...	0635	0705	0719	0735	0805	0819	same minutes	2135	2205	2219	2235	2305	2219	2305	2319	2319	2335	0005
Bulle a.	...	...	0629	0644	...	0659	0729	0744	0759	0829	0844	past each	2159	2229	2244	2259	2329	2244	2329	2344	2344	2359	0029
Bulle d.	0550	0607	0644	0650	0650	0720	0750	0750	0820	0850	0850	hour until	2220	2250	2250	2320	...	2250	...	...	2350	...	...
Gruyères d.	0558	0615	0652	0658	0658	0728	0758	0758	0828	0858	0858		2228	2258	2258	2328	...	2258	...	...	2358	...	...
Montbovon a.	0619	0635	0712	0719	0719	...	0819	0819	...	0919	0919		...	2319	2319	...	...	2319	...	...	0019	...	...

BROC - BULLE - ROMONT - FRIBOURG - BERN

km																						
0	**Broc** Chocolaterie d.	...	...	0603	0633		1803	1833	1903	1933	2003	2033	2103	2133	2203	2233	2303	2333	...	...	...	...	...
1	Broc Village d.	...	...	0605	0635	and at the	1805	1835	1905	1935	2005	2035	2105	2135	2205	2235	2305	2335	...	...	...	...	...
5	**Bulle** a.	...	...	0613	0643	same minutes	1813	1843	1912	1943	2012	2043	2112	2143	2212	2243	2312	2343	...	...	...	...	...
5	**Bulle** d.	0520	0550	0620	0650	past each	1820	1850	1920	1950	2020	2050	2120	2150	2220	2250	2320	2350	...	...	...	...	...
23	Romont **500** a.	0537	0607	0637	0707	hour until	1837	1907	1937	2007	2037	2107	2137	2207	2237	2307	2337	0007	...	...	...	...	...
49	Fribourg **500** a.	0555	0625	0655	0725		1855	1925	1954	2025	2054	2125	2154	2225	2254	2325	2354	0025	...	...	...	...	...
80	**Bern** **500** a.	...	0651	...	0751		...	1951	...	...	...	...	...	...	...	...	...	...	...	...	...	...	...

			Ⓐ																			
Bern **500** d.	...	...	...	...	...	...	0709		...	2009	...	...	...	...	...	...	...	...	...	...	...	...
Fribourg **500** d.	...	...	0534	0604	0634	0704	0734	and at the	2004	2034	2104	2134	2204	2234	2304	2334	0004	...	...	...	...	...
Romont **500** d.	...	...	0552	0622	0652	0722	0752	same minutes	2022	2052	2122	2152	2222	2252	2322	2352	0023	...	...	...	...	...
Bulle a.	...	...	0611	0641	0711	0741	0811	past each	2041	2111	2141	2211	2241	2311	2341	0011	0041	...	...	...	...	...
Bulle d.	0547	0617	0617	0647	0717	0747	0817	hour until	2047	2117	2147	2217	2247	2317	...	...	...	...	...	...	...	...
Broc Village d.	0553	0623	0623	0653	0723	0753	0823		2053	2123	2153	2223	2253	2323	...	...	...	...	...	...	...	...
Broc Chocolaterie a.	0557	0627	0627	0657	0727	0757	0827		2057	2127	2157	2227	2257	2327	...	...	...	...	...	...	...	...

r – Bulle - Montbovon journeys at 1250, 1650, 1850 run 6 minutes **earlier** on Ⓐ.

△ – Journeys at 1238, 1638, 1838 run 7 minutes later Montbovon - Bulle on Ⓐ.

569 MONTREUX - CAUX - ROCHERS DE NAYE
MVR (narrow gauge rack railway; 2nd class only)

km													
0	**Montreux** d.	0528	0628	0728	0828	0934		1534	1634	1734	1834		2334
3	Glion ▲ d.	0538	0638	0738	0838	0944	and	1544	1644	1744	1844	and	2344
5	Caux a.	0549	0649	0749	0849	0956	hourly	1556	1656	1756	1855	hourly	2355
6	Haut-de-Caux ⊗ a.	0553	0653	0753	0853	1002	until	1602	1702	1802	1859	until	2359
10	**Rochers de Naye** a.	...	...	...	0914**r**	1022**r**		1622**r**	1722**b**	1822**b**	...		...

Rochers de Naye d.	...	...	...	...	0927**r**		1627**r**	1727**b**	1827**b**	...		...
Haut-de-Caux ⊗ d.	0554	0654	0754	...	0949	and	1649	1749	1849	2001	and	0001
Caux d.	0558	0658	0758	0857	0957	hourly	1657	1757	1857	2005	hourly	0005
Glion ▲ d.	0609	0709	0809	0909	1009	until	1709	1809	1909	2016	until	0016
Montreux a.	0624	0724	0824	0924	1024		1724	1824	1924	2031		0031

b – May 17 - Oct. 26.
r – No service Haut-de-Caux - Rochers de Naye or v.v. on ①② Jan. 6 - Feb.11 or ①② Feb. 24 - Mar. 25. Also may be suspended in bad weather.
⊗ – Haut-de-Caux is a request stop.
▲ – Funicular railway operates **Glion** - **Territet** and v.v. Journey 6 minutes. Operator MVR. **No service Apr. 22, 23, Oct. 20 - 24**. Subject to alteration Apr. 24, Oct. 25. Simultaneous departures from both **Glion** and **Territet** every 15 minutes 0511 - 2111, every 30 minutes 2141 - 0111.
Note: Local stopping trains run hourly from Territet to Montreux, Vevey, Lausanne and Aigle.

SBB **GENÈVE - LAUSANNE - SION - BRIG** **570**

km		IR 1705	IR 1805	EC 41	IR 1707	RE 18457	IR 1807	IR 1709	RE 18459	IR 1809	EC 143	EC 43	IR 1711	RE 18461	IR 1811	IR 1713	RE 18463	IR 1813	IR 1715	RE 18465	IR 1815	IR 1717	RE 18467	IR 1817	IR 1719
				◧ A✕					⊖		①–⑤ r◧	⑥⑦ r◧													
0	**Genève** Aéroport ✈ 500 d.	...	...	...	0511	0530c	...	0614	0630c	0655	✕	✕	0711	0730c	0755	0814	0830c	0855	0914	0930c	0955	1014	1030c	1055	1114
6	**Genève** 500 d.	0408	0446	0527	0522	0538	0605	0624	0638t	0705	0727	0727	0723	0738t	0805	0824	0838t	0905	0924	0938t	1005	1024	1038t	1105	1124
27	Nyon 500 d.	0425	0508	|	0539	0555	|	0639	0655	|	|	|	0739	0755	|	0839	0855	|	0939	0955	|	1039	1055	|	1139
53	Morges 500 d.	0447	0524	|	0601h	0616	|	0655	0716	|	|	|	0801h	0816	|	0855	0916	|	0955	1016	|	1055	1116	|	1155
61	Renens 500 d.	0454	0532	|	|	0624	0638	|	0724	0738	|	|	|	0824	0838	|	0924	0938	|	1024	1038	|	1124	1138	|
66	**Lausanne** 500 a.	0459	0538	0606	0612	0629	0644	0707	0729	0744	0806	0806	0812	0829	0844	0907	0929	0944	1007	1029	1044	1107	1129	1144	1207
66	**Lausanne** ▷ d.	0504	0541	0610	0614	0631	0648	0714	0731	0748	0810	0810	0814	0831	0848	0914	0931	0948	1014	1031	1048	1114	1131	1148	1214
84	Vevey ▷ d.	0519	0556	|	0629	0646	0703	0729	0746	0803	|	|	0829	0846	0903	0929	0946	1003	1029	1046	1103	1129	1145	1203	1229
91	**Montreux** ▷ d.	0526	0603	0631	0636	0651	0710	0736	0751	0810	0831	0831	0836	0851	0910	0936	0951	1010	1036	1051	1110	1136	1151	1210	1236
95	Villeneuve ▷ d.	0532	|	|	|	0656	|	|	0756	|	|	|	|	0856	|	|	0956	|	|	1056	|	|	1156	|	|
105	Aigle ▷ d.	0542	0615	|	0647	0703	0722	0747	0803	0822	|	|	0847	0903	0922	0947	1003	1022	1047	1103	1122	1147	1203	1222	1247
114	Bex ▷ d.	0549	|	|	|	0709	|	|	0809	|	|	|	|	0909	|	|	1009	|	|	1109	|	|	1209	|	|
118	St Maurice ▷ d.	0554	0624	|	|	0713	0732	|	0813	0832	|	|	|	0913	0932	|	1013	1032	|	1113	1132	|	1213	1232	|
133	Martigny d.	0605	0635	|	0705	0723	0743	0805	0823	0843	|	|	0905	0923	0943	1005	1023	1043	1105	1123	1143	1205	1223	1243	1305
158	**Sion** d.	0620	0653	0709	0720	...	0757	0820	...	0857	0909	0909	0920	...	0957	1020	...	1057	1120	...	1157	1220	...	1257	1320
174	Sierre / Siders d.	0630	0704	|	0731	...	0808	0831	...	0908	|	|	0931	...	1008	1031	...	1108	1131	...	1208	1231	...	1308	1331
184	Leuk d.	0638	0712	|	0739	...	|	0839	...	|	|	|	0939	...	|	1039	...	|	1139	...	|	1239	...	|	1339
203	Visp 560 d.	0654j	0724	|	0754j	...	0824	0854j	...	0924	|	|	0954j	...	1024	1054j	...	1124	1154j	...	1224	1254j	...	1324	1354j
212	**Brig** 560 a.	0702	0732	0738	0802	...	0832	0902	...	0932	0938	0941	1002	...	1032	1102	...	1132	1202	...	1232	1302	...	1332	1402
	Milano Centrale **590** a.	...	...	0943r	...	...	...	...	...	...	d	1143	...	...	...	...	...	...	...	...	...	...	...	...	...

	RE 18469	IR 1819	IR 1721	RE 18471	IR 1821	EC 45	IR 1723	RE 18473	IR 1823	IR 1725	RE 18475	IR 1825	IR 1727	RE 18477	IR 1827	IR 1729	RE 18479	IR 1829	IR 1731	RE 18481	IR 1831	EC 47	IR 1733	RE 18483	IR 1833
						◧ r✕																◧ r✕			
Genève Aéroport ✈ 500 d.	1130c	1155	1214	1230c	1255	...	1311	1330c	1355	1414	1430c	1455	1514	1530c	1555	1614	1630c	1655	1714	1730c	1755	...	1811	1830c	1855
Genève 500 d.	1138t	1205	1224	1238t	1305	1327	1323	1338t	1405	1424	1438t	1505	1524	1538t	1605	1624	1638t	1705	1724	1738t	1805	1827	1823	1838t	1905
Nyon 500 d.	1155	|	1239	1255	|	|	1339	1355	|	1439	1455	|	1539	1555	|	1639	1655	|	1739	1755	|	|	1839	1855	|
Morges 500 d.	1216	|	1255	1316	|	|	1401h	1416	|	1455	1516	|	1555	1616	|	1655	1716	|	1755	1816	|	|	1901h	1916	|
Renens 500 d.	1224	1238	|	1324	1338	|	|	1424	1438	|	1524	1538	|	1624	1638	|	1724	1738	|	1824	1838	|	|	1924	1938
Lausanne 500 a.	1229	1244	1307	1329	1344	1406	1412	1429	1444	1507	1529	1544	1607	1629	1644	1707	1729	1744	1807	1829	1844	1906	1912	1929	1944
Lausanne ▷ d.	1231	1248	1314	1331	1348	1410	1414	1431	1448	1514	1531	1548	1614	1631	1648	1714	1731	1748	1814	1831	1848	1910	1914	1931	1948
Vevey ▷ d.	1246	1303	1329	1346	1403	|	1429	1446	1503	1529	1546	1603	1629	1646	1703	1729	1746	1803	1829	1846	1903	|	1929	1946	2003
Montreux ▷ d.	1251	1310	1336	1351	1410	1431	1436	1451	1510	1536	1551	1610	1636	1651	1710	1736	1751	1810	1836	1851	1910	1931	1936	1951	2010
Villeneuve ▷ d.	1256	|	|	1356	|	|	|	1456	|	|	1556	|	|	1656	|	|	1756	|	|	1856	|	|	|	1956	|
Aigle ▷ d.	1303	1322	1347	1403	1422	|	1447	1503	1522	1547	1603	1622	1647	1703	1722	1747	1803	1822	1847	1903	1922	|	1947	2003	2022
Bex ▷ d.	1309	|	|	1409	|	|	|	1509	|	|	1609	|	|	1709	|	|	1809	|	|	1909	|	|	|	2009	|
St Maurice ▷ d.	1313	1332	|	1413	1432	|	|	1513	1532	|	1613	1632	|	1713	1732	|	1813	1832	|	1913	1932	|	|	2013	2032
Martigny d.	1323	1343	1405	1423	1443	|	1505	1523	1543	1605	1623	1643	1705	1723	1743	1805	1823	1843	1905	1923	1943	|	2005	2023	2043
Sion d.	...	1357	1420	...	1457	1509	1520	...	1557	1620	...	1657	1720	...	1757	1820	...	1857	1920	...	1957	2009	2020	...	2057
Sierre / Siders d.	...	1408	1431	...	1508	|	1531	...	1608	1631	...	1708	1731	...	1808	1831	...	1908	1931	...	2008	|	2031	...	2108
Leuk d.	...	|	1439	...	|	|	1539	...	|	1639	...	|	1739	...	|	1839	...	|	1939	...	|	|	2039	...	|
Visp 560 d.	...	1424	1454j	...	1524	|	1554j	...	1624	1654j	...	1724	1754j	...	1824	1854j	...	1924	1954j	...	2024	|	2054j	...	2124
Brig 560 a.	...	1432	1502	...	1532	1538	1602	...	1632	1702	...	1732	1802	...	1832	1902	...	1932	2002	...	2032	2038	2102	...	2132
Milano Centrale **590** a.	...	...	...	...	...	1743	...	...	...	...	...	...	...	...	...	...	...	...	...	...	...	2243	...	...	...

	IR 1735	RE 18485	IR 1835	IR 1737	RE 18487	RE 18487	24485	IR 1837	IR 1837	IR 1739	IR 1739	RE 18489	RE 18489	24489	IR 1839	IR 1741	IR 1741	RE 18491	24493	IR 1841	IR 1841	IR 1743	IR 1743	RE 18493	24497
						⑤⑥ f		⑤⑥	⑦–④	⑤⑥	⑦–④		⑤⑥ f			⑤⑥	⑦–④			⑤⑥	⑦–④	⑤⑥	⑦–④		
Genève Aéroport ✈ 500 d.	1914	1930c	1955	2014	2030c	2030k	...	2055	...	2111	2111	...	...	...	2155z	2211	2211	2230	...	2255	...	2311	2311	2330	...
Genève 500 d.	1924	1938t	2005	2024	2038t	2038q	...	2105	...	2121	2121	2138	2138	...	2205z	2221	2220	2238	...	2305	...	2321	2321	2338	...
Nyon 500 d.	1939	1955	|	2039	2055	2055	...	|	...	2136	2136	2155	2155	...	|	2236	2236	2255	...	|	...	2336	2338	2355	...
Morges 500 d.	1955	2016	|	2055	2116	2116	...	|	...	2152	2152	2217	2217	...	|	2252	2254	2317	...	|	...	2352	2355	0017	...
Renens 500 d.	|	2024	2038	|	2124	2124	...	2138	...	2201	2201	2224	2224	...	2238z	2301	2303	2324	...	2338	...	0001	0004	0024	...
Lausanne 500 a.	2007	2029	2044	2107	2129	2129	...	2144	...	2207	2207	2229	2229	...	2244z	2307	2308	2329	...	2344	...	0007	0009	0029	...
Lausanne ▷ d.	2014	2031	2048	2114	...	2131	2134	2148	2148	2214	2214	...	2231	2234	2248	2314	2314	...	2334	2348	2348	0014	0014	...	0034
Vevey ▷ d.	2029	2046	2103	2129	...	2146	2154	2203	2203	2229	2229	...	2245	2254	2303	2329	2329	...	2355	0003	0003	0032	0032	...	0055
Montreux ▷ d.	2036	2051	2110	2136	...	2151	2203	2210	2212	2236	2241	...	2251	2303	2310	2336	2341	...	0004	0010	0010	0039	0039	...	0104
Villeneuve ▷ d.	|	2056	|	|	...	2156	2210	|	|	|	|	...	2255	2310	|	|	|	...	0011	|	|	|	|	...	0111
Aigle ▷ d.	2047	2103	2122	2147	...	2203	2216	2222	2230	2247	2301	...	2303	2316	2322	2348	0000	...	0017	0022	0022	0051	0051	...	0118
Bex ▷ d.	|	2109	|	|	...	2209	2223	|	|	|	|	...	2309	2323	|	2355	0007	...	0023	|	|	0058	0058	...	0124
St Maurice ▷ d.	|	2113	2132	|	...	2213	2227v	2232	2239	|	|	...	2313	2327v	2332	0001	0013	...	0027	0032	0032	0103	0103	...	0129
Martigny d.	2105	2123	2143	2205	...	2223	...	2243	2250	2305	2318	...	2323	...	2343	0012	0024	...	...	0043	0043	0114	0114	...	...
Sion d.	2120	...	2157	2220	...	...	...	2257	2305	2319	2333	...	...	...	2357	0027	0038	...	...	0057	0057	0128	0128	...	...
Sierre / Siders d.	2131	...	2208	2231	...	...	...	2308	2316	...	2343	...	...	...	0008	0038	0048	...	...	0107	0108	...	...	...	...
Leuk d.	2139	...	|	2239	...	...	...	|	|	...	2351	...	...	...	0016	0046	0056	...	...	0115	0115	...	...	...	...
Visp 560 d.	2154j	...	2224	2254j	...	...	...	2324	2339	...	0004	...	...	...	0028	0058	0108	...	...	0127	0127	...	...	...	...
Brig 560 a.	2202	...	2232	2302	...	...	...	2332	2347	...	0012	...	...	...	0036	0106	0117	...	...	0134	0135	...	...	...	...
Milano Centrale **590** a.	...	...	...	...	...	...	...	...	...	...	...	...	...	...	...	...	...	...	...	...	...	...	...	...	...

	IR 1702	IR 1702	IR 1804	24406	RE 18452	IR 1704	IR 1904	IR 1806	RE 18454	IR 1706	IR 1808	RE 18456	IR 1708	IR 1810	RE 18458	IR 1710	IR 1812	RE 18460	IR 1712	IR 1814	RE 18462	IR 1714	EC 40	IR 1816	RE 18464
	①–⑤	⑥⑦					Ⓐ															⊡	◧ r✕		
Milano Centrale **590** d.	...	...	...	...	...	...	...	...	...	...	...	...	...	...	...	...	...	...	...	...	...	...	0805	...	...
Brig 560 d.	...	...	0420	...	...	0438	...	0522	...	0557	0622	...	0657	0726	...	0757	0826	...	0857	0926	...	0957	1020	1026	...
Visp 560 d.	...	...	0428	...	...	0445	...	0531	...	0609j	0631	...	0709j	0736	...	0809j	0836	...	0909j	0936	...	1009j	|	1036	...
Leuk d.	...	...	0439	...	...	0459	...	0542	...	0620	0642	...	0720	|	...	0820	|	...	0920	|	...	1020	|	|	...
Sierre / Siders d.	...	...	0447	...	...	0507	...	0551	...	0628	0651	...	0728	0751	...	0828	0851	...	0928	0951	...	1028	|	1051	...
Sion d.	0430	0433	0458	...	...	0533	0544	0602	...	0639	0702	...	0739	0802	...	0839	0902	...	0939	1002	...	1039	1051	1102	...
Martigny d.	0444	0447	0513	...	...	0547	0559	0617	0635	0654	0717	0735	0754	0817	0833	0854	0917	0935	0954	1017	1035	1054	|	1117	1135
St Maurice ▷ d.	0455	0458	0524	0532	...	0558	0616p	0628	0646	|	0728	0746	|	0828	0846j	|	0928	0946	|	1028	1046	|	|	1128	1146
Bex ▷ d.	0500	0504	0530	0536	...	0604	0624	|	0650	|	|	0750	|	|	0850	|	|	0950	|	|	1050	|	|	|	1150
Aigle ▷ d.	0508	0512	0538	0543	...	0612	0632	0638	0657	0712	0738	0757	0812	0838	0857	0912	0938	0957	1012	1038	1057	1112	|	1138	1157
Villeneuve ▷ d.	|	|	|	0549	...	|	|	|	0703	|	|	0803	|	|	0903	|	|	1003	|	|	1103	|	|	|	1203
Montreux ▷ d.	0520	0523	0549	0556	...	0623	0643	0649	0708	0723	0749	0808	0823	0849	0908	0923	0949	1008	1023	1049	1108	|	1129	1149	1208
Vevey ▷ d.	0528	0530	0556	0605	...	0630	0650	0656	0713	0730	0756	0813	0830	0856	0913	0930	0956	1013	1030	1056	1113	1127	|	1156	1213
Lausanne ▷ a.	0543	0546	0612	0625	...	0646	0708	0712	0728	0746	0812	0828	0846	0912	0928	0946	1012	1028	1046	1112	1128	1142	1150	1212	1228
Lausanne 500 d.	0552	0552	0616	...	0630	0652	0713	0716	0730	0752	0816	0830	0852	0916	0930	0952	1016	1030	1052	1116	1130	1145	1152	1216	1230
Renens 500 d.	|	|	0623	...	0635	|	|	0723	0735	|	0823	0835	|	0923	0935	|	1023	1035	|	1123	1135	|	|	1223	1235
Morges 500 d.	0604	0604	|	...	0643	0704	0730	|	0743	0804	|	0843	0904	|	0943	1004	|	1043	1104	|	1143	1204p	|	|	1243
Nyon 500 d.	0620	0620	|	...	0705	0720	|	|	0805	0820	|	0905	0920	|	1005	1020	|	1105	1120	|	1205	1221	|	|	1305
Genève 500 a.	0635	0635	0655	...	0721	0735	0759	0755	0821	0835	0855	0921	0935	0955	1021	1035	1055	1121	1135	1155	1221	1236	1231	1255	1321
Genève Aéroport ✈ 500 a.	0644	0644	0705	...	0730c	0744	...	0805	0830c	0844	0905	0930c	0944	1005	1030c	1044	1105	1130c	1144	1205	1230c	1244	...	1305	1330c

A – (12) and ✕ Genève - Milano - Venezia and v.v.
c – © only.
d – To Domodossola (a. 1011).
e – 10–12 minutes later on ⑦–④.
f – Not Aug. 1.
h – Arrives 6 minutes earlier.
j – Arrives 4 minutes earlier.
k – ⑥ only.
m – From Domodossola (d. 1448).
p – Arrives 8 minutes earlier.
q – 2039 on ⑥.
r – Not June 8 - July 27, Aug. 31 - Sept. 12.
t – 1 minute later on ©.
v – ⑦–④ only.
z – ⑤⑥ only.

⊖ – On © until Apr. 6 conveys through cars Genève Aéroport - Martigny - Le Châble and v.v. (Table **574**).
⊡ – June 8 - July 27 and Aug. 31 - Sept. 12 departs Lausanne xx52, arrives Morges xx03.
▷ – Additional trains run Lausanne - Aigle - St Maurice and v.v.
◧ – Ⓡ. Supplement payable for journeys from / to Italy.

TABLE CONTINUES ON NEXT PAGE →

570 BRIG - SION - LAUSANNE - GENÈVE — SBB

	IR 1716	*IR* 1818	*RE* 18466	*IR* 1718	*IR* 1820	*RE* 18468	*IR* 1720	*IR* 1822	*RE* 18470	*IR* 1722	*IR* 1824	*RE* 18472	*IR* 1724	*EC* 142	*EC* 42	*IR* 1826	*RE* 18474	*IR* 1726	*IR* 1828	*RE* 18476	*IR* 1728	*IR* 1830	*RE* 18478	*IR* 1730	*IR* 1832
													⊡	①–⑤ r◧ m✕	⑥⑦r ◧✕					⊖					
Milano Centrale **590** d.	...	...	...	...	...	...	...	...	...	...	...	...	...		1305	...	...	...	...	...	...	...	...	...	...
Brig 560 d.	1057	1126	...	1157	1226	...	1257	1326	...	1357	1426	...	1457	1520	1520	1526	...	1557	1626	...	1657	1726	...	1757	1826
Visp 560 d.	1109j	1136	...	1209j	1236	...	1309j	1336	...	1409j	1436	...	1509j	|	|	1536	...	1609j	1636	...	1709j	1736	...	1809j	1836
Leuk d.	1120	|	...	1220	|	...	1320	|	...	1420	|	...	1520	|	|	|	...	1620	|	...	1720	|	...	1820	|
Sierre / Siders d.	1128	1151	...	1228	1251	...	1328	1351	...	1428	1451	...	1528	|	|	1551	...	1628	1651	...	1728	1751	...	1828	1851
Sion d.	1139	1202	...	1239	1302	...	1339	1402	...	1439	1502	...	1539	1551	1551	1602	...	1639	1702	...	1739	1802	...	1839	1902
Martigny d.	1154	1217	1235	1254	1317	1335	1354	1417	1433	1454	1517	1535	1554	|	|	1617	1635	1654	1717	1735	1754	1817	1835	1854	1917
St Maurice ▷ d.	|	1228	1246	|	1328	1346	|	1428	1446j	|	1528	1546	|	|	|	1628	1646	|	1728	1746	|	1828	1846	|	1928
Bex ▷ d.	|	|	1250	|	|	1350	|	|	1450	|	|	1550	|	|	|	|	1650	|	|	1750	|	|	1850	|	|
Aigle ▷ d.	1212	1238	1257	1312	1338	1357	1412	1438	1457	1512	1538	1557	1612	|	|	1638	1657	1712	1738	1757	1812	1838	1857	1912	1938
Villeneuve ▷ d.	|	|	1303	|	|	1403	|	|	1503	|	|	1603	|	|	|	|	1703	|	|	1803	|	|	1903	|	|
Montreux ▷ d.	1223	1249	1308	1323	1349	1408	1423	1449	1508	1523	1549	1608	|	1629	1629	1649	1708	1723	1749	1808	1823	1849	1908	1923	1949
Vevey ▷ d.	1230	1256	1313	1330	1356	1413	1430	1456	1513	1530	1556	1613	1627	|	|	1656	1713	1730	1756	1813	1830	1856	1913	1930	1956
Lausanne ▷ a.	1246	1312	1328	1346	1412	1428	1446	1512	1528	1546	1612	1628	1642	1650	1650	1712	1728	1746	1812	1828	1846	1912	1928	1946	2012
Lausanne 500 d.	1252	1316	1330	1352	1416	1430	1452	1516	1530	1552	1616	1630	1645	1652	1652	1716	1730	1752	1816	1830	1852	1916	1930	1952	2016
Renens 500 d.	|	1323	1335	|	1423	1435	|	1523	1535	|	1623	1635	|	|	|	1723	1735	|	1823	1835	|	1923	1935	|	2023
Morges 500 d.	1304	|	1343	1404	|	1443	1504	|	1543	1604	|	1643	1704p	|	|	|	1743	1804	|	1843	1904	|	1943	2004	|
Nyon 500 d.	1320	|	1405	1420	|	1505	1520	|	1605	1620	|	1705	1721	|	|	|	1805	1820	|	1905	1920	|	2005	2020	|
Genève 500 a.	1335	1355	1421	1435	1455	1521	1535	1555	1621	1635	1655	1721	1736	1731	1731	1755	1821	1835	1855	1921	1935	1955	2021	2035	2055
Genève Aéroport ✈ 500 a.	1344	1405	1430c	1444	1505	1530c	1544	1605	1630c	1644	1705	1730c	1744	...	...	1805	1830c	1844	1905	1930c	1944	2005	...	2047	2105

	RE 18480	*IR* 1732	*EC* 44	*EC* 144	*IR* 1834	*RE* 18482	*IR* 1734	*IR* 1836	*IR* 1836	24480	*RE* 18484	*RE* 18484	*IR* 1736	*IR* 1736	*EC* 146	*IR* 1838	*EC* 46	*RE* 18486	*RE* 18486	24484	*IR* 1738	*IR* 1738	*IR* 1840	*IR* 1840	*RE* 18488
		⊡	①–⑤ r◧✕	⑥⑦r ◧✕					⑤⑥		⑤⑥ f		⑤⑥	⑦–④	⑤⑥ ◧A	⑤⑥	⑦–④ ◧A		⑤⑥ f	⑦–④	⑤⑥	⑦–④	⑤⑥	⑦–④	
Milano Centrale **590** d.	...	...	1705	1705	...	...	...	...	...	...	...	...	...	...	1905r	...	1905r	...	...	...	...	...	...	...	...
Brig 560 d.	...	1857	1920	1920	1926	...	1957	2026	2026	...	...	...	2057	2057	2120	2126	2126	...	...	...	2157	2157	2226	2226	...
Visp 560 d.	...	1909j	|	|	1936	...	2009j	2036	2036	...	...	...	2109j	2109j	|	2136	2136	...	...	...	2209j	2209j	2236	2236	...
Leuk d.	...	1920	|	|	|	...	2020	|	|	...	...	...	2120	2120	|	|	|	...	...	...	2220	2225	|	|	...
Sierre / Siders d.	...	1928	|	|	1951	...	2028	2051	2051	...	...	...	2128	2128	|	2151	2151	...	...	...	2228	2233	2251	2256	...
Sion d.	...	1939	1951	1951	2002	...	2039	2102	2102	...	...	...	2139	2139	2151	2202	2202	...	...	...	2239	2245	2302	2307	...
Martigny d.	1933	1954	|	|	2017	2035	2054	2117	2117	...	2135	...	2154	2154	|	2217	2217	...	2235	...	2254	2259	2317	2321	...
St Maurice ▷ d.	1946j	|	|	|	2028	2046	|	2128	2128	2132v	2146	...	|	2205	|	2228	2227	...	2246	2232	|	|	2328	2332	...
Bex ▷ d.	1950	|	|	|	|	2050	|	|	|	2136	2150	...	|	|	|	|	|	...	2250	2238	|	|	|	|	...
Aigle ▷ d.	1957	2012	|	|	2038	2057	2112	2138	2138	2142	2157	...	2212	2215	|	2238	2241	...	2257	2246	2312	2320	2338	2342	...
Villeneuve ▷ d.	2003	|	|	|	|	2103	|	|	|	2148	2203	...	|	|	|	|	|	...	2303	2252	|	|	|	|	...
Montreux ▷ d.	2008	|	2029	2029	2049	2108	2123	2149	2149	2155	2208	...	|	2227	2229	2249	2253	...	2308	2259	2323	2331	2349	2353	...
Vevey ▷ d.	2013	2028	|	|	2056	2113	2130	2156	2156	2204	2213	...	2227	2233	|	2256	2300	...	2313	2308	2330	2338	2356	0000	...
Lausanne ▷ a.	2028	2043	2050	2050	2112	2128	2146	2212	2212	2225	2228	...	2242	2248	2250	2312	2316	...	2328	2329	2346	2353	0012	0015	...
Lausanne 500 d.	2030	2045	2052	2052	2116z	2130	2151	...	2216	...	2230	2230	2245	2252	2252	2316	2318	2330	2330	*2334*	2351	2355	0016	...	0030
Renens 500 d.	2035	|	|	|	2123z	2135	2157	...	2223	...	2235	2235	|	2258	|	2323	2325	2335	2335	*2339*	2357	|	0023	...	0035
Morges 500 d.	2043	2104p	|	|	|	2143e	2204	...	|	...	2242	2242	2305p	2305	|	2330	2332	2343	2343	*2348*	0004	0005	|	...	0042
Nyon 500 d.	2105	2121	|	|	|	2204e	2222	...	|	...	2305	2305	2323	2323	|	2346	2350	0005	0005	...	0020	0022	|	...	0105
Genève 500 a.	2121	2136	2131	2131	2155z	2221e	2238	...	2255	...	2321	2321	2339	2338	2331	2400	0005	0022	0022	...	0035	0038	0054	...	0122
Genève Aéroport ✈ 500 a.	2130	2146	...	...	2205z	2229e	2248	...	2305	...	2330	2330	2348	2348	...	0011	...	0030	0030	...	...	...	...	...	...

← FOR FOOTNOTES SEE PREVIOUS PAGE

571 Local services from VEVEY, AIGLE and BEX — 2nd class only

VEVEY - BLONAY - LES PLÉIADES: Narrow gauge (rack Blonay - Les Pléiades). **Operator**: MVR. Additional services run Vevey - Blonay and v.v. on Ⓐ

km						Ⓐz																	
0	Vevey d.	0532	0605	0635	0705	0720	0735	0805	0835	and at the same	1905	1935	2005	2035	2105	2135	2205	2235	2305	...	...	...	...
6	Blonay a.	0548	0621	0651	0721	0739	0751	0823	0851	minutes past	1923	1951	2021	2051	2121	2151	2221	2251	2321	...	...	...	...
10	Les Pléiades a.	...	...	...	...	0755	...	0839	...	each hour until	1939	...	...	...	...	...	...	...	...	...	...	...	...

								Ⓐz														
Les Pléiades d.	...	...	...	...	...	...	...	0758	...	0844	...	and at the same	1944	...	...	...	...	...	...	...	...	...
Blonay d.	0510	0537	0610	0640	0710	0740	0810	0825	0840	0910	0940	minutes past	2010	2040	2110	2140	2210	2240	2310	...	...	...
Vevey a.	0525	0552	0625	0655	0725	0755	0825	0840	0855	0925	0955	each hour until	2025	2055	2125	2155	2225	2255	2325	...	...	...

AIGLE - LEYSIN: Narrow gauge rack railway. *6 km*. The Leysin terminus station is Grand Hotel, but all trains also call at Leysin Village and Feydey stations. **Operator**: TPC.

From Aigle (journey time 29 minutes): 0532 Ⓐ, 0552 Ⓒ, 0612 Ⓐ, 0652, 0732 Ⓐ, 0752 Ⓒ, 0812 Ⓐ, 0832 Ⓒ, 0852 Ⓐ, 0912 Ⓒ, 0952, 1052 and hourly until 1552; then 1632, 1712, 1752, 1832 Ⓐ, 1852 Ⓒ, 1912 Ⓐ, 1952, 2052, 2152 and 2252 (also 2352 to Feydey).

From Leysin Grand Hotel (journey time 39 minutes): 0529 Ⓐ, 0549 Ⓒ, 0609 Ⓐ, 0649, 0729 Ⓐ, 0749 Ⓒ, 0809 Ⓐ, 0829 Ⓒ, 0849 Ⓐ, 0909 Ⓒ, 0949, 1049 and hourly until 1549; then 1629, 1709, 1749, 1829 Ⓐ, 1849 Ⓒ, 1909 Ⓐ, 1949, 2049, 2149, 2249 and 2333.

AIGLE - LES DIABLERETS: Narrow gauge. *23 km*. Journey time: 50 minutes Aigle - Les Diablerets / 54 minutes Les Diablerets - Aigle. **Operator**: TPC.

From Aigle at 0510, 0625, 0725, 0829, 0929 and hourly until 2129; then 2234.

From Les Diablerets at 0607, 0707, 0734, 0834 and hourly until 2134; then 2239.

AIGLE - CHAMPÉRY: Narrow gauge rack railway. 2nd class only. **Operator**: TPC. Additional trains operate Aigle - Monthey and v.v. on ⚒.

km		Ⓐ		Ⓐ		Ⓐ							⚒					⚒						⑤⑥v		⑤⑥v
0	**Aigle** d.	0508	...	0608	0638	0708	0738	0808	0838	0938	and	1438	1508	1538	1638	1708	1738	1808	1838	1938	2038	2138	2238	2238	2338	2338
11	Monthey Ville a.	0529	...	0629	0659	0729	0759	0829	0859	0959	hourly	1459	1529	1559	1659	1729	1759	1829	1859	1959	2059	2159	2259	2259	2359	2359
11	Monthey Ville d.	0534	0604	0634	0704	0734	0804	0834c	0904	1004	until	1504	1534	1604	1704	1734e	1804	1834e	1904	2004	2104	2204	...	2304	...	0004
23	**Champéry** a.	0610	0640	0710	0740	0810	0840	0910c	0940	1040		1540	1610	1640	1740	1810e	1840	1910e	1940	2040	2140	2240	...	2340	...	0040

	Ⓐ		Ⓐ		Ⓐ				⚒		⑥							Ⓐ		Ⓐ					⑤⑥v
Champéry d.	...	...	0520	0550	0620	0650	0720e	0750	0820e	0850	0920	0950	and	1550	1620	1650	1750	1820	1850	1920	1950	2050	2150	2250	2350
Monthey Ville a.	...	...	0555	0625	0655	0725	0755e	0825	0855e	0925	0955	1025	hourly	1625	1655	1725	1825	1855	1925	1955	2025	2125	2225	2325	0025
Monthey Ville d.	0445	0545	0559	0629	0659	0729	0759	0829	0859	0929	0959	1029	until	1629	1659	1729	1829	1859	1929	1959	2029	2129	2229	2329	0029
Aigle a.	0507	0607	0621	0651	0721	0751	0821	0851	0921	0951	1021	1051		1651	1721	1751	1851	1921	1951	2021	2051	2151	2251	2351	0051

BEX - VILLARS-SUR-OLLON - COL-DE-BRETAYE: Narrow gauge rack railway. 2nd class only. **Operator**: TPC. Additional trains operate Villars - Col-de-Bretaye and v.v. (see note ⊡).

km					W		r§				r§											D				D
0	**Bex** d.	0617	0717	0817	0837	0917	...	1017	1117	1217	...	1317	...	1417	...	1517	...	1617	...	1717	1817	...	1917	2017	2117	...
3	Bévieux ⊗ d.	0627	0727	0827	|	0927	...	1027	1127	1227	...	1327	...	1427	...	1527	...	1627	...	1727	1827	...	1927	2027	2127	...
12	Villars-sur-Ollon a.	0655	0755	0855	0912	0955	...	1055	1155	1255	...	1355	...	1455	...	1555	...	1655	...	1755	1855	...	1955	2055	2155	...
12	Villars-sur-Ollon d.	...	*0805*r	*0900*	0930	*1000*	1030	*1100*	*1200*	*1300*	1330	*1400*r	1430	*1500*r	1530	*1600*r	1630	*1710*r	1735	*1802*r	...	1903	...	...	...	2205
17	**Col-de-Bretaye** a.	...	*0823*r	*0918*	0948	*1018*	1048	*1118*	*1218*	*1318*	1348	*1418*r	1448	*1518*r	1548	*1618*r	1648	*1728*r	1754	*1820*r	...	1921	...	...	...	2223

																r‡				r			D		
Col-de-Bretaye d.	...	...	...	...	*0830*r	0925	*0955*r	1025	*1055*r	1125	*1155*r	1225	*1255*r	1325	*1355*r	1425	*1455*	*1555*	*1655*	1730	*1755*	*1825*r	1925	...	...
Villars-sur-Ollon a.	...	...	...	...	*0851*r	0947	*1017*r	1047	*1117*r	1147	*1217*r	1247	*1317*r	1347	*1417*r	1447	*1517*	*1617*	*1716*	1753	*1817*	*1847*r	1947	...	...
Villars-sur-Ollon d.	0512	0625	0725	0825	0925	...	1025	...	1125	...	1225	...	1325	...	1425	...	1525	1625	1725	...	1825	1925	...	2025	2125
Bévieux ⊗ d.	0547	0700	0800	0900	1000	...	1100	...	1200	...	1300	...	1400	...	1500	...	1600	1700	1800	...	1900	2000	...	2100	2200
Bex a.	0558	0711	0811	0911	1011	...	1111	...	1211	...	1311	...	1411	...	1511	...	1611	1711	1811	...	1911	2011	...	2111	2211

D – ⑤⑥ Dec. 20 - Apr. 19; ⑤⑥ June 28 - Sept. 27.
W – ⑥⑦ Dec. 15 - Apr. 6.

c – Ⓒ only.
e – Ⓐ only.

r – Daily Dec. 15 - Apr. 21 and June 28 - Aug. 31; ⑥⑦ Sept. 6 – 28.
v – Not Aug. 1.
z – Not Sept. 22.

⊗ – Trains call at Bévieux on request.

⊡ – Additional trains operate Villars - Col-de-Bretaye and v.v. Dec. 21 - Mar. 23.
§ – Also at 1130 **r** and 1230 **r**.
‡ – Also at 1525 **r** and 1625 **r**.

TMR (2nd class only); narrow gauge rack railway — MARTIGNY - VALLORCINE — 572

For services Vallorcine - Chamonix - St Gervais and v.v. see Table **365a**.

km		W			Ⓐ											Ⓐ			Ⓐ						® §
0	**Martigny** d.	0014	...	0547	0631	0656	0814	0914	1014	1114	1214	1314	1414	1514	1614	1656	1714	1814	1856	1914	2014	2114	2214	...	2314
7	Salvan d.	0030	...	0604	0648	0712	0830	0930	1030	1130	1230	1330	1430	1530	1630	1713	1730	1830	1913	1930	2030	2130	2230	...	2330
9	Les Marécottes d.	0034	...	0608	0652	0716	0834	0934	1034	1134	1234	1334	1434	1534	1634	1717	1734	1834	1917	1934	2034	2134	2234	...	2334
14	Finhaut d.	0047	...	0622	0709	0729	0847	0947	1047	1147	1247	1347	1447	1547	1647	1731	1747	1847	1931	1947	2047	2147	2247	...	2347
18	Le Châtelard Frontière 🏛 d.	0058	...	0632	...	0740	0858	0958	1058	1158	1258	1358	1458	1558	1658	1741	1758	1858	1941	1958	2058	2158	2258	...	2358
21	**Vallorcine** a.	...	...	...	...	0748	0905	1005	1105	1205	1305	1405	1505	1605	1705	...	1805	1905	...	2005	...	...	...	...	...

	Ⓐ			Ⓐ											Ⓐ			Ⓐ						
Vallorcine d.	...	...	...	...	0813	0913	1013	1113	1213	1313	1413	1513	1613	1713	...	1813	1913	...	2013	2113	...	...	...	...
Le Châtelard Frontière 🏛 d.	...	0554	0642	...	0819	0919	1019	1119	1219	1319	1419	1519	1619	1719	1800	1819	1919	2000	2019	2119	2219	2319	...	...
Finhaut d.	0521	0605	0652	0713	0830	0930	1030	1130	1230	1330	1430	1530	1630	1730	1810	1830	1930	2010	2030	2130	2230	2330	...	...
Les Marécottes d.	0535	0620	0707	0727	0844	0944	1044	1144	1244	1344	1444	1544	1644	1744	1825	1844	1944	2025	2044	2144	2244	2344	...	...
Salvan d.	0539	0624	0711	0731	0849	0949	1049	1149	1249	1349	1449	1549	1649	1749	1829	1849	1949	2029	2049	2149	2249	2349	...	...
Martigny a.	0600	0644	0734	0750	0909	1009	1109	1209	1309	1409	1509	1609	1709	1809	1852	1909	2009	2052	2109	2209	2309	0009	...	...

W – ⑥⑦ only. ® (to reserve telephone +41 27 764 1271 before 2400).

§ – To reserve telephone +41 27 764 1271 before 2300.

SION VALLEY RESORTS — 573

LE CHÂBLE - VERBIER. Cable car. Journey time: 13 minutes. www.televerbier.ch No service Apr. 28 - May 25, Oct. 21–25, 28–31, Nov. 1.
From Le Châble and Verbier: continuous service 0510-2355. A 🚌 service also operates between Le Châble Gare and Verbier Post (approx 8 journeys per day).

🚌 **MARTIGNY - AOSTA** via Grand St Bernard tunnel. Journey time: ± 1 hour 50 minutes. **Operator**: TMR / Arriva Italia. Subject to alteration
From Martigny Gare at 0830 Ⓐ.
From Aosta Autostazione at 1615 Ⓐ.

🚌 **SION - CRANS-MONTANA** Journey time: ± 45 minutes. On Mar. 19, June 19, Aug. 15, Nov. 1, Dec. 8 services run as on ⑦. On Apr. 18 services run as on Ⓐ. **Operator**: CarPostal SA.
From Sion Gare: 0555 Ⓐ, 0705, 0805, 0905 Ⓐ, 0910 ⑥, 1005 Ⓐ, 1010 Ⓒ, 1105 ⚒, 1205, 1305 Ⓐ, 1405, 1505, 1605, 1705, 1805 ⚒, 1810 †, 1905 Ⓐ, 1918 Ⓒ, 2010 and 2105.
From Crans-Montana Le Mèrignou: 0605 Ⓐ, 0645, 0755, 0905, 1005 ⚒, 1105, 1205 ⚒, 1300, 1405 Ⓐ, 1505, 1611, 1705, 1803 Ⓒ, 1805 Ⓐ, 1905, 2005 and 2105.

SIERRE - MONTANA. Funicular railway. *4 km*. Journey time: 13–14 minutes. **Closed for maintenance Apr. 28 - May 2 and Oct. 3–7.** 🚌 services also available. **Operator**: SMC.
From Sierre funi: 0604, 0624, 0644 and every 20 minutes (⊗) until 2104, 2124, 2144; then 2204 and 2224.
From Montana Gare: 0604, 0624, 0644 and every 20 minutes (⊗) until 2104, 2124, 2144; then 2204 and 2224.

🚌 **BRIG - SAAS-FEE**. Journey time: 68–91 minutes. Services call at **Visp** (Bahnhof Süd) ± 20 minutes from Brig, and **Saas Grund** (Post) ± 7 minutes from Saas Fee. **Operator**: PA.
From Brig Bahnhof: 0420, 0515, 0545 and every 30 minutes (△) until 1815, 1845; then 1945, 2045 and 2215. Also at 2315 (change at Visp).
From Saas-Fee Busterminal: 0530, 0600, 0630, 0700, 0730, 0750, 0820, 0850 and every 30 minutes until 1820, 1850; then 1930, 1956, 2130, 2330. Also at 2246 (change at Visp).

△ – Brig d. 1140 (not 1145).

⊗ – Not at 0804, 1104, 1604, 2004.

RA — MARTIGNY - LE CHÂBLE and ORSIÈRES — 574

km										G							n				H	H	③e	③e				
0	**Martigny** d.	0607	...	0717	...	0751	...	0817	...	0827	0851t	...	0917	...	0951	...	1017	...	1051	...	1151	...	1200	...	1251	...	1351	...
13	Sembrancher a.	0624	0625	0733	0734	0807	0809	0832	0834	|	0907	0909	0932	0934	1007	1009	1032	1034	1107	1109	1207	1209	1216	1218	1307	1309	1407	1409
19	**Orsières** a.	|	0634	|	0742	|	0818	|	0842	|	|	0918	|	0942	|	1018	|	1042	|	1118	|	1218	|	1227	|	1318	|	1418
19	**Le Châble** a.	0634	...	0742	...	0817	...	0841	...	0851	0917	...	0941	...	1017	...	1041	...	1117	...	1217	...	1226	...	1317	...	1417	...

					n				n				n				n				n							
Martigny d.	1449	...	1551	...	1617	...	1651	...	1717	...	1751	...	1817	...	1851	...	1917	...	1951	...	2017	...	2051	...	2156	...	2324	...
Sembrancher a.	1507	1509	1607	1609	1632	1634	1707	1709	1732	1734	1807	1809	1832	1834	1907	1909	1932	1934	2007	2009	2032	2034	2107	2109	2211	2212	2339	2341
Orsières a.	|	1518	|	1618	|	1642	|	1718	|	1742	|	1818	|	1842	|	1918	|	1942	|	2018	|	2042	|	2118	|	2221	|	2350
Le Châble a.	1517	...	1617	...	1641	...	1717	...	1741	...	1817	...	1841	...	1917	...	1941	...	2017	...	2041	...	2117	...	2222	...	2350	...

																		n				H	③e	Ⓒ	Ⓒ	Ⓐ	Ⓐ	
Le Châble d.	...	0535	...	0639	...	0711	...	0748	...	0823	...	0848j	...	0923	...	0948	...	1023	...	1048	...	1148	1213	...	1248	...	1300	...
Orsières d.	0534	|	0638	|	0710	|	0746	|	0822	|	0846	|	0922	|	0946	|	1022	|	1046	|	1146	|	|	1246	|	1256	|	1346
Sembrancher d.	0543	0544	0647	0648	0719	0722	0755	0757	0830	0832	0855	0857	0930	0932	0955	0957	1030	1032	1055	1057	1155	1157	1222	1255	1257	1305	1309	1355
Martigny a.	...	0600	...	0706	...	0738	...	0813	...	0847	...	0913	...	0947	...	1013	...	1047	...	1113	...	1213	1238	...	1313	...	1325	...

							n			G		n				n				n				n				
Le Châble d.	1348	...	1448	...	1548	...	1623	...	1648	1658	...	1723	...	1748	...	1823	...	1848	...	1923	...	1948	...	2023	...	2048	...	2244
Orsières d.	|	1446	|	1546	|	1622	|	1646	|	|	1722	|	1746	|	1822	|	1846	|	1922	|	1946	|	2022	|	2046	|	2241	|
Sembrancher d.	1357	1455	1457	1555	1557	1630	1632	1655	1657	|	1730	1732	1755	1757	1830	1832	1855	1857	1930	1932	1955	1957	2030	2032	2055	2057	2251	2253
Martigny a.	1413	...	1513	...	1613	...	1647	...	1713	1727	...	1747	...	1813	...	1847	...	1913	...	1947	...	2013	...	2047	...	2113	...	2309

G – Ⓒ Dec. 15 - Apr. 6. From / to Genève (Table **570**).
H – ①②④⑤⑥⑦ to June 10; daily June 12 - Aug. 26; ①②④⑤⑥⑦ from Aug. 28 (also Oct. 22).
e – Not June 18 - Aug. 20, Oct. 22.
j – Ⓐ to Apr. 25; daily from Apr. 28.
n – Not Sept. 26 - Oct. 5.
t – 0848 on Ⓒ Dec. 15 - Apr. 6.

MGB, RhB* — GLACIER EXPRESS — 575

Glacier Express through services. ®. Supplement payable. For local services see Tables **545** and **576**. Narrow gauge railway (part rack).

km		WINTER SERVICE →	920 ® a ✕	902 ® ✕	SUMMER SERVICE →	900 ® ✕	902 ® ✕	904 ® ✕	906 ® ✕
0	**Zermatt** d.		0752	0852		0752	0852	0952	...
45	**Brig** Bahnhofplatz a.		0906	1006		0906	1006	1106	...
45	**Brig** Bahnhofplatz d.		0914	1014		0914	1014	1114	1414
113	**Andermatt** a.	**Dec. 15**	1046	1146	**May 3**	1046	1146	1246	1546
113	**Andermatt** d.	**to**	1054	1154	**to**	1054	1154	1254	1554
142	**Disentis / Mustér** a.	**May 2**	1156	1256	**Oct. 11**	1156	1256	1356	1656
142	**Disentis / Mustér** d.		1211	1311		1219	1311	1411	1711
201	**Chur** a.	⊡	1325	1425		1325	1425	1525	1825
201	**Chur** d.		1334	1434		...	1434	1534	1858
242	Tiefencastel ▽ a.		1429	|		...	|	1629	1944
252	**Filisur** ▽ a.		|	1542		...	1542	|	2000
285	**Samedan** ▽ a.		1530	1630		...	1630	1730	2045
290	**St Moritz** a.		1537	1637		...	1637	1737	2053

	WINTER SERVICE →	923 ® ✕	925 ® a ✕	SUMMER SERVICE →	901 ® ✕	903 ® ✕	905 ® ✕	907 ® ✕
St Moritz d.		0839	0939		0707	0839	0939	...
Samedan △ d.		0846	0946		0716	0846	0946	...
Filisur △ d.		0929	|		0800	0929	|	...
Tiefencastel △ d.	**Dec. 15**	|	1101	**May 3**	0815	|	1101	...
Chur a.	**to**	1045	1156	**to**	0904	1045	1156	...
Chur d.	**May 2**	1105	1214	**Oct. 11**	0926	1105	1214	1426
Disentis / Mustér a.		1227	1328		1028	1218	1328	1528
Disentis / Mustér d.	⊡	1237	1337		1037	1237	1337	1537
Andermatt a.		1346	1446		1146	1346	1446	1646
Andermatt d.		1354	1454		1208	1408	1508	1708
Brig Bahnhofplatz a.		1540	1640		1340	1540	1640	1840
Brig Bahnhofplatz d.		1550	1650		...	1550	1650	1850
Zermatt a.		1707	1807		...	1707	1807	2007

All Glacier Express trains convey (12) [panorama cars]. Reservations can be made at any Swiss station. Reservations for ✕ are obligatory and must be made in advance of travel: RhB, ✆ 081 300 15 15. Meals are served between 1100 and 1330 at your seat. Further information: www.glacierexpress.ch

a – Not Jan. 6–31, Dec. 6–12.

⊡ – Also Dec. 6–13, 2025.
△ – Calls to pick up only.
▽ – Calls to set down only.

* – Operators:
MGB: Zermatt - Brig - Andermatt - Disentis;
RhB: Disentis - Chur - St Moritz.

☛ No service Oct. 12 - Dec. 5, 2025.

576 Local services ZERMATT - BRIG - ANDERMATT - DISENTIS (also ANDERMATT - GÖSCHENEN) MGB

Narrow gauge railway (part rack). For *Glacier Express* through services see Table **575**

ZERMATT - VISP - BRIG

km																							
0	**Zermatt** d.	0537	0606	0637	0706	0737	and at	1706	1737	1806	1837	1906	1937	2006	...	2106	...	2206	...	...	...	...	...
8	Täsch d.	0551	0621	0651	0721	0751	the same	1721	1751	1821	1851	1921	1951	2021	...	2121	...	2221	...	...	...	...	...
21	St Niklaus d.	0617	0647	0717	0747	0817	minutes	1747	1817	1847	1917	1947	2017	2047	...	2147	...	2247	...	...	...	...	...
29	Stalden-Saas d.	0638	0708	0738	0808	0838	past each	1808	1838	1908	1938	2008	2038	2108	...	2208	...	2308	...	...	...	...	...
36	Visp a.	0650	0721	0747	0821	0847	hour until	1821	1847	1921	1950	2021	2050	2121	...	2221	...	2321	...	...	...	...	...
36	Visp **560 570** d.	0702	0734	*0808*	0834	*0908*		1834	*1908*	1934	2002	2034	2102	2134	...	2234	...	2334	...	...	...	...	...
45	**Brig** Bahnhofplatz **560 570** a.	0713	0745	*0820*	0845	*0920*		1845	*1920*	1945	2013	2045	2113	2145	...	2245	...	2345	...	...	...	...	...

																	①–⑥	⑦					
Brig Bahnhofplatz **560 570** d.	0517	0551	0622	0651	0722	*0738*	0822	*0838*	and at	1822	*1838*	...	1951	...	2051	...	2222	2322	...	...	...	...	...
Visp **560 570** a.	0528	0602	0633	0702	0733	*0750*	0833	*0850*	the same	1833	*1850*	...	2002	...	2102	...	2232	2332	...	...	...	...	...
Visp d.	0530	0611	0637	0711	0737	0811	0837	0911	minutes	1837	1911	...	2011	...	2111	...	2237	2333	...	...	...	...	...
Stalden-Saas d.	0539	0621	0650	0721	0750	0821	0850	0921	past each	1850	1921	...	2021	...	2121	...	2250	2342	...	...	...	...	...
St Niklaus d.	0555	0638	0709	0738	0809	0838	0909	0938	hour until	1909	1938	...	2038	...	2138	...	2309	2358	...	...	...	...	...
Täsch d.	0620	0702	0736	0802	0836	0902	0936	1002		1936	2002	...	2102	...	2202	...	2336	0017	...	...	...	...	...
Zermatt a.	0633	0717	0750	0817	0850	0917	0950	1017		1950	2017	...	2117	...	2217	...	2348	0028	...	...	...	...	...

VISP - BRIG - ANDERMATT

km									①–⑥	⑦	
	Visp d.	...	0708		1808	*1908*	2008	2108	2238	2255	...
	Brig Bahnhofplatz a.	...	0720		1820	*1920*	2020	2120	2249	2306	...
0	**Brig** Bahnhofplatz d.	0623	0723	and	1823	1923	2023	2123	2250	2316	...
7	Mörel d.	0633	0733		1833	1933	2033	2133	2300	2325	...
10	Bettmeralp Talstation d.	0639	0739	hourly	1839	1939	2039	2139	2306	2332	...
17	Fiesch d.	0656	0756		1856	1956	2056	2155	2322	2349	...
41	Oberwald 🚗 d.	0742	0842	until	1942	2042	2139	*2235**	...	...	...
59	Realp 🚗 ⊗ d.	0805	0905		2005	2105	...	...	...	...	...
68	**Andermatt** a.	0820	0920		2020	2120	...	...	...	...	...

									①–⑥	⑦
Andermatt d.	...	0637		1637	1737	1837	1925	2025	...	...
Realp 🚗 ⊗ d.	...	0650		1650	1750	1850	1936	2036	...	...
Oberwald 🚗 d.	*0612**	0712	and	1712	1812	1912	1956	2056	*2250**	*2250**
Fiesch d.	0655	0755		1755	1855	1955	2031	2131	2325	2353
Bettmeralp Talstation d.	0715	0815	hourly	1815	1915	2015	2047	2147	2344	0010
Mörel d.	0722	0822		1822	1922	2022	2057	2157	2351	0017
Brig Bahnhofplatz a.	0733	0833	until	1833	1933	2033	2106	2206	0001	0026
Brig Bahnhofplatz d.	0738	0838		1838	*1938*	*2038*	2120	2209	...	...
Visp a.	0750	0850		1850	*1950*	*2050*	2133	22221	...	...

ANDERMATT - GÖSCHENEN

km																								
	Realp d.	...	0605	...	...	0731	...	0831	...	0931	...	...	and at the same	...	...	...	1831	...	...	...	...	...	2131	2231
0	**Andermatt** d.	0550	0629	0650	0729	0750	0829	0850	0929	0950	1029	1050	minutes past	1729	1750	1829	1850	1929	1950	2029	2050	2129	2150	2250
4	**Göschenen** a.	0605	0644	0705	0744	0806	0844	0906	0944	1006	1044	1106	each hour until	1744	1806	1844	1906	1944	2006	2044	2106	2144	2206	2306

Göschenen d.	0608	0654	0714	0754	0814	0854	0914	0954	and at the same	1614	1654	1714	1754	1814	1854	1914	1954	2014	2054	2114	2154	2214	2314
Andermatt a.	0618	0706	0724	0806	0824	0906	0924	1006	minutes past	1624	1706	1724	1806	1824	1906	1922	2006	2022	2106	2122	2206	2224	2324
Realp a.	...	0721	...	0821	...	0921	...	...	each hour until	...	...	...	1821	...	...	...	...	...	2121	...	2221	...	...

ANDERMATT - DISENTIS

km						🚌	🚌	🚌	
		B				C	A		
0	**Andermatt** d.	0628	0728	and	1928	...	2125	...	...
10	Oberalppass d.	0650	0750	hourly	1950	...	2135	...	...
19	Sedrun d.	0716	0816	until	2016	2055	2155	2155	...
29	**Disentis / Mustér** a.	0739	0839		2039	2110	2210	2210	...

					🚌	🚌		🚌		🚌
	B					A		C		
Disentis / Mustér d.	0614	0714	and	1914	2015	2015	...	2115	...	2225
Sedrun d.	0631	0731	hourly	1931	2030	2030	...	2130	...	2238
Oberalppass d.	0653	0753	until	1953	...	2051	...	...	...	...
Andermatt a.	0722	0822		2022	...	2105	...	...	...	...

REALP - FURKA - OBERWALD ⊡

km		H 🚂		D 🚂		J 🚂				
0	**Realp** DFB d.	1020	...	1120	...	1420	...	...	...	...
7	Furka DFB a.	1105	...	1205	...	1510	...	...	...	...
7	Furka DFB d.	1130	...	1245	...	1530	...	...	...	...
13	Gletsch d.	1210	...	1320	...	1610	...	...	...	...
18	**Oberwald** a.	1235	...	1345	...	1635	...	...	...	...

	E 🚂		H 🚂		D 🚂						
Oberwald d.	1050	...	1350	...	1450	...	...	...	...	...	...
Gletsch d.	1120	...	1420	...	1520	...	...	...	...	...	...
Furka DFB a.	1158	...	1455	...	1555	...	...	...	...	...	...
Furka DFB d.	1220	...	1530	...	1625	...	...	...	...	...	...
Realp DFB a.	1305	...	1615	...	1705	...	...	...	...	...	...

A – May 1 - Oct. 31.
B – May 3 - Oct. 12.
C – Until Apr. 30 and from Nov. 1.
D – ④–⑦ July 17 - Aug. 17.
E – ⑤–⑦ June 20 - Sept. 28.
H – ④–⑦ June 19 - Sept. 28.
J – ④–⑥ June 19 - Sept. 27.

⊗ – Realp is a request stop.
* – By 🚌 from / to Fiesch.
🚂 – Steam train. Ⓡ. Special fares.
⊡ – Summer only tourist service. Special fares. Operator: Dampfbahn Furka-Bergstrecke ✆ 0848 000 144. www.dfb.ch
🚗 – For car-carrying shuttle trains Oberwald - Realp and v.v. see www.matterhorngotthardbahn.ch ✆ +41 (0) 848 642 442.

578 ZERMATT - GORNERGRAT Narrow gauge rack railway. GGB

Journey ±33 minutes uphill, ±44 minutes downhill, *9 km. Services may be suspended in bad weather.* ***No service Nov. 3–9.***

DEC. 15 - APR. 21. From Zermatt: 0824, 0848, 0912, 0936, 1000, 1024, 1048, 1112, 1136, 1200, 1224, 1248, 1312, 1336, 1400, 1424, 1448, 1512, 1536, 1600, 1624, 1724, 1824, 1924.
From Gornergrat: 0735, 0907, 0931, 0955, 1019, 1043, 1107, 1131, 1155, 1219, 1243, 1307, 1331, 1355, 1419, 1443, 1507, 1531, 1555, 1619, 1638, 1718, 1818, 1918, 2007.

APR. 22 - JUNE 13 and OCT. 20 - NOV. 2. From Zermatt: 0700, 0805, 0835, 0910, 0945, 1020, 1055, 1130, 1205, 1240, 1315, 1350, 1425, 1500, 1535, 1610, 1645, 1740.
From Gornergrat: 0742, 0847, 0922, 0957, 1032, 1107, 1142, 1217, 1252, 1327, 1402, 1437, 1512, 1547, 1622, 1657, 1732, 1837.

JUNE 14 - OCT. 19. From Zermatt: 0700, 0800, 0824, 0848, 0912, 0936, 1000, 1024, 1048, 1112, 1136, 1200, 1224, 1248, 1312, 1336, 1400, 1424, 1448, 1512, 1536, 1600, 1624, 1724, 1824, 1924 **c**. **From Gornergrat**: 0735, 0843, 0907, 0931, 0955, 1019, 1043, 1107, 1131, 1155, 1219, 1243, 1307, 1331, 1355, 1419, 1443, 1507, 1531, 1555, 1619, 1638, 1718, 1818, 1918, 2007 **c**.

NOV. 10–28: **From Zermatt**: 0700 Ⓐ, 0824, 1024, 1136, 1224, 1336, 1424, 1624. **From Gornergrat**: 0735 Ⓐ, 0931, 1131, 1219, 1331, 1419, 1531, 1718.

NOV. 29 - DEC. 13. From Zermatt: 0824, 0848, 0912, 0936, 1000, 1024, 1048, 1112, 1136, 1200, 1224, 1248, 1312, 1336, 1400, 1424, 1448, 1512, 1536, 1600, 1624, 1724 **e**, 1824 **e**, 1924 **e**.
From Gornergrat: 0735, 0907, 0931, 0955, 1019, 1043, 1107, 1131, 1155, 1219, 1243, 1307, 1331, 1355, 1419, 1443, 1507, 1531, 1555, 1619, 1638, 1718, 1818 **e**, 1918 **e**, 2007 **e**.

c – June 20 - Sept. 22.
e – Dec. 12, 13 only.

European Rail Timetable Subscription

Keep up to date with the latest changes to European rail schedules with a subscription.

See page 12 for details of our various subscription options

Order on-line at **www.europeanrailtimetable.eu**

✆ +44 (0) 1832 270198 (Monday to Friday 1000–1600)

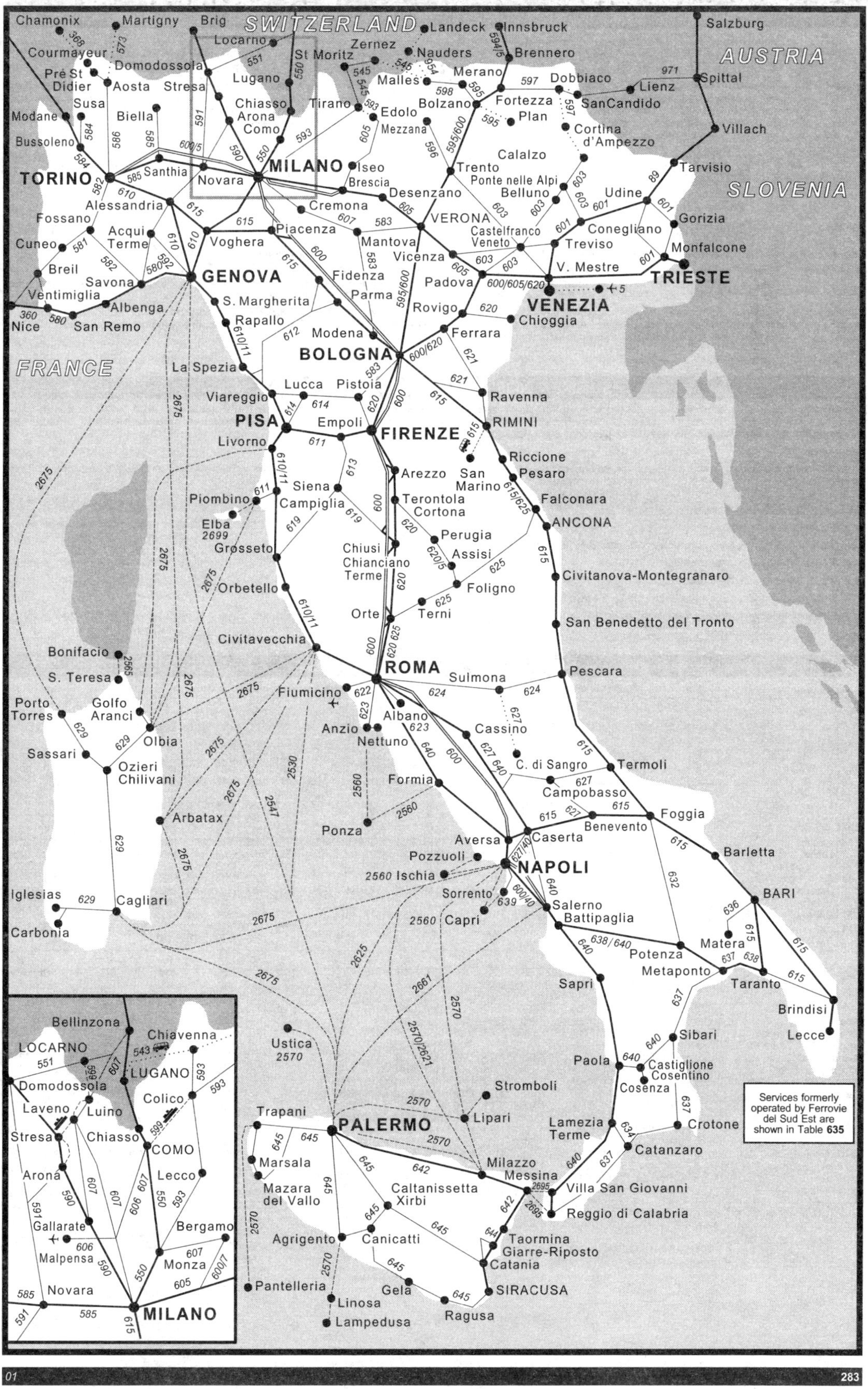
SWITZERLAND
AUSTRIA
SLOVENIA
FRANCE
Chamonix
Martigny
Brig
Locarno
Landeck
Innsbruck
Salzburg
Courmayeur
Domodossola
Zernez
Nauders
St Moritz
Brennero
Pré St Didier
Aosta
Stresa
Lugano
Malles
Merano
Dobbiaco
Lienz
Spittal
Susa
Chiasso
Arona
Como
Tirano
Edolo
Bolzano
Fortezza
Plan
San Candido
Modane
Biella
Mezzana
Cortina d'Ampezzo
Villach
Bussoleno
Iseo
Trento
Calalzo
Tarvisio
TORINO
Santhia
Novara
MILANO
Brescia
Ponte nelle Alpi
Belluno
Udine
Alessandria
Cremona
Desenzano
VERONA
Fossano
Acqui Terme
Piacenza
Mantova
Castelfranco Veneto
Conegliano
Gorizia
Voghera
Vicenza
Treviso
Cuneo
Monfalcone
Breil
GENOVA
Fidenza
Padova
V. Mestre
TRIESTE
Savona
Parma
Ventimiglia
S. Margherita
Rovigo
VENEZIA
Albenga
Chioggia
Nice
San Remo
Rapallo
Modena
Ferrara
BOLOGNA
La Spezia
Lucca
Pistoia
Ravenna
Viareggio
PISA
Empoli
RIMINI
FIRENZE
Livorno
Riccione
Arezzo
San Marino
Pesaro
Siena
Piombino
Campiglia
Terontola Cortona
Falconara
ANCONA
Elba 2699
Perugia
Grosseto
Chiusi Chianciano Terme
Assisi
Civitanova-Montegranaro
Orbetello
Foligno
Orte
Terni
San Benedetto del Tronto
Civitavecchia
Bonifacio
ROMA
Pescara
S. Teresa
Sulmona
Porto Torres
Golfo Aranci
Fiumicino
Albano
Olbia
Anzio
Nettuno
Cassino
Sassari
C. di Sangro
Termoli
Ozieri Chilivani
Formia
Campobasso
Arbatax
Ponza
Benevento
Foggia
Aversa
Caserta
Pozzuoli
Barletta
NAPOLI
2560 Ischia
Iglesias
Cagliari
Sorrento
Salerno
Battipaglia
BARI
Carbonia
2560 Capri
Matera
Potenza
Metaponto
Taranto
Sapri
Brindisi
Lecce
Ustica 2570
Sibari
Paola
Castiglione Cosentino
Cosenza
Stromboli
Trapani
PALERMO
Lipari
Lamezia Terme
Crotone
Catanzaro
Marsala
Milazzo
Messina
Mazara del Vallo
Caltanissetta Xirbi
Villa San Giovanni
Reggio di Calabria
Agrigento
Canicattì
Taormina Giarre-Riposto
Catania
Pantelleria
Gela
SIRACUSA
Linosa
Ragusa
Lampedusa
Bellinzona
Chiavenna
LOCARNO
LUGANO
Domodossola
Colico
Laveno
Luino
Stresa
Chiasso
COMO
Arona
Lecco
Gallarate
Bergamo
Malpensa
Monza
Novara
MILANO
Services formerly operated by Ferrovie del Sud Est are shown in Table 635

ITALY

Operator: Services are operated by Trenitalia, a division of Ferrovie dello Stato Italiane S.p.a. (FS), unless otherwise noted: www.trenitalia.com.
Trenord is a joint venture between Trenitalia and Ferrovie Nord Milano (LeNord) that operates local services, mainly in the Lombardia region: www.trenord.it.
Nuovo Trasporto Viaggiatori (NTV) is an open-access operator providing alternative services over the high-speed network: www.italotreno.it.

Services: All trains convey First and Second classes of travel unless otherwise shown by a figure "2" at the top of the column, or in a note in the Table heading. Four classes of accommodation is available on Frecciarossa (*FR*) services: Executive, Business, Premium and Standard class. Overnight sleeping car (🛏) or couchette (▬) trains do not necessarily convey seating accommodation or may convey only second class seats - refer to individual footnotes. Excelsior sleeping cars offer en-suite facilities. Descriptions of sleeping and couchette cars appear on page 10. Refreshment services (✕ or 🍸) where known, may only be available for part of the journey, and may be added to or taken away from trains during the currency of the timetable.

Train Categories: There are eight categories of express train:

EC	**EuroCity**	international express; supplement payable.
FA	**Frecciargento**	tilting trains used on both high-speed and traditional lines.
FB	**Frecciabianca**	fast premium fare services using traditional lines.
FR	**Frecciarossa**	fast premium fare services using high-speed lines.
IC	**InterCity**	internal day express; supplement payable.
ICN	**InterCity Notte**	internal night express.
ITA	**.italo**	high-speed service (operated by NTV).
RJ(X)	**Railjet**	Austrian express; supplement payable.

Timings: Long-distance services (those shown with train numbers) are valid **June 16 - September 14** unless otherwise stated. All other services should be regarded as subject to confirmation.

Tickets: Tickets must be date-stamped by the holder before boarding the train using the self-service validating machines – this applies to all tickets except passes.

Reservations: Reservations are **compulsory** for all journeys by services for which a train category (*EC, FA, FB, FR, IC, ICN, ITA, NJ, RJ, RJX*) is shown in the timing column and passengers boarding without a prior reservation may be surcharged. Reservations for sleeping and couchette car accommodation on domestic night trains are valid only when presented with personal identification. *ITA* services are 'global' price trains with compulsory reservation - Trenitalia tickets are not valid.

Supplements: Supplements are calculated according to class of travel and total distance travelled (minimum 10km, maximum 3000km), and are payable on all *EC* and *IC* trains, regardless of the number of changes of train. A higher fare (including supplement) is payable for travel by *FA, FB* and *FR* trains. Some trains are only available to passengers holding long distance tickets and the restrictions applying to these are noted in the tables.

SUMMER 2025 - IMPORTANT INFORMATION

Except where otherwise noted, long-distance services (those shown with train numbers) are valid **June 16 - September 14**. All other services should be regarded as subject to confirmation - we hope to have them fully updated in time for the July digital edition. There is a large amount of engineering work taking place this summer, with most routes affected at some point. We recommend that you confirm all journeys using the Trenitalia journey planner at www.trenitalia.com.

Major changes include:

Tables **580** and **610**: Maintenance work taking place on the Bressana Bottarone bridge over the river Po will result in changes to Milano - Genova trains from June 1 to September 28. Trains between Milano and Voghera will either be diverted or replaced by buses.

Table **590**: The railway will be closed June 8 - July 27 and August 30 - September 13. During this period *EC* trains will be replaceed by buses (Ⓡ required) between Domodossola and Milan with extended journey times. Local trains are subject to alteration.

Table **593**: Engineering work takes place July 28 - August 24.

Table **595**: Engineering work takes place Bolzano - Merano June 15 - August 9.

Table **600**: Engineering work takes place August 11 – 31.

Table **605**: Engineering work takes place August 4 – 24.

Table **620**: Engineering work takes place August 11 – 22 and from September 15.

Table **640**: Engineering work until July 6 and from October 13.

580 VENTIMIGLIA - SAVONA - GENOVA

Subject to alteration. For Ventimiglia - Monaco - Nice - Cannes and v.v. see Table **361**.

km		*IC*				*IC*		*IC*	*IC*		*IC*		*IC*			*IC*		*IC*	*IC*			*IC*		
		653	2	2	2	**505**	2	**631**	**515**	2	**745**	2	**1539**		2	**635**	2	**681**	**681**	2	2	**639**	2	2
				Ⓐ	Ⓐ								⑥⑦					①–⑤	⑥⑦	Ⓑ	⑥			
						A			**C**					...										
0	**Ventimiglia** 🏛 d.	0445	0509	0530	0550	0637	0757	0910	...	0957	1059	1157	...	...	1357	1510	1557	1659	1659	1757	1757	1910	1957	2120
5	Bordighera d.	0454	0516	0537	0558	0644	0804	|	...	1004	1107	1204	...	...	1404	|	1604	1707	1707	1804	1804	|	2004	2128
16	San Remo d.	0504	0524	0545	0606	0653	0812	0923	...	1012	1116	1212	...	...	1412	1523	1612	1716	1716	1812	1812	1923	2012	2136
24	Taggia Arma d.	0510	0530	0551	0612	0700	0819	|	...	1019	1123	1219	...	...	1419	|	1619	1722	1722	1819	1819	|	2019	2142
39	Imperia d.	0520	0540	0601	0622	0710	0829	0935	...	1029	1132	1229	...	...	1429	1535	1629	1732	1732	1829	1829	1934	2029	2152
46	Diano d.	0525	0545	0606	0627	0717	0835	0941	...	1035	1138	1235	...	...	1435	1541	1635	1736	1736	1835	1835	1940	2035	2157
61	Alassio d.	0537	0556	0622	0644	0730	0848	0952	...	1048	1152	1248	...	...	1448	1552	1648	1752	1752	1848	1848	1950	2048	2212
67	Albenga d.	0545	0603	0630	0650	0737	0855	0959	...	1055	1159	1255	...	...	1455	1600	1655	1800	1800	1855	1855	1957	2055	2219
76	Loano d.	|	0612	0649	0659	|	0903	|	...	1103	|	1303	...	...	1503	|	1703	|	1808	1903	1903	|	2103	2230
79	Pietra Ligure d.	|	0616	0653	|	|	0908	|	...	1108	|	1308	...	...	1508	|	1708	|	1813	1908	1908	|	2108	2234
85	Finale Ligure Marina d.	0600	0623	0659	0708	0752	0914	1017	...	1114	1219	1314	...	...	1514	1617	1714	1814	1820	1914	1914	2018	2114	2242
108	**Savona** d.	0617	0645	0717	0724	0805	0933	1033	1100	1133	1233	1333	1432	...	1533	1633	1733	1833	1835	1933	1933	2035	2133	2305
120	Varazze d.	|	0654	|	0732	|	|	|	|	|	|	|	|	...	|	|	|	|	1843	|	|	|	2146	...
151	**Genova** Piazza Principe a.	0655	0738	0805	0812	0850	1021	1105	1141	1217	1305	1417	1504	...	1617	1705	1817	1908	1908	2017	2017	2108	2224	...
154	**Genova** Brignole a.	|	|	0813	0820	0859	1029	|	...	1225	|	1425	|	...	1625	|	1825	|	|	2025	...	|	2232	...
	Milano Centrale **610** a.	0900	0935	...	...	...	...	1255	...	...	1455	...	1655		...	1855	...	2100	2100	...	...	2255	...	...

				IC	*IC*			*IC*	*IC*	*IC*			*IC*	*IC*			*IC*		*IC*		*IC*	*IC*
	2	2	2	2	**503**	**633**	2	2	**659**	**659**	**1549**	2		**1549**	**637**	2	2	**641**	2	**675**	2	**518**	**689**
			⚒	Ⓐ			Ⓐ	⑥	①–⑤	⑥⑦	⑥	Ⓑ		⑦									
					C																	**B**	
Milano Centrale **610** d.	...	...	...	...	...	0700	...	...	0910	0910	0930	...	...	1005	1110	...	...	1510	...	1705	...	...	2005
Genova Brignole d.	0515	0600	0638	0732	...	|	0935	...	|	|	|	1135	...	|	|	1335	1535	|	1735	|	1935	2129	|
Genova Piazza Principe d.	0522	0607	0646	0740	0814	0858	0943	1035	1058	1058	1124	1143	...	1150	1258	1343	1543	1658	1743	1858	1943	2137	2158
Varazze d.	0605	0653	0729	|	|	|	|	|	|	1123	|	|	...	|	|	|	|	|	|	|	|	|	|
Savona d.	0621	0710	0745	0828	0856	0931	1029	1112	1131	1131	1210	1228	...	1243	1331	1428	1628	1731	1828	1931	2028	2207	2232
Finale Ligure Marina d.	0636	0729	0801	0843	...	0943	1043	1133	1143	1144	...	1243	...	...	1343	1443	1643	1743	1843	1943	2046	2219	2245
Pietra Ligure d.	0642	0737	0807	0849	...	|	1049	1140	|	1153	...	1249	...	...	|	1449	1649	|	1849	|	2051	|	|
Loano d.	0647	0742	0812	0853	...	|	1053	1146	|	1159	...	1253	...	...	|	1453	1653	|	1853	|	2054	|	|
Albenga d.	0704	0804	0824	0901	...	0959	1101	1159	1159	1211	...	1301	...	...	1358	1501	1701	1759	1901	1957	2102	2232	2301
Alassio d.	0711	0811	0832	0908	...	1007	1108	1206	1208	1226	...	1311	...	...	1407	1508	1708	1809	1908	2004	2108	2240	2308
Diano d.	0725	0825	0846	0920	...	1021	1120	1218	1218	1236	...	1324	...	...	1421	1520	1720	1821	1920	2019	2120	2253	2319
Imperia d.	0732	0832	0851	0928	...	1028	1128	1226	1225	1244	...	1332	...	...	1428	1528	1728	1828	1928	2027	2128	2302	2326
Taggia Arma d.	0742	0842	0901	0938	...	|	1138	1236	1236	1254	...	1342	...	...	|	1538	1738	|	1938	2038	2138	2313	2335
San Remo d.	0748	0848	0906	0945	...	1042	1145	1243	1243	1301	...	1349	...	...	1442	1545	1745	1842	1945	2045	2145	2321	2342
Bordighera d.	0756	0857	0915	0954	...	|	1154	1252	1253	1310	...	1402	...	...	|	1554	1754	1852	1954	2055	2154	2331	2353
Ventimiglia 🏛 a.	0806	0906	0925	1006	...	1059	1206	1303	1307	1322	...	1412	...	...	1459	1606	1806	1904	2006	2107	2206	2339	0007

A – To La Spezia on Ⓐ, to Roma on Ⓒ (Table **610**).
B – From Roma (Table **610**).
C – To / from Torino (Table **610**).
D – To Voghera (Table **610**).

Additional local trains:
Ventimiglia - Savona and v.v. hourly on Ⓐ / every two hours on Ⓒ. Journey 2 hours.
Savona - Genova and v.v. every 30 minutes on Ⓐ / hourly on Ⓒ. Journey 70 minutes.

2nd class VENTIMIGLIA and NICE - CUNEO 581

Service until November 23. Additional 🚌 services are available Nice - Breil and v.v., and to Sospel - please check locally. Subject to alteration on and around French holiday dates (see page 4).

km			🚌		🚌		🚌			
**	**Ventimiglia** d.	0618	...	1039	...	1620	...	1849	...	...
0	**Nice** Ville d.	|	0915	|	1430	|	1730	|	...	...
34	Sospel d.	|	|	|	|	|	|	|	...	...
43	Breil sur Roya a.	0655	1035	1117	1600	1655	1900	1925	...	...
43	Breil sur Roya d.	0656	...	1119	...	1700	...	1926	...	...
71	Tende d.	0751	...	1220	...	1802	...	2017	...	...
89	Limone 🏛 a.	0825	...	1246	...	1835	...	2045	...	...
89	Limone 🏛 582 d.	0840	...	1247	...	1840	...	2046	...	...
118	**Cuneo** 582 a.	0919	...	1319	...	1919	...	2119	...	...

		🚌		🚌		🚌		🚌	
Cuneo 582 d.	0641	...	0841	...	1441	...	1715	...	...
Limone 🏛 582 a.	0718	...	0918	...	1518	...	1754	...	...
Limone 🏛 d.	0720	...	0919	...	1520	...	1756	...	...
Tende d.	0750	...	0947	...	1550	...	1832	...	...
Breil sur Roya a.	0841	...	1036	...	1643	...	1922	...	...
Breil sur Roya d.	0842	0850	1037	1040	1657	1720	1927	1930	...
Sospel d.	|	|	|	|	|	|	|	|	...
Nice Ville a.	|	1010	|	1200	|	1840	|	2040	...
Ventimiglia a.	0921	...	1121	...	1733	...	2005	...	...

** – Ventimiglia - Breil sur Roya is *20 km*.

2nd class TORINO - CUNEO, LIMONE and SAVONA 582

km							Ⓑ			†										Ⓐ			⚒			
0	**Torino** Porta Nuova d.	0525	0625	...	0720	0825	...	0925	1025	...	1125	1225	...	1325	1425	...	1525	1625	...	1725	1825	...	1925	2025	2125
52	Savigliano d.	0603	0703	...	0803	0903	...	1003	1103	...	1203	1303	...	1403	1503	...	1603	1703	...	1803	1903	...	2003	2103	2203
64	Fossano d.	0612	0713	0725	0812	0913	0925	1012	1113	1125	1212	1313	1325	1412	1513	1525	1612	1713	1725	1812	1913	1925	2012	2113	2212
90	Cuneo 581 d.	0636	|	0750	0836	|	0950	1036	|	1150	1236	|	1350	1436	|	1550	1636	|	1750	1836	|	1950	2036	|	2236
119	**Limone** 581 a.	...	|	0828	...	|	1028	...	|	1228	...	|	1428	...	|	1628	...	|	1828	...	|	2028	...	|	...
83	Mondovi d.	...	0728	...	...	0928	...	...	1128	...	...	1328	...	...	1528	...	...	1728	...	...	1928	...	...	2128	...
103	Ceva d.	...	0742	...	...	0942	...	...	1142	...	...	1342	...	...	1542	...	...	1742	...	...	1942	...	...	2142	...
132	S.Giuseppe di Cairo d.	...	0813	...	...	1013	...	...	1213	...	...	1413	...	...	1613	...	...	1813	...	...	2013	...	...	2213	...
153	**Savona** a.	...	0836	...	...	1036	...	...	1241	...	...	1441	...	...	1636	...	...	1841	...	...	2041	...	...	2241	...

	⚒	†						Ⓑ			Ⓑ							A		Ⓐ			⚒	
Savona d.	...	...	0731	...	...	0931	...	...	1131	...	...	1330	...	...	1531	...	...	1731	...	...	1927	...	...	2131
S.Giuseppe di Cairo d.	...	...	0753	...	...	0953	...	...	1153	...	...	1353	...	...	1553	...	...	1753	...	...	1953	...	...	2153
Ceva d.	...	...	0817	...	...	1017	...	...	1217	...	...	1417	...	...	1617	...	...	1817	...	...	2017	...	...	2217
Mondovi d.	...	...	0832	...	...	1032	...	...	1232	...	...	1432	...	...	1632	...	...	1832	...	...	2032	...	...	2232
Limone 581 d.	...	0732	|	...	0932	|	...	1132	|	...	1332	|	...	1532	|	...	1732	|	...	1932	|	...	2132	|
Cuneo 581 d.	0724	0812	|	0924	1012	|	1124	1212	|	1324	1412	|	1524	1612	|	1724	1812	|	1924	2012	|	2124	2212	|
Fossano d.	0744	0835	0844	0944	1035	1044	1144	1235	1244	1344	1435	1444	1544	1635	1644	1744	1835	1844	1944	2035	2044	2144	2235	2244
Savigliano d.	0752	...	0852	0952	...	1052	1152	...	1252	1352	...	1452	1552	...	1652	1752	...	1852	1952	...	2052	2152	...	2252
Torino Porta Nuova a.	0835	...	0940	1035	...	1140	1235	...	1340	1435	...	1540	1635	...	1740	1835	...	1940	2035	...	2140	2235	...	2345

A – Runs 18–25 minutes later on Ⓒ.

☛ Other trains: Limone - Torino at 0524; Savona - Torino at 0531.

2nd class MANTOVA and PORRETTA TERME 583

An *FR* train is available Mantova - Bologna - Firenze - Roma and v.v. (Table **600**).

BOLOGNA - PORRETTA TERME *59 km* Journey 75 minutes

From **Bologna Centrale** at 0617 ⚒, 0717 and hourly until 2217.

From **Porretta Terme** at 0629 and hourly until 2132.

MANTOVA - MODENA *61 km* Journey 60–90 minutes

From **Mantova** at 0535 ⚒, 0629, 0732 ⚒, 0829, 0929, 1129, 1229 ⚒, 1329, 1429 ⚒, 1529, 1629 ⚒, 1729, 1829 ⚒, 1929, 2029 ⚒, 2129.

From **Modena** at 0545 ⚒, 0630 ⚒, 0706, 0806 ⚒, 0906, 1106 †, 1206 ⚒, 1306, 1406 ⚒, 1506, 1606 ⚒, 1706, 1805 ⚒, 1906, 2005, 2106 ⚒, 2207.

PORRETTA TERME - PISTOIA *40 km* Journey 60–75 minutes

From **Porretta Terme** at 0655 ⚒, 0714, 0926 ⚒, 1022 †, 1322, 1524, 1824.

From **Pistoia** at 0600, 0823 ⚒, 0921 †, 1220, 1420, 1718, 1926.

VERONA - MANTOVA *37 km* Journey 45–50 minutes

From **Verona Porta Nuova** at 0631 ⚒, 0731 ⚒, 0831 ⚒, 0931 ⚒, 0940 †, 1231 ⚒, 1331, 1431 ⚒, 1531, 1631 ⚒, 1731, 1831 ⚒, 1931, 2031 ⚒, 2131 †.

From **Mantova** at 0629 ⚒, 0729 ⚒, 0829, 0929 ⚒, 1229, 1329 ⚒, 1429, 1529 ⚒, 1629, 1729 ⚒, 1829, 1929 ⚒, 2029.

2nd class TORINO - SUSA and BARDONECCHIA 584

For Italy - France high-speed trains via Oulx and Modane see Table **44**. Oulx-Claviere is the station for Cesana, Claviere and Sestriere.

km		⚒	⚒	†	⚒		⚒	⚒	†	⑥		⑥		⚒	†	⚒		⚒	⚒	†	⚒		⚒	⚒
0	**Torino** Porta Nuova d.	0515	0545	0545	0615	0645	0715	0745	0745	0815	0845	0915	...	0945	0945	1015	1045	1115	1145	1145	1215	1245	1315	1345
46	Bussoleno d.	0559	0643	0632	0712	0743	0759	0843	0832	0859	0943	0959	...	1043	1032	1059	1143	1159	1243	1232	1259	1343	1359	1443
54	**Susa** a.	|	0653	|	|	0753	|	0853	|	|	0953	|	...	1053	|	|	1153	|	1253	|	|	1353	|	1453
76	Oulx-Claviere-Sestriere d.	0628	...	0701	0742	...	0828	...	0901	0928	...	1028	...	...	1101	1128	...	1228	...	1301	1328	...	1428	...
87	**Bardonecchia** a.	0642	...	0715	0756	...	0842	...	0915	0942	...	1042	...	...	1115	1144	...	1244	...	1315	1342	...	1442	...

	†	⚒		⚒	⚒	†	⚒		⚒	⚒	†		⚒		⚒	⚒	†	⚒		⚒	⚒	†	⚒
Torino Porta Nuova d.	1345	1415	1445	1515	1545	1545	1615	1645	1715	1745	1745	...	1815	1845	1915	1945	1945	2015	2045	2115	2145	2145	2215
Bussoleno d.	1432	1459	1543	1559	1643	1632	1657	1743	1759	1843	1832	...	1859	1943	1959	2043	2032	2059	2143	2159	2243	2232	2259
Susa a.	|	|	1553	|	1653	|	|	1753	|	1853	|	...	|	1953	|	2053	|	|	2153	|	2253	|	|
Oulx-Claviere-Sestriere d.	1501	1528	...	1628	...	1701	1726	...	1828	...	1901	...	1928	...	2028	...	2101	2128	...	2228	...	2301	2328
Bardonecchia a.	1515	1542	...	1642	...	1715	1746	...	1842	...	1915	...	1942	...	2042	...	2115	2142	...	2242	...	2315	2342

	†	⚒	⚒	⚒	⚒	†	⚒		⚒	⚒	†		⑥		⑥	⚒	†	⚒	⚒	⚒	⚒	†	⚒
Bardonecchia d.	0508	0520	...	0620	...	0647	0720	...	0818	...	0847	...	0920	...	1020	...	1047	1118	...	1214	...	1247	1306
Oulx-Claviere-Sestriere d.	0520	0532	...	0632	...	0659	0732	...	0830	...	0859	...	0932	...	1032	...	1059	1130	...	1226	...	1259	1318
Susa d.	|	|	0609	|	0709	|	|	0809	|	0909	|	...	|	1009	|	1109	|	|	1209	|	1309	|	|
Bussoleno d.	0549	0601	0619	0701	0719	0728	0801	0819	0901	0919	0928	...	1001	1019	1101	1119	1128	1201	1219	1300	1319	1328	1349
Torino Porta Nuova a.	0645	0645	0715	0745	0815	0815	0845	0915	0945	1015	1015	...	1045	1120	1145	1215	1215	1245	1315	1345	1415	1415	1445

		⚒	⚒	†	⚒		⚒	⚒	†	⚒			⚒	⚒	†	⚒		⚒	⚒	†	⚒		⚒
Bardonecchia d.	...	1420	...	1447	1520	...	1620	...	1647	1720	...	...	1820	...	1847	1920	...	2014	...	2047	2120	...	2220
Oulx-Claviere-Sestriere d.	...	1432	...	1459	1532	...	1632	...	1659	1732	...	...	1832	...	1859	1932	...	2026	...	2059	2132	...	2232
Susa d.	1409	|	1509	|	|	1609	|	1709	|	|	1809	...	|	1909	|	|	2009	|	2109	|	|	2209	|
Bussoleno d.	1419	1501	1519	1528	1601	1619	1701	1719	1728	1801	1819	...	1901	1919	1928	2001	2019	2100	2119	2128	2201	2219	2301
Torino Porta Nuova a.	1515	1545	1615	1615	1645	1715	1745	1815	1815	1845	1915	...	1945	2015	2015	2045	2115	2145	2215	2215	2245	2315	2345

🚌 service **BARDONECCHIA - MODANE** and v.v. Journey 30 minutes. Route **902** www.extrato.it.

From **Bardonecchia** at 0650 ⚒, 0810 ⚒, 1200 ⚒, 1400 ⚒, 1510 ⚒, 1700 ⚒, 1850 ⚒.

From **Modane** at 0730 ⚒, 0840 ⚒, 1230 ⚒, 1440 ⚒, 1540 ⚒, 1740 ⚒, 1930 ⚒.

585 TORINO - BIELLA S. PAOLO and MILANO

For high-speed trains see Tables **600** and **605**

km																								
							Ⓐ d												Ⓐ d					
0	**Torino** Porta Nuova **586** d.	0454	0554	0654	0754	...	...	0854	1054	1154	...	1254	1354	1454	1554	...	1654	1754	...	1854	...	1954	2054	...
6	**Torino** Porta Susa **586** d.	0505	0605	0705	0805	...	0859	0905	1105	1205	...	1305	1405	1505	1605	...	1705	1805	1859	1905	...	2005	2105	...
29	Chivasso **586** d.	0520	0620	0720	0820	...	0913	0920	1120	1220	...	1320	1420	1520	1620	...	1720	1820	1913	1920	...	2020	2120	...
60	Santhià d.	0538	0638	0738	0838	...	0931	0938	1138	1238	...	1338	1438	1538	1638	...	1738	1838	1931	1938	...	2038	2138	...
79	Vercelli d.	0549	0649	0749	0849	...	...	0949	1149	1249	...	1349	1449	1549	1649	...	1749	1849	...	1949	...	2049	2149	...
101	Novara d.	0605	0705	0805	0905	...	...	1005	1205	1305	...	1405	1505	1605	1705	...	1805	1905	...	2005	...	2105	2205	...
140	Rho Fiera Milano d.	0631	0731	0831	0931	...	...	1031	1231	1331	...	1431	1531	1631	1731	...	1831	1931	...	2031	...	2131	2231	...
153	**Milano** Centrale a.	0650	0750	0850	0950	...	...	1050	1250	1350	...	1450	1550	1650	1750	...	1850	1950	...	2050	...	2150	2250	...

		Ⓐ d						Ⓐ d															
Milano Centrale d.	0615	...	0715	0815	...	0915	1115	...	1215	...	1315	1415	1515	1615	...	1715	1815	1915	2015	...	2115	2215	...
Rho Fiera Milano d.	0629	...	0729	0829	...	0929	1129	...	1229	...	1329	1429	1529	1629	...	1729	1829	1929	2029	...	2129	2229	...
Novara d.	0656	...	0756	0856	...	0956	1156	...	1256	...	1356	1456	1556	1656	...	1756	1856	1956	2056	...	2156	2256	...
Vercelli d.	0709	...	0809	0909	...	1009	1209	...	1309	...	1409	1509	1609	1709	...	1809	1909	2009	2109	...	2209	2309	...
Santhià d.	0721	0731	0821	0921	...	1021	1221	1245	1321	...	1421	1521	1621	1721	...	1821	1921	2021	2121	...	2221	2321	...
Chivasso **586** d.	0742	0758	0842	0942	...	1042	1242	1305	1342	...	1442	1542	1642	1742	...	1842	1942	2042	2142	...	2242	2342	...
Torino Porta Susa **586** a.	0754	0823	0854	0954	...	1058	1254	1324	1354	...	1454	1554	1654	1754	...	1854	1954	2054	2154	...	2254	2354	...
Torino Porta Nuova **586** a.	0811	...	0911	1011	...	1115	1311	...	1411	...	1511	1611	1711	1811	...	1911	2011	2111	2211	...	2311	0011	...

km																								
		Ⓐ	Ⓐ	Ⓐ	Ⓒ	Ⓐ	Ⓐ d	Ⓒ	Ⓐ	Ⓒ	Ⓐ	Ⓐ	Ⓒ	Ⓐ	Ⓐ	Ⓒ	Ⓐ	Ⓐ	Ⓒ	Ⓐ	Ⓐ d	Ⓐ		Ⓐ
0	**Santhià** d.	0609	0648	0746	0750	0850	0932	0950	1150	1250	1250	1350	1450	1450	1550	1650	1650	1750	1850	1854	1932	1952	2050	2150
27	**Biella S. Paolo** a.	0631	0710	0814	0815	0918	0951	1015	1218	1315	1318	1418	1515	1518	1618	1715	1718	1818	1915	1918	1951	2020	2118	2218

	Ⓐ	Ⓐ	Ⓒ	Ⓐ d	Ⓐ	Ⓒ	Ⓐ	Ⓐ	Ⓒ	Ⓐ d	Ⓐ		Ⓐ	Ⓒ	Ⓐ	Ⓐ	Ⓒ	Ⓐ	Ⓐ	Ⓒ	Ⓐ	Ⓐ	Ⓐ
Biella S. Paolo d.	0602	0641	0648	0713	0747	0848	0851	0953	1148	1227	1251	1348	1451	1548	1551	1651	1748	1751	1849	1948	1953	2051	2151
Santhià a.	0628	0707	0712	0730	0809	0912	0913	1015	1212	1244	1313	1413	1513	1612	1613	1713	1812	1813	1915	2012	2015	2113	2213

d – (2) Biella S. Paolo - Torino and v.v.

586 TORINO - AOSTA

2nd class

Services are operated by 🚌 Ivrea - Aosta and v.v.

km																								
			⚒							⚒		†		⚒		†		⚒		⚒			Ⓐ	
0	**Torino** Porta Nuova **585** d.	0525	...	0725	...	0825	0925	1125	...	1225	1325	1425	...	1425	1625	1725	...	1725	1825	...	...	2025	...	2225
6	**Torino** Porta Susa **585** d.	0534	...	0734	...	0834	0934	1134	...	1234	1334	1434	...	1434	1634	1734	...	1734	1834	...	...	2034	...	2234
29	Chivasso **585** d.	0552	0652	0752	...	0852	0952	1152	...	1300	1352	1452	...	1452	1652	1752	...	1752	1852	1923	...	2052	2123	2252
62	**Ivrea** a.	0614	0739	0823	...	0923	1023	1223	...	1324	1423	1518	...	1523	1722	1818	...	1823	1923	2008	...	2123	2208	2314
62	**Ivrea** d.	0623	0740	0832	...	0932	1032	1232	...	1330	1432	1527	...	1532	1732	1827	...	1832	1932	2013	...	2132	2217	2332
79	Pont Saint Martin d.	0648	0805	0857	...	0957	1057	1257	...	1355	1457	1552	...	1557	1757	1852	...	1857	1957	2038	...	2157	2242	2357
91	Verrès d.	0703	0825	0912	...	1012	1112	1312	...	1415	1512	1609	...	1612	1812	1909	...	1912	2012	2058	...	2212	2302	0012
104	Chatillon-Saint Vincent d.	0728	0850	0937	...	1037	1137	1337	...	1440	1537	1634	...	1637	1837	1934	...	1937	2037	2123	...	2237	2327	0037
129	**Aosta** a.	0800	0920	1009	...	1109	1209	1409	...	1510	1609	1704	...	1707	1909	2004	...	2007	2109	2153	...	2309	2357	0109

		†	⚒								⚒		†				⚒	⚒	†				
Aosta d.	0449	0549	0551	...	0642	0749	0949	...	1103	1149	1240	...	1303	1349	1449	...	1540	1640	1649	...	1749	1849	1949
Chatillon-Saint Vincent d.	0519	0619	0621	...	0712	0819	1019	...	1133	1219	1310	...	1333	1419	1519	...	1610	1710	1719	...	1819	1919	2019
Verrès d.	0544	0644	0646	...	0737	0844	1044	...	1158	1244	1335	...	1358	1444	1544	...	1635	1735	1744	...	1844	1944	2044
Pont Saint Martin d.	0601	0701	0701	...	0757	0901	1101	...	1218	1301	1355	...	1418	1501	1601	...	1655	1755	1801	...	1901	2001	2101
Ivrea a.	0626	0726	0726	...	0826	0926	1126	...	1243	1326	1420	...	1443	1526	1626	...	1720	1820	1826	...	1926	2026	2126
Ivrea d.	0641	0741	0741	...	0841	0941	1141	...	1250	1341	1425	...	1450	1541	1641	...	1748	1841	1841	...	1941	2041	2141
Chivasso **585** a.	0706	0806	0806	...	0906	1006	1206	...	1337	1406	1448	...	1531	1606	1706	...	1837	1906	1906	...	2006	2106	2206
Torino Porta Susa **585** a.	0725	0825	0830	...	0925	1025	1225	...	...	1425	1515	...	...	1625	1725	...	1914	1925	1925	...	2025	2125	2225
Torino Porta Nuova **585** a.	0735	0835	0840	...	0935	1035	1235	...	...	1435	1525	...	...	1635	1735	...	1925	1935	1935	...	2035	2135	2235

589 BRIG - DOMODOSSOLA

2nd class BLS

For *EC* services Genève, Lausanne, Basel and Bern - Milano see Table **82**.

km																								
					Ⓐ				③–⑦		Ⓒ						Ⓐ							
0	**Brig** 🚗 d.	0020	0520	...	0720	0720	...	0920	1044	...	1120	1320	...	1520	1720	...	1844	1920	...	2220	...	...	...	...
23	Iselle di Trasquera § 🚗 d.	0034	0534	...	|	0734	...	0934	|	...	1134	1334	...	1534	1734	...	1858	1934	...	2234	...	...	...	...
42	**Domodossola** a.	0053	0553	...	0753	0753	...	0953	1115	...	1153	1353	...	1553	1753	...	1924	1953	...	2253	...	...	...	...

		Ⓐ			Ⓐ					⑥	Ⓒ												
Domodossola d.	0435	0542	...	0558	0658	...	0758	0958	...	1046	1158	...	1358	1558	...	1758	1958	...	2258	...	...	...	...
Iselle di Trasquera § 🚗 d.	0454	0559	...	0618	0721	...	0818	1018	...	|	1218	...	1418	1618	...	1818	2018	...	2318	...	...	...	...
Brig 🚗 a.	0510	0615	...	0633	0736	...	0833	1033	...	1115	1233	...	1433	1633	...	1833	2033	...	2333	...	...	...	...

§ – Ticket point is **Iselle**.

🚗 – Car-carrying shuttle available. www.bls.ch.

590 DOMODOSSOLA - MILANO

Trenord

Subject to alteration June 8 - July 27 and August 30 - September 13. For *EC* services Genève, Lausanne, Basel and Bern - Milano see Table **82**.

km																								
				2		2⚒		2†		2Ⓒ	2Ⓒ	Ⓒ		2Ⓒ			2				2		2	
0	**Domodossola** d.	0456	0556	0607	0654	0726	...	0807	0856	1007	1207	1256	...	1407	1456	1556	1607	1656	...	1756	1807	1856	2007	2056
30	Verbània-Pallanza d.	0516	0616	0634	0706	0749	...	0834	0916	1034	1234	1316	...	1434	1516	1616	1634	1716	...	1816	1834	1916	2034	2116
35	Baveno d.	|	|	0639	|	|	...	0839	|	1039	1239	|	...	1439	|	|	1639	|	...	|	1839	|	2039	|
39	Stresa d.	0523	0623	0645	0723	0758	...	0845	0923	1045	1245	1323	...	1445	1523	1623	1645	1723	...	1823	1845	1923	2045	2123
56	Arona d.	0535	0635	0709	0735	0815	...	0915	0935	1115	1315	1335	...	1515	1535	1635	1715	1735	...	1835	1915	1935	2115	2135
82	Gallarate d.	0557	0657	0742	0757	0847	...	0947	0957	1147	1347	1357	...	1547	1557	1657	1747	1757	...	1857	1947	1957	2147	2157
89	Busto Arsizio FS d.	0603	0703	0748	0803	0853	...	0953	1003	1153	1353	1403	...	1553	1603	1703	1753	1803	...	1903	1953	2003	2153	2203
112	Rho-Fiera Milano d.	0621	0721	0811	0821	0911	...	1011	1021	1211	1411	1421	...	1611	1621	1721	1811	1821	...	1921	2011	2021	2211	2221
123	**Milano** Porta Garibaldi a.	|	|	0825	|	0925	...	1025	|	1225	1425	|	...	1625	|	|	1825	|	...	|	2025	|	2225	|
125	**Milano** Centrale a.	0640	0740	...	0840	...	...	...	1040	...	...	1440	...	...	1640	1740	...	1840	...	1940	...	2040	...	2240

	2		2			Ⓒ	2Ⓒ		Ⓒ	2				2				2				2	
Milano Centrale d.	...	0725	...	...	0825	0925	...	...	1325	...	1425	...	1525	...	1625	...	1725	...	1825	...	1925	...	2125
Milano Porta Garibaldi d.	0610	|	0740	...	|	|	1140	...	|	1340	|	...	|	1540	|	...	|	1740	|	...	|	1940	|
Rho-Fiera Milano d.	0619	0738	0749	...	0838	0938	1149	...	1338	1349	1438	...	1538	1549	1638	...	1738	1749	1838	...	1938	1949	2138
Busto Arsizio FS d.	0636	0757	0807	...	0857	0957	1207	...	1357	1407	1457	...	1557	1607	1657	...	1757	1807	1857	...	1957	2007	2157
Gallarate d.	0642	0802	0813	...	0902	1002	1213	...	1402	1413	1502	...	1602	1613	1702	...	1802	1813	1902	...	2002	2013	22022
Arona d.	0717	0825	0845	...	0925	1025	1245	...	1425	1454	1525	...	1625	1645	1725	...	1825	1845	1925	...	2025	2045	2225
Stresa d.	0737	0837	0906	...	0937	1037	1306	...	1437	1514	1537	...	1637	1706	1737	...	1837	1906	1937	...	2037	2106	2237
Baveno d.	0742	|	0911	...	|	|	1311	...	|	1519	|	...	|	1711	|	...	|	1911	|	...	|	2111	|
Verbània-Pallanza d.	0747	0844	0916	...	0944	1044	1316	...	1444	1524	1544	...	1644	1716	1744	...	1844	1916	1944	...	2044	2116	2244
Domodossola a.	0820	0904	0953	...	1004	1104	1353	...	1504	1553	1604	...	1704	1753	1804	...	1904	1953	2004	...	2104	2153	2304

DOMODOSSOLA and ARONA - NOVARA - ALESSANDRIA — 591

2nd class

km		Ⓐ	⚒			⚒	⚒			
0	**Domodossola** d.	0520	0617	0648	1245	1343	1545	1747	1848	...
38	Omegna d.	0614	0657	0752	1337	1444	1641	1842	1940	...
44	Pettenasco d.	0621	0704	0759	1343	1451	1648	1849	1947	...
47	Orta-Miasino d.	0626	0712	0804	1351	1456	1653	1854	1952	...
60	Borgomanero d.	0641	0724	0815	1406	1507	1704	1905	2004	...
90	**Novara** a.	0716	0754	0843	1437	1541	1740	1943	2039	...

	⚒		†	⚒			Ⓐ	⚒	
Novara d.	0546	0645	1223	1345	1515	1734	1818	1915	...
Borgomanero d.	0621	0725	1249	1420	1550	1811	1851	1950	...
Orta-Miasino d.	0645	0740	1306	1432	1608	1826	1911	2006	...
Pettenasco d.	0649	0744	1311	1437	1613	1831	1915	2011	...
Omegna d.	0656	0751	1318	1443	1619	1843	1922	2018	...
Domodossola a.	0748	0849	1417	1542	1714	1938	2004	2114	...

km		†	†	†	Ⓐ	†	⚒	†	⚒	⚒
0	**Arona** ◧ d.	0915	1115	1315	1348	1515	1548	1715	1748	1848
20	Oleggio ◧ d.	0932	1132	1332	1412	1532	1612	1732	1812	1917
37	**Novara** ◧ a.	0948	1148	1348	1432	1548	1632	1748	1832	1932

	†	†	†	†	⚒	⚒	†	⚒	†
Novara ◧ d.	0812	1012	1212	1412	1423	1523	1612	1723	1812
Oleggio ◧ d.	0826	1026	1226	1426	1441	1541	1626	1741	1826
Arona ◧ a.	0845	1045	1245	1445	1512	1612	1645	1812	1845

km		⚒	⚒		⑥	†	⚒	⚒	⚒	†
0	**Novara** ⊡ d.	0608	0708	0808	0908	1408	1423	1608	1708	1908
25	Mortara ⊡ d.	0632	0732	0832	0932	1432	1452	1632	1732	1932
67	**Alessandria** ⊡ a.	0713	0813	0913	1013	1513	1532	1713	1813	2013

	†	Ⓒ	Ⓐ	⑥			⚒		Ⓐ
Alessandria ⊡ d.	0647	1247	1347	1347	1647	1747	1847	1947	2047
Mortara ⊡ d.	0728	1328	1428	1428	1728	1828	1928	2028	2128
Novara ⊡ a.	0752	1352	1452	1452	1752	1852	1952	2052	2152

◧ – Also from Arona at 0648 ⚒, 0748 ⚒, 1915 †, 1948 ⚒, 2115 †; also from Novara at 0650 ⚒, 0750 Ⓐ, 1823 ⚒, 1923 ⚒, 2012 †.
⊡ – Additional trains are available Novara - Mortara and v.v. and Mortara - Alessandria and v.v.

ALESSANDRIA - ACQUI TERME - SAVONA and GENOVA — 592

2nd class

km				⚒	⚒			⚒	⚒	
0	**Alessandria** d.	0740	0935	1140	...	1340	1540	1740	1940	...
34	**Acqui Terme** d.	0816	1017	1217	1324	1417	1617	1817	2017	...
84	S. Giuseppe di Cairo d.	0922	1122	1322	1437	1522	1721	1922	2122	...
105	**Savona** a.	0952	1154	1355	1504	1550	...	2000	2201	...

	⚒	⚒			⚒				
Savona d.	0611	0800	1002	1207	1407	1602	...	2010	...
S. Giuseppe di Cairo d.	0637	0839	1039	1239	1439	1639	1839	2039	...
Acqui Terme a.	0736	0937	1136	1336	1536	1736	1936	2137	...
Alessandria a.	0820	...	1220	1420	1620	1820	2020	...	...

km		Ⓐ					Ⓐ		Ⓐ	
0	**Acqui Terme** ⊖ d.	0740	0917	1117	1217	1317	1417	1617	1717	1817
59	**Genova** Piazza Principe ⊖ a.	0845	1043	1243	1343	1443	1543	1743	1843	1942
61	**Genova** Brignole ⊖ a.	0854	1051	1251	1351	1451	1551	1751	1851	1950

	⚒		Ⓐ		Ⓐ		Ⓐ		
Genova Brignole ⊖ d.	1013	1113	1213	1313	1413	1613	1713	1813	1913
Genova Piazza Principe ⊖ d.	1021	1121	1221	1321	1421	1621	1721	1821	1921
Acqui Terme ⊖ a.	1139	1239	1339	1439	1539	1739	1839	1939	2039

⊖ – Also from Acqui Terme at 0607, 0703 ⚒, 2040; also from Genova Brignole at 0600 Ⓐ, 0706, 0913, 1513 Ⓐ, 2035.

MILANO - COLICO - CHIAVENNA and TIRANO — 593

Trenord

Additional trains are available Milano Porta Garibaldi - Lecco and v.v., and Lecco - Sondrio and v.v. For Tirano - St Moritz see Table **545**.

km																								
0	**Milano** Centrale d.	0620	0720	...	0820	0920	...	1020	1120	...	1220	1320	...	1420	1520	...	1620	1720	...	1820	1920	...	2020	2120
12	Monza d.	0632	0732	...	0832	0932	...	1032	1132	...	1232	1332	...	1432	1532	...	1632	1732	...	1832	1932	...	2032	2132
50	Lecco d.	0702	0802	...	0902	1002	...	1102	1202	...	1302	1402	...	1502	1602	...	1702	1802	...	1902	2002	...	2102	2201
72	Varenna-Esino d.	0725	0825	...	0925	1025	...	1125	1225	...	1325	1425	...	1525	1625	...	1725	1825	...	1925	2025	...	2125	*2247**
75	Bellano-Tartavalle Terme d.	0730	0830	...	0930	1030	...	1130	1230	...	1330	1430	...	1530	1630	...	1730	1830	...	1930	2030	...	2130	*2254**
89	**Colico** a.	0746	0846	...	0946	1046	...	1146	1246	...	1346	1446	...	1546	1646	...	1746	1846	...	1946	2046	...	2146	*2317**
130	Sondrio a.	0820	0920	...	1020	1120	...	1220	1320	...	1420	1520	...	1620	1720	...	1820	1921	...	2020	2119	...	2221	*0013**
156	**Tirano** a.	0852	0952	...	1052	1152	...	1252	1352	...	1452	1552	...	1652	1752	...	1852	1952	...	2052	2152	...	...	...

					⊕																		
Tirano d.	...	0612	...	0700	*0737**	...	0908	1008	...	1108	1208	...	1308	1408	...	1508	1608	...	1708	1808	...	1908	2008
Sondrio d.	0530	0641	...	0741	0841	...	0941	1041	...	1141	1241	...	1341	1441	...	1541	1641	...	1741	1841	...	1941	2041
Colico d.	0601	0715	...	0815	0915	...	1015	1115	...	1215	1315	...	1415	1515	...	1615	1715	...	1815	1915	...	2015	2115
Bellano-Tartavalle Terme d.	0615	0730	...	0830	0930	...	1030	1130	...	1230	1330	...	1430	1530	...	1630	1730	...	1830	1930	...	2030	2130
Varenna-Esino d.	0620	0735	...	0835	0935	...	1035	1135	...	1235	1335	...	1435	1535	...	1635	1735	...	1835	1935	...	2035	2135
Lecco d.	0654	0801	...	0901	1001	...	1101	1201	...	1301	1401	...	1501	1601	...	1701	1801	...	1901	2001	...	2101	2201
Monza d.	0727	0827	...	0927	1027	...	1127	1227	...	1327	1427	...	1527	1627	...	1727	1827	...	1927	2027	...	2127	2227
Milano Centrale a.	0740	0840	...	0940	1040	...	1140	1240	...	1340	1440	...	1540	1640	...	1740	1840	...	1940	2040	...	2140	2240

km	*2nd class only*	⚒	†						
0	**Colico** ● d.	0618	0653	0753	0853	and hourly	1853	1953	2053
27	**Chiavenna** ● a.	0649	0725	0825	0925	until	1925	2025	2125

2nd class only	†	†						🚌
Chiavenna ● d.	0635	0735	0835	0935	and hourly	1835	1935	2031
Colico ● a.	0707	0807	0907	1007	until	1907	2007	2107

🚌 TIRANO - EDOLO 🚌 — Route **A061** (Bus Perego / Autoservizi Gelmi)

	⚒	⚒	⚒	⑥	Ⓐ
Tirano d.	0840	1040	1440	1635	1700
Aprica S Pietro d.	0915	1115	1515	1715	1745
Edolo a.	0945	1145	1545	1745	1810

	⚒	⚒	⚒	⚒	⚒
Edolo d.	*0615*	0915	1115	1515	1715
Aprica S Pietro d.	0650	0940	1140	1540	1740
Tirano a.	0735	1020	1220	1620	1820

● – Also from Colico at 0553 🚌, 0701 ⚒, 0930 †; also from Chiavenna at 0519 Ⓐ 🚌, 0544 ⚒, 0614 ⚒, 0657 ⚒, 0740 ⚒, 1754 †.
* – Connection by 🚌.
⊕ – Connecting bus runs on ⚒ only.

INNSBRUCK - BRENNERO — 594

ÖBB, SAD

km									
0	**Innsbruck** Hbf 595 d.	0549	0649	0749	and	1949	2105	2205	2305
18	Matrei d.	0606	0706	0806	hourly	2006	2122	2222	2322
23	Steinach in Tirol d.	0610	0710	0810	until	2010	2126	2226	2326
37	**Brennero / Brenner** 🛂 595 a.	0627	0727	0827	⊙	2027	2143	2243	2343

Brennero / Brenner 🛂 595 d.	0733	0833	0933	and	1833	1933	2033	2154
Steinach in Tirol d.	0749	0849	0949	hourly	1849	1949	2049	2208
Matrei d.	0754	0854	0954	until	1854	1954	2054	2213
Innsbruck Hbf 595 a.	0811	0911	1011	⊙	1911	2011	2111	2230

⊙ – Also from Innsbruck at 0005, 0519, 0619, 0719, 0819, 1219, 1419, 1619, 1819; also from Brennero / Brenner at 0527, 0558, 0628, 0648 Ⓐ, 0703, 0803, 0902, 1303, 1503, 1703, 1903, 2303.

INNSBRUCK - BOLZANO / BOZEN - VERONA - BOLOGNA — 595

For high-speed trains see Table **600**. For ÖBB Nightjet trains see Table **71**. All *EC* and *RJ / RJX* services convey ✕ and are available to passengers without reservation.
Running days, timings and numbers of *ICN* trains may vary - please check your reservation. For confirmed timings please consult the *Trenitalia* journey planner at www.trenitalia.com.

km																					*EC* **1281**	*EC* **81**				*IC* **611**
					Ⓐ	Ⓐ	⚒	⚒		⚒	Ⓒ	Ⓐ			Ⓒ	Ⓒ	Ⓒ	Ⓒ			⑥⑦	①–⑤		†		A
	München Hbf **951** d.	...	...	...	...	...	...	...	...	...	...	...	...	...	...	...	...	...	...	...	0732	0732	...	...	...	...
0	**Innsbruck** Hbf 594 d.	...	...	...	...	...	...	...	...	...	...	...	...	...	...	...	...	...	...	...	0924	0924	...	...	...	...
37	**Brennero / Brenner** 🛂 594 a.	...	...	...	...	...	...	...	...	...	...	...	...	...	...	...	...	...	...	...	1000	1000	...	...	...	...
37	**Brennero / Brenner** 🛂 d.	...	...	...	...	...	...	0534	0608	0708	...	...	0738	0808	...	0838	0908	...	...	0938	1014	1014	...	...	...	...
60	Vipiteno / Sterzing d.	...	...	...	...	...	...	0553	0627	0727	...	...	0757	0827	...	0857	0927	...	...	0957	|	|	...	...	...	...
78	Fortezza / Franzensfeste d.	...	...	...	...	...	0536	0611	0645	0745	...	...	0815	0845	...	0915	0945	...	...	1015	|	|	...	...	...	...
89	Bressanone / Brixen d.	...	...	...	...	...	0545	0621	0655	0755	...	...	0825	0855	...	0925	0955	...	...	1025	1056	1056	...	...	...	...
99	Chiusa / Klausen d.	...	...	...	...	...	0553	0629	0703	0803	...	...	0833	0903	...	0933	1003	...	...	1033	|	|	...	...	...	...
127	**Bolzano / Bozen** a.	...	...	...	...	...	0617	0653	0729	0829	...	...	0859	0929	...	0959	1029	...	...	1059	1127	1127	...	...	...	...
127	**Bolzano / Bozen** 600 ⊕ d.	...	...	0500	...	0536	0620	0655	0731	0831	...	0836	0901	...	0936	1001	...	1031	...	1101	1131	1131	...	...	1136	1145
	Merano / Meran ⊕ d.	...	...	|	...	|	|	0743	|	|	...	|	0945	...	|	1045	...	|	...	1145	|	|	...	...	|	|
143	Ora / Auer d.	...	...	0512	...	0555	0633	...	0743	0843	...	0855	...	...	0955	...	...	1043	...	...	|	|	...	...	1155	1203
165	Mezzocorona d.	...	...	0525	...	0622	0650	...	0756	0856	...	0916	...	...	1016	...	...	1056	...	...	|	|	...	...	1216	1222
182	Trento 600 d.	...	...	0537	...	0638	0705	...	0810	0910	...	0937	...	...	1033	...	...	1110	...	...	1204	1204	...	...	1233	1238
206	Rovereto 600 d.	...	...	0551	...	0654	0721	...	0825	0927	...	0953	...	...	1048	...	...	1127	...	...	1219	1219	...	...	1249	1254
274	**Verona** Porta Nuova 600 a.	...	...	0646	...	0759	0817	...	0917	1017	...	1101	...	...	1154	...	...	1217	...	...	1256	1258	...	...	1354	1358
274	**Verona** Porta Nuova 600 d.	0518	0605	0703	0742	...	...	...	...	...	1026	...	...	...	...	...	...	...	1226	...	1313	1313	1326	1345	...	1415
388	**Bologna** Centrale 600 a.	0653	0739	0842	0824	...	...	...	...	...	1158	...	...	...	...	...	...	...	1358	...	|	|	1458	1524	...	1537
	Venezia Santa Lucia **605** a.	...	...	...	...	...	...	...	...	...	...	...	...	...	...	...	...	...	...	...	1425	1514	...	...	...	...

FOR ADDITIONAL TRAINS AND FOOTNOTES SEE NEXT PAGE →

595 INNSBRUCK - BOLZANO / BOZEN - VERONA - BOLOGNA

For high-speed trains see Table **600**. For ÖBB Nightjet trains see Table **71**. All *EC* and *RJ* / *RJX* services convey ✕ and are available to passengers without reservation.
Running days, timings and numbers of *ICN* trains may vary - please check your reservation. For confirmed timings please consult the *Trenitalia* journey planner at www.trenitalia.com.

				RJ 83 E	⚒					RJ 85	⚒					Ⓐ		RJ 87				Ⓐ		Ⓐ	RJ 89	Ⓐ
München Hbf **951**	d.	...	...	...	0933	...	...	...	...	...	1132	...	...	...	...	...	...	...	1333	...	...	...	...	...	...	1533	...
Innsbruck Hbf **594**	d.	...	...	...	1124	...	...	...	...	...	1324	...	...	...	...	...	...	...	1524	...	...	...	...	...	...	1724	...
Brennero / Brenner 🏛 **594**	a.	...	...	...	1200	...	...	...	...	...	1400	...	...	...	...	...	...	...	1600	...	...	...	...	...	...	1800	...
Brennero / Brenner 🏛	d.	1038	...	1138	1214	...	...	1238	1300	1338	1414	...	...	...	1438	1508	...	1538	1614	...	1638	1708	...	1738	...	1814	1800
Vipiteno / Sterzing	d.	1057	...	1157	│	...	...	1257	1320	1357	│	...	...	...	1457	1527	...	1557	│	...	1657	1727	...	1757	...	│	1819
Fortezza / Franzensfeste	d.	1115	...	1215	│	...	...	1315	1338	1415	│	...	...	...	1515	1545	...	1615	│	...	1715	1745	...	1815	...	│	1838
Bressanone / Brixen	d.	1125	...	1225	1256	...	...	1325	1348	1425	1456	...	...	...	1525	1555	...	1625	1656	...	1725	1755	...	1825	...	1856	1849
Chiusa / Klausen	d.	1133	...	1233	│	...	...	1333	1356	1433	│	...	...	...	1533	1603	...	1633	│	...	1733	1803	...	1833	...	│	1857
Bolzano / Bozen	a.	1159	...	1259	1327	...	...	1359	1423	1459	1527	...	...	...	1559	1629	...	1659	1727	...	1759	1829	...	1859	...	1927	1921
Bolzano / Bozen **600** ⊕	d.	1201	1231	1301	1331	...	1336	1401	1425	1501	1531	...	1536	...	1601	1631	1636	1701	1731	1736	1801	1831	1836	1901	1906	1931	1935
Merano / Meran ⊕	d.	1245	│	1345	│	...	│	1445	│	1545	│	...	│	...	1645	│	│	1745	│	│	1845	│	│	1944	│	│	2015
Ora / Auer	d.	...	1243	...	│	...	1401	...	1437	...	│	...	1555	...	...	1643	1655	...	│	1755	...	1843	1855	...	1922	│	...
Mezzocorona	d.	...	1256	...	│	...	1416	...	1450	...	│	...	1616	...	...	1656	1716	...	│	1816	...	1856	1916	...	1942	│	...
Trento **600**	d.	...	1310	...	1404	...	1433	...	1504	...	1604	...	1633	...	...	1710	1733	...	1804	1833	...	1910	1933	...	1955	2004	...
Rovereto **600**	d.	...	1325	...	1419	...	1449	...	1519	...	1619	...	1649	...	...	1725	1749	...	1819	1848	...	1925	1949	...	2012	2019	...
Verona Porta Nuova **600**	a.	...	1414	...	1501	...	1554	...	1614	...	1658	...	1754	...	...	1814	1857	...	1901	1954	...	2014	2054	...	2111	2059	...
Verona Porta Nuova **600**	d.	...	1426	...	1513	1516	...	...	1626	...	1710	1717	...	...	...	1826	...	...	1915	...	...	2104	...	...	...	2114	...
Bologna Centrale **600**	a.	...	1603	...	1608	1658	...	...	1803	...	│	1857	...	...	...	2003	...	...	2016	...	...	2243	...	...	...	2211	...
Venezia Santa Lucia **605**	a.	...	...	...	...	...	...	...		...	1825	...	...	...	...	...	...	...	...	...	...	...	...	...	...	...	...

					Ⓐ		ICN 763 ⑥⑦ C	†		RJX 185 D	
München Hbf **951**	d.	...	...	...	...	...	...	...	...	...	...
Innsbruck Hbf **594**	d.	...	...	...	...	...	...	...	...	2004	...
Brennero / Brenner 🏛 **594**	a.	...	...	...	...	...	...	...	...	2040	...
Brennero / Brenner 🏛	d.	...	1838	1908	...	1938	1954	...	2038	2050	2151
Vipiteno / Sterzing	d.	...	1857	1927	...	1957	2018	...	2056	2116	2210
Fortezza / Franzensfeste	d.	...	1915	1945	...	2015	2037	...	2122	│	2228
Bressanone / Brixen	d.	...	1925	1955	...	2025	2048	...	2132	2144	2238
Chiusa / Klausen	d.	...	1933	2003	...	2033	2059	...	2139	│	2246
Bolzano / Bozen	a.	...	1959	2029	...	2059	2126	...	2200	2215	2310
Bolzano / Bozen **600** ⊕	d.	1936	2001	2031	2036	2101	2130	2136	2201	...	2315
Merano / Meran ⊕	d.	│	2044	│	│	2144	│	│	2244	...	│
Ora / Auer	d.	1955	...	2043	2055	...	2144	2155	...	...	2331
Mezzocorona	d.	2016	...	2056	2116	...	2200	2216	...	...	2351
Trento **600**	d.	2033	...	2110	2133	...	2216	2233	...	...	0009
Rovereto **600**	d.	2049	...	2125	2149	...	2232	2249	...	...	...
Verona Porta Nuova **600**	a.	2154	...	2217	2254	...	2319	2351	...	...	...
Verona Porta Nuova **600**	d.	...	...	...	...	...	2336	...	...	...	...
Bologna Centrale **600**	a.	...	...	...	...	...	...	...	...	...	...
Venezia Santa Lucia **605**	a.	...	...	...	...	...	...	...	...	...	...

		⚒		⚒		⚒			RJX 184 D		ICN 764 ⑥⑦ C
Venezia Santa Lucia **605**	d.	...	...	...	...	...	...	...	...	...	...
Bologna Centrale **600**	d.	...	...	...	...	...	...	...	...	...	...
Verona Porta Nuova **600**	a.	...	...	...	...	...	...	...	...	...	0530
Verona Porta Nuova **600**	d.	...	...	...	...	0520	...	...	...	...	0600
Rovereto **600**	d.	...	...	...	...	0607	...	...	...	...	0701
Trento **600**	d.	...	0528a	0555	...	0632	0632	0640	...	...	0717
Mezzocorona	d.	...	0544a	0610	...	0646	0646	0653	...	...	0730
Ora / Auer	d.	...	0603a	0629	...	0706	0706	0711	...	...	0747
Merano / Meran ⊕	d.	...	│	│	0600f	│	│	│	...	0713	│
Bolzano / Bozen **600** ⊕	a.	...	0618a	0645	0650f	0725	0725	0728	...	0800	0808
Bolzano / Bozen	d.	0602	0632	...	0702	...	...	0732	0750	0802	0811
Chiusa / Klausen	d.	0625	0655	...	0725	...	...	0755	│	0825	0837
Bressanone / Brixen	d.	0633	0703	...	0733	...	...	0803	0818	0833	0847
Fortezza / Franzensfeste	d.	0645	0715	...	0745	...	...	0815	│	0845	0857
Vipiteno / Sterzing	d.	0703	0733	...	0803	...	...	0833	0847	0903	0916
Brennero / Brenner 🏛	a.	0722	0752	...	0822	...	...	0852	0910	0922	0935
Brennero / Brenner 🏛 **594**	d.	...	...	...	...	...	...	...	0920	...	...
Innsbruck Hbf **594**	a.	...	...	...	...	...	...	...	0956	...	...
München Hbf **951**	a.	...	...	...	...	...	...	...	...	...	...

		⚒		⚒	Ⓐ					Ⓐ	RJ 88	Ⓒ	⑥			†		RJ 86		⚒		Ⓒ			⚒	RJ 84	
Venezia Santa Lucia **605**	d.	...	...	...	...	...	...	...	...	...	...	...	...	...	...	...	...	...	...	...	...	...	...	...	...	1135	...
Bologna Centrale **600**	d.	...	...	...	0520	0605	...	...	0710	...	0745	...	...	...	0810	...	...	0952	...	...	...	1010	...	...	1110	│	...
Verona Porta Nuova **600**	a.	...	...	...	0659	0743	...	...	0835	...	0847	...	...	...	0935	...	...	1049	...	...	...	1135	...	...	1240	1252	...
Verona Porta Nuova **600**	d.	0606	...	0706	...	...	0750	...	...	0849	0901	...	0906	...	...	0953	...	1101	...	1106	1150	1150	...	1206	...	1301	...
Rovereto **600**	d.	0707	...	0807	...	...	0839	...	...	0936	0943	...	1007	...	...	1041	...	1143	...	1207	1239	1239	...	1307	...	1343	...
Trento **600**	d.	0732	...	0832	...	...	0854	...	...	0952	0959	...	1032	...	...	1058	...	1159	...	1232	1254	1254	...	1332	...	1359	...
Mezzocorona	d.	0746	...	0846	...	...	0905	...	...	1004	│	...	1046	...	...	1109	...	│	...	1246	1305	1305	...	1346	...	│	...
Ora / Auer	d.	0806	...	0906	...	...	0919	...	...	1019	│	...	1106	...	...	1123	...	│	...	1306	1319	1319	...	1406	...	│	...
Merano / Meran ⊕	d.	│	0816	│	...	...	│	0916	...	│	│	1016	│	...	...	│	1116	│	1216	│	│	│	1316	│	...	│	1416
Bolzano / Bozen **600** ⊕	a.	0823	0900	0925	...	...	0930	1000	...	1041	1034	1100	1125	...	...	1135	1200	1231	1300	1325	1330	1330	1400	1423	...	1431	1500
Bolzano / Bozen	d.	...	0902	...	...	...	0932	1002	...	...	1036	1102	...	...	...	...	1202	1234	1302	...	1332	1332	1402	...	...	1434	1502
Chiusa / Klausen	d.	...	0925	...	...	...	0955	1025	...	...	│	1125	...	...	...	...	1225	│	1325	...	1355	1355	1425	...	...	│	1525
Bressanone / Brixen	d.	...	0933	...	...	...	1003	1033	...	...	1104	1133	...	...	...	...	1233	1304	1333	...	1403	1403	1433	...	...	1504	1533
Fortezza / Franzensfeste	d.	...	0945	...	...	...	1015	1045	...	...	│	1145	...	...	...	...	1245	│	1345	...	1415	1415	1445	...	...	│	1545
Vipiteno / Sterzing	d.	...	1003	...	...	...	1033	1103	...	...	│	1203	...	...	...	...	1303	│	1403	...	1433	1433	1503	...	...	│	1603
Brennero / Brenner 🏛	a.	...	1022	...	...	...	1101	1122	...	...	1148	1222	...	...	...	...	1322	1348	1422	...	1456	1456	1522	...	...	1548	1622
Brennero / Brenner 🏛 **594**	d.	...	...	...	...	...	...	...	...	...	1200	...	...	...	...	...	...	1400	...	...	...	...	...	...	...	1600	...
Innsbruck Hbf **594**	a.	...	...	...	...	...	...	...	...	...	1236	...	...	...	...	...	...	1436	...	...	...	...	...	...	...	1636	...
München Hbf **951**	a.	...	...	...	...	...	...	...	...	...	1427	...	...	...	...	...	...	1627	...	...	...	...	...	...	...	1828	...

		Ⓐ	Ⓒ			Ⓐ	RJ 82 F					Ⓐ	EC 80							Ⓒ	IC 610 G			Ⓑ	Ⓐ		
Venezia Santa Lucia **605**	d.	...	...	...	...	...	...	...	...	...	...	...	1535	...	...	...	...	...	...	...	...	...	...	...	...	...	...
Bologna Centrale **600**	d.	1205	1210	...	...	...	1352	...	1410	...	...	...	│	...	...	1610	...	...	...	...	1703	1810	...	1910	...	2005	2105
Verona Porta Nuova **600**	a.	1335	1338	...	...	...	1446	...	1535	...	...	...	1652	...	...	1735	...	...	...	...	1835	1935	...	2048	...	2135	2235
Verona Porta Nuova **600**	d.	1350	1350	...	1406	...	1458	...	1550	...	1606	...	1701	...	...	1750	...	1806	...	...	1845	1950	2006	...	2106	2155	...
Rovereto **600**	d.	1439	1439	...	1507	...	1543	...	1639	...	1707	...	1743	...	...	1839	...	1907	...	...	1933	2039	2107	...	2207	2246	...
Trento **600**	d.	1454	1454	...	1532	...	1559	...	1654	...	1732	...	1759	...	...	1854	...	1932	...	...	1949	2054	2132	...	2232	2301	...
Mezzocorona	d.	1505	1505	...	1546	...	│	...	1705	...	1746	...	│	...	...	1905	...	1946	...	...	2001	2105	2146	...	2246	2312	...
Ora / Auer	d.	1519	1519	...	1606	...	│	...	1719	...	1806	...	│	...	...	1919	...	2006	...	...	2018	2119	2206	...	2306	2326	...
Merano / Meran ⊕	d.	│	│	1516	│	1546	│	1616	│	1716	│	1746	│	...	1816	│	1916	│	...	1946	│	│	│	...	│	│	...
Bolzano / Bozen **600** ⊕	a.	1530	1530	1600	1625	1625	1631	1700	1730	1800	1825	1825	1831	...	1900	1930	2000	2025	...	2027	2031	2130	2225	...	2330	2339	...
Bolzano / Bozen	d.	1532	1532	1602	...	1627	1634	1701	1732	1802	...	1827	1834	...	1902	1932	2002	...	2032	2032	...	2132	...	...	...	...	...
Chiusa / Klausen	d.	1555	1555	1625	...	1649	│	1722	1755	1825	...	1849	│	...	1925	1955	2025	...	2055	2055	...	2155	...	...	...	...	...
Bressanone / Brixen	d.	1603	1603	1633	...	1657	1704	1730	1803	1833	...	1857	1904	...	1933	2003	2033	...	2103	2103	...	2203	...	...	...	...	...
Fortezza / Franzensfeste	d.	1615	1615	1645	...	1707	│	1745	1815	1845	...	1907	│	...	1945	2015	2045	...	2115	2115	...	2215	...	...	...	...	...
Vipiteno / Sterzing	d.	1633	1633	1703	...	1723	│	1803	1833	1903	...	1932	│	...	2003	2033	2103	...	2133	2133	...	2233	...	...	...	...	...
Brennero / Brenner 🏛	a.	1656	1656	1722	...	1744	1748	1822	1856	1922	...	1958	1952	...	2022	2056	2122	...	2151	2151	...	2256	...	...	...	...	...
Brennero / Brenner 🏛 **594**	d.	...	...	...	...	...	1800	...	...	...	...	...	2000	...	...	...	...	...	...	...	...	...	...	...	...	...	...
Innsbruck Hbf **594**	a.	...	...	...	...	...	1836	...	...	...	...	...	2036	...	...	...	...	...	...	...	...	...	...	...	...	...	...
München Hbf **951**	a.	...	...	...	...	...	2026	...	...	...	...	...	2228	...	...	...	...	...	...	...	...	...	...	...	...	...	...

A – To Bari (Table **615**).
C – 🛏 1, 2 cl., ▬ 2 cl. (4 berth) 🚃2 Brennero - Roma Termini (a. 0615 ①⑦ / d. 2300⑤⑥) and v.v.
D – 🚃12 ✕ Wien - Bolzano and v.v.
E – To Ancona Apr. 17 - Oct. 5.
F – From Ancona Apr. 18 - Oct. 6.
G – From Lecce (Table **615**).
a – Ⓐ only.
e – Venezia **Mestre**.
f – ⚒ only.

⊕ – **Bolzano - Merano is subject to alteration June 15 - August 9.**
Other trains Bolzano - Merano at 0545⚒, 0624⚒, 0655†, 0735⚒, 0801, 0835⚒, 0935, 1001Ⓐ, 1035, 1135, 1235, 1335, 1435†, 1535, 1635, 1735, 1835⚒, 1935⑥. Other trains Merano - Bolzano at 0633⚒, 0654Ⓐ, 0746⚒, 0846⚒, 0946, 1046, 1146, 1246, 1346, 1446, 1546Ⓒ, 1646, 1746Ⓒ, 1846⚒, 1946Ⓐ, 2046, 2146.

FOR OTHER TRAINS SEE PREVIOUS PAGE.

FOR 🚌 SERVICE BOLZANO - PLAN AND V.V. SEE NEXT PAGE →

595 BOLZANO - PLAN

www.suedtirolmobil.info Route 350

km									
		⚒							
0	**Bolzano / Bozen** bus station d.	0628	0728	0828	0928	and hourly until	1728	1828	1928
	Ponte Gardena / Waidbruck d.	0657	0757	0857	0957		1757	1857	1957
	Ortisei / St Ulrich d.	0727	0827	0927	1027		1827	1927	2027
	Santa / St Cristina d.	0736	0836	0936	1036		1836	1936	2036
	Selva / Wolkenstein d.	0748	0848	0948	1048		1848	1948	2048
	Plan a.	0752	0852	0952	1052		1852	1952	2052

	⚒							
Plan d.	0559	0634	0732	0834	and hourly until	1634	1734	1834
Selva / Wolkenstein d.	0602	0637	0735	0837		1637	1737	1837
Santa / St Cristina Rathaus d.	0614	0649	0749	0849		1649	1749	1849
Ortisei / St Ulrich d.	0626	0701	0801	0901		1701	1801	1901
Ponte Gardena / Waidbruck a.	0654	0729	0829	0929		1729	1829	1929
Bolzano / Bozen bus station a.	0722	0757	0857	0957		1757	1857	1957

596 TRENTO - MALÉ - MEZZANA

Trentino Trasporti

Mezzocorona Ferrovia is adjacent to Mezzocorona FS station. Operator Trentino Trasporti (www.trentinotrasporti.it).

km																								
		†	⚒	⚒	†	⚒	⚒	†	⚒	⚒	⚒	†	⚒	⚒	†	⚒	⚒	†	⚒	⚒	†	⚒	⚒	†
0	**Trento** d.	0610	0612	0710	0810	0810	0932	1010	1021	1104	1206	1210	1326	1345	1410	1454	1555	1610	1718	1809	1810	1842	1935	2010
17	Mezzocorona Ferrovia d.	0637	0639	0740	0837	0839	0958	1037	1047	1130	1232	1237	1352	1414	1437	1521	1622	1637	1739	1935	1837	1908	2001	2040
22	Mezzolombardo d.	0644	0647	0753	0844	0847	1006	1044	1055	1138	1240	1244	1400	1422	1444	1528	1631	1644	1746	1943	1844	1616	2008	2044
45	Cles d.	0722	0729	0831	0922	0925	1043	1122	1132	1222	1320	1322	1435	1459	1522	1611	1709	1722	1819	1918	1922	1953	2044	2122
56	Malé d.	0746	0755	0857	0946	0951	1109	1146	1157	1250	1347	1346	1455	1527	1546	1637	1736	1746	1840	1936	1944	2016	2104	2144
66	**Mezzana** a.	0803	...	0913	1003	1007	1125	1203	1213	1309	1408	1403	...	1544	1603	1653	1753	1803	1857	...	...	...	...	...

	⚒	†	⚒	⚒	⚒	†	⚒	⚒	†	⚒	⚒	†	⚒	⚒	†	⚒	⚒	†	⚒	⚒	†	⚒	†
Mezzana d.	...	...	0600	0657	...	0842	0933	1036	1042	1137	1230	1242	1346	1425	1442	...	1619	1642	1715	1806	1842	1921	...
Malé d.	0530	0600	0618	0717	0820	0900	0953	1055	1100	1156	1251	1300	1407	1444	1500	1511	1639	1700	1735	1825	1900	1943	2000
Cles d.	0550	0624	0637	0755	0847	0924	1019	1121	1124	1223	1319	1324	1433	1512	1524	1533	1707	1724	1801	1853	1924	2008	2024
Mezzolombardo d.	0626	0701	0711	0832	0926	1001	1056	1159	1021	1302	1359	1401	1512	1550	1601	1609	1747	1801	1842	1931	2001	2044	2101
Mezzocorona Ferrovia d.	0633	0708	0717	0840	0933	1008	1103	1207	1208	1310	1406	1408	1520	1557	1608	1616	1755	1808	1849	1938	2008	2052	2108
Trento a.	0700	0734	0737	0806	0959	1034	1129	1233	1234	1339	1434	1434	1544	1623	1634	1646	1824	1834	1915	2004	2034	2117	2134

597 BRESSANONE / BRIXEN - CORTINA, S. CANDIDO / INNICHEN and LIENZ

ÖBB, SAD 2nd class

Due to engineering work the railway is closed Fortezza / Franzensfeste - Brunico / Bruneck until December 2025. Subject to alteration on and around Italian and Austrian holiday dates.

BRESSANONE / BRIXEN - S. CANDIDO / INNICHEN - LIENZ

km																								
				Ⓐ																				
	Bressanone / Brixen ⊖ d.	...	...	*0510**	...	*0610**	*0710**	*0810**	...	*0910**	*1010**	*1110**	...	*1210**	*1310**	*1410**	...	*1510**	*1610**	*1710**	...	*1810**	*1910**	...
0	**Fortezza / Franzensfeste** d.	...	...	|	...	|	|	|	...	|	|	|	...	|	|	|	...	|	|	|	...	|	|	...
33	Brunico / Bruneck ⊖ ● d.	...	...	0615	...	0715	0815	0915	...	1015	1115	1215	...	1315	1415	1515	...	1615	1715	1815	...	1915	2015	...
61	Dobbiaco / Toblach ● d.	...	...	0651	...	0751	0851	0951	...	1051	1151	1251	...	1351	1451	1551	...	1651	1751	1851	...	1951	2051	...
65	**S. Candido / Innichen** ● a.	...	...	0655	...	0755	0855	0955	...	1055	1155	1255	...	1355	1455	1555	...	1655	1755	1855	...	1955	2055	...
65	**S. Candido / Innichen** 🏛 d.	0644	0716	0716	...	0805	0905	1005	...	1105	1205	1305	...	1405	1505	1605	...	1705	1805	1916	...	2016	...	...
78	Sillian 🏛 d.	0658	0730	0730	...	0830	0930	1030	...	1130	1230	1330	...	1430	1530	1630	...	1730	1830	1930	...	2030	...	...
108	**Lienz** a.	0735	0809	0809	...	0909	1009	1109	...	1209	1309	1409	...	1509	1609	1709	...	1809	1909	2009	...	2109	...	...

Lienz d.	...	0550	0645	...	0750	0850	0950	...	1050	1150	1250	...	1350	1450	1550	...	1650	1750	1850	...	...	1950	...
Sillian d.	...	0630	0730	...	0842	0942	1042	...	1142	1242	1342	...	1442	1542	1642	...	1742	1842	1930	...	...	2030	...
S. Candido / Innichen 🏛 a.	...	0643	0743	...	0855	0955	1055	...	1155	1255	1355	...	1455	1555	1655	...	1755	1855	1943	...	...	2043	...
S. Candido / Innichen 🏛 d.	0605	0705	0805	...	0905	1005	1105	...	1205	1305	1405	...	1505	1605	1705	...	1805	1905	...	...	2035	...	...
Dobbiaco / Toblach d.	0610	0710	0810	...	0910	1010	1110	...	1210	1310	1410	...	1510	1610	1710	...	1810	1910	...	...	2040	...	...
Brunico / Bruneck ⊖ a.	0644	0744	0844	...	0944	1044	1144	...	1244	1344	1444	...	1544	1644	1744	...	1844	1944	...	...	2114	...	...
Fortezza / Franzensfeste a.	|	|	|	...	|	|	|	...	|	|	|	...	|	|	|	...	|	|	...	...	|	...	...
Bressanone / Brixen ⊖ a.	*0743**	*0843**	*0943**	...	*1043**	*1143**	*1243**	...	*1343**	*1443**	*1543**	...	*1643**	*1743**	*1843**	...	*1943**	*2043**	...	...	*2213**	...	...

🚌 DOBBIACO / TOBLACH - CORTINA 🚌

Route 445 www.suedtirolmobil.info

km										
0	Dobbiaco / Toblach bus station d.	0705	0920	1120	1420	1620	1820	...	...	...
	Dobbiaco / Toblach Bahnhof d.	0710	0925	1125	1425	1625	1825	...	...	...
	Cortina a.	0755	1010	1210	1510	1710	1910	...	...	...

Cortina d.	0820	1020	1320	1520	1720	1920	...	...	...
Dobbiaco Bahnhof a.	0900	1100	1400	1600	1800	2000	...	...	...
Dobbiaco bus station a.	0905	1105	1405	1605	1805	2005	...	...	...

⊖ – Full 🚌 service Bressanone / Brixen - Brunico / Bruneck and v.v.: from Bressanone / Brixen at 0510 Ⓐ, 0540 Ⓐ, 0610 and every 30 minutes until 1940, 2040; from Brunico / Bruneck at 0521 Ⓐ, 0551 Ⓐ, 0621 Ⓐ, 0651 and every 30 minutes until 2021, 2121.

● – Also: Brunico / Bruneck - S. Candido / Innichen at 0645 and hourly until 2145; S. Candido / Innichen - Brunico / Bruneck at 0635 and hourly until 1935.

598 MERANO / MERAN - MALLES / MALS

SAD 2nd class

'Ferrovia della Val Venosta'. Operator SAD (www.sad.it).

km																							
		Ⓐ					Ⓐ											Ⓐ			🚌	🚌	🚌
0	**Merano / Meran** d.	0534	0636	0716	0746	0816	0846	0916	0946	and at	1516	1546	1616	1646	1716	1746	1816	1846	1916	1946	2052	2152	2252
	Töll d.	0546	0652	0731	0800	0830	0900	0930	1000	the same	1530	1600	1630	1700	1730	1800	1830	1900	1930	2000	2105	2205	2305
37	Silandro / Schlanders d.	0621	0729	0814	0844	0914	0944	1014	1044	minutes	1614	1644	1714	1744	1814	1844	1914	1944	2014	2044	2145	2245	2345
	Laas a.	0629	0735	0821	0851	0921	0951	1021	1051	past each	1621	1651	1721	1751	1821	1851	1921	1951	2021	2051	2156	2256	2356
60	**Malles / Mals** a.	*0700**	*0807**	*0852**	*0922**	*0952**	*1022**	*1052**	*1122**	hour until	*1652**	*1722**	*1752**	*1822**	*1852**	*1922**	*1952**	*2022**	*2052**	*2122**	2222	2322	0022

	Ⓐ					Ⓐ									Ⓐ				🚌	🚌	🚌⚒
Malles / Mals d.	*0500**	*0522**	*0602**	*0648**	*0706**	*0736**	*0806**	*0836**	and at	*1506**	*1536**	*1606**	*1636**	*1706**	*1736**	*1806**	*1836**	...	*1906**	2006	2106	2216
Laas	0531	0553	0633	0719	0737	0807	0837	0907	the same	1537	1607	1637	1707	1737	1807	1837	1907	...	1937	2032	2132	2240
Silandro / Schlanders d.	0538	0601	0641	0727	0749	0819	0849	0917	minutes	1549	1619	1649	1719	1749	1819	1849	1919	...	1949	2045	2145	2255
Töll a.	0610	0636	0717	|	0829	0859	0929	0959	past each	1629	1659	1729	1759	1829	1859	1929	1959	...	2029	2123	2223	2333
Merano / Meran a.	0626	0650	0732	0813	0843	0913	0943	1013	hour until	1643	1713	1743	1813	1843	1913	1943	2013	...	2043	2136	2236	2346

* – Connection by 🚌.

599 ITALIAN LAKES (LAGO MAGGIORE, GARDA, COMO)

Lago Maggiore: ⛴ services link Arona, Stresa, Baveno, Laveno, Luino and Locarno throughout the year on an irregular schedule.
Operator: Navigazione sul Lago Maggiore, P. le Baracca 1, 28041 Arona, Italy. ✆ +39 (0)322 233 200. www.navigazionelaghi.it

Lago di Garda: ⛴ services link Desenzano, Peschiera, Garda, Salo, Gardone and Riva, (April to October only), on an irregular schedule with a very limited service at other times.
Operator: Navigazione sul Lago di Garda, Piazza Matteotti 1, 25015 Desenzano del Garda, Italy. ✆ +39 (0)30 914 9511. www.navigazionelaghi.it

Lago di Como: ⛴ services link Como, Bellagio, Menaggio, Varenna, Bellano and Colico (April to September only) on an irregular schedule.
Operator: Navigazione Lago di Como, Via Per Cernobbio 18, 22100 Como, Italy. ✆ +39 (0)31 579 211. www.navigazionelaghi.it

Hydrofoil service (valid until May 31):

	⚒⊡		†	⚒	⚒	†	⚒	⊖			
Como d.	0733	0840	1100	1215	1330	1400	1420	1710	1840	1910	...
Tremezzo d.	0820	|	1148	1252	1417	1439	1459	1757	1919	1957	...
Bellagio d.	0814	0920	1158	1303	1425	1447	1507	1816	1926	2004	...
Menaggio d.	0808	0928	1206	1310	1433	1455	1515	1806	1932	2011	...
Bellano d.	...	0937	1216	...	1443	1507	1527	...	1944	...	...
Colico a.	...	1010	1248	...	...	1535	1555	...	2012	...	...

	⚒	⚒	†	⚒	†		⚒	†	⚒		
Colico d.	0601	...	0706	...	...	1015	...	1355	...	1603	...
Bellano d.	0624	...	0730	...	...	1040	...	1429	1443	1636	...
Menaggio d.	0635	0703	0741	0808	0848	|	1310	1448	1517	1654	1808
Bellagio d.	0642	0712	0747	0814	0856	1057	1326	1500	1527	1704	1820
Tremezzo d.	0647	0718	0753	0820	0902	|	1331	1508	|	1710	|
Como a.	0728	0805	0830	0857	0940	1142	1409	1555	1602	1750	1858

⊡ – Calling order is Menaggio, Bellagio, Tremezzo.
⊖ – Calling order is Tremezzo, Menaggio, Bellagio.

ITALY

600 HIGH-SPEED SERVICES

Italo, Trenitalia

Subject to alteration August 11–31. All trains Ⓡ and 🍸. *FR* trains are operated by Trenitalia (www.trenitalia.com). *ITA* trains are operated by Italo (www.italotreno.it). Trenitalia tickets and passes are not valid on Italo trains. Italo tickets are not valid on Trenitalia trains. Trains may use different numbers for part of their journey.

TORINO - MILANO - BOLOGNA - FIRENZE - ROMA - NAPOLI - SALERNO

km		*FA* 8333	*FR* 9503	*FA* 8863	*FR* 9505	*FR* 9601	*ITA* 9907	*ITA* 9907	*FR* 9603	*FR* 9511	*ITA* 9967	*FR* 9605	*FR* 9301	*ITA* 8111	*ITA* 9969	*FR* 9607	*FR* 9303	*FR* 9515	*ITA* 9971	*ITA* 9971	*FR* 9604	*ITA* 9917	*FR* 9611	*FR* 9519	*ITA* 9998
			⚒			Ⓐ		⑦	Ⓐ			⚒	⚒		①–⑥					①–⑥					
		B		B						E			A	B			⊡	R				Q ❦			
0	**Torino** Porta Nuova ..... **605** d.	...	...	...	...	...	...	...	...	...	...	...	...	...	...	0550	...	...	...	0600	...	0625	0650	0700	...
6	**Torino** Porta Susa △ .. **605** d.	...	...	...	...	...	...	...	...	...	...	...	...	...	...	0600	...	...	...	0610	...	0635	0700	0710	...
148	**Milano** Centrale .... **605** a.	...	...	...	...	...	...	...	...	...	...	...	...	...	...	0650	...	...	...	0657	...	0730	0750	0800	...
148	**Milano** Centrale .... **605** d.	...	...	...	0510	0520	0540	0540	0600	0610	0615	0635	...	0640	0645	0700	...	0710	0715	0715	0730	0740	0800	0810	0815
158	**Milano** Rogoredo .... d.	...	...	...	0520**u**	0530**u**	0550	0550	|	0620**u**	0625	|	...	|	|	|	...	0720	0725	0725	0740	|	|	0820	0825
299	Reggio Emilia AV .... d.	...	...	...	0556	0610	0628	0628	|	0656	|	|	...	0728	|	|	...	0756	|	|	|	0828	|	0856	|
363	**Bologna** Centrale ● .... **620** a.	...	...	...	0624	0634	0654	0654	0704	0724	|	|	...	0754	0749	0804	...	0824	|	|	|	0854	0904	0924	|
363	**Bologna** Centrale ● .... **620** d.	...	...	...	0627	0637	0657	0657	0707	0727	|	|	0712	0757	0752	0807	0812	0827	|	|	|	0857	0907	0927	|
455	**Firenze** SMN .... **620** a.	...	...	...	0704	|	0735	0735	|	0804	|	|	0750	0835	|	|	0850	0904	|	|	|	0935	|	1004	|
455	**Firenze** SMN .... **620** d.	...	0600	...	0714	|	0743	0743	|	0814	|	|	0759	0843	|	|	0859	0914	|	|	|	0943	|	1014	|
	Roma Tiburtina .... **620** a.	...	|	...	0854	|	0910	0910	|	|	|	|	0924**s**	1009	0950	|	|	|	|	|	|	1108	|	|	|
716	**Roma** Termini .... **620** a.	...	0749	...	0904	0840	0919	0919	0910	0949	0924	0934	0940	1019	1000	1011	1035	1049	1025	1025	1040	1119	1110	1149	1125
716	**Roma** Termini .... **640** d.	0730	0805	0858	0915	0853	...	0930	0925	...	0941	0953	...	1030	...	1025	...	1100	1040	1040	1053	...	1125	1200	1140
926	**Napoli** Afragola .... **640** a.	0834	0904**s**	1001	|	0948**s**	...	1027	|	...	1036	1051**s**	...	|	...	|	...	1156	1139	1139	1148**s**	...	|	1257	1236
938	**Napoli** Centrale .... **640** a.	|	0918	|	1028	1003	...	1043	1033	...	1053	1103	...	1143	...	1138	...	1213	1153	1153	1203	...	1233	1315	1253
938	**Napoli** Centrale .... **640** d.	|	...	|	1050	...	...	...	...	...	...	...	...	1200	...	...	...	1225	1205	1205	...	...	...	1325	...
988	**Salerno** .... **640** a.	0905	...	1030	1127	...	...	...	...	...	...	...	...	1244	...	...	...	1302	1251	1251	...	...	...	1406	...

	FR 9613	*ITA* 9919	*FR* 9391	*FR* 9615	*FR* 9583	*ITA* 9975	*FR* 9617	*ITA* 9923	*FR* 9311	*FR* 9619	*FR* 9527	*FR* 9805	*ITA* 9977	*ITA* 9927	*FR* 9623	*FR* 9587	*ITA* 9979	*FR* 9625	*ITA* 9931	*FR* 9627	*FR* 9535	*ITA* 9981	*ITA* 9935	*FR* 9631
				Ⓐ						Ⓐ								Ⓐ		①–⑥				Ⓑ
		g			B							E			B	B					B			
Torino Porta Nuova .... **605** d.	...	0730	0740	...	0800	...	...	0830	0840	...	...	0910	...	0930	...	1000	...	...	...	...	1100	...	1130	...
Torino Porta Susa △ .... **605** d.	...	0740	0750	...	0810	...	...	0840	0850	...	...	0920	...	0940	...	1010	...	...	...	...	1110	...	1140	...
Milano Centrale .... **605** a.	...	0830	0845**d**	...	0902	...	...	0930	0945**d**	...	...	1010**d**	...	1030	...	1102	...	...	...	...	1202	...	1230	...
Milano Centrale .... **605** d.	0830	0840	0848**d**	0858	0910	0915	0935	0940	0948**d**	0958	1010	1013**d**	1015	1040	1058	1110	1115	1125	1140	1158	1210	1220	1240	1300
Milano Rogoredo .... d.	|	0850	0905	|	0920	0925	|	0950	1005	|	1020**u**	1045	1025	1050	|	1120	1125	1140**u**	1150	|	1220	1230	1250	|
Reggio Emilia AV .... d.	|	0928	0940	|	0956	|	|	1028	1042	|	1056	1120	|	1128	|	1156	|	|	1228	|	1256	|	1328	|
Bologna Centrale ● .... **620** a.	0934	0954	1009	1004	1024	|	|	1054	1109	1104	1124	1142	|	1154	1204	1224	|	1234	1254	1304	1324	|	1354	1404
Bologna Centrale ● .... **620** d.	0937	0957	1012	1007	1027	|	|	1057	1112	1107	1127	...	|	1157	1207	1227	|	1237	1257	1307	1327	|	1357	1407
Firenze SMN .... **620** a.	|	1035	1050	|	1104	|	|	1135	1150	|	1204	...	|	1235	|	1304	|	|	1335	|	1404	|	1435	|
Firenze SMN .... **620** d.	|	1043	1059	|	1114	|	|	1143	1159	|	1214	...	|	1243	|	1314	|	|	1343	|	1414	|	1443	|
Roma Tiburtina .... **620** a.	|	1209	1224	|	1240	|	|	1309	1322	|	1340	...	|	1409	|	1440	|	|	1509	|	1540	|	1609	|
Roma Termini .... **620** a.	1140	1219	1235	1215	1249	1225	1239	1319	1335	1310	1349	...	1325	1419	1410	1449	1425	1443	1519	1510	1549	1525	1619	1615
Roma Termini .... **640** d.	1155	1230	1255	...	1300	1240	...	...	1353	1325	1400	...	1340	1430	1425	1505	...	1453	1530	1525	1605	1540	1630	1625
Napoli Afragola .... **640** a.	1250**s**	1327	1348**s**	...	1356	1335	...	...	1448**s**	|	1456	...	1437	1527	1520	1604	...	1548**s**	1625	|	1703	1636	1727	|
Napoli Centrale .... **640** a.	1310	1343	1408	...	1413	1353	...	...	1503	1433	1512	...	1453	1543	|	1620	...	1603	1643	1633	|	1653	1743	1733
Napoli Centrale .... **640** d.	...	...	...	...	1425	...	...	...	...	...	1525	...	1505	...	|	1630	...	...	1700	...	|	...	...	...
Salerno .... **640** a.	...	...	...	...	1503	...	...	...	...	...	1606	...	1552	...	1614	1708	...	...	1739	...	1752	...	...	...

	FR 9539	*ITA* 9983	*FR* 9633	*ITA* 9939	*FR* 9637	*FR* 9543	*ITA* 9985	*FR* 9639	*ITA* 8103	*ITA* 8143	*FR* 9321	*FR* 9641	*FR* 9547	*ITA* 9987	*FR* 9643	*ITA* 9947	*FR* 9323	*FR* 9323	*FR* 9645	*FR* 9551	*ITA* 9989	*FR* 9647	*ITA* 9951	*FR* 9325
			Ⓐ		Ⓑ				①–⑥	⑦					Ⓑ		①–④	⑤–⑦						
				F ❦				B	C	B			S					T				J		
Torino Porta Nuova .... **605** d.	...	...	...	1220	...	1300	...	...	1320	1320	1340	1350	...	...	...	1430	1440	...	1450	...	...	...	1530	1540
Torino Porta Susa △ .... **605** d.	...	...	...	1230	...	1310	...	...	1330	1330	1350	1400	...	...	...	1440	1450	1450	1500	...	...	...	1540	1550
Milano Centrale .... **605** a.	...	...	...	1330	...	1402	...	...	1430	1430	1445**d**	1450	...	...	...	1530	1545**d**	1545**d**	1550	...	...	...	1630	1645**d**
Milano Centrale .... **605** d.	1310	1320	1330	1340	1358	1410	1420	1430	1440	1440	1448**d**	1500	1510	1515	1525	1540	1548**d**	1548**d**	1600	1610	1615	1630	1640	1648**d**
Milano Rogoredo .... d.	1320**u**	1330	1340**u**	|	|	1420	1430	|	|	|	1505	|	1520**u**	1525	1540**u**	1550	1605	1605	|	1620**u**	1625	1640**u**	1650	1705
Reggio Emilia AV .... d.	1356	|	|	1428	|	1456	|	|	1528	1528	1542	|	1556	|	|	1628	1642	1642	|	1656	|	|	1728	1742
Bologna Centrale ● .... **620** a.	1424	|	|	1454	1504	1524	|	1534	1554	1554	1609	1604	1624	|	1634	1654	1709	1709	1704	1724	|	|	1754	1809
Bologna Centrale ● .... **620** d.	1427	|	|	1457	1507	1527	|	1537	1557	1557	1612	1607	1627	|	1637	1657	1712	1712	1707	1727	|	|	1757	1812
Firenze SMN .... **620** a.	1504	|	|	1535	|	1604	|	|	1635	1635	1650	|	1704	|	|	1735	1750	1750	|	1804	|	|	1835	1850
Firenze SMN .... **620** d.	1514	|	|	1543	|	1614	|	|	1643	1643	1659	|	1714	|	|	1743	1759	1759	|	1814	|	|	1843	1859
Roma Tiburtina .... **620** a.	1640	|	|	1709	|	|	|	|	1809	1809	|	|	1840	|	|	1909	|	|	|	|	|	|	2009	2024
Roma Termini .... **620** a.	1649	1625	1640	1719	1710	1749	1725	1740	1819	1819	1835	1815	1849	1825	1840	1919	1935	1935	1915	1949	1925	1940	2019	2035
Roma Termini .... **640** d.	1700	...	1650	...	1725	1805	...	1753	1830	1830	...	...	1900	1840	1853	1930	...	...	...	2000	1940	...	2030	2053
Napoli Afragola .... **640** a.	|	...	1747**s**	...	|	1904	...	1848	1928	1928	...	...	2005	1940	1948**s**	2025	...	...	...	2056	2038	...	2125	2148**s**
Napoli Centrale .... **640** a.	1853	...	1803	...	1833	1918	...	|	|	|	...	...	|	1955	2005	2043	...	...	...	2113	2053	...	2143	2203
Napoli Centrale .... **640** d.	...	...	...	...	...	1930	...	|	|	|	...	...	|	...	...	2055	...	...	...	2125	...	...	2155	...
Salerno .... **640** a.	...	...	...	...	...	2010	...	1919	2016	2016	...	...	2036	...	...	2132	...	...	...	2205	...	...	2232	...

	FR 9649	*FR* 9555	*ITA* 9991	*FR* 9651	*ITA* 9955	*ITA* 9993	*FR* 9653	*FR* 9559	*ITA* 9995	*FR* 9657	*ITA* 9959	*ITA* 9997	*FR* 9329	*FR* 9661	*FR* 9563	*FR* 9663	*ITA* 9961	*ITA* 9961	*FR* 9567	*FR* 9681	*ITA* 9963	*FR* 9573	*FR* 9573	*FR* 9549
						Ⓑ						Ⓑ	Ⓑ					⑥		Ⓑ				
		K	L										M									Be	Bf	
Torino Porta Nuova .... **605** d.	1550	...	...	...	1630	...	...	1700	...	...	1720	...	1740	...	...	...	...	1830	1900	...	1925	...	...	2200
Torino Porta Susa △ .... **605** d.	1600	...	...	...	1640	...	...	1710	...	...	1730	...	1750	...	...	...	...	1840	1910	...	1935	...	...	2210
Milano Centrale .... **605** a.	1650	...	...	...	1730	...	...	1802	...	...	1830	...	1845**d**	...	...	...	...	1930	2002	...	2030	...	...	2300
Milano Centrale .... **605** d.	1658	1710	1715	1735	1740	1745	1800	1810	1820	1830	1840	1845	1848**d**	1900	1910	1935	1940	1940	2010	2035	2040	2120	2120	...
Milano Rogoredo .... d.	|	1720**u**	1725	|	1750	|	|	1820	1830	|	|	|	1905	|	1920**u**	|	1950	1950	2020	|	|	2130**u**	2130**u**	...
Reggio Emilia AV .... d.	|	1756	|	|	1828	|	|	1856	|	|	1928	|	1942	|	1956	|	2028	2028	2056	|	2128	2206	2206	...
Bologna Centrale ● .... **620** a.	1804	1824	|	|	1854	1849	1904	1924	|	1934	1954	1949	2009	2004	2024	|	2054	2054	2124	|	2154	2234	2234	...
Bologna Centrale ● .... **620** d.	1807	1827	|	|	1857	1852	1907	1927	|	1937	1957	1952	2012	2007	2027	|	2057	2057	2127	|	2157	2237	2237	...
Firenze SMN .... **620** a.	|	1904	|	|	1935	|	|	2004	|	|	2035	|	2050	|	2104	|	2135	2135	2204	|	2235	2314	|	...
Firenze SMN .... **620** d.	|	1914	|	|	1943	|	|	2014	|	|	2043	|	...	|	2114	|	2143	2143	2214	|	2243	2324	|	...
Roma Tiburtina .... **620** a.	|	|	|	|	2109	2048	|	2140**s**	|	|	2209	2149	...	|	2254**s**	|	2309	2309	2340**s**	|	0009	|	|	...
Roma Termini .... **620** a.	2015	2050	2025	2039	2119	2100	2110	2154	2125	2140	2220	2200	...	2210	2310	2239	2319	2319	2354	2325	0019	|	|	...
Roma Termini .... **640** d.	...	2100	...	...	2130	...	2125	...	2140	2153	2230	...	...	2220	...	...	...	...	...	...	...	|	|	...
Napoli Afragola .... **640** a.	...	2156	...	...	2225	...	|	...	2237	2248**s**	|	...	...	|	...	...	...	...	...	...	...	|	|	...
Napoli Centrale .... **640** a.	...	2213	...	...	2243	...	2233	...	2253	2303	2343	...	...	2333	...	...	...	...	...	...	...	|	|	...
Napoli Centrale .... **640** d.	...	2223	...	...	...	...	2245	...	...	...	...	...	...	...	...	...	...	...	...	...	...	|	|	...
Salerno .... **640** a.	...	2300	...	...	...	...	2322	...	...	...	...	...	...	...	...	...	...	...	...	...	...	◧	◧	...

NOTES FOR PAGES 290 and 291:

- **A** – From Mantova (d. 0600 ⚒) and Modena (d. 0647 ⚒).
- **B** – To/from Reggio di Calabria (Table **640**).
- **C** – To Rosarno on ①–⑤, to Reggio di Calabria on ⑥ (Table **640**).
- **E** – To/from Lecce (Table **615**).
- **F** – To/from Bari (Table **615**).
- **J** – To/from Foggia (Table **615**).
- **K** – To/from Battipaglia (Table **640**).
- **L** – To/from Caserta (Table **615**).
- **M** – To/from Perugia (Table **620**).
- **N** – To Modena (a. 2216) and Mantova (a. 2303).
- **P** – From Pompei (Table **640**).
- **Q** – To/from Benevento (Table **615**).
- **R** – To/from Sapri on ⑤–⑦ (Table **640**).
- **S** – To/from Taranto (Table **640**).
- **T** – From Bardonecchia (d. 1340) and Oulx (d. 1351).
- **U** – To Oulx (a. 1207) and Bardonecchia (a. 1220).

- **d** – Milano **Porta Garibaldi**.
- **e** – ④⑤ until Sept. 12 (also June 21, 22, 28, 29, Aug. 9, 30, 31, Sept. 6, 7, 13, 14).
- **f** – July 5 - Aug. 3.
- **g** – Not July 10 - Sept. 7.
- **s** – Calls to set down only.
- **u** – Calls to pick up only.

- ⊡ – To/from Milano via Table **620**.
- ◧ – Next station is Paola (Table **640**).
- ⊖ – Previous station is Paola (Table **640**).
- ❦ – Subject to confirmation.
- △ – Most trains call to pick up only.
- ▽ – Most trains call to set down only.
- ● – Most services use underground platforms 16–19; allow a minimum of 10 minutes when connecting with services from/to the main station.

Subject to alteration August 11 – 31. All trains 🄡 and 🍷. *FR* trains are operated by Trenitalia (www.trenitalia.com). *ITA* trains are operated by Italo (www.italotreno.it). Trenitalia tickets and passes are not valid on Italo trains. Italo tickets are not valid on Trenitalia trains. Trains may use different numbers for part of their journey.

SALERNO - NAPOLI - ROMA - FIRENZE - BOLOGNA - MILANO - TORINO

km		*FR* 9782	*ITA* 9900	*FR* 9600	*FR* 9574	*FR* 9574	*FR* 9504	*FR* 9682	*FR* 9300	*ITA* 9904	*ITA* 9904	*FR* 9508	*FR* 9508	*FR* 9606	*ITA* 9966	*ITA* 9908	*FR* 9608	*ITA* 9968	*FR* 9512	*FR* 9610	*FR* 9304	*ITA* 9970	*ITA* 9912	*FR* 9612	*ITA* 9972
			①–⑥		⑤⑥	⑥⑦		②–⑤	①–⑥ M	①–⑥		①–④	⑤–⑦ U	Ⓐ	①–⑥		①–⑥							K	L
	Salerno 640 d.	...	...	...	⊖	⊖	...	...	...	...	...	...	...	...	...	...	0516	...	...	...	...	...	...	0538	...
	Napoli Centrale 640 a.	...	...	...	|	|	...	...	...	...	...	...	...	...	...	...	|	...	...	...	...	...	...	0617	...
	Napoli Centrale 640 d.	...	...	...	|	|	...	...	...	...	...	...	...	0509	...	0514	|	0535	...	...	0523	0602	0614	0630	...
	Napoli Afragola 640 d.	...	...	...	|	|	...	...	...	...	...	...	...	0521**u**	...	0529	0542	0550	...	...	|	0616	0628	|	...
	Roma Termini 640 a.	...	...	...	|	|	...	...	...	...	...	...	...	0615	...	0630	0640	0646	...	...	0715	0720	0730	0740	...
0	**Roma** Termini 620 d.	...	...	...	|	|	0510	0538	...	0540	...	0600	0600	0625	0630	0640	0650	0705	0710	0720	0725	0730	0740	0750	0805
4	**Roma** Tiburtina 620 d.	...	...	...	|	|	0520**u**	|	...	0550	...	0610**u**	0610**u**	|	0638	0648	|	|	0720**u**	|	0735	0740	0750	|	|
261	**Firenze** SMN 620 a.	...	...	...	0646	0646	0646	|	...	0717	...	0746	0746	|	|	0817	|	|	0846	|	0901	|	0917	|	|
	Firenze SMN 620 d.	...	...	...	0655	0655	0655	|	0710	0725	...	0755	0755	|	|	0825	|	|	0855	|	0910	|	0925	|	|
	Bologna Centrale ● 620 a.	...	...	...	0728	0728	0728	|	0748	0803	...	0833	0833	|	0838	0903	0853	0908	0933	0923	0948	|	1003	0953	1008
	Bologna Centrale ● 620 d.	...	...	...	0731	0731	0731	|	0751	0806	...	0836	0836	|	0841	0906	0856	0911	0936	0926	0951	|	1006	0956	1011
	Reggio Emilia AV d.	...	...	...	0800	0800	0800	|	0815	0830	...	0900	0900	|	|	0930	|	|	1000	|	1015	|	1030	|	|
	Milano Rogoredo a.	...	...	...	0839**s**	0839**s**	0839**s**	|	0854	0909	...	0939	0939	|	|	|	|	|	1039**s**	1021**s**	1054	1034	|	|	|
	Milano Centrale 605 a.	...	...	...	0850	0850	0850	0830	0912**d**	0920	...	0950	0950	0924	0945	1020	1000	1015	1050	1035	1112**d**	1045	1120	1058	1115
	Milano Centrale 605 d.	0653	0730	0753	...	...	...	...	0915**d**	0930	0930	1002	1002	...	...	1030	...	...	...	...	1115**d**	...	1130	1110	...
	Torino Porta Susa ▽ 605 a.	0743	0818	0843	...	...	...	...	1008	1018	1018	1053	1053	...	...	1124	...	...	...	...	1208	...	1229	1159	...
	Torino Porta Nuova 605 a.	0801	0830	0855	...	...	...	...	1026	1030	1030	1111	...	...	...	1135	...	...	...	...	1226	...	1240	1216	...

	FR 9516	*FR* 9616	*ITA* 9916	*FR* 9618	*ITA* 9974	*FR* 9520	*FR* 9308	*ITA* 9920	*FR* 9622	*ITA* 9976	*ITA* 9976	*FR* 9524	*FR* 9624	*FR* 9310	*ITA* 9924	*FR* 9626	*ITA* 9978	*FR* 9514	*FR* 9628	*ITA* 9928	*FR* 9630	*ITA* 9980	*ITA* 9980	*FR* 9532
		⚒							Ⓐ		⑦							S	Ⓐ	F ❦	⚒		⑦	
Salerno 640 d.	0550	...	0620	...	...	...	...	0720	...	...	...	0744	...	...	...	...	...	0923	...	...	...	...	...	...
Napoli Centrale 640 a.	0628	...	0658	...	...	...	...	0758	...	...	...	0822	...	...	...	...	...	|	...	...	...	...	...	...
Napoli Centrale 640 d.	0640	0655	0720	...	0740	0745	...	0820	0825	...	0825	0840	...	0855	0920	...	...	|	0955	...	1030	...	1035	1040
Napoli Afragola 640 d.	0656	0710**u**	0735	...	|	0801**u**	...	0835	|	...	|	0855	...	0909**u**	0934	...	...	0956	1010**u**	...	|	...	1050	1057**u**
Roma Termini 640 a.	0755	0804	0830	...	0851	0900	...	0930	0940	...	0940	0950	...	1008	1030	...	...	1058	1105	...	1140	...	1147	1200
Roma Termini 620 d.	0810	0820	0840	0850	0905	0910	0925	0943	0950	1005	1005	1010	1020	1025	1040	1050	1105	1110	1120	1140	1150	1210	1210	1210
Roma Tiburtina 620 d.	|	|	0850	|	|	0920	0935**u**	0951	|	|	|	|	|	|	1050	|	|	1120	|	1150	|	|	|	1220
Firenze SMN 620 a.	0946	|	1017	|	|	1046	1101	1117	|	|	|	1146	|	1201	1217	|	|	1246	|	1317	|	|	|	1346
Firenze SMN 620 d.	0955	|	1025	|	|	1055	1110	1125	|	|	|	1155	|	1210	1225	|	|	1255	|	1325	|	|	|	1355
Bologna Centrale ● 620 a.	1033	1023	1103	1053	1108	1133	1148	1203	1153	1208	1208	1233	1223	1248	1303	1253	1308	1333	1323	1403	1353	|	|	1433
Bologna Centrale ● 620 d.	1036	1026	1106	1056	1111	1136	1151	1206	1156	1211	1211	1236	1226	1251	1306	1256	1311	1336	1326	1406	1356	|	|	1436
Reggio Emilia AV d.	1100	|	1130	|	|	1200	1215	1230	|	|	|	1300	|	1315	1330	|	|	1400	|	1435	|	|	|	1500
Milano Rogoredo a.	1139	1121**s**	1209	|	|	1239**s**	1254	1309	|	|	|	1339	1321**s**	1354	1409	|	|	1439	1421**s**	|	|	1504	1504	1539
Milano Centrale 605 a.	1150	1135	1220	1158	1215	1250	1312**d**	1320	1258	1315	1315	1350	1335	1412**d**	1420	1358	1415	1450	1435	1520	1458	1515	1515	1550
Milano Centrale 605 d.	1202	...	1230	...	...	...	1315**d**	1330	...	...	...	...	...	1415**d**	1430	1410	...	1502	...	1530	...	...	...	1602
Torino Porta Susa ▽ 605 a.	1249	...	1318	...	...	...	1408	1418	...	...	...	...	...	1508	1520	1459	...	1549	...	1629	...	...	...	1649
Torino Porta Nuova 605 a.	1300	...	1330	...	...	...	1426	1430	...	...	...	...	...	1526	1530	1516	...	1606	...	1640	...	...	...	1706

	FR 9632	*ITA* 9930	*ITA* 9930	*FR* 9634	*ITA* 9982	*FR* 9584	*FR* 9636	*ITA* 8134	*FR* 9638	*ITA* 9984	*FR* 9540	*FR* 9640	*ITA* 9940	*FR* 9642	*ITA* 9986	*FR* 9544	*FR* 9644	*FR* 9320	*ITA* 9946	*FR* 9646	*ITA* 9950	*FR* 9588	*FR* 9648	*ITA* 9948
	Ⓑ		⑥			B	Ⓐ	B	Ⓑ	❦	B	Ⓑ		B					g			B		
Salerno 640 d.	...	...	...	...	...	1051	...	1122	...	...	1215	...	...	1305	...	1250	...	...	...	...	1343	1354	...	...
Napoli Centrale 640 a.	...	...	...	...	...	1127	...	1158	...	...	|	...	...	|	...	1328	...	...	...	...	1423	1428	...	...
Napoli Centrale 640 d.	1055	1120	1120	1130	1135	1140	1155	1215	1230	...	|	1255	1320	|	...	1340	...	1355	1420	1430	1435	1440	1500	1520
Napoli Afragola 640 d.	1110**u**	1135	1135	|	1150	1158	1210**u**	1230	|	...	1253	1310**u**	1335	1341	...	1358	...	1410**u**	1435	|	1450	1458	1515**u**	1535
Roma Termini 640 a.	1210	1230	1230	1239	1245	1300	1305	1330	1340	...	1355	1405	1430	1440	...	1455	...	1505	1530	1540	1545	1555	1610	1630
Roma Termini 620 d.	1220	1240	1240	1250	1305	1310	1320	1340	1350	1410	1410	1420	1440	1450	1505	1510	1520	1525	1540	1550	1610	1610	1625	1640
Roma Tiburtina 620 d.	|	1250	1250	|	|	|	|	1350	|	|	1420	|	1450	|	|	|	|	|	1550	|	|	1620	|	1650
Firenze SMN 620 a.	|	1417	1417	|	|	1446	|	1517	|	|	1546	|	1617	|	|	1646	|	1701	1717	|	|	1746	|	1817
Firenze SMN 620 d.	|	1425	1425	|	|	1455	|	1525	|	|	1555	|	1625	|	|	1655	|	1710	1725	|	|	1755	|	1825
Bologna Centrale ● 620 a.	1423	1503	1503	1453	1508	1533	|	1603	1553	|	1633	|	1703	1653	1708	1733	|	1748	1803	1753	|	1833	|	1903
Bologna Centrale ● 620 d.	1426	1506	1506	1456	1511	1536	|	1606	1556	|	1636	|	1706	1656	1711	1736	|	1751	1806	1756	|	1836	|	1906
Reggio Emilia AV d.	|	1530	1530	|	|	1600	|	1635	|	|	1700	|	1730	|	|	1800	|	1815	1835	|	|	1900	|	1930
Milano Rogoredo a.	1521**s**	1609	1609	|	|	1639	1619**s**	|	|	1704	1739**s**	1719**s**	1809	|	|	1839**s**	1819**s**	1854	1909	|	1904	1939	|	2009
Milano Centrale 605 a.	1535	1620	1620	1600	1615	1650	1630	1720	1658	1715	1750	1730	1820	1758	1815	1850	1830	1912**d**	1920	1900	1915	1950	1924	2020
Milano Centrale 605 d.	...	...	1630	...	...	1702	...	1730	...	...	...	...	1830	1810	...	...	...	1915**d**	1930	...	...	2002	...	...
Torino Porta Susa ▽ 605 a.	...	...	1718	...	...	1749	...	1824	...	...	...	...	1919	1859	...	...	...	2008	2019	...	...	2049	...	...
Torino Porta Nuova 605 a.	...	...	1730	...	...	1806	...	1835	...	...	...	...	1930	1916	...	...	...	2026	2030	...	...	2106	...	...

	FR 9650	*ITA* 9990	*FR* 9808	*FR* 9552	*FR* 9652	*ITA* 9958	*FR* 9658	*ITA* 9992	*FR* 9556	*FR* 9660	*FR* 9326	*ITA* 9954	*FR* 9662	*ITA* 9994	*FR* 9560	*FR* 9328	*ITA* 8158	*FR* 9668	*FR* 9330	*ITA* 9996	*FR* 9592	*ITA* 9962	*FR* 9568	*FR* 9674
	Ⓑ		E		Ⓑ	Q ❦	B								E	Ⓑ N	B		⊡	Ⓑ	R		⑦ P	
Salerno 640 d.	...	...	...	1445	...	...	1617	...	...	...	...	1625	...	...	...	...	1722	...	...	...	1753	1814	...	...
Napoli Centrale 640 a.	...	...	...	1523	...	...	|	...	...	...	...	1705	...	...	...	...	1758	...	...	...	1828	1858	...	...
Napoli Centrale 640 d.	...	...	...	1540	1555	...	|	1620	1640	1655	...	1720	1725	1730	...	...	1820	1830	...	1835	1840	1920	1940	2030
Napoli Afragola 640 d.	...	...	...	1558	1610**u**	...	1641	1634	1658**u**	1709**u**	...	1734	|	1748	...	...	|	|	...	1850	1858	1935	1958	2044**u**
Roma Termini 640 a.	...	...	...	1700	1710	...	1740	1730	1755	1805	...	1830	1835	1846	...	...	1930	1940	...	1946	1955	2030	2055	2138
Roma Termini 620 d.	1650	1705	...	1710	1720	1740	1750	1805	1810	1820	1825	1840	1850	1905	1911	1925	1940	1950	1950	2005	2010	2040	2110	2148
Roma Tiburtina 620 d.	|	|	...	|	|	1750	|	|	|	|	1835**u**	1851	|	|	1920	1935**u**	1950	|	2000**u**	|	|	2050	2120	2155
Firenze SMN 620 a.	|	|	...	1846	|	1917	|	|	1946	|	2001	2017	|	|	2046	2101	2117	|	2127	|	2146	2217	2258	2320
Firenze SMN 620 d.	|	|	...	1855	|	1925	|	|	1955	|	2010	2025	|	|	2055	2110	2125	|	2136	|	2155	2225	...	...
Bologna Centrale ● 620 a.	|	1908	...	1933	1923	2003	1953	|	2033	2023	2048	2103	2053	2108	2133	2148	2203	2153	2213	|	2235	2303	...	...
Bologna Centrale ● 620 d.	|	1911	1918	1936	1926	2006	1956	|	2036	2026	2051	2106	2056	2111	2136	...	2206	2156	...	|	2238	2306	...	...
Reggio Emilia AV d.	|	|	1942	2000	|	2030	|	|	2100	|	2115	2130	|	|	2200	...	2235	|	...	|	2300	2330	...	...
Milano Rogoredo a.	1949**s**	|	2015	2039	|	|	|	2104	2139**s**	|	2154	2209	|	|	2238**s**	...	|	|	...	2304	2339**s**	0009	...	...
Milano Centrale 605 a.	1958	2015	2047**d**	2050	2030	2120	2100	2115	2150	2130	2212**d**	2220	2200	2215	2250	...	2320	2300	...	2315	2350	0020	...	...
Milano Centrale 605 d.	...	...	2050**d**	2102	...	2130	...	...	...	...	2215**d**	...	...	2230	...	...	...	...	...	...	...	...	...	...
Torino Porta Susa ▽ 605 a.	...	...	2138	2149	...	2229	...	...	...	...	2308	...	...	2319	...	...	...	...	...	...	...	...	...	...
Torino Porta Nuova 605 a.	...	...	2156	2206	...	2240	...	...	...	...	2326	...	...	2330	...	...	...	...	...	...	...	...	...	...

OR RETURN AND FOOTNOTES SERVICE SEE PREVIOUS PAGE. FOR SERVICES FROM / TO BRESCIA, BOLZANO AND VENEZIA SEE NEXT TWO PAGES →

600 HIGH-SPEED SERVICES

Italo, Trenitalia

Subject to alteration August 11–31. All trains 🅁 and 🍸. *FR* trains are operated by Trenitalia (www.trenitalia.com). *ITA* trains are operated by Italo (www.italotreno.it). Trenitalia tickets and passes are not valid on Italo trains. Italo tickets are not valid on Trenitalia trains. Trains may use different numbers for part of their journey.

BRESCIA and BOLZANO - VERONA - MILANO - BOLOGNA - FIRENZE - ROMA - NAPOLI - SALERNO

km		*FR* **8505**	*ITA* **8951**	*FR* **9604**		*ITA* **9938** ①–⑥	*FR* **8513** ①–⑥	*ITA* **8953**		*FR* **8507**	*FR* **8503**	*FR* **9721** ①–⑤		*ITA* **8959**	*FR* **8519**	*ITA* **8963**		*FR* **8525**	*FR* **8527**	*ITA* **8967**		*FR* **8529**	*FR* **8701** ⑥⑦	
															A									
0	**Brescia** 605 d.	...	0627	0642	...	0647	...	...	...	...	0847	...	...	1329	...	...	...	...	1700	1729	...	...	...	...
28	Desenzano-Sirmione 605 d.	...	0643	│	...	│	...	...	...	...	│	...	...	1344	...	...	...	...	│	1743	...	...	...	...
42	Peschiera del Garda 605 d.	...	0652	│	...	│	...	...	...	...	0909	...	...	1353	...	...	...	...	1725	1752	...	...	...	...
	Bolzano / Bozen 595 d.	0512	│	│	...	│	0550	0642	...	0712	│	0845	...	│	1312	1442	...	1512	│	│	...	1710	1745	...
	Trento 595 d.	0543	│	│	...	│	0622	0713	...	0743	│	0919	...	│	1343	1514	...	1543	│	│	...	1743	1821	...
	Rovereto 595 d.	0557	│	│	...	│	0636	0727	...	0757	│	0934	...	│	1357	1528	...	1557	│	│	...	1757	1838	...
65	**Verona** Porta Nuova 595 a.	0640	0711	│	...	│	0744	0810	...	0840	0924	1020	...	1411	1440	1610	...	1640	1741	1811	...	1840	1920	...
65	**Verona** Porta Nuova 595 d.	0652	0722	│	...	│	0753	0822	...	0852	0937	1032	...	1422	1452	1620	...	1652	1752	1822	...	1852	1932	...
	Peschiera del Garda ‡ d.	│	│	│	...	│	│	│	...	│	│	1048	...	│	│	│	...	│	│	│	...	│	1948	...
	Desenzano-Sirmione d.	│	│	│	...	│	│	│	...	│	│	│	...	│	│	│	...	│	│	│	...	│	│	...
	Brescia d.	│	│	│	...	│	│	│	...	│	│	1109	...	│	│	│	...	│	│	│	...	│	2009	...
	Milano Centrale 605 a.	│	│	0720	...	0730	│	│	...	│	│	1145	...	│	│	│	...	│	│	│	...	│	2045	...
	Milano Centrale 605 d.	│	│	0730	...	0745	│	│	...	│	│	...	...	│	│	│	...	│	│	│	...	│	...	...
	Milano Rogoredo d.	│	│	0740	...	│	│	│	...	│	│	...	...	│	│	│	...	│	│	│	...	│	...	...
179	**Bologna** Centrale ● 620 a.	0744	0814	│	...	0849	0844	0914	...	0944	1044	...	...	1514	1544	1714	...	1744	1844	1914	...	1944	...	...
179	**Bologna** Centrale ● 620 d.	0747	0817	│	...	0852	0847	0917	...	0947	1047	...	...	1517	1547	1717	...	1747	1847	1917	...	1947	...	...
271	**Firenze** SMN 620 a.	0824	0854	│	...	│	0924	0954	...	1024	1124	...	...	1554	1624	1754	...	1824	1924	1954	...	2024	...	...
271	**Firenze** SMN 620 d.	0833	0903	│	...	│	0933	1003	...	1033	1133	...	...	1603	1633	1803	...	1833	1933	2003	...	2033	...	...
	Roma Tiburtina 620 a.	1000**s**	│	│	...	1049	1058**s**	│	...	1159**s**	│	...	...	│	│	│	...	│	2059**s**	2132	...	2159**s**	...	...
532	**Roma** Termini 620 a.	1015	1035	1040	...	1100	1115	1135	...	1215	1310	...	...	1735	1810	1935	...	2010	2115	2143	...	2215	...	...
532	**Roma** Termini 640 d.	...	...	1053	...	...	...	...	...	...	...	...	...	...	1820	...	...	2025	...	2205	...	...	...	...
742	**Napoli** Afragola 640 a.	...	...	1148**s**	...	...	...	...	...	...	...	...	...	...	1920	...	...	│	...	│	...	...	...	...
754	**Napoli** Centrale 640 a.	...	...	1203	...	...	...	...	...	...	...	...	...	...	│	...	...	2133	...	2318	...	...	...	...
804	**Salerno** 640 a.	...	...	...	...	...	...	...	...	...	...	...	...	...	1948	...	...	...	...	...	...	...	...	...

km		*FR* **8703** ⑥⑦	*FR* **8502**	*ITA* **8954**		*ITA* **8956**	*FR* **8506**	*FR* **8508**		*FR* **8509**	*ITA* **8960**	*FR* **8520** Ⓑ		*FR* **9751** ①–⑤	*FR* **8524**	*FR* **8526**		*FR* **9660**	*ITA* **8966**	*ITA* **9944** Ⓑ		*FR* **8528**	*ITA* **8968**	
										A														
	Salerno 640 d.	...	...	...	...	...	...	...	...	0911	...	...	...	...	...	...	...	...	...	...	...	...	...	...
	Napoli Centrale 640 d.	...	...	0550	...	0702	0730	...	...	│	...	...	...	...	...	...	...	1655	...	...	...	...	1755	...
	Napoli Afragola 640 d.	...	...	│	...	│	│	...	...	0941	...	...	...	...	...	...	...	1709**u**	...	...	...	...	│	...
	Roma Termini 640 a.	...	...	0705	...	0815	0840	...	...	1040	...	...	...	...	...	...	...	1805	...	...	...	...	1910	...
0	**Roma** Termini 620 d.	...	0645	0725	...	0825	0850	0950	...	1050	1225	1450	...	...	1650	1750	...	1820	1825	1830	...	1850	1925	...
4	**Roma** Tiburtina 620 d.	...	0655**u**	│	...	│	│	1000**u**	...	1100	│	1500**u**	...	...	1700**u**	1800**u**	...	│	│	1839	...	1901**u**	│	...
261	**Firenze** SMN 620 a.	...	0827	0857	...	0957	1027	1127	...	1227	1357	1627	...	...	1827	1927	...	│	1957	│	...	2027	2057	...
—	**Firenze** SMN 620 d.	...	0836	0905	...	1005	1036	1136	...	1236	1405	1636	...	...	1836	1936	...	│	2005	│	...	2036	2105	...
	Bologna Centrale ● 620 a.	...	0913	0943	...	1043	1113	1213	...	1313	1443	1713	...	...	1913	2013	...	2023	2043	2038	...	2113	2143	...
0	**Bologna** Centrale ● 620 d.	...	0916	0946	...	1046	1116	1216	...	1316	1446	1716	...	...	1916	2016	...	2026	2046	2041	...	2116	2146	...
	Milano Rogoredo a.	...	│	│	...	│	│	│	...	│	│	│	...	...	│	│	...	│	│	│	...	│	│	...
	Milano Centrale 605 a.	...	│	│	...	│	│	│	...	│	│	│	...	...	│	│	...	2130	│	2145	...	│	│	...
	Milano Centrale 605 d.	0815	│	│	...	│	│	│	...	│	│	│	...	1745	│	│	...	2145	│	2155	...	│	│	...
	Brescia d.	0853	│	│	...	│	│	│	...	│	│	│	...	1823	│	│	...	│	│	│	...	│	│	...
	Desenzano-Sirmione d.	│	│	│	...	│	│	│	...	│	│	│	...	│	│	│	...	│	│	│	...	│	│	...
	Peschiera del Garda ‡ d.	0914	│	│	...	│	│	│	...	│	│	│	...	1844	│	│	...	│	│	│	...	│	│	...
114	**Verona** Porta Nuova 595 a.	0928	1008	1038	...	1138	1208	1308	...	1408	1538	1808	...	1858	2008	2108	...	│	2138	│	...	2208	2238	...
114	**Verona** Porta Nuova 595 d.	0938	1020	1050	...	1149	1220	1320	...	1420	1549	1820	...	1920	2020	2120	...	│	2150	│	...	2220	2249	...
182	Rovereto 595 d.	1015	1103	1132	...	│	1303	│	...	1503	│	1903	...	2003	2103	2203	...	│	2232	│	...	│	│	...
206	Trento 595 d.	1029	1117	1146	...	│	1317	│	...	1517	│	1917	...	2017	2117	2217	...	│	2246	│	...	│	│	...
261	**Bolzano / Bozen** 595 a.	1111	1156	1223	...	│	1348	│	...	1548	│	1958	...	2048	2148	2248	...	│	2323	│	...	│	│	...
	Peschiera del Garda 605 d.	...	...	...	...	1207	...	1336	...	...	1607	...	...	...	...	...	...	│	...	│	...	2236	2307	...
	Desenzano-Sirmione 605 d.	...	...	...	...	1216	...	│	...	...	1616	...	...	...	...	...	...	│	...	│	...	│	2316	...
	Brescia 605 a.	...	...	...	...	1233	...	1400	...	...	1633	...	...	...	...	...	...	2223	...	2236	...	2300	2333	...

NOTES FOR PAGE 292:

A – To / from Sibari (Table **640**).

s – Calls to set down only.
u – Calls to pick up only.

‡ – Station for Gardaland Park. Free shuttle bus available.
● – Most services use underground platforms 16–19; allow a minimum of 10 minutes when connecting with services from / to the main station.

FOR SERVICES TO / FROM TORINO SEE PREVIOUS TWO PAGES; FOR SERVICES TO / FROM VENEZIA SEE NEXT PAGE.

Subject to alteration August 11 – 31. All trains 🅁 and 🍷. *FR* trains are operated by Trenitalia (www.trenitalia.com). *ITA* trains are operated by Italo (www.italotreno.it).
Trenitalia tickets and passes are not valid on Italo trains. Italo tickets are not valid on Trenitalia trains. Trains may use different numbers for part of their journey.

VENEZIA - BOLOGNA - FIRENZE - ROMA - NAPOLI - SALERNO

km		*FR* 9401	*FR* 9403	*FR* 8801	*ITA* 8903	*FR* 9405	*ITA* 8905	*FR* 9466	*FR* 9409	*ITA* 8907	*FR* 9411	*ITA* 8902	*FR* 9413	*ITA* 8911	*FR* 9415	*ITA* 8929
				A					B							
	Trieste Central **601** d.	...	...	...	...	...	...	0638	...	...	...	0802	...	...	...	...
	Udine **601** d.	...	...	...	...	...	...	|	0647	0723	...	|	...	...	...	...
0	**Venezia** Santa Lucia d.	0526	0626	0653	0705	0726	0805	|	|	|	0926	|	1026	1105	1126	1205
9	**Venezia** Mestre △ **620** d.	0538	0638	0705	0717	0738	0817	0834	0840	0920	0938	1017	1038	1117	1138	1217
37	Padova **620** d.	0556	0656	0723	0735	0756	0835	0850	0856	0935	0956	1035	1056	1135	1156	1235
81	Rovigo **620** d.	0617	|	0747	|	0816	0857	|	|	|	|	|	|	1157	|	|
113	Ferrara **620** d.	|	0729	0805	0811	|	|	|	0929	1011	1029	1110	1129	|	1229	1311
160	**Bologna** Centrale ● **620** a.	0659	0759	0842	0839	0859	0939	0949	0959	1039	1059	1139	1159	1239	1259	1339
160	**Bologna** Centrale ● **620** d.	0702	0802	...	0842	0902	0942	0952	1002	1042	1102	1142	1202	1242	1302	1342
252	**Firenze** SMN **620** a.	0739	0839	...	0920	0939	1020	|	1039	1120	1139	1220	1239	1320	1339	1420
252	**Firenze** SMN **620** d.	0748	0848	...	0928	0948	1028	|	1048	1128	1148	1228	1248	1328	1348	1428
	Roma Tiburtina **620** a.	0915**s**	|	...	1054	|	1154	1149**s**	|	1254	|	1354	|	1454	1514**s**	1557
513	**Roma** Termini **620** a.	0933	1025	...	1105	1122	1205	1207	1225	1305	1330	1405	1425	1505	1525	1605
513	**Roma** Termini **640** d.	...	1035	...	1115	1135	...	...	1250	1330	...	1415	1438	...	...	1615
723	**Napoli** Afragola **640** a.	...	|	...	|	|	...	...	|	1427	...	|	|	...	...	|
735	**Napoli** Centrale **640** a.	...	1148	...	1228	1248	...	...	1403	1443	...	1528	1548	...	...	1728
735	**Napoli** Centrale **640** d.	...	...	...	...	...	...	...	...	...	...	...	...	...	...	...
788	**Salerno** **640** a.	...	...	...	...	...	...	...	...	...	...	...	...	...	...	...

	FR 8419	*ITA* 8913	*FR* 9421	*ITA* 8915	*FR* 9425	*FR* 8815	*ITA* 8919	*FR* 9427	*ITA* 8923	*FR* 9431	*ITA* 8925	*FR* 9433	*ITA* 8927	*FR* 9435	*FR* 9437
	C	C				A							≋		
Trieste Central **601** d.	...	...	...	...	...	...	...	...	...	...	...	...	...	...	...
Udine **601** d.	...	...	...	...	...	...	...	...	...	...	...	...	...	...	...
Venezia Santa Lucia d.	1226	1305	1326	1405	1426	1452	1505	1526	1605	1626	1705	1726	1805	1826	1926
Venezia Mestre △ **620** d.	1238	1317	1338	1417	1438	1504	1517	1538	1617	1638	1717	1738	1817	1838	1938
Padova **620** d.	1256	1335	1356	1435	1456	1521	1535	1556	1635	1656	1735	1756	1835	1856	1956
Rovigo **620** d.	|	|	1417	|	|	1546	|	|	1656	1717	|	|	|	|	|
Ferrara **620** d.	1329	1411	|	1511	1529	1602	1611	1629	|	|	1811	1829	1911	1929	2029
Bologna Centrale ● **620** a.	1359	1439	1459	1539	1559	1637	1639	1659	1739	1759	1839	1859	1939	1959	2059
Bologna Centrale ● **620** d.	1402	1442	1502	1542	1602	...	1642	1702	1742	1802	1842	1902	1942	2002	2102
Firenze SMN **620** a.	1439	1520	1539	1620	1639	...	1720	1739	1820	1839	1920	1939	2020	2039	2139
Firenze SMN **620** d.	1448	1528	1548	1628	1648	...	1728	1748	1828	1848	1928	1948	2028	2048	2148
Roma Tiburtina **620** a.	|	1653	1714	1754	|	...	1854	|	1954	|	2054	2114**s**	2154	|	2314**s**
Roma Termini **620** a.	1624	1705	1724	1805	1825	...	1905	1925	2005	2025	2105	2130	2205	2225	2330
Roma Termini **640** d.	1635	1715	1735	1815	1835	...	1915	1935	2015	2035	2115	...	...	2235	...
Napoli Afragola **640** a.	1736	1816	|	|	|	...	|	|	|	|	|	...	...	2334**s**	...
Napoli Centrale **640** a.	|	|	1848	1928	1948	...	2028	2048	2147	2148	2228	...	...	2348	...
Napoli Centrale **640** d.	|	|	...	...	...	...	2040	2101	...	...	...	...	...	...	...
Salerno **640** a.	1809	1854	...	...	...	...	2117	2138	...	...	...	...	...	...	...

	FR 9400	*ITA* 8900	*FR* 9404	*ITA* 8924	*FR* 9406	*ITA* 8904	*FR* 9490	*ITA* 8906	*FR* 9414	*ITA* 8908	*FR* 9416	*ITA* 8910	*FR* 8418	*FR* 8816	*ITA* 8914
		≋										≋	C	A	
Salerno **640** d.	...	...	...	...	...	...	0610	...	0713	...	...	0838	0959	...	...
Napoli Centrale **640** a.	...	...	...	...	...	...	0647	...	0753	...	...	0923	|	...	...
Napoli Centrale **640** d.	...	...	...	...	0609	0607	0709	...	0809	0830	...	0935	|	...	...
Napoli Afragola **640** d.	...	...	...	...	|	|	|	...	|	|	...	|	1025	...	...
Roma Termini **640** a.	...	...	...	...	0725	0735	0820	...	0925	0945	...	1045	1125	...	...
Roma Termini **620** d.	0535	0555	0635	0655	0735	0755	0835	0855	0935	0955	1035	1055	1135	...	1155
Roma Tiburtina **620** d.	0545**u**	0605	0643**u**	0706	0745	0805	|	0905	|	1005	1045**u**	1105	|	...	1203
Firenze SMN **620** a.	0711	0731	0811	0831	0911	0931	1011	1031	1111	1131	1211	1231	1311	...	1331
Firenze SMN **620** d.	0720	0739	0820	0839	0920	0939	1020	1039	1120	1139	1220	1239	1320	...	1339
Bologna Centrale ● **620** a.	0758	0818	0858	0918	0958	1018	1058	1118	1158	1218	1258	1318	1358	...	1418
Bologna Centrale ● **620** d.	0801	0821	0901	0921	1001	1021	1101	1121	1201	1221	1301	1321	1401	1418	1421
Ferrara **620** d.	0829	0849	0929	0949	1029	|	|	1149	1229	1249	1329	1349	1429	1440	|
Rovigo **620** d.	|	|	|	|	|	1106	1145	|	|	|	|	|	|	1457	1506
Padova **620** d.	0906	0927	1006	1027	1106	1127	1206	1227	1306	1327	1406	1427	1506	1533	1527
Venezia Mestre ▽ **620** a.	0923	0942	1023	1042	1123	1142	1223	1242	1323	1342	1423	1442	1523	1556	1542
Venezia Santa Lucia a.	0934	0955	1034	1055	1134	1155	1234	1255	1334	1355	1434	1455	1534	1608	1555
Udine **601** a.	...	...	...	...	...	...	...	...	...	...	...	...	...	...	...
Trieste Centrale **601** a.	...	...	...	...	...	...	...	...	...	...	...	...	...	...	...

	FR 9420	*ITA* 8916	*FR* 9422	*FR* 9423	*ITA* 8918	*FR* 9426	*ITA* 8928	*FR* 9480	*FR* 9428	*ITA* 8920	*FR* 9430	*FR* 8828	*ITA* 8922	*FR* 9432	*FR* 9434
		④–①									B	A			
Salerno **640** d.	...	...	...	...	...	...	...	...	...	...	...	...	...	...	...
Napoli Centrale **640** a.	...	...	...	...	...	...	...	...	...	...	...	...	...	...	...
Napoli Centrale **640** d.	1109	...	1209	...	1335	1410	...	...	1509	1535	1609	...	1635	1705	1809
Napoli Afragola **640** d.	|	...	|	...	|	|	...	...	|	1550	|	...	|	|	|
Roma Termini **640** a.	1219	...	1320	...	1446	1520	...	...	1620	1645	1719	...	1745	1815	1920
Roma Termini **620** d.	1236	1255	1335	1435	1455	1535	1555	1630	1635	1655	1735	...	1755	1835	1935
Roma Tiburtina **620** d.	|	1305	|	|	1505	|	1605	1640**u**	1645	1705	|	...	1805	1847	|
Firenze SMN **620** a.	1411	1431	1511	1611	1631	1711	1731	|	1811	1831	1911	...	1931	2032	2111
Firenze SMN **620** d.	1420	1439	1520	1620	1639	1720	1739	|	1820	1839	1920	...	1939	2041	2120
Bologna Centrale ● **620** a.	1458	1518	1558	1658	1718	1758	1818	1838	1858	1918	1958	...	2018	2118	2158
Bologna Centrale ● **620** d.	1501	1521	1601	1701	1721	1801	1821	1841	1901	1921	2001	2018	2021	2121	2201
Ferrara **620** d.	|	1552	1629	|	1752	1829	1849	|	1929	1949	|	2042	|	2152	2229
Rovigo **620** d.	1545	|	|	1745	|	|	|	|	|	|	2045	2108	2101	|	|
Padova **620** d.	1606	1627	1706	1806	1827	1906	1927	1942	2006	2027	2106	2140	2127	2229	2306
Venezia Mestre ▽ **620** a.	1623	1642	1723	1823	1842	1923	1942	1956	2023	2040	2123	2156	2142	2242	2323
Venezia Santa Lucia a.	1634	1655	1734	1834	|	1934	1955	|	2034	|	|	2209	2155	2255	2334
Udine **601** a.	...	...	...	...	|	...	...	|	...	2217	2303	...	...	...	...
Trieste Centrale **601** a.	...	...	...	...	2056	...	...	2155	...	...	...	...	...	...	...

NOTES FOR PAGE 293:

A – To / from Lecce (Table **615**).
B – To / from Gorizia (Table **601**).
C – To / from Reggio di Calabria (Table **640**).

s – Calls to set down only.
u – Calls to pick up only.

△ – Most trains call to pick up only.
▽ – Most trains call to set down only.
≋ – Subject to confirmation.
● – Most services use underground platforms 16 – 19; allow a minimum of 10 minutes when connecting with services from / to the main station.

FOR SERVICES TO / FROM TORINO SEE PAGES 290 / 291.
FOR SERVICES TO / FROM BRESCIA AND BOLZANO SEE PAGE 292.

601 VENEZIA - TRIESTE and UDINE

Subject to alteration August 11–31. For *IC* trains Roma - Trieste and v.v. see Table **620** For *ICN* night trains Trieste - Udine - Venezia - Rome and v.v. see Table **641**.

VENEZIA - TRIESTE

Additional slower trains are available

km		⚒				⑥⑦		*FR* **9707**							*FR* **9737**			*ITA* **8918** **A**	*FR* **9749**		*FR* **9480**	Ⓑ	*FR* **9759** **B**	
	Roma Termini **600 620** d.	...	...	...	...	...	...	...	...	...	...	...	...	...	...	...	...	1455	...	...	1630	...	...	...
	Bologna C **600 620** d.	...	...	...	...	...	...	...	...	...	...	...	...	...	...	...	...	1721	...	...	1841	...	...	...
	Milano Centrale **605** d.	...	...	...	...	...	...	0745	...	...	...	...	...	...	1515	...	...	|	1715	...	|	...	1943d	...
0	**Venezia** Santa Lucia	...	...	0639	0739	0839	0939	|	1039	1239	1339	1439	1539	1639	|	1739	1839	|	|	1939	|	2101	|	2239
9	**Venezia** Mestre d.	...	0551	0651	0751	0851	0951	1011	1051	1251	1351	1451	1551	1651	1740	1751	1851	1855	1940	1951	2010	2114	2210	2251
42	S. Dona di Piave-Jesolo ◧ d.	...	0615	0715	0815	0915	1015	1039	1115	1315	1415	1515	1615	1715	|	1815	1915	1926	|	2015	|	|	|	2315
69	Portogruaro-Caorle d.	0529	0635	0735	0835	0935	1035	1057	1135	1335	1435	1535	1635	1735	1827	1835	1935	1949	2029	2035	|	|	|	2335
83	Latisana-Lignano-Bibione d.	0540	0646	0746	0846	0946	1046	1108	1146	1346	1446	1546	1646	1746	|	1846	1946	1958	2037	2046	2058	2154	2248	2346
101	S. Giorgio di Nogaro d.	0552	0658	0758	0858	0958	1058	|	1158	1358	1458	1558	1658	1758	|	1858	1958	|	|	2058	|	2204	|	2358
112	Cervignano-Aquileia-Grado d.	0601	0707	0807	0907	1007	1107	1126	1207	1407	1507	1607	1707	1807	|	1907	2007	|	|	2107	|	2212	2306	0007
124	Trieste Airport ✈ d.	0609	0715	0815	0915	1015	1115	1135	1215	1415	1515	1615	1715	1815	1857	1915	2015	2024	2059	2115	2125	2220	2315	0015
129	Monfalcone d.	0615	0721	0821	0921	1021	1121	1142	1221	1421	1521	1621	1721	1821	1904	1921	2021	2032	2105	2121	|	2226	2322	0021
157	**Trieste** Centrale a.	0642	0744	0844	0944	1044	1144	1205	1244	1444	1544	1644	1744	1844	1927	1944	2044	2056	2127	2144	2155	2255	2345	0044

		FR **9712** **B**		*FR* **9466**	*FR* **9718**		*ITA* **8902** **A**			*FR* **9726**	⑥⑦						*FR* **9758**				Ⓐ		
Trieste Centrale d.	0516	0600	0616	0638	0707	0716	0802	0816	0916	0939	1016	1216	1316	1416	1516	1616	1705	1716	1816	1916	2016	2116	2206
Monfalcone d.	0540	0623	0640	|	0732	0740	0827	0840	0940	1004	1040	1240	1340	1440	1540	1640	1730	1740	1840	1940	2042	2142	2229
Trieste Airport ✈ d.	0545	0629	0645	0706	0738	0745	0834	0845	0945	1010	1045	1245	1345	1445	1545	1645	1736	1745	1845	1945	2047	2147	2234
Cervignano-Aquileia-Grado d.	0553	0637	0653	|	|	0753	|	0853	0953	|	1053	1253	1353	1453	1553	1653	1743	1753	1853	1953	2055	2154	2242
S. Giorgio di Nogaro d.	0601	|	0701	|	|	0801	|	0901	1001	|	1101	1301	1401	1501	1601	1701	|	1801	1901	2001	2103	2203	2249
Latisana-Lignano-Bibione d.	0614	0653	0714	0725	0758	0814	0900	0914	1014	|	1114	1314	1414	1514	1614	1714	1759	1814	1914	2014	2116	2216	2300
Portogruaro-Caorle d.	0625	|	0725	|	0808	0825	0910	0925	1025	1038	1125	1325	1425	1525	1625	1725	1809	1825	1925	2025	2126	2226	2310
S. Dona di Piave-Jesolo ◧ d.	0643	|	0743	|	|	0843	0929	0943	1043	|	1143	1343	1443	1543	1643	1743	1825	1843	1943	2043	*2201*	*2300*	2327
Venezia Mestre a.	0709	0741	0809	0819	0850	0909	0955	1009	1109	1115	1209	1409	1509	1609	1709	1809	1850	1909	2009	2109	*2328*	*2338*	2350
Venezia Santa Lucia a.	0721	|	0821	|	|	0921	|	1021	1121	|	1221	1421	1521	1621	1721	1821	|	1921	2021	2121	*2251*	*2351*	...
Milano Centrale **605** a.	...	0955d	...	|	1115	...	|	...	...	1345	...	...	...	...	...	...	2115	...	...	...	...	...	...
Bologna Centrale **600 620** a.	...	...	...	0949	...	...	1139	...	...	...	...	...	...	...	...	...	...	...	...	...	...	...	...
Roma Termini **600 620** a.	...	...	...	1207	...	...	1405	...	...	...	...	...	...	...	...	...	...	...	...	...	...	...	...

VENEZIA - UDINE - TRIESTE

Due to engineering work timings of Wien trains are subject to alteration

km		Ⓐ	⚒	⚒	†	Ⓐ	*FR* **9703**	*RJ* **132**				Ⓐ	*RJ* **130**		2 **F**	Ⓐ		Ⓑ ⊖	*ITA* **8993**		*ITA* **8920** **C**	*FR* **9755**	*NJ* **1236** **D**	*FR* **9430** **E**	
	Roma Termini **600 620** d.	...	...	...	...	...	...	...	...	...	...	...	...	...	...	...	...	...	...	...	1655	...	...	1735	...
	Bologna C **600 620** d.	...	...	...	...	...	...	...	...	...	...	...	...	...	...	...	...	...	...	...	1921	...	...	2001	...
	Milano Centrale **605** d.	...	...	...	...	...	0645	...	...	...	...	...	...	...	...	...	...	...	1735	...	|	1845	...	|	...
0	**Venezia** Santa Lucia ⊙ d.	0501	0701	0801	0801	0901	|	0956	1001	1201	1401	1501	1552	1601	...	1701	1801	1901	|	2001	|	|	2105	|	2201
9	**Venezia** Mestre ⊙ d.	0514	0714	0814	0814	0914	0924	1008	1014	1214	1414	1514	1604	1614	...	1714	1814	1914	2000	2014	2051	2110	2117	2137	2214
30	Treviso Centrale ⊙ d.	0534	0734	0834	0834	0934	0944	1028	1034	1234	1434	1534	1628	1634	...	1734	1834	1934	2028	2034	2109	2130	2136	2158	2235
57	Conegliano ⊙ d.	0552	0752	0852	0852	0952	1002	|	1052	1252	1452	1552	|	1652	...	1752	1852	1952	2046	2052	2127	2148	2156	2217	2253
74	Sacile ⊙ d.	0603	0803	0903	0903	1003	|	|	1103	1303	1503	1603	|	1703	...	1803	1903	2003	|	2103	|	|	|	|	2304
87	Pordenone ⊙ d.	0615	0815	0915	0915	1015	1025	1105	1115	1315	1515	1615	1705	1715	...	1815	1915	2015	2106	2115	2147	2208	2214	2238	2316
136	**Udine** ⊙ a.	0651	0851	0951	0951	1051	1056	1142	1151	1351	1551	1651	1742	1751	...	1851	1951	2051	2140	2151	2217	2237	2245	2303	2353
	Villach **83** a.	|	|	...	|	...	...	1311	|	|	|	|	1911	...	...	|	|	|	...	|	...	...	0027	|	...
	Wien Hbf **83** a.	|	|	...	|	...	...	1736	|	|	|	|	2336	...	...	|	|	|	...	|	...	...	0819	|	...
136	**Udine** d.	0654	0854	...	0954	...	...	...	1154	1354	1554	1654	...	...	1755	1854	1954	2120	...	2154	...	...	...	2305	...
169	Gorizia Centrale ⊡ d.	0718	0918	...	1018	...	...	...	1218	1418	1618	1718	...	...	1829	1918	2018	2151	...	2218	...	...	...	2328	...
192	Monfalcone d.	0739	0939	...	1039	...	...	...	1239	1439	1639	1739	...	...	1834	1939	2041	2215	...	2239	...	...	...	...	...
219	**Trieste** Centrale a.	0802	1002	...	1102	...	...	...	1302	1502	1702	1802	...	...	1857	2002	2104	2244	...	2302	...	...	...	...	...

	Ⓐ		*FR* **9713**	*NJ* **1237** **D**	*FR* **9409** **E**	⚒	*ITA* **8971**	*ITA* **8907** **C**		2 **F**		*FR* **9729**		*RJ* **131**	Ⓐ		Ⓐ			*RJ* **133**	Ⓐ		Ⓐ	
Trieste Centrale d.	...	...	...	...	...	0528	...	...	0658	0852	0858	...	1058	...	1128	1258	1332	1458	1658	...	1758	1858	...	2032
Monfalcone d.	...	...	...	...	...	0558	...	...	0722	0916	0922	...	1122	...	1158	1322	1402	1522	1722	...	1822	1922	...	2058
Gorizia Centrale ⊡ d.	...	...	...	...	0612	0620	...	...	0743	0921	0943	...	1143	...	1220	1343	1424	1543	1743	...	1843	1943	...	2120
Udine a.	...	...	...	...	0645	0652	...	...	0806	0954	1006	...	1206	...	1252	1406	1456	1606	1806	...	1906	2006	...	2152
Wien Hbf **83** d.	...	...	...	2149	|	|	...	...	|	...	|	...	|	0624	|	|	|	|	|	1224	|	|	...	|
Villach **83** d.	...	...	...	0500	|	|	...	...	|	...	|	...	|	1049	|	|	|	|	|	1649	|	|	...	|
Udine ⊙ d.	0509	0601	0615	0625	0647	0658	0716	0723	0809	...	1009	1123	1209	1218	1309	1409	1509	1609	1809	1818	1909	2009	2109	2209
Pordenone ⊙ d.	0544	0636	0646	0700	0721	0737	0749	0800	0844	...	1044	1159	1244	1252	1344	1444	1544	1644	1844	1851	1944	2044	2144	2244
Sacile ⊙ d.	0555	0647	|	|	|	0752	|	|	0855	...	1055	|	1255	|	1355	1455	1555	1655	1855	|	1955	2055	2155	2254
Conegliano ⊙ d.	0607	0659	0706	0725	0750	0803	0811	0823	0907	...	1107	1223	1307	|	1407	1507	1607	1707	1907	|	2007	2107	2207	2307
Treviso Centrale ⊙ d.	0627	0723	0731	0758	0813	0823	0831	0845	0927	...	1127	1243	1327	1333	1427	1527	1627	1727	1927	1932	2027	2127	2227	2327
Venezia Mestre ⊙ a.	0646	0746	0749	0822	0827	0846	0855	0908	0946	...	1146	1310	1346	1402	1446	1546	1646	1746	1946	1952	2046	2146	2246	2346
Venezia Santa Lucia ⊙ a.	0659	0759	|	0834	|	0859	|	|	0959	...	1159	|	1359	1414	1459	1559	1659	1759	1959	2004	2059	2159	2259	2359
Milano Centrale **605** a.	...	...	1015	...	|	...	1125	|	...	...	...	1545	...	...	...	...	...	...	...	...	...	...	...	...
Bologna C **600 620** a.	...	...	...	...	0959	...	...	1039	...	...	...	...	...	...	...	...	...	...	...	...	...	...	...	...
Roma Termini **600 620** a.	...	...	...	...	1225	...	...	1305	...	...	...	...	...	...	...	...	...	...	...	...	...	...	...	...

🚋 service **Trieste** (Piazza Dalmazia) - **Villa Opicina** (Stazione Trenovia) and v.v. Operator: Trieste Trasporti S.p.A. Journey 31 minutes.

From **Trieste**: 0722, 0750, 0818, 0846, 0914, 0942, 1010, 1038, 1106, 1134, 1202, 1230, 1258, 1326, 1354, 1422, 1450, 1518, 1546, 1614, 1642, 1710, 1738, 1806, 1834, 1920, 1930, 1958, 2026. Also by 🚌 from Trieste Piazza Oberdan (Line **2**) 0711, 0731, 0751 and every 20 minutes until 2011. Journey 12 minutes.

From **Villa Opicina**: 0700, 0728, 0756, 0824, 0852, 0920, 0948, 1016, 1044, 1112, 1140, 1208, 1236, 1304, 1332, 1400, 1428, 1456, 1524, 1552, 1620, 1648, 1716, 1744, 1812, 1840, 1908, 1936, 2004. Also by 🚌 from Villa Opicina (Line **2**) 0700, 0720, 0740 and every 20 minutes until 2000. Journey 12 minutes.

Walking times: Trieste Centrale railway station - Piazza Dalmazia 7 minutes / Piazza Oberdan 9 minutes; Villa Opicina Stazione Trenovia - Villa Opicina railway station 20 minutes.

VENEZIA - NOVA GORICA

	Ⓒ	Ⓒ
Venezia Mestre d.	0716	1600
S. Dona di Piave-Jesolo d.	0743	1624
Portogruaro-Caorle d.	0803	1649
Latisana-Lignano-Bibione d.	0813	1701
Cervignano-Aquileia-Grado d.	0836	1718
Trieste Airport d.	0844	1727
Gorizia Centrale a.	0907	1750
Gorizia Centrale d.	0920	1800
Nova Gorica a.	0939	1820

	Ⓒ	Ⓒ
Nova Gorica d.	1240	1840
Gorizia Centrale a.	1300	1859
Gorizia Centrale d.	1312	1909
Trieste Airport d.	1339	1931
Cervignano-Aquileia-Grado d.	1347	1939
Latisana-Lignano-Bibione d.	1407	1955
Portogruaro-Caorle d.	1417	2004
S. Dona di Piave-Jesolo d.	1435	2020
Venezia Mestre a.	1500	2050

A – (12) 🍷 Napoli - Trieste and v.v.
B – (12) 🍷 Torino - Trieste and v.v.
C – (12) 🍷 Napoli - Udine and v.v.
D – *ÖBB Nightjet* 🛏 1,2 cl., 🛌 2 cl. (4,6 berth), (2) Wien - Venezia and v.v.
E – (12) 🍷 Napoli - Gorizia and v.v.
F – (2) Ljubljana - Villa Opicina - Udine and v.v. (Table **1305**).

d – Milano **Porta Garibaldi**.

⊖ – By connecting trains on Ⓐ.

⊙ – Also from Venezia Santa Lucia at 0601 Ⓐ, 1301 ⚒, 1701 †.
Also from Udine at 0909 †, 1109 Ⓐ, 1709 Ⓐ, 1909 †.

◧ – 🚌 S. Dona di Piave-Jesolo - Lido di Jesolo and v.v. ATVO route **19A**. 1–2 journeys per hour 0600 - 2300. Journey 35 minutes. www.atvo.it.

⊡ – 🚌 Gorizia Centrale - Nova Gorica (Slovenia) and v.v. TPL-FVG route **1**. Frequent service. Bus stop for Nova Gorica is 100 metres from station on Italian side. Total journey time ± 20 minutes. www.mycicero.it.

2nd class

NORTH EAST ITALY LOCAL SERVICES 603

ENZIA - TREVISO - BELLUNO

km		Ⓐ	⑥			Ⓐ	Ⓒ			Ⓐ 🚌	Ⓐ 🚌			Ⓐ		Ⓐ			⚒			Ⓑ		🚌
0	**Venezia** Santa Lucia 601 d.	...	...	...	...	0743	0748	0843	...	...	...	...	...	...	...	1443	...	...	1643	1743	...	1843	1931	...
9	**Venezia** Mestre 601 d.	...	...	...	...	0756	0800	0856	...	...	...	...	...	...	...	1456	...	...	1656	1756	...	1856	1944	...
30	**Treviso** Centrale 601 d.	0622	...	...	...	0822	0821	0922	...	...	...	...	...	1314	...	1522	...	...	1722	1822	...	1922	2007	...
57	Conegliano 601 d.	0639	0639	0741	...	0840	0841	0940	...	1040	1140	1241	...	1341	1441	1540	...	1641	1740	1846	...	1940	2031	2201
71	Vittorio Veneto a.	0657	0957	0802	...	0902	0902	1002	...	1103	1203	1302	...	1402	1502	1602	...	1702	1802	1903	...	2002	2047	2224
98	Ponte nelle Alpi-Polpet a.	0731	0731	0831	...	0931	0931	1031	...	1148	1248	1331	...	1431	1531	1631	...	1731	1831	1931	...	2031	2115	2309
98	Ponte nelle Alpi-Polpet d.	0739	0739	0839	...	0939	0932	1039	...	1148	1248	1339	...	1439	1539	1639	...	1739	1839	1939	...	2039	2116	2310
105	**Belluno** a.	0747	0747	0847	...	0947	0939	1047	...	1201	1301	1347	...	1447	1547	1647	...	1747	1847	1947	...	2047	2124	2322

	⚒	⚒	†	⚒			Ⓐ 🚌		Ⓐ 🚌	Ⓐ				⑥	Ⓐ	Ⓐ	†			Ⓒ	Ⓐ	Ⓐ	🚌
elluno d.	0536	0615	0620	0720	0820	...	0920	1020	1120	1220	1320	...	1420	1520	1520	1620	1620	...	1720	1820	1820	1920	2020
onte nelle Alpi-Polpet a.	0544	0623	0628	0728	0828	...	0933	1028	1133	1228	1328	...	1428	1528	1528	1628	1628	...	1728	1828	1828	1928	2033
onte nelle Alpi-Polpet d.	0545	0624	0633	0733	0833	...	0933	1033	1133	1233	1333	...	1433	1533	1533	1633	1633	...	1733	1833	1833	1933	2033
ittorio Veneto d.	0613	0656	0701	0759	0901	...	1011	1101	1211	1301	1401	...	1501	1601	1601	1701	1701	...	1801	1904	1904	2001	2111
onegliano 601 a.	0630	0711	0718	0816	0920	...	1041	1118	1241	1318	1418	...	1520	1618	1618	1720	1718	...	1818	1918	1924	2018	2141
reviso Centrale 601 a.	0653	0737	0737	0837	0940	...	...	1137	...	...	...	...	1540	...	1643	1740	...	...	1837	1940	1949	2037	...
enezia Mestre 601 a.	0716	0804	0804	0904	1004	...	...	1204	...	...	...	...	1604	...	...	1804	...	...	1904	2004	...	...	...
enezia Santa Lucia 601 a.	0729	0817	0817	0917	1017	...	...	1217	...	...	...	...	1617	...	...	1817	...	...	1917	2017	...	...	...

🚌 CALALZO - BELLUNO - MONETBELLUNA 🚌

A limited number of trains run Calalzo - Belluno and v.v., please check locally for times

km		⚒		⚒		⚒		†		Ⓐ		⚒			Ⓐ	⚒	Ⓑ	Ⓐ		Ⓑ	⑥			
0	**Calalzo** ◧ d.	...	...	0558	...	0643	...	0658	0858	1057	...	1158	...	1258	1357	...	1458	1557	...	...	1558	1658	1758	1928
37	Ponte nelle Alpi-Polpet d.	...	...	0644	...	0729	...	0744	0944	1148	...	1244	...	1344	1448	...	1544	1648	...	...	1627	1744	1844	2014
44	**Belluno** d.	0507	0607	0707	0707	0747	...	0807	1007	1202	1207	1307	...	1407	1502	1507	1607	1702	...	1707	1707	1807	1907	2032
75	Feltre d.	0554	0654	0754	0751	0844	...	0854	1054	...	1254	1354	...	1454	...	1554	1654	...	...	1754	1754	1854	1954	...
110	**Montebelluna** a.	0651	0751	0851	0851	0936	...	0951	1151	...	1351	1451	...	1551	...	1651	1751	...	...	1851	1851	1951	2051	...

	⚒	⚒			Ⓐ	Ⓒ		Ⓐ	†	⚒	⚒					Ⓐ	Ⓐ	Ⓐ		⑥	Ⓑ		
ontebelluna d.	0533	0609	0709	0809	...	...	1009	...	1209	1215	1309	...	1409	1509	1609	...	1715	...	1809	1909	1909	2009	2219
eltre d.	0630	0708	0806	0906	...	...	1106	...	1306	1306	1406	...	1506	1606	1706	...	1806	...	1906	2006	2006	2106	2316
elluno d.	0715	0756	0856	0956	1030	1030	1151	1230	1356	1356	1456	...	1556	1651	1756	1830	1856	1926	1956	2051	2056	2151	0001
onte nelle Alpi-Polpet d.	...	0809	0909	1009	1041	1041	...	1241	1409	1409	1509	...	1609	...	1809	1841	1909	1939	2009	...	2109	...	...
alalzo ◧ a.	...	0900	1000	1100	1135	1134	...	1335	1500	1500	1600	...	1700	...	1900	1935	2000	2030	2100	...	2200	...	...

🚌 CALALZO - CORTINA 🚌

www.dolomitibus.it Route **30**

km		⚒	⚒			⚒	⚒	⚒		⚒	⚒	Ⓐ		⑥	†	⚒		⚒	⚒	†		⚒	⚒	
0	**Calalzo** Stazione FS d.	0622	0647	0658	...	0740	0820	0935	...	1118	1215	1310	...	1320	1400	1410	...	1450	1745	1835	...	1905	2035	...
35	**Cortina** Autostazione a.	0718	0745	0756	...	0838	0918	1033	...	1216	1313	1408	...	1418	1458	1508	...	1548	1843	1933	...	2003	2128	...

	⚒	⚒	⚒		⚒	⚒	⚒		⚒		⚒		⚒	†	⚒		⚒	⚒	⚒		†	⚒	
ortina Autostazione d.	0545	0650	0720	...	0820	0930	1115	...	1220	1240	1315	...	1402	1505	1620	...	1705	1750	1910	...	1940	2010	...
alalzo Stazione FS a.	0643	0748	0818	...	0918	1028	1213	...	1318	1338	1413	...	1500	1603	1718	...	1803	1848	2005	...	2035	2103	...

MONTEBELLUNA - TREVISO

km		Ⓐ	⚒	⚒		† 🚌		†			🚌			⚒ 🚌		⚒		Ⓑ						
0	**Montebelluna** d.	0601	0701	0801	...	0801	0901	1001	...	1201	1245	1401	...	1518	1601	1701	...	1801	1901	2001	...	2101	...	...
21	**Treviso** Centrale a.	0625	0725	0825	...	0843	0925	1025	...	1225	1327	1425	...	1600	1625	1725	...	1825	1925	2025	...	2125	...	...

	⚒	⚒	⚒		Ⓐ 🚌		⚒ 🚌		†	⚒					Ⓐ						⚒ 🚌		
reviso Centrale d.	0535	0635	0735	...	0835	0935	1110	...	1135	1235	1335	...	1435	1535	1658	...	1735	1835	1935	...	2035	...	...
ontebelluna a.	0559	0659	0759	...	0917	0959	1152	...	1159	1259	1359	...	1459	1559	1727	...	1759	1859	1959	...	2117	...	...

PADOVA - CASTELFRANCO VENETO - MONTEBELLUNA

km						†		⚒		⚒		⚒			⚒	⚒			Ⓑ					
0	**Padova** d.	0604	0704	0804	...	0904	1104	1125	...	1204	1304	1404	...	1504	1604	1625	...	1704	1804	1904	...	2004	2125	...
31	Castelfranco Veneto d.	0636	0736	0836	...	0936	1136	1152	...	1236	1336	1436	...	1536	1636	1652	...	1736	1836	1936	...	2036	2156	...
48	**Montebelluna** a.	0652	0752	0852	...	0952	1152	1205	...	1252	1352	1452	...	1552	1652	1705	...	1752	1852	1952	...	2052	2209	...

	⚒					⚒	†			⚒			⚒	⚒			⚒	Ⓑ					
ontebelluna d.	0541	0708	0808	...	0908	0946	1008	...	1208	1308	1408	...	1457	1508	1608	...	1708	1808	1908	...	2008	2108	...
astelfranco Veneto d.	0554	0725	0825	...	0925	0959	1025	...	1225	1325	1425	...	1510	1525	1625	...	1725	1825	1925	...	2025	2125	...
adova a.	0628	0756	0856	...	0956	1033	1056	...	1256	1356	1456	...	1534	1556	1656	...	1756	1856	1956	...	2056	2156	...

TRENTO - BASSANO DEL GRAPPA

km		⚒		⚒		⚒		⚒		†		⚒		⚒				⚒				⚒		
0	**Trento** ⊡ d.	0455	...	0535	...	0655	...	0755	...	0855	...	0955	...	1055	...	1255	...	1355	...	1655	...	1955	...	...
31	Levico Terme ⊡ d.	0546	...	0626	...	0746	...	0846	...	0946	...	1046	...	1146	...	1346	...	1446	...	1746	...	2046	...	...
44	Borgo Valsugana Centro ⊡ a.	0603	...	0643	...	0803	...	0903	...	1003	...	1103	...	1203	...	1403	...	1503	...	1803	...	2103	...	...
97	**Bassano del Grappa** ⊡ a.	0712	...	...	...	0916	...	1016	...	1116	...	1216	...	1316	...	1516	...	1616	...	1916	...	2216	...	...

	⚒				⚒		⚒		†		⚒		⚒		†		⚒		⚒		🚌		🚌
assano del Grappa ⊡ d.	0500	...	0725	...	0925	...	1025	...	1125	...	1225	...	1325	...	1525	...	1625	...	...	...	1925	...	2125
orgo Valsugana Centro ⊡ d.	0603	...	0833	...	1033	...	1133	...	1233	...	1333	...	1433	...	1633	...	1733	...	1823	...	2033	...	2233
evico Terme ⊡ d.	0619	...	0849	...	1049	...	1149	...	1249	...	1349	...	1439	...	1639	...	1739	...	1839	...	2049	...	2249
rento ⊡ a.	0709	...	0939	...	1139	...	1239	...	1339	...	1439	...	1539	...	1739	...	1839	...	1929	...	2139	...	2339

VENEZIA - CASTELFRANCO VENETO - BASSANO DEL GRAPPA

Additional trains are available on ⚒

km		⚒																						
0	**Venezia** Santa Lucia d.	0557	0657	0757	...	0857	0957	1057	...	1157	1257	1357	...	1457	1557	1657	...	1757	1857	1957	...	2057	2157	...
9	**Venezia** Mestre d.	0609	0709	0809	...	0909	1009	1109	...	1209	1309	1409	...	1509	1609	1709	...	1809	1909	2009	...	2109	2210	...
45	Castelfranco Veneto d.	0646	0746	0846	...	0946	1046	1146	...	1246	1346	1446	...	1546	1646	1746	...	1846	1946	2046	...	2146	2252	...
64	**Bassano del Grappa** a.	0711	0811	0911	...	1011	1111	1211	...	1311	1411	1511	...	1611	1711	1811	...	1911	2011	2111	...	2211	2314	...

	⚒																						
assano del Grappa d.	0521	0621	0721	...	0821	0921	1021	...	1121	1221	1321	...	1421	1521	1621	...	1721	1821	1921	...	2021	2121	...
astelfranco Veneto d.	0545	0646	0746	...	0846	0946	1046	...	1146	1246	1346	...	1446	1546	1646	...	1746	1846	1946	...	2046	2146	...
enezia Mestre a.	0621	0721	0821	...	0921	1021	1121	...	1221	1321	1421	...	1521	1621	1721	...	1821	1921	2021	...	2121	2226	...
enezia Santa Lucia a.	0633	0733	0833	...	0933	1033	1133	...	1233	1333	1433	...	1533	1633	1733	...	1833	1933	2033	...	2133	2239	...

VICENZA - CASTELFRANCO VENETO - TREVISO

km		⚒			⚒	†		Ⓐ			⚒			⚒			⚒	⚒						
0	**Vicenza** d.	0614	0714	...	0814	0914	...	1114	1214	...	1314	1414	...	1514	1614	...	1714	1814	...	1914	2014	...	...	...
24	Cittadella d.	0639	0739	...	0839	0939	...	1139	1239	...	1339	1439	...	1539	1639	...	1739	1839	...	1939	2039	...	...	...
36	Castelfranco Veneto d.	0655	0755	...	0855	0955	...	1155	1255	...	1355	1455	...	1555	1655	...	1755	1855	...	1955	2055	...	...	...
60	**Treviso** Centrale a.	0722	0822	...	0922	1022	...	1222	1322	...	1422	1522	...	1622	1722	...	1822	1922	...	2022	2122	...	...	...

	⚒	⚒			⚒		†	Ⓑ		⚒			⚒			⚒			⚒				
reviso Centrale d.	0538	0638	...	0738	0838	...	0938	1138	...	1238	1338	...	1438	1538	...	1638	1738	...	1838	2038	...	...	...
astelfranco Veneto d.	0607	0707	...	0807	0907	...	1007	1207	...	1307	1407	...	1507	1607	...	1707	1807	...	1907	2107	...	...	...
ittadella d.	0621	0721	...	0821	0921	...	1021	1221	...	1321	1421	...	1521	1621	...	1721	1821	...	1921	2121	...	...	...
icenza a.	0649	0749	...	0849	0949	...	1049	1249	...	1349	1449	...	1549	1649	...	1749	1849	...	1949	2149	...	...	...

◧ – Calalzo-Pieve di Cadore-Cortina.

⊡ – By 🚌 Trento - Castelnuovo in Valsugana (not shown) and v.v.

605 TORINO - MILANO - VERONA - VENEZIA

Subject to alteration August 4–31. For other high-speed trains see Table **600**.

km		*FR* 9703	*FR* 9705	*ITA* 8973		*FR* 9707	*FR* 9709	*FR* 9710		*FR* 9715	*ITA* 8977	*FR* 9717		*EC* 41	*FR* 9709	*ITA* 8981		*FR* 9723	*EC* 1281	*EC* 81		*EC* 33	*ITA* 8983	*FR* 9727
				④–①			①–⑤								⑥⑦				⑥⑦	①–⑤				
														B					**C** ♠	**C** ♠		**D**		
	Torino Porta Nuova d.	...	...	...	...	...	...	...	...	0805	...	...	...	...	...	...	...	...	...	...	...	...	...	...
	Torino Porta Susa △ d.	...	...	...	...	...	...	...	...	0815	...	...	...	...	...	...	...	...	...	...	...	...	...	...
	Rho-Fiera Milano d.	...	...	...	...	...	...	...	...	0858	...	...	...	...	...	...	...	...	...	...	...	...	...	...
	Milano Porta Garibaldi d.	...	...	...	...	...	...	...	...	0913	...	...	...	...	...	...	...	...	...	...	...	...	...	...
0	**Milano** Centrale d.	0645	0715	0735	...	0745	0815	0845	...	|	0935	0945	...	1005	1045	1135	...	1145	...	...	...	1205	1235	1245
83	Brescia d.	0723	0753	0813	...	0823	0853	0923	...	0953	1013	1023	...	1053	1123	1213	...	1223	...	...	...	1253	1313	1323
111	Desenzano-Sirmione d.	0738	|	|	...	|	0908	|	...	1008	1027	|	...	|	1138	|	...	1238	...	...	...	|	1327	1338
125	Peschiera del Garda ‡ d.	|	0814	0833	...	0844	|	0944	...	|	|	1044	...	1114	|	1234	...	|	...	...	...	1314	|	|
148	**Verona** Porta Nuova d.	0800	0830	0849	...	0900	0930	1000	...	1030	1049	1100	...	1130	1200	1249	...	1300	1313	1313	...	1330	1349	1400
200	Vicenza d.	0827	0857	0917	...	0927	0957	1027	...	1057	1117	1127	...	1157	1227	1317	...	1327	1338s	1343s	...	1357	1417	1427
230	Padova d.	0846	0916	0934	...	0946	1016	1046	...	1116	1134	1146	...	1216	1246	1334	...	1346	1357s	1427s	...	1416	1434	1446
258	**Venezia** Mestre ▽ a.	0900	0930	0952	...	1000	1030	1100	...	1130	1152	1200	...	1230	1300	1352	...	1400	1413	1502	...	1430	1452	1500
267	**Venezia** Santa Lucia a.	|	0942	1003	...	|	1042	1112	...	1142	1203	1212	...	1242	1312	1403	...	1412	1425	1514	...	1442	1503	1512
	Udine **601** a.	1056	...	...	...	|	...	...	...	...	...	...	...	...	...	...	...	...	...	...	...	...	...	...
	Trieste Centrale **601** a.	...	...	...	...	1205	...	...	...	...	...	...	...	...	...	...	...	...	...	...	...	...	...	...

	FR 9731	*FR* 9733	*ITA* 8987		*FR* 9735	*FR* 9737	*FR* 9741		*RJ* 85	*FR* 9743	*FR* 9747		*FR* 9749	*ITA* 8993	*FR* 9753		*ITA* 8995	*FR* 9755	*FR* 9757		*ITA* 8997	*FR* 9759	*FR* 9763
			④–①								Ⓑ												Ⓑ
			❋						**C** ♠														
Torino Porta Nuova d.	...	...	...	...	...	...	...	...	...	1510	...	...	...	...	1705	...	...	...	...	...	...	1840	...
Torino Porta Susa △ d.	...	...	...	...	...	...	...	...	...	1520	...	...	...	...	1715	...	...	...	...	...	...	1850	...
Rho-Fiera Milano d.	...	...	...	...	...	...	...	...	...	1558	...	...	...	...	1758	...	...	...	...	...	...	1928	...
Milano Porta Garibaldi d.	...	...	...	...	...	...	...	...	...	1613	...	...	...	...	1813	...	...	...	...	...	...	1943	...
Milano Centrale d.	1345	1415	1435	...	1445	1515	1545	...	...	|	1645	...	1715	1735	|	...	1835	1845	1915	...	1935	|	2045
Brescia d.	1423	1453	1513	...	1523	1553	1623	...	...	1653	1723	...	1753	1813	1853	...	1913	1923	1953	...	2013	2023	2123
Desenzano-Sirmione d.	|	1508	|	...	1538	|	|	...	...	1708	|	...	1807	1827	1908	...	|	|	2008	...	2027	|	2138
Peschiera del Garda ‡ d.	1444	|	1533	...	|	1614	1644	...	...	|	1744	...	|	|	|	...	1934	1944	|	...	|	|	2147
Verona Porta Nuova d.	1500	1530	1549	...	1600	1630	1700	...	1710	1730	1800	...	1830	1849	1930	...	1949	2000	2030	...	2049	2055	2203
Vicenza d.	1527	1557	1617	...	1627	1657	1727	...	1735s	1757	1827	...	1857	1917	1957	...	2017	2027	2057	...	2117	2124	2230
Padova d.	1546	1616	1634	...	1646	1716	1746	...	1756s	1816	1846	...	1916	1934	2016	...	2034	2046	2116	...	2134	2144	2249
Venezia Mestre ▽ a.	1600	1630	1652	...	1700	1730	1800	...	1812	1830	1900	...	1928	1950	2030	...	2052	2100	2130	...	2152	2200	2303
Venezia Santa Lucia a.	1612	1642	1703	...	1712	|	1812	...	1825	1842	1912	...	|	|	2042	...	2103	|	2142	...	2203	|	2315
Udine **601** a.	...	...	...	...	...	|	...	...	...	...	...	...	|	2140	...	...	...	2237	...	...	...	|	...
Trieste Centrale **601** a.	...	...	...	...	...	1927	...	...	...	...	...	...	2127	...	...	...	...	...	...	...	...	2345	...

	FR 9700	*ITA* 8970	*FR* 9702		*FR* 9706	*FR* 9708	*FR* 9712		*FR* 9713	*ITA* 8974	*FR* 9716		*FR* 9718	*ITA* 8971	*FR* 9724		*ITA* 8978	*FR* 9726	*RJ* 84		*FR* 9728	*FR* 9732	
																	④–①						
																	❋		**C** ♠				
Trieste Centrale **601** d.	...	...	...	...	...	...	0600	...	...	...	...	...	0707	...	...	...	...	0939	...	...	...	...	...
Udine **601** d.	...	...	...	...	...	...	|	...	0615	...	...	...	|	0716	...	...	...	|	...	...	...	...	...
Venezia Santa Lucia d.	0539	0557	0618	...	0648	0718	|	...	|	0757	0818	...	|	|	1048	...	1057	|	1135	...	1148	1248	...
Venezia Mestre △ d.	0551	0609	0630	...	0700	0730	0749	...	0800	0809	0830	...	0900	0909	1100	...	1109	1130	1147	...	1200	1300	...
Padova d.	0607	0626	0646	...	0716	0746	|	...	0816	0826	0846	...	0916	0926	1116	...	1126	1146	1203u	...	1216	1316	...
Vicenza d.	0626	0644	0704	...	0734	0804	|	...	0834	0844	0904	...	0934	0944	1134	...	1144	1204	1224u	...	1234	1334	...
Verona Porta Nuova d.	0652	0712	0732	...	0802	0832	0846	...	0902	0912	0932	...	1002	1012	1202	...	1212	1232	1252	...	1302	1402	...
Peschiera del Garda ‡ d.	0707	|	0748	...	|	0848	|	...	|	|	0948	...	|	|	|	...	1226	|	...	...	1318	|	...
Desenzano-Sirmione d.	0716	0733	|	...	0823	|	|	...	0923	0926	|	...	1023	1033	1223	...	|	1253	...	...	|	1423	...
Brescia d.	0734	0749	0809	...	0839	0909	|	...	0939	0949	1009	...	1039	1049	1239	...	1249	1309	...	...	1339	1439	...
Milano Centrale a.	0812	0825	|	...	0915	0945	|	...	1015	1025	|	...	1115	1125	1315	...	1325	1345	...	...	1415	1515	...
Milano Porta Garibaldi a.	...	...	0847	...	...	...	0955	...	...	...	1047	...	...	...	...	...	...	...	...	...	...	...	...
Rho-Fiera Milano a.	...	...	0901	...	...	...	|	...	...	...	1101	...	...	...	...	...	...	...	...	...	...	...	...
Torino Porta Susa ▽ a.	...	...	0938	...	...	...	1048	...	...	...	1143	...	...	...	...	...	...	...	...	...	...	...	...
Torino Porta Nuova a.	...	...	0956	...	...	...	1106	...	...	...	1201	...	...	...	...	...	...	...	...	...	...	...	...

	FR 9729	*FR* 9736	*ITA* 8984		*FR* 9740	*ITA* 8986	*EC* 32		*EC* 80	*FR* 9744	*ITA* 8988		*EC* 46 146	*FR* 9748	*FR* 9750		*FR* 9752	*ITA* 8992	*FR* 9754		*FR* 9758	*FR* 9762	
																		④–①	①–⑤			Ⓑ	
							D		**C** ♠				**B**										
Trieste Centrale **601** d.	...	...	...	...	...	...	...	...	...	...	...	...	...	...	...	...	...	...	...	...	1705	...	...
Udine **601** d.	1123	...	...	...	...	...	...	...	...	...	...	...	...	...	...	...	...	...	...	...	|	...	...
Venezia Santa Lucia d.	|	1348	1357	...	1448	1457	1518	...	1535	1548	1557	...	1618	1648	1718	...	1748	1757	1818	...	|	1948	...
Venezia Mestre △ d.	1330	1400	1409	...	1500	1509	1530	...	1547	1600	1609	...	1630	1700	1730	...	1800	1809	1830	...	1900	2000	...
Padova d.	1346	1416	1426	...	1516	1526	1546	...	1603u	1616	1626	...	1646	1716	1746	...	1816	1826	1846	...	1916	2016	...
Vicenza d.	1404	1434	1444	...	1534	1544	1604	...	1624u	1634	1644	...	1704	1734	1804	...	1834	1844	1904	...	1934	2034	...
Verona Porta Nuova d.	1432	1502	1512	...	1602	1612	1632	...	1652	1702	1712	...	1732	1802	1832	...	1902	1912	1932	...	2002	2102	...
Peschiera del Garda ‡ d.	|	|	|	...	|	1626	1648	...	...	|	|	...	1748	|	1848	...	1918	1926	|	...	2018	|	...
Desenzano-Sirmione d.	1454	1523	1533	...	1623	|	|	...	...	1723	1733	...	|	1823	|	...	|	|	1953	...	|	2123	...
Brescia d.	1509	1539	1549	...	1639	1649	1709	...	...	1739	1749	...	1809	1839	1909	...	1939	1949	2009	...	2039	2139	...
Milano Centrale a.	1545	1615	1625	...	1715	1725	1755	...	...	1815	1825	...	1855	1915	|	...	2015	2025	2045	...	2115	2215	...
Milano Porta Garibaldi a.	...	...	...	...	...	...	...	...	...	...	...	...	...	...	1947	...	...	...	...	...	...	...	...
Rho-Fiera Milano a.	...	...	...	...	...	...	...	...	...	...	...	...	...	...	2001	...	...	...	...	...	...	...	...
Torino Porta Susa ▽ a.	...	...	...	...	...	...	...	...	...	...	...	...	...	...	2044	...	...	...	...	...	...	...	...
Torino Porta Nuova a.	...	...	...	...	...	...	...	...	...	...	...	...	...	...	2101	...	...	...	...	...	...	...	...

MILANO - VERONA LOCAL TRAINS

Trenord

km									⑤⑥
0	**Milano** Centrale d.	0625	0725	0825		2025	2125	2225	2325
4	**Milano** Lambrate d.	0633	0733	0833	and	2033	2133	2233	2333
34	Treviglio d.	0656	0756	0856	hourly	2056	2156	2256	2356
83	Brescia d.	0733	0833	0933	until	2133	2233	2333	0033
111	Desenzano-Sirmione d.	0749	0849	0949	◧ ⊡	2149	2249	2349	0049
125	Peschiera del Garda ‡ d.	0758	0858	0958		2158	2258	2358	0058
148	**Verona** Porta Nuova a.	0817	0917	1017		2217	2317	0017	0117

Verona Porta Nuova d.	0543	0643	0743		1843	1943	2043	2143
Peschiera del Garda ‡ d.	0557	0657	0757	and	1857	1957	2057	2157
Desenzano-Sirmione d.	0607	0707	0807	hourly	1907	2007	2107	2207
Brescia d.	0628	0728	0828	until	1928	2028	2128	2228
Treviglio d.	0705	0805	0905	◧ ⊡	2005	2105	2205	2305
Milano Lambrate d.	0728	0828	0928		2028	2128	2228	2320
Milano Centrale a.	0735	0835	0935		2035	2135	2235	2327

VERONA - VENEZIA LOCAL TRAINS

2nd class Trenord

km		Ⓐ	⚒					Ⓒ	
0	**Verona** Porta Nuova d.	0522	0622	0722	and	1822	1922	2022	2222
52	Vicenza d.	0603	0703	0803	hourly	1903	2003	2103	2303
82	Padova **600** d.	0622	0722	0822	until	1922	2022	2124	2322
100	**Venezia** Mestre **600** a.	0637	0737	0837	⊡	1937	2037	2150	2337
109	**Venezia** Santa Lucia **600** a.	0650	0750	0850		1950	2050	2203	2350

	⚒							Ⓒ
Venezia Santa Lucia **600** d.	0610	0710	0810	and	1910	2010	2110	2215
Venezia Mestre **600** d.	0623	0723	0823	hourly	1923	2023	2123	2227
Padova **600** d.	0640	0740	0840	until	1940	2040	2140	2244
Vicenza d.	0658	0758	0858	⊙ ⊡	1958	2058	2158	2301
Verona Porta Nuova a.	0738	0838	0938		2038	2138	2238	2340

B – To / from Genève (Table **82**).
C – To / from München (Table **70**).
D – To / from Zürich (Table **82**).

s – Stops to set down only.
u – Stops to pick up only.

♠ – Also available to passengers without reservation.
‡ – Station for Gardaland Park. Free shuttle bus available.

⊖ – For 🚌 Edolo - Tirano see Table **593**.
◧ – 1025 from Milano and 1243 from Verona run on Ⓒ only.
⊙ – 1210 from Venezia runs Ⓐ only.
⊡ – Timings may vary by a few minutes.
△ – Most trains call to pick up only.
▽ – Most trains call to set down only.
❋ – Subject to confirmation.

FOR BRESCIA - EDOLO SEE NEXT PAGE →

BRESCIA - EDOLO 605

BRESCIA - EDOLO Services are operated by 🚌 Marone-Zone - Edolo and v.v. until September 7 2nd class Trenord

km																								
		Ⓐ	†										⚒								Ⓐ	Ⓐ		Ⓐ		
0	**Brescia** d.	0553	0707	0756	...	0907	0956	1107	...	1156	1307	1322	...	1356	1507	1556	...	1707	1714	1756	...	1907	2039	2139
	Iseo d.	0632	0730	0830	...	0930	1031	1130	...	1230	1330	1405	...	1430	1530	1630	...	1730	1752	1830	...	1930	2113	2213
	Marone-Zone a.	0647	0745	0845	...	0945	1045	1145	...	1245	1345	1423	...	1445	1545	1645	...	1745	1809	1845	...	1945	...	...
103	**Edolo** ⊖ a.	0829	0923	1029	...	1123	1229	1323	...	1429	1523	...	...	1629	1723	1829	...	1923	...	2029	...	2123	...	...

	Ⓐ	⚒	Ⓐ	†		⚒		Ⓐ 🚌				⚒									Ⓐ	Ⓐ	†
Edolo ⊖ d.				0600	...	0625	0735	0825	...	...	0935	1025	1135	1225	...	1335	1425	1535	1625	...	1735	1825	1925
Marone-Zone d.	0616	0650	0730	0747	...	0815	0914	1002	1015	...	1114	1215	1314	1415	...	1514	1615	1714	1815	...	1914	2015	2114
Iseo d.	0633	0709	0747	0806	...	0833	0930	...	1033	...	1130	1233	1330	1433	...	1530	1633	1730	1833	...	1930	2033	2136
Brescia a.	0711	0744	0821	0840	...	0905	0953	...	1105	...	1153	1305	1353	1505	...	1553	1705	1753	1905	...	1953	2105	2200

MILANO MALPENSA AEROPORTO ✈ 606

Trenord

Services from / to Milano Cadorna operate as *Malpensa Express* - special fare payable. Trains crossing the Swiss / Italian border are subject to alteration on and around public holidays.

km									
0	**Milano** Cadorna d.	0427	0457	0527	0557	and at	2227	2257	2327
	Milano Bovisa d.	0433	0503	0533	0603	the same	2233	2303	2333
	Busto Arsizio FN d.	0455	0525	0555	0625	minutes	2255	2325	2355
	Malpensa Aeroporto T1 ✈ a.	0504	0534	0604	0634	past each	2304	2334	0004
	Malpensa Aeroporto T2 ✈ a.	0510	0540	0610	0640	hour until	2310	2340	0010

Malpensa Aeroporto T2 ✈ d.	0520	0550	0620	0650	and at	2320	2350	0020
Malpensa Aeroporto T1 ✈ d.	0526	0556	0626	0656	the same	2326	2356	0026
Busto Arsizio FN d.	0533	0603	0633	0703	minutes	2333	0003	0033
Milano Bovisa a.	0556	0626	0656	0726	past each	2356	0026	0056
Milano Cadorna a.	0604	0634	0704	0734	hour until	0004	0034	0104

km									
									A
0	**Milano** Centrale d.	0525	0555	0625	0655	and at	1925	1955	2025
	Milano Porta Garibaldi d.	0535	0605	0635	0705	the same	1935	2005	2035
	Milano Bovisa d.	0542	0612	0642	0712	minutes	1942	2012	2042
	Busto Arsizio FN d.	0607	0637	0707	0737	past each	2007	2037	2107
	Malpensa Aeroporto T1 ✈ a.	0616	0646	0716	0746	hour until	2016	2046	2116
	Malpensa Aeroporto T2 ✈ a.	0622	0652	0722	0752		2022	2052	2122

								B
Malpensa Aeroporto T2 ✈ d.	0537	0607	0637	0707	and at	2037	2107	2137
Malpensa Aeroporto T1 ✈ d.	0543	0613	0643	0713	the same	2043	2113	2143
Busto Arsizio FN d.	0552	0622	0652	0722	minutes	2052	2122	2152
Milano Bovisa a.	0618	0648	0718	0748	past each	2118	2148	2218
Milano Porta Garibaldi a.	0625	0655	0725	0755	hour until	2125	2155	2225
Milano Centrale a.	0637	0707	0737	0807		2137	2207	2237

km									
			⑥⑦						
	Malpensa Aeroporto T2 ✈ d.	...	...	0613	0713	and	2113	2213	2313
0	**Malpensa** Aeroporto T1 ✈ d.	...	...	0619	0719	at	2119	2219	2319
	Busto Arsizio FN d.	...	...	0630	0730	the	2130	2230	2330
17	Busto Arsizio FS d.	...	...	0640	0740	same	2140	2240	2340
25	Gallarate d.	...	...	0647	0747	minutes	2147	2247	2347
44	Varese d.	0500	0606	0706	0806	past	2206	2306	0006
56	Stabio d.	0516	0623	0723	0823	each	2223	2323	0023
60	Mendrisio a.	0520	0627	0727	0827	hour	2227	2327	0027
79	Lugano 550 a.	0554	0654	0754	0854	until	2254	2354	0054
108	**Bellinzona** 550 a.	0619	0713	0813	0913		2313	0026	0126

Bellinzona 550 d.	0433	0533	0641	0746	and	1946	2046	2146
Lugano 550 d.	0506	0606	0706	0806	at	2006	2106	2206
Mendrisio d.	0533	0633	0733	0833	the	2033	2133	2233
Stabio d.	0537	0637	0737	0837	same	2037	2137	2237
Varese d.	0600	0700	0800	0900	minutes	2100	2200	2254
Gallarate d.	0614	0714	0814	0914	past	2114	2214	...
Busto Arsizio FS d.	0625	0725	0825	0925	each	2125	2225	...
Busto Arsizio FN d.	0631	0731	0831	0931	hour	2131	2231	...
Malpensa Aeroporto T1 ✈ a.	0641	0741	0841	0941	until	2141	2241	...
Malpensa Aeroporto T2 ✈ a.	0647	0747	0847	0947		2147	2247	...

A – Also at 2125, 2225, 2325.

B – Also at 2237.

LOMBARDIA REGIONAL SERVICES 607

Trenord

Trains crossing the Swiss / Italian border are subject to alteration on and around public holiday dates.

km									
0	**Milano** Porta Garibaldi d.	0532	0632	0732	0832	and at	1832	1932	2032
13	Rho-Fiera Milano d.	0544	0644	0744	0844	the same	1844	1944	2044
36	Busto Arsizio FS d.	0602	0702	0802	0902	minutes	1902	2002	2102
44	Gallarate d.	0608	0708	0808	0908	past each	1908	2008	2108
63	Varese FS d.	0625	0725	0825	0925	hour until	1925	2025	2125
77	**Porto Ceresio** a.	0645	0745	0845	0945		1945	2045	2145

Porto Ceresio d.	0516	0616	0716	0816	and at	1816	1916	2016
Varese FS d.	0536	0636	0736	0836	the same	1836	1936	2036
Gallarate d.	0552	0701	0752	0852	minutes	1852	1952	2052
Busto Arsizio FS d.	0558	|	0758	0858	past each	1858	1958	2058
Rho-Fiera Milano d.	0616	0731	0816	0916	hour until	1916	2016	2116
Milano Porta Garibaldi a.	0633	0746	0833	0933		1933	2033	2133

km									
		⚒	⑥	⚒	⚒		⚒	⚒	⚒
0	**Varese** FS d.	0536	0636	0736	0836	and at	1736	1836	1936
12	Stabio d.	0553	0653	0753	0853	the same	1753	1853	1953
16	Mendrisio a.	0557	0657	0757	0857	minutes	1757	1857	1957
23	Chiasso a.	0610	0710	0810	0910	past each	1810	1910	2010
27	**Como** San Giovanni a.	0624	0724	0824	0924	hour until	1824	1924	2024

	⚒	⚒	⚒	⚒		⚒	⚒	⚒
Como San Giovanni d.	0541	0636	0736	0836	and at	1736	1836	1936
Chiasso d.	0550	0650	0750	0850	the same	1750	1850	1950
Mendrisio d.	0603	0703	0803	0903	minutes	1803	1903	2003
Stabio d.	0607	0707	0807	0907	past each	1807	1907	2007
Varese FS a.	0624	0724	0824	0924	hour until	1824	1924	2024

km																								
																					Ⓒ		Ⓐ	
0	**Milano** Cadorna d.	0639	0752	...	0852	0952	...	1052	1152	...	1252	1352	...	1452	1552	...	1652	1752	...	1852	1939	...	1952	2039
	Milano Bovisa d.	0646	0759	...	0859	0959	...	1059	1159	...	1259	1359	...	1459	1559	...	1659	1759	...	1859	1946	...	1959	2046
	Varese FN d.	0747	0847	...	0947	1047	...	1147	1247	...	1347	1447	...	1547	1647	...	1747	1847	...	1947	2047	...	2047	2147
72	**Laveno Mombello** Lago a.	0823	0923	...	1023	1123	...	1223	1323	...	1423	1523	...	1623	1723	...	1823	1923	...	2023	2123	...	2123	2223

	Ⓐ																						
Laveno Mombello Lago d.	0538	0638	...	0738	0838	...	0938	1038	...	1138	1238	...	1338	1438	...	1538	1638	...	1738	1838	...	1938	2038
Varese FN d.	0620	0716	...	0816	0916	...	1016	1116	...	1216	1316	...	1416	1516	...	1616	1716	...	1816	1916	...	2020	2120
Milano Bovisa a.	0713	0800	...	0900	1000	...	1100	1200	...	1300	1400	...	1500	1600	...	1700	1800	...	1900	2000	...	2113	2213
Milano Cadorna a.	0722	0809	...	0909	1009	...	1109	1209	...	1309	1409	...	1509	1609	...	1709	1809	...	1909	2009	...	2122	2222

km																								
		①–⑤	⚒		Ⓐ			⑥⑦	⑥⑦								Ⓐ		Ⓐ		⚒			
0	**Gallarate** d.	...	0608	...	0719	0819	0842	1019	1219	...	1319	1419	...	1519	1619	1719	1742	1819	1842	1919	1942	2019	2219	2330
31	Laveno Mombello FS d.	...	0641	...	0801	0901	0925	1101	1301	...	1401	1501	...	1601	1701	1801	1825	1901	1925	2001	2025	2101	2301	0039
46	**Luino** a.	...	0706	...	0815	0915	0943	1115	1315	...	1415	1515	...	1615	1715	1815	1843	1915	1943	2015	2043	2115	2315	0103
46	**Luino** d.	0540	...	0718	...	0918	...	1118	1318	1318	...	1518	...	...	1718	...	...	1918	...	...	...	2118	...	...
59	Pino-Tronzano 🏛 a.	0558	...	0730	...	0930	...	1130	1330	1330	...	1530	...	...	1730	...	...	1930	...	...	...	2130	...	...
77	**Cadenazzo** 548 a.	0622	...	0756	...	0956	...	1156	1356	1356	...	1556	...	...	1756	...	...	1956	...	...	...	2156	...	...
86	**Bellinzona** 548 a.	0633	...	*0811*	...	*1011*	...	*1211*	*1411*	*1411*	...	*1611*	...	...	*1811*	...	...	*2011*	...	...	...	*2211*	...	...

	⚒	Ⓐ	Ⓒ	Ⓐ		⚒			Ⓐ	⑥⑦		⑥⑦	Ⓒ						①–⑤	⑥⑦			
Bellinzona d.	...	...	...	...	0553	...	*0749*	...	...	*0949*	*1149*	*1149*	...	...	*1349*	...	...	*1549*	1654	...	*1749*	...	*1949*
Cadenazzo d.	...	...	...	...	0604	...	0804	...	...	1004	1204	1204	...	...	1404	...	...	1604	1704	...	1804	...	2004
Pino-Tronzano 🏛 d.	...	...	...	...	0628	...	0828	...	...	1028	1228	1228	...	...	1428	...	...	1628	|	...	1828	...	2028
Luino a.	...	...	...	...	0642	...	0842	...	...	1042	1242	1242	...	...	1442	...	...	1642	1744	...	1842	...	2042
Luino d.	0500	0534	0604	0619	0645	0719	0845	...	1000	1045	...	1245	1319	1345	1445	...	1545	1645	1745	1745	1845	1945	2045
Laveno Mombello FS d.	0515	0550	0618	0642	0700	0734	0900	...	1032	1100	...	1300	1334	1405	1500	...	1600	1700	1800	1800	1900	2000	2100
Gallarate a.	0552	0627	0651	0718	0741	0802	0935	...	1146	1141	...	1341	1418	1441	1541	...	1641	1741	1841	1841	1941	2041	2141

km										
0	**Milano** Centrale ◧ d.	0620	0820	1020	1220	1420	1620	1820	1915	2020
60	Codogno ◧ d.	0702	0902	1102	1302	1502	1702	1902	1957	2102
88	Cremona ◧ d.	0730	0930	1130	1330	1530	1730	1930	2025	2130
151	**Mantova** ◧ a.	0844	1038	1238	1438	1638	1838	2048	2138	2244

Mantova ◧ d.	0530	0607	0813	1013	1213	1413	1613	1813	2007
Cremona ◧ d.	0653	0730	0930	1130	1330	1530	1730	1930	2130
Codogno ◧ d.	0716	0756	0953	1153	1353	1553	1753	1953	2153
Milano Centrale ◧ a.	0810	0842	1040	1240	1440	1640	1840	2040	2240

MILANO - BERGAMO *56 km.* Journey 1 hour. 2nd class
From **Milano Centrale** at 0605, 0705, 0805, 0905, 1005, 1105, 1205, 1305, 1405, 1505, 1605, 1705, 1805, 1905, 2005, 2105, 2205.
From **Bergamo** at 0602, 0702, 0802, 0902, 1002, 1102, 1202, 1302, 1402, 1502, 1602, 1702, 1802, 1902, 2002, 2102, 2207.

MILANO - COMO LAGO *46 km.* Journey: 1 hour. 2nd class
From **Milano Cadorna**: 0613 ⚒, 0643, 0743, 0843, 0943, 1043, 1143, 1243, 1343, 1443, 1543, 1643, 1743, 1843, 1943, 2043, 2143, 2243.
From **Como Lago**: 0616, 0716, 0816, 0916, 1016, 1116, 1216, 1316, 1416, 1516, 1616, 1716, 1816, 1916, 2016, 2116, 2216.

◧ – All services are operated by 🚌 Bozzolo (not shown) - Mantova and v.v.

610 TORINO and MILANO - GENOVA - PISA - ROMA

Subject to alteration from July 21. For local trains see Table **611**. For *ICN* night trains see Tables **615** and **641**.

km		*IC* 501 ①–⑤	*IC* 501 ⑥⑦	*FB* 8601	*FA* 8583 ①–⑥	*FB* 8605	*FA* 8551 ①–⑥	*IC* 651	*IC* 503 A	2 ⚒	*IC* 633 B	*IC* 505 Ⓒ B	*IC* 505 Ⓐ B	2 Ⓐ	2 Ⓒ	*IC* 657 ⑥⑦	*IC* 659 B	*IC* 1549 ⑥ A	*IC* 1549 ⑦ A	*FB* 8613	*IC* 511	*IC* 637 B	*EC* 155 C
0	**Torino** Porta Nuova d.	...	...	...	...	...	...	...	0605	...	...	...	...	...	...	...	...	...	...	...	1040	...	...
56	Asti d.	...	...	...	...	...	...	...	0641	...	...	...	...	...	...	...	...	...	...	...	1113	...	...
91	Alessandria d.	...	...	...	...	...	...	...	0702	...	...	...	...	...	...	...	...	...	...	...	1136	...	...
112	Novi Ligure d.	...	...	...	...	...	...	...	0718	...	...	...	...	...	...	...	...	...	...	...	|	...	...
	Milano Centrale d.	...	...	...	...	...	...	0610	|	0625	0710	...	...	0725	0725	0805	0910	0930	1005	...	|	1110	1015r
	Pavia d.	...	...	...	...	...	...	0636	|	0659	0728	...	...	0759	0759	0836	0936	0959	1036	...	|	1136	|
	Voghera d.	...	...	...	...	...	...	|	|	0716	0751	...	...	0816	0816	0851	|	1016	1051	...	|	1151	1211
	Tortona d.	...	...	...	...	...	...	0702	|	0726	|	...	...	0826	0826	|	1002	|	|	...	|	|	|
166	**Genova** Piazza Principe a.	...	...	...	...	...	...	0744	0800	0816	0844	...	...	0908	0921	0944	1044	1112	1138	...	1221	1244	1304
166	**Genova** Piazza Principe d.	...	...	0516	0553	0705	0720	0747	...	0818	...	0853	0853	0911	0923	0947	...	...	...	1210	1224	...	1306
169	**Genova** Brignole d.	...	...	0523u	0600u	0712u	0728u	0756	...	0831	...	0901	0901	0923	0932	0956	...	...	...	1217u	1233	...	1314
194	S. Margherita-Portofino d.	...	...	|	|	|	|	0824	...	...	...	|	|	0959	1022	1016	...	...	...	|	|	...	1345
196	Rapallo d.	...	...	|	|	0737	0757	0829	...	...	...	0922	0922	1003	1027	1021	...	...	...	|	1303	...	1350
205	Chiavari d.	...	...	0547	|	0746	|	0838	...	...	...	0931	0931	1013	1037	1030	...	...	...	1246	1312	...	1395
212	Sestri Levante d.	0453	0453	|	|	|	|	0845	...	...	...	0938	0938	1028	1050	1039	...	...	...	|	1320	...	1406
235	Levanto d.	0510	0510	|	|	|	|	0901	...	...	...	|	|	...	...	1100	...	...	...	|	|	...	|
240	Monterosso d.	0516	0516	|	|	|	|	0907	...	...	...	0956	0956	...	...	1107	...	...	...	|	|	...	|
256	**La Spezia** Centrale d.	0532	0532	0618	0651	0816	0832	0923	...	...	...	1014	1017	...	...	1123	...	...	...	1316	1350	...	1454
272	Sarzana d.	0547	0547	|	|	|	|	|	...	...	...	|	...	...	...	|	...	...	...	|	|	...	|
282	Carrara-Avenza d.	0556	0556	|	|	|	|	0942	...	...	...	|	...	...	...	1141	...	...	...	|	1409	...	|
289	Massa Centro d.	0604	0604	0638	|	0836	|	0949	...	...	...	1036	...	...	...	1148	...	...	...	1336	1417	...	1522
310	Viareggio d.	0618	0618	0650	|	0848	|	1003	...	...	...	1049	...	...	...	1209	...	...	...	1348	1432	...	1541
331	**Pisa** Centrale a.	0634	0634	0704	0730	0904	0912	1020	...	...	...	1103	...	...	...	1223	...	...	...	1404	1447	...	1600
331	**Pisa** Centrale d.	0647	0637	0707	0733	0907	0915	1023	...	...	...	1111	...	...	...	1226	...	...	...	1407	1450	...	...
	Firenze Campo di Marte d.	|	|	|	0826	|	1006	|	...	...	...	|	...	...	...	|	...	...	...	|	|	...	...
351	**Livorno** Centrale a.	0655	0655	0724	|	0924	|	1041	...	...	...	1127	...	...	...	1244	...	...	...	1423	1504	...	...
351	**Livorno** Centrale d.	0657	0657	0726	|	0926	|	1044	...	...	...	1129	...	...	...	1259	...	...	...	1425	1506	...	...
385	Cecina d.	0722	0722	|	|	|	|	1109	...	...	...	1153	...	...	...	1327	...	...	...	|	|	...	...
420	Campiglia Marittima d.	0740	0740	0801	|	1001	|	1130	...	...	...	|	...	...	...	1345	...	...	...	1501	1542	...	...
437	Follonica d.	0750	0751	|	|	|	|	1140	...	...	...	1218	...	...	...	1356	...	...	...	|	1553	...	...
479	Grosseto d.	0817	0817	0834	|	1034	|	1215	...	...	...	1244	...	...	...	1429	...	...	...	1534	1618	...	...
589	Civitavecchia d.	0916	0916	0931	|	1131	|	...	...	...	...	1343	...	...	...	...	...	...	...	1632	1714	...	...
660	**Roma** Ostiense a.	0957	1003	|	0946t	|	1124t	...	...	...	...	1435	...	...	...	...	...	...	...	|	1754	...	...
667	**Roma** Termini a.	|	|	1016	1005	1233	1137	...	...	...	...	1448	...	...	...	...	...	...	...	1718	1805	...	...
	Napoli Centrale **640** a.	1229	1234	...	...	...	...	...	...	...	...	...	...	...	...	...	...	...	...	...	2031	...	...
	Salerno **640** a.	...	...	...	...	...	...	...	...	...	...	...	...	...	...	...	...	...	...	...	2126	...	...

	IC 665	2	*FB* 8619	*IC* 669	2	*IC* 641 B	*FB* 8623	*IC* 673	*FA* 8591 ①–⑤	2 Ⓒ	2 Ⓐ	*IC* 675 B	*IC* 679	*IC* 519	2 Ⓒ	2 Ⓐ	*IC* 685	*IC* 689 B	2 Ⓐ	2 Ⓒ	*IC* 887 ②–④	*IC* 687 ⑤–①
Torino Porta Nuova d.	...	...	...	...	...	...	1515	...	...	...	...	...	...	1805	...	...	...	...	...	...	...	...
Asti d.	...	...	...	...	...	...	1555	...	...	...	...	...	...	1841	...	...	...	...	...	...	...	...
Alessandria d.	...	...	...	...	...	...	1616	...	...	...	...	...	...	1902	...	...	...	...	...	...	...	...
Novi Ligure d.	...	...	...	...	...	...	|	...	...	...	...	...	...	1916	...	...	...	...	...	...	...	...
Milano Centrale d.	1210	1225	1310	1405	1425	1510	|	1605	...	1625	1625	1705	1805	|	1825	1825	1905	2005	2025	2025	2110	2110
Pavia d.	1236	1259	1336	1436	1459	1536	|	1636	...	1659	1659	1736	1836	|	1903	1903	1936	2036	2059	2059	2136	2136
Voghera d.	|	1316	|	1451	1516	1551	|	1651	...	1716	1716	1751	1851	|	1921	1921	1951	2051	2116	2116	2151	2151
Tortona d.	1302	1326	|	|	1526	|	|	|	...	1726	1726	|	1902	|	1931	1931	|	|	2126	2126	|	|
Genova Piazza Principe a.	1344	1418	1437	1544	1618	1644	1700	1744	...	1814	1818	1844	1944	2002s	2014	2021	2044	2144	2218	2232	2240	2244
Genova Piazza Principe d.	1347	1420	1502	1547	...	...	1705	1747	1835	...	1820	...	1947	|	...	2024	2047	...	...	...	2243	2247
Genova Brignole d.	1356	1427	1512	1556	...	...	1712	1756	1842u	...	1827	...	1955	2012	...	2030	2056	...	...	...	2252	2256
S. Margherita-Portofino d.	1416	...	|	|	...	...	|	1816	|	...	...	...	2016	...	...	...	|	...	...	...	2315	2319
Rapallo d.	1421	...	1537	1621	...	...	1737	1821	|	...	...	...	2021	...	...	...	2126	...	...	...	2320	2324
Chiavari d.	1430	...	1546	1630	...	...	1746	1830	|	...	...	...	2030	...	...	...	2135	...	...	...	2329	2333
Sestri Levante d.	1438	...	|	1638	...	...	|	1838	|	...	...	...	2038	...	...	...	2142	...	...	...	2341	2345
Levanto d.	1501	...	|	1701	...	...	|	1901	|	...	...	...	2100	...	...	...	|	...	...	...	2356	0001
Monterosso d.	1507	...	|	1707	...	...	|	1907	|	...	...	...	2107	...	...	...	|	...	...	...	0001	0007
La Spezia Centrale d.	1521	...	1616	1724	...	...	1816	1923	1948	...	...	...	2123	...	...	...	2223	...	...	...	0014	0025
Sarzana d.	...	...	|	|	...	...	1828	|	2000	...	...	...	|	...	...	...	2235	...	...	...	...	...
Carrara-Avenza d.	...	...	|	1749	...	...	|	1943	|	...	...	...	|	...	...	...	2243	...	...	...	...	...
Massa Centro d.	...	...	1636	1757	...	...	1840	1950	2012	...	...	...	2145	...	...	...	2250	...	...	...	...	...
Viareggio d.	...	...	1648	1815	...	...	1852	2003	|	...	...	...	2200	...	...	...	2303	...	...	...	...	...
Pisa Centrale a.	...	...	1704	1830	...	...	1908	2017	2036	...	...	...	2217	...	...	...	2317	...	...	...	...	...
Pisa Centrale d.	...	...	1707	1832	...	...	1911	2020	2038	...	...	...	2220	...	...	...	2320	...	...	...	...	...
Firenze Campo di Marte d.	...	...	|	|	...	...	|	|	2131	...	...	...	|	...	...	...	|	...	...	...	...	...
Livorno Centrale a.	...	...	1724	1848	...	...	1930	2035	|	...	...	...	2235	...	...	...	2335	...	...	...	...	...
Livorno Centrale d.	...	...	1726	...	...	...	1932	...	|	...	...	...	...	...	...	...	...	...	...	...	...	...
Cecina d.	...	...	|	...	...	...	1953	...	|	...	...	...	...	...	...	...	...	...	...	...	...	...
Campiglia Marittima d.	...	...	1801	...	...	...	2010	...	|	...	...	...	...	...	...	...	...	...	...	...	...	...
Follonica d.	...	...	|	...	...	...	|	...	|	...	...	...	...	...	...	...	...	...	...	...	...	...
Grosseto d.	...	...	1834	...	...	...	2043	...	|	...	...	...	...	...	...	...	...	...	...	...	...	...
Civitavecchia d.	...	...	1931	...	...	...	2137	...	|	...	...	...	...	...	...	...	...	...	...	...	...	...
Roma Ostiense a.	...	...	|	...	...	...	|	...	2247t	...	...	...	...	...	...	...	...	...	...	...	...	...
Roma Termini a.	...	...	2025	...	...	...	2233	...	2301	...	...	...	...	...	...	...	...	...	...	...	...	...
Napoli Centrale **640** a.	...	...	...	...	...	...	...	...	...	...	...	...	...	...	...	...	...	...	...	...	...	...
Salerno **640** a.	...	...	...	...	...	...	...	...	...	...	...	...	...	...	...	...	...	...	...	...	...	...

TORINO - GENOVA LOCAL TRAINS — 2nd class

km								
0	**Torino** Porta Nuova d.	0530	0630	0730	and	1830	1930	2130
56	Asti d.	0607	0707	0807	hourly	1907	2007	2207
91	Alessandria d.	0631	0731	0831	until	1931	2031	2231
112	Novi Ligure d.	0644	0744	0844	◧	1944	2044	2244
166	**Genova** Piazza Principe a.	0736	0835	0938		2030	2130	2330

Genova Piazza Principe d.	0527	0627	0727	and	1827	2027	2127
Novi Ligure d.	0614	0714	0814	hourly	1914	2114	2214
Alessandria d.	0631	0731	0831	until	1931	2131	2231
Asti d.	0654	0754	0854	◧	1954	2154	2254
Torino Porta Nuova a.	0733	0833	0933		2033	2233	2338

A – To / from Savona (Table **580**).
B – To / from Ventimiglia (Table **580**).
C – Until Sept. 28. [12] Zürich - Pisa and v.v.

e – Arrives 2117.
r – Milano **Rogoredo**.
s – Calls to set down only.
t – Roma **Tiburtina**.
u – Calls to pick up only.

⊡ – Runs up to 10 minutes later Grosseto - Pisa July 4 – 20.

◧ – No train from Torino at 0930, 1630; no train from Genova at 1127, 1527.
Some trains continue to / from Genova Brignole. Timings may vary by up to 8 minutes.

FOR RETURN SERVICE SEE NEXT PAGE →

ROMA - PISA - GENOVA - MILANO and TORINO 610

Subject to alteration from July 21. For local trains see Table **611**. For *ICN* night trains see Tables **615** and **641**.

km		2 ⑥–②	2 ③–⑤	*IC* 652	*IC* 500	*IC* 653 B	2 B	*IC* 658	*IC* 662	*FA* 8588	*IC* 631 B	*IC* 515 A		*FB* 8606	*IC* 666	*IC* 745 B	2 Ⓐ	2 Ⓒ	*IC* 670	*IC* 670 ⑥⑦	*IC* 1539 ⑥⑦ A	*IC* 510	2
	Salerno **640** d.	...	...	...	...	...	...	...	...	...	...	...	...	...	...	...	...	...	...	...	...	0639	...
	Napoli Centrale **640** d.	...	...	...	...	...	...	...	...	...	...	...	...	...	...	...	...	...	...	...	...	0731	...
0	**Roma** Termini d.	...	...	...	...	...	...	...	...	0623	...	...	...	0642	...	...	...	...	...	...	...	0957	...
7	**Roma** Ostiense d.	...	...	...	...	...	...	...	...	0632**t**	...	...	...	|	...	...	...	...	...	...	...	1007	...
81	Civitavecchia d.	...	...	...	...	...	...	...	...	|	...	...	...	0731	...	...	...	...	...	...	...	1047	...
188	Grosseto d.	...	...	...	...	...	...	...	...	|	...	...	...	0825	...	...	...	...	...	...	...	1141	...
230	Follonica d.	...	...	...	...	...	...	...	...	|	...	...	...	|	...	...	...	...	...	...	...	1200	...
247	Campiglia Marittima d.	...	...	...	...	...	...	...	...	|	...	...	...	0851	...	...	...	...	...	...	...	1211	...
282	Cecina d.	...	...	...	...	...	...	...	...	|	...	...	...	0906	...	...	...	...	...	...	...	|	...
316	**Livorno** Centrale a.	...	...	...	...	...	...	...	...	|	...	...	...	0931	...	...	...	...	...	...	...	1251	...
316	**Livorno** Centrale d.	...	...	...	...	...	...	0525	0620	|	...	...	...	0933	0830	...	...	...	...	1124	...	1253	...
	Firenze Campo di Marte d.	...	...	...	...	...	...	|	|	0754	...	...	...	|	|	...	...	...	...	|	...	|	...
336	**Pisa** Centrale a.	...	...	...	...	...	...	0539	0639	0848	...	...	...	0950	0855	...	...	...	...	1139	...	1309	...
336	**Pisa** Centrale d.	...	...	...	...	...	...	0542	0642	0850	...	...	...	0953	0857	...	...	...	...	1142	...	1312	...
357	Viareggio d.	...	...	...	...	...	...	0557	0657	|	...	...	...	1008	0923	...	...	...	...	1200	...	1327	...
378	Massa Centro d.	...	...	...	...	...	...	0613	0709	0916	...	...	...	1021	0937	...	...	...	...	1212	...	1340	...
385	Carrara-Avenza d.	...	...	...	...	...	...	|	0716	|	...	...	...	|	0952	...	...	...	...	1219	...	1349	...
395	Sarzana d.	...	...	...	...	...	...	|	0724	|	...	...	...	|	|	...	...	...	...	|	...	|	...
411	**La Spezia** Centrale d.	...	...	0456	...	...	...	0638	0738	0939	...	...	...	1045	1010	...	...	...	1238	1238	...	1411	...
418	Monterosso d.	...	...	0514	...	...	...	0654	|	|	...	...	...	|	1033	...	...	...	1255	1255	...	|	...
423	Levanto d.	...	...	0521	...	...	...	0700	0757	|	...	...	...	|	1040	...	...	...	1302	1302	...	|	...
446	Sestri Levante d.	0432	0437	0540	...	...	...	0716	0814	|	...	...	...	|	1122	...	...	...	1324	1324	...	1444	...
453	Chiavari d.	0443	0448	0552	...	...	...	0724	0824	|	...	...	...	1117	1132	...	...	...	1332	1332	...	1451	...
462	Rapallo d.	0451	0456	0601	...	...	...	0733	0833	|	...	...	...	|	1141	...	...	...	1341	1341	...	1500	...
464	S. Margherita-Portofino d.	0455	0500	0607	...	...	...	0739	|	|	...	...	...	|	|	...	...	...	1346	1346	...	|	...
498	**Genova** Brignole d.	0536	0538	0635	0648	...	...	0810	0909	1038**s**	...	...	...	1145	1210	...	1336	...	1410	1410	...	1529	...
501	**Genova** Piazza Principe a.	0542	0544	0641	|	...	...	0816	0915	1045	...	...	...	1150	1216	...	1342	...	1416	1416	...	1535	...
501	**Genova** Piazza Principe d.	0544	0546	0644	0656**u**	0719	0750	0819	0918	...	1119	1153	...	1159	1219	1319	1344	1344	1419	1419	1520	1538	1544
573	Tortona d.	0633	0633	|	|	|	0833	0859	|	...	|	|	...	|	|	|	1433	1433	|	|	|	|	1633
590	Voghera d.	0644	0644	0735	|	0810	0844	0910	1010	...	1210	|	...	|	1310	1410	1444	1444	1510	1510	1610	|	1644
616	Pavia d.	0701	0701	0752	|	0826	0901	0926	1026	...	1226	|	...	|	1326	1426	1501	1501	1526	1526	1626	|	1701
655	**Milano** Centrale a.	0735	0735	0822	|	0900	0935	1000	1055	...	1255	|	...	|	1355	1455	1535	1535	1555	1555	1655	|	1735
	Novi Ligure d.	...	...	...	0734	...	...	...	...	...	...	1233	...	|	...	...	...	...	...	...	...	|	...
	Alessandria d.	...	...	...	0748	...	...	...	...	...	...	1252	...	1244	...	...	...	...	...	...	...	1636	...
	Asti d.	...	...	...	0807	...	...	...	...	...	...	1318	...	1302	...	...	...	...	...	...	...	1700	...
	Torino Porta Nuova a.	...	...	...	0845	...	...	...	...	...	...	1410	...	1340	...	...	...	...	...	...	...	1740	...

	IC 674	*EC* 156 C	*FB* 8616	*IC* 635 B	2 Ⓒ	2 Ⓐ	*IC* 680	*FB* 8620	*IC* 681 B	2	*IC* 684 ⑥⑦ ⊡		*IC* 684 ①–⑤ ⊡	*FA* 8556 Ⓑ	*IC* 639 B	*IC* 518 B	2 Ⓑ	*FB* 8626	*FB* 8630	*FA* 8596 Ⓑ	*IC* 822 ②–④	*IC* 522 ⑤–①
Salerno **640** d.	...	...	...	...	...	...	...	...	...	...	...	...	...	...	...	...	...	...	...	...	...	...
Napoli Centrale **640** d.	...	...	...	...	...	...	...	...	...	...	...	...	...	...	...	...	...	...	...	...	1601	1731
oma Termini d.	...	...	1145	...	...	...	...	1342	...	...	...	...	...	1620	...	1542	...	1642	1812	2023	|	|
oma Ostiense d.	...	...	|	...	...	...	...	|	...	...	...	...	...	|	...	1552**u**	...	|	|	2033**t**	1904	1943
vitavecchia d.	...	...	1231	...	...	...	...	1431	...	...	...	...	...	|	...	1632	...	1731	1901	|	2009	2023
rosseto d.	...	...	1326	...	...	...	...	1528	...	...	1554	...	1600	|	...	1730	...	1827	1956	|	2109	2123
ollonica d.	...	...	|	...	...	...	...	|	...	...	1614	...	1621	|	...	1750	...	|	|	|	2129	2143
ampiglia Marittima d.	...	...	1354	...	...	...	...	1554	...	...	1626	...	1632	|	...	|	...	1856	2022	|	2139	2153
ecina d.	...	...	|	...	...	...	...	|	...	...	1645	...	1650	|	...	1814	...	|	|	|	2157	2212
vorno Centrale a.	...	...	1433	...	...	...	...	1634	...	...	1712	...	1718	|	...	1842	...	1934	2101	|	2224	2242
vorno Centrale d.	1321	...	1435	...	...	...	...	1636	...	...	1714	...	1720	|	...	1844	...	1936	2103	|	2226	2243
Firenze Campo di Marte d.	|	...	|	...	...	...	...	|	...	...	|	...	|	1744	...	|	...	|	|	2154	|	|
isa Centrale a.	1336	...	1453	...	...	...	...	1653	...	...	1733	...	1739	1837	...	1903	...	1953	2120	2240	2242	2301
isa Centrale d.	1339	1320	1456	...	...	...	...	1656	...	...	1736	...	1742	1840	...	1906	...	1956	2123	2243	2245	2301
areggio d.	1359	1342	1511	...	...	...	...	1712	...	...	1753	...	1802	|	...	1922	...	2012	2140	|	2302	2318
assa Centro d.	1411	1359	1524	...	...	...	...	1725	...	...	1814	...	1814	|	...	1937	...	2025	2154	|	2321	2331
arrara-Avenza d.	1418	|	|	...	...	...	...	|	...	...	1821	...	|	|	...	|	...	|	|	|	2330	2339
arzana d.	|	|	|	...	...	...	...	|	...	...	|	...	|	|	...	|	...	|	|	|	2339	2348
Spezia Centrale d.	1438	1432	1546	...	...	...	1638	1746	...	...	1838	...	1838	1927	...	2003	...	2046	2216	2327	2354	0013
onterosso d.	1455	|	|	...	...	...	1655	|	...	...	1855	...	1855	|	...	|	...	|	|	|	0009	0026
evanto d.	1502	|	|	...	...	...	1702	|	...	...	1902	...	1902	|	...	|	...	|	|	|	0016	0032
estri Levante d.	1524	1538	|	...	...	...	1725	|	...	...	1925	...	1925	|	...	2030	...	|	|	|	0035	0055
hiavari d.	1532	1551	1616	...	...	...	1732	1817	...	...	1932	...	1932	|	...	2038	...	|	2246	2358	...	...
apallo d.	1541	1601	1625	...	...	...	1741	|	...	...	1941	...	1941	2002	...	2046	...	2123	|	|	...	...
Margherita-Portofino d.	1546	1607	|	...	...	...	1746	|	...	...	1946	...	1946	|	...	|	...	|	|	|	...	...
enova Brignole d.	1608	1646	1651**s**	...	...	1736	1809	1847	...	1926	2010	...	2010	2023**s**	...	2129**e**	...	2143**s**	2313**s**	0024**s**	...	...
enova Piazza Principe a.	1614	1653	1658	...	...	1742	1815	1852	...	1932	2016	...	2016	2032	...	2134	...	2150	2320	0032	...	...
enova Piazza Principe d.	1619	1656	...	1719	1734	1744	1818	1854	1922	1934	2019	...	2019	...	2122	...	2144	...	...	...	...	...
Tortona d.	1659	|	...	|	1833	1833	1859	|	1959	2033	|	...	|	...	|	...	2233	...	...	...	...	...
Voghera d.	|	1805	...	1810	1844	1844	|	|	|	2044	2110	...	2110	...	2210	...	2244	...	...	...	...	...
Pavia d.	1726	|	...	1826	1901	1901	1926	2006	2026	2101	2126	...	2126	...	2226	...	2301	...	...	...	...	...
Milano Centrale a.	1755	1955**r**	...	1855	1935	1935	2000	2040	2100	2135	2155	...	2155	...	2255	...	2335	...	...	...	...	...
ovi Ligure d.	...	...	...	...	...	...	...	...	...	...	...	...	...	...	...	...	...	...	...	...	...	...
lessandria d.	...	...	...	...	...	...	...	...	...	...	...	...	...	...	...	...	...	...	...	...	...	...
sti d.	...	...	...	...	...	...	...	...	...	...	...	...	...	...	...	...	...	...	...	...	...	...
orino Porta Nuova a.	...	...	...	...	...	...	...	...	...	...	...	...	...	...	...	...	...	...	...	...	...	...

OR FOOTNOTES SEE PREVIOUS PAGE.

611 GENOVA - LA SPEZIA - PISA, FIRENZE and ROMA

2nd class

Subject to alteration from July 21. Regional trains. For long distance trains see Table **610**.

GENOVA - SESTRI LEVANTE - LA SPEZIA

km																										
					⚒	†					Ⓐ				Ⓐ					Ⓐ	Ⓒ		⑤-①			
0	**Genova** Brignole d.	0500	0606	...	0720	0720	...	1045	1245	...	1322	1445	...	1645	1738	...	1845	1930	...	2045	2045	...	2300	...	...	...
25	S. Margherita-Portofino d.	0528	0637	...	0759	0759	...	1115	1315	...	1403	1515	...	1715	1809	...	1915	2009	...	2112	2112	...	2336	...	...	...
27	Rapallo d.	0532	0641	...	0803	0803	...	1119	1319	...	1408	1519	...	1719	1814	...	1919	2014	...	2116	2116	...	2340	...	...	...
36	Chiavari d.	0540	0650	...	0813	0811	...	1127	1327	...	1418	1527	...	1727	1823	...	1927	2023	...	2125	2125	...	2348	...	...	...
43	**Sestri Levante** d.	0549	0700	...	0826	0820	...	1135	1335	...	1429	1535	...	1735	1840	...	1937	2032	...	2133	2135	...	2359	...	...	...
66	Levanto d.	0615	0725	...	0853	0847	...	1150	1350	...	1511	1550	...	1750	1914	...	1952	2052	...	2148	2150	...	0021	...	...	...
71	Monterosso d.	0620	0730	...	0858	0953	...	|	1355	...	1517	1555	...	1755	1919	...	1957	2057	...	2153	2155	...	0026	...	...	...
80	Riomaggiore d.	0635	|	...	0908	0909	...	1203	|	...	1533	1604	...	|	1935	...	2004	2106	...	2202	2203	...	0042	...	...	...
87	**La Spezia** Centrale a.	0645	0745	...	0914	0917	...	1213	1410	...	1540	1610	...	1810	1940	...	2010	2112	...	2210	2210	...	0052	...	...	...

		Ⓐ		⑥	Ⓐ		Ⓐ	Ⓒ												Ⓒ		Ⓑ			
La Spezia Centrale d.	0500	0540	...	0600	0625	...	0704	0704	...	0750	0950	...	1150	1350	...	1550	1750	...	1945	2145	...	2310	...	...	...
Riomaggiore d.	0509	0549	...	0608	|	...	0712	0712	...	|	|	...	|	1358	...	1558	1758	...	1953	2153	...	2319	...	...	...
Monterosso d.	0525	0604	...	0623	|	...	0727	0727	...	|	|	...	|	1406	...	1606	|	...	2005	2201	...	2335	...	...	...
Levanto d.	0530	0609	...	0628	0641	...	0732	0732	...	0811	1011	...	1211	1411	...	1611	1811	...	2011	2206	...	2340	...	...	...
Sestri Levante d.	0605	0636	...	0657	0657	...	0758	0758	...	0826	1026	...	1226	1426	...	1626	1826	...	2036	2224	...	0005	...	...	...
Chiavari d.	0617	0645	...	0707	0706	...	0808	0808	...	0833	1033	...	1234	1434	...	1634	1834	...	2044	2231	...	0014	...	...	...
Rapallo d.	0628	0656	...	0716	|	...	0818	0816	...	0841	1041	...	1242	1442	...	1642	1842	...	2055	2239	...	0025	...	...	...
S. Margherita-Portofino d.	0632	0700	...	|	|	...	0822	0820	...	0845	1045	...	1246	1446	...	1646	1846	...	2059	2243	...	0029	...	...	...
Genova Brignole a.	0709	0753	...	0753	0740	...	0856	0856	...	0915	1115	...	1315	1515	...	1715	1915	...	2139	2309	...	0123	...	...	...

LA SPEZIA - PISA

Additional trains are available

km																										
		⚒e	⚒	⚒	†	⚒	⚒		†	⑥	Ⓒ	Ⓐ 🚌	ⒸA		†A	⚒A		A	A		A	A	A	⚒A		
0	**La Spezia** Centrale d.	0600	0628	0656	0712	0715	0740	0821	0915	0915	1021	1030	1235	1319	1332	1335	1415	1435	1540	1621	1640	1740	1840	1916	2015	222
16	Sarzana d.	0615	0647	0717	0733	0736	0800	0838	0932	0932	1036	|	1300	1335	1352	1355	1430	1501	1600	1637	1700	1800	1900	1933	2030	224
26	Carrara-Avenza d.	0623	0656	0725	0743	0746	0807	0847	0940	0940	1044	|	1308	1343	1359	1402	1440	1509	1608	1645	1708	1808	1908	1942	2038	224
33	Massa Centro d.	0630	0702	0732	0749	0753	0814	0853	0946	0947	1050	1118	1314	1349	1405	1408	1446	1515	1614	1651	1714	1814	1914	1948	2044	225
54	Viareggio d.	0653	0724	0755	0810	0814	0825	0913	1007	1010	1110	1158	1333	1406	1425	1427	1503	1534	1633	1708	1733	1833	1933	2007	2104	231
75	**Pisa** Centrale a.	0721	0749	0818	0827	0832	0849	0940	1038	1043	1140	1235	1352	1427	1444	1452	1527	1552	1652	1727	1752	1852	1951	2032	2127	233

	⚒	⚒	ⒸA	⚒f	†	†A	⑥A	†	ⒸA		⚒A	A	A	⚒	A	Ⓒ	A	Ⓐ	Ⓒ	Ⓐ	†A		⚒		⚒
Pisa Centrale d.	0619	0702	0736	0819	0840	1006	1106	1106	1206	1234	1306	1406	1506	1550	1606	1634	1706	1736	1743	1748	1806	1834	1934	2034	214
Viareggio d.	0640	0724	0758	0837	0900	1023	1123	1123	1223	1254	1328	1423	1523	1612	1623	1655	1723	1757	1804	1807	1823	1859	1954	2055	220
Massa Centro d.	0701	0745	0821	0858	0923	1044	1144	1144	1244	1312	1351	1444	1544	1630	1644	1712	1744	1817	1822	1824	1844	1917	2012	2113	222
Carrara-Avenza d.	0707	0751	0828	0905	0930	1050	1150	1150	1250	1318	1357	1450	1550	1637	1650	1718	1750	1823	1828	1831	1850	1923	2018	2119	223
Sarzana d.	0715	0802	0837	0913	0939	1058	1158	1158	1258	1326	1405	1458	1558	1647	1658	1726	1758	1830	1836	1841	1858	1932	2031	2128	223
La Spezia Centrale a.	0733	0826	0858	0933	0957	1127	1220	1220	1320	1341	1425	1520	1620	1707	1720	1739	1820	1858	1858	1904	1920	1958	2058	2143	225

LIVORNO - PISA - FIRENZE

Additional trains are available

km																										
			⚒		⚒	†	⚒				ⒸA		A	⚒	A		A		A			A	A		⚒A	
0	**Livorno** Centrale d.	0609	0712	0808	0909	0909	1009	1106	1209	1308	...	1409	...	1509	...	1609	...	1708	...	1809	1846	...	...	2012	...	210
20	**Pisa** Centrale a.	0627	0735	0829	0928	0928	1029	1127	1229	1329	...	1428	...	1529	...	1629	...	1729	...	1829	1906	...	...	2029	...	212
20	**Pisa** Centrale d.	0629	0738	0832	0932	0932	1032	1130	1232	1332	1354	1432	1454	1532	1554	1632	1654	1730	1754	1832	1909	1854	1954	2032	2042	213
67	Empoli **613** d.	0659	0808	0904	1004	1017	1104	1202	1304	1404	1432	1504	1532	1604	1632	1704	1732	1802	1832	1904	1937	1932	2032	2107	2117	220
	Firenze Rifredi **613** a.	0720	0829	0926	1025	1038	1125	1226	1325	1425	1459	1525	1559	1625	1659	1725	1759	1825	1859	1925	|	1959	2059	2129	2148	222
101	**Firenze** SMN **613** a.	0728	0838	0933	1033	1047	1133	1233	1333	1433	1508	1533	1608	1633	1708	1733	1808	1833	1908	1933	2001	2008	2108	2139	2157	223

	ⒸA				†A		⑥A		ⒸA		⚒A		A	⚒	A		A		⑥A	ⒷA		†A			B
Firenze SMN **613** d.	0608	0653	0728	0828	0850	0928	0953	1028	1053	1128	1153	1228	1253	1328	1353	1428	1453	1528	1546	1553	1628	1653	1728	1828	192
Firenze Rifredi **613** d.	0614	0659	0734	0834	0856	0934	0959	1034	1059	1134	1159	1234	1259	1334	1359	1434	1459	1534	1552	1559	1634	1659	1734	1834	193
Empoli **613** d.	0645	0730	0758	0858	0925	0958	1027	1058	1127	1157	1227	1258	1327	1358	1427	1458	1528	1558	1626	1627	1658	1728	1758	1858	195
Pisa Centrale a.	0732	0806	0832	0928	1004	1028	1104	1128	1204	1226	1304	1328	1404	1428	1504	1528	1604	1628	1704	1704	1728	1804	1828	1928	202
Pisa Centrale d.	...	0809	0832	0932	...	1032	...	1132	...	1227	...	1332	...	1432	...	1532	...	1632	...	...	1732	...	1837	1932	203
Livorno Centrale a.	...	0830	0855	0952	...	1055	...	1152	...	1247	...	1352	...	1452	...	1551	...	1652	...	...	1752	...	1855	1952	205

PISA - LIVORNO - GROSSETO - ROMA

Additional trains are available Civitavecchia - Roma and v.v.

km																										
		⑥	†	Ⓐ	⚒			†			Ⓐ			⚒	Ⓐ	Ⓒ				⚒		Ⓐ				Ⓑ
0	**Pisa** Centrale d.	...	...	...	...	0532	0642	0837	...	0735	0840	1049	1135	1201	1227	1229	1325	...	...	1400	1535	1632	1735	1837	1935	214
20	**Livorno** Centrale a.	...	...	...	...	0551	0700	0855	...	0753	0902	1109	1152	1219	1246	1247	1343	...	...	1417	1553	1652	1753	1855	1953	220
20	**Livorno** Centrale d.	...	...	...	0500	0554	0702	0857	...	0756	0904	1111	1155	1222	1248	1249	1345	...	...	1420	1556	1654	1756	1857	1956	220
43	Rosignano d.	...	...	...	0517	0611	0718	0919	...	0813	0925	1133	1212	1245	1309	1310	1401	...	...	1440	1613	|	1813	1919	2013	222
54	Cecina d.	...	...	...	0525	0620	0726	0927	...	0822	0932	1143	1221	1256	1319	1320	1409	...	...	1451	1622	1719	1822	1927	2022	223
89	Campiglia Marittima a.	...	...	...	0554	0640	|	|	...	0844	1003	1217	1242	1326	1344	1351	1429	...	...	1525	1643	1735	1843	1950	2043	225
89	Campiglia Marittima ⊡ d.	...	...	...	0602	0641	|	|	...	0844	1004	1218	1243	1336	1345	1352	1430	...	...	1533	1644	1746	1844	1951	2044	230
103	**Piombino** ⊡ a.	...	...	...	0614	|	0802	1002	...	|	|	|	|	1352	|	|	|	...	...	1547	|	|	|	|	|	|
105	**Piombino** Marittima ⊡ a.	...	...	...	0630	|	0820	1020	...	|	|	|	|	1405	|	|	|	...	...	1600	|	|	|	|	|	|
106	Follonica d.	...	...	...	...	0651	...	...	...	0855	1023	1230	1254	...	1356	1401	1440	...	...	...	1655	1746	1855	2001	2055	231
148	**Grosseto** d.	0611	0615	0641	...	0723	...	...	...	0929	1100	1312	1328	...	1434	1445	1513	1642	...	...	1729	1816	1935	2048	2129	234
186	Orbetello-Monte Argentario d.	0639	0644	0709	...	0748	...	...	...	0952	...	...	1351	...	...	...	1536	1708	...	...	1752	1846	2003	...	2154	...
225	Tarquinia d.	0712	0717	0744	...	0824	...	...	...	1028	...	...	1427	...	...	...	1609	1744	...	...	1828	...	2042	...	2231	...
255	Civitavecchia d.	0730	0734	0758	...	0842	...	...	...	1044	...	...	1444	...	...	...	1644	1758	...	...	1844	...	2059	...	2245	...
264	S. Marinella d.	0737	0741	0805	...	0849	...	...	...	1051	...	...	1451	...	...	...	1651	1805	...	...	1851	...	2106	...	2252	...
286	Ladispoli-Cerveteri d.	0754	0757	0824	...	0904	...	...	...	1105	...	...	1505	...	...	...	1705	1825	...	...	1905	...	2120	...	2306	...
329	**Roma** Ostiense a.	0838	0837	0906	...	0936	...	...	...	1139	...	...	1536	...	...	...	1736	1906	...	...	1936	...	2151	...	2337	...
336	**Roma** Termini a.	0850	0850	0918	...	0948	...	...	...	1150	...	...	1548	...	...	...	1748	1918	...	...	1948	...	2203	...	2349	...

	⚒	†	⚒				†	⑥	Ⓐ				⚒	⚒				Ⓒ	†	Ⓐ		†	Ⓐ		
Roma Termini d.	...	...	...	...	0612	...	...	...	...	1027	...	1212	...	1327	1412	1612	...	...	...	1727	1827	...	1859	2000	205
Roma Ostiense d.	...	...	...	...	0623	...	...	...	...	1038	...	1223	...	1338	1423	1623	...	...	...	1739	1838	...	1910	2011	210
Ladispoli-Cerveteri d.	...	...	...	...	0651	...	...	...	...	1106	...	1251	...	1417	1451	1651	...	...	...	1815	1910	...	1948	2040	214
S. Marinella d.	...	...	...	...	0707	...	...	...	...	1122	...	1307	...	1434	1507	1707	...	...	...	1836	1926	...	2005	2055	215
Civitavecchia d.	...	...	...	...	0715	...	...	...	...	1133	...	1315	...	1443	1515	1717	...	...	...	1847	1936	...	2016	2108	220
Tarquinia d.	...	...	...	...	0728	...	...	...	...	1146	...	1327	...	1455	1528	1730	...	...	...	1900	1948	...	2092	2120	221
Orbetello-Monte Argentario d.	0552	...	...	...	0804	...	...	...	...	1219	...	1400	...	1527	1601	1803	...	...	...	1941	2021	...	2110	2154	225
Grosseto d.	0620	0637	...	0730	0831	...	...	1133	1150	1246	1340	1428	...	1556	1628	1833	...	...	1925	2017	2047	...	2142	2221	232
Follonica d.	0643	0700	...	0802	0853	...	...	1156	1212	1310	1411	1452	...	...	1652	1857	...	...	1948	...	2111	...	...	2245	...
Piombino Marittima ⊡ d.	|	|	0638	|	|	0916	1128	|	|	|	|	|	1515	...	|	|	1845	1915	|	...	|	2132	...	|	...
Piombino ⊡ d.	|	|	0649	|	|	0927	1139	|	|	|	|	|	1527	...	|	|	1856	1928	|	...	|	2143	...	|	...
Campiglia Marittima ⊡ a.	0655	0710	0707	0816	0902	0943	1155	1204	1225	1320	1423	1502	1548	...	1706	1909	1909	|	1958	...	2121	|	...	2259	...
Campiglia Marittima d.	0657	0712	0722	0817	0903	0956	1205	1205	1226	1321	1424	1503	1558	...	1707	1910	1919	|	1959	...	2122	|	...	2300	...
Cecina d.	0723	0736	0755	0855	0924	1020	1230	1230	1252	1344	1452	1526	1624	...	1730	1933	1940	2006	2022	...	2142	2218	...	2323	...
Rosignano d.	0731	0744	0806	0903	0935	1030	1238	1238	1259	1352	1503	1534	1635	...	1738	1941	|	2014	2032	...	2150	2227	...	2332	...
Livorno Centrale a.	0751	0806	0836	0925	1001	1104	1306	1306	1325	1417	1533	1559	1707	...	1800	2003	2009	2035	2056	...	2215	2255	...	2357	...
Livorno Centrale d.	0753	0808	0839	0928	1004	1106	1308	1308	1327	1420	1536	1602	1708	...	1803	2006	2012	2037	2108	...	2218	2258	...	0000	...
Pisa Centrale a.	0811	0829	0900	0951	1027	1127	1329	1329	1347	1439	1554	1623	1729	...	1823	2026	2029	2054	2129	...	2238	2317	...	0020	...

A – (2) La Spezia - Pisa - Firenze and v.v.
B – Also from Firenze SMN at 2053, 2128, 2200.

e – To Livorno (a. 0746).
f – From Livorno (d. 0800).

⊡ – Also from Campiglia Marittima at 1533 †, 1645, 1736 Ⓑ, 1804, 1839 Ⓒ, 2055 †; also from Piombino Marittima at 1608, 1724, 1812 Ⓑ.

2nd class PARMA and MILANO - PONTREMOLI - LA SPEZIA, PISA and FIRENZE 612

PARMA - PONTREMOLI - LA SPEZIA

km			⚒						⚒			⚒							⚒					⚒	†	
0	**Parma** d.	...	...	0542	0647	...	0750	0847	...	1147	...	1247	1347	1447	1547	...	1647	1747	1847	1947	...	2047	2147	2220	2247	...
23	Fornovo d.	...	...	0608	0713	...	0813	0913	...	1213	...	1313	1413	1513	1613	...	1713	1813	1913	2013	...	2113	2213	2248	2313	...
61	Borgo Val di Taro d.	...	0616	0651	0751	...	0851	0951	...	1251	...	1351	1451	1551	1651	...	1751	1851	1951	2051	...	2151	2251	2322	2351	...
79	**Pontremoli** d.	0531	0634	0709	0809	...	0909	1009	1209	1309	...	1409	1509	1609	1709	...	1809	1909	2009	2109	...	2209	2309	2340	0009	...
100	Aulla Lunigiana d.	0557	0657	0728	0828	...	0927	1028	1228	1328	...	1428	1528	1628	1728	...	1828	1928	2028	2128	...	2228	...	...	0028	...
108	S. Stefano di Magra d.	0603	0703	0734	0834	...	0933	1034	1234	1334	...	1434	1534	1634	1734	...	1834	1934	2034	2134	...	2234	...	...	0034	...
120	**La Spezia** Centrale a.	0622	0724	0756	0853	...	0947	1056	1256	1353	...	1453	1555	1654	1752	...	1855	1953	2052	2154	...	2254	...	...	0052	...

		⚒					⚒						⚒			⚒									
La Spezia Centrale d.	...	...	0508	0608	...	0706	0808	0908	1002	...	1208	1308	...	1406	1508	1606	...	1705	1806	1908	...	2008	2114	2208	...
S. Stefano di Magra d.	...	...	0525	0625	...	0725	0825	0925	1022	...	1225	1325	...	1425	1525	1625	...	1725	1825	1925	...	2025	2125	2225	...
Aulla Lunigiana d.	...	...	0532	0632	...	0732	0832	0932	1030	...	1232	1332	...	1432	1532	1632	...	1732	1832	1932	...	2032	2132	2232	...
Pontremoli d.	0405	0508	0552	0652	...	0752	0852	0951	1053	...	1252	1352	...	1452	1552	1652	...	1752	1852	1952	...	2052	2152	2253	...
Borgo Val di Taro d.	0423	0526	0609	0709	...	0809	0909	...	...	...	1309	1409	...	1509	1609	1709	...	1809	1909	2009	...	2109	2209	...	...
Fornovo d.	0459	0609	0647	0747	...	0847	0947	...	...	...	1347	1447	...	1547	1647	1747	...	1847	1947	2047	...	2147	2247	...	...
Parma a.	0531	0631	0714	0814	...	0914	1014	...	...	...	1414	1514	...	1614	1714	1816	...	1914	2014	2114	...	2214	2316	...	...

MILANO - PONTREMOLI - PISA - FIRENZE

km		⚒	⚒		Ⓒ		Ⓐ			
0	**Milano** Centrale d.	...	...	0650	...	...	...	...	1714f	...
10	**Milano** Rogoredo d.	...	...	0701	...	...	...	...	1741	...
72	Piacenza d.	...	...	0759	...	...	...	...	1843	...
107	Fidenza d.	...	...	0821	0916	...	...	...	1906	...
132	Fornovo d.	...	...	0838	0932	...	...	...	1926	...
170	Borgo Val di Taro d.	0530	...	0925	1007	...	1415	...	2006	...
188	**Pontremoli** d.	0552	0716	0953	1027	...	1435	...	2025	...
209	Aulla Lunigiana d.	0613	0749	1019	1048	...	1504	...	2050	...
217	S. Stefano di Magra d.	0620	0756	1026	1055	...	1513	...	2059	...
225	Sarzana d.	0629	0807	1043	1103	...	1526	...	2111	...
235	Carrara-Avenza d.	0636	0814	1052	1111	...	1534	...	2119	...
242	Massa Centro d.	0647	0820	1100	1119	...	1541	...	2130	...
263	Viareggio d.	0711	0840	1124	1141	...	1602	...	2151	...
284	**Pisa** Centrale 613 d.	0744	0859	1200	1216	...	1623	...	2218	...
304	**Livorno** Centrale a.	|	...	...	...	...	...	...	2240	...
331	Empoli 613 d.	0815	...	...	...	...	...	...	...	...
	Firenze Rifredi 613 a.	0839	...	...	...	...	...	...	...	...
365	**Firenze** SMN 613 a.	0848	...	...	...	...	...	...	...	...

			Ⓐ		Ⓐ	⑥⑦			
Firenze SMN 613 d.	...	...	...	...	...	...	...	1853	...
Firenze Rifredi 613 d.	...	...	...	...	...	...	...	1859	...
Empoli 613 d.	...	...	...	...	...	...	...	1927	...
Livorno Centrale d.	0530	...	...	...	...	...	...	|	...
Pisa Centrale 613 d.	0548	...	1155	...	1635	1752	1845	2006	...
Viareggio d.	0608	...	1213	...	1653	1812	1905	2023	...
Massa Centro d.	0629	...	1234	...	1714	1830	1921	2044	...
Carrara-Avenza d.	0635	...	1240	...	1720	1837	1928	2050	...
Sarzana d.	0644	...	1249	...	1728	1845	1936	2058	...
S. Stefano di Magra d.	0704	...	1300	...	1737	1852	1958	2105	...
Aulla Lunigiana d.	0712	...	1307	...	1743	1859	2006	2111	...
Pontremoli d.	0734	...	1338	...	1808	1925	2040	2135	...
Borgo Val di Taro d.	0754	...	1357	...	...	1952	2059	2155	...
Fornovo d.	0841	...	...	...	...	2032	2136	...	...
Fidenza d.	0905	...	...	...	...	2050	2158	...	...
Piacenza d.	0930	...	...	...	...	...	2225	...	...
Milano Rogoredo a.	1017	...	...	...	...	...	2310	...	...
Milano Centrale a.	1045f	...	...	...	...	...	2322	...	...

– Milano **Porta Garibaldi**.

☛ Services between Parma and La Spezia is subject to alteration.

2nd class FIRENZE - SIENA 613

For additional trains Firenze - Empoli see Table **611**.

km						⚒	⚒		⚒			⚒			⚒	⚒		⚒	⚒		⚒				⚒
0	**Firenze** SMN d.	0620	...	0810	...	0910	1010	1110	...	1210	...	1310	...	1410	...	1510	...	1610	...	1710	...	1810	1910	2010	2138
	Firenze Rifredi d.	0626	...	0816	...	0916	1016	1116	...	1216	...	1316	...	1416	...	1516	...	1616	...	1716	...	1816	1916	2016	2144
34	Empoli ◧ d.	0650	0806	0840	0908	0940	1040	1140	1208	1240	1308	1340	1408	1440	1508	1540	1608	1640	1708	1740	1808	1840	1940	2040	2208
72	Poggibonsi-S. Gimignano ◧ d.	0724	0844	0915	0945	1015	1115	1215	1245	1315	1345	1415	1445	1514	1545	1615	1645	1715	1749	1815	1845	1915	2015	2115	2246
97	**Siena** ◧ a.	0755	0917	0938	1016	1040	1140	1238	1315	1340	1416	1440	1517	1537	1614	1640	1714	1738	1815	1840	1916	1938	2040	2139	2316

	⚒	†	⚒	⚒	†			⚒	⚒	⚒			⚒		⚒	⚒			⚒			⚒		
Siena ◧ d.	0543	0636	0636	0702	0715	0818	0848	0918	1041	1118	1145	1218	1241	1318	1341	1418	1441	1518	1618	1718	1818	1918	2018	2140
Poggibonsi-S. Gimignano ◧ d.	0606	0659	0659	0728	0742	0842	0909	0942	1108	1142	1212	1242	1308	1342	1408	1442	1508	1542	1642	1742	1842	1942	2042	2207
Empoli ◧ d.	0645	0735	0750	0820	0820	0921	0945	1021	1154	1221	1254	1321	1354	1421	1454	1521	1554	1621	1721	1821	1921	2021	2121	2241
Firenze Rifredi a.	0713	0753	0822	0850	0850	0943	1007	1043	...	1243	...	1343	...	1443	...	1543	...	1643	1743	1843	1943	2043	2143	2310
Firenze SMN a.	0723	0804	0832	0859	0859	0952	1017	1052	...	1252	...	1352	...	1452	...	1552	...	1652	1752	1852	1952	2052	2152	2319

◧ – Also from Siena at 0621 ⚒, 0726 ⚒, 1908, 2008 ⚒, 2108 ⚒, 2208 †; also from Firenze SMN at 0733 ⚒, 1541 ⚒, 1641, 1741, 1842 ⚒, 1941.

2nd class FIRENZE - PRATO - BOLOGNA, VIAREGGIO and PISA 614

Frequent additional trains are available Firenze - Pistoia and v.v.

km		⚒	⚒				†	⚒							†	Ⓐ								
0	**Firenze** SMN 613 d.	0510	...	0603	...	0709	...	...	...	0809	...	0909	...	...	1009	...	...	1209	...	1309	...	...	1409	...
	Firenze Rifredi 613 d.	0516	...	0609	...	0715	...	...	...	0815	...	0915	...	...	1015	...	...	1215	...	1315	...	...	1415	...
17	Prato Centrale d.	0533	...	0623	...	0728	...	...	...	0830	...	0930	...	...	1030	...	...	1230	...	1330	...	...	1430	...
	Bologna Centrale a.	|	...	|	...	|	...	...	...	|	...	|	...	...	|	...	...	|	...	|	...	...	|	...
34	Pistoia d.	0551	...	0640	...	0745	...	...	...	0844	...	0944	...	...	1044	...	...	1244	...	1344	...	...	1444	...
47	Montecatini Centro d.	0604	...	0658	...	0801	...	...	...	0901	...	1001	...	...	1101	...	...	1301	...	1401	...	...	1501	...
78	Lucca d.	0646	0652	0755	0759	0830	0842	0849	...	0930	0942	1033	1042	...	1130	1242	1312	1330	1340	1430	1442	...	1530	1542
101	**Viareggio** a.	0707	|	|	0826	0850	|	|	...	0950	|	1056	|	...	1150	|	|	1350	|	1450	|	...	1550	|
102	**Pisa** Centrale 613 a.	...	0717	0825	...	...	0913	0918	...	...	1014	...	1113	...	...	1313	1342	...	1413	...	1513	...	...	1613

										†	⚒						⚒					
Firenze SMN 613 d.	1509	...	...	1609	...	...	1709	...	...	1809	...	...	...	1909	...	...	2009	...	...	2109	...	2209	...
Firenze Rifredi 613 d.	1515	...	...	1615	...	...	1715	...	...	1815	...	...	...	1915	...	...	2015	...	...	2115	...	2215	...
Prato Centrale d.	1530	...	...	1630	...	...	1730	...	...	1830	...	...	...	1930	...	...	2030	...	...	2130	...	2230	...
Bologna Centrale a.	|	...	...	|	...	...	|	...	...	|	...	...	...	|	...	...	|	...	...	|	...	|	...
Pistoia d.	1544	...	...	1644	...	...	1744	...	...	1844	...	...	...	1944	...	...	2044	...	...	2144	...	2246	...
Montecatini Centro d.	1601	...	...	1701	...	...	1801	...	...	1901	...	...	...	2001	...	...	2101	...	...	2200	...	2301	...
Lucca d.	1630	1642	...	1730	1742	...	1830	1842	...	1930	1941	1945	...	2030	2042	...	2130	2142	...	2249	...	2330	...
Viareggio a.	1650	|	...	1750	|	...	1850	|	...	1950	|	|	...	2050	|	...	2150	|	...	2309	...	2350	...
Pisa Centrale 613 a.	...	1713	...	...	1813	...	...	1917	...	...	2013	2015	...	...	2113	...	...	2213	...	...	...	...	...

	⚒		⚒		⚒												⚒			⚒	†	
Pisa Centrale 613 d.	...	0525	...	...	0613	...	...	...	...	0750	...	...	0850	...	0950	...	...	1020	...	...	1220	1250	...
Viareggio d.	...	|	0545	...	|	0628	...	0710	...	|	0810	...	|	0910	|	1010	...	|	1207	...	|	|	1310
Lucca d.	0505	0559	0609	...	0640	0648	...	0727	...	0823	0831	...	0920	0931	1018	1031	...	1048	1231	...	1247	1317	1331
Montecatini Centro d.	0533	...	0641	...	...	0715	...	0753	...	...	0857	...	...	0957	...	1057	...	...	1257	...	...	...	1357
Pistoia d.	0552	...	0709	...	...	0732	...	0813	...	...	0913	...	...	1013	...	1113	...	...	1313	...	...	...	1413
Bologna Centrale d.	|	...	|	...	...	|	...	|	...	...	|	...	...	|	...	|	...	...	|	...	...	...	|
Prato Centrale d.	0612	...	0728	...	...	0747	...	0830	...	...	0930	...	...	1030	...	1130	...	...	1330	...	...	...	1430
Firenze Rifredi 613 a.	0632	...	0746	...	...	0801	...	0846	...	...	0946	...	...	1046	...	1146	...	...	1346	...	...	...	1446
Firenze SMN 613 a.	0638	...	0752	...	...	0807	...	0852	...	...	0952	...	...	1052	...	1152	...	...	1352	...	...	...	1452

																			⚒			
Pisa Centrale 613 d.	1343	...	1450	...	...	1550	...	...	1650	...	1750	...	...	1850	...	...	1950	...	2050	...	...	2150	...
Viareggio d.	|	1410	|	1510	...	|	1610	...	|	1710	|	1810	...	|	1910	...	|	2010	|	2110	...	|	2210
Lucca d.	1409	1431	1517	1531	...	1617	1631	...	1717	1731	1817	1831	...	1917	1931	...	2017	2031	2118	2131	...	2217	2231
Montecatini Centro d.	...	1457	...	1557	...	...	1657	...	...	1757	...	1857	...	...	1957	...	...	2057	...	2157	...	...	2257
Pistoia d.	...	1513	...	1613	...	...	1713	...	...	1813	...	1913	...	...	2013	...	...	2113	...	2213	...	...	2313
Bologna Centrale d.	...	|	...	|	...	...	|	...	...	|	...	|	...	...	|	...	...	|	...	|	...	...	|
Prato Centrale d.	...	1530	...	1630	...	...	1730	...	...	1830	...	1930	...	...	2030	...	...	2130	...	2230	...	...	2330
Firenze Rifredi 613 a.	...	1546	...	1646	...	...	1746	...	...	1846	...	1946	...	...	2046	...	...	2146	...	2246	...	...	2344
Firenze SMN 613 a.	...	1552	...	1652	...	...	1752	...	...	1852	...	1952	...	...	2052	...	...	2152	...	2252	...	...	2350

615 MILANO, BOLOGNA, RIMINI, ANCONA and ROMA - BARI - LECCE

Subject to alteration August 11 – 31. High-speed and long-distance trains. For local trains Milano - Bologna see Table **620**. For other local trains see page 304.
Running days, timings and numbers of *ICN* trains may vary - please check your reservation. For confirmed timings please consult the *Trenitalia* journey planner at www.trenitalia.com.

HIGH SPEED TRAINS

km		*FA* 8303	*FR* 9511	*FR* 9803 ⑥⑦	*FR* 8801 A	*ITA* 9917 B 🍴	*FR* 8803 ①⑦	*FR* 8803 ②–⑥	*FR* 9805 B	*FA* 8311 ⑧	*FR* 8807	*FA* 8315	*FR* 8809	*FA* 8317	*FR* 8811	*FA* 8319 ⑤	*ITA* 9939 B 🍴	*FR* 8813	*FA* 8323	*FR* 8815 A	*FR* 9809	*FR* 8819	*FR* 9647	*ITA* 9991	*FR* 981
0	**Milano** Centrale d.	...	0610	0705	...	0740	0735	0750	1013**d**	...	1135	...	1150	...	1335	...	1340	1435	...	...	1535	1550	1630	1715	173
10	**Milano** Rogoredo △ d.	...	0620	|	...	|	|	|	1045	...	|	...	|	...	|	...	|	|	...	...	|	|	1640	1725	|
72	Piacenza d.	...	|	|	...	|	|	|	|	...	|	...	|	...	|	...	|	|	...	...	|	|	|	|	|
129	Parma d.	...	|	|	...	|	0842	0843	|	...	|	...	1243	...	|	...	|	|	...	...	|	1643	|	|	|
157	Reggio Emilia d.	...	|	|	...	|	0900	0900	|	...	|	...	1300	...	|	...	|	|	...	...	|	1700	|	|	|
	Reggio Emilia AV d.	...	0656	|	...	0828	|	|	1120	...	1220	...	|	...	1420	...	1428	1520	...	...	1621	|	|	|	181
182	Modena d.	...	|	|	...	|	0916	0916	|	...	|	...	1316	...	|	...	|	|	...	...	|	1716	|	|	|
219	**Bologna** Centrale ● a.	...	0724	0812	...	0854	0942	0942	1142	...	1242	...	1342	...	1442	...	1454	1542	...	...	1650	1742	|	|	184
219	**Bologna** Centrale ● d.	...	0727	0815	0845	0857	0945	0945	1145	...	1245	...	1345	...	1445	...	1457	1545	...	1645	1655	1745	|	|	184
269	Faenza d.	...	|	|	|	|	|	|	|	...	|	...	|	...	|	...	|	|	...	|	|	1808	|	|	|
284	Forlì d.	...	|	|	|	|	|	|	|	...	|	...	1416	...	|	...	|	|	...	|	|	1817	|	|	191
302	Cesena d.	...	|	|	|	|	|	|	|	...	1324	...	|	...	|	...	|	1624	...	|	|	1829	|	|	|
331	**Rimini** ⊡ a.	...	|	0915	0938	|	1038	1038	1238	...	1341	...	1441	...	1541	...	|	1641	...	1741	1754	1849	|	|	194
331	**Rimini** ⊡ d.	...	|	0917	0940	|	1040	1040	1240	...	1343	...	1443	...	1543	...	|	1643	...	1743	1756	1851	|	|	194
340	Riccione d.	...	|	0925	0948	|	1047	1047	|	...	|	...	|	...	|	...	|	1650	...	|	1804**f**	|	|	|	|
364	Pesaro d.	...	|	0942	1002	|	1102	1102	1302	...	1405	...	1502	...	1602	...	|	1706	...	1802	|	1910	|	|	200
423	**Ancona** a.	...	◧	1013	1031	◧	1131	1131	1334	...	1434	...	1534	...	1631	...	◧	1734	...	1833	1847	1939	◧	◧	203
423	**Ancona** d.	...	|	1016	1034	|	1134	1134	1337	...	1437	...	1537	...	1634	...	|	1737	...	1836	1850	1942	|	|	203
466	C. Marche-Montegranaro d.	...	|	|	|	|	1157	1157	|	...	|	...	|	...	|	...	|	|	...	|	|	|	|	|	|
508	S. Benedetto del Tronto d.	...	|	|	|	|	|	|	|	...	1516	...	1616	...	|	...	|	1815	...	|	|	2022	|	|	211
569	**Pescara** Centrale a.	...	|	1134	1144	|	1244	1244	1444	...	1547	...	1647	...	1747	...	|	1847	...	1944	1957	2054	|	|	214
569	**Pescara** Centrale d.	...	|	...	1147	|	1247	1247	1447	...	1550	...	1650	...	1750	...	|	1850	...	1947	2000	2057	|	|	...
659	Termoli d.	...	|	...	1236	|	1339	1339	1536	...	1639	...	1737	...	1837	...	|	1939	...	2036	2048	2145	|	|	...
	Roma Termini d.	0800	1000	...	|	1145	|	|	|	1315	|	1458	|	1557	|	1655	1743	|	1758	|	|	|	1953	2040	...
	Caserta d.	0907	1109	...	|	1253	|	|	|	1424	|	1612	|	1706	|	1804	1857	|	1912	|	|	|	2102	2148	...
	Benevento d.	1003	1203	...	|	1338	|	|	|	1521	|	1702	|	1759	|	1857	1942	|	2004	|	|	|	2202	...	...
746	**Foggia** a.	1112	1308	...	1319	...	1421	1421	1619	1626	1721	1757	1821	1905	1921	2005	2045	2021	2108	2119	2129	2228	2305	...	...
746	**Foggia** d.	1121	1317	...	1322	...	1424	1424	1622	1635	1724	1806	1824	1914	1924	2014	2054	2024	2117	2124	2132	2231	...	...	...
814	Barletta d.	1152	1346	...	1354	...	1453	1453	1651	1703	1753	1837	1853	1946	1953	2044	2128	2053	2147	2156	|	2300	...	...	...
869	**Bari** Centrale a.	1222	1423	...	1431	...	1530	1530	1727	1739	1830	1912	1930	2020	2030	2114	2207	2130	2218	2227	2232	2336	...	...	...
869	**Bari** Centrale d.	1226	1427	...	1435	...	...	...	1731	...	1840	1916	1934	2024	2034	2118	...	2134	2222	2231	...	...	...	...	...
923	Gioia del Colle d.	|	|	...	|	...	...	...	|	...	1912	|	|	|	|	|	...	|	|	|	...	...	...	...	...
984	**Taranto** a.	|	|	...	|	...	...	...	|	...	1946	|	|	|	|	|	...	|	|	|	...	...	...	...	...
910	Monopoli d.	1252	|	...	1501	...	...	...	|	...	...	1940	1956	|	|	|	...	|	|	|	...	...	...	...	...
924	Fasano d.	|	|	...	1511	...	...	...	|	...	...	|	|	|	|	|	...	|	|	|	...	...	...	...	...
944	Ostuni d.	1310	|	...	1524	...	...	...	|	...	...	|	2015	|	|	|	...	|	|	|	...	...	...	...	...
980	**Brindisi** a.	1331	1528	...	1542	...	...	...	1824	...	...	2015	2034	2120	2129	2241	...	2232	2320	2329	...	...	...	...	...
1019	**Lecce** a.	1358	1551	...	1608	...	...	...	1850	...	...	2040	2100	2148	2157	2306	...	2256	2346	2357	...	...	...	...	...

LONG DISTANCE TRAINS

	FR 8823	*FR* 8825	*FR* 8829	*FR* 9561 ⑤⑥		*IC* 558 Hg	*ICN* 789 ⑤ C	*IC* 558 Hh	*ICN* 765 C	*ICN* 755 ④–① C	*ICN* 755 ②③ C	*ICN* 757 CE	*IC* 564 G	*IC* 703	*IC* 603	*IC* 542 ①–⑥ L	*IC* 605	*IC* 607	*IC* 1545 ⑥		*IC* 609	*IC* 611 D	*RJ* 83 J	*IC* 613
Milano Centrale d.	1750	1835	1950	2245	...	...	...	...	2115	2150	2150	...	...	...	0525	...	0705	0910**d**	1000	...	...	...	...	1505
Milano Rogoredo △ d.	|	|	|	2255	...	...	...	...	|	|	|	...	...	...	0535	...	0715	0938	1013	...	...	...	...	1515
Piacenza d.	1820	1904	|	|	...	...	...	...	2201	2237	2237	...	...	...	0615	...	0808	1020	1048	...	...	...	...	1608
Fidenza d.	|	|	|	|	...	...	...	...	|	|	|	...	...	...	0638	...	0836	1042	1105	...	...	...	...	1631
Parma d.	1843	1943	2043	2341	...	...	...	...	2233	2307	2307	...	...	...	0651	...	0853	1054	1118	...	...	...	...	1650
Reggio Emilia d.	1900	2000	2100	2357	...	...	...	...	2251	2325	2325	...	...	...	0710	...	0908	1109	1133	...	...	...	...	1707
Reggio Emilia AV d.	|	|	|	|	...	...	...	...	|	|	|	...	...	...	|	...	|	|	|	...	...	...	...	|
Modena d.	1916	2016	2116	0013	...	...	...	...	2308	2341	2341	...	...	...	0728	...	0926	1126	1149	...	...	...	...	1724
Bologna Centrale ● a.	1942	2042	2142	0037	...	...	...	...	2335	0006	0006	...	...	...	0757	...	0954	1156	1219	...	...	...	...	1752
Bologna Centrale ● d.	1945	2045	2145	0040	...	...	...	...	2339	0010	0010	0027	...	...	0800	...	0958	1200	1225	...	1400	1600	1612	1758
Faenza d.	2008	2108	|	|	...	...	...	...	0008	0040	0040	|	...	...	0828	...	1028	1228	1256	...	1428	1628	|	1828
Forlì d.	2017	2117	2216	|	...	...	...	...	0019	0058	|	|	...	...	0838	...	1038	1238	1306	...	1438	1638	|	1838
Cesena d.	2029	2129	|	|	...	...	...	...	0031	0112	|	|	...	...	0851	...	1052	1251	1319	...	1451	1651	1704	1851
Rimini ⊡ a.	2049	2149	2241	|	...	...	...	...	0059	0140	0145	0153	...	...	0911	...	1113	1313	1348	...	1513	1713	1730	1913
Rimini ⊡ d.	2051	2151	2243	|	...	...	...	...	0119	0155	0155	0201	...	...	0919	...	1115	1315	1351	...	1515	1715	1759	1915
Riccione d.	2059	|	|	|	...	...	...	...	|	|	|	|	...	...	0930	...	1124	1324	1400	...	1524	1724	1810	1924
Pesaro d.	2114	2210	2302	|	...	...	...	...	0158	|	|	|	...	...	0947	...	1142	1342	1418	...	1542	1742	1830	1942
Fano d.	|	|	|	|	...	...	...	...	|	|	|	|	...	...	0956	...	1151	1351	1427	...	1551	1751	|	1951
Senigallia d.	|	|	|	|	...	...	...	...	|	|	|	|	...	...	1010	...	1203	1403	1439	...	1603	1803	1847	2003
Ancona a.	2142	2242	2338	|	...	...	...	...	0242	0247	0247	0252	...	...	1036	...	1223	1423	1456	...	1623	1823	1910	2023
Ancona d.	2145	...	...	|	...	...	...	...	0246	0250	0250	0256	...	...	1039	1128	1226	1426	1458	...	1626	1826	...	2026
C. Marche-Montegranaro d.	|	...	...	|	...	...	...	...	|	|	|	|	...	...	1101	1205	1255	1452	1523	...	1652	1852	...	2052
S. Benedetto del Tronto d.	2225	...	...	|	...	...	...	...	|	|	|	|	...	...	1126	1235	1323	1523	1548	...	1723	1928	...	2129
Pescara Centrale a.	2305	...	...	|	...	...	...	...	0404	0411	0411	0426	...	...	1201	...	1359	1559	1631	...	1759	2008	...	2205
Pescara Centrale d.	...	...	...	|	...	...	...	...	0406	0413	0413	0428	...	...	1203	...	1401	1601	1635	...	1801	2010	...	...
Termoli d.	...	...	...	|	...	...	...	...	|	0513	0513	0521	...	...	1254	...	1452	1652	1750	...	1852	2102	...	...
Roma Termini d.	...	...	...	|	...	...	2356	...	|	|	|	|	...	0728	|	...	|	|	|	...	|	|	...	...
Napoli Centrale d.	...	...	...	|	...	...	|	...	|	|	|	|	...	|	|	...	|	|	|	...	|	|	...	...
Caserta d.	...	...	...	|	...	...	0236	...	|	|	|	|	...	0959	|	...	|	|	|	...	|	|	...	...
Benevento d.	...	...	...	|	...	...	0332	...	|	|	|	|	...	1111	|	...	|	|	|	...	|	|	...	...
Foggia a.	...	...	...	0509	...	...	0449	...	0544	0606	0606	0617	...	1231	1349	...	1549	1741	1848	...	1949	2151	...	...
Foggia d.	...	...	...	0512	...	...	0504	...	0547	0609	0609	0638	...	1242	1352	...	1552	1744	1851	...	1952	2159	...	...
Barletta d.	...	...	...	0541	...	...	0536	...	0618	0651	0651	0721	...	1313	1421	...	1621	1819	1925	...	2021	2232	...	...
Bari Centrale a.	...	...	...	0616	...	...	0628	...	0700	0740	0740	0810	...	1357	1505	...	1705	1858	2013	...	2105	2316	...	...
Bari Centrale d.	...	...	...	0624	...	0615	0632	0703	0710	0744	0744	0814	...	1411	1509	...	1717	1902	2017	...	2109	...	...	...
Gioia del Colle d.	...	...	...	|	...	⊖	|	0735	0745	|	|	|	...	1443	|	...	1753	|	|	...	|	...	...	...
Taranto a.	...	...	...	|	...	0823	|	0810	0820	|	|	|	1441	1518	|	...	1827	|	|	...	|	...	...	...
Monopoli d.	...	...	...	0653	...	...	0704	...	|	0819	0819	0852	|	...	1537	...	|	1927	2105	...	2137	...	...	...
Fasano d.	...	...	...	0704	...	...	0715	...	|	0828	0828	0904	|	...	1549	...	|	1936	2114	...	2148	...	...	...
Ostuni d.	...	...	...	0718	...	...	0730	...	|	0841	0841	0919	|	...	1604	...	|	1948	2126	...	2201	...	...	...
Brindisi a.	...	...	...	0742	...	...	0752	...	0919	0905	0905	0943	1551	...	1625	...	1928	2008	2145	...	2223	...	...	...
Lecce a.	...	...	...	0809	...	...	0815	...	1002	0930	0930	1010	1621	...	1651	...	1955	2035	2207	...	2249	...	...	...

TORINO and GENOVA - BOLOGNA

km		2	2	*ICN* 757 E
0	**Torino** Porta Nuova d.	...	...	2050
56	Asti d.	...	...	2129
91	Alessandria d.	...	...	2152
	Genova Brignole d.	1117	1706	|
	Genova Piazza Principe d.	1125	1714	|
113	Tortona d.	1238	1848	2208
130	Voghera d.	1250	1900	2220
188	Piacenza a.	1340	1949	2257
335	**Bologna** Centrale a.	*1525*	2125	0022

	ICN 754 ②–⑥ E	*ICN* 754 ①⑦ E	2	2
Bologna Centrale d.	0535	0545	0633	*1150*
Piacenza d.	0710	0710	0809	1409
Voghera d.	0756	0756	0856	1456
Tortona d.	0807	0807	0907	1507
Genova Piazza Principe a.	|	|	1014	1612
Genova Brignole a.	|	|	1024	1620
Alessandria d.	0825	0825	...	...
Asti d.	0847	0847	...	...
Torino Porta Nuova a.	0925	0925	...	...

FOR FOOTNOTES AND RETURN SERVICE SEE NEXT PAGE →

LECCE - BARI - ROMA, ANCONA, RIMINI, BOLOGNA and MILANO 615

Subject to alteration August 11 – 31. High-speed and long-distance trains. For local trains Milano - Bologna see Table **620**. For other local trains see page 304.
Running days, timings and numbers of *ICN* trains may vary - please check your reservation. For confirmed timings please consult the *Trenitalia* journey planner at www.trenitalia.com.

km				*FR* 8802	*FR* 9802	*FR* 8804	*FR* 8806	*ITA* 9972	*FR* 9620	*FR* 8810	*FA* 8348 ①–⑥	*FR* 9806	*FR* 8814	*ITA* 9928 B ❦	*FR* 8302	*FR* 8816 A	*FA* 8306	*FR* 8818	*FR* 8820	*FA* 8312 ⑥	*FR* 8824	*FA* 8314	*FR* 9808 B	*ITA* 9958 B ❦	*FR* 8828 A	*FR* 9810 ⑥⑦	*FR* 9560
0	**Lecce**	d.		...	...	...	...	...	...	...	...	...	0555	...	0607	0700	0710	0804	...	0935	0958	1113	1206	...	1257	...	1242
39	**Brindisi**	d.		...	...	...	...	...	...	...	...	...	0617	...	0629	0723	0735	0827	...	0957	1019	1135	1229	...	1318	...	1303
75	Ostuni	d.		...	...	...	...	...	...	...	...	...	|	...	|	|	|	|	...	|	1040	|	|	...	1339	...	|
95	Fasano	d.		...	...	...	...	...	...	...	...	...	|	...	|	|	|	|	...	|	|	|	|	...	1352	...	|
109	Monopoli	d.		...	...	...	...	...	...	...	...	...	|	...	0703	|	|	|	...	|	1059	|	|	...	1401	...	|
	Taranto	d.		...	...	...	...	...	...	...	...	...	|	...	|	|	|	|	0915	|	|	|	|	...	|	...	|
	Gioia del Colle	d.		...	...	...	...	...	...	...	...	...	|	...	|	|	|	|	0948	|	|	|	|	...	|	...	|
150	**Bari** Centrale	a.		...	...	...	...	...	...	...	...	...	0726	...	0732	0826	0834	0924	1020	1059	1124	1236	1326	...	1426	...	1406
150	**Bari** Centrale	d.		...	...	...	...	...	...	0530	0605	0635	0730	0650	0740	0830	0840	0928	1030	1103	1128	1240	1330	...	1430	...	1410
205	Barletta	d.	H	...	...	...	...	...	...	0606	0637	|	0805	0737	0811	0906	0914	1005	1106	1134	1205	1311	1406	...	1506	...	1445
273	**Foggia**	a.	I	...	...	...	...	...	...	0633	0708	0736	0831	0806	0841	0933	0946	1031	1133	1209	1231	1341	1433	...	1533	...	1513
273	**Foggia**	d.	G	...	...	...	...	...	0600	0636	0717	0739	0834	0815	0850	0936	0955	1034	1136	1218	1234	1350	1436	...	1536	...	1522
374	Benevento	d.	H	...	...	...	...	...	0703	|	0813	|	|	0922	0956	|	1100	|	|	1319	|	1453	|	1520	|	...	1634
437	Caserta	d.		...	...	...	...	0645	0759	|	0903	|	|	1006	1052	|	1144	|	|	1410	|	1552	|	1609	|	...	1747
653	**Roma** Termini	a.	S	...	...	...	...	0750	0915	|	1013	|	|	1115	1205	|	1315	|	|	1525	|	1705	|	1715	|	...	1858
	Termoli	d.	P	...	...	...	...	|	|	0720	...	0824	0919	|	...	1020	...	1119	1220	...	1319	...	1520	|	1620	...	|
	Pescara Centrale	a.	E	...	...	...	...	|	|	0807	...	0909	1008	|	...	1107	...	1205	1307	...	1405	...	1607	|	1707	...	|
	Pescara Centrale	d.	E	...	0500	...	0600	|	|	0810	...	0912	1011	|	...	1110	...	1208	1310	...	1408	...	1610	|	1710	1754	|
	S. Benedetto del Tronto	d.	D	...	0532	...	0636	|	|	0841	...	|	|	|	...	|	...	1242	1341	...	1439	...	|	|	|	|	|
	C. Marche-Montegranaro	d.		...	|	...	|	|	|	|	...	|	1057	|	...	|	...	|	|	...	|	...	|	|	|	|	|
	Ancona	a.	T	...	0612	...	0717	|	|	0922	...	1025	1122	|	...	1222	...	1323	1422	...	1520	...	1722	|	1822	1907	|
	Ancona	d.	R	0520	0615	0620	0720	◧	◧	0925	...	1028	1125	◧	...	1225	...	1326	1425	...	1523	...	1725	◧	1825	1910	◧
	Pesaro	d.	A	0547	0641	0647	0749	|	|	0952	...	|	1152	|	...	1252	...	1354	1452	...	1554	...	1752	|	1852	1946	|
	Riccione	d.	I	|	|	|	0804	|	|	1006	...	1111f	|	|	...	|	...	|	|	...	|	...	1806	|	1906	2004	|
	Rimini ⊡	a.	N	0608	0701	0708	0810	|	|	1015	...	1118	1214	|	...	1313	...	1414	1515	...	1614	...	1815	|	1915	2012	|
	Rimini ⊡	d.	S	0610	0703	0710	0812	|	|	1017	...	1120	1216	|	...	1315	...	1416	1517	...	1616	...	1817	|	1917	2014	|
	Cesena	d.		0627	|	0727	0828	|	|	|	...	|	|	|	...	|	...	|	1534	...	|	...	|	|	|	|	|
	Forlì	d.		0640	0733	0739	0840	|	|	1042	...	|	|	|	...	|	...	1442	|	...	1642	...	|	|	|	|	|
	Faenza	d.		0649	|	0749	0849	|	|	|	...	|	|	|	...	|	...	|	|	...	|	...	|	|	|	|	|
	Bologna Centrale ●	a.		0715	0810	0815	0915	1008	|	1115	...	1215	1315	1403	...	1415	...	1515	1615	...	1715	...	1915	2003	2015	2115	2133
	Bologna Centrale ●	d.		0718	0813	0818	0918	1011	|	1118	...	1218	1318	1406	...	...	...	1518	1618	...	1718	...	1918	2006	...	2118	2136
	Modena	d.		0740	|	0840	0940	|	|	|	...	|	|	|	...	...	...	1540	1640	...	1740	...	|	|	...	|	|
	Reggio Emilia AV	d.		|	0842	|	|	|	|	1142	...	1242	1342	1435	...	...	...	|	|	...	|	...	1942	2030	...	2142	2200
	Reggio Emilia	d.		0757	|	0857	0957	|	|	|	...	|	|	|	...	...	...	1557	1657	...	1757	...	|	|	...	|	|
	Parma	d.		0815	|	0915	1015	|	|	|	...	|	|	|	...	...	...	1615	1715	...	1815	...	|	|	...	|	|
	Piacenza	d.		0846	|	|	|	|	|	|	...	|	|	|	...	...	...	|	|	...	|	...	|	|	...	|	|
	Milano Rogoredo ▽	a.		0919	|	|	|	|	|	|	...	|	|	|	...	...	...	|	|	...	|	...	2015	|	...	|	2238
	Milano Centrale	a.		0930	0935	1010	1110	1115	1224	1230	...	1325	1425	1520	...	...	...	1710	1810	...	1910	...	2047d	2120	...	2230	2250

(The letters in the fourth column read downwards: HIGH SPEED TRAINS.)

		FR 8830	*FR* 8326	*FR* 9562 ⑥⑦			*IC* 604	*IC* 606	*RJ* 82 K	*IC* 608	*IC* 610 F	*IC* 544 ①–⑥ L	*IC* 612 j	*IC* 1546 ⑦	*IC* 612 k	*IC* 566 G	*IC* 614	*IC* 704	*IC* 562 Hg	*IC* 562 Hh	*ICN* 758 C	*ICN* 752 C	*ICN* 754 ①–⑤ CE	*ICN* 754 ⑥ CE	*ICN* 754 ⑦ CE	*ICN* 788 ⑦ C
ecce	d.	...	1700	2055	...		...	...	...	0623	0820	...	0842	0935	1006	1135	1154	...	...	...	1831	1950	2025	2025	2025	2215
rindisi	d.	...	1723	2117	...		...	...	...	0647	0842	...	0921	0956	1028	1200	1214	...	...	...	1901	2019	2053	2053	2053	2240
stuni	d.	...	1744	2142	...		...	...	...	0710	0904	...	|	1018	1049	|	1235	...	...	...	|	2044	2116	2116	2116	2302
asano	d.	...	|	2155	...		...	...	...	0723	0917	...	|	1030	1101	|	1247	...	...	...	|	2059	2131	2131	2131	2315
onopoli	d.	...	1803	2204	...		...	...	...	0733	0928	...	|	1040	1112	|	1257	...	...	...	|	2109	2140	2140	2140	2326
Taranto	d.	...	|	|	...		...	...	...	|	|	...	1028	|	|	1304	|	1450	1841	1850	2004	|	|	|	|	|
Gioia del Colle	d.	...	|	|	...		...	...	...	|	|	...	1104	|	|	...	|	1522	⊙	1921	2037	|	|	|	|	|
ari Centrale	a.	...	1826	2231	...		...	...	...	0802	0951	...	1143	1105	1145	...	1344	1555	2103	1956	2115	2137	2206	2206	2206	2355
ari Centrale	d.	1630	1830	2235	...		...	0550	...	0806	0955	...	1155	1108	1155	...	1355	1605	...	...	2128	2145	2210	2210	2210	0001
arletta	d.	1706	1905	2317	...		...	0629	...	0851	1038	...	1238	1151	1238	...	1438	1648	...	...	2213	2238	2246	2246	2256	0048
oggia	a.	1733	1933	2351	...	L	...	0702	...	0918	1107	...	1307	1221	1307	...	1507	1728	...	...	2249	2315	2321	2321	2328	0132
oggia	d.	1736	1942	2354	...	O	...	0710	...	0921	1110	...	1310	1223	1310	...	1510	1741	...	...	2259	2318	2325	2325	2331	0200
Benevento	d.	|	2047	|	...	N	...	|	...	|	|	...	|	|	|	...	|	1855	...	...	|	|	|	|	|	0312
Caserta	d.	|	2148	|	...	G	...	|	...	|	|	...	|	|	|	...	|	2000	...	...	|	|	|	|	|	0407
Napoli Centrale	a.	|	|	|	...		...	|	...	|	|	...	|	|	|	...	|	|	...	...	|	|	|	|	|	|
Roma Termini	a.	|	2305	|	...	D	...	|	...	|	|	...	|	|	|	...	|	2227e	...	...	|	|	|	|	|	0611
ermoli	d.	1820	...	|	...	I	...	0805	...	1009	1205	...	1405	1332	1405	...	1605	...	...	...	|	0015	0023	0023	0023	...
escara Centrale	a.	1907	...	|	...	S	...	0900	...	1100	1300	...	1500	1430	1500	...	1700	...	...	...	0105	0114	0122	0122	0122	...
escara Centrale	d.	1910	...	|	...	T	0702	0902	...	1102	1302	...	1502	1432	1502	...	1702	...	...	...	0108	0117	0126	0126	0126	...
. Benedetto del Tronto	d.	1941	...	|	...	A	0736	0936	...	1148	1348	1422	1536	1512	1536	...	1748	...	...	...	|	0200	|	|	|	...
. Marche-Montegranaro	d.	|	...	|	...	N	0809	1009	...	1213	1413	1450	1606	1539	1606	...	1813	...	...	...	|	|	|	|	|	...
ncona	a.	2022	...	|	...	C	0835	1037	...	1235	1435	1527	1635	1610	1635	...	1835	...	...	...	0256	0303	0309	0309	0309	...
ncona	d.	2025	...	|	...	E	0838	1040	1130	1238	1438	...	1638	1614	1638	...	1838	...	...	...	0306	0312	0317	0317	0317	...
enigallia	d.	|	...	|	...		0856	1057	1146	1256	1456	...	1656	1630	1656	...	1856	...	...	...	|	|	|	|	|	...
ano	d.	|	...	|	...	T	0909	1110	|	1309	1509	...	1709	1643	1709	...	1909	...	...	...	|	|	|	|	|	...
esaro	d.	2052	...	|	...	R	0919	1119	1204	1317	1517	...	1717	1655	1717	...	1917	...	...	...	|	|	0354	0354	|	...
iccione	d.	2107	...	|	...	A	0938	1138	1223	1338	1538	...	1738	1718	1738	...	1938	...	...	...	|	|	|	|	|	...
imini ⊡	a.	2115	...	|	...	I	0945	1145	1232	1345	1545	...	1745	1727	1745	...	1945	...	...	...	0357	0407	0417	0417	0417	...
imini ⊡	d.	2117	...	|	...	N	0947	1147	1234	1347	1547	...	1747	1729	1747	...	1947	...	...	...	0359	0409	0419	0419	0419	...
esena	d.	|	...	|	...	S	1009	1207	1253	1407	1607	...	1807	1747	1807	...	2007	...	...	...	|	|	0440	0440	|	...
orlì	d.	|	...	|	...		1021	1219	|	1419	1619	...	1819	1759	1819	...	2019	...	...	...	|	|	0453	0453	|	...
aenza	d.	|	...	|	...		1031	1229	|	1429	1629	...	1829	1810	1829	...	2029	...	...	...	|	|	0503	0503	|	...
ologna Centrale ●	a.	2215	...	0531	...		1101	1300	1348	1500	1700	...	1901	1840	1901	...	2100	...	...	...	0452	0502	0530	0540	0540	...
ologna Centrale ●	d.	2218	...	0534	...		1105	1303	...	1504	...	...	1905	1845	1905	...	2104	...	...	...	0456	0506	...	...	...	...
odena	d.	2240	...	0600	...		1133	1325	...	1528	...	...	1936	1913	1936	...	2135	...	...	...	|	0526	...	...	...	...
Reggio Emilia AV	d.	|	...	|	...		|	|	...	|	...	...	|	|	|	...	|	...	...	...	|	|	...	...	...	...
eggio Emilia	d.	2257	...	0617	...		1204	1340	...	1547	...	...	1956	1926	1956	...	2151	...	...	...	|	0541	...	...	...	...
arma	d.	2315	...	0634	...		1220	1356	...	1606	...	...	2013	1941	2013	...	2210	...	...	...	|	0556	...	...	...	...
idenza	d.	|	...	|	...		1232	1409	...	1620	...	...	2025	1954	2025	...	2224	...	...	...	|	|	...	...	...	...
iacenza	d.	|	...	|	...		1252	1429	...	1644	...	...	2046	2019	2046	...	2243	...	...	...	|	0628	...	...	...	...
ilano Rogoredo ▽	a.	|	...	0724	...		|	1516	...	1738	...	...	2124	2100	2124	...	2325	...	...	...	|	|	...	...	...	...
ilano Centrale	a.	0010	...	0740	...		1340	1530	...	1750	...	...	2140	2115	2140	...	2340	...	...	...	0705	0717	...	...	...	...

(The letters in the sixth column read downwards: LONG DISTANCE TRAINS.)

– To/from Venezia (Table **600**).
– To/from Torino (Table **600**).
– Conveys 🛏 1, 2 cl., 🛏 2 cl. (4 berth).
– (12) Bolzano - Bologna - Bari.
– 🛏 1, 2 cl., 🛏 2 cl. (4 berth) Torino - Lecce and v.v.
– (12) Lecce - Bologna - Bolzano.
– (12) Reggio di Calabria - Taranto - Lecce and v.v.
– (12) Reggio di Calabria - Taranto - Bari and v.v.
– Apr. 17 - Oct. 5: (12) München - Bologna - Ancona.
– Apr. 18 - Oct. 6: (12) Ancona - Bologna - München.
– (12) Roma - Falconara - Ancona - S. Benedetto del Tronto and v.v.

– Milano **Porta Garibaldi**.
– Arrives 2220 on ⑦.
– ⑤–⑦ only.
– July 1 - Aug. 31.
– Not July 1 - Aug. 31.

j – Until June 30.
k – From July 1.

◧ – Via Table **600**.
⊖ – Via Monopoli (d. 0646) and Brindisi (a. 0724 / d. 0734).
⊙ – Via Brindisi (a. 1941 / d. 1950) and Monopoli (d. 2028).
❦ – Subject to confirmation.
△ – Most trains call here to pick up only.
▽ – Most trains call here to set down only.
● – Most high-speed services use underground platforms 16 – 19; allow a minimum of 10 minutes when connecting with services from/to the main station.

⊡ – 🚌 **Rimini - San Marino**. **June 7 - Sept. 14.** *27 km*. Journey 70 minutes. www.bonellibus.it.
From **Rimini** FS station at 0730, 0900, 0945, 1030, 1115, 1200, 1315, 1445, 1530, 1615, 1700, 1745, 1830, 1915, 2000, 2045.
From **San Marino** centro storico (ex stazione) - park 2 bus at 0715, 0845, 0930, 1015, 1100, 1145, 1300, 1430, 1515, 1600, 1645, 1730, 1815, 1900, 1945, 2030.

615 BOLOGNA - ANCONA - PESCARA and BARI - TARANTO - LECCE

Local trains. For high-speed and long-distance trains see previous two pages.

km																										
					⑥⑦		©	Ⓐ			⑥		†	⚒			Ⓐ									
	Milano Centrale **620** d.	...	...	...	0630	...	...	...	...	...	0920	...	...	...	...	...	...	...	...	...	...	...	...	1815	...	...
	Piacenza **620** d.	...	0530	0646	0727	0749	0846	0846	...	0946	1014	1046	*1146*	1146	1246	1345	...	1446	...	1546	1646	1746	1846	1909	1949	...
0	**Bologna** Centrale a.	0634	0734	0834	0912	0934	1034	1034	...	1134	1212	1234	1334	1334	1434	1534	...	1634	...	1734	1834	1934	2034	2110	2134	223
35	Imola d.	0655	0802	0855	0944	0955	1058	1058	...	1155	1243	1255	1355	1355	1455	1555	...	1655	...	1756	1855	1955	2055	2129	2155	|
42	Castelbolognese-Riolo T. d.	0702	0808	0902	|	1002	1104	1104	...	1202	1257	1302	1402	1402	1502	1602	...	1702	...	1802	1902	2002	2102	2136	2202	|
48	Faenza d.	0717	0817	0917	0954	1017	1117	1115	...	1217	1304	1317	1417	1417	1517	1617	...	1717	...	1817	1917	2017	2117	|	2217	230
63	Forlì d.	0728	0828	0928	1003	1033	1128	1129	...	1228	1319	1328	1428	1428	1528	1628	...	1734	...	1828	1928	2029	2128	|	2228	231
81	Cesena d.	0742	0842	0942	1015	1059	1142	1156	...	1244	1335	1342	1442	1442	1542	1642	...	1748	...	1844	1942	2046	2142	|	2245	233
110	**Rimini** a.	0801	0901	1001	1044	1120	1201	1219	...	1309	1359	1403	1502	1501	1601	1701	...	1805	...	1901	2001	2112	2201	2318	2322	235
110	**Rimini** d.	0803	0903	1003	1046	...	1203	1221	...	1319	...	1405	1503	1503	1603	1703	1720	1807	...	1903	2003	...	2203	...	...	...
119	Riccione d.	0812	0912	1012	1057	...	1212	1230	...	1331	...	1414	1511	1511	1612	1713	1731	1815	...	1910	2012	...	2212	...	...	...
128	Cattolica-Gabicce d.	0820	0920	1020	1104	...	1220	1238	...	1341	...	1422	1519	1519	1620	1722	1740	1823	...	1919	2020	...	2220	...	...	...
143	Pesaro d.	0830	0930	1030	1116	...	1230	1248	...	1352	...	1432	1530	1530	1630	1735	1751	1834	...	1931	2030	...	2230	...	...	...
155	Fano d.	0838	0938	1038	|	...	1238	1257	...	1402	...	1440	1539	1539	1638	...	1759	1842	...	1939	2038	...	2238	...	...	...
177	Senigallia d.	0853	0954	1053	1134	...	1253	1313	...	1425	...	1454	1554	1554	1653	...	1817	1857	...	1952	2053	...	2252	...	...	...
194	Falconara Marittima d.	0906	1011	1104	|	...	1304	1331	...	1439	...	1504	1607	1607	1704	...	1832	1911	...	2006	2104	...	2306	...	...	...
202	**Ancona** a.	0920	1022	1116	1154	...	1316	1350	...	1450	...	1516	1620	1620	1716	...	1844	1922	...	2026	2116	...	2323	...	...	...

									†									Ⓐ		⑥⑦		A	⚒		
Ancona d.	...	...	0445	0545	0645	0745	0845	...	0945	1045	1145	1245	...	...	1445	...	1645	1715	...	1757	1845	...	1945	2045	223
Falconara Marittima d.	...	...	0454	0555	0655	0756	0854	...	0954	1054	1154	1256	...	...	1455	...	1654	1726	...	1807	1855	...	1955	2056	224
Senigallia d.	...	...	0506	0605	0707	0808	0904	...	1007	1104	1204	1305	...	...	1505	...	1704	1744	...	1821	1905	...	2012	2108	225
Fano d.	...	...	0520	0620	0721	0823	0919	...	1021	1119	1219	1319	...	...	1518	...	1719	1759	...	1835	1918	...	2026	2123	231
Pesaro d.	...	...	0527	0628	0730	0832	0927	...	1029	1127	1227	1327	...	...	1526	...	1726	1812	1823	1845	1926	...	2034	2131	232
Cattolica-Gabicce d.	...	...	0538	0639	0741	0843	0938	...	1040	1138	1238	1328	...	...	1536	...	1736	...	1834	1903	1936	...	2045	2142	233
Riccione d.	...	...	0546	0645	0750	0849	0946	...	1048	1146	1246	1347	...	...	1544	...	1745	...	1842	1911	1944	...	2054	2150	233
Rimini a.	...	...	0556	0651	0800	0857	0956	...	1057	1156	1256	1356	...	...	1556	...	1756	...	1853	1918	1956	...	2105	2202	234
Rimini d.	...	0520	0558	0653	0802	0859	0958	1041	1059	1158	1258	1358	...	1441	1558	1640	1758	...	1854	1923	1958	2050	...	2204	...
Cesena d.	...	|	0618	0709	0819	0919	1019	1110	1121	1219	1319	1419	...	1510	1619	1708	1819	...	1919	1944	2019	2113	...	2223	...
Forlì d.	...	|	0631	0720	0831	0931	1033	1127	1135	1231	1331	1431	...	1528	1631	1726	1831	...	1933	1956	2031	2127	...	2236	...
Faenza d.	...	|	0641	0736	0841	0941	1043	1140	1146	1241	1341	1441	...	1540	1641	1735	1841	...	1943	2007	2041	2139	...	2247	...
Castelbolognese-Riolo Terme d.	0546	0710	0647	0742	0847	0947	1049	1147	1158	1247	1347	1447	...	1548	1647	1748	1847	...	1949	|	2047	2146	...	2253	...
Imola d.	0555	0716	0700	0800	0900	1000	1100	1200	1210	1300	1400	1500	...	1600	1700	1756	1900	...	2000	2017	2100	2200	...	2300	...
Bologna Centrale a.	0626	0738	0726	0826	0926	1026	1126	1226	1234	1326	1426	1526	...	1626	1726	1826	1926	...	2026	2046	2126	2224	...	2321	...
Piacenza **620** a.	0807	0950	...	1016	1116	1216	1316	1416	...	1516	1616	1713	...	1810	1918	2012	2110	...	2213	2231	2315	...	...	...	...
Milano Centrale **620** a.	...	1045	...	...	...	...	...	...	...	...	...	...	...	...	...	2115	...	...	...	2330	...	...	...	...	...

km																										
		⚒	⚒	⚒	⚒	†	Ⓐ	†		Ⓐ	⚒		Ⓐ	⚒	†	⑥	Ⓑ	⚒			Ⓐ	⑥	⚒		Ⓑ	⚒
0	**Ancona** d.	0515	0600	0625	0733	0810	0845	0945	...	0945	1045	1145	1245	1345	1345	1440	1445	1545	...	1645	1745	1745	1841	1945	2045	215
43	Civitanova ◧ d.	0549	0628	0700	0808	0845	0921	1012	...	1021	1121	1221	1321	1421	1421	1516	1521	1621	...	1722	1821	1821	1922	2019	2117	222
85	S. Benedetto del Tronto d.	0621	0702	0732	0840	0919	1000	1047	...	1054	1154	1253	1354	1454	1454	1554	1554	1654	...	1756	1854	1855	1954	2051	2147	230
146	**Pescara** Centrale a.	0720	...	0824	0916	1010	...	...	...	...	...	1350	...	1540	1556	1656	1656	...	...	1856	1941	...	2050	2145	...	...

	⚒	⚒	Ⓐ	†	⚒	⚒	⚒	Ⓐ	†	⚒	Ⓐ	†	⚒	⚒	Ⓑ	⚒	⚒	†	⚒		Ⓐ	⑥	†	⚒	Ⓐ
Pescara Centrale d.	0505	...	...	0550	...	0653	...	...	0915	1015	...	1145	1158	...	...	1415	...	1520	1602	1720	1817	...	1913	1915	...
S. Benedetto del Tronto d.	0556	0611	0645	0649	0714	0752	0854	0951	1007	1102	1153	1240	1256	1355	1456	1506	1558	1612	1700	1813	1908	1908	2007	2007	212
Civitanova ◧ d.	0626	0644	0711	0723	0753	0826	0928	1023	1039	1135	1226	1318	1330	1430	1519	1539	1629	1645	1732	1848	1939	1938	2039	2039	215
Ancona a.	0705	0725	0745	0804	0827	0907	1010	1100	1115	1217	1302	1358	1410	1510	1550	1615	1705	1730	1809	1930	2010	2010	2120	2120	223

km																										
		⚒	Ⓐ	⚒	⚒	Ⓐ		⚒	Ⓐ	⚒		⚒		⚒	⚒	Ⓐ		⚒		⚒🚌		⚒	⚒🚌	⚒		†
0	**Pescara** Centrale d.	...	...	0605	...	...	...	0805	0905	...	...	1210	...	1405	...	...	1505	1705	...	...	...	1905	...	2015	...	202
90	Termoli d.	0648	...	0720	0747	...	...	0920	1020	1242	...	1325	...	1520	1619	...	1620	1824	...	1940	...	2020	2120	2125	...	213
177	**Foggia** ⊡ d.	0749	0802	...	0903	0932	...	...	...	1403	1430	...	...	...	1715	1732	...	...	...	2140	2206	...	2320	...	...	...
245	Barletta ⊡ d.	...	0844	...	...	1014	...	...	...	...	1513	...	...	...	...	1811	...	...	...	...	2249	...	...	...	...	...
300	**Bari** Centrale ⊡ a.	...	0925	...	...	1121	...	...	...	...	1604	...	...	...	...	1855	...	...	...	...	2343	...	...	...	...	...

	⚒	⚒	⚒	†	⑥		Ⓐ	⚒🚌	⚒	Ⓐ	⚒		⚒	⚒	⚒	Ⓐ	⚒			⚒	Ⓐ	⚒	⚒		⚒
Bari Centrale ⊡ d.	...	...	...	...	0415	...	0425	...	...	...	0811	...	...	...	...	1305	...	...	...	...	1735	...	...	...	...
Barletta ⊡ d.	...	...	...	...	0503	...	0512	...	...	...	0859	...	...	...	...	1344	...	...	...	...	1814	...	...	...	...
Foggia ⊡ d.	...	...	...	...	0548	...	0557	0610	...	...	1005	...	1048	...	...	1428	1441	...	...	...	1858	1936	...	...	204
Termoli d.	0600	0635	0733	0740	...	...	...	0800	0940	1140	...	...	1146	1340	1540	...	1546	...	1640	1840	...	2033	2040	...	214
Pescara Centrale a.	0715	0750	0843	0855	...	...	...	...	1055	1255	...	...	...	1455	1655	...	...	...	1755	1955	...	...	2155	...	...

km																										
		⚒	⚒	†		⚒	⚒	⚒		⚒		⚒		†	⚒	⚒			⚒			⚒	Ⓐ	⑥		
0	**Bari** d.	0623	0720	0822	...	0950	1050	1305	...	1335	1440	1524	...	1600	1625	1744	...	1820	1945	2050	...	2126	2239	2350	...	...
54	Gioia del Colle d.	0706	0802	0905	...	1033	1132	1349	...	1418	1523	1606	...	1641	1707	1826	...	1900	2027	2133	...	2209	2321	0033	...	...
115	**Taranto** a.	0745	0842	0944	...	1112	1212	1422	...	1457	1602	1646	...	1722	1747	1906	...	1940	2107	2212	...	2249	2359	0112	...	...

	⚒	⚒			⚒	⚒	⚒		†	⚒	⚒			⚒	⚒			⚒	†		⚒	⚒	⚒		
Taranto d.	0440	0530	0616	...	0703	0756	0955	...	1040	1135	1300	...	1340	1432	1530	...	1650	1805	1910	...	1930	2015	2100	...	...
Gioia del Colle d.	0517	0609	0655	...	0742	0836	1034	...	1119	1216	1340	...	1420	1512	1610	...	1730	1838	1950	...	2005	2055	2140	...	...
Bari a.	0557	0652	0739	...	0825	0918	1117	...	1202	1257	1420	...	1502	1554	1652	...	1810	1922	2032	...	2047	2137	2226	...	...

km											
		⚒	⚒	⚒	⚒	⚒	⚒	⚒	⚒		
0	**Taranto** d.	0535	0608	0845	1244	1402	1523	1652	1849	...	...
34	Francavilla Fontana d.	0602	0637	0918	1312	1429	1551	1722	1917	...	...
70	**Brindisi** a.	0635	0719	0957	1350	1506	1634	1759	2002	...	...

	⚒	⚒	⚒	⚒	⚒	⚒	⚒	⚒		
Brindisi d.	0645	0754	1100	1401	1519	1644	1809	2018	...	...
Francavilla Fontana d.	0722	0832	1138	1440	1554	1719	1846	2051	...	...
Taranto a.	0750	0907	1206	1513	1625	1755	1922	2123	...	...

km																										
		Ⓐ	Ⓐ	⑥	Ⓐ	©	Ⓐ	Ⓐ	©	Ⓐ	©	©	Ⓐ	Ⓐ	Ⓐ	⑥	Ⓐ	©	Ⓐ	⑥	Ⓐ	Ⓐ	©	Ⓐ	⑥	
0	**Bari** Centrale d.	0602	0632	0708	0732	0801	0802	0902	0902	1002	1035	1220	1232	1302	1332	1335	1402	1440	1502	1555	1602	1632	1635	1702	1735	1745
41	Monopoli d.	0629	0659	0745	0802	0838	0830	0930	0939	1029	1112	1257	1259	1329	1359	1412	1429	1517	1529	1632	1629	1659	1712	1729	1820	1809
55	Fasano d.	0637	0707	0754	0811	0847	0838	0938	0948	1037	1121	1306	1307	1337	1407	1421	1437	1526	1537	1641	1637	1707	1721	1737	1829	|
75	Ostuni d.	0651	0718	0808	0825	0901	0852	0952	1001	1048	1136	1321	1318	1351	1418	1436	1451	1541	1551	1656	1651	1720	1736	1748	1843	|
111	**Brindisi** d.	0713	0743	0830	0844	0926	0915	1015	1025	1112	1157	1342	1343	1412	1443	1457	1514	1602	1614	1717	1714	1743	1757	1811	1904	1846
150	**Lecce** a.	0743	0813	0901	0915	0956	0945	1045	1058	1143	1228	1413	1413	1443	1513	1528	1543	1633	1645	1748	1743	1813	1828	1845	1938	1910

	Ⓐ	©	Ⓐ	©	Ⓐ	©	Ⓐ		
Bari Centrale d.	1802	1818	1832	1950	2040	2040	2102	2302	...
Monopoli d.	1829	1854	1859	2026	2111	2117	2129	2339	...
Fasano d.	1837	1902	1907	2034	2120	2125	2137	2347	...
Ostuni d.	1851	1917	1918	2049	2133	2139	2151	0001	...
Brindisi d.	1914	1941	1943	2112	2156	2202	2214	0024	...
Lecce a.	1943	2013	2013	2144	2225	2234	2243	0055	...

	Ⓐ			Ⓐ		©	Ⓐ	⑥	Ⓐ
Lecce d.	0611	0631	0720	0725	...	0725	0751	0847	1017
Brindisi d.	0639	0655	0744	0754	...	0756	0818	0918	1045
Ostuni d.	0659	0718	|	0816	...	0818	0840	0941	1107
Fasano d.	0713	0740	|	0828	...	0832	0900	0955	1121
Monopoli d.	0722	0750	0820	0838	...	0840	0910	1003	1130
Bari Centrale a.	0759	0823	0845	0908	...	0919	0944	1041	1158

	©	Ⓐ	Ⓐ	©	Ⓐ	⑥	Ⓐ	Ⓐ	©	Ⓐ	Ⓐ	©		Ⓐ	©	Ⓐ	Ⓐ	©	©	Ⓐ	⚒	©	Ⓐ	Ⓐ	⑥
Lecce d.	1017	1120	1217	1217	1317	1317	1347	1417	1417	1447	1517	1517	...	1547	1605	1617	1720	1725	1800	1817	1905	2000	2017	2117	2117
Brindisi d.	1048	1147	1246	1248	1345	1348	1416	1445	1448	1516	1545	1548	...	1615	1635	1645	1747	1752	1832	1845	1933	2032	2045	2146	2148
Ostuni d.	1111	1209	1307	1311	1407	1411	1439	1507	1511	1537	1607	1611	...	1637	1658	1707	1809	1815	1855	1907	1956	2055	2107	2207	2211
Fasano d.	1125	1223	1321	1325	1421	1425	1451	1521	1525	1548	1621	1625	...	1651	1712	1721	1823	1831	1909	1921	2010	2109	2121	2218	2225
Monopoli d.	1133	1231	1330	1333	1430	1433	1500	1530	1533	1558	1630	1633	...	1700	1720	1730	1831	1839	1917	1930	2019	2117	2130	2227	2233
Bari Centrale a.	1211	1300	1358	1411	1458	1511	1528	1558	1611	1628	1658	1711	...	1728	1758	1758	1900	1918	1954	1958	2058	2154	2158	2308	2311

A – To Parma (Table **620**).

◧ – Full name is Civitanova Marche-Montegranaro.

⊡ – Other trains Foggia - Bari and v.v.: from Foggia at 0602, 0630 ⚒, 0702 Ⓐ, 0732 Ⓐ, 0830, 1026 © 1032 Ⓐ, 1130 ⚒, 1202 Ⓐ, 1217 ©, 1330 ⚒, 1532 Ⓐ, 1632 Ⓐ, 1640 ©, 1830, 1932 Ⓐ, 2030; from Bari Centrale at 0540 Ⓐ, 0620 Ⓐ, 0639 ©, 0835 ©, 0905 Ⓐ, 1018 ©, 1035 Ⓐ, 1218 ©, 1319 Ⓐ, 1405 ⚒, 1445 ©, 1505 Ⓐ, 1535 Ⓐ, 1618 †, 1635 Ⓐ, 1705 Ⓐ, 1720 ©, 1805 Ⓐ, 1852 ⑥, 1905 Ⓐ, 2015 †, 2022 ⑥, 2035 Ⓐ, 2105 Ⓐ, 2135 ⑥, 2215.

SIENA - GROSSETO and CHIUSI — 619

2nd class

km				⚒							🚌						🚌							
0	**Siena** d.	0545	...	0707	...	0802	1010	...	1205	...	...	...	1332	1544	...	...	...	1725	...	1745	1917	...	1950	...
29	Buonconvento d.	0622	...	0746	...	0841	1045	...	1237	...	1247	...	1404	1616	...	1247	...	1801	...	1825	1952	...	2022	...
102	**Grosseto** a.	...	...	...	...	0952	...	...	...	...	1357	...	1517	...	...	1357	...	...	...	1937	...	...	2135	...

		⚒ 🚌	⚒	⚒				⚒ 🚌										† 🚌	⚒ 🚌			Ⓐ 🚌	† 🚌	
	Grosseto d.	0434	...	...	...	0605	0700	0740	...	...	...	...	...	1345	...	1618	...	1640	1710	...	...	1908	1954	...
	Buonconvento d.	0544	0554	0703	...	0719	0812	0850	...	0900	1102	1247	...	1458	1627	1729	...	|	1820	1830	...	2018	|	2028
	Siena a.	...	0623	0732	...	0751	0846	...	...	0935	1140	1322	...	1530	1702	1813	...	1815	...	1907	...	...	2100	2105

SIENA - CHUSI-CHIANCIANO TERME. *89 km.* Journey 75–90 minutes.
From **Siena** at 0554 ⚒, 0600 †, 0802 †, 0813 ⚒, 1002 †, 1215 ⚒, 1325 ⚒, 1352 ⚒, 1402 †, 1443 ⚒, 1602, 1648 ⚒, 1743 ⚒, 1802 †, 1816 ⚒, 1926 ⚒, 2002 †, 2023 ⚒.
From **Chiusi-Chianciano Terme** at 0556 ⚒, 0629 †, 0645 ⚒, 0710 ⚒, 0830 †, 0900 ⚒, 1030 †, 1046 ⚒, 1230 †, 1348 ⚒, 1511 ⚒, 1630 †, 1713 ⚒, 1830 †, 1835 ⚒, 1955 ⚒, 2030 †, 2200 ⚒.

MILANO, TRIESTE and VENEZIA - BOLOGNA - FIRENZE - ROMA — 620

For high-speed trains see Tables **600** and **601**. For other long-distance trains Milano - Bologna see Table **615**. For *ICN* night trains see Table **641**. For other local trains see next page.

km		2 ⚒	*IC* **581** ①–⑥	2	2	*FR* **9303**	*IC* **583** Ⓐ	*IC* **583** Ⓒ	*IC* **1589** ⑥ **A**	2	*IC* **584** Ⓒ	2		2	*IC* **584** Ⓐ	*IC* **597**	2	2	*IC* **594**	2 Ⓐ	*FR* **9329** Ⓑ **B**	2 Ⓐ	*IC* **599** **C**
	Milano Centrale 615 d.	...	...	...	...	0550	0545	0605	0655	...	...	...	...	...	...	1348	...	...	...	...	1848**p**	...	1740
	Milano Rogoredo △ 615 d.	...	...	...	...	0600	0554	0614	0705	...	...	...	...	...	...	1400	...	...	...	...	1905	...	1800
	Piacenza 615 d.	...	...	...	...	0624	0644	0713	0744	...	...	...	...	...	...	1438	...	...	...	...	|	...	1837
	Fidenza 615 d.	...	...	...	...	|	0705	0734	0805	...	...	...	...	...	...	1456	...	...	...	...	|	...	1854
	Parma 615 d.	...	...	...	...	0705	0721	0747	0819	...	...	...	...	...	...	1509	...	...	...	...	|	...	1906
	Reggio Emilia 615 d.	...	...	...	...	0723	0738	0805	0835	...	...	...	...	...	...	1526	...	...	...	...	1942**r**	...	1922
	Modena 615 d.	...	...	...	...	0742	0754	0824	0855	...	...	...	...	...	...	1548	...	...	...	...	|	...	1938
	Trieste Centrale 601 d.	...	...	...	...	|	|	|	|	...	0721	...	...	...	1047	|	...	...	1327	...	|	...	|
	Monfalcone 601 d.	...	...	...	...	|	|	|	|	...	0747	...	...	...	1112	|	...	...	1351	...	|	...	|
	Trieste Airport ✈ 601 d.	...	...	...	...	|	|	|	|	...	0753	...	...	...	1118	|	...	...	1357	...	|	...	|
	Cervignano-Aquileia-Grado 601 d.	...	...	...	...	|	|	|	|	...	0802	...	...	...	1127	|	...	...	1406	...	|	...	|
	Latisana-Lignano-Bibione 601 d.	...	...	...	...	|	|	|	|	...	0821	...	...	...	1145	|	...	...	1422	...	|	...	|
	Portogruaro-Caorle 601 d.	...	...	...	...	|	|	|	|	...	0832	...	...	...	1157	|	...	...	1432	...	◧	...	|
	S. Dona di Piave-Jesolo 601 d.	...	...	...	...	|	|	|	|	...	0850	...	...	...	1215	|	...	...	1450	...	|	...	|
	Venezia Mestre 601 a.	...	...	...	...	|	|	|	|	...	0919	...	...	...	1246	|	...	...	1514	...	|	...	|
0	**Venezia** Mestre d.	...	...	...	...	|	|	|	|	...	0934	...	...	...	1305	|	...	...	1534	...	|	...	|
28	Padova d.	...	...	...	...	|	|	|	|	...	0950	...	...	...	1321	|	...	...	1550	...	|	...	|
72	Rovigo d.	...	...	...	...	|	|	|	|	...	1023	...	...	...	1351	|	...	...	1630	...	|	...	|
104	Ferrara d.	...	...	...	...	|	|	|	|	...	1042	...	...	...	1417	|	...	...	1650	...	|	...	|
151	**Bologna** Centrale 615 a.	...	...	...	...	0809	0820	0850	0933	...	1112	...	...	...	1451	1614	...	...	1721	...	2009	...	2002
151	**Bologna** Centrale d.	...	...	...	...	0812	0824	0854	0937	...	1121	...	...	...	1455	1621	...	...	1725	...	2012	...	2006
232	Prato Centrale d.	...	...	...	...	|	0959	0959	1057	...	1212	...	...	...	1600	1712	...	...	1814	...	|	...	2105
248	**Firenze** SMN a.	...	...	...	...	0850	|	|	|	...	|	...	...	...	|	|	...	...	|	...	2050	...	2122
248	**Firenze** SMN d.	...	0545	0635	0904	0859	|	|	|	1114	|	1314	...	1514	|	|	1714	...	|	1914	2059	2114	2152
	Firenze Rifredi d.	...	|	|	|	|	1015	1015	1116	|	1230	|	...	|	1622	1730	|	...	1828	|	|	|	|
336	Arezzo d.	...	0625	0738	1007	|	1113	1113	|	1217	1312	1417	...	1617	1710	1811	1817	...	1907	2017	2133	2217	2230
354	Castiglion Fiorentino d.	...	|	0752	1020	|	|	|	|	1228	|	1428	...	1628	|	|	1828	...	|	2028	|	2228	|
370	Terontola-Cortona d.	0600	0645	0809	1035	|	1134	1134	|	1241	1330	1441	...	1641	1735	1835	1842	...	1929	2042	2154	2241	2251
413	**Perugia** d.	|	|	|	|	◧	|	|	|	|	|	|	...	|	|	|	|	...	|	|	2230	|	2317
381	Castiglione del Lago d.	0610	|	0816	1042	|	|	|	|	1248	|	1448	...	1648	|	|	1849	...	|	2049	...	2248	...
399	Chiusi-Chianciano Terme d.	0622	0704	0831	1054	|	1152	1152	1230	1301	1349	1500	...	1700	1758	1856	1900	1915	1950	2102	...	2259	...
449	Orvieto d.	0652	0725	0857	1120	|	1217	1217	1253	1327	1413	1527	...	1727	1839	1921	...	1943	2015	2129	...	2325	...
481	Orte d.	0728	|	0940	1154	|	1249	1249	|	1401	1450	1611	...	1811	1920	1952	...	2021	2051	2211	...	0001	...
559	**Roma** Tiburtina ▽ a.	0803	|	1049	1236	|	1327	1327	1336	1430	|	1648	...	1848	|	2035	...	2121	|	2243	...	0102	...
564	**Roma** Termini a.	0814	0820	...	1248	1035	|	|	|	1448	1535	1705	...	1900	2000	2100	...	2130	2135	2300	...	0112	...
	Napoli Centrale **640** a.	...	...	...	...	...	1534	1534	1609	...	...	...	...	...	...	2332	...	...	...	...	...	...	...
	Salerno **640** a.	...	...	...	...	...	...	...	1704	...	...	...	...	...	...	0022	...	...	...	...	...	...	...

	FR **9300** ①–⑥ **B**	*IC* **580** **C**	2 ②–⑥	2	2		*IC* **588**	2	*IC* **590**	2 ⚒	2 †		2	2	*IC* **592**	*IC* **596**		*IC* **1588** ⑦ **A**	2	*IC* **598** Ⓑ	*FR* **9330**	2
Salerno **640** d.	...	...	...	...	...	...	...	...	0858	...	...	...	...	...	...	...	...	1337	...	...	...	...
Napoli Centrale **640** d.	...	...	...	...	...	...	...	...	1031	...	...	...	...	...	...	1420	...	1446	...	...	...	...
Roma Termini d.	...	...	0606	0702	0902	...	1022	...	|	1302	1302	...	...	1502	1530	|	...	|	1720	1815	1950	2002
Roma Tiburtina △ d.	...	...	0615	0712	0912	...	|	1111	1240	1313	1313	...	...	1513	|	1633	...	1712	1730	|	2000	2012
Orte d.	...	...	0650	0747	0952	...	1102	1149	1314	1346	1346	...	...	1552	1613	1705	...	|	1803	1854	|	2047
Orvieto d.	...	...	0724	0820	1029	...	1139	1229	1345	1419	1421	...	...	1626	1648	1743	...	1819	1837	1923	|	2121
Chiusi-Chianciano Terme d.	...	...	0758	0848	1058	...	1210	1258	1410	1514	1511	...	...	1658	1717	1814	...	1845	1906	1946	|	2149
Castiglione del Lago d.	...	...	0809	0900	1109	...	|	1310	|	1531	1529	...	...	1709	|	|	...	|	1918	|	|	2200
Perugia d.	0524	0637	|	|	|	...	|	|	|	|	|	...	...	|	|	|	...	|	|	|	◧	|
Terontola-Cortona d.	0556	0710	0819	0908	1119	...	1230	1319	1427	1540	1536	...	1619	1719	1737	1836	...	1903	1927	2004	|	2207
Castiglion Fiorentino d.	|	|	0831	0923	1131	...	|	1332	|	...	1549	...	1631	1731	|	|	...	|	1939	|	|	2220
Arezzo d.	0625	0732	0844	0943	1145	...	1252	1345	1452	...	1603	...	1644	1744	1802	1901	...	1929	1952	2026	|	2233
Firenze Rifredi d.	|	|	|	|	|	...	1333	|	1533	...	...	...	|	|	1845	1941	...	2017	|	|	|	|
Firenze SMN a.	0701	0806	0952	1048	1250	...	|	1448	|	...	...	...	1757	1848	|	|	...	|	2055	2125	2127	2342
Firenze SMN d.	0710	0821	...	...	...	...	|	...	|	...	...	...	...	...	|	|	...	|	...	...	2136	...
Prato Centrale d.	|	0833	...	...	...	...	1352	...	1552	...	...	...	...	...	1901	1952	...	2038	...	...	|	...
Bologna Centrale a.	0748	0938	...	...	...	...	1447	...	1650	...	...	...	...	...	1956	2042	...	2130	...	...	2213	...
Bologna Centrale 615 d.	0751	0946	...	...	...	...	1451	...	1654	...	...	...	...	...	2000	2046	...	2138	...	...	2216	...
Ferrara d.	|	|	...	...	...	...	1515	...	|	...	...	...	...	...	2034	|	...	|	...	...	|	...
Rovigo d.	|	|	...	...	...	...	1532	...	|	...	...	...	...	...	2053	|	...	|	...	...	|	...
Padova d.	|	|	...	...	...	...	1600	...	|	...	...	...	...	...	2122	|	...	|	...	...	|	...
Venezia Mestre a.	|	|	...	...	...	...	1616	...	|	...	...	...	...	...	2136	|	...	|	...	...	|	...
Venezia Mestre 601 d.	|	|	...	...	...	...	1640	...	|	...	...	...	...	...	2151	|	...	|	...	...	|	...
S. Dona di Piave-Jesolo 601 d.	|	|	...	...	...	...	1706	...	|	...	...	...	...	...	2212	|	...	|	...	...	|	...
Portogruaro-Caorle 601 d.	|	|	...	...	...	...	1730	...	|	...	...	...	...	...	2230	|	...	|	...	...	|	...
Latisana-Lignano-Bibione 601 d.	|	|	...	...	...	...	1741	...	|	...	...	...	...	...	2241	|	...	|	...	...	|	...
Cervignano-Aquileia-Grado 601 d.	|	|	...	...	...	...	1759	...	|	...	...	...	...	...	2259	|	...	|	...	...	|	...
Trieste Airport ✈ 601 d.	|	|	...	...	...	...	1809	...	|	...	...	...	...	...	2309	|	...	|	...	...	|	...
Monfalcone 601 d.	|	|	...	...	...	...	1815	...	|	...	...	...	...	...	2315	|	...	|	...	...	|	...
Trieste Centrale 601 a.	|	|	...	...	...	...	1837	...	|	...	...	...	...	...	2338	|	...	|	...	...	|	...
Modena 615 d.	|	1010	...	...	...	...	...	...	1717	...	...	...	...	...	...	2110	...	2207	...	...	2246	...
Reggio Emilia 615 d.	0815**r**	1024	...	...	...	...	...	...	1731	...	...	...	...	...	...	2124	...	2225	...	...	2303	...
Parma 615 d.	|	1039	...	...	...	...	...	...	1746	...	...	...	...	...	...	2140	...	2243	...	...	2322	...
Fidenza 615 d.	|	1054	...	...	...	...	...	...	1759	...	...	...	...	...	...	2154	...	2304	...	...	|	...
Piacenza 615 d.	|	1119	...	...	...	...	...	...	1824	...	...	...	...	...	...	2219	...	2322	...	...	2352	...
Milano Rogoredo ▽ 615 a.	0854	1200	...	...	...	...	...	...	1914	...	...	...	...	...	...	2300	...	0001	...	...	|	...
Milano Centrale 615 a.	0912**p**	1220	...	...	...	...	...	...	1925	...	...	...	...	...	...	2317	...	0015	...	...	0025	...

A – To/from Reggio di Calabria (Table **640**).
B – To/From Torino (Table **600**).
C – To/from Terni (Table **625**).
p – Milano **Porta Garibaldi**.
r – Reggio Emilia **AV**.
◧ – Via Table **600**.
△ – Most trains call to pick up only.
▽ – Most trains call to set down only.

620 VENEZIA and MILANO - BOLOGNA and FIRENZE - PERUGIA - FOLIGNO

2nd class

Local trains. For long-distance trains see previous page.

VENEZIA - BOLOGNA

km																								
		⚒																						
0	**Venezia** Santa Lucia d.	0540	0640	0740	...	0840	0940	1040	...	1140	1240	1340	...	1440	1540	1640	...	1740	1840	1940	...	2140	...	...
9	**Venezia** Mestre d.	0553	0653	0753	...	0853	0953	1053	...	1153	1253	1353	...	1453	1553	1653	...	1753	1853	1953	...	2153	...	...
37	Padova d.	0612	0709	0809	...	0909	1009	1109	...	1209	1309	1409	...	1509	1609	1709	...	1809	1909	2009	...	2210	...	...
81	Rovigo a.	0642	0741	0845	...	0947	1042	1142	...	1242	1345	1442	...	1552	1645	1742	...	1850	1944	2044	...	2244	...	...
81	Rovigo d.	0644	0758	0847	...	0958	1044	1144	...	1244	1347	1444	...	1558	1647	1744	...	1858	1946	2046	...	2246	...	...
113	Ferrara d.	0705	0818	0905	...	1018	1105	1205	...	1305	1405	1505	...	1618	1705	1805	...	1918	2014	2111	...	2308	...	...
160	**Bologna** Centrale a.	0746	0855	0946	...	1050	1146	1246	...	1346	1446	1546	...	1652	1746	1846	...	1950	2046	2146	...	2340	...	...
			⚒																					
	Bologna Centrale d.	0520	0610	0710	...	0810	0910	1010	...	1110	1210	1310	...	1423	1510	1610	...	1710	1810	1910	...	2110	...	...
	Ferrara d.	0553	0643	0743	...	0843	0943	1043	...	1143	1243	1343	...	1500	1543	1643	...	1743	1843	1943	...	2143	...	...
	Rovigo a.	0609	0701	0801	...	0901	1001	1101	...	1201	1301	1401	...	1516	1601	1701	...	1801	1901	2001	...	2201	...	...
	Rovigo d.	0611	0703	0803	...	0903	1003	1103	...	1203	1303	1403	...	1518	1603	1703	...	1803	1903	2003	...	2203	...	...
	Padova d.	0651	0753	0853	...	0953	1053	1153	...	1253	1353	1453	...	1553	1653	1753	...	1853	1953	2053	...	2253	...	...
	Venezia Mestre a.	0707	0807	0907	...	1007	1107	1207	...	1307	1407	1507	...	1607	1707	1807	...	1907	2007	2107	...	2307	...	...
	Venezia Santa Lucia a.	0720	0820	0920	...	1020	1120	1220	...	1320	1420	1520	...	1620	1720	1820	...	1920	2020	2120	...	2320	...	...

🚌 ROVIGO - CHIOGGIA 🚌

Additional connections may be available - please check locally

km																								
		⚒	†			⚒		Ⓑ	Ⓒ		⚒	⚒		†	⚒		Ⓑ	Ⓐ		Ⓐ			Ⓐ	Ⓑ
0	**Rovigo** d.	0610	...	...	0710	0810	...	0910	1110	...	1310	1410	...	1510	1610	...	1710	...	...	1810	1910	...	2010	2115
25	Adria d.	0657	0657	...	0757	0857	...	0957	1157	...	1357	1457	...	1557	1657	...	1757	1815	...	1857	1957	...	2057	2200
57	**Chioggia** a.	0750	0750	...	0850	0950	...	1050	1250	...	1450	1550	...	1650	1750	...	1850	1907	...	1950	2050	...	2150	...
		†	⚒	⚒		⚒		†		⚒	†	⚒	Ⓐ	⑥	†	Ⓐ		Ⓐ	†	Ⓐ	⑥	†	Ⓐ	
	Chioggia d.	...	0510	0554	0654	0830	0854	0954	...	1154	1254	1354	1454	1454	...	...	...	1654	1754	1854	1930	1954	1954	2000
	Adria d.	0546	0604	0646	0746	0921	0946	1045	...	1246	1346	1446	1546	1545	1546	1722	...	1746	1846	1946	2022	2046	2045	2052
	Rovigo a.	0634	0639	0734	0834	...	1034	...	...	1334	1434	1534	1634	...	1634	1805	...	1834	1934	2034	2110	2134	...	...

MILANO - BOLOGNA

km																								
						①	⑥⑦				Ⓒ	Ⓐ			⑥			⑥		⚒			†	
0	**Milano** Centrale d.	...	0515	...	...	0615	0630	...	...	0720	...	...	...	0920	0920	...	...	0920	...	...	...	...	1120	...
10	**Milano** Rogoredo d.	...	0525	...	...	0628	|	...	...	0733	...	...	...	0933	0933	...	...	0933	...	...	...	...	1133	...
72	Piacenza d.	0530	0609	0646	...	0717	0727	0749	...	0814	0846	0846	...	1014	1014	0946	...	1014	1046	1146	...	1146	1217	1246
107	Fidenza d.	0558	0631	0713	...	0742	0751	0814	...	0845	0913	0913	...	1037	1037	1013	...	1037	1113	1213	...	1213	1248	1313
129	Parma d.	0615	0645	0727	...	0755	0806	0827	...	0900	0927	0927	...	1100	1100	1027	...	1100	1127	1227	...	1227	1302	1327
157	Reggio Emilia d.	0642	0704	0744	...	0814	0821	0844	...	0922	0944	0944	...	1120	1120	1044	...	1120	1144	1244	...	1244	1321	1344
182	Modena d.	0700	0722	0758	...	0834	0840	0858	...	0940	0958	0958	...	1146	1146	1058	...	1138	1158	1258	...	1258	1347	1358
219	**Bologna** Centrale a.	0729	0805	0825	...	0910	0904	0925	...	1013	1025	1025	...	1210	1210	1125	...	1209	1225	1325	...	1325	1410	1425
	Rimini **615** a.	0901	...	1001	...	...	1044	1120	...	...	1201	1219	...	...	1359	1309	...	1359	1403	1501	...	...	...	1601
	Ancona **615** a.	1022	...	1116	...	...	1154	...	...	...	1316	1355	...	...	...	1450	...	...	1516	1620	...	...	...	1716
	Milano Centrale d.	1215	...	1320	...	...	...	1520	...	...	1615	...	...	1720	...	1815	...	...	1920	...	...	...	2120	2205d
	Milano Rogoredo d.	1225	...	1333	...	...	...	1533	...	...	1628	...	...	1733	...	1825	...	...	1933	...	...	...	2133	2228
	Piacenza d.	1307	1345	1414	...	1446	1546	1614	...	1646	1707	1746	...	1814	1846	1909	...	1949	2014	2046	...	2146	2214	2305
	Fidenza d.	1327	1412	1437	...	1513	1613	1637	...	1713	1727	1813	...	1843	1913	1932	...	2014	2037	2111	...	2211	2240	|
	Parma d.	1343	1427	1500	...	1527	1627	1700	...	1727	1743	1827	...	1900	1927	1952	...	2027	2100	2127	...	2227	2257	2334
	Reggio Emilia d.	...	1444	1520	...	1544	1644	1719	...	1744	...	1844	...	1927	1944	2010	...	2044	2118	2143	...	2243	...	2349
	Modena d.	...	1458	1538	...	1558	1658	1738	...	1801	...	1858	...	1946	1958	2027	...	2058	2138	2158	...	2257	...	0005
	Bologna Centrale a.	...	1525	1610	...	1625	1725	1810	...	1825	...	1925	...	2016	2025	2105	...	2125	2210	2227	...	2328	...	0033
	Rimini **615** a.	...	1701	...	...	1805	1901	...	...	2001	...	2112	...	...	2201	2318	...	2322	...	...	...	...	...	...
	Ancona **615** a.	...	...	...	...	1922	2026	...	...	2116	...	...	...	...	2323	...	...	...	...	...	...	...	...	...
					⚒	A																		
	Ancona **615** d.	...	...	...	...	...	...	...	...	...	0545	0645	...	...	0745	...	0845	...	...	...	1045	...	...	1145
	Rimini **615** d.	...	...	...	...	...	...	...	0520	...	0653	0802	...	...	0859	...	0958	...	...	1041	1158	...	...	1258
	Bologna Centrale d.	...	0528	...	0540	0633	...	0658	0750	...	0833	0933	...	0950	1033	...	1133	1150	...	1233	1333	...	1350	1433
	Modena d.	...	0555	...	0607	0700	...	0731	0823	...	0900	1000	...	1023	1100	...	1200	1223	...	1300	1400	...	1423	1500
	Reggio Emilia d.	...	0610	...	0622	0718	...	0750	0841	...	0916	1016	...	1041	1116	...	1216	1241	...	1316	1417	...	1441	1516
	Parma d.	0610	0627	...	0640	0733	...	0808	0900	...	0933	1033	...	1100	1133	...	1233	1300	...	1333	1433	...	1500	1533
	Fidenza d.	0624	0639	...	0656	0745	...	0821	0917	...	0946	1046	...	1117	1146	...	1346	1317	...	1346	1446	...	1517	1546
	Piacenza d.	0650	0703	...	0725	0807	...	0853	0950	...	1016	1116	...	1150	1216	...	1316	1350	...	1416	1516	...	1550	1616
	Milano Rogoredo a.	0731	0745	...	0801	...	...	0931	1031	...	...	...	...	1231	...	...	...	1431	...	...	...	...	1631	...
	Milano Centrale a.	0745	0800	...	0833**d**	...	...	0945	1045	...	...	...	...	1245	...	...	...	1445	...	...	...	...	1645	...
														⑤				B		⑥⑦				
	Ancona **615** d.	1245	...	...	...	...	...	1445	...	...	...	...	...	...	1645	...	...	...	...	1757	1845	...	...	...
	Rimini **615** d.	1358	...	...	1441	...	...	1558	...	...	1640	...	...	...	1758	...	...	1854	...	1923	1958	...	2050	...
	Bologna Centrale d.	1533	1550	...	1633	...	...	1733	1750	...	1833	1850	...	1850	1933	...	1950	2033	...	2054	2133	...	2233	...
	Modena d.	1600	1623	...	1700	...	...	1800	1823	...	1900	1923	...	1923	2000	...	2023	2100	...	2120	2200	...	2300	...
	Reggio Emilia d.	1616	1641	...	1716	...	...	1816	1841	...	1916	1941	...	1941	2016	...	2041	2116	...	2136	2216	...	2315	...
	Parma d.	1633	1700	...	1733	1810	...	1833	1902	...	1933	2000	...	2000	2033	...	2100	2133	...	2153	2233	...	2329	...
	Fidenza d.	1646	1717	...	1746	1824	...	1846	1919	...	1946	2017	...	2017	2046	...	2117	2146	...	2206	2246	...	...	...
	Piacenza d.	1713	1750	...	1810	1853	...	1918	1950	...	2012	2050	...	2050	2110	...	2150	2213	...	2231	2315	...	...	...
	Milano Rogoredo a.	...	1831	...	...	1931	...	...	2031	...	2045	...	...	2131	...	...	2231	...	...	2318	...	...	...	...
	Milano Centrale a.	...	1845	...	...	1945	...	...	2045	...	2115	...	...	2145	...	...	2245	...	...	2330	...	...	...	...

FIRENZE - PERUGIA - FOLIGNO

km																								
		⚒	⚒			⚒		⚒		⚒	⚒				Ⓐ				Ⓐ	†		⚒	⑥	Ⓑ
0	**Firenze** SMN d.	...	...	0640	...	...	0802	0948	...	...	...	1214	...	1414	...	1614	...	1714	...	1814	...	1814	2014	2014
88	Arezzo d.	...	...	0743	...	...	0913	1049	...	...	...	1317	...	1517	...	1717	...	1817	...	1917	...	1917	2117	2117
106	Castiglion Fiorentino d.	...	...	0755	...	...	0924	1102	...	...	...	1328	...	1528	...	1728	...	1828	...	1928	...	1928	2128	2128
122	Terontola-Cortona d.	0625	0710	0809	...	0830	0941	1121	...	1139	1226	1341	...	1541	1620	1741	...	1841	1850	1941	...	1941	2141	2141
134	Passignano sul Trasimeno d.	0639	0721	...	...	0842	0950	...	...	1149	1235	1350	...	1550	1630	1750	...	...	1900	1950	...	1950	2151	2150
165	**Perugia** a.	0714	0758	...	...	0912	1017	...	...	1225	1314	1425	...	1621	1701	1826	...	...	1939	2021	...	2021	2219	2218
165	**Perugia** 625 d.	0718	0804	...	...	0914	1019	...	...	1227	1316	1427	...	1623	1703	1828	...	...	1941	2023	...	2023	2221	2239
176	**Perugia** P. S. Giovanni 625 d.	0727	0814	...	...	0924	1030	...	...	1236	1327	1436	...	1632	1714	1840	...	...	1950	2034	...	2034	2230	2248
189	Assisi 625 d.	0739	0828	...	...	0938	1043	...	...	1247	1343	1448	...	1646	1728	1852	...	...	2001	2047	...	2047	2242	2259
200	Spello 625 d.	0749	0840	...	...	0946	1052	...	...	1255	1354	1459	...	1655	1737	1906	...	...	2010	2057	...	2057	2251	2307
205	**Foligno** 625 a.	0758	0850	...	...	0952	1057	...	...	1301	1402	1508	...	1703	1744	1915	...	...	2016	2105	...	2109	2257	2315
		⚒	⚒	†		⚒					⚒				⚒			Ⓐ				Ⓐ		⑥
	Foligno 625 d.	0530	0636	0645	...	0722	...	...	0910	1108	1150	...	...	1303	1345	...	1456	1533	...	...	1706	1812	1903	2054
	Spello 625 d.	0536	0641	0650	...	0728	...	...	0915	1114	1156	...	...	1309	1351	...	1502	1538	...	...	1711	1817	1909	2100
	Assisi 625 d.	0545	0649	0700	...	0742	...	...	0924	1122	1205	...	...	1317	1404	...	1511	1549	...	...	1721	1826	1917	2111
	Perugia Ponte San Giovanni 625 d.	0600	0708	0711	...	0753	...	...	0936	1134	1216	...	...	1330	1417	...	1526	1603	...	...	1733	1843	1929	2125
	Perugia 625 a.	0613	0716	0721	...	0802	...	...	0948	1142	1225	...	...	1339	1425	...	1536	1618	...	...	1742	1852	1939	2136
	Perugia d.	0615	0718	0723	...	0804	...	...	0950	1144	1227	...	...	1341	1427	...	1540	1623	...	...	1744	1854	1941	2138
	Passignano sul Trasimeno d.	0642	0755	0748	...	0839	...	...	1019	1212	1256	...	...	1409	1459	...	1609	1659	...	...	1812	1923	2009	2207
	Terontola-Cortona d.	0656	0805	0758	0819	0859	...	0908	1036	1221	1309	1319	...	1419	1511	1517	1619	1714	...	1719	1825	1936	2019	2220
	Castiglion Fiorentino d.	0710	...	...	0831	...	...	0923	|	1234	...	1332	...	1431	...	1531	1631	...	...	1731	1837	...	2031	...
	Arezzo d.	0725	...	...	0844	...	...	0943	1100	1245	...	1345	...	1444	...	1543	1644	...	...	1744	1849	...	2044	...
	Firenze SMN a.	0838	...	...	0952	...	...	1048	1155	1351	...	1448	...	1548	...	1648	1757	...	...	1848	1952	...	2150	...

A – From Castelbolognese-Riolo Terme (Table **615**). B – From Pesaro (Table **615**). d – Milano **Porta Garibaldi**. * – Connection by 🚌.

RIMINI - RAVENNA - BOLOGNA and FERRARA — 621

2nd class

km																									
							⚒			⚒	†	⚒	⚒			†	⚒		†		⚒	†			⚒
0	**Ferrara**	d.	...	0520	...	0545	0610	...	...	...	...	0708	...	...	...	0827	0829	...	...	...	0916	1005	...	...	1134
	Bologna Centrale	d.	...	|	...	|	|	...	...	0650	...	|	...	...	0805	|	|	0905	...	...	|	|	1005	1105	|
	Imola	d.	...	|	...	|	|	...	...	0712	...	|	...	...	0826	|	|	0926	...	...	|	|	1026	1126	|
	C'bolognese-Riolo Terme	d.	...	|	...	|	|	...	...	0718	...	|	...	...	0833	|	|	0933	...	...	|	|	1033	1133	|
	Lugo	d.	...	|	...	|	|	...	...	0733	...	|	...	...	0848	|	|	0948	...	...	|	|	1048	1148	|
74	**Ravenna**	d.	0530	0622	0627	0702	0733	...	0747	0804	0819	0833	0847	...	0919	0942	0947	1017	1020	...	1027	1119	1117	1219	1248
95	Cervia-Milano Marittima	d.	0550	...	0645	...	...	...	0808	...	0838	...	0908	...	0938	...	1008	...	1038	...	...	1138	...	1238	...
103	Cesenatico	d.	0558	...	0651	...	...	...	0816	...	0846	...	0916	...	0946	...	1016	...	1046	...	...	1146	...	1246	...
124	**Rimini**	a.	0630	...	0723	...	...	...	0842	...	0915	...	0942	...	1020	...	1042	...	1117	...	...	1217	...	1320	...

					⚒					Ⓐ		⚒		⚒		⚒							
Ferrara	d.	...	1234	...	1335	...	...	1435	...	1633	...	1637	...	...	...	1737	...	1835	...	...	...	2037	...	...
Bologna Centrale	d.	1205	|	1305	|	1405	...	|	1505	|	1605	|	...	1650	1705	|	1805	|	...	1905	2005	|	2110	2206
Imola	d.	1226	|	1326	|	1426	...	|	1526	|	1626	|	...	|	1726	|	1826	|	...	1926	2026	|	2129	2239
Castelbolognese-Riolo Terme	d.	1233	|	1333	|	1433	...	|	1533	|	1633	|	...	|	1733	|	1833	|	...	1933	2033	|	2136	2245
Lugo	d.	1248	|	1348	|	1448	...	|	1548	|	1648	|	...	1730	1748	|	1848	|	...	1948	2048	|	2150	2301
Ravenna	d.	1319	1348	1419	1448	1519	...	1548	1619	|	1719	1748	...	1752	1819	1848	1919	1950	...	2019	2119	2150	2219	2330
Cervia-Milano Marittima	d.	1338	...	1438	...	1538	...	...	1638	|	1738	...	...	...	1838	...	1938	...	...	2038	2138	...	2237	...
Cesenatico	d.	1346	...	1446	...	1546	...	...	1646	|	1746	...	...	...	1846	...	1946	...	...	2046	2146	...	2244	...
Rimini	a.	1420	...	1517	...	1619	...	...	1719	1855	1820	...	...	...	1919	...	2020	...	...	2120	2217	...	2318	...

km																									
					⚒					⚒	⚒		⚒			†		⚒			†		†	⚒	
	Rimini	d.	...	...	...	0601	...	...	0652	...	0735	...	...	...	0843	...	0918	...	...	...	1043	...	...	...	...
	Cesenatico	d.	...	...	...	0632	...	...	0721	...	0800	...	...	...	0916	...	0946	...	...	...	1116	...	...	...	...
	Cervia-Milano Marittima	d.	...	...	...	0646	...	...	0727	...	0809	...	...	...	0922	...	0952	...	...	...	1122	...	...	...	...
0	**Ravenna**	d.	0503	0623	0626	0707	0712	...	0755	0757	0831	0843	0843	...	0943	0955	1016	1040	1043	...	1140	1143	1147	1210	1243
28	Lugo	d.	0528	0652	|	...	|	...	0815	|	...	0912	|	...	1012	|	...	|	1112	...	...	1212	|	|	1312
42	C'bolognese-Riolo Terme	d.	0546	0710	|	...	|	...	|	|	...	0928	|	...	1028	|	...	|	1128	...	...	1228	|	|	1328
50	Imola	d.	0555	0716	|	...	|	...	|	|	...	0935	|	...	1034	|	...	|	1134	...	...	1234	|	|	1334
84	**Bologna** Centrale	a.	0626	0738	|	...	|	...	0855	|	...	0955	|	...	1055	|	...	|	1155	...	...	1255	|	|	1355
	Ferrara	a.	...	...	0741	...	0827	...	...	0905	...	...	1001	...	...	1110	...	1201	...	...	...	...	1301	1325	...

						⚒								⚒									
Rimini	d.	...	1243	...	1343	...	...	1443	1520	1543	...	1643	...	...	1743	1843	...	1943	...	2043	...	2143	2242	...
Cesenatico	d.	...	1316	...	1416	...	...	1516	1546	1616	...	1716	...	...	1816	1916	...	2016	...	2116	...	2216	2315	...
Cervia-Milano Marittima	d.	...	1322	...	1422	...	...	1522	1552	1622	...	1722	...	...	1822	1922	...	2022	...	2122	...	2222	2321	...
Ravenna	d.	1310	1343	1425	1443	1512	...	1543	1616	1643	1712	1743	...	1812	1843	1943	2012	2043	...	2143	2217	2242	2340	...
Lugo	d.	|	1406	|	1512	|	...	1612	|	1712	|	1812	...	|	1912	2012	|	2112	...	2220	|	...	...	...
Castelbolognese-Riolo Terme	d.	|	1428	|	1528	|	...	1628	|	1728	|	1828	...	|	1928	2028	|	2128	...	2234	|	...	...	...
Imola	d.	|	1434	|	1534	|	...	1634	|	1734	|	1834	...	|	1934	2034	|	2134	...	2240	|	...	...	...
Bologna Centrale	a.	|	1455	|	1555	|	...	1655	|	1755	|	1855	...	|	1955	2055	|	2155	...	2300	|	...	...	...
Ferrara	a.	1425	...	1547	...	1625	...	...	1724	...	1825	...	...	1925	...	...	2125	...	...	...	2326	...	...	...

ROMA AIRPORTS ✈ — 622

ROMA CIAMPINO AIRPORT ✈. Rail service Roma Termini - Ciampino and v.v. (Table **623**). A 🚌 connects Ciampino station and the airport. Overall journey time approximately 1 hour.

ROMA FIUMICINO AIRPORT ✈. *Leonardo Express* rail service Roma Termini - Roma Fiumicino ✈ and v.v. *31 km.* Journey time 32 minutes. Special fare payable.
From **Roma Termini** at 0450 and at least every 30 minutes until 2335. Some services are classified *FR* with 🅁.
From **Roma Fiumicino** ✈ at 0538 and at least every 30 minutes until 2353. Some services are classified *FR* with 🅁.
Additional suburban rail services operate Roma Tiburtina - Roma Ostiense - Fiumicino ✈. *39 km.* Journey time: Tiburtina - Fiumicino ✈ ± 45 minutes; Ostiense - Fiumicino ✈ ± 30 minutes. From Roma Tiburtina 0545 - 2200 (approx. every 15 minutes on Ⓐ / every 30 minutes on Ⓒ); from Roma Fiumicino ✈ 0557 - 2242 (approx. every 15 minutes on Ⓐ / every 30 minutes on Ⓒ).

ROMA - ALBANO LAZIALE and ANZIO — 623

2nd class

km																									
			⚒								†	⚒	⚒		†	⚒	⚒		†	⚒	⚒		†	⚒	⚒
0	**Roma** Termini	d.	0542	0721	0821	...	0900	1221	1321	...	1421	1421	1521	...	1621	1621	1721	...	1821	1821	1921	...	2021	2021	2121
14	Ciampino	d.	0558	0740	0837	...	0918	1237	1337	...	1437	1437	1537	...	1637	1637	1737	...	1837	1837	1937	...	2037	2037	2137
23	Marino Laziale	d.	0614	0801	0857	...	0936	1257	1400	...	1456	1500	1600	...	1656	1700	1800	...	1856	1900	2000	...	2056	2100	2157
26	Castel Gandolfo	d.	0621	0807	0903	...	0942	1303	1406	...	1503	1507	1606	...	1703	1706	1806	...	1903	1906	2007	...	2102	2106	2203
29	**Albano Laziale**	a.	0627	0815	0912	...	0951	1312	1415	...	1511	1515	1615	...	1711	1715	1815	...	1911	1915	2015	...	2111	2115	2213

		⚒	⚒		⚒				⚒			⚒			⚒			⚒			⚒		⚒	†
Albano Laziale	d.	0629	0700	...	0743	0838	...	1023	1144	...	1343	1443	...	1543	1643	...	1743	1843	...	1943	2043	...	2140	2145
Castel Gandolfo	d.	0636	0707	...	0750	0845	...	1030	1151	...	1351	1451	...	1551	1651	...	1751	1851	...	1951	2051	...	2148	2152
Marino Laziale	d.	0643	0720	...	0802	0858	...	1036	1157	...	1359	1459	...	1559	1659	...	1759	1859	...	1959	2059	...	2158	2158
Ciampino	d.	0703	0739	...	0823	0917	...	1057	1218	...	1419	1519	...	1619	1719	...	1819	1919	...	2019	2119	...	2219	2219
Roma Termini	a.	0720	0754	...	0841	0934	...	1113	1234	...	1434	1534	...	1634	1734	...	1834	1934	...	2034	2134	...	2234	2234

ROMA - ANZIO *57 km* Journey 60 – 80 minutes. All services continue to Nettuno (*3 km* and 4 – 7 minutes from Anzio).

From **Roma Termini** at 0506 ⚒, 0640, 0742 ⚒, 0812, 0942, 1042 ⚒, 1142, 1242 ⚒, 1342, 1412 Ⓐ, 1442, 1542 ⚒, 1642, 1742 ⚒, 1812 Ⓐ, 1842, 1912 Ⓐ, 1942, 2042 ⚒, 2142.

From **Anzio** at 0559 ⚒, 0635, 0703 Ⓐ, 0731, 0816 ⚒, 0912, 1012, 1112 ⚒, 1212 ⚒, 1310, 1412 ⚒, 1510, 1612 ⚒, 1630 Ⓐ, 1705 †, 1712 ⚒, 1810, 1912 ⚒, 2010, 2112 Ⓐ, 2201.

ROMA - PESCARA — 624

2nd class

Additional trains are available Roma - Avezzano and v.v., Avezzano - Sulmon and v.v., and Sulmona - Pescara and v.v.

km											
				†	⚒		†	⚒			
0	**Roma** Termini	d.	...	0710t	1420	1640	1725t	1813t	1847	...	...
40	Tivoli	d.	...	0811	1458	1720	1803	1900	1922	...	...
108	Avezzano	d.	0630	0920	1601	1819	1903	1957	2020	...	...
172	Sulmona ⊖	d.	0740	1020	1652	1908	1958	2046	2111	...	...
226	Chieti	d.	0849	1107	1737	1951	2037	2122	2201	...	...
240	**Pescara** Centrale	a.	0905	1120	1750	2007	2052	2139	2214	...	...

		⚒	†		⚒	⚒	†	†	†	⚒
Pescara Centrale	d.	0525	...	0730	0925	1020	1040	1438	1627	1714
Chieti	d.	0538	...	0744	0937	1033	1053	1458	1648	1738
Sulmona ⊖	d.	0619	0619	0826	1019	1111	1131	1542	1736	1845
Avezzano	d.	0712	0711	0919	1112	1201	1223	1637	1837	2010
Tivoli	d.	0812	0810	1023	1210	1258	1323	1750	1951	*2232*
Roma Termini	a.	0845	0845	1055t	1250	1344t	1359t	1825	2035t	*2315*

t – Roma **Tiburtina**.

⊖ – For 🚌 service Sulmona - Castel di Sangro see Table **627**.

ROMA - RAVENNA, ANCONA and PERUGIA — 625

km																									
										IC **534**							*IC* **540**				*FA* **8852**				
			2⚒	2†	2⚒				⚒	A	⚒	⚒	†		2⚒				⚒			⚒	†		
0	**Roma** Termini	d.	...	...	...	0552	...	...	0652	0750	0930	1158	1222	...	...	1322	1522	1558	1702	...	1725	1831	1855	2102	...
5	**Roma** Tiburtina △	d.	...	...	...	0600	...	...	0700	0758	0938	1207	1232	...	...	1331	1529	1609	1713	...	|	1842	1906	2112	...
83	Orte	d.	...	...	...	0634	...	...	0738	0830	1013	1244	1308	...	...	1405	1601	1644	|	...	|	1917	1940	2148	...
112	Terni	d.	...	...	...	0653	...	...	0801	0852	1036	1314	1332	...	...	1428	1622	1706	1807	...	1830	1938	2001	2212	...
141	Spoleto	d.	...	...	...	0717	...	...	0831	0917	1103	1339	1356	...	...	1457	1648	1739	1832	...	1853	2005	2029	2238	...
167	**Foligno**	d.	0545	0615	0640	0739	0744	...	0850	0935	1125	1401	1413	...	1420	1520	1706	1759	1851	...	1909	2025	2048	2256	2303
224	Fabriano	d.	0647	0714	0736	...	0838	...	...	1031	1218	...	...	...	1523	1614	1755	1849	...	...	1950	2123	2139	...	2357
268	Jesi	d.	0733	0756	0821	...	0915	...	...	1101	1257	...	...	...	1606	1706	1828	1923	...	...	2019	2200	2213	...	0033
286	Falconara Marittima **615**	d.	0751	0813	0839	...	0928	...	...	1115	1316	...	...	...	1626	1722	1852	1940	...	...	2042	2213	2228	...	0048
	Pesaro **615**	d.	|	|	|	...	|	...	...	|	|	...	...	...	|	|	|	|	...	...	2105	|	|	...	|
	Rimini **615**	d.	|	|	|	...	|	...	...	|	|	...	...	...	|	|	|	|	...	...	2129	|	|	...	|
	Ravenna	a.	|	|	|	...	|	...	...	|	|	...	...	...	|	|	|	|	...	...	2212	|	|	...	|
295	**Ancona**	a.	0805	0828	0855	...	0940	...	...	1125	1328	...	...	...	1637	1740	1905	1956	...	...	...	2225	2245	...	0100

FOR RETURN SERVICE AND FOOTNOTES SEE NEXT PAGE →

625 ANCONA, RAVENNA and PERUGIA - ROMA

						IC 533	*IC* 533		*FA* 8851							*IC* 544							
		⚒		2⚒		†	⚒					2⚒				①–⑥ A					2		
Ancona d.	0333	...	...	0505	...	0550	0550	...	...	...	0905	1250	...	1350	...	1555	1850	...	1950	...	2130	...	...
Ravenna d.	|	...	...	|	...	|	|	...	0608	...	|	|	...	|	...	|	|	...	|	...	|	...	...
Rimini **615** d.	|	...	...	|	...	|	|	...	0652	...	|	|	...	|	...	|	|	...	|	...	|	...	...
Pesaro **615** d.	|	...	...	|	...	|	|	...	0716	...	|	|	...	|	...	|	|	...	|	...	|	...	...
Falconara Marittima **615** d.	0346	...	...	0513	...	0600	0600	...	0750	...	0914	1305	...	1403	...	1604	1900	...	2001	...	2141	...	...
Jesi d.	0400	...	...	0526	...	0615	0615	...	0807	...	0928	1323	...	1417	...	1616	1914	...	2016	...	2154	...	...
Fabriano d.	0434	...	...	0605	...	0651	0651	...	0838	...	1007	1412	...	1457	...	1652	1953	...	2051	...	2235	...	...
Foligno d.	0522	0555	...	0705	...	0750	0750	...	0920	...	1105	1509	...	1554	...	1758	2046	...	2147	...	2327	...	...
Spoleto d.	0540	0616	...	...	...	0811	0811	...	0938	...	1124	...	...	1614	...	1815	2059	...	2205	...	...	...	...
Terni d.	0611	0648	...	...	...	0837	0843	...	1002	...	1152	...	...	1647	...	1853	2126	...	2238	...	...	...	...
Orte d.	0634	|	...	...	...	0858	0900	...	|	...	1216	...	...	1710	...	1914	2147	...	2300	...	...	...	...
Roma Tiburtina ▽ a.	0708	0743	...	...	...	0931	0935	...	|	...	1248	...	...	1747	...	1944	2221	...	2334	...	...	...	...
Roma Termini a.	0718	0800	...	...	...	0945	0948	...	1100	...	1300	...	...	1805	...	1955	2232	...	2345	...	...	...	...

km		*IC* 580								*IC* 546
		B	2⚒	2⚒	●	†		Ⓑ	⚒	Ⓑ
0	**Roma** Termini d.	...	...	...	0802	1005	1428	1758	1902	1955
5	**Roma** Tiburtina △ d.	...	...	...	0813	1013	1436	1812	1912	2006
83	Orte d.	...	...	...	0847	1047	1509	1847	1946	2037
112	Terni d.	0505	0545	0620	0908	1107	1529	1910	2009	2056
141	Spoleto d.	0537	0613	0656	0935	1139	1556	1941	2035	2130
167	**Foligno** **620** d.	0557	0636	0722	0955	1156	1614	2001	2054	2147
172	Spello **620** d.	|	0641	0728	|	|	1620	2007	2100	|
183	Assisi **620** d.	0610	0649	0742	1011	1210	1630	2018	2111	2200
196	**Perugia** PSG ⊡ ▽ **620** d.	0624	0708	0753	1027	1220	1645	2037	2125	2209
207	**Perugia** **620** a.	0635	0716	0802	1044	1230	1658	2048	2137	2222

		IC 531								*IC* 599
	①–⑥	①–⑥	2⚒	†	†	●	d●	⚒		B
Perugia **620** d.	0552	0640	0652	0723	0922	1105	1347	1555	1815	2319
Perugia PSG ⊡ △ **620** d.	0603	0652	0705	0732	0933	1115	1357	1606	1826	2329
Assisi **620** d.	0615	0703	0720	0745	0945	1130	1415	1627	1839	2339
Spello **620** d.	0626	|	0731	0754	|	1138	1426	1637	1848	|
Foligno **620** d.	0636	0717	0737	0802	1006	1150	1438	1645	1856	2354
Spoleto d.	0659	0736	0759	0822	1032	1214	1500	1705	1912	0013
Terni d.	0740	0801	0831	0846	1055	1247	1527	1734	1938	0040
Orte d.	0805	0818	...	0905	1115	1313	1555	1756	2001	...
Roma Tiburtina ▽ a.	0839	0845	...	0936	1144	1344	1629	1830	2039	...
Roma Termini a.	0852	0855	...	0955	1200	1355	1643	1845	2050	...

A – 🚆12 Roma - Ancona - S. Benedetto del Tronto and v.v.
B – 🚆12 Terni - Perugia - Milano and v.v. (Table **620**).
d – Does not call at Spello on †.
△ – Numbered trains call to pick up only.
▽ – Numbered trains call to set down only.
⊡ – Full name is Perugia Ponte San Giovanni.
● – Runs 13 – 20 minutes later on †.

FOR RETURN SERVICE ANCONA and RAVENNA - ROMA SEE PREVIOUS PAGE.

627 ROMA and NAPOLI - CAMPOBASSO - TERMOLI
2nd class

Additional journeys Roma / Napoli - Campobasso and v.v. may be available by changing to / from 🚌 at Venafro or Roccaravindola - please enquire locally.

km					⚒	⚒		†	⚒		⑤	⑥–④		⚒	†		†			⚒	†			
0	**Roma** Termini ◧ d.	0615	0907	...	...	1307	...	...	...	...	1435	1435	...	...	...	...	1740	...	...	2007	2014	...	...	...
138	Cassino ◧ d.	0742	1033	...	...	1445	...	...	...	...	1600	1603	...	...	...	...	|	...	...	|	|	...	...	...
	Napoli Centrale d.	|	|	...	1200	|	...	1400	1400	...	|	|	...	1658	1706	...	|	1930	...	|	|	...	...	...
	Caserta d.	|	|	...	1240	|	...	1440	1446	...	|	|	...	1740	1738	...	|	2003	...	|	|	...	...	...
	Vairano-Caianello d.	|	|	...	1321	|	...	1516	1521	...	|	|	...	1824	1820	...	|	2044	...	|	|	...	...	...
162	Venafro a.	0808	1051	...	1341	1502	...	1538	1542	...	1619	1625	...	1843	1840	...	1923	2104	...	2005	2202	...	...	...
187	Isernia a.	0829	1115	...	1407	1524	...	1601	1605	...	1640	1647	...	1905	1905	...	1950	2127	...	2227	2223	...	...	...
246	**Campobasso** Centro a.	*0935**	*1225**	...	*1520**	*1635**	...	*1715**	*1715**	...	*1755**	*1755**	...	*2015**	*2015**	...	*2105**	*2235**	...	*2335**	*2335**	...	...	...

	⚒			⚒	†			⚒			⚒		†	†		⚒	†		⚒				
Campobasso C d.	*0500**	*0530**	...	*0615**	*0730**	...	*0730**	*1215**	...	*1245**	*1350**	...	*1405**	*1615**	...	*1645**	*1800**	...	*1800**	*1920**	...	...	...
Isernia d.	0605	0640	...	0729	0831	...	0838	1328	...	1411	1503	...	1520	1730	...	1800	1919	...	1919	2032	...	...	...
Venafro d.	0628	0704	...	0750	0854	...	0859	1358	...	1435	1531	...	1541	1750	...	1822	1948	...	1948	2055	...	...	...
Vairano-Caianello d.	0646	|	...	0809	0913	...	|	|	...	1456	|	...	|	|	...	|	2013	...	2013	|	...	...	...
Caserta d.	0717	|	...	0847	0945	...	|	|	...	1530	|	...	|	|	...	|	2051	...	2100	|	...	...	...
Napoli Centrale a.	0754	|	...	0929	1020	...	|	|	...	1609	|	...	|	|	...	|	2122	...	2132	|	...	...	...
Cassino ◧ d.	...	0724	...	...	...	...	0918	1417	...	...	1550	...	1558	1808	...	1841	...	...	...	2117	...	...	...
Roma Termini ◧ a.	...	0853	...	...	...	...	1047	1554	...	...	1727	...	1727	1934	...	2025	...	...	...	2254	...	...	...

km		⚒	⚒	⚒	⚒	⚒	⚒	†	⚒	†	⚒	⚒		⚒	⚒	⚒	Ⓐ		⚒	†		†	⚒	Ⓐ
0	**Roma** Termini ◧ d.	...	...	...	...	...	...	...	...	...	...	1235	...	...	...	...	...	...	1642	1655	1807	...	...	...
138	Cassino ◧ d.	0503	0550	...	0703	...	0838	...	1005	1305	1343	1406	...	1435	1514	...	1710	1805	1858	1857	1946	...	...	2100
170	Vairano-Caianello d.	0536	0621	0704	0736	0809	0911	0913	1033	1338	1415	1430	1456	1505	1547	1605	1742	1836	1928	1928	2008	2013	2013	2127
216	Caserta d.	0620	0705	0750	0821	0947	0955	0945	1117	1422	1500	1505	1530	1549	1635	1650	1826	1925	2020	2018	2045	2051	2100	2206
250	**Napoli** Centrale a.	0705	0746	0835	0905	0929	1040	1020	...	1505	...	...	1609	1635	...	1735	1910	...	...	...	...	2122	2132	...

	Ⓐ	†	⚒		⚒	⚒	⚒	⚒		⚒	⚒	⚒	†	⚒	⚒	†	⚒	†	Ⓐ	⚒	⚒		Ⓐ
Napoli Centrale d.	...	...	0510	...	...	...	...	...	0755	1154	...	1340	1400	...	...	1550	1658	1706	1712	1755	1855	1930	1955
Caserta d.	0500	0512	0551	0610	0620	0730	0742	0755	0836	1245	1336	1423	1440	1536	1626	1631	1740	1738	1754	1838	1936	2044	2038
Vairano-Caianello d.	0547	0557	0638	0646	0703	0808	0823	0834	0921	1327	1420	1510	1515	1620	1711	1715	1823	1819	1838	1922	2023	2127	2122
Cassino ◧ d.	0618	0627	...	0711	0740	0837	0852	0900	0957	1403	1453	...	...	1656	1746	1750	...	...	1913	1957	...	...	2157
Roma Termini ◧ a.	0820	0834	...	0848	...	1013	...	...	...	...	...	...	...	...	...	...	...	...	...	...	...	...	...

OTHER 🚌 SERVICES

CAMPOBASSO - BENEVENTO and v.v. : from **Campobasso** at 0620 ⚒, 1305 ⚒, 1416 ⚒, 1750 ⚒; from **Benevento** at 0640 ⚒, 0745 ⚒, 1420 ⚒, 1740 ⚒. Journey time 70 minutes.

CAMPOBASSO - TERMOLI and v.v.: from **Campobasso** at 0600, 1415, 1825; from **Termoli** at 0600, 1410, 1750. Journey 105 minutes.

SULMONA - CASTEL DI SANGRO and v.v. : from **Sulmona** at 1030, 1950 ⚒; from **Castel di Sangro** at 0600 ⚒, 1625 †, 1640 ⚒. Journey time 60 – 70 minutes.

◧ – Trains run approximately hourly.
* – Connection by 🚌.

629 SARDINIA
2nd class

CAGLIARI - CARBONIA and IGLESIAS

km		⚒	⚒	⚒	Ⓐ						⚒	⚒	Ⓑ	Ⓑ		⚒	⚒	Ⓑ	Ⓑ		⚒	⚒	
0	**Cagliari** d.	0526	0545	...	0614	...	0644	...	0744	...	...	0844	...	0944	...	...	1044	...	1145	...	...	1244	...	1344
7	Elmas Aeroporto ✈ d.	0532	0551	...	0620	...	0650	...	0750	...	...	0850	...	0950	...	...	1050	...	1150	...	...	1250	...	1350
17	Decimomannu d.	0541	0604	...	0635	...	0704	...	0804	...	...	0903	...	1003	...	...	1103	...	1203	...	...	1304	...	1403
46	Villamassargia d.	0603	0635	0635	0703	...	0731	0734	0831	0834	...	0931	0934	1031	1034	...	1131	1134	1231	1234	...	1331	1334	1431
69	**Carbonia** Serbariu a.	|	0656	|	|	...	|	0756	0852	|	...	|	0956	1052	|	...	|	1155	1252	|	...	|	1355	1452
55	**Iglesias** a.	0611	...	0644	0712	...	0741	...	...	0843	...	0940	...	...	1043	...	1140	...	...	1243	...	1340	...	...

		⚒	⚒🚌	⚒		⚒			Ⓑ		Ⓑ			Ⓐ		Ⓐ🚌	Ⓐ	Ⓐ					🚌
Cagliari d.	...	1418	...	1444	...	...	1544	...	1644	...	...	1744	...	1810	...	...	1844	...	1944	...	...	2044	...
Elmas Aeroporto ✈ d.	...	1424	...	1450	...	...	1550	...	1650	...	...	1750	...	1816	...	...	1850	...	1950	...	...	2050	...
Decimomannu d.	...	1432	...	1503	...	...	1603	...	1703	...	...	1803	...	1830	...	...	1903	...	2004	...	...	2103	...
Villamassargia a.	1434	1500	1504	1531	...	1534	1631	1634	1731	...	1734	1831	1834	1858	...	1901	1931	1934	2031	...	2034	2130	2135
Carbonia Serbariu a.	|	|	1527	|	...	1555	1652	|	|	...	1755	1852	|	|	...	1924	|	1955	2052	...	|	|	2158
Iglesias a.	1443	1509	...	1540	...	...	...	1643	1740	...	...	...	1843	1906	...	...	1940	...	...	...	2043	2140	...

FOR OTHER SERVICES AND FOOTNOTES SEE NEXT PAGE →

SARDINIA 629

2nd class

CARBONIA and IGLESIAS - CAGLIARI. See previous page for return service.

	Ⓐ🚌	⚒	⚒	†	⚒		⚒🚌	⚒			Ⓐ🚌		Ⓐ			⚒	⚒		Ⓑ	Ⓑ	⚒	⚒	Ⓑ
Iglesias d.	...	0553	0623	0627	...	...	...	0653	...	0721	...	...	0754	0818	...	...	0921	...	1018	...	...	1121	1218
Carbonia Serbariu d.	0532	|	|	|	0608	...	0632	|	0705	|	0732	...	|	|	0805	0905	|	...	|	1005	1105	|	|
Villamassargia d.	0558	0603	0630	0636	0635	...	0658	0703	0726	0731	0758	...	0803	0826	0831	0926	0931	...	1026	1031	1126	1131	1226
Decimomannu d.	...	0633	...	0703	0702	...	...	0732	...	0756	...	...	0831	...	0856	...	0956	...	...	1058	...	1156	...
Elmas Aeroporto ✈ d.	...	0645	...	0716	0717	...	...	0744	...	0807	...	...	0844	...	0909	...	1009	...	...	1110	...	1208	...
Cagliari a.	...	0652	...	0723	0724	...	...	0750	...	0815	...	...	0850	...	0915	...	1015	...	...	1117	...	1215	...

	Ⓑ	⚒	⚒		†		⚒	⚒	⚒	⚒				Ⓑ	Ⓑ				Ⓐ	Ⓐ	Ⓐ		
Iglesias d.	...	...	1321	1418	...	...	...	...	1521	1552	1618	...	...	...	1721	1818	...	...	...	1921	1953	2018	...
Carbonia Serbariu d.	1205	1305	|	|	1405	...	1405	1505	|	|	|	...	1605	1705	|	|	1805	...	1905	|	|	|	2005
Villamassargia d.	1231	1326	1331	1426	1431	...	1431	1526	1531	1601	1626	...	1631	1726	1731	1826	1831	...	1926	1931	2003	2026	2031
Decimomannu d.	1257	...	1356	...	1456	...	1500	...	1556	1631	...	...	1656	...	1756	...	1857	...	...	1956	2030	...	2059
Elmas Aeroporto ✈ d.	1310	...	1409	...	1509	...	1515	...	1607	1639	...	...	1711	...	1807	...	1911	...	...	2009	|	...	2113
Cagliari a.	1317	...	1415	...	1516	...	1522	...	1614	1645	...	...	1717	...	1814	...	1917	...	...	2015	2043	...	2120

CAGLIARI - ORISTANO - OLBIA, SASSARI and PORTO TORRES Service until May 31

km		⚒	⚒	⚒	⚒	⚒	⚒	⚒	⚒	⚒	⚒	⚒	⚒	⚒	⚒	⚒	⚒	⚒	⚒	⚒	⚒	⚒	⚒	⚒	⚒	⚒	⚒
0	**Cagliari** d.		...	...	...	0627	...	0722	0835	...	0925	...	1040	1112	...	...	1222	...	1325	1430	...	1522	1630	1720	1830	...	1920
7	Elmas Aeroporto ✈ d.		...	...	...	0633	...	0729	0842	...	0931	...	1046	1117	...	...	1229	...	1332	1437	...	1529	1636	1726	1836	...	1926
17	Decimomannu d.		...	...	...	0641	...	0737	|	...	0939	...	|	1131	...	...	1237	...	1341	|	...	1537	|	1739	|	...	1940
95	**Oristano** d.		...	...	...	0730	...	0830	0931	...	1048	...	1134	1232	...	...	1330	...	1438	1534	...	1632	1731	1841	1936	...	2050
154	Macomer d.		...	...	...	0824	...	...	1024	...	1144	...	1227	▬	...	...	1431	...	1535	1631	...	...	1819	▬	2024	2036	▬
214	Ozieri-Chilivani a.		...	...	...	0903	...	...	1104	...	...	...	|	...	...	...	1516	...	...	1709	...	...	1858	⚒	|	2123	⚒
214	Ozieri-Chilivani d.		...	0642	0644	0906	0910	...	1109	1109	...	1212	|	...	1441	...	1524	1522	...	1717	1714	...	1901	1903	|	2125	2128
	Olbia Terranova a.		...	|	0742	0957	|	...	1201	|	...	1310	|	⚒	|	...	1628	|	...	|	1818	...	1953	|	|	2222	|
261	**Sassari** a.		0650	0731	...	...	0950	...	...	1149	...	...	1339	1345	1525	1530	...	1601	...	1756	...	...	...	1947	2134	...	2208
280	**Porto Torres** a.		0704	0758	...	...	...	...	...	...	...	...	...	1400	...	1545	...	...	...	1811	...	...	...	...	...	...	...
281	**Porto Torres** Marittima a.		0707	0801	...	...	...	...	...	...	...	...	...	1404	...	1549	...	...	...	1816	...	...	...	...	...	...	...

	⚒		†	†	†	†	†	†	†	†	†	†	†	†	†	†	†	†	†	†	†	†	†	†	†
Cagliari d.	2035	...		...	...	...	...	0624	...	...	...	0933	1014	1110	1222	...	1413	...	1640	...	1713	...	1820	...	1915	2040
Elmas Aeroporto ✈ d.	2041	...		...	...	...	...	0630	...	...	...	0939	1020	1116	1229	...	1419	...	1647	...	1719	...	1826	...	1921	2046
Decimomannu d.	2050	...		...	...	...	...	0638	...	...	...	0947	1032	1129	1238	...	1428	...	|	...	1732	...	1834	...	1934	2055
Oristano d.	2154	...		...	...	...	...	0730	...	...	...	1046	1136	1225	1331	...	1531	...	1742	...	1829	...	1928	...	2034	2201
Macomer d.	...	...		...	...	...	...	0821	...	...	...	1142	...	...	1431	...	1629	...	1830	...	...	...	2028	...	...	...
Ozieri-Chilivani a.	...	...		...	...	...	...	0904	...	...	...	...	...	...	1516	...	1712	...	1908	...	...	...	2117	...	...	...
Ozieri-Chilivani d.	...	...		...	0745	...	0748	0914	0912	1105	1105	...	...	...	1521	1521	1719	1718	1915	1913	...	1954	2125	2130	...	...
Olbia Terranova a.	...	...		...	|	...	0846	|	1009	|	1205	...	...	...	1617	|	|	1817	|	1953	...	|	2219	|	...	...
Sassari a.	...	...		0650	0824	0835	...	0952	...	1146	...	...	...	...	...	1600	1757	...	1954	...	...	2030	...	2210	...	...
Porto Torres a.	...	...		0704	...	0848	...	...	...	...	...	...	...	...	...	...	1812	...	...	...	...	...	...	...	...	...
Porto Torres Marittima a.	...	...		0707	...	0852	...	...	...	...	...	...	...	...	...	...	1816	...	...	...	...	...	...	...	...	...

	⚒	⚒	⚒	⚒	⚒	⚒	⚒	⚒	⚒	⚒	⚒	⚒	⚒	⚒	⚒	⚒	⚒	⚒	⚒	⚒	⚒	⚒	⚒	⚒🚌	⚒	⚒
Porto Torres Marittima d.		...	...	...	...	...	0718	...	...	...	0952	...	...	...	...	...	1415	...	1605	...	...	...	...	...	1830	...
Porto Torres d.		...	...	...	...	...	0721	...	...	...	0955	...	...	...	...	...	1418	...	1608	...	...	...	...	...	1833	...
Sassari d.		...	...	0600	...	0627	0736	0820	...	...	1010	1023	1120	...	...	...	1433	1439	1623	1628	...	1815	...	...	1848	1900
Olbia Terranova d.		...	...	|	0541	|	▬	|	0806	1007	...	|	|	...	1334	1414	...	|	▬	|	1611	|	1800	1820	...	|
Ozieri-Chilivani a.		...	...	0639	0640	|	...	0859	0902	1103	...	1100	1210	...	1449	1520	...	1518	...	1708	1707	1855	1856	1940	...	|
Ozieri-Chilivani d.		...	...	▬	0644	|	...	...	0905	...	...	1108	▬	...	...	...	...	1525	⚒	...	1713	▬	1900	...	...	|
Macomer d.		...	...	⚒	0731	0743	⚒	...	0945	...	...	1146	⚒	1341	...	...	...	1605	1632	...	1752	⚒	1940	...	...	2024
Oristano d.		0530	0625	0730	...	0831	0930	...	1031	...	...	1233	1330	1437	...	...	...	1649	1732	...	1848	1936	2032	...	...	2116
Decimomannu d.		0629	0717	0821	...	|	1027	...	|	...	...	|	1422	1538	...	...	...	|	1833	...	|	2036	|	...	...	2216
Elmas Aeroporto ✈ d.		0637	0727	0830	...	0921	1041	...	1118	...	...	1320	1430	1546	...	...	...	1737	1847	...	1936	2043	2121	...	...	2225
Cagliari a.		0643	0737	0837	...	0928	1048	...	1125	...	...	1327	1438	1554	...	...	...	1744	1853	...	1943	2049	2128	...	...	2232

	⚒	⚒		†	†	†	†	†	†	†	†	†	†	†	†	†	†	†	†	†	†	†	†	†	†	†
Porto Torres Marittima d.	...	...	...		...	...	...	...	0718	...	...	...	...	1005	...	...	...	...	...	...	...	...	1840	...	...	...
Porto Torres d.	...	...	...		...	...	...	...	0721	...	...	...	...	1008	...	...	...	...	...	...	...	...	1843	...	...	...
Sassari d.	2031	...	...		...	...	...	0704	0736	0826	...	0924	...	1022	...	...	1433	...	...	...	1630	...	1858	1904	2038	...
Olbia Terranova d.	|	2018	...		...	...	0636	|	...	|	0800	|	0950	|	...	1413	|	...	...	1558	|	1838	...	|	|	2121
Ozieri-Chilivani a.	2120	2123	...		...	...	0740	0742	...	0905	0909	1013	1101	1100	...	1514	1511	...	...	1710	1712	1949	...	1949	2119	2124
Ozieri-Chilivani d.	...	...	...		...	...	...	0750	...	...	0911	...	...	1108	...	▬	1519	...	...	...	...	...	...	1956	...	...
Macomer d.	...	...	...		...	...	...	0839	...	...	0956	...	...	1151	...	†	1558	1729	...	...	...	...	...	2048	...	...
Oristano d.	...	...	...		0530	0730	...	0925	...	...	1046	...	...	1237	1430	1530	1654	1830	1930	...	...	...	...	2137	...	...
Decimomannu d.	...	...	...		0629	0829	...	1015	...	...	1144	...	...	1343	1530	1624	1745	1939	2029	...	...	...	...	2235	...	...
Elmas Aeroporto ✈ d.	...	...	...		0637	0837	...	1022	...	...	1152	...	...	1351	1545	1639	1752	1947	2043	...	...	...	...	2248	...	...
Cagliari a.	...	...	...		0643	0843	...	1029	...	...	1159	...	...	1358	1552	1646	1800	1954	2050	...	...	...	...	2258	...	...

🚌 OLBIA - GOLFO ARANCI 🚌 Service February 1 - May 31

	⚒	⚒	†	⚒	⚒	⚒				
Olbia Terranova d.	0640	1020	1250	1350	1420	1450	1650	1850	...	...
Golfo Aranci a.	0721	1101	1331	1431	1501	1531	1731	1931	...	...

	⚒	⚒	†	⚒	⚒	⚒	†			
Golfo Aranci d.	0700	1050	1315	1405	1515	1650	1725	1915	...	...
Olbia Terranova a.	0741	1131	1356	1456	1556	1731	1806	1956	...	...

Narrow gauge services on Sardinia are operated by ARST (www.arst.sardegna.it). Regular services operate on the following routes: Alghero - Sassari, Sassari - Sorso, Macomer - Nuoro and Monserrato Gottardo - Isili. Tram connections are available Monserrato Gottardo - Cagliari Repubblica and v.v. *Trenino Verde della Sardegna* operates tourist trains (www.treninoverde.com).

FOGGIA - POTENZA 632

2nd class

Service May 11 - December 13. Additional trains are available Melfi - Potenza and v.v.

km					⚒	⚒		†			†	†			⚒		†	⚒			🚌			
0	**Foggia** d.	0506	0534	...	0620	0645	...	0645	0842	...	1029	1137	...	1424	1752	...	1752	1830	...	2057	2250	...	...	...
67	Melfi d.	0555	0633	...	0723	0757	...	0748	0942	...	1124	1232	...	1534	1849	...	1800	1930	...	2156	2340	...	...	...
119	**Potenza** Centrale a.	0705	0800	...	0837	0917	...	0919	1101	...	1237	1347	...	1644	2000	...	2000	2051	...	2256	0053	...	...	...

		⚒		†	⚒		†			⚒	†												
Potenza Centrale d.	0528	0618	...	0715	0840	...	0842	1128	...	1330	1330	...	1704	1816	...	2010	2111	...	...	...	...	...	...
Melfi d.	0636	0726	...	0826	0945	...	0945	1229	...	1448	1452	...	1815	1933	...	2119	2224	...	...	...	...	...	...
Foggia a.	0746	0823	...	0935	1040	...	1040	1329	...	1558	1558	...	1931	2032	...	2222	2321	...	...	...	...	...	...

CATANZARO - LAMEZIA TERME 634

2nd class

km			⚒					Ⓐ	†		⑥	⚒		†	⚒		Ⓐ							
0	**Catanzaro** Lido d.	0628	0735	...	0829	0935	...	1031	1038	...	1140	1338	...	1428	1431	...	1528	1628	...	1738	1938	...	...	...
9	**Catanzaro** d.	0636	0743	...	0837	0943	...	1039	1046	...	1148	1346	...	1436	1439	...	1536	1636	...	1746	1946	...	...	...
47	**Lamezia Terme** C a.	0720	0824	...	0920	1020	...	1122	1120	...	1230	1420	...	1520	1523	...	1620	1720	...	1823	2020	...	...	...

	⚒	Ⓒ			Ⓑ		Ⓐ	Ⓒ		⚒	Ⓑ		Ⓑ	⑥		Ⓑ	⚒		⚒				
Lamezia Terme Centrale d.	0640	0740	...	0840	0940	...	1040	1240	...	1340	1435	...	1540	1640	...	1740	1840	...	1940	2040	...	...	...
Catanzaro a.	0716	0819	...	0915	1020	...	1118	1315	...	1420	1515	...	1615	1715	...	1820	1916	...	2021	2115	...	...	...
Catanzaro Lido a.	0725	0828	...	0925	1030	...	1127	1325	...	1430	1525	...	1625	1724	...	1830	1925	...	2030	2125	...	...	...

635 SUD EST SERVICES

Line 1 : BARI - TARANTO

km		⚒	⚒	⚒	⚒	†	⚒	†	⚒	⚒	⚒	⚒	†	⚒	⚒	⚒	†	⚒	⚒	⚒	†	⚒	⚒	†	
0	**Bari** Centrale d.	0514	0621	0721	0821	0844	0921	1012	1021	1114	1221	1321	1336	1421	1521	1621	1702	1721	1821	1921	1940	2021	2051	2138	...
1	Bari Sud Est d.	0518	0625	0725	0825	0848	0925	1016	1028	1118	1225	1325	1340	1425	1525	1625	1706	1725	1825	1925	1944	2025	2055	2142	...
4	Mungivacca d.	0526	0635	0735	0835	0855	0933	1023	1035	1126	1235	1335	1347	1435	1535	1635	1713	1735	1835	1935	1951	2035	2105	2149	...
24	Casamassima d.	0608	0708	0808	0908	0922	1006	1050	1107	1204	1308	1408	1414	1508	1608	1708	1744	1808	1908	2008	2018	2108	2138	2216	...
44	**Putignano** a.	0639	0739	0839	0939	0948	1039	1116	1139	1239	1339	1439	1440	1539	1639	1739	1810	1839	1939	2039	2048	2139	2209	2242	...

	⚒	⚒	⚒	⚒	†	⚒	†	⚒	⚒	⚒	⚒	†	⚒	⚒	⚒	†	⚒	⚒	†	⚒	⚒	⚒	†	
Putignano d.	0533	0554	0613	0654	0730	0754	0853	0911	1014	1113	1154	1204	1254	1354	1454	1527	1554	1654	1701	1754	1854	1954	2024	...
Casamassima d.	0601	0628	0646	0728	0756	0828	0923	0945	1046	1145	1228	1230	1328	1428	1528	1557	1628	1728	1727	1828	1928	2028	2052	...
Mungivacca d.	0634	0704	0734	0804	0821	0904	0948	1020	1127	1217	1304	1256	1404	1504	1604	1621	1704	1804	1753	1904	2004	2104	2117	...
Bari Sud Est d.	0640	0710	0740	0810	0828	0910	0954	1027	1134	1226	1310	1302	1410	1510	1610	1627	1710	1810	1759	1910	2010	2110	2123	...
Bari Centrale a.	0644	0714	0744	0814	0834	0914	0958	1031	1138	1231	1314	1308	1414	1514	1614	1633	1714	1814	1805	1914	2014	2114	2128	...

km			⚒	⚒	⚒🚌	⚒🚌	⚒	⚒	†	†	⚒	⚒	⚒🚌	⚒	†	⚒	⚒🚌	⚒	⚒🚌	†	⚒	⚒	†	⚒	
0	**Putignano** d.	...	0505	0633	0705	0745	0815	0949	0956	1124	1135	1235	1255	1359	1448	1524	1600	1635	1735	1818	1855	2023	2056	2116	...
35	Martina Franca **2** a.	...	0600	0728	0803	0843	0908	1047	1049	1219	1230	1333	1353	1454	1541	1622	1658	1730	1833	1912	1950	2118	2149	2214	...
		⚒	⚒	⚒					⚒🚌				⚒	⚒			⚒	⚒							
35	Martina Franca **2** d.	0530	0635	0744	...	...	...	...	1210	...	...	...	1354	1504	...	...	1716	1803	...	...	...	...	...	...	...
68	**Taranto** a.	0625	0734	0840	...	...	...	...	1302	...	...	...	1453	1602	...	...	1815	1902	...	...	...	...	...	...	...

						⚒	⚒	⚒										⚒	⚒			⚒	⚒	
Taranto d.	...	...	...	...	...	0635	0741	0848	...	...	...	...	...	...	...	...	...	1504	1610	...	...	1823	1911	...
Martina Franca **2** a.	...	...	...	...	...	0736	0841	0942	...	...	...	...	...	...	...	...	...	1605	1708	...	...	1925	2009	...
	⚒	⚒🚌	⚒🚌	⚒	†	⚒		⚒	†	⚒	⚒🚌	⚒	⚒🚌	⚒	†	⚒	†	⚒	⚒🚌	⚒	†	⚒	⚒	
Martina Franca **2** d.	0442	0510	0610	0704	0750	0821	...	1025	1102	1112	1223	1247	1325	1407	1423	1505	1557	1643	1730	1832	1922	2000	2128	...
Putignano a.	0540	0608	0708	0803	0853	0917	...	1120	1204	1210	1321	1342	1423	1505	1527	1600	1701	1741	1828	1930	2024	2058	2223	...

Line 2 : MARTINA FRANCA - LECCE (all services Francavilla Fontana - Lecce and v.v. are currently operated by 🚌)

km		⚒	⚒🚌	⚒	⚒🚌	⚒	⚒🚌	⚒	⚒🚌	†	†🚌		⚒	⚒🚌	⚒	⚒🚌		⚒	⚒🚌	†	†🚌	⚒	⚒🚌	⚒	⚒🚌
0	**Martina Franca 1** d.	0457	...	0554	...	0723	...	0850	...	0900	...	...	1200	...	1308	...	...	1522	...	1630	...	1741	...	1902	...
41	Francavilla Fontana d.	0555	0605	0659	0709	0825	0835	0949	0959	0956	1006	...	1258	1308	1408	1418	...	1621	1631	1725	1735	1840	1850	2002	2012
92	Novoli **3** d.	...	0728	...	0832	...	0958	...	1122	...	1129	...	...	1431	...	1541	...	...	1754	...	1858	...	2013	...	2135
103	**Lecce 5** a.	...	0748	...	0852	...	1018	...	1142	...	1149	...	...	1451	...	1601	...	...	1814	...	1918	...	2033	...	2155

	⚒🚌	⚒	⚒🚌	⚒	⚒🚌	⚒	⚒🚌	⚒	†🚌	†		⚒🚌	⚒	⚒🚌	⚒	⚒🚌	⚒		†🚌	†	⚒🚌	⚒	⚒🚌	⚒
Lecce 5 d.	0421	...	0545	...	0710	...	0856	...	0910	...	...	1221	...	1340	...	1440	...	...	1610	...	1719	...	1853	...
Novoli **3** d.	0441	...	0605	...	0730	...	0916	...	0930	...	...	1241	...	1400	...	1500	...	...	1630	...	1739	...	1913	...
Francavilla Fontana d.	0601	0611	0725	0735	0850	0900	1036	1046	1050	1100	...	1401	1411	1520	1530	1620	1630	...	1750	1800	1859	1909	2033	2043
Martina Franca 1 a.	...	0713	...	0837	...	1001	...	1148	...	1157	...	...	1511	...	1633	...	1731	...	...	1857	...	2018	...	2140

Line 3 : LECCE - NOVOLI - NARDÒ - GAGLIANO

km		⚒	⚒	⚒	†	⚒	⚒	⚒	†	⚒	⚒	⚒
0	**Lecce 5** d.	0525	0635	0810	0937	0950	1135	1305	1455	1535	1643	1930
11	Novoli **2** d.	0546	0657	0832	0958	1011	1157	1325	1516	1555	1705	1951
36	Nardò Centrale **5** d.	0633	0745	0916	1037	1055	1245	1408	1555	1641	1754	2037
60	Casarano **4** d.	0730	0836	1003	1119	1151	1334	1457	1638	1732	1841	2127
85	**Gagliano Leuca 6** a.	0811	0917	1046	1208	1234	1417	1540	1721	1815	1930	2210

	⚒	⚒	⚒	†	⚒	⚒	⚒	⚒	†	⚒	⚒
Gagliano Leuca 6 d.	0629	0832	1000	1219	1245	1351	1548	1644	1730	1825	1940
Casarano **4** d.	0713	0922	1050	1304	1333	1441	1631	1733	1814	1912	2025
Nardò Centrale **5** d.	0800	1009	1132	1344	1420	1526	1713	1823	1853	1954	2112
Novoli **2** d.	0853	1103	1221	1428	1509	1616	1803	1912	1939	2045	2200
Lecce 5 a.	0908	1119	1237	1445	1526	1632	1819	1927	1956	2101	2216

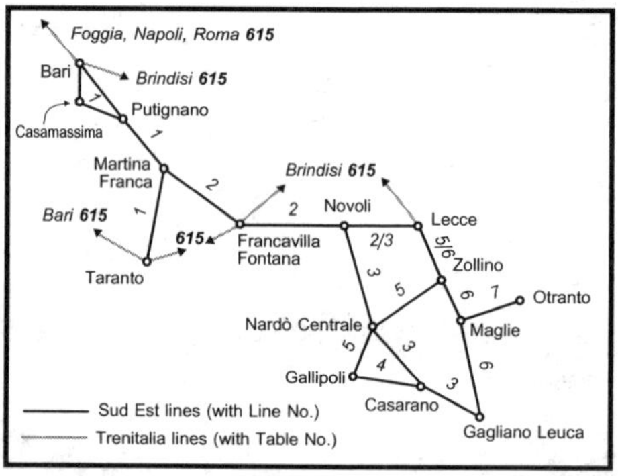

Line 4 : CASARANO - GALLIPOLI

km		⚒	⚒		†	⚒	⚒	⚒	†	⚒	†	⚒
0	Casarano **3** d.	0721	0925	...	1145	1325	1500	1643	1728	1819	1912	1959
22	Gallipoli **5** a.	0758	1002	...	1226	1401	1537	1720	1810	1856	1954	2036

	⚒	⚒	⚒	⚒	†	⚒	†	⚒	⚒	†	⚒
Gallipoli **5** d.	0503	0630	0813	1230	1242	1412	1550	1557	1733	1820	1913
Casarano **3** a.	0540	0707	0850	1307	1323	1449	1631	1634	1810	1901	1950

Line 5 : LECCE - GALLIPOLI

km		⚒🚌		⚒	⚒🚌		⚒	⚒🚌		⚒	⚒🚌		⚒🚌	⚒🚌	⚒🚌	†🚌	⚒🚌		⚒	⚒🚌		⚒🚌		⚒🚌	
0	**Lecce 2** d.	0600	...	0700	...	...	0900	...	...	1040	...	...	1310	1400	1500	1640	1703	...	1802	...	...	1900	...	2100	...
19	Zollino **6** d.	0639	...	0734	0744	...	0935	0945	...	1121	1131	...	1349	1439	1539	1710	1742	...	1841	1851	...	1939	...	2139	...
36	Nardò Centrale **3** d.	0712	...	...	0817	...	...	1018	...	...	1204	...	1422	1512	1612	1745	1815	...	...	1924	...	2012	...	2212	...
53	**Gallipoli 4** a.	0745	...	...	0850	...	...	1051	...	...	1237	...	1455	1545	1645	1805	1848	...	...	1957	...	2045	...	2245	...

	⚒🚌	⚒🚌	⚒		⚒🚌	⚒🚌		⚒🚌	⚒		⚒🚌	⚒🚌	⚒🚌		⚒🚌	⚒		⚒🚌	⚒		†🚌		⚒🚌	
Gallipoli 4 d.	0555	0640	...	...	0807	0907	...	1055	...	...	1307	1407	1507	...	1655	...	...	1820	...	...	1835	...	2007	...
Nardò Centrale **3** d.	0628	0713	...	...	0840	0940	...	1128	...	...	1340	1440	1540	...	1728	...	...	1853	...	...	1855	...	2040	...
Zollino **6** d.	0701	0746	0754	...	0913	1013	...	1201	1214	...	1413	1513	1613	...	1801	1814	...	1926	1938	...	1930	...	2113	...
Lecce 2 a.	0746	...	0837	...	0958	1058	...	...	1248	...	1458	1558	1658	...	...	1850	...	...	2014	...	2000	...	2158	...

Line 6 : LECCE - ZOLLINO - GAGLIANO

km		⚒	⚒		⚒	⚒		⚒		†	⚒		⚒	†	⚒	†		⚒	⚒	†	⚒		⚒		
0	**Lecce 2** d.	0510	0545	...	0700	0815	...	0900	...	1030	1040	...	1250	1307	1330	1410	...	1519	1622	1700	1802	...	1924	...	...
19	Zollino **5** d.	0545	0621	...	0735	0852	...	0936	...	1108	1122	...	1324	1335	1409	1447	...	1555	1658	1734	1842	...	2006	...	...
29	Maglie **7** d.	0604	0646	...	0756	0916	...	1001	...	1125	1138	...	1346	1353	1426	1508	...	1616	1721	1755	1903	...	2024	...	...
	Otranto **7** a.	...	|	...	|	|	...	|	...	1155	|	...	|	|	|	|	...	|	...	1824	|	...	|	...	...
66	**Gagliano Leuca 3** a.	...	0755	...	0904	1031	...	1117	...	...	1248	...	1459	1454	1531	1613	...	1722	...	...	2009	...	2132	...	...

	⚒	⚒		⚒	⚒		†	⚒		⚒	†	⚒		⚒		⚒		†	⚒		⚒	†	⚒	
Gagliano Leuca 3 d.	0515	0622	...	0824	0925	...	1035	1040	...	1210	...	1323	...	1544	...	1641	...	1655	...	...	1810	...	...	...
Otranto **7** d.	|	|	...	|	|	...	|	|	...	|	1330	|	...	|	...	|	...	|	...	...	|	2002	2007	...
Maglie **7** d.	0623	0730	...	0937	1039	...	1138	1155	...	1322	1359	1445	...	1658	...	1755	...	1803	1835	...	1922	2033	2039	...
Zollino **5** d.	0641	0754	...	0956	1055	...	1156	1214	...	1342	1418	1501	...	1717	...	1814	...	1824	1901	...	1938	2052	2055	...
Lecce 2 a.	0720	0837	...	1031	1131	...	1224	1248	...	1417	1456	1539	...	1751	...	1850	...	1900	1944	...	2014	2127	2130	...

Line 7 : MAGLIE - OTRANTO

km		⚒		⚒		⚒		†L	⚒		†	⚒		⚒		⚒		†L	⚒		†	⚒			
0	Maglie **6** d.	0630	...	0800	...	1010	...	1125	1145	...	1245	1330	...	1510	...	1635	...	1755	1800	...	1920	1927	...	...	...
18	Otranto a.	0700	...	0829	...	1040	...	1155	1215	...	1315	1400	...	1540	...	1705	...	1824	1830	...	1950	1957	...	...	...

	⚒		⚒		⚒		†	⚒		†L	⚒		⚒		⚒		⚒	†		†L	⚒L			
Otranto d.	0710	...	0838	...	1050	...	1205	1240	...	1330	1430	...	1555	...	1715	...	1840	1840	...	2002	2007	...	...	...
Maglie **6** a.	0740	...	0908	...	1120	...	1235	1310	...	1358	1500	...	1625	...	1745	...	1910	1910	...	2030	2036	...	...	...

L – From / to Lecce (see Line 6).

BARI - MATERA 636

FAL (www.ferrovieappulolucane.it) 2nd class

km																								
		⚒	⚒	⚒		⚒	⚒	⚒		⚒	⚒	⚒		⚒	⚒	⚒		⚒	⚒	⚒		⚒		
0	**Bari** Centrale d.	0506	0617	0749	...	0959	1048	1139	...	1244	1409	1518	...	1600	1655	1809	...	1855	1917	2003	...	2122	...	...
48	Altamura a.	0619	0729	0903	...	1110	1204	1256	...	1354	1522	1632	...	1712	1810	1920	...	1949	2030	2112	...	2234	...	...
		⚒	⚒	⚒		⚒	⚒	⚒		⚒	⚒	⚒		⚒	⚒	⚒		|	⚒	⚒		⚒		
48	Altamura d.	0621	0742	0909	...	1117	1207	1303	...	1402	1523	1635	...	1718	1812	1923	...	1952	2035	2119	...	2240	...	...
76	**Matera** Centrale a.	0650	0816	0937	...	1148	1236	1333	...	1432	1552	1703	...	1750	1841	1953	...	2018	2106	2150	...	2308	...	...

	⚒	⚒	⚒		⚒	⚒	⚒		⚒	⚒	⚒		⚒	⚒	⚒		⚒	⚒	⚒		⚒	⚒	
Matera Centrale d.	0545	0621	0705	...	0748	0834	1000	...	1114	1206	1323	...	1422	1522	1607	...	1717	1828	1922	...	2038	2122	...
Altamura a.	0611	0651	0733	...	0814	0900	1026	...	1142	1235	1350	...	1449	1552	1633	...	1745	1856	1951	...	2106	2150	...
	⚒	⚒	⚒		|	⚒	⚒		⚒	⚒	⚒		⚒	⚒	⚒		⚒	⚒	⚒		⚒	⚒	
Altamura d.	0624	0655	0738	...	0816	0907	1033	...	1147	1239	1358	...	1501	1558	1637	...	1749	1900	1957	...	2113	2155	...
Bari Centrale a.	0735	0805	0849	...	0911	1015	1152	...	1300	1355	1508	...	1616	1711	1756	...	1909	2017	2112	...	2224	2310	...

REGGIO DI CALABRIA - SIBARI - TARANTO 637

2nd class (except where noted)

Subject to confirmation. Additional trains are available Reggio di Calabria - Roccella Jonica and v.v. Additional 🚌 are available Catanzaro - Crotone and v.v., and Crotone - Sibari and v.v.

km																								
		🚌	🚌		🚌				*IC* **564**	🚌			🚌		🚌		*IC* **562**		🚌			🚌		
		⚒	†				Ⓐ		**A**			⚒			⚒		**B**			Ⓐ		Ⓐ		⚒
0	**Reggio di Calabria** C.le d.	...	...	0500	...	...	0547	0700	0800	...	...	1008	...	1108	...	...	1209	1308	...	1506	...	...	1708	1925
30	Melito di Porto Salvo d.	...	...	0522	...	...	0619	0725	0828	...	...	1032	...	1134	...	...	1235	1331	...	1529	...	...	1731	1950
96	Locri d.	...	...	0616	...	...	0735	0825	0921	...	...	1120	...	1219	...	...	1323	1424	...	1624	...	...	1824	2051
101	Siderno d.	...	...	0627	...	...	0740	0830	0927	...	...	1126	...	1224	...	...	1335	1430	...	1630	...	...	1830	2058
112	Roccella Jonica d.	...	...	0642	...	...	0756	0842	0942	...	...	1138	...	1234	...	...	1354	1444	...	1642	...	...	1842	2120
160	Soverato d.	...	...	0717	...	...	0836	0912	1028	...	...	1207	...	1315	...	...	1426	1520	...	1712	...	...	1917	2151
178	Catanzaro Lido a.	...	...	0730	...	...	0850	0928	1042	...	...	1227	...	1330	...	...	1439	1533	...	1733	...	...	1933	2205
178	Catanzaro Lido d.	0515	0615	...	0836	...	...	...	1052	1200	...	...	1235	...	1340	...	1450	...	1540	...	...	1740	...	...
238	**Crotone** d.	0644	0744	...	1007	...	...	...	|	1335	...	...	1418	...	1509	...	|	...	1709	...	...	1909	...	...
325	Rossano d.	0859	0959	...	1158	...	...	...	|	1550	...	...	1609	...	1724	...	|	...	1924	...	...	2124	...	...
336	Corigliano Calabro d.	0919	1019	...	1225	...	...	...	|	1610	...	...	1621	...	1744	...	|	...	1944	...	...	2144	...	...
351	**Sibari** a.	0944	1044	...	1255	...	...	...	1307	1635	...	...	1656	...	1809	...	1700	...	2009	...	...	2209	...	...
351	**Sibari** d.	...	...	...	...	...	...	...	1310	...	...	...	...	...	...	...	1711	...	...	...	...	...	...	...
366	Trebisacce d.	...	...	...	...	...	...	...	1322	...	...	...	...	...	...	...	1723	...	...	...	...	...	...	...
430	Metaponto **638** d.	...	...	...	...	...	...	...	1404	...	...	...	...	...	...	...	1812	...	...	...	...	...	...	...
473	**Taranto** **638** a.	...	...	...	...	...	...	...	1437	...	...	...	...	...	...	...	1840	...	...	...	...	...	...	...

				🚌	*IC* **558**	🚌	⚒		🚌			🚌		🚌	🚌		*IC* **566**	🚌		🚌	🚌		🚌
	⚒				**B**	⑥						†	Ⓐ	⚒			**A**					Ⓐ	
Taranto **638** d.	...	...	...	...	0841	...	...	...	...	...	...	...	...	...	...	...	1307	...	...	...	...	...	...
Metaponto **638** d.	...	...	...	...	0913	...	...	...	...	...	...	...	...	...	...	...	1335	...	...	...	...	...	...
Trebisacce d.	...	...	...	...	0952	...	...	...	...	...	...	...	...	...	...	...	1429	...	...	...	...	...	...
Sibari a.	...	...	...	...	1002	...	...	...	...	...	...	...	...	...	...	...	1440	...	...	...	...	...	...
Sibari d.	...	...	...	0620	1005	0800	...	...	1017	...	...	1200	...	1215	1400	...	1443	...	...	1455	1600	...	1715
Corigliano Calabro d.	...	...	...	0645	|	0825	...	...	1049	...	...	1225	...	1240	1425	...	|	...	...	1527	1625	...	1740
Rossano d.	...	...	...	0705	|	0845	...	...	1116	...	...	1245	...	1300	1445	...	|	←	...	1554	1645	...	1800
Crotone d.	...	...	...	0920	|	1100	...	...	1307	...	...	1500	...	1515	1659	...	|	1700	...	1745	1900	...	2030
Catanzaro Lido a.	...	...	...	1049	1216	1229	...	...	1436	...	...	1629	...	1644	→	...	1702	1829	...	1914	2029	...	2159
Catanzaro Lido d.	0530	0734	0934	...	1228	...	1335	...	...	1440	1552	...	1635	...	...	...	1712	...	1830	...	...	2035	...
Soverato d.	0543	0757	0948	...	1244	...	1355	...	...	1455	1606	...	1649	...	...	...	1731	...	1843	...	...	2049	...
Roccella Jonica d.	0614	0843	1018	...	1321	...	1443	...	...	1526	1643	...	1732	...	...	...	1803	...	1914	...	...	2119	...
Siderno d.	0626	0856	1031	...	1334	...	1455	...	...	1537	1656	...	1747	...	...	...	1816	...	1926	...	...	2136	...
Locri d.	0631	0901	1036	...	1340	...	1502	...	...	1544	1702	...	1756	...	...	...	1825	...	1931	...	...	2143	...
Melito di Porto Salvo d.	0724	1035	1130	...	1431	...	1620	...	...	1631	1803	...	1905	...	...	...	1924	...	2025	...	...	2235	...
Reggio di Calabria C.le a.	0755	1040	1158	...	1459	...	1644	...	...	1702	1839	...	1938	...	...	...	1950	...	2050	...	...	2306	...

A – (12) Reggio di Calabria - Lecce and v.v.

B – (12) Villa S. Giovanni - Reggio di Calabria - Bari and v.v.

SALERNO - POTENZA - TARANTO 638

Service from July 1. Local trains. For long distance trains see Table **640**.

km																								
		⚒		⚒	⚒		†		⚒	⚒		⚒	⚒	⚒		⚒	⚒					⚒	†	⚒
				🚌					🚌	🚌		🚌					🚌							🚌
0	**Salerno** d.	0540	...	0750	0955	...	1008	...	1135	...	...	1240	...	1400	...	1510	...	1621	1701	...	...	1954	2029	2100
20	Battipaglia d.	0555	...	|	1011	...	1024	...	|	...	...	|	...	1415	...	1525	...	1635	1717	...	...	2010	2045	|
112	**Potenza** Centrale d.	0749	0806	0914	1147	...	1208	1252	1305	1310	...	1405	1428	1544	...	1659	1735	1813	1848	...	2112	2147	2223	2257
219	Metaponto **637** d.	...	0931	...	...	...	...	1428	...	1441	...	...	1553	...	...	...	1908	...	2008	...	2237	...	...	...
263	**Taranto** **637** a.	...	1013	...	...	...	...	1505	...	1523	...	...	1629	...	...	...	1950	...	2049	...	2308	...	...	...

	⚒	⚒		†		⚒			⚒			⚒			⚒	⚒		⚒	⚒	†			⚒
	🚌								🚌						🚌								
Taranto **637** d.	...	...	...	...	0525	...	...	0626	...	...	1010	1101	...	...	1230	...	...	...	...	...	...	1830	...
Metaponto **637** d.	...	...	...	...	0557	...	...	0658	...	...	1047	1136	...	...	1310	...	...	...	...	...	...	1903	...
Potenza Centrale d.	0600	0623	...	0713	0721	0722	...	0823	0900	...	1217	1315	1339	...	1445	1702	...	1820	1904	1926	...	2048	2056
Battipaglia d.	|	0803	...	0845	...	0851	...	...	|	...	1345	...	1525	...	...	1856	...	1945	2042	2110	...	...	2233
Salerno a.	0720	0824	...	0903	...	0905	...	...	1030	...	1358	...	1542	...	...	1913	...	2025	2103	2141	...	...	2259

NAPOLI - SORRENTO, BAIANO and SARNO 639

Circumvesuviana Ferrovia 2nd class

Additional slower trains are available. SITA operates 🚌 services along the Amalfi Coast between Sorrento and Salerno (change buses at Amalfi). For details see www.sitasudtrasporti.it.

km																												
				★Ⓡ					★Ⓡ					★Ⓡ						★Ⓡ								
	Napoli Porta Nolana d.	0617	0805	0822	0841	0953	1029	1105	1122	1141	1253	1329	1405	1422	1441	1517	1553	1629	1705	1722	1817	1853	1929	2005	2041	2117	2153	2211
0	**Napoli** P. Garibaldi d.	0620	0808	0826	0844	0956	1032	1108	1126	1144	1256	1332	1408	1426	1444	1520	1556	1632	1708	1726	1820	1856	1932	2008	2044	2120	2156	2214
10	Ercolano Scavi d.	|	|	0841	|	|	|	|	1141	|	|	|	|	1441	|	|	|	|	|	1741	|	|	|	|	|	|	|	2226
20	Torre Annunziata d.	0643	0831	|	0907	1019	1055	1131	|	1207	1319	1355	1431	|	1507	1543	1619	1655	1731	|	1843	1919	1955	2034	2107	2143	2219	2238
23	Pompei S. Villa Misteri d.	0649	0837	0902	0913	1025	1101	1137	1202	1213	1325	1404	1437	1502	1513	1549	1625	1701	1737	1802	1849	1925	2001	2037	2113	2149	2225	2244
29	Castellammare d.	0706	0854	0913	0930	1043	1118	1154	1213	1230	1342	1418	1454	1513	1530	1606	1643	1718	1754	1813	1906	1943	2018	2054	2130	2206	2243	2259
42	**Sorrento** a.	0729	0917	0935	0953	1105	1141	1217	1235	1253	1405	1441	1517	1535	1553	1629	1705	1741	1817	1835	1929	2005	2041	2117	2153	2229	2304	2318

							★Ⓡ						★Ⓡ					★Ⓡ				★Ⓡ					
Sorrento d.	0626	0702	0814	0850	0926	1002	1020	1038	1114	1150	1226	1302	1320	1338	1414	1450	1526	1620	1638	1750	1902	1920	1938	2014	2050	2126	2202
Castellammare d.	0648	0724	0837	0913	0949	1025	1045	1101	1137	1213	1249	1325	1345	1401	1437	1513	1549	1645	1701	1813	1925	1945	2001	2037	2113	2149	2225
Pompei S. Villa Misteri d.	0706	0742	0853	0929	1005	1041	1101	1117	1153	1229	1305	1341	1401	1417	1453	1529	1605	1701	1717	1829	1941	2001	2017	2053	2129	2205	2240
Torre Annunziata d.	0713	0749	0859	0935	1011	1047	|	1123	1159	1235	1311	1347	|	1423	1459	1535	1611	|	1723	1835	1947	|	2023	2059	2135	2211	2247
Ercolano Scavi d.	0726	0802	|	|	|	|	1122	|	|	|	|	|	1422	|	|	|	|	1722	|	|	|	2022	|	|	|	|	2258
Napoli P. Garibaldi a.	0741	0817	0924	0959	1036	1112	1135	1148	1224	1300	1336	1412	1435	1448	1524	1600	1636	1735	1748	1900	2012	2035	2048	2124	2200	2235	2311
Napoli Porta Nolana a.	0743	0819	0926	1001	1038	1114	1137	1150	1226	1302	1338	1414	1437	1450	1526	1602	1638	1737	1750	1902	2014	2037	2050	2126	2202	2237	2313

NAPOLI - BAIANO Journey: 70 minutes. **WARNING!** Until September 30 services are operated by 🚌 with different departure times. Please check www.eavsrl.it for schedules.

From Napoli San Giorgio a Cremano at 0616⚒, 0652, 0728, 0804, 0842, 0918⚒, 0954, 1030, 1106, 1142, 1218, 1254, 1330, 1406, 1442, 1518⚒, 1554, 1630, 1706, 1742, 1818⚒, 1930, 2006.
From Baiano Parco del Partenio at 0619, 0703, 0815, 0851, 0927, 1003, 1039⚒, 1115, 1151, 1227, 1303, 1339⚒, 1415, 1451, 1527, 1603, 1639⚒, 1715, 1751, 1827, 1903, 1939⚒, 2017.

NAPOLI - SARNO Journey: 75 minutes. All services call at Poggiomarino (58 minutes from Napoli, 17 minutes from Sarno).

From Napoli Porta Nolana ◇ at 0546, 0622, 0658, 0734, 0810, 0846, 0922, 1034⚒, 1110, 1222, 1258⚒, 1334, 1446, 1522, 1558, 1634, 1710, 1746, 1822, 1858, 1934.
From Sarno at 0602, 0638, 0714, 0750, 0826, 0902, 0938, 1014, 1050, 1126, 1238⚒, 1314†, 1338⚒, 1426, 1502⚒, 1538, 1650, 1726, 1802, 1838, 1914, 1950.

★ – *Campania Express* tourist train. Advance reservation required (on-line or at EAV ticket offices).
◇ – Trains call at Napoli Porta Garibaldi 2–3 minutes later.

Operator: Circumvesuviana Ferrovia. www.eavsrl.it.

640 ROMA - NAPOLI - TARANTO and REGGIO DI CALABRIA

For *ICN* overnight trains see Table **641**.

km			FR 9573	FR 9573 ⑤–⑦	FR 9573 ⑥⑦	ITA 8191	FA 8333	FR 9693 ⑦	FA 8863	ITA 8111	FR 9515 ⑤–⑦	FR 9583	FR 9623	FR 9587	FR 9535	FR 8419	ITA 8913	FR 9639 ⑥⑦	FR 9639 ①–⑤	FR 8519	ITA 8143 ⑦	ITA 8103 ①–⑥	ITA 8103 ⑥	FR 9547	FR 9555
			H	d	e											A	A			B				r	
	Torino P Nuova **600 610** d.		...	...	...	...	...	...	...	...	...	0800	...	1000	1100	...	...	...	...	...	1320	1320	1320	...	...
	Milano C **600 610 620** d.		2120	2120	2120	...	...	...	...	0640	0710	0910	1058	1110	1210	...	...	1430	1430	...	1440	1440	1440	1510	1710
	Bologna Centrale **600 620** d.		2237	2237	2237	...	...	...	...	0757	0827	1027	1207	1227	1327	1402	1442	1537	1537	...	1557	1557	1557	1627	1827
0	**Roma** Termini **600** d.	H	|	|	|	0600	0730	0853	0858	1030	1100	1300	1425	1505	1605	1635	1715	1753	1753	1820	1830	1830	1830	1900	2100
	Napoli Afragola **600** a.	I	|	|	|	|	0832	0948	0959	|	1156	1356	1520	1604	1703	1736	1815	1848	1848	1920	1928	1928	1928	2005	2156
	Napoli Afragola **600** d.	G	|	|	|	|	0834	0950	1001	|	1158	1358	1522	1606	1705	1738	1818	1850	1850	1922	1930	1930	1930	2007	2158
214	**Napoli** Centrale **600** a.	H	|	|	|	0712	|	1003	|	1143	1213	1413	|	1620	|	|	|	|	|	|	|	|	|	|	2213
214	**Napoli** Centrale **600** d.		|	|	|	0725	|	1013	|	1200	1225	1425	|	1630	|	|	|	|	|	|	|	|	|	|	2223
	Pompei a.	S	|	|	|	|	|	1040	|	|	|	|	|	|	|	|	|	|	|	|	|	|	|	|	|
268	**Salerno** **600** a.	P	|	|	|	0804	0905	...	1030	1244	1302	1503	1614	1708	1752	1809	1854	1919	1919	1948	2016	2016	2016	2036	2300
268	**Salerno** **638** d.	E	|	|	|	0806	0908	...	1033	1246	1305	1505	1616	1710	1755	1811	1856	1921	1921	1950	2019	2019	2019	2038	2303
288	Battipaglia **638** d.	E	|	|	|	|	|	...	1044	|	|	|	1630	|	|	|	|	|	|	|	|	|	|	|	2319
380	Potenza Centrale **638** d.	D	|	|	|	|	|	...	|	|	|	|	|	|	|	|	|	|	|	|	|	|	|	2159	...
487	Metaponto **638** d.		|	|	|	|	|	...	|	|	|	|	|	|	|	|	|	|	|	|	|	|	|	2313	...
531	**Taranto** **638** a.	T	|	|	|	|	|	...	|	|	|	|	|	|	|	|	|	|	|	|	|	|	|	2342	...
318	Agropoli-Castellabate d.	R	|	|	|	0830	|	...	|	1310	1358	|	|	1736	|	|	|	|	|	|	2045	2045	2045	...	...
395	Sapri d.	A	|	|	|	0919	|	...	1140	1355	1432	|	1728	1823	1913	|	|	|	|	|	2130	2130	2130	...	...
489	Paola d.	I	0629	0659	0712	1007	1101	...	1229	1447	...	1704	1826	1919	2004	1957	2050	2117	2117	2143	2225	2225	2225	...	...
546	**Lamezia Terme** Centrale a.	N	0656	0736	0743	1033	1127	...	1255	1514	...	1730	1851	1947	2029	2023	2116	2144	2144	...	2251	2251	2251	...	...
546	**Lamezia Terme** Centrale d.	S	0659	0741	0746	1036	1130	...	1258	1517	...	1732	1854	1950	2032	2026	2119	2147	2147	...	2254	2254	2254	...	...
606	Rosarno d.		0728	0811	0817	1108	1158	...	1329	1551	...	1800	1932	2022	2110	2056	2151	2217	2257	...	2324	0005	0007	...	...
616	Gioia Tauro d.		|	|	|	|	|	...	1337	|	...	|	1940	|	|	|	|	|	|	...	|	...	|	...	...
652	Villa S. Giovanni a.		0758	0847	0847	1139	1228	...	1405	1621	...	1830	2003	2053	2141	2124	2222	2246	2326	...	2352	...	0035	...	...
652	Villa S. Giovanni d.		0801	0850	0850	1142	1231	...	1408	1624	...	1832	2006	2056	2144	2127	2225	2249	2329	...	2355	...	0038	...	...
667	**R di Calabria** Centrale a.		0817	0908	0907	1202	1250	...	1432	1646	...	1856	2024	2114	2200	2144	2245	2309	2349	...	0012	...	0055	...	...

		IC 701	IC 562	IC 721	IC 723		IC 551	IC 501 ①–⑤	IC 501 ⑥⑦	IC 727		IC 729	IC 553	IC 583		IC 1589 ⑥	IC 555	IC 707	IC 561 ⑥⑦		IC 811 ①–⑤	IC 591	IC 511	IC 597
		r	J					C	C					D		D		r					E	D
Roma Termini **600** d.		0626	...	0726	0726	...	0926	1004**n**	1010**n**	1126	...	1126	1226	1329**t**	...	1344**t**	1426	1526	1626	...	1626	1726	1828	2115
Latina d.	L	0700	...	0800	0800	...	1000	1057	1103	1200	...	1200	1300	1400	...	1424	1500	1600	1700	...	1700	1800	1902	2156
Formia-Gaeta d.	O	0735	...	0835	0835	...	1035	1134	1140	1235	...	1235	1335	1435	...	1506	1535	1635	1735	...	1735	1835	1937	2236
Aversa d.	N	0811	...	0911	0911	...	1111	1209	1215	1311	...	1311	1411	1511	...	1545	1611	1711	1811	...	1811	1911	2013	2312
Napoli Centrale **600** a.	G	0829	...	0929	0929	...	1129	1229	1234	1329	...	1329	1429	1534	...	1609	1629	1729	1829	...	1829	1929	2031	2332
Napoli Centrale **600** d.		0845	...	0950	0950	...	1145	...	...	1345	...	1345	1445	...	...	1625	1645	1745	1855	...	1855	1945	2047	2346
Salerno **600** a.	D	0923	...	1037	1037	...	1219	...	...	1421	...	1421	1524	...	...	1704	1726	1823	1932	...	1932	2030	2126	0022
Salerno **638** d.	I	0925	...	1039	1039	...	1222	...	...	1424	...	1424	1526	...	...	1718	1729	1825	1934	...	1934	...	...	...
Battipaglia **638** d.	S	0939	...	|	|	...	1235	...	...	|	...	|	1538	...	...	|	1743	1839	1948	...	1948	...	...	...
Potenza Centrale **638** d.	T	1102	...	|	|	...	|	...	...	|	...	|	|	...	...	|	|	2008	|	...	|	...	...	...
Metaponto **638** d.	A	1223	...	|	|	...	|	...	...	|	...	|	|	...	...	|	|	2128	|	...	|	...	...	...
Taranto **638** a.	N	1255	...	|	|	...	|	...	...	|	...	|	|	...	...	|	|	2200	|	...	|	...	...	...
Agropoli-Castellabate d.	C	...	...	|	|	...	1255	...	...	|	...	|	1600	...	...	|	1806	...	|	...	|	...	...	...
Sapri d.	E	...	...	1150	1150	...	1344	...	...	1533	...	1533	1707	...	...	1840	1920	...	2102	...	2102	...	...	...
Paola d.		...	...	1237	1237	...	1506	...	...	1630	...	1630	1808	...	...	1940	2022	...	2203	...	2202	...	...	...
Lamezia Terme Centrale a.	T	...	...	1303	1303	...	1545	...	...	1656	...	1656	1839	...	...	2012	2053	...	2234	...	2233	...	...	...
Lamezia Terme Centrale d.	R	...	...	1305	1305	...	1547	...	...	1659	...	1659	1842	...	...	2015	2056	...	2237	...	2236	...	...	...
Rosarno d.	A	...	...	|	|	...	1741	...	...	|	...	|	1915	...	...	2147	2130	...	2309	...	2346	...	...	...
Gioia Tauro d.	I	...	...	1344	1344	...	1750	...	...	1735	...	1735	1923	...	...	2156	2138	...	2317	...	2354	...	...	...
Villa S. Giovanni a.	N	...	...	1410	1410	...	1818	...	...	1805	...	1805	1947	...	...	2220	2202	...	2339	...	0017	...	...	...
Villa S. Giovanni d.	S	...	1152	1425	1425	...	1821	...	...	1820	...	1820	1950	...	...	2223	2205	...	2342	...	0020	...	...	...
Reggio di Calabria Centrale a.		...	1209	|	|	...	1846	...	...	|	...	|	2007	...	...	2239	2220	...	2358	...	0041	...	...	...
Siracusa **642** ▲ a.		...	...	1828	|	...	...	...	...	2238	...	|	...	...	...	...	...	...	...	...	...	...	...	...
Palermo Centrale **642** ▲ a.		...	...	...	1902	...	...	...	...	...	...	2255	...	...	...	...	...	...	...	...	...	...	...	...

REGIONAL TRAINS

2nd class

km			⚒	⚒	†	Ⓐ	†	⚒	†	⚒	†	Ⓐ	⑥		Ⓐ	†	Ⓐ	†	⚒	†	Ⓐ	†	⚒		⚒
0	**Roma** Termini d.	0531	0656	0736	0736	0750**t**	1036	1036	1136	1156	1238	1256	1256	...	1440**t**	1536	1556	1636	1656	1736	1756	1836	1856	1956	2054
62	Latina d.	0608	0731	0820	0820	0839	1118	1118	1218	1233	1321	1331	1331	...	1538	1618	1631	1718	1731	1818	1832	1918	1931	2032	2131
129	Formia-Gaeta d.	0656	0821	0913	0908	0925	1207	1212	1311	1321	1413	1421	1421	...	1625	1708	1721	1807	1821	1907	1921	2007	2021	2110	2221
195	Aversa d.	0750	0914	1012	1008	|	1300	1314	1400	1414	1507	1514	|	...	1718	1807	1814	1900	1918	2006	2014	2100	2114	|	2313
216	**Caserta** **626** a.	|	|	|	|	1027	|	|	|	|	|	|	1516	...	|	|	|	|	|	|	|	|	|	2209	|
214	**Napoli** Centrale **626** a.	0812	0950	1036	1040	1116	1323	1340	1423	1440	1535	1548	1551	...	1741	1843	1840	1923	1944	2043	2040	2123	2140	2252	2342

km		⚒			Ⓒ	Ⓐ				Ⓐ		†		⚒		⚒	Ⓐ	Ⓐ		⑥		Ⓑ			Ⓑ
0	**Napoli** Centrale **638** d.	...	...	0540	0650	0650	0735	0850	...	...	...	1150	1250	...	1350	...	...	...	...	...	1714	...	1914	2025	2116
54	Salerno **638** d.	...	0551	0637	0733	0733	0818	0934	...	...	...	1232	1333	...	1433	...	...	1712	...	1734	1803	...	2001	2108	2203
74	Battipaglia **638** d.	...	0610	0654	0749	0749	0835	0949	...	...	...	1247	1348	...	1450	...	...	1731	...	1753	1822	...	2018	2126	2221
104	Agropoli-Castellabate d.	...	0632	0717	0810	0811	0857	1011	...	...	...	1317	1410	...	1512	...	...	1751	...	1816	1850	...	2041	2150	2241
135	Ascea d.	...	0656	0745	0834	0836	0922	1036	...	...	...	1341	1434	...	1536	...	...	1814	...	1842	1914	...	2113	2216	2304
181	Sapri d.	0622	0735	0838	0906	0908	1009	1110	...	1246	1410	1420	1513	1544	1639	1721	1831	1903	...	1954	1959	2007	2150	2257	2340
193	Maratea d.	0635	0747	...	0917	0920	...	1122	...	1259	1423	1433	1526	1557	...	1733	1843	...	...	...	...	2019	2202	...	...
241	Belvedere Marittimo d.	0712	0832	...	0949	1000	...	1153	...	1337	1505	1511	|	1636	...	1814	1919	...	...	...	...	2056	2237	...	...
275	Paola a.	0744	0908	...	1023	1029	...	1214	...	1408	1535	1542	1641	1720	...	1844	1951	...	...	...	...	2132	2304	...	...
275	Paola ⊡ d.	0748	...	...	1025	...	...	1216	...	...	1552	...	1646	...	...	1848	1953	...	...	...	...	2150	2306	...	...
296	Castiglione Cosentino ⊡ d.	0803	...	...	1040	...	...	1231	...	...	1607	...	1701	...	...	1902	2006	...	...	...	...	2209	2324	...	...
301	**Cosenza** ⊡ a.	0809	...	...	1052	...	...	1241	...	...	1613	...	1707	...	...	1907	2012		......	...	...	2217	2335	...	...

km		Ⓐ	⑥			Ⓐ		⚒	†		Ⓐ	⚒		†	Ⓐ		⚒	Ⓐ		⚒					
0	**Cosenza** ⊡ d.	0523	0523	...	0623	0723	...	0923	1033	...	1223	1323	...	1323	1423	...	1523	1623	...	1723	1823	...	...	...	...
5	Castiglione Cosentino ⊡ d.	0530	0530	...	0630	0732	...	0930	1043	...	1233	1330	...	1330	1430	...	1535	1630	...	1729	1830	...	...	...	...
26	Paola ⊡ a.	0545	0545	...	0645	0747	...	0945	1100	...	1250	1344	...	1346	1445	...	1551	1645	...	1745	1845	...	...	...	...
26	Paola d.	0555	0555	...	0655	0757	...	0955	1110	...	1300	1354	...	1356	1455	...	1601	1655	...	1755	1857	...	...	...	...
83	**Lamezia Terme** Centrale d.	0630	0632	...	0732	0832	...	1026	1144	...	1337	1436	...	1432	1532	...	1635	1736	...	1832	1932	...	...	...	...
143	Rosarno d.	0703	0705	...	0805	0905	...	1059	1216	...	1410	1507	...	1503	1605	...	1708	1810	...	1905	2005	...	...	...	...
153	Gioia Tauro d.	0710	0712	...	0812	0912	...	1106	1223	...	1417	1514	...	1510	1612	...	1715	1817	...	1912	2012	...	...	...	...
189	Villa S. Giovanni d.	0743	0744	...	0844	0944	...	1147	1257	...	1449	1546	...	1544	1644	...	1747	1852	...	1944	2044	...	...	...	...
204	**R. di Calabria** Centrale a.	0801	0802	...	0902	1002	...	1208	1315	...	1507	1602	...	1602	1702	...	1804	1910	...	2002	2102	...	...	...	...

km		⚒		⚒		†		Ⓑ		⚒		Ⓑ				Ⓐ									
0	**Cosenza** d.	0516	...	0716	...	0815	...	1139	...	1415	...	1539	...	1739	...	1939	...	...	...	...	...	...	...	...	...
5	Castiglione Cosentino d.	0522	...	0726	...	0821	...	1145	...	1421	...	1545	...	1745	...	1945	...	...	...	...	...	...	...	...	...
70	**Sibari** a.	0614	...	0813	...	0908	...	1232	...	1508	...	1632	...	1832	...	2032	...	...	...	...	...	...	...	...	...

A – To / from Venezia (Table **605**).
B – 12 🍸 Bolzano - Sibari (a. 2233).
C – To / from Sestri Levante (Table **610**). Subject to alteration from July 21.
D – To / from Milano (Table **620**).
E – To / from Torino (Table **610**). Subject to alteration from July 21.
F – 12 🍸 Sibari (d. 0624) - Bolzano.
G – To Firenze (Table **600**).
H – ④⑤ July 3 - Aug. 8 (also June 19, 26, Aug. 9); ④–⑦ Aug. 29 - Sept. 14.
J – 12 Villa S. Giovanni - Reggio di Calabria - Bari and v.v.

d – June 20 – 29.
e – July 5 - Aug. 3.
n – Roma **Ostiense**.
p – Milano **Porta Garibaldi**.
r – From July 1.
s – Calls to set down only.
t – Roma **Tiburtina**.
u – Calls to pick up only.

TABLE AND NOTES CONTINUE ON NEXT PAGE →

REGGIO DI CALABRIA and TARANTO - NAPOLI - ROMA 640

Subject to alteration August 11–31. For *ICN* overnight trains see Table **641**.

HIGH SPEED TRAINS

	FR	*FR*	*FR*	*FR*		*FR*	*FR*	*ITA*	*FR*		*FR*	*FR*	*FR*		*ITA*	*FA*	*FR*	*FA*		*FR*	*ITA*	*FR*	*FR*
	8334	**9612**	**8509**	**9514**		**8418**	**9584**	**8134**	**9540**		**9642**	**9588**	**9658**		**8158**	**8868**	**9592**	**8332**		**9568**	**8192**	**9574**	**9574**
																	⑤–⑦			⑦		④⑤	⑥⑦
			F	**r**		**A**														**G**			
Reggio di Calabria Centrale d.	...	...	...	...	...	0607	0640	0720	0815	...	0901	1007	1226	...	1324	1336	...	1516	...	...	1730	2122	2219
Villa S. Giovanni a.	...	...	...	...	...	0622	0656	0737	0833	...	0914	1022	1240	...	1340	1351	...	1531	...	...	1746	2137	2234
Villa S. Giovanni d.	...	...	...	...	...	0625	0659	0740	0836	...	0917	1025	1243	...	1343	1354	...	1534	...	...	1749	2140	2237
Gioia Tauro d.	...	...	...	...	...	|	|	|	|	...	0940	|	|	...	|	1417	...	|	...	...	|	|	|
Rosarno d.	...	...	...	...	...	0652	0728	0810	0906	...	0948	1055	1313	...	1414	1425	...	1602	...	...	1817	2213	2306
Lamezia Terme Centrale a.	...	...	...	...	...	0725	0800	0841	0937	...	1018	1125	1345	...	1446	1454	...	1627	...	...	1850	2342	2336
Lamezia Terme Centrale d.	...	...	...	...	...	0728	0803	0843	0940	...	1021	1128	1348	...	1448	1457	...	1630	...	...	1852	2345	2339
Paola d.	...	...	0714	...	...	0759	0833	0915	1012	...	1053	1159	1421	...	1519	1533	...	1703	...	...	1925	0017	0014
Sapri d.	...	...	|	...	...	|	0932	1008	1103	...	1146	|	|	...	1608	1625	1613	|	...	...	2011	|	|
Agropoli-Castellabate d.	...	...	|	...	...	|	1021	1053	|	...	|	|	|	...	1655	1711	1723	|	...	...	2056	|	|
Taranto 638 d.	...	...	|	0610	...	|	|	|	|	...	|	|	|	...	|	|	|	|	...	...	|	|	|
Metaponto 638 d.	...	...	|	0638	...	|	|	|	|	...	|	|	|	...	|	|	|	|	...	...	|	|	|
Potenza Centrale 638 d.	...	...	|	0755	...	|	|	|	|	...	|	|	|	...	|	|	|	|	...	...	|	|	|
Battipaglia 638 d.	...	0512	|	|	...	|	|	|	|	...	1250	|	|	...	|	1731	|	|	...	...	|	|	|
Salerno 638 a.	...	0530	0909	0921	...	0956	1048	1119	1212	...	1302	1351	1614	...	1719	1743	1751	1852	...	...	2125	|	|
Salerno 600 d.	...	0538	0911	0923	...	0959	1051	1122	1215	...	1305	1354	1617	...	1722	1745	1753	1854	...	...	2128	|	|
Pompei d.	...	|	|	|	...	|	|	|	|	...	|	|	|	...	|	|	|	|	...	1840	|	|	|
Napoli Centrale 600 a.	...	0617	|	|	...	|	1127	1158	|	...	|	1428	|	...	1758	|	1828	|	...	1923	2208	|	|
Napoli Centrale 600 d.	0545	0630	|	|	...	|	1140	1215	|	...	|	1440	|	...	1820	|	1840	|	...	1940	2218	|	|
Napoli Afragola 600 a.	|	|	0939	0954	...	1023	1156	1228	1251	...	1339	1456	1639	...	|	1810	1856	1920	...	1956	|	|	|
Napoli Afragola 600 d.	0557**u**	|	0941	0956	...	1025	1158	1230	1253	...	1341	1458	1641	...	|	1812	1858	1922	...	1958	|	|	|
Roma Termini 600 a.	0700	0740	1040	1058	...	1125	1300	1330	1355	...	1440	1555	1740	...	1930	1915	1955	2025	...	2055	2330	|	|
Bologna Centrale 600 620 a.	...	0953	1313	1333	...	1358	1533	1603	1633	...	1653	1833	1953	...	2203	...	2235	...	...	...	...	0728	0728
Milano Centrale 600 610 620 a.	...	1058	...	1450	...	...	1650	1720	1750	...	1758	1950	2100	...	2320	...	2350	...	...	...	...	0850	0850
Torino Porta Nuova 600 610 a.	...	1216	...	1606	...	...	1806	1835	...	...	1916	2106	...	...	...	...	...	...	...	...	...	...	...

LONG DISTANCE TRAINS

	IC	*IC*	*IC*		*IC*	*IC*	*IC*		*IC*	*IC*	*IC*		*IC*	*IC*	*IC*		*IC*	*IC*	*IC*		*IC*	*IC*	*IC*
	582	**510**	**590**		**550**	**700**	**552**		**596**	**1588**	**556**		**822**	**722**	**728**		**522**	**702**	**724**		**730**	**560**	**558**
										⑦			②–④				⑤–①						
		E	**D**			**r**			**D**	**D**			**C**				**C**	**r**					**J**
Palermo Centrale 642 ▲ d.	...	...	...	...	...	...	...	...	...	...	...	...	...	...	0705	...	...	...	...	...	1015	...	...
Siracusa 642 ▲ d.	...	...	...	...	...	...	...	...	...	...	...	...	...	0738	|	...	...	...	1025	...	|	...	...
Reggio di Calabria Centrale d.	...	...	...	...	0617	...	0750	...	...	0841	1000	...	...	|	|	...	...	...	|	...	|	1425	1504
Villa S. Giovanni a.	...	...	...	...	0635	...	0805	...	...	0900	1015	...	...	1130	1130	...	...	...	1435	...	1435	1441	1521
Villa S. Giovanni d.	...	...	...	...	0637	...	0807	...	...	0902	1017	...	...	1150	1150	...	...	...	1450	...	1450	1444	...
Gioia Tauro d.	...	...	...	...	0701	...	0834	...	...	0927	1055	...	...	1217	1217	...	...	...	1515	...	1515	1508	...
Rosarno d.	...	...	...	...	0709	...	0842	...	...	0936	1105	...	...	|	|	...	...	...	|	...	|	1516	...
Lamezia Terme Centrale a.	...	...	...	...	0741	...	0914	...	...	1053	1138	...	...	1253	1253	...	...	...	1555	...	1559	1641	...
Lamezia Terme Centrale d.	...	...	...	...	0744	...	0917	...	...	1055	1141	...	...	1256	1256	...	...	...	1557	...	1601	1643	...
Paola d.	...	...	...	...	0817	...	0952	...	...	1128	1214	...	...	1330	1330	...	...	...	1632	...	1636	1714	...
Sapri d.	...	...	...	...	0916	...	1055	...	...	1221	1312	...	...	1420	1420	...	...	...	1726	...	1729	1815	...
Agropoli-Castellabate d.	...	...	...	...	|	...	1144	...	...	|	1404	...	...	|	|	...	...	...	|	...	|	1902	...
Taranto 638 d.	...	...	...	...	|	0800	|	...	...	|	|	...	...	|	|	...	...	1347	|	...	|	|	...
Metaponto 638 d.	...	...	...	...	|	0831	|	...	...	|	|	...	...	|	|	...	...	1429	|	...	|	|	...
Potenza Centrale 638 d.	...	...	...	...	|	0856	|	...	...	|	|	...	...	|	|	...	...	1548	|	...	|	|	...
Battipaglia 638 d.	...	...	...	...	1024	1127	1208	...	...	|	1424	...	...	|	|	...	...	1717	|	...	|	1922	...
Salerno 638 a.	...	...	...	...	1037	1138	1220	...	...	1334	1434	...	...	1534	1534	...	...	1730	1837	...	1837	1934	...
Salerno 600 d.	0528	0639	0858	...	1040	1140	1223	...	...	1337	1437	...	...	1537	1537	...	...	1733	1839	...	1839	1937	...
Napoli Centrale 600 a.	0606	0718	0948	...	1117	1218	1305	...	...	1418	1517	...	...	1617	1617	...	...	1817	1913	...	1913	2017	...
Napoli Centrale 600 d.	0631	0731	1031	...	1131	1231	1331	...	1420	1446	1531	...	1601	1631	1631	...	1731	1831	1931	...	1931	2031	...
Aversa d.	0648	0749	1049	...	1149	1249	1349	...	1438	1506	1549	...	1622	1649	1649	...	1749	1849	1949	...	1949	2049	...
Formia-Gaeta d.	0722	0822	1122	...	1222	1322	1422	...	1511	1544	1622	...	1714	1722	1722	...	1822	1922	2022	...	2022	2122	...
Latina d.	0800	0900	1200	...	1300	1400	1500	...	1549	1627	1700	...	1814	1800	1800	...	1900	2000	2100	...	2100	2200	...
Roma Termini 600 a.	0834	0934	1238**t**	...	1334	1434	1534	...	1631**t**	1707**t**	1734	...	1902**n**	1834	1834	...	1941**n**	2034	2134	...	2134	2234	...

REGIONAL TRAINS 2nd class

	Ⓐ		⚒		†		⚒		†		⚒		Ⓑ		⚒		Ⓐ		†					
Sibari d.	0535	...	0640	...	0725	...	0832	...	0932	...	1332	...	1532	...	1732	...	1932	...	2130	...	...	...	...	...
Castiglione Cosentino d.	0619	...	0725	...	0810	...	0917	...	1017	...	1417	...	1624	...	1824	...	2024	...	2224	...	...	...	...	...
Cosenza a.	0626	...	0733	...	0818	...	0927	...	1025	...	1427	...	1632	...	1832	...	2032	...	2231	...	...	...	...	...

	⚒	⚒		⚒	†		Ⓐ			⚒	⚒		Ⓑ	⑥		Ⓐ	Ⓑ		⚒	Ⓐ				
Reggio di Calabria Centrale d.	0500	0550	...	0658	0658	...	0800	1158	...	1258	1358	...	1453	1558	...	1658	1758	...	1858	1958	...	...	...	...
Villa S. Giovanni d.	0518	0606	...	0716	0716	...	0849	1216	...	1316	1416	...	1509	1616	...	1716	1816	...	1916	2016	...	...	...	...
Gioia Tauro d.	0549	0635	...	0747	0747	...	0850	1247	...	1347	1447	...	1538	1647	...	1747	1847	...	1947	2047	...	...	...	...
Rosarno d.	0555	0650	...	0755	0755	...	0856	1255	...	1355	1455	...	1545	1655	...	1755	1855	...	1955	2055	...	...	...	...
Lamezia Terme Centrale d.	0632	0734	...	0832	0832	...	0932	1332	...	1438	1532	...	1635	1736	...	1832	1932	...	2032	2130	...	...	...	...
Paola a.	0708	0806	...	0904	0901	...	1005	1406	...	1507	1606	...	1706	1805	...	1905	2005	...	2105	...	...	...	...	...
Paola ⊡ d.	0718	0816	...	0915	0916	...	1016	1416	...	1519	1616	...	1716	1817	...	1916	2015	...	...	...	...	...	...	...
Castiglione Cosentino ⊡ d.	0732	0831	...	0931	0931	...	1031	1431	...	1534	1631	...	1731	1831	...	1931	2031	...	...	...	...	...	...	...
Cosenza ⊡ a.	0737	0837	...	0937	0937	...	1037	1437	...	1542	1637	...	1737	1837	...	1937	2037	...	...	...	...	...	...	...

	②–⑥	①⑦		⚒	Ⓑ		⚒	⚒	†	Ⓐ	Ⓒ		⚒		†	Ⓐ	Ⓐ	†	⚒	⑥	⚒	†		Ⓐ
Cosenza ⊡ d.	...	...	0558	0610	0823	...	...	...	...	...	1314	...	1353	1453	...	...	1653	...	...	1653	...	1753	1853	2046
Castiglione Cosentino ⊡ d.	...	...	0604	0616	0830	...	...	...	...	...	1321	...	1400	1459	...	...	1700	...	...	1700	...	1800	1901	2053
Paola ⊡ a.	...	...	0619	0631	0845	...	...	...	...	...	1337	...	1414	1515	...	...	1715	...	...	1715	...	1814	1915	2108
Paola d.	...	...	0621	0634	0847	...	1146	1240	1245	1337	1339	...	1424	1517	...	1612	1719	1719	...	1725	1815	1815	1917	2118
Belvedere Marittimo d.	...	...	0649	0705	0917	...	1217	1308	1311	1408	1408	...	1456	1545	...	1642	1749	1749	...	1755	1846	1846	1943	2145
Maratea d.	...	...	0724	0745	1005	...	1249	1346	1350	1443	1443	...	1533	1629	...	1730	1826	1825	...	1832	1925	1923	2014	2218
Sapri d.	0552	0600	0738	0759	1019	1255	1259	1400	1403	1458	1458	...	1547	1642	1714	1742	1839	1839	1842	1845	1938	1936	2026	2228
Ascea d.	0638	0638	0814	...	...	1347	...	1452	1453	1542	1542	...	...	1722	1803	...	...	1920	1917	...	...	...	2107	...
Agropoli-Castellabate d.	0705	0705	0847	...	...	1414	...	1517	1518	1612	1612	...	...	1750	1836	...	...	1947	1946	...	...	...	2132	...
Battipaglia 638 d.	0729	0729	0910	...	...	1440	...	1540	1540	1639	1641	...	...	1813	1859	...	...	2011	2011	...	...	...	2159	...
Salerno 638 d.	0750	0750	0931	...	...	1501	...	1601	1601	1701	1701	...	...	1831	1920	...	...	2031	2031	...	...	...	2217	...
Napoli Centrale 638 a.	0827	0827	1018	...	...	1538	...	1638	1638	1738	1738	...	...	1908	2000	...	...	2108	2108	...	...	...	2258	...

	⚒	†	⚒	⚒	†	⚒	†	Ⓐ	†	⚒	⚒	⚒	†	⚒	†	⚒	†	†	⚒	⚒	†	⚒	f	g
Napoli Centrale 626 d.	0500	0500	0509	0619	0637	0820	0830	0935	1117	1120	1220	1320	1345	1425	1430	1520	1540	1617	1620	1720	1817	1820	1952	2045
Caserta 626 d.	|	|	|	|	|	|	|	|	|	|	|	|	|	|	|	|	|	|	|	|	|	|	|	|
Aversa d.	0525	0525	0531	0637	0659	0838	0856	0954	1145	1136	1236	1338	1402	1445	1456	1538	1559	1645	1638	1738	1844	1838	2018	2109
Formia-Gaeta d.	0611	0614	0625	0739	0752	0938	0949	1041	1249	1238	1340	1438	1448	1540	1553	1638	1652	1752	1738	1838	1952	1938	2125	2209
Latina d.	0655	0710	0717	0829	0842	1028	1041	1115	1338	1337	1438	1528	1536	1628	1640	1728	1742	1842	1828	1937	2042	2028	2212	2257
Roma Termini a.	0734	0754	0807	0904	0924	1104	1124	1153**t**	1422	1422	1524	1604	1624	1712	1724	1804	1824	1924	1904	2024	2129	2112	2305	2340

⊡ – All trains **Paola - Cosenza** and v.v.:

From **Paola** at 0718 ⚒, 0748 ⚒, 0816 ⚒, 0915, 1016 Ⓐ, 1025 Ⓒ, 1116 †, 1216, 1245 †, 1306 ⑥, 1345 Ⓐ, 1416, 1519 ⚒, 1552, 1616 Ⓐ, 1646, 1716 Ⓑ, 1817 ⑥, 1848, 1916 ⚒, 1956 Ⓐ, 2015, 2150 Ⓑ, 2306.

From **Cosenza** at 0523 ⚒, 0558, 0610 ⚒, 0623, 0723, 0823 Ⓑ, 0923, 1033 †, 1050 ⚒, 1123 ⚒, 1223 Ⓐ, 1323, 1353 ⚒, 1423 Ⓐ, 1453, 1523 ⚒, 1623, 1653 ⚒, 1723 ⚒, 1753 †, 1823, 1853, 1923 ⑥, 2046 Ⓐ.

▲ – Through trains are conveyed by ⛴ Villa S. Giovanni - Messina and v.v. See Table **2695** for other sailings.

FOR RETURN SERVICE AND ADDITIONAL NOTES SEE PREVIOUS PAGE.

Trains without numbers are subject to confirmation.

641 OVERNIGHT TRAINS

WARNING! All trains are subject to frequent variations. Outline timings are shown. For confirmed timings please consult the *Trenitalia* journey planner at www.trenitalia.com.
Trains generally convey 🛏 1, 2 cl., ▬ 2 cl. (4 berth). Running days, timings and numbers may vary - please check your reservation.

TRIESTE - ROMA

Subject to confirmation

		ICN 770
Trieste Centrale	d.	1847
Monfalcone	d.	1911
Gorizia Centrale	d.	1935
Udine	d.	1959
Pordenone	d.	2033
Sacile	d.	2043
Conegliano	d.	2056
Treviso Centrale	d.	2119
Venezia Santa Lucia	d.	2205
Venezia Mestre	d.	2217
Padova	d.	2233
Rovigo	d.	2304
Ferrara	d.	2323
Bologna Centrale	d.	0148
Arezzo	d.	0423
Terontola-Cortona	a.	0443
Chiusi-Chianciano Terme	a.	0505
Roma Termini	a.	0635

		ICN 774
Roma Termini	d.	2235
Chiusi-Chianciano Terme	d.	0007
Terontola-Cortona	d.	0025
Arezzo	d.	0047
Bologna Centrale	a.	0421
Ferrara	a.	0456
Rovigo	a.	0514
Padova	a.	0545
Venezia Mestre	a.	0608
Venezia Santa Lucia	a.	0620
Treviso Centrale	a.	0712
Conegliano	a.	0735
Sacile	a.	0749
Pordenone	a.	0759
Udine	a.	0838
Gorizia Centrale	a.	0908
Monfalcone	a.	0929
Trieste Centrale	a.	0957

TORINO - SALERNO - REGGIO DI CALABRIA

Subject to confirmation

		ICN 795	ICN 899 ②–④	ICN 797	ICN 799 ⑤–⑦	ICN 799 ①
Torino Porta Nuova	d.	1520	2015	2030	2155	2155
Torino Porta Susa	d.	|	|	2040	|	|
Vercelli	d.	|	|	2126	|	|
Novara	d.	|	|	2142	|	|
Milano Porta Garibaldi	d.	|	|	2218	|	|
Piacenza	d.	|	|	2319	|	|
Parma	d.	|	|	2352	|	|
Asti	d.	1601	2056	|	2236	2236
Alessandria	d.	1622	2119	|	2259	2259
Genova Piazza Principe	d.	1711	2207	|	2353	2353
Genova Brignole	d.	1717	2216	|	0002	0002
Rapallo	d.	1750	2255	|	0028	0028
Chiavari	d.	1802	2307	|	0038	0038
La Spezia Centrale	d.	1912	0008	|	0127	0127
Viareggio	d.	1952	|	|	|	|
Pisa Centrale	d.	2011	0311	|	0221	0311
Livorno Centrale	d.	2028	|	|	0240	|
Grosseto	d.	2142	0442	|	0407	0442
Civitavecchia	d.	2237	0535	|	0500	0535
Orvieto	a.	|	|	0446	|	|
Orte	a.	|	|	0518	|	|
Roma Tiburtina	a.	|	|	0552	|	|
Roma Ostiense	d.	2326	0620	|	0546	0620
Latina	a.	|	0705	|	0635	0705
Formia-Gaeta	a.	|	0745	|	0715	0745
Aversa	a.	|	0834	|	0756	0834
Napoli Centrale	a.	|	0901	0846	0817	0901
Salerno	a.	0259	0955	0946	0911	0955
Sapri	a.	0423	...	...	...	...
Paola	a.	0520	...	...	...	...
Lamezia Terme Centrale	a.	0600	...	...	...	...
Rosarno	a.	0737	...	...	...	...
Gioia Tauro	a.	0745	...	...	...	...
Villa S. Giovanni	a.	0822	...	...	...	...
Reggio di Calabria Centrale	a.	0845	...	...	...	...

		ICN 798	ICN 796	ICN 794
Reggio di Calabria Centrale	d.	...	...	2143
Villa S. Giovanni	d.	...	...	2203
Gioia Tauro	d.	...	...	2237
Rosarno	d.	...	...	2247
Lamezia Terme Centrale	d.	...	...	0010
Paola	d.	...	...	0054
Sapri	d.	...	...	0153
Salerno	d.	2038	2052	0310
Napoli Centrale	d.	2135	2143	|
Aversa	d.	|	2202	|
Formia-Gaeta	d.	|	2241	0454
Latina	d.	|	2318	0530
Roma Ostiense	a.	|	0015	0604
Roma Tiburtina	d.	2351	|	|
Orte	d.	0026	|	|
Orvieto	d.	0103	|	|
Civitavecchia	a.	|	0052	0653
Grosseto	a.	|	0151	0754
Livorno Centrale	a.	|	0306	0905
Pisa Centrale	a.	|	0323	0922
Viareggio	a.	|	|	0945
La Spezia Centrale	a.	|	0423	1039
Chiavari	a.	|	0510	1147
Rapallo	a.	|	0519	1200
Genova Brignole	a.	|	0548	1241
Genova Piazza Principe	a.	|	0601	1249
Alessandria	a.	|	0655	1335
Asti	a.	|	0721	1359
Parma	a.	0522	|	|
Piacenza	a.	0554	|	|
Milano Porta Garibaldi	a.	0655	|	|
Novara	a.	0800	|	|
Vercelli	a.	0814	|	|
Torino Porta Susa	a.	0905	|	|
Torino Porta Nuova	a.	0920	0810	1440

MILANO and ROMA - SIRACUSA and PALERMO

Subject to confirmation

		ICN 1955 A	ICN 1957 A	ICN 1959 ①–⑤	ICN 1961 ①–⑤	ICN 1959 ⑥⑦	ICN 1961 ⑥⑦	ICN 1963	ICN 1965
Milano Centrale	d.	...	...	...	...	...	...	2010	2010
Piacenza	d.	...	...	...	...	...	...	2107	2107
Fidenza	d.	...	...	...	...	...	...	2131	2131
Parma	d.	...	...	...	...	...	...	2149	2149
Reggio Emilia	d.	...	...	...	...	...	...	2211	2211
Modena	d.	...	...	...	...	...	...	2233	2233
Bologna Centrale	d.	...	...	...	...	...	...	2305	2305
Prato Centrale	d.	...	...	...	...	...	...	2353	2353
Firenze Campo di Marte	d.	...	...	...	...	...	...	0012	0012
Roma Termini	d.	2012	2012	2222	2222	2300	2300	|	|
Latina	d.	2047	2047	|	|	|	|	|	|
Formia-Gaeta	d.	2132	2132	|	|	|	|	|	|
Napoli Centrale	d.	2237	2237	|	|	|	|	|	|
Salerno	a.	2314	2314	|	|	|	|	0613	0613
Battipaglia	a.	|	|	|	|	|	|	0628	0628
Agropoli-Castellabate	a.	|	|	|	|	|	|	0645	0645
Sapri	a.	|	|	|	|	|	|	0741	0741
Paola	a.	|	|	|	|	|	|	0850	0850
Lamezia Terme Centrale	a.	|	|	0446	0446	0459	0459	0929	0929
Rosarno	a.	|	|	|	|	|	|	1004	1004
Gioia Tauro	a.	|	|	|	|	|	|	1012	1012
Villa S. Giovanni	a.	0330	0330	0620	0620	0610	0610	1040	1040
Messina Centrale	a.	0515	0515	0805	0805	0805	0805	1245	1245
Taormina-Giardini	a.	0647	|	0929	|	0929	|	1351	|
Giarre-Riposto	a.	0712	|	0946	|	0946	|	1408	|
Catania Centrale	a.	0740	|	1010	|	1010	|	1432	|
Augusta	a.	0836	|	1105	|	1105	|	1524	|
Siracusa	a.	0901	|	1129	|	1129	|	1548	|
Milazzo	a.	...	0615	...	0942	...	0857	...	1341
S. Agata di Militello	a.	...	0720	...	1041	...	0952	...	1443
Cefalù	a.	...	0831	...	1140	...	1049	...	1557
Termini Imerese	a.	...	0852	...	1200	...	1118	...	1617
Palermo Centrale	a.	...	0922	...	1231	...	1157	...	1655

		ICN 1964 B	ICN 1962 B	ICN 1954	ICN 1956	ICN 1958 C	ICN 1960 ⑥⑦	ICN 1958 ①–⑤	ICN 1960 ①–⑤
Palermo Centrale	d.	1258	...	1848	...	2025	...	2025	...
Termini Imerese	d.	1325	...	1917	...	2057	...	2057	...
Cefalù	d.	1346	...	1940	...	2123	...	2123	...
S. Agata di Militello	d.	1449	...	2032	...	2219	...	2214	...
Milazzo	d.	1558	...	2128	...	2314	...	2314	...
Siracusa	d.	|	1335	|	1910	|	2145	|	2145
Augusta	d.	|	1400	|	1932	|	2213	|	2213
Catania Centrale	d.	|	1454	|	2026	|	2258	|	2258
Giarre-Riposto	d.	|	1522	|	2051	|	2320	|	2320
Taormina-Giardini	d.	|	1539	|	2112	|	2335	|	2335
Messina Centrale	d.	1645	1645	2210	2210	0035	0035	0035	0035
Villa S. Giovanni	d.	1845	1845	2355	2355	|	|	|	|
Gioia Tauro	d.	1914	1914	|	|	|	|	|	|
Rosarno	d.	1922	1922	|	|	|	|	|	|
Lamezia Terme Centrale	d.	2000	2000	0105	0105	|	|	|	|
Paola	d.	2052	2052	|	|	|	|	|	|
Sapri	d.	2154	2154	|	|	|	|	|	|
Agropoli-Castellabate	d.	2253	2253	|	|	|	|	|	|
Battipaglia	d.	2313	2313	|	|	|	|	|	|
Salerno	a.	2330	2330	|	|	0642	0642	0753	0753
Napoli Centrale	a.	|	|	|	|	0722	0722	0833	0833
Formia-Gaeta	a.	|	|	0548	0548	0831	0831	0958	0958
Latina	a.	|	|	0623	0633	0910	0910	1046	1046
Roma Termini	a.	|	|	0724	0724	0951	0951	1134	1134
Firenze Campo di Marte	a.	0536	0536	...	...	...	...	...	...
Prato Centrale	a.	0604	0604	...	...	...	...	...	...
Bologna Centrale	a.	0707	0707	...	...	...	...	...	...
Modena	a.	0741	0741	...	...	...	...	...	...
Reggio Emilia	a.	0804	0804	...	...	...	...	...	...
Parma	a.	0821	0821	...	...	...	...	...	...
Fidenza	a.	0834	0834	...	...	...	...	...	...
Piacenza	a.	0901	0901	...	...	...	...	...	...
Milano Centrale	a.	1010	1010	...	...	...	...	...	...

A – Runs 18–35 minutes later Roma - Salerno on ⑥⑦.
B – Runs up to 2 hours later on Firenze - Milano on ⑥⑦ until Aug. 3.
C – ⑥⑦. On ⑦: Palermo d. 2110, Termini Imerese d. 2137, Cefalù d. 2206, S. Agata di Militello d. 2256, Milazzo d. 2350.

ROMA - MESSINA - SIRACUSA and PALERMO 642

For *ICN* overnight trains see Table **641**.

INTERCITY TRAINS ROMA - SIRACUSA and PALERMO — For other station calls see Table **640**

km		*IC* 721	*IC* 723	*IC* 729	*IC* 727					
	Roma Termini .... **640** d.	0726	0726	1126	1126	...	...	...	...	...
	Villa S. Giovanni .... **640** a.	1410	1410	1805	1805	...	...	...	...	...
0	**Villa S. Giovanni** .... ▲ d.	1425	1425	1820	1820	...	...	...	...	...
9	**Messina** Centrale .... ▲ a.	1535	1535	1935	1935	...	...	...	...	...
9	**Messina** Centrale .... d.	1550	1600	1950	2000	...	...	...	...	...
56	Taormina-Giardini .... d.	1626	|	|	2045	...	...	...	...	...
74	Giarre-Riposto .... d.	1642	|	|	2102	...	...	...	...	...
104	**Catania** Centrale .... a.	1709	|	|	2124	...	...	...	...	...
104	**Catania** Centrale .... d.	1712	|	|	2127	...	...	...	...	...
160	Augusta .... d.	1802	|	|	2213	...	...	...	...	...
191	**Siracusa** .... a.	1828	|	|	2238	...	...	...	...	...
45	Milazzo .... d.	...	1622	2011	...	...	...	...	...	...
115	S. Agata di Militello .... d.	...	1719	2110	...	...	...	...	...	...
173	Cefalù .... d.	...	1813	2205	...	...	...	...	...	...
204	Termini Imerese .... **645** d.	...	1832	2225	...	...	...	...	...	...
241	**Palermo** Centrale .... **645** a.	...	1902	2255	...	...	...	...	...	...

	IC 728	*IC* 722	*IC* 724	*IC* 730					
Palermo Centrale .... **645** d.	0705	...	...	1015	...	...	...	...	...
Termini Imerese .... **645** d.	0730	...	...	1051	...	...	...	...	...
Cefalù .... d.	0755	...	...	1112	...	...	...	...	...
S. Agata di Militello .... d.	0843	...	...	1158	...	...	...	...	...
Milazzo .... d.	0933	...	...	1249	...	...	...	...	...
Siracusa .... d.	|	0738	1025	|	...	...	...	...	...
Augusta .... d.	|	0804	1049	|	...	...	...	...	...
Catania Centrale .... a.	|	0849	1131	|	...	...	...	...	...
Catania Centrale .... d.	|	0852	1134	|	...	...	...	...	...
Giarre-Riposto .... d.	|	0915	1158	|	...	...	...	...	...
Taormina-Giardini .... d.	|	0930	1217	|	...	...	...	...	...
Messina Centrale .... a.	0955	1005	1300	1310	...	...	...	...	...
Messina Centrale .... ▲ d.	1015	1015	1320	1320	...	...	...	...	...
Villa S. Giovanni .... ▲ a.	1130	1130	1435	1435	...	...	...	...	...
Villa S. Giovanni .... **640** d.	1150	1150	1450	1450	...	...	...	...	...
Roma Termini .... **640** a.	1834	1834	2134	2134	...	...	...	...	...

MESSINA - CATANIA - SIRACUSA — 2nd class

km		⚒	†	⚒	⚒	†		⑥	⚒	†	⚒	†		⑥	Ⓐ	⚒	†	⚒		⚒	†	⚒	†	⚒
0	**Messina** Centrale .... d.	...	0513	0513	...	0539	...	0539	0630	0652	0725	0755	...	0755	0755	0915	0915	...	...	1025	1055	1115	1146	1200
47	Taormina-Giardini .... d.	...	0552	0552	...	0631	...	0632	0733	0756	0805	0857	...	0902	0902	1001	1001	...	...	1121	1137	1156	1246	1310
65	Giarre-Riposto .... d.	0530	0610	0610	0639	0657	...	0657	0751	0814	0820	0916	...	0924	0924	1017	1016	...	...	1140	1204	1216	1311	1331
95	**Catania** Centrale .... a.	0559	0630	0630	0712	0730	...	0737	0830	0847	0846	0952	...	0956	1000	1037	1037	...	...	1213	1224	1236	1340	1403
95	**Catania** Centrale .... **645** d.	0601	0635	0635	0714	...	...	...	...	0852	0851	0957	...	0958	...	...	1042	1050	...	1218	1226	1240	...	...
101	**Catania** F'narossa ✈ .... **645** d.	0610	0644	0646	0724	...	...	...	...	0859	0901	1003	...	1004	...	...	1052	1058	...	1225	1235	1249	...	...
151	Augusta .... d.	0705	0724	0730	0817	...	...	...	...	...	0941	...	...	...	...	...	1132	1145	...	...	1313	1333	...	...
182	**Siracusa** .... a.	0731	0748	0755	0840	...	...	...	...	...	1002	...	...	...	...	...	1154	1208	...	...	1339	1400	...	...

	⚒	⚒	⚒	†		⚒		⑥	Ⓐ	†	⚒			⚒		⚒			⚒	⚒	†	†	⚒
essina Centrale .... d.	1320	1335	1415	1435	...	1438	...	...	...	1614	1618	...	1715	1745	...	1825	...	...	1927	2018	2018	2134	2215
aormina-Giardini .... d.	1405	1448	1505	1539	...	1539	...	...	...	1723	1722	...	1758	1850	...	1931	...	...	2026	2126	2126	2237	2311
iarre-Riposto .... d.	1422	1509	1534	1559	...	1601	...	...	...	1741	1741	...	1814	1909	...	1950	...	...	2052	2143	2144	2256	2328
atania Centrale .... a.	1443	1539	1609	1625	...	1632	...	...	...	1818	1815	...	1833	1934	...	2022	...	...	2115	2215	2218	2329	2359
atania Centrale .... **645** d.	1503	...	1614	1630	...	...	...	1650	1650	1823	1818	...	1837	...	...	2024	2059	...	2120	2220	...	...	...
atania Fontanarossa ✈ .... **645** d.	1512	...	1623	1637	...	...	...	1658	1658	1832	1825	...	1845	...	...	2032	2108	...	2126	2228	...	...	...
ugusta .... d.	1551	...	...	...	...	...	...	1748	1740	...	...	...	1931	...	...	2113	2143	...	...	2308	...	...	...
racusa .... a.	1610	...	...	...	...	...	...	1808	1812	...	...	...	2000	...	...	2135	2210	...	...	2330	...	...	...

	⚒		⚒		†		†		⚒				⚒		†		⚒				Ⓐ		⚒
iracusa .... d.	...	...	...	...	...	...	0505	...	0506	...	0552	...	0640	...	...	...	0849	...	...	...	...	...	...
ugusta .... d.	...	...	...	...	...	...	0526	...	0526	...	0613	...	0706	...	...	...	0911	...	...	...	...	...	...
atania Fontanarossa ✈ .... **645** d.	...	...	0519	...	...	...	0604	...	0604	...	0651	...	0758	...	...	...	1000	...	...	...	...	...	...
atania Centrale .... **645** a.	...	...	0527	...	...	...	0611	...	0612	...	0705	...	0806	...	...	...	1010	...	...	...	...	...	...
atania Centrale .... d.	0501	...	0529	...	0530	...	0616	...	0617	...	...	...	0808	...	0915	...	1015	...	...	...	1105	...	1254
iarre-Riposto .... d.	0530	...	0603	...	0600	...	0639	...	0640	...	...	...	0831	...	0944	...	1037	...	...	...	1133	...	1327
aormina-Giardini .... d.	0552	...	0632	...	0631	...	0703	...	0701	...	...	...	0848	...	1010	...	1103	...	...	...	1156	...	1352
essina Centrale .... a.	0703	...	0742	...	0742	...	0753	...	0747	...	...	...	0942	...	1107	...	1159	...	...	...	1252	...	1506

	⚒		⚒		†		†		⚒						⑥		Ⓐ				⚒		⚒
iracusa .... d.	1253	...	1415	...	1416	...	...	...	...	...	1601	...	...	...	1712	...	1712	...	1815	...	1925	...	2005
ugusta .... d.	1316	...	1435	...	1438	...	...	...	...	...	1622	...	...	...	1732	...	1740	...	1841	...	1954	...	2025
atania Fontanarossa ✈ .... **645** d.	1356	...	1522	...	1517	...	...	...	...	...	1702	...	...	...	1823	...	1823	...	1919	...	2029	...	2107
atania Centrale .... **645** a.	1404	...	1528	...	1524	...	...	...	...	...	1708	...	...	...	1830	...	1830	...	1927	...	2035	...	2117
atania Centrale .... d.	1409	...	1531	...	1529	...	1535	...	1535	...	...	...	1719	...	1836	...	1836	...	1932	...	2037	...	2118
iarre-Riposto .... d.	1432	...	1552	...	1551	...	1608	...	1608	...	...	...	1741	...	1900	...	1900	...	1953	...	2112	...	2149
aormina-Giardini .... d.	1448	...	1611	...	1608	...	1641	...	1643	...	...	...	1758	...	1919	...	1920	...	2010	...	2140	...	2212
essina Centrale .... a.	1546	...	1656	...	1701	...	1759	...	1759	...	...	...	1840	...	2002	...	2003	...	2108	...	...	...	2303

MESSINA - PALERMO — Additional slower trains are available Messina - S. Agata di Militello and v.v. — 2nd class

km		⚒	⚒	⚒	†		⚒	⚒	†	⚒		⚒	⚒	⚒	†		⚒	†	⚒	⑥		Ⓐ	⚒	†	
0	**Messina** Centrale .... d.	0453	...	0636	0745	...	0756	1043	...	...	...	1227	...	1437	1437	...	...	1708	1714	...	...	...	...	1857	...
36	Milazzo .... d.	0511	...	0657	0804	...	0817	1101	...	...	...	1248	...	1453	1453	...	...	1725	1731	...	...	...	...	1915	...
106	S. Agata di Militello .... d.	0604	0641	0755	0909	...	0918	1159	1213	1217	...	1351	1415	1545	1545	...	1602	1818	1830	1850	...	1859	1950	2021	...
164	Cefalù .... d.	0657	0734	0846	1009	...	1005	1240	1309	1318	...	1432	1522	1636	1638	...	1710	1907	1911	2002	...	2002	2101	2109	...
195	Termini Imerese .... **645** d.	0720	0803	0903	1026	...	1023	1303	1332	1342	...	1455	1555	1700	1700	...	1736	1928	1936	2034	...	2034	2124	2128	...
232	**Palermo** Centrale .... **645** a.	0747	0845	0929	1055	...	1052	1332	1402	1412	...	1523	1622	1729	1729	...	1805	1955	2005	2106	...	2106	2154	2157	...

	⚒	⚒		†		⚒	⚒	⚒	†		⚒	⚒	⚒	†		⑥	Ⓐ	†	⚒		⚒	⚒	†	
alermo Centrale .... **645** d.	0507	0622	0827	0933	...	0936	1152	1338	1430	...	1430	1552	1632	1738	...	1752	1752	1833	1833	...	1938	2018	2033	...
ermini Imerese .... **645** d.	0532	0649	0852	1001	...	1003	1223	1406	1501	...	1505	1620	1659	1806	...	1821	1821	1858	1900	...	2006	2043	2058	...
efalù .... d.	0548	0707	0910	1022	...	1024	1251	1441	1526	...	1532	1646	1719	1835	...	1845	1845	1919	1921	...	2029	2100	2119	...
. Agata di Militello .... d.	0641	0758	1004	1125	...	1133	1345	1539	1623	...	1621	1750	1812	1944	...	1946	1948	2007	2007	...	2133	2152	2211	...
ilazzo .... d.	0735	0856	1051	...	...	...	...	...	1718	...	1718	...	1900	...	...	...	...	2054	2054	...	...	2246	2300	...
essina Centrale .... a.	0803	0920	1111	...	...	...	...	...	1738	...	1738	...	1920	...	...	...	...	2116	2116	...	...	2312	2322	...

▲ – Through trains are conveyed by ⛴ Villa S. Giovanni - Messina and v.v. See Table **2695** for other sailings.

CATANIA - RANDAZZO - RIPOSTO 644

Ferrovia Circumetnea

km		⚒	⚒ 🚌		⚒	⚒ 🚌		⚒	⚒ 🚌		⚒	⚒		⚒ 🚌	⚒		⚒	⚒ 🚌		⚒	⚒ 🚌		⚒	
	Catania Nesima .... d.	...	0645	...	...	0820	...	...	0920	...	...	...	...	1215	...	...	...	1330	...	...	1555	...	...	...
0	Paternò .... d.	...	0720	...	0725	0855	...	0859	0955	...	...	...	...	1250	1256	...	...	1405	...	1410	1630	...	1635	...
16	Adrano Nord .... d.	...	...	...	0755	...	...	0927	1035	...	1046	...	...	...	1325	...	...	...	...	1438	...	...	1703	...
32	Bronte .... d.	...	...	...	0818	...	...	0954	...	...	1113	...	...	...	1352	...	...	...	...	...	...	...	1730	...
51	**Randazzo** .... d.	0632	...	...	0846	...	...	1021	...	...	1141	1145	...	...	1419	...	1510	...	...	...	...	...	1757	...
89	Giarre .... a.	0738	...	...	...	...	...	...	...	...	...	1251	...	...	...	...	1616	...	...	...	...	...	...	...
91	**Riposto** .... a.	0742	...	...	...	...	...	...	...	...	...	1255	...	...	...	...	1620	...	...	...	...	...	...	...

	⚒	⚒ 🚌		⚒	⚒ 🚌		⚒	⚒ 🚌		⚒	⚒		⚒ 🚌	⚒		⚒ 🚌	⚒	⚒		⚒ 🚌		⚒	
iposto .... d.	...	...	...	...	...	...	...	...	...	0856	...	...	...	...	...	...	1341	...	...	...	...	1641	...
iarre .... d.	...	...	...	...	...	...	...	...	...	0900	...	...	...	...	...	...	1345	...	...	...	...	1645	...
andazzo .... d.	0547	...	...	0700	...	...	0858	...	...	1004	1043	...	...	1230	...	...	1449	1451	...	...	...	1749	...
ronte .... d.	0616	...	...	0730	...	...	0928	...	...	...	1113	...	...	1259	...	...	...	1520	...	...	...	...	...
drano Nord .... d.	0641	...	...	0754	...	...	0954	1000	...	...	1138	...	...	1324	...	...	...	1545	...	...	...	...	...
aternò .... d.	0711	0715	...	0825	0830	...	...	1040	...	...	1208	...	1210	1353	...	1355	...	1615	...	1620	...	...	...
atania Nesima .... a.	...	0755	...	...	0910	...	...	1120	...	...	...	...	1250	...	...	1435	...	...	...	1700	...	...	...

Metropolitana di Catania operates a metro service Nesima - San Nullo - Milo - Catania Borgo - Giuffrida - Galatea - Giovanni XXIII (for Catania Centrale) - Stesicoro and v.v. (9 km). Services run every 10–15 minutes 0640⚒/0830† - 2230 (later trains run on Friday and Saturday evenings).

645 SICILY

2nd class

For Messina - Siracusa and Palermo see Table **642**.

PALERMO - CALTANISSETTA - CATANIA

km		⚒	†	⚒		⚒	†	⚒		⚒	⚒	⚒		†	†	⚒		⚒	⚒	†		†A	⚒	
0	**Palermo** Centrale 642 d.	...	...	...	...	0729	0734	0931	...	...	...	1327	...	...	1531	1531	...	...	1731	1731	...	1925	1945	...
37	Termini Imerese 642 d.	...	...	...	...	0756	0759	0956	...	...	...	1353	...	...	1555	1555	...	...	1755	1755	...	1949	2012	...
70	Roccapalumba-Alia d.	...	...	...	...	|	|	|	...	...	...	1416	...	...	|	1617	...	...	1817	|	...	2017	2036	...
	Caltanissetta Centrale d.	0515	0705	0800	...	|	|	|	...	1306	1420	|	...	1512	|	|	...	1721	|	|	...	|	|	...
127	**Caltanissetta** Xirbi d.	0525	0713	0808	...	0901	0904	1101	...	1314	1428	1501	...	1520	1701	1701	...	1729	1905	1905	...	2100	2120	...
154	Enna d.	0556	0736	0834	...	0925	0928	1123	...	1342	1501	1524	...	1544	1723	1724	...	1754	1927	1927	...	...	2144	...
175	Dittaino a.	0618	0758	0855	...	0945	0948	1145	...	1403	1524	1545	...	1603	1745	1745	...	1812	1947	1947	...	...	2205	...
237	**Catania** Fontanarossa ✈ 642 a.	0725*	0905*	1002*	...	...	...	...	...	1510*	1631*	...	...	1710*	...	...	...	1919*	...	...	...	...	...	...
243	**Catania** Centrale 642 a.	0751*	0931*	1028*	...	...	...	...	...	1536*	1657*	...	...	1736*	...	...	...	1945*	...	...	...	...	...	...

	⚒	⚒	†		†	⚒	⚒		⚒	⚒	†A		⚒	†	⚒		†	⚒	⚒			⚒	
Catania Centrale 642 d.	...	...	...	...	0832*	...	0922*	...	...	...	...	...	...	...	1519*	...	...	...	1724*	...	1942*	2042*	...
Catania Fontanarossa ✈ 642 d.	...	...	...	...	0857*	...	0947*	...	...	...	...	...	...	...	1544*	...	...	...	1749*	...	2007*	2107*	...
Dittaino d.	0536	0810	0817	...	1010	1040	1100	...	1155	1418	...	...	1616	1616	1657	...	1818	1818	1902	...	2120	2220	...
Enna d.	0555	0835	0838	...	1030	1101	1124	...	1214	1437	...	...	1637	1637	1725	...	1837	1837	1928	...	2145	2241	...
Caltanissetta Xirbi d.	0617	0901	0904	...	1056	1126	1147	...	1237	1501	...	...	1701	1701	1757	...	1901	1901	1953	...	2209	2306	...
Caltanissetta Centrale a.	|	|	|	...	1104	|	1156	...	1245	|	1606	...	|	|	1804	...	|	|	2000	...	2220	2314	...
Roccapalumba-Alia d.	0709	|	|	...	...	|	...	...	...	|	|	...	|	1743	...	...	1943	|	...	...	...	...	...
Termini Imerese 642 d.	0732	1005	1014	...	...	1236	...	...	...	1606	|	...	1805	1807	...	...	2012	2012	...	...	...	...	...
Palermo Centrale 642 a.	0759	1029	1036	...	...	1258	...	...	...	1630	1751	...	1829	1831	...	...	2037	2037	...	...	...	...	...

AGRIGENTO and ROCCAPALUMBA-ALIA - CALTANISSETTA

km		⚒B	⚒	⚒	†	⚒				
0	**Agrigento** Centrale d.	0505	1250	1358	1700	1912	...	...	...	...
13	Aragona-Caldare d.	0519	1306	1414	1716	1928	...	...	...	...
43	Canicattì d.	|	1347	1451	1758	2007	...	...	...	...
78	**Caltanissetta** Centrale a.	|	1415	1520	1828	2037	...	...	...	...
84	**Caltanissetta** Xirbi a.	0718	...	...	1843	2050	...	...	...	...

	⚒	⚒	⚒	†	⚒				
Caltanissetta Xirbi d.	...	0636	1510	1910	...	...	...	...	...
Caltanissetta Centrale d.	0558	0646	1523	1923	1935	...	...	...	...
Canicattì d.	0635	0725	1605	2005	2015	...	...	...	...
Aragona-Caldare d.	0705	0754	1643	2043	2052	...	...	...	...
Agrigento Centrale a.	0730	0810	1659	2059	2109	...	...	...	...

km		⚒B	⚒	⚒	⑥	⚒	†A			
0	**Roccapalumba-Alia** d.	0620	0730	1455	1553	1954	2017	...	...	...
57	**Caltanissetta** Xirbi a.	0718	0821	1556	1643	2044	2100	...	...	...
63	**Caltanissetta** Centrale a.	0737	0838	1613	1704	2100	2120	...	...	...

	⚒	⚒	⚒	†A	⚒				
Caltanissetta Centrale d.	0502	1256	1405	1606	1806	...	...	...	...
Caltanissetta Xirbi d.	0517	1311	1423	1624	1822	...	...	...	...
Roccapalumba-Alia a.	0609	1405	1533	...	1933	...	...	...	...

PALERMO - AGRIGENTO

km		⚒	⚒		⚒	†		Ⓐ	⚒		Ⓐ				Ⓐ		⚒							
0	**Palermo** Centrale 642 d.	0543	0743	...	0843	0850	...	1043	1143	...	1243	1343	...	1443	1543	...	1643	1743	...	1843	2043	...	...	...
37	Termini Imerese 642 d.	0612	0812	...	0912	0917	...	1112	1212	...	1312	1412	...	1512	1612	...	1712	1812	...	1912	2112	...	...	...
70	Roccapalumba-Alia a.	0642	0842	...	0939	0946	...	1139	1242	...	1342	1442	...	1540	1642	...	1739	1842	...	1942	2142	...	...	...
70	Roccapalumba-Alia d.	0643	0843	...	0943	0947	...	1143	1243	...	1343	1443	...	1544	1643	...	1743	1843	...	1943	2143	...	...	...
125	Aragona-Caldare d.	0732	0932	...	1032	1032	...	1232	1332	...	1432	1532	...	1632	1732	...	1832	1932	...	2032	2232	...	...	...
139	**Agrigento** Centrale a.	0747	0947	...	1047	1049	...	1247	1347	...	1447	1547	...	1647	1747	...	1847	1947	...	2047	2247	...	...	...

	⚒	⚒	⚒		Ⓐ	†	⚒		†	⚒	Ⓐ			⚒	Ⓑ						⚒		
Agrigento Centrale d.	0454	0522	0615	...	0715	0815	0815	...	1015	1015	1215	...	1315	1415	1515	...	1615	1715	1815	...	2015	...	...
Aragona-Caldare d.	0508	0536	0632	...	0732	0830	0832	...	1032	1032	1232	...	1332	1432	1532	...	1632	1732	1832	...	2032	...	...
Roccapalumba-Alia a.	0551	0616	0716	...	0815	0913	0916	...	1114	1116	1316	...	1413	1514	1613	...	1716	1813	1916	...	2116	...	...
Roccapalumba-Alia d.	0552	0617	0717	...	0819	0914	0917	...	1115	1117	1317	...	1417	1517	1617	...	1717	1817	1917	...	2117	...	...
Termini Imerese 642 d.	0623	0651	0749	...	0849	0942	0949	...	1144	1149	1349	...	1449	1549	1649	...	1749	1849	1949	...	2149	...	...
Palermo Centrale 642 a.	0655	0717	0822	...	0917	1010	1017	...	1212	1217	1417	...	1517	1617	1717	...	1817	1917	2017	...	2217	...	...

PALERMO - TRAPANI

Service until May 31

km		⚒	⚒	⚒	⚒		†	⚒	⚒	†		⚒	†	⚒	⚒		⚒	⚒	†	⚒			†	⚒
0	**Palermo** Centrale ▲ d.	...	...	...	...	...	...	...	...	...	...	...	...	...	...	...	...	...	...	...	...	...	...	...
32	Piraineto d.	...	...	...	...	...	...	...	...	0930	...	1121	1231	...	...	...	1522	...	...	...	...	1835	2122	2135
73	Castellammare del Golfo d.	...	...	...	0727	...	...	...	...	1013	...	1201	1311	...	...	...	1605	...	...	...	...	1917	2201	2214
79	Alcamo Diramazione d.	...	...	...	0734	...	...	...	...	1021	...	1209	1318	...	1503	...	1613	...	...	...	...	1925	2208	2221
121	Castelvetrano d.	0600	0620	0728	0819	...	0830	0949	1100	1104	...	1247	1359	1414	1540	...	1657	1735	1750	1910	...	2010	2250	2303
144	Mazara del Vallo d.	0621	0652	0755	0842	...	0852	1010	1124	1126	...	1318	...	1441	1608	...	...	1801	1814	1940	...	2033	...	...
165	Marsala d.	0654	0720	0820	0912	...	0912	1030	1149	1154	...	1348	...	1505	1626	...	...	1823	1837	2001	...	2056	...	...
196	**Trapani** a.	0746*	0819*	0912*	1006*	...	1006*	1130*	1308*	1314*	...	1440*	...	...	1722*	...	...	1916*	1932*	2100*	...	2157*	...	...

	⚒	⚒	†	⚒	⚒		†	⚒	⚒	⚒	⚒		⚒	†	⚒ 🚌	⚒	⚒ 🚌		Ⓐ 🚌		⚒ 🚌	⚒ 🚌	
Trapani d.	...	0528*	0503*	0634*	0733*	...	0818*	0945*	1111*	1146*	1303*	...	1348*	1426*	1438	...	1600	...	1730	...	1815	1920	...
Marsala d.	...	0627	0629	0724	0846	...	0945	1058	1225	1314	1416	...	1515	1553	1521	1636	1659	...	1813	1847	1914	2019	2124
Mazara del Vallo d.	...	0651	0652	0756	0912	...	1007	1123	1246	1346	1442	...	1537	1615	1554	1657	1746	...	1846	1908	2001	...	2148
Castelvetrano d.	0500	0718	0718	0818	0939	...	1029	1152	1314	1412	1510	...	1606	1645	1623	1724	1824	...	1915	1937	2038	...	2216
Alcamo Diramazione d.	0541	...	0756	0857	...	...	1111	...	1353	1452	...	...	1644	1724	...	...	...	...	...	2015	...	...	...
Castellammare del Golfo d.	0548	...	0803	0904	...	...	1119	...	1401	...	...	...	1651	1731	...	...	...	...	...	2022	...	...	...
Piraineto d.	0630	...	0848	0946	...	...	1205	...	1444	...	...	...	1735	1815	...	...	...	...	...	2109	...	...	...
Palermo Centrale ▲ a.	...	...	...	...	...	...	...	...	...	...	...	...	...	...	...	...	...	...	...	...	...	...	...

SIRACUSA - GELA - CALTANISSETTA

km		⚒	⚒	⚒d	⚒	⚒	⚒	⚒	⚒	⚒
0	**Siracusa** ◧ d.	...	0533	...	...	1032	...	1435	1540	1739
62	Pozzallo ◧ d.	...	0646	...	...	1137	...	1541	1653	1850
92	Modica ◧ d.	0540	0720	0734	0918	1213	1347	1616	1733	1926
112	Ragusa d.	0602	0744	0756	0941	1235	1409	1648	1755	1955
153	Vittoria d.	0645	...	0838	1022	1323	1447	1729	1836	...
183	**Gela** d.	0708	...	0904	1049	1350	1509	1753	...	...
218	Licata d.	0736	...	0931	...	...	1536	...	...	...
264	Canicattì d.	0816	...	1010	...	...	1615	...	...	...
293	**Caltanissetta** Centrale a.	0841	...	1040	...	...	1642	...	...	...
299	**Caltanissetta** Xirbi a.	0852	...	1054	...	...	1655	...	...	...

	⚒	⚒	⚒	⚒	⚒	⚒	⚒	⚒d	⚒
Caltanissetta Xirbi d.	...	...	...	...	...	...	...	1710	1911
Caltanissetta Centrale d.	...	...	0510	...	...	...	...	1720	1920
Canicattì d.	...	...	0538	...	...	...	...	1747	1946
Licata d.	...	...	0613	...	...	...	...	1822	2021
Gela d.	...	...	0642	0725	1254	1515	1818	1849	2048
Vittoria d.	...	...	...	0749	1322	1541	1845	1913	2112
Ragusa d.	...	0759	...	0839	1410	1626	1931	1958	2158
Modica d.	0552	0820	...	0901	1431	1647	1954	2020	2221
Pozzallo d.	0624	0853	...	...	1503	1720	2026	...	...
Siracusa a.	0737	0956	...	...	1618	1834	2135	...	...

A – 2nd class Palermo - Caltanissetta Centrale and v.v.
B – 2nd class Agrigento - Caltanissetta Centrale.
d – Not on days before public holidays.
◧ – Also Siracusa - Modica at 2035 ⚒.
▲ – Please check locally for connections from/to Palermo.
* – By 🚌.

MALTA

Bus services on Malta and Gozo are operated by Malta Public Transport www.publictransport.com.mt. Travellers will also find useful information on the unofficial website www.maltabybus.com

649 PRINCIPAL BUS SERVICES

Routes from Valletta: **X4** Airport - Hal Far, **1** L'Isla (Senglea), **2/4** Birgu (Vittoriosa), **3** Birgu - Smart City - Rinella - Kalkara, **13-15** Sliema - San Giljan (St Julian's), **13** Bahar ic-Caghaq, **31/45/48** Mosta - Bugibba (**45** via Qawra seafront), **31/43/45** Naxxar, **41/42** Mosta - St Paul's Bay - Mellieha - Ghadira - Cirkewwa (for Gozo ferry), **44** Ghajn Tuffieha (Golden Bay), **49** Armier Bay (summer) **51-53** Rabat/Mdina, **52/56** Dingli, **61** Zebbug, **62** Siggiewi, **71/73** Zurrieq, **72** Qrendi, **74** Hagar Qim - Blue Grotto, **80/82/X4** Birzebbuga, **81/85** Marsaxlokk, **91-93** Marsaskala, **94** Xghajra.

Other routes: **X1** Airport - Cirkewwa, **X2** Airport - Sliema, **X3** Airport - Rabat - Bugibba, **186** Bugibba - Ta' Qali - Rabat, **202** Sliema - Naxxar - Mosta - Rabat, **203** Sliema - Naxxar - Mosta - Bugibba **212** Sliema - San Giljan - Bugibba, **221** Bugibba - Mellieha - Cirkewwa, **222** Sliema - St Paul's Bay - Mellieha - Cirkewwa, **223** Bugibba - Ghajn Tuffieha, **225** Sliema - St Paul's Bay - Ghajn Tuffieha

Gozo: routes from Rabat (Victoria): **301/303** Mgarr (for Cirkewwa ferry), **302** Ramla, **305** Sannat, **306/330** Xlendi, **307** Xaghra, **308** Ta' Pinu - Ghasri, **309** Zebbug, **310** Marsalforn, **311** Dwejra

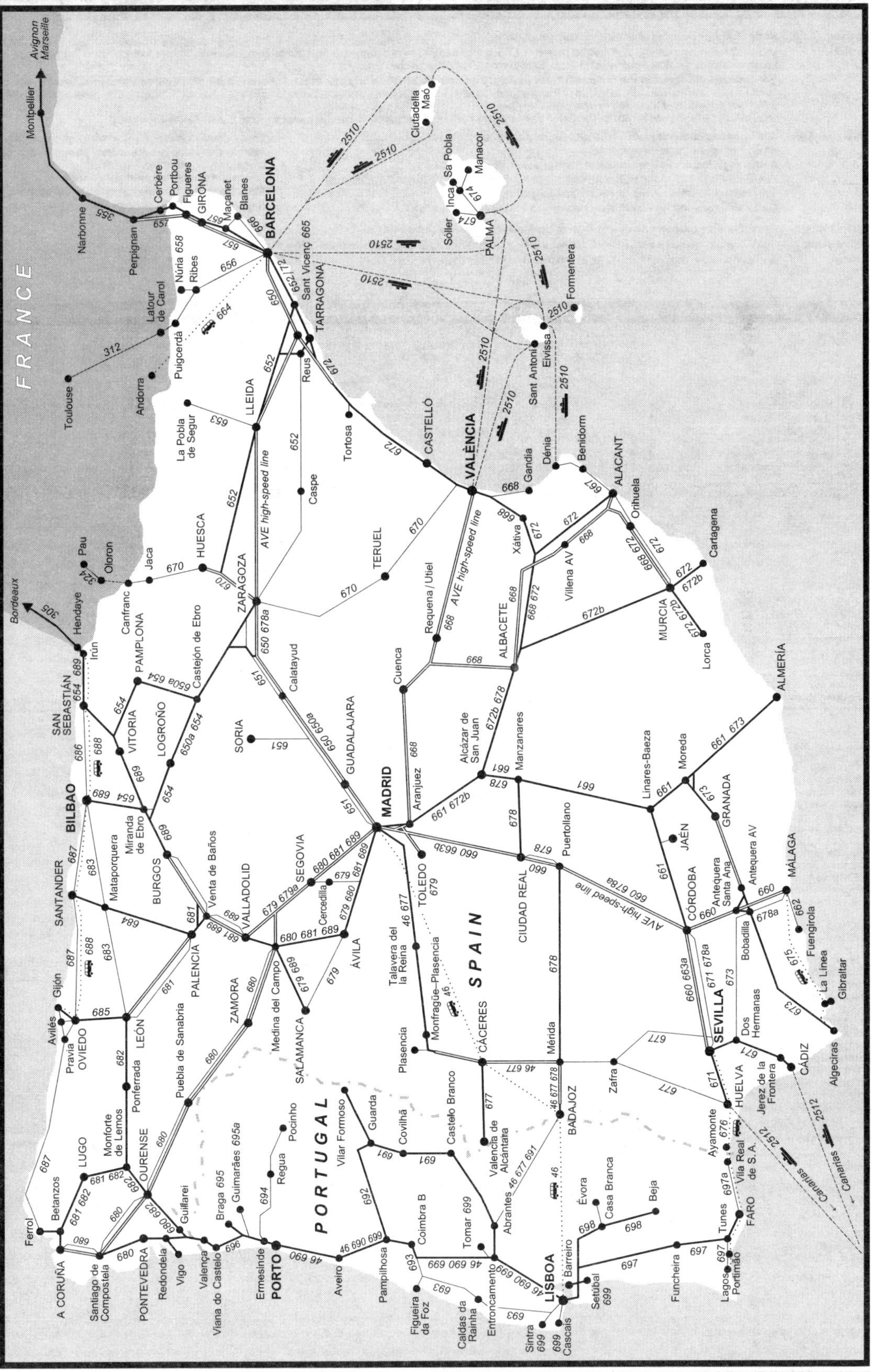
FRANCE
SPAIN
PORTUGAL
MADRID
BARCELONA
VALÈNCIA
BILBAO
SEVILLA
LISBOA
PORTO
ZARAGOZA
MÁLAGA
GRANADA
CÓRDOBA
ALACANT
MURCIA
VALLADOLID
SALAMANCA
BADAJOZ
CÁCERES
SANTANDER
OVIEDO
LEÓN
BURGOS
PALENCIA
ZAMORA
SEGOVIA
ÁVILA
TOLEDO
GUADALAJARA
LLEIDA
TARRAGONA
GIRONA
HUESCA
PAMPLONA
VITORIA
LOGROÑO
SORIA
TERUEL
CASTELLÓ
ALBACETE
CIUDAD REAL
JAÉN
ALMERÍA
CÁDIZ
HUELVA
FARO
A CORUÑA
LUGO
OURENSE
PONTEVEDRA
PALMA
AVE high-speed line
Toulouse
Narbonne
Montpellier
Avignon
Marseille
Perpignan
Bordeaux
Hendaye
Irún
SAN SEBASTIÁN
Pau
Oloron
Canfranc
Jaca
Andorra
Puigcerdà
Latour de Carol
Núria
Ribes
Cerbère
Portbou
Figueres
Maçanet
Blanes
Sant Vicenç
Reus
Tortosa
Caspe
La Pobla de Segur
Calatayud
Castejón de Ebro
Miranda de Ebro
Mataporquera
Venta de Baños
Medina del Campo
Cercedilla
Gijón
Avilés
Pravia
Ponferrada
Monforte de Lemos
Puebla de Sanabria
Ferrol
Betanzos
Santiago de Compostela
Redondela
Vigo
Guillarei
Valença
Viana do Castelo
Braga
Guimarães
Ermesinde
Regua
Pocinho
Aveiro
Pampilhosa
Coimbra B
Figueira da Foz
Caldas da Rainha
Entroncamento
Tomar
Abrantes
Sintra
Cascais
Barreiro
Setúbal
Évora
Casa Branca
Beja
Funcheira
Tunes
Lagos
Portimão
Vila Real de S. A.
Ayamonte
Vilar Formoso
Guarda
Covilhã
Castelo Branco
Valencia de Alcántara
Plasencia
Monfragüe–Plasencia
Talavera de la Reina
Mérida
Zafra
Aranjuez
Cuenca
Requena / Utiel
Alcázar de San Juan
Manzanares
Puertollano
Linares-Baeza
Moreda
Antequera AV
Antequera Santa Ana
Bobadilla
Fuengirola
La Línea
Gibraltar
Algeciras
Dos Hermanas
Jerez de la Frontera
Villena AV
Xàtiva
Gandia
Dénia
Benidorm
Orihuela
Cartagena
Lorca
Sant Antoni
Eivissa
Formentera
Sóller
Inca
Sa Pobla
Manacor
Ciutadella
Maó
Canarias

SPAIN

Operator: **Renfe Operadora** – unless otherwise indicated. www.renfe.es

Services: Unless otherwise indicated (by '2' in the train column or 2 in the notes), all trains convey both first- and second-class seating accommodation. Up to four classes of accommodation is available on services: Prémiun, Elige Confort, Elige Estándar and Básico.
🍸 indicates a buffet car (*cafetería*) or a mobile trolley service. ✕ indicates the availability of hot meals served from the buffet car. Meals are served free of extra charge, on Mondays to Fridays and Sundays, to holders of *Prémiun* tickets on all *AVE* and *Euromed* trains. Note that catering services may not be available throughout a train's journey particularly in the case of trains with multiple origins / destinations.
Local (*Media Distancia*) and suburban (*Cercanías*) trains are shown without an indication of category except for some fast ***Media Distancia*** (*MD*).

Train categories:
Alta Velocidad Española (*AVE*): High-speed trains running on the standard-gauge lines.
Alvia: High-speed gauge-changing trains.
Avant (*Av*): Medium-distance high-speed trains on the standard-gauge lines.
Euromed (*Em*): *AVE*-like trains running on the broad-gauge Barcelona - València - Alacant route.
iryo: High-speed trains running on the standard-gauge lines.
Ouigo, avlo: Low-cost high-speed trains running on the standard-gauge lines.
Train à Grande Vitesse (*TGV*): French high-speed trains.
Intercity (*IC*): Long distance express trains, including gauge-changing trains and Talgo stock. Also certain medium and short distance trains.
Media Distancia (*MD*): Medium distance regional trains.
Regional Exprés (*RE*): Medium distance regional trains.

Reservations: Reservations are compulsory in all long distance trains, ***Avant*** and ***Media Distancia*** trains.

Supplements: Higher fares, incorporating a supplement, are payable for travel by *Alvia*, *AVE*, *Euromed*, *Intercity* and *TGV* services.

Timings: Timings have been compiled from the latest information supplied by operators.

650 MADRID - ZARAGOZA - BARCELONA — High-speed services

km		*Av* 8077 ①–⑤	*avlo* 6301 ①–④	*iryo* 6061 ①–⑤	*Av* 8087	*avlo* 6301 ⑤⑥⑦	*AVE* 3063 ①–④	*AVE* 3071 ①–⑤	*Ouigo* 6471	*iryo* 6071 ①–⑤	*AVE* 3073	*AVE* 3081 ①–⑤	*iryo* 6081 ⑥⑦	*AVE* 3083 ①②③④⑥⑦	*iryo* 6081 ①–⑤	*AVE* 3091 ①–⑥	*iryo* 6091 U	*iryo* 6091 T
	Sevilla **660** d.	...	...	...	...	...	...	...	...	...	...	...	...	...	...	...	...	...
	Málaga **660** d.	...	...	...	...	...	...	...	...	...	...	...	...	...	...	...	...	...
0	**Madrid** Puerta de Atocha d.	...	0616	0622	...	0627	0627	0657	0702	0722	0727	0757	0807	0827	0832	0857	0922	0922
64	Guadalajara - Yebes d.	...	|	|	...	|	|	|	|	|	0753	|	|	|	|	|	|	|
221	Calatayud d.	...	|	|	...	0727	0727	|	|	|	|	|	|	|	|	|	|	|
307	**Zaragoza** Delicias d.	...	|	|	...	0753	0753	|	0823	|	0852	|	0926	0946	|	|	1041	1041
447	Lleida d.	0705	|	|	0800	|	|	|	|	|	0937	|	|	|	|	|	|	|
526	Camp de Tarragona d.	0735	|	|	0831	|	|	|	|	|	1006	|	|	|	|	1103	|	1139
621	**Barcelona** Sants a.	0811	0853	0859	0905	0925	0925	0934	0954	0959	1046	1034	1059	1119	1109	1141	1214	1221
	Girona **657** a.	...	...	...	...	...	...	...	...	...	1132	...	...	...	...	...	...	...
	Figueres Vilafant **657** a.	...	...	...	...	...	...	...	...	...	1149	...	...	...	...	...	...	...

	AVE 2561	*iryo* 6011	*Ouigo* 6501	*avlo* 6303	*AVE* 3993	*AVE* 3943	*iryo* 6111	*AVE* 3113	*iryo* 6121	*AVE* 3123 Ⓑ	*AVE* 3123 ⑥	*AVE* 3131 Ⓑ	*AVE* 9725 M	*AVE* 3141 ④⑤	*iryo* 6141 Ⓑ	*Ouigo* 6541		
Sevilla **660** d.	0600	0654	...	...	...	0837	...	...	...	...	...	...	...	...	...	...	...	...
Málaga **660** d.	|	|	...	...	0822	|	...	...	...	...	...	...	...	...	...	...	...	...
Madrid Puerta de Atocha d.	0927	0957	1002	1027	|	|	1122	1127	1222	1227	1230	1257	1318	1357	1402	1412	...	...
Guadalajara - Yebes d.	|	|	|	|	|	|	|	|	|	|	|	|	1346	|	|	|	...	...
Calatayud d.	|	|	|	|	|	|	|	1226	|	|	|	|	|	|	|	|	...	...
Zaragoza Delicias d.	1047	1118	1125	1148	1237	1237	1241	1252	1341	1346	1346	|	1446	|	1523	|	...	...
Lleida d.	1134	|	|	|	1319	1319	|	1337	|	1431	1431	|	|	|	|	|	...	...
Camp de Tarragona d.	1202	|	1221	|	1345	1345	|	1406	|	|	|	|	1542	|	|	|	...	...
Barcelona Sants a.	1241	1249	1304	1319	1425	1425	1414	1446	1514	1544	1544	1534	1622	1634	1654	1649	...	...
Girona **657** a.	1330	...	...	...	...	...	...	...	...	1632	...	...	1713	...	...	...	...	...
Figueres Vilafant **657** a.	1347	...	...	...	...	...	...	...	...	1649	...	...	1730	...	...	...	...	...

	AVE 3143 Ⓑ	*iryo* 6021	*AVE* 3151 ①–⑤	*avlo* 6305	*AVE* 3161 Ⓑ	*Av* 8187	*AVE* 3163 ①–⑤	*AVE* 3163 ⑥⑦	*iryo* 6161	*AVE* 3171 Ⓑ	*Ouigo* 6571	*iryo* 6171 Ⓑ	*Av* 8207 ①–⑤	*AVE* 3173 ①–④	*avlo* 6373 ⑤⑥⑦	*AVE* 2553 Ⓑ		
Sevilla **660** d.	...	...	...	...	...	...	...	...	...	...	...	...	...	...	...	...	...	...
Málaga **660** d.	...	1133	...	...	...	...	...	...	...	...	...	...	...	...	...	1458	...	...
Madrid Puerta de Atocha d.	1427	1442	1457	1527	1557	...	1627	1627	1637	1657	1717	1722	...	1727	1727	1757	...	...
Guadalajara - Yebes d.	|	|	|	|	|	...	|	|	|	|	|	|	...	1754	1754	|	...	...
Calatayud d.	1526	|	|	1626	|	...	|	|	|	|	|	|	...	|	|	|	...	...
Zaragoza Delicias d.	1552	1603	|	1652	|	...	1746	1746	|	|	|	1841	...	1852	1852	|	...	...
Lleida d.	|	|	|	1737	|	1755	|	|	|	|	|	|	1923	1937	1937	|	...	...
Camp de Tarragona d.	|	|	|	1806	|	1827	|	|	|	|	|	|	1955	2006	2006	|	...	...
Barcelona Sants a.	1724	1741	1734	1846	1834	1903	1919	1919	1914	1934	1954	2014	2035	2046	2046	2034	...	...
Girona **657** a.	1816	...	...	...	...	...	2011	...	...	...	...	...	...	...	...	...	...	...
Figueres Vilafant **657** a.	1834	...	...	...	...	...	2028	...	...	...	...	...	...	...	...	...	...	...

	AVE 3183	*iryo* 6181 Ⓑ	*AVE* 3931 G	*AVE* 2861 H	*AVE* 3191 ①②③④⑦	*AVE* 3191 ⑤	*iryo* 6013	*AVE* 3991	*AVE* 3941	*avlo* 6309	*AVE* 3201 Ⓑ	*iryo* 6201	*AVE* 3203	*Ouigo* 6611	*AVE* 2883 Ⓑ			
Sevilla **660** d.	...	...	...	1545	...	...	1627	...	1636	...	...	...	...	...	...	...	...	...
Málaga **660** d.	...	...	...	|	...	...	|	1620	|	...	...	...	...	...	1755	...	...	...
Madrid Puerta de Atocha d.	1827	1832	...	1850	1857	1857	1929	|	|	1934	2005	2022	2027	2102	2107	...	...	...
Guadalajara - Yebes d.	|	|	...	1917	|	|	|	|	|	2001	|	|	2053	|	|	...	...	...
Calatayud d.	|	|	...	2004	|	|	|	|	|	2037	|	|	2133	|	|	...	...	...
Zaragoza Delicias d.	1946	|	2001	2030	|	|	2048	2037	2037	2103	|	2142	2158	2219	2227	...	...	...
Lleida d.	|	|	2050	...	|	|	|	2119	2119	2148	|	|	2242	|	|	...	...	...
Camp de Tarragona d.	2046	|	2118	...	|	|	|	2152	2152	2217	|	|	2309	|	|	...	...	...
Barcelona Sants a.	2124	2109	2154	...	2134	2134	2221	2233	2233	2255	2242	2314	2348	2354	2359	...	...	...
Girona **657** a.	...	...	...	...	2222	...	...	...	...	2343	...	...	...	...	...	...	...	...
Figueres Vilafant **657** a.	...	...	...	...	2239	...	...	...	...	2359	...	...	...	...	...	...	...	...

A – ①④⑤⑥⑦ until June 29; daily from June 30.
G – From Granada (Table **660**).
H – To Huesca (Tables **650a**).
M – To Marseille (Table **13**).
T – June 15 - Sept. 14.
U – Until June 14 and Sept. 15 - Dec. 13.

Ouigo – Low-cost ***TGV*** Euroduplex services branded **Ouigo**: www.ouigo.com.
avlo – Low-cost ***AVE*** Renfe services branded **avlo**: www.avlorenfe.com
iryo – ***ETR*** 1000 services branded **iryo**: www.iryo.eu Services subject to alteration during holiday periods.
☛ *AVE* trains convey ✕ and 🍸. *Avant* trains (*Av*) are *Turista* class only.

High-speed services — BARCELONA - ZARAGOZA - MADRID — 650

	AVE 3052 ①–④	*iryo* 6060 ①–⑤	*AVE* 3862 ①–⑤	*AVE* 3062 ⑥	*AVE* 3060 ①–④	*Ouigo* 6470	*avlo* 6302	*AVE* 3930 G	*AVE* 3270 ①–④	*iryo* 6070 ①–⑤	*AVE* 3662 ①–⑤	*AVE* 3872 ①–⑥ H	*AVE* 3272 ⑦ H	*iryo* 6080 ⑥⑦	*iryo* 6080 ①–⑤	*AVE* 3882 Ⓑ	*AVE* 3082 ⑥	
Figueres Vilafant **657** d.	...	...	...	...	...	...	0530	...	...	...	0620	...	...	...	...	...	...	...
Girona **657** d.	...	...	...	...	...	...	0546	...	...	...	0636	...	...	...	...	...	...	...
Barcelona Sants d.	0540	0545	0550	0550	0620	0625	0635	0645	0700	0705	0727	...	...	0750	0755	0800	0800	...
Camp de Tarragona d.	|	|	0624	0624	|	|	|	0719	|	|	0800	...	...	|	|	0834	0834	...
Lleida d.	|	|	0652	0652	|	|	|	0748	|	|	|	...	...	|	|	0902	0902	...
Zaragoza Delicias d.	0705	0709	0736	0736	|	0757	0801	0835	|	|	|	0855	0855	0914	|	0945	0945	...
Calatayud d.	|	|	0801	0801	|	|	|	...	|	|	|	0921	0921	|	|	1010	1010	...
Guadalajara - Yebes d.	|	|	0840	0840	|	|	|	...	|	|	|	1003	1003	|	|	|	|	...
Madrid Puerta de Atocha a.	0832	0837	0915	0910	0857	0917	0927	...	0937	0942	1012	1038	1038	1042	1032	1119	1119	...
Málaga **660** a.	...	...	1226	...	...	...	...	...	...	...	...	|	...	...	...	1423	...	...
Sevilla **660** a.	...	...	...	...	...	...	...	...	...	...	...	1345	...	...	...	...	...	...

	AVE 3940	*AVE* 3990	*iryo* 6090	*AVE* 3092 ①–⑥	*AVE* 3092 ⑦	*iryo* 6010	*avlo* 6304	*Ouigo* 6500	*iryo* 6110 Ⓑ	*AVE* 3112	*iryo* 6020	*avlo* 6322 ⑤⑥⑦	*AVE* 3122 ①–④	*AVE* 9730 C	*iryo* 6130	*AVE* 3130 ①–⑤	*iryo* 6014	
Figueres Vilafant **657** d.	...	...	...	0755	...	...	...	...	...	...	...	...	...	1142	...	...	...	...
Girona **657** d.	...	...	...	0811	...	...	...	...	...	...	...	...	...	1159	...	...	...	...
Barcelona Sants d.	0830	0830	0845	0900	0900	0943	0955	1040	1045	1100	1150	1200	1200	1250	1305	1325	1345	...
Camp de Tarragona d.	0905	0905	|	|	|	|	1029	|	|	|	|	1234	1234	1323	|	|	|	...
Lleida d.	0934	0934	|	|	|	|	1056	|	|	|	|	1301	1301	|	|	|	|	...
Zaragoza Delicias d.	1020	1020	1009	1026	1026	1114	1141	1206	|	1226	1313	1345	1345	1425	1429	|	1509	...
Calatayud d.	|	|	|	|	|	|	1206	|	|	|	|	|	|	|	|	|	|	...
Guadalajara - Yebes d.	|	|	|	|	|	|	1246	|	|	|	|	1445	1445	|	|	|	|	...
Madrid Puerta de Atocha a.	|	|	1137	1152	1152	1242	1319	1332	1322	1352	1442	1519	1519	1552	1557	1602	1637	...
Málaga **660** a.	|	1454	...	...	...	|	...	...	...	...	1742	...	...	...	...	...	|	...
Sevilla **660** a.	1422	...	...	...	...	1537	...	...	...	...	...	...	...	...	...	...	1937	...

	Ouigo 6540	*avlo* 6308	*AVE* 3140 ④⑤	*iryo* 6150 Ⓑ	*AVE* 3152	*AVE* 3942	*AVE* 3992	*AVE* 3150 ①–⑤	*iryo* 6160 Ⓑ	*AVE* 3162	*Av* 8166	*AVE* 3160 Ⓑ	*AVE* 3172	*AVE* 3170 Ⓑ	*iryo* 6180 Ⓑ	*Ouigo* 6570	*AVE* 3182	
Figueres Vilafant **657** d.	...	...	...	...	...	...	...	...	...	1455	...	...	...	...	...	...	...	...
Girona **657** d.	...	...	...	...	...	...	...	...	...	1511	...	...	...	...	...	...	...	...
Barcelona Sants d.	1350	1400	1425	1455	1500	1517	1517	1525	1552	1600	1605	1625	1700	1725	1735	1740	1800	...
Camp de Tarragona d.	|	1432	|	|	|	1553	1553	|	|	1634	1642	|	|	|	|	|	1834	...
Lleida d.	|	1500	|	|	|	1626	1626	|	|	1701	1713	|	|	|	|	|	1901	...
Zaragoza Delicias d.	|	1544	|	|	1626	1712	1712	|	1719	1745	...	|	1826	|	|	|	1945	...
Calatayud d.	|	1610	|	|	|	|	|	|	|	1810	...	|	|	|	|	|	2010	...
Guadalajara - Yebes d.	|	|	|	|	|	|	|	|	|	|	...	|	|	|	|	|	|	...
Madrid Puerta de Atocha a.	1627	1719	1701	1732	1752	|	|	1802	1851	1919	...	1902	1952	2002	2012	2017	2119	...
Málaga **660** a.	...	...	...	...	...	|	2143	...	...	...	...	...	...	...	...	...	...	...
Sevilla **660** a.	...	...	...	...	...	2124	...	...	...	...	...	...	...	...	...	...	...	...

	Av 8186 ①–⑤	*AVE* 3180 Ⓑ	*AVE* 3192	*iryo* 6190	*AVE* 3190 Ⓑ	*avlo* 6310	*Av* 8206	*Ouigo* 6610	*iryo* 6210	*AVE* 3212	*AVE* 3610 ⑤⑦	*Av* 8216 Ⓐ						
Figueres Vilafant **657** d.	...	...	1735	...	...	...	...	...	...	...	...	...	...	...	...	...	...	...
Girona **657** d.	...	...	1751	...	...	...	...	...	...	...	...	...	...	...	...	...	...	...
Barcelona Sants d.	1805	1825	1840	1905	1925	2000	2005	2040	2055	2105	2115	2125	...	...	...	...	...	...
Camp de Tarragona d.	1842	|	1914	|	|	2034	2042	2113	|	|	|	2202	...	...	...	...	...	...
Lleida d.	1913	|	1942	|	|	2101	2113	|	|	|	|	2233	...	...	...	...	...	...
Zaragoza Delicias d.	...	|	2026	2029	|	2145	...	2215	2219	2230	|	...	...	...	...	...	...	...
Calatayud d.	...	|	|	|	|	|	...	|	|	|	|	...	...	...	...	...	...	...
Guadalajara - Yebes d.	...	|	|	|	|	2245	...	|	|	|	|	...	...	...	...	...	...	...
Madrid Puerta de Atocha a.	...	2102	2152	2157	2202	2319	...	2342	2347	2358	2352	...	...	...	...	...	...	...
Málaga **660** a.	...	...	...	...	...	...	...	...	...	...	...	...	...	...	...	...	...	...
Sevilla **660** a.	...	...	...	...	...	...	...	...	...	...	...	...	...	...	...	...	...	...

A – ①④⑤⑥⑦ until June 29; daily from June 30.

C – From Marseille (Table **13**).

G – To Granada (Table **660**).

H – From Huesca (Tables **670**).

Ouigo – Low-cost ***TGV*** Euroduplex services branded **Ouigo**: www.ouigo.com

avlo – Low-cost ***AVE*** Renfe services branded **avlo**: www.avlorenfe.com

iryo – ***ETR*** 1000 services branded **iryo**: www.iryo.eu Services subject to alteration during holiday periods.

☛ *AVE* trains convey ✕ and 🍸. *Avant* trains (*Av*) are *Turista* class only.

European Rail Timetable Subscription

Keep up to date with the latest changes to European rail schedules with a subscription.

See page 12 for details of our various subscription options

Order on-line at **www.europeanrailtimetable.eu**

✆ +44 (0) 1832 270198 (Monday to Friday 1000 – 1600)

650a MADRID – LOGROÑO, PAMPLONA / IRUÑA, HUESCA – BARCELONA

		Alvia **533**	*Alvia* **601** ①–⑤	*Alvia* **705** ⑥⑦	*Alvia* **603** ⑥	*Alvia* **605** Ⓑ		*IC* **563** ⑦	*Alvia* **631**	*Alvia* **621** **625**	*Alvia* **437**	*Alvia* **609**		*Alvia* **613** ⑤⑦	*Alvia* **701**	*AVE* **2861**	*Alvia* **801** Ⓑ			
		K							**B**	**J**	**F**			...		**A**				
Madrid Puerta de Atocha ... d.	...	...	0735	0805	0935	1135	...	...	...	...	...	1505	...	1735	1815	1905	1935	...	...	...
Guadalajara - Yebes ... d.	...	...	|	0831	1002	1201	...	...	...	...	...	1531	...	|	1840	1928	|	...	...	...
Calatayud ... d.	...	...	|	0917	1106	1248	...	...	...	...	...	1619	...	|	1934	2006	|	...	...	...
Logroño **654** ... a.	...	...	|	1132	|	|	...	...	...	...	1753	|	...	|	2142	|	|	...	...	...
Pamplona / Iruña **654** ... a.	...	0905	1042	...	1303	1452	...	1610	1725	1725	|	1828	...	2043	...	|	2240	...	...	...
Zaragoza Delicias ... d.	...	1109	...	...	...	...	...	1747	1924	1924	1952	...	...	...	...	2033	...	...	...	...
Huesca **670** ... a.	...	|	...	...	...	...	...	|	|	|	|	...	...	...	...	2122	...	...	...	...
Lleida ... d.	...	1200	...	...	...	...	...	1839	2014	2014	2057	...	...	...	...	...	...	...	...	...
Camp de Tarragona ... d.	...	1233	...	...	...	...	...	1910	2054	2054	2133	...	...	...	...	...	...	...	...	...
Barcelona Sants ... a.	...	1309	...	...	...	...	...	1955	2139	2139	2214	...	...	...	...	...	...	...	...	...
	Alvia **802** ①–⑤	*AVE* **3872** ①–⑥	*AVE* **3272** ⑦	*Alvia* **702**	*Alvia* **800** ①	*Alvia* **600** ⑥	*Alvia* **602** Ⓑ	*Alvia* **438**	*Alvia* **632**	*Alvia* **622** **626**		*Alvia* **606**		*Alvia* **608** ⑤	*Alvia* **612** ⑦	*Alvia* **706** ⑥⑦	*Alvia* **530**	*Alvia* **610** Ⓑ	*IC* **562** ⑤	
		A						**F**	**B**	**J**							**K**			
Barcelona Sants ... d.	...	...	...	...	...	...	...	0850	0905	0905	...	...	...	...	...	...	1530	...	1638	...
Camp de Tarragona ... d.	...	...	...	...	...	...	...	0927	0941	0941	...	...	...	...	...	...	1608	...	1715	...
Lleida ... d.	...	...	...	...	...	...	...	0959	1013	1013	...	...	...	...	...	...	1639	...	1748	...
Huesca **670** ... d.	...	0810	0810	...	...	...	...	|	|	|	...	...	...	...	...	...	|	...	|	...
Zaragoza Delicias ... d.	...	0900	0900	...	...	...	...	1048	1106	1106	...	...	...	...	...	...	1729	...	1842	...
Pamplona / Iruña **654** ... d.	0640	|	|	...	0810	0900	1130	|	1305	1305	...	1537	...	1828	1828	...	1925	1935	2032	...
Logroño **654** ... d.	|	|	|	0730	|	|	|	1242	...	...	...	|	...	|	|	1845	...	|	...	...
Calatayud ... d.	|	0925	0925	0936	|	1113	1323	...	...	...	...	|	...	|	|	2055	...	2131	...	...
Guadalajara - Yebes ... d.	|	1005	1005	1022	|	1202	1411	...	...	...	...	|	...	|	|	2157	...	2221	...	...
Madrid Puerta de Atocha ... a.	0950	1030	1030	1050	1124	1230	1448	...	...	...	...	1845	...	2135	2135	2225	...	2250	...	...

A – From / to Sevilla (Table **660**).
B – (12) Salamanca - Valladolid - Barcelona and v.v. (Tables **654, 689**).
F – (12) Bilbao - Barcelona and v.v. (Table **654**).
J – (12) Vigo / A Coruña - Barcelona and v.v. (Table **680**).
K – (12) San Sebastián / Donostia - Barcelona and v.v. (Table **654**).

651 MADRID - SORIA and ZARAGOZA

Engineering work until December 2025. 🚌 serve all routes.

km	*For high-speed trains see Tables **650** and **650a***																			
		2 Ⓐ 🚌	2 Ⓒ 🚌	2 Ⓐ 🚌	2 Ⓐ 🚌	2 Ⓐ 🚌	2 Ⓐ 🚌	2 Ⓒ 🚌	2 Ⓒ 🚌	2 Ⓐ 🚌	2 Ⓒ 🚌		2 🚌	2 🚌	2 ⑤ 🚌		2 🚌	2 🚌	2 Ⓐ 🚌	2 ⑦ 🚌
0	**Madrid**-Chamartín-Clara Campoamor ... d.	...	...	...	0643	0746	0800	0808	0817	...	0838	...	...	1507	1546	...	1837	1902	1907	1908
55	Guadalajara ... d.	...	...	...	0809	0920	0920	0937	0937	...	1003	...	...	1633	1706	...	2022	2022	2050	2038
138	Sigüenza ... d.	...	...	0908	0956	1015	1045	1032	1102	...	1150	...	1728	1820	1831	...	2117	2147	2209	2157
248	**Soria** ... a.	...	...	|	|	...	1233	...	1250	...	|	...	|	|	1954	...	...	2310	...	...
178	Arcos de Jalón ... d.	0600	...	0959	1047	...	...	...	...	...	1241	...	1819	1911	...	...	...	...	...	...
241	Calatayud ... d.	0730	0930	1056	1142	...	...	...	...	1325	1346	...	1935	2026	...	...	...	...	...	...
339	**Zaragoza** Delicias ♣ ... a.	0855	1118	1151	1237	...	...	...	...	1455	1441	...	2100	2121	...	...	...	...	...	...

*For high-speed trains see Tables **650** and **650a***																			
	2 Ⓐ 🚌	2 Ⓐ 🚌	2 Ⓐ 🚌	2 Ⓐ 🚌	2 Ⓐ 🚌	2 Ⓒ 🚌	2 Ⓒ 🚌	2 🚌		2 🚌		2 Ⓑ 🚌	2 ⑦ 🚌		2 🚌	2 🚌	2 🚌			
Zaragoza Delicias ♥ ... d.	0630	...	...	...	...	...	...	0800	...	1400	...	1600	...	...	...	...	2000	...	...	...
Calatayud ... d.	0901	...	...	...	...	...	...	0915	...	1505	...	1715	...	...	...	...	2115	...	...	...
Arcos de Jalón ... d.	...	...	...	...	...	...	...	1034	...	1558	...	...	...	...	...	...	2250	...	...	...
Soria ... d.	...	...	0726	...	0726	...	0837	|	...	|	...	...	1659	...	1830	...	...	...	...	...
Sigüenza ... d.	...	0648	|	0851	0908	1002	1019	1125	...	1650	...	...	1841	...	2012	2046	...	...	...	...
Guadalajara ... d.	...	0807	|	0946	1021	1057	1202	1256	...	1825	...	...	2013	...	2210	2141	...	...	...	...
Madrid-Chamartín-Clara Campoamor ... a.	...	0944	1012	1142	1211	1241	1322	1413	...	1941	...	...	2133	...	2330	0013	...	...	...	...

652 ZARAGOZA - BARCELONA

Engineering work March 3 - June 16. 🚌 serve Sant Vicenç de Calders to / from local station Torredembarra.

km	*For high-speed trains see Tables **650** and **650a***																								
		2 Ⓐ	2	2	2	2	2	2	2	2	2	2 ⑥	2 ⑦	2	2 Ⓐ	2 Ⓒ	2	2 Ⓐ	2	2	2 Ⓐ	2	2	2 Ⓑ	2
	Madrid Chamartín ‡ **651** . d.	...	...	...	...	...	...	...	...	...	...	...	...	...	...	...	...	...	...	...	...	...	...	...	...
0	**Zaragoza** Delicias ♣ ... d.	...	...	...	...	...	...	...	...	...	...	0857	1027	...	1121	1121	...	...	...	...	1515	...	1630	2040	2015
114	Caspe ... d.	...	...	...	...	...	0705	...	...	...	...	|	|	...	1253	1253	...	...	...	...	|	...	1800	|	2152
★	Lleida ... d.	...	...	...	0606	...	|	0815	...	...	...	1121	1237	1238	|	|	...	...	1545	...	1727	1808	|	2308	...
239	Reus ... d.	0535	0605	0705	0735	0804	0905	0935	1035	1205	1335	...	...	1405	1452	1452	1535	1605	1705	1835	...	1935	2005	...	...
257	Tarragona ... **672** d.	0555	0625	0725	0755	0825	0925	0955	1055	1225	1355	...	...	1425	1512	1512	1555	1625	1725	1855	...	1955	2025	...	...
282	Sant Vicenç de Calders . **672** d.	|	|	|	|	|	|	|	|	|	|	...	...	|	|	|	|	|	|	|	...	|	|	...	...
342	**Barcelona** Sants ... **672** a.	0708	0739	0839	0909	0939	1137	1109	1209	1339	1509	...	...	1539	1637	1637	1709	1739	1839	2009	...	2109	2137	...	...
345	Barcelona Pass. de Gràcia .. a.	0714	0744	0844	0914	0944	1143	1114	1214	1344	1514	...	...	1544	1643	1643	1714	1744	1844	2014	...	2114	2143	...	...
350	**Barcelona** França ... a.	0724	0754	0854	0924	0954	1154	1124	1224	1354	1524	...	...	1554	1654	1654	1724	1754	1854	2024	...	2124	2154	...	...

*For high-speed trains see Tables **650** and **650a***																									
	2 Ⓐ	2 Ⓐ	2	2 Ⓒ	2	2 ⑥	2 Ⓐ	2	2	2	2	2 ⑦	2	2	2	2 Ⓑ	2	2	2	2	2	2	2	2	2
Barcelona França ... d.	...	...	0615	...	0645	...	0715	0845	0915	1015	1115	...	1145	1315	1415	...	1545	1645	1715	1815	1845	1945	2012	2115	2145
Barcelona Pass. de Gràcia .. d.	...	...	0626	...	0656	...	0726	0856	0926	1026	1126	...	1156	1326	1426	...	1556	1656	1726	1826	1856	1956	2023	2126	2156
Barcelona Sants ... **672** d.	...	...	0633	...	0703	...	0733	0903	0933	1033	1133	...	1203	1333	1433	...	1603	1703	1733	1833	1903	2003	2030	2133	2203
Sant Vicenç de Calders **672** d.	...	...	|	...	|	...	|	|	|	|	|	...	|	|	|	...	|	|	|	|	|	|	|	|	|
Tarragona ... **672** d.	...	...	0745	...	0815	...	0845	1012	1045	1145	1245	...	1315	1445	1545	...	1715	1815	1845	1945	2015	2115	2142	2245	2315
Reus ... d.	...	...	0805	...	0835	...	0904	1029	1104	1204	1305	...	1334	1505	1605	...	1739	1835	1905	2004	2039	2135	2201	2304	2334
Lleida ... d.	...	0625	...	...	1009	1025	...	|	...	...	1431	1515	...	...	1739	1748	|	2001	|	...	2211	...	...	...	...
Caspe ... d.	0653	|	...	1039	...	|	...	1230	...	...	...	|	...	...	...	|	1944	...	2108	...	...	...	...	...	...
Zaragoza Delicias ♥ ... a.	0825	0856	...	1215	...	1253	...	1406	...	...	...	1731	...	...	...	2005	2114	...	...	...	...	...	...	...	...
Madrid Chamartín ‡ **651** .. a.	...	...	...	...	...	...	...	...	...	...	...	...	...	...	...	...	...	...	...	...	...	...	...	...	...

★ – Leida - Reus: *90 km.*
Zaragoza - Lleida: *189 km.*
Lleida - Sant Vicenç: *106 km.*

♥ – All trains call 5 – 8 minutes earlier at Zaragoza **Goya** and 3 – 5 minutes earlier at Zaragoza **Portillo**.
♣ – All trains call 4 – 5 minutes later at Zaragoza **Portillo** and 6 – 8 minutes later at Zaragoza **Goya**.
‡ – Full name is Madrid-Chamartín-Clara Campoamor.

653 LLEIDA - LA POBLA DE SEGUR

FGC 2nd class

km		Ⓐ		Ⓐ	Ⓒ	H	P	Ⓑ	Ⓐ	⑥	†	①–④	⑤
0	**Lleida** ... d.	0459	0620	0732	0747	1040	1047	1047	1339	1505	1705	1730	1925
27	Balaguer ... d.	0525	0646	0800	0815	1110	1115	1115	1407	1531	1731	1756	1951
77	Tremp ... d.	0632	...	0854	0922	|	|	1209	1501	1625	1825	1850	2045
90	**La Pobla de Segur** ... a.	0645	...	0907	0935	1235	1222	1222	1514	1638	1838	1903	2058

	Ⓐ	Ⓑ	⚒	⑦	Ⓐ	P	H	†	⑥	①–④	B	⑤
La Pobla de Segur d.	0653	1008	1300	1515	1530	1635	1700	1900	1921	1946	...	2146
Tremp ... d.	0704	1019	1311	1526	1541	|	|	1911	1932	1957	...	2157
Balaguer ... d.	0800	1115	1407	1622	1637	1757j	1830f	2007	2028	2053	2202	2253
Lleida ... a.	0826	1141	1433	1648	1703	1823	1900	2033	2054	2119	2228	2319

H – Tren dels Llacs - Tren Històric: ⑥ Apr. 26 - July 12, Aug. 16 - Oct. 25.
P – Tren dels Llacs - Tren Panoràmic: ⑥ July 19 - Aug. 9.
T – Runs 19 minutes earlier on ⑥.
f – Arrive 1815.
j – Arrive 1742.

ZARAGOZA - IRÚN and BILBAO 654

km					*Alvia*		*Alvia*	*Alvia*	*Alvia*	*Alvia*	*Alvia*		*IC*				*Alvia*		*Alvia*		*IC*	*Alvia*		
		18071	**16071**		**601**		**438**	**603**	**622**	**632**	**605**	**18021**	**4786**	**18073**	**16015**		**609**	**18023**	**530**	**16017**	**562**	**613**	**18075**	
		2	2						**626**			2	**M**	2	2			2		2			2	
		①–⑥	①–⑤		①–⑤			⑥	**J**	**S**	Ⓑ		Ⓑ					⑤		①–⑥	⑤	⑤⑦		
	Barcelona Sants **652** d.	...	...	...	...	...	0845	...	0905	0905	...	...	...	...	...	...	...	...	1530	...	1638	...	...	...
	Madrid PA ‡ **650a** d.	...	...	...	0735	...	|	0935	|	|	1135	...	...	...	...	...	1505	...	|	...	|	1735	...	...
0	**Zaragoza** Delicias d.	0625	...	...	|	...	1048	|	1106	1106	|	1309	...	1435	...	...	|	1652	1729	...	1842	|	1742	...
94	Castejón de Ebro ★ d.	0729	0730	...	0944	...	1200	1210	1211	1211	|	1417	...	1540	...	...	|	1748	1828	...	1933	|	1849	...
182	**Pamplona / Iruña** d.	0837	|	...	1042	...	|	1303	1308	1308	1452	1526	...	|	1642	...	1828	1859	1930	1958	2032	2043	|	...
234	Altsasu **689** d.	0918**t**	|	...	...	...	|	...	|	|	...	...	...	|	1718**t**	...	...	...	1959	2034**t**	...	...	|	...
275	Vitoria / Gasteiz **689** d.	0950	|	...	...	...	|	...	1403	1403	...	...	...	|	1753	...	...	...	|	2107	...	...	|	...
321	San Sebastián / Donostia d.	|	|	...	...	...	|	...	|	|	...	...	...	|	|	...	...	...	2116	...	...	...	|	...
337	**Irún** **689** a.	|	|	...	...	...	|	...	|	|	...	...	...	|	|	...	...	...	...	...	...	...	|	...
171	**Logroño 650a** d.	|	0829	...	...	...	1253	...	|	|	...	...	1612	1635	|	...	...	...	...	...	...	...	1945	...
242	Miranda de Ebro **689** d.	1016	...	...	...	...	1354	...	1424	1424	...	...	1717	...	1820	...	...	...	...	...	...	...	...	...
347	**Bilbao** Abando **689** a.	...	...	...	...	...	1536	...	...	...	...	...	...	...	....	...	...	...	...	...	...	...	...	...

				Alvia	*Alvia*				
	16027		**18077**	**701**	**801**	**18079**			
	2		2			2			
	⑦			Ⓑ	Ⓑ	⑤⑥⑦			
Barcelona Sants **652** d.	...	...	...	...	...	...	...	...	...
Madrid PA ‡ **650a** d.	...	...	...	1815	1935	...	...	...	...
Zaragoza Delicias d.	...	...	1921	|	|	2109	...	...	...
Castejón de Ebro ★ d.	1852	...	2031	|	|	2215	...	...	...
Pamplona / Iruña d.	2005	...	2138	|	2240	|	...	...	...
Altsasu **689** d.	2046**t**	...	...	|	...	|	...	...	...
Vitoria / Gasteiz **689** d.	2118	...	...	|	...	|	...	...	...
San Sebastián / Donostia d.	|	...	...	|	...	|	...	...	...
Irún **689** a.	|	...	...	|	...	|	...	...	...
Logroño 650a d.	|	...	...	2136	...	2312	...	...	...
Miranda de Ebro **689** d.	2143	...	...	...	...	...	...	...	...
Bilbao Abando **689** a.	...	...	...	...	...	...	...	...	...

			Alvia	*Alvia*		*Alvia*	*Alvia*	*Alvia*		
	18068	**18072**	**802**	**702**	**18074**	**800**	**600**	**533**		
	2	2			2					
	①–⑤	①–⑤	①–⑤	①–⑥		①	⑥			
Bilbao Abando **689** d.	...	...	...	...	...	...	...	...	...	...
Miranda de Ebro **689** d.	...	...	...	...	...	...	...	...	...	...
Logroño 650a d.	...	0615	...	0735	...	...	...	...	...	...
Irún **689** d.	...	|	...	|	...	...	...	...	...	...
San Sebastián / Donostia d.	...	|	...	|	...	...	...	0710	...	...
Vitoria / Gasteiz **689** d.	...	|	...	|	...	...	...	|	...	...
Altsasu **689** d.	...	|	...	|	...	...	...	0830	...	...
Pamplona / Iruña d.	...	|	0640	|	0743**z**	0810	0900	0905	...	...
Castejón de Ebro d.	0605	0720**e**	0730	|	0850	|	0952	1002	...	...
Zaragoza Delicias a.	0715	0836	|	|	0956	|	|	1106	...	...
Madrid PA ‡ **650a** a.	...	...	0950	1050	...	1124	1230	|	...	...
Barcelona Sants **652** a.	...	...	...	...	...	...	...	1309	...	...

		Alvia	*IC*			*Alvia*	*IC*			*Alvia*	*Alvia*	*Alvia*	*Alvia*	*Alvia*	*Alvia*									
	16019	**602**	**4687**		**18076**	**606**	**563**	**18070**	**18029**	**621**	**631**	**437**	**608**	**612**	**610**	**16111**	**16011**	**18078**						
	2**b**		**M**		2			2	2	**625**						2	2	2						
	①–⑥	Ⓑ	①–⑥				⑦	⑤⑥⑦	**b**	**J**	**S**		⑤	⑦	Ⓑ	①–⑥	⑦							
Bilbao Abando **689** d.	...	...	...	...	...	...	...	...	...	...	...	1520	...	...	...	...	...	...	...	...	...	...	...	...
Miranda de Ebro **689** d.	0925	...	1139	...	...	...	...	...	1501	1557	1557	1652	...	...	...	...	...	...	...	...	...	...	...	...
Logroño 650a d.	|	...	1241	...	1415	...	...	1642	|	|	|	1753	...	...	...	...	...	2023	...	...	...	...	...	...
Irún **689** d.	|	...	...	...	|	...	...	|	|	|	|	|	...	...	...	...	...	|	...	...	...	...	...	...
San Sebastián / Donostia d.	|	...	...	...	|	...	...	|	|	|	|	|	...	...	...	...	...	|	...	...	...	...	...	...
Vitoria / Gasteiz **689** d.	0952	...	...	...	|	...	...	|	1530	1626	1626	|	...	...	...	1900	1921	|	...	...	...	...	...	...
Altsasu **689** d.	1025**t**	...	...	...	|	...	...	|	1601**t**	|	|	|	...	...	...	1931**t**	1952**t**	|	...	...	...	...	...	...
Pamplona / Iruña d.	1057	1130	...	...	|	1537	1610	|	1638	1725	1725	|	1828	1828	1935	2015	2026	|	...	...	...	...	...	...
Castejón de Ebro d.	...	|	...	...	1510	|	1659	1741	1744	1824	1824	1854	|	|	|	2111	2123	2127	...	...	...	...	...	...
Zaragoza Delicias a.	...	|	...	...	1611	|	1744	...	1851	1921	1921	1949	|	|	|	...	2217	2235	...	...	...	...	...	...
Madrid PA ‡ **650a** a.	...	1448	...	...	...	1845	|	...	...	|	|	|	2135	2135	2250	...	...	...	...	...	...	...	...	...
Barcelona Sants **652** a.	...	...	...	...	...	...	1955	...	...	2139	2139	2220	...	...	...	...	...	...	...	...	...	...	...	...

J – 12 🍷 Barcelona - Vigo / A Coruña and v.v. (Table **680**).

M – To / from Madrid (Table **689**).

S – 12 Salamanca - Valladolid - Barcelona and v.v. (Tables **680, 689**).

b – From Burgos Rosa Manzano on ①–⑥ (Table **689**).

e – Arrive 0709.

t – Altsasu Pueblo (*230 km*).

z – ①–⑤.

★ – Calatayud - Castejón: *140 km*.

‡ – Full name is Madrid Puerta de Atocha.

2nd class BARCELONA - PUIGCERDÀ - LATOUR DE CAROL 656

km		Ⓐ							Ⓒ							Ⓐ	Ⓒ							
0	**Barcelona** Sants d.	0501	0531	0601	0701	0731	0801	0831	0901	0931	1031	1131	1201	1231	1301	1331	1331	1431	1501	1531	1631	1701	1731	1801
	La Sagrera-Meridiana d.	0515	0545	0615	0715	0745	0815	0845	0915	0945	1045	1145	1215	1245	1315	1345	1345	1445	1515	1545	1645	1715	1745	1815
	Fabra i Puig d.	0518	0548	0618	0718	0748	0818	0848	0918	0948	1048	1148	1218	1248	1318	1348	1348	1448	1518	1548	1648	1718	1748	1818
33	Granollers - Canovelles d.	0550	0620	0650	0750	0820	0850	0920	0951	1020	1120	1220	1250	1320	1350	1420	1420	1520	1550	1620	1720	1750	1820	1850
74	Vic d.	0627	0657	0728	0828	0857	0927	0958	1028	1058	1158	1258	1327	1358	1427	1458	1458	1558	1627	1658	1758	1827	1858	1928
90	Torelló d.	...	...	0743	0843	...	...	1013	1044	1113	1213	1313	...	1413	...	1513	1513	1613	...	1713	1813	...	1913	1943
110	Ripoll d.	...	...	0810	0911	...	...	1040	1115	1139	1239	1340	...	1439	...	1541	1541	1640	...	1739	1840	...	1944	2010
124	Ribes de Freser **658** a.	...	...	0831	0926	...	...	1101	...	...	...	1401	...	...	...	...	1556	1701	...	...	1901	...	...	2031
145	La Molina a.	...	...	0858	...	...	...	1131	...	...	...	1431	...	...	...	...	...	1731	...	...	1928	...	...	2058
159	Puigcerdà a.	...	...	0917	...	...	...	1150	...	...	...	1450	...	...	...	...	...	1750	...	...	1946	...	...	2116
163	**Latour de Carol** 🏛 **312** a.	...	...	0923	...	...	...	1156	...	...	...	1456	...	...	...	...	...	1756	...	...	...	...	...	...

		Ⓐ							
Barcelona Sants d.	1831	1852	1901	1931	2001	2031	2101	2131	2231
La Sagrera-Meridiana d.	1845	1906	1915	1945	2015	2045	2115	2145	2245
Fabra i Puig d.	1848	1909	1918	1948	2018	2048	2118	2148	2248
Granollers - Canovelles d.	1920	1933	1950	2020	2050	2120	2150	2220	2320
Vic d.	1957	2015	2027	2057	2128	2157	2228	2257	2357
Torelló d.	...	2027	...	...	2143	...	2243	...	...
Ripoll d.	...	2050	...	...	2209	...	2309	...	...
Ribes de Freser **658** a.	...	2107	...	...	...	...	...	...	...
La Molina a.	...	2135	...	...	...	...	...	...	...
Puigcerdà a.	...	2154	...	...	...	...	...	...	...
Latour de Carol 🏛 **312** a.	...	...	...	...	...	...	...	...	...

	Ⓐ				Ⓐ				
Latour de Carol 🏛 **312** d.	...	...	...	...	...	...	...	...	...
Puigcerdà d.	...	...	...	...	0529	...	...	...	0708
La Molina d.	...	...	...	...	0549	...	...	...	0728
Ribes de Freser **658** d.	...	...	...	...	0616	...	...	...	0755
Ripoll d.	...	...	0544	...	0634	...	0715	...	0814
Torelló d.	...	...	0611	...	0655	...	0742	...	0841
Vic d.	0529	0559	0628	0659	0710	0729	0759	0829	0859
Granollers - Canovelles d.	0606	0636	0706	0736	0750	0806	0836	0906	0936
Fabra i Puig d.	0638	0708	0738	0808	0826	0838	0908	0938	1008
La Sagrera-Meridiana d.	0641	0711	0741	0811	0829	0841	0911	0941	1011
Barcelona Sants a.	0655	0725	0755	0825	0843	0855	0925	0955	1025

											Ⓒ	Ⓐ				Ⓒ							
Latour de Carol 🏛 **312** d.	...	0830	...	1030	...	...	...	...	1330	...	...	...	...	...	1630	...	...	...	...	1900	...	...	...	...
Puigcerdà d.	...	0837	...	1037	...	...	...	...	1337	...	...	...	...	...	1637	...	...	...	...	1907	...	...	...	...
La Molina d.	...	0857	...	1057	...	...	...	...	1357	...	...	...	...	...	1657	...	1755	...	...	1927	...	...	...	...
Ribes de Freser **658** d.	...	0924	1026	1126	...	...	...	...	1426	...	...	1626	...	...	1726	...	1823	...	...	1954	...	...	...	...
Ripoll d.	...	0946	1044	1145	...	1244	...	1344	1445	...	1544	1644	1644	...	1745	...	1842	1912	...	2013	...	2114	...	...
Torelló d.	...	1011	1112	1211	...	1312	...	1412	1511	...	1612	1712	1712	...	1811	...	1912	1942	...	2043	...	2142	...	...
Vic d.	0959	1029	1129	1229	1259	1329	1359	1429	1529	1559	1629	1729	1729	1759	1829	1859	1929	1959	2029	2059	2129	2159	2229	...
Granollers - Canovelles d.	1036	1106	1206	1306	1336	1406	1436	1506	1606	1636	1706	1806	1806	1836	1906	1936	2006	2036	2106	2136	2206	2236	2306	...
Fabra i Puig d.	1108	1138	1238	1338	1408	1438	1508	1538	1638	1708	1738	1838	1838	1908	1938	2008	2038	2108	2138	2208	2238	2308	2338	...
La Sagrera-Meridiana d.	1111	1141	1241	1341	1411	1441	1511	1541	1641	1711	1741	1841	1841	1911	1941	2011	2041	2111	2141	2211	2241	2311	2341	...
Barcelona Sants a.	1125	1155	1255	1355	1425	1455	1525	1555	1655	1725	1755	1855	1855	1925	1955	2025	2055	2125	2155	2225	2255	2325	2355	...

657 BARCELONA - GIRONA - FIGUERES - PORTBOU / PERPIGNAN

Reservations are not compulsory on *Media Distancia* (*MD*) services on the Barcelona - Girona - Portbou - Cebère route. All stopping services convey 2nd class only.

km	km		*MD* Ⓐ	Ⓐ	*Av* 34609*	*MD* Ⓐ	*MD* Ⓒ	Ⓐ	*MD* Ⓒ	*Av* 8287	*MD* Ⓐ	*AVE* 9737 34137* B	Ⓒ	Ⓐ	*TGV* 9708 P	*Av* 8297 Ⓑ	*MD* Ⓒ	*MD* Ⓐ	*MD* Ⓒ	*AVE* 3073 34073*	Ⓐ	*MD* Ⓐ	*MD* Ⓒ	*MD* Ⓐ	Ⓒ	*AVE* 2561 34093* K	Ⓐ
		Madrid ⊠ **650** d.	...	...	...	...	...	...	...	...	...	...	...	...	...	...	...	...	...	0727	...	...	...	...	...	0927	...
0	0	**Barcelona** Sants ... **666** d.	0556	0616	0645	0646	0646	0716	0746	0810	0816	0819	0846	0916	0928	0939	0946	1016	1046	1054	1116	1146	1146	1246	1246	1249	1316
		Sant Andreu d.	|	0629	|	|	0659	0730	|	|	|	|	0859	0929	|	|	|	|	1059	|	1129	|	|	|	1259	|	1329
31		Granollers Centre d.	|	0648	|	0710	0718	0753	|	|	|	|	0918	0948	|	|	|	|	1118	|	1148	|	|	|	1318	|	1348
72		Maçanet - Massanes **666** d.	0657	0721	|	0744	0751	0831	0844	|	0914	|	0951	1021	|	|	1045	1114	1151	|	1221	1244	1244	1344	1351	|	1421
86		Caldes de Malavella d.	0705	0733	|	0756	0803	0843	0856	|	0925	|	1003	1033	|	|	1057	1126	1203	|	1233	1256	1256	1356	1403	|	1433
102	95	**Girona** d.	0717	0748	0727	0807	0818	0853	0907	0855	0937	0901	1018	1048	1010	1022	1108	1137	1218	1134	1248	1307	1307	1410	1418	1332	1448
118		Flaçà d.	0730	0803	|	0820	0833	0913	0920	|	0950	|	1033	1103	|	|	1121	1150	1233	|	1303	1320	1320	1422	1433	|	1503
143		Figueres § d.	0747	0827	|	0837	0857	0935	0937	|	1007	|	1057	1127	|	|	1138	1207	1257	|	1327	1337	1337	1444	1457	|	1527
	129	Figueres Vilafant § d.	...	|	0743	...	|	|	|	0910	|	0918	|	|	1027	1037	|	|	|	1149	|	...	|	...	|	1347	|
162		Llançà d.	...	0841	...	...	0911	0949	0951	...	1021	|	1111	1141	|	...	1152	1221	1311	...	1341	...	1351	...	1511	...	1541
169		**Portbou** **355** a.	...	0852	...	...	0922	1000	0959	...	1029	|	1122	1152	|	...	1200	1229	1322	...	1352	...	1359	...	1522	...	1552
171		**Cerbère** **355** a.	...	0904	...	...	0926	1004	...	...	...	|	1126	1204	|	...	...	...	1326	...	1404	...	...	...	1526	...	1604
	177	**Perpignan** **355** a.	...	...	...	...	...	...	...	...	...	0943	...	...	1052	...	...	...	...	...	...	...	...	...	...	...	...

	⑦	*MD* Ⓐ	*MD* ⑥	*MD* ⑦	*Av* 34113*		*TGV* 9704 A P	*AVE* 3123 34123* Ⓑ	*MD*	*TGV* 9706 P	*AVE* 9725 34125* C	*Av* 8377 Ⓑ		*AVE* 3143 34143* Ⓑ	*MD* Ⓐ	*MD* Ⓐ	*MD* Ⓒ	*Em/Av* 1152 34153* ①–④ ⑦	*MD* Ⓐ		*AVE* 3163 34163* ①–⑤	*MD* Ⓐ	Ⓒ	*MD* Ⓑ	*AVE* 3191 S	*MD*	*avlo* 6309 34309*
Madrid ⊠ **650** d.	...	...	...	...	...	...	...	1227	...	...	1318	...	...	1427	...	...	...		...	...	1627	...	...	...	1857	...	1934
Barcelona Sants ... **666** d.	1346	1416	1416	1446	1500	1516	1520	1554	1616	1625	1634	1705	1716	1734	1746	1816	1819	1829	1846	1916	1925	1946	2016	2046	2144	2146	2305
Sant Andreu d.	|	|	|	|	|	1529	|	|	|	|	|	|	1729	|	|	|	|	|	|	1929	|	|	|	|	|	|	|
Granollers Centre d.	|	|	|	|	|	1545	|	|	|	|	|	|	1748	|	|	|	|	|	|	1948	|	|	|	|	|	|	|
Maçanet - Massanes . **666** d.	1444	1514	1514	1544	|	1621	|	|	1714	|	|	|	1821	|	1844	1914	1921	|	1944	2021	|	2044	2114	2150	|	2250	|
Caldes de Malavella d.	1456	1526	1526	1556	|	1633	|	|	1726	|	|	|	1833	|	1856	1926	1933	|	1956	2033	|	2056	2126	2206	|	2302	|
Girona d.	1507	1537	1537	1607	1543	1648	1602	1637	1737	1707	1716	1750	1848	1821	1907	1937	1944	1920	2009	2048	2016	2107	2137	2217	2224	2313	2347
Flaçà d.	1520	1550	1550	1620	|	1703	|	|	1750	|	|	|	1903	|	1920	1950	1957	|	2022	2103	|	2120	2150	2230	|	...	|
Figueres § d.	1537	1607	1607	1637	|	1727	|	|	1807	|	|	|	1927	|	1937	2007	2014	|	2040	2127	|	2137	2210	2249	|	...	|
Figueres Vilafant § d.	|	...	|	|	1558	|	1619	1652	...	1724	1733	1805	|	1837	|	...	...	1934	...	|	2031	...	...	...	2239	...	0002
Llançà d.	1551	...	1621	1651	...	1741	|	...	...	|	|	...	1941	...	1951	...	...	...	...	2141	...	...	...	...	...	...	...
Portbou **355** a.	1559	...	1629	1659	...	1752	|	...	...	|	|	...	1951	...	1959	...	...	...	...	2151	...	...	...	...	...	...	...
Cerbère **355** a.	...	...	...	...	...	1804	|	...	...	|	|	...	...	...	...	...	...	...	...	...	...	...	...	...	...	...	...
Perpignan **355** a.	...	...	...	...	...	...	1646	...	...	1747	1800	...	...	...	...	...	...	...	...	...	...	...	...	...	...	...	...

	avlo 6302 34302*	*MD* Ⓐ	*MD*	*AVE* 3662 34662* ①–⑤	*Em/Av* 1081 34082* ①–⑤	*MD*	*MD* Ⓐ		†	*AVE* 3092 34092* ①–⑥	*MD*	*Em/Av* 1101 34102*		*MD*		*Av* 8316	*AVE* 9730 34130* C	*MD*	*TGV* 9711 A P	*Av* 8336		*TGV* 9713 P	*MD*	*MD* Ⓐ	*AVE* 3162 34262*		*MD* Ⓐ
Perpignan **355** d.	...	...	...	...	...	...	...	...	...	...	...	...	...	...	...	...	1118	...	1206	...	...	1307	...	...	...	...	...
Cerbère **355** d.	...	...	...	...	...	...	...	...	...	...	...	...	...	...	...	...	|	...	|	...	...	|	...	...	...	...	...
Portbou **355** d.	...	...	...	...	...	...	...	0705	...	...	...	...	0835	...	1035	...	|	1124	|	...	1235	|	1324	...	...	1435	...
Llançà d.	...	...	...	...	...	...	...	0714	...	...	...	...	0844	...	1044	...	|	1132	|	...	1244	|	1332	...	...	1444	...
Figueres Vilafant § d.	0530	...	...	0620	0710	...	...	|	...	0755	...	0910	|	...	|	1135	1142	|	1232	1310	|	1330	|	...	1455	|	...
Figueres § d.	|	...	0552	|	|	0641	0708	0729	0746	|	0816	|	0859	0946	1059	|	|	1146	|	|	1259	|	1346	1416	|	1459	1546
Flaçà d.	|	...	0612	|	|	0700	0728	0752	0805	|	0835	|	0922	1005	1122	|	|	1205	|	|	1322	|	1405	1435	|	1522	1605
Girona d.	0546	0614	0627	0636	0726	0714	0744	0809	0819	0811	0849	0926	0939	1019	1139	1153	1159	1219	1249	1326	1339	1347	1419	1449	1511	1539	1619
Caldes de Malavella d.	|	0625	0639	|	|	0725	0755	0824	0830	|	0900	|	0954	1030	1154	|	|	1230	|	|	1354	|	1430	1500	|	1554	1630
Maçanet - Massanes **666** d.	|	0636	0651	|	|	0736	0806	0835	0841	|	0911	|	1005	1041	1205	|	|	1241	|	|	1405	|	1441	1511	|	1605	1641
Granollers Centre d.	|	|	|	|	|	|	|	0908	|	|	|	|	1038	|	1238	|	|	|	|	|	1438	|	|	|	|	1638	|
Sant Andreu d.	|	|	|	|	|	|	|	0925	|	|	|	|	1055	|	1255	|	|	|	|	|	1455	|	|	|	|	1655	|
Barcelona Sants ... **666** a.	0625	0740	0755	0715	0805	0840	0910	0940	0940	0850	1010	1005	1110	1140	1310	1232	1238	1340	1328	1405	1510	1429	1540	1610	1550	1710	1740
Madrid ⊠ **650** a.	0927	...	...	1012	...	...	...	...	...	1152	...	...	...	...	...	...	1552	...	...	...	...	...	...	...	1919	...	...

	MD Ⓒ	*MD* Ⓐ	Ⓑ	*Av* 34182* ①–⑤	*Av* 34712*	⑥	*MD* Ⓐ	*MD* ⑦	*AVE* 3192 34192*	*MD* Ⓒ	*MD* Ⓐ	Ⓐ	*MD* †	*AVE* 9742 34142* B	*MD*	*Av* 8396	*AVE* 34292* Ⓑ	†	*TGV* 9715 P	Ⓐ	Ⓒ	*MD* Ⓐ	Ⓐ	Ⓒ			
Perpignan **355** d.	...	...	...	...	...	...	...	...	...	...	...	...	...	1811	...	...	...	...	2007	...	...	...	...	...	...	...	...
Cerbère **355** d.	...	...	...	...	...	...	...	...	...	...	...	...	...	|	...	...	...	...	|	...	...	...	...	...	...	...	...
Portbou **355** d.	1524	...	1605	...	...	1635	...	...	...	1724	...	1735	1754	|	...	...	...	1839	|	1905	1945	...	2024	2025	...	...	...
Llançà d.	1532	...	1614	...	...	1644	...	...	...	1732	...	1744	1802	|	...	...	...	1848	|	1914	1954	...	2032	2034	...	...	...
Figueres Vilafant § d.	|	...	|	1710	1716	|	...	...	1735	|	...	|	|	1838	...	1906	1935	|	2030	|	|	...	|	|	...	...	...
Figueres § d.	1546	...	1629	|	|	1659	1716	...	|	1746	...	1759	1816	|	1846	|	|	1903	|	1929	2009	2026	2046	2049	...	...	...
Flaçà d.	1605	...	1652	|	|	1722	1735	...	|	1805	...	1822	1835	|	1905	|	|	1926	|	1952	2032	2045	2105	2108	...	...	...
Girona d.	1619	1649	1709	1726	1732	1739	1749	1749	1751	1819	1819	1839	1849	1855	1919	1924	1952	1943	2047	2009	2049	2059	2119	2123	...	...	...
Caldes de Malavella d.	1630	1700	1724	|	|	1754	1800	1800	|	1830	1830	1854	1900	|	1930	|	|	1958	|	2024	2104	2110	2130	2137	...	...	...
Maçanet - Massanes **666** d.	1641	1711	1735	|	|	1805	1811	1811	|	1841	1841	1905	1911	|	1941	|	|	2009	|	2035	2115	2121	2141	2148	...	...	...
Granollers Centre d.	|	|	1808	|	|	1838	|	|	|	|	|	1938	|	|	|	|	|	|	|	2108	2148	|	|	2221	...	...	...
Sant Andreu d.	|	|	1825	|	|	1855	|	|	|	|	|	1955	|	|	|	|	|	|	|	2125	2205	|	|	2237	...	...	...
Barcelona Sants ... **666** a.	1740	1810	1840	1805	1814	1910	1910	1910	1830	1940	1940	2010	2010	1934	2040	2003	2030	2110	2129	2140	2220	2220	2239	2252	...	...	...
Madrid ⊠ **650** a.	...	...	...	...	...	...	...	...	2152	...	...	...	...	...	...	...	...	...	...	...	...	...	...	...	...	...	...

		Ⓒ	Ⓐ	Ⓒ	Ⓐ	Ⓒ	Ⓐ	Ⓐ	Ⓒ	Ⓐ	
Portbou d.	...	1104	1204	1303	1404	1455	1604	1804	1904	2004	...
Cerbère a.	...	1110	1210	1309	1410	1501	1610	1810	1910	2010	...

	Ⓐ	Ⓒ	Ⓐ	Ⓒ	Ⓒ	Ⓐ	Ⓒ	Ⓐ	Ⓒ	Ⓐ	Ⓒ	Ⓒ	Ⓐ	Ⓐ
Cerbère d.	0923	0934	1012	1041	1134	1204	1239	1404	1440	1541	1636	1804	1840	1941
Portbou a.	0927	0938	1016	1045	1138	1208	1245	1408	1445	1545	1640	1808	1845	1945

A – ⑥⑦ May 3 - June 29 (also May 9, 30). Daily July 5 - Aug. 31. ⑥⑦ Sept. 6 - Nov. 2.
B – To / from Lyon (Table **13**).
C – To / from Marseille (Table **13**).
K – From Sevilla (Table **660**).
P – To / from Paris (Table **13**).
S – ①②③④⑦.
⊠ – Madrid Puerta de Atocha.
* – Train number for *Turista class (classified Av)*.

§ – **FIGUERES VILAFANT - FIGUERES BUS STATION (150m from Figueres)**. *5 km*. By bus. Journey time: 15 – 20 minutes.

From **Figueres Vilafant**: 0810, 0915, 1010, 1030 Ⓐ, 1150, 1345, 1600, 1655 Ⓑ, 1745, 1840, 1935 ①②③④⑦, 2035 Ⓐ, 2105, 2245 ①②③④⑦, 0000.

From **Figueres Bus Station**: 0505, 0605 Ⓐ, 0645 Ⓐ, 0725 ⚒, 0840, 0940, 1110, 1240, 1425 ⚒, 1515, 1635 Ⓐ, 1725, 1810, 1910 Ⓑ.

658 VALL DE NÚRIA *2nd class*

Ribes Enllaç - **Ribes** Vila - **Queralbs** - **Núria** rack railway

HIGH SEASON:

⑥⑦ June 3 - Oct. 29 (also May 1, daily July 31 - Sept. 1, also Sept. 11, Oct. 12, 13):
From **Ribes** Enllaç: 0730 **v**, 0820, 0930, 1020, 1110, 1205, 1255, 1340, 1430, 1535, 1625, 1715, 2010 ⑤.
From **Núria**: 0820, 0930, 1020, 1110, 1205, 1255, 1340, 1430, 1535, 1625, 1715, 1805, 2100 ⑤.

LOW SEASON:

①–⑤ May 2 - Nov. 3 (daily May 2 - June 2, also ⑥⑦ Nov. 4 - 26; not July 31 - Sept. 1, Sept. 11, Oct. 12, 13):
From **Ribes** Enllaç: 0835, 0930, 1110, 1255, 1430, 1625.
From **Núria**: 0820, 1020, 1205, 1340, 1535, 1715.

Journey times **Ribes** – **Queralbs** (*6 km*) 24 minutes, **Ribes** – **Núria** (*12 km*) 44 minutes.
Ferrocarrils de la Generalitat de Catalunya (FGC) ✆ +34 972 732 020. www.valldenuria.cat
v – From Ribes Vila.

659 AEROPORT BARCELONA *2nd class*

Local rail service *Cercanías* (suburban) line **R2 Nord**. *14km*
Aeroport - **Barcelona Sants** – **Barcelona Passeig de Gràcia**
Journey time: 23 minutes Sants, 28 minutes Passeig de Gràcia

From Aeroport del Prat:
0542, 0608, 0638, 0708, 0738 and every 30 minutes until 2208, 2238, 2308, 2338

From Barcelona Sants:
0513, 0535, 0609, 0639, 0709 and every 30 minutes until 2139, 2206, 2239, 2311

High-speed services — MADRID - CÓRDOBA - SEVILLA and MÁLAGA — 660

km		avlo 2068	iryo 6066	AVE 2070	Alvia 2074	Ouigo 6478	AVE 2072	AVE 2076	Ouigo 6476	iryo 6078	AVE 2080	Alvia 9366	AVE 2082	iryo 6086	avlo 2096	IC 2494	AVE 2092 3862	AVE 3930	AVE 2100	Alvia 2104	avlo 2108	AVE 3982	AVE 3872	Ouigo xxxx	AVE 3882	iryo 6118	AVE 3940	AVE 3990
													①–⑥				Ⓑ			①④⑤⑦		V	①–⑥ H		Ⓑ			
	Barcelona Sants **650** d.	...	...	...	...	...	...	...	...	...	...	...	...	...	...	...	0550f	0645	...	...	...	...	...	...	0800	...	0830	0830
0	**Madrid** Puerta de Atocha d.	0615	0650	0700	0705	0719	0735	0735	0740	0755	0800	0805	0830	0855	0900	0923	0935	|	1000	1005	1035	...	1100	1108	1135	1155	|	|
171	Ciudad Real d.	0711	|	0756	0804	|	|	|	|	|	|	0906	|	|	0956	|	|	|	|	|	1131	1140	|	|	|	|	1217	1217
210	Puertollano d.	0728	|	0812	0821	|	|	|	|	|	|	0923	|	|	1011	|	|	|	|	|	1148	1157	|	|	|	|	1234	1234
	Villanueva de CLP ⊠ d.	0753	|	|	|	|	|	|	|	|	|	|	|	|	1037	|	|	|	|	|	1212	|	|	|	|	|	|	|
345	**Córdoba** d.	0819	0838	0858	0907	0913	0925	0925	|	0944	0949	1010	|	1043	1102	1119	1124	1139	1150	|	1238	1246	1249	1302	1324	1334	1324	1336
470	**Sevilla** a.	|	0932	0952	1016	|	|	|	1025	|	1043	|	|	1137	1156	1225	|	|	1244	1307	|	1340	1345	|	|	|	1422	|
	Cádiz **671** a.	|	...	...	1145	|	|	|	...	|	...	|	|	...	...	|	|	|	...	1443	|	...	...	|	|	|	...	|
	Huelva **671** a.	|	...	...	...	|	|	|	...	|	...	|	|	...	...	1402	|	|	...	...	|	...	...	|	|	|	...	|
419	Puente Genil - Herrera ¶ a.	0845	...	...	...	|	0950	0950	...	|	...	|	|	...	...	...	|	|	...	...	1304	...	...	|	|	|	...	1400
455	Antequera - Santa Ana § a.	0858	...	...	...	|	1007	1007	...	|	...	1058	|	...	...	...	1155	|	...	...	1317	...	...	|	|	|	...	1423
	Algeciras **673** a.	|	...	...	...	|	|	|	...	|	...	1337	|	...	...	...	|	|	...	...	|	...	...	|	|	|	...	|
	Antequera AV a.	|	...	...	...	|	|	1018	...	|	...	...	|	...	...	...	|	1219	...	...	|	...	...	|	|	|	...	|
	Granada **678a** a.	|	...	...	...	|	|	1106	...	|	...	...	|	...	...	...	|	1311	...	...	|	...	...	|	|	|	...	|
513	**Málaga** María Zambrano a.	0929	...	...	...	1017	1049	...	...	1042	...	...	1112	...	...	...	1226	...	...	...	1348	...	...	1401	1423	1432	...	1454

	AVE 2120	Alvia 2134	AVE 2122	iryo 6010	AVE 2130	AVE 2136	iryo 6136	AVE 2140	AVE 2142	iryo 6016	avlo 2156	Ouigo 6566	Ouigo 6568	AVE 2152	AVE 2160	Alvia 2164	Alvia 2366	AVE 2360	iryo 6168	AVE 2162	iryo 6014	avlo 2176	AVE 2172	Ouigo 6586	AVE 2180	Alvia 2384	AVE 3942	AVE 3992
								Ⓑ									A	Ⓑ					C					
Barcelona Sants **650** d.	...	...	...	0950	...	...	...	...	...	1150	...	...	...	...	...	...	...	...	...	...	1345	...	...	...	...	...	1517	1517
Madrid Puerta de Atocha d.	1200	1205	1235	1255	1300	1335	1355	1400	1435	1455	1500	1514	1523	1535	1600	1605	1610	1625	1630	1635	1655	1700	1730	1737	1800	1805	|	|
Ciudad Real d.	|	1304	|	|	|	|	|	|	|	|	1556	|	|	|	|	|	|	|	|	1732	|	1756	|	|	|	|	1919	1919
Puertollano d.	|	1321	|	|	|	|	|	|	|	|	1611	|	|	|	|	|	|	|	|	1748	|	1811	|	|	|	|	|	|
Villanueva de CLP ⊠ d.	|	|	|	|	|	|	|	|	|	|	1637	|	|	|	|	|	|	|	|	|	|	1837	|	|	|	|	|	|
Córdoba d.	1350	1407	1424	1443	1449	1524	1543	1549	1626	1644	1702	1708	|	|	1749	|	1806	|	1819	1834	1843	1902	|	1930	1949	1958	2023	2033
Sevilla a.	1444	1515	|	1537	1543	|	1637	1643	|	|	1756	1802	|	|	1842	|	|	1858	|	|	1937	1956	|	2030	2043	|	2124	|
Cádiz **671** a.	...	1641	|	...	...	|	...	...	|	|	...	...	|	|	...	2029	|	...	|	|	...	...	|	...	...	|	...	|
Huelva **671** a.	...	...	|	...	...	|	...	...	|	|	...	...	|	|	...	...	|	...	|	|	...	...	|	...	...	2202	...	|
Puente Genil - Herrera ¶ a.	...	...	|	...	...	|	...	...	|	|	...	...	|	|	...	...	|	...	|	1859	...	...	|	...	...	...	...	2057
Antequera - Santa Ana § a.	...	...	|	...	...	|	...	...	|	|	...	...	|	|	...	...	|	...	|	1914	...	...	|	...	...	...	...	2113
Algeciras **673** a.	...	...	|	...	...	|	...	...	|	|	...	...	|	|	...	...	|	...	|	|	...	...	|	...	...	...	...	|
Antequera AV a.	...	...	|	...	...	1603	...	...	|	|	...	...	|	|	...	...	1904	...	|	|	...	...	|	...	...	...	...	|
Granada **678a** a.	...	...	|	...	...	1652	...	...	|	|	...	...	|	|	...	...	1955	...	|	|	...	...	|	...	...	...	...	|
Málaga María Zambrano a.	...	...	1522	...	...	...	...	...	1726	1742	...	...	1811	1817	...	...	...	...	1917	1945	...	...	2012	...	...	...	...	2143

	avlo 2188	AVE 2190	iryo 6196	AVE 5862	Ouigo xxxx	AVE 2200	AVE 2196	AVE 2202	iryo 6208	AVE 2210	AVE 2212
				Ⓑ M		Ⓑ				B	⑤ J
Barcelona Sants **650** d.	...	...	...	...	...	...	...	...	...	...	...
Madrid Puerta de Atocha d.	1835	1900	1905	1935	1950	2000	2005	2035	2055	2105	2125
Ciudad Real d.	1931	|	|	|	|	|	|	|	|	2201	|
Puertollano d.	1948	|	|	|	|	|	|	|	|	2217	|
Villanueva de CLP ⊠ d.	2012	|	|	|	|	|	|	|	|	|	|
Córdoba d.	2038	|	2053	2129	2144	2149	2155	2224	2244	2303	|
Sevilla a.	|	2137	2147	|	|	2243	|	|	|	2357	|
Cádiz **671** a.	|	...	...	|	|	...	|	|	|	...	|
Huelva **671** a.	|	...	...	|	|	...	|	|	|	...	|
Puente Genil - Herrera ¶ a.	2104	...	...	|	|	...	|	2250	|	...	|
Antequera - Santa Ana § a.	2117	...	...	|	|	...	|	2304	|	...	|
Algeciras **673** a.	|	...	...	|	|	...	|	|	|	...	|
Antequera AV a.	|	...	...	|	|	...	2234	|	|	...	|
Granada **678a** a.	|	...	...	|	|	...	2328	|	|	...	|
Málaga María Zambrano a.	2148	...	...	2236	2243	...	...	2335	2342	...	0007

	AVE 2561	avlo 2069	AVE 2261	iryo 6011	AVE 2063	AVE 2077	AVE 2071	Ouigo xxxx	Ouigo 6477	AVE 2073	AVE 2913	iryo 6089
	F		①–④		①–⑤	E					①–⑥ M	
Málaga María Zambrano d.	...	0548	...	...	0648	...	...	0725	...	0741	0755	0805
Granada **678a** d.	...	|	...	...	|	0612	...	|	...	|	|	|
Antequera AV d.	...	|	...	...	|	0702	...	|	...	|	|	|
Algeciras **673** d.	...	|	...	...	|	|	...	|	...	|	|	|
Antequera - Santa Ana § d.	...	0609	...	...	|	0713	...	|	...	|	|	|
Puente Genil - Herrera ¶ d.	...	0623	...	...	|	|	...	|	...	|	|	|
Huelva **671** d.	...	|	...	...	|	|	...	|	...	|	|	|
Cádiz **671** d.	...	|	...	...	|	|	...	|	...	|	|	|
Sevilla d.	0600	|	0630	0654	|	|	0718	|	0738	|	|	|
Córdoba d.	0645	0650	0714	0738	0747	0747	0802	0818	0823	0833	|	0856
Villanueva de CLP ⊠ d.	|	0713	|	|	|	|	|	|	|	|	|	|
Puertollano d.	0734	0740	|	|	|	|	0847	|	|	|	|	|
Ciudad Real d.	0751	0757	|	|	|	|	0904	|	|	|	|	|
Madrid Puerta de Atocha a.	0856	0903	0913	0936	0944	0944	1010	1020	1024	1032	1039	1054
Barcelona Sants **650** a.	1241	...	...	1249	...	...	...	...	...	...	...	...

	Alvia 2075	AVE 2081	AVE 3993	AVE 3943	Alvia 2285	AVE 2091	AVE 2093	iryo 6107	AVE 2101	avlo 2109	Ouigo 6517	Ouigo 6529	AVE 2111	iryo 6015	Alvia 2087	AVE 2123	iryo 6127	avlo 2137	AVE 2141	avlo 2149	AVE 2553	Alvia 2135	AVE 2151	iryo 6159	AVE 2861	Ouigo xxxx	AVE 2167	AVE 2163
		①–⑥			①–⑥		Ⓑ								A						Ⓑ		Ⓑ		H			
Málaga María Zambrano d.	...	...	0822	...	...	...	0932	...	...	1033	...	1115	...	1133	...	1159	...	...	...	1420	1458	...	...	1528	...	1535	...	1541
Granada **678a** d.	...	...	|	...	...	...	|	...	...	|	...	|	...	|	1113	|	...	...	...	|	|	...	...	|	...	|	1506	|
Antequera AV d.	...	...	|	...	...	...	|	...	...	|	...	|	...	|	1158	|	...	...	...	|	|	...	...	|	...	|	1555	|
Algeciras **673** d.	...	...	|	...	...	...	|	...	...	|	...	|	...	|	|	|	...	...	...	|	|	...	...	|	...	|	|	|
Antequera - Santa Ana § d.	...	...	0843	...	...	...	0953	...	...	1054	...	|	...	|	|	|	...	...	...	1441	|	...	...	|	...	|	1604	1604
Puente Genil - Herrera ¶ d.	...	...	0858	...	...	...	1008	...	...	1108	...	|	...	|	|	|	...	...	...	1455	|	...	...	|	...	|	|	|
Huelva **671** d.	...	...	|	...	0800	...	|	...	...	|	...	|	...	|	|	|	...	...	...	|	|	...	...	|	...	|	|	|
Cádiz **671** d.	0635	...	|	...	|	...	|	...	...	|	...	|	...	|	|	|	...	...	...	|	|	1330	...	|	...	|	|	|
Sevilla d.	0803	0832	|	0837	|	0936	|	1020	1030	|	1114	|	1132	|	|	|	1225	1315	1430	|	|	1456	1534	|	1545	|	|	|
Córdoba d.	0904	0916	0933	0933	1001	|	1035	1104	1113	1135	|	1207	1216	1226	1246	1250	1309	1359	1514	1522	|	1559	|	1620	1628	|	1644	1644
Villanueva de CLP ⊠ d.	|	|	|	|	|	|	|	|	|	1158	|	|	|	|	|	|	|	1422	|	1545	|	|	|	|	|	|	|	|
Puertollano d.	0949	|	|	|	|	|	1119	|	|	1225	|	|	|	|	|	|	|	1449	|	1612	|	1644	|	|	|	|	|	|
Ciudad Real d.	1006	|	1034	1034	|	|	1136	|	|	1242	|	|	|	|	|	|	|	1506	|	1629	|	1701	|	|	|	|	|	|
Madrid Puerta de Atocha a.	1111	1116	|	|	1202	1213	1242	1302	1315	1348	1356	1410	1415	1424	1457	1450	1507	1612	1712	1735	1742	1803	1813	1818	1827	1838	1843	1843
Barcelona Sants **650** a.	...	...	1425	1425	...	...	...	...	...	...	...	...	...	1741	...	...	...	...	...	...	2034	...	...	...	...	...	...	...

	iryo 6013	AVE 3931	AVE 2361	AVE 3991	AVE 3941	AVE 3981	AVE 2173	Alvia 2365	AVE 2171	AVE 2883	Alvia 2165	iryo 6177	Alvia 9331	iryo 6189	avlo 2187	AVE 2197	AVE 2193	IC 2375	AVE 2191	Ouigo 6607	Alvia 2175	Ouigo 6599	AVE 2203	iryo 6217	iryo 6209	avlo 2217	AVE 2213	
			Ⓑ			V		⑦		Ⓑ	①④⑤⑦								Ⓑ								⑦ D	
Málaga María Zambrano d.	...	...	...	1620	...	...	1700	...	...	1755	...	...	...	1840	...	...	1850	...	...	...	...	1950	2005	...	2040	...	2120	...
Granada **678a** d.	...	1535	...	|	...	...	|	...	...	|	...	...	...	|	...	1815	|	...	...	...	...	|	|	...	|	...	|	...
Antequera AV d.	...	1621	...	|	...	...	|	...	...	|	...	...	...	|	...	1903	|	...	...	...	...	|	|	...	|	...	|	...
Algeciras **673** d.	...	|	...	|	...	...	|	...	...	|	...	...	1552	|	...	|	|	...	...	...	...	|	|	...	|	...	|	...
Antequera - Santa Ana § d.	...	|	...	1642	...	...	|	...	...	|	...	...	1825	|	...	1913	1913	...	...	...	...	|	|	...	|	...	|	...
Puente Genil - Herrera ¶ d.	...	|	...	1657	...	...	|	...	...	|	...	...	|	|	...	1932	1932	...	...	...	...	|	|	...	|	...	|	...
Huelva **671** d.	...	|	...	|	...	...	|	1605	...	|	...	...	|	|	...	|	|	1750	...	...	...	|	|	...	|	...	|	...
Cádiz **671** d.	...	|	...	|	...	...	|	|	...	|	1615	...	|	|	...	|	|	|	...	...	1810	|	|	...	|	...	|	...
Sevilla d.	1627	|	1631	|	1636	1653	|	|	1746	|	1748	1808	|	|	1855	|	|	1925	1933	1944	|	|	|	2028	|	2054	|	...
Córdoba d.	1704	1709	1715	1728	1728	1741	|	1810	1830	1846	|	1852	1904	1931	1939	2000	2000	2021	|	2029	|	|	2057	2112	2131	2138	|	...
Villanueva de CLP ⊠ d.	|	|	|	|	|	|	|	|	|	|	|	|	|	|	2002	|	|	|	|	|	|	|	|	|	|	2200	|	...
Puertollano d.	|	|	|	1815	1815	1836	|	|	1915	|	|	|	1950	|	2029	|	|	|	|	|	|	|	2141	|	|	2227	|	...
Ciudad Real d.	|	|	|	1832	1832	1900	|	|	1933	|	|	|	2009	|	2046	|	|	|	|	|	|	|	2158	|	|	2244	|	...
Madrid Puerta de Atocha a.	1902	|	1914	|	|	...	1944	2013	2040	2045	2055	2050	2120	2129	2152	2159	2159	2223	2213	2232	2242	2253	2304	2310	2329	2350	0004	...
Barcelona Sants **650** a.	2221	2154	...	2233	2233	...	...	...	...	2359	...	...	...	...	...	...	...	...	...	...	...	...	...	...	...	...	...	...

A – To/from Almería (Table **661**).
B – ③④⑤⑥⑦.
C – ①③④⑤⑦.
D – ⑦ (⑤⑦ June 6–29; daily July 1 - Sept. 7).
E – On ⑥⑦ departs Granada 0655 and runs 41–46 mins. later.
F – To Figueres (Table **657**).
H – From/to Huesca (Table **670**).
J – ⑤ (⑤⑦ June 8–29; daily July 1 - Sept. 7).

M – From/to Murcia (Table **668**).
V – From/to València (Table **668**).

f – Ⓐ.

§ – ± *17 km* from Antequera.
¶ – ± *8 km* from Puente Genil.

⊠ – Full name: Villanueva de Córdoba-Los Pedroches.
avlo – Low-cost ***AVE*** Renfe services branded **avlo**: www.avlorenfe.com
iryo – ***ETR*** 1000 services branded **iryo**: www.iryo.eu
Ouigo – Low-cost ***TGV*** Euroduplex services branded **Ouigo**: www.ouigo.com.
☛ – All trains convey 🍸. *AVE* trains also convey ✕.

661 MADRID - ALMERÍA and JAÉN

km		MD	MD		MD	IC	MD		MD	MD		Alvia	MD	MD		MD	Alvia	MD		MD		MD	
		17008	13331		13079	276	18030		18170	13083		697	13035	13073		18032	2366	18034		18036		17000	
		2	2		2		2		2	2		🍷	2	2		2		2		2		2	
		Ⓐ	Ⓐ													Ⓐ		Ⓑ					
					E				C	E		T	E	E									
0	**Madrid** Chamartín ‡ **669 672b** d.	...	...	...	...	0802	0904	...	1257	...	...	...	...	...	...	1545	...	1725	...	1919	...	2114	...
8	**Madrid** Atocha Cercanías **669 672b** d.	0713	...	...	...	0820	0916	...	1311	...	...	...	...	...	...	1558	1610	1739	...	1931	...	2128	...
57	Aranjuez **669 672b** d.	0751	...	...	...	|	1000	...	1345	...	...	...	...	...	...	1635	|	|	...	2011	...	2207	...
	Barcelona Sants **672** d.	|	...	...	...	|	|	...	|	...	...	0745	...	...	...	|	|	|	...	|	...	|	...
	València Joaquín Sorolla **668** d.	|	...	...	...	|	|	...	|	...	...	1143	...	...	...	|	|	|	...	|	...	|	...
157	Alcázar de San Juan **678** d.	0840	...	...	...	0943	1055	...	1435	...	...	1501	...	...	...	1724	|	1904	...	2102	...	2301	...
206	Manzanares **678** d.	...	...	...	...	|	1118	...	1501	...	...	1539	...	...	...	1748	◧	1929	...	2125	...	...	...
323	Linares - Baeza a.	...	...	...	...	1118	1246	...	...	...	...	1701	...	...	...	1917	|	2047	...	2242	...	...	...
323	Linares - Baeza d.	...	...	...	...	1120	1247	...	...	...	...	1703	...	...	...	1918	|	2048	...	2243	...	...	...
441	Moreda d.	...	...	...	...	|	|	...	...	...	...	|	...	...	...	|	|	|	...	|	...	...	...
466	Guadix **673** d.	...	...	...	...	1315	|	...	...	...	...	|	...	...	...	|	2120	|	...	|	...	...	...
565	**Almería** **673** a.	...	...	...	...	1457**x**	|	...	...	...	...	|	...	...	...	|	2303	|	...	|	...	...	...
¶	**Jaén** d.	...	0518	...	0729	...	1328	...	...	1435	...	|	1700	1818	...	1959	...	2130	...	2324	...	...	...
371	Andújar d.	...	0559	...	0809	...	...	...	...	1515	...	1737	1745	1858	...	...	...	...	...	...	...	...	...
450	**Córdoba** a.	...	0705	...	0917	...	...	...	...	1626	...	1827	1852	2000	...	...	...	...	...	...	...	...	...

	MD		MD		MD		Alvia	MD		MD	MD	Alvia	MD	MD		MD	MD	MD	IC	MD		MD	
	18047		18031		18033		2087	13337		13001	13003	694	18171	17041		18035	13009	18037	279	13011		13017	
	2		2		2			2		2	2	🍷	2	2		2	2	2		2		2	
	Ⓐ		Ⓐ		Ⓑ			Ⓐ		Ⓐ	Ⓒ												
										E	E	T		C			E			N		E	
Córdoba d.	...	...	...	...	...	...	...	0717	...	0914	1024	1016	...	...	...	...	1423	...	...	1604	...	2101	...
Andújar d.	...	...	...	...	...	...	...	0832	...	1024	1129	1113	...	...	...	...	1532	...	...	1716	...	2207	...
Jaén d.	...	...	0612	...	0832	...	...	0919	...	1105	1208	|	...	...	...	1522	1612	1720	...	1810	...	2246	...
Almería **673** d.	...	...	|	...	|	...	0808**x**	...	...	...	...	|	...	...	...	|	...	|	1530**x**	...	...	...	...
Guadix **673** d.	...	...	|	...	|	...	0954	...	...	...	...	|	...	...	...	|	...	|	1716	...	...	...	...
Moreda d.	...	...	|	...	|	...	|	...	...	...	...	|	...	...	...	|	...	|	|	...	...	...	...
Linares - Baeza a.	...	...	0650	...	0912	...	|	...	...	...	...	1147	...	...	...	1602	...	1758	1908	...	...	...	...
Linares - Baeza d.	...	...	0651	...	0913	...	|	...	...	...	...	1150	...	...	...	1603	...	1759	1910	...	...	...	...
Manzanares **678** d.	...	...	0815	...	1032	...	◧	...	...	...	...	1313	...	1521	...	1723	...	1920	|	...	...	...	...
Alcázar de San Juan **678** d.	0527	...	0842	...	1055	...	|	...	...	...	...	1342	1355	1547	...	1745	...	1943	2102	...	...	...	...
València Joaquín Sorolla **668** a.	|	...	|	...	|	...	|	...	...	...	...	1654	|	|	...	|	...	|	|	...	...	...	...
Barcelona Sants **672** a.	|	...	|	...	|	...	|	...	...	...	...	2047	|	|	...	|	...	|	|	...	...	...	...
Aranjuez **669 672b** d.	0621	...	0936	...	1143	...	|	...	...	...	...	...	1447	1642	...	1830	...	2030	|	...	...	...	...
Madrid Atocha Cercanías **669 672b** a.	0656	...	1013	...	1213	...	1457	...	...	...	...	...	1526	1723	...	1909	...	2108	2226	...	...	...	...
Madrid Chamartín ‡ **669 672b** a.	...	...	1028	...	1227	...	...	...	...	...	...	...	1541	1737	...	1924	...	2122	2242	...	...	...	...

C – To/from Ciudad Real (Table **678**).
E – To/from Cádiz (Table **671**).
N – Daily from Sevilla. From Cádiz on ①–⑤. Table **671**.
T – TORRE DEL ORO – [12] 🍷 Barcelona - València - Córdoba - Sevilla - Cádiz and v.v. (Table **672a**).
x – 🚌 Almería - Huercal-Viator and v.v. (6 km.).
◧ – Via Córdoba (Table **660**).
¶ – Linares - Jaen: *59 km*. Jaen - Andújar: *54 km*.
‡ – Full name is Madrid-Chamartín-Clara Campoamor.

662 MÁLAGA - TORREMOLINOS - FUENGIROLA

2nd class

km					❦							
0	**Málaga** María Zambrano d.	0523	0558	0633	0653	and	2133	2203	2233	2303	2333	...
8	Málaga Aeropuerto ✈ d.	0532	0607	0642	0702	every	2142	2212	2242	2312	2342	...
16	**Torremolinos** d.	0543	0618	0653	0713	20	2153	2223	2253	2323	2353	...
20	Benalmádena d.	0554	0629	0704	0724	mins.	2204	2234	2304	2334	0004	...
31	**Fuengirola** a.	0606	0641	0716	0736	until	2216	2246	2316	2346	0016	...

				❦							
Fuengirola d.	0610	0645	0720	0740	and	2220	2250	2320	2350	0020	...
Benalmádena d.	0624	0659	0734	0754	every	2234	2304	2334	0004	0034	...
Torremolinos d.	0633	0708	0743	0803	20	2243	2313	2343	0013	0043	...
Málaga Aeropuerto ✈ d.	0644	0719	0754	0814	mins.	2254	2324	2354	0024	0054	...
Málaga María Zambrano a.	0652	0727	0802	0822	until	2302	2332	0002	0032	0102	...

❦ – 0653, 0733, 0813 from Málaga and 0740, 0820, 0900 from Fuengirola do not run on ⑥⑦.

663a MÁLAGA - CÓRDOBA - SEVILLA

Avant high-speed shuttle services, Turista class 🍷

	8654	8664	8694		8744	8764	8784	8704	
	Ⓐ	Ⓐ				Ⓐ			
Málaga María Zambrano d.	...	0635	0917	...	1425	1522	1818	2015	...
Antequera - Santa Ana § d.	...	0658	0940	...	1448	1545	1841	2038	...
Puente Genil - Herrera ¶ d.	...	0712	0954	...	1502	1603	1855	2052	...
Córdoba a.	...	0741	1022	...	1530	1631	1923	2121	...
Córdoba d.	0620	0746	1027	...	1535	1636	1928	2126	...
Sevilla a.	0712	0838	1119	...	1627	1728	2024	2227	...

	8075	8085		8125	8155	8175	8195	8215		
	Ⓐ					Ⓐ		Ⓐ		
Sevilla d.	0620	0754	...	1300	1539	1740	2016	2136	...	...
Córdoba a.	0704	0838	...	1343	1623	1822	2100	2224	...	...
Córdoba d.	0709	0843	...	1348	1628	1827	2105	...	...	...
Puente Genil - Herrera ¶ d.	0737	0917	...	1427	1657	1855	2132	...	...	...
Antequera - Santa Ana § d.	0753	0933	...	1443	1712	1911	2148	...	...	...
Málaga María Zambrano a.	0821	1000	...	1511	1741	1940	2215	...	...	...

§ – ± *17 km* from Antequera.
¶ – ± *8 km* from Puente Genil.

663b MADRID - PUERTOLLANO

Avant high-speed shuttle services, Turista class 🍷

		8260		8080		8100			8130	8140	8150		8170	8180	8190	8200		8220		
		Ⓐ		Ⓐ						Ⓐ				Ⓐ		Ⓑ				
Madrid Puerta de Atocha d.	...	0625	...	0810	...	1010	...	...	1310	1410	1540	...	1710	1810	1910	2010	...	2215	...	...
Ciudad Real d.	...	0730	...	0914	...	1114	...	...	1414	1514	1644	...	1814	1914	2013	2113	...	2319	...	...
Puertollano a.	...	0750	...	0932	...	1132	...	...	1432	1532	1702	...	1832	1932	2032	2132	...	2337	...	...

		8261	8271	8471	8081		8101		8111			8151	8161	8171	8181	8191		8211		
		Ⓐ	Ⓐ	Ⓐ								⚒	Ⓐ		⑦			Ⓑ		
Puertollano d.	...	0630	0700	0720	0805	...	1005	...	1205	...	...	1505	1630	1730	1805	1905	...	2132	...	...
Ciudad Real d.	...	0648	0718	0738	0823	...	1023	...	1223	...	...	1523	1648	1748	1823	1923	...	2150	...	...
Madrid Puerta de Atocha a.	...	0753	0822	0842	0927	...	1127	...	1327	...	...	1627	1752	1852	1927	2027	...	2254	...	...

664 🚌 BARCELONA - ANDORRA

From **Barcelona** Nord bus station: 0630*, 0700, 0730*, 1030, 1500, 1700*, 1900.
From **Andorra la Vella** bus station: 0600, 0815*, 1100, 1500, 1700*, 1915.
Journey 3 hr 15 min (* 4 hours). Operator: Alsina Graells, Barcelona (ALSA) ✆ (+34) 91 327 05 40.

From **Barcelona Airport** ✈ (T1 and T2): 0730, 0930, 1100, 1300, 1500, 1730, 2000, 2130, 2300.
From **Barcelona** Sants railway station: 0615, 0815, 1015, 1145, 1345, 1545, 1815, 2045, 2215, 2345.
From **Andorra la Vella** bus station: 0330, 0615, 0815, 1115, 1315, 1515, 1630, 1815, 2015, 2215.
Journey 3 hours (3 hrs 30 mins to/from Barcelona ✈). Operator: Autocars Nadal ✆ +376 805 151.

665 BARCELONA - SITGES - SANT V de CALDERS

2nd class

Local rail service **Barcelona - Sitges - Sant Vicenç de Calders**.

From Barcelona Sants: 0606, 0636 and every 30 minutes until 2206; then 2306.

From Sant Vicenç: 0601, 0616 ⚒, 0631 Ⓐ, 0659, 0729, 0751, 0831, 0902, 0932 and every 30 minutes until 2102, 2132 Ⓐ, then 2200.

Additional trains operate **Barcelona - Sitges** and v.v.

Journey times: **Barcelona** – **Sitges** (*34 km*) 30 minutes,
Barcelona – **Sant Vicenç** (*60 km*) 57 minutes.

2nd class BARCELONA - MATARÓ, BLANES and MAÇANET 666

Cercanías (suburban) line **R1**. For faster services Barcelona - Maçanet via Granollers, see Table **657**.
Approximate journey times (in mins) to / from **Barcelona** Sants: Mataró (46), Arenys de Mar (57), Calella (69), Pineda de Mar (73), Malgrat de Mar (79), Blanes (84), Maçanet-Massanes (97).

Barcelona Sants – **Mataró** and v.v. *35 km*
Ⓐ: 4–6 trains per hour.
From Barcelona 0555 – 2318; from Mataró 0501 – 2301.
Ⓒ: 2–4 trains per hour.
From Barcelona 0555 – 2318; from Mataró 0501 – 2231.

Barcelona Sants – **Blanes** *67 km*
0555, 0625 and every 30 mins. until 2155 Ⓒ, 2255 Ⓐ.

Blanes - **Barcelona** Sants
Daily: 0603, 0623 and every 30 mins. until 2153.

Barcelona Sants – Blanes – **Maçanet-Massanes** *82 km*
Daily: 0555, 0655 and every 30 mins. until 2155.
Maçanet-Massanes – Blanes – **Barcelona** Sants
Ⓐ: 0609, 0639 and every 30 mins until 1109 then hourly until 1909, 1939, 2009, 2039, 2109, 2139.
Ⓒ: 0609, 0639, 0709 and hourly until 1909, 2009, 2139.

2nd class ALACANT - BENIDORM - DÉNIA 667

◐ *By tram (route L1)*		①–⑤							
Alacant Luceros ⊙ d.	...	0541	0611	0711	every	1911	2011	2111	2211
El Campello d.	...	0609	0639	0739	30 mins.	1939	2039	2139	2239
La Vila Joiosa d.	0612	0635	0705	0805	◐	2005	2105	2205	2305
Benidorm a.	0630	0653	0723	0823	until	2023	2123	2223	2323

✣ *By tram (route L1)*	①–⑤								
Benidorm d.	0635	0705	0805	every	1905	2005	2105	2205	2235
La Vila Joiosa d.	0653	0723	0823	30 mins.	1923	2023	2123	2223	2253
El Campello d.	0723	0753	0853	✣	1953	2053	2153	2253	...
Alacant Luceros ⊙ a.	0751	0821	0921	until	2021	2121	2221	2321	...

By train (route L9)									
Benidorm d.	0535	0635	0735		1935	2035	2135	2235	...
Altea d.	0550	0650	0750	every	1950	2050	2150	2250	...
Calpe d.	0611	0711	0811	hour	2011	2111	2211	...	...
Teulada d.	0630	0730	0830	until	2030	2130	2230	...	...
Gata 🚌 d.	0641	0741	0841		2041	2141	2241	...	...
Dénia 🚌 a.	0626	0756	0856		2056	2156	2256	...	...

By train (route L9)									
Dénia 🚌 d.	...	0602	0702	0802		2002	2102	...	2202
Gata d.	...	0617	0717	0817	every	2017	2117	...	2217
Teulada d.	...	0629	0729	0829	hour	2029	2129	...	2229
Calpe d.	...	0648	0748	0848	until	2048	2148	...	2248
Altea d.	0609	0709	0809	0909		2109	2209	2259	2309
Benidorm a.	0624	0724	0824	0924		2124	2224	2314	2324

◐ – Alacant - Benidorm runs every 30 minutes 0641 - 2141 (also 0025, 0155 night of ⑤⑥ June 30 - Aug. 26).
⊙ – ± 400 m from Alacant Renfe station.
✣ – Benidorm - Alacant runs every 30 minutes 0635 - 2205 (also 0211, 0441 night of ⑤⑥ June 30 - Aug. 26).
Operator: Tram Metropolitano / FGV ✆ 900 72 04 72 www.fgvalicante.com

MADRID - ALACANT, MURCIA and VALÈNCIA 668

km		*avlo* 5668	*avlo* 5064	*iryo* 6062 ①–⑤	18024 ①–⑤ B	*AVE* 5072	18018 ⑥⑦ J	*Ouigo* 6472	*AVE* 5070 ①–⑤	*iryo* 6074	*Ouigo* 6484	*AVE* 5080 C	*MD* 14404 ①–⑥	*AVE* 5092 V	*iryo* 6092	*AVE* 5102	*AVE* 5962	*AVE* 5890	*Ouigo* 6504	*avlo* 5104	*iryo* 6102	*MD* 18081 2 h	*AVE* 2913 ①–⑥ M
	Madrid Chamartín ¶ d.	0615	0630	0645	...	0700	...	0715	0730	0745	0815	0830	...	0900	0930	0945	1000	...	1015	1030	1045	...	...
0	**Madrid** Puerta de Atocha d.	|	|	|	...	|	...	|	|	|	|	|	...	|	|	|	|	0944	|	|	|	...	1100
189	Cuenca Fernando Zóbel d.	0720	0735	|	...	0806	...	|	0836	0850	|	|	...	1006	1035	|	|	1045	|	1136	1150	...	1202
321	Requena / Utiel d.	|	0809	|	...	|	...	|	|	|	|	|	...	|	|	|	|	1122	|	1211	|	...	|
322*	**Albacete** d.	0755	|	|	0832	0840	0918	|	|	0923	0949	|	1010	1040	|	|	|	|	1149	|	|	1220	1236
436	Villena AV d.	0829	|	|	|	0915	|	|	|	|	|	|	|	|	|	|	|	|	|	|	|	1315v	1311
486	**Alacant** Terminal d.	0856	|	|	|	0934	|	|	|	1010	|	|	|	1129	|	1210	|	|	1237	|	|	1409	1339
	Elche AV / Elx AV d.	0918	|	|	|	...	|	|	|	...	1037	|	|	...	|	...	1215	|	...	|	|	...	1407
	Orihuela d.	0934	|	|	|	...	|	|	|	...	|	|	|	...	|	...	1230	|	...	|	|	...	1422
	Murcia a.	0950	|	|	|	...	|	|	|	...	1101	|	|	...	|	...	1245	|	...	|	|	...	1437
477	Xátiva d.	...	|	|	1002	...	1042	|	|	...	...	|	1135	...	|	...	...	|	...	|	|	...	...
391	**València** Joaquín Sorolla a.	...	0831	0839	|	...	|	0909	0930	...	...	1024	|	...	1129	...	...	1147	...	1236	1243	...	...
	València Nord △ a.	...	...	...	1053	...	1125	...	...	...	...	...	1219	...	...	...	...	|	...	...	...	...	...
	Castelló de la Plana **672** a.	...	...	...	...	...	...	...	...	...	...	...	...	...	...	...	...	1315	...	...	...	...	...

	AVE 5912 ⑦	*Ouigo* 6512	*AVE* 5110 ①–⑤	*Alvia* 4072 S	*AVE* 5312 ⑥⑦ N	*AVE* 5124	*iryo* 6122	*Ouigo* 6532	*Alvia* 694 🍸 T	*AVE* 5142 ①–⑤	*Ouigo* 6544 A	*AVE* 5742	*avlo* 5144	*iryo* 6142	*AVE* 5152 Ⓑ	*iryo* 6152	*AVE* 5750 G	*MD* 14406	*iryo* 6154	*AVE* 5162	*Ouigo* 6564	*AVE* 5160 Ⓑ	
Madrid Chamartín ¶ d.	...	1115	1130	1145	1200	1230	1245	1315	...	1400	1415	...	1430	1445	1500	1515	1530	...	1545	1600	1615	1630	...
Madrid Puerta de Atocha d.	1100	|	|	|	|	|	|	|	...	|	|	1425	|	|	|	|	|	...	|	|	|	|	...
Cuenca Fernando Zóbel d.	1203	|	|	1258	1306	1336	|	|	...	|	1520	1526	1535	|	|	|	1636	...	1650	1706	|	|	...
Requena / Utiel d.	|	|	|	|	|	1410	|	|	...	|	|	|	1610	|	|	|	|	...	|	|	|	|	...
Albacete d.	1237	|	|	1337	1340	|	|	|	1459	1534	1554	1600	|	|	|	|	|	1700	1723	1740	1749	|	...
Villena AV d.	1311	|	|	1424	|	|	|	|	|	1608	|	1633	|	|	|	|	|	|	|	1815	|	|	...
Alacant Terminal d.	1339	|	|	1443	1428	|	|	|	|	1628	1644	1700	|	|	1717	|	|	|	1810	1834	|	|	...
Elche AV / Elx AV d.	1407	|	|	...	...	|	|	|	|	...	...	1722	|	|	...	|	|	|	...	...	1839	|	...
Orihuela d.	1422	|	|	...	...	|	|	|	|	...	...	1737	|	|	...	|	|	|	...	...	|	|	...
Murcia a.	1437	|	|	...	...	|	|	|	|	...	...	1752	|	|	...	|	|	|	...	...	1903	|	...
Xátiva d.	...	|	|	...	...	|	|	|	1616	...	...	...	|	|	...	|	|	1834	...	...	...	|	...
València Joaquín Sorolla a.	...	1309	1324	...	...	1434	1439	1509	1654	...	...	...	1634	1639	...	1709	1730	|	...	...	...	1824	...
València Nord △ a.	...	...	...	...	...	...	...	...	|	...	...	...	...	...	...	...	|	1923	...	...	...	...	...
Castelló de la Plana **672** a.	...	...	...	...	...	...	...	...	1756	...	...	...	...	...	...	...	1836	...	...	...	...	...	...

	iryo 6162	*avlo* 5178 A	*MD* 18181 2 h	*Ouigo* 6572	*AVE* 5170	*Av* 8163 Ⓐ H	*AVE* 5182	*Av* 8173 Ⓒ H	*AVE* 5180	*iryo* 6182	*AVE* 5382 Y	*AVE* 5990	*AVE* 3981 P	*AVE* 5792 Ⓑ E	*Alvia* 4140 G	*AVE* 5192 Ⓑ	*Ouigo* 6604	*AVE* 5200 N	*iryo* 6202	*avlo* 5214	*Ouigo* 6612 A		
Madrid Chamartín ¶ d.	1645	1700	...	1715	1730	...	1800	...	1830	1845	1900	...	...	1915	1945	2000	2015	2030	2045	2100	2115	...	...
Madrid Puerta de Atocha d.	|	|	...	|	|	1730	|	1750	|	|	|	1940	...	|	|	|	|	|	|	|	|	...	...
Cuenca Fernando Zóbel d.	1750	1806	...	|	|	1846	|	1927	|	|	2006	2042	2031	|	2058	2106	|	|	|	2206	2221	...	...
Requena / Utiel d.	|	|	...	|	|	|	|	|	|	|	|	2118	|	|	|	|	|	|	|	2241	|	...	...
Albacete d.	|	1840	1849	|	|	1924	1936	2006	|	|	2040	|	|	|	2136	2140	2149	|	|	|	|	...	...
Villena AV d.	|	1915	1959v	|	|	...	|	...	|	|	|	|	|	|	2224	2215	|	|	|	|	|	...	...
Alacant Terminal d.	|	1934	2047	|	|	...	2023	...	|	|	2128	|	|	|	2245	2234	2239	|	|	|	|	...	...
Elche AV / Elx AV d.	|	...	...	|	|	...	...	...	|	|	...	|	|	2138	...	...	...	|	|	|	|	...	...
Orihuela d.	|	...	...	|	|	...	...	...	|	|	...	|	|	2154	...	...	...	|	|	|	|	...	...
Murcia a.	|	...	...	|	|	...	...	...	|	|	...	|	|	2209	...	...	...	|	|	|	|	...	...
Xátiva d.	|	...	...	|	|	...	...	...	|	|	...	|	|	...	...	...	...	|	|	|	|	...	...
València Joaquín Sorolla a.	1840	...	...	1909	1924	...	...	...	2024	2039	...	2142	2215	...	...	...	...	2224	2237	2305	2315	...	...
València Nord △ a.	...	...	...	...	...	...	...	...	...	...	...	|	...	...	...	...	...	...	...	...	...	...	...
Castelló de la Plana **672** a.	...	...	...	...	...	...	...	...	...	...	...	2242	...	...	...	...	...	...	...	...	...	...	...

A – From Valladolid (Table **679a**).
B – From Alcázar de San Juan on ②–⑤. From Ciudad Real on ① (Table **678**).
C – On ①–⑥ from Burgos (Table **689**).
E – From Burgos (Table **689**).
G – From Gijón (Table **685**).
H – From Toledo (Table **679**).
J – From Alcázar de San Juan.
M – From Málaga (Table **660**).
N – From Leon (Table **681**).
P – From Sevilla (Table **660**).
S – From Santander (Table **684**).
T – TORRE DEL ORO – 12 🍸 Cádiz - Barcelona (Table **672a**).
V – On ①–⑤ from Leon (Table **681**).
Y – On ①–⑥ From Ourense (Table **680**).
h – From Ciudad Real (Table **678**).
v – Villena.
* – Albacete - Xátiva - València: *203 km*.
¶ – Full name is Madrid-Chamartín-Clara Campoamor.

Av – ***Avant*** high-speed services. Single class.
avlo – Low-cost high-speed ***AVE*** Renfe services branded **avlo**: www.avlorenfe.com
Ouigo – Low-cost high-speed ***TGV*** services branded **Ouigo**: www.ouigo.com
iryo – ***ETR*** 1000 high-speed services branded **iryo**: www.iryo.eu

668 VALÈNCIA, MURCIA and ALACANT - MADRID

	Av	AVE	avlo	AVE	iryo	AVE	Ouigo	AVE	AVE	AVE	Ouigo	AVE	Av	AVE	AVE	avlo	iryo	AVE	Ouigo	AVE	MD	Alvia	
	8072	**5063**	**5065**	**5763**	**6073**	**5871**	**6473**	**5071**	**5273**	**5073**	**6485**	**5081**	**8082**	**3982**	**5083**	**5095**	**6103**	**5093**	**6503**	**5101**	**18183**	**4143**	
	①-⑤	①-⑤	①-⑤	①-⑥	①-⑤					①-⑥		①-⑥	⑥⑦								2		
	H			**B**					**Y**		**V**		**H**	**P**						**N**	**h**	**S**	
Castelló de la Plana **672** d.	...	...	...	...	...	0602	...	...	...	...	...	...	...	...	...	...	...	...	...	...	...	...	...
València Nord △ d.	...	...	...	...	...	|	...	...	...	...	...	...	...	...	...	...	...	...	...	...	...	...	...
València Joaquín Sorolla d.	...	...	0632	...	0653	0657	0727	0742	...	...	...	0842	...	0914	...	0932	0957	...	1027	1032	...	...	...
Xátiva d.	...	...	|	...	|	|	|	|	...	...	...	|	...	|	...	|	|	...	|	|	...	...	...
Murcia d.	...	...	|	0630	|	|	|	|	...	...	...	|	...	|	...	|	|	...	|	|	...	...	...
Orihuela d.	...	...	|	0645	|	|	|	|	...	...	...	|	...	|	...	|	|	...	|	|	...	...	...
Elche AV / Elx AV d.	...	...	|	0659	|	|	|	|	...	...	...	|	...	|	...	|	|	...	|	|	...	...	...
Alacant Terminal d.	...	0552	|	|	|	|	|	|	0724	0740	0753	|	...	|	0835	|	|	0940	|	|	1012	1026	...
Villena AV d.	...	0612	|	|	|	|	|	|	|	|	|	|	...	|	0855	|	|	1000	|	|	1053v	1048	...
Albacete d.	0540	0645	|	|	|	|	|	|	0814	|	0844	|	0854	|	0929	|	|	1034	|	|	1150	1125	...
Requena / Utiel d.	|	|	0659	|	|	0725	|	|	|	|	|	|	|	|	|	0959	|	|	|	1059	...	|	...
Cuenca Fernando Zóbel d.	0623	0719	0735	|	0748	0802	|	|	0848	|	0919	|	0934	1006	1003	1034	|	|	|	1135	...	1203	...
Madrid Puerta de Atocha a.	0752	|	|	|	|	0908	|	|	|	|	|	|	1101	...	|	|	|	|	|	|	...	|	...
Madrid Chamartín ¶ a.	...	0823	0838	0913	0853	...	0923	0938	0952	1000	1022	1038	...	...	1108	1138	1153	1208	1223	1238	...	1323	...

	iryo	avlo	AVE	iryo	AVE	Alvia	Ouigo	AVE	iryo	Ouigo	MD	AVE	Ouigo	AVE	AVE	avlo	iryo	Alvia	AVE	AVE	AVE	MD	
	6123	**5817**	**5721**	**6125**	**5113**	**697**	**6535**	**5131**	**6143**	**6545**	**14405**	**5843**	**6553**	**5143**	**5951**	**5155**	**6163**	**4181**	**5153**	**5161**	**5862**	**18083**	
						🍷													Ⓑ			2	
		V	**G**			**T**							**V**					**G**			**M**	**h**	
Castelló de la Plana **672** d.	...	...	1117	...	...	1025	...	...	...	...	...	...	...	...	1411	...	...	...	...	...	...	...	...
València Nord △ d.	...	...	|	...	...	|	...	...	...	...	1353	...	...	...	|	...	...	...	...	...	...	...	...
València Joaquín Sorolla d.	1200	...	1231	...	...	1143	...	1331	1357	...	|	...	1451	...	1509	1532	1557	...	...	1635	...	...	...
Xátiva d.	|	...	|	...	...	1233	...	|	|	...	1444	...	|	...	|	|	|	...	...	|	...	...	...
Murcia d.	|	1032	|	...	...	|	1239	|	|	...	|	1353	|	...	|	|	|	...	...	|	1532	...	...
Orihuela d.	|	1047	|	...	...	|	|	|	|	...	|	1408	|	...	|	|	|	...	...	|	1548	...	...
Elche AV / Elx AV d.	|	1103	|	...	...	|	1302	|	|	...	|	1422	|	...	|	|	|	...	...	|	1602	...	...
Alacant Terminal d.	|	1136	|	1225	1245	|	|	|	|	1400	|	|	|	1434	|	|	|	1526	1550	|	1635	1655	...
Villena AV d.	|	1156	|	|	|	|	|	|	|	|	|	|	|	1455	|	|	|	1547	|	|	1654	1740v	...
Albacete d.	|	1230	|	1313	1335	1344	1350	|	|	1451	1605	|	|	1529	|	|	|	1623	|	|	1730	1839	...
Requena / Utiel d.	|	|	|	|	|	...	|	1358	|	|	...	|	|	|	1536	1559	|	|	|	|	|	...	...
Cuenca Fernando Zóbel d.	|	1304	1331	1347	|	...	|	1434	|	|	...	|	1550	1604	1613	1634	|	1701	|	|	1803	...	...
Madrid Puerta de Atocha a.	|	|	|	|	|	...	|	|	|	|	...	|	|	|	1718	|	|	|	|	|	1908	...	...
Madrid Chamartín ¶ a.	1353	1407	1437	1450	1508	...	1523	1537	1553	1623	...	1638	1654	1708	...	1738	1752	1821	1808	1838	...	...	...

		Ouigo	AVE	iryo	AVE	Ouigo	AVE	AVE	AVE	iryo	iryo	AVE	Ouigo	AVE	avlo	Ouigo	avlo	MD	iryo				
	18027	**6573**	**5171**	**6183**	**5183**	**6985**	**5181**	**5193**	**5191**	**6203**	**6195**	**5203**	**6603**	**5903**	**5215**	**6615**	**5217**	**14407**	**6163**				
			Ⓑ					⑤⑦	Ⓑ									Ⓑ	Ⓑ				
	A		**B**		**N**																		
Castelló de la Plana **672** d.	...	...	...	...	...	...	...	...	...	...	...	...	...	...	...	...	...	...	...	...	...	...	...
València Nord △ d.	1650	...	...	...	...	...	...	...	...	...	...	...	...	...	...	...	...	2050	...	...	...	...	...
València Joaquín Sorolla d.	|	1728	1742	1757	...	...	1831	...	1942	2000	...	...	2027	...	2112	...	...	|	2157	...	...	...	...
Xátiva d.	1734	|	|	|	...	...	|	...	|	|	...	...	|	...	|	...	...	2114	|	...	...	...	...
Murcia d.	|	|	|	|	...	...	|	...	|	|	...	...	|	1858	|	2039	...	|	|	...	...	...	...
Orihuela d.	|	|	|	|	...	...	|	..	|	|	...	...	|	1915	|	|	...	|	|	...	...	...	...
Elche AV / Elx AV d.	|	|	|	|	...	...	|	...	|	|	...	...	|	1929	|	2102	...	|	|	...	...	...	...
Alacant Terminal d.	|	|	|	|	1743	1800	|	1850	|	|	1935	1945	|	2001	|	|	2104	2234	|	...	...	...	...
Villena AV d.	|	|	|	|	|	|	|	|	|	|	|	|	|	2021	|	|	2125	...	|	...	...	...	...
Albacete d.	1913	|	|	|	1832	1851	|	|	|	|	2023	2035	|	2055	|	2150	2159	...	|	...	...	...	...
Requena / Utiel d.	...	|	|	|	|	|	1858	|	|	|	|	|	|	|	2139	|	|	...	|	...	...	...	...
Cuenca Fernando Zóbel d.	...	|	|	|	1906	|	1934	|	|	2053	2057	|	|	2129	2214	|	2234	...	|	...	...	...	...
Madrid Puerta de Atocha a.	...	|	|	|	|	|	|	|	|	|	|	|	|	2234	|	|	|	...	|	...	...	...	...
Madrid Chamartín ¶ a.	...	1923	1937	1953	2008	2023	2038	2108	2138	2155	2202	2208	2223	...	2318	2323	2338	...	2353	...	...	...	...

A – To Alcázar de San Juan on ①-⑥. To Ciudad Real on ⑦ (Table **678**).
B – To Burgos (Table **689**).
G – To Gijón (Table **685**).
H – To Toledo (Table **679**).
M – To Málaga (Table **660**).
N – To Leon (Table **682**).
P – To Sevilla (Table **660**).
S – To Santander (Table **684**).
T – TORRE DEL ORO – 🛏12 🍷 Barcelona - Cádiz (Table **672a**).
V – To Valladolid (Table **679a**).
Y – To Ourense on ①-⑥ (Table **680**).
h – To Ciudad Real (Table **678**).
v – Villena.
* – Albacete - Xátiva - València: *203 km*.
¶ – Full name is Madrid-Chamartín-Clara Campoamor.

Av – ***Avant*** high-speed services. Single class.
avlo – Low-cost high-speed ***AVE*** Renfe services branded **avlo**: www.avlorenfe.com
Ouigo – Low-cost high-speed ***TGV*** services branded **Ouigo**: www.ouigo.com
iryo – ***ETR*** 1000 high-speed services branded **iryo**: www.iryo.eu

674 PALMA DE MALLORCA - INCA - SA POBLA and MANACOR

SFM 2nd class

Table temporarily relocated from page 330

km		Ⓐ		Ⓐ	Ⓒ	Ⓐ	Ⓒ	Ⓐ	Ⓐ	Ⓒ		Ⓐ	Ⓒ	Ⓐ	Ⓒ	Ⓐ	Ⓐ		Ⓒ		Ⓐ		Ⓒ		Ⓐ	Ⓐ	Ⓒ
0	**Palma** d.	0550	0610	0632	0640	0650	0710	0710	0730	0740	0810	0832	0840	0850	0910	0930	0950	1010	1040	1110	1130	1210	1240	1310	1332	1350	1410
7	Marratxi d.	0603	0623	0640	0654	0703	0724	0723	0743	0754	0823	0840	0854	0903	0924	0943	1003	1023	1054	1123	1143	1223	1254	1323	1340	1403	1424
29	**Inca** d.	0624	0644	0705	0715	0724	0745	0744	0804	0815	0844	0905	0915	0924	0945	1004	1024	1044	1115	1144	1204	1244	1315	1344	1405	1424	1446
***	sa Pobla a.	0621	|	0722	0732	|	|	0801	|	0832	|	0922	0932	|	|	|	1041	|	1132	|	1221	|	1332	|	1422	|	|
64	**Manacor** a.	...	0715	...	...	0755	0815	...	0835	...	0915	...	...	0955	1015	1035	...	1115	...	1214	...	1314	...	1414	...	1455	1515

	Ⓐ	Ⓒ	Ⓐ		Ⓐ	Ⓒ	Ⓐ	Ⓐ	Ⓒ		Ⓐ	Ⓒ	Ⓒ	Ⓐ	Ⓒ	Ⓒ	Ⓐ	Ⓒ	Ⓒ	Ⓐ	Ⓒ	Ⓒ	Ⓐ	Ⓒ	Ⓒ	Ⓐ	
Palma d.	1430	1440	1450	1510	1550	1610	1612	1630	1640	1710	1730	1740	1810	1835	1840	1910	1935	1940	2010	2035	2040	2110	2135	2140	2210	2220	...
Marratxi d.	1443	1454	1503	1523	1603	1624	1620	1643	1654	1723	1743	1754	1824	1848	1854	1924	1948	1954	2024	2048	2054	2124	2148	2154	2224	2233	...
Inca d.	1504	1515	1524	1544	1624	1646	1645	1704	1715	1744	1804	1815	1846	1909	1915	1946	2009	2015	2046	2109	2115	2146	2209	2215	2246	2254	...
sa Pobla a.	|	1532	1541	|	|	|	1702	|	1732	|	1821	1832	|	1926	1932	|	2026	2032	|	2126	2132	|	2226	2232	|	|	...
Manacor a.	1535	...	...	1615	1655	1715	...	1735	...	1815	...	...	1915	...	...	2015	...	...	2115	...	...	2215	...	...	2315	2324	...

	Ⓐ	Ⓐ	Ⓒ	Ⓐ	Ⓐ	Ⓒ	Ⓐ	Ⓒ	Ⓐ	Ⓒ	Ⓒ	Ⓐ	Ⓐ	Ⓒ	Ⓐ	Ⓐ	Ⓒ	Ⓐ	Ⓒ	Ⓐ	Ⓒ	Ⓐ	Ⓐ	Ⓒ	Ⓐ	Ⓒ	Ⓐ
Manacor d.	...	0616	0624	0656	...	0724	0736	...	0816	0824	...	0856	...	0924	0936	1016	1024	...	...	1056	1124	1138	...	1224	1238	1324	1338
sa Pobla d.	0600	|	|	|	0730	|	|	0807	|	|	0907	|	0930	|	|	|	|	1050	1107	|	|	|	1230	|	|	|	|
Inca d.	0618	0647	0654	0728	0748	0754	0808	0823	0848	0854	0923	0928	0948	0954	1008	1048	1054	1108	1123	1128	1154	1210	1248	1254	1310	1354	1410
Marratxi d.	0637	0707	0715	0748	0811	0815	0828	0844	0908	0915	0944	0948	1011	1015	1028	1108	1115	1128	1144	1148	1215	1230	1308	1315	1330	1415	1430
Palma a.	0652	0715	0729	0802	0819	0829	0842	0858	0922	0929	0958	1002	1019	1029	1042	1122	1129	1142	1158	1202	1229	1244	1322	1329	1344	1429	1444

	Ⓒ	Ⓒ	Ⓐ	Ⓐ	Ⓐ	Ⓒ	Ⓐ	Ⓒ	Ⓐ	Ⓒ	Ⓐ	Ⓒ	Ⓐ	Ⓐ	Ⓒ	Ⓐ	Ⓒ	Ⓐ	Ⓒ	Ⓒ	Ⓐ	Ⓒ	Ⓐ	Ⓐ	Ⓒ	Ⓒ	Ⓐ
Manacor d.	...	1424	1436	...	1516	1524	1556	1624	1636	...	1716	1724	...	1756	1824	1828	1924	1928	...	2024	2028	2124	2128	...	...	2224	2230
sa Pobla d.	1407	|	|	1510	|	|	|	|	|	1707	|	|	1750	|	|	|	|	|	2007	|	|	|	|	2202	2207	|	|
Inca d.	1423	1454	1508	1528	1548	1554	1628	1654	1708	1723	1748	1754	1808	1828	1854	1900	1954	2000	2023	2054	2100	2154	2200	2220	2223	2254	2301
Marratxi d.	1444	1515	1528	1551	1608	1615	1648	1715	1728	1744	1808	1815	1828	1848	1915	1920	2015	2020	2044	2115	2120	2215	2220	2240	2244	2315	2321
Palma a.	1458	1529	1542	1559	1622	1629	1702	1729	1742	1758	1822	1829	1842	1902	1929	1934	2029	2034	2058	2129	2134	2229	2234	2254	2258	2329	2335

Additional services Palma to Manacor Ⓐ 1815, 1915, 2015, 2115.
Additional services Palma to Sa Pobla Ⓐ 0750, 0910, 1030, 1230, 1412, 1530, 1650.
Additional services Palma to Sa Pobla Ⓒ 0940, 1140, 1340, 1540.
*** – *19 km* Inca - sa Pobla.

Additional services Sa Pobla to Palma Ⓐ 0650, 0810, 0850, 1010, 1130, 1330, 1430, 1550, 1630, 1710, 1857, 2002, 2102.
Additional services Sa Pobla to Palma Ⓒ 1007, 1207, 1307, 1507, 1607, 1807, 1907, 2107.

Operator: Serveis Ferroviaris de Mallorca (SFM) ✆ +34 971 752 245.

PALMA DE MALLORCA - SÓLLER *28 km* Journey time: 55 minutes. **Operator**: Ferrcarril de Sóller (FS) ✆ +34 971 752 051. **SÓLLER - PALMA DE MALLORCA**

Nov. - Mar.: 1000, 1250, 1510, 1800. Apr. - Oct.: 1010, 1050, 1215, 1330, 1510, 1940.

Nov. - Mar.: 0900, 1140, 1400, 1700. Apr. - Oct.: 0900, 1050, 1215, 1400, 1800, 1830, 1930.

A connecting tram service operates **Sóller - Port de Sóller**. *5 km*. Journey time: 15–20 minutes. Not all services shown.

From Sóller: 0800, 0900, 1000, 1130, 1200, 1300, 1330, 1400, 1430, 1500, 1530, 1600, 1700, 1800, 1900.
From Port de Sóller: 0830, 0930, 1030, 1130, 1230, 1330, 1430, 1500, 1530, 1630, 1700, 1730, 1830, 1930, 2000.

2nd class (except *AVE* trains) VALÈNCIA - TERUEL - ZARAGOZA - HUESCA - CANFRANC 670

km												
					MD			*MD*		*AVE*	*MD*	
		Ⓐ			**18502**			**18504**		**2861**	**18506**	
				🚌	🚌			🚌		**T**	🚌	
0	**València** Nord .... d.	...	...	...	0820	...	...	1215	...	...	1515	...
34	Sagunt .... d.	...	...	...	0853	...	...	1248	...	...	1548	...
65	Segorbe .... d.	...	...	...	0918	...	...	1313	...	...	1613	...
171	**Teruel** .... d.	...	...	0610	1104	...	...	1457	...	...	1758	...
242	Calamocha .... d.	...	...	0745	1228	...	...	1621	...	...	1929	...
305	Cariñena .... d.	...	...	0830	1312	...	...	1705	...	...	2013	...
	Madrid ◇ **650** ...... d.	...	...	|	|	...	...	|	...	1850	|	...
359	**Zaragoza** Delicias .... d.	0624	0843	0924	1400	1432	1620	1745	1902	2033	2101	2139
361	**Zaragoza** Portillo ..... d.	0627	0847	...	...	1436	1624	...	1905	|	...	2142
363	**Zaragoza** Goya .... d.	0629	0851	...	...	1439	1626	...	1907	|	...	2144
417	Tardienta .... d.	0711	0931	...	...	1512	1713	...	1948	2106	...	2223
439	**Huesca** .... a.	0725	0946	...	...	1528	1728	...	2003	2122	...	2238
439	**Huesca** .... d.	...	0951	...	...	...	1733	...	...	...	...	...
474	Ayerbe .... d.	...	1019	...	...	...	1801	...	...	...	...	...
533	Sabiñánigo .... d.	...	1117	...	...	...	1859	...	...	...	...	...
549	Jaca .... d.	...	1131	...	...	...	1917	...	...	...	...	...
574	**Canfranc 324** .... a.	...	1202	...	...	...	1948	...	...	...	...	...

		MD		*AVE*			*MD*			*MD*			
	Ⓐ	**18511**	Ⓐ	**3272**	Ⓒ	Ⓐ	**18523**	Ⓒ		**18515**			
		🚌		**S**			🚌			🚌	🚌		
Canfranc 324 ...... d.	...	...	...	...	...	0635		0842	...	...	...	...	1819
Jaca .... d.	...	...	...	...	...	0704		0911	...	...	...	...	1848
Sabiñánigo .... d.	...	...	...	...	...	0718		0925	...	...	...	...	1902
Ayerbe .... d.	...	...	...	...	...	0819		1029	...	...	...	...	2007
Huesca .... a.	...	...	...	...	...	0846		1056	...	...	...	...	2034
Huesca .... d.	0623	...	0738	0805	0833	0851	...	1101	1602	...	...	1838	2039
Tardienta .... d.	0638	...	0753	0818	0850	0904	...	1117	1618	...	...	1856	2053
Zaragoza Goya .... d.	0716	...	0831	|	0932	0949	...	1158	1702	...	...	1941	2138
Zaragoza Portillo.. d.	0719	...	0833	|	0935	0952	...	1201	1705	...	...	1943	2141
Zaragoza Delicias d.	0723	0815	0836	0855	0938	0955	1030	1205	1710	1725	1915	1946	2147
Madrid ◇ **650**... a.	...	|	...	1038	...	...	|	...	...	|	|	...	...
Cariñena .... d.	...	0904	...	...	...	...	1119	...	...	1814	2012	...	...
Calamocha .... d.	...	0948	...	...	...	...	1203	...	...	1858	2056	...	...
Teruel .... d.	...	1134	...	...	...	...	1343	...	...	2038	2229	...	...
Segorbe .... d.	...	1306	...	...	...	...	1506	...	...	2200	...	...	...
Sagunt .... d.	...	1331	...	...	...	...	1531	...	...	2225	...	...	...
València Nord...... a.	...	1401	...	...	...	...	1600	...	...	2255	...	...	...

S – To Sevilla on ①–⑥ as Train **3872** (Table **660**).

T – From Sevilla (Table **660**).

◇ – Madrid Puerta de Atocha.

☛ See Table **324** for 🚌 Canfranc - Bedous for connections to / from Pau.

CÓRDOBA - SEVILLA - HUELVA and CÁDIZ 671

km																									
		MD	*MD*	*MD*	*MD*	*MD*		*MD*	*Alvia*	*MD*	*IC*	*MD*	*MD*	*Alvia*		*MD*	*MD*	*MD*	*Alvia*	*MD*	*MD*	*MD*	*MD*	*Alvia*	
		13000	**13002**	**13030**	**13030**	**13099**		**13020**	**2074**	**13079**	**2494**	**13008**	**13097**	**2104**		**13010**	**13032**	**13032**	**2134**	**13032**	**13014**	**13039**	**13083**	**2164**	
		2	2	2	2	2		2		2		2	2	①④		2	2	2		2	2	2	2		
		Ⓐ	⚒	Ⓐ	Ⓒ					**J**		Ⓐ		⑤⑦			Ⓒ	Ⓐ		Ⓐ			**J**		
	Madrid PA ✣ **660** .... d.	...	...	...	...	...	...	...	0705	...	0923	...	...	1005	...	...	...	...	1205	...	...	...	...	1605	...
0	**Córdoba** .... **660** d.	...	...	0640	...	...	...	0814	0907	0921	1119	...	...	|	...	...	1403	1403	1407	←	...	...	1628	|	...
51	Palma del Río .... d.	...	...	0716	...	...	...	0849	|	0956	|	...	...	|	...	...	1438	1437	|	1438	...	...	1701	|	...
129	**Sevilla** .... **660** a.	...	...	0815	...	...	...	0948	1016	1056	1225	...	...	1307	...	...	1537	→	1515	1537	...	...	1802	|	...
129	**Sevilla** .... **673** § d.	0640	0745	0832	0832	0845	...	1012	1018	1105	1240	1245	1248	1309	...	1445	...	...	1517	1549	1645	1700	1809	|	...
204	La Palma del Condado .... d.	|	|	|	|	0959	...	|	|	|	1334	|	1353	|	...	|	...	...	|	|	|	1759	|	|	...
244	**Huelva** .... a.	|	|	|	|	1033	...	|	|	|	1402	|	1423	|	...	|	...	...	|	|	|	1832	|	|	...
145	Dos Hermanas .... **673** § d.	0654	0758	0846	0846	...	...	1025	|	1118	...	1258	...	|	...	1500	...	...	|	1603	1658	...	1822	|	...
162	Utrera .... § d.	0705	|	0858	0858	...	...	1036	|	1131	...	1308	...	|	...	|	...	...	|	1613	|	...	1834	|	...
224	Aeropuerto de Jerez....... ▲ d.	0739	|	0933	0933	...	...	|	|	1206	...	1345	...	|	...	1540	...	...	|	|	1741	...	1910	|	...
236	Jerez de la Frontera....... ▲ d.	0746	0846	0940	0940	...	...	1113	1107	1214	...	1353	...	1357	...	1548	...	...	1604	1655	1749	...	1918	1952	...
251	Puerto de Santa María .... d.	0756	0855	0950	0950	...	...	1124	1118	1223	...	1402	...	1408	...	1558	...	...	1615	1704	1758	...	1927	2003	...
270	San Fernando - Bahía Sur ... d.	0812	0911	1006	1006	...	...	1140	1132	1237	...	1418	...	1422	...	1615	...	...	1629	1718	1813	...	1943	2017	...
285	**Cádiz** .... a.	0826	0923	1017	1017	...	...	1154	1145	1249	...	1430	...	1443	...	1627	...	...	1641	1730	1825	...	1957	2029	...

	MD	*Alvia*	*MD*	*Alvia*	*MD*		*MD*				
	13394	**697**	**13035**	**2384**	**13095**		**13073**				
	2		2		2		2				
		A	**J**				**J**				
Madrid PA ✣ **660** .... d.	...	...	...	1805	...	...	...	...	...	...	...
Córdoba .... **660** d.	...	1832	1854	1958	...	...	2003	...	...	...	...
Palma del Río .... d.	...	|	1930	|	...	...	2053	...	...	...	...
Sevilla .... **660** a.	...	1932	2031	|	...	...	2153	...	...	...	...
Sevilla .... **673** § d.	1930	1937	2050	|	2050	...	2210	...	...	...	...
La Palma del Condado ..... d.	|	|	|	2135	2151	...	|	...	...	...	...
Huelva .... a.	|	|	|	2202	2220	...	|	...	...	...	...
Dos Hermanas .... **673** § d.	1944	|	2103	...	...	...	2223	...	...	...	...
Utrera .... § d.	|	|	2114	...	...	...	2233	...	...	...	...
Aeropuerto de Jerez .... ▲ d.	|	|	|	...	...	...	2308	...	...	...	...
Jerez de la Frontera .... ▲ d.	2035	2042	2153	...	...	...	2316	...	...	...	...
Puerto de Santa María .... d.	2044	2053	2202	...	...	...	2325	...	...	...	...
San Fernando - Bahía Sur .... d.	2059	2109	2217	...	...	...	2341	...	...	...	...
Cádiz .... a.	2112	2120	2228	...	...	...	2358	...	...	...	...

	MD	*Alvia*	*MD*	*Alvia*	*MD*	*Alvia*	*MD*	*Alvia*	*MD*
	13001	**2075**	**13041**	**2285**	**13003**	**694**	**13005**	**2285**	**13007**
	2 **J**		2		2		2		2
	Ⓐ			⚒	**M**	**A**		⑥	Ⓐ
Cádiz .... d.	0540	0635	...	...	0645	0735	0840	...	0940
San Fernando - Bahía Sur. d.	0553	0646	...	...	0656	0748	0851	...	0951
Puerto de Santa María ..... d.	0608	0700	...	...	0711	0804	0905	...	1006
Jerez de la Frontera .... ▲ d.	0617	0711	...	...	0720	0814	0914	...	1015
Aeropuerto de Jerez .... ▲ d.	0624	|	...	...	0728	|	|	...	1023
Utrera .... § d.	0702	|	...	...	0806	|	|	...	|
Dos Hermanas .... **673** § d.	0712	|	...	...	0816	|	1005	...	1107
Huelva .... d.	|	|	0630	0800	|	|	|	1007	|
La Palma del Condado . d.	|	|	0700	0828	|	|	|	1035	|
Sevilla .... **673** § a.	0728	0800	0806	|	0832	0908	1020	|	1120
Sevilla .... **660** d.	0735	0803	...	|	0840	0912	...	|	...
Palma del Río .... d.	0830	|	...	|	0935	|	...	|	...
Córdoba .... **660** a.	0910	0902	...	0959	1021	1011	...	1205	...
Madrid PA ✣ **660** .... a.	...	1111	...	1202	...	...	...	1408	...

	MD	*MD*		*MD*	*MD*	*Alvia*	*MD*	*MD*	*MD*	*Alvia*	*MD*	*Alvia*	*IC*	*MD*	*Alvia*	*MD*	*MD*	*MD*	*MD*						
	13045	**13009**		**13011**	**13011**	**2135**	**13393**	**13013**	**13043**	**2365**	**13015**	**2165**	**2375**	**13017**	**2175**	**13031**	**13049**	**13019**	**13021**						
	2	2		2 **J**	2 **J**		2	2	2		2	①④		2		2	2	2	2						
		J		Ⓐ	Ⓒ			Ⓐ		⑦		⑤⑦		**J**											
Cádiz .... d.	...	1050	...	1240	...	1330	1340	1440	...	...	1540	1615	...	1724	1810	1840	...	1940	2040	...	...	...	...	...	...
San Fernando - Bahía Sur ... d.	...	1101	...	1251	...	1341	1351	1451	...	...	1551	1627	...	1735	1822	1851	...	1951	2052	...	...	...	...	...	...
Puerto de Santa María .... d.	...	1116	...	1306	...	1355	1404	1506	...	...	1606	1641	...	1749	1836	1905	...	2006	2106	...	...	...	...	...	...
Jerez de la Frontera .... ▲ d.	...	1125	...	1315	...	1406	1413	1515	...	...	1615	1651	...	1758	1846	1914	...	2015	2115	...	...	...	...	...	...
Aeropuerto de Jerez .... ▲ d.	...	1133	...	|	...	|	|	1523	...	...	1623	|	...	1806	|	1921	...	|	|	...	...	...	...	...	...
Utrera .... § d.	...	|	...	1356	...	|	1453	|	...	...	1700	|	...	|	|	|	...	2102	2156	...	...	...	...	...	...
Dos Hermanas .... **673** § d.	...	1216	...	1406	...	|	1503	1606	...	...	1710	|	...	1850	|	2005	...	2112	2206	...	...	...	...	...	...
Huelva .... d.	1051	|	...	|	...	|	|	|	1500	1605	|	|	1750	|	|	|	1857	|	|	...	...	...	...	...	...
La Palma del Condado .... d.	1124	|	...	|	...	|	|	|	1531	1633	|	|	1817	|	|	|	1929	|	|	...	...	...	...	...	...
Sevilla .... **673** § a.	1237	1231	...	1420	...	1453	1517	1620	1627	|	1725	1746	1914	1904	|	2017	2035	2128	2220	...	...	...	...	...	...
Sevilla .... **660** d.	...	1245	...	1430	1430	1456	...	...	...	|	1730	1748	1925	1920	|	2034	...	...	...	...	...	...	...	...	...
Palma del Río .... d.	...	1340	...	1525	1525	|	...	...	...	|	1825	|	|	2015	|	2134	...	...	...	...	...	...	...	...	...
Córdoba .... **660** a.	...	1421	...	1601	1601	1557	...	...	...	1808	1907	|	2019	2058	|	2208	...	...	...	...	...	...	...	...	...
Madrid PA ✣ **660** .... a.	...	...	...	...	...	1803	...	...	...	2013	...	2055	2223	...	2242	...	...	...	...	...	...	...	...	...	...

A – TORRE DEL ORO – 🚃12 🍷 Barcelona - Córdoba - Cádiz and v.v. (Table **672a**).

J – From / to Jaén (Table **661**).

M – To Jaén on Ⓒ (Table **661**).

t – ①–⑤.

✣ – Madrid Puerta de Atocha.

§ – Frequent suburban services operate Sevilla - Utrera and v.v.

▲ – Additional suburban services operate Jerez de la Frontera - Aeropuerto de Jerez and v.v.: depart Aeropuerto 0720 Ⓐ, 0820 Ⓒ, 1325, 1920; depart Jerez 0657 Ⓐ, 0757 Ⓒ, 1257, 1857.

672 BARCELONA - VALÈNCIA - ALACANT - CARTAGENA

km		MD 14123 ⑦ 2	MD 14123 ①-⑥ 2	AVE 5871	Ⓐ 2	Em 1071 ①-⑤	Em 1071 ⑥	⑥ 2	Alvia 697 A	2	Em 1081 ①-⑤	Em 1081 ⑥	AVE 5721 G	Em 1101	IC 463 🍷	AVE 5951	IC 1463 🍷	IC 1463 🚌	Ⓑ 2	2	2	MD 35623 2
	Figueres Vilafant d.	...	...	...	...	...	...	...	...	...	0710	...	...	0910	...	...	...	...	...	...	...	...
	Girona d.	...	...	...	...	...	...	...	...	...	0726	...	...	0926	...	...	...	...	...	...	...	...
0	**Barcelona** França d.	...	...	...	...	...	...	...	...	0745	|	...	...	|	...	...	...	...	...	0945	...	...
5	Barcelona Passeig de Gràcia d.	...	...	...	...	...	...	...	...	0756	|	...	...	|	...	...	...	...	...	0956	...	...
8	**Barcelona** Sants 652 d.	...	...	...	...	0715	0715	...	0745	0803	0815	0815	...	1015	1105	...	...	...	...	1003	...	...
68	Sant Vicenç de Calders 652 d.	...	...	...	...	|	|	...	|	|	|	|	...	|	|	...	...	...	...	|	...	...
82	Altafulla - Tamarit d.	...	...	...	...	|	|	...	|	0903	|	|	...	|	|	...	...	...	...	1103	...	...
	Camp de Tarragona d.	...	...	...	...	0750	0750	...	0822	|	0851	0851	...	1051	1143	...	...	...	...	|	...	...
93	Tarragona 652 d.	...	...	...	...	|	|	...	|	0915	|	|	...	|	|	...	...	...	...	1115	...	...
103	Vila-Seca ¶ d.	...	...	...	...	|	|	...	|	0923	|	|	...	|	|	...	...	...	...	1123	...	...
105	Cambrils-AV d.	...	...	...	...	|	|	...	0844	0936	|	|	...	|	|	...	...	...	...	1136	...	...
	Tortosa d.	...	...	...	0605	|	|	0800	|	|	|	|	...	|	|	...	...	...	...	|	1335	...
163	L'Aldea - Amposta d.	...	...	...	0615	|	|	0810	0909	1021	|	|	...	|	1234	...	...	...	...	1221	1346	...
176	Tortosa a.	...	...	...	|	|	|	|	|	1033	|	|	...	|	|	...	...	...	...	1233	|	...
202	Vinaròs d.	...	...	...	0641	|	|	0847	0929	...	|	|	...	|	1250	...	...	...	...	1323	1414	...
208	Benicarló - Peñíscola d.	...	...	...	0647	|	|	0853	0937	...	|	|	...	|	1258	...	...	...	...	1329	1420	...
268	Benicàssim d.	...	...	...	0727	|	|	0931	|	...	|	|	...	|	|	...	...	...	...	1419	1458	...
280	Castelló de la Plana d.	...	...	0602	0739	0921	0921	0942	1025	...	1016	1015	1117	1219	1332	1411	...	...	...	1431	1507	...
353	**València** Nord a.	...	...	|	0901	1010	1010	1103	|	...	1120	|	|	1313	1432	|	...	...	...	1545	1621	...
353	**València** Nord 668 d.	0630	0645	|	...	1020	...	...	|	...	...	|	|	1323	...	|	1505	...	1525	...	...	1628
	València Joaquín Sorolla a.	|	|	0649	...	|	...	...	1138	...	...	1119	1212	|	...	1457	|	...	|	...	...	|
	València Joaquín Sorolla 668 d.	|	|	0657	...	|	...	...	1143	...	...	...	1231	|	...	1509	|	...	|	...	...	|
409	Xàtiva 668 d.	0705	0720	|	...	|	...	...	1233	...	...	...	|	|	...	|	1546	...	1614	...	...	1712
	Madrid P de Atocha 668 a.	|	|	0908	...	|	...	...	|	...	...	...	1437j	|	...	1718	|	...	|	...	...	|
	Cádiz 671 a.	|	|	...	...	|	...	...	2120	...	...	...	...	|	...	...	|	...	|	...	...	|
495	Elda - Petrer d.	0813	0837	...	...	|	...	...	...	...	...	...	...	|	...	...	1702	...	1728	...	...	1810
536	**Alacant** a.	0857	0913	...	...	1239	...	...	...	...	...	...	...	1540	...	...	1739	...	1803	...	...	1843
536	**Alacant** d.	0910	0920	...	...	...	...	...	...	...	...	...	...	...	...	...	1751	...	...	...	...	1849
614	Murcia 673 a.	1042	1058	...	...	...	...	...	...	...	...	...	...	...	...	...	1918	1945	...	...	...	2016
677	**Lorca** Sutullena a.	...	...	...	...	...	...	...	...	...	...	...	...	...	...	...	|	2102	...	...	...	|
679	**Cartagena** 673 a.	...	...	...	...	...	...	...	...	...	...	...	...	...	...	...	2034	...	...	...	...	2117

	2		2	IC 1371 ⑤	2		Em 1161	2	IC 5201	IC 5811	2		2	Em 1181	Av 35968 2	2	IC 1201 Ⓑ	2				
Figueres Vilafant d.	...	...	...	...	...	...	...	...	...	...	...	...	...	...	...	...	...	...	...	...	...	...
Girona d.	...	...	...	...	...	...	...	...	...	...	...	...	...	...	...	...	...	...	...	...	...	...
Barcelona França d.	1045	...	1245	...	1445	...	...	1615	...	...	...	...	1745	...	...	1915	...	2045	...	...	...	...
Barcelona Passeig de Gràcia d.	1056	...	1256	...	1456	...	...	1626	...	...	...	...	1756	...	...	1926	...	2056	...	...	...	...
Barcelona Sants 652 d.	1103	...	1303	1408	1503	...	1615	1633	...	...	...	...	1803	1815	1830	1933	2015	2103	...	...	...	...
Sant Vicenç de Calders 652 d.	|	...	|	|	|	...	|	|	...	...	...	...	|	|	|	|	|	|	...	...	...	...
Altafulla - Tamarit d.	1203	...	1403	|	1603	...	|	1733	...	...	...	...	1903	|	|	2033	|	2203	...	...	...	...
Camp de Tarragona d.	|	...	|	1445	|	...	1651	|	...	...	...	...	|	1851	1907	|	2050	|	...	...	...	...
Tarragona 652 d.	1215	...	1415	|	1615	...	|	1745	...	...	...	...	1915	|	|	2045	|	2215	...	...	...	...
Vila-Seca ¶ d.	1223	...	1423	|	1623	...	|	1753	...	...	...	...	1923	|	|	2053	|	2223	...	...	...	...
Cambrils-AV d.	1236	...	1436	1508	1636	...	|	1806	...	...	...	...	1936	|	1929	2106	|	2236	...	...	...	...
Tortosa d.	|	...	|	|	|	...	|	|	...	...	1822	...	|	|	|	|	|	|	...	...	...	...
L'Aldea - Amposta d.	1324	...	1521	1533	1724	...	|	1851	...	...	1842	...	2021	|	2006	2154	|	2321	...	...	...	...
Tortosa a.	1348	...	1533	|	1743	...	|	1905	...	...	|	...	2037	|	2017	2213	|	2333	...	...	...	...
Vinaròs d.	...	...	...	1550	...	...	|	...	1814t	...	1910	...	...	|	...	...	|	...	...	...	...	...
Benicarló - Peñíscola d.	...	...	...	1555	...	...	|	...	1821t	...	1915	...	...	|	...	...	|	...	...	...	...	...
Benicàssim d.	...	...	...	1628	...	...	|	...	1856t	...	1954	...	...	|	...	...	|	...	...	...	...	...
Castelló de la Plana d.	...	...	...	1638	...	...	1812	...	1908	2007	2004	...	...	2019	...	...	2230	...	...	...	...	...
València Nord a.	...	...	...	1740	...	...	1902	...	|	|	2134	...	...	2109	...	...	2334	...	...	...	...	...
València Nord 668 d.	...	...	...	1752	...	...	1912	...	|	|	...	...	...	2119	...	...	...	...	...	...	...	...
València Joaquín Sorolla a.	...	...	...	|	...	...	|	...	1959	2055	...	...	...	|	...	...	...	...	...	...	...	...
València Joaquín Sorolla 668 d.	...	...	...	|	...	...	|	...	2012	2105	...	...	...	|	...	...	...	...	...	...	...	...
Xàtiva 668 d.	...	...	...	1844	...	...	|	...	|	|	...	...	...	|	...	...	...	...	...	...	...	...
Madrid P de Atocha 668 a.	...	...	...	|	...	...	|	...	2227j	2332	...	...	...	|	...	...	...	...	...	...	...	...
Cádiz 671 a.	...	...	...	|	...	...	|	...	...	...	...	...	...	|	...	...	...	...	...	...	...	...
Elda - Petrer d.	...	...	...	1948	...	...	|	...	...	...	...	...	...	|	...	...	...	...	...	...	...	...
Alacant a.	...	...	...	2024	...	...	2133	...	...	...	...	...	...	2340	...	...	...	...	...	...	...	...
Alacant d.	...	...	...	...	...	...	...	...	...	...	...	...	...	...	...	...	...	...	...	...	...	...
Murcia 673 a.	...	...	...	...	...	...	...	...	...	...	...	...	...	...	...	...	...	...	...	...	...	...
Lorca Sutullena a.	...	...	...	...	...	...	...	...	...	...	...	...	...	...	...	...	...	...	...	...	...	...
Cartagena 673 a.	...	...	...	...	...	...	...	...	...	...	...	...	...	...	...	...	...	...	...	...	...	...

	2	Av 35869 2	IC 1072 ①-⑥	2	2	2	Em 1092		Em 1112	2		AVE 5890	2	MD 18504 ①-⑥ 2	2	Em 1152 Ⓑ	Em 1162 ①-⑤	2		2		
Cartagena 673 d.	...	...	...	...	...	...	...	...	...	...	...	...	...	0650z	...	...	...	...	...	...	...	...
Lorca Sutullena d.	...	...	...	...	...	...	...	...	...	...	...	...	...	|	...	...	...	...	...	...	...	...
Murcia 673 d.	...	...	...	...	...	...	...	...	...	...	...	...	...	0752	...	...	...	...	...	...	...	...
Alacant a.	...	...	...	...	...	...	...	...	...	...	...	...	...	0909	...	...	...	...	...	...	...	...
Alacant d.	...	...	...	...	...	...	0655	...	0915	...	...	...	...	0917	...	...	1330	...	...	...	...	...
Elda - Petrer d.	...	...	...	...	...	...	|	...	|	...	...	...	...	0957	...	...	|	...	...	...	...	...
Cádiz 671 d.	...	...	...	...	...	...	|	...	|	...	...	...	...	|	...	...	|	...	...	...	...	...
Madrid P de Atocha 668 d.	...	...	...	...	...	...	|	...	|	...	...	0944	...	|	...	...	|	...	...	...	...	...
Xàtiva 668 d.	...	...	...	...	...	...	|	...	|	...	...	|	...	1052	...	...	|	...	...	...	...	...
València Joaquín Sorolla 668 a.	...	...	...	...	...	...	|	...	|	...	...	1147	...	|	...	...	|	...	...	...	...	...
València Joaquín Sorolla d.	...	...	...	...	...	...	|	...	|	...	...	1147	...	|	...	...	|	...	...	...	...	...
València Nord 668 a.	...	...	...	...	...	...	0855	...	1115	...	...	|	...	1137	...	...	1526	...	...	...	...	...
València Nord d.	...	...	0630	...	...	0815	0905	...	1125	...	...	|	...	...	1400	1502	1536	...	...	...	...	...
Castelló de la Plana d.	...	...	0719	...	...	0941	0952	...	1211	...	...	1315	...	...	1518	1550	1621	...	...	...	...	...
Benicàssim d.	...	...	|	...	...	0951	|	...	|	...	...	...	...	...	1532	|	|	...	...	...	...	...
Benicarló - Peñíscola d.	...	...	|	...	...	1033	|	...	|	...	...	...	...	...	1617	|	|	...	...	...	...	...
Vinaròs d.	...	...	|	...	...	1040	|	...	|	...	...	...	...	...	1623	|	|	...	...	...	...	...
Tortosa d.	0540	0635	|	0734	0910	|	|	...	|	1208	...	...	1410	...	|	|	|	1634	...	1810	...	...
L'Aldea - Amposta d.	0552	0646	|	0748	0922	1105	|	...	|	1222	...	...	1422	...	1653	|	|	1648	...	1822	...	...
Tortosa a.	|	|	|	|	|	1132	|	...	|	|	...	...	|	...	1723	|	|	|	...	|	...	...
Cambrils-AV d.	0634	0724	|	0834	1004	...	|	...	|	1304	...	...	1504	...	...	|	|	1734	...	1904	...	...
Vila-Seca ¶ d.	0644	|	|	0844	1014	...	|	...	|	1314	...	...	1514	...	...	|	|	1744	...	1914	...	...
Tarragona 652 d.	0655	|	|	0855	1025	...	|	...	|	1325	...	...	1525	...	...	|	|	1755	...	1925	...	...
Camp de Tarragona d.	|	0747	0856	|	|	...	1131	...	1354	|	...	...	|	...	...	1730	1807	|	...	|	...	...
Altafulla - Tamarit d.	0704	|	|	0904	1034	...	|	...	|	1334	...	...	1534	...	...	|	|	1804	...	1934	...	...
Sant Vicenç de Calders 652 d.	|	|	|	|	|	...	|	...	|	|	...	...	|	...	...	|	|	|	...	|	...	...
Barcelona Sants 652 a.	0809	0823	0935	1007	1139	...	1208	...	1450	1439	...	...	1642	...	...	1819	1900	1909	...	2039	...	...
Barcelona Passeig de Gràcia a.	0814	...	...	1013	1144	...	...	...	...	1444	...	...	1647	...	...	...	...	1914	...	2044	...	...
Barcelona França a.	0824	...	...	1024	1154	...	...	...	...	1454	...	...	1657	...	...	...	...	1924	...	2054	...	...
Girona a.	...	...	...	...	...	...	...	...	...	...	...	...	...	...	...	...	...	...	...	...	...	...
Figueres Vilafant a.	...	...	...	...	...	...	...	...	...	...	...	...	...	...	...	...	...	...	...	...	...	...

FOR NOTES SEE NEXT PAGE →

CARTAGENA - ALACANT - VALÈNCIA - BARCELONA 672

	Alvia	*IC*	*IC*	*IC*			*AVE*	*Em*	*IC*	*Em*		*IC*		*MD*	*AVE*							
	694	**1460**	**1460**	**460**			**5750**	**1182**	**1382**	**1192**		**1402**	Ⓑ	**14202**	**5990**	Ⓑ						
	A	🚌			2	2	**G**	⑦	⑦		2	⑦	2	2		2						
Cartagena .... **673** ¦ d.	...	...	1155	...	...	...	...	...	...	...	...	...	...	1613	...	...	...	...	...	...	...	...
Lorca Sutullena .... ¦ d.	...	1103	│	...	...	...	...	...	...	...	...	...	...	│	...	...	...	...	...	...	...	...
Murcia .... **673** ¦ d.	...	1220	1303	...	...	...	...	...	...	...	...	...	...	1710	...	...	...	...	...	...	...	...
Alacant .... ¦ a.	...	...	1430	...	...	...	...	...	...	...	...	...	...	1841	...	...	...	...	...	...	...	...
Alacant .... d.	...	...	1440	...	...	...	...	...	...	1637	...	1705	...	1848	...	1930	...	...	...	...	...	...
Elda - Petrer .... d.	...	...	1523	...	...	...	...	...	...	│	...	1747	...	1919	...	2002	...	...	...	...	...	...
Cádiz **671** .... d.	0735	...	│	...	...	...	...	...	...	│	...	│	...	│	...	│	...	...	...	...	...	...
Madrid P de Atocha .... **668** d.	│	...	│	...	...	...	1530**j**	...	...	│	...	│	...	│	1940	│	...	...	...	...	...	...
Xátiva .... **668** d.	1616	...	1623	...	...	...	│	...	...	│	...	1849	...	2027	│	2113	...	...	...	...	...	...
València Joaquín Sorolla ... **668** a.	1654	...	│	...	...	...	1730	...	...	│	...	│	...	│	2142	│	...	...	...	...	...	...
València Joaquín Sorolla .... d.	1659	...	│	...	...	...	1740	...	...	│	...	│	...	│	2152	│	...	...	...	...	...	...
València Nord .... **668** a.	│	...	1709	...	...	...	│	...	...	1832	...	1937	...	2110	│	2205	...	...	...	...	...	...
València Nord .... ¦ d.	│	...	...	1730	...	1717	│	1802	1837	1842	...	1947	2005	...	│	...	...	...	...	...	...	...
Castelló de la Plana .... ¦ d.	1758	...	...	1821	...	1830	1836	1844	1927	1935	...	2043	2107	...	2242	...	...	...	...	...	...	...
Benicàssim .... ¦ d.	│	...	...	│	...	1846	...	│	│	│	...	2054	2118	...	...	...	...	...	...	...	...	...
Benicarló - Peñíscola .... ¦ d.	1839	...	...	1903	...	1926	...	│	│	│	...	2125	2157	...	...	...	...	...	...	...	...	...
Vinaròs .... ¦ d.	1845	...	...	1908	...	1932	...	│	│	│	←	2131	2203	...	...	...	...	...	...	...	...	...
Tortosa .... d.	│	...	...	│	1934	2030	...	│	│	│	2040	│	│	...	...	...	...	...	...	...	...	...
L'Aldea - Amposta .... d.	1902	...	...	1924	1948	→	...	│	│	│	2052	2147	2227	...	...	...	...	...	...	...	...	...
Tortosa .... a.	│	...	...	│	│	...	...	│	│	│	│	│	2253	...	...	...	...	...	...	...	...	...
Cambrils-AV .... d.	1932	...	...	│	2034	...	...	│	│	│	2134	2222	...	...	...	...	...	...	...	...	...	...
Vila–Seca ¶ .... d.	│	...	...	│	2044	...	...	│	│	│	2144	│	...	...	...	...	...	...	...	...	...	...
Tarragona .... **652** d.	│	...	...	│	2055	...	...	│	│	│	2155	│	...	...	...	...	...	...	...	...	...	...
Camp de Tarragona .... d.	1956	...	...	2013	│	...	...	2029	2106	2117	│	2249	...	...	...	...	...	...	...	...	...	...
Altafulla - Tamarit .... d.	│	...	...	│	2104	...	...	│	│	│	2204	│	...	...	...	...	...	...	...	...	...	...
Sant Vicenç de Calders ..... **652** d.	│	...	...	│	│	...	...	│	│	│	│	│	...	...	...	...	...	...	...	...	...	...
Barcelona Sants .... **652** a.	2047	...	...	2057	2209	...	...	2115	2210	2204	2307	2325	...	...	...	...	...	...	...	...	...	...
Barcelona Passeig de Gràcia .... a.	...	...	...	...	2214	...	...	...	...	...	2313	...	...	...	...	...	...	...	...	...	...	...
Barcelona França .... a.	...	...	...	...	2224	...	...	...	...	...	2324	...	...	...	...	...	...	...	...	...	...	...
Girona .... a.	...	...	...	...	...	...	...	...	...	...	...	...	...	...	...	...	...	...	...	...	...	...
Figueres Vilafant .... a.	...	...	...	...	...	...	...	...	...	...	...	...	...	...	...	...	...	...	...	...	...	...

Alacant - Orihuela - Murcia - Cartagena

		Av	*Av*	*avlo*		*MD*	*Av*			*Av*		*Av*		*Av*	*Av*	*Av*		*IC*	*MD*	*Av*		*Av*		
	Ⓐ	**9075**	**9085**	**5668**		**14123**	**9105**	⚒		**9125**	Ⓐ	**34912**	Ⓐ	**9155**	**34442**	**9175**		**1463**	**18523**	**9195**	Ⓑ	**9215**		
	2	Ⓐ		**M**	2	**V**		2	2		2	⚒	2				2	**V**	**f**		2			
Alacant Terminal .... d.	...	0700	0840	0856	...	0920	1037	...	...	1250	...	1339	...	1457	1700	1715	...	1751	1849	1950	...	2155	...	...
Elche AV / Elx AV .... d.	...	0721	0901	0918	...	1004**p**	1058	...	...	1311	...	1407	...	1518	1722	1736	...	1827**p**	1930**p**	2010	...	2215	...	...
Orihuela .... d.	...	0736	0916	0934	...	1040	1113	...	...	1326	...	1422	...	1533	1737	1751	...	1856	2001	2027	...	2231	...	...
Murcia .... d.	0720	0755	0935	0950	1015	1058	1132	1158	1315	1345	1430	1437	1535	1558	1752	1810	1815	1928	2023	2045	2140	2250	...	...
Cartagena .... a.	0825	...	...	...	1116	...	...	1304	1418	...	1529	...	1641	...	...	...	1913	2029	2122	...	2240	...	...	...

		Av	*MD*	*Av*		*Av*	*avlo*		*Av*	*IC*		*Av*	*Av*		*Av*	*MD*		*Av*	*Av*	*Av*				
	⚒	**9067**	**18504**	**9087**		**9107**	**5817**		**9127**	**1460**	Ⓑ	**9157**	**34863**	Ⓐ	**9167**	**14202**		**34903**	**9197**	**9217**	Ⓐ			
	2	Ⓐ	Ⓐ**f**		2		**M**			**V**	2			2	Ⓐ		2	Ⓑ			2	2		
Cartagena .... d.	0509	...	0650	...	0900	...	...	...	...	1155	1325	...	...	1430	...	1613	1720	...	...	...	2015	2135	...	...
Murcia .... d.	0605	0640	0752	0815	0958	1010	1032	...	1250	1303	1428	1458	1532	1531	1650	1710	1825	1858	1950	2120	2123	2245	...	...
Orihuela .... d.	...	0658	0811	0832	...	1028	1047	...	1308	1328	...	1516	1548	...	1708	1728	...	1915	2008	2138	...	...	...	...
Elche AV / Elx AV .... d.	...	0713	0843**p**	0848	...	1043	1103	...	1323	1353**p**	...	1531	1602	...	1723	1804**p**	...	1929	2023	2153	...	...	...	...
Alacant Terminal .... a.	...	0734	0909	0909	...	1104	1125	...	1344	1430	...	1552	1623	...	1744	1841	...	1949	2044	2214	...	...	...	...

A – TORRE DEL ORO – (12) 🍷 Barcelona - València - Córdoba - Sevilla - Cádiz and v.v. (Table **672a**).
G – To / from Gijón (Tables **681**, **685**).
M – To / from Madrid (Table **668**).
V – To / from Valencia.

j – Depart / arrive Madrid ‡.
p – Elche Parque / Elx Parc.
t – ⑤⑦.

x – 🚌.
y – ⑦.
z – Ⓐ.

¦ – Additional local trains operate between these stations.
¶ – Station for Port Aventura.
‡ – Madrid-Chamartín-Clara Campoamor.

BARCELONA - SEVILLA - CADIZ 672a

	Alvia		*Alvia*
	697		**694**
	A		**A**
Barcelona Sants .... d.	0745	**Cádiz** .... d.	0735
Camp de Tarragona .... d.	0822	San Fernando - Bahía Sur ..... d.	0748
Cambrils-AV .... d.	0844	Puerto de Santa María .... d.	0804
L'Aldea - Amposta .... d.	0909	Jerez de la Frontera .... d.	0814
Vinaròs .... d.	0929	**Sevilla** .... a.	0908
Benicarló - Peñíscola .... d.	0937	**Sevilla** .... d.	0912
Castelló de la Plana .... d.	1025	**Córdoba** .... a.	1011
València Joaquín Sorolla .... a.	1138	**Córdoba** .... d.	1016
València Joaquín Sorolla .... d.	1143	Andújar .... d.	1113
Xátiva .... d.	1233	Linares - Baeza .... d.	1150
Albacete .... d.	1349	Manzanares .... d.	1313
Alcázar de San Juan .... d.	1501	Alcázar de San Juan .... d.	1342
Manzanares .... d.	1539	Albacete .... d.	1459
Linares - Baeza .... d.	1703	Xátiva .... d.	1616
Andújar .... d.	1737	**València** Joaquín Sorolla ...... a.	1654
Córdoba .... a.	1827	**València** Joaquín Sorolla ...... d.	1659
Córdoba .... d.	1832	Castelló de la Plana .... d.	1758
Sevilla .... a.	1932	Benicarló - Peñíscola .... d.	1839
Sevilla .... d.	1937	Vinaròs .... d.	1845
Jerez de la Frontera .... d.	2042	L'Aldea - Amposta .... d.	1902
Puerto de Santa María .... d.	2053	Cambrils-AV .... d.	1932
San Fernando - Bahía Sur .... d.	2109	Camp de Tarragona .... d.	1956
Cádiz .... a.	2120	**Barcelona** Sants .... a.	2047

A – TORRE DEL ORO – (12) 🍷 Barcelona - Cádiz and v.v. (Tables **661**, **668**, **671**, **672**, **678**).

MADRID - CARTAGENA 672b

km		*AVE*	*IC*		*MD*		*AVE*	*IC*			*MD*
		5092	**11092**		**18040**		**5182**	**11182**		**18044**	**18042**
			🚌					🚌		⑤	Ⓑ
0	**Madrid** Chamartín ¶ . ‡ d.	0900	...	...	1419	...	1800	...	...	1643	1818
8	**Madrid** Atocha C ◧ .. ‡ d.	│	...	...	1432	...	│	...	...	1657	1832
57	Aranjuez .... ‡ d.	│	...	...	1509	...	│	...	...	1731	1908
157	Alcázar de San Juan ‡ d.	│	...	...	1604	...	│	...	...	1828	2000
288	**Albacete** .... d.	1037	1055	...	1715	...	1931	1945	...	1941	2106
354	Hellín .... d.	...	1140	...	...	...	...	2030	...	...	...
	Archena-Fortuna .... d.	...	1240	...	...	...	...	2130	...	...	...
450	Murcia .... **672** ¦ d.	...	1307	...	...	...	...	2155	...	...	...
	Lorca Sutullena ... ¦ a.	...	│	...	...	...	...	│	...	...	...
562	Aguilas .... ¦ a.	...	│	...	...	...	...	│	...	...	...
515	**Cartagena** .... **672** ¦ a.	...	1435	...	...	...	...	2315	...	...	...

	MD	*MD*	*MD*		*IC*	*AVE*		*MD*		*IC*	*AVE*	
	18041	**18049**	**18049**		**11093**	**5093**		**18043**		**11183**	**5183**	
	Ⓐ	⑥	⑦		🚌					🚌		
Cartagena .... **672** ¦ d.	...	...	...	...	0625	...	...	...	...	1420	...	...
Aguilas .... ¦ d.	...	...	...	...	│	...	...	...	...	│	...	...
Lorca Sutullena . ¦ d.	...	...	...	...	│	...	...	...	...	│	...	...
Murcia .... **672** ¦ d.	...	...	...	...	0755	...	...	...	...	1550	...	...
Archena-Fortuna .... d.	...	...	...	...	0815	...	...	...	...	1620	...	...
Hellín .... d.	...	...	...	...	0925	...	...	...	...	1720	...	...
Albacete .... d.	0605	0730	...	...	1015	1034	...	1740	...	1813	1828	...
Alcázar de San Juan ‡ d.	0711	0837	0837	...	...	│	...	1851	...	...	│	...
Aranjuez .... ‡ d.	0807	0933	0933	...	...	│	...	1948	...	...	│	...
Madrid Atocha C ◧ ‡ a.	0844	1008	1008	...	...	│	...	2022	...	...	│	...
Madrid Chamartín ¶ ‡ a.	0858	1022	1022	...	...	1208	...	2036	...	...	2005	...

‡ – See also Table **661**. ◧ – Madrid **Atocha Cercanías**. ¶ – Full name is Madrid-Chamartín-Clara Campoamor. ¦ – Additional local trains operate between these stations.

673 SEVILLA and ALGECIRAS - MÁLAGA, GRANADA and ALMERÍA — 2nd class

For trains **Sevilla – Málaga** and v.v. via **Córdoba**, see Table **660**. For trains **Sevilla – Granada** and v.v. via **Córdoba**, see Table **678a**.

km		*MD* 13063	*MD* 13900	*MD* 13940	*MD* 13902		*MD* 13904	*MD* 13065	*MD* 13942		*MD* 13944	*MD* 13077	*MD* 13906 ⑤⑦	*Alvia* 9331	*Alvia* 2366 M	*MD* 13946	*MD* 13908		*MD* 13910	
0	**Sevilla** d.	...	0701	...	0822	...	1032	...	...	...	...	...	1612	...	...	...	1834	...	2012	...
15	Dos Hermanas d.	...	0722	...	0843	...	1051	...	...	...	...	...	1633	...	...	...	1901	...	2039	...
	Algeciras d.	0545	|	...	|	...	|	1017	...	...	...	1424	|	1552	...	...	|	...	|	...
	San Roque - La Línea d.	0601	|	...	|	...	|	1034	...	...	...	1440	|	1605	...	...	|	...	|	...
	Ronda d.	0737	|	...	|	...	|	1224	...	...	...	1617	|	1721	...	...	|	...	|	...
	Antequera - Santa Ana § d.	|	0906	...	1033	...	1238	|	...	...	...	|	1811	1825	...	...	2039	...	2219	...
167	Bobadilla d.	0836	0915	...	1042	...	1247	1325	...	...	...	1724	1820	|	...	...	2048	...	2228	...
236	**Málaga** M. Zambrano a.	|	1026	...	1147	...	1410	|	...	...	...	|	1932	|	...	...	2154	...	2331	...
	Antequera - Santa Ana § a.	0846	...	...	...	...	...	1335	...	...	...	1734	...	|	...	...	...	...	...	...
	Madrid Pta de Atocha **660** a.	|	...	...	...	...	...	|	...	...	...	|	...	2120	...	...	...	...	...	...
183	Antequera AV d.	0903	...	...	...	...	...	1353	...	...	...	1752	...	...	1906	...	...	...	...	...
290	**Granada** a.	...	...	1113	...	...	...	...	1508	...	1812	...	...	...	1955	2205	...	...	...	...
372	Guadix **661** d.	...	...	1219	...	...	...	...	1619	...	1924	...	...	...	2118	2313	...	...	...	...
471	**Almería** **661** a.	...	...	1352**x**	...	...	...	...	1811**x**	...	2100**x**	...	...	...	2303**x**	0052**x**	...	...	...	...

km		*MD* 13901		*MD* 13951	*MD* 13903	*MD* 13062	*Alvia* 9366	*Alvia* 2087 M	*MD* 13953	*MD* 13905	*MD* 13064		*MD* 13907 ⑤⑦	*MD* 13955	*MD* 13909		*MD* 13957	*MD* 13076	*MD* 13911	
0	**Almería** **661** d.	...	...	0559**x**	...	...	...	0808	0919**x**	...	...	...	...	1310**x**	...	...	1806**x**	...	...	...
99	Guadix **661** d.	...	...	0739	...	...	...	0954	1057	...	...	...	...	1454	...	...	1959	...	...	...
181	**Granada** d.	...	...	0846	...	...	...	1115	1209	...	...	...	...	1559	...	...	2107	...	...	...
288	Antequera AV d.	...	...	...	...	0954	...	1158	...	...	1451	...	...	...	...	...	...	1925	...	...
	Madrid Pta de Atocha **660** d.	...	...	...	...	|	0805	...	...	...	|	...	...	...	...	...	...	|	...	...
	Antequera - Santa Ana § d.	...	...	...	...	1008	|	...	...	...	1505	...	...	...	...	...	...	1939	...	...
	Málaga M. Zambrano d.	0702	...	...	0905	|	|	...	...	1326	|	...	1527	...	1708	...	...	|	2018	...
304	Bobadilla d.	0809	...	...	1023	1022	|	...	...	1441	1519	...	1639	...	1822	...	...	1953	2126	...
	Antequera - Santa Ana § d.	0817	...	...	1031	|	1057	...	...	1449	|	...	1647	...	1830	...	...	|	2134	...
376	Ronda d.	|	...	...	|	1120	1206	...	...	|	1620	...	|	...	|	...	...	2051	|	...
468	San Roque - La Línea d.	|	...	...	|	1304	1324	...	...	|	1807	...	|	...	|	...	...	2227	|	...
480	**Algeciras** a.	|	...	...	|	1319	1337	...	...	|	1823	...	|	...	|	...	...	2242	|	...
456	Dos Hermanas a.	1010	...	...	1211	...	...	...	...	1626	...	...	1827	...	2012	...	...	...	2311	...
471	**Sevilla** a.	1030	...	...	1234	...	...	...	...	1643	...	...	1844	...	2029	...	...	...	2332	...

M – From/to Madrid (Table **660**).
x – Almeria - Huercal-Viator and v.v. (6 km.).
§ – ± *17 km* from Antequera.
For Granada - Córdoba - Sevilla *Avant* services, see Table **678a**.

674 PALMA DE MALLORCA - INCA - SA POBLA and MANACOR — SFM 2nd class

Temporarily moved to page 326

675 MÁLAGA and ALGECIRAS - LA LÍNEA (for Gibraltar)

There are no cross-border services: passengers to/from Gibraltar must cross the frontier on foot (walking-time about 5 minutes) and transfer to/from Gibraltar local services

MÁLAGA bus stn – **LA LÍNEA** bus station (for **Gibraltar**)

From Málaga: 0830, 1130 ▽, 1315, 1430, 1545, 1730, 2025.
From La Línea: 0745, 1105, 1235, 1530, 1630 ▽, 1925, 2015.
Journey time: 3 hours. Operator: Avanza, Málaga ✆ (+34) 91 272 28 32.
▽ – Journey operated by ALSA (see Table **664** for contact details).

ALGECIRAS bus station - **LA LÍNEA** bus station (for **Gibraltar**) Route M-120

From Algeciras: Ⓐ: 0700 and every 30 minutes until 2130, also 2230.
⑥: every 45 mins 0700 – 2115, also 2230. †: every 45 mins 0800 – 2130, also 2230.
From La Línea: Ⓐ: 0645, 0745 and every 30 minutes until 2215, also 2315.
⑥: every 45 mins 0700 – 2200, also 2315. †: 0700, 0845 then every 45 mins until 2215, also 2315.
Journey time: 45 mins. Operator: Transportes Generales Comes SA, Algeciras ✆ (+34) 902 450 550.

676 SEVILLA - AYAMONTE - FARO - LAGOS — DAMAS ☆

		⚒	†	⚒		Ⓐ	Ⓒ		⚒				⚒	†			Ⓐ				Ⓐ	Ⓐ		
Sevilla ⊖ d.	Summer July 1 - Sept. 4 2022	0730	...	0930	1130	...		1530	1730	1930	...	Winter Sept. 9 - June 30, 2025	0730	...	0930	1130	...	1330	...	1530	1730	...	1930	...
Huelva d.		0900	0900	1100	1300	1400	1500	1700	1900	2100	...		0900	0900	1100	1300	1400	1500	...	1700	1900	2000	2100	...
Ayamonte a.		1000	1000	1200	1400**t**	1505	1600**t**	1800	2000	2240	...		1035	1040	1200**j**	1400**j**	1505	1600**j**	...	1800**j**	2000	2135	2240	...

		⚒	⚒	⚒			⚒			Ⓐ	Ⓒ		Ⓐ	⚒		⑥	†	Ⓐ			†	Ⓐ	Ⓐ	Ⓒ
Ayamonte d.	Summer July 1 - Sept. 4 2022	0640	0700	0800	0930**h**	1100	1230	1500	1730	2000	2000	Winter Sept. 9 - June 30, 2025	0640	0700	0930**h**	1100	1100	1130	1300**f**	1530**h**	1700	1730	1900	1930
Huelva d.		0800	0900	1000	1100	1300	1400	1700	1900	2100	2130		0800	0900	1100	1300	1245	1300	1500	1700	1900	1830	2100	2130
Sevilla ⊖ a.		0915	1015	1115	1215	1415	1515	1815	2015	...	2245		0915	1015	1215	1415	...	1415	1615	1815	2015	2015	2215	2245

h – 30 mins. earlier on Ⓒ. **j** – 35–40 mins. later on Ⓒ. **t** – 30 mins. later on ⑦.

Ayamonte - Vila Real de Santo António Guadiana Journey time: 10 minutes. ✆ (+34) 959 470 617.
Sept. 16 - Apr. 30: hourly from Ayamonte 1000 - 1900 ⚒, 1100 - 1800 †. From Vila Real de Santo António Guadiana 0945 then hourly 1030 - 1730, 1900 ⚒, 1100 - 1800 †.

INTERNATIONAL SERVICE Joint ALSA △/REDE EXPRESSOS ☆ service *for international journeys only* No service Dec. 25, Jan. 1

	→ Summer July 1 - Sept. 4, 2022					→ Winter 2022-2023		
Sevilla Santa Justa d.		0930	1130	1530	1800		0930	1530
Huelva, Estación de Autobuses d.		|	1315	|	|		|	|
Ayamonte 🏛 ES d.		|	|	|	|		|	|
Vila Real de Santo António 🏛 PT a.		|	|	|	|		|	|
Faro, Aeroporto a.		1115	1400	1745	2015		1145	1745
Albufeira, Terminal Rodoviário a.		1215	1500	1845	2115		1245	1845
Portimão, Av. Guanaré a.		1315	1530	1915	2145		1315	1915
Lagos, Terminal Rodoviário a.		1345	1600	1945	2215		1345	1945

	→ Summer July 1 - Sept. 4, 2022					→ Winter 2022-2023		
Lagos, Terminal Rodoviário d.		0800	1030	1530	1700		0800	1530
Portimão, Av. Guanaré d.		0830	1100	1600	1730		0830	1600
Albufeira, Terminal Rodoviário d.		0900	1130	1630	1800		0900	1630
Faro, Aeroporto d.		0945	1215	1715	1845		0945	1715
Vila Real de Santo António 🏛 PT d.		|	|	|	|		|	|
Ayamonte 🏛 ES a.		|	|	|	|		|	|
Huelva, Estación de Autobuses a.		|	|	|	2145		|	|
Sevilla Santa Justa a.		1415	1645	2145	2330		1415	2145

☆ – REDE EXPRESSOS ✆ +707 22 33 44. www.rede-expressos.pt
△ – ALSA, ✆ +34 919 914 030. www.alsa.com
ES – Spain (Central European Time).
PT – Portugal (West European Time).
Huelva bus station is ± 1.7 km from the rail station.
Ayamonte bus station is ± 1.5 km from the ferry terminal.

MADRID - CÁCERES - BADAJOZ 677

km		13084				Alvia 190		5500 482	IC 512	MD 17902	17028	MD 13086			5502 486	IC 528	MD 17012		Alvia 192		17823	Alvia 194	17018	17706
		2	2	2	🚌	2	🚌	2	R	2	2	2	2	2	2	R	2	🚌			2		2	2
		⚒			⚒	⚒	⚒				③⑤⑦	⑤⑥⑦		Ⓑ			Ⓑ			🚌	Ⓑ	Ⓑ	Ⓑ	
0	**Madrid** Chamartín ‡ d.	...	...	...	...	0830	...	...	...	...	...	...	...	...	...	...	...	...	1617	...	...	1749	...	...
8	**Madrid** Atocha Cercanías d.	...	...	...	...	0851	...	...	...	1055	...	...	...	...	...	...	1450	...	1638	...	...	1809	1908	2109
146	Talavera de la Reina d.	...	...	...	...	1017	...	...	...	1229	...	...	...	...	...	...	1614	...	1800	...	...	1934	2035	2237
	Navalmoral de La Mata d.	...	...	...	...	1100	...	...	...	1309	...	...	...	...	...	...	1649	...	1839	...	...	2014	2121	...
	Plasencia d.	...	...	...	1045	|	...	...	...	|	...	...	...	...	...	...	|	1825	|	...	...	|	|	...
	Monfragüe–Plasencia d.	...	...	...	1109	1132	1135	...	...	1337	...	...	...	...	...	...	1731	1849	1908	1915	...	|	2152	...
278	Plasencia a.	...	...	...	...	|	1159	...	...	1351	...	...	...	...	...	...	1745	...	|	1939	...	2058	2207	...
278	Plasencia d.	...	0630x	...	...	|	...	...	...	1355	...	...	...	...	...	...	1750	...	|	...	...	2103	2210	...
343*	**Cáceres** d.	...	0709	...	...	1210	...	...	...	1437	1436	...	...	...	...	...	1830	...	1947	...	...	2139	2319	...
	San Vicente de Alcántara d.	...	|	...	...	|	...	...	...	|	1550	...	...	...	...	...	|	...	|	...	...	|	...	...
430	Valencia de Alcántara d.	...	|	...	...	|	...	...	...	|	1605	...	...	...	...	...	|	...	|	...	...	|	...	...
409	Mérida a.	...	0748	...	...	1242	...	...	...	1515	...	...	...	...	...	...	1910	...	2019	...	...	|	...	...
409	Mérida 678 d.	...	0754	0804	...	1247	...	...	...	1523	...	...	1531	1820	...	...	...	...	2024	...	2034	|	...	...
469	**Badajoz** 🏛 678 ES a.	...	|	0848	...	1326	...	1409	...	|	...	...	1605	1905	1941	...	...	...	2056	...	|	2228	...	...
	Elvas 🏛 PT a.	...	|	...	...	...	...	1325	...	|	...	...	...	...	1857	...	...	...	...	...	|	...	...	...
	Abrantes 691 a.	...	|	...	...	...	...	1521	...	|	...	...	...	...	2052	...	...	...	...	...	|	...	...	...
	Entroncamento 691 a.	...	|	...	...	...	...	1555	1559	|	...	...	...	...	2126	2159	...	...	...	...	|	...	...	...
	Lisboa Oriente 691 a.	...	|	...	...	...	...	...	1652	|	...	...	...	...	...	2252	...	...	...	...	|	...	...	...
742	**Lisboa** S Apolónia 691 a.	...	|	...	...	...	...	...	1700	|	...	...	...	...	...	2300	...	...	...	...	|	...	...	...
475	Zafra d.	...	0846	...	...	...	...	...	...	1617	...	1625	...	...	...	...	...	...	...	...	2124	...	...	...
649	Sevilla a.	...	1117	...	...	...	...	...	...	1858	...	|	...	...	...	...	...	...	...	...	...	...	...	...
521	Fregenal de la Sierra d.	...	...	...	...	...	...	...	...	...	...	1710	...	...	...	...	...	...	...	...	...	...	...	...
	Jabugo-Galaroza d.	0735	...	...	...	...	...	...	...	...	...	1815	...	...	...	...	...	...	...	...	...	...	...	...
660	Huelva a.	0932	...	...	...	...	...	...	...	...	...	2040	...	...	...	...	...	...	...	...	...	...	...	...

	17703	17021	17705	Alvia 291		Alvia 293		Alvia 299			17026	IC 511	AP 121	481 5501	MD 13087	MD 17907	IC 513	485 5503	17029		Alvia 295	Alvia 297	13089	
	2	2	2		2				2	2	2	R	R	2	2	2	R	2	2	🚌	2	2	2	2
	Ⓐ	⚒	⑦	Ⓐ	⚒	Ⓐ	🚌	Ⓒ	⑥	Ⓐ	Ⓑ				⑤⑥⑦				③⑤⑦	Ⓑ	Ⓑ	⑥	Ⓑ	
Huelva d.	...	...	...	...	...	...	...	...	...	...	...	...	...	...	0940	...	...	...	...	...	...	...	1940	...
Jabugo-Galaroza d.	...	...	...	...	...	...	...	...	...	...	...	...	...	...	1205	...	...	...	...	...	...	...	2133	...
Fregenal de la Sierra d.	...	...	...	...	...	...	...	...	...	...	...	...	...	...	1310	...	...	...	...	...	...	...	▬	...
Sevilla d.	...	...	...	...	...	...	...	...	...	...	...	...	...	...	|	1150	...	...	...	...	...	...	...	1654
Zafra d.	...	...	...	...	0655	...	...	...	...	...	...	...	...	...	1355	1421	...	...	...	...	...	...	...	1925
Lisboa S Apolónia 691 d.	...	...	...	...	|	...	...	...	...	...	...	0730	0800	...	▬	|	1230	...	...	...	...	...	...	|
Lisboa Oriente 691 d.	...	...	...	...	|	...	...	...	...	...	...	0739	0809	...	...	|	1239	...	...	...	...	...	...	|
Entroncamento 691 d.	...	...	...	...	|	...	...	...	...	...	...	0832	0857	0906	...	|	1332	1336	...	...	...	...	...	|
Abrantes 691 d.	...	...	...	...	|	...	...	...	...	...	...	...	...	0938	...	|	...	1408	...	...	...	...	...	|
Elvas 🏛 PT d.	...	...	...	...	|	...	...	...	...	...	...	...	...	1140	2	|	...	1616	...	...	...	...	2	|
Badajoz 🏛 678 ES d.	...	...	...	0636	|	0721	...	0830	1151	1156	...	...	...	1254	1420	|	...	1726	...	...	1748	1810	1933	|
Mérida 678 a.	...	...	...	|	0742	0751	...	0900	1232	1237	...	...	...	...	1506	1513	...	...	...	...	1823	|	2016	2015
Mérida d.	...	...	...	|	▬	0756	...	0909	...	...	1313	...	...	...	...	1521	...	...	...	...	1828	|	▬	2039
Valencia de Alcántara d.	...	...	...	|	...	|	...	|	...	...	|	...	...	...	...	|	...	...	1720	...	|	|	...	|
San Vicente de Alcántara d.	...	...	...	|	...	|	...	|	...	...	|	...	...	...	...	|	...	...	1735	...	|	|	...	|
Cáceres d.	...	0610	...	0724	...	0830	...	0944	...	...	1350	...	...	...	...	1602	...	...	1849	...	1903	1859	...	2119
Plasencia a.	...	0714	...	0758	🚌	|	...	|	...	...	1428	...	...	...	...	1643	...	...	...	...	|	1933	🚌	2158z
Plasencia d.	...	0718	...	0803	0840	|	...	|	...	...	1432	...	...	...	...	1646	...	...	...	1900	|	1938	Ⓑ	...
Monfragüe–Plasencia d.	...	0733	...	|	0904	0907	0925	1022	...	...	1448	...	...	...	...	1703	...	...	...	1924	1941	|	1950	...
Plasencia a.	...	|	...	|	...	|	0949	|	...	...	|	...	...	...	...	|	...	...	...	...	|	|	2014	...
Navalmoral de La Mata d.	...	0804	...	0844	...	0935	...	1051	...	...	1515	...	...	...	...	1737	...	...	...	...	2010	2017	...	...
Talavera de la Reina d.	0623	0844	0844	0923	...	1017	...	1137	...	...	1553	...	...	...	...	1822	...	...	...	...	2055	2056	...	...
Madrid Atocha Cercanías a.	0751	1017	1017	1046	...	1143	...	1258	...	...	1733	...	...	...	...	2003	...	...	...	...	2218	2218	...	...
Madrid Chamartín ‡ a.	...	...	...	1107	...	1207	...	1321	...	...	...	...	...	...	...	...	...	...	...	...	2239	2239	...	...

x – ⚒. **z** – Ⓑ. * – Madrid - Cáceres via Plasencia *363 km*. ‡ – Full name is Madrid-Chamartín-Clara Campoamor. ES – Spain (Central European Time). PT – Portugal (West European Time).

ALBACETE - ALCÁZAR DE SAN JUAN - BADAJOZ 678

km				MD 17042	MD 17044		MD 18183	MD 18170	Alvia 697	MD 18330	MD 18083	18027	18027
							w		T		w	v	A
		2	2	2	2	2	2	2		2	2	2	2
		Ⓐ	Ⓒ	Ⓐ	Ⓒ							①–⑥	⑦
	Madrid § **661 668** d.	...	...	...	...	...	...	1257	...	...	...	...	...
	Albacete d.	...	...	...	...	...	1152	|	1349	...	1841	1915	1915
0	**Alcázar de San Juan** 661 d.	...	...	0725	0852	...	1305	1435	1501	1524	1957	2054	2054
50	Manzanares 661 d.	...	...	0750	0917	...	1331	1502	1537	1548	2024	...	2121
114	Ciudad Real 660 d.	...	...	0830	0957	...	1418	1549	...	1636	2108	...	2202
153	Puertollano 660 d.	...	...	...	...	1200	...	...	...	1704	...	...	...
265	Cabeza del Buey d.	0614	0720	...	...	1346	...	...	...	1850	...	...	...
392	Mérida 677 d.	0804	0905	...	...	1531	...	...	...	2037	...	...	...
451	**Badajoz** 677 a.	0848	0949	...	...	1605	...	...	...	2128	...	...	...

	18024	18024	18018	MD 18081	MD 18331	Alvia 694	MD 17041	MD 18181		
	B	v	v	w		T		w		
	2	2	2	2	2		2	2	2	2
	①	②–⑤	⑥⑦							
Badajoz 677 d.	...	...	...	...	0650	...	...	...	1420	1933
Mérida 677 d.	...	...	...	...	0750	...	...	...	1520	2040
Cabeza del Buey d.	...	...	...	...	0922	...	...	...	1703	2214
Puertollano 660 d.	...	...	...	...	1108	...	...	...	1858	...
Ciudad Real 660 d.	0552	...	...	1002	1136	...	1435	1624	...	...
Manzanares 661 d.	0632	...	...	1042	1225	1313	1521	1710	...	...
Alcázar de San Juan 661 a.	0700	0705	0750	1107	1250	1337	1546	1733	...	...
Albacete a.	0831	0831	0917	1218	...	1454	|	1847	...	...
Madrid § **661 668** a.	...	...	...	...	...	...	1737	...	...	...

A – ⑦: (2) València - Albacete - Ciudad Real (Table **668**).
B – ①: (2) Ciudad Real - Albacete - València (Table **668**).
T – TORRE DEL ORO – (12) 🍸 Barcelona - Albacete - Manzanares - Cádiz and v.v. (Table **672a**).
v – From/to València (Table **668**).
w – From/to Alacant (Table **668**).
§ – Madrid-Chamartín-Clara Campoamor.

Avant high-speed shuttle services, *Turista* class — GRANADA - MÁLAGA / CÓRDOBA - SEVILLA 678a

For trains **Sevilla** – **Málaga** and v.v. via **Córdoba**, see Table **663a**.

	8475	8915		8525	8935		8575		8505	8955
Granada d.	0625	0736	...	1220	1325	...	1622	...	1822	1829
Loja d.	0647	0758	...	1248	1347	...	1653	...	1845	1852
Antequera AV d.	0716	0827	...	1321	1416	...	1719	...	1913	1921
Málaga M. Zambrano a.	|	0900	...	|	1449	...	|	...	|	1954
Antequera - Santa Ana § d.	0726	...	...	1331	...	...	1729	...	1924	...
Puente Genil - Herrera ¶ d.	0741	...	...	1345	...	...	1743	...	1939	...
Córdoba a.	0809	...	...	1413	...	...	1813	...	2009	...
Córdoba d.	0815	...	...	1418	...	...	1818	...	2014	...
Sevilla a.	0908	...	...	1511	...	...	1916	...	2109	...

	8275	8815		8295		8335	8835		8395	8855
Sevilla d.	0742	...	...	1011	...	1217	...	...	1755	...
Córdoba a.	0826	...	...	1055	...	1301	...	...	1839	...
Córdoba d.	0831	...	...	1100	...	1306	...	...	1844	...
Puente Genil - Herrera ¶ d.	0901	...	...	1134	...	1337	...	...	1917	...
Antequera - Santa Ana § d.	0917	...	...	1151	...	1352	...	...	1933	...
Málaga M. Zambrano d.	|	0925	...	|	...	|	1640	...	|	2020
Antequera AV d.	0928	0953	...	1201	...	1403	1708	...	1944	2048
Loja d.	0955	1021	...	1229	...	1430	1735	...	2010	2115
Granada a.	1017	1043	...	1251	...	1452	1758	...	2032	2137

§ – ± *17 km* from Antequera. ¶ – ± *8 km* from Puente Genil.

679 MADRID - TOLEDO, SEGOVIA, VALLADOLID, SALAMANCA and EL ESCORIAL — 2nd class

km		Av 8062 Ⓐ	Av 8072 Ⓐ B	Av 8082	Av 8292	Av 8102	Av 8312 Ⓐ	Av 8312 Ⓒ B	Av 8322		Av 8132	Av 8142 Ⓐ	Av 8152	Av 8162 Ⓐ	Av 8172	Av 8182 Ⓐ	Av 8192	Av 8212					
0	**Madrid** Puerta de Atocha d.	0642	0747	0835	0915	1015	1115	1115	1215	...	1345	1445	1550	1645	1745	1845	1945	2045	...	...	...	...	...
75	**Toledo** a.	0718	0823	0911	0951	1051	1151	1151	1251	...	1421	1521	1626	1721	1821	1921	2021	2121	...	...	...	...	...

	Av 8063 Ⓐ	Av 8273 Ⓐ	Av 8073 Ⓐ	Av 8283 Ⓐ		Av 8093	Av 8103		Av 8123	Av 8133		Av 8153	Av 8163 Ⓐ B	Av 8173 Ⓐ	Av 8173 Ⓒ B	Av 8183	Av 8193	Av 8203	Av 8213				
Toledo d.	0625	0650	0728	0755	...	0930	1028	...	1230	1334	...	1525	1625	1711	1711	1838	1912	2021	2126	...	...	...	...
Madrid Puerta de Atocha a.	0701	0726	0804	0831	...	1006	1104	...	1306	1410	...	1601	1701	1747	1747	1914	1948	2057	2202	...	...	...	...

km	km		Av 8079 Ⓐ	Alvia 4899		Av 8109		Av 8129	Alvia 4929 Ⓐ	Av 34149 Ⓑ	Av 8139 ⑤		Alvia 4969	Av 8159 ⑤	Av 8359	Av 8169 Ⓐ	Av 8179	Av 8389 Ⓑ	Av 8189 A	Av 8199 Ⓐ	Av 8209	Av 34209 Ⓑ	Av 8219	Alvia 4909	
0	0	**Madrid** Chamartín ‡ d.	0752	0850	...	1014	...	1205	1240	1303	1347	...	1550	1525	1540	1626	1700	1810	1845	1930	2002	2024	2130	2047	...
68	68	**Segovia** Guiomar d.	0820	0918	...	1042	...	1233	1309	1333	1415	...	1618	1553	1608	1654	1728	1838	1913	1959	2030	|	2158	2115	...
		Medina del Campo AV d.	|	0947	...	|	...	|	|	|	|	...	1647	|	|	|	|	|	|	|	|	|	|	2144	...
180		**Valladolid** Campo Grande a.	0857	|	...	1125	...	1310	|	1406	1452	...	|	1630	1645	1731	1805	1915	1950	2036	2107	2119	2241	|	...
	230	**Salamanca** a.	...	1031	...	...	...	...	1421	...	...	...	1731	...	...	...	...	...	...	...	...	...	...	2227	...

	Av 8058 Ⓐ	Av 8068 Ⓐ	Alvia 4868 Ⓐ	Av 34080 ①–⑥	Av 8078 Ⓐ	Av 34078 Ⓐ	Av 8278 Ⓐ	Alvia 4898 Ⓒ	Av 8088	Av 34088 Ⓐ	Av 8318 ⑥	Av 8098 ⑦	Alvia 4918 Ⓐ	Av 8118 Ⓐ		Av 8148 Ⓐ	Alvia 4958	Av 8158	Av 8168 ⑦	Av 8178 Ⓑ	Av 8178 ⑥	Alvia 4988	Av 34178 Ⓑ	Av 8198	Av 8208
Salamanca d.	...	...	0625	...	...	...	...	0810	...	...	...	...	1050	...	...	...	1525	...	...	...	...	1850	...	...	...
Valladolid Campo Grande d.	0623	0645	|	0718	0727	0745	0755	|	0815	0925	0930	0950	|	1130	...	1405	|	1520	1622	1750	1758	|	1929	1946	2035
Medina del Campo AV d.	|	|	0708	|	|	|	|	0854	|	|	|	|	|	|	...	|	1609	|	|	|	|	1933	|	|	|
Segovia Guiomar d.	0700	0722	0738	|	0804	|	0832	0923	0852	|	1007	1027	1159	1207	...	1443	1639	1557	1659	1827	1835	2003	2005	2023	2112
Madrid Chamartín ‡ a.	0728	0750	0805	0813	0832	0839	0900	0950	0920	1035	1035	1055	1226	1235	...	1510	1706	1625	1727	1855	1903	2030	2032	2051	2140

km		Ⓐ	Ⓒ	Ⓒ	Ⓐ	Ⓒ		⑤	Ⓒ	Ⓐ	Ⓒ
0	**Madrid** Chamartín ‡ d.	...	0845	*1015*	*1116*	*1215*	...	*1545*	*1615*	*1814*	*1915*
58	Cercedilla d.	0648	0952	1134	1230	1332	...	1659	1732	1930	2031
100	**Segovia** a.	0742	1036	1217	1314	1416	...	1742	1815	2014	2115

	Ⓐ	Ⓒ	Ⓒ			⑤	Ⓒ	Ⓐ	Ⓒ	
Segovia d.	*0743*	*1042*	*1243*	*1442*	...	*1746*	*1843*	*2046*	2123	...
Cercedilla d.	0832	1131	1333	1532	...	1833	1931	2133	2207	...
Madrid Chamartín ‡ a.	0935	1234	1436	1635	...	1936	2034	2235	...	...

km		MD 18001 Ⓐ	MD 18901 Ⓐ	MD 18921 Ⓒ	MD 18903	MD 18905 Ⓐ	MD 18907	MD 18913	MD 18909	MD 18909	MD 18911 Ⓑ
0	**Madrid** Principe Pio ◧ d.	0640	0740	0826	1110	1340	1525	1753	1937	1937	2110
122	Ávila ◧ d.	0818	0909	0955	1239	1510	1711	1939	2115	2115	2238
233	**Salamanca** a.	...	1040	1123	1353	1619	1828	2049	2225	2225	2344

	Ⓐ	MD 18910 ①–⑥	MD 18900	MD 18912	MD 18902	MD 18004 Ⓐ	MD 18904	MD 18006	MD 18906 Ⓐ	MD 18908
Salamanca d.	...	0547	0735	0944	1228	...	1642	...	1802	2001
Ávila ◧ d.	0555	0654	0843	1055	1339	1547	1812	1854	1912	2112
Madrid Principe Pio ◧ a.	0743	0825	1017	1240	1510	1729	1947	2041	2056	2246

MADRID ATOCHA CERCANÍAS - VILLALBA - EL ESCORIAL. *45 km.* Line C8. Journey time: Villalba, 53 minutes; El Escorial, 66-67 minutes. Depart 14 minutes later from Madrid Chamartín; arrive 15 minutes earlier at Madrid Charmartín. Additional services operate.

From **Madrid Atocha Cercanías**: 0621 Ⓐ, 0635 Ⓒ, 0651 Ⓐ, 0709 Ⓐ, 0723 Ⓐ, 0737 Ⓒ, 0750 Ⓐ, 0835 Ⓒ, 0839 Ⓐ, 0935 Ⓒ, 0941 Ⓐ, 1036, 1135, 1235, 1335, 1407 Ⓐ, 1436 Ⓒ, 1450 Ⓐ, 1521 Ⓐ, 1536 Ⓒ, 1547 Ⓐ, 1635, 1715 Ⓐ, 1736 Ⓒ, 1745 Ⓐ, 1827 Ⓐ, 1836 Ⓒ, 1847 Ⓐ, 1920, 1936, Ⓒ, 1944 Ⓐ, 2036 Ⓐ, 2042 Ⓒ, 2139, 2236, 2334.

From **El Escorial**: 0548, 0616 Ⓒ, 0631 Ⓐ, 0658 Ⓐ, 0706 Ⓐ, 0716 Ⓒ, 0736 Ⓐ, 0802 Ⓐ, 0817 Ⓒ, 0831 Ⓐ, 0915, 1015, 1115, 1215, 1315, 1414, 1515, 1601 Ⓐ, 1615 Ⓒ, 1624 Ⓐ, 1713, 1815, 1858 Ⓐ, 1912 Ⓐ, 1915 Ⓒ, 1930 Ⓐ, 1959 Ⓐ, 2013 Ⓒ, 2029 Ⓐ, 2115, 2215.

A – ①②③④⑥.
B – From / to Albacete (Table **668**).
MD – Medium Distance Plus.
Av – ***Avant*** high-speed services. Single class.
◧ – See also Tables **680**, **681**, **689**.
‡ – Full name is Madrid-Chamartín-Clara Campoamor.

679a MADRID - VALLADOLID

High-speed services. For Avant high-speed services, see Table **679**.

km		Alvia 4261 ①–⑤	Alvia 4187 ①–⑥	Alvia 4087	Alvia 4071 ⑥	Alvia 4073 ①–⑥	IC 4687 ①–⑥ Q	Alvia 4091 Ⓑ C	AVE 5763 ①–⑥ MB	Alvia 4101	Ouigo 6485	avlo 4121	AVE 5101 VL	Alvia 4143	avlo 5817 M	IC 4257 Ⓑ	AVE 5721 V	AVE 4161 Ⓑ	Ouigo 6543 D	IC 4179 Ⓑ P	Alvia 4167	Alvia 4267 Ⓑ H	Alvia 4181	Alvia 4193	AVE 5171 Ⓑ BV	AVE 5183 L
	Alacant Terminal **668** d.	...	...	...	...	...	...	...	...	...	0753	...	...	1026	...	...	...	...	...	...	...	...	1526	...	...	1743
0	**Madrid** Chamartín ‡ d.	0649	0720	0720	0732	0745	0840	0915	0925	1024	1039	1145	1303	1340	1422	1446	1459	1637	1716	1732	1737	1737	1835	1908	1953	2024
68	Segovia Guiomar d.	|	0745	0750	|	|	0909	|	0952	1055	1108	1213	1333	1410	|	|	1526	|	1744	1801	1806	1806	|	|	|	|
180	**Valladolid** Campo Grande a.	0752	0825	0825	0833	0900	0943	1016	1024	1132	1140	1245	1406	1445	1518	1552	1559	1731	1817	1835	1841	1841	1939	2020	2047	2119
	Gijón Sanz Crespo **685** a.	1039	|	|	1122	|	...	...	...	1421	...	1533	...	|	...	|	1842	2011	...	...	|	|	2227	|	...	...
	Santander **684** a.	...	|	|	...	1206	...	...	...	...	...	...	...	1747	...	|	...	...	...	...	|	|	...	2328	...	...
	Bilbao Abando **689** a.	...	1200	|	...	...	...	...	...	...	...	...	...	...	...	|	...	...	...	...	|	2221	...	...	...	...
	Irún **689** a.	...	...	1409	...	...	...	...	...	...	...	...	...	...	...	2037	...	...	...	...	2300	...	...	...	...	...

	AVE 5080 ①–⑥ BV	AVE 5092 ①–⑤ L	AVE 4060 ①–⑤	IC 4056 Ⓐ S	IC 4088 ①–⑥ P	Alvia 4072	Alvia 4186 ①–⑥ J	AVE 5312 ⑥⑦ L	Alvia 4080 Z	Alvia 4086	Ouigo 6544	AVE 5750 V	avlo 5178	Alvia 4142	AVE 5792 Ⓑ BM	Alvia 4140	IC 4166 ⑦	IC 4786 Ⓑ Q	Alvia 4170 Ⓑ C	Alvia 4176	Alvia 4366 Ⓑ	AVE 5210 LV	Ouigo 6612 D	AVE 4398 ⑦	Alvia 4192 Ⓑ	avlo 4190
Irún **689** d.	...	...	...	...	...	...	...	...	...	0830	...	...	...	...	...	...	1318	...	...	1523	...	...	...	...	...	...
Bilbao Abando **689** d.	...	...	...	...	...	...	0700	...	...	|	...	...	...	...	...	...	|	...	...	|	1735	...	...	...	...	...
Santander **684** d.	...	...	...	...	...	0648	|	...	...	|	...	...	...	1358	...	...	|	...	...	|	|	...	...	...	1900	...
Gijón Sanz Crespo **685** d.	...	...	0600	...	...	|	|	...	0900	|	...	1109	...	|	...	1530	|	...	...	|	|	...	...	...	|	1925
Valladolid Campo Grande d.	0718	0745	0841	0847	0911	0955	1022	1051	1150	1250	1300	1358	1550	1703	1800	1823	1827	1911	2007	2106	2106	1929	2000	2138	2207	2216
Segovia Guiomar d.	|	|	|	|	0948	1054	1100	|	|	1328	1335	1434	|	|	1835	|	1905	1948	|	2144	2144	2005	2035	2213	|	2251
Madrid Chamartín ‡ a.	0813	0839	0937	0953	1015	1123	1128	1145	1252	1356	1400	1500	1645	1814	1900	1924	1934	2015	2109	2213	2213	2032	2100	2239	2324	2318
Alacant Terminal **668** a.	...	1129	...	...	...	1443	...	1428	...	...	1644	...	1934	...	...	2245	...	...	...	...	...	...	...	...	...	...

B – To / from Burgos (Table **689**).
C – To / from Avilés (Table **685**).
D – To / from València (Table **668**).
H – Ⓑ (daily June 18 - Oct. 15).
J – ①–⑥ (daily June 18 - Oct. 15).
L – To / from Leon (Table **681**).
M – From / to Murcia (Table **668**).
P – To / from Ponferrada (Table **682**).
Q – To / from Logroño (Tables **654, 689**).
S – From San Sebastián / Donostia (Table **689**).
V – To / from Castelló (Table **668**).
Z – ①②③④⑥⑦. On ⑥ is *AVE* **4282** depart Valladolid 1144, arrive Madrid 1240.

‡ – Full name is Madrid-Chamartín-Clara Campoamor.
☛ All trains convey 🍸. *AVE* trains also convey ✕.

MADRID - ZAMORA - VIGO, PONTEVEDRA and A CORUÑA 680

For services to / from A Coruña via León, see Table **682**

Additional connections between Vigo and Ourense can be made by changing trains at Santiago de Compostela

km			*Av*	*MD*	*Av*	*MD*	*Av*		*AVE*	*MD*	*AVE*		*avlo*		*AVE*	*AVE*	*AVE*	*Av*	*MD*	*MD*	*AVE*	*Av*	*Av*
			9470	**9072**	**9480**	**9082**	**9090**		**4494**	**9112**	**4475**		**4295**		**4254**	**5273**	**4505**	**9120**	**9132**	**9142**	**4515**	**9140**	**9550**
				Ⓡ		Ⓡ				Ⓡ									Ⓡ	Ⓡ			
		2	2	2	2	2	2	2	**E**	2	**B**	2		2	**G**	**A**		2	2	2	**E**	2	2
		①–⑤	①–⑤				①–⑤				①–⑥		①–⑥			①–⑥	⑦			①–⑤	①–⑥		①–⑤
0	**Madrid** Chamartín ‡ ... **681 689** d.	...	...	...	...	...	...	...	...	...	0714	...	0825	...	...	1004	1004	...	...	...	1117	...	...
68	Segovia Guiomar ... **679 679a** d.	...	...	...	...	...	...	...	...	...	|	...	0852	...	...	|	|	...	...	...	|	...	...
	Irún **689** ... d.	...	...	...	...	...	...	...	...	...	|	...	|	...	...	|	|	...	...	...	|	...	...
	Barcelona Sants **650a** ... d.	...	...	...	...	...	...	...	...	...	|	...	|	...	...	|	|	...	...	...	|	...	...
	Miranda de Ebro **681 689** ... d.	...	...	...	...	...	...	...	...	...	|	...	|	...	...	|	|	...	...	...	|	...	...
207*	Medina AV ... **681 689** d.	...	...	...	...	...	...	...	...	...	|	...	0919	...	...	|	|	...	...	...	|	...	...
297	**Zamora** ... d.	...	...	...	...	...	...	...	...	...	0822	...	0943	...	...	1109	1110	...	...	...	1223	...	...
404	Sanabria AV ... d.	...	...	...	...	...	...	...	...	...	|	...	1012	...	...	|	|	...	...	...	|	...	...
547	**Ourense** ... d.	...	0640	...	0750	...	0955	...	...	...	0939	1005	1111	...	...	1218	1227	1240	...	...	1342	1425	1530
641	Guillarei ... d.	...	|	...	|	...	|	...	...	...	|	1127	|	...	...	...	|	|	...	...	|	|	|
	Vigo Urzáiz ... d.	0508	|	0634	|	0800	|	0915**c**	0944	1035	1109	|	|	1231**c**	1337	...	1411	|	1340	1430	1526	|	|
666	Redondela AV ... d.	0516	|	0642	|	|	|	0927**r**	|	|	|	1150**r**	|	1244**r**	|	...	|	|	1348	|	|	|	|
678	**Vigo** Guixar ... a.	|	|	|	|	|	|	|	|	|	|	1205	|	|	|	...	|	|	|	|	|	|	|
684	**Pontevedra** ... d.	0532	|	0654	|	0817	|	0946	1001	1052	1053	...	|	1304	1354	...	1355	|	1402	1447	1510	|	|
717	Vilagarcía de Arousa ... d.	0550	|	0712	|	0833	|	1005	1020	1108	...	...	|	1323	|	...	1337	|	1420	1503	1452	|	|
677§	Santiago de Compostela ... d.	0635	0722	0742	0832	0858	1037	1057	1044	1133	...	...	1155	1410	1437	...	1311	1322	1448	1528	1426	1507	1612
751§	**A Coruña** ... a.	0717	0753	0818	0903	0929	1108	1135	...	1204	...	...	1227	1449	...	...	...	1353	1519	1559	...	1538	1643

		Alvia	*Av*	*MD*		*AVE*	*AVE*	*MD*	*MD*	*Av*		*MD*	*AVE*	*AVE*		*avlo*	*Alvia*	*Alvia*	*Av*		*AVE*	*MD*	*avlo*
		4325	**9160**	**9162**		**4345**	**4384**	**9172**	**9182**	**9590**		**9192**	**4565**	**4375**		**4975**	**622**	**626**	**9610**		**4395**	**9212**	**4405**
			Ⓡ	Ⓡ				Ⓡ	Ⓡ			Ⓡ					🍷	🍷				Ⓡ	
	2	**q**	2	2	2		**H**	2	2	2	2	2	**B**		2	**E**	**P**	**Q**	2	2		2	
													Ⓑ	Ⓑ			✣	✣	⑦	**J**	Ⓑ		Ⓑ
Madrid Chamartín ‡ ... **681 689** d.	...	1320	...	...	...	1440	...	...	...	...	...	...	1605	1710	...	1806	...	...	...	...	1917	...	2023
Segovia Guiomar ... **679 679a** d.	...	|	...	...	...	|	...	...	...	...	...	...	|	|	...	|	...	...	...	...	|	...	|
Irún **689** ... d.	...	|	...	...	...	|	...	...	...	...	...	...	|	|	...	|	...	...	...	...	|	...	|
Barcelona Sants **650a** ... d.	...	|	...	...	...	|	...	...	...	...	...	...	|	|	...	|	0905	0905	...	...	|	...	|
Miranda de Ebro **681 689** ... d.	...	|	...	...	...	|	...	...	...	...	...	...	|	|	...	|	1426	1426	...	...	|	...	|
Medina AV ... **681 689** d.	...	1415	...	...	...	|	...	...	...	...	...	...	|	|	...	1855	|	|	...	1829**x**	|	...	|
Zamora ... d.	...	1442	...	...	...	1545	...	...	...	...	...	...	1711	1819	...	1918	|	|	...	1923	2022	...	2128
Sanabria AV ... d.	...	1515	...	...	...	|	...	...	...	...	...	...	|	|	...	1947	|	|	...	2048**p**	|	...	|
Ourense ... d.	...	1615	1640	...	1647	1703	...	...	...	1900	...	...	1828	1940	...	2045	2101	2101	2116	...	2140	...	2246
Guillarei ... d.	...	...	|	...	|	|	...	...	...	|	...	...	|	|	...	|	|	|	|	...	|	...	|
Vigo Urzáiz ... d.	1500**c**	...	|	1630	|	|	1725	1735	1815	|	1815**c**	1926	1958	|	2028**c**	2229	|	|	|	...	|	2150	|
Redondela AV ... d.	1511**r**	...	|	|	|	|	|	|	|	|	1828**r**	|	|	|	2041**r**	|	2239**r**	|	|	...	|	2158	|
Vigo Guixar ... a.	|	...	|	|	|	|	|	|	|	|	|	|	|	|	|	|	2251	|	|	...	|	|	|
Pontevedra ... d.	1533	...	|	1647	|	|	1742	1750	1832	|	1848	1943	1942	|	2101	2213	...	|	|	...	|	2212	|
Vilagarcía de Arousa ... d.	1552	...	|	1703	|	|	1800	1806	1848	|	1911	1959	...	|	2121	2155	...	|	|	...	|	2230	|
Santiago de Compostela ... d.	1638	...	1722	1728	1827	1745	...	1831	1913	1942	1954	2024	...	2021	2207	2129	...	2151	2158	...	2219	2258	2328
A Coruña ... a.	1717	...	1753	1759	...	1817	...	1903	1944	2013	...	2057	...	2054	2245	...	...	2224	2229	...	2254	2329	2359

km		*avlo*			*Av*	*avlo*		*MD*	*AVE*	*MD*	*Alvia*	*Alvia*	*MD*	*avlo*		*MD*	*AVE*	*Av*	*Alvia*	*MD*			
		4154			**9061**	**4864**		**9073**	**4064**	**9083**	**621**	**625**	**9093**	**4454**		**9113**	**4314**	**9111**	**4114**	**9123**			
			2				2	Ⓡ		Ⓡ	🍷	🍷	Ⓡ			Ⓡ				Ⓡ			
			J	2	2	**B**	**J**	2		2	**R**	**S**	2	**E**	2	2		2	**q**	2	2		
		①–⑥	Ⓐ	①–⑤	①–⑤		Ⓒ		①–⑥		✣	✣				①–⑤	Ⓑ						
0	**A Coruña** ... d.	0514	...	0530	0550	...	...	0700	0715	0800	...	0812	0900	...	0939	1106	1115	1125	...	1200	1245	...	...
74	Santiago de Compostela ... d.	0547	...	0612	0623	...	...	0733	0748	0833	...	0843	0933	1049	1024	1139	1148	1158	...	1233	1330	...	...
116	Vilagarcía de Arousa ... d.	|	...	0650	|	...	...	0802	|	0856	...	|	0956	1020	1102	1202	|	|	...	1256	1410	...	...
149	**Pontevedra** ... d.	|	...	0711	|	0617	...	0820	|	0913	...	|	1013	1001	1121	1219	|	|	...	1313	1429	...	...
	Vigo Guixar ... d.	|	...	|	|	|	...	|	|	|	0748	|	|	|	|	|	|	|	...	|	|	...	...
167	Redondela AV ... d.	|	...	0729**r**	|	|	...	0832	|	|	0800**r**	|	|	|	1140**r**	|	|	|	...	|	1447**r**	...	...
179	**Vigo** Urzáiz ... d.	|	...	0741**c**	|	0600	...	0840	|	0927	|	|	1027	0944	1153**c**	1233	|	|	...	1327	1500**c**	...	...
192	Guillarei ... d.	|	...	...	|	|	...	...	|	...	0817	|	...	|	...	...	|	|	...	...	...	...	...
	Ourense ... d.	0624	...	...	0703	0726	...	...	0825	...	0925	0925	...	1127	...	...	1225	1238	1257	...	...	...	...
	Sanabria AV ... d.	|	0708**p**	...	...	|	0730**p**	...	|	...	|	|	...	1227	...	...	|	...	1401	...	...	...	...
	Zamora ... d.	0741	0832	...	...	0843	0854	...	0943	...	|	|	...	1256	...	...	1343	...	1436	...	...	...	...
	Medina AV ... **681 689** d.	|	0926**x**	...	...	|	0947**x**	...	|	...	|	|	...	1320	...	...	|	...	1503	...	...	...	...
	Miranda de Ebro **681 689** ... a.	|	...	...	...	|	...	...	|	...	1555	1555	...	|	...	...	|	...	|	...	...	...	...
	Barcelona Sants **650a** ... a.	|	...	...	...	|	...	...	|	...	2139	2139	...	|	...	...	|	...	|	...	...	...	...
	Hendaye **689** ... a.	|	...	...	...	|	...	...	|	...	...	...	...	|	...	...	|	...	|	...	...	...	...
	Segovia Guiomar ... **679 679a** d.	|	...	...	...	|	...	...	|	...	...	...	...	|	...	...	|	...	|	...	...	...	...
	Madrid Chamartín ‡ ... **681 689** a.	0849	...	...	...	0950	...	...	1050	...	...	...	...	1408	...	...	1450	...	1600	...	...	...	...

	Av	*AVE*		*AVE*	*MD*	*MD*	*Av*	*AVE*		*avlo*	*MD*	*Av*	*AVE*	*MD*			*AVE*	*avlo*	*Av*	*MD*			
	9131	**4254**		**4115**	**9133**	**9153**	**9351**	**5182**		**4334**	**9173**	**9171**	**4384**	**9183**			**4404**	**4975**	**9201**	**9213**			
			2		Ⓡ	Ⓡ					Ⓡ			Ⓡ						Ⓡ			
	2	**G**	**h**	**E**	2	2	2	**A**	2		2	2	**H**	2	2	2		**E**	2	2	2		
	①–⑤	Ⓑ		①–⑥				Ⓑ						Ⓑ			Ⓑ						
A Coruña ... d.	1335	...	...	...	1405	1500	1510	...	1539	1554	1700	1715	...	1800	...	1908	1933	...	2100	2125	...	...	...
Santiago de Compostela ... d.	1408	1437	...	...	1438	1533	1543	...	1624	1626	1733	1748	...	1833	1847	1953	2005	2129	2133	2201	2210	...	...
Vilagarcía de Arousa ... d.	|	|	...	1452	1507	1556	|	...	1702	|	1756	|	1800	1856	|	2037	|	2155	|	2230	2252	...	...
Pontevedra ... d.	|	1354	...	1510	1525	1613	|	...	1721	|	1813	|	1742	1912	|	2059	|	2213	|	2248	2311	...	...
Vigo Guixar ... d.	|	|	1407	|	|	|	|	...	|	|	|	|	|	|	|	|	|	|	|	|	|	...	...
Redondela AV ... d.	|	|	1420**r**	|	1534	|	|	...	1740**r**	|	|	|	|	|	|	2120**r**	|	|	|	2300	2331**r**	...	...
Vigo Urzáiz ... d.	|	1337	|	1526	1542	1627	|	...	1754**c**	|	1827	|	1725	1926	|	2131**c**	|	2229	|	2308	2344**c**	...	...
Guillarei ... d.	|	|	1441	...	...	...	|	...	...	|	...	|	|	...	|	...	|	...	|	...	...	...	...
Ourense ... d.	1448	1513	1615	...	...	...	1623	1625	...	1704	...	1828	1855	...	2028	...	2043	...	2213	...	...	...	...
Sanabria AV ... d.	...	|	...	...	...	...	...	|	...	1804	...	...	|	...	...	...	|	...	...	...	...	...	...
Zamora ... d.	...	1630	...	...	...	...	...	1736	...	1833	...	...	2011	...	...	...	2200	...	...	...	...	...	...
Medina AV ... **681 689** d.	...	|	...	...	...	...	...	|	...	1857	...	...	|	...	...	...	|	...	...	...	...	...	...
Miranda de Ebro **681 689** ... a.	...	|	...	...	...	...	...	|	...	|	...	...	|	...	...	...	|	...	...	...	...	...	...
Barcelona Sants **650a** ... a.	...	|	...	...	...	...	...	|	...	|	...	...	|	...	...	...	|	...	...	...	...	...	...
Hendaye **689** ... a.	...	|	...	...	...	...	...	|	...	|	...	...	|	...	...	...	|	...	...	...	...	...	...
Segovia Guiomar ... **679 679a** d.	...	|	...	...	...	...	...	|	...	1923	...	...	|	...	...	...	|	...	...	...	...	...	...
Madrid Chamartín ‡ ... **681 689** a.	...	1737	...	...	...	...	...	1840	...	1951	...	...	2120	...	...	...	2307	...	...	...	...	...	...

A – From / to Alacant (Table **668**).
B – Routeing is Madrid - Ourense - Pontevedra - Vigo and v.v.
D – Routeing is Madrid - Ourense - Santiago de Compostela - Vilagarcía de Arousa - Pontevedra - Vigo and v.v.
E – Routeing is Madrid - Ourense - Santiago de Compostela - Vilagarcía de Arousa - Pontevedra - Vigo and v.v. See opposite direction for further stops.
G – Routeing is Vigo - Pontevedra - Santiago de Compostela - Ourense. See opposite direction for further stops.
H – Routeing is Vigo - Pontevedra - Vilagarcía de Arousa - Ourense.
J – [2] Valladolid - Medina del Campo - Puebla de Sanabria and v.v. (Table **689**).
P – ③⑤⑦ [12] 🍷 Barcelona - Ourense - Vigo ✣.
Q – ①②④⑥ [12] 🍷 Barcelona - Ourense - A Coruña ✣.
R – ①④⑥ [12] 🍷 Vigo - Ourense - Barcelona ✣.
S – ②③⑤⑦ [12] 🍷 A Coruña - Ourense - Barcelona ✣.

c – Vigo **Guixar**.
h – To Ponferrada (Table **682**).
p – Puebla de Sanabria.
q – To / from Lugo (Table **682**).
r – Redondela **de Galica**.
x – Medina del Campo.

◐ – Via Lugo (Table **682**).

‡ – Full name is Madrid-Chamartín-Clara Campoamor.
* – *153 km* Madrid - Medina del Campo via high-speed line.
§ – *636 km* Madrid - Santiago de Compostela via high-speed line. *697 km* Madrid - A Coruña via high-speed line.
✣ – On days of indirect service, connections are available between Ourense and Vigo / A Coruña and v.v. in similar timings.

681 MADRID - LEÓN

km	km via HSL				Alvia	Alvia	Alvia	Alvia	AVE	Alvia	avlo		AVE	Alvia	Alvia	AVE	AVE	MD	IC	Alvia	MD	Alvia	AVE			
					4261	**4071**	**4073**	**4091**	**4399**	**4101**	**4121**		**5101**	**4143**	**622** **626**	**5721**	**4161**	**18003**	**4179**	**4181**	**18005**	**4193**	**5183**			
			Ⓐ	Ⓒ	①–⑤	⑥	①–⑥	Ⓑ	⑦								Ⓑ	2	Ⓑ		2					
			2	2				**B**					**V**	**E**	**L**	**V**				**Q**			**Q**			
0	0	**Madrid** Chamartín ¶ ... **680 689** d.	...	...	0649	0732	0745	0915	0942	1024	1145	...	1303	1340	...	1459	1637	1626**p**	1732	1835	1827**p**	1908	2024	...	...	...
121		Ávila ... **680 689** d.	...	...	|	|	|	|	|	|	|	...	|	|	...	|	|	1759	|	|	2009	|	|	...	...	...
207		Medina del Campo .. **680 689** d.	...	...	|	|	|	|	|	|	|	...	|	|	...	|	|	1845	|	|	2054	|	|	...	...	...
249	180	**Valladolid** C. Grande ... **689** d.	0700	0718	0752	0835	0902	1018	1044	1132	1247	...	1409	1448	...	1601	1733	1913	1837	1938	2120	2020	2121	...	...	...
286		Venta de Baños ... **689** d.	0733	0751	|	|	|	|	|	|	|	...	|	|	...	|	|	1938	|	|	2147	|	|	...	...	...
		Barcelona Sants **652** ... d.	|	|	|	|	|	|	|	|	|	...	|	|	0905	|	|	|	|	|	|	|	|	...	...	...
		Irún **689** ... d.	|	|	|	|	|	|	|	|	|	...	|	|	|	|	|	|	|	|	|	|	|	...	...	...
		Miranda de Ebro ... **689** d.	|	|	|	|	|	|	|	|	|	...	|	|	1426	|	|	|	|	|	|	|	|	...	...	...
		Burgos Rosa Manzano **689** d.	|	|	|	|	|	|	|	|	|	...	|	|	1535	|	|	|	|	|	|	|	|	...	...	...
		Palencia ... **689** d.	0747	0805	0818	0902	0937	1045	1108	1157	1312	...	1435	1520	1612	1625	|	1949	1904	2004	2158	2055	2146	...	...	...
297	233	*Santander* **684** ... a.	|	|	|	|	1206	|	|	|	|	...	|	1747	|	|	|	|	|	|	|	2328	|	...	...	...
		León ... a.	0916	0927	0903	0946	...	1136	1143	1242	1353	...	1510	...	1654	1707	1836	2058	1941	2048	2307	...	2222	...	...	...
420	345	*Gijón Sanz Crespo* **685** ... a.	1220	1233	1039	1122	...	...	...	1421	1533	...	...	...	|	1842	2011	...	|	2227	...	...	...	...	...	...
		Ponferrada **682** ... a.	...	...	...	...	...	...	...	...	...	...	...	...	1837	...	...	...	2134	...	...	...	...	...	...	...
		Vigo Guixar **682** ... a.	...	...	...	...	...	...	...	...	...	...	...	...	2251	...	...	...	...	...	...	...	...	...	...	...
		A Coruña **682** ... a.	...	...	...	...	...	...	...	...	...	...	...	...	2224	...	...	...	...	...	...	...	...	...	...	...
		Ferrol **682** ... a.	...	...	...	...	...	...	...	...	...	...	...	...	...	...	...	...	...	...	...	...	...	...	...	...

	AVE	MD	MD	AVE	IC	Alvia	AVE	AVE	Alvia		AVE	Alvia		MD	Alvia	Alvia	AVE		Alvia	Alvia		AVE	Alvia	avlo		
	5092	**18002**	**18002**	**4060**	**4088**	**4072**	**5312**	**4280**	**4080**		**5750**	**625** **621**		**18006**	**4142**	**4140**	**5210**		**4170**	**10160**		**4398**	**4192**	**4190**		
	①–⑤	Ⓐ	Ⓒ	①–⑤	①–⑥		⑥⑦	⑥	①–④					2				†	Ⓑ	⑦		⑦	Ⓑ			
	Q	2	2			**E**	**Q**		⑦		**V**	**L**				**Q**	**V**	2	**B**							
Ferrol **682** ... d.	...	...	...	...	...	...	...	...	...	...	...	...	...	...	...	...	...	...	...	...	...	...	...	...	...	...
A Coruña **682** ... d.	...	...	...	...	...	...	...	...	...	...	...	0812	...	...	...	...	...	...	...	...	...	...	...	...	...	...
Vigo Guixar **682** ... d.	...	...	...	...	...	...	...	...	...	...	...	0748	...	...	...	...	...	...	...	...	...	...	...	...	...	...
Ponferrada **682** ... d.	...	...	...	...	0615	...	...	...	...	...	...	1152	...	...	...	...	...	1620	...	...	...	...	...	...	...	...
Gijón Sanz Crespo **685** ... d.	...	...	...	0600	|	...	...	0900	0900	...	1109	|	...	...	...	1530	...	|	...	1719	...	...	...	1925	...	...
León ... d.	0645	0640	0650	0738	0806	...	0950	1041	1040	...	1246	1335	...	1542	...	1711	1828	1841	1850	1855	...	2037	...	2110	...	...
Santander **684** ... d.	|	|	|	|	|	0648	|	|	|	...	|	|	...	|	1358	|	|	|	|	|	...	|	1900	|	...	...
Palencia ... **689** d.	0720	0750	0805	|	0845	0915	1025	|	1124	...	1334	1419	...	1654	1630	1757	1904	2007	1942	|	...	2113	2130	2152	...	...
Burgos Rosa Manzano . **689** d.	|	|	|	|	|	|	|	|	|	...	|	1458	...	|	|	|	|	|	|	|	...	|	|	|	...	...
Miranda de Ebro ... **689** a.	|	|	|	|	|	|	|	|	|	...	|	1555	...	|	|	|	|	|	|	|	...	|	|	|	...	...
Hendaye **689** ... a.	|	|	|	|	|	|	|	|	|	...	|	|	...	|	|	|	|	|	|	|	...	|	|	|	...	...
Barcelona Sants **652** ... a.	|	|	|	|	|	|	|	|	|	...	|	2139	...	|	|	|	|	|	|	|	...	|	|	|	...	...
Venta de Baños ... **689** d.	|	0803	0818	|	|	|	|	|	|	...	|	...	...	1706	|	|	|	2023	|	|	...	|	|	|	...	...
Valladolid C. Grande ... **689** d.	0745	0833	0848	0841	0911	0955	1051	1144	1150	...	1358	...	...	1742	1703	1823	1929	2057	2007	|	...	2138	2207	2216	...	...
Medina del Campo .... **680 689** a.	|	0859	0914	|	|	|	|	|	|	...	|	...	...	1807	|	|	|	...	|	|	...	|	|	|	...	...
Ávila ... **680 689** a.	|	0943	0958	|	|	|	|	|	|	...	|	...	...	1852	|	|	|	...	|	|	...	|	|	|	...	...
Madrid Chamartín ¶ ... **680 689** a.	0839	1126**p**	1141**p**	0937	1015	1123	1145	1240	1252	...	1500	...	...	2041**p**	1814	1924	2032	...	2109	2059	...	2239	2324	2318	...	...

☛ **FOR NOTES**, SEE TABLE **682** BELOW.

682 LEÓN - VIGO, FERROL and A CORUÑA

km		MD		MD	MD				MD	MD		MD		Alvia		MD	Alvia	Alvia		MD	IC	IC	
		33163		**12641**	**12681**				**12683**	**12694**		**12685**		**4325**		**12687**	**626**	**622**		**12646**	**4179**	**560**	
		2		2	2	2	2	2	2	2	2	2				2			2	2	Ⓑ	Ⓑ	
		①–⑥								**J**				**M**			**L**	**L**	⑤	**H**		2**JZ**	
	Madrid Chamartín ¶ ... ‡ d.	...	...	...	...	...	...	...	...	...	...	...	...	1332	...	...	...	...	...	...	1732	...	...
	Barcelona Sants ... ‡ d.	...	...	...	...	...	...	...	...	...	...	...	...	|	...	...	0905	0905	...	...	|	...	...
	Irún ... ‡ d.	...	...	...	...	...	...	...	...	...	...	...	...	|	...	...	|	|	...	...	|	...	...
	Bilbao Abando ... ‡ d.	...	...	...	...	...	...	...	...	...	...	...	...	|	...	...	|	|	...	...	|	...	...
0	**León** ... d.	...	...	...	...	...	...	0709	...	...	1230	...	...	|	...	...	1659	1659	1815	...	1946	...	...
52	Astorga ... d.	...	...	...	...	...	...	0758	...	...	1323	...	...	|	...	...	1739	1739	1859	...	2023	...	...
128	**Ponferrada** ... d.	...	...	...	...	0615	...	0907	...	...	1434	...	...	|	...	...	1838	1838	2017	...	2135	...	...
238	Monforte de Lemos ... a.	...	...	...	...	0801	...	...	...	...	...	...	...	1701	...	...	2014	2014	...	...	...	...	...
238	Monforte de Lemos ... d.	...	...	0730	...	0810	...	...	...	1316	...	...	...	1703	...	...	2016	2016	...	2035	...	2342	...
285	Ourense ... **680** d.	...	...	|	...	0900	1005	...	...	1230	...	...	...	1620	...	...	2101	2101	...	1950	...	2300	...
416	**Vigo** Guixar ... **680** a.	...	...	|	...	...	1205	...	...	|	...	...	...	|	...	...	|	2251	...	|	...	|	...
309	Lugo ... d.	...	...	0825	...	...	...	...	...	1416	...	...	...	1751	...	...	|	...	...	2129	...	0045	...
445	**Ferrol** ... d.	0540	...	|	0910	...	...	...	1415	...	...	1741	...	...	...	2036	▲	...	...	|	...	...	...
402	Betanzos - Infesta ... d.	0623	...	0946	0959	...	...	...	1504	...	...	1831	...	...	...	2125	|	...	...	2253	...	...	...
428	**A Coruña** ... **680** a.	0647	...	1013	1027	...	...	...	1532	...	...	1900	...	...	...	2158	2224	...	...	2331	...	...	...
445	**Ferrol** ... a.	...	...	...	...	...	...	...	...	...	...	...	...	...	...	...	...	...	...	...	...	...	...

	IC	MD	MD	Alvia	Alvia		Alvia	MD	MD		MD				MD		IC	MD	MD				
	4088	**12644**	**12680**	**621**	**625**		**4114**	**12682**	**12696**		**12684**				**12690**		**558**	**12642**	**37145**				
	①–⑤	2	2					2	2	2	2	2	2	2	2		Ⓑ	2	2				
		H		**L**	**L**		**M**		**J**			†**y**		**h**			2**JZ**						
Ferrol ... d.	...	...	...	...	...	...	...	...	...	...	...	...	...	...	...	...	...	...	...	...	...	...	...
A Coruña ... **680** d.	...	0705	0730	...	0812	...	...	1240	...	...	1504	...	...	...	1832	...	...	1935	2305	...	...	...	...
Betanzos - Infesta ... d.	...	0735	0801	...	|	...	...	1313	...	...	1533	...	...	...	1904	...	...	2005	2332	...	...	...	...
Ferrol ... a.	...	|	0848	...	▲	...	...	1358	...	...	1620	...	...	...	1949	...	...	|	0012	...	...	...	...
Lugo ... d.	...	0855	...	...	|	...	1118	...	1425	...	...	...	...	...	...	...	1845	2128	...	...	...	...	...
Vigo Guixar ... **680** d.	...	|	...	0748	|	...	|	...	|	...	...	...	...	1407	...	...	|	|	...	...	...	...	...
Ourense ... **680** d.	...	1049	...	0925	0925	...	1257	...	1615	...	...	...	...	1630	...	...	2030	|	...	...	...	...	...
Monforte de Lemos ... a.	...	0944	...	1013	1013	...	1207	...	1526	...	...	...	...	1726	...	...	1946	2226	...	...	...	...	...
Monforte de Lemos ... d.	...	...	...	1015	1015	...	1209	...	...	...	...	...	...	1730	...	...	...	...	...	...	...	...	...
Ponferrada ... d.	0615	...	...	1152	1152	...	|	...	...	1604	...	1630	1813	1925	...	...	...	...	...	...	...	...	...
Astorga ... d.	0720	...	...	1252	1252	...	|	...	...	1719	...	1756	1938	...	...	...	...	...	...	...	...	...	...
León ... a.	0757	...	...	1330	1330	...	|	...	...	1804	...	1847	2021	...	...	...	...	...	...	...	...	...	...
Bilbao Abando ... ‡ a.	|	...	...	|	|	...	|	...	...	...	...	...	...	...	...	...	...	...	...	...	...	...	...
Hendaye ... ‡ a.	|	...	...	|	|	...	|	...	...	...	...	...	...	...	...	...	...	...	...	...	...	...	...
Barcelona Sants ... ‡ a.	|	...	...	2139	2139	...	|	...	...	...	...	...	...	...	...	...	...	...	...	...	...	...	...
Madrid Chamartín ¶ ... ‡ a.	1015	...	...	...	...	...	1600	...	...	...	...	...	...	...	...	...	...	...	...	...	...	...	...

B – [12] Madrid - León - Avilés and v.v. (Table **685**).
E – [12] Alacant - Madrid - Santander and v.v.
H – Routeing is A Coruña - Lugo - Monforte de Lemos - Ourense and v.v., with connections at Ourense to and from Madrid (Table **680**).
J – Routeing is Ourense - Monforte de Lemos - Lugo and v.v., with connections at Ourense to and from Madrid (Table **680**).
L – [12] 🍷 Barcelona - A Coruña and Vigo and v.v. For days of running see Table **680**.
M – [12] Madrid - Zamora - Ourense - Monforte de Lemos - Lugo and v.v. (Table **680**).
Q – From/to Alacant (Table **668**).
V – To/from Castelló (Table **668**).

Z – Until further notice: 🚌 Ourense - Lugo and v.v.

h – From Vigo **Guixar**.
p – Madrid **Principe Pio**.
y – To Valladolid (Table **681**).

▲ – Via Santiago (Table **680**).
‡ – See Table **681**.
¶ – Full name is Madrid-Chamartín-Clara Campoamor.

683 LEÓN - BILBAO

FEVE narrow-gauge

1350 ✣ →	1410 →	1445 →	1535 →	1636 →	1715 →	1801 →	1935 →	2044 →	2134
León	San Feliz	La Vecilla	Cistierna	Guardo	Vado Cervera	Mataporquera	Espinosa	Balmaseda	**Bilbao** Concordia
2203 ✣	← 2138	← 2059	← 2018	← 1921	← 1841	← 1800	← 1623	← 1520	← 1430

✣ – Journey may be by 🚌 between León and Asunción-Universidad y León, due to construction of a new tunnel.

PALENCIA - SANTANDER 684

km		Alvia 4073 ①–⑥	2		Alvia 4143 A		2		Alvia 4193	
	Madrid CCC ¶ **681 689** d.	0745	...	...	1340	...	...	...	1908	...
	Valladolid C G **681 689** d.	0902	0952	...	1448	...	1830	...	2020	...
0	**Palencia** d.	0937	1039	...	1520	...	1917	...	2055	...
98	Aguilar de Campoo d.	1028	1153	...	|	...	2032	...	2148	...
110	Mataporquera **683** ‡ d.	|	1202	...	|	...	2043	...	|	...
129	Reinosa § d.	1051	1218	...	|	...	2059	...	2213	...
188	Torrelavega § d.	1140	1315	...	1722	...	2200	...	2302	...
218	**Santander** § a.	1206	1343	...	1747	...	2229	...	2328	...

	Alvia 4072 A	Ⓒ 2	Ⓐ 2		Alvia 4142		2	Alvia 4192 Ⓑ	
Santander § d.	0648	0714	0920	...	1358	...	1627	1900	...
Torrelavega § d.	0712	0745	0953	...	1422	...	1655	1923	...
Reinosa § d.	0759	0839	1046	...	|	...	1759	2010	...
Mataporquera **683** ‡ d.	|	0855	1112	...	|	...	1816	|	...
Aguilar de Campoo d.	0823	0905	1122	...	|	...	1824	2032	...
Palencia a.	0913	1022	1234	...	1628	...	1933	2128	...
Valladolid C G **681 689** a.	0951	1108	1320	...	1701	...	2013	2205	...
Madrid CCC ¶ **681 689** a.	1123	...	...	...	1814	...	...	2324	...

– From/to Alacant (Table **668**).
‡ – Narrow gauge station is 600 metres.
§ – Additional local services operate between these stations.
¶ – Full name is Madrid-Chamartín-Clara Campoamor.

LEÓN - OVIEDO - GIJÓN 685

km	km via HSL		Alvia 4261 ①–⑤	Ⓐ 2 A	Ⓒ 2 A	Alvia 4071 ⑥	Alvia 4091 Ⓑ D	avlo 4121	AVE 5721 V	AVE 4161 Ⓑ	Alvia 4181 C	
		Madrid CCC ¶ **681** d.	0649	...	...	0732	0915	1145	1459	1637	1835	...
0	0	**León** d.	0905	0918	0929	0948	1138	1355	1710	1838	2051	...
109	75	Pola de Lena § a.	|	1112	1125	|	|	|	|	|	|	...
140	106	**Oviedo** ▽ § a.	1010	1151	1205	1053	1244	1503	1812	1941	2159	...
172	138	**Gijón** Sanz Crespo. § a.	1039	1220	1233	1122	...	1533	1842	2011	2227	...

	AVE 4060 ①–⑤	AVE 4280 ⑥	Alvia 4080 ①–④ ⑦	AVE 5750 V	Alvia 4140 C	Alvia 4170 Ⓑ E	avlo 4180	2		
Gijón Sanz Crespo § d.	0600	0900	0900	1109	1530	...	1925	2025	...	...
Oviedo ▽ § d.	0631	0931	0930	1140	1559	1737	1956	2055	...	...
Pola de Lena § d.	|	|	|	|	|	|	|	2130	...	...
León a.	0736	1039	1038	1244	1709	1848	2107	2337	...	...
Madrid CCC ¶ **681** a.	0937	1240	1252	1500	1924	2109	2318	...	...	...

– From Valladolid (Table **681**).
– From/to Alacant (Table **668**).
D – To Avilés (a. 1311).
E – From Avilés (d. 1707).
V – To/from Castelló (Table **668**).
¶ – Full name is Madrid-Chamartín-Clara Campoamor.

– **OVIEDO – AVILÉS** and v.v. ***Renfe Cercanías*** (suburban) service. *31 km.* Journey time: ± 38 minutes. **Additional services on Ⓐ.**
From Oviedo: Approximately 1 train each hour 0550 Ⓐ, 0616 Ⓐ, then 0716 until 2216. **From Avilés**: Approximately 1 train each hour 0641 Ⓐ, 0741 Ⓐ, then 0841 until 2311.

– **GIJÓN – OVIEDO – POLA de LENA** and v.v. ***Renfe Cercanías*** (suburban) service. *63 km.* Journey time: ± 78 minutes.
From Pola de Lena: Approximately 1–2 trains each hour from 0630 until 2200. **From Gijón**: Approximately 1–2 trains each hour from 0600 until 2230.

SAN SEBASTIÁN - BILBAO 686

Euskotren (narrow gauge)

	Ⓐ	Ⓐ	Ⓒ					
an Sebastián ⊡ Amara d.	0550	0650	0650	0750	0850		1950	2050
arautz d.	0620	0720	0720	0820	0920		2020	2120
umaia d.	0629	0729	0729	0829	0929	and	2029	2129
ibar d.	0711	0811	...	0911	1011	hourly	2111	2211
urango d.	0741	0841	...	0941	1041	until	2141	2241
ilbao Casco Viejo § ⊖ a.	0821	0921	...	1021	1121		2221	2321**z**
ilbao Matiko a.	0825	0925	...	1024	1124		2225	2325**z**

	Ⓐ	Ⓐ	Ⓒ					
Bilbao Matiko d.	...	0555	...	0655**x**	0755**x**		1855**x**	1955**x**
Bilbao Casco Viejo § ⊖ d.	...	0558	...	0658**x**	0758**x**		1858**x**	1958**x**
Durango d.	0539	0639	...	0739	0839	and	1939	2039
Eibar d.	0614	0714	...	0814	0914	hourly	2014	2114
Zumaia d.	0700	0800	0800	0900	1000	until	2100	2200
Zarautz d.	0708	0808	0808	0908	1008		2108	2208
San Sebastián ⊡ Amara a.	0738	0838	0838	0938	1038		2138	2238

– 3 minutes earlier on Ⓒ.
– Ⓒ.
⊡ – San Sebastián/Donostia.
⊖ – Metro interchange.
§ – Bilbao Casco Viejo ⇆ Bilbao Abando (*Renfe*): ± *400 m.* Linked by tram approx every 3-5 minutes, journey 2 minutes.
Operator: Euskotren. 2nd class, narrow gauge. Distance: San Sebastian - Bilbao *108* km.

BILBAO - SANTANDER - OVIEDO - FERROL 687

FEVE (narrow gauge)

			Ⓐ		Ⓐ					
ilbao Concordia § d.	...	...	...	0800	...	...	1300	...	1934	...
larrón d.	...	...	0710	0942	...	...	1439	...	2115	...
reto d.	...	...	0721	0953	...	...	1450	...	2126	...
antander a.	...	...	0830	1056	...	...	1556	...	2230	...
antander ▽ d.	...	0829	...	...	...	1528	...	...	...	...
orrelavega ▽ d.	...	0900	...	...	...	1559	...	...	...	...
abezón de la Sal ▽ d.	...	0941	...	...	...	1634	...	...	...	...
nquera d.	...	1023	...	...	...	1718	...	...	...	...
lanes d.	0710	1101	...	...	1427	1758	...	...	...	...
ibadesella d.	0749	1138	...	...	1506	1837	...	...	...	...
viedo a.	1022	1356	...	...	1731	2101	...	...	...	...

					Ⓐ			Ⓐ		
Oviedo d.	...	...	0757	...	1110	...	1444	...	1839	...
Ribadesella d.	...	...	1021	...	1337	...	1712	...	2105	...
Llanes d.	...	...	1104	...	1416	...	1754	...	2144	...
Unquera d.	...	...	1134	...	...	...	1824	...	...	...
Cabezón de la Sal ▽ d.	...	...	1221	...	...	...	1909	...	...	...
Torrelavega ▽ d.	...	...	1302	...	...	...	1947	...	...	...
Santander ▽ a.	...	...	1334	...	...	...	2019	...	...	...
Santander d.	0754	...	...	1400	...	1900	...	2037	...	...
Treto d.	0858	...	...	1507	...	2003	...	2144	...	...
Marrón d.	0910	...	...	1519	...	2014	...	2155	...	...
Bilbao Concordia § a.	1108	...	...	1659	...	2205	...	...	...	...

viedo △ d.	...	...	0719	...	...	...	...	...	1418	...
Gijón Sanz Crespo △ d.	...	0701	|	0931	...	1131	...	1421	|	1831
Avilés △ d.	...	0740	|	1018	...	1218	...	1500	|	1918
ravia △ d.	...	0812	0839	1048	...	1248	...	1529	1540	1948
uarca d.	...	...	1003	...	...	...	...	...	1708	...
avia d.	...	...	1033	...	...	...	...	...	1739	...
ibadeo d.	0655	...	1134	...	1500	...	...	...	1840	...
iveiro d.	0803	...	1244	...	1609	...	...	...	1949	...
rtigueira d.	0843	...	1324	...	1650	...	1840	...	2028	...
errol a.	1000	...	1444	...	1810	...	1957	...	2144	...

Ferrol d.	...	...	0820	...	1045	...	1445	1530	...	1905
Ortigueira d.	...	...	0938	...	1204	...	1601	1649	...	2027
Viveiro d.	...	...	1018	...	1245	...	...	1729	...	2106
Ribadeo d.	...	...	1130	...	1353	...	...	1842	...	2218
Navia d.	...	...	1225	...	...	...	...	1940	...	...
Luarca d.	...	...	1256	...	...	...	...	2012	...	...
Pravia △ d.	0848	1148	1428	1448	...	1648	...	2152	2155	...
Avilés △ d.	0926	1226	|	1526	...	1726	...	|	2229	...
Gijón Sanz Crespo △ a.	1008	1308	|	1608	...	1808	...	|	2309	...
Oviedo △ a.	...	...	1542	...	...	...	...	2305	...	...

– Additional trains run Santander - Cabezón de al Sal and v.v.
– Additional trains run Oviedo/Gijón - Pravia and v.v.
§ – Bilbao Concordia is adjacent to Bilbao Abando (*Renfe*).
Operator: FEVE. 2nd class, narrow gauge.

IRÚN - BILBAO - SANTANDER - GIJÓN 688

ALSA ★

🚌	▽ ①–⑥			♡ Ⓑ	♡ ⑥	①–⑥	⑦				♡ Ⓑ	⑥		♡ Ⓑ		♡	⑤⑦					⊖ ⑤⑦		⑦	
ún RENFE rail station d.	...	...	...	0645	...	0745	...	...	0845	...	...	...	1100	...	1345	1445	...	...	1615	...	1830	...	2045	2115	2355
an Sebastián/Donostia d.	...	...	...	0710	...	0810	...	...	0910	...	...	...	1125	...	1410	1510	...	...	1640	...	1855	...	2110	2140	0020
ilbao TermiBus d.	0600	...	0700	0830	0830	0930	0930	1000	1030	1130	1230	1230	1330	1430	1530	1630	1730	1730	1800	1845	2030	2115	2230	2300	0145
antander d.	0715	0830	0830	0950	0950	1100	1115	1130	1215	1300	1350	1400	1530	1550	1700	1750	1900	1900	1930	2015	2200	2235	2350	0020	0330
viedo a.	1000*	1145	...	1205	1205	...	...	...	1530	...	1605	...	1845	1805	...	2005	2145	...	2230	2230	...	0050	...	...	0600
ijón a.	0930	1215	...	1230	1230	...	...	...	1600	...	1635	...	1915	1835	...	2030	2215	...	2300	2300	...	0120	...	...	0700

🚌		①–⑥			①–⑥	♡	♡ ①–⑥	⑤	⑦	①–⑥	♡ ①–⑥		⑤⑦	♡			⑥	♡ Ⓑ				▽ Ⓑ	⑤⑦	▽ ⑤	▽ ⑦
ijón d.	0014	...	...	...	...	0715	...	...	0815	0815	0915	1130	...	1315	...	1515	1545	1630	...	1715	...	1915	2015	2115	2115
viedo d.	0100	...	...	...	...	0745	...	...	0845	0845	0945	|	...	1345	...	|	1615	1700	...	1745	...	1945	2045	2145	2145
antander d.	0345	0600	0700	0800	0930	1005	1200	...	1200	1230	1200	1400	1545	1605	1700	1900	1900	1920	...	2030	2100	2205	2340	0005	2359
ilbao TermiBus d.	0515	0730	0840	0930	1100	1120	1315	1400	1400	1415	1315	1530	1745	1720	1830	2045	2030	2035	2045	2200	2230	2320	...	0120	0115
an Sebastián/Donostia a.	0640	0845	1000	...	1210	1230	...	1510	1600	1615	...	...	1855	1830**z**	1940	2155	...	2145**r**	2155	2310	...	...	...	...	0225
ún RENFE rail station a.	0700	0915	1030	...	1240	1305	...	1545	1630	1645	...	...	1925	1905**z**	2010	2225	...	2220**r**	2225	2340	...	...	...	...	0300

– *Clase Supra+* luxury coach.
– *Clase Supra Economy* luxury coach.
– *Supra+ on* ⑤, *Supra Economy* on ⑦.
r – ①–④ only.
z – ⑥ only.
* – Calls after Gijon.
★ – ALSA: ✆ +34 913 270 540 www.alsa.es
Frequent services operate Bilbao - Santander and Oviedo - Gijon.

689 MADRID and SALAMANCA - BILBAO and IRÚN

km △		RE 16207 2 Ⓐ	RE 16001 2	RE 16019 2 N	MD 18310 2 Ⓐ	17227 2	17201 2 Ⓐ	Alvia 4187 ①–⑥	Alvia 4087	RE 18302 2	MD 18001 2 Ⓐ	IC 4187 L ①–⑥	RE 18321 Y 2 Ⓐ	RE 17203 2 Ⓒ	RE 18321 Y 2 Ⓒ	AVE 5763 M ⚒	Alvia 438	MD 18061 2	18029 2 Z	2	MD 18011 2 Ⓒ		
0	**Madrid** Chamartín ‡ 680 681 d.	...	...	...	...	...	...	0720	0720	...	...	0840	...	...	...	0925	...	...	...	...	...	...	...
	Madrid Principe Pio d.	...	...	...	...	...	...	|	|	...	0643	|	...	...	...	|	...	0906	...	...	0940	...	...
121	Ávila 680 681 d.	...	...	...	...	...	0645	|	|	...	0823	|	...	0833	...	|	...	1038	...	...	1118	...	...
	Salamanca d.	...	...	...	0600	...	|	|	|	0715	|	|	...	|	...	|	...	|	...	...	|	...	...
207	Medina del Campo 680 681 d.	...	...	...	0639	0655	0733	|	|	0802	0911	|	0927	0923	0948	|	...	1125	...	...	1206	...	...
250	**Valladolid** Campo Grande 681 d.	...	...	...	0705	0730	0807	0827	0827	0828	0939	0945	1013	0959	1025	1026	...	1150	...	1225	1235	...	...
286	Venta de Baños 681 d.	...	...	...	...	...	...	|	|	...	...	|	...	...	...	|	...	1215	...	1300	...	...	...
298	Palencia 681 d.	...	...	...	...	...	...	|	|	...	...	|	...	...	...	|	...	|	...	1313	...	...	...
371	**Burgos** Rosa Manzano 681 d.	...	...	0823	...	...	...	0915	0915	...	...	1028	...	...	...	1103	...	1328	...	...	...	...	...
460	Miranda de Ebro 654 d.	0720	0825	0925	...	...	...	1019	1030	...	...	1132	...	...	...	...	1341	1427	1501	...	...	...	...
565	**Bilbao** Abando 654 a.	|	|	|	...	...	...	1200	|	...	...	...	...	...	...	...	1522	|	|	...	...	...	...
494	Vitoria / Gasteiz 654 d.	0747	0857	0952	...	...	...	...	1051	...	...	...	...	...	...	...	...	1450	1530	...	...	...	...
	Barcelona Sants **653** a.	...	|	|	...	...	...	...	|	...	...	...	...	...	...	...	...	|	|	...	...	...	...
537	Altsasu 654 d.	...	0926	1025**n**	...	...	...	...	|	...	...	...	...	...	...	...	...	1519	1601**n**	...	...	...	...
624	**San Sebastián / Donostia** ▲ 654 a.	...	1048	...	...	...	...	...	1243	...	...	...	...	...	...	...	...	1648	...	...	...	...	...
641	**Irún** ▲ 654 a.	...	1137	...	...	...	...	...	1409	...	...	...	...	...	...	...	...	1811	...	...	...	...	...
643	Hendaye ▲ 654 a.	...	...	...	...	...	...	...	...	...	...	...	...	...	...	...	...	...	...	...	...	...	...

	Alvia 631	Alvia 621 625 X	IC 280	IC 282 🚌	MD 18063 2 Ⓑ	MD 18063 2 ⑥	MD 18306 2	IC 4257 Ⓑ		MD 18905 2 Ⓐ	RE 17221 2	MD 18314 2	16111 2 Z	RE 18009 2 ⑤	MD 18003 2	Alvia 4167	Alvia 4267 H Ⓑ	MD 18003 2	MD 18065 2 Ⓑ	AVE 5171 A Ⓑ	MD 18065 2 Ⓑ	RE 18312 2	MD 18007 2 Ⓑ
Madrid Chamartín ‡ 680 681 d.	...	...	...	...	...	...	...	1446	...	...	...	...	...	...	...	1737	1737	...	...	1953	...	...	...
Madrid Principe Pio d.	...	...	...	...	1225	1225	...	|	...	1340	...	...	...	1455	1626	|	|	...	1711	|	...	...	2028
Ávila 680 681 d.	...	...	...	...	1406	1406	...	|	...	1510	1535	...	...	1641	1759	|	|	...	1850	|	...	...	2209
Salamanca d.	1228	...	...	...	|	|	1400	|	...	1619	|	1608	...	|	|	|	|	←	|	|	...	2050	|
Medina del Campo 680 681 d.	1306	...	...	...	1453	1453	1504	|	...	...	1624	1648	...	1734	1844	|	|	1845	1938	|	...	2145	2256
Valladolid Campo Grande 681 d.	1334	...	...	...	1517	1517	1528	1554	...	...	1657	1716	...	1806	→	1843	1843	1913	2006	2050	←	2220	2321
Venta de Baños 681 d.	|	...	...	...	1542	1542	1608	|	...	...	...	...	...	1834	...	|	|	1938	2030	|	2031	...	2347
Palencia 681 d.	|	1419	...	...	|	|	1620	|	...	...	...	...	...	|	...	|	|	1948	→	|	2050	...	2358
Burgos Rosa Manzano 681 d.	1458	1458	...	...	1655	1700	...	1636	...	...	...	...	...	1927	...	1934	1931	...	...	2129	2143	...	...
Miranda de Ebro 654 d.	1557	1557	1625	...	1755	1803	...	1737	...	...	...	...	...	2027	...	2038	2043	...	...	...	2239	...	...
Bilbao Abando 654 a.	|	|	1815	...	|	|	...	|	...	...	...	...	...	|	...	|	2221	...	...	...	|	...	...
Vitoria / Gasteiz 654 d.	1626	1626	...	1645	1816	1822	...	1759	...	...	...	...	1900	2050	...	2100	...	...	...	...	2300	...	...
Barcelona Sants **653** a.	2139	2139	...	|	|	|	...	|	...	...	...	...	|	...	...	|	...	...	...	...	...	...	...
Altsasu 654 d.	...	...	...	1725	1843	1850	...	|	...	...	...	...	1931**n**	...	...	|	...	...	...	...	...	...	...
San Sebastián / Donostia ▲ 654 a.	...	...	...	1850	2018	2023	...	1952	2034	...	...	...	...	...	...	2247	...	...	...	...	...	...	...
Irún ▲ 654 a.	...	...	...	...	2109	2109	...	...	2109	...	...	...	...	...	...	2315	...	...	...	...	...	...	...
Hendaye ▲ 654 a.	...	...	...	...	...	...	...	...	...	...	...	...	...	...	...	...	...	...	...	...	...	...	...

km		MD 18066 2 ⚒	AVE 5080 A ⚒	MD 18300 2 Ⓐ	IC 4056 Ⓐ	2	MD 18304 2	MD 18010 2 ⚒	Alvia 4186 J ①–⑥	MD 18010 2 ⚒	RE 16000 2 ⚒	RE 18071 Z 2 ⚒	Alvia 4086	RE 17218 2	MD 18308 2	MD 18004 2	MD 18012 2 ⚒	MD 18012 2 †	IC 281 🚌	IC 283 2	Alvia 622 626 X	Alvia 632	
0	**Irún** ▲ 654 d.	...	...	...	...	...	...	...	...	...	0551	...	0830	...	...	...	1018	1018	...	...	...	...	...
17	**San Sebastián / Donostia** ▲ 654 d.	...	...	...	0450	...	...	...	...	...	0618	...	0852	...	...	...	1106	1105	1130	...	...	...	...
104	Altsasu 654 d.	...	...	...	|	...	...	...	...	...	0736	0918**n**	|	...	...	...	1237	1236	1245	...	...	...	...
	Barcelona Sants **653** d.	...	...	...	|	...	...	...	...	...	|	|	|	...	...	...	|	|	|	...	0905	0905	...
147	Vitoria / Gasteiz 654 d.	...	...	...	0648	...	...	0740	...	...	0808	0950	1043	...	...	...	1307	1306	1335	...	1403	1403	...
	Bilbao Abando 654 d.	...	...	...	|	...	...	|	0700	...	...	|	|	...	...	...	|	|	...	1215	|	|	...
180	Miranda de Ebro 654 d.	...	...	...	0710	0716	...	0801	0837	...	...	1016	1105	...	...	...	1327	1326	...	1404	1426	1445	...
270	**Burgos** Rosa Manzano 681 d.	...	0640	...	0806	0816	...	0900	0934	...	...	...	1208	...	...	...	1425	1423	...	...	1535	1541	...
353	Palencia 681 d.	0545	|	...	|	...	...	0959	|	←	...	...	|	...	1335	...	|	|	...	...	1610	|	...
355	Venta de Baños 681 d.	0558	|	...	|	...	...	1011	|	1011	...	...	|	...	1348	...	1537	1537	...	...	...	|	...
391	**Valladolid** Campo Grande 681 d.	0626	0718	0735	0847	...	0940	→	1022	1038	...	...	1250	1300	1419	1424	1602	1603	...	...	...	1700	...
434	Medina del Campo 680 681 d.	0652	|	0814	|	...	1007	...	|	1105	...	...	|	1338	1448	1500	1628	1628	...	...	...	1727	...
511	**Salamanca** a.	|	|	0911	|	...	1046	...	|	|	...	...	|	|	1552	|	|	|	...	...	...	1806	...
	Ávila 680 681 d.	0740	|	...	|	...	...	...	|	1155	...	...	|	1429	...	1547	1718	1715	...	...	...	...	...
	Madrid Principe Pio a.	0928	|	...	|	...	...	...	|	1325	...	...	|	...	...	1731	1855	1855	...	...	...	...	...
	Madrid Chamartín ‡ 680 681 a.	...	0813	...	0953	...	...	...	1128	...	...	...	1356	...	...	...	...	...	...	...	...	...	...

	2	MD 18006 2	RE 17226 2 Y	AVE 5792 M Ⓑ	MD 18014 2	IC 4166 ⑦	MD 18014 2	RE 18318 2	IC 4786 L Ⓑ	RE 17200 2	RE 18008 2 †	16015 2 N	Alvia 4176	Alvia 4366 Ⓑ	RE 18316 2	17226 2	16017 2 N ⚒	16027 2 b †	RE 16004 2 Ⓑ	RE 16004 2 ⑥			
Irún ▲ 654 d.	...	...	...	...	1318	1318	...	...	...	...	...	...	1523	...	...	...	...	...	1916	1954	...	...	...
San Sebastián / Donostia ▲ 654 d.	...	...	...	...	1400	1412	...	...	...	...	...	...	1652	...	...	...	...	...	2012	2040	...	...	...
Altsasu 654 d.	...	...	...	...	1531	|	...	...	...	...	...	1715**n**	|	...	...	...	2034**n**	2047**n**	2131	2200	...	...	...
Barcelona Sants **653** d.	...	...	...	...	|	|	...	...	...	...	...	|	|	...	...	...	|	|	|	|	...	...	...
Vitoria / Gasteiz 654 d.	...	...	...	...	1601	1610	...	...	...	...	1720	1750	1846	...	...	...	2107	2119	2205	2234	...	...	...
Bilbao Abando 654 d.	...	...	...	...	|	|	...	...	...	...	|	|	|	1735	...	...	...	|	|	|	...	...	...
Miranda de Ebro 654 d.	...	...	...	...	1621	1635	...	...	1723	...	1744	1817	1911	1911	...	...	...	2144	2230	2259	...	...	...
Burgos Rosa Manzano 681 d.	...	...	...	1718	1720	1742	...	...	1829	...	1843	...	2018	2018	...	...	...	...	...	...	...	...	...
Palencia 681 d.	1633	1654	...	|	|	|	←	...	|	...	|	...	|	|	...	...	...	...	...	...	...	...	...
Venta de Baños 681 d.	1646	1706	...	|	1829	|	1830	...	|	...	1933	...	|	|	...	...	...	...	...	...	...	...	...
Valladolid Campo Grande 681 d.	1720	1742	1750	1800	→	1827	1850	1856	1911	1948	2005	...	2106	2106	2122	2240	...	...	...	...	...	...	...
Medina del Campo 680 681 d.	...	1808	1828	|	...	|	1915	1934	|	2025	2040	...	|	|	2201	2314	...	...	...	...	...	...	...
Salamanca a.	...	|	...	|	...	|	|	2027	|	|	|	...	|	|	2241	...	...	...	...	...	...	...	...
Ávila 680 681 d.	...	1854	...	|	...	|	2001	...	|	2115	2137	...	|	|	...	...	...	...	...	...	...	...	...
Madrid Principe Pio a.	...	2041	...	|	...	|	2142	...	|	...	2340	...	|	|	...	...	...	...	...	...	...	...	...
Madrid Chamartín ‡ 680 681 a.	...	...	...	1900	...	1934	...	...	2015	...	...	...	2213	2213	...	...	...	...	...	...	...	...	...

▲ – **SAN SEBASTIÁN - IRÚN** and v.v. ***Renfe Cercanías*** (suburban) service. Additional journeys can be made by changing trains at Pasaia. *17 km.* Journey time: ± 27 minutes

From San Sebastián: 0626 ⑦, 0701 ⚒, 0726 Ⓒ, 0751 Ⓐ, 0816 ⑥, 0838 Ⓐ, 0946 ⑦, 0951 ⚒, 1036 ⚒, 1100 ⑦, 1116 ⑥, 1126 ⑦, 1146 Ⓐ, 1218 ⑦, 1226 ⚒, 1346, 1421 ⚒, 1516 ⚒, 1546 1639 Ⓑ, 1648 ⑥, 1743, 1816 ⑦, 1931 ⚒, 1954 ⑦, 2001 ⚒, 2046 ⚒, 2144.

From Irún: 0648 ⚒, 0738 Ⓐ, 0810 ⑥, 0828 Ⓑ, 0928 Ⓑ, 1028 ⚒, 1042 ⑦, 1128 Ⓐ, 1158 Ⓒ, 1218 Ⓐ, 1258 Ⓒ, 1333, 1453, 1535 ⑦, 1618, 1713 ⑦, 1723 ⑥, 1727 Ⓐ, 1733 ⑦, 1813 ⑥ 1858 Ⓑ, 1918, 2033, 2128, 2215.

SAN SEBASTIÁN / DONOSTIA (Amara) - **IRÚN** (Colón, near Renfe station) - **HENDAYE** (SNCF station) and v.v. ***EuskoTren*** (narrow-gauge). *22 km.* Journey time: ± 37 minutes.

From San Sebastián: 0615 Ⓐ, 0645 Ⓐ, 0715, 0745 and every 30 mins until 2215, 2245. **From Hendaye** (⊙): 0533 Ⓐ, 0603 Ⓐ, 0633 Ⓐ, 0703, 0733 and every 30 mins until 2233.

A – From / to València (Table **668**).
H – Ⓑ (daily June 18 - Oct. 15).
J – ①–⑥ (daily June 18 - Oct. 15).
L – To / from Logroño (Table **654**).
M – From / to Murcia (Table **668**).
N – To / from Pamplona (Table **654**).
X – 🚃 Vigo / A Coruña - Palencia - Barcelona and v.v. (Table **680**).
Y – 🚃 Valladolid - Medina del Campo - Puebla de Sanabria and v.v. (Table **689**).
Z – To / from Pamplona and Zaragoza (Table **654**).
b – From / to Castejón de Ebro and Pamplona / Iruña (Table **654**).
n – Altsasu Pueblo.
⊙ – 4 minutes later from Irún.
△ – Distance via Ávila.
‡ – Full name is Madrid-Chamartín-Clara Campoamor.

PORTUGAL

SEE MAP PAGE 317

perator: **CP** – Comboios de Portugal (www.cp.pt).

rain categories: ***Alfa Pendular*** – *AP* – high-quality tilting express trains. ***Intercidades*** – *IC* – high-quality express trains linking the main cities. ***Interregional*** – *IR* – 'semi-fast' links usually calling at principal stations only. ***Celta*** – International services between Porto and Vigo. ***Regional*** and ***Suburbano*** – local stopping trains (shown without train numbers). Higher fares are payable for travel by *AP* and *IC* trains, and there is an additional supplement for travel by *AP* trains.

ervices: All services shown with a train number convey first and second class accommodation (on *Alfa Pendular* trains termed, respectively, *Conforto* and *Turística*) unless otherwise indicated. *Regional* and *Suburbano* trains convey second-class seating only. *AP*, *IC*, *IR* and international trains convey a buffet car (*carruagem-bar*) and there is an at-seat service of meals to passengers in 1st class on *AP* and certain *IC* trains.

eservations: Reservations are **compulsory** for travel by *AP*, *IC* and international trains. Seat reservation is not normally available on other services.

imings: Timings are the latest received. Amendments to timetables may come into effect at short notice, especially during the Christmas and New Year period.

LISBOA - COIMBRA - PORTO — 690

Subject to alteration on and around public holidays (see page 4). Additional local trains run approximately hourly Aveiro - Porto and v.v.
Other services: Table **691** Lisboa - Entroncamento; Table **692** Lisboa - Entroncamento - Coimbra - Pampilhosa; Tables **699** local trains Lisboa - Entroncamento - Coimbra - Aveiro.

km	🅁 on *AP* and *IC* trains	*IR* **831** ⊡	*IC* **521** ①–⑥	*AP* **131**	*AP* **121**	*AP* **123** Ⓐ	*IC* **721**	*AP* **182**	*IC* **621** ☆	*AP* **125** ⚒	*AP* **133**	*IR* **821** ⑤	*IC* **523**	*AP* **135** Ⓑ	*IC* **525** ⑤	*AP* **127**	*IC* **527** ⑥	*IC* **731** Ⓑ ⊡	*AP* **137**	*AP* **186**	*IC* **723**	*AP* **129** Ⓑ	Ⓑ	*IC* **529**
0	**Lisboa** Santa Apolónia d.	...	0630	0700	0800	0900	0930	...	1130	1200	1400	...	1530	1600	1630	1700	1730	1730	1800	...	1930	2000	...	2200
	Faro **697** d.	...	|	|	|	|	|	0700	|	|	|	...	|	|	|	|	|	|	|	1600	|	|	...	|
7	**Lisboa** Oriente d.	...	0639	0709	0809	0909	0939	1009	1139	1209	1409	...	1539	1609	1639	1709	1739	1739	1809	1909	1939	2009	...	2209
31	Vila Franca de Xira d.	...	0652	|	|	|	0952	|	1152	|	|	...	1552	|	1652	|	1752	1752	|	|	1952	|	...	2222
75	Santarém d.	...	0713	|	0839	|	1013	|	1213	|	|	...	1613	|	1713	|	1813	1813	|	|	2013	|	...	2243
107	**Entroncamento** d.	...	0733	|	0858	|	1033	|	1233	|	|	1408	1633	|	1733	|	1833	1833	|	|	2033	|	2132	2303
140	Caxarias d.	...	|	|	|	|	1051	|	|	|	|	1431	|	|	1751	|	1851	1851	|	|	|	|	2202	2321
171	Pombal d.	...	0805	|	0927	|	1108	|	1306	|	|	1451	1706	|	1808	|	1908	1908	|	|	2105	|	2225	2338
199	Alfarelos d.	...	|	|	|	|	|	|	1320	|	|	1508	1720	|	|	|	|	|	|	|	|	|	2248	|
218	**Coimbra** B d.	0726	0833	0847	0953	1047	1135	1147	1336	1347	1547	1525	1735	1747	1835	1847	1935	1935	1947	2047	2133	2147	2313	0005
232	Pampilhosa d.	0737	|	|	|	|	|	|	1346	|	|	1536	1746	|	|	|	|	|	|	|	|	|	2325	|
273	Aveiro d.	0806	0904	0915	1020	1115	1204	1215	1406	1415	1615	1608	1806	1815	1904	1915	2004	2004	2015	2115	2204	2215	2359	0034
318	Espinho d.	0833	0928	|	1040	|	1228	|	1428	|	|	1644	1828	|	1928	|	2028	2028	|	|	2228	|	0028	0058
334	Vila Nova de Gaia d.	0845	0938	0943	1050	1143	1238	1243	1438	1443	1643	1655	1838	1843	1938	1943	2038	2038	2043	2143	2238	2243	0040	0108
337	**Porto** Campanhã a.	0849	0943	0948	1055	1148	1243	1248	1443	1448	1648	1700	1843	1848	1943	1948	2043	2043	2048	2148	2243	2248	0045	0113
	Braga **695** a.	...	...	1027	...	...	1325	...	...	...	1727	...	...	1927	...	...	...	...	2127	...	2325	...	...	...

🅁 on *AP* and *IC* trains	①–⑥	*AP* **180**	*AP* **130**	*IC* **520** ①–⑥	*AP* **128** ①–⑥	*IC* **522** ⑦	*IC* **730** ①–⑥ ⊡	*AP* **120** ⚒	*IC* **720**	*AP* **122** Ⓑ	*IC* **524**	*AP* **132**	*AP* **184**	*IC* **722**	*AP* **124**	*IC* **526** ⑦	*AP* **126** Ⓑ	*IC* **620** ☆	*AP* **134**	*IC* **528**	*IR* **820** ⑦	*IR* **830** ⊡	*AP* **136** Ⓑ
Braga **695** d.	...	...	0602	...	...	...	...	...	1006	...	...	1302	...	1406	...	...	...	...	1802	...	...	...	2002
orto Campanhã d.	0108	0540	0640	0645	0740	0845	0845	0940	1045	1140	1245	1340	1440	1445	1640	1645	1740	1745	1840	1954	1954	2030	2040
la Nova de Gaia d.	0114	0545	0645	0650	0745	0850	0850	0945	1050	1145	1250	1345	1445	1450	1645	1650	1745	1750	1854	1950	1959	2035	2045
spinho d.	0135	|	|	0700	|	0900	0900	|	1100	|	1300	|	|	1500	|	1700	1754	1800	|	2000	2009	2046	|
veiro d.	0213	0616	0716	0727	0816	0927	0927	1016	1126	1216	1327	1416	1516	1525	1716	1727	1817	1827	1916	2027	2040	2121	2116
ampilhosa d.	0244	|	|	|	|	|	|	|	1142	|	|	|	|	1542	|	|	|	|	|	|	2106	2143	|
oimbra B d.	0255	0643	0743	0757	0843	0954	0954	1043	1156	1243	1356	1443	1543	1556	1743	1756	1843	1856	1943	2056	2117	2154	2143
farelos d.	0309	|	|	|	|	|	|	|	1209	|	|	|	|	1609	|	|	|	|	|	|	2131	...	|
ombal d.	0331	|	|	0826	|	1022	1022	|	1225	|	1424	|	|	1625	|	1824	1909	1924	|	2124	2150	...	|
axarias d.	0351	|	|	|	|	1040	1040	|	|	|	1440	|	|	|	|	1840	|	1940	|	2140	|	...	|
ntroncamento d.	0414	|	|	0859	|	1059	1059	|	1259	|	1459	|	|	1659	|	1859	1940	1959	|	2159	2236	...	|
antarém d.	0441	|	|	0919	|	1119	1119	|	1319	|	1519	|	|	1719	|	1919	1959	2019	|	2219	2258	...	|
la Franca de Xira d.	0524	|	|	0939	|	1139	1139	|	1339	|	1539	|	|	1739	|	1939	|	2039	|	2239	2326	...	|
sboa Oriente a.	0551	0823	0923	0953	1023	1152	1152	1223	1353	1423	1553	1623	1723	1753	1923	1953	2033	2053	2123	2253	2343	...	2323
Faro **697** a.	|	1123	|	|	|	|	|	|	|	|	|	|	2023	|	|	|	|	|	|	|	|	...	|
sboa Santa Apolónia a.	0559	...	0930	1000	1030	1200	1200	1230	1400	1430	1600	1630	...	1800	1930	2000	2040	2100	2130	2300	2350	...	2330

– To / from Guimarães (Table **695a**). ⊡ – To / from Valença (Table **696**).

LISBOA - ENTRONCAMENTO - COVILHÃ - GUARDA — 691

Linha da Beira Baixa

Subject to alteration on and around public holidays (see page 4). See Tables **690**, **692** and **699** for other services Lisboa - Entroncamento and v.v.

km			Ⓐ			*IC* **511**	*AP* **121**		*IC* **541**					*IC* **513**		*IC* **543**				*IR* **933** Ⓐ		*IC* **545**		
0	**Lisboa** Santa Apolónia d.	...	0550	...	...	0730	0800	...	0815	0945	...	...	...	1230	...	1315	1615	...	1745	1815	...	1915	1945	...
7	**Lisboa** Oriente d.	...	0558	...	...	0739	0809	...	0823	0953	...	...	...	1239	...	1323	1623	...	1753	1823	...	1923	1953	...
31	Vila Franca de Xira d.	...	0616	...	...	0752	|	...	0838	1011	...	...	...	1252	...	1338	1639	...	1811	1838	...	1938	2011	...
75	Santarém d.	...	0653	...	...	0813	0839	...	0904	1054	...	...	...	1313	...	1402	1706	...	1854	1907	...	2004	2054	...
107	**Entroncamento** a.	...	0719	...	...	0832	0857	...	0923	1120	...	...	...	1332	...	1422	1728	...	1920	1929	...	2025	2120	...
107	**Entroncamento** d.	...	▬	0735	...	...	...	0906	0924	...	1134	...	...	...	1336	1423	1729	...	...	...	1936	2026	...	2154
135	Abrantes d.	...	...	0805	...	...	...	0938	0947	...	1204	...	...	...	1408	1444	1758	...	...	...	2005	2047	...	2230
	Portalegre d.	...	...	|	...	...	...	1056	|	...	|	...	...	...	1532	|	|	...	...	...	|	|	...	...
	Elvas 🏛 d.	...	...	|	...	...	...	1140	|	...	|	...	...	...	1616	|	|	...	...	...	|	|	...	...
	Badajoz 🏛 ⊙ a.	...	...	|	...	...	...	1254	|	...	|	...	...	...	1726	|	|	...	...	...	|	|	...	...
199	Ródão d.	...	...	0915	...	...	...	...	1039	...	1304	...	...	...	...	1535	1903	...	...	...	2111	2149	...	...
229	Castelo Branco a.	...	...	0944	...	...	...	...	1103	...	1333	...	...	...	...	1605	1935	...	...	...	2139	2213	...	...
229	Castelo Branco d.	0649	...	...	0955	...	...	...	1104	...	...	1440	...	...	...	1606	...	1940	...	...	...	2214	...	...
283	Fundaõ d.	0737	...	...	1043	...	...	...	1139	...	...	1534	...	...	...	1641	...	2033	...	...	...	2249	...	...
301	**Covilhã** a.	0758	...	...	1059	...	...	...	1153	...	...	1550	...	...	...	1655	...	2049	...	...	...	2303	...	...
301	**Covilhã** d.	...	0800	...	...	...	...	...	1155	...	...	...	1555	...	...	1656	...	...	...	...	...	2304	...	...
347	**Guarda** a.	...	0845	...	...	...	...	...	1245	...	...	...	1640	...	...	1742	...	...	...	...	...	2350	...	...

km		Ⓐ	*IR* **930** Ⓐ	⚒	①	①–⑥	*IC* **540**					*IC* **512**					*IC* **542**						*IC* **544**	*IC* **528**
	Guarda d.	...	...	...	...	...	0702	...	...	...	...	...	1147	...	...	...	1407	...	...	...	1743	...	1825	...
	Covilhã a.	...	...	...	...	...	0747	...	...	...	...	...	1230	...	...	...	1452	...	...	...	1826	...	1910	...
	Covilhã d.	...	...	...	0450	...	0748	0850	...	...	...	...	...	1245	...	...	1453	...	...	...	...	1827	1911	...
	Fundaõ d.	...	...	...	0506	...	0802	0906	...	...	...	...	...	1301	...	...	1507	...	...	...	...	1843	1925	...
	Castelo Branco a.	...	...	...	0553	...	0837	0954	...	...	...	...	...	1349	...	...	1542	...	...	...	...	1931	2003	...
	Castelo Branco d.	...	...	...	...	0555	0838	...	1006	...	...	...	...	...	1400	...	1543	1820	...	...	...	...	2004	...
	Ródão d.	...	...	...	...	0623	0902	...	1039	...	...	...	...	...	1428	...	1607	1848	...	...	...	...	2030	...
0	**Badajoz** 🏛 ⊙ d.	...	...	...	...	|	|	...	|	...	1409	...	...	...	|	...	|	|	...	1941	...	...	|	...
10	Elvas 🏛 d.	...	...	...	...	|	|	...	|	...	1325	...	...	...	|	...	|	|	...	1857	...	...	|	...
59	Portalegre d.	...	...	...	...	|	|	...	|	...	1410	...	...	...	|	...	|	|	...	1942	...	...	|	...
141	Abrantes d.	0540	...	...	...	0722	1000	...	1138	...	1523	...	...	...	1533	...	1659	1948	...	2054	...	...	2121	...
169	**Entroncamento** a.	0613	...	...	...	0757	1020	...	1214	...	1555	...	...	...	1603	...	1720	2024	...	2126	...	...	2142	...
	Entroncamento ▷ d.	...	0625	0641	...	0807	1021	...	...	1236	...	1559	...	...	...	1636	1721	...	2041	...	...	...	2143	2159
	Santarém ▷ d.	...	0647	0708	...	0829	1041	...	...	1303	...	1619	...	...	...	1703	1741	...	2108	...	...	...	2203	2219
	Vila Franca de Xira ▷ d.	...	0717	0747	...	0856	1101	...	...	1347	...	1639	...	...	...	1747	1801	...	2147	...	...	...	2227	2239
	Lisboa Oriente ▷ a.	...	0734	0806	...	0912	1114	...	...	1406	...	1653	...	...	...	1806	1814	...	2206	...	...	...	2241	2253
	Lisboa Santa Apolónia ▷ a.	...	0741	0813	...	0920	1120	...	...	1413	...	1700	...	...	...	1830	1820	...	2213	...	...	...	2250	2300

– Spanish time (one hour ahead of Portugal).

692 LISBOA - COIMBRA - GUARDA - VILAR FORMOSO *Linha da Beira Alta*

Subject to alteration on and around public holidays (see page 4).

km		IC 511 R	🚌			🚌 ⚒		🚌	IC 513 R		🚌			🚌 Ⓐ	🚌 Ⓑ		🚌	🚌		IC 515 R	🚌			
	Lisboa Santa Apolónia ▷ d.	0730	...	...	...	...	...	...	1230	...	...	...	...	...	...	...	...	...	...	1830	...	...	...	...
	Lisboa Oriente ▷ d.	0739	...	...	...	...	...	...	1239	...	...	...	...	...	...	...	...	...	...	1839	...	...	...	...
	Vila Franca de Xira ▷ d.	0752	...	...	...	...	...	...	1252	...	...	...	...	...	...	...	...	...	...	1852	...	...	...	...
	Santarém ▷ d.	0813	...	...	...	...	...	...	1313	...	...	...	...	...	...	...	...	...	...	1913	...	...	...	...
	Entroncamento ▷ d.	0833	...	...	...	...	...	...	1333	...	...	...	...	...	...	...	...	...	...	1933	...	...	...	...
	Fátima ✣ d.	0846	...	...	...	...	...	...	1346	...	...	...	...	...	...	...	...	...	...	1946	...	...	...	...
	Caxarias d.	0853	...	...	...	...	...	...	1353	...	...	...	...	...	...	...	...	...	...	1953	...	...	...	...
	Pombal d.	0910	...	...	...	...	...	...	1410	...	...	...	...	...	...	...	...	...	...	2010	...	...	...	...
	Alfarelos d.	0924	...	...	...	...	...	...	1424	...	...	...	...	...	...	...	...	...	...	2024	...	...	...	...
0	**Coimbra** B d.	0938	0945	...	...	1225	...	1225	1438	...	1445	...	...	1625	1625	...	1835	1835	...	2038	2045	...	...	...
14	Pampilhosa d.	...	|	...	...	|	...	1245	...	...	|	...	...	|	1645	...	|	1855	...	...	|	...	...	...
49	Santa Comba Dão d.	...	1030	...	...	1325	...	1340	...	...	1530	...	...	1725	1740	...	1935	1950	...	...	2130	...	...	...
81	Nelas d.	...	1055	...	...	1400	...	1425	...	...	1555	...	...	1800	1830	...	2010	2040	...	...	2155	...	...	...
93	Mangualde d.	...	1115	...	1214	1420	...	1445	...	...	1615	1714	...	1820	1850	...	2030	2100	...	...	2215	...	...	...
169	**Guarda** a.	...	1215	...	1310	1520	...	1600	...	...	1715	1810	...	1920	2005	...	2130	2230	...	...	2315	...	...	...
216	Vilar Formoso 🏛 a.	...	...	...	1350	...	...	...	...	...	...	1850	...	...	...	...	...	...	...	...	...	...	...	...

	🚌 ⚒	🚌			🚌	IC 510 R	🚌		🚌 Ⓐ	🚌	IC 512 R			🚌 ⑦	🚌 ⚒		🚌 ⑦	⑦	🚌		IC 514 R		
Vilar Formoso 🏛 d.	...	...	0550	...	...	...	...	...	...	...	...	...	1500	...	...	...	...	...	...	...	...	...	...
Guarda d.	0415	0600	0630	...	0640	...	0900	...	0945	1210	...	...	1540	1515	1530	...	1545	...	1740	...	...	...	...
Mangualde d.	0530	0715	0724	...	0740	...	1030	...	1045	1310	...	...	1634	1645	1645	...	1655	...	1840	...	...	...	...
Nelas d.	0550	0735	...	...	0800	...	1050	...	1105	1330	...	...	...	1705	1705	...	1715	...	1900	...	...	...	...
Santa Comba Dão d.	0640	0810	...	...	0825	...	1140	...	1140	1355	...	...	...	1750	1750	...	1750	...	1925	...	...	...	...
Pampilhosa d.	0735	|	...	...	|	...	1235	...	|	|	...	...	...	1845	1845	...	|	...	|	...	...	...	...
Coimbra B d.	0750	0910	...	...	0910	0921	1250	...	1240	1440	1452	...	...	1900	1900	...	1850	1911	2010	...	2020	...	...
Alfarelos d.	...	...	...	...	...	0935	...	...	...	...	1506	...	...	...	...	...	...	1927	...	...	2034	...	...
Pombal d.	...	...	...	...	...	0951	...	...	...	...	1522	...	...	...	...	...	...	1946	...	...	2051	...	...
Caxarias d.	...	...	...	...	...	1007	...	...	...	...	1538	...	...	...	...	...	...	2006	...	...	2107	...	...
Fátima ✣ d.	...	...	...	...	...	1014	...	...	...	...	1545	...	...	...	...	...	...	2013	...	...	2114	...	...
Entroncamento ▷ d.	...	...	...	...	...	1029	...	...	...	...	1559	...	...	...	...	...	...	2036	...	...	2129	...	...
Santarém ▷ d.	...	...	...	...	...	1049	...	...	...	...	1619	...	...	...	...	...	...	2059	...	...	2149	...	...
Vila Franca de Xira ▷ d.	...	...	...	...	...	1109	...	...	...	...	1639	...	...	...	...	...	...	2126	...	...	2209	...	...
Lisboa Oriente ▷ a.	...	...	...	...	...	1123	...	...	...	...	1653	...	...	...	...	...	...	2143	...	...	2223	...	...
Lisboa Santa Apolónia ▷ a.	...	...	...	...	...	1130	...	...	...	...	1700	...	...	...	...	...	...	2150	...	...	2230	...	...

▷ – See also Tables **690**, **691**, **699**.

✣ – Chão de Maçãs - Fátima (*20 km* from Fátima).

693 LISBOA - CALDAS DA RAINHA - FIGUEIRA DA FOZ and COIMBRA *Linha do Oeste*

For connecting suburban services Lisboa - Mira Sintra - Meleças see Table **699**.

km							IR 811 Ⓐ	IR 813 Ⓒ			
	Lisboa Santa Apolónia d.	0535	...	...	1150	...	1653	1653	...	...	...
0	Entrecampos d.	0545	...	...	1201	...	1703	1703	...	...	...
2	Sete Rios d.	0549	...	...	1204	...	1707	1707	...	...	...
15	Agualva - Cacém d.	0604	...	...	1221	...	1725	1725	...	...	...
19	Mira Sintra - Meleças d.	0609	0755	0927	1227	1408	1730	1730	1833	1930	...
65	Torres Vedras d.	0720	0859	1027	1327	1511	1821	1821	1935	2031	...
88	Bombarral d.	0746	0922	1049	1354	1533	1843	1843	2002	2053	...
107	**Caldas da Rainha** a.	0808	0944	1111	1416	1555	1859	1859	2023	2115	...

		IR 810								
Caldas da Rainha d.	0520	0621	0725	...	1116	1316	...	1616	1735	192
Bombarral d.	0541	0638	0747	...	1138	1337	...	1638	1756	194
Torres Vedras d.	0700	0700	0809	...	1200	1400	...	1700	1820	200
Mira Sintra - Meleças d.	0703	0754	0916	...	1302	1502	...	1803	1923	211
Agualva - Cacém d.	...	0758	...	...	...	1507	...	...	...	211
Sete Rios a.	...	0813	...	...	...	1523	...	...	...	213
Entrecampos a.	...	0816	...	...	...	1527	...	...	...	213
Lisboa Santa Apolónia a.	...	0830	...	...	...	1541	...	...	...	214

km		IR 801 ①–⑥			IR 803			IR 805			
0	**Caldas da Rainha** d.	0613	...	0830	1115	...	1420	1612	...	1906	...
12	São Martinho do Porto d.	0621	...	0841	1123	...	1430	1620	...	1916	...
46	Marinha Grande d.	0650	...	0916	1152	...	1503	1649	...	1949	...
56	Leiria d.	0658	...	0924	1200	...	1511	1657	...	1957	...
109	Verride a.	0743	...	...	1245	...	|	1742	...	2042	...
109	Verride d.	0744	0752	...	1250	1250	|	1748	1747	2048	2048
123	Bifurcação de Lares a.	|	0800	...	|	1257	1553	|	1754	|	2055
129	**Figueira da Foz** a.	|	0812	...	|	1312	1601	|	1812	|	2107
117	Alfarelos d.	0752	...	...	1258	...	...	1757	...	2056	...
136	**Coimbra** B a.	0808	...	...	1314	...	...	1814	...	2114	...

			IR 800				IR 802			IC 804 Ⓑ
Coimbra B d.	0515	...	0852	...	...	...	1358	...	...	194
Alfarelos d.	0531	...	0907	...	...	...	1414	...	...	200
Figueira da Foz d.	|	0858	|	...	1358	...	|	1717	1959	|
Bifurcação de Lares d.	|	0912	|	...	1412	...	|	1726	2012	|
Verride a.	0539	0920	0916	...	1419	...	1423	|	2019	201
Verride d.	0539	...	0921	...	...	...	1424	|	...	202
Leiria d.	0625	...	1009	1213	...	...	1513	1813	...	211
Marinha Grande d.	0635	...	1019	1224	...	...	1522	1823	...	212
São Martinho do Porto d.	0711	...	1046	1256	...	...	1549	1854	...	214
Caldas da Rainha a.	0723	...	1055	1308	...	...	1558	1905	...	215

LOCAL TRAINS **FIGUEIRA DA FOZ - COIMBRA**

km		⚒	Ⓐ	831 A	⚒	Ⓐ																		
0	**Figueira da Foz** d.	0558	0631	0647	0655	0736	...	0858	0958	1058	1158	1256	1358	1458	...	1603	1658	1758	1858	1959	...	2156	...	...
8	Bifurcação de Lares d.	0610	0641	|	0707	0746	...	0912	1014	1112	1212	1312	1412	1512	...	1616	1712	1812	1912	2012	...	2208	...	...
20	Verride d.	0618	0648	|	0719	0753	...	0921	1022	1120	1220	1320	1424	1520	...	1624	1720	1820	1920	2020	...	2220	...	...
28	Alfarelos **699** d.	0629	0657	0707	0729	0802	...	0939	1034	1134	1234	1334	1435	1534	...	1634	1734	1834	1934	2034	...	2231	...	...
47	**Coimbra** B **699** a.	0659	0717	0721	0758	0824	...	1009	1104	1204	1305	1404	1504	1604	...	1704	1804	1904	2004	2103	...	2300	...	...

			⚒			Ⓐ								Ⓐ		Ⓑ	Ⓐ			830 A			
Coimbra B **699** d.	0028	...	0533	0701	...	0807	0902	1007	...	1207	1307	1407	1507	1607	1708	1807	1912	2002	...	2155	2248	...	...
Alfarelos **699** d.	0055	...	0601	0729	...	0834	0939	1035	...	1234	1334	1435	1534	1634	1735	1834	1934	2036	...	2211	2316	...	...
Verride d.	0107	...	0618	0752	...	0847	0952	1047	...	1250	1346	1446	1551	1646	1747	1846	1943	2048	...	|	2328	...	...
Bifurcação de Lares d.	0114	...	0626	0800	...	0854	0959	1054	...	1257	1354	1454	1559	1654	1754	1854	|	2055	...	|	2335	...	...
Figueira da Foz a.	0126	...	0642	0812	...	0912	1014	1112	...	1312	1411	1511	1616	1711	1812	1911	1957	2107	...	2232	2347	...	...

A – 🚃2 Valença - Porto - Figueira da Foz and v.v. Classified *IR*.

Linha do Douro PORTO - RÉGUA - TUA - POCINHO 694

km				IR 861	IR 21861		IR 865			IR 867		IR 869					IR 871	IR 873	IR 875				IR 877	
		⚒	⚒										A											
0	**Porto** São Bento ◧ d.	0630	...	...	0820	...	...	0930	...	...	...	1320	...	1330	...	...	1520	...	...	1830	...	...	1920	2220
3	**Porto** Campanhã ◧ d.	0635	...	0725	0825	...	0925	0935	...	1125	...	1325	...	1335	...	...	1525	...	1725	1835	...	...	1925	2225
12	Ermesinde ◧ d.	0647	...	0736	0838	...	0935	0947	...	1134	...	1335	...	1347	...	...	1534	...	1737	1847	...	...	1936	2238
50	Caíde ◧ d.	0722	...	0811	0913	...	1008	1023	...	1208	...	1408	...	1422	...	...	1608	...	1810	1922	...	...	2008	2317
59	Livração ◧ d.	0733	...	0820	|	...	1020	1036	...	1219	...	1419	...	1435	...	...	1619	...	1825	1937	...	...	2016	2326
64	Marco de Canaveses ◧ d.	0738	0741	0826	0933	...	1026	1041	1050	1225	...	1425	...	1440	1450	...	1625	...	1831	1942	1948	...	2022	2332
107	**Régua** a.	...	0836	0922	1019	...	1117	...	1153	1325	...	1516	...	...	1551	...	1712	...	1923	...	2046	...	2109	0030
107	**Régua** d.	...	...	0923	1024	...	1118	...	...	...	...	1518	1530	...	1557	...	...	1719	1925	...	...	...	...	...
130	Pinhão d.	...	...	0949	1048	...	1143	...	...	...	...	1544	1620	...	1624	...	...	1744	1951	...	...	...	...	...
143	Tua d.	...	...	1004	1104	...	1158	...	...	...	...	1558	1640	...	...	...	...	1759	2008	...	...	...	...	...
175	**Pocinho** a.	...	...	1048	1151	...	1241	...	...	...	...	1642	...	...	...	...	...	1842	2051	...	...	...	...	...

		IR 860	IR 862				IR 864	IR 866				IR 868	IR 21860	IR 874					IR 876				
				⚒														A					
Pocinho d.	...	...	0708	...	...	...	...	1110	...	...	...	1310	1512	...	...	...	...	...	1712	1926	...	...	...
Tua d.	...	...	0751	...	...	...	...	1157	...	...	...	1353	1559	...	...	...	...	1707	1758	2010	...	...	...
Pinhão d.	...	...	0807	...	...	...	...	1212	...	...	...	1409	1625	1641	...	...	...	1751	1813	2025	...	...	...
Régua a.	...	...	0832	...	...	...	...	1237	...	...	...	1434	1646	1707	...	...	...	1825	1838	2050	...	...	...
Régua d.	0526	0646	0837	0900	...	...	1035	1238	1302	...	...	1435	1647	1713	...	1806	...	...	1839	...	...	2110	...
Marco de Canaveses ◧ d.	0625	0739	0928	1002	...	1015	1129	1330	1402	...	1414	1529	1745	1802	...	1907	1913	...	1930	...	...	2208	2210
Livração ◧ d.	0635	0745	0936	...	...	1021	1140	1336	...	...	1420	1536	|	1808	...	...	1918	...	1936	...	...	...	2215
Caíde ◧ d.	0647	0755	0947	...	...	1037	1150	1347	...	...	1437	1547	1803	1821	...	...	1934	...	1945	...	...	...	2227
Ermesinde ◧ d.	0725	0830	1021	...	...	1114	1225	1421	...	...	1514	1621	1836	1852	...	...	2010	...	2017	...	...	...	2314
Porto Campanhã ◧ a.	0735	0840	1030	...	...	1125	1235	1430	...	...	1525	1630	1845	1900	...	...	2020	...	2025	...	...	...	2325
Porto São Bento ◧ a.	...	0845	...	...	...	1130	1240	...	...	...	1530	...	1850	1905	...	...	2025	...	2030	...	...	...	2330

A – COMBOIO HISTORICO – ⑥⑦ June - Oct. 2025 (also certain ③ July - Sept). Excursion train. 🅁. Special fare payable.

◧ – Local trains run hourly Porto São Bento - Marco de Canaveses and v.v.

PORTO - BRAGA 695

Subject to alteration on and around public holidays (see page 4).

km											AP 131								IC 721					
				Ⓐ		Ⓐ		Ⓐ			🅁						Ⓐ		🅁					
	Lisboa Santa Apolónia **690** d.	...	...	...	...	...	...	...	...	...	0700	...	...	...	...	...	...	...	0930	...	...	...	...	...
0	**Porto** São Bento ... **695a 696** d.	0050	...	0615	0645	0715	0745	0815	0850	...	|	0950	...	1045	...	1145	1215	...	|	1245	...	1345	...	1445
3	**Porto** Campanhã ... **695a 696** d.	0055	...	0620	0650	0720	0750	0820	0855	...	0950	0955	...	1050	...	1150	1220	...	1245	1250	...	1350	...	1450
12	Ermesinde **695a 696** d.	0107	...	0632	0702	0732	0802	0832	0908	...	|	1008	...	1102	...	1202	1232	...	|	1302	...	1402	...	1502
26	Trofa **695a 696** d.	0120	...	0644	0716	0744	0816	0844	0922	...	|	1022	...	1116	...	1216	1244	...	|	1316	...	1416	...	1516
35	Famalicão **696** d.	0128	...	0652	0727	0752	0827	0852	0933	...	1011	1033	...	1127	...	1227	1252	...	1309	1327	...	1427	...	1527
42	Nine **696** d.	0132	...	0656	0735	0756	0835	0856	0941	...	1016	1041	...	1135	...	1235	1256	...	1314	1335	...	1435	...	1535
57	**Braga** a.	0153	...	0709	0756	0817	0856	0909	1002	...	1027	1102	...	1156	...	1256	1309	...	1325	1356	...	1456	...	1556

				AP 133						AP 135					AP 137					IC 723			
		Ⓐ		🅁		Ⓐ		Ⓐ		Ⓑ 🅁					🅁			Ⓐ		🅁			
Lisboa Santa Apolónia **690** d.	...	...	...	1400	...	...	...	...	...	1600	...	...	...	...	1800	...	...	...	...	1930	...	...	...
Porto São Bento **695a 696** d.	1545	1615	...	|	1650	1715	1745	1815	...	|	1850	1915	1945	...	|	2105	...	2145	...	|	2310	...	...
Porto Campanhã **695a 696** d.	1550	1620	...	1650	1655	1720	1750	1820	...	1850	1855	1920	1950	...	2050	2110	...	2150	...	2245	2315	...	...
Ermesinde **695a 696** d.	1602	1632	...	|	1708	1732	1802	1832	...	|	1907	1932	2002	...	|	2122	...	2202	...	|	2327	...	...
Trofa **695a 696** d.	1616	1644	...	|	1722	1744	1816	1844	...	|	1918	1946	2016	...	|	2136	...	2216	...	|	2341	...	...
Famalicão **696** d.	1627	1652	...	1711	1733	1752	1827	1852	...	1911	1926	1957	2027	...	2111	2147	...	2227	...	2309	2352	...	...
Nine **696** d.	1635	1656	...	1716	1741	1756	1835	1856	...	1916	1933	2002	2035	...	2116	2155	...	2235	...	2314	0000	...	...
Braga a.	1656	1709	...	1737	1802	1809	1856	1909	...	1927	1954	2014	2056	...	2127	2216	...	2256	...	2325	0021	...	...

				AP 130												IC 720						AP 132	
			⚒	🅁	Ⓐ			Ⓐ	Ⓒ	Ⓐ						🅁						🅁	Ⓐ
Braga d.	0434	...	0528	0602	0621	0635	...	0721	0728	0750	0804	0834	...	0934	...	1006	1034	...	1134	...	1228	1302	1321
Nine **696** d.	0454	...	0548	0612	0633	0655	...	0733	0748	0800	0824	0854	...	0954	...	1017	1054	...	1154	...	1248	1312	1333
Famalicão **696** d.	0502	...	0556	0617	0638	0703	...	0738	0756	0805	0832	0902	...	1002	...	1022	1102	...	1202	...	1256	1317	1338
Trofa **695a 696** d.	0513	...	0607	|	0646	0714	...	0746	0807	0812	0844	0913	...	1013	...	|	1113	...	1213	...	1307	|	1346
Ermesinde **695a 696** d.	0528	...	0623	|	0659	0729	...	0759	0823	0824	0859	0928	...	1028	...	|	1128	...	1229	...	1323	|	1359
Porto Campanhã **695a 696** d.	0541	...	0635	0638	0711	0741	...	0811	0835	0836	0911	0941	...	1041	...	1044	1141	...	1241	...	1335	1338	1411
Porto São Bento **695a 696** a.	0545	...	0640	|	0715	0745	...	0815	0840	0840	0915	0945	...	1045	...	|	1145	...	1245	...	1340	|	1415
Lisboa Santa Apolónia **690** a.	...	...	...	0930	...	...	...	...	...	...	...	...	...	...	...	1400	...	...	...	...	...	1630	...

		IC 722							AP 134					AP 136								
		🅁						Ⓐ		🅁	Ⓐ				Ⓑ 🅁				Ⓒ		Ⓐ		
Braga d.	1334	1406	1434	...	1534	...	1634	1721	1737	1802	1821	1834	...	1937	2002	...	2039	...	2139	...	2239	...	2332
Nine **696** d.	1354	1417	1454	...	1554	...	1654	1733	1757	1812	1833	1854	...	1957	2012	...	2059	...	2159	...	2259	...	2352
Famalicão **696** d.	1402	1422	1502	...	1602	...	1702	1738	1805	1817	1838	1902	...	2005	2017	...	2107	...	2207	...	2307	...	2357
Trofa **695a 696** d.	1413	|	1513	...	1613	...	1713	1746	1816	|	1846	1913	...	2016	|	...	2118	...	2218	...	2318	...	0005
Ermesinde **695a 696** d.	1428	|	1528	...	1628	...	1728	1759	1839	|	1859	1928	...	2039	|	...	2133	...	2233	...	2333	...	0019
Porto Campanhã **695a 696** d.	1441	1444	1541	...	1641	...	1741	1811	1851	1838	1911	1941	...	2051	2038	...	2145	...	2245	...	2345	...	0031
Porto São Bento **695a 696** a.	1445	|	1545	...	1645	...	1745	1815	1855	|	1915	1945	...	2055	|	...	2150	...	2250	...	2350	...	0035
Lisboa Santa Apolónia **690** a.	...	1800	...	...	...	...	...	...	...	2130	...	...	...	...	2330	...	...	...	...	...	...	...	...

PORTO - GUIMARÃES 695a

km											IC 621													
		Ⓐ			Ⓐ		Ⓐ				🅁			Ⓐ		Ⓐ	Ⓐ			Ⓒ		Ⓐ		
	Lisboa Santa Apolónia **690** d.	...	...	...	...	...	...	...	...	...	1130	...	...	...	...	...	...	...	...	...	...	...	...	...
0	**Porto** São Bento **695 696** d.	0620	0725	0825	0925	1025	1125	1225	...	1420	|	...	1620	1725	1825	1910	1925	2020	...	2120	...	2225	...	2320
3	**Porto** Campanhã **695 696** d.	0625	0730	0830	0930	1030	1130	1230	...	1425	1445	...	1625	1730	1830	1915	1930	2025	...	2125	...	2230	...	2325
12	Ermesinde **695 696** d.	0637	0742	0842	0940	1042	1142	1242	...	1437	|	...	1637	1742	1842	1925	1942	2037	...	2137	...	2242	...	2337
26	Trofa **695 696** d.	0652	0757	0857	0951	1057	1157	1257	...	1452	1503	...	1652	1757	1857	1936	1957	2052	...	2152	...	2257	...	2352
59	**Guimarães** a.	0742	0837	0941	1027	1138	1241	1341	...	1532	1539	...	1744	1837	1943	2009	2044	2138	...	2236	...	2337	...	0032

														IC 620									
	Ⓐ	Ⓒ	Ⓐ	Ⓐ	Ⓐ					Ⓐ				🅁	Ⓐ	Ⓒ	Ⓐ	Ⓐ	Ⓒ	Ⓐ			
Guimarães d.	0553	0653	0702	0721	0802	0853	0953	...	1153	1253	1353	...	1553	1649	1707	1758	1813	1921	1953	2020	...	2148	2257
Trofa **695 696** d.	0633	0733	0739	0802	0840	0933	1036	...	1233	1333	1433	...	1633	1724	1750	1838	1900	2007	2033	2105	...	2229	2342
Ermesinde **695 696** d.	0649	0749	0751	0819	0851	0949	1053	...	1249	1349	1449	...	1649	|	1808	1854	1918	2023	2049	2122	...	2247	2358
Porto Campanhã **695 696** d.	0701	0801	0801	0831	0901	1001	1106	...	1301	1401	1501	...	1701	1743	1821	1906	1931	2035	2101	2136	...	2301	0010
Porto São Bento **695 696** a.	0705	0805	0805	0835	0905	1005	1110	...	1305	1405	1505	...	1705	|	1825	1910	1935	2040	2105	2140	...	2305	0015
Lisboa Santa Apolónia **690** a.	...	...	...	...	...	...	...	...	...	...	...	...	...	2100	...	...	...	...	...	...	...	...	...

696 PORTO - VIANA DO CASTELO - VALENÇA - VIGO *Linha do Minho*

km																								
		IR 851					421	*IR* 831			*IR* 853					*IR* 855			*IR* 857	423			*IC* 731	
			Ⓐ			①–⑥								Ⓐ									Ⓑ	
							A [R]	**B**												**A** [R]			[R]	
	Lisboa Santa Apolónia **690** d.	...	...	...	...	...	...	...	...	...	...	...	...	...	...	...	...	...	...	...	...	...	1730	...
	Coimbra B **690** d.	...	...	...	...	...	...	0726	...	...	...	...	...	...	...	...	...	...	...	...	...	...	1935	...
0	**Porto** São Bento ... **695 695a** d.	...	0615	...	0645	...	...	|	0950	...	1305	1345	...	1445	...	...	1650	...	...	...	1915	...	|	...
3	**Porto** Campanhã ... **695 695a** d.	0605	0620	...	0650	...	0813	0850	0955	...	1310	1350	...	1450	...	1610	1655	...	1815	1910	1920	...	2053	2210
15	Ermesinde **695 695a** d.	0615	0632	...	0702	...	|	0859	1008	...	1321	1402	...	1502	...	1621	1708	...	1824	|	1932	...	|	2220
26	Trofa **695 695a** d.	0625	0644	...	0716	...	|	0911	1022	...	1331	1416	...	1516	...	1631	1722	...	1834	|	1946	...	2122	2231
35	Famalicão **695** d.	0632	0652	...	0727	...	|	0919	1033	...	1338	1427	...	1527	...	1638	1733	...	1841	|	1957	...	2119	2240
42	**Nine** **695** a.	0637	0656	...	0735	...	0843	0924	1041	...	1343	1435	...	1535	...	1643	1741	...	1846	1940	2002	...	2124	2245
42	**Nine** d.	0637	...	0659	...	0746	0843	0928	...	1057	1344	...	1503	...	1559	1644	...	1745	1847	1940	...	2005	2125	2246
54	Barcelos d.	0648	...	0711	...	0804	|	0942	...	1109	1353	...	1515	...	1611	1654	...	1757	1856	|	...	2017	2140	2258
85	**Viana do Castelo** a.	0721	...	0753	...	0851	0915	1024	...	1146	1423	...	1557	...	1647	1722	...	1838	1825	2012	...	2100	2207	2336
85	**Viana do Castelo** d.	0723	...	0804	...	...	0917	1025	...	1148	1424	...	...	...	1650	1723	...	1847	1927	2014	...	2115	2208	...
119	Vila Nova de Cerveira d.	0751	...	0847	...	...	|	1053	...	1225	1455	...	...	...	1727	1750	...	1821	1959	|	...	2155	2231	...
133	**Valença** 🏛 PT a.	0801	...	0900	...	...	0950	1102	...	1238	1505	...	...	...	1740	1759	...	1943	2009	2046	...	2209	2240	...
137	Tui 🏛 ES a.	...	...	...	...	...	|	...	...	...	...	...	...	...	...	...	...	...	...	|	...	...	...	...
177	**Vigo** Guixar a.	...	...	...	...	...	1135	...	...	...	...	...	...	...	...	...	...	...	...	2234	...	...	...	...

						IC 730	*IR* 850	420		*IR* 852					*IR* 854					*IR* 830		422	*IR* 856
		Ⓐ	①–⑥			①–⑥						Ⓐ	Ⓐ	Ⓒ			Ⓐ						
						[R]		**A** [R]												**B**		**A** [R]	
Vigo Guixar d.	...	...	...	...	...	...	...	0858	...	...	...	...	...	...	...	...	...	...	...	...	...	1956	...
Tui 🏛 ES d.	...	...	...	...	...	...	...	|	...	...	...	...	...	...	...	...	...	...	...	...	...	|	...
Valença 🏛 PT d.	...	...	...	...	0550	0656	0722	0836	...	0926	1141	...	1254	1254	1430	1510	...	...	...	1810	1840	1933	2024
Vila Nova de Cerveira d.	...	...	...	...	0604	0703	0732	|	...	0940	1155	...	1308	1308	1440	1524	...	...	...	1820	1854	|	2037
Viana do Castelo a.	...	...	...	...	0641	0736	0802	0908	...	1006	1237	...	1345	1346	1505	1605	...	...	...	1846	1943	2006	2106
Viana do Castelo d.	0511	...	0557	...	0642	0737	0803	0917	0928	1007	1238	...	1346	▬	1508	1607	...	1745	...	1858	...	2014	2108
Barcelos d.	0548	...	0634	...	0733	0803	0832	|	1007	1036	1315	...	1429	...	1538	1654	...	1821	...	1928	...	|	2140
Nine a.	0600	...	0651	...	0744	0811	0840	0950	1020	1045	1327	...	1441	...	1547	1707	...	1833	...	1936	...	2047	2152
Nine **695** d.	...	0633	...	0655	0744	0812	0841	0951	...	1046	...	1333	...	1454	1548	...	1733	...	1854	1937	...	2048	2156
Famalicão **695** d.	...	0638	...	0703	0750	0819	0847	|	...	1052	...	1338	...	1502	1554	...	1738	...	1902	1943	...	|	2202
Trofa **695 695a** d.	...	0646	...	0714	0758	0826	0854	|	...	1059	...	1346	...	1513	1601	...	1746	...	1913	1950	...	|	2209
Ermesinde **695 695a** d.	...	0659	...	0729	0810	|	0906	|	...	1111	...	1359	...	1528	1612	...	1759	...	1928	2001	...	|	2220
Porto Campanhã **695 695a** a.	...	0710	...	0740	0820	0843	0915	1020	...	1119	...	1410	...	1540	1620	...	1810	...	1940	2010	...	2118	2230
Porto São Bento **695 695a** a.	...	0715	...	0745	...	|	...	...	...	1125	...	1415	...	1545	...	...	1815	...	1945	|	...	...	...
Coimbra B **690** a.	...	...	...	...	...	0952	...	...	...	...	...	...	...	...	...	...	...	...	...	2154	...	...	...
Lisboa Santa Apolónia **690** a.	...	...	...	...	...	1200	...	...	...	...	...	...	...	...	...	...	...	...	...	...	...	...	...

A – *Celta.* (2) [R]. **B** – (2) Valença - Figueira da Foz and v.v. ES – Spain (Central European Time). PT – Portugal (West European Time).

697 LISBOA - PINHAL NOVO - TUNES - FARO

km		*AP* 180	*IC* 570		*IC* 572		*AP* 184	*IC* 574		
	Porto Campanhã **690** d.	0540	...	...	...	...	1440	...	...	...
	Coimbra B **690** d.	0643	...	...	...	...	1543	...	...	...
0	**Lisboa** Oriente ⊙ d.	0823	1002	...	1402	...	1723	1832	...	...
7	Entrecampos ⊙ d.	0831	1010	...	1410	...	1731	1840	...	...
9	Sete Rios ⊙ d.	|	1014	...	1414	...	|	1844	...	...
18	Pragal ⊙ d.	|	1026	...	1426	...	|	1855	...	...
47	Pinhal Novo ⊙ d.	0906	1048	...	1448	...	1806	1921	...	...
118	Grândola d.	|	1121	...	1517	...	|	1950	...	...
180	Funcheira d.	|	1157	...	1554	...	|	2026	...	...
264	**Tunes** ▷ d.	1054	1302	...	1707	...	1955	2134	...	...
269	Albufeira ▷ d.	1101	1308	...	1712	...	2002	2139	...	...
286	Loulé ▷ d.	1113	1320	...	1724	...	2014	2151	...	...
302	**Faro** ▷ a.	1123	1330	...	1735	...	2023	2202	...	...

	AP 182	*IC* 670		*IC* 672	*AP* 186		*IC* 674		
Faro ▷ d.	0700	0822	...	1415	1600	...	1815	...	...
Loulé ▷ d.	0710	0833	...	1426	1611	...	1825	...	...
Albufeira ▷ d.	0723	0845	...	1438	1624	...	1837	...	...
Tunes ▷ d.	0729	0851	...	1444	1630	...	1844	...	...
Funcheira d.	0821	1001	...	1554	|	...	1954	...	...
Grândola d.	0853	1037	...	1636	|	...	2032	...	...
Pinhal Novo ⊙ d.	0923	1108	...	1707	1823	...	2105	...	...
Pragal ⊙ a.	|	1134	...	1734	|	...	2134	...	...
Sete Rios ⊙ a.	|	1144	...	1744	|	...	2144	...	...
Entrecampos ⊙ a.	0957	1147	...	1747	1857	...	2147	...	...
Lisboa Oriente ⊙ a.	1005	1156	...	1756	1905	...	2156	...	...
Coimbra B **690** a.	1145	...	...	...	2045	...	...	...	...
Porto Campanhã **690** a.	1248	...	...	...	2148	...	...	...	...

LOCAL TRAINS **LAGOS - TUNES - FARO**

km			⚒						Ⓐ	
0	**Lagos** ◧ d.	0610	0654	0747	1110	1323	1509	1720	1827	2011
18	Portimão ◧ d.	0631	0714	0806	1130	1349	1529	1744	1847	2031
29	Silves d.	0648	0731	0823	1148	1405	1547	1801	1905	2049
42	Algoz d.	0704	0747	0840	1205	1422	1604	1818	1926	2105
46	**Tunes** ▷ d.	0711	0754	0851	1212	1428	1611	1824	1933	2112
52	Albufeira ▷ d.	0722	0800	0858	1219	1438	1623	1837	1939	2123
69	Loulé ▷ d.	0743	0815	0919	1242	1453	1638	1859	1955	2138
85	**Faro** ▷ a.	0759	0835	0934	1257	1508	1654	1916	2010	2154

	⚒						Ⓐ		
Faro ▷ d.	0711	0902	1023	1225	1617	1741	1825	1918	2050
Loulé ▷ d.	0728	0919	1039	1242	1638	1758	1842	1935	2107
Albufeira ▷ d.	0743	0935	1100	1307	1655	1814	1900	2001	2123
Tunes ▷ d.	0754	0942	1106	1313	1707	1824	1908	2007	2133
Algoz d.	0800	0947	1112	1318	1713	1830	1914	2013	2138
Silves d.	0823	1004	1129	1334	1729	1846	1933	2029	2152
Portimão ◧ d.	0838	1020	1148	1349	1744	1906	1948	2049	2207
Lagos ◧ a.	0858	1040	1209	1410	1805	1926	2008	2109	2226

◧ – Also Lagos - Portimão at 0903 Ⓐ; Portimão - Lagos at 0931 Ⓐ.
▷ – Also see other section of table above or below.
⊙ – See Table **698** for other fast trains, Table **699** for local services, including connections Barreiro - Pinhal Novo.

697a FARO - VILA REAL DE SANTO ANTÓNIO

km		Ⓐ								
0	**Faro** d.	0857	0955	1130	1355	1515	1713	1927	2030	2216
10	Olhão d.	0908	1006	1141	1406	1531	1729	1939	2040	2227
32	Tavira d.	0939	1033	1208	1433	1558	1756	2010	2106	2254
56	**Vila Real** § a.	1008	1102	1237	1503	1627	1825	2039	2135	2319

Vila Real § d.	0639	0706	0840	1108	1243	1430	1633	1753	2107
Tavira d.	0708	0735	0909	1135	1312	1504	1702	1831	2138
Olhão d.	0735	0802	0936	1204	1339	1531	1729	1901	2201
Faro a.	0746	0813	0946	1214	1349	1542	1739	1912	2211

§ – ± 1500 metres from bus station/ferry terminal.

ADDITIONAL JOURNEYS: Faro - Villa Real at 0720, 1300 Ⓐ, 1753, 1826 Ⓐ; Villa Real - Faro at 0548, 1524 Ⓐ, 1910 Ⓐ.

698 LISBOA - PINHAL NOVO - ÉVORA and BEJA *Linha do Alentejo*

km	All services [R]	*IC* 590	*IC* 592	*IC* 594		*IC* 790		*IC* 596	*IC* 598	
		Ⓐ	Ⓐ	Ⓒ		Ⓐ				
0	**Lisboa** Oriente ⊡ d.	0702	0902	0958	...	1335	...	1702	1902	...
7	Entrecampos ⊡ d.	0710	0910	1006	...	1343	...	1710	1910	...
9	Sete Rios ⊡ d.	0714	0914	1010	...	1347	...	1714	1914	...
18	Pragal ⊡ d.	0726	0926	1020	...	1359	...	1726	1926	...
47	**Pinhal Novo** ⊡ d.	0748	0948	1041	...	1421	...	1748	1948	...
88	Vendas Novas d.	0818	1010	1111	...	1443	...	1810	2010	...
122	Casa Branca d.	0832	1024	1125	...	1457	...	1824	2024	...
148	**Évora** a.	0842	1035	1135	...	1508	...	1835	2035	...

All services [R]	*IC* 690	*IC* 692		*IC* 698		*IC* 694		*IC* 696	
	Ⓐ			Ⓐ					
Évora d.	0706	0906	...	1135	...	1657	...	1906	...
Casa Branca d.	0716	0916	...	1145	...	1707	...	1916	...
Vendas Novas d.	0731	0931	...	1200	...	1722	...	1931	...
Pinhal Novo ⊡ d.	0753	0953	...	1223	...	1751	...	1953	...
Pragal ⊡ a.	0814	1014	...	1244	...	1814	...	2014	...
Sete Rios ⊡ a.	0824	1024	...	1254	...	1824	...	2024	...
Entrecampos ⊡ a.	0828	1028	...	1258	...	1828	...	2028	...
Lisboa Oriente ⊡ a.	0836	1036	...	1306	...	1836	...	2036	...

km	All services [R]	*IC* 682	*IC* 581	*IC* 585	*IC* 583		*IC* 686	*IC* 587	*IC* 588	
		Ⓐ	Ⓐ	Ⓒ	Ⓐ		Ⓐ			
0	**Évora** d.	0809	...	...	...	...	1433	...	2001	...
26	Casa Branca d.	0835	1027	1128	1150	...	1503	1829	2026	...
89	**Beja** a.	0926	1118	1219	1241	...	1554	1920	2116	...

All services [R]	*IC* 680	*IC* 580	*IC* 582		*IC* 684		*IC* 584	*IC* 688	
	Ⓐ		Ⓐ		Ⓐ				
Beja d.	0623	0822	1045	...	1310	...	1611	1815	...
Casa Branca a.	0711	0914	1141	...	1358	...	1700	1908	...
Évora a.	0736	...	...	...	1423	...	...	1937	...

⊡ – See Table **697** for other fast trains and Table **699** for local services, including connections Barreiro - Pinhal Novo.

LISBOA - ESTORIL - CASCAIS

km			Ⓐ		Ⓐ		Ⓒ		Ⓒ
0	**Lisboa** C do Sodre ◧ d.	Ⓐ	0700	and every	2110	Ⓒ	0820	and every	1900
24	Estoril ◧ d.		0729	15–20	2146		0856	20	1936
26	**Cascais** ◧ a.		0733	min. until	2150		0900	min. until	1940

		Ⓐ		Ⓐ		Ⓒ		Ⓒ
Cascais ◧ d.	Ⓐ	0651	and every	2100	Ⓒ	0844	and every	1904
Estoril ◧ d.		0655	15–20	2104		0848	20	1908
Lisboa C do Sodre ◧ a.		0724	min. until	2140		0924	min. until	1944

◧ – Earlier and later services are available operated by 🚌 with extended journey times. Please check locally for schedules.

LISBOA ORIENTE - SINTRA

km		Ⓒ	Ⓐ			Ⓒ	Ⓐ	Ⓐ		
0	**Lisboa Oriente** ⊡ d.	0608	0618	0638	and	2008	2018	2038	2138	2238
6	Roma Areeiro ⊡ d.	0615	0625	0645	at	2015	2025	2045	2145	2245
7	Entrecampos ⊡ d.	0617	0627	0647	least	2017	2027	2047	2147	2247
9	Sete Rios ⊡ d.	0620	0630	0650	every	2020	2030	2050	2150	2250
19	Monte Abraão ⊡ d.	0635	0645	0705	30	2035	2045	2105	2205	2305
23	Agualva-Cacém ⊡ d.	0641	0651	0711	minutes	2041	2051	2111	2211	2311
33	**Sintra** ⊡ a.	0655	0705	0725	until	2055	2105	2125	2225	2325

			Ⓐ		Ⓒ	Ⓐ			
Sintra ⊡ d.	0536	0606	0616	and	2006	2016	2036	2106	2206
Agualva-Cacém ⊡ d.	0549	0619	0629	at	2019	2029	2049	2119	2219
Monte Abraão ⊡ d.	0554	0624	0634	least	2024	2034	2054	2124	2224
Sete Rios ⊡ d.	0609	0639	0649	every	2039	2049	2109	2139	2239
Entrecampos ⊡ d.	0612	0642	0652	30	2042	2052	2112	2142	2242
Roma Areeiro ⊡ d.	0614	0644	0654	minutes	2044	2054	2114	2144	2244
Lisboa Oriente ⊡ a.	0622	0652	0702	until	2052	2102	2122	2152	2252

⊡ – Also from Lisboa at 0008, 0038, 0108, 0558 Ⓐ, 0648 Ⓐ, 2108 Ⓒ, 2208, 2308, 2338; also from Sintra at 0006, 0506, 2136, 2236, 2306, 2336.

LISBOA ROSSIO - SINTRA and MIRA SINTRA-MELEÇAS

km		Ⓐ	Ⓒ	Ⓐ	Ⓒ		Ⓐ	Ⓒ	Ⓐ	Ⓒ
0	**Lisboa Rossio** d.	0541	0601	0626	0631	and	1941	2001	2026	2031
13	Monte Abraão d.	0601	0621	0646	0651	hourly	2001	2021	2046	2051
17	Agualva-Cacém d.	0607	0627	0652	0657	until	2007	2027	2052	2057
20	**Mira Sintra-M'ças** a.	|	|	0655	0700	⊖	|	|	2055	2100
27	**Sintra** a.	0621	0641	...	...		2021	2041	...	...

	Ⓐ	Ⓒ	Ⓒ	Ⓐ		Ⓐ	Ⓒ	Ⓒ	Ⓐ
Sintra d.	0640	0650	...	...	and	1940	1950	...	...
Mira Sintra-M'ças d.	|	|	0730	0735	hourly	|	|	2030	2035
Agualva-Cacém d.	0653	0703	0733	0738	until	1953	2003	2033	2038
Monte Abraão d.	0659	0709	0739	0744	●	1959	2009	2039	2044
Lisboa Rossio a.	0719	0729	0759	0804		2019	2029	2059	2104

⊖ – Lisboa Rossio - Mira Sintra-Meleças trains run 5 minutes earlier 1021 Ⓐ - 1621 Ⓐ. Other trains: **Lisboa Rossio - Sintra** at 0001, 0031, 0101, 0611 Ⓐ, 0711 Ⓐ, 0811 Ⓐ, 0911 Ⓐ, 1001 Ⓐ, 1101 Ⓐ, 1201 Ⓐ, 1301 Ⓐ, 1401 Ⓐ, 1501 Ⓐ, 1601 Ⓐ, 1711 Ⓐ, 1811 Ⓐ, 1911 Ⓐ, 2011 Ⓐ, 2041 Ⓐ, 2101, 2131, 2201, 2231, 2301, 2331; **Lisboa Rossio - Mira Sintra-Meleças** at 0656 Ⓐ, 0756 Ⓐ, 0856 Ⓐ, 1656 Ⓐ, 1756 Ⓐ, 1856 Ⓐ, 1956 Ⓐ.

● – Mira Sintra-Meleças - Lisboa Rossio trains run 5 minutes earlier 1030 Ⓐ - 1630 Ⓐ. Other trains: **Sintra - Lisboa Rossio** at 0020, 0520, 0550, 0620, 0710 Ⓐ, 0810 Ⓐ, 0910 Ⓐ, 1000 Ⓐ, 1100 Ⓐ, 1200 Ⓐ, 1300 Ⓐ, 1400 Ⓐ, 1500 Ⓐ, 1600 Ⓐ, 1710 Ⓐ, 1810 Ⓐ, 1910 Ⓐ, 2010 Ⓐ, 2050, 2120, 2150, 2220, 2250, 2320, 2350; **Mira Sintra-Meleças - Lisboa Rossio** at 0705 Ⓐ, 0805 Ⓐ, 0905 Ⓐ, 1705 Ⓐ, 1805 Ⓐ, 1905 Ⓐ, 2005 Ⓐ.

LISBOA - PINHAL NOVO - SETÚBAL

Fertagus (CP tickets not valid)

km								Ⓐ		
0	**Roma-Areeiro** d.	0713	0733	0753	and	2113	2133	2153	...	...
	Entrecampos d.	0715	0735	0755	every	2115	2135	2155	...	...
	Sete Rios d.	0719	0739	0759	20	2119	2139	2159	...	...
	Pragal d.	0730	0750	0810	minutes	2130	2150	2210	...	...
	Pinhal Novo d.	0758	0818	0838	until	2158	2218	2238	...	...
	Setúbal a.	0811	0831	0851	⊙	2211	2231	2251	...	...

							Ⓐ		
Setúbal d.	0603	0623	0643	and	2003	2023	2043	...	...
Pinhal Novo d.	0616	0636	0656	every	2016	2036	2056	...	...
Pragal d.	0649	0709	0729	20	2049	2109	2129	...	...
Sete Rios d.	0700	0720	0740	minutes	2100	2120	2140	...	...
Entrecampos d.	0704	0724	0744	until	2104	2124	2144	...	...
Roma-Areeiro a.	0706	0726	0746	⊙	2106	2126	2146	...	...

⊙ – Also from Roma-Areeiro at 0553 Ⓐ, 0613, 0633 Ⓐ, 0653, 2213 Ⓒ, 2223 Ⓐ, 2233 Ⓒ, 2253 Ⓐ, 2313 Ⓒ, 2323Ⓐ, 2333 Ⓒ, 2353 Ⓐ; also from Setúbal at 0543 Ⓐ, 2103, 2123 Ⓒ, 2143 Ⓐ, 2203, 2223 Ⓒ, 2243 Ⓐ, 2303, 2343 Ⓐ.

Catamaran LISBOA - BARREIRO

Transtejo Soflusa — Certain Ⓐ peak journeys do not run in July and August

From Lisboa Terreiro do Paço: By ⛴ journey time 20–25 minutes. *10* km

Ⓐ: 0000, 0030, 0100, 0200, 0530, 0550, 0620, 0640, 0700 and every 5–15 minutes until 0920, 0940, 0955 and every 30 minutes until 1455, 1520, 1535, 1600, 1625, 1640 and every 5–15 minutes until 2035, 2100, 2125, 2155, 2230, 2255, 2330.

Ⓒ: 0000, 0030, 0100, 0200, 0545, 0615, 0647, 0715, 0755, 0825 ⑥, 0855, 0925 ⑥, 0955, 1025 ⑥, 1055, 1155, 1255, 1355, 1455, 1525, 1555, 1625, 1655, 1725, 1755, 1825, 1855, 1925, 1955, 2055, 2125, 2155, 2255.

From Barreiro Barcos: By ⛴ journey time 20–25 minutes. *10* km

Ⓐ: 0005, 0030, 0130, 0505, 0520, 0555, 0615, 0635 and every 5–15 minutes until 0910, 0925, 0940, 0955, 1025 and every 30 minutes until 1455, 1510, 1535, 1600 and every 5–15 minutes until 1950, 2000, 2010, 2035, 2100, 2125, 2200, 2225, 2300, 2330.

Ⓒ: 0005, 0030, 0130, 0515, 0545, 0622, 0650, 0725, 0755 ⑥, 0825, 0855⑥, 0925, 0955 ⑥, 1025, 1125, 1225, 1325, 1425, 1455, 1525, 1555, 1625, 1655, 1725, 1755, 1825, 1855, 1925, 2025, 2055, 2125, 2225, 2330.

BARREIRO - SETÚBAL

km		Ⓐ				Ⓐ	Ⓒ		
0	**Barreiro** d.	0555	0625	and every	2125	2225	2225	2325	...
15	Pinhal Novo d.	0614	0644	30 mins. on Ⓐ /	2144	2244	2244	2344	...
28	**Setúbal** d.	0626	0656	hourly on Ⓒ	2156	2256	2256	2356	...
	Praias do Sado A a.	0633	0703	until	2203	2303	...	...	...

	Ⓒ	Ⓐ					Ⓐ	Ⓒ
P. do Sado A d.	0540	0610	0640	and every	2140	2240	2340	...
Setúbal d.	0548	0618	0648	30 mins. on Ⓐ /	2148	2248	2348	2348
Pinhal Novo d.	0600	0630	0700	hourly on Ⓒ	2200	2300	0000	0000
Barreiro a.	0618	0648	0718	until	2218	2318	0018	0018

LISBOA - ENTRONCAMENTO - TOMAR

Local trains — For fast trains see Table **690**

km			Ⓐ	⚒		Ⓐ			Ⓐ	Ⓐ		Ⓐ			Ⓐ			Ⓐ §			Ⓐ §					Ⓐ	
0	**Lisboa** S. Apolónia d.	0015	0550	0645	0745	0845	...	0945	1045	1145	1245	1345	...	1445	1545	1615	1645	1715	...	1745	1815	1845	1945	2045	...	2145	2245
7	**Lisboa** Oriente d.	0025	0558	0653	0753	0853	...	0953	1053	1153	1253	1353	...	1453	1553	1623	1653	1723	...	1753	1823	1853	1953	2053	...	2153	2253
31	Vila Franca de Xira d.	0051	0616	0711	0811	0911	...	1011	1111	1211	1311	1411	...	1511	1611	1639	1711	1739	...	1811	1838	1911	2011	2111	...	2211	2311
75	Santarém d.	0135	0653	0754	0854	0957	...	1054	1148	1254	1348	1448	...	1549	1654	1706	1754	1806	...	1854	1907	1954	2054	2149	...	2259	2349
107	**Entroncamento** a.	0201	0719	0820	0919	1023	...	1120	1214	1321	1414	1520	...	1616	1720	1728	1820	1828	...	1920	1929	2020	2120	2215	...	2325	0015
130	**Tomar** a.	...	0751	0847	0946	...	...	1151	1242	...	1442	1551	...	1643	1751	...	1854	1859	...	1947	1958	2051	2148	2246	...	2352	0042
		Ⓐ §	⚒	†	Ⓐ §	⚒		†		Ⓐ		⚒		†			Ⓐ					Ⓐ		Ⓐ		⑦ §	
	Tomar d.	0510	0614	...	0650	0711	...	...	0801	...	1009	1111	...	...	...	1313	...	1511	...	1600	1711	1903	2011	...	...	...	2206
	Entroncamento d.	0541	0641	0641	0710	0741	...	0741	0836	0941	1036	1141	...	1141	1236	1341	1436	1541	...	1636	1741	1942	2041	2150	...	2236	2240
	Santarém d.	0608	0708	0708	0733	0808	...	0808	0903	1008	1103	1208	...	1208	1303	1408	1503	1607	...	1703	1808	2009	2108	2213	...	2258	2306
	Vila Franca de Xira d.	0647	0747	0747	0802	0847	...	0847	0947	1047	1147	1247	...	1247	1347	1447	1547	1654	...	1747	1847	2055	2147	2252	...	2326	2344
	Lisboa Oriente d.	0706	0806	0803	0819	0906	...	0906	1006	1106	1206	1306	...	1306	1406	1506	1606	1713	...	1806	1906	2113	2206	2311	...	2343	0003
	Lisboa S. Apolónia a.	0713	0813	0813	0828	0913	...	0913	1013	1113	1213	1313	...	1313	1413	1513	1613	1720	...	1813	1913	2120	2213	2318	...	2350	0010

§ – *IR* train.

ENTRONCAMENTO - COIMBRA

Local trains — For fast trains see Table **690**

km		†		Ⓐ							Ⓑ
0	**Entroncamento** d.	...	0640	0740	0840	1037	1237	1537	1737	1940	2132
24	Fátima ⊙ d.	...	0700	0807	0900	1057	1257	1557	1757	2007	2153
64	Pombal d.	...	0732	0839	0938	1135	1335	1629	1835	2039	2225
91	Alfarelos d.	0711	0756	0902	1001	1158	1358	1652	1858	2102	2248
111	**Coimbra B** a.	0735	0820	0926	1025	1222	1422	1716	1923	2126	2311

	①–⑥	Ⓐ					Ⓐ			Ⓑ
Coimbra B d.	0612	0712	0823	1022	1330	1627	1722	1823	1922	2022
Alfarelos d.	0635	0735	0846	1045	1353	1649	1745	1845	1945	2044
Pombal d.	0700	0800	0917	1117	1418	1715	1817	1918	2017	2110
Fátima ⊙ d.	0741	0847	0949	1149	1459	1747	1849	1958	2049	2148
Entroncamento a.	0801	0907	1009	1209	1519	1807	1909	2018	2109	2208

⊙ – Station is *20 km* from Fátima (full name of station is Chão de Maçãs-Fátima).

☛ Additional trains: **Entroncamento - Coimbra B** at 0555 Ⓐ and 1840 Ⓐ. **Coimbra B - Entroncamento** at 0518 Ⓐ.

AVEIRO - COIMBRA

Local trains — For fast trains see Table **690**

km							Ⓐ				
0	**Aveiro** d.	0644	0744	0944	1139	1344	1444	1539	1744	1953	2153
41	Pampilhosa d.	0720	0820	1020	1216	1420	1520	1616	1820	2029	2229
55	**Coimbra B** a.	0736	0836	1036	1231	1436	1536	1632	1835	2045	2245

		⚒								
Coimbra B d.	0633	0750	0850	1100	1350	1456	1642	1850	1954	2215
Pampilhosa d.	0649	0806	0906	1116	1406	1512	1658	1907	2014	2231
Aveiro a.	0727	0844	0945	1154	1445	1550	1735	1945	2052	2310

☛ Additional trains: **Aveiro - Coimbra B** at 0544 ⚒, 0735 Ⓐ, 0854 Ⓐ, 1044 Ⓐ, 1224 Ⓐ, 1640 Ⓐ, 1844 Ⓐ and 2045 Ⓐ.
Coimbra B - Aveiro at 0540 Ⓐ, 1013 Ⓐ, 1150 Ⓐ, 1250 Ⓐ, 1550 Ⓐ, 1750 Ⓐ and 2050 Ⓐ.

FINLAND
SWEDEN
NORWAY
DENMARK
GERMANY
For 🚌 routes north of Narvik, see page 369.
For 🚌 to/from Svolvær see note ♣ in Table 787.
København - Malmø: Tables 703, 730, 735, 745 and 746
see inset above
Aarhus
Ebeltoft
Skanderborg
Samsø
Sj. Odde
Helsingborg
Helsingør
KØBENHAVN
Lund
MALMÖ
Vejle
Fredericia
Kalundborg
Roskilde
Odense
Ringsted
Trelleborg
Korsør
Nyborg
Bøjden
Vordingborg
Nakskov
Nykøbing
Fynshav
Maribo
Rødby
Sønderborg
Gedser
Kirkenes
Svolvær
Narvik
Kiruna
Moskenes
Bodø
Fauske
Gällivare
Mo i Rana
Boden
Haparanda
Kemi
Luleå
Arvidsjaur
Sandnessjøen
Mosjøen
Brønnøysund
Skellefteå
Bastuträsk
Storuman
Rørvik
Vännäs
Umeå
Steinkjer
Örnsköldsvik
TRONDHEIM
Duved
Åre
Hell
Storlien
Östersund
Kristiansund
Støren
Bräcke
Härnösand
Molde
Ånge
Sundsvall
Røros
Oppdal
Sveg
Ljusdal
Ålesund
Åndalsnes
Hudiksvall
Geiranger
Dombås
Orsa
Bollnäs
Söderhamn
Mora
Eckerö
Måløy
Rättvik
Mariehamn
Sogndal
Lillehammer
Falun
Gävle
Balestrand
Lærdal
Elverum
Borlänge
Grisslehamn
Hamar
Flåm
Gjøvik
Avesta
Eidsvoll
Ludvika
Kapellskär
Voss
Myrdal
Gol
Oslo
Kongsvinger
Sala
Uppsala
Roa
Fagersta
Arlanda
BERGEN
Geilo
Charlottenberg
Västerås
STOCKHOLM
Hønefoss
Lillestrøm
Nykroppa
Frövi
Eskilstuna
Södertälje
Drammen
OSLO
Kil
Örebro
Nynäshamn
Notodden
Karlstad
Katrineholm
Nordagutu
Kristinehamn
Hallsberg
Skien
Fredrikstad
Laxå
Larvik
Mariestad
Norrköping
Strömstad
Motala
Skövde
Linköping
Nelaug
Öxnered
Mjölby
Stavanger
Uddevalla
Falköping
Västervik
Trollhättan
Arendal
Herrljunga
Visby
Egersund
Moi
Kristiansand
Jönköping
Nässjö
Hirtshals
Skagen
Borås
Hjørring
GÖTEBORG
Berga
Oskarshamn
Frederikshavn
Aalborg
Varberg
Alvesta
Växjö
Kalmar
Thisted
Emmaboda
Randers
Halmstad
Karlskrona
Struer
Langå
Karlshamn
Holstebro
Kristianstad
Hässleholm
Skjern
Herning
Bramming
Simrishamn
Esbjerg
Lunderskov
Ystad
Fanø
Rønne
Tønder
Tinglev
Westerland
Padborg
Niebüll
Flensburg
Puttgarden
Kiel
Rostock

DENMARK

Operators: Principal operator is Danske Statsbaner (*DSB*): www.dsb.dk. GoCollective (*GC*) operate many local services in Jutland: www.gocollective.dk. Midttrafik operate services Skjern - Holstebro (Table **708**): www.midttrafik.dk. Nordjyske Jernbaner operates services north of Aalborg: www.nj.dk. Local trains over the Øresund bridge are operated by *Øtåg*.

Services: InterCity (*IC*) and InterCityLyn (*Lyn*) trains offer *Business* (first class), *Standard* (second class), and on some services *Hvilepladser* ('quiet' seats) and *Familiepladser* ('family' seats). These services often consist of two or more portions for different destinations and care should be taken to join the correct portion. Other trains convey first and second (standard) classes of accommodation unless otherwise shown.

Timings: **Valid until December 13, 2025** (unless otherwise stated). Note that minor amendments may be made at any time, especially on and around the dates of public holidays (Jan. 1, Apr. 17, 18, 20, 21, May 29, June 8, 9, Dec. 25, 26) and during the high-summer period from mid-June to mid-August.
In our Danish tables Ⓐ = ①–⑤, Ⓒ = ⑥⑦. See the panel on page 348 for service provision on holiday dates.
Engineering work often affects schedules (particularly late evening / early morning services and also during the summer months) and readers are advised to check locally.

Reservations: Seat reservations (currently 30 DKK) are recommended for travel on *IC* and *Lyn* trains (especially at peak times) and may be purchased a maximum of two months and a minimum of 15 minutes before departure of the train from its *originating* station. Passengers may board the train without a reservation but are not guaranteed a seat. Reservations are also available on EuroCity (*EC*) trains. It is not possible to reserve seats on other types of train. Special reservation rules may apply during holiday periods.

KØBENHAVN - ODENSE - FREDERICIA - AARHUS 700

Most Aarhus services run to / from Aalborg (Table **701**). For through cars to / from Struer, see Table **715**.

km		*IC*	*IC*		*IC*	*IC*		*IC*	*IC*	*Lyn*	*IC*	*IC*	*IC*	*Lyn*	*IC*	*IC*	*IC*	*IC*	*Lyn*	*IC*	*Lyn*	*IC*	*Lyn*	*IC*
		101	**103**		**107**	**109**		**411**	**113**	**15**	**117**	**417**	**819**	**19**	**121**	**121**	**421**	**823**	**23**	**125**	**625**	**827**	**27**	**129**
		Ⓐ	Ⓒ		Ⓐ	Ⓒ		Ⓒ	Ⓐ	Ⓐ	Ⓐ		Ⓐ	Ⓐ	Ⓒ	Ⓐ		Ⓐ			Ⓐ			
													⊖	⊡				⊖		⊗	r	⊖	⊡	
	København Lufthavn ✈ d.	0012	0020	...	0212	0229	...	...	0327	...	0427	...	...	0531	0521	...	...	...	0631	...	...	...	0731	...
0	**København** H 710 720 § d.	0035	0050	...	0235	0250	...	...	0350	...	0450	...	0532	0552	0550	0550	...	0632	0652	0650	0722	0732	0752	0750
20	Høje Taastrup 720 § d.	0052	0105	...	0252	0305	...	...	0405	...	0505	...	|	|	0605	0605	...	|	|	0705	|	|	|	0805
31	Roskilde 720 § d.	0102	0114	...	0301	0314	...	...	0413	...	0513	...	|	|	0613	0613	...	|	|	0713	|	|	|	0813
64	Ringsted 710 720 d.	0121	0132	...	0321	0332	...	...	0430	...	0530	...	0606	|	0630	0630	...	0706	|	0730	|	0806	|	0830
93	Slagelse d.	0141	0151	...	0342	0351	...	...	0449	...	0549	...	0625	|	0649	0649	...	0725	|	0749	|	0824	|	0849
108	Korsør d.	0151	0200	...	0353	0401	...	...	0459	...	0559	...	0633	|	0659	0659	...	0733	|	0759	|	0833	|	0859
132	Nyborg d.	0206	0214	...	0408	0415	...	...	0512	...	0612	...	0647	|	0712	0712	...	0747	|	0812	|	0846	|	0912
160	**Odense** 710 a.	0221	0225	...	0423	0428	...	...	0528	...	0628	...	0700	0703**c**	0728	0728	...	0800	0803**c**	0828	0833	0900	0903**c**	0928
160	**Odense** d.	0223	0230	...	0426	0431	...	...	0531	0606	0631	...	0709	0706	0731	0731	...	0809	0806	0831	0836	0909	0906	0931
210	Middelfart d.	0249	0255	...	0453	0455	...	...	0555	|	0654	...	0732	|	0754	0754	...	0832	|	0854	|	0932	|	0954
220	**Fredericia** a.	0257	0303	...	0502	0503	...	...	0602	0634	0702	...	...	0734	0802	0802	...	...	0834	0902	0907	...	0934	1002
220	**Fredericia** 705 715 d.	0303	0309	...	0509	0509	...	0601	*0609*	0639	...	0709	...	0739	...	...	0809	...	0839	0908	...	...	0939	*1009*
246	Vejle 705 715 d.	0321	0325	...	0525	0525	...	0621	*0625*	0655	...	0725	...	0755	...	...	0825	...	0855	0923	...	...	0955	*1025*
277	Horsens 705 d.	0339	0342	...	0541	0541	...	0640	*0641*	0711	...	0741	...	0811	...	...	0841	...	0911	0940	...	...	1011	*1041*
306	Skanderborg 705 713 d.	0356	0358	...	0556	0556	...	0655	*0656*	0726	...	0756	...	0826	...	...	0856	...	0926	0956	...	...	1026	*1056*
329	**Aarhus** 705 713 a.	0412	0412	...	0612	0612	...	0712	*0712*	0742	...	0812	...	0842	...	...	0912	...	0942	1012	...	...	1042	*1112*

	IC	*Lyn*	*IC*	*IC*	*Lyn*	*IC*	*IC*	*Lyn*	*IC*	*IC*	*Lyn*	*IC*	*IC*	*Lyn*	*IC*	*Lyn*	*IC*	*Lyn*	*IC*	*IC*	*Lyn*	*IC*	*Lyn*	*IC*
	831	**31**	**133**	**835**	**35**	**137**	**839**	**39**	**141**	**843**	**43**	**145**	**847**	**47**	**149**	**649**	**851**	**51**	**153**	**855**	**55**	**157**	**657**	**859**
																Ⓐ							Ⓐ	
	⊖			⊖	⊡		⊖			⊖	⊡		⊖			r	⊖	⊡		⊖			r	⊖
København Lufthavn ✈ d.	...	0831	...	...	0931	...	...	1031	...	...	1131	...	...	1231	...	...	...	1331	...	...	1431	...	...	...
København H 710 720 § d.	0832	0852	0850	0932	0952	0950	1032	1052	1050	1132	1152	1150	1232	1252	1250	1322	1332	1352	1350	1432	1452	1450	1522	1532
Høje Taastrup 720 § d.	|	|	0905	|	|	1005	|	|	1105	|	|	1205	|	|	1304	|	|	|	1405	|	|	1505	|	|
Roskilde 720 § d.	|	|	0913	|	|	1013	|	|	1113	|	|	1213	|	|	1313	|	|	|	1413	|	|	1513	|	|
Ringsted 710 720 d.	0906	|	0930	1006	|	1030	1106	|	1130	1206	|	1230	1306	|	1330	|	1406	|	1430	1506	|	1530	|	1606
Slagelse d.	0925	|	0949	1025	|	1049	1124	|	1149	1225	|	1249	1325	|	1349	|	1424	|	1449	1525	|	1549	|	1625
Korsør d.	0933	|	0959	1033	|	1058	1133	|	1159	1233	|	1259	1333	|	1358	|	1433	|	1459	1533	|	1559	|	1633
Nyborg d.	0947	|	1012	1047	|	1112	1146	|	1212	1247	|	1312	1347	|	1411	|	1446	|	1512	1547	|	1612	|	1647
Odense 710 a.	1000	1003**c**	1028	1100	1103**c**	1128	1200	1203**c**	1228	1300	1303**c**	1328	1400	1403**c**	1428	1433	1500	1503**c**	1528	1600	1603**c**	1628	1633	1700
Odense d.	1009	1006	1031	1109	1106	1131	1209	1206	1231	1309	1306	1331	1409	1406	1431	1436	1509	1506	1531	1609	1606	1631	1636	1709
Middelfart d.	1032	|	1054	1132	|	1154	1232	|	1254	1332	|	1354	1432	|	1454	|	1532	|	1554	1632	|	1654	|	1732
Fredericia a.	...	1034	1102	...	1134	1202	...	1234	1302	...	1334	1402	...	1434	1502	1507	...	1534	1602	...	1634	1702	1707	...
Fredericia 705 715 d.	...	1039	*1109*	...	1139	*1209*	...	1239	*1309*	...	1339	*1409*	...	1439	*1509*	...	...	1539	*1609*	...	1639	1708	...	...
Vejle 705 715 d.	...	1055	*1125*	...	1155	*1225*	...	1255	*1325*	...	1355	*1425*	...	1455	*1525*	...	...	1555	*1625*	...	1655	1723	...	...
Horsens 705 d.	...	1111	*1141*	...	1211	*1241*	...	1311	*1341*	...	1411	*1441*	...	1511	*1541*	...	...	1611	*1641*	...	1711	1740	...	...
Skanderborg 705 713 d.	...	1126	*1156*	...	1226	*1256*	...	1326	*1356*	...	1426	*1456*	...	1526	*1556*	...	...	1626	*1656*	...	1726	1756	...	...
Aarhus 705 713 a.	...	1142	*1212*	...	1242	*1312*	...	1342	*1412*	...	1442	*1512*	...	1542	*1612*	...	...	1642	*1712*	...	1742	1812	...	...

	Lyn	*IC*	*IC*	*Lyn*	*IC*	*IC*	*Lyn*	*IC*	*IC*	*Lyn*	*IC*	*IC*	*Lyn*	*IC*	*IC*	*Lyn*	*IC*	*IC*	*IC*	*IC*		*IC*		*IC*
	59	**161**	**863**	**63**	**165**	**867**	**67**	**169**	**871**	**71**	**173**	**875**	**75**	**177**	**879**	**79**	**181**	**883**	**185**	**185**		**189**		**193**
																				⑤⑥				
	⊡		⊖			⊖	⊡		⊖			⊖	⊡				⊙							
København Lufthavn ✈ d.	1531	...	...	1631	...	...	1731	...	...	1831	...	...	1931	...	...	2031	...	...	2131	2131	...	2223	...	2325
København H 710 720 § d.	1552	1550	1632	1652	1650	1732	1752	1750	1832	1852	1850	1932	1952	1950	2032	2052	2050	2132	2150	2150	...	2250	...	2350
Høje Taastrup 720 § d.	|	1605	|	|	1705	|	|	1805	|	|	1905	|	|	2005	|	|	2105	|	2205	2205	...	2305	...	0005
Roskilde 720 § d.	|	1613	|	|	1713	|	|	1813	|	|	1913	|	|	2013	|	|	2113	|	2213	2213	...	2313	...	0013
Ringsted 710 720 d.	|	1630	1706	|	1730	1806	|	1830	1906	|	1930	2006	|	2030	2106	|	2130	2206	2230	2230	...	2330	...	0031
Slagelse d.	|	1649	1724	|	1749	1825	|	1849	1925	|	1949	2025	|	2049	2125	|	2149	2225	2249	2249	...	2349	...	0049
Korsør d.	|	1659	1733	|	1759	1833	|	1859	1933	|	1958	2033	|	2059	2134	|	2159	2233	2259	2259	...	2359	...	0059
Nyborg d.	|	1712	1746	|	1812	1847	|	1912	1947	|	2012	2047	|	2112	2147	|	2212	2247	2312	2312	...	0012	...	0112
Odense 710 a.	1703**c**	1728	1800	1803**c**	1828	1900	1903**c**	1928	2000	2003**c**	2028	2100	2103**c**	2128	2200	2203	2228	2300	2328	2328	...	0028	...	0128
Odense d.	1706	1731	1809	1806	1831	1909	1906	1931	2009	2006	2031	2109	2106	2131	...	2206	2231	...	...	2331	...	0031	...	...
Middelfart d.	|	1754	1832	|	1854	1932	|	1954	2032	|	2054	2132	|	2154	...	|	2254	...	...	2354	...	0054	...	...
Fredericia a.	1734	1802	...	1834	1902	...	1934	2002	...	2034	2102	...	2134	2202	...	2234	2302	...	...	0002	...	0102	...	...
Fredericia 705 715 d.	1739	*1809*	...	1839	*1909*	...	1939	*2009*	...	2039	*2109*	...	2139	*2209*	...	2239	2308	...	...	0008	...	0108	...	...
Vejle 705 715 d.	1755	*1825*	...	1855	*1925*	...	1955	*2025*	...	2055	*2125*	...	2154	*2229*	...	2254	2328	...	...	0028	...	0123	...	...
Horsens 705 d.	1811	*1841*	...	1911	*1941*	...	2011	*2041*	...	2111	*2141*	...	2211	*2249*	...	2311	2348	...	...	0048	...	0140	...	...
Skanderborg 705 713 d.	1826	*1856*	...	1926	*1956*	...	2026	*2056*	...	2126	*2156*	...	2226	*2304*	...	2326	0004	...	...	0104	...	0156	...	...
Aarhus 705 713 a.	1842	*1912*	...	1942	*2012*	...	2042	*2112*	...	2142	*2212*	...	2242	*2322*	...	2342	0022	...	...	0122	...	0212	...	...

	IC	*IC*		*IC*	*IC*		*IC*	*IC*	*IC*	*Lyn*	*IC*	*IC*	*Lyn*	*IC*	*Lyn*	*IC*	*IC*	*Lyn*	*IC*	*IC*	*IC*	*IC*	*Lyn*	*IC*
	188	**188**		**100**	**102**		**802**	**104**	**104**	**6**	**806**	**108**	**10**	**810**	**612**	**112**	**112**	**14**	**814**	**414**	**416**	**116**	**18**	**818**
	⑥⑦	①–⑤		Ⓐ	Ⓒ		Ⓐ	Ⓒ	Ⓐ	Ⓐ	Ⓐ		Ⓐ	Ⓐ	Ⓐ		Ⓐ			Ⓒ	Ⓐ			
	d	**e**									⊖		⊡	⊖	r				⊖				⊡	⊖
Aarhus 705 713 d.	0037	0037	...	...	0245	...	...	...	...	0415	...	...	0515	...	...	...	0545	0615	...	0637	0645	...	0715	...
Skanderborg 705 713 d.	0054	0054	...	...	0301	...	...	...	...	0432	...	...	0532	...	...	...	0602	0632	...	0656	0702	...	0732	...
Horsens 705 d.	0112	0112	...	...	0317	...	...	...	...	0448	...	...	0548	...	...	...	0618	0648	...	0711	0718	...	0748	...
Vejle 705 715 d.	0131	0131	...	...	0334	...	...	...	...	0505	...	...	0604	...	...	...	0634	0704	...	0731	0734	...	0804	...
Fredericia 705 715 a.	0149	0149	...	...	0349	...	...	...	...	0521	...	...	0621	...	...	...	0649	0721	...	0749	0749	...	0821	...
Fredericia d.	0156	0156	...	...	0356	...	...	...	0456	0527	...	0556	0627	...	0652	...	0656	0727	...	...	...	0756	0827	...
Middelfart d.	0205	0206	...	...	0405	...	...	...	0505	|	0528	0605	|	0628	|	...	0705	|	0728	...	...	0805	|	0828
Odense a.	0228	0232	...	...	0427	...	...	...	0527	0554	0552**c**	0627	0654	0652**c**	0723	...	0727	0754	0752**c**	...	...	0827	0854	0852**c**
Odense d.	0230	0234	...	0409	0430	...	0500	0529	0529	0557	0600	0629	0657	0700	0726	0729	0729	0757	0800	...	...	0829	0857	0900
Nyborg d.	0245	0251	...	0427	0445	...	0514	0547	0547	|	0614	0647	|	0714	|	0747	0747	|	0814	...	...	0847	|	0914
Korsør d.	0259	0306	...	0440	0459	...	0527	0601	0601	|	0627	0701	|	0727	|	0801	0801	|	0827	...	...	0901	|	0927
Slagelse d.	0309	0318	...	0450	0509	...	0536	0611	0611	|	0636	0711	|	0736	|	0811	0811	|	0836	...	...	0911	|	0936
Ringsted 720 a.	0326	0337	...	0507	0527	...	0552	0628	0628	|	0652	0728	|	0752	|	0828	0828	|	0852	...	...	0928	|	0952
Roskilde § 720 a.	0344	0357	...	0525	0544	...	|	0645	0645	|	|	0745	|	|	|	0845	0845	|	|	...	...	0945	|	|
Høje Taastrup § 720 a.	0353	0406	...	0533	0553	...	|	0654	0654	|	|	0754	|	|	|	0854	0854	|	|	...	...	0954	|	|
København H § 720 a.	0410	0417	...	0550	0610	...	0628	0710	0710	0706	0728	0810	0806	0828	0838	0910	0910	0906	0928	...	...	1010	1006	1028
København Lufthavn ✈ a.	0432	0453	...	...	0631	...	...	0731	...	...	...	...	0831	...	0902	...	...	0935	...	...	...	...	1031	...

c – Connects with train in previous column.
d – Also Apr. 21, June 9; not May 30.
e – Also May 30; not Apr. 21, June 9.
r – Not Apr. 14 – 16, May 30, July 7 - Aug. 8.

⊡ – Conveys (12) København - Fredericia - Sønderborg and v.v. (Table **710**).
⊙ – Conveys (12) København - Fredericia - Lunderskov (Table **710**); conveys (12) København - Fredericia - Esbjerg (Table **705**).
⊗ – Change trains at Fredericia on Ⓒ.

⊖ – To / from Esbjerg (Table **705**).
§ – *IC* and *Lyn* trains are not available for local journeys. Frequent local trains run between Roskilde and København.

700 AARHUS - FREDERICIA - ODENSE - KØBENHAVN

Most services from Aarhus start from Aalborg (Table **701**). For through cars from Struer, see Table **715**.

	IC 418 Ⓒ	*IC* 420 Ⓐ	*IC* 120	*Lyn* 22	*IC* 822 ⊖	*IC* 124	*Lyn* 26 ⊡	*IC* 826 ⊖	*IC* 128	*Lyn* 30	*IC* 830 ⊖	*IC* 132	*Lyn* 34 ⊡	*IC* 834 ⊖	*IC* 136	*Lyn* 38	*IC* 838 ⊖	*IC* 140	*Lyn* 42 ⊡	*IC* 842 ⊖	*IC* 144	*Lyn* 46	*IC* 846 ⊖
Aarhus 705 713 d.	0737	0745	...	0815	...	*0845*	0915	...	*0945*	1015	...	*1045*	1115	...	*1145*	1215	...	*1245*	1315	...	1345	1415	...
Skanderborg 705 713 d.	0756	0802	...	0832	...	*0902*	0932	...	*1002*	1032	...	*1102*	1132	...	*1201*	1232	...	*1302*	1332	...	1402	1432	...
Horsens 705 d.	0811	0818	...	0848	...	*0918*	0948	...	*1018*	1048	...	*1118*	1148	...	*1218*	1248	...	*1318*	1348	...	1418	1448	...
Vejle 705 715 d.	0831	0834	...	0904	...	*0934*	1004	...	*1034*	1104	...	*1134*	1204	...	*1234*	1304	...	*1334*	1404	...	1434	1504	...
Fredericia 705 715 a.	0849	0849	...	0921	...	*0949*	1021	...	*1049*	1121	...	*1149*	1221	...	*1249*	1321	...	*1349*	1421	...	1449	1521	...
Fredericia d.	...	...	0856	0927	...	0956	1027	...	1056	1127	...	1156	1227	...	1256	1327	...	1356	1427	...	1456	1527	...
Middelfart d.	...	...	0905	│	0928	1005	│	1028	1105	│	1128	1205	│	1228	1305	│	1328	1405	│	1428	1505	│	1528
Odense a.	...	...	0927	0954	0952**c**	1027	1054	1052**c**	1127	1154	1152**c**	1227	1254	1252**c**	1327	1354	1352**c**	1427	1454	1452**c**	1527	1554	1552**c**
Odense d.	...	...	0929	0957	1000	1029	1057	1100	1129	1157	1200	1229	1257	1300	1329	1357	1400	1429	1457	1500	1529	1557	1600
Nyborg d.	...	...	0947	│	1014	1047	│	1114	1147	│	1214	1247	│	1314	1347	│	1414	1447	│	1514	1547	│	1614
Korsør d.	...	...	1001	│	1027	1101	│	1127	1201	│	1227	1301	│	1327	1401	│	1427	1501	│	1527	1601	│	1627
Slagelse d.	...	...	1011	│	1036	1111	│	1136	1211	│	1236	1311	│	1336	1411	│	1436	1511	│	1536	1611	│	1636
Ringsted 720 a.	...	...	1028	│	1052	1128	│	1152	1228	│	1252	1328	│	1352	1428	│	1452	1528	│	1552	1628	│	1652
Roskilde § 720 a.	...	...	1045	│	│	1145	│	│	1245	│	│	1345	│	│	1445	│	│	1545	│	│	1645	│	│
Høje Taastrup § 720 a.	...	...	1054	│	│	1154	│	│	1254	│	│	1354	│	│	1454	│	│	1554	│	│	1654	│	│
København H § 720 a.	...	...	1110	1106	1128	1210	1206	1228	1310	1306	1328	1410	1406	1428	1510	1506	1528	1610	1606	1628	1710	1706	1728
København Lufthavn ✈ a.	...	...	...	1131	...	...	1235	...	...	1331	...	...	1435	...	...	1531	...	...	1646**h**	...	...	1731	...

	IC 148	*Lyn* 50 ⊡	*IC* 850 ⊖	*Lyn* 652 Ⓐ r	*IC* 152	*Lyn* 54	*IC* 854 ⊖	*IC* 156	*Lyn* 58 ⊡	*IC* 858 ⊖	*IC* 160	*Lyn* 62	*IC* 862 ⊖	*IC* 164	*Lyn* 66 ⊡	*IC* 866 ⊖	*IC* 168	*Lyn* 70	*IC* 172	*Lyn* 74	*IC* 176	*IC* 180 ⑤⑥ k⊕	*IC* 182 ⑦–④ m
Aarhus 705 713 d.	*1445*	1515	...	...	*1545*	1615	...	*1645*	1715	...	*1745*	1815	...	*1845*	1915	...	*1945*	2015	*2045*	2115	2145	2245	2245
Skanderborg 705 713 d.	*1502*	1532	...	...	*1602*	1632	...	*1702*	1732	...	*1802*	1832	...	*1902*	1932	...	*2002*	2032	*2102*	2132	2202	2302	2302
Horsens 705 d.	*1518*	1548	...	...	*1618*	1648	...	*1718*	1748	...	*1818*	1848	...	*1918*	1948	...	*2018*	2048	*2118*	2148	2218	2318	2318
Vejle 705 715 d.	*1534*	1604	...	...	*1634*	1704	...	*1734*	1804	...	*1834*	1904	...	*1934*	2004	...	*2034*	2104	*2134*	2204	2234	2334	2334
Fredericia 705 715 a.	*1549*	1621	...	...	*1649*	1721	...	*1749*	1821	...	*1849*	1921	...	*1949*	2021	...	*2049*	2121	*2149*	2221	2249	2349	2349
Fredericia d.	1556	1627	...	1652	1656	1727	...	1756	1827	...	1856	1927	...	1956	2027	...	2056	2127	2156	...	2256	2356	2356
Middelfart d.	1605	│	1628	│	1705	│	1728	1805	│	1828	1905	│	1928	2005	│	2028	2105	│	2205	...	2305	0005	0006
Odense a.	1627	1654	1652**c**	1724	1727	1754	1752**c**	1827	1854	1852**c**	1927	1954	1952**c**	2027	2054	2052**c**	2127	2154	2227	...	2327	0027	0031
Odense d.	1629	1657	1700	1727	1729	1757	1800	1829	1857	1900	1929	1957	2000	2029	2057	2100	2129	2157	2229	...	2329	0029	0033
Nyborg d.	1647	│	1714	│	1747	│	1814	1847	│	1914	1947	│	2014	2047	│	2114	2147	│	2247	...	2347	0047	0053
Korsør d.	1701	│	1727	│	1801	│	1827	1901	│	1927	2001	│	2027	2101	│	2127	2201	│	2301	...	0001	0101	0108
Slagelse d.	1711	│	1736	│	1811	│	1836	1911	│	1936	2011	│	2036	2111	│	2136	2211	│	2311	...	0011	0111	0119
Ringsted 720 a.	1728	│	1752	│	1828	│	1852	1928	│	1952	2028	│	2052	2128	│	2152	2228	│	2328	...	0028	0128	0138
Roskilde § 720 a.	1745	│	│	│	1845	│	│	1945	│	│	2045	│	│	2145	│	│	2245	│	2345	...	0045	0145	0157
Høje Taastrup § 720 a.	1754	│	│	│	1854	│	│	1954	│	│	2054	│	│	2154	│	│	2254	│	2354	...	0054	0154	0207
København H § 720 a.	1810	1806	1828	1838	1910	1906	1928	2010	2006	2028	2110	2106	2128	2210	2206	2228	2310	2306	0010	...	0110	0210	0225
København Lufthavn ✈ a.	...	1835	...	...	...	1931	...	...	2031	...	...	2131	...	...	2231	...	...	2331	0032	...	0132	0232	0252

c – Connects with train in previous column.
h – 1635 on Ⓒ.
k – Also Apr. 21, June 9.
m – Not Apr. 21, June 9.
r – Not Apr. 14–16, May 30, July 7 - Aug. 8.
⊖ – From Esbjerg (Table **705**).
⊕ – Conveys 🛏 Esbjerg - Fredericia - København (Table **705**).
⊡ – Conveys 🛏 Sønderborg - Fredericia - København (Table **710**).
§ – *IC* and *Lyn* trains are not available for local journeys. Frequent local trains run between Roskilde and København.

701 AARHUS - AALBORG

Note: Train numbers may differ south of Aarhus

km		*IC* 4103 Ⓐ	*IC* 4103 Ⓒ		*IC* 4105 4305 Ⓐ◧	*Lyn* 4007 Ⓐ	*IC* 4109 Ⓐ	*IC* 4109 Ⓒ	*Lyn* 4011 Ⓐ	*IC* 4113 Ⓒ	*IC* 4113 Ⓐ	*Lyn* 4015 Ⓐ	*IC* 4117 4317 ◧	*Lyn* 4019 Ⓐ	*Lyn* 4019	*IC* 4121 4321 ◧	*Lyn* 4023	*IC* 4125 Ⓒ	*IC* 4125 4135 Ⓐ◧	*Lyn* 4027	*IC* 4129 4329 ◧	*Lyn* 4031	*IC* 4133 4333 ◧
	København H 700 d.	0035	0050	...	...	...	0235	0250	...	...	...	...	...	0552	...	...	0652	...	...	0752	...	0852	...
	Odense 700 d.	0223	0230	...	...	...	0426	0431	...	...	...	0606	...	0706	...	...	0806	...	...	0906	...	1006	...
	Fredericia 700 705 d.	0303	0309	...	...	...	0509	0509	...	0601	0609	0639	0709	0739	...	0809	0839	0909	...	0939	1009	1039	1109
0	**Aarhus** 712 d.	0419	0419	...	0519	0549	0619	0619	0649	0719	0719	0749	0819	0849	0849	0919	0949	1019	1019	1049	1119	1149	1219
46	Langå 712 d.	0445	0445	...	0545	│	0645	0645	│	0745	0745	│	0845	│	│	0945	│	1045	1045	│	1145	│	1245
59	Randers d.	0454	0454	...	0554	0619	0654	0654	0719	0754	0754	0818	0854	0918	0918	0954	1018	1054	1054	1118	1154	1218	1254
91	Hobro d.	0510	0510	...	0610	0634	0710	0710	0734	0810	0810	0834	0910	0934	0934	1010	1034	1110	1110	1134	1210	1234	1310
140	**Aalborg** ‡ a.	0546	0546	...	0646	0700	0746	0746	0800	0846	0846	0857	0946	0957	0957	1046	1057	1146	1146	1157	1246	1257	1346
145	Aalborg Lufthavn ✈ ‡ a.	0559	0559	...	...	0712	...	0759	0812	0859	...	0912	...	1012	1012	...	1112	...	...	1212	...	1312	...

	Lyn 4035	*IC* 4137 4337 ◧	*Lyn* 4039	*IC* 4141 4341 ◧	*Lyn* 4043	*IC* 4145 4345 ◧	*Lyn* 4047	*IC* 4149 4349 ◧	*Lyn* 4051	*IC* 4153 4353 ◧	*Lyn* 4055	*IC* 4157	*Lyn* 4059	*IC* 4161	*Lyn* 4063	*IC* 4165	*Lyn* 4067	*IC* 4169	*IC* 4173	*IC* 4177 ⑤⑥	*IC* 4179 ⑦–④	*IC* 4181 ⑤⑥	*IC* 4189 ⑤⑥
København H 700 d.	0952	...	1052	...	1152	...	1252	...	1352	...	1452	...	1552	...	1652	...	1752	...	...	...	2052	2050	2250
Odense 700 d.	1106	...	1206	...	1306	...	1406	...	1506	...	1606	...	1706	...	1806	...	1906	...	...	...	2206	2231	0031
Fredericia 700 705 d.	1139	1209	1239	1309	1339	1409	1439	1509	1539	1609	1639	...	1739	1809	1839	1909	1939	2009	2109	2209	2239	2308	0108
Aarhus 712 d.	1249	1319	1349	1419	1449	1519	1549	1619	1649	1719	1749	1819	1849	1919	1949	2019	2049	2119	2219	2329	2349	0029	0221
Langå 712 d.	│	1345	│	1445	│	1545	│	1645	│	1745	│	1845	│	1945	│	2045	│	2145	2245	2354	0015	0054	0246
Randers d.	1318	1354	1418	1454	1518	1554	1618	1654	1718	1754	1818	1854	1918	1954	2018	2054	2118	2154	2254	0004	0025	0104	0255
Hobro d.	1334	1410	1434	1510	1534	1610	1634	1710	1734	1810	1834	1910	1934	2010	2034	2110	2134	2210	2310	0021	0042	0121	0311
Aalborg ‡ a.	1357	1446	1457	1546	1557	1646	1657	1746	1757	1846	1857	1946	1957	2046	2057	2146	2157	2246	2346	0057	0119	0157	0347
Aalborg Lufthavn ✈ ‡ a.	1412	...	1512	...	1612	...	1712	...	1812	...	1912	...	2012	...	2112	...	2212	2312	...	...	...	...	...

	IC 4102 Ⓒm		*Lyn* 4014 Ⓐ	*IC* 4116 4316 Ⓐ◐	*Lyn* 4018 Ⓐ	*IC* 4118 Ⓒ	*IC* 4120 4320 Ⓐ◐		*Lyn* 4022	*IC* 4124 4324 ◐	*Lyn* 4026	*IC* 4128 4328 ◐	*Lyn* 4030	*IC* 4132 4332 ◐	*Lyn* 4034	*IC* 4136 4336 ◐	*Lyn* 4038	*IC* 4140 4340 ◐	*Lyn* 4042	*IC* 4144 4344 ◐	*Lyn* 4046	*IC* 4148 4348 ◐	*Lyn* 4050
Aalborg Lufthavn ✈ ‡ d.	...	...	...	...	0542	0550	...	...	0642	...	0742	...	0842	...	0942	...	1042	...	1142	...	1242	...	1342
Aalborg ‡ d.	0109	...	0459	0509	0559	0602	0609	...	0659	0709	0759	0809	0859	0909	0959	1009	1059	1109	1159	1209	1259	1309	1359
Hobro d.	0146	...	0521	0546	0621	0639	0646	...	0721	0746	0821	0846	0921	0946	1021	1046	1121	1146	1221	1246	1321	1346	1421
Randers d.	0202	...	0537	0602	0637	0655	0702	...	0737	0802	0837	0902	0937	1002	1037	1102	1137	1202	1237	1302	1337	1402	1437
Langå 712 d.	0211	...	│	0611	│	0703	0711	...	│	0811	│	0911	│	1011	│	1111	│	1211	│	1311	│	1411	│
Aarhus 712 a.	0238	...	0608	0638	0708	0730	0738	...	0808	0838	0908	0938	1008	1038	1108	1138	1208	1238	1308	1338	1408	1438	1508
Fredericia 700 705 a.	0349	...	0721	0749	0821	0849	0849	...	0921	0949	1021	1049	1121	1149	1221	1249	1321	1349	1421	...	1521	1549	1621
Odense 700 a.	0427	...	0754	...	0854	...	...	...	0954	...	1054	...	1154	...	1254	...	1354	...	1454	...	1554	...	1654
København H 700 a.	0610	...	0906	...	1006	...	...	...	1106	...	1206	...	1306	...	1406	...	1506	...	1606	...	1706	...	1806

	IC 4152 4352 ◐	*Lyn* 4054	*IC* 4156 4356 ◐	*Lyn* 4058	*IC* 4160 4360 ◐	*Lyn* 4062	*IC* 4164 4364 ◐	*Lyn* 4066	*IC* 4168	*Lyn* 4070	*IC* 4172	*Lyn* 4074	*IC* 4176		*IC* 4180 ⑤⑥ k	*IC* 4182 ⑦–④ m		*IC* 4184		*IC* 4188 ⑤⑥ d	*IC* 4188 ⑦–④ e		*IC* 4192
Aalborg Lufthavn ✈ ‡ d.	...	1442	...	1542	...	1642	...	1742	...	1842	...	1942	...	...	2055	2055	...	2155	...	2250	2250	...	2350
Aalborg ‡ d.	1409	1459	1509	1559	1609	1659	1709	1759	1809	1859	1909	1959	2009	...	2109	2109	...	2209	...	2302	2302	...	0002
Hobro d.	1446	1521	1546	1621	1646	1721	1746	1821	1846	1921	1946	2021	2046	...	2146	2146	...	2246	...	2339	2339	...	0039
Randers d.	1502	1537	1602	1637	1702	1737	1802	1837	1902	1937	2002	2037	2102	...	2202	2202	...	2302	...	2355	2355	...	0055
Langå 712 d.	1511	│	1611	│	1711	│	1811	│	1911	│	2011	│	2111	...	2211	2211	...	2311	...	0004	0004	...	0104
Aarhus 712 a.	1538	1608	1638	1708	1738	1808	1838	1908	1938	2008	2038	2108	2138	...	2238	2238	...	2338	...	0030	0030	...	0130
Fredericia 700 705 a.	1649	1721	1749	1821	1849	1921	1949	2021	2049	2121	2149	2221	2249	...	2349	2349	...	0049	...	0149	0149	...	...
Odense 700 a.	...	1754	...	1854	...	1954	...	2054	...	2154	...	...	2327	...	0027	0031	...	...	...	0228	0232	...	...
København H 700 a.	...	1906	...	2006	...	2106	...	2206	...	2306	...	...	0110	...	0210	0225	...	...	...	0410	0425	...	...

d – Also Apr. 20, June 8; not May 29.
e – Also May 29; not Apr. 20, June 8.
k – Also Apr. 21, June 9.
m – Not Apr. 21, June 9.
◧ – Timings Langå - Aalborg are 2–3 minutes later on Ⓐ from Mar. 31.
◐ – Timings Aalborg - Langå are 2–3 minutes **earlier** on Ⓐ from Mar. 31.
‡ – Additional trains run Aalborg - Aalborg Lufthavn ✈ and v.v.

HELSINGØR - KØBENHAVN - KØBENHAVN LUFTHAVN ✈ - MALMÖ 703

EASTBOUND

Services operate every 20 minutes (less frequent 0000 - 0400 hours) **Helsingør** - Østerport - København H - København Lufthavn ✈ - **Malmö C**.

Journey times:
Helsingør - København H: 47 minutes;
København H - København Lufthavn ✈: 13 minutes;
København Lufthavn ✈ - Malmö C: 26 minutes.

København H - København Lufthavn ✈ services operate every 10 minutes.

WESTBOUND

Services operate every 20 minutes (less frequent 0000 - 0400 hours) **Malmö C** - København Lufthavn ✈ - København H - Østerport - **Helsingør**.

Journey times:
Malmö C - København Lufthavn ✈: 21 minutes;
København Lufthavn ✈ - København H: 13 minutes;
København H - Helsingør: 46 minutes.

København Lufthavn ✈ - København H services operate every 10 minutes.

KØBENHAVN - HOLBÆK - KALUNDBORG 704

km		Ⓐ	Ⓐ	Ⓒ	Ⓐ	Ⓒ	Ⓐ		Ⓐ	Ⓒ		Ⓐ		Ⓐ	Ⓒ	Ⓐ	Ⓒ	Ⓐ	Ⓒ	Ⓐ					Ⓐr	Ⓐr	Ⓐr
0	**København** H d.	0511	0603	0630	0703	0730	0803	0811	0841	0843	and at	1903	1911	1941	1943	2003	2011	2041	2043	2103	2134	2230	2330		1438	1538	1638
20	Høje Taastrup d.	0525	0615	0645	0715	0746	0815	0825	0855	0855	the same	1915	1925	1955	1955	2015	2025	2055	2055	2115	2149	2245	2345	A	1450	1550	1650
31	Roskilde .... d.	0538	0624	0658	0724	0758	0824	0838	0908	0904	minutes	1924	1938	2008	2004	2024	2038	2108	2104	2124	2202	2258	2358	L	1459	1559	1659
67	**Holbæk**.......... a.	0606	0641	0727	0741	0825	0841	0906	0936	0927	past each	1941	2006	2036	2027	2041	2106	2136	2127	2141	2231	2327	0027	S	1520	1620	1720
67	**Holbæk**.......... d.	...	0643	0730	0743	...	0843	...	...	0930	hour until	1943	...	...	2030	2043	...	...	2130	2143	2234	2330	0030	O	1522	1622	1722
111	**Kalundborg**... a.	...	0725	0813	0825	...	0925	...	...	1013		2025	...	...	2113	2125	...	...	2213	2226	2313	0013	0110		1600	1700	1800

	Ⓐ	Ⓒj	Ⓐr	Ⓐ	Ⓐ	Ⓒ	Ⓐr	Ⓐ	Ⓐ	Ⓒ	Ⓐr	Ⓐ	Ⓐ	Ⓐ	Ⓒ			Ⓐ	Ⓐ	Ⓒ		Ⓐ	Ⓒ				⑤⑥
Kalundborg ....d.	0430	...	0501	...	0537	0550	0601	...	0637	0650	0659	...	0737	...	0750	...	and at	1937	...	1950	...	2037	2050	...	2150	2247	2350
Holbæk...........a.	0508	...	0536	...	0615	0629	0636	...	0715	0729	0736	...	0815	...	0829	...	the same	2015	...	2029	...	2115	2129	...	2229	2329	0029
Holbæk...........d.	0509	0535	0538	0553	0617	0632	0638	0653	0717	0732	0738	0753	0817	0823	0832	0853	minutes	2017	2023	2032	2053	2117	2132	2153	2232	2332	0032
Roskilde ....d.	0540	0604	0601	0622	0637	0702	0701	0722	0737	0802	0801	0822	0837	0852	0857	0922	past each	2037	2052	2057	2122	2137	2157	2222	2303	0003	0103
Høje Taastrup..a.	0551	0615	0608	0633	0643	0714	0708	0733	0743	0814	0808	0833	0843	0903	0903	0933	hour until	2043	2103	2104	2133	2143	2204	2233	2315	0015	0115
København H .a.	0607	0630	0622	0649	0657	0730	0722	0749	0757	0830	0822	0849	0857	0919	0917	0949		2057	2119	2117	2149	2157	2217	2249	2330	0030	0130

j – Also May 30; not Apr. 21, June 9.

r – Not Apr. 14 – 16, May 30, June 5, July 7 - Aug. 8.

AARHUS - FREDERICIA - ESBJERG 705

km		*IC* 404		*IC* 408	*IC* 815	3312	2912	*IC* 412	*IC* 819	*IC* 414	*IC* 416	*IC* 823	*IC* 823	*IC* 418	*IC* 420	*IC* 827	*IC* 424	*IC* 831	*IC* 428	*IC* 835	*IC* 432	*IC* 839	*IC* 436	*IC* 843
		Ⓐ			Ⓐ	Ⓐ A	Ⓐ B		Ⓐ	Ⓒ	Ⓐ		Ⓐ	Ⓒ	Ⓐ									
	Aarhus.................. **700 713** d.	...	...	...	...	0533	0533	...	...	0637	0645	...	...	0737	0745	...	0845	...	0945	...	1045	...	1145	...
	Skanderborg.......... **700 713** d.	...	...	...	...	0550	0552	...	...	0656	0702	...	...	0756	0802	...	0902	...	1002	...	1102	...	1201	...
	Horsens........................ **700** d.	...	...	...	...	0606	0607	...	...	0711	0718	...	...	0811	0818	...	0918	...	1018	...	1118	...	1218	...
	Vejle...................... **700 715** d.	...	...	...	...	0625	0627	...	...	0731	0734	...	...	0831	0834	...	0934	...	1034	...	1134	...	1234	...
	København H **700** ....d.	...	...	...	...	|	|	...	0532	|	|	...	0632	|	|	0732	|	0832	|	0932	|	1032	|	1132
	Odense .... **700** d.	...	...	...	0609	|	|	...	0709	|	|	0809	0809	|	|	0909	|	1009	|	1109	|	1209	|	1309
0	Middelfart.................. **700** d.	...	...	...	0632	|	|	...	0732	|	|	0832	0832	|	|	0932	|	1032	|	1132	|	1232	|	1332
	Fredericia .... **700 710 715** d.	0505	...	0605	|	0644	0646	0651	|	0751	0751	|	|	0851	0851	|	0951	|	1051	|	1151	|	1251	|
23	Kolding .... **710** d.	0520	...	0620	0648	...	...	0706	0748	0806	0806	0848	0848	0906	0906	0948	1006	1048	1106	1148	1206	1248	1306	1348
36	Lunderskov.................. **710** d.	0528	...	0628	0656	...	...	0714	|	0814	0814	|	|	0914	0914	|	1014	|	1114	|	1214	|	1314	|
47	Vejen..................................d.	0535	...	0635	0703	...	...	0721	0802	0827	0827	0902	0902	0921	0921	1002	1021	1102	1121	1202	1221	1302	1321	1402
75	Bramming..................... **709** d.	0558	...	0658	0724	...	...	0744	0818	0844	0844	0918	0918	0944	0944	1018	1044	1118	1144	1218	1244	1318	1344	1418
91	**Esbjerg**...................... **709** a.	0608	...	0708	0734	...	...	0754	0828	0854	0854	0928	0928	0954	0954	1028	1054	1128	1154	1228	1254	1328	1354	1428

	IC 440	*IC* 847	*IC* 3344 444 A	*IC* 2944 444 B	*IC* 851	*IC* 448	*IC* 855	*IC* 452	*IC* 859	*IC* 456	*IC* 863	*IC* 460	*IC* 867	*IC* 464	*IC* 871	*IC* 468	*IC* 875	*IC* 472		*IC* 176	*IC* 181 476			
Aarhus.................. **700 713** d.	1245	...	1333	...	...	1445	...	1545	...	1645	...	1745	...	1845	...	1945	...	2045	...	2145	...	...	...	...
Skanderborg.......... **700 713** d.	1302	...	1350	1352	...	1502	...	1602	...	1702	...	1802	...	1902	...	2002	...	2102	...	2202	...	...	...	...
Horsens........................ **700** d.	1318	...	1406	1407	...	1518	...	1618	...	1718	...	1818	...	1918	...	2018	...	2118	...	2218	...	...	...	...
Vejle...................... **700 715** d.	1334	...	1425	1427	...	1534	...	1634	...	1734	...	1834	...	1934	...	2034	...	2134	...	2234	...	...	...	...
København H **700** ....d.	|	1232	|	|	1332	|	1432	|	1532	|	1632	|	1732	|	1832	|	1932	|	...	|	2050	...	...	...
Odense.................... **700** d.	|	1409	|	|	1509	|	1609	|	1709	|	1809	|	1909	|	2009	|	2109	|	...	|	2231	...	...	...
Middelfart.................. **700** d.	|	1432	|	|	1532	|	1632	|	1732	|	1832	|	1932	|	2032	|	2132	|	...	|	2254	...	...	...
Fredericia .... **700 710 715** d.	1351	|	1451	1451	|	1551	|	1651	|	1751	|	1851	|	1951	|	2051	|	2151	...	2249	2312	...	...	...
Kolding .... **710** d.	1406	1448	1506	1506	1548	1606	1648	1706	1748	1806	1848	1906	1948	2006	2048	2106	2148	2206	...	...	2327	...	...	...
Lunderskov.................. **710** d.	1414	|	1514	1514	|	1614	|	1714	|	1814	|	1914	|	2014	|	2114	|	2214	...	...	2335	...	...	...
Vejen..................................d.	1421	1502	1521	1521	1602	1621	1702	1721	1802	1821	1902	1921	2002	2021	2102	2121	2202	2221	...	...	2342	...	...	...
Bramming..................... **709** d.	1444	1518	1544	1544	1618	1644	1718	1744	1818	1844	1918	1944	2018	2044	2118	2144	2218	2244	...	...	0005	...	...	...
Esbjerg...................... **709** a.	1454	1528	1554	1554	1628	1654	1728	1754	1828	1854	1928	1954	2028	2054	2128	2154	2228	2254	...	...	0015	...	...	...

	IC 806	*IC* 413	*IC* 810	*IC* 417	*IC* 814	*IC* 421	*IC* 818	*IC* 423	*IC* 425 2925	*IC* 425 3325	*IC* 822	*IC* 429	*IC* 826	*IC* 433	*IC* 830	*IC* 437	*IC* 834	*IC* 441	*IC* 838	*IC* 445	*IC* 842	*IC* 449	*IC* 846	*IC* 453
	Ⓐ	Ⓐ	Ⓐ					Ⓒ	Ⓐ B	Ⓐ A														
Esbjerg...................... **709** d.	0433	0502	0533	0602	0633	0702	0733	0804	0804	0804	0833	0904	0933	1004	1033	1104	1133	1204	1233	1304	1333	1404	1433	1504
Bramming..................... **709** d.	0444	0513	0544	0613	0644	0713	0744	0815	0815	0815	0844	0915	0944	1015	1044	1115	1144	1215	1244	1315	1344	1415	1444	1515
Vejen..................................d.	0458	0535	0558	0635	0658	0735	0758	0837	0837	0837	0858	0937	0958	1037	1058	1137	1158	1237	1258	1337	1358	1437	1458	1537
Lunderskov.................. **710** d.	|	0543	|	0643	|	0743	|	0845	0845	0845	|	0945	|	1045	|	1145	|	1245	|	1345	|	1445	|	1545
Kolding .... **710** d.	0513	0552	0613	0652	0713	0752	0813	0854	0854	0854	0913	0954	1013	1054	1113	1154	1213	1254	1313	1354	1413	1454	1513	1554
Fredericia .... **700 710 715** d.	|	0609	|	0709	|	0809	|	0909	0912	0912	|	1009	|	1109	|	1209	|	1309	|	1409	|	1509	|	1609
Middelfart.................. **700** d.	0528	|	0628	|	0728	|	0828	|	|	|	0928	|	1028	|	1128	|	1228	|	1328	|	1428	|	1528	|
Odense..................... **700** a.	0552	|	0652	|	0752	|	0852	|	|	|	0952	|	1052	|	1152	|	1252	|	1352	|	1452	|	1552	|
København H **700** ....a.	0728	|	0828	|	0928	|	1028	|	|	|	1128	|	1228	|	1328	|	1428	|	1528	|	1628	|	1728	|
Vejle...................... **700 715** d.	...	0625	...	0725	...	0825	...	0925	0931	0932	...	1025	...	1125	...	1225	...	1325	...	1425	...	1525	...	1625
Horsens........................ **700** d.	...	0641	...	0741	...	0841	...	0941	0951	0952	...	1041	...	1141	...	1241	...	1341	...	1441	...	1541	...	1641
Skanderborg.......... **700 713** d.	...	0656	...	0756	...	0856	...	0956	1005	1007	...	1056	...	1156	...	1256	...	1356	...	1456	...	1556	...	1656
Aarhus.................. **700 713** a.	...	0712	...	0812	...	0912	...	1012	...	1023	...	1112	...	1212	...	1312	...	1412	...	1512	...	1612	...	1712

	IC 850	*IC* 457 2957 B	*IC* 457 3357 A	*IC* 854	*IC* 461	*IC* 858	*IC* 465	*IC* 862	*IC* 469	*IC* 866	*IC* 473		*IC* 477		*IC* 483	*IC* 483 180 ⑤⑥c	*IC* 485 185		*IC* 487	*IC* 189				
Esbjerg...................... **709** d.	1533	1604	1604	1633	1704	1733	1804	1833	1904	1933	2004	...	2104	...	2241	2241	...	...	2341	...	...	...	...	...
Bramming..................... **709** d.	1544	1615	1615	1644	1715	1744	1815	1844	1915	1944	2015	...	2115	...	2252	2252	...	...	2352	...	...	...	...	...
Vejen..................................d.	1558	1637	1637	1658	1737	1758	1837	1858	1937	1958	2037	...	2137	...	2314	2314	...	...	0014	...	...	...	...	...
Lunderskov.................. **710** d.	|	1644	1644	|	1745	|	1845	|	1945	|	2045	...	2145	...	2322	2322	...	...	0022	...	...	...	...	...
Kolding .... **710** d.	1613	1653	1653	1713	1754	1813	1854	1913	1954	2013	2054	...	2154	...	2331	2331	...	...	0031	...	...	...	...	...
Fredericia .... **700 710 715** d.	|	1712	1712	|	1809	|	1909	|	2009	|	2109	...	2209	...	2345	2356	0008	...	0045	0108	...	...	...	...
Middelfart.................. **700** d.	1628	|	|	1728	|	1828	|	1928	|	2028	|	...	|	...	...	0005	|	...	...	|	...	...	...	...
Odense..................... **700** a.	1652	|	|	1752	|	1852	|	1952	|	2052	|	...	|	...	...	0027	|	...	...	|	...	...	...	...
København H **700** ....a.	1828	|	|	1928	|	2028	|	2128	|	2228	|	...	|	...	...	0210	|	...	...	|	...	...	...	...
Vejle...................... **700 715** d.	...	1731	1732	...	1825	...	1925	...	2025	...	2125	...	2229	...	...	...	0028	...	...	0123	...	...	...	...
Horsens........................ **700** d.	...	1751	1752	...	1841	...	1941	...	2041	...	2141	...	2249	...	...	...	0048	...	...	0140	...	...	...	...
Skanderborg.......... **700 713** d.	...	1805	1807	...	1856	...	1956	...	2056	...	2156	...	2304	...	...	...	0104	...	...	0156	...	...	...	...
Aarhus.................. **700 713** a.	...	...	1823	...	1912	...	2012	...	2112	...	2212	...	2322	...	...	...	0122	...	...	0212	...	...	...	...

A – Until Mar. 29.

B – From Mar. 30.

c – Also Apr. 21, June 9.

707 ESBJERG - SKJERN

Operator: *GC* (2nd class only)

km		Ⓐ	Ⓐ	Ⓐ	Ⓐ	Ⓐ	Ⓐ		Ⓐ	Ⓐ	Ⓐ	Ⓐ	Ⓐ	Ⓐ	Ⓐ	Ⓐ	Ⓒ	⑥	⑦	⑥	Ⓒ		Ⓒ	Ⓒ	Ⓒ
0	**Esbjerg** ▷ d.		0443	0540	0633	0759	0859		1559	1659	...	1838	...	2038	...	2238		...	...	0616	0816		2016	2216	2317
17	Varde ▷ a.		0502	0558	0651	0816	0918	and	1618	1718	...	1856	...	2056	...	2256		...	...	0635	0835	and every	2035	2235	2335
17	Varde d.		0503	0600	0653	0829	0929	hourly	1629	...	1729	...	1904	...	2104	2304		0436	0636	0636	0836	**two** hours	2036	2236	...
60	**Skjern** a.		0540	0637	0733	0911	1011	until	1711	...	1811	...	1941	...	2141	2341		0512	0712	0712	0912	until	2112	2312	...
	Herning **713** a.		0622	0722	0822	0954	1054		1754	...	...	...	2021	...	2221	0021		0554	0754	0754	0954		2154	2354	...
	Aarhus **713** a.		...	...	...	1131e	1231		1931	...	...	...	...	...	...	...		0731	0931	0931	1131		2331	...	...

	Ⓐ	Ⓐ	Ⓐ	Ⓐ	Ⓐ	Ⓐ		Ⓐ	Ⓐ	Ⓐ	Ⓐ	Ⓐ	Ⓐ	Ⓐ	Ⓐ	Ⓐ	Ⓐ	Ⓒ	⑥	⑦	⑥	Ⓒ		Ⓒ	Ⓒ
Aarhus **713** d.		...	...	...	0623	0723		1423	...	1523	...	...	1723	...	1923	...	2123		...	...	0523	0723		1923	2123
Herning **713** d.		0434	0556	0656	0756	0902	and	1602	...	1702	...	...	1902	...	2102	...	2302		0502	0702	0702	0902	and every	2102	2302
Skjern d.		0513	0642	0738	0841	0941	hourly	1641	...	1741	1816	...	1955	...	2155	...	2349		0542	0742	0742	0942	**two** hours	2142	2342
Varde a.		0552	0725	0817	0918	1018	until	1718	...	1818	1853	...	2032	...	2232	...	0026		0618	0818	0818	1018	until	2218	0018
Varde ▷ d.		0607	0726	0819	0919	1019		1719	1757	...	...	1857	...	2040	...	2240	...		0619	0819	0819	1019		2219	...
Esbjerg ▷ a.		0628	0744	0837	0937	1037		1737	1815	...	...	1915	...	2058	...	2258	...		0637	0837	0837	1037		2237	...

e – Until Mar. 31.

▷ – Additional services operate Esbjerg - Varde and v.v.

708 SKJERN - HOLSTEBRO

Operator: *Midttrafik* (2nd class only)

km		Ⓐ	Ⓐ	Ⓐ	Ⓐ	Ⓐ	Ⓐ	Ⓐ	Ⓐ	Ⓐ	Ⓐ	Ⓐ	Ⓐ	Ⓐ	Ⓐ	Ⓐ	Ⓐ	Ⓐ		Ⓒ	Ⓒ		Ⓒ	Ⓒ	Ⓒ
0	**Skjern** d.		0504	0619	0715	0800	0905	1044	1138	1238	1338	1438	1538	1638	1738	1911	2011	2136	...		0716	and every	1916	2015	2216
23	Ringkøbing d.		0524	0639	0736	0819	0923	1102	1156	1256	1405	1505	1557	1657	1757	1930	2030	2154	...		0736	**two** hours	1936	2033	2236
71	**Holstebro** a.		0605	0721	0821	0859	1008	1142	1240	1340	1446	1546	1640	1737	1840	2010	2110	2234	...		0816	until	2016	2113	2316

	Ⓐ	Ⓐ	Ⓐ	Ⓐ	Ⓐ	Ⓐ	Ⓐ	Ⓐ	Ⓐ	Ⓐ	Ⓐ	Ⓐ	Ⓐ	Ⓐ	Ⓐ	Ⓐ	Ⓐ		Ⓒ	Ⓒ	Ⓒ		Ⓒ	Ⓒ	Ⓒ
Holstebro d.		0443	0533	0636	0737	0936	1021	1108	1208	1308	1415	1515	1608	1807	1849	2025	2242	...		0736	0836	and every	1836	2036	2136
Ringkøbing d.		0524	0617	0716	0819	1016	1102	1157	1257	1357	1457	1557	1657	1848	1930	2108	2323	...		0826	0916	**two** hours	1916	2123	2216
Skjern a.		0542	0637	0734	0837	1034	1120	1215	1315	1415	1515	1615	1715	1906	1948	2126	2341	...		0844	0934	until	1934	2141	2234

709 ESBJERG - TØNDER - NIEBÜLL

Operator: *GC* (2nd class only)

km		Ⓐ	Ⓐ	Ⓐ	Ⓐ	Ⓐ		Ⓐ	Ⓐ	Ⓐ	Ⓐ	Ⓐ	Ⓐ	Ⓐ	Ⓐ	Ⓐ	Ⓒ	⑦	⑥	Ⓒ		Ⓒ	Ⓒ	Ⓒ	Ⓒ
0	**Esbjerg** ▷ **705** d.		0523	0623	0718	0754	and	1454	1554	1710	1810	1910	2010	2110	2210	2310		...	0609	0809	and every	2009	2053	2209	2253
16	Bramming ▷ **705** d.		0538	0638	0733	0810	hourly	1510	1610	1725	1825	1925	2025	2125	2225	2325		...	0624	0824	**two** hours	2024	2108	2224	2308
33	Ribe ▷ d.		0603	0703	0750	0830	until	1530	1636	1744	1844	1944	2044	2143	2244	2343		0641	0641	0841	until	2041	2125	2241	2325
80	**Tønder** a.		0650	0754	...	0921		1621	1728	1831	1931	2031	2131	...	2331	...		0728	0728	0928		2128	...	2328	...

	Ⓐ	Ⓐ	Ⓐ	Ⓐ	Ⓐ		Ⓐ	Ⓐ	Ⓐ	Ⓐ	Ⓐ	Ⓐ	Ⓐ	Ⓐ	Ⓐ	⑤	Ⓒ	⑥	Ⓒ		Ⓒ	Ⓒ		⑦	⑥
Tønder d.		...	0553	0658	0826	and	1526	1633	1736	1836	1936	2036	2136	...	2336	2336		0534	0734	and every	2134	...	...	2334	2334
Ribe ▷ d.		0545	0644	0751	0913	hourly	1613	1721	1824	1924	2024	2124	2224	2348	0022	0023		0621	0821	**two** hours	2221	2330	...	0020	0021
Bramming ▷ **705** d.		0603	0703	0808	0929	until	1629	1749j	1849j	1949j	2049j	2149j	2249j	0010	...	0041		0645	0849j	until	2249j	2348	...	...	0039
Esbjerg ▷ **705** a.		0618	0718	0822	0944		1644	1804	1904	2004	2104	2204	2304	0025	...	0057		0700	0904		2304	0003	...	...	0055

TØNDER - NIEBÜLL. *17 km.* Journey time: 18 – 19 minutes. Operated by Norddeutsche Eisenbahn. Danish public holiday dates apply.
From Tønder: On Ⓐ at 0704 **b**, 0832 **b**, 1032, 1232, 1344 **c**, 1432, 1532, 1632, 1836, 1936 and 2136. On Ⓒ at 0732 ⑥, 0932 and every **two** hours until 2132.
From Niebüll: On Ⓐ at 0636 **b**, 0733 **b**, 1006, 1206, 1322 **d**, 1406, 1506, 1607, 1807, 1907 and 2107. On Ⓒ at 0707 ⑥, 0907 and every **two** hours until 2107.

b – Also Apr. 17.
c – 1332 Apr. 11 – 25, July 28 - Sept. 5 and Oct. 20 – 31.
d – 1306 Apr. 11 – 25, July 28 - Sept. 5 and Oct. 20 – 31.

j – Arrives 6 – 9 minutes earlier.

▷ – Additional services operate Esbjerg - Ribe and v.v. See Table **705** for other services Esbjerg - Bramming and v.v.

710 KØBENHAVN - FREDERICIA - SØNDERBORG and FLENSBURG

See Table **705** for other *IC* services København - Odense - Kolding - Lunderskov and v.v.

km		*IC* **5751** ①–⑥		*Lyn* **911** Ⓐ	*IC* **5753**	*Lyn* **19** **919** Ⓐ	**921** Ⓒ	*EC* **391** **R**	*IC* **5755**	*Lyn* **27** **927**	*EC* **393** **R**	*IC* **5757**	*Lyn* **35** **935**	*EC* **395** **R**	*IC* **5759**	*Lyn* **43** **943**	*EC* **1197** **S** **R**	*IC* **5761**	*Lyn* **51** **951**	*EC* **397** **R**	*IC* **5763**	*Lyn* **59** **959**	*EC* **399** **R**	*IC* **5765**
	København H **700** d.	...	...	...	...	0552	...	0622	...	0752	0822	...	0952	1022	...	1152	1207	...	1352	1422	...	1552	1622	...
	Ringsted **700** d.	...	...	...	...	|	...	0652	...	|	0852	...	|	1052	...	|	1250	...	|	1452	...	|	1652	...
	Odense **700** d.	...	...	0506	...	0706	...	0735	...	0906	0935	...	1106	1135	...	1306	1335	...	1506	1535	...	1706	1735	...
0	**Fredericia** **700 705** d.	0430	...	0542	0630	0742	0742	|	0830	0942	|	1030	1142	|	1230	1342	|	1430	1542	|	1630	1742	|	1830
20	Kolding **705** d.	0443	...	0555	0643	0755	0755	0815	0843	0955	1015	1043	1155	1215	1243	1355	1415	1443	1555	1615	1643	1755	1815	1843
33	Lunderskov **705** d.	0451	...	0603	0651	0803	0803	|	0851	1003	|	1051	1203	|	1251	1403	|	1451	1603	|	1651	1803	|	1851
60	Vojens d.	0508	...	0620	0708	0820	0820	|	0908	1020	|	1108	1220	|	1308	1420	|	1508	1620	|	1708	1820	|	1908
95	Tinglev d.	0529	...	0641	0729	0841	0841	|	0929	1041	|	1129	1241	|	1329	1441	|	1529	1641	|	1729	1841	|	1929
136	**Sønderborg** a.	|	...	0713	|	0913	0913	|	|	1113	|	|	1313	|	|	1513	|	|	1713	|	|	1913	|	|
110	Padborg 🏛 a.	0539	...	...	0739	...	...	0857	0939	...	1057	1139	...	1257	1339	...	1459	1539	...	1657	1739	...	1857	1939
122	**Flensburg** 🏛 a.	0553	...	...	0753	...	...	|	0953	...	|	1153	...	|	1353	...	|	1553	...	|	1753	...	|	1953
302	*Hamburg Hbf* **50 823** a.	...	...	...	...	...	...	1101	...	...	1302	...	...	1500	...	...	1703	...	...	1902	...	...	2108	...

	Lyn **67** **967**	*EC* **1199** **T** **R**	*IC* **5767**	*Lyn* **75** **975**	*IC* **181** **476**	**983**		*EC* **1195** Ⓑ**C** **R**	
København H **700** d.	1752	1822	...	1952	2050	...	...	2335	...
Ringsted **700** d.	|	1852	...	|	2130	...	...	0007	...
Odense **700** d.	1906	1935	...	2106	2231	...	...	0055	...
Fredericia **700 705** d.	1942	|	2030	2142	2312	2356	...	|	...
Kolding **705** d.	1955	2015	2043	2155	2327	0009	...	0144	...
Lunderskov **705** d.	2003	|	2051	2203	2335	0017	...	|	...
Vojens d.	2020	|	2108	2220	...	0034	...	|	...
Tinglev d.	2041	|	2129	2241	...	0055	...	|	...
Sønderborg a.	2113	|	|	2313	...	0127	...	|	...
Padborg 🏛 a.	...	2057	2139	...	...	...	...	0301	...
Flensburg 🏛 a.	...	|	2153	...	...	...	...	0337	...
Hamburg Hbf **50 823** a.	...	2303	...	...	...	...	...	0546	...

	Lyn **910** **10** Ⓐ		*IC* **5750** ①–⑥	*Lyn* **918** **18**	*IC* **5752**	*EC* **1198** **T** **R**	*Lyn* **926** **26**	*IC* **5754**	*EC* **398** **R**
Hamburg Hbf **50 823** d.	...	...	...	...	...	0703	...	...	0850
Flensburg 🏛 d.	...	...	0605	...	0805	|	...	1005	|
Padborg 🏛 d.	...	...	0621	...	0821	0903	...	1021	1103
Sønderborg d.	0445	...	|	0645	|	|	0845	|	|
Tinglev d.	0520	...	0632	0720	0832	|	0920	1032	|
Vojens d.	0540	...	0652	0740	0852	|	0940	1052	|
Lunderskov **705** d.	0556	...	0709	0756	0909	|	0956	1109	|
Kolding **705** d.	0605	...	0718	0805	0918	0946	1005	1118	1146
Fredericia **700 705** a.	0617	...	0730	0817	0930	|	1017	1130	|
Odense **700** a.	0654	...	...	0854	...	1023	1054	...	1223
Ringsted **700** a.	|	...	...	|	...	1107	|	...	1307
København H **700** a.	0806	...	...	1006	...	1138	1206	...	1338

	Lyn **934** **34**	*IC* **5756**	*EC* **396** **R**	*Lyn* **942** **42**	*IC* **5758**	*EC* **394** **R**	*Lyn* **950** **50**	*IC* **5760**	*EC* **392** **R**	*Lyn* **958** **58**	*IC* **5762**	*EC* **390** **R**	*Lyn* **966** **66**		*IC* **5764**	*EC* **1190** **S** **R**	**974** **2776**		*IC* **5766**	**982**		*EC* **1194** Ⓑ**A** **R**		
Hamburg Hbf **50 823** d.	...	...	1053	...	...	1253	...	...	1456	...	...	1655	...	...	...	1850	...	...	...	...	...	2356	...	...
Flensburg 🏛 d.	...	1205	|	...	1405	|	...	1605	|	...	1805	|	...	...	2005	|	...	...	2205	...	...	0240	...	...
Padborg 🏛 d.	...	1221	1303	...	1421	1503	...	1621	1703	...	1821	1903	...	...	2021	2103	...	...	2221	...	...	0332	...	...
Sønderborg d.	1045	|	|	1245	|	|	1445	|	|	1645	|	|	1845	...	|	|	2045	...	|	2245	...	|	...	...
Tinglev d.	1120	1232	|	1320	1432	|	1520	1632	|	1720	1832	|	1920	...	2032	|	2120	...	2232	2320	...	|	...	...
Vojens d.	1140	1252	|	1340	1452	|	1540	1652	|	1740	1852	|	1940	...	2052	|	2140	...	2252	2340	...	|	...	...
Lunderskov **705** d.	1156	1309	|	1356	1509	|	1556	1709	|	1756	1909	|	1956	...	2109	|	2156	...	2309	2356	...	|	...	...
Kolding **705** d.	1205	1318	1346	1405	1518	1546	1605	1718	1746	1805	1918	1946	2005	...	2118	2146	2205	...	2318	0005	...	0423	...	...
Fredericia **700 705** a.	1217	1330	|	1417	1530	|	1617	1730	|	1817	1930	|	2017	...	2130	|	2217	...	2330	0017	...	|	...	...
Odense **700** a.	1254	...	1423	1454	...	1623	1654	...	1823	1854	...	2023	2054	...	...	2223	2324	...	...	...	...	0508	...	...
Ringsted **700** a.	|	...	1507	|	...	1707	|	...	1907	|	...	2107	|	...	...	2307	...	...	...	...	...	0605	...	...
København H **700** a.	1406	...	1538	1606	...	1738	1806	...	1938	2006	...	2138	2206	...	...	2346	...	...	...	...	...	0638	...	...

A – Ⓑ May 23 - Aug. 31 (also May 29) departing Hamburg (following morning from Flensburg).
C – Ⓑ May 23 - Aug. 31 (also May 29).

R – 🅁 for international journeys.
S – Apr. 11 - Nov. 2.

T – May 23 - Aug. 31.

AARHUS - VIBORG - STRUER 712

Operator: GC (2nd class only)

km			Ⓐ	Ⓐ	Ⓐ	Ⓐ	Ⓐ	Ⓐ		Ⓐ	Ⓐ	Ⓐ	Ⓐ	Ⓐ	Ⓐ	Ⓐ	Ⓐ	Ⓐ	Ⓐ	Ⓐ		Ⓐ		
0	**Aarhus** 701 d.	Ⓐ	0434	0506	0552	*0619*	0703	*0719*	and at	1503	*1519*	1603	*1619*	1703	*1719*	1803	1903	2003	2103	2203	...	2306	...	...
46	Langå 701 a.		0507	0539	0625	*0646*	0736	*0746*	the same	1536	*1547*	1636	*1646*	1736	*1746*	1836	1936	2036	2136	2236	...	2336	...	...
46	Langå d.		0512	0545	0630	0700	0741	0759	minutes	1541	1559	1641	1659	1741	1759	1841	1941	2041	2141	2241	...	2341	...	...
86	Viborg d.		0544	0616	0701	0730	0814	0830	past each	1614	1630	1714	1746j	1814	1830	1914	2014	2114	2214	2314	...	0013	...	...
116	Skive d.		0609	...	0725	...	0842	...	hour until	1642	...	1742	1812	1842	...	1942	2042	2137	2242	2338	...	...	...	...
148	**Struer** a.		0632	...	0749	...	0908	...		1708	...	1808	1834	1908	...	2008	2108	...	2308	2359	...	...	...	...

		⑥	⑥	⑥	⑦	Ⓒ	Ⓒ	Ⓒ	⑦	⑥	Ⓒ		Ⓒ	⑥	⑦	Ⓒ	⑥	⑦	Ⓒ	Ⓒ	Ⓒ		
Aarhus 701 d.	Ⓒ	...	0458	0558	...	0658	0758	0858	0958	0958	1058		1658	1758	1758	1858	1958	1958	2058	2158	2258	...	...
Langå 701 a.		...	0531	0631	...	0731	0831	0931	1031	1031	1131	and	1731	1831	1831	1931	2031	2031	2131	2231	2331	...	...
Langå d.		...	0536	0636	...	0736	0836	0936	1036	1036	1136	hourly	1736	1836	1836	1936	2036	2036	2136	2236	2336	...	...
Viborg d.		0509	0609	0709	0709	0809	0909	1009	1109	1109	1209	until	1809	1909	1909	2009	2109	2109	2209	2309	0008	...	...
Skive d.		0533	0632	0733	0733	0833	0933	1033	1132	1133	1233		1833	1932	1933	2033	2132	2133	2233	2333	...	...	...
Struer a.		0557	...	0757	0757	0857	0957	1057	...	1157	1257		1857	...	1957	2057	...	2157	2257	2357	...	...	...

		Ⓐ	Ⓐ	Ⓐ	Ⓐ	Ⓐ	Ⓐ	Ⓐ	Ⓐ	Ⓐ	Ⓐ		Ⓐ	Ⓐ	Ⓐ	Ⓐ	Ⓐ	Ⓐ	Ⓐ	Ⓐ			
Struer d.	Ⓐ	...	0455	...	0546	0611	0650	...	0754	...	0848	and at	...	1648	1748	1848	1948	2048	...	2248	...	...	...
Skive d.		...	0517	...	0610	0635	0713	...	0816	...	0912	the same	...	1712	1812	1912	2012	2112	2212	2312	...	...	...
Viborg d.		0442	0543	0624	0640r	0710t	0740	0820	0840	0920	0940	minutes	1720	1740	1840	1940	2040	2140	2240	2340	...	...	...
Langå a.		0511	0613	0655	0713	0740	0812	0854	0912	0954	1012	past each	1754	1812	1912	2012	2112	2212	2312	0012	...	...	...
Langå 701 d.		0518	0618	*0709*	0718	*0809*	0818	*0909*	0918	*1009*	1018	hour until	*1809*	1818	1918	2018	2118	2218	2318	0018	...	...	...
Aarhus 701 a.		0551	0651	*0738*	0751	*0838*	0851	*0938*	0951	*1038*	1051		*1838*	1851	1951	2051	2151	2251	2351	0051	...	...	...

		⑥	⑥	⑦	⑥	⑥	⑦	Ⓒ	Ⓒ	Ⓒ	Ⓒ	⑦	⑥	Ⓒ		Ⓒ	⑥	⑦	Ⓒ	⑦	⑥	⑦	⑥
Struer d.	Ⓒ	...	0444	...	0536	...	0644	0736	0836	0936	1036	...	1136	1236		1836	...	1936	2036	2136	...	2236	2236
Skive d.		...	0507	...	0607r	0707	0707	0807r	0907r	1007r	1107r	1207	1207r	1307r	and	1907r	2007	2007r	2107r	2207r	2207	2307r	2307r
Viborg d.		0435	0535	0635	0635	0735	0735	0835	0935	1035	1135	1235	1235	1335	hourly	1935	2035	2035	2135	2235	2235	2334	2335
Langå a.		0507	0607	0707	0707	0807	0807	0907	1007	1107	1207	1307	1307	1407	until	2007	2107	2107	2207	2307	2307	...	0007
Langå 701 d.		0514	0614	0714	0714	0814	0814	0914	1014	1114	1214	1314	1314	1414		2014	2114	2114	2214	2312	2314	...	0014
Aarhus 701 a.		0547	0647	0747	0747	0847	0847	0947	1047	1147	1247	1347	1347	1447		2047	2147	2147	2247	2345	2347	...	0047

j – Arrives 1730. r – Arrives 5–7 minutes earlier. t – Arrives 0700.

AARHUS - HERNING - SKJERN and STRUER 713

Operator: GC (2nd class only)

km					Ⓐ	Ⓐ	Ⓐ	Ⓐ	Ⓐ	Ⓐ	Ⓐ	Ⓐ	Ⓐ		Ⓐ	Ⓐ	Ⓐ	Ⓐ	Ⓐ	Ⓐ	Ⓐ	Ⓐ	Ⓐ	Ⓐ	Ⓐ
0	**Aarhus** 700 705 d.	Ⓐ	...	...	...	...	0453	...	0557	0623	0657	0723	0757	and at	1523	1557	1623	1657	1723	1723	1757	1823	1923	2023	2123
23	Skanderborg 700 705 d.		...	...	...	...	0514	...	0618	0645	0718	0745	0818		1545	1618	1645	1718	1745	1745	1818	1845	1945	2045	2145
53	Silkeborg d.		...	...	...	...	0546	...	0645	0715	0745	0815	0845	the same	1615	1645	1715	1745	1815	1815	1845	1915	2015	2115	2215
94	**Herning** a.		...	...	...	...	0626	...	0725	0753	0823	0853	0923	minutes	1653	1723	1753	1823	1853	1853	1923	1953	2053	2153	2253
94	**Herning** 715 d.		0434	...	0527	0556	0627	0656	0727	0756	0827	0902	0927		1702	1727	...	1827	...	1902	...	...	2102	...	2302
	Holstebro 715 d.		│	...	0605	│	0705	│	0805	│	0905	│	1005	past each	│	1805	...	1905	...	│	...	...	│	...	│
	Struer 715 a.		│	...	0618	│	0718	│	0818	│	0918	│	1018		│	1818	...	1918	...	│	...	...	│	...	│
136	**Skjern** a.		0508	...	...	0630	...	0730	...	0830	...	0936	...	hour until	1736	...	...	...	...	1936	...	...	2136	...	2336

	Ⓐ	Ⓐ			⑥		⑦	⑥	⑥	Ⓒ	Ⓒ	Ⓒ	Ⓒ	Ⓒ	Ⓒ	Ⓒ	Ⓒ	Ⓒ	Ⓒ	Ⓒ	Ⓒ	Ⓒ	Ⓒ	Ⓒ	Ⓒ	⑥
Aarhus 700 705 d.	2223	2336	...	Ⓒ	...	...	...	0523	0623	0723	0823	0923	1023	1123	1223	1323	1423	1523	1623	1723	1823	1923	2023	2123	2223	2323
Skanderborg 700 705 d.	2245	0000	...		...	...	...	0545	0645	0745	0845	0945	1045	1145	1245	1345	1445	1545	1645	1745	1845	1945	2045	2145	2245	2345
Silkeborg d.	2315	0026	...		...	...	...	0615	0715	0815	0915	1015	1115	1215	1315	1415	1515	1615	1715	1815	1915	2015	2115	2215	2315	0014
Herning a.	2352	0104	...		...	...	...	0653	0753	0853	0953	1053	1153	1253	1353	1453	1553	1653	1753	1853	1953	2053	2153	2253	2352	0051
Herning 715 d.	...	...	...		0502	...	0702	0702	...	0902	...	1102	...	1302	...	1502	...	1702	...	1902	...	2102	...	2302	...	...
Holstebro 715 d.	...	...	...		│	...	│	│	...	│	...	│	...	│	...	│	...	│	...	│	...	│	...	│	...	...
Struer 715 a.	...	...	...		│	...	│	│	...	│	...	│	...	│	...	│	...	│	...	│	...	│	...	│	...	...
Skjern a.	...	...	...		0536	...	0736	0736	...	0936	...	1136	...	1336	...	1536	...	1736	...	1936	...	2136	...	2336	...	...

		Ⓐ	Ⓐ	Ⓐ	Ⓐ	Ⓐ	Ⓐ	Ⓐ	Ⓐ	Ⓐ	Ⓐ	Ⓐ	Ⓐ	Ⓐ	Ⓐ	Ⓐ	Ⓐ		Ⓐ	Ⓐ	Ⓐ	Ⓐ	Ⓐ	Ⓐ	Ⓐ
Skjern d.	Ⓐ	...	...	0517	0545	...	...	0645	...	...	0745	...	...	...	0918	...	1018	and at	...	1718	...	...	...	1946	...
Struer 715 d.		...	...	│	│	0532	...	│	0632	...	│	0723	...	0832	│	0932	│		1632	│	1732	...	...	│	...
Holstebro 715 d.		...	...	│	│	0548	...	│	0648	...	│	0748	...	0848	│	0948	│	the same	1648	│	1748	...	...	│	...
Herning 715 a.		...	...	0552	0622	0623	...	0722	0724	...	0822	0824	...	0924	0954	1024	1054		1724	1754	1824	...	...	2021	...
Herning d.		0502	0536	0602	...	0636	0702	...	0730	0802	...	0830	0902	0930	1002	1030	1102	minutes	1730	1802	...	1902	2002	...	2102
Silkeborg d.		0542	0613	0642	...	0713	0742	...	0813	0842	...	0913	0942	1013	1047	1113	1142	past each	1813	1842	...	1942	2042	...	2142
Skanderborg 700 705 d.		0610	0636	0710	...	0736	0810	...	0836	0910	...	0936	1010	1036	1110	1136	1210		1836	1910	...	2010	2110	...	2210
Aarhus 700 705 a.		0631	0657	0731	...	0757	0831	...	0857	0931	...	0957	1031	1057	1131e	1157	1231	hour until	1857	1931	...	2031	2131	...	2231

	Ⓐ	Ⓐ	Ⓐ	Ⓐ			⑥	⑥	Ⓒ	Ⓒ	Ⓒ	Ⓒ	Ⓒ	Ⓒ	Ⓒ	Ⓒ	Ⓒ	Ⓒ	Ⓒ	Ⓒ	Ⓒ	Ⓒ	Ⓒ	Ⓒ	Ⓒ	Ⓒ
Skjern d.	...	2146	...	2346	...	Ⓒ	...	0518	...	0718	...	0918	...	1118	...	1318	...	1518	...	1718	...	1918	...	2118	...	2318
Struer 715 d.	...	│	...	│	...		...	│	...	│	...	│	...	│	...	│	...	│	...	│	...	│	...	│	...	│
Holstebro 715 d.	...	│	...	│	...		...	│	...	│	...	│	...	│	...	│	...	│	...	│	...	│	...	│	...	│
Herning 715 a.	...	2221	...	0021	...		...	0554	...	0754	...	0954	...	1154	...	1354	...	1554	...	1754	...	1954	...	2154	...	2354
Herning d.	2202	...	2335	...	...		0502	0602	0702	0802	0902	1002	1102	1202	1302	1402	1502	1602	1702	1802	1902	2002	2102	2202	2335	...
Silkeborg d.	2242	...	0015	...	...		0542	0642	0742	0842	0942	1042	1142	1242	1342	1442	1542	1642	1742	1842	1942	2042	2142	2242	0015	...
Skanderborg 700 705 d.	2310	...	0041	...	...		0610	0710	0810	0910	1010	1110	1210	1310	1410	1510	1610	1710	1810	1910	2010	2110	2210	2310	0041	...
Aarhus 700 705 a.	2331	...	0105	...	...		0631	0731	0831	0931	1031	1131	1231	1331	1431	1531	1631	1731	1831	1931	2031	2131	2231	2331	0105	...

e – Until Mar. 28.

☛ See Table **715** for other connecting services Herning - Struer and v.v.

VEJLE - HERNING - STRUER 715

Operators: GC (2nd class only), DSB

km								Lyn 23		Lyn 31				Lyn 47				Lyn 63					
		2		2	2	2	2	**723**	2	**731**	2	2	2	**747**	2	2	2	**763**	2	2	2		2
		Ⓒ			Ⓒ	Ⓐ																	
	København H **700** d.	...	...	...	...	...	...	0652	...	0852	...	...	...	1252	...	...	...	1652	...	...	...	...	...
	Odense **700** d.	...	...	...	...	...	...	0806	...	1006	...	...	...	1406	...	...	...	1806	...	...	...	...	...
	Fredericia **700** d.	...	...	...	...	...	...	0843	...	1043	...	...	...	1443	...	...	...	1843	...	...	...	...	...
0	**Vejle** d.	...	...	0503	0603	0603	0703	0803	0903	1003	1103	1203	1303	1403	1503	1603	1703	1803	1903	2003	2103	2203	...	2303
73	Herning a.	...	...	0557	0657	0657	0757	0857	0957	1057	1157	1257	1357	1457	1557	1657	1757	1857	1957	2057	2157	2257	...	2357
73	Herning 713 d.	0459	...	0559	0659	0659	0759	0859	0959	1059	1159	1259	1359	1459	1559	1659	1759	1859	1959	2059	2159	2309	...	...
114	Holstebro 708 713 d.	0534	...	0634	0734	0737	0834	0934	1034	1134	1234	1334	1434	1534	1634	1734	1834	1934	2034	2134	2234	2347	...	...
129	**Struer** 708 713 a.	0548	...	0648	0748	0750	0848	0948	1048	1148	1248	1348	1448	1548	1648	1748	1848	1948	2048	2148	2248	2400	...	...

				Lyn 724	Lyn 722				Lyn 740	Lyn 738		Lyn 748	Lyn 746				Lyn 764	Lyn 762						
	2	2	2	22	22	2	2	2	38	38	2	46	46	2	2	2	62	62	2	2	2	2	2	2
				Ⓒ	Ⓐ				Ⓒ	Ⓐ		Ⓒ	Ⓐ				Ⓒ	Ⓐ						
Struer 708 713 d.	...	0504	0604	0704	0704	0804	0904	1004	1104	1104	1204	1304	1304	1404	1504	1604	1704	1704	1804	1904	2004	2104	2204	2304
Holstebro 708 713 d.	...	0518	0618	0718	0718	0818	0918	1018	1118	1118	1218	1318	1318	1418	1518	1618	1718	1718	1818	1918	2018	2118	2218	2318
Herning 713 a.	...	0552	0652	0751	0752	0852	0952	1052	1151	1152	1252	1351	1352	1452	1552	1652	1751	1752	1852	1951	2051	2151	2251	2351
Herning d.	0459	0559	0659	0759	0759	0859	0959	1059	1159	1159	1259	1359	1359	1459	1559	1659	1759	1759	1859	1959	2059	2159	2301	...
Vejle a.	0555	0655	0755	0855	0855	0955	1055	1155	1256	1256	1355	1455	1455	1555	1655	1755	1855	1855	1955	2055	2155	2255	2356	...
Fredericia **700** a.	...	...	...	0914	0914	...	...	...	1314	1314	...	1514	1514	...	...	...	1914	1914	...	...	...	...	...	...
Odense **700** a.	...	...	...	0954	0954	...	...	...	1354	1354	...	1554	1554	...	...	...	1954	1954	...	...	...	...	...	...
København H **700** a.	...	...	...	1106	1106	...	...	...	1506	1506	...	1706	1706	...	...	...	2106	2106	...	...	...	...	...	...

716 STRUER - THISTED

Operator: *GC* (2nd class only)

km			Ⓐ	Ⓐ	Ⓐ	Ⓐ		Ⓐ	Ⓐ	Ⓐ	Ⓐ	Ⓐ	Ⓐ	Ⓐ	Ⓐ	Ⓐ			⑥	Ⓒ		Ⓒ	⑦	⑥
0	Struer d.	Ⓐ	0415	0516	0607	0707	...	1006	1206	1306	1406	1506	1606	1806	2006	2206	...	Ⓒ	0503	0703	and every	2103	2221	2303
74	Thisted a.		0532	0633	0733	0833	...	1124	1324	1424	1524	1624	1724	1923	2123	2323	...		0621	0821	**two** hours until	2221	2342	0021

		Ⓐ	Ⓐ	Ⓐ	Ⓐ		Ⓐ	Ⓐ	Ⓐ	Ⓐ	Ⓐ	Ⓐ	Ⓐ	Ⓐ	Ⓐ			⑦		⑥	Ⓒ		Ⓒ	⑦
Thisted d.	Ⓐ	0538	0638	0738	0838	...	1138	1329	1429	1529	1629	1735	1935	2135	2330	...	Ⓒ	0029	...	0629	0829	and every	2229	2347
Struer a.		0654	0754	0854	0954	...	1254	1453	1553	1653	1745	1853	2053	2253	0046	...		0148	...	0751	0951	**two** hours until	2351	0106

720 KØBENHAVN - NYKØBING (FALSTER)

km		Ⓐ	Ⓐ	Ⓒ	Ⓐ	Ⓐ	Ⓐ	Ⓐ	Ⓐ		Ⓐ			Ⓐ		Ⓐ			Ⓐ				
0	**København H** 700 704 d.	0456	...	0530	0556	0606	...	...	0626	0656	0707	...	...	0726	0756	0807	...	...	0826	0856	0907	...	...
20	Høje Taastrup 700 704 d.	0510	...	0544	0610	|	←	...	0640	0710	|	←	...	0740	0810	|	←	...	0840	0910	|	←	...
31	Roskilde 700 704 d.	0523	...	0557	0622	|	0623	...	0653	0722	|	0723	...	0753	0822	|	0823	...	0853	0922	|	0923	...
64	Ringsted 700 d.	0545	...	0619	→	0637	0645	...	0715	→	0738	0745	...	0815	→	0838	0845	...	0915	→	0938	0945	...
91	Næstved d.	0601	0613	0636	...	0651	0701	0713	0731	...	0752	0801	0813	0831	...	0852	0901	0913	0931	...	0952	1001	1013
118	Vordingborg d.	...	0630	0653	...	0707	...	0730	...	...	0806	...	0830	...	...	0906	...	0930	...	...	1006	...	1030
147	**Nykøbing** (Falster) ⊙ a.	...	0652	0715	...	0729	...	0752	...	...	0822	...	0852	...	...	0922	...	0952	...	...	1022	...	1052

		Ⓐ																				
København H 700 704 d.	and at	1726	1756	1807	...	...	1856	1907	...	...	1956	2007	...	2056	2107	...	2207	2210	2307	2310	0010	0110
Høje Taastrup 700 704 d.	the same	1740	1810	|	←	...	1910	|	←	...	2010	|	←	2110	|	←	|	2224	|	2324	0024	0124
Roskilde 700 704 d.	minutes	1753	1822	|	1823	...	1922	|	1923	...	2022	|	2023	2122	|	2123	|	2237	|	2337	0037	0137
Ringsted 700 d.	past each	1815	→	1838	1845	...	→	1938	1945	...	→	2038	2045	→	2138	2145	2242	2259	2342	2359	0059	0159
Næstved d.	hour until	1831	...	1852	1901	1913	...	1952	2001	2013	...	2052	2101	...	2152	2201	2256	2314	2356	0014	0116	0214
Vordingborg d.		...	...	1906	...	1930	...	2006	...	2030	...	2109	...	...	2209	...	2313	...	0013	...	0133	...
Nykøbing (Falster) ⊙ a.		...	...	1922	...	1952	...	2022	...	2052	...	2131	...	...	2231	...	2335	...	0035	...	0155	...

	Ⓐ	Ⓐ	Ⓒ	Ⓐ	Ⓐ	Ⓐ	Ⓐ	Ⓒ	Ⓐ	Ⓐ	Ⓐ	Ⓐ			Ⓐ	Ⓐ			Ⓐ	Ⓐ			
Nykøbing (Falster) ⊙ d.	...	*0443*	0504	0508	...	0538	...	0604	0606	...	0638	...	0708	...	0738	...	0808	...	0838	...	0908	...	0938
Vordingborg d.	...	0510	0526	0531	...	0555	0610	0628	0629	...	0655	...	0731	...	0755	...	0831	...	0855	...	0931	...	0955
Næstved d.	0428	0528	0545	0547	0558	0610	0628	0645	0645	0658	0710	0728	0747	0758	0810	0828	0847	0858	0910	0928	0947	0958	1010
Ringsted 700 d.	0444	0544	0601	...	0614	0624	0644	0701	...	0714	0724	0744	...	0814	0824	0844	...	0914	0924	0944	...	1014	1024
Roskilde 700 704 d.	0507	0607	0623	...	0637	|	0707	0723	...	0737	|	0807	...	0837	|	0907	...	0937	|	1007	...	1037	|
Høje Taastrup 700 704 a.	0518	0618	0634	...	0648	|	0718	0734	...	0748	|	0818	...	0848	|	0918	...	0948	|	1018	...	1048	|
København H 700 704 a.	0533	0633	0650	...	0703	0654	0733	0750	...	0803	0754	0833	...	0903	0854	0933	...	1003	0954	1033	...	1103	1054

	Ⓐ					Ⓐ																
Nykøbing (Falster) ⊙ d.	...		1608	...	1638	...	1708	...	1738	1808	...	1838	1908	...	1938	...	2029	...	2126	...	2226	2326
Vordingborg d.	...	and at	1631	...	1655	...	1731	...	1755	1831	...	1855	1931	...	1955	...	2052	...	2149	...	2249	2349
Næstved d.	1028	the same	1647	1658	1710	1728	1747	1758	1810	1847	1858	1910	1947	1958	2010	2058	2110	2158	2207	2245	2307	0007
Ringsted 700 d.	1044	minutes	...	1714	1724	1744	...	1814	1824	...	1914	1924	...	2014	2024	2114	2124	2214	2221	2301	2321	0021
Roskilde 700 704 d.	1107	past each	...	1737	|	1807	...	1837	|	...	1937	|	...	2037	|	2137	|	2237	|	2324	|	|
Høje Taastrup 700 704 a.	1118	hour until	...	1748	|	1818	...	1848	|	...	1948	|	...	2048	|	2148	|	2248	|	2335	|	|
København H 700 704 a.	1133		...	1803	1754	1833	...	1903	1854	...	2003	1954	...	2103	2054	2203	2154	2303	2254	2350	2354	0054

⊙ – **NYKØBING FALSTER - NAKSKOV** and v.v. Journey time: 46–47 minutes. Operator: Lokaltog A/S.
All trains call at Maribo (25 minutes from Nykøbing Falster/22 minutes from Nakskov); operates every 30 minutes on Ⓐ, hourly on Ⓒ, connecting with most rail services listed below (journey time: 40 minutes).
From Nykøbing on Ⓐ at 0506, 0536 and every 30 minutes until 1936; then 2028, 2142, 2242, 2342 and 0042.
From Nykøbing on Ⓒ at 0707, 0807 and hourly until 1807; then 1917, 2028, 2142, 2242, 2342 and 0042.
From Nakskov on Ⓐ at 0408, 0438 and every 30 minutes until 1908; then 2031, 2131, 2231 and 2331.
From Nakskov on Ⓒ at 0557, 0708 and hourly until 1808; then 1934, 2031, 2131, 2231 and 2331.

LINKS TO FERRY PORTS.

Bus 720R Maribo – Rødby Færge and v.v.
Journey time: 40 minutes. Runs every 30 minutes on Ⓐ, hourly on Ⓒ.

Bus 740 Nykøbing Falster – Gedser Færge and v.v.
Journey time: 40 minutes. Runs approximately hourly on Ⓐ, approximately every 2 hours on Ⓒ.

728 AALBORG - SKAGEN and HIRTSHALS

Nordjyske Jernbaner (2nd class only)

km			Ⓐ	Ⓐ	Ⓐ	Ⓐ	Ⓐ	Ⓐ	Ⓐ	★	Ⓐ	Ⓐ		Ⓐ	Ⓐ	Ⓐ	Ⓐ	Ⓐ	Ⓐ	Ⓐ	Ⓐ	Ⓐ	Ⓐ	Ⓐ	Ⓐ
0	**Aalborg** d.	Ⓐ	...	...	0356	...	...	0506	0536	and at	1606	1636	1706	...	1806	...	1906	...	2016	...	2116	...	2216	...	2316
48	Hjørring a.	♥	...	...	0431	...	...	0541	0611	the same	1641	1711	1741	...	1841	...	1941	...	2051	...	2151	...	2251	...	2351
48	Hjørring d.		...	...	0446	0447	0516	0546	0619	minutes	1646	1719	1746	1747	1846	1903	1959	2003	2059	2103	2159	2203	2259	2303	2359
66	**Hirtshals** a.		...	...	...	0509	|	|	0641	past each	|	1742	|	1811	|	1925	|	2025	|	2125	|	2225	|	2325	|
85	**Frederikshavn** a.		...	...	0518	...	0548	0618	...	hour until	1718	...	1818	...	1918	...	2027	...	2127	...	2227	...	2327	...	0027
85	**Frederikshavn** d.		0427	0457	0527	...	0557	0627	...		1727	...	1827	...	1927	...	2038	...	2138	...	2238	...	2338	...	...
125	**Skagen** a.		0504	0534	0604	...	0634	0704	...		1804	...	1904	...	2004	...	2115	...	2215	...	2315	...	0015	...	...

		Ⓒ	Ⓒ	Ⓒ	Ⓒ		Ⓒ	Ⓒ	Ⓒ
Aalborg d.	Ⓒ	0416	...	0616	...	and at	2216	...	2316
Hjørring a.		0451	...	0651	...	the same	2251	...	2351
Hjørring d.		0459	0559	0659	0703	minutes	2259	2303	2359
Hirtshals a.		|	|	|	0725	past each	|	2325	|
Frederikshavn a.		0527	0627	0727	...	hour until	2327	...	0027
Frederikshavn d.		0538	0638	0738	...		2338	...	...
Skagen a.		0615	0715	0815	...		0015	...	...

		Ⓐ	Ⓐ	Ⓐ	Ⓐ	Ⓐ	Ⓐ	Ⓐ	Ⓐ	Ⓐ	
Skagen d.	Ⓐ	...	...	0512	0542	...	0612	...	0712	...	and at
Frederikshavn a.	♣	...	...	0552	0622	...	0652	...	0752	...	the same
Frederikshavn d.		0504	...	0604	0634	...	0704	...	0804	...	minutes
Hirtshals d.		|	0541	|	|	0641	|	0741	|	0842	past each
Hjørring a.		0537	0605	0637	0707	0705	0737	0805	0837	0905	hour until
Hjørring d.		0541	0611	0641	...	0711	0741	0811	0841	0911	
Aalborg a.		0619	0649	0719	...	0749	0819	0849	0919	0949	

	Ⓐ	Ⓐ	Ⓐ	Ⓐ	Ⓐ	Ⓐ	Ⓐ	Ⓐ	Ⓐ	Ⓐ	Ⓐ	Ⓐ	Ⓐ	Ⓐ	Ⓐ	Ⓐ		Ⓒ	Ⓒ	Ⓒ	Ⓒ		Ⓒ	Ⓒ	Ⓒ
Skagen d.	1612	...	1712	...	1742	...	1842	...	1942	...	2042	...	2142	...	2242	2342	Ⓒ	...	...	...	0642	and at	...	2242	2342
Frederikshavn a.	1652	...	1752	...	1822	...	1919	...	2019	...	2119	...	2219	...	2319	0019		...	...	...	0719	the same	...	2319	0019
Frederikshavn d.	1704	...	1804	...	1834	...	1928	...	2028	...	2128	...	2228	...	2328	0028		0528	0628	...	0728	minutes	...	2328	0028
Hirtshals d.	|	1742	|	1830	|	1930	|	2030	|	2130	|	2230	|	2330	|	|		|	|	0730	|	past each	2330	|	|
Hjørring a.	1737	1805	1837	1852	1907	1952	1956	2052	2056	2152	2156	2252	2256	2352	2356	0056		0556	0656	0752	0756	hour until	2352	2356	0056
Hjørring d.	1741	1811	1841	...	1911	...	2004	...	2104	...	2204	...	2304	...	0004	...		0604	0704	...	0804		...	0004	...
Aalborg a.	1819	1849	1919	...	1949	...	2045	...	2145	...	2245	...	2345	...	0045	...		0645	0745	...	0845		...	0045	...

★ – Hjørring d. 0949/1049/1149/1249 (not 0946/1046/1146/1246).
♥ – Additional trains on Ⓐ: Hjørring - Frederikshavn - Skagen at 0616, 0716, 1316, 1416, 1516 and 1616 (departing Frederikshaven at 0657, 0757, 1357, 1457, 1557 and 1657); Hjørring - Hirtshals at 0519, 0547, 0647, 0747, 1347, 1447, 1547 and 1647.
♣ – Additional trains on Ⓐ: Skagen - Frederikshavn - Hjørring at 0642, 0742, 1442, 1542 and 1642 (departing Frederikshavn at 0734, 0834, 1534, 1634 and 1734); Hirtshals - Hjørring at 0610, 0710, 0810, 1411, 1511, 1611, 1711 and 1811.

TRAIN SERVICES IN DENMARK ON AND AROUND PUBLIC HOLIDAYS

On the following dates the service provided is as per the day of the week indicated

Date	DSB	GC	Date	DSB	GC	Date	DSB	GC
Dec. 24	⑥	⑦	Apr. 16	⑤	⑤	May 28	⑤	⑤
Dec. 25	⑦	⑦	Apr. 17	⑥	⑦	May 29	⑥	⑦
Dec. 26	⑦	⑦	Apr. 18	⑥	⑦	June 8	⑦	⑦
Dec. 31	⑥	⑦	Apr. 19	⑥	⑥	June 9	⑦	⑦
Jan. 1	⑦	⑦	Apr. 20	⑦	⑦			
			Apr. 21	⑦	⑦			

ICELAND

There are no railways in Iceland but bus services serve most major settlements. Principal services along road number 1 around the country and some other important routes are shown below. Buses have scheduled stops in all settlements (often at N1 filling stations) but stops at other points along the route are possible with prior agreement with the operator. For comprehensive information on all bus routes, including local services and ferries, see www.publictransport.is and the websites of operators (see bottom of page). Confirm all timings with operators as schedules may change at short notice. Buses may be cancelled, delayed or run to amended schedules during adverse weather conditions, particularly in winter.

Scheduled public bus services (*STR*, *FAS*) and buses to Keflavík airport run all year, although there are no long-distance *STR* services on Dec. 24, 25, 31, Jan. 1. Advance reservation is not possible; tickets must be purchased from the driver. Travelling a full circle around the country by bus is only possible in summer and involves use of local buses in the east.

Scheduled touristic buses operated by private companies (*RE*, *TRX* and *SCA*) run only in summer, serving a few popular tourist destinations in the highlands. These have to be pre-booked, although tickets can also be obtained from the driver if there is space available. Tourist excursions and day tours to other destinations are available all year.

Public holidays in 2025: Jan. 1, Apr. 17, 18, 20, 21, 24, May 1, 29, June 8, 9, 17, Aug. 4, Dec. 25, 26.
No services run on Dec. 25, Jan. 1. Only a limited service runs on Dec. 24, 31.

PRINCIPAL BUS SERVICES 729

REYKJAVÍK - AKUREYRI - EGILSSTADIR

km	*STR Route 57*		④‡	x	⑥‡	⑥‡	†		Ⓑ
0	Reykjavík (BSÍ terminal) ■ ▷ d.	...	*0832***c**	*0832***c**	*0832***c**	...	0840	...	*1700***c**
7	Reykjavík (Mjódd) ■ ▷ d.	...	0900	0900	0900	...	0900	...	1730
89	Borgarnes (N1) ▷ d.	...	1021	1028	1021**b**	1028	1028	...	1858
426	Akureyri (Hof) a.	...	...	1529	...	1529	1529	...	2359
	STR Route 56 ⊙	v							
426	Akureyri (Hof) d.	0800	...	...	...	...	...	...	...
513	Reykjahlíd (Mývatn) N1 d.	0915	...	...	...	...	...	...	...
676	Egilsstadir (Campsite) d.	1122	...	...	...	...	...	...	...

STR Route 56 ⊙			v						
Egilsstadir (Campsite) d.	...	...	1230	...	...	...	...	...	...
Reykjahlíd (Mývatn) N1 d.	...	...	1436	...	...	...	...	...	...
Akureyri (Hof) a.	...	...	1551**b**	...	...	...	...	...	...
STR Route 57	Ⓑ			y	④‡				
Akureyri (Hof) d.	1015	...	...	1620	...	...	...	...	...
Borgarnes (N1) ▷ d.	1523	...	...	2128	2128	...	...	...	...
Reykjavík (Mjódd) ■ ▷ a.	1643	...	...	2243	2243	...	...	...	...
Reykjavík (BSÍ terminal) ■ ▷ a.	*1702***c**	...	...	*2301***c**	*2301***c**	...	...	...	...

EGILSSTADIR - HÖFN

No winter service Breiddalsvík - Djúpivogur and v.v.

km	*STR/FAS Route 91*			Ⓐ	⑥			Ⓐ	
0	Egilsstadir (Campsite) d.	...	...	0902	1002	...	...	1602	...
36	Reydarfjördur (Molinn) a.	...	...	0935	1035	...	...	1635	...
	STR Route 96		Ⓐ	▬	▬	Ⓐ	Ⓐ	Ⓐ	Ⓐ
36	Reydarfjördur (Molinn) d.	...	0757	...	...	1506	1624	1744	1917
56	Fáskrúdsfjördur (Kirkjugardur) a.	...	0817	...	...	1526	1644**b**	1804**b**	1937
	STR Route 92	Ⓐ	▬			▬	Ⓐ**g**	Ⓐ**g**	
56	Fáskrúdsfjördur (Kirkjugardur) d.	0715	...	...	...	...	1648	1815	...
105	Breiddalsvík (Kaupfjelagid) a.	0755	...	...	...	...	1728	1855	...
	STR Route 94	▬	†**R**	**zA**	**wR**	④**A**			
105	Breiddalsvík (Kaupfjelagid) d.	④**R**	...	1220	...	1440	...	...	...
166	Djúpivogur (Hótel Framtíd) d.	1220	1320	1345	1500	1605	...	...	...
269	Höfn í Hornafirdi ★ a.	1415	1515	1515	1650	1735	...	...	...

STR Route 94		①⑤**A**	†**A**	③**A**	④**A**		④**R**	†**R**	**wR**
Höfn í Hornafirdi ★ d.	...	0930	0950	1015	1150	...	1415	1515	1650
Djúpivogur (Hótel Framtíd) d.	...	1115	1135	1200	1335	...	1545	1645	1820
Breiddalsvík (Kaupfjelagid) a.	...	1210	1230	1255	1430	...	▬	▬	...
STR Route 92	Ⓐ	▬	▬	▬	▬		Ⓐ**g**	Ⓐ**g**	
Breiddalsvík (Kaupfjelagid) d.	0625	...	...	...	...	...	1600	1730	...
Fáskrúdsfjördur (Kirkjugardur) a.	0705**b**	...	...	...	...	...	1640	1810**b**	...
STR Route 96	Ⓐ		Ⓐ		Ⓐ	Ⓐ	Ⓐ	Ⓐ	
Fáskrúdsfjördur (Kirkjugardur) d.	0712	...	0822	...	1432	1552	1722	1812	...
Reydarfjördur (Molinn) a.	0722**b**	...	0842	...	1452	1612	1742	1822	...
STR/FAS Route 91	Ⓐ	⑥		Ⓐ					
Reydarfjördur (Molinn) d.	0735	0853	...	1433	...	...	...	...	...
Egilsstadir (Campsite) a.	0805	0926	...	1506	...	...	...	...	...

HÖFN - REYKJAVÍK

km	*operator*	*RE*	*STR*	*STR*	*STR*	*STR*	*STR*	*STR*	*RE*
	route number	HB03	51	51	51	51	51	51	HB03
		B [R]	†	Ⓒ	Ⓒ	**u**	Ⓐ	Ⓐ	**B** [R]
0	Höfn í Hornafirdi ★ d.	...	1025	...	...	1155	...	...	...
79	Jökulsárlón glacier lagoon d.	...	1125	...	...	1255	...	...	...
135	Skaftafell (Service centre) d.	...	1220	...	...	1350	...	...	...
274	Vík í Mýrdal (N1) d.	...	1415**b**	1442	...	1545**b**	1600	...	...
308	Skógar (Waterfall) ● d.	1015	...	1507	...	...	1625	...	...
357	Hvolsvöllur (N1) ● ▷ d.	1115**r**	...	1547	...	...	1705	...	1740
405	Selfoss (N1) ▷ d.	...	...	1627**b**	1629	...	1745**b**	1750	1830
458	Reykjavík (Mjódd) ■ ▷ a.	...	...	...	1724	...	...	1845	|
465	Reykjavík (BSÍ) ■ ▷ a.	...	...	...	*1802***c**	...	...	*1902***c**	1930

operator	*RE*		*STR*	*STR*	*STR*	*STR*	*STR*	*STR*	
route number	HB03		51	51	51	51	51	51	
	B [R]		Ⓒ	Ⓒ	†	Ⓐ	Ⓐ	**u**	
Reykjavík (BSÍ) ■ ▷ d.	0700	...	*1102***c**	...	...	*1232***c**	...	...	...
Reykjavík (Mjódd) ■ ▷ d.	|	...	1130	...	...	1300	...	...	...
Selfoss (N1) ▷ d.	0740	...	1224**b**	1227	...	1354**b**	1357	...	...
Hvolsvöllur (N1) ● ▷ d.	0900	...	...	1307	...	...	1437	...	...
Skógar (Waterfall) ● d.	0945	...	...	1342	...	...	1512	...	...
Vík í Mýrdal (N1) d.	...	...	...	1412**b**	1445	...	1542**b**	1615	...
Skaftafell (Service centre) d.	...	...	...	...	1650	...	...	1820	...
Jökulsárlón glacier lagoon d.	...	...	...	...	1735	...	...	1905	...
Höfn í Hornafirdi ★ a.	...	...	...	...	1835	...	...	2005	...

OTHER SERVICES

Reykjavík - Keflavík Airport: *50 km*, journey ±50 minutes. From BSÍ terminal ■: *flybus*, operator *RE*, connecting with all flights. Optional connecting shuttle services to/from hotels and other locations in the capital area.
Additional stopping services: *STR* route 55, BSÍ (Vatnsmýrarvegur ■) - KEF Airport and v.v. on Ⓐ peak hours only. During off-peak hours and on Ⓒ route 55 only operates Hafnarfjördur (Fjördur) – KEF Airport and v.v. From Reykjavík, use *STR* city route 1 from Skúlagata via Gamla Hringbraut ■ direction Hfj. Skardshlíd and change to route 55 at Hafnarfjördur (Fjördur). 7 – 13 services per day with a total journey time of 75 – 90 minutes.

Reykjavík - Blue Lagoon: *48 km*, journey ±45 minutes. From BSÍ terminal ■: operator *RE*, daily, [R]. From Reykjavík Terminal (Skógarhlíd 10) ■: 'Destination Blue Lagoon', operator *BL*, daily, [R]. Both operators also provide infrequent services KEF Airport - Blue Laggon and v.v. **Note: Blue Lagoon services may be suspended owing to ongoing volcanic activity (check with operator).**

Egilsstadir - Seydisfjördur: *27 km*, journey ±40 minutes, *STR* route 93, operated by *FAS*. Services connect with Smyril Line ferry (Table **2285**). Confirm departure point with operator.
Summer (June 5 - Sept. 4, 2025): From **Egilsstadir** (Campsite) at 0900 Ⓐ, 1005 ⑥, 1050 ④, 1605 Ⓐ. From **Seydisfjördur** (Herdubreid, Austurvegur 4) at 0745 Ⓐ, 0845 ⑥, 1000 ④ **s**, 1430 Ⓐ.
Winter (Sept. 9, 2024 - June 4, 2025): From **Egilsstadir** (Campsite) at 0900 Ⓐ, 1005 ⑥, 1105 **D**, 1605 Ⓐ. From **Seydisfjördur** (Herdubreid, Austurvegur 4) at 0745 Ⓐ, 0845 ⑥, 1010 **D s**, 1430 Ⓐ.

LAUGAVEGUR HIKING TRAIL. **Reykjavík - Landmannalaugar** (*215 km*, journey ± 4 h 15 m): *RE Highland Bus* daily June 14 - Sept. 14, 2025; *TRX Highland Bus* daily June 20 - Sept. 5, 2025. **Reykjavík - Thórsmörk** (*158 km*, journey ± 4 h 30 m): *RE Highland Bus* daily June 2 - Sept. 14, 2025; *TRX Highland Bus* daily June 22 - Sept. 7, 2025. **Hvolsvöllur - Thórsmörk - Skógar**: *SCA* daily May 1 - Nov. 1, 2025. [R] on all routes with operation dependent on weather and highland road conditions (*RE* services are cancelled if no bookings received 24 hours before departure). Departure points: *RE* services from Reykjavík BSÍ terminal; *TRX* services from Reykjavík City Hall (Vonarstræti 4); *SCA* services from Hvolsvöllur N1 and from Skógar waterfall.

A – May 1 - Aug. 31, 2025.
B – June 15 - Sept. 11, 2024 (service cancelled if no bookings received 24 hours before departure).
D – ② Sept. 10 - Nov. 5, 2024 (also Nov. 13, 20); ③ Mar. 19 - May 28, 2025. Connects with Smyril Line ferry; confirm with operator.
R – Nov. 1, 2024 - Apr. 30, 2025. A similar service expected from Sept. 1, 2025 (please check with operator).

b – Passengers connecting with onward services should inform operator/bus driver.
c – Connection with *STR* city route 3 from/to Gamla Hringbraut (next to BSÍ), change at Mjódd (see ■).
g – Runs on demand only. ✆ +354 892 0955 at least six hours before departure.
r – Continues to Reykjavík at 1750 (see later column).
s – Seydisfjördur Smyril Line terminal.
u – ①②④⑤ (not holidays).
v – ①②⑤† Sept. 1, 2024 - June 1, 2025; Ⓑ June 2 - Aug. 31, 2025. From Sept. 1, 2025 services are expected to run on ①②⑤† (please check with operator).
w – ①③⑤.
x – ①②③⑤ (not holidays).
y – ①②③⑤⑥⑦ (also holidays).
z – ①③⑤†. 20 minutes later on †. 45 minutes later on ③.

‡ – Not holidays.
★ – Höfn swimming pool.
● – Additional *SCA* services operate.
▷ – Additional *STR* services operate.
⊙ – Operated by *SBA*.

N1 – Bus stop is at N1 filling station.

Operators:

BL Destination Blue Lagoon ✆ +354 420 8800 www.destinationbluelagoon.is
FAS Ferdathjónusta Austurlands ✆ +354 472 1515 www.straeto.is
RE Reykjavik Excursions ✆ +354 580 5400 www.re.is or www.ioyo.is
SBA SBA Nordurleid ✆ +354 550 0700 www.sba.is
SCA Southcoast Adventure ✆ +354 867 3535 www.southadventure.is
STR Straetó ✆ +354 540 2700 www.straeto.is
TRX TREX ✆ +354 587 6000 www.trex.is

■ – Reykjavík terminals

City Hall, Vonarstræti 4 (city centre)
- *TRX*
- Nearby bus stops Rádhús/MR and Lækjartorg (*STR* city services)

BSÍ/Umferdarmidstödin (city centre, south side)
- BSÍ terminal (*RE*, also certain *STR* services on route 57)
- Bus stop "BSÍ" 50 m north of BSÍ at Vatnsmýrarvegur (*STR* route 55)
- Bus stop "Gamla Hringbraut" 100 m north of BSÍ (*STR* city services)

Reykjavík Terminal, Skógarhlíd 10 (1 km southeast of city centre)
- *BL*
- Bus stop "Klambratún" 400 m north of Skógarhlíd (*STR* city services)

Mjódd bus terminal (7 km southeast of city centre)
- *STR* long distance routes 51, 52, 27 and *STR* city services

Connections between city centre and bus terminals: *STR* city service 3 runs at least every 30 minutes from Grandi to Sel/Fell via Lækjartorg, Rádhús/MR (near city hall), Gamla Hringbraut (near BSÍ), Klambratún (near Skógarhlíd) and Mjódd. Journey time to Mjódd: approximately 28 minutes from Lækjartorg, 17 – 21 minutes from Gamla Hringbraut. Note that long distance services do not wait for delayed city buses. Connections Mjódd - city centre: *STR* city service 3 (direction Grandi), departs at xx21 and xx51 past each hour until 2321. Note that there are no city services on ⑦ and public holiday mornings before 0950.

SWEDEN

SEE MAP PAGE 342

Operators: Most services are operated by Swedish State Railways (SJ): www.sj.se. There are, however, a number of other operators that run services and these are indicated by their initials in the relevant table heading, or at the top of each train column where more than one operator runs services on the same route.

AEX – Arlanda Express; *IB* – Inlandsbanan AB; *NT* – Norrtåg; *Øtåg* – Øresundståg; *ST* – Snälltåget; *Tab* – Tågab; *TiB* – Tåg i Bergslagen; *VRS* – VR Snabbtåg Sverige; Vy – Vy Tåg AB

The Regional Public Transport Authority is responsible for many local services, known collectively as Länstrafik (*LT*). Those shown within these pages are abbreviated as follows: *Krösa* – Krösatågen; *Mal* – Mälartåg; *Skåne* – Skånetrafiken; *V* – Västtågen; *VTAB* – Värmlandstrafik; *XT* – X-Trafik

Services: Trains convey first and second classes of accommodation, unless otherwise shown. The fastest SJ trains are classified *Snabbtåg (Sn)* and *InterCity (IC)*. On overnight trains, sleeping cars (🛏) offer the following accommodation: First-class compartments (one or two berths) with shower and WC. These can only be booked as a private compartment and include breakfast in either the bistro car or at a nearby hotel at your destination. Second-class compartments (three berths) have shared shower and WC facilities in each coach. These can be booked as a private compartment for one, two or three persons, or as a single berth in a shared compartment (male or female). Couchette cars (▬) have six berths which can be booked as a single berth in a shared compartment or as a private compartment when four or more passengers are travelling together.

Timings: Valid until **August 31** unless otherwise stated. **Warning!** Due to widespread engineering work and numerous variations, timings are given as a guide but may alter, and readers are advised to confirm timings and days of running when booking or before travel. Services may be cancelled or retimed during the summer period and it has not been possible to show full details in the tables. In addition, service amendments on and around the dates of public holidays are not always shown, so readers are advised to confirm journey plans if travelling during holiday periods.

Catering: Most long-distance services convey a bistro-car (🍷) serving drinks, snacks and light meals. First-class tickets on *Sn* services includes access to complimentary tea, coffee and snacks, with breakfast also served on departures before 0900. First-class tickets on *MTR* services include a complimentary meal and drinks.

Tickets: Travellers must ensure they are in possession of a valid ticket before joining a train; a penalty fare will be charged if you do not have a valid ticket. Note that there are no staffed ticket offices in Sweden and automatic ticket machines have also been phased out. Readers are therefore advised to purchase tickets on-line at www.sj.se before travelling. However, it is possible to purchase and collect SJ tickets at all Pressbyrån shops and certain 7-Eleven stores (some of which are located at rail stations).

Reservations: Seat reservation is compulsory on all *Snabbtåg*, *InterCity*, *MTRX*, *Snälltåget* and overnight trains. Reserved seats are not labelled and, if occupied, should be claimed by presenting the seat ticket on the train.

730 STOCKHOLM - MALMÖ - KØBENHAVN

Subject to alteration due to engineering work. See Table **730a** for other regional and *IC* services Stockholm - Norrköping - Linköping.
Trains in this table are not available for local journeys Stockholm - Södertälje Syd and v.v. or København Lufthavn ✈ - København H and v.v.

km	All trains Ⓡ	*Sn* **519** 🍷 Ⓐ	*Sn* **521** 🍷	*Sn* **523** 🍷 Ⓑ	*ST* **3941** ✕	*Sn* **527** 🍷 **E**	*Sn* **529** 🍷	*Sn* **531** 🍷	*Sn* **533** 🍷	*Sn* **535** 🍷	*Sn* **537** 🍷	*Sn* **539** 🍷	*Sn* **541** 🍷	*ST* **3943** ✕
0	**Stockholm** Central d.	0519	0620	0721	0913	0921	1020	1123	1225	1325	1425	1524	1617	1620
36	Södertälje Syd d.	|	0640	|	0931	0941	|	1142	|	|	1444	|	1636	1640
162	**Norrköping** 754 d.	0639	0743	0841	1035	1043	1140	1242	1340	1440	1543	1640	1738	1745
209	Linköping 754 d.	0704	0807	0906	1100	1109	1205	1309	1405	1505	1609	1707	1805	1810
241	**Mjölby** d.	|	|	|	|	|	|	|	1421	|	|	|	1821	|
277	Tranås d.	|	|	0934	|	|	|	|	|	|	|	|	|	|
329	**Nässjö** d.	0753	0856	0958	1155	1158	1254	1358	1458	1553	1658	1755	1858	1905
416	Alvesta 746 d.	0827	0932	1032	1241	1232	1330	1432	1532	1630	1732	1828	1932	1942
463	Älmhult 746 d.	0849	|	|	|	|	|	|	|	|	|	1850	|	|
514	Hässleholm 745 746 d.	0911	1012	1112	1325**s**	1312	1412	1512	1612	1712	1812	1912	2012	2025**s**
581	Lund ● a.	0940	1040	1140	1356**s**	1340	1440	1540**s**	1640	1740**s**	1840	1940	2040	2100**s**
597	**Malmö** C ● a.	0952	1052	1152	1408	1352	1452	1552	1652	1752	1852	1952	2052	2115
626	København Lufthavn ✈ ● a.	...	...	...	...	...	...	...	...	...	...	...	...	...
638	**København** H ● a.	...	...	...	...	...	...	...	...	...	...	...	...	...

All trains Ⓡ	*Sn* **543** 🍷 Ⓑ	*EN* **345** **H**	*Sn* **545** 🍷	*Sn* **547** 🍷 Ⓑ	**1** **N** Ⓑ**p** ⊙
Stockholm Central d.	1726	1734	1824	1913	2317
Södertälje Syd d.	|	|	|	1933	|
Norrköping 754 d.	1841	1859	1940	2042	0056
Linköping 754 d.	1906	1928	2005	2109	0127
Mjölby d.	|	|	2021	|	|
Tranås d.	1934	|	|	|	|
Nässjö d.	1958	2026	2058	2158	0316**z**
Alvesta 746 d.	2032	2108	2132	2232	0404
Älmhult 746 d.	|	|	|	|	|
Hässleholm 745 746 d.	2112	2154	2212	2312	0509**s**
Lund ● a.	2140	2229	2240**s**	2340**s**	0645**s**
Malmö C ● a.	2152	2242	2252	2352	0659
København Lufthavn ✈ ● a.	...	2354	...	...	...
København H ● a.	...	...	...	...	...

All trains Ⓡ	*EN* **346** **H**	*Sn* **520** 🍷 Ⓐ**J**	*Sn* **522** 🍷 Ⓐ	*Sn* **524** 🍷 ⚒	*Sn* **526** 🍷
København H ● d.	...	...	...	...	...
København Lufthavn ✈ ● d.	0341	...	...	...	...
Malmö C ● d.	0401**s**	0404	0507	0607	0707
Lund ● d.	0435**s**	0416**u**	0520**u**	0620**u**	0720**u**
Hässleholm 745 746 d.	0509**s**	0444	0548	0648	0748
Älmhult 746 d.	|	0505	|	0709	|
Alvesta 746 d.	0602**s**	0529	0629	0731	0829
Nässjö d.	0645**s**	0605	0702	0805	0902
Tranås d.	|	0629	|	|	|
Mjölby d.	|	|	|	|	0939
Linköping 754 d.	0748**s**	0703	0759	0856	0956
Norrköping 754 d.	0827**s**	0730	0822	0919	1019
Södertälje Syd a.	|	|	0919	|	|
Stockholm Central a.	0955	0842	0938	1036	1142

All trains Ⓡ	*Sn* **528** 🍷	*Sn* **530** 🍷	*ST* **3940** ✕ **E**	*Sn* **532** 🍷	*Sn* **534** 🍷	*Sn* **536** 🍷	*Sn* **538** 🍷 Ⓑ**q**	*Sn* **542** 🍷	*Sn* **544** 🍷	*Sn* **546** 🍷	*ST* **3942** ✕	*Sn* **548** 🍷 Ⓑ	*Sn* **550** 🍷	**2** **N** Ⓑ**p** ⊡
København H ● d.	...	...	...	...	...	...	...	...	...	...	...	...	...	...
København Lufthavn ✈ ● d.	...	...	...	...	...	...	...	...	...	...	...	...	...	...
Malmö C ● d.	0807	0907	0920	1007	1107	1207	1307	1507	1607	1707	1714	1807	1907	2217
Lund ● d.	0820	0920**u**	0930**u**	1020	1120	1220	1320	1520	1620	1720	1725**u**	1820**u**	1920	2233**u**
Hässleholm 745 746 d.	0848	0948	1005**u**	1048	1148	1248	1348	1548	1648	1748	1758**u**	1848	1948	0005**u**
Älmhult 746 d.	|	|	|	|	|	|	|	|	1709	|	|	|	|	|
Alvesta 746 d.	0929	1029	1047	1129	1229	1329	1429	1629	1731	1829	1841	1931	2029	0109
Nässjö d.	1002	1102	1124	1202	1302	1402	1502	1702	1805	1902	1917	2005	2102	0241**t**
Tranås d.	|	|	|	|	|	|	1525	|	|	|	|	|	|	|
Mjölby d.	|	|	|	|	1339	|	|	1739	|	1939	|	|	|	|
Linköping 754 d.	1053	1153	1222	1253	1356	1453	1557	1756	1856	1957	2020	2056	2153	0348
Norrköping 754 d.	1116	1216	1248	1316	1419	1516	1620	1819	1919	2021	2048	2119	2216	0417
Södertälje Syd a.	1215	|	1355	1417	|	1615	|	|	|	|	2155	|	2315	|
Stockholm Central a.	1245	1334	1415	1435	1531	1634	1733	1932	2032	2136	2215	2231	2334	0553

E – Days of running and timings vary - please check when booking.
H – 🛏, ▬ and (2) Stockholm - Hamburg - Berlin and v.v. (see Table **50**).
J – Ⓐ to June 13 and Ⓐ from Aug. 18.
N – Conveys 🛏, ▬ and (2).

p – Also ⑥ July 5 - Aug. 9.
q – Also ⑥ July 5 - Aug. 16.
s – Calls to set down only.
t – Arrives 0158.
u – Calls to pick up only.
z – Arrives 0233.

⊙ – Also calls at Helsingborg Central (a. 0612) on most dates.
⊡ – Also calls at Helsingborg Central (d. 2307) on most dates.
● – See also Tables **735**, **745** and **746** for other trains Lund - Malmö - København and v.v.

☛ **Warning!** Trains in this table are subject to variations in timings (particularly departure times from Stockholm) - please check when booking.

For further information on trains operated by Snälltåget see www.snalltaget.se.

(GÄVLE -) STOCKHOLM - LINKÖPING 730a

Subject to alteration due to engineering work. Certain trains may not run mid-June to mid-August. See Table **730** for other fast services Stockholm - Linköping and v.v.

	◇	◇	*IC* 257	*IC* 259	◇	*IC* 261	◇	*IC* 263	*IC* 263	◇	*IC* 265	◇	*IC* 267	◇	*IC* 269	◇	◇		*IC* 273	◇	*IC* 275	◇	*IC* 277	◇	◇	
	Ⓐ	Ⓐ	⚒	Ⓐ J		⚒	Ⓐ	Ⓐ	†		⑥	Ⓐ	Ⓐ		Ⓑ	Ⓐ			⑥	Ⓐ	H			Ⓐ	Ⓒ	
	2	2	🅁	🅁	2	L 🅁	2	🅁	🅁	2	L 🅁	2	🅁	2	L 🅁	2	2		🅁	2	🅁	2	🅁	2	2	
Gävle C **760** d.	...	...	...	0601	...	0701	...	0801	...	...	0901	...	1001	...	1101	...	...	...	1301	...	1401	...	1501	...	...	...
Stockholm Central d.	0543	0642	0638	0740	0742	0837	0842	0941	0940	0944	1037	1043	1137	1143	1234	1244	1340	...	1440	1443	1537	1540	1637	1643	1721	...
Flemingsberg d.	0554	0653	0649	0750	0754	0848	0852	0951	0951	0954	1047	1053	1148	1154	1244	1254	1351	...	1450	1454	1548	1550	1647	1654	1731	...
Södertälje Syd d.	0604	0703	0659	0800	0804	0859	0903	1001	1001	1004	1058	1103	1159	1204	1254	1304	1401	...	1500	1504	1558	1601	1700	1704	1743	...
Nyköping d.	0645	0745	|	|	0845	|	0945	|	|	1045	|	1145	|	1245	|	1345	1445	...	|	1545	|	1645	|	1745	1825	...
Norrköping **754** d.	0726	0826	0808	0907	0926	1004	1026	1107	1107	1126	1204	1226	1305	1326	1405	1426	1526	...	1607	1626	1707	1726	1806	1826	1906	...
Linköping **754** a.	...	...	0835	0932	...	1029	...	1133	1131	...	1230	...	1332	...	1430	...	...	...	1633	...	1733	...	1831	...	...	...

	IC 279	◇	*IC* 281	◇	◇	◇	◇	◇	◇	◇	◇	
	Ⓐ	Ⓐ	†	Ⓐ	†	Ⓐ	⑥	①–④	Ⓑ	⑥	⑤	
	L 🅁	2	🅁	2	2	2	2	2				
Gävle C **760** d.	1600	...	1701	...	...	...	...	...	...	...	...	...
Stockholm Central d.	1737	1743	1837	1843	1927	1943	2023	2043	2143	2325	2343	...
Flemingsberg d.	1747	1754	1848	1854	1937	1954	2034	2054	2154	2336	2354	...
Södertälje Syd d.	1758	1804	1858	1904	1947	2004	2044	2104	2204	2346	0004	...
Nyköping d.	|	1845	|	1945	2026	2045	2125	2145	2245	0027	0045	...
Norrköping **754** d.	1905	1926	2005	2026	2106	2126	2206	2226	2326	0108	0126	...
Linköping **754** a.	1929	...	2029	...	...	...	...	...	...	...	...	...

	◇	*IC* 262		◇	◇		◇	◇	
	Ⓐ	Ⓐ J		Ⓐ	Ⓐ				
	2	🅁		2	2		2	2	
Linköping **754** d.	...	0530	...	...	...	...	...	...	...
Norrköping **754** d.	0531	0556	...	0552	0634	...	0734	0834	...
Nyköping d.	0612	|	...	0633	0714	...	0814	0914	...
Södertälje Syd d.	0654	0700	...	0718	0751	...	0853	0952	...
Flemingsberg d.	0703	0710	...	0727	0801	...	0902	1001	...
Stockholm Central a.	0713	0721	...	0738	0812	...	0912	1011	...
Gävle C **760** a.	...	0856	...	...	...	...	...	...	...

	◇	*IC* 270	◇	*IC* 272	◇	*IC* 274		◇	*IC* 276	◇	*IC* 278	◇	*IC* 280	◇	*IC* 282	◇	*IC* 284	◇	*IC* 286	◇	*IC* 288	◇	*IC* 290	◇	◇	
	Ⓐ			Ⓐ J	Ⓐ				†	Ⓐ	Ⓒ		Ⓐ	Ⓐ	Ⓐ		Ⓑ	Ⓐ			H	Ⓐ	F		Ⓐ	
	2	🅁	2	🅁	2	L 🅁		2	🅁	2	🅁	2	L 🅁	2	🅁	2	🅁	2	L 🅁	2	🅁	2	🅁	2	2	
Linköping **754** d.	...	0934	...	1030	...	1127	...	...	1231	...	1329	...	1429	...	1525	...	1633	...	1726	...	1833	...	1928	...	...	...
Norrköping **754** d.	0934	0959	1034	1056	1133	1155	...	1234	1256	1334	1356	1434	1455	1534	1553	1634	1702	1734	1754	1834	1858	1934	1954	2034	2134	...
Nyköping d.	1014	|	1114	|	1214	|	...	1314	|	1414	|	1514	|	1614	|	1714	|	1814	|	1914	|	2014	|	2114	2214	...
Södertälje Syd d.	1052	1101	1156	1159	1252	1301	...	1358	1402	1451	1501	1553	1602	1654	1702	1801	1806	1855	1859	1951	2002	2051	2059	2151	2251	...
Flemingsberg d.	1102	1111	1208	1209	1301	1311	...	1408	1412	1501	1511	1603	1613	1704	1713	1812	1816	1905	1909	2000	2012	2101	2109	2200	2301	...
Stockholm Central a.	1112	1122	1221	1220	1311	1322	...	1418	1425	1512	1522	1614	1624	1714	1724	1823	1827	1915	1921	2010	2023	2112	2122	2211	2312	...
Gävle C **760** a.	...	1256	...	1356	...	1456	...	...	1556	...	1656	...	1756	...	1856	...	1956	...	2056	...	2156	...	...	...	...	...

F – Ⓑ to June 13 / from Aug. 15 (also ⑦ June 22 - Aug. 3).
H – ①–④ (not June 14 - Aug. 17).
J – Not June 14 - Aug. 17.
L – From / to Ljusdal (Table **761**).
◇ – Operated by Mälartåg.

LUND - MALMÖ - YSTAD - SIMRISHAMN and TRELLEBORG 731

Operator: *Skåne*

km		Ⓐ	Ⓐ	Ⓐ	Ⓒ	Ⓐ		Ⓐ				⊡			⚒		⚒		⚒	⚒	†	⚒		⑥⑦	⑥⑦
0	**Lund** C d.	...	...	0534	...	0604	0634	0704	0734	0804	0834	and at the	1904	1934	2004	2034	2104	2134	2204	2234	2234	2304	2334	0004	0034
16	**Malmö** C d.	0453	...	0553	0553	0623	0653	0723	0753	0823	0853	same minutes	1923	1953	2023	2053	2123	2153	2223	2257	2257	2327	2353	0023	0053
86	Ystad d.	0546	0616	0646	0646	0716	0746	0814	0846	0914	0946	past each	2014	2046	2114	2146	2214	2246	2314	2346	2344	0014	0044	0114	0144
132	**Simrishamn** a.	0625	0653	0725	0725	0753	0825	...	0925	...	1025	hour until	...	2125	...	2225	...	2325	...	0025	...	...	...	...	...

		Ⓐ		Ⓐ		Ⓐ		Ⓐ				◧				⚒		⚒	⚒	†	⚒	①–④	⑤⑥	⚒	⑤⑥
Simrishamn d.	...	...	0535a	0607	0635r	0707	0735	0807	...	0835	...	and at the	1835	...	1935	...	2035	...	2135	2135	...	2235	2235	...	2335
Ystad d.	0516	0546	0616	0646	0716	0746	0816	0846	0846	0916	0946	same minutes	1916	1946	2016	2046	2116	2146	2216	2216	2246	2316	2314	2346	0016
Malmö C a.	0607	0637	0707	0737	0807	0837	0907	0937	0937	1007	1037	past each	2007	2037	2107	2137	2207	2237	2307	2303	2337	0003	...	0037	0107
Lund C a.	0626	0656	0726	0756	0826	0856	0926	0956	0956	1026	1056	hour until	2026	2056	2126	2156	2226	2256	2326	...	2356	...	...	0056	...

km		Ⓐ§							⑥⑦
0	**Malmö** C d.	0638	0708	0738	and every	2308	2338	0008	0038
44	**Trelleborg** C a.	0710	0740	0810	30 minutes until	2340	0010	0040	0110

	Ⓐ§							⚒	⚒	⑥⑦
Trelleborg C d.	0520	0550	0620	0650	and every	2220	2250	2320	2350	0050
Malmö C a.	0552	0622	0652	0722	30 minutes until	2252	2322	2352	0022	0122

a – Ⓐ only.
r – ⚒ only.
⊡ – Journeys at 1404 and 1504 extend to Simrishamn on Ⓐ.
◧ – On Ⓐ, journeys at 1646 and 1746 start from Simrishamn at 1607 and 1707.
§ – Also at 0538Ⓐ, 0608 from Malmö, 0450Ⓐ from Trelleborg.
☛ Additional journeys Ystad - Simrishamn: 0446Ⓐ, 0516Ⓐ, 0546⚒.

STOCKHOLM - ESKILSTUNA - ÖREBRO 732

Operator: *Mälartåg* (2nd class only)

km	⊡	Ⓐ H	Ⓐ	Ⓒ	Ⓐ	Ⓐ		Ⓐ		Ⓐ		Ⓐ	Ⓒ	Ⓐ		Ⓐ J	Ⓒ	Ⓐ	Ⓐ	Ⓐ	Ⓒ	Ⓐ		Ⓐ	†	Ⓐ
0	**Stockholm** Central d.	...	0554	0644	0656	0755	0855	0955	1056	1155	1256	1355	1454	1454	1552	1610	1655	1654	1753	1857	1856	1955	2055	2155	2255	2255
36	Södertälje Syd d.	...	0615	0704	0716	0816	0915	1015	1116	1215	1316	1415	1513	1513	1612	|	1716	1716	1814	1916	1916	2014	2114	2215	2316	2316
67	Läggesta ● d.	...	0633	0720	0733	0833	0933	1033	1133	1233	1333	1433	1533	1533	1633	|	1733	1733	1833	1933	1933	2033	2133	2233	2333	2333
83	Strängnäs d.	...	0641	0729	0741	0841	0941	1041	1141	1241	1341	1441	1541	1541	1641	|	1741	1741	1841	1941	1941	2041	2141	2241	2341	2341
115	**Eskilstuna** a.	...	0656	0744	0756	0856	0956	1056	1156	1256	1356	1456	1556	1556	1656	1700	1756	1756	1856	1956	1956	2056	2156	2256	2356	2356
115	**Eskilstuna** d.	0602	0702	0759	0759	0859	0959	1059	1159	1259	1359	1459	1559	1603	...	1703	1759	1805	1859	1959	1959	2059	2159	...	...	2359
141	Kungsör d.	0618	0717	0815	0815	0915	1015	1115	1216	1316	1415	1515	1615	1619	...	1719	1815	1819	1915	2015	2015	2114	2215	...	...	0015
159	Arboga **756** d.	0628	0729	0825	0825	0925	1026	1125	1226	1327	1426	1525	1625	1629	...	1729	1826	1829	1925	2025	2026	2124	2225	...	...	0025
205	**Örebro** C **756** a.	0650	0752	...	0845	...	...	...	...	...	...	1545	...	1649	...	1751	...	1850	1946	2045	...	...	2245a	...	...	0045

⊡	Ⓐ	Ⓐ J		Ⓐ H	Ⓒ	Ⓐ	⑥		⚒		Ⓐ	Ⓒ		Ⓐ	†	Ⓐ	Ⓒ	Ⓐ	†	Ⓐ	Ⓒ	Ⓐ		Ⓐ		⑤
Örebro C **756** d.	0510	0608	...	0708	...	0813	...	...	...	...	...	...	...	...	...	1513	...	1608	...	1708	...	1808	1913a	2013	...	2213
Arboga **756** d.	0531	0629	...	0730	0734	0834	...	0934	1034a	1134	1234	...	1333	1434	...	1534	1534	1629	...	1729	1734	1829	1934	2034	2134	2234
Kungsör d.	0542	0640	...	0739	0745	0845	...	0945	1045a	1145	1245	...	1344	1445	...	1545	1545	1640	...	1740	1745	1840	1945	2045	2145	2245
Eskilstuna a.	0557	0655	...	0755	0800	0900	...	1000	1100a	1200	1300	...	1400	1500	...	1600	1600	1655	...	1755	1800	1858	2000	2100	2200	2300
Eskilstuna d.	0604	0700	0703	0804	0804	0904	0904	1004	1104	1204	1304	1304	1404	1504	1504	1602	1604	1702	1704	1804	1804	1904	2004	2104	2204	2304
Strängnäs d.	0618	|	0717	0818	0818	0918	0918	1018	1118	1218	1318	1318	1418	1518	1518	1616	1618	1716	1718	1818	1818	1918	2018	2118	2218	2318
Läggesta ● d.	0627	|	0728	0827	0827	0927	0927	1027	1126	1227	1327	1327	1427	1527	1527	1625	1627	1725	1727	1827	1827	1927	2027	2127	2227	2327
Södertälje Syd d.	0644	|	0744	0844	0844	0943	0944	1044	1143	1244	1344	1344	1444	1544	1544	1644	1644	1744	1744	1844	1844	1944	2044	2144	2244	2344
Stockholm Central a.	0705	0748	0805	0905	0904	1004	1005	1105	1205	1304	1405	1405	1505	1606	1607	1705	1704	1805	1805	1905	1905	2005	2105	2205	2305	0005

H – Not June 10 - Aug. 3.
J – Not June 14 - Aug. 17.
a – Ⓐ only.
⊡ – Subject to alteration due to engineering work.
● – Narrow gauge service operates Mariefred - Läggesta (nedre) - Taxinge-Näsby. Summer only. Operator: Östra Södermanlands Järnväg, Box 53, SE-647 22 Mariefred. ✆ +46 (0) 159 210 00. www.oslj.nu
☛ Additional journeys Stockholm - Eskilstuna and v.v.:
From Stockholm Central 0525Ⓐ, 0628Ⓐ, 0730Ⓐ, 0827Ⓐ **J**, 0955⑥, 1355Ⓒ, 1521Ⓐ, 1622Ⓐ, 1723Ⓐ, 1754†, 2355⑤⑥.
From Eskilstuna 0504Ⓐ, 0534Ⓐ, 0634Ⓐ, 0734Ⓐ, 0835Ⓐ **J**, 1634Ⓐ **J**.

SKÖVDE - JÖNKÖPING - NÄSSJÖ 733

Operator: *Västtågen* (2nd class only)

km		Ⓐ	Ⓐ	Ⓐ		Ⓐ J		†	⚒	⚒					Ⓐ J	Ⓐ§		Ⓐ J			Ⓑ		Ⓐ J	⑦	Ⓑ	⑥
0	**Skövde** **740** d.	...	0551	0626	0657	0716	0758	0853	0857	0957	1058	1152	1256	1354	1421	...	1453	1524	1554	1655	1755	1855	1952	1952	2058	2159
30	Falköping **740** a.	...	0608	0643	0714	0734	0815	0910	0914	1014	1115	1209	1313	1411	1438	...	1512	1541	1611	1712	1812	1912	2009	2009	2115	2216
30	Falköping d.	0502	0613	0645	0717	0738	0819	0916	0916	1017	1117	1217	1317	1415	1444	...	1515	1548	1617	1719	1818	1918	2017	2017	2121	2221
100	Jönköping a.	0544	0657	0728	0800	0827	0900	1000	1000	1100	1200	1300	1400	1500	1525	...	1559	1629	1703	1803	1902	2001	2101	2101	2207	2308
100	Jönköping d.	0546	0705	*0739*	0807	*0841*	0907	1004	1004	1105	1205	1307	1406	1505	...	1535	1607	...	1707	1806	1908	2004	2106	2106	2209	2316
143	**Nässjö** a.	0617	0736	*0814*	0840	*0913*	0939	1038	1038	1137	1238	1339	1437	1538	...	1609	1639	...	1738	1839	1940	2036	2140	2140	2239	2347

	Ⓐ E	Ⓐ F	Ⓐ	Ⓐ J	⚒	Ⓐ J	⚒		⚒					Ⓐ J	Ⓒ	Ⓐ	Ⓐ J			Ⓑ d	Ⓑ	⑥	Ⓑ d	Ⓐ§		Ⓐ§
Nässjö d.	0412	0428	0555	...	0715	...	0819	0917	1019	1118	1218	1317	1424	...	1515	1524	...	1619	1718	1819	1919	1919	2022	2047	2118	2218
Jönköping a.	0442	0459	0626	...	0750	...	0852	0948	1050	1150	1250	1348	1458	...	1546	1601	...	1652	1752	1851	1953	1955	2059	2118	2150	2249
Jönköping d.	0445	0501	0628	0733	0801	0832	0901	1001	1101	1201	1300	1401	1500	1532	1602	1603	1636	1703	1804	1903	2002	2002	2103	...	2153	...
Falköping a.	0529	0545	0714	0819	0845	0916	0944	1045	1145	1245	1344	1444	1543	1615	1646	1646	1727	1746	1846	1946	2046	2046	2148	...	2237	...
Falköping **740** d.	0532	0552	0721	0824	0847	0918	0947	1052	1146	1248	1347	1450	1548	1622	1652	1649	1729	1749	1850	1949	2050	...	...	...	2240	...
Skövde **740** a.	0611	0608	0737	0840	0904	0935	1004	1108	1203	1306	1403	1506	1605	1639	1709	1706	1748	1806	1906	2005	2106	...	...	...	2256	...

E – From July 14.
F – Until July 11.
J – Not June 30 - Aug. 15.
d – Runs daily Nässjö - Jönköping.
§ – Operated by Jönköpings Länstrafik.

734 KRISTIANSTAD - HÄSSLEHOLM - HELSINGBORG

Operator: *Skåne*

km		Ⓐ	Ⓐ	Ⓐ	⚒	Ⓐ		Ⓐ		Ⓐ				Ⓐ			Ⓐ		Ⓐ						⑤⑥
0	**Kristianstad** ..... **745** d.	...	*0504*	0543	*0604*	0643	*0704*	0743	*0804*	0843	*0904*	and at	*1404*	1443	*1504*	and at	1743	*1804*	1843	*1904*	*2004*	*2104*	*2204*	*2304*	*0004*
30	Hässleholm .... **745** a.	...	*0526*	0604	*0626*	0704	*0726*	0804	*0826*	0904	*0926*	the same	*1426*	1504	*1526*	the same	1804	*1826*	1904	*1926*	*2026*	*2126*	*2226*	*2326*	*0026*
30	Hässleholm ....d.	0506	0536	0606	0636	0706	0736	0806	0836	0906	0936	minutes	1436	1506	1536	minutes	1806	1836	...	1936	2036	2136	2236	2336	0041
83	Åstorp ....d.	0544	0614	0644	0714	0744	0814	0844	0914	0944	1014	past each	1514	1544	1614	past each	1844	1914	...	2014	2114	2214	2314	0014	0124
107	**Helsingborg** ....a.	0610	0640	0710	0740	0810	0840	0910	0940	1010	1040	hour until	1540	1610	1640	hour until	1910	1940	...	2040	2140	2240	2340	0040	0150

	Ⓐ	Ⓐ	D	⚒	Ⓐ	D		Ⓐ		Ⓐ				Ⓐ			Ⓐ							
Helsingborg ....d.	...	0419	0449	0519	...	0549	0619	0649	0719	0749	0819	and at	1319	1349	1419	and at	1649	1719	1819	1919	2019	2119	2219	2319
Åstorp ....d.	...	0443	0513	0543	...	0613	0643	0713	0743	0813	0843	the same	1343	1413	1443	the same	1713	1743	1843	1943	2043	2143	2243	2343
Hässleholm ....a.	...	0523	0553	0623	...	0653	0723	0753	0823	0853	0923	minutes	1423	1453	1523	minutes	1753	1823	1923	2023	2123	2223	2323	0023
Hässleholm .... **745** d.	0455	*0534*	0555	...	0634	0655	*0734*	0755	*0834*	0855	*0934*	past each	*1434*	1455	*1534*	past each	1755	*1834*	*1934*	*2034*	*2134*	*2234*	*2334*	...
Kristianstad .... **745** a.	0516	*0556*	0616	...	0656	0716	*0756*	0816	*0856*	0916	*0956*	hour until	*1456*	1516	*1556*	hour until	1816	*1856*	*1956*	*2056*	*2156*	*2256*	*2356*	...

D – Ⓐ Helsingborg - Hässleholm; daily Hässleholm - Kristianstad.

☛ Additional journeys Helsingborg - Hässleholm: 0849Ⓐ, 1749Ⓐ, 0019⑤⑥.

735 GÖTEBORG - MALMÖ - KØBENHAVN

Operator: *Øtåg* (except *Sn* trains)

Fast *Sn* services Göteborg - Malmö. Subject to alteration due to engineering work - see note ❦.

All trains Ⓡ		*Sn* 481 Ⓐ 🍷		*Sn* 485 Ⓒ 🍷		*Sn* 487 Ⓐ 🍷		*Sn* 489 🍷		107 385 E§ 🍷		*Sn* 491 🍷		*Sn* 493 † 🍷		*Sn* 495 ⚒ 🍷		*Sn* 497 Ⓑ 🍷		*Sn* 439 Ⓑs 🍷		123 395 F§ 🍷		
Oslo S **770** ....d.	...	...	...	...	...	...	...	...	...	0814	...	...	...	...	...	...	...	...	...	...	...	1615	...	...
Göteborg C..........................d.	...	0624	...	0824	...	0924	...	1024	...	1155	...	1324	...	1524	...	1619	...	1724	...	1854	...	1954	...	...
Varberg ....d.	...	0705r	...	0905r	...	1005r	...	1105r	...	|	...	1405r	...	|	...	|	...	1805r	...	|	...	|	...	...
Halmstad ....d.	...	0739	...	0935	...	1037	...	1135	...	1310	...	1435	...	1635	...	1738	...	1838	...	2008	...	2110	...	...
Helsingborg ....d.	...	0814	...	1014	...	1111	...	1211	...	1346	...	1515	...	1711	...	1814	...	1913	...	2045	...	2145	...	...
Lund .... ▽ a.	...	0840	...	1040	...	1140	...	1240	...	1414	...	1545	...	1743	...	1844	...	1942	...	2114	...	2212	...	...
Malmö C ....a.	...	0853	...	1055	...	1155	...	1254	...	1425	...	1557	...	1755	...	1856	...	1954	...	2127	...	2227	...	...

All trains Ⓡ		*Sn* 480 Ⓐ 🍷		386 118 G§ 🍷		*Sn* 430 ⚒t 🍷		*Sn* 484 🍷		*Sn* 486 Ⓒ 🍷		*Sn* 488 Ⓐ 🍷		*Sn* 490 🍷		396 134 E§ 🍷		*Sn* 448 Ⓑt 🍷		*Sn* 492 ⑥ 🍷		*Sn* 494 ⑦ 🍷		*Sn* 496 Ⓐ 🍷
Malmö C ....d.	...	0604	...	0719	...	0731	...	1004	...	1201	...	1301	...	1404	...	1534	...	1638	...	1701	...	1901	...	2001
Lund .... △ d.	...	0616	...	0741	...	0746	...	1017	...	1217	...	1317	...	1417	...	1549	...	1650	...	1717	...	1917	...	2014
Helsingborg ....d.	...	0643	...	0815	...	0814	...	1043	...	1243	...	1343	...	1443	...	1615	...	1714	...	1743	...	1943	...	2043
Halmstad ....d.	...	0720	...	0851	...	0849	...	1121	...	1321	...	1421	...	1521	...	1652	...	1751	...	1821	...	2021	...	2121
Varberg ....d.	...	0754r	...	|	...	|	...	1154r	...	1354r	...	1453r	...	1554r	...	|	...	1821r	...	1853r	...	|	...	2154r
Göteborg C..........................a.	...	0835	...	1005	...	1005	...	1235	...	1435	...	1535	...	1635	...	1755	...	1905	...	1935	...	2135	...	2235
Oslo S **770** ....a.	...	...	...	1345	...	...	...	...	...	...	...	...	...	...	...	2144	...	...	...	...	...	...	...	...

Regional services operated by Øresundståg. See panel below for additional trains Helsingborg - Malmö - København and v.v.

km		Ⓐ		Ⓐ			Ⓐ																		
0	**Göteborg** C..........................d.	...	...	...	0440a	...	0540	0640	0740	0840	0940	1040	1140	1240	1340	1440	1540	1640	1740	1840	1940	2040	2140	2240	2340
28	Kungsbacka ....d.	...	...	...	0459a	...	0559	0659	0759	0859	0959	1059	1159	1259	1359	1459	1559	1659	1759	1859	1959	2059	2159	2259	2359
76	Varberg ....d.	...	...	...	0529a	...	0629	0729	0829	0929	1029	1129	1229	1329	1429	1529	1629	1729	1829	1929	2029	2129	2229	2329	0029
106	Falkenberg ....d.	...	...	...	0545a	...	0645	0745	0845	0945	1045	1145	1245	1345	1445	1545	1645	1745	1845	1945	2045	2145	2245	2345	0045
150	**Halmstad** ....a.	...	...	...	0603a	...	0703	0803	0903	1003	1103	1203	1303	1403	1503	1603	1703	1803	1903	2003	2103	2203	2303	0003	0103
150	**Halmstad** ....d.	...	...	0513	0613	0713	0713	0813	0913	1013	1113	1213	1313	1413	1513	1613	1713	1813	1913	2013	2113	2213	2313	...	...
173	Laholm ....d.	...	...	0525	0625	0725	0725	0825	0925	1025	1125	1225	1325	1425	1525	1625	1725	1825	1925	2025	2125	2225	2325	...	...
185	Båstad ....d.	...	...	0532	0632	0732	0732	0832	0932	1032	1132	1232	1332	1432	1532	1632	1732	1832	1932	2032	2132	2232	2332	...	...
210	Ängelholm ....d.	...	...	0543	0643	0743	0743	0843	0943	1043	1143	1243	1343	1443	1543	1643	1743	1843	1943	2043	2143	2243	2343	...	...
237	**Helsingborg** ....a.	...	...	0604	0704	0804	0804	0904	1004	1104	1204	1304	1404	1504	1604	1704	1804	1904	2004	2104	2204	2300	2400	...	...
237	**Helsingborg** ....d.	0507	0607	0607	0707	0807	0807	0907	1007	1107	1207	1307	1407	1507	1607	1707	1807	1907	2007	2107	2207	2307	...	...	...
259	Landskrona ....d.	0519	0619	0619	0719	0819	0819	0919	1019	1119	1219	1319	1419	1519	1619	1719	1819	1919	2019	2119	2219	2319	...	...	...
290	Lund .... ● d.	0538	0638	0638	0738	0838	0838	0938	1038	1138	1238	1338	1438	1538	1638	1738	1838	1938	2038	2138	2238	2338	...	...	...
306	**Malmö** C .... ● a.	0548	0648	0648	0748	0848	0848	0948	1048	1148	1248	1348	1448	1548	1648	1748	1848	1948	2048	2148	2248	2348	...	...	...
306	**Malmö** C .... ● d.	0550	0650	0650	0750	0850	0850	0950	1050	1150	1250	1350	1450	1550	1650	1750	1850	1950	2050	2150	2250	...	...	...	...
335	København Lufthavn ✈ .... ● a.	0613	0713	0713	0813	0913	0913	1013	1113	1213	1313	1413	1513	1613	1713	1813	1913	2013	2113	2213	2313	...	...	...	...
347	**København** H................. ● a.	0627	0727	0727	0827	0927	0927	1027	1127	1227	1327	1427	1527	1627	1727	1827	1927	2027	2127	2227	2327	...	...	...	...

	Ⓐ	Ⓒ	Ⓐ	Ⓒ	Ⓐ																		⑤⑥		
København H .... ● d.	...	...	...	...	...	0530	0630	0730	0830	0930	1030	1130	1230	1330	1430	1530	1630	1730	1830	1930	2030	2130	2130	2223	2330
København Lufthavn ✈ ... ● d.	...	...	...	...	...	0544	0644	0745	0844	0944	1044	1144	1244	1344	1444	1544	1644	1744	1844	1944	2044	2144	2144	2240	2344
Malmö C .... ● a.	...	...	...	...	...	0610	0710	0810	0910	1010	1110	1210	1310	1410	1510	1610	1710	1810	1910	2010	2110	2210	2210	2304	0010
Malmö C .... ● d.	...	...	...	...	0512	0612	0712	0812	0912	1012	1112	1212	1312	1412	1512	1612	1712	1812	1912	2012	2112	2212	2212	2312	0012
Lund .... ● d.	...	...	...	...	0524	0624	0724	0824	0924	1024	1124	1224	1324	1424	1524	1624	1724	1824	1924	2024	2124	2224	2224	2324	0024
Landskrona ....d.	...	...	...	...	0539	0639	0739	0839	0939	1039	1139	1239	1339	1439	1539	1639	1739	1839	1939	2039	2139	2239	2239	2339	0040
Helsingborg ....a.	...	...	...	...	0553	0653	0753	0853	0953	1053	1153	1253	1353	1453	1553	1653	1753	1853	1953	2053	2153	2253	2253	2353	0053
Helsingborg ....d.	...	...	0500	0600	0600	0700	0800	0900	1000	1100	1200	1300	1400	1500	1600	1700	1800	1900	2000	2100	2200	2300	2300	0000	...
Ängelholm ....d.	...	...	0515	0616	0616	0716	0816	0916	1016	1116	1216	1316	1416	1516	1616	1716	1816	1916	2016	2116	2216	2316	2316	0014	...
Båstad ....d.	...	...	0528	0628	0628	0728	0828	0928	1028	1128	1228	1328	1428	1528	1628	1728	1828	1928	2028	2128	2228	2328	2328	0028	...
Laholm ....d.	...	...	0535	0635	0635	0735	0835	0935	1035	1135	1235	1335	1435	1535	1635	1735	1835	1935	2035	2135	2235	2335	2335	0035	...
Halmstad ....a.	...	...	0546	0646	0646	0746	0846	0946	1046	1146	1246	1346	1446	1546	1646	1746	1846	1946	2046	2146	2246	2346	2346	0046	...
Halmstad ....d.	0445	0556	0556	0656	0656	0756	0856	0956	1056	1156	1256	1356	1456	1556	1656	1756	1856	1956	2056	2156	2256	...	2356	...	...
Falkenberg ....d.	0502	0613	0613	0713	0713	0813	0913	1013	1113	1213	1313	1413	1513	1613	1713	1813	1913	2013	2113	2213	2313	...	0013	...	...
Varberg ....d.	0519	0633	0630	0733	0735	0833	0933	1033	1133	1233	1333	1433	1533	1633	1733	1833	1933	2033	2133	2233	2333	...	0033	...	...
Kungsbacka ....d.	0544	0659	0659	0759	0759	0859	0959	1059	1159	1259	1359	1459	1559	1659	1759	1859	1959	2059	2159	2259	2359	...	0059	...	...
Göteborg C..........................a.	0605	0720	0720	0820	0820	0920	1020	1120	1220	1320	1420	1520	1620	1720	1820	1920	2020	2120	2220	2320	0020	...	0120	...	...

Other Øresundståg regional services Helsingborg - Malmö - København.

	Ⓐ	Ⓐ	Ⓐ	Ⓐ	Ⓐ			
Helsingborg ....d.	0507	0535	0635	0735	0835	0935		1735
Landskrona ....d.	0519	0549	0649	0749	0849	0949	and	1749
Lund ....d.	0538	0608	0708	0808	0908	1008	hourly	1808
Malmö C ....d.	0550	0620	0720	0820	0920	1020	until	1820
København Lufthavn ✈ ....a.	0613	0643	0743	0843	0943	1043		1843
København H ....a.	0627	0657	0757	0857	0957	1057		1857

		Ⓐ	Ⓐ	Ⓐ	Ⓐ	Ⓐ				Ⓐ	⚒
København H ....d.	...	0659	0759	0859	0959	1059		1759	1859	...
København Lufthavn ✈ ... d.	...	0714	0814	0914	1014	1114	and	1814	1914	...
Malmö C ....d.	0642	0742	0842	0942	1042	1142	hourly	1842	1942	0039
Lund ....d.	0654	0754	0854	0954	1054	1154	until	1854	1954	0058
Landskrona ....d.	0708	0809	0909	1009	1109	1209		1909	2009	0120
Helsingborg ....a.	0723	0823	0923	1023	1123	1223		1923	2023	0138

E – July 14 - Aug. 8 (not Aug. 1 - 3).
F – July 14 - Aug. 7 (not July 31 - Aug. 3).
G – Ⓑ July 14 - Aug. 8 (not Aug. 1 - 4).
a – Ⓐ only.

r – Calls on certain dates in July and August.
s – From Stockholm (Table **740**).
t – To Stockholm (Table **740**).
§ – Operated by Vy.

▽ – Trains call to set down only.
△ – Trains call to pick up only.
❦ – Times and days of running are subject to variation - please check when booking. On certain dates *Sn* trains are diverted via Borås and Alvesta with extended journey times.
● – See also Tables **745** and **746**.

TABLE 739 (continued from opposite page). **Service June 30 - July 13:**

No rail service Varberg - Borås or v.v.

Borås - Herrljunga on Ⓐ at 0605, 0658, 0805, 0901, 1034, 1205, 1403, 1605, 1703, 1806, 2003; on Ⓒ at 0804, 1001, 1207, 1401⑥, 1402⑦, 1604, 1804⑥, 1806⑦, 2001⑥.

Herrljunga - Borås on Ⓐ at 0646, 0754, 0917, 1022, 1118, 1257, 1518, 1621, 1723, 1918, 2120; on Ⓒ at 0920, 1129, 1319, 1519⑦, 1520⑥, 1720, 1902, 1923⑥, 2120.

Herrljunga - Uddevalla on Ⓐ at 0645, 0900, 1123, 1320, 1522, 1602, 1719, 1824, 1920, 2120; on Ⓒ at 0901, 1121⑥, 1122⑦, 1321, 1520⑥, 1611⑦, 1727, 1921.

Uddevalla - Herrljunga on Ⓐ at 0533, 0632, 0820, 0915, 1140, 1307, 1434, 1538, 1725; on Ⓒ at 0736, 0920, 1136, 1335, 1536, 1712, 1935⑦.

Operator: *Västtågen* (2nd class only) ÖREBRO - HALLSBERG - MARIESTAD - GÖTEBORG 736

Service to July 13. For service July 14 - August 17 see page 605.

km		Ⓐ§	Ⓐ	⑥	Ⓐ	⑦J	ⒶJ	⑥d	⑦J	Ⓐ	⑥J	⑦	Ⓐ	⑥	Ⓐ	⑥	⑦	Ⓐ	ⒶJ	⑥	Ⓐ	⑦	Ⓐ	⑥	⑦	ⒶK	⑥J
	Örebro C .... **755 756** d.	...	...	...	...	...	...	...	...	0737	...	...	...	...	...	...	...	...	...	...	...	...	1635	...	...	...	...
0	**Hallsberg** .... **755 756** d.	...	...	...	...	...	...	...	...	0816r	...	...	...	1123	...	...	*1246*	...	...	...	...	...	1656	1719	1906	2003	...
30	Laxå .... **756** d.	...	...	...	...	...	...	...	...	0833	...	...	...	1140	1210	...	*1303*	...	...	...	...	...	1713	1736	1923	2021	...
92	Mariestad .... a.	...	...	...	...	...	...	...	...	0920	...	...	...	1228	1256	...	*1353*	...	...	...	...	...	1759	1822	2008	2107	...
92	Mariestad .... d.	...	0524	...	0655	...	0753	0815	0849	0926	...	...	1112	1230	1300	1407	1407	1442	...	1605*	1624	1703	1807	1824	2010	2110	2119
146	Lidköping .... a.	...	0606	...	0744	...	0845	0900	0931	1013	...	...	1159	1317	1346	1451	1449	1530	...	1652*	1711	1750	1854	1911	2057	2157	2206
146	Lidköping .... d.	0514	0614	0712	0747	0814	...	0903	0934	1023	1108	1147	1215	1328	1353	1453	1452	1531	1610	1714	1716	1753	2010	1914	...	2210	2209
201	**Herrljunga** ..... **740 756** a.	0600	0700	0759	0835	0900	...	0948	1020	1109	1154	1237	1258	1416	1439	1540	1538	1622	1658	1800	1800	1841	2056	2000	...	2256	2255
	Göteborg C ... **740 756** a.	...	0754	...	0925	...	...	1040	1110	1200	...	1330	...	1505	1530	1630	1630	...	...	...	...	1930t	...	...	...	...	...

	Ⓐ	Ⓐ	Ⓐ	⑥	⑦J	Ⓐ	⑦L	⑦J	⑥	Ⓐ	⑥	⑦	Ⓐ	⑥J	Ⓐ	⑦	⑥	Ⓐ	ⒶJ	Ⓐ	⑥	⑦	Ⓐ	⑥J	⑦	⚒	⚒
Göteborg C..... **740 756** d.	...	...	...	...	...	0835	...	...	...	1030	1130	1130	...	...	1350	1430	1535	...	...	1725	1730	1730	...	...	1950	...	...
Herrljunga ...... **740 756** d.	...	...	0702	...	...	0922	...	1000	1002	1117	1224	1221	1303	1401	1439	1519	1624	1627	1728	1814u	1823	1826	1903	2005	2043	2103	2303
Lidköping .... a.	...	...	0746	...	...	1010	...	1051	1052	1202	1312	1313	1349	1448	1525	1608	1713	1714	1817	1857	1908	1912	1949	2051	2127	2149	2348
Lidköping .... d.	0440f	0607	0751	0807	0937	1016	1043	...	1054	1206	1318	1316	1352	1454	1530	1611	1716	1719	...	1901	1912	1916	1952f	...	...	...	...
Mariestad .... a.	0523f	0651	0839	0858	1024	1103	1130	...	1142	1253	1400	1358	1439	1543	1619	1658	1803	1806	...	1947	1954	1958	2039f	...	...	...	...
Mariestad .... d.	0537	...	...	0858	1026	1105	1132	...	...	...	*1415*	...	1453	...	...	*1705*	...	1809f	...	...	...	...	...	...	...	...	...
Laxå .... **756** d.	0626	...	...	0949	1114	1152	1220	...	...	...	*1504**	...	1541	...	...	*1756*	...	1858f	...	...	...	...	...	...	...	...	...
Hallsberg .... **755 756** a.	0644	...	...	1007	1130	...	1236	...	...	...	*1520**	...	1558	...	...	*1812*	...	1915f	...	...	...	...	...	...	...	...	...
Örebro C......... **755 756** a.	0716	...	...	...	...	...	...	...	...	...	...	...	1619	...	...	...	...	...	...	...	...	...	...	...	...	...	...

J – Not June 30 - July 13.
K – Not June 30 - July 13 (runs daily Lidköping - Herrljunga).
L – From June 30.

d – Also runs on ⑦ from July 6.
f – Not June 30 - July 13.
r – Arrives 0757.
t – 1940 from July 6.

u – Calls to pick up only.
§ – Runs 28 minutes later June 30 - July 13.
* – 11–15 minutes later June 30 - July 13.

Operator: *Krösatågen* South-eastern SECONDARY LINES 738

km		Ⓐ		Ⓒ				Ⓐ			
0	**Västervik** .... d.	0537	...	0739	...	1355	...	1810	...	...	...
77	Åtvidaberg .... d.	0642	...	0844	...	1500	...	1915	...	...	...
116	**Linköping** .... a.	0719	...	0921	...	1536	...	1949	...	...	...

				Ⓐ							
Linköping .... d.	1208	...	1618	...	2027	...	...	...	...	...	...
Åtvidaberg .... d.	1239	...	1652	...	2101	...	...	...	...	...	...
Västervik .... a.	1345	...	1758	...	2207	...	...	...	...	...	...

km		Ⓐ	Ⓐ	⑥						Ⓑ	Ⓑ
0	**Linköping** .... d.	...	0523	...	0820	1020	1220	1420	1623	1820	2020
41	Rimforsa .... d.	...	0559	...	0900	1103	1303	1503	1703	1903	2103
123	Hultsfred .... d.	0607	0705	0705	1004	1204	1404	1604	1804	2004	2204
159	Berga .... ▷ a.	0632	0730	0730	1029	1229	1429	1629	1829	2029	...
159	Berga .... ▷ d.	0638	0735	0735	1034	1234	1434	1634	1834	2034	...
235	**Kalmar** .... a.	0738	0837	0837	1138	1338	1538	1738	1938	2138	...

	Ⓐ	Ⓐ	⑥						Ⓑ	Ⓑ	
Kalmar .... d.	...	0537	...	0832	1035	1235	1435	1635	1835	2035	...
Berga .... ▷ a.	...	0635	...	0933	1133	1333	1533	1733	1933	2133	...
Berga .... ▷ d.	...	0640	...	0938	1138	1338	1538	1738	1938	2138	...
Hultsfred .... d.	0535	0705	0706	1004	1204	1404	1604	1804	2004	2202	...
Rimforsa .... d.	0634	0804	0804	1103	1303	1503	1703	1903	2103	...	...
Linköping .... a.	0711	0842	0842	1140	1340	1540	1740	1940	2140	...	...

▷ – Connecting 🚌 service **Berga - Oskarshamn** and v.v. (route 155). *29 km.* Journey 31 – 38 minutes. Service to August 17.
From Berga station on Ⓐ: 0533◇, 0608◇, 0643, 0740, 0838◇, 0938◇, 1040, 1238◇**b**, 1338◇, 1408◇, 1440, 1508◇, 1608◇, 1708◇, 1738◇, 1840, 1938◇, 2053◇.
On ⑥: 0738◇, 0940, 1040, 1240, 1340, 1440, 1640, 1740, 1840, 1040, 2153◇, 2353◇. On ⑦: 0940, 1040, 1140, 1240, 1440, 1540, 1040, 1740, 2153◇, 2353◇.
From Oskarshamn station on Ⓐ: 0625◇, 0655◇, 0725◇, 0755◇, 0855, 0955, 1055, 1255, 1355, 1555◇, 1620◇, 1655, 1755, 1855, 1955, 2055.
On ⑥: 0855, 0955, 1055, 1255, 1355, 1455, 1555, 1655, 1855, 2055◇, 2255◇. On ⑦: 0855, 0955, 1055, 1155, 1255, 1455, 1655, 1755, 2055◇.

b – On school holidays departs from rail station at 1240.
◇ – Serves Berga **affären** bus stop (approx. 200 m from rail station).

Operator: *Västtågen* (2nd class only) VARBERG - HEERLJUNGA - UDDEVALLA 739

Service from July 14. For service June 30 - July 13 see foot of page 352 opposite (no rail service Varberg - Borås or v.v. June 8 - July 13).

km		⑦ H	Ⓐ J	Ⓐ H	Ⓐ J	Ⓐ N	Ⓐ H	Ⓐ J	Ⓐ N	Ⓒ △	Ⓐ	Ⓐ J	Ⓐ H	⑥ △	⑦ △	Ⓐ H	Ⓒ △	Ⓐ J	Ⓐ H	⑥ △	⑦ △	Ⓐ J	Ⓐ	Ⓒ △	Ⓐ H
0	**Varberg** .... d.	0218	...	...	...	...	0608	...	...	...	0706	0813	0813	0841	...	1040	1040	1040	1239	1240	1240	1337	1437	1442	...
84	Borås .... a.	0335	...	...	...	...	0728	...	...	...	0830	0936	0936	0958	...	1156	1200	1156	1356	1400	1400	1456	1557	1558	...
84	Borås .... d.	...	0445	0605	0606	0658	0755	0805	...	0825	0838	1009	1034	1029	1029	1205	1217	1221	1428	1431	1432	1502	1620	1608	...
127	**Herrljunga** .... a.	...	0520	0640	0641	0736	0833	0842	...	0902	0913	1047	1112	1107	1107	1240	1254	1256	1507	1510	1510	1540	1655	1643	...
127	**Herrljunga** .... d.	...	...	0645	0646	...	...	0853	0900	0947	...	1150	1149	1250	1250	1320	1344	1320	1546	1551	1551	1550	...	1653	1655
191	Vänersborg .... d.	...	...	0731	0732	...	...	0939	0946	1034	...	1240	1238	1337	1337	1412	1431	1412	1643	1645	1639	1643	...	1740	1751
195	Öxnered .... d.	...	...	0737	0738	...	...	0945	0953	1041	...	1245	1244	1344	1344	1419	1438	1419	1647	1650	1645	1650	...	1746	1757
217	**Uddevalla** C .... a.	...	...	0752	0753	...	...	1004	1007	1055	...	1301	1300	1358	1359	1434	1452	1434	1702	1704	1659	1712	...	1801	1812

	①–④ J	Ⓐ P	①–④ J	Ⓐ J	⑥	⑦ △	Ⓐ J	Ⓐ	⑦	⑥ H	
Varberg .... d.	1541	1643	1643	1739	1839	1840	1840	2042	2043	2043	...
Borås .... a.	1701	1803	1803	1905	2000	2000	2001	2201	2159	2159	...
Borås .... d.	1703	1806	1829	1926	2003	2003	2004	...	...	...	...
Herrljunga .... a.	1741	1841	1904	2001	2038	2038	2042	...	...	...	...
Herrljunga .... d.	1843	1917	2013	2054	...	2103	...	...	...	...	...
Vänersborg .... d.	1932	2014	2059	2140	...	2154	...	...	...	...	...
Öxnered .... d.	1937	2020	2103	2146	...	2158	...	...	...	...	...
Uddevalla C .... a.	...	2035	...	...	...	2214	...	...	...	...	...

	Ⓐ J	Ⓐ	Ⓐ	⑥	Ⓐ J	Ⓐ N	Ⓐ J	Ⓒ △	
Uddevalla C .... d.	...	...	0533	...	0628	0632	0722	0747	...
Öxnered .... d.	...	...	0549	...	0644	0648	0741	0801	...
Vänersborg .... d.	...	...	0554	...	0656	0656	0747	0809	...
Herrljunga .... a.	...	...	0640	...	0741	0741	0833	0856	...
Herrljunga .... d.	...	...	0646	...	0753	0754	0855	0902	...
Borås .... a.	...	...	0724	...	0832	0832	0930	0940	...
Borås .... d.	0526	0624	0731	0759	0837	...	0958	1002	...
Varberg .... a.	0647	0749	0852	0920	0954	...	1118	1120	...

	Ⓐ H	Ⓐ J	Ⓐ H	Ⓐ J	Ⓒ △	Ⓒ △	Ⓐ		Ⓐ J	Ⓒ △	Ⓐ	Ⓐ	Ⓐ J		⑦ △	Ⓐ	⑥ △		Ⓒ △	Ⓐ H	Ⓐ J	⚒	⑦ △		
Uddevalla C .... d.	0817	0902	0915	0946	1000	1138	1140	...	...	1302	1307	...	1436	...	1536	1537	1540	...	1706	1710	1721	...	1902	...	...
Öxnered .... d.	0832	0922	0931	1002	1015	1154	1156	...	...	1319	1323	...	1452	...	1552	1553	1556	...	1722	1726	1744	...	1918	...	...
Vänersborg .... d.	0839	0928	0937	1011	1022	1200	1202	...	...	1325	1329	...	1458	...	1558	1559	1602	...	1728	1732	1751	...	1924	...	...
Herrljunga .... a.	0928	1013	1022	1059	1108	1245	1250	...	...	1412	1417	...	1543	...	1651	1647	1651	...	1813	1817	1836	...	2009	...	...
Herrljunga .... d.	1023	1050	1118	1145	1122	1257	1257	...	1344	1450	...	1521	1610	...	1658	1702	1658	...	1850	1847	1913	2055	2055	...	...
Borås .... a.	1101	1128	1156	1220	1159	1332	1332	...	1420	1530	...	1559	1647	...	1733	1740	1733	...	1925	1925	1951	2132	2130	...	...
Borås .... d.	...	1159	1159	...	1201	1400	1358	...	1457	1601	...	1602	1704	...	1804	1805	1803	...	2000	2002	2002	...	...	...	...
Varberg .... a.	...	1316	1316	...	1320	1519	1518	...	1621	1721	...	1721	1820	...	1920	1921	1919	...	2120	2121	2121	...	...	...	...

GÖTEBORG - UDDEVALLA - STRÖMSTAD

Timings may vary June 7 - 29 and from August 2

km		Ⓐ	⚒	⚒		⚒							Ⓐb		Ⓐb	Ⓐ		Ⓐb				⑥		Ⓑ		
0	**Göteborg** C .. § d.	0525	0640	0740	0840	0940	1040	1140	1240	1340	1440	1540	1545	1640	1645	1710	1740	1745	1840	1940	2040	2140	2240	2340	...	...
	Trollhättan .. § d.	|	|	|	|	|	|	|	|	|	|	|	1622	|	1721	|	|	1819	|	|	|	|	|	|	...	...
89	Uddevalla C ...... a.	0637	0753	0853	0953	1053	1153	1253	1353	1453	1553	1653	1641	1753	1742	1827	1853	1840	1953	2053	2153	2253	2353	0052	...	...
89	Uddevalla C ...... d.	...	0806	...	1011	...	1206	...	1407	...	1606	...	...	1808	1754	...	...	...	2000	...	...	...	...	...	...	...
180	**Strömstad** .... a.	...	0926	...	1132	...	1323	...	1529	...	1724	...	...	1930	1915	...	...	...	2117	...	...	...	...	...	...	...

	Ⓐ	Ⓐ	Ⓐ	Ⓐb	⚒	⑥	Ⓐ	⑦	⚒								Ⓐb							⑤⑥		
Strömstad .... d.	...	...	...	...	...	...	0642	...	...	0832	...	1037	...	1226	...	1433	...	...	1626	...	1835	...	...	2245	...	...
Uddevalla C .... a.	...	...	...	...	...	...	0800	...	...	0952	...	1155	...	1348	...	1551	...	...	1748	...	1955	...	...	0003	...	...
Uddevalla C .... d.	0534	0607	0637	0648	0707	0801	0807	0807	0907	1007	1107	1207	1307	1407	1507	1607	1654	1707	1807	1907	2007	2107	2207	0007	...	...
Trollhättan ... § d.	|	|	|	0708	|	|	|	|	|	|	|	|	|	|	|	|	1713	|	|	|	|	|	|	|	...	...
Göteborg C .... § a.	0650	0720	0750	0745	0820	0920	0920	0920	1020	1120	1220	1320	1420	1520	1620	1720	1745	1820	1920	2020	2120	2220	2320	0120	...	...

H – July 14 - Aug. 17.
J – From Aug. 18.
N – June 30 - Aug. 15.
P – July 14 - Aug. 1.
b – Not June 23 - Aug. 15.

x – Until July 27.

△ – From Aug. 2 there is no rail service Öxnered - Uddevalla or v.v. and timings may vary.
§ – For other trains see Table **740**.

☛ For service Borås - Herrljunga and Herrljunga - Uddevalla **June 30 - July 13** see foot of page 352 opposite. For service **June 8 - 29** see www.vasttrafik.se. There is no rail service Varberg - Borås or v.v. June 8 - July 13.

740 STOCKHOLM - GÖTEBORG

Subject to alteration (especially evenings and weekends) due to engineering work. Some journeys may be diverted with longer journey times.
Times and days of running vary - please confirm timings when booking. See Table **756** for slower regional services via Västerås and Örebro.

km	All trains 🅁	Sn 419	VRS 2019	Sn 421	Sn 419	Sn 423	VRS 2023	Sn 425	VRS 2025		Sn 427	VRS 2027	Sn 429	VRS 2029		Sn 431	VRS 2031		Sn 433	VRS 2033	Sn 435	VRS 2035	Sn 437	VRS 2037
		🍷 Ⓐ E	🍷 Ⓐ	🍷 ⚒	🍷 Ⓐ B	🍷 Ⓐ D	🍷 Ⓐ ⊠	🍷	🍷 ⑥⑦ ⊠		🍷	🍷 ⚒ ⊠	🍷	🍷 ⑦ ⊠		🍷	🍷 ⚒ ⊠		🍷	🍷 ⑦ ⊠	🍷	🍷 ⑥ ⊠	🍷	🍷 ⊠
0	**Stockholm** C 750/6 d.	0505	0522	0601	0621	0704	0720	0805	0827	...	0900	0928	1007	1018	...	1112	1127	...	1200	1226	1307	1328	1407	1428
16	Flemingsberg △ 750 d.	|	0532	|	|	|	0730	|	0837	...	|	0938	|	1028	...	|	1137	...	|	1236	|	1338	|	1438
36	Södertälje Syd △ 750 d.	|	|	|	|	|	|	|	|	...	0920	|	|	|	...	|	|	...	1219	|	|	|	|	|
131	Katrineholm 750 d.	0602	|	0658	0718	0805	|	0858	|	...	0958	|	1100	|	...	1206	|	...	1258	|	1400	|	1500	|
197	**Hallsberg** 750 756 d.	|	|	|	|	|	|	|	|	...	|	|	|	|	...	|	|	...	|	|	|	|	|	|
272	Töreboda 756 d.	|	|	|	|	|	|	|	|	...	|	|	|	|	...	|	|	...	|	|	|	|	|	|
311	**Skövde** 733 756 d.	0721	0739	0817	0842	0922	0939	1015	1039	...	1115	1141	1218	1237	...	1322	1340	...	1415	1439	1518	1539	1617	1639
341	Falköping 733 756 d.	|	|	|	|	|	|	|	|	...	|	1156	|	|	...	|	|	...	|	1455	|	|	|	|
375	Herrljunga 756 d.	|	0811	0846	|	|	1011	|	1111	...	|	|	1246	1308	...	|	1410	...	|	|	1549	1610	1645	1710
410	Alingsås ▽ 756 a.	|	0830	|	|	|	1030	|	1129	...	|	1230	|	1327	...	|	1430	...	|	1527	|	1627	|	1727
455	**Göteborg** C 756 a.	0840	0900	0930	1000	1035	1100	1140	1200	...	1240	1300	1341	1400	...	1441	1500	...	1540	1600	1635	1700	1741	1800
	Trollhättan a.	...	...	...	...	...	...	...	...	...	...	...	...	...	...	...	...	...	...	...	...	...	...	...
	Uddevalla a.	...	...	...	...	...	...	...	...	...	...	...	...	...	...	...	...	...	...	...	...	...	...	...

All trains 🅁	Sn 439	Sn 439		Sn 441	VRS 2001	VRS 2041		Sn 443		VRS 2003	VRS 2043		Sn 445	VRS 2045		Sn 447	VRS 2047		Sn 449	VRS 2049	VRS 2049	Sn 451	Sn 453	
	🍷 Ⓐ m	🍷 † m		🍷	🍷 Ⓐ ⊠	🍷 ⑦ ⊠		🍷 Ⓑ		🍷 ①–④ ⊠	🍷 ⑥ ⊠		🍷	🍷 ⑦ ⊠		🍷 Ⓑ	🍷 Ⓑ ⊠		🍷 Ⓑ	🍷 ④⑤ ⊠	🍷 ⑦ ⊠	🍷 Ⓑ B	🍷 ⑦ E	
Stockholm C 750/6 d.	1501	1502	...	1603	1626	1626	...	1701	...	1729	1729	...	1805	1827	...	1907	1930	...	2005	2032	2032	2112	2206	...
Flemingsberg △ 750 d.	|	|	...	|	1636	1636	...	|	...	1739	1739	...	|	1837	...	|	|	...	|	|	|	|	|	...
Södertälje Syd △ 750 d.	1521	1521	...	|	|	|	...	1721	...	|	|	...	|	|	...	1927	|	...	|	|	|	|	|	...
Katrineholm 750 d.	1559	1600	...	1657	|	|	...	1804	...	|	|	...	1900	|	...	2005	|	...	2058	|	|	2205	2259	...
Hallsberg 750 756 d.	1633	|	...	|	|	|	...	|	...	|	|	...	|	|	...	|	|	...	|	|	|	|	|	...
Töreboda 756 d.	|	|	...	|	|	|	...	|	...	|	|	...	|	|	...	|	|	...	|	|	|	|	|	...
Skövde 733 756 d.	1721	1716	...	1823	1839	1839	...	1923	...	1940	1939	...	2018	2039	...	2122	2141	...	2215	2245	2242	2322	0015	...
Falköping 733 756 d.	1740	1733	...	|	|	|	...	|	...	1956	1954	...	|	2055	...	|	2156	...	|	2300	2257	|	|	...
Herrljunga 756 d.	|	|	...	1851	1911	1910	...	|	...	|	|	...	2045	|	...	|	2211	...	|	2314	2311	|	|	...
Alingsås ▽ 756 a.	|	|	...	|	1930	1927	...	2008	...	2030	2030	...	|	2127	...	|	2227	...	|	2329	2327	|	|	...
Göteborg C 756 a.	1841	1840	...	1935	2000	2000	...	2040	...	2100	2100	...	2130	2200	...	2230	2300	...	2340	2400	2400	0041	0130	...
Trollhättan a.	...	...	...	...	...	...	...	...	...	...	...	...	...	...	...	...	...	...	...	...	...	...	...	...
Uddevalla a.	...	...	...	...	...	...	...	...	...	...	...	...	...	...	...	...	...	...	...	...	...	...	...	...

All trains 🅁	Sn 420	VRS 2020		Sn 400	VRS 2002		Sn 422		Sn 424		VRS 2026	VRS 2026		Sn 426		VRS 2028	Sn 428		VRS 2030	Sn 430		VRS 2032	Sn 432	
	🍷 Ⓐ	🍷 ②–⑤ ⊠		🍷 Ⓐ J	🍷 Ⓐ ⊠		🍷 ⚒		🍷 ⚒		🍷 ①–④ ⊠	🍷 ⑥⑦ ⊠		🍷		🍷 ⑤–⑦ ⊠	🍷 J		🍷 ⑥⑦ ⊠	🍷 m		🍷 Ⓐ ⊠	🍷	
Uddevalla d.	...	...	...	...	...	...	...	...	...	...	...	...	...	...	...	...	...	...	...	...	...	...	...	...
Trollhättan d.	...	...	...	...	...	...	...	...	...	...	...	...	...	...	...	...	...	...	...	...	...	...	...	...
Göteborg C 756 d.	0434	0459	...	0518	0559	...	0624	...	0719	...	0759	0759	...	0819	...	0859	0919	...	0959	1019	...	1059	1119	...
Alingsås △ 756 d.	0512	0529	...	|	0627	...	|	...	0758	...	0830	0830	...	|	...	0930	|	...	1030	|	...	1128	|	...
Herrljunga 756 d.	0528	0544	...	|	0643	...	0704	...	|	...	0845	0845	...	0910	...	0945	|	...	1046	|	...	|	|	...
Falköping 733 756 d.	0544	0558	...	|	|	...	|	...	|	...	|	|	...	|	...	1001	|	...	1101	|	...	1158	|	...
Skövde 733 756 d.	0600	0613	...	|	0710	...	0730	...	0834	...	0912	0912	...	0936	...	1015	1032	...	1115	1131	...	1212	1231	...
Töreboda 756 d.	0616	|	...	|	|	...	|	...	|	...	|	|	...	|	...	|	|	...	|	|	...	|	|	...
Hallsberg 750 756 d.	0653	|	...	|	|	...	|	...	|	...	|	|	...	|	...	|	|	...	|	|	...	|	|	...
Katrineholm 750 d.	0728	|	...	|	|	...	0851	...	0954	...	|	|	...	1056	...	|	1152	...	|	1251	...	|	1351	...
Södertälje Syd ▽ 750 a.	0806	|	...	|	|	...	0933	...	|	...	|	|	...	|	...	|	|	...	|	|	...	|	1427	...
Flemingsberg ▽ 750 a.	|	|	...	|	|	...	|	...	|	...	|	1117	...	|	...	|	|	...	|	|	...	1417	|	...
Stockholm C 750/6 a.	0825	0828	...	0831	0924	...	0952	...	1046	...	1129	1129	...	1148	...	1231	1244	...	1331	1346	...	1429	1445	...

All trains 🅁	VRS 2034	Sn 434	VRS 2036		Sn 436	VRS 2038	Sn 438	VRS 2040	Sn 440	VRS 2042		Sn 442	VRS 2044	Sn 444	VRS 2076	Sn 446	VRS 2048	VRS 2048		Sn 448	VRS 2050	Sn 450	VRS 2092	VRS 2092
	🍷 ⑦ ⊠	🍷	🍷 ⚒ ⊠		🍷	🍷 ⑦ ⊠	🍷	🍷 ⚒ ⊠	🍷	🍷 ⑦ ⊠		🍷	🍷 ⚒ ⊠	🍷	🍷 ⑦ ⊠	🍷	🍷 Ⓐ ⊠	🍷 ⑥ ⊠		🍷 Ⓑ m	🍷 ⑦ ⊠	🍷 Ⓑ	🍷 ④⑤ ⊠	🍷 ⑦ ⊠
Uddevalla d.	...	...	...	...	...	...	...	...	...	...	...	...	...	...	...	...	...	...	...	...	...	...	...	...
Trollhättan d.	...	...	...	...	...	...	...	...	...	...	...	...	...	...	...	...	...	...	...	...	...	...	...	...
Göteborg C 756 d.	1159	1218	1259	...	1324	1359	1419	1459	1519	1559	...	1619	1659	1719	1759	1819	1924	1918	...	1919	1959	2019	2118	2118
Alingsås △ 756 d.	1230	|	1327	...	|	1430	|	1527	|	1630	...	1650	1730	|	1829	|	1953	1952	...	|	2030	|	2149	2149
Herrljunga 756 d.	|	1310	|	...	|	|	|	1543	|	|	...	1705	1745	1810	|	|	2018	2018	...	|	2045	|	|	|
Falköping 756 d.	|	|	1356	...	|	1458	|	|	|	1658	...	|	1801	|	1858	|	|	|	...	|	2101	|	2218	2218
Skövde 756 d.	1309	1335	1410	...	1427	1512	1531	1610	1631	1712	...	1731	1816	1835	1912	1931	2031	2032	...	2035	2115	2127	2233	2233
Töreboda 756 d.	|	|	|	...	|	|	|	|	|	|	...	|	|	|	|	|	|	|	...	|	|	|	|	|
Hallsberg 750 756 d.	|	|	|	...	|	|	|	|	|	|	...	|	|	|	|	|	|	|	...	2126	|	|	|	|
Katrineholm 750 d.	|	1455	|	...	1547	|	1651	|	1751	|	...	1851	|	1955	|	2051	|	|	...	2201	|	2247	|	|
Södertälje Syd ▽ 750 a.	|	|	|	...	1625	|	|	|	|	|	...	|	|	|	|	2129	|	|	...	|	|	|	|	|
Flemingsberg ▽ 750 a.	1514	|	1616	...	|	1717	|	1819	|	1916	...	|	2021	|	2116	|	2236	2236	...	|	2320	|	0037	0037
Stockholm C 750/6 a.	1527	1550	1629	...	1644	1729	1743	1832	1843	1929	...	1943	2033	2048	2128	2148	2248	2248	...	2257	2332	2343	0050	0048

B – Until June 13.
D – From June 16.
E – From Aug. 17.
J – Not June 16 - Aug. 15.
m – To / from Malmö (Table **735**) on certain dates.

△ – Trains call to pick up only.
▽ – Trains call to set down only.
⊠ – Timings may vary. *VRS* reservations: https://vrresa.se ✆ +46 (0)8-580 971 66

☛ **First-class tickets**: On *Sn* services includes complimentary tea, coffee and snacks with breakfast served on departures before 0900.
On *VRS* services a complimentary meal and drink is included.

742 KRISTINEHAMN - KARLSTAD - GÖTEBORG

Subject to alteration due to engineering work

km	All trains 🅁	351 Ⓐ	355	359 ⑥	359 Ⓐ	363 †	363 ⚒	367	371 Ⓑ	Tab 7067 ⑥ b	Tab 7067 ⑦ b	375	379 ⑦–④
0	Kristinehamn § d.	0547	...	0943	...	1145	...	...	...	1603	1635	...	...
40	**Karlstad** § d.	0613	0812	1006	1011	1210	1212	1408	1611	1635	1700	1808	2232
59	Kil § d.	0627	0827	1025	1029	1226	1226	1426	1625	1648	1714	1830	2245
110	Säffle d.	0659	0900	1100	1100	1258	1259	1459	1701	1724	|	1901	2317
127	Åmål d.	0710	0911	1111	1110	1310	1310	1511	1711	1735	1800	1913	2327
168	Mellerud d.	0736	0936	1135	1135	1336	1336	1538	1738	1800	1825	1939	2352
209	Öxnered d.	0759	0958	1158	1158	1358	1358	1559	1759	1830s	|	2000	0014
219	Trollhättan d.	0806	1005	1205	1205	1405	1405	1606	1806	1845s	1849s	2007	0020
291	**Göteborg** C a.	0845	1040	1240	1240	1440	1440	1645	1845	1925	1945	2040	0050

All trains 🅁	350 Ⓐ	352 Ⓐ	356	360 ⚒	Tab 7034 ⑦ c	364	368	372 Ⓑ	378	Tab 7038 ⑦
Göteborg C d.	0514	0714	0914	1114	1115	1314	1514	1714	1914	2035
Trollhättan d.	0548	0752	0952	1151	1150u	1346	1552	1751	1945	2108
Öxnered d.	0556	0759	1000	1158	1156u	1359	1559	1758	1958	|
Mellerud d.	0617	0821	1022	1221	1220	1420	1622	1823	2020	2135
Åmål d.	0642	0845	1046	1245	1243	1444	1646	1847	2044	2158
Säffle d.	0658	0859	1059	1258	1255	1459	1659	1859	2056	2208
Kil § d.	0730	0932	1134	1330	1326	1531	1732	1934	2128	2243
Karlstad § a.	0746	0945	1147	1343	1342	1544	1746	1947	2143	2257
Kristinehamn § a.	...	...	...	...	1404	...	...	2014	2205z	2322

b – From Stockholm (Table **750**).
c – To Stockholm (Table **750**).
s – Calls to set down only.
u – Calls to pick up only.
z – ⑥ only.
§ – See also Table **750**.

Operator: *Øresundståg*

KØBENHAVN - MALMÖ - KRISTIANSTAD - KARLSKRONA 745

For other trains København - Malmö - Lund see Tables **735** and **746**. For other trains København - Hässleholm see Tables **730** and **746**.

km		Ⓐ	Ⓐ	Ⓐ	Ⓐ	⚒																			②–⑦
0	**København** H ⊖ d.	...	...	...	0444	0544	0544	0644	0744	0844	0944	1044	1144	1244	1344	1444	1544	1644	1744	1844	1944	2044	2144	2249	...
12	København Lufthavn ✈ ⊖ d.	...	...	...	0459	0559	0559	0659	0759	0859	0959	1059	1159	1259	1359	1459	1559	1659	1759	1859	1959	2059	2159	2304	...
47	**Malmö** C ⊖ a.	...	...	...	0525	0625	0625	0725	0825	0925	1025	1125	1225	1325	1425	1525	1625	1725	1825	1925	2025	2125	2225	2325	...
47	**Malmö** C ⊖ d.	...	0427	...	0527	0627	0627	0727	0827	0927	1027	1127	1227	1327	1427	1527	1627	1727	1827	1927	2027	2127	2227	2327	0024
63	Lund ⊖ d.	...	0447	...	0541	0641	0641	0741	0841	0941	1041	1141	1241	1341	1441	1541	1641	1741	1841	1941	2041	2141	2241	2341	0047
130	Hässleholm **734** ⊖ d.	0516	0534	...	0616	0716	0716	0816	0916	1016	1116	1216	1316	1416	1516	1616	1716	1816	1916	2016	2116	2216	2316	0016	0131
160	**Kristianstad** **734** a.	0533	0556	...	0633	0733	0733	0833	0933	1033	1133	1233	1333	1433	1533	1633	1733	1833	1933	2033	2133	2233	2333	0033	...
160	**Kristianstad** d.	0540	...	0602	0640	0740	...	0840	0940	1040	1140	1240	1340	1440	1540	1640	1740	1840	1940	2040	2140	2240	...	...	...
191	Sölvesborg d.	0559	...	0626	0659	0759	...	0859	0959	1059	1159	1259	1359	1459	1559	1659	1759	1859	1959	2059	2159	2259	...	...	...
222	**Karlshamn** d.	0621	...	0651	0721	0821	...	0921	1021	1121	1221	1321	1421	1521	1621	1721	1821	1921	2021	2121	2221	2321	...	...	...
260	Ronneby d.	0648	...	...	0748	0848	...	0948	1048	1148	1248	1348	1448	1548	1648	1748	1848	1948	2048	2148	2248	2348	...	...	...
290	**Karlskrona** a.	0712	...	...	0812	0912	...	1012	1112	1212	1312	1412	1512	1612	1712	1812	1912	2012	2112	2212	2312	0012	...	...	...

	Ⓐ				Ⓐ		⚒		⚒															②–⑦
arlskrona d.	...	...	...	...	0447	...	0547	...	0647	0747	0847	0947	1047	1147	1247	1347	1447	1547	1647	1747	1847	1947	2047	2147	...
onneby d.	...	...	...	...	0508	...	0608	...	0708	0808	0908	1008	1108	1208	1308	1408	1508	1608	1708	1808	1908	2008	2108	2208	...
arlshamn d.	...	...	...	...	0535	...	0635	...	0735	0835	0935	1035	1135	1235	1335	1435	1535	1635	1735	1835	1935	2035	2135	2235	...
ölvesborg d.	...	...	...	...	0558	...	0658	...	0758	0858	0958	1058	1158	1258	1358	1458	1558	1658	1758	1858	1958	2058	2158	2258	...
ristianstad a.	...	...	...	...	0620	...	0720	...	0820	0920	1020	1120	1220	1320	1420	1520	1620	1720	1820	1920	2020	2120	2220	2320	...
ristianstad **734** d.	0404	...	0525	0625	0625	0725	0725	0825	0825	0925	1025	1125	1225	1325	1425	1525	1625	1725	1825	1925	2025	2125	2225	2325	0004
ässleholm **734** ⊖ d.	0428	0504	0545	0645	0645	0745	0745	0845	0845	0945	1045	1145	1245	1345	1445	1545	1645	1745	1845	1945	2045	2145	2245	2345	0031
ınd ⊖ d.	0519	0549	0621	0721	0721	0821	0821	0921	0921	1021	1121	1221	1321	1421	1521	1621	1721	1821	1921	2021	2121	2221	2321	0021	0119
almö C ⊖ a.	0536	0606	0633	0733	0733	0833	0833	0933	0933	1033	1133	1233	1333	1433	1533	1633	1733	1833	1933	2033	2133	2233	2333	0033	0136
almö C ⊖ d.	...	...	0635	0735	0735	0835	0835	0935	0935	1035	1135	1235	1335	1435	1535	1635	1735	1835	1935	2035	2135	2235	2335	0035	...
øbenhavn Lufthavn ✈ ⊖ a.	...	...	0655	0755	0755	0855	0855	0955	0955	1055	1155	1255	1355	1455	1555	1655	1755	1855	1955	2055	2155	2255	0002	0118	...
øbenhavn H ⊖ a.	...	...	0709	0810	0810	0909	0909	1009	1009	1109	1209	1309	1409	1509	1611	1709	1811	1909	2009	2109	2209	2309	0017	0132	...

⊖ – *Øresundståg* trains run every 30 minutes København - Hässleholm and v.v. (see also Table **746**).

Operator: *Øresundståg*

KØBENHAVN, MALMÖ and GÖTEBORG - KALMAR 746

Other trains: København - Malmö - Lund see Tables **735** and **745**; København - Lund - Hässleholm see Table **745**; København - Lund - Hässleholm - Alvesta see Table **730**.

km		Ⓐ	Ⓐ	Ⓐ	Ⓐ	Ⓐ			Ⓐ			Ⓐ			Ⓐ	†			Ⓐ			Ⓑ		
0	**København** H ⊖ d.	...	...	0444	0514	0614	0614	0714	0814	0814	0914	1014	1014	1114	1214	1214	1214	1314	1414	1414	1514	1614	1614	...
12	København Lufthavn ✈ ⊖ d.	...	...	0459	0529	0629	0629	0729	0829	0829	0929	1029	1029	1129	1229	1229	1229	1329	1429	1429	1529	1629	1629	...
47	**Malmö** C ⊖ a.	...	...	0525	0555	0655	0655	0755	0855	0855	0955	1055	1055	1155	1255	1255	1255	1355	1455	1455	1555	1655	1655	...
47	**Malmö** C ⊖ d.	...	...	0527	0557	0657	0657	0757	0857	0857	0957	1057	1057	1157	1257	1257	1257	1357	1457	1457	1557	1657	1657	...
63	Lund ⊖ d.	...	...	0541	0611	0711	0711	0811	0911	0911	1011	1111	1111	1211	1311	1311	1311	1411	1511	1511	1611	1711	1711	...
80	Eslöv ⊖ d.	...	...	0550	0619	0719	0719	0819	0919	0919	1019	1119	1119	1219	1319	1319	1319	1419	1519	1519	1619	1719	1719	...
130	Hässleholm ⊖ a.	...	...	0614	0644	0744	0744	0844	0944	0944	1044	1144	1144	1244	1344	1344	1344	1444	1544	1544	1644	1744	1744	...
130	Hässleholm d.	...	...	...	0652	0752	...	0852	0952	...	1052	1152	...	1252	1352	1352	...	1452	1552	1552	1652	1752	...	...
181	Älmhult d.	...	...	...	0715	0815	...	0915	1015	...	1115	1215	...	1315	1415	1415	...	1515	1615	1615	1715	1815	...	...
228	Alvesta d.	...	0640	...	0740	0841	...	0940	1040	...	1140	1241	...	1340	1440	1441	...	1540	1640	1641	1740	1837	...	...
246	**Växjö** d.	0552	0652	...	0752	0852	...	0952	1052	...	1152	1252	...	1352	1452	1452	...	1552	1652	1652	1752	1852	...	...
302	Emmaboda ⊡ d.	0630	0730	...	0830	...	...	1030	1130	...	1230	...	...	1430	1530	...	...	1630	1730	...	1830	...	...	...
330	Nybro d.	0643	0743	...	0843	...	...	1043	1143	...	1243	...	...	1443	1543	...	...	1643	1743	...	1843	...	...	...
359	**Kalmar** a.	0659	0759	...	0859	...	...	1059	1159	...	1259	...	...	1459	1559	...	...	1659**z**	1759	...	1859	...	...	...

		Ⓑ			Ⓑ			Ⓐ	
øbenhavn H ⊖ d.	1714	1814	1814	1914	2014	2014	2114	2214	2249
øbenhavn Lufthavn ✈ ⊖ d.	1729	1829	1829	1929	2029	2029	2129	2229	2304
almö C ⊖ a.	1755	1855	1855	1955	2055	2055	2155	2255	2325
almö C ⊖ d.	1757	1857	1857	1957	2057	2057	2157	2257	2327
und ⊖ d.	1811	1911	1911	2011	2111	2111	2211	2311	2341
slöv ⊖ d.	1819	1919	1919	2019	2119	2119	2219	2319	2350
ässleholm ⊖ a.	1844	1944	1944	2044	2144	2144	2244	2344	0014
ässleholm d.	1852	1952	...	2052	2152	...	2252	...	...
lmhult d.	1915	2015	...	2115	2215	...	2315	...	...
lvesta d.	1940	2041	...	2140	2241	...	2344	...	...
äxjö d.	1952	2052	...	2152	2252	...	2355	...	...
mmaboda ⊡ d.	2030	...	...	2230	...	...	...	...	...
ybro d.	2043	...	...	2243	...	...	...	...	...
almar a.	2059	...	...	2259	...	...	...	...	...

	Ⓐ	Ⓒ	Ⓐ	Ⓒ	Ⓐ	⑥	⑦		Ⓐ
Kalmar d.	...	...	...	...	0600	...	...	0700	0800
Nybro d.	...	...	...	...	0615	...	...	0715	0815
Emmaboda ⊡ d.	...	...	...	...	0631	...	...	0731	0831
Växjö d.	0511	...	0611	...	0709	0711	...	0809	0909
Alvesta d.	0523	...	0623	...	0723	0723	...	0823	0923
Älmhult d.	0544	...	0644	...	0744	0744	...	0844	0944
Hässleholm a.	0609	...	0709	...	0809	0809	...	0909	1009
Hässleholm ⊖ d.	0616	0616	0716	0716	0816	0816	0816	0916	1016
Eslöv ⊖ d.	0639	0639	0739	0739	0839	0839	0839	0939	1039
Lund ⊖ d.	0651	0651	0751	0751	0851	0851	0851	0951	1051
Malmö C ⊖ a.	0703	0703	0803	0803	0903	0903	0903	1003	1103
Malmö C ⊖ d.	0705	0705	0805	0805	0905	0905	0905	1005	1105
København Lufthavn ✈ ⊖ a.	0725	0725	0825	0825	0925	0925	0925	1025	1125
København H ⊖ a.	0739	0739	0839	0839	0939	0939	0939	1039	1139

	⑥	⑦		⚒			Ⓐ			Ⓐ	⑦			Ⓐ			Ⓐ	⑦			Ⓐ	⑦		Ⓐ
almar d.	...	...	0900	...	...	1100	...	...	1300	1400	...	...	1500	...	...	1700	1800	...	...	1900	2000	...	...	2100
ybro d.	...	...	0915	...	...	1115	...	...	1315	1415	...	...	1515	...	...	1715	1815	...	...	1915	2015	...	...	2115
mmaboda ⊡ d.	...	...	0931	...	...	1131	...	...	1331	1431	...	...	1531	...	...	1731	1831	...	...	1931	2031	...	...	2132
äxjö d.	0911	...	1009	1111	...	1209	1311	...	1409	1509	1511	...	1609	1711	...	1809	1909	1911	...	2009	2109	2111	...	2206
lvesta d.	0923	...	1023	1123	...	1223	1323	...	1423	1523	1523	...	1623	1723	...	1823	1923	1923	...	2023	2123	2123	...	...
lmhult d.	0944	...	1044	1144	...	1244	1344	...	1444	1544	1544	...	1644	1744	...	1844	1944	1944	...	2044	2144	2144	...	...
ässleholm a.	1009	...	1109	1209	...	1309	1409	...	1509	1609	1609	...	1709	1809	...	1909	2009	2009	...	2109	2209	2209	...	...
ässleholm ⊖ d.	1016	1016	1116	1216	1216	1316	1416	1416	1516	1616	1616	1616	1716	1816	1816	1916	2016	2016	2016	2116	2216	2216	2216	...
slöv ⊖ d.	1039	1039	1139	1239	1239	1339	1439	1439	1539	1639	1639	1639	1739	1839	1839	1939	2039	2039	2039	2139	2239	2239	2239	...
und ⊖ d.	1051	1051	1151	1251	1251	1351	1451	1451	1551	1651	1651	1651	1751	1851	1851	1951	2051	2051	2051	2151	2251	2251	2251	...
almö C ⊖ a.	1103	1103	1203	1303	1303	1403	1503	1503	1603	1703	1703	1703	1803	1903	1903	2003	2103	2103	2103	2203	2303	2303	2303	...
almö C ⊖ d.	1105	1105	1205	1305	1305	1405	1505	1505	1605	1705	1705	1705	1805	1905	1905	2005	2105	2105	2105	2205	2305	2305	2305	...
øbenhavn Lufthavn ✈ ⊖ a.	1125	1125	1225	1325	1325	1425	1525	1525	1625	1725	1725	1725	1825	1925	1925	2025	2125	2125	2125	2225	2337	2337	2337	...
øbenhavn H ⊖ a.	1139	1139	1239	1339	1339	1439	1539	1539	1639	1739	1739	1739	1839	1939	1939	2039	2139	2139	2139	2239	2351	2351	2351	...

GÖTEBORG - VÄXJÖ - KALMAR (operator: SJ) *Subject to alteration - please confirm times when booking* ❦

km	All trains 🅁	**319** Ⓐ	**327** ⚒		**331** †	**335** Ⓒ		**339** ⚒	**343** Ⓑ	
0	**Göteborg** C ⊗ d.	0559	0959**r**	...	1219	1354	...	1604	1804	...
73	Borås ⊗ d.	0704	1103**r**	...	1318	1459	...	1700	1859	...
112	Limmared d.	0733	1132	...	1347	1529	...	1729	1929	...
173	Värnamo d.	0811	1211	...	1431	1611	...	1811	2012	...
222	Alvesta d.	0838	1238	...	1458	1638	...	1838	2038	...
239	**Växjö** d.	0850	1250	...	1510	1650	...	1850	2050	...
296	Emmaboda d.	0930	1330	...	1550	1730	...	1930	2130	...
324	Nybro d.	0944	1344	...	1604	1744	...	1944	2144	...
353	**Kalmar** a.	1005	1405	...	1631	1805	...	2005	2205	...

All trains 🅁	**328** E	**332** ⚒		**336** Ⓑ		**344** ⚒		**348** †	
Kalmar d.	0747	0955	...	1152	...	1552	...	1755	...
Nybro d.	0804	1013	...	1213	...	1613	...	1813	...
Emmaboda d.	0821	1030	...	1230	...	1630	...	1830	...
Växjö d.	0856	1107	...	1307	...	1707	...	1907	...
Alvesta d.	0909	1119	...	1319	...	1719	...	1919	...
Värnamo d.	0936	1146	...	1345	...	1746	...	1946	...
Limmared d.	1015	1228	...	1428	...	1828	...	2028	...
Borås ⊗ d.	1046	1258	...	1458	...	1859	...	2058	...
Göteborg C ⊗ a.	1140	1355	...	1551	...	1955	...	2155	...

MMABODA - KARLSKRONA (2nd class only) Operator: *Krösatågen*

km		Ⓐ	⚒	⚒	⚒		⚒				Ⓑ		Ⓑ		Ⓑ		Ⓑ
0	Emmaboda d.	0634	0734	0834	0934	1034	1134	1234	1334	1434	1534	1634	1734	1834	1934	2034	2134
57	Karlskrona a.	0716	0816	0916	1016	1116	1216	1316	1416	1516	1616	1716	1816	1916	2016	2116	2216

	Ⓐ	⚒	⚒	⚒		⚒				Ⓑ		Ⓑ		Ⓑ		Ⓑ
arlskrona a.	0542	0642	0742	0842	0942	1042	1142	1242	1342	1442	1542	1642	1742	1842	1942	2042
mmaboda d.	0625	0725	0825	0925	1025	1125	1225	1325	1425	1525	1625	1725	1825	1925	2025	2125

E – Ⓒ from July 12.

r – On ①–⑥ June 9 - July 5 (not June 14, 21) Goteborg d. 0854, Boras a. 1025.

⊡ – See panel below main table for connecting trains Emmaboda - Karlskrona and v.v.

⊖ – *Øresundståg* trains run every 30 minutes København - Hässleholm and v.v. (see also Table **745**).

⊗ – Additional local trains run Göteborg - Borås.

❦ – Journey times may be extended by up to 1 hour on certain dates.

747 STOCKHOLM - STOCKHOLM ARLANDA ✈

Operator: A-Train AB (*AEX* – Arlanda Express)

Journey time: 18 minutes. All services stop at Arlanda Södra (17 minutes from Stockholm, 2 minutes from Arlanda Norra). Södra serves terminals 2, 3 and 4; Norra serves terminal 5.

From **Stockholm** Central: 0420, 0435, 0450, 0505, 0520, 0535, 0550 and every 15 minutes until 2335; then 0005 and 0035.

From **Arlanda** Norra: 0450, 0505, 0520, 0535, 0550 and every 15 minutes until 2350; then 0005, 0035 and 0105.

750 STOCKHOLM - HALLSBERG - KARLSTAD - OSLO

Swedish holiday dates apply. **Subject to alteration due to engineering work - please check times and days of running when booking.**

km		*Tab*	*Sn*	*Tab*	*IC*	*IC*	*Tab*	*Sn*	*Tab*	*IC*	*Tab*	*Tab*	*Tab*	*Tab*	*IC*	*Sn*	*Sn*	*Sn*	*Tab*	*Sn*	*Sn*	*Tab*	*Tab*	*IC*	*IC*
		7059	**621**	**7051**	**653**	**653**	**7063**	**629**	**7055**	**665**	**7067**	**7041**	**7053**	**7053**	**669**	**639**	**643**	**643**	**7024**	**645**	**645**	**7028**	**7047**	**677**	**677**
		⑥	Ⓐ	④⑤	Ⓐ	Ⓒ	⑥ **J**		⑤ **J**		⑥	⑦ **z**	**C**	**B**	Ⓑ	⑥	Ⓐ	⑦	⑤ **J**	Ⓑ	⑥	⑦ **J**	⑦ **H**	Ⓐ	†
			[R] 🍷		[R] 🍷	[R] 🍷	[R]	[R] 🍷	[R] 🍷	[R]	[R] 🍷	[R] 🍷	[R] 🍷	[R] 🍷	[R] 🍷	[R] 🍷	[R] 🍷	[R] 🍷	[R] 🍷	[R] 🍷	[R] 🍷	[R] 🍷	[R]	[R] 🍷	[R] 🍷
0	**Stockholm** C ⊖ d.	...	0540	...	0727	0733	0900	1023	1153	1235	1341	1417	1438	1450	1530	1533	1707	1707	...	1809	1810	...	1901	1939	2022
36	Södertälje Syd △ ⊖ d.	...	0558	...	0747	0753	|	1041	|	1254	|	|	|	|	1550	1551	1726	1726	...	1827	1828	...	|	1959	2044
131	Katrineholm ⊖ d.	...	0640	...	0830	0836	0957	1130	1250	1341	1439	1515	1538	1550	1633	1633	1813	1813	⊗	1910	1910	⊗	1959	2042	2127
197	**Hallsberg** ⊖ d.	...	0717	...	0907	0913	1033	1205	1327	1417	1515	1550	1624	1627	1709	1708	1847	1847	1858	1945	1945	2015	2039	2119	2203
261	Degerfors d.	...	0747	...	0939	0945	1106	1235	1400	1448	1545	1619	1657	1657	1740	1738	1917	1917	1928	2015	2015	2050	2110	2151	2234
287	Kristinehamn 742 d.	0728	0805	0913	0957	1003	1127	1252	1417	1517	1603	1635	1715	1714	1757	1754	1935	1935	1954	2033	2033	2107	2127	2209	2252
327	**Karlstad** 742 a.	0754	0827	0942	1019	1025	1148	1315	1441	1542	1627	1658	1740	1740	1820	1815	2000	2000	2019	2054	2055	2126	2149	2231	2314
327	**Karlstad** 742 d.	...	0833	...	1027	1027	...	1317	...	...	1635	1700	...	...	1822	1820	...	|	...	2056	|	...	...	...	...
347	Kil 742 d.	...	|	...	|	|	...	|	...	...	1648	1712	...	...	|	|	...	2025**f**	...	|	2110**f**	...	...	...	...
395	Arvika d.	...	0916	...	1110	1110	...	1403	...	...	**g**	**g**	...	...	1905	1905	...	...	...	2138	...	...	...	...	...
430	Charlottenberg 🏛 d.	...	|	...	|	|	...	|	...	...	...	...	...	...	|	|	...	...	...	|	...	...	...	...	...
472	Kongsvinger d.	...	1006	...	1159	1159	...	1450	...	...	...	...	...	...	2006	2006	...	...	...	2228	...	...	...	...	...
572	**Oslo** Sentral a.	...	1110	...	1323	1323	...	1609	...	...	...	...	...	...	2123	2122	...	...	...	0002	...	...	...	...	...

	Sn	*Sn*	*IC*	*Tab*	*IC*	*Sn*		*Tab*	*Tab*	*Tab*	*IC*	*Tab*	*Tab*	*Sn*	*Tab*	*Tab*	*Sn*		*Tab*	*Tab*	*IC*	*IC*	*Sn*	*Tab*	
	620	**622**	**652**	**7060**	**656**	**626**		**7040**	**7052**	**17052**	**660**	**7023**	**7064**	**634**	**7027**	**7034**	**638**		**7054**	**7054**	**642**	**674**	**648**	**7038**	
	Ⓐ	⑥	Ⓐ	⑥ **u**	⑦	Ⓐ		⑦ **J**	**C**	⑦ **H**		⑤ **J**	⑥ **J**	⑦	⑦ **J**	⑦			⑤ **J**	④ **J**		**Y**		† **J**	
	[R] 🍷	[R] 🍷	[R] 🍷	[R] 🍷	[R] 🍷	[R] 🍷		[R] 🍷	[R] 🍷	[R] 🍷	[R] 🍷	[R] 🍷	🍷	[R] 🍷	[R] 🍷	[R] 🍷	[R] 🍷		[R] 🍷	[R] 🍷	[R] 🍷	[R] 🍷	[R] 🍷	[R] 🍷	
Oslo Sentral d.	...	...	...	...	...	0556	...	...	...	...	0727	...	...	...	...	...	1146	...	...	...	...	1436	1652	...	...
Kongsvinger d.	...	...	...	...	...	0706	...	...	...	...	0857	...	...	...	...	...	1257	...	...	...	...	1555	1804	...	...
Charlottenberg 🏛 d.	...	...	...	...	...	|	...	...	...	...	|	...	...	...	...	...	|	...	...	...	...	|	|	...	...
Arvika d.	...	...	...	...	...	0752	...	...	...	...	0943	...	...	...	...	**g**	1342	...	...	...	...	1642	1847	**g**	...
Kil 742 d.	0550	0625	...	...	...	|	...	...	...	...	|	1024	...	1245	...	1326	|	...	...	...	...	|	|	2243	...
Karlstad 742 a.	|	|	...	...	...	0832	...	...	...	...	1026	1039	...	|	...	1342	1422	...	...	...	...	1723	1930	2257	...
Karlstad 742 d.	0611	0644	0648	0822	0823	0834	...	0943	1004	1010	1027	1041	1205	1303	1249	1343	1424	...	1508	1515	1616	1730	1932	2259	...
Kristinehamn 742 d.	0632	0705	0711	0846	0845	0856	...	1005	1029	1034	1051	1105	1228	1329	1318	1404	1445	...	1532	1540	1639	1755	1955	2322	...
Degerfors d.	0650	0723	0730	0901	0904	0913	...	1022	1045	1050	1109	1121	...	1345	1334	1419	1503	...	1548	1556	1657	1814	2012	...	...
Hallsberg ⊖ d.	|	0755	0808	0935	0938	0950	...	1054	1122	1136	1143	1155	...	1421	1405	1500	1535	...	1627	1627	1731	1847	2046	...	...
Katrineholm ⊖ d.	|	0831	0846	1011	1015	1026	...	1139	1157	1213	1223	⊗	...	1457	⊗	1539	1610	...	1706	1706	1809	1924	2122	...	...
Södertälje Syd ▽ ⊖ a.	|	0912	0927	|	1057	1105	...	|	|	|	1306	...	...	1538	...	|	1651	...	|	|	1851	2006	2203	...	...
Stockholm C ⊖ a.	0850	0930	0948	1115	1117	1125	...	1245	1300	1310	1326	...	...	1556	...	1649	1711	...	1808	1808	1911	2026	2221	...	...

Local trains **Stockholm - Hallsberg** (operated by Mälartåg; 2nd class only)

⊡	Ⓐ	⚒		†	Ⓐ	Ⓒ **e**	Ⓐ	Ⓒ		Ⓐ	Ⓒ	Ⓐ	Ⓐ		Ⓐ	Ⓐ	Ⓒ	Ⓐ	**E**	⑤	①–④	†	⑤⑥	
Stockholm C d.	0633	0758	...	0851	0853	0958	1046	1151	...	1259	1358	1449	1533	1558	1650	1759	1759	1851	1952	2102	2158	2158	2328	...
Flemingsberg d.	0644	0809	...	0901	0903	1009	1056	1201	...	1309	1408	1459	1544	1608	1700	1809	1809	1901	2002	2112	2208	2208	2339	...
Södertälje Syd d.	0653	0819	...	0911	0913	1018	1106	1211	...	1319	1418	1515	1553	1618	1710	1819	1819	1911	2011	2122	2218	2218	2349	...
Flen 754 d.	0728	0901	...	0946	0948	1056	1147	1246	...	1357	1456	1555	1628	1656	1748	1903	1903	1946	2047	2200	2254	2254	0024	...
Katrineholm 754 d.	0740	0913	...	0958	0959	1107	1159	1258	...	1409	1507	1607	1639	1708	1800	1915	1914	1958	2059	2212	2306	2306	0036	...
Hallsberg a.	0817	0949	...	1034	...	...	1235	1334	...	1445	...	1643	1715	1744	1836	1951	...	2034	2135	2248	2342	2342	0112	...

⊡	Ⓐ	Ⓐ		Ⓐ	⑥	Ⓐ	Ⓒ		Ⓐ	⑥	Ⓒ **e**	Ⓐ	Ⓒ	Ⓐ		Ⓐ	Ⓒ		Ⓐ	⑦	Ⓐ	Ⓒ	Ⓑ	
Hallsberg d.	0516	0616	...	0721	0746	0832	0906	...	...	1017	...	1219	1317	1405	...	1516	...	1617	1721	1806	1821	...	2011	...
Katrineholm 754 d.	0553	0654	...	0759	0823	0909	0942	...	1053	1054	1149	1256	1355	1442	...	1554	1554	1654	1757	1843	1857	1954	2048	...
Flen 754 d.	0604	0705	...	0812	0834	0920	0958	...	1104	1105	1203	1308	1406	1457	...	1605	1605	1705	1808	1854	1908	2005	2059	...
Södertälje Syd d.	0641	0741	...	0847	0908	0959	1033	...	1139	1140	1237	1342	1441	1535	...	1640	1640	1740	1842	1928	1942	2041	2137	...
Flemingsberg d.	0651	0751	...	0856	0917	1010	1042	...	1149	1149	1246	1351	1451	1545	...	1650	1650	1750	1851	1937	1951	2051	2146	...
Stockholm C a.	0702	0802	...	0907	0927	1021	1052	...	1200	1200	1256	1402	1502	1555	...	1700	1701	1801	1902	1947	2002	2102	2156	...

Local trains **Kristinehamn - Karlstad - Charlottenberg** (operated by Värmlandstrafik; 2nd class only). **Subject to alteration**

	Ⓐ	Ⓐ	Ⓐ	⑥	Ⓐ	⑦	Ⓐ	⑥	Ⓐ	⑦	⑥	Ⓐ		Ⓐ	⑥		②–⑤	⑦	①	⑥	Ⓐ	Ⓐ	Ⓐ	⑦	
Degerfors d.	...	...	...	...	0653	...	...	...	...	...	...	...	...	...	...	...	...	...	...	...	...	...	...	...	...
Kristinehamn 742 d.	...	...	0607	0633	0709	...	0735	...	0836	0845	0905	1032	...	1221	1330	...	1424	1426	1424	1542	...	1627	1653**v**	1658	...
Karlstad 742 a.	...	...	0642	0700	0735	...	0801	...	0905	0911	0933	1058	...	1247	1354	...	1454	1452	1454	1607	...	1654	1723**v**	1722	...
Karlstad 742 d.	0519	0633	...	0702	0735	0752	...	0846	0911	0913	...	1100	...	1250	1355	...	1455	1454	1455	1608	1624	1654	1725	1725	...
Kil 742 d.	0537	0647	...	0716	0755	0809	...	0900	0929	0926	...	1113	...	1302	1416	...	1508	1507	1529**t**	1621	1645	1711	1738	1739	...
Arvika d.	0611	0724	...	0753	0831	0846	...	0941	1003	1007	...	1147	...	1337	1451	...	1547	1541	1608	1700	1723	1746	1817	1816	...
Charlottenberg a.	0636	0749	...	0819	0854	0911	...	1008	1028	1033	...	1213	...	...	1518	...	1612	1605	1639	1724	1748	...	1843	1843	...

	Ⓐ	①	②–⑤	⑥	③	**G**	⑥	⑦	Ⓐ	⑥	⑦
Degerfors d.	...	...	...	...	...	...	...	...	...	...	...
Kristinehamn 742 d.	1734	1825	1825	1835	1917	1917	2107	2136	2142	2146	2333
Karlstad 742 a.	1758	1850	1852	1902	1951	1951	2139	2200	2208	2211	2356
Karlstad 742 d.	...	1901	1914	1904	1955	2001	2140	2200	2210	...	...
Kil 742 d.	...	1917	1942	1919	2013	2015	2159	2220	2223	...	...
Arvika d.	...	1954	2018	1955	2112**r**	2112**r**	2235	2256	2316**x**	...	...
Charlottenberg a.	...	...	...	...	2144	2144	2300	2321	2343	...	...

	Ⓐ	⑥	Ⓐ	Ⓐ	⑦	Ⓐ	⑥	Ⓐ	⑥	Ⓐ
Charlottenberg d.	...	...	...	0549	0636	0639	0644	0808	...	1007
Arvika d.	0503	...	...	0612	0700	0703	0708	0832	...	1031
Kil 742 d.	0540	...	...	0650	0737	0743	0744	0912	...	1113
Karlstad 742 a.	0552	...	...	0701	0749	0755	0801	0924	...	1126
Karlstad 742 d.	0553	0603	0652	0703	0750	0756	0802	0925	0935	1127
Kristinehamn 742 d.	0619	0627	0720	0730	0816	0824	0828	0950	1001	1153
Degerfors a.	0634	...	...	...	...	...	...	...	...	...

	⑥	Ⓐ	⑦	Ⓐ	⑦	⑥		**G**	③	⑦	Ⓐ	Ⓐ	Ⓐ	⑥	⑤	②④	①③	Ⓐ	⑦	⑥	Ⓐ	⑥	⑦	Ⓐ	
Charlottenberg d.	1024	...	1113	1151	...	1237	...	1404	1424	1514	1521	1658	...	1732	...	...	...	1910	1914	1932	...	...	2113	2114	...
Arvika d.	1048	...	1139	1216	...	1259	...	1429	1447	1540	1546	1722	1752	1755	...	...	...	1935	1938	2001	2031	2047	2141	2139	...
Kil 742 d.	1124	...	1218	1257	...	1335	...	1508	1537	1619	1624	1806	1839	1830	...	...	...	2008	2017	2037	2108	2122	2220	2227	...
Karlstad 742 a.	1136	...	1231	1310	...	1347	...	1522	1555	1632	1637	1819	1854	1842	...	...	...	2021	2030	2049	2125	2135	2232	2243	...
Karlstad 742 d.	1137	1143	1232	1314	1349	1352	...	1523	1557	1633	1640	1820	...	1843	1904	1907	1913	2025	2034	2052	...	...	2234	2249	...
Kristinehamn 742 d.	1202	1214	1304	1340	1412	1418	...	1552	1622	1656	1711	1846	...	1909	1928	1945	1945	2051	2105	2118	...	...	2303	2318	...
Degerfors a.	...	...	...	...	...	...	...	...	...	...	...	...	...	...	...	...	...	...	...	...	...	...	...	...	...

B – ④⑤ to July 11 (not June 20).
C – ③④⑤ July 16 - Aug. 15 (not Aug. 13).
E – Daily except ⑤.
G – ①②④⑤.
H – July 13 - Aug. 10.
J – Not June 16 - Aug. 16.
Y – Please check days of running when booking.

e – Not June 14 - Aug. 17.
f – Extends to Kil on certain dates.
g – To/from Göteborg (Table **742**).
r – Arrives 2050.
t – Arrives 1508.

u – Not June 20, 28.
v – On ④ Kristinehamn d. 1638, Karlstad a. 1712.
x – Arrives 2259.
z – Not June 21, July 6.

⊖ – See also Table **740** and panel below main table.
⊗ – From/to Alvesta.
△ – Trains call to pick up only.
▽ – Trains call to set down only.
⊡ – Timings and days of running may vary - please check before travel.
Tab - Operated by Tågab.

VÄSTERÅS - LUDVIKA 752

Operator: *TiB* (2nd class only)

km		Ⓐ	Ⓐ	ⒶJ	Ⓒ	Ⓐ	Ⓐ	Ⓒ	Ⓐ	Ⓒ	Ⓐ	Ⓒ	Ⓐ	Ⓒ	Ⓐ	Ⓒ	Ⓐ	Ⓒ	Ⓐ	ⒶJ	Ⓒ	Ⓐ	ⒶJ	Ⓒ	Ⓐ	
0	**Västerås** d.	0529	0630	0707	0726	0739	0840	0926	0940	1026	1040	1127	1141	1226	1241	1326	1342	1426	1443	1514	1526	1547	1616	1626	1648	...
80	Fagersta C d.	0634	0733	0805	0827	0837	0941	1027	1039	1129	1139	1227	1239	1326	1340	1428	1442	1526	1542	1616	1627	1646	1718	1726	1747	...
129	**Ludvika** a.	0718	...	...	0914	0921	...	1114	1124	...	...	1314	...	...	1424	1514	...	...	1626	...	1714	...	...	...	1831	...

	Ⓒ	Ⓐ	Ⓐ	Ⓒ		Ⓐ	Ⓐ				
ästerås d.	1726	1749	1850	1927	...	1951	2052	2219	...	...	...
agersta C d.	1827	1848	1949	2027	...	2050	2150	2319	...	...	...
udvika a.	1915	...	2033	2114	...	...	2234	...	...	...	...

	Ⓐ	ⒶJ	Ⓐ	ⒶJ	Ⓐ	Ⓒ	Ⓐ	Ⓒ	Ⓐ	Ⓒ	
Ludvika d.	...	...	0522	...	...	0644	0728	...	...	0845	...
Fagersta C d.	0503	0537	0607	0637	0708	0730	0813	0831	0914	0930	...
Västerås a.	0602	0637	0707	0740	0811	0832	0912	0932	1013	1032	...

	Ⓐ	Ⓒ	Ⓐ	Ⓒ	Ⓐ	Ⓒ	Ⓐ	Ⓒ	Ⓐ	Ⓒ	ⒶJ	Ⓐ	Ⓒ	Ⓐ	Ⓒ	Ⓐ	Ⓒ	Ⓐ	Ⓐ	Ⓒ	Ⓐ	Ⓐ					
udvika d.	0930	...	...	1043	...	...	1232	1245	...	...	...	1432	1445	...	...	1636	1645	...	1839	1845	...	2103	...	...	...	...	...
agersta C d.	1015	1030	1115	1129	1216	1231	1317	1331	1417	1431	1444	1517	1531	1622	1631	1722	1731	1824	1925	1931	2026	2149	...	...	...	...	...
ästerås a.	1113	1132	1213	1232	1313	1331	1414	1431	1515	1531	1551	1619	1631	1720	1731	1821	1831	1922	2023	2031	2123	2251	...	...	...	...	...

– Not June 29 - Aug. 10.

LINKÖPING - NORRKÖPING - VÄSTERÅS - SALA - UPPSALA 754

Operator: *Mälartåg* (2nd class only)

km		Ⓐ	Ⓐ	Ⓐ	Ⓒ	Ⓐ	ⒶH	Ⓐ		ⒶJ		Ⓐ		ⒶH	ⒶJ	ⒶH		Ⓐ	Ⓐ	ⒶH		Ⓐ		Ⓐ‡	‡	Ⓐ‡
	Linköping 730 d.	...	...	...	...	0610	...	0710	0810	0910	1010	...	1210	...	1310	...	1410	...	1510	...	1610	1710	1810	1910	2010	...
0	**Norrköping** 730 d.	...	0538	...	...	0638	...	0738	0838	0938	1038	1136	1238	...	1338	...	1438	...	1538	...	1638	1738	1838	1938	2038	2138
48	Katrineholm 750 d.	...	0604	...	...	0704	...	0805	0904	1005	1104	1201	1304	...	1404	...	1504	...	1605	...	1704	1804	1905	2005	2104	2205
71	Flen 750 d.	...	0615	...	...	0715	...	0816	0915	1016	1115	1215	1315	...	1415	...	1515	...	1616	...	1715	1815	1916	2016	2115	2216
112	Eskilstuna ⊡ d.	0622	0652	0722	0752	0752	0822	0852	0952	1052	1152	1252	1352	1422	1452	1522	1552	1622	1652	1722	1752	1852	1952	2052	2152	2252
160	**Västerås** ⊡ d.	0656	0726	0756	0826	0826	0856	0926	1026	1126	1226	1326	1426	1456	1526	1556	1626	1656	1726	1756	1826	1926	2026	2126	2226	2326
199	Sala a.	0724	0754	0823	0853	0854	0924	0954	1054	1154	1254	1354	1454	1524	1554	1624	1654	1724	1754	1824	1854	1954	2053	...	...	...
	Sala d.	0737	...	0831	...	...	0932	...	...	...	...	...	...	1531	...	1631	...	1734	...	1831	...	...	...	...	...	...
	Uppsala a.	0820	...	0909	...	...	1008	...	...	...	...	...	...	1620	...	1708	...	1816	...	1919	...	...	...	...	...	...

	Ⓐ	Ⓐ	ⒶH	J	Ⓐ‡	Ⓐ	ⒶH	Ⓐ	ⒶH	Ⓐ	J	Ⓐ		Ⓐ	Ⓐ		ⒶH	Ⓐ	ⒶH		ⒶH	Ⓐ		Ⓐ‡	‡	Ⓐ‡
ppsala d.	...	...	0541	...	0634	...	0741	...	0842	...	...	...	...	...	...	...	1435	...	1539	...	1638	...	...	...	...	2120
ala a.	...	...	0625	...	0722	...	0825	...	0827	...	...	...	...	...	...	...	1525	...	1622	...	1727	...	...	...	...	2200
ala d.	...	0603	0632	0703t	0732	0803	0832	0903t	0932	1003	1103t	1203	1303t	1403	...	1503t	1532	1603	1632	1703t	1732	1803	1903t	2005	2105	2205
ästerås ⊡ d.	0533	0634	0704	0734	0804	0834	0904	0934	1004	1034	1134	1234	1334	1434	1504	1534	1604	1634	1704	1734	1804	1834	1934	2034	2134	2234
skilstuna ⊡ d.	0608	0708	0737	0808	0837	0908	0937	1008	1037	1108	1208	1308	1408	1508	1537	1608	1637	1708	1738	1808	1838	1908	2008	2108	2207	2308
len 750 d.	0642	0742	...	0842	...	0942	...	1042	...	1142	1242	1342	1442	1542	...	1642	...	1742	...	1842	...	1942	2042	2142	...	...
atrineholm 750 d.	0657	0757	...	0857	...	0957	...	1057	...	1157	1257	1357	1457	1557	...	1657	...	1757	...	1857	...	1957	2057	2157	...	...
orrköping 730 d.	0724	0824	...	0924	...	1022	...	1124	...	1224	1324	1424	1524	1624	...	1724	...	1824	...	1924	...	2024	2124	2222	...	...
inköping 730 a.	0749	0849	...	0949	...	...	...	1149	...	1249	1349	1449	1549	1649	...	1749	...	1849	...	1952	...	2049	2149	...	...	...

– Not June 10 - Aug. 30.
– Not on Ⓐ June 16 - Aug. 15.
t – Departs 2 minutes later on Ⓒ.
‡ – Subject to alteration.
⊡ – Additional journeys run Eskilstuna - Västerås and v.v.

MJÖLBY - HALLSBERG - ÖREBRO - GÄVLE 755

Operator: *TiB* (2nd class only)

Warning! A revised service operates July 14 - August 10 – see note ❦. There is no service Mjölby - Hallsberg or v.v. July 7 - August 10 – see note ◧.

km		Ⓐ	Ⓐ	⚒	Ⓐ	Ⓐ	⑥	⑦	Ⓐ	Ⓐ		ⒶJ	⑥	ⒶJ	Ⓐ	Ⓒ	⑦	ⒶJ		Ⓐ	Ⓐ	Ⓒ	Ⓐ		ⒶJ	Ⓒ
0	**Mjölby** d.	...	...	...	...	...	...	...	...	0547	...	...	...	...	...	...	...	...	1001	...	...	1201	...	1401	...	...
27	Motala d.	...	...	...	...	...	...	...	...	0604	...	...	...	...	...	...	...	...	1018	...	...	1218	...	1418	...	...
96	**Hallsberg** a.	...	...	...	...	...	...	...	...	0640	...	...	...	...	...	...	...	...	1107	...	...	1307	...	1510	...	...
96	**Hallsberg** 756 d.	...	...	...	...	0515	...	...	0615	0650	0725	0800	...	0830	_0859_*	0932	...	_0959_	1117	_1159_*	_1258_*	1317	_1403_*	1517	1550	...
121	**Örebro** C 756 a.	...	...	...	...	0535	...	...	0635	0710	0745	0820	...	0852	_0919_*	0952	...	_1019_	1137	_1219_*	_1318_*	1337	_1423_*	1537	1611	...
121	**Örebro** C d.	...	...	...	...	0550	0553	...	0650	...	0750	...	0853	0853	0953	0953	1053	1053	1153	1253*	1353	1353	1453	1553	1623	1653
146	Frövi d.	...	...	...	...	0608	0608	...	0708	...	0808	...	0909	0908	1008	1008	1109	1108	1208	1308*	1408	1408	1508	1608	1641	1709
204	Kopparberg d.	...	...	...	...	0651	0651	...	0756	...	0856	...	|	0956	1056	1056	|	1157	1257	1401*	1458	1458	1559	1700	...	|
232	Grängesberg d.	...	...	...	...	0712	0712	...	0816	...	0916	...	|	1016	1121	1122	|	1217	1317	1421*	1520	1520	1618	1721	...	|
247	Ludvika d.	...	...	...	0636	0728	0728	...	0827	...	0927	...	|	1027	1133	1133	|	1228	1328	1433*	1531	1531	1632	1732	...	|
295	**Borlänge** a.	...	...	...	0708	0757	0757	...	0856	...	0954	...	|	1106	1209	1200	|	1255	1358	1511*	1602	1602	1701	1811	...	|
295	**Borlänge** 758 d.	0526	...	0628	0708	0811	0812	0812	0912*	...	1012	...	|	1112	1212	1212	|	1312	1411	1512	1612	1612	1711	1812	...	|
317	Falun 758 d.	0547	...	0646	0726	0829	0830	0830	0930*	...	1030	...	|	1130	1230	1230	|	1330	1429	1530	1630	1630	1730	1830	...	|
	Fagersta d.	|	0610	|	|	|	|	|	|	...	|	...	0957	|	|	|	1157	|	|	|	|	|	|	|	...	1757
	Avesta Krylbo d.	|	0635	|	|	|	|	|	|	...	|	...	1022	|	|	|	1222	|	|	|	|	|	|	|	...	1822
371	Storvik d.	0626	0714	0726	0803	0907	0907	0907	1007*	...	1108	...	1101	1207	1307	1307	1301	1406	1506	1606	1707	1707	1807	1907	...	1901
385	Sandviken d.	0636	0724	0737	0814	0917	0917	0917	1017*	...	1118	...	1111	1217	1317	1317	1311	1417	1517	1617	1717	1718	1818	1917	...	1911
408	**Gävle** a.	0651	0738	0752	0828	0931	0931	0931	1031*	...	1132	...	1126	1232	1331	1331	1326	1431	1532	1631	1731	1731	1831	1931	...	1925

	ⒶJ	Ⓐ	⑥	⑦	Ⓐ	ⒶJ	⑦	Ⓐ	Ⓐ	⑦
jölby d.	...	...	1601	1601	...	...	1801	1801	2001	2001
otala d.	...	...	1618	1618	...	...	1818	1818	2018	2018
allsberg a.	...	...	1710	1710	...	...	1907	1907	2109	2108
allsberg 756 d.	1640	...	1717	1717	1732	1850	1917	1917	2109	2109
rebro C 756 a.	1700	...	1737	1737	1752	1910	1937	1937	2129	2129
rebro C d.	1701	1705	1753	1753	1753	...	1953	1953	2153*	...
rövi d.	1716	1721	1808	1808	1808	...	2008	2008	2208*	...
opparberg d.	1801	|	1856	1856	1856	...	2056	2056	2256*	...
rängesberg d.	1822	|	1917	1917	1917	...	2117	2117	2317*	...
udvika d.	1837	|	1928	1928	1928	...	2128	2128	2328*	...
orlänge a.	1907	|	1956	1956	1956	...	2157	2157	2400*	...
orlänge 758 d.	1911	|	...	2011	2011	...	...	2210	...	...
alun 758 d.	1931	|	...	2029	2029	...	...	2228	...	...
Fagersta d.	|	1806	...	|	|	...	...	|	...	...
Avesta Krylbo d.	|	1831	...	|	|	...	...	|	...	...
torvik d.	2006	...	...	2106	2106	...	...	2303	...	...
andviken d.	2016	...	...	2117	2117	...	...	2313	...	...
ävle a.	2035	...	...	2131	2131	...	...	2332	...	...

km		Ⓐ	ⒶJ	Ⓐ	Ⓐ	Ⓐ	⑥	⑦	ⒶJ	Ⓐ	Ⓐ	⑥
0	**Gävle** d.	...	...	...	...	0409	...	...	...	0522	0618	0618
23	Sandviken d.	...	...	...	...	0424	...	...	...	0537	0635	0637
37	Storvik d.	...	...	...	...	0434	...	...	...	0547	0647	0647
95	Avesta Krylbo d.	...	...	...	0557	|	...	...	...	|	|	|
130	Fagersta d.	...	...	...	0631	|	...	...	...	|	|	|
	Falun 758 d.	...	...	...	|	0515	...	...	...	0628	0724	0724
	Borlänge 758 a.	...	...	...	|	0540	...	...	...	0650	0741	0741
	Borlänge d.	...	0456	...	|	0553	0553	...	...	0653	0756	0756
	Ludvika d.	...	0524	...	|	0621	0621	...	...	0725	0826	0826
	Grängesberg d.	...	0535	...	|	0632	0632	...	...	0736	0837	0837
	Kopparberg d.	...	0555	...	|	0659	0659	...	...	0759	0859	0859
202	Frövi d.	0608	0638	0709	0715	0742	0742	...	...	0842	0942	0942
228	**Örebro** C a.	0624	0654	0725	0730	0758	0758	...	...	0858	0958	0958
228	**Örebro** C 756 d.	0625	0655	0726	_0748_*	0820	0820	0820	0842	_0947_*	_1044_*	0959
252	**Hallsberg** 756 a.	0645	0715	0746	_0808_*	0840	0840	0840	0902	_1007_*	_1104_*	1019
	Hallsberg d.	...	...	...	...	0846	0847	0846	...	...	...	...
	Motala d.	...	...	...	...	0928	0928	0928	...	...	...	...
	Mjölby a.	...	...	...	...	0944	0944	0944	...	...	...	...

	⑦	Ⓐ	⑥		ⒶJ	⑦	Ⓐ	Ⓒ	ⒶJ		ⒶJ	ⒶJ	ⒶJ	⑥	Ⓑ	Ⓐ	Ⓒ	Ⓐ	⑥	Ⓑ	Ⓐ	⑥	Ⓑ§	ⒶJ	Ⓑ	Ⓐ
ävle d.	...	0715	0828	0824	0924	1028	1024	1024	1124	1224	...	1324	...	1424	1424	1524	1628	1628	1624	1624	1724	1824	1824	1924	2022	...
andviken d.	...	0736	0843	0839	0938	1043	1040	1038	1138	1238	...	1338	...	1438	1438	1538	1643	1643	1638	1638	1738	1838	1838	1938	2036	...
torvik d.	...	0746	0853	0849	0948	1053	1050	1048	1148	1248	...	1348	...	1448	1448	1548	1653	1653	1648	1648	1748	1848	1848	1948	2046	...
Avesta Krylbo d.	...	|	0933	|	|	1133	|	|	|	|	...	|	...	|	|	|	1733	1733	|	|	|	|	|	|	|	...
Fagersta d.	...	|	0959	|	|	1159	|	|	|	|	...	|	...	|	|	|	1759	1758	|	|	|	|	|	|	|	...
alun 758 d.	...	0828	|	0931	1030	|	1132	1131	1230	1330	...	1430	...	1530	1530	1630	|	▬	1730	1730	1830	1930	1932	2030	2132	...
orlänge 758 a.	...	0845	|	0948	1047	|	1149	1148	1247	1347	...	1447	...	1547	1547	1647	|	...	1747	1747	1847	1947	1950	2047	2149	...
orlänge d.	0756	0856*	|	0956	1053	|	1156	1159	1256	1357	...	1456	...	1602	1602	1700	|	...	1756	1756	...	▬	2014	...	...	2214
udvika d.	0826	0926*	|	1026	1127	|	1227	1227	1327	1431	...	1530	...	1631	1631	1731	|	...	1824	1824	...	...	2042	...	...	2242
rängesberg d.	0837	0937*	|	1037	1138	|	1238	1238	1338	1442	...	1541	...	1642	1642	1742	|	...	1835	1835	...	...	2053	...	...	...
opparberg d.	0859	0959*	|	1059	1159	|	1259	1259	1402	1501	...	1600	...	1707	1707	1802	|	...	1859	1859	...	...	2119	...	...	...
rövi d.	0942	1042*	1043	1142	1242	1243	1342	1342	1444	1543	1624	1642	1732	1750	1750	1850	1843	...	1942	1942	...	...	2202	...	...	...
rebro C a.	0958	1058*	1058	1158	1258	1258	1358	1358	1500	1558	1639	1658	1748	1806	1806	1906	1858	ⒶJ	1958	1958	...	Ⓐ	2218	...	...	...
rebro C 756 d.	0959	_1147_*	...	1220	_1344_	...	_1447_*	1420	_1541_	1619	1653	...	1748	1807	1819	...	...	1946	1959	2019	...	2129	...	...	...	...
allsberg 756 a.	1019	_1207_*	...	1240	_1404_	...	_1507_*	1440	_1600_	1640	1713	...	1808	1827	1841	...	...	2006	2019	2039	...	2149	...	...	...	...
allsberg d.	...	...	...	1244	...	...	...	1447	...	1646	...	...	...	...	1843	...	...	...	...	2045	...	...	...	...	...	...
otala d.	...	...	...	1328	...	...	...	1528	...	1728	...	...	...	...	1919	...	...	...	...	2128	...	...	...	...	...	...
jölby a.	...	...	...	1344	...	...	...	1544	...	1744	...	...	...	...	1937	...	...	...	...	2144	...	...	...	...	...	...

– Not June 29 - Aug. 10.

– **July 7 - Aug. 10**: no service Mjölby - Hallsberg or v.v. Most Mjölby trains are diverted to run from / to Norrköping (running 15 minutes later Hallsberg to Örebro and up to 21 minutes **earlier** Örebro to Hallsberg).

❦ – **July 14 - August 10**: service is by 🚌 Borlänge - Ludvika and v.v. with extended journey times and revised timings.

* – Not June 29 - Aug. 10.

§ – Runs 11 – 18 minutes later Borlänge - Örebro July 7 - 13.

756 STOCKHOLM - VÄSTERÅS - ÖREBRO - HALLSBERG - GÖTEBORG

Subject to alteration. See Table **740** for fast services Stockholm - Skövde - Göteborg and v.v. See Table **732** for Stockholm - Örebro via Eskilstuna.

km																										
		Ⓐ	Ⓐ	⑥	⚒	⚒	Ⓐ						Ⓐ						⚒	†	Ⓑ		†	⚒	Ⓑ	k
0	**Stockholm** C ‡ d.	...	...	...	...	0614	...	0714r	0814	0914	1014	1114	...	1214	1314	1414	1514	1614	1714	1714	1814	1914	1958	2014	2214	2314
72	Enköping ‡ d.	...	...	...	...	0655	...	0755r	0855	0955	1055	1155	...	1254	1355	1455	1555	1655	1756	1755	1855	1955	2042	2055	2255	2355
107	**Västerås** ‡ d.	...	0512	0520	0612	0712	...	0812	0912	1012	1112	1212	...	1311	1412	1512	1612	1712	1812	1812	1912	2012	2108	2112	2312	0010
141	Köping d.	...	0529	0537	0629	0729	...	0829	0929	1029	1129	1229	...	1328	1429	1529	1629	1729	1829	1829	1929	2029	2128	2129	2329	...
159	Arboga d.	...	0541	0549	0641	0741	...	0841	0941	1041	1141	1241	...	1340	1441	1541	1641	1741	1841	1841	1941	2041	2140	2141	2341	...
205	**Örebro** C a.	...	0602	0610	0703	0803	...	0902	1002	1102	1202	1302	...	1401	1503	1602	1702	1802	1902	1902	2002	2102	2204	2202	0002	...
205	**Örebro** C 755 d.	...	0614	0614	0715	0804	0815	0915	1015	1115	1214	1304	1316	1414	1516	1614	1715	1804	1915	1904	2003	2103	2205	2203	0003	...
230	**Hallsberg** 755 a.	...	0635	0635	0737	0826	0836	0936	1036	1136	1236	1325	1335	1435	1536	1635	1736	1825	1936	1925	2025	2124	2226	2224	0024	...
230	**Hallsberg** 736 d.	0543	0637	0637	0741	...	0841	0939	1039	1139	1241	...	1341	1440	1541	1637	1741	...	1941	1941	...	...	...	...	...	...
260	Laxå 736 d.	0600	0653	0653	0758	...	0857	0955	1055	1156	1257	...	1357	1457	1557	1653	1757	...	1957	1957	...	...	...	...	...	...
305	Töreboda d.	0622	0716	0716	0820	...	0919	1018	1120	1218	1320	...	1419	1520	1620	1716	1820	...	2020	2020	...	...	...	...	...	...
344	**Skövde** d.	0638	0732	0732	0836	...	0935	1034	1136	1233	1336	...	1436	1536	1636	1732	1836	...	2036	2036	...	...	...	...	...	...
374	Falköping d.	0654	0748	0748	0852	...	0952	1050	1152	1249	1352	...	1453	1552	1652	1748	1852	...	2052	2052	...	...	...	...	...	...
408	Herrljunga d.	0710	0807	0807	0907	...	1006	1105	1207	1304	1407	...	1508	1606	1706	1808	1906	...	2106	2106	...	...	...	...	...	...
443	Alingsås d.	0729	0826	0826	0926	...	1026	1124	1226	1323	1426	...	1527	1624	1724	1826	1924	...	2124	2124	...	...	...	...	...	...
488	**Göteborg** C a.	0800	0857	0857	0957	...	1057	1157	1257	1357	1457	...	1557	1700	1757	1857	1957	...	2157z	2157	...	...	...	...	...	...

	Ⓐ	⚒	Ⓐ	⑥	⚒	⑦	Ⓐ	⚒									Ⓐ	Ⓒ			①–④	⑦	⑤⑥	⑦–④	⑤⑥	Ⓑ b
Göteborg C d.	...	...	0503	...	0602	...	0702	...	0802v	0902	1002	1102	1203	1302	1402	1502	1559	1602	1703	1802	1902	1902	1903	2002	2003	2103
Alingsås d.	...	...	0532	...	0631	...	0731	...	0833	0933	1031	1132	1234	1331	1433	1531	1628	1633	1736	1834	1931	1931	1932	2034	2034	2132
Herrljunga d.	...	...	0551	...	0651	...	0751	...	0853	0953	1051	1152	1252	1351	1452	1551	1648	1652	1754	1853	1951	1951	1951	2053	2052	2150
Falköping d.	...	...	0613	...	0707	...	0809	...	0909	1008	1107	1208	1310	1407	1508	1607	1704	1707	1810	1909	2007	2007	2007	2108	2115	2209
Skövde d.	...	...	0632	...	0722	...	0823	...	0924	1023	1122	1223	1324	1422	1523	1622	1719	1722	1824	1924	2023	2023	2023	2123	2134	2227
Töreboda d.	...	...	0647	...	0738	...	0845	...	0944	1044	1144	1244	1340	1444	1544	1644	1735	1738	1840	1944	2049	2045	2039f	2144	2149	—
Laxå 736 d.	...	...	—	...	0808x	...	0909	...	1008	1108	1208	1308	—	1508	1608	1708	1808	1808	—	2008	2112	2109	—	2208	...	...
Hallsberg 736 a.	...	...	Ⓑ	...	0824x	...	0924	...	1024	1124	1224	1324	...	1525	1625	1725	1825	1825	...	2025	2128	2126	...	2225	...	...
Hallsberg 755 d.	0534	0634	0734	0731	0826	0834	0926	0930t	1029	1129	1228	1329	1428	1528	1628	1728	1828	1828	1928	2028	2130	2128	...	2228	...	...
Örebro C 755 a.	0555	0655	0755	0751	0848	0855	0946	0950	1050	1150	1250	1350	1450	1550	1649	1749	1849	1849	1949	2049	2150	2149	...	2248	...	...
Örebro C d.	0557	0657	0757	0753	0857	0857	...	0957	1057	1157	1257	1357	1456	1556	1656	1756	1856	1856	1956	2056	2156	2156	...	2256	...	...
Arboga d.	0618	0718	0818	0817	0918	0918	...	1018	1118	1218	1318	1418	1518	1618	1718	1818	1918	1918	2018	2118	2218	2218	...	2318	...	Ⓐ
Köping d.	0628	0729	0829	0828	0929	0929	...	1029	1129	1229	1329	1429	1528	1629	1729	1829	1929	1929	2029	2129	2229	2229	⑥	2329	...	0529
Västerås ‡ d.	0647	0748	0848	0847	0948	0948	...	1048	1148	1248	1348	1448	1548	1648	1748	1848	1948	1948	2048	2148	2247	2249	2249	2346	...	0548
Enköping ‡ d.	0702	0803	0903	0905	1003	1003	...	1103	1203	1303	1403	1503	1603	1703	1803	1903	2003	2003	2103	2203	...	2304	2304	...	...	0603
Stockholm C ‡ a.	0744	0844	0944	0952	1044	1044	...	1144	1244	1344	1444	1544	1644	1744	1844	1944	2044	2044	2144	2244	...	2344	2344	...	...	0644

b – An additional journey runs to Skövde at 2303Ⓑ.
f – ⑤ only.
k – On ⑤⑥ Stockholm 2343, Enköping 0024, Vesterås 0039.
r – ⚒ only.
t – 0927 on ⑥.
v – ①–⑥ only.
x – On ⑥ Laxå d. 0802, Hallsberg a. 0818.
z – ①–⑤ only.
‡ – Additional trains operate Stockholm - Västerås and v.v.

758 STOCKHOLM - BORLÄNGE - FALUN and MORA

Warning! Subject to alteration - please check timings and days of running when booking.

Subject to alteration July 14 - August 10 with 🚌 substitution Säter - Borlänge - Falun and v.v. From Aug. 11 trains are diverted via Västerås with extended journey times.

km																									
		IC		*IC*	*IC*		*IC*	*IC*		*IC*	*IC*		*IC*	*IC*	*TiB*		*IC*	*IC*		*IC*	*TiB*		*IC*		
		12		**14**	**32**		**16**	**42**		**18**	**36**		**20**	**46**			**22**	**54**		**48**			**26**		
		Ⓐ		⚒	⚒									⑦				Ⓐ			Ⓑ		Ⓑ		
		B						**B**		**B**															
		🅁🍷		🅁🍷	🅁🍷		🅁🍷	🅁🍷		🅁🍷	🅁🍷		🅁🍷	🅁🍷	2		🅁🍷	🅁🍷		🅁🍷	2		🅁🍷		
0	**Stockholm** C ♠ d.	0613	...	0744	0744	...	0942	0942	...	1144	1144	...	1343	1343	...	...	1544	1644	...	1744	...	...	1944	...	...
39	Arlanda C ✈ ♠ d.	0635	...	0804	0804	...	1005	1005	...	1205	1205	...	1405	1405	...	...	1605	1705	...	1805	...	...	2005	...	...
69	**Uppsala** ♠ d.	0654	...	0823	0823	...	1025	1025	...	1225	1225	...	1424	1424	...	...	1624	1724	...	1824	...	...	2024	...	...
131	Sala d.	0736	...	0900	0900	...	1100	1100	...	1259	1259	...	1500	1500	...	...	1700	1802	...	1900	...	...	2100	...	...
164	Avesta Krylbo d.	0756	...	0920	0920	...	1120	1120	...	1320	1320	...	1520	1520	...	...	1720	1823	...	1920	...	...	2120	...	...
229	**Borlänge** a.	0837	...	1007	1007	...	1207	1207	...	1407	1407	...	1607	1607	...	...	1807	1903	...	2001	...	...	2201	...	...
229	**Borlänge** □ 755 d.	0838	...	1007	1014	...	1207	1211	...	1407	1422	...	1607	1611	1612	...	1807	1903	...	2004	2011	...	2201	...	...
253	**Falun** 755 a.	0900	...	1027	|	...	1226	|	...	1426	|	...	1626	|	1629	...	1826	1922	...	|	2029	...	2220	...	...
	Leksand □ d.	...	...	...	1050	...	...	1248	...	...	1456	...	...	1646	...	...	...	...	...	2041	...	...	...	...	...
	Rättvik □ d.	...	...	...	1107	...	...	1306	...	...	1513	...	...	1707	...	...	...	...	...	2059	...	...	...	...	...
	Mora C □ a.	...	...	...	1132	...	...	1332	...	...	1537	...	...	1732	...	...	...	...	...	2124	...	...	...	...	...

	IC	*IC*	*IC*		*TiB*	*IC*	*IC*	*TiB*	*IC*	*IC*		*IC*	*IC*	*TiB*	*IC*	*IC*	*TiB*	*IC*	*TiB*	*IC*	*IC*		*IC*	*IC*	
	13	**51**	**51**			**41**	**15**		**43**	**17**		**45**	**19**		**31**	**21**		**47**		**39**	**25**		**49**	**27**	
	Ⓐ	Ⓐ	⑥		Ⓐ	Ⓐ	⑥		⑥	Ⓑ		⑦							⚒				⑦	Ⓐ	
		B	**B**									**B**				**B**		**B**			**B**			**B**	
	🅁🍷	🅁🍷	🅁🍷		2	🅁🍷	🅁🍷	2	🅁🍷	🅁🍷		🅁🍷	🅁🍷	2	🅁🍷	🅁🍷	2	🅁🍷	2	🅁🍷	🅁🍷		🅁🍷	🅁🍷	...
Mora C □ d.	...	...	...	...	...	0628	...	...	0828	...	...	1028	...	...	1232	...	...	1431	...	1621	...	...	1824	...	...
Rättvik □ d.	...	...	...	...	...	0652	...	...	0852	...	...	1052	...	...	1256	...	...	1455	...	1646	...	...	1848	...	...
Leksand □ d.	...	...	...	...	...	0709	...	...	0910	...	...	1109	...	...	1315	...	...	1513	...	1707	...	...	1908	...	...
Falun 755 d.	0532	0602	0608	...	0724	|	0735	0931	|	0934	...	|	1135	1330	|	1335	1530	|	1730	|	1733	...	|	1929	...
Borlänge □ 755 a.	0551	0620	0626	...	0741	0748	0757	0948	0952	0954	...	1145	1154	1347	1353	1354	1547	1551	1747	1748	1751	...	1946	1947	...
Borlänge d.	0552	0621	0627	...	...	0751	0758	...	0955	0955	...	1155	1155	...	1355	1355	...	1555	...	1755	1755	...	1948	1948	...
Avesta Krylbo d.	0634	0703	0709	...	...	0838	0838	...	1038	1038	...	1238	1238	...	1437	1437	...	1638	...	1837	1838	...	2038	2038	...
Sala d.	0654	0723	0729	...	...	0900	0859	...	1059	1059	...	1259	1259	...	1458	1458	...	1659	...	1900	1859	...	2100	2100	...
Uppsala ♠ d.	0733	0805	0805	...	...	0935	0935	...	1137	1136	...	1335	1334	...	1535	1535	...	1735	...	1935	1935	...	2138	2139	...
Arlanda C ✈ ♠ a.	0753	0824	0824	...	...	0954	0958	...	1155	1155	...	1354	1353	...	1554	1554	...	1754	...	1954	1954	...	2157	2158	...
Stockholm C ♠ a.	0816	0845	0845	...	...	1015	1020	...	1217	1215	...	1415	1415	...	1615	1615	...	1815	...	2015	2015	...	2220	2219	...

Other local services **BORLÄNGE - MORA** (2nd class only) ✣ **Warning!** Service is by 🚌 July 14 - August 10 – see note ❦.

km																										
		Ⓐ	Ⓐ	Ⓐ	Ⓐ	Ⓐ			⚒	⑦	Ⓐ	Ⓐ	Ⓐ			Ⓐ	Ⓐ	⚒	Ⓐ	⑦	⑦	⚒	⚒	①–④	⑤	Ⓑ
		J	J	K	J	J			n	n	J	b	J	n		n	J		J	J	K	J	K	J	J	
0	**Borlänge** d.	0507	0557	0557	0701	0751	0853	...	1018	1018	1129	1226	1318	1422	...	1533	1540	1620	1727	1822	1820	1822	1822	1917	1917	2220
43	Leksand d.	0542	0634	0634	0737	0825	0926	...	1051	1051	1202	1300	1400	1454	...	1612	1612	1653	1800	1853	1852	1856	1856	1950	1950	2255
63	Rättvik d.	0602	0651	0651	0756	0843	0941	...	1106	1108	1217	1318	1415	1512	...	1632	1632	1708	1815	1912	1910	1912	1912	2005	2005	2311
103	**Mora** C a.	0627	0716	0716	0820	0908	1005	...	1129	1131	1246	1341	1454	1540	...	1702	1702	1736	1839	1936	1934	1936	1936	2037	2047	2334
104	Morastrand a.	0630	...	0719	0823	0912	1009*	...	...	...	1249	...	1458	...	...	...	...	1740*	1842	...	...	...	1939	2040	2050	2338

	Ⓐ	Ⓐ	⑥	⑦	Ⓐ	Ⓑ	Ⓑ	Ⓐ	Ⓐ	Ⓐ	⑥	⑦		Ⓐ		Ⓐ	Ⓐ		Ⓐ	Ⓐ	Ⓐ		Ⓐ	⚒	Ⓑ	Ⓐ
		J		n	J	J	K	J	n	J	J	J	K	J	n	n	J	E	b	n	b	n	J			J
Morastrand d.	0459	0535	0626	0626	0708	...	0816	0906	1003	1002	1019	1022	...	1058	...	1300	1310	...	...	1512	1507	...	...	1808*	2009a	2212
Mora C d.	0504	0539	0631	0631	0716	0820	0820	0914	1008	1007	1024	1027	1024	1103	1222	1305	1315	1423	1429	1516	1511	1610	1712	1812	2014	2217
Rättvik d.	0528	0603	0655	0655	0740	0844	0844	0940	1032	1031	1047	1051	1047	1133	1246	1345	1345	1447	1453	1541	1541	1633	1741	1842	2038	2241
Leksand d.	0543	0618	0710	0710	0755	0859	0859	0955	1050	1048	1106	1106	1105	1147	1304	1401	1401	1505	1511	1557	1557	1652	1759	1857	2057	2256
Borlänge a.	0614	0653	0741	0741	0830	0934	0934	1034	1122	1122	1141	1141	1137	1227	1335	1438	1438	1536	1541	1636	1636	1724	1837	1933	2128	2327

A – Aug. 11-29.
B – Until June 14.
E – June 15, 20-22, 28-30, July 1-13.
J – Not June 29 - July 13.
K – June 29 - July 13.

a – Ⓐ June 30 - July 11.
b – June 15 - July 13.
n – Not June 15 - July 13.

□ – See also panel below main table.
♠ – For additional *Sn* and *IC* trains Stockholm - Uppsala and v.v. see Table **760**. Local trains (operated by Mälartåg) also operate approx. hourly.
✣ – Operated by Tåg i Bergslagen.
* – Not June 29 - July 13.

❦ – 🚌 service **July 14 - Aug. 10**: **Borlänge - Morastrand**: 0520Ⓐ, 0825, 1027, 1227, 1427, 1630, 1830, 2027⑤⑦, 2048①–④⑥, 2248Ⓑ. **Morastrand - Borlänge** (timings vary July 27 - Aug. 1): 0428Ⓐ, 0528, 0725, 0925, 1125, 1325, 1525, 1725⑤⑦, 1807①–④, 2007Ⓑ. Journey approx 2 hours. Subject to alteration from Aug. 11.

STOCKHOLM - GÄVLE - SUNDSVALL - UMEÅ 760

Subject to alteration due to engineering work. Some trains may be cancelled mid-June to mid-August. For overnight services see Table **767**.

km		Sn	XT	IC	Sn	XT	XT	IC	XT	IC	Sn	Sn		Sn	IC	XT	Sn	XT	IC	IC	XT		IC	XT	IC	IC	
		590		**260**	**560**			**262**		**80**	**564**	**564**		**566**	**266**		**568**		**268**	**268**			**270**		**10**	**10**	
		Ⓐ**Q**	Ⓐ	Ⓐ**P**	⚒**t**	†	⑥	Ⓐ**Q**	Ⓐ	**Bd**	Ⓒ	Ⓒ**T**		**C**	**D**	Ⓐ	⑥⑦	†	⑥	Ⓐ	Ⓐ			⑥	Ⓒ**E**	Ⓐ**E**	
		🅁🍷	2	🅁	🅁🍷	2	2	🅁	2	🅁	🅁🍷	🅁🍷		🅁🍷	🅁🍷	2	🅁🍷	2	🅁	L🅁	2		🅁	2	🅁🍷	🅁🍷	
	Linköping **730a** d.	...	...	...	...	...	...	0530	...	...	...	...	...	...	0727	...	...	...	...	...	...	...	0934	...	...	...	...
0	**Stockholm** C d.	0350	...	0559	0622	...	...	0730	...	0755	0821	0821	...	0922	0931	...	1021	...	1027	1028	...	...	1132	...	1211	1212	...
39	Arlanda C ✈ △ d.	|	...	0621	0642	...	...	0751	...	0820	0842	0842	...	0942	0952	...	1041	...	1051	1051	...	...	1152	...	1234	1234	...
69	Uppsala △ d.	0428	...	0639	0700	...	...	0810	...	0838	0900	0900	...	1000	1010	...	1100	...	1109	1109	...	...	1210	...	1255	1255	...
182	**Gävle** C d.	0512	0612	0726	0745	0745	0851	0856	0920	0927	0945	0945	...	1045	1056	1127	1145	1157	1156	1156	1257	...	1256	1300	1347	1347	...
260	Söderhamn d.	0556	0705	...	0830	0831	0942	...	1006	...	1030	1030	...	1130	...	1213	1230	1257	...	...	1348	...	...	1347	1430	1430	...
314	Hudiksvall d.	0630	0738	...	0858	0900	1013	...	1040	...	1058	1058	...	1158	...	1244	1258	1327	...	...	1421	...	...	1416	1500	1500	...
402	**Sundsvall** C a.	0740	0843	...	0953	0959	1118	...	1143	...	1154	1154	...	1256	...	1347	1353	1428	...	...	1540	...	...	1519	1554	1554	...
715	*Umeå C* ⊡ a.	...	...	...	1237	...	...	...	...	...	...	1440	...	...	...	...	...	...	...	...	...	...	...	...	...	...	...

	IC	Sn	IC	XT	Sn	IC	XT	Sn	XT	IC	XT	XT		Sn	IC	Sn	Sn	IC		Sn	IC	IC	XT	IC			
	272	**574**	**274**		**576**	**276**		**578**		**278**				**580**	**280**	**598**	**582**	**282**		**584**	**284**	**286**		**288**	**92**		
	Ⓐ**Q**	**F**		†		†	Ⓐ	†**e**	⑥	Ⓒ	Ⓐ	†		**G**	Ⓐ		Ⓑ**Q**	Ⓐ			Ⓑ			**H**	**N**		
	🅁	🅁🍷	L🅁	2	🅁🍷	🅁	2	🅁🍷	2	🅁	2	2		🅁🍷	L🅁	🅁🍷	🅁🍷	🅁		🅁🍷	🅁	L🅁	2	🅁	🅁🍷		
Linköping **730a** d.	1030	...	1127	...	...	1231	...	...	...	1329	...	...	...	...	1429	...	...	1525	...	...	1633	1726	...	1833	...	...	...
Stockholm C d.	1231	1321	1331	...	1421	1431	...	1521	...	1530	...	...	...	1623	1632	1650	1723	1732	...	1823	1831	1928	...	2031	2155	...	...
Arlanda C ✈ △ d.	1252	1341	1351	...	1441	1451	...	1541	...	1551	...	...	...	1642	1652	1712	1742	1752	...	1842	1851	1951	...	2051	2221	...	...
Uppsala △ d.	1310	1400	1410	...	1500	1510	...	1600	...	1609	...	...	...	1700	1710	1730	1800	1810	...	1900	1910	2009	...	2109	2245	...	...
Gävle C d.	1356	1445	1456	1510	1545	1556	1612	1645	1648	1656	1708	1708	...	1745	1756	1813	1845	1856	...	1945	1956	2056	2116	2156	2353	...	...
Söderhamn d.	...	1530	...	1558	1630	...	1702	1726	1741	...	1757	1757	...	1830	...	**n**	1930	...	...	2028	...	...	2158	...	0042	...	...
Hudiksvall d.	...	1558	...	1638	1658	...	1743	1758	1813	...	1827	1829	...	1858	...	...	1958	...	...	2054	...	...	2228	...	0130	...	...
Sundsvall C a.	...	1653	...	1742	1756	...	1844	1854	1920	...	1928	1937	...	1953	...	...	2053	...	...	2151	...	...	2325	...	0244	...	...
Umeå C ⊡ a.	...	1940	...	...	...	...	...	2138	...	...	...	...	...	2239	...	...	2340	...	...	...	...	...	...	...	0712	...	...

	IC	IC	Sn	XT	IC	Sn	IC	Sn	Sn	IC	Sn	IC	XT	Sn	Sn		XT	Sn	XT	Sn	IC	Sn	IC	Sn	XT	IC	
	259	**261**	**561**		**263**	**563**	**265**	**565**	**591**	**267**	**567**	**269**		**569**	**597**			**571**		**595**	**273**	**573**	**275**	**575**		**277**	
	Ⓐ**Q**	⚒	Ⓐ**Q**	Ⓐ	Ⓐ**Q**	Ⓐ	⑥	Ⓐ**M**	Ⓐ	Ⓐ**Q**		Ⓑ	Ⓒ	Ⓐ	⑥		Ⓐ	Ⓒ	†	⑦	⑥	⑦**M**	**H**	⑦	Ⓐ		
	🅁	L🅁	🅁🍷	2	🅁	🅁🍷	L🅁	🅁🍷	🅁🍷	🅁	🅁🍷	L🅁	2	🅁🍷	🅁🍷		2	🅁🍷	2	🅁🍷	🅁	🅁🍷	🅁	🅁🍷	2	🅁	
Umeå C ⊡ d.	...	...	...	...	...	...	...	0421	...	...	...	...	...	0615	...	...	...	0719	...	...	...	...	...	0915	...	...	...
Sundsvall C d.	...	...	0509	0536	...	0606	...	0704	...	...	0806	...	0837	0902	...	...	0930	1006	1028	...	...	1104	...	1204	1230	...	...
Hudiksvall d.	...	...	0603	0633	...	0700	...	0800	...	...	0900	...	0942	1000	...	...	1038	1100	1132	...	...	1200	...	1300	1332	...	...
Söderhamn d.	...	...	0631	0703	...	0728	...	0828	**n**	...	0928	...	1014	1028	**n**	...	1105	1128	1203	**n**	...	1228	...	1328	1404	...	...
Gävle C d.	0601	0701	0714	0746	0801	0814	0901	0914	0931	1001	1014	1101	1107	1114	1114	...	1149	1213	1248	1259	1301	1314	1401	1414	1448	1501	...
Uppsala ▽ d.	0651	0751	0759	...	0851	0859	0951	0959	1017	1050	1059	1151	...	1159	1159	...	...	1259	...	1347	1351	1359	1450	1459	...	1551	...
Arlanda C ✈ ▽ d.	0710	0810	0818	...	0909	0919	1010	1019	1036	1109	1119	1210	...	1218	1219	...	...	1319	...	|	1410	1419	1509	1519	...	1610	...
Stockholm C a.	0731	0828	0838	...	0927	0937	1028	1037	1058	1127	1137	1228	...	1238	1237	...	...	1337	...	1422	1429	1437	1527	1537	...	1630	...
Linköping **730a** a.	0932	1029	...	...	1133	...	1230	...	...	1332	...	1430	...	...	...	...	...	...	...	...	1633	...	1733	...	...	1831	...

	Sn	XT	IC	Sn	IC	XT	XT	IC		XT	IC	Sn	XT	IC	Sn	XT	Sn		IC	Sn	XT	XT	XT	XT			
	577		**279**	**579**	**281**			**11**			**283**	**583**		**285**	**585**		**587**		**85**	**589**					**91**		
	⑦**M**	⑥	Ⓐ		†	Ⓐ	†	**E**		⑥	⑥	Ⓒ**f**	Ⓐ		Ⓑ	†	⑥**e**		**E**	**T**	Ⓐ	⑥	†	Ⓐ	**N**		
	🅁🍷	2	L🅁	🅁🍷	🅁	2	2	🅁🍷		2	🅁	🅁🍷	2	L🅁	🅁🍷	2	🅁🍷		🅁🍷	🅁🍷	2	2	2	2	🅁🍷		
Umeå C ⊡ d.	...	...	...	...	...	...	...	...	...	...	...	...	...	...	1420	...	1517	...	...	1610	...	...	...	...	2116	...	...
Sundsvall C d.	1306	1306	...	1404	...	1423	1436	1455	...	1531	...	1604	1615	...	1704	1756	1802	...	...	1904	1955	2000	2008	2134	0117	...	...
Hudiksvall d.	1400	1414	...	1500	...	1532	1544	1558	...	1632	...	1700	1717	...	1800	1858	1856	...	...	2000	2057	2057	2116	2245	0300	...	...
Söderhamn d.	1428	1447	...	1528	...	1603	1615	1630	...	1704	...	1728	1745	...	1828	1927	1924	...	...	2028	2126	2126	2158	2313	0335	...	...
Gävle C d.	1514	1535	1600	1614	1701	1658	1708	1725	...	1746	1801	1814	1835	1901	1914	2009	2014	...	2106	2113	2212	2212	2244	2356	0451	...	...
Uppsala ▽ d.	1559	...	1650	1659	1751	...	...	1820	...	...	1851	1859	...	1951	1959	...	2059	...	2202	2159	...	...	...	...	0553	...	...
Arlanda C ✈ ▽ d.	1619	...	1709	1719	1810	...	...	|	...	...	1910	1919	...	2010	2019	...	2119	...	2223	2219	...	...	...	...	0635	...	...
Stockholm C a.	1637	...	1727	1737	1828	...	...	1902	...	...	1928	1937	...	2028	2037	...	2137	...	2246	2237	...	...	...	...	0701	...	...
Linköping **730a** a.	...	...	1929	...	2029	...	...	...	...	...	...	...	...	...	...	...	...	...	...	...	...	...	...	...	...	...	...

SUNDSVALL - UMEÅ

km		NT	NT	NT	NT	NT	NT	NT	Sn	NT	NT	Sn	NT	NT	NT	NT	NT	NT	Sn	NT	Sn	NT	Sn	NT	Sn	NT	
									560			**564**							**574**		**578**		**580**		**582**		**92**
		Ⓐ	Ⓐ**J**	Ⓐ**J**	Ⓐ**K**	Ⓐ**J**	Ⓐ**J**	**A**	⚒**t**	⚒**J**	Ⓐ**K**	Ⓒ**T**	**J**	Ⓒ**K**	Ⓐ		Ⓑ	Ⓐ	**F**	Ⓒ	†**e**	Ⓐ	**G**	⑤	Ⓑ**Q**	Ⓐ	**N**
		2	2	2	2	2	2	2	🅁🍷	2	2	🅁🍷	2	2	2	2	2	2	🅁🍷	2	🅁🍷	2	🅁🍷	2	🅁🍷	2	🅁🍷
0	*Stockholm C* ⊙ d.	...	...	...	...	...	...	...	0622	...	...	0821	...	...	...	...	...	...	1321	...	1521	...	1623	...	1723	...	2155
402	**Sundsvall** C d.	0415	0515	...	0715	0815	...	0915	0957	1015	1015	1200	1215	1215	1315	1415	1515	1615	1657	1815	1858	1915	1957	2015	2058	...	0311
470	Härnösand d.	0507	0605	0805	0805	0911	...	1010	1044	1107	1107	1246	1309	1309	1409	1508	1608	1709	1744	1910	1947	2010	2048	2111	2146	...	0417
516	Kramfors d.	0531	0634	0832	0832	0936	1036	1036	1113	1130	1130	1309	1332	1332	1436	1531	1631	1733	1808	1934	2011	2037	2111	2134	2210	...	0446
603	Örnsköldsvik C d.	0616	0719	0917	0917	1014	1115	1115	1147	1217	1217	1347	1414	1414	1519	1619	1713	1817	1851	2015	2049	2115	2147	2216	2250	2254	0540
713	**Umeå** Östra a.	0722	0822	1022	1022	1123	1223	1223	1231	1320	1320	1434	1521	1521	1624	1725	1822	1922	1936	2115	2134	2223	2235	2322	2335	2354	0705
715	**Umeå** C a.	0724	0825	1024	1024	1125	1225	1225	1237	1324	1324	1440	1524	1524	1626	1728	1824	1925	1940	2118	2138	2226	2239	2325	2340	2358	0712

	Sn	NT	NT	NT	Sn	NT	Sn	NT	NT	NT	Sn	NT	NT	NT	Sn	NT	Sn	NT	NT	NT	Sn	NT	NT	NT	NT		NT
	565				**569**		**571**				**575**				**585**		**587**				**589**					**91**	
	Ⓐ**M**	Ⓐ	Ⓐ**J**	Ⓐ**K**	Ⓐ	Ⓐ	Ⓒ	Ⓐ	**J**	**K**	⑦		Ⓐ**J**		Ⓐ	⚒	⑥**e**	Ⓐ**J**	Ⓐ**K**	⑦	**T**	⚒**J**	⑥**K**	Ⓑ	Ⓑ**J**	**N**	Ⓐ
	🅁🍷	2	2	2	🅁🍷	2	🅁🍷	2	2	2	🅁🍷	2	2	2	🅁🍷	2	🅁🍷	2	2	2	🅁🍷	2	2	2	2	🅁🍷	2
Umeå C d.	0421	0437	0536	0536	0615	0636	0719	0737	0837	0837	0915	1037	1137	1237	1420	1433	1517	1537	1537	1537	1610	1636	1636	1737	1837	2116	2137
Umeå Östra d.	0425	0442	0541	0541	0621	0641	0724	0742	0842	0842	0920	1042	1142	1242	1425	1438	1524	1542	1542	1542	1615	1640	1640	1742	1842	2123	2143
Örnsköldsvik C d.	0508	0538	0636	0636	0709	0738	0807	0836	0937	0937	1003	1142*	1236	1336	1508	1534	1609	1637	1637	1637	1702	1734	1734	1837	1940	2235	2247
Kramfors d.	0544	0623	0720	0720	0745	0821	0843	0916	1020	1020	1046	1224	1314	1418	1544	1620	1645	1724	1724	1724	1738	1817	1817	1922	2021	2328	...
Härnösand d.	0607	0645	0744	0744	0807	0843	0904	0946	1043**c**	1043	1106	1246	1343	1442	1607	1645	1707	1747	1747	1747	1804	1840	1840	1947	2045	0007	...
Sundsvall C a.	0658	0739	...	0839	0857	0941	0958	1048	1139**c**	1139	1159	1340	1440	1540	1659	1743	1759	...	1839	1839	1900	1948	1948	2041**r**	2147	0102	...
Stockholm C. ⊙ a.	1037	...	...	...	1238	...	1337	...	...	...	1537	...	...	...	2037	...	2137	...	...	...	2237	...	...	...	...	0701	...

A – Ⓒ (daily June 23 - Aug. 10).
B – June 9 - July 6, July 12, 13, 19, 20, 26, 27, Aug. 5, 9 - 15, 18 - 29.
C – Ⓐ to Aug. 15; Ⓑ from Aug. 24.
D – June 16 - July 13, July 21 - 31, Aug. 1 - 3, 9, 10.
E – To / from Duved (Table **761**).
F – ⚒ to June 14; ⑥ June 28 - Aug. 9 (also June 20); ⚒ from Aug. 18.
G – June 15 - Aug. 14.
H – ①–④ (not June 14 - Aug. 17).
J – Not June 23 - Aug. 10.
K – June 23 - Aug. 10.
L – To / from Ljusdal (Table **761**).
M – Not June 14 - Aug. 24.
N – 🛏, 🛏, 2 and ✕ Stockholm - Umeå - Boden - Luleå and v.v. Subject to alteration. For further information and additional night trains see Table **767**.
P – Not June 30 - Aug. 8.
Q – Not June 15 - Aug. 17.
T – ⑥⑦ June 15 - Aug.10 (also Aug. 20).

c – Ⓒ only.
d – To / from Duved (Table **761**).
e – Not June 15 - Aug. 31.
f – Ⓒ (not on ⑥ July 5 - Aug. 16).
n – To / from Östersund (Table **761**).
r – 2052 on ⑤**J**.
t – Not Aug. 18 - 22 or ⑥ June 21 - Aug. 30.

△ – *Sn* trains call to pick up only.
▽ – *Sn* trains call to set down only (times are arrival times).
⊡ – See lower part of table.
⊙ – See upper part of table.
* – 1137 on ⑥**J**.

761 STOCKHOLM and SUNDSVALL - ÖSTERSUND - TRONDHEIM

See Table **760** for Stockholm - Gävle - Sundsvall and v.v. For overnight services, see Table **767**.

km		*NT*	*NT*	*NT*	*NT*	*NT*	*NT*	*NT*	*IC* 80	*NT*	*NT*	*IC* 268	*IC* 10	*IC* 10	*NT*	*IC* 10	*NT*	*NT*	*IC* 274	*NT*	*NT*	*IC* 280	*Sn* 598	*NT*	*IC* 286	70
		Ⓒ	Ⓐ	⑥	Ⓐ	†	Ⓐ		n	⑥		Ⓐ v	⑥	Ⓐ	⑦	⑦	⑥	Ⓐ		Ⓐ	†	Ⓐ		Ⓐ J		N
		2	2	2	2	2	2	2	🅁 🍷	2	2	🅁	🅁 🍷	🅁 🍷	2	🅁 🍷	2	2	⊖ 🅁	2	2	⊖ 🅁	🅁 🍷	2	⊖ 🅁	🅁 🍷
0	**Stockholm** C ◇ d.	...	...	...	...	...	...	...	0755	...	...	1028	1211	1212	...	1211	...	...	1331	...	...	1631	1650	...	1928	2238
39	Arlanda C ✈ ◇ d.	...	...	...	...	...	...	...	0820	...	...	1051	1234	1234	...	1234	...	...	1351	...	...	1653	1712u	...	1951	2304u
69	Uppsala ◇ d.	...	...	...	...	...	...	...	0838	...	...	1109	1255	1255	...	1259	...	...	1410	...	...	1710	1730u	...	2009	2325u
182	**Gävle** C ◇ d.	...	...	...	...	...	...	...	0928	...	...	1159	1347	1347	...	1347	...	...	1502	...	...	1758	1814	...	2101	0121
281	Bollnäs d.	...	...	...	...	...	...	...	1033	...	...	1301	|	|	...	|	...	...	1604	...	...	1910	1905	...	2203	0232
344	Ljusdal d.	...	...	...	...	...	...	...	1113	...	...	1343	|	|	...	|	...	...	1646	...	...	2003	1941	...	2246	0335
	Sundsvall d.	...	0456	0609	0610	0803	0810	1010	|	1210	1410	...	1558	1558	1603	1605	1609	1639	...	1810	1909	...	|	2009	...	|
450	Ånge d.	...	0607	0723	0723	0914	0924	1124	1213	1322	1524	...	1706	1706	1714	1720	1722	1756	...	1927	2022	...	2038	2121	...	0501
480	Bräcke d.	...	0626	0741	0741	0931	0942	1142	1233	1341	1542	...	1729	1729	1731	1739	1740	1814	...	1944	2040	...	2056	2139	...	0526
551	**Östersund** C a.	...	0722	0833	0837	1034	1034	1237	1317	1433	1631	...	1818	1823	1822	1838	1835	1905	...	2035	2138	...	2139	2232	...	0625
551	**Östersund** C d.	0718	0724	0844	...	...	1040	1240	1322	...	1633	...	1820	1825	1823	1840	...	...	...	2037	...	...	...	...	...	0636
656	Åre d.	0833	0837	1010	...	...	1159	1359	1441	...	1744	...	1939	1941	1938	2001	...	...	...	2200	...	...	...	...	...	0803
665	Duved d.	0841	0845	1018	...	...	...	1407	1453	...	1752	...	1951	1953	1948	2013	...	...	...	2208	...	...	...	...	...	0815
713	Storlien 🛃 a.	0914	0917	...	...	...	...	...	...	...	1825	...	...	...	...	...	...	...	...	...	...	...	...	...	...	...
713	Storlien 🛃 ◧ d.	*0929*	*0929*	...	...	...	...	...	...	...	*1849*	...	...	...	...	...	...	...	...	...	...	...	...	...	...	...
819	**Trondheim** ◧ a.	*1104*	*1104*	...	...	...	...	...	...	...	*2028*	...	...	...	...	...	...	...	...	...	...	...	...	...	...	...

km		*IC* 261	*IC* 265	*NT*	*Sn* 591	*IC* 269	*NT*	*Sn* 597	*Sn* 595	*NT*	*NT*	*IC* 279		*NT*	*IC* 11	*IC* 11	*IC* 285	*NT*	*NT*	*NT*	*NT*	*IC* 85	*NT*		*NT*	
		Ⓐ §	⑥	Ⓐ	Ⓐ n	Ⓑ §	Ⓐ	⑥	⑦	Ⓑ	⑥	Ⓐ §			Ⓑ	⑥		⑥	Ⓐ	†			Ⓐ J			
		⊖ 🅁	⊖ 🅁	2	🅁 🍷	⊖ 🅁	2	🅁 🍷	🅁 🍷	2	2	⊖ 🅁	2	2	🅁 🍷	🅁 🍷	🅁	2	2	2	2	🅁 🍷	2	2	2	
	Trondheim ◧ d.	...	...	...	...	...	...	...	...	...	...	...	0731	...	...	...	...	...	...	...	...	...	...	1648	...	...
	Storlien 🛃 ◧ a.	...	...	...	...	...	...	...	...	...	...	...	0908	...	...	...	...	...	...	...	...	...	...	1826	...	...
	Storlien 🛃 d.	...	...	...	...	...	...	...	...	...	...	...	...	0928	...	...	...	...	...	...	...	...	...	...	1839	...
	Duved d.	...	...	...	...	...	0600	...	...	...	0802	...	...	1004	1030	1032	...	1204	...	...	1506	1532	...	...	1912	...
	Åre d.	...	...	...	...	...	0607	...	...	...	0809	...	...	1011	1048	1050	...	1210	1212	...	1512	1550	...	...	1919	...
	Östersund C a.	...	...	...	...	...	0721	...	...	...	0927	...	...	1126	1213	1213	...	1324	1325	...	1626	1715	...	...	2035	...
	Östersund C d.	...	...	0513	0604	...	0729	0733	0923	0927	0929	...	...	1129	1217	1217	...	1327	1327	1325	1632	1720	1925	...	2037	...
	Bräcke d.	...	...	0602	0645	...	0818	0813	1003	1018	1018	...	...	1217	1305	1305	...	1417	1417	1417	1720	1804	2018	...	2127	...
0	Ånge d.	...	...	0623	0703	...	0837	0832	1020	1035	1037	...	...	1233	1325	1325	...	1435	1435	1435	1736	1824	2035	...	2143	...
94	**Sundsvall** a.	...	...	0738	|	...	0954	|	|	1153	1153	...	...	1353	1450	1450	...	1553	1553	1553	1851	|	2152	...	2257b	...
	Ljusdal d.	0526	0711	...	0802	0914	...	0932	1127	...	...	1410	...	...	|	|	1710	...	...	...	...	1922	...	...	...	...
	Bollnäs d.	0602	0753	...	0836	0958	...	1007	1201	...	...	1454	...	...	|	|	1754	...	...	...	...	2009	...	...	...	...
	Gävle C ◇ a.	0701	0901	...	0929	1101	...	1108	1258	...	...	1559	...	...	1722	1722	1900	...	...	...	...	2105	...	...	...	...
	Uppsala ◇ a.	0750	0950	...	1017s	1149	...	1159s	1347s	...	...	1649	...	...	1820	1820	1950	...	...	...	...	2156	...	...	...	...
	Arlanda C ✈ ◇ a.	0810	1009	...	1036s	1208	...	1219s	|	...	...	1708	...	...	|	|	2010	...	...	...	...	2223	...	...	...	...
	Stockholm C ◇ a.	0831	1031	...	1058	1227	...	1237	1422	...	...	1727	...	...	1902	1900	2028	...	...	...	...	2246	...	...	...	...

J – Not June 23 - Aug. 10.
N – For further details and additional night trains see Table **767**.
b – Not ⑥.
n – Not on ①–⑤ July 7 - Aug. 8.
s – Calls to set down only.
u – Calls to pick up only.
v – Not July 7 - Aug. 15.
⊖ – From / to Linköping (Table **730a**).
◧ – Storlien - Trondheim trains are operated by SJ Nord.
◇ – For other trains Stockholm - Gävle and v.v. see Table **760**.
§ – Subject to cancellation on certain dates.

763 UMEÅ - LULEÅ

Operator: *NT* (2nd class only)

km		N § 🅁	⚒		Ⓑ J	⑦ K
0	**Umeå** Östra ♣ d.	0705	0809	1325	1833	1833
2	**Umeå** C ♣ d.	0717	0815	1332	1841	1841
33	Vännäs ♣ d.	|	0843	1400	1910	1910
142	Bastuträsk d.	0900	0950	1511	2023	2023
269	Älvsbyn d.	1021	1108	1630	2143	2143
315	Boden a.	1051	1135	1657	2209	2209
315	Boden 765 d.	1115	1142	1702	2214	2214
351	**Luleå** 765 a.	1153	1214	1732	2243	2243

	⚒	Ⓐ	Ⓒ	N § 🅁	Ⓑ J	⑦ K
Luleå 765 d.	0828	1331	1331	1702	1854	1854
Boden 765 a.	0901	1356	1356	1731	1922	1922
Boden d.	0913	1407	1407	1754	1932	1932
Älvsbyn d.	0938	1431	1431	1821	2004	2004
Bastuträsk d.	1048	1544	1544	1938	2120	2120
Vännäs ♣ d.	1204	|	1706	|	2241	2241
Umeå C ♣ a.	1227	1719	1729	2111	2304	2304
Umeå Östra ♣ a.	1233	1725	1735	2122	2310	2310

♣ – Other local journeys Umeå Östra - Umeå C - Vännäs and v.v.:
From Umeå Östra at 0501 Ⓐ, 0632 Ⓐ, 0734 ⚒, 0913 Ⓑ, 1133 ⚒, 1227 Ⓐ, 1405 Ⓐ **J**, 1405 ⑦, 1515 Ⓐ, 1629, 1753 Ⓐ, 1947 Ⓐ **J**, 2148 Ⓐ.
From Vännäs at 0553 Ⓐ, 0657 Ⓐ, 0830 Ⓐ, 0914 ⚒, 1054 Ⓑ, 1310 ⚒, 1412 Ⓐ, 1552 Ⓐ **J**, 1552 ⑦, 1711 Ⓐ, 1825, 1928 Ⓐ, 2130 Ⓐ **J**, 2323 Ⓐ.
§ – Subject to cancellation on certain dates.

J – Not June 23 - Aug. 10.
K – June 23 - Aug. 10.
N – Overnight train Stockholm - Luleå and v.v. – see Table **767**.

765 LULEÅ - KIRUNA - NARVIK

km	Service to Sept. 21	*NT*	94	*NT*	*NT*		96	*NT*		*NT*	
			🅁				🅁 🍷				
		⚒		⚒	Ⓑ E			Ⓑ D			
		2	⊙ ‡	2 △	2		‡	2		2 ▽	
0	**Luleå** 763 768 d.	0505	...	0610	0847	...	1040	1111	...	1647	...
36	Boden 763 768 a.	0532	...	0636	0913	...	1105	1143	...	1723	...
36	Boden d.	...	0605	0638	0915	...	1114	1145	...	1725	...
204	Gällivare a.	...	0758	0832	1113	...	1340	1353	...	1934	...
204	Gällivare d.	...	0758	0848	1115	...	1359	1353	...	1934	...
304	**Kiruna** a.	...	0913	0949t	1303	...	1512	1502	...	2053	...
304	**Kiruna** d.	...	0944	...	...	...	1530	...	...	...	...
397	Abisko Östra d.	...	1102r	...	...	...	1645	...	...	...	...
406	Björkliden d.	...	1119	...	...	...	1658	...	...	...	...
426	Vassijaure d.	...	|	...	...	...	1717	...	...	...	...
433	Riksgränsen 🛃 d.	...	1147	...	...	...	1728	...	...	...	...
473	**Narvik** a.	...	1245	...	...	...	1830	...	...	...	...

Service to Sept. 21	*NT*	*NT*	*NT*	*NT*	*NT*	95	*NT*	*NT*	99	*NT*
						🅁 🍷			🅁 ✕	
	⚒ E	⚒ D	D	Ⓐ E	Ⓒ E		Ⓑ E	Ⓑ D		G
	2	2	2	2 △	2 △	‡	2	2	⊙ ‡	2
Narvik d.	...	...	...	...	...	1025	...	...	1511	...
Riksgränsen 🛃 d.	...	...	...	...	...	1123	...	...	1558	...
Vassijaure d.	...	...	...	...	...	1134	...	...	|	...
Björkliden d.	...	...	...	...	...	1222	...	...	1627	...
Abisko Östra d.	...	...	...	...	...	1236	...	...	1643	...
Kiruna a.	...	...	...	...	...	1347	...	...	1754	...
Kiruna d.	▽	0550	1048	1038	1048	1404	1433	1612	1809	...
Gällivare a.	▽	0705	1153	1155	1153	1515	1552	1720	2004	...
Gällivare d.	0613	0711	1153	1158	1153	1534	1555	1720	2004	...
Boden a.	0857	0906	1353	1354	1352	1740	1802	1923	2150	...
Boden 763 768 d.	0902	0912	1354	1356	1354	1748	1807	1934	...	2215
Luleå 763 768 a.	0930	0936	1421	1421	1421	1825	1838	2005	...	2246

D – Until June 22.
E – From June 23.
G – Ⓒ (daily from June 23).
r – Arrives 1044.
t – 1012 on ⑥ June 28 - Aug. 2 and ⑥ Sept. 6 - 20.
△ – By 🚌 Gällivare - Kiruna and v.v. Aug. 4 - 31.
▽ – By 🚌 Gällivare - Kiruna and v.v. June 23 - Sept. 21.
⊙ – Overnight service from / to Stockholm (see Table **767**).
‡ – Timings and days of running may vary.

766 KRISTINEHAMN - MORA - ÖSTERSUND - GÄLLIVARE

INLANDSBANAN

km		*TiB* M △	*TiB* L §	F	G
	Kristinehamn 750 d.	0655	...	...	...
	Karlstad 750 d.	0718	...	...	...
	Kil 750 d.	0750	...	...	...
0	**Kristinehamn** 750 d.	|	0834	...	...
131	Grängesberg 755 d.	0933	|	...	...
146	Ludvika 755 d.	0944	1027	...	...
192	Borlänge 755 758 d.	1057	1115	...	...
296	**Mora** 758 d.	1210	1232	1336	1346
310	Orsa d.	...	...	1350	1402
433	Sveg d.	...	...	1609	1619
617	**Östersund** C a.	...	...	1955	2008

	C	*TiB* M	*TiB* L	
Östersund C d.	0700	...	...	...
Sveg d.	1002	...	...	...
Orsa d.	1221	...	...	...
Mora 758 d.	1236	1257	1341	...
Borlänge 755 758 d.	...	1424	1511	...
Ludvika 755 d.	...	1500	1544	...
Grängesberg 755 d.	...	1510	|	...
Kristinehamn 750 a.	...	1704r	|	...
Kil 750 a.	...	|	1736	...
Karlstad 750 a.	...	1731t	1810	...
Kristinehamn 750 a.	...	...	1838	...

km		D	
0	**Östersund** C 761 d.	0729	...
115	Ulriksfors d.	0919	...
244	Vilhelmina d.	1116	...
247	Vilhelmina Norra a.	1120	...
247	Vilhelmina Norra d.	1220	...
312	Storuman d.	1318	...
384	Sorsele d.	1437	...
420	Slagnäs d.	1507	...
473	Arvidsjaur d.	1627v	...
646	Jokkmokk d.	1941	...
746	**Gällivare** 765 a.	2103	

	E	
Gällivare 765 d.	0805	...
Jokkmokk d.	0932	...
Arvidsjaur d.	1312z	...
Slagnäs d.	1358	...
Sorsele d.	1446	...
Storuman d.	1550	...
Vilhelmina Norra a.	1645	...
Vilhelmina Norra d.	1735	...
Vilhelmina d.	1741	...
Ulriksfors d.	1937	...
Östersund C 761 a.	2135	

C – June 16 - Aug. 24.
D – June 16 - Aug. 23.
E – June 17 - Aug. 24.
F – July 14, 21, 28.
G – June 16 - Aug. 24 (not July 14, 21, 28).
L – ③–⑤ June 18 - July 11 (not June 20).
M – ⑦ June 22 - July 13.
r – 1650 on July 6; 1654 on July 13.
t – 1745 on July 6; 1720 on July 13.
v – Arrives approx 1555.
z – Arrives approx 1240.
△ – Kristinehamn to Ludvika times are approx. 25 mins later on July 13.
§ – Departs Ludvika 1045 on ③ (also June 19, 26, 27). Times from Borlänge vary. Arrives Mora 1309 on June 18, 19, 25 - 27; arrives 1256 on July 2, 9.

Operator: Inlandsbanan AB, Box 561, 831 27 Östersund ✆ + 46 (0) 771 53 53 53 (except connecting *TiB* services).

LONG DISTANCE SLEEPER TRAINS 767

All services Ⓡ		*SJ* 94		*SJ* 92*		*SJ* 70		*ST* 3920	*ST* 3920		
		⊡ A		♥ D◧		♥ E		✣ H	✣ G		
Malmö C d.	...	...	...	...	...	...	...	1505	1635	...	...
Lund C △ d.	...	...	...	...	...	...	...	1515	1655	...	...
Hässleholm C △ d.	...	...	...	...	...	...	...	|	1735	...	...
Alvesta △ d.	...	...	...	...	...	...	...	|	1830	...	...
Nässjö C △ d.	...	...	...	...	...	...	...	|	1920	...	...
Linköping C △ d.	...	...	...	...	...	...	...	|	2030	...	...
Norrköping C △ d.	...	...	...	...	...	...	...	|	2100	...	...
Helsingborg △ d.	...	...	...	...	...	...	...	1545	|	...	...
Halmstad △ d.	...	...	...	...	...	...	...	1625	|	...	...
Göteborg C △ d.	...	...	...	...	...	...	...	1830	|	...	...
Skövde C △ d.	...	...	...	...	...	...	...	1950	|	...	...
Stockholm C △ d.	...	1809	...	2155	...	2239	...	2255	2255	...	...
Arlanda C ✈ △ d.	...	1834	...	2221	...	2304	...	|	|	...	...
Uppsala △ d.	...	1902	...	2245	...	2325	...	2340	2340	...	...
Gävle △ d.	...	2000	...	2353	...	0121	...	|	|	...	...
Söderhamn d.	...	2055	...	0042	...	|	...	|	|	...	...
Hudiksvall d.	...	2136	...	0130	...	|	...	|	|	...	...
Sundsvall a.	...	2232	...	0244	...	|	...	|	|	...	...
Sundsvall d.	...	2244	...	0311	...	|	...	|	|	...	...
Härnösand d.	...	2338	...	0417	...	|	...	|	|	...	...
Kramfors d.	...	0008	...	0446	...	|	...	|	|	...	...
Ånge a.	...	|	...	|	...	0501	...	|	|	...	...
Bräcke a.	...	|	...	|	...	0526	...	|	|	...	...
Östersund C a.	...	|	...	|	...	0625	...	0615	0615	...	...
Åre a.	...	|	...	|	...	0758	...	0735	0735	...	...
Duved a.	...	|	...	|	...	0815	...	0755	0755	...	...
Storlien a.	...	|	...	|	...	...	...	0855	0855	...	...
Örnsköldsvik d.	...	0055	...	0540	...	...	...	...	...	...	...
Umeå C a.	...	0202	...	0712	...	...	...	...	...	...	...
Umeå C d.	...	0210	...	0717	...	...	...	...	...	...	...
Bastuträsk d.	...	0345	...	0900	...	...	...	...	...	...	...
Älvsbyn d.	...	0514	...	1021	...	...	...	...	...	...	...
Boden a.	...	0542	...	1051	...	...	...	...	...	...	...
Boden d.	...	0605	...	1115	...	...	...	...	...	...	...
Luleå a.	...	|	...	1153	...	...	...	...	...	...	...
Narvik 765 a.	...	1245	...	...	...	...	...	...	...	...	...

All services Ⓡ		*SJ* 71		*SJ* 91		*SJ* 93		*ST* 3921	*ST* 3921
		♥ E		♥ D		⊙ A		✣ J	✣ K
Narvik 765 d.	...	...	...	...	...	1511	...	...	...
Luleå d.	...	...	...	1702	...	|	...	...	...
Boden a.	...	...	...	1731	...	2150	...	...	...
Boden d.	...	...	...	1754	...	2218	...	...	...
Älvsbyn d.	...	...	...	1821	...	2246	...	...	...
Bastuträsk d.	...	...	...	1938	...	0008	...	...	...
Umeå C a.	...	...	...	2111	...	0141	...	...	...
Umeå C d.	...	...	...	2116	...	0144	...	...	...
Örnsköldsvik d.	...	...	...	2235	...	0241	...	...	...
Storlien d.	...	...	...	|	...	|	...	1525	1525
Duved d.	...	1950	...	|	...	|	...	1620	1620
Åre d.	...	2005	...	|	...	|	...	1640	1640
Östersund C d.	...	2144	...	|	...	|	...	1820	1820
Bräcke d.	...	2236	...	|	...	|	...	|	|
Ånge d.	...	2258	...	|	...	|	...	|	|
Kramfors d.	...	|	...	2328	...	0328	...	|	|
Härnösand d.	...	|	...	0007	...	0356	...	|	|
Sundsvall a.	...	|	...	0102	...	0450	...	|	|
Sundsvall d.	...	|	...	0117	...	0537	...	|	|
Hudiksvall d.	...	|	...	0300	...	0649	...	|	|
Söderhamn d.	...	|	...	0335	...	0734	...	|	|
Gävle ▽ a.	...	0152	...	0431	...	0825	...	|	|
Uppsala ▽ a.	...	0410	...	0553	...	0923	...	2315	2315
Arlanda C ✈ ▽ a.	...	0435	...	0635	...	0954	...	|	|
Stockholm C ▽ a.	...	0505	...	0701	...	1017	...	2355	2355
Skövde ▽ a.	...	...	...	...	...	...	...	|	0400
Göteborg ▽ a.	...	...	...	...	...	...	...	|	0535
Halmstad ▽ a.	...	...	...	...	...	...	...	|	0745
Helsingborg ▽ a.	...	...	...	...	...	...	...	|	0830
Norrköping C ▽ a.	...	...	...	...	...	...	...	0215	|
Linköping C ▽ a.	...	...	...	...	...	...	...	0245	|
Nässjö C ▽ a.	...	...	...	...	...	...	...	0430	|
Alvesta ▽ a.	...	...	...	...	...	...	...	0525	|
Hässleholm C ▽ a.	...	...	...	...	...	...	...	0620	|
Lund C ▽ a.	...	...	...	...	...	...	...	0655	0910
Malmö C a.	...	...	...	...	...	...	...	0715	0925

A – 🛏, ▬, (2) and ✕ Stockholm - Boden - Narvik and v.v.
D – 🛏, ▬, (2) and ✕ Stockholm - Boden - Luleå and v.v.
E – 🛏, ▬, (2) and ✕ Stockholm - Sundsvall - Duved and v.v.
G – ③⑥ June 25 - July 12; ③⑥ Aug. 20 - Sept. 27.
H – ~~③⑥ July 16 - Aug. 16.~~
J – ④⑦ June 26 - July 13; ④⑦ Aug. 21 - Sept. 28.
K – ④⑦ July 17 - Aug. 17.

△ – Trains call to pick up only.
▽ – Trains call to set down only.

♥ – May be cancelled on certain dates - please confirm times and days of running when booking.
◧ – Departure times from Stockholm vary between 2051 and 2155 (also 1854 on June 24).
✣ – Conveys ▬, (12) and ✕. Operated by Snälltåget.
⊡ – June 18-21, 27, 28, July 11-26, 31, Aug. 1, 2. §
⊙ – ~~June 19-22, 28, 29, July 12-31. §~~
§ – Further dates may be added. Please confirm when booking.
* – Train **94** on certain dates.

UMEÅ - LULEÅ - HAPARANDA-TORNIO - KEMI 768

Rail service **LULEÅ - BODEN - HAPARANDA** (operated by Norrtåg). Service to Sept. 21.

km		⚒	†	†	Ⓐ	⑥		Ⓐ	Ⓒ F	Ⓒ E	
0	**Luleå** 763 765 d.	0505	0544	1023	1130	1315	...	1635	1829	1839	...
36	**Boden** 763 765 a.	0532	0613	1050	1202	1342	...	1713	1854	1904	...
36	**Boden** d.	0534	0613	1052	1204	1343	...	1716	1907	1907	...
195	**Haparanda** a.	0700	0741	1217	1329	1509	...	1840	2032	2032	...

		⚒	†	†	Ⓐ	⑥	Ⓐ E	Ⓒ E	F	
Haparanda d.	...	0712	0757	1225	1428	1521	1930	2050	2050	...
Boden a.	...	0838	0923	1350	1553	1647	2101	2215	2215	...
Boden 763 765 d.	...	0840	0925	1402	1555	1649	2108	2215	2215	...
Luleå 763 765 a.	...	0919	0951	1426	1625	1722	2152	2246	2246	...

Until Dec. 13, 2025 — 🚌 **UMEÅ - LULEÅ - HAPARANDA-TORNIO** ⊠ — Länstrafiken Norrbotten, routes 11/20/Express 100

	11 Ⓐ	20 Ⓐ	20 Ⓐ	20 Ⓐ	100 Ⓐ	11 Ⓐ	100 ⑥	20 Ⓐ	20 †		20 ⑥	20 Ⓐ	100 †	100 Ⓒ	100 Ⓐ	11 Ⓐ	100 ⑥	100 Ⓐ	20 †	20 ⑥	100 †	20 Ⓐ	100 †	100 Ⓐ	100 ⑥
Umeå d.	...	...	...	0515	0715	...	0815	0815	0830	...	1015	1005	1100	1200	1205	...	1415	1430	1430	1515	1530	1605	1715	1805	1815
Skellefteå d.	...	0525	0640	0750	0930	...	1030	1055	1050	...	1235	1245	1315	1415	1430	...	1630	1645	1650	1735	1745	1845	1930	2030	2030
Piteå d.	...	0655	0755	0910	1050	...	1150	1220	1210	...	1355	1410	1435	1535	1550	...	1750	1805	1810	1855	1905	2010	2050	2150	2150
Luleå a.	...	0755	0855	1005	1150	...	1240	1315	1305	...	1450	1505	1525	1625	1640	...	1840	1905	1905	1950	1955	2105	2140	2240	2240
Luleå d.	0520	0810	...	1020	...	1200	...	1400	1310	...	1455	1520	...	...	...	1710	...	...	1925	1955	...	2120	...	...	...
Haparanda-Tornio 🚉 § d.	0800	1040	...	1245	...	1430	...	1635	1540	...	1725	1755	...	...	...	1940	...	...	2145	2225	...	2345	...	...	...

	100 Ⓐ	100 Ⓐ	100 ⑥	100 †	20 Ⓐ	100 Ⓐ	100 ⑥	20 Ⓐ	20 †		11 Ⓐ	100 †	100 ⑥	100 Ⓐ	20 ⑥	20 Ⓐ	100 †	20 Ⓐ	100 Ⓐ	100 †	11 Ⓐ	100 ⑥	20 †	20 ⑥	20 Ⓐ
Haparanda-Tornio 🚉 § d.	...	...	...	...	0515	...	...	0650	0730	...	0900	...	...	...	1130	1215	...	1345	...	...	1510	...	1605	1615	1650
Luleå a.	...	...	...	...	0745	...	...	0940	0955	...	1135	...	...	...	1355	1445	...	1610	...	...	1735	...	1830	1840	1910
Luleå d.	0535	0705	0730	0805	0805	0935	0945	1000	1000	...	...	1205	1305	1355	1400	1500	1535	1625	1705	1715	...	1805	1845	1845	1925
Piteå d.	0635	0805	0830	0905	0915	1035	1045	1110	1105	...	...	1305	1405	1455	1505	1615	1635	1730	1805	1815	...	1905	1950	1950	2035
Skellefteå d.	0755	0925	0950	1025	1040	1155	1205	1240	1225	...	...	1425	1525	1615	1625	1740	1755	1850	1925	1935	...	2025	2110	2110	2155
Umeå a.	1010	1140	1155	1230	1305	1410	1410	1505	1440	...	...	1630	1730	1830	1840	2005	2000	2115	2130	2140	...	2230	2325	2325	0020

🚌 **HAPARANDA - TORNIO - KEMI** ⊠ **Subject to alteration from August 4**

		EJK Ⓐ s		*EJK* Ⓐ s		*NTM* Ⓐ	*HEI* Ⓐ	*NTM* ⑤ s		*NTM* Ⓐ			*NTM* ⑥					*MLJ* ⑦		*MLJ* ⑦		*MLJ* ⑦			
Haparanda-Tornio 🚉 § ⊡ d.	Ⓐ	0705	...	1150	...	1440	1545	1550	...	1710	...	⑥	1230	...	...	⑦	...	1205	...	1405	...	1545	...	...	...
Tornio Centre Kaupungintalo d.		0712	...	1200	...	1445	1547	1600	...	1715	...		1235	...	...		...	1210	...	1410	...	1550	...	...	...
Kemi a.		0750	...	1240	...	1515r	1620	1630	...	1745r	...		1300	...	...		...	1245r	...	1445r	...	1625r	...	...	...

		HEI Ⓐ	*NTM* Ⓐ	*EJK* Ⓐ s		*NTM* Ⓐ		*EJK* Ⓐ s		*NTM* ①–④ s			*NTM* ⑥				*MLJ* ⑦		*MLJ* ⑦		*MLJ* ⑦				
Kemi d.	Ⓐ	0630	0710	0800	...	1100	...	1600	...	1850	...	⑥	1100	...	...	⑦	1300t	...	1500	...	1635v	...	...	...	...
Tornio Centre Kaupungintalo d.		|	0745	0847	...	1125	...	1645	...	1915	...		1125	...	...		1335	...	1535	...	1705	...	...	...	...
Haparanda-Tornio 🚉 § ⊡ a.		0655	0800	0900	...	1130	...	1650	...	1920	...		1130	...	...		1340	...	1540	...	1710	...	...	...	...

E – Until June 22.
F – From June 23.

r – Also calls at Kemi rail station upon request.
s – Schooldays only (subject to confirmation).
t – Also calls at Kemi rail station.
v – From Kemi rail station (d. 1630).

⊠ – All stops refer to bus stations except where shown otherwise.

⊡ – Finnish time (one hour later than Swedish time).
§ – Swedish name: Haparanda-Tornio.
Finnish name: Tornio-Haaparanta.

☛ Haparanda-Tornio bus station is located on the Swedish side of the border (distance to border approximately 200 metres). Walking distance between Haparanda-Tornio bus station and the Tornio Centre Puutarhakatu stop is 600 metres. Walking distance between Kemi bus and rail stations is 200 metres. See www.matkahuolto.fi for all Finnish long-distance bus services, including extra services on the Haparanda-Tornio - Kemi route.

Operators:
EJK – E. Jussila Oy: www.jussilanbussilla.fi
HEI – Heiskasen Liikenne Oy: heiskasen.fi
LOH – Liikenne Lohiniva Oy: www.lohiniva.fi
MLJ – Meri-Lapin Joukkoliikenne.
NTM – North Travels MAP Oy.

NORWAY

SEE MAP PAGE 342

Operator: The principal and national operator is Vy (www.vy.no). Long distance services (and connecting local trains) between Oslo and Stavanger are operated by GoAhead Nordic (www.go-aheadnordic.no). Services Oslo - Åndalsnes / Trondheim, Hamar - Røros - Trondheim and Trondheim - Bodø are operated by SJ NORD (www.sj.no).

Services: All trains convey second class seating accommodation. Many services, as identified in the notes, also convey *Komfort* accommodation (see below). Sleeping-cars (🛏) have one and two-berth compartments; the sleeper supplement is 950 NOK per compartment (for two people travelling together, or sole use for single travellers). Most long distance express trains convey a bistro car (✕) serving hot and cold meals, drinks and snacks. 🍸 indicates that drinks and light refreshments are available from automatic vending machines.

Timings: **Valid until December 13, 2025** (unless otherwise specified in individual tables). Dec. 25, 26, Jan. 1, Apr. 17, 18, 20, 21, May 1, 17, 29, June 8, 9 are Norwegian public holidays and services are subject to alteration on and around these dates. Alterations to internal Norwegian services during holiday periods are not usually shown in the tables and readers are advised to confirm timings before travelling (✆ +47 61 05 19 10).

Reservations: Seat reservation is highly recommended on long-distance route Oslo - Kristiansand - Stavanger (Table **775**), and is compulsory on other major routes as shown in the tables.

Komfort class: *Vy Komfort / Go Ahead Komfort / SJ NORD Premium / SJ NORD Premium Pluss* are dedicated coaches with complimentary food, drink and newspapers; a supplement is payable per single journey.

770 OSLO - HALDEN - GÖTEBORG

All trains convey *Vy Komfort* and 🍸

km	Norwegian train number	103	105	107	109	111	113	115	117	119	121	141	123	123	143	125	145	127	129	131	133	135	137		139
	Swedish train number	383		385		387		389		391		393		395				397							
		Ⓐ	⚒									Ⓐ	Ⓐ	Ⓒ	Ⓐ		Ⓐ								
0	**Oslo** Sentral d.	0611	0714	0814	0914	1014	1114	1214	1314	1414	1514	1545	1615	1615	1648	1715	1744	1810	1914	2014	2114	2214	2314	...	0022
60	Moss d.	0643	0750	0846	0947	1046	1147	1246	1347	1447	1547	1619	1649	1649	1721	1749	1816	1844	1947	2045	2147	2247	2347	...	0103
94	Fredrikstad d.	0710	0817	0913	1015	1114	1215	1313	1414	1514	1614	1645	1716	1716	1748	1818	1845	1914	2014	2112	2216	2315	0015	...	0130
109	Sarpsborg d.	0725	0831	0927	1030	1126	1230	1326	1430	1527	1629	1657	1730	1730	1802	1833	1857	1926	2029	2127	2232	2327	0027	...	0142
137	**Halden** ★ d.	0747	0850	0947	1049	1147	1249	1347	1449	1547	1648	1718	1748	1750	1824	1852	1919	1947	2048	2146	2251	2346	0046	...	0201
268	Öxnered **751** d.	|	...	|	...	|	...	|	...	|	...	|	...	|	...	...	...	|	...	...	...	...	...	...	...
278	Trollhättan **751** d.	0912	...	1112	...	1312	...	1512	...	1711	...	1843	...	1912	...	...	...	2112	...	...	...	...	...	...	...
350	**Göteborg 751** a.	0945	...	1145	...	1345	...	1545	...	1740	...	1915	...	1945	...	...	...	2145	...	...	...	...	...	...	...

Swedish train number								382			384			386		388		390		392	394		396		398
Norwegian train number	102	104	142	106	144	108	146	110	110	112	114	114	116	118	120	122	124	126	128	130	130	132	134	136	138
	Ⓐ	⚒	Ⓐ		Ⓐ		Ⓐ	Ⓐ	Ⓒ		⚒	⑦								Ⓐ	Ⓒ				
Göteborg 751 d.	...	...	...	...	...	...	...	0615	...	...	0813	...	...	1015	...	1215	...	1415	...	1613	1613	...	1813	...	2010
Trollhättan **751** d.	...	...	...	...	...	...	...	0644	...	...	0844	...	...	1044	...	1244	...	1444	...	1644	1644	...	1844	...	2044
Öxnered **751** d.	...	...	...	...	...	...	...	|	...	...	|	...	...	|	...	|	...	|	...	|	|	...	|	...	|
Halden ★ d.	0405	0505	0531	0602	0632	0706	0725	0812	0812	0903	1011	1011	1103	1211	1303	1411	1504	1611	1703	1814	1814	1903	2011	2108	2213
Sarpsborg d.	0426	0526	0552	0623	0653	0727	0748	0832	0832	0925	1031	1031	1125	1231	1325	1432	1526	1630	1728	1834	1834	1926	2031	2128	2233
Fredrikstad d.	0440	0540	0606	0637	0708	0741	0801	0845	0845	0939	1045	1045	1139	1244	1339	1445	1539	1643	1746	1846	1846	1940	2044	2141	2246
Moss d.	0508	0608	0632	0705	0734	0808	0833	0913	0913	1007	1113	1113	1207	1313	1408	1515	1606	1710	1814	1914	1914	2008	2112	2208	2315
Oslo Sentral a.	0543	0640	0707	0740	0807	0840	0907	0945	0945	1040	1145	1145	1240	1345	1440	1547	1638	1744	1846	1946	1946	2040	2144	2240	2347

★ – 🏛 at Kornsjø (*km169*).

771 OSLO - OSLO LUFTHAVN GARDERMOEN ✈

*See also Tables **783** and **785***

Operated by Flytoget AS.
Special fares apply.
✆ +47 23 15 90 00
www.flytoget.no

Daily services (journey time: 19–22 minutes)
Trains call at Lillestrøm 10 minutes from Oslo.
From Oslo Sentral: every 20 minutes 0440 - 2400.
From Gardermoen ✈: every 20 minutes 0530 - 2350 (also at 0010, 0030, 0050).

773 OSLO - GJØVIK

All trains convey 🍸

Service until August 10

km		Ⓐ	Ⓐ						Ⓐ			
0	**Oslo** Sentral d.	0604	0704	0804	0904	and	1804	1904	2004	2104	2204	0004
56	Roa d.	0704	0805	0904	1005		1905	2005	2105	2205	2312	0107
70	Jaren d.	0721	0821	0921	1021	hourly	1921	2021	2121	2221	2328	0123
99	Eina d.	0744	0844	0948	1044		1944	2044	2144	2244	2351	0146
110	Raufoss d.	0756	0856	0959	1056	until	1956	2056	2156	2256	0003	0158
122	**Gjøvik** a.	0807	0907	1009	1107		2007	2107	2207	2307	0014	0209

	Ⓐ	Ⓐ						Ⓐ				
Gjøvik d.	0434	0534	0634	0734	and	1534	1634	1734	1834	1934	2034	2134
Raufoss d.	0445	0545	0645	0745		1545	1645	1745	1845	1945	2045	2145
Eina d.	0456	0556	0656	0756	hourly	1556	1656	1756	1856	1956	2056	2156
Jaren d.	0520	0620	0720	0820		1620	1720	1820	1920	2020	2120	2220
Roa d.	0536	0636	0736	0836	until	1636	1736	1836	1936	2036	2136	2236
Oslo Sentral a.	0632	0745t	0845t	0932		1745	1845	1945	2045	2145	2246	2346

t – Arrives 13 minutes later on ⑥⑦.

775 OSLO - KRISTIANSAND - STAVANGER

Long distance services are not available for local journeys Oslo - Drammen and v.v. or Sandnes - Stavanger and v.v.
Operated by GoAhead Nordic (except for local trains Oslo - Kongsberg shown in notes § and ‡).

km		701	705	705	707	709	711	713	715	719	721	725
		Ⓐ	Ⓒ	Ⓐ			Ⓑ			c	⑦	Ⓑ
		⊡	✕⊡	✕⊡	✕⊡	✕⊡	✕⊡	✕⊡	✕⊡	✕⊡	✕⊡	♣✕
0	**Oslo** Sentral § d.	...	...	0419	0725	0925	1125	1325	1523	1825	2125	2225
41	Drammen △ § d.	...	...	0454	0800	1000	1200	1400	1600	1900	2200	2300
87	Kongsberg § d.	...	...	0530	0836	1036	1236	1436	1648	1947	2247	2343
134	Nordagutu ⊗ d.	...	...	0604	0909	|	1313	1513	|	2020	2326	0021
151	Bø d.	...	...	0619x	0924	1124	1327	1527	1744	2035	2341	0037x
209	Neslandsvatn ⊗ d.	...	...	0711	1006	1208	1409	1609	1827	2118	0024	0126
270	Nelaug d.	...	...	0756	1052	1255	1455	1656	1911	2215	0111	0216x
353	**Kristiansand** a.	...	...	0853	1151	1358	1553	1753	2009	2312	0209	0330
353	**Kristiansand** d.	0502	0905	0905	1200	1414	1608	1801	2016	...	...	0345
457	Sira ⊗ d.	0623	1025	1025	1325	1543	1727	1921	2121	...	...	0512
465	Moi ⊗ d.	0630	1032	1032	1332	1551	1734	1928	2128	...	...	0520
514	Egersund ◇ d.	0709	1107x	1107	1406	1635	1814	2007	2209	...	...	0607
573	Sandnes S ▽ ⊗ a.	0805	1152	1152	1452	1734	1904	2102	2301	...	...	0704
587	**Stavanger** ◇ a.	0820	1205	1205	1505	1749	1919	2115	2317	...	...	0720

	702	704	706	708	710	712	714	716	716	720	726
	Ⓐ	A	B				⑦	Ⓑ	⑥	Ⓐ	Ⓑ
	⊡	✕⊡	✕⊡	✕⊡	✕⊡	✕⊡	✕⊡	✕⊡	✕⊡	✕⊡	♣✕
Stavanger ◐ d.	...	0431	0647	0847	1016	1247	1447	1634	1634	1936	2215
Sandnes S △ ◐ d.	...	0445	0701	0901	1031	1301	1500	1648	1648	1950	2231
Egersund ◐ d.	...	0535	0744	0943	1118	1342	1547	1754	1754	2032	2318
Moi ⊗ d.	...	0616	0819	1019	1158	1423	1630	1830	1830	2110	2400
Sira ⊗ d.	...	0623	0826	1026	1206	1430	1637	1837	1837	2117	0008
Kristiansand a.	...	0742	0942	1143	1331	1545	1802	1952	1952	2239	0137
Kristiansand d.	0443	0751	0954	1155	1347	1556	1811	1959	...	...	0217
Nelaug d.	0541	0854	1054	1254	1456	1655	1910	2058	...	...	0331x
Neslandsvatn. ⊗ d.	0625	0938	1140	1341	|	1740	|	|	...	...	0418
Bø d.	0713	1023	1226	1427	1629	1828	2034	2223	...	...	0507
Nordagutu ⊗ d.	0727	|	1241	1441	|	1842	2049	2239	...	...	0523
Kongsberg ‡ d.	0802	1117	1317	1517	1718	1917	2126	2317	...	...	0610
Drammen ▽ ‡ a.	0851	1151	1351	1551	1751	1951	2207	2352	...	...	0650
Oslo S ‡ a.	0925	1225	1425	1625	1825	2025	2245	0025	...	...	0726

Nelaug - Arendal

km		Ⓐ	⚒							⑥	Ⓑ	
0	Nelaug d.	0700	0900	1100	1300	1500	1700	1915	...	2208	2220	...
36	Arendal a.	0737	0937	1137	1337	1537	1737	1952	...	2245	2257	...

	Ⓐ		⚒						Ⓑ	⑥	
Arendal d.	0459	...	0810	1010	1210	1410	1610	1825	2010	2120	...
Nelaug a.	0536	...	0847	1047	1247	1447	1647	1902	2047	2157	...

A – Ⓐ (also ⑥ Kristiansand - Oslo).
B – ⚒ (daily Kristiansand - Oslo).

c – Train **723** on ⑥, Nelaug d. 2203, Kristiansand a. 2303.
x – Calls on request.

♣ – Conveys 🛏 and 🛋2 (also reclining seats). Reservation recommended.
⊡ – Reservation recommended. Conveys *Go Ahead Komfort*.
⊗ – Trains call on request.
△ – Calls to pick up only.
▽ – Calls to set down only.

§ – Other local trains (operated by Vy) **Oslo** S - **Drammen** (34 minutes) - **Kongsberg** (75–80 minutes): 0609 Ⓐ, 0709, 0809 and hourly until 2309, then 0009 (also 1549 Ⓐ, 1649 Ⓐ).

‡ – Other local trains (operated by Vy) **Kongsberg** - **Drammen** (42–43 minutes) - **Oslo** S (76–77 minutes): 0334 Ⓐ, 0434 Ⓐ, 0534, 0550 Ⓐ, 0634, 0649 Ⓐ, 0734, 0835, 0935, 1035, 1134, 1235, 1334, 1435, 1534, 1635, 1734, 1834, 1934, 2034, 2134, 2234.

◇ – Other local trains **Egersund** - **Sandnes** S (51–58 minutes) - **Stavanger** (67–71 minutes): 0439 Ⓐ, 0505 Ⓐ, 0540 Ⓐ, 0615 ⚒, 0646 Ⓐ, 0717 ⚒, 0817 ⚒, 0916, 1019, 1120, 1217, 1315, 1418, 1449 Ⓐ, 1519, 1549 Ⓐ, 1619, 1649 Ⓐ, 1720, 1818, 1920, 2019, 2122, 2222, 2319, 0019 ⑤⑥, 0119 ⑤⑥.

◐ – Other local trains **Stavanger** - **Sandnes** S (15 minutes) - **Egersund** (70–80 minutes): 0440 Ⓐ, 0514 Ⓐ, 0547 ⚒, 0645 ⚒, 0754 ⚒, 0854, 0954, 1054, 1154, 1254, 1324 Ⓐ, 1354, 1424 Ⓐ, 1454, 1524 Ⓐ, 1554, 1624 Ⓐ, 1654, 1754, 1854, 1954, 2054, 2154, 2256, 2354, 0054 ⑤⑥, 0154 ⑤⑥.

PORSGRUNN - NOTODDEN 779

km		Ⓐ	Ⓐn	Ⓐ	Ⓐ	Ⓐn	Ⓐ	Ⓐn	Ⓐ
0	**Porsgrunn** ..... **783** d.	...	0639	0749	1151	1307	1441	1606	1751
9	Skien .... **783** d.	0527	0649	0759	1201	1321	1455	1620	1801
43	Nordagutu .... a.	0557	0719	0829	1231	1351	1526	1651	1831
43	Nordagutu .... d.	0606	0720	0830	1232	1352	1527	1652	1832
62	**Notodden** .... a.	0626	0740	0850	1252	1412	1547	1712	1852

	Ⓐ	Ⓐn	Ⓐ	Ⓐ	Ⓐn	Ⓐ	Ⓐn	Ⓐ
Notodden .... d.	0636	0807	0907	1308	1443	1608	1809	2009
Nordagutu .... a.	0655	0826	0926	1327	1502	1627	1828	2028
Nordagutu .... d.	0656	0829	0927	1328	1503	1628	1831	2029
Skien .... **783** d.	0731	0900	0958	1404	1539	1703	1902	2059
Porsgrunn ... **783** a.	0739	0908	1006	1412	1553	1711	1910	...

n – Not June 30 - Aug. 8.

☛ No service on Ⓒ.

OSLO - BERGEN 780

Warning! From June 28 to Aug. 10 services are diverted between Oslo and Hønefoss, not calling at Drammen; during this period most Oslo departures are up to 21 minutes **earlier** and arrivals are up to 37 minutes later (note that trains **607**, **608** and **610** are unaffected); train numbers may also vary during this period.

km		61 D ⊡ R	61 E ⊡ R	63 ⊡ R	1825 C	607 ⒷJ 🍷	601 ⊡ R	65 B 🍷	67 ⊡ R		605 Ⓑ N R
0	**Oslo** Sentral .... **783** d.	0625	0625	0825	...	0918	1203	1425	1623	...	2303
41	Drammen .... **783** d.	0700**u**	0700**u**	0900**u**	...	|	1238**u**	1500**u**	1700**u**	...	2338**u**
112	Hønefoss .... d.	0759	0759	0955	...	1104	1339	1600	1801	...	0041
208	Nesbyen .... d.	0907	0907	1103	...	1230	1451	1708	1912	...	0157
225	Gol .... d.	0920	0920	1116	...	1243	1504	1721	1927	...	0209
250	Ål .... d.	0939	0939	1135	...	1318	1526	1740	1948	...	0231
275	Geilo .... d.	0959	0959	1156	1331	1351	1549	1801	2011	...	0307
286	Ustaoset .... d.	1010	|	1208	1341	1403	1602	1812	2022	...	0319
324	Finse .... d.	1050	1049	1237	1408	1437	1635	1853	2049	...	0349
354	**Myrdal** .... **781** d.	1121	1121	1306	1438	1501	1704	1925	2119	...	0421
403	**Voss** .... **781** d.	1207	1207	1351	1530	...	1754	2011	2205	...	0510
443	Dale .... **781** a.	|	|	|	1600	...	1825	2049	2234	...	0540**s**
480	Arna .... **781** a.	1302**s**	1302**s**	1449**s**	1647	...	1858**s**	2122**s**	2308**s**	...	0617**s**
489	**Bergen** .... **781** a.	1312	1312	1459	1654	...	1910	2132	2317	...	0627

	60 🍷	62 ⊡ R	1810 C	602 ⊡ R	608 ⒶJ 🍷	610 ⑦J 🍷	64 ⊡ R	66 ⊡ R		606 Ⓑ N R
Bergen .... **781** d.	0621	0808	0921	1149	...	...	1537	1646	...	2300
Arna .... **781** d.	0630**u**	0817**u**	0929	1158**u**	...	...	1545**u**	1655**u**	...	2311**u**
Dale .... **781** d.	|	|	1006	1232	...	...	|	1732	...	2345
Voss .... **781** d.	0728	0920	1056	1303	...	...	1657	1807	...	0028
Myrdal .... **781** d.	0812	1002	1215	1352	1514	1544	1740	1855	...	0120
Finse .... d.	0838	1031	1248	1420	1551	1615	1806	1927	...	0200
Ustaoset .... d.	0903	1057	1314	1450	1636	1646	1835	1959	...	0230
Geilo .... d.	0916	1112	1324	1504	1650	1659	1848	2013	...	0242
Ål .... d.	0939	1135	...	1525	1710	1738	1909	2033	...	0306
Gol .... d.	0958	1154	...	1545	1745	1758	1928	2055	...	0325
Nesbyen .... d.	1010	1206	...	1558	1759	1810	1941	2108	...	0337
Hønefoss .... d.	1129	1317	...	1718	1939**r**	1939	2057	2226	...	0454
Drammen .... **783** a.	1228**s**	1427**s**	...	1828**s**	|	|	2151**s**	2327**s**	...	0551**s**
Oslo Sentral ..... **783** a.	1305	1505	...	1905	2116	2116	2227	0005	...	0627

– Daily until Oct. 3; Ⓑ from Oct. 5.
– May 1 - Sept. 30.
– ①–⑥ from Oct. 1.
– Daily until Sept. 30.

J – May 8 - Sept. 30.
N – Conveys 🛏, 🛏 (see note ★), 2nd class seats and ✕. Also conveys *PlussNatt* (a fully reclining lie-flat seat).
r – 1927 June 30 - Aug. 8.

s – Calls to set down only.
u – Calls to pick up only.
⊡ – Conveys ✕. Also conveys *Pluss* seating.
★ – 🛏 (6-berth). Whole compartment must be booked.

Local services MYRDAL - VOSS - BERGEN and FLÅM 781

Local trains convey 🍷

See Table **780** for long-distance services.

km		⚒		Ⓐ		Ⓐ M	Ⓐ N		C	B	D	J				C	B	Ⓐ	D	Ⓐ			⚒		
0	**Myrdal** .... d.	...	...	...	...	...	...	...	0928	...	1037	...	1152	1313	...	1438	...	...	1556	...	...	1848	...	...	...
18	Mjølfjell .... d.	...	...	...	...	0737	...	...	|	...	|	...	1212	1335	...	|	...	...	1615**x**	...	...	1907	...	...	...
49	**Voss** .... a.	...	...	...	...	0815	...	...	1014	...	1126	...	1255	1403	...	1527	...	...	1651	...	...	1943	...	...	...
49	**Voss** .... d.	0451	0555	0637	0726	0832	0832	...	1016	1016	1127	1127	1259	1406	...	1530	1530	1600	1700	1805	1913	1951	2108	...	2302
89	Dale .... d.	0523	0630	0714	0800	0911	0911	...	1050	1050	1158	1158	1332	1438	...	1600	1600	1636	1733	1839	1950	2029	2142	...	2343
104	Vaksdal .... d.	0538	0648	0731	0816	0934	0934	...	1105	1105	1216	1216	1348	1454	...	1621	1621	1651	1748	1858	2013	2045	2202	...	2359
126	Arna .... ‡ d.	0557	0708	0750	0838	0953	0953	...	1124	1124	1235	1235	1407	1516	...	1647	1647	1715	1809	1917	2032	2107	2221	...	0018
135	**Bergen** .... ‡ a.	0604	0716	0758	0846	1001	1001	...	1132	1132	1243	1243	1414	1524	...	1654	1654	1722	1817	1925	2040	2115	2229	...	0026

	Ⓐ	Ⓐ	L	J	L	J	C	B			C	B		Ⓐ			Ⓐ		Ⓐ		Ⓑ	⚒		
Bergen .... ‡ d.	...	0548	0704	0704	0830	0830	0921	0921	1035	...	1232	1232	1317	1423	1515	1619	1738	1831	1923	2039	2137	2238	...	0035
Arna .... ‡ d.	...	0557	0712	0712	0838	0838	0929	0929	1043	...	1240	1240	1325	1431	1523	1627	1746	1839	1931	2047	2145	2246	...	0043
Vaksdal .... d.	...	0616	0731	0731	0856	0856	0951	0951	1105	...	1303	1303	1347	1453	1542	1650	1807	1858	1954	2105	2203	2308	...	0104
Dale .... d.	...	0635	0746	0746	0911	0911	1006	1006	1120	...	1318	1318	1402	1508	1600	1710	1825	1913	2009	2126	2218	2323	...	0119
Voss .... a.	...	0710	0818	0818	0942	0942	1047	1047	1158	...	1350	1350	1439	1541	1634	1749	1856	1948	2046	2158	2253	2400	...	0151
Voss .... d.	0655	...	0825	...	0944	0951	1056	...	1204	...	1414	...	1441	...	...	1751	...	...	...	...	...	...	...	...
Mjølfjell .... d.	0729	...	0859**x**	...	|	1025**x**	1136	...	1237**x**	...	1453**x**	...	1517	...	...	1822**x**	...	...	...	...	...	...	...	...
Myrdal .... a.	...	...	0917	...	1029	1043	1152	...	1256	...	1512	...	1535	...	...	1840	...	...	...	...	...	...	...	...

MYRDAL - FLÅM ⊠

km		J	J	J	ⒸJ	ⒶJ		K	K	K	K	K	K	④⑤K		ⒶC	C	C	C	C	C	C	C	C	C
0	Myrdal .... d.	1015	1315	1539	1805	1928	...	0930	1045	1206	1324	1607	1722	1928	...	0817	0930	1045	1206	1324	1448	1607	1722	1837	1953
20	Flåm .... a.	1105	1405	1625	1855	2018	...	1028	1143	1304	1422	1705	1820	2018	...	0913	1028	1143	1304	1422	1546	1705	1820	1935	2049

	J		J	J	J		K	K	K	K	K	K	④⑤K		ⒶC	C	C	C	C	C	C	C	C	C
Flåm .... d.	0900	...	1145	1430	1650	...	0820	0935	1050	1210	1455	1615	1730	...	0720	0820	0935	1050	1210	1330	1455	1615	1730	1845
Myrdal .... a.	0944	...	1228	1514	1735	...	0917	1032	1147	1308	1551	1710	1825	...	0802	0917	1032	1147	1308	1426	1551	1710	1825	1941

– From Oct. 1.
– May 1 - Sept. 30.
– May 2 - Sept. 30.
– From Nov. 1.

K – Oct. 1–31.
L – May 1 - Oct. 31.
M – May 2 - June 20 and from Aug. 11.
N – June 23 - Aug. 8.

x – Request stop.

‡ – Additional local services operate.
⊠ – Flåmsbana. Operated by Vy.

🚢 FLÅM - GUDVANGEN and 🚌 GUDVANGEN - VOSS 781a

Service until March 31, 2026

	🚢	🚌 t	🚌 v	🚢 s		🚢 f	🚌 t	🚌 v	🚢 s	
Flåm .... d.	0930	...	...	1130	...	1445	...	...	1700	...
Gudvangen ferjekai .... a.	1130	...	...	1330	...	1645	...	...	1900	...
Gudvangen ferjekai .... d.	...	1140	1140	...	1450	...	1650	1725	...	...
Voss .... a.	...	1230	1255	...	1545	...	1748	1845	...	...

	🚢 s	🚌 t	🚌 v	🚢 f	🚢 s		🚌 t	🚌	🚢 f	
Voss .... d.	...	1010	1010	...	...	...	1445	1550	...	...
Gudvangen ferjekai ... a.	...	1100	1125	...	...	...	1545	1650	...	...
Gudvangen ferjekai ... d.	0900	...	...	1200	1430	...	...	...	1715	...
Flåm .... a.	1100	...	...	1400	1630	...	...	...	1915	...

– 15 minutes later May 1 - Sept. 30.
– May 1 - Sept. 30.

t – Until Apr. 30.
v – From May 1.

🚌 operator: Skyss ✆ +47 5555 9070.
🚢 operator: The Fjords ✆ +47 5763 1400.

🚢 / 🚌 SOGNEFJORD AREA 782

	🚢 ⚒	🚌 Ⓐ	🚌	🚢 ⑦S	🚌 Ⓑ	🚌 ⚒	🚢 ⑦W	🚢 S	🚌	🚌	🚌 ⑦	🚌 c
Lillehammer skysst. d.	...	...	...	...	...	0915	...	...	...	...	1305	...
Gjøvik skysstasjon .. d.	...	...	...	...	...	1000	...	...	...	...	1350	...
Sogndal ⊕ .... d.	...	...	0955	...	...	|	...	...	...	...	|	...
Kaupangsenteret.... d.	...	...	1010	...	...	|	...	...	...	...	|	...
Gol Skysstasjon .... d.	...	...	|	...	...	|	...	...	1320	...	|	1845
Lærdal Rådhus .... d.	...	...	1045	...	...	|	...	...	1522	...	|	2035
Kaupangsenteret ...... d.	...	...	|	...	...	|	...	...	1600	...	|	2120
Sogndal ⊕ .... a.	...	...	|	...	...	|	...	...	1615	...	|	2135
Sogndal ⊕ .... d.	0705	0855	|	1040	1450	|	1540	...	...	1620	|	2205
Flåm .... d.	|	|	1135	|	|	1508	|	1530	...	|	1902	|
Leikanger Kai .... d.	0730	0920	|	1105	1515	|	1605	1630	...	1645	|	2230
Balestrand Kai .... d.	0750	1010	|	1127	1605	|	1625	1650	...	1735	|	2315
Voss .... **781** d.	|	...	1245	|	...	1618	|	|	...	...	2012	...
Bergen ⊡ .... **781** a.	1150	...	...	1520	...	1803	2015	2045	...	...	2200	...

	🚌 c	🚢 S	🚌	🚌	🚌	🚌 Ⓐ	🚢 ⑥	🚌	🚌	🚢 Ⓑ	🚌 Ⓑ
Bergen ⊡ .... **781** d.	...	0800	0910	...	...	...	1415	...	...	1630	...
Voss .... **781** d.	...	|	1047	...	...	...	|	...	1805	|	...
Balestrand Kai .... d.	1005	1158	|	1310	...	1540	1820	1815	|	2031	2120
Leikanger Kai .... d.	1055	1218	|	1355	...	1630	1835	1900	|	2051	2200
Flåm .... d.	|	1340	1200	|	...	|	|	|	1910	|	|
Sogndal ⊕ .... a.	1125	...	|	1425	...	1655	1900	1930	|	2120	2225
Sogndal ⊕ .... d.	1130	...	|	...	1430	...	...	...	|	...	...
Kaupangsenteret .... d.	1145	...	|	...	1445	...	...	...	|	...	...
Lærdal Rådhus .... d.	1225	...	|	...	1525	...	...	...	1956	...	...
Gol skysstasjon .... a.	1415	...	|	...	1715	...	...	...	|	...	...
Kaupangsenteret .... a.	...	...	|	...	...	...	...	...	2040	...	...
Sogndal ⊕ .... a.	...	...	|	...	...	...	...	...	2055	...	...
Gjøvik skysstasjon ... a.	...	...	1710	...	...	...	...	...	...	...	...
Lillehammer skysst . a.	...	...	1755	...	...	...	...	...	...	...	...

S – Apr. 1 - Oct. 31.
W – Nov. 1 - Mar. 31.
c – Change buses at Sogndal.

⊕ – 🚌: Sogndal skysstasjon. 🚢: Sogndal kai.
⊡ – 🚌: Bus station. 🚢: Strandkaiterminal.

🚌 operators: Vy Buss AS ✆ +47 4070 5070. Nor-way Bussekspress ✆ +47 2231 3150. Skyss ✆ +47 5555 9070.
🚢 operator: Norled AS ✆ +47 5186 8700.

783 EIDSVOLL - OSLO - SKIEN

All trains convey *Vy Komfort* and 🍷

Service until June 27

km																									
		Ⓐ	⚒								Ⓐ		Ⓐ	Ⓐ		Ⓐ	Ⓐ								
0	**Eidsvoll** 785 d.	0501	0601	0701	0801	0901	1001	1101	1201	1301	...	1401	...	...	1501	...	...	1601	1701	1801	1901	2001	2101	2201	2301
16	Oslo Lufthavn ✈ ¶ 785 d.	0513	0613	0713	0813	0913	1013	1113	1213	1313	...	1413	...	...	1513	...	...	1613	1713	1813	1913	2013	2113	2213	2313
47	Lillestrøm 785 d.	0526	0626	0726	0826	0926	1026	1126	1226	1326	...	1426	...	...	1526	...	...	1626	1726	1826	1926	2026	2126	2226	2326
68	**Oslo** S 785 a.	0536	0636	0736	0836	0936	1036	1136	1236	1336	...	1436	...	...	1536	...	...	1636	1736	1836	1936	2036	2136	2236	2336
68	**Oslo** S 785 d.	0539	0639	0739	0839	0939	1039	1139	1239	1339	1405	1439	1505	1533	1539	1605	1633	1639	1739	1839	1939	2039	2139	2239	2339
108	Drammen 785 d.	0613	0713	0813	0913	1013	1113	1213	1313	1413	1445	1513	1545	|	1613	1645	|	1713	1813	1913	2013	2113	2213	2313	0013
142	Holmestrand d.	0636	0732	0832	0932	1032	1132	1232	1332	1432	1506	1532	1606	|	1632	1706	|	1732	1832	1932	2032	2132	2232	2332	0032
156	Skoppum d.	0649	0741	0840	0940	1040	1140	1240	1340	1440	1518	1540	1618	|	1640	1718	|	1740	1840	1940	2040	2140	2240	2340	0040
172	Tønsberg d.	0705	0752	0852	0952	1052	1152	1252	1352	1452	1529	1552	1629	1642	1652	1729	1742	1752	1852	1952	2052	2152	2252	2352	0052
191	Torp ✈ d.	0720	0812	0912	1012	1112	1212	1312	1412	1512	|	1612	|	|	1712	|	|	1812	1912	2012	2112	2212	2312	0011	|
196	**Sandefjord** d.	0726	0818	0918	1018	1118	1218	1318	1418	1518	1549	1618	1649	1706	1718	1749	1806	1818	1918	2018	2118	2218	2318	0016	0111
215	Larvik d.	0746	0833	0933	1033	1133	1233	1333	1433	1533	1604	1633	1704	1720	1733	1804	1820	1833	1933	2033	2133	2233	2333	0030	0125
240	Porsgrunn 779 d.	0758	0845	0945	1045	1145	1245	1345	1445	1545	1622	1645	1722	1734	1745	1822	1834	1845	1945	2045	2145	2245	2345	0042	0137
249	**Skien** 779 a.	0807	0853	0953	1053	1153	1253	1353	1453	1553	1630	1653	1730	1742	1753	1830	1842	1853	1953	2053	2153	2253	2353	0050	0145

	Ⓐ	Ⓐ	⚒	Ⓐ	Ⓐ		Ⓐ	Ⓐ																Ⓑ
Skien 779 d.	0410	0426	0511	0525	0537	0607	0617	0625	0709	0809	0909	1009	1109	1209	1309	1409	1509	1608	1708	1808	1909	2009	2109	2209	2309
Porsgrunn 779 d.	0418	0435	0519	0534	0546	0615	0626	0634	0717	0817	0917	1017	1117	1217	1317	1417	1517	1617	1717	1817	1917	2017	2117	2217	2317
Larvik d.	0431	0449	0532	0547	0600	0629	0640	0648	0732	0832	0932	1032	1132	1232	1332	1432	1532	1632	1732	1832	1932	2032	2132	2232	2332
Sandefjord d.	0446	0504	0547	0602	0615	0645	0654	0702	0747	0847	0947	1047	1147	1247	1347	1447	1547	1647	1747	1847	1947	2047	2147	2247	2347
Torp ✈ d.	0450	0508	0551	0606	|	0649	|	0707	0751	0851	0951	1051	1151	1251	1351	1451	1551	1651	1751	1851	1951	2051	2151	2251	2351
Tønsberg d.	0508	0528	0608	0624	0638	0707	0718	0727	0808	0908	1008	1108	1208	1308	1408	1508	1608	1708	1808	1908	2008	2108	2208	2308	0008
Skoppum d.	0518	0538	0618	0635	|	0718	|	0740	0818	0918	1018	1118	1218	1318	1418	1518	1618	1718	1818	1918	2018	2118	2218	2318	0018
Holmestrand d.	0526	0547	0626	0644	|	0726	|	0749	0826	0926	1026	1126	1226	1326	1426	1526	1626	1726	1826	1926	2026	2126	2226	2326	0026
Drammen 785 d.	0547	0609	0647	0710	|	0747	|	0812	0847	0947	1047	1147	1247	1347	1447	1547	1647	1747	1847	1947	2047	2147	2247	2347	0045
Oslo S 785 a.	0621	0645	0721	0745	0747	0821	0826	0845	0921	1021	1121	1221	1321	1421	1521	1621	1721	1821	1921	2021	2121	2221	2321	0021	...
Oslo S 785 d.	0624	0647	0724	...	0752	0824	...	...	0924	1024	1124	1224	1324	1424	1524	1624	1724	1824	1924	2024	2124	2224	2324	0024	...
Lillestrøm 785 d.	0635	|	0735	...	0802	0835	...	...	0935	1035	1135	1235	1335	1435	1535	1635	1735	1835	1935	2035	2135	2235	2335	0035	...
Oslo Lufthavn ✈ ¶ 785 d.	0649	0707	0749	...	...	0849	...	...	0949	1049	1149	1249	1349	1449	1549	1649	1749	1849	1949	2049	2149	2249	2349	0049	...
Eidsvoll 785 a.	0659	...	0759	...	...	0859	...	...	0959	1059	1159	1259	1359	1459	1559	1659	1759	1859	1959	2059	2159	2259	2359	0059	...

¶ – Oslo Lufthavn Gardermoen ✈.

784 HAMAR - RØROS - TRONDHEIM

Operated by SJ NORD

km													
		Ⓐ [R]	⑥ [R]	Ⓐ [R]	⚒ [R]	Ⓐ [R]	⑦ [R]	⑥ [R]		[R]	Ⓑ [R]	Ⓑ [R]	
0	**Hamar** d.	...	...	0810	1011	1211	1211	...	...	1609	1815	2011	...
32	Elverum d.	...	...	0836	1037	1237	1237	...	...	1636	1841	2037	...
64	Rena d.	...	...	0857	1059	1258	1258	...	...	1658	1902	2058	...
120	Koppang d.	...	...	0941	1147	1341	1341	...	...	1742	1948	2142	...
273	**Røros** a.	...	...	1138	1342	1538	1538	...	...	1939	2143	2337	...
273	**Røros** d.	0502	0700	...	...	1544	1607	1628	...	1945	...	...	...
384	Støren 785 d.	0646	0837	...	...	1727	1743	1803	...	2126	...	...	...
435	**Trondheim** S 785 a.	0744	0934	...	...	1826	1836	1856	...	2226	...	...	...

	Ⓐ [R]	⚒ [R]	Ⓐ [R]		[R]	Ⓑ [R]	[R]	⑦ [R]	Ⓐ [R]	⑦ [R]
Trondheim S 785 d.	...	...	0537	...	0934	...	...	1329	1621	2020
Støren 785 d.	...	...	0640	...	1033	...	...	1429	1724	2127
Røros a.	...	...	0817	...	1210	...	...	1605	1902	2305
Røros d.	0418	0618	0822	...	1220	1417	1623	1623	...	...
Koppang d.	0612	0811	1022	...	1421	1613	1823	1823	...	...
Rena d.	0655	0856	1105	...	1505	1658	1906	1906	...	...
Elverum d.	0718	0919	1127	...	1527	1721	1928	1928	...	...
Hamar a.	0742	0943	1151	...	1552	1746	1952	1952	...	...

785 OSLO - LILLEHAMMER - ÅNDALSNES and TRONDHEIM

Services to / from Trondheim and Åndalsnes are operated by SJ NORD. Local services Drammen - Oslo - Lillehammer are operated by Vy.

km		43	2343	45	2345		47	2347	49	2349		51	329		405
				Ⓐ	Ⓐ				Ⓑ	Ⓑ		Ⓑ	Ⓑ f		Ⓑ
		[R] p	[R]	[R]	[R]		[R]	[R]	[R]	[R]		[R]	◇		[R] n
		✕ ⊕	🍷	✕ ⊙	🍷		✕ ⊕	🍷	✕ ⊙	🍷		✕ ⊙	🍷		✕ ⊕
0	**Oslo** Sentral ★ d.	0802	...	1002	...	...	1402	...	1602	...	...	1802	1834	...	2250
21	Lillestrøm ★ d.	0813u	...	1012u	...	...	1413u	...	1613u	...	...	1813u	1845	...	2320u
52	Oslo ✈ ⊖ ★ d.	0829u	...	1027u	...	...	1429u	...	1629u	...	...	1828u	1859	...	2338u
127	**Hamar** ★ d.	0912	...	1110	...	...	1512	...	1712	...	...	1911	1952	...	0024
185	**Lillehammer** ★ d.	1001	...	1200	...	...	1602	...	1809	...	...	2003	2045	...	0117
243	Ringebu d.	1045	...	1246	...	...	1655	...	1851	...	...	2045	2126	...	0207
267	Vinstra d.	1102	...	1303	...	...	1713	...	1916	...	...	2102	2141	...	0226
298	Otta d.	1129	...	1334	...	...	1737	...	1939	...	...	2126	2205	...	0304
344	Dombås d.	1201	1208	1405	1422	...	1814	1826	2010	2015	...	2159	2235	...	0339
458	**Åndalsnes** ♥ a.	|	1330	|	1554	...	|	1948	|	2137	...	|	...	...	|
430	Oppdal ♥ d.	1306	...	1516	...	...	1914	...	2108	...	...	2315	...	...	0445
502	Støren 784 d.	1356	...	1606	...	...	2006	...	2210	...	...	0009	...	...	0540
553	**Trondheim** S 784 a.	1440	...	1653	...	...	2055	...	2253	...	...	0052	...	...	0640

	308	2340	40	2342	42	44		2346	46		2348	48		406
	⚒	Ⓐ	Ⓐ			Ⓑ		Ⓑ	Ⓑ					Ⓑ
	◇	[R]	[R]	[R]	[R] q	[R]		[R]	[R]		[R]	[R] p		[R] n
	🍷	🍷	✕ ⊙	🍷	✕ ⊙	✕ ⊕		🍷	✕ ⊙		🍷	✕ ⊕		✕ ⊕
Trondheim S 784 d.	...	...	0555	...	0817	0952	...	...	1306	...	...	1527	...	2317
Støren 784 d.	...	...	0645	...	0902	1043	...	...	1354	...	...	1618	...	0009
Oppdal ♥ d.	...	...	0742	...	0953	1136	...	...	1444	...	...	1711	...	0110
Åndalsnes ♥ d.	...	0718	|	0924	|	|	...	1423	|	...	1629	|	...	|
Dombås d.	0523	0842	0847	1048	1054	1243	...	1547	1552	...	1753	1812	...	0231
Otta d.	0554	...	0918	...	1127	1315	...	...	1623	...	...	1842	...	0312
Vinstra d.	0616	...	0942	...	1150	1339	...	...	1646	...	...	1904	...	0336
Ringebu d.	0632	...	0959	...	1206	1357	...	...	1710	...	...	1920	...	0353
Lillehammer ★ d.	0715	...	1046	...	1250	1442	...	...	1751	...	...	2005	...	0439
Hamar ★ d.	0812	...	1134	...	1344	1530	...	...	1838	...	...	2051	...	0534
Oslo ✈ ⊖ ★ a.	0903	...	1222s	...	1423s	1623s	...	...	1926s	...	...	2134s	...	0619s
Lillestrøm ★ a.	0916	...	1238s	...	1438s	1638s	...	...	1939s	...	...	2152s	...	0638s
Oslo Sentral ★ a.	0926	...	1248	...	1448	1648	...	...	1948	...	...	2202	...	0649

e – ⑦ only.
f – Not June 8.
n – Conveys 🛏 and 2 (also reclining seats).
p – Does **not** convey Premium Pluss on ②⑥.
q – Conveys Premium Pluss on ⑥.
s – Calls to set down only.
u – Calls to pick up only.

◇ – Operated by Vy.
⊙ – Conveys *SJ NORD Premium.*
⊕ – Conveys *SJ NORD Premium Pluss.*
⊖ – Oslo Lufthavn Gardermoen.
★ – See also panel below main table.
♥ – See Table **785a** for connecting 🚌 services to / from Molde, Ålesund and Kristiansund.

Local services Drammen - Oslo - Lillehammer (operated by Vy).

	Ⓐ									Ⓐ			Ⓑ	Ⓐ		Ⓐ							①–④	⑦
Drammen 783 d.	0557	0657	0757e	...	...	...	...	...	...	...	1457e	...	1557	...	...	1657	...	...	...	...	...	...	2347	2347
Oslo Sentral 771 783 d.	0634	0734	0834	0934	1034	1134	1234	1334	1434	1502	1534	1634	1634	1702	1734	1734	1834	1934	2034	2134	2234	2334	0024	0024
Lillestrøm 783 d.	0645	0745	0845	0945	1045	1145	1245	1345	1445	1513	1545	1645	1645	1713	1745	1745	1845	1945	2045	2145	2245	2345	0035	0035
Oslo ✈ ⊖ 771 783 d.	0659	0759	0859	0959	1059	1159	1259	1359	1459	1527	1559	1659	1659	1727	1759	1759	1859	1959	2059	2159	2259	2359	0049	0049
Eidsvoll 783 d.	0708	0808	0908	1008	1108	1208	1308	1408	1508	1536	1608	1708	1708	1736	1808	1808	1910	2008	2108	2208	2308	0008	0102	0102
Hamar a.	0745	0843	0943	1045	1145	1243	1343	1444	1543	1611	1647	1743	1743	1809	1850	1850	1945	2043	2143	2243	2343	0043	0137	0137
Hamar d.	0752	0852	0952	1052	1152	1252	1352	1452	1552	...	1652	1752	1752	...	1852	1852	1952	2052	2152	2244	2344	0044	0139	...
Lillehammer a.	0841	0941	1041	1141	1245	1341	1441	1538	1641	...	1741	1841	1841	...	1941	1941	2041	2141	2237	2329	0029	0129	0224	...

	Ⓐ	Ⓐ		Ⓐ		Ⓐ								Ⓑ		Ⓐ								
Lillehammer d.	0336	0419	0531	...	0615	...	0715	0815	0915	1015	1111	1215	1315	1315	1411	1411	1507	1615	1715	1815	1915	2011	2115	...
Hamar a.	0422	0504	0616	...	0705	...	0805	0905	1005	1105	1205	1305	1405	1405	1505	1505	1605	1705	1805	1905	2005	2105	2205	...
Hamar d.	0424	0506	0618	0636	0712	0734	0812	0912	1012	1112	1212	1312	1412	1412	1512	1512	1612	1712	1813	1909	2008	2112	2212	...
Eidsvoll 783 d.	0501	0542	0653	0712	0753	0813	0853	0953	1053	1153	1253	1353	1453	1453	1553	1553	1653	1753	1853	1953	2053	2153	2253	...
Oslo ✈ ⊖ 771 783 d.	0513	0603	0703	0723	0803	0823	0903	1003	1103	1203	1303	1403	1503	1503	1603	1603	1703	1803	1903	2003	2103	2203	2303	...
Lillestrøm 783 d.	0526	0616	0716	0738	0816	0838	0916	1016	1116	1216	1316	1416	1516	1516	1616	1616	1716	1816	1916	2016	2116	2216	2316	...
Oslo Sentral 771 783 a.	0536	0626	0726	0748	0826	0848	0926	1026	1126	1226	1326	1426	1526	1526	1626	1626	1726	1826	1926	2026	2126	2226	2326	...
Drammen 783 a.	0611	0702	0802e	...	...	...	...	...	...	...	...	1502e	...	1602	...	1702	...	...	...	...	...	...	0002	...

🚌 ÅNDALSNES - MOLDE and ÅLESUND; 🚌 OPPDAL - KRISTIANSUND 785a

FRAM 🚌 routes 420 and 681 — **ÅNDALSNES - MOLDE and ÅLESUND**

🚌	⑦	Ⓐ	Ⓐ			Ⓐ	Ⓐt	Ⓐ		⑥⑦		⑥	Ⓐ	Ⓐs	Ⓐ	⑦				Ⓑ			
ndalsnes Stasjon d.	0605	0610	0725	...	1000	1140	1240	1340	1340	1400	...	1600	1620	1720	1820	1820	...	1955	2000	2155	...	...	...
Molde Trafikkterminal a.	0732	0742	0849	...	1127	1307	1407	1512	|	1527	...	1727	1747	1847	1942	1947	...	2117	|	2317	...	...	...
lesund (Skateflukaia) a.	...	...	...	...	...	...	...	...	1545	...	...	...	...	...	...	...	...	...	2205	...	...	...	...

🚌	Ⓐh	Ⓐs	Ⓐ	⑥⑦		⚒	⑦	⑦	Ⓐ		Ⓐ	⑥⑦	Ⓐ	⑥	Ⓐs	Ⓐ	Ⓐ	Ⓐs	⑥⑦	Ⓐ	Ⓑ		
lesund (Skateflukaia) d.	...	...	0703	0705	...	...	...	1150	...	...	...	...	1350	1405	...	...	...	...	...	...	...	...	...
Molde Trafikkterminal d.	0600	0630	|	|	0750	0955	1235	|	1255	...	1425	1435	|	|	1510	1545	1630	1750	1755	1935	2030	2150	...
ndalsnes Stasjon a.	0714	0752	0910	0915	0915	1115	1355	1414	1415	...	1555	1555	1605	1615	1635	1715	1755	1915	1912	2055	2150	2307	...

FRAM 🚌 route 901 — **OPPDAL - KRISTIANSUND**

🚌	Ⓐ	⑥	Ⓐ		Ⓐ	⑦		⑤⑦	Ⓑ
ppdal Skysstasjon § d.	0515	0530	1055	...	1315	1315	...	1810	2120
ristiansund Trafikkterminal a.	0855	0845	1425	...	1631	1625	...	2125	0025

🚌	Ⓐ		Ⓐ	⑥	Ⓑ	⑤	⑦		Ⓑ
Kristiansund Trafikkterminal d.	0630	...	1045	1125	1330	1635	1640	...	2125
Oppdal Skysstasjon § a.	0935	...	1425	1445	1645	2005	2005	...	0035

h – School holidays only.
s – Schooldays only.
t – On schooldays d. 1255, a. 1427.
§ – Bus terminal adjacent to railway station.

Operator: FRAM www.frammr.no

🚌 BERGEN - STAVANGER 786

ERGEN (Busstasjon) - **STAVANGER** (Bussterminal)

perator: NOR-WAY Bussekspress ✆ +47 2231 3150. www.nor-way.no *Journey time: 4½ – 5½ hours.*

rom Bergen on Ⓐ at 0715, 0840, 0920, 0940⑤, 1040, 1120, 1240, 1300, 1400, 1435, 1530, 1635, 1655.
rom Bergen on ⑥ at 0820, 0935, 1050, 1230, 1435, 1550.
rom Bergen on ⑦ at 0940, 1040, 1200, 1240, 1320, 1440, 1520, 1620, 1640, 1740, 1820.
rom Stavanger on Ⓐ at 0645, 0800, 0830, 0945, 1045⑤, 1130, 1200, 1345, 1430, 1525, 1615, 1645, 1800.
rom Stavanger on ⑥ at 0935, 1015, 1215, 1415, 1555, 1615.
rom Stavanger on ⑦ at 0945, 1045, 1145, 1230, 1400, 1500, 1530, 1600, 1630, 1700, 1800.

TRONDHEIM - BODØ and NARVIK 787

Operated by SJ NORD

km		1797		1781	1783		475	🚌	483	473	1785		1787		1789	471	🚌	1791		479	1793		477	
		⑥⑦ R 🍷		Ⓐ R 🍷	Ⓐ R 🍷		❋ R N 🍴★	◇ g	⚒ R 🍷	⚒ R 🍷	Ⓐ R 🍷		Ⓐ R 🍷		Ⓐ R 🍷	R 🍴★	◇ h	Ⓐ R 🍷		Ⓑ R 🍷	Ⓐ R 🍷		Ⓑ R	
0	**Trondheim** S d.	...	...	...	...	...	2305	...	...	...	...	...	...	...	...	0749	...	...	...	...	...	...	1600	...
33	Trondheim ✈ ‡ d.	...	...	...	...	...	2337	...	...	...	...	...	...	...	...	0824	...	...	...	...	...	...	1636**u**	...
34	Stjørdal d.	...	...	...	...	...	2341	...	...	...	...	...	...	...	...	0828	...	...	...	...	...	...	1641**u**	...
126	Steinkjer d.	...	...	...	...	...	0057	...	...	...	...	...	...	...	...	0951	...	...	...	...	...	...	1807**u**	...
220	Grong d.	...	...	...	...	...	0207	...	...	...	...	...	...	...	...	1058	...	...	...	...	...	...	1914	...
406	Mosjøen d.	...	...	...	...	...	0444	...	0642	...	...	...	...	...	...	1317	...	...	...	1657	...	...	2145**z**	...
498	Mo i Rana d.	...	...	...	...	...	0555	...	0746	0756	...	...	...	...	...	1431	...	...	...	1801	...	...	2248	...
648	Rognan d.	0205	...	0535	0631	...	0750	...	...	0947	1124	...	...	...	...	1631	...	1801	...	2001	2048	...	...	...
	Bodø ⊖ d.	|	...	|	|	...	|	0719	...	|	|	...	...	...	...	|	1644	|	...	|	|	...	...	...
674	Fauske d.	0225	...	0555	0651	...	0811	0840	...	1009	1144	...	1424	...	1612	1652	1800	1830	...	2022	2108	...	...	...
	Narvik ⊡ ♣ a.	|	...	|	|	...	|	1335	...	|	|	...	|	...	|	|	2315	|	...	|	|	...	...	...
729	**Bodø** a.	0306	...	0636	0732	...	0905	...	...	1051	1225	...	1505	...	1659	1744	...	1910	...	2103	2155	...	...	...

	1796		478		470		1784		🚌	472	1786		1788	1790		474	1792		🚌	476		1794	
	⑥⑦ R 🍷		R 🍴		Ⓐ R 🍴		Ⓐ R 🍷		◇ j	R 🍴★	Ⓐ R 🍷		Ⓐ R 🍷	Ⓐ R 🍷		R 🍷	Ⓐ R 🍷		◇ k	❋ R N 🍴★		Ⓑ R 🍷	
odø d.	0055	...	...	...	0734	...	1012	...	...	1227	1335	...	1513	1616	...	1746	1925	...	...	2109	...	2315	...
Narvik ⊡ ♣ d.	|	...	...	...	|	...	|	...	0705	|	|	...	|	|	...	|	|	...	1625	|	...	|	...
auske d.	0137	...	...	...	0821	...	1056	...	1210	1316	1416	...	1555	1700	...	1828	2022	...	2125	2202	...	2358	...
Bodø ⊖ a.	|	...	...	...	|	...	|	...	1307	|	...	...	...	|	...	|	|	...	2223	|	...	|	...
ognan d.	0156	...	...	...	0839	...	1115	...	...	1336	...	...	...	1719	...	1846	2040	...	...	2222	...	0016	...
lo i Rana d.	...	...	0811	...	1025	...	...	...	...	1545	...	...	...	...	...	2035	...	...	...	0024	...	...	...
losjøen d.	...	...	0916	...	1128	...	...	...	...	1655	...	...	...	...	...	2138	...	...	...	0142	...	...	...
rong d.	...	...	1129	...	...	...	...	...	...	1914	...	...	...	...	...	...	...	...	...	0405	...	...	...
teinkjer a.	...	...	1231**x**	...	...	...	...	...	...	2021**x**	...	...	...	...	...	...	...	...	...	0517	...	...	...
tjørdal a.	...	...	1342**x**	...	...	...	...	...	...	2145**x**	...	...	...	...	...	...	...	...	...	0640	...	...	...
rondheim ✈ ‡ a.	...	...	1345**x**	...	...	...	...	...	...	2148	...	...	...	...	...	...	...	...	...	0643	...	...	...
rondheim a.	...	...	1413	...	...	...	...	...	...	2213	...	...	...	...	...	...	...	...	...	0715	...	...	...

Local services **Støren - Trondheim - Steinkjer**

From May 3 to June 15 services between 1000 and 2000 are affected by engineering work with rail replacement 🚌 services operating for all or part of the journey as follow: May 3 – 24 between Trondheim and Stjørdal; May 25 - June 1 between Trondheim and Steinkjer; June 2 – 15 between Stjørdal and Steinkjer.

km		Ⓐ	Ⓐ	⚒	⚒		⚒		⚒			Ⓐ		Ⓐ	Ⓑ		Ⓑ	Ⓐ	⑥		Ⓑ		Ⓑ		Ⓑ
0	**Støren** 784 785 d.	0409	0513	0606	0712	0811**c**	...	...	...	...	1317**e**	...	...	...	...	1613**a**	...	1727	1803	...	...	...	...	2126	...
30	Melhus Skysstasjon d.	0437	0542	0642	0747	0847	0939	1048	1147	1248	1348	...	1448	...	1541	1644	1748	1757	1832	1847	1948	2049	2149	2202	2248
51	**Trondheim** S **784 785** a.	0500	0612	0711	0814	0914	1014	1114	1214	1314	1414	...	1514	...	1614	1714	1814	1826	1856	1914	2014	2115	2215	2226	2314
51	**Trondheim** S d.	0505	0615	0714	0816	0916	1017	1117	1217	1317	1417	1442	1517	1541	1617	1716	1817	...	...	1916	2017	2117	2217	...	2317
82	Hell ● d.	0542	0650	0750	0850	0950	1050	1150	1250	1350	1450	1520	1550	1620	1650	1750	1850	...	...	1950	2051	2150	2250	...	2350
84	Trondheim ✈ ‡ d.	0545	0653	0753	0853	0953	1053	1153	1253	1353	1453	1523	1553	1623	1653	1753	1853	...	...	1953	2054	2153	2253	...	2353
85	Stjørdal d.	0551	0657	0759	0900	1000	1100	1200	1300	1400	1500	1528	1600	1628	1700	1800	1900	...	...	2000	2101	2200	2300	...	2356
177	**Steinkjer** a.	0723	0822	0922	1025	1125	1225	1326	1425	1525	1624	1652	1725	1752	1825	1924	2024	...	...	2125	2227	2321	0021	...	0117

	Ⓐ	Ⓐ	Ⓐ	Ⓐ	Ⓐ			⚒		⚒	⑦			Ⓐ		Ⓐ			Ⓑ		Ⓑ		Ⓑ	
teinkjer d.	0429	0506	0534	0602	0632	...	0734	0833	0930	1037	...	1137	1238	...	1337	...	1437	1537	1632	1732	1837	1932	2024	2134
tjørdal d.	0551	0623	0657	0724	0759	...	0900	1000	1100	1200	...	1300	1400	1420	1500	...	1600	1700	1800	1900	2000	2101	2200	2300
rondheim ✈ ‡ d.	0554	0626	0700	0727	0802	...	0903	1003	1103	1203	...	1303	1403	1423	1503	...	1603	1703	1803	1903	2003	2104	2203	2303
ell ● d.	0557	0629	0703	0730	0805	...	0906	1006	1106	1206	...	1306	1406	1426	1506	...	1606	1706	1806	1906	2009	2107	2206	2306
rondheim S a.	0629	0703	0741	0803	0841	...	0941	1041	1141	1241	...	1341	1441	1506	1541	...	1641	1741	1841	1941	2043	2141	2241	2341
rondheim S **784 785** d.	0632	...	0744	...	...	0934	0944	1044	1144	1244	1332	1344	1444	1509	1544	1621	1645	1744	1844	1944	2045	2145	2244	2344
lelhus Skysstasjon d.	0657	...	0808	...	...	1001	1008	1108	1208	1308	1357	1408	1511	1534	1608	1651	1708	1812	1908	2008	2109	2215	2308	0008
tøren **784 785** a.	0740	...	...	...	...	1033	...	...	...	...	1428	...	...	1602	1637**a**	1724	...	...	...	...	...	2241**f**	2336	0042

N – Conveys 🛏, (2) (and (2) reclining) and 🍴. Service suspended – see note ❋.
a – Ⓐ only.
c – Ⓒ only.
e – ⑦ only.
f – ⑥ only.
g – Change bus at Bognes ferjekai (a. 1130 / d. 1140).
h – Change bus at Storjord (a. 2053 / d. 2100).
j – Change bus at Storjord (a. 0913 / d. 0917).
k – Change bus at Storjord (a. 1828 / d. 1832).
u – Calls to pick up only.
x – Calls on request.
z – Arrives 2127.

❋ – Service suspended until further notice due to shortage of locomotives.
★ – Conveys *SJ NORD Premium Pluss.*
● – Trains call at Hell on request.
‡ – Trondheim Lufthavn (station for Trondheim Værnes Airport).
⊡ – Bus terminal.
⊖ – Bodø Sentrum Regionbuss (bus terminal). Also serves Bodø lufthavn (airport), d. 0710 and 1630; a. 1320 and 2235.
◇ – Operator: Nordlandsbuss AS (Line 100).
♣ – 🚌 **Narvik - Svolvær** (Lofoten) *253 km.* Journey approx 4 hours.
From Narvik bussterminal at 0945 and 1545.
From Svolvær sentrum (Avisgata) at 0935 and 1505.

FINLAND

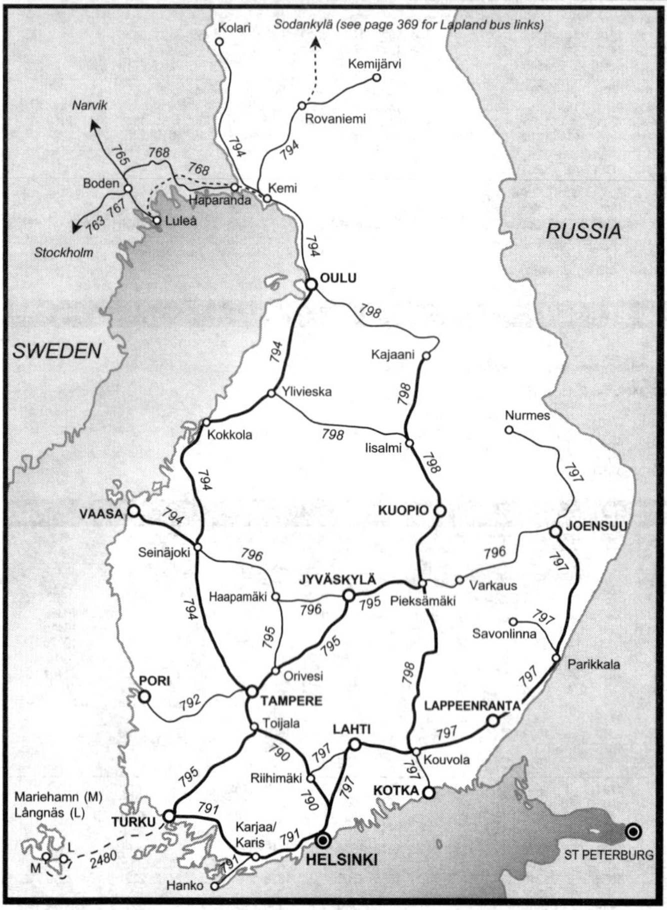

Operator: VR – VR-Yhtymä Oy www.vr.fi

Tickets and train types: Travel classes in Finland are referred to as *Extra* (1st) and *Eco* (2nd). For all except purely local journeys, tickets are always sold for travel by a specific train or combination of trains with seat reservations included. Standard *Eco* fares are referred to as 'Basic', whilst cheaper advance puchase 'Saver' fares are also available in limited numbers. In both cases tickets can be changed to a different date / departure time for a €5 fee (plus any price difference). Both ticket types can be upgraded to a seat in *Extra* class for a variable fee (€4 – 17, dependent on the length of journey). Tickets may be purchased on board long-distance trains (also regional trains outside of the Helsinki area), although an additional charge of €3 (for short journeys up to 76km) or €6 (for journeys over 76km) will be added to the 'Basic' fare. Please note that cash is no longer accepted for on board ticket purchase (only debit / credit cards are accepted). On board ticket purchase is **not** permitted on local trains (shown as 2nd class only in tables) Helsinki - Riihimäki - Tampere (Table **790**), Helsinki - Lahti - Kouvola - Kotka (Table **797**) and Riihimäki - Lahti (Table **797**).

- **S Pendolino** (e.g. *S* **123**) – high-speed tilting trains with *Extra* and *Eco* class seats, all reservable.
- **InterCity** (e.g. *IC* **124**) – quality fast trains between major centres, with *Eco* class seats (most also convey *Extra* class seats), all reservable.
- **Express**, *pikajunat* (train number only shown, e.g. **128**) – other fast trains, with *Eco* class seats, all reservable. Night expresses convey sleeping-cars and *Eco* class seats only (marked ★ in the tables).
- **Regional**, *taajamajunat* (no train number shown) - stopping-trains, normally with *Eco* class seats only. Regional fares apply.

Rail tickets are **not** valid on 🚌 services (except Seinäjoki - Vaasa).

Services: ✕ indicates a train with a restaurant car. Trains marked 🍸 convey a *MiniBistro* trolley. A variable supplement is payable for travel in sleeping-cars (🛏) in addition to the relevant *Eco* class fare – the price to be paid depends on the date of travel and the type of accommodation required. A higher supplement is charged for occupancy of a single-berth cabin.

Timings: **Valid from June 16.** Services are subject to confirmation – please check before travelling. In these tables Ⓐ = ①–⑤, ⚒ = ①–⑥, Ⓑ = ①–⑤ and ⑦.

Changes to the normal service pattern are likely to occur on and around the dates of public holidays (see page 4).

790 HELSINKI - TAMPERE

See next page for other regional services Helsinki - Riihimäki

For through journeys to / from **Oulu** and **Rovaniemi**, see Table **794**. For through journeys to / from **Jyväskylä** and **Pieksämäki**, see Table **795**.

km				*S* 35		*IC* 21	*IC* 155		*IC* 41	*IC* 165	*IC* 165	*IC* 23	*IC* 93		*IC* 43	*S* 143	*S* 33	*IC* 45		*S* 171	*IC* 25	*IC* 145		*IC* 37	*S* 87	*IC* 87
				⚒	⚒	⚒				Ⓐ	⑦									⑤–⑦					Ⓑ	⑥
		2		✕◐	2	✕	✕◐	2	✕◐	P✕◐	✕	✕	✕◐	2	✕	✕◐	✕◐	✕	2	✕◐	✕	✕◐	2	✕	✕	P✕
0	**Helsinki** d.	0040	...	0500	0509	0620	0700	0709	0720	0800	0800	0820	0900	0909	0920	1000	1020	1100	1109	1200	1220	1300	1309	1320	1400	1400
3	Pasila d.	0045	...	0506	0514	0626	0706	0714	0726	0806	0806	0826	0906	0914	0926	1006	1026	1106	1114	1206	1226	1306	1314	1326	1406	1406
16	Tikkurila d.	0054	...	0516	0524	0636	0716	0723	0736	0816	0816	0836	0916	0923	0936	1016	1036	1116	1123	1216	1236	1316	1323	1336	1416	1416
71	Riihimäki d.	0136	...	0552	0625f	|	0752	0815j	|	0852	0852	|	0952	1015j	|	1052	|	1152	1215j	1252	|	1352	1415j	|	1452	1452
108	Hämeenlinna d.	...	...	0611	0648	|	0811	0838	|	0911	0911	|	1011	1038	|	1111	|	1211	1238	1311	|	1411	1438	|	1511	1511
147	Toijala d.	...	...	0631	0711	|	0831	0901	|	0931	0931	|	1031	1101	|	1131	|	1231	1301	1331	|	1431	1501	|	1531	1531
187	**Tampere** a.	...	...	0653	0735	0758	0853	0925	0858	0953	0953	0958	1053	1125	1058	1153	1158	1253	1325	1353	1358	1453	1525	1458	1553	1553

	IC 27	*IC* 151		*IC* 47	*IC* 147	*IC* 51	*S* 59	*S* 59	*IC* 177		*IC* 49	*S* 89	*IC* 29	*IC* 149		**265**	*IC* 183	*S* 53	**269**	*S* 185		*IC* 187		**273**	
		Ⓑ					⑦	Ⓐ										Ⓑ		⑦					
	✕	✕	2	✕	✕	✕	✕	✕	✕	2	✕	✕◐	✕◐	✕	2	★	✕◐	✕	★	✕	2	✕◐	2	★	
Helsinki d.	1420	1500	1509	1520	1600	1620	1627	1627	1700	1709	1720	1800	1820	1900	1909	1929	2000	2020	2029	2100	2109	2200	2239	2313	...
Pasila d.	1426	1506	1514	1526	1606	1626	1633	1633	1706	1714	1726	1806	1826	1906	1914	1937	2006	2026	2036	2106	2114	2206	2244	2320	...
Tikkurila d.	1436	1516	1523	1536	1616	1636	|	|	1716	1723	1736	1816	1836	1916	1923	2030	2016	2036	2129	2116	2123	2216	2253	0001	...
Riihimäki d.	|	1552	1615j	|	1652	|	1725	1725	1752	1815j	|	1852	|	1952	2015j	2116	2052	|	2218j	2151	2215j	2251	2345j	0044	...
Hämeenlinna d.	|	1611	1638	|	1711	|	1745	1745	1811	1838	|	1911	|	2011	2038	2140	2111	|	2244	2211	2238	2311	0008	0106	...
Toijala d.	|	1631	1701	|	1731	|	|	|	1831	1901	|	1931	|	2031	2101	|	2131	|	|	2231	2301	2331	0031	0130	...
Tampere a.	1558	1653	1725	1658	1753	1758	1821	1821	1853	1925	1858	1953	1958	2053	2125	2231	2153	2158	2334	2253	2325	2353	0055	0155	...

	266		*IC* 160	*IC* 162	*IC* 166	**274**	*IC* 40	*IC* 80	**276**	*IC* 42	*S* 140		*IC* 150	*S* 44	*IC* 20		*IC* 36	*IC* 142	*IC* 22	*IC* 94		*S* 46	*IC* 38	*IC* 178	*IC* 178
			Ⓐ	⚒	Ⓐ		Ⓐ			⚒			⚒				⚒							①–④	⑤⑦
	★		✕◐	✕◐	✕	★	✕	✕	★	✕	✕◐	2	✕	✕	✕◐	2	✕◐	✕	✕	✕◐	2	✕◐	✕	✕	P✕
Tampere d.	0345	...	0504	0545	0610	0614	0700	0704	0734	0800	0804	0835	0900	0904	1000	1035	1100	1104	1200	1204	1235	1300	1400	1404	1404
Toijala d.	0412	...	0526	0607	|	0642	|	0726	0802	|	0826	0859	|	0926	|	1059	|	1126	|	1226	1259	|	|	1426	1426
Hämeenlinna d.	0438	...	0547	0628	0648	0708	|	0747	0835	|	0847	0922	|	0947	|	1122	|	1147	|	1247	1322	|	|	1447	1447
Riihimäki d.	0503	...	0608	0647	0708	0739	|	0808	0900	|	0906	0952j	|	1008	|	1152j	|	1208	|	1308	1352j	|	|	1508	1508
Tikkurila a.	0543	...	0643	0722	0743	0815	0822	0843	0948	0922	0943	1035	1022	1043	1122	1235	1222	1243	1322	1343	1435	1422	1522	1543	1543
Pasila a.	0619	...	0652	0732	0752	0906	0832	0852	1024	0932	0952	1044	1032	1052	1132	1244	1232	1252	1332	1352	1444	1432	1532	1552	1552
Helsinki a.	0627	...	0659	0739	0759	0914	0839	0859	1032	0939	0959	1050	1039	1059	1139	1250	1239	1259	1339	1359	1450	1439	1539	1559	1559

		IC 48	*IC* 144	*IC* 24	*IC* 86		*IC* 50	*IC* 180		*IC* 26	*S* 146	*IC* 54	*IC* 184	*IC* 34	*S* 88	*IC* 88		*S* 56	*IC* 148	*S* 28		*S* 58			
								⑤–⑦	Ⓐ				⑤⑦		Ⓑ	⑥			⑤⑦			⑤⑦			
	2	✕◐	✕◐	✕	✕◐	2	✕	✕	2	✕	✕◐	✕	✕	✕	✕	P✕	2	✕◐	✕◐	✕◐	2	✕			
Tampere d.	1435	1500	1504	1600	1604	1635	1700	1704	1735	1800	1804	1900	1904	2000	2004	2004	2035	2100	2104	2200	2235	2300	...	...	...
Toijala d.	1459	|	1526	|	1628	1659	|	1728	1759	|	1826	|	1928	|	2026	2026	2059	|	2126	|	2259	|	...	...	...
Hämeenlinna d.	1522	|	1547	|	1649	1722	|	1749	1822	|	1847	|	1949	|	2047	2047	2122	|	2147	|	2322	|	...	...	...
Riihimäki d.	1552j	|	1608	|	1708	1752j	|	1808	1852j	|	1908	|	2008	|	2108	2108	2152j	|	2208	|	2352j	|	...	...	...
Tikkurila a.	1635	1622	1643	1722	1743	1835	1822	1843	1935	1922	1943	2022	2043	2122	2143	2143	2235	2222	2243	2322	0035	0022	...	...	...
Pasila a.	1644	1632	1652	1732	1752	1844	1832	1852	1944	1932	1952	2032	2052	2132	2152	2152	2244	2232	2252	2332	0044	0032	...	...	...
Helsinki a.	1650	1639	1659	1739	1759	1850	1839	1859	1950	1939	1959	2039	2059	2139	2159	2159	2250	2239	2259	2339	0050	0039	...	...	...

FOR NOTES AND OTHER REGIONAL SERVICES, SEE TOP OF NEXT PAGE →

HELSINKI - TAMPERE 790

Other selected regional trains HELSINKI - RIIHIMÄKI (2nd class only)

km		Ⓐ		Ⓐ	⚒		⚒						
0	**Helsinki** d.	0409	0609	0639	0739	0809	0839	0939		2139	2209	...	2339
3	Pasila d.	0414	0614	0644	0744	0814	0844	0944	and	2144	2214	...	2344
16	Tikkurila d.	0423	0623	0653	0753	0823	0853	0953	hourly	2153	2223	...	2353
37	Järvenpää d.	0441	0641	0709	0809	0841	0909	1009	until	2209	2241	...	0009
59	Hyvinkää d.	0458	0658	0730	0830	0858	0930	1030		2230	2258	...	0027
71	**Riihimäki** a.	0506	0706	0738	0838	0906	0938	1038		2238	2305	...	0035

	Ⓐ		Ⓐ			⚒					
Riihimäki d.	0519	0552	0620	0652	0752	0819	0852	0919		2219	2252
Hyvinkää d.	0527	0600	0629	0700	0800	0827	0900	0927	and	2227	2300
Järvenpää d.	0549	0616	0649	0716	0816	0849	0916	0949	hourly	2249	2316
Tikkurila d.	0606	0636	0706	0736	0836	0906	0936	1006	until	2306	2336
Pasila d.	0615	0645	0715	0744	0845	0915	0945	1015		2315	2345
Helsinki a.	0620	0650	0720	0750	0850	0920	0950	1020		2320	2350

– To / from Pori (Table **792**).

– Arrives 0606.

– Arrives 7 – 10 minutes earlier.

◐ – Train classification may vary on certain days.

★ – Overnight train to / from northern Finland. For through cars and days of running see Table **794**.

HELSINKI - KARJAA - TURKU and KARJAA - HANKO 791

km		*IC* **941**	*IC* **943**	*S* **979**		*S* **945**	*IC* **945**	*S* **945**		*IC* **947**	*IC* **949**	*IC* **951**	*IC* **953**	*S* **955**	*IC* **957**	*IC* **959**	*IC* **961**	*IC* **963**	*IC* **965**	*S* **971**			*S* **967**		*IC* **973**
			Ⓐ	Ⓐ		⑦	⑤⑥	①–④		Ⓐ	⑤⑥		Ⓐ				Ⓑ		Ⓐ	⑥⑦					
		🍷◐	🍷	✕		✕	🍷	✕		🍷◐	🍷◐	🍷◐	🍷	✕◐	🍷◐	🍷	🍷◐	🍷	🍷	🍷◐		**A**	✕◐		🍷◐
0	**Helsinki** d.	0528	0628	0735	...	0833	0835	0835	...	0935	1035	1135	1235	1335	1435	1535	1635	1735	1835	1935	...	2053	2105	...	2252
3	Pasila d.	0534	0634	0741	...	0839	0841	0841	...	0941	1041	1141	1241	1341	1441	1541	1641	1741	1841	1941	...	2057	2111	...	2258
87	Karjaa / Karis d.	0630	0730	0837	...	0937	0937	0937	...	1037	1137	1237	1337	1437	1537	1637	1737	1837	1937	2037	...	2157	2207	...	2357
138	Salo d.	0658	0804	0907	...	1007	1007	1007	...	1107	1207	1307	1407	1507	1607	1707	1807	1907	2007	2107	...	...	2237	...	0027
194	**Turku** a.	0729	0834	0939	...	1039	1039	1039	...	1139	1239	1339	1439	1539	1639	1739	1839	1939	2039	2139	...	...	2309	...	0059
197	Turku satama a.	0739	...	...	...	...	...	1050**e**	...	...	...	...	...	...	...	1749**k**	1849**n**	1949	...	...	...	...	...	...	...

	S **942**	*IC* **944**		*IC* **946**	*IC* **948**	*IC* **950**		*S* **954**	*IC* **956**	*S* **958**	*IC* **960**	*IC* **962**	*S* **964**	*IC* **966**	*IC* **968**	*IC* **974**			*IC* **972**					
	Ⓐ	⚒		⚒		⚒									Ⓑ									
	✕	🍷		🍷◐	🍷◐	🍷		✕◐	🍷◐	✕◐	🍷◐	🍷◐	✕◐	🍷◐	🍷	🍷◐	**A**		🍷					
Turku satama d.	...	...	...	...	0805	...	...	1110**e**	...		...	...	...	...	...	1910**r**	...	...	2030	...	...	...	...	...
Turku d.	0525	0625	...	0734	0834	0934	...	1134	1234	1334	1434	1534	1634	1734	1834	1934	...	...	2057	...	...	...	...	...
Salo d.	0557	0657	...	0806	0906	1006	...	1206	1306	1406	1506	1606	1706	1806	1906	2006	...	...	2136	...	...	...	...	...
Karjaa / Karis d.	0628	0728	...	0836	0936	1036	...	1236	1336	1436	1536	1636	1736	1836	1936	2036	2052	...	2206	...	...	...	...	...
Pasila a.	0721	0821	...	0934	1034	1134	...	1334	1434	1534	1634	1734	1834	1934	2034	2134	2148	...	2304	...	...	...	...	...
Helsinki a.	0727	0827	...	0940	1040	1140	...	1340	1440	1540	1640	1740	1840	1940	2040	2140	2154	...	2310	...	...	...	...	...

KARJAA / KARIS - HANKO

km		Ⓐ							**A**	**D**	
0	**Karjaa / Karis** d.	0742	0949	1249	1449	1649	1849	...	2210	2219	...
16	Tammisaari d.	0754	1001	1301	1501	1701	1901	...	2222	2231	...
49	**Hanko** a.	0822	1029	1329	1529	1729	1929	...	2250	2259	...

	Ⓐ								**A**	**D**
Hanko d.	0634	0840	...	1140	1340	1540	1740	...	2010	2110
Tammisaari d.	0701	0907	...	1207	1407	1607	1807	...	2037	2137
Karjaa / Karis a.	0714	0920	...	1220	1420	1620	1820	...	2050	2150

A – ③⑤⑦. 2nd class Helsinki - Karjaa - Hanko and v.v.

D – ①②④⑥.

e – ③ only.

k – ⑥ only.

n – ①③④⑤⑦.

r – ①③④⑤⑥⑦.

◐ – Train classification may vary on certain days.

TAMPERE - PORI 792

Most trains convey ✕

km		*IC* **477**	*IC* **461**	*IC* **165**	*S* **165**	*IC* **465**	*IC* **467**	*IC* **469**	*IC* **175**	*IC* **471**	*IC* **473**	*IC* **475**
		Ⓐ	⚒	①–④	⑤			Ⓑ	⑥		Ⓑ	**e** 🚌
	Helsinki **790** d.	...	...	0803	0803	...	...	...	1403	...	...	...
0	**Tampere** d.	0600	0808	1011	1011	1211	1411	1611	1611	1811	2009	2220
17	Nokia d.	0616	0824	1027	1027	1227	1427	1627	1627	1827	2027	2250
59	Vammala d.	0658	0854	1102	1102	1258	1458	1658	1658	1858	2059	2339
135	**Pori** a.	0747	0940	1148	1148	1344	1544	1744	1744	1944	2145	0105

	IC **460**	*IC* **462**	*IC* **466**	*IC* **476**	*IC* **464**	*IC* **474**	*S* **178**	*IC* **468**	*IC* **470**	*IC* **472**	*IC* **186**
	⚒	⚒		Ⓐ		①–④	⑤			Ⓑ	⑥
Pori d.	0517	0612	0717	0804	1003	1212	1212	1412	1612	1812	1812
Vammala d.	0604	0659	0804	0853	1050	1259	1259	1459	1659	1859	1859
Nokia d.	0633	0728	0838	0922	1119	1328	1328	1528	1728	1928	1928
Tampere a.	0650	0745	0855	0939	1136	1345	1345	1545	1745	1946	1946
Helsinki **790** a.	...	...	...	...	...	...	1554	...	...	...	2154

– Rail replacement 🚌 operates until Aug. 3.

☛ Frequent 🚌 services operate Turku - Rauma - Pori and v.v. See www.matkahuolto.fi.

TAMPERE - VAASA, OULU, KOLARI and ROVANIEMI 794

Warning! Rail replacement 🚌 in operation Oulu - Rovaniemi and v.v until September 25.

km		*S* **52**	*S* **35**	*S* **55**	*IC* **21**	*S* **35**	*S* **411**	*IC* **41**	*IC* **23**	*IC* **43**	*S* **33**	*IC* **45**	*IC* **25**	*IC* **37**	*S* **445**	*IC* **27**	*IC* **415**	*IC* **47**	*IC* **51**	*S* **447**	*S* **59**	*IC* **49**	*IC* **29**	*S* **187**	*IC* **53**	**265**	**269**	**273**
		Ⓐ	⚒	Ⓐ	⚒	⚒	⑦										⑥			Ⓑ	Ⓑ			⑥	Ⓑ	⚒	**d**	
		◇✕	✕◐	✕	✕	✕◐	✕	✕◐	✕	✕	✕◐	✕	✕	✕	✕	✕	🍷	✕	✕	✕	✕	✕	✕◐	✕	✕	★	★	★⊕
	Helsinki **790** d.	...	0503	0503**j**	0623	...	...	0723	0824	0924	1024	1103	1224	1324	...	1424	...	1524	1624	...	1640**r**	1724	1824	2003	2024	1929	2029	2313
0	**Tampere** d.	...	0702	0702**j**	0802	...	...	0902	1002	1102	1202	1302	1402	1502	...	1602	...	1702	1802	...	1825	1902	2002	2202	2202	2309	2359	0237
75	Parkano d.	...	0746	0746**j**	|	...	...	|	|	1144	|	|	|	1542	...	|	...	1736	|	...	1859	|	2036	2235	2235	0001	|	0323
159	Seinäjoki a.	...	0827	0827**j**	0918	...	...	1007	1105	1229	1305	1416	1509	1625	...	1711	...	1810	1905	...	1933	2005	2117	2307	2307	0056	0138	0411
159	Seinäjoki d.	0650	0834	0837	0922	...	...	1011	1109	1233	1309	1420	1513	1635	1632	1723	...	1814	1909	1927	1937	2008	2127	2310	2310	0107	0155	0415
233	**Vaasa** a.	0753	|	0927	|	...	...	1107	|	1322	|	1517	|	|	1728	|	...	1910	|	2017	|	2102	|	2359	2359	|	|	|
292	Kokkola d.	...	0949	...	1040	...	...	...	1229	...	1412	...	1614	1750	...	1828	...	...	2014	...	2057	...	2233	...	...	0238	0334	0551
371	Ylivieska d.	...	1030	...	1120	...	...	...	1309	...	1449	...	1652	1830	...	1905	...	...	2055	...	...	...	2310	...	...	0326	0424	0642
493	**Oulu** a.	...	1142	...	1216	←	...	...	1422	...	1545	...	1748	1941	...	2012	...	...	2215	...	...	...	0016	...	...	0444	0542	0806
493	**Oulu** d.	...	1223	...	...	1223	1223	...	1427	...	...	...	1800**b**	...	...	2024**b**	2024	...	...	...	...	...	...	...	...	0456	0630	0826
599	Kemi d.	...	→	...	...	1326	1326	...	1532	...	...	...	1905**b**	...	...	2126**b**	2126	...	...	...	...	...	...	...	...	0602	0756	0936
808	**Kolari** a.	...	...	...	...	|	|	...	|	...	...	...	|	...	...	|	|	...	...	...	...	...	...	...	...	|	1055	|
713	**Rovaniemi** a.	...	...	...	...	1441	1441	...	1646	...	...	...	2023**b**	...	...	2245**b**	2245	...	...	...	...	...	...	...	...	0720	...	1103
796	Kemijärvi a.	...	...	...	...	...	...	...	...	...	...	...	...	...	...	...	...	...	...	...	...	...	...	...	...	0850	...	...

	IC **40**	*S* **52**	*IC* **42**	*S* **44**	*S* **440**	*IC* **20**	*S* **20**	*S* **446**	*IC* **36**	*IC* **412**	*IC* **22**	*S* **46**	*S* **444**	*IC* **38**	*IC* **48**	*IC* **24**	*IC* **50**	*IC* **26**	*IC* **54**	*IC* **34**	*S* **442**	*S* **56**	*S* **418**	*S* **28**	*S* **58**	**266**	**274**	**276**
	Ⓐ	Ⓐ	⚒		②–⑤	⚒	⑦	②–⑤	Ⓐ¶	⑥			⑥⑦		Ⓑ								⑥		⑤⑦			**h**
	✕	◇✕	✕	✕	✕	✕	✕	✕	✕	✕	✕	✕◐	✕	✕	✕	✕	✕	✕	✕	✕	✕	✕◐	✕	✕◐	✕	★⊕	★	★
Kemijärvi d.	...	...	...	...	...	...	...	...	...	...	...	...	...	...	...	...	...	...	...	...	...	...	...	...	...	...	1900	...
Rovaniemi d.	...	...	...	...	...	...	...	...	...	0515	0515**t**	...	...	...	...	0922	...	...	...	1302	...	...	1535	1535**b**	...	1752	2100	...
Kolari d.	...	...	...	...	...	...	...	...	...	|	|	...	...	...	...	|	...	...	...	|	...	...	|	|	...	|	|	1942
Kemi d.	...	...	...	...	...	...	...	...	...	0639	0639**t**	...	...	...	...	1040	...	...	...	1424	...	...	1659	1659**b**	...	1924	2228	2250
Oulu a.	...	...	...	...	...	...	...	...	...	0737	0737**t**	...	...	...	...	1140	...	...	...	1523	...	...	1800	1800**b**	...	2024	2349	0010
Oulu d.	...	...	...	...	...	0521	...	...	0620	...	0749	...	...	0916	...	1155	...	1333	...	1530	...	1611	...	1808	...	2055	2353	0057
Ylivieska d.	...	...	...	...	...	0643	...	...	0735	...	0848	...	...	1030	...	1259	...	1441	...	1634	...	1725	...	1904	...	2231	0109	0233
Kokkola d.	...	0517	...	...	...	0727	0727	...	0815	...	0927	...	...	1117	...	1338	...	1521	...	1713	...	1806	...	1941	...	2331	0157	0335
Vaasa d.	0444	|	0544	0644	0723	|	|	0820	|	...	|	1035	1135	|	1245	|	1445	|	1625	|	1807	|	...	|	2031	|	|	|
Seinäjoki a.	0533	0626	0633	0733	0812	0831	0831	0915	0922	...	1031	1124	1223	1227	1341	1434	1534	1624	1714	1820	1857	1921	...	2041	2120	0058	0345	0509
Seinäjoki d.	0537	...	0637	0737	...	0835	0835	...	0926	...	1035	1128	...	1231	1345	1438	1538	1628	1726	1828	...	1928	...	2044	2124	0115	0356	0519
Parkano d.	0615	...	0715	0815	...	|	|	...	|	...	|	1205	...	1310	|	|	1612	1709	|	|	...	2009	...	|	2158	0205	|	|
Tampere a.	0654	...	0751	0851	...	0951	0951	...	1051	...	1151	1251	...	1351	1454	1551	1651	1751	1854	1954	...	2051	...	2151	2245	0250	0535	0713
Helsinki **790** a.	0835	...	0935	1054	...	1135	1135	...	1235	...	1335	1435	...	1535	1635	1735	1835	1935	2035	2135	...	2235	...	2335	0035	0627	0915	1045

– Not ⑥.

– ③⑤ Apr. 23 - June 13 (also June 9, 14).

– ④⑦ Apr. 24 - June 15 (also June 7, 10, 14; not June 8).

– ① only.

– 1630 on ⑦.

– Ⓐ only.

¶ – Also runs Kokkola - Helsinki on ⑥ (as *S* **36**).

◐ – Train classification may vary on certain days.

◇ – 12 Kokkola - Seinäjoki - Vaasa.

★ – Conveys 🛏, 2nd class and ✕.

⊕ – Also conveys 🛏 Turku - Tampere - Rovaniemi and v.v. See Table **795**.

795 TURKU - TAMPERE - PIEKSÄMÄKI

km		*IC* 81 Ⓐ ✕	⚒ 2	*IC* 905 ⚒ 🍷	*IC* 155 ✕◐	*IC* 909 🍷	*IC* 93 ✕◐	2	*S* 143 ✕◐	*S* 915 ⑤ K✕	*S* 171 ⑦ K✕	*IC* 917 🍷	*IC* 145 ✕◐	*S* 87 Ⓑ ✕	2	*IC* 921 ⑤⑦ 🍷	*IC* 151 Ⓑ ✕	*IC* 923 🍷	*IC* 147 K✕	*IC* 927 🍷	*S* 89 Ⓑ ✕	*IC* 149 ✕	*IC* 931 🍷	2	933 C
	Turku satama d.	...	...	...	...	0810	...	...	...	...	...	1250	...	...	...	...	...	...	...	...	...	...	1950**e**	...	2020
0	**Turku** d.	...	...	0654	...	0905	...	...	...	1205	...	1305	...	...	...	1456	...	1605	...	1805	...	...	2005	...	2108
66	Loimaa d.	...	...	0740	...	0944	...	...	...	1244	...	1344	...	...	...	1542	...	1644	...	1844	...	...	2044	...	2149
86	Humppila d.	...	...	0753	...	0959	...	...	...	1259	...	1357	...	...	...	1559	...	1659	...	1859	...	...	2057	...	2204
	Helsinki **790** d.	...	...	|	0703	|	0903	...	1003	|	1203	|	1303	1403	...	|	1503	|	1603	|	1803	1903	|	...	|
128	Toijala **790** d.	...	...	0819	0831	1025	1031	...	1131	1325	1331	1425	1431	1531	...	1625	1631	1725	1731	1925	1931	2031	2125	...	2234
168	**Tampere** **790** a.	...	...	0842	0853	1047	1053	...	1153	1347	1353	1447	1453	1553	...	1647	1653	1747	1753	1947	1953	2053	2146	...	2258
168	**Tampere** d.	0707	0806	...	0907	...	1107	1206	1212	1407	1407	...	1507	1607	1616	...	1706	...	1807	...	2007	2107	...	2207	...
210	Orivesi d.	0731	0832	...	0932	...	1132	1232	1237	1432	1432	...	1532	1632	1642	...	1730	...	1832	...	2032	2132	...	2233	...
257	Vilppula d.	|	0907	...	|	...	|	1307	|	|	|	...	|	|	1717	...	|	...	|	...	|	|	...	2308	...
282	**Haapamäki** a.	|	0925	...	|	...	|	1325	|	|	|	...	|	|	1735	...	|	...	|	...	|	|	...	2326	...
266	Jämsä d.	0813	...	...	1012	...	1207	...	1312	1515	1515	...	1607	1714	...	...	1805	...	1912	...	2108	2213	...	|	...
323	Jyväskylä **796** d.	0843	...	...	1045**b**	...	1240	...	1343	1550	1550	...	1638	1744	...	...	1833	...	1941	...	2135	2243	...	0039	...
403	**Pieksämäki** **796** a.	...	...	...	1205**b**	...	...	...	1437	1650	1650	...	1730	...	...	...	...	...	2041	...	...	...	...	...	...

	904 D	*IC* 80 Ⓐ ✕	⚒ 2	*S* 140 ⚒ ✕◐	*IC* 150 ⚒ ✕	*IC* 910 🍷	*S* 912 ⑥ ✕	⑦ 2	*IC* 142 K✕	⚒ 2	*IC* 94 ✕◐	*IC* 916 🍷	*IC* 920 ⑤⑦ 🍷	*IC* 144 ✕◐	*IC* 922 🍷	2	*IC* 86 🍷◐	*IC* 924 🍷	*S* 146 ✕◐	*IC* 928 🍷	*S* 88 Ⓑ ✕	2	*IC* 148 ✕◐	*IC* 934 Ⓑ 🍷	*S* 152 ⑤⑦ K✕
Pieksämäki **796** d.	...	...	...	...	...	...	...	...	0820	...	0830**b**	...	...	1218	...	...	...	...	1516	...	...	...	1810	...	2008
Jyväskylä **796** d.	...	0524	0505	0617	0719	...	...	0805	0919	...	1015**b**	...	...	1315	...	...	1420	...	1612	...	1810	...	1915	...	2114
Jämsä d.	...	0555	|	0648	0748	...	...	|	0948	...	1051	...	...	1352	...	...	1451	...	1650	...	1848	...	1951	...	2149
Haapamäki d.	...	|	0619	|	|	...	...	0919	|	1019	|	...	...	|	...	1419	|	...	|	...	|	1831	|	...	|
Vilppula d.	...	|	0640	|	|	...	...	0940	|	1040	|	...	...	|	...	1440	|	...	|	...	|	1852	|	...	|
Orivesi d.	...	0630	0715	0725	0825	...	...	1015	1023	1115	1126	...	...	1427	...	1515	1526	...	1725	...	1923	1927	2026	...	2224
Tampere a.	...	0654	0740	0749	0849	...	...	1040	1049	1140	1150	...	...	1451	...	1540	1550	...	1749	...	1949	1955	2050	...	2250
Tampere **790** d.	0550	0704	...	0804	0900	0910	1015	...	1104	...	1204	1210	1410	1504	1510	...	1604	1610	1804	1810	2004	...	2104**f**	2112	...
Toijala **790** d.	0614	0726	...	0826	|	0935	1039	...	1126	...	1226	1235	1435	1526	1535	...	1628	1635	1826	1835	2026	...	2126**f**	2135	...
Helsinki **790** a.	|	0854	...	0954	1035	|	|	...	1254	...	1354	|	|	1654	|	...	1754	|	1954	|	2154	...	2254**f**	|	...
Humppila d.	0641	...	...	...	...	1000	1107	...	...	...	...	1300	1500	...	1600	...	...	1700	...	1900	...	...	...	2202	...
Loimaa d.	0655	...	...	...	...	1013	1120	...	...	...	...	1313	1513	...	1613	...	...	1713	...	1915	...	...	...	2215	...
Turku a.	0733	...	...	...	...	1050	1157	...	...	...	...	1355	1550	...	1655	...	...	1750	...	1955	...	...	...	2252	...
Turku satama a.	0752	...	...	...	...	...	...	...	...	...	...	...	...	...	...	...	...	1811**e**	...	2005	...	...	...	...	...

C – Also conveys 🛏 Turku - Tampere (**273**) - Rovaniemi (Table **794**).
D – Also conveys 🛏 Rovaniemi (**266**) - Tampere - Turku (Table **794**).
K – To / from Kuopio (Table **798**).

b – Rail replacement 🚌 June 16 - Aug. 1.
e – ①③④⑤⑥⑦ (also June 3, 10).
f – ⑤⑦ only.

◐ – Train classification may vary on certain days.

796 JOENSUU - PIEKSÄMÄKI - JYVÄSKYLÄ - SEINÄJOKI

km		Ⓐ	Ⓐ	⚒	⑦		*IC* 142 ✕			*IC* 148 ✕◐	
0	**Joensuu** d.	...	...	...	...	0600	...	...	1540	...	...
134	Varkaus d.	...	...	...	...	0736	...	...	1717	...	...
183	**Pieksämäki** **795** d.	...	...	...	...	0810	0820	...	1752	1810	...
263	**Jyväskylä** **795** d.	...	...	0505	0805	...	0919	1223	...	1915	1947
	Tampere **795** a.	...	...	|	|	...	1049	|	...	2050	|
341	Haapamäki d.	...	...	0611	0911	...	...	1330	...	...	2054
414	Alavus d.	0657	0818	...	...	...	...	1430	...	...	2155
459	**Seinäjoki** d.	0729	0850	...	...	...	...	1502	...	...	2227

	Ⓐ	Ⓐ	*IC* 155 ◐			*S* 143 ✕◐	*IC* 145 ✕◐	⑥		*IC* 147 ✕	Ⓑ	
Seinäjoki d.	0525	0740	...	...	0930	...	...	...	1652	...	...	...
Alavus d.	0556	0810	...	...	1001	...	...	...	1724	...	...	...
Haapamäki d.	...	...	...	...	1103	...	...	...	1827	...	...	2334
Tampere **795** d.	...	...	0907	...	|	1212	1507	...	|	1807	...	|
Jyväskylä **795** d.	...	...	1041	...	1208	1343	1638	...	1932	1941	...	0039
Pieksämäki **795** d.	...	...	1133	1145	...	1437	1730	1807	...	2041	2050	...
Varkaus d.	...	...	...	1222	...	...	...	1844	...	...	2126	...
Joensuu a.	...	...	...	1356	...	...	...	2018	...	...	2300	...

◐ – Train classification may vary on certain days.

797 HELSINKI - KOUVOLA - JOENSUU - NURMES

km		⚒ 2	*S* 61 ⚒ ✕	*IC* 1 ✕	2	*IC* 63 K✕	*IC* 3 ✕	2	*IC* 65 K✕	*IC* 5 ✕	2	2	*S* 109 ⑤–⑦ ✕	*IC* 67 K✕	*IC* 7 Ⓑ ✕	Ⓐ 2	*S* 69 Ⓑ K✕	*S* 9 ✕	*S* 9 Ⓑ ✕	Ⓑ 2	Ⓐ 2	*IC* 111 Ⓑ ✕	*IC* 11 ✕	2	*IC* 73 ◐ K✕	*IC* 115 ◐ 🍷
0	**Helsinki** ▷ d.	...	0557	0654	...	0814	1014	...	1114	1314	...	...	1356	1414	1514	1535	1614	1614	1614	...	1635	1714	1829	...	1914	2120
3	Pasila ▷ d.	...	0603	0700	...	0820	1020	...	1120	1320	...	...	1402	1420	1520	1540	1620	1620	1620	...	1640	1720	1835	...	1920	2126
16	Tikkurila ▷ d.	...	0613	0711	...	0831	1031	...	1131	1336	...	...	1413	1431	1531	1549	1631	1631	1631	...	1649	1731	1845	...	1931	2137
104	**Lahti** ▷ d.	...	0651	0751	...	0913	1113	...	1216	1413	...	...	1451	1513	1613	1650	1713	1713	1713	...	1750	1813	1923	...	2013	2213
166	**Kouvola** a.	...	0719	0819	...	0941	1141	...	1245	1441	...	...	1519	1541	1641	1733	1741	1741	1741	...	1833	1841	1951	...	2041	2241
166	**Kouvola** d.	...	...	0823	...	▬	1143	...	...	1443	...	...	1523	...	1643	...	...	1748	1748	...	...	1844	2000	...	...	2244
252	Lappeenranta d.	...	...	0906	...	...	1223	...	...	1523	...	...	1605	...	1723	...	...	1828	1828	...	...	1927	2041	...	...	2327
288	Imatra d.	...	...	0935	...	...	1254	...	...	1554	...	...	...	...	1745	...	...	1854	1856	...	...	1955	2114	...	...	2355
352	Parikkala d.	0730	...	1018	1026	...	1333	1337	...	1633	1637	...	...	...	|	...	...	...	1938	1942	...	...	2156	2200	...	...
411	Savonlinna a.	0823	...	|	1119	2	|	1430	...	|	1730	...	...	...	|	...	...	...	|	2035	...	...	|	2253	...	...
482	**Joensuu** d.	...	...	1136	...	1154	1451	...	...	1751	...	1800	...	...	1929	...	...	...	2056	...	...	...	2314	...	...	...
586	Lieksa d.	...	...	...	...	1315	...	...	...	...	...	1921	...	...	...	...	...	...	...	...	...	...	...	...	...	...
642	**Nurmes** a.	...	...	...	...	1400	...	...	...	...	...	2006	...	...	...	...	...	...	...	...	...	...	...	...	...	...

	2	*IC* 102 ⚒ ✕	*IC* 104 ⚒ ✕	⚒ 2	*S* 2 ⚒ ✕	*S* 2 ✕	*IC* 62 ⚒◐ K✕	*IC* 4 ⚒ ✕	*S* 4 ⑦ ✕	*S* 64 ◐ K✕	2	2	*IC* 6 ✕	*IC* 66 ◐ K✕	2	*IC* 8 ✕	*S* 114 ⑤–⑦ ✕	*IC* 68 K✕	2	*IC* 10 ✕	*S* 72 Ⓑ K✕	*IC* 70 K✕	2	2	*IC* 12 ✕	Ⓑ 2
Nurmes d.	...	...	...	...	...	...	...	...	...	...	0635	...	...	...	...	...	...	...	...	...	...	...	1540	...	...	...
Lieksa d.	...	...	...	...	...	...	...	...	...	...	0722	...	...	...	...	...	...	...	...	...	...	...	1626	...	...	...
Joensuu d.	...	...	...	...	0500	...	...	0600	...	...	0850	...	0900	...	...	1210	...	...	...	1510	...	...	1745	...	1810	...
Savonlinna d.	...	...	...	0515	|	...	...	|	...	...	...	0919	|	...	1230	|	...	...	1530	|	...	...	...	1835	|	2056
Parikkala d.	...	...	...	0608	0615	...	...	0719	...	...	...	1012	1020	...	1323	1331	...	...	1623	1631	...	...	...	1928	1936	2149
Imatra d.	...	0502	0602	...	0702	0702	...	0802	0802	...	...	...	1102	...	...	1409	...	...	...	1709	...	...	...	...	2018	...
Lappeenranta d.	...	0531	0631	...	0725	0725	...	0831	0831	...	...	...	1131	...	...	1436	1622	...	...	1741	...	...	...	...	2043	...
Kouvola a.	...	0612	0712	...	0805	0805	...	0912	0912	...	...	...	1212	...	...	1515	1704	...	...	1821	...	...	...	...	2123	...
Kouvola d.	0500	0619	0719	...	0809	0809	0819	0919	0919	1119	...	...	1219	1419	...	1519	1708	1719	...	1824	1919	2015	...	...	2126	...
Lahti ▷ d.	0529	0649	0749	...	0840	0840	0849	0949	0949	1149	...	...	1249	1449	...	1549	1738	1749	...	1854	1949	2047	...	...	2155	...
Tikkurila ▷ a.	0619	0727	0827	...	0914	0914	0927	1027	1027	1227	...	...	1327	1527	...	1627	1814	1827	...	1929	2027	2130	...	...	2230	...
Pasila ▷ a.	0628	0737	0837	...	0923	0923	0937	1037	1037	1237	...	...	1337	1537	...	1637	1823	1837	...	1938	2037	2139	...	...	2239	...
Helsinki ▷ a.	0634	0744	0844	...	0930	0930	0944	1044	1044	1244	...	...	1344	1544	...	1644	1829	1844	...	1945	2044	2145	...	...	2245	...

Local trains **LAHTI - KOUVOLA - KOTKA** and v.v. 2nd class only.

km		⚒		Ⓐ							Ⓐ		⑥⑦			
	Lahti d.	...	...	0711	...	...	...	...	...	...	1500	...	1620	...	...	1930
0	**Kouvola** d.	0600	0653	0800	0800	0900	...	1200	...	1527	1618	1618	1718	1718	...	2037
51	**Kotka** a.	0644	0737	0844	0844	0944	...	1244	...	1611	1702	1702	1802	1802	...	2121
52	**Kotka** satama a.	0647	0740	0847	0847	0947	...	1247	...	1614	1705	1705	1805	1805	...	2124

	⚒										Ⓐ					
Kotka satama d.	0654	0752	0855	...	...	1200	...	...	1513	1621	1712	1712	...	2033	...	2215
Kotka d.	0657	0755	0858	...	...	1203	...	...	1516	1624	1715	1715	...	2036	...	2218
Kouvola a.	0742	0840	0943	1030	...	1248	1330	...	1601	1709	1800	1800	...	2121	...	2303
Lahti a.	0834	...	...	1113	...	...	1413	...	1652	...	1845	...	...	...	...	...

Local trains **RIIHIMÄKI - LAHTI** and v.v. 2nd class only.
59 km. Journey time: 42 – 43 minutes.

From Riihimäki at 0440 Ⓐ, 0513 ⑥, 0613, 0700 Ⓐ, 0713 ⑥, 0813 and hourly until 1913; then 2113 and 2213.

From Lahti at 0535 ⚒, 0704 ⚒, 0804 and hourly until 2004; then 2204.

K – To / from stations in Table **798**.

◐ – Train classification may vary on certain days.

▷ – Other local journeys Helsinki - Lahti and v.v. (2nd class only, journey 65 – 70 minutes):
From Helsinki at 0010, 0110 ⑥⑦, 0630 Ⓐ, 0640 ⑥⑦, 0730 Ⓐ, 0735 ⑥, 0740 ⑦, 0835 ⚒, 0840 ⑦, 0935, 1035 and hourly until 2135; then 2310.
From Lahti at 0024, 0613 Ⓐ, 0614 ⑥⑦, 0713 Ⓐ, 0714 ⑥⑦, 0800 Ⓐ, 0814 ⑦, 0819 ⑥ 0919, 1019 and hourly until 2219; then 2314.

KOUVOLA - KUOPIO - OULU 798

km		*IC*711	*S*61	*IC*63		*IC*65	*S*171	*S*915	*IC*67	*IC*67	*S*69	*IC*147		*IC*73	*S*73	*IC*73	
			⚒				⑦	⑤	Ⓑ		Ⓑ			C	④	⑥	
		✕	✕	✕		✕	✕	T✕	✕	✕	✕	✕		✕	✕	✕	
	Helsinki **797** d.	...	0557	0814	...	1114	1203	...	1414	1414	1619	1603	...	1914	1914	1914	...
0	**Kouvola** d.	...	0731	0950	...	1303	|	...	1550	1550	1750	|	...	2051	2051	2051	...
113	Mikkeli d.	...	0843	1057	...	1406	|	...	1654	1654	1853	|	...	2154	2154	2154	...
	Tampere **795** d.	...	|	|	...	|	1407	1407	|	|	|	1807	...	|	|	|	...
184	Pieksämäki d.	...	0923	1140	...	1445	1702	1702	1737	1737	1932	2043	...	2233	2233	2233	...
273	**Kuopio** a.	...	1012	1229	...	1535	1727	1727	1830	1830	2024	2135	...	2325	2325	2325	...
273	**Kuopio** d.	0715	...	1239	...	1539	1755	1755	1838	1838	2029	...	...	2329	2329	...	...
358	Iisalmi d.	0822	...	1342	...	1641	...	...	1939	1939	2130	...	...	0035	0035	...	...
441	**Kajaani** a.	0915	...	1435	...	1734	...	...	2032	2032	2223	...	...	0128	0128	...	...
441	**Kajaani** d.	0917	...	1437	...	1737	...	...	2102	...	...	...	...	...	...	...	...
484	Paltamo d.	0951	...	1511	...	1811	...	...	2136	...	...	...	...	...	...	...	...
633	**Oulu** a.	1125	...	1645	...	1945	...	...	2310	...	...	...	...	...	...	...	...
	Rovaniemi **794** a.	...	...	...	...	...	...	...	...	...	...	...	...	...	...	...	...

	*IC*62	*S*62	*IC*142	*S*64	*IC*64		*IC*66	*IC*66		*IC*68		*S*72	*IC*70		*S*152	*IC*710	
	D	⑤		⚒	⑦		⚒					Ⓑ			⑤⑦		
	✕◐	✕◐	✕◐	✕	✕		✕	✕		✕		✕	✕		✕	✕	
Rovaniemi **794** d.	...	...	...	...	...	...	...	...	...	...	...	...	...	...	...	...	...
Oulu d.	...	...	...	...	...	...	0707	...	...	1003	...	...	1227	...	...	1822	...
Paltamo d.	...	...	...	...	...	...	0838	...	...	1136	...	...	1358	...	...	1956	...
Kajaani a.	...	...	...	...	...	...	0911	...	...	1208	...	...	1431	...	...	2029	...
Kajaani d.	0333	0333	...	0625	...	...	0915	0915	...	1211	...	...	1435	...	...	2032	...
Iisalmi d.	0428	0428	...	0720	...	...	1010	1010	...	1306	...	...	1534	...	...	2128	...
Kuopio a.	0528	0528	...	0820	...	...	1110	1110	...	1406	...	...	1643	...	...	2228	...
Kuopio d.	0532	0532	0728	0826	0826	...	1115	1115	...	1411	...	1612	1700	...	1908	...	...
Pieksämäki d.	0628	0628	0820	0920	0920	...	1213	1213	...	1520	...	1707	1804	...	2008	...	...
Tampere **795** a.	|	|	1049	|	|	...	|	|	...	|	...	|	|	...	2250	...	...
Mikkeli d.	0709	0709	|	1003	1003	...	1253	1253	...	1600	...	1757	1851	...	...	...	...
Kouvola a.	0811	0811	|	1109	1109	...	1403	1403	...	1709	...	1907	1952	...	...	...	...
Helsinki **797** a.	0944	0944	1254	1244	1244	...	1544	1544	...	1844	...	2044	2145	...	...	...	...

IISALMI - YLIVIESKA

km		⚒ 2		2	
0	**Iisalmi** d.	0830	...	1645	...
99	Haapajärvi d.	0937	...	1748	...
154	**Ylivieska** a.	1013	...	1824	...

		2		Ⓑ 2	
	Ylivieska d.	1337	...	1912	...
	Haapajärvi d.	1413	...	1948	...
	Iisalmi a.	1518	...	2055	...

C – ①②③⑤⑦.
D – ①②③④⑥.
T – From Turku (Table **795**).

LAPLAND 🚌 LINKS 799

Subject to alteration on and around public holiday dates

Narvik – Tromsø – Alta

Operator: Torghatten www.tromskortet.no

km		①–⑤	⑥	①–⑤	Ⓑ	Ⓑ				⑦	⑦
0	**Narvik** bussterminal d.	0535	...	...	...	...	...	1310	1545	...	1900
181	Nordkjosbotn balsfjord d.	0825	0810	1040	1320	1620	...	1620	1845	2035	2200
252	**Tromsø** Prostneset d.	0944	0929	1158	1435	|	1545	1736	2001	|	2316
241	Lyngseidet ferjekai d.	...	...	...	...	1730	1740	...	...	2145	...
465	**Alta** sentrum a.	...	...	...	...	...	2220	...	...	...	...

km		①–⑤		①–⑤	①–⑥	Ⓑ□		⑦	⑦	⑦
0	**Alta** sentrum d.	...	...	...	1055	...	...	1415	...	...
224	Lyngseidet ferjekai d.	...	...	...	1555	1550	...	1915	1920	...
293	**Tromsø** Prostneset d.	0605	1015	1355	1744	|	1545	2109	|	1915
	Nordkjosbotn balsfjord d.	0725	1135	1512	...	1657	1705	...	2027	2035
	Narvik bussterminal a.	1010	1420	...	...	...	1950	...	...	2320

Alta – Hammerfest – Karasjok – Kirkenes

Operator: Snelandia www.snelandia.no

km		①–⑤ t	①–⑤	⑥ t	①–⑤	⑦	①–⑤	①–⑤		Ⓑ	⑥	
0	**Alta** sentrum d.	0640	...	0900	0900	...	1155	...	...	...	1600	1610
	Hammerfest d.	|	0710	|	|	1125	|	1219	...	1634	|	|
87	Skaidi d.	0810	0811	1030	1038	1226	1325	1320	...	1735	1738	1740
144	Hammerfest a.	|	|	|	1133	|	|	|	...	|	1833	|
112	Olderfjord d.	0845	0845	1105	...	1246	1400	1400	...	1815	...	1815
212	Honningsvåg ★ a.	1023	|	1243	...	|	1538	|	...	|	...	1953
	Nordkapp a.	...	|	▬	...	|	▬	|	...	|	...	...
174	Lakselv d.	...	0957	①–⑤	...	1413	⑦	1456	...	1911	...	...
248	Karasjok d.	...	|		...	|	...	1607	...	2013	...	...
	Varangerbotn d.	...	1357	1435	...	1754	1805	...	...	...	...	...
571	**Kirkenes** AMFI a.	...	...	1639	...	...	2004	...	...	...	...	...

	①–⑤	①–⑤	⑥	①–⑤	①–⑤	①–⑤	①–⑤		Ⓑ t	Ⓑ	⑦	⑦
Kirkenes AMFI d.	...	...	...	0615	...	...	...	...	...	...	1205	...
Varangerbotn d.	...	...	...	0819	0830	...	...	...	...	...	1404	1415
Karasjok d.	...	0610	...	▬	|	...	...	...	...	1550	...	|
Lakselv d.	...	0731	...	⑥	1245	...	...	...	...	1701	...	1807
Nordkapp d.	...	|	...		|	...	...	...	...	|	...	|
Honningsvåg ★ d.	0657	|	...	0917	|	1212	...	...	1627	|	...	|
Olderfjord d.	0845	0845	...	1105	1400	1400	...	...	1815	1815	...	1915
Hammerfest d.	|	|	0920	|	|	|	1330	...	|	|	...	|
Skaidi d.	0905	0905	1021	1125	1420	1420	1431	...	1835	1835	...	1935
Hammerfest a.	|	1006	|	|	1524	|	|	...	|	1936	...	2039
Alta sentrum a.	1030	...	1150	1250	...	1545	1600	...	2000	...	...	...

Rovaniemi – Muonio – Tromsø

www.matkahuolto.fi

km	*Operator:*	*E*		*G*
0	**Rovaniemi** bus station d.	1140	...	1710
	Rovaniemi rail station d.	1120*	...	1720
152	Kittila, (Hotel) d.	1335	...	1925
232	Muonio d.	1505	...	2030
320	Karesuvanto d.	1630	...	...
424	Kilpisjärvi ⊡ FI d.	1805	...	...
538	Nordkjosbotn ⊕ NO d.	1825**v**	...	...
611	**Tromsø** Prostneset a.	1930**v**	...	...

	G		*E*
Tromsø Prostneset d.	...	...	0710**z**
Nordkjosbotn ⊕ NO d.	...	...	0805**z**
Kilpisjärvi ⊡ FI d.	...	...	1050
Karesuvanto d.	...	...	1230
Muonio d.	0855	...	1400
Kittila, (Hotel) d.	1010	...	1525
Rovaniemi rail station a.	1210	...	1720
Rovaniemi bus station a.	1215	...	1725

Rovaniemi – Karasjok and Nordkapp

www.matkahuolto.fi

km	*Operator:*	*G*		*E*		*J* ①–⑤		*E*		*L* ⑦–④	
0	**Rovaniemi** bus station d.	0900	...	1145	...	1315	...	1720	...	2035	...
	Rovaniemi rail station d.	0840*	...	1120*	...	|	...	1705*	...	2045	...
130	Sodankylä d.	1055**f**	...	1345**f**	...	1505	...	1905**f**	...	2230	...
305	Ivalo, bus station FI d.	1315	...	1630**e**	...	...	...	2110	...	0030	...
346	Inari, K-market FI d.	...	...	1710	...	...	...	2145	...	...	...
461	Karasjok ⊖ NO a.	...	...	1740**n**	...	...	...	...	...	...	...
536	Lakselv, Circle K a.	...	...	...	...	...	...	...	...	...	...
	Honningsvåg ◇ a.	...	...	...	...	...	...	...	...	...	...
735	**Nordkapp** a.	...	...	...	...	...	...	...	...	...	...

Operator:	*J* ①–⑤		*E*		*L* ①–⑤		*E*		*G*	
Nordkapp d.	...	...	...	...	...	...	...	...	...	...
Honningsvåg ◇ d.	...	...	...	...	...	...	...	...	...	...
Lakselv, Circle K d.	...	...	...	...	...	...	...	...	...	...
Karasjok ⊖ NO d.	...	...	...	...	...	...	0915**j**	...	...	...
Inari, K-market FI d.	...	...	0720**k**	...	...	...	1210	...	...	...
Ivalo, bus station FI d.	...	...	0810**f**	...	1210	...	1315**e**	...	1600	...
Sodankylä d.	0910	...	1030**f**	...	1445**f**	...	1540**f**	...	1825**f**	...
Rovaniemi rail station a.	1105**x**	...	1210	...	1640•	...	1715	...	2005	...
Rovaniemi bus station a.	1110	...	1215	...	1635	...	1725	...	2010	...

Operator codes:

E – J M Eskelisen Lapin Linjat Oy.
G – OnniBus FLEX.
L – Liikenne O. Niemelä Oy.
J – Jbus Oy.

Time Zones:

FI – Finland (East European Time).
NO – Norway (Central European Time).

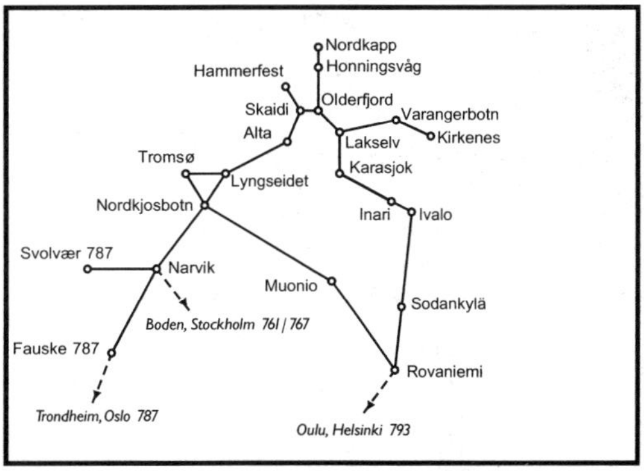

e – Arrives 30 minutes earlier.
f – Arrives 10–20 minutes earlier.
j – Not Dec. 25, 26, 31, Jan. 7.
k – Not Dec. 25.
n – Not Dec. 24, 25, 30, Jan. 6.
t – Honningsvåg - Nordkapp and v.v in summer only.
v – Kilpisjärvi to Tromsø June 2 to Sept. 19.
z – Tromsø to Kilpisjärvi June 3 to Sept. 20.
x – Stops on request.

* – Serves Rovaniemi rail station before bus station.
• – Serves Rovaniemi rail station after bus station.
□ – Runs 50 minutes earlier on ⑦.
◇ – Scandic Hotel, stops by request.
⊕ – Nordkjosbotn Gjestgiveri.
⊡ – K-Market.
⊖ – Karasjok, Scandic Hotel.
★ – Honningsvåg (Nordkapp).
Honningsvåg - **Nordkapp** and v.v. *34 km*.
Journey: 35 minutes. Operates May 1 - Sept. 30.
From Honningsvåg at 1115¶.
From Nordkapp at 1430¶.
¶ – Service operated by North Cape Tours (from Honningsvåg tourist information office). Bus route 406 Timings may vary. Special fares apply. www.northcapetours.com

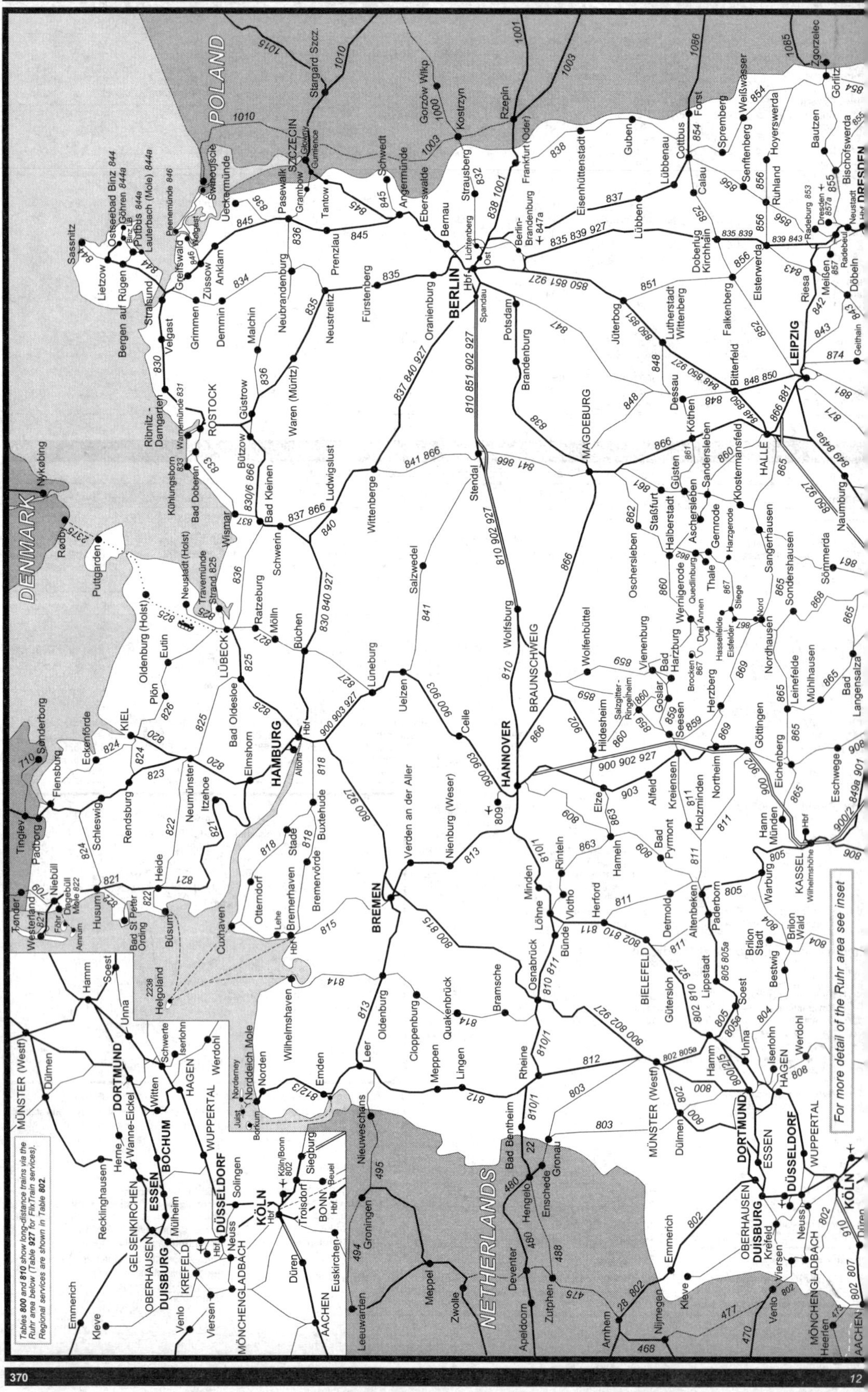
DENMARK
POLAND
NETHERLANDS
BERLIN
HAMBURG
HANNOVER
BREMEN
LEIPZIG
HALLE
MAGDEBURG
BRAUNSCHWEIG
ROSTOCK
LÜBECK
KIEL
SZCZECIN
BIELEFELD
MÜNSTER (Westf)
DORTMUND
ESSEN
DUISBURG
DÜSSELDORF
KÖLN
WUPPERTAL
BOCHUM
GELSENKIRCHEN
OBERHAUSEN
KREFELD
MÖNCHENGLADBACH
HAGEN
AACHEN
BONN
KASSEL
DRESDEN
Tables 800 and 810 show long-distance trains via the Ruhr area below (Table 927 for FlixTrain services). Regional services are shown in Table 802.
For more detail of the Ruhr area see inset

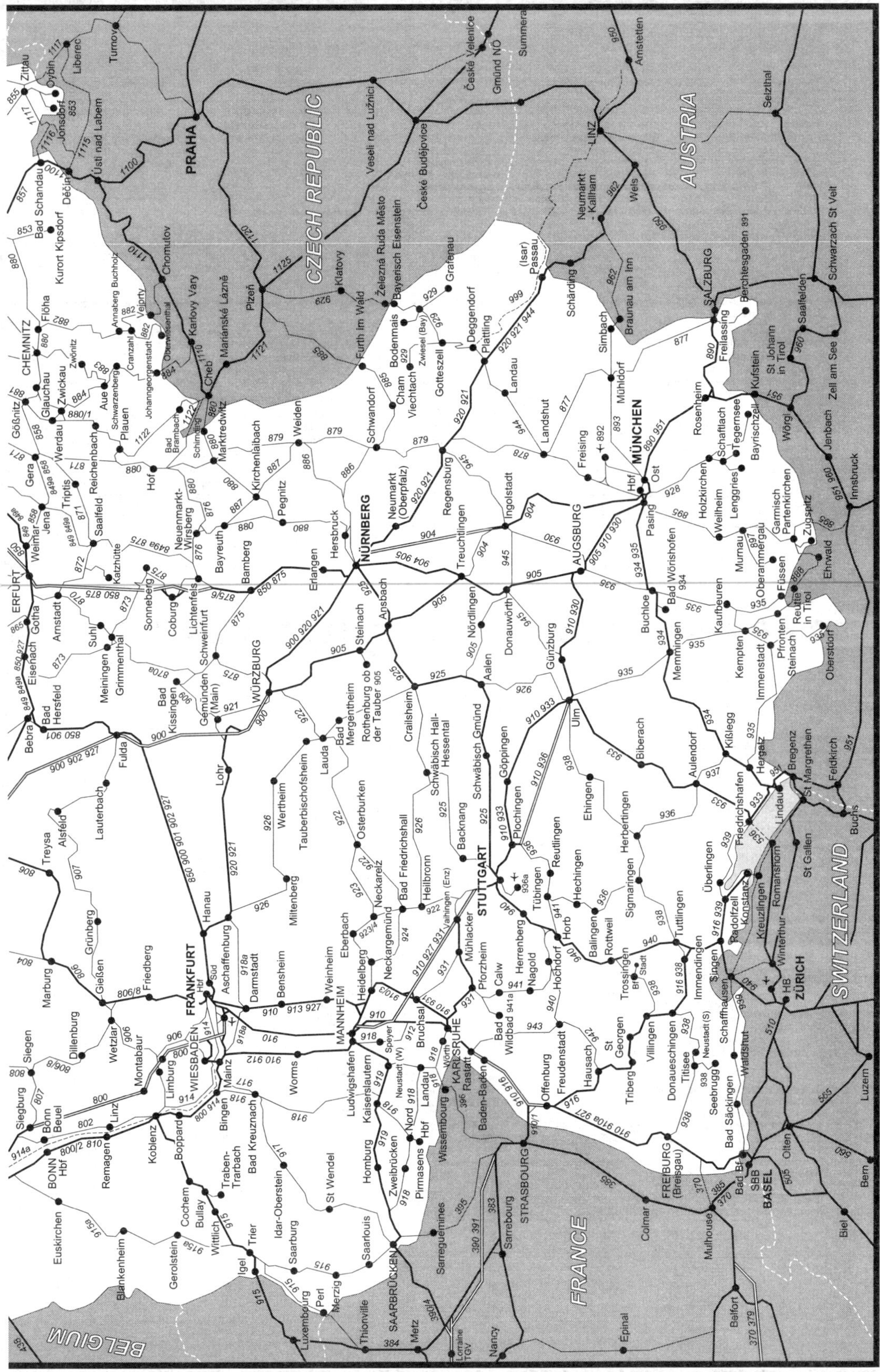
CZECH REPUBLIC
AUSTRIA
SWITZERLAND
FRANCE
BELGIUM
PRAHA
ERFURT
CHEMNITZ
NÜRNBERG
WÜRZBURG
FRANKFURT
MANNHEIM
STUTTGART
KARLSRUHE
AUGSBURG
MÜNCHEN
SALZBURG
LINZ
ZÜRICH
BASEL
STRASBOURG
SAARBRÜCKEN
WIESBADEN
BONN Hbf
FREIBURG (Breisgau)
Fulda
Hanau
Aschaffenburg
Darmstadt
Heidelberg
Ludwigshafen
Mainz
Koblenz
Trier
Kaiserslautern
Pforzheim
Offenburg
Ulm
Ingolstadt
Regensburg
Passau
Bamberg
Bayreuth
Hof
Plauen
Zwickau
Gera
Jena
Weimar
Gotha
Eisenach
Bebra
Marburg
Gießen
Siegen
Innsbruck
Kufstein
Bregenz
Lindau
Konstanz
Schaffhausen
Luxembourg
Metz
Nancy
Colmar
Mulhouse
Belfort
Bern
Luzern
Olten
St Gallen

GERMANY

See map on pages 370 and 371

Operator: Principal operator is Deutsche Bahn AG (DB) www.bahn.de
Many regional services are run by private operators – these are specified in the table heading (or by footnotes for individual trains).

Services: Trains convey first- and second-class seating accommodation unless otherwise shown (by '2' in the column heading, a footnote or a general note in the table heading). Overnight sleeping car (🛏) and couchette (🛏) trains do not necessarily convey seating accommodation - refer to individual footnotes for details. Descriptions of sleeping and couchette cars appear on page 10.

There are various categories of trains in Germany. The type of train is indicated by the following letter codes above each column (or by a general note in the table heading):

ICE	**InterCity Express**	German high-speed (230 – 320 km/h) train.
EC/ECE	**EuroCity**	International express train.
IC	**InterCity**	Internal express train.
ALX	**alex**	Regional express train operated by *Vogtlandbahn*.
FLX	**Flixtrain**	Independent long-distance operator – see Table **927**.
WB	**WESTbahn**	Independent Austrian operator running services from/to Wien.
RJ/RJX	**Railjet**	Austrian express train. Conveys first and economy (second) class. *Business class* also available to first class ticket holders (supplement payable).
TGV	**Train à Grande Vitesse**	French high-speed (320 km/h) train. Reservation compulsory for all international journeys.
IRE	**InterRegio Express**	Regional express train.
RE	**Regional Express**	Regional semi-fast train.
RB	**Regional Bahn**	Regional stopping train.
S-Bahn		Suburban stopping train.

Overnight services:

NJ	**ÖBB nightjet**	Quality overnight express train operated by Austrian Railways. Conveys *Deluxe* sleeping cars (1/2/3 berth) with en-suite shower and WC, standard sleeping cars (1/2/3 berth), couchettes (4/6 berth) and second class seats (in a compartment). Reservation compulsory. New rolling stock is gradually being introduced which includes single berth couchette accommodation in mini capsule style compartments.
EN	**EuroNight**	Other international overnight express train.

Timings: **Valid June 7 - Dec. 13, 2025.** Engineering work frequently affects services and we are not always able to show amended timings. **Readers are strongly advised to confirm timings before travelling.**

Many long distance trains operate on selected days only for part of the journey. These are often indicated in the train composition footnote by showing the dated journey segment within brackets. For example '12 Leipzig - Hannover (- Dortmund ⑦)' means that the train runs daily (or as shown in the column heading) between Leipzig and Hannover, but only continues to Dortmund on Sundays. Additional footnotes/symbols are often used to show more complex running dates, e.g. '12 (München ⊡ -) Nürnberg - Hamburg' means that the train runs only on dates in note ⊡ between München and Nürnberg, but runs daily (or as shown in the column heading) between Nürnberg and Hamburg. Please note that international overnight trains that are not intended for internal German journeys are not usually shown in the German section (refer to the International section).

Engineering work may occasionally disrupt services at short notice (especially at weekends and during holiday periods), so it is advisable to check timings locally before travelling. Information regarding major and longer-term alterations will be included in the relevant tables.

Tickets: There are three standard levels of fares, corresponding to travel by (in ascending order of price): ○ Regional trains. ○ *IC/EC* trains. ○ High-speed *ICE*, *TGV*, *RJ/RJX* and *ECE* trains. A variable supplement is payable for sleeping car and couchette accommodation (and sometimes seating) on overnight *EN/NJ* trains, the cost of which depends on the type required. Please note that Interrail and Eurail pass holders may have to pay a special fare or supplement for travel on overnight trains.

Catering: Two types of catering are indicated in the tables: 🍸 Bordbistro – hot and cold drinks, snacks and light meals (or an at-seat trolley service on certain *IC* trains); ✕ Bordrestaurant – full restaurant car service (bordbistro also available). First class passengers on *ICE* and *IC* trains benefit from an at-seat service. On overnight *NJ/EN* trains 🍸 indicates that drinks and light snacks are available, usually from the sleeping or couchette car attendant (the refreshment service may only be available to sleeping and couchette car passengers).

Reservations: Reservation is compulsory for travel in sleeping car and couchette accommodation on overnight trains (also in the seating accommodation of *ÖBB nightjet* services). Optional seat reservations are available on *ICE*, *EC* and *IC* trains (€5,20 in second class, €6,50 in first class).

Holidays: Dec. 25, 26, Jan. 1, Apr. 18, 21, May 1, 29, June 9 and Oct. 3 are German national public holidays (trains marked ⚒ or Ⓐ do not run). In addition there are other regional holidays as follows: Jan. 6 – Heilige Drei Könige (Epiphany), Mar. 8 – Weltfrauentag (International Women's Day), June 19 – Fronleichnam (Corpus Christi), Aug. 15 – Mariä Himmelfahrt (Assumption), Sept. 20 – Weltkindertag (World Children's Day), Oct. 31 – Reformationstag (Reformation Day), Nov. 1 – Allerheiligen (All Saints Day) and Nov. 19 – Buß und Bettag (Repentance Day). On these days the regional service is usually that applicable on ⑦ (please refer to individual footnotes).

800 FRANKFURT - KÖLN - DORTMUND - HAMBURG

See Table **802** for Rhein-Ruhr regional services. See Table **810** for services to Berlin via Bielefeld and Hannover. See Table **927** for FlixTrain services.

km	km	IMPORTANT! SEE NOTE ⊠	*ICE*	*IC*	*IC*	*IC*	*NJ*	*ICE*	*ICE*	*ICE*	*ICE*	*ICE*	*IC*	*ICE*	*ICE*	*IC*	*IC*	*ICE*	*ICE*	*ICE*	*ICE*	*ICE*	*ICE*	*IC*	
			1028	**2445**	**2214**	**2208**	**402**	**618**	**1038**	**222**	**222**	**208**	**2443**	**826**	**18**	**2206**	**2306**	**616**	**824**	**1223**	**1223**	**220**	**1014**	**2310**	
			①–⑤	①–⑥		⊡					Ⓐ						♠		①–⑥	①–⑤	⑥⑦		⑥		
			✕	J🍸	Y	N🍸	♦	K✕	✕	⊗✕	⊗✕	Q✕	J🍸	✕	✕	N🍸	🍸	✕	✕	P✕	P✕	⊗✕	N✕	Y	
		München Hbf **904 910** d.	...	...	...	...	...	0000	...	...	...	...	...	...	...	...	...	0331	...	...	...	...	...	...	...
		Stuttgart Hbf **910** d.	...	...	...	...	...	0222	...	...	...	...	...	...	...	...	...	0551	...	...	...	...	0636	...	...
		Basel SBB 🚇 **910** d.	...	...	...	...	2313**z**	│	...	...	...	...	...	...	...	...	...	│	...	...	...	...	│	...	...
		Karlsruhe Hbf **910** d.	...	...	...	...	0120	│	...	...	...	...	...	...	...	...	...	│	...	...	...	...	│	...	...
		Mannheim Hbf **910** d.	...	...	...	...	0152	0401	...	...	...	...	...	...	...	...	...	0635	...	...	...	...	0720	...	...
		Wien Hbf **950** d.	...	...	...	...	│	│	...	...	...	...	...	...	...	...	...	│	...	...	...	...	│	...	...
		Passau Hbf **920** d.	...	...	...	...	│	│	...	...	...	...	...	...	...	...	...	│	...	...	...	...	│	...	...
		Nürnberg Hbf **920** d.	...	...	...	...	│	│	...	...	...	...	...	...	...	...	...	│	...	...	...	...	│	...	...
0		**Frankfurt** (Main) Hbf **914** d.	...	...	...	...	0313	0446	...	...	0526	...	...	0538	0627	...	...	│	0708	0558	...	0727	│	...	...
11		**Frankfurt** Flughafen ✈ §**914** d.	...	...	...	...	0330	0500	...	...	0538	...	...	0552	0641	...	...	0710	0723	0610	...	0741	0754	...	...
	0	**Mainz** Hbf **914** d.	...	...	...	...	0349	│	...	...	│	...	...	│	│	...	...	│	│	0635	...	│	│	...	...
	10	Wiesbaden Hbf d.	...	...	...	...	│	│	...	...	│	...	...	│	│	...	...	│	│	0710**t**	...	│	│	...	...
		Koblenz Hbf **914** d.	...	...	...	...	0443	│	...	...	│	...	0605	│	│	...	...	│	│	│	...	│	│	...	...
		Andernach d.	...	...	...	...	│	│	...	...	│	...	0618	│	│	...	...	│	│	│	...	│	│	...	...
		Remagen d.	...	...	...	...	│	│	...	...	│	...	0631	│	│	...	...	│	│	│	...	│	│	...	...
		Bonn Hbf d.	...	...	...	...	0530**b**	│	...	...	│	...	0645	│	│	...	...	│	│	│	...	│	│	...	...
70	*65*	Limburg Süd d.	...	...	...	...	│	│	...	...	│	...	│	0610	│	...	...	│	│	0734	...	│	│	...	...
92	*87*	Montabaur d.	...	...	...	...	│	│	...	...	│	...	│	0621	│	...	...	│	│	0749	...	│	│	...	...
155	*150*	Siegburg/Bonn 🚌 **801** d.	...	...	...	...	│	0546	...	...	0616	...	│	0642	│	...	...	│	│	0808	...	│	0832	...	...
	166	Köln/Bonn Flughafen ✈ **801** d.	...	...	...	...	│	│	...	...	│	...	│	│	│	...	...	│	│	│	...	│	│	...	...
179	*180*	**Köln** Messe/Deutz **801** a.	...	...	...	...	│	│	...	...	│	...	│	│	│	...	...	│	0814	0822	...	│	0849	...	...
180	*181*	**Köln** Hbf **801** a.	...	...	...	...	0557	0603	...	...	0633	...	0705	0705	0733	...	...	0805	│	│	...	0833	│	...	...
180		**Köln** Hbf **802 806** d.	0358	0511	0508	0541	0602	0609	0615	0641	0641	0710	0711	0714	0742	0746	0801	0811	│	│	...	0839	│	0905	...
		Aachen Hbf **802 806** a.	│	│	│	│	│	│	│	│	│	│	│	│	0816	│	│	│	│	│	...	│	│	│	...
		Brussels Midi/Zuid **21** a.	│	│	│	│	│	│	│	│	│	│	│	│	0935	│	│	│	│	│	...	│	│	│	...
181		**Köln** Messe/Deutz d.	0403	│	│	│	│	│	│	│	│	│	│	│	...	│	│	│	0817	0824	...	│	0851	│	...
		Solingen Hbf d.	│	0530	│	│	│	│	│	│	│	│	0730	│	...	│	│	│	│	│	...	│	│	│	...
		Wuppertal Hbf d.	│	0544	│	│	│	│	│	│	│	│	0744	│	...	│	│	│	│	│	...	│	│	│	...
		Hagen Hbf d.	│	0601	│	│	│	│	│	│	│	│	0801	│	...	│	│	│	│	│	...	│	│	│	...
220		**Düsseldorf** Hbf d.	0425	│	0533	0607	│	0633	0641	0708	0708	0734	│	0738	...	0812	0829	0834	0840	0848	...	0908	0915	0928	...
227		Düsseldorf Flughafen ✈ d.	0433	│	│	0614	│	│	│	│	│	│	│	│	...	│	│	│	│	│	...	│	│	│	...
244		**Duisburg** Hbf d.	0443	│	0547	0625	│	0647	0654	0725	0725	0747	│	0751	...	0827	0844	0847	0854	0902	...	0925	0929	0941	...
		Oberhausen Hbf d.	│	│	│	0633	│	│	│	0733	0733	│	│	│	...	0834	│	│	│	│	0854	0933	│	│	...
		Amsterdam Centraal **28** a.	│	│	│	│	0932**v**	│	│	0929	0929	│	│	│	...	│	│	│	│	│	│	1129	│	│	...
263		**Essen** Hbf d.	0500	│	0600	│	...	0700	0706	...	...	0800	│	0802	...	│	0858	0900	0905	0917	0917	...	│	0954	...
		Gelsenkirchen Hbf d.	│	│	│	0643	...	│	│	...	...	│	│	...	...	0844	0911	│	...	│	│	...	0945	│	...
		Wanne-Eickel Hbf d.	│	│	│	0650	...	│	│	...	...	│	│	...	...	0851	│	│	...	│	│	...	0951	│	...
		Recklinghausen Hbf d.	│	│	│	0657	...	│	│	...	...	│	│	...	...	0858	0921	│	...	│	│	...	0959	│	...
279		Bochum Hbf d.	0510	│	0610	│	...	0710	│	...	...	0810	│	...	...	│	│	0910	...	0927	0927	...	│	│	...
297		**Dortmund** Hbf a.	0521	0621	0621	│	...	0721	│	...	...	0821	0821	...	...	│	│	0921	...	0939	0939	...	│	│	...
297		**Dortmund** Hbf **805** d.	0525	0628	0625	│	...	0725	│	...	...	0825	0828	...	...	│	│	0925	...	0941	0941	...	│	│	...
		Hamm (Westf) **805** a.	│	0643	│	│	...	│	│	...	...	│	0843	...	...	│	│	│	...	0957	0957	...	│	│	...
353		Münster (Westf) Hbf **802** d.	0557	...	0657	0728	...	0757	│	...	...	0857	...	...	...	0929	0952	0957	...	...	...	...	1028	1047	...
403		Osnabrück Hbf **802 815** d.	0623	...	0723	...	...	0823	│	...	...	0923	...	...	...	...	...	1023	...	...	...	...	...	│	...
		Berlin Hbf **810** a.	│	...	│	...	...	│	│	...	...	│	...	...	...	...	...	│	...	...	...	...	...	│	...
525		**Bremen** Hbf **815** ☆ d.	0727	...	0818	...	...	0917	│	...	...	1018	...	...	...	...	...	1117	...	...	...	...	...	│	...
628		**Hamburg** Harburg ☆ a.	0819	...	0901	...	...	1001	│	...	...	1101	...	...	...	...	...	1201	...	...	...	...	...	1246	...
640		**Hamburg** Hbf ☆ a.	0834	...	0914	...	...	1014	0951	...	...	1114	...	...	...	...	...	1214	...	...	...	...	...	1259	...
647		**Hamburg** Altona a.	0848	...	...	...	...	...	1004	...	...	1129**g**	...	...	...	...	...	1230	...	...	...	...	...	...	...

FOR NOTES, SEE PAGE 375 →

FRANKFURT - KÖLN - DORTMUND - HAMBURG 800

See Table **802** for Rhein-Ruhr regional services. See Table **810** for services to Berlin via Bielefeld and Hannover. See Table **927** for FlixTrain services.

IMPORTANT! SEE NOTE ⊠	IC 2441 V J⊙	IC 2441 W J⊙	ICE 206 V ✕	ICE 206 W ✕	ICE 822 ①–⑥ ✕	IC 2155 V G	IC 2155 W G	ICE 316 ✕	ICE 1122 ①–⑤ L✕	IC 2204 E🍷	IC 5107 X	ICE 614 ✕	ICE 1022 ✕	ICE 820 ①–⑥ ✕	ICE 128 ⊗✕	ICE 1012 ①–⑥ ✕	ICE 1012 ⊖ ✕	ICE 1656 ◇	IC 2049 C J🍷	IC 2049 D J🍷	ICE 202 V ✕	ICE 202 W ✕	ICE 728 ✕	ICE 759 e ✕	ICE 16 ✕
München Hbf **904 910** d.	...	...	...	...	0447	...	...	...	0533	...	...	0532	...	0553	...	0625	0625	...	...	...	...	...	0647	...	...
Stuttgart Hbf **910** d.	...	...	...	...	│	...	...	...	│	...	...	0751	...	│	...	0839	0839	...	0736	...	...	...	│	...	...
Basel SBB 🏛 **910** d.	...	...	0513n	0513	│	...	...	...	│	...	...	│	...	│	...	│	│	...	│	...	0713n	0713	│	...	...
Karlsruhe Hbf **910** d.	...	...	0701	0701	│	...	...	...	│	...	...	│	...	│	...	│	│	...	│	0752	0901	0901	│	...	...
Mannheim Hbf **910** d.	...	...	0735	0735	│	...	...	...	│	...	...	0836	...	│	...	0920	0920	...	0839	0839	0935	0935	│	...	...
Wien Hbf **950** d.	...	...	│	│	│	...	...	...	│	...	...	│	...	│	...	│	│	...	│	│	│	│	│	...	...
Passau Hbf **920** d.	...	...	│	│	│	...	...	...	│	...	...	│	...	│	...	│	│	...	│	│	│	│	│	...	...
Nürnberg Hbf **920** d.	...	...	│	│	0600	...	...	...	0639	...	...	│	0528	0703	...	│	│	...	│	│	│	│	0757	...	...
Frankfurt (Main) Hbf **914** d.	0642	0642	│	│	0809	...	...	0815	│	...	...	│	0742	0909	0927	│	│	0842	│	│	│	│	1009	...	1025
Frankfurt Flughafen ✈ § **914** d.	0657	0657	0810	0810	0823	...	...	0830	0842	...	...	0910	0757	0923	0941	0954	0954	0857	│	│	1010	1010	1023	...	1041
Mainz Hbf **914** d.	0717	0717	│	│	│	...	...	│	│	...	...	│	0820	│	│	│	│	0915a	0920	0920	│	│	│	...	│
Wiesbaden Hbf d.	│	│	│	│	│	...	...	│	│	...	...	│	│	│	│	│	│	0933	│	│	│	│	│	...	│
Koblenz Hbf **914** d.	0813	0813	│	│	│	...	...	│	│	...	0841	│	0913	│	│	│	│	...	1013	1013	│	│	│	...	│
Andernach d.	│	│	│	│	│	...	...	│	│	...	0856	│	│	│	│	│	│	...	│	│	│	│	│	...	│
Remagen d.	│	│	│	│	│	...	...	│	│	...	0908	│	│	│	│	│	│	...	│	│	│	│	│	...	│
Bonn Hbf d.	0845	0845	│	│	│	...	...	│	│	...	0923	│	0945	│	│	│	│	...	1045	1045	│	│	│	...	│
Limburg Süd d.	│	│	│	│	│	...	...	0848	│	...	│	│	│	│	│	│	│	...	│	│	│	│	│	...	│
Montabaur d.	│	│	│	│	│	...	...	0859	│	...	│	│	│	│	│	│	│	...	│	│	│	│	│	...	│
Siegburg/Bonn 🚋 **801** d.	│	│	│	│	0901	...	...	│	│	...	│	│	│	1001	│	1032	1032	...	│	│	│	│	│	...	│
Köln/Bonn Flughafen ✈ **801** d.	│	│	│	│	│	...	...	│	│	...	│	│	│	│	│	│	│	...	│	│	│	│	│	...	│
Köln Messe/Deutz **801** a.	│	│	│	│	0915	...	...	│	0936	...	│	│	│	1015	│	1048	1048	...	│	│	│	│	1114	...	│
Köln Hbf **801** a.	0906	0906	0905	0905	│	...	...	0933	│	...	0943	1005	1006	│	1033	│	│	...	1106	1106	1105	1105	│	...	1133
Köln Hbf **802 806** d.	0909	0909	0911	0911	│	0919	0918	0941	│	0938	0946	1011	1011	│	1041	│	│	...	1111	1111	1111	1111	│	1137	1142
Aachen Hbf **802 806** a.	│	│	│	│	│	│	│	1016	│	│	│	│	│	│	│	│	│	...	│	│	│	│	│	│	1216
Brussels Midi/Zuid **21** a.	│	│	│	│	│	│	│	1135	│	│	│	│	│	│	│	│	│	...	│	│	│	│	│	│	1335
Köln Messe/Deutz d.	│	│	│	│	0917	│	│	...	0939	│	│	│	│	1017	│	1050	1050	...	│	│	│	│	1117	│	...
Solingen Hbf d.	│	0930	0930	│	│	│	│	...	│	│	│	1030	│	│	│	│	│	...	1130	1130	│	│	│	│	...
Wuppertal Hbf d.	│	0944	0944	│	│	│	│	...	│	│	│	1044	│	│	│	│	│	...	1144	1144	│	│	│	│	...
Hagen Hbf d.	│	1001	1001	│	│	│	1008	...	│	│	│	1101	│	│	│	│	│	...	1201	1201	│	│	│	│	...
Düsseldorf Hbf d.	0934	│	│	0934	0938	0943	│	...	1005	1012	1012	│	1034	1040	1108	1110	1111	...	│	│	1134	1134	1138	1206	...
Düsseldorf Flughafen ✈ d.	│	│	│	│	│	0950	│	...	...	│	...	│	│	│	│	...	│	...	│	│	│	│	│	│	...
Duisburg Hbf d.	0948	│	│	0947	0951	1002	│	...	...	1027	...	│	1047	1054	1125	...	1129	...	│	│	1147	1147	1151	1221	...
Oberhausen Hbf d.	│	│	│	│	│	│	│	...	...	1034	...	│	│	│	1133	...	│	...	│	│	│	│	│	│	...
Amsterdam Centraal **28** a.	│	│	│	│	│	│	│	...	...	│	...	│	│	│	1329	...	│	...	│	│	│	│	│	│	...
Essen Hbf d.	1000	│	│	1000	1002	1016	│	...	...	│	...	│	1100	1105	...	...	1142	...	│	│	1200	1200	1202	1233	...
Gelsenkirchen Hbf d.	│	│	│	│	...	│	│	...	...	1044	...	│	│	...	...	...	│	...	│	│	│	│	...	│	...
Wanne-Eickel Hbf d.	│	│	│	│	...	│	│	...	...	1051	...	│	│	...	...	...	│	...	│	│	│	│	...	1247	...
Recklinghausen Hbf d.	│	│	│	1021	...	│	│	...	...	1058	...	│	│	...	...	...	│	...	│	│	│	1221	...	│	...
Bochum Hbf d.	1010	│	│	│	...	1028	│	...	...	│	...	│	1110	...	...	...	1152	...	│	│	1210	│	...	│	...
Dortmund Hbf a.	1021	1021	1021	│	...	1040	1040	...	...	│	...	1121	1121	...	...	...	1204	...	1221	1221	1221	│	...	│	...
Dortmund Hbf **805** d.	1028	1028	1025	│	...	...	...	...	...	│	...	1125	...	...	...	...	...	...	1228	1228	1225	│	...	│	...
Hamm (Westf) **805** a.	1043	1043	│	│	...	...	...	...	...	│	...	│	...	...	...	...	...	...	1243	1243	│	│	...	│	...
Münster (Westf) Hbf **802** d.	...	...	1057	1057	...	...	...	...	...	1128	...	1157	...	...	...	...	...	...	...	...	1257	1257	...	1327	...
Osnabrück Hbf **802 815** d.	...	...	1123	1123	...	...	...	...	...	...	...	1223	...	...	...	...	...	...	...	...	1323	1323	...	1352	...
Berlin Hbf **810** a.	...	...	│	│	...	...	...	...	...	...	...	│	...	...	...	...	...	...	...	...	│	│	...	1651	...
Bremen Hbf **815** ☆ d.	...	...	1218	1218	...	...	...	...	...	...	...	1317	...	...	...	...	...	...	...	...	1417	1417	...	...	...
Hamburg Harburg ☆ a.	...	...	1301	1301	...	...	...	...	...	...	...	1401	...	...	...	...	...	...	...	...	1501	1501	...	...	...
Hamburg Hbf ☆ a.	...	...	1314	1314	...	...	...	...	...	...	...	1414	...	...	...	...	...	...	...	...	1514	1514	...	...	...
Hamburg Altona a.	...	...	1330	1330	...	...	...	...	...	...	...	1430	...	...	...	...	...	...	...	...	1530	1530	...	...	...

IMPORTANT! SEE NOTE ⊠	IC 2202 N🍷	ICE 904 ✕	ICE 1020 ✕	ICE 612 K✕	ICE 726 ✕	ICE 126 ⊗✕	ICE 1010 ✕	ICE 1654 ◇	IC 2047 J 🍷♦	ICE 200 ✕	ICE 724 ✕		ICE 314 ✕	IC 2200 N🍷	ICE 928 ✕	ICE 902 ✕	ICE 610 ✕	ICE 722 ✕	ICE 124 ⊗✕	ICE 918 ✕	ICE 108 ✕	ICE 1652 ◇	IC 2045 C J✕	IC 2045 D J🍷	
München Hbf **904 910** d.	...	...	...	0727	0746	...	0827	...	...	...	0847	...	...	...	...	...	0927	0950	...	1029	...	...	...	...	...
Stuttgart Hbf **910** d.	...	...	...	0951	│	...	1039	...	0937	...	│	...	...	...	...	...	1151	│	...	1238	...	...	1137	...	...
Basel SBB 🏛 **910** d.	...	...	...	│	│	...	│	...	│	0913n	│	...	...	...	...	...	│	│	...	│	1113h	...	│	...	...
Karlsruhe Hbf **910** d.	...	...	...	│	│	...	│	...	│	1101	│	...	...	...	...	...	│	│	...	│	1301	...	│	1152	...
Mannheim Hbf **910** d.	...	...	...	1036	│	...	1120	...	1039	1135	│	...	...	...	...	...	1236	│	...	1320	1335	...	1239	1239	...
Wien Hbf **950** d.	...	...	...	│	│	...	│	...	│	│	│	...	...	...	...	...	│	│	...	│	│	...	│	│	...
Passau Hbf **920** d.	...	...	0511	│	│	...	│	...	│	│	│	...	...	...	0717	...	│	│	...	│	│	...	│	│	...
Nürnberg Hbf **920** d.	...	...	0730	│	0858	...	│	...	│	│	0957	...	...	...	0929	...	│	1058	...	│	│	...	│	│	...
Frankfurt (Main) Hbf **914** d.	...	1031	0942	│	1109	1127	│	1042	│	│	1209	...	1225	...	1142	1231	│	1309	1327	│	│	1242	│	│	...
Frankfurt Flughafen ✈ § **914** d.	...	1050	0957	1110	1123	1141	1154	1057	│	1210	1225	...	1241	...	1157	1250	1310	1323	1341	1354	1410	1257	│	│	...
Mainz Hbf **914** d.	...	│	1020	│	│	│	│	1115a	1120	│	│	...	│	...	1220	│	│	│	│	│	│	1315a	1320	1320	...
Wiesbaden Hbf d.	...	│	│	│	│	│	│	1133	│	│	│	...	│	...	│	│	│	│	│	│	│	1333	│	│	...
Koblenz Hbf **914** d.	...	│	1113	│	│	│	│	...	1213	│	│	...	│	...	1313	│	│	│	│	│	│	...	1413	1413	...
Andernach d.	...	│	│	│	│	│	│	...	│	│	│	...	│	...	│	│	│	│	│	│	│	...	│	│	...
Remagen d.	...	│	│	│	│	│	│	...	│	│	│	...	│	...	│	│	│	│	│	│	│	...	│	│	...
Bonn Hbf d.	...	│	1145	│	│	│	│	...	1245	│	│	...	│	...	1345	│	│	│	│	│	│	...	1445	1445	...
Limburg Süd d.	...	1109	│	│	│	│	│	...	│	│	│	...	│	...	│	1309	│	│	│	│	│	...	│	│	...
Montabaur d.	...	1120	│	│	│	│	│	...	│	│	│	...	│	...	│	1320	│	│	│	│	│	...	│	│	...
Siegburg/Bonn 🚋 **801** d.	...	1140	│	│	1201	│	1232	...	│	│	│	...	│	...	│	1340	│	1401	│	1432	│	...	│	│	...
Köln/Bonn Flughafen ✈ **801** d.	...	│	│	│	│	│	│	...	│	│	│	...	│	...	│	│	│	│	│	│	│	...	│	│	...
Köln Messe/Deutz **801** a.	...	1155	│	│	1215	│	1248	...	│	│	1314	...	│	...	│	1354	│	1415	│	1448	│	...	│	│	...
Köln Hbf **801** a.	...	1200	1206	1205	│	1233	│	...	1306	1305	│	...	1333	...	1406	...	1405	│	1433	│	1505	...	1506	1506	...
Köln Hbf **802 806** d.	1146	...	1211	1211	│	1241	│	...	1311	1311	│	...	1342	1346	1411	...	1411	│	1441	│	1511	...	1511	1511	...
Aachen Hbf **802 806** a.	│	...	│	│	│	│	│	...	│	│	│	...	1416	│	│	...	│	│	│	│	│	...	│	│	...
Brussels Midi/Zuid **21** a.	│	...	│	│	│	│	│	...	│	│	│	...	1535	│	│	...	│	│	│	│	│	...	│	│	...
Köln Messe/Deutz d.	│	...	│	│	1217	│	1250	...	│	│	1317	...	...	│	│	...	│	1417	│	1450	│	...	│	│	...
Solingen Hbf d.	│	...	│	1230	│	│	│	...	1330	│	│	...	...	│	│	...	1430	│	│	│	│	...	1530	1530	...
Wuppertal Hbf d.	│	...	│	1244	│	│	│	...	1344	│	│	...	...	│	│	...	1444	│	│	│	│	...	1544	1544	...
Hagen Hbf d.	│	...	│	1301	│	│	│	...	1401	│	│	...	...	│	│	...	1501	│	│	│	│	...	1601	1601	...
Düsseldorf Hbf d.	1212	...	1234	│	1238	1308	1312	...	│	1334	1338	...	...	1412	1434	...	│	1438	1508	1511	1534	...	│	│	...
Düsseldorf Flughafen ✈ d.	│	...	│	│	│	│	│	...	│	│	│	...	...	│	│	...	│	│	│	│	│	...	│	│	...
Duisburg Hbf d.	1227	...	1247	│	1251	1325	1329	...	│	1347	1351	...	...	1427	1447	...	│	1451	1525	1528	1547	...	│	│	...
Oberhausen Hbf d.	1234	...	│	│	│	1333	│	...	│	│	│	...	...	1434	│	...	│	│	1533	│	│	...	│	│	...
Amsterdam Centraal **28** a.	│	...	│	│	│	1529	│	...	│	│	│	...	...	│	│	...	│	│	1729	│	│	...	│	│	...
Essen Hbf d.	│	...	1300	│	1302	...	1342	...	│	1400	1402	...	...	│	1500	...	│	1502	...	1542	1600	...	│	│	...
Gelsenkirchen Hbf d.	1245	...	│	│	...	...	│	...	│	│	...	...	...	1444	│	...	│	...	...	│	│	...	│	│	...
Wanne-Eickel Hbf d.	1252	...	│	│	...	...	│	...	│	│	...	...	...	1451	│	...	│	...	...	│	│	...	│	│	...
Recklinghausen Hbf d.	1259	...	│	│	...	...	│	...	│	│	...	...	...	1459	│	...	│	...	...	│	│	...	│	│	...
Bochum Hbf d.	│	...	│	│	...	...	1352	...	│	1410	...	...	...	│	│	...	│	...	...	1552	1610	...	│	│	...
Dortmund Hbf a.	│	...	│	1321	...	...	1404	...	1421	1421	...	...	...	│	│	...	1521	...	...	1604	1621	...	1621	1621	...
Dortmund Hbf **805** d.	│	...	│	1325	...	...	...	...	1428	1425	...	...	...	│	│	...	1525	...	...	...	1625	...	1628	1628	...
Hamm (Westf) **805** a.	│	...	│	│	...	...	...	...	1443	│	...	...	...	│	│	...	│	...	...	...	│	...	1643	1643	...
Münster (Westf) Hbf **802** d.	1328	...	1347	1357	...	...	...	...	...	1457	...	...	...	1528	1547	...	1557	...	...	...	1657	...	...	...	...
Osnabrück Hbf **802 815** d.	...	...	│	1423	...	...	...	...	...	1523	...	...	...	...	│	...	1623	...	...	...	1723	...	...	...	...
Berlin Hbf **810** a.	...	...	│	│	...	...	...	...	...	│	...	...	...	...	│	...	│	...	...	...	│	...	...	...	...
Bremen Hbf **815** ☆ d.	...	...	│	1517	...	...	...	...	...	1617	...	...	...	...	│	...	1717	...	...	...	1817	...	...	...	...
Hamburg Harburg ☆ a.	...	...	1537	1601	...	...	...	...	...	1701	...	...	...	...	1738	...	1801	...	...	...	1901	...	...	...	...
Hamburg Hbf ☆ a.	...	...	1551	1614	...	...	...	...	...	1714	...	...	...	...	1751	...	1814	...	...	...	1914	...	...	...	...
Hamburg Altona a.	...	...	1606	...	...	...	...	...	...	1730	...	...	...	...	1804	...	1830	...	...	...	1930	...	...	...	...

FOR NOTES, SEE PAGE 375 →

800 FRANKFURT - KÖLN - DORTMUND - HAMBURG

See Table **802** for Rhein-Ruhr regional services. See Table **810** for services to Berlin via Bielefeld and Hannover. See Table **927** for FlixTrain services.

IMPORTANT! SEE NOTE ⊠	ICE 720	IC 2157	IC 2157	ICE 14	IC 2004	IC 2006	ICE 900	ICE 1030	ICE 518	ICE 518	ICE 628	ICE 122	IC 2012	IC 2012	ICE 818	ICE 106	IC 2043	ICE 1650	EC 8	EC 8	ICE 626	ICE 12	IC 2002	ICE 816	
		V	W		⑧	⑥			V	W			V	W					V	W					
	✕	♦	♦	✕	E🍷	🍷	✕	✕	✕	✕	✕	⊗✕	♦	♦	✕	✕	🍷♦	◇	✕♦	✕♦	✕	✕	E🍷	✕	
München Hbf **904 910** d.	1048	...	...	...	...	...	...	...	1127	1127	1150	...	...	...	...	...	...	...	...	...	1247	...	...	...	...
Stuttgart Hbf **910** d.	|	...	...	...	...	...	...	...	1351	1351	|	...	1312	1312	...	...	...	...	...	...	|	...	...	...	...
Basel SBB 🚍 **910** d.	|	...	...	...	...	...	...	...	|	|	|	...	|	|	...	1313	...	...	1220	1220	|	...	...	...	...
Karlsruhe Hbf **910** d.	|	...	...	...	...	...	...	...	|	|	|	...	|	|	...	1501	...	...	1412	1412	|	...	...	...	...
Mannheim Hbf **910** d.	|	...	...	...	...	...	...	...	1436	1436	|	...	1408	1408	...	1535	...	...	1438	1438	|	...	...	...	...
Wien Hbf **950** d.	|	...	...	...	...	...	...	...	|	|	|	...	|	|	...	|	...	...	|	|	|	...	...	...	...
Passau Hbf **920** d.	|	...	...	...	...	...	...	...	|	|	|	...	|	|	...	|	...	...	|	|	|	...	...	...	...
Nürnberg Hbf **920** d.	1157	...	...	...	...	...	...	...	|	|	1258	...	|	|	...	|	...	...	|	|	1357	...	...	...	...
Frankfurt (Main) Hbf **914** d.	1409	...	...	1427	...	...	1431	...	|	|	1509	1527	|	|	1515	|	...	1442	|	|	1609	1627	...	1615	...
Frankfurt Flughafen ✈ § **914** d.	1423	...	...	1441	...	...	1450	...	1510	1510	1523	1541	|	|	1530	1610	...	1457	|	|	1623	1641	...	1630	...
Mainz Hbf **914** d.	|	...	...	|	...	...	|	...	|	|	|	|	1449	1449	|	|	...	1515**a**	1520	1520	|	|	...	|	...
Wiesbaden Hbf d.	|	...	...	|	...	...	|	...	|	|	|	|	|	|	|	|	...	1533	|	|	|	|	...	|	...
Koblenz Hbf **914** d.	|	...	...	|	...	...	|	...	|	|	|	|	1544	1544	|	|	...	...	1613	1613	|	|	...	|	...
Andernach d.	|	...	...	|	...	...	|	...	|	|	|	|	1556	1556	|	|	...	...	|	|	|	|	...	|	...
Remagen d.	|	...	...	|	...	...	|	...	|	|	|	|	1608	1608	|	|	...	...	|	|	|	|	...	|	...
Bonn Hbf d.	|	...	...	|	...	...	|	...	|	|	|	|	1623	1623	|	|	...	...	1645	1645	|	|	...	|	...
Limburg Süd d.	|	...	...	|	...	...	1509	...	|	|	|	|	|	|	1548	|	...	...	|	|	|	|	...	1648	...
Montabaur d.	|	...	...	|	...	...	1520	...	|	|	|	|	|	|	1605**r**	|	...	...	|	|	|	|	...	1705**r**	...
Siegburg/Bonn 🚊 **801** d.	|	...	...	|	...	...	1540	...	|	|	|	|	|	|	1625	|	...	...	|	|	|	|	...	1726	...
Köln/Bonn Flughafen ✈ **801** d.	|	...	...	|	...	...	|	...	|	|	|	|	|	|	|	|	...	...	|	|	|	|	...	|	...
Köln Messe/Deutz **801** a.	1514	...	...	|	...	...	|	...	|	|	1614	|	|	|	|	|	...	...	|	|	1714	|	...	|	...
Köln Hbf **801** a.	|	...	...	1533	...	...	1556	...	1605	1605	|	1633	1644	1644	1644	1705	...	...	1706	1706	|	1733	...	1743	...
Köln Hbf **802 806** d.	|	1519	1518	1541	1546	1546	...	1604	1611	1611	|	1641	1647	1647	...	...	1711	...	1709	1709	|	1742	1745	...	...
Aachen Hbf **802 806** a.	|	|	|	1616	|	|	...	|	|	|	|	|	|	|	...	...	|	...	|	|	|	1816	|	...	...
Brussels Midi/Zuid **21** a.	|	|	|	1735	|	|	...	|	|	|	|	|	|	|	...	...	|	...	|	|	|	1935	|	...	...
Köln Messe/Deutz d.	1517	|	|	...	|	|	...	|	|	|	1617	|	|	|	...	...	|	...	|	|	1717	...	|	...	...
Solingen Hbf d.	|	|	|	...	|	|	...	|	|	1630	|	|	|	|	...	...	1730	...	|	|	|	...	|	...	...
Wuppertal Hbf d.	|	|	|	...	|	|	...	|	|	1644	|	|	|	|	...	...	1744	...	|	|	|	...	|	...	...
Hagen Hbf d.	|	|	1610	...	|	|	...	|	|	1701	|	|	|	|	...	...	1801	...	|	|	|	...	|	...	...
Düsseldorf Hbf d.	1538	1543	|	...	1612	1612	...	1629	1634	|	1640	1708	1712	1712	...	...	|	...	1733	1733	1738	...	1812	...	...
Düsseldorf Flughafen ✈ d.	|	1550	|	...	|	|	...	|	|	|	|	|	|	|	...	...	|	...	|	|	|	...	|	...	...
Duisburg Hbf d.	1551	1602	|	...	1627	1626	...	1643	1647	|	1654	1725	1728	1728	...	...	|	...	1747	1747	1751	...	1826	...	...
Oberhausen Hbf d.	|	|	|	...	1634	1634	...	|	|	|	|	1733	|	|	...	...	|	...	|	|	|	...	1833	...	...
Amsterdam Centraal **28** a.	|	|	|	...	|	|	...	|	|	|	|	1929	|	|	...	...	|	...	|	|	|	...	|	...	...
Essen Hbf d.	1602	1616	|	...	|	|	...	1657	1700	|	1705	...	1742	|	...	...	|	...	1800	1800	1817**j**	...	|	...	...
Gelsenkirchen Hbf d.	...	|	|	...	1645	1645	...	|	|	|	...	...	|	1744	...	...	|	...	|	|	|	...	1843	...	...
Wanne-Eickel Hbf d.	...	|	|	...	1652	1653	...	|	|	|	...	...	|	|	...	...	|	...	|	|	|	...	1851	...	...
Recklinghausen Hbf d.	...	|	|	...	1659	|	...	|	|	|	...	...	|	|	...	...	|	...	|	1822	|	...	1858	...	...
Bochum Hbf d.	...	1628	|	...	|	|	...	|	1710	|	...	...	1752	|	...	...	|	...	1810	|	1828	...	|	...	...
Dortmund Hbf a.	...	1640	1634	...	|	1708	...	|	1721	1721	...	...	1803	1804	...	...	1821	...	1821	|	1840	...	|	...	...
Dortmund Hbf **805** d.	...	...	...	...	|	...	...	|	1725	1725	...	...	...	...	...	...	1828	...	1825	|	...	...	|	...	...
Hamm (Westf) **805** a.	...	...	...	...	|	...	...	|	|	|	...	...	...	...	...	...	1843	...	|	|	...	...	|	...	...
Münster (Westf) Hbf **802** d.	...	...	...	...	1729	...	...	|	1757	1757	...	...	...	...	...	...	...	...	1857	1857	...	...	1928	...	...
Osnabrück Hbf **802 815** d.	...	...	...	...	...	...	...	|	1823	1823	...	...	...	...	...	...	...	...	1923	1923	...	...	...	...	...
Berlin Hbf **810** a.	...	...	...	...	...	...	...	|	|	|	...	...	...	...	...	...	...	...	|	|	...	...	...	...	...
Bremen Hbf **815** ☆ d.	...	...	...	...	...	...	...	|	1917	1917	...	...	...	...	...	...	...	...	2017	2017	...	...	...	...	...
Hamburg Harburg ☆ a.	...	...	...	...	...	...	...	|	2001	2001	...	...	...	...	...	...	...	...	2100	2100	...	...	...	...	...
Hamburg Hbf ☆ a.	...	...	...	...	...	...	...	1949	2014	2014	...	...	...	...	...	...	...	...	2114	2114	...	...	...	...	...
Hamburg Altona a.	...	...	...	...	...	...	...	2005	2030	2030	...	...	...	...	...	...	...	...	2130	2130	...	...	...	...	...

IMPORTANT! SEE NOTE ⊠	ICE 710	ICE 28	ICE 516	ICE 624	ICE 118	ICE 814	ICE 120	ICE 814	ICE 914	ICE 1558	IC 2041	ICE 104	EC 6		ICE 622	ICE 114	ICE 812	ICE 10	ICE 812	ICE 26	ICE 514	ICE 620	ICE 224	ICE 912	
	①–⑤										⑦												⊕	△	
	✕	✕	✕	✕	✕♦	✕	⊗✕	✕	✕	◇	H🍷	✕	✕♦		✕	✕♦	✕	✕	✕	✕	✕	✕	✕	✕	
München Hbf **904 910** d.	...	...	1327	1350	...	...	...	...	1427	...	...	...	...	...	1447	1347	...	...	...	...	1527	1550	1628	1628	...
Stuttgart Hbf **910** d.	1435	...	1551	|	1512	...	...	...	1637	...	...	...	...	...	|	1607	...	...	...	...	1751	|	1838	1838	...
Basel SBB 🚍 **910** d.	|	...	|	|	|	...	...	...	|	...	...	1513	1427	...	|	|	...	...	...	...	|	|	|	|	...
Karlsruhe Hbf **910** d.	|	...	|	|	|	...	...	...	|	...	...	1701	1612	...	|	|	...	...	...	...	|	|	|	|	...
Mannheim Hbf **910** d.	1533	...	1636	|	1607	...	...	...	1720	...	...	1735	1639	...	|	1657	...	...	...	...	1836	|	1921	1921	...
Wien Hbf **950** d.	|	0913	|	|	|	...	...	...	|	...	...	|	|	...	|	|	...	...	...	1113	|	|	|	|	...
Passau Hbf **920** d.	|	1134	|	|	|	...	...	...	|	...	...	|	|	...	|	|	...	...	...	1337	|	|	|	|	...
Nürnberg Hbf **920** d.	|	1329	|	1458	|	...	...	...	|	...	...	|	|	...	1557	|	...	...	...	1530	|	1658	|	|	...
Frankfurt (Main) Hbf **914** d.	|	1541	|	1709	|	1715	1727	...	|	1642	...	|	|	...	1809	|	1815	1827	...	1741	|	1909	|	|	...
Frankfurt Flughafen ✈ § **914** d.	|	1558	1710	1723	|	1730	1741	...	1754	1657	...	1810	|	...	1823	|	1830	1841	...	1758	1910	1923	1954	1954	...
Mainz Hbf **914** d.	1622	1620	|	|	1652	|	|	...	|	1715**a**	...	|	1720	...	|	1742	|	|	...	1820	|	|	|	|	...
Wiesbaden Hbf d.	1645	|	|	|	1711	|	|	...	|	1733	...	|	|	...	|	1810	|	|	...	|	|	|	|	|	...
Koblenz Hbf **914** d.	|	1713	|	|	|	|	|	...	|	...	...	|	1813	...	|	|	|	|	...	1913	|	|	|	|	...
Andernach d.	|	|	|	|	|	|	|	...	|	...	...	|	|	...	|	|	|	|	...	|	|	|	|	|	...
Remagen d.	|	|	|	|	|	|	|	...	|	...	...	|	|	...	|	|	|	|	...	|	|	|	|	|	...
Bonn Hbf d.	|	1745	|	|	|	|	|	...	|	...	...	|	1845	...	|	|	|	|	...	1945	|	|	|	|	...
Limburg Süd d.	1708	|	|	|	|	1748	|	←	|	...	...	|	|	...	|	|	1848	|	←	|	|	1941	|	|	...
Montabaur d.	1718	|	|	|	1747**r**	1758	|	1805	|	...	...	|	|	...	|	1847**r**	1858	|	1905	|	|	1952	|	|	...
Siegburg/Bonn 🚊 **801** d.	1739	|	|	|	1811	→	|	1825	1832	...	...	|	|	...	1901	1910	→	|	1925	|	|	2013	2032	2032	...
Köln/Bonn Flughafen ✈ **801** d.	1749	|	|	|	|	...	|	|	|	...	...	|	|	...	|	|	...	|	1939	|	|	|	|	|	...
Köln Messe/Deutz **801** a.	|	|	|	1814	1825	...	|	|	1848	...	...	|	|	...	1915	1927	...	|	|	|	|	2027	2048	2048	...
Köln Hbf **801** a.	1801	1806	1805	|	|	...	1833	1844	|	...	...	1905	1906	...	|	|	...	1933	1955	2006	2005	|	|	|	...
Köln Hbf **802 806** d.	...	1811	1811	|	|	...	1841	...	|	...	1909	1911	1912	...	|	|	...	1942	...	2011	2011	|	|	|	...
Aachen Hbf **802 806** a.	...	|	|	|	|	...	|	...	|	...	|	|	|	...	|	|	...	2016	...	|	|	|	|	|	...
Brussels Midi/Zuid **21** a.	...	|	|	|	|	...	|	...	|	...	|	|	|	...	|	|	...	2135	...	|	|	|	|	|	...
Köln Messe/Deutz d.	...	|	|	1817	1830	...	|	...	1850	...	|	|	|	...	1917	1931	...	...	...	|	|	2030	2050	2050	...
Solingen Hbf d.	...	|	1830	|	|	...	|	...	|	...	1926	|	1931	...	|	|	...	...	...	|	2030	|	|	|	...
Wuppertal Hbf d.	...	|	1844	|	|	...	|	...	|	...	1943	|	1948	...	|	|	...	...	...	|	2044	|	|	|	...
Hagen Hbf d.	...	|	1901	|	|	...	|	...	|	...	2001	|	2007	...	|	|	...	...	...	|	2101	|	|	|	...
Düsseldorf Hbf d.	...	1834	|	1838	1859**r**	...	1908	...	1914	...	|	1934	|	...	1938	1957	...	...	...	2034	|	2051	2111	2111	...
Düsseldorf Flughafen ✈ d.	...	|	|	|	|	...	|	...	|	...	|	|	|	...	|	|	...	...	...	|	|	|	|	|	...
Duisburg Hbf d.	...	1847	|	1851	1915	...	1925	...	1928	...	|	1947	|	...	1951	2017	...	...	...	2047	|	2104	2126	2129	...
Oberhausen Hbf d.	...	|	|	|	1923	...	1933	...	|	...	|	|	|	...	|	|	...	...	...	|	|	|	|	|	...
Amsterdam Centraal **28** a.	...	|	|	|	|	...	2129	...	|	...	|	|	|	...	|	|	...	...	...	|	|	|	2329	|	...
Essen Hbf d.	...	1900	|	1904	|	...	...	...	1942	...	|	2000	|	...	2004	2034	...	...	...	2100	|	2117	...	2142	...
Gelsenkirchen Hbf d.	...	|	|	|	1935	...	...	...	|	...	|	|	|	...	|	|	...	...	...	|	|	|	...	|	...
Wanne-Eickel Hbf d.	...	|	|	|	1941	...	...	...	|	...	|	|	|	...	|	|	...	...	...	|	|	|	...	|	...
Recklinghausen Hbf d.	...	|	|	|	1949	...	...	...	|	...	|	|	|	...	|	|	...	...	...	|	|	|	...	|	...
Bochum Hbf d.	...	1910	|	1914	|	...	...	...	1951	...	|	2010	|	...	2014	2045	...	...	...	2110	|	2127	...	2151	...
Dortmund Hbf a.	...	1921	1921	1927	|	...	...	...	2003	...	2021	2021	2030	...	2027	2057	...	...	...	2121	2121	2140	...	2203	...
Dortmund Hbf **805** d.	...	...	1925	...	|	...	...	...	...	...	2028	2025	...	...	...	...	...	...	...	...	2125	...	...	...	...
Hamm (Westf) **805** a.	...	...	|	...	|	...	...	...	...	...	2043	|	...	...	...	...	...	...	...	...	|	...	...	...	...
Münster (Westf) Hbf **802** d.	...	...	1957	...	2026	...	...	...	...	...	...	2057	...	...	...	...	...	...	...	...	2157	...	...	...	...
Osnabrück Hbf **802 815** d.	...	...	2023	...	...	...	...	...	...	...	...	2123	...	...	...	...	...	...	...	...	2223	...	...	...	...
Berlin Hbf **810** a.	...	...	|	...	...	...	...	...	...	...	...	|	...	...	...	...	...	...	...	...	|	...	...	...	...
Bremen Hbf **815** ☆ d.	...	...	2117	...	...	...	...	...	...	...	...	2219	...	...	...	...	...	...	...	...	2317	...	...	...	...
Hamburg Harburg ☆ a.	...	...	2201	...	...	...	...	...	...	...	...	2303	...	...	...	...	...	...	...	...	0001	...	...	...	...
Hamburg Hbf ☆ a.	...	...	2214	...	...	...	...	...	...	...	...	2316	...	...	...	...	...	...	...	...	0014	...	...	...	...
Hamburg Altona a.	...	...	2230	...	...	...	...	...	...	...	...	2331	...	...	...	...	...	...	...	...	0030	...	...	...	...

FOR NOTES, SEE PAGE 375 →

FRANKFURT - KÖLN - DORTMUND - HAMBURG 800

See Table **802** for Rhein-Ruhr regional services. See Table **810** for services to Berlin via Bielefeld and Hannover. See Table **927** for FlixTrain services.

IMPORTANT! SEE NOTE ⊠	*ICE* **1556**	*IC* **2349**	*IC* **2349**	*ICE* **102**	*ICE* **102**		*ICE* **528**	*ICE* **1120**	*ICE* **318**	*ICE* **810**		*ICE* **1222**	*ICE* **512**	*ICE* **526**	*ICE* **512**	*ICE* **910**	*ICE* **1554**	*IC* **2347**	*ICE* **100**	*ICE* **524**		*ICE* **510**	*ICE* **522**	*ICE* **920**	
		A	**R**	**F**	**Z**			Ⓑ	⑦■	①–⑥								**C**						**B**	
	◇			H✕	H✕		✕	L✕	✕	U✕		✕	✕	✕		✕	◇		✕	✕		✕	✕		
München Hbf **904 910** d.	...	...	...	...	...	...	1648	1733	...	...	...	1618	1727	1751	...	1827	...	...	...	1847	...	1927	1947	...	...
Stuttgart Hbf **910** d.	...	1737	1737	...	...	...	│	│	...	...	...	│	1951	│	...	2038	...	1915y	...	│	...	2151	│	...	...
Basel SBB 🏛 **910** d.	...	│	│	1713	1713	...	│	│	...	...	...	│	│	│	...	│	...	│	1913	│	...	│	│	...	...
Karlsruhe Hbf **910** d.	...	│	│	1901	1901	...	│	│	...	...	...	│	│	│	...	│	...	│	2102	│	...	│	│	...	...
Mannheim Hbf **910** d.	...	1839	1839	1935	1935	...	│	│	...	...	...	│	2035	│	...	2120	...	2039	2135	│	...	2236	│	...	...
Wien Hbf **950** d.	...	│	│	│	│	...	│	│	...	...	...	│	│	│	...	│	...	│	│	│	...	│	│	...	...
Passau Hbf **920** d.	...	│	│	│	│	...	│	│	...	...	...	│	│	│	...	│	...	│	│	│	...	│	│	...	...
Nürnberg Hbf **920** d.	...	│	│	│	│	...	1757	1841	...	...	...	1736	│	1903	...	│	...	│	│	1958	...	│	2058	...	...
Frankfurt (Main) Hbf **914** d.	1842	│	│	│	│	...	2009	│	2015	2031	...	1942	│	2109	...	│	2043	│	│	2209	...	│	2309	2324	...
Frankfurt Flughafen ✈ § **914** d.	1857	│	│	2010	2010	...	2024	2042	2030	2050	...	1957	2109	2123	...	2154	2059	│	2208	2223	...	2309	2324	2339	...
Mainz Hbf **914** d.	1915a	1920	1920	│	│	...	│	│	│	│	...	2020	│	│	...	│	2115a	2120	│	│	...	│	│	0001	...
Wiesbaden Hbf d.	1933	│	│	│	│	...	│	│	│	│	...	│	│	│	...	│	2133	│	│	│	...	│	│	│	...
Koblenz Hbf **914** d.	...	2013	2013	│	│	...	│	│	│	│	...	2113	│	│	...	│	...	2213	│	│	...	│	│	0058	...
Andernach d.	...	│	│	│	│	...	│	│	│	│	...	│	│	│	...	│	...	│	│	│	...	│	│	0110	...
Remagen d.	...	│	│	│	│	...	│	│	│	│	...	│	│	│	...	│	...	│	│	│	...	│	│	0122	...
Bonn Hbf d.	...	2045	2045	│	│	...	│	│	│	│	...	2145	│	│	...	│	...	2245	│	│	...	│	│	0138	...
Limburg Süd d.	...	│	│	│	│	...	│	│	2048	2109	...	│	│	│	...	│	...	│	│	2241	...	│	2343	│	...
Montabaur d.	...	│	│	│	│	...	│	│	2106	2120	...	│	│	│	...	│	...	│	│	2252	...	│	2353	│	...
Siegburg/Bonn 🚋 **801** d.	...	│	│	│	│	...	│	│	│	2140	...	│	2151	│	...	2232	...	│	2251	2313	...	2351	0013	│	...
Köln/Bonn Flughafen ✈ **801** d.	...	│	│	│	│	...	│	│	│	│	...	│	│	│	...	│	...	│	│	2327	...	│	│	│	...
Köln Messe/Deutz **801** a.	...	│	│	│	│	...	2114	2130	│	2154	...	│	│	2214	...	2247	...	│	│	2336	...	│	│	│	...
Köln Hbf **801** a.	...	2106	2106	2105	2105	...	│	│	2139	2202	...	2206	2206	│	...	│	...	2306	2306	│	...	0006	0029	0205	...
Köln Hbf **802 806** d.	...	2111	2109	2111	2111	...	│	│	2142	...	...	2210	2212	│	...	│	...	...	2312	│	...	...	...	0209	...
Aachen Hbf **802 806** a.	...	│	│	│	│	...	│	│	2216	...	...	│	│	│	...	│	...	...	│	│	...	...	...	│	...
Brussels Midi/Zuid **21** a.	...	│	│	│	│	...	│	│	2335	...	...	│	│	│	...	│	...	...	│	│	...	...	...	│	...
Köln Messe/Deutz d.	...	│	│	│	│	...	2117	2132	...	...	...	│	│	2217	...	2249	...	...	│	2338	...	...	...	│	...
Solingen Hbf d.	...	2130	│	│	2130	...	│	│	...	...	...	2230	│	│	...	│	...	...	│	│	...	...	...	│	...
Wuppertal Hbf d.	...	2144	│	│	2144	...	│	│	...	...	...	2244	│	│	...	│	...	...	│	│	...	...	...	│	...
Hagen Hbf d.	...	2201	│	│	2201	...	│	│	...	...	...	2301	│	│	...	│	...	...	│	│	...	...	...	│	...
Düsseldorf Hbf d.	...	│	2134	2134	│	...	2138	2151	...	...	...	│	2235	2238	...	2312	...	...	2335	2359	...	...	...	0233	...
Düsseldorf Flughafen ✈ d.	...	│	│	│	│	...	│	...	...	...	...	│	│	│	...	│	...	...	2342	│	...	...	...	0240	...
Duisburg Hbf d.	...	│	2147	2147	│	...	2151	...	...	...	...	│	2248	2251	...	2327	...	...	2352	0012	...	...	...	0251	...
Oberhausen Hbf d.	...	│	│	│	│	...	│	...	...	...	...	│	│	│	...	│	...	...	│	│	...	...	...	│	...
Amsterdam Centraal **28** a.	...	│	│	│	│	...	│	...	...	...	...	│	│	│	←	│	...	...	│	│	...	...	...	│	...
Essen Hbf d.	...	│	2200	2200	│	...	2204	...	...	...	...	│	2259	2304	2308	2342	...	...	0004	0025	...	...	...	0306	...
Gelsenkirchen Hbf d.	...	│	│	│	│	...	│	...	...	...	...	│	→	│	2321	│	...	...	│	│	...	...	...	│	...
Wanne-Eickel Hbf d.	...	│	│	│	│	...	│	...	...	...	...	│	...	│	│	│	...	...	│	│	...	...	...	│	...
Recklinghausen Hbf d.	...	│	│	│	│	...	│	...	...	...	...	│	...	│	2334	│	...	...	│	│	...	...	...	│	...
Bochum Hbf d.	...	│	│	2210	│	...	2214	...	...	...	...	│	...	2314	│	2351	...	...	0014	0035	...	...	...	0316	...
Dortmund Hbf a.	...	2221	2233	2221	2221	...	2227	...	...	...	...	2321	...	2327	│	0003	...	...	0027	0048	...	...	...	0327	...
Dortmund Hbf **805** d.	...	...	...	2228	2228	...	...	...	...	...	...	...	...	...	│	...	...	...	0033	...	...	...	...	0332	...
Hamm (Westf) **805** a.	...	...	...	2243	2243	...	...	...	...	...	...	...	...	...	│	...	...	...	0049	...	...	...	...	0350	...
Münster (Westf) Hbf **802** d.	...	...	...	...	...	...	...	...	...	...	...	...	...	...	0001	...	...	...	│	...	...	...	...	0415	...
Osnabrück Hbf **802 815** d.	...	...	...	...	...	...	...	...	...	...	...	...	...	...	...	...	...	...	│	...	...	...	...	0450	...
Berlin Hbf **810** a.	...	...	...	...	...	...	...	...	...	...	...	...	...	...	...	...	...	...	0536	...	...	...	...	│	...
Bremen Hbf **815** ☆ d.	...	...	...	...	...	...	...	...	...	...	...	...	...	...	...	...	...	...	...	...	...	...	...	0554	...
Hamburg Harburg ☆ a.	...	...	...	...	...	...	...	...	...	...	...	...	...	...	...	...	...	...	...	...	...	...	...	0638	...
Hamburg Hbf ☆ a.	...	...	...	...	...	...	...	...	...	...	...	...	...	...	...	...	...	...	...	...	...	...	...	0650	...
Hamburg Altona a.	...	...	...	...	...	...	...	...	...	...	...	...	...	...	...	...	...	...	...	...	...	...	...	0706	...

♦ – **NOTES** (LISTED BY TRAIN NUMBER) FOR PAGES 372 – 375.

6 – 🚃12 ✕ Interlaken - Bern - Basel - Dortmund.
8 – 🚃12 ✕ Zürich - Basel - Hamburg.
114 – WÖRTHERSEE – 🚃12 ✕ Klagenfurt - Salzburg - München - Dortmund.
118 – BODENSEE – 🚃12 ✕ Innsbruck - Lindau - Ulm - Stuttgart - Münster.
402 – 🛏 1, 2 cl. and 🛏 2 cl. (Ⓡ) Zürich - Amsterdam. Also conveys 🚃2 (*IC* **60402**).
2012 – ALLGÄU – 🚃12 Oberstdorf (Table **935**) - Ulm - Stuttgart - Köln - Dortmund. Also calls at Bingen (Rhein) Hbf (d. 1507).
2043 – 🚃12 Köln - Hannover (- Magdeburg Ⓑ) (- Leipzig ⑤⑦). Until Aug. 8 runs only to Bielefeld.
2047 – 🚃12 Tübingen - Stuttgart - Köln - Hannover - Leipzig - Dresden.
2157 – 🚃12 Köln - Paderborn - Kassel - Erfurt (- Gera Ⓑ).

A – ①②④⑤⑦ June 8 - July 25 and Oct. 31 - Dec. 12.
B – Also calls at Bingen (Rhein) Hbf (d. 0019).
C – Not July 26 - Sept. 5.
D – July 26 - Sept. 5.
E – To Emden (Table **812**).
F – Not Sept. 5 - Oct. 30.
G – To Gera via Paderborn and Kassel (Tables **805** and **849a**).
H – To Hannover (Table **810**).
J – To Dresden via Hannover and Leipzig (Table **810**). Until Aug. 8 runs only to Bielefeld.
K – To Kiel (Table **820**).
L – From Aug. 9.
N – To Norddeich Mole (Table **812**).
P – To München via Kassel (Tables **805** and **900**).
Q – To Ostseebad Binz via Stralsund until July 31 (Tables **844** and **845**).
R – ①②④⑤⑦ Sept. 7 - Oct. 30.
T – From Tübingen (Table **936**).
U – From Nov. 3.
V – Not Sept. 6 - Oct. 31.
W – Sept. 6 - Oct. 31.
X – From Luxembourg (Table **915**).
Y – To Westerland (Table **821**).
Z – Sept. 5 - Oct. 30.

a – Arrival time.
b – Bonn **Beuel**.
d – Also operates on June 13, Dec. 5.
e – From Sept. 24.
f – 5 – 6 minutes later on ⑤.
g – From Aug. 1.
h – Not June 7 - 14.
j – Arrives 1802.
n – Not June 7 - July 23.
r – Arrives 7 – 9 minutes earlier.
t – Arrives 0648.
v – 0944 on ⑤–⑦. 1044 on June 21, Oct. 4, 10, 11, 13, 17, 18.
y – 1936 on ⑤–⑦.
z – 2117 on ⑦.

⊖ – ①②③④⑥.
⊡ – ④⑤⑥ to Nov. 1; ⑥ from Nov. 8.
♠ – ⑥⑦ to Nov. 2; ⑥ from Nov. 8. To Emden (Table **912**).
■ – Runs daily until Nov. 2.
◇ – From stations in Table **850**.
△ – On June 13 - 15, June 27 - Aug. 24, Oct. 20 - Nov. 2, Dec. 5 - 7 runs with train number **1212**, departs Siegburg/Bonn 2038 and does not call at Köln Messe/Deutz.
⊙ – Also calls at Boppard Hbf (d. 0758).
⊗ – Subject to alteration June 14, 15, June 28 - Aug. 24, Oct. 20 - Nov. 2, Dec. 6, 7 (see panel below for amended Amsterdam services during these periods). Note that international journeys to / from Amsterdam are Ⓡ May 28 - Aug. 31.
⊕ – Subject to alteration Oct. 20 - Nov. 2, Dec. 5 - 7 (see panel below for amended timings).
§ – Frankfurt Flughafen Fernbahnhof.
🚋 – Frequent light-rail services operate from / to Bonn Hbf.
☆ – Local trains Bremen - Hamburg (operated by *metronom*). Journey time: 70 – 90 minutes. **From Bremen** Hbf at 0015 Ⓒ, 0114 Ⓒ, 0314 Ⓒ, 0433 Ⓐ, 0458, 0528 Ⓐ, 0558, 0626 Ⓐ, 0633 Ⓒ, 0658, 0733, 0758, 0833, 0859, 0933, 0958 and at 33 and 58 minutes past each hour until 2033, 2058; then 2133 ⑤⑥, 2158 and 2312.
⊠ – **WARNING!** The section of line between Essen and Dortmund will be closed **from Sept. 6 to Oct. 31** (also from late evening on Sept. 5) with trains diverted via alternative routes. Only local S-Bahn services will serve Bochum during this period. Many long-distance services between Köln and Dortmund will affected by this closure including diversions and amended timings (earlier departures possible); **station calls at Essen and Dortmund may also be omitted**. Unfortunately we do not have space to include all of these changes in our tables so readers are strongly advised to check journey plans during this period.

Amended Amsterdam service June 14, 15, June 28 - Aug. 24, Oct. 20 - Nov. 2, Dec. 6, 7

	ICE **250**	*ICE* **158**	*ICE* **156**	*ICE* **154**	*ICE* **152**	*ICE* **152**	*ICE* **252**		*ICE* **254**
					⑥⑦	①–⑤			**d**
	✕	✕	✕	✕	✕	✕	✕		✕
München Hbf **910** d.	...	...	...	...	...	...	...	...	1628
Frankfurt (Main) Hbf d.	0727	0927	1127	1327	1527	1527	1727	...	│
Frankfurt Flughafen Fernbf ✈ d.	0741	0941	1141	1341	1541	1541	1741	...	1954
Siegburg/Bonn d.	│	│	│	│	│	│	│	...	2035
Köln Hbf d.	0839	1039	1239	1440	1639	1639	1839	...	2105
Mönchengladbach Hbf d.	0944	1131	1330	1530	1732	1732	1930	...	2151
's-Hertogenbosch a.	1125	1254	1454	1651	1854	1854	2054	...	2308
Utrecht Centraal a.	1154	1324	1524	1723	1924	1924	2124	...	2338
Amsterdam Centraal a.	1222	1353	1552f	1752f	1952	1958	2153	...	0015

800 FRANKFURT - KÖLN - DORTMUND - HAMBURG

See Table 802 for Rhein-Ruhr regional services. See Table 810 for services from Berlin via Hannover and Bielefeld. See Table 927 for FlixTrain services.

km	km	IMPORTANT! SEE NOTE ⊠	ICE	ICE	ICE	ICE	ICE	ICE	ICE	ICE	ICE	ICE		IC	IC	ICE	ICE		ICE	ICE	ICE	ICE	ICE	
			827	827	521	523	511	811	711	1121	525	101		2040	2040	1557	913		813	813	527	1621	513	
			①–⑥			①–⑥		①–⑤	①–⑤	①–⑤				C	D		①–⑥			①–⑤				
							✕	✕	L✕	✕L	✕	✕		🍷	🍷	◇	✕		✕	✕	✕	✕	✕	
0		**Hamburg** Altona d.	...	...	...	...	...	...	...	...	...	...	...	...	...	...	...	...	...	...	...	...	...	...
7		**Hamburg** Hbf ☆ d.	...	...	...	...	...	...	...	...	...	...	...	...	...	...	...	...	...	...	...	...	...	...
19		**Hamburg** Harburg ☆ d.	...	...	...	...	...	...	...	...	...	...	...	...	...	...	...	...	...	...	...	...	...	...
122		**Bremen** Hbf 815 ☆ d.	...	...	...	...	...	...	...	...	...	...	...	...	...	...	...	...	...	...	...	...	...	...
		Berlin Hbf **810** d.	...	...	...	...	...	...	...	...	...	0022	...	...	...	...	...	...	...	...	...	...	...	...
244		Osnabrück Hbf **802 815** d.	...	...	...	...	...	...	...	...	...	|	...	...	...	...	...	...	...	...	...	...	...	...
294	0	Münster (Westf) Hbf **802** d.	...	...	...	...	...	...	...	...	...	|	...	0502	0502	...	...	...	...	...	...	...	0603	...
		Hamm (Westf) **805** d.	...	...	...	...	...	...	...	...	...	0503	...	|	|	...	...	...	...	...	...	...	|	...
350		**Dortmund** Hbf **805** a.	...	...	...	...	...	...	...	...	...	0521	...	0532	0532	...	...	...	...	...	...	...	0632	...
350		**Dortmund** Hbf d.	...	...	...	0405	...	...	...	...	0523	0536	...	0536	0536	...	0548	...	...	0555	0623	0636	0636	...
		Bochum Hbf d.	...	...	...	0418	...	...	...	...	0536	0548	...	|	|	...	0602	...	...	|	0636	|	0648	...
	58	Recklinghausen Hbf d.	...	...	...	|	...	...	...	...	|	|	...	|	|	...	|	...	...	|	|	|	|	...
	68	Wanne-Eickel Hbf d.	...	...	...	|	...	...	...	...	|	|	...	|	|	...	|	...	...	|	|	|	|	...
	73	Gelsenkirchen Hbf d.	...	...	...	|	...	...	...	...	|	|	...	|	|	...	|	...	...	|	|	|	|	...
		Essen Hbf d.	...	...	...	0430	...	...	...	...	0553	0600	...	|	|	...	0614	...	...	|	0654	|	0700	...
		Amsterdam Centraal **28** d.	...	...	...	|	...	...	...	...	|	|	...	|	|	...	|	...	...	|	|	|	|	...
	89	Oberhausen Hbf d.	...	...	...	|	...	...	...	...	|	|	...	|	|	...	|	...	...	|	|	|	|	...
	97	**Duisburg** Hbf d.	...	...	...	0443	...	...	...	...	0607	0613	...	|	|	...	0627	...	...	|	0708	|	0713	...
	114	Düsseldorf Flughafen ✈ d.	...	...	...	|	...	...	...	...	|	|	...	|	|	...	|	...	...	|	|	|	|	...
	121	**Düsseldorf** Hbf d.	...	...	...	0457	...	...	...	0607	0621	0627	...	|	|	...	0647	...	...	|	0721	|	0727	...
381		**Hagen** Hbf d.	...	...	...	|	...	...	...	|	|	|	...	0558	0558	...	|	...	...	0619	|	0658	|	...
408		Wuppertal Hbf d.	...	...	...	|	...	...	...	|	|	|	...	0615	0615	...	|	...	...	0636	|	0715	|	...
426		Solingen Hbf d.	...	...	...	|	...	...	...	|	|	|	...	0627	0627	...	|	...	...	0647	|	0727	|	...
453	160	**Köln** Messe/Deutz a.	...	...	...	0518	...	...	...	0627	0642	|	...	|	|	...	0708	...	...	|	0742	|	|	...
		Brussels Midi/Zuid **21** d.	...	...	...	|	...	...	...	|	|	|	...	|	|	...	|	...	...	|	|	|	|	...
		Aachen Hbf **802 806** d.	...	...	...	|	...	...	...	|	|	|	...	|	|	...	|	...	...	|	|	|	|	...
454	161	**Köln** Hbf **802 806** a.	...	...	...	|	...	...	...	|	|	0649	...	0647	0647	...	|	...	...	0708	|	0747	0749	...
454		**Köln** Hbf **801** d.	0321	0321	0420	|	0548	0600	0601	|	|	0655	...	0653	0653	...	|	...	0718	0718	|	0753	0755	...
		Köln Messe/Deutz **801** d.	|	|	|	0520	|	|	|	0629	0644	|	...	|	|	...	0710	...	|	|	0744	|	|	...
		Köln/Bonn Flughafen ✈ **801** d.	0334	0334	|	0531	|	|	|	|	|	|	...	|	|	...	|	...	|	|	|	|	|	...
		Siegburg/Bonn 🚋 **801** d.	0343	0343	0437	0541	0604	0615	0624	|	|	|	...	|	|	...	0724	...	0735	0735	|	|	|	...
		Montabaur d.	0403	0403	0457	0602	|	0636	0644	|	|	|	...	|	|	...	|	...	0756	0756	|	|	|	...
		Limburg Süd d.	0414	0414	0508	0613	|	0647	0654	|	|	|	...	|	|	...	|	...	0807	0807	|	|	|	...
488		**Bonn** Hbf d.	|	|	|	|	|	|	|	|	|	|	...	0715	0715	...	|	...	|	|	|	0815	|	...
508		Remagen d.	|	|	|	|	|	|	|	|	|	|	...	|	|	...	|	...	|	|	|	|	|	...
529		Andernach d.	|	|	|	|	|	|	|	|	|	|	...	|	|	...	|	...	|	|	|	|	|	...
547		**Koblenz** Hbf **914** d.	|	|	|	|	|	|	|	|	|	|	...	0748	0748	...	|	...	|	|	|	0848	|	...
		Wiesbaden Hbf **914** a.	|	|	|	|	|	|	0720	|	|	|	...	|	|	0826	|	...	|	|	|	|	|	...
638		**Mainz** Hbf a.	|	|	|	|	|	|	0744	|	|	|	...	0839	0839	0843**d**	|	...	|	|	|	0939	|	...
664		**Frankfurt** Flughafen ✈ § **914** a.	0433	0433	0526	0633	0649	0708	|	0717	0733	0749	...	|	|	0859	0806	...	0826	0826	0833	0958	0849	...
675		**Frankfurt** (Main) Hbf **914** a.	0448	0448	0540	0648	|	0723	|	|	0748	|	...	|	|	0913	|	...	0841	0841	0848	1013	|	...
		Nürnberg Hbf **920** a.	0658	...	0756	0858	|	...	|	0915	0956	|	...	|	|	...	|	...	...	...	1100	1224	|	...
		Passau Hbf **920** a.	|	...	|	|	|	...	|	|	|	|	...	|	|	...	|	...	...	...	|	|	|	...
		Wien Hbf **950** a.	|	...	|	|	|	...	|	|	|	|	...	|	|	...	|	...	...	...	|	|	|	...
		Mannheim Hbf **910** a.	|	...	|	|	0723	...	0824	|	|	0823	...	0921	0921	...	0840	...	...	...	|	|	0923	...
		Karlsruhe Hbf **910** a.	|	...	|	|	|	...	|	|	|	0858	...	|	1016	...	|	...	...	...	|	|	|	...
		Basel SBB 🏛 **910** a.	|	...	|	|	|	...	|	|	|	1048**e**	...	|	...	...	|	...	...	...	|	|	|	...
		Stuttgart Hbf **910** a.	|	...	|	|	0808	...	0918	|	|	...	...	1024	...	...	0922	...	...	...	|	|	1008	...
		München Hbf **904 910** a.	0806	...	0906	1006	1026	...	...	1020	1107	...	...	...	...	...	1126	...	...	...	1210	1343	1226	...

♦ – **NOTES** (LISTED BY TRAIN NUMBER) FOR PAGES 376–379.

7 – [12] ✕ Hamburg - Basel - Bern - Interlaken.
9 – [12] ✕ Dortmund - Basel - Zürich.
115 – WÖRTHERSEE – [12] ✕ Münster - München - Salzburg - Schwarzach-St Veit.
119 – BODENSEE – [12] ✕ Dortmund - Stuttgart - Ulm - Lindau - Innsbruck.
403 – 🛏 1, 2 cl. and 🛏 2 cl. ([R]) Amsterdam - Zürich. Also conveys [2] (*IC* **60403**).
2013 – ALLGÄU – [12] Dortmund - Köln - Stuttgart - Ulm (*RE* **2013**) - Oberstdorf (Table **935**). Also calls at Bingen (Rhein) Hbf (d. 1252).
2042 – [12] (Leipzig ① -) (Magdeburg ①–⑥ -) Hannover - Köln. Until Aug. 8 starts from Bielefeld.
2048 – [12] Dresden - Leipzig - Hannover - Hamm - Köln - Stuttgart - Tübingen. Until Aug. 8 starts from Bielefeld.
2156 – [12] (Gera ①–⑥ -) Erfurt - Kassel - Paderborn - Köln.

A – To Düren (a. 1823) and Aachen Hbf (a. 1846).
B – Runs Aug. 9 - Dec. 13. To Düren (a. 1851) and Aachen Hbf (a. 1912). On ①②③ runs with train number **1546** and terminates at Düsseldorf.
C – Not July 26 - Sept. 5.
D – July 26 - Sept. 5.
E – From Emden (Table **812**).
F – Aug. 9 - Dec. 13.
G – From Gera via Paderborn and Kassel (Tables **805** and **849a**).
H – From Hannover (Table **810**).
J – From Dresden via Leipzig and Hannover (Table **810**). Until Aug. 8 starts from Bielefeld.
K – From Kiel (Table **820**).
L – From Aug. 9.
M – From München via Kassel and Paderborn (Tables **805** and **900**).
N – From Norddeich Mole (Table **812**).
Q – From Ostseebad Binz via Stralsund (Tables **844** and **845**).
R – Not Aug. 9 - Sept. 5.
S – Aug. 9 - Sept. 5.
V – Not Sept. 6 - Oct. 31.
W – Sept. 6 - Oct. 31.
X – To Luxembourg (Table **915**).
Y – From Westerland (Table **821**).
Z – From Stralsund on ⑥⑦ to July 27 (Table **830**).

a – ①–⑤ (daily from July 28).
b – Bonn **Beuel**.
c – Arrives 8–12 minutes earlier.
d – Departure time.
e – From June 15.
f – July 26 - Aug. 8 terminates at Karlsruhe (2216) not serving Stuttgart.
j – Arrives 0457.
k – 1625 on ⑥⑦.
n – From July 23.
q – Not Oct. 2.
t – Mornings of ②–⑦ only. Arrives 0059 on mornings of ⑥⑦.
v – ⑦ only.

⊖ – ①②③④⑥⑦.
♣ – ③④⑤⑦ to Nov. 2; ⑤⑦ from Nov. 7.
♠ – ⑥⑦ to Nov. 2; ⑥ from Nov. 8.
■ – On ①–⑥ Nov. 3 - Dec. 13 runs Köln Hbf - Frankfurt only (numbered *ICE* **909**).
⊡ – Also calls at Bingen (Rhein) Hbf (d. 2123).
⊙ – Also calls at Bingen (Rhein) Hbf (d. 0608).
⊗ – Subject to alteration June 14, 15, June 28 - Aug. 24, Oct. 20 - Nov. 2, Dec. 6, 7 (see panel below for amended Amsterdam services during these periods). Note that international journeys to / from Amsterdam are [R] May 28 - Aug. 31.
◇ – To stations in Table **850**.
§ – Frankfurt Flughafen Fernbahnhof.
* – Calls before Düsseldorf.
🚋 – Frequent light-rail services operate from / to Bonn Hbf.
☆ – Local trains Hamburg - Bremen (operated by *metronom*). Journey time: 70–90 minutes. **From Hamburg** Hbf at 0057 ©, 0256 ©, 0457, 0536, 0558 Ⓐ, 0615 ©, 0637, 0715, 0736, 0815, 0837 and at 15 and 37 minutes past each hour until 2115, 2137; then 2237 and 2337.
⊠ – **WARNING!** The section of line between Dortmund and Essen will be closed **from Sept. 6 to Oct. 31** (also from late evening on Sept. 5) with trains diverted via alternative routes. Only local S-Bahn services will serve Bochum during this period. Many long-distance services between Dortmund and Köln will affected by this closure including diversions and amended timings (earlier departures possible); **station calls at Dortmund and Essen may also be omitted**. Unfortunately we do not have space to include all of these changes in our tables so readers are strongly advised to check journey plans during this period.

Amended Amsterdam service June 14, 15, June 28 - Aug. 24, Oct. 20 - Nov. 2, Dec. 6, 7

	ICE	ICE	ICE	ICE	ICE	ICE	ICE	ICE	ICE
	253	253	255	255	153	155	157	159	251
	①–⑥	⑦	①–④	⑤–⑦					
	✕	✕	✕	✕	✕	✕	✕	✕	✕
Amsterdam Centraal d.	0601	0604	0737	0746	1001	1201	1401	1601	1801
Utrecht Centraal d.	0627	0638	0808	0813	1027	1227	1427	1627	1827
Venlo d.	0752	0752	|	|	1152	1352	1552	1752	1952
Mönchengladbach Hbf a.	0831	0831	|	|	1229	1431	1631	1831	2031
Köln Hbf a.	0921	0921	1103	1103	1321	1521	1721	1923	2121
Siegburg/Bonn a.	|	|	1125	1125	|	|	|	|	|
Frankfurt Flughafen Fernbf ✈ a.	1017	1017	1206	1206	1417	1617	1817	2017	2217
Frankfurt (Main) Hbf a.	1031	1031	|	|	1431	1631	1831	2031	2231
München Hbf **910** a.	...	...	1527	1527	...	...	...	...	...

HAMBURG - DORTMUND - KÖLN - FRANKFURT 800

See Table **802** for Rhein-Ruhr regional services. See Table **810** for services from Berlin via Hannover and Bielefeld. See Table **927** for FlixTrain services.

IMPORTANT! SEE NOTE ⊠	ICE 815	ICE 11	ICE 815	ICE 115	ICE 529	EC 7	EC 7	ICE 1559	ICE 103	ICE 915	ICE 119	ICE 121	ICE 621	ICE 1031	ICE 515	ICE 27	ICE 27	ICE 817	ICE 13	IC 2005	ICE 623	EC 9	EC 9	IC 2042	ICE 1651
	①–⑤		①–⑤			V	W							①–④		W	V			①–⑥		W	V		
	✗	✗	✗	✗◆	✗	✗◆	✗◆	◇	H✗	✗	✗◆	⊗✗	✗	q✗	✗	✗	✗	✗	✗	E🍷	✗	✗◆	✗◆	◆🍷	◇
Hamburg Altona d.	...	...	...	...	...	0421	0421	...	...	...	...	...	...	0556	0529	...	...	...	...	...	...	...	...	...	...
Hamburg Hbf ☆ d.	...	...	...	...	...	0438	0438	...	...	...	...	...	...	0611	0546	...	...	...	...	...	...	...	...	...	...
Hamburg Harburg ☆ d.	...	...	...	...	...	0450	0450	...	...	...	...	...	...	|	0557	...	...	...	...	...	...	...	...	...	...
Bremen Hbf **815** ☆ d.	...	...	...	...	...	0540	0540	...	...	...	...	...	...	|	0644	...	...	...	...	...	...	...	...	...	...
Berlin Hbf **810** d.	...	...	...	...	...	|	|	...	...	...	...	...	...	|	|	...	...	...	...	...	...	...	...	...	...
Osnabrück Hbf **802 815** d.	...	...	...	...	...	0637	0637	...	...	...	...	...	...	|	0737	...	...	...	...	...	...	...	...	...	...
Münster (Westf) Hbf **802** d.	...	...	...	0631	...	0703	0703	...	...	...	...	...	...	|	0803	...	...	...	...	0832	...	...	...	...	...
Hamm (Westf) **805** d.	...	...	...	|	...	|	|	...	0715	...	...	...	...	|	|	...	...	...	...	|	...	...	...	0917	...
Dortmund Hbf **805** a.	...	...	...	|	...	0732	|	...	0731	...	...	...	...	|	0832	...	...	...	...	|	...	...	...	0932	...
Dortmund Hbf d.	...	...	...	|	0723	0736	|	...	0736	0750	0753	...	...	|	0836	0823	0835	...	...	|	0915**v**	0924	0925	0936	...
Bochum Hbf d.	...	...	...	|	0736	0748	|	...	|	0802	|	...	...	|	|	|	0848	...	...	|	0929**v**	|	0937	|	...
Recklinghausen Hbf d.	...	...	...	0701	|	|	|	...	|	|	|	...	...	|	|	|	|	...	...	0900	|	|	|	|	...
Wanne-Eickel Hbf d.	...	...	...	0709	|	|	|	...	|	|	|	...	...	|	|	0843	|	...	...	0909	|	0944	|	|	...
Gelsenkirchen Hbf d.	...	...	...	0715	|	|	0744	...	|	|	|	...	...	|	|	|	|	...	...	0914	|	|	|	|	...
Essen Hbf d.	...	...	...	|	0753	0800	0800	...	|	0814	|	...	0849	0856	|	|	0900	...	...	|	0939	|	0951	|	...
Amsterdam Centraal **28** d.	...	...	...	|	|	|	|	...	|	|	|	0638	|	|	|	|	|	...	...	|	|	|	|	|	...
Oberhausen Hbf d.	...	...	...	0726	|	|	|	...	|	|	|	0833	|	|	|	0902	|	...	...	0926	|	1002	|	|	...
Duisburg Hbf d.	...	...	...	0734	0808	0813	0813	...	|	0827	|	0841	0903	0909	|	0913	0913	...	...	0934	0953	|	1005	|	...
Düsseldorf Flughafen ✈ d.	...	...	...	|	|	|	|	...	|	|	|	|	|	|	|	|	|	...	...	|	|	|	|	|	...
Düsseldorf Hbf d.	...	...	...	0749	0821	0827	0827	...	|	0844	|	0855	0918	0923	|	0927	0927	...	...	0949	1007	1022	1020	|	...
Hagen Hbf d.	...	...	...	|	|	|	|	...	0758	|	0817	|	|	|	0858	|	|	...	...	|	|	|	|	0958	...
Wuppertal Hbf d.	...	...	...	|	|	|	|	...	0815	|	0835	|	|	|	0915	|	|	...	...	|	|	|	|	1015	...
Solingen Hbf d.	...	...	...	|	|	|	|	...	0827	|	0849	|	|	|	0927	|	|	...	...	|	|	|	|	1027	...
Köln Messe/Deutz a.	...	...	...	0817	0842	|	|	...	|	0908	0918	|	0938	|	|	|	|	...	...	|	1031	|	|	|	...
Brussels Midi/Zuid **21** d.	...	0623	...	|	|	|	|	...	|	|	|	|	|	|	|	|	|	...	0825	|	|	|	|	|	...
Aachen Hbf **802 806** d.	...	0739	...	|	|	|	|	...	|	|	|	|	|	|	|	|	|	...	0939	|	|	|	|	|	...
Köln Hbf **802 806** a.	...	0815	...	|	|	0849	0849	...	0847	|	|	0918	|	0946	0947	0949	0949	...	1015	1015	|	1046	1046	1047	...
Köln Hbf **801** d.	0758	0818	...	|	|	0853	0853	...	0855	|	|	0928	|	...	0955	0953	0953	0959	1020	...	|	1053	1053	...	...
Köln Messe/Deutz **801** d.	|	|	...	0829	0844	|	|	...	|	0910	0921	|	0944	...	|	|	|	|	|	...	1033	|	|	...	...
Köln/Bonn Flughafen ✈ **801** d.	0811	|	...	|	|	|	|	...	|	|	|	|	|	...	|	|	|	|	|	...	1044	|	|	...	...
Siegburg/Bonn 🚌 **801** d.	0821	0832	...	0857**c**	|	|	|	...	|	0924	0942**c**	|	|	...	|	|	|	1017	1034	...	|	|	|	...	...
Montabaur d.	0845	|	←	|	|	|	|	...	|	|	1014**c**	|	|	...	|	|	|	1038	|	...	|	|	|	...	...
Limburg Süd d.	0855	|	0902	|	|	|	|	...	|	|	|	|	|	...	|	|	|	1049	|	...	|	|	|	...	...
Bonn Hbf d.	→	|	|	|	|	0915	0915	...	|	|	|	|	|	...	|	1015	1015	|	|	...	|	1115	1115	...	...
Remagen d.	...	|	|	|	|	|	|	...	|	|	|	|	|	...	|	|	|	|	|	...	|	|	|	...	...
Andernach d.	...	|	|	|	|	|	|	...	|	|	|	|	|	...	|	|	|	|	|	...	|	|	|	...	...
Koblenz Hbf **914** d.	...	|	|	|	|	0948	0948	...	|	|	|	|	|	...	|	1048	1048	|	|	...	|	1148	1148	...	...
Wiesbaden Hbf **914** a.	...	|	|	0944	|	|	|	1026	|	|	1043	|	|	...	|	|	|	|	|	...	|	|	|	...	1226
Mainz Hbf a.	...	|	|	1014	|	1039	1039	1043**d**	|	|	1108	|	|	...	|	1139	1139	|	|	...	|	1239	1239	...	1243**d**
Frankfurt Flughafen ✈ § **914** a.	...	0917	0926	|	0933	|	|	1059	0949	1006	|	1017	1033	...	1049	1158	1158	1108	1117	...	1133	|	|	...	1259
Frankfurt (Main) Hbf **914** a.	...	0931	0941	|	0948	|	|	1113	|	|	|	1031	1048	...	|	1212	1212	1123	1131	...	1148	|	|	...	1313
Nürnberg Hbf **920** a.	...	...	...	|	1156	|	|	...	|	|	|	...	1258	...	|	1427	1427	...	...	...	1404	|	|	...	...
Passau Hbf **920** a.	...	...	...	|	|	|	|	...	|	|	|	...	|	...	|	1625	1625	...	...	...	|	|	|	...	...
Wien Hbf **950** a.	...	...	...	|	|	|	|	...	|	|	|	...	|	...	|	1847	1847	...	...	...	|	|	|	...	...
Mannheim Hbf **910** a.	...	...	...	1100	|	1121	1121	...	1023	1039	1152	...	|	...	1123	...	...	...	...	...	|	1321	1321	...	...
Karlsruhe Hbf **910** a.	...	...	...	|	|	1147	1147	...	1058	|	|	...	|	...	|	...	...	...	...	...	|	1347	1347	...	...
Basel SBB 🏛 **910** a.	...	...	...	|	|	1333	1333	...	1248	|	|	...	|	...	|	...	...	...	...	...	|	1536	1536	...	...
Stuttgart Hbf **910** a.	...	...	...	1153	|	...	...	...	...	1122	1248	...	|	...	1208	...	...	...	...	...	|	...	...	...	...
München Hbf **904 910** a.	...	...	...	1411	1305	...	...	...	...	1326	...	...	1406	...	1426	...	...	...	...	...	1512	...	...	...	...

IMPORTANT! SEE NOTE ⊠	ICE 105	IC 2013	ICE 225	ICE 625	ICE 517	ICE 819	ICE 731	ICE 15	IC 2009	IC 2156	IC 2156	ICE 627	IC 2044	IC 2044	ICE 107	ICE 123	ICE 629	ICE 519	ICE 519	ICE 1653	ICE 229	ICE 229	ICE 901	IC 5106	IC 2201
			⊗							V	W		C	D				V	W		W	V			
	✗	◆	✗	✗	✗	✗	✗	✗	E🍷	◆	◆	✗	J✗	J✗	✗	⊗✗	✗	✗	✗	◇	✗	✗	✗	X	N🍷
Hamburg Altona d.	0629	...	...	...	0728	...	0737	...	...	...	...	...	...	...	0829	...	...	0929	0929	...	...	...	...	...	...
Hamburg Hbf ☆ d.	0646	...	...	...	0746	...	0754	...	...	...	...	...	...	...	0845	...	...	0946	0946	...	...	...	...	...	...
Hamburg Harburg ☆ d.	0657	...	...	...	0757	...	|	...	...	...	...	...	...	...	0856	...	...	0957	0957	...	...	...	...	...	...
Bremen Hbf **815** ☆ d.	0744	...	...	...	0844	...	0852	...	...	...	...	...	...	...	0944	...	...	1044	1044	...	...	...	...	...	...
Berlin Hbf **810** d.	|	...	...	...	|	...	|	...	...	...	...	...	...	...	|	...	...	|	|	...	...	...	...	...	...
Osnabrück Hbf **802 815** d.	0837	...	...	...	0937	...	|	...	...	...	...	...	...	...	1037	...	...	1137	1137	...	...	...	...	...	...
Münster (Westf) Hbf **802** d.	0903	...	...	...	1003	...	1009	...	1032	...	...	...	...	...	1103	...	...	1203	1203	...	...	...	...	...	1229
Hamm (Westf) **805** d.	|	...	...	...	|	...	|	...	|	1057	1057	...	1117	1117	|	...	...	|	|	...	...	...	...	...	|
Dortmund Hbf **805** a.	0932	...	...	...	1032	...	|	...	|	1113	1116	...	1132	1132	1132	...	...	1232	1232	...	...	...	...	...	|
Dortmund Hbf d.	0936	0950	...	1023**v**	1036	...	|	...	|	1116	1119	1123**v**	1136	1136	1136	...	...	1236	1236	...	1220	1235	...	...	|
Bochum Hbf d.	0948	1003	...	1036**v**	|	...	|	...	|	1130	|	1136**v**	|	|	1148	...	...	1248	|	...	|	|	...	...	|
Recklinghausen Hbf d.	|	|	...	|	|	...	1038	...	1100	|	|	|	|	|	|	...	...	|	|	...	|	|	...	...	1259
Wanne-Eickel Hbf d.	|	|	...	|	|	...	|	...	1109	|	|	|	|	|	|	...	...	|	|	...	|	|	...	...	1308
Gelsenkirchen Hbf d.	|	|	...	|	|	...	1049	...	1114	|	|	|	|	|	|	...	...	|	|	...	|	|	...	...	1313
Essen Hbf d.	1000	1014	...	1054	|	...	1103	...	|	1140	|	1153	|	|	1200	...	1254	1300	|	...	1300	|	...	...	|
Amsterdam Centraal **28** d.	|	|	0830	|	|	...	|	...	|	|	|	|	|	|	|	1037	|	|	|	...	|	|	...	...	|
Oberhausen Hbf d.	|	|	|	|	|	...	|	...	1126	|	|	|	|	|	|	1233	|	|	|	...	|	|	...	...	1325
Duisburg Hbf d.	1013	1030	1040	1107	|	...	1117	...	1134	1156	|	1207	|	|	1213	1241	1307	1313	|	...	1313	|	...	...	1334
Düsseldorf Flughafen ✈ d.	|	|	|	|	|	...	|	...	|	1206	|	|	|	|	|	|	|	|	|	...	|	|	...	...	|
Düsseldorf Hbf d.	1027	1044	1053	1121	|	...	1131	...	1149	1214	|	1221	|	|	1227	1254	1321	1327	|	...	1327	|	...	1345	1349
Hagen Hbf d.	|	|	|	|	1058	...	|	...	|	|	1141	|	1158	1158	|	|	|	|	1257	...	|	1257	...	|	|
Wuppertal Hbf d.	|	|	|	|	1115	...	|	...	|	|	|	|	1215	1215	|	|	|	|	1315	...	|	1315	...	|	|
Solingen Hbf d.	|	|	|	|	1127	...	|	...	|	|	|	|	1227	1227	|	|	|	|	1327	...	|	1327	...	|	|
Köln Messe/Deutz a.	|	|	1112	1142	|	...	|	...	|	|	|	1242	|	|	|	|	1342	|	|	...	|	|	...	|	|
Brussels Midi/Zuid **21** d.	|	|	|	|	|	...	|	1025	|	|	|	|	|	|	|	|	|	|	|	...	|	|	...	|	|
Aachen Hbf **802 806** d.	|	|	|	|	|	...	|	1139	|	|	|	|	|	|	|	|	|	|	|	...	|	|	...	|	|
Köln Hbf **802 806** a.	1049	1111	|	|	1147	...	1158	1215	1215	1240	1239	|	1247	1247	1249	1315	|	1349	1346	...	1349	1347	...	1410	1415
Köln Hbf **801** d.	1055	1114	|	|	1155	1159	...	1220	...	...	...	|	1253	1253	1255	1321	|	1355	1355	...	1353	1353	1359	1417	...
Köln Messe/Deutz **801** d.	|	|	1114	1144	|	|	...	|	...	...	...	1244	|	|	|	|	1344	|	|	...	|	|	|	|	...
Köln/Bonn Flughafen ✈ **801** d.	|	|	|	|	|	|	...	|	...	...	...	|	|	|	|	|	|	|	|	...	|	|	|	|	...
Siegburg/Bonn 🚌 **801** d.	|	|	1126	|	|	1217	...	1234	...	...	...	|	|	|	|	1336	|	|	|	...	|	|	1417	|	...
Montabaur d.	|	|	|	|	|	1238	...	|	...	...	...	|	|	|	|	|	|	|	|	...	|	|	1438	|	...
Limburg Süd d.	|	|	|	|	|	1249	...	|	...	...	...	|	|	|	|	|	|	|	|	...	|	|	1449	|	...
Bonn Hbf d.	|	1136	|	|	|	|	...	|	...	...	...	|	1315	1315	|	|	|	|	|	...	1415	1415	|	1438	...
Remagen d.	|	1152	|	|	|	|	...	|	...	...	...	|	|	|	|	|	|	|	|	...	|	|	|	1451	...
Andernach d.	|	1204	|	|	|	|	...	|	...	...	...	|	|	|	|	|	|	|	|	...	|	|	|	1503	...
Koblenz Hbf **914** d.	|	1218	|	|	|	|	...	|	...	...	...	|	1348	1348	|	|	|	|	|	...	1448	1448	|	1516	...
Wiesbaden Hbf **914** a.	|	|	|	|	|	|	...	|	...	...	...	|	|	|	|	|	|	|	|	1426	|	|	|	...	...
Mainz Hbf a.	|	1311	|	|	|	|	...	|	...	...	...	|	1439	1439	|	|	|	|	|	1443**d**	1539	1539	|	...	...
Frankfurt Flughafen ✈ § **914** a.	1149	|	1206	1233	1249	1308	...	1317	...	...	...	1333	|	|	1349	1417	1433	1449	1449	1459	1558	1558	1508	...	...
Frankfurt (Main) Hbf **914** a.	|	|	|	1248	|	1323	...	1331	...	...	...	1348	|	|	|	1431	1448	|	|	1513	1613	1613	1523	...	...
Nürnberg Hbf **920** a.	|	|	|	1500	|	...	...	...	...	...	...	1556	|	|	|	...	1658	|	|	...	1827	1827	...	...	...
Passau Hbf **920** a.	|	|	|	|	|	...	...	...	...	...	...	|	|	|	|	...	|	|	|	...	2026	2026	...	...	...
Wien Hbf **950** a.	|	|	|	|	|	...	...	...	...	...	...	|	|	|	|	...	|	|	|	...	2305	2305	...	...	...
Mannheim Hbf **910** a.	1223	1352	1239	|	1323	...	...	...	...	...	...	|	1521	1521	1423	...	|	1523	1523	...	...	...	...	...	...
Karlsruhe Hbf **910** a.	1258	|	|	|	|	...	...	...	...	...	...	|	|	1616	1458	...	|	|	|	...	...	...	...	...	...
Basel SBB 🏛 **910** a.	1448	|	|	|	|	...	...	...	...	...	...	|	|	...	1648	...	|	|	|	...	...	...	...	...	...
Stuttgart Hbf **910** a.	...	1450	1320	|	1408	...	...	...	...	...	...	|	1622	...	...	...	|	1608	1608	...	...	...	...	...	...
München Hbf **904 910** a.	...	...	1527	1607	1626	...	...	...	...	...	...	1706	...	...	...	...	1807	1826	1826	...	...	...	...	...	...

← **FOR NOTES, SEE PAGE 376**

GERMANY

800 HAMBURG - DORTMUND - KÖLN - FRANKFURT

See Table **802** for Rhein-Ruhr regional services. See Table **810** for services from Berlin via Hannover and Bielefeld. See Table **927** for FlixTrain services.

IMPORTANT! SEE NOTE ⊠	ICE 1050	ICE 315	ICE 721	IC 2046	IC 2046	ICE 1655	ICE 109	ICE 1011	ICE 1011	ICE 125	ICE 723	ICE 611	ICE 927	ICE 903	IC 2203	ICE 1123	ICE 17	ICE 17	ICE 725	IC 2048	IC 2048	ICE 1657	ICE 201	IC 2311	ICE 1013
	F			C	D				⊖							Ⓑ L	⑥	Ⓑ		R	S				
	✕	✕	✕	J 🍷	J 🍷	◇	✕	✕	✕	⊗✕	✕	✕	✕	✕	N 🍷	✕	✕	✕	✕	🍷♦	J 🍷	◇	✕	Y	✕
Hamburg Altona d.	...	...	...	...	...	...	1027	...	...	...	...	1129	1139	...	...	...	...	...	...	...	...	...	1229	...	...
Hamburg Hbf ☆ d.	...	...	...	...	...	...	1046	...	...	...	...	1146	1153	...	...	...	...	...	...	...	...	...	1246	1250	...
Hamburg Harburg ☆ d.	...	...	...	...	...	...	1056	...	...	...	...	1157	│	...	...	...	...	...	...	...	...	...	1256	│	...
Bremen Hbf **815** ☆ d.	...	...	...	...	...	...	1144	...	...	...	...	1244	1252	...	...	...	...	...	...	...	...	...	1344	1348	...
Berlin Hbf **810** d.	0909	...	...	...	...	...	│	...	...	...	...	│	│	...	...	...	...	...	...	...	...	...	│	│	...
Osnabrück Hbf **802 815** d.	1206	...	...	...	...	...	1237	...	...	...	...	1337	│	...	...	...	...	...	...	...	...	...	1437	1443	...
Münster (Westf) Hbf **802** d.	1232	...	...	...	...	...	1303	...	...	...	...	1403	1409	...	1432	...	...	...	...	...	...	...	1503	1509	...
Hamm (Westf) **805** d.	│	...	...	1317	1317	...	│	...	...	...	...	│	│	...	│	...	...	...	...	1517	1517	...	│	│	...
Dortmund Hbf **805** a.	│	...	...	1332	1332	...	1332	...	...	...	...	1432	│	...	│	...	...	...	...	1532	1532	...	1532	│	...
Dortmund Hbf d.	│	...	...	1336	1336	...	1336	...	1350	...	...	1436	│	...	│	...	...	...	...	1536	1536	...	1536	│	1550
Bochum Hbf d.	│	...	...	│	│	...	1348	...	1403	...	...	│	│	...	│	...	...	...	...	│	│	...	1548	│	1602
Recklinghausen Hbf d.	1305	...	...	│	│	...	│	...	│	...	...	│	1439	...	1500	...	...	...	...	│	│	...	│	1538	│
Wanne-Eickel Hbf d.	│	...	...	│	│	...	│	...	│	...	...	│	│	...	1509	...	...	...	...	│	│	...	│	│	│
Gelsenkirchen Hbf d.	│	...	...	│	│	...	│	...	│	...	...	│	│	...	1514	...	...	...	...	│	│	...	│	1549	│
Essen Hbf d.	1325	...	1354	│	│	...	1400	...	1414	...	1454	│	1500	...	│	...	...	...	1554	│	│	...	1600	1603	1614
Amsterdam Centraal **28** d.	│	...	│	│	│	...	│	...	│	1238	│	│	│	...	│	...	...	...	│	│	│	...	│	│	│
Oberhausen Hbf d.	│	...	│	│	│	...	│	...	│	1433	│	│	│	...	1526	...	...	...	│	│	│	...	│	│	│
Duisburg Hbf d.	1338	...	1407	│	│	...	1413	...	1428	1441	1507	│	1513	...	1534	...	...	...	1607	│	│	...	1613	1618	1627
Düsseldorf Flughafen ✈ d.	│	...	│	│	│	...	│	...	│	│	│	│	│	...	│	...	...	...	│	│	│	...	│	│	│
Düsseldorf Hbf d.	1352	...	1421	│	│	...	1427	1446	1446	1455	1521	│	1527	...	1549	1607	...	...	1621	│	│	...	1627	1632	1646
Hagen Hbf d.	│	...	│	1358	1358	...	│	│	│	│	│	1458	│	...	│	│	...	...	│	1558	1558	...	│	│	│
Wuppertal Hbf d.	│	...	│	1415	1415	...	│	│	│	│	│	1515	│	...	│	│	...	...	│	1615	1615	...	│	│	│
Solingen Hbf d.	│	...	│	1427	1427	...	│	│	│	│	│	1527	│	...	│	│	...	...	│	1627	1627	...	│	│	│
Köln Messe/Deutz a.	│	...	1442	│	│	...	│	1508	1508	│	1542	│	│	...	│	1627	...	...	1642	│	│	...	│	│	1708
Brussels Midi/Zuid **21** d.	│	1225	│	│	│	...	│	│	│	│	│	│	│	...	│	│	1425	1425	│	│	│	...	│	│	│
Aachen Hbf **802 806** d.	│	1339	│	│	│	...	│	│	│	│	│	│	│	...	│	│	1539	1539	│	│	│	...	│	│	│
Köln Hbf **802 806** a.	1421	1415	│	1447	1447	...	1449	│	│	1518	│	1547	1549	...	1614	│	1615	1615	│	1647	1647	...	1649	1657	│
Köln Hbf **801** d.	...	1427	│	1453	1453	...	1455	│	│	1528	│	1555	1553	...	...	│	1620	1623	│	1653	1653	...	1655	...	│
Köln Messe/Deutz **801** d.	...	│	1444	│	│	...	│	1510	1510	│	1544	│	│	1600	...	1629	│	│	1644	│	│	...	│	...	1710
Köln/Bonn Flughafen ✈ **801** d.	...	│	│	│	│	...	│	│	│	│	│	│	│	│	...	│	│	│	│	│	│	...	│	...	│
Siegburg/Bonn 🚌 **801** d.	...	│	│	│	│	...	│	1524	1524	│	│	│	│	1617	...	│	│	│	│	│	│	...	│	...	1724
Montabaur d.	...	│	│	│	│	...	│	│	│	│	│	│	│	1638	...	│	│	│	│	│	│	...	│	...	│
Limburg Süd d.	...	│	│	│	│	...	│	│	│	│	│	│	│	1649	...	│	│	│	│	│	│	...	│	...	│
Bonn Hbf d.	...	│	│	1515	1515	...	│	│	│	│	│	│	1615	│	...	│	│	│	│	1715	1715	...	│	...	│
Remagen d.	...	│	│	│	│	...	│	│	│	│	│	│	│	│	...	│	│	│	│	│	│	...	│	...	│
Andernach d.	...	│	│	│	│	...	│	│	│	│	│	│	│	│	...	│	│	│	│	│	│	...	│	...	│
Koblenz Hbf **914** d.	...	│	│	1548	1548	...	│	│	│	│	│	│	1648	│	...	│	│	│	│	1748	1748	...	│	...	│
Wiesbaden Hbf **914** a.	...	│	│	│	│	1626	│	│	│	│	│	│	│	│	...	│	│	│	│	│	│	1826	│	...	│
Mainz Hbf a.	...	│	│	1639	1639	1643**d**	│	│	│	│	│	│	1739	│	...	│	│	│	│	1839	1839	1843**d**	│	...	│
Frankfurt Flughafen ✈ § **914** a.	...	1517	1533	│	│	1659	1549	1606	1606	1617	1633	1649	1758	1708	...	1717	1717	1726	1733	│	│	1859	1749	...	1806
Frankfurt (Main) Hbf **914** a.	...	1531	1548	│	│	1713	│	│	│	1631	1648	│	1813	1723	...	│	1731	1740	1748	│	│	1913	│	...	│
Nürnberg Hbf **920** a.	...	...	1756	│	│	...	│	│	│	...	1859	│	2028	...	...	1915	...	...	1956	│	│	...	│	...	│
Passau Hbf **920** a.	...	...	│	│	│	...	│	│	│	...	│	│	2242	...	...	│	...	...	│	│	│	...	│	...	│
Wien Hbf **950** a.	...	...	│	│	│	...	│	│	│	...	│	│	...	...	...	│	...	...	│	│	│	...	│	...	│
Mannheim Hbf **910** a.	...	...	│	1721	1721	...	1623	1639	1639	...	│	1723	...	...	...	│	...	...	│	1921	1921	...	1823	...	1839
Karlsruhe Hbf **910** a.	...	...	│	│	1815	...	1658	│	│	...	│	│	...	...	...	│	...	...	│	│	2015	...	1858	...	│
Basel SBB 🚉 **910** a.	...	...	│	│	...	...	1848	│	│	...	│	│	...	...	...	│	...	...	│	│	...	...	2048**n**	...	│
Stuttgart Hbf **910** a.	...	...	│	1827	...	...	...	1721	1721	...	│	1808	...	...	...	│	...	...	│	2023	...	...	...	...	1922
München Hbf **904 910** a.	...	...	1907	...	...	...	...	1927	1927	...	2006	2029	...	...	...	2020	...	...	2107	...	...	...	...	...	2126

IMPORTANT! SEE NOTE ⊠	ICE 127	ICE 713	IC 2305	ICE 1224	ICE 727	ICE 613	ICE 929	ICE 929	ICE 905	ICE 735	IC 2205	ICE 756	ICE 317	IC 2152	IC 2152	ICE 729	ICE 203	IC 2440	ICE 1659	ICE 1015	ICE 1015	ICE 129	ICE 821		ICE 615
		Ⓑ	♠				W	V		⑤⑦		B		V	W				Ⓑ	Ⓑ	⑥				
	⊗✕	✕	E 🍷	M✕	✕	K✕	✕	✕	✕	A✕	N 🍷	✕	✕	G	G	✕	Q✕	J 🍷	◇	✕	N✕	⊗✕	✕		✕
Hamburg Altona d.	...	...	...	...	...	...	...	...	...	1338	...	...	...	...	...	...	...	...	...	...	...	...	...	...	1529
Hamburg Hbf ☆ d.	...	...	...	...	...	1346	...	...	...	1353	...	...	...	...	...	...	1445	...	...	...	...	...	...	...	1545
Hamburg Harburg ☆ d.	...	...	...	...	...	1357	...	...	...	1404	...	...	...	...	...	...	1457	...	...	...	...	...	...	...	1557
Bremen Hbf **815** ☆ d.	...	...	...	...	...	1444	...	...	...	1452	...	...	...	...	...	...	1544	...	...	...	...	...	...	...	1644
Berlin Hbf **810** d.	...	...	...	...	...	│	...	...	...	│	...	1306	...	...	...	...	│	...	...	...	...	...	...	...	│
Osnabrück Hbf **802 815** d.	...	...	...	...	...	1537	...	...	...	│	...	1606	...	...	...	...	1637	...	...	...	...	...	...	...	1737
Münster (Westf) Hbf **802** d.	...	...	1533	...	...	1603	...	...	...	│	1630	1633	...	...	...	...	1703	...	...	...	1729	...	...	...	1803
Hamm (Westf) **805** d.	...	...	│	1556	...	│	...	...	...	│	│	│	...	...	1657	...	│	1717	...	...	│	...	...	...	│
Dortmund Hbf **805** a.	...	...	│	1616	...	1632	...	...	...	│	│	│	...	...	1714	...	1732	1732	...	...	│	...	...	...	1832
Dortmund Hbf d.	...	...	│	1620	...	1636	1635	1636	...	│	│	│	...	1716	1717	...	1736	1736	...	1750	│	...	...	...	1836
Bochum Hbf d.	...	...	│	│	...	│	│	1648	...	│	│	│	...	1730	│	...	1748	│	...	1803	│	...	...	...	│
Recklinghausen Hbf d.	...	...	1604	│	...	│	│	│	...	1638	1659	1707	...	│	│	...	│	│	...	│	1800	...	...	...	│
Wanne-Eickel Hbf d.	...	...	1613	1637	...	│	│	│	...	│	1708	│	...	│	│	...	│	│	...	│	1809	...	...	...	│
Gelsenkirchen Hbf d.	...	...	1618	1643	...	│	│	│	...	│	1713	│	...	│	│	...	│	│	...	│	1815	...	...	...	│
Essen Hbf d.	...	...	1630	│	1654	│	│	1700	...	1704	│	1728	...	1740	│	1754	1800	│	...	1815	│	...	1839	...	│
Amsterdam Centraal **28** d.	1438	...	│	│	│	│	│	│	...	│	│	│	...	│	│	│	│	│	...	│	│	1638	│	...	│
Oberhausen Hbf d.	1633	...	│	1658	│	│	│	│	...	│	1725	│	...	│	│	│	│	│	...	│	│	1833	│	...	│
Duisburg Hbf d.	1641	...	1643	...	1707	│	1713	1713	...	1718	1734	│	...	1755	│	1807	1813	│	...	1830	1831	1841	1853	...	│
Düsseldorf Flughafen ✈ d.	│	...	│	...	│	│	│	│	...	│	│	│	...	1806	│	│	│	│	...	│	│	│	│	...	│
Düsseldorf Hbf d.	1655	...	1702	...	1721	│	1727	1727	...	1732	1749	1754	...	1812	1833	1821	1827	│	...	1843	1843	1855	1907	...	│
Hagen Hbf d.	│	...	│	...	│	1658	│	│	...	│	│	│	...	...	1742*	│	│	1758	...	│	│	│	│	...	1858
Wuppertal Hbf d.	│	...	│	...	│	1715	│	│	...	│	│	│	...	...	...	│	│	1815	...	│	│	│	│	...	1915
Solingen Hbf d.	│	...	│	...	│	1727	│	│	...	│	│	│	...	...	...	│	│	1827	...	│	│	│	│	...	1927
Köln Messe/Deutz a.	│	...	│	...	1742	│	│	│	...	│	│	│	...	...	...	1842	│	│	...	1908	1908	│	1928	...	│
Brussels Midi/Zuid **21** d.	│	...	│	...	│	│	│	│	...	│	│	│	1622**k**	...	...	│	│	│	...	│	│	│	│	...	│
Aachen Hbf **802 806** d.	│	...	│	...	│	│	│	│	...	│	│	│	1739	...	...	│	│	│	...	│	│	│	│	...	│
Köln Hbf **802 806** a.	1719	...	1731	...	│	1747	1749	1749	...	1757	1814	1818	1815	...	...	│	1849	1847	...	│	│	1918	│	...	1947
Köln Hbf **801** d.	1728	1731	...	...	│	1755	1753	1753	1800	...	...	...	1820	...	...	│	1855	1853	...	│	│	1928	│	...	1955
Köln Messe/Deutz **801** d.	│	│	...	...	1744	│	│	│	│	...	...	...	│	...	...	1844	│	│	...	1910	1910	│	1933	...	│
Köln/Bonn Flughafen ✈ **801** d.	│	│	...	...	│	│	│	│	│	...	...	...	│	...	...	│	│	│	...	│	│	│	│	...	│
Siegburg/Bonn 🚌 **801** d.	│	1746	...	...	│	│	│	│	1817	...	...	...	1834	...	...	│	│	│	...	1924	1924	│	│	...	│
Montabaur d.	│	1805	...	...	│	│	│	│	1838	...	...	...	│	...	...	│	│	│	...	│	│	│	2003	...	│
Limburg Süd d.	│	1820	...	...	│	│	│	│	1849	...	...	...	│	...	...	│	│	│	...	│	│	│	2014	...	│
Bonn Hbf d.	│	│	...	...	│	│	1815	1815	│	...	...	...	│	...	...	│	│	1915	...	│	│	│	│	...	│
Remagen d.	│	│	...	...	│	│	│	│	│	...	...	...	│	...	...	│	│	│	...	│	│	│	│	...	│
Andernach d.	│	│	...	...	│	│	│	│	│	...	...	...	│	...	...	│	│	│	...	│	│	│	│	...	│
Koblenz Hbf **914** d.	│	│	...	...	│	│	1848	1848	│	...	...	...	│	...	...	│	│	1948	...	│	│	│	│	...	│
Wiesbaden Hbf **914** a.	│	1840	...	...	│	│	│	│	│	...	...	...	│	...	...	│	│	│	2026	│	│	│	│	...	│
Mainz Hbf a.	│	1855	...	...	│	│	1939	1939	│	...	...	...	│	...	...	│	│	2039	2043**d**	│	│	│	│	...	│
Frankfurt Flughafen ✈ § **914** a.	1817	1928	...	...	1833	1849	1958	1958	1908	...	...	...	1917	...	...	1933	1949	│	2059	2006	2006	2017	2033	...	2049
Frankfurt (Main) Hbf **914** a.	1831	1940	...	...	1848	│	2013	2013	1923	...	...	...	1931	...	...	1948	│	│	2113	│	│	2031	2048	...	│
Nürnberg Hbf **920** a.	...	...	...	...	2100	│	2228	2228	...	...	...	...	...	...	...	2157	│	│	...	│	│	...	2300	...	│
Passau Hbf **920** a.	...	...	...	...	│	│	0050	0050	...	...	...	...	...	...	...	│	│	│	...	│	│	...	│	...	│
Wien Hbf **950** a.	...	...	...	...	│	│	...	...	...	...	...	...	...	...	...	│	│	│	...	│	│	...	│	...	│
Mannheim Hbf **910** a.	...	...	...	...	│	1923	...	...	...	...	...	...	...	..	..	│	2023	2121	...	2039	2039	...	│	...	2124
Karlsruhe Hbf **910** a.	...	...	...	...	│	│	...	...	...	...	...	...	...	...	...	│	2058	**f**	...	│	│	...	│	...	│
Basel SBB 🚉 **910** a.	...	...	...	...	│	│	...	...	...	...	...	...	...	...	...	│	2255**n**	│	...	│	│	...	│	...	│
Stuttgart Hbf **910** a.	...	...	...	...	│	2008	...	...	...	...	...	...	...	...	...	│	...	2223**f**	...	2122	2122	...	│	...	2208
München Hbf **904 910** a.	...	...	...	...	2210	2226	...	...	...	...	...	...	...	...	...	2318	...	...	...	2326	...	...	0020	...	0026

← **FOR NOTES, SEE PAGE 376**

HAMBURG - DORTMUND - KÖLN - FRANKFURT 800

See Table **802** for Rhein-Ruhr regional services. See Table **810** for services from Berlin via Hannover and Bielefeld. See Table **927** for FlixTrain services.

MPORTANT! SEE NOTE ⊠	*ICE* 1021 Z ⊡✕	*ICE* 19 ✕	*IC* 2207 E🍷	*ICE* 823 ✕	*ICE* 205 V ✕	*ICE* 205 W ✕	*IC* 2442 V J🍷	*IC* 2442 W J🍷		*IC* 2215 Y	*ICE* 221 ⊗✕	*ICE* 617 ✕	*IC* 2209 ♣ N🍷	*ICE* 319 ■ ✕	*IC* 2444 J🍷		*ICE* 207 V ✕	*ICE* 207 W ✕	*NJ* 403 ♦	*ICE* 619 K✕	*ICE* 209 ✕		*ICE* 921 ⊙		
amburg Altona ... d.	1555**a**	...	...	...	1629	1629	...	...	...	...	...	1729	...	...	...	...	1829	1829	...	...	2029	...	2229	...	...
amburg Hbf ... ☆ d.	1610	...	...	...	1646	1646	...	...	...	1650	...	1746	...	...	...	...	1846	1846	...	1946	2046	...	2246	...	...
amburg Harburg ... ☆ d.	│	...	...	...	1656	1656	...	...	...	│	...	1757	...	...	...	...	1857	1857	...	1957	2056	...	2256	...	...
remen Hbf ... **815** ☆ d.	│	...	...	...	1745	1745	...	...	...	1749	...	1844	...	...	...	...	1944	1944	...	2044	2144	...	2344	...	...
Berlin Hbf **810** ... d.	│	...	...	...	│	│	...	...	...	│	...	│	...	...	...	...	│	│	...	│	│	...	│	...	...
snabrück Hbf ... **802 815** d.	│	...	...	...	1837	1837	...	...	...	1843	...	1937	...	...	...	...	2037	2037	...	2137	2237	...	0037	...	...
ünster (Westf) Hbf ... **802** d.	│	...	1832	...	1902	1902	...	...	...	1909	...	2003	2032	...	...	...	2103	2102	...	2203	2303	...	0104	...	...
Hamm (Westf) ... **805** d.	│	...	│	...	│	│	1917	1917	...	│	...	│	│	...	2117	...	│	│	...	│	│	...	0124	...	...
ortmund Hbf ... **805** a.	│	...	│	...	1932	│	1932	1932	...	│	...	2032	│	...	2132	...	2132	│	...	2232	2332	...	0143	...	...
ortmund Hbf ... d.	│	...	│	...	1936	│	1934	1936	...	│	...	2036	│	...	2136	...	2136	│	...	2236	2335	...	0145	...	...
ochum Hbf ... d.	│	...	│	...	│	│	1946	│	...	│	...	2048	│	...	│	...	2148	│	...	2248	│	...	0157	...	...
Recklinghausen Hbf ... d.	1837	...	1900	...	│	│	│	│	...	1938	...	│	2100	...	│	...	│	│	...	│	│	...	│	...	...
Wanne-Eickel Hbf ... d.	│	...	1909	...	│	1939	│	│	...	│	...	│	2109	...	│	...	│	2139	...	│	│	...	│	...	...
Gelsenkirchen Hbf ... d.	│	...	1914	...	│	│	│	│	...	1949	...	│	2114	...	│	...	│	│	...	│	│	...	│	...	...
ssen Hbf ... d.	1900	...	│	1939	│	1957	1959	│	...	2003	...	2100	│	...	│	...	2200	2157	...	2300	│	...	0209	...	...
Amsterdam Centraal **28** ... d.	│	...	│	│	│	│	│	│	...	│	1838	│	│	...	│	...	│	│	2015	│	│	...	│	...	...
Oberhausen Hbf ... d.	│	...	1926	│	│	│	│	│	...	│	2033	│	2126	...	│	...	│	│	│	│	│	...	│	...	...
uisburg Hbf ... d.	1913	...	1934	1953	│	2013	2012	│	...	2018	2041	2113	2134	...	│	...	2213	2213	│	2313	│	...	0222	...	...
üsseldorf Flughafen ✈ ... d.	│	...	│	│	│	│	│	│	...	│	│	│	│	...	│	...	│	│	│	│	│	...	0232	...	...
üsseldorf Hbf ... d.	1927	...	1949	2007	│	2027	2026	│	...	2033	2055	2127	2149	...	│	...	2227	2227	│	2327	│	...	0240	...	...
Hagen Hbf ... d.	│	...	│	│	1958	│	│	1958	...	│	│	│	│	...	2158	...	│	│	│	│	2358	...	│	...	...
Wuppertal Hbf ... d.	│	...	│	│	2015	│	│	2015	...	│	│	│	│	...	2215	...	│	│	│	│	0015	...	│	...	...
Solingen Hbf ... d.	│	...	│	│	2027	│	│	2027	...	│	│	│	│	...	2227	...	│	│	│	│	0027	...	│	...	...
öln Messe/Deutz ... a.	│	...	│	2028	│	│	│	│	...	│	│	│	│	...	│	...	│	│	│	│	│	...	│	...	...
Brussels Midi/Zuid **21** ... d.	│	1825	│	│	│	│	│	│	...	│	│	│	│	2025	│	...	│	│	│	│	│	...	│	...	...
Aachen Hbf ... **802 806** d.	│	1939	│	│	│	│	│	│	...	│	│	│	│	2139	│	...	│	│	│	│	│	...	│	...	...
öln Hbf ... **802 806** a.	1949	2015	2015	│	2047	2049	2049	2046	...	2057	2118	2149	2214	2215	2247	...	2249	2249	2338	2349	0047	...	0302	...	...
öln Hbf ... **801** d.	1953	2020	...	│	2055	2055	2053	2053	...	...	2128	2155	...	2227	2253	...	...	...	2342	2355	...	...	0349	...	...
öln Messe/Deutz ... **801** d.	│	│	...	2033	│	│	│	│	...	...	│	│	...	│	│	...	...	...	│	│	...	...	│	...	...
Köln/Bonn Flughafen ✈ **801** d.	│	│	...	│	│	│	│	│	...	...	│	│	...	2240	│	...	...	...	│	│	...	...	│	...	...
iegburg/Bonn 🚌 ... **801** d.	│	2034	...	│	│	│	│	│	...	...	│	2209	...	2249	│	...	...	...	│	0009	...	...	│	...	...
ontabaur ... d.	│	│	...	2104	│	│	│	│	...	...	│	│	...	2310	│	...	...	...	│	│	...	...	│	...	...
mburg Süd ... d.	│	│	...	2115	│	│	│	│	...	...	│	│	...	2321	│	...	...	...	│	│	...	...	│	...	...
Bonn Hbf ... d.	2015	│	...	│	│	│	2115	2115	...	...	│	│	...	│	2314	...	...	...	0004**b**	│	...	...	0413	...	...
Remagen ... d.	│	│	...	│	│	│	│	│	...	...	│	│	...	│	2328	...	...	...	│	│	...	...	0427	...	...
Andernach ... d.	│	│	...	│	│	│	│	│	...	...	│	│	...	│	2341	...	...	...	│	│	...	...	0442	...	...
Koblenz Hbf ... **914** d.	2048	│	...	│	│	│	2148	2148	...	...	│	│	...	│	2354	...	...	...	0049	│	...	...	0531**j**	...	...
Wiesbaden Hbf ... **914** a.	│	│	...	│	│	│	│	│	...	...	│	│	...	│	...	...	...	...	│	│	...	...	│	...	...
Mainz Hbf ... a.	2142	│	...	│	│	│	2239	2239	...	...	│	│	...	│	...	...	...	...	0140	│	...	...	0626	...	...
rankfurt Flughafen ✈ § **914** a.	2159	2117	...	2134	2149	2149	2259	2259	...	...	2217	2253	...	2340	...	...	...	...	0203	0054	...	...	0646	...	...
rankfurt (Main) Hbf ... **914** a.	2213	2131	...	2149	│	│	2313	2313	...	...	2231	│	...	2356	...	...	...	...	0220	0110	...	...	0702	...	...
Nürnberg Hbf **920** ... a.	0042	...	...	...	│	│	...	...	...	...	...	│	...	...	...	...	...	...	│	│	...	...	...	...	...
Passau Hbf **920** ... a.	...	...	...	...	│	│	...	...	...	...	...	│	...	...	...	...	...	...	│	│	...	...	...	...	...
Wien Hbf **950** ... a.	...	...	...	...	│	│	...	...	...	...	...	│	...	...	...	...	...	...	│	│	...	...	...	...	...
Mannheim Hbf **910** ... a.	...	...	...	...	2223	2223	...	...	...	...	...	2327	...	...	...	...	...	...	0331	0202	...	...	...	...	...
Karlsruhe Hbf **910** ... a.	...	...	...	...	2259	2259	...	...	...	...	...	│	...	...	...	...	...	...	0401	│	...	...	...	...	...
Basel SBB 🏛 **910** ... a.	...	...	...	...	0104**t**	0104**t**	...	...	...	...	...	│	...	...	...	...	...	...	0620	│	...	...	...	...	...
Stuttgart Hbf **910** ... a.	...	...	...	...	...	...	...	...	...	...	...	0008	...	...	...	...	...	...	...	0333	...	...	...	...	...
München Hbf **904 910** ... a.	...	...	...	...	...	...	...	...	...	...	...	...	...	...	...	...	...	...	...	0603	...	...	...	...	...

– **FOR NOTES, SEE PAGE 376**

S-Bahn 19 KÖLN - KÖLN/BONN FLUGHAFEN ✈ - SIEGBURG/BONN 801

		Ⓐ	⊗	Ⓐ		⑥		⑥	⑥	⑥		⑥		†		†				
öln Hbf ... d.	Ⓐ	0401		2041	⑥	0411		0741	0811	0821		2041	†	0411		2041	D	2111		0341
öln Messe/Deutz ... d.		0403	and every	2043		0413	and every	0743	0813	0823	and every	2043		0413	and every	2043	A	2113	and every	0343
öln/Bonn Flughafen ✈ ... d.		0416	20 minutes	2056		0426	30 minutes	0756	0826	0836	20 minutes	2056		0426	30 minutes	2056	I	2126	30 minutes	0356
roisdorf ... d.		0427	until	2107		0437	until	0807	0837	0847	until	2107		0437	until	2107	L	2137	until	0407
iegburg/Bonn ... a.		0431		2111		0441		0811	...	0851		2111		0441		2111	Y	2141		0411

		Ⓐ	⊕	Ⓐ		⑥		⑥		⑥	⊠	⑥		†		†				
iegburg/Bonn ... d.	Ⓐ	0427		2107	⑥	0437		0707	...	0747		2107	†	0437		2107	D	2137		0407
roisdorf ... d.		0432	and every	2112		0442	and every	0712	...	0752	and every	2112		0442	and every	2112	A	2142	and every	0412
öln/Bonn Flughafen ✈ ... d.		0443	20 minutes	2123		0453	30 minutes	0723	...	0803	20 minutes	2123		0453	30 minutes	2123	I	2153	30 minutes	0423
öln Messe/Deutz ... a.		0456	until	2136		0506	until	0736	...	0816	until	2136		0506	until	2136	L	2206	until	0436
öln Hbf ... a.		0459		2139		0509		0739	...	0819		2139		0509		2139	Y	2209		0439

) – The 0441 from Köln Hbf terminates at Troisdorf.

) – No service from Siegburg/Bonn at 0507 (starts from Troisdorf, d. 0512).

⊠ – No service from Siegburg/Bonn at 0847 (starts from Troisdorf, d. 0853, then Köln/Bonn Flughafen d. 0904).

RE / RB services RHEIN – RUHR LOCAL SERVICES 802

ervices in this table (pages 380 – 382) are shown route by route. Sub-headings indicate the route number and principal stations served. See Tables **800** and **810** for *ICE, EC and IC* services.

RE1 Aachen - Köln - Düsseldorf - Dortmund - Hamm ♣ ⊡ ❖ *RE6* Köln - Neuss - Düsseldorf - Bielefeld - Minden ♣ ⊡ ❖

km	*SEE NOTE* ❖		Ⓒ		⚒			⚒			Ⓐ	Ⓒ		Ⓐ										
0	**Aachen** Hbf ... **807** d.	...	0051	...	...	...	...	...	...	...	...	...	...	0451	...	0551	...	▲	1851	...	1951	...	2051	...
31	Düren ... **807** d.	...	0117	...	...	...	...	...	...	...	...	...	...	0517	...	0617	...		1917	...	2017	...	2117	...
	Köln/Bonn Flughafen ✈ ... d.	...	│	...	...	0320	...	...	...	0448	0448	...	...	│	0548	│	0648		│	1948	│	2048	│	2148
70	**Köln** Hbf ... **807** a.	...	0144	...	...	0335	...	...	...	0501	0501	...	...	0544	0602	0644	0701		1944	2001	2042	2101	2143	2201
70	**Köln** Hbf ... d.	...	0149	...	...	0349	...	...	0449	0507	0507	...	0549	0549	0607	0649	0707		1949	2007	2049	2107	2149	2207
71	**Köln** Messe/Deutz ... d.	...	0153	...	...	0353	...	...	0453	│	│	...	0553	0553	│	0653	│		1953	│	2053	│	2153	│
83	Leverkusen Mitte ... d.	...	0204	...	...	0404	...	...	0504	│	│	...	0604	0604	│	0704	│	and at	2004	│	2104	│	2204	│
	Neuss Hbf ... d.	...	│	...	...	│	...	...	│	0534	0534	...	│	│	0634	│	0735		│	2036	│	2136	│	2236
110	**Düsseldorf** Hbf ... a.	...	0220	...	...	0420	...	...	0520	0547	0547	...	0620	0620	0647	0720	0748	the same	2020	2048	2120	2149	2220	2248
110	**Düsseldorf** Hbf ... ▷ d.	0222	0222	...	...	0422	...	...	0522	...	0555	...	0622	0622	0655	0722	0755		2022	2054	2122	2155	2222	2254
117	Düsseldorf Flughafen ✈ .. ▷ d.	0228	0228	...	...	0428	...	...	0528	...	0603	...	0628	0628	0703	0728	0803	minutes	2028	2102	2128	2203	2228	2302
134	**Duisburg** Hbf ... ▷ d.	0238	0238	...	...	0438	...	...	0538	...	0615	...	0638	0638	0715	0738	0815		2038	2115	2138	2215	2238	2315
144	Mülheim (Ruhr) Hbf ... ▷ d.	0244	0244	...	...	0444	...	...	0544	...	0621	...	0644	0644	0721	0744	0821	past each	2044	2121	2144	2221	2244	2321
153	**Essen** Hbf ... ▷ d.	0252	0252	...	...	0452	...	...	0552	...	0629	...	0652	0652	0729	0752	0829		2052	2129	2152	2229	2252	2329
169	Bochum Hbf ... ❖ ▷ d.	0303	0303	...	...	0503	...	...	0603	...	0640	...	0703	0703	0741	0803	0840	hour until	2103	2142	2203	2240	2303	2342
187	**Dortmund** Hbf ... ▷ d.	0314	0316	...	0455**t**	0516	0555	0555	0616	...	0655	0654	0716	0716	0755	0816	0855		2116	2155	2216	2255	2316	2353
218	**Hamm** (Westf) ... ▷ d.	...	0340	...	0515	0540	0615	0615	0639	...	0715	0715	0740	0740	0815	0839	0915		2139	2215	2240	2315	2340	...
268	Gütersloh Hbf ... d.	...	...	...	0548	...	0648	0648	...	...	0749	0749	...	...	0848	...	0948		...	2248	...	2348	...	...
285	**Bielefeld** Hbf ... **811** d.	...	...	...	0600	...	0657	0700	...	...	0800	0800	...	...	0900	...	1000		...	2300	...	2400	...	...
299	Herford ... **811** d.	...	...	...	0607	...	...	0707	...	...	0808	0808	...	...	0908	...	1008		...	2308	...	...	...	...
309	Löhne ... **811** d.	...	...	...	0614	...	...	0714	...	...	0814	0814	...	...	0914	...	1014		...	2315	...	...	...	...
315	Bad Oeynhausen ... **811** d.	...	...	...	0619	...	...	0719	...	...	0819	0819	...	...	0919	...	1019		...	2320	...	...	...	...
330	**Minden** (Westf) ... **811** a.	...	...	...	0630	...	...	0730	...	...	0830	0830	...	...	0930	...	1030		...	2330	...	...	...	...

❖ – From Sept. 6 to Oct. 31 (also from approx. 2100 on Sept. 5) the following changes apply: *RE1* services are diverted between Essen and Dortmund (not calling at Bochum); Dortmund timings may vary by up to 5 minutes during this period. *RE6* services do not call at Mülheim and are suspended between Essen and Dortmund (minor timing variations may also apply).

OR OTHER NOTES, SEE NEXT PAGE →

802 RHEIN – RUHR LOCAL SERVICES

RE / RB services

Services in this table (pages 380 – 382) are shown route by route. Sub-headings indicate the route number and principal stations served. See Tables **800** and **810** for *ICE, EC and IC services*

RE1 Aachen - Köln - Düsseldorf - Dortmund - Hamm ♣ ⊡ ❖

km	SEE NOTE ❖				⑤⑥			
	Aachen Hbf .... **807** d.	2151	...	2251	2251	...	2351	...
	Düren .... **807** d.	2217	...	2317	2317	...	0017	...
0	Köln/Bonn Flughafen ✈ ..... d.	|	2248	|	|	2348	|	...
15	**Köln** Hbf .... **807** a.	2244	2301	2344	2344	0002	0044	...
15	**Köln** Hbf .... d.	2249	2307	2349	2349	0007	0049	...
	Köln Messe/Deutz .... d.	2253	|	2353	2353	|	0053	...
	Leverkusen Mitte .... d.	2304	|	0004	0004	|	0104	...
51	Neuss Hbf .... d.	|	2336	|	|	0036	|	...
62	**Düsseldorf** Hbf .... a.	2320	2348	0019	0019	0048	0120	...
	Düsseldorf Hbf .... ▷ d.	2322	2354	0022	0022	0054	0122	...
	Düsseldorf Flughafen ✈ ... ▷ d.	2328	0002	0028	0028	0102	0128	...
	Duisburg Hbf .... ▷ d.	2338	0017	0038	0038	0115	0138	...
	Mülheim (Ruhr) Hbf .... ▷ d.	2344	0023	0044	0044	0121	0144	...
	Essen Hbf .... ▷ d.	2352	0031	0052	0052	0129	0152	...
	Bochum Hbf .... ❖ ▷ d.	0003	0043	0103	0103	0142	0203	...
	Dortmund Hbf .... ▷ d.	0016	0055	0114	0116	0153	0216	...
	Hamm (Westf) .... **810** ▷ d.	0042	...	...	0140	...	0242	...
	Gütersloh Hbf .... **810** d.	...	...	...	...	...	...	...
	Bielefeld Hbf .... **810/1** d.	...	...	...	...	...	...	...
	Herford .... **810/1** d.	...	...	...	...	...	...	...
	Löhne .... **811** d.	...	...	...	...	...	...	...
	Bad Oeynhausen .... **810/1** d.	...	...	...	...	...	...	...
	Minden (Westf) .... **810/1** a.	...	...	...	...	...	...	...

RE6 Köln - Neuss - Düsseldorf - Bielefeld - Minden ♣ ⊡ ❖

SEE NOTE ❖	Ⓒ	Ⓐ					Ⓐ			⚒	
Minden (Westf) .... **810/1** d.	...	...	...	...	...	...	...	...	...	...	...
Bad Oeynhausen .... **810/1** d.	...	...	...	...	...	...	...	...	...	...	...
Löhne .... **811** d.	...	...	...	...	...	...	...	...	...	...	...
Herford .... **810/1** d.	...	...	...	...	...	...	...	...	...	...	...
Bielefeld Hbf .... **810/1** d.	...	...	...	...	...	...	...	...	...	0459	...
Gütersloh Hbf .... **810** d.	...	...	...	...	...	...	...	...	...	0508	...
Hamm (Westf) .... **810** ▷ d.	0018	...	...	0317	...	0417	...	...	0518	0544	...
Dortmund Hbf .... ▷ d.	0045	0045	...	0345	...	0445	0507	...	0545	0607	...
Bochum Hbf .... ❖ ▷ d.	0055	0055	...	0355	...	0455	0519	...	0555	0619	...
Essen Hbf .... ▷ d.	0109	0109	...	0408	...	0509	0532	...	0609	0632	...
Mülheim (Ruhr) Hbf .... ▷ d.	0115	0115	...	0415	...	0515	0538	...	0615	0638	...
Duisburg Hbf .... ▷ d.	0123	0123	...	0422	...	0523	0548	...	0623	0648	...
Düsseldorf Flughafen ✈ . ▷ d.	0132	0132	...	0431	...	0532	0557	...	0632	0657	...
Düsseldorf Hbf .... ▷ a.	0138	0138	...	0437	...	0538	0605	...	0638	0705	...
Düsseldorf Hbf .... d.	0140	0140	0413	0439	0513	0540	0613	0613	0640	0713	0713
Neuss Hbf .... d.	|	|	0424	|	0524	|	0624	0624	|	0724	0724
Leverkusen Mitte .... d.	0155	0155	|	0454	|	0555	|	|	0655	|	|
Köln Messe/Deutz .... d.	0208	0208	|	0507	|	0608	|	|	0708	|	|
Köln Hbf .... a.	0212	0211	0450	0512	0552	0612	0650	0650	0712	0750	0750
Köln Hbf .... **807** d.	0215	0222	0457	0515**t**	0556	0615	0652	0652	0715	0801	0801
Köln/Bonn Flughafen ✈ .. a.	|	0234	0511	|	0611	|	0711	0711	|	0812	0812
Düren .... **807** d.	0239	...	...	0541**t**	...	0641	...	...	0741	...	...
Aachen Hbf .... **807** a.	0307	...	...	0607**t**	...	0707	...	...	0807	...	...

SEE NOTE ❖			Ⓐ					⚒			▲☒											⑤⑥f	
Minden (Westf) .... **810/1** d.	...	...	0528	...	0628	...	...	0728	...	0828		...	1828	...	1928	...	2028	...	...	2128	...	...	2228
Bad Oeynhausen .... **810/1** d.	...	...	0539	...	0639	...	...	0739	...	0839		...	1839	...	1939	...	2039	...	...	2139	...	...	2239
Löhne .... **811** d.	...	...	0544	...	0644	...	...	0744	...	0844		...	1844	...	1944	...	2044	...	...	2144	...	...	2244
Herford .... **810/1** d.	...	...	0552	...	0652	...	...	0751	...	0852		...	1852	...	1951	...	2052	...	...	2152	...	...	2252
Bielefeld Hbf .... **810/1** d.	...	0601	0601	...	0701	...	0759	0759	...	0901		...	1901	...	1959	...	2101	...	...	2201	...	...	2301
Gütersloh Hbf .... **810** d.	...	0610	0610	...	0710	...	0810	0810	...	0910		...	1910	...	2010	...	2110	...	...	2210	...	...	2310
Hamm (Westf) .... **810** ▷ d.	0618	0644	0644	0720	0744	0820	0844	0844	0920	0944	and at	1920	1944	2020	2045	2120	2144	2218	...	2244	2320	2320	2344
Dortmund Hbf .... ▷ d.	0645	0707	0707	0745	0807	0845	0907	0907	0945	1007		1945	2007	2045	2107	2145	2207	2245	...	2307	2345	2345	0007
Bochum Hbf .... ❖ ▷ d.	0655	0719	0719	0755	0819	0855	0917	0917	0955	1019	the same	1955	2019	2055	2119	2155	2219	2255	...	2319	2356	2356	0019
Essen Hbf .... ▷ d.	0709	0732	0732	0809	0832	0909	0929	0929	1009	1032		2009	2032	2109	2132	2209	2232	2309	...	2332	0009	0009	0032
Mülheim (Ruhr) Hbf .... ▷ d.	0715	0738	0738	0815	0838	0915	0935	0935	1015	1038	minutes	2015	2038	2115	2138	2215	2238	2315	...	2338	0015	0015	0038
Duisburg Hbf .... ▷ d.	0723	0748	0748	0823	0848	0923	0945	0945	1023	1048		2023	2048	2123	2148	2223	2248	2324	...	2348	0023	0023	0048
Düsseldorf Flughafen ✈ ..... ▷ d.	0732	0757	0757	0832	0857	0932	0955	0955	1032	1057	past each	2032	2057	2132	2157	2232	2257	2332	...	2357	0032	0032	0057
Düsseldorf Hbf .... ▷ a.	0738	0805	0805	0838	0905	0938	1004	1004	1038	1105		2038	2105	2138	2205	2238	2305	2338	...	0005	0038	0038	0105
Düsseldorf Hbf .... d.	0740	0813	0813	0840	0913	0940	1013	1013	1040	1113	hour until	2040	2113	2140	2213	2240	2313	2340	...	...	...	0040	...
Neuss Hbf .... d.	|	0824	0824	|	0924	|	1024	1024	|	1124		|	2124	|	2224	|	2324	|	...	...	...	|	...
Leverkusen Mitte .... d.	0755	|	|	0855	|	0955	|	|	1055	|		2055	|	2155	|	2255	|	2355	...	...	...	0055	...
Köln Messe/Deutz .... d.	0808	|	|	0908	|	1008	|	|	1108	|		2108	|	2208	|	2308	|	0008	...	...	...	0108	...
Köln Hbf .... a.	0812	0852	0852	0912	0950	1012	1052	1052	1112	1150		2112	2150	2212	2252	2312	2352	0012	...	...	...	0112	...
Köln Hbf .... **807** d.	0815	0858	0858	0915	0952	1015	1058	1058	1115	1152		2115	2152	2215	2258	2315	2358	0015	...	...	...	0115	...
Köln/Bonn Flughafen ✈ ..... a.	|	0911	0911	|	1011	|	1111	1111	|	1211		|	2211	|	2311	|	0011	|	...	...	...	|	...
Düren .... **807** d.	0841	...	...	0941	...	1039	...	...	1139	...		2139	...	2239	...	2339	...	0040	...	...	...	0139	...
Aachen Hbf .... **807** a.	0907	...	...	1007	...	1107	...	...	1207	...		2207	...	2307	...	0007	...	0107	...	...	...	0207	...

RE2 Düsseldorf - Essen - Gelsenkirchen - Münster ⊡ *RE42* Mönchengladbach - Essen - Münster

km	SEE NOTE ⊗		⚒	⚒	⚒		⚒							●										
0	**Düsseldorf** Hbf .... d.	0006	...	0506	...	...	0606	...	0706	...	0806	...	0906		...	1906	...	2006	...	2106	...	2206	...	2306
7	Düsseldorf Flughafen ✈ d.	0013	...	0513	...	...	0613	...	0713	...	0813	...	0913		...	1913	...	2013	...	2113	...	2213	...	2313
	Mönchengladbach . d.	|	...	|	0522	...	|	0622	|	0722	|	0822	|		1823	|	1922	|	2022	|	2122	|	2222	|
	Viersen .... d.	|	...	|	0531	...	|	0631	|	0731	|	0831	|	and at	1831	|	1931	|	2031	|	2131	|	2231	|
	Krefeld Hbf .... d.	|	...	|	0541	...	|	0641	|	0741	|	0841	|		1841	|	1941	|	2041	|	2141	|	2241	|
24	**Duisburg** Hbf .... d.	0024	...	0524	0602	...	0624	0702	0724	0802	0824	0902	0924	the same	1902	1924	2002	2024	2102	2124	2202	2224	2302	2324
34	Mülheim (Ruhr) Hbf ..... d.	0030	...	0530	0609	...	0630	0709	0730	0809	0830	0909	0930		1909	1930	2009	2030	2109	2130	2209	2230	2309	2330
43	**Essen** Hbf .... d.	0046	0446	0541	0617	0641	0641	0717	0741	0817	0841	0917	0941	minutes	1917	1941	2017	2041	2117	2141	2217	2241	2317	2346
53	Gelsenkirchen Hbf ...... d.	0054	0455	0550	0626	0650	0650	0726	0750	0826	0850	0926	0950	past each	1926	1950	2026	2050	2126	2150	2226	2250	2326	2354
58	Wanne-Eickel Hbf .... d.	0100	0500	0556	0631	0656	0656	0731	0756	0831	0856	0931	0956	hour until	1931	1956	2031	2056	2131	2156	2231	2256	2331	0000
68	Recklinghausen Hbf .... d.	0109	0509	0604	0639	0704	0704	0739	0804	0839	0904	0939	1004		1939	2004	2039	2104	2139	2204	2239	2304	2339	0009
84	Haltern am See .... d.	0120	0519	0613	0650	0713	0713	0750	0813	0850	0913	0950	1013		1950	2013	2050	2113	2151	2213	2251	2313	2351	0020
97	Dülmen .... d.	0129	0528	0620	0659	0720	0720	0759	0820	0859	0920	0959	1020		1959	2020	2059	2120	...	2220	...	2320	...	0029
126	**Münster** (Westf) Hbf ★ d.	0153	0549	0637	0722	0737	0737	0822	0837	0922	0938	1022	1037		2022	2037	2122	2137	...	2237	...	2335	...	0053
176	**Osnabrück** Hbf ...... ★ a.	...	...	0712	...	0819	0819	...	0910	...	1015	...	1110		...	2110	...	2215	...	2310**f**	...	...	...	...

SEE NOTE ⊗			⚒	⚒	⚒										♥									⑤⑥
Osnabrück Hbf ...... ★ d.	...	...	...	...	...	...	0545**r**	...	0648	...	0748	...	0849	...		1849	...	1948	...	2049	...	...	...	...
Münster (Westf) Hbf ★ d.	0007	0209	0425	...	0525	0536**t**	0625	0636**r**	0725	0736**r**	0825	0836	0925	0936		1925	1936	2025	2036	2125	...	2209	2309	2309
Dülmen .... d.	0029	0232	0439	...	0539	0558**t**	0639	0658**r**	0739	0758**r**	0839	0858	0939	0958		1939	1958	2039	2058	2139	...	2232	2332	2332
Haltern am See .... d.	0039	0244	0446	0507	0546	0607	0646	0707	0746	0807	0846	0907	0946	1007	and at	1946	2007	2046	2107	2146	2207	2244	2344	2344
Recklinghausen Hbf ..... d.	0050	0255	0455	0519	0555	0619	0655	0719	0755	0819	0855	0919	0955	1018		1955	2019	2055	2119	2155	2219	2255	2355	2355
Wanne-Eickel Hbf .... d.	0059	0304	0503	0528	0603	0628	0703	0728	0803	0828	0903	0929	1003	1027	the same	2003	2027	2103	2128	2203	2228	2304	0004	0004
Gelsenkirchen Hbf .... d.	0104	0309	0509	0533	0609	0633	0709	0733	0809	0833	0909	0934	1009	1032		2009	2032	2109	2133	2209	2233	2309	0009	0009
Essen Hbf .... d.	0114	0321	0521	0545	0621	0645	0721	0745	0821	0845	0921	0945	1021	1045	minutes	2021	2045	2121	2145	2221	2245	2321	0019	0021
Mülheim (Ruhr) Hbf .... d.	...	0327	0527	0552	0627	0652	0727	0752	0827	0852	0927	0952	1027	1052	past each	2027	2052	2127	2152	2227	2252	2327	...	0027
Duisburg Hbf .... d.	...	0336	0536	0601	0636	0701	0736	0801	0836	0901	0936	1001	1036	1101		2036	2101	2136	2201	2236	2301	2336	...	0036
Krefeld Hbf .... d.	...	|	|	0618	|	0718	|	0818	|	0918	|	1018	|	1118	hour until	|	2118	|	2218	|	2318	|	...	|
Viersen .... d.	...	|	|	0633	|	0733	|	0833	|	0933	|	1033	|	1133		|	2133	|	2233	|	2333	|	...	|
Mönchengladbach .. a.	...	|	|	0642	|	0742	|	0842	|	0942	|	1042	|	1142		|	2142	|	2242	|	2342	|	...	|
Düsseldorf Flughafen ✈ .d.	...	0346	0546	...	0646	...	0746	...	0846	...	0946	...	1046	...		2046	...	2146	...	2246	...	2346	...	0046
Düsseldorf Hbf .... a.	...	0353	0553	...	0653	...	0753	...	0853	...	0953	...	1053	...		2053	...	2153	...	2253	...	2353	...	0053

RE3 Düsseldorf - Duisburg - Gelsenkirchen - Dortmund - Hamm ⊡ ◇

km											
0	**Düsseldorf** Hbf .... d.	0445	0545	0645		1845	1945	2045	2145	2245	2345
7	Düsseldorf Flughafen ✈ d.	0453	0553	0653		1853	1953	2053	2153	2253	2353
24	**Duisburg** Hbf .... d.	0510	0610	0710	and	1910	2010	2110	2210	2310	0010
32	Oberhausen Hbf .... d.	0516	0616	0716	hourly	1916	2016	2116	2216	2316	0016
48	Gelsenkirchen Hbf ...... d.	0529	0629	0729		1929	2029	2129	2229	2329	0029
53	Wanne-Eickel Hbf .... d.	0534	0634	0734	until	1934	2034	2134	2234	2334	0034
57	Herne .... d.	0538	0638	0738		1938	2038	2138	2238	2338	0038
78	**Dortmund** Hbf .... a.	0556	0656	0756		1956	2056	2156	2256	2356	0056
109	**Hamm** (Westf) .... a.	0629**t**	0729**r**	0829		2029	...	...	...	...	...

Hamm (Westf) .... d.	...	0530**t**	0630**t**	0730**r**	0830		2030	...	...
Dortmund Hbf .... d.	0503	0603	0703	0803	0903		2103	2203	2303
Herne .... d.	0519	0619	0719	0819	0919	and	2119	2219	2319
Wanne-Eickel Hbf .... d.	0524	0624	0724	0824	0924	hourly	2124	2224	2324
Gelsenkirchen Hbf .... d.	0529	0629	0729	0829	0929		2129	2229	2329
Oberhausen Hbf .... d.	0543	0643	0743	0843	0943	until	2143	2243	2343
Duisburg Hbf .... d.	0553	0653	0753	0853	0953		2153	2253	2353
Düsseldorf Flughafen ✈ ..... d.	0604	0704	0804	0904	1004		2204	2304	0004
Düsseldorf Hbf .... a.	0612	0712	0812	0912	1012		2212	2312	0012

r – ⚒ only.
t – Ⓐ only.

◇ – Operated by *eurobahn*.
♣ – Operated by National Express.
▲ – Timings may vary by up to 3 minutes.
☒ – Köln Hbf d. 1258, 1458, 1858 and 2058 (not xx52).

● – Osnabrück arrivals vary – subsequent arrivals are at 1219, 1310, 1419, 1510, 1618, 1711, 1819, 1910 and 2015.
♥ – Timings may vary by 1 – 2 minutes. Osnabrück departures vary – subsequent departures are at 0947, 1049, 1145, 1249, 1346, 1449, 1547, 1649 and 1747.
⊗ – Timings may vary by up to 3 minutes Sept. 6 - Oct. 31.

★ – Additional trains (◇) Münster - Osnabrück and v.v. (journey time 36 minutes): **From Münster** at 0503 Ⓐ, 0603 ⚒, 0703, 0803 and hourly until 0003. **From Osnabrück** at 0519 Ⓐ, 0619 ⚒, 0719, 0819 and hourly until 0019; also at 2145 (operated by DB).
▷ – See Table **805** for *RE11* services Düsseldorf - Hamm - Paderborn - Kassel and v.v
⊡ – See shaded panel on page 382 for a summary of the principal Rhein-Ruhr *RE* routes.
❖ – Subject to alteration Sept. 6 - Oct. 31 (see note at bottom of page 379).

Services in this table (pages 380–382) are shown route by route. Sub-headings indicate the route number and principal stations served. See Tables **800** and **810** for *ICE, EC and IC* services.

RE4 Aachen - Mönchengladbach - Düsseldorf - Wuppertal - Dortmund ♣ ⊡ *RE13* Venlo - Mönchengladbach - Düsseldorf - Wuppertal - Hamm ◇ ⊡

km			Ⓐ	⚒	Ⓐ	⚒	⚒		⚒														
0	**Aachen** Hbf .... **473** d.	0253	0421	0421	...	...	0521	0521	...	0621	...		1721	...	1821	...	1921	...	2022	...	2121	...	2237	2337
14	Herzogenrath .... **473** d.	0307	0436	0436	...	...	0536	0536	...	0636	...	⊖	1736	...	1836	...	1936	...	2036	...	2136	...	2252	2352
58	Rheydt Hbf .... d.	0343	0507	0507	...	...	0607	0607	...	0707	...		1807	...	1907	...	2007	...	2107	...	2207	...	2332	0032
	Venlo 🏛 .... d.	|	|	|	0505	0505	|	|	0605	|	0705	and at	|	1805	|	1905	|	2005	|	2105	|	2205	|	|
	Kaldenkirchen .... d.	|	|	|	0510	0510	|	|	0610	|	0710		|	1810	|	1910	|	2010	|	2110	|	2210	|	|
	Viersen .... d.	|	|	|	0527	0527	|	|	0627	|	0727	the same	|	1827	|	1927	|	2027	|	2127	|	2227	|	|
62	**Mönchengladbach** Hbf a.	0348	0511	0511	0536	0536	0611	0611	0636	0711	0736		1811	1836	1911	1936	2011	2036	2111	2136	2211	2236	2337	0037
62	**Mönchengladbach** Hbf d.	0350	0512	0512	0545	0545	0612	0612	0645	0712	0745	minutes	1812	1845	1912	1945	2012	2045	2112	2145	2212	...	...	...
79	Neuss Hbf .... d.	0403	0527	0527	0557	0557	0627	0627	0657	0727	0757		1827	1857	1927	1957	2027	2057	2127	2157	2227	...	...	...
90	**Düsseldorf** Hbf .... a.	0413	0539	0539	0610	0610	0639	0639	0710	0739	0810	past each	1839	1910	1939	2010	2039	2110	2139	2210	2239	...	...	...
90	**Düsseldorf** Hbf .... d.	d	0542	...	0612	...	0642	▬	0712	0742	0812		1842	1912	1942	2012	2042	...	2142	...	2242	...	...	...
117	**Wuppertal** Hbf .... d.	...	0602	...	0632	...	0702	...	0732	0802	0832	hour until	1902	1932	2002	2032	2102	...	2202	...	2302	...	...	...
144	**Hagen** Hbf.......... **804** d.	...	0627	...	0657	...	0727	0758	0758	0827	0858		1927	1958	2027	2055	2127	...	2227	...	2327	...	...	...
159	Witten Hbf .... d.	...	0640	...	|	...	0740	|	|	0840	|		1940	|	2040	...	2140	...	2240	...	2340	...	...	...
175	**Dortmund** Hbf............ d.	...	0651	...	|	...	0751	|	|	0851	|		1951	|	2051	...	2151	...	2251	...	2351	...	...	...
	Schwerte.......... **804** d.	...	...	...	0706	...	...	0808	0808	...	0908		...	2008	...	...	...	...	...	...	...	...	...	...
	Unna........................ d.	...	...	...	0720	...	...	0820	0820	...	0920		...	2020	...	...	...	...	...	...	...	...	...	...
	Hamm (Westf) .... a.	...	...	...	0734	...	...	0834	0834	...	0934		...	2035	...	...	...	...	...	...	...	...	...	...

km		⚒	Ⓐ	⚒	⚒			Ⓐ	⚒			⚒													
0	**Hamm** (Westf) .... d.	...	...	...	...	...	...	...	0625	...	...	...	0725r	...	0824	...	0925		...	1925	...	...	...	...
19	Unna........................ d.	...	...	...	...	...	...	...	0637	...	...	...	0737r	...	0839	...	0937	⊗	...	1937	...	...	...	...
35	Schwerte.......... **804** d.	...	...	...	...	...	...	...	0648	...	...	...	0749r	...	0850	...	0949		...	1949	...	...	...	...
	Dortmund Hbf............ d.	...	...	...	...	...	...	0609	|	...	...	0709	|	0809	|	0909	|	and at	1909	|	2009	...	2109	2209
	Witten Hbf .... d.	...	...	...	...	...	...	0620	|	...	...	0720	|	0820	|	0920	|		1920	|	2020	...	2120	2220
48	**Hagen** Hbf.......... **804** d.	...	...	...	...	0602t	...	0634	0702	...	...	0734	0802	0834	0902	0934	1002	the same	1934	2002	2034	...	2134	2234
75	**Wuppertal** Hbf .... d.	...	...	...	...	0625t	...	0657	0725	...	...	0757	0825	0857	0925	0957	1025		1957	2025	2057	...	2157	2257
102	**Düsseldorf** Hbf .... a.	...	...	...	...	0646t	...	0718	0746	...	...	0818	0846	0918	0946	1018	1046	minutes	2018	2046	2118	...	2218	2318
102	**Düsseldorf** Hbf .... d.	...	0521	0548	0621	0648r	0721	0721	0748	0748	0821	0821	0848	0921	0948	1021	1048		2021	2048	2121	2148	2221	2321
113	Neuss Hbf .... d.	...	0536	0601	0636	0701r	0736	0736	0801	0801	0836	0836	0901	0936	1001	1036	1101	past each	2036	2101	2136	2201	2236	2336
130	**Mönchengladbach** Hbf a.	...	0549	0611	0649	0711r	0749	0749	0811	0811	0849	0849	0911	0949	1011	1049	1111		2049	2111	2149	2211	2249	2349
130	**Mönchengladbach** Hbf d.	0525	0550	0625	0650	0725	0750	0750	0825	0825	0850	0850	0925	0950	1025	1050	1125	hour until	2050	2125	2150	2225	2250	2350
139	Viersen .... d.	0533	|	0633	|	0733	|	|	0833	0833	|	|	0933	|	1033	|	1133		|	2133	|	2233	|	|
157	Kaldenkirchen .... d.	0550	|	0650	|	0750	|	|	0850	0850	|	|	0950	|	1050	|	1150		|	2150	|	2250	|	|
167	**Venlo** 🏛 .... a.	0556	|	0656	|	0756	|	|	0856	0856	|	|	0956	|	1056	|	1156		|	2156	|	2256	|	|
	Rheydt Hbf .... d.	...	0554	...	0654	...	0754	0754	...	...	0854	0854	...	0954	...	1054	...		2054	...	2154	...	2254	2354
	Herzogenrath....... **473** d.	...	0624	...	0724	...	0824	0824	...	...	0924	0924	...	1024	...	1124	...		2124	...	2224	...	2324	0024
	Aachen Hbf......... **473** a.	...	0636	...	0739	...	0836	0836	...	...	0936	0936	...	1036	...	1136	...		2137	...	2236	...	2336	0037

RE5 Koblenz - Bonn - Köln - Düsseldorf - Duisburg - Oberhausen ♣ ⊡ *RE19* Düsseldorf - Emmerich - Arnhem ⊙

km				⚒◐	⚒	Ⓐ		◐		⚒											⑤⑥f				◐
0	**Koblenz** Hbf.............. d.	...	...	0429	...	0516	...	0530	...	0616	...	0716	...		1916	...	2016	...	2116	2116	...	2216	...	2326
18	Andernach .... d.	...	...	0446	...	0528	...	0545	...	0628	...	0728	...		1928	...	2028	...	2128	2128	...	2228	...	2344
29	Bad Breisig................. d.	...	...	0455	...	0534	...	0555	...	0634	...	0734	...		1934	...	2034	...	2134	2134	...	2234	...	2354
39	Remagen..................... d.	...	...	0511j	...	0544	...	0611j	...	0644	...	0744	...	and at	1944	...	2044	...	2144	2144	...	2244	...	0011j
59	**Bonn** Hbf .... d.	...	...	0533	...	0604	...	0633	...	0704	...	0804	...		2004	...	2104	...	2204	2204	...	2304	...	0033
93	**Köln** Hbf .... a.	...	...	0602	...	0628	...	0702	...	0728	...	0828	...	the same	2028	...	2128	...	2228	2228	...	2328	...	0102
	Köln Hbf .... d.	...	...	|	0631	0631	...	|	0731	0731	...	0831	...		2031	...	2131	...	2231	2231	*2249*	2331	2349	0105
94	**Köln** Messe/Deutz...... d.	...	...	0608	0634	0634	...	0708	0734	0734	...	0834	...	minutes	2034	...	2134	...	2233	2234	*2253*	2333	2353	0108
106	Leverkusen Mitte .... d.	...	...	...	0645	0645	...	...	0745	0745	...	0845	...		2045	...	2145	...	...	2245	*2304*	...	0004	▬
133	**Düsseldorf** Hbf .... d.	...	0626	...	0703	0703	0726	...	0803	0803	0826	0903	0926	past each	2103	2126	2203	2226	...	2303	2326	...	0022	...
140	Düsseldorf Flughafen ✈ d.	...	0633	...	0709	0709	0733	...	0809	0809	0833	0909	0933		2109	2133	2209	2233	...	2309	2333	...	0028	...
157	**Duisburg** Hbf............. d.	0544	0644	...	0719	0719	0744	...	0819	0819	0844	0919	0944	hour until	2119	2144	2219	2244	...	2317	2344	...	0036	0044
165	Oberhausen Hbf .... d.	0550	0650	...	0724	0724	0750	...	0824	0824	0850	0924	0950		2124	2150	2224	2250	...	...	2350	...	...	0050
192	Wesel.......................... d.	0616	0716	...	...	...	0816	...	...	...	0916	...	1016		...	2216	...	2316	...	...	0016	...	...	0116
226	**Emmerich** 🏛 .... d.	0646b	0746	...	...	...	0846	...	...	...	0946	...	1046		...	2246	...	2346	...	...	0047	...	...	0147
256	**Arnhem** Centraal........ a.	0713b	0813	...	...	...	0913	...	...	...	1013	...	1113		...	2313	...	0013	...	...	...	...	...	...

	Ⓐ	◐		⚒	◐			⚒												◐				
rnhem Centraal......... d.	...	...	...	...	...	...	...	...	0545r	...	0645	...	0745	...		1845	...	1945	...	...	2045	2145	...	2245
mmerich 🏛 .... d.	...	...	0409	...	...	0509	...	...	0609	...	0709	...	0809	...		1909	...	2009	...	...	2109	2209	...	2309
'esel .... d.	...	...	0443	...	...	0543	...	...	0643	...	0743	...	0843	...		1943	...	2043	...	...	2143	2243	...	2343
berhausen Hbf .... d.	...	...	0508	0533t	...	0608	...	0633	0708	0733	0808	0828	0908	0933	and in	2008	2028	2108	2133	...	2208	2308	...	0008
uisburg Hbf .... d.	...	...	0516	0541	...	0616	...	0641	0716	0741	0816	0835	0916	0941		2016	2035	2116	2141	...	2216	2315	2324	0015
üsseldorf Flughafen ✈ d.	...	...	0525	0550	...	0625	...	0650	0725	0750	0825	0850	0925	0950	the same	2025	2050	2125	2150	...	2225	▬	2332	...
üsseldorf Hbf .... d.	...	...	0533	0558	...	0633	...	0658	0733	0758	0833	0858	0933	0958		2033	2058	2133	2158	...	2233	...	2340	...
everkusen Mitte .... d.	...	...	...	0613	...	...	...	0713	...	0813	...	0913	...	1013	pattern	...	2113	...	2213	...	...	◐	2355	...
öln Messe/Deutz....... d.	0526	0549	...	0626	0649	...	0726	0726	...	0826	...	0926	...	1026		...	2126	...	2226	2249	...	2349	0008	...
öln Hbf .... a.	0529	0553	...	0629	0653	...	0729	0729	...	0829	...	0929	...	1029	every two	...	2129	...	2229	2253	...	2353	0012	...
öln Hbf .... d.	0532	0556	...	0632	0656	...	0732	0732	...	0832	...	0932	...	1032		...	2132	...	2232	2256	...	2356	...	...
onn Hbf .... d.	0557	0627	...	0657	0727	...	0757	0757	...	0857	...	0957	...	1057	hours until	...	2157	...	2257	2327	...	0027	...	...
emagen....................... d.	0615	0654j	...	0716	0754j	...	0816	0816	...	0916	...	1016	...	1116		...	2216	...	2316	2351	...	0054j	...	...
ad Breisig.................... d.	0622	0702	...	0723	0802	...	0823	0823	...	0923	...	1023	...	1123		...	2223	...	2323	2359	...	0102	...	...
ndernach..................... d.	0629	0712	...	0730	0813	...	0830	0830	...	0930	...	1030	...	1130		...	2230	...	2330	0009	...	0112	...	...
oblenz Hbf................. a.	0642	0727	...	0742	0828	...	0842	0842	...	0942	...	1042	...	1142		...	2242	...	2342	0026	...	0132	...	...

RE7 Krefeld - Köln - Wuppertal - Hamm - Münster (- Rheine: Table 812) ♣ ⊡

km		Ⓐ								⑤⑥f	
0	**Krefeld** Hbf .... d.	...	...	0535r	0635		2035	2135	2235	2235	...
18	Neuss Hbf .... d.	...	...	0552r	0652		2052	2152	2252	2252	...
54	**Köln** Hbf .... a.	...	...	0618r	0718		2118	2218	2318	2318	...
54	**Köln** Hbf .... d.	...	0521t	0621r	0721	and	2121	2221	...	2321	2352
55	**Köln** Messe/Deutz...... d.	...	0524t	0624r	0724		2124	2224	...	2324	2355
82	Solingen Hbf................ d.	...	0543t	0643r	0743	hourly	2143	2243	...	2343	0020
100	**Wuppertal** Hbf .... d.	...	0556t	0656r	0756		2156	2256	...	2356	0036
127	**Hagen** Hbf.................. d.	0521	0621	0721	0821	until	2221	2321	...	0021	...
140	Schwerte (Ruhr) ... **808** d.	0532	0632	0732	0832		2232	2332	...	0032	...
156	Unna .... **808** d.	0543	0643	0743	0843		2243	2343	...	0043	...
175	**Hamm** (Westf) .. **805/8** d.	0559	0659	0759	0859		2259	2357	...	0057	...
211	**Münster** Hbf..... **805/8** a.	0622	0722	0822	0922		2322	...	...	...	...

	Ⓐ	⚒v			❖			⑤⑥f		⑤⑥f
Münster Hbf.. **805/8** d.	...	...	0531t	0635		2035	2135	2135	2235	2234
Hamm (Westf) **805/8** d.	...	0500	0600	0700		2100	2203	2203	2300	2300
Unna..................... **808** d.	...	0512	0612	0712		2112	2214	2214	2312	2312
Schwerte (Ruhr) **808** d.	...	0525	0625	0725	and	2125	2225	2225	2325	2325
Hagen Hbf.................. d.	0439	0539	0639	0739		2139	2237	2239	2337	2339
Wuppertal Hbf.......... d.	0504	0604	0704	0804	hourly	2204	▬	2304	...	0002
Solingen Hbf............... d.	0515	0615	0715	0815		2215	...	2315	...	...
Köln Messe/Deutz ... d.	0535	0635	0735	0835	until	2235	...	2335	...	...
Köln Hbf.................. a.	0538	0638	0738	0838		2238	...	2338	...	...
Köln Hbf.................. d.	0541	0641	0741	0841		2241	2341	2341	...	...
Neuss Hbf.................. d.	0607	0707	0807	0907		2307	0007	0007	...	...
Krefeld Hbf .... a.	0624	0724	0824	0924		2324	0024	0024	...	...

– On ⑦ Emmerich a. 0646, d. 0707, Arnhem a. 0729.
– To Düsseldorf Flughafen Terminal (a. 0425).
– Also June 8, 18, Oct. 2.
– Arrives 7–8 minutes earlier.
– ⚒ only.
– Ⓐ only.
– Runs daily Köln Messe/Deutz - Krefeld.

⊖ – Aachen Hbf d. 0820 (not 0821). The 1105 and 1705 from Venlo depart Hagen and Schwerte 1–2 minutes earlier.
⊗ – Hamm d. 1422 (not 1425) / Unna d. 1434 (not 1437).
❖ – Certain services depart Hamm and Unna 2–3 minutes later.
◐ – Operated by Mittelrheinbahn.
◇ – Operated by *eurobahn*.
♣ – Operated by National Express.
⊙ – *RE19* operated by VIAS Rail. See below for details of 🚌 substitution June 28 - Aug. 24.
⊡ – See shaded panel on page 382 for a summary of the principal Rhein-Ruhr *RE* routes.

☛ **June 28 - Aug. 24** (also evening of June 27): trains are replaced by 🚌 between Oberhausen and Zevenaar or Arnhem. Arrivals at Arnhem are approx. 70 minutes later; departures from Arnhem are approx. 76 minutes earlier.

802 RHEIN – RUHR LOCAL SERVICES *RE / RB services*

Services in this table (pages 380 – 382) are shown route by route. Sub-headings indicate the route number and principal stations served. See Tables **800** and **810** for *ICE, EC and IC services*

Düsseldorf - Krefeld - Kleve ⊖

km		Ⓐ	⚒	Ⓐ			Ⓐ			
0	**Düsseldorf** Hbf .... d.	0538	0608	0638	0708		2038	2108	2208	2308
27	**Krefeld** Hbf .... d.	0606	0636	0706	0736	and at	2106	2136	2236	2336
57	Geldern .... d.	0631	0701	0731	0801	the same	2131	2201	2301	0001
66	Kevelaer .... d.	0638	0708	0738	0808	minutes	2138	2208	2308	0008
72	Weeze .... d.	0645	0715	0745	0815	past each	2145	2215	2315	0015
79	Goch .... d.	0651	0721	0751	0821	hour until	2151	2221	2321	0021
92	**Kleve** .... a.	0705	0735	0805	0835		2205	2235	2335	0035

	Ⓐ	⚒	Ⓐ			Ⓐ			●
Kleve .... d.	0454	0524	0554	0624		1854	1924	2024	2124
Goch .... d.	0508	0538	0608	0638	and at	1908	1938	2038	2138
Weeze .... d.	0515	0545	0615	0645	the same	1915	1945	2045	2145
Kevelaer .... d.	0521	0551	0621	0651	minutes	1921	1951	2051	2151
Geldern .... d.	0528	0558	0628	0658	past each	1928	1958	2058	2158
Krefeld Hbf .... d.	0556	0626	0656	0726	hour until	1956	2026	2126	2226
Düsseldorf Hbf .... a.	0624	0653	0723	0753		2023	2053	2153	2253

RE8 / RB27 Mönchengladbach - Köln - Königswinter - Koblenz ⊠

km	*SEE NOTE* ⊠	Ⓒ	Ⓐ	⚒		⚒	⚒	Ⓐ			⚒				⚒						⑤⑥f			⑤⑥
0	**Mönchengladbach** Hbf d.	0041	...	...	...	0441	...	0507	0541	...	0607	0641		...	2007	2041	...	2141	...	2241	2241	...	2341	2341
3	Rheydt Hbf .... d.	0046	...	...	...	0446	...	0512	0546	...	0612	0646		...	2012	2046	...	2146	...	2246	2246	...	2346	2346
22	Grevenbroich .... d.	0103	...	...	...	0503	...	0529	0603	...	0629	0703	and at	...	2029	2103	...	2203	...	2303	2303	...	0003	0003
56	**Köln** Hbf .... a.	0135	...	...	...	0535	...	0600	0635	...	0700	0735		...	2100	2135	...	2235	...	2335	2335	...	0035	0035
56	**Köln** Hbf .... **807** d.	0138	...	...	...	0538	0603	0603	0638	0703	0703	0738	the same	2103	2103	2138	2203	2238	2303	2338	2338	0003	0038	0038
57	**Köln** Messe/Deutz ...... d.	0142	...	...	...	0542	0607	0607	0642	0707	0707	0742		2107	2107	2142	2207	2242	2307	2342	2342	0007	0042	0042
71	Köln/Bonn Flughafen ✈ d.	0151	...	...	...	0551	|	|	0651	|	|	0751	minutes	|	|	2151	|	2251	|	2351	2351	|	0051	0051
83	Troisdorf .... **807** d.	0200	...	...	...	0600	0623	0623	0700	0723	0723	0800		2123	2123	2200	2223	2300	2323	0000	0000	0023	0100	0100
92	**Bonn** Beuel .... d.	0212	...	...	...	0612	0635	0635	0712	0735	0735	0812	past each	2135	2135	2212	2235	2312	2335	0012	0012	0035	0112	0112
100	Königswinter .... d.	0221	...	...	...	0621	0644	0644	0721	0744	0744	0821		2144	2144	2221	2244	2321	2344	0021	0021	0044	0121	0121
105	Bad Honnef .... d.	0226	...	...	...	0626	0651	0651	0726	0751	0751	0826	hour until	2151	2151	2226	2251	2326	2351	0026	0026	0051	0126	0126
115	Linz (Rhein) .... d.	0236	0437	0537	0637	0637	0701	0701	0737	0801	0801	0837		2201	2201	2237	2301	2337	0002	0036	0037	0100	0136	0137
122	Bad Hönningen .... d.	...	0444	0544	0644	0644	0706	0706	0744	0806	0806	0844		2206	2206	2244	2306	2344	...	...	0044	...	...	0144
138	Neuwied .... **914** d.	...	0458	0558	0658	0658	0719	0719	0758	0819	0819	0858		2219	2219	2258	2319	2358	...	...	0058	...	...	0158
153*	**Koblenz** Hbf .... **914** a.	...	0519	0619	0719	0719	0740	0740	0819	0840	0840	0919		2240	2240	2319	2340	0019	...	...	0119	...	...	0219

SEE NOTE ⊠	Ⓒ		⚒	⚒d	⚒		Ⓐ	⑥	†		⚒				⚒								
Koblenz Hbf .... **914** d.	0040	...	...	0440t	0516t	0540r	0611	0611	...	0640	0700	0700	0740		1800	1800	1840	1900	1940		2200	2240	2340
Neuwied .... **914** d.	0101	...	...	0501t	0535t	0602r	0633	0635	...	0701	0734	0734	0801		1834	1834	1901	1934	2001		2234	2301	0001
Bad Hönningen .... d.	0114	...	...	0514t	0547t	0615r	0645	0647	...	0714	0747	0747	0814	and at	1847	1847	1914	1947	2014	and at	2247	2314	0014
Linz (Rhein) .... d.	0122	...	...	0522	0553	0622	0652	0653	0653	0722	0753	0753	0822		1853	1853	1922	1953	2022		2253	2322	0022
Bad Honnef .... d.	0132	...	...	0532	0602	0632	0702	0702	0702	0731	0802	0802	0832	the same	1902	1902	1932	2002	2032	the same	2302	2332	0032
Königswinter .... d.	0138	...	...	0538	0608	0638	0708	0708	0708	0737	0808	0808	0838		1908	1908	1938	2008	2038		2308	2338	0038
Bonn Beuel .... d.	0147	...	...	0547	0617	0647	0717	0717	0717	0746	0817	0817	0847	minutes	1917	1917	1947	2017	2047	minutes	2317	2347	0047
Troisdorf .... **807** d.	0159	...	...	0559	0628	0659	0728	0728	0728	0757	0828	0828	0859		1928	1928	1959	2028	2059		2328	2359	0059
Köln/Bonn Flughafen ✈ d.	0209	...	...	0609	|	0709	|	|	|	0809	|	|	0909	past each	|	|	2009	|	2109	past each	|	0009	0109
Köln Messe/Deutz .... d.	0219	...	0519	0619	0650	0719	0750	0750	0750	0819	0850	0850	0919		1950	1950	2019	2050	2119		2350	0019	0119
Köln Hbf .... **807** a.	0222	...	0522	0622	0653	0722	0753	0753	0753	0822	0853	0853	0922	hour until	1953	1953	2022	2053	2122	hour until	2353	0022	0122
Köln Hbf .... d.	...	...	0525	0625	0659	0725	0759	0759	...	0825	0859	...	0925		1959	...	2025	...	2126		...	0025	0125
Grevenbroich .... d.	...	...	0555	0655	0729	0755	0829	0829	...	0855	0929	...	0955		2029	...	2055	...	2155		...	0055	0155
Rheydt Hbf .... d.	...	...	0612	0712	0746	0812	0846	0846	...	0912	0946	...	1012		2046	...	2112	...	2212		...	0112	0212
Mönchengladbach Hbf . a.	...	...	0619	0719	0751	0819	0851	0851	...	0919	0951	...	1019		2051	...	2119	...	2219		...	0119	0219

Dortmund - Unna - Soest ◇

km		Ⓒ		⚒	⚒	Ⓐ		♣		
0	**Dortmund** Hbf..... **805** d.	0103	...	0503	0603	0633	0703	and	0003	...
23	Unna .... d.	0130	...	0530	0630	0700	0730	hourly	0030	...
53	**Soest** .... **805** a.	0152	...	0552	0652	0722	0752	until	0052	...

	Ⓒ		⚒	Ⓐ	⚒	Ⓐ		♠	
Soest .... **805** d.	0106	...	0506	0536	0606	0636	0706	and	0006
Unna .... d.	0129	...	0529	0559	0629	0659	0729	hourly	0029
Dortmund Hbf.. **805** a.	0156	...	0556	0626	0656	0726	0756	until	0056

RB 53 Dortmund - Schwerte - Iserlohn

km		Ⓒ	Ⓒ	Ⓐ	Ⓐ		Ⓐ		⊡	
0	**Dortmund** Hbf .... d.	0023	0223	0523	0553	0623	0653	0723	and	2323
18	Schwerte (Ruhr) .... d.	0045	0245	0545	0615	0645	0715	0745	hourly	2345
38	**Iserlohn** .... a.	0109	0309	0609	0639	0709r	0739	0809	until	0009

	Ⓒ	Ⓐ	Ⓐ		Ⓐ		⊙		⑤⑥
Iserlohn .... d.	0050	0520	0620	0650r	0720	0750	and	2250	2350
Schwerte (Ruhr) .... d.	0117	0547	0647	0717	0747	0817	hourly	2317	0017
Dortmund Hbf .... a.	0138	0607	0707	0738	0807	0838	until	2338	0038

Summary of principal Rhein - Ruhr *RE* routes

	RE1	*RE2*	*RE3*	*RE4*	*RE5*	*RE6*	*RE7*	*RE11*	*RE13*	*RE42*
Aachen Hbf	●	...	...	●	...	...	...	...	...	...
Köln Hbf	●	...	...	|	●	●	●	...	...	...
Mönchengladbach Hbf...	|	...	...	●	|	|	|	...	●	●
Düsseldorf Hbf	●	●	●	●	●	●	|	●	●	|
Duisburg Hbf	●	●	●	|	●	●	|	●	|	●
Essen Hbf	●	●	|	|	...	●	|	●	|	●
via Gelsenkirchen	|	●	●	|	...	|	|	|	|	●
via Wuppertal and Hagen	|	|	|	●	...	|	●	|	●	|
Dortmund Hbf	●	|	●	●	...	●	|	●	|	|
Hamm (Westf)	●	|	●	...	...	●	●	●	●	|
Münster (Westf) Hbf	...	●	...	...	...	...	●	...	...	●

OTHER S-BAHN LINKS

Services operate every 20 – 30 minutes

Service	*Route (journey time in minutes)*
S 1	Solingen Hbf - Düsseldorf Hbf (22) - Düsseldorf Flughafen ✈ (35) - Duisburg Hbf (53) - Essen Hbf (72) - Bochum Hbf (90) - Dortmund Hbf (113)
S 3	Oberhausen Hbf - Mülheim Hbf (8) - Essen Hbf (17).
S 9	Essen Hbf - Wuppertal Hbf (46).
S11	Düsseldorf Flughafen Terminal ✈ - Düsseldorf Hbf (12) - Neuss Hbf (31) - Köln Hbf (82).

c – Mornings of Ⓒ.
d – Runs daily Köln Messe/Deutz - Mönchengladbach.
f – Also June 8, 18, Oct. 2.
r – ⚒ only.
t – Ⓐ only.

● – Also from Kleve at 2224.
♣ – Trains run every 30 minutes 0703 - 2003 on Ⓐ, 1003 - 2003 on ⑥.
♠ – Trains run every 30 minutes 0706 - 1906 on Ⓐ, 0906 - 1906 on ⑥.
⊡ – On Ⓐ trains run every 30 minutes 0723 - 1723.
⊙ – On Ⓐ trains run every 30 minutes 0750 - 1750.
⊖ – Operated by Rhein Ruhr Bahn.
◇ – Operated by *eurobahn* (2nd class only).
⊠ – Timings may vary by up to 4 minutes (earlier departures possible).

803 DORTMUND and MÜNSTER - ENSCHEDE

2nd class only; German holiday dates apply

DORTMUND - ENSCHEDE

km		⑥	Ⓐ	⚒						
0	**Dortmund** Hbf .... d.	...	0553	0653	0753r	0853		2053	2153	2253
44	Dülmen .... d.	...	0639	0739	0839r	0939	and	2139	2239	2339
61	Coesfeld (Westf) .... a.	...	0653	0753	0853r	0953		2153	2253	2353
61	Coesfeld (Westf) .... d.	0700	0705	0800	0900	1000	hourly	2200	...	...
96	Gronau (Westf) .... a.	0734	0738	0834	0934	1034		2234	...	...
96	Gronau (Westf) ...... 🚌 d.	0746	0745	0845	0946	1046	until	2246	...	...
103	**Enschede** .... a.	0757	0756	0856	0957	1057		2257	...	...

	⚒	⚒		Ⓐ	⑥				
Enschede .... d.	...	0556t	...	0656	0703	0803	0903		2103
Gronau (Westf).... 🚌 a.	...	0607t	...	0707	0714	0814	0914	and	2114
Gronau (Westf) .... d.	0522t	0622	...	0708	0722	0822	0922		2122
Coesfeld (Westf) .... a.	0557t	0657	...	0757	0757	0857	0957	hourly	2157
Coesfeld (Westf) .... d.	0603	0703	0803	0803	0803	0903	1003		2203
Dülmen .... d.	0617	0717	0817	0817	0817	0917	1017	until	2217
Dortmund Hbf .... a.	0706	0806	0906	0906	0906	1006	1106		2306

MÜNSTER - ENSCHEDE June 7 - 13 and Oct 10 - Dec. 13 ❦

km			⑥⑦		Ⓐ	Ⓐ	⚒			
0	**Münster** (Westf) Hbf.... d.	0008	0008	...	0508	0608	0708	0808	and	2308
56	Gronau (Westf) .... a.	0105	0105	...	0605	0704	0805	0905	hourly	0005
56	Gronau (Westf) ...... 🚌 d.	...	0116	...	0609	0716	0816	0916	until	0016
63	**Enschede** .... a.	...	0127	...	0620	0727	0827	0927		0027

	Ⓐ	⚒	⚒						⑤⑥
Enschede .... d.	...	...	0626	0733r	0833	and	2233	2333	2333
Gronau (Westf).... 🚌 a.	...	...	0637	0744r	0844	hourly	2244	2344	2344
Gronau (Westf) .... d.	0445	0545	0645	0745	0845	until	2245	...	2345
Münster (Westf) Hbf . a.	0544	0644	0744	0844	0944		2344	...	0044

f – Also Apr. 17, 20, 30, May 28, June 8; not June 6.
r – ⚒ only.
t – Ⓐ only.

❦ – No service June 14 - Oct. 9. Alternative connections are available via Rheine and Hengelo (Tables **812** and **811**) or via Coesfeld (Tables **802** and **803**).

RE services — HAGEN and DORTMUND - WARBURG and BRILON — 804

SERVICE UNTIL JUNE 21 AND FROM SEPTEMBER 2. For amended service June 22 - September 1 see page 606.

km		Ⓐ	Ⓐ	⑥	⚒	⚒b	Ⓐ	Ⓒ	Ⓐ																
0	**Hagen** Hbf .... **802** d.	0502	...	...	0602	0602	...	0700	0717	...	...	0817	...	0917	...	...	1017	...	1117	...	...	1215	...	1317	...
	Dortmund Hbf . **802** d.	|	...	...	|	|	0641	|	|	...	0741	|	0841	|	...	0941	|	1041	|	...	1141	|	1241	|	...
14	Schwerte (Ruhr) ... **802** d.	0512	...	...	0612	0612	|	0712	0728	...	|	0828	|	0928	...	|	1028	|	1128	...	|	1228	|	1328	...
57	Arnsberg (Westf) .... d.	0541	...	...	0641	0641	0725	0741	0758	...	0825	0858	0925	0958	...	1025	1058	1125	1158	...	1225	1258	1325	1358	...
77	Meschede .... d.	0558	...	0609	0658	0658	0742	0758	0816	...	0842	0916	0942	1016	...	1042	1116	1142	1216	...	1242	1316	1342	1416	...
85	Bestwig .... d.	0605	...	0616	0705	0705	0754**k**	0805	0823	...	0854**k**	0923	0954**k**	1023	...	1054**k**	1123	1154**k**	1223	...	1254**k**	1323	1354**k**	1423	...
	Marburg (Lahn) .... d.	|	...	|	|	|	|	|	|	0629**t**	|	|	|	|	0829	|	|	|	|	1029	|	|	|	|	1229
100	Brilon Wald .... a.	0619	...	0630	0719	0719	0808	0819	0836	0841**t**	0908	0936	1008	1036	1041	1108	1136	1208	1236	1241	1315	1336	1408	1436	1441
	Brilon Wald .... d.	0622	0626	0630	0722	0726	0819	0819	...	0844	0919	0944	1019	...	1044	1119	1144	1219	...	1244	1319	1344	1419	...	1444
	Brilon Stadt .... a.	|	0634	|	|	0734	|	|	...	0852	|	0952	|	...	1052	|	1152	|	...	1252	|	1354	|	...	1452
126	Marsberg .... d.	0650	...	0656	0747	...	0845	0845	...	...	0945	...	1045	...	...	1145	...	1245	...	...	1345	...	1445	...	...
151	**Warburg** (Westf) .... d.	0709	...	0715	0808	...	0907	0907	...	...	1007	...	1107	...	...	1207	...	1307	...	...	1407	...	1507	...	...

																								¶	¶
agen Hbf .... **802** d.	...	1417	...	...	1517	...	...	...	1615	...	...	1717	...	...	1817	...	1917	...	...	2017	...	...	...	...	...
Dortmund Hbf .. **802** d.	1341	|	1441	...	|	...	1541	...	|	1641	...	|	...	1741	|	1841	|	...	1941	|	...	2041	2123	2223	2323
hwerte (Ruhr) .... **802** d.	|	1428	|	...	1528	...	|	...	1628	|	...	1728	...	|	1828	|	1928	...	|	2028	...	|	2149	2249	2349
nsberg (Westf) .... d.	1425	1458	1525	...	1558	...	1625	...	1658	1725	...	1758	...	1825	1858	1925	1958	...	2025	2058	...	2125	2221	2321	0021
eschede .... d.	1442	1516	1542	...	1616	...	1642	...	1716	1742	...	1816	...	1842	1916	1942	2016	...	2042	2116	...	2142	2239	2339	0039
estwig .... d.	1454**k**	1523	1554**k**	...	1623	...	1654**k**	...	1723	1754**k**	...	1823	...	1854**k**	1923	1954**k**	2023	...	2053**k**	2123	...	2148	2245	2345	0045
Marburg (Lahn) .... d.	|	|	|	...	|	1429	|	...	|	|	...	|	1629	|	|	|	|	1829	|	|	1929	...	...	...	...
ilon Wald .... a.	1508	1536	1608	...	1636	1641	1708	...	1737	1808	...	1836	1841	1908	1936	2008	2036	2041	2108	2136	2141	...	...	...	...
ilon Wald .... d.	1517	1544	1619	1617	...	1644	1717	1720	1745	1819	1817	...	1844	1919	1944	2019	...	2044	2119	...	2144	...	...	...	...
Brilon Stadt .... a.	|	1554	|	1625	...	1652	|	1728	1752	|	1825	...	1852	|	1952	|	...	2052	|	...	2152	...	...	...	...
arsberg .... d.	1545	...	1645	...	...	...	1745	...	...	1845	...	...	...	1945	...	2045	...	...	2145	...	...	...	...	...	...
arburg (Westf) .... d.	1607	...	1707	...	...	...	1807	...	...	1907	...	...	...	2007	...	2107	...	...	2207	...	...	...	...	...	...

km		⚒	Ⓐ	⚒		⚒	⚒b	Ⓐ	⑥																
	Warburg (Westf) .... d.	...	...	0535	...	...	...	0631	0635	...	...	...	0752	...	...	0852	...	0952	...	...	1052	...	1152	...	...
	Marsberg .... d.	...	...	0555	...	...	...	0650	0656	...	...	...	0812	...	...	0912	...	1012	...	...	1112	...	1212	...	...
0	**Brilon** Stadt .... d.	...	0543	|	...	0643**t**	0706	|	|	...	0739**t**	0806	|	0906	...	|	1006	|	1106	...	|	1206	|	1306	...
4	Brilon Wald .... a.	...	0551	0619	...	0651**t**	0714	0716	0719	...	0747**t**	0814	0839	0914	...	0939	1014	1039	1114	...	1139	1214	1239	1314	...
	Brilon Wald .... d.	...	0552	0620	...	0653**t**	0727	0720	0720	...	0749**t**	0820	0849	0922	0920	0949	1020	1049	1122	1120	1149	1220	1249	1322	1320
98	**Marburg** (Lahn) .... a.	...	|	|	...	|	0923	|	|	...	|	|	|	1123	|	|	|	|	1323	|	|	|	|	1523	|
—	Bestwig .... d.	0534	0610	0634	0634	0710	...	0734	0734	0734	0810**k**	0834	0910	...	0934	1010**k**	1034	1110**k**	...	1134	1210**k**	1234	1310**k**	...	1334
	Meschede .... d.	0541	0616	0641	0641	0717	...	0741	0741	0741	0817	0841	0917	...	0941	1017	1041	1117	...	1141	1217	1241	1317	...	1341
0	Arnsberg (Westf) .... d.	0559	0634	0659	0659	0734	...	0759	0759	0759	0834	0859	0934	...	0959	1034	1059	1134	...	1159	1234	1259	1334	...	1359
	Schwerte (Ruhr) .... **802** a.	0628	|	0728	0728	|	...	0828	0828	0828	|	0928	|	...	1028	|	1128	|	...	1228	|	1328	|	...	1428
59	**Dortmund** Hbf ... **802** a.	|	0717	|	|	0817	...	|	|	|	0917	|	1017	...	|	1117	|	1217	...	|	1317	|	1417	...	|
	Hagen Hbf .... **802** a.	0642	...	0742	0742	...	...	0842	0842	0842	...	0942	...	...	1042	...	1142	...	...	1242	...	1342	...	...	1442

arburg (Westf) .... d.	1252	...	1352	...	...	1452	...	...	1552	...	...	...	1652	...	...	1752	...	...	1852	...	1952	...	2052	...	2152
arsberg .... d.	1312	...	1412	...	...	1512	...	...	1612	...	...	...	1712	...	...	1812	...	...	1912	...	2012	...	2112	...	2212
Brilon Stadt .... d.	|	1406	|	1506	...	|	1606	1634	|	1706	...	1734	|	1806	1834	|	1906	...	|	2006	|	2106	|	2224	|
ilon Wald .... a.	1339	1414	1439	1514	...	1539	1614	1642	1639	1714	...	1742	1739	1814	1842	1839	1914	...	1939	2014	2039	2114	2139	2232	2237
ilon Wald .... d.	1349	1420	1449	1522	1520	1549	1620	...	1649	1722	1720	...	1749	1820	...	1849	1922	1920	1949	2020	2049	...	2149	▬	2238
Marburg (Lahn) .... a.	|	|	|	1723	|	|	|	...	|	1923	|	...	|	|	...	|	2123	|	|	|	|	...	|	...	|
estwig .... d.	1410**k**	1434	1510**k**	...	1534	1610**k**	1634	...	1710**k**	...	1734	...	1810**k**	1834	...	1910**k**	...	1934	2010**k**	2034	2104	...	2210**k**	...	2253
eschede .... d.	1417	1441	1517	...	1541	1617	1641	...	1717	...	1741	...	1817	1841	...	1917	...	1941	2017	2041	2111	...	2217	...	2300
nsberg (Westf) .... d.	1434	1459	1534	...	1559	1634	1659	...	1734	...	1759	...	1834	1859	...	1934	...	1959	2034	2059	...	...	2234	...	...
hwerte (Ruhr) .... **802** a.	|	1528	|	...	1628	|	1728	...	|	...	1828	...	|	1928	...	|	...	2028	|	2128	...	...	2303	2325	...
Dortmund Hbf .. **802** a.	1517	|	1617	...	|	1717	|	...	1817	...	|	...	1917	|	...	2017	...	|	2117	|	...	...	2329	|	...
agen Hbf .... **802** a.	...	1542	...	...	1642	...	1742	...	...	...	1842	...	...	1942	...	...	...	2042	...	2142	...	...	...	2337	...

– Change trains at Brilon Wald on ⑥. **k** – Arrives 5–7 minutes earlier. **t** – Ⓐ only. ¶ – By 🚌 Arnsberg - Bestwig from July 1 (arrives 33 minutes later).

(KÖLN -) DÜSSELDORF - PADERBORN - KASSEL — 805

km		⊙ Ⓐ	⊙ ⚒	⊙ Ⓐ n	⊙ Ⓒ	⊙ n	⊙ n	⊙ n	*ICE* **1223** ①–⑤ J✕	*ICE* **1223** ⑥⑦ K✕	⊙	*IC* **2155** G△	⊙ n	*IC* **1959** ⑤⑦ L△	⊙ n	⊙ n	⊙ n	⊙ n	*IC* **2157** G△	⊙ n	⊙ n	⊙ n	⊙ n	⊙ u
	Köln Hbf .... **800 802** d.	...	...	...	...	...	...	...	0824•	...	...	0919	...	1044x	...	...	...	...	1519	...	...	...	...	...
	Düsseldorf Hbf .... **800 802** d.	...	...	0536	...	0636	0736	0836	0848	...	...	0943	1036	1118	1136	1236	1336	1436	1543	1636	1736	1836	1936	2036
	Düsseldorf Flug ✈ ... **800 802** d.	...	...	0543	...	0643	0743	0843	|	...	...	0950	1043	|	1143	1243	1343	1443	1550	1643	1743	1843	1943	2043
	Duisburg Hbf .... **800 802** d.	...	...	0559	...	0659	0759	0859	0902	...	...	1002	1059	1134	1159	1259	1359	1459	1602	1659	1758	1859	1959	2059
	Mülheim (Ruhr) Hbf .... **802** d.	...	...	0605	...	0705	0805	0905	|	...	...	|	1105	|	1205	1305	1405	1505	|	1705	1804	1905	2005	2105
	Essen Hbf .... **800 802** d.	...	...	0613	...	0713	0813	0913	0917**r**	0917**r**	...	1016	1113	1147	1213	1313	1413	1513	1616	1713	1811	1913	2013	2113
	Bochum Hbf .... **800 802** d.	...	...	0624	...	0724	0824	0924	0927**r**	0927**r**	...	1028	1124	1158	1224	1324	1424	1524	1628	1724	1824	1924	2024	2124
0	**Dortmund** Hbf .... **800 802** d.	0433	...	0639*	0639*	0739	0839	0937	0941	0941	←	1043	1139	1210	1239*	1339*	1439*	1539*	1644	1739	1839*	1939*	2039	2139*
31	Hamm (Westf) .... **800 802** a.	0453	...	0702	0702	0756	0902	0955	0957	0957	0955	1101	1156	1226	1302	1356	1502	1556	|	1756	1902	1956	2102	2156
31	Hamm (Westf) .... **805a** d.	0501	0607	0707	0707	0807	0907	→	1005	1005	1011	1107	1207	1232	1307	1407	1507	1607	|	1807	1907	2007	2107	2207
57	Soest .... **802 805a** d.	0516	0621	0721	0721	0821	0921	...	1020	1020	1027	1121	1221	1248	1321	1421	1521	1621	1715	1821	1921	2021	2121	2221
77	Lippstadt .... **805a** d.	0526	0631	0731	0731	0831	0931	...	1030	1030	1038	1131	1231	1300	1331	1431	1531	1631	1731	1832	1931	2031	2131	2231
109	**Paderborn** Hbf **805a 809 811** d.	0543	0648	0748	0748	0848	0948	...	1047	1047	1058	1147	1248	1316	1348	1448	1548	1648	1748	1848	1948	2048	2148	2248
126	Altenbeken .... **809 811** d.	0556	0701	0801	0801	0901	1001	...	1100	1100	1113	1159	1301	1330	1401	1501	1601	1701	1802	1901	2001	2101	2201	2301
163	Warburg (Westf) .... d.	0618	0724	0824	0824	0923	1024	...	1126	1126	1136	1224	1323	|	1423	1524	1624	1724	1827	1924	2024	2124	2224	2324
189	Hofgeismar .... d.	0633	0738	0838	0838	0938	1038	...	|	|	1154	|	1338	|	1438	1538	1638	1738	|	1938	2038	2138	2238	2338
214	**Kassel** Wilhelmshöhe .... a.	0652	0756	0856	0856	0956	1056	...	1156	1156	1217	1255	1356	1417	1456	1556	1656	1756	1857	1956	2055	2155	2256	2356

	⊙ Ⓐ n		⊙ Ⓐ n	⊙ ⚒	⊙ n	⊙ n	*IC* **2156** G△	⊙ n	⊙ n	⊙ n	⊙ n	*ICE* **1224** H✕	⊙	*IC* **2152** G▽	⊙ n	⊙ n	⊙ n	⊙ n	*IC* **1952** ⑤⑦ L△	⊙	⊙	⊙	
ssel Wilhelmshöhe .... d.	...	...	0555	...	0703	0803	0902	1003	1103	1203	1303	1403	1403	1502	1603	1703	1803	1903	1942	2003	2103	2203	...
fgeismar .... d.	...	...	0611	...	0720	0820	|	1020	1120	1220	1321	|	1423	|	1620	1720	1820	1920	|	2020	2120	2220	...
arburg (Westf) .... d.	0533	...	0634	...	0734	0834	0934	1034	1134	1234	1335	1434	1438	1534	1634	1734	1834	1934	2018	2034	2134	2234	...
tenbeken .... **809 811** d.	0558	...	0658	...	0758	0858	|	1058	1158	1258	|	|	1501	|	1658	1758	1858	1958	2040	2058	2158	2258	...
aderborn Hbf .... **805a 809 811** d.	0610	...	0712	0712	0812	0912	1010	1112	1211	1312	1410	1510	1514	1610	1712	1810	1912	2011	2053	2112	2212	2312	...
pstadt .... **805a** d.	0625	...	0727	0727	0825	0927	1026	1127	1225	1327	1425	1525	1530	1629	1727	1825	1927	2025	2109	2127	2227	2327	...
est .... **802 805a** d.	0640	...	0738	0738	0835	0938	1042	1138	1235	1338	1440	1537	1542	1641	1738	1840	1938	2035	2121	2138	2238	2338	...
amm (Westf) .... **805a** a.	0653	...	0752	0752	0850	0952	|	1152	1250	1352	1453	1551	1555	|	1752	1853	1952	2050	2134	2152	2252	2352	...
amm (Westf) .... **800 802** d.	0658	...	0757	0757	0855	0957	|	1157	1255	1357	1458	1556	...	|	1757	1858	1957	2055	2140	...	2258	...	...
rtmund Hbf .... **800 802** d.	0721	...	0821	0821	0921	1021	1116	1221	1321	1421	1521	1616	...	1716	1821	1921	2021	2121	2200	...	2319	...	...
chum Hbf .... **800 802** d.	0733	...	0833	0833	0933	1033	1130	1233	1333	1433	1533	...	...	1730	1833	1933	2033	2133	2212	...	...	...	...
sen Hbf .... **800 802** d.	0747	...	0847	0847	0947	1047	1140	1247	1347	1447	1547	...	...	1740	1847	1947	2047	2147	2225	...	...	...	...
ilheim (Ruhr) Hbf .... **802** d.	0753	...	0853	0853	0953	1053	|	1253	1353	1453	1553	...	...	|	1853	1953	2053	2153	|	...	...	...	...
isburg Hbf .... **800 802** d.	0807**t**	...	0907	0907	1007	1106	1156	1307	1407	1507	1607	...	...	1755	1907	2007	2107	2207**f**	2241	...	...	...	...
isseldorf Flug ✈ .... **800 802** d.	0816	...	0916	0916	1016	1116	1206	1316	1416	1516	1616	...	...	1806	1916	2016	2116	2216	2251	...	...	...	...
isseldorf Hbf .... **800 802** a.	0824	...	0924	0924	1024	1124	1212	1324	1424	1524	1624	...	...	1812	1924	2024	2124	2224	2257	...	...	...	...
ln Hbf .... **800 802** a.	...	...	...	...	...	...	1240	...	...	...	...	...	...	...	...	...	...	...	2325	...	...	...	...

– To / from Gera via Weimar (Table **849a**).
– From München (Table **900**). To Oberhausen (Table **800**).
– From Frankfurt via Wiesbaden (Table **800**). To München (Table **900**).
– From Oberhausen (Table **800**). To München (Table **900**).
– To / from Weimar (Table **849a**).
· Arrives 2201.

n – Will not run Düsseldorf - Dortmund or v.v. Sept. 6 - Oct. 31.
r – Not Sept. 6 - Oct. 31.
t – Arrives 0759.
u – Will not run Düsseldorf - Dortmund or v.v. Sept. 5 - Oct. 30.

x – 1027 on ⑤.
⊙ – Operated by National Express.
• – Köln **Messe/Deutz**.
* – 2 minutes **earlier** Sept. 6 - Oct. 31 (also Sept. 5 after 2100).
△ – Sept. 6 - Oct. 31 service is diverted Köln - Dortmund and v.v.
▽ – Sept. 6 - Oct. 31 service is diverted Dortmund - Düsseldorf.

805a DÜSSELDORF and MÜNSTER - PADERBORN - KASSEL

Operator: *eurobahn* (2nd class

	Ⓐ	⚒	Ⓐ		Ⓐ	Ⓐ	⑥	†	Ⓐ	Ⓐ	Ⓒ						Ⓐ		Ⓐ	Ⓐ	Ⓒ			Ⓐ	
Münster (Westf) Hbf...... 802 d.	...	0510	...	0610	0640	*0708*	0708	0710	0740	*0810*	0810	0908	1010	1108	...	1210	1240	1308	1340	*1410*	1410	1508	1610	1640	...
Hamm (Westf)............... 802 a.	...	0537	...	0636	0707	*0734*	0734	0737	0807	*0837*	0837	0934	1037	1134	...	1237	1307	1334	1407	*1436*	1436	1534	1637	1707	...
Hamm (Westf)............... 805 d.	0446	0546	0616	0646	0716	0746	0746	0746	...	0846	0846	0946	1046	1146	...	1246	1316	1346	1416	1446	1446	1546	1646	1716	...
Soest.......................802 805 d.	0503	0603	0633	0703	0733	0803	0803	0803	...	0903	0903	1003	1103	1203	...	1303	1333	1403	1433	1503	1503	1603	1703	1733	...
Lippstadt..................... 805 d.	0515	0615	0645	0715	0745	0815	0815	0815	...	0915	0915	1015	1115	1215	...	1315	1345	1415	1445	1515	1515	1615	1715	1745	...
Paderborn Hbf............ 805 a.	0540	0640	0710	0740	0810	0840	0840	0840	...	0940	0940	1040	1140	1240	...	1340	1410	1440	1510	1540	1540	1640	1740	1810	...

		Ⓐ								Ⓒn
Münster (Westf) Hbf...... 802 d.	1708	1740	1810	1908	2010	2110	2210	2310	0010	0010
Hamm (Westf)............... 802 a.	1734	1807	1836	1934	2037	2137	2237	2337	0037	0037
Hamm (Westf)............... 805 d.	1746	1816	1846	1946	2046	2146	2309	0009	...	0109
Soest.......................802 805 d.	1803	1833	1903	2003	2103	2203	2326	0026	...	0126
Lippstadt..................... 805 d.	1815	1845	1915	2015	2115	2215	2338	0038	...	0138
Paderborn Hbf............ 805 a.	1840	1910	1940	2040	2140	2240	0003	0103	...	0203

		Ⓐ	⚒	Ⓐ		Ⓐ		⚒	†	Ⓐ
Paderborn Hbf......... 805 d.	...	0451	0521	...	0621	0651	0721	0821	0821	092
Lippstadt.................. 805 d.	...	0514	0544	...	0644	0714	0744	0844	0844	094
Soest.................802 805 d.	...	0526	0556	...	0656	0726	0756	0856	0856	095
Hamm (Westf)........... 805 a.	...	0544	0614	...	0714	0744	0814	0914	0914	101
Hamm (Westf)........... 802 d.	0520	0550	0620	0650	0722	0750	0824	*0920*	0920	*102*
Münster (Westf) Hbf.. 802 a.	0547	0617	0647	0717	0748	0817	0850	*0947*	0947	*105*

	Ⓒ	⊗		Ⓐ				Ⓐ		Ⓐ	Ⓐ	Ⓒ	Ⓐ			Ⓐ									
Paderborn Hbf............ 805 d.	0921	1021	1121	1151	1221	1321	1421	1451	1521	1551	1621	1621	1651	1721	1821	1851	1921	2015	2115	2215	2315	0015	...	...	...
Lippstadt..................... 805 d.	0944	1044	1144	1214	1244	1344	1444	1514	1544	1614	1644	1644	1714	1744	1844	1914	1944	2038	2138	2238	2338	0038	...	...	...
Soest.......................802 805 d.	0956	1056	1156	1226	1256	1356	1456	1526	1556	1626	1656	1656	1726	1756	1856	1926	1956	2050	2150	2250	2350	0050	...	...	...
Hamm (Westf)............... 805 a.	1014	1114	1214	1244	1314	1414	1514	1544	1614	1644	1714	1714	1744	1814	1914	1944	2014	2108	2208	2308	0008	0108	...	...	...
Hamm (Westf)............... 802 d.	1024	1122	1224	1250	1320	1424	1520	1550	1624	1650	*1720*	1720	...	1824	1922	...	2024	2120	2224	2320	0010	0110	...	...	...
Münster (Westf) Hbf...... 802 a.	1050	1149	1250	1317	1347	1450	1547	1617	1650	1717	*1747*	1747	...	1850	1948	...	2050	2147	2250	2347	0037	0137	...	...	...

n – Mornings of ⑥ and ⑦.

⊗ – Change trains at Hamm on Ⓑ.

806 FRANKFURT - GIESSEN - KASSEL and SIEGEN

ICE/IC trains **KARLSRUHE - FRANKFURT - GIESSEN - KASSEL - HAMBURG - STRALSUND** (see below for regional services).

ICE/IC trains	*ICE* 1674 ①–⑥ ✕	*ICE* 1672 B✕	*IC* 2374 A		*ICE* 1578 ①–④ ✕	*ICE* 1578 ⑤–⑦ E✕	*ICE* 1576 ✕	*ICE* 1574 ✕	*ICE* 1572 ✕	
Stuttgart Hbf **910**......d.	...	...	0857	...	1103	...	...	...	1654	...
Karlsruhe Hbf **910**......d.	...	0702**p**	|	...	|	1110	1310	1510	|	...
Heidelberg Hbf **910**..d.	...	0746**p**	0946	...	1146	1146	1346	1546	1746	...
Frankfurt (Main) Hbf....d.	0650	0851	1051	...	1251	1251	1448	1648	1848	...
Friedberg (Hess)..........d.	0716	0916	1116	...	1316	1316	1516	1716	1916	...
Gießen........................d.	0734	0934	1134	...	1334	1334	1534	1734	1934	...
Marburg (Lahn)............d.	0752	0952	1151	...	1352	1352	1552	1752	1952	...
Treysa..........................d.	0816	1016	1216	...	1416	1416	1616	1816	2016	...
Wabern.........................d.	0833	1033	1234	...	|	|	1633	1833	2033	...
Kassel Wilhelmshöhe..a.	0854	1054	1254	...	1454	1454	1654	1855	2054	...
Hannover Hbf **900**.....a.	0956	1156	1356	...	1556	1556	1756	1956	2156	...
Hamburg Hbf **900**.....a.	1129	1330	1530	...	1732	1732	1929	2130	2329**f**	...
Rostock Hbf **830**.......a.	...	1532**r**	...	...	1932**r**	1932**r**	2132**b**	2332**v**	...	...
Stralsund Hbf **830**.....a.	...	1627**r**	...	...	2028**r**	2028**r**	2229**v**	...	...	...

ICE/IC trains	*ICE* 1573 ①–⑥ ✕		*ICE* 1575 ①–⑥ ✕	*ICE* 1577 ✕	*ICE* 1579 D✕	*ICE* 1671 B✕	*IC* 2375* A		*ICE* 1675 B✕	*ICE* 167 ⑤⑦ ✕
Stralsund Hbf **830**...........d.	...	...	...	0521**x**	0727**h**	0926**r**	...	...	1325**r**	152
Rostock Hbf **830**.............d.	...	...	...	0625**x**	0825**h**	1025**r**	...	...	1425**r**	162
Hamburg Hbf **900**...........d.	...	...	0624	0828	1028	1228	1428	...	1628	182
Hannover Hbf **900**...........d.	0557**a**	...	0801	1001	1201	1401	1601	...	1801	200
Kassel Wilhelmshöhe........d.	0701	...	0903	1104	1303	1503	1703	...	1903	210
Wabern..............................d.	0720	...	|	1123	|	1523	1722	...	1923	212
Treysa...............................d.	0737	...	0937	1140	1337	1540	1739	...	1940	213
Marburg (Lahn)...................d.	0803	...	1003	1204	1403	1604	1804	...	2004	220
Gießen..............................d.	0824	...	1024	1224	1424	1624	1824	...	2024	222
Friedberg (Hess)..................d.	0843	...	1043	1243	1443	1643	1843	...	2043	224
Frankfurt (Main) Hbf..........a.	0908	...	1108	1308	1508	1708	1908	...	2108	230
Heidelberg Hbf **910**.........a.	1013	...	1213	1413	1613	1813	2013	...	...	...
Karlsruhe Hbf **910**..........a.	1051	...	1251	|	1651	1852	|	...	...	...
Stuttgart Hbf **910**............a.	...	...	...	1503	...	...	2057	...	...	...

Regional trains **FRANKFURT - GIESSEN - KASSEL / SIEGEN** (see above for *ICE / IC* services to / from Kassel). See Table **808** for other *IC* services Frankfurt - Wetzlar - Siegen and v.v.

km			◇ ⚒	◇ Ⓐ	◇ Ⓐ	◇	◇ Ⓒ		◇ ⚒	◇	◇ ⚒	◇	◇		◇	◇	◇	◇		◇	◇	◇	◇		◇	◇
0	**Frankfurt** (Main) Hbf.. d.	0520	...	0550	...	0616**k**	...	0718	...	0749	0749	0820	0820**t**	0920	...	0950	1020	1020	1120	...	1150	1220	1220	1320	...	135
34	Friedberg (Hess)........ d.	0544	...	0614	...	0645	...	0744	...	0814	0814	0845	0845**t**	0944	...	1014	1045	1045	1144	...	1214	1245	1245	1344	...	141
39	Bad Nauheim............ d.	|	...	0618	...	|	...	|	...	0818	0818	|	|	|	...	1018	|	|	|	...	1218	|	|	|	...	141
66	**Gießen**..................... a.	0602	...	0634	...	0702	...	0802	...	0834	0834	0902	0902**t**	1002	...	1034	1102	1102	1202	...	1234	1302	1302	1402	...	143
66	**Gießen**............. **906** d.	0604	0615	0640	0652	0705	0709	0804	0815	0839	0840	0905	0909	1004	1015	1040	1105	1109	1204	1215	1240	1305	1309	1404	1415	144
79	Wetzlar.......... **906** d.	|	0624	0650	0703	|	0718	|	0824	|	0850	|	0918	|	1024	1050	|	1118	|	1224	1250	|	1318	|	1424	145
101	Herborn................. d.	|	0637	0714	0730	|	0733	|	0837	|	0914	|	0933	|	1037	1114	|	1133	|	1237	1314	|	1333	|	1437	151
107	Dillenburg.............. d.	|	0642	0722	0738	|	0738	|	0843	|	0922	|	0938	|	1043	1122	|	1138	|	1243	1322	|	1338	|	1443	152
139	**Siegen** Hbf............ a.	|	0713	...	0805	|	0805	|	0913	|	...	|	1005	|	1113	...	|	1205	|	1313	...	|	1405	|	1513	...
96	Marburg (Lahn).......... d.	0621	...	...	...	0721	...	0821	...	0907	...	0921	...	1021	...	...	1121	...	1221	...	...	1321	...	1421	...	...
118	Stadtallendorf........... d.	0636	...	...	...	0737	...	0836	...	0926	...	0937	...	1036	...	...	1137	...	1236	...	...	1337	...	1436	...	...
138	Treysa.................... d.	0649	...	...	...	0755	...	0849	...	...	...	0955	...	1049	...	...	1155	...	1249	...	...	1355	...	1449	...	...
166	Wabern.................... d.	0707	...	...	...	0818	...	0907	...	...	...	1018	...	1107	...	...	1218	...	1307	...	...	1418	...	1507	...	...
196	**Kassel** Wilhelmshöhe a.	0726	...	...	...	0846	...	0926	...	...	...	1046	...	1126	...	...	1247	...	1326	...	...	1446	...	1526	...	...
200	**Kassel** Hbf............... a.	0734	...	...	...	0854	...	0934	...	...	...	1055	...	1134	...	...	1254	...	1334	...	...	1454	...	1534	...	...

	◇	◇		◇	◇	◇	◇		◇	◇	◇	◇		◇	◇	◇	◇		◇	◇	◇	◇		⑤⑥†	◇	
Frankfurt (Main) Hbf.... d.	1420	1420	1518**n**	...	1550	1617	1617	1718**n**	...	1750	1817	1817	1918**n**	...	1950	2020	2020	2120	...	2150	2220	2220	2320	2320	...	...
Friedberg (Hess)......... d.	1445	1445	1544	...	1614	1645	1645	1744	...	1814	1845	1845	1944	...	2014	2045	2045	2144	...	2214	2245	2245	2344	2344	...	...
Bad Nauheim.............. d.	|	|	|	...	1618	|	|	|	...	1818	|	|	|	...	2018	|	|	|	...	2218	|	|	|	|	...	...
Gießen....................... a.	1502	1502	1602	...	1634	1702	1702	1802	...	1834	1902	1902	2002	...	2034	2102	2102	2202	...	2234	2302	2302	0002	0002	...	...
Gießen.................**906** d.	1505	1509	1604	1609	1640	1705	1709	1804	1809	1840	1905	1909	2004	2015	2040	2105	2109	2204	2209	2239	2305	2309	0008	0008	0011	...
Wetzlar.............**906** d.	|	1518	|	1621	1650	|	1718	|	1821	1850	|	1918	|	2024	2050	|	2118	|	2218	|	|	2318	|	|	0021	...
Herborn.................. d.	|	1533	|	1637	1714	|	1733	|	1837	1914	|	1933	|	2037	2114	|	2133	|	2233	|	|	2333	|	|	0044	...
Dillenburg............... d.	|	1538	|	1643	1722	|	1738	|	1843	1922	|	1938	|	2043	2122	|	2138	|	2238	|	|	2338	|	|	0051	...
Siegen Hbf.............. a.	|	1605	|	1713	...	|	1805	|	1913	...	|	2005	|	2113**y**	...	|	2205	|	2304	|	|	0005	|	|	0122	...
Marburg (Lahn).......... d.	1521	...	1621	...	...	1721	...	1821	...	...	1921	...	2021	...	...	2121	...	2221	...	2307	2321	...	0033	0033	...	...
Stadtallendorf............ d.	1537	...	1636	...	...	1737	...	1836	...	...	1937	...	2036	...	...	2137	...	2236	...	...	2340	...	0050	0050	...	...
Treysa..................... d.	1555	...	1649	...	...	1755	...	1849	...	...	1955	...	2049	...	...	2155	...	2249	...	...	2355	...	0104	0105	...	...
Wabern..................... d.	1618	...	1707	...	...	1818	...	1907	...	...	2018	...	2107	...	...	2218	...	2307	...	...	0018	...	...	0124	...	...
Kassel Wilhelmshöhe . a.	1646	...	1726	...	...	1846	...	1926	...	...	2047	...	2126	...	...	2245	...	2326	...	...	0048	...	...	0141	...	...
Kassel Hbf................ a.	1655	...	1734	...	...	1854	...	1934	...	...	2054	...	2134	...	...	2252	...	2334	...	...	0054	...	...	0149	...	...

A – To / from Westerland (Table **821**).
B – To / from Ostseebad Binz (Table **844**) until Aug. 1.
D – To Konstanz (Table **916**) on ⑤⑥.
E – Also June 9, 19, July 28 - 31, Aug. 4 - Sept. 4. From Konstanz (Table **916**) on ⑥⑦ (also Oct. 3).

a – ①–⑤ only.
b – Ⓑ to Aug. 1.
f – ⑤–⑦ only.
h – ⑥ until July 26.
k – 0620 on Ⓒ.

n – 2 minutes later on Ⓒ.
p – ①–⑥ only.
r – Until Aug. 1.
t – Ⓐ only.
v – ⑦ to July 27.
x – Ⓐ until Aug. 1.
y – 2105 on Ⓐ.

◇ – Operated by Hessische Landesbahn.
* – Train number *IC* **2393** on certain dates.

KASSEL and SIEGEN - GIESSEN - FRANKFURT 806

Regional trains **KASSEL / SIEGEN - GIESSEN - FRANKFURT** (continued from previous page). See Table **808** for other *IC* services Siegen - Wetzlar - Frankfurt.

	Ⓐ	Ⓒ	◇ Ⓐ	◇ ⑥	Ⓐ	◇ Ⓒ	◇ Ⓐ	◇ ⚒	◇ ⑥	Ⓐ	Ⓒ	◇ Ⓐ A	◇	◇ †	◇ ⚒	◇	◇		◇	◇	◇	◇		◇	◇	◇
ssel Hbf d.	0403	0423	...	...	...	...	...	...	...	0608	0615	...	...	...	0705	...	...	0823	...	0905	...	...	1023	...	1105	...
ssel Wilhelmshöhe d.	0408	0429	...	...	...	...	...	...	...	0613	0620	...	...	...	0710	...	...	0829	...	0910	...	...	1029	...	1110	...
abern d.	0427	0449	...	...	...	...	...	...	...	0638	0649	...	...	...	0738	...	...	0849	...	0938	...	...	1049	...	1138	...
eysa d.	0446	0507	...	...	0559	0559	...	...	...	0658	0707	...	...	0753	0802j	...	...	0907	...	1002	...	...	1107	...	1202	...
adtallendorf d.	0500	0521	...	...	0613	0614	...	...	...	0714	0721	...	...	0808	0817j	...	...	0921	...	1017	...	...	1121	...	1217	...
arburg (Lahn) d.	0516	0536	...	...	0635	0635	...	...	...	0733	0736	...	...	0835	0835	...	...	0936	...	1035	...	...	1136	...	1235	...
Siegen Hbf d.	|	|	0458	0554	|	|	0600	...	0645	|	|	0645	0754	|	|	...	0845	|	0954	|	...	1045	|	1154	|	...
Dillenburg d.	|	|	0525	0617	|	|	0626	0631	0717	|	|	0717	0817	|	|	0831r	0917	|	1017	|	1031e	1117	|	1217	|	1231
Herborn d.	|	|	0530	0622	|	|	0631	0639	0722	|	|	0736y	0822	|	|	0839r	0922	|	1022	|	1039	1122	|	1222	|	1239
Wetzlar **906** d.	|	|	0547	0637	|	|	0649	0703	0737	|	|	0752	0837	|	|	0903	0937	|	1037	|	1103	1137	|	1237	|	1303
eßen **906** a.	0536	0552	|	0646	0652	0651	0659	0714	0746	0752	0752	0801	0847	0851	0851	0914	0946	0952	1046	1051	1114	1146	1152	1246	1251	1314
eßen d.	0538	0554	|	0655	0654	0655	0709	0722	...	0754	0754	*0808*	0855	0855	0855	0922	...	0954	1055	1055	1122	...	1154	1255	1255	1322
d Nauheim d.	0559	|	0611	|	|	|	0728	0741	...	|	|	*0829*	|	|	|	0941	...	|	|	|	1141	...	|	|	|	1341
edberg (Hess) d.	0603	0614	|	0713	0714	0713	0733	0745	...	0814	0814	*0834*	0913	0913	0913	0945	...	1014	1113	1113	1145	...	1214	1313	1313	1345
ankfurt (Main) Hbf a.	0625	0639	0640	0735	0738	0738	0800	0807	...	0839	0838	*0857*	0940	0940	0939	1007	...	1039	1138	1138	1207	...	1239	1338	1338	1407

	◇		◇	◇	◇	◇		◇	◇	◇	◇		◇	◇	◇	◇		◇	◇	◇	◇		◇	◇	◇	
ssel Hbf d.	...	1223	...	1305	...	...	1423	...	1505	...	...	1623	...	1705	...	...	1823	...	1905	...	...	2023	2105	...	...	2223
ssel Wilhelmshöhe d.	...	1229	...	1310	...	...	1429	...	1510	...	...	1629	...	1710	...	...	1829	...	1910	...	...	2032	2110	...	...	2229
abern d.	...	1249	...	1338	...	...	1449	...	1538	...	...	1649	...	1738	...	...	1849	...	1938	...	...	2052	2138	...	...	2253
eysa d.	...	1307	...	1402	...	...	1507	...	1602	...	...	1707	...	1802	...	...	1907	...	2002	...	...	2109	2202	...	...	2311
adtallendorf d.	...	1321	...	1417	...	...	1521	...	1617	...	...	1721	...	1817	...	...	1921	...	2017	...	...	2123	2217	...	...	2325
arburg (Lahn) d.	...	1336	...	1435	...	...	1536	...	1635	...	...	1736	...	1835	...	...	1936	...	2035	...	...	2139	2235	...	...	2341
Siegen Hbf d.	1245	|	1354	|	...	1445	|	1554	|	...	1645	|	1754	|	...	1845	|	1954	|	...	2052	|	|	2154	2310	|
Dillenburg d.	1317	|	1417	|	1431	1517	|	1617	|	1631	1717	|	1817	|	1831	1917	|	2017	|	2031	2117	|	|	2217	2334	|
Herborn d.	1322	|	1422	|	1439	1522	|	1622	|	1639	1722	|	1822	|	1839	1922	|	2022	|	2039	2122	|	|	2222	2339	|
Wetzlar **906** d.	1337	|	1437	|	1503	1537	|	1637	|	1703	1737	|	1837	|	1903	1937	|	2037	|	2103	2137	|	|	2237	2352	|
eßen **906** a.	1346	1352	1446	1451	1514	1546	1552	1646	1651	1714	1746	1752	1846	1851	1914	1946	1952	2046	2051	2114	2147	2155	2251	2246	0001	0004
eßen d.	...	1354	1455	1455	1522	...	1554	1655	1655	1722	...	1754	1855	1855	1922	...	1954	2055	2055	2122	...	2157	...	2255	...	0008
d Nauheim d.	...	|	|	|	1541	...	|	|	|	1741	...	|	|	|	1941	...	|	|	|	2141	...	|	...	|	...	0032
edberg (Hess) d.	...	1414	1513	1513	1545	...	1614	1713	1713	1745	...	1814	1913	1913	1945	...	2014	2113	2113	2145	...	2216	...	2313	...	0036
ankfurt (Main) Hbf a.	...	1439	1538	1538	1607	...	1639	1738	1738	1807	...	1839	1938	1938	2007	...	2039	2138	2138	2207	...	2241	...	2338	...	0101

– From Au (Table **807**).

– 1035 on †.

j – 2 minutes earlier on ⑥.

r – ⚒ only.

y – Arrives 0721.

◇ – Operated by Hessische Landesbahn.

E / *S-Bahn* services AACHEN - KÖLN - SIEGEN 807

m		⓪	Ⓐ2	Ⓐg	⑥	⑥	Ⓐ		○	†															
0	**Aachen** Hbf **802 910** d.	...	...	◇	◇	...	0518	0617t	0718r	0818	0818r	0918	1018	1118	1218	1318	1418	1518	1618	1718	1818	1918	2018	2118	...
31	Düren **802** d.	...	...	...	...	...	0546	0646t	0746r	0845	0846r	0946	1046	1146	1245	1346	1446	1546	1646	1746	1846	1946	2046	2146	...
70	**Köln** Hbf **802 910** a.	...	...	...	...	...	0611	0711t	0812r	0912	0912r	1012	1112	1212	1312	1412	1512	1619	1712	1812	1912	2012	2112	2211	...
70	**Köln** Hbf **802 910** d.	0023	0431	...	...	0623	0623	0723	0823	0915	0923	1023	1123	1223	1323	1423	1523	1623	1723	1823	1923	2023	2121	2223	2323
71	**Köln** Messe/Deutz **802 910** d.	0027	0433	...	...	0627	0627	0727	0827	0918	0927	1027	1127	1227	1327	1427	1527	1627	1727	1827	1927	2026	2124	2226	2327
91	Troisdorf **802** d.	0041	0454	...	...	0641	0641	0741	0841	...	0941	1041	1141	1241	1341	1441	1541	1641	1741	1841	1941	2042	2141	2242	2341
95	Siegburg/Bonn **910** d.	0046	0459	...	...	0646	0646	0746	0845	...	0946	1046	1146	1246	1346	1446	1546	1646	1746	1846	1946	2046	2146	2246	2346
02	Hennef (Sieg) d.	0050	0505	...	...	0650	0651	0750	0850	...	0950	1050	1150	1250	1351	1450	1550	1650	1750	1850	1950	2051	2150	2251	2350
14	Eitorf d.	0059	0518	...	...	0659	0701	0759	0859	...	0959	1059	1159	1259	1359	1459	1559	1659	1759	1859	1959	2100	2159	2300	2359
36	Au (Sieg) d.	0116	0539	0556	0605	0716	0717	0816	0916	...	1016	1116	1216	1316	1416	1516	1616	1716	1816	1916	2016	2117	2216	2316	0016
42	Wissen (Sieg) d.	0124	...	0603	0612	0721	0722	0821	0921	...	1021	1121	1221	1321	1421	1521	1621	1721	1821	1921	2021	2122	2224	2324	0024
54	Betzdorf (Sieg) d.	0138	...	0618	0626	0731	0732	0831	0931	...	1031	1131	1231	1331	1431	1531	1631	1731	1831	1931	2031	2132	2238	2338	0038
71	**Siegen** Hbf a.	0200	...	0643	0651	0750	0750	0850	0950	...	1050	1150	1250	1350	1450	1550	1650	1750	1850	1950	2048	2150	2300	2400	0100

	⚒2	Ⓐ	Ⓐ	⑥																		◇	2	2
egen Hbf d.	...	...	0454	0500	0610	0710	0810	0910	1010	1110	1210	1310	1410	1510	1610	1710	1810	1910	2010	2110	...	2210	2231	...	...
tzdorf (Sieg) d.	...	...	0522	0522	0628	0728	0828	0928	1028	1128	1228	1328	1428	1528	1628	1728	1828	1928	2028	2128	...	2228	2255	...	...
issen (Sieg) d.	...	...	0535	0535	0637	0737	0837	0937	1037	1137	1237	1337	1437	1537	1637	1737	1837	1937	2037	2137	...	2237	2308	...	...
(Sieg) d.	0420	...	0543	0543	0643	0743	0843	0943	1043	1143	1243	1343	1443	1543	1643	1743	1843	1943	2043	2143	...	2243	2316	2320	...
orf d.	0439	...	0600	0600	0700	0800	0900	1000	1100	1200	1300	1400	1500	1600	1700	1800	1900	2000	2100	2200	...	2300	...	2339	...
nnef (Sieg) d.	0453	...	0609	0609	0709	0809	0909	1009	1109	1209	1309	1409	1509	1609	1709	1809	1909	2009	2109	2209	...	2309	...	2352	0002
egburg/Bonn **910** d.	0458	...	0614	0614	0714	0814	0914	1014	1114	1214	1314	1414	1514	1614	1714	1814	1914	2014	2114	2214	...	2314	...	2358	0007
oisdorf **802** d.	0503	...	0618	0618	0718	0818	0918	1018	1118	1218	1318	1418	1518	1618	1718	1818	1918	2018	2118	2218	...	2318	...	0003	0012
ln Messe/Deutz **802 910** d.	0527	0533	0633	0633	0733	0836	0933	1035	1133	1233	1333	1436	1533	1633	1733	1834	1936	2033	2133	2233	2237	2333	...	0027	0037
ln Hbf **802 910** a.	0529	0536	0636	0636	0736	0839	0936	1038	1136	1236	1336	1439	1536	1636	1736	1837	1939	2036	2137	2236	2240	2336	...	0029	0039
ln Hbf **802 910** d.	...	0547	0648	...	0747t	0847r	0947	1047	1147	1247	1345	1447	1547	1647	1747	1847	1947	2047	2147	...	2247	2347	...	...	0040
ren **802** d.	...	0613	0713	...	0813t	0913r	1013	1113	1213	1313	1413	1513	1613	1713	1813	1913	2013	2113	2213	...	2314	0013	...	...	0118
chen Hbf **802 910** a.	...	0641	0741	...	0841t	0941r	1041	1141	1241	1341	1441	1541	1641	1741	1841	1941	2041	2141	2241	...	2346	0041	...	...	0143

– To Gießen (Table **806**).

– ⚒ only.

– Ⓐ only.

⊙ – Change trains at Köln Hbf on ⑥.

◇ – Operated by Hessische Landesbahn.

MÜNSTER - DORTMUND - SIEGEN - FRANKFURT and ESSEN - HAGEN - SIEGEN 808

IC services ⊙	*IC* **2223** ⚒	*IC* **2223** Ⓐ	*IC* **2225**	*IC* **2225** ⚒	*IC* **2225** Ⓐ	*IC* **2229**		*IC* **2323**	*IC* **2325**	*IC* **2327** Ⓒ	
nster (Westf) Hbf **802** d.	...	...	...	...	0619	...	...	1419	...	1819	...
mm (Westf) **802** d.	...	...	...	...	0641	...	...	1441	...	1841	...
rtmund Hbf **802** d.	...	0502	...	0702	0702	1102	...	1502	1702	1902	...
tten Hbf **802** d.	...	0514	...	0714	0714	1114	...	1514	1714	1914	...
tmathe d.	...	0539	...	0739	0739	1139	...	1539	1739	1940	...
ena (Westf) d.	...	0548	...	0748	0748	1148	...	1548	1748	1949	...
erdohl d.	...	0557	...	0757	0757	1157	...	1557	1757	1958	...
nentrop d.	...	0615	...	0815	0815	1215	...	1615	1815	2016	...
nnestadt-Altenhundem d.	...	0628	...	0828	0828	1228	...	1628	1828	2028	...
euztal d.	...	0645	...	0845	0845	1245	...	1645	1845	2045	...
egen Hbf a.	...	0655	...	0855	0855	1255	...	1655	1855	2055	...
egen Hbf **806** d.	0701	0701	0901	0901	0901	1301	...	1701	1901	...	...
llenburg **806** d.	0725	0725	0925	0925	0925	1325	...	1725	1925	...	...
etzlar **806** d.	0742	0742	0942	0942	0942	1342	...	1742	1942	...	...
d Nauheim d.	0804	0804	1004	1004	1004	1404	...	1804	2004	...	...
ankfurt (Main) Hbf **806** a.	0835	0835	1035	1035	1035	1435	...	1835	2035	...	...

IC services ⊙	*IC* **2326** ⚒ S	*IC* **2324**	*IC* **2324** ⚒		*IC* **2320**		*IC* **2226**	*IC* **2224**	*IC* **2222** Ⓒ
Frankfurt (Main) Hbf **806** d.	0527	...	0726	...	1126	...	1526	1726	1926
Bad Nauheim d.	0556	...	0756	...	1156	...	1556	1756	1956
Wetzlar **806** d.	0618	...	0818	...	1218	...	1618	1818	2018
Dillenburg **806** d.	0636	...	0836	...	1236	...	1636	1836	2036
Siegen Hbf **806** a.	0658	...	0858	...	1258	...	1658	1858	2101
Siegen Hbf d.	0704	0904	0904	...	1304	...	1704	1904	...
Kreutztal d.	0716	0916	0916	...	1316	...	1716	1916	...
Lennestadt-Altenhundem d.	0734	0934	0934	...	1334	...	1734	1934	...
Finnentrop d.	0746	0946	0946	...	1346	...	1746	1946	...
Werdohl d.	0804	1004	1004	...	1404	...	1804	2004	...
Altena (Westf) d.	0813	1013	1013	...	1413	...	1813	2013	...
Letmathe d.	0823	1023	1023	...	1423	...	1823	2023	...
Witten Hbf **802** d.	0847	1047	1047	...	1447	...	1847	2047	...
Dortmund Hbf **802** a.	0856	1056	1056	...	1456	...	1856	2056	...
Hamm (Westf) **802** a.	...	1117	1117	...	...	...	1917	...	...
Münster (Westf) Hbf **802** a.	...	1139	1139	...	...	...	1939	...	...

– From Stuttgart via Karlsruhe (Tables **910** and **931**).

⊙ – Most *IC* services convey 🍷. Regional tickets valid Dortmund - Siegen - Dillenburg and v.v.

☛ See next page for regional services.

808 MÜNSTER - DORTMUND - SIEGEN - FRANKFURT and ESSEN - HAGEN - SIEGEN

Regional services **DORTMUND and HAGEN - SIEGEN**. See previous page for *IC* services.

km		Ⓒ ◇		Ⓐ	Ⓐ	Ⓐ ◇		⚒ ◇	Ⓐ ◇	† ◇	⚒ ◇		◇	⚒ ◇		◇	⚒ ◇		◇	⚒ ◇		◇	⚒ ◇		◇
	Dortmund Hbf d.	...	...	...	...	...	0559	...	...	...	...	0759	...	...	0959	...	...	1159	...	...	1359	...	...	1559	...
	Witten Hbf d.	...	...	...	...	...	0610	...	...	...	...	0810	...	...	1010	...	...	1210	...	...	1410	...	...	1610	...
0	**Hagen** Hbf d.	0033	...	...	0414	0542	|	...	0642	0715	0742	|	0842	0942	|	1042	1142	|	1242	1342	|	1442	1542	|	164
21	Letmathe d.	0050	...	...	0430	0600	0636	...	0700	0732	0800	0836	0900	1000	1036	1100	1200	1236	1300	1400	1436	1500	1600	1636	170
30	Altena (Westf) d.	0058	...	...	0438	0608	0644	...	0708	0743	0808	0844	0908	1008	1044	1108	1208	1244	1308	1408	1444	1508	1608	1644	170
39	Werdohl d.	0107	...	...	0446	0616	0652	...	0716	0752	0816	0852	0916	1016	1052	1116	1216	1252	1316	1416	1452	1516	1616	1652	171
61	Finnentrop d.	0125	...	0400	0504	0633	0710	0733	0733	0810	0833	0910	0933	1033	1110	1133	1233	1310	1333	1433	1510	1533	1633	1710	173
74	Lennestadt ♥ d.	0138	...	0413	0516	0645	0722	0745	0745	0822	0845	0922	0945	1045	1122	1145	1245	1322	1345	1445	1522	1545	1645	1722	174
96	Kreuztal d.	0202	...	0435	0539	0708	0741	0808	0808	0840	0908	0941	1008	1108	1141	1208	1308	1341	1408	1508	1541	1608	1708	1741	180
107	**Siegen** Hbf a.	0214	...	0448	0550	0720	0750	0820	0820	0850	0920	0950	1020	1120	1150	1220	1320	1350	1420	1520	1550	1620	1720	1750	182

	⚒ ◇		◇	Ⓐ	⚒ ◇		◇	◇		◇
Dortmund Hbf d.	...	1759	...	1859	...	1959	...	...	2159	...
Witten Hbf d.	...	1810	...	1910	...	2010	...	...	2210	...
Hagen Hbf d.	1742	|	1842	|	1942	|	2042	2115	|	2315
Letmathe d.	1800	1836	1900	1936	2000	2036	2100	2132	2236	2332
Altena (Westf) d.	1808	1844	1908	1944	2008	2044	2108	2140	2244	2340
Werdohl d.	1816	1852	1916	1952	2016	2052	2116	2149	2252	2349
Finnentrop d.	1833	1910	1933	2010	2033	2110	2133	2207	2310	0007
Lennestadt ♥ d.	1845	1922	1945	2022	2045	2122	2145	2219	2322	0019
Kreuztal d.	1908	1941	2008	2040	2108	2141	2208	2243	2345	0043
Siegen Hbf a.	1920	1950	2020	2050	2120	2150	2220	2254	2356	0054

	Ⓐ		Ⓒ ◇	⑥ ◇	Ⓐ ◇		Ⓐ ◇	† ◇	⚒ ◇	
Siegen Hbf d.	0401	...	...	0501	0540	0608	0640	0708	0740	080
Kreuztal d.	0412	...	...	0513	0552	0618	0652	0718	0752	081
Lennestadt ♥ d.	0435	...	...	0535	0614	0636	0714	0736	0814	083
Finnentrop d.	0448	...	0548	0548	0626	0648	0726	0748	0826	084
Werdohl d.	0505	...	0605	0605	0643	0705	0743	0805	0843	090
Altena (Westf) d.	0513	...	0614	0614	0651	0713	0751	0814	0851	091
Letmathe d.	0523	...	0627	0627	0703	0723	0803	0827	0903	092
Hagen Hbf a.	|	...	0643	0643	0720	|	0820	0843	0919	|
Witten Hbf d.	0549	...	...	...	...	0749	...	...	...	094
Dortmund Hbf a.	0559	...	...	...	...	0759	...	...	...	095

	◇	⚒ ◇		◇	⚒ ◇		◇	⚒ ◇		◇	⚒ ◇		◇	⚒ ◇		◇	⚒ ◇		◇	◇	⑦–④ b	⑤⑥ c	◇	⑤⑥ d ◇	
Siegen Hbf d.	0840	0940	1008	1040	1140	1208	1240	1340	1408	1440	1540	1608	1640	1740	1808	1840	1940	2008	2040	2140	2208	2208	2240	2240	230
Kreuztal d.	0852	0952	1018	1052	1152	1218	1252	1352	1418	1452	1552	1618	1652	1752	1818	1852	1952	2018	2052	2152	2218	2218	2252	2252	232
Lennestadt ♥ d.	0914	1014	1036	1114	1214	1236	1314	1414	1436	1514	1614	1636	1714	1814	1836	1914	2014	2036	2114	2214	2236	2236	2314	2314	234
Finnentrop d.	0926	1026	1048	1126	1226	1248	1326	1426	1448	1526	1626	1648	1726	1826	1848	1926	2026	2048	2126	2226	2248	2248	2326	2326	235
Werdohl d.	0943	1043	1105	1143	1243	1305	1343	1443	1505	1543	1643	1705	1743	1843	1905	1943	2043	2105	2143	2243	2305	2305	2343	2343	...
Altena (Westf) d.	0951	1051	1113	1151	1251	1313	1351	1451	1513	1551	1651	1713	1751	1851	1913	1951	2051	2113	2151	2251	2313	2313	2351	2351	...
Letmathe d.	1003	1103	1123	1203	1303	1323	1403	1503	1523	1603	1703	1723	1803	1903	1923	2003	2103	2123	2203	2303	2323	2323	2400	0003	...
Hagen Hbf a.	1019	1119	|	1219	1319	|	1419	1519	|	1619	1719	|	1819	1919	|	2019	2119	|	2219	2319	2339	|	...	0019	...
Witten Hbf d.	...	...	1149	...	...	1349	...	...	1549	...	...	1749	...	...	1949	...	...	2149	...	...	...	2349	...	...	...
Dortmund Hbf a.	...	...	1159	...	...	1359	...	...	1559	...	...	1759	...	...	1959	...	...	2159	...	...	...	2359	...	...	...

Regional services **ESSEN - HAGEN - LETMATHE - ISERLOHN**. SEE NOTE ⊗.

		◇		Ⓐ ◇	Ⓒ ◇		Ⓐ ◇	◇		⚒ ◇	◇		◇			◇		◇		◇		◇		
Essen Hbf ⊗ d.	0507	...	0607	0634	...	0707	0734	...	0807	0834	...	0907	0934	and at	1907	1934	2007	...	2107	...	2207	...	2307	001
Bochum Hbf ⊗ d.	0521	...	0621	0647	...	0721	0747	...	0821	0847	...	0921	0947	the same	1921	1947	2021	...	2121	...	2221	...	2321	002
Witten Hbf ⊗ d.	0533	...	0633	0657	...	0733	0757	...	0833	0857	...	0933	0957	minutes	1933	1957	2033	...	2133	...	2233	...	2333	003
Hagen Hbf ⊗ a.	0547	...	0647	0710	...	0747	0810	...	0847	0910	...	0947	1010	past each	1947	2010	2047	...	2147	...	2247	...	2347	005
Hagen Hbf d.	...	0615	...	0715	0715	...	0815	0815	...	0915	0915	...	1015	hour until	...	2015	...	2115	...	2215	...	2315	...	...
Letmathe a.	...	0630	...	0730	0730	...	0830	0830	...	0930	0930	...	1030		...	2030	...	2130	...	2230	...	2330	...	...
Iserlohn a.	...	0638	...	0738	0738e	...	0838	0838	...	0938	0938	...	1038		...	2038	...	2143	...	2238	...	2343	...	...

			Ⓐ ◇		◇	Ⓐ ◇		† ◇	⚒ ◇		◇			◇			◇		◇		◇		◇	
Iserlohn d.	...	...	0620	...	0720	0720	...	0814	0820	...	0920	and at	...	1920	...	...	2020	...	2120	...	2220	...	2320	...
Letmathe d.	...	...	0627	...	0727	0727	...	0827	0827	...	0927	the same	...	1927	...	...	2027	...	2127	...	2227	...	2327	...
Hagen Hbf a.	...	...	0641	...	0743	0743	...	0843	0843	...	0943	minutes	...	1943	...	...	2043	...	2143	...	2243	...	2343	...
Hagen Hbf ⊗ d.	0516	0616	0648	0716	...	0748	0816	...	0848	0916	0948	past each	1916	1948	...	2016	...	2116	...	2216	...	2316	...	001
Witten Hbf ⊗ d.	0531	0631	0701	0731	...	0801	0831	...	0901	0931	1001	hour until	1931	2001	...	2031	...	2131	...	2231	...	2331	...	003
Bochum Hbf ⊗ d.	0543	0643	0713	0743	...	0813	0843	...	0913	0943	1013		1943	2013	...	2043	...	2143	...	2243	...	2343	...	004
Essen Hbf ⊗ a.	0558	0658	0727	0758	...	0827	0858	...	0927	0958	1027		1958	2027	...	2058	...	2158	...	2258	...	2358	...	005

b – Also Oct. 3, Nov. 1.
c – Not Oct. 3, Nov. 1.
d – Also June 9, 19, Oct. 3.
e – 0743 on †.
◇ – Operated by VIAS Rail.
♥ – Lennestadt-Altenhundem.
⊗ – Services do not run Essen - Hagen and v.v. Sept. 6 - Oct. 31 (also from approx 2100 on Sept. 5).

809 PADERBORN - HAMELN - HANNOVER - HANNOVER FLUGHAFEN ✈ *S-Bahn*

km										Ⓐ	⑥			⚒§	†								§		
0	**Paderborn** Hbf **805 811** d.	...	...	...	...	...	...	...	...	0512	...	...	...	0611	...	...	0715	...	0815	...	0915	...	1011	...	111
17	Altenbeken **805 811** d.	...	...	...	...	...	...	...	...	0524	...	...	...	0624	...	...	0727	...	0827	...	0927	...	1023	...	112
56	Bad Pyrmont d.	...	...	...	...	...	...	0505r	...	0602	0605	...	0635t	0657	0705	0735t	0802	...	0902	...	1002	...	1056	...	120
75	Hameln a.	...	...	...	...	...	...	0518r	...	0616	0618	...	0649t	0710	0718	0749t	0816	...	0916	...	1016	...	1110	...	121
75	Hameln d.	...	...	...	...	0420t	0450r	0520	0550r	0620	0620	0620	0650r	0714	0720	0750r	0820	0850r	0920	0950r	1020	1050r	1114	1150r	122
133	**Hannover** Hbf a.	...	...	...	...	0503t	0533r	0603	0633r	0703	0703	0703	0733r	0803	0803	0833r	0903	0933r	1003	1033r	1103	1133r	1203	1233r	130
133	**Hannover** Hbf d.	0234	0335	0411	0435	0505	0535	0605	0635	0705	0705	0705	0735	0805	0805	0835	0905	0935	1005	1035	1105	1135	1205	1235	130
148	**Hannover** Flughafen ✈ a.	0253	0353	0429	0453	0523	0553	0623	0653	0723	0723	0723	0753	0823	0823	0853	0923	0953	1023	1053	1123	1153	1223	1253	132

		§				§				§								§						⑤⑥	A
Paderborn Hbf **805 811** d.	...	1211	...	1313	...	1411	...	1515	...	1611	...	1715	...	1815	...	1915	...	2011	...	2115	...	2215	...	2307	...
Altenbeken **805 811** d.	...	1223	...	1327	...	1423	...	1527	...	1623	...	1727	...	1827	...	1927	...	2023	...	2127	...	2227	...	2321	...
Bad Pyrmont d.	...	1257	1335t	1402	...	1457	...	1602	1635t	1657	1735t	1802	1835t	1902	...	2002	...	2057	...	2202	...	2302	...	0002	000
Hameln a.	...	1310	1349t	1416	...	1510	...	1616	1649t	1710	1749t	1816	1849t	1916	...	2016	...	2110	...	2216	...	2316	...	0016	001
Hameln d.	1250r	1314	1350r	1420	1450r	1514	1550	1620	1650	1714	1750	1820	1850	1920	1950	2020	2050t	2114	...	2220	...	2320	...	0020	002
Hannover Hbf a.	1333r	1403	1433r	1503	1533r	1603	1633	1703	1733	1803	1833	1903	1933	2003	2033	2103	2133t	2203	...	2303	...	0003	...	0103	010
Hannover Hbf d.	1335	1405	1435	1505	1535	1605	1635	1705	1735	1805	1835	1905	1935	2005	2035	2105	2135	2205	2235	2305	2335	0005	0035	0105	010
Hannover Flughafen ✈ a.	1353	1423	1453	1523	1553	1623	1653	1723	1753	1823	1853	1923	1953	2023	2053	2123	2153	2223	2253	2323	2353	0023	0053	0123	012

		An					⚒		Ⓐ		⚒														
Hannover Flughafen ✈ d.	0006	0036	0106	0209	0306	0406	0436	0436	0506	0506	0536	0536	0606	0636	0706	0736	0806	0836	0906	0936	1006	1036	1106	1136	120
Hannover Hbf a.	0023	0053	0124	0226	0324	0423	0453	0453	0523	0523	0553	0553	0623	0653	0723	0753	0823	0853	0923	0953	1023	1053	1123	1153	122
Hannover Hbf d.	...	0055	...	...	...	...	0455	...	0525	...	0555	...	0625r	0655	0725r	0755	0825r	0855	0925r	0955	1025r	1055	1125r	1155	122
Hameln a.	...	0143	...	...	...	...	0540	...	0610	...	0646*	...	0710r	0740	0810r	0846*	0910r	0940	1010r	1046*	1110r	1140	1210r	1246*	131
Hameln d.	...	...	...	...	...	...	0544	...	0611	...	0650*	...	0711t	0744	...	0850*	...	0944	...	1050*	...	1144	...	1250*	131
Bad Pyrmont d.	...	...	...	...	...	...	0600	...	0625	...	0704*	...	0725t	0800	...	0904*	...	1000	...	1104*	...	1200	...	1304*	132
Altenbeken **805 811** d.	...	...	...	...	...	...	0633	...	...	...	0737*	...	...	0833	...	0937*	...	1033	...	1137*	...	1233	...	1337*	...
Paderborn Hbf **805 811** a.	...	...	...	...	...	...	0646	...	...	...	0752*	...	...	0846	...	0949*	...	1046	...	1152*	...	1246	...	1349*	...

																					B	⑤⑥		Ⓐ	
Hannover Flughafen ✈ d.	1236	1306	1336	1406	1436	1506	1536	1606	1636	1706	1736	1806	1836	1906	1936	2006	2036	2106	2136	2206	2236	2236	2306	2336	233
Hannover Hbf a.	1253	1323	1353	1423	1453	1523	1553	1623	1653	1723	1753	1823	1853	1923	1953	2023	2053	2123	2153	2223	2253	2253	2323	2353	235
Hannover Hbf d.	1255	1325r	1355	1425r	1455	1525	1555	1625	1655	1725	1755	1825	1855	1925	1955	2025r	2055	2125t	2155	...	2255	2255	...	2355	235
Hameln a.	1340	1410r	1446*	1510r	1540	1610	1646*	1710	1740	1810	1846*	1910	1940	2010	2046*	2110r	2141	2210t	2246*	...	2340	2340	...	0040	004
Hameln d.	1344	...	1450*	...	1544	1611t	1650*	1711t	1744	1811t	1850*	...	1944	...	2050*	...	2144	...	2250*	...	2341	2344	...	0042	...
Bad Pyrmont d.	1400	...	1504*	...	1600	1625t	1704*	1725t	1800	1825t	1904*	...	2000	...	2104*	...	2200	...	2304*	...	2355	0000	...	0058	...
Altenbeken **805 811** d.	1433	...	1537*	...	1633	...	1737*	...	1833	...	1937*	...	2033	...	2137*	...	2233	...	2337*	...	...	0033	...	0133	...
Paderborn Hbf **805 811** a.	1446	...	1549*	...	1646	...	1752*	...	1846	...	1949*	...	2046	...	2149*	...	2246	...	2349*	...	...	0046	...	0145	...

A – Mornings of Ⓐ.
B – ⑦–④ only.
n – Runs daily Hannover Flughafen - Hannover.
r – ⚒ only.
t – Ⓐ only.
* – 4–6 minutes **earlier** from Aug. 9.
§ – Runs 4–6 minutes later Paderborn - Hannover from Aug. 9.

KOBLENZ - KÖLN - HANNOVER - BERLIN and BAD BENTHEIM - HANNOVER - BERLIN 810

For other services Koblenz - Köln - Dortmund - Hamm, see Tables **800** (long distance) and **802/805** (regional).
Independent operator **FlixTrain** also run services Köln - Berlin (see Table **927**). **WARNING!** Timings Köln - Dortmund may vary Sept. 6 - Oct. 31 – SEE NOTE ⊠.

km	km	See note ⊠	ICE 674	ICE 649	ICE 841	ICE 751	ICE 541	ICE 551	ICE 741	IC 2445	ICE 843	ICE 853	ICE 1155	ICE 553	ICE 553	ICE 543	IC 141	IC 2443	ICE 845	ICE 855	ICE 1545	ICE 555	ICE 555	ICE 545	IC 143
				①–⑤		E	①–⑥	①–⑥		①–⑥			①–⑥	D	C		D				①–⑥	D	C		n
			F		O	H	m	C	D	A			D					A			T				≋
				✕	✕	✕	✕	✕	✕	🍷	✕	✕	✕	✕	✕	✕		🍷	✕	✕	✕	✕	✕	✕	
		Koblenz Hbf d.	...	...	...	...	...	...	...	...	...	...	...	0541	0541	...	...	0605	...	...	...	...	...	...	...
		Andernach d.	...	...	...	...	...	...	...	...	...	...	...	0555	0555	...	...	0618	...	...	...	...	...	...	...
		Remagen d.	...	...	...	...	...	...	...	...	...	...	...	0608	0608	...	...	0631	...	...	...	...	...	...	...
		Bonn Hbf d.	...	...	...	...	...	...	...	...	...	...	0549	0623	0623	...	...	0645	...	...	...	...	...	...	...
		Aachen Hbf **802** d.	...	...	...	...	...	...	...	...	...	...	|	|	|	...	...	|	...	...	0707	...	...	...	...
	0	**Köln** Hbf **802** d.	...	...	...	...	0424	...	...	0511	0526	0544	0618	0646	0646	0626	...	0711	0726	0745	|	0845	0845	0825	...
		Solingen Hbf d.	...	...	...	...	|	...	...	0530	|	0603	|	|	|	|	...	0730	|	|	|	|	|	|	...
		Wuppertal Hbf d.	...	...	...	...	|	...	...	0544	|	0616	|	0716	0716	|	...	0744	|	0816	|	0916	0916	|	...
		Hagen Hbf d.	...	...	...	...	|	...	...	0601	|	0632	|	0733	0733	|	...	0801	|	0832	|	0933	0933	|	...
	40	**Düsseldorf** Hbf d.	...	...	...	...	0448	...	...	|	0550	|	|	|	|	0651	...	|	0750	|	|	|	|	0851	...
	47	Düsseldorf Flughafen ✈ d.	...	...	...	...	0456j	...	...	|	0559j	|	|	|	|	0700	...	|	0759j	|	|	|	|	0900j	...
		Mönchengladbach Hbf **802** d.	...	...	...	...	|	...	...	|	|	|	|	|	|	|	...	|	|	|	0759	|	|	|	...
	64	**Duisburg** Hbf **802** d.	...	...	...	...	0506	...	...	|	0609	|	|	|	|	0710	...	|	0809j	|	0835	|	|	0910	...
	83	**Essen** Hbf d.	...	...	...	...	0518	...	...	|	0621	|	|	|	|	0722	...	|	0821	|	0848	|	|	0922	...
	99	Bochum Hbf d.	...	...	...	...	0529j	...	...	|	0632j	|	|	|	|	0733j	...	|	0832j	|	0859	|	|	0933j	...
	117	**Dortmund** Hbf a.	...	...	...	...	0541	...	...	0621	0643	|	|	|	|	0745	...	0821	0843	|	0909	|	|	0945	...
	117	**Dortmund** Hbf d.	...	...	...	...	0543	...	...	0628	0645	|	|	|	|	0747	...	0828	0845	|	0911	|	|	0947	...
	148	**Hamm** (Westf) a.	...	...	...	...	|	...	...	0643	0707	0702	|	|	|	|	...	0843	0907	0902	0932	|	|	1005f	...
	148	**Hamm** (Westf) **802** d.	...	...	...	...	|	...	...	0645	0711	0711	|	|	|	|	...	0845	0911	0911	0934	|	|	1007f	...
	198	Gütersloh Hbf **802** d.	...	...	...	...	0622	...	...	0708	|	|	|	|	|	|	...	0908	|	|	0954	|	|	|	...
	215	**Bielefeld** Hbf **802 811** d.	...	...	...	...	0635	...	...	0719	0728f	0738f	|	0827	|	0835	...	0919	0938f	0938f	1005	1027	|	1035	...
	229	Herford **811** d.	...	...	...	...	|	...	...	0728	|	|	|	|	|	|	...	0928	|	|	1015	|	|	|	...
0		*Amsterdam Cent.* **22** ⊖ d.	...	...	...	...	|	...	...	|	|	|	|	|	|	|	0600	|	|	|	|	|	|	|	0800
182		Bad Bentheim 🏛 **811** d.	...	...	...	...	|	...	...	|	|	|	|	|	|	|	0812	|	|	|	|	|	|	|	1012
203		Rheine **811** d.	...	...	...	...	|	...	...	|	|	|	|	|	|	|	0826	|	|	|	|	|	|	|	1026
		Münster (Westf) Hbf **800** d.	...	...	...	...	|	0517	0617	|	|	|	|	|	|	|	|	|	|	|	|	|	|	|	|
251		**Osnabrück** Hbf **800 811** d.	...	...	...	...	|	|	0652	|	|	|	|	|	|	|	0854	|	|	|	|	|	|	|	1054
288		Bünde (Westf) **811** d.	...	...	...	...	|	|	0715	|	|	|	|	|	|	|	0916	|	|	|	|	|	|	|	1116
304	245	Bad Oeynhausen **811** d.	...	...	...	...	|	|	|	0738	|	|	|	|	|	|	|	0938	|	|	|	|	|	|	|
319	260	Minden (Westf) **811** d.	...	...	...	...	0700	|	|	0748	|	|	|	|	|	0900	|	0948	|	|	|	|	|	1100	|
384	325	**Hannover** Hbf **811** a.	...	...	...	...	0728	0804	0801	0820	0828	0828	|	0919	1004	0928	1001	1019	1028	1028	1101	1119	1204	1128	1201
	325	**Hannover** Hbf d.	0418	0527	0631	0703	0731	0806	0804	0835	0831	0831	|	0922	1006	0931	1004	1036	1031	1031	1104	1122	1206	1131	1204
		Magdeburg Hbf **866** a.	|	|	|	|	|	|	|	0954	|	|	|	|	|	|	|	1154	|	|	|	|	|	|	|
		Leipzig Hbf **866** a.	|	▽	|	|	|	|	|	1118	|	|	|	|	|	|	|	1318	|	|	|	|	|	|	|
		Dresden Hbf **842** a.	|	|	|	|	|	|	|	1257*	|	|	|	|	|	|	|	1457*	|	|	|	|	|	|	|
	400	Wolfsburg **902** d.	0513	0619	0704	0737	0803	|	|	...	0904	0904	|	|	|	1003	|	...	1104	1104	|	|	|	1203	|
	475	Stendal Hbf **838** d.	0540	0648	0734	0804	|	|	|	...	|	|	|	|	|	|	|	...	|	|	|	|	|	|	|
	567	**Berlin** Spandau **838 902** a.	0627	0727	0811	0839	0858	0930	0930	...	0958	0958	1004	1047	1129	1058	1130	...	1158	1158	1230	1247	1329	1258	1330
	579	**Berlin** Zoo a.	0641	|	|	|	|	|	|	...	|	|	|	|	|	|	|	...	|	|	|	|	|	|	|
	583	**Berlin** Hbf **838 902** a.	0649	0747	0829	0853	0918	0949	0949	...	1018	1018	1014	1103	1149	1118	1151	...	1218	1218	1251	1303	1349	1318	1351
	588	**Berlin** Ostbahnhof **838 902** a.	0659	0758	0840	0904	0927	1002	1002	...	1028	1028	...	1113	1200	1127	1202	...	1227	1227	1302	1314	1400	1327	1402

See note ⊠	IC 2441	IC 2441	ICE 847	ICE 857	ICE 757	ICE 557	ICE 557	ICE 547	IC 145	IC 2049	ICE 849	ICE 859	ICE 1157	ICE 759	ICE 559	ICE 559	ICE 549	IC 147	IC 2047	ICE 941	ICE 951	ICE 1051	ICE 1051	ICE 651	ICE 651
	J	K			U	D	C		n				D	D	D	C		v				J	K	D	C
	AF	F							≋	AS								≋	AS						
	🍷	🍷	✕	✕	✕	✕	✕	✕		🍷	✕	✕	✕	✕	✕	✕	✕		🍷	✕	✕	✕	✕	✕	✕
Koblenz Hbf d.	0813	0813	...	...	...	...	...	...	...	1013	...	...	...	...	...	...	...	...	1213	...	...	...	...	...	...
Bonn Hbf d.	0845	0845	...	...	...	...	...	...	...	1045	...	...	1149	...	...	...	...	...	1245	...	...	...	...	...	...
Aachen Hbf **802** d.	|	|	...	...	0906	...	...	...	...	|	...	...	|	...	...	...	...	...	|	...	...	1247	1247	...	...
Köln Hbf **802** d.	0909	0909	0926	0945	|	1045	1045	1026e	...	1111	1126e	1145	1218	1137	1245	1245	...	...	1311	...	1345	1335	1335	1445	1445
Solingen Hbf d.	|	0930	|	|	|	|	|	|	...	1130	|	|	|	|	|	|	...	...	1330	...	|	|	|	|	|
Wuppertal Hbf d.	|	0944	|	1016	|	1116	1116	|	...	1144	|	1216	|	|	1316	1316	...	...	1344	...	1416	|	1422	1516	1516
Hagen Hbf d.	|	1001	|	1032	|	1133	1133	|	...	1201	|	1232	|	|	1333	1333	...	...	1401	...	1432	|	1440	1533	1533
Düsseldorf Hbf d.	0934	|	0950	|	|	|	|	1051	...	|	1150	|	|	1206	|	|	1251	...	|	1350	|	1417	|	|	|
Düsseldorf Flughafen ✈ d.	|	|	0959j	|	|	|	|	1100j	...	|	1159j	|	|	|	|	|	1300	...	|	1359	|	|	|	|	|
Mönchengladbach Hbf **802** d.	|	|	|	|	0958	|	|	|	...	|	|	|	|	|	|	|	|	...	|	|	|	|	|	|	|
Duisburg Hbf **802** d.	0948	|	1009	|	1035j	|	|	1110	...	|	1209	|	|	1221	|	|	1310	...	|	1409	|	1431	|	|	|
Essen Hbf d.	1000	|	1021	|	1048j	|	|	1122	...	|	1221	|	|	1233	|	|	1322	...	|	1421	|	1445	|	|	|
Bochum Hbf d.	1010	|	1032j	|	1059j	|	|	1133j	...	|	1232j	|	|	|	|	|	1333j	...	|	1432j	|	1456	|	|	|
Dortmund Hbf a.	1021	1021	1043	|	1109	|	|	1145	...	1221	1243	|	|	|	|	|	1345	...	1421	1443	|	1508	1507	|	|
Dortmund Hbf d.	1028	1028	1045	|	1111	|	|	1147	...	1228	1245	|	|	|	|	|	1347	...	1428	1445	|	1510	1510	|	|
Hamm (Westf) a.	1043	1043	1107	1102	1132	|	|	|	...	1243	1307	1302	|	|	|	|	1405f	...	1443	1507	1502	1532	1532	|	|
Hamm (Westf) **802** d.	1045	1045	1111	1111	1134	|	|	|	...	1245	1311	1311	|	|	|	|	1407f	...	1445	1511	1511	1534	1534	|	|
Gütersloh Hbf **802** d.	1108	1109	|	|	1154	|	|	|	...	1309	|	|	|	|	|	|	|	...	1509	|	|	1554	1554	|	|
Bielefeld Hbf **802 811** d.	1119	1119	1138f	1138f	1205	1227	|	1235	...	1319	1338f	1338f	|	|	1427	|	1435	...	1519	1538f	1538f	1605	1605	1627	|
Herford **811** d.	1128	1128	|	|	1215	|	|	|	...	1328	|	|	|	|	|	|	|	...	1528	|	|	1615	1615	|	|
Amsterdam Cent. **22** ⊖ d.	|	|	|	|	|	|	|	|	1000	|	|	|	|	|	|	|	|	1200	|	|	|	|	|	|	|
Bad Bentheim 🏛 **811** d.	|	|	|	|	|	|	|	|	1212	|	|	|	|	|	|	|	|	1412	|	|	|	|	|	|	|
Rheine **811** d.	|	|	|	|	|	|	|	|	1226	|	|	|	|	|	|	|	|	1426	|	|	|	|	|	|	|
Münster (Westf) Hbf **800** d.	|	|	|	|	|	|	|	|	|	|	|	|	|	1327	|	|	|	|	|	|	|	|	|	|	|
Osnabrück Hbf **800 811** d.	|	|	|	|	|	|	|	|	1254	|	|	|	|	1352	|	|	|	1454	|	|	|	|	|	|	|
Bünde (Westf) **811** d.	|	|	|	|	|	|	|	|	1316	|	|	|	|	|	|	|	|	1516	|	|	|	|	|	|	|
Bad Oeynhausen **811** d.	1138	1138	|	|	|	|	|	|	|	1338	|	|	|	|	|	|	|	|	1538	|	|	|	|	|	|
Minden (Westf) **811** d.	1147	1147	|	|	|	|	|	1300	|	1348	|	|	|	|	|	|	1500	|	1547	|	|	|	|	|	|
Hannover Hbf **811** a.	1220	1220	1228	1228	1301	1319	1404	1328	1401	1418	1428	1428	|	1501	1519	1604	1528	1601	1620	1628	1628	1702	1702	1718	1804
Hannover Hbf d.	1236	1236	1231	1231	1304	1322	1407	1331	1404	1436	1431	1431	|	1504	1522	1606	1531	1604	1636	1631	1631	1705	1705	1721	1806
Magdeburg Hbf **866** a.	1354	1354	|	|	|	|	|	|	|	1554	|	|	|	|	|	|	|	|	1754	|	|	|	|	|	|
Leipzig Hbf **866** a.	1519	1519	|	|	|	|	|	|	|	1718	|	|	|	|	|	|	|	|	1919	|	|	|	|	|	|
Dresden Hbf **842** a.	1638	1639	|	|	|	|	|	|	|	1840	|	|	|	|	|	|	|	|	2040	|	|	|	|	|	|
Wolfsburg **902** d.	...	...	1305	1305	|	|	|	1403	|	...	1504	1504	|	|	|	|	1603	|	...	1704	1704	|	|	|	|
Stendal Hbf **838** d.	...	...	|	|	|	|	|	|	|	...	|	|	|	|	|	|	|	|	...	|	|	|	|	|	|
Berlin Spandau **838 902** a.	...	...	1358	1358	1430	1447	1529	1458	1530	...	1557	1557	1605	1630	1647	1729	1658	1730	...	1758	1758	1830	1830	1847	1929
Berlin Zoo a.	...	...	|	|	|	|	|	|	|	...	|	|	|	|	|	|	|	|	...	|	|	|	|	|	|
Berlin Hbf **838 902** a.	...	...	1417	1417	1449	1503	1549	1518	1551	...	1618	1618	1615	1651z	1704	1749	1718	1751	...	1818	1818	1851	1851	1903	1949
Berlin Ostbahnhof **838 902** a.	...	...	1428	1428	1503	1517	1600	1528	1602	...	1628	1628	...	1702	1716	1800	1727	1802	...	1828	1828	1904	1904	1913	2000

A – On June 7 - Aug. 8 runs to Bielefeld only (will not run Bielefeld - Hannover - Dresden).
C – June 7 - Aug. 8.
D – Aug. 9 - Dec. 13.
E – ①–⑤ (daily from July 28).
F – From Frankfurt (Table **800**).
H – From Hamburg (Table **900**).
J – Not Sept. 6 - Oct. 31.
K – Sept. 6 - Oct. 31.
O – From Oldenburg via Bremen on ①–⑤ (Table **813**).
S – From Stuttgart (Tables **800** and **910**).
T – ①–⑥ from Aug. 9: KAROLINGER – Also calls at Herzogenrath (d. 0723), Rheydt Hbf (d. 0753), Viersen (d. 0807) and Krefeld Hbf (d. 0819). **Does not run Aachen - Dortmund Sept. 6 - Oct. 31**.
U – Runs from Aug. 10. Also calls at Herzogenrath (d. 0923), Rheydt Hbf (d. 0952), Viersen (d. 1006j) and Krefeld Hbf (d. 1018j).
e – ⑦ (also Oct. 4).

f – Until June 13.
j – Not Sept. 6 - Oct. 31.
m – Runs earlier on June 11 (Köln d. 0407).
n – Not June 28 - 30.
v – Not June 28, 29.
z – On Aug. 9 - Sept. 23 calls at Berlin **Zoo** (1644) not Hbf.

▽ – Via Braunschweig (Table **902**).
⊖ – Ⓡ for international journeys May 28 - Aug. 31.
⊠ – **From Sept. 6 to Oct. 31** (also from late evening on Sept. 5) timings Köln - Dortmund via Essen may vary by up to 11 minutes (earlier departures possible). **Trains do not call at Bochum Hbf during this period**.
≋ – Diverted June 7 - Aug. 8, not calling at Osnabrück or Bünde (Hannover and Berlin times are 70 - 80 minutes later).
* – For revised Dresden times from Aug. 10 see Table **842** on page 607.

810 KOBLENZ - KÖLN - HANNOVER - BERLIN and BAD BENTHEIM - HANNOVER - BERLIN

For other services Koblenz - Köln - Dortmund - Hamm and v.v., see Tables **800** (long distance) and **802**/**805** (regional).
Independent operator **FlixTrain** also run services Köln - Berlin (see Table **927**). **WARNING!** Timings Köln - Dortmund and v.v. may vary Sept. 6 - Oct. 31 – SEE NOTE ⊠.

See note ⊠	ICE	IC	ICE	ICE	ICE	ICE	ICE	ICE	ICE	IC	IC	ICE	ICE	ICE	ICE	ICE	ICE	IC	IC	ICE	ICE	ICE	ICE	ICE	ICE
	641	**149**	**2045**	**943**	**953**	**1059**	**653**	**653**	**643**	**241**	**2043**	**945**	**955**	**1159**	**655**	**655**	**645**	**243**	**2041**	**947**	**957**	**657**	**102**	**102**	**100**
		v				⑤⑦	D	C		v		Ⓑ		D	D	C		v	⑦		R	V	Y	W	
		≋	A S			T				≋	A							≋	D				B	B	B
	✕		✕	✕	✕	✕	✕	✕	✕		🍷	✕	✕	✕	✕	✕	✕		🍷	✕	✕	✕	✕	✕	♥
Koblenz Hbf d.	...	...	1413	...	...	...	...	...	...	...	...	...	...	...	...	...	...	...	...	...	...	...	...	...	...
Bonn Hbf d.	...	...	1445	...	...	...	...	...	...	...	...	...	...	1749	...	...	...	...	...	...	...	...	...	...	...
Aachen Hbf **802** d.	...	...	|	...	...	...	...	...	...	...	...	...	...	|	...	...	...	...	...	...	...	1957	...	...	...
Köln Hbf **802** d.	...	...	1511	...	1545	1618	1644	1645	...	...	1711	...	1745	1818	1845	1845	...	...	1909	1926r	1946	2047	2111	2111	2312
Solingen Hbf d.	...	...	1530	...	|	|	|	|	...	...	1730	...	|	|	|	|	...	...	1926	|	|	|	|	2130	|
Wuppertal Hbf d.	...	...	1544	...	1616	|	1715	1716	...	...	1744	...	1816	|	1916	1916	...	...	1943	|	2016	2117	|	2144	|
Hagen Hbf d.	...	...	1601	...	1632	|	1732	1733	...	...	1801	...	1832	|	1933	1933	...	...	2001	|	2032	2134	|	2201	|
Düsseldorf Hbf d.	1451	...	|	1550	|	|	|	|	1651	...	|	1750	|	|	|	|	1851	...	|	1950	|	|	2134	|	2335
Düsseldorf Flughafen ✈ d.	1500j	...	|	1559j	|	|	|	|	1700j	...	|	1759j	|	|	|	|	1900j	...	|	1959j	|	|	|	|	2342
Mönchengladbach Hbf. **802** d.	|	...	|	|	|	|	|	|	|	...	|	|	|	|	|	|	|	...	|	|	|	|	|	|	|
Duisburg Hbf **802** d.	1510	...	|	1609	|	|	|	|	1710	...	|	1809	|	|	|	|	1910	...	|	2009	|	|	2147	|	2352
Essen Hbf d.	1522	...	|	1621	|	|	|	|	1722	...	|	1821	|	|	|	|	1922	...	|	2021	|	|	2200	|	0004
Bochum Hbf d.	1533j	...	|	1632j	|	|	|	|	1733j	...	|	1832j	|	|	|	|	1933j	...	|	2032j	|	|	2210	|	0014j
Dortmund Hbf a.	1545	...	1621	1643	|	|	|	|	1745	...	1821	1843	|	|	|	|	1945	...	2021	2043	|	|	2221	2221	0027
Dortmund Hbf d.	1547	...	1628	1645	|	|	|	|	1747	...	1828	1845	|	|	|	|	1947	...	2028	2045	|	|	2228	2228	0033
Hamm (Westf) a.	1605f	...	1643	1707	1702	|	|	|	1805f	...	1843	1907	1902	|	|	|	2005f	...	2043	2107	2102	2202	2243	2243	0049
Hamm (Westf) **802** d.	1607f	...	1645	1711	1711	|	|	|	1807f	...	1845	1911	1911	|	|	|	2007f	...	2045	2111	2111	2205	2245	2245	0051
Gütersloh Hbf **802** d.	|	...	1709	|	|	|	|	|	|	...	1908	|	|	|	|	|	|	...	2109	|	|	|	2308	2308	0111j
Bielefeld Hbf **802 811** d.	1635	...	1719	1738f	1738f	|	1827	|	1835	...	1919	1938f	1938f	|	2027	|	2035	...	2119	2138f	2138f	2235	2318	2318	0123
Herford **811** d.	|	...	1728	|	|	|	|	|	|	...	1928	|	|	|	|	|	|	...	2128	|	|	|	2328	2328	|
Amsterdam Cent. **22** ⊖ d.	|	1400	|	|	|	|	|	|	|	1600	|	|	|	|	|	|	|	1759	|	|	|	|	|	|	|
Bad Bentheim 🏛 **811** d.	|	1612	|	|	|	|	|	|	|	1812	|	|	|	|	|	|	|	2012	|	|	|	|	|	|	|
Rheine **811** d.	|	1626	|	|	|	|	|	|	|	1826	|	|	|	|	|	|	|	2026	|	|	|	|	|	|	|
Münster (Westf) Hbf **800** d.	|	|	|	|	|	|	|	|	|	|	|	|	|	|	|	|	|	|	|	|	|	|	|	|	|
Osnabrück Hbf **800 811** d.	|	1654	|	|	|	|	|	|	|	1854	|	|	|	|	|	|	|	2054	|	|	|	|	|	|	|
Bünde (Westf) **811** d.	|	1716	|	|	|	|	|	|	|	1916	|	|	|	|	|	|	|	2116	|	|	|	|	|	|	|
Bad Oeynhausen **811** d.	|	|	1738	|	|	|	|	|	|	|	1939	|	|	|	|	|	|	|	2138	|	|	|	2338	2338	|
Minden (Westf) **811** d.	1700	|	1747	|	|	|	|	|	1900	|	1948	|	|	|	|	|	2100	|	2147	|	|	|	2347	2347	0151
Hannover Hbf **811** a.	1728	1801	1820	1828	1828	|	1918	2004	1928	2001	2020	2028	2028	|	2119	2204	2128	2201	2220	2228	2228	2328	0018	0018	0223
Hannover Hbf d.	1731	1804	1836	1831	1831	|	1922	2006	1931	2004	2036b	2031	2031	|	2122	2206	2131	...	...	2231	2231	2331	...	...	0240
Magdeburg Hbf **866** a.	|	|	1954	|	|	|	|	|	|	|	2154b	|	|	|	|	|	|	...	...	|	|	|	...	...	0402
Leipzig Hbf **866** a.	|	|	2119	|	|	|	|	|	|	|	2318h	|	|	|	|	|	|	...	...	|	|	|	...	...	|
Dresden Hbf **842** a.	|	|	2240b	|	|	|	|	|	|	|	...	|	|	|	|	|	|	...	...	|	|	|	...	...	|
Wolfsburg **902** d.	1803	|	...	1904	1904	|	|	|	2003	|	...	2104	2104	|	|	|	2203	...	...	2304	2304	0003	...	...	|
Stendal Hbf **838** d.	|	|	...	|	|	|	|	|	|	|	...	2132	2132	|	|	|	|	...	...	|	|	|	...	...	|
Berlin Spandau **838 902** a.	1858	1929	...	1958	1958	2012	2046	2130	2057	2130	...	2207	2207	2203	2244	2330	2258	...	...	2359	2359	0057	...	...	|
Berlin Zoo a.	|	|	...	|	|	2023	|	|	2110	2144	...	2219	2219	2214y	2255	|	2310	...	...	0011	0011	0109	...	...	0530
Berlin Hbf **838 902** a.	1918	1951	...	2018	2018	2029	2103	2149	2118	2151	...	2226x	2226x	2221	2303	2349	2317	...	...	0018	0018	0114	...	...	0536
Berlin Ostbahnhof **838 902** a.	1927	2002	...	2028	2028	2040	2115	2201	2128	2202	...	2236	2236	2231	2315	2400	2327	...	...	0028	0028	0127	...	...	0547

See note ⊠	ICE	ICE	IC	ICE	ICE	IC	ICE	ICE	IC	IC	ICE	ICE	IC	ICE	ICE	ICE	ICE	IC	ICE	ICE	ICE	IC	ICE	ICE	ICE
	101	**103**	**242**	**646**	**656**	**240**	**956**	**946**	**2042**	**240**	**654**	**644**	**148**	**654**	**954**	**944**	**2044**	**148**	**652**	**642**	**652**	**146**	**1050**	**952**	**942**
				①–⑥	①–⑤	C		①–⑥		D	C		C	D			E	D	C		D	C	D		
	B	B	△		§								v				S					v			
	★	✕	v	✕	✕		✕	✕	🍷		✕	✕		✕	✕	✕	✕		✕	✕	✕		✕	✕	✕
Berlin Ostbahnhof **838 902** d.	0011	...	...	0410	...	0442	0516	0516	...	0553	0554	0633	0643	0644	0732	0732	...	0753	0753	0832	0844	0843	0856	0932	0932
Berlin Hbf **838 902** d.	0022	...	...	0421	...	0453	0527	0527	...	0606	0608	0646	0655	0657	0746	0746	...	0806	0807	0846	0857	0855	0909	0946	0946
Berlin Zoo d.	0028	...	...	0430	...	0459	0535	0535	...	|	|	|	|	|	|	|	...	|	|	|	|	|	|	|	|
Berlin Spandau **838 902** d.	|	...	...	0441	...	0626	0547	0547	...	0626	0626	0700t	|	0712	0800t	0800t	...	0826	0826	0900t	0912	|	0927	1000t	1000t
Stendal Hbf **838** d.	|	...	...	0515	...	|	0624	0624	...	|	|	|	|	|	|	|	...	|	|	|	|	|	|	|	|
Wolfsburg **902** d.	|	...	...	0547	...	|	0653	0653	...	|	|	0753	|	|	0853	0853	...	|	|	0953	|	|	|	1053	1053
Dresden Hbf **842** d.	|	...	...	|	...	|	|	|	...	|	|	|	|	|	|	|	0509	|	|	|	|	|	|	|	|
Leipzig Hbf **866** d.	|	...	...	|	...	|	|	|	...	|	|	|	|	|	|	|	0638	|	|	|	|	|	|	|	|
Magdeburg Hbf **866** d.	0148	...	...	|	...	|	|	|	0603z	|	|	|	|	|	|	|	0804	|	|	|	|	|	|	|	|
Hannover Hbf a.	0309	...	...	0618	...	0637	0728	0728	0723z	0753	0752	0828	0837	0837	0928	0928	0923	0953	0952	1028	1037	1037	1053	1128	1128
Hannover Hbf **811** d.	0313	0541	0556	0621	0640q	0646	0731	0731	0740	0756	0758	0831	0847	0840	0931	0931	0940	0956	0958	1031	1040	1046	1056	1131	1131
Minden (Westf) **811** d.	0400	0613	|	0650	|	|	|	|	0813	|	|	0902	|	|	|	|	1013	|	|	1102	|	|	|	|	|
Bad Oeynhausen **811** d.	|	0624	|	|	|	|	|	|	0823	|	|	|	|	|	|	|	1023	|	|	|	|	|	|	|	|
Bünde (Westf) **811** d.	|	|	0643	|	|	|	|	|	|	0843	|	|	|	|	|	|	|	1043	|	|	|	|	|	|	|
Osnabrück Hbf **800 811** d.	|	|	0706	|	|	|	|	|	|	0906	|	|	|	|	|	|	|	1106	|	|	|	|	1206	|	|
Münster (Westf) Hbf **800** a.	|	|	|	|	|	|	|	|	|	|	|	|	|	|	|	|	|	|	|	|	|	|	1230	|	|
Rheine **811** d.	|	|	0736	|	|	0936	|	|	|	0936	|	|	1136	|	|	|	|	1136	|	|	|	1336	|	|	|
Bad Bentheim 🏛 **811** a.	|	|	0748	|	|	0948	|	|	|	0948	|	|	1148	|	|	|	|	1148	|	|	|	1348	|	|	|
Amsterdam Cent. **22** ⊖ a.	|	|	0959	|	|	1159	|	|	|	1159	|	|	1359	|	|	|	|	1359	|	|	|	1558	|	|	|
Herford **811** d.	|	|	...	0713	|	...	|	|	|	...	|	|	...	|	|	|	|	...	|	|	|	...	|	|	|
Bielefeld Hbf **802 811** d.	0428	0641	...	0722	|	...	|	|	0840	...	|	0928	...	|	|	|	1040	...	|	1128	|	...	|	|	|
Gütersloh Hbf **802** d.	0437	0653	...	|	|	...	|	|	0851	...	|	|	...	|	|	|	1051	...	|	|	|	...	|	|	|
Hamm (Westf) **802** a.	0501	0713	...	0750	|	...	0849	0849	0915	...	|	|	...	|	1049	1049	1115	...	|	|	|	...	|	1249	1249
Hamm (Westf) d.	0503	0715	...	0752	|	...	0856	0854	0917	...	|	|	...	|	1056	1054	1117	...	|	|	|	...	|	1256	1254
Dortmund Hbf a.	0521	0731	...	0809	|	...	|	0910	0932	...	|	1011	...	|	|	1110	1132	...	|	1211	|	...	|	|	1310
Dortmund Hbf d.	0536	0736	...	0812	|	...	|	0913	0936	...	|	1014	...	|	|	1113	1136	...	|	1214	|	...	|	|	1313
Bochum Hbf d.	0548	|	...	0825j	|	...	|	0925j	|	...	|	1025j	...	|	|	1125j	|	...	|	1225j	|	...	|	|	1325j
Essen Hbf d.	0600	|	...	0837	|	...	|	0937	|	...	|	1037	...	|	|	1137	|	...	|	1237	|	...	1325	|	1337
Duisburg Hbf **802** d.	0613	|	...	0850	|	...	|	0950	|	...	|	1050	...	|	|	1150	|	...	|	1250	|	...	1338	|	1350
Mönchengladbach Hbf **802** a.	|	|	...	|	|	...	|	|	|	...	|	|	...	|	|	|	|	...	|	|	|	...	|	|	|
Düsseldorf Flughafen ✈ d.	|	|	...	0859j	|	...	|	|	|	...	|	1058j	...	|	|	1158j	|	...	|	1258j	|	...	|	|	1358j
Düsseldorf Hbf d.	0627	|	...	0907	|	...	|	1002	|	...	|	1108	...	|	|	1207	|	...	|	1308	|	...	1352	|	1407
Hagen Hbf d.	|	0758	...	...	|	...	0926	...	0958	...	1029	...	...	1029	1126	...	1158	...	1229	...	1229	...	|	1326	...
Wuppertal Hbf d.	|	0815	...	...	0844	...	0943	...	1015	...	1046	...	...	1046	1143	...	1215	...	1246	...	1246	...	|	1343	...
Solingen Hbf d.	|	0827	...	...	|	...	|	...	1027	...	|	...	...	|	|	...	1227	...	|	...	|	...	|	|	...
Köln Hbf **802** a.	0649	0847	...	...	0915	...	1012	...	1047	...	1115	...	...	1115	1212	...	1247	...	1319	...	1319	...	1421	1412	...
Aachen Hbf **802** a.	...	...	...	...	...	...	...	...	...	...	...	...	...	...	...	...	|	...	...	...	...	...	...	...	...
Bonn Hbf a.	...	...	...	...	...	...	...	...	...	...	...	...	...	...	...	...	1313	...	...	...	...	...	...	...	...
Koblenz Hbf a.	...	...	...	...	...	...	...	...	...	...	...	...	...	...	...	...	1346	...	...	...	...	...	...	...	...

A – On June 7 - Aug. 8 runs to Bielefeld only (will not run Bielefeld - Hannover - Dresden).
B – From/to Basel (Table **910**).
C – June 7 - Aug. 8.
D – Aug. 9 - Dec. 13.
E – On June 7 - Aug. 8 starts from Bielefeld (will not run Dresden - Hannover - Bielefeld).
R – ⑤⑥ to Aug. 2; ⑤–⑦ from Aug. 8 (also Oct. 2).
S – From/to Stuttgart (Tables **800** and **910**).
T – ⑤⑦ Sept. 26 - Dec. 12 (also Oct. 2; not Oct. 3).
V – ⑤⑦ (also Oct. 2; not Oct. 3). Also runs on ①–④ to Hannover.
W – Sept. 5 - Oct. 30.
Y – Not Sept. 5 - Oct. 30.

b – Not ⑥.
f – Until June 13.
h – ⑤⑦ only.
j – Not Sept. 6 - Oct. 31.
q – 0558 until Aug. 8.
r – ①–④ only.
t – Not June 7 - Aug. 8.
v – Not June 28, 29.
x – Sept. 24 - Dec. 13.
y – Not Aug. 9 - Sept. 23.
z – ①–⑥ only.

⊖ – 🄁 for international journeys May 28 - Aug. 31.
△ – On ①–⑥ June 7 - Aug. 8 departs Hannover 0446, not calling at Bünde or Osnabrück.
§ – Starts from Berlin Ost on ① (Berlin Hbf d. 0404 ① **C**, 0454 ① **D**).
⊠ – **From Sept. 6 to Oct. 31** (also from late evening on Sept. 5) timings Köln - Dortmund and v.v. via Essen may vary by up to 13 minutes (earlier departures possible). **Trains do not call at Bochum Hbf during this period**.
♥ – Also calls at Braunschweig Hbf (a. 0314), Brandenburg Hbf (a. 0445), Potsdam Hbf (a. 0505) and Berlin Wannsee (a. 0517).
★ – Also calls at Potsdam Hbf (d. 0048), Brandenburg Hbf (d. 0106) and Braunschweig Hbf (d. 0236).
≋ – Diverted June 7 - Aug. 8, not calling at Osnabrück or Bünde (Hannover and Berlin times are 70 - 80 minutes later).

BERLIN - HANNOVER - KÖLN - KOBLENZ and BERLIN - HANNOVER - BAD BENTHEIM 810

For other services Hamm - Dortmund - Köln - Koblenz, see Tables **800** (long distance) and **802/805** (regional).
Independent operator **FlixTrain** also run services Berlin - Köln (see Table **927**). **WARNING!** Timings Dortmund - Köln may vary Sept. 6 - Oct. 31 – SEE NOTE ⊠.

See note ⊠	*IC* **2046** E S 🍷	*ICE* **1132** C L ✕	*IC* **146** D	*ICE* **640** ✕	*ICE* **650** D ✕	*ICE* **758** H ✕	*ICE* **758** G ✕	*ICE* **1156** D ✕	*ICE* **950** ✕	*ICE* **940** ✕	*IC* **2048** E S 🍷	*IC* **144** D	*ICE* **558** C ✕	*ICE* **548** ✕	*IC* **142** C v	*ICE* **558** D ✕	*ICE* **756** D¶ ✕	*ICE* **858** ✕	*ICE* **848** ✕	*IC* **2440** E S 🍷	*ICE* **1091** ⑤⑦ T ✕	*IC* **142** D	*ICE* **546** ✕	*IC* **140** C v	*ICE* **556** D ✕
Berlin Ostbahnhof **838 902** d.	...	0941	0953	1033	1045	1053	1053	...	1132	1132	...	1153	1154	1232	1243	1244	1253	1332	1332	...	1345	1353	1432	1443	1444
Berlin Hbf **838 902** d.	...	0955	1006	1046	1057	1106	1106	1141**f**	1146	1146	...	1206	1207	1246	1255	1257	1306	1346	1346	...	1355	1406	1446	1455	1457
Berlin Zoo d.	...	|	|	|	|	|	|	|	|	|	...	|	|	|	|	|	|	|	|	...	|	|	|	|	|
Berlin Spandau **838 902** d.	...	1012	1026	1100**t**	1112	1126	1126	1151	1200**t**	1200**t**	...	1226	1227	1300**t**	|	1312	1326	1400**t**	1400**t**	...	1412	1426	1500**t**	|	1512
Stendal Hbf **838** d.	...	|	|	|	|	|	|	|	|	|	...	|	|	|	|	|	|	|	|	...	|	|	|	|	|
Wolfsburg **902** d.	...	|	|	1153	|	|	|	|	1253	1253	...	|	|	1353	|	|	|	1453	1453	...	1508	|	1553	|	|
Dresden Hbf **842** d.	0709**z**	|	|	|	|	|	|	|	|	|	0909*	|	|	|	|	|	|	|	|	1109*	|	|	|	|	|
Leipzig Hbf **866** d.	0838	|	|	|	|	|	|	|	|	|	1038	|	|	|	|	|	|	|	|	1238	|	|	|	|	|
Magdeburg Hbf **866** d.	1004	|	|	|	|	|	|	|	|	|	1204	|	|	|	|	|	|	|	|	1404	|	|	|	|	|
Hannover Hbf a.	1123	1137	1153	1228	1237	1253	1253	|	1328	1328	1323	1353	1352	1428	1437	1437	1453	1528	1528	1523	1544	1553	1628	1637	1637
Hannover Hbf **811** d.	1140	...	1156	1231	1240	1256	1256	|	1331	1331	1340	1356	1358	1431	1446	1440	1456	1531	1531	1540	...	1556	1631	1646	1640
Minden (Westf) **811** d.	1213	...	|	1302	|	|	|	|	|	|	1413	|	|	1502	|	|	|	|	|	1613	...	|	1702	|	|
Bad Oeynhausen **811** d.	1223	...	|	|	|	|	|	|	|	|	1423	|	|	|	|	|	|	|	|	1623	...	|	|	|	|
Bünde (Westf) **811** d.	|	...	1243	|	|	|	|	|	|	|	|	1443	|	|	|	|	|	|	|	|	...	1643	|	|	|
Osnabrück Hbf **800 811** d.	|	...	1306	|	|	|	|	|	|	|	|	1506	|	|	|	|	1606	|	|	|	...	1706	|	|	|
Münster (Westf) Hbf **800** a.	|	...	|	|	|	|	|	|	|	|	|	|	|	|	|	|	1631	|	|	|	...	|	|	|	|
Rheine **811** d.	|	...	1336	|	|	|	|	|	|	|	|	1536	|	|	1736	|	|	|	|	|	...	1736	|	1936	|
Bad Bentheim 🏛 **811** a.	|	...	1348	|	|	|	|	|	|	|	|	1548	|	|	1748	|	|	|	|	|	...	1748	|	1948	|
Amsterdam Cent. **22** ⊖ a.	|	...	1559	|	|	|	|	|	|	|	|	1759	|	|	1959	|	|	|	|	|	...	1959	|	2159	|
Herford **811** d.	|	...	...	|	|	1345	1345	|	|	|	|	...	|	|	...	|	|	|	|	|	...	...	|	...	|
Bielefeld Hbf **802 811** d.	1240	...	...	1328	|	1355	1355	|	|	|	1440	...	|	1528	...	|	|	|	|	1640	...	...	1728	...	|
Gütersloh Hbf **802** d.	1251	...	...	|	|	|	|	|	|	|	1451	...	|	|	...	|	|	|	|	1651	...	...	|	...	|
Hamm (Westf) **802** a.	1315	...	...	|	|	1423	1423	|	1449	1449	1515	...	|	|	...	|	|	1650	1650	1715	...	...	|	...	|
Hamm (Westf) d.	1317	...	...	|	|	1425	1431	|	1456	1454	1517	...	|	|	...	|	|	1656	1654	1717	...	...	|	...	|
Dortmund Hbf a.	1332	...	...	1411	|	1448	|	|	|	1510	1532	...	|	1612	...	|	|	|	1710	1732	...	...	1811	...	|
Dortmund Hbf d.	1336	...	...	1414	|	1450	|	|	|	1513	1536	...	|	1615	...	|	|	|	1713	1736	...	...	1814	...	|
Bochum Hbf d.	|	...	...	1425**j**	|	1503	|	|	|	1525**j**	|	...	|	1627**j**	...	|	|	|	1725**j**	|	...	...	1825**j**	...	|
Essen Hbf d.	|	...	...	1437	|	1514	|	|	|	1537	|	...	|	1639	...	|	1728	|	1737	|	...	...	1837	...	|
Duisburg Hbf **802** d.	|	...	...	1450	|	1530	|	|	|	1550	|	...	|	1652**j**	...	|	|	|	1750	|	...	...	1850**j**	...	|
Mönchengladbach Hbf **802** a.	|	...	...	|	|	|	|	|	|	|	|	...	|	|	...	|	|	|	|	|	...	...	|	...	|
Düsseldorf Flughafen ✈ d.	|	...	...	1458**j**	|	|	|	|	|	1558**j**	|	...	|	1700**j**	...	|	|	|	1800**j**	|	...	...	1903**j**	...	|
Düsseldorf Hbf d.	|	...	...	1507	|	1544	|	|	|	1607	|	...	|	1708	...	|	1754	|	1809	|	...	...	1912	...	|
Hagen Hbf d.	1358	...	...	...	1429	|	|	|	1526	...	1558	...	1629	...	...	1629	|	1726	|	1758	...	...	|	...	1829
Wuppertal Hbf d.	1415	...	...	...	1446	|	1530	|	1543	...	1615	...	1646	...	...	1646	|	1743	|	1815	...	...	|	...	1846
Solingen Hbf d.	1427	...	...	...	|	|	1546	|	|	...	1627	...	|	...	...	|	|	|	|	1827	...	...	|	...	|
Köln Hbf **802** a.	1447	...	...	...	1515	1618	1617	1540	1612	...	1647	...	1715	...	...	1715	1818**h**	1812	1832**r**	1847	...	...	1936	...	1915
Aachen Hbf **802** a.	|	...	...	...	...	1708	1708	|	...	...	|	...	...	...	...	...	1912**h**	...	...	|	...	...	...	...	|
Bonn Hbf a.	1513	...	...	...	...	...	...	1610	...	...	1713	...	...	...	...	...	...	...	...	1913	...	...	...	...	1938**z**
Remagen a.	|	...	...	...	...	...	...	...	...	...	|	...	...	...	...	...	...	...	...	|	...	...	...	...	1951**z**
Andernach a.	|	...	...	...	...	...	...	...	...	...	|	...	...	...	...	...	...	...	...	|	...	...	...	...	2004**z**
Koblenz Hbf a.	1546	...	...	...	...	...	...	...	...	...	1746	...	...	...	...	...	...	...	...	1946	...	...	...	...	2019**z**

See note ⊠	*ICE* **1544** ⑧ J ✕	*ICE* **856** ✕	*ICE* **846** ✕	*IC* **2442** E F 🍷	*IC* **140** D	*ICE* **554** C ✕	*ICE* **544** ✕	*ICE* **554** D ✕	*ICE* **854** ✕	*ICE* **844** ✕	*IC* **2444** E 🍷	*ICE* **742** D ✕	*ICE* **542** ✕	*ICE* **552** D ✕	*ICE* **872** R ✕	*ICE* **892** R ✕	*ICE* **842** ①–④ C ✕	*ICE* **842** ①–④ D ✕	*ICE* **740** ⑤⑦ D ✕	*ICE* **550** C ✕	*ICE* **540** O ✕	*ICE* **840** ⑧ ✕	*ICE* **840** ⑦	*IC* **2448** ⑤ D	*ICE* **271** Y
Berlin Ostbahnhof **838 902** d.	1454	1532	1532	...	1553	1554	1632	1645	1732	1732	...	1753	1832	1844	1933	1933	1934	1934	1953	1956	2032	2113	2113	...	2315
Berlin Hbf **838 902** d.	1506	1546	1546	...	1606	1607	1646	1657	1746	1746	...	1806	1846	1857	1946	1946	1948	1946	2006	2008	2045	2123	2123	...	2328
Berlin Zoo d.	|	|	|	...	|	|	|	|	|	|	...	|	|	|	|	|	|	|	|	2015	2052**x**	2131	2131	...	2335
Berlin Spandau **838 902** d.	1526	1600**t**	1600**t**	...	1626	1627	1700**t**	1712	1800**t**	1800**t**	...	1826	1900**t**	1912	2000	2000	|	2000	2027	2027	2100**y**	2142**t**	2142**t**	...	2345
Stendal Hbf **838** d.	|	|	|	...	|	|	|	|	|	|	...	1859	|	|	|	|	|	|	|	|	2138	2218	2218	...	0025
Wolfsburg **902** d.	1620	1653	1653	...	|	|	1753	|	1853	1853	...	|	1953	|	2053	2053	2053	2053	|	|	2208	2248	2248	...	0100
Dresden Hbf **842** d.	|	|	|	1245*	|	|	|	|	|	|	1509	|	|	|	|	|	|	|	|	|	|	|	|	1845*	|
Leipzig Hbf **866** d.	|	|	|	1438	|	|	|	|	|	|	1638	|	|	|	|	|	|	|	|	|	|	|	|	2038	|
Magdeburg Hbf **866** d.	|	|	|	1604	|	|	|	|	|	|	1804	|	|	|	|	|	|	|	|	|	|	|	|	2204	|
Hannover Hbf a.	1652	1728	1728	1723	1753	1752	1828	1837	1928	1928	1923	1953	2028	2037	2128	2128	2128	2128	2153	2152	2242	2322	2322	2326	0137
Hannover Hbf **811** d.	1656	1731	1731	1740	1756	1758	1831	1840	1931	1931	1940	1956	2031	2040	2131	2136	2131	2136	2156	2158	...	...	2331	2331	...
Minden (Westf) **811** d.	|	|	|	1813	|	|	1902	|	|	|	2013	|	2102	|	|	2212	|	2212	|	|	...	...	|	0005	...
Bad Oeynhausen **811** d.	|	|	|	1823	|	|	|	|	|	|	2023	|	|	|	|	|	|	|	|	|	...	...	|	0015	...
Bünde (Westf) **811** d.	|	|	|	|	1843	|	|	|	|	|	|	2043	|	|	|	|	|	|	2243	|	...	...	|	|	...
Osnabrück Hbf **800 811** d.	|	|	|	|	1906	|	|	|	|	|	|	2110	|	|	|	|	|	|	2306	|	...	...	|	|	...
Münster (Westf) Hbf **800** a.	|	|	|	|	|	|	|	|	|	|	|	2135	|	|	|	|	|	|	2333	0031●	...	...	|	|	...
Rheine **811** d.	|	|	|	|	1936	|	|	|	|	|	|	...	|	|	|	|	|	|	...	|	...	...	|	|	...
Bad Bentheim 🏛 **811** a.	|	|	|	|	1948	|	|	|	|	|	|	...	|	|	|	|	|	|	...	|	...	...	|	|	...
Amsterdam Cent. **22** ⊖ a.	|	|	|	|	2159	|	|	|	|	|	|	...	|	|	|	|	|	|	...	|	...	...	|	|	...
Herford **811** d.	1745	|	|	|	...	|	|	|	|	|	|	...	|	|	|	2232	|	2234	...	|	...	...	0018	0027	...
Bielefeld Hbf **802 811** d.	1755	|	|	1840	...	|	1928	|	|	|	2040	...	2128	|	2225	2244	|	2244	...	|	...	...	0028	0035	...
Gütersloh Hbf **802** d.	|	|	|	1851	...	|	|	|	|	|	2051	...	|	|	|	2254	|	2254	...	|	...	...	0037	0046	...
Hamm (Westf) **802** a.	1824	1850	1850	1915	...	|	|	|	2049	2049	2115	...	|	|	2253	2314	2250	2314	...	0009	...	...	0100	0110	...
Hamm (Westf) d.	1826	1856	1854	1917	...	|	|	|	2056	2054	2117	...	|	|	2255	2316	2254	2316	...	...	...	...	0102	0112	...
Dortmund Hbf a.	1847	|	1910	1932	...	|	2011	|	|	2110	2132	...	2211	|	|	2333	2310	2332	...	...	...	...	0119	0127	...
Dortmund Hbf d.	1851	|	1913	1934	...	|	2014	|	|	2113	2136	...	2214	|	|	2337	2313	2337	...	...	...	...	0122	...	...
Bochum Hbf d.	1904	|	1925**j**	1946	...	|	2025**j**	|	|	2125**t**	|	...	2225**k**	|	|	2349**k**	2325	2349**k**	...	...	...	...	0133**j**	...	...
Essen Hbf d.	1915	|	1937	1959	...	|	2037	|	|	2138	|	...	2237	|	|	0001	2337	0001	...	...	...	...	0146	...	...
Duisburg Hbf **802** d.	1929	|	1951	2012	...	|	2050	|	|	2151	|	...	2250	|	|	0015	2350	0015	...	...	...	...	0159	...	...
Mönchengladbach Hbf **802** a.	2001	|	2042‡	|	...	|	|	|	|	|	|	...	|	|	|	|	|	|	...	...	...	...	|	...	...
Düsseldorf Flughafen ✈ d.	|	|	|	|	...	|	2100**j**	|	|	2201	|	...	2300**k**	|	|	0025	0001	0025	...	...	...	...	0209	...	...
Düsseldorf Hbf d.	|	|	2015	2026	...	|	2109	|	|	2209	|	...	2309	|	|	0034	0009	0034	...	...	...	...	0218	...	...
Hagen Hbf d.	|	1926	|	|	...	2029	|	2029	2126	|	2158	...	|	2229	2325	|	|	|	...	...	...	...	|	...	...
Wuppertal Hbf d.	|	1943	|	|	...	2046	|	2046	2143	|	2215	...	|	2246	2342	|	|	|	...	...	...	...	|	...	...
Solingen Hbf d.	|	|	|	|	...	|	|	|	|	|	2227	...	|	|	|	|	|	|	...	...	...	...	|	...	...
Köln Hbf **802** a.	|	2012	|	2049	...	2114	2133	2115	2212	2233	2247	...	2333	2315	0011	0057	0033	0057	...	...	...	...	0242	...	...
Aachen Hbf **802** a.	2052	...	2134**e**	|	...	|	...	...	...	...	|	...	...	|	...	...	...	...	...	...	...	...	...	...	...
Bonn Hbf a.	...	...	...	2113	...	2142**z**	...	...	...	...	2312	...	...	2341**e**	...	...	...	...	...	...	...	...	...	...	...
Remagen a.	...	...	...	|	...	2156**z**	...	...	...	...	2326	...	...	2357**e**	...	...	...	...	...	...	...	...	...	...	...
Andernach a.	...	...	...	|	...	2211**z**	...	...	...	...	2339	...	...	0013**e**	...	...	...	...	...	...	...	...	...	...	...
Koblenz Hbf a.	...	...	...	2146	...	2226**z**	...	...	...	...	2354	...	...	0028**e**	...	...	...	...	...	...	...	...	...	...	...

C – June 7 - Aug. 8.
D – Aug. 9 - Dec. 13.
E – On June 7 - Aug. 8 starts from Bielefeld (will not run Dresden - Hannover - Bielefeld).
F – To Frankfurt (Table **800**).
G – Sept. 6 - Oct. 31.
H – From Aug. 9 (not Sept. 6 - Oct. 31).
J – To Dortmund on ⑧ from Aug. 9; extends to Aachen on ①②③ Aug. 11 - Sept. 3 and ⑧ from Nov. 2. Also calls at Krefeld Hbf (a. 1941), Viersen (a. 1953), Rheydt Hbf (a. 2007) and Herzogenrath (a. 2037). Train number **750** on certain dates.
L – To Bremen (Table **813**).
O – To Oldenburg via Bremen (Table **813**).
R – ⑤–⑦ from Aug. 9 (also Oct. 2).

S – To Stuttgart (Tables **800** and **910**).
T – ⑤⑦ (also Oct. 4; not Oct. 3). To Stuttgart via Frankfurt (Tables **900** and **910**).
Y – To Chur via Frankfurt, Basel and Zürich (Tables **900**, **910** and **520**).

e – ⑦ only.
f – 1133 on ⑦.
h – ④–⑦ from Aug. 9.
j – Not Sept. 6 - Oct. 31.
k – Not Sept. 5 - Oct. 30.
r – ①–④ (also ⑦ to Aug. 3).
t – Not June 7 - Aug. 8.
v – Not June 28, 29.
x – June 7 - Aug. 2.
y – Aug. 3 - Dec. 13.
z – ①–⑥ only.

● – Calls after Hamm.
¶ – Train number **1546** on ①–③.
‡ – Calls after Düsseldorf. Also calls at Neuss Hbf (a. 2028). On ⑦ continues to Rheydt Hbf (a. 2048) and Aachen Hbf (a. 2134).
⊖ – 🅁 for international journeys May 28 - Aug. 31.
⊠ – **From Sept. 6 to Oct. 31** (also from late evening on Sept. 5) timings Dortmund - Köln via Essen may vary by up to 14 minutes. **Trains do not call at Bochum Hbf during this period**.
* – For revised times from Aug. 10 see Table **842** on page 607.

811 Regional services BIELEFELD and HENGELO - HANNOVER and PADERBORN

See Table **22** for international *IC* services Amsterdam - Hengelo - Bad Bentheim - Hannover and v.v. See Table **810** for fast *ICE* / *IC* services Bielefeld / Bad Bentheim - Hannover and v.v.

RHEINE and BIELEFELD - HANNOVER - BRAUNSCHWEIG ⊡

km		⚒	Ⓐ	Ⓒ		⚒					●														
0	**Bielefeld** Hbf ... **802** d.	...	0424	0432	...	...	0631	...	0831	...	...	1031	...	1231	...	1431	...	1631	...	1831	...	2031	...	2231	...
14	Herford ... **802** d.	...	0433	0441	...	...	0641	...	0841	...	...	1041	...	1241	...	1441	...	1641	...	1841	...	2041	...	2241	...
	Rheine ... ● d.	...	|	|	...	...	|	0638	|	0838	0939	|	1038	|	1238	|	1438	|	1638	|	1838	|	2038	|	2238
	Ibbenbüren ... ● d.	...	|	|	...	...	|	0654	|	0854	0951	|	1054	|	1254	|	1454	|	1654	|	1854	|	2054	|	2254
	Osnabrück Hbf ... ● a.	...	|	|	...	...	|	0713	|	0913	1006	|	1113	|	1313	|	1513	|	1713	|	1913	|	2113	|	2313
	Osnabrück Hbf ... ● d.	...	|	|	...	0517	|	0718	|	0917	1008	|	1117	|	1317	|	1517	|	1717	|	1917	|	2117	|	2317
	Bünde (Westf) ... ● d.	...	|	|	...	0539	|	0740	|	0939	1030	|	1139	|	1339	|	1539	|	1739	|	1939	|	2139	|	2339
24	Löhne ... **802** ● d.	...	0440	0448	...	0551	0648	0751	0848	0951	1038	1048	1151	1248	1351	1448	1551	1648	1751	1848	1951	2048	2151	2248	2351
30	Bad Oeynhausen ... **802** d.	...	0445	0452	...	0557	0652	0757	0852	0957	...	1052	1157	1252	1357	1452	1557	1652	1757	1852	1957	2052	2157	2252	2357
45	Minden (Westf) ... **802** a.	...	0457	0507	...	0607	0707	0807	0908	1007	...	1107	1207	1308	1407	1507	1607	1707	1807	1908	2007	2107	2207	2308	0007
45	Minden (Westf) ... ▷ d.	0403	0508	0508	0608	0608	0708	0808	0908	1008	...	1108	1208	1308	1408	1508	1608	1708	1808	1909	2009	2108	2208	2309	...
110	**Hannover** Hbf ... ▷ a.	0450	0550	0550	0650	0650	0750	0852	0949	1050	...	1150	1250	1349	1453	1550	1650	1750	1853	1950	2052	2150	2250	2350	...
110	**Hannover** Hbf ... **866** d.	0454	0555	0555	0655	0655	0755	0855	0955	1055	...	1155	1255	1355	1456	1555	1655	1755	1855	1955	2055	2155	2255	0014	...
145	Peine ... **866** d.	0524	0623	0623	0723	0723	0823	0924	1023	1123	...	1223	1323	1423	1524	1623	1723	1823	1923	2023	2123	2223	2323	0040	...
171	**Braunschweig** Hbf ... **866** a.	0540	0640	0640	0740	0740	0840	0940	1040	1140	...	1240	1340	1440	1540	1640	1740	1840	1940	2040	2140	2240	2340	0059	...

km			⚒				●																◇		⑤⑥
0	**Braunschweig** Hbf ... **866** d.	0020	0420	0520	0620	0720	...	0820	0920	1020	1120	1220	1320	1420	1520	1620	1720	1820	1920	2020	2120	2220	...	2320	2320
26	Peine ... **866** d.	0038	0438	0538	0637	0738	...	0837	0938	1038	1138	1237	1338	1438	1538	1638	1738	1837	1938	2038	2138	2238	...	2338	2338
61	**Hannover** Hbf ... **866** a.	0106	0505	0605	0703	0805	...	0904	1005	1105	1205	1303	1405	1505	1605	1705	1805	1903	2005	2105	2205	2305	...	0005	0005
61	**Hannover** Hbf ... ▷ d.	—	0509	0609	0708	0809	...	0909	1009	1109	1209	1305	1409	1509	1609	1709	1809	1905	2009	2109	2209	2309	...	0009	0009
126	Minden (Westf) ... ▷ a.	...	0551	0654	0752	0851	...	0951	1051	1151	1251	1350	1451	1551	1651	1751	1851	1951	2051	2151	2251	2351	...	0051	0051
126	Minden (Westf) ... **802** d.	...	0552	0655	0753	0852	...	0952	1052	1152	1252	1351	1452	1552	1652	1752	1852	1952	2052	2152	2252	2352	0010	...	0100
141	Bad Oeynhausen ... **802** d.	...	0604	0706	0804	0904	...	1004	1104	1204	1304	1403	1504	1604	1704	1804	1904	2003	2104	2204	2304	0004	0022	...	0112
147	Löhne ... **802** ● d.	...	0609	0710	0809	0909	0918	1009	1109	1209	1309	1408	1509	1609	1709	1809	1909	2008	2109	2209	2309	0009	0027	...	0117
157	Bünde (Westf) ... ● d.	...	0620	|	0820	|	0927	1020	|	1220	|	1420	|	1620	|	1820	|	2020	|	2220	|	0020	|	...	|
194	**Osnabrück** Hbf ... ● a.	...	0641	|	0841	|	0948	1041	|	1241	|	1441	|	1641	|	1841	|	2041	|	2241	|	0041	|	...	|
194	**Osnabrück** Hbf ... ● d.	0646	0646	|	0846	|	0950	1046	|	1246	|	1446	|	1646	|	1846	|	2046	|	2246	|	...	|	...	|
220	Ibbenbüren ... ● d.	0705	0705	|	0905	|	1006	1105	|	1305	|	1505	|	1704	|	1905	|	2105	|	2305	|	...	|	...	|
242	**Rheine** ... ● d.	0722	0722	|	0922	|	1018	1121	|	1322	|	1522	|	1721	|	1922	|	2122	|	2322	|	...	|	...	|
	Herford ... **802** d.	...	...	0720	...	0917	...	...	1117	...	1317	...	1517	...	1717	...	1917	...	2117	...	2320	...	0040	...	0125
	Bielefeld Hbf ... **802** a.	...	...	0732v	...	0931	...	...	1131	...	1331	...	1531	...	1731	...	1931	...	2131	...	2328	...	0050	...	0136

HENGELO - BAD BENTHEIM - OSNABRÜCK - BIELEFELD ◇

km		⚒	⚒		Ⓐ		⚒					⑤⑥f
0	**Hengelo** ... d.	...	...	...	0534	...	0634	0734	⊠	2134	2234	2234
11	Oldenzaal ... d.	...	...	...	0542	...	0642	0742		2142	2242	2242
26	Bad Bentheim 🏛 ... d.	...	...	...	0556	...	0656	0756	and	2156	2256	2256
47	**Rheine** ... d.	...	0514	...	0614	...	0714	0814		2214	2314	2314
69	Ibbenbüren ... d.	...	0528	...	0628	...	0728	0828	hourly	2228	2328	2328
95	**Osnabrück** Hbf ... d.	0447	0547	0647	0647	0747	0747	0847		2247	2345	2347
132	Bünde (Westf) ... d.	0512	0612	0712	0712	0812	0812	0912	until	2312	...	0012
146	Herford ... a.	0527	0627	0727	0727	0827	0827	0927		2327	...	0027
146	Herford ... d.	0536	0636	0736	0736	0836	0836	0936		2336	...	0036
160	**Bielefeld** Hbf ... a.	0547	0647	0747	0747	0847	0847	0947		2347	...	0047

	Ⓐ	⚒	⚒h					⑤⑥f		⑤⑥f
Bielefeld Hbf ... d.	...	0511	0611	0712	⊠	2112	2212	2212	2312	2312
Herford ... a.	...	0521	0621	0723		2123	2223	2223	2323	2323
Herford ... d.	...	0532	0633	0732	and	2132	2233	2233	2332	2332
Bünde (Westf) ... d.	...	0546	0648	0746		2146	2247	2247	2346	2346
Osnabrück Hbf ... d.	0514	0614	0714	0814	hourly	2214	2314	2314	0012	0014
Ibbenbüren ... d.	0530	0630	0731	0830		2230	2330	2330	...	0031
Rheine ... d.	0549	0649	0748	0849	until	2249	2346	2349	...	0048
Bad Bentheim 🏛 ... d.	0608	0708	0808	0908		2308	...	0004	...	...
Oldenzaal ... d.	0618	0718	0818	0918		2318	...	...	...	...
Hengelo ... a.	0626	0726	0826	0926		2326	...	...	...	...

BIELEFELD - PADERBORN ⊖

44 km. Journey time: 53 – 54 minutes.

From Bielefeld Hbf on Ⓐ at 0434, 0534, 0604, 0634, 0704, 0734, 0804, 0834, 0934, 1034, 1134, 1234, 1304 and every 30 minutes until 1904; then 1943, 2043, 2143, 2243 and 2343.
From Bielefeld Hbf on ⑥ at 0543 and hourly until 2343. **From Bielefeld** Hbf on † at 0843 and hourly until 2343.

From Paderborn Hbf on Ⓐ at 0513, 0543, 0613, 0643, 0713, 0743, 0813, 0843, 0913, 1013, 1113, 1213, 1313, 1343 and every 30 minutes until 1913; then 2023, 2123, 2223 and 2323.
From Paderborn Hbf on ⑥ at 0523 and hourly until 2323. **From Paderborn** Hbf on † at 0823 and hourly until 2323.

PADERBORN - HOLZMINDEN - KREIENSEN ⊖

km		⚒	Ⓐ	⚒	⚒		⚒								Ⓐ		Ⓐ	Ⓒ	Ⓐ				†		
0	**Paderborn** Hbf ... **805 809** d.	0453	0453	...	0553	0653	0753	0853	0953	1053	1153	1253	1353	1453	1553	1553	1653	1653	...	1753	1853	1953	2053	2053	2206
17	Altenbeken ... **805 809** d.	0507	0507	...	0607	0707	0807	0907	1007	1107	1207	1307	1407	1507	1607	1607	1707	1707	...	1807	1907	2007	2107	2107	2219
48	Höxter-Ottbergen ... a.	0532	0532	...	0632	0732	0832	0932	1032	1132	1232	1332	1432	1532	1632	1632	1732	1732	...	1832	1932	2032	2132	2132	2244
48	Höxter-Ottbergen ... d.	—	0536	...	0636	0736	0836	0936	1036	1136	1236	1336	1436	1536	1636	1636	1736	1736	...	1836	1936	2036	2136	2136	2245
58	Höxter Rathaus ... d.	...	0545	...	0645	0745	0845	0945	1045	1145	1245	1345	1445	1545	1645	1645	1745	1745	...	1845	1945	2045	2145	2145	2254
66	Holzminden ... a.	Ⓐ	0554	...	0654	0754	0854	0954	1054	1154	1254	1354	1454	1554	1654	1654	1754	1754	...	1854	1954	2054	2154	2154	2302
66	Holzminden ... d.	0545	...	0633	...	0758	...	0958	...	1158	...	1358	...	1558	1654	...	1754	1758	1831	...	1958	...	2158	...	...
110	**Kreiensen** ... a.	0619	...	0706	...	0832	...	1032	...	1232	...	1432	...	1632	1728	...	1828	1832	1905	...	2032	...	2232	...	...

	Ⓐ	⚒	⚒	Ⓐ		⚒										Ⓐ	Ⓒ	Ⓐ		Ⓐ			†	⚒	†
Kreiensen ... d.	...	...	...	0627	...	0723	...	0923	...	1123	...	1323	...	1523	...	*1652*	1723	1752	...	1828	1923	...	2125	2127	2241
Holzminden ... a.	...	...	...	0700	...	0756	...	0956	...	1156	...	1356	...	1556	...	*1725*	1756	1825	...	1900	1956	...	2158	2200	2314
Holzminden ... d.	0506	0606	0701	0701	0801	0801	0901	1001	1101	1201	1301	1401	1501	1601	1701	1801	1801	...	1901	1901	2001	2101	2201	2201	2316
Höxter Rathaus ... d.	0515	0615	0710	0710	0810	0810	0910	1010	1110	1210	1310	1410	1510	1610	1710	1810	1810	...	1910	1910	2010	2110	2210	2210	2322
Höxter-Ottbergen ... a.	0524	0624	0719	0719	0819	0819	0919	1019	1119	1219	1319	1419	1519	1619	1719	1819	1819	...	1919	1919	2019	2119	2219	2219	2330
Höxter-Ottbergen ... d.	0526	0626	0726	0726	0826	0826	0926	1026	1126	1226	1326	1426	1526	1626	1726	1826	1826	...	1926	1926	2026	2126	2226	2226	2331
Altenbeken ... **805 809** d.	0552	0652	0752	0752	0852	0852	0952	1052	1152	1252	1352	1452	1552	1652	1752	1852	1852	...	1952	1952	2052	2152	2252	2252	2357
Paderborn Hbf ... **805 809** a.	0605	0705	0805	0805	0905	0905	1005	1105	1205	1305	1405	1505	1605	1705	1805	1905	1905	...	2005	2005	2105	2205	2305	2305	0010

(PADERBORN -) OTTBERGEN - GÖTTINGEN ⊖

km		⚒	⚒		⚒		⚒		⑥	Ⓐk	Ⓐr	Ⓒ			Ⓐ		Ⓐ								
	Paderborn Hbf ★ ... d.	0453	0553	0653	0753	0853	0953	1053	1153	1153	1153	1253	...	1453	1553	1653	1753	1853	1953	...	...	...	...	...	...
0	Höxter-Ottbergen ... d.	0534	0634	0734	0834	0934	1034	1134	1234	1234	1234	1334	...	1534	1634	1734	1834	1934	2034	...	...	...	...	...	...
63	**Göttingen** ... a.	0644	0754	0845	0954	1045	1154	1245	1354	1354	1417	1445	...	1645	1754	1845	1954	2045	2154	...	...	...	...	...	...

	⚒	⚒	†	⚒	⚒	†	⚒	⚒	†	⚒	⑥	†	Ⓐr	Ⓐk	⑥	Ⓐ	Ⓒ	Ⓐ	Ⓐ	Ⓒ	Ⓐ	Ⓐ	Ⓒ	Ⓐk	r
Göttingen ... d.	0557	0710	0715	0801	0910	0915	1001	1110	1115	1201	1310	1315	1331	1401	1401	1510	1515	1601	1710	1715	1801	1910	1915	2000	2110
Höxter-Ottbergen ... a.	0723	0824	0824	0924	1024	1024	1124	1224	1224	1324	1424	1424	1524	1524	1524	1624	1624	1724	1824	1824	1924	2024	2024	2123	2224
Paderborn Hbf ★ ... a.	0805	0905	0905	1005	1105	1105	1205	1305	1305	1405	1505	1505	1605	1605	1605	1705	1705	1805	1905	1905	2005	2105	2105	2205	2305

HERFORD - PADERBORN ◇

km		Ⓐ	⚒					A	⑤⑥f	
0	**Herford** ... d.	0530	0633	0733	and	2133	2233	2233	2336	...
8	Bad Salzuflen ... d.	0537	0640	0740		2140	2240	2240	2343	...
19	Lage (Lippe) ... d.	0549	0652	0752	hourly	2152	2252	2252	2355	...
28	Detmold ... d.	0559	0702	0802		2202	2258	2302	0002	...
57	Altenbeken ... **805 809** d.	0624	0727	0827	until	2227	...	2327	0027	...
74	**Paderborn** Hbf ... **805 809** a.	0638	0741	0841		2241	...	2341	0041	...

	Ⓐ	⚒						⑤⑥f
Paderborn Hbf ... **805 809** d.	...	0518	0621	and	2021	2121	...	2221
Altenbeken ... **805 809** d.	...	0530	0633		2033	2133	...	2233
Detmold ... d.	0458	0558	0701	hourly	2101	2201	...	2301
Lage (Lippe) ... d.	0506	0606	0709		2109	2209	...	2309
Bad Salzuflen ... d.	0517	0617	0720	until	2120	2220	...	2320
Herford ... a.	0524	0624	0727		2127	2227	...	2327

A – ⑤⑥†.

f – Also Oct. 2.
h – Runs daily Rheine - Hengelo.
k – ①–⑤ June 10, July 3 - Aug. 13, Oct. 13 - 24, Oct. 31.
r – Not dates in note **k**.

v – 0729 on Ⓒ.

⊡ – Operated by WestfalenBahn.
◇ – Operated by eurobahn.
⊖ – Operated by NordWestBahn. 2nd class only.
⊠ – Timings may vary by 1 – 2 minutes.

★ – Through trains from / to Paderborn are combined with services to / from Holzminden between Paderborn and Höxter-Ottbergen (see previous panel).
▷ – Additional S-Bahn services operate Minden - Hannover and v.v. (journey 55 minutes):
From Minden at 0535 and hourly until 2335.
From Hannover Hbf at 0628 and hourly until 0028.
● – Additional trains (operated by DB) run Rheine - Löhne and v.v.
From Rheine at 0539 Ⓐ, 0739 ⚒, 0939 (as shown) and then every **two** hours until 2139.
From Löhne at 0518 Ⓐ, 0718 ⚒, 0918 (as shown) and then every **two** hours until 2118.

MÜNSTER - EMDEN - NORDDEICH 812

km				IC					IC					IC	IC			ICE			IC	IC				
		◇	◇	2438	◇	⊡	◇	⊡	2208	◇	⊡	◇	⊡	2206	2306	◇	⊡	1014	◇	⊡	2204	2432	◇	◇	⊡	◇
		⚒	Ⓐ	①–⑥	⚒	Ⓐ		Ⓐ					Ⓐ		C			⑥		Ⓐ			Ⓒ	Ⓐ		
									D 🍷					🍷	🍷			S ✕			🍷					
	Köln Hbf **800 802** d.	...	...	...	...	...	...	0521	0541	...	0621r	...	0721	0746	0801	...	0821	0851x	...	0921	0938	...	...	...	1021	...
	Düsseldorf Hbf **800** d.	...	...	...	...	...	...	|	0607	...	|	...	|	0812	0829	...	|	0915	...	|	1012	...	...	...	|	...
	Hagen Hbf **802** d.	...	...	...	...	0521	...	0621	|	...	0721	...	0821	|	|	...	0921	|	...	1021	|	...	...	...	1121	...
0	**Münster** (Westf) Hbf d.	...	0502	...	0602	0624	0702	0724	0731	0805	0824	0905	0924	0932	0955	1005	1024	1031	1105	1124	1131	...	1205	1205	1224	1305
15	Greven d.	...	0513	...	0613	0636	0712	0734	|	0815	0834	0915	0934	|	|	1015	1034	|	1115	1134	|	...	1215	1215	1234	1315
26	Emsdetten d.	...	0521	...	0621	0644	0721	0741	|	0822	0841	0922	0941	|	|	1022	1041	|	1122	1141	|	...	1222	1222	1241	1322
39	**Rheine** d.	0534	0534	...	0634	0657	0733	0751	0756	0834	0851	0933	0951	0956	1025	1033	1051	1056	1133	1151	1156	...	1233	1233	1251	1333
70	Lingen (Ems) d.	0555	0555	...	0655	▬	0755	...	0815	0855	▬	0955	...	1015	|	1055	▬	|	1155	...	1215	...	1255	1255	▬	1355
90	Meppen d.	0609	0609	...	0709	...	0809	...	0829	0909	...	1009	...	1030	|	1109	...	|	1209	...	1229	...	1309	1327k	...	1409
136	Papenburg (Ems) d.	0642	0642	...	0742	**H**	0842	...	0856	0942	**H**	1042	...	1056	|	1142	**H**	|	1242	...	1256	...	1342	1404	**H**	1442
153	Leer (Ostfriesl) **813** d.	0653	0653	0722	0753	0824	0853	...	0908	0953	1024	1053	...	1108	1126	1153	1224	|	1253	...	1308	1322	1353	1417	1424	1453
180	**Emden** Hbf ◧ **813** a.	0709	0709	0738	0809	0841	0909	...	0925	1009	1041	1109	...	1125	1144	1209	1241	1215	1309	...	1326	1338	1409	1433	1441	1509
180	**Emden** Hbf **813** d.	...	...	0742	...	0842	...	...	0944	...	1042	...	...	1142	...	...	1242	1220	...	...	...	1342	...	...	1442	...
209	Norden **813** d.	...	...	0808	...	0906	...	...	1009	...	1106	...	...	1205	...	...	1306	1247	...	...	...	1408	...	...	1506	...
215	**Norddeich** **813** a.	...	...	0814	...	0912	...	...	1015	...	1112	...	...	1211	...	...	1312	|	...	...	...	1414	...	...	1512	...
	Norddeich Mole ‡ **813** a.	...	...	0820	...	0916	...	...	1020	...	1116	...	...	1216	...	...	1316	1259	...	...	...	1420	...	...	1516	...

		IC					IC					IC	IC					IC								
	⊡	2202	◇	⊡	◇	⊡	2200	◇	⊡	◇	⊡	2004	2036	◇	⊡	◇	⊡	2002		◇	⊡	◇	⊙	◇	◇	⊙
	Ⓐ					Ⓐ					Ⓐ	Ⓑ	Ⓑ				Ⓐ									
		🍷					🍷					🍷														
Köln Hbf **800 802** d.	1121	1146	...	1221	...	1321	1346	...	1421	...	1521	1546	...	...	1621	...	1721	1745	...	...	1821	...	...	...	...	...
Düsseldorf Hbf **800** d.	|	1212	...	|	...	|	1412	...	|	...	|	1612	...	...	|	...	|	1812	...	...	|	...	...	...	...	...
Hagen Hbf **802** d.	1221	|	...	1321	...	1421	|	...	1521	...	1621	|	...	...	1721	...	1821	|	...	...	1921	...	...	...	...	...
Münster (Westf) Hbf d.	1324	1331	1405	1424	1505	1524	1531	1605	1624	1705	1724	1732	...	1805	1824	1905	1924	1931	...	2005	2024	2105	2135	2212	2312	0013
Greven d.	1334	|	1415	1434	1515	1534	|	1615	1634	1715	1734	|	...	1815	1834	1915	1934	|	...	2015	2034	2115	2147	2223	2324	0025
Emsdetten d.	1341	|	1422	1441	1522	1541	|	1622	1641	1722	1741	|	...	1822	1841	1922	1941	|	...	2022	2041	2122	2155	2231	2332	0033
Rheine d.	1351	1356	1434	1451	1533	1551	1556	1633	1651	1733	1751	1756	...	1833	1851	1933	1951	1956	...	2033	2051	2133	2208	2252j	2356h	0046
Lingen (Ems) d.	...	1415	1455	▬	1555	...	1615	1655	▬	1755	...	1815	...	1855	▬	1955	...	2015	...	2055	▬	2155	...	2313	0017	...
Meppen d.	...	1429	1509	...	1609	...	1629	1709	...	1809	...	1829	...	1909	...	2009	...	2029	...	2109	...	2209	...	2327	0031	...
Papenburg (Ems) d.	...	1456	1542	**H**	1642	...	1656	1742	**H**	1842	...	1856	...	1942	**H**	2042	...	2056	...	2142	**H**	2242	...	0000	...	...
Leer (Ostfriesl) **813** d.	...	1509	1553	1624	1653	...	1709	1753	1824	1853	...	1909	1922	1953	2024	2053	...	2110	2122	2153	2224	2253	...	0012	...	...
Emden Hbf ◧ **813** a.	...	1525	1609	1641	1709	...	1726	1809	1841	1909	...	1926	1938	2009	2041	2109	...	2126	2138	2209	2241	2309	...	0028	...	...
Emden Hbf **813** d.	...	1542	...	1642	...	...	1728	...	1842	...	...	...	1942	...	2042	...	...	...	2142	...	2242	...	...	...	...	...
Norden **813** d.	...	1605	...	1706	...	...	1751	...	1906	...	...	...	2008	...	2106	...	...	...	2208	...	2306	...	...	...	...	...
Norddeich **813** a.	...	1611	...	1712	...	...	1757	...	1912	...	...	...	2014	...	2112	...	...	...	2214	...	2312	...	...	...	...	...
Norddeich Mole ‡ **813** a.	...	1616	...	1716	...	...	1802	...	1916	...	...	...	2020	...	2116	...	...	...	...	...	...	...	...	...	...	...

						IC						IC	IC					IC						IC		
	⊙	⊡	◇		◇	2005	⊡	◇	◇		◇	2037	2009	⊡	◇		◇	2201	⊡	◇		◇	◇	2203	⊡	◇
	⚒	Ⓐ	⚒	⚒		①–⑥	Ⓐ	Ⓐ	Ⓒ			①–⑥		Ⓐ					Ⓐ				Ⓐ		Ⓐ	Ⓐ
				H		🍷				**H**		🍷				**H**		🍷			**H**			🍷		
Norddeich Mole ‡ **813** d.	...	...	...	...	...	...	...	...	...	...	...	0736	...	...	...	0839	...	0951	...	...	1039	...	...	1136	...	...
Norddeich **813** d.	...	...	...	0445	...	*0535*	...	...	...	0641	...	0739	...	...	...	0841	...	0957	...	...	1041	...	...	1139	...	...
Norden **813** d.	...	...	...	0451	...	*0542*	...	...	...	0647	...	0746	...	...	...	0847	...	1007	...	...	1047	...	...	1146	...	...
Emden Hbf **813** a.	...	...	...	0517	...	*0606*	...	...	...	0717	...	0814	...	...	...	0917	...	1029	...	...	1117	...	...	1214	...	...
Emden Hbf ◧ **813** d.	...	...	0452	0517	0552r	0634	...	0642	0651	0717	0752	0816	0833	...	0852	0917	0952	1034	...	1052	1117	1152	1224	1234	...	...
Leer (Ostfriesland) **813** d.	...	...	0509	0534	0609r	0652	...	0659	0707	0734	0809	0833	0853	...	0909	0934	1009	1053	...	1109	1134	1209	1241	1252	...	...
Papenburg (Ems) d.	...	...	0519	▬	0619r	0704	...	0709	0716	▬	0819	...	0904	...	0919	▬	1019	1104	...	1119	▬	1219	1251	1304	...	←
Meppen d.	...	...	0550	⊡	0650	0730	...	0750j	0747	⊡	0850	...	0930	...	0950	⊡	1050	1131	...	1150	⊡	1250	1325	1330	...	1337
Lingen (Ems) d.	...	...	0604	...	0704	0744	...	0804	0801	...	0904	...	0944	...	1004	...	1104	1144	...	1204	...	1304	→	1344	...	1351
Rheine d.	0453	0608	0629	0708	0729	0804	0808	0829	0829	0908	0929	...	1004	1008	1029	1108	1129	1204	1208	1229	1308	1329	...	1404	1408	1429j
Emsdetten d.	0502	0616	0637	0716	0738	|	0816	0838	0838	0916	0938	...	|	1016	1038	1116	1138	|	1216	1238	1316	1338	...	|	1416	1438
Greven d.	0510	0623	0644	0723	0745	|	0823	0845	0845	0923	0945	...	|	1023	1045	1123	1145	|	1223	1245	1323	1345	...	|	1423	1445
Münster (Westf) Hbf a.	0524	0633	0655	0733	0756	0829	0833	0856	0855	0933	0956	...	1029	1033	1056	1133	1156	1227	1233	1256	1333	1356	...	1429	1433	1455
Hagen Hbf **802** a.	...	0737	...	0837	...	|	0937	...	...	1037	...	...	|	1137	...	1237	...	|	1337	...	1437	...	...	|	1537	...
Düsseldorf Hbf **800** a.	...	|	...	|	...	0947	|	...	...	|	...	...	1147	|	...	|	...	1347	|	...	|	...	...	1547	|	...
Köln Hbf **800 802** a.	...	0838	...	0938	...	1015	1038	...	...	1138	...	...	1215	1238	...	1338	...	1415	1438	...	1538	...	...	1614	1638	...

			IC			IC				ICE			IC	IC					IC							
	◇		2305	⊡	◇	2205	⊡	◇		1015	⊡	◇	2435	2207	⊡	◇		◇	2209	⊡	◇		◇	◇		◇
	Ⓒ		C				Ⓐ			⑥					Ⓐ					Ⓐ						
		H	🍷			🍷			**H**	S ✕				🍷			**H**		E 🍷			**H**			**H**	
Norddeich Mole ‡ **813** d.	...	1239	...	...	...	1351	...	...	1439	1454	...	...	1536	...	...	...	1639	...	1758	...	...	1839	...	...	2039	...
Norddeich **813** d.	...	1241	...	...	...	1357	...	...	1441	|	...	...	1539	...	...	...	1641	...	1801	...	...	1841	...	...	2041	...
Norden **813** d.	...	1247	...	...	...	1407	...	...	1447	1506	...	...	1546	...	...	...	1647	...	1808	...	...	1847	...	...	2047	...
Emden Hbf **813** a.	...	1317	...	...	...	1429	...	...	1517	1528	...	...	1614	...	...	...	1717	...	1830	...	...	1917	...	...	2117	...
Emden Hbf ◧ **813** d.	1252	1317	1341	...	1352	1434	...	1452	1517	1531	...	1552	1616	1633	...	1652	1717	1752	1834	...	1852	1917	1952	2052	2117	2214
Leer (Ostfriesland) **813** d.	1309	1334	|	...	1409	1452	...	1509	1534	1552	...	1609	1633	1652	...	1709	1734	1809	1852	...	1909	1934	2009	2109	2134	2231
Papenburg (Ems) d.	1319	...	|	...	1419	1504	...	1519	...	1603	...	1619	...	1703	...	1719	▬	1819	1904	...	1919	...	2019	2119	▬	2241
Meppen d.	1350	...	|	...	1450	1530	...	1550	...	1630	...	1650	...	1730	...	1750	⊡	1850	1930	...	1950	...	2050	2150	⊙	2313
Lingen (Ems) d.	1404	...	|	...	1504	1544	...	1604	...	1643	...	1704	...	1744	...	1804	...	1904	1944	...	2004	...	2104	2204	...	2327
Rheine d.	1429	...	1459	1508	1529	1604	1608	1629	...	1703	1708	1729	...	1804	1808	1829	1908	1929	2004	2008	2029	...	2129	2229	2253	2353
Emsdetten d.	1438	...	|	1516	1538	|	1616	1638	...	|	1716	1738	...	|	1816	1838	1916	1938	|	2016	2038	...	2138	2238	2302	0002
Greven d.	1445	...	|	1523	1545	|	1623	1645	...	|	1723	1745	...	|	1823	1845	1923	1945	|	2023	2046	...	2146	2245	2310	0010
Münster (Westf) Hbf a.	1456	...	1527	1533	1556	1627	1633	1656	...	1727	1733	1756	...	1829	1833	1856	1933	1956	2029	2033	2056	...	2156	2256	2324	0024
Hagen Hbf **802** a.	...	...	|	1637	...	|	1737	...	...	|	1837	...	...	|	1937	...	2037	...	|	2137	...	...	...	...	...	...
Düsseldorf Hbf **800** a.	...	...	1659	|	...	1747	|	...	...	1842	|	...	...	1947	|	...	|	...	2147	|	...	...	...	...	...	...
Köln Hbf **800 802** a.	...	...	1731	1738	...	1814	1838	...	...	1908x	1938	...	...	2015	2038	...	2138	...	2214	2238	...	...	...	...	...	...

C – ⑥⑦ to Nov. 2; ⑥ from Nov. 8.
D – ④⑤⑥ to Nov. 1; ⑥ from Nov. 8.
E – ③④⑤⑦ to Nov. 2; ⑤⑦ from Nov. 7.
H – From/to Hannover (Table **813**).
S – From/to Stuttgart (Table **910**).

h – Arrives 2344.
j – Arrives 8–10 minutes earlier.
k – Arrives 1307.
r – ⚒ only.
x – Köln **Messe/Deutz**.

⊡ – Operated by National Express.
◇ – Operated by WestfalenBahn.
⊙ – Operated by *eurobahn*.
‡ – For ⛴ to/from Juist and Norderney. See www.reederei-frisia.de for latest timings.
◧ – For train/🚌/⛴ connections to/from Borkum via Emden Außenhafen (certain Emden trains may be extended to/from Emden Außenhafen to connect with sailings). See www.ag-ems.de for latest timings.

813 NORDDEICH - EMDEN - BREMEN - HANNOVER

Regional tickets are valid on *IC* services Norddeich - Emden - Oldenburg - Bremen and v.v.

km		RE 4447 ©	RE 4441	ICE 841 ①-⑤	RE 4443	IC 2033 ①-⑥	IC 2033 🍷	RE 4405 B	RE 4407	ICE 533 ①-⑥ ✕	RE 4407	IC 2035 ①-⑥ 🍷	IC 2035 🍷	RE 4409 B	RE 4411	ICE 535 ⑥⑦ ✕	ICE 535 ✕	RE 4411	IC 2037 🍷	RE 4413 B	RE 4415	ICE 537 ⑦ ✕	ICE 537 ✕	RE 4415	IC 2039 🍷
	Norddeich Mole ‡ **812** d.	...	...	...	...	...	...	...	...	...	...	...	...	...	...	...	...	...	0736e	...	0839	...	...	...	0936
0	**Norddeich** **812** d.	...	...	...	...	...	...	...	0445r	...	...	0535	...	...	0641	...	...	...	0739e	...	0841	...	...	...	0939
6	Norden **812** d.	...	...	...	...	...	...	...	0451r	...	...	0542	...	...	0647	...	...	...	0746e	...	0847	...	...	...	0946
35	**Emden** Hbf ◧ **812** d.	...	...	...	...	0416	...	...	0517	...	...	0608	...	...	0717	...	...	...	0816	...	0917	...	...	...	1016
62	Leer (Ostfriesland) **812** a.	...	...	...	...	0433	...	...	0534	...	...	0625	...	...	0734	...	...	...	0833	...	0934	...	...	...	1033
62	Leer (Ostfriesland) d.	...	...	...	...	0441	...	...	0541	...	...	0634	...	...	0741	...	...	...	0841	...	0941	...	...	...	1041
101	Bad Zwischenahn d.	...	...	...	...	0513	...	...	0612	...	...	0713	...	...	0812	...	...	...	0913	...	1012	...	...	...	1113
116	**Oldenburg** (Oldb) a.	...	...	...	...	0523	...	...	0623	...	...	0723	...	...	0823	...	...	...	0923	...	1023	...	...	...	1123
116	**Oldenburg** (Oldb) d.	...	...	0440	...	0535	...	...	0635	0640	...	0735	0735	...	0835	0842	...	...	0935	...	1035	1040	...	...	1135
147	Delmenhorst d.	...	...	0458	...	0554	...	...	0654	0659	...	0754	0754	...	0854	0900	...	...	0954	...	1054	1059	...	...	1154
161	**Bremen** Hbf a.	...	...	0508	...	0605	...	...	0705	0709	←	0805	0805	...	0905	0910	...	←	1005	...	1105	1109	...	←	1205
161	**Bremen** Hbf d.	0208	0408	0510	0517	0609	0609	0617	→	0715	0717	0809	0809	0817	→	0915	0915	0917	1009	1017	→	1115	1115	1117	1209
196	Verden (Aller) d.	0239	0441	0531	0541	0630	0630	0641		|	0741	0830	0830	0841		|	|	0941	1030	1041	...	|	|	1141	1230
227	Nienburg (Weser) d.	0301	0503	0548	0603	0646	0646	0703	...	|	0803	0846	0846	0903	...	|	|	1003	1046	1103	...	|	|	1203	1246
283	**Hannover** Hbf a.	0341	0538	0615	0638	0713	0713	0738	...	0814	0838	0913	0913	0938	...	1014	1014	1038	1113	1138	...	1214	1214	1238	1313
	Magdeburg Hbf **866** a.	...	...	|	...	0858	0858	...	...	|	...	1057	1057	...	...	|	|	...	1257	...	...	|	|	...	1457
	Berlin Hbf **810** a.	...	...	0829	...	|	|	...	...	|	...	1231t	1231t	...	...	|	|	...	|	...	...	|	|	...	|
	Leipzig Hbf **866** a.	...	...	...	...	1016	1016	...	...	|	...	1216v	1216v	...	...	|	|	...	1416	...	...	|	|	...	1616
	Nürnberg Hbf **900** a.	...	...	...	...	...	...	...	...	1125	...	...	...	...	...	1325	1325	...	...	...	...	1525	1525	...	...
	München Hbf **900** a.	...	...	...	...	...	...	...	...	1240	...	...	...	...	...	1439	1441	...	...	...	...	1641	1641	...	...

	RE 4417 B	IC 1931 ⑤t D🍷	RE 4419	IC 2431 C🍷	RE 4421 B	ICE 631 ✕	RE 4423	IC 2433 🍷	RE 4425 B	ICE 633 ✕	RE 4427	IC 2435 🍷	RE 4429 B	ICE 635 ✕	RE 4431	IC 2437 ⑥	IC 2437 Ⓑ 🍷	RE 4433 B	RE 4435	IC 2439 🍷	RE 4437 B	RE 4439	♣	RE 4445	♣
Norddeich Mole ‡ **812** d.	...	...	1039	...	...	...	1239	...	...	...	1439	1536	...	...	1639	...	...	...	1839	...	...	2039	...	...	...
Norddeich **812** d.	...	...	1041	...	...	...	1241	...	...	...	1441	1539	...	...	1641	...	...	...	1841	...	...	2041	...	...	...
Norden **812** d.	...	...	1047	...	...	...	1247	...	...	...	1447	1546	...	...	1647	...	...	...	1847	...	...	2047	...	...	...
Emden Hbf ◧ **812** d.	...	...	1117	1216	...	...	1317	1417	...	...	1517	1616	...	...	1717	1816	1816	...	1917	2016	...	2117	...	...	...
Leer (Ostfriesland) **812** a.	...	...	1134	1233	...	...	1334	1433	...	...	1534	1633	...	...	1734	1833	1833	...	1934	2033	...	2134	...	...	...
Leer (Ostfriesland) d.	...	...	1141	1241	...	...	1341	1441	...	...	1541	1641	...	...	1741	1841	1841	...	1941	2041	...	2141	...	...	...
Bad Zwischenahn d.	...	...	1212	1313	...	...	1412	1513	...	...	1612	1713	...	...	1812	1913	1913	...	2012	2113	...	2212	2245	...	2345
Oldenburg (Oldb) a.	...	...	1223	1323	...	...	1423	1523	...	...	1623	1723	...	...	1823	1923	1923	...	2023	2123	...	2223	2257	...	2357
Oldenburg (Oldb) d.	...	1230	1235	1335	...	...	1434	1535	...	...	1635	1735	...	...	1835	1935	1935	...	2035	2135	...	2235	2305	...	0005
Delmenhorst d.	...	1249	1254	1354	...	...	1454	1554	...	...	1654	1754	...	...	1854	1954	1954	...	2054	2154	...	2254	2329	...	0029
Bremen Hbf a.	...	1300	1305	1405	...	...	1505*	1605	...	...	1705*	1805	...	...	1905*	2005	2005	...	2105	2205	...	2305	2343	...	0043
Bremen Hbf d.	1217	1305	1317	1409	1417	1515	1517	1608	1617	1715	1717	1809	1817	1915	1917	...	2009	2017	2117	...	2217	2313	...	0013	...
Verden (Aller) d.	1241	|	1341	1430	1441	|	1541	1630	1641	|	1741	1830	1841	|	1941	...	2030	2041	2141	...	2241	2346	...	0046	...
Nienburg (Weser) d.	1303	|	1403	1446	1503	|	1603	1646	1703	|	1803	1846	1903	|	2003	...	2046	2103	2203	...	2303	0008	...	0108	...
Hannover Hbf a.	1338	1407	1438	1513	1538	1614	1638	1713	1738	1814	1838	1913	1938	2014	2038	...	2113	2138	2238	...	2338	0040	...	0140	...
Magdeburg Hbf **866** a.	...	1533	...	1657	...	|	...	1857	...	|	...	2057	...	|	...	...	2300	...	...	...	...	...	...	...	...
Berlin Hbf **810** a.	...	|	...	1830	...	|	...	|	...	|	...	|	...	|	...	...	...	...	...	...	...	...	...	...	...
Leipzig Hbf **866** a.	...	1647	...	...	...	|	...	2015	...	|	...	2216	...	|	...	...	...	...	...	...	...	...	...	...	...
Nürnberg Hbf **900** a.	...	...	...	...	...	1925	...	...	...	2125	...	...	...	2325b	...	...	...	...	...	...	...	...	...	...	...
München Hbf **900** a.	...	...	...	...	...	2045	...	...	...	2240	...	...	...	0045k	...	...	...	...	...	...	...	...	...	...	...

	♣ Ⓐ	RE 4438 ⚒	RE 4446 ©	RE 4400 B	IC 2438 ①-⑥ 🍷	RE 4402	RE 4404 B	IC 2436 ⑦	IC 2436 ⑥	IC 2436 ①-⑤ 🍷	RE 4406	ICE 636 ①-⑤ ✕	RE 4408 B	IC 2434 ⑦	IC 2434 ①-⑥ 🍷	RE 4410	ICE 634 ①-⑥ ✕	RE 4412 B	IC 2432 C🍷	RE 4414	RE 4416 B	IC 2430 🍷	RE 4418	ICE 630 ✕	RE 4420 B
München Hbf **900** d.	...	...	...	...	...	...	...	...	...	...	...	...	...	...	...	...	0514	...	...	...	...	...	...	0917	...
Nürnberg Hbf **900** d.	...	...	...	...	...	...	...	...	...	...	...	...	...	...	...	...	0632	...	...	...	...	...	...	1033	...
Leipzig Hbf **866** d.	...	...	...	...	...	...	...	...	...	...	...	...	...	...	0542	...	|	...	...	...	...	0942	...	|	...
Berlin Hbf **810** d.	...	...	...	...	...	...	...	...	...	...	...	...	...	...	|	...	|	...	0732	...	...	|	...	|	...
Magdeburg Hbf **866** d.	...	...	...	...	...	...	...	...	...	0500	...	...	...	...	0701	...	|	...	0902	...	...	1101	...	|	...
Hannover Hbf d.	...	...	0217	0420	...	0520	0618h	...	0645	0645	0720	0745	0820	0845	0845	0920	0945	1020	1045	1120	1220	1245	1320	1345	1420
Nienburg (Weser) d.	...	...	0258	0454	...	0554	0654	...	0713	0713	0754	|	0854	0913	0913	0954	|	1054	1113	1154	1254	1313	1354	|	1454
Verden (Aller) d.	...	...	0320	0515	...	0615	0715	...	0730	0730	0815	|	0915	0930	0930	1015	|	1115	1130	1215	1315	1330	1415	|	1515
Bremen Hbf a.	...	...	0351	0539	...	0639	0739	...	0750	0750	0839	0845*	0939	0950	0950	1039	1045*	1139	1150	1239	1339	1350	1439	1445*	1539
Bremen Hbf d.	0415	...	...	...	0553	0653	...	0753	0753	0753	0853	...	...	0953	0953	1053	...	...	1153	1253	...	1353	1453	...	...
Delmenhorst d.	0427	...	...	...	0604	0703	...	0804	0804	0804	0903	...	...	1004	1004	1103	...	...	1204	1303	...	1404	1503	...	...
Oldenburg (Oldb) a.	0453	...	...	...	0623	0723	...	0823	0823	0823	0923	...	...	1023	1023	1123	...	...	1223	1323	...	1423	1523	...	...
Oldenburg (Oldb) d.	0458	0533	...	...	0633	0733	...	0833	0833	0833	0933	...	...	1033	1033	1133	...	...	1233	1333	...	1433	1533	...	...
Bad Zwischenahn d.	0511	0544	...	...	0644	0744	...	0844	0844	0844	0944	...	...	1044	1044	1144	...	...	1244	1344	...	1444	1544	...	...
Leer (Ostfriesland) a.	...	0613	...	...	0714	0813	...	0914	0914	0914	1013	...	...	1114	1114	1213	...	...	1314	1413	...	1514	1613	...	...
Leer (Ostfriesland) **812** d.	...	0624	...	...	0722	0824	...	0922	0922	0922	1024	...	...	1122	1122	1224	...	...	1322	1424	...	1522	1624	...	...
Emden Hbf ◧ **812** d.	...	0642	...	...	0742	0842	...	0938	0938	0938	1042	...	...	1138	1138	1242	...	...	1342	1442	...	1538	1642	...	...
Norden **812** d.	...	0706	...	...	0808	0906	...	...	...	...	1106	...	...	...	...	1306	...	...	1408	1506	...	...	1706	...	...
Norddeich **812** a.	...	0712	...	...	0814	0912	...	...	...	...	1112	...	...	...	...	1312	...	...	1414	1512	...	...	1712	...	...
Norddeich Mole ‡ **812** a.	...	0716	...	...	0820	0916	...	...	...	...	1116	...	...	...	...	1316	...	...	1420	1516	...	...	1716	...	...

	IC 2038 🍷	RE 4422	ICE 538 ✕	RE 4424 B	IC 2036 🍷	IC 2036 Ⓑ 🍷	RE 4426	ICE 536 ✕	RE 4428 B	IC 2034 🍷	IC 1934 ⑦t D🍷	RE 4430	ICE 776 F✕	RE 4430	RE 4432 B	IC 2032 🍷	IC 2032 Ⓑ 🍷	♣	RE 4434	RE 4434 ⑥	ICE 532 ✕	RE 4442	ICE 540	RE 4444	RE 4440
München Hbf **900** d.	...	...	1117	...	...	...	...	1317	...	...	...	...	...	...	...	...	...	...	...	...	1716	...	...	...	...
Nürnberg Hbf **900** d.	...	...	1233	...	...	...	...	1434	...	...	...	...	...	...	...	...	...	...	...	...	1833	...	...	...	...
Leipzig Hbf **866** d.	1142	...	|	...	1342	1342	...	|	...	1542v	1602	...	...	...	...	1740	1740	...	...	...	|	...	...	...	...
Berlin Hbf **810** d.	|	...	|	...	|	|	...	|	...	1528t	|	...	...	...	...	|	|	...	...	...	|	...	2045	...	...
Magdeburg Hbf **866** d.	1301	...	|	...	1501	1501	...	|	...	1700	1725	...	...	...	...	1901	1901	...	...	...	|	...	|	...	...
Hannover Hbf d.	1445	1520	1545	1620	1645	1645	1720	1745	1820	1845	1901	1920	1951	...	2020	2045	2045	...	2120	2120	2145	2220	2245	2320	0020
Nienburg (Weser) d.	1513	1554	|	1654	1713	1713	1754	|	1854	1913	1930	1954	|	...	2054	2113	2113	...	2154	2154	2213	2254	2314	2354	0054
Verden (Aller) d.	1530	1615	|	1715	1730	1730	1815	|	1915	1930	1948	2015	|	...	2115	2130	2130	...	2215	2215	2233	2315	2332	0015	0115
Bremen Hbf a.	1550	1639	1645*	1739	1750	1750	1839	1845*	1939	1950	2009	2040	2047	←	2139	2150	2150	...	2239	2239	2259	2347	2351	0047	0147
Bremen Hbf d.	1553	1653	...	...	1753	1753	1853	...	...	1953	2012	→	2050	2054	...	2153	2153	2215	2253	2253	2303	...	2353	...	...
Delmenhorst d.	1604	1703	...	...	1804	1804	1903	...	...	2004	2024	...	|	2104	...	2204	2204	2227	2304	2304	2315	...	0005	...	...
Oldenburg (Oldb) a.	1623	1723	...	...	1823	1823	1923	...	...	2023	2040	...	2117	2123	...	2223	2223	2253	2323	2323	2332	...	0023	...	...
Oldenburg (Oldb) d.	1633	1733	...	...	1833	1833	1933	...	...	2033	2042	...	...	2133	...	...	2233	2258	...	2333	...	...	...	...	...
Bad Zwischenahn d.	1644	1744	...	...	1844	1844	1944	...	...	2044	2055	...	...	2144	...	...	2245	2311	...	2344	...	...	...	...	...
Leer (Ostfriesland) a.	1714	1813	...	...	1914	1914	2013	...	...	2114	2128	...	...	2213	...	...	2314	...	...	0013	...	...	...	...	...
Leer (Ostfriesland) **812** d.	1722	1824	...	...	1922	1922	2024	...	...	2122	2136	...	...	2224	...	...	2322	...	...	0024	...	...	...	...	...
Emden Hbf ◧ **812** d.	1738	1842	...	...	1938	1942	2042	...	...	2142	2152	...	...	2242	...	...	2338	...	...	0041	...	...	...	...	...
Norden **812** d.	...	1906	...	...	...	2008	2106	...	...	2208	...	...	...	2306	...	...	...	...	...	...	...	...	...	...	...
Norddeich **812** a.	...	1912	...	...	...	2014	2112	...	...	2214	...	...	...	2312	...	...	...	...	...	...	...	...	...	...	...
Norddeich Mole ‡ **812** a.	...	1916	...	...	...	2020	2116	...	...	...	...	...	...	...	...	...	...	...	...	...	...	...	...	...	...

B – To / from Bremerhaven (Table **815**).
C – To / from Cottbus on dates in Table **837**.
D – From / to Dresden (Table **842**).
F – From Frankfurt (Table **900**).

b – Not ⑥.
e – Not ⑦.

h – 0620 on ⑦ (also June 9).
k – Nürnberg - München on ⑤⑦ only.
r – ⚒ only.
t – Until Aug. 1.
v – From Aug. 2.

* – Connects with train in previous column.
‡ – For sailings from / to Juist and Norderney (www.reederei-frisia.de).
◧ – For train / 🚌 / ⛴ connections from / to Borkum via Emden Außenhafen (www.ag-ems.de).
♣ – Operated by Nord West Bahn (2nd class only).

OSNABRÜCK - OLDENBURG - WILHELMSHAVEN — 814

Nord West Bahn

Warning! Cloppenburg - Oldenburg and v.v. is by 🚌 July 2 - Aug. 13 (through passengers will arrive in Wilhelmshaven or Osnabruck one hour later than shown).

km		⚒	⚒	Ⓐ					†
0	**Osnabrück** Hbf d.	...	...	0459	0601	and	2201	2301	2301
20	Bramsche d.	...	...	0518	0618	hourly	2218	2318	2318
50	Quakenbrück d.	...	...	0540	0640	until	2240	2340	2340
72	Cloppenburg d.	...	...	0556	0656		2256	2356	2356
113	**Oldenburg** (Oldb) a.	...	...	0629	0729		2329	0029	0029
113	**Oldenburg** (Oldb) d.	0536	0636	0636	0736		2336	...	0037
143	Varel (Oldb) d.	0601	0701	0701	0801		0001	...	0103
165	**Wilhelmshaven** Hbf a.	0621	0721	0721	0821		0021	...	0122

	Ⓐ	⚒		⚒	Ⓐ		❖	⑤⑥		
Wilhelmshaven Hbf d.	...	0440	...	0540	...	0640	and	2140	2310	2310
Varel (Oldb) d.	...	0458	...	0558	...	0658	hourly	2158	2328	2328
Oldenburg (Oldb) a.	...	0524	...	0624	...	0724	until	2224	2351	2351
Oldenburg (Oldb) d.	0403	0529	0629	0629	0659	0729		2229	2359	...
Cloppenburg d.	0435	0605	0705	0705	0735	0805		2305	0033	...
Quakenbrück d.	0450	0621	0721	0721	0751	0821		2321	...	...
Bramsche d.	0513	0641	0741	0741	0811	0841		2341	...	...
Osnabrück Hbf a.	0531	0658	0758	0758	0829	0858		2358	...	...

❖ – On ⑥ Wilhelmshaven d. *1328* (not 1340) and change trains at Sande (a. *1335*, d. 1347).

OSNABRÜCK - BREMEN - BREMERHAVEN - CUXHAVEN — 815

RE services

km		⚒¶	⚒	ⒶH	⚒	Hr	r	Hr	r	Hr	r	Hr	t	Ht	t	Ht	t	Ht	t	Ht	¶		¶		¶	
0	**Osnabrück** Hbf 800 d.	...	0417	...	0527	*0627*	0729	*0827*	0927	*1027*	1127	*1227*	1327	*1427*	1527	*1627*	1727	*1827*	1927	*2027*	...	2127	...	2227	...	2327
53	Diepholz d.	...	0450	...	0559	*0659*	0801	*0859*	0959	*1059*	1159	*1259*	1359	*1459*	1559	*1659*	1759	*1859*	1959	*2059*	...	2159	...	2259	...	2359
122	**Bremen** Hbf 800 a.	...	0546	...	0645	*0744*	0845	*0944*	1044	*1144*	1244	*1344*	1444	*1544*	1644	*1745*	1844	*1944*	2044	*2144*	...	2244	...	2344	...	0044
122	**Bremen** Hbf d.	0540	...	0557	0657	0757	0857	0957	1057	1157	1257	1357	1457	1557	1657	1757	1857	1957	2057	2157	2240	...	2312	...	0012	...
143	Osterholz-Scharmbeck d.	0556	...	0611	0711	0811	0911	1011	1111	1211	1311	1411	1511	1611	1711	1811	1911	2011	2111	2211	2256	...	2328	...	0028	...
185	**Bremerhaven** Hbf a.	0626	...	0631	0731	0831	0931	1031	1131	1231	1331	1431	1531	1631	1731	1831	1931	2031	2131	2231	2326	...	2357	...	0057	...
188	**Bremerhaven**-Lehe a.	0630	...	0636	0736	0836	0936	1036	1136	1236	1336	1436	1536	1636	1736	1836	1936	2036	2136	2236	2330	...	0002	...	0102	...

	⚒	⚒¶	⚒	⚒H		⚒		Hr	r	Hr	r	Hr	r	Hr	t	Ht	t	Ht	t	Ht	t	Ht	¶		¶
Bremerhaven-Lehe d.	...	0407	...	0523	...	0623	...	0723	0823	0923	1023	1123	1223	1323	1423	1523	1623	1723	1823	1923	2023	2123	2156	...	2256
Bremerhaven Hbf d.	...	0412	...	0528	...	0628	...	0728	0828	0928	1028	1128	1228	1328	1428	1528	1628	1728	1828	1928	2028	2128	2201	...	2301
Osterholz-Scharmbeck d.	...	0444	...	0550	...	0650	...	0750	0850	0950	1050	1150	1250	1350	1450	1550	1650	1750	1850	1950	2050	2150	2233	...	2333
Bremen Hbf a.	...	0502	...	0603	...	0703	...	0803	0903	1003	1103	1203	1303	1403	1503	1603	1703	1803	1903	2003	2103	2203	2250	...	2350
Bremen Hbf 800 d.	0414	...	0514	...	0614	0714	0714	*0814*	0914	*1014*	1114	*1214*	1314	*1414*	1514	*1614*	1714	*1814*	1914	*2014*	2114	*2215*	...	2315	...
Diepholz d.	0458	...	0558	...	0658	0758	0758	*0858*	0958	*1058*	1158	*1258*	1358	*1458*	1603	*1659*	1758	*1858*	1958	*2058*	2158	*2304*	...	0004	...
Osnabrück Hbf 800 a.	0527	...	0627	...	0727	0827	0827	*0927*	1027	*1127*	1227	*1327*	1427	*1527*	1632	*1728*	1827	*1927*	2027	*2127*	2227	*2333*	...	0033	...

BREMERHAVEN - CUXHAVEN

km	⊡	⑥⑦	Ⓐ	⚒			
0	**Bremerhaven** Hbf d.	0003	0506	0636	0736	and	2236
3	Bremerhaven-Lehe d.	0008	0511	0641	0741	hourly	2241
43	**Cuxhaven** a.	0050	0557	0727	0827	until	2327

⊡	Ⓐ	⚒			
Cuxhaven d.	0509	0639	0739	and	2239
Bremerhaven-Lehe d.	0549	0719	0819	hourly	2319
Bremerhaven Hbf a.	0553	0723	0823	until	2323

H – From/to Hannover (Table **813**).

r – ①–⑥ (daily to July 12 and from Oct. 6), also Aug. 17. Runs daily Osnabrück - Bremen and v.v. ❖

t – ①–⑤ (daily to July 11 and from Oct. 6), also Aug. 16, 17. Runs daily Osnabrück - Bremen and v.v. ❖

⊡ – Operated by Eisenbahnen und Verkehrsbetriebe Elbe-Weser.

¶ – Operated by Nord West Bahn (2nd class only).

❖ – Note that daily stopping trains run Bremen to Bremerhaven Lehe at xx40 (arrive xx30) and Bremerhaven Lehe to Bremen at xx37 (arrive xx30).

HAMBURG - CUXHAVEN and BREMERHAVEN — 818

Regionalverkehre Start Deutschland; Elbe-Weser

HAMBURG - CUXHAVEN (operated by Regionalverkehre Start Deutschland).

km		Ⓐ	⑥	Ⓐ		⑥	Ⓐ	†	⚒																
0	**Hamburg** Hbf ⊖ d.	...	0422*	0442*	...	0522*	*0558*	0622*	0706r	0806r	0906r	1006r	1106r	1206r	1306r	1406r	1507r	1606x	1706r	1806t	1906r	2006r	2106r	2205r	2306r
12	**Hamburg** Harburg ⊖ d.	...	0438*	0458*	...	0538*	0623	0638*	0723	0823	0923	1023	1123	1223	1323	1423	1523	1623	1723	1823	1923	2023	2123	2223	2323
33	**Buxtehude** ⊖ d.	...	0504*	0524*	...	0604*	0638	0704*	0738	0838	0938	1038	1138	1238	1338	1438	1538	1638	1738	1838	1938	2038	2138	2238	2338
54	Stade ⊖ d.	0447	0540	0553	...	0640	0657	0740	0757	0857	0957	1057	1157	1257	1357	1457	1557	1657	1757	1857	1957	2057	2157	2257	2357
102	Otterndorf d.	0529	0622	0635	...	0722	0737	0822	0837	0937	1037	1137	1237	1337	1437	1537	1637	1737	1837	1937	2037	2137	2237	2337	0037
116	**Cuxhaven** a.	0542	0635	0648	...	0735	0750	0835	0850	0950	1050	1150	1250	1350	1450	1550	1650	1750	1850	1950	2050	2150	2250	2350	0050

	*	Ⓐ	⚒	Ⓐ		Ⓐ	Ⓒ															⑤⑥f	v	*	
Cuxhaven d.	...	0430	0509	0549	0609	0649	0709	0809	0909	1009	1109	1209	1309	1409	1509	1609	1709	1809	1909	2009	2109	2209	2237	...	...
Otterndorf d.	...	0442	0521	0601	0621	0701	0721	0821	0921	1021	1121	1221	1321	1421	1521	1621	1721	1821	1921	2021	2121	2221	2250	...	...
Stade ⊖ d.	0436	0525	0605	0645	0705	0745	0805	0905	1005	1105	1205	1305	1405	1505	1605	1705	1805	1905	2005	2105	2205	2305	2332	2336	...
Buxtehude ⊖ d.	0456	0540	0620	0700	0720	0800	0820	0920	1020	1120	1220	1320	1420	1520	1620	1720	1820	1920	2020	2120	2220	2320	...	2356	...
Hamburg Harburg ⊖ a.	0523	0558	0638	0717	0738	0816	0838	0938	1038	1138	1238	1338	1438	1538	1638	1738	1838	1938	2038	2138	2238	2338	...	0023	...
Hamburg Hbf ⊖ a.	0539	*0622*	0656z	0733	0756z	0834z	0858z	0956z	1058z	1156z	1257z	1356z	1458z	1555z	1656z	1759z	1855z	1957z	2056z	2157z	2256z	2356z	...	0039	...

BUXTEHUDE - BREMERHAVEN (operated by Eisenbahnen und Verkehrsbetriebe Elbe-Weser). See panel above for connections from/to Hamburg.

km		Ⓐ	Ⓐ	⚒		Ⓐ		Ⓐ	Ⓐ	Ⓒ					Ⓑ									
0	**Buxtehude** d.	...	...	...	...	0543	...	0643	0717	0743	0843	and	2043	2143	2243	...	...	...	...	...	...	...	...	...
39	Bremervörde a.	...	...	...	...	0623	...	0723	0823	0823	0923	hourly	2123	2223	2323	...	...	...	...	...	...	...	...	...
39	Bremervörde d.	0408	0436	0536	0636	0636	0736	0736	0836	0836	0936	until	2136	...	...	...	...	...	...	...	...	...	...	...
78	**Bremerhaven** Hbf a.	0450	0520	0620	0720	0720	0820	0820	0920	0920	1020		2220	...	...	...	...	...	...	...	...	...	...	...

	Ⓐ		Ⓐ		⚒					Ⓐ	Ⓒ	Ⓐ	Ⓒ	b	⑤⑥†			Ⓑ		⑤⑥			
Bremerhaven Hbf d.	...	...	0536	...	0636	0736	and	1336	1436	1536	1536	1636	1636	1736	1736	1836	1936	2036	2036	2136	2136	2236	2354
Bremervörde a.	...	...	0617	...	0717	0817	hourly	1417	1517	1617	1617	1717	1717	1817	1817	1917	2017	2117	2117	2217	2217	2316	0034
Bremervörde d.	0531	0631	0631	0731	0731	0831	until	1431	1531•	1624	1631	1724	1731	1824	1831	1931	2031	2131	...	2231	...	...	...
Buxtehude a.	0612	0712	0712	0812	0812	0912		1512	1612	1712	1712	1812	1812	1912	1912	2012	2112	2212	...	2312	...	...	...

b – ①–④ (not June 9).

f – Also June 8, Oct. 2, 30.

r – From June 23. Until June 22 connecting train departs 9–10 minutes earlier.

t – ①–④ (daily from June 23). Connecting train departs *1757* on other days.

v – ⑦–④ (not June 8, Oct. 2, 30).

x – ⑤ (daily from June 23). Connecting train departs *1557* on other days.

z – From June 23. Until June 22 connecting train arrives approx 7 minutes later.

• – 1524 on ⑤ (not Oct. 3, 31).

* – Hamburg S-Bahn.

⊖ – Additional S-Bahn trains operate.

HAMBURG - KIEL — 820

RE services except where shown

km		Ⓐ		Ⓒ	Ⓐ	⚒	†	⚒			❖				R		R		R		R			R
0	**Hamburg** Hbf 823 d.	0436	0536	0636	0640	0719	0736	0737	0822	0843	and at the same	1722	1743	1822	1843	1922	1943	2022	2043	2122	2146	2222	2324	2343
34	Elmshorn 823 d.	0504	0604	0704	0709	0747	0804	0808	0847	0909	minutes past	1747	1809	1847	1909	1947	2009	2047	2109	2147	2214	2248	2349	0011
78	Neumünster 823 d.	0532	0632	0734	0734	0814	0834	0834	0914	0934	each hour until	1814	1834	1914	1934	2014	2034	2114	2134	2213	2240	2316	0016	0040
109	**Kiel** Hbf a.	0555	0655	0757	0757	0834	0857	0857	0934	0957		1834	1857	1935	1957	2035	2057	2135	2157	2234	2303	2337	0037	0103

	Ⓐ		S	⚒			⚒	†						R		R		R		R				
Kiel Hbf d.	0312	0402	0502	0521	0602	0623	0702	0702	0723	0802	and at the same	1702	1723	1802	1823	1902	1921	2002	2021	2102	2121	2205	2305	0005
Neumünster 823 d.	0331	0428	0528	0542	0628	0642	0728	0735	0742	0828	minutes past	1728	1742	1828	1842	1928	1942	2028	2042	2128	2142	2233	2333	0033
Elmshorn 823 d.	0400	0454	0548	0611	0649	0711	0749	0756	0811	0849	each hour until	1749	1811	1849	1912	1949	2011	2049	2111	2149	2212	2258	2358	0058
Hamburg Hbf 823 a.	0426	0521	0615	0637	0715	0735	0815	0827	0837	0915		1816	1837	1916	1937	2015	2037	2116	2137	2217	2237	2325	0025	0125

Long-distance *ICE* and *EC* services

	ICE 1088 ①–⑥ G	*ICE* 618 F	*ICE* 474 B	*ICE* 804 ♥ E	*ICE* 882 M	*ICE* 612 F	*ICE* 74 D	*EC* 378 ♠ P	*ICE* 1094 Ⓑ A	
Hamburg Hbf 823 d.	0900	1017	1139	1226	1357	1617	1739	1915	2033	...
Elmshorn 823 d.	|	|	|	|	|	|	|	|	|	...
Neumünster 823 d.	0952	1106	1225	1327	1500	1705	1826	2004	2124	...
Kiel Hbf a.	1009	1123	1244	1348	1517	1722	1843	2022	2141	...

	ICE 573 ①–⑥ A	*ICE* 73 ①–⑤ D	*EC* 379 ♥ P	*ICE* 705 ♣ E	*ICE* 75 ⑥⑦ D	*ICE* 77 D	*ICE* 613 F	*ICE* 801 ♥ E	*ICE* 1171 B	*ICE* 885 M	*ICE* 619 F
Kiel Hbf d.	0613	0713	0742	0742	0912	1111	1237	1413	1512	1634	1833*
Neumünster 823 d.	0632	0733	0759	0759	0931	1134	1256	1432	1532	1651	1851*
Elmshorn 823 d.	|	|	|	|	|	|	|	|	|	|	|
Hamburg Hbf 823 a.	0720	0819	0848	0849	1020	1221	1342	1532	1620	1758	1942

A – (12) ✕ Kiel - Hannover - Frankfurt - Stuttgart and v.v.

B – (12) ✕ Basel - Frankfurt - Hannover - Kiel and v.v.

D – (12) ✕ Zürich - Basel - Frankfurt - Hannover - Kiel and v.v.

E – (12) ✕ München - Nürnberg - Erfurt - Berlin - Kiel and v.v.

F – (12) ✕ München - Stuttgart - Köln - Kiel and v.v.

G – (12) ✕ Frankfurt - Hannover - Kiel.

M – (12) ✕ München - Nürnberg - Hannover - Kiel and v.v.

P – (12) ✕ Praha - Dresden - Berlin - Kiel and v.v.

R – June 20 - Dec. 13.

S – June 21 - Dec. 13.

❖ – Timings may vary by 1–2 minutes.

♥ – Until Aug. 1.

♣ – From Aug. 2.

♠ – Until July 31.

* – 5 minutes later from June 21.

821 HAMBURG - WESTERLAND

See Tables **820** and **823** for connecting *RE* services Hamburg Hbf - Elmshorn and v.v. Frequent S-Bahn services operate Hamburg Hbf - Altona and v.v.

km		A		⚒		A		Ⓐ	Ⓒ	Ⓐ	⑥⑦ Y		Ⓒ Y		*IC*• 2214	D	Ⓒ T	① P	*IC*• 2074 ♥	Ⓒ T	D			*IC*• 2310	S
	Köln Hbf **800** d.	...	...	...	...	...	...	...	...	...	...	...	...	...	0508	...	...	...	...	...	...	...	...	0905	...
	Berlin Hbf **840** d.	...	...	...	...	...	...	...	...	...	...	...	...	...	|	...	...	...	0804	...	...	...	...	|	...
	Hamburg Hbf **820** d.	...	...	...	...	...	...	...	...	...	...	...	...	...	0917	...	...	...	1009	...	...	...	...	1302	...
0	**Hamburg** Altona d.	...	...	...	...	...	...	0526	0628	0636	0729	0736	0831	0838	|	0935	0935	1008	|	1035	1035	1135	1236	|	1336
30	Elmshorn **820** d.	...	...	...	...	...	...	0549	0649	0701	|	0801	|	0901	|	1001	1001	1032	|	1101	1101	1201	1301	|	1401
64	Itzehoe a.	...	...	...	...	...	...	0611	0713	0723	|	0823	|	0923	1002	1023	1023	1055	1100	1123	1123	1223	1323	1354	1423
64	Itzehoe d.	...	...	0508	...	...	...	0612	0714	0724	|	0824	|	0924	1016	1024	1024	1056	1113	1124	1124	1224	1324	1414	1424
123	Heide (Holst) a.	...	...	0548	...	...	...	0656	0758	0758	|	0858	|	0958	1050	1058	1058	1129	1148	1158	1158	1258	1358	1449	1458
123	Heide (Holst) d.	...	...	0549	...	...	...	0701	0801	0801	|	0901	|	1001	1052	1101	1101	1131	1150	1201	1201	1301	1401	1451	1501
157	Husum d.	0458	0558	0614	0630	0658	0730	0730	0830	0830	0905	0930	1005	1030	1118	1130	1130	1200	1217	1230	1230	1330	1430	1516	1530
197	Niebüll a.	0527	0627	...	0659	0727	0759	0759	0859	0859	0928	0959	1028	1059	1145	1206	1206	1225	1243	1306	1306	1359	1459	1544	1606
197	Niebüll 🚗 d.	0530	0630	...	0700	0730	0800	0800	0900	0900	0930	1000	1030	1100	1200	1215	1230	1230	1300	1315	1330	1400	1500	1600	1615
237	**Westerland** (Sylt) 🚗 a.	0604	0703	...	0734	0804	0834	0834	0934	0935	1004	1034	1106	1134	1233	1250	1304	1304	1335	1350	1404	1434	1534	1634	1650

	①–④ R			*IC*• 2374 J							
Köln Hbf **800** d.	...	...	...	...	...	...	...	...	...	...	...
Berlin Hbf **840** d.	...	...	...	...	...	...	...	...	...	...	...
Hamburg Hbf **820** d.	...	...	...	1533	...	...	...	...	...	...	...
Hamburg Altona d.	1336	1435	1536	|	1635	1735	1835	1936	2035	2136	2243
Elmshorn **820** d.	1401	1501	1601	|	1701	1801	1901	2001	2101	2201	2306
Itzehoe a.	1423	1523	1623	1628	1723	1823	1925	2025	2125	2225	2330
Itzehoe d.	1424	1524	1624	1644	1724	1824	1926	2026	2126	2226	2331
Heide (Holst) a.	1458	1558	1658	1718	1758	1858	2000	2100	2200	2310	0015
Heide (Holst) d.	1501	1601	1701	1720	1801	1901	2001	2101	2201	2311	0016
Husum d.	1530	1630	1730	1744	1830	1930	2030	2130	2230	2340	0044
Niebüll a.	1606	1659	1759	1809	1859	1959	2059	2159	2259	0009	...
Niebüll 🚗 d.	1630	1700	1800	1830	1900	2000	2100	2200	2300	0010	...
Westerland (Sylt) 🚗 a.	1704	1734	1834	1903	1934	2034	2134	2234	2334	0050**g**	...

	Ⓐ	Ⓐ			†	⚒				*IC*• 2311
Westerland 🚗 d.	...	0419	...	0520	0620	0620	0720	0820	0907	0921
Niebüll 🚗 a.	...	0453	...	0559	0659	0659	0759	0859	0944	0959
Niebüll d.	...	0454	...	0601	0701	0701	0801	0901	1000	1013
Husum d.	0424	0524	0524	0631	0729	0731	0831	0931	1031	1042
Heide (Holst) a.	0449	0549	0549	0657	0752	0757	0857	0957	1057	1106
Heide (Holst) d.	0450	0550	0550	0658	0753	0802	0902	1002	1102	1108
Itzehoe a.	0533	0633	0633	0733	0836	0836	0936	1036	1136	1143
Itzehoe d.	0534	0634	0634	0734	0837	0837	0937	1037	1137	1158
Elmshorn **820** d.	0600	0700	0700	0800	0900	0900	1000	1100	1200	|
Hamburg Altona a.	...	0721	0721	0823	0921	0921	1022	1121	1221	|
Hamburg Hbf **820** a.	...	...	...	...	...	...	...	...	...	1245
Berlin Hbf **840** a.	...	...	...	...	...	...	...	...	...	|
Köln Hbf **800** a.	...	...	...	...	...	...	...	...	...	1657

		IC• 2375 J		⑤ E			*IC*• 2215		*IC*• 2075 ♥			⑦ N		Ⓒ Y		⑥ L					⑤⑥ d	⑦–④ e	⊙		
Westerland (Sylt) 🚗 d.	1020	1052	1120	1150	1220	1307	1321	1350	1420	1520	1620	1650	1720	1750	1820	1850	1920	2020	...	2120	2120	...	...	2220	2320
Niebüll 🚗 a.	1059	1129	1159	1229	1259	1344	1359	1429	1459	1559	1659	1729	1759	1829	1859	1929	1959	2059	...	2159	2159	...	...	2259	2355
Niebüll d.	1101	1145	1201	1234	1301	1355	1413	1455	1513	1601	1701	1731	1801	1831	1901	1931	2001	2101	...	2201	2201	...	...	2301	0001
Husum d.	1131	1211	1231	1301	1331	1431**f**	1442	1531**f**	1542	1631	1731	1756	1831	1856	1931	1956	2031	2131	...	2229	2231	2248	...	2329	0029
Heide (Holst) a.	1157	1234	1257	1323	1357	1457	1506	1557	1606	1657	1757	|	1857	|	1957	|	2057	2157	...	...	2257	2313	...	...	...
Heide (Holst) d.	1202	1236	1302	1325	1402	1502	1508	1602	1608	1702	1802	|	1902	|	2002	|	2104	2204	...	...	2304	2314	...	...	...
Itzehoe a.	1236	1311	1336	1359	1436	1536	1542	1636	1642	1736	1836	|	1936	|	2036	|	2138	2247	...	...	2347	2354	...	...	...
Itzehoe d.	1237	1327	1337	1403	1437	1537	1555	1637	1658	1737	1837	|	1937	|	2037	|	2139	2248	...	...	2348	...	0002	...	...
Elmshorn **820** d.	1300	|	1400	1433	1500	1600	|	1700	|	1800	1900	|	2000	|	2100	|	2202	2310	...	...	0010	...	0033	...	...
Hamburg Altona a.	1321	|	1423	1502	1523	1621	|	1721	|	1822	1922	1928	2022	2035	2122	2128	2223	2331	...	...	0031	...	0057	...	...
Hamburg Hbf **820** a.	...	1425	...	...	...	...	1645	...	1748	...	...	...	...	...	...	...	...	...	...	...	...	...	...	...	...
Berlin Hbf **840** a.	...	...	...	...	...	...	|	...	1955	...	...	...	...	...	...	...	...	...	...	...	...	...	...	...	...
Köln Hbf **800** a.	...	...	...	...	...	...	2057	...	...	...	...	...	...	...	...	...	...	...	...	...	...	...	...	...	...

A – Daily to Nov. 7; Ⓐ from Nov. 10.
D – Ⓐ to Nov. 7; daily from Nov. 8.
E – ⑤ until Oct. 24 (also Oct. 2, 30).
J – WATTENMEER – [12] Stuttgart - Frankfurt - Hamburg - Westerland and v.v.
L – ⑥ May 10 - Sept. 27 (also June 8).
N – ⑦ until Nov. 2 (also June 9; not June 8).
P – ① until Oct. 27 (also June 10; not June 9).
R – ①–④ until Oct. 30 (not June 9).

S – ⑤⑥† until Nov. 2; daily from Nov. 3.
T – Until Nov. 2.
Y – May 10 - Sept. 28.

d – Also June 8, Oct. 2, 30.
e – Not June 8, Oct. 2, 30.
f – Arrives 7 minutes earlier.
g – 0043 on the mornings of ⑦.

• – Conveys [2] to/from Dagebüll Mole on dates in Table **822**.
♥ – Until Aug. 1.
⊙ – Operated by *nordbahn*.

🚗 – Regular car-carrying shuttle services also operate between Niebüll and Westerland (18–28 per day in summer, 12–14 in winter).

822 SCHLESWIG-HOLSTEIN BRANCH LINES

NEUMÜNSTER - HEIDE - BÜSUM (operated by *nordbahn*)

km		⚒			⚒																				
0	Neumünster d.	...	...	...	0535	...	0735	...	0935	...	1135	...	1335	...	1535	...	1735	...	1935	...	2135	...	...	...	...
63	Heide (Holst) a.	...	...	...	0646	...	0846	...	1046	...	1246	...	1446	...	1646	...	1846	...	2046	...	2246	...	...	...	...
63	Heide (Holst) d.	0449	0556	0701	0701	0801	0901	1001	1101	1201	1301	1401	1501	1601	1701	1801	1901	2003	2103	2203	2313	...	...	...	...
87	Büsum a.	0515	0622	0727	0727	0827	0927	1027	1127	1227	1327	1427	1527	1627	1727	1827	1927	2029	2129	2229	2339	...	...	...	...

	⚒	⚒																						
Büsum d.	...	0519	0626	0731	0831	0931	1031	1131	1231	1331	1431	1531	1631	1731	1831	1931	2032	2132	2232	2342	...	...	...	...
Heide (Holst) a.	...	0545	0652	0757	0857	0957	1057	1157	1257	1357	1457	1557	1657	1757	1857	1957	2058	2158	2258	0008	...	...	...	...
Heide (Holst) d.	0515	...	0715	...	0915	...	1115	...	1315	...	1515	...	1715	...	1915	...	2115	...	2315	...	...	...	...	...
Neumünster a.	0625	...	0825	...	1025	...	1225	...	1425	...	1625	...	1825	...	2025	...	2225	...	0025	...	...	...	...	...

HUSUM - BAD ST PETER ORDING (operated by *nordbahn*)

km										
0	Husum d.	0436	0536	and	2236	...	...	...	...	...
21	Tönning d.	0501	0601	hourly	2301	...	...	...	...	...
43	Bad St Peter Ording a.	0527	0627	until	2327	...	...	...	...	...

Bad St Peter Ording d.	0533	0633	and	2333	...	...	...	...	...
Tönning d.	0604	0704	hourly	0004	...	...	...	...	...
Husum a.	0625	0725	until	0025	...	...	...	...	...

NIEBÜLL - DAGEBÜLL MOLE *See note* ⊡

km	*Until Nov. 2* ♥					★	★ n	n	★			n
	Hamburg Hbf a.	...	...	...	...	0917	1009**t**	...	1302	...	...	...
0	Niebüll NEG d.	0635	0735	0905	1010	1205	1335	1435	1605	1710	1825	1910
14	Dagebüll Mole a.	0653	0753	0923	1028	1223	1353	1453	1623	1728	1843	1928

Until Nov. 2 ♥		★	★			★	★			v	
Dagebüll Mole d.	0815	0930	1035	1145	1245	1340	1440	1635	1735	1845	1935
Niebüll NEG a.	0833	0948	1053	1225	1303	1357	1457	1653	1753	1903	1953
Hamburg Hbf a.	...	1245	1425	...	...	1645	1748**t**	...	...	...	...

km	*From Nov. 3*		Ⓐ		Ⓐ		Ⓐ					
0	Niebüll NEG d.	0635	0735	0905	1010	1120	1245	1340	1440	1605	1820	1910
14	Dagebüll Mole a.	0653	0753	0923	1028	1138	1303	1358	1458	1623	1838	1928

From Nov. 3		Ⓐ		Ⓐ		Ⓐ					
Dagebüll Mole d.	0700	0815	0930	1035	1145	1310	1415	1505	1635	1845	1935
Niebüll NEG a.	0718	0833	0948	1053	1203	1328	1433	1523	1653	1903	1953

E – ⑥⑦ Aug. 2 - Sept. 14.
n – Runs 25–30 minutes later on ⑥⑦ June 28 - Sept. 14.
t – Until Aug. 1.
v – Runs 15 minutes later on ⑥⑦ June 28 - Sept. 14.

⊡ – **Operator**: Norddeutsche Eisenbahngesellschaft Niebüll GmbH (NEG) ✆ +49 (0) 4661 980 880. Niebüll NEG station is situated a short distance from the Niebüll DB station forecourt. Dagebüll Mole is the station for ferries to/from the islands of Föhr and Amrum (see www.faehre.de).

★ – Conveys [2] (*IC*) from/to Hamburg and beyond (Table **821**).

♥ – **Additional journeys June 7–27 and Sept. 15 - Nov. 2**:
Niebüll NEG → Dagebüll Mole at 1120 and 1230; Dagebüll Mole → Niebüll NEG at 0700 and 1505.
Additional journeys June 28 - Sept. 14:
Niebüll NEG → Dagebüll Mole at 1025 ⑤–⑦, 1105 ⑤, 1120 (not ⑤), 1230, 2035 ⑥⑦.
Dagebüll Mole → Niebüll NEG at 0700 ①–⑤, 0705 ⑥⑦, 1055 ⑥⑦, 1105 ⑤, 1420**E**, 1505 ①–⑤, 1530 ⑥⑦, 2100 ⑥⑦.

HAMBURG - NEUMÜNSTER - FLENSBURG — 823

RE / RB services except where shown

km		①–⑥	⚒		⑥	Ⓐ	†	⚒	†										*EC* 174 ♥ A✕						⑦	①–⑤
0	**Hamburg** Hbf ..... **820** d.	...	...	...	0636	0640	...	0737r	...	0843	0943	1042	1143	1243	1343	1443	1543	1643	1714	1743	1843e	1943e	2043e	2146e	2230e	2243c
34	Elmshorn .... **820** d.	...	...	...	0704	0709	...	0808	...	0909	1010	1109	1209	1309	1409	1509	1609	1709	|	1809	1909e	2009e	2109e	2214e	2302e	2314c
78	Neumünster .... **820** d.	0040	0534	0646	0732	0732	0734	0832	0834	0932	1032	1132	1232	1332	1432	1532	1632	1732	1808	1832	1932	2032	2132	2237	2331	2337
117	Rendsburg .... **824** d.	0111	0600	0715	0759	0759	0759	0859	0859	0959	1059	1159	1259	1359	1459	1559	1659	1759	1831	1859	1959	2059	2159	2304	2359	0003
141	Schleswig .... **824** d.	0126	0615	0731	0815	0815	0815	0915	0915	1015	1115	1215	1315	1415	1515	1615	1715	1815	1847	1915	2015	2115	2215	2320	0019	0020
179	**Flensburg** .... a.	0148	0640	0756	0840	0840	0840	0940	0940	1040	1140	1240	1340	1440	1540	1640	1740	1840	1907	1940	2040	2140	2240	2345	0044	0045

	⑥ d		Ⓐ	⑥	⚒	⚒	†			*EC* 175 ♣ A✕												Ⓑ				Ⓑ
Flensburg .... d.	0015	...	0415	0415	0515	0615	0623	0716	0815	0846	0915	1015	1115	1215	1315	1415	1515	1615	1715	1815	1915	2015	2015	2115	2215	2315
Schleswig .... **824** d.	0039	...	0439	0439	0539	0639	0647	0740	0839	0914	0939	1039	1139	1239	1339	1439	1539	1639	1739	1839	1939	2039	2039	2139	2239	2339
Rendsburg .... **824** d.	0057	...	0457	0457	0557	0657	0704	0757	0857	0932	0957	1057	1157	1257	1356	1457	1557	1657	1757	1857	1957	2057	2057	2157	2257	2357
Neumünster .... **820** a.	0122	...	0522	0522	0622	0722	0730	0822	0922	0953	1022	1122	1222	1322	1422	1522	1622	1722	1822	1922	2022	2122	2122	2222	2322	0022
Elmshorn .... **820** a.	...	...	0546f	...	0648	0748	0755	0848	0948	|	1048	1148	1248	1347	1448	1548	1648	1748	1848e	1948e	2048e	2148e	...	...	...	...
Hamburg Hbf ...... **820** a.	...	...	0613f	...	0715	0815	0827	0915	1015	1048	1115	1215	1315	1415	1515	1615	1716	1816	1916e	2015e	2116e	2217e	...	...	...	...

A – (12) ✕ Praha - Dresden - Berlin - Flensburg and v.v.
c – ①–⑤ from June 20 (also June 21, 28, Oct. 4).
d – Also June 9, 22, 29, Oct. 3, 31.
e – From June 20.
f – From June 23.
r – 0740 from Aug. 2.
♥ – Until July 31.
♣ – Until Aug. 1.

KIEL - HUSUM and FLENSBURG — 824

Operated by *nordbahn*

KIEL - HUSUM

km		①–⑥	①–⑥	①–⑥				Ⓑ		
0	**Kiel** Hbf .... d.	0355	0503	0603	0703	and	2203	2303	...	...
40	Rendsburg .... **823** d.	0438	0535	0635	0735	hourly	2235	2335	...	...
65	Schleswig .... **823** d.	0457	0554	0654	0754	until	2254	2354	...	...
102	**Husum** .... a.	0526	0625	0725	0825		2325	0025	...	...

	①–⑥	①–⑥				Ⓑ	Ⓑ		
Husum .... d.	0435	0535	0635	and	2135	2235	2335	...	...
Schleswig .... **823** d.	0506	0606	0706	hourly	2206	2306	0006	...	...
Rendsburg .... **823** d.	0526	0626	0726	until	2226	2326	0026	...	...
Kiel Hbf .... a.	0557	0657	0757		2257	2357	0057	...	...

KIEL - FLENSBURG

km		Ⓐ	⚒							
0	**Kiel** Hbf .... d.	0408	0508	0608		2208	2308	...	...	...
29	Eckernförde .... d.	0441	0541	0641	and	2241	2341	...	...	...
	Schleibrücke Süd ..... ‡ a.	0454	0554	0654		2254	2354	...	...	...
		Ⓐ	⚒		hourly					
	Schleibrücke Nord ... ‡ d.	0510	0610	0710		2310	0024	...	...	...
50	Süderbrarup .... d.	0531	0631	0731	until	2331	0031	...	...	...
81	**Flensburg** .... a.	0557	0657	0757		2357	0057	...	...	...

	Ⓐ	⚒							
Flensburg .... d.	0404	0504	0604		2204	2304	...	...	...
Süderbrarup .... d.	0443	0543j	0643j	and	2243j	2343j	...	...	...
Schleibrücke Nord . ‡ a.	0450	0550	0650		2250	2350	...	...	...
	Ⓐ	⚒		hourly					
Schleibrücke Süd .. ‡ d.	0505	0605	0705		2305	...	...	...	...
Eckernförde .... d.	0520	0620	0720	until	2320	...	...	...	...
Kiel Hbf .... a.	0551	0651	0751		2351	...	...	...	...

j – Arrives 14 minutes earlier.

‡ – Temporary station during major upgrade work on the Schlei Bridge. Passengers must transfer on foot across the bridge (350 metres).

HAMBURG - LÜBECK - PUTTGARDEN and TRAVEMÜNDE — 825

RB / RE services

HAMBURG - LÜBECK - TRAVEMÜNDE STRAND

km		k		©	©		k	Ⓐ	k	Ⓐ	k	⚒	k		k			k			D	E	A
0	**Hamburg** Hbf .... d.	0006	0106	0206	0306	...	0506	0534	0606	0634	0706	0734	0806	0834	0906	0934	and at	2306	2334	A	1201	1301	2104
40	Bad Oldesloe .... ● d.	0032	0132	0232	0332	...	0532	0605	0632	0705	0732	0805	0832	0905	0932	1005	the same	2332	0005	L	|	|	|
63	**Lübeck** Hbf .... a.	0052	0152	0252	0352	...	0552	0624	0652	0724	0752	0824	0852	0923	0952	1024	minutes	2352	0024	S	1241	1340	2142
	Lübeck Hbf .... d.	0103	...	...	...	0503	0603	...	0703	...	0803	...	0903	...	1003	...	past each	0003	...	O	...	...	...
81	Travemünde Skandinavienkai a.	0120	...	...	...	0520	0620	...	0720	...	0820	...	0920	...	1020	...	hour until	0020	...		...	...	...
84	**Travemünde** Strand .... a.	0126	...	...	...	0526	0626	...	0726	...	0826	...	0926	...	1026	...		0026	...		...	...	...

	k	k	©	Ⓐ		Ⓐ	k	⚒	Ⓐ	k		Ⓐ	k		k	⊡		k	k		B	C	F
Travemünde Strand .... d.	0034	0134	...	...	...	...	0534	...	0634	0634z	...	0734	0734z	...	0834	and at	...	2234	2334		...	...	...
Travemünde Skandinavienkai. d.	0040	0140	...	...	...	...	0540	...	0640	0640z	...	0740	0740z	...	0840	the same	...	2240	2340	A	...	...	...
Lübeck Hbf .... a.	0056	0156	...	...	...	...	0556	...	0656	0656z	...	0756	0756z	...	0856	minutes	...	2256	2356	L	...	...	...
Lübeck Hbf .... d.	0109	0209z	0409	0437	0509	0537	0609	0637	0700	0709	0737	0800	0809	0837	0909	past each	2237	2309	0009	S	0816	1317	1416
Bad Oldesloe .... ● d.	0129	0229z	0429	0457	0529	0557	0629	0657	|	0729	0757	|	0828	0857	0929	hour until	2257	2329	0029	O	|	|	|
Hamburg Hbf .... a.	0159v	0253z	0453	0525	0553	0625	0653	0725	0741	0753	0825	0841	0852	0925	0953		2325	2353	0053		0855	1358	1455

LÜBECK - NEUSTADT (Holst) and PUTTGARDEN

km		Ⓐ		🚌 Ⓐ		🚌		🚌		🚌		🚌			🚌		🚌		🚌		🚌		🚌	
0	**Lübeck** Hbf .... d.	0412	0512	0512	0612	0612	0712	0712	0812	0812	0912	0912	and at	1912	1912	2012	2012	2112	2112	2212	2212	2312	2312	0012
30	Neustadt (Holst) .... a.	0446	0546	|	0650	|	0750	|	0846	|	0950	|	the same	1950	|	2046	|	2146	|	2246	|	2346	|	0046
	Oldenburg (Holst) .... d.	...	...	0613	...	0713	...	0813	...	0913	...	1013	minutes	...	2013	...	2113	...	2213	...	2313	...	0013	...
	Fehmarn-Burg .... d.	...	...	0649	...	0749	...	0849	...	0949	...	1049	past each	...	2049	...	2149	...	2249	...	2349	...	0049	...
	Puttgarden .... a.	...	...	0701	...	0801	...	0901	...	1001	...	1101	hour until	...	2101	...	2201	...	2301	...	0001	...	0101	...

			Ⓐ		🚌 Ⓐ	Ⓐ		🚌	Ⓐ		🚌		🚌			🚌		🚌					
Puttgarden .... d.	...	...	...	...	0456	...	...	0556	...	...	0656	...	0756	and at	...	2156	...	2256	...	...	...	...	...
Fehmarn-Burg.......................... d.	...	...	...	...	0508	...	...	0608	...	...	0708	...	0808	the same	...	2208	...	2308	...	...	...	...	...
Oldenburg (Holst) .... d.	...	...	...	...	0544	...	...	0644	...	...	0744	...	0844	minutes	...	2244	...	2344	...	...	...	...	...
Neustadt (Holst) .... d.	0115	...	0515	0615	|	0645	0715	|	0745	0815	|	0915	|	past each	2315	|	0015	|	...	...	...	...	...
Lübeck Hbf .... a.	0148	...	0548	0648	0650	0718	0748	0750	0818	0848	0850	0948	0950	hour until	2348	2350	0048	0050	...	...	...	...	...

A – *ICE* **584**. From München (Table **900**).
B – *ICE* **585**. To München (Table **900**).
C – *ICE* **1007**. Until Aug. 1. To München via Berlin (Tables **840** and **850**).
D – *ICE* **1008**. Until Aug. 1. From München via Berlin (Tables **840** and **850**).
E – *ICE* **682**. From Aug. 2. From München (Table **900**).
F – *ICE* **681**. From Aug. 2. To München (Table **900**).
k – Change trains at Lübeck from Aug. 2.
v – 0153 on ©.
z – © only.
⊡ – The 1534 and 1634 from Travemünde Strand arrive Hamburg 3 minutes later.
● – Connecting trains (operated by nordbahn) Bad Oldesloe - Neumünster (*45 km*). Journey: 44 – 54 minutes.
From Bad Oldesloe at 0537 Ⓐ, 0637 ⚒, 0737 and hourly until 0037
From Neumünster at 0427 Ⓐ, 0527 ⑥, 0537 Ⓐ, 0627 †, 0637 ⚒, 0737 and hourly until 2337.

KIEL - LÜBECK — 826

Operator: erixx

km		Ⓐ	Ⓐ	⑥	Ⓐ	⑥	†	Ⓐ	⚒										
0	**Kiel** Hbf .... d.	0405	0443	0438	0505	0538	0538	0543	0605	0643	0705	0743	and at the same	2305	2343	...	0005	0043	0109
33	Plön .... d.	0445	0515	0515	0545	0615	0615	0615	0645	0715	0745	0815	minutes past	2345	0015	...	0045	0115	0145
47	Eutin .... d.	0500	0530	0530	0600	0630	0630	0630	0700	0730	0800	0830	each hour until	0000	0030	...	0100	0130	0200
80	**Lübeck** Hbf ...... a.	0532	0553	0559	0632	0652	0658	0652	0732	0752	0832	0852		0032	0052	...	0132	0152	0232

	Ⓐ	Ⓐ	©	Ⓐ	Ⓐ	©	Ⓐ	⚒	©	Ⓐ										
Lübeck Hbf .... d.	0351	0428	0500	0505	0528	0600	0606	0628	0706	0706	0728	0806	0828	and at the same	2306	2328	0006	0028	0106
Eutin .... d.	0424	0458	0530	0529	0600	0630	0629	0659	0729	0730	0759	0829	0859	minutes past	2329	2359	0029	0059	0129
Plön .... d.	0443	0515	0545	0545	0615	0645	0644	0714	0744	0745	0814	0844	0914	each hour until	2344	0014	0044	0114	0144
Kiel Hbf .... a.	0519	0556	0617	0617	0656	0716	0716	0756	0816	0817	0856	0916	0956		0016	0056	0120	0156	0216

827 LÜBECK - BÜCHEN - LÜNEBURG

Operator: erixx

km																									
		Ⓐ	Ⓐ	Ⓒ	Ⓐ	Ⓒ	Ⓐ	Ⓒ																	
0	**Lübeck** Hbf d.	0401	0501	0510	0601	0610	0705	0710	0810	0910	1010	1110	1210	1310	1410	1510	1610	1710	1810	1910	2010	2110	2210	2310	0010
9	Lübeck Flughafen ✈ ▷ d.	0410	0510	0520	0610	0620	0714	0720	0820	0920	1020	1120	1220	1320	1420	1520	1620	1720	1820	1920	2020	2120	2220	2320	0020
22	Ratzeburg d.	0420	0523	0530	0627	0630	0730	0730	0830	0930	1030	1130	1230	1330	1430	1530	1630	1730	1830	1930	2030	2130	2230	2330	0030
31	Mölln (Lauenburg) d.	0427	0530	0537	0634	0636	0736	0736	0836	0936	1036	1136	1236	1336	1436	1536	1636	1736	1836	1936	2036	2136	2236	2336	0036
50	Büchen a.	0439	0543	0550	0646	0648	0748	0748	0848	0948	1048	1148	1248	1348	1448	1548	1648	1748	1848	1948	2048	2148	2248	2348	0048
50	Büchen d.	0451	0553	0551	0655	0707	0756	0750	0907	0950	1107	1150	1307	1350	1507	1550	1707	1750	1907	1950	2107	2150	2307	2350	0050
79	**Lüneburg** a.	0515	0617	0615	0718	0730	0823	0815	0930	1015	1130	1215	1330	1415	1530	1615	1730	1815	1930	2015	2130	2215	2330	0015	0115

	Ⓐ	Ⓐ	Ⓒ	Ⓐ	Ⓒ																		
Lüneburg d.	0420	0524	0545	0628	0630	0745	0830	0945	1030	1145	1230	1345	1430	1545	1630	1745	1830	1945	2030	2145	2230	...	2345	0045
Büchen a.	0442	0545	0608	0650	0652	0808	0852	1008	1052	1208	1252	1408	1452	1608	1652	1808	1852	2008	2052	2208	2252	...	0008	0108
Büchen d.	0453	0553	0609	0657	0709	0809	0909	1009	1109	1209	1309	1409	1509	1609	1709	1809	1909	2009	2109	2209	2309	...	0009	0114
Mölln (Lauenburg) d.	0505	0605	0622	0709	0722	0822	0922	1022	1122	1222	1322	1422	1522	1622	1722	1822	1922	2022	2122	2222	2322	...	0022	0126
Ratzeburg d.	0512	0612	0632	0717	0732	0832	0932	1032	1132	1232	1332	1432	1532	1632	1732	1832	1932	2032	2132	2232	2332	...	0032	0134
Lübeck Flughafen ✈ ▷ d.	0521	0621	0640	0725	0740	0840	0940	1040	1140	1240	1340	1440	1540	1640	1740	1840	1940	2040	2140	2240	2340	...	0040	0142
Lübeck Hbf a.	0532	0632	0652	0736	0752	0852	0952	1052	1152	1252	1352	1452	1552	1652	1752	1852	1952	2052	2152	2252	2352	...	0052	0153

▷ – Trains call at Lübeck Flughafen on request only.

830 HAMBURG - ROSTOCK - STRALSUND

RE services except where shown

SERVICE JUNE 7 - AUGUST 1. See page 607 for amended service August 2 - December 13 (diverted via Lübeck).

km										*ICE*			*ICE*			*ICE*	*ICE*			*ICE*				*ICE*		
		◇	◇		◇				◇	**1678**		◇	**1676**		◇	**208**	**208**		◇	**1672**	◇		◇	**1074**		◇
			Ⓐ			Ⓐ	Ⓐ									①–⑤	⑥⑦				Ⓐ					
		S	S		S				S	H✕		S	✕◆		S	✕◆	✕◆		S	A✕	P		S	R✕		S
0	**Hamburg** Hbf d.	...	...	...	...	...	0511	0621	...	0739	0821	...	0942	1021	...	1142	1142	1221	...	1343	...	1421	...	1543	1621	...
47	Büchen d.	...	...	0458a	...	...	0552t	0658t	...	|	0858t	...	|	1058t	...	|	|	1258t	...	|	...	1458t	...	|	1658t	...
123	**Schwerin** Hbf 837 d.	...	...	0548	...	0642	0647	0748	...	0837	0948	...	1037	1148	...	1238	1238	1348	...	1437	...	1548	...	1637	1748	...
140	Bad Kleinen 836 837 d.	...	...	0603	...	0659	▬	0803	...	|	1003	...	|	1203	...	|	|	1403	...	|	...	1603	...	|	1803	...
181	Bützow 836 d.	...	...	0629	...	0723	◇	0829	...	0910	1029	...	1110	1229	...	|	|	1429	...	1510	...	1629	...	1710	1829	...
211	**Rostock** Hbf a.	...	...	0650	...	0750	Ⓐ P	0850	...	0932	1050	...	1132	1252	...	1332	1332	1450	...	1532	...	1650	...	1732	1850	...
211	**Rostock** Hbf d.	0454	0553	...	0700	...	0811	...	0900	0938	...	1100	1138	...	1300	1338	1342	...	1500	1538	1610	...	1700	1738	...	1900
240	Ribnitz-D'garten West d.	0517	0616	...	0725	...	0849	...	0922	0959	...	1122	1200	...	1322	1400	1416	...	1522	1600	1650	...	1722	1758	...	1922
265	Velgast d.	0539	0638	...	0742	...	0903	...	0940	1015	...	1140	1215	...	1340	1415	1435	...	1540	1614	1711t	...	1740	1814	...	1940
283	**Stralsund** Hbf a.	0555	0655	...	0758	...	0917	...	0957	1029	...	1157	1229	...	1357	1430	1447	...	1557	1627	1723	...	1757	1828	...	1957
	Ostseebad Binz **844** a.	...	...	...	...	...	...	...	...	1123r	...	...	...	...	...	1529	1539	...	...	1720v	...	...	...	...	...	...

	ICE			*ICE*	*ICE*			*ICE*		
	1578		◇	**1576**	**1576**		◇	**1574**		
				Ⓑ	⑦			⑦		
	A✕		S	A✕	A✕			A		
Hamburg Hbf d.	1741	1821	...	1943	1943	2021	...	2143	2254	0036
Büchen d.	|	1858t	...	|	|	2058t	...	|	2328	0108
Schwerin Hbf 837 d.	1837	1948	...	2037	2037	2148	...	2237	0019	0157
Bad Kleinen 836 837 d.	1848	2003	...	2048	2048	2203	...	2248	0029	...
Bützow 836 d.	1912	2029	...	2112	2112	2229	...	2312	0054	...
Rostock Hbf a.	1932	2050	...	2132	2132	2250	...	2332	0115	...
Rostock Hbf d.	1938	...	2100	...	2138	...	2300	...	...	...
Ribnitz-Damgarten West d.	2000	...	2122	...	2200	...	2322	...	...	...
Velgast d.	2015	...	2140	...	2215	...	2340	...	...	...
Stralsund Hbf a.	2028	...	2157	...	2229	...	2357	...	...	...
Ostseebad Binz **844** a.	...	...	...	...	...	...	...	...	...	...

					ICE		*ICE*				*ICE*
					1599	◇	**1577**	◇		◇	**1179**
	Ⓐ	Ⓒ	Ⓐ		①–⑤	Ⓐ	①–⑤			Ⓐ	①–⑤
					✕	S	A✕	S		P	R✕
Ostseebad Binz **844** d.	...	...	...	...	...	...	...	...	...	...	...
Stralsund Hbf d.	...	...	...	...	...	0449	0521	0558	...	0637	0727
Velgast d.	...	...	...	...	...	0505	0536	0614	...	0651	0741
Ribnitz-Damgarten West d.	...	...	...	...	...	0524	0552	0632	...	0706	0758
Rostock Hbf a.	...	...	...	...	...	0547	0617	0654	...	0746	0818
Rostock Hbf d.	...	...	...	0508	0545	...	0625	...	0708	...	0825
Bützow 836 d.	...	...	...	0529	0605	...	0645	...	0729	...	0845
Bad Kleinen 836 837 d.	...	...	...	0558	0629	...	0708	...	0758	...	|
Schwerin Hbf 837 d.	0350	0443	0452	0611	0641	...	0720	...	0811	...	0920
Büchen d.	0448	0540	0551	0707t	0717	...	|	...	0907t	...	|
Hamburg Hbf a.	0518	0610	0626	0738	0746	...	0816	...	0938	...	1016

	ICE	*ICE*			*ICE*			*ICE*			*ICE*	*ICE*				*ICE*					*ICE*					
	1579	**1683**	◇		**1671**	◇		**203**	◇		**1021**	**1675**	◇		◇	**1677**	◇		◇	◇	**1679**	◇		◇		◇
	⑥	⑥									⑥⑦				Ⓐ					Ⓐ	⑦					
	RA	F✕	S		A✕	S		✕◆			✕◆	A✕	S		P	✕◆	S				L✕			S		S
Ostseebad Binz **844** d.	✕	...	...	...	0826	...	...	1043	1104	...	...	1226	...	...	...	...	...	...	1602	...	...	1703	...	...	...	...
Stralsund Hbf d.	0727	...	0759	...	0926	0959	...	1137	1159	...	1303	1325	1359	...	1451	1526	1559	...	1659	...	1726	1759	...	1959	...	2200
Velgast d.	0741	...	0815	...	0940	1015	...	1156	1215	...	1317	1340	1415	...	1505	1540	1615	...	1712	...	1740	1815	...	2015	...	2215
Ribnitz-Damgarten West d.	0758	...	0833	...	0958	1033	...	1214	1233	...	1337	1359	1433	...	1522	1558	1633	...	1737t	...	1758	1833	...	2033	...	2233
Rostock Hbf a.	0818	...	0855	...	1019	1055	...	1238	1255	...	1359	1419	1455	...	1547	1618	1655	...	1801	...	1818	1855	...	2055	...	2255
Rostock Hbf d.	0825	0859	...	0908	1025	...	1108	1244	...	1308	1412	1425	...	1508	...	1625	▬	1708	▬	1809	1825	...	1908	...	2108	*2313*
Bützow 836 d.	0845	0921	...	0929	1045	...	1129	|	...	1329	1434	1445	...	1529	...	1645	...	1729	...	1830	1845	...	1929	...	2129	*2334*
Bad Kleinen 836 837 d.	|	0946	...	0958	|	...	1158	|	...	1358	|	|	...	1558	...	|	...	1758	Ⓐ	1903t	|	...	1958	...	2158	*0000*
Schwerin Hbf 837 d.	0920	1005	...	1011	1120	...	1211	1339	...	1411	1508	1520	...	1611	...	1720	1724	1811	1911	1914	1920	...	2011	...	2211	*0010*
Büchen d.	|	|	...	1107t	|	...	1307t	|	...	1507t	|	|	...	1707t	...	|	1822	1907t	2007t	...	|	...	2107t	...	2303	...
Hamburg Hbf a.	1016	1120	...	1138	1216	...	1338	1433	...	1538	1603	1616	...	1738	...	1816	1855	1938	2038	...	2019	...	2138	...	2337	...

◆ – **NOTES** (LISTED BY TRAIN NUMBER)

203 – [12] ✕ Ostseebad Binz - Hamburg - Köln - Karlsruhe - Basel.
208 – [12] ✕ Köln - Hamburg - Ostseebad Binz.
1021 – [12] ✕ Stralsund - Hamburg - Köln - Frankfurt - Nürnberg.
1676 – [12] ✕ (Kassel ①–⑤ -) (Hannover ①–⑥ -) Hamburg - Stralsund.
1677 – [12] ✕ Stralsund - Hamburg - Hannover (- Frankfurt ⑤⑦).

A – From/to Frankfurt via Gießen, Kassel, Hannover (Tables **806** and **900**).
F – To Frankfurt via Fulda (Table **900**).
H – ①–⑥ until Aug. 1. From Hannover (Table **900**) on ①–⑤. To Bergen auf Rügen (Table **844**) on ⑥.
L – To Kassel (Table **900**).
P – To/from Pasewalk (Table **845**).

R – To/from Greifswald (Table **846**).
S – To/ from Sassnitz (Table **844**).

a – Ⓐ only.
n – Not Jan. 3 - Feb. 25.
r – ①–⑤.
t – Arrives 6–7 minutes earlier.
v – Not ⑦.

◇ – Operated by Ostdeutsche Eisenbahn.

☛ See Table **866** for *IC* services Leipzig - Magdeburg - Schwerin - Rostock - Warnemünde and v.v.

831 ROSTOCK - WARNEMÜNDE

S-Bahn

ROSTOCK - WARNEMÜNDE and v.v. *13 km*. Journey time: 21 minutes. On June 9, Oct. 3, 31 services run as on ⑦.

From Rostock Hbf at 0003, 0033 ①Ⓒ, 0103 Ⓒ, 0133, 0203 Ⓒ, 0233 Ⓒ, 0303 Ⓒ, 0333 Ⓒ, 0403 Ⓒ, 0433, 0448 Ⓐ, 0503, 0518 Ⓐ, 0533, 0548 Ⓐ, 0603, 0618 Ⓐ, 0633, 0648 Ⓐ, 0703, 0718 Ⓐ, 0733, 0748 Ⓐ, 0757 ⚒, 0807, 0817 ⚒, 0827, 0837 ⚒, 0847, 0857 ⚒ and then every 10 minutes on ⚒, every 20 minutes on † until 1757 ⚒, 1807, 1817 ⚒, 1827, 1837 ⚒, 1847; then 1903, 1918 ⚒, 1933, 1948 ⚒, 2003, 2018 ⚒, 2033, 2048 ⚒, 2103, 2118 ⚒, 2133, 2148 ⚒, 2203, 2233, 2303, 2333. **From Warnemünde** at 0003, 0033, 0103 Ⓒ, 0133 Ⓒ, 0203 Ⓒ, 0233 Ⓒ, 0303 Ⓒ, 0333 Ⓒ, 0403, 0433, 0448 Ⓐ, 0503, 0518 Ⓐ, 0533, 0548 Ⓐ, 0603, 0618 Ⓐ, 0633, 0648 Ⓐ, 0703, 0718 Ⓐ, 0733, 0748 Ⓐ, 0803, 0819 ⚒, 0829, 0839 ⚒ 0849, 0859 ⚒, 0909 and then every 10 minutes on ⚒, every 20 minutes on † until 1759 ⚒, 1809, 1819 ⚒, 1829, 1839 ⚒, 1849; then 1903, 1918 ⚒, 1933, 1948 ⚒, 2003, 2018 ⚒, 2033, 2048 ⚒, 2103, 2118 ⚒, 2133, 2148, 2203, 2233, 2303, 2333.

832 BERLIN - KOSTRZYN

Niederbarnimer Eisenbahn (2nd class only)

km																				
		⚒																		
0	**Berlin** Ostkreuz ⊡ d.	0533	0633**r**	0733	0833	0933	1033**r**	1133	1233	1333	1433	1533**r**	1633**r**	1733	1833**r**	1933	2033	2133	2233	2333
26	Strausberg d.	0558	0658	0758	0858	0958	1058	1158	1258	1358	1458	1558	1658	1758	1858	1958	2058	2158	2258	2358
44	Müncheberg (Mark) ¶ d.	0614	0714	0814	0914	1014	1114	1214	1314	1414	1514	1614	1714	1814	1914	2014	2114	2214	2314	0014
79	Küstrin-Kietz 🏛 d.	0650	0740	0851	0947	1050	1147	1251	1347	1451	1547	1651	1747	1851	1947	2051	2147	2251	2347	0051
83	**Kostrzyn** 🏛 a.	0657	0745	0857	0953	1054	1153	1257	1353	1457	1553	1657	1753	1857	1953	2057	2153	2257	2353	0057

	⚒																		
Kostrzyn 🏛 d.	0402	0502	0602	0702	0802	0904	1002	1104	1202	1304	1402	1504	1602	1704	1802	1904	2002	2104	2202	2304
Küstrin-Kietz 🏛 d.	0409	0509	0609	0707	0809	0911	1009	1111	1209	1311	1409	1511	1609	1711	1809	1911	2009	2111	2209	2311
Müncheberg (Mark) ¶ d.	0445	0549	0649	0749	0849	0949	1049	1149	1249	1349	1449	1549	1649	1749	1849	1949	2049	2149	2249	2349
Strausberg d.	0505	0605	0705	0805	0905	1005	1105	1205	1305	1405	1505	1605	1705	1805	1905	2005	2105	2205	2305	0005
Berlin Ostkreuz ⊙ a.	0529**r**	0629	0730	0829	0929**r**	1029	1129	1229	1329	1429**r**	1529**r**	1629	1729**r**	1829	1929	2029	2129	2229	2329	0028

r – Berlin Lichtenberg on Ⓐ
⊡ – All trains also call at Berlin Lichtenberg (5 minutes later).
⊙ – All trains also call at Berlin Lichtenberg (5–6 minutes earlier).
¶ – Station for Buckower Kleinbahn (operates on Ⓒ May 1 - Oct. 5).

☛ **Warning! Subject to alteration until July 4.**

WISMAR - ROSTOCK 833

RE services

km		⚒	Ⓐ				
0	**Wismar** d.	0442	0542	0642	and	2042	2142
22	Neubukow d.	0511	0611	0711	hourly	2111	2211
41	Bad Doberan ▲ d.	0530	0630	0730	until	2130	2230
57	**Rostock** Hbf a.	0551	0651	0751		2151	2251

	Ⓐ		⚒				
Rostock Hbf d.	0412	0506	0606	0706	and	2006	2106
Bad Doberan ▲ d.	0432	0532r	0632r	0732r	hourly	2032r	2132r
Neubukow d.	0451	0551	0651	0751	until	2051	2151
Wismar a.	0515	0615	0715	0815		2115	2215

r – Arrives 5–7 minutes earlier.

▲ – **BAD DOBERAN - OSTSEEBAD KÜHLUNGSBORN WEST**. All services worked by steam locomotive. Journey time: 43–45 minutes.
Operator: Mecklenburgische Bäderbahn Molli GmbH, Am Bahnhof, 18209 Bad Doberan. ✆ +49 (0) 38293 431331. www.molli-bahn.de **Service April 12 - Nov. 2.**
From **Bad Doberan** at 0835 Ⓐ, 0936, 1036, 1135, 1236, 1336, 1436, 1536, 1636, 1745 and 1845. From **Kühlungsborn West** at 0640 Ⓐ, 0828, 0935, 1035 and hourly until 1735.

STRALSUND - NEUBRANDENBURG - NEUSTRELITZ 834

km			Ⓐ			Ⓐ									Ⓑ			Ⓑ			Ⓑ					⑤⑥
0	**Stralsund** Hbf d.	...	0406	...	0501	0604	...	0701	0804r	0901	1004r	1101	1204r	1301	1404	...	1501	1604	...	1701	1804	...	1901	...	2103	2103
23	Grimmen d.	...	0427	...	0523	0624	...	0723	0824r	0923	1024r	1123	1224r	1323	1424	...	1523	1624	...	1723	1824	...	1923	...	2128	2128
47	Demmin d.	...	0445	...	0546	0646	...	0746	0846r	0946	1046r	1146	1246r	1346	1446	...	1546	1646	...	1746	1846	...	1946	...	2146	2146
89	**Neubrandenburg** a.	...	0529	...	0629	0729	...	0829	0929r	1029	1129r	1229	1329r	1429	1529	...	1629	1729	...	1829	1929	...	2029	...	2229	2229
89	**Neubrandenburg** d.	0427	0529	0529	0630	0730	0730	0830	0930	1030	1130	1230	1330	1430	1530	1530	1630	1730	1730	1830	1930	1930	2030	2130	2230	2230
124	**Neustrelitz** Hbf a.	0457	0557	0557	0659	0756	0756	0859	0956	1059	1155	1259	1356	1459	1556	1556	1659	1756	1756	1859	1956	1956	2059	2156	2259	2259
	Berlin Hbf **835** a.	0609	...	...	0812	...	...	1013	...	1212	...	1409	...	1613	...	...	1811	...	...	2009	...	...	2209	...	...	0009

	Ⓐ		Ⓐ	Ⓐ									Ⓑ			Ⓑ			Ⓑ							⑤⑥
Berlin Hbf **835** d.	...	...	...	...	...	0547	...	0747	...	0947	...	1147	...	...	1347	...	...	1547	...	...	1747	...	1948v	...	2147	2347
Neustrelitz Hbf d.	...	...	0501	0602	0602	0701	0803	0901	1003	1101	1203	1301	1403	1403	1501	1603	1603	1701	1803	1803	1901	2003	2101	2203	2301	0111
Neubrandenburg a.	...	...	0529	0629	0629	0729	0829	0929	1029	1129	1229	1329	1429	1429	1529	1629	1629	1729	1829	1829	1929	2029	2129	2229	2329	0139
Neubrandenburg d.	0431	0531	0531	0631	...	0731	0831r	0931	1031r	1131	1231r	1331	1431	...	1531	1631	...	1731	1831	...	1931	...	2131	...	...	...
Demmin d.	0510	0610	0610	0710	...	0810	0910r	1010	1110r	1210	1310r	1410	1510	...	1610	1710	...	1810	1910	...	2010	...	2210	...	...	...
Grimmen d.	0529	0629	0629	0729	...	0829	0929r	1029	1129r	1229	1329r	1429	1529	...	1629	1729	...	1829	1929	...	2029	...	2229	...	...	...
Stralsund Hbf a.	0551	0651	0651	0751	...	0851	0951r	1051	1149r	1251	1351r	1451	1551	...	1651	1751	...	1851	1951	...	2051	...	2251	...	...	...

– ⚒ only.

v – 1947 on ⑥.

ROSTOCK - BERLIN - ELSTERWERDA 835

km		*RE* 4351 Ⓐ	*RE* 3503	*RE* 4353	*RE* 3505	*IC* 2173 🍷	*RE* 4355	*RE* 3507	*IC* 2175 🍷	*RE* 4357	*RE* 3509	*IC* 2177 🍷	*RE* 4359	*ICE* 691 F✕	*RE* 3511	*IC* 2179 🍷	*RE* 4361	*IC* 2479 K	*RE* 3513	*IC* 2271 C🍷	*RE* 4363	*IC* 2475 J	*ICE* 1971 H✕	*RE* 3515
	Warnemünde 831 ▷ d.	...	...	...	...	...	...	...	...	...	...	...	...	...	...	...	...	...	...	...	...	...	...	...
0	**Rostock** Hbf 831 ▷ d.	...	...	0434a	...	0621	0634	...	0821	0834	...	1021	1034	1121	...	1221	1234	1321	...	1421	1434	1521	1522	...
34	Güstrow ▷ d.	...	...	0456a	...	|	0656*	...	|	0856*	...	|	1056*	|	...	|	1256*	|	...	|	1456*	|	|	...
85‡	Waren (Müritz) d.	...	...	0530a	...	0701	0730	...	0901	0930	...	1101	1130	1203	...	1301	1330	1401	...	1501	1530	1600	1602	...
	Stralsund Hbf **834** d.	...	...	|	0501	|	|	0701	|	|	0901	|	|	|	1101	|	|	|	1301	|	|	|	|	1501
	Neubrandenburg **834** d.	...	0427	|	0630	|	|	0830	|	|	1030	|	|	|	1230	|	|	|	1430	|	|	|	|	1630
120	**Neustrelitz** Hbf a.	...	0457	0552a	0659	0718	0752	0859	0918	0952	1059	1118	1152	|	1259	1318	1352	1418	1459	1518	1552	1618	1619	1659
120	**Neustrelitz** Hbf d.	0349	0458	0600	0700	0719	0800	0900	0919	1000	1100	1119	1200	|	1300	1319	1400	1419	1500	1519	1600	1619	1621	1700
141	Fürstenberg (Havel) d.	0401	0509	0612	0712	|	0812	0912	|	1012	1112	|	1212	|	1312	|	1412	|	1512	|	1612	|	|	1712
162	Gransee d.	0415	0523	0626	0723	|	0826	0923	|	1026	1123	|	1226	|	1323	|	1426	|	1523	|	1626	|	|	1723
191	Oranienburg d.	0440	0540	0640	0740	0755	0840	0940	0955	1040	1140	1155	1240	|	1340	1355	1440	1455	1540	1555	1640	1655	1657	1740
223	**Berlin** Gesundbrunnen a.	0503	0603	0704	0803	0817	0904	1004	1017	1104	1204	1217	1304	|	1402	1417	1504	1518	1606	1617	1704	1718	|	1802
227	**Berlin** Hbf a.	0510	0609	0713	0812	0823r	0912	1013	1023r	1112	1212	1223r	1311	1322	1409	1423r	1512	...	1613	1623r	1712	1724	1722	1811
233	**Berlin** Südkreuz a.	0520	0620	0726	0824	0831t	0923	1024	1031t	1123	1223	1231t	1323	1331	1421	1431t	1523	...	1628	1631t	1722	...	1736	1824v
	Dresden Hbf **839** a.	...	...	...	...	1027j	...	...	1227j	...	...	1427j	...	...	...	1627j	...	...	...	1827j	...	...	...	...

	IC 2273 C🍷	*RE* 4365	*RE* 3517	*IC* 2275 Ⓑ 🍷	*IC* 2275 🍷	*RE* 4367	*RE* 3519	*IC* 495 Ⓑ A	*ICE* 1975 ⑥	*RE* 4369	*RE* 3521 ⑤⑥	*RE* 3525
Warnemünde 831 ▷ d.	...	...	...	...	...	...	...	...	...	...	...	...
Rostock Hbf 831 ▷ d.	1621	1634	...	1821	1821	1834	...	2021	2021	2034	...	2334
Güstrow ▷ d.	|	1656*	...	|	|	1856*	...	|	|	2056*	...	2356
Waren (Müritz) d.	1701	1730	...	1901	1901	1930	...	2101	2100	2130	...	0030
Stralsund Hbf **834** d.	|	|	1701	|	|	|	1901	|	|	|	2103	|
Neubrandenburg **834** d.	|	|	1830	|	|	|	2030	|	|	|	2230	|
Neustrelitz Hbf a.	1718	1752	1859	1918	1918	1952	2059	2118	2118	2152	2259	0052
Neustrelitz Hbf d.	1719	1800	1900	1919	1919	2000	2100	2119	2120	2200	2300	...
Fürstenberg (Havel) d.	|	1812	1912	|	|	2012	2112	|	|	2212	2312	...
Gransee d.	|	1826	1923	|	|	2026	2123	|	|	2226	2323	...
Oranienburg d.	1755	1840	1940	1955	1955	2040	2140	2155	2154	2240	2340	...
Berlin Gesundbrunnen a.	1817	1904	2003	2017	2017	2104	2203	2217	2218	2304	0003	...
Berlin Hbf a.	1823r	1912	2009	2023r	2023	2110	2209	2223	2225	2310	0009	...
Berlin Südkreuz a.	1831t	1923	2020	2031t	...	2121	2220	2231	2233	2322	...	...
Dresden Hbf **839** a.	2027j	...	...	2227j	...	...	...	...	...	...	...	...

	RE 4350 Ⓐ	*RE* 3504	*IC* 494 ①–⑥ A	*RE* 4352	*IC* 2274 E 🍷	*RE* 3506	*ICE* 1974 H✕
Dresden Hbf **839** d.	...	...	...	...	0530k	...	...
Berlin Südkreuz d.	...	0536	0626	0636	0728	0736	0814
Berlin Hbf d.	0448	0547	0636	0646	0736	0747	0835
Berlin Gesundbrunnen d.	0455	0555	0644	0655	0744	0755	0843
Oranienburg d.	0516	0616	0704	0716	0804	0816	|
Gransee d.	0533	0635	|	0733	|	0835	|
Fürstenberg (Havel) d.	0547	0647	|	0747	|	0847	|
Neustrelitz Hbf a.	0559	0659	0740	0759	0840	0859	0937
Neustrelitz Hbf d.	0606	0701	0741	0806	0841	0901	0939
Neubrandenburg **834** a.	|	0729	|	|	|	0929	|
Stralsund Hbf **834** a.	|	0851	|	|	|	1051	|
Waren (Müritz) d.	0630	...	0759	0830	0858	...	0957
Güstrow ▷ d.	0701*	...	|	0901*	|	...	|
Rostock Hbf 831 ▷ a.	0723	...	0836	0923	0936	...	1036
Warnemünde 831 ▷ a.	...	...	...	...	...	...	...

	RE 4354	*IC* 2272 C🍷	*RE* 3508	*RE* 4356	*IC* 2270 C🍷	*RE* 3510	*IC* 2474 G🍷	*RE* 4358	*IC* 2178 🍷	*RE* 3512	*RE* 4360	*IC* 2176 🍷	*RE* 3514	*ICE* 690 F✕	*RE* 4362	*IC* 2174 🍷	*RE* 3516	*RE* 4364	*IC* 2172 🍷	*RE* 3518	*RE* 4366	*RE* 3520	*RE* 4368	*RE* 3522 ⑤⑥
Dresden Hbf **839** d.	...	0730k	...	...	0930k	...	...	...	1130k	...	...	1330k	...	...	...	1530k	...	...	1726k	...	...	...	...	...
Berlin Südkreuz d.	0836	0928t	0935	1036	1127t	1136	...	1236	1328t	1336	1436	1527t	1536	1627	1636	1728t	1735	1836	1927t	1935	2036	2135	2236	2336
Berlin Hbf d.	0846	0936r	0947	1047	1136r	1147	1237	1246	1337r	1347	1446	1536r	1547	1637	1646	1737r	1747	1847	1936r	1947	2047	2147	2246	2347
Berlin Gesundbrunnen d.	0855	0944	0955	1055	1144	1155	1244	1255	1343	1355	1455	1544	1555	1643	1655	1744	1755	1855	1944	1955	2055	2155	2254	2355
Oranienburg d.	0916	1004	1016	1116	1204	1216	1304	1316	1404	1416	1516	1604	1616	|	1716	1804	1816	1916	2004	2016	2116	2216	2316	0016
Gransee d.	0933	|	1035	1133	|	1235	|	1333	|	1435	1533	|	1635	|	1733	|	1835	1933	|	2035	2133	2235	2332	0043
Fürstenberg (Havel) d.	0947	|	1047	1147	|	1247	|	1347	|	1447	1547	|	1647	|	1747	|	1847	1947	|	2047	2147	2247	2347	0058
Neustrelitz Hbf a.	0959	1040	1059	1159	1240	1259	1339	1359	1440	1459	1559	1640	1659	|	1759	1840	1859	1959	2040	2059	2159	2259	2359	0110
Neustrelitz Hbf d.	1006	1041	1101	1206	1241	1301	1340	1406	1441	1501	1606	1641	1701	|	1806	1841	1901	2006	2041	2101	2206	2301	0004	0111
Neubrandenburg **834** a.	|	|	1129	|	|	1329	|	|	|	1529	|	|	1729	|	|	|	1929	|	|	2129	|	2329	|	0139
Stralsund Hbf **834** a.	|	|	1251	|	|	1451	|	|	|	1651	|	|	1851	|	|	|	2051	|	|	2251	|	...	|	...
Waren (Müritz) d.	1030	1058	...	1230	1258	...	1357	1430	1458	...	1630	1658	...	1758	1830	1858	...	2030	2058	...	2230	...	0027	...
Güstrow ▷ d.	1101*	|	...	1301*	|	...	|	1501*	|	...	1701*	|	...	|	1901*	|	...	2101*	|	...	2301*	...	0059	...
Rostock Hbf 831 ▷ a.	1123	1137	...	1323	1337	...	1436	1523	1537	...	1723	1736	...	1836	1923	1936	...	2123	2136	...	2323	...	0121	...
Warnemünde 831 ▷ a.	...	...	...	...	...	...	...	...	...	...	...	...	...	...	...	...	...	...	...	...	...	...	...	...

BERLIN - ELSTERWERDA. Operated by Ostdeutsche Eisenbahn. See also Table **839**.

	Ⓐ									
Berlin Hbf d.	...	0542	0742	0942	1142	1342	1542	1742	1942	2142
Berlin Südkreuz d.	...	0554	0753	0953	1153	1353	1553	1753	1953	2153
Doberlug-Kirchhain d.	0523	0732	0929	1129	1329	1529	1729	1929	2129	2323
Elsterwerda a.	0538	0746	0942	1142	1342	1542	1742	1942	2142	2338

		⚒							
Elsterwerda d.	0413	0624	0812	1012	1212	1412	1612	1812	2005
Doberlug-Kirchhain d.	0429	0634	0827	1027	1227	1427	1627	1827	2021
Berlin Südkreuz a.	0559	0726	0959	1159	1359	1559	1759	1959	2158
Berlin Hbf a.	0611	0733	1009	1209	1409	1611	1812	2009	2207

A – From/to Wien via Nürnberg (Tables **849a**, **850** and **920**).
C – From/to Chemnitz (Table **880**).
E – ①–⑥ (daily from Berlin Hbf).
F – To/from München via Erfurt, Frankfurt and Stuttgart (Tables **850** and **910**).
G – From Aug. 2. 🚌12 Magdeburg (Table **838**) - Rostock - Stralsund - Ostseebad Binz (Tables **830**/**844**). Runs only to Rostock Sept. 6 - Nov. 7.
H – ⑥ Aug. 2-30. 🚌12 Berlin - Stralsund - Ostseebad Binz (Tables **830**/**844**) and v.v.
J – Ⓐ from Aug. 4. To Magdeburg (Table **838**).
K – From Aug. 2. Starts from Ostseebad Binz on dates in Table **844**.

a – Ⓐ only.
j – Until Aug. 9 arrives Dresden 10–19 mins earlier.
k – Until Aug. 9 departs Dresden 13–17 mins later.
r – Not Sept. 24 - Dec. 13.
t – Berlin **Ostkreuz** Sept. 24 - Dec. 13 (not calling at Südkreuz).
v – 1828 on ⑦ (also June 9; not June 8).
‡ – Rostock to Waren is 78 km direct.
▷ – S-Bahn services run Warnemünde - Rostock - Güstrow (hourly Ⓐ, two-hourly Ⓒ).
* – Trains will not call at Güstrow Aug. 2 - Dec. 13 (but see page 608).

836 LÜBECK - BAD KLEINEN - PASEWALK - SZCZECIN

RE services

km		Ⓑ	Ⓐ	T												♥	♣				V			♣	
	Lübeck Hbf ★ d.	...	...	...	...	...	...	...	...	...	...	...	...	...	...	...	...	...	...	...	...	...	...	...	...
0	**Bad Kleinen** 830 d.	...	...	0504z	0603	0705*	0803	0904*	1003	1102*	1203	1304*	1403	1504*	1603	1705	1703	1803	1902*	2003	2003	2104*	2203	2303	...
41	Bützow 830 d.	...	...	0533z	0633	0733	0833	0933	1033	1137	1233	1333	1433	1533	1633	1733	1733	1833	1937	2033	2033	2133	2233	2333	...
55	Güstrow a.	...	...	0542z	0642	0742	0842	0942	1042	1146	1242	1342	1442	1542	1642	1742	1742	1842	1946	2042	2042	2142	2242	2342	...
55	Güstrow d.	...	...	0604	0704	0804	0904	1004	1104	1204	1304	1404	1504	1604	1704	1804	1804	1904	2004	2104	2104	2204	2304	...	...
84	Teterow a.	...	...	0627	0727	0827	0927	1027	1127	1227	1327	1427	1527	1627	1727	1827	1827	1927	2027	2127	2127	2227	2327	...	...
84	Teterow d.	...	...	0633	0733	0833	0933	1033	1133	1233	1333	1433	1533	1633	1733	1833	1833	1933	2033	2133	2133	2233	2328	...	...
98	Malchin d.	...	0529	0644	0744	0844	0944	1044	1144	1244	1344	1444	1544	1644	1744	1844	1844	1944	2044	2144	2144	2243	2338	...	...
142	**Neubrandenburg** a.	...	0601	0721	0821	0921	1021	1121	1221	1321	1421	1521	1621	1721	1821	1921	1921	2021	2121	2221	2221	2315	0010	...	...
142	**Neubrandenburg** d.	0513t	0606	0733	0833r	0933	1033	1133	1233	1333	1433	1533	1633	1733	1833	1933	1933	2033	2133	...	2233	...	...	...	...
195	**Pasewalk** a.	0559t	0654	0815	0915r	1015	1115	1215	1315	1415	1515	1615	1715	1815	1915	2015	2015	2115	2215	...	2314	...	...	...	...
195	**Pasewalk** ▷ d.	0616	0700	0816	...	1016	...	1216	...	1416	1525t	1616	...	1816	...	2016	2016	...	...	...	2316f	...	...	...	...
	Ueckermünde S ¶ ▷ a.	|	0731	|	...	|	...	|	...	|	1556t	|	...	|	...	|	|	...	...	...	|	...	...	...	...
222	Grambow d.	0638	...	0838	...	1038	...	1238	...	1438	...	1638	...	1838	...	2038	2038	...	...	...	2338f	...	...	...	...
232	Szczecin Gumience 🏛 d.	0648	...	0848	...	1048	...	1248	...	1448	...	1648	...	1848	...	2048	2048	...	...	...	2348f	...	...	...	...
237	**Szczecin** Głowny a.	0655	...	0855	...	1055	...	1255	...	1455	...	1655	...	1855	...	2055	2055	...	...	...	2355f	...	...	...	...

	①♥	♥	♣			Ⓐ	Ⓒ	Ⓐ			Ⓐ											c	S		
Szczecin Głowny d.	...	...	...	...	...	0501	...	...	...	0701	...	...	0901	...	1101	...	1301	...	1501	...	1701	...	1901	...	2101
Szczecin Gumience 🏛 d.	...	...	...	...	...	0507	...	...	...	0707	...	...	0907	...	1107	...	1307	...	1507	...	1707	...	1907	...	2107
Grambow d.	...	...	...	...	...	0518	...	...	...	0718	...	...	0918	...	1118	...	1318	...	1518	...	1718	...	1918	...	2118
Ueckermünde S ¶ ▷ d.	...	...	...	...	...	|	...	0600	...	|	0738	...	|	...	|	...	|	...	|	1601t	|	...	|	...	|
Pasewalk ⊙ ▷ a.	...	...	...	...	...	0539	...	0632	...	0739	0810	...	0939	...	1139	...	1339	...	1539	1632t	1739	...	1939	...	2139
Pasewalk ⊙ d.	0301	...	...	...	...	0541	0541	0638	...	0743	0843	0843r	0944	1043	1144	1243	1343	1443	1543	1643	1743	1843	1943	2043	2143
Neubrandenburg a.	0339	...	...	...	...	0623	0623	0723	...	0826	0926	0926r	1026	1126	1226	1326	1426	1526	1626	1726	1826	1926	2026	2126	2226
Neubrandenburg d.	0340	...	...	0447	0544	0641	0641	0741	0741	0841	0941	0941	1041	1141	1241	1341	1441	1541	1641	1741	1841	1941	2041	2141	...
Malchin d.	0410	...	...	0531	0620	0713	0713	0813	0813	0913	1013	1013	1113	1213	1313	1413	1513	1613	1713	1813	1913	2013	2113	2213	...
Teterow a.	0420	...	...	0540	0630	0723	0723	0823	0823	0923	1023	1023	1123	1223	1323	1423	1523	1623	1723	1823	1923	2023	2123	2223	...
Teterow d.	0421	...	...	0541	0631	0730	0730	0830	0830	0930	1030	1030	1130	1230	1330	1430	1530	1630	1730	1830	1930	2030	2130	2230	...
Güstrow a.	0439	...	...	0603	0653	0753	0753	0853	0853	0953	1053	1053	1153	1253	1353	1453	1553	1653	1753	1853	1953	2053	2153	2253	...
Güstrow d.	0440	0451	0508	0608	0708	0805	0805	0908	0908	1008	1108	1108	1208	1308	1405	1508	1608	1708	1808	1908	2008	2108	2208	2308	...
Bützow 830 a.	0450	0500	0518	0618	0718	0815	0815	0918	0918	1018	1118	1118	1218	1318	1415	1518	1618	1718	1818	1918	2018	2118	2218	2318	...
Bad Kleinen 830 a.	0517	0554	0554	0646*	0754	0842*	0842*	0954	0954	1046*	1154	1154	1246*	1354	1442*	1554	1646*	1754	1846*	1954	2046*	2154	2246	2359	...
Lübeck Hbf ★ a.	...	...	...	...	...	...	...	...	...	...	...	...	...	...	...	...	...	...	...	...	...	...	...	...	...

km		🚌 Until Aug. 1 →					△	and hourly until				From Aug. 2 →			and hourly until	
0	**Lübeck** Hbf d.		0436	0533	0602	0703	0802		2002	2103	2202		0502	0602		2302
39	Grevesmühlen d.		0518	0618	0644	0744	0844		2044	2144	2244		0536	0636		2336
62	**Bad Kleinen** a.		0558	0658	0724	0824	0924		2124	2224	2324		0551	0651		2351

	🚌 Until Aug. 1 →						and hourly until				From Aug. 2 →	s		and hourly until	
Bad Kleinen d.		...	0528	0628	0728	0828		2028	2128	2230		0405	0501		2201
Grevesmühlen d.		0520	0616	0716	0816	0916		2116	2216	2320		0420	0515		2215
Lübeck Hbf a.		0556	0656	0756	0856	0956		2156	2256	2356		0456	0556		2256

S – To Schwerin a. 2318 (2259 ♣).
T – From Schwerin (d. 0451**z**).
V – ⑤–⑦ (also Oct. 2, 30).
c – Change at Neubrandenburg until Aug. 1.
f – ⑤ (also Oct. 2, 30).
r – ⚒ only.
s – From Schwerin (depart 0345).
t – Ⓐ only.
z – 7-8 minutes later from Aug. 2
¶ – Ueckermünde Stadthafen.

♥ – Until Aug. 1.
♣ – From Aug. 2.
★ – See panel for full service Lübeck - Bad Kleinen and v.v.
▷ – For **PASEWALK - UECKERMÜNDE** see panel at foot of page.
🚌 – By 🚌 Grevesmühlen - Bad Kleinen and v.v. until Aug. 1.
△ – 1 minute later from Lübeck on uneven hours.
* – Change trains at Bützow Aug. 2 - Dec. 13 (departures may be 1-2 minutes earlier from Bad Kleinen; arrivals 8 minutes later).

837 WISMAR - BERLIN - COTTBUS

SERVICE UNTIL AUGUST 1. See page 608 for amended service Wismar - Schwerin and Schwerin - Berlin from August 2

km	◇				Ⓐ	Ⓐ	⚒	†									and in the same pattern every two hours until								
0	**Wismar** d.	...	...	...	0417	...	0522	...	...	0624	0733	...	0824	0924	...	1024		1724	...	1824	1924	...	2024	2125	2224
16	Bad Kleinen 830 d.	...	...	...	0431	...	0536	...	...	0639	0747	...	0839	0938	...	1039		1738	...	1839	1938	...	2039	2139	2239
32	**Schwerin** Hbf 830 a.	...	...	...	0444	...	0549	...	...	0652	0759	...	0851	0951	...	1051		1751	...	1851	1950	...	2051	2151	2251
32	**Schwerin** Hbf d.	...	...	0500	0500	0531	0600	...	...	0700	0800	...	0853	1000	...	1100		1800	...	1900	2000	...	2100	2200	2300
72	Ludwigslust 840 d.	...	...	0533	0533	0605	0633	...	...	0734	0833	...	0935	1033	...	1134		1833	...	1935	2033	...	2134	2233	2334
116	Wittenberge 840 d.	0406	0506	0606f	0606f	...	0703f	0705	0806	...	0903f	1006	...	1103f	1206	...		1903f	2006	...	2103f	2206	...	2307k	...
207	Nauen d.	0501	0601	0701	0701	...	0801	0801	0901	...	1001	1101	...	1201	1301	...		2001	2101	...	2201	2301	...	0003	...
229	**Berlin** Spandau 840 d.	0518	0623	0723	0723	...	0823	0823	0923	...	1023	1123	...	1223	1323	...		2022	2123	...	2223	2323	...	0023	...
241	**Berlin** Zoo ‡ d.	0527	0633	0733	0733	...	0833	0833	0933	...	1033	1133	...	1233	1333	...		2033	2133	...	2233	2333	...	0033	...
245	**Berlin** Hbf 840 ‡ d.	0532	0640	0740	0740	...	0840	0840	0940	...	1040	1140	...	1240	1340	...		2040	2140	...	2240	2340	...	0040	...
250	**Berlin** Ostbahnhof ‡ d.	0544	0653	0753	0753	...	0853	0853	0953	...	1053	1153	...	1253	1353	...		2053	2153	...	2253	2353	...	0053	...
252	**Berlin** Ostkreuz ‡ d.	0551	0657	0757	0757	...	0857	0857	0957	...	1057	1157	...	1257	1357	...		2057	2158	...	2257	2357	...	0057	...
269	**Flughafen Berlin** ✈ ‡ a.	0611	0715	0815	0815	...	0915	0915	1015	...	1115	1215	...	1315	1415	...		2115	2215	...	2315	0015	...	0115	...

◇	Ⓐ			⚒									and in the same pattern every two hours until												
Flughafen Berlin ✈ ‡ d.	...	0342	0444	0444	...	0544	0644	...	0744	0844	...	0944		1444	...	1544	1644	...	1744	1844	...	1944	2044	2144	2244
Berlin Ostkreuz ‡ d.	...	0400	0503	0503	...	0603	0703	...	0803	0903	...	1003		1503	...	1603	1703	...	1803	1903	...	2003	2103	2204	2303
Berlin Ostbahnhof ‡ d.	...	0404	0507	0507	...	0607	0707	...	0807	0907	...	1007		1507	...	1607	1707	...	1807	1907	...	2007	2107	2209	2307
Berlin Hbf 840 ‡ d.	...	0416	0519	0519	...	0620	0720	...	0820	0920	...	1020		1520	...	1620	1720	...	1820	1920	...	2020	2120	2222	2320
Berlin Zoo ‡ d.	...	0425	0525	0525	...	0626	0726	...	0826	0926	...	1026		1526	...	1626	1726	...	1826	1926	...	2026	2126	2228	2326
Berlin Spandau 840 d.	...	0434	0536	0536	...	0638	0738	...	0838	0938	...	1038		1538	...	1638	1738	...	1838	1938	...	2038	2138	2238	2338
Nauen d.	...	0459	0559	0559	...	0656	0756	...	0856	0956	...	1056		1556	...	1656	1756	...	1856	1956	...	2056	2156	2256	2356
Wittenberge 840 d.	...	0603k	0659	0701	...	0757	0901	...	0957	1101	...	1157		1701	...	1757	1901	...	1957	2101	...	2157	2301	2357	0056
Ludwigslust 840 d.	0526	0628	...	0726	0826	...	0926	1036	...	1126	1226	...		1726	1823	...	1926	2026	...	2126	2256	...	2326	...	...
Schwerin Hbf a.	0559	0658	...	0757	0859	...	0957	1109	...	1157	1259	...		1757	1900	...	1957	2105x	...	2157	2330	...	2357	...	...
Schwerin Hbf 830 d.	0604	0659	...	0806	0904	...	1006	1110	...	1206	1304	...		1806	1904	...	2006	2107	...	2206	...	...	0006	...	...
Bad Kleinen 830 d.	0617	0711	...	0818	0917	...	1018	1122	...	1218	1317	...		1818	1917	...	2018	2119	...	2218	...	...	0032z	...	...
Wismar a.	0637	0726	...	0837	0937	...	1037	1138	...	1237	1337	...		1837	1937	...	2037	2138	...	2237	...	...	0046	...	...

BERLIN - COTTBUS

km				Ⓐ				and hourly until					ALSO	2431 ⒷE
0	Nauen d.	...	0537t	...	0637t	0737t	0837t		2037t	2208t	2322t	0008t		...
22	**Berlin** Spandau d.	...	0604	...	0704	0804	0904		2104	2233	2354	0035		...
34	**Berlin** Zoo d.	0517	0617	0659	0717	0817	0921		2121	2245	0006	0047		...
38	**Berlin** Hbf d.	0523	0623	0705	0723	0823	0927*		2127*	2251	0013	0053		1831
43	**Berlin** Ostbahnhof d.	0535	0635	0716	0735	0835	0935r		2135r	2303	0024	0105		1840
45	**Berlin** Ostkreuz d.	0539	0639	0721	0739	0839	0939		2139	2308	0028	0110		1845
76	Königs Wusterhausen d.	0603	0703	0744	0803	0903	1003		2203	2331	0054	0131		1909
123	Lübben (Spreewald) d.	0626	0726	0806	0826	0926	1026		2226	0009	0131	0209		1933
134	Lübbenau (Spreew) d.	0633	0733	0828j	0833	0933	1033		2233	0016	0138	0216		1942
163	**Cottbus** Hbf a.	0657	0756	0846	0855	0955	1055		2255	0039	0202	0239		1959

			Ⓐ	2432 ⚒E		Ⓐ			and hourly until				
Cottbus Hbf d.	0401	0501	0526	0601	0607	0613	0703	0804		2004	2104	2203	2305
Lübbenau (Spreew) d.	0425	0527	0546	0620	0627	0646j	0727	0827		2027	2127	2225	2328
Lübben (Spreewald) d.	0432	0534	0553	0628	0634	0653	0734	0834		2034	2134	2232	2335
Königs Wusterhausen d.	0458	0558	0617	0652	0658	0716	0758	0858		2058	2158	2258	0013
Berlin Ostkreuz d.	0520	0620	0639	0712	0720	0740	0820	0920		2120	2220	2319	0034
Berlin Ostbahnhof d.	0525r	0625r	...	0718	0725r	...	0825r	0925r		2125r	2225r	2323	0039
Berlin Hbf d.	0535	0635	...	0729	0735	...	0835	0935		2135	2235	2335	0051
Berlin Zoo d.	0542	0642	...	0736	0742	...	0842	0942		2142	2242	2342	0058
Berlin Spandau d.	0556	0656	...	...	0756	...	0856	0956		2156	2256	2356	...
Nauen a.	0621t	0721t	...	...	0821t	...	0921t	1021t		2221t	2321t	0021t	...

E – *IC* **2431/2**. (12) Emden - Bremen - Hannover - Magdeburg Berlin - Cottbus and (12) Cottbus - Berlin - Magdeburg - Hannover - Bremen - Norddeich.
f – Arrives 5–6 minutes earlier.
j – Arrives 14–15 minutes earlier.
k – Arrives 8–9 minutes earlier.
r – Calls at Ostbhf from Aug. 9 (from Sept. 24 towards Cottbus
t – Not Aug. 2 - Dec. 13.
x – 2059 on Ⓒ.
z – Arrives 0017.
‡ – See also Table **847**.
◇ – Operated by Ostdeutsche Eisenbahn.
* – 4 minutes earlier from Sept. 24.
☛ See Table **866** for *IC* services Leipzig - Magdeburg - Wittenberge - Schwerin - Bad Kleinen - Rostock - Warnemünde and v.v.

PASEWALK - UECKERMÜNDE *30 km.* Journey 31–35 mins.
From Pasewalk at 0518 Ⓐ, 0610 ⚒, 0700 Ⓐ, 0822, 1022, 1222, 1422, 1525 Ⓐ, 1608, 1822 and 2022.
From Ueckermünde Stadthafen at 0600 Ⓐ, 0700 ⚒, 0738 Ⓐ, 0900, 1100, 1300, 1500, 1601 Ⓐ, 1700, 1900 and 2100.

Ostdeutsche Eisenbahn / DB — MAGDEBURG - BERLIN - FRANKFURT (ODER) - COTTBUS — 838

km																									
		Ⓒ			Ⓐ				Ⓐ			Ⓐ				❖							Ⓐ★	△	A♣
0	**Magdeburg** Hbf .... d.	0042	...	...	...	0419	0512	...	0554	0612c	...	0619	0712	...	0812		...	2012	2106	2206	2321		0704	1104	...
79	**Brandenburg** Hbf ..... d.	0141	0315c	0417	0505	0519	0605	0619	0645	0705	0719	0719	0805	0819	0905	and at	2019	2105	2159	2259	0023	A	0741	1142	1945s
114	Potsdam Hbf .... d.	0211	0345c	0450	0527	0550	0631	0650	0710	0731	0750	0750	0831	0850	0931		2050	2131	2230	2330	0054		0803	1204	2006s
123	Berlin Wannsee .... d.	0218	0352c	0457	0535	0557	0640	0657	0716	0740	0757	0757	0840	0857	0939	the same	2057	2140	2237	2339	0101	L	0810s	1212	2030s
138	**Berlin** Zoo .... d.	0231	0405	0508	0548	0608	0653	0708	...	0753	0808	0808	0855	0908	0952	minutes	2108	2153	2250	2352	0116		|	|	2042s
142	**Berlin** Hbf .... **1001** d.	0237	0411	0514	0556	0614	0659	0714	...	0759	0814	0814	0901	0914	0958		2114	2159	2256	2358	0123	S	0830	1230	2047s
147	**Berlin** Ostbahnhof .... d.	0249	0422	0525	0606	0625	0710	0725	...	0810	0825	0825	0911	0925	1009	past each	2125	2210	2310	0009	0134		0840r	...	2100
149	**Berlin** Ostkreuz .... d.	0253	0429	0532	0611	0632	0715	0732	...	0815	0832	0832	0915	0932	1015		2132	2215	2315	0014	0138	O	...	...	...
194	Fürstenwalde (Spree) d.	0327	0503	0605	0648	0703	0748	0803	...	0848	0903	0903	0948	1003	1048	hour until	2203	2248	2348	0047	0210		...	...	...
228	**Frankfurt** (Oder) **1001** a.	0355	0531	0633	0705	0731	0805	0831	...	0905	0931	0931	1005	1031	1105		2231	2315	0015	0114	0237		...	...	...

		Ⓒ	Ⓒ		Ⓐ		Ⓒ		Ⓐ										⑤⑥			Ⓒ♣	Ⓐ♥	Ⓐ◐	⑦♣
rankfurt (Oder) **1001** d.	0024	0024	...	...	...	0341	0424	0444	0518	0526	0555		1926	1955	2026	2124	2224	2324	2324	...		...	...	...	...
ürstenwalde (Spree). d.	0052	0052	...	...	...	0409	0452	0512	0536	0554	0612	and at	1954	2012	2054	2152	2252	2352	2352	...	A	...	...	...	...
erlin Ostkreuz .... d.	0125	0125	0251	...	...	0444	0526	0545	0607	0626	0645		2026	2045	2125	2225	2325	0025	0025	...		...	...	...	...
erlin Ostbahnhof ..... d.	0130	0130	0256	...	...	0449	0530	0549	0612	0630	0649	the same	2030	2049	2130	2230	2330	0030	0030	...	L	0711	1717	...	2120
erlin Hbf ....**1001** d.	0141	0141	0307	...	...	0501	0541	0601	0624	0641	0701		2041	2100	2141	2241	2341	0044	0044	...		0723u	1728u	1734	2131u
erlin Zoo .... d.	0146	0147	0313	...	...	0508	0547	0608	0630	0647	0708	minutes	2047	2107	2147	2247	2347	0050	0050	...		0730u	1735u	|	2137u
erlin Wannsee .... d.	...	0200	0327	...	...	0523	0559	0623	0643	0659	0723	past each	2059	2123	2159	2300	0000	0103	0103	...	S	0742u	1751u	|	2148u
otsdam Hbf.............. d.	...	0208	0336	...	...	0531	0607	0631	0654	0707	0731		2107	2131	2207	2308	0008	0111	0111	...		0753u	1801	1801	2157u
randenburg Hbf...... d.	...	0239	0408	0408	0451	0555	0638	0655	0716	0738	0755	hour until	2139	2155	2241	2341	0039	0142	0144	...	O	0813u	1819	1819	2217u
agdeburg Hbf......... a.	...	...	0508	0508	0550	0647	...	0747	...	...	0847		...	2247	2340	0034	...	...	0237	...		...	1855	1855	...

FRANKFURT (ODER) - COTTBUS (operated by DB; certain services run to / from Leipzig as shown in Table **852**).

km											
		Ⓒ	Ⓐ		Ⓐ		Ⓐ				
0	**Frankfurt (Oder)** .... d.	0031	0438	0536	0601	0638	0712	0736	and	2136	2322
23	Eisenhüttenstadt .... d.	0052	0459	0557	0619	0659	0734	0757	hourly	2157	2343
48	Guben........................ d.	0113	0520	0618	0635	0720	0750	0818	until	2218	0005
86	**Cottbus** Hbf .... a.	0150	0556	0654	0659	0756	0814	0854		2254	0042

			Ⓐ					Ⓐ	
Cottbus Hbf........... d.	0402	0502	0527	0602	and	2102	...	2202	2302
Guben...................... d.	0439	0539	0609	0639	hourly	2139	...	2239	2339
Eisenhüttenstadt..... d.	0500	0600	0630	0700	until	2200	...	2300	0000
Frankfurt (Oder) .... a.	0521	0621	0652	0721		2221	...	2321	0021

A – ⑤–⑦.
c – Ⓒ only.
r – From Sept. 24.
s – Calls to set down only.
u – Calls to pick up only.

❖ – Timings may vary by 1 – 2 minutes.
★ – *IC* **2231**. Operated by DB.
♥ – *IC* **2232**. Operated by DB. Runs until Aug. 1.
◐ – *IC* **2475**. Operated by DB. Runs from Aug. 4. From Rostock (Table **835**).

△ – *IC* **2474**. Operated by DB. Runs from Aug. 2. To Rostock (Table **830**) or Ostseebad Binz.
♣ – 2 Berlin - Halberstadt - Thale / Ilsenburg / Goslar and v.v. (Tables **860** and **862**). Until Sept. 21 diverted to serve Berlin **Lichtenberg** (arrives 2051; departures are at 0656 and 2100). Operated by Start Mitteldeutschland. **DB tickets not valid**.

☛ See Table **866** for other *IC* services.

See Table 927 for services operated by FlixTrain — BERLIN - DRESDEN — 839

SERVICE UNTIL SEPTEMBER 23. For amended service September 24 - December 13 see page 608.

km	*For night trains see Table* **60**	*RJ*	*EC*	*IC*		*EC*	*IC*		*EC*	*IC*		*EC*	*IC*		*EC*	*IC*		*EC*	*IC*		*RJ*	*IC*		
		257	**171**	**2173**		**173**	**2175**		**379**	**2177**		**175**	**2179**		**177**	**2271**		**179**	**2273**		**2079**	**2275**		
		M																				Ⓑ		
		G✕	✕	🍷		B✕	🍷		K✕	🍷		F✕	🍷		✕	C🍷		✕	C🍷		✕	🍷		
	Hamburg Hbf **840** .... d.	...	...	...	...	0648x	...	...	0851x	...	...	1051x	...	...	1252x	...	...	...	...	...	1651x	...	...	...
	Rostock Hbf **835** .... d.	...	...	0621	...	|	0821	...	|	1021	...	|	1221	...	|	1421	...	...	1621	...	|	1821	...	...
0	**Berlin** Hbf .... **835** d.	0615	0715f	0826	...	0915f	1026	...	1116f	1226	...	1316f	1426	...	1516f	1626	...	1716f	1826	...	1915f	2026	...	...
6	**Berlin** Südkreuz .... **835** d.	0520	0723f	0833	...	0923f	1033	...	1123f	1233	...	1323f	1433	...	1523f	1633	...	1723f	1833	...	1923f	2033	...	...
120	Doberlug-Kirchhain .... **835** d.	0724	|	0924	...	|	1124	...	|	1324	...	|	1524	...	|	1724	...	|	1924	...	|	2124	...	...
140	Elsterwerda .... **843 835** d.	0735	|	0937	...	|	1137	...	|	1337	...	|	1537	...	|	1737	...	|	1937	...	|	2137	...	...
193	**Dresden** Neustadt .... a.	0800	0900	1002*	...	1100	1202*	...	1300	1402*	...	1500	1602*	...	1700	1805*	...	1900	2005*	...	2100	2202*	...	...
197	**Dresden** Hbf .... **843** a.	0806	0906	1008*	...	1106	1208*	...	1306	1408*	...	1506	1608*	...	1706	1817*	...	1906	2017*	...	2107	2208*	...	...
	Praha hl.n. **1100** .... a.	1026	1127	...	...	1323	...	...	1523	...	...	1723	...	...	1923	...	...	2123	...	...	...	...	...	...

km	*For night trains see Table* **60**	*IC*		*ICE*	*RJ*	*IC*		*EC*	*IC*		*EC*	*IC*		*EC*	*IC*		*EC*	*IC*		*EC*	*IC*	*EC*	*RJ*	*EC*
		2274		**870**	**2078**	**2272**		**178**	**2270**		**176**	**2178**		**174**	**2176**		**378**	**2174**		**172**	**2172**	**170**	**256**	**258**
		①–⑥		**N**	**P**																		**L**	**V**
		🍷		✕	✕	C🍷		✕	C🍷		✕	🍷		F✕	🍷		K✕	🍷		B✕	🍷	✕	G✕	✕
	Praha hl.n. **1100** .... d.	...	...	...	...	...	...	0628	...	...	0828	...	...	1028	...	...	1233	...	...	1433	...	1628	1728	2028
0	**Dresden** Hbf .... **843** d.	0543z	...	0700	0700	0745z	...	0855	0945z	...	1055	1143z	...	1255	1343z	...	1455	1543z	...	1655	1743z	1855	1955	2253
4	**Dresden** Neustadt .... d.	0550z	...	0707	0707	0753z	...	0902	0953z	...	1102	1150z	...	1302	1350z	...	1502	1550z	...	1702	1750z	1902	2002	2300
57	Elsterwerda .... **843 835** d.	0624	...	|	|	0824	...	|	1024	...	|	1224	...	|	1424	...	|	1624	...	|	1824	|	2028	|
77	Doberlug-Kirchhain .... **835** d.	0634	...	|	|	0834	...	|	1034	...	|	1234	...	|	1434	...	|	1634	...	|	1834	|	2038	|
205	**Berlin** Südkreuz .... **835** a.	0726	...	0837	0837t	0926	...	1035t	1126	...	1236t	1326	...	1436t	1526	...	1636t	1726	...	1836t	1926	2036t	2137	0050
211	**Berlin** Hbf .... **835** a.	0733	...	0845	0845t	0933	...	1043t	1133	...	1243t	1333	...	1443t	1533	...	1643t	1733	...	1843t	1933	2043t	2146	0057
	Rostock Hbf **835** .... a.	0936	...	|	...	1137	...	...	1337	...	|	1537	...	|	1736	...	|	1936	...	|	2136	...	...	...
	Hamburg Hbf **840** .... a.	...	...	1116x	...	...	...	...	...	...	1512x	...	...	1711x	...	...	1912x	...	...	2117x	...	...	...	...

B – To / from Budapest (Table **60**).
C – To / from Chemnitz (Table **880**).
F – From / to Flensburg until Aug. 1 (Table **823**).
G – From / to Graz via Wien (Table **60**).
K – From / to Kiel until Aug. 1 (Table **820**).
L – Until June 28.

M – Until June 29.
N – Until Aug. 2.
P – From Aug. 3.
V – Until Sept. 14.
f – Departs 19 – 20 mins **earlier** Aug. 10 - Sept. 23.

r – Berlin **Ostkreuz**.
t – 16 – 19 mins later from Aug. 10.
x – Not Aug. 2 - Dec. 13.
z – 13 – 16 mins **earlier** Aug. 10 - Sept. 23.
* – Arrives 19 mins later Aug. 10 - Sept. 23.

See Table 927 for services operated by FlixTrain — HAMBURG - BERLIN — 840

SERVICE TO AUGUST 1. For amended service from August 2 (diverted via Salzwedel and Stendal) see page 608.

km		*ICE*	*ICE*	*EC*	*ICE*	*ICE*	*ICE*	*EC*	*ICE*	*ICE*	*ICE*	*EC*	*ICE*	*ICE*	*ICE*	*EC*	*ICE*	*ICE*	*ICE*	*ICE*	*ICE*	*ICE*	*ICE*	*ICE*	*ICE*	*ICE*
		701	**505**	**173**	**703**	**93**	**507**	**379**	**705**	**1005**	**509**	**175**	**707**	**95**	**1601**	**177**	**709**	**1007**	**603**	**935**	**801**	**1009**	**1605**	**1605**	**1705**	**871**
		①–⑤																						Ⓑ	Ⓑ	
		M✕	M✕	B✕	M✕	G✕	M✕	✕	M✕	M✕	M✕	F✕	M✕	G✕	M✕	✕	M✕	L✕	M✕	S✕	M✕	M✕	✕	M✕	J✕	✕
	Kiel Hbf **820** .... d.	...	...	...	...	...	...	0742	...	...	...	...	...	...	...	...	...	...	...	...	1413	...	...	...	...	...
0	**Hamburg** Altona .... d.	0512	0617	0635	0718	0751	0818	|	0919	0950	1017	...	1118	1150	1215	1238	1318	...	1419	1438	1521	1537	1616	1616	1616	1637
7	**Hamburg** Hbf .... **830** d.	0527	0634	0648	0735	0805	0835	0851	0936	1005	1034	1051	1136	1204	1232	1252	1336	1404	1435	1451	1536	1551	1634	1634	1634	1651
54	Büchen .... **830** d.	|	|	0715	|	|	|	0915	|	|	|	1115	|	|	|	1315	|	|	|	1514	|	|	|	|	|	1715
122	Ludwigslust .... **837** d.	0612	|	0741	|	|	|	0941	|	|	|	1141	|	|	|	1341	|	|	|	1541	|	1645	|	|	|	1741
167	Wittenberge .... **837** d.	0631	|	0801	|	|	|	1001	|	|	|	1201	|	|	|	1401	|	|	|	1601	|	|	|	|	|	1801
280	**Berlin** Spandau . **837** a.	0710	0808	0844	0910	0943	1008	1044	1110	1143	1208	1244	1310	1343	1408	1444	1510	1543	1608	1644	1710	1743	1808	1808	1808	1844
293	**Berlin** Hbf .... **837** a.	0722	0820	0855	0922	0953	1020	1055	1122	1155	1220	1255	1322	1353	1420	1455	1522	1555	1620	1655	1722	1755	1820	1820	1820	1855
299	**Berlin** Südkreuz......... a.	0739	0833	0921	0939	1009	1033	1121	1139	1209	1233	1321	1339	1409	1434	1521	1539	1617	1633	1706	1739	1817	...	1834	1834	1920
	Dresden Hbf **839** ... a.	...	...	1106	...	...	...	1306	...	...	...	1506	...	...	...	1706	...	...	...	...	...	...	...	...	...	2107
	Praha hl.n. **1100** .... a.	...	...	1323	...	...	...	1523	...	...	...	1723	...	...	...	1923	...	...	...	...	...	...	...	...	...	...

	ICE	*IC*	*ICE*	*IC*	*ICE*	*ICE*		*ICE*		*ICE*	
	803	**2075**	**1607**	**2073**	**699**	**609**		**805**		**907**	
						Ⓑ		**z**		⑤⑦	
	N✕	U	D✕		A✕	✕		✕		✕z	
Kiel Hbf **820** .... d.	...	...	...	...	...	...	...	...	...	...	...
amburg Altona .... d.	1720	...	1818	1835	1920	2017	...	2134	...	2235	...
amburg Hbf ......**830** d.	1735	1751	1835	1851	1937	2034	...	2151	...	2252	...
üchen ....**830** d.	|	|	|	1915	|	|	...	2215	...	2315	...
udwigslust..........**837** d.	|	1843	|	1941	|	2118	...	2242	...	2341	...
ittenberge ....**837** d.	1834	|	|	2001	|	|	...	2303	...	0001	...
erlin Spandau ...**837** a.	1910	1943	2008	2044	2110	2211	...	2343	...	0042	...
erlin Hbf ....**837** a.	1923	1955	2020	2055	2122	2224	...	2354	...	0053	...
erlin Südkreuz .... a.	1936	2003	2034b	2104	2131	2233	...	0002	...	0103	...
Dresden Hbf **839** .... a.	...	...	...	...	...	...	...	...	...	...	...
Praha hl.n. **1100** ..... a.	...	...	...	...	...	...	...	...	...	...	...

	ICE	*ICE*		*ICE*	*IC*	*ICE*	*IC*	*ICE*	*ICE*	*ICE*	*ICE*
	908	**608**		**808**	**2070**	**1606**	**2074**	**806**	**870**	**1604**	**1704**
	①	①–⑤		①–⑥							①–⑤
	✕	✕		✕	✕	C✕	U	E✕	✕	N✕	J✕
Praha hl.n. **1100** . d.	..	...	...	...	...	...	...	...	...	...	...
Dresden Hbf **839** d.	...	...	...	...	...	...	...	...	0700	...	...
Berlin Südkreuz..... d.	0457	0519	...	0627	0656	0724	0752	0828	0839	0924	0924
Berlin Hbf........ **837** d.	0507	0530	...	0636	0706	0741	0804	0836	0906	0938	0938
Berlin Spandau **837** d.	0516	0540	...	0647	0716	|	0814	0846	0917	0947	0947
Wittenberge ..... **837** d.	0600	0621	...	|	0801	|	|	|	1001	|	|
Ludwigslust...... **837** d.	0618	0641	...	0742	0820	|	0913	|	1020	|	|
Büchen .... **830** d.	|	|	...	|	0850	|	|	|	1050	|	|
Hamburg Hbf .. **830** a.	0712	0725	...	0825	0912	0924	1003	1022	1116	1124	1124
Hamburg Altona.... a.	0726	0740	...	0840	0924	0939	...	1038	1130	1139	1139
Kiel Hbf **820** .... a.	...	...	...	...	...	...	...	...	...	...	...

840 (continued from previous page) BERLIN - HAMBURG

See Table **927** for services operated by FlixTrain

SERVICE TO AUGUST 1. For amended service from August 2 (diverted via Salzwedel and Stendal) see page 608.

	ICE 1008	ICE 804	ICE 934	ICE 602	ICE 1006	ICE 802	EC 176	ICE 1600	ICE 94	ICE 800	EC 174	ICE 508	ICE 1004	ICE 708	EC 378	ICE 506	ICE 92	ICE 706	EC 172	ICE 504		ICE 704		ICE 502		ICE 700
															d				d			z		z		⑤⑦
	L✕	M✕	H✕	M✕	M✕	M✕	✕	M✕	G✕	M✕	F✕	M✕	M✕	M✕	✕	M✕	G✕	M✕	B✕	M✕		M✕		M✕		✕z
Praha hl.n. **1100** d.	...	...	...	...	...	...	0828	...	...	...	1028	...	...	...	1233	...	...	..	1433	...	...	...	...	...	...	...
Dresden Hbf **839** d.	...	...	...	...	...	...	1055	...	...	...	1255	...	...	...	1455	...	...	...	1655	...	...	...	...	...	...	...
Berlin Südkreuz d.	0948	1017	1054	1124	1135	1217	1238	1324	1347	1417	1438	1524	1535	1617	1638	1725	1747	1817	1838	1925	...	2017	...	2125	...	2227
Berlin Hbf **837** d.	1005	1036	1106	1138	1205	1236	1306	1338	1405	1436	1506	1538	1605	1636	1706	1738	1805	1836	1906	1938	...	2037	...	2137	...	2238
Berlin Spandau **837** d.	1014	1046	1117	1147	1214	1246	1316	1347	1415	1446	1516	1547	1614	1646	1716	1748	1815	1846	1916	1947	...	2046	...	2147	...	2248
Wittenberge **837** d.	|	|	1201	|	|	|	1401	|	|	|	1601	|	|	|	1801	|	|	|	2001	|	...	|	...	2229	...	2328
Ludwigslust **837** d.	|	|	1220	|	|	|	1420	|	|	|	1620	|	|	|	1820	|	|	|	2020	|	...	|	...	2248	...	2347
Büchen **830** d.	|	|	1249	|	|	|	1450	|	|	|	1650	|	|	|	1850	|	|	|	2050	|	...	|	...	|	...	|
Hamburg Hbf **830** a.	1151	1222	1311	1324	1351	1423	1512	1524	1600	1622	1711	1724	1757	1822	1912	1924	1951	2023	2117	2125	...	2222	...	2334	...	0032
Hamburg Altona a.	...	1236	1324	1341	1404	1438	1524	1539	1620	1638	...	1740	1812	1838	|	1940	2013	2038	2135	2139	...	...	...	2349	...	0047
Kiel Hbf **820** a.	...	1348	...	...	...	...	...	...	...	...	...	...	...	...	2022	...	...	...	...	...	...	...	...	...	...	...

A – [12] Hamburg - Berlin - Leipzig - Erfurt - Frankfurt - Stuttgart - München.
B – To/from Budapest (Table **60**).
C – [12] (Erfurt ①–⑤ -) Leipzig - Berlin - Hamburg.
D – [12] Hamburg - Berlin (- Leipzig - Erfurt Ⓑ) (- München ⑤).
E – [12] (Eisenach ①–⑤ -) Leipzig - Berlin - Hamburg.
F – From/to Flensburg (Table **823**).
G – [12] Hamburg - Halle - Erfurt - Nürnberg - Wien and v.v.
H – [12] (Stuttgart ① -) Darmstadt - Frankfurt - Erfurt - Berlin - Hamburg.
J – To/from Jena (Table **849a**).
L – [12] München - Nürnberg - Berlin - Hamburg - Lübeck and v.v.
M – To/from München via Erfurt (Table **850**).
N – To/from Nürnberg via Erfurt (Table **850**).
S – [12] Hamburg - Halle - Erfurt - Frankfurt - Saarbrücken.
U – From/to Westerland (Table **821**).
b – Not ⑥.
d – Not Aug. 1.
z – Diverted via Salzwedel on Aug. 1 (see page 608).

841 MAGDEBURG - STENDAL - UELZEN and WITTENBERGE

RE/*S-Bahn* services

SERVICE TO AUGUST 1. For amended service from August 2 see page 606.

km																											
		Ⓐ	①–⑥	Ⓐ			⚒	Ⓐ			A				⚒			★			Ⓐ					Ⓐ	
0	**Magdeburg** Hbf d.	...	0347	...	0447	0510	0540	0610	0610	0640	0659	...	0710	0740	0810	0810	0840	0857	0910	0940	1010	1010	1040	1110	1140	1210	1210
58	Stendal Hbf a.	...	0430	...	0530	0558	0625	0658	0658	0725	0734	...	0758	0825	0858	0858	0925	0933	0958	1025	1058	1058	1125	1158	1225	1258	1258
58	Stendal Hbf d.	0408	0432	0508	0532	0601	0633	0701	...	0726	0736	...	0801	0833	0901	...	0932	0935	1001	1033	1101	...	1132	1201	1233	1301	...
113	**Wittenberge** a.	0452	|	0551	|	0648	|	0746	...	|	|	←	0848	|	0945	...	|	1009	1048	|	1148	...	|	1248	|	1348	...
116	Salzwedel d.	...	0508	...	0608	...	0708	...	...	0800	0804	0809	...	0908	...	...	1008	...	...	1108	...	...	1208	...	1308	...	...
167	**Uelzen** a.	...	0541	...	0641	...	0741	...	...	→	0830	0841	...	0941	...	...	1041	...	...	1141	...	...	1241	...	1341	...	...

				Ⓐ					Ⓐ			★			Ⓐ					Ⓐ							
Magdeburg Hbf d.	1240	1310	1340	1410	1410	1440	1510	1540	1610	1610	1640	1658	1710	1740	1810	1810	1840	1910	1940	2010	2010	2040	2110	2140	2210	...	2310
Stendal Hbf a.	1325	1358	1425	1458	1458	1525	1558	1625	1658	1658	1725	1733	1758	1825	1858	1858	1925	1958	2025	2058	2058	2125	2158	2225	2258	...	2358
Stendal Hbf d.	1332	1401	1433	1501	...	1532	1601	1633	1701	...	1732	...	1801	1833	1901	...	1932	2001	2033	2101	...	2132	2201	2233	...	...	...
Wittenberge a.	|	1448	|	1545	...	|	1648	|	1746	...	|	...	1848	|	1948	...	|	2048	|	2148	...	|	2248	|	...	...	...
Salzwedel d.	1408	...	1508	...	...	1608	...	1708	...	...	1808	...	...	1908	...	...	2008	...	2108	...	...	2208	...	2308	...	...	...
Uelzen a.	1441	...	1541	...	...	1641	...	1748	...	...	1841	...	...	1941	...	...	2041	...	...	...	...	2241	...	...	...	...	...

	Ⓐ		①–⑥		Ⓐ			Ⓐ	①–⑥				Ⓐ			★			⚒					Ⓐ			
Uelzen d.	...	...	...	...	...	...	...	...	0617	...	0717	...	...	0809	...	...	0917	...	...	1017	...	1117	...	...	1217	...	1317
Salzwedel d.	...	...	0454	...	...	0550	...	...	0651	...	0751	...	...	0851	...	...	0951	...	...	1051	...	1151	...	...	1251	...	1351
Wittenberge d.	...	...	|	...	0500	|	...	0610	|	0710	|	...	0810	|	0910	0949	|	...	1010	|	1110	|	...	1210	|	1310	|
Stendal Hbf a.	...	...	0530	...	0542	0628	...	0652	0726	0752	0828	...	0852	0926	0952	1020	1028	...	1052	1126	1152	1228	...	1252	1326	1352	1428
Stendal Hbf d.	0357	0457	0532	0557	0557	0632	0657	0657	0732	0757	0832	0857	0857	0932	0957	1022	1032	1057	1057	1132	1157	1232	1257	1257	1332	1357	1432
Magdeburg Hbf a.	0445	0545	0615	0645	0645	0715	0745	0745	0815	0845	0915	0945	0945	1015	1045	1057	1115	1145	1145	1215	1245	1315	1345	1345	1415	1445	1515

		Ⓐ			★			Ⓐ			ⒷB			Ⓐ					Ⓐ					Ⓐ			
Uelzen d.	...	...	1417	...	...	1517	...	...	1617	...	1730	1717	...	...	1817	...	1917	...	...	2017	...	2102	...	...	...	...	2302
Salzwedel d.	...	...	1451	...	...	1551	...	...	1651	...	1758	1751	...	...	1851	...	1951	...	...	2051	...	2135	...	...	...	...	2335
Wittenberge d.	...	1410	|	1510	1549	|	...	1610	|	1710	|	|	...	1810	|	1910	|	...	2010	|	2110	|	...	2210	...	2307	|
Stendal Hbf a.	...	1452	1526	1552	1620	1628	...	1652	1726	1752	1824	1832	...	1852	1926	1952	2028	...	2052	2126	2152	2212	...	2252	...	2348	0005
Stendal Hbf d.	1457	1457	1532	1557	1622	1632	1657	1657	1732	1757	1826	1833	1857	1857	1932	1957	2032	2057	2057	2132	2157	2223	2257	2257	...	...	0007
Magdeburg Hbf a.	1545	1545	1615	1645	1657	1715	1745	1745	1815	1845	1904	1915	1945	1945	2015	2045	2115	2145	2145	2212	2245	2302	2345	2345	...	...	0046

A – ①–⑥ (not June 9). *IC* **2230**. To Hamburg (Table **900**).
B – Ⓑ (not June 8). *IC* **2233**. From Hamburg (Table **900**).
★ – *IC* service (see also Table **866**).

842 LEIPZIG - DRESDEN

SERVICE UNTIL AUGUST 9. For amended service from August 10 see page 607.

	EN 40459	EC 459		IC 2249	IC 2449	ICE 1553	IC 2447	ICE 1555	IC 2245	ICE 1557	IC 2243	ICE 1559	IC 2241	ICE 1651	IC 1931	IC 2059	ICE 1653	IC 2057	ICE 1655	IC 2055	ICE 1657			
				①–⑤		①–⑥									⑤					Ⓑ				
	Ⓡ A	B		🍷	M 🍷	E ✕	H 🍷	✕	K 🍷	✕	K 🍷	✕	K 🍷	✕	F 🍷	K 🍷	✕	K 🍷	✕	K ✕				
Wiesbaden Hbf **911** d.	...	...	...	...	...	...	...	0627	...	0826	...	1026	...	1226	...	...	1426	...	1626	...	1826	...	...	...
Frankfurt (Main) Hbf **850** d.	0027●	0027●	...	...	...	...	...	0718	...	0918	...	1118	...	1318	...	...	1518	...	1718	...	1918	...	...	...
Leipzig Hbf d.	0545	0545	...	0631	0731	0831	0931	1031	1131	1231	1331	1431	1531	1631	1653	1731	1831	1931	2031	2131	2231	...	...	...
Riesa d.	0623	0623	...	0701	0801	0901	1001	1101	1201	1301	1401	1501	1601	1701	1732	1801	1901	2001	2101	2201	2301	...	...	...
Dresden Neustadt a.	0659	0659	...	0730	0830	0930	1051	1130	1251	1330	1451	1530	1630	1730	1829	1831f	1930	2030	2130	2230	2330	...	...	...
Dresden Hbf a.	0706	0706	...	0738	0838	0939	1057	1139	1257	1339	1457	1539	1638	1739	1836	1840f	1938	2039	2139	2238	2339	...	...	...

	IC 2054	ICE 1654	IC 2056	ICE 1652	IC 2058	ICE 1650	IC 2240	ICE 1558	IC 2242	ICE 1556	IC 1934	IC 2244	ICE 1554	IC 2446	ICE 1552	IC 2448	IC 2448		EN 40458	EC 458				
			①–⑥								⑦					Ⓑ	⑥							
	K ✕	✕	K 🍷	✕	K 🍷	✕	K 🍷	✕	K 🍷	✕	G 🍷	K 🍷	✕	H	✕	H 🍷	🍷		Ⓡ A	B				
Dresden Hbf d.	0511	0610	0711	0810	0845	1010	1045	1210	1245	1410	1444	1511	1610	1712	1810	1845	1845	...	2102	2102	...	...	...	...
Dresden Neustadt d.	0519	0619	0719	0819	0852	1019	1052	1219	1252	1419	1449	1519	1619	1720	1819	1852	1852	...	2109	2109	...	...	...	...
Riesa d.	0547	0649	0747	0849	0947	1049	1147	1249	1347	1449	1524	1547	1649	1747	1849	1947	1947	...	2143	2143	...	...	...	...
Leipzig Hbf a.	0621	0726	0821	0926	1021	1126	1221	1326	1421	1526	1554	1621	1726	1821	1926	2021	2021	...	2218	2218	...	...	...	...
Frankfurt (Main) Hbf **850** a.	...	1036	...	1236	...	1436	...	1636	...	1836	...	...	2036	...	2236	...	...	...	0335●	0335●	...	...	...	...
Wiesbaden Hbf **911** a.	...	1133	...	1333	...	1533	...	1733	...	1933	...	...	2133	...	...	...	...	...	...	...	...	...	...	...

RE services until Aug. 9. For service from August 10 see page 607.

km		⚒		⚒				
0	**Leipzig** Hbf d.	0400	0500	0600	0700		2200	2308
26	Wurzen d.	0418	0518	0618	0718	and	2218	2326
53	Oschatz d.	0436	0536	0636	0736		2236	2344
66	Riesa d.	0454r	0554r	0654r	0754r	hourly	2254r	2354
102	Coswig **843 856 857** d.	0527	0627	0727	0827		2327	0027
110	Radebeul Ost **857** d.	|	|	|	|	until	|	|
116	**Dresden** Neustadt **856/7** a.	0535	0635	0735	0835		2335	0035
120	**Dresden** Hbf **843 856 857** a.	0543	0643	0743	0843		2343	0043

	⚒		⚒				Ⓐ	Ⓒ	
Dresden Hbf. **843 856 857** d.	0410	0507	0607	0707		2107	2207	2207	2307
Dresden Neustadt **856/7** d.	0417	0515	0615	0715	and	2115	2215	2215	2315
Radebeul Ost **857** d.	0423	|	|	|		|	|	|	|
Coswig **843 856 857** d.	0429	0529	0624v	0729	hourly	2124	2224	2229	2324
Riesa d.	0506r	0606r	0706r	0806r		2206r	2306r	2306r	0006
Oschatz d.	0514	0614	0714	0814	until	2214	2314	2314	0014
Wurzen d.	0532	0632	0732	0832		2232	2332	2332	0032
Leipzig Hbf a.	0550	0650	0750	0850		2250	2350	2350	0050

A – CANOPUS – 1, 2 cl. and 2 cl. Zürich - Basel - Leipzig - Dresden - Praha and v.v.
B – [2] Zürich - Basel - Leipzig - Dresden - Praha and v.v.; also conveys [1] and ✕ Leipzig - Dresden - Praha and v.v.
E – From Erfurt on ⑥ (Table **850**).
F – From Oldenburg via Bremen and Hannover (Tables **813** and **866**).
G – [12] Dresden - Magdeburg - Hannover - Bremen - Emden.
H – To/from Hannover (Table **866**).
K – To/from Köln via Hannover on Aug. 9 (Tables **800**, **810** and **866**). To/from Hannover (Table **866**) on June 7 - Aug. 8.
M – From Magdeburg (Table **866**).
f – 12–16 minutes later on ⑤.
r – Arrives 8–10 minutes earlier.
v – 0629 on ⑥.
● – Frankfurt (Main) **Süd** (not Hbf).
☛ Dresden times may vary June 24 - July 11.

ƎE / RB services ELSTERWERDA - CHEMNITZ and DRESDEN; DÖBELN - LEIPZIG 843

ELSTERWERDA - CHEMNITZ *Operated by Mitteldeutsche Regiobahn*

km																									
		Ⓐ	Ⓐ		Ⓐ		Ⓐ		Ⓐ		Ⓐ		Ⓐ		Ⓐ		Ⓐ		Ⓐ						
0	**Elsterwerda** d.	...	0513	...	0613	...	0713	0813	...	1013	...	1213	...	1413	1513	1613	1713	1813	1913	2013	...	...	2213	...	...
24	Riesa a.	...	0538	...	0638	...	0738	0838	...	1038	...	1238	...	1438	1538	1638	1738	1838	1938	2038	...	...	2238	...	...
24	Riesa d.	0448	0548	0548	0648	0648	0748	0848	0948	1048	1148	1248	1348	1448	1548	1648	1748	1848	1948	2048	...	2153	2253	...	...
50	Döbeln Hbf d.	0509	0609	0609	0709	0709	0809	0909	1009	1109	1209	1309	1409	1509	1609	1709	1809	1909	2009	2109	...	2218	2318	...	...
91	**Chemnitz** Hbf a.	0544	0645	0644	0745	0745	0845	0945	1045	1145	1245	1345	1445	1545	1645	1745	1845	1945	2045	2145	...	2258	2358	...	...

	Ⓐ		Ⓐ		Ⓐ		Ⓐ		Ⓐ		Ⓐ		Ⓐ		Ⓐ					Ⓐ				
hemnitz Hbf d.	0409	0509	0509	0609	0709	0809	0909	1009	1109	1209	1309	1409	1509	1609	1709	1809	1909	2009	...	2137	2237	...	...	...
öbeln Hbf d.	0447	0547	0547	0647	0749	0847	0947	1047	1147	1247	1347	1447	1547	1647	1747	1847	1947	2047	...	2219	2319	...	...	...
esa a.	0509	0609	0609	0709	0810	0909	1009	1109	1209	1309	1409	1509	1609	1709	1809	1909	2009	2109	...	2240	2340	...	...	...
esa d.	0514	...	0614	0714	...	0914	...	1114	...	1314	1414	1514	1614	1714	1814	1914	2014	...	...	2249	...	...	...	...
sterwerda a.	0536	...	0636	0736	...	0936	...	1136	...	1337	1436	1536	1636	1736	1836	1936	2036	...	...	2311	...	...	...	...

ELSTERWERDA - DRESDEN

km									
		Ⓐ		Ⓐ	Ⓐ				
0	**Elsterwerda-Biehla** d.	0439	...	0539	0639	0739	0937	and every	2337
2	Elsterwerda d.	0445	0545	0545	0645	0744	0945	**two** hours	2345
41	Coswig ▷ d.	0523	0623	0623	0723	0823	1023	until	0023
59	**Dresden** Neustadt ▷ a.	0545	0647	0647	0745	0845r	1047		0047

	§	Ⓐ	n	K	J		⊠		Ⓐ	
Dresden Neustadt ▷ d.	0457	0607	0707	0907	0910	1107	and every	2107	2207	2307
Coswig ▷ d.	0520	0630	0730	0930	0942j	1130	**two** hours	2130	2230	2330
Elsterwerda a.	0558	0708	0808	1008	1032	1208	until	2208	2308	0008
Esterwerda-Biehla a.	0613	0713	0813	1013	1037	1213		2213	2321e	...

DÖBELN - LEIPZIG *Operated by Mitteldeutsche Regiobahn*

km										
		Ⓐ	Ⓐ		Ⓐ		Ⓐ			
0	**Döbeln** Hbf d.	0450	0550	0650	0750	and hourly	1850	1950	2050	...
13	Leisnig d.	0502	0602	0702	0802	on Ⓐ,	1902	2002	2102	...
28	Großbothen d.	0517	0617	0717	0817	every **two**	1917	2017	2117	...
35	Grimma ob Bf d.	0526	0626	0726	0826	hours on	1926	2026	2126	2308
66	**Leipzig** Hbf a.	0600	0700	0800	0900	Ⓒ until	2000	2100	2200	2342

	Ⓐ		Ⓐ			Ⓐ			
Leipzig Hbf d.	0506	0606	0706	and hourly	1806	1906	2006	2106	2206
Grimma ob Bf d.	0541	0641	0741	on Ⓐ,	1841	1941	2041	2139	2240
Großbothen d.	0547	0647	0747	every **two**	1847	1947	2047	...	2246
Leisnig d.	0604	0704	0804	hours on	1904	2004	2104	...	2300
Döbeln Hbf a.	0617	0717	0817	Ⓒ until	1917	2017	2117	...	2313

– Until Aug. 9.
– From Aug. 10.
– Change trains at Elsterwerda on ⑤.

j – Arrives 7 minutes earlier.
n – Timings vary until Aug. 9 (Dresden N. d. 0657Ⓒ, 0710Ⓐ).
r – 0852 from Aug. 10.

⊠ – Additional service runs at 1607 on Ⓐ.
▷ – See also Tables **842**, **856**, **857**.
§ – Runs up to 10 mins later from Aug. 10.

ɔstdeutsche Eisenbahn (except *ICE* / *IC* services) STRALSUND - OSTSEEBAD BINZ / SASSNITZ 844

km																										
												ICE **1678** ⑥ R	*ICE* **1678** Ⓐ D	*ICE* **1078** ⑥t B			*ICE* **1974** ⑥ U§			*ICE* **1636** ⑤⑥ E	*IC* **2260** ♣ Tr	*ICE* **1714** ⑥ J♥	*ICE* **1714** ⑥ BU	*ICE* **714** ⑦ B		
		⚒	Ⓐ		Ⓐ	Ⓐ																				
	Rostock Hbf **830** d.	...	...	0454r	...	0553r	0700r	...	...	...	0900r	0938	0938	...	...	...	1049	1100r	...	...	1138	...	...	...	...	...
0	**Stralsund** Hbf d.	0000	0459	0559	...	0659	0800	...	0859	...	0959	1031	1031	1044	1059	...	1142	1159	...	1204	1238	1246	1244	1246	1259	...
29	Bergen auf Rügen d.	0030	0529	0629	...	0729	0830	...	0929	...	1029	1053	1055	1116	1129	...	1206	1229	...	1239	1305	1314	1316	1315	1329	...
39	Lietzow (Rügen) d.	0039	0538	0638	0640	0738	0839	0841	0937	0939	1038	...	|	|	1137	1139	|	1238	1241	|	|	|	|	|	1337	1339
	Ostseebad Binz a.	|	|	|	0654	*0755*	|	0855	0951	|	*1055*	...	1123	1137	1151	|	1232	|	1255	1300	1329	1333	1357	1335	1352	|
51	**Sassnitz** a.	0055	0554	0654	...	0753	0855	...	...	0954	1054	...	...	...	...	1154	...	1254	...	...	...	...	...	...	...	1354

			ICE **208** ①–⑤ G	*ICE* **1076** U B	*ICE* **1076** V B	*ICE* **208** ⑥⑦ G			*IC* **2474** ⑥⑦ ♣r§		*ICE* **932** ⑥⑦ C	*ICE* **1672** ①–⑥ F	*IC* **2262** ♣ Tr	*ICE* **1710** ♥ M	*ICE* **1074** ♣ B				*ICE* **1072** B	Y	Ⓐ			Ⓐ	Ⓐ	
Rostock Hbf **830** d.	1300r	...	1338	...	...	1342	...	...	1445	1500r	...	1538	1538	...	...	...	...	1700r	...	...	...	1900r	...	...	...	2100r
ralsund Hbf d.	1359	...	1437	1439	1449	1452	1459	...	1542	1559	1605	1631	1631	1640	1646	1659	...	1759	1840	1859	...	1959	...	2101	...	2159
ergen auf Rügen d.	1429	...	1504	1504	1514	1516	1529	...	1607	1629	1638	1655	1655	1706	1715	1729	...	1829	1906	1929	...	2029	...	2130	...	2229
etzow (Rügen) d.	1438	1441	|	|	|	|	1537	1539	|	1638	|	|	|	|	|	1737	1739	1838	|	1937	1939	2038	2041	2138	2140	2238
Ostseebad Binz a.	|	1455	1529	1530	1537	1539z	1552	|	1631	*1655*	1700	1720	1720	1733	1735	1752	|	*1855*	1929	1952	|	|	2055	2153	|	*2255*
ssnitz a.	1454	...	...	...	...	...	...	1554	...	1654	...	...	...	...	...	...	1754	1854	...	...	1954	2054	...	...	2155	2254

km																										
										ICE **1073** B	*ICE* **1671** F					*ICE* **1711** ♥ M	*ICE* **1071** ♣ B	*ICE* **203** ♥ Q	*IC* **2263** ♣ Tr	*ICE* **933** ⑥⑦ A			*IC* **2479** 🍷 r§			*ICE* **1075** Bf
		Ⓐ		Ⓐ	⚒			Ⓐ	Ⓐ																	
	Sassnitz d.	0350	0501	...	0601	...	0701	0758	...	...	...	...	0901	0959	...	...	...	...	...	...	1059	...	...	1159	...	...
0	**Ostseebad Binz** d.	|	|	0600	|	0659	|	|	0803	0819	0826	0900	|	|	1002	1021	1021	1043	1043	1055	|	1104	1114	|	1203	1219
12	Lietzow (Rügen) d.	0406	0517	0614	0618	0713	0717	0813	0818	0842	0855	0913	0917	1014	1019	|	|	|	|	|	1114	1120	|	1214	1219	|
22	Bergen auf Rügen d.	0415	0526	...	0627	...	0726	...	0827	|	|	...	0926	...	1028	1043	1043	1108	1108	1118	...	1129	1144	...	1228	1242
51	**Stralsund** Hbf a.	0445	0556	...	0656	...	0756	...	0857	0905	0921	...	0956	...	1057	1109	1109	1132	1132	1144	...	1157	1210	...	1257	1306
	Rostock Hbf **830** a.	0547r	0654r	...	...	...	0855r	...	...	...	1019	...	1055r	...	...	...	...	...	1240	...	...	1255r	1314	...	...	...

	ICE **1675** F			*ICE* **1971** ⑥ U§			*ICE* **1715** ⑤–⑦ B¶	*IC* **2265** ♣ Tr					*ICE* **1077** ⑤⑦ B	*ICE* **1717** ⑥ L							Ⓐ	Ⓐ			Ⓐ	Y
ssnitz d.	...	...	1302	...	1359	...	...	...	...	1502	1559	...	...	...	1659	...	1759	...	...	1902	1959	...	...	2101	2200	...
Ostseebad Binz d.	1226	1300	|	1318	|	1403	1420	1427	1500	|	|	1602	1620	1620	|	1703	|	1803	1900	|	|	2003	2100	|	|	2204
etzow (Rügen) d.	|	1314	1318	|	1414	1419	|	|	1514	1518	1614	1618	|	|	1714	1719	1814	1819	1914	1918	2014	2019	2114	2118	2215	2220
ergen auf Rügen d.	1255	...	1327	1350	...	1428	1443	1457	...	1527	...	1627	1642	1642	...	1728	...	1828	...	1927	...	2028	...	2127	...	2229
ralsund Hbf a.	1321	...	1357	1413	...	1457	1506	1521	...	1557	...	1657	1705	1705	...	1757	...	1857	...	1957	...	2057	...	2158	...	2258
Rostock Hbf **830** a.	1419	...	1455r	1514	...	...	...	1627	...	1655r	...	1801r	...	...	...	1855r	...	...	...	2055r	...	...	...	2255r	...	...

– 🄬 ✕ Ostseebad Binz - Berlin - Erfurt - Frankfurt.
– From/to Berlin (Table **845**).
– 🄬 ✕ Saarbrücken - Frankfurt - Erfurt - Berlin - Ostseebad Binz.
– ①–⑤ until Aug. 1. 🄬 ✕ (Hannover ①–⑤ -) Hamburg - Ostseebad Binz.
– From Eisenach via Berlin (Tables **845** and **850**).
– Until Aug. 1. 🄬 ✕ Ostseebad Binz - Hamburg - Hannover - Frankfurt and v.v.
– Until Aug. 1. 🄬 ✕ Köln - Hamburg - Ostseebad Binz.

J – 🄬 ✕ Jena - Leipzig - Berlin - Ostseebad Binz.
L – To Leipzig via Berlin (Tables **845** and **850**).
M – 🄬 ✕ München - Nürnberg - Berlin - Ostseebad Binz and v.v.
Q – 🄬 ✕ Ostseebad Binz - Hamburg - Köln - Karlsruhe - Basel.
R – ⑥ until July 26. From Hamburg (Table **830**).
T – From/to Hamburg (Table **830**).
U – ⑥ Aug. 2-30.
V – Daily except dates in note **U**.
Y – ①–⑤ (daily June 23 - Sept. 6).

f – Daily to Nov. 1; ⑥ Nov. 8 - Dec. 13.
r – Not Sept. 6 - Nov. 7.
t – Also Oct. 3; not Oct. 4.
z – 1557 on ⑥.

¶ – Train number **715** on ⑦.
§ – From/to Berlin via Rostock (Table **835**).
♥ – Until Aug. 1.
♣ – From Aug. 2.

ɾeßnitztalbahn BERGEN AUF RÜGEN - PUTBUS - LAUTERBACH and RÜGENSCHE BÄDERBAHN 844a

km										
		Ⓐ	Ⓐ							
0	**Bergen** auf Rügen d.	0640	0740	0840	and	1840	...	2040	...	...
10	**Putbus** a.	0649	0749	0849	hourly	1849	...	2049	...	...
12	**Lauterbach** Mole a.	0654	0754	0854	until	1854	...	...	...	...

	Ⓐ	Ⓐ	Ⓐ						
Lauterbach Mole d.	0600	0700	0800	...	0900	and	1900	...	...
Putbus d.	0611	0711	0811	0811	0911	hourly	1911	...	...
Bergen auf Rügen a.	0620	0720	0820	0820	0920	until	1920	...	...

ÜGENSCHE BÄDERBAHN **SERVICE MAY 10 - NOVEMBER 2.** Steam train service. Please note that Binz Lokalbahn station is situated approx. 2 km from Ostseebad Binz DB station.

km											
											A
0	**Lauterbach** Mole d.	...	...	...	1122	1322	1522	...	1722	1922	...
2	**Putbus** a.	...	...	...	1129	1329	1529	...	1729	1929	...
2	**Putbus** d.	0808	...	1008	1208	1408	1608	...	1808	2008	...
14	Binz Lokalbahn ♥ d.	0840	0944	1040	1240	1440	1640	1744	1840	2040	2244
22	Sellin (Rügen) Ost ♥ d.	0909	1013	1109	1309	1509	1709	1813	1909	2109	2313
27	**Göhren** (Rügen) ♥ a.	0923	1027	1123	1323	1523	1723	1827	1923	2123	2327

										A
Göhren (Rügen) ♥ d.	0849	0953	1153	1353	1553	1649	1753	1849	1953	2149
Sellin (Rügen) Ost ♥ d.	0907	1011	1211	1411	1611	1707	1811	1907	2011	2207
Binz Lokalbahn ♥ d.	0933	1040	1240	1440	1640	1733	1840	1936	2040	2233
Putbus a.	...	1106	1306	1506	1706	...	1906	2002	2106	...
Putbus d.	...	1111	1311	1511	1711	...	1911	...	...	...
Lauterbach Mole a.	...	1117	1317	1517	1717	...	1917	...	...	...

– May 24 - Aug. 31.

♥ – Additional journeys Binz Lokalbahn - Göhren: **From Binz** at 1144, 1344 and 1544. **From Göhren** at 1049, 1249 and 1449.

845 BERLIN - ANGERMÜNDE - STRALSUND and SZCZECIN

RE services except where shown

km		●	⚒	R◇	*ICE* 1179 ①–⑥ T§		◇		●		*ICE* 1078 ⑥b ✕	Ⓑ ◇	⑥ ◇	Ⓒ A	G	*ICE* 1636 ⑤⑥r E✕	*ICE* 1636 ⑤⑥t E✕		Ⓒ ◇	Ⓐ ◇	*ICE* 1714 ⑥ J✕	*ICE* 714 ⑦ ✕	Ⓒ A	●		*ICE* 107… ✕
0	**Berlin** Südkreuz d.	0028	...	...	...	...	...	0520	0623	0721	0736	...	...	...	0825	0852	0852	0920	...	...	0935*	0936	...	1024	1119z	...
6	**Berlin** Hbf d.	0036	...	...	...	0426	...	0532	0633	0731	0744	...	...	0803	0833	0909	0903	0931	...	...	0943	0944	0957	1033	1132	114…
10	**Berlin** Gesundbrunnen d.	0043	...	...	...	0433	...	0538	0639	0737	0750	...	...	0809	0839	0916	0909	0937	...	...	0951	0951	1009j	1039	1139	115…
31	Bernau (b. Berlin) d.	0057	...	...	...	0448	...	0553	0654	0754	|	...	...	0823	0854	|	0923	0952	...	...	1005	1005	1023	1054	1153	120…
53	Eberswalde Hbf d.	0118	...	...	...	0509	...	0609	0709	0809	0823	...	...	0838	0909	0955	0945	1008	...	...	1023	1023	1038	1109	1209	122…
79	Angermünde a.	0138c	...	...	...	0528	...	0628	0729	0828	0838	...	...	0858	0929	1009	1000	1028	...	...	1039	1039	1054	1129	1228	123…
	Angermünde d.	0140c	...	...	...	0533	...	0634	0733	0834	0840	...	...	0900	0933	1012	1002	1033	...	...	1041	1041	1056	1133	1234	124…
102	**Schwedt** (Oder) a.	0202c	...	...	...	|	...	0656	|	0856	|	...	...	|	|	|	|	1056	...	...	|	|	|	|	1256	|
	Prenzlau d.	...	...	...	...	0601	...	...	0801	...	0905	...	...	0930	1001	|	|	...	...	...	1105	1105	1126	1201	...	130…
	Pasewalk d.	...	0418	0511	...	0620	0713	...	0819	...	0921	0907	0907	0951	1019	1049	1039	...	1107	1108	1121	1121	1148j	1219	...	132…
	Anklam d.	...	0451	0544	...	0651	0745	...	0850	...	0947	0944	1000j	1022	1050	1115	1105	...	1141	1144	1152j	1152j	1231v	1250	...	134…
	Züssow d.	...	0505	0556	...	0704	0800	...	0903	...	0959	1000	1014	1035	1103	1129	1119	...	1154	1157	1204	1204	1244	1303	...	135…
	Greifswald d.	...	0522	0611	0702	0720	0815	...	0919	...	1012	1015	1029	1052	1119	1143	1133	...	1228x	1213	1216	1216	1303	1319	...	141…
	Stralsund Hbf a.	...	0544	0635	0724	0744	0840	...	0941	...	1037	1043	1053	1113	1141	1202	1153	...	1253	1237	1237	1237	1324	1341	...	143…
	Ostseebad Binz **844** a.	...	...	...	...	...	...	...	...	...	1137	...	...	...	...	1309	1300	...	...	...	1333e	1335	...	...	...	153…

	R◇	●	*ICE* 932 ⑥⑦ S✕		*ICE* 1710 Y M✕	*ICE* 1074 Z ✕	◇	●		*ICE* 1072 ✕	◇	●		⑥ ◇	*ICE* 1070 Ⓑ ✕	Ⓑ ◇	●		◇	●		⑦–④ ●	⑤⑥ ●	⑦–④	⑦	
Berlin Südkreuz d.	...	1224	1252	1319	1324	...	...	1424	1519	...	...	1624	1720	...	1735	...	1824	1920k	...	2024	2119z	2224	2224	...	...	...
Berlin Hbf d.	...	1233	1304	1331	1342	1342	...	1433	1531	1544	...	1633	1732	...	1743	...	1833	1941	...	2033	2133	2233	2233	...	...	233…
Berlin Gesundbrunnen d.	...	1239	1310	1338	1349	1349	...	1439	1538	1550	...	1639	1738	...	1749	...	1839	1949	...	2039	2139	2238	2238	...	...	233…
Bernau (b. Berlin) d.	...	1254	|	1353	1402	1402	...	1454	1553	1605	...	1653	1753	...	1803	...	1854	2002	...	2054	2153	2253	2253	...	...	235…
Eberswalde Hbf d.	...	1309	1337	1409	1417	1417	...	1509	1609	1623	...	1709	1809	...	1823	...	1909	2017	...	2109	2214	2314	2314	...	...	001…
Angermünde a.	...	1329	1353	1428	1433	1433	...	1529	1629	1640	...	1729	1828	...	1839	...	1929	2035	...	2129	2234	2332	2332	...	...	...
Angermünde d.	...	1333	1355	1434	1435	1435	...	1533	1634	1642	...	1733	1834	...	1842	...	1933	2037	...	2133	2236	2334	2334	2340	2340	...
Schwedt (Oder) a.	...	|	|	1456	|	|	...	|	1656	|	...	|	1856	...	|	...	|	2059	...	|	2258	2357	|	|	|	...
Prenzlau d.	...	1401	1418	...	1500	1500	...	1601	...	1705	...	1801	...	...	1905	...	2001	...	...	2201	...	...	0003	0008	0008	...
Pasewalk d.	1309	1419	1435	...	1517	1520	1505	1619	...	1721	1709	1819	...	1907	1921	1907	2019	...	2109	2219	...	...	0019	0024	0026	...
Anklam d.	1357	1450	1504	...	1543	1553	1555	1650	...	1747	1757	1850	...	1943	1947	1958	2051	...	2140	2250	...	...	...	...	0058	...
Züssow d.	1409	1503	1516	...	1557	1605	1607	1703	...	1759	1810	1903	...	1959	1959	2011	2104	...	2153	2303	...	...	...	...	0111	...
Greifswald d.	1423	1519	1532	...	1610	1618	1622	1719	...	1812	1826	1919	...	2015	2012	2027	2120	...	2209	2319	...	...	...	...	0126	...
Stralsund Hbf a.	1447	1541	1552	...	1630	1638	1647	1741	...	1833	1850	1941	...	2040	2033	2051	2142	...	2233	2341	...	...	...	...	0148	...
Ostseebad Binz **844** a.	...	...	1700	...	1733	1735	...	...	...	...	...	...	...	...	...	...	...	...	...	...	...	...	...	...	...	...

km			●	①	Ⓐ	⚒		●	◇		●	Ⓒ ◇	Ⓐ ◇	*ICE* 839 ①–⑤ F✕		*ICE* 1073 ✕	●	R◇		*ICE* 1711 Y M✕	*ICE* 1071 Z ✕	●	◇	*ICE* 933 ⑥⑦d F✕	*ICE* 933 ⑥⑦s F✕	
	Ostseebad Binz **844** d.	...	...	...	...	...	...	...	...	...	...	...	...	...	...	0819	...	...	...	1021	1021	...	...	1055	1056	...
0	**Stralsund** Hbf d.	...	...	0402	...	0416	...	...	0516	0616	...	0726	0726	0804	0816	0914	...	0926	1016	1115	1115	...	1127	1150	1207	121…
31	Greifswald d.	...	...	0422	...	0438	...	...	0542	0638	...	0752	0752	0828	0838	0938	...	0952	1038	1140	1140	...	1152	1214	1229	124…
49	Züssow d.	...	...	0437	...	0455	...	...	0557	0655	...	0807	0819v	0847	0857	0953	...	1007	1055	1155	1154	...	1218v	1234	1242	125…
66	Anklam d.	...	...	0448	...	0507	...	...	0608	0707	...	0819	0831	|	0909	1007	...	1020	1107	1208	1207	...	1232	1246	1253	130…
109	**Pasewalk** d.	...	...	0517j	0517	0544j	0544	...	0642	0744j	...	0853	0902	0925	0944j	1038	...	1051	1144j	1238	1238	...	1300	1321	1321	134…
133	Prenzlau d.	...	...	0534	0534	0601	0601	...	...	0801	...	...	...	0942	1003	1054	...	...	1201	1254	1254	...	...	1337	1337	140…
	Schwedt (Oder) d.	...	0506	|	|	|	|	0706	...	|	0906	...	...	|	|	|	1106	...	|	|	|	1306	...	|	|	|
170	Angermünde a.	...	0528	0601	0601	0628	0628	0728	...	0828	0928	...	...	1003	1030	1115	1128	...	1228	1315	1315	1328	...	1359	1359	143…
	Angermünde d.	0427a	0533	0603	0603	0633	0633	0733	...	0833	0933	...	...	1005	1032	1117	1133	...	1233	1317	1317	1333	...	1401	1401	143…
196	Eberswalde Hbf d.	0448	0553	0623	0623	0654	0654	0753	...	0854	0953	...	...	1022	1053	1134	1153	...	1254	1334	1335	1353	...	1418	1418	145…
218	Bernau (b. Berlin) d.	0509	0607	0640	0640	0708	0708	0807	...	0908	1007	...	...	|	1107	|	1207	...	1308	1349	1349	1407	...	|	|	150…
239	**Berlin** Gesundbrunnen a.	0522	0621	0656	0656	0722	0722	0821	...	0922	1021	...	...	1047	1120	1159	1222	...	1322	1407	1406	1422	...	1444	1444	152…
243	**Berlin** Hbf a.	0528	0628	0706	0706	0730	0730	0828	...	0928	1028	...	...	1056	1126	1208	1228	...	1328	1413	1413	1428	...	1450	1450	152…
249	**Berlin** Südkreuz a.	0541	0639	0717	0717	0742	0742	0839	...	0942	1039	...	...	1105	1142	1218	1239	...	1342	1434	...	1439	...	1505	1505	154…

	Ⓒ A	*ICE* 1075 ✕	●	Ⓒ ◇	Ⓐ ◇		Ⓒ A	*ICE* 1715 ⑤⑥ m✕	*ICE* 715 ⑦ ✕	●	◇		*ICE* 1077 ⑤⑦ ✕n	*ICE* 1717 ⑥ L✕	●	R◇		*ICE* 1074 Ⓑ T	●	◇	●		⑤⑥ H	◇	⑤⑥ V	⑦
Ostseebad Binz **844** d.	...	1219f	...	...	...	...	...	1420	1420	...	...	...	1620	1620	...	...	...	...	...	...	...	...	...	...	...	...
Stralsund Hbf d.	1245	1314	...	1327	1327	1416	1441	1515	1515	...	1528	1616	1714	1714	...	1726	1816	1830	...	1923	2016	...	...	2126	2216	223…
Greifswald d.	1312	1337	...	1352	1352	1438	1503	1541	1541	...	1553	1638	1739	1739	...	1751	1838	1849	...	1949	2038	...	...	2152	2238	230…
Züssow d.	1328	1352	...	1406	1406	1455	1520	1556	1556	...	1618v	1655	1753	1753	...	1806	1855	...	...	2004	2055	...	...	2207	2255	231…
Anklam d.	1340	1406	...	1421	1431	1507	1533	1609	1609	...	1632	1707	1806	1806	...	1818	1907	...	...	2016	2107	...	...	2219	2307	232…
Pasewalk d.	1414	1438	...	1450	1500	1544j	1605	1639	1639	...	1700	1744j	1838	1838	...	1851	1944j	...	...	2049	2144j	...	...	2251	2344	240…
Prenzlau d.	1430	1454	...	...	...	1601	1623	1655	1655	...	...	1801	1854	1854	...	...	2001	...	...	...	2201	...	...	...	0001	...
Schwedt (Oder) d.	|	|	1506	...	...	|	|	|	|	1706	...	|	|	|	1905	...	|	...	2106	...	|	2306	2306	...	|	...
Angermünde a.	1456	1515	1528	...	...	1628	1650	1716	1716	1728	...	1828	1915	1915	1928	...	2028	...	2128	...	2228	2329	2329	...	0028	...
Angermünde d.	1458	1517	1533	...	...	1633	1655	1718	1718	1733	...	1833	1917	1917	1932	...	2033	...	2133	...	2233	2333	2333	...	0033	...
Eberswalde Hbf d.	1521	1534	1553	...	...	1654	1716	1736	1736	1753	...	1854	1934	1934	1952	...	2054	...	2153	...	2254	2353	2353	...	0054	...
Bernau (b. Berlin) d.	1536	|	1607	...	...	1708	1732	1751	1750	1808	...	1908	1949	1949	2007	...	2108	...	2207	...	2313	0008	0008	...	0113	...
Berlin Gesundbrunnen a.	1553	1559	1621	...	...	1722	1745	1808	1805	1822	...	1921	2007	2007	2021	...	2121	...	2222	...	2327	0021	0021	...	0127	...
Berlin Hbf a.	...	1605	1628	...	...	1728	...	1816	1816	1829	...	1928	2016	2015	2028	...	2127	...	2228	...	2332	0028	0028	...	0134	...
Berlin Südkreuz a.	...	1613	1639	...	...	1740	...	1823	1824	1839	...	1942	...	2034	2039	...	2142	...	2238	...	2341	...	0049	...	...	...

ANGERMÜNDE - SZCZECIN (all services are currently operated by 🚌).

	🚌 ⚒	🚌	🚌		🚌	🚌	🚌	🚌	🚌	🚌	
Angermünde d.	0438	0538	0638	and in the	1738	1838	1938	2038	2145	2345	...
Tantow d.	0550	0650	|	same pattern	1850	|	2050	|	2257	0057	...
Szczecin Gumience ▦ d.	0615	0715	0740	every **two**	1915	1940	2115	2140	2322	0122	...
Szczecin Głowny a.	0633	0733	0758	hours until	1933	1958	2133	2158	2340	0140	...

	🚌 ⚒	🚌	🚌		🚌	🚌	🚌	🚌
Szczecin Głowny d.	0326	0506	0526	and in the	1906	1926	2106	212…
Szczecin Gumience ▦ d.	0344	0524	0544	same pattern	1924	1944	2124	214…
Tantow d.	0409	|	0609	every **two**	|	2009	|	220…
Angermünde a.	0521	0626	0721	hours until	2026	2121	2226	232…

A – Until Nov. 2.
E – From Eisenach (Table **850**).
F – To Frankfurt (Table **850**).
G – From Lutherstadt Wittenberg (Table **851**). Starts from Halle on Ⓒ (Table **848**).
H – To Halle via Lutherstadt Wittenberg (Tables **848** and **851**).
J – From Jena via Leipzig (Tables **849a** and **850**).
L – To Leipzig (Table **850**). Also runs Oct. 3.
M – From/to München via Nürnberg (Table **850**).
R – To/from Rostock on dates in Table **830**.
S – From Saarbrücken via Frankfurt (Tables **850** and **919**).
T – Until Aug. 1. To/from Hamburg (Table **830**).
V – Runs ①–⑥ Stralsund - Pasewalk.
Y – Until Aug. 1.
Z – From Aug. 2.

a – Ⓐ only.
b – Also Oct. 3; not Oct. 4.
c – Ⓒ only.
d – ⑥⑦ Aug. 2 - 31.

e – 1357 on ⑥ Aug. 2 - 30; 1337 on ⑥ from Sept. 6.
f – Daily to Nov. 1; ⑥ Nov. 8 - Dec. 13.
j – Arrives 5 – 7 minutes earlier.
k – ⑥ only.
m – To München via Nürnberg (Table **850**) on ⑥ until July 26.
n – Also Oct. 2; not Oct. 3.
r – ⑤⑥ until July 26.
s – ⑥⑦ to Nov. 1 (not Aug. 2 - 31).
t – ⑤⑥ from Aug. 1 (also Oct. 2; not Oct. 4). On Aug. 1 does not call at Bernau.
v – Arrives 11 – 14 minutes earlier.
x – Arrives 1208.
z – Ⓒ only.

§ – Train number **1579** on ⑥.
■ – From Jüterbog (also Falkenberg on Ⓒ). See Table **851**.
● – From/to Lutherstadt Wittenberg (see Table **851**).
◇ – Operated by Ostdeutsche Eisenbahn.
* – 0924 until July 26.

ZÜSSOW - ŚWINOUJŚCIE — 846

2nd class only

km													
			⊠	⊕								A	⑦b
0	**Züssow** d.	0508	and	1508	1612	1708	1812	1908	2012	2108	2208	2308	2320
18	Wolgast d.	0531	hourly	1531	1631	1731	1831	1931	2031	2131	2231	2331	2338
28	Zinnowitz ▲ d.	0549	until	1549	1649	1749	1849	1949	2049	2149	2249	2349	2354
55	Seebad Heringsdorf a.	0625		1625	1725	1825	1925	2025	2125	2225	2325	0025	0028
57	Seebad Ahlbeck a.	0635		1635	1735	1835	1935	2035	*2135*	2235	...	...	...
61	**Świnoujście** Centrum a.	0640		1640	1740	1840	1940	2040	*2140*	2240	...	...	...
			Ⓐ	Ⓒ						✣		
	Świnoujście Centrum d.	...	0516	0555	0616	0716	0816	0916	1016	1116	and	2116	2216
	Seebad Ahlbeck d.	...	0522	0600	0622	0722	0822	0922	1022	1122	hourly	2122	2222
	Seebad Heringsdorf d.	0433	0533	0610	0633	0733	0833	0933	1033	1133	until	2133	2233
	Zinnowitz ▲ d.	0511	0611	0650	0711	0811	0911	1011	1110	1211		2211	2311
	Wolgast d.	0528	0630	0730j	0730	0826	0930	1030	1125	1230		2230	2325
	Züssow a.	0546	0648	0748	0748	0844	0948	1048	1143	1248		2248	...

A – ①–⑥ (also June 8).
b – Not June 8.
j – Arrives 0704.
⊠ – Züssow d. 1212 / 1412 (not 1208 / 1408). On ⑥ May 3 - Oct. 4 Züssow d. 1106 (not 1108).
✣ – Wolgast d. 1526 (not 1530), Züssow a. 1544 (not 1548).
⊕ – Change trains at Seebad Heringsdorf May 3 - Oct. 5.
▲ – **Zinnowitz - Peenemünde** (*12 km,* journey 14 minutes). **From Zinnowitz** at 0434 Ⓐ, 0513 Ⓐ, 0613, 0659 Ⓐ, 0713 Ⓒ, 0813, 0913 and hourly until 2113. **From Peenemünde** at 0453 Ⓐ, 0532 Ⓐ, 0632, 0718 Ⓐ, 0732 Ⓒ, 0832, 0932 and hourly until 2132.

BERLIN - DESSAU — 847

RE services

km		Ⓐ		Ⓐ						
0	**Berlin** Ostbahnhof d.	0359	0502	0602	0702	and	2102	2204	2302	0016
5	**Berlin** Hbf d.	0411	0514	0614	0714	hourly	2114	2216	2314	0029
9	**Berlin** Zoo d.	0417	0520	0620	0720	until	2120	2222	2320	0035
24	Berlin Wannsee d.	0434	0534	0634	0734		2134	2236	2334	0048
33	Potsdam Rehbrücke d.	0443	0543	0643	0743		2143	2245	2343	0058
76	Bad Belzig d.	0519	0619	0719	0819		2219	2319	0019	0133
120	Roßlau (Elbe) **848** d.	0548	0648	0748	0848		2248	...	0048	...
125	**Dessau** Hbf **848** a.	0553	0653	0753	0853		2252	...	0053	...

	Ⓐ		Ⓐ		Ⓐ				
Dessau Hbf **848** d.	0405	0505	0605	0705	0805	0905	and	2205	2323
Roßlau (Elbe) **848** d.	0410	0510	0610	0710	0810	0910	hourly	2210	2328
Bad Belzig d.	0441	0541	0641	0741	0841	0941	until	2241	2359
Potsdam Rehbrücke d.	0516	0616	0716	0816	0916	1016		2316	0034
Berlin Wannsee d.	0525	0626	0726	0826	0926	1026		2326	0045
Berlin Zoo d.	0539	0640	0740	0840	0940	1040		2340	0058
Berlin Hbf a.	0543	0644	0744	0844	0944	1044		2344	0103
Berlin Ostbahnhof a.	0554	0656	0756	0856	0956	1056		2356	0115

FLUGHAFEN BERLIN BRANDENBURG ✈ - BERLIN — 847a

RE / RB services

Flughafen Berlin ✈ **837** d.	0002	0040	0115	0139	0239	0342	0425	0444	0458	0514	0528	0544	0558	0614	0628	0644	0658	and at	2214	2228	2244	2258	2314	2328	2343
Berlin Ostkreuz **837** a.	0018	0056	0131	0156	0256	0358	0442	0501	0516	0529	0546	0601	0616	0629	0646	0701	0716	the same	2229	2246	2301	2316	2329	2346	2359
Berlin Ostbahnhof **837** a.	0024	0103	0137	0202	0301	0404	│	0507	│	0538	│	0607	│	0638	│	0707	│	minutes	2238	│	2307	│	2338	│	0005
Berlin Gesundbrunnen a.	│	│	│	│	│	│	0458	│	0529	│	0558	│	0629	...	0658	│	0729	past each	...	2258	│	2331	...	2358	│
Berlin Hbf **837** a.	0033	0113	0146	0212	0311	0414	0504	0517	0533	0548a	0603	0618	0633	...	0703	0718	0733	hour until	...	2303	2318	2336	...	0003	0015
Berlin Zoo **837** a.	0041	0121	0153	0220	0319	0425	...	0525	...	0556a	...	0626	...	...	...	0726	...		...	...	2326	...	...	...	0022
Berlin Zoo **837** d.	0033	0142	0240	0309	0323	0339	...	...	0435	...	0501	...	0527	...	...	...	0633	and at	...	...	...	2233	...	...	2333
Berlin Hbf **837** d.	0040	0148	0246	0315	0329	0346	0351	0421	0441	0451	0507	0521	0532	0551	...	0621	0640	the same	2151	...	2221	2240	...	2321	2340
Berlin Gesundbrunnen d.	│	│	│	│	│	│	0400	0429	│	0500	│	0529	│	0600	...	0629	│	minutes	2200	...	2229	│	...	2329	│
Berlin Ostbahnhof **837** d.	0053	0159	0257	0326	0340	0356	│	│	0452	│	0518	│	0544	│	0620	│	0653	past each	│	2220	│	2253	2323	│	2353
Berlin Ostkreuz **837** d.	0057	0204	0302	0330	0343	0400	0412	0441	0457	0512	0523	0541	0551	0612	0626	0641	0657	hour until	2212	2226	2241	2257	2328	2341	2357
Flughafen Berlin ✈ **837** a.	0115	0221	0318	0346	0400	0418	0430	0500	0515	0530	0546	0600	0611	0630	0646	0700	0715		2230	2246	2300	2315	2347	2400	0015

a – Ⓐ only.

☛ Subject to alteration from Sept. 23. The airport is also linked with Berlin Osthbf, Hbf, Zoo and Spandau by S-Bahn route S9.

MAGDEBURG - DESSAU - LEIPZIG and HALLE (SAALE) — 848

RE / RB / S-Bahn services

km		Ⓐ								
0	**Magdeburg** Hbf d.	0427	0517	0615j	0717	and	2017	2112	2203	2317
56	Roßlau (Elbe) **847** d.	0510	0605	0705	0805	hourly	2105	2153	2252	0005
61	**Dessau** Hbf **847** d.	0519	0612	0712	0812	until	2112	2158	2258	0009
87	Bitterfeld a.	0541	0628	0728	0828		2128	2219	2319	...
87	Bitterfeld d.	0545	0631	0731	0831		2131	2221	2320	...
120	**Leipzig** Hbf a.	0613	0656	0756	0856		2159	2243	2347	...

	Ⓐ			Ⓐ						
Leipzig Hbf d.	...	...	0502	...	0602	0704	and	2004	*2048*	2218
Bitterfeld a.	...	...	0525	...	0625	0725	hourly	2025	*2115*	2247
Bitterfeld d.	...	0418t	0527	...	0627	0727	until	2027	2118	2249
Dessau Hbf **847** d.	0358	0449	0548	0627	0648	0748		2048	2148	2314
Roßlau (Elbe) **847** d.	0403	0453	0553	0632	0653	0753		2053	2153	2318
Magdeburg Hbf a.	0452	0542	0642	0723	0742	0842		2142	2234	0006

DESSAU / LUTHERSTADT WITTENBERG - BITTERFELD - HALLE / LEIPZIG

	ⒸB	Ⓒ		Ⓐ	§	Ⓐ§	Ⓒ§	Ⓐ§	Ⓐ§		⑥	Ⓐ	Ⓐ			Ⓐ	Ⓐ								
Lutherstadt Wittenberg d.	0159r	...	...	...	...	...	0413	0416	0440	...	0504	0543e	...	...	0604	0616	...	...	0704	0804	...	...	0904	1004	...
Dessau Hbf d.	0226	...	...	...	0417	...	│	0450	│	0519	│	│	0547	0618	│	0650	...	0720	│	│	0820	0920	│	│	1020
Bitterfeld a.	0239	...	...	...	0439	...	0441	0511	0508	0541	0540	0611	0609	0640	0643	0711	...	0742	0740	0843	0842	0942	0940	1043	1042
Bitterfeld d.	0241	0246	...	0412	0446	0442	0445	0512	0516	0545	0547	0612	0616	0646	0645	0712	0716	0745	0747	0845	0847	0945	0947	1045	1047
Leipzig Hbf a.	│	0314	...	0443	│	0513	0513	0543	│	0613	│	0643	│	│	0713	0743	│	0813	│	0913	│	1013	│	1113	│
Leipzig-Stötteritz ♥ a.	│	0326	...	0457	│	0527	0527	0557	│	0627	│	0657	│	│	0727	0757	│	0827	│	0927	│	1027	│	1127	│
Halle (Saale) Hbf a.	0312	...	...	...	0507	...	...	...	0537	...	0607	...	0637	0707	...	...	0738	...	0807	...	0907	...	1007	...	1107
													Ⓐ									§	§	§	
Lutherstadt Wittenberg d.	...	1104	1204	...	...	1304	1404	...	...	1504	1604	...	1616	...	1705	1804	...	...	1905	2004	...	...	2104	2217	...
Dessau Hbf d.	1120	│	│	1220	1320	│	│	1418	1520	│	│	1620	1650	1720	│	│	1820	1920	│	│	2020	2120	│	│	*2258*
Bitterfeld a.	1142	1140	1243	1242	1342	1340	1443	1440	1542	1540	1643	1642	1711	1742	1740	1843	1842	1942	1940	2043	2042	2142	2140	2244	*2319*
Bitterfeld d.	1145	1147	1245	1247	1345	1347	1445	1447	1545	1547	1645	1647	1712	1745	1747	1845	1847	1945	1947	2045	2047	2145	2147	2247	2320
Leipzig Hbf a.	1213	│	1313	│	1413	│	1513	│	1613	│	1713	│	1743	1813	│	1913	│	2013	│	2113	│	2213	│	│	│
Leipzig-Stötteritz ♥ a.	1227	│	1327	│	1427	│	1527	│	1627	│	1727	│	1757	1827	│	1927	│	2027	│	2127	│	2227	│	│	│
Halle (Saale) Hbf a.	...	1207	...	1307	...	1407	...	1507	...	1607	...	1707	...	...	1807	...	1907	...	2007	...	2107	...	2207	2307	2353

	Ⓒ§		Ⓐ§	Ⓐ§	§	§	Ⓐ§	ⒸA	Ⓐ		Ⓐ														
Halle (Saale) Hbf d.	0026	...	0355	0355	0452	...	...	0551	0553	...	...	0652	...	0752	...	0852	...	0952	...	1052	...	1152	...	1252	...
Leipzig-Stötteritz ♥ d.	│	0006	│	│	│	0434	0504	│	│	0534	0604	│	0634	│	0734	│	0834	│	0934	│	1034	│	1134	│	1234
Leipzig Hbf d.	│	0020	│	│	│	0448	0518	│	│	0548	0618	│	0648	│	0748	│	0848	│	0948	│	1048	│	1148	│	1248
Bitterfeld a.	0046	0047	0416	0416	0513	0515	0548	0615	0613	0615	0647	0713	0715	0813	0815	0913	0915	1013	1015	1113	1115	1213	1215	1313	1315
Bitterfeld d.	0055	0054z	0418	0421	0518	0516	0550	0620	0620	0618	0648	0718	0716	0820	0818	0918	0916	1020	1018	1118	1116	1220	1218	1318	1316
Dessau Hbf a.	│	0117z	0441	│	0541	│	0613	│	│	0641	0708	0741	│	│	0841	0941	│	│	1041	1141	│	│	1241	1341	│
Lutherstadt Wittenberg a.	0124	...	...	0450	...	0551	0654	0658	0655	...	0742	...	0757	0855	...	...	0957	1055	...	...	1157	1255	...	...	1357
	Ⓐ	Ⓐ	Ⓒ						Ⓐ											§	§	Ⓐ§	§	§	§
Halle (Saale) Hbf d.	1350	1350	1352	...	1452	...	1552	...	...	1652	...	1752	...	1852	...	1950	...	2052	...	2152	...	2220	...	2326	...
Leipzig-Stötteritz ♥ d.	│	│	│	1334	│	1434	│	1534	1604	│	1634	│	1734	│	1834	│	1934	│	2034	│	2134	│	2204	│	2306
Leipzig Hbf d.	│	│	│	1348	│	1448	│	1548	1618	│	1648	│	1748	│	1848	│	1948	│	2048	│	2148	│	2218	│	2320
Bitterfeld a.	1410	1410	1413	1415	1513	1515	1613	1615	1647	1713	1715	1813	1815	1913	1915	2011	2015	2113	2115	2213	2215	2243	2247	2346	2346
Bitterfeld d.	1412	1420	1420	1418	1518	1516	1620	1618	1648	1718	1716	1820	1818	1918	1916	2020	2018	2118	2116	2220	2218	...	2249	2352	2352
Dessau Hbf a.	1432	│	│	1441	1541	│	│	1641	1708	1741	│	│	1841	1941	│	│	2041	2141	│	│	2241	...	2312	0015	│
Lutherstadt Wittenberg a.	1505	1455	1455	...	...	1556	1655	...	1742	...	1756	1855	...	...	1957	2055	...	...	2157	2255	...	...	...	...	0028

LUTHERSTADT WITTENBERG - DESSAU

km		Ⓐ	Ⓐ	Ⓒ	Ⓐ	⚒	Ⓐ									Ⓐ			Ⓐ						
0	**Lutherstadt Wittenberg** d.	0413	0502	0516	0557	0616	0652	0716	0816	0916	1016	1116	1216	1316	1416	1452	1516	1616	1652	1716	1816	1916	2016	...	2216
32	Roßlau (Elbe) d.	0441	0532	0544	0626	0644	0717	0744	0844	0944	1044	1144	1244	1344	1444	1517	1544	1644	1717	1744	1844	1944	2044	...	2244
37	**Dessau** Hbf a.	0448	0536	0548	0631	0648	0721	0748	0848	0948	1048	1148	1248	1348	1448	1521	1548	1648	1721	1748	1848	1948	2048	...	2248

	Ⓐ		Ⓐ			⚒							Ⓐ		Ⓐ		Ⓐ		Ⓐ						
Dessau Hbf d.	0422	0510	0622	0710	...	0810	0910	1010	1110	1210	1310	1410	1435	1510	1532	1610	1635	1710	1732	1810	1910	2010	2110	...	2300
Roßlau (Elbe) d.	0426	0514	0626	0714	...	0814	0914	1014	1114	1214	1314	1414	1440	1514	1537	1614	1640	1714	1737	1814	1914	2014	2114	...	2304
Lutherstadt Wittenberg a.	0454	0542	0654	0742	...	0842	0942	1042	1142	1242	1342	1442	1505	1542	1602	1642	1705	1742	1802	1842	1942	2042	2142	...	2332

A – To Stralsund via Berlin (Tables **851** and **845**).
B – From Schwedt via Berlin (Tables **851**).
e – 0537 on ① (also June 10).
j – 0617 on Ⓒ.
r – Not Sept. 27 - Dec. 13.
t – Ⓐ only.
z – Ⓒ July 5 - Sept. 6.
♥ – Trains also call at City Tunnel stations Markt, Wilhelm-Leuschner-Platz, Bayerischer Bahnhof and MDR.
§ – Times may vary by up to 7 minutes June 7 - 28.

849 Local services HALLE and LEIPZIG - EISENACH and SAALFELD

Operated by ABELLIO Rail Mitteldeutschland. See Tables **849a** and **850** for faster *ICE* and *IC* trains.

HALLE / LEIPZIG - ERFURT - EISENACH *See lower panel for other connecting services Halle - Naumburg and v.v.*

km																								
		Ⓐ	Ⓐ									▽											⑤⑥f	
0	**Halle** (Saale) Hbf .... d.	...	...	0424	0524	...	0606	...	0706	...		1606	...	1706	...	1806	...	1906	...	2006	...	...	...	...
	Leipzig Hbf .... d.	...	...	|	|	0519	|	0619	|	0719	and in	|	1619	|	1719	|	1819	|	1919	|	2019	2119	2219	2319
24	Großkorbetha .... d.	...	...	0445	0545	0551	|	0651	|	0751		|	1651	|	1751	|	1851	|	1951	|	2051	2151	2251	2351
32	Weißenfels .... d.	...	...	0452	0552	0558	0628	0658	0728	0758	the same	1628	1658	1728	1758	1828	1858	1928	1958	2028	2058	2158	2258	2358
46	Naumburg (Saale) Hbf a.	...	...	0502	0603	0607	0636	0707	0736	0807		1636	1707	1736	1807	1836	1907	1936	2007	2036	2107	2207	2307	0007
46	Naumburg (Saale) Hbf d.	...	...	0503	▬	0608	0638	0708	0738	0808	pattern	1638	1708	1738	1808	1838	1908	1938	2008	2038	2108	2208	2308	0009
72	Apolda .... d.	...	...	0525	...	0629	0657	0729	0758	0829	every	1657	1729	1758	1829	1857	1929	1958	2029	2057	2129	2229	2329	0030
87	Weimar .... **858** d.	...	...	0538	...	0642	0708	0742	0809	0842	**two hours**	1708	1742	1809	1842	1908	1942	2009	2042	2108	2142	2242	2342	0044
108	**Erfurt** Hbf .... **858** a.	...	...	0553	Ⓐ	0657	0723	0758	0823	0858		1723	1758	1823	1858	1923	1958	2023	2058	2123	2158	2259	2357	0100
108	**Erfurt** Hbf .... **865** d.	0423	0507	0554	0625	0705	...	0800	...	0905	until	...	1800	...	1905	...	2000	...	*2104*	...	2218	*2310*	...	0007
121	Neudietendorf .... **865** d.	0435	0515	0603	0633	0715	...	0809	...	0915		...	1809	...	1915	...	2009	...	*2114*	...	2228	*2320*	...	0017
136	Gotha .... **865** d.	0453	0535	0615	0642	0727	...	0821	...	0927		...	1821	...	1927	...	2021	...	*2126*	...	2240	*2332*	...	0029
165	**Eisenach** .... a.	0519	0558	0636	0705	0749	...	0843	...	0949		...	1843	...	1949	...	2043	...	*2148*	...	2302	*2354*	...	0051

Note on the table above: in the columns after "until", the printed ⑤⑥f column and the final column carry these values in the Leipzig–Erfurt a. rows: ⑤⑥f column 2219, 2251, 2258, 2307, 2308, 2329, 2342, 2357; final column 2319, 2351, 2358, 0007, 0009, 0030, 0044, 0100.

				Ⓐ	Ⓐ		Ⓐ	⊖				⚒												⊕
Eisenach .... d.	...	...	...	0411	...	...	0458	...	0604	...	0642	0713	...	0806	...	0913	...		1806	...	1913	...	2006	2113	2209
Gotha .... **865** d.	...	...	...	0434	...	...	0522	...	0628	...	0705	0736	...	0830	...	0936	...		1830	...	1936	...	2030	2136	2233
Neudietendorf ...... **865** d.	...	...	...	0447	...	...	0535	...	0641	...	0718	0749	...	0843	...	0949	...	and in	1843	...	1949	...	2043	2149	2246
Erfurt Hbf .... **865** a.	...	...	...	0456	...	...	0545	...	0650	...	0728	0758	...	0853	...	0958	...	the same	1853	...	1958	...	2053	2158	2256
Erfurt Hbf .... **858** d.	...	...	...	0458	0458	0530	0601	0634	0701	0736	0736	0801	0837	0901	0936	1001	1036		1901	1936	2001	2036	2101	2201	2309
Weimar .... **858** d.	...	...	...	0518	0518	0545	0618	0650	0718	0752	0752	0818	0852	0918	0952	1018	1052	pattern	1918	1952	2018	2052	2118	2218	2325
Apolda .... d.	...	...	...	0529	0529	0555	0629	0700	0729	0802	0802	0829	0902	0929	1002	1029	1102	every	1929	2002	2029	2102	2129	2229	2336
Naumburg (Saale) Hbf . a.	...	...	...	0551	0551	0615	0651	0719	0751	0821	0821	0851	0921	0951	1021	1051	1121		1951	2021	2051	2121	2151	2251	2355
Naumburg (Saale) Hbf d.	0446	0446	0509	0552	0552	0616	0652	0720	0752	0822	0822	0852	0922	0952	1022	1052	1122	**two hours**	1952	2022	2052	2122	2152	2252	0003
Weißenfels .... d.	0457	0457	0520	0602	0602	0626	0702	0730	0802	0832	0832	0902	0932	1002	1032	1102	1132	until	2002	2032	2102	2132	2202	2302	0014
Großkorbetha .... d.	0506	0508	0527	0608	0608	|	0708	|	0808	|	|	0908	|	1008	|	1108	|		2008	|	2108	|	2208	2308	0020
Leipzig Hbf .... a.	|	0541	|	0639	0639	|	0739	|	0839	|	|	0939	|	1039	|	1139	|		2039	|	2139	|	2239	2339	|
Halle (Saale) Hbf .... a.	0528		0549	...	...	0648		0753	...	0856	0856	...	0954	...	1056	...	1154		...	2056	...	2154	...	...	0041

HALLE / LEIPZIG - JENA - SAALFELD

km																								
		Ⓐ	Ⓐ	Ⓐ		Ⓐ			⚒			**E**				**E**							⑤⑥f	
	Halle (Saale) Hbf .... d.	...	0424	...	...	...	...	0524	...	...	0624			...	2024		...	...	2124	...	2224	...	2324	2324	...
0	**Leipzig** Hbf .... d.	...	|	...	...	...	0519	|	...	0619	|	0650	and at	2019	|	2050	...	2119	|	2219	|	2319	|	|	...
32	Großkorbetha .... d.	...	0445	...	...	...	0551	0545	...	0651	0645	|	the same	2051	2045	|	...	2151	2145	2251	2245	2351	2345	2345	...
40	Weißenfels .... d.	...	0452	...	...	...	0558	0552	...	0658	0652	0722		2058	2052	2122	...	2158	2152	2258	2252	2358	2352	2352	...
56	Naumburg (Saale) Hbf a.	...	0502	...	...	...	0607	0603	...	0707	0703	0731	minutes	2107	2103	2131	...	2207	2203	2307	2303	0007	0003	0003	...
56	Naumburg (Saale) Hbf d.	...	...	0508	...	...	...	0612	...		0712	0732		...	2112	2132	...	...	2212	...	2312	...	0013	0013	...
95	**Jena** Paradies .... d.	0507	...	0543	0543	0612	...	0645	0716		0745	0759	past each	...	2145	2159	...	...	2245	...	2345	...	0046	0046	...
100	Jena-Göschwitz .... d.	0512	...	0548	0548	0617	...	0650	0721		0750	0804	hour until	...	2150	2204	...	...	2250	...	2350	...	0050	0051	...
132	Rudolstadt (Thür) .... d.	0536	|	0614	0614	0640	...	0716	0745		0816	0826		...	2216	2226	...	...	2316	...	0016	...	...	0117	...
142	**Saalfeld** (Saale) .... a.	0546	...	0623	0623	0649	...	0726	0754		0826	0838		...	2226	2235	...	...	2326	...	0027	...	...	0127	...

											G				**G**							⑤⑥f		
Saalfeld (Saale) .... d.	0433	...	0519	...	0633	...	0733	...	0833	...	0922	0933	...		1922	1933	...	...	2033	...	2133	...	2233	2233	...
Rudolstadt (Thür) .... d.	0442	...	0527	...	0642	...	0742	...	0842	...	0933	0942	...	and at	1933	1942	...	...	2042	...	2142	...	2242	2242	...
Jena-Göschwitz .... d.	0508	...	0555	...	0708	...	0808	...	0908	...	0955	1008	...	the same	1955	2008	...	...	2108	...	2208	...	2308	2308	...
Jena Paradies .... d.	0515	...	0601	...	0715	...	0815	...	0915	...	1001	1015	...		2001	2015	...	...	2115	...	2215	...	2314	2314	...
Naumburg (Saale) Hbf a.	0547	...	0627	...	0747	...	0847	...	0947	...	1027	1047	...	minutes	2027	2047	...	...	2147	...	2247	...	2346	2348	...
Naumburg (Saale) Hbf d.	0556	0552	0628	0652	0756	0752	0856	0852	0956	0952	1028	1056	1052		2028	2056	2052	...	2156	2152	2256	2252	2347	...	0003
Weißenfels .... d.	0607	0602	0637	0702	0807	0802	0907	0902	1007	1002	1037	1107	1102	past each	2037	2107	2102	...	2207	2202	2307	2302	2357	...	0014
Großkorbetha .... d.	0613	0608	0652	0708	0813	0808	0913	0908	1013	1008	|	1113	1108	hour until	|	2113	2108	...	2213	2208	2313	2308	0003	...	0020
Leipzig Hbf .... a.	|	0639	0709	0739	|	0839	|	0939	|	1039	1108	|	1139		2108	|	2139	...	|	2239	|	2339	0034	...	|
Halle (Saale) Hbf .... a.	0635	...	...	...	0834	...	0934	...	1037	...	...	1134	...		...	2134	...	...	2234	...	2334	...	...	...	0041

EISENACH - BEBRA *45km.* Journey time: 35 – 41 minutes. Operated by CANTUS Verkehrsgesellschaft (2nd class only).

From Eisenach at 0436 Ⓐ, 0530 Ⓐ, 0613 ⚒, 0713 ⚒, 0814, 0915 ⚒, 1013, 1115 Ⓐ, 1213, 1315 Ⓐ, 1413, 1515 Ⓐ, 1613, 1715 Ⓐ, 1813, 1915 Ⓐ, 2013, 2115 Ⓐ and 2213 Ⓒ.
From Bebra at 0504 Ⓐ, 0559 ⚒, 0704 Ⓒ, 0716 Ⓐ, 0804 ⚒, 0904, 1004 Ⓐ, 1104, 1204 Ⓐ, 1304 Ⓒ, 1315 Ⓐ, 1404 Ⓐ, 1504 **d**, 1604 Ⓐ, 1704, 1804 Ⓐ, 1904, 2004 Ⓐ and 2104.

E – Runs every **two** hours (from Leipzig **even** hours 0650 to 2050).
G – Runs every **two** hours (from Saalfeld **uneven** hours 0922 to 1922).
d – 3 minutes later on ⑤⑦.
f – Also June 8, Oct. 2, 30.
⊕ – Change trains at Erfurt on ⑤⑥.
⊖ – Change trains at Erfurt on ①–⑤.
▽ – On Ⓐ the 1606 journey continues to Eisenach (a. 1809).

849a GERA - WEIMAR - ERFURT - KASSEL and LEIPZIG - JENA - SAALFELD - NÜRNBERG

	IC 2156 ①–⑥	*IC* 2156 ⑦	*IC* 2152	*IC* 1952 ⑤⑦	*IC* 2150 Ⓑ
Gera Hbf .... **858** d.	0604	...	1204	...	1804
Jena Göschwitz .... **858** d.	0638	...	1238	...	1838
Jena West .... **858** d.	0645	...	1245	...	1845
Weimar .... **849 858** d.	0704	...	1304	1747	1904
Erfurt Hbf......... **849 850 858** a.	0716	...	1316	1759	1916
Erfurt Hbf................ **849 850** d.	0718	0725	1318	1801	1918
Gotha .... **849 850** a.	0735	0741	1335	1814	1935
Gotha .... **849 850** d.	0748	0748	1348	1816	1948
Eisenach................. **849 850** d.	0804	0804	1404	1836	2004
Bebra .... **849 901** d.	|	|	|	1902	2028
Kassel Wilhelmshöhe ..... **901** a.	0900	0900	1500	1939	2107
Dortmund Hbf **805** .... ▷ a.	1114	1114	1714	2157	...
Düsseldorf Hbf **805** .... ▷ a.	1212**t**	1212**t**	1812	2257**v**	...
Köln Hbf **805** .... ▷ a.	1240	1240	...	2325	...

	IC 2151 ①–⑥	*IC* 2155	*IC* 1959 ⑤⑦	*IC* 2157 ⑥	*IC* 2157 Ⓑ
Köln Hbf **805** .... ▷ d.	...	0919	1027**r**	1519	1519
Düsseldorf Hbf **805** .... ▷ d.	...	0943**t**	1118**t**	1543**t**	1543**t**
Dortmund Hbf **805** .... ▷ d.	...	1043	1210	1644	1644
Kassel Wilhelmshöhe.. **901** d.	0648	1257	1419	1859	1859
Bebra .... **849 901** d.	0728	|	1503	|	|
Eisenach .... **849 850** d.	0752	1356	1527	1956	1956
Gotha .... **849 850** a.	0807	1410	1540	2010	2010
Gotha .... **849 850** d.	0825	1425	1542	2022	2025
Erfurt Hbf .... **849 850** a.	0842	1442	1556	2039	2042
Erfurt Hbf ...... **849 850 858** d.	0844	1444	1558	...	2044
Weimar .... **849 858** d.	0859	1459	1613	...	2059
Jena West .... **858** a.	0913	1513	...	...	2113
Jena Göschwitz .... **858** a.	0919	1519	...	...	2119
Gera Hbf .... **858** a.	0955	1555	...	...	2155

C – Not Aug. 1 - Oct. 16.
D – Aug. 1 - Oct. 16.
H – To / from Hamburg (Table **840**).
O – To Ostseebad Binz (Tables **844/845**).
T – From Rostock on Ⓑ (Table **835**). To Wien via Passau (Tables **920/950**).
U – From Wien via Passau (Tables **920/950**). To Rostock on ①–⑥ (Table **835**).
b – Not June 27 - July 11.
d – Not June 26 - July 11.
r – 1044 on ⑦.
s – Arrival time. Calls to set down only.
t – Not Sept. 6 - Oct. 31.
v – Not Sept. 5 - Oct. 31.
▷ – Timings may vary Sept. 6 - Oct. 31.

	IC 495 C T	*IC* 495 D T		*IC* 2162 🍷	*IC* 2160 b 🍷	*IC* 2066 b 🍷	*IC* 2064 b 🍷	*IC* 2062 Ⓑd 🍷	*ICE* 1705 Ⓑ H✕	
Berlin Hbf **850** ....d.	2228	2228	...	...	...	...	...	...	1829	...
Leipzig Hbf .... **849 850** d.	0035	0035	...	0749	0949	1349	1549	1749	1951	...
Halle (Saale) Hbf... **849 850** d.	0110	0110	...	|	|	|	|	|	|	...
Weißenfels .... **849** d.	|	|	...	0816	1016	1416	1616	1816	2020	...
Naumburg (Saale) Hbf ..... **849** d.	0143	|	...	0826	1026	1426	1626	1826	2031	...
Jena Paradies .... **849** d.	0215	|	...	0856	1056	1456	1656	1856	2057**s**	...
Jena Göschwitz .... **849** d.	0221	|	...	0902	1102	1502	1702	1902	2104	...
Rudolstadt (Thür) .... **849** d.	|	|	...	0923	1123	1523	1723	1923	...	...
Saalfeld (Saale)........ **849 875** d.	0249	|	...	0934	1134	1534	1734	1934	...	...
Kronach .... **875** d.	|	|	...	1026	1226	1626	1826	2026	...	...
Lichtenfels .... **875** d.	0350	|	...	1040	1240	1640	1840	2040	...	...
Bamberg................... **850 875** d.	0421	|	...	1058	1257	1658	1858	2057	...	...
Erlangen .... **850 875** d.	0443	|	...	1120	1320	1720	1920	2120	...	...
Nürnberg Hbf.......... **850 875** a.	0502	0557	...	1134	1334	1735	1934	2134	...	...
Stuttgart Hbf **925** ....a.	...	...	...	1352	1552	1953	2153	...	...	...
Karlsruhe Hbf **931** ....a.	...	...	...	1453	1652	2053	2300	...	...	...

	IC 494 D U	*IC* 494 C U	*ICE* 1704 ①–⑤ H✕	*ICE* 1704 ⑥ O✕	*IC* 2061 ①–⑥ 🍷b	*IC* 2065 b 🍷	*IC* 2067 d 🍷	*IC* 2161 b 🍷	*IC* 2163 🍷
Karlsruhe Hbf **931** ....d.	...	...	...	...	...	0707	0906	1306	1506
Stuttgart Hbf **925** ....d.	...	...	...	...	...	0808	1009	1409	1609
Nürnberg Hbf...... **850 875** d.	0003	0026	...	...	0619	1024	1224	1622	1824
Erlangen................. **850 875** d.	|	0043	...	...	0634	1040	1238	1636	1839
Bamberg.................. **850 875** d.	|	0105	...	...	0659	1100	1300	1701	1900
Lichtenfels .... **875** d.	|	0126	...	...	0715	1117	1317	1717	1917
Kronach .... **875** d.	|	|	...	...	0730	1131	1331	1731	1931
Saalfeld (Saale).... **849 875** d.	|	0235	...	...	0825	1225	1425	1825	2025
Rudolstadt (Thür)......... **849** d.	|	|	...	...	0834	1234	1434	1834	2034
Jena Göschwitz .... **849** d.	|	0302	0652	0652	0855	1255	1455	1855	2055
Jena Paradies .... **849** d.	|	0310	0659	0659	0902	1302	1502	1902	2102
Naumburg (Saale) Hbf . **849** d.	|	0338	0726	0726	0930	1330	1530	1930	2130
Weißenfels..................... **849** d.	|	|	0735	0735	0939	1339	1539	1939	2139
Halle (Saale) Hbf **849 850** a.	0413	0413	|	|	|	|	|	|	|
Leipzig Hbf .... **849 850** a.	0453	0453	0804	0804	1009	1409	1609	2009	2209
Berlin Hbf **850** .... a.	0631	0631	0929	0929	...	...	...	...	...

BERLIN - HALLE / LEIPZIG - ERFURT - FRANKFURT / NÜRNBERG 850

See Table **902** for other services Berlin - Frankfurt via Braunschweig. See Table **927** for services operated by FlixTrain.
Other regional services: Table **845** Berlin - Lutherstadt Wittenberg. Table **848** Lutherstadt Wittenberg - Bitterfeld - Leipzig / Halle. Table **849** Leipzig / Halle - Weimar - Erfurt - Eisenach.

km		*ICE* 1656	*ICE* 601	*ICE* 501	*ICE* 593	*ICE* 1701	*ICE* 1001	*ICE* 833	*ICE* 1654	*ICE* 503	*ICE* 835	*ICE* 1103	*ICE* 595	*ICE* 701	*ICE* 1003	*ICE* 1003	*ICE* 1652	*ICE* 505	*ICE* 837	*ICE* 1105	*ICE* 597	*ICE* 703	*ICE* 93	*ICE* 1650
		①–⑥	Ⓐ	①–⑥		①–⑤		①–⑤							Z	Y				Y				
		✕	L✕	✕	M✕	✕	✕	✕	✕	✕	✕	✕	M✕	✕	G✕	G✕	✕	✕	✕	✕	M✕	✕	A✕	✕
	Hamburg Hbf **840** d.	...	...	...	...	...	...	...	...	...	...	...	...	0527a	...	...	...	0634r	...	...	...	0735r	0805x	...
0	**Berlin** Hbf d.	...	...	0429	0526	0534	0559	0559	...	0628	0700	0704	0726	0734	0711	0811	...	0828	0900	0904	0926	0934	1004	...
6	**Berlin** Südkreuz d.	...	...	0437	0533	0540	0606	0606	...	0635	0707	0711	0733	0741	|	0818	...	0836	0907	0911	0933	0941	1011	...
97	Lutherstadt Wittenberg d.	...	...	0511	0610	|	|	|	...	0712	|	|	0810	|	|	|	...	0911	|	|	1010	|	|	...
134	Bitterfeld d.	...	...	|	|	0634	|	|	...	|	|	|	|	0834	|	|	...	|	|	|	|	1034	|	...
	Halle (Saale) Hbf d.	...	...	|	|	0652	0712	0712	...	|	0815	0821	|	0852	0918	|	...	|	1015	1021	|	1052	1118	...
	Dresden Hbf **842** d.	...	...	|	|	|	|	|	0610	|	|	|	|	|	|	|	0810	|	|	|	|	|	|	1010
167	**Leipzig** Hbf a.	...	...	0542	0642	|	|	|	0726	0742	|	|	0842	|	|	|	0926	0942	|	|	1042	|	|	1126
167	**Leipzig** Hbf d.	0533	...	0548	0648	|	|	|	0733	0748	|	|	0848	|	|	|	0933	0948	|	|	1048	|	|	1133
287	**Erfurt** Hbf a.	0616	...	0629	0728	0724p	0740	0740	0816	0829	0845	0848	0928	0924p	0945	|	1016	1029	1045	1048	1128	1124p	1152	1216
287	**Erfurt** Hbf **849a** d.	0618	...	0631	0730	0732	0745	0749	0818	0831	0847	0850	0930	0932	0947	|	1018	1031	1047	1050	1130	1132	1154	1218
	Coburg **875** d.	|	...	0705	|	|	|	|	|	|	|	|	|	|	|	|	|	|	|	|	|	|	1228	|
	Bamberg **875** d.	|	0643	0726	|	0817	|	|	|	0916	|	|	|	1016	|	|	|	1116	|	|	|	1216	|	|
	Erlangen **875** d.	|	0709	0753	|	|	|	|	|	0938	|	|	|	|	|	|	|	1139	|	|	|	|	|	|
	Nürnberg Hbf **875** a.	|	0725	0808	|	0852	0856	|	|	0952	|	1000	|	1052	1056	1056	|	1152	|	1200	|	1250	1323	|
	München Hbf **904 905** a.	|	0845	0918	|	1042	1002	|	|	1103	|	1111	|	1242	1202	1202	|	1301	|	1309	|	1402	...	|
315	Gotha **849a** d.	0633	...	...	|	...	...	|	0833	...	|	...	|	...	...	...	1033	...	|	...	|	...	...	1233
344	**Eisenach** **849a** d.	0648	...	...	0755	...	...	|	0848	...	|	...	0956	...	...	...	1048	...	|	...	1155	...	...	1248
401	Bad Hersfeld d.	0716	...	...	|	...	...	|	0916	...	|	...	|	...	...	...	1115	...	|	...	|	...	...	1316
443	Fulda **900/1/2** d.	0742	...	...	0849	...	...	|	0942	...	|	...	1049	...	...	...	1142	...	|	...	1250	...	...	1342
524	Hanau Hbf **901** d.	|	...	...	|	...	...	|	|	...	|	...	|	...	...	...	|	...	|	...	|	...	...	|
547	**Frankfurt** (M) Hbf **900/1/2** ◇ a.	0836	...	...	0944	...	...	0956	1036	...	1056	...	1144	...	...	...	1236	...	1256	...	1344	...	...	1436
558	**Frankfurt** Flughafen ✈ §. ◇ a.	0854	...	...	|	...	...	...	1054	...	...	...	|	...	...	...	1254	...	...	...	|	...	...	1454
	Stuttgart Hbf **910** a.	|	...	...	1108	...	...	...	|	...	...	...	1308	...	...	...	|	...	...	...	1508	...	...	|
586	**Mainz** Hbf ◇ a.	0915	...	...	...	...	...	...	1115	...	...	...	...	...	...	...	1315	...	...	...	...	...	...	1515
596	**Wiesbaden** Hbf ◇ a.	0933	...	...	...	...	...	...	1133	...	...	...	...	...	...	...	1333	...	...	...	...	...	...	1533

	ICE 507	*ICE* 839	*ICE* 1107	*ICE* 1219	*ICE* 705	*ICE* 1005	*ICE* 1558	*ICE* 509	*ICE* 931	*ICE* 1109	*ICE* 691	*ICE* 707	*ICE* 1556	*ICE* 95	*ICE* 1695	*ICE* 1601	*ICE* 1711	*ICE* 933	*ICE* 1111	*ICE* 693	*ICE* 709	*ICE* 1554	*ICE* 1007	*ICE* 603
			Y								⊙				U		W							
	✕	S✕	✕	M✕	✕	✕	✕	✕	✕	✕	M✕	✕	✕	A✕	✕	✕	O✕	B✕	✕	P✕	✕	✕	D✕	✕
Hamburg Hbf **840** d.	0835r	...	...	...	0936r	1005x	...	1034r	...	...	...	1136r	...	1204x	...	1232r	...	...	...	...	1336r	...	1404x	1435r
Berlin Hbf d.	1028	1100	1104	1126	1134	1204	...	1228	1300	1304	1326	1334	...	1404	1404	1429	1429	1500	1504	1526	1534	...	1611	1628
Berlin Südkreuz d.	1036	1108	1111	1133	1141	1211	...	1236	1307	1311	1333	1341	...	1411	1411	1436	1436	1508	1511	1533	1541	...	1618	1636
Lutherstadt Wittenberg d.	1111	|	|	1210	|	|	...	1311	|	|	1410	|	...	|	|	1511	1511	|	|	1610	|	...	|	1711
Bitterfeld d.	|	|	|	|	1234	|	...	|	|	|	|	1434	...	|	|	|	|	|	|	|	1634	...	|	|
Halle (Saale) Hbf d.	|	1215	1221	|	1252	1318	...	|	1415	1421	|	1452	...	1518	1518	|	|	1615	1621	|	1652	...	|	|
Dresden Hbf **842** d.	|	|	|	|	|	|	1210	|	|	|	|	|	1410	|	|	|	|	|	|	|	|	1610	|	|
Leipzig Hbf a.	1142	|	|	1242	|	|	1326	1342	|	|	1442	|	1526	|	|	1542	1542	|	|	1642	|	1726	|	1742
Leipzig Hbf d.	1148	|	|	1248	|	|	1333	1348	|	|	1448	|	1533	|	|	1548	1548	|	|	1648	|	1733	|	1748
Erfurt Hbf a.	1229	1245	1248	1328	1324p	1345	1416	1429	1445	1448	1528	1524p	1616	1552	1552	1629	1629	1645	1648	1728	1724p	1816	|	1829
Erfurt Hbf **849a** d.	1231	1247	1250	1330	1332	1347	1418	1431	1447	1450	1530	1532	1618	1554	1554	1631	1631	1647	1650	1730	1732	1818	|	1831
Coburg **875** d.	|	|	|	|	|	|	|	|	|	|	|	|	|	1628	1628	|	|	|	|	|	|	|	|	|
Bamberg **875** d.	1315	|	|	|	1416	|	|	1516	|	|	|	1617	|	|	|	|	|	|	|	|	1816	|	|	1917
Erlangen **875** d.	1338	|	|	|	|	|	|	1538	|	|	|	|	|	|	|	1738	1738	|	|	|	|	|	|	1938
Nürnberg Hbf **875** a.	1352	|	1357	|	1452	1456	|	1552	|	1600	|	1652	|	1724	1724	1752	1752	|	1800	|	1852	|	1856	1952
München Hbf **904 905** a.	1504	|	1508	|	1642	1601	|	1701	|	1710	|	1803	|	...	1917	1903	1903	|	1911	|	2042	|	2002	2103
Gotha **849a** d.	...	|	...	|	...	...	1433	...	|	...	|	...	1633	...	...	...	...	|	...	|	...	1833	...	...
Eisenach **849a** d.	...	|	...	1356	...	...	1448	...	|	...	1555	...	1648	...	...	...	...	|	...	1755	...	1848	...	...
Bad Hersfeld d.	...	|	...	|	...	...	1515	...	|	...	|	...	1716	...	...	...	...	|	...	|	...	1916	...	...
Fulda **900/1/2** d.	...	|	...	1449	...	...	1542	...	|	...	1649	...	1742	...	...	...	...	|	...	1849	...	1942	...	...
Hanau Hbf **901** d.	...	|	...	|	...	...	|	...	|	...	|	...	|	...	...	...	...	|	...	|	...	|	...	...
Frankfurt (M) Hbf **900/1/2** ◇ a.	...	1456	...	1544	...	...	1636	...	1656	...	1744	...	1836	...	...	...	...	1856	...	1944	...	2036	...	...
Frankfurt Flughafen ✈ § ◇ a.	...	...	...	|	...	...	1654	...	...	...	|	...	1854	...	...	...	...	...	...	|	...	2056	...	...
Stuttgart Hbf **910** a.	...	...	...	1708	...	...	|	...	...	...	1908	...	|	...	...	...	...	...	...	2108	...	|	...	...
Mainz Hbf ◇ a.	...	...	...	...	...	...	1715	...	...	...	...	...	1915	...	...	...	...	...	...	...	...	2115	...	...
Wiesbaden Hbf ◇ a.	...	...	...	...	...	...	1733	...	...	...	...	...	1933	...	...	...	...	...	...	...	...	2133	...	...

	ICE 935	*ICE* 1113	*ICE* 695	*ICE* 801	*ICE* 1009	*ICE* 1552	*ICE* 1705	*ICE* 1605	*ICE* 1715	*ICE* 937	*ICE* 1115	*ICE* 697	*ICE* 803	*ICE* 1019	*ICE* 1607	*ICE* 1607	*ICE* 1717	*ICE* 699	*EN* 40458	*NJ* 408	*IC* 495	*IC* 495	*IC* 495	
						Ⓑ	Ⓑ	T	⑥W					Y	Ⓑ	⑤	⑥				b	c	d	
	H✕	✕	M✕	K✕	✕	✕	J✕	✕	O✕	✕	✕	✕	✕	✕	✕	✕	O✕	M	N	♣	R	R	R	
Hamburg Hbf **840** d.	1451x	...	...	1536r	1551x	...	1634r	1634r	...	...	...	...	1735r	...	1835r	1835r	...	1937r	...	...	...	...	...	...
Berlin Hbf d.	1701	1704	1726	1734	1812	...	1829	1829	1828	1900	1904	1927	1931	2004	2029	2029	2029	2127	...	2103s	2228	2228	2235	...
Berlin Südkreuz d.	1708	1711	1733	1741	1818	...	1836	1836	1836	1907	1911	1934	1938	2010	2036	2036	2036	2133	...	2110*	2234	2234	|	...
Lutherstadt Wittenberg d.	|	|	1810	|	|	...	1911	1911	1911	|	|	2010	|	|	2111	2111	2111	2213	...	2149*	2317	2317	|	...
Bitterfeld d.	|	|	|	1834	|	...	|	|	|	|	|	|	2034	|	|	|	|	2229	...	2209	2334	2334	0004	...
Halle (Saale) Hbf d.	1815	1821	|	1852	|	...	|	|	|	2015	2021	|	2052	2118	|	|	|	|	...	|	0110z	0110z	0110z	...
Dresden Hbf **842** d.	|	|	|	|	|	1810	|	|	|	|	|	|	|	|	|	|	|	|	2102	|	|	|	|	...
Leipzig Hbf a.	|	|	1842	|	|	1926	1942	1942	1942	|	|	2042	|	|	2142	2142	2142	2248	2218	2229	2355	2355	0025	...
Leipzig Hbf d.	|	|	1848	|	|	1933	...	1948	1948	|	|	2048	|	|	2148	2148	...	2255	2345	2345	0035	0035	0035	...
Erfurt Hbf a.	1845	1848	1928	1924	|	2016	...	2029	2029	2045	2048	2128	2124p	2145	2229	2229	...	2335	0121	0121	|	0143	0143	...
Erfurt Hbf **849a** d.	1847	1850	1930	1932	|	2018	...	2031	2031	2047	2050	2130	2132	2147	...	2235	...	2341	0123	0123	|	0145	0145	...
Coburg **875** d.	|	|	|	|	|	|	...	|	|	|	|	|	2206	|	...	|	...	|	|	|	|	|	|	...
Bamberg **875** d.	|	|	|	2017	|	|	...	|	|	|	|	|	2228	|	...	2320	...	|	|	|	0421	|	|	...
Erlangen **875** d.	|	|	|	|	|	|	...	2137	2137	|	|	|	2252	|	...	2342	...	|	|	|	0443	|	|	...
Nürnberg Hbf **875** a.	|	2000	|	2052	2056	|	...	2152	2152	|	2158	|	2309	2256	...	2357	...	|	|	|	0502	0557	0557	...
München Hbf **904 905** a.	|	2112	|	2243	2202	|	...	2305	2305	|	2309	|	...	0001	...	0114	...	|	|	|	...	...	...	...
Gotha **849a** d.	|	...	|	...	...	2033	...	...	...	|	...	|	...	...	...	...	...	|	|	|	...	...	...	...
Eisenach **849a** d.	|	...	1956	...	...	2048	...	...	...	|	...	2155	...	...	...	...	...	0012	|	|	...	...	...	...
Bad Hersfeld d.	|	...	|	...	...	2116	...	...	...	|	...	|	...	...	...	...	...	|	|	|	...	...	...	...
Fulda **900/1/2** d.	|	...	2050	...	...	2142	...	...	...	|	...	2251	...	...	...	...	...	|	|	|	...	...	...	...
Hanau Hbf **901** d.	|	...	|	...	...	|	...	...	...	|	...	|	...	...	...	...	...	|	|	|	...	...	...	...
Frankfurt (M) Hbf **900/1/2** ◇ a.	2056	...	2144	...	...	2236	...	...	...	2256	...	2348	...	...	...	...	...	0211	0335•	0335•	...	...	...	...
Frankfurt Flughafen ✈ § ◇ a.	...	...	|	...	...	...	...	...	...	|	...	...	...	...	...	...	...	0237	...	...	...	...	...	...
Stuttgart Hbf **910** a.	...	...	2308	...	...	...	...	...	...	0051	...	...	...	...	...	...	...	0452	...	...	...	...	...	...
Mainz Hbf ◇ a.	...	...	...	...	...	...	...	...	...	...	...	...	...	...	...	...	...	...	...	...	...	...	...	...
Wiesbaden Hbf ◇ a.	...	...	...	...	...	...	...	...	...	...	...	...	...	...	...	...	...	...	...	...	...	...	...	...

A – To Wien via Passau (Tables **920** and **950**).
B – From Ostseebad Binz on ⑥⑦ (Tables **844** and **845**).
D – From Lübeck Hbf until Aug. 1 (d. 1317; Table **825**).
G – To Garmisch on ⑥ (Table **895**).
H – To Saarbrücken (Table **919**).
J – To Jena (Table **849a**).
K – From Kiel (Table **820**).
L – From Lichtenfels (d. 0622).
M – To München via Ulm (Table **910**).
N – CANOPUS – 🛏 1, 2 cl. and 🛋 2 cl. (Ⓡ) Praha - Dresden - Leipzig - Basel - Zürich. Also conveys 🚲 (*EC* **458**).
O – From Ostseebad Binz (Tables **844** and **845**).
P – To München via Ulm on Ⓑ (Table **910**).

R – From Rostock on Ⓑ (Table **835**). To Wien via Jena and Passau (Tables **849a**, **920** and **950**).
S – From Stralsund on ①–⑤ (Table **845**).
T – Ⓑ (daily from Aug. 2).
U – Until June 13 (not June 10, 12).
W – Until Aug. 1.
Y – Until Sept. 23.
Z – From Sept. 24.

a – ①–⑤. Departs 0449 from Aug. 2 (see note **r**).
b – June 5 - July 31.
c – Aug. 1 - Sept. 23.
d – Sept. 24 - Dec. 13.
p – Connects with train in previous column.

r – Departs approx. 50 minutes earlier from Aug. 2 (diverted via Salzwedel and Stendal; see amended version of Table **840** on page 608).
s – Departs 2024 Sept. 24 - Dec. 13.
x – Not Aug. 2 - Dec. 13.
z – Arrives 0056 (calls after Leipzig).

⊙ – From Warnemünde / Rostock (Table **835**).
♣ – To Zürich via Basel (Table **910**). Conveys 🛏 1, 2 cl. and 🛋 2 cl. (Ⓡ). Also conveys 🚲 (*IC* **60408**).
• – Frankfurt (Main) **Süd** (not Hbf).
§ – Frankfurt Flughafen Fernbahnhof ✈.
◇ – See Tables **914**, **917** and **917a** for other local services.
* – Not June 26 - 28, Sept. 24 - Dec. 13.

850 FRANKFURT and NÜRNBERG - ERFURT - LEIPZIG / HALLE - BERLIN

km		IC 494	IC 494	NJ 409	EN 40459	ICE 1606	ICE 698	ICE 806	ICE 806	ICE 1636	ICE 1604	ICE 1604	ICE 1704	ICE 1714	ICE 1553	ICE 1008	ICE 804	ICE 696	ICE 1114	ICE 934	ICE 602	ICE 1555	ICE 1006	ICE 802	ICE 694
		Z	V						①–⑤	①–⑥	⑦	①–⑥	F	⑥W	⑥d										
		T	T	♣	N	✕	M✕	✕	✕	L✕	✕	✕	J✕	JO✕	✕	D✕	K✕	H✕	✕	✕	✕	✕	✕	✕	✕
	Wiesbaden Hbf ◇ d.	...	...	...	...	...	...	...	...	...	...	...	...	...	...	...	...	...	...	...	...	0627	...	...	...
	Mainz Hbf ◇ d.	...	...	...	...	...	...	...	...	...	...	...	...	...	...	...	...	...	...	...	...	|	...	...	...
	Stuttgart Hbf **910** d.	...	...	...	...	...	0011	...	...	...	...	...	...	...	...	...	...	...	...	0456g	...	|	...	...	0650
	Frankfurt Flughafen ✈ § ◇ d.	...	...	...	...	...	0229	...	...	...	...	...	...	...	...	...	...	...	...	|	...	0702	...	...	|
	Frankfurt (M) Hbf **900/1/2** ◇ d.	...	...	0027•	0027•	...	0249	...	...	...	...	...	...	...	...	...	...	0614	...	0702	...	0718	...	...	0814
	Hanau Hbf **901** d.	...	...	|	|	...	|	...	...	...	...	...	...	...	...	...	...	|	...	|	...	|	...	...	|
	Fulda **900/1/2** d.	...	...	0124	0124	...	|	...	...	...	...	...	...	...	...	...	...	0711	...	|	...	0815	...	...	0911
	Bad Hersfeld d.	...	...	|	|	...	|	...	...	...	...	...	...	...	...	...	...	|	...	|	...	0841	...	...	|
	Eisenach **849a** d.	...	...	|	|	...	0447	...	0553	0638	...	...	...	...	...	...	...	0801	...	|	...	0908	...	...	1001
	Gotha **849a** d.	...	...	|	|	...	0503	...	0610u	0653	...	...	...	...	...	...	...	|	...	|	...	0922	...	...	|
	München Hbf **904 905** d.	...	...	|	|	...	|	...	|	|	...	...	...	...	...	0553	0506a	|	0651	|	0657	|	0756	0713	|
0	**Nürnberg** Hbf **875** d.	0003	0026	|	|	...	|	...	|	|	...	0542	...	...	...	0659	0706	|	0801	|	0805	|	0902	0905	|
24	Erlangen **875** d.	|	0043	|	|	...	|	...	|	|	...	0558	...	...	...	|	|	|	|	|	0819	|	|	|	|
62	**Bamberg** **875** d.	|	0105	|	|	...	|	...	|	|	...	0622	...	...	...	|	0742	|	|	|	0842	|	|	0942	|
	Coburg **875** d.	|	|	|	|	...	|	...	|	|	...	0644	...	...	...	|	|	|	|	|	|	|	|	|	|
190	**Erfurt** Hbf **849a** a.	0336	|	0244	0244	...	0518	...	0626	0708	...	0724	...	...	...	0809	0824	0826p	0909	0909	0926	0938	|	1024	1026p
190	**Erfurt** Hbf d.	0338	|	0246	0246	0527a	0522	...	0628	0710	...	0727	...	...	0740	0811	0832	0828	0911	0912	0928	0940	|	1032	1028
	Leipzig Hbf a.	0453	0453	0448	0448	0609a	|	...	0710	|	...	0810	...	...	0824	|	|	0910	|	|	1010	1024	|	|	1110
	Leipzig Hbf d.	0514	0514	0518	0545	0617	◧	0716	0716	|	0818	0818	0818	0818	0831	|	|	0916	|	|	1016	1031	|	|	1116
	Dresden Hbf **842** a.	|	|	|	0706	|	|	|	|	|	|	|	|	|	0939	|	|	|	|	|	|	1140	|	|	|
284	**Halle** (Saale) Hbf d.	0431y	0431y	0537s	...	|	0640	|	|	0744	|	|	|	|	...	0840	0906	|	0941	0946	|	...	|	1106	|
314	Bitterfeld d.	0532	0532	0602s	...	|	0656	|	|	0801	|	|	|	|	...	|	0924	|	|	|	|	...	|	1124	|
351	Lutherstadt Wittenberg d.	0547	0547	0619s	...	0648	|	0748	0748	|	0848	0848	0848	0848	...	|	|	0948	|	|	1048	...	|	|	1148
442	**Berlin** Südkreuz a.	0624	0624	0711	...	0722	0747	0826	0826	0850	0922	0922	0922	0922	...	0946	1015	1025	1046	1050	1122	...	1133	1215	1225
448	**Berlin** Hbf a.	0631	0631	0720	...	0729	0755	0833	0833	0857	0929	0929	0929	0929	...	0953	1022	1032	1056	1059	1130	...	1142	1222	1234
	Hamburg Hbf **840** a.	...	...	...	...	0924r	...	1022r	1022r	...	1124r	1124r	1124r	...	...	1151x	1222r	...	...	1311x	1324r	...	1351x	1423r	...

	ICE 1112	ICE 932	ICE 1600	ICE 1710	ICE 1557	ICE 94	ICE 1694	ICE 800	ICE 692	ICE 1110	ICE 930	ICE 508	ICE 1559	ICE 1004	ICE 708	ICE 690	ICE 1108	ICE 838*	ICE 506	ICE 1651	ICE 92	ICE 706	ICE 1218	ICE 1106	ICE 836
				W												⊙								Y	
	✕	B✕	✕	O✕	✕	A✕	✕	✕	M✕	✕	✕	✕	✕	✕	k✕	M✕	✕	✕	✕	✕	A✕	✕	M✕	✕	✕
Wiesbaden Hbf ◇ d.	...	...	...	...	0826	...	...	...	...	...	...	...	1026	...	...	...	...	...	...	1226	...	...	...	...	...
Mainz Hbf ◇ d.	...	...	...	...	0843	...	...	...	...	...	...	...	1043	...	...	...	...	...	...	1243	...	...	...	...	...
Stuttgart Hbf **910** d.	...	...	...	...	|	...	...	...	0851	...	...	...	|	...	...	1051	...	...	...	|	...	...	1251	...	...
Frankfurt Flughafen ✈ § . ◇ d.	...	...	...	...	0902	...	...	...	|	...	...	...	1102	...	...	|	...	...	...	1302	...	...	|	...	...
Frankfurt (M) Hbf **900/1/2** ◇ d.	...	0902	...	...	0918	...	...	...	1014	...	1102	...	1118	...	...	1214	...	1302	...	1318	...	...	1414	...	1502
Hanau Hbf **901** d.	...	|	...	...	|	...	...	...	|	...	|	...	|	...	...	|	...	|	...	|	...	...	|	...	|
Fulda **900/1/2** d.	...	|	...	...	1015	...	...	...	1111	...	|	...	1215	...	...	1311	...	|	...	1415	...	...	1511	...	|
Bad Hersfeld d.	...	|	...	...	1041	...	...	...	|	...	|	...	1241	...	...	|	...	|	...	1441	...	...	|	...	|
Eisenach **849a** d.	...	|	...	...	1108	...	...	...	1201	...	|	...	1308	...	...	1401	...	|	...	1508	...	...	1601	...	|
Gotha **849a** d.	...	|	...	...	1122	...	...	...	|	...	|	...	1322	...	...	|	...	|	...	1522	...	...	|	...	|
München Hbf **904 905** d.	0851	|	0854	0854	|	...	0838	0954	|	1051	|	1056	|	1156	1113	|	1251	|	1254	|	...	1353	|	1451	|
Nürnberg Hbf **875** d.	1001	|	1006	1006	|	1035	1035	1106	|	1201	|	1205	|	1302	1305	|	1401	|	1405	|	1436	1505	|	1601	|
Erlangen **875** d.	|	|	1020	1020	|	|	|	|	|	|	|	1219	|	|	|	|	|	|	1419	|	|	|	|	|	|
Bamberg **875** d.	|	|	|	|	|	|	|	1142	|	|	|	1242	|	|	1342	|	|	|	1442	|	|	1542	|	|	|
Coburg **875** d.	|	|	|	|	|	1129	1129	|	|	|	|	|	|	|	|	|	|	|	|	|	1529	|	|	|	|
Erfurt Hbf **849a** a.	1109	1109	1126	1126	1138	1202	1202	1224	1226p	1309	1308	1326	1338	|	1424	1426p	1509	1509	1526	1538	1602	1624	1626p	1709	1709
Erfurt Hbf d.	1111	1111	1128	1128	1140	1205	1205	1232	1228	1311	1310	1328	1340	|	1432	1428	1511	1512	1528	1540	1605	1632	1628	1711	1712
Leipzig Hbf a.	|	|	1210	1210	1224	|	|	|	1310	|	|	1410	1424	|	|	1510	|	|	1610	1624	|	|	1710	|	|
Leipzig Hbf d.	|	|	1216	1216	1231	|	|	|	1316	|	|	1416	1431	|	|	1516	|	|	1616	1631	|	|	1716	|	|
Dresden Hbf **842** a.	|	|	|	|	1340	|	|	|	|	|	|	|	1540	|	|	|	|	|	|	1740	|	|	|	|	|
Halle (Saale) Hbf d.	1141	1146	|	|	...	1240	1240	1306	|	1341	1346	|	...	|	1506	|	1541	1546	|	...	1640	1706	|	1741	1746
Bitterfeld d.	|	|	|	|	...	|	|	1324	|	|	|	|	...	|	1524	|	|	|	|	...	|	1724	|	|	|
Lutherstadt Wittenberg d.	|	|	1248	1248	...	|	|	|	1348	|	|	1448	...	|	|	1548	|	|	1648	...	|	|	1748	|	|
Berlin Südkreuz a.	1246	1250	1322	1322	...	1345	1345	1415	1425	1447	1450	1522	...	1533	1615	1625	1646	1650	1722	...	1745	1815	1825	1846	1850
Berlin Hbf a.	1256	1257	1329	1329	...	1353	1353	1422	1432	1456	1459	1530	...	1542	1622	1632	1656	1657	1732	...	1752	1822	1832	1856	1857
Hamburg Hbf **840** a.	...	...	1524r	...	...	1600x	...	1622r	...	...	...	1724r	...	1757x	1822r	...	...	...	1924r	...	1951x	2023r	...	...	...

	ICE 504	ICE 1653	ICE 1002	ICE 704	ICE 596	ICE 1104	ICE 834	ICE 502	ICE 1655	ICE 1000	ICE 702	ICE 594	ICE 1102	ICE 832	ICE 500	ICE 1657	ICE 1018	ICE 592	ICE 592	ICE 592	ICE 1500	ICE 1100	ICE 600	ICE 1659	ICE 1659
						Y											△	⑦	⑤⑥		Ⓑ	⑤Y	⑦f	Ⓑ	⑦
	✕	✕	G✕	✕	M✕	✕	✕	✕	✕	✕	✕	M✕	✕	✕	✕	✕	✕	M✕	M✕	M✕	✕	✕	✕	✕	✕
Wiesbaden Hbf ◇ d.	...	1426	...	...	...	...	...	...	1626	...	...	...	...	...	...	1826	...	...	...	...	...	...	...	2026	2026
Mainz Hbf ◇ d.	...	1443	...	...	...	...	...	...	1643	...	...	...	...	...	...	1843	...	...	...	...	...	...	...	2043	2043
Stuttgart Hbf **910** d.	...	|	...	...	1451	...	...	...	|	...	...	1651	...	...	...	|	...	1851	1851	1851	...	...	...	|	|
Frankfurt Flughafen ✈ § . ◇ d.	...	1502	...	...	|	...	...	...	1702	...	...	|	...	...	...	1902	...	|	|	|	...	...	...	2102	2102
Frankfurt (M) Hbf **900/1/2** ◇ d.	...	1518	...	...	1614	...	1702	...	1718	...	...	1814	...	1902	...	1918	...	2014	2014	2014	...	...	...	2118	2118
Hanau Hbf **901** d.	...	|	...	...	|	...	|	...	|	...	...	|	...	|	...	|	...	|	|	|	...	...	...	|	|
Fulda **900/1/2** d.	...	1615	...	...	1711	...	|	...	1815	...	...	1911	...	|	...	2015	...	2111	2111	2111	...	...	...	2215	2215
Bad Hersfeld d.	...	1641	...	...	|	...	|	...	1841	...	...	|	...	|	...	2041	...	|	|	|	...	...	...	2241	2241
Eisenach **849a** d.	...	1708	...	...	1801	...	|	...	1908	...	...	2001	...	|	...	2108	...	2201	2201	2201	...	...	...	2308	2308
Gotha **849a** d.	...	1722	...	...	|	...	|	...	1922	...	...	|	...	|	...	2122	...	|	|	|	...	...	...	2322	2322
München Hbf **904 905** d.	1456	|	1556	1513	|	1649v	|	1654	|	1751	1709	|	1851	|	1855	|	1955	|	|	|	1909	2052	2055	|	|
Nürnberg Hbf **875** d.	1605	|	1702	1705	|	1801	|	1805	|	1900	1906	|	2002	|	2007	|	2102	|	|	|	2105	2203	2205	|	|
Erlangen **875** d.	1619	|	|	|	|	|	|	1819	|	|	|	|	|	|	2021	|	|	|	|	|	2120	|	2220	|	|
Bamberg **875** d.	1642	|	|	1742	|	|	|	1842	|	|	1942	|	|	|	2043	|	|	|	|	|	2142	|	2243	|	|
Coburg **875** d.	|	|	|	|	|	|	|	|	|	|	|	|	|	|	|	|	|	|	|	|	2205	|	|	|	|
Erfurt Hbf **849a** a.	1726	1738	|	1824	1826p	1909	1909	1926	1938	2009	2024	2026p	2109	2109	2126	2138	2209	2226	2226	2226	2239	2309	2325	2338	2338
Erfurt Hbf d.	1728	1740	|	1832	1828	1911	1912	1928	1940	2011	2032	2028	2111	2112	2128	2140	2211	2228	2228	...	2243	2311	2327	...	2343
Leipzig Hbf a.	1810	1824	|	|	1910	|	|	2010	2024	|	|	2110	|	|	2210	2224	|	2310	2310	...	2326	|	0007	...	0027
Leipzig Hbf d.	1816	1831	|	|	1916	|	|	2016	2031b	|	|	2116	|	|	2216	2231	|	2316	...	...	...	|	0013	...	...
Dresden Hbf **842** a.	|	1940	|	|	|	|	|	|	2140b	|	|	|	|	|	|	2343	|	|	...	...	...	|	|	...	...
Halle (Saale) Hbf d.	|	...	|	1906	|	1941	1946	|	...	2040	2106	|	2141	2146	|	...	2242	|	...	...	...	2342	|	...	...
Bitterfeld d.	|	...	|	1924	|	|	|	|	...	|	2124	|	|	|	2234	...	|	2334	...	...	...	|	|	...	...
Lutherstadt Wittenberg d.	1848	...	|	|	1948	|	|	2048	...	|	|	2148	|	|	2250	...	|	2351	...	...	...	|	0044	...	...
Berlin Südkreuz a.	1922	...	1933	2015	2025	2046	2050	2122	...	2146	2215	2225	2245	2248	2325	...	2343	0029	...	...	...	0107	0121	...	...
Berlin Hbf a.	1930	...	1943c	2022	2032	2056	2057	2130	...	2153	2222	2232	2252	2256	2332	...	2350	0036	...	...	...	0114	0128	...	...
Hamburg Hbf **840** a.	2125r	...	...	2222r	...	...	...	2334r	...	...	...	...	...	...	...	...	...	...	...	...	...	...	...	...	...

A – From Wien via Passau (Tables **950** and **920**).
B – From Saarbrücken (Table **919**). To Ostseebad Binz on ⑥⑦ (Tables **844** and **845**).
D – To Lübeck Hbf until Aug. 1 (a. 1241).
F – ①–⑤ (also ⑥ from Aug. 2).
G – From Garmisch on ⑥ (Table **895**).
H – From Karlsruhe on ① (Table **910**).
J – From Jena (Table **849a**).
K – To Kiel until Aug. 1 (Table **820**).
L – To Ostseebad Binz on ⑤⑥ (Tables **844** and **845**).
M – From München via Ulm (Table **910**).
N – CANOPUS – 🛏 1, 2 cl. and ▬ 2 cl. (Ⓡ) Zürich - Basel - Leipzig - Dresden - Praha. Also conveys [2] (*EC* **459**).
O – To Ostseebad Binz (Tables **844** and **845**).
T – From Wien via Passau and Jena (Tables **849a**, **920** and **950**). To Rostock / Warnemünde (Table **835**).
V – Not Aug. 1 - Oct. 16. Times may vary.

W – Until Aug. 1.
Y – Until Sept. 23.
Z – Aug. 1 - Oct. 16. Times may vary.

a – Ⓐ only.
b – Not ⑥.
c – 1945 on ⑥.
d – Also Oct. 3; not Oct. 4.
f – Not Aug. 10.
g – ① (also June. 9; not June 10).
k – Continues to Kiel from Aug. 2.
p – Connects with train in previous column.
r – Arrives approx. 50 - 55 minutes later from Aug. 2, also after 2200 on Aug. 1 (diverted via Stendal and Salzwedel; see amended version of Table **840** on page 608).
s – Calls to set down only.

u – Calls to pick up only.
v – 1652 on Ⓒ.
x – Not Aug. 2 - Dec. 13.
y – Arrives 0413 (calls before Leipzig).

* – Train number **938** on ⑥⑦.
⊙ – To Rostock / Warnemünde (Table **835**).
△ – Until June 28 runs via Leipzig (a. 2247 / d. 2303), not Halle (Berlin Hbf a. 0017).
◧ – Also calls at Weimar (d. 0537) and Naumburg (d. 0605).
• – Frankfurt (Main) **Süd** (not Hbf).
♣ – From Zürich via Basel (Table **910**). Conveys 🛏 1, 2 cl. and ▬ 2 cl. (Ⓡ). Also conveys [2] (*IC* **60409**). Berlin a. 0752 from Sept. 23, not calling at Lutherstadt Wittenberg.
◇ – See Tables **914**, **917** and **917a** for other local services.
§ – Frankfurt Flughafen Fernbahnhof ✈.

RE services — STENDAL - BERLIN - LUTHERSTADT WITTENBERG and FALKENBERG — 851

km																							
																							⑤⑥
0	**Stendal** d.	...	0444r	...	0546t	0640	...	...	0845	...	...	1044v	...	and in	...	1844v	...	...	2050x	...	...	...	2245	H
34	Rathenow d.	0406t	0508	...	0606	0706	...	0806	0906	...	1002	1103	...	the same	1802	1903	...	2002	2112	...	2206	...	2306	...
92	**Berlin** Spandau d.	0452t	0552	...	0652	0751	...	0853	0951	...	1052	1151	...	pattern	1852	1951	...	2052	2151	...	2252	...	2352	...
	Stralsund Hbf **845** d.	|	|	...	|	|	...	|	|	...	|	|	...	every	|	|	...	|	|	...	|	2016	|	...
	Schwedt **845** d.	|	|	0506	|	|	0706	|	|	0906	|	|	1106	**two** hours	|	|	1905	|	|	2106	|	|	|	2306
104	**Berlin** Hbf a.	0502t	0602	0628	0702	0801	0828	0902	1001	1028	1102	1201	1228	until	1902	2001	2028	2102	2201	2228	2302	2332	0003	0028
104	**Berlin** Hbf **850** ◇ d.	0505	0604	0632	0705	0803	0832	0905	1003	1032	1105	1203	1232	⊠	1905	2003	2032	2105	2203f	2231	▬	2333	...	0042
110	**Berlin** Südkreuz **850** ◇ d.	0514	0614	0641	0714	0811	0841	0914	1014	1041	1114	1214	1241		1914	2014	2041	2114	2214f	2240	...	2343	...	0051
156	Luckenwalde ◇ d.	0546	0648	0716	0746	0849	0916	0946	1048	1116	1146	1248	1316		1946	2048	2116	2147	2248f	2323	...	0024	...	0134
169	Jüterbog ◇ d.	0554	0656	0724	0754	0856	0924	0954	1056	1124	1154	1256	1324		1954	2056	2124	2156	2256f	2332	2340	0034	...	0142
218	**Falkenberg** (Elster) a.	0634	...	|	0834	...	|	1034	...	|	1234	...	|		2034	...	|	*2244*	...	|	0021	|	...	|
	Lutherstadt Wittenberg 850 a.	...	...	0759	...	...	0959	...	...	1159	...	...	1359		...	...	2156	....	...	0001	...	0103z	...	0158

km																							
		©	Ⓐ		©																P			E
0	**Lutherstadt Wittenberg 850** d.	0034	...	...	...	...	0505	...	...	0700	...	...	and in	1700	...	...	...	1905	...	...	2100		...	2300
	Falkenberg (Elster) d.	|	...	...	0350	...	|	0514	...	|	0708*	...	the same	|	1714	...	...	|	1914	...	|	2114	...	|
32	Jüterbog ◇ d.	0102	...	0432	0432	0503	0537	0555	0703	0736	0755	0903	pattern	1736	1755	1903	...	1936	1955	2103	2136	2153	2203	2329
45	Luckenwalde ◇ d.	0111	...	0440	0440	0516	0545	0610j	0711	0744	0810j	0911	every	1744	1810j	1918	...	1944	2010j	2111	2144	...	2211	2337
91	**Berlin** Südkreuz **850** ◇ d.	0153	...	0520	0520	0549	0623	0645	0745	0824	0845	0945	**two** hours	1824	1845	1945	...	2024	2045	2145	2224	...	2258	0028
97	**Berlin** Hbf **850** ◇ a.	0201	...	0527	0527	0555	0630	0653	0752	0832	0853	0952	until	1831	1853	1952	...	2031	2053	2152	2231	...	2305	0034
	Berlin Hbf d.	...	0457	0532	0532	0557	0633	0657	0755	0833	0857	0957	⊠	1833	1857	1957	...	2033	2057	2157	2233h	...	2307	...
	Schwedt **845** a.	...	|	0656	0656	|	|	|	|	|	|	|		|	|	|	...	|	|	|	2357h	...	|	...
	Stralsund Hbf **845** a.	...	|	...	...	|	0941	|	|	1141	|	|		2142	|	|	...	2341	|	|	...	...	|	...
	Berlin Spandau d.	...	0508	...	...	0609	...	0708	0809	...	0908	1009		...	1908	2009	...	...	2108	2209	...	...	2318	...
	Rathenow a.	...	0552	...	...	0656	...	0755	0856	...	0955	1053		...	1955	2056	...	...	2152	2252	...	...	2358	...
	Stendal a.	...	0613	...	...	0715	...	...	0915•	...	...	1114•		...	...	2126•	...	...	...	2313	...	...	0017	...

E – To Eberswalde (also Schwedt on ©). See Table **845**.
H – ⑤⑥ from Schwedt (⑥⑦ from Berlin). To / from Halle on dates in Table **848**.
P – To Pasewalk (Table **845**) on ⑤⑥.
f – ⑤⑥.
h – ⑦–④.
j – Arrives 8 mins earlier.
r – ⚒ only.
t – Ⓐ only.
v – 12 mins earlier from Aug. 2.
x – 2033 from Aug. 2.
z – Mornings of © only.
• – From Aug. 2 arrives every 2 hours 0929 - 2129.
◇ – Additional trains run Berlin - Jüterbog and v.v.
⊠ – Timings may vary by 2 - 3 minutes.
* – Following departures: 0914, 1114, 1314, 1514.

RE services — COTTBUS - LEIPZIG — 852

km											
		◐	◐	◐	◐	◐	◐	◐	◐		
	Frankfurt (Oder) **838** d.	...	0536	0736	0936	1136	1336	1536	1736	1936	...
0	**Cottbus** Hbf d.	0459	0703	0903	1103	1303	1503	1703	1903	2105	2303
24	Calau (Niederl) d.	0516	0719	0919	1119	1319	1519	1719	1919	2122	2322
46	Finsterwalde d.	0529	0733	0933	1133	1333	1533	1733	1933	2136	2339
56	Doberlug-Kirchhain d.	0537	0741	0941	1141	1341	1541	1741	1941	2144	2347
79	Falkenberg (Elster) a.	0554	0758	0958	1158	1358	1558	1758	1958	2158	0013
	Falkenberg (Elster) d.	0557	0801	1001	1201	1401	1601	1801	2001	2159	...
97	Torgau d.	0610	0814	1014	1214	1414	1614	1814	2014	2211	...
124	Eilenburg d.	0631	0831	1031	1231	1431	1631	1831	2031	2228	...
149	**Leipzig** Hbf a.	0650	0850	1050	1250	1450	1650	1850	2050	2248	...

		◐	◐	◐	◐	◐	◐	◐		
Leipzig Hbf d.	0507	0712	0912	1112	1312	1512	1712	1912	2112	2333
Eilenburg d.	0526	0731	0931	1131	1331	1531	1731	1931	2131	2352
Torgau d.	0544	0749	0949	1149	1349	1549	1749	1949	2149	0014
Falkenberg (Elster) a.	0555	0800	1000	1200	1400	1600	1800	2000	2200	0026
Falkenberg (Elster) d.	0558	0803	1003	1203	1403	1603	1803	2003	2203	0027
Doberlug-Kirchhain d.	0617	0816	1016	1216	1416	1616	1816	2016	2216	0041
Finsterwalde d.	0624	0825	1025	1225	1425	1625	1825	2025	2225	0048
Calau (Niederl) d.	0639	0839	1039	1239	1439	1639	1839	2039	2239	0102
Cottbus Hbf a.	0657	0855	1055	1255	1455	1655	1855	2055	2255	0119
Frankfurt (Oder) **838** a.	0821	1021	1221	1421	1621	1821	2021	2221	0021	...

◐ – Also conveys 12 Hoyerswerda - Falkenberg - Leipzig and v.v. (see Table **856**).

☛ Additional trains: **Cottbus** - **Falkenberg** at 0605 Ⓐ, 0805, 1005 and every **two** hours until 2205.
Falkenberg - **Cottbus** at 0346 Ⓐ, 0447, 0655, 0855, 1055, 1255, 1455, 1652 Ⓐ, 1655 ©, 1852 Ⓐ, 1855 © and 2055.

STEAM TRAINS IN SACHSEN — 853

Lößnitzgrundbahn. SDG Sächsische Dampfeisenbahngesellschaft mbH, Am Bahnhof 1, 01468 Moritzburg. ✆ +49 (0) 35207 8929. SEE NOTES ⊠ AND ⊖. www.loessnitzgrundbahn.de

km											
0	Radebeul Ost **842 857** d.	0856	...	1026	...	1326	...	1456	...	1756	...
8	Moritzburg d.	0925	...	1057	...	1355	...	1527	...	1825	...
16	Radeburg a.	...	...	1121	...	...	...	1551	...	...	...

Radeburg d.	...	...	1136	...	...	...	1606	...	...
Moritzburg d.	0933	...	1203	...	1403	...	1633	...	1833
Radebeul Ost **842 857** a.	1000	...	1230	...	1430	...	1700	...	1900

Weißeritztalbahn. SDG Sächsische Dampfeisenbahngesellschaft mbH, Am Bahnhof 1, 01468 Moritzburg. ✆ +49 (0) 35207 89290. SEE NOTE ⊠ AND ⊕. www.weisseritztalbahn.com

km											
		△			△			△			
	Dresden Hbf d.	0834	...	...	1234	...	...	1634	...	...	...
0	Freital-Hainsberg d.	0847	0925	...	1247	1325	...	1647	1705	...	...
15	Dippoldiswalde d.	...	1018	...	...	1418	...	...	1750	...	...
26	Kurort Kipsdorf a.	...	1051	...	...	1451	...	...	...	...	...

		△			△			△	
Kurort Kipsdorf d.	1111	...	...	1511	...	...	...	...	...
Dippoldiswalde d.	1145	...	...	1545	...	...	1802	...	...
Freital-Hainsberg a.	1230	1237	...	1630	1637	...	1847	1908	...
Dresden Hbf a.	...	1250	...	...	1650	...	...	1922	...

Zittauer Schmalspurbahn. SOEG - Sächisch Oberlausitzer Eisenbahngesellschaft mbH, Bahnhofstraße 41, 02763 Zittau. ✆ +49 (0) 3583 540540. www.soeg-zittau.de

km																										
				🍷	Cd	C	🍷		Cd	C	🍷		Cd	C	🍷		C		C		🍷	🍷	🍷	🍷	🍷	🍷
0	Zittau d.	High	0847	0909	1020	...	1109	...	1220	...	1309	...	1420	...	1509	...	1620	...	...	Low	0907	...	...	1307	...	...
9	Bertsdorf d.	season	0946r	0946t	1053	1053	1146t	1146	1253	1253	1346t	1346	1453	1453	1546t	1546	1653	1655	1742	season	0938	1039	1135	1338	1439	1535
12	Kurort Oybin a.	♥	|	0957	1104	|	1157	|	1304	|	1357	|	1504	|	1557	|	|	1704	1754	♣	0949	|	1146	1349	|	1546
13	Kurort Jonsdorf a.	→	0959	...	...	1105	...	1159	...	1305	...	1359	...	1505	...	1559	1705	...	...	→	...	1051	...	...	1451	...

			🍷	C	Cd		🍷	C	Cd		🍷	C	Cd		🍷	C		C		🍷	🍷	🍷	🍷	🍷	🍷
Kurort Jonsdorf d.	High	1008	...	1115	...	1208	...	1315	...	1408	...	1515	...	1608	...	1715	...	...	Low	...	1101	...	...	1501	...
Kurort Oybin d.	season	|	1007	|	1115	|	1207	|	1315	|	1407	|	1515	|	1607	|	1728	1804	season	0959	|	1156	1359	|	1556
Bertsdorf d.	♥	1019	1020	1126	1129	1219	1220	1326	1329	1419	1420	1526	1529	1619	1620	1726	1740	1815	♣	1010	1112	1208	1410	1512	1608
Zittau a.	→	...	1050	...	1158	...	1250	...	1358	...	1450	...	1558	...	1650	...	1810	1845	→	...	...	1237	...	...	1637

C – ⑥⑦ until Nov. 2 (also June 9, Oct. 3, 31). Diesel train.
d – Runs daily Bertsdorf - Oybin and v.v.
r – Arrives 0916.
t – Arrives 6 minutes earlier.
♣ – Nov. 29 - Dec. 14.
♥ – Apr. 5 - Nov. 2.
⊠ – No service Nov. 3 - 21.
⊖ – A special service operates June 8, 9, Oct. 3 - 5.
⊕ – A special service operates June 8, 9.
△ – Suggested main-line connecting service.

Ostdeutsche Eisenbahn (ODEG); 2nd class only — FORST - COTTBUS - GÖRLITZ - ZITTAU — 854

km															
		⑥⑦		Ⓐ	Ⓐ	⑥	⚒		⚒						
0	**Cottbus** Hbf d.	0048	...	...	0503	...	0603	0703	0803	...	0903		2103	2204	2304
24	Spremberg d.	0106	...	...	0521	...	0621	0722	0822	...	0922	and	2122	2222	2322
42	Weißwasser d.	0121	...	...	0535	...	0635	0735	0835	...	0935		2135	2235	2336
72	Horka d.	0142	...	...	0559	...	0659	0759	0859	...	0959	hourly	2159	2259	2358
93	**Görlitz** a.	0157	...	...	0614	...	0714	0814	0914	...	1014		2214	2314	0013
93	**Görlitz** d.	...	...	0512	0618	0618	0718	0818	0918	0918	1018	until	2218	...	...
127	**Zittau** a.	...	...	0549	0655	0655	0755	0855	0955	0955	1055		2255	...	...

	Ⓐ	⚒		⚒	⚒	Ⓐ			⚒					⑤⑥
Zittau d.	...	...	...	0458	...	0604	0704	...	0804	0904		2104	2204	2204
Görlitz a.	...	...	...	0533	...	0639	0739	...	0839	0939	and	2139	2239	2239
Görlitz d.	0344	0437	0543	0543	0643	0643	0743	0843	0843	0943		2143	...	2243
Horka d.	0359	0453	0559	0559	0659	0659	0759	0859	0859	0959	hourly	2159	...	2259
Weißwasser d.	0420	0520	0620	0620	0720	0720	0820	0920	0920	1020		2220	...	2320
Spremberg d.	0434	0538	0638	0638	0738	0738	0838	0938	0938	1038	until	2238	...	2338
Cottbus Hbf a.	0453	0557	0656	0656	0756	0756	0856	0956	0956	1056		2256	...	2356

h – Also June 19, Aug. 15, Nov. 11.
k – Not June 19, Aug. 15, Nov. 11.

FORST (Lausitz) - **COTTBUS** and v.v. *22 km*. Journey time: 18 – 20 minutes.

From Forst at 0429 Ⓐ, 0533, 0633, 0733, 0830 ①–⑤ **k**, 0833 ⑥⑦ **h**, 0933, 1033, 1130 ①–⑤ **k**, 1133 ⑥⑦ **h**, 1233, 1333, 1430 ①–⑤ **k**, 1433 ⑥⑦ **h**, 1533, 1633, 1730 ①–⑤ **k**, 1733 ⑥⑦ **h**, 1833, 1933, 2030 ①–⑤ **k**, 2033 ⑥⑦ **h** and 2133.

From Cottbus Hbf at 0507 Ⓐ, 0607 ⑥⑦ **h**, 0609 ①–⑤ **k**, 0707, 0807 and hourly until 2107; then 2308.

855 DRESDEN - BISCHOFSWERDA - GÖRLITZ and ZITTAU

Trilex (2nd class only)

km																										
		⚒	Ⓐ			⚒ ◧			⚒			⚒									⚒					
0	**Dresden** Hbf ● d.	0356	*0522*	0623	0653	0723	0823	0853	*0923*	1023	1053	*1123*	1223	*1323*	1423	*1523*	1623	*1723*	1823	1853	*1923*	2023	2053	*2123*	2223	*2347*
4	Dresden Neustadt ● d.	0402	*0530*	0635	0702	0735	0835	0906	*0935*	1035	1106	*1135*	1235	*1335*	1435	*1535*	1635	*1735*	1835	1906	*1935*	2035	2106	*2135*	2235	*2355*
41	Bischofswerda ● d.	0438	0602	0706	0741	0808	0904	0941	1008	1104	1141	1208	1304	1408	1504	1608	1704	1808	1904	1941	2008	2104	2141	2208	2304	0032
60	Bautzen d.	0453	0614	0718	0756	0820	0916	0956	1020	1116	1156	1220	1316	1420	1516	1620	1716	1820	1916	1956	2020	2116	2156	2220	2320	0046
82	Löbau (Sachs) d.	0511	0628	0732	0813	0834	0930	1013	1033	1130	1213	1233	1330	1433	1530	1633	1730	1833	1930	2013	2033	2130	2213	2233	2337	0104
105	**Görlitz** 1083 a.	0531	0643	0747	0833	0849	0945	1033	1049	1145	1233	1248	1345	1448	1545	1648	1745	1848	1945	2033	2048	2145	2233	2248	2358	0124
106	Zgorzelec 🏛 1083 a.	...	0649	0756	...	...	0954	...	...	1156	...	1254	1356	1454	1556	1654	...	1854	1958	...	...	...	...	...	...	...

	Ⓐ	Ⓒ	Ⓐ		Ⓐ																⚒					
Zgorzelec 🏛 1083 d.	...	...	...	...	...	0715t	0804	...	1004	...	1204	1304	...	1404	1502	...	1604	1702	...	...	1904	*1904*	2004	...	...	...
Görlitz 1083 d.	0358	0523	0539	0612	0652	0723	0813	0923	1013	1123	1213	1310	1323	1413	1510	1523	1613	1710	1723	1813	1910	1923	2013	2118	2218	2318
Löbau (Sachs) d.	0418	0543	0554	0627	0707	0743	0828	0943	1028	1143	1228	1325	1343	1428	1525	1543	1628	1725	1743	1828	1925	1943	2028	2138	2238	2338
Bautzen d.	0435	0600	0608	0640	0721	0800	0842	1000	1042	1200	1242	1339	1400	1442	1539	1600	1642	1739	1800	1842	1939	2000	2042	2155	2255	2355
Bischofswerda d.	0452	0621k	0621	0654	0734	0821k	0856	1021k	1056	1221k	1256	1351	1421k	1456	1551	1621k	1656	1751	1821k	1856	1951	2021k	2056	2218k	2316k	0018k
Dresden Neustadt a.	0525	0655	0654	0724	0804	0855	0924	1055	1124	1255	1324	*1424*	1455	1524	*1624*	1655	1724	*1824*	1855	1924	*2024*	2055	2124	2251	2350	0053
Dresden Hbf a.	0533	0703	0702	0732	0812	0903	0932	1103	1132	1303	1332	*1432*	1503	1532	*1632*	1703	1732	*1832*	1903	1932	*2032*	2103	2132	2257	2355	0059

km																										
		⚒	Ⓐ	v		v							v												⑤⑥	
0	**Dresden** Hbf ● d.	0356	...	...	0522	...	0553	0723	0753	0923	0953	1123	...	1153	1323	1353	1523	1553	1723	1753	1923	1953	2123	2205	...	2347
4	Dresden Neustadt ● d.	0402	...	...	0530	...	0602	0735	0802	0935	1002	1135	...	1202	1335	1402	1535	1602	1735	1802	1935	2002	2135	2211	...	2355
41	Bischofswerda ● d.	0436	0438	...	0559	...	0637	0806	0837	1004	1037	1204	...	1237	1404	1437	1604	1637	1804	1837	2004	2037	2204	2246	...	0030
79	Ebersbach (Sachs) d.	...	0521	...	0630	...	0726	0835	0926	1034	1126	1234	...	1326	1434	1526	1634	1726	1834	1926	2034	2128	2234	2327	...	0106
83	Neugersdorf d.	...	0525	...	0634	...	0730	0839	0930	1038	1130	1238	...	1330	1438	1530	1638	1730	1838	1930	2038	2132	2238	2331	...	0110
105	**Zittau** a.	...	0546	...	0653	...	0751	0858	0951	1056	1151	1256	...	1351	1456	1551	1656	1751	1856	1951	2056	2153	2256	2352	...	0132
	Zittau 🏛 ≋ 1117 d.	...	...	0612	0656c	0721	*0839*v	0901*	...	1100*	*1216*e	1301c	1318	*1418*v	1500c	*1614*v	1701*	*1836*e	1900*	...	2101c	*2158**	...	...	2358	...
132	Liberec 🏛 ≋ 1117 a.	...	...	0649	0727c	0755	*0912*v	0928*	...	1127*	*1249*e	1329c	1355	*1455*v	1527c	*1649*v	1729*	*1910*e	1927*	...	2131c	*2229**	...	...	0030	...

	Ⓐ		e	Ⓐ								e			e		e									
Liberec 🏛 ≋ 1117 d.	...	...	0454	...	...	0628*	*0731*c	0828*	...	1028*	*1131*c	1228	1228c	*1302*e	1402	1428c	1502	*1531*c	1628*	*1708*e	1829*	*1931**	2028c	*2140*	...	...
Zittau 🏛 ≋ 1117 a.	...	...	0526	...	...	0655*	*0803*c	0859*	...	1056*	*1203*c	1259	1256c	*1341*e	1441	1456c	1541	*1603*c	1658*	*1741*e	1859*	*2003**	2056c	*2218*	...	...
Zittau d.	0411	0457	...	0528	0603	0702	0806	0903	1006	1103	1206	...	1303	1406	...	1503	...	1606	1703	1806	1903	2006	2101	2301	...	...
Neugersdorf d.	0433	0515	...	0551	0625	0720	0828	0921	1028	1121	1228	...	1321	1428	...	1521	...	1628	1721	1828	1922	2028	2123	2322	...	...
Ebersbach (Sachs) d.	0437	0520	...	0555	0633	0724	0836	0925	1036	1125	1236	...	1325	1436	...	1525	...	1636	1725	1836	1926	2036	2126	2326	...	...
Bischofswerda d.	0520k	0556k	...	0632	0723k	0756	0921k	0956	1121k	1156	1321k	...	1356	1521k	...	1556	...	1721k	1756	1921k	1957	2121k	2218r	0001	0018	...
Dresden Neustadt a.	0555	0623	...	0706	0755	0824	0954	1024	1154	1224	1354	...	1424	1554	...	1624	...	1754	1824	1954	2025	2154	2251	...	0053	...
Dresden Hbf a.	0603	0632	...	0712	0802	0832	1003	1032	1203	1232	1403	...	1432	1603	...	1632	...	1803	1832	2003	2033	2203	2257	...	0059	...

c – ⑥⑦ from Oct. 4 (also Oct. 28, Nov. 17).
e – ①–⑤ from Oct. 1 (not Oct. 28, Nov. 17).
k – Arrives 6–8 minutes earlier.
r – Arrives 2201.

t – Ⓐ only.
v – ①–⑤ from Oct. 1 (not Oct. 2, 3, 27, 28, 30, 31, Nov. 17).
* – From Oct. 1.

● – Trains between Dresden and Bischofswerda may convey portions for two separate destinations. Please take care to join the correct portion for your destination.
≋ – By 🚌 to Sept. 30: from Zittau on Ⓐ at 0425, 0525, 0610, 0640, 0710, hourly until 2010, 2140; on Ⓒ hourly 0605 - 2205. From Liberec on Ⓐ at 0425, 0505, 0526, 0605, hourly to 2005, also 2126, 2235; on Ⓒ hourly 0505 to 1805, also 1856, 1956, 2105, 2235. Journey 50 mins.

856 DRESDEN and FALKENBERG - RUHLAND - COTTBUS and HOYERSWERDA

RE / *RB* services

See Tables **842**, **843** and **857** for other services Dresden - Coswig. See Table **852** for faster services Falkenberg - Cottbus (via Doberlug).

km																									
			Ⓐ					Ⓐ					Ⓐ						Ⓐ						
0	**Dresden** Hbf d.	...	...	...	...	...	...	...	...	...	...	...	...	...	...		...	...	...	...	...	...	...	...	...
4	**Dresden** Neustadt d.	...	...	...	0558	...	0658	...	...	0758	...	0858	...	...	0958		...	1858	...	...	1958	...	2058	...	2158
18	Coswig d.	...	...	...	0607	...	0707	...	...	0807	...	0907	...	...	1007	and in	...	1907	...	...	2007	...	2107	...	2207
	Leipzig Hbf **852** d.	...	...	...	|	...	|	...	0712t	|	...	|	...	0912	|	the same	...	|	...	1912	|	...	|	...	|
	Falkenberg (Elster) d.	0516	...	0614	|	0716	|	...	0812	|	0916	|	...	1012	|		1916	|	...	2012	|	2116	|	2216	|
	Elsterwerda d.	|	0602	|	|	|	|	0802	|	|	|	|	1002	|	|	pattern	|	|	2002	|	|	|	|	|	|
	Elsterwerda-Biehla d.	0534	0605	0633	|	0734	|	0805	0833	|	0934	|	1005	1033	|		1934	|	2005	2033	|	2134	|	2234	|
73	Ruhland a.	0555	0627	0655	0656*	0755	0756*	0827	0855	0856*	0955	0956*	1027	1055	1056*	every **two**	1955	1956*	2027	2055	2056*	2155	2156*	2255	2253*
73	Ruhland d.	0559	0628	0702	0659	0759	0802	0828	0902	0859	0959	1002	1028	1102	1059	hours until	1959	2002	2028	2102	2100	2159	2202	2259	2306
	Hoyerswerda a.	|	|	0725	|	|	0825	|	0925	|	|	1025	|	1125	|		|	2025	|	2125	|	|	2225	|	2329
86	Senftenberg d.	0610	0641	...	0709	0810	...	0841	...	0909	1010	...	1041	...	1109		2010	...	2041	...	2110	2210	...	2310	...
120	**Cottbus** Hbf a.	0642	0708	...	0743	0842	...	0908	...	0939	1042	...	1108	...	1137		2040	...	2108	...	2139	2240	...	2340	...

km																									
					Ⓐd			Ⓐ					Ⓐ						Ⓐ						
	Cottbus Hbf d.	...	0414	...	0514	...	0614	0650	...	0714	...	0818	0850	⊠	...	1714	...	1816	1850	...	1916	...	2016	2116	2216
	Senftenberg d.	...	0447	...	0547	...	0647	0717	...	0747	...	0848	0917		...	1747	...	1848	1917	...	1947	...	2047	2147	2247
0	**Hoyerswerda** d.	0430	|	0533	|	0633	|	|	0733	|	0833	|	|	and in	1733	|	1833	|	|	1933	|	2033	|	|	|
25	Ruhland a.	0452	0458*	0555	0558*	0655	0658*	0726	0755	0758*	0855	0857*	0926	the same	1755	1758*	1855	1857*	1926	1955	1958*	2055	2058*	2158	2258
25	Ruhland d.	0502	0501	0601	0605	0702	0701	0727	0801	0805	0902	0901	0927		1801	1805	1902	1901	1927	2001	2005	2101	2105	2205	2305f
51	Elsterwerda-Biehla d.	0524	|	|	0627	0724	|	0751	|	0827	0924	|	0950	pattern	|	1827	1924	|	1950	|	2027	|	2127	2227	2327f
	Elsterwerda a.	|	|	|	|	|	|	0754	|	|	|	|	0953		|	|	|	|	1953	|	|	|	|	|	|
75	**Falkenberg** (Elster) a.	0546	|	|	0646	0746	|	...	|	0846	0946	|	...	every **two**	|	1846	1946	|	...	|	2046	|	2146	2246	2346f
	Leipzig Hbf **852** a.	0650t	|	|	...	0850	|	...	|	...	1050	|	...	hours until	|	...	2050y	|	...	|	...	|	...	...	...
	Coswig d.	...	0547	0647	...	...	0747	...	0847	...	...	0947	...		1847	...	...	1947	...	2047	...	2147	...	...	...
	Dresden Neustadt a.	...	0555	0655	...	...	0755	...	0855	...	...	0955	...		1855	...	...	1955	...	2055	...	2155	...	...	...
	Dresden Hbf a.	...	...	...	...	...	...	...	...	...	...	...	...		...	...	...	...	...	...	...	...	...	...	...

HOYERSWERDA - GÖRLITZ. *72 km.* Journey time: 52 – 59 minutes. Operated by Ostdeutsche Eisenbahn. **No rail service July 1 - Aug. 22.**
Until June 30: **From Hoyerswerda** 0501 Ⓐ, 0643 ⚒, 0843, every **two** hours until 2043, also 2243 ⑥. **From Görlitz** 0520 Ⓐ, 0620 ⚒, 0820, every **two** hours until 1820, also 2028, 2228 ⑥.
From Aug. 23: **From Hoyerswerda** 0631 ⚒, 0731Ⓐ, 0831, every **two** hours until 2031, also 2231 ⑥. **From Görlitz** 0634 ⚒, 0732Ⓐ, 0834, every **two** hours until 2034, also 1532Ⓐ, 2234 ⑥.

d – Runs daily Ruhland - Falkenberg.
f – ⑤⑥ (also June 8).

t – Ⓐ only.
y – † only.

* – Connects with train in preceding column.
⊠ – Cottbus departure variations: 1416 (not 1418) and 1616 (not 1618).

857 BAD SCHANDAU - DRESDEN - MEISSEN

S-Bahn

km																		
				Ⓐ			⚒											
0	**Bad Schandau** ⊡ 1100 d.	...	...	0444	...	0514	0544	...	0614	0644		2114	2144	2214	2244	2314	...	0014
23	Pirna d.	...	0436	0506	0506	0536	0606	0606	0636	0706	and every	2136	2206	2236	2306	2336	0006	0036
40	**Dresden** Hbf 842 843 856 1100 d.	0430	0500	0530	0530	0600	0630	0630	0700	0730		2200	2230	2300	2330	0000	0028	0058
44	**Dresden** Neustadt 842 856 d.	0437	0507	0537	0537	0607	0637	0637	0707	0737	30 minutes	2207	2237	2307	2337	0007	...	...
50	Radebeul Ost d.	0446	0516	0546	0546	0616	0646	0646	0716	0746		2216	2246	2316	2346	0016	...	...
58	Coswig 842 843 856 d.	0456	0526	0556	0556	0626	0656	0656	0726	0756	until	2226	2256	2326	2356	0030j	...	...
68	**Meißen** a.	0504	0534	0604	0604	0634	0704	0704	0734	0804		2234	2304	2334	0005	0039	...	...

f – Arrives 2357.
j – Arrives 0025.

		Ⓐ			⚒													
Meißen d.	...	...	0421	0451	0451	0521	0551		2021	2051	2121	2151	2221	2251	2321	...	0021	...
Coswig 842 843 856 d.	...	...	0430	0500	0500	0530	0600	and every	2030	2100	2130	2200	2230	2300	2330	...	0030	...
Radebeul Ost d.	...	...	0440	0510	0510	0540	0610		2040	2110	2140	2210	2240	2310	2340	...	0040	...
Dresden Neustadt 842 856 d.	...	...	0450	0520	0520	0550	0620	30 minutes	2050	2120	2150	2220	2250	2320	2350	...	0050	...
Dresden Hbf 842 843 856 1100 d.	0429	0429	0459	0529	0529	0559	0629		2059	2129	2159	2229	2259	2329	0012f	...	0057	0100
Pirna d.	0451	0452	0522	0551	0552	0622	0652	until	2122	2152	2222	2252	2322	2351	0035	...	...	0122
Bad Schandau ⊡ 1100 a.	...	0513	0543	...	0613	0643	0713		2143	2213	2243	2313	2343	...	0056	...	...	...

⊡ – A frequent ferry services links the railway station with Bad Schandau town centre. **Operator**: Oberelbische Verkehrsgesellschaft Pirna - Sebnitz mbH. ✆ + 49 (0) 3501 7920. www.ovps.de

857a DRESDEN - DRESDEN FLUGHAFEN ✈

S-Bahn

km									
0	**Dresden** Hbf d.	0418	0448	and at the same	2218	2248	2318	...	...
4	**Dresden** Neustadt d.	0425	0455	minutes past	2225	2255	2325	...	...
15	**Dresden** Flughafen ✈ a.	0439	0509	each hour until	2239	2309	2339	...	...

Dresden Flughafen ✈ d.	0448	0518	0548	and at the same	2318	2348	...
Dresden Neustadt a.	0500	0530	0600	minutes past	2330	2400	...
Dresden Hbf a.	0508	0538	0608	each hour until	2338	0008	...

RE services

GLAUCHAU - GERA - ERFURT 858

WARNING! Journeys from/to Glauchau are subject to alteration Apr. 6 - Aug. 8. See note △.

km		Ⓐ ◧	Ⓒ ◧	⚒		①–⑥ e★	⑦ v						★							⑥ h	Ⓑ b★				◧	◧	
0	**Glauchau** (Sachs) △ d.	...	...	...	...	...	...	0607**r**	...	0807	...	1007	...	1207	...	1407	...	1607	...	...	1807	...	2007	...	...	...
16	Gößnitz a.	...	...	...	...	...	...	0621**r**	...	0821	...	1021	...	1221	...	1421	...	1621	...	...	1821	...	2021	...	...	...
16	Gößnitz d.	...	...	...	...	...	...	0631	...	0831	...	1031	...	1231	...	1431	...	1631	...	...	1831	...	2031	...	...	...
51	**Gera** Hbf a.	...	...	...	...	...	...	0700	...	0900	...	1100	...	1300	...	1500	...	1700	...	...	1900	...	2100	...	...	...
51	**Gera** Hbf d.	...	...	0503	0555	0604	0617	0705	0805	0905	1005	1105	1204	1305	1405	1505	1605	1705	1805	1804	1905	2005	2105	2207	2341	...
91	Jena-Göschwitz d.	0412	0414	0532	0623	0638	0644	0732	0832	0932	1032	1132	1238	1332	1432	1532	1632	1732	1832	1838	1932	2032	2132	2237	0017	...
96	**Jena** West d.	0418	0419	0538	0629	0645	0650	0738	0838	0938	1038	1138	1245	1338	1438	1538	1638	1738	1838	1845	1938	2038	2138	2243	0022	...
119	Weimar **849 850** d.	0439	0436	0554	0646	0704	0706	0754	0854	0954	1054	1154	1304	1354	1454	1554	1654	1754	1854	1904	1954	2054	2154	2300	0041	0048
140	**Erfurt** Hbf **849 850** a.	0455	0450	0607	0700	0716	0721	0807	0909	1007	1109	1207	1316	1407	1512	1607	1712	1807	1909	1916	2007	2107	2207	2314	...	0105
	Göttingen **865** a.	...	...	0751	...	...	...	0951	...	1151	...	1351	...	1551	...	1751	...	1951	...	...	2150	2250	...	...	...	...

	◧	†	⚒	Ⓐ				①–⑥ e★	⑦ v						★						Ⓑ	Ⓑ b★	⑥ h			◧
Göttingen **865** d.	...	...	...	...	...	...	0604	...	...	0808	...	1008	...	1208	...	1408	...	1608	...	1808	1808	...	...	2008	2108	...
Erfurt Hbf **849 850** d.	0037	0437	0436	0543	...	0653	0752	0844	0850	0952	1050	1152	1250	1352	1444	1552	1650	1752	1850	1952	1952	2044	2050	2152	2301	2351
Weimar **849 850** d.	0055	0451	0449	0557	...	0706	0806	0859	0904	1006	1104	1206	1304	1406	1459	1606	1704	1806	1904	2006	2006	2059	2104	2206	2316	0006
Jena West d.	0114	0505	0503	0612	...	0720	0822	0914	0920	1022	1120	1222	1320	1422	1514	1622	1720	1822	1920	2022	2022	2114	2120	2222	2332	0026
Jena-Göschwitz d.	0120	0513	0517**j**	0625**j**	...	0725	0827	0920	0925	1027	1125	1227	1325	1427	1520	1627	1725	1827	1925	2027	2027	2120	2125	2227	2337	0032
Gera Hbf a.	0152**z**	0541	0545	0654	...	0754	0855	0955	0954	1055	1154	1255	1354	1455	1555	1655	1754	1855	1954	2055	2055	2155	2154	2255	0005	0105
Gera Hbf d.	...	0547	...	0658	0658	...	0858	...	...	1058	...	1258	...	1458	...	1658	...	1858	...	...	2058	...	...	...	...	...
Gößnitz a.	...	0623	...	0728	0728	...	0928	...	...	1128	...	1328	...	1528	...	1728	...	1928	...	...	2128	...	...	...	...	...
Gößnitz d.	...	...	...	0736	0736	...	0936	...	...	1136	...	1336	...	1536	...	1736	...	1936	...	...	2136	...	...	...	...	...
Glauchau (Sachs) △ a.	...	...	...	0750	0750	...	0950	...	...	1150	...	1350	...	1550	...	1750	...	1950	...	...	2150	...	...	...	...	...

b – Not June 8, 23, 30, Oct. 3.
e – Not June 9, 30, Oct. 4.
h – Also June 8, Oct. 3.
j – Arrives 9–10 minutes earlier.
r – ⚒ only.
v – Also June 9, Oct. 4.
z – Ⓒ only.
◧ – Operated by Erfurter Bahn.
★ – *IC* service (see Table **849a**). Regional tickets are valid Gera - Erfurt and v.v.
△ – Apr. 6 - Aug. 8 a rail replacement 🚌 service operates Glauchau - Schmölln (km 26) and v.v. (Glauchau departures are at xx06); please check locally for journeys Glauchau - Gößnitz and v.v. during this period.

DB (*RB* services); *erixx*

BRAUNSCHWEIG - BAD HARZBURG, GOSLAR and HERZBERG 859

BRAUNSCHWEIG - GOSLAR and BAD HARZBURG ⊠

km		⚒	Ⓐ	⚒	⚒					
0	**Braunschweig** Hbf d.	0524	0524	0624	0624	0724	0724	and	2324	2324
12	Wolfenbüttel d.	0533	0533	0633	0633	0733	0733	hourly	2333	2333
39	Vienenburg **860** d.	0601	0602	0700	0702	0800	0802		0000	0002
47	**Bad Harzburg 860** a.	|	0611	|	0711	|	0811	until	|	0011
52	**Goslar 860** a.	0616	...	0712	...	0812	...		0012	...

	⚒	⚒	⚒	Ⓐ		Ⓒ					
Goslar 860 d.	0445	...	0545	...	0645	...	...	0745	and	...	2245
Bad Harzburg 860 d.	|	0545	|	0626	|	0645	0745	|	hourly	2245	|
Vienenburg **860** d.	0503	0603	0603	0635	0700**h**	0703	0803	0803		2303	2303
Wolfenbüttel d.	0526	0626	0626	0659	0726	0726	0826	0826	until	2326	2326
Braunschweig Hbf a.	0535	0635	0635	0709	0735	0735	0835	0835		2335	2335

BRAUNSCHWEIG - HERZBERG

km		Ⓒ z B		Ⓐ		⚒				K
0	**Braunschweig** Hbf d.	0005	...	0505	0605	0605	0705	and	2205	2305
31	Salzgitter-Ringelheim d.	0029	...	0529	0629	0629	0729	hourly	2229	2329
52	Seesen d.	0043	...	0544	0643	0644	0744		2244	2344
71	Osterode (Harz) Mitte d.	...	...	0606	...	0706	0806	until	2306	...
83	**Herzberg** (Harz) a.	...	...	0620	...	0720	0820		2320	...

	D		Ⓐ B	⑥ B	Ⓐ			⚒			
Herzberg (Harz) d.	...	...	...	...	0534	...	...	0634	0734	and	2234
Osterode (Harz) Mitte d.	...	...	...	...	0548	...	...	0648	0748	hourly	2248
Seesen d.	0011	...	0511	0611	0611	...	0711	0711	0811		2311
Salzgitter-Ringelheim d.	0028	...	0528	0628	0628	...	0728	0728	0828	until	2328
Braunschweig Hbf a.	0050	...	0550	0650	0650	...	0750	0750	0850		2350

BAD HARZBURG - KREIENSEN - GÖTTINGEN

km		Ⓒ z B	Ⓐ	⚒	Ⓒ	Ⓐ			Ⓐ	Ⓒ															H B
0	**Bad Harzburg 860** d.	...	...	0548	...	0628	0736	0748	...	0822	0936	1022	1136	1222	1336	1422	1536	1622	1736	1822	1936	2022	2136	2222	...
11	Goslar **860** d.	...	0544	0600	0636	0641	0757	0801	0836	0836	0956	1036	1156	1236	1356	1436	1556	1636	1756	1836	1956	2036	2156	2236	...
34	Seesen d.	0044	0603	...	0655	0700	0816	...	0855	0855	1016	1055	1216	1255	1416	1455	1616	1655	1816	1855	2016	2055	2216	2255	2344
48	Bad Gandersheim d.	0054	0613	...	0705	0711	0826	...	0905	0905	1026	1105	1226	1305	1426	1505	1626	1705	1826	1905	2026	2105	2226	2305	2355
54	**Kreiensen** a.	0100	0618	...	0711	0716	0831	...	0911	0911	1031	1111	1231	1311	1431	1511	1631	1711	1831	1911	2031	2111	2231	2311	2400
54	**Kreiensen 903** d.	...	*0624*	...	*0719*	*0723*	0839	...	*0919*	*0919*	1039	*1119*	1239	*1319*	1439	*1519*	1639	*1719*	1839	*1919*	2039	*2119*	2239	*2322*	*0023*
73	Northeim (Han) **903** d.	...	*0637*	...	*0733*	*0736*	0855	...	*0933*	*0933*	1055	*1133*	1255	*1333*	1455	*1533*	1655	*1733*	1855	*1933*	2055	*2133*	2255	*2336*	*0036*
93	**Göttingen 903** a.	...	*0650*	...	*0747*	*0749*	0909	...	*0946*	*0946*	1109	*1146*	1309	*1346*	1509	*1546*	1709	*1746*	1909	*1946*	2109	*2146*	2309	*2349*	*0049*

	Ⓐ B	Ⓐ	⑥ B		Ⓒ	Ⓐ																		
Göttingen 903 d.	*0408*	*0504*	*0504*	*0604*	0648	0719	...	*0809*	0848	*1009*	1048	*1209*	1248	*1407*v	1448	*1609*	1648	*1809*	1848	*2009*	2048	...	*2209*	...
Northeim (Han) **903** d.	*0421*	*0517*	*0517*	*0617*	0702	0734	...	*0823*	0902	*1023*	1102	*1223*	1302	*1421*v	1502	*1623*	1702	*1823*	1902	*2023*	2102	...	*2223*	...
Kreiensen 903 a.	*0434*	*0530*	*0530*	*0631*	0718	0750	...	*0836*	0918	*1036*	1118	*1236*	1318	*1434*v	1518	*1636*	1718	*1836*	1918	*2036*	2118	...	*2236*	...
Kreiensen d.	0456	0535	0556	0642	0724	0750	...	0842	0924	1042	1124	1242	1324	1442	1524	1642	1724	1842	1924	2042	2124	...	2242	...
Bad Gandersheim d.	0501	0540	0601	0647	0729	0756	...	0847	0929	1047	1129	1247	1329	1447	1529	1647	1729	1847	1929	2047	2129	...	2247	...
Seesen d.	0511	0551	0611	0658	0739	0806	...	0858	0939	1058	1139	1258	1339	1458	1539	1658	1739	1858	1939	2058	2139	...	2258	...
Goslar **860** d.	...	0610	...	0718	0800	0826	0856	0918	1000	1118	1200	1318	1400	1518	1600	1718	1800	1918	2000	2118	2200	...	2316	2356
Bad Harzburg 860 a.	...	0623	...	0730	0814	...	0907	0930	1014	1130	1214	1330	1414	1530	1614	1730	1814	1930	2014	2130	2214	...	...	0007

B – 🚲12 Braunschweig - Seesen - Kreiensen and v.v.
D – ①⑥⑦ (also June 10, Oct. 3, 31).
H – ①–④ (not June 9, Oct. 2, 30).
K – Daily. Continues to Kreisensen on dates in note **H** (see lower panel).
h – 0703 on Ⓒ.
v – 2 minutes later on Ⓒ.
z – Also June 9, Oct. 3, 31.
⊠ – Operated by *erixx*.

erixx; *Start Mitteldeutschland*

HANNOVER - BAD HARZBURG and GOSLAR - HALLE 860

HANNOVER - BAD HARZBURG ⊠

km		Ⓐ	⚒							
0	**Hannover** Hbf d.	0448	0548	0648	0746	0848		2248	2348	...
36	**Hildesheim** Hbf d.	0515	0614	0714	0814	0914	and	2314	0015	...
70	Salzgitter-Ringelheim d.	0542	0641	0741	0841	0941	hourly	2341	0042	...
89	Goslar **859** d.	0556	0656	0756	0856	0956	until	2356	0057	...
100	**Bad Harzburg 859** a.	0607	0707	0807	0907	1007		0007	0108	...

	Ⓐ	Ⓐ	⚒	⚒		Ⓐ				⚒	†
Bad Harzburg 859 d.	...	0448	...	0548	...	...	0648		2148	2248	2248
Goslar **859** d.	0403	0503	0503	0603	0603	0635	0703	and	2202	2303	2303
Salzgitter-Ringelheim d.	0416	0516	0516	0616	0616	0648	0716	hourly	2215	2316	2316
Hildesheim Hbf d.	0444	0544	0544	0644	0644	0717	0744	until	2244	2344	2344
Hannover Hbf a.	0510	0610	0610	0710	0710	0741	0810		2310	0010	0013

GOSLAR - HALBERSTADT - HALLE ◇

km			Ⓐ t	Ⓐ t	Ⓒ z	Ⓐ t			Ⓒ	⑥	Ⓐ														
0	**Goslar 859** d.	...	...	...	...	...	...	...	...	0606	0606	0705	...	0806	0904	...	1006	1105	...	1206	1305	...	1406	1505	...
13	Vienenburg **859** d.	...	...	...	...	...	...	...	...	0616	0616	0715	...	0816	0915	...	1016	1115	...	1216	1315	...	1416	1515	...
29	Ilsenburg d.	...	0411	...	...	...	0529	...	0629	0629	0629	0731	...	0831	0931	...	1031	1131	...	1231	1331	...	1431	1531	...
38	Wernigerode d.	...	0422	...	...	...	0540	...	0640	0640	0640	0742	...	0840	0942	...	1040	1142	...	1240	1342	...	1440	1542	...
62	**Halberstadt** a.	...	0438	...	...	...	0555	...	0656	0656	0656	0755	...	0856	0955	...	1056	1155	...	1256	1355	...	1456	1555	...
62	**Halberstadt** d.	0339	...	0446	0446	0528	0602	0607	0657	0657	0701	0801	0802	0901	1001	1002	1101	1201	1202	1301	1401	1402	1501	1601	1602
	Magdeburg Hbf **862** a.	|	...	|	|	|	0700	|	|	|	|	0848	|	|	1048	|	|	1248	|	|	1448	|	|	1649	|
	Berlin Hbf **838** a.	|	...	|	|	|	...	|	|	|	|	...	|	|	...	|	|	...	|	|	...	|	|	...	|
94	Aschersleben d.	0404	...	0520**e**	0520**e**	0557	...	0641	0726	0726	0726	...	0824	0926	...	1024	1126	...	1224	1326	...	1424	1526	...	1624
105	Sandersleben (Anh) d.	0419	...	0537	0537	0606	...	0656	0737	0737	0737	...	0837	0937	...	1037	1137	...	1237	1337	...	1437	1537	...	1637
122	Könnern d.	0433	...	0550	0550	0620	...	0710	0750	0750	0750	...	0850	0950	...	1050	1150	...	1250	1350	...	1450	1550	...	1650
152	**Halle** (Saale) Hbf a.	0459	...	0608	0619	0637	...	0737	0811	0811	0811	...	0911	1011	...	1111	1211	...	1311	1411	...	1511	1611	...	1711

e – Arrives 0513.
t – Not June 9, Oct. 3, 31.
z – Also June 9, Oct. 3, 31.
⊠ – Operated by *erixx*.
◇ – Operated by *Start Mitteldeutschland*.

CONTINUES ON NEXT PAGE →

860 HANNOVER - BAD HARZBURG and GOSLAR - HALLE *Start Mitteldeutschland*

			⑤–⑦									
Goslar 859 d.	1606	1705	1705	...	1806	1905	...	2006	2105	2206	2305	...
Vienenburg **859** d.	1616	1715	1715	...	1816	1915	...	2016	2115	2216	2315	...
Ilsenburg d.	1631	1731	1731	...	1831	1931	...	2031	2131	2232	2331	...
Wernigerode d.	1640	1742	1742	...	1840	1942	...	2040	2142	2243	2342	...
Halberstadt a.	1656	1755	1755	...	1856	1955	...	2056	2155	2258	2355	...
Halberstadt d.	1701	1801	1801	1802	1901	2001	2002	2101	2202	2305	...	...
Magdeburg Hbf **862** a.	|	1848	1848	|	|	2058	|	|	2258	|	...	...
Berlin Hbf **838** a.	|	...	2047**z**	|	|	...	|	|	...	|	...	...
Aschersleben d.	1726	...	...	1824	1926	...	2024	2126	...	2333	...	...
Sandersleben (Anh) d.	1737	...	...	1837	1937	...	2037	2137	...	2347	...	...
Könnern d.	1750	...	...	1850	1950	...	2050	2150	...	0000	...	...
Halle (Saale) Hbf a.	1811	...	...	1911	2011	...	2111	2208	...	0028	...	...

	⚒	Ⓐ						
Halle (Saale) Hbf d.	...	0345	...	0525	0638	...	0749	0849
Könnern d.	...	0405	...	0551	0710	...	0810	0910
Sandersleben (Anh) d.	...	0418	...	0606	0724	...	0823	0923
Aschersleben d.	...	0429	...	0627**c**	0737	...	0835	0937
Berlin Hbf **838** d.	...	|	...	|	|	...	|	|
Magdeburg Hbf **862** d.	...	|	...	|	|	0707	|	|
Halberstadt a.	...	0458	...	0657	0757	0757	0900	0957
Halberstadt d.	0459	0459	0559	0702	...	0804	0904	...
Wernigerode d.	0516	0516	0616	0719	...	0818	0921	...
Ilsenburg d.	0530	0530	0630	0730	...	0829	0930	...
Vienenburg **859** d.	0541	0541	0643	0741	...	0842	0941	...
Goslar 859 a.	0552	0552	0653	0752	...	0853	0952	...

		Ⓒ																				Ⓐ		⚒	⑦
Halle (Saale) Hbf d.	...	...	0949	1049	...	1149	1249	...	1349	1449	...	1549	1649	...	1749	1849	...	1949	2049	...	...	2207	2309	...	...
Könnern d.	...	...	1010	1110	...	1210	1310	...	1410	1510	...	1610	1710	...	1810	1910	...	2010	2110	...	...	2246**e**	2329	...	...
Sandersleben (Anh) d.	...	...	1023	1123	...	1223	1323	...	1423	1523	...	1623	1723	...	1823	1923	...	2023	2123	...	...	2300	2347	...	...
Aschersleben d.	...	...	1035	1137	...	1235	1337	...	1435	1537	...	1635	1737	...	1835	1937	...	2035	2137	...	...	2309	0001	...	...
Berlin Hbf **838** d.	...	0723**v**	|	|	...	|	|	...	|	|	...	|	|	...	|	|	...	|	|	...	...	|	|	...	2131**x**
Magdeburg Hbf **862** d.	0908	0908	|	|	1107	|	|	1307	|	|	1507	|	|	1707	|	|	1907	|	|	2107	...	|	|	2318	2319
Halberstadt a.	0957	0957	1100	1157	1157	1300	1357	1357	1500	1557	1557	1700	1757	1757	1900	1957	1957	2102	2157	2159	...	2338	0028	0009	0009
Halberstadt d.	1004	1004	1104	...	1204	1304	...	1404	1504	...	1604	1704	...	1804	1904	...	2004	2105	...	2206	...	...	...	0035	0035
Wernigerode d.	1018	1018	1121	...	1218	1321	...	1418	1521	...	1618	1721	...	1818	1921	...	2018	2121	...	2220	...	...	...	0051	0051
Ilsenburg d.	1029	1029	1130	...	1229	1330	...	1429	1530	...	1629	1730	...	1829	1930	...	2029	2129	...	2230	...	...	...	0101	0101
Vienenburg **859** d.	1042	1042	1141	...	1242	1341	...	1442	1541	...	1642	1741	...	1842	1941	...	2042	2141	...	2243	...	...	...	...	...
Goslar 859 a.	1053	1053	1152	...	1253	1352	...	1453	1552	...	1653	1752	...	1853	1952	...	2053	2152	...	2253	...	...	...	...	...

c – Arrives 0618. **e** – Arrives 2239. **v** – Berlin **Lichtenberg** 0656 to Sept. 21. **x** – Berlin **Lichtenberg** 2100 to Sept. 21. **z** – Berlin **Lichtenberg** 2051 to Sept. 21.

861 MAGDEBURG - SANGERHAUSEN - ERFURT and DESSAU - ASCHERSLEBEN *Start Mitteldeutschland*

Magdeburg - Erfurt and Aschersleben

km																										
		Ⓒ	Ⓐ	Ⓐ		Ⓐ	Ⓒ								Ⓐ	Ⓒ	Ⓐ		Ⓐ							
0	**Magdeburg** Hbf d.	0050	0435	0510	0607	0708	0711	0825	0911	1025	1110	1225	1310	1425	1456	1510	1529	1625	1711	1710	1825	1910	2025	2110	2225	2255
17	Schönebeck (Elbe) d.	0106	0450	0526	0623	0726	0726	0839	0926	1039	1126	1239	1326	1439	1510	1526	1542	1639	1726	1726	1839	1926	2039	2126	2239	2316
37	Staßfurt d.	0130	0509	0550	0649**r**	0750	0747	0853	0950	1053	1150	1253	1350	1453	1534	1550	1607	1653	1750	1750	1853	1950	2053	2150	2253	2338
44	Güsten d.	0137	0515	0558	0657	0758	0754	0859	0958	1059	1158	1259	1358	1459	1541	1558	1615	1659	1803**r**	1759	1859	1958	2059	2158	2259	2345
	Aschersleben a.	0149	|	0610	|	0810	*0816*	|	1010	|	1210	|	1410	|	|	1610	1627	|	|	1810	|	2010	|	2210	|	2356
60	Sandersleben d.	—	0546**k**	—	0712	...	—	0912	—	1112	—	1312	—	1512	1555	—	—	1712	1816	—	1912	—	2112	...	2312	...
66	Hettstedt d.	...	0554	...	0719	...	...	0919	...	1119	...	1319	...	1519	1602	...	...	1719	1822	...	1919	...	2119	...	2319	...
75	Klostermansfeld d.	...	0603	...	0728	...	...	0928	...	1128	...	1328	...	1528	1611	Ⓒ	Ⓐ	1728	1831	...	1928	...	2128	...	2328	...
97	**Sangerhausen** d.	0547	0623	0641	0748	...	0852	0948	1052	1148	1252	1348	1452	1548	1636	1652	1652	1748	1854	1905	1956**f**	2100	2159**n**	...	2345	...
142	Sömmerda d.	0633	0701	0731	0829	...	0931	1029	1131	1229	1331	1429	1531	1629	...	1731	1736**r**	1829	...	1953	2037	2142	2244	...	...	...
167	**Erfurt** Hbf a.	0654	0721	0752	0850	...	0951	1050	1151	1250	1351	1451	1551	1650	...	1751	1756	1850	...	2014	2058	2203	2305	...	...	...

	Ⓐ	Ⓐ	Ⓒ	Ⓐ	Ⓐ			Ⓐ																
Erfurt Hbf d.	...	...	...	...	...	0503	...	0612	0704	0809	0910	1009	1110	1209	1310	1409	1509	1609	1710	1809	1906	...	2018	2136	2328
Sömmerda d.	...	...	...	...	...	0523	...	0633	0730	0829	0932	1029	1132	1229	1332	1429	1532	1629	1732	1829	1928	...	2038	2155	2349
Sangerhausen d.	...	...	...	0511	...	0618**f**	...	0723	0818	0909	1018	1109	1218	1309	1418	1509	1618	1709	1818	1909	2018**r**	...	2123	2243	0033
Klostermansfeld d.	...	...	...	0529	...	0637	...	...	0837	—	1037	—	1237	—	1437	—	1637	—	1837	—	2037	...	...	...	...
Hettstedt d.	...	...	...	0538	...	0645	...	...	0845	...	1045	...	1245	...	1445	...	1645	...	1845	...	2045	...	...	...	...
Sandersleben d.	...	...	...	0545	...	0653	...	...	0853	...	1053	...	1253	...	1453	...	1653	...	1853	...	2053	...	...	...	...
Aschersleben d.	0448	0530	0544	|	0623	|	0746	...	|	0946	|	1146	|	1346	|	1546	|	1746	|	1946	|	2146	...	...	...
Güsten d.	0501	0541	0556	0559	0635	0708	0758	...	0908	0958	1108	1158	1308	1358	1508	1558	1708	1758	1908	1958	2108	2158	...	...	...
Staßfurt d.	0509	0553	0604	0612	0644	0715	0808	...	0915	1008	1115	1208	1315	1408	1515	1608	1715	1808	1915	2008	2115	2208	...	...	...
Schönebeck (Elbe) d.	0529	0615	0626	0629	0705	0730	0829	...	0930	1029	1130	1229	1330	1429	1530	1629	1730	1829	1930	2029	2130	2232	...	...	...
Magdeburg Hbf a.	0543	0627	0640	0643	0718	0744	0843	...	0943	1043	1143	1243	1343	1443	1543	1643	1743	1843	1943	2043	2143	2245	...	...	...

Dessau - Aschersleben (- Halberstadt) Warning! No rail service June 18 - August 7

km																										
		Ⓐ	Ⓒ	Ⓐ	Ⓐ	Ⓒ	Ⓐ	Ⓒ	Ⓐ								Ⓐ	Ⓒ								
0	**Dessau** Hbf d.	0428	0454	0515	0553	0559	0643	0712	0730	0802	0902	1002	1102	1202	1302	1402	1502	1502	1602	1702	1802	1902	2002	2102	2212	*2329*
21	Köthen a.	0448	0515	0536	0619	0620	0707	0732	0754	0822	0922	1022	1122	1222	1322	1422	1522	1522	1622	1722	1822	1922	2022	2122	2231	*2349*
21	Köthen d.	0451	0517	0539	0632	0632	0723	0733	0754	0832	0923	1032	1123	1232	1323	1432	1523	1523	1632	1723	1832	1923	2032	2123	2232	*2351*
42	Bernburg Hbf d.	0512	0539	0558	0651	0653	0743	0754	0813	0853	0942	1053	1142	1253	1342	1453	1542	1542	1653	1742	1853	1942	2053	2142	2253	0023
54	Güsten d.	0524	0550	0610	0703	0704	0754	0805	0824	0904	0954	1104	1154	1304	1354	1504	1553	1554	1704	1754	1904	1954	2104	2153	2304	0034
66	**Aschersleben** ... **860** a.	0535	0602	0621	0712	0715	0802**v**	0816	0832	0915	1002**v**	1115	1202**v**	1315	1402**v**	1515	1604	1602**v**	1715	1802**v**	1915	2002**v**	2115	2202**v**	2315	0046
	Halberstadt **860** a.	...	...	...	...	...	...	...	...	0951	...	...	...	1351	...	1551	...	...	1751	...	...	...	...	...	...	0115

		Ⓐ											Ⓐ	Ⓒ										
Halberstadt **860** d.	...	...	...	...	...	...	...	1011	...	...	...	1411	...	...	1611	...	...	...	...	...	...	...	...	...	...
Aschersleben **860** d.	0421	0516	0557	0649	0753**v**	0849	0953**v**	1049	1153**v**	1249	1353**v**	1449	1537	1553**v**	1649	1753**v**	1849	1953**v**	2049	2153**v**	...	...	...	...	...
Güsten d.	0433	0527	0607	0701	0801	0902	1001	1102	1201	1302	1401	1502	1549	1601	1702	1801	1902	2001	2102	2201	...	...	...	...	...
Bernburg Hbf d.	0454**f**	0538	0617	0713	0813	0913	1013	1113	1213	1313	1413	1513	1600	1613	1713	1813	1913	2013	2113	2213	...	...	...	...	...
Köthen a.	0516	0600	0638	0735	0834	0935	1034	1135	1234	1335	1434	1535	1622	1634	1735	1834	1935	2034	2135	2234	...	...	...	...	...
Köthen d.	0518	0603	0640	0737	0835	0937	1035	1137	1235	1337	1435	1537	1635	1635	1737	1835	1937	2035	2137	2235	...	...	...	...	...
Dessau Hbf a.	0542	0622	0700	0756	0854	0956	1054	1156	1254	1356	1454	1556	1654	1654	1756	1854	1956	2054	2156	2254	...	...	...	...	...

f – Arrives 11 minutes earlier.
k – Arrives 0529.
n – Arrives 2145.
r – Arrives 5–7 minutes earlier.
v – Change at Ashersleben until Sept. 21 (connections arrive Aschersleben 11 minutes later and depart Aschersleben 7 minutes earlier).

862 MAGDEBURG - HALBERSTADT - THALE *Start Mitteldeutschland*

km																										
			Ⓐ					Ⓐ	Ⓒ																①–⑥	⑦
						◧		◧	▲		◧		◧		◧		◧			◧		◧			◐¶	▲¶
	Berlin Hbf **838** d.	...	...	...	...	...	...	...	0723**v**	...	...	...	...	...	...	...	...	...	...	...	...	...	...	...	...	2131**x**
0	**Magdeburg** Hbf d.	...	0425	...	0543	0707	0807	0908	0908	1007	1107	1207	1307	1407	1507	1607	1707	1807	1843	1907	2007	2107	2207	2318	2318
39	Oschersleben (Bode) d.	...	0502	...	0624	0742	0842	0942	0942	1042	1142	1242	1342	1442	1542	1642	1742	1842	1924	1942	2045	2145	2247	2355	2355
59	**Halberstadt** a.	...	0516	...	0640	0757	0857	0957	0957	1057	1157	1257	1357	1457	1557	1657	1757	1857	1939	1957	2100	2159	2302	0009	0009
59	**Halberstadt** d.	0517	0517	0610	0708	0808	*0908*	1008	1008	*1108*	1208	*1308*	1408	*1508*	1608	*1708*	1808	*1908*	...	2008	*2109*	2202	...	0029	0029
77	Quedlinburg a.	0532	0532	0625	0723	0823	*0923*	1023	1023	*1123*	1223	*1323*	1423	*1523*	1623	*1723*	1823	*1923*	...	2023	*2124*	2217	...	0043	0043
77	Quedlinburg ❦ d.	0536	0536	0630	0730	0830	*0930*	1030	1030	*1130*	1230	*1330*	1430	*1530*	1630	*1730*	1830	*1930*	...	2030	*2130*	2218	...	0044	0044
87	**Thale** Hbf ❦ a.	0549	0549	0643	0743	0843	*0943*	1043	1043	*1143*	1243	*1343*	1443	*1543*	1643	*1743*	1843	*1943*	...	2043	*2143*	2229	...	0056	0056

	Ⓐ																⑤–⑦							
				◐		◧		◧		◧		◧		◧		◧	▲		◧		◧			§
Thale Hbf ❦ d.	...	...	...	0521	0616	*0716*	0816	*0916*	1016	*1116*	1216	*1316*	1416	*1516*	1616	*1716*	1716	1816	*1916*	2016	*2116*	...	2230**r**	2341
Quedlinburg ❦ a.	...	...	...	0533	0628	*0728*	0828	*0928*	1028	*1128*	1228	*1328*	1428	*1528*	1628	*1728*	1728	1828	*1928*	2028	*2128*	...	2240	2352
Quedlinburg d.	...	...	...	0535	0633	*0733*	0833	*0932*	1033	*1133*	1233	*1336*	1433	*1532*	1633	*1733*	1733	1833	*1936*	2033	*2133*	...	2241	2353
Halberstadt a.	...	...	...	0551	0649	*0749*	0849	*0948*	1049	*1149*	1249	*1351*	1449	*1548*	1649	*1749*	1749	1849	*1951*	2049	*2149*	...	2257	0009
Halberstadt d.	0356	0440	0540	0602	0701	0801	0901	1001	1101	1201	1301	1401	1501	1601	1701	1801	1801	1901	2001	2103	2202	...	...	...
Oschersleben (Bode) d.	0414	0457	0555	0618	0717	0817	0917	1017	1117	1217	1317	1417	1517	1617	1717	1817	1817	1917	2017	2119	2219	...	...	...
Magdeburg Hbf a.	0455	0535	0635	0648	0748	0848	0948	1048	1148	1248	1348	1448	1548	1648	1748	1848	1848	1948	2058	2154	2258	...	...	...
Berlin Hbf **838** a.	...	...	...	...	...	...	...	...	...	...	...	...	...	...	...	...	2047**z**	...	...	...	...	...	...	...

r – 🚌 connection June 16 - Aug. 1 is at 2210.
v – Berlin **Lichtenberg** 0656 until Sept. 21.
x – Berlin **Lichtenberg** 2100 until Sept. 21.
z – Berlin **Lichtenberg** 2051 until Sept. 21.
◧ – Conveys (12) Magdeburg - Halberstadt - Goslar and v.v. (Table **860**).
◐ – Conveys (12) Magdeburg - Halberstadt - Ilsenburg and v.v. (Table **860**).
▲ – DB tickets not valid for journeys from / to Berlin. Conveys (2) Berlin - Halberstadt - Ilsenburg / Goslar and v.v. (Table **860**).
❦ – By 🚌 June 16 - Aug. 1 (arr. Thale 4 minutes later; departs Thale 7 minutes earlier, except note **r**).
§ – Not June 16 - Aug. 1.
¶ – 6 mins earlier from Halberstadt June 16 - Aug. 1.

Regionalverkehre Start Deutschland

HILDESHEIM - HAMELN - HERFORD 863

km		Ⓐ	⚒	⑥	Ⓐ	†																			
0	**Hildesheim** Hbf d.	...	0537	0634	0637	...	0737	0834	0937	1034	1137	1234	1337	1434	1537	1634	1737	1834	1937	2034	2137	2234	...	...	...
18	Elze a.	...	0553	0650	0652	...	0753	0851	0954	1050	1153	1250	1353	1450	1553	1650	1753	1850	1953	2050	2153	2250	...	...	...
18	Elze d.	...	0602	0702	0702	...	0802	0902	1002	1102	1202	1302	1402	1502	1602	1702	1802	1902	2002	2102	2202	2307	...	...	...
47	**Hameln** d.	0529	0629	0729	0729	0729	0828	0928	1028	1128	1228	1328	1429	1528	1628	1728	1828	1928	2028	2128	2228	2332	...	...	...
71	Rinteln d.	0546	0646	0746	0746	0746	0846	0946	1046	1146	1246	1346	1446	1546	1646	1746	1846	1946	2046	2146	2246	...	...	...	...
88	Vlotho d.	0600	0700	0800	0800	0800	0900	1000	1100	1200	1300	1400	1500	1600	1700	1800	1900	2000	2100	2200	2300	...	...	...	...
94	Bad Oeynhausen Süd d.	0605	0705	0805	0805	0805	0905	1005	1105	1205	1305	1405	1505	1605	1705	1805	1905	2005	2105	2205	2305	...	...	...	...
100	Löhne (Westf) **811** a.	0612	0712	0812	0812	0812	0912	1012	1112	1212	1312	1412	1512	1612	1712	1812	1912	2012	2112	2212	2312	...	...	...	...
110	**Herford** **811** a.	0623	0723	0823	0823	0823	0923	1023	1123	1223	1323	1423	1523	1623	1723	1823	1923	2023	2123	2223	...	...	...	...	...

	Ⓐ	⚒	Ⓐ	⚒	⚒																			
Herford **811** d.	*0433*	...	0536	...	0636	...	0736	0836	0936	1036	1136	1236	1336	1436	1536	1636	1736	1836	1936	2035	2136	...	...	...
Löhne (Westf) **811** d.	0446	...	0546	...	0646	...	0746	0846	0946	1046	1146	1246	1346	1446	1546	1646	1746	1846	1946	2046	2146	...	...	...
Bad Oeynhausen Süd d.	0451	...	0551	...	0652	...	0751	0852	0951	1052	1151	1252	1351	1452	1551	1652	1751	1852	1951	2051	2151	...	...	...
Vlotho d.	0459	...	0559	...	0659	...	0759	0859	0959	1059	1159	1259	1359	1500	1559	1659	1759	1859	1959	2059	2159	...	...	...
Rinteln d.	0510	...	0610	...	0710	...	0810	0910	1010	1110	1210	1310	1410	1511	1610	1710	1810	1910	2010	2110	2210	...	...	...
Hameln d.	0528	0528	0628	0628	0729	0729	0828	0929	1028	1128	1228	1328	1428	1529	1628	1728	1828	1928	2028	2128	2228	...	...	...
Elze a.	0553	0553	0653	0653	0754	0754	0852	0953	1052	1153	1252	1353	1452	1551	1652	1752	1852	1952	2052	2153	2252	...	...	...
Elze d.	0602	0602	0702	0702	0803	0803	0909	1003	1109	1202	1309	1401	1509	1602	1709	1802	1909	2002	2109	2202	2309	...	...	...
Hildesheim Hbf a.	0620	0620	0720	0720	0820	0820	0926	1021	1126	1220	1326	1423	1526	1619	1726	1820	1926	2020	2126	2220	2326	...	...	...

☛ June 7 - 13: change trains at Löhne (timings vary).

DB (*RE* / *RB* services); Abellio

ERFURT and HALLE - LEINEFELDE - KASSEL and GÖTTINGEN 865

km		Ⓐ‡	Ⓐ	Ⓐ‡	Ⓐ		Ⓐ	‡	G	Ⓐ‡			‡	A	⚒‡			‡	A	‡			‡	A	‡
0	**Erfurt** Hbf **849 850 870/2** d.	...	...	...	...	0423	0502	...	0609	...	0622	0707	...	0809	...	0833	0907	...	1009	...	1033	1107	...	1209	...
13	Neudietendorf **849 870/2** d.	...	...	...	...	0435	|	...	0618	...	|	|	...	0818	...	|	|	...	1018	...	|	|	...	1218	...
27	Gotha **849 850** d.	...	...	...	...	0458**f**	◇	...	0635**e**	...	|	◇	...	0835**e**	...	|	◇	...	1035**e**	...	|	◇	...	1235**e**	...
48	Bad Langensalza d.	...	...	...	0446	0509	0555**f**	...	0647	...	0710**e**	0800**e**	...	0847	...	0914	1000	...	1047	...	1114	1200	...	1247	...
67	Mühlhausen (Thür) d.	...	...	...	0503	0524	0611	...	0701	...	0726	0815	...	0900	...	0926	1015	...	1100	...	1126	1215	...	1300	...
	Halle (Saale) Hbf d.	...	...	...	|	|	|	0455	|	0527	|	|	0702	|	0757	|	|	0902	|	0957	|	|	1102	|	1157
	Röblingen am See d.	...	...	...	|	|	|	0516	|	0600	|	|	0721	|	0818	|	|	0921	|	1018	|	|	1121	|	1218
	Lutherstadt Eisleben d.	...	...	...	|	|	|	0525	|	0610	|	|	0730	|	0826	|	|	0930	|	1026	|	|	1130	|	1226
	Sangerhausen d.	...	...	0412	|	|	|	0544	|	0631	|	|	0752	|	0843	|	|	0952	|	1043	|	|	1152	|	1243
	Nordhausen d.	...	...	0449	|	|	|	0619	|	0705	|	|	0826	|	0917	|	|	1026	|	1117	|	|	1226	|	1317
94	**Leinefelde** d.	0423	0502	0529	0533	0544	0634	0655	0719	0745	0751	0840	0858	0918	0948	0953	1040	1058	1118	1148	1153	1240	1258	1318	1348
110	Heilbad Heiligenstadt d.	0438	0513	...	0547	0556	...	0705	0730	...	0801	...	0908	0929	...	1004	...	1108	1129	...	1204	...	1308	1329	...
144	**Göttingen** a.	|	0539	...	|	0625	...	|	0751	...	|	...	|	0951	...	|	...	|	1151	...	|	...	|	1351	...
125	Eichenberg **865a** d.	0501**f**	...	...	0602	...	...	0719	...	...	0816	...	0919	...	...	1018	...	1119	...	...	1218	...	1319	...	...
148	Hann Münden **865a** d.	0520	...	...	0622	...	...	0736	...	...	0833	...	0936	...	...	1035	...	1136	...	...	1235	...	1336	...	...
172	**Kassel** Hbf **865a** a.	0540	...	...	0643	...	...	|	...	...	|	...	|	...	...	|	...	|	...	...	|	...	|	...	...
176	**Kassel** Wilhelmshöhe a.	...	...	...	0655	...	...	0753	...	...	0853	...	0953	...	...	1054	...	1153	...	...	1254	...	1356	...	...

			‡	A	‡			‡	A	‡			‡	A	‡		‡		A		‡	G		‡	‡
Erfurt Hbf **849 850 870/2** d.	1233	1307	...	1409	...	1433	1507	...	1609	...	1633	1707	...	1809	...	1833	...	1907	2009	2033	...	2111	2258	...	...
Neudietendorf **849 870/2** d.	|	|	...	1418	...	|	|	...	1619	...	|	|	...	1818	...	|	...	|	2018	|	...	2120	2307	...	...
Gotha **849 850** d.	|	◇	...	1435**e**	...	|	◇	...	1635**e**	...	|	◇	...	1835**e**	...	|	...	◇	2035**e**	|	...	2135**e**	2326**f**	...	...
Bad Langensalza d.	1314	1400	...	1447	...	1514	1600	...	1647	...	1714	1800	...	1847	...	1914	...	2000	2047	2112	...	2147	2339	...	...
Mühlhausen (Thür) d.	1326	1415	...	1500	...	1526	1615	...	1700	...	1726	1815	...	1900	...	1926	...	2016	2100	2127	...	2158	2353	...	...
Halle (Saale) Hbf d.	|	|	1302	|	1357	|	|	1502	|	1557	|	|	1702	|	1757	|	1902	...	|	|	1957	|	|	2108	2321
Röblingen am See d.	|	|	1321	|	1418	|	|	1521	|	1618	|	|	1721	|	1818	|	1921	...	|	|	2018	|	|	2127	2340
Lutherstadt Eisleben d.	|	|	1330	|	1426	|	|	1530	|	1626	|	|	1730	|	1826	|	1930	...	|	|	2026	|	|	2136	2349
Sangerhausen d.	|	|	1352	|	1443	|	|	1552	|	1643	|	|	1752	|	1843	|	1952	...	|	|	2043	|	|	2156	0009
Nordhausen d.	|	|	1426	|	1517	|	|	1626	|	1717	|	|	1826	|	1917	|	2026	...	|	|	2123**f**	|	|	2229	0043
Leinefelde d.	1353	1440	1456	1518	1548	1553	1640	1658	1718	1748	1753	1840	1858	1918	1948	1953	2058	...	2118	2147	2204	2217	0010	...	...
Heilbad Heiligenstadt d.	1404	...	1507	1529	...	1604	...	1708	1729	...	1804	...	1908	1929	...	2004	2108	...	2129	2158	▬	2228	...	...	...
Göttingen a.	|	...	|	1551	...	|	...	|	1751	...	|	...	|	1951	...	|	|	...	2150	|	...	2250	...	...	...
Eichenberg **865a** d.	1418	...	1519	...	...	1618	...	1719	...	...	1818	...	1919	...	...	2018	2119	...	...	2212	2233	...	...	...	...
Hann Münden **865a** d.	1435	...	1536	...	...	1635	...	1736	...	...	1835	...	1936	...	...	2035	2136	...	...	...	2253	...	...	...	...
Kassel Hbf **865a** a.	|	...	|	...	...	|	...	|	...	...	|	...	|	...	...	|	2154	...	...	...	2313	...	...	...	...
Kassel Wilhelmshöhe a.	1454	...	1553	...	...	1655	...	1756	...	...	1854	...	1953	...	...	2054	...	...	...	...	...	...	...	...	...

km		‡		Ⓐ‡	Ⓐ	⚒‡	A	Ⓐ‡	Ⓒ‡			‡	A	‡			‡	A	‡			‡	A	‡	
0	**Kassel** Wilhelmshöhe d.	...	...	...	...	...	...	...	...	...	0706**t**	...	...	0805	...	0906	...	...	1006	...	1106	...	...	1206	...
	Kassel Hbf **865a** d.	...	...	0416	...	...	...	0546	0606	...	|	...	...	|	...	|	...	...	|	...	|	...	...	|	...
23	Hann Münden **865a** d.	...	...	0436	...	...	...	0605	0623	...	0722**t**	...	...	0823	...	0922	...	...	1023	...	1122	...	...	1223	...
46	Eichenberg **865a** d.	...	...	0457	...	...	...	0633**f**	0640	...	0741**t**	...	...	0840	...	0941	...	...	1040	...	1141	...	...	1240	...
	Göttingen d.	...	...	|	...	...	0604	|	|	...	|	...	0808	|	...	|	...	1008	|	...	|	...	1208	|	...
61	Heilbad Heiligenstadt d.	...	0444**t**	0509	...	...	0628	0647	0652	...	0755**t**	...	0831	0852	...	0955	...	1031	1052	...	1155	...	1231	1252	...
77	**Leinefelde** d.	0440**t**	0502	0523	0547	0551**b**	0640	0702	0703	0719**t**	0807	0810**r**	0843	0903	0919	1007	1010**r**	1043	1103	1119	1207	1209	1243	1303	1319
119	**Nordhausen** d.	0531**j**	|	0557	|	0638	|	0734	0734	|	|	0843**r**	|	0934	|	|	1043**r**	|	1134	|	|	1243	|	1334	|
157	Sangerhausen d.	0611	|	0634	|	0717	|	0813	0813	|	|	0919	|	1013	|	|	1119	|	1213	|	|	1319	|	1413	|
179	Lutherstadt Eisleben d.	0629	|	0652	|	0735	|	0834	0834	|	|	0936	|	1034	|	|	1136	|	1234	|	|	1336	|	1434	|
190	Röblingen am See a.	0638	|	0702	|	0743	|	0841	0841	|	|	0943	|	1041	|	|	1143	|	1241	|	|	1343	|	1441	|
217	**Halle** (Saale) Hbf a.	0658	|	0734	|	0803	|	0859	0859	|	|	1003	|	1059	|	|	1203	|	1259	|	|	1403	|	1459	|
—	Mühlhausen (Thür) d.	...	0522	...	0612	...	0657	...	...	0742	0832	...	0859	...	0942	1032	...	1059	...	1142	1232	...	1259	...	1342
0	Bad Langensalza d.	...	0535	...	0630	...	0710	...	...	0759	0844	...	0910	...	0959	1044	...	1110	...	1159	1244	...	1310	...	1359
	Gotha **849 850** a.	...	0551	...	⊙	...	0722	...	...	⊙	|	...	0922	...	⊙	|	...	1122	...	⊙	|	...	1322	...	⊙
	Neudietendorf **849 870/2** a.	...	0606	...	|	...	0737	...	...	|	|	...	0937	...	|	|	...	1137	...	|	|	...	1337	...	|
38	**Erfurt** Hbf **849 850 870/2** a.	...	0615	...	0720	...	0746	...	...	0846	0921	...	0946	...	1046	1121	...	1146	...	1246	1321	...	1346	...	1446

		‡	A	‡			‡	A	‡			‡	A	‡			‡	G	‡	G		‡	⑤–⑦		
Kassel Wilhelmshöhe d.	1306	...	...	1406	...	1506	...	...	1606	...	1706	...	...	1806	...	1905	...	...	2004	...	2106	...	...	...	...
Kassel Hbf **865a** d.	|	...	...	|	...	|	...	...	|	...	|	...	...	|	...	|	...	...	|	...	|	...	...	*2146*	...
Hann Münden **865a** d.	1322	...	...	1423	...	1523	...	...	1623	...	1722	...	...	1823	...	1922	...	...	2023	...	2122	...	...	*2206*	...
Eichenberg **865a** d.	1341	...	...	1440	...	1541	...	...	1640	...	1741	...	...	1840	...	1941	...	...	2040	...	2141	...	...	2242	...
Göttingen d.	|	...	1408	|	...	|	...	1608	|	...	|	...	1808	|	...	|	...	2008	|	2108	|	...	2218	|	2308
Heilbad Heiligenstadt d.	1355	...	1431	1452	...	1555	...	1631	1652	...	1755	...	1831	1852	...	1955	...	2031	2052	2132	2155	...	2244	2254	2331
Leinefelde d.	1407	1409	1443	1503	1519	1607	1609	1643	1703	1719	1807	1809	1843	1903	1919	2007	2013	2043	2103	2148	2220**k**	2223	2257	2304	2342
Nordhausen d.	|	1443	|	1534	|	|	1643	|	1734	|	|	1843	|	1934	|	|	2053	|	2137	|	|	2302	|	...	...
Sangerhausen d.	|	1519	|	1613	|	|	1719	|	1813	|	|	1919	|	2013	|	|	2132	|	2215	|	|	2339	|	...	...
Lutherstadt Eisleben d.	|	1536	|	1634	|	|	1736	|	1834	|	|	1936	|	2034	|	|	2150	|	2234	|	|	2359	|	...	...
Röblingen am See a.	|	1543	|	1641	|	|	1743	|	1841	|	|	1943	|	2041	|	|	2159	|	2241	|	|	0008	|	...	...
Halle (Saale) Hbf a.	|	1603	|	1659	|	|	1803	|	1859	|	|	2003	|	2059	|	|	2234	|	2301	|	|	0040	|	...	...
Mühlhausen (Thür) d.	1432	...	1459	...	1542	1632	...	1659	...	1742	1832	...	1859	...	1942	2027	...	2059	...	2212	2239	...	2313	...	...
Bad Langensalza d.	1444	...	1510	...	1559	1644	...	1710	...	1759	1844	...	1910	...	1959	2042	...	2110	...	2222	2255	...	2324	...	...
Gotha **849 850** a.	|	...	1522	...	⊙	|	...	1722	...	⊙	|	...	1922	...	⊙	|	...	2122	...	2235	|	...	2346	...	...
Neudietendorf **849 870/2** a.	|	...	1537	...	|	|	...	1737	...	|	|	...	1937	...	|	|	...	2140	...	2250	|	...	0001	...	...
Erfurt Hbf **849 850 870/2** a.	1521	...	1546	...	1646	1721	...	1746	...	1846	1921	...	1946	...	2051	2121	...	2149	...	2258	2334	...	0010	...	...

A – From / to Glauchau (Table **858**).
G – From / to Gera (Table **858**).

b – 0558 on ⑥.
e – Arrives 6 – 7 minutes earlier.
f – Arrives 8 – 10 minutes earlier.
j – Arrives 0520.
k – Arrives 2206.
r – ⚒ only.
t – Ⓐ only.

‡ – Operated by Abellio Rail Mitteldeutschland.
◇ – Connecting trains Gotha - Bad Langensalza (journey time: 18 – 21 minutes). **From Gotha** at 0530 Ⓐ, 0737, 0937, 1137, 1337, 1537, 1737 and 1937.
⊙ – Connecting trains Bad Langensalza - Gotha (journey time: 19 minutes). **From Bad Langensalza** at 0650 Ⓐ, 0801, 1001, 1201, 1401, 1601, 1801 and 2001.

865a GÖTTINGEN - KASSEL local services

CANTUS Verkehrsgesellschaft (2nd class only)

km		Ⓒ	Ⓐ	⚒	⚒	Ⓒ	Ⓐ	Ⓐ						Ⓒ	Ⓐ			Ⓐ								
0	**Göttingen** .... **908** d.	0026	0414	0514	0614	0714	0718	0748	0814	0914	1014	1114	1214	1314	1325	1414	1514	1543	1614	1714	1814	1914	2014	2114	2214	2314
20	Eichenberg .... **908** a.	0040	0428	0528	0628	0728	0732	0802	0828	0928	1028	1128	1228	1328	1339	1428	1528	1557	1628	1728	1828	1928	2028	2128	2228	2328
20	Eichenberg .... **865** d.	0041	0433	0533	0633	0733	0733	0803	0833	0933	1033	1133	1233	1333	1342	1433	1533	1603	1633	1733	1833	1933	2033	2133	2233	2333
43	Hann Münden .... **865** d.	0101	0453	0553	0653	0753	0753	0823	0853	0953	1053	1153	1253	1353	1402	1453	1553	1623	1653	1753	1853	1953	2053	2153	2253	2353
67	**Kassel** Hbf ⊡ .... **865** a.	0121	0513	0613	0713	0813	0813	0843	0913	1013	1113	1213	1313	1413	1426	1513	1613	1643	1713	1813	1913	2013	2113	2213	2313	0013

	Ⓒ	Ⓐ	Ⓐ	⑥	Ⓐ								Ⓐ				Ⓐ		Ⓐ							
Kassel Hbf ⊡ ...... **865** d.	0115	0416	0518	0546	0616	0646	0746	0846	0946	1046	1146	1246	1316	1346	1446	1546	1616	1646	1716	1746	1846	1946	2046	2146	2246	2346
Hann Münden ...... **865** d.	0135	0436	0537	0606	0636	0706	0806	0906	1006	1106	1206	1306	1336	1406	1506	1606	1636	1706	1736	1806	1906	2006	2106	2206	2306	0006
Eichenberg .... **865** a.	0154	0456	0557	0626	0656	0726	0826	0926	1026	1126	1226	1326	1356	1426	1526	1626	1656	1726	1756	1826	1926	2026	2126	2225	2326	0026
Eichenberg .... **908** d.	0155	*0502*	0605	0631	0704	0731	0831	0931	1031	1131	1231	1331	1357	1431	1531	1631	1659	1731	1806	1831	1931	2031	2131	2229	2331	0027
Göttingen .... **908** a.	0209	*0515*	0619	0645	0717	0745	0845	0945	1045	1145	1245	1345	1411	1445	1545	1645	1713	1745	1820	1845	1945	2045	2145	2243	2345	0041

⊡ – See Tables **806** and **901** for connecting trains to / from Kassel Wilhelmshöhe.

866 HANNOVER - MAGDEBURG - LEIPZIG

See panels below main table for regional trains Braunschweig - Magdeburg - Halle (Saale) and v.v. See Table **848** for other regional trains between Magdeburg and Leipzig via Dessau.

km		*IC* **2449** ①–⑤	*IC* **2031** ①–⑤ 🍷	*IC* **2447** ①–⑥ 🍷	*IC* **2033** 🍷	*IC* **2445** 🍷	*IC* **2035** A 🍷	*IC* **2035** B 🍷	*IC* **2235** A D🍷	*IC* **2443** K🍷	*IC* **2037** 🍷	*IC* **2441** F🍷	*IC* **2039** 🍷	*IC* **1931** ⑤A 🍷	*IC* **2049** S🍷	*IC* **2431** C🍷	*IC* **2239** △ D🍷	*IC* **2047** S🍷	*IC* **2433** 🍷	*IC* **2045** S🍷	*IC* **2435** 🍷	*IC* **2043** Ⓑ 🍷	*IC* **2043** ⑤⑦ 🍷	*IC* **2437** Ⓑ 🍷	
	Köln Hbf **800** .... d.	...	...	...	...	0511**v**	...	...	...	0711**r**	...	0909**r**	...	...	1111**r**	...	...	1311**r**	...	1511**r**	...	1711**r**	1711**r**	...	...
	Dortmund Hbf **800** .... d.	...	...	...	...	0628**r**	...	...	...	0828**r**	...	1028**r**	...	...	1228**r**	...	...	1428**r**	...	1628**r**	...	1828**r**	1828**r**	...	...
	Norddeich **813** .... d.	...	...	...	...	|	0535**e**	0535**e**	...	|	0739**e**	|	0939	...	|	...	...	|	...	|	1539	|	|	...	...
	Emden Hbf **813** .... d.	...	...	...	0416**e**	|	0608**e**	0608**e**	...	|	0816	|	1016	...	|	1216	...	|	1417	|	1616	|	|	1816	...
	Oldenburg (Oldb) **813** ... d.	...	...	...	0535**e**	|	0735	0735	...	|	0935	|	1135	1230	|	1335	...	|	1535	|	1735	|	|	1935	...
	Bremen Hbf **813** .... d.	...	...	...	0609	|	0809	0809	...	|	1009	|	1209	1305	|	1409	...	|	1608	|	1809	|	|	2009	...
0	**Hannover** Hbf .... **811** d.	...	0534	0636	0735	0835	0936	0936	...	1036	1136	1236	1336	1411	1436	1536	...	1636	1736	1836	1936	2036	2036	2136	...
35	Peine .... **811** d.	...	0555	|	|	|	|	|	...	|	|	|	|	|	|	|	...	|	|	|	|	|	|	2157	...
61	**Braunschweig** Hbf ...... **811** d.	...	0610	0710	0811	0910	1010	1010	...	1110	1210	1310	1410	1447	1511	1610	...	1710	1810	1910	2010	2110	2110	2213	...
97	Helmstedt .... d.	...	0631	|	0831	|	1031	1031	...	|	1231	|	1431	|	|	1631	...	|	1831	|	2031	|	|	2234	...
145	**Magdeburg** Hbf .... a.	...	0657	0754	0858	0954	1057	1057	...	1154	1257	1354	1457	1533	1554	1657	...	1754	1857	1954	2057	2154	2154	2300	...
145	**Magdeburg** Hbf .... **839** d.	0600	0704	0801	0905	1001	1104	1104	1104	1201	1304	1401	1504	1538	1601	1704	1704	1801	1904	2001	2104	...	2201	...	2307
	Brandenburg Hbf ...... **839** a.	|	|	|	|	|	1140	|	|	|	|	|	|	|	|	1740	|	|	|	|	|	...	|	...	|
	Potsdam Hbf .... **839** a.	|	|	|	|	|	1200	|	|	|	|	|	|	|	|	1759	|	|	|	|	|	...	|	...	|
	Berlin Wannsee .... **839** a.	|	|	|	|	|	1210	|	|	|	|	|	|	|	|	1810	|	|	|	|	|	...	|	...	|
	Berlin Hbf .... **839** a.	|	|	|	|	|	1231**z**	|	|	|	|	|	|	|	|	1830**z**	|	|	|	|	|	...	|	...	|
	Berlin Ostbahnhof .... **839** a.	|	|	|	|	|	1240	|	|	|	|	|	|	◐	|	1840	|	|	|	|	|	...	|	...	|
195	Köthen .... d.	0629	0733	0829	0933	1029	...	1133	1133	1229	1333	1429	1533	|	1630	...	1733	1830	1933	2029	2133	...	2229	...	2347
231	**Halle** (Saale) Hbf .... a.	0648	0753	0848	0953	1048	...	1153	1153	1248	1353	1448	1553	|	1648	...	1753	1848	1953	2048	2153	...	2247	...	0014
231	**Halle** (Saale) Hbf .... ⊡ d.	0655	0755	0855	0955	1055	...	1155	1155	1255	1355	1455	1555	|	1655	...	1755	1855	1955	2055	2155	...	2255	...	*0025*
249	Leipzig/Halle Flughafen ✈ ⊡ a.	0705	|	0905	|	1105	...	|	|	1305	|	1505	|	|	1705	...	|	1905	|	2105	|	...	2305	...	|
268	**Leipzig** Hbf .... ⊡ a.	0718	0815	0919	1016	1118	...	1216	1216	1318	1416	1519	1616	1647	1718	...	1816	1918	2015	2118	2216	...	2318	...	*0102*
	Dresden Hbf **842** .... a.	0838*	...	1057*	...	1257*	...	...	...	1457*	...	1638*	...	1836	1840**g**	...	...	2039*	...	2240**b**	...	...	...	...	...

	IC **2436** ①–⑤ 🍷	Ⓐ d	*IC* **2042** ①	*IC* **2042** ①–⑥ 🍷	*IC* **2434** ①–⑥ 🍷	*IC* **2044** S🍷	*IC* **2238** D🍷	*IC* **2432** C🍷	*IC* **2046** S🍷	*IC* **2430** 🍷	*IC* **2048** S🍷	*IC* **2038** 🍷	*IC* **2440** S🍷	*IC* **2036** 🍷	*IC* **2442** F🍷	*IC* **2234** A D🍷	*IC* **2034** B 🍷	*IC* **2034** A 🍷	*IC* **1934** ⑦A 🍷	*IC* **2444** K🍷	*IC* **2032** 🍷	*IC* **2446**	*IC* **2030** ⑤ 🍷	*IC* **2448** Ⓑ 🍷	*IC* **2448** ⑤**r** 🍷
Dresden Hbf **842** .... d.	...	...	...	...	...	0511*	...	...	0711**e**	...	0845*	...	1045*	...	1245*	...	...	...	1444	1511*	...	1712*	...	1845*	1845*
Leipzig Hbf .... ⊡ d.	...	*0358*	0441	...	0542	0638	0742	...	0838	0942	1038	1142	1238	1342	1438	1542	1542	...	1602	1638	1740	1838	1942	2038	2038
Leipzig/Halle Flughafen ✈ ⊡ d.	...	*0412*	0453	...	|	0650	|	...	0850	|	1050	|	1250	|	1450	|	|	...	|	1650	|	1850	|	2050	2050
Halle (Saale) Hbf .... ⊡ a.	...	*0422*	0504	...	0600	0701	0800	...	0901	1000	1101	1200	1301	1400	1501	1600	1600	...	|	1701	1759	1901	2000	2101	2101
Halle (Saale) Hbf .... d.	...	0442	0507	...	0606	0709	0806	...	0909	1006	1109	1206	1309	1406	1509	1606	1606	...	|	1709	1806	1909	2006	2109	2109
Köthen .... d.	...	0510	0527	...	0627	0728	0827	...	0927	1027	1127	1227	1327	1427	1527	1627	1627	...	|	1727	1827	1927	2027	2127	2127
Berlin Ostbahnhof .... d.	...	|	|	...	|	|	|	0718	|	|	|	|	|	|	|	|	|	1517	◧	|	|	|	|	|	|
Berlin Hbf .... d.	...	|	|	...	|	|	|	0729**z**	|	|	|	|	|	|	|	|	|	1528**z**	|	|	|	|	|	|	|
Berlin Wannsee .... d.	...	|	|	...	|	|	|	0750	|	|	|	|	|	|	|	|	|	1549	|	|	|	|	|	|	|
Potsdam Hbf .... d.	...	|	|	...	|	|	|	0801	|	|	|	|	|	|	|	|	|	1601	|	|	|	|	|	|	|
Brandenburg Hbf .... d.	...	|	|	...	|	|	|	0821	|	|	|	|	|	|	|	|	|	1620	|	|	|	|	|	|	|
Magdeburg Hbf .... a.	...	0550	0555	...	0655	0757	0855	0900	0957	1054	1157	1254	1357	1454	1557	1655	1654	1657	1723	1757	1854	1957	2054	2156	2156
Magdeburg Hbf .... d.	0500	...	0603	0603	0701	0804	...	0902	1004	1101	1204	1301	1404	1501	1604	...	1701	1700	1725	1804	1901	2004	2101	2204	2204
Helmstedt .... d.	0526	...	0628	0628	0726	|	...	0928	|	1126	|	1326	|	1526	|	...	1726	1726	|	|	1926	|	2126	|	|
Braunschweig Hbf .... **811** d.	0549	...	0649	0649	0749	0849	...	0951	1049	1149	1249	1349	1449	1549	1649	...	1749	1749	1816	1849	1949	2049	2149	2250	2250
Peine .... **811** d.	0606	...	|	|	|	|	...	|	|	|	|	|	|	|	|	...	|	|	|	|	|	|	|	|	|
Hannover Hbf .... **811** a.	0626	...	0723	0723	0823	0923	...	1025	1123	1223	1323	1423	1523	1623	1723	...	1823	1823	1850	1923	2023	2122	2221	2326	2326
Bremen Hbf **813** .... a.	0750	...	|	|	0950	|	...	1150	|	1350	|	1550	|	1750	|	...	1950	1950	2009	|	2150	...	...	...	|
Oldenburg (Oldb) **813** .... a.	0823	...	|	|	1023	|	...	1223	|	1423	|	1623	|	1823	|	...	2023	2023	2040	|	2223	...	...	...	|
Emden Hbf **813** .... a.	0938	...	|	|	1138	|	...	1338	|	1538	|	1738	|	1938	|	...	2138	2138	2152	|	2338**b**	...	...	...	|
Norddeich **813** .... a.	...	...	|	|	...	|	...	1414	|	...	|	...	|	2014**b**	|	...	2214	2214	...	|	...	...	...	...	|
Dortmund Hbf **800** .... a.	...	...	0932**r**	0932**r**	...	1132**r**	...	...	1332**r**	...	1532**r**	...	1732**r**	...	1932**r**	...	...	...	...	2132**r**	...	...	...	...	0127
Köln Hbf **800** .... a.	...	...	1047**r**	1047**r**	...	1247**r**	...	...	1447**r**	...	1647**r**	...	1847**r**	...	2049**r**	...	...	...	...	2247**r**	...	...	...	...	...

Other regional stopping trains **BRAUNSCHWEIG - MAGDEBURG**

	†			Ⓐ	Ⓐ	Ⓐ	Ⓒ	①–⑥	Ⓐ					Ⓑ	⑥	Ⓑ								
Braunschweig Hbf .... d.	0106	...	...	...	0529	...	0542	...	0616	...	0716	and	2016	2116	2147	2216	...	2347	...	...	...	...	...	...
Helmstedt .... d.	0136	...	0405	0505	0602	0606	0610	0645	0645	...	0745	hourly	2045	2145	2216	2245	...	0016	...	...	...	...	...	...
Magdeburg Hbf .... a.	0218	...	0447	0547	...	0652	0652	0728	0728	...	0828	until	2128	2228	2259	2328	...	...	...	...	...	...	...	...

	Ⓒ		Ⓐ	Ⓒ	Ⓐ	Ⓐ																		
Magdeburg Hbf .... d.	0250	...	0432	0532	...	0530	0632	0732	0832	and	2032	...	2205	...	2314	...	...	...	...	...	...	...	...	...
Helmstedt .... d.	0330	...	0513	0613	0612	0635**p**	0713	0813	0913	hourly	2113	...	2245	...	2355	...	...	...	...	...	...	...	...	...
Braunschweig Hbf .... a.	0359	...	0541	0641	0642	0705	0741	0841	0941	until	2141	...	2313	...	...	...	...	...	...	...	...	...	...	...

Other regional trains **MAGDEBURG - HALLE**

		Ⓐ						
Magdeburg Hbf .... d.	0411	0458	0534	0634	and	2034	2215	2307
Schönebeck (Elbe) .... d.	0422	0511	0546	0646	hourly	2046	2226	2320
Köthen .... d.	0447	0536	0614	0714	until	2114	2254	2347
Halle (Saale) Hbf .... a.	0514	0600	0642	0741		2141	2318	0014

	Ⓐ			Ⓐ						
Halle (Saale) Hbf .... d.	0442	...	0542	0614	0714	and	2014	2125	2259	0008
Köthen .... d.	0510	0510	0610	0643	0743	hourly	2043	2154	2328	0036
Schönebeck (Elbe) .... d.	0537	0537	0637	0710	0809	until	2109	2220	2354	0102
Magdeburg Hbf .... a.	0550	0550	0651	0725	0823		2123	2238	0006	0114

A – Until Aug. 1.
B – From Aug. 2.
C – To / from Cottbus on dates in Table **837**.
D – To / from Rostock until Aug. 1 (see panel).
F – From / to Frankfurt from Aug. 9 (Table **800**).
K – From / to Koblenz from Aug. 9 (Table **800**).
S – From / to Stuttgart or Karlsruhe from Aug. 9 (Tables **800** and **910**).

b – Not ⑥.
d – Daily from Köthen.
e – Not ⑦.
g – 1856 on ⑤ to Aug. 8.
p – Arrives 0610.
r – From Aug. 9.

v – ①–⑥ from Aug. 9.
z – Also calls at Berlin Zoo.

◐ – Via Dessau Hbf (d. 1615) and Bitterfeld (d. 1630).
◧ – Via Bitterfeld (d. 1626) and Dessau Hbf (d. 1646).
⊡ – See Table **881** for other S-Bahn services.
△ – Train *IC* **2479** from Aug. 2 (from Berlin).
* – Times may vary June 24 - July 11. For times from Aug. 10 see amended version of Table **842** on page 607.

☛ Trains starting from / finishing at Hannover (instead of Köln and beyond) until Aug. 8 have different train numbers to those shown (e.g. **2443** is **2243**, **2043** is **2053**, **2045** is **1945** etc).

Through services **WARNEMÜNDE - ROSTOCK - LEIPZIG**

	IC **2235** A 🍷	*IC* **2239** A 🍷
Warnemünde .... d.	...	...
Rostock Hbf .... d.	0805	1405
Bützow .... d.	0827	1427
Bad Kleinen .... d.	0849	1450
Schwerin Hbf .... d.	0901	1502
Ludwigslust .... d.	0927	1526
Wittenberge .... d.	0949	1549
Stendal Hbf .... d.	1022	1622
Magdeburg Hbf .... a.	1057	1657
Leipzig Hbf ★ ... a.	1216	1816

	IC **2238** A 🍷	*IC* **2234** A 🍷
Leipzig Hbf ★ .... d.	0742	1542
Magdeburg Hbf .... d.	0857	1658
Stendal Hbf .... d.	0935	1735
Wittenberge .... d.	1011	|
Ludwigslust .... d.	1032	1830
Schwerin Hbf .... d.	1056	1856
Bad Kleinen .... d.	1109	1909
Bützow .... d.	1136	1936
Rostock Hbf .... a.	1156	1956
Warnemünde .... a.	...	...

★ – See main table for full timings to / from Leipzig.

HARZER SCHMALSPURBAHNEN 867

2nd class only

SUMMER SERVICE APRIL 25 - NOVEMBER 11, 2025

km		🚂		🚂	🚂	🚂	🚂		🚂	🚂	🚂 r	
0	**Wernigerode** § d.	0900	...	1000	1046	1157	...	1400	1454	...	1632	1725
15	Drei Annen Hohne a.	0937	...	1037	1123	1234	...	1443	1531	e	1712	1806
15	Drei Annen Hohne ◇ d.	0957	1004	1050	1136	1244	1248	1510	1548	1600	1731	1807
20	Schierke ◇ a.	1009	|	1102	1148	|	1300	1522	|	1612	1743	|
20	Schierke ◇ d.	1016	|	1110	1203	|	1308	1530	|	1622	1748	|
34	**Brocken** ◇ a.	1049	|	1143	1236	|	1341	1603	|	1655	1821	|
19	Elend d.	...	1016	...	...	1256	☛	...	1600	...	...	1825
28	Sorge d.	...	1035	...	...	1316	...	...	1619	...	...	1844
31	Benneckenstein d.	...	1044	...	...	1325	...	...	1628	...	...	1853
44	Eisfelder Talmühle a.	...	1112	...	...	1356	...	...	1656	...	...	1921
44	Eisfelder Talmühle d.	...	1116	...	...	...	1417	...	1715	...	...	1933
50	Ilfeld d.	...	1131	...	...	...	1432	...	1730	...	...	1948
61	**Nordhausen** Nord § a.	...	1152	...	...	...	1453	...	1752	...	...	2013

		🚂	🚂	🚂		🚂	🚂	🚂 s			
Nordhausen Nord § d.	0754‡	1033	...	...	1325	...	...	...	1626	...	...
Ilfeld d.	0815	1059	...	...	1347	...	...	...	1647	h	...
Eisfelder Talmühle a.	0829	1113	...	...	1412	...	...	...	1702	1713	...
Eisfelder Talmühle d.	0830	1120	...	...	☛	1414	...	...	☛	1722	...
Benneckenstein d.	0943	1150	...	...	...	1443	...	...	...	1752	...
Sorge d.	☛	1158	...	...	...	1451	...	...	...	1800	...
Elend d.	🚂	1217	...	...	🚂	1511	...	...	🚂	1824	...
Brocken d.	1107	|	1200	1305	1358	|	1451	1619	1711	|	1833
Schierke a.	1150	|	1255	1348	1441	|	1523	1702	1743	|	1905
Schierke d.	1207	|	1304	1355	1443	|	1524	1703	1745	|	1906
Drei Annen Hohne a.	1218	1228	1315	1406	1454	1522	1536	1715	1756	1835	1918
Drei Annen Hohne d.	...	1238	...	1422	1510	b	1551	1727	1813	1836	1923
Wernigerode § a.	...	1315	...	1502	1550	...	1627	1803	1849	1912	1959

km				🚂					🚂		🚂	
0	**Quedlinburg** § d.	0730	1042	1130	...	1310	...	...	...	1545	1749	1940
8	**Gernrode** a.	0745	1057	1146	...	1325	...	...	...	1600	1804	1956
8	**Gernrode** d.	0746	1058	1147	...	1326	...	...	...	1608	☛	...
18	Mägdesprung d.	0817	1129	1218	...	1357	...	...	...	1642	...	...
	Harzgerode △ d.	|	|	|	...	|	...	...	...	|	...	...
23	Alexisbad a.	0831	1143	1232	...	1411	...	...	...	1656	...	...
23	Alexisbad d.	0832	1147	1239	...	1412	...	...	...	1703	...	...
26	**Harzgerode** △ a.	|	|	|	...	|	...	...	...	|	...	...
26	Silberhütte d.	0841	1156	1248	...	1422	...	...	...	1712	...	...
30	Straßberg (Harz) d.	0852	1208	1300	...	1434	...	...	...	1723	...	...
35	Güntersberge d.	...	1218	1310	...	1444	...	...	...	1733	...	...
	Hasselfelde d.	...	|	|	...	|	n	1639	...	|	1826	...
44	Stiege a.	...	1237	1329	...	1503	1621	1652	...	1803	1839	...
44	Stiege d.	...	1238	1334	...	1508	1622	1653	...	1804	1840	...
48	**Hasselfelde** a.	...	1251	|	...	|	1635	|	...	1817	|	...
53	Eisfelder Talmühle d.	...	...	1356	1417	1529	...	1713	1715	...	1901	...
59	Ilfeld d.	...	...	...	1432	1548	...	w	1730	...	1917	...
70	**Nordhausen** Nord § a.	...	...	...	1453	1613	...	...	1752	...	1939	...

							🚂	🚂			
Nordhausen Nord § d.	...	...	0925	...	...	1325	...	...	1525	...	1626
Ilfeld d.	...	...	0946	...	...	1347	...	...	1546	...	1647
Eisfelder Talmühle d.	...	...	1001	...	...	1412	1414	...	1601	...	1715
Hasselfelde d.	...	...	|	1040	1317	...	|	1509	|	1639	|
Stiege a.	...	...	1021	1053	1330	...	1434	1522	1621	1652	1735
Stiege d.	...	...	1022	1054	1332	...	1446	1523	1622	1653	1739
Hasselfelde a.	...	...	1035	|	|	...	1459	|	1635	w	|
Güntersberge d.	...	...	☛	1112	1348	...	...	1541	...	...	1802
Straßberg (Harz) d.	...	0856	...	1123	1401	...	...	1552	...	...	1812
Silberhütte d.	...	0907	...	1135	1423	...	...	1603	...	...	1824
Harzgerode △ d.	...	|	...	|	|	...	...	|	...	...	|
Alexisbad a.	...	0917	...	1145	1433	...	...	1613	...	...	1833
Alexisbad d.	...	0918	...	1202	1434	...	...	1627	...	...	1834
Harzgerode △ a.	...	|	...	|	|	...	...	|	...	...	|
Mägdesprung d.	...	0933	...	1219	1448	...	...	1641	...	...	1848
Gernrode a.	...	1003	🚂	1249	1518	...	...	1711	...	...	1918
Gernrode d.	0710	1004	1100	1250	1519	...	...	1714	...	...	1919
Quedlinburg § a.	0725	1019	1115	1305	1533	...	...	1729	...	...	1933

b – To Brocken.
e – From Eisfelder Talmühle.
h – To / from Hasselfelde.
n – From Nordhausen.
r – Diesel loco from Drei Annen Hohne.
s – Diesel loco to Drei Annen Hohne.
w – To Wernigerode.

§ – Adjacent to DB station.
‡ – Nordhausen **Bahnhofsplatz**.
◇ – Additional journey by 🚂: Drei Annen Hohne d. 1341 - Brocken a. 1434.
△ – No service to / from Harzgerode due to reconstruction work.
🚂 – Steam train.
☛ Simultaneous departure of two 🚂 departs Eisfelder Talmühle at 1414.

Operator: Harzer Schmalspurbahnen GmbH.
Friedrichstraße 151, 38855 Wernigerode.
✆ + 49 (0) 3943 558 0.
Fax + 49 (0) 3943 558 148.

Nordhausen - Wernigerode: *Die Harzquerbahn*.
Eisfelder Talmühle - Quedlinburg: *Die Selketalbahn*.
Drei Annen Hohne - Brocken: *Die Brockenbahn*.

ERFURT - NORDHAUSEN 868

RE / RB services

km		Ⓐ																	
0	**Erfurt** Hbf d.	0448	0559	0700	0802	0902	1002	1102	1202	1302	1402	1502	1602	1702	1802	1902	2016	...	2213
27	Straußfurt d.	0514	0624	0724	0828	0924	1029	1124	1229	1324	1429	1524	1629	1724	1829	1924	2045	...	2245
60	Sondershausen d.	0547	0657	0757	0857	0957	1057	1157	1257	1357	1457	1557	1657	1757	1857	1957	2113	...	2317
80	**Nordhausen** a.	0609	0714	0819	0915	1019	1115	1219	1315	1419	1515	1619	1715	1819	1915	2019	2130	...	2338

	Ⓐ	Ⓐ																
Nordhausen d.	0420	0522	0623	0729	0834	0929	1034	1129	1234	1329	1434	1529	1634	1729	1834	1929	...	2137
Sondershausen d.	0443	0548	0640	0757	0857	0957	1057	1157	1257	1357	1457	1557	1657	1757	1857	1957	...	2158
Straußfurt d.	0515	0625	0709	0830	0924	1030	1124	1230	1324	1430	1524	1630	1724	1830	1924	2030	...	2230
Erfurt Hbf a.	0541	0650	0738	0856	0950	1056	1150	1256	1350	1456	1550	1656	1750	1856	1950	2056	...	2256

NORDHAUSEN - GÖTTINGEN 869

RB services

km		Ⓐ	⚒																	
0	**Nordhausen** d.	...	0539	0639	0739	0839	0939	1039	1139	1239	1339	1439	1539	1639	1739	1839	1939	2039	2139	...
20	Walkenried d.	0503	0603	0703	0803	0903	1003	1103	1203	1303	1403	1503	1603	1703	1803	1903	2003	2103	2203	...
23	Bad Sachsa d.	0508	0608	0708	0808	0908	1008	1108	1208	1308	1408	1508	1608	1708	1808	1908	2008	2108	2208	...
37	Bad Lauterberg ⊡ d.	0519	0619	0719	0819	0919	1019	1119	1219	1319	1419	1519	1619	1719	1819	1919	2019	2119	2219	...
43	Herzberg (Harz) d.	0526	0626	0726	0826	0926	1026	1126	1226	1326	1426	1526	1626	1726	1826	1926	2026	2126	2226	2326
70	Northeim **859 903** a.	0550	0650	0750	0850	0950	1050	1150	1250	1350	1450	1550	1650	1750	1850	1950	2050	2150	2250	2350
90	**Göttingen** **859 903** a.	0608	0710	0809	*0909*	1009	*1109*	1209	*1309*	1409	*1509*	1609	*1709*	1809	*1909*	2009	*2109*	2209	*2309*	0008

	Ⓐ	⚒	Ⓒ	Ⓐ															⑤⑥ f	
Göttingen **859 903** d.	*0408*	0549	*0648*	0649	0749	*0848*	0949	*1048*	1149	*1248*	1349	*1448*	1549	*1648*	1749	*1848*	1949	*2048*	2149	2249
Northeim **859 903** d.	0506	0606	0706	0706	0806	0906	1006	1106	1206	1306	1406	1506	1606	1706	1806	1906	2006	2106	2206	2306
Herzberg (Harz) d.	0530	0630	0730	0730	0830	0930	1030	1130	1230	1330	1430	1530	1630	1730	1830	1930	2030	2130	2230	2330
Bad Lauterberg ⊡ d.	0536	0636	0736	0736	0836	0936	1036	1136	1236	1336	1436	1536	1636	1736	1836	1936	2036	2136	2236	...
Bad Sachsa d.	0547	0647	0747	0747	0847	0947	1047	1147	1247	1347	1447	1547	1647	1747	1847	1947	2047	2147	2247	...
Walkenried d.	0551	0651	0751	0751	0851	0951	1051	1151	1251	1351	1451	1551	1651	1751	1852	1951	2051	2151	2251	...
Nordhausen a.	0615	0715	0815	0815	0915	1015	1115	1215	1315	1415	1515	1615	1715	1815	1915	2015	2115	2215	2315	...

f – Runs daily Göttingen - Herzberg.

⊡ – Bad Lauterberg im Harz Barbis.

ERFURT - MEININGEN 870

DB (*RE* services); *STB* ▽

km			⊙	⚒		Ⓐ								Ⓐ									
0	**Erfurt** Hbf **872** d.	0500	...	0602	...	0701	0735	...	0805	and in the same pattern every **two** hours until	1535	...	1605	1702	1735	...	1805	1935	...	2005	2118	2250	0009
13	Neudietendorf **872** d.	0508	...	0611	...	0710	0743	...	0814		1543	...	1614	1711	1743	...	1814	1943	...	2014	2127	2259	0019
23	Arnstadt Hbf **872** d.	0515	...	0620	...	0718	0751	...	0822		1551	...	1622	1719	1751	...	1822	1951	...	2026	2135	2307	0029
31	Plaue (Thür) d.	0522	...	0628	...	0726	0758	...	0830		1558	...	1630	1727	1758	...	1830	1958	...	2034	2143	2316	0038
37	Gräfenroda d.	0527	...	0633	...	0731	|	...	0835		|	...	1635	1732	|	...	1835	2003	...	2039	2147	2321	0043
58	Zella-Mehlis d.	0543	...	0652	...	0749	0816	...	0857		1616	...	1657	1751	1816	...	1857	2018	...	2101	2205	2338	0101
64	Suhl d.	0548	...	0658	...	0755	0822	...	0903		1622	...	1703	1758	1822	...	1903	2024	...	2107	2211	2344	0107
84	Grimmenthal **873** a.	0559	0603	0714	0718	0811	0832	0842	0918		1632	1642	1718	1811	1832	1842	1918	2035	2043	2123	2228	2357	0124
	Schweinfurt Hbf **870a** a.	0713	|	0842t	|	|	0926	|	|		1725	|	|	|	1926	|	|	2126	|	|	|	|	|
	Würzburg Hbf **870a** a.	0745	|	...	|	|	0955	|	|		1755	|	|	|	1955	|	|	2157	|	|	|	|	|
92	**Meiningen** **873** a.	...	0609	...	0724	0819	...	0849	0933		...	1649	1733	1819	...	1849	1934	...	2050	2132	2241	0003	0132

	Ⓐ	Ⓐ				⚒	e								Ⓐ								⑤⑥ r
Meiningen **873** d.	0403	0503	0524	0609	...	...	0710	0819	0901	...	and in the same pattern every **two** hours until	1619	1701	...	1736	1819	1901	...	2019	2110	...	...	2320
Würzburg Hbf **870a** d.	|	|	|	|	...	...	|	|	|	0801		|	|	1601	|	|	|	1801	|	|	2001	...	|
Schweinfurt Hbf **870a** d.	|	|	|	|	0530	...	|	|	|	0830		|	|	1630	|	|	|	1830	|	|	2030	...	|
Grimmenthal **873** d.	0414	0511	0531	0616	0621	0628	0717	0833j	0908	0920		1633j	1708	1720	1744	1833j	1908	1920	2036k	2117	2127	...	2335j
Suhl d.	0431	0524	0549	...	0633	0645	0730	0850	...	0933		1650	...	1733	1759	1850	...	1933	2053	...	2144	...	2356
Zella-Mehlis d.	0438	0531	0556	...	0639	0654	0736	0901	...	0939		1701	...	1739	1805	1901	...	1939	2101	...	2150	...	0002
Gräfenroda d.	0455	0548	0614	...	0654	0712	0752	0919	...	|		1719	...	|	1822	1919	...	|	2119	...	2205	...	0018
Plaue (Thür) d.	0506	0553	0626j	...	0659	0717	|	0924	...	0957		1724	...	1757	1828	1924	...	1957	2124	...	2210	...	0027
Arnstadt Hbf **872** d.	0514	0603	0634	...	0706	0726	0804	0934	...	1005		1734	...	1805	1838	1934	...	2005	2133	...	2217	...	0036
Neudietendorf **872** a.	0524	0611	0645	...	0713	0736	0811	0942	...	1012		1742	...	1812	1847	1942	...	2012	2143	...	2224	...	0043
Erfurt Hbf **872** a.	0535	0620	0654	...	0722	0747	0820	0951	...	1021		1751	...	1821	1856	1951	...	2021	2153	...	2233	...	0053

e – From Eisenach (Table **873**).
j – Arrives 6 – 7 minutes earlier.
k – Arrives 2027.
r – ⑤⑥ (also June 8, Oct. 2, 30). From Eisenach (Table **873**).
t – Ⓐ only.

⊙ – 20 minutes later on Ⓒ.
▽ – Most services to / from Meiningen are operated by Süd Thüringen Bahn (2nd class only).

870a MEININGEN - SCHWEINFURT - WÜRZBURG

DB (*RE* services); Erfurter Bahn (2nd class only)

km																									
		Ⓐ	Ⓐ				⚒	Ⓐ	Ⓒ																
0	**Meiningen** .... **873** d.	0413	...	0521	0548	...	0642t	◧	0719	0819	...	*0918*	◧	*1118*	◧	*1318*	◧	*1518*	◧	*1718*	◧	1901	◧	2110	*2226*
	Erfurt Hbf **870** ....d.	|	...	|	|	0500	|	0602	|	|	0735	|	0935	|	1135	|	1335	|	1535	|	1735	|	1935	|	|
	Grimmenthal..... **873** d.	|	...	|	0555	0603	|	0726	|	0827	0835	0930	1035	1130	1235	1330	1435	1530	1635	1730	1835	1930v	2035	2130k	2238
25	Mellrichstadt ....d.	0437	0506	0548	...	0623	0709	0747	0747	...	0849	0948	1049	1148	1249	1348	1449	1549	1649	1748	1849	1948	2049	2148	2256
39	Bad Neustadt (Saale) .. d.	0446	0514	0559	...	0633	0718	0759	0759	...	0857	0959	1057	1159	1257	1358	1457	1610k	1657	1759	1857	1959	2057	2159	2305
49	Münnerstadt................d.	0454	0522	0607	...	0642	0726	0807	0807	...	0903	1007	1103	1207	1304	1406	1504	1619	1703	1807	1903	2007	2103	2207	2313
64	Ebenhausen (Unterfr) .. a.	0505	0533	0618	...	0653	0736	0818	0818	...	0912	1018	1112	1218	1312	1417	1512	1630	1712	1818	1912	2018	2112	2218	2325
	Ebenhausen (Unterfr) .. d.	*0509*	0540	0625	...	0657	0742	0826	0826	...	0917	1025	1117	1225	1317	1425	1517	1639	1717	1825	1917	2025	2117	2225	2328
78	**Schweinfurt** Hbf . **875** a.	*0521*	0552	0637	...	0713	0753	0842	0842	...	0926	1042	1126	1241	1326	1440	1525	1652	1725	1841	1926	2041	2126	2236	2339
121	**Würzburg** Hbf..... **875** a.	...	*0648*	*0721*	...	0745	*0821*	*0921*	*0921*	...	0955	*1121*	1155	*1320*	1355	*1521*	1555	*1721*	1755	*1921*	1955	*2121*	2157	...	*0016*

km																									
				⚒r																				e	⑤⑥f
	Würzburg Hbf..... **876** d.	*0454r*	...	...	*0623h*	0801	*0835*	1001	*1035*	1201	*1235*	1401	*1435*	*1508*	1601	*1635*	1801	...	*1835*	2001	...	*2035*	...	*2143*	*2143*
	Schweinfurt Hbf . **876** d.	0530	...	0610	0700	0830	0912	1029	1112	1230	1312	1430	1512	1543	1630	1712	1830	...	1912	2030	...	2113	...	2224	2224
	Ebenhausen (Unterf) ... a.	0539	...	0622	0712	0838	0928	1039	1128	1238	1328	1439	1528	1555	1638	1728	1838	...	1928	2038	...	2128	...	2239	2239
	Ebenhausen (Unterf) ... d.	0541	...	0629	0714	0840	0932	1040	1132	1240	1331	1441	1532	1603	1640	1732	1840	...	1932	2040	...	2132	...	2242	2242
	Münnerstadt................d.	0550	...	0646	0726	0849	0944	1049	1144	1249	1342	1450	1544	1619	1649	1744	1849	...	1944	2049	...	2144	...	2253	2253
	Bad Neustadt (Saale) .. d.	0557	...	0654	0737	0857	0958	1057	1158	1257	1358	1457	1558	1627	1657	1758	1857	...	1958	2057	...	2157	...	2305	2305
0	Mellrichstadt ....d.	0605	...	0707	0746	0906	1007	1106	1207	1306	1407	1506	1607	1635t	1706	1807	1906	...	2007	2106	...	2206	...	2313	2313
21	Grimmenthal..... **873** a.	0619	0623	|	|	0919	1024	1119	1224	1319	1424	1519	1624	...	1719	1824	1919	1927	2024	2121	2126	2224	2234	|	2331
	Erfurt Hbf **870** ....a.	0722	|	|	|	1021	|	1221	|	1421	|	1621	|	...	1821	|	2021	|	|	2233	|	...	|	|	|
	Meiningen .... **873** a.	...	0629	0731t	0810	◧	*1033*	◧	*1233*	◧	*1433*	◧	*1633*	...	◧	*1833*	...	1934	*2034*	...	2132	...	2241	2338	2342

e – ⑦–④ (not June 8, Oct. 2, 30).
f – ⑤⑥ (also June 8, Oct. 2, 30).
h – 0603 on Ⓒ.
k – Arrives 13 minutes earlier.
r – ⚒ only.
t – Ⓐ only.
v – Arrives 1908.
◧ – Connecting trains Meiningen - Grimmenthal and v.v. (journey 7 minutes): **From Meiningen** at 0710, 1019, 1219 and every **two** hours until 2019. **From Grimmenthal** at 0926, 1126 and every **two** hours until 1726.

871 LEIPZIG - GERA - SAALFELD

Erfurter Bahn (2nd class only)

km																									
		Ⓒ		Ⓐ	Ⓐ		Ⓐ			⚒				⊠											
0	**Leipzig** Hbf.......d.	0034	...	...	...	...	0508	0557	...	0654	0753	0753	0854	and in	1553	1553	1654	1753	1753	1854	1955	2054	...	2157	2306
45	Zeitz..................d.	0111	...	...	...	...	0553	0635	...	0735	0834	0834	0934	the same	1634	1634	1734	1834	1834	1934	2034	2132	...	2236	2347
72	**Gera** Hbf...........a.	0136	...	...	...	...	0617	0659	...	0800	0858	0858	0958		1658	1658	1758	1858	1858	1959	2058	2157	...	2300	0010
72	**Gera** Hbf...........d.	...	...	0447	0527	0629	0629	0702	0802	0802	0902	0902	1002	pattern	1702	1702	1802	1902	1902	2002	2110	...	2208	2310	...
84	Weida..................d.	...	...	0459	0538	0643	0643	0715	0813	0813	0916	0918	1013		1716	1718	1813	1916	1918	2014	2122	...	2220	2322	...
156	**Hof** Hbf...........a.	...	...	|	|	|	|	0825	|	|	1025	|	|	every	1825	|	|	2025	|	|	|	...	...	|	...
99	Triptis ....d.	...	...	0511	0552	0700j	0700j	...	0826	0826	...	0934	1027	two hours	...	1734	1827	...	1934	2026	2136	...	...	2334	...
108	Neustadt (Orla)...d.	...	...	0517	0558	0707	0707	...	0832	0832	...	0940	1033		...	1740	1833	...	1941	2037	2142	...	...	2341	...
139	**Saalfeld** (Saale) . a.	...	...	0547	0626	0738	0738	...	0854	0854	...	1009	1055	until	...	1809	1855	...	2008	2104	2211	...	...	0008	...

		⚒		Ⓐ	†	⑥	Ⓐ							⊠										
Saalfeld (Saale) .d.	...	...	...	0509	...	0552	0551	0657	0751	...	0905	0947	...	and in	1503	1547	...	1703	1747	...	1904	2008	...	2104	2213
Neustadt (Orla)...d.	...	...	...	0542	...	0619	0623	0724	0818	...	0926	1019	...	the same	1526	1619	...	1726	1819	...	1927	2035	...	2128	2239
Triptis ....d.	...	...	...	0551	...	0625	0630	0730	0826	...	0933	1026	...		1533	1626	...	1733	1826	...	1934	2042	...	2135	2246
Hof Hbf...........d.	...	...	...	|	...	|	|	|	|	0734	|	|	0934	pattern	|	|	1534	|	|	1734	|	|	2036	|	|
Weida..................d.	...	...	...	0603	0642	0642j	0642	0742	0844j	0844	0945	1044j	1044		1545	1644j	1644	1745	1844j	1844	1946	2054	2140	2147	2258
Gera Hbf...........a.	...	...	...	0615	0655	0655	0655	0754	0856	0856	0956	1056	1056	every	1556	1656	1656	1756	1856	1856	1957	2106	2152	2157	2309
Gera Hbf...........d.	0443	0535	0623	0623	0700	0700	0700	0801	0901	0901	1001	1101	1101	two hours	1601	1700	1700	1801	1901	1901	2001	...	...	2158	2312f
Zeitz..................d.	0514	0605	0654	0654	0725	0725	0725	0825	0925	0925	1025	1125	1125		1625	1725	1725	1825	1925	1925	2025	...	...	2222	2337f
Leipzig Hbf.......a.	0551	0650	0734	0734	0808	0808	0808	0905	1005	1005	1105	1205	1205	until	1705	1805	1805	1905	2005	2005	2105	...	...	2259	0022f

f – Gera - Leipzig on ⑤⑥ (also June 8, Oct. 3, 30).
j – Arrives 5–6 minutes earlier.
⊠ – Certain timings vary by ± 1 minute.
☛ An amended service Leipzig - Saalfeld and v.v. operates June 28 - July 13 with partial 🚌 substitution.

872 ERFURT - SAALFELD and ROTTENBACH - KATZHÜTTE

DB; Erfurter Bahn; 2nd class only

km		Ⓐ	Ⓐ							
0	**Erfurt** Hbf.......... **870** d.	0431	0526	0638		2038	2145	...	2324	...
13	Neudietendorf ...... **870** d.	0442	0537	0648	and	2048	2155	...	2334	...
23	Arnstadt Hbf......... **870** d.	0453	0548	0700		2100	2207	...	2345	...
38	Stadtilm ....d.	0506	0601	0713	hourly	2113	2220	...	2358	...
54	Rottenbach ....d.	0520	0613	0727		2127	2235	...	0011	...
62	Bad Blankenburg.......d.	0528	0621	0735	until	2135	2243	...	0019	...
70	**Saalfeld** (Saale)........a.	0536	0629	0742		2142	2250	...	0026	...

	Ⓐ								
Saalfeld (Saale)..............d.	0504	0612	0712		2112	...	2220	...	...
Bad Blankenburg ....d.	0511	0622	0719	and	2119	...	2227	...	...
Rottenbach ....d.	0519	0629	0727		2127	...	2235	...	...
Stadtilm ....d.	0533	0642	0740	hourly	2140	...	2247	...	...
Arnstadt Hbf............ **870** d.	0549	0659	0756		2156	...	2301	...	...
Neudietendorf .... **870** a.	0559	0706	0805	until	2205	...	2308	...	...
Erfurt Hbf.................. **870** a.	0610	0716	0817		2217	...	2317	...	...

km		Ⓐ						⑤⑦r		
0	Rottenbach ....d.	0535	...	0641	and	1941	...	2041	...	...
15	Obstfelderschmiede .. a.	0558	...	0705	hourly	2005	...	2105	...	...
25	Katzhütte ....a.	0615	...	0722	until	2022	...	2122	...	...

	Ⓐ						⑤⑦r		
Katzhütte ....d.	0529	...	0636	and	1936	...	2036	...	...
Obstfelderschmiede ....d.	0546	...	0653	hourly	1953	...	2053	...	...
Rottenbach ....a.	0609	...	0716	until	2016	...	2116	...	...

r – Also June 9; not June 8, Oct. 3, 31.

☛ **Thüringer Bergbahn**. Obstfelderschmiede - Lichtenhain - Cursdorf. www.thueringerbergbahn.com. Journey: 28–44 minutes.
From Obstfelderschmiede at 0630, 0700, 0730 and every 30 minutes until 1730; then 1808, 1830, 1908, 1930.
From Cursdorf at 0614, 0640, 0706, 0734, 0814, 0844 and every 30 minutes until 1944.

873 EISENACH - MEININGEN - SONNEBERG

Süd Thüringen Bahn (2nd class only)

km																										
		⚒	Ⓐ		Ⓐ	E																				E
0	**Eisenach**..................d.	...	0353	...	0500	0603	0716	0816	0916	1016	1116	...	...	1216	1316	...	...	1416	1516	1616	1716	1816	1916	2016	2121	2216
27	Bad Salzungen.......... d.	...	0418	...	0531	0632	0742	0842	0942	1042	1142	...	...	1242	1342	...	...	1442	1542	1642	1742	1842	1942	2042	2152	2242
41	Wernshausen............ d.	...	0435	...	0547	0649	0758	0858	0958	1058	1158	...	...	1258	1358	...	...	1458	1558	1658	1758	1858	1958	2058	2208	2301
61	**Meiningen**................ a.	...	0452	...	0604	0706	0815	0915	1015	1115	1215	...	...	1315	1415	...	...	1515	1615	1715	1815	1915	2015	2115	2224	2317
		Ⓐ	|		|	▽	▽	|	▽	|		Ⓒ	Ⓐ	|		Ⓒ	Ⓐ	|	▽	|	▽	▽	▽		|	
61	**Meiningen**......... **870** d.	0403	0455	0609	0609	0725	0834	0918	1034	1118	...	1234	1234	1318	...	1434	1434	1518	1634	1718	1834	1919	2035	...	2226	...
68	Grimmenthal ...... **870** d.	0412	0506	0623j	0623j	0734	0842	0930	1042	1130	...	1242	1242	1330	...	1442	1442	1530	1642	1730	1842	1930	2045	...	2234	...
82	Themar .... d.	0425	0519	0636	0636	0747	0859	0943	1059	1143	...	1259	1259	1343	...	1459	1459	1543	1659	1743	1859	1943	2058	...	2247	...
94	Hildburghausen .... d.	0437	0535	0652j	0652j	0801	0911	1001j	1111	1201j	...	1311	1325k	1401j	...	1511	1528r	1601j	1711	1801j	1911	2004f	2114j	...	2302	...
109	**Eisfeld**..................... d.	0452	0550	0707	0707	0816	0926	1016	1126	1216	...	1326	1340	1416	...	1526	1543	1616	1726	1816	1926	2019	2129	...	2317	...
141	**Sonneberg** (Thür) Hbf a.	0536	0638	...	...	0900	...	1100	...	1300	...	...	...	1500	...	...	...	1700	...	1900	...	2103	...	...	...	...

		Ⓐ		Ⓐ																
Sonneberg (Thür) Hbf d.	...	...	...	...	...	0546t	0702	...	0902	...	1102	...	1302	...	1502	...	1702	...	1902	2012
Eisfeld .... d.	...	0418	...	0518	...	0632	0746	0830	0946	1030	1146	1230	1346	1430	1546	1630	1746	1830	1949	2059
Hildburghausen.......... d.	...	0440j	...	0534	...	0649	0801	0846	1001	1046	1201	1246	1401	1446	1601	1646	1801	1846	2004	2114
Themar...................... d.	...	0452	...	0545	...	0659	0812	0858	1012	1058	1212	1258	1412	1458	1612	1658	1812	1858	2015	2125
Grimmenthal........**870** d.	...	0510j	...	0603j	0623	0718j	0828	0911	1028	1111	1228	1311	1428	1511	1628	1711	1828	1911	2028	2138
Meiningen...........**870** a.	...	0517	...	0609	0629	0724	0833	0917	1033	1117	1233	1317	1433	1517	1633	1717	1833	1917	2034	2145
	Ⓐ	|			|	|	|	▽	|	▽	|	▽	|	▽	|	▽	|	▽	|	▽
Meiningen................. d.	0415	0526	0526	...	0630	0738	0838	0938	1038	1138	1238	1338	1438	1538	1638	1738	1838	1938	2038	2150
Wernshausen.............. d.	0435	0547	0547	...	0649	0758	0858	0958	1058	1158	1258	1358	1458	1558	1658	1758	1858	1958	2058	2210
Bad Salzungen .... d.	0449	0602	0602	...	0712f	0812	0912	1012	1112	1212	1312	1412	1512	1612	1712	1812	1912	2012	2112	2224
Eisenach.................. a.	0517	0629	0629	...	0743	0843	0943	1043	1143	1243	1343	1443	1543	1643	1743	1843	1943	2043	2138	2255

E – To Erfurt (Table **870**).
f – Arrives 10–11 minutes earlier
j – Arrives 6–8 minutes earlier.
k – Arrives 1310.
r – Arrives 1510.
t – Ⓐ only.
▽ – Change trains.

874 LEIPZIG - CHEMNITZ

Mitteldeutsche Regiobahn

km			⚒				
0	**Leipzig** Hbf ....d.	0518	0621	0721		2221	2337
33	Bad Lausick..................d.	0547	0647	0747	and	2247	0000
44	Geithain.......................d.	0556	0656	0756	hourly	2256	0009
66	Burgstädt......................d.	0613	0713	0813	until	2313	0026
81	**Chemnitz** Hbf............a.	0625	0725	0825		2325	0039

		⚒				
Chemnitz Hbf..........d.	0421	0531	0631		2131	2231
Burgstädt ....d.	0433	0543	0643	and	2143	2243
Geithain ....d.	0451	0600	0700	hourly	2200	2300
Bad Lausick ....d.	0500	0610	0710	until	2210	2310
Leipzig Hbf...............a.	0525	0633	0733		2233	2333

RE services NÜRNBERG - BAMBERG - SONNEBERG, ERFURT, SAALFELD and WÜRZBURG 875

km																								
				⚒																				¶
0	**Nürnberg** Hbf .... **850** d.	0610	...	0710	0810	...	0910	1010	1110	1210	...	1310	1410	1510	1610	...	1710	1810	...	1910	2010	2110	2209	...	2310
8	Fürth (Bay) Hbf .... d.	0616	...	0716	0816	...	0916	1016	1116	1216	...	1316	1416	1516	1616	...	1716	1816	...	1916	2016	2116	2216	...	2316
24	Erlangen .... **850** d.	0627	...	0727	0827	...	0927	1027	1127	1227	...	1327	1427	1527	1627	...	1727	1827	...	1927	2027	2127	2227	...	2327
39	Forchheim (Oberfr) .... d.	0636	...	0735	0836	...	0935	1035	1135	1235	...	1335	1435	1535	1635	...	1735	1835	...	1935	2035	2136	2236	...	2335
62	**Bamberg** .... **850 876** d.	0654	...	0755	0855	...	0954	1055	1154	1255	...	1354	1455	1554	1656	...	1754	1855	...	1955	2056	2154	2256	...	2355
108	**Coburg** .... **850** a.	0720	...	0816	0922	...	1020	1122	1220	1322	...	1420	1521	1620	1722	...	1820	1922	...	2021	2121	...	2321	...	0042
108	**Coburg** .... **850** d.	0727	0734	0832	0927	0934	1032	1134	1232	1327	1334	1432	1534	1632	1727	1734	1832	1927	1934	2032	2134	...	2335	...	0043
195	**Erfurt** Hbf .... **850** a.	0803	|	|	1003	|	|	|	|	1403	|	|	|	|	1803	|	|	2003	|	|	|	...	|	...	|
129	**Sonneberg** (Thür) Hbf .... a.	...	0755	0853	...	0955	1053	1155	1253	...	1355	1453	1555	1653	...	1755	1853	...	1955	2054	2155	...	2356	...	0104

	Ⓐ¶	⚒	‡																						
Sonneberg (Thür) Hbf .... d.	0420	0515	...	...	0605	0703	0802	...	0903	1002	...	1103	1202	1303	1402	...	1503	1602	1703	1802	...	...	1903	2003	...
Erfurt Hbf .... **850** d.	|	|	...	...	|	|	|	0752	|	|	0952	|	|	|	|	1352	|	|	|	|	1752	...	|	|	1952
Coburg .... **850** a.	0442	0536	...	...	0627	0725	0823	0828	0924	1023	1028	1124	1223	1324	1423	1428	1524	1623	1724	1823	1828	...	1924	2024	2028
Coburg .... **850** d.	0444	0538	0544	...	0636	0737	...	0836	0937	...	1035	1137	1235	1337	...	1435	1537	1635	1737	...	1835	...	1937	...	2035
Bamberg .... **850** d.	0539	0603	0636	...	0703	0803	...	0903	1003	...	1103	1203	1303	1403	...	1503	1603	1703	1803	...	1903	...	2003	...	2103
Forchheim (Oberfr) .... d.	0554	0619	0652	...	0719	0819	...	0920	1020	...	1120	1220	1320	1420	...	1520	1620	1720	1820	...	1920	...	2020	...	2120
Erlangen .... **850** d.	0603	0629	0701	...	0729	0829	...	0929	1030	...	1129	1229	1329	1430	...	1529	1629	1729	1831	...	1929	...	2029	...	2129
Fürth (Bay) Hbf .... d.	0612	0640	0712	...	0741	0841	...	0940	1041	...	1141	1241	1340	1441	...	1541	1640	1742	1841	...	1941	...	2040	...	2141
Nürnberg Hbf .... **850** a.	0619	0648	0718	...	0748	0848	...	0948	1047	...	1148	1248	1348	1449	...	1548	1647	1749	1849	...	1948	...	2048	...	2148

NÜRNBERG - BAMBERG - LICHTENFELS - SAALFELD

km																									
		Ⓐ	Ⓐ	Ⓒ◧	Ⓐ◧	Ⓐ	Ⓒ	◧		◧		Ⓒ◧	Ⓐ◧		◧		◧		◧		◧			¶	
0	**Nürnberg** Hbf ..... **849a 850** d.	...	...	0529	0529	0628	0636	0738	0838	0938	1040	1138	1138	1238	1338	1440	1538	1638	1740	1838	1938	2038	2138	2310	0010
8	Fürth (Bay) Hbf .... d.	...	...	0536	0536	0635	0643	0744	0844	0944	1046	1144	1144	1244	1344	1447	1544	1644	1746	1844	1944	2044	2144	2316	0016
24	Erlangen .... **849a 850** d.	...	...	0546	0546	0647	0652	0754	0854	0954	1055	1154	1154	1254	1354	1455	1554	1654	1755	1854	1954	2054	2154	2327	0027
39	Forchheim (Oberfr) .... d.	...	...	0556	0556	0657	0701	0805	0902	1002	1103	1202	1202	1302	1402	1503	1602	1702	1804	1902	2002	2102	2202	2335	0035
62	**Bamberg** .... **849a 850** d.	0500	0543	0627**f**	0627**f**	0722	0722	0822	0922	1022	1122	1222	1222	1322	1422	1522	1622	1722	1822	1922	2022	2136**j**	2238**j**	2355	0055
94	Lichtenfels .... **849a** d.	0527	0604	0651	0654	0747	0747	0847	0947	1047	1147	1247	1247	1349	1447	1547	1647	1747	1847	1947	2046	2203	2304	0021	0121
118	Kronach .... **849a** d.	0551	...	0706	0715	0804	0804	0903	1003	1103	1203	1303	1309**e**	1404	1503	1603	1703	1803	1903	2003	2107	2224	2324	...	...
181	**Saalfeld** (Saale) .... **849a** a.	0649	...	0807	0815	0900	0859	1004	1100	1204	1300	1404	1409	1500	1604	1700	1804	1900	2004	2100	2207	2325**v**	...	...	...

			¶	‡	Ⓐ	Ⓐ◇	◧	Ⓐ			◧		◧		◧		◧		◧		◧				
Saalfeld (Saale) .... **849a** d.	...	...	...	...	...	...	...	0609	...	0657	0755	0900	0955	1100	1155	1300	1355	1500	1555	1700	1755	1900	1947	2047	2147
Kronach .... **849a** d.	...	...	...	...	0538	...	0647	0710	...	0756	0855	0956	1055	1156	1254	1356	1455	1556	1655	1756	1855	1955	2047	2147	2247
Lichtenfels .... **849a** d.	0411**t**	...	0511	0609	0609**e**	0622	0709	0732	...	0814	0908	1015	1108	1215	1308	1415	1508	1615	1708	1815	1908	2013	2107	2212**e**	2310
Bamberg .... **849a 850** d.	0439	...	0539	0636	0636	0643	0739	0758	0803	0839	0939**e**	1039	1139**e**	1239	1339**e**	1439	1539**e**	1638	1739**e**	1839	1939**e**	2038	2139**e**	2239	2339
Forchheim (Oberfr) .... d.	0454	...	0554	0652	0652	|	0754	...	0819	0854	0954	1054	1154	1254	1354	1454	1554	1654	1754	1854	1954	2054	2154	2254	2354
Erlangen .... **849a 850** d.	0502	...	0603	0701	0701	0709	0803	...	0829	0903	1003	1103	1203	1303	1403	1503	1603	1703	1803	1903	2003	2103	2203	2303	0003
Fürth (Bay) Hbf .... d.	0511	...	0612	0712	0712	|	0812	...	0841	0912	1012	1112	1212	1312	1412	1512	1612	1712	1812	1912	2012	2113	2213	2313	0012
Nürnberg Hbf .... **849a 850** a.	0518	...	0619	0718	0718	0725	0819	...	0848	0919	1019	1119	1219	1319	1419	1519	1619	1719	1819	1919	2019	2119	2220	2320	0019

(NÜRNBERG -) BAMBERG - WÜRZBURG

km																									
		Ⓐ	Ⓒ	⑥	Ⓐ		☉			☉			☉		☉		☉		☉		☉				
	Nürnberg Hbf ⊡ .... d.	...	...	...	...	0529	...	0738	...	...	...	0938	...	1138	...	1338	...	1538	...	1740	...	1938	...	...	...
0	**Bamberg** .... d.	0445	0445	0515	0520	0625	0725	0827	0841	0920	0941	1027	1120	1227	1320	1427	1520	1627	1720	1827	1926	2027	2042	2141	2304
32	Haßfurt .... d.	0506	0506	0536	0548	0642	0742	0844	0902	0942	1002	1044	1142	1244	1342	1443	1542	1644	1742	1844	1942	2044	2102	2202	2326
57	Schweinfurt Hbf .... **870** d.	0526	0526	0556	0610	0657	0756	0857	0919	0956	1019	1057	1156	1257	1356	1456	1556	1657	1756	1857	1956	2057	2119	2220	2345
100	**Würzburg** Hbf .... **870** a.	0548	0557	0618	0648	0721	0821	0921	0951	1021	1051	1121	1221	1320	1421	1521	1621	1721	1821	1921	2021	2121	2150	2251	0016

	⚒		⚒	☉			☉			☉		☉		☉		☉			☉			☉			
Würzburg Hbf .... **870** d.	0454	0603	0635	0739	0835	0907	0939	1008	1035	1139	1235	1339	1435	1539	1635	1739	1808	1835	1939	2008	2035	2139	2143	2235	2307
Schweinfurt Hbf .... **870** d.	0537**f**	0634	0700	0802	0900	0938	1003	1038	1100	1202	1300	1403	1500	1603	1700	1803	1838	1900	2003	2038	2100	2203	2219	2300	2345
Haßfurt .... d.	0554	0652	0712	0814	0912	0955	1016	1055	1112	1215	1312	1415	1512	1616	1712	1816	1855	1912	2016	2055	2112	2216	2236	2312	0004
Bamberg .... a.	0615	0715	0732	0832	0930	1016	1032	1116	1130	1232	1330	1432	1530	1632	1730	1832	1916	1930	2032	2116	2130	2232	2257	2330	0028
Nürnberg Hbf ⊡ .... a.	...	...	0819	...	1019	...	...	...	1219	...	1419	...	1619	...	1819	...	...	2019	...	...	...	...	...	...	...

LICHTENFELS - COBURG - SONNEBERG

km																									
		Ⓐ		Ⓐ																					¶
0	**Lichtenfels** .... ▷ d.	0515	0609	0636	0702	0802	0900	1002	1101	1202	1230	1300	1359	1500	1602	1630	1700	1801	1900	2002	2111	2139	2311	...	0022
20	**Coburg** .... ▷ a.	0535	0629	0700	0724	0822	0917	1025	1117	1224	1250	1317	1425	1516	1625	1650	1717	1825	1917	2025	2128	2200	2330	...	0042
20	**Coburg** .... d.	0546	0634**r**	0705	0734	*0832*	*0934*	*1032*	*1134*	*1232*	*1303***t**	*1334*	*1432*	*1534*	*1632*	*1703***t**	*1734*	*1832*	*1934*	*2032*	*2134*	*2211*	2335	...	0043
41	**Sonneberg** (Thür) Hbf .... a.	0614	0656**r**	0733	0755	*0853*	*0955*	*1053*	*1155*	*1253*	*1332***t**	*1355*	*1453*	*1555*	*1653*	*1732***t**	*1755*	*1853*	*1955*	*2054*	*2155*	*2232*	*2356*	...	0104

	Ⓐ¶	⚒	‡		Ⓐ				⊕			Ⓐ	Ⓒ												
Sonneberg (Thür) Hbf .... d.	0420	0515	...	*0605*	0625	*0703*	*0802*	*0903*	1002	*1103*	*1202*	*1303*	1303	1402	*1503*	*1602*	1623**t**	*1703*	*1802*	*1903*	2003	2108	...	2202	2308
Coburg .... a.	0442	0536	...	*0627*	0656	*0725*	*0823*	*0924*	1023	*1124*	*1223*	*1324*	1324	1423	*1524*	*1623*	1650**t**	*1724*	*1823*	*1924*	2024	2130	...	2230	2330
Coburg .... ▷ d.	0444	...	0544	0632	0701	0743	0833	0934	1041	1134	1241	1331	1334	1441	1534	1641	1710	1734	1841	1934	2041	...	2211	2232	2332
Lichtenfels .... ▷ a.	0505	...	0605	0657	0722	0801	0852	0957	1059	1156	1259	1357	1357	1459	1557	1659	1730	1757	1859	1957	2059	...	2231	2253	2353

e – Arrives 6–7 minutes earlier.
f – Arrives 11–13 minutes earlier.
j – Arrives 16–18 minutes earlier.
r – ⚒ only.
t – Ⓐ only.
v – ⑤⑥ (not June 27, 28, Oct. 3).
z – Ⓒ only.

◇ – Ⓐ (not June 9, 19, 20, Aug. 15, Oct. 3). *ICE* **601**. To München (Table **904**).
⊕ – Change trains at Coburg on ⑥.
☉ – From / to Frankfurt (Table **921**).
¶ – [12] Nürnberg - Lichtenfels - Sonneberg and v.v.
‡ – [12] Coburg - Lichtenfels - Nürnberg.

◧ – Conveys [12] Nürnberg - Bamberg - Würzburg and v.v. (see lower panel).
⊡ – See Nürnberg - Saalfeld panel for intermediate calling points.
▷ – Additional trains Lichtenfels - Coburg and v.v. (journey 19–26 minutes): **From Lichtenfels** at 0543 Ⓐ, 0731 Ⓐ, 0834, 0938, 1030, 1138, 1338, 1430, 1538, 1738, 1830, 1938 and 2030. **From Coburg** at 0603 Ⓐ, 0756, 0910, 1002, 1110, 1202, 1310, 1402, 1509, 1602, 1802, 1910, 2002 and 2105.

RE services BAMBERG - HOF and BAYREUTH 876

km																									
		Ⓐ◐	Ⓐ◐	Ⓐn	Ⓒn	n	n		n	n		n	✣⊡	n	n		n		n				n	◐	n
0	**Bamberg** .... **875** d.	...	...	...	...	...	0640	0640	0746	...	0846	...		1746	...	1846	...	1946	...	2047	...	*2136*	...	*2238*	...
32	Lichtenfels .... **875** d.	0516	...	0549	0550	...	0703	0703	0806	...	0908	0908	and in	1806	...	1908	1908	2006	...	2108	2108	2209	...	2313	...
62	Kulmbach .... d.	0540	...	0612	0613	...	0726	0726	0824	...	0928	0928	the same	1824	...	1928	1928	2024	...	2127	2127	2227	...	2337	...
74	Neuenmarkt-Wirsberg a.	0551	...	0623	0627	...	0734	0734	0834	...	0936	0936	pattern	1834	...	1936	1936	2034	...	2135	2135	2239	...	2348	...
74	Neuenmarkt-Wirsberg d.	0551	0600	0624	0627	...	0736	0738	0835	...	0938	0949	every	1835	...	1938	1949	2035	...	2138	2140	2240	...	2348	...
	Trebgast .... a.	0556	|	0629	0632	...	0741	|	0839	...	|	|	two hours	1839	...	|	|	2039	...	|	2144	2245	...	2352	...
	Trebgast .... d.	0556	|	0634	0640	0637**r**	0745	|	0843	0842	|	|	until	1843	1842	|	|	2044	2042	|	2145	2249	2248	2353	0025
96	**Bayreuth** Hbf .... a.	0612	|	0653	0656	|	0754	|	0855	|	|	1002		1855	|	|	2003	2055	|	|	2155	2304	|	0007	|
103	Münchberg .... **880** d.	...	0630	...	...	0702**r**	...	0802	...	0906	1002	...		...	1906	2002	...	...	2106	2202	...	...	2315	...	0053
116	Schwarzenbach .... d.	...	0643	...	...	0711	...	0811	...	|	1011	...		...	|	2011	...	...	|	2211	...	...	2327	...	0102
127	**Hof** Hbf .... **880** a.	...	0654	...	...	0724	...	0821	...	0924	1021	...		...	1924	2021	...	...	2124	2223	...	...	2338	...	0114

	Ⓐ	Ⓐ	Ⓒn	Ⓒ	Ⓐn	Ⓐ	Ⓒn	Ⓒn		n	n	n		n	✣		n	n	n		n	n	n		n
Hof Hbf .... **880** d.	0523	...	0523	...	...	0623	0632	...	0736	...	0836	...	0936	...		1736	...	1836	...	1936	...	2036	...	2136	...
Schwarzenbach .... d.	0533	...	0533	...	...	0634	0642	...	0744	...	|	...	0944	...	and in	1744	...	|	...	1944	...	|	...	2144	...
Münchberg .... **880** d.	0542	...	0542	...	...	0645	0651	...	0755	...	0855	...	0955	...	the same	1755	...	1855	...	1955	...	2055	...	2155	...
Bayreuth Hbf .... d.	|	0550	|	0550	0701	|	|	0702	|	0801	|	0903	|	1004	pattern	|	1804	|	1903	|	2004	|	2103	|	2204
Trebgast .... a.	|	0607	0610	0606	0714	|	0717	0715	|	|	0917	0916	|	|	every	|	|	1917	1916	|	|	2117	2116	|	2218
Trebgast .... d.	|	0609	...	0613	0715	|	...	0719	|	|	...	0920	|	|	two hours	|	|	...	1920	|	|	...	2120	|	2219
Neuenmarkt-Wirsberg a.	0611	0615	...	0618	0720	0716	...	0724	0818	0822	...	0925	1018	1022	until	1818	1822	...	1925	2018	2022	...	2125	2218	2224
Neuenmarkt-Wirsberg d.	0618	0618	...	0621	0723	0723	...	0725	0824	0824	...	0926	1024	1024		1824	1824	...	1926	2024	2024	...	2126	2227	2227
Kulmbach .... d.	0631	0631	...	0631	0733	0733	...	0735	0832	0832	...	0936	1032	1032		1832	1832	...	1936	2032	2032	...	2136	2238	2238
Lichtenfels .... **875** a.	0653	0653	...	0651	0750	0750	...	0752	0852	0852	...	0954	1052	1052		1852	1852	...	1954	2052	2052	...	2154	2302	2302
Bamberg .... **875** a.	0714	0714	...	0714	...	0811	...	0811	0912	...	...	1012	1112	...		1912	...	...	2012	2112	2112	...	...	*2336*	*2336*

n – To / from Nürnberg via Pegnitz (Table **880**).
r – On Ⓐ Trebgast d. 0632, Münchberg d. 0658.

t – Ⓐ only.
z – Ⓒ only.

◐ – Operated by *agilis* (2nd class only).
✣ – Certain timings vary by 1–3 minutes (earlier departures possible).
⊡ – The 1308 from Lichtenfels to Bayreuth arrives Bayreuth 1413.

877 LANDSHUT - MÜHLDORF - SALZBURG — *RB* services

km					e				⊠		⊕
0	**Landshut** (Bay) Hbf... d.	0608f	*0737*	0837	*0937*	1037	*1137*	1237	and hourly until	2037	2137
55	Mühldorf (Oberbay).... a.	0712f	*0826*	0928	*1025*	1128	*1225*	1329		2129	2228
55	Mühldorf (Oberbay).... d.	0743	0843	0944	1043	1143	1243	1342		2146	2249
120	Freilassing ...... **890/1** a.	0835	0944	1044	1142	1243	1343	1443		2240	2344
126	**Salzburg** Hbf.. **890/1** a.	0855	0955	1055	1155	1255z	1354	1455		2254	0017

	⊗	⊗		⊠					⊠		
Salzburg Hbf **890/1** d.	0605	0742	0908	and hourly until	1208	*1305*	1408	1508	and hourly until	2008	2108
Freilassing .... **890/1** d.	0628	0813	0924		1224	1324	1424	1524		2024	2124
Mühldorf (Oberbay). a.	0723	0915	1015		1315	1415	1515	1616		2116	2222
Mühldorf (Oberbay). d.	0730	0932	1030		*1332*	1430	*1532*	1630		*2134*	2240
Landshut (Bay) Hbf a.	0821	1021	1121		*1421*	1521	*1620*	1721		*2221*	2328

e – Change trains at Mühldorf on ⑤.
f – On ⓒ: Landshut d. 0637, Mühldorf a. 0726.
z – ⓒ only.
⊠ – Timings may vary by up to 4 minutes. Certain services require a change of trains at Mühldorf.
⊕ – Change trains at Mühldorf and Freilassing.
⊗ – Change trains at Freilassing and Mühldorf.

878 MÜNCHEN - REGENSBURG - SCHWANDORF — DB (*RE* services); *ALX*

See Table **892** for services Regensburg - Landshut - Freising - München Flughafen ✈ and v.v. **Warning!** No through trains to / from Praha June 15 - Aug. 22.

km		*ALX* P		Ⓐ	*ALX* P		*ALX* P		*ALX* P		*ALX* P		*ALX* P		*ALX* ⒶK	*ALX* P	*ALX*	Ⓐ		*ALX*		*ALX*		*ALX*	
0	**München** Hbf...... **944** d.	0444	0544	0604	0644	0744	0844	0944	1044	1144	1244	1342	1444	1542	1604	1644	1644	1701	1742	1844	1944	2044	2144	2244	0004
42	Freising .... **944** d.	0508	0608	0634	0708	0808	0908	1008	1108	1208	1308	1408	1508	1608	1628	1708	1708	1734	1808	1908	2008	2108	2208	2308	0028
76	Landshut (Bay) Hbf **944** d.	0529	0630	0711v	0729	0830	0929	1030	1129	1230	1329	1430	1529	1630	1649	1729	1729	1800	1830	1929	2030	2129	2230	2334	0052
99	Neufahrn (Niederbay) .. d.	0544	0647	0728	0744	0847	0944	1047	1144	1247	1344	1447	1544	1647	|	1744	1744	1818	1847	1946	2047	2146	2247	2351	0109
138	**Regensburg** Hbf . **879** a.	0607	0712	0800	0807	0912	1007	1112	1207	1312	1407	1512	1609	1712	1727	1808	1808	1845	1912	2010	2112	2210	2312	0017	0134
	Schwandorf .... **879** a.	0644r	0746r	...	0844r	0946r	1044r	1146r	1244r	1346r	1444r	1546r	1644r	1746r	...	1845r	1845r	...	1946r	2052r	2146r	2252r	2355r	0058r	...
	Hof Hbf **879** .... a.	...	0920*	...	...	1120*	...	1320*	...	1520*	...	1720*	...	1920*	...	...	2026*	...	2120*	...	2322*	...	...	...	...

		ALX	Ⓐ	ⓒ	Ⓐ	*ALX* ⒶK	*ALX*		*ALX* P		*ALX* P		*ALX* P		*ALX* P		*ALX* P		*ALX* P		*ALX* P		N	*ALX*
Hof Hbf **879**...................... d.	...	...	...	...	0438*	...	0538*	0640*	...	0840*	...	1040*	...	1240*	...	1440*	...	1640*	...	1840*	...	2040*	...	...
Schwandorf..................... **879** d.	0402t	0502t	...	0602r	0608r	0622	0711r	0810r	0913r	1010r	1113r	1210r	1313r	1410r	1513r	1610r	1713r	1810r	1913r	2010r	2113r	2210r	...	2301r
Regensburg Hbf .... **879** d.	0445	0546	0624	0645	0651	0705	0751	0846	0951	1046	1151	1246	1351	1446	1551	1646	1751	1846	1951	2046	2151	2246	2319	2349
Neufahrn (Niederbay) .... d.	0511	0610	0652	0711	0715	0731	0816	0912	1015	1112	1215	1313	1415	1512	1615	1712	1815	1912	2015	2112	2215	2312	2350	0016
Landshut (Bay) Hbf.......... **944** d.	0530	0628	0710	0730	0733	0750	0832	0930	1032	1130	1232	1330	1432	1530	1632	1730	1832	1930	2032	2130	2232	2335	0006	0035
Freising .... **944** d.	0551	0649	0731	0751	|	0810	0851	0951	1051	1151	1251	1351	1451	1551	1651	1751	1851	1951	2051	2151	2251	2356	...	0054
München Hbf................. **944** a.	0616	0717	0758	0818	0821	0837	0918	1018	1118	1216	1318	1416	1518	1616	1718	1816	1918	2016	2118	2216	2318	0021	...	0119

K – Not June 15 - Aug. 22.
N – From Nürnberg (Table **921**).
P – To / from Praha (Tables **76** and **885**). See note **r**.
r – By 🚌 June 15 - Aug. 22 (most 🚌 arrive Schwandorf 16 - 18 mins later, depart Schwandorf 55 minutes earlier).
t – Ⓐ only. Note **r** applies.
v – Arrives 0702.
* – Use previous train from München / following train to München June 15 - Aug. 22 (see note **r**).
ALX – *alex* train. Operated by Die Länderbahn.

879 REGENSBURG - HOF — DB (*RE* services); *Oberpfalzbahn*

km		Ⓐ	Ⓐ		Ⓐ									ⓒ	Ⓐ							Ⓐ			
	München Hbf **878**.... d.	...	...	...	...	...	0544*	...	...	0744*	...	...	0944*	...	...	...	1144*	...	...	1342*	...	...	...	1542*	...
0	**Regensburg** Hbf . **878** d.	0514r	...	...	0623r	0650r	0720r	0750r	0850r	0920r	0951r	1050r	1120r	1151r	1151r	1250r	1320r	1351r	1451r	1520r	1551r	1622r	1650r	1720r	1751r
42	Schwandorf .... **878** d.	0547	0553	0622n	0658	0720	0747	0820	0920	0947	1020	1120	1147	1220	1220	1320	1347	1420	1520	1547	1620	1653	1721	1747	1820
86	Weiden (Oberpf)..........d.	0614	0630	0701	0737	0801	0814	0901	1001	1014	1101	1201	1214	1301	1321e	1401	1414	1501	1601	1614	1701	1715	1802	1814	1901
137	Marktredwitz .... **880** a.	0652	0712	0743	...	0843	0852	0943	1043	1052	1142	1243	1252	1343	1402	1443	1452	1542	1642	1652	1742	1750	1844	1852	1943
179	**Hof** Hbf .... **880** a.	0720	*0750*	*0817*	...	...	0920	*1017*	...	1120	*1217*	...	1320	*1417*	*1438*	...	1520	*1617*	...	1720	*1817*	*1817*	...	1920	...

	◇									
München Hbf **878**..... d.	1644*	...	1742*	...	...	1944*	...	...	2144*	...
Regensburg Hbf .. **878** d.	1817r	1851r	1920r	1950r	2050r	2120r	2150r	2250r	2322r	...
Schwandorf........... **878** d.	1852	1920	1947	2020	2120	2147	2220	2320	2355	0002
Weiden (Oberpf)...........d.	1917	2001	2014	2100	2200	2214	2300	2359	...	0039
Marktredwitz .... **880** a.	1957	2042	2052	2143	2243	2254	2343	...	...	...
Hof Hbf .... **880** a.	2026	...	2120	*2236*	...	2322	*0025*	...	...	...

	Ⓐ	⚒	ⓒ	Ⓐ	Ⓐ	◇		Ⓐ		
Hof Hbf....................... **880** d.	...	...	...	0438	...	0538	...	*0555*	0640	...
Marktredwitz .... **880** d.	...	...	...	0504	0515	0604	0613	0635	0707	0717
Weiden (Oberpf) ....d.	0459	0518	...	0543	0558	0645	0656	0717	0744	0800
Schwandorf................. **885** d.	0536	0557	0602	0608	0700e	0711	0733	0754	0810	0840
Regensburg Hbf .... **885** a.	0606r	0629f	0637r	0639r	0729r	0743r	0804r	...	0838r	0911r
München Hbf **878** ....a.	...	...	0818*	0821*	...	0918*	...	...	1018*	...

	Ⓐ	ⓒ															†								
Hof Hbf .... **880** d.	*0740*	*0740*	0840	...	*0940*	1040	...	*1140*	1240	...	*1340*	1440	...	*1540*	1640	...	1740	*1740*	1840	...	*1940*	2040	...	...	*2241*
Marktredwitz .... **880** d.	0806	0817	0907	0917	1017	1107	1117	1217	1307	1320	1417	1507	1517	1617	1707	1717	1810	1817	1907	1917	2017	2107	2117	...	2320
Weiden (Oberpf)...........d.	0900k	0900	0944	1000	1100	1144	1200	1300	1344	1359	1500	1544	1600	1700	1744	1800	1843	1900	1944	2000	2100	2144	2220e	...	2400
Schwandorf........... **885** d.	0939	0939	1010	1039	1139	1210	1239	1339	1410	1440	1539	1610	1639	1739	1810	1839	1907	1939	2010	2039	2139	2210	2257	2301	...
Regensburg Hbf .. **885** a.	1011r	1011r	1038r	1111r	1210r	1238r	1311r	1410r	1438r	1511r	1611r	1638r	1711r	1811r	1838r	1911r	1936r	2011r	2038r	2111r	2211r	2238r	...	2335r	...
München Hbf **878**.....a.	...	...	1216*	...	...	1416*	...	...	1616*	...	...	1816*	...	...	2016*	...	...	...	2216*	...	...	0021*	...	0119*	...

e – Arrives 22 – 25 mins earlier.
f – Ⓐ only. Note **r** applies.
k – Arrives 0846.
n – ⚒ only.
r – By 🚌 June 15 - Aug. 22 (most 🚌 dep Regensburg 30 - 34 mins earlier, arr Regensburg 27 - 44 mins later).
* – No through trains June 15 - Aug. 22 (see note **r**).
◇ – Operated by Die Länderbahn.

880 NÜRNBERG - HOF - DRESDEN — *RE* / *RB* services

NÜRNBERG - HOF

km	km		Ⓐ	Ⓐ	ⓒ	ⓒ	Ⓐ	Ⓐ	B	Ⓐ	⊡	L			B		⊡	L				B		⊡
0	0	**Nürnberg** Hbf .... ● d.	...	...	0529	0529	0529	0529	0559	0635	0635	0703	0737	0737	0805	0837	0837	0905	0937	0937	and in the same pattern every **two** hours until	1405	1437	1437
28	28	Hersbruck (r Pegnitz) .... ● d.	...	...	0548	0548	0551	0551	0618	0650	0650	0718	|	|	0820	|	|	0920	|	|		1421	|	|
67	67	Pegnitz.......................... ● a.	...	...	0609	0609	0612	0612	0640	0714	0714	0739	0814	0814	0841	0914	0914	0943	1014	1014		1442	1514	1514
67	67	Pegnitz..............................d.	...	...	0611	0615	0614	0618	0641	0716	0720	0740	0816	0820	0843	0916	0920	0944	1016	1020		1443	1516	1520
	94	**Bayreuth** Hbf ....d.	0540	0621	0627	|	0637	|	0700	0740	|	0759	0832	|	0900	0941	|	0959	1032	|		1500	1541	|
	142	Münchberg................ **876** d.	|	0658	0702	|	...	|	...	...	|	...	0906	|	...	...	|	...	1106	|		...	...	|
94		Kirchenlaibach.......................d.	0601	|	|	0630	...	0632	...	...	0734	...	|	0834	...	...	0934	...	|	1034		...	...	1534
125		Marktredwitz................. **879** d.	0633r	|	|	0653r	...	0649	...	...	0753	...	|	0857	...	...	0953	...	|	1052		...	...	1553
167	166	**Hof** Hbf................. **876 879** a.	0707	0724	0724	0716	...	*0720*	...	...	0817	...	0924	*0938*	...	...	1017	...	1124	*1138*		...	...	1617

	L			B		⊡	L			B		⊡	B			L			L						
Nürnberg Hbf.................. ● d.	1505	1537	1537	1605	1637	1637	1705	1737	1737	1805	1837	1837	1905	1937	1937	2005	2037	2037	2105	2137	2137	2237	2237	2311	0022
Hersbruck (r Pegnitz)........ ● d.	1521	|	|	1621	|	|	1721	|	|	1821	|	|	1920	|	|	2020	2054	2054	2120	2154	2154	2253	2253	2327	0040
Pegnitz .... ● a.	1543	1614	1614	1641	1714	1714	1743	1814	1814	1842	1914	1914	1943	2014	2014	2042	2117	2117	2143	2217	2217	2317	2317	2351	0105
Pegnitz .... d.	1544	1616	1620	1643	1716	1720	1744	1816	1820	1843	1916	1920	1944	2016	2020	2043	2119	2123	2144	2219	2223	2319	2323	2352	0106
Bayreuth Hbf.................... d.	1558	1632	|	1700	1741	|	1758	1832	|	1900	1941	|	1959	2032	|	2100	2146	|	2159	2235	|	2338	|	0011	0125
Münchberg .... **876** d.	...	1706	|	...	...	|	...	1906	|	...	...	|	...	2106	|	...	...	|	...	2315	|	...	|	0053	...
Kirchenlaibach .... d.	...	|	1634	...	...	1734	...	|	1834	...	...	1934	...	|	2034	...	...	2137	...	|	2237	...	2338	|	...
Marktredwitz .... **879** d.	...	|	1652	...	...	1753	...	|	1852	...	...	1953	...	|	2052	...	...	2201	...	|	2303	...	2359	|	...
Hof Hbf ....**876 879** a.	...	1724	*1738*	...	...	1817	...	1924	*1938*	...	...	2017	...	2124	*2138*	...	...	2236	...	2338	*2342*	...	0025	0114	...

HOF - DRESDEN ⊠

km						★					★													◇
0	**Hof** Hbf........................ **881** d.	...	...	...	0428	...	...	0528	...	0628	...	...	0728	...	and at the same minutes past each hour until	1928	...	...	2030	...	...	...	...	2248
48	Plauen (Vogtl) ob Bf ..... **881** d.	...	...	...	0500	...	...	0600	...	0700	...	...	0800	...		2000	...	...	2102	...	...	...	...	2328
73	Reichenbach (Vogtl) ob Bf **881** d.	...	...	...	0516	...	...	0616	...	0716	...	...	0816	...		2016	...	...	2118	...	...	...	...	2351
96	**Zwickau** (Sachs) Hbf.... **881** d.	...	...	0439	0532	...	0539	0632	...	0732	...	0739	0832	0839		2032	2039	...	2134	2139	...	2239	...	0017
112	Glauchau (Sachs) .... **858** d.	...	...	0455	0542	...	0555	0642	...	0742	...	0755	0842	0855		2042	2055	...	2144	2155	...	2255	...	...
144	**Chemnitz** Hbf............. **858** a.	...	...	0525	0603	...	0625	0703	...	0803	...	0825	0903	0925		2103	2125	...	2205	2225	...	2325	...	...
144	**Chemnitz** Hbf.......................d.	0430	0504	0530	0604	0626	0630	0704	...	0804	0826	0830	0904	0930		2104	2130	...	...	2230	...	2330	...	...
157	Flöha ....d.	0443	0514	0543	0614	|	0643	0714	...	0814	|	0843	0914	0943		2114	2143	...	...	2243	...	2343	...	...
183	Freiberg (Sachs)....................d.	0507	0531	0607	0631	0654	0707	0731	...	0831	0854	0907	0931	1007		2131	2207	...	...	2307	...	0007	...	...
223	**Dresden** Hbf.........................a.	0550	0604	0650	0704	0725	0750	0804	...	0904	0925	0950	1004	1050		2204	2250	...	...	2350	...	0050	...	...

B – To Bamberg (Table **876**).
L – To Lichtenfels (Table **876**).
N – From Nürnberg (see main table).
r – Arrives 7 minutes earlier.
⊡ – Conveys (12) Nürnberg - Marktredwitz - Cheb. See panel for timings from Marktredwitz.
◇ – Operated by Vogtlandbahn.
⊠ – Operated by Mitteldeutsche Regiobahn (2nd class only).
★ – *IC* service to Warnemünde via Berlin and Rostock (Tables **835** and **840**). Operated by DB.
● – Certain trains between Nürnberg and Pegnitz convey portions for two separate destinations. Passengers should take care to join the correct portion for their destination.

MARKTREDWITZ - CHEB (operated by DB / *agilis*; journey 21 – 25 minutes)

From Marktredwitz at 0703, 0800 **N**, 0903, 1000 **N**, 1103, 1200 **N**, 1302, 1400 **N**, 1502, 1600 **N**, 1702, 1800 **N**, 1902, 2002 **N** and 2102.

RE / RB services

DRESDEN - HOF - NÜRNBERG 880

DRESDEN - HOF ⊠

										★					◇	★								
Dresden Hbf d.	...	...	0452	0508	0552	and at	1708	1752	1808	1832	1852	1908	1952	2008	...	2032	2108	2152	2208	...	2308	...	...	...
Freiberg (Sachs) d.	...	...	0525	0551	0625	the same	1751	1825	1851	1906	1925	1951	2025	2051	...	2105	2151	2225	2251	...	2351	...	...	...
Flöha d.	...	...	0543	0614	0643	minutes	1814	1843	1914	|	1943	2014	2043	2114	...	|	2214	2243	2314	...	0014	...	...	...
Chemnitz Hbf a.	...	...	0552	0625	0652	past each	1825	1852	1925	1931	1952	2025	2052	2125	...	2131	2225	2252	2325	...	0025	...	...	...
Chemnitz Hbf **858** d.	0409	...	0554	0630	0654	hour until	1830	1854	1930	...	1954	2030	2054	2130	...	...	2230	2254	2330	...	...	...	...	...
Glauchau (Sachs) **858** d.	0441	...	0615	0702	0715		1902	1915	2002	...	2015	2102	2115	2202	...	...	2302	2315	0002	...	...	...	...	...
Zwickau (Sachs) Hbf **881** d.	0511	...	0627	0718	0727		1918	1927	2018	...	2027	2118	2127	2218	2245	...	2318	2326	0018	...	...	...	...	...
Reichenbach (Vogtl) ob Bf **881** d.	0527	...	0642	...	0742		...	1942	...	...	2042	...	2142	...	2313	...	...	...	...	...	...	...	...	...
Plauen (Vogtl) ob Bf **881** d.	0544	...	0659	...	0759		...	1959	...	...	2059	...	2159	...	2335	...	...	...	...	...	...	...	...	...
Hof Hbf **881** a.	0618	...	0731	...	0831		...	2031	...	...	2131	...	2231	...	...	...	...	...	...	...	...	...	...	...

HOF - NÜRNBERG

		Ⓐ				L			B	⊡		B			L	⊡		B			L	⊡		B		
Hof Hbf **876 879** d.	...	0421	...	*0515*t	0523	...	...	0623k	...	0739	...	...	*0840*	0836	...	0940	...	...	*1040*	1036	...	1140	...	...	*1240*	1236
Marktredwitz **879** d.	...	0443	...	0551	|	...	0702	|	...	0806	...	...	0909	|	...	1007	...	...	1109	|	...	1207	...	...	1309	|
Kirchenlaibach d.	...	0511	...	0620	|	...	0723	|	...	0826f	...	...	0926	|	...	1025	...	...	1126	|	...	1225	...	...	1326	|
Münchberg **876** d.	...	|	...	|	0542	...	|	0645k	...	|	...	...	|	0855	...	|	...	...	|	1055	...	|	...	...	|	1255
Bayreuth Hbf d.	0452	|	0555	|	0624e	0702	|	0726	0803	|	0816	0901	|	0929	1003	|	1016	1101	|	1129	1203	|	1216	1301	|	1327h
Pegnitz a.	0512	0527	0611	0638	0642	0717j	0740	0744	0817	0840	0844	0918	0940	0944	1017	1038	1042	1118	1140	1144	1218	1238	1243	1318	1340	1344
Pegnitz d.	0516	0537	0612	0644	0644	0718j	0746	0746	0818	0846	0846	0919	0947	0947	1018	1045	1045	1119	1146	1146	1218	1245	1245	1319	1346	1346
Hersbruck (r Pegnitz) d.	0538	0603	0635	0708t	0708t	0741	|	|	0840	|	|	0940	|	|	1040	|	|	1140	|	|	1240	|	|	1340z	|	|
Nürnberg Hbf a.	0554	0618	0651	0722	0722	0756	0822	0822	0855	0922	0922	0955	1023	1023	1055	1120	1120	1155	1222	1222	1255	1320	1320	1355	1422	1422

		⊡	L	B			L	⊡		B			L	⊡		B			L	⊡						
Hof Hbf **876 879** d.	...	1340	...	...	*1440*	1436	...	1540	...	...	*1640*	1636	...	1740	...	...	*1840*	1836	...	1940	...	2036	*2022*	...	2140	2237
Marktredwitz **879** d.	...	1407	...	...	1509	|	...	1607	...	...	1709	|	...	1807	...	...	1909	|	...	2007	...	|	2101	...	2205	|
Kirchenlaibach d.	...	1425	...	...	1526	|	...	1625	...	...	1726	|	...	1825	...	...	1926	|	...	2025	...	|	2125	...	2226	|
Münchberg **876** d.	...	|	...	...	|	1455	...	|	...	...	|	1655	...	|	...	...	|	1855	...	|	...	2055	|	...	|	2303
Bayreuth Hbf d.	1403	|	1416	1501	|	1529	1604	|	1616	1701	|	1729	1804	|	1816	1901	|	1929	2004	|	2016	2129	|	2214	|	2339
Pegnitz a.	1417	1438	1443	1518	1540	1544	1617	1638	1643	1718	1740	1744	1817	1838	1843	1918	1940	1944	2017	2038	2043	2144	2140	2237	2241	2358
Pegnitz d.	1418	1445	1445	1519	1546	1546	1618	1645	1645	1719	1746	1746	1818	1845	1845	1919	1946	1946	2018	2045	2045	2146	2146	2244	2244	2359
Hersbruck (r Pegnitz) d.	1440	|	|	1540	|	|	1640	|	|	1740	|	|	1840	|	|	1940	|	|	2040	|	|	|	|	2309	2309	0021
Nürnberg Hbf a.	1456	1520	1520	1555	1622	1622	1655	1720	1720	1755	1822	1822	1855	1920	1920	1955	2022	2022	2055	2120	2120	2222	2222	2324	2324	0038

B – From Bamberg (Table **876**).
L – From Lichtenfels (Table **876**).
N – To Nürnberg (see main table).

e – Arrives 0620. Departs 0627 on ©.
f – Arrives 0821.
h – 1329 on ©.

j – 2 minutes later on ©.
k – On © Hof d. 0632, Münchberg d. 0651.
t – Ⓐ only.
z – © only.

◇ – Operated by Vogtlandbahn.

⊡ – Conveys (12) Cheb - Marktredwitz - Cheb. See panel for timings from Cheb.
⊠ – Operated by Mitteldeutsche Regiobahn (2nd class only).
★ – *IC* service from Warnemünde via Berlin and Rostock (Tables **835** and **840**). Operated by DB.

CHEB - MARKTREDWITZ (operated by DB / *agilis*; journey 23 – 27 minutes)

From Cheb at 0631, 0736 **N**, 0831, 0937 **N**, 1031, 1137 **N**, 1231, 1337 **N**, 1431, 1537 **N**, 1631, 1737 **N**, 1831, 1937 **N** and 2031.

S-Bahn 5

ZWICKAU - LEIPZIG - HALLE 881

km																						
0	**Zwickau** (Sachs) Hbf d.	0349	...	0507t	0524	0604	...	0704t	0720	0804	...	0904	and in	1720	1804	...	1904	1920	2004	...	2104t	2120	2230
9	Werdau d.	0400	...	0518t	0535	0613	...	0714t	0735j	0813	...	0914	the same	1735j	1813	...	1914	1935j	2013	...	2114t	2135j	2241
29	Gößnitz d.	0418	...	0533t	0553	0633j	...	0733t	0753	0833j	...	0933j	pattern	1753	1833j	...	1933j	1953	2033j	...	2133t	2153	2259
44	Altenburg d.	0431	0508	0543	0608	0643	0708	0743	0808	0843	0908	0943	every	1808	1843	1908	1943	2008	2043	2109	2143	2208	2312
80	Leipzig-Connewitz ★ d.	0511	0541	0611	0641	0711	0741	0811	0841	0911	0941	1011	**two** hours	1841	1911	1941	2011	2041	2111	2141	2211	2241	2351
85	**Leipzig** Hbf ★ **866** d.	0523	0553	0623	0653	0723	0753	0823	0853	0923	0953	1023	until	1853	1923	1953	2023	2053	2123	2153	2223	2251	0002
104	Leipzig/Halle Flughafen ✈ **866** d.	0536	0606	0636	0706	0736	0806	0836	0906	0936	1006	1036		1906	1936	2006	2036	2106	2136	2207	2236	*2321*	*0026*
122	**Halle** (Saale) Hbf **866** a.	0545	0620t	0645	0716	0745	0816	0845	0916	0945	1016	1045		1916	1945	2016	2045	2116	2145	2216	2245	...	*0036*

	Ⓐd										⊠												
Halle (Saale) Hbf **866** d.	0410	...	0515	0540t	0615	0640t	0715	0741	0815	0841	and in	1915	1941	2015	2041	2115	2141	2215	2234	...	...	2359	0059
Leipzig/Halle Flughafen ✈ **866** d.	0421	0456	0526	0552	0626	0652	0726	0752	0826	0852	the same	1926	1952	2026	2052	2126	2152	2226	2245	2328	2344	0010	0110
Leipzig Hbf ★ **866** d.	0435	0509	0540	0609	0640	0709	0740	0809	0840	0909	pattern	1940	2009	2040	2109	2140	2209	2240	2307k	2341	2357	0028	0123
Leipzig-Connewitz ★ d.	0445	0519	0550	0619	0650	0719	0750	0819	0850	0919	every	1950	2019	2050	2119	2150	2219	2250	2317	2351	...	0038	...
Altenburg d.	0516	0552	0616	0649	0716	0752	0816	0849	0916	0952	**two** hours	2016	2049	2116	2152	2216	2250	...	2356	...	...	...	...
Gößnitz d.	0533j	0605	0628t	...	0733j	0805	0828	...	0933j	1005	until	2028	...	2133j	2205	2228	...	...	0009	...	...	...	...
Werdau d.	0548	0632j	0647t	...	0747	0832j	0847j	...	0947	1032j		2047j	...	2147	2225	2247j	...	...	0028	...	...	...	...
Zwickau (Sachs) Hbf a.	0556	0644	0656t	...	0756	0844	0856	...	0956	1044		2056	...	2156	2235	2256	...	...	0039	...	...	...	...

PLAUEN - WERDAU ◇

km		Ⓐ	⚒						
	Plauen (Vogt) ob Bf **880** d.	0433	0526	0633	0727	and in the	1927	2033	2158
0	Reichenbach (Vogt) ¶ **880** d.	0455	0549	0655	0750	same pattern	1950	2055	2221
17	**Werdau** a.	0508	0601	0708	0802	every **two**	2002	2108	2233
	Zwickau (Sachs) Hbf **880** a.	0521	0615	0722	0815	hours until	2015	2121	2246

	Ⓐ	⚒							
Zwickau (Sachs) Hbf **880** d.	0543	0636	0743	0836	and in the	1943	2036	2143	2245
Werdau d.	0556	0651	0756	0851	same pattern	1956	2051	2156	2300
Reichenbach (Vogt) ¶ **880** d.	0609	0704	0809	0904	every **two**	2009	2104	2217n	2313
Plauen (Vogt) ob Bf **880** a.	0631	0726	0831	0926	hours until	2031	2126	2245	2335

d – Runs daily Halle - Leipzig-Connewitz.
j – Arrives 5 – 8 minutes earlier.
k – Arrives 2257.

n – Arrives 2208.
t – Ⓐ only.

¶ – Reichenbach (Vogtl) ob Bf.
⊠ – The 1841 from Halle arrives Zwickau 2047 (not 2044).
◇ – Operated by Vogtlandbahn (2nd class only). Certain services run from / to Cheb (see Table **1122**).
★ – All trains also call at Leipzig MDR, Bayerischer Bahnhof, Wilhelm-Leuschner-Platz and Markt.

DB (*RB* services)

CHEMNITZ - CRANZAHL - VEJPRTY - CHOMUTOV 882

km												
0	**Chemnitz** Hbf **880** d.	0636	0836	0936	1136	1236	1336	1436	1636	1836	2036	2236
13	Flöha **880** d.	0647	0847	0947	1147	1247	1347	1447	1647	1847	2047	2247
31	Zschopau d.	0708	0908	1008	1208	1309	1410	1509	1708	1910	2108	2308
57	Annaberg-Buchholz ¶ d.	0743	0943	1049	1243	1349	1445	1544	1743	1945	2143	2343
64	Cranzahl ⊖ a.	...	0955	1101	1255	1402z	1501	1556	1755	...	...	...
			C⊙			C⊙			C⊙			
64	Cranzahl d.	...	1007	...	...	1407	...	...	1807	...	...	...
75	Vejprty 🏛 d.	...	1026	...	...	1426	...	...	1826	...	...	...
133	**Chomutov** a.	...	1145	...	...	1545	...	...	1945	...	...	...

			C⊙			C⊙			C⊙	
Chomutov d.	...	...	0810	...	...	1210	...	...	1610	...
Vejprty 🏛 d.	...	...	0935	...	...	1345	...	...	1735	...
Cranzahl a.	...	...	0948	...	...	1358	...	...	1748	...
			d			E			d	
Cranzahl ⊖ d.	...	...	1001	1155	1301	1445z	1558	1651	1801	...
Annaberg-Buchholz ¶ d.	0607	0807	1013	1207	1313	1508	1610	1707	1813	2007
Zschopau d.	0644	0844	1047	1245	1347	1545	1645	1744	1847	2045
Flöha **880** a.	0708	0908	1108	1308	1408	1608	1708	1808	1908	2108
Chemnitz Hbf **880** a.	0720	0920	1120	1320	1420	1620	1720	1820	1920	2120

⊖ – **Cranzahl - Kurort Oberwiesenthal** *Fichtelbergbahn* (17 km, narrow gauge steam). Journey: ± 55 minutes. A special service operates June 7, 8, Nov. 29, 30, Dec. 6, 7, Dec. 13. **No service Nov. 3 – 21**. Operator: SDG Sächsische Dampfeisenbahngesellschaft, Bahnhofstraße 7, 09484 Kurort Oberwiesenthal. ✆ + 49 (0) 37348 151 0.
From Cranzahl at 1000, 1256, 1521 and 1811. **From Kurort Oberwiesenthal** at 0845, 1148, 1413 and 1703.

C – ⑥⑦ Mar. 29 - Nov. 2 (also Apr. 18, 21, May 1, 8, Oct. 28).
E – ⑥⑦ **z** from Cranzahl; daily from Annaberg-Buchholz.
d – Daily.
z – ⑥⑦ (also June 9, Oct. 3, 28, 31, Nov. 19).
¶ – Annaberg-Buchholz unterer Bf.
⊙ – Operated by Die Länderbahn CZ.

City-Bahn Chemnitz

CHEMNITZ - AUE 883

km		⚒						
0	**Chemnitz** Hbf d.	0551	0651	and	2051	...	2203	...
27	Thalheim d.	0646	0746	hourly	2146	...	2301	...
36	Zwönitz d.	0658	0758	until	2158	...	2313	...
51	**Aue** (Sachs) a.	0716	0816		2216	...	2330	...

	Ⓐ						
Aue (Sachs) d.	0359	0439	and	2039	...	2221	...
Zwönitz d.	0417	0458	hourly	2058	...	2239	...
Thalheim d.	0428	0509	until	2109	...	2250	...
Chemnitz Hbf a.	0522	0602		2202	...	2345	...

884 ZWICKAU - JOHANNGEORGENSTADT - KARLOVY VARY

DB; ČD (2nd class only)

km		Ⓐ								⑤⑥
0	**Zwickau** (Sachs) Hbf . d.	0503	...	0603	and	1903	2003	2103	2203	2303
27	Aue (Sachs) .... d.	0537	0537	0637	hourly	1937	2037	2137	2235	2337
37	Schwarzenberg (Erzg) . d.	0553	0553	0653	until	1953	2053	2150	...	2350
56	**Johanngeorgenstadt** . a.	0618	0618	0718		2018	2118	...	...	...

	Ⓐ	Ⓐ							⑤⑥
Johanngeorgenstadt ...... d.	...	0427	...	0527	and	1927	2027	2127	2127
Schwarzenberg (Erzg) ...... d.	0354	0454	0454	0554	hourly	1954	2054	2154	2154
Aue (Sachs) .... d.	0407	0507	0507	0607	until	2007	2107	2206	2207
Zwickau (Sachs) Hbf .... a.	0439	0539	0539	0640		2040	2139	...	2239

km	*SEE NOTE* ▶		Ⓐ	⊗						Ⓒ	
0	**Johanngeorgenstadt** . d.	...	...	0730	0930	1230	1449	1630	2054	2054	...
1	Potučky 🏛 .... d.	0434	0615	0733	0933	1233	1452	1633	2057	2057	...
28	Nejdek .... d.	0520	0658	0816	1016	1316	1537	1716	2138	2139	2225
44	**Karlovy Vary** .... a.	0545	0723	0841	1041	1341	1601	1741	...	2205	2250
47	**Karlovy Vary** dolní ... a.	0552	0731	0847	1047	1347	1606	1747	...	...	...

SEE NOTE ▶					Ⓐ	Ⓒ	Ⓐ	Ⓒ		
Karlovy Vary dolní .... d.	0605t	0807	1007	1303	1407	1503	1703	1803	2107	...
Karlovy Vary .... d.	0610	0813	1013	1313	1413	1511	1713	1810	2113	...
Nejdek .... d.	0635	0839	1039	1339	1439	1539	1739	1839	2137	2221
Potučky 🏛 .... d.	0719	0921	1121	1421	1521	1621	1821	1921	...	2303
Johanngeorgenstadt ...... a.	0721	0923	1123	1423	1523	1623	1823	1923	...	...

t – Ⓐ only. ⊗ – Change trains at Nejdek on Ⓐ. ▶ – Czech holiday dates apply (see page 4). Subject to alteration until July 18 with 🚌 substitution Potučky - Nejdek.

885 REGENSBURG - SCHWANDORF - FURTH IM WALD - PLZEŇ

km				◇	◇	**365**	◇	**353**	◇	**355**	◇	**357**	◇	◇	**359**	◇	◇	**361**	◇		◇	**363**	◇		◇
		Ⓒ	Ⓐ	Ⓐ	⚒¶	‡🍷		‡🍷		‡🍷		‡🍷	Ⓒ		‡🍷			‡🍷		**DN**		‡🍷		**N**	
	München Hbf **878** .... d.	...	...	...	...	0444*	...	0644*	...	0844*	...	1044*	...	...	1244*	...	...	1444*	...	...	...	1644*	...	...	...
0	**Regensburg** Hbf . **879** d.	...	...	...	...	0617**r**	...	0817**r**	...	1017**r**	...	1217**r**	...	...	1417**r**	...	...	1617**r**	...	...	...	1817**r**	...	...	...
42	**Schwandorf** .... **879** d.	...	...	0550	0623	0653	0802	0853	1001	1053	1201	1253	1310	1401	1453	1510	1601	1653	1710	1732	*1801*	1853	2001	2108	2310
90	Cham (Oberpf) .... d.	...	...	0632	0707	0724	0841	0925	1038	1125	1238	1325	1346	1438	1525	1546	1641	1725	1744	1814	1841	1925	2038	2147	2346
109	**Furth im Wald** 🏛 .... d.	...	...	0649	0725	0740	0900	0940	1055	1140	1255	1340	1405	1455	1540	1605	1658	1740	1801	1834	1858	1940	2055	2205	0005
131	Domažlice .... ⊠ d.	0635	0651	...	...	0801	0922**c**	1001	...	1201	...	1401	...	...	1601	...	...	1801	1824**c**	...	...	2001	...	...	...
190	**Plzeň** hl.n. .... ⊠ a.	0740	0748	...	...	0847	...	1047	...	1247	...	1447	...	...	1647	...	...	1847	...		...	2047	...	...	...
	Praha hl.n. **1120** ...... a.	...	...	...	...	1022	...	1222	...	1422	...	1622	...	...	1822	...	...	2022	...	...	...	2222	...	...	...

			◇	◇	**362**	◇	**360**	◇	◇	**358**	◇	◇	**356**	◇	◇	**354**	◇	◇	**352**	◇	**364**	◇		
	ⒶN	N			‡🍷		‡🍷		Ⓐ	‡🍷			‡🍷		Ⓐ	‡🍷			‡🍷		‡🍷			
Praha hl.n. **1120** .... d.	...	...	...	...	0535	...	0735	...	...	0935	...	...	1135	...	...	1335	...	...	1535	...	1735	...	...	...
Plzeň hl.n. .... ⊠ d.	...	...	...	...	0711	...	0911	...	...	1111	...	...	1311	...	...	1511	...	...	1711	...	1911	...	2120	2247
Domažlice .... ⊠ d.	...	...	...	...	0801	...	1001	1036**c**	...	1201	...	...	1401	...	...	1601	...	...	1801	1836**c**	2001	...	2221	2347
Furth im Wald 🏛 .... d.	0440	0554	0657	0755	0823	0903	1023	1103	1153	1223	1303	1353	1423	1503	1553	1623	1703	1751	1823	1903	2023	2103	...	...
Cham (Oberpf) .... d.	0456	0612	0724	0816	0837	0926	1037	1126	1215	1237	1326	1415	1437	1526	1615	1637	1725	1815	1837	1926	2037	2126	...	...
Schwandorf .... **879** a.	0527	0649	0757	0851	0905	0959	1105	1159	1251	1305	1359	1451	1505	1559	1651	1705	1759	1851	1905	1959	2105	2159	...	...
Regensburg Hbf .... **879** a.	...	...	...	...	0941**r**	...	1141**r**	...	...	1341**r**	...	...	1541**r**	...	...	1741**r**	...	...	1941**r**	...	2141**r**	...	...	...
München Hbf **878** .... a.	...	...	...	...	1118*	...	1318*	...	...	1518*	...	...	1718*	...	...	1918*	...	...	2118*	...	2318*	...	...	...

D – ①–④ (not June 19).
N – From / to Nürnberg (Table **886**).
c – ⑥⑦ only.
r – By 🚌 June 15 - Aug. 22 (most 🚌 dep Regensburg 27 mins earlier, arr Regensburg 24 mins later).

¶ – Change trains at Cham on Ⓐ.
◇ – Operated by Oberpfalzbahn (2nd class only).
‡ – BAVORSKÝ EXPRES. Train category *ALX* in Germany (operated by Die Länderbahn).
* – No through trains June 15 - Aug. 22 (see note **r** and refer to Table **878** for revised connections, generally one hour earlier / later).

⊠ – Other local trains Domažlice - Plzeň and v.v. (journey 60 – 78 minutes):
From Domažlice at 0345, 0430 Ⓐ, 0530, 0612 Ⓐ, 0726 Ⓐ, 0835, 1035, 1235, 1326 Ⓐ, 1435, 1528 Ⓐ, 1634 Ⓒ, 1636 Ⓐ, 1738 Ⓐ, 1835 Ⓒ, 1925 Ⓐ and 2035 Ⓒ.
From Plzeň hl.n. at 0505 Ⓐ, 0605 Ⓐ, 0620 Ⓒ, 0820, 1020, 1220, 1320 Ⓐ, 1418, 1518 Ⓐ, 1620, 1720 Ⓐ, 1820, 1920 Ⓐ and 2020 Ⓒ.

886 NÜRNBERG - SCHWANDORF and WEIDEN

RE services

km				Ⓐ	Ⓒ	Ⓐ											ⒶF		①–④			F				
0	**Nürnberg** Hbf .... ◧ d.	0022	...	0426	0529	0559	0630	0743	0843	0943	1043	1143	1243	1343	1443	1543	1605	1643	1705	1743	1843	1943	2037	2137	2237	2345
28	Hersbruck (r Pegnitz) ◧ d.	0039	...	0442	0545	0622	0645	0758	0858	0958	1058	1158	1258	1358	1458	1558	1625	1658	1725	1758	1858	1958	2058	2158	2258	0000
56	Sulzbach-Rosenberg . d.	0104	...	0504	0615	0651	0721	0825	0925	1025	1125	1225	1325	1425	1525	1625	1649	1725	1749	1825	1925	2026	2125	2225	2325	0027
68	Amberg .... d.	0112	...	0517	0623	0704	0729	0833	0933	1033	1133	1233	1333	1433	1533	1633	1701	1733	1801	1833	1933	2033	2133	2233	2333	0035
94	**Schwandorf** .... a.	0126**z**	...	0530	0639	0727	0751	0847	0947	1047	1147	1247	1349	1447	1547	1648	1725	1747	1825	1847	1947	2049	2147	2247	2348	0050

			Ⓐ	⚒	ⒶF		Ⓐ	F	Ⓐ																
Schwandorf .... d.	0010	...	0403	0459	0533	0605	0634	0707	0733	0808	0908	1008	1108	1208	1308	1408	1508	1608	1708	1808	1908	2008	2108	2208	2308
Amberg .... d.	0025	...	0418	0519	0549	0621	0651	0725	0749	0822	0922	1022	1122	1222	1322	1422	1522	1622	1722	1822	1922	2022	2122	2222	2322
Sulzbach-Rosenberg .... d.	0034	...	0427	0527	0557	0630	0658	0732	0757	0830	0930	1030	1130	1230	1330	1430	1530	1630	1729	1830	1930	2030	2129	2230	2330
Hersbruck (r pegnitz) .... d.	0100	...	0503	0559	|	0703	|	0759	|	0900	1000	1100	1200	1300	1400	1500	1600	1700	1800	1900	2000	2059	2159	2309**j**	0000
Nürnberg Hbf .... a.	0115	...	0518	0614	0639	0719	0740	0815	0840	0915	1015	1115	1215	1315	1415	1515	1615	1715	1815	1915	2015	2115	2215	2324	0015

km											
0	**Nürnberg** Hbf .... ◧ d.	0529	0630	0743	0843	and	1943	2037	2137	2237	2345
28	Hersbruck (r Pegnitz) ◧ d.	0545	0645	0758	0858	hourly	1958	2058	2158	2258	0000
97	**Weiden** (Oberpf) .... a.	0640	0747	0853	0952	until	2052	2152	2252	2352	0053

	Ⓐ				△				
Weiden (Oberpf) ..... d.	0500	0605	0701	0806	and	2006	2106	2206	2306
Hersbruck (r Pegnitz) a.	0558	0702	0758	0859	hourly	2058	2158	2300	2359
Nürnberg Hbf .... a.	0614	0719	0815	0915	until	2115	2215	2324	0015

F – To / from Furth im Wald (Table **885**).
j – Arrives 2300.
z – Ⓒ only.

△ – Weiden d. 1604 / 1704 (not 1606 / 1706).

◧ – Certain trains from Nürnberg and Hersbruck convey portions for two separate destinations. Passengers should take care to join the correct portion of the train.
☛ Subject to alteration June 7 - 13.

887 BAYREUTH - WEIDEN

Operated by *agilis* (2nd class only)

km		Ⓐ	Ⓐ								Ⓐ	Ⓒ									
0	**Bayreuth** Hbf.. d.	0450	0540	0640	0718	0804	0901	0959	1101	1159	1301	1301	1401	1501	1601	1701	1801	1901	2018	2206	0014
19	Kirchenlaibach d.	0511	0603**j**	0657	0740	0826	0922**j**	1022**j**	1122**j**	1222**j**	1320	1322**j**	1422**j**	1522**j**	1622**j**	1722**j**	1822**j**	1922**j**	2044	2226	0031
59	**Weiden**.......... a.	0540	0637	0728	...	0856	0956	1056	1156	1256	1356	1356	1456	1556	1656	1756	1856	1956	2114	2255	...

	Ⓐ	Ⓐ		Ⓐ							Ⓒ	Ⓐ									
Weiden ....d.	...	0548	...	0645	...	0804	0906	1006	1106	1206	1306	1323	1406	1506	1606	1706	1806	1906	2022	2222	...
Kirchenlaibach ..d.	0514	0618	0720	0720	0805	0841	0942	1042	1142	1242	1342	1355	1442	1542	1642	1742	1842	1942	2058	2257	2340
Bayreuth Hbf ...a.	0530	0634	0736	0736	0822	0857	0957	1058	1157	1258	1357	1416	1457	1557	1657	1757	1857	1957	2114	2313	2356

j – Arrives 7 minutes earlier.

888 KEMPTEN - REUTTE IN TIROL - GARMISCH-PARTENKIRCHEN

RB services

km		Ⓐ	Ⓒ						❖				
0	**Kempten** (Allgäu) Hbf d.	0614	0630	0731	0831	0931	1031	1131	1231	1335		2035	2258
18	Oy-Mittelberg .... d.	0700**r**	0658	0800	0858	1000	1100	1200	1300	1403	and	2103	2329
24	Nesselwang .... d.	0711	0709	0811	0910	1011	1111	1211	1311	1414	hourly	2114	2340
31	Pfronten-Ried .... d.	0721	0719	0821	0920	1021	1121	1224	1321	1424	until	2124	2350
33	**Pfronten-Steinach** ... a.	0725	0723	0825	0924	1025	1125	1227	1325	1428		2128	2354

Pfronten-Steinach . d.	0633	0734		1234	1334	1436		1936	2136
Pfronten-Ried .... d.	0637	0738	and	1238	1338	1440	and	1940	2140
Nesselwang .... d.	0646	0747	hourly	1247	1347	1449	hourly	1949	2149
Oy-Mittelberg .... d.	0657	0759	until	1259	1403	1503	until	2003	2203
Kempten Hbf .... a.	0725	0825		1329	1429	1529		2029	2229

km		a		⚒						c	a							
0	**Pfronten-Steinach** ... d.	...	0636	...	0837**c**	0936	1036	1133**j**	1236	1336	1336	1436	1536	1636	1736	1836	2036	2136
5	**Vils** Stadt ⊗ .... ‡ d.	...	0643	...	0845	0943	1043	1140**j**	1243	1343	1343	1443	1543	1643	1743	1843	2043	2143
15	**Reutte in Tirol** .... ‡ d.	0526	0701	0750**e**	0901	0958	1101	1158**j**	1301	1401	1401	1501	1601	1701	1801	1901	2101	2158
35	Lermoos.................. ‡ d.	0550	0725	0825	0925	...	1125	1225	1325	1425	1436	1525	1625	1725	1825	1925	2125	...
38	Ehrwald Zugspitzbahn ‡ d.	0556	0731	0831	0931	...	1131	1231	1331	1431	1441	1531	1631	1731	1831	1931	2131	...
60	**Garmisch**-Partenk. ... a.	0623	0757	0857**e**	0957	...	1157	1257	1357	1457	...	1557	1659	1757	1857	1957	2157	...
	München Hbf **895** .. a.	...	0926**z**	1026	1126	...	1326**z**	1426	1526	1626	...	1726**z**	1826	1926	2026	2126**k**	2326**f**	...

		⚒	c	a	ad			cd				a	c				Ⓑw	
München Hbf **895** ... d.	...	...	0532	...	0632**z**	0732	0834	0932	1032**z**	1132	1232	...	1332	1432**z**	1530	1632	1729	1832**x**
Garmisch-Partenk. .... d.	...	0637	0704	0722	0804	0904	1004	1104	1204	1304	1404	...	1504	1604	1704	1804	1904	2004
Ehrwald Zugspitzbahn ‡ d.	...	0702	0731	0752	0831	0931	1031	1131	1231	1331	1431	1520	1531	1631	1731	1831	1931	2031
Lermoos .... ‡ d.	...	0706	0735	0756	0835	0935	1035	1135	1235	1335	1435	1526	1535	1635	1735	1835	1935	2035
Reutte in Tirol .... ‡ d.	0602	0736	0802	0823	0902	1004	1102	1202	1302	1402	1502	1602	1602	1702	1802	1902	2002	2102
Vils Stadt ⊗ .... ‡ d.	0617	...	0817	0838	0917	1019	1117	1217	1317	1417	1517	1617	1617	1717	1817	1917	2017	2117
Pfronten-Steinach .... a.	0624	...	0824	...	0924	1026	1124	1224	1324	1424	1524	1624	1624	1724	1824	1924	2024	2124

a – ①–⑤ (not June 9, 19, Aug. 15).
c – ⑥⑦ (also June 9, 19, Aug. 15).
d – Runs daily Reutte - Pfronten-Steinach.
e – On ⑥ Reutte d. 0801, Garmisch a. 0901.
f – ⑤ only.
j – 3 minutes later on ⑥⑦ **c**.
k – ①②③④⑥⑦ (also Oct. 3).
r – Arrives 0641.
w – Not June 8, 18, Aug. 14, Oct. 31, Dec. 7.
x – ⑥⑦ (also June 19, Aug. 15).
z – ⑥⑦ (also June 9, 19, Aug. 15, Oct. 3).
❖ – Runs 29 – 37 mins later on Ⓐ June 23 - July 31, Sept. 16 - Oct. 31, Nov. 10 - Dec. 12.
⊗ – Most services call on request.
‡ – Station is in Austria. Germany holiday dates apply.

MÜNCHEN - SALZBURG 890

Bayerische Oberlandbahn; DB

km		◇ Ⓐ		◇	RJX 265 ✕	◇	RJX 61 B✕	WB 961 ⊙ 🍷	◇	RJ 111 ✕♦	◇	RJX 63 B✕	WB 963 ⊙ 🍷	◇	EC 217 ♦	◇	RJX 65 B✕	WB 965 ⊙ 🍷	◇	EC 113 ♦	◇	RJX 67 B✕	◇	IC 2083 ♦	ICE 115 ✕♦
	Frankfurt (Main) Hbf **910** d.	...	...	...	...	...	...	...	...	...	...	...	...	...	...	...	...	...	...	0821	...	...	...	...	...
	Stuttgart Hbf **910** d.	...	...	...	...	...	...	...	...	...	...	...	0712	...	0759	...	...	...	...	0958	...	...	...	...	1159
0	**München** Hbf **951** d.	...	...	0552	0621	0655	0722	0749	0756	0816	0856	0928	0947	0955	1016	1055	1127	1145	1155	1217	1255	1328	1355	...	1417
10	München Ost **951** d.	...	...	0601	0631	0704	|	0758	0804	0826	0904	|	0958	1004	1025	1104	|	1158	1204	1226	1304	|	1404	1413	1426
65	Rosenheim **951** d.	0532	...	0639	0703	0735	0803	0828	0835	0855	0935	|	1028	1035	1054	1135	|	1228	1235	1254	1335	|	1435	1442	1454
82	Bad Endorf d.	0543	...	0650	|	0746	|	|	0846	|	0946	|	|	1046	|	1146	|	|	1246	|	1346	|	1446	1455	|
90	Prien am Chiemsee d.	0549	...	0657	|	0752	|	|	0852	0913	0952	|	|	1052	1111	1152	|	|	1252	1311	1352	|	1452	1503	1511
118	Traunstein d.	0612	...	0720	|	0816	|	|	0916	0932	1016	|	|	1116	1131	1216	|	|	1316	1331	1416	|	1516	1525	1532
147	Freilassing **891** d.	0630	...	0742	|	0835	|	|	0935	0952	1035	|	|	1135	1152	1235	|	|	1335	1352	1435	|	1535	1542	1552
153	**Salzburg** Hbf 🏛 **891** a.	0638	...	0752	0758	0842	0858	0921	0942	0959	1042	1058	1121	1142	1159	1242	1258	1321	1342	1359	1442	1458	1542	...	1559
	Wien Westbahnhof **950** a.	...	...	...	|	...	|	1152	...	...	...	|	1352	...	...	...	|	1552	...	...	...	|	...	...	...
	Wien Hbf **950** a.	...	...	...	1032	...	1132	...	...	...	...	1332	...	...	...	...	1532	...	...	...	...	1732	...	...	...

	◇	RJX 69 ✕	WB 967 ⊙ 🍷	◇	EC 219 🍷♦	◇	RJX 261 B✕	WB 969 ⊙ 🍷	◇	ICE 117 ✕♦	EN 406 ♦	◇	RJ 1299 Ⓑ ✕	◇	NJ 295 [R] ♦	IC 1291 🍷	◇	RJ 1295 ①–④ m✕	RJ 263 ⑤–⑦ v✕	◇	◇		EN 50237 [R] K	NJ 237 [R] ♦	◇
Frankfurt (Main) Hbf **910** d.	...	...	...	...	1219	...	...	...	...	1419	...	...	...	...	...	1620	...	...	...	...	...	...	...	...	...
Stuttgart Hbf **910** d.	...	...	...	...	1359	...	...	1512	...	1559	...	...	...	...	...	1759	...	...	...	...	...	...	2029	2029	...
München Hbf **951** d.	1455	1528	1548	1555	1617	1655	1729	1749	1756	1817	1835	1855	1916	1955	2008	2017	2054	2116	2116	2143	2243	2328	|	|	2351
München Ost **951** d.	1504	|	1558	1604	1625	1704	|	1759	1804	1826	1845	1904	1927	2004	2020**u**	2028	2102	2125	2125	2152	2252	2337	2354	2354	0002
Rosenheim **951** d.	1535	|	1628	1635	1654	1735	|	1828	1835	1854	1922	1935	1957	2035	2050**u**	2055	2135	2154	2154	2232	2335**j**	...	0033	0033	0038
Bad Endorf d.	1546	|	|	1646	|	1746	|	|	1846	|	|	1946	2009	2046	|	2108	2146	|	|	2246	2346	...	|	|	0049
Prien am Chiemsee d.	1552	|	|	1652	1711	1752	|	|	1852	1911	|	1952	2016	2052	|	2116	2152	2211	2211	2252	2352	...	|	|	0055
Traunstein d.	1616	|	|	1716	1731	1816	|	|	1916	1932	|	2016	2035	2116	|	2136	2219	2231	2231	2319	0016	...	|	|	0120
Freilassing **891** d.	1635	|	|	1735	1752	1835	|	|	1935	1952	|	2035	2054	2135	|	2155	2238	2252	2252	2338	0035	...	|	|	0139
Salzburg Hbf 🏛 **891** a.	1642	1658	1721	1742	1759	1842	1858	1921	1942	1959	2026	2042	2100	2142	2152	2201	2245	2259	2259	2345	0042	...	0128	0128	0146
Wien Westbahnhof **950** a.	...	|	1952	...	...	...	|	2152	...	...	|	...	...	...	...	...	...	...	|	...	...	...	|	...	...
Wien Hbf **950** a.	...	1932	...	...	...	...	2132	...	...	...	2316	...	...	...	...	...	...	...	0220	...	...	...	0632	...	...

	◇ Ⓐ	NJ 236 [R] ♦	EN 50462 [R] K			◇	IC 1296	◇	◇ Ⓐ	NJ 294 [R] ♦	RJ 1298 ①–⑥ ✕t	◇	ICE 1290 ✕	◇	WB 960 ⊙🍷	EN 407 ♦	RJX 260 ✕	◇	IC 2082 ♦	EC 218 ♦	◇	WB 962 ⊙🍷	RJX 262 ✕	◇	ICE 114 ✕♦
Wien Hbf **950** d.	...	...	2328	...	...	...	...	...	...	...	...	...	...	...	...	0539	0628	...	...	...	...	...	0828	...	...
Wien Westbahnhof **950** d.	...	...	|	...	...	...	...	...	...	...	...	...	...	...	0608	|	|	...	...	...	...	0808	|	...	...
Salzburg Hbf 🏛 **891** d.	0347	0405	0405	...	...	0505	0543	0605	0646	0701	0710	0704**z**	0800	0805	0839	0833	0900	0905	...	1000	1005	1039	1100	1108	1200
Freilassing **891** d.	0356	|	|	...	...	0524**r**	0551	0624**r**	0654	|	0716	0722**r**	0808	0824**r**	|	|	|	0924**r**	0947	1008	1024**r**	|	|	1124**r**	1208
Traunstein d.	0415	|	|	...	...	0544	0609	0644	0721**j**	|	0736	0744	0825	0844	|	|	|	0944	1006	1025	1044	|	|	1144	1225
Prien am Chiemsee d.	0437	|	|	...	...	0606	0627	0706	0743	|	0755	0806	0844	0906	|	|	|	1006	1027	1044	1106	|	|	1206	1244
Bad Endorf d.	0444	|	|	...	...	0613	0634	0713	0750	|	0803	0813	|	0913	|	|	|	1013	1035	|	1113	|	|	1213	|
Rosenheim **951** d.	0504**j**	0517**s**	0517**s**	...	...	0629	0649	0729	0806	0834**s**	0819	0829	0902	0929	0932	0942**s**	|	1029	1047	1102	1129	1132	|	1229	1302
München Ost **951** a.	0531	0550	0550	0559	...	0656	0717	0756	0841	|	0849	0856	0930	0956	1000	1013	|	1056	1115	1131	1156	1200	|	1256	1331
München Hbf **951** a.	0541	|	|	0007	...	0700	0730	0800	0850	0921	0902	0900	0941	1000	1014	1024	1033	1100	...	1141	1200	1214	1232	1300	1341
Stuttgart Hbf **910** a.	...	0838	0838	...	...	...	0959	...	...	...	...	...	1159	...	...	...	...	...	...	1359	...	1437	...	...	1559
Frankfurt (Main) Hbf **910** a.	...	...	...	...	...	...	1140	...	...	...	...	...	1340	...	...	...	...	...	...	1540	...	...	...	...	...

	◇	WB 964 ⊙ 🍷	RJX 60 B✕	◇	EC 112 ♦	◇	RJX 62 B✕	◇	EC 216 ♦	◇	RJX 64 B✕	◇	RJ 268 ✕	◇	WB 966 ⊙ 🍷	RJX 66 B✕	◇	RJ 110 ✕♦	◇	WB 968 ⊙ 🍷	RJX 68 B✕	◇		◇	◇
Wien Hbf **950** d.	...	...	1028	...	...	...	1228	...	...	...	1428	...	1455	...	...	1628	...	...	...	...	1828	...	...	...	...
Wien Westbahnhof **950** d.	...	1008	|	...	...	...	|	...	...	...	|	...	|	...	1608	|	...	...	...	1808	|	...	...	...	...
Salzburg Hbf 🏛 **891** d.	1205	1239	1300	1305	1400	1407	1500	1505	1600	1605	1700	1705	1800	1808	1839	1900	1905	2000	2005	2039	2100	2108	...	2208	2252
Freilassing **891** d.	1224**r**	|	|	1324**r**	1408	1424**r**	|	1524**r**	1608	1624**r**	|	1724**r**	1808	1824**r**	|	|	1924**r**	2008	2024**r**	|	|	2127**r**	...	2226**r**	2310**r**
Traunstein d.	1244	|	|	1346	1425	1444	|	1544	1625	1644	|	1744	1825	1844	|	|	1944	2025	2044	|	|	2147	...	2245	2329
Prien am Chiemsee d.	1306	|	|	1408	1444	1506	|	1606	1644	1706	|	1806	1844	1906	|	|	2006	2043	2106	|	|	2209	...	2307	2350
Bad Endorf d.	1313	|	|	1414	|	1513	|	1613	|	1713	|	1813	|	1913	|	|	2013	|	2113	|	|	2216	...	2314	2356
Rosenheim **951** d.	1329	1332	|	1429	1502	1529	|	1629	1702	1729	|	1829	1902	1929	1932	|	2032**j**	2102	2132**j**	2132	2155	2233	...	2332**j**	0012
München Ost **951** a.	1355	1400	|	1456	1530	1556	|	1655	1731	1756	|	1856	|	1956	2000	|	2106	2131	2206	2202	|	2307	...	0006	0048
München Hbf **951** a.	1405	1412	1432	1506	1541	1606	1634	1706	1741	1806	1831	1906	1938	2006	2016	2031	2116	2141	2217	2213	2232	2317	...	0018	0058
Stuttgart Hbf **910** a.	...	...	...	...	1758	...	...	...	1958	...	...	...	...	...	2239	...	...	...	...	...	...	...	...	...	...
Frankfurt (Main) Hbf **910** a.	...	...	...	...	1940	...	...	...	...	...	...	...	...	...	...	...	...	...	...	...	...	...	...	...	...

♦ – **NOTES** (LISTED BY TRAIN NUMBER)

110 – HOHE TAUERN – [12] ✕ Schwarzach-St Veit - München.
111 – HOHE TAUERN – [12] ✕ München - Schwarzach-St Veit.
112/3 – BLAUER ENZIAN – [12] Schwarzach-St Veit - München - Frankfurt and v.v.
114 – WÖRTHERSEE – [12] ✕ Schwarzach-St Veit - München - Mannheim - Köln - Dortmund.
115 – WÖRTHERSEE – [12] ✕ Münster - Köln - Mannheim - München - Schwarzach-St Veit .
117 – SALZACH – [12] ✕ Frankfurt - München - Schwarzach-St Veit.
216/7 – DACHSTEIN – [12] Graz - Salzburg - Mannheim - Saarbrücken and v.v.
218/9 – CHIEMGAU – [12] Graz - Bischofshofen - Salzburg - Frankfurt and v.v.
236 – 🛏 1, 2 cl., ▬ 2 cl. and [2] Venezia - Villach - München - Stuttgart; 🛏 1, 2 cl., ▬ 2 cl. and [2] (**414** – LISINSKI) Zagreb - Ljubljana - Jesenice 🏛 - Villach - München - Stuttgart. **The Venezia portion (236) is suspended until July 13. The Zagreb portion (414) is diverted via Graz until July 13 (not serving Ljubljana, Jesenice or Villach).**
237 – 🛏 1, 2 cl., ▬ 2 cl. and [2] Stuttgart - München - Villach - Venezia; 🛏 1, 2 cl., ▬ 2 cl. and [2] (**40237** – LISINSKI) Stuttgart - München - Villach - Jesenice 🏛 - Ljubljana - Zagreb. **The Venezia portion (237) is suspended until July 13. The Zagreb portion (40237) is diverted via Graz until July 13 (not serving Villach, Jesenice or Ljubljana).**
294/5 – 🛏 1, 2 cl., ▬ 2 cl. and [2] Roma - Firenze - Bologna - München and v.v.; 🛏 1, 2 cl., ▬ 2 cl. and [2] La Spezia (**40235/40295**) - Genova - Milano - München and v.v. **Service suspended until July 13.**

406/7 – 🛏 1, 2 cl. and ▬ 2 cl. München - Wien - Břeclav - Ostrava - Kraków - Warszawa and v.v. Also conveys [2] (*IC* **60406/7**).
2082 – Until Oct. 8: KÖNIGSSEE – [12] Berchtesgaden - Augsburg - Hamburg.
2083 – Until Oct. 9: KÖNIGSSEE – [12] Hamburg - Augsburg - Berchtesgaden.

B – To / from Budapest (Table **1250**).
K – KÁLMÁN IMRE – 🛏 1, 2 cl., ▬ 2 cl. and [2] Budapest - München - Stuttgart and v.v.

j – Arrives 6 – 9 minutes earlier.
m – Not Aug. 14, Dec. 8.
r – Arrives 10 – 14 minutes earlier.
s – Calls to set down only.
t – Not Oct. 4.
u – Calls to pick up only.
v – Also Aug. 14, Dec. 8.
z – Ⓒ only.

◇ – *Meridian* regional service (operated by Bayerische Regiobahn; German holiday dates apply).
⊙ – Operated by *WESTbahn* (special fares).

SALZBURG - FREILASSING - BERCHTESGADEN 891

Bayerische Regiobahn *

km		◇	Ⓐ	Ⓐ	Ⓒ										⚒		⚒		c					A ◇
0	**Salzburg** Hbf **890** ⊡ d.	0505	0612	0657	0712	0805	0842	0905	0942	and at	1808	1842	1908	1942	2012	2042	2112	2142	2229	2242	2308	2342	A	1605
6	Freilassing **890** ⊡ a.	0513	0624	0710	0724	0813	0854	0913	0954	the same	1814	1854	1918	1954	2024	2054	2124	2154	2241	2254	2321	2354	L	1613
6	Freilassing d.	0553	0636	0718	0741	0840	0857	0939	0957	minutes	1840	1857	1939	...	...	2058	...	2158	2246	...	2342**t**	...	S	1618
21	Bad Reichenhall d.	0616	0655	0739	0801	0859	0920	1001	1020	past each	1901	1920	2001	...	...	2122	...	2215	2306	...	0009**t**	...	O	1631
39	**Berchtesgaden** Hbf a.	0658	0723	0808	0828	0928	...	1028	...	hour until	1928	...	2028	...	...	2150	...	2244	2334	...	0036**t**	...		1707

		Ⓐ	Ⓒ	Ⓐ		Ⓐ b	A ◇								J ◇										
Berchtesgaden Hbf d.	0621	0703	0730	0732	...	0830	0850	...	0932	...	and at	1632	...	1732	1750	...	1832	...	1932	...	2032	...	2207	...
Bad Reichenhall d.	0654	0738	0759	0808	0834	0858	0927	0934	1000	1034	the same	1700	1734	1800	1827	1834	1900	1934	2000	...	2100	...	2242	...
Freilassing a.	0712	0757	0818	0831	0857	0918	0939	0957	1018	1057	minutes	1718	1757	1818	1839	1857	1918	1957	2018	...	2118	...	2304	...
Freilassing **890** ⊡ d.	0742	0807	0835	0835	0907	0927	0946	1007	1035	1107	past each	1735	1807	1835	1846	1907	1935	2007	2035	2107	2135	2207	2307	0007
Salzburg Hbf **890** ⊡ a.	0752	0817	0842	0842	0917	0939	0955	1017	1042	1117	hour until	1742	1817	1842	1855	1917	1942	2033	2042	2117	2142	2217	2317	0017

A – Until Oct. 8 (next day from Berchtesgaden): *IC* **2082/3**: KÖNIGSSEE – [12] Berchtesgaden - Hamburg and v.v. (train category *RE* in this table).
J – Until Oct. 8.
b – Runs daily Berchtesgaden - Freilassing from Oct. 11.

c – Change at Freilassing on Ⓒ.
t – Night of ⑤⑥⑦.
***** – 2nd class only. German holiday dates apply.
◇ – Operated by DB.

⊡ – Other local trains Salzburg - Freilassing and v.v.: **From Salzburg** 0042Ⓒ, 0142Ⓒ, 0542, 0612⑥, 0642, 0712, 0742, 0755⚒, 1523Ⓐ. **From Freilassing** at 0607, 0637, 0707, 0807.

892 MÜNCHEN FLUGHAFEN ✈

S-Bahn services S1 and S8 from / to München (2nd class only). Services on both routes run approximately every 20 minutes.

S1 München Hbf (low level) - Freising - München Flughafen Terminal ✈ (41 km). **From München Hbf** 0501 to 2321. **From München Flughafen** 0531 to 0011. Journey: ± 45 minutes. **S1** trains from München Hbf are often combined with a Freising service - travel in the rear portion for the Airport.

S8 München Pasing - München Hbf (low level) - München Ost - München Flughafen Terminal ✈ (44 km). **From München Pasing** 0303 to 0003 (10 minutes later from München Hbf, 19 minutes later from München Ost). **From München Flughafen** 0404 to 0004. Journey: 50 minutes from / to Pasing, 40 minutes from / to Hbf, 31 minutes from / to Ost.

Direct *RE* services Regensburg - Landshut - Freising - München Flughafen. Certain services run as through from / to Nürnberg (see Table **921**).

					Ⓒz	Ⓐt			
Regensburg Hbf ...... **878** d.	0319	0419	0528	0614	0720	0728	0819	and	2219
Neufahrn (Niederbay) ...... **878** d.	0348	0448	0557	|	0749	0801	0848	hourly	2248
Landshut (Bay) Hbf ...... **878** d.	0405	0505	0617	0703	0806	0819	0905		2305
Freising ...... **878** d.	0428	0528	0640	0726	0828	0840	0928	until	2328
München Flughafen ⊡ ✈ ...... a.	0441	0541	0653	0741	0841	0853	0941		2341

	Ⓒz	Ⓐt	Ⓐt	Ⓒz	Ⓐt	Ⓒz				
München Flughafen ⊡ ✈ .. d.	0428	0512	0528	0608	0616	0708	0716	0816	and	2316	0021
Freising ...... **878** d.	0439	0523	0539	0619	0628	0719	0728	0828	hourly	2329	0034
Landshut (Bay) Hbf ...... **878** d.	0505	0546	0614f	0642	0653	0742	0753	0853		2353	0059
Neufahrn (Niederbay) ...... **878** d.	0521	0602	0630	0658	0710	0758	0811	0910	until	0010	0115
Regensburg Hbf ...... **878** a.	0554	0636	0701	0732	0741	0832	0841	0941		0041	0148

f – Arrives 0601. t – Not June 19, Aug. 15. z – Also June 19, Aug. 15. ⊡ – München Flughafen Terminal.

893 MÜNCHEN - MÜHLDORF - SIMBACH

On June 19, Aug. 15 services run as on ⑦

km		Ⓐ	Ⓒ									Ⓐ		Ⓐ	Ⓒ	Ⓐ	Ⓒ	Ⓐ		Ⓐ		Ⓐ				
0	**München** Hbf ...... d.	0605	0605	0707	0807c	0907	1007	1107	1207	1307	1406	1425	1506	1521	1607	1627	1707	1726	1808	1831	1907	1948	2028	2128	2228	2328
10	**München** Ost ...... d.	0615	0617	0716	0816	0917	1017	1117	1217	1317	1417	1439	1516	1533	1617	1638	1717	1738	1818	1840	1917	1957	2039	2138	2238	2338
85	**Mühldorf** (Oberbay) .. a.	0721	0722	0819	0919	1017	1117	1217	1317	1417	1517	1535	1619	1630	1717	1731	1816	1830	1920	1930	2020	2102	2140	2235	2335	0038
			d									d	Ⓒ	|		d	Ⓒ	|		d						
85	**Mühldorf** (Oberbay) .. d.	...	0737	0837	0937	1037	1137	1227f	1337	1437	...	1538	1637	1634	...	1737	1839	1834	...	1937	2037	...	2147	2247	2342	...
124	**Simbach** (Inn) .... **962** a.	...	0813	0913	1013	1113	1213	1258f	1413	1513	...	1613	1713	1708	...	1813	1913	1907	...	2013	2113	...	2219	2319	0014	...

			Ⓐ	⑥	Ⓐ	Ⓐ	Ⓒ											Ⓐ	Ⓒ		Ⓐ	Ⓒ				
Simbach (Inn) ...... **962** d.	...	...	0507	0540	0554	0648	0648	0749	0849	0949	1049	1149	1249e	1349	1449	1549	...	1641	1649	1749	1841	1849	1949	2049	2154	2254
Mühldorf (Oberbay) ... a.	...	...	0540	0611	0628	0722	0722	0822	0921	1022	1123	1221	1321e	1422	1523	1622	...	1718	1722	1822	1918	1922	2022	2126	2229	2329
		⚒	Ⓐ	Ⓒ	|	|	Ⓒ									Ⓒ	Ⓐ	Ⓐ	Ⓒ			d				
Mühldorf (Oberbay) ... d.	0429	0518	0546	0623	0637	0732	0732	0832	0937	1030	1140	1231	1340	1430	1538	1630	1634	1737	1737	1843	...	1940	2034	2146	2246	...
München Ost ...... a.	0524	0623	0640	0724	0722	0823	0826	0926	1045	1126	1244	1326	1443	1524	1643	1725	1744	1844	1843	1943	...	2044	2143	2248	2349	...
München Hbf ...... a.	0534	0634	0651	0734	0733	0835	0837	0937	1056	1137	1254	1337	1454	1535	1654	1737	1754	1854	1854	1955	...	2053	2154	2259	2400	...

c – Ⓒ only. d – Daily from Mühldorf. e – On Ⓐ Simbach d. 1259, Mühldorf a. 1332. f – On Ⓒ Mühldorf d. 1237, Simbach a. 1313.

895 MÜNCHEN - GARMISCH - INNSBRUCK

DB; ÖBB (2nd class only in Austria)

km																*ICE*					*ICE*				
				◧		◧			◧		◧		◧	◧		◧	**1003**	◧	◧	◧		**1207**	◧			◧
			Ⓐ	Ⓒ	Ⓐ	Ⓒ		Ⓒ		Ⓒ		Ⓒ					⑥					⑥h			Ⓐ	
			t	z	t	z		z		z		z					♥					♣			t	
0	**München** Hbf ...... d.	...	0451	0532	0631	0632	...	0713	0732	0814	0834	0914	0932	1032	...	1132	1213	1232	1332	1432	...	1511	1530	...	1610	1632
7	München Pasing ...... d.	...	0458	0538	0638	0638	...	0720	0738	0821	0842	0921	0938	1038	...	1138	|	1238	1338	1438	...	|	1537	...	1617	1638
40	Tutzing ...... d.	...	0525	0601	0701	0701	...	|	0801	|	0901	|	1001	1101	...	1201	1244	1301	1401	1501	...	|	1601	...	|	1700
54	Weilheim (Oberbay) ... d.	...	0545	0612	0712	0712	...	0749	0814	0849	0912	0949	1012	1112	...	1212	1259	1312	1412	1512	...	1549	1612	...	1649	1712
75	Murnau ...... d.	...	0604	0628	0729	0728	...	0801	0832	0901	0928	1001	1028	1128	...	1228	1314	1328	1428	1528	...	1610	1628	...	1702	1728
101	**Garmisch**-Partenk. ¶ a.	...	0630	0655	0759	0755	...	0823	0856	0924	0955	1024	1055	1155	...	1255	1343	1355	1455	1555	...	1634	1655	...	1724	1755
101	**Garmisch**-Partenk. ¶ d.	0632	0632	▬	▬	...	0802	0828	0906	0927	1002	1026	1102	▬	1202	1302	▬	1402	1502	▬	1602	1636	1702	...	1726	1802
118	**Mittenwald** ...... a.	0653	0653	...	...	...	0823	0854	0927	0954	1023	1053	1123	...	1223	1323	...	1423	1523	...	1623	1702	1723	...	1752	1823
118	**Mittenwald** 🏛 ...... d.	0655	0655	⚒	...	...	0826	...	0936	▬	1025	...	1136c	...	1225	1336c	...	1425	1536	...	1625	1714	1736c	...	...	1825
125	Scharnitz 🏛 ...... ⊡ d.	0703	0703	0733	0803	...	0833	...	0944	...	1033	...	1144c	1203a	1233	1344c	1403a	1433	1544	...	1633	|	1744c	1803a	...	1833
135	Seefeld in Tirol ...... ⊡ d.	0716	0716	0746	0816	...	0846	...	0956	1016	1046	...	1156c	1216	1246	1356c	1416	1446	1556	1616	1646	1746	1756c	1816	...	1846
160	**Innsbruck** Hbf ...... ⊡ a.	0753	0753	0823	0853	...	0923	...	...	1053	1123	...	...	1253	1323	...	1453	1523	...	1653	1723	1816	...	1853	...	1923

							ICE				
		◧		◧			**1205**				
	Ⓐ		Ⓐ				⑤g				
	t		t				♣				
München Hbf ...... d.	1713	1729	1813	1832	...	1932	2013	2032	2132	2232	2332
München Pasing ...... d.	1719	1735	1819	1838	...	1938	|	2039	2138	2238	2338
Tutzing ...... d.	|	1801	|	1901	...	2001	2043	2101	2201	2301	0001
Weilheim (Oberbay) ...... d.	1749	1813	1849	1912	...	2012	2058	2112	2212	2312	0012
Murnau ...... d.	1802	1828	1902	1928	...	2028	2112	2128	2228	2328	0028
Garmisch-Partenk. . ¶ a.	1824	1855	1924	1955	...	2055	2135	2155	2255	2355	0055
Garmisch-Partenk. . ¶ d.	1826	1902	1926	...	2002	2102	2137	2202	2302	0002	▬
Mittenwald ...... a.	1852	1923	1952	...	2023	2123	2204	2223	2323	0023	...
Mittenwald 🏛 ...... d.	...	1936	▬	...	2025	...	2211	...	...	...	...
Scharnitz 🏛 ...... ⊡ d.	...	1944	...	...	2033	...	|	...	...	...	2203
Seefeld in Tirol ...... ⊡ d.	...	1956	2016	...	2046	...	2232	...	...	...	2216
Innsbruck Hbf ...... ⊡ a.	...	...	2053	...	2123	...	2311	...	...	...	2253

											◧
	⚒	Ⓐ	Ⓐ	Ⓒ	Ⓐ	Ⓐ	Ⓒ	Ⓐ			
		t	t	z	t	t	z	t			
Innsbruck Hbf ... ⊡ d.	...	...	...	...	...	...	...	...	0638	0708	...
Seefeld in Tirol ... ⊡ d.	...	...	...	...	...	...	...	...	0715	0745	...
Scharnitz 🏛 ...... ⊡ d.	...	...	...	...	...	...	...	...	0728	0757	...
Mittenwald 🏛 ...... a.	...	...	...	...	...	...	...	...	0735	▬	...
Mittenwald ...... d.	...	0507	0530	0536	0603	0634	0634	*0658*	0736	...	0836
Garmisch-Partenk. ¶ a.	...	0528	0551	0557	0630	0700	0700	*0720*	0757	◧	0857e
Garmisch-Partenk. ¶ d.	0458	0535	0558	0607	0635	0702	0707	0732	...	0805e	0905e
Murnau ...... d.	0522	0554	0626	0632	0654	0728	0732	0757	...	0832	0932
Weilheim (Oberbay) d.	0541	0610	0645	0649	0711	0746	0749	0812	...	0849	0949
Tutzing ...... d.	0553	|	0700	0700	|	0800	0800	|	...	0900	1000
München Pasing .... a.	0615	0638	0718	0719	0742	0819	0819	0844	...	0919	1019
München Hbf ...... a.	0621	0646	0727	0726	0749	0827	0826	0850	...	0926	1026

			ICE				*ICE*		*ICE*																	
	◧		**1206**			◧	**1204**	◧	**1002**		◧		◧	◧		◧			◧			◧			◧	
			⑥k				⑦k		⑥						Ⓒ		Ⓒ			Ⓒ						
			♣				♣		♥						z		z			z						
Innsbruck Hbf ...... ⊡ d.	0838	*0908*	1018	1038	1108	...	1218	1238	...	1308	...	1438	...	*1508*	...	1638	...	1708	...	...	1838	...	1908	...	2038	...
Seefeld in Tirol ...... ⊡ d.	0915	1004	1104	1115	1145	1204c	1304	1315	...	1345	1404c	1515	...	1604	...	1715	...	1745	1804c	...	1915	...	1944	2004	2115	...
Scharnitz 🏛 ...... ⊡ d.	0928	1016	|	1128	1157a	1216c	|	1328	...	1357a	1416c	1528	...	1616	...	1728	...	1757a	1816c	...	1928	...	...	2016	2128	...
Mittenwald 🏛 ...... a.	0935	1025	1122	1135	▬	1225c	1322	1335	...	...	1425c	1535	...	1625	...	1735	...	...	1825c	...	1935	...	...	2025	2135	...
Mittenwald ...... d.	0936	1036	1127	1136	...	1236	1326	1336	...	...	1436	1536	...	1634	1704	1736	1804	...	1836	1904	1936	...	...	2036	2136	2236
Garmisch-Partenk. . ¶ a.	1000	1057	1148	1157	◧	1300	1348	1400	...	...	1500	1557	...	1656	1730	1800	1830	...	1900	1930	1957	...	...	2057	2200	2257
Garmisch-Partenk. . ¶ d.	1005e	1107	1154	...	1207	1307	1359	1407	1415	...	1507	...	1605	1705	1735	1805	1835	...	1905	1935	...	2005	...	2107	2207	2307
Murnau ...... d.	1032	1132	1216	...	1231	1332	1427	1432	1444	...	1532	...	1632	1732	1758	1832	1858	...	1932	1958	...	2032	...	2132	2232	2332
Weilheim (Oberbay) .... d.	1049	1149	1235	...	1249	1349	1442	1449	1500	...	1549	...	1649	1749	1812	1849	1912	...	1949	2012	...	2049	...	2149	2249	2349
Tutzing ...... d.	1100	1200	1251	...	1300	1400	1453	1500	|	...	1600	...	1700	1800	|	1900	|	...	2000	|	...	2100	...	2200	2300	0000
München Pasing ...... a.	1119	1219	|	...	1319	1419	|	1519	|	...	1619	...	1719	1819	1841	1919	1941	...	2019	2042	...	2119	...	2219	2319	0019
München Hbf ...... a.	1126	1226	1334	...	1326	1426	1536	1526	1548	...	1626	...	1726	1826	1848	1926	1948	...	2026	2050	...	2126	...	2226	2326	0026

a – ①–⑤ (not June 9, 19, Aug. 15, Dec. 8).
c – ⑥⑦ (also June 9, 19, Aug. 15, Dec. 8).
e – 2–3 minutes later on Ⓐ (not June 19, Aug. 15).
f – 1507 from Oct. 11.
g – Not July 11 - Aug. 29, Oct. 3.
h – Also Oct. 3, Nov. 15; not July 12 - Aug. 30. Departs München 1507 from Oct. 11.
k – Not July 12 - Aug. 31.
t – Not June 19, Aug. 15.
z – Also June 19, Aug. 15.

♥ – [12] ✕ Garmisch - Nürnberg - Berlin and v.v. (Table **850**).
♣ – [12] ✕ Hamburg - Hannover - München - Innsbruck and v.v. (Table **900**).
◧ – Conveys [12] to / from stations in Table **888**.
⊡ – Other local trains Scharnitz - Innsbruck and v.v.:
From Scharnitz at 0633, 0903, 1103 Ⓑ, 1303 ⚒, 1503, 1703, 1903, 2103, 2303 and 0003.
From Innsbruck at 0808, 1008 Ⓑ, 1208 ⚒, 1408, 1608, 1808, 2008, 2108, 2208 and 2308.
¶ – Bayerische Zugspitzbahn (rack railway) operates Garmisch - Zugspitzplatt: Departures at 0815 and hourly until 1415, returning from Zugspitzplatt at 0930 and hourly until 1630.

897 MURNAU - OBERAMMERGAU

RB services

km		Ⓐt	⑥v	Ⓐt												
0	**Murnau** ...... d.	0505	0548	0558	0648	0742	0842	0942	1042	1142	1234	1334	1442	and	2242	2334
12	Bad Kohlgrub ...... d.	0523	0606	0617	0706	0800	0900	1000	1100	1200	1253	1353	1500	hourly	2300	2353
24	**Oberammergau** .... ♥ a.	0541	0625	0635	0725	0819	0919	1019	1119	1219	1312	1412	1519	until	2319	0012

	Ⓐt	⑥v	Ⓐt												
Oberammergau ...... ♥ d.	0500	0543	0553	0643	0738	0838	0938	1038	1138	1229	1329	1438	and	2238	2329
Bad Kohlgrub ...... d.	0522	0605	0616	0705	0800	0900	1000	1100	1200	1252	1352	1500	hourly	2300	2352
Murnau ...... a.	0540	0623	0634	0724	0819	0919	1019	1119	1219	1311	1411	1519	until	2319	0011

t – Not Aug. 15.
v – Not Nov. 1.

♥ – Trains call at Unterammergau (*km 20*) 4–5 minutes from Oberammergau.

NÜRNBERG and FRANKFURT - HAMBURG 900

km		ICE 1080		NJ 470 ♦	ICE 1678 ①–⑤ T✕		NJ 40420 Ⓡ B	NJ 490 Ⓡ ♦		ICE 1088 ①–⑥ K✕	IC 2230 ①–⑥ M🍷	ICE 1676 ①–⑤ T✕	ICE 1676 ①–⑥ T✕	ICE 672 Y✕	ICE 888 ①–⑤ ✕		ICE 774 ✕	ICE 684 ✕	ICE 634 ①–⑥ ✕	ICE 1674 ①–⑥ ✕	ICE 474 K✕	ICE 886 ✕	ICE 772 ✕
	Basel SBB **910** 🏛 d.	...	...	2213y	...	...	...	...	...	...	...	...	...	...	...	...	...	...	...	...	0508‡	...	...
	Karlsruhe Hbf **910** d.	...	...	0019	...	...	...	...	...	...	...	...	...	...	...	...	...	...	...	...	0651	...	...
	Stuttgart Hbf **910** d.	...	...	|	...	...	...	...	...	...	...	...	...	...	...	...	0502	...	...	...	|	...	0724
	Mannheim Hbf **910** d.	...	...	|	...	...	...	...	...	...	...	...	...	...	...	...	0603	...	...	...	0717	...	0805
	Frankfurt Flughafen Fernbf ✈ **910** d.	...	...	|	...	...	...	...	...	...	...	...	...	0532	...	...	0641	...	...	...	|	...	0841
	Frankfurt (Main) Hbf **850 901 902** d.	...	...	0213•	...	...	...	...	...	0505	...	...	...	0550	...	...	0658	...	...	0650	0758	...	0858
	Hanau Hbf **850 901 902** d.	...	...	0230	...	...	...	...	...	0520	...	...	...	0607	...	...	|	...	...	|	|	...	|
	München Hbf **904 905** d.	2300	...	|	...	...	2252	...	...	|	...	...	...	|	0412	...	|	0514	0514	|	|	0612	|
	Augsburg Hbf **905** d.	|	...	|	...	...	2325	...	...	|	...	...	...	|	|	...	|	|	|	◧	|	|	|
0	**Nürnberg** Hbf **905 920 921** d.	0017	...	|	...	...	0142	0142	...	|	...	...	...	|	0532	...	|	0632	0632	|	|	0733	|
102	**Würzburg** Hbf **920 921** d.	0118	...	|	...	...	0236	0236	...	|	...	...	...	|	0627	...	|	0729	0729	|	|	0827	|
195	Fulda **850 901 902** d.	|	...	|	...	...	|	|	...	0605	...	...	...	0649	0703	...	|	0803	0803	|	|	0903	|
285	**Kassel** Wilhelmshöhe **901 902** d.	|	...	|	...	...	0544	0544	...	0637	...	0656	...	0725	0736	...	0823	0836	0836	0856	0922	0936	1023
330	Göttingen **902 903** d.	0405	...	0433	...	...	0609	0609	...	0656	...	0717	...	0744	0756	...	0841	0856	0856	0917	0941	0956	1041
430	**Hannover** Hbf **903** a.	0506	...	0529	...	...	0650	0650	...	0732	...	0756	...	0819	0832	...	0917	0932	0932	0956	1017	1032	1117
430	**Hannover** Hbf **903** d.	0510	...	0532	0554	...	0705	0705	...	0736	...	0759	0759	0822	0836	...	0920	0936	0945	0959	1020	1036	1120
	Bremen Hbf **813** a.	|	...	0642	|	...	|	|	...	|	...	|	|	|	|	...	|	|	1045	|	|	|	|
471	Celle **903** d.	0531	...	|	0617	...	|	|	...	|	...	0818	0818	|	|	...	|	|	...	1019	|	|	|
523	Uelzen **903** d.	0555	...	|	0642	...	|	|	...	|	0832	0842	0842	|	|	...	|	|	...	1043	|	|	|
559	Lüneburg **903** d.	0613	...	|	0659	...	|	|	...	|	0851	0902	0902	|	|	...	|	|	...	1059	|	1127	|
596	**Hamburg** Harburg **903** a.	0629	...	0736	0716	...	0830	0830	...	0843	0913	0919	0919	|	0941	...	|	1041	...	1116	|	1144	|
608	**Hamburg** Hbf **903** a.	0642	...	0753	0730	...	0847	0847	...	0856	0926	0932	0932	0936	0953	...	1036	1055	...	1129	1136	1158	1236
615	**Hamburg** Altona a.	...	...	0809	...	...	0906	0905	...	...	0942	...	...	...	...	...	...	...	...	1145	...	...	...

	ICE 682 L✕		ICE 1672 ✕♦	ICE 78 Z✕	ICE 882 K✕	ICE 1586 Ⓑ ✕	ICE 770 ✕	ICE 680 ✕	ICE 630 ✕		IC 2374 ♣	ICE 76 Z✕	ICE 880 ✕	ICE 1084 ⑤⑥ ✕	ICE 1224 ✕♦	ICE 578 ✕	ICE 588 ✕	ICE 538 ✕		ICE 1578 ①–④ T✕	ICE 1578 ⑤–⑦ q T✕	ICE 74 ✕♦	ICE 788 ✕
Basel SBB **910** 🏛 d.	...	...	...	0706	...	...	...	...	...	...	...	0906	...	...	...	...	...	...	...			1106	...
Karlsruhe Hbf **910** d.	...	...	0702h	0851	...	...	...	...	...	...	...	1051	...	...	...	...	...	...	...	...	1110	1251	...
Stuttgart Hbf **910** d.	...	...	|	|	...	...	0923	...	...	...	0857	|	...	1014	...	1123	...	...	...	1103	|	|	...
Mannheim Hbf **910** d.	...	...	|	0917	...	...	1004	...	...	...	|	1117	...	|	...	1203	...	...	...	|	|	1317	...
Frankfurt Flughafen Fernbf ✈ **910** d.	...	...	|	|	...	...	1041	...	...	...	|	|	...	|	...	1241	...	...	...	|	|	|	...
Frankfurt (Main) Hbf **850 901 902** d.	...	...	0851	0958	...	...	1058	...	...	...	1051	1158	...	1215	...	1258	...	...	...	1251	1251	1358	...
Hanau Hbf **850 901 902** d.	...	...	|	|	...	...	|	...	...	...	|	|	...	1241	...	|	...	...	...	|	|	|	...
München Hbf **904 905** d.	0717	...	|	|	0817	0814	|	0917	0917	...	|	|	1020	|	1048	|	1117	1117	...	|	|	|	1220
Augsburg Hbf **905** d.	|	...	◧	|	|	0847	|	|	|	...	◧	|	|	|	|	|	|	|	...	◧	◧	|	|
Nürnberg Hbf **905 920 921** d.	0832	...	|	|	0933	|	|	1033	1033	...	|	|	1133	|	1157	|	1233	1233	...	|	|	|	1333
Würzburg Hbf **920 921** d.	0927	...	|	|	1027	1039	|	1127	1127	...	|	|	1227	|	1300t	|	1327	1327	...	|	|	|	1427
Fulda **850 901 902** d.	1003	...	|	|	1103	1123	|	1203	1203	...	|	|	1303	1325	1333	|	1403	1403	...	|	|	|	1503
Kassel Wilhelmshöhe **901 902** d.	1036	...	1056	1122	1136	1157	1223	1236	1236	...	1256	1322	1336	1356	1401	1423	1436	1436	...	1456	1456	1523	1536
Göttingen **902 903** d.	1056	...	1117	1141	1156	1219	1241	1256	1256	...	1317	1341	1356	1422	...	1441	1456	1456	...	1517	1517	1542	1556
Hannover Hbf **903** a.	1132	...	1156	1217	1232	1258	1317	1332	1332	...	1356	1417	1432	1456	...	1517	1532	1532	...	1556	1556	1617	1632
Hannover Hbf **903** d.	1136	...	1159	1220	1236	1301	1320	1336	1345	...	1359	1420	1436	1459	...	1520	1536	1545	...	1559	1559	1620	1636
Bremen Hbf **813** a.	|	...	|	|	|	|	|	|	1445	...	|	|	|	|	...	|	|	1645	...	|	|	|	|
Celle **903** d.	|	...	1218	|	|	1319	|	|	...	...	1418	|	|	1519	...	|	|	...	...	1618	1618	|	|
Uelzen **903** d.	|	...	1242	|	|	1342	|	|	...	...	1442	|	|	1543	...	|	|	...	...	1642	1642	|	|
Lüneburg **903** d.	|	...	1259	|	|	1358	|	|	...	...	1459	|	|	|	...	|	|	...	...	1702	1702	|	|
Hamburg Harburg **903** a.	1241	...	1316	|	1341	1416	|	1441	...	...	1517	|	1540	1616	...	|	1641	...	...	1719	1719	|	1740
Hamburg Hbf **903** a.	1254	...	1330	1336	1354	1429	1436	1455	...	...	1530	1536	1555	1628	...	1636	1655	...	...	1732	1732	1735	1753
Hamburg Altona a.	...	...	1344e	...	...	1444	...	...	...	...	...	...	...	1643	...	...	...	...	...	...	...	...	...

	IC 2082 D	ICE 576 ✕	ICE 586 ✕	ICE 536 ✕		ICE 1576 V ✕	ICE 1576 U ✕	ICE 72 ✕	ICE 786 ✕	ICE 1206 ⑥ R✕	ICE 1284 ⑤⑦ S✕	ICE 1594 Ⓑ ✕	ICE 1594 ⑦–④ ✕	ICE 1094 K✕	ICE 1594 ⑦–④ ✕	ICE 584 L✕	ICE 776 N✕	ICE 1574 J ✕	ICE 1574 H ✕	ICE 70 ✕♦	ICE 620 ✕	ICE 90 ✕♦	
Basel SBB **910** 🏛 d.	...	...	...	...	...	...	...	1306	...	...	...	...	...	...	...	...	...	...	...	1506	...	...	...
Karlsruhe Hbf **910** d.	...	...	...	...	...	1310	1310	1451	...	...	...	...	...	...	...	...	...	1510	1510	1651	...	...	...
Stuttgart Hbf **910** d.	...	1323	...	...	...	|	|	|	...	...	...	...	...	1523	...	...	...	|	|	|	...	...	...
Mannheim Hbf **910** d.	...	1403	...	...	...	|	|	1517	...	...	...	...	...	1604	...	...	...	|	|	1717	...	...	...
Frankfurt Flughafen Fernbf ✈ **910** d.	...	1441	...	...	...	|	|	|	...	...	...	...	...	1641	...	...	...	|	|	|	...	...	...
Frankfurt (Main) Hbf **850 901 902** d.	...	1458	...	...	...	1448	1448	1558	...	...	...	1615	1615	1658	...	...	1701	1648	1648	1758	...	...	...
Hanau Hbf **850 901 902** d.	...	|	...	...	...	|	|	|	...	...	...	1639	1639	|	...	...	1733	|	|	|	...	...	...
München Hbf **904 905** d.	1117o	|	1317	1317	...	|	|	|	1420	1356	1356	|	|	|	...	1517	|	|	|	|	1550	...	...
Augsburg Hbf **905** d.	1230	|	|	|	...	◧	◧	|	|	1425	1425	|	|	|	...	|	|	◧	◧	|	|	...	...
Nürnberg Hbf **905 920 921** d.	|	|	1434	1434	...	|	|	|	1534	|	|	|	|	|	...	1633	|	|	|	|	1658	1731	...
Würzburg Hbf **920 921** d.	1440	|	1527	1527	...	|	|	|	1628	1634	1633	|	|	|	...	1727	|	|	|	|	1752	1826	...
Fulda **850 901 902** d.	1518	|	1603	1603	...	|	|	|	1703	1720	1719	1727	1727	|	...	1803	1820	|	|	|	...	1904	...
Kassel Wilhelmshöhe **901 902** d.	1555	1623	1636	1636	...	1656	1656	1722	1736	1758	1758	1801	1801	|	...	1836	1852	1857	1857	1922	...	1938	...
Göttingen **902 903** d.	1615	1641	1656	1656	...	1718	1718	1741	1756	1820	1820	1823	1823	|	...	1856	1912	1917	1917	1941	...	1958	...
Hannover Hbf **903** a.	1654	1717	1732	1732	...	1756	1756	1817	1832	1858	1858	1902	1902	1912	←	1932	1948	1956	1956	2017	...	2033	...
Hannover Hbf **903** d.	1657	1720	1736	1745	...	1759	1759	1820	1836	1901	1901	...	1918	1915	1918	1936	1951	1959	1959	2020	...	2036	...
Bremen Hbf **813** a.	|	|	|	1845	...	|	|	|	|	|	|	...	→	|	|	|	2047	|	|	|	...	|	...
Celle **903** d.	1717	|	|	...	...	1817	1817	|	|	1920	1921	...	...	|	1938	|	...	2018	2018	|	...	|	...
Uelzen **903** d.	1743	|	|	...	...	1842	1842	|	|	1943	1943	...	...	|	|	|	...	2042	2042	|	...	|	...
Lüneburg **903** d.	1759	|	|	...	...	1858	1858	|	|	2008j	2008j	...	...	|	2015	2028	...	2058	2058	|	...	|	...
Hamburg Harburg **903** a.	1816	|	1841	...	...	1916	1916	|	1941	2025	2025	...	...	|	2033	2044	...	2116	2116	2126	...	2141	...
Hamburg Hbf **903** a.	1830	1836	1856	...	...	1929	1929	1936	1954	2038	2038	...	...	2030	2047	2058	...	2129	2130	2139	...	2155	...
Hamburg Altona a.	1847	...	...	...	...	1944	...	...	...	2054	2053	...	...	...	2103	...	...	2150	...	...	...	2211	...

♦ – **NOTES** (LISTED BY TRAIN NUMBER)

70 – [12] ✕ Chur - Zürich - Basel - Hamburg.
74 – [12] ✕ Zürich - Basel - Hamburg - Kiel.
90 – DONAUWALZER – [12] ✕ Wien - Linz - Passau - Regensburg - Hamburg.
470 – 🛏 1, 2 cl. and ▬ 2 cl. Zürich (d. 1934 ⑦ / 2059 ①–⑥) - Basel - Hamburg. Also conveys [2] (*IC* **60470**).
490 – 🛏 1, 2 cl., ▬ 2 cl. (1, 4 berth) and [2] (*ÖBB nightjet* new generation) Wien - Passau 🏛 - Hamburg.
1224 – [12] ✕ München - Paderborn - Hamm - Oberhausen.
1672 – [12] ✕ (Karlsruhe ①–⑥ -) Frankfurt - Hamburg (- Rostock - Stralsund - Ostseebad Binz until Aug. 1).

B – 🛏 1, 2 cl., ▬ 2 cl. (1, 4 berth) and [2] (*ÖBB nightjet* new generation) Innsbruck - Hamburg (Table **53**).
D – June 7 - Oct. 9. [12] Berchtesgaden - München Ost - Hamburg; [12] Oberstdorf (**2084**) - Augsburg (**2082**) - Hamburg.
H – ⑦ to July 27. To Rostock (Table **830**).
J – ①–⑥ (daily from July 28).
K – To Kiel (Table **820**).
L – To Lübeck on dates in Table **825**.
M – From Magdeburg (Table **841**). Arrives Hamburg Hbf 0929 on ⑥.
N – To Oldenburg (Table **813**).
R – From Innsbruck via Garmisch (Table **895**).
S – From Schwarzach-St Veit via Wörgl on ⑦ (Table **960**).
T – To Stralsund via Rostock on dates in Table **830**.
U – Ⓑ to Aug. 1. To Rostock (Table **830**), also Stralsund on ⑦.
V – ⑥ (daily from Aug. 2).
Y – From Wiesbaden Hbf (d. 0500) and Mainz Hbf (d. 0512).
Z – From Zürich (Table **510**).

e – From Aug. 2.
h – ①–⑥.
j – Arrives 1958.
o – München **Ost**.
q – From Konstanz on dates in Table **916**.
t – Arrives 1252.
y – 2058 on ⑦.

• – Frankfurt (Main) **Süd**.
‡ – Basel **Badischer Bahnhof**.
♣ – WATTENMEER – To Westerland (Table **821**).
◧ – Via Gießen (Table **806**).

900 NÜRNBERG and FRANKFURT - HAMBURG

	ICE 1204 ⑦ R✕	ICE 1204 ①–⑤ ✕	ICE 572 ✕	ICE 582 ✕	ICE 532 M✕		ICE 1572 ⑤–⑦ ✕	ICE 1572 ✕		ICE 376 Ⓑ ✕♦	ICE 782 ✕		ICE 570 ⑦ ✕	ICE 580 Ⓑ ✕	ICE 580 ⑦ ✕	ICE 292 ⑦ ✕♦	ICE 580 ⑦	ICE 272 ⑥ Z✕	ICE 272 ①–⑤ Z✕		ICE 780 ⑦ ✕		ICE 674 ♦
Basel SBB **910** 🏛 d.	...	...	...	...	...	...	...	...	...	1707	...	...	...	...	...	1813	...	1813	1813	...	...	...	...
Karlsruhe Hbf **910** d.	...	...	...	...	...	...	...	...	...	1851	...	...	...	...	...	2000	...	2000	2000	...	...	...	...
Stuttgart Hbf **910** d.	...	...	1723	...	...	...	1654	1654	...	|	...	...	1923	...	...	|	...	|	|	...	...	...	...
Mannheim Hbf **910** d.	...	...	1803	...	...	...	|	|	...	1917	...	...	2004	...	...	2032	...	2032	2032	...	...	...	...
Frankfurt Flughafen Fernbf ✈ **910** d.	...	...	1841	...	...	...	|	|	...	|	...	...	2041	...	...	|	...	|	|	...	...	...	0004*
Frankfurt (Main) Hbf **850 901 902** d.	...	...	1858	...	...	...	1848	1848	...	1958	...	...	2058	...	...	2114	...	2114	2114	...	...	...	2335
Hanau Hbf **850 901 902** d.	...	...	1913	...	...	...	|	|	...	|	...	...	2113	...	...	2129	...	2129	2129	...	...	...	0030
München Hbf **904 905** d.	1552	1618	|	1716	1716	...	|	|	...	|	1818	...	|	1917	1917	|	...	|	|	...	2017	...	|
Augsburg Hbf **905** d.	1624	|	|	|	|	...	◧	◧	...	|	|	...	|	|	|	|	...	|	|	...	|	...	|
Nürnberg Hbf **905 920 921** d.	|	1736	|	1833	1833	...	|	|	...	|	1934	...	|	2032	2032	|	...	|	|	...	2134	...	|
Würzburg Hbf **920 921** d.	1833	1833	|	1927	1927	...	|	|	...	|	2027	...	|	2127	2127	|	...	|	|	...	2228	...	|
Fulda **850 901 902** d.	1921	1921	|	2003	2003	...	|	|	...	|	2103	...	|	2204	2204	2214	...	2214	2214	...	2303	...	0116
Kassel Wilhelmshöhe **901 902** d.	1956	1956	2025	2036	2036	...	2056	2056	...	2122	2136	...	2225	2234	2236	2245	←	2245	2245	...	2334	...	|
Göttingen **902 903** d.	2016	2016	2046	2056	2056	...	2117	2117	...	2141	2156	...	2245	...	2255	2303	2307	2306	2306	...	...	...	0245
Hannover Hbf **903** a.	2053	2053	2119	2132	2132	...	2156	2156	...	2217	2231	...	2318	...	→	...	2341	2341	0002	...	...	...	0352
Hannover Hbf **903** d.	2058	2058	2122	2136	2145	...	2159	...	...	2220	2236	...	2321	...	...	...	2345	2344	0005	...	...	...	...
Bremen Hbf **813** a.	|	|	|	|	2259	...	|	...	...	|	|	...	|	...	...	...	|	|	|	...	...	...	...
Celle **903** d.	2118	2118	|	|	...	...	2218	...	...	|	2256	...	|	...	...	...	0005	|	0026	...	...	...	...
Uelzen **903** d.	2143	2143	|	|	...	...	2242	...	...	|	2317	...	|	...	...	...	0026	0025	0050	...	...	...	...
Lüneburg **903** d.	2200	2200	2214	|	...	...	2259	...	...	|	2335	...	0014	...	...	...	0044	0041	0106	...	...	...	...
Hamburg Harburg **903** a.	2216	2216	2232	2241	...	...	2316	...	...	|	2351	...	0030	...	...	...	0100	0100	0122	...	...	...	...
Hamburg Hbf **903** a.	2229	2229	2246	2255	...	...	2329	...	...	2339	0005	...	0044	...	...	...	0113	0113	0136	...	...	...	...
Hamburg Altona a.	2247	2247	...	...	...	...	2346	...	...	2359	...	...	...	...	...	...	...	...	...	...	...	...	...

	ICE 271 ♦		ICE 591 ①–⑥ N✕	ICE 781 ① ✕	ICE 781 ①–⑥ ✕		ICE 1573 ①–⑤ ✕		ICE 581 ①–⑥ ✕	ICE 571 ✕	ICE 751 J ✕	ICE 1097 ①–⑤ ✕	ICE 783 ①–⑤ ✕	ICE 783 ⑥⑦ ✕		ICE 71 ✕	ICE 1575 ①–⑥ ✕	ICE 533 ①–⑥ M✕	ICE 583 ✕		ICE 573 K✕	IC 2083 D	
Hamburg Altona d.	...	...	0303	...	...	...	...	...	...	...	0503	0550	...	...	...	...	0608	...	...	...	...	0712	...
Hamburg Hbf **903** d.	...	...	0320	0349	...	...	...	...	0454	0514	0523	0606	0554	0554	...	0618	0624	...	0701	...	0724	0729	...
Hamburg Harburg **903** d.	...	...	0332	|	...	...	...	...	0506	0527	0535	|	0606	0606	...	0630	0636	...	0713	...	|	0741	...
Lüneburg **903** d.	...	...	0351	0421	...	...	...	...	0525	0546	0554	|	0625	0625	...	0648	0655	...	|	...	|	0801	...
Uelzen **903** d.	...	...	0408	0438	...	...	...	...	0542	|	0613	|	|	0641	...	|	0715	...	|	...	|	0816	...
Celle **903** d.	...	...	0437	0501	...	...	...	...	0604	|	0637	|	|	0704	...	|	0738	...	|	...	|	0839	...
Bremen Hbf **813** d.	...	...	|	|	...	...	...	...	|	|	|	|	|	|	...	|	|	0715	|	...	|	|	...
Hannover Hbf **903** a.	...	...	0456	0520	...	...	...	...	0623	0638	0657	0719	0723	0723	...	0738	0758	0814	0822	...	0838	0859	...
Hannover Hbf **903** d.	0210	...	0519	0526	...	...	0557	...	0626	0641	▽	0722	0726	0726	...	0741	0801	0826	0826	...	0841	0903	...
Göttingen **902 903** d.	0308	...	0554	0602	...	...	0636	...	0702	0716	...	|	0802	0802	...	0816	0839	0902	0902	...	0916	0944	...
Kassel Wilhelmshöhe **901 902** d.	|	...	0615	0623	0623	...	0701	...	0723	0737	...	|	0823	0823	...	0837	0903	0924	0924	...	0937	1007	...
Fulda **850 901 902** d.	0433	...	0646	0656	0656	...	|	...	0756	|	...	|	0856	0856	...	|	|	0956	0956	...	|	1042	...
Würzburg Hbf **920 921** d.	|	...	|	0729	0729	...	|	...	0829	|	...	|	0929	0929	...	|	|	1030	1030	...	|	1123	...
Nürnberg Hbf **905 920 921** a.	|	...	|	0824	0824	...	◧	...	0925	|	...	|	1023	1023	...	|	◧	1125	1125	...	|	|	...
Augsburg Hbf **905** a.	|	...	|	|	|	...	|	...	|	|	...	|	|	|	...	|	|	|	|	...	|	1330	...
München Hbf **904 905** a.	|	...	|	0943	0943	...	|	...	1045	|	...	|	1144	1144	...	|	|	1240	1240	...	|	1411o	...
Hanau Hbf **850 901 902** d.	0521	...	0730	...	...	...	|	...	...	|	...	|	...	...	...	|	|	...	...	...	|	...	...
Frankfurt (Main) Hbf **850 901 902** a.	0537	...	0744	...	...	...	0908	...	...	0900	...	0932	...	...	...	1000	1108	...	...	...	1100	...	...
Frankfurt Flughafen Fernbf ✈ **910** a.	|	...	|	...	...	...	|	...	...	0918	...	0951	...	...	...	|	|	...	...	...	1118	...	...
Mannheim Hbf **910** a.	0625	...	0827	...	...	...	|	...	...	0956	...	...	...	...	...	1044	|	...	...	...	1156	...	...
Stuttgart Hbf **910** a.	|	...	0908	...	...	...	|	...	...	1038	...	...	...	...	...	|	|	...	...	...	1238	...	...
Karlsruhe Hbf **910** a.	0656	...	...	...	...	...	1051	...	...	...	...	...	...	...	...	1109	1251	...	...	...	...	...	...
Basel SBB **910** a.	0848	...	...	...	...	...	...	...	...	...	...	...	...	...	...	1310	...	...	...	...	...	...	...

	ICE 91 ✕♦	ICE 621 ✕	ICE 73 ✕♦	ICE 1577 T ✕	ICE 1577 U ✕	ICE 1207 ⑥ R✕		ICE 535 M✕	ICE 585 L✕	ICE 575 ✕	ICE 1083 ⑥ ✕	ICE 1223 ✕♦	ICE 1083 ⑥ ✕	ICE 787 ✕	ICE 75 ✕♦	ICE 1579 ✕♦	ICE 537 M✕	ICE 587 ✕	ICE 577 ✕	ICE 1285 Ⓑ S✕	ICE 1683 Ⓑ ✕	ICE 1683 ⑥ E✕	ICE 789 ✕
Hamburg Altona d.	0745	...	...	...	0809	0809	...	...	...	...	...	...	...	...	...	1013t	...	...	...	1111	1111	1111t	...
Hamburg Hbf **903** d.	0802	...	0824	0828	0828	0828	...	...	0901	0924	0929	...	...	1001	1024	1028	...	1101	1124	1128	1128	1128	1201
Hamburg Harburg **903** d.	0813	...	|	0841	0841	0841	...	...	0914	|	|	...	...	1013	|	1041	...	1113	|	|	|	|	1213
Lüneburg **903** d.	|	...	|	0859	0859	0859	...	...	|	|	|	...	...	|	|	1059	...	|	|	1155	1155	1155	|
Uelzen **903** d.	|	...	|	0916	0916	0916	...	...	|	|	|	...	...	|	|	1115	...	|	|	|	|	|	|
Celle **903** d.	|	...	|	0938	0938	0938	...	...	|	|	|	...	...	|	|	1138	...	|	|	|	|	|	|
Bremen Hbf **813** d.	|	...	|	|	|	|	...	0915	|	|	|	...	...	|	|	|	1115	|	|	|	|	|	|
Hannover Hbf **903** a.	0921	...	0938	0958	0958	0958	...	1014	1022	1038	1046	...	...	1120	1138	1158	1214	1222	1238	1246	1246	1246	1320
Hannover Hbf **903** d.	0926	...	0941	1001	1001	1001	...	1026	1026	1041	1052	...	...	1126	1141	1201	1226	1226	1241	1255	1255	1255	1326
Göttingen **902 903** d.	1003	...	1016	1037	1037	1037	...	1102	1102	1116	1127	...	←	1202	1216	1239	1302	1302	1316	1333	1333	1333	1402
Kassel Wilhelmshöhe **901 902** d.	1024	...	1037	1104	1104	1107	...	1123	1123	1137	1145	1158	1204	1223	1237	1303	1323	1323	1337	1354	1354	1354	1423
Fulda **850 901 902** d.	1057	...	|	|	|	1139	...	1156	1156	|	→	1228	1235	1256	|	|	1356	1356	|	1431	1435	1435	1456
Würzburg Hbf **920 921** d.	1133	1203	|	|	|	1216	...	1230	1230	|	...	1312j	|	1329	|	|	1430	1430	|	1512	|	|	1529
Nürnberg Hbf **905 920 921** a.	1228	1258	|	◧	◧	|	...	1325	1325	|	...	1404	|	1424	|	◧	1525	1525	|	|	|	|	1624
Augsburg Hbf **905** a.	...	|	|	|	|	1407	...	|	|	|	...	|	|	|	|	|	|	|	|	1731	|	|	|
München Hbf **904 905** a.	...	1406	|	|	|	1449	...	1441	1441	|	...	1512	|	1544	|	|	1641	1641	|	1803	|	|	1745
Hanau Hbf **850 901 902** d.	...	...	|	|	|	...	...	...	...	|	...	...	1319	...	|	|	...	...	|	...	1516	1516	...
Frankfurt (Main) Hbf **850 901 902** a.	...	...	1200	1308	1308	...	...	...	...	1300	...	...	1340	...	1400	1508	...	...	1500	...	1543	1543	...
Frankfurt Flughafen Fernbf ✈ **910** a.	...	...	|	|	|	...	...	...	...	1318	...	...	...	...	|	|	...	...	1518	...	...	...	...
Mannheim Hbf **910** a.	...	...	1244	|	|	...	...	...	...	1356	...	...	...	...	1444	|	...	...	1556	...	...	...	...
Stuttgart Hbf **910** a.	...	...	|	1503	1503	...	...	...	...	1438	...	...	...	...	|	|	...	...	1638	...	...	...	...
Karlsruhe Hbf **910** a.	...	...	1309	...	...	...	...	...	...	...	...	...	...	...	1509	1651	...	...	...	...	...	...	...
Basel SBB **910** a.	...	...	1455	...	...	...	...	...	...	...	...	...	...	...	1655	...	...	...	...	...	...	...	...

♦ – **NOTES** (LISTED BY TRAIN NUMBER)

73 – 🚃12 ✕ (Kiel ①–⑤ -) Hamburg - Basel - Zürich.
75 – 🚃12 ✕ (Kiel ⑥⑦ -) Hamburg - Basel - Zürich.
91 – DONAUWALZER – 🚃12 ✕ Hamburg - Regensburg - Passau - Linz - Wien.
271 – 🚃12 Berlin - Hannover - Basel - Zürich - Chur.
292 – 🚃12 ✕ Zürich - Basel - Berlin.
376 – 🚃12 ✕ Interlaken - Bern - Basel - Hamburg.
674 – 🚃12 Frankfurt - Hannover - Berlin.
1223 – On ①–⑤: 🚃12 ✕ Köln - Hamm - Paderborn - Kassel - München.
On ⑥⑦: 🚃12 ✕ (Oberhausen to Aug. 31 -) Dortmund - Hamm - Paderborn - Kassel - München.
1579 – 🚃12 ✕ (Greifswald - Stralsund ⑥ to July 26 -) Hamburg - Frankfurt - Karlsruhe (- Konstanz ⑤⑥).

D – June 7 - Oct. 8. 🚃12 Hamburg - München Ost - Berchtesgaden; 🚃12 Hamburg - Augsburg (**2085**) - Oberstdorf.
E – From Rostock until July 26 (Table **830**).
J – ①–⑤ (daily from July 28).
K – From Kiel on ①–⑥ (Table **820**).
L – From Lübeck (Table **825**).
M – To/from Oldenburg on dates in Table **813**.

N – To München (Table **910**).
R – From/to Innsbruck via Garmisch (Table **895**).
S – Continues to Schwarzach via Wörgl on ⑤ (Table **960**). From Oct. 10 Würzburg d. 1507, Nürnberg a. 1609, München a. 1759, not calling at Augsburg.
T – ①–⑤ to Aug. 1. From Stralsund via Rostock (Table **830**).
U – ⑥⑦ (daily from Aug. 2).
Z – From Zürich (Table **510**).

j – Arrives 1300.
o – München **Ost**.
t – From Aug. 2.

***** – Calls after Frankfurt (Main) Hbf.
▽ – Continues to Berlin (Table **810**).
◧ – Via Gießen (Table **806**).

HAMBURG - FRANKFURT and NÜRNBERG — 900

	ICE 77	ICE 1671		ICE 689	ICE 579	ICE 1205	ICE 1597		ICE 881	ICE 79	ICE 1091	IC 2375		ICE 631	ICE 681	ICE 771	ICE 883	ICE 1171	ICE 1675	IC 2233	ICE 803	ICE 633	ICE 683
						Ⓑ	⑦				⑤⑦												
	L✕	O✕		✕	✕	S✕	✕		✕	Z✕	R✕	W		✕	✕	✕	✕	K✕	Y✕	M🍸	U✕	✕	✕
Hamburg Altona d.	...	1213t	...	...	...	1311	1311	...	...	...	...	...	...	...	...	...	...	...	1610t	1623	1616	...	...
Hamburg Hbf 903 d.	1224	1228	...	1301	1324	1328	1328	...	1401	1424	...	1428	...	...	1501	1524	1601	1624	1628	1638	1638	...	1701
Hamburg Harburg 903 d.	|	1240	...	1313	|	1339	1339	...	1413	|	...	1440	...	...	1513	|	1612	|	1640	1653	1654	...	1712
Lüneburg 903 d.	|	1259	...	|	|	1359	1359	...	1429	|	...	1458	...	...	|	|	|	|	1659	1712	1714	...	|
Uelzen 903 d.	|	1315	...	|	|	1414	1414	...	|	|	...	1515	...	...	|	|	|	|	1715	1728	1735	...	|
Celle 903 d.	|	1338	...	|	|	|	|	...	|	|	...	1538	...	...	|	|	|	|	1737	...	...	...	|
Bremen Hbf **813** d.	|	|	...	|	|	|	|	...	|	|	...	|	...	1515	|	|	|	|	|	...	...	1715	|
Hannover Hbf 903 a.	1338	1358	...	1422	1438	1451	1451	...	1520	1538	...	1558	...	1614	1622	1638	1720	1738	1757	...	...	1814	1822
Hannover Hbf 903 d.	1341	1401	...	1426	1441	1454	1454	...	1526	1541	1551	1601	...	1626	1626	1641	1726	1741	1801	...	...	1826	1826
Göttingen 902 903 d.	1417	1439	...	1502	1516	1535	1535	...	1602	1616	1631	1640	...	1702	1702	1716	1802	1816	1839	...	...	1902	1902
Kassel Wilhelmshöhe 901 902 d.	1437	1503	...	1523	1537	1558	1558	...	1623	1637	1654	1703	...	1723	1723	1737	1823	1837	1903	...	...	1923	1923
Fulda 850 901 902 d.	|	|	...	1556	|	1632	1636	...	1656	|	1729	|	...	1756	1756	|	1856	|	|	...	...	1956	1956
Würzburg Hbf 920 921 d.	|	|	...	1629	|	1711	|	...	1729	|	|	|	...	1831	1831	|	1929	|	|	...	...	2030	2030
Nürnberg Hbf 905 920 921 a.	|	◧	...	1725	|	|	|	...	1823	|	|	◧	...	1925	1925	|	2024	|	◧	...	...	2125	2125
Augsburg Hbf 905 a.	|	|	...	|	|	1930	|	...	|	|	|	|	...	|	|	|	|	|	|	...	...	|	|
München Hbf **904 905** a.	|	|	...	1842	|	2002	|	...	1945	|	|	|	...	2045	2045	|	2143	|	|	...	...	2240	2240
Hanau Hbf 850 901 902 d.	|	|	...	...	|	...	|	...	...	|	|	|	...	...	...	|	...	|	|	...	...	...	...
Frankfurt (Main) Hbf 850 901 902 a.	1600	1708	...	...	1701	...	1740	...	...	1800	1831	1908	...	...	...	1900	...	2000	2108	...	...	...	...
Frankfurt Flughafen Fernbf ✈ **910** a.	|	|	...	...	1718	...	...	...	...	|	|	|	...	...	...	1918	...	|	...	...	...	...	...
Mannheim Hbf **910** a.	1644	|	...	...	1755	...	...	...	...	1844	1916	|	...	...	...	1955	...	2044	...	...	...	...	...
Stuttgart Hbf **910** a.	|	|	...	...	1838	...	...	...	...	|	1958	2057	...	...	...	2038	...	|	...	...	...	...	...
Karlsruhe Hbf **910** a.	1709	1852	...	...	...	...	...	...	...	1909	...	...	...	...	...	...	...	2109	...	...	...	...	...
Basel SBB **910** a.	1855	...	...	...	...	...	...	...	...	2055	...	...	...	...	...	...	...	2304	...	...	...	...	...

	ICE 773	ICE 1687	ICE 1687		ICE 885	ICE 273	ICE 273	ICE 1677	ICE 1677	ICE 635	ICE 635	ICE 685	ICE 685	ICE 775		ICE 887	ICE 1087	NJ 491	NJ 40491	ICE 1679		NJ 471	ICE 1081
		①–⑤	Ⓑ				⑤⑥	Ⓑ	⑤⑦	Ⓑ	⑤⑦		⑤–⑦			Ⓑ	⑥	[R]	[R]	⑦		[R]	
	✕	✕	✕		K✕	✕	✕	T✕	T✕	✕	✕	✕	✕	✕		N✕	N✕	H	A	T✕		D	
Hamburg Altona d.	...	1711	1711	...	...	...	...	1813t	1813t	...	...	...	...	...	...	...	...	1956	1956	2009t	...	2152	...
Hamburg Hbf 903 d.	1724	1728	1728	...	1801	1824	1824	1828	1828	...	...	1901	1901	1924	...	2001	2001	2010	2010	2024	...	2208	2228
Hamburg Harburg 903 d.	|	1738	1738	...	1812	|	|	1840	1840	...	...	1912	1912	|	...	|	|	2023	2023	|	...	2221	2241
Lüneburg 903 d.	|	1758	1758	...	|	|	|	1859	1859	...	...	|	|	|	...	2028	2028	|	|	2051	...	|	2259
Uelzen 903 d.	|	1818	1818	...	|	|	|	1915	1915	...	...	|	|	|	...	2044	2044	|	|	2108	...	|	2314
Celle 903 d.	|	1840	1840	...	|	|	|	1938	1938	...	...	|	|	|	...	|	|	|	|	2140	...	|	2340
Bremen Hbf **813** d.	|	|	|	...	|	|	|	|	|	1915	1915	|	|	|	...	|	|	|	|	|	...	2311	|
Hannover Hbf 903 a.	1838	1905	1905	...	1920	1938	1938	1958	1958	2014	2014	2022	2022	2038	...	2123	2123	2150	2150	2159	...	0026	2400
Hannover Hbf 903 d.	1841	1909	...	...	1926	1941	1941	...	2001	2026	2026	2026	2026	2041	...	2126	2126	2153	2153	2202	...	0030	0003
Göttingen 902 903 d.	1916	1945	...	...	2002	2018	2018	...	2040	2102	2102	2102	2102	2116	...	2202	2202	2239	2239	2244	...	0132	0113
Kassel Wilhelmshöhe 901 902 d.	1937	2009	...	...	2023	2039	2039	...	2103	2123	2123	2123	2123	2137	...	2223	2223	2303	2303	2307	...	|	|
Fulda 850 901 902 d.	|	...	...	...	2056	|	|	...	|	2156	2156	2156	2156	|	...	2255	2256	|	|	...	...	|	|
Würzburg Hbf 920 921 d.	|	...	...	...	2129	|	|	...	|	2229	2229	2229	2229	|	...	|	|	0148j	0148j	...	...	|	0354
Nürnberg Hbf 905 920 921 a.	|	...	...	...	2225	|	|	...	◧	2325	2325	2325	2325	|	...	|	|	0315	0315	...	...	|	0447
Augsburg Hbf 905 a.	|	...	...	...	|	|	|	...	|	...	|	...	|	|	...	|	|	...	0624	...	...	|	|
München Hbf **904 905** a.	|	...	...	...	2344	|	|	...	|	...	0045	...	0045	|	...	|	|	...	0706	...	...	|	0604
Hanau Hbf 850 901 902 d.	|	...	...	...	...	|	|	...	|	...	...	...	...	|	...	2336	2336	...	...	...	...	0416	...
Frankfurt (Main) Hbf 850 901 902 a.	2100	...	...	...	...	2200	2200	...	2308	...	...	...	...	2300	...	2352	2355	...	...	...	...	0428•	...
Frankfurt Flughafen Fernbf ✈ **910** a.	2118	...	...	...	...	|	|	...	...	...	...	...	...	2318	...	0026	0026	...	...	...	...	|	...
Mannheim Hbf **910** a.	2155	...	...	...	...	2244	2244	...	...	...	...	...	...	2356	...	...	...	...	...	...	...	|	...
Stuttgart Hbf **910** a.	2251	...	...	...	...	|	|	...	...	...	...	...	...	|	...	...	...	...	...	...	...	|	...
Karlsruhe Hbf **910** a.	...	...	...	...	...	2309	2309	...	...	...	...	...	...	0032	...	...	...	...	...	...	...	0603	...
Basel SBB **910** a.	...	...	...	...	...	...	0104	...	...	...	...	...	...	...	...	...	...	...	...	...	...	0810	...

A – 🛏 1, 2 cl., ▬ 2 cl. (1, 4 berth) and [2] (*ÖBB nightjet* new generation) Hamburg - Innsbruck (Table **53**).
D – 🛏 1, 2 cl. and ▬ 2 cl. ([R]) Hamburg - Basel - Zürich (a. 1005). Also conveys [2] (*IC* **60471**).
H – 🛏 1, 2 cl., ▬ 2 cl. (1, 4 berth) and [2] (*ÖBB nightjet* new generation) Hamburg - Passau - Wien.
J – From Lübeck from Aug. 2 (Table **825**).
K – From Kiel (Table **820**).
L – [12] ✕ Kiel - Hamburg - Basel - Zürich.
M – Ⓑ to Aug. 1. To Magdeburg (Table **841**).
N – To Mainz Hbf (a. 0044) and Wiesbaden Hbf (a. 0058).
O – From Ostseebad Binz via Stralsund until Aug. 1 (Tables **830** and **844**).
R – From Berlin (Table **902**).
S – On ⑤ continues to Innsbruck via Garmisch (Table **895**). On ⑦–④ Oct. 12 - Dec. 11 terminates at Nürnberg (a. 1804); on ⑤ Oct. 10 - Dec. 12 via Nürnberg (a. 1804), München a. 1958, not calling at Augsburg.
T – Until Aug. 1 starts from Stralsund via Rostock (Table **830**).
U – From Aug. 2. To Nürnberg via Stendal and Berlin.

W – WATTENMEER – From Westerland (Table **821**).
Y – Until Aug. 1 conveys [12] ✕ Ostseebad Binz - Stralsund - Hamburg - Frankfurt.
Z – To Zürich (Table **510**).

j – Arrives 0133.
t – From Aug. 2.

• – Frankfurt (Main) **Süd**.
◧ – Via Gießen (Table **806**).

RE / RB services — Local services FRANKFURT - FULDA - KASSEL — 901

On June 19 services run as on ⑦.

Other *ICE / IC* services: Table **850** for Bebra - Kassel Wilhelmshöhe and v.v., also Frankfurt - Fulda - Bad Hersfeld and v.v. Tables **900 / 902** for Frankfurt - Fulda - Kassel Wilhelmshöhe and v.v.

km							F			ⒶB	B
0	**Frankfurt** (Main) Hbf 921 d.	0519	0626		2126	2226	2326		A	1542	2018
4	**Frankfurt** (Main) Süd 921 d.	0525	0633	and	2133	2233	2333		L	1548	2023
10	Offenbach (Main) Hbf 921 d.	0530	0638	hourly	2138	2238	2338		S	1553	|
23	Hanau Hbf 921 d.	0539	0647	until	2147	2247	2347		O	1602	2039
104	**Fulda** a.	0642	0750		2250	2350	0050			1729	2132

	†	⚒	ⒶB		ⒶD				
Fulda d.	0400	0507	0512	0559	0606	0658	0707		2207	2310
Hanau Hbf 921 d.	0502	0609	0616	0655	0709	0749	0809	and	2309	0013
Offenbach (Main) Hbf. 921 d.	0510	0617	0624	|	0717	|	0817	hourly	2317	0021
Frankfurt Main) Süd . 921 d.	0515	0623	0631	0710	0723	0803	0823	until	2323	0026
Frankfurt (Main) Hbf.. 921 a.	0520	0628	0636	0715	0728	0808	0828		2328	0031

FULDA - KASSEL. Operated by CANTUS Verkehrsgesellschaft (except trains marked with notes **B**, **D** and **E**). 2nd class only. Additional trains run Bad Hersfeld - Kassel and v.v.

km		Ⓐ	Ⓐ												ⒶB	Ⓐ					B			⑤⑥f	E
0	**Fulda** d.	...	...	...	0616	0720	0820	0920	1020	1120	1220	1320		1720	1731	...	1820	1920	2020	2122	2132	2221	2309	2356	2357
42	Bad Hersfeld d.	...	0505	0543a	0644	0748	0848	0948	1048	1148	1248	1348	and	1748	1803	1810	1848	1948	2048	2149	2203	2249	2335	0027	0028
56	Bebra a.	...	0515	0554a	0654	0758	0858	0959	1057	1158	1258	1358		1758	1813	1820	1858	1958	2058	2159	2213	2258	2345	0041	0041
56	Bebra d.	0415	0518	0559	0659	0759	0859	1000	1059	1159	1259	1359	hourly	1759	...	1833	1859k	1959	2059	2200	...	2302	2348	...	...
62	Rotenburg (Fulda) d.	0421	0524	0605	0705	0806	0905	1006	1105	1205	1305	1405		1805	...	1838	1905k	2005	2105	2206	...	2308	2354	...	...
84	Melsungen d.	0440	0543	0624	0724	0824	0924	1024	1124	1224	1324	1424	until	1824	...	1852	1924k	2024	2124	2224	...	2326	0012	...	...
110	**Kassel** Wilhelmshöhe 804/6 d.	0507	0610	0643	0743	0843	0943	1043	1143	1243	1342	1443		1843	...	1913	1943k	2043	2144	2252	...	2352	0038	...	...
114	**Kassel** Hbf 804/6 a.	0512	0616	0648	0747	0847	0947	1047	1147	1247	1347	1447		1847	...	1917	1947k	2048	2148	2256	...	2356	0043	...	...

		Ⓐ	ⒶB	⚒◐	ⒶD	Ⓒ	Ⓐ																		
Kassel Hbf 804/6 d.	...	0355	...	0505	0535	0606	0611	0711	0811c	0911	1011	1111	1210	1311	1410	1511	1611	1710	1811	1911	2010	2111	2211	2311	0011
Kassel Wilhelmshöhe 804/6 d.	...	0359	...	0510	0540	0615	0618	0715	0815	0915	1015	1115	1215	1315	1415	1515	1615	1715	1815	1915	2015	2115	2216	2316	0015
Melsungen d.	...	0418	...	0528	0557	0634	0635	0734	0834	0934	1034	1134	1234	1334	1434	1534	1634	1734	1834	1934	2034	2134	2234	2334	0034
Rotenburg (Fulda) d.	...	0437	...	0547	0611	0653	0653	0753	0853	0953	1053	1153	1253	1353	1453	1553	1653	1753	1853	1953	2052	2153	2253	2353	0053
Bebra a.	...	0443	...	0554	0617	0658	0659	0758	0859	0958	1058	1158	1258	1358	1459	1558	1658	1758	1858	1958	2058	2158	2258	2358	0058
Bebra d.	0314	0446	0522	0559	0618	0659	0701	0759	0859	0959	1059	1159	1259	1359	1459	1559	1659	1759	1859	1959	2059	2159	2259	2359	0059
Bad Hersfeld d.	0324	0456	0531	0609	0627	0709	0725j	0809	0909	1009	1109	1209	1309	1409	1509	1609	1709	1809	1909	2009	2109	2209	2310	0011	0110
Fulda a.	0353	...	0558	0637	0657	0737	0755	0837	0937	1036	1138	1237	1338	1437	1537	1637	1737	1837	1937	2037	2137	2237	2337f	...	...

B – [12] Bebra - Fulda - Frankfurt.
D – [12] Kassel - Fulda - Frankfurt.
E – ⑦–④ (also Oct. 3). Starts from Frankfurt; see upper panel.
F – Continues to Bebra on ⑦–④ (also Oct. 3); see lower panel.

a – Ⓐ only.
c – 0806 on †.
f – ⑤⑥ (not Oct. 3).
j – Arrives 0711.

k – 6–7 minutes later on ⑤⑦ (also June 9, Oct. 2; not June 8, Oct. 3).

◐ – Runs daily Bebra - Fulda.

902 FRANKFURT - BRAUNSCHWEIG - BERLIN

See Table **850** for additional services Frankfurt - Berlin and v.v. Independent operator **FlixTrain** also run services Stuttgart - Berlin and v.v. (Table **927**).

km		*ICE* 649	*ICE* 876	*ICE* 998	*ICE* 996	*ICE* 270	*ICE* 1136	*ICE* 994	*ICE* 374	*ICE* 992	*ICE* 372	*ICE* 798	*ICE* 370	*ICE* 9591	*ICE* 796	*ICE* 278	*ICE* 1034	*ICE* 794	*ICE* 276	*ICE* 792	*ICE* 274	*ICE* 790	*ICE* 292	*ICE* 674
		①–⑤		①–⑤	①–⑥																		⑦	
		✕	✕	✕	✕	✕	✕	✕	✕	✕	L✕	✕	✕	P✕	✕	L✕	A✕	✕	✕	✕	✕	✕	Z✕	
	Basel SBB **910** d.	...	...	...	...	...	...	...	0606	...	0813	...	1013	...	...	1213	...	...	1413	...	1613	...	1813	...
	Karlsruhe Hbf **910** d.	...	...	...	...	0557	...	...	0800	...	1000	...	1200	1236	...	1400	...	...	1600	...	1800	...	2000	...
	Frankfurt Flughafen ✈ d.	...	...	...	...	|	...	0809	|	1009	|	1209	|	|	1409	|	...	1609	|	1809	|	2009	|	0004
0	**Frankfurt** (Main) Hbf **850 900** d.	...	...	0558	...	0714	0802	|	0914	|	1114	|	1314	|	|	1514	1602	|	1714	|	1914	|	2114	2335*
4	**Frankfurt** (Main) Süd d.	...	...	|	...	|	|	0820	|	1020	|	1220	|	1406	1420	|	|	1620	|	1820	|	2020	|	0016
23	Hanau Hbf **850 900** d.	...	...	|	...	0729	|	|	0929	|	1129	|	1329	|	|	1529	|	|	1729	|	1929	|	2129	0030
104	Fulda **850 900** d.	...	...	|	...	0814	|	0917	1014	1115	1214	1315	1414	|	1517	1614	|	1715	1814	1915	2014	2115	2214	0116
194	**Kassel** Wilhelmshöhe **900** d.	...	0643	|	0748	0846	|	0949	1046	1149	1246	1349	1445	|	1549	1645	|	1749	1845	1949	2045	2149	2245	|
239	Göttingen **900** d.	...	0706	|	0809	0906	|	1009	1106	1209	1306	1409	1506	|	1609	1706	|	1809	1906	2009	2106	2210	2304	0245
317	Hildesheim Hbf ▷ d.	...	0736	|	0837	0936	|	1037	1136	1237	1336	1437	1536	|	1637	1736	|	1837	1936	2037	2136	2242	2333	|
360	**Braunschweig** Hbf ▷ d.	0601	0801	|	0903	1001	|	1103	1201	1303	1401	1503	1601	|	1703	1801	|	1903	2001	2103	2201	2305	0001	|
	Hannover Hbf **900** a.	|	|	|	|	|	|	|	|	|	|	|	|	|	|	|	|	|	|	|	|	|	|	0352
392	Wolfsburg **810** ▷ d.	0619	0818	|	0920	1019	|	1120	1219	1320	1419	1520	1619	|	1720	1819	|	1920	2019	2120	2219	2323	0018	0513
467	Stendal Hbf **810** d.	0648	|	|	0947	|	|	1147	|	1347	|	1547	|	|	1747	|	|	1947	|	|	|	2353	|	0540
559	**Berlin** Spandau **810** a.	0727	0915	0940	1022	1115	1146	1222	1315	1422	1515	1622	1716	1746	1822	1915	1946	2023	2115	2217	2314	0026	0113	0627
575	**Berlin** Hbf **850 810** a.	0741	0931	1003	1032	1130	1203	1234	1331	1432	1531	1632	1731	1803	1832	1929	2004	2033	2133	2231	2330	0043	0132	0649
580	**Berlin** Ostbahnhof **810** a.	0758	0944	1016	...	1144	1214	...	1341	...	1542	...	1741	1816	...	1940	2014	...	2145	2242	2342	0056	0142	0659

	ICE 275	*ICE* 277	*ICE* 791	*ICE* 1035	*ICE* 279	*ICE* 793	*ICE* 371	*ICE* 795	*ICE* 9590	*ICE* 373	*ICE* 797	*ICE* 1091	*ICE* 375	*ICE* 799	*ICE* 1131	*ICE* 1095	*ICE* 377	*ICE* 995	*ICE* 995	*ICE* 877	*ICE* 997	*ICE* 1279	*ICE* 271
	①–⑤											⑤⑦			①–⑥	⑦		⑦	①–⑥		⑥	⑦	
	L✕	✕	✕	A✕	✕	✕	L✕	✕	P✕	L✕	✕	S✕	✕	✕	✕	S✕	✕	S✕	✕	✕	✕	✕	C
Berlin Ostbahnhof **810** d.	0416	0615	...	0744	0815	...	1014	...	1145	1217	...	1345	1415	...	1545	1545	1615	...	...	1815	...	2016	2315
Berlin Hbf **850 810** d.	0428	0629	0722	0755	0828	0925	1028	1124	1155	1230	1323	1355	1428	1524	1555	1555	1628	1723	1723	1828	1924	2028	2328
Berlin Spandau **810** d.	0446	0645	0735	0811	0845	0936	1045	1135	1212	1245	1334	1412	1446	1535	1612	1612	1645	1735	1735	1845	1935	2046	2345
Stendal Hbf **810** d.	|	|	0812	|	|	1012	|	1210	|	|	1412	|	|	1612	|	|	|	1810	1810	|	2012	|	0025
Wolfsburg **810** ▷ d.	0538	0738	0839	|	0938	1039	1138	1236	|	1338	1439	1508	1538	1639	|	1708	1738	1836	1836	1938	2039	2139	0100
Hannover Hbf **900** d.	|	|	|	|	|	|	|	|	|	|	|	1551	|	|	|	1751	|	|	|	|	|	|	0210
Braunschweig Hbf ▷ d.	0557	0757	0859	|	0957	1059	1157	1259	|	1357	1459	|	1557	1659	|	|	1757	1857	1857	1957	2059	2157	|
Hildesheim Hbf ▷ d.	0619	0819	0921	|	1019	1121	1219	1321	|	1419	1521	|	1619	1721	|	|	1819	1919	1919	2019	2121	2219	|
Göttingen **900** d.	0652	0852	0952	|	1052	1152	1252	1352	|	1452	1552	1631	1652	1752	|	1831	1852	1952	1952	2052	2152	2252	0308
Kassel Wilhelmshöhe **900** d.	0714	0914	1014	|	1114	1214	1314	1414	|	1514	1614	1654	1714	1814	|	1853	1914	2014	2014	2114	2212	2314	|
Fulda **850 900** d.	0746	0946	1046	|	1147	1245	1346	1445	|	1546	1646	1729	1746	1847	|	1925	1946	2045	2045	2146	...	2347	0433
Hanau Hbf **850 900** d.	0829	1029	|	|	1229	|	1429	|	|	1629	|	|	1829	|	|	2014	2028	|	|	2229	...	0028	0521
Frankfurt (Main) Süd a.	|	|	1139	|	|	1339	|	1539	1552	|	1739	|	|	1939	|	|	|	|	|	|	...	|	|
Frankfurt (Main) Hbf **850 900** a.	0844	1044	|	1156	1244	|	1444	|	|	1644	|	1831	1844	|	1956	2031	2043	2140	2140	2244	...	0044	0537
Frankfurt Flughafen Fernbf ✈ a.	|	|	1151	...	|	1351	|	1551	|	|	1751	...	|	1951	...	...	|	...	...	...	...	|	|
Karlsruhe Hbf **910** a.	0957	1157	...	...	1358	...	1557	...	1706	1758	...	...	1958	...	...	...	2158	...	...	...	...	0153	0656
Basel SBB **910** a.	1148	1348	...	...	1548	...	1748	...	...	1948	...	...	2149	...	...	...	2359	...	...	...	...	...	0848

Regional trains **WOLFSBURG - BRAUNSCHWEIG - HILDESHEIM** (operated by *enno*; additional trains operate).

km		Ⓐt	Ⓐt	⚒t						
0	**Wolfsburg** Hbf d.	0518	0548	0618	0718	and	2218	...	2318	...
32	**Braunschweig** Hbf d.	0541	0611	0641	0741	hourly	2241	...	2341	...
75	**Hildesheim** Hbf a.	0608	0638	0708	0808	until	2308	...	0008	...

	Ⓐt	⚒t		⚒t		Ⓐt			
Hildesheim Hbf d.	0450	...	...	0550	...	0620	0650	and	2250
Braunschweig Hbf d.	0521	0521	...	0621	0621	0651	0721	hourly	2321
Wolfsburg Hbf a.	0541	0541	...	0641	0641	0711	0741	until	2341

A – To / from Saarbrücken (Table **919**).
C – To Chur via Zürich (Tables **510** and **520**).
L – From / to Interlaken via Bern (Table **560**).
P – To / from Paris (Table **910**).
S – To Stuttgart (Table **910**).
Z – From Zürich (Table **510**).
t – Not Oct. 31.
* – Calls before Frankfurt Flughafen.
▷ – See also panel below main table.
☛ Berlin timings may vary by up to 4 minutes.

903 Local services GÖTTINGEN - HANNOVER - UELZEN - HAMBURG *metronom*

Services below are operated by ***metronom***. On Oct. 31 services run as on ⑦. See Table **900** for faster *ICE* and *IC* services (operated by DB).
Note: July 3 - Aug. 13 certain services may require a change of trains at Hannover (where shown as normally running as a through train).

km																											
			⚒			⊖		Ⓒ	Ⓐ																	†	⚒
0	**Göttingen** d.	...	0408	...	...	0504	0604	0704	0707	0809	0904	1009	1104	1209	1304	1407**p**	1504	1609	1704	1809	1904	...	2009	2104	2209	2309	2311
20	Northeim (Han) d.	...	0421	...	...	0517	0617	0717	0720	0823	0917	1023	1117	1223	1317	1421**p**	1517	1623	1717	1823	1917	...	2023	2117	2223	2322	2324
39	Kreiensen d.	...	0435	...	...	0531	0631	0731	0733	0837	0931	1037	1131	1237	1331	1437	1531	1637	1733**q**	1837	1931	...	2037	2131	2237	2339	2338
58	Alfeld (Leine) d.	...	0448	...	...	0544	0644	0744	0746	0850	0944	1050	1144	1250	1344	1450	1544	1650	1746**q**	1850	1944	...	2050	2144	2250	2352	2351
75	Elze (Han) d.	...	0503	...	...	0558	0659	0759	0759	0903	0959	1103	1159	1303	1359	1503	1559	1703	1759	1903	1959	...	2103	2159	2303	0004	0003
108	**Hannover** Hbf. a.	...	0526	...	...	0624	0723	0823	0823	0926	1023	1126	1223	1326	1423	1526	1623	1726	1823	1926	2023	...	2127	2223	2326	0027	0026
			▽			|	▽	|	|	▽	|	▽	|	▽	|	▽	|	▽	|	▽	|		▽	|	▽	|	|
			Ⓐ	⑥			◇																		⊙		
108	**Hannover** Hbf. d.	...	0540	0540	...	0640	0740	0840	0840	0940	1040	1140	1240	1340	1440	1540	1640	1740	1840	1940	2040	...	2140	2248	2340	0040	0040
149	Celle d.	...	0608	0608	...	0708	0808	0908	0908	1008	1108	1208	1308	1408	1508	1608	1708	1808	1908	2008	2108	...	2208	2316	0008	0106	0106
201	**Uelzen** a.	...	0639	0639	...	0739	0839	0939	0939	1039	1138	1239	1338	1439	1539	1639	1738	1839	1939	2039	2139	...	2239	2347	0039	0138	0138
			|	|		▽	|		▽	|	▽	|	▽	|	▽	|	▽	|	▽	|	▽		▽	▽			
																					⚒	†					
201	**Uelzen** d.	0605	0647	0704	0704	0801	0901	...	1001	1101	1201	1301	1401	1501	1601	1701	1801	1901	2002	2101	2201	2201	2306	2359	...	...	...
214	Bad Bevensen d.	0614	0655	0713	0713	0809	0910	...	1009	1109	1209	1309	1409	1509	1609	1709	1809	1909	2010	2109	2209	2209	2314	0007	...	...	...
237	Lüneburg d.	0629	0709	0727	0727	0828	0928	...	1028	1130**j**	1228	1328	1428	1528	1628	1728	1828	1928	2031**j**	2128	2228	2232**j**	2338**k**	0021	...	...	...
256	Winsen (Luhe) d.	0640	0720	0739	0739	0839	0939	...	1039	1141	1239	1339	1439	1539	1639	1739	1839	1939	2042	2139	2239	2248	2354	0036	...	...	...
274	Hamburg Har ¶ d.	0651	0731	0752	0752	0850	0951	...	1051	1152	1251	1351	1451	1551	1651	1751	1852	1951	2053	2151	2250	2309	0016	0057	...	...	...
286	**Hamburg** Hbf a.	0703	0741**v**	0803	0803	0902	1003	...	1103	1204	1303	1403	1503	1603	1703	1803	1903	2003	2104	2202	2302	2321	0027	0109	...	...	...

					Ⓐ		Ⓐ	Ⓒ																		⑤⑥ f	
Hamburg Hbf d.	...	...	...	...	0433	...	0542	0558	0657	0757	0857	0957	1057	1157	1257	1357	1457	1557	1657	1757	1857	1957	2057	2157	2234	2234	2333
Hamburg Har ¶ d.	...	...	...	...	0445	...	0553	0611	0708	0808	0908	1008	1108	1208	1308	1408	1508	1608	1708	1808	1908	2008	2107	2211	2245	2245	2345
Winsen (Luhe) d.	...	...	...	...	0506	...	0604	0623	0720	0820	0920	1020	1120	1220	1320	1420	1520	1620	1720	1820	1920	2020	2119	2223	2306	2306	0006
Lüneburg d.	...	...	...	...	0532**k**	...	0615**e**	0634	0733	0834	0934	1034	1134	1234	1334	1434	1534	1634	1734	1834	1934	2034	2130	2234	2324	2324	0023
Bad Bevensen d.	...	...	...	...	0549	...	0632	0648	0747	0848	0948	1048	1148	1248	1348	1448**z**	1548	1648	1748	1848	1948	2048	2145	2249	2338	2338	0037
Uelzen a.	...	...	...	...	0559	...	0640	0656	0756	0856	0956	1056	1156	1256	1356	1456**z**	1555	1656	1756	1856	1956	2056	2153	2256	2346	2346	0045
					|		▽	▽	|	▽	|	▽	|	▽	|	▽	|	▽	|	▽	|	▽	|	▽	▬	|	
		Ⓐ	Ⓒ	Ⓐ			Ⓐ	Ⓒ																	⑤⑥ f		
Uelzen d.	...	0412	0513	0513	0609	0609	0651	0709	0809	0909	1009	1109	1209	1309	1409	1509	1609	1709	1809	1909	2009	2114	2209	2309	2309	2349	...
Celle d.	...	0446	0547	0547	0647	0647	0747**r**	0747	0848	0947	1048	1147	1247	1348	1447	1547	1647	1747	1847	1947	2048	2147	2247	2349	2349	0028	...
Hannover Hbf a.	...	0514**t**	0615	0615	0715	0715	0815**t**	0815**t**	0915**t**	1015**t**	1115**t**	1215**t**	1315**t**	1415**t**	1515**t**	1615**t**	1715**t**	1815**t**	1915**t**	2015**t**	2115**t**	2215	2315	0017	0017	0057	...
		▽	|	|		▽	|	|	▽	|	▽	|	▽	|	▽	|	▽	|	▽	|	▽	|	▽		|		
	Ⓐ	⚒															⊡										
Hannover Hbf d.	0432	0536	0633	0633	...	0736	0833	0833	0936	1033	1136	1233	1336	1433	1536	1633	1736	1833	1936	2033	2136**n**	2236	2336	...	0038	...	...
Elze (Han) d.	0455	0558	0655	0655	...	0800	0855	0855	1000	1055	1200	1255	1400	1455	1600	1655	1758	1855	2000	2055	2200	2258	2358	...	0100	...	...
Alfeld (Leine) d.	0507	0610	0706	0706	...	0812	0906	0906	1012	1106	1212	1306	1412	1506	1612	1706	1810	1906	2012	2106	2212	2309	0010	...	0112	...	...
Kreiensen d.	0520	0624	0719	0723**j**	...	0825	0919	0919	1025	1119	1225	1319	1425	1519	1625	1719	1823	1919	2025	2119	2225	2322	0023	...	0125	...	...
Northeim (Han) d.	0533	0637	0733	0736	...	0838	0933	0933	1038	1133	1238	1333	1438	1533	1638	1733	1836	1933	2038	2133	2238	2336	0036	...	0138	...	...
Göttingen a.	0546	0650	0747	0749	...	0851	0946	0946	1051	1146	1251	1346	1451	1546	1651	1746	1849	1946	2051	2146	2251	2349	0049	...	0153	...	...

e – 0618 from Aug. 4.
f – Also June 8, Oct. 2, 30.
j – Arrives 5–8 minutes earlier.
k – Arrives 9–11 minutes earlier.
n – 2134 on ⑥.
p – 2 minutes later on Ⓒ.
q – 2 minutes **earlier** on Ⓒ.
r – Arrives 0729.
t – 2–3 minutes later July 3 - Aug. 13.
v – From June 23.
z – 3 minutes later on ⑤ (also Oct. 2; not Oct. 3).
⊖ – Timings Göttingen - Elze are 2–4 minutes later on †.
⊡ – Timings Elze - Göttingen are 2 minutes later on Ⓒ.
⊙ – Runs 8 minutes later on Ⓒ.
▽ – Change trains.
◇ – Change trains at Uelzen on Ⓐ.
¶ – Hamburg Harburg.

MÜNCHEN - INGOLSTADT - NÜRNBERG 904

km	Most *ICE* trains convey ✕	*ICE* 888	*ICE* 822	*ICE* 684	*ICE* 1008	*ICE* 820	*ICE* 886	*ICE* 728	*ICE* 602	*ICE* 682	*ICE* 726	*ICE* 1006	*ICE* 882	*ICE* 724	*ICE* 1600	*ICE* 680	*ICE* 722	*ICE* 800	*ICE* 880	*ICE* 720	*ICE* 508	*ICE* 588	*ICE* 628	*ICE* 1004	*ICE* 788	*ICE* 626	*ICE* 506
		①–⑤	①–⑥			①–⑥																					
			K		**D**	**K**		**K**			**K**		**L**	**K**			**K**			**K**			**K**			**K**	
0	**München** Hbf ⊡ d.	0412	0447	0514	0553	0553	0612	0647	0657	0717	0746	0756	0817	0847	0854	0917	0950	0954	1020	1048	1056	1117	1150	1156	1220	1247	1254
81	**Ingolstadt** Hbf d.	0451	0527	0557	|	|	0654	|	|	0758	0825	|	0900	|	|	0958	|	1032	1100	|	|	1158	|	|	1300	|	|
171	**Nürnberg** Hbf ⊡ a.	0522	0557	0629	0655	0655	0726	0753	0802	0829	0855	0859	0930	0953	1003	1030	1055	1103	1130	1153	1202	1230	1255	1259	1330	1353	1402
	Würzburg Hbf **900 920** a.	0625	0652	0724	|	0754	0825	0852	|	0924	0952	|	1025	1052	|	1126	1152	|	1225	1252	|	1325	1352	|	1425	1452	|
	Frankfurt (Main) Hbf **920** a.	|	0804	|	|	0904	|	1004	|	|	1104	|	|	1204	|	|	1304	|	|	1404	|	|	1504	|	|	1604	|
	Leipzig Hbf **850** a.	|	...	|	|	...	|	...	1010	|	...	|	|	...	1210	|	...	|	|	...	1410	|	...	|	|	...	1610
	Berlin Hbf **850** ⊡ a.	|	...	|	0953	...	|	...	1130	|	...	1142	|	...	1329	|	...	1422	|	...	1530	|	...	1542	|	...	1732
	Hamburg Hbf **840 900** a.	0953	...	1055	1151**x**	...	1158	...	1324**r**	1254	...	1351**x**	1354	...	1524**r**	1455	...	1622**r**	1555	...	1724**r**	1655	...	1757**x**	1753	...	1924**r**

Most *ICE* trains convey ✕	*ICE* 586	*ICE* 624	*ICE* 706	*ICE* 786	*ICE* 622	*ICE* 504	*ICE* 584	*ICE* 620	*ICE* 1002	*ICE* 1222	*ICE* 528	*ICE* 502	*ICE* 582	*ICE* 1000	*ICE* 526	*ICE* 782	*ICE* 524	*ICE* 500	*ICE* 580	*ICE* 522	*ICE* 1018	*ICE* 780	*ICE* 520	*ICE* 520	*ICE* 1100	*ICE* 600	*ICE* 1080
																			Ⓑ			⑦	⑦	①–⑥	⑤	⑦	
		K			**K**		**D**	**K**	**G**	**K**	**K**				**K**		**K**		**A**	**K**		**B**			**w**	**s**	
München Hbf ⊡ d.	1317	1350	1353	1420	1447	1456	1517	1550	1556	1618	1648	1654	1716	1751	1751	1818	1847	1855	1917	1947	1955	2017	2045	2048	2052	2055	2300
Ingolstadt Hbf d.	1358	|	1431	1500	|	|	1558	|	|	1659	|	|	1756	|	|	1900	|	|	1958	2025	|	2100	2124	2129	|	|	2337
Nürnberg Hbf ⊡ a.	1431	1455	1502	1531	1554	1602	1630	1655	1659	1733	1754	1802	1828	1856	1856	1931	1955	2004	2029	2055	2059	2131	2153	2157	2200	2202	0013
Würzburg Hbf **900 920** a.	1526	1552	|	1626	1652	|	1726	1752	|	1827	1852	|	1925	|	1953	2026	2052	|	2124	2152	|	2226	2254	2254	|	|	0115
Frankfurt (Main) Hbf **920** a.	|	1704	|	|	1804	|	|	1904	|	1936	2004	|	|	|	2104	|	2204	|	|	2304	|	...	0004	0004	|	|	|
Leipzig Hbf **850** a.	|	...	|	|	...	1810	|	...	|	...	...	2010	|	|	...	|	...	2210	|	...	2247	...	...	...	|	0007	|
Berlin Hbf **850** ⊡ a.	|	...	1822	|	...	1930	|	...	1943**h**	...	...	2130	|	2153	...	|	...	2332	|	...	0017	...	...	...	0114	0128	|
Hamburg Hbf **840 900** a.	1856	...	2023**r**	1954	...	2125**r**	2058	...	...	...	...	2334**r**	2255	...	...	0005	...	...	0113‡	...	...	...	...	...	...	...	0642

Most *ICE* trains convey ✕	*ICE* 1081	*ICE* 825	*ICE* 985	*ICE* 827	*ICE* 601	*ICE* 521	*ICE* 501	*ICE* 781	*ICE* 1001	*ICE* 523	*ICE* 581	*ICE* 503	*ICE* 525	*ICE* 783	*ICE* 1003	*ICE* 527	*ICE* 583	*ICE* 505	*ICE* 529	*ICE* 1621	*ICE* 703	*ICE* 621	*ICE* 585	*ICE* 507	*ICE* 623	*ICE* 787	*ICE* 1005
		①–⑤	①–⑤	①–⑥	Ⓐ		①–⑥	①–⑥		①–⑥	①–⑥																
		n	**n**	**K**	**E**	**K**		**M**		**K**			**K**		**G**	**K**			**K**	**K**		**K**	**D**		**K**		
Hamburg Hbf **840 900** d.	2228	...	...	...	...	...	...	0349**g**	...	...	0454	...	...	0554	...	...	0701	0634**r**	...	...	0735**r**	...	0901	0835**r**	...	1001	1005**x**
Berlin Hbf **850** ⊡ d.	|	...	...	...	...	...	0429	|	0559	...	|	0628	...	|	0811**e**	...	|	0828	...	...	0934	...	|	1028	...	|	1204
Leipzig Hbf **850** d.	|	...	...	...	...	...	0548	|	|	...	|	0748	...	|	|	...	|	0948	...	...	|	...	|	1148	...	|	|
Frankfurt (Main) Hbf **920** d.	|	...	...	0454	...	0554	|	|	|	0654	|	|	0754	|	|	0854	|	|	0954	1022	|	1054	|	|	1154	|	|
Würzburg Hbf **900 920** d.	0354	...	...	0603	...	0703	|	0729	|	0803	0829	|	0903	0929	|	1003	1030	|	1103	1131	|	1203	1230	|	1312	1329	|
Nürnberg Hbf ⊡ d.	0452	0554	0630	0701	0728	0759	0811	0826	0859	0903	0930**j**	0955	0959	1026	1059	1103	1128	1155	1159	1227	1253	1303	1328	1355	1407	1427	1459
Ingolstadt Hbf d.	0524	0626	0704	0729	0802	|	|	0901	|	|	1006**j**	|	|	1101	|	1132	1201	|	|	1301	1323	|	1401	|	|	1501	|
München Hbf ⊡ a.	0604	0705	0741	0806	0845	0906	0918	0943	1002	1006	1045	1103	1107	1144	1202	1210	1240	1301	1305	1343	1402	1406	1441	1504	1512	1544	1601

Most *ICE* trains convey ✕	*ICE* 625	*ICE* 587	*ICE* 509	*ICE* 627	*ICE* 789	*ICE* 707	*ICE* 629	*ICE* 689	*ICE* 1601	*ICE* 721	*ICE* 881	*ICE* 1007	*ICE* 723	*ICE* 681	*ICE* 603	*ICE* 725	*ICE* 883	*ICE* 1009	*ICE* 727	*ICE* 683	*ICE* 1605	*ICE* 729	*ICE* 885	*ICE* 1019	*ICE* 821	*ICE* 685	*ICE* 1607
																					◧					⑤–⑦	⑤
	K			**K**			**K**			**K**		**D**	**K**			**K**			**K**			**K**	**L**		**K**		
Hamburg Hbf **840 900** d.	...	1101	1034**r**	...	1201	1136**r**	...	1301	1232**r**	...	1401	1404**x**	...	1501	1435**r**	...	1601	1551**x**	...	1701	1634**q**	...	1801	...	...	1901	1835**r**
Berlin Hbf **850** ⊡ d.	...	|	1228	...	|	1334	...	|	1429	...	|	1611	...	|	1628	...	|	1812	...	|	1829	...	|	2004	...	|	2029
Leipzig Hbf **850** d.	...	|	1348	...	|	|	...	|	1548	...	|	|	...	|	1748	...	|	|	...	|	1948	...	|	|	...	|	2148
Frankfurt (Main) Hbf **920** d.	1254	|	|	1354	|	|	1454	|	|	1554	|	|	1654	|	|	1754	|	|	1854	|	|	1954	|	|	2054	|	|
Würzburg Hbf **900 920** d.	1403	1430	|	1503	1529	|	1603	1629	|	1703	1729	|	1803	1831	|	1903	1929	|	2003	2030	|	2103	2129	|	2203	2229	|
Nürnberg Hbf ⊡ d.	1503	1528	1555	1559	1627	1655	1703	1728	1755	1759	1827	1859	1903	1931	1955	1959	2027	2059	2104	2128	2155	2206	2228	2259	2313	2331	0000
Ingolstadt Hbf d.	|	1602	|	|	1702	1725	|	1803	|	|	1903	|	|	2006	|	|	2101	|	2132	2201	|	2240	2301	|	2342	0004	0033
München Hbf ⊡ a.	1607	1641	1701	1706	1745	1803	1807	1842	1903	1907	1945	2002	2006	2045	2103	2107	2143	2202	2210	2240	2305	2318	2344	0001	0020	0045	0114

RE services via the high-speed line

km																												
			⑥**b**		Ⓒ**z**	Ⓐ**t**		Ⓒ**z**	Ⓐ**t**		Ⓐ**t**	Ⓒ**z**		**Y**	**R**		**Y**	**R**	Ⓒ**z**	Ⓐ**t**	**Y**	**R**		**N**	**Y**		⑤⑥	**Q**
0	**München** Hbf d.	0501	...	0705	0805	0805	0904	1004	1005	1105	1203	1204	1304	1400	1404	1504	1601	1604	1704	1710	*1801*	1804	1905	2005	*2003*	2105	2227	*2226*
50	Pfaffenhofen (Ilm) d.	0531	...	0732	0832	0834	0931	1032	1034	1132	1233	1232	1331	1430	1432	1531	1627	1632	1731	1742	*1832*	1832	1932	2032	*2034*	2132	2301	*2300*
81	**Ingolstadt** Hbf a.	0551	...	0752	0851	0854	0951	1050	1055	1152	1254	1251	1351	1451	1450	1551	1646	1650	1751	1801	*1852*	1852	1951	2051	*2055*	2151	2322	*2321*
81	**Ingolstadt** Hbf d.	0601	0658	0801	0852	...	1004	1052	...	1204	...	1252	1404	...	1452	1604	1648	1652	1802	1802	1904	1904	2001	2053	2104	2157	2324	2331
112	Kinding d.	0622	0714	0818	0914	...	1020	1113	...	1220	...	1313	1420	...	1513	1620	1704	1713	1823	1823	1920	1920	2018	2109	2120	2213	2340	2353
146	Allersberg d.	0637	0729	0833	0929	...	1035	1129	...	1235	...	1329	1435	...	1529	1635	1729	1729	1838	1838	1935	1935	2033	2124	2135	2228	2355	0008
171	**Nürnberg Hbf** a.	0652	0743	0851	0943	...	1051	1143	...	1251	...	1343	1451	...	1545	1651	1745	1745	1852	1852	1951	1951	2051	2138	2151	2242	0008	0022

	Ⓐ**t**	⑥**b**	Ⓐ**t**	†**z**	Ⓒ**z**	Ⓐ**t**	Ⓐ**t**	⑥**b**	Ⓒ	Ⓐ	Ⓒ**z**	Ⓐ**t**		Ⓒ**z**	Ⓐ**t**		Ⓐ**t**	Ⓒ**z**		**R**		**R**	**Y**		⊕		⊗	⑤⑥
Nürnberg Hbf d.	0509	0557	0607	0607	0706	0732	...	0815	0907	0907	1007	...	1107	1207	...	1307	...	1415	1507	1607	1707	1808	1808	1907	2007	2107	2233	2337
Allersberg d.	0522	0615	0620	0620	0719	0746	...	0829	0921	0925	1021	...	1121	1221	...	1321	...	1428	1521	1621	1721	1822	1822	1921	2021	2121	2246	2350
Kinding d.	0538	0630	0635	0635	0735	0801	...	0849	0936	0941	1037	...	1137	1237	...	1336	...	1448	1536	1637	1736	1838	1838	1938	2036	2136	2301	0005
Ingolstadt Hbf a.	0556	0648	0655	0653	0753	0818	...	0907	0955	1001	1054	...	1155	1254	...	1355	...	1506	1557	1657	1757	1857	1857	2001	2054	2154	2319	0023
Ingolstadt Hbf d.	0600	*0707*	0657	0701	0803	0820	0904	0909	1004	1009	1104	1104	1204	1304	1304	1404	1504	1508	1605	1705	1806	1906	*1907*	2009	2104	2204	2336	0024
Pfaffenhofen (Ilm) d.	0619	*0727*	0712	0720	0824	0838	0926	0928	1025	1031	1126	1125	1226	1326	1327	1426	1525	1526	1627	1726	1828	1927	*1928*	2030	2126	2226	0005	0042
München Hbf a.	0647	*0756*	0736	0748	0854	0902	0956	0955	1055	1059	1154	1155	1254	1355	1358	1454	1556	1555	1655	1754	1856	1955	*1958*	2057	2153	2254	0041	0110

RE services via EICHSTÄTT and TREUCHTLINGEN

km																												
		†**z**	⑥**b**	Ⓐ**t**	Ⓐ**t**	Ⓒ**z**	Ⓐ**t**															Ⓐ	†	⑥		**Q**	⑤⑥**d**	
0	**München** Hbf d.	...	...	...	0519	...	0558	0618	0724	0823	0926	1027	1126	1226	1324	1426	1526	1626	1722	1826	1924	2022	2023	2027	2126	2226	*2227*	2326
50	Pfaffenhofen (Ilm) d.	...	0500	0500	0601	...	0627	0653	0801	0859	1003	1102	1202	1302	1359	1501	1602	1702	1803	1902	2000	2101	2058	2102	2202	2300	*2301*	0003
81	**Ingolstadt** Hbf a.	...	0523	0521	0624	...	0647	0716	0822	0921	1025	1125	1224	1323	1421	1523	1624	1723	1825	1924	2022	2124	2120	2124	2223	2321	*2322*	0027
81	**Ingolstadt** Hbf d.	0524	0524	0523	0627	0627	0650	0730	0830	0930	1027	1129	1226	1326	1428	1526	1628	1727	1826	1926	2030	2125	2125	2125	2225	2322	2343	...
108	Eichstätt Bahnhof ♥ d.	0556	0556	0556	0656	0656	0710	0758	0857	0957	1056	1157	1256	1356	1457	1557	1657	1757	1857	1953	2057	2156	2156	2156	2256	2348	0009	...
137	Treuchtlingen a.	0620	0620	0620	0719	0719	...	0820	0919	1020	1119	1220	1319	1420	1520	1620	1720	1821	1919	2016	2119	2219	2219	2219	2319	0012	0034	...
137	Treuchtlingen **905** d.	0629	*0629*	*0629*	0725	0728	...	*0828*	0928	*1028*	1128	*1228***c**	1328	*1428*	1528	*1628*	1728	*1829*	1928	*2029*	2127	*2228*	*2228*	*2228*	2325	...	...	...
146	Weißenburg **905** d.	0635	*0635*	*0635*	0731	0734	...	*0834*	0934	*1034*	1134	*1234***c**	1334	*1434*	1534	*1635*	1734	*1835*	1934	*2036*	2133	*2234*	*2234*	*2234*	2331	...	...	...
199	**Nürnberg** Hbf **905** a.	0718	*0718*	*0719*	0817	0818	...	*0917*	1016	*1116*	1217	*1316***c**	1420	*1517*	1617	*1718*	1817	*1918*	2017	*2118*	2216	*2316*	*2316*	*2316*	0015	...	...	...

	Ⓐ**t**	Ⓒ**z**	⚒**t**	†**z**	Ⓐ**t**	Ⓒ**z**	Ⓐ**t**	Ⓒ**z**	Ⓐ**t**					Ⓒ**z**	Ⓐ**t**										**Q**		⊖	
Nürnberg Hbf **905** d.	...	...	*0441*	0441	0526	0539	...	*0639*	*0650*	0738	*0838*	0939	*1039*	1139	1139	*1238*	1339	*1438*	1538	*1639*	1739	*1838*	1937	*2039*	2138	2138	2244	2344
Weißenburg **905** d.	...	...	*0521*	0523	0608	0621	...	*0721*	*0723*	0821	*0920*	1021	*1120*	1221	1221	*1320*	1421	*1520*	1621	*1720*	1821	*1920*	2019	*2120*	2221	2221	2326	0025
Treuchtlingen **905** a.	...	...	*0527*	0530	0616	0628	...	*0726*	*0730*	0827	*0927*	1027	*1127*	1227	1227	*1327*	1427	*1527*	1627	*1727*	1830	*1927*	2025	*2127*	2227	2227	2332	0031
Treuchtlingen d.	0443	...	0532	0532	0632	0635	...	0735	0735	0835	0935	1035	1135	1235	1240	1336	1435	1535	1635	1735	1835	1935	2035	2135	2235	2235	2334	...
Eichstätt Bahnhof ♥ d.	0507	...	0556	0556	0655	0658	0720	0759	0759	0900	0959	1058	1159	1258	1303	1400	1458	1559	1658	1759	1858	1959	2105*	2159	2258	2258	2359	...
Ingolstadt Hbf a.	0532	...	0622	0622	0721	0724	0746	0825	0825	0936	1038	1136	1239	1327	1336	1439	1536	1639	1736	1841	1936	2038	2136	2224	2330	2330	0028	...
Ingolstadt Hbf d.	0534	0539	0631	0631	0734	0734	0750	0831**y**	0835	0937	1040	1137	1240	1333	1338	1440	1537	1640	1737	1842	1937	2040	2137	2234	2336	...	...	...
Pfaffenhofen (Ilm) d.	0555	0559	0655	0655	0758	0758	0811	0854**y**	0903	1005**v**	1104	1159	1304	1356	1401	1505	1600	1704	1801	1906	2005	2103	2200	2303	0005	...	...	...
München Hbf a.	0630	0634	0732	0732	0833	0834	0837	0932**y**	0939	1041**v**	1140	1235	1339	1433	1437	1541	1636	1741	1838	1941	2041	2139	2236	2340	0041	...	...	...

A – [12] München - Kassel (- Hamburg ⑦).
B – To Kassel (Table **900**).
D – To / from Lübeck (Table **825**).
E – From Lichtenfels (Tables **850** and **875**).
G – From / to Garmisch on ⑥ (Table **895**).
K – To / from Köln, Essen or Dortmund (Table **800**).
L – To / from Kiel (Table **820**).
M – [12] (Hamburg ① -) Kassel - München.
N – ⑤⑥† (5 minutes later Kinding - Nürnberg on ⑦).
Q – ⑦–④ (also Aug. 15, Oct. 3).
R – ⑤⑥† only.
Y – ①–④ (not June 9, Oct. 3).

b – Not Nov. 1.
c – On Ⓐ Treuchtlingen d. *1238*, Weißenburg d. *1245*, Nürnberg a. *1329*.
d – Not Aug. 15, Oct. 3.
e – 0711 from Sept. 24.
g – ① only.
h – 1945 on ⑥.
j – On ⑥ Nürnberg d. 0928, Ingolstadt d. 1001.
n – Not June 9, 19, Aug. 15, Oct. 3.
q – Not ⑥. Note **r** applies.
r – Arrives later / departs earlier from Aug. 2, (diverted via Stendal and Salzwedel; see amended version of Table **840** on page 608).
s – Not Aug. 10.
t – Not Aug. 15.
v – 5 minutes earlier on ⑦.
w – Until Sept. 19.
x – Not Aug. 2 - Dec. 13.

y – On ⑥ Ingolstadt Hbf d. 0835, Pfaffenhofen d. 0903, München a. 0939.
z – Also Aug. 15.

‡ – Kassel - Hamburg on ⑦ only.
◧ – Train number **1715** on ⑥.
⊕ – Change trains at Ingolstadt Hbf on ①–④ **Y** (connecting train arrives München 2158).
⊗ – Change trains at Ingolstadt Hbf on ⑦–④ (also Aug. 15).
⊖ – Change trains at Treuchtlingen on ⑤⑥ (also Aug. 14, Oct. 2); connecting train departs Treuchtlingen *2337*.
⊡ – Additional trains run München - Nürnberg - Berlin and v.v. (see Table **850**).
♥ – Connecting trains run Eichstätt Bahnhof - Eichstätt Stadt (*5 km*; operated by Bayerische Regiobahn).
* – Arrives 2058.

905 MÜNCHEN - AUGSBURG - NÜRNBERG and WÜRZBURG

ICE / IC services (also fast *RE* services). See Table **904** for services via Ingolstadt.

km		*ICE* **804** Ⓐ ✕		*ICE* **802** ✕	*ICE* **1586** ⒷF ✕	*ICE* **1694** ✕	*RE* **57022**	*RE* **3285** H		*ICE* **708** ✕	*IC* **2082** F K	*ICE* **1284** ⑦D	*ICE* **1206** ⑥F ♣✕	*ICE* **1284** ⑤ G	*ICE* **1284** ⑦F ♥✕	*ICE* **704** ✕	*ICE* **1204** ⑦ ♣✕		*ICE* **702** ✕		*RB* **57170** Ⓒz	*RB* **57072** Ⓐt	*RE* **3299** H	*ICE* **1500** Ⓑ L✕
	München Ost d.	...	...	...	...	...	...	...	...	...	1117	...	...	...	1338	...	...	...	...	...	...	...	...	...
0	**München** Hbf 910 930 d.	0506	...	0713	0814	0838	0834	...	...	1113	|	1342	1356	1356	1356	1513	1552	...	1709	...	1803	1815	...	1909
7	München Pasing 910 930 d.	0515	...	0721	|	0849	0843	...	...	1122	1130	|	|	|	|	1522	1601	...	1717	...	1811	1823	...	1918
62	**Augsburg** Hbf. 900 910 930 d.	0540	...	0746	0847	0913	0918	0926	...	1146	1230**h**	1412	1425	1425	1425	1546	1624	...	1741	...	1854**v**	1902	1919	1943
103	Donauwörth d.	0602	...	0808	|	0933	...	0949	...	1208	1248	|	1443	1444	1444	1608	1645	...	1803	...	1934	1938	1945	2007
137	Treuchtlingen d.	0622	...	|	|	|	...	1008	...	|	1311	|	1504	1505	1505	|	1704	...	1824	...	...	...	2004	2026
199	**Nürnberg** Hbf 900 920 a.	0657	...	0859	|	1023	...	1045	...	1259	|	1521	|	|	|	1659	|	...	1859	...	...	...	2035	2059
	Berlin Hbf **850** a.	1022	...	1222	|	1353	...	...	...	1622	|	|	|	|	|	2022	|	...	2222	...	...	...	...	...
	Ansbach d.	|	...	|	0948	...	...	...	...	|	1345	|	1534	1534	1534	|	1734	...	...	...	...	...	...	...
	Steinach (b. Rothenb) d.	|	...	|	|	...	...	...	...	|	1404	|	|	|	|	|	|	...	...	...	...	...	...	...
	Würzburg Hbf 900 920 a.	|	...	|	1038	...	...	...	...	|	1437	1629	1629	1629	1629	|	1831	...	...	...	...	...	...	...
	Hamburg Hbf **840 900** a.	1222**r**	...	1423**r**	1429	...	...	...	...	1822**r**	1830	2038	2035	2038	2038	2222**r**	2229	...	...	...	...	...	...	...

	ICE **1581** Ⓐ ✕	*ICE* **987** Ⓐ ✕	*RE* **3284** H	*RE* **57033**		*ICE* **1701** ①-⑤ ✕		*ICE* **701** ✕	*ICE* **701** ①-⑤ ✕		*IC* **2083** P K	*ICE* **1207** ⑥F ♣✕		*ICE* **705** ✕	*ICE* **1285** ⒷF	*ICE* **1285** ⑤F ♥✕	*RE* **3298** H	*RE* **57075**	*ICE* **1695** ✕	*ICE* **1205** ⒷF ●✕	*ICE* **709** ✕		*ICE* **801** ✕	
Hamburg Hbf **840 900** d.	...	...	...	...	...	...	...	...	0527**r**	...	0729	0828	...	0936**r**	1128	1128	...	...	...	1328	1336**r**	...	1536**r**	...
Würzburg Hbf 900 920 d.	...	...	...	...	...	...	...	...	|	...	1123	1216	...	|	1512	1512	...	...	...	1711	|	...	|	...
Steinach (b. Rothenb) d.	...	...	...	...	...	...	...	...	|	...	1156	|	...	|	|	|	...	...	...	|	|	...	|	...
Ansbach d.	...	...	...	...	...	...	...	...	|	...	1216	|	...	|	1608	1608	...	...	...	1813	|	...	|	...
Berlin Hbf **850** d.	...	...	...	...	...	0534	...	0734	0734	...	|	|	...	1134	|	|	...	...	1404	|	1534	...	1734	...
Nürnberg Hbf 900 920 d.	...	0547	0719**e**	...	...	0900	...	1059	1059	...	|	|	...	1459	|	|	1713	...	1732	|	1859	...	2100	...
Treuchtlingen d.	...	0622	0750	...	...	|	...	|	|	...	1246	|	...	|	1639	1639	1746	...	|	1845	|	...	|	...
Donauwörth d.	0557	0642	0808	...	...	0950	...	1150	1150	...	1308	|	...	1550	1706	1706	1806	...	1826	1906	1950	...	2151	...
Augsburg Hbf 900 910 930 a.	0617	0706	0832	0838	...	1009	...	1208	1208	...	1330	1407	...	1608	1731	1731	1829	1838	1846	1930	2009	...	2210	...
München Pasing 910 930 a.	0641	0730	...	0914	...	1032	...	1232	1232	...	1358	|	...	1632	|	|	...	1913	|	1953	2032	...	2233	...
München Hbf 910 930 a.	0652	0740	...	0923	...	1042	...	1242	1242	...	|	1449	...	1642	1803	1803	...	1921	1917	2002	2042	...	2243	...
München Ost a.	...	...	...	...	...	...	...	...	...	...	1411	...	...	...	...	1835	...	...	...	...	...	...	...	...

RE services **MÜNCHEN - TREUCHTLINGEN - WÜRZBURG** (operated by Arverio Bayern). **SERVICE TO OCT. 9**. See note ★ for connecting trains Steinach - Rothenburg ob der Tauber

km		Ⓒ	Ⓐ	Ⓒ	Ⓐ	Ⓐ	Ⓐ	Ⓒ			▽		▽		▽		▽		▽		A		▽			N	
0	**München** Hbf 930 d.	0005	...	...	...	...	...	...	0528	...	0736	...	0935	...	1135	...	1335	...	1536	...	1735	...	1935	...	2057	2159	2258
7	München Pasing 930 d.	0014	...	...	...	...	...	...	0536	...	0744	...	0943	...	1143	...	1343	...	1544	...	1743	...	1943	...	2105	2207	2305
62	**Augsburg** Hbf 930 a.	0053	...	...	...	...	...	...	0618	...	0818	...	1019	...	1219	...	1419	...	1619	...	1819	...	2020	...	2146	2246	2346
62	**Augsburg** Hbf d.	*0057*	...	...	...	...	...	...	0628	...	0828	...	1028	...	1224	...	1428	...	1628	...	1828	...	2028	...	2154	2256	*0000*
103	Donauwörth d.	*0139*	...	...	...	...	...	...	0659	...	0859	...	1059	...	1259	...	1459	...	1659	...	1859	...	2059	...	2239	2334	*0040*
137	Treuchtlingen a.	▬	...	...	...	...	...	...	0720	...	0920	...	1120	...	1320	...	1520	...	1720	...	1920	...	2120	...	2301	...	...
137	Treuchtlingen d.	...	...	0502	0512	0549	0625	0625	0726	0825	0928	1025	1128	1225	1328	1425	1528	1625	1728	1826	1928	2024	2128	2225	...	...	...
161	Gunzenhausen d.	...	...	0516	0526	0603	0638	0638	0741	0840	0940	1040	1140	1240	1340	1440	1541	1640	1740	1840	1940	2040	2140	2240	...	...	...
188	Ansbach a.	⚒	...	0536	0547	0623	0658	0658	0801	0901	1001	1101	1201	1301	1401	1501	1601	1701	1801	1901	2001	2101	2201	2259	...	...	...
188	Ansbach d.	0440	0524	0537	0601	0631	0659	0711	0811	0910	1011	1111	1211	1311	1411	1511	1611	1711**y**	1811	1911	2011	2111	...	2311	...	...	...
220	Steinach ★ d.	0503	0547	0601	0624	0653	0722	0733	0833	0932	1033	1133	1233	1333	1433	1533	1633	1733**y**	1833	1933	2033	2133	...	2333	...	...	...
277	**Würzburg** Hbf a.	0547	0631	0644	0708	0736	0805	0817	0918	1016	1116	1216	1317	1417	1517	1617	1717	1816**y**	1916	2017	2117	2217	...	0017	...	...	...

	Ⓒ	Ⓐ	Ⓐ	⑥	Ⓐ		Ⓐ	Ⓒ	Ⓐ	▽		▽		▽		▽		▽		▽		▽				⚒	
Würzburg Hbf d.	...	...	0430	0441	...	...	0522	0522	0555	0641	0741	0841	0941	1041	1141	1241	1341	1441	1541	1641	1741	1841	1941	2041	2141	2304	2304
Steinach ★ d.	...	...	0513	0524	...	...	0606	0606	0637	0724	0824	0924	1024	1124	1224	1326	1424	1525	1626	1724	1824	1925	2024	2124	2223	2347	2347
Ansbach a.	...	...	0535	0545	...	...	0627	0627	0700	0747	0845	0945	1045	1145	1246	1347	1445	1545	1646	1745	1845	1945	2045	2145	2245	0009	0009
Ansbach d.	...	...	0537	0554	0601	...	0628	0654	0710	0754	0854	0954	1054	1154	1254	1354	1454	1554	1654	1754	1854	1954	2054	2154	2254	0010	...
Gunzenhausen d.	...	...	0556	0616	0620	...	0648	0719	0730	0819	0915	1019	1115	1219	1315	1419	1515	1619	1715	1819	1915	2019	2116	2219	2315	0029	...
Treuchtlingen a.	...	...	0609	0629	0633	...	0700	0730	0744	0830	0928	1030	1128	1230	1328	1430	1528	1630	1728	1830	1928	2030	2128	2230	2328	0044	...
Treuchtlingen d.	...	...	...	0634	0634	0634	...	...	...	0834	...	1034	...	1234	...	1434	...	1634	...	1834	...	2034	...	2234	...	...	...
Donauwörth d.	0528	0530	...	0659	0659	0659	...	...	...	0859	...	1059	...	1259	...	1459	...	1658	...	1859	...	2059	...	2259	...	...	...
Augsburg Hbf a.	0608	0608	...	0728	0728	0728	...	...	...	0928	...	1128	...	1328	...	1528	...	1728	...	1928	...	2128	...	2340	...	...	...
Augsburg Hbf 930 d.	0613	0619	...	0737	0737	0737	...	...	...	0938	...	1137	...	1337	...	1538	...	1738	...	1938	...	2139	...	*2349*	...	...	...
München Pasing 930 a.	0653	0653	...	0811	0811	0811	...	...	...	1012	...	1212	...	1412	...	1612	...	1812	...	2012	...	2223	...	*0029*	...	...	...
München Hbf 930 a.	0701	0701	...	0819	0819	0819	...	...	...	1020	...	1220	...	1420	...	1620	...	1821	...	2020	...	2231	...	*0037*	...	...	...

RE services **MÜNCHEN - DONAUWÖRTH - AALEN** (operated by Arverio Bayern). *On Aug. 15 service is as on ⑦.*

km		Ⓐ	Ⓐ	Ⓒ	Ⓐ												Ⓐ		Ⓐ	Ⓐ	Ⓐ	Ⓒ					
	München Hbf d.	...	...	...	...	...	...	0736**z**	...	0935	...	1135	...	1335	...	1536	...	...	1641	...	...	1735	...	1935	...	...	2159
	Augsburg Hbf d.	...	...	...	0521	...	...	0828	...	1028	...	1224	...	1428	...	1628	...	...	1733	...	...	1828	...	2028	...	...	2256
0	Donauwörth d.	...	...	0607	0607	0710	0812	0906	1012	1105	1212	1312	1405	1512	1611	1712	1754	1812	1826	1900	1912	1912	2008	2105	2212	...	2339
29	Nördlingen d.	0441	0534	0641	0641	0742	0842	0942**f**	1042	1142**v**	1242	1342	1442**v**	1542	1642	1742	1820	1842	1859	1921	1939	1942	2049**v**	2142**f**	2242	...	0012**v**
68	**Aalen** Hbf a.	0519	0613	0722	0723	0824	0924	1024	1124	1224	1324	1424	1524	1624	1724	1824	...	1924	...	1950	2016	2024	2125	2224	2324	...	0048

	Ⓐ	Ⓐ		Ⓐ	Ⓐ	Ⓒ	Ⓐ										Ⓐ				Ⓒ	Ⓐ				⑤⑥	
Aalen Hbf d.	...	...	...	0537	0608	0631	0631	0733	0833	0933	1033	1133	1233	1333	1433	1533	...	1633	1733	1833	1933	1944	2033	2133	2233	2233	2331
Nördlingen d.	0520	0557	0623	0623	0640	0708	0708	0821**v**	0915	1021**v**	1117	1221**v**	1321**v**	1421**v**	1521**v**	1621**v**	1703	1721**v**	1821**v**	1921**v**	2025**f**	2025	2114	2221**v**	2310	2318	0008
Donauwörth a.	0546	0630	0652	0652	0706	0734	0737	0851	0947	1051	1149	1251	1351	1449	1551	1651	1734	1751	1851	1951	2051	2051	2146	2252	...	2350	...
Augsburg Hbf a.	...	0710	...	...	0800	...	0821	0928	...	1128	...	1328	...	1528	...	1728	...	...	1928	...	2128	2128	...	...	...	...	...
München Hbf a.	...	0802	...	...	0854	...	...	1020	...	1220	...	1420	...	1620	...	1821	...	...	2020	...	2231	2231	...	...	...	...	...

RE services **AUGSBURG - TREUCHTLINGEN - NÜRNBERG** (operated by DB). *On Aug. 15 service is as on ⑦.*

	Ⓒ	⑥	Ⓐ			Ⓒ	Ⓐ					
Augsburg Hbf d.	0310	0528	0557	0719**c**	0932	1126	1126	1326	1527	1726	1926	2128
Donauwörth d.	0350	0559	0627	0757	1000	1159	1159	1359	1559	1758	1959	2159
Treuchtlingen a.	0411	0619	0647	0818	1020	1220	1220	1420	1620	1818	2019	2220
Treuchtlingen 904 d.	0412	0629	0649	0828	1028	1228	1238	1428	1628	1829	2029	2228
Weißenburg 904 d.	0418	0635	0655	0834	1034	1234	1245	1434	1635	1835	2036	2234
Nürnberg Hbf 904 a.	0502	0718	0730	0917	1116	1316	1329	1517	1718	1918	2118	2316

	⑥	Ⓐ	Ⓒ	Ⓐ							
Nürnberg Hbf 904 d.	0441	0441	0639	0650	0838	1039	1238	1438	1639	1838	2039
Weißenburg 904 d.	0521	0521	0721	0723	0920	1120	1320	1520	1720	1920	2120
Treuchtlingen 904 a.	0527	0527	0726	0730	0927	1127	1327	1527	1727	1927	2127
Treuchtlingen d.	0528	0528	0735	0735	0934	1134	1335	1534	1734	1935	2135
Donauwörth d.	0549	0604**j**	0758	0758	0958	1158	1358	1558	1758	1958	2158
Augsburg Hbf a.	0620	0635	0828	0828	1027	1228	1428	1629	1827	2029	2228

A – Change trains at Ansbach on Ⓐ. On Ⓒ conveys (12) München - Donauwörth - Aalen (see panel).
D – ⑦ Oct. 12 - Dec. 7.
F – Until Oct. 9.
G – ⑤ to Oct. 3 (also June 15, Oct. 2).
H – From / to Lindau and Oberstdorf (Table **935**).
K – KÖNIGSSEE – (12) Berchtesgaden - Augsburg - Hamburg and v.v.
L – To Leipzig (Table **850**).
N – To Aalen (see panel).
P – Until Oct. 8.

c – 0728 on Ⓒ.
e – 3 minutes earlier from Oct. 10.
f – Arrives 10–12 minutes earlier.
h – Arrives 1159.
j – Arrives 0549.

r – For Hamburg times from Aug. 2 (also Aug. 1 after 2200) see amended Table **840** on page 608 (trains are diverted via Salzwedel with journey times extended).
v – Arrives 6–9 minutes earlier.
y – 3 minutes later on ⑥.
z – Ⓒ only.

♣ – From / to Innsbruck via Garmisch on dates in Table **895**.
♥ – From / to Schwarzach-St Veit via Wörgl (Table **960**).
● – Continues to Innsbruck via Garmisch on ⑤ (Table **895**).
▽ – Conveys (12) München - Augsburg - Donauwörth - Aalen and v.v. (see panel below).

★ – Steinach (b. Rothenburg). Connecting trains Steinach - Rothenburg ob der Tauber and v.v. Operated by DB. 2nd class only. *12 km*. Journey time: 15 minutes.
From Steinach at 0422 Ⓐ, 0517 ⚒, 0627, 0727 Ⓐ, 0736 Ⓒ, 0836, 0936 and hourly until 1636; then 1739, 1836 Ⓒ, 1845 Ⓐ, 1936, 2036, 2136 Ⓒ and 2236.
From Rothenburg ob der Tauber at 0444 Ⓐ, 0540 ⑥, 0547 Ⓐ, 0658 Ⓐ, 0705 Ⓒ, 0805, 0905, 1005, 1105, 1205, 1309, 1405 and hourly until 2005; then 2105 Ⓒ, 2205 and 2305.

906 GIESSEN - KOBLENZ; LIMBURG - FRANKFURT and WIESBADEN

DB (*RE* services); HLB★

GIESSEN - KOBLENZ (additional stopping trains operate).

km												
				⚒								
0	**Gießen** .... **807** d.	...	0618	0716	0916	1116	1316	1516	1716	1916	2116	2122	2222
13	Wetzlar .... **807** d.	...	0631	0726	0926	1126	1326	1526	1726	1926	2126	2136	2236
36	Weilburg .... d.	...	0655	0743	0943	1143	1343	1543	1743	1943	2143	2200	2300
65	**Limburg** (Lahn) .. a.	...	0734	0808	1008	1208	1408	1608	1808	2008	2208	2237	2337
			◧	|	|	|	|	|	|	|	|	◧ Ⓒ	◧ ⑤⑥ f
65	**Limburg** (Lahn) .. d.	0638	0745	0809	1009	1209	1409	1609	1809	2009	2209	2245	2345
68	Diez .... d.	0642	0749	0813	1013	1213	1413	1613	1813	2013	2213	2250	2350
91	Nassau (Lahn) .... d.	0716	0819	0833	1033	1233	1433	1633	1833	2033	2233	2316	0016
99	Bad Ems .... d.	0725	0828	0841	1040	1240	1440	1640	1841	2040	2240	2325	0025
112	Niederlahnstein ... d.	0742	0844	0853	1053	1253	1453	1653	1853	2053	2253	2342	0042
117	**Koblenz** Hbf ...... a.	0750	0850	0901	1102	1300	1500	1701	1900	2101	2300	2351	0050

	Ⓐ										Ⓒ
Koblenz Hbf .... d.	0509	0657	0857	1057	1257	1457	1657	1857	1909	2109	2209
Niederlahnstein .... d.	0516	0704	0904	1104	1304	1504	1704	1904	1916	2116	2216
Bad Ems .... d.	0532	0716	0916	1116	1316	1516	1716	1916	1932	2132	2232
Nassau (Lahn) ...... d.	0541	0726	0926	1126	1326	1526	1726	1926	1941	2141	2244
Diez .... d.	0608	0747	0947	1147	1347	1547	1747	1947	2008	2208	2315
Limburg (Lahn) .... a.	0614	0750	0950	1150	1350	1550	1750	1950	2014	2214	2320
	◧ d	|	|	|	|	|	|	|	◧	◧	
Limburg (Lahn) .... d.	0618	0751	0951	1151	1351	1551	1751	1951	2023	2223	...
Weilburg .... d.	0655	0816	1016	1216	1416	1616	1816	2016	2100	2300	...
Wetzlar .... **807** d.	0720	0832	1032	1232	1432	1632	1832	2032	2127	2327	...
Gießen .... **807** a.	0732	0842	1042	1242	1442	1642	1842	2042	2138	2338	...

LIMBURG - NIEDERNHAUSEN - FRANKFURT and WIESBADEN.

km																									
		Ⓒ	Ⓒ		⚒	Ⓐ	Ⓐ			Ⓐ	Ⓐ	Ⓐ	Ⓒ	Ⓒ	Ⓐ	Ⓐ	Ⓐ	Ⓐ			Ⓐ	Ⓐ			
0	**Limburg** (Lahn) .... d.	0019	...	0419	...	0449	...	0519	...	0556	...	0612	0619	...	0633	0640	0656	...	0719	...	0756	...	0819	...	and at
21	Bad Camberg .... d.	0043	...	0443	...	0513	...	0543	...	0615	...	0636	0643	...	0657	0704	0715	...	0743	...	0815	...	0843	...	the same
30	Idstein .... d.	0052	...	0452	...	0522	...	0552	...	0622	...	0646	0652	...	0706	0715	0722	...	0752	...	0822	...	0852	...	minutes
38	Niedernhausen .... ‡ d.	0059	0105	0459	0504	0529	0535	0559	0605	0629	0635	0653	0659	0705	0713	0723	0729	0735	0759	0803	0829	0835	0859	0905	past each
58	**Wiesbaden** Hbf ..... a.	|	0127	|	0525	|	0557	|	0627	|	0656	0715	|	0727	|	0745	|	0759	|	0828	|	0857	|	0927	hour until
70	**Frankfurt** (Main) Hbf ‡ a.	0131	...	0531	...	0601	...	0631	...	0701	...	...	0731	...	0743	...	0759	...	0831	...	0859	...	0931	...	

			Ⓐ			Ⓐ	Ⓐ	◇			Ⓐ	Ⓐ			Ⓐ									
Limburg (Lahn) .... d.	1219	...	1250	1319	...	1356	...	and at	1719	...	1756	...	1819	...	1849	1919	...	2019	...	2119	...	2219	...	2319	...
Bad Camberg .... d.	1243	...	1314	1343	...	1415	...	the same	1743	...	1815	...	1843	...	1913	1943	...	2043	...	2143	...	2243	...	2343	...
Idstein .... d.	1252	...	1324	1352	...	1422	...	minutes	1752	...	1822	...	1852	...	1923	1952	...	2052	...	2152	...	2252	...	2352	...
Niedernhausen .... ‡ d.	1259	1305	1335	1359	1405	1429	1435	past each	1759	1805	1829	1835	1859	1905	1935	1959	2005	2059	2105	2159	2205	2259	2305	2359	0005
Wiesbaden Hbf ...... a.	|	1327	1357	|	1427	|	1457	hour until	|	1827	|	1857	|	1927	1957	|	2027	|	2127	|	2227	|	2327	|	0027
Frankfurt (Main) Hbf ‡ a.	1331	...	...	1430	...	1501	...		1830	...	1901	...	1931	...	...	2030	...	2131	...	2229	...	2331	...	0031	...

			⚒		Ⓐ	Ⓐ	Ⓒ	Ⓒ	Ⓐ	Ⓐ	Ⓐ	Ⓒ		Ⓐ			⊠			Ⓐ	Ⓐ		Ⓐ	Ⓐ
Frankfurt (Main) Hbf ‡ d.	...	0029	...	0530	...	0559	...	0629	...	0659	...	...	0728	...	...	0829	and at	...	1329	...	1359	...	1429	...	1459
Wiesbaden Hbf ...... d.	0036	|	0536	|	0606	|	0636	|	0653	|	0723	0736	|	0806	0836	|	the same	1336	|	1406	|	1436	|	1506	|
Niedernhausen .... ‡ d.	0058	0101	0558	0601	0628	0631	0658	0701	0714	0731	0758	0758	0801	0831	0858	0901	minutes	1358	1401	1428	1431	1458	1501	1528	1531
Idstein .... d.	...	0107	...	0607	...	0637	...	0707	...	0737	...	...	0807	0838	...	0907	past each	...	1407	...	1437	...	1507	...	1537
Bad Camberg .... d.	...	0117	...	0616	...	0646	...	0716	...	0744	...	...	0816	0847	...	0916	hour until	...	1416	...	1444	...	1516	...	1544
Limburg (Lahn) .... a.	...	0142	...	0639	...	0709	...	0741	...	0803	...	...	0841	0911	...	0941		...	1441	...	1503	...	1541	...	1603

	Ⓒ	Ⓒ	Ⓐ	Ⓐ	Ⓐ	Ⓒ	Ⓒ	Ⓐ	Ⓐ	Ⓐ	Ⓐ		Ⓒ	Ⓐ	Ⓐ	Ⓐ			Ⓐ	Ⓐ					
Frankfurt (Main) Hbf ‡ d.	...	1529	...	...	1559	...	1629	...	1643	...	1658	...	1729	1743	...	1759	...	1829	...	1900	...	1929	and at	...	2329
Wiesbaden Hbf ...... d.	1536	|	1536	1606	|	1636	|	1636	|	1706	|	1736	|	|	1806	|	1836	|	1906	|	1936	|	the same	2336	|
Niedernhausen .... ‡ d.	1558	1601	1601	1628	1631	1658	1701	1701	1716	1728	1731	1758	1801	1816	1828	1831	1858	1901	1928	1931	1958	2001	minutes	2358	0001
Idstein .... d.	...	1607	1608	...	1637	...	1707	1708	1722	...	1737	...	1807	1822	...	1837	...	1907	...	1937	...	2007	past each	...	0007
Bad Camberg .... d.	...	1616	1617	...	1644	...	1716	1717	1731	...	1744	...	1816	1831	...	1844	...	1916	...	1944	...	2016	hour until	...	0016
Limburg (Lahn) .... a.	...	1641	1641	...	1703	...	1741	1741	1755	...	1803	...	1841	1854	...	1903	...	1941	...	2003	...	2041		...	0041

d – Daily. Runs 5 – 7 minutes later on Ⓒ.
f – Not Oct. 3.
◧ – Change trains at Limburg.
★ – Hessische Landesbahn.
⊠ – Frankfurt (Main) Hbf d. 0926 (not 0929).
◇ – Timings may vary by 1 – 2 minutes.
‡ – Frequent S-Bahn *S2* services also run Frankfurt - Niedernhausen and v.v.

907 GIESSEN - FULDA

Hessische Landesbahn

km																										
		Ⓐ	Ⓐ	Ⓐ	⑥	Ⓐ		Ⓐ	Ⓒ	Ⓐ					Ⓐ	Ⓒ										
0	**Gießen** .... d.	...	...	0521	...	...	...	0613	0744	0748	0844	0947	1044	1147	1241	1244	1347	1444**t**	1547	1644**t**	1747	1844**t**	1947	2111	2211	2311
23	Grünberg (Oberhess). d.	...	...	0547	...	0613	...	0704	0811	0811	0911	1013	1111	1213	1311	1311	1411**v**	1511	1611**v**	1711	1811**v**	1911	2015	2135	2239	2336
60	Alsfeld (Oberhess) ..... d.	0515	0558	0631**j**	0650	0715**r**	0750	0750	0850	0850	0950	1050	1150	1250	1350	1350	1450	1550	1650	1750	1850	1950	2056**j**	2219**j**	2319	0010
79	Lauterbach (Hess) ..... d.	0528	0611	0647	0704	0729	0804	0804	0904	0904	1004	1104	1204	1304	1404	1404	1504	1604	1704	1804	1904	2008	2109	2237	...	...
106	**Fulda** .... a.	0553	0637	0717	0730	0759	0830	0830	0930	0930	1030	1130	1230	1330	1430	1430	1530	1630	1730	1830	1930	2039	2139	2301	...	...

	Ⓐ	Ⓐ	Ⓐ	⑥	Ⓐ	Ⓒ	Ⓐ	Ⓐ	Ⓒ	⑥	Ⓐ														
Fulda .... d.	...	...	...	...	0526	...	0610	0650	...	0733	0732	0833	0933	1033	1133	1233	1333	1433	1533	1633	1733	1833	2010	2101	2209	2309
Lauterbach (Hess) ...... d.	...	...	...	...	0557	...	0652**k**	0731**h**	...	0805	0805	0905	1005	1105	1205	1305	1405	1505	1605	1705	1805	1905	2037	2127	2236	2336
Alsfeld (Oberhess) ...... d.	0417	0530	0550	0612	0626**k**	0712	0714**j**	0744	0819	0819	0819	0919	1019	1119	1219	1319	1419	1519	1619	1719	1819	1919	2058**j**	2141	2249	2349
Grünberg (Oberhess) .. d.	0451	0611	0636	0647	0701	0747	0750	...	0851	0851	0853	0953	1051	1153	1251**t**	1353	1451**t**	1553	1651**t**	1753	1851**t**	1953	2137	2217	...	...
Gießen .... a.	0516	0637	0700	0710	0731	0816	0817	...	0916	0916	0916	1018	1116	1218	1316	1416**v**	1516	1616**v**	1716	1817	1916	2018	2202	2242	...	...

h – Arrives 0716.
j – Arrives 7 – 9 minutes earlier.
k – Arrives 10 – 12 minutes earlier.
r – Arrives 0658.
t – 2 – 3 minutes later on Ⓐ.
v – 2 minutes later on Ⓒ.

908 GÖTTINGEN - BEBRA

CANTUS Verkehrsgesellschaft (2nd class only)

km											
		Ⓐ	⚒	⚒	Ⓐ	Ⓒ d					
0	**Göttingen** .... **864** d.	0414	0514	0614	0646	0714	0814		2114	2214	2314
20	Eichenberg .... **864** d.	0430	0530	0630	0701	0730	0830	and	2130	2230	2330
35	Bad Sooden-Allendorf ...... d.	0440	0540	0640	0710	0740	0840	hourly	2140	2240	2340
49	Eschwege .... a.	0451	0551	0651	0721	0751	0851	until	2151	2251	2351
49	Eschwege .... d.	0521	0621	0725	|	0821	0921		2221	2313	2357
87	**Bebra** .... a.	0550	0650	0754	*0754*e	0850	0950		2250	2342	0027

	Ⓐ	⚒							
Bebra .... d.	0400	0530	0631	0708	0808		2008	2108	2208
Eschwege .... a.	0428	0558	0659	0737	0836	and	2036	2136	2236
Eschwege .... d.	0434	0605	0705	0805	0905	hourly	2105	2205	2305
Bad Sooden-Allendorf ... d.	0445	0616	0716	0816	0916	until	2116	2216	2316
Eichenberg .... **864** d.	0502	0631	0731	0831	0931		2131	2229	2331
Göttingen .... **864** a.	0515	0645	0745	0845	0945		2145	2243	2345

d – Runs daily Eschwege - Bebra.
e – Change trains at Eschwege-Niederhone (a. 0718, d. *0728*).

909 WÜRZBURG - BAD KISSINGEN - GEMÜNDEN

DB (*RE* services); EB★

On June 19 services run as on ⑦.

km																									
								Ⓒ	Ⓐ		Ⓐ														
0	**Würzburg** Hbf .... **870 876** ‡ d.	...	...	0801	...	...	1001	...	...	1201	...	...	1401	...	...	1601	...	...	1801	...	...	2001	...	...	...
43	**Schweinfurt** Hbf. **870 876** ‡ d.	0610	0812	0830	0912	1012	1029	1205	1205	1230	1302	1412	1430	1512	1612	1630	1712	1812	1830	1912	2012	2030	2113	2224	2351
57	Ebenhausen (Unterf) ... **870** ‡ d.	0624	0825	0843	0929	1025	1043	1226	1226	1243	1316	1425	1443	1529	1625	1643	1729	1825	1843	1929	2025	2043	2129	2240	0005
66	**Bad Kissingen** .... a.	0633	0834	0853	0938	1034	1053	1235	1235	1253	1325	1434	1453	1538	1634	1653	1738	1834	1853	1938	2034	2053	2138	2249	0014
66	**Bad Kissingen** .... d.	0637	0841	...	...	1041	...	1241	1241	...	1343	1441	...	1543**t**	1641	...	1743**t**	1841	...	1943	2043	...	2142	...	...
85	Hammelburg .... d.	0659	0908	...	...	1105	...	1306	1313	...	1406	1506	...	1606**t**	1706	...	1807**t**	1906	...	2006	2107	...	2207	...	...
113	**Gemünden** (Main) .... a.	0737	0941	...	...	1140	...	1340	1350	...	1441	1540	...	1641**t**	1741	...	1841**t**	1941	...	2039	2143	...	...	...	...

	Ⓐ		Ⓒ	Ⓐ							Ⓒ	Ⓐ	Ⓐ												
Gemünden (Main) .... d.	...	...	...	*0614*	0707**r**	...	0811	...	1011	...	1211	1211	1320	...	1411	1510**t**	...	1610	1710**t**	...	1810	1910**t**	...	2113	2211
Hammelburg .... d.	0545	*0612***t**	0636	*0700*	0748**r**	...	0844	...	1044	...	1244	1244	1407**e**	...	1444	1543**t**	...	1644	1743**t**	...	1845	1943**t**	...	2146	2248
Bad Kissingen .... a.	0607	*0636***t**	0702	*0722*	0810**r**	...	0907	...	1107	...	1307	1307	1429	...	1507	1609**t**	...	1707	1808**t**	...	1907	2008**t**	...	2208	2309
Bad Kissingen .... d.	0612	0641	0706	0730	0814	0900	0918	1100	1118	1300	1318	1326	...	1500	1518	1614	1700	1718	1813	1900	1918	2013	2100	2213	2313
Ebenhausen (Unterf) ..... **870** a.	0621	0650	0715	0740	0823	0909	0927	1109	1127	1309	1327	1336**k**	...	1509	1527	1623	1709	1727	1822	1909	1927	2022	2109	2222	2321
Schweinfurt Hbf ....**870 876** a.	0637	0713	0730	0753	0842	0926	0942	1126	1144	1326	1342	1407	...	1525	1542	1641	1725	1743	1841	1926	1942	2041	2126	2236	2339
Würzburg Hbf ....**870 876** a.	...	0745	...	...	...	0955	...	1155	...	1355	...	...	...	1555	...	...	1755	...	...	1955	...	...	2157	...	...

e – Arrives 1353.
k – Departs 1356.
r – ⚒ only.
t – Ⓐ only.
★ – Erfurter Bahn (2nd class only).
‡ – Trains between Würzburg, Schweinfurt and Ebenhausen are often combined with a service to Meiningen or Erfurt. Passengers should take care to join the correct portion for their destination.

See Table **927** for services operated by FlixTrain

910 FRANKFURT - STUTTGART - MÜNCHEN and FRANKFURT - KARLSRUHE - BASEL - ZÜRICH

km	km		ICE 1279	ICE 619		ICE 699	NJ 403	NJ 408	ICE 3	NJ 471	ICE 1061	ICE 1063	ICE 561	IC 481	ICE 991	ICE 271	TGV 9578	ICE 911	WB 963	RJX 897	EC 217	ICE 511	ICE 5	ICE 9568
			①						①–⑤		①–⑤		①–⑤	①–⑤			①–⑥	①–⑥					①–⑥	Ⓑ b
				K		✕	♦	♦	✕	♦	✕	✕	✕	Z	✕	H✕	Ⓡ 🍷	✕	E 🍷	✕♦	♦	✕	✕	Ⓡ✕
		Hamburg Hbf **800 900** d.	...	1946	...	1937f	...	...	...	2208	...	...	...	...	...	...	...	...	...	...	...	...	...	...
		Berlin Hbf **810 850 902** d.	2028p	|	...	2127	...	2103	...	|	...	...	...	...	...	2328	...	...	...	...	...	...	...	...
		Hannover Hbf **810 900** d.	|	|	...	|	...	|	...	0030	...	...	...	...	...	0210	...	...	...	...	...	...	...	...
		Dortmund Hbf **800** ⊠ d.	|	2236	...	|	...	|	...	|	...	...	...	...	...	|	...	...	...	...	...	...	...	...
		Köln Hbf **800** d.	|	2355	...	|	2342	|	...	|	...	...	...	...	...	|	...	...	...	...	...	0548	...	...
		Köln Messe/Deutz **800** d.	|	|	...	|	|	|	...	|	...	...	...	...	...	|	...	...	...	...	...	|	...	...
		Koblenz Hbf **800** d.	|	|	...	|	0049	|	...	|	...	...	...	...	...	|	...	...	...	...	...	|	...	...
		Wiesbaden Hbf **917a 918a** d.	|	|	...	|	|	|	...	|	...	...	...	...	0526	|	...	...	...	...	...	|	...	...
		Mainz Hbf **912 917a 918a** d.	|	|	...	|	0142	|	...	|	...	...	...	...	0540	|	...	...	...	...	...	|	...	...
		Worms Hbf **912** d.	|	|	...	|	|	|	...	|	...	...	...	...	0608	|	...	...	...	...	...	|	...	...
0	0	**Frankfurt** (Main) Hbf **913** d.	0050	0119	...	0225	0245	0341•	...	0432•	...	...	...	0518	|	0550	...	0602	...	0553	...	|	0650	0656
		Frankfurt Flughafen ✈ ◧ d.	|	0056*	...	0246	0209*	|	...	|	...	...	...	|	|	|	...	|	...	|	...	0651	|	|
78		**Mannheim** Hbf **912 913** a.	0127	0202	...	0323	0331	0420	...	|	...	...	...	|	0623	0625	...	|	...	|	...	0723	0727	0736
78		**Mannheim** Hbf **913** d.	0130	0204	...	0325	0333	0422	...	|	...	...	...	|	0629	0632	...	|	...	|	0711	0731	0734	0737
	28	Darmstadt Hbf **913 918a** d.	|	|	...	|	|	|	...	0450	...	...	...	0536	|	|	...	|	...	0613	|	|	|	|
	50	Bensheim **913** d.	|	|	...	|	|	|	...	|	...	...	...	0550	|	|	...	|	...	0625	|	|	|	|
	64	Weinheim **913** d.	|	|	...	|	|	|	...	|	...	...	...	0600	|	|	...	|	...	0636	|	|	|	|
	87	**Heidelberg** Hbf **913** d.	|	0219	...	0340	|	|	...	0534	...	...	...	0615	|	|	...	|	...	0652	|	|	|	|
		Karlsruhe Hbf **913 931** d.	|	|	...	|	|	|	...	|	...	...	0600	|	|	|	...	|	...	|	|	|	|	|
	120	Bruchsal **913 931** d.	|	|	...	|	|	|	...	|	...	...	0616	|	|	|	...	|	...	|	|	|	|	|
		Vaihingen (Enz) **931** d.	|	|	...	|	|	|	...	|	...	...	|	|	|	|	...	|	...	|	|	|	|	|
		Stuttgart Hbf **931** a.	|	0333	...	0452	|	|	...	|	...	...	0644	0702	0708	|	...	0720	...	0737	0753n	0808	|	|
		Stuttgart Hbf **933** ▷ d.	|	0339	...	0512	|	|	...	|	0552	0624	0650	...	0715	|	0652	0728	0712	0744	0759n	0814	|	|
		Ulm Hbf **930 933** ▷ d.	|	0440	...	0608	|	|	...	|	0638	0712	0736	...	0801	|	|	0812	0807	0902	0855	0912	|	|
		Günzburg **930** d.	|	0455	...	0623	|	|	...	|	0652	0729	|	...	0816	|	|	|	0828	|	0910	|	|	|
		Augsburg Hbf **930** d.	|	0532	...	0655	|	|	...	|	0723	0759	0819	...	0848	|	|	0855	0907	|	0941	0955	|	|
		München Pasing **930** a.	|	0553	...	0717	|	|	...	|	0742	0821	0840	...	0908	|	|	0919	|	|	|	1017	|	|
		München Hbf **930** a.	|	0603	...	0728	|	|	...	|	0754	0830	0849	...	0918	|	|	0928	0938	|	1010	1026	|	|
		Salzburg Hbf **890** a.	|	...	...	...	|	|	...	|	...	...	...	...	...	|	|	...	1121	1502	1159	...	|	|
138	141	**Karlsruhe** Hbf **913** a.	0153	...	...	...	0401	0507	...	0603	...	...	...	...	...	0656	0731	...	...	...	...	...	0757	0805
		Karlsruhe Hbf **910a 916** d.	...	...	...	...	0403	0509	0556	0605	...	...	...	...	...	0658	0732	...	...	...	...	...	0759	0806
167	172	Baden-Baden **910a 916** d.	...	...	...	...	0427	0528	0613	|	...	...	...	...	...	0716	|	...	...	...	...	...	|	|
207		Offenburg **910a 911 916** d.	...	...	...	...	0452	0548	0630	0643j	...	...	...	...	...	0733	|	...	...	...	...	...	0831	|
	225	**Strasbourg** ⊖ **390 911** a.	...	...	...	...	|	|	|	|	...	...	...	...	...	|	0814	...	...	...	...	...	|	0847
	664	**Paris** Est **390** a.	...	...	...	...	|	|	|	|	...	...	...	...	...	|	1006	...	...	...	...	...	|	1038
270		**Freiburg** (Brsg) Hbf **910a** d.	...	...	...	...	0528	0619	0702	0723	...	...	...	...	...	0804	...	...	...	...	...	...	0902	...
327		**Basel** Bad Bf 🏛 **910a** a.	...	...	...	...	0610	0656	0736	0759	...	...	...	...	...	0837	...	...	...	...	...	...	0936	...
332		**Basel** SBB **510 910a** a.	...	...	...	...	0620	0720	0748	0810	...	...	...	...	...	0848	...	...	...	...	...	...	0948	...
423		**Zürich** HB **510** a.	...	...	...	...	0805	0904	0900	1005	...	...	...	...	...	1000	...	...	...	...	...	...	...	...

	ICE 1511	ICE 267	ICE 1178	ICE 591	ICE 591	ICE 711	ICE 1513	ICE 101	ICE 913	ECE 151	TGV 9576	EC 113	IC 2040	IC 2040	ICE 513	ICE 275	ICE 275	ICE 9566	ICE 571	ICE 1573	ICE 563	ICE 593	ICE 103	ICE 915
	①–⑤		①–⑤		①–⑥	①–⑤	⑥s		①–⑥		Ⓡ		R	S		⑥⑦	①–⑤	⑥		①–⑥				
	✕	✕♦	✕v	✕		✕	✕	✕	✕	L✕	A 🍷	♦	M 🍷	M 🍷	M✕	N✕	N✕	Ⓡ✕	✕	✕♦	B✕	✕	✕	✕
Hamburg Hbf **800 900** d.	...	...	...	...	0320	...	...	...	...	...	...	...	...	...	...	...	...	...	0514	...	...	...	...	...
Berlin Hbf **810 850 902** d.	...	...	...	...	|	...	...	0022	...	...	...	...	...	...	...	...	0428	...	|	...	...	0526	...	...
Hannover Hbf **810 900** d.	...	...	...	...	0519	...	...	0313	...	...	...	...	...	...	...	...	|	...	0641	0557a	...	|	0541	...
Dortmund Hbf **800** ⊠ d.	...	...	...	...	|	...	...	0536	0548	...	...	...	0536	0536	0636	...	|	...	|	|	...	|	0736	0750
Köln Hbf **800** d.	...	...	...	...	|	0601	...	0655	|	...	...	...	0653	0653	0755	...	|	...	|	|	...	|	0855	|
Köln Messe/Deutz **800** d.	...	...	...	...	|	|	...	|	0710	...	...	...	|	|	|	...	|	...	|	|	...	|	|	0910
Koblenz Hbf **800** d.	...	...	...	...	|	|	...	|	|	...	...	...	0748	0748	|	...	|	...	|	|	...	|	|	|
Wiesbaden Hbf **917a 918a** d.	...	...	...	...	|	0732	0731	|	|	...	...	...	|	|	|	...	|	...	|	|	...	|	|	|
Mainz Hbf **912 917a 918a** d.	...	...	...	...	|	0746	0746	|	|	...	...	...	0842	0842	|	...	|	...	|	|	...	|	|	|
Worms Hbf **912** d.	...	...	...	...	|	|	|	|	|	...	...	...	|	|	|	...	|	...	|	|	...	|	|	|
Frankfurt (Main) Hbf **913** d.	0705	...	...	0749	0749	|	|	|	|	0805	...	0821	|	|	|	0848	0850	0856	0905	0919	...	0950	|	|
Frankfurt Flughafen ✈ ◧ d.	|	...	...	|	|	|	|	0751	0808	|	...	|	|	|	0851	|	|	|	0924	|	...	|	0951	1008
Mannheim Hbf **912 913** a.	0748	...	...	0827	0827	0824	0824	0823	0840	0844	...	|	0921	0921	0923	0927	0927	0936	0956	|	...	1027	1023	1039
Mannheim Hbf **913** d.	0750	...	0818	0830	0830	0826	0826	0835	0843	0847	...	|	0923	0923	0931	0934	0934	0938	0959	|	1002	1030	1035	1043
Darmstadt Hbf **913 918a** d.	|	...	|	|	|	|	|	|	|	|	...	0838	|	|	|	|	|	|	|	0937	|	|	|	|
Bensheim **913** d.	|	...	|	|	|	|	|	|	|	|	...	0849	|	|	|	|	|	|	|	0950	|	|	|	|
Weinheim **913** d.	|	...	|	|	|	|	|	|	|	|	...	0859	|	|	|	|	|	|	|	1000	|	|	|	|
Heidelberg Hbf **913** d.	|	...	|	|	|	0839	0839	|	|	|	...	0913	0936	0935	|	|	|	|	|	1015	|	|	|	|
Karlsruhe Hbf **913 931** d.	|	0805	|	|	|	|	|	|	|	|	...	|	|	|	|	|	|	|	|	|	|	|	|	|
Bruchsal **913 931** d.	|	0817	|	|	|	|	|	|	|	|	...	|	|	0956	|	|	|	|	|	1035	|	|	|	|
Vaihingen (Enz) **931** d.	|	|	|	|	|	|	|	|	|	|	...	|	1004	|	|	|	|	|	|	|	|	|	|	|
Stuttgart Hbf **931** a.	0829	0845	0905	0908	0908	0918	0919	|	0922	|	...	0952	1024	|	1008	|	|	|	1038	|	1045	1108	|	1122
Stuttgart Hbf **933** ▷ d.	...	0851	...	0915	0915	...	0933r	|	0928	|	0910	0958	...	|	1014	|	|	|	...	|	1051	1115	|	1128
Ulm Hbf **930 933** ▷ d.	...	0936	...	1001	1001	...	1040r	|	1012	|	|	1056	...	|	1112	|	|	|	...	|	1136	1201	|	1213
Günzburg **930** d.	...	|	...	|	|	...	1059r	|	|	|	|	1110	...	|	|	|	|	|	...	|	|	|	|	|
Augsburg Hbf **930** d.	...	1019	...	1043	1043	...	1133r	|	1055	|	|	1141	...	|	1155	|	|	|	...	|	1219	1243	|	1255
München Pasing **930** a.	...	1040	...	1104	1104	...	|	|	1117	|	|	|	...	|	1217	|	|	|	...	|	1240	1304	|	1317
München Hbf **930** a.	...	1049	...	1113	1113	...	1202r	|	1129	|	|	1210	...	|	1226	|	|	|	...	|	1249	1313	|	1326
Salzburg Hbf **890** a.	...	...	...	...	...	...	...	|	...	|	|	1359	...	|	...	|	|	|	...	|	...	...	|	...
Karlsruhe Hbf **913** a.	...	...	...	...	...	...	...	0858	...	0909	0951	...	...	1016	...	0957	0957	1002	...	1051	...	...	1058	...
Karlsruhe Hbf **910a 916** d.	...	...	...	...	...	...	...	0900e	...	0911	0953	...	...	...	...	0959	0959	1003	...	...	...	...	1100	...
Baden-Baden **910a 916** d.	...	...	...	...	...	...	...	0917e	...	|	|	...	...	...	...	|	|	|	...	...	...	...	|	...
Offenburg **910a 911 916** d.	...	...	...	...	...	...	...	0935e	...	|	|	...	...	...	...	1032	1032	|	...	...	...	...	1133	...
Strasbourg ⊖ **390 911** a.	...	...	...	...	...	...	...	|	...	|	1037	...	...	...	...	|	|	1047	...	...	...	...	|	...
Paris Est **390** a.	...	...	...	...	...	...	...	|	...	|	1231	...	...	...	...	|	|	1238	...	...	...	...	|	...
Freiburg (Brsg) Hbf **910a** d.	...	...	...	...	...	...	...	1006e	...	1015	...	...	...	...	...	1102	1102	...	...	...	...	...	1203	...
Basel Bad Bf 🏛 **910a** a.	...	...	...	...	...	...	...	1037e	...	1045	...	...	...	...	...	1136	1136	...	...	...	...	...	1236	...
Basel SBB **510 910a** a.	...	...	...	...	...	...	...	1048e	...	1055	...	...	...	...	...	1148	1148	...	...	...	...	...	1248	...
Zürich HB **510** a.	...	...	...	...	...	...	...	...	...	1200	...	...	...	...	...	...	...	...	...	...	...	...	...	...

♦ – **NOTES** (LISTED BY TRAIN NUMBER)

113 – BLAUER ENZIAN – 🚃12 Frankfurt - Salzburg - Schwarzach-St Veit - Klagenfurt.
217 – DACHSTEIN – 🚃12 Saarbrücken - München Ost - Salzburg - Graz. Not Sept. 13 - Oct. 17.
267 – BADEN-KURIER – 🚃12 ✕ (Basel ①–⑥ -) Karlsruhe - München.
403 – 🛏 1, 2 cl. and 🛌 2 cl. (Ⓡ) Amsterdam - Utrecht - Basel - Zürich. Also conveys 🚃2 (*IC* **60403**).
408 – 🛏 1, 2 cl. and 🛌 2 cl. (Ⓡ) Berlin - Leipzig - Basel - Zürich. Also conveys 🚃2 (*IC* **60408**).
🛏 1, 2 cl. and 🛌 2 cl. (*EN* **40458** Ⓡ) and 🚃2 (*EC* **458**) Praha - Dresden - Leipzig - Basel - Zürich.
471 – 🛏 1, 2 cl. and 🛌 2 cl. (Ⓡ) Hamburg - Basel - Zürich. Also conveys 🚃2 (*IC* **60471**).
897 – BREGENZERWALD – 🚃12 ✕ Frankfurt - Ulm - Lindau - Bregenz (**867**) - Innsbruck - Wien.
1573 – ①–⑥. 🚃12 ✕ (Hannover ①–⑤ -) Kassel - Gießen - Frankfurt - Karlsruhe.

A – From München (Table **32** or other direction of this table).
B – From Saarbrücken (Table **919**).
E – To Wien (Table **950**). Operated by *WESTbahn* (special fares).
H – To Chur (Table **520**).
K – From Kiel (Table **820**).
L – To Milano via Chiasso (Table **550**).
M – From Münster (Table **800**).
N – To Interlaken via Bern (Table **560**).
R – Not July 26 - Sept. 5.
S – July 26 - Sept. 5.
Z – To Zürich via Singen (Table **940**). Terminates at Stuttgart July 28 - Sept. 5 (train *IC* **2297**).

a – ①–⑤.
b – Conveys 🚃12 Frankfurt - Strasbourg - Poitiers - Bordeaux on ⑥ July 5 - Aug. 30 (not July 19) as *TGV* **9594**.
e – From June 15.
f – 1849 from Aug. 2.
j – Arrives 0637.
n – Not July 26 - Sept. 5.
p – Previous day (⑦).
r – ⑥ June 21 - July 19; ⑥ Sept. 6 - Oct. 4.
s – Wiesbaden - Stuttgart (- St Anton am Arlberg on dates in note **r**).
v – From Basel (see other direction of this table).
***** – Calls at Frankfurt Flughafen before Frankfurt (Main) Hbf.
• – Frankfurt (Main) **Süd**.
⊖ – 🏛 is at Kehl (8 km from Strasbourg). See Table **911** for local journeys Offenburg - Strasbourg.
▷ – For regional services via Wendlingen, see Table **936**.
◧ – Frankfurt Flughafen Fernbahnhof.
⊠ – Services between Dortmund and Köln are subject to alteration Sept. 6 - Oct. 31 (also from late evening on Sept. 5) with many trains retimed or diverted via alternative routes. Please check for journeys from Dortmund during this period.

FRANKFURT - STUTTGART - MÜNCHEN and FRANKFURT - KARLSRUHE - BASEL - ZÜRICH 910

SEE NOTE ⊠	ICE 71	ICE 9574	ICE 999	ICE 115	EC 7	ICE 515	ICE 277	ICE 119	ICE 573	ICE 565	ICE 1575	ICE 1575 ①–⑥		ICE 595	ICE 105	ICE 225	ICE 73	EC 219	EC 9	ICE 517	ICE 279	ICE 575	ICE 567	
	✕	[R] ✕	✕	✕♦	N✕	✕	✕	✕♦	K✕	✕	✕	✕		✕	✕	A✕	K✕	♦	✕	✕	✕	✕	✕	
Hamburg Hbf **800 900** d.	0618	...	...	...	0438	0546	...	...	0724	...	...	0624	...	...	0646	...	0824	...	...	0746	...	0924	...	...
Berlin Hbf **810 850 902** d.	|	...	...	...	|	|	0629	...	|	...	...	|	...	0726	|	...	|	...	...	|	0829	|	...	...
Hannover Hbf **810 900** d.	0741	...	...	...	|	|	|	...	0841	...	...	0801	...	|	|	...	0941	...	...	|	|	1041	...	...
Dortmund Hbf **800** ⊠ d.	|	...	...	...	0736t	0836	|	0753	|	...	...	|	...	|	0936t	...	|	...	0924	1036	|	|	...	...
Köln Hbf **800** d.	|	...	...	...	0853	0955	|	|	|	...	...	|	...	|	1055	...	|	...	1053	1155	|	|	...	...
Köln Messe/Deutz **800** d.	|	...	...	0829	|	|	|	0921	|	...	...	|	...	|	|	1114	|	...	|	|	|	|	...	...
Koblenz Hbf **800** d.	|	...	...	|	0948	|	|	|	|	...	...	|	...	|	|	|	|	...	1148	|	|	|	...	...
Wiesbaden Hbf ... **917a 918a** d.	|	...	...	0959	|	|	|	1057	|	...	...	|	...	|	|	|	|	...	|	|	|	|	...	...
Mainz Hbf ...... **912 917a 918a** d.	|	...	...	1017	1042	|	|	1113	|	...	...	|	...	|	|	|	|	...	1242	|	|	|	...	...
Worms Hbf **912** d.	|	...	...	1045	|	|	|	|	|	...	...	|	...	|	|	|	|	...	|	|	|	|	...	...
Frankfurt (Main) Hbf .... **913** d.	1005	...	1019	|	|	|	1050	|	1105	...	1119	1119	...	1150	|	|	1205	1219	|	|	1250	1305	...	...
Frankfurt Flughafen ✈ ◧ ... d.	|	...	|	|	|	1051	|	|	1124	...	|	|	...	|	1151	1208	|	|	|	1251	|	1324	...	...
Mannheim Hbf .... **912 913** a.	1044	...	|	1100	1121	1123	1127	1152	1156	...	|	|	...	1227	1223	1239	1244	|	1321	1323	1327	1356	...	...
Mannheim Hbf **913** d.	1046	...	|	1102	1123	1131	1134	1154	1159	...	|	|	...	1230	1235	1243	1246	|	1323	1331	1335	1359	...	...
Darmstadt Hbf .... **913 918a** d.	|	...	1037	|	|	|	|	|	|	...	1137	1137	...	|	|	|	|	1237	|	|	|	|	...	...
Bensheim **913** d.	|	...	|	|	|	|	|	|	|	...	1150	1150	...	|	|	|	|	1249	|	|	|	|	...	...
Weinheim **913** d.	|	...	1056	|	|	|	|	|	|	...	1200	1200	...	|	|	|	|	1259	|	|	|	|	...	...
Heidelberg Hbf **913** d.	|	...	1111	|	|	|	|	1206	|	...	1215	1215	...	|	|	|	|	1313	|	|	|	|	...	...
Karlsruhe Hbf .. **913 931** d.	|	...	|	|	|	|	|	|	|	1205	|	|	...	|	|	|	|	|	|	|	|	|	1405	...
Bruchsal **913 931** d.	|	...	|	|	|	|	|	|	|	1217	1236	1236	...	|	|	|	|	|	|	|	|	|	1417	...
Vaihingen (Enz) **931** d.	|	...	|	1137	|	|	|	|	|	|	|	|	...	|	|	|	|	|	|	|	|	|	|	...
Stuttgart Hbf **931** a.	|	...	1151	1153	|	1208	|	1248	1238	1245	|	|	...	1308	|	1320	|	1353	|	1408	|	1438	1445	...
Stuttgart Hbf .... **933** ▷ d.	|	1052	...	1159	|	1214	|	1257	...	1251	|	|	...	1315	|	1328	|	1359	|	1414	|	...	1451	...
Ulm Hbf ....**930 933** ▷ d.	|	|	...	1256	|	1312	|	1404	...	1336	|	|	...	1401	|	1412	|	1456	|	1512	|	...	1536	...
Günzburg **930** d.	|	|	...	1311	|	|	|	...	...	|	|	|	...	|	|	|	|	1510	|	|	|	...	|	...
Augsburg Hbf **930** d.	|	|	...	1341	|	1355	|	...	...	1419	|	|	...	1443	|	1455	|	1541	|	1555	|	...	1619	...
München Pasing **930** a.	|	|	...	|	|	1417	|	...	...	1440	|	|	...	1504	|	1518	|	|	|	1617	|	...	1640	...
München Hbf **930** a.	|	|	...	1411	|	1426	|	...	...	1449	|	|	...	1514	|	1527	|	1610	|	1626	|	...	1649	...
Salzburg Hbf **890** a.	|	|	...	1559	|	...	|	...	...	...	|	|	...	...	|	...	|	1759	|	...	|	...	...	...
Karlsruhe Hbf **913** a.	1109	1131	...	...	1147	...	1157	...	...	...	1251	1251	...	...	1258	...	1309	...	1347	...	1358	...	...	...
Karlsruhe Hbf .... **910a 916** d.	1111	1132	...	...	1149	...	1159	...	...	...	...	...	...	...	1300	...	1311	...	1349	...	1400	...	...	...
Baden-Baden .... **910a 916** d.	1128	|	...	...	|	...	1216	...	...	...	...	...	...	...	|	...	1328	...	1406	...	|	...	...	...
Offenburg ....**910a 911 916** d.	|	|	...	...	|	...	1232	...	...	...	...	...	...	...	1332	...	|	...	|	...	1431	...	...	...
Strasbourg ⊖ ..... **390 911** a.	|	1215	...	...	|	...	|	...	...	...	...	...	...	...	|	...	|	...	|	...	|	...	...	...
Paris Est **390** a.	|	1406	...	...	|	...	|	...	...	...	...	...	...	...	|	...	|	...	|	...	|	...	...	...
Freiburg (Brsg) Hbf .... **910a** d.	1214	...	...	...	1251	...	1303	...	...	...	...	...	...	...	1403	...	1414	...	1456	...	1502	...	...	...
Basel Bad Bf 🏛 .... **910a** a.	1245	...	...	...	1323	...	1337	...	...	...	...	...	...	...	1436	...	1445	...	1528	...	1536	...	...	...
Basel SBB .... **510 910a** a.	1310	...	...	...	1333	...	1348	...	...	...	...	...	...	...	1448	...	1455	...	1536	...	1548	...	...	...
Zürich HB **510** a.	...	...	...	...	...	...	...	...	...	...	...	...	...	...	...	...	1600	...	1700	...	...	...	...	...

SEE NOTE ⊠	IC 2013	ICE 1577	ICE 597	ICE 919	WB 969	ICE 107	TGV 9580 [R]	ICE 75	TGV 9580 [R]	ICE 9572	ICE 117	IC 2044 D	IC 2044 D	ICE 519	ICE 371	ICE 577	ICE 569	ICE 1579	ICE 1219	ICE 109	ICE 1011	ICE 9590	ICE 77	
	♦	C✕	✕	✕	E🍷	✕	M🍷	K✕	M🍷	◇ [R]	✕♦	R✕	S✕	✕	N✕	✕	✕	✕♦	B✕	✕	✕	[R] ✕	K✕	
Hamburg Hbf **800 900** d.	...	0828	...	...	...	0845	...	1024	...	...	...	...	...	0946	...	1124	...	1028	...	1046	...	...	1224	...
Berlin Hbf **810 850 902** d.	...	|	0926	...	...	|	...	|	...	...	...	...	...	|	1028	|	...	|	1126	|	...	1154	|	...
Hannover Hbf **810 900** d.	...	1001	|	...	...	|	...	1141	...	...	...	0940r	0940r	|	|	1241	...	1201	|	|	...	|	1341	...
Dortmund Hbf **800** ⊠ d.	0950	|	|	...	...	1136t	...	|	...	...	...	1136	1136	1236	|	|	...	|	|	1336t	1350v	|	|	...
Köln Hbf **800** d.	1114	|	|	...	...	1255	...	|	...	...	...	1253	1253	1355	|	|	...	|	|	1455	|	|	|	...
Köln Messe/Deutz **800** d.	|	|	|	...	...	|	...	|	...	...	...	|	|	|	|	|	...	|	|	|	1510	|	|	...
Koblenz Hbf **800** d.	1218	|	|	...	...	|	...	|	...	...	...	1348	1348	|	|	|	...	|	|	|	|	|	|	...
Wiesbaden Hbf ... **917a 918a** d.	|	|	|	...	...	|	...	|	...	...	...	|	|	|	|	|	...	|	|	|	|	|	|	...
Mainz Hbf ...... **912 917a 918a** d.	1313	|	|	...	...	|	...	|	...	...	...	1442	1442	|	|	|	...	|	|	|	|	|	|	...
Worms Hbf **912** d.	|	|	|	...	...	|	...	|	...	...	...	|	|	|	|	|	...	|	|	|	|	|	|	...
Frankfurt (Main) Hbf .... **913** d.	|	1319	1350	...	...	|	1356	1405	...	...	1419	|	|	|	1450	1505	...	1519	1550	|	|	1553•	1605	...
Frankfurt Flughafen ✈ ◧ ... d.	|	|	|	...	...	1351	|	|	...	...	|	|	|	1451	|	1524	...	|	|	1551	1608	|	|	...
Mannheim Hbf .... **912 913** a.	1352	|	1427	...	...	1423	1437	1444	...	...	|	1521	1521	1523	1527	1556	...	|	1627	1623	1639	|	1644	...
Mannheim Hbf **913** d.	1354	|	1430	...	...	1435	1439	1446	...	...	|	1523	1523	1531	1534	1559	...	|	1630	1635	1643	|	1646	...
Darmstadt Hbf .... **913 918a** d.	|	1337	|	...	...	|	|	|	...	...	1437	|	|	|	|	|	...	1537	|	|	|	|	|	...
Bensheim **913** d.	|	1350	|	...	...	|	|	|	...	...	1449	|	|	|	|	|	...	1550	|	|	|	|	|	...
Weinheim **913** d.	|	1400	|	...	...	|	|	|	...	...	1459	|	|	|	|	|	...	1600	|	|	|	|	|	...
Heidelberg Hbf **913** d.	1406	1415	|	...	...	|	|	|	...	...	1513	1536	1536	|	|	|	...	1615	|	|	|	|	|	...
Karlsruhe Hbf .. **913 931** d.	|	|	|	...	...	|	|	|	...	...	|	|	|	|	|	|	1605	|	|	|	|	|	|	...
Bruchsal **913 931** d.	|	|	|	...	...	|	|	|	...	...	|	|	1557	|	|	|	1617	1636	|	|	|	|	|	...
Vaihingen (Enz) **931** d.	|	|	|	...	...	|	|	|	...	...	|	1604	|	|	|	|	|	|	|	|	|	|	|	...
Stuttgart Hbf **931** a.	1450	1503	1508	...	...	|	|	|	...	...	1553	1622	|	1608	|	1638	1645	|	1708	|	1721	|	|	...
Stuttgart Hbf .... **933** ▷ d.	1459	...	1515	1528	1512	|	|	|	...	1452	1559	...	|	1614	|	...	1651	|	1714	|	1728	|	|	...
Ulm Hbf ....**930 933** ▷ d.	1614	...	1600	1611	1607	|	|	|	...	|	1657	...	|	1712	|	...	1736	|	1801	|	1812	|	|	...
Günzburg **930** d.	...	...	|	|	1628	|	|	|	...	|	1711	...	|	|	|	...	|	|	|	|	|	|	|	...
Augsburg Hbf **930** d.	...	...	1643	1655	1708	|	|	|	...	|	1741	...	|	1755	|	...	1819	|	1843	|	1856	|	|	...
München Pasing **930** a.	...	...	1704	1717	|	|	|	|	...	|	|	...	|	1817	|	...	1840	|	1903	|	1918	|	|	...
München Hbf **930** a.	...	...	1716	1726	1738	|	|	|	...	|	1810	...	|	1826	|	...	1849	|	1912	|	1927	|	|	...
Salzburg Hbf **890** a.	...	...	...	...	1921	|	|	|	...	|	1959	...	|	...	|	...	...	|	...	|	...	|	|	...
Karlsruhe Hbf **913** a.	...	...	...	...	...	1458	1505	1509	←	1531	...	...	1616	...	1557	...	...	1651	...	1658	...	1706	1709	...
Karlsruhe Hbf .... **910a 916** d.	...	...	...	...	...	1500	1512	1511	1512	1532	...	...	...	...	1559	...	...	1654f	...	1700	...	1707	1711	...
Baden-Baden .... **910a 916** d.	...	...	...	...	...	|	→	1528	1535	|	...	...	...	...	|	...	...	|	...	1718	...	|	|	...
Offenburg ....**910a 911 916** d.	...	...	...	...	...	1533	...	|	|	|	...	...	...	...	1631	...	...	1727f	...	1736	...	|	|	...
Strasbourg ⊖ ..... **390 911** a.	...	...	...	...	...	|	...	|	1604	1614	...	...	...	...	|	...	...	...	...	|	...	1753	|	...
Paris Est **390** a.	...	...	...	...	...	|	...	|	...	1805	...	...	...	...	|	...	...	...	...	|	...	1955	|	...
Freiburg (Brsg) Hbf .... **910a** d.	...	...	...	...	...	1603	...	1614	...	...	...	...	...	...	1702	...	...	...	...	1806	...	...	1814	...
Basel Bad Bf 🏛 .... **910a** a.	...	...	...	...	...	1636	...	1645	...	...	...	...	...	...	1736	...	...	...	...	1837	...	...	1845	...
Basel SBB .... **510 910a** a.	...	...	...	...	...	1648	...	1655	...	...	...	...	...	...	1748	...	...	...	...	1848	...	...	1855	...
Zürich HB **510** a.	...	...	...	...	...	...	...	1800	...	...	...	...	...	...	...	...	...	...	...	...	...	...	2000	...

♦ – **NOTES** (LISTED BY TRAIN NUMBER)

115 – WÖRTHERSEE – [12] ✕ Münster - München - Salzburg - Schwarzach St Veit.
117 – SALZACH – [12] ✕ Frankfurt - München - Salzburg - Schwarzach-St Veit (- Klagenfurt from July 14).
119 – BODENSEE – [12] ✕ Dortmund - Stuttgart - Ulm - Lindau - Bregenz - Innsbruck.
219 – CHIEMGAU – [12] Frankfurt - München - Salzburg - Bischofshofen - Graz.
1579 – [12] ✕ (Greifswald ⑥ until July 26 -) Hamburg - Frankfurt - Karlsruhe (- Konstanz ⑤⑥).
2013 – ALLGÄU – [12] Dortmund - Köln - Stuttgart - Ulm (*RE* **2013**) - Oberstdorf (Table **935**). Also calls at Plochingen (d. 1519) and Göppingen (d. 1533).

A – From Amsterdam (Table **28**). On June 14, 15, June 28 - Aug. 24, Oct. 20 - Nov. 2, Dec. 6, 7 runs with train number **255** and is diverted to run via Köln Hbf (d. 1108; not calling at Köln Messe/Deutz). [R] for international journeys.
B – To Innsbruck (Table **953**).
C – From Stralsund (Table **830**).
D – From Dresden via Leipzig from Aug. 10 (Table **866**). Until Aug. 9 starts from Bielefeld.
E – To Wien (Table **950**). Operated by *WESTbahn* (special fares).
K – From Kiel (Table **820**).
M – To Marseille via Lyon (Tables **350** and **379**).
N – To Interlaken via Bern (Table **560**).
R – Not July 26 - Sept. 5.
S – July 26 - Sept. 5.

f – ⑤⑥ only.
r – Aug. 10 - Dec. 13.
t – Not Sept. 6 - Oct. 31.
v – ①②③④⑥⑦. On ⑤ starts from Düsseldorf.

• – Frankfurt (Main) **Süd** (not Hbf).
⊠ – Services between Dortmund and Köln are subject to alteration Sept. 6 - Oct. 31 (also from late evening on Sept. 5) with many trains retimed or diverted via alternative routes. Please check for journeys from Dortmund during this period.
◇ – Runs as *TGV* **9592** on ⑥ to June 28 and from Sept. 6 (also July 19). *ICE* ✕, *TGV* 🍷.
⊖ – 🏛 is at Kehl (8 km from Strasbourg). See Table **911** for local journeys Offenburg - Strasbourg.
▷ – For regional services via Wendlingen, see Table **936**.
◧ – Frankfurt Flughafen Fernbahnhof.

910 FRANKFURT - STUTTGART - MÜNCHEN and FRANKFURT - KARLSRUHE - BASEL - ZÜRICH

SEE NOTE ⊠	*IC* 1291	*IC* 2046	*IC* 2046	*ICE* 611	*ICE* 373	*TGV* 9560	*ICE* 1064		*ICE* 579	*ICE* 1069	*ICE* 1671	*ICE* 691	*ICE* 201	*ICE* 1013	*TGV* 9577	*ICE* 79	*TGV* 9570	*ICE* 1099	*ICE* 1099	*ICE* 1091	*IC* 2048	*IC* 2048	*ICE* 613	*EN* 50237
		D	D												Ⓑ			Ⓑ		⑤⑦	D	D		Ⓡ
		R	S	✕	N✕	Ⓡ🍷	✕		✕	✕	T✕	✕	✕	✕	Q🍷	✕	Ⓡ🍷	✕	✕	✕	Wy	X	K✕	♦
Hamburg Hbf **800 900** d.	...	...	...	1146	...	...	...	...	1324	...	1228	...	1246	...	...	1424	...	...	...	...	...	...	1346	...
Berlin Hbf **810 850 902** d.	...	...	...	|	1230	...	...	...	|	...	|	1326	|	...	...	|	...	...	...	1355	...	...	|	...
Hannover Hbf **810 900** d.	...	1140**r**	1140**r**	|	|	...	...	...	1441	...	1401	|	|	...	...	1541	...	...	...	1551	1340**r**	1340**r**	|	...
Dortmund Hbf **800** ⊠ d.	...	1336	1336	1436	|	...	...	...	|	...	|	|	1536**t**	1550	...	|	...	...	...	|	1536	1536	1636	...
Köln Hbf **800** d.	...	1453	1453	1555	|	...	...	...	|	...	|	|	1655	|	...	|	...	...	...	|	1653	1653	1755	...
Köln Messe/Deutz **800** d.	...	|	|	|	|	...	...	...	|	...	|	|	|	1710	...	|	...	...	...	|	|	|	|	...
Koblenz Hbf **800** d.	...	1548	1548	|	|	...	...	...	|	...	|	|	|	|	...	|	...	...	...	|	1748	1748	|	...
Wiesbaden Hbf **917a 918a** d.	...	|	|	|	|	...	...	...	|	...	|	|	|	|	...	|	...	...	...	|	|	|	|	...
Mainz Hbf **912 917a 918a** d.	...	1642	1642	|	|	...	...	...	|	...	|	|	|	|	...	|	...	...	...	|	1842	1842	|	...
Worms Hbf **912** d.	...	|	|	|	|	...	...	...	|	...	|	|	|	|	...	|	...	...	...	|	|	|	|	...
Frankfurt (Main) Hbf **913** d.	1620	|	|	|	1650	1656	...	...	1705	...	1719	1750	|	|	...	1805	...	1818	1818	1838	|	|	|	...
Frankfurt Flughafen ✈ ◧ d.	|	|	|	1651	|	|	...	...	1724	...	|	|	1751	1808	...	|	...	|	|	|	|	|	1851	...
Mannheim Hbf **912 913** a.	|	1721	1721	1723	1727	1736	...	...	1755	...	|	1827	1823	1839	...	1844	...	|	|	1916	1921	1921	1923	...
Mannheim Hbf **913** d.	|	1723	1723	1731	1734	1738	...	...	1759	...	|	1830	1835	1843	...	1846	...	|	|	1918	1923	1923	1931	...
Darmstadt Hbf **913 918a** d.	1638	|	|	|	|	|	...	...	|	...	1737	|	|	|	...	|	...	1837	1837	|	|	|	|	...
Bensheim **913** d.	1649	|	|	|	|	|	...	...	|	...	1750	|	|	|	...	|	...	1849	1849	|	|	|	|	...
Weinheim **913** d.	1659	|	|	|	|	|	...	...	|	...	1800	|	|	|	...	|	...	1859	1859	|	|	|	|	...
Heidelberg Hbf **913** d.	1713	1736	1736	|	|	|	...	...	|	...	1815	|	|	|	...	|	...	1913	1913	|	1936	1936	|	...
Karlsruhe Hbf **913 931** d.	|	|	|	|	|	|	...	...	|	1805	|	|	|	|	1828	|	...	|	|	|	|	|	|	...
Bruchsal **913 931** d.	|	|	1756	|	|	|	...	...	|	1817	1835	|	|	|	|	|	...	|	|	|	|	1956	|	...
Vaihingen (Enz) **931** d.	|	1810	|	|	|	|	...	...	|	|	|	|	|	|	|	|	...	|	|	|	2005	|	|	...
Stuttgart Hbf **931** a.	1753	1827	|	1808	|	|	...	...	1838	1851	|	1908	|	1922	1904	|	...	1952	1952	1958	2023	|	2008	...
Stuttgart Hbf **933** ▷ d.	1759	...	|	1814	|	|	1734	...	...	1857	|	1915	|	1928	1920	|	1852	1958	...	...	...	|	2014	2029
Ulm Hbf **930 933** ▷ d.	1856	...	|	1912	|	|	|	...	...	1939	|	2001	|	2012	2023	|	|	2056	...	...	...	|	2112	2153
Günzburg **930** d.	1911	...	|	|	|	|	|	...	...	|	|	|	|	|	|	|	|	2111	...	...	...	|	|	|
Augsburg Hbf **930** d.	1941	...	|	1955	|	|	|	...	...	2024	|	2043	|	2056	2107	|	|	2141	...	...	...	|	2155	2302
München Pasing **930** a.	|	...	|	2017	|	|	|	...	...	2047	|	2104	|	2117	|	|	|	2203	...	...	...	|	2217	|
München Hbf **930** a.	2010	...	|	2029	|	|	|	...	...	2056	|	2113	|	2126	2136	|	|	2212	...	...	...	|	2226	|
Salzburg Hbf **890** a.	2201	...	|	...	|	|	|	...	...	...	|	...	|	...	...	|	|	...	...	...	...	|	...	0128
Karlsruhe Hbf **913** a.	...	...	1815	...	1758	1804	1820	...	...	...	1852	...	1858	...	...	1909	1931	...	...	...	...	2015	...	...
Karlsruhe Hbf **910a 916** d.	...	...	...	...	1800	1805	1824	...	...	...	...	...	1900**n**	...	...	1911	1932	...	...	...	...	...	...	...
Baden-Baden **910a 916** d.	...	...	...	...	|	|	1845	...	...	...	...	...	|	...	...	1928	|	...	...	...	...	...	...	...
Offenburg **910a 911 916** d.	...	...	...	...	1831	|	1902	...	...	...	...	...	1932**n**	...	...	|	|	...	...	...	...	...	...	...
Strasbourg ⊖ **390 911** a.	...	...	...	...	|	1848	|	...	...	...	...	...	|	...	...	|	2015	...	...	...	...	...	...	...
Paris Est **390** a.	...	...	...	...	|	2041	|	...	...	...	...	...	|	...	...	|	2213	...	...	...	...	...	...	...
Freiburg (Brsg) Hbf **910a** d.	...	...	...	...	1902	...	1932	...	...	...	...	...	2003**n**	...	...	2014	...	...	...	...	...	...	...	...
Basel Bad Bf 🏛 **910a** a.	...	...	...	...	1936	...	2008	...	...	...	...	...	2036**n**	...	...	2045	...	...	...	...	...	...	...	...
Basel SBB **510 910a** a.	...	...	...	...	1948	...	2018	...	...	...	...	...	2048**n**	...	...	2055	...	...	...	...	...	...	...	...
Zürich HB **510** a.	...	...	...	...	...	...	...	...	...	...	...	...	...	...	...	2200	...	...	...	...	...	...	...	...

SEE NOTE ⊠	*ICE* 266	*ICE* 375	*ICE* 266	*ICE* 771	*IC* 2375*		*ICE* 693	*ICE* 693	*TGV* 9579	*ICE* 203	*ICE* 1015	*ICE* 1015	*ICE* 1171	*IC* 2299	*ICE* 1095	*IC* 2440	*IC* 2440	*ICE* 615	*ICE* 377		*ICE* 773		*ICE* 695	*ICE* 695
	Ⓑ		Ⓑ				Ⓑ		⑥		Ⓑ	⑥		§	⑦	D	D						⑤–⑦	
	✕♦	✕	♦	✕	♣		✕	✕	Q🍷	T✕	✕	C✕	K✕		✕	Uz	V	✕	✕		✕			
Hamburg Hbf **800 900** d.	...	...	...	1524	1428	...	...	...	...	1445	...	...	1624	...	...	...	...	1545	...	...	1724	...	...	...
Berlin Hbf **810 850 902** d.	...	1432	...	|	|	...	1526	1526	...	|	...	...	|	...	1555	...	...	|	1630	...	|	...	1726	1726
Hannover Hbf **810 900** d.	...	|	...	1641	1601	...	|	|	...	|	...	...	1741	...	1751	1540**r**	1540**r**	|	|	...	1841	...	|	|
Dortmund Hbf **800** ⊠ d.	...	|	...	|	|	...	|	|	...	1736**t**	1750	...	|	...	|	1736	1736	1836	|	...	|	...	|	|
Köln Hbf **800** d.	...	|	...	|	|	...	|	|	...	1855	|	...	|	...	|	1853	1853	1955	|	...	|	...	|	|
Köln Messe/Deutz **800** d.	...	|	...	|	|	...	|	|	...	|	1910	1910	|	...	|	|	|	|	|	...	|	...	|	|
Koblenz Hbf **800** d.	...	|	...	|	|	...	|	|	...	|	|	|	|	...	|	1948	1948	|	|	...	|	...	|	|
Wiesbaden Hbf **917a 918a** d.	...	|	...	|	|	...	|	|	...	|	|	|	|	...	|	|	|	|	|	...	|	...	|	|
Mainz Hbf **912 917a 918a** d.	...	|	...	|	|	...	|	|	...	|	|	|	|	...	|	2042	2042	|	|	...	|	...	|	|
Worms Hbf **912** d.	...	|	...	|	|	...	|	|	...	|	|	|	|	...	|	|	|	|	|	...	|	...	|	|
Frankfurt (Main) Hbf **913** d.	...	1850	...	1905	1918	...	1950	1950	...	|	|	|	2005	2019	2038	|	|	|	2050	...	2105	...	2150	2150
Frankfurt Flughafen ✈ ◧ d.	...	|	...	1924	|	...	|	|	...	1951	2008	2008	|	|	|	|	|	2051	|	...	2124	...	|	|
Mannheim Hbf **912 913** a.	...	1927	...	1955	|	...	2027	2027	...	2023	2039	2039	2044	|	2116	2121	2121	2124	2127	...	2155	...	2227	2227
Mannheim Hbf **913** d.	...	1934	...	1959	|	...	2030	2030	...	2035	2043	2043	2046	|	2118	2123	2123	2131	2134	...	2158	...	2230	2230
Darmstadt Hbf **913 918a** d.	...	|	...	|	1937	...	|	|	...	|	|	|	|	2037	|	|	|	|	|	...	|	...	|	|
Bensheim **913** d.	...	|	...	|	1950	...	|	|	...	|	|	|	|	2049	|	|	|	|	|	...	|	...	|	|
Weinheim **913** d.	...	|	...	|	2000	...	|	|	...	|	|	|	|	2059	|	|	|	|	|	...	|	...	|	|
Heidelberg Hbf **913** d.	...	|	...	|	2015	...	|	|	...	|	|	|	|	2114	|	2136	2135	|	|	...	2211	...	|	|
Karlsruhe Hbf **913 931** d.	...	|	...	|	|	...	|	|	2027	|	|	|	|	|	|	|	|	|	|	...	|	...	|	|
Bruchsal **913 931** d.	...	|	...	|	|	...	|	|	|	|	|	|	|	|	|	|	2156	|	|	...	|	...	|	|
Vaihingen (Enz) **931** d.	...	|	...	|	|	...	|	|	|	|	|	|	|	|	|	2205	|	|	|	...	|	...	|	|
Stuttgart Hbf **931** a.	...	|	...	2038	2057	...	2108	2108	2104	|	2122	2122	|	2156	2159	2223	|	2208	|	...	2255	...	2308	2308
Stuttgart Hbf **933** ▷ d.	1912	|	...	...	...	...	2115	...	2114	|	2128	...	|	...	...	...	|	2214	|	...	...	...	2315	...
Ulm Hbf **930 933** ▷ d.	|	|	...	...	...	...	2201	...	2212	|	2212	...	|	...	...	...	|	2312	|	...	...	...	0001	...
Günzburg **930** d.	|	|	...	...	...	...	|	...	|	|	|	...	|	...	...	...	|	|	|	...	...	...	0017	...
Augsburg Hbf **930** d.	|	|	...	...	...	...	2242	...	2258	|	2256	...	|	...	...	...	|	2355	|	...	...	...	0048	...
München Pasing **930** a.	|	|	...	...	...	...	2304	...	|	|	2317	...	|	...	...	...	|	0017	|	...	...	...	0109	...
München Hbf **930** a.	|	|	...	...	...	...	2313	...	2326	|	2326	...	|	...	...	...	|	0026	|	...	...	...	0118	...
Salzburg Hbf **890** a.	|	|	...	...	...	...	...	...	...	|	...	...	|	...	...	...	|	...	|	...	...	...	...	...
Karlsruhe Hbf **913** a.	1952	1958	...	...	...	...	...	...	...	2058	...	...	2109	...	...	...	2216	...	2158	...	...	...	...	...
Karlsruhe Hbf **910a 916** d.	1955	2000	...	...	...	...	...	...	...	2102**n**	...	...	2112	...	...	...	...	...	2200	...	...	...	...	...
Baden-Baden **910a 916** d.	2012	2017	...	...	...	...	...	...	...	2120**n**	...	...	2129	...	...	...	...	...	2217	...	...	...	...	...
Offenburg **910a 911 916** d.	2029	2036	...	...	...	...	...	...	...	2138**n**	...	...	2147	...	...	...	...	...	2236	...	...	...	...	...
Strasbourg ⊖ **390 911** a.	|	|	...	...	...	...	...	...	...	|	...	...	|	...	...	...	...	...	|	...	...	...	...	...
Paris Est **390** a.	|	|	←	...	...	...	...	...	...	|	...	...	|	...	...	...	...	...	|	...	...	...	...	...
Freiburg (Brsg) Hbf **910a** d.	2101	2107	2110	...	...	...	...	...	...	2209**n**	...	...	2217	...	...	...	...	...	2309	...	...	...	...	...
Basel Bad Bf 🏛 **910a** a.	→	2139	2147	...	...	...	...	...	...	2242**n**	...	...	2251	...	...	...	...	...	2346	...	...	...	...	...
Basel SBB **510 910a** a.	...	2149	2200	...	...	...	...	...	...	2255**n**	...	...	2304	...	...	...	...	...	2359	...	...	...	...	...
Zürich HB **510** a.	...	...	...	...	...	...	...	...	...	...	...	...	...	...	...	...	...	...	...	...	...	...	...	...

♦ – **NOTES** (LISTED BY TRAIN NUMBER)

266 – BADEN-KURIER – [12] ✕ München - Stuttgart - Basel. Also calls at Müllheim (Baden), a. 2128.

50237 – KÁLMÁN IMRE – 🛏 1,2 cl., ▬ 2 cl. and [2] Stuttgart - Wien - Budapest; 🛏 1,2 cl., ▬ 2 cl. and [2] (*EN* **40237** - LISINSKI) Stuttgart - Graz - Maribor - Dobova - Zagreb. From July 14 conveys 🛏 1,2 cl., ▬ 2 cl. and [2] Stuttgart - Villach - Venezia. Also calls at Göppingen (d. 2113).

C – From Norddeich Mole via Münster (Tables **800** and **812**).
D – From Dresden via Leipzig from Aug. 9 (Table **866**). Until Aug. 8 starts from Bielefeld.
K – From Kiel (Table **820**).
N – To Interlaken via Bern (Table **560**).
Q – From Paris via Strasbourg (Table **32**). Ⓡ for international journeys.
R – Not July 26 - Sept. 5.
S – July 26 - Sept. 5.
T – From Ostseebad Binz via Stralsund (Tables **830** and **844**). Starts from Hamburg from Aug. 2.
U – Not July 26 - Aug. 8.
V – July 26 - Aug. 8.
W – Not Aug. 9 - Sept. 5.
X – Aug. 9 - Sept. 5.

n – Not June 7 - July 22.
r – Aug. 9 - Dec. 13.
t – Not Sept. 6 - Oct. 31.
y – To Tübingen (Table **936**) until Aug. 8.
z – To Tübingen (Table **936**) from Aug. 9.

♣ – WATTENMEER – From Westerland (Table **821**).
⊠ – Services between Dortmund and Köln are subject to alteration Sept. 6 - Oct. 31 (also from late evening on Sept. 5) with many trains retimed or diverted via alternative routes. Please check for journeys from Dortmund during this period.
⊖ – 🏛 is at Kehl (8 km from Strasbourg). See Table **911** for local journeys Offenburg - Strasbourg.
▷ – For regional services via Wendlingen, see Table **936**.
◧ – Frankfurt Flughafen Fernbahnhof.
§ – *ICE* **1999** on ⑤ July 4 - Aug. 29 (not July 18).
* – Train number *IC* **2393** on certain dates.

FRANKFURT - STUTTGART - MÜNCHEN and FRANKFURT - KARLSRUHE - BASEL - ZÜRICH 910

SEE NOTE ⊠	*ICE* 205	*ICE* 205 ①–④	*ICE* 205 ⑤⑥	*ICE* 995 ⑦w	*ICE* 273	*ICE* 273 ⑤⑥	*ICE* 205 ①–④	*ICE* 617	*ICE* 775	*ICE* 937
	✗	n✗	n✗		✗	✗	n	✗		
Hamburg Hbf **800 900** d.	1646	1646	1646	...	1824	1824	...	1746	1924	...
Berlin Hbf **810 850 902** d.	|	|	|	1723	|	|	...	|	|	1900
Hannover Hbf **810 900** d.	|	|	|	|	1941	1941	...	|	2041	|
Dortmund Hbf **800** ⊠ d.	1936t	1936t	1936t	|	|	|	...	2036t	|	|
Köln Hbf **800** d.	2055	2055	2055	|	|	|	...	2155	|	|
Köln Messe/Deutz **800** d.	|	|	|	|	|	|	...	|	|	|
Koblenz Hbf **800** d.	|	|	|	|	|	|	...	|	|	|
Wiesbaden Hbf **917a 918a** d.	|	|	|	|	|	|	...	|	|	|
Mainz Hbf **912 917a 918a** d.	|	|	|	|	|	|	...	|	|	|
Worms Hbf **912** d.	|	|	|	|	|	|	...	|	|	|
Frankfurt (Main) Hbf **913** d.	|	|	|	2154	2206	2206	...	|	2305	2308
Frankfurt Flughafen ✈ ◧ d.	2151	2151	2151	|	|	|	...	2255	2324	|
Mannheim Hbf **912 913** a.	2223	2223	2223	|	2244	2244	...	2327	2356	|
Mannheim Hbf **913** d.	2235	2235	2235	|	2246	2246	...	2330	2359	|
Darmstadt Hbf **913 918a** d.	|	|	|	2212	|	|	...	|	|	2326
Bensheim **913** d.	|	|	|	2224	|	|	...	|	|	2339
Weinheim **913** d.	|	|	|	2235	|	|	...	|	|	2350
Heidelberg Hbf **913** d.	|	|	|	2249	|	|	...	|	|	0006
Karlsruhe Hbf **913 931** d.	|	|	|	|	|	|	...	|	|	|
Bruchsal **913 931** d.	|	|	|	|	|	|	...	|	|	|
Vaihingen (Enz) **931** d.	|	|	|	2321	|	|	...	|	|	0035
Stuttgart Hbf **931** a.	|	|	|	2337	|	|	...	0008	|	0051
Stuttgart Hbf **933** ▷ d.	|	|	|	...	|	|	...	...	|	...
Ulm Hbf **930 933** ▷ d.	|	|	|	...	|	|	...	...	|	...
Günzburg **930** d.	|	|	|	...	|	|	...	...	|	...
Augsburg Hbf **930** d.	|	|	|	...	|	|	...	...	|	...
München Pasing **930** a.	|	|	|	...	|	|	...	...	|	...
München Hbf **930** a.	|	|	|	...	|	|	...	...	|	...
Salzburg Hbf **890** a.	|	|	|	...	|	|	...	...	|	...
Karlsruhe Hbf **913** a.	2259	2259	2259	...	2309	2309	←	...	0032	...
Karlsruhe Hbf **910a 916** d.	...	2313	2302	...	...	2313	2313	...	...	...
Baden-Baden **910a 916** d.	...	→	2321	...	...	2330	2330	...	...	...
Offenburg **910a 911 916** d.	...	...	2340	...	...	2348	2348	...	...	...
Strasbourg ⊖ **390 911** a.	...	...	|	...	...	|	|	...	...	...
Paris Est **390** a.	...	...	|	...	...	|	|	...	...	...
Freiburg (Brsg) Hbf **910a** d.	...	...	0015	...	...	0018	0018	...	...	...
Basel Bad Bf 🏛 **910a** a.	...	...	0046	...	...	0052	0050	...	...	...
Basel SBB **510 910a** a.	...	...	0059	...	...	0104	0104	...	...	...
Zürich HB **510** a.	...	...	...	...	...	...	...	...	...	...

SEE NOTE ⊠	*ICE* 618	*IC* 2326 Ⓐ		*ICE* 696 ①		*ICE* 934	*ICE* 934 ①g	*ICE* 774
	K	♦		✗		✗	✗	✗
Zürich HB **510** d.	...	...	...	...	...	...	...	...
Basel SBB **510 910a** d.	...	...	...	...	...	...	...	...
Basel Bad Bf 🏛 **910a** d.	...	...	...	...	...	...	...	...
Freiburg (Brsg) Hbf **910a** d.	...	...	...	...	...	...	...	...
Paris Est **390** d.	...	...	...	...	...	...	...	...
Strasbourg ⊖ **390 911** d.	...	...	...	...	...	...	...	...
Offenburg **910a 911 916** d.	...	...	...	...	...	...	...	...
Baden-Baden **910a 916** d.	...	...	...	...	...	...	...	...
Karlsruhe Hbf **910a 916** a.	...	...	...	...	...	...	...	...
Karlsruhe Hbf **913** d.	...	0335	...	0500	...	...	...	...
Salzburg Hbf **890** d.	...	|	...	|	...	...	...	...
München Hbf **930** d.	0000	|	...	|	...	...	...	...
München Pasing **930** d.	0008	|	...	|	...	...	...	...
Augsburg Hbf **930** d.	0031	|	...	|	...	...	...	...
Günzburg **930** d.	0102	|	...	|	...	...	...	...
Ulm Hbf **930 933** ▷ d.	0116	|	...	|	...	...	...	...
Stuttgart Hbf **933** ▷ a.	0216	|	...	|	...	...	...	...
Stuttgart Hbf **931** d.	0222	0226z	...	|	...	...	0456	0502
Vaihingen (Enz) **931** d.	|	|	...	|	...	...	|	0518
Bruchsal **913 931** d.	|	0347	...	|	...	...	|	|
Karlsruhe Hbf **913 931** a.	|	|	...	|	...	...	|	|
Heidelberg Hbf **913** d.	0343	0410	...	|	...	...	0542	0547
Weinheim **913** d.	|	|	...	|	...	...	0601	|
Bensheim **913** d.	|	|	...	|	...	...	0615	|
Darmstadt Hbf **913 918a** d.	|	|	...	|	...	0637	0637	|
Mannheim Hbf **913** a.	0355	0422	...	0525	...	|	|	0559
Mannheim Hbf **912 913** d.	0401	0424	...	0528	...	|	|	0603
Frankfurt Flughafen ✈ ◧ a.	0457*	0500	...	|	...	|	|	0635
Frankfurt (Main) Hbf **913** a.	0438	0518	...	0608	...	0656	0656	0652
Worms Hbf **912** d.	|	|	...	|	...	|	|	|
Mainz Hbf **912 917a 918a** a.	|	|	...	|	...	|	|	|
Wiesbaden Hbf **917a 918a** a.	|	|	...	|	...	|	|	|
Koblenz Hbf **800** a.	|	|	...	|	...	|	|	|
Köln Messe/Deutz **800** a.	|	|	...	|	...	|	|	|
Köln Hbf **800** a.	0603	|	...	|	...	|	|	|
Dortmund Hbf **800** ⊠ a.	0721	0856	...	|	...	|	|	|
Hannover Hbf **810 900** a.	|	...	...	|	...	|	|	0917
Berlin Hbf **810 850 902** a.	|	...	...	1032	...	1059	1059	|
Hamburg Hbf **800 900** a.	1014	...	...	...	...	1311x	1311x	1036

km ♥	km ♥	SEE NOTE ⊠	*ICE* 270 ①	*ICE* 270	*ICE* 616	*ICE* 474	*IC* 2298 ①–⑥	*ICE* 1014 ①–⑥	*ICE* 1118 ①–⑤	*ICE* 206	*ICE* 694	*ICE* 1672 ①–⑥	*ICE* 1178 ①–⑤	*ICE* 1068 ①–⑥	*ICE* 772	*IC* 2388	*ICE* 267 ①–⑥	*ICE* 374	*ICE* 614	*IC* 2049	*IC* 2049	*ICE* 1098 ①–⑥	*ICE* 78	*EN* 50462 Ⓡ
			✗	✗	✗	K✗		N✗	✗	✗	✗	H✗	✗	✗	✗	Λ	♦✗	✗	✗	W	X	✗	✗	♦
		Zürich HB **510** d.	...	...	...	...	...	...	...	...	...	...	...	...	...	...	...	...	...	...	...	...	0559	...
		Basel SBB **510 910a** d.	...	...	...	...	...	...	...	0513n	...	...	0537	...	...	...	0550	0606	...	...	...	...	0706	...
		Basel Bad Bf 🏛 **910a** d.	...	...	...	0508	...	...	...	0521n	...	...	0546	...	...	...	0600	0615	...	...	...	...	0714	...
		Freiburg (Brsg) Hbf **910a** d.	...	...	...	0541	...	...	...	0553n	...	...	0619	...	...	...	0644	0650	...	...	...	...	0747	...
		Paris Est **390** d.	...	...	...	|	...	...	...	|	...	...	|	...	...	...	|	|	...	...	...	...	|	...
		Strasbourg ⊖ **390 911** d.	...	...	...	|	...	...	...	|	...	...	|	...	...	...	|	|	...	...	...	...	|	...
		Offenburg **910a 911 916** d.	0517	...	...	|	...	...	...	0625n	...	...	0654	...	...	...	0730	0723	...	...	...	...	|	...
		Baden-Baden **910a 916** d.	0535	...	...	0632	...	...	...	0641n	...	...	0713	...	...	...	0746	0740	...	...	...	...	0832	...
		Karlsruhe Hbf **913** d.	0554	...	...	0649	...	...	...	0658n	...	...	0731	...	...	...	0803	0757	...	...	...	...	0849	...
		Karlsruhe Hbf **910a 916** d.	0557	0557	...	0651	...	...	...	0701	...	0702	0736	...	...	...	0805	0800	...	...	0752	...	0851	...
		Salzburg Hbf **890** d.	|	|	...	|	...	...	...	|	...	|	|	...	...	...	|	|	...	...	|	...	|	0405
0		**München** Hbf **930** d.	|	|	0331	|	...	...	...	|	...	|	|	0459	...	...	|	|	0532	...	|	0544	|	|
7		München Pasing **930** d.	|	|	0340	|	...	...	...	|	...	|	|	0508	...	...	|	|	0541	...	|	0553	|	|
62		**Augsburg** Hbf **930** d.	|	|	0404	|	...	...	...	|	...	|	|	0535	...	...	|	|	0604	...	|	0616	|	0648
124		Günzburg **930** d.	|	|	|	|	...	...	...	|	...	|	|	|	...	...	|	|	|	...	|	0648	|	|
148		**Ulm** Hbf **930 933** ▷ d.	|	|	0447	|	...	...	...	|	...	|	|	0619	...	...	|	|	0647	...	|	0703	|	0738
237		**Stuttgart** Hbf **933** ▷ a.	|	|	0545	|	...	...	...	|	...	|	|	0704	...	...	0845	|	0745	...	|	0759	|	0838
237	0	**Stuttgart** Hbf **931** d.	|	|	0551	|	0605	0636	0626	|	0650	|	|	0710	0724	0727	...	|	0751	0736	|	0805	|	...
	29	Vaihingen (Enz) **931** d.	|	|	|	|	0625	|	0643	|	|	|	|	|	|	|	...	|	|	0754	|	|	|	...
		Bruchsal **913 931** d.	|	|	|	|	|	|	|	|	|	0722	|	0739	|	|	...	|	|	|	0805	|	|	...
		Karlsruhe Hbf **913 931** a.	|	|	|	|	|	|	|	|	|	|	|	0753	|	|	...	|	|	|	|	|	|	...
	92	**Heidelberg** Hbf **913** d.	|	|	|	|	0659	|	0720	|	|	0746	|	...	|	|	...	|	|	0825	0826	0846	|	...
		Weinheim **913** d.	|	|	|	|	0715	|	|	|	|	0800	|	...	|	0823	...	|	|	|	|	0900	|	...
		Bensheim **913** d.	|	|	|	|	0728	|	|	|	|	0809	|	...	|	0833	...	|	|	|	|	0909	|	...
		Darmstadt Hbf **913 918a** d.	|	|	|	|	0742	|	|	|	|	0824	|	...	|	0847	...	|	|	|	|	0924	|	...
344	109	**Mannheim** Hbf **913** a.	0624	0624	0628	0715	|	0718	0732	0724	0728	|	0759	...	0802	|	...	0824	0828	0837	0837	|	0915	...
344	109	**Mannheim** Hbf **913** d.	0632	0632	0635	0717	|	0720	0734	0735	0732	|	0818	...	0805	|	...	0832	0836	0839	0839	|	0917	...
416		**Frankfurt** Flughafen ✈ ◧ a.	|	|	0707	|	|	0751	|	0807	|	|	v	...	0835	|	...	|	0907	|	|	|	|	...
	187	**Frankfurt** (Main) Hbf **913** a.	0708	0708	|	0752	0758	|	|	|	0808	0840	...	...	0852	0910	...	0908	|	|	|	0940	0952	...
		Worms Hbf d.	|	|	|	|	...	|	|	|	|	|	...	...	|	...	...	|	|	|	|	...	|	...
		Mainz Hbf **917a 918a** a.	|	|	|	|	...	|	0815	|	|	|	...	...	|	...	...	|	|	0918	0918	...	|	...
		Wiesbaden Hbf **917a 918a** a.	|	|	|	|	...	|	0833	|	|	|	...	...	|	...	...	|	|	|	|	...	|	...
		Koblenz Hbf **800** a.	|	|	|	|	...	|	...	|	|	|	...	...	|	...	...	|	|	1011	1011	...	|	...
		Köln Messe/Deutz **800** a.	|	|	|	|	...	0849	...	|	|	|	...	...	|	...	...	|	|	|	|	...	|	...
		Köln Hbf **800** a.	|	|	0805	|	...	...	...	0905	|	|	...	...	|	...	...	|	1005	1106	1106	...	|	...
		Dortmund Hbf **800** ⊠ a.	|	|	0921	|	...	...	...	1021t	|	|	...	...	|	...	...	|	1121	1221	1221	...	|	...
		Hannover Hbf **810 900** a.	|	|	|	1017	...	...	...	|	|	1156	...	...	1117	...	...	|	|	1418r	1418r	...	1217	...
		Berlin Hbf **810 850 902** a.	1130	1130	|	|	...	...	...	|	1234	|	...	...	|	...	...	1331	|	...	...	...	|	...
		Hamburg Hbf **800 900** a.	...	...	1214	1136	...	...	...	1314	...	1330	...	...	1236	...	...	...	1414	...	...	...	1336	...

♦ – **NOTES** (LISTED BY TRAIN NUMBER)

267 – BADEN-KURIER – 🚃12 ✗ Basel - Stuttgart - München. Also calls at Müllheim (Baden), d. 0624.

2326 – 🚃12 Stuttgart - Karlsruhe - Frankfurt - Siegen - Dortmund. See Table **808** for timings Frankfurt - Dortmund.

50462 – KÁLMÁN IMRE – 🛏 1, 2 cl., 🛌 2 cl. and 🚃2 Budapest - Wien - Stuttgart; 🛏 1, 2 cl., 🛌 2 cl. and 🚃2 (*EN* **414** – LISINSKI) Zagreb - Dobova - Maribor - Graz - Salzburg - Stuttgart. From July 14 conveys 🛏 1, 2 cl., 🛌 2 cl. and 🚃2 Venezia (*NJ* **236**) - Villach - München Ost - Stuttgart. Also calls at Göppingen (a. 0812).

A – Oct. 6 - 9, 13 - 16, 20 - 23 and ① Oct. 27 - Dec. 8. Also runs via Mannheim (a. 0817 / d. 0825), not calling at Weinheim, Bensheim or Darmstadt on June 16, 17, 23 - 26, 30, July 1 - 3, 7, 21, Sept. 8, 15 - 18, 21 - 25, 29. From Rottweil (Table **940**).

H – To Ostseebad Binz via Stralsund until Aug. 1 (Tables **830** / **844**).

K – To Kiel (Table **820**).

N – To Düsseldorf on ①-⑤. To Norddeich Mole on ⑥ (Tables **800** and **812**).

W – Not Aug. 9 - Sept. 5.

X – Aug. 9 - Sept. 5.

g – ① (also June 10; not June 9).

n – Not June 7 - July 23.

r – Aug. 9 - Dec. 13 (to Dresden or Leipzig, Table **866**). Until Aug. 8 terminates at Bielefeld.

t – Not Sept. 6 - Oct. 31.

v – To Stuttgart (a. 0905).

w – Also June 9; not June 8.

x – Not Aug. 1 - Dec. 13.

z – Via Karlsruhe (Table **931**).

* – Calls at Frankfurt Flughafen after Frankfurt (Main) Hbf.

⊠ – Services Dortmund - Köln and v.v. are subject to alteration Sept. 6 - Oct. 31 (also from late evening on Sept. 5) with many trains retimed or diverted via alternative routes. Please check for journeys from / to Dortmund during this period.

▷ – For regional services via Wendlingen, see Table **936**.

♥ – Via high-speed lines.

⊖ – 🏛 is at Kehl (8 km from Strasbourg). See Table **911** for local journeys Strasbourg - Offenburg.

◧ – Frankfurt Flughafen Fernbahnhof.

910 ZÜRICH - BASEL - KARLSRUHE - FRANKFURT and MÜNCHEN - STUTTGART - FRANKFURT

SEE NOTE ⊠	*ICE*	*ICE*	*ICE*	*IC*		*TGV*	*ICE*	*ICE*	*TGV*	*ICE*	*ICE*	*IC*	*IC*	*ICE*	*ICE*	*ICE*	*ICE*	*ICE*	*ICE*	*ICE*	*ICE*	*ICE*	*ICE*	
	1012	**202**	**692**	**2374**		**9576**	**770**	**9571**	**9561**	**372**	**612**	**2047**	**1296**	**1067**	**76**	**1084**	**1010**	**200**	**690**	**1578**	**1578**	**568**	**578**	
	①–⑥								①–⑥							▲				①–④	⊡			
	✕	✕	✕	♣		Q🍷	✕	[R]✕	[R]🍷	N✕	K✕	T D	🍷	✕	✕	✕	✕	✕	✕	A ✕	✕	✕	✕	
Zürich HB .... **510** d.	...	...	...	...	...	...	...	...	...	...	...	...	...	...	0759	...	...	...	...		...	...	...	...
Basel SBB .... **510 910a** d.	...	0713**n**	...	...	...	...	...	...	...	0813	...	...	...	0827	0906	...	...	0913**n**	...	...	...	...	...	...
Basel Bad Bf 🏛 .... **910a** d.	...	0721**n**	...	...	...	...	...	...	...	0821	...	...	...	0836	0914	...	...	0922**n**	...	...	...	...	...	...
Freiburg (Brsg) Hbf .... **910a** d.	...	0755**n**	...	...	...	...	...	...	...	0855	...	...	...	0923	0948	...	...	0956**n**	...	...	...	...	...	...
Paris Est .... **390** d.	...	|	...	...	...	...	...	0654	0718**y**	|	...	...	...	|	|	...	...	|	...	...	...	...	...	...
Strasbourg ⊖ ..... **390 911** d.	...	|	...	...	...	...	...	0845	0908	|	...	...	...	|	|	...	...	|	...	...	...	...	...	...
Offenburg .... **910a 911 916** d.	...	0825**n**	...	...	...	...	...	|	|	0928	...	...	...	0957	|	...	...	1028**n**	...	...	1018**c**	...	...	...
Baden-Baden .... **910a 916** d.	...	0841**n**	...	...	...	...	...	|	|	|	...	...	...	|	1030	...	...	|	...	...	|	...	...	...
Karlsruhe Hbf .... **910a 916** a.	...	0858**n**	...	...	...	...	...	0926	0953	0958	...	...	...	1025	1049	...	...	1058**n**	...	...	1056**c**	...	...	...
Karlsruhe Hbf .... **913** d.	...	0901	...	...	...	...	...	0928	0955	1000	...	...	...	1027	1051	...	...	1101	...	...	1110	...	...	...
Salzburg Hbf **890** .... d.	...	|	...	...	...	...	...	|	|	|	...	...	...	|	|	...	...	|	...	...	|	...	...	...
München Hbf .... **930** d.	0625	|	0641	...	...	0651	...	|	|	|	0727	...	0746	|	|	...	0827	|	0846	...	|	0902	...	...
München Pasing .... **930** d.	0634	|	0650	...	...	|	...	|	|	|	0736	...	|	|	|	...	0836	|	0855	...	|	0911	...	...
Augsburg Hbf .... **930** d.	0700	|	0714	...	...	0720	...	|	|	|	0801	...	0815	|	|	...	0901	|	0918	...	|	0935	...	...
Günzburg .... **930** d.	|	|	|	...	...	|	...	|	|	|	|	...	0848	|	|	...	|	|	|	...	|	|	...	...
Ulm Hbf .... **930 933** ▷ d.	0746	|	0758	...	...	0804	...	|	|	|	0847	...	0902	|	|	...	0946	|	1001	...	|	1019	...	...
Stuttgart Hbf .... **933** ▷ a.	0831	|	0844	...	...	0901	...	1004	|	|	0945	...	0959	1103	|	...	1031	|	1043	...	|	1102	...	...
Stuttgart Hbf .... **931** d.	0839	|	0851	0857	...	0910	0923	...	|	|	0951	0937	1005	...	|	1014	1039	|	1051	1103	|	1112	1123	...
Vaihingen (Enz) .... **931** d.	|	|	|	|	...	|	|	...	|	|	|	0954	|	...	|	|	|	|	|	|	|	|	|	...
Bruchsal .... **913 931** d.	|	|	|	|	...	|	|	...	|	|	|	|	|	...	|	|	|	|	|	|	1122	1138	|	...
Karlsruhe Hbf .. **913 931** a.	|	|	|	|	...	0951	|	...	|	|	|	|	|	...	|	|	|	|	|	|	|	1152	|	...
Heidelberg Hbf .... **913** d.	|	|	|	0946	...	...	|	...	|	|	|	1025	1046	...	|	|	|	|	|	1146	1146	...	|	...
Weinheim .... **913** d.	|	|	|	1000	...	...	|	...	|	|	|	|	1100	...	|	|	|	|	|	1200	1200	...	|	...
Bensheim .... **913** d.	|	|	|	1009	...	...	|	...	|	|	|	|	1109	...	|	|	|	|	|	1209	1209	...	|	...
Darmstadt Hbf .... **913 918a** d.	|	|	|	1024	...	...	|	...	|	|	|	|	1124	...	|	|	|	|	|	1224	1224	...	|	...
Mannheim Hbf .... **913** a.	0918	0924	0929	|	...	...	1001	...	1018	1024	1028	1037	|	...	1115	1059	1118	1124	1129	|	|	...	1201	...
Mannheim Hbf .... **912 913** d.	0920	0935	0932	|	...	...	1004	...	1020	1032	1036	1039	|	...	1117	1108	1120	1135	1132	|	|	...	1203	...
Frankfurt Flughafen ✈ ◧ ... a.	0951	1007	|	|	...	...	1035	...	|	|	1107	|	|	...	|	|	1151	1207	|	|	|	...	1235	...
Frankfurt (Main) Hbf .... **913** a.	|	|	1008	1040	...	...	1052	...	1059	1108	|	|	1140	...	1152	1208	|	|	1208	1240	1240	...	1252	...
Worms Hbf .... **912** d.	|	|	|	|	...	...	|	...	...	|	|	|	...	...	|	|	|	|	|	|	|	...	|	...
Mainz Hbf ...... **912 917a 918a** a.	|	|	|	|	...	...	|	...	...	|	|	1118	...	...	|	|	|	|	|	|	|	...	|	...
Wiesbaden Hbf ... **917a 918a** a.	|	|	|	|	...	...	|	...	...	|	|	|	...	...	|	|	|	|	|	|	|	...	|	...
Koblenz Hbf **800** .... a.	|	|	|	|	...	...	|	...	...	|	|	1211	...	...	|	|	|	|	|	|	|	...	|	...
Köln Messe/Deutz **800** .... a.	1048	|	|	|	...	...	|	...	...	|	|	|	...	...	|	|	1248	|	|	|	|	...	|	...
Köln Hbf **800** .... a.	|	1105	|	|	...	...	|	...	...	|	1205	1306	...	...	|	|	|	1305	|	|	|	...	|	...
Dortmund Hbf **800** .... ⊠ a.	1204**j**	1221**t**	|	|	...	...	|	...	...	|	1321	1421	...	...	|	|	1404**t**	1421**t**	|	|	|	...	|	...
Hannover Hbf **810 900** .... a.	...	|	|	1356	...	...	1317	...	...	|	|	1620**r**	...	...	1417	1456	...	|	|	1556	1556	...	1517	...
Berlin Hbf **810 850 902** .... a.	...	|	1432	|	...	...	|	...	...	1529	|	...	...	...	|	|	...	|	1632	|	|	...	|	...
Hamburg Hbf **800 900** .... a.	...	1514	...	1530	...	...	1436	...	...	...	1614	...	...	...	1536	1628	...	1714	...	1732	1732	...	1636	...

SEE NOTE ⊠	*ICE*	*ICE*	*ICE*	*ICE*	*ICE*	*ICE*	*ICE*	*ICE*	*ICE*	*ICE*	*ICE*	*ICE*	*IC*	*ICE*	*ICE*	*TGV*	*ICE*	*ICE*	*EC*	*EC*	*TGV*	*ICE*	*TGV*	
	370	**610**	**2045**	**2045**	**1290**	**9591**	**74**	**918**	**108**	**1218**	**1576**	**566**	**2012**	**576**	**9573**	**9593**	**278**	**518**	**8**	**218**	**9583**	**72**	**9583**	
			D	**D**											Ⓑ	⑥					[R]		[R]	
	✕	✕	R🍷	S🍷	✕	[R]✕	K✕	✕	✕	B✕	✕♦	✕	♦	✕	[R]✕	[R]🍷	N✕	✕	✕	♦	M🍷	✕	M🍷	
Zürich HB .... **510** d.	...	...	...	...	...	...	0959	...	...	...	...	...	...	...	...	...	...	...	1059	...	...	...	...	...
Basel SBB .... **510 910a** d.	1013	...	...	...	...	...	1106	...	1113**e**	...	...	...	...	...	...	...	1213	...	1220	...	...	1306	...	...
Basel Bad Bf 🏛 .... **910a** d.	1022	...	...	...	...	...	1114	...	1122**e**	...	...	...	...	...	...	...	1222	...	1228	...	...	1314	...	...
Freiburg (Brsg) Hbf .... **910a** d.	1055	...	...	...	...	...	1147	...	1156**e**	...	...	...	...	...	...	...	1255	...	1304	...	...	1347	...	...
Paris Est .... **390** d.	|	...	...	...	...	0955	|	...	|	...	...	...	...	...	1054	1054	|	...	|	...	...	|	...	...
Strasbourg ⊖ ..... **390 911** d.	|	...	...	...	...	1146	|	...	|	...	...	...	...	...	1245	1245	|	...	|	...	1355	|	...	...
Offenburg .... **910a 911 916** d.	1128	...	...	...	...	|	|	...	1228**e**	...	...	...	...	...	|	|	1329	...	|	...	|	|	...	...
Baden-Baden .... **910a 916** d.	|	...	...	...	...	|	1232	...	|	...	...	...	...	...	|	|	|	...	1352	...	1424	1432	...	...
Karlsruhe Hbf .... **910a 916** a.	1158	...	...	...	...	1234	1249	...	1258**e**	...	...	...	...	...	1325	1325	1358	...	1410	...	1446	1449	←	...
Karlsruhe Hbf .... **913** d.	1200	...	...	1152	...	1236	1251	...	1301	...	1310	...	...	...	1327	1327	1400	...	1412	...	1454	1451	1454	...
Salzburg Hbf **890** .... d.	|	...	...	|	0800	|	|	...	|	...	|	...	...	...	|	|	|	...	|	1000	→	|	|	...
München Hbf .... **930** d.	|	0927	...	|	0947	|	|	1029	|	1047	|	1102	...	...	|	|	|	1127	|	1148	...	|	|	...
München Pasing .... **930** d.	|	0936	...	|	|	|	|	|	|	1055	|	1111	...	...	|	|	|	1136	|	|	...	|	|	...
Augsburg Hbf .... **930** d.	|	1001	...	|	1015	|	|	1101	|	1118	|	1135	...	...	|	|	|	1201	|	1216	...	|	|	...
Günzburg .... **930** d.	|	|	...	|	1048	|	|	|	|	|	|	|	...	...	|	|	|	|	|	1248	...	|	|	...
Ulm Hbf .... **930 933** ▷ d.	|	1047	...	|	1103	|	|	1146	|	1201	|	1219	1157	...	|	|	|	1247	|	1303	...	|	|	...
Stuttgart Hbf .... **933** ▷ a.	|	1145	...	|	1159	|	|	1232	|	1243	|	1302	1259	...	1404	1404	|	1345	|	1359	...	|	|	...
Stuttgart Hbf .... **931** d.	|	1151	1137	|	1205	|	|	1238	|	1251	|	1309	1312	1323	...	...	|	1351	|	1405	...	|	|	...
Vaihingen (Enz) .... **931** d.	|	|	1154	|	|	|	|	|	|	|	|	|	|	|	...	...	|	|	|	|	...	|	|	...
Bruchsal .... **913 931** d.	|	|	|	|	|	|	|	|	|	|	1322	1337	|	|	...	...	|	|	|	|	...	|	|	...
Karlsruhe Hbf .. **913 931** a.	|	|	|	|	|	|	|	|	|	|	|	1352	|	|	...	...	|	|	|	|	...	|	|	...
Heidelberg Hbf .... **913** d.	|	|	1225	1225	1246	|	|	|	|	|	1346	...	1355	|	...	...	|	|	|	1446	...	|	|	...
Weinheim .... **913** d.	|	|	|	|	1300	|	|	|	|	|	1400	...	|	|	...	...	|	|	|	1500	...	|	|	...
Bensheim .... **913** d.	|	|	|	|	1309	|	|	|	|	|	1409	...	|	|	...	...	|	|	|	1509	...	|	|	...
Darmstadt Hbf .... **913 918a** d.	|	|	|	|	1324	|	|	|	|	|	1424	...	|	|	...	...	|	|	|	1524	...	|	|	...
Mannheim Hbf .... **913** a.	1224	1228	1237	1237	|	|	1315	1318	1324	1329	|	...	1406	1401	...	...	1424	1428	1436	|	...	1515	1518	...
Mannheim Hbf .... **912 913** d.	1232	1236	1239	1239	|	|	1317	1320	1335	1332	|	...	1408	1403	...	...	1432	1436	1438	|	...	1517	1521	...
Frankfurt Flughafen ✈ ◧ ... a.	|	1307	|	|	|	|	|	1351	1407	|	|	...	|	1435	...	...	|	1507	|	|	...	|	|	...
Frankfurt (Main) Hbf .... **913** a.	1308	|	|	|	1340	1404•	1352	|	|	1408	1440	...	|	1452	...	...	1508	|	|	1540	...	1552	1559	...
Worms Hbf .... **912** d.	|	|	|	|	...	|	|	|	|	|	|	...	|	|	...	...	|	|	|	...	...	|	...	...
Mainz Hbf ...... **912 917a 918a** a.	|	|	1318	1318	...	|	|	|	|	|	|	...	1447	|	...	...	|	|	1518	...	...	|	...	...
Wiesbaden Hbf ... **917a 918a** a.	|	|	|	|	...	|	|	|	|	|	|	...	|	|	...	...	|	|	|	...	...	|	...	...
Koblenz Hbf **800** .... a.	|	|	1411	1411	...	|	|	|	|	|	|	...	1542	|	...	...	|	|	1611	...	...	|	...	...
Köln Messe/Deutz **800** .... a.	|	|	|	|	...	|	|	1448	|	|	|	...	|	|	...	...	|	|	|	...	...	|	...	...
Köln Hbf **800** .... a.	|	1405	1506	1506	...	|	|	|	1505	|	|	...	1644	|	...	...	|	1605	1706	...	...	|	...	...
Dortmund Hbf **800** .... ⊠ a.	|	1521	1621	1621	...	|	|	1604**t**	1621**t**	|	|	...	1803	|	...	...	|	1721	1821**t**	...	...	|	...	...
Hannover Hbf **810 900** .... a.	|	|	1820**r**	1820**r**	...	|	1617	...	|	|	1756	...	...	1717	...	...	|	|	|	...	...	1817	...	...
Berlin Hbf **810 850 902** .... a.	1731	|	...	...	...	1803	|	...	|	1832	|	...	...	|	...	...	1930	|	|	...	...	|	...	...
Hamburg Hbf **800 900** .... a.	...	1814	...	...	...	...	1735	...	1914	...	1929	...	...	1836	...	...	...	2014	2114	...	...	1936	...	...

♦ – **NOTES** (LISTED BY TRAIN NUMBER)

218 – CHIEMGAU – 🚃12 Graz - Bischofshofen - Salzburg - München - Frankfurt.
1576 – 🚃12 ✕ Karlsruhe - Frankfurt - Hamburg (- Rostock Ⓑ to Aug. 1) (- Stralsund ⑦ to July 27).
2012 – ALLGÄU – 🚃12 Oberstdorf (Table **935**) - Ulm - Stuttgart - Köln - Dortmund.

A – To Stralsund until July 24 (Table **830**).
B – From Innsbruck (Table **953**).
D – To Dresden via Leipzig from Aug. 9 (Table **866**). Until Aug. 8 terminates at Bielefeld.
K – To Kiel (Table **820**).
M – From Marseille via Lyon (Tables **350** and **379**).
N – From Interlaken via Bern (Table **560**).
Q – To Paris via Strasbourg (Table **32**). [R] for international journeys.
R – Not July 26 - Sept. 5.
S – July 26 - Sept. 5.
T – From Tübingen (Table **936**).

c – ⑥⑦ (also Oct. 3).
e – Not June 7 - 14.
j – ①②③④⑥. On ⑤ (daily Sept. 6 - Oct. 30) terminates at Düsseldorf.
n – Not June 7 - July 23.
r – Aug. 9 - Dec. 13.
t – Not Sept. 6 - Oct. 31.
y – 0715 on ①.

• – Frankfurt (Main) **Süd** (not Hbf).
⊡ – ⑤–⑦ (also June 9, 19, July 28 - 31, Aug. 4 - Sept. 4). 🚃12 ✕ (Konstanz ⑥⑦ -) Karlsruhe - Frankfurt - Hamburg - Stralsund (- Greifswald on ⑦ to July 27).
♣ – WATTENMEER – To Westerland (Table **821**).
▲ – ⑤⑥ June 7 - Sept. 27.
⊠ – Services between Köln and Dortmund are subject to alteration Sept. 6 - Oct. 31 (also from late evening on Sept. 5) with many trains retimed or diverted via alternative routes. Please check for journeys to Dortmund during this period.
⊖ – 🏛 is at Kehl (8 km from Strasbourg). See Table **911** for local journeys Strasbourg - Offenburg.
▷ – For regional services via Wendlingen, see Table **936**.
◧ – Frankfurt Flughafen Fernbahnhof.

ZÜRICH - BASEL - KARLSRUHE - FRANKFURT and MÜNCHEN - STUTTGART - FRANKFURT 910

SEE NOTE ⊠	*ICE* 106	*ICE* 710	*WB* 962	*ICE* 596	*ICE* 710	*ICE* 1574	*ICE* 564	*ICE* 118	*ICE* 1094	*ICE* 276	*ICE* 516	*EC* 6	*ICE* 1168	*ICE* 114	*TGV* 9575	*ICE* 70	*ICE* 914	*ICE* 104	*ICE* 594	*ICE* 1512	*ICE* 1572	*ICE* 562	*ECE* 150	*ICE* 572
		①–⑤			①–⑤															①–④				
	✕	✕	E🍷	✕	✕	✕	✕	✕◆	K✕	✕	✕	N✕	✕	✕◆	🅁🍷	C✕	✕	✕	✕	✕	✕	B✕	L✕	✕
Zürich HB ... **510** d.	...	...	...	...	...	...	...	...	...	...	...	...	...	...	...	1359	...	...	...	...	...	...	1434	...
Basel SBB ... **510 910a** d.	1313	...	...	...	...	...	...	...	...	1413	...	1427	...	...	...	1506	...	1513	...	...	...	...	1538	...
Basel Bad Bf 🏛 ... **910a** d.	1322	...	...	...	...	...	...	...	...	1422	...	1435	...	...	...	1514	...	1522	...	...	...	...	1552	...
Freiburg (Brsg) Hbf ... **910a** d.	1356	...	...	...	...	...	...	...	...	1455	...	1506	...	...	...	1547	...	1556	...	...	...	...	1624	...
Paris Est ... **390** d.	│	...	...	...	...	...	...	...	...	│	...	│	...	...	1354	│	...	│	...	...	...	...	│	...
Strasbourg ⊖ ... **390 911** d.	│	...	...	...	...	...	...	...	...	│	...	│	...	...	1545	│	...	│	...	...	...	...	│	...
Offenburg ... **910a 911 916** d.	1428	...	...	...	...	...	...	...	...	1528	...	│	...	...	│	│	...	1628	...	...	...	...	│	...
Baden-Baden ... **910a 916** d.	│	...	...	...	...	...	...	...	...	│	...	│	...	...	│	1632	...	│	...	...	...	...	│	...
Karlsruhe Hbf ... **910a 916** a.	1458	...	...	...	...	...	...	...	...	1558	...	1610	...	...	1625	1649	...	1658	...	...	...	...	1729	...
Karlsruhe Hbf ... **913** d.	1501	...	...	...	...	1510	...	...	...	1600	...	1612	...	...	1627	1651	...	1701	...	...	...	...	1731	...
Salzburg Hbf **890** ... d.	│	...	1039	...	...	│	...	...	...	│	...	│	...	1200	│	│	...	│	...	...	...	...	│	...
München Hbf ... **930** d.	│	...	1222	1246	...	│	1302	...	...	│	1327	│	...	1347	│	│	1427	│	1446	...	...	1502	│	...
München Pasing ... **930** d.	│	...	│	1255	...	│	1311	...	...	│	1336	│	...	│	│	│	1436	│	1455	...	...	1511	│	...
Augsburg Hbf ... **930** d.	│	...	1251	1318	...	│	1335	...	...	│	1401	│	...	1415	│	│	1501	│	1518	...	...	1535	│	...
Günzburg ... **930** d.	│	...	1332	│	...	│	│	...	...	│	│	│	...	1448	│	│	│	│	│	...	...	│	│	...
Ulm Hbf ... **930 933** ▷ d.	│	...	1353	1401	...	│	1419	1354	...	│	1447	│	...	1503	│	│	1546	│	1601	...	...	1619	│	...
Stuttgart Hbf ... **933** ▷ a.	│	...	1437	1443	...	│	1502	1459	...	│	1545	│	...	1559	1704	│	1631	│	1643	...	...	1702	│	...
Stuttgart Hbf ... **931** d.	│	1435	...	1451	...	│	1509	1512	1523	│	1551	│	1602	1607	...	│	1637	│	1651	1623	1654	1708	│	1723
Vaihingen (Enz) ... **931** d.	│	1454	...	│	...	│	│	│	│	│	│	│	│	1624	...	│	│	│	│	│	│	│	│	│
Bruchsal ... **913 931** d.	│	│	...	│	...	1522	1537	│	│	│	│	│	│	│	...	│	│	│	│	│	│	│	│	│
Karlsruhe Hbf .. **913 931** a.	│	│	...	│	←	│	1552	│	│	│	│	│	│	│	...	│	│	│	│	│	│	│	│	│
Heidelberg Hbf ... **913** d.	│	1518	...	│	1520	1546	...	1555	│	│	│	│	1646	│	...	│	│	│	│	1720	1746	│	│	│
Weinheim ... **913** d.	│	→	...	│	│	1600	...	│	│	│	│	│	1700	│	...	│	│	│	│	│	1800	│	│	│
Bensheim ... **913** d.	│	...	...	│	│	1609	...	│	│	│	│	│	1709	│	...	│	│	│	│	│	1809	│	│	│
Darmstadt Hbf ... **913 918a** d.	│	...	...	│	│	1624	...	│	│	│	│	│	1724	│	...	│	│	│	│	│	1824	│	│	│
Mannheim Hbf ... **913** a.	1524	...	...	1529	1531	│	...	1605	1601	1624	1628	1637	│	1655	...	1715	1718	1724	1729	1736	│	1746	1758	1801
Mannheim Hbf ... **912 913** d.	1535	...	...	1532	1533	│	...	1607	1604	1632	1636	1639	│	1657	...	1717	1720	1735	1732	1738	│	...	1800	1803
Frankfurt Flughafen ✈ ◧ ... a.	1607	...	...	│	│	│	...	│	1635	│	1707	│	│	│	...	│	1751	1807	│	│	│	...	│	1835
Frankfurt (Main) Hbf ... **913** a.	│	...	...	1608	│	1640	...	│	1652	1708	│	│	1740	│	...	1752	│	│	1808	│	1840	...	1844	1852
Worms Hbf ... **912** d.	│	...	...	│	│	│	...	│	│	│	│	│	...	1714	...	│	│	│	│	│	│	...	...	│
Mainz Hbf ... **912 917a 918a** a.	│	...	...	│	1615	│	...	1647	│	│	│	1718	...	1740	...	│	│	│	│	1815	│	...	...	│
Wiesbaden Hbf ... **917a 918a** a.	│	...	...	│	1633	│	...	1702	│	│	│	│	...	1800	...	│	│	│	│	1832	│	...	...	│
Koblenz Hbf **800** ... a.	│	...	...	│	│	│	...	│	│	│	│	1811	...	│	...	│	│	│	│	...	│	...	...	│
Köln Messe/Deutz **800** ... a.	│	...	...	│	│	│	...	1825	│	│	│	│	...	1927	...	│	1848	│	│	...	│	...	...	│
Köln Hbf **800** ... a.	1705	...	...	│	1801	│	...	...	│	│	1805	1906	...	│	...	│	│	1905	│	...	│	...	...	│
Dortmund Hbf **800** ... ⊠ a.	...	...	...	│	...	│	...	...	│	│	1921	2030	...	2057	...	│	2003	2021t	│	...	│	...	...	│
Hannover Hbf **810 900** ... a.	...	...	...	│	...	1956	...	...	1912	│	│	...	...	...	...	2017	...	│	│	...	2156	...	...	2119
Berlin Hbf **810 850 902** ... a.	...	...	...	2032	...	│	...	...	│	2133	│	...	...	...	...	│	...	│	2232	...	│	...	...	│
Hamburg Hbf **800 900** ... a.	...	...	...	...	...	2130	...	...	2030	...	2214	...	...	...	...	2139	...	2316	...	...	2329f	...	...	2246

SEE NOTE ⊠	*ICE* 9563	*ICE* 274	*ICE* 514	*IC* 2349	*IC* 2349	*EC* 112	*TGV* 9577	*ICE* 376	*ICE* 376	*ICE* 224	*ICE* 912	*ICE* 102	*ICE* 592	*ICE* 592	*ICE* 266	*ICE* 570	*ICE* 570	*ICE* 272	*ICE* 272	*ICE* 292	*ICE* 512	*IC* 2343	*IC* 2343	**IC** 2347
							Ⓑ	Ⓑ	⑥		△		①–⑥	⑦		⑦		⑥	①–⑤	⑦		①–④	⑤–⑦	
	🅁✕	✕	✕	R	S	◆	D🅁🍷	N✕	N✕	A✕	✕	✕	F✕	✕	✕◆	✕	✕	✕	✕	✕	M✕	R	R	S
Zürich HB ... **510** d.	...	...	...	...	...	...	...	...	...	...	...	...	...	...	...	...	...	1659	1659	1659	...	...	...	...
Basel SBB ... **510 910a** d.	...	1613	...	...	...	...	...	1707	1707	...	...	1713	...	...	...	...	...	1813	1813	1813	...	...	...	...
Basel Bad Bf 🏛 ... **910a** d.	...	1622	...	...	...	...	...	1715	1715	...	...	1721	...	...	...	...	...	1822	1822	1822	...	...	...	...
Freiburg (Brsg) Hbf ... **910a** d.	...	1655	...	...	...	...	...	1747	1747	...	...	1755	...	...	...	...	...	1855	1855	1855	...	...	...	...
Paris Est ... **390** d.	1521	│	...	...	...	...	1554	│	│	...	...	│	...	...	...	...	...	│	│	│	...	...	...	...
Strasbourg ⊖ ... **390 911** d.	1713	│	...	...	...	...	1746	│	│	...	...	│	...	...	...	...	...	│	│	│	...	...	...	...
Offenburg ... **910a 911 916** d.	│	1727	...	...	...	...	│	│	│	...	...	1826	...	...	...	...	...	1928	1928	1928	...	...	...	...
Baden-Baden ... **910a 916** d.	│	│	...	...	...	...	│	1832	1832	...	...	1841	...	...	...	...	...	│	│	│	...	...	...	...
Karlsruhe Hbf ... **910a 916** a.	1753	1758	...	...	...	...	1826	1849	1849	...	...	1858	...	...	...	...	...	1958	1958	1958	...	...	...	...
Karlsruhe Hbf ... **913** d.	1755	1800	...	...	1739	...	1828	1851	1851	...	...	1901	...	...	...	...	...	2000	2000	2000	...	...	...	1958
Salzburg Hbf **890** ... d.	│	│	...	...	│	1400	│	│	│	...	...	│	...	...	...	...	...	│	│	│	...	...	...	│
München Hbf ... **930** d.	│	│	1527	...	│	1547	│	│	│	1628	1628	│	1646	1646	1658	...	...	│	│	│	1727	...	...	│
München Pasing ... **930** d.	│	│	1536	...	│	│	│	│	│	1637	1637	│	1654	1654	1707	...	...	│	│	│	1736	...	...	│
Augsburg Hbf ... **930** d.	│	│	1601	...	│	1615	│	│	│	1701	1701	│	1718	1718	1731	...	...	│	│	│	1801	...	...	│
Günzburg ... **930** d.	│	│	│	...	│	1648	│	│	│	│	│	│	│	│	1804	...	...	│	│	│	│	...	...	│
Ulm Hbf ... **930 933** ▷ d.	│	│	1647	...	│	1703	│	│	│	1746	1746	│	1801	1801	1819	...	...	│	│	│	1847	...	...	│
Stuttgart Hbf ... **933** ▷ a.	│	│	1745	...	│	1758	1904	│	│	1832	1832	│	1843	1843	1902	...	...	│	│	│	1945	...	...	│
Stuttgart Hbf ... **931** d.	│	│	1751	1737	│	1804	...	│	│	1838	1838	│	1851	1851	1912	1923	1923	│	│	│	1951	1915	1936	│
Vaihingen (Enz) ... **931** d.	│	│	│	│	│	│	...	│	│	│	│	│	│	│	│	│	│	│	│	│	│	│	1954	│
Bruchsal ... **913 931** d.	│	│	│	│	1758	│	...	│	│	│	│	│	│	│	1940	│	│	│	│	│	│	│	│	│
Karlsruhe Hbf .. **913 931** a.	│	│	│	│	│	│	...	│	│	│	│	│	│	│	1952	│	│	│	│	│	│	│	│	│
Heidelberg Hbf ... **913** d.	│	│	│	1825	1825	1846	...	│	│	│	│	│	│	│	...	│	│	│	│	│	│	2025v	2025	2025
Weinheim ... **913** d.	│	│	│	│	│	1900	...	│	│	│	│	│	│	│	...	│	│	│	│	│	│	│	│	│
Bensheim ... **913** d.	│	│	│	│	│	1909	...	│	│	│	│	│	│	│	...	│	│	│	│	│	│	│	│	│
Darmstadt Hbf ... **913 918a** d.	│	│	│	│	│	1924	...	│	│	│	│	│	│	│	...	│	│	│	│	│	│	│	│	│
Mannheim Hbf ... **913** a.	1818	1824	1828	1837	1837	│	...	1915	1915	1918	1918	1924	1929	1929	...	2002	2002	2024	2024	2024	2028	2037	2037	2037
Mannheim Hbf ... **912 913** d.	1820	1832	1836	1839	1839	│	...	1917	1917	1921	1921	1935	1932	1932	...	2004	2004	2032	2032	2032	2035	2039	2039	2039
Frankfurt Flughafen ✈ ◧ ... a.	│	│	1907	│	│	│	...	│	│	1951	1951	2007	│	│	...	2035	2035	│	│	│	2107	│	│	│
Frankfurt (Main) Hbf ... **913** a.	1859	1908	│	│	│	1940	...	1952	1955	│	│	│	2008	2008	...	2052	2052	2108	2108	2108	│	│	│	│
Worms Hbf ... **912** d.	...	│	│	│	│	...	...	│	...	│	│	│	...	│	...	│	...	│	│	│	│	│	│	│
Mainz Hbf ... **912 917a 918a** a.	...	│	│	1918	1918	...	...	│	...	│	│	│	...	│	...	│	...	│	│	│	│	2118	2118	2118
Wiesbaden Hbf ... **917a 918a** a.	...	│	│	│	│	...	...	│	...	│	│	│	...	│	...	│	...	│	│	│	│	│	│	│
Koblenz Hbf **800** ... a.	...	│	│	2011	2011	...	...	│	...	│	│	│	...	│	...	│	...	│	│	│	│	2211	2211	2211
Köln Messe/Deutz **800** ... a.	...	│	│	│	│	...	...	│	...	2048	2048	│	...	│	...	│	...	│	│	│	│	│	│	│
Köln Hbf **800** ... a.	...	│	2005	2106	2106	...	...	│	...	...	│	2105	...	│	...	│	...	│	│	│	2206	2306	2306	2306
Dortmund Hbf **800** ... ⊠ a.	...	│	2121	2221	2221	...	...	│	...	...	2203	2221	...	│	...	│	...	│	│	│	...	...	...	...
Hannover Hbf **810 900** ... a.	...	│	│	...	...	...	...	2217	...	...	...	0018	...	│	...	2318	...	2341	0002	│	...	...	...	...
Berlin Hbf **810 850 902** ... a.	...	2331	│	...	...	...	...	│	...	...	...	...	...	0036	...	│	...	│	│	0132	...	...	...	...
Hamburg Hbf **800 900** ... a.	...	...	0014	...	...	...	...	2339	...	...	...	...	...	...	...	0044	...	0113	0136	...	...	...	...	...

◆ – **NOTES** (LISTED BY TRAIN NUMBER)

112 – BLAUER ENZIAN – 🚃12 Schwarzach-St Veit - Salzburg - Frankfurt.

114 – WÖRTHERSEE – 🚃12 ✕ (Kalgenfurt from July 14 -) Schwarzach-St Veit - Salzburg - München - Dortmund.

118 – BODENSEE – 🚃12 ✕ Innsbruck - Bregenz - Lindau - Ulm - Stuttgart - Münster.

266 – BADEN-KURIER – 🚃12 ✕ München - Karlsruhe (- Basel Ⓑ).

A – To Amsterdam (Table **28**). On June 13 - 15, June 27 - Aug. 24, Oct. 20 - Nov. 2, Dec. 5 - 7 runs with train number **254** and is diverted to run via Köln Hbf (a. 2102; not calling at Köln Messe/Deutz). 🅁 for international journeys.

B – To Saarbrücken (Table **919**).

C – From Chur (Table **520**).

D – To München (Table **32** or other direction of this table).

E – From Wien (Table **950**). Operated by *WESTbahn* (special fares).

F – To Erfurt / Leipzig (Table **850**).

K – To Kiel (Table **820**).

L – From Milano via Chiasso (Table **550**).

M – To Münster (Table **800**).

N – From Interlaken via Bern (Table **560**).

R – Not July 26 - Sept. 5.

S – July 26 - Sept. 5.

f – ⑤–⑦.

t – Not Sept. 6 - Oct. 31.

v – Arrives 2005.

△ – On June 13 - 15, June 27 - Aug. 24, Oct. 20 - Nov. 2, Dec. 5 - 7 runs with train number **1212** and does not call at Köln Messe/Deutz.

⊠ – Services between Köln and Dortmund are subject to alteration Sept 6 - Oct. 31 (also from late evening on Sept. 5) with many trains retimed or diverted via alternative routes. Please check for journeys to Dortmund during this period.

⊖ – 🏛 is at Kehl (8 km from Strasbourg). See Table **911** for local journeys Strasbourg - Offenburg.

▷ – For regional services via Wendlingen, see Table **936**.

◧ – Frankfurt Flughafen Fernbahnhof.

910 ZÜRICH - BASEL - KARLSRUHE - FRANKFURT and MÜNCHEN - STUTTGART - FRANKFURT

	EC 216	RJX 890	ICE 910	TGV 9579		ICE 100	ICE 590	ICE 560		ICE 4	ICE 510		WB 966	ICE 990	NJ 409	IC 1998		NJ 470	NJ 470	ICE 698	NJ 402	NJ 402		ICE 1060
SEE NOTE ⊠								⑧								⑥		⑦	①–⑥		⑦	①–⑥		
	♦	✕♦	✕	D 🅁		✕	F✕	✕		✕	✕		E🍸	✕	♦			♦z	♦	✕	♦	♦		
Zürich HB ... 510 d.	...	...	...	🍸	...	...	...	...	...	1859	...	...	...	...	1959	...	...	1934	2059	...	1936	2134j	...	...
Basel SBB ... 510 910a d.	...	...	...	...	...	1913	...	...	...	2013	...	...	...	...	2113	...	...	2058	2213	...	2117	2313	...	...
Basel Bad Bf 🏛 ... 910a d.	...	...	...	...	...	1921	...	...	...	2021	...	...	...	...	2122	...	...	2129	2222	...	2137	2323	...	...
Freiburg (Brsg) Hbf ... 910a d.	...	...	...	...	...	1955	...	...	...	2055	...	...	...	...	2158	...	...	2205	2258	...	2213	0005	...	...
Paris Est ... 390 d.	...	...	...	1754	...	│	...	...	...	│	...	...	...	...	│	...	...	│	│	...	│	│	...	...
Strasbourg ⊖ ... 390 911 d.	...	...	...	1945	...	│	...	...	...	│	...	...	...	...	│	...	...	│	│	...	│	│	...	...
Offenburg ... 910a 911 916 d.	...	...	...	│	...	2026	...	...	...	2127	...	...	...	...	2231	...	...	2240	2333	...	2249	0041	...	...
Baden-Baden ... 910a 916 d.	...	...	...	│	...	2042	...	...	...	2144	...	...	...	...	│	...	...	2301	2354	...	2314	0102	...	...
Karlsruhe Hbf ... 910a 916 a.	...	...	...	2025	...	2100	...	...	...	2200	...	...	...	...	2305	...	...	2318	0012	...	2336	0118	...	...
Karlsruhe Hbf ... 913 d.	...	...	...	2027	...	2102	...	...	...	2202	...	...	...	...	2307	...	...	0019	0019	...	0120	0120	...	...
Salzburg Hbf **890** ... d.	1600	1256	...	│	...	│	...	...	...	│	...	...	1839	...	│	...	...	│	│	...	│	│	...	...
München Hbf ... 930 d.	1747	│	1827	│	...	│	1846	1900	...	│	1927	...	2032	2043	│	...	...	│	│	2151	│	│	...	2245
München Pasing ... 930 d.	│	│	1836	│	...	│	1855	1909	...	│	1936	...	│	2052	│	...	...	│	│	│	│	│	...	2254
Augsburg Hbf ... 930 d.	1815	│	1901	│	...	│	1918	1933	...	│	2001	...	2102	2115	│	...	...	│	│	2218	│	│	...	2317
Günzburg ... 930 d.	1848	│	│	│	...	│	│	2005	...	│	│	...	2133	2145	│	...	...	│	│	2249	│	│	...	│
Ulm Hbf ... 930 933 ▷ d.	1903	1910	1946	│	...	│	2001	2019	...	│	2047	...	2151	2201	│	...	...	│	│	2303	│	│	...	0001
Stuttgart Hbf ... 933 ▷ a.	1958n	2005	2032	2104	...	│	2043	2103	...	│	2145	...	2239	2243	│	...	...	│	│	0001	│	│	...	0043
Stuttgart Hbf ... 931 d.	2004n	2012	2038	...	...	│	2051	2111	...	│	2151	...	...	2251	│	2309	...	│	│	0011	│	│	...	...
Vaihingen (Enz) ... 931 d.	│	│	│	...	...	│	│	│	...	│	│	...	...	│	│	2326	...	│	│	│	│	│	...	...
Bruchsal ... 913 931 d.	│	│	│	...	...	│	│	2139	...	│	│	...	...	│	│	│	...	│	0038	│	│	│	...	...
Karlsruhe Hbf .. 913 931 a.	│	│	│	...	...	│	│	2152	...	│	│	...	...	│	│	│	...	│	│	│	│	│	...	...
Heidelberg Hbf ... 913 d.	│	2055	│	...	...	│	│	...	...	│	│	...	...	│	│	0002	...	│	0108	0127	│	│	...	...
Weinheim ... 913 d.	│	2109	│	...	...	│	│	...	...	│	│	...	...	│	│	0018	...	│	│	│	│	│	...	...
Bensheim ... 913 d.	│	2119	│	...	...	│	│	...	...	│	│	...	...	│	│	0028	...	│	│	│	│	│	...	...
Darmstadt Hbf ... 913 918a d.	│	2133	│	...	...	│	│	...	...	│	│	...	...	│	│	0051	...	│	0153	│	│	│	...	...
Mannheim Hbf ... 913 a.	2047	│	2118	...	...	2125	2129	...	...	2224	2228	...	...	2329	2340	│	...	│	│	0142	0149	0149	...	...
Mannheim Hbf ... 912 913 d.	...	│	2120	...	...	2135	2132	...	...	2232	2236	...	...	2332	2342	│	...	│	│	0144	0152	0152	...	...
Frankfurt Flughafen ✈ ◧ ... a.	...	│	2151	...	...	2206	│	...	...	│	2307	...	...	│	│	│	...	│	│	0219	0325*	0325*	...	...
Frankfurt (Main) Hbf ... 913 a.	...	2152	│	...	...	│	2208	...	...	2308	│	...	...	0008	0023•	0106	...	│	0209•	0240	0245	0245	...	...
Worms Hbf ... 912 d.	...	...	│	...	...	│	...	...	...	...	│	...	...	...	│	...	...	│	│	│	│	│	...	...
Mainz Hbf ... 912 917a 918a a.	...	...	│	...	...	│	...	...	...	...	│	...	...	...	│	...	...	│	│	│	0347	0347	...	...
Wiesbaden Hbf ... 917a 918a a.	...	...	│	...	...	│	...	...	...	...	│	...	...	...	│	...	...	│	│	│	│	│	...	...
Koblenz Hbf **800** ... a.	...	...	│	...	...	│	...	...	...	...	│	...	...	...	│	...	...	│	│	│	0441	0441	...	...
Köln Messe/Deutz **800** ... a.	...	...	2247	...	...	│	...	...	...	...	│	...	...	...	│	...	...	│	│	│	│	│	...	...
Köln Hbf **800** ... a.	...	...	│	...	...	2306	...	...	...	...	0006	...	...	...	│	...	...	│	│	│	0557	0557	...	...
Dortmund Hbf **800** ... ⊠ a.	...	...	0003	...	...	0027	...	...	...	...	...	...	...	...	│	...	...	│	│	│	...	...	...	...
Hannover Hbf **810 900** ... a.	...	...	...	...	...	0223	...	...	...	...	...	...	...	...	│	...	...	0529	0529	│	...	...	...	...
Berlin Hbf **810 850 902** ... a.	...	...	...	...	...	0536	...	...	...	...	...	...	...	...	0720	...	...	│	│	0755	...	...	...	...
Hamburg Hbf **800 900** ... a.	...	...	...	...	...	...	...	...	...	...	...	...	...	...	...	...	...	0753	0753	...	...	...	...	...

♦ – **NOTES** (LISTED BY TRAIN NUMBER)

216 – DACHSTEIN – 🚃12 Graz - Bischofshofen - Salzburg - München Ost - Saarbrücken. Not Sept. 13 - Oct. 17.
402 – 🛏 1,2 cl. and 🛌 2 cl. (🅁) Zürich - Basel - Amsterdam. Also conveys 🚃2 (*IC* **60402**).
409 – 🛏 1,2 cl. and 🛌 2 cl. (🅁) Zürich - Basel - Leipzig - Berlin. Also conveys 🚃2 (*IC* **60409**).
🛏 1,2 cl. and 🛌 2 cl. (*EN* **40459** 🅁) and 🚃2 (*EC* **459**) Zürich - Basel - Leipzig - Dresden - Praha.
470 – 🛏 1,2 cl. and 🛌 2 cl. (🅁) Zürich - Basel - Hannover - Hamburg. Also conveys 🚃2 (*IC* **60470**).
890 – BREGENZERWALD – 🚃12 ✕ Wien (**860**) - Innsbruck - Bregenz (**890**) - Lindau - Ulm - Frankfurt.

D – Continues to München on ⑥ (see Table **32** or other direction of this table).
E – From Wien (Table **950**). Operated by *WESTbahn* (special fares).
F – To Erfurt on ⑦ (Table **850**).

j – 2159 on ⑥.

n – Not July 26 - Sept. 5.
z – On June 15, 22 runs Zürich - Karlsruhe in times in next column.

• – Frankfurt (Main) **Süd**.
***** – Calls after Frankfurt (Main) Hbf.
⊠ – Services between Köln and Dortmund are subject to alteration Sept. 6 - Oct. 31 (also from late evening on Sept. 5) with many trains retimed or diverted via alternative routes. Please check for journeys to Dortmund during this period.
▷ – For regional services via Wendlingen, see Table **936**.
⊖ – 🏛 is at Kehl (8 km from Strasbourg). See Table **911** for local journeys Strasbourg - Offenburg.
◧ – Frankfurt Flughafen Fernbahnhof.

910a Regional trains KARLSRUHE - OFFENBURG - BASEL

Selected services. **German holiday dates apply**. On June 19 services between Karlsruhe and Basel Bad Bf run as on ⑦. See Table **910** for long-distance *ICE*/*IC*/*EC* services.

	Ⓒ	Ⓐ		Ⓐ											§				§		⚒y			w	e
Karlsruhe Hbf ... 916 d.	0006	...	...	...	...	...	...	0733	...	...	...	...	1239	...	1439	1539	1639	1739	1839	...	...	...	...	*2209*	2309
Rastatt ... 916 d.	0026	...	...	...	...	...	...	0748	...	...	...	...	1252	...	1452	1552	1652	1752	1852	...	...	...	...	*2229*	2329
Baden-Baden ... 916 d.	0033	...	...	...	...	...	...	0755	...	...	...	...	1259	...	1459	1600	1659	1759	1859	...	...	...	...	*2237*	2335
Offenburg ... 916 a.	0102	...	...	...	...	...	...	0821	...	...	...	...	1326	...	1526	1626	1726	1826	1926	...	...	...	...	*2306*	0003
Offenburg ... d.	0107	0423	...	0511	0552	0634	0742	0836	0946	1035	1147	1226	1347	1435	1547	1635	1747	1836	1937	2046	...	2141	2246e	2317	0007
Freiburg (Brsg) Hbf ... a.	0150	0522	...	0607	0644	0716	0829	0914	1031	1115	1230	1315	1430	1515	1630	1715	1830	1915	2032	2130	...	2232	2336e	0010	0051
Freiburg (Brsg) Hbf ... d.	0152	0532	0600	0627	0646	0718	0832	0918	1034	1118	1232	1317	1432	1518	1632	1718	1832	1918	2033	2132	...	2234	2343	0027	▬
Müllheim (Baden) ... d.	0212	0553	0625	0649	0711	0737	0852	0937	1053	1137	1251	1338	1451	1537	1651	1737	1851	1937	2052	2151	...	2253	0008	0052	Ⓒf
Basel Bad Bf 🏛 ... ▷ a.	0244	0624	0701	0721	0746	0803	0929	1003	1130	1201	1323	1402	1523	1601	1723	1801	1924	2001	2129	2223	2245	2323	0043	0128	0150
Basel SBB ... ▷ a.	...	*0650*	*0725*	0730	0801t	*0825*	*0950*r	*1025*	*1150*r	1219v	*1350*r	*1425*	*1550*r	1619v	*1750*r	1819v	*1950*r	*2025*	*2150*r	2231t	2250	...	...	...	0155

		⚒		Ⓐ	‡	‡				⚒	†			¶	¶	‡						z		z	
Basel SBB ... ▷ d.	...	...	...	*0501*	*0603*r	0734	0737t	*0804*r	*0934*	*1004*	...	*1134*	1225t	*1334*	*1404*r	*1534*	1628t	*1734*	1828t	*1934*	*2006*r	*2134*	2240	2259t	...
Basel Bad Bf 🏛 ... ▷ d.	0406	...	...	0537	0636	0740	0758	0828	0958	1028	1028	1158	1233	1358	1427	1558	1638	1758	1837	1958	2028	2158	2245	2308	2353
Müllheim (Baden) ... d.	0444	...	...	0607	0705	...	0821	0904	1022	1104	1102	1222	1306	1422	1501	1622	1707	1822	1907	2021	2104	2222	...	2337	0027
Freiburg (Brsg) Hbf ... a.	0510	...	...	0630	0724	...	0839	0927	1040	1124	1121	1240	1325	1440	1523	1640	1726	1840	1926	2040	2124	2240	...	2357	0053
Freiburg (Brsg) Hbf ... d.	...	0520	0626	...	0726	...	0843	0929	1042	1126	1129	1242	1327	1442	1527	1642	1729	1842	1929	2042	2127	2242	...	0010	...
Offenburg ... a.	...	0612	0712	...	0812	...	0922	1013	1121	1211	1214	1321	1412	1529	1613	1721	1814	1921	2014	2121	2213	2321	...	0106	...
Offenburg ... 916 d.	...	0627	0734	...	...	...	...	...	...	...	...	1334	1434	1534	1634	1734	...	...	2034	...	...	2334	...	...	...
Baden-Baden ... 916 d.	...	0653	0801	...	...	...	...	...	...	...	...	1401	1501	1601	1701	1801	...	...	2100	...	...	0001	...	...	...
Rastatt ... 916 d.	...	0700	0808	...	...	...	...	...	...	...	...	1408	1508	1608	1708	1808	...	...	2107	...	...	0008	...	...	...
Karlsruhe Hbf ... 916 a.	...	0714	0821	...	...	...	...	...	...	...	...	1421	1521	1621	1721	1821	...	...	2121	...	...	0021	...	...	...

e – Daily until June 28; ①–⑥ from June 30.
f – Not Aug. 2 - Sept. 14.
r – ⚒ only.
t – Ⓐ only.
v – On Ⓒ arrives 4–6 minutes later (change trains at Basel Bad Bf).
w – Daily until June 28; ①–⑥ from June 30. Runs daily Freiburg - Basel Bad Bf.

y – Not July 31 - Sept. 13.
z – Terminates at Freiburg on ⑦ from June 29.
§ – Connecting trains arrive Basel SBB *1756*r and *2203*r July 31 - Sept. 13.
‡ – Connecting train Basel SBB - Basel Bad will not run July 31 - Sept. 14.
¶ – Connecting train Basel SBB - Basel Bad departs 4 minutes earlier July 31 - Sept. 14.
▷ – Frequent local tram services operate Basel Bad - Basel SBB and v.v. (rail tickets not valid).

911 STRASBOURG - OFFENBURG

Südwestdeutsche Landesverkehrs / SNCF (2nd class only)

On June 9 services run as on ⑦.

km																												
		②–⑦			①–⑤		①–⑤	①–⑤		①–⑤					①–⑤		①–⑤		①–⑤			①–⑤	①–⑤					①–⑥
0	**Strasbourg** . d.	0006	...	0622	0722	0752	0822	0852	0922	0952	1052	...	1252	1322	1422	1452	1522	1622	1652	1722	1755	1822	1852	1922	2022	...	2152	2252
21	Kehl 🏛 ... d.	0017	...	0633	0733	0803	0833	0903	0933	1003	1103	...	1303	1333	1433	1503	1533	1633	1703	1733	1806	1833	1903	1933	2033	...	2203	2303
29	**Offenburg** .. a.	0035	...	0652	0752	0822	0852	0922	0952	1022	1122	...	1322	1355	1452	1522	1552	1652	1722	1752	1825	1852	1922	1952	2052	...	2222	2322

		①–⑤		①–⑤		①–⑤	①–⑤	⑥⑦	①–⑤		⑥⑦		①–⑤	①–⑤	⑥⑦	①–⑤			①–⑤		①–⑤	①–⑤		①–⑤			①–⑥	①–⑥
Offenburg ... d.	0635	0705	0735	0805	0843	0905	0935	1005	1035	...	1205	1235	1305	1335	1405	1435	1505	1605	1635	1705	1735	1805	1835	1905	2005	2105	2205	2328
Kehl 🏛 ... d.	0654	0724	0754	0824	0901	0924	0954	1024	1054	...	1224	1254	1324	1355	1424	1454	1524	1624	1654	1724	1754	1824	1854	1924	2024	2124	2224	2347
Strasbourg . a.	0704	0734	0804	0834	0909	0934	1004	1033	1102	...	1234	1304	1334	1406	1434	1504	1534	1634	1704	1734	1804	1833	1904	1934	2034	2134	2234	2358

RE / S-Bahn services

Local services MAINZ - MANNHEIM and MAINZ - SPEYER - KARLSUHE 912

On June 19, Nov. 1 services run as on ⑦. See Table **910** for long-distance *ICE / IC / EC* services.
Warning! From Sept. 30, services in this table do not run Frankfurt - Mainz and v.v.

km		Ⓐ	⚒	Ⓐ	Ⓐ§		Ⓐ																	Ⓒ	Ⓐ	Ⓒ
	Frankfurt (Main) Hbf ‡ d.	...	...	...	...	...	0608	...	...	...	0738**t**	...	0838	0938**z**	...	1038	1138	...	1238	1338	...	1438	1538**z**	...	1538	1638
0	**Mainz** Hbf ‡ d.	0456	0515	0545	...	0552**t**	0647	0622	0656	0722	0813	...	0913	1013	...	1117	1213	...	1317	1413	...	1517	1613	...	1617	1717
46	Worms Hbf a.	0540	0556	0614	...	0634**t**	0714	0706	0739	0806	0839	...	0940	1039	...	1144	1239	...	1344	1439	...	1544	1639	...	1652	1744
46	Worms Hbf d.	0541	0556	0615	...	0635	0715	0717	0746	0816	0840	0848	0941	1040	1048	1145	1240	1249	1345	1440	1448	1545	1640	1648	1653	1745
67	Ludwigshafen Hbf **918** d.	0600	0616	0637	0654	0653	0731	0735	0804	0836	0857	0909	│	1057	1109	│	1257	1309	│	1457	1509	│	1655	1709	1708	1804
78	Schifferstadt ... **918** d.	│	│	│	0706	│	│	│	│	│	0906	│	│	1106	│	│	1306	│	│	1506	│	│	1705	│	│	│
87	Speyer Hbf ..... **918** d.	│	│	│	0713	│	│	│	│	│	0913	│	│	1113	│	│	1313	│	│	1513	│	│	1713	│	│	│
101	Germersheim .. **918** d.	│	│	│	0723	│	│	│	│	│	0923	│	│	1123	│	│	1323	│	│	1523	│	│	1723	│	│	│
138	**Karlsruhe** Hbf a.	│	│	│	0753	│	│	│	│	│	0953	│	│	1153	│	│	1353	│	│	1553	│	│	1753	│	│	│
68	Ludwigshafen Mitte ... d.	0602	0619	│	...	0655	0734	0738	0809	0838	...	0912	1000	...	1111	1204	...	1311	1402	...	1511	1603	...	1711	1711	1807
70	**Mannheim** Hbf a.	0604	0621	0641	...	0658	0737	0741	0813	0841	...	0915	1003	...	1115	1207	...	1314	1405	...	1514	1606	...	1714	1715	1810

	Ⓐ											
Frankfurt (Main) Hbf ‡ d.	1638	...	1738**z**	...	1838	...	1938**z**	...	...	2038	...	...
Mainz Hbf ‡ d.	1713	...	1813	...	1917	1925	2013	...	2052	2117	2206	2308
Worms Hbf a.	1744	...	1839	...	1944	2008	2039	...	2136	2155	2251	2351
Worms Hbf d.	1745	1749	1840	1848	1945	2018	2040	2048	2148	2156	2251	2351
Ludwigshafen Hbf **918** d.	1800	1809	1857	1909	2002	2037	2057	2109	2208	2215	2309	0009
Schifferstadt **918** d.	1811	│	1906	│	│	│	2106	│	│	│	│	│
Speyer Hbf **918** d.	1819	│	1913	│	│	│	2113	│	│	│	│	│
Germersheim ...**918** d.	1828	│	1923	│	│	│	2123	│	│	│	│	│
Karlsruhe Hbf a.	...	│	1953	│	│	│	2153	│	│	│	│	│
Ludwigshafen Mitte .... d.	...	1811	...	1913	2005	2039	...	2111	2211	2218	2311	0012
Mannheim Hbf a.	...	1814	...	1916	2007	2042	...	2114	2214	2221	2314	0014

			⑥	Ⓐ	Ⓐ	⚒	Ⓐ	Ⓐ	
Mannheim Hbf d.	0018	...	0424	0425	0459	0530	0540	...	0650
Ludwigshafen Mitte d.	0020	...	0427	0428	0501	0533	0542	...	0653
Karlsruhe Hbf d.	│	...	│	│	│	│	│	...	│
Germersheim **918** d.	│	...	│	│	│	│	│	0619	│
Speyer Hbf **918** d.	│	...	│	│	│	│	│	0632	│
Schifferstadt **918** d.	│	...	│	│	│	│	│	0641	│
Ludwigshafen Hbf **918** d.	0023	...	0433	0433	0504	0535	0546	0656**c**	0659
Worms Hbf a.	0039	...	0451	0451	0522	0553	0607	0712	0718
Worms Hbf d.	0040**z**	...	0452	0452	0523	0555	0607	0713	0725
Mainz Hbf ‡ a.	0122**z**	...	0538	0538	0608	0638	0641	0747	0808
Frankfurt (Main) Hbf ‡ a.	...	...	...	...	...	...	0722	0822	...

	Ⓐ	Ⓒ	Ⓐ																							
Mannheim Hbf d.	...	0751	0749	0844	...	0915	0958	1044	...	1151	1244	...	1351	1447	...	1549	1644	...	1752	1844	...	1951	2044	...	2144	2247
Ludwigshafen Mitte .... d.	...	0753	0751	0847	...	0917	1000	1047	...	1154	1248	...	1354	1449	...	1552	1646	...	1754	1847	...	1954	2047	...	2146	2249
Karlsruhe Hbf d.	0655	│	│	│	0806	│	│	│	1006	│	│	1206	│	│	1406	│	│	1606	│	│	1806	│	│	2006	│	│
Germersheim ...**918** d.	0724	│	│	│	0838	│	│	│	1038	│	│	1238	│	│	1438	│	│	1638	│	│	1838	│	│	2038	│	│
Speyer Hbf **918** d.	0733	│	│	│	0847	│	│	│	1047	│	│	1247	│	│	1447	│	│	1647	│	│	1847	│	│	2047	│	│
Schifferstadt **918** d.	0740	│	│	│	0854	│	│	│	1054	│	│	1254	│	│	1454	│	│	1654	│	│	1854	│	│	2054	│	│
Ludwigshafen Hbf **918** d.	0751	0756	0755	0850	0904	0920	1003	1050	1104	│	1250	1304	│	1452	1504	│	1649	1704	│	1850	1904	│	2050	2104	2150	2252
Worms Hbf a.	0804	0816	0814	0914	0919	0938	1019	1111	1119	1216	1311	1319	1416	1514	1519	1616	1714	1719	1816	1913	1919	2016	2114	2119	2213	2309
Worms Hbf d.	0809	0817	0825	...	0920	0955	1020	...	1120	1217	...	1320	1417	...	1520	1617	...	1720	1817	...	1920	2017	...	2120	2218	2310
Mainz Hbf a.	0836	0843	0908	...	0947	1036	1046	...	1147	1243	...	1347	1443	...	1547	1643	...	1747	1843	...	1947	2043	...	2147	2301	2353
Frankfurt (Main) Hbf ‡ a.	...	0922	...	...	1022	...	1122	...	1222	1322	...	1422	1522	...	1623	1722**z**	...	1822**z**	1922**z**	...	2022	2122	...	2222	...	...

c – Arrives 0649.
t – Ⓐ only.
z – Ⓒ only.

§ – From Mannheim Hbf (d. 0647).
‡ – From Sept. 30, services in this table do not run Frankfurt - Mainz and v.v.
See Tables **800**, **914**, **917** and **917a** for other services Frankfurt - Mainz and v.v.

RE / RB / S-Bahn services

Local trains FRANKFURT - HEIDELBERG - KARLSRUHE 913

On June 19, Nov. 1 services run as on ⑦. See Table **910** for long-distance *ICE / IC / EC* services.

FRANKFURT - DARMSTADT - HEIDELBERG and MANNHEIM

			Ⓒ			Ⓐ		Ⓒ	Ⓐ		Ⓒ	Ⓐ		Ⓐ											
Frankfurt (Main) Hbf d.	0006	...	0206	...	0406	0406	0506	0506	0533	0606	0606	0632	0706	0736	0806	0834	0906	0935	1006	1034	1106	1131	1206	1234	1306
Darmstadt Hbf d.	0030	...	0235**b**	...	0427	0427	0530	0530	0553	0630	0630	0652	0734	0758	0830	0853	0930	0955	1030	1053	1130	1150	1230	1253	1330
Bensheim d.	0054	...	0257	...	0456	0456	0557	0557	0610	0655	0655	0710	0758	0813	0857	0910	0957	1011	1057	1110	1158	1211	1257	1310	1357
Weinheim (Bergstr) d.	0109	...	0311	...	0512	0512	0612	0612	0622	0711	0711	0722	0813	0826	0913	0922	1014	1023	1113	1122	1213	1223	1313	1322	1413
Mannheim Hbf a.	│	...	│	...	│	0546	│	0645	0646	│	0745	0743	│	0847	│	0945	│	1046	│	1145	│	1246	│	1344	│
Heidelberg Hbf a.	0134	...	0333	...	0540	...	0637	...	...	0736	...	...	0842	...	0939	...	1039	...	1139	...	1238	...	1339	...	1439

									Ⓒ	Ⓐ														Ⓒ	
Frankfurt (Main) Hbf d.	1334	1406	1434	1506	1534	1606	1634	1706	1734	1734	1806	1834	1906	1906	1931	2006	2034	2106	2106	...	2206	2206	...	2234	2312
Darmstadt Hbf d.	1353	1430	1453	1530	1553	1630	1653	1730	1753	1757	1830	1853	1930	1930	1951	2031	2053	2130	2130	...	2230	2230	...	2253	2333
Bensheim d.	1410	1457	1510	1558	1612	1657	1710	1757	1810	1831	1857	1910	1957	1957	2011	2057	2110	2155	2155	...	2255	2255	...	2310	2355
Weinheim (Bergstr) d.	1422	1513	1522	1613	1624	1713	1722	1813	1822	1844	1913	1922	2012	2012	2023	2113	2122	2210	2210	...	2310	2310	...	2322	0010
Mannheim Hbf a.	1446	│	1545	│	1645	│	1745	│	1844	1905	│	1945	│	2041	2045	│	2142	│	2243	...	│	2344	...	2341	│
Heidelberg Hbf a.	...	1540	...	1640	...	1739	...	1836	...	...	1939	...	2039	...	...	2140	...	2237	...	...	2337	...	...	...	0034

	Ⓒ	Ⓒ	Ⓒ	Ⓐ	Ⓐ			Ⓐ			Ⓐ	Ⓐ	Ⓒ	Ⓒ	Ⓐ										
Heidelberg Hbf d.	0020	...	0220	0423	...	...	0520	...	...	0622	...	...	...	0723	0724	...	0820	...	0920	...	1020	...	1120	...	1220
Mannheim Hbf d.	│	0016	│	│	0445	0514	│	0606	0617	│	0650	0715	0715	│	│	0815	│	0915	│	1015	│	1115	│	1215	│
Weinheim (Bergstr) d.	0046	0046	0248	0451	0518	0546	0546	0626	0647	0647	0720	0739	0748	0748	0748	0839	0846	0936	0946	1039	1046	1139	1146	1239	1246
Bensheim d.	0104	0104	0303	0506	0534	0603	0603	0640	0702	0702	0735	0752	0802	0802	0802	0851	0901	0949	1001	1051	1101	1151	1201	1251	1301
Darmstadt Hbf d.	0128	0128	0330	0530	0600	0630	0630	0658	0730	0730	0757	0810	0830	0830	0830	0907	0930	1005	1030	1107	1130	1207	1230	1307	1330
Frankfurt (Main) Hbf a.	0149	0149	0349	0548	0620	0648	0648	0716	0748	0748	0816	0832**e**	0848	0848	0848	0924	0948	1024	1048	1124	1148	1224	1248	1324	1348

						Ⓒ	Ⓐ													Ⓒ	Ⓒ	Ⓐ	Ⓐ		
Heidelberg Hbf d.	...	1320	...	1420	...	1520	1523	...	1620	...	1717	...	1820	...	1920	...	2020	...	2120	...	2220	2220	...	...	2320
Mannheim Hbf d.	1315	│	1415	│	1515	│	│	1615	│	1715	│	1815	│	1915	│	2015	│	2117	│	2214	│	│	2216	2316	│
Weinheim (Bergstr) d.	1339	1346	1439	1446	1539	1548	1548	1639	1646	1739	1746	1839	1846	1939	1946	2039	2046	2146	2146	2238	2246	2246	2246	2346	2346
Bensheim d.	1350	1401	1451	1501	1551	1602	1602	1651	1701	1751	1801	1851	1901	1951	2001	2051	2102	2203	2203	2251	2301	2301	2301	0003	0003
Darmstadt Hbf d.	1407	1430	1507	1530	1607	1630	1630	1707	1730	1807	1830	1907	1930	2007	2030	2107	2130	2230	2230	2307	2330	2331	2331	0030	0030
Frankfurt (Main) Hbf a.	1424	1448	1524	1548	1624	1648	1648	1724	1748	1824	1848	1924	1948	2024	2048	2124	2148	2248	2248	2324	2348	2348	2348	0048	0048

MANNHEIM - HEIDELBERG - KARLSUHE ⊠

	Ⓐ	Ⓐ	Ⓒ		Ⓒ	Ⓐ			†F											◧		⚒	†			
Mannheim Hbf ⊡ d.	...	0454	0506	0555	*0634*	0646	0701**z**	*0748***k**	0812	*0837*	*0938*	*1038*	*1138*	*1238*	*1338*	*1438*	*1538*	*1638*	*1738*	*1838*	*1938*	*2038*	2055	2202	2258	0021
Heidelberg Hbf ⊡ a.	...	0505	0516	0605	*0647*	0704	0715**z**	*0801***k**	0828	*0853*	*0954*	*1055*	*1154*	*1254*	*1354*	*1454*	*1554*	*1654*	*1754*	*1855*	*1954*	*2054*	2106	2213	2309	0037
Heidelberg Hbf d.	0420	0510	0518	0610	0700	0707	0722	0810	0830	0907	1010	1105	1210	1305	1410	1506	1608	1707	1810	1903	2010	2107	2107	2215	2310	0044
Bruchsal d.	0442	0530	0543	0633	0728	0734	0744	0830	0850	0930	1030	1130	1230	1330	1430	1530	1630	1730	1830	1930	2030	2130	2130	2235	2330	0113
Karlsruhe Hbf a.	0458	0544	0557	0647	0746	0751	0800	0844	0902	0944	1044	1144	1244	1344	1444	1543	1643	1744	1844	1944	2044	2143	2143	2249	2344	0131

	Ⓐ	Ⓐ	Ⓒ		Ⓐ	†	⑥	Ⓐ												†F	⚒					
Karlsruhe Hbf d.	0420	0512	0522	0610	0648	0715	0715	0717	0817	0913	1012	1113	1215	1313	1415	1513	1612	1713	1813	1917	1917	2013	2115	2218	2318	0011
Bruchsal d.	0437	0530	0540	0623	0703	0728	0728	0733	0833	0930	1032	1129	1232	1330	1432	1530	1632	1730	1830	1930	1930	2026	2130	2230	2332	0027
Heidelberg a.	0505	0549	0607	0642	0731	0748	0748	0751	0853	0949	1051	1151	1252	1349	1454	1549	1652	1751	1852	1949	1949	2046	2149	2249	2350	0055
Heidelberg Hbf ⊡ d.	0506	*0559*	0607	0643**h**	0731	0750	*0804*	*0804*	*0903*	*1003*	*1103*	*1203*	*1303*	*1403*	*1503*	*1603*	*1703*	*1803*	*1903*	1950	*2003*	2050	2152	2252	2350	0056
Mannheim Hbf ⊡ a.	0523	*0615*	0627	0653**h**	0748	0803	*0819*	*0819*	*0920*	*1019*	*1119*	*1219*	*1318*	*1419*	*1520*	*1619*	*1719*	*1819*	*1920*	2004	*2019*	2106	2203	2305	0006	0114

F – To / from Freudenstadt (Table **943**).

b – Arrives 0224.
e – 0825 until Sept. 30.
h – Ⓒ only. On Ⓐ connecting train departs Heidelberg Hbf *0650*, arrives Mannheim Hbf *0706*.
k – On Ⓒ Mannheim Hbf d. *0738*, Heidelberg Hbf a. *0753*.
z – Ⓒ only.

◧ – On † Heidelberg Hbf d. 1909, Bruchsal d. 1934, Karlsruhe Hbf a. 1950.
⊠ – Most trains shown are limited stop *RE* services. Additional stopping S-Bahn services operate.
⊡ – See also Tables **918**, **919**, **923**, **924**.

914 Local trains KOBLENZ - FRANKFURT

On June 19 services run as on ⑦

Koblenz - Bingen - Mainz - Frankfurt *(Linke Rheinstrecke)* ⊠

km			Ⓐ	Ⓐ	Ⓐ	Ⓒ	K		K		K		K		K		K				Ⓒ		✣			
0	**Koblenz** Hbf	d.	0507	0606	0617	0652	0707	0803	0904	1003	1104	1203	1304	1403	1504	1603	1704	1803	1902	2104		0628	0730		1930	2029	2130
19	Boppard Hbf	d.	0519	0618	0632	0704	0719	0815	0916	1015	1116	1215	1316	1415	1516	1615	1716	1815	1916	2116		0643	0744		1944	2043	2145
24	Boppard-Bad Salzig	d.	|	|	0636	|	|	|	|	|	|	|	|	|	|	|	|	|	|	|		0647	0748		1948	2046	2149
34	St Goar	d.	|	|	0645	|	|	|	|	|	|	|	|	|	|	|	|	|	|	|	A	0655	0756	and	1956	2054	2157
41	Oberwesel	d.	0533	0633	0651	0718	0733	0829	0930	1029	1130	1229	1330	1429	1530	1629	1730	1829	1930	2130	L	0700	0801		2001	2100	2202
47	Bacharach	d.	0537	|	0656	0723	0737	|	0936	|	1136	|	1336	|	1536	|	1736	|	1936	2136	S	0706	0806	hourly	2006	2104	2207
61	Bingen (Rhein) Hbf	a.	0546	0646	0709	0733	0746	0842	0946	1042	1146	1242	1346	1442	1546	1642	1746	1842	1946	2146	O	0720	0819		2018	2116	2219
61	Bingen (Rhein) Hbf	d.	0547	0647	0713	0734	0747	0855t	0947	1056t	1147	1256t	1347	1455t	1547	1656t	1747	1856t	1947	2147		0724	0824	until	2024	2127	2229
62	Bingen (Rhein) Stadt	d.	|	|	0716	|	|	0858t	|	1059t	|	1259t	|	1458t	|	1659t	|	1859t	|	|	⊡	0727	0827		2027	2130	2231
73	Ingelheim	d.	0556	0655	0722	0745	0755	0908t	0955	1109t	1155	1309t	1355	1508t	1555	1710t	1755	1909t	1955	2155		0737	0839		2037	2140	2240
91	**Mainz** Hbf	a.	0608	0708	0736	0757	0808	0926t	1008	1126t	1208	1326t	1408	1525t	1608	1727t	1808	1926t	2008	2208		0757	0858		2057	2157	2257
119	Frankfurt Flughafen ◧	a.	0633	0733	0804	0819	0833	...	1033	...	1233	...	1433	...	1633	...	1833	...	2033	2235		...	...		...	...	...
130	**Frankfurt** (Main) Hbf	a.	0648	0748	0824	0836	0848	...	1048	...	1248	...	1448	...	1648	...	1847	...	2047	2249		...	...		...	...	...

		Ⓐ		K		K		K		K		K	Ⓐ		ⒸK	Ⓐ											
Frankfurt (Main) Hbf	d.	0456	0659	...	0908	...	1108	...	1308	...	1508	...	1624	1708	...	1824	1908	2108		...	...	...		...	...	...	...
Frankfurt Flughafen ◧	d.	0508	0709	...	0924	...	1124	...	1324	...	1524	...	1638	1724	...	1838	1924	2124		...	...	...		...	...	...	...
Mainz Hbf	d.	0532	0732	0832t	0951	1032t	1151	...	1351	1432t	1551	1632t	1700	1751	...	1900	1951	2151		0547	0701	0802		2003	2102	2203	2302
Ingelheim	d.	0547	0747	0850t	1002	1050t	1202	...	1402	1450t	1602	1650t	1711	1802	...	1911	2002	2202	A	0605	0719	0820	and	2020	2120	2221	2320
Bingen (Rhein) Stadt	d.	|	|	0901t	|	1101t	|	...	|	1459t	|	1701t	|	|	...	|	|	|	L	0615	0735	0830		2030	2130	2231	2330
Bingen (Rhein) Hbf	a.	0555	0755	0903t	1011	1103t	1211	...	1411	1503t	1611	1703t	1721	1811	...	1921	2011	2211	S	0618	0738	0833	hourly	2033	2133	2234	2333
Bingen (Rhein) Hbf	d.	0556	0756	0913	1013	1113	1213	1313	1413	1513	1613	1713	1722	1813	1913	1922	2013	2216	O	0626	0739	0839		2039	2139	...	2339
Bacharach	d.	0604	0804	|	1021	|	1221	|	1421	|	1621	|	1734	1821	|	1930	2021	2228		0638	0750	0850	until	2050	2150	...	2350
Oberwesel	d.	0609	0809	0925	1026	1125	1226	1325	1426	1525	1626	1725	1739	1826	1925	1935	2026	2232	⊡	0649	0754	0854		2054	2154	...	2354
St Goar	d.	|	|	|	|	|	|	|	|	|	|	|	1745	|	|	|	|	2238		0655	0800	0900		2100	2200	...	0000
Boppard-Bad Salzig	d.	|	|	|	|	|	|	|	|	|	|	|	|	|	|	|	|	2247		0703	0808	0908		2108	2208	...	0008
Boppard Hbf	d.	0623	0823	0939	1040	1139	1240	1339	1440	1539	1640	1739	1754	1840	1939	1949	2040	2251		0707	0812	0912		2112	2212	...	0012
Koblenz Hbf	a.	0638	0838	0953	1054	1153	1254	1353	1454	1553	1654	1753	1809	1855	1953	2004	2054	2309		0723	0827	0927		2127	2227	...	0027

Neuwied - Koblenz - St Goarshausen - Wiesbaden - Frankfurt *(Rechte Rheinstrecke). Operated by VIAS.*

km			Ⓐ	Ⓐ	Ⓐ	⚒		Ⓐ	Ⓐ		Ⓐ							Ⓐd		Ⓐd		Ⓐd					⑤⑥e
0	**Neuwied** 802	d.	...	...	0433	...	...	...	0528	...	...	0627z	0733	0827	0933		1433	...	1533	...	1633	...	1733		2133	2233	2233
15	**Koblenz** Hbf 802 906	d.	...	...	0452	...	...	...	0552	...	...	0652	0752	0852	0952		1452	...	1552	1622	1652	1723	1752		2152	2252	2252
20	Niederlahnstein 906	d.	...	...	0459	...	...	...	0559	...	...	0659	0759	0859	0959		1459	...	1559	1629	1659	1729	1759		2159	2259	2259
26	Braubach	d.	...	...	0505	...	...	...	0605	...	...	0705	0805	0905	1005	and	1505	...	1605	1635	1706	1736	1805	and	2205	2305	2305
38	Kamp-Bornhofen	d.	...	...	0516	...	...	...	0616	...	...	0716	0816	0916	1016		1516	...	1616	1646	1716	1746	1816		2216	2316	2316
50	St Goarshausen	d.	...	...	0527	...	...	...	0627	...	...	0727	0827	0927	1027	hourly	1527	...	1627	1657	1727	1757	1827	hourly	2227	2327	2327
61	Kaub	d.	...	0506	0536	...	...	0606	0636	0636	0706	0736	0836	0936	1036		1536	1606	1636	1706	1736	1806	1836		2236	2335	2336
67	Lorch (Rhein)	d.	...	0512	0542	...	...	0612	0642	0642	0712	0742	0842	0942	1042	until	1542	1612	1642	1712	1742	1812	1842	until	2242	...	2342
79	Rüdesheim (Rhein)	d.	0453	0523	0553	0553	...	0623	0653	0653	0723	0753	0853	0953	1053		1553	1623	1653	1723	1753	1823	1853		2253	...	2353
109	**Wiesbaden** Hbf	a.	0525	0555	0625	0625	...	0655	0725	0725	0755	0825	0925	1025	1125		1625	1655	1725	1755	1825	1855	1925		2325	...	0025
109	**Wiesbaden** Hbf	d.	0532	0602	0632	0632	0632	0702	0732	0732	0802	0832	0932	1032	1132		1632	1702	1732	1802	1832	1902	1932		2332	...	0032
117	**Mainz** Kastel	d.	0539	0609	0639	0639	0639	0709	0739	0739	0809	0839	0939	1039	1139		1639	1709	1739	1809	1839	1909	1939		2339	...	0039
150	**Frankfurt** (Main) Hbf	a.	0604	0634f	0704	0704	0704	0734f	0804	0804	0834f	0904	1004	1104	1204		1704	1734f	1804	1834f	1904	1934f	2004		0004	...	0104

		Ⓐ	Ⓐ		Ⓐ						Ⓐ		Ⓐd		Ⓐd		Ⓐd		Ⓐd		Ⓐ				⑤⑥e		⑤⑥e
Frankfurt (Main) Hbf	d.	...	...	...	0523j	0554t	0654		1354	1424j	1424j	1454	1525j	1553	1624j	1654	1724j	1754	1824j	1854	1924j	1954	2054	2153	2153	2253	2253
Mainz Kastel	d.	...	...	...	0549j	0619t	0719		1419	1449j	1449j	1519	1549j	1619	1649j	1719	1749j	1819	1849j	1919	1949j	2019	2119	2219	2219	2319	2319
Wiesbaden Hbf	a.	...	...	...	0558	0628t	0728		1428	1458	1458	1528	1558	1628	1658	1728	1758	1828	1858	1928	1958	2028	2128	2228	2228	2328	2328
Wiesbaden Hbf	d.	...	...	0533t	0603	0633r	0733	and	1433	1503	1503	1533	1603	1633	1703	1733	1803	1833	1903	1933	2003	2033	2133	2233	2233	2333	2333
Rüdesheim (Rhein)	d.	...	0535	0605t	0635	0705r	0805		1505	1534	1535	1605	1635	1705	1735	1805	1835	1905	1935	2005	2034	2105	2205	2305	2305	0004	0005
Lorch (Rhein)	d.	...	0546	0616t	0646	0716r	0816	hourly	1516	...	1546	1616	1646	1716	1746	1816	1846	1916	1946	2016	...	2116	2216	2316	2316	...	0016
Kaub	d.	0453	0553	0623	0653	0723	0823		1523	...	1552	1623	1653	1723	1753	1823	1853	1923	1953	2023	...	2123	2223	2322	2323	...	0022
St Goarshausen	d.	0502	0602	0632	0702	0732	0832	until	1532	...	...	1632	1702	1732	1802	1832	1902	1932	2002	2032	...	2132	2232	...	2332	...	...
Kamp-Bornhofen	d.	0512	0612	0642	0712	0742	0842		1542	...	...	1642	1712	1742	1812	1842	1912	1942	2012	2042	...	2142	2242	...	2342	...	...
Braubach	d.	0523	0623	0653	0723	0753	0853		1553	...	...	1653	1723	1753	1823	1853	1923	1953	2023	2053	...	2153	2253	...	2353	...	...
Niederlahnstein 906	d.	0529	0629	0659	0729	0759	0859		1559	...	...	1659	1729	1759	1829	1859	1929	1959	2029	2059	...	2159	2259	...	2359	...	...
Koblenz Hbf 802 906	a.	0536	0636	0706	0736	0806	0906		1606	...	...	1706	1736	1806	1836	1906	1936	2006	2036	2106	...	2206	2306	...	0006	...	...
Neuwied 802	a.	0555	...	0725	...	0825	0925		1626	...	...	1725	...	1826	...	1925	...	2028	...	2126	...	2225	2325	...	...	...	...

K – To/from Kaiserslautern (Table **918**). Operated by Vlexx.

d – Runs daily Rüdesheim - Frankfurt and v.v.
e – Also June 8, 18, Oct. 2.
f – 8 minutes later Sept. 15 - Nov. 21.
j – Sept. 15 - Nov. 21 departs Frankfurt 5–6 minutes earlier, Mainz Kastel 3 minutes later.
r – ⚒ only.
t – Ⓐ only.
z – Ⓒ only.

◧ – Frankfurt Flughafen Regionalbahnhof ✈.
⊡ – Stopping services (operated by Mittelrheinbahn).
✣ – Timings Bingen (Rhein) Hbf - Mainz may vary by up to 3 minutes.
⊠ – See Table **800** for long-distance *ICE / IC / EC* services.
See Table **917** for other services Ingelheim - Mainz - Frankfurt and v.v.
See Table **917a** for S-Bahn services Mainz - Frankfurt Flughafen ✈ - Frankfurt (Main) Hbf and v.v.

914a *2025 service* KÖLN - KOBLENZ - MAINZ

Köln Düsseldorfer Deutsche Rheinschiffahrt

◐			A	A	B ⛴	E	A	E	A	B	B	B	E
750	**Köln** (Rheingarten)	d.	...	...	...	...	...	...	...	...	0930	...	...
1600	**Bonn**	d.	...	...	...	...	...	...	...	1030	1230	1430	...
900	Königswinter Fähre	d.	...	...	...	...	...	...	...	1130	1330	1530	...
750	Bad Honnef (Rhein)	d.	...	...	...	...	...	...	...	1150	1350	1550	...
400	Remagen	d.	...	...	...	...	...	...	...	1220	1420	1620	...
750	Linz am Rhein	d.	...	...	...	...	...	...	...	1250	1450	1650	...
1500	Bad Breisig	d.	...	...	...	...	...	...	...	▬	...	...	...
400	Bad Hönningen	d.	...	...	...	...	...	...	...	...	...	...	...
1200	Andernach	d.	...	...	...	...	...	...	...	...	...	...	...
2200	**Koblenz** ⊙	d.	...	...	0900	...	...	1200	...	...	...	...	1750
150	Oberlahnstein	d.	...	...	0940	...	...	1240	...	...	...	...	1830
450	Braubach	d.	...	...	1005	...	...	1305	...	A	...	...	1855
400	**Boppard**	d.	...	1000	1100	...	1300	1400	...	1600	...	...	1945
400	Kamp-Bornhofen	d.	...	1010	1110	...	1310	1410	...	1610	...	...	...
300	Bad Salzig	d.	...	1025	1125	...	1325	1425	...	1625	...	...	...
450	**St Goarshausen** ★	d.	1045	|	1210	1250	|	|	1600	|	...	...	...
250	**St Goar** ★	d.	1055	1120	1220	1315	1420	1520	1610	1720	...	...	...
450	Oberwesel	d.	1125	...	1250	1350	...	...	1640	...	...	...	...
900	Kaub	d.	1140	...	1305	1405	...	...	1655	...	...	...	...
600	Bacharach	d.	1205	...	1330	1430	...	...	1720	...	...	...	...
400	**Bingen** (Rhein) ♥	d.	1335	...	1500	1600	...	...	1850	...	...	...	...
900	**Rüdesheim** ♥	a.	1350	...	1515	1620	...	...	1900	...	...	...	...
1500	Wiesbaden-Biebrich	a.	...	...	...	1810t	...	...	...	...	...	...	...
1600	**Mainz**	a.	...	...	...	1840t	...	...	...	...	...	...	...

		A	E	B	A	E	A	E	A	A	B ⛴
Mainz	d.	...	...	...	...	0915t	...	...	...	...	...
Wiesbaden-Biebrich	d.	...	...	...	...	0930t	...	...	...	...	...
Rüdesheim ♥	d.	0900	...	...	...	1100	...	...	1415	...	1615
Bingen (Rhein) ♥	d.	0915	...	...	...	1115	...	...	1430	...	1630
Bacharach	d.	1000	...	...	...	1200	...	...	1515	...	1715
Kaub	d.	1010	...	...	...	1210	...	...	1525	...	1725
Oberwesel	d.	1020	...	...	...	1220	...	...	1535	...	1735
St Goar ★	d.	|	...	...	1130	|	1430	1530	|	1730	1755
St Goarshausen ★	d.	1045	...	...	1140	1250	1440	1540	1600	1740	1805
Bad Salzig	d.	...	...	...	1205	▬	1505	1605	...	1805	1830
Kamp-Bornhofen	d.	...	...	...	1215	...	1515	1615	...	1815	1840
Boppard	d.	...	1015	...	1230	...	1530	1630	...	1830	1850
Braubach	d.	...	1045	...	▬	...	▬	1700	...	...	1915
Oberlahnstein	d.	...	1100	...	...	...	...	1715	...	...	1930
Koblenz ⊙	d.	...	1145	...	...	...	...	1740	...	...	2000
Andernach	d.	...	...	...	...	...	...	...	...	...	...
Bad Hönningen	d.	...	...	...	...	...	...	...	...	...	...
Bad Breisig	d.	...	...	...	D	C	B	...	...	...	...
Linz am Rhein	d.	...	...	1250	1450	1550	1650	...	...	...	...
Remagen	d.	...	...	1300	1500	1600	1700	...	...	...	...
Bad Honnef (Rhein)	d.	...	...	1325	1525	1625	1725	...	...	...	...
Königswinter Fähre	d.	...	...	1340	1540	1640	1740	...	...	...	...
Bonn	d.	...	...	1415	1615	1715	1815	...	...	...	...
Köln (Rheingarten)	a.	...	...	...	1800	1900	...	...	...	...	...

A – Apr. 5 - Oct. 26.
B – ②–⑦ Apr. 26 - Oct. 5.
C – ②③④⑦ Apr. 27 - Oct. 5.
D – ⑤⑥ Apr. 26 - Oct. 4.
E – ②–⑦ Apr. 26 - Oct. 26.

t – Not Oct. 6–26.

⊙ – Koblenz (Konrad-Adenauer-Ufer).
◐ – Distance in metres from rail station to river landing stage.
⛴ – Operated by paddlesteamer *Goethe*.

★ – A frequent ferry service sails between St Goar and St Goarshausen operated by Rheinschifffahrt Goar. ✆ + 49 (0) 6771 26 20. www.faehre-loreley.de

♥ – A frequent ferry service sails between Bingen and Rüdesheim operated by Bingen-Rüdesheimer Fähr- und Schiffahrtsgesellschaft. ✆ + 49 (0) 6721 30808. www.bingen-ruedesheimer.de

Operator: Köln Düsseldorfer Deutsche Rheinschiffahrt, Frankenwerft 35, D-50667 Köln. ✆ +49 (0) 221 20 88 318. www.k-d.com

RE services except where shown — KOBLENZ - TRIER - LUXEMBOURG and SAARBRÜCKEN — 915

Many Saarbrücken services continue to / start from stations in Table **919**.

km		Ⓐ	†	Ⓐ				†	⚒			⑥				⊠			A						
0	**Koblenz** Hbf ... d.	...	...	...	...	...	0525	...	0603	...	0706	0706	...	0806	0806		1506	1506	1520	1606	1606	1706	1706	1806	1806
47	Cochem (Mosel) ... d.	...	...	0515	...	...	0615	...	0638	...	0741	0741	...	0841	0841	and at	1541	1541	1555	1641	1641	1741	1741	1841	1841
59	Bullay ... d.	...	...	0526	...	...	0626	...	0648	...	0751	0751	...	0851	0851		1551	1551	1603	1651	1651	1751	1751	1851	1851
76	Wittlich Hbf ... d.	...	...	0542	...	...	0642	...	0700	...	0803	0803	...	0903	0903	the same	1603	1603	1616	1703	1703	1803	1803	1903	1903
112	**Trier** Hbf ... a.	...	...	0620	...	...	0720	...	0731	...	0830	0830	...	0930	0930		1630	1630	1643	1730	1730	1830	1830	1930	1930
112	**Trier** Hbf ... ≋ d.	0456	0533	...	0633	0637	...	0733	0733	0737	0833	0837	0837	0933	0937	minutes	1633	1637	1646	1733	1737	1833	1837	1933	1937
163	**Luxembourg** ... ≋ a.	|	|	...	|	0723	...	|	|	0823	|	0923	0923	|	1023		|	1723	1748	|	1823	|	1923	|	2023
135	Saarburg ... d.	0514	0551	...	0651	...	...	0751	0751	...	0851	...	...	0951	...	past each	1651	...	...	1751	...	1851	...	1951	...
161	Merzig (Saar) ... d.	0534	0610	...	0710	...	...	0810	0810	...	0910	...	...	1010	...		1710	...	...	1810	...	1910	...	2010	...
173	Dillingen (Saar) ... d.	0543	0619	...	0720	...	...	0820	0820	...	0920	...	...	1020	...	hour until	1720	...	...	1820	...	1920	...	2020	...
177	Saarlouis Hbf ... d.	0547	0623	...	0724	...	...	0824	0824	...	0924	...	...	1024	...		1724	...	...	1824	...	1924	...	2024	...
190	Völklingen ... d.	0557	0632	...	0732	...	...	0832	0832	...	0932	...	...	1032	...		1732	...	...	1832	...	1932	...	2032	...
200	**Saarbrücken** Hbf ... a.	0606	0641	...	0741	...	...	0841	0841	...	0941	...	...	1041	...		1741	...	...	1841	...	1941	...	2041	...

									⑥⑦				
Koblenz Hbf ... d.	1825	...	...	1919	...	2019	2019	2119	2119	...	2219	2219	2321
Cochem (Mosel) ... d.	1915	...	...	1954	...	2054	2054	2154	2154	...	2254	2254	2356
Bullay ... d.	1926	...	...	2002	...	2102	2102	2202	2202	...	2302	2302	0004
Wittlich Hbf ... d.	1942	...	...	2014	...	2114	2114	2214	2214	...	2314	2314	0016
Trier Hbf ... a.	2020	...	...	2040	...	2140	2140	2240	2240	...	2340	2340	0042
Trier Hbf ... ≋ d.	...	...	2033	2043	2101	2143	2149	2249	2243	2243	2345	2349	...
Luxembourg ... ≋ a.	...	...	|	2129	|	2229	|	|	2329	2329	|	0035	...
Saarburg ... d.	...	...	2051	...	2125	...	2210	2310	...	...	0010	...	...
Merzig (Saar) ... d.	...	...	2110	...	2151	...	2230	2330	...	...	0036	...	...
Dillingen (Saar) ... d.	...	...	2120	...	2201	...	2240	2340	...	...	0046	...	...
Saarlouis Hbf ... d.	...	...	2124	...	2205	...	2244	2344	...	...	0050	...	...
Völklingen ... d.	...	...	2132	...	2216	...	2252	2352	...	...	0101	...	...
Saarbrücken Hbf ... a.	...	...	2141	...	2229	...	2301	0001	...	...	0114	...	...

	Ⓐ		Ⓐ	Ⓒ	①–⑤ r	Ⓐ	⚒		A
Saarbrücken Hbf ... d.	...	...	...	...	...	0458	...	0516	...
Völklingen ... d.	...	...	...	...	...	0506	...	0528	...
Saarlouis Hbf ... d.	...	...	...	...	...	0514	...	0539	...
Dillingen (Saar) ... d.	...	...	...	...	...	0518	...	0542	...
Merzig (Saar) ... d.	...	...	...	...	...	0526	...	0553	...
Saarburg ... d.	...	...	...	...	...	0545	...	0619	...
Luxembourg .. ≋ d.	...	...	...	...	0510	|	...	|	0610
Trier Hbf ... ≋ a.	...	...	...	...	0601	0605	...	0646	0706
Trier Hbf ... d.	0410	...	0510	0453	0610	0610	0610	...	0710
Wittlich Hbf ... d.	0436	0501	0536	0540e	0636	0636	0636	...	0736
Bullay ... d.	0449	0516	0549	0556	0649	0649	0649	...	0749
Cochem (Mosel) ... d.	0458	0528	0558	0624	0658	0658	0658	...	0758
Koblenz Hbf ... a.	0536	0618	0636	0716	0736	0736	0736	...	0836

								⑥⑦										⑤	⑥	⑤⑥ h						
Saarbrücken Hbf ... d.	0619	...	0719		...	1719	...	...	1819	...	1919	...	2019	...	2119	...	...	2222	...	2222	2232	...	2335	0034	0120
Völklingen ... d.	0627	...	0727	and at	...	1727	...	...	1827	...	1927	...	2027	...	2127	...	...	2231	...	2231	2244	...	2347	0045	0131
Saarlouis Hbf ... d.	0635	...	0735		...	1735	...	...	1835	...	1935	...	2035	...	2135	...	...	2239	...	2239	2255	...	2358	0056	0141
Dillingen (Saar) ... d.	0639	...	0739	the same	...	1739	...	...	1839	...	1939	...	2039	...	2139	...	...	2242	...	2242	2258	...	0001	0059	0145
Merzig (Saar) ... d.	0647	...	0747		...	1747	...	...	1847	...	1947	...	2047	...	2147	...	...	2250	...	2250	2309	...	0012	0111	0156
Saarburg ... d.	0707	...	0807	minutes	...	1807	...	...	1907	...	2007	...	2107	...	2207	...	...	2309	...	2309	2335	...	0038	...	...
Luxembourg ... ≋ d.	|	0733	|		1733	|	1833	1833	|	1933	|	2033	|	2133	|	2233	2233	|	...	|	|	2333	|	...	...
Trier Hbf ... ≋ a.	0727	0823	0827	past each	1823	1827	1923	1923	1927	2023	2027	2123	2127	2223	2227	2323	2323	2328	...	2328	0002	0023	0105	...	...
Trier Hbf ... d.	0731	0831	0831		1831	1831	...	1931	1931	2031	2031	2131	2131	...	2231	...	2331	2331	2331	...	...	...	...	...	...
Wittlich Hbf ... d.	0756	0856	0856	hour until	1856	1856	...	1956	1956	2056	2056	2156	2156	...	2256	...	2356	2356	2356	...	...	...	...	...	...
Bullay ... d.	0809	0909	0909		1909	1909	...	2009	2009	2109	2109	2209	2209	...	2309	...	0009	0009	0009	...	...	...	...	...	...
Cochem (Mosel) ... d.	0818	0918	0918		1918	1918	...	2018	2018	2118	2118	2218	2218	...	2318	...	0018	0018	0018	...	...	...	...	...	...
Koblenz Hbf ... a.	0856	0956	0956		1956	1956	...	2056	2056	2156	2156	2256	2256	...	2356	...	0056	0056	0056	...	...	...	...	...	...

A – To / from Düsseldorf (Table **800**). Train classification is *IC* Koblenz - Düsseldorf and v.v.
S – ⑥⑦ until Aug. 31 (also Aug. 15).

e – Arrives 0530.
h – Also June 18.
r – Not June 9, 19, Aug. 15, Oct. 3.

⊠ – The 0906 from Koblenz to Luxembourg requires a change of trains at Trier.
The 1306 from Koblenz to Luxembourg requires a change of trains at Trier on Ⓒ.

≋ – Trier - Luxembourg and v.v. is by 🚌 **Aug. 23 - Sept. 14**:
From Trier at 0558 ⚒, 0644, 0744 and hourly until 1944, then 2050, 2150, 2250, 2350.
From Luxembourg at 0510 ⚒, 0610, 0731, 0831, and hourly until 2331.
Journey time 50 minutes. Additional buses operate (those shown connect with trains above).

BULLAY - TRABEN-TRARBACH — *13 km* — Journey time: 18 minutes

Operated by Rhenus Veniro.
From Bullay at 0600 ⚒, 0658, 0838, 0938 and hourly until 2138.
From Traben-Trarbach at 0625 ⚒, 0741, 0901, 1001 and hourly until 2201.

TRIER - PERL - METZ

km		S		S			S		S	
0	**Trier** Hbf ... d.	1042	...	1942	...	**Metz** ... d.	0851	...	1738	...
49	Perl 🏢 ... d.	1119	...	2019	...	Thionville . d.	0909	...	1808	...
70	Thionville ... a.	1153	...	2053	...	Perl 🏢 ... d.	0944	...	1844	...
100	**Metz** ... a.	1215	...	2117	...	**Trier** Hbf.. a.	1018	...	1918	...

Local *RB* services **Trier** - **Perl** and v.v. Journey time: 48 – 53 minutes.
From Trier Hbf at 0446 Ⓐ, 0541 ⚒, 0614 Ⓐ, 0641, 0741, 0841, 0941, 1045, 1141, 1241, 1322 Ⓐ, 1341, 1441, 1541, 1641, 1741, 1841, 1945, 2047, 2207, 2307 and 2357.
From Perl at 0456 Ⓐ, 0618 ⚒, 0645 Ⓐ, 0726, 0826, 0919, 1026, 1129, 1226, 1326, 1426, 1526, 1626, 1726, 1819, 1926, 2029, 2126 and 2226.

RE / RB services — KÖLN - GEROLSTEIN - TRIER — 915a

SERVICE FROM JUNE 16 *On June 19, Oct. 3 services in this table run as on ⑦.*

Warning! The section of line between Gerolstein and Trier is closed for electrification work until September 29 (please check for rail replacement 🚌 timings).
From October 13 journeys between Kall and Gerolstein (between Euskichen and Gerolstein November 8 – 16) will once again be subject to alteration due to ongoing electrification work.

km		⚒		Ⓐ	Ⓒ	Ⓐ	Ⓒ														Ⓒ	Ⓐ			⑤⑥ f
0	**Köln** Messe/Deutz ... d.	...	...	0505	...	0605	0615	0715	0815	0915	1015	1115	1215	1314	1414	1515	1615	1714	1815	1915	2015	2015	2115	2213	2316
1	**Köln** Hbf ... d.	...	...	0512	...	0612	0621	0721	0821	0921	1021	1121	1221	1321	1421	1521	1621	1721	1821	1922	2021	2021	2121	2221	2322
6	**Köln** Süd ... d.	...	...	0519	...	0619	0629	0729	0829	0929	1029	1129	1229	1329	1429	1529	1629	1729	1829	1929	2029	2029	2129	2229	2330
41	Euskirchen ... d.	...	...	0556	...	0656	0700	0800	0900	1000	1100	1200	1300	1400	1500	1600	1700	1800	1900	2000	2100	2100	2200	2300	0000
56	Mechernich ... d.	...	...	0608	...	0708	0709	0809	0909	1009	1109	1209	1309	1409	1509	1609	1709	1809	1909	2009	2109	2109	2209	2309	0009
65	Kall ... d.	...	...	0617	...	0717	0717	0817	0917	1017	1117	1217	1317	1417	1517	1617	1717	1817	1917	2017	2117	2116	2217	2317	0017
81	Blankenheim ... d.	...	...	0633	...	0733	0733	0833	0932	1033	1133	1233	1333	1433	1533	1633	1733	1833	1933	2033	2133	...	...	...	...
94	Jünkerath ... d.	...	...	0646	...	0746	0746	0846	0946	1046	1146	1246	1346	1446	1546	1646	1746	1846	1946	2046	2146	...	...	...	...
113	**Gerolstein** ... d.	0503	0603	0703	0703	0803	0803	0903	1003	1103	1203	1303	1403	1503	1603	1703	1803	1903	2003	2102	2203	...	...	...	...
143	Bitburg-Erdorf ... ▲ d.	0540	0640	0740	0740	0840	0840	0940	1040	1140	1240	1340	1440	1540	1640	1740	1840	1940	2040	...	...	...	...	...	...
182	**Trier** Hbf ... ▲ a.	0627	0727	0827	0827	0927	0927	1027	1127	1227	1327	1427	1527	1627	1727	1827	1927	2027	2127	...	...	...	...	...	...

	Ⓐ	Ⓐ	⑥ t	Ⓐ	Ⓐ	⚒ v	Ⓐ	⚒ v	†													Ⓐ	Ⓒ		
Trier Hbf ... ▲ d.	...	...	...	...	...	...	...	0536	...	0636	0736	0836	0936	1036	1136	1236	1336	1436	1536	1636	1736	1836	1836	1936	2036
Bitburg-Erdorf ... ▲ d.	...	...	...	...	...	...	...	0619	...	0719	0819	0919	1019	1119	1219	1319	1419	1519	1619	1719	1819	1919	1919	2019	2119
Gerolstein ... d.	...	...	...	0512	...	0556	...	0656	0656	0756	0856	0956	1056	1156	1256	1356	1456	1556	1656	1756	1856	1953	1956	2053	2153
Jünkerath ... d.	...	...	...	0529	...	0613	...	0713	0713	0813	0913	1013	1113	1213	1313	1413	1513	1613	1713	1813	1913	...	2013	...	...
Blankenheim ... d.	...	...	...	0543	...	0627	...	0727	0727	0827	0927	1027	1127	1227	1327	1427	1527	1627	1727	1827	1927	...	2027	...	...
Kall ... d.	0505	0529	0538	0559	0613	0642	0700	0742	0742	0842	0942	1042	1142	1242	1342	1442	1542	1642	1742	1842	1942	...	2042	...	...
Mechernich ... d.	0514	0538	0547	0607	0622	0649	0709	0749	0749	0849	0949	1049	1149	1249	1349	1449	1549	1649	1749	1849	1949	...	2049	...	...
Euskirchen ... d.	0530	0556	0603	0626	0639	0703	0722	0803	0803	0903	1003	1103	1203	1303	1403	1503	1603	1703	1803	1903	2003	...	2103	...	...
Köln Süd ... a.	0603	0631	0631	0703	0708	0731	0748	0831	0831	0931	1031	1131	1231	1332	1431	1531	1631	1731	1829	1932	2031	...	2131	...	...
Köln Hbf ... a.	0612	0639	0639	0712	0716	0739	0757	0839	0839	0939	1039	1139	1239	1339	1439	1539	1639	1739	1839	1940	2039	...	2139	...	...
Köln Messe/Deutz ... a.	0618	0646	0645	0718	0722	0745	0803	0846	0846	0945	1045	1145	1245	1345	1445	1545	1645	1745	1845	1946	2045	...	2145	...	...

f – Also June 18, Oct. 2.
t – Not Nov. 1.
v – Not June 19, Nov. 1.

▲ – Journeys to / from Bitburg-Erdorf and Trier are subject to alteration until Sept. 29.

916 KARLSRUHE - OFFENBURG - KONSTANZ

RE services except where shown

km																									
			Ⓐ t	Ⓒ z				⑥ B									*ICE* 1579 ⑤⑥ T✕						Ⓑ h	⑥ k	A
0	**Karlsruhe** Hbf 910 910a 943 d.	...	...	0456	0606	0702	0810	...	0907	1007	1107	1207	1307	1407	1507	1607	1654	1707	1810	1907	2010	2107	2107	2209	*2209*
21	Rastatt 910a 943 d.	...	...	0510	0620	0719	0824	...	0924	1024	1124	1224	1324	1422	1524	1624	|	1724	1824	1924	2024	2124	2124	2229	*2229*
29	Baden-Baden 910 910a d.	...	...	0516	0627	0726	0832	...	0932	1032	1132	1232	1332	1432	1532	1632	|	1732	1832	1932	2032	2132	2132	2237	*2237*
69	**Offenburg** 910 910a a.	...	...	0540	0653	0755	0857	...	0956	1057	1156	1257	1356	1457	1556	1657	1727	1756	1857	1956	2057	2157	2157	2306	*2306*
69	**Offenburg** 942 d.	...	0523	0556	0656	0759	0859	0908	0959	1059	1159	1259	1359	1459	1559	1659	1729	1759	1859	1959	2059	2159	2159	2328	2328
102	Hausach 942 d.	...	0548	0622	0722	0821	0922	0928	1022	1122	1222	1322	1422	1522	1622	1722	|	1822	1922	2022	2122	2222	2222	2350	2351
112	Hornberg (Schwarzw) d.	...	0556	0630	0730	0829	0929	0936	1029	1129	1229	1329	1429	1529	1629	1729	|	1829	1929	2029	2129	2229	2229	...	2359
125	Triberg d.	...	0609	0643	0743	0843	0943	0950	1043	1143	1243	1343	1443	1543	1643	1743	|	1843	1943	2043	2143	2243	2243	...	0013
140	St Georgen (Schwarzw) d.	...	0625	0657	0757	0857	0957	1004	1057	1157	1257	1357	1457	1557	1657	1757	1833	1857	1957	2057	2157	2257	2257	...	0028
155	Villingen (Schwarzw) 938 d.	0549	0635	0706	0806	0906	1006	1013	1106	1206	1306	1406	1506	1606	1706	1806	1844	1906	2006	2106	2206	2305	2306	...	0036
169	Donaueschingen 938 d.	0600	0645	0716	0816	0916	1016	1022	1116	1216	1316	1416	1516	1616	1716	1816	1900	1916	2016	2116	2216	...	2316	...	...
188	Immendingen 938 d.	0617	0657	0728	0828	0928	1028	|	1128	1228	1328	1428	1528	1628	1728	1828	|	1928	2028	2128	2229	...	2328	...	...
204	Engen 940 d.	0631	0710	0740	0840	0940	1040	|	1140	1240	1340	1440	1540	1640	1740	1840	|	1940	2040	2140	2242	...	|	...	...
218	**Singen** 940 a.	0646	0723	0751	0850	0950	1050	1106	1150	1250	1350	1450	1550	1650	1750	1850	1936	1950	2050	2150	2251	...	2349	...	...
218	**Singen** 939 940 d.	0654	0725	0752	0852	0952	1052	1111	1152	1252	1352	1452	1552	1652	1752	1852	1940	1952	2052	2152	2256	...	2352	...	...
228	Radolfzell 939 940 d.	0705	0737	0800	0900	1000	1100	1122	1200	1300	1400	1500	1600	1700	1800	1900	1954	2001	2100	2200	2304	...	0000	...	...
248	**Konstanz** 940 a.	0727	0759	0816	0916	1016	1116	1144	1216	1316	1416	1516	1616	1716	1816	1916	2012	2016	2116	2216	2320	...	0014	...	...

			①–⑥					*ICE* 1578 ⑥⑦ S✕								◇	⑦ C						D		
Konstanz 940 d.	...	...	0451	...	0520	0640	0736	0746	0839	0939	1039	1139	1239	1339	1439	1539	1610	1639	1739	1839	1939	2039	2039	2158	2323
Radolfzell 939 940 d.	...	...	0505	...	0534	0656	0753	0806	0856	0956	1056	1156	1256	1356	1456	1556	1626	1656	1756	1856	1956	2056	2056	2222	2346
Singen 939 940 a.	...	...	0511	...	0545	0703	0801	0817	0903	1003	1103	1203	1303	1403	1503	1603	1632	1703	1803	1903	2003	2103	2103	2233	2356
Singen 940 d.	...	...	0512	...	0546	0706	0806	0821	0907	1007	1107	1207	1307	1407	1507	1607	1639	1707	1807	1907	2007	2106	2106	2234	0000
Engen 940 d.	...	...	0523	...	0555	0715	0816	|	0916	1016	1116	1216	1316	1416	1516	1616	|	1716	1816	1916	2016	2115	2115	2250	0012
Immendingen 938 d.	...	...	0536	...	0612	0728	0830	|	0930	1030	1130	1230	1330	1430	1530	1630	|	1730	1830	1930	2030	2128	2128	2307	...
Donaueschingen 938 d.	0502	...	0551	...	0624	0740	0840	0858	0940	1040	1140	1240	1340	1440	1540	1640	1711	1740	1840	1940	2040	2140	2140	2319	...
Villingen (Schwarzw) 938 d.	0520	0531	0600	...	0635	0750	0850	0911	0950	1050	1150	1250	1350	1450	1550	1650	1722	1750	1850	1950	2050	2150	2150	2328	...
St Georgen (Schwarzw) d.	...	0540	0610	...	0644	0759	0859	0922	0959	1059	1159	1259	1359	1459	1559	1659	1732	1759	1859	1959	2059	2159	2159	...	...
Triberg d.	...	0555	0625	...	0659	0815	0914	|	1014	1114	1214	1314	1414	1514	1614	1714	1746	1814	1914	2014	2114	2214	2214	...	...
Hornberg (Schwarzw) d.	...	0610	0639	...	0712	0826	0926	|	1026	1126	1226	1326	1426	1526	1626	1726	1800	1826	1926	2026	2128	2228	2228	...	...
Hausach 942 d.	...	0619	0649	...	0720	0837	0937	|	1037	1137	1237	1337	1437	1537	1637	1737	1809	1837	1937	2037	2137	2236	2237	...	...
Offenburg 942 a.	...	0644	0721	...	0744	0859	0959	1016	1059	1159	1259	1359	1459	1559	1659	1759	1828	1859	1959	2059	2159	...	2259	...	...
Offenburg 910 910a d.	...	0658	...	0734	0753	0902	1002	1018	1102	1202	1302	1402	1502	1602	1702	1802	...	1902	2002	2102	2202	...	*2302*	...	...
Baden-Baden 910 910a a.	...	0724	...	0800	0818	0927	1027	|	1127	1227	1327	1427	1527	1627	1727	1827	...	1927	2027	2127	2227	...	*2327*	...	...
Rastatt 943 910a a.	...	0731	...	0807	0826	0933	1033	|	1133	1233	1333	1433	1533	1633	1733	1833	...	1933	2033	2133	2233	...	*2334*	...	...
Karlsruhe Hbf 910 910a 943 a.	...	0749	...	0821	0839	0949	1049	1056	1149	1249	1349	1449	1549	1649	1749	1849	...	1949	2049	2149	2249	..	*2349*	...	...

A – Ⓑ to June 27; ①–⑤ from June 30 (also Nov. 1)
B – ⑥ until Sept. 13 (also June 19). Operated by SBB.
C – ⑦ until Sept. 14 (also June 19). Operated by SBB.
D – Daily until June 28; ①–⑥ from June 30.
S – ⑥⑦ (also June 9, Oct. 3). 12 ✕ Konstanz - Karlsruhe - Frankfurt - Hannover - Hamburg - Stralsund.
T – ⑤⑥ (also June 8, Oct. 2). 12 ✕ (Greifswald ⑥ -) Hamburg - Hannover - Frankfurt - Karlsruhe - Konstanz.

h – Also Nov. 1.
k – Not Nov. 1.
t – Not June 19.
z – Also June 19.

◇ – Change trains at Offenburg on Ⓐ (not June 19).

917 FRANKFURT - MAINZ - IDAR OBERSTEIN - SAARBRÜCKEN

Operator: *Vlexx*

On June 19 services run as on ⑦.

km																								
			Ⓐ	Ⓐ	⚒												Ⓒ	Ⓐ		Ⓒ	Ⓐ			
0	**Frankfurt** (Main) Hbf 914 ‡ d.	...	...	0456	...	0608t	0708	0808	*0908*	1008	*1108*	1202k	*1308*	1408	*1508*	1608	*1708*	1720	1808	*1908*	1924	2008	*2108*	2208
11	Frankfurt Flughafen ✈ § 914 ‡ d.	...	...	0508	...	0624t	0724	0824	*0924*	1024	*1124*	1224	*1324*	1424	*1524*	1624	*1724*	1738	1824	*1924*	1938	2024	*2124*	2224
39	**Mainz** Hbf 914 ‡ a.	...	...	0530	...	0649t	0749	0849	*0949*	1049	*1149*	1249	*1349*	1449	*1549*	1649	*1749*	1758	1849	*1949*	1958	2049	*2149*	2249
39	**Mainz** Hbf 914 d.	...	0408	▬	0542	0655	0751	0853	0956	1053	1156	1254	1356	1453	1556	1653	1756	1800	1853	1956	2000	2053	2156	2253
57	Ingelheim 914 d.	...	0423	...	0555	0710	0805	0905	1010	1105	1210	1305	1410	1505	1610	1705	1810	1811	1905	2010	2011	2105	2210	2305
80	Bad Kreuznach d.	...	0503g	...	0611	0724	0822	0922	1024	1122	1224	1322	1424	1522	1624	1722	1824	1829	1922	2024	2026	2122	2224	2322
102	Bad Sobernheim d.	...	0526	...	0634	0744	0843	0943	1045	1143	1244	1343	1444	1543	1644	1743	1844	1849	1943	2044	2046	2143	2244	2343
117	Kirn d.	...	0540	...	0645	0754	0853	0953	1055	1153	1254	1353	1454	1553	1654	1753	1854	1859	1953	2054	2056	2153	2254	2353
131	Idar-Oberstein d.	...	0602j	...	0657	0805	0905	1005	1106	1205	1305	1405	1505	1605	1705	1805	1905	1910	2005	2105	2107	2205	2305	0005
170	St Wendel d.	0557	0651	0659	0735	0836	0936	1036	1137	1236	1336	1436	1536	1636	1736	1836	1936	1941	2036	2136	2138	2236	2336	0036
179	Ottweiler (Saar) d.	0606	0658	0709	0742	0842	0942	1042	1143	1242	1342	1442	1542	1642	1742	1842	1942	1947	2042	2142	2144	2242	2342	0042
184	Neunkirchen (Saar) d.	0613	0705	0717	0751	0851	0951	1051	1151	1251	1351	1451	1551	1651	1751	1851	1951	1954	2051	2151	2151	2251	2351	0051
205	**Saarbrücken** Hbf a.	0638	0723	0742	0810	0910	1010	1110	1210	1310	1410	1510	1610	1710	1810	1910	2010	2013	2110	2210	2210	2310	0010	0110

			Ⓐ	Ⓒ																			
Saarbrücken Hbf d.	0342	0442	0545	0551	0651	0751	0851	0951	1051	1151	1251	1351	...	1451	1551	...	1651	1751	1851	1951	2035	2151	2235	2351
Neunkirchen (Saar) d.	0400	0500	0603	0610	0711	0810	0911	1010	1111	1210	1311	1410	...	1511	1609	...	1711	1810	1911	2010	2100	2214	2323e	0016
Ottweiler (Saar) d.	0406	0506	0609	0615	0716	0815	0916	1015	1116	1215	1316	1415	...	1516	1614	...	1716	1815	1916	2015	2107	2219	2330	0023
St Wendel d.	0413	0513	0616	0622	0723	0822	0923	1022	1123	1222	1323	1422	...	1523	1621	...	1723	1822	1923	2022	2117	2226	2339	0033
Idar-Oberstein d.	0445	0545	0648	0652	0754	0852	0954	1052	1154	1252	1354	1453	...	1554	1653	...	1754	1852	1954	2052	...	2259	...	...
Kirn d.	0456	0556	0659	0703	0806	0903	1006	1103	1206	1303	1406	1504	...	1606	1704	...	1806	1903	2006	2103	...	2310	...	...
Bad Sobernheim d.	0506	0606	0709	0712	0816	0912	1016	1112	1216	1312	1416	1513	...	1616	1713	...	1816	1912	2016	2112	...	2319	...	...
Bad Kreuznach d.	0527	0627	0737h	0733	0839	0933	1039	1133	1239	1331	1439	1533	...	1639	1733	...	1839	1933	2039	2133	...	2341	...	...
Ingelheim 914 d.	0544	0644	0754	0747	0854	0947	1054	1147	1254	1347	1454	1547	...	1654	1747	...	1854	1947	2054	2147	...	0001	...	...
Mainz Hbf 914 a.	0556	0656	0806	0759	0906	0959	1106	1159	1306	1359	1506	1557	...	1706	1757	...	1906	1959	2106	2159	...	0019	...	...
Mainz Hbf 914 ‡ d.	0558	0658	0810	*0810*	0910	*1010*	1110	*1210*	1310	*1410*	1510	1559t	1610	1710	1759t	1810	1910	*2010*	2110	2214	...	...	...	...
Frankfurt Flughafen ✈ § 914 ‡ a.	0620	0720	0833	*0833*	0933	*1033*	1133	*1233*	1333	*1433*	1533	1620t	1633	1733	1820t	1833	1933	*2033*	2133	2235	...	...	...	...
Frankfurt (Main) Hbf 914 ‡ a.	0636	0736	0848	*0848*	0948	*1048*	1148	*1248*	1348	*1448*	1548	1636t	1648	1748	1836t	1847	1948	*2047*	2148	2249	...	...	...	...

e – Arrives 2259.
g – Arrives 0445.
h – Arrives 0731.
j – Arrives 0555.
k – 1208 on Ⓒ.
t – Ⓐ only.
‡ – See also Tables **800** and **917a**.
§ – Frankfurt Flughafen Regionalbahnhof.

917a FRANKFURT - FRANKFURT FLUGHAFEN ✈ - MAINZ - WIESBADEN

S-Bahn 8/9

					Ⓒz		Ⓒz																		
Frankfurt (Main) Hbf d.	0002	0017	0047	0117	0147	0217	0247	0317	0347	0417	0432	0447	0502	0517	0532	0547	and at	2202	2217	2232	2247	2302	2317	2332	2347
Frankfurt Flughafen ★ d.	0015	0030	0100	0130	0200	0230	0300	0330	0400	0430	0445	0500	0515	0530	0545	0600	the same	2215	2230	2245	2300	2315	2330	2345	0000
Mainz Hbf d.	|	0059	0129	0159	0229	0259	0329	0359	|	0459	|	0529	|	0559	|	0629	minutes	|	2259	|	2329	|	2359	|	0029
Mainz-Kastel d.	0040	|	|	|	|	|	|	|	0425	|	0510	|	0540	|	0610	|	past each	2240	|	2310	|	2340	|	0010	|
Wiesbaden Hbf a.	0048	0113	0143	0213	0243	0313	0343	0413	0433	0513	0518	0543	0548	0613	0618	0643	hour until	2248	2313	2318	2343	2348	0013	0018	0043

			Ⓒz		Ⓒz																				
Wiesbaden Hbf d.	0018	0048	0118	0148	0218	0248	0318	0339	0348	0409	0418	0439	0448	and at	2109	2118	2139	2148	2209	2218	2239	2248	2309	2318	2348
Mainz-Kastel d.	|	|	|	|	|	|	|	0347	|	0417	|	0447	|	the same	2117	|	2147	|	2217	|	2247	|	2317	|	|
Mainz Hbf d.	0032	0102	0132	0202	0232	0302	0332	|	0402	|	0432	|	0502	minutes	|	2132	|	2202	|	2232	|	2302	|	2332	0002
Frankfurt Flughafen ★ d.	0100	0130	0200	0230	0300	0330	0400	0415	0430	0445	0500	0515	0530	past each	2145	2200	2215	2230	2245	2300	2315	2330	2345	0000	0030
Frankfurt (Main) Hbf a.	0113	0143	0213	0243	0313	0343	0413	0428	0443	0458	0513	0528	0543	hour until	2158	2213	2228	2243	2258	2313	2328	2343	2358	0013	0043

z – Also June 19.

★ – Frankfurt Flughafen Regionalbahnhof ✈.

RB / S-Bahn services

RHEINLAND-PFALZ LOCAL SERVICES — 918

PIRMASENS - SAARBRÜCKEN

km		Ⓐ	⚒	Ⓐ	⚒					
0	**Pirmasens** Hbf ... d.	0510	0552	*0622*	*0732*	0832	and	1832	1932	2032
7	Pirmasens Nord ... d.	0517	0559	0641	0743	0843	hourly	1843	1943	2043
31	Zweibrücken Hbf ... d.	0547	0640	0713	0813	0913	until	1913	2013	2113
67	**Saarbrücken** Hbf ... a.	0627	0724	0752	0852	0952		1952	2051	2153

	Ⓐ	⑥	Ⓐ						
Saarbrücken Hbf ... d.	0602	0602	0633	0705	0807	and	1907	2007	2107
Zweibrücken Hbf ... d.	0643	0643	0713	0745	0845	hourly	1945	2045	2145
Pirmasens Nord ... a.	0715	0715	0741	0815	0915	until	2015	2115	...
Pirmasens Hbf ... a.	*0728*	*0757*	0753	0826	0926		2026	2126	...

PIRMASENS - LANDAU (Pfalz)

km		Ⓐ	⑥Y	Ⓐ	ⒶY					
0	**Pirmasens** Hbf ... d.	0438	0542	0544	0622	0702	and	1802	1902	2002
7	Pirmasens Nord ... d.	0450	0555	0609	0636	0718	hourly	1818	1918	2018
55	**Landau** (Pfalz) Hbf ... a.	0546	0659	0708	0734	0818	until	1918	2018	2118

	ⒶN	Ⓐ	⑥						
Landau (Pfalz) Hbf ... d.	0527	0608	0641	...	0741	and	1841	1941	2041
Pirmasens Nord ... a.	0632	0715	0740	...	0840	hourly	1940	2040	2140
Pirmasens Hbf ... a.	0657	0728	0757	...	0857	until	1957	2057	2157

PIRMASENS - KAISERSLAUTERN

km		Ⓐ	Ⓐ	⚒	†	⚒	†			
0	**Pirmasens** Hbf ... d.	0528	0610	0637	0641	0732	0741	0841	and	2041
7	Pirmasens Nord ... d.	0535	0617	0645	0652	0750	0750	0850	hourly	2050
36	**Kaiserslautern** Hbf ... a.	0607	0649	0722	0724	0826	0826	0926	until	2126

	Ⓒ		Ⓐ	⚒					
Kaiserslautern Hbf .. d.	0053	...	0514	0616	0735	and	2035	...	2300
Pirmasens Nord ... a.	0125	...	0554	0702	0809	hourly	2109	...	2332
Pirmasens Hbf ... a.	0134	...	0608	0719	0818	until	2118	...	2341

(KOBLENZ -) BINGEN - KAISERSLAUTERN

km		Ⓐ	Ⓐ	Ⓒ		◇			◇			◇			◇			◇	Ⓒ	Ⓐ	Ⓒ	◇		m		⑤⑥f
	Koblenz Hbf **914** ... d.	...	...	...	...	0803	...	...	1003	...	...	1203	...	...	1403	...	...	1603	...	...	...	1803	...	...	...	...
0	**Bingen** (Rhein) Hbf ... d.	0546	0646	0701**h**	0755	0843	0855	0955	1043	1055	1204	1243	1255	1355	1443	1455	1555	1643	1655	1734	1803**r**	1843	1855	1955	2057	2258
16	Bad Kreuznach ... a.	0606	0706	0721**h**	0815	0855	0915	1015	1055	1115	1224	1255	1315	1415	1455	1515	1615	1655	1715	1754	1821	1855	1915	2015	2117	2318
16	Bad Kreuznach ... d.	0607	0707	0729	0828	0857	0928**k**	1028	1057	1128	1228	1257	1328	1418	1457	1527	1618	1657	1727	1755	1828**r**	1857	1927	2032	2127	2329
43	Rockenhausen ... d.	0634	0735	0756	0856	0926	0956	1056	1126	1156	1256	1326	1356	1456	1526	1556	1656	1726	1756	1820	1856	1926	1956	2059	2156	2356
79	**Kaiserslautern** Hbf ... a.	0711	0808	0827	0926	0954	1027	1126	1154	1227	1327	1354	1427	1527	1554	1627	1726	1754	1827	1856	1926	1954	2026	2130	2226	0026

	⑥	⚒	Ⓐ		◇			◇			◇			◇			◇		⑥	†	Ⓐ	◇				
Kaiserslautern Hbf ... d.	0516	0624	0637	0737	0804	0831	0931	1004	1031	1131	1204	1231	1331	1403	1431	1531	1603	1634	1731	1731	1736	1804	1840	1931	2032	2153
Rockenhausen ... d.	0550	0653	0711	0807	0830	0900	1000	1030	1100	1200	1230	1300	1400	1429	1500	1600	1629	1703	1800	1800	1809	1830	1909	2000	2101	2223
Bad Kreuznach ... a.	0632	0722	0742	0843	0859	0929	1029	1059	1129	1229	1259	1337	1429	1451	1529	1629	1651	1738	1829	1843	1842	1859	1938	2030	2137	2253
Bad Kreuznach ... d.	0633	0722	0743	0844	0900	0941	1041	1100	1141	1241	1300	1342	1441	1501	1541	1641	1701	1741	1841	1843	1842	1900	1941	2044	2142	2312
Bingen (Rhein) Hbf ... a.	0654	0744	0804	0905	0912	1003	1103	1112	1203	1303	1312	1403	1503	1512	1603	1703	1712	1802	1903	1904	1903	1912	2004	2105	2204	2334
Koblenz Hbf **914** ... a.	...	...	...	...	0953	...	...	1153	...	...	1353	...	...	1553	...	...	1753	...	...	...	...	1953**z**	...	...	...	...

(KAISERSLAUTERN -) NEUSTADT - KARLSRUHE and WISSEMBOURG

km		Ⓐ	Ⓐ	Ⓐ	Ⓐ	Ⓐ	⚒	⚒	Ⓐ	Ⓐ	†	⑥		⑥	Ⓑ					D	†E		D	†E
	Kaiserslautern Hbf ... **919** d.	...	...	...	...	...	...	...	...	0629	...	0629	...	...	...	...	...	...	0941	...	...	...	...	...
0	**Neustadt** (Weinstr) Hbf ... **919** d.	0427	...	0504	...	...	0529	0608	0636	0659	0700	0709	0736	0805	0809	0836	0909	0936	1009	1036	1045	1109	1136	1145
18	Landau (Pfalz) Hbf ... d.	0449	...	0525	0535	...	0555	0634	0658	0713	0722	0722	0758	0822	0822	0858	0922	0958	1022	1058	1058	1122	1158	1158
31	Winden (Pfalz) ... d.	0503	0505	...	0550	0555	0603	0650	0708	0722	0731	0731	0809	0831	0831	0909	0931	1009	1031	1109	1109	1131	1209	1209
47	**Wissembourg** 🏛 ◐ ... a.	|	0521	...	|	0615	|	|	0726	|	|	|	0827	|	|	0927	|	1027	|	1127	1127	|	1227	1227
44	Wörth (Rhein) ... d.	0520	...	...	0607	...	0616	0708	...	0735	0744	0744	...	0844	0844	...	0944	...	1044	...	...	1144	...	...
58	**Karlsruhe** Hbf ... a.	0534	...	...	0619	...	0636	0725	...	0753	0754	0754	...	0854	0854	...	0954	...	1054	...	...	1154	...	...

			Ⓐ	Ⓒ																				⑥
Kaiserslautern Hbf ... **919** d.	1141	...	...	...	...	...	...	...	...	1541**z**	...	...	...	...	...	...	...	...	...	...	...	...	...	...
Neustadt (Weinstr) Hbf ... **919** d.	1209	1236	1305	1309	1336	1409	1436	1509	1536	1609	1636	1709	1736	1809	1836	1909	1936	2009	2104	2136	...	2230	2336	2336
Landau (Pfalz) Hbf ... d.	1222	1258	1319	1322	1358	1422	1458	1522	1558	1622	1658	1722	1758	1822	1858	1922	1958	2022	2122	2158	...	2252	2358	2359
Winden (Pfalz) ... d.	1231	1309	1331	1331	1409	1431	1509	1531	1609	1631	1709	1731	1808	1831	1908	1931	2008	2031	2131	2213	2231	2306	...	0023**e**
Wissembourg 🏛 ◐ ... a.	|	1327	|	|	1427	|	1527	|	1627	|	1727	|	1826	|	1926	|	2026	|	|	...	|	|	...	|
Wörth (Rhein) ... d.	1244	...	1344	1344	...	1444	...	1544	...	1644	...	1744	...	1844	...	1944	...	2044	2144	...	2244	2319	...	0038
Karlsruhe Hbf ... a.	1254	...	1354	1354	...	1454	...	1554	...	1654	...	1754	...	1854	...	1954	...	2054	2154	...	2254	2336	...	0049

	Ⓐ	Ⓐ	⑥	Ⓐ	Ⓐ	⑥	Ⓐ	Ⓒ	Ⓐ		Ⓐ		Ⓑ	⑥									Ⓐ	Ⓒ
Karlsruhe Hbf ... d.	0430	...	0528	0557	...	0611	0642	0705	0717	...	...	0805	...	...	0905	...	1005	...	1105	...	1205	...	1305	1306
Wörth (Rhein) ... d.	0447	...	0546	0616	...	0628	0652	0715	0736	...	...	0816	...	...	0916	...	1016	...	1116	...	1216	...	1316	1316
Wissembourg 🏛 ◐ ... d.	|	0527	|	|	0625	|	|	|	|	...	0733	|	0832	0833	|	0933	|	1033	|	1133	|	1233	|	|
Winden (Pfalz) ... d.	0502	0547	0600	0631	0647	0641	0706	0727	0749	...	0758	0829	0853	0853	0929	0953	1029	1053	1129	1153	1229	1253	1330	1329
Landau (Pfalz) Hbf ... d.	0518	0601	0615	0645	0705**j**	0703**e**	0721	0736	0758	0807	0807	0838	0903	0903	0938	1003	1038	1103	1138	1203	1238	1303	1339	1338
Neustadt (Weinstr) Hbf ... **919** a.	0540	0622	0637	0704	0726	0724	0744	0751	0812	0826	0826	0851	0924	0924	0951	1024	1051	1124	1151	1224	1251	1324	1351	1351
Kaiserslautern Hbf ... **919** a.	...	...	...	...	...	...	0818	0818**h**	...	...	...	...	...	...	1016	...	...	...	...	...	...	...	...	1416

						Ⓐ	Ⓒ	†E	D	Ⓐ	Ⓒ	†E	D							Ⓑ	⑥			
Karlsruhe Hbf ... d.	...	1405	...	1505	...	1601	1605	...	...	1705	1705	...	...	1805	...	1905	...	2005	...	...	...	2106	2206	2318
Wörth (Rhein) ... d.	...	1416	...	1516	...	1616	1616	...	...	1716	1716	...	...	1816	...	1916	...	2016	...	...	...	2116	2216	2331
Wissembourg 🏛 ◐ ... d.	1333	|	1433	|	1533	|	|	1633	1633	|	|	1733	1733	|	1832	|	1933	|	...	2033	2103	|	|	|
Winden (Pfalz) ... d.	1353	1429	1453	1529	1553	1629	1629	1653	1653	1729	1729	1753	1753	1829	1853	1929	1953	2029	...	2053	2123	2131	2229	2344
Landau (Pfalz) Hbf ... d.	1403	1438	1503	1538	1603	1638	1638	1701	1703	1738	1738	1801	1803	1838	1903	1938	2003	2038	2103	2103	2131	2140	2238	2353
Neustadt (Weinstr) Hbf ... **919** a.	1424	1451	1524	1551	1624	1651	1651	1712	1724	1751	1754	1815	1824	1851	1924	1951	2024	2051	2124	2124	...	2201	2256	0012
Kaiserslautern Hbf ... **919** a.	...	...	...	...	...	...	...	...	...	...	...	...	...	1919	...	...	...	...	...	...	...	2226**b**	...	...

GERMERSHEIM - SPEYER - MANNHEIM - HEIDELBERG

km		Ⓐ	Ⓒ	Ⓐ	Ⓐ	⑥	Ⓐ	Ⓒ	Ⓐ				▲									
0	**Germersheim** ... **912** d.	0409	0409	0514	0559	0622	0704	0703	0727	0749	0812	0849	and at	1912	1949	2014	2049	2114	2211	2257	2322	0008	...
14	Speyer Hbf ... **912** d.	0423	0423	0527	0613	0635	0713	0716	0740	0802	0825	0902	the same	1925	2002	2027	2102	2127	2224	2310	2335	0021	...
23	Schifferstadt ... **912 919** d.	0434	0433	0537	0627	0647	|	0729	0751	0811	0835	0911	minutes	1935	2011	2046	2119**j**	2148**e**	2238	2320	2351	0031	...
34	Ludwigshafen Hbf ... **912 919** d.	0450	0455**e**	0545	0640	0659	0726	0742	0806	0820	0847	0921	past each	1948	2022	2057	2131	2201	2250	2331	0002	0042	0111
35	Ludwigshafen Mitte ... **919** d.	0453	0457	0548	0643	0702	0729	0745	0808	0823	0850	0923	hour until	1950	2025	2059	2133	2203	2254	2333	0006	...	0113
37	**Mannheim** Hbf ... **919** ⊡ a.	0456	0500	0552	0645	0705	0732	0748	0810	0826	0853	0926		1953	2027	2102	2136	2205	2258	2336	0009	...	0116
54	**Heidelberg** Hbf ... **919** ⊡ a.	0515	*0516*	0622	0704	0723	0753	0816	...	0844	0916	0945		2017	2046	2123	2154	2223	2322	2354	0037	...	0140

	Ⓐ	Ⓒ	Ⓒ	Ⓐ	Ⓐ	⑥	†	Ⓐ	⚒					▲									
Heidelberg Hbf ... **919** ⊡ d.	0506	0534	...	0602	...	0607	0607	*0643*	0712	0734	0743**t**	0813	0843	and at	1913	1943	2013	2033	2113	2144	2214	2244	2314
Mannheim Hbf ... **919** ⊡ d.	0526	0554	...	0622	0647	0648	0656	0705	0731	0756	0804	0831	0904	the same	1931	2004	2031	2056	2137	2206	2243	2309	2338
Ludwigshafen Mitte ... **919** d.	0528	0556	...	0625	0650	0651	0659	0707	0733	0758	0806	0833	0907	minutes	1933	2007	2033	2058	2139	2209	2246	2311	2340
Ludwigshafen Hbf ... **912 919** d.	0531	0600	0610	0637**e**	0654	0654	0702	0710	0736	0804	0810	0836	0910	past each	1936	2010	2038	2103	2142	2214	2248	2315	2343
Schifferstadt ... **912 919** d.	0545	0611	0623	0650	0706	0717**n**	0717	0725	0750	0814	0824	0847	0924	hour until	1947	2024	2047	2120**j**	2159	2234	2302	2326	2358
Speyer Hbf ... **912** d.	0555	...	0632	0700	0713	0726	0726	0733	0759	...	0832	0856	0932		1956	2032	2056	2129	2208	2243	2311	2336	0007
Germersheim ... **912** a.	0609	...	0645	0712	0722	0740	0740	0745	0812	...	0845	0909	0945		2009	2045	2109	2142	2221	2256	2323	2349	0020

D – ⚒ until Nov. 1; daily from Nov. 2.
E – † until Oct. 26.
N – From Neustadt (Weinstr) Hbf, d. 0504.
Y – To Neustadt (Weinstr) Hbf, arrives 23–25 minutes after Landau.

b – Not ⑥. Runs Nov. 1.
e – Arrives 9–12 minutes earlier.
f – Also June 8, 18, Oct. 2.
h – ⑥ (not Nov. 1).
j – Arrives 6–8 minutes earlier.
k – 0918 on †.

m – Change trains at Bad Kreuznach on Ⓐ (departs Bingen 1956).
n – Arrives 0704.
r – On Nov. 1 departs Bingen 1802, Bad Kreuznach 1822.
t – Ⓐ only.
z – Ⓒ only.

◇ – Operated by Vlexx.
▲ – Timings may vary by 1–2 minutes.
◐ – For Strasbourg connections see Table **396**.
⊡ – See also Tables **913**, **923** and **924**.

☛ **Note**: on June 19, Nov. 1 services in this table run as on ⑦.

918a WIESBADEN - MAINZ - DARMSTADT - ASCHAFFENBURG *Hessische Landesbahn*

km		⚒	Ⓐ	⚒		Ⓒ	Ⓐ							Ⓒ
0	**Wiesbaden** Hbf d.	...	0437	0536	0536	0637	0637	0736		2036	2136	2236	2336	...
10	**Mainz** Hbf d.	...	0449	0549	0549	0649	0649	0749	and	2049	2149	2249	2349	...
43	Darmstadt Hbf a.	...	0521	0621	0621	0720	0720	0821	hourly	2120	2221	2321	0021	...
43	Darmstadt Hbf d.	0530	0530	0630	...	0731	0735	0831	until	2131	2231	2331	...	0033
87	**Aschaffenburg** Hbf a.	0614	0614	0712	...	0812	0815	0912		2212	2312	0012	...	0114

	Ⓐ		Ⓐ		⚒	⚒	†						Ⓒ
Aschaffenburg Hbf d.	...	...	0443	...	0540	0643	...	0747		2147	2247	2347	...
Darmstadt Hbf a.	...	...	0527	...	0626	0730	...	0827	and	2227	2327	0027	...
Darmstadt Hbf d.	0438	0538	0538	0638	0638	0738	0740	0838	hourly	2238	2338	...	0038
Mainz Hbf d.	0512	0613	0613	0713	0713	0814	0813	0913	until	2313	0013	...	0113
Wiesbaden Hbf a.	0527	0625	0625	0727	0727	0827	0824	0927		2327	0027	...	0126

☛ Additional services run Wiesbaden - Darmstadt and v.v. on ⚒, Darmstadt - Aschaffenburg and v.v. on Ⓐ.

919 SAARBRÜCKEN - MANNHEIM - FRANKFURT and STUTTGART

Additional S-Bahn services run Kaiserslautern - Mannheim - Heidelberg and v.v.

km		Ⓒ	Ⓒ	Ⓐ	⚒	*EC* **217** Gy			Ⓐ		*ICE* **932** ⊖ E✗	†				*ICE* **563** M✗	Ⓐ	†				*TGV* **9551** R🍷			
	Trier Hbf **915** d.	...	...	...	...	...	...	...	0456	...	...	0533	...	0633	...	...	0733	0733	...	0833	...	...	...	1033	...
	Paris Est **30** d.	...	...	...	...	...	...	...	|	...	...	|	...	|	...	...	|	|	...	|	...	0906	...	|	...
0	**Saarbrücken** Hbf d.	...	...	0444	...	0536	...	0550	0608	...	0628	0647	*0700*	0747	*0801*	0827	0847	0847	*0902*	0947	*1002*	1058	*1102*	1147	*1202*
31	Homburg (Saar) Hbf d.	...	...	0505	0538	0557	...	0620	0632	...	0650	0709	*0727*	0809	*0828*	0849	0909	0909	*0928*	1009	*1028*	|	*1128*	1209	*1228*
67	**Kaiserslautern** Hbf a.	...	...	0527	0607	0618	...	0650	0653	...	0710	0729	*0755*	0829	*0855*	0909	0929	0936	*0954*	1029	*1054*	1135	*1154*	1229	*1254*
67	**Kaiserslautern** Hbf d.	0009	0511	0528	0611	0620	←	...	0654	0702	0714	0730	0758	0834	0858	0911	...	0937	0958	1034	1058	1137	1158	1234	1258
100	Neustadt (Weinstr) Hbf d.	0042j	0544	0551	0641	0647	0650	...	0717	0732	0740	0759	0830	0859	0930	0937	...	1000	1031j	1059	1130	|	1230j	1259	1330
117	Schifferstadt **918** d.	0057	0559	|	→	|	0707	...	|	0747	|	|	0845	|	0945	|	...	|	1045	|	1145	|	1245	|	1345
128	Ludwigshafen Hbf **918** d.	0111	0612	0609	...	0705	0719	...	0738	0800	|	|	0857	|	0957	|	...	|	1057	|	1158	|	1257	|	1357
129	Ludwigshafen Mitte **918** d.	0113	0614	|	...	|	0722	...	|	0803	|	0817	0900	0917	1000	|	...	1017	1100	1117	1200	|	1300	1319	1400
131	**Mannheim** Hbf **918** a.	0116	0617	0616	...	0709	0724	...	0743	0805	0800	0821	0903	0921	1003	0957	...	1021	1103	1121	1203	1216	1303	1321	1403
131	**Mannheim** Hbf . **910 918** ▽ d.	0121	0628	*0629*t	...	0711	0728	...	0748	0807	0802	*0830*	0907	*0930*	1007	1002	...	*1030*	1107	*1130*	1207	1218	1308	*1330*	1407
	Heidelberg Hbf . **910 918** a.	0140	0645	*0642*t	...	|	0744	...	0801	0823	|	*0844*	0923	*0945*	1023	|	...	*1045*	1123	*1144*	1223	|	1323	*1345*	1423
	Stuttgart Hbf **910** a.	...	...	...	...	0753r	...	...	...	...	|	...	...	...	...	1045	...	...	...	...	...	|	...	...	...
191	Darmstadt Hbf ▽ a.	...	...	...	...	...	...	...	...	...	0838	...	...	...	...	...	...	...	...	...	...	|	...	...	...
219▲	**Frankfurt** (Main) Hbf ▽ a.	...	...	...	...	...	...	...	...	...	0856	...	...	...	...	...	...	...	...	...	...	1259	...	...	...

			ICE **1034** B✗			*ICE* **9553** R✗								⑥ s	*ICE* **9555** Ⓑ R✗				Ⓑ	*ICE* **9557** ⊡ R✗			⑦	①–⑥	
Trier Hbf **915** d.	1133	...	...	1233	...	...	...	1433	...	1533	...	1633	...	1733	...	...	1833	...	1933	...	...	...	2033	2033	...
Paris Est **30** d.	|	...	...	|	...	1310	...	|	...	|	...	|	...	|	1710	...	|	...	|	1907e	...	...	|	|	...
Saarbrücken Hbf d.	1247	*1302*	1324	1347	*1402*	1500	*1504*	1547	*1601*	1647	*1702*	1747	*1802*	1847	1900	*1903*	1947	*2002*	2047	2059	...	2103	2147	2147	...
Homburg (Saar) Hbf d.	1309	*1328*	1350	1409	*1428*	|	*1528*	1609	*1628*	1709	*1728*	1809	*1828*	1909	|	*1928*	2009	*2028*	2109	|	...	2128	2209	2209	...
Kaiserslautern Hbf a.	1329	*1354*	1412	1429	*1454*	1535	*1554*	1629	*1654*	1729	*1754*	1829	*1854*	1929	1935	*1954*	2029	*2054*	2130	2135	...	2200	2229	2229	...
Kaiserslautern Hbf d.	1334	1358	1414	1434	1458	1537	1558	1634	1658	1734	1800	1834	1858	1934	1937	1958	2034	2058	...	2137	2145	...	2230	2230	2300
Neustadt (Weinstr) Hbf d.	1359	1430	1440	1459	1530j	|	1630	1659	1730	1759	1830	1859	1930	1959	|	2030	2059	2130	...	|	2214	...	2300	2302	2330
Schifferstadt **918** d.	|	1445	|	|	1545	|	1645	|	1745	|	1845	|	1945	|	|	2046	|	2148	...	|	2238k	...	2315	2316	2351
Ludwigshafen Hbf **918** d.	|	1457	|	|	1557	|	1657	|	1757	|	1858	|	1957	|	|	2057	|	2201	...	|	2250	...	|	|	0002
Ludwigshafen Mitte **918** d.	1417	1500	|	1517	1600	|	1700	1717	1800	1817	1900	1917	2000	2017	|	2059	2117	2203	...	|	2254	...	2327	2326	0006
Mannheim Hbf **918** a.	1421	1502	1500	1520	1602	1616	1703	1721	1803	1821	1903	1921	2003	2020	2016	2102	2121	2205	...	2216	2258	...	2330	2331	0009
Mannheim Hbf ...**910 918** ▽ d.	*1430*	1507	1502	*1530*	1607	1618	1707	*1730*	1807	*1830*	1907	*1930*	2007	*2030*	2018	2107	*2137*	2207	...	2218	2304	...	*2336*	*2336*	0021
Heidelberg Hbf ...**910 918** a.	*1443*	1523	|	*1546*	1623	|	1723	*1745*	1823	*1845*	1923	*1945*	2023	*2046*	|	2123	*2154*	2223	...	|	2322	...	*2354*	*2354*	0037
Stuttgart Hbf **910** a.	...	...	|	...	...	|	...	...	...	...	...	...	...	...	|	...	...	...	...	|	...	...	...	...	...
Darmstadt Hbf ▽ a.	...	...	1537	...	..	|	...	...	...	...	...	...	...	...	|	...	...	...	...	|	...	...	...	...	...
Frankfurt (Main) Hbf ▽ a.	...	...	1556	...	...	1659	...	...	...	...	...	...	...	...	2059	...	...	...	...	2259	...	...	...	...	...

	⚒	⚒	①–⑤	Ⓒ	Ⓐ	*ICE* **9558** F R✗	Ⓐ	⑥		⑥ s	*ICE* **9586** ⑥f R✗	Ⓑ n				*ICE* **9556** ①–⑤ R✗		⑥⑦				*ICE* **9554** ⑥⑦ R✗	Ⓐ		
Frankfurt (Main) Hbf ▽ d.	...	...	...	...	...	0556	...	...	...	...	0656	...	...	...	...	0856	...	...	...	...	...	1056	...	...	...
Darmstadt Hbf ▽ d.	...	...	...	...	...	|	...	...	...	...	|	...	...	...	...	|	...	...	...	...	...	|	...	...	...
Stuttgart Hbf **910** d.	...	...	...	...	...	|	...	...	...	...	|	...	...	...	...	|	...	...	...	...	...	|	...	...	...
Heidelberg Hbf ...**910 918** d.	...	0413	...	0534	0536t	|	*0602*t	...	0631x	*0643*	|	*0712*	0734	0817v	0834	|	...	*0913*	0933	*1013*	1033	|	*1113*	1133	*1213*
Mannheim Hbf ...**910 918** ▽ a.	...	0429	...	0553	0552t	0639	*0621*t	...	0650x	*0653*	0738	*0729*	0753	0836v	0851	0939	...	*0929*	0951	*1029*	1051	1139	*1130*	1151	*1229*
Mannheim Hbf **918** d.	...	0430	...	0554	0554	0640	0628	...	0656	0702	0740	0738	0756	0839	0856	0940	...	0939	0954	1036	1056	1140	1139	1156	1236
Ludwigshafen Mitte **918** d.	...	0433	...	0556	0557	|	0631	...	0659	0705	|	0741	0758	0842	0858	|	...	0942	0956	1040	1058	|	1142	1158	1240
Ludwigshafen Hbf **918** d.	...	0436	...	0600	0600	|	|	...	0702	|	|	0744	0804	|	0903	|	...	|	1002	|	1103	|	|	1202	|
Schifferstadt **918** d.	...	0448	...	0613	0611	|	|	...	0713	|	|	|	0815	|	0915	|	...	|	1015	|	1115	|	|	1215	|
Neustadt (Weinstr) Hbf d.	...	0506	...	0631	0631	|	0648	...	0731	0728	|	0800	0832	0900	0932	|	...	1000	1032	1100	1132	|	1200	1232	1300
Kaiserslautern Hbf a.	...	0533	...	0658	0658	0721	0716	...	0759	0753	0821	0824	0859	0924	0959	1021	...	1024	1059	1124	1159	1221	1224	1259	1324
Kaiserslautern Hbf d.	0425	0534	0621	...	...	0722	0731	0731	*0803*	0803	0822	0831	*0903*	0931	*1003*	1022	1031	1031	*1103*	1131	*1203*	1222	1231	*1303*	1331
Homburg (Saar) Hbf d.	0501	0606	0653	...	...	|	0752	0752	*0831*	0830	|	0852	*0930*	0952	*1030*	|	1052	1052	*1130*	1152	*1230*	|	1252	*1330*	1352
Saarbrücken Hbf a.	0535	...	0716	...	...	0759	0818	0816	*0857*	0856	0859	0915	*0956*	1015	*1056*	1059	1115	1115	*1156*	1215	*1256*	1259	1315	*1356*	1415
Paris Est **30** a.	...	...	|	...	...	0952	|	|	...	|	1052	|	...	|	...	1252	|	|	...	|	...	1452	|	...	|
Trier Hbf **915** a.	...	...	0827	...	...	...	0927	0927	...	1027	...	1027	...	1127	...	...	1227	1227	...	1327	...	...	1427	...	1527

	ICE **1035** B✗		*TGV* **9552** R🍷									*ICE* **562** M✗				*ICE* **9550** Ⓑ R✗	⑥ s		*EC* **216** Gy			*ICE* **935** ⊙ E✗			
Frankfurt (Main) Hbf ▽ d.	1202	...	1256	...	...	...	...	...	...	...	...	...	...	...	...	1856	...	...	...	...	...	2102	...	...	...
Darmstadt Hbf ▽ d.	1220	...	|	...	...	...	...	...	...	...	...	...	...	...	...	|	...	...	...	...	...	2120	...	...	...
Stuttgart Hbf **910** d.	|	...	|	...	...	...	...	...	...	...	...	1708	...	...	...	|	...	...	2004r	...	...	|	...	...	...
Heidelberg Hbf ...**910 918** d.	|	1233	|	1334	*1413*	1433	*1513*	1533	*1613*	1633	*1713*	|	1733	*1813*	1833	|	*1913*	1933	|	2033	2113	|	...	*2214*	2314
Mannheim Hbf ...**910 918** ▽ a.	1302	1251	1338	1350	*1429*	1451	*1529*	1549	*1629*	1649	*1729*	1746	1751	*1829*	1851	1939	*1929*	1950	2047	2051	2129	2155	...	*2230*	2330
Mannheim Hbf **918** d.	1304	1256	1342	1356	1439	1456	1539	1556	1636	1656	1735	1748	1756	1836	1856	1940	1939	1956	2049	2056	2137	2157	...	2239	2338
Ludwigshafen Mitte **918** d.	|	1258	|	1358	1442	1458	|	1558	|	1658	1739	|	1758	1840	1858	|	1942	1958	|	2058	2139	|	...	2242	2340
Ludwigshafen Hbf **918** d.	|	1303	|	1403	|	1503	1544	1603	1644	1703	|	|	1805	|	1903	|	|	2002	|	2103	2142	|	...	|	2343
Schifferstadt **918** d.	|	1315	|	1415	|	1515	|	1616	|	1715	|	|	1816	|	1915	|	|	2015	|	2115	2157	|	←	|	0002j
Neustadt (Weinstr) Hbf d.	1324	1332	|	1432	1500	1532	1600	1632	1700	1732	1800	1811	1832	1900	1932	|	2000	2032	2111	2132	2215	2219	2224	2302	0019
Kaiserslautern Hbf a.	1350	1359	1423	1459	1524	1559	1624	1659	1724	1759	1824	1833	1859	1924	1959	2021	2024	2100	2132	2159	→	2243	2252	2327	0047
Kaiserslautern Hbf d.	1352	*1403*	1424	*1503*	1531	*1603*	1631	*1703*	1731	*1803*	1830	1835	*1903*	1931	*2003*	2022	2031	*2105*	2134	*2205*	...	2245	2253	2329	...
Homburg (Saar) Hbf d.	1419	*1430*	|	*1530*	1552	*1631*	1652	*1730*	1752	*1830*	1850	1856	*1930*	1952	*2030*	|	2052	*2133*	2155	*2233*	...	2306	2322	2356	...
Saarbrücken Hbf a.	1440	*1456*	1459	*1558*	1615	*1659*	1715	*1758*	1815	*1856*	1912	1917	*1956*	2015	*2056*	2059	2115	*2159*	2216	*2259*	...	2329	...	0019	...
Paris Est **300** a.	...	...	1652	...	|	...	|	...	|	...	|	...	...	|	...	2252	|	...	...	...	...	...	...	...	...
Trier Hbf **915** a.	...	...	...	...	1727	...	1827	...	1927	...	2027	...	...	2127	...	...	2227	...	...	...	...	...	...	...	...

B – From/to Berlin (Table **902**).
E – From/to Berlin (Table **850**).
F – ①–⑤ (also July 5, 12 and ⑥ July 26 - Aug. 30).
G – DACHSTEIN – 🚌12 Graz - Salzburg - München - Saarbrücken and v.v.
M – From/to München (Table **910**).
R – Ⓡ for international journeys.

e – Departs 1903 on certain dates.

f – Not July 5, 12, July 26 - Aug. 30.
j – Arrives 5–7 minutes earlier.
k – Arrives 2229.
n – Also Nov. 1.
r – Not July 26 - Sept. 5.
s – Not Nov. 1.
t – Not June 19.
v – On Ⓒ Heidelberg d. *0813*, Mannheim a. *0829* (change trains at Mannheim).

x – On Ⓒ Heidelberg d. 0607, Mannheim a. 0625.
y – Not Sept. 13 - Oct. 17.

⊖ – Also calls at Bensheim (a. 0825).
⊙ – Also calls at Bensheim (d. 2132).
⊡ – On most ⑥ runs as *TGV* **9559** (🍷).
▽ – See also Table **910** (*ICE* trains) and Table **913** (local trains).
▲ – *209 km* for trains running non-stop Mannheim - Frankfurt.

FRANKFURT - NÜRNBERG - PASSAU (- WIEN) 920

See Table **921** for other regional trains.

km		NJ 491 [R] N	NJ 40491 [R] NL		IC 495 A	ICE 827 ①–⑥ ✕		ICE 521 ✕	ICE 21 ✕	ICE 523 ①–⑥ ✕	ICE 523 ⑦ ✕	ICE 1121 ①–⑤ P✕	ICE 525 R ✕	ICE 525 Q ✕	ICE 23 ✕		ICE 527 ✕	ICE 529 R ✕	ICE 529 Q ✕	ICE 1621 ✕	ICE 91 ✕	ICE 621 ✕	ICE 93 ✕	ICE 623 ✕
	Hamburg Hbf **800 900** d.	2010	2010	...	...	...	...	...	...	...	...	...	...	...	...	...	...	...	...	...	0802	...	0805**x**	...
	Berlin Hbf **850** d.	|	|	...	...	...	...	...	...	...	...	...	...	...	...	...	...	...	...	...	|	...	1004	...
	Dortmund Hbf **800** d.	|	|	...	...	...	...	...	...	0405**r**	...	...	0512	0523	...	...	0623**r**	0712	0723	0636	|	...	|	0915**v**
	Essen Hbf **800** d.	|	|	...	...	...	...	...	...	0430	...	...	0550	0553	...	...	0654	0750	0753	|	|	0849	|	0939
	Düsseldorf Hbf **800** d.	|	|	...	...	...	...	...	...	0457	...	0607	0621	0621	...	...	0721	0821	0821	|	|	0918	|	1007
	Köln Hbf **800** d.	|	|	...	...	0321	...	0420	...	|	...	|	|	|	...	...	|	|	|	0753	|	|	|	|
	Köln Messe/Deutz **800** d.	|	|	...	...	|	...	|	...	0520	...	0629	0644	0644	...	...	0744	0844	0844	|	|	0944	|	1033
	Bonn Hbf **800** d.	|	|	...	...	|	...	|	...	|	...	|	|	|	...	...	|	|	|	0815	|	|	|	|
	Koblenz Hbf **800** d.	|	|	...	...	|	...	|	...	|	...	|	|	|	...	...	|	|	|	0848	|	|	|	|
	Mainz Hbf **800** d.	|	|	...	...	|	...	|	...	|	...	|	|	|	...	...	|	|	|	0942	|	|	|	|
0	**Frankfurt** Flughafen ✈ § d.	|	|	...	...	0435	...	0528	...	0635	...	0719	0735	0735	...	...	0835	0935	0935	1001	|	1035	|	1135
11	**Frankfurt** (Main) Hbf d.	|	|	...	...	0454	...	0554	0619	0654	0654	|	0754	0754	0822	...	0854	0954	0954	1022	|	1054	|	1154
35	Hanau Hbf d.	|	|	...	...	0510	...	0611	0637	|	|	|	|	|	0838	...	|	|	|	1038	|	|	|	|
57	Aschaffenburg Hbf d.	|	|	...	...	0524	...	0624	0652	0723	0723	|	0823	0823	|	...	0923	1023	1023	|	|	1123	|	1223
136	**Würzburg** Hbf **900** d.	0148	0148	...	...	0603	...	0703	0734	0803	0803	|	0903	0903	0933	...	1003	1103	1103	1131	1133	1203	|	1312**k**
238	**Nürnberg** Hbf **900** a.	0315	0315	...	...	0658	...	0756	0827	0858	0858	0915	0956	0956	1027	...	1100	1156	1156	1224	1228	1258	1323	1404
238	**Nürnberg** Hbf d.	0408	0436	...	0600	0701	...	0759	0831	0903	0903	0917	0959	0959	1031	...	1103	1159	1159	1227	1231	1303	1332	1407
	Augsburg Hbf **905** a.	|	0624	...	|	|	...	|	|	|	|	|	|	|	|	...	|	|	|	|	|	|	|	|
	München Hbf **904** a.	|	0706	...	|	0806	...	0906	|	1006	1006	1020	1107	1107	|	...	1210	1305	1305	1343	|	1406	|	1512
335	**Regensburg** Hbf d.	0509	...	...	0711	...	...	...	0925	...	...	...	...	...	1125	...	...	...	...	...	1325	...	1425	...
375	Straubing d.	|	...	...	0735	...	...	...	|	...	...	...	...	...	|	...	...	...	...	...	|	...	1449	...
400	Plattling **944** d.	|	...	...	0753	...	...	...	0958	...	...	...	...	...	1159	...	...	...	...	...	1359	...	|	...
452	**Passau** Hbf ⊞ **944** a.	0613	...	...	0822	...	...	...	1023	...	...	...	...	...	1225	...	...	...	...	...	1425	...	1526	...
	Linz Hbf **950** a.	0743	...	...	0926	...	...	...	1126	...	...	...	...	...	1326	...	...	...	...	...	1526	...	1626	...
	Wien Hbf **950** a.	0917	...	...	1047	...	...	...	1247	...	...	...	...	...	1447	...	...	...	...	...	1647	...	1747	...

	ICE 27 R ✕	ICE 27 Q ✕	ICE 625 ✕	ICE 627 ✕	ICE 29 ✕	ICE 629 ✕	ICE 95 ✕		ICE 721 ✕	ICE 229 R ✕	ICE 229 Q ✕	ICE 723 ✕	ICE 1123 Ⓑ P ✕	ICE 725 ✕	ICE 927 ✕		ICE 727 ✕	ICE 729 ✕	ICE 929 R ✕	ICE 929 Q ✕	ICE 821 ✕		ICE 1021 ✕	
Hamburg Hbf **800 900** d.	...	...	...	...	...	...	1204**x**	...	...	...	...	...	...	...	1153	...	...	...	...	...	...	...	1610	...
Berlin Hbf **850** d.	...	...	...	...	...	...	1404	...	...	...	...	...	...	...	|	...	...	...	...	...	..	...	|	...
Dortmund Hbf **800** d.	0823	0835	1023**v**	1123**v**	...	...	|	...	...	1220	1235	...	...	...	|	...	...	...	1635	1636	...	...	|	...
Essen Hbf **800** d.	|	0900	1054	1153	...	1254**r**	|	...	1354	1300	|	1454	...	1554	1500	...	1654**r**	1754	|	1700	1839	...	1900	...
Düsseldorf Hbf **800** d.	0927	0927	1121	1221	...	1321	|	...	1421	1327	|	1521	1607	1621	1527	...	1721	1821	1727	1727	1907	...	1927	...
Köln Hbf **800** d.	0953	0953	|	|	...	|	|	...	|	1353	1353	|	|	|	1553	...	|	|	1753	1753	|	...	1953	...
Köln Messe/Deutz **800** d.	|	|	1144	1244	...	1344	|	...	1444	|	|	1544	1629	1644	|	...	1744	1844	|	|	1933	...	|	...
Bonn Hbf **800** d.	1015	1015	|	|	...	|	|	...	|	1415	1415	|	|	|	1615	...	|	|	1815	1815	|	...	2015	...
Koblenz Hbf **800** d.	1048	1048	|	|	...	|	|	...	|	1448	1448	|	|	|	1648	...	|	|	1848	1848	|	...	2048	...
Mainz Hbf **800** d.	1142	1142	|	|	...	|	|	...	|	1542	1542	|	|	|	1742	...	|	|	1942	1942	|	...	2144	...
Frankfurt Flughafen ✈ § d.	1201	1201	1235	1335	...	1435	|	...	1535	1601	1601	1635	1719	1735	1801	...	1835	1935	2001	2001	2035	...	2202	...
Frankfurt (Main) Hbf d.	1222	1222	1254	1354	1421	1454	|	...	1554	1621	1621	1654	|	1754	1821	...	1854	1954	2022	2022	2054	...	2222	...
Hanau Hbf d.	1238	1238	|	|	1438	|	|	...	|	1638	1638	|	|	|	1837	...	|	|	2037	2037	|	...	2238	...
Aschaffenburg Hbf d.	|	|	1323	1423	|	1523	|	...	1623	1652	1652	1723	|	1823	1852	...	1923	2023	2053	2053	2123	...	2253	...
Würzburg Hbf **900** d.	1334	1334	1403	1503	1533	1603	|	...	1703	1733	1733	1803	|	1903	1934	...	2003	2103	2134	2134	2203	...	2346	...
Nürnberg Hbf **900** a.	1427	1427	1500	1556	1628	1658	1724	...	1756	1827	1827	1859	1915	1956	2028	...	2100	2157	2228	2228	2300	...	0042	...
Nürnberg Hbf d.	1431	1431	1503	1559	1631	1703	1732	...	1759	1831	1831	1903	1917	1959	2031	...	2104	2206	2237	2237	2313	...	...	...
Augsburg Hbf **905** a.	|	|	|	|	|	|	|	...	|	|	|	|	|	|	|	...	|	|	|	|	|	...	...	...
München Hbf **904** a.	|	|	1607	1706	|	1807	|	...	1907	|	|	2006	2020	2107	|	...	2210	2318	|	|	0020	...	...	...
Regensburg Hbf d.	1525	1525	...	...	1725	...	1825	...	...	1925	1925	...	...	...	2133	...	...	...	2340	2340	...	...	...	...
Straubing d.	|	|	...	...	|	...	|	...	...	|	|	...	...	...	|	...	...	...	|	|	...	...	...	...
Plattling **944** d.	1559	1559	...	...	1759	...	1858	...	...	1959	1959	...	...	...	2209	...	...	...	0017	0017	...	...	...	...
Passau Hbf ⊞ **944** a.	1625	1625	...	...	1826	...	1923	...	...	2026	2026	...	...	...	2242	...	...	...	0050	0050	...	...	...	...
Linz Hbf **950** a.	1726	1726	...	...	1926	...	2026	...	...	2138	2138	...	...	...	...	...	...	...	...	...	...	...	...	...
Wien Hbf **950** a.	1847	1847	...	...	2047	...	2147	...	...	2305	2305	...	...	...	...	...	...	...	...	...	...	...	...	...

	ICE 1022 Q ✕	ICE 1022 R ✕	Ⓐ t◐	ICE 822 ①–⑥ ✕	ICE 1122 ①–⑤ P✕		Ⓒ z◐	Ⓐ t◐	ICE 820 ①–⑥ ✕	ICE 1020 ✕	ICE 728 ✕		ICE 726 ✕	ICE 928 ✕	ICE 724 ✕		ICE 94 ✕	ICE 722 ✕	ICE 228 ✕	ICE 720 ✕	ICE 628 ✕	ICE 28 Q ✕	ICE 28 R ✕	
Wien Hbf **950** d.	...	...	...	...	...	...	...	...	...	...	...	...	...	...	...	...	0613	...	0713	...	...	0913	0913	...
Linz Hbf **950** d.	...	...	...	...	...	...	...	...	...	...	...	...	...	...	...	...	0734	...	0834	...	...	1034	1034	...
Passau Hbf ⊞ **944** d.	...	...	...	...	...	...	...	...	...	0511	...	...	...	0717	...	...	0836	...	0934	...	...	1134	1134	...
Plattling **944** d.	...	...	...	...	...	...	0450	...	...	0543	...	...	...	0751	...	...	|	...	1004	...	...	1201	1201	...
Straubing d.	...	...	...	...	...	...	0505	0517	...	0557	...	...	...	0805	...	...	|	...	|	...	...	|	|	...
Regensburg Hbf d.	...	...	0430	...	...	...	0533	0546	...	0622	...	...	...	0827	...	...	0935	...	1035	...	...	1235	1235	...
München Hbf **904** d.	...	...	|	0447	0533	...	|	|	0553	|	0647	...	0746	|	0847	...	|	0950	|	1048	1150	|	|	...
Augsburg Hbf **905** d.	...	...	|	|	|	...	|	|	|	|	|	...	|	|	|	...	|	|	|	|	|	|	|	...
Nürnberg Hbf a.	...	...	0546	0557	0637	...	0647	0647	0655	0721	0753	...	0855	0926	0953	...	1030	1055	1127	1153	1255	1327	1327	...
Nürnberg Hbf **900** d.	0528	0528	...	0600	0639	...	...	...	0703	0730	0757	...	0858	0929	0957	...	1035	1058	1129	1157	1258	1329	1329	...
Würzburg Hbf **900** d.	0624	0624	...	0654	|	...	...	...	0755	0824	0854	...	0954	1024	1054	...	|	1154	1224	1256	1354	1424	1424	...
Aschaffenburg Hbf d.	0705	0705	...	0733	|	...	...	...	0833	|	0933	...	1033	|	1133	...	|	1233	|	1333	1433	|	|	...
Hanau Hbf d.	|	|	...	|	|	...	...	...	|	0915	|	...	|	1116	|	...	|	|	1316	|	|	1516	1516	...
Frankfurt (Main) Hbf a.	0736	0736	...	0804	|	...	...	...	0904	0936	1004	...	1104	1136	1204	...	|	1304	1336	1404	1504	1536	1536	...
Frankfurt Flughafen ✈ § a.	0755	0755	...	0820	0839	...	...	...	0920	0955	1020	...	1120	1155	1222	...	|	1320	...	1420	1520	1555	1555	...
Mainz Hbf **800** a.	0818	0818	...	|	|	...	...	...	|	1018	|	...	|	1218	|	...	|	|	...	|	|	1618	1618	...
Koblenz Hbf **800** a.	0911	0911	...	|	|	...	...	...	|	1111	|	...	|	1311	|	...	|	|	...	|	|	1711	1711	...
Bonn Hbf **800** a.	0943	0943	...	|	|	...	...	...	|	1143	|	...	|	1343	|	...	|	|	...	|	|	1743	1743	...
Köln Messe/Deutz **800** a.	|	|	...	0915	0936	...	...	...	1015	|	1114	...	1215	|	1314	...	|	1415	...	1514	1614	|	|	...
Köln Hbf **800** a.	1006	1006	...	|	|	...	...	...	|	1206	|	...	|	1406	|	...	|	|	...	|	|	1806	1806	...
Düsseldorf Hbf **800** a.	1032	1032	...	0936	1005	...	...	...	1038	1232	1136	...	1236	1432	1336	...	|	1436	...	1536	1638	1832	1832	...
Essen Hbf **800** a.	1058	1058	...	1002	...	...	...	...	1105	1258	1202	...	1302	1458	1402	...	|	1502	...	1602	1705	1858	1858	...
Dortmund Hbf **800** a.	1121	1137	...	...	...	...	...	...	...	|	...	...	...	|	...	...	|	...	...	...	...	1921	1933	...
Berlin Hbf **850** a.	...	...	...	...	...	...	...	...	...	|	...	...	...	|	...	...	1353	...	...	...	...	...	...	...
Hamburg Hbf **800 900** a.	...	...	...	...	...	...	...	...	...	1551	...	...	...	1751	...	...	1600**x**	...	...	...	...	...	...	...

A – From / to Rostock / Berlin via Jena (Tables **835**, **849a**, **850**).
L – To / from Innsbruck (Table **53**).
N – Conveys 🛏 1, 2 cl., 🛏 2 cl. (1, 4 berth) and 2 (*ÖBB nightjet* new generation). See Table **53** for through cars from / to Amsterdam.
P – From Aug. 9.
Q – Not Sept. 6 - Oct. 31.
R – Sept. 6 - Oct. 31.

e – 12 minutes later Sept. 6 - Oct. 31.
f – 13 – 19 minutes later Sept. 5 - Oct. 31.
g – Arrives 2333 Sept. 5 - Oct. 30.
k – Arrives 1305.
r – 3 – 7 minutes earlier Sept. 6 - Oct. 31.
t – Not June 19.
v – ⑦ (not Sept. 7 - Oct. 26).
x – Not Aug. 2 - Dec. 13.
z – Also June 19.

◐ – Regional service operated by *agilis*.
§ – Frankfurt Flughafen Fernbahnhof.

☛ See Table **53** for overnight service Brussels - Köln - München Ost - Wien and v.v.

920 (WIEN -) PASSAU - NÜRNBERG - FRANKFURT

See Table **921** for other regional trains

	ICE	ICE	ICE	ICE	ICE	ICE	ICE		ICE	ICE	ICE	ICE	ICE	ICE	ICE		ICE	ICE	ICE		IC	NJ	NJ	
	626	**92**	**624**	**26**	**622**	**620**	**90**		**1222**	**528**	**1120**	**526**	**22**	**524**	**522**		**20**	**520**	**520**		**494**	**40420**	**490**	
				Q							⑧ P							⑦	①–⑥			Ⓡ	Ⓡ	
	✗	✗	✗	✗	✗	✗	✗		✗	✗	✗	✗	✗	✗	✗		✗	✗	✗		A	N L	N	
Wien Hbf **950** d.	...	1013	...	1113	...	...	1313	...	...	...	...	...	1513	...	...	...	1713	...	...	...	1913	...	2010	...
Linz Hbf **950** d.	...	1134	...	1234	...	...	1434	...	...	...	...	...	1634	...	...	...	1834	...	...	...	2034	...	2134	...
Passau Hbf 🚌 **944** d.	...	1233	...	1337	...	...	1537	...	...	...	...	...	1737	...	...	...	1937	...	...	...	2147	...	2253	...
Plattling **944** d.	...	|	...	1404	...	...	1604	...	...	...	...	...	1804	...	...	...	2004	...	...	...	2217	...	|	...
Straubing d.	...	1312	...	|	...	...	|	...	...	...	...	...	|	...	...	...	|	...	...	...	2237	...	|	...
Regensburg Hbf d.	...	1333	...	1435	...	...	1635	...	...	...	...	...	1835	...	...	...	2035	...	...	...	2259	...	2357	...
München Hbf **904** d.	1247	|	1350	|	1447	1550	|	...	1618	1648	1733	1751	|	1847	1947	...	|	2045	2048	...	|	2252	|	...
Augsburg Hbf **905** d.	|	|	|	|	|	|	|	...	|	|	|	|	|	|	|	...	|	|	|	...	|	2325	|	...
Nürnberg Hbf a.	1353	1430	1455	1528	1554	1655	1729	...	1733	1754	1839	1856	1928	1955	2055	...	2128	2153	2157	...	2400	0053	0057	...
Nürnberg Hbf **900** d.	1357	1436	1458	1530	1557	1658	1731	...	1736	1757	1841	1903	1930	1958	2058	...	2130	2201	2201	...	...	0142	0142	...
Würzburg Hbf **900** d.	1454	|	1554	1624	1654	1754	1826	...	1831	1855	|	1954	2024	2054	2154	...	2224	2255	2255	...	...	0236	0236	...
Aschaffenburg Hbf d.	1533	|	1633	|	1733	1833	|	...	|	1933	|	2033	|	2133	2233	...	2305	2335	2335	...	...	|	|	...
Hanau Hbf d.	|	|	|	1716	|	|	|	...	1919	|	|	|	2116	|	2247	...	2320	|	|	...	...	|	|	...
Frankfurt (Main) Hbf a.	1604	|	1704	1736	1804	1904	|	...	1936	2004	|	2104	2136	2204	2304	...	2337	0004	0004	...	...	|	|	...
Frankfurt Flughafen ✈ § a.	1620	|	1720	1755	1820	1920	|	...	1955	2020	2042	2120	...	2220	2321	...	...	...	...	...	...	|	|	...
Mainz Hbf **800** a.	|	|	|	1818	|	|	|	...	2018	|	|	|	...	|	|	...	...	...	...	...	...	|	|	...
Koblenz Hbf **800** a.	|	|	|	1911	|	|	|	...	2111	|	|	|	...	|	|	...	...	...	...	...	...	|	|	...
Bonn Hbf **800** a.	|	|	|	1943	|	|	|	...	2143	|	|	|	...	|	|	...	...	...	...	...	...	|	|	...
Köln Messe/Deutz **800** a.	1714	|	1814	|	1915	2027	|	...	|	2114	2130	2214	...	2336	|	...	...	...	...	...	...	|	|	...
Köln Hbf **800** a.	|	|	|	2006	|	|	|	...	2206	|	|	|	...	|	0029	...	...	...	...	...	...	|	|	...
Düsseldorf Hbf **800** a.	1736	|	1836	2032	1936	2049	|	...	|	2136	2151	2236	...	2357	...	...	...	...	...	...	...	|	|	...
Essen Hbf **800** a.	1802	|	1902	2058	2002	2115	|	...	|	2202	...	2302	...	0023	...	...	...	...	...	...	...	|	|	...
Dortmund Hbf **800** a.	1840	|	1927**e**	2121**f**	2027**e**	2140**f**	|	...	2321	2227**f**	...	2327**g**	...	0048**e**	...	...	...	...	...	...	...	|	|	...
Berlin Hbf **850** a.	...	1752	...	...	...	...	|	...	...	...	...	...	...	...	...	...	...	...	...	...	...	|	|	...
Hamburg Hbf **800 900** a.	...	1951**x**	...	...	...	...	2155	...	...	...	...	...	...	...	...	...	...	...	...	...	...	0847	0847	...

← FOR NOTES, SEE PREVIOUS PAGE.

921 Regional trains FRANKFURT - WÜRZBURG - NÜRNBERG - REGENSBURG - PASSAU *RE* services

See Table **920** for faster *ICE* / *IC* trains

km			Ⓒ	Ⓐ										Ⓒ	Ⓐ		Ⓒ	Ⓐ							⑤⑥ **f**	
0	**Frankfurt** (Main) Hbf d.	...	*0450*k	0524	0634	0730	0834	0930	1034	1130	1234	1330	1434	1530	1534	1634	1730	1734	1834	1930	2034	2130	2230	2330	2330	0030
4	**Frankfurt** (Main) Süd d.	...	*0457*k	0530	0640	0736	0840	0936	1040	1135	1240	1336	1440	1535	1540	1640	1736	1740	1840	1935	2040	2136	2236	2336	2336	0036
10	Offenbach (Main) Hbf d.	...	|	0535	0645	|	0845	|	1045	|	1245	|	1445	|	1545	1645	|	1745	1846	|	2045	|	|	|	|	|
24	Hanau Hbf d.	...	*0521*k	0545	0658	0758	0858	0958	1058	1158	1258	1358	1458	1558	1558	1658	1758	1758	1859	1958	2058	2158	2259	2359	2359	0058
46	Aschaffenburg Hbf d.	0501	0612	0612**j**	0716	0816	0916	1016	1116	1216	1316	1416	1516	1616	1616	1716	1816	1816	1916	2016	2116	2218	2322	0022	0022	0122
84	Lohr Bahnhof d.	0530	0640	0640	0741	0841	0941	1041	1141	1241	1341	1441	1541	1641	1641	1741	1841	1841	1941	2041	2141	2247	2350	0051	0051	...
96	Gemünden (Main) d.	0542	0654	0654	0752	0852	0952	1052	1152	1252	1356	1452	1552	1652	1652	1752	1852	1852	1952	2053	2152	2300	0002	0101	0102	...
109	Karlstadt (Main) d.	0554	0703	0703	0801	0900	1000	1100	1200	1300	1404	1500	1600	1700	1700	1800	1900	1900	2000	2101	2200	2310	0010	...	0112	...
134	**Würzburg** Hbf a.	0616	0721	0721	0821	0921	1021	1121	1221	1321	1421	1521	1621	1721	1721	1821	1921	1921	2021	2121	2221	2333	0025	...	0128	...
	Bamberg **875** a.	...	0832	0832	...	1032	...	1232	...	1432	...	1632	...	1832	1832	...	2032	2032	...	2232	...	...	...	...	...	...

		Ⓒ **z**			Ⓐ	Ⓒ		Ⓐ	Ⓒ																	
Bamberg **875** d.	...	...	...	...	...	...	...	..	...	...	0725	...	0926	...	1126	...	1326	...	1526	...	1726	...	1926	...	...	...
Würzburg Hbf d.	0044	0044	...	...	0419	...	0515	0637	0637	0737	0837	0937	1037	1137	1237	1337	1437	1537	1637	1737	1837	1937	2037	2135	2236	2340
Karlstadt (Main) d.	0110	0110	...	...	0443	...	0538	0653	0653	0755	0855	0955	1055	1155	1255	1355	1454	1555	1655	1755	1855	1955	2055	2156	2258	0003
Gemünden (Main) d.	0120	0121	...	...	0453	...	0548	0703	0703	0805	0905	1005	1105	1205	1305	1405	1505	1605	1705	1805	1905	2005	2105	2207	2309	0013
Lohr Bahnhof d.	...	0132	...	...	0504	...	0559	0714	0714	0817	0915	1015	1115	1215	1315	1415	1515	1615	1715	1816	1915	2015	2115	2217	2319	0023
Aschaffenburg Hbf d.	...	0202	...	0428	0536	0536	0637**j**	0743	0743	0843	0943	1043	1143	1243	1343	1443	1543	1643	1743	1843	1943	2043	2143	2251	2351	0054
Hanau Hbf d.	...	...	...	0453	0600	0603	0702	0804	0802	0902	1003	1101	1203	1303	1403	1502	1603	1702	1803	1902	2003	2102	2209	2315	0015	...
Offenbach (Main) Hbf d.	...	...	...	|	0611	|	0712	0812	|	0912	|	1112	|	1312	|	1512	|	1712	|	1912	|	2112	|	|	|	...
Frankfurt (Main) Süd a.	...	...	...	0515	0615	0625	0716	0816	0824	0916	1025	1116	1225	1316	1425	1516	1625	1716	1825	1916	2025	2116	2231	2338	0040	...
Frankfurt (Main) Hbf a.	...	...	...	0524	0624	0632	0724	0826	0832	0924	1032	1124	1232	1324	1432	1524	1632	1724	1832**e**	1924	2032**p**	2124	2240	2344	0048	...

WÜRZBURG - NÜRNBERG

km		Ⓐ **t**	⚒ **t**	Ⓐ **t**						
0	**Würzburg** Hbf d.	0438	0536	0608	0636	0741	and hourly until	2041	2148	2304
23	Kitzingen d.	0456	0554	0623	0655	0801		2101	2208	2323
61	Neustadt (Aisch) Bf d.	0518	0616	0645	0718	0826		2126	2240**j**	2346
94	Fürth (Bay) Hbf d.	0547	0644	0714	0744	0847		2147	2309	0015
102	**Nürnberg** Hbf a.	0553	0652	0721	0752	0854		2154	2316	0024

	⚒ **t**									
Nürnberg Hbf d.	0428	0604	0703	0805	and hourly until	1904	2005	2105	2206	2335
Fürth (Bay) Hbf d.	0436	0611	0711	0811		1911	2011	2111	2212	2344
Neustadt (Aisch) Bf d.	0506	0634	0734	0834		1934	2034	2134	2234	0013
Kitzingen d.	0528	0657	0758	0857		1957	2057	2157	2256	0035
Würzburg Hbf a.	0548	0715	0817	0916		2016	2116	2219	2315	0054

NÜRNBERG - REGENSBURG - PLATTLING (- PASSAU) ◇ **Warning!** Ingolstadt - Regensburg – see note ❦

	Ⓐ **t**		Ⓐ **t**	Ⓒ **z**	Ⓒ **z**	Ⓐ **t**		¶			¶			¶		Ⓐ **t**	Ⓒ **z**	Ⓐ **t**	¶			Ⓐ **t**	Ⓒ **z** ¶			Ⓐ **t**
Nürnberg Hbf d.	...	...	0548	...	0611	0611	0711	...	0807	0911	...	1011	1111	...	1211	...	1311	1311	...	1411	1511	...	...	1611	1711	...
Neumarkt (Oberpf) d.	0447	0516	0609	...	0631	0631	0731	...	0831	0931	...	1031	1131	...	1231	1316	1331	1331	...	1431	1531	1610	...	1631	1731	1810
Ingolstadt Hbf **945** ❦ d.	|	|	|	0602	|	|	|	0805**n**	|	|	1005	|	|	1205	|	|	|	|	1405	|	|	|	1605	|	|	|
Regensburg Hbf a.	0539	0610	0655	0707	0716	0720	0810	0908	0913	1010	1108	1113	1210	1308	1313	1408	1410	1421	1508	1513	1610	1703	1708	1713	1810	1903
Regensburg Hbf d.	0541	0618	0655	0715	0720	0728	0812	0910	0919	1012	1110	1119	1212	1310	1319	1410	1412	...	1510	1519	1612	1710	1710	1719	1812	1910
München Flug ✈ ⊡ a.	|	|	|	|	0841	0853	|	|	1041	|	|	1241	|	|	1441	|	|	...	|	1641	|	|	|	1841	|	|
Straubing d.	0608	0645	0723	0743	...	...	0838	0938	...	1038	1138	...	1238	1338	...	1438	1438	...	1538	...	1638	1738	1738	...	1838	1938
Plattling **944** a.	0623	0700	0740	0756	...	...	0852	0952	...	1052	1152	...	1252	1352	...	1452	1452	...	1552	...	1652	1752	1752	...	1852	1952
Passau Hbf **944** a.	...	...	...	...	...	...	0929**c**	...	...	1129**c**	...	...	...	...	...	...	...	...	...	...	...	...	...	...	...	...

	Ⓒ **z** ¶			¶			¶	L		
Nürnberg Hbf d.	...	1812	1911	...	2011	2111	...	2211	2307	0011
Neumarkt (Oberpf) d.	...	1832	1931	...	2031	2131	...	2231	2331	0031
Ingolstadt Hbf **945** ❦ d.	1804	|	|	2005**n**	|	|	2205	|	|	|
Regensburg Hbf a.	1908	1913	2010	2108	2113	2210	2308	2317	0012	0116
Regensburg Hbf d.	1910	1919	2012	2110	2119	2212	2310	...	0014	...
München Flug ✈ ⊡ a.	|	2041	|	|	2241	|	|	...	|	...
Straubing d.	1938	...	2038	2138	...	2238	2338	...	0040	...
Plattling **944** a.	1952	...	2052	2152	...	2252	2352	...	0056	...
Passau Hbf **944** a.	...	...	...	...	...	...	...	...	...	...

	Ⓐ **t**	Ⓒ **z**	Ⓐ **t**	Ⓐ **t**		Ⓐ **t**	Ⓐ **t**	Ⓐ **t**	Ⓒ **z**	Ⓐ **t**	
Passau Hbf **944** d.	...	...	...	...	...	...	...	...	...	...	...
Plattling **944** d.	...	0450	...	0530	0558**z**	0606	0643	0704	0706	0734	...
Straubing d.	...	0505	0517	0545	0613**z**	0621	0658	0719	0721	0749	...
München Flug ✈ ⊡ d.	...	|	|	|	|	|	|	|	|	|	0708**b**
Regensburg Hbf a.	...	0532	0544	0612	0643**z**	0647	0724	0746	0746	0818	0832**b**
Regensburg Hbf d.	0430	0533	0546	0614	0645	0651	0726	0748	0748	0817	0845
Ingolstadt Hbf **945** ❦ a.	|	|	|	|	|	0755	|	|	|	|	|
Neumarkt (Oberpf) d.	0526	0625	0627	0720	0726	...	0820	0826	0826	0917	0926
Nürnberg Hbf a.	0546	0647	0647	...	0747	...	...	0847	0847	...	0947

	¶	¶		¶			¶			¶			¶	Ⓐ **t**		Ⓐ **t**		¶			¶					
Passau Hbf **944** d.	...	...	...	...	...	...	...	...	...	...	...	...	...	...	1631**c**	...	...	...	1831**c**	...	...	...	...	...	...	...
Plattling **944** d.	0808	0908	...	1008	1106	...	1208	1306	...	1408	1506	...	1608	1638	1706	1732	...	1808	1906	...	2008	2106	...	2208	...	2308
Straubing d.	0823	0922	...	1023	1122	...	1223	1322	...	1423	1522	...	1623	1653	1722	1747	...	1823	1922	...	2023	2122	...	2223	...	2323
München Flug ✈ ⊡ d.	|	|	0916	|	|	1116	|	|	1316	|	|	1516	|	|	|	|	1716	|	|	1916	|	|	2116	|	...	|
Regensburg Hbf a.	0850	0947	1041	1050	1146	1241	1250	1346	1441	1450	1546	1641	1650	1720	1746	1813	1840	1850	1946	2040	2050	2147	2241	2250	...	2350
Regensburg Hbf d.	0853	0948	1045	1053	1148	1245	1253	1348	1445	1453	1548	1645	1653	1722	1748	1822	1845	1853	1948	2045	2053	2149	2245	2253	2330	...
Ingolstadt Hbf **945** ❦ a.	0954	|	|	1154	|	|	1354	|	|	1554	|	|	1754	|	|	|	|	1954	|	|	2153	|	|	2353	|	...
Neumarkt (Oberpf) d.	...	1026	1126	...	1226	1326	...	1426	1526	...	1626	1726	...	1816	1826	1921	1926	...	2026	2126	...	2228	2326	...	0025	...
Nürnberg Hbf a.	...	1047	1147	...	1247	1347	...	1447	1549	...	1647	1749	...	...	1847	...	1947	...	2047	2147	...	2250	2347	...	0046	...

L – To Landshut (Table **878**).

b – 8–9 minutes later on Ⓒ **z**.
c – Ⓒ until Oct. 19.
e – 1840 on ⑤⑦ (also June 9, Oct. 2).
f – Also June 8, 18, Oct. 2.

j – Arrives 9 minutes earlier.
k – ⑥ only.
n – 1–2 minutes later on Ⓐ **t**.
p – 2040 on †.
t – Not June 19, Aug. 15.
z – Ⓒ (also June 19, Aug. 15).

¶ – To / from Ulm on Ⓒ **z** (Table **945**) except July 5 - Aug. 31.
◇ – Operated by *agilis* (except trains to / from München Flughafen). See Table **944** for connecting regional trains Plattling - Passau and v.v.
⊡ – München Flughafen Terminal ✈ (see also Table **892**).
❦ – Ingolstadt - Regensburg journeys are by 🚌 July 5 - Sept. 1 between Sinzing and Regensburg. Arrival in Regensburg is approx. 15 minutes later (no onward connection). Regensburg - Ingolstadt journeys depart approx. 23 minutes earlier.

WÜRZBURG - HEILBRONN - STUTTGART 922

Operators: Arverio Baden-Württemberg and SWEG Bahn

km		Ⓐ	Ⓐ	Ⓒ	Ⓐ	Ⓐ																				
0	**Würzburg** Hbf .... d.	...	...	...	0505	...	0630t	0736	0837	0936	1037	1137	1237	1337	1437	1537	1637	1737	1837	1937	2037	2137		...		...
43	Lauda .... d.	...	0458	0537	0550	0609	0708	0809	0909	1009	1109	1209	1309	1409	1509	1609	1709	1809	1909	2009	2109	2207		...		...
78	Osterburken .... d.	0500	0526	0605	0617	0631	0730	0831	0931	1031	1131	1231	1331	1431	1531	1631	1731	1831	1931	2031	2131	2229		0836		2036
94	Möckmühl .... d.	0516	0540	0621	...	0643	0743	0843	0943	1043	1144	1243	1343	1443	1543	1643	1743	1843	1943	2042	2142	2241	A	0851	and	2051
116	Bad Friedrichshall Hbf d.	0539	0558	0645	...	0702	0801	0901	1001	1101	1201	1301	1401	1501	1601	1701	1801	1901	2001	2101	2201	2301	L	0916		2116
127	**Heilbronn** Hbf .... ★d.	0557	0612	0657	...	0720	0814	0912	1012	1112	1212	1312	1412	1512	1612	1712	1812	1912	2012	2112	2212	2312	S	0930	hourly	2130
140	Lauffen (Neckar) .... ★d.	0607	|	0707	...	|	|	|	|	|	|	|	|	|	|	|	|	|	|	|	|	|	O	0940		2140
157	Bietigheim-Bissingen ★d.	0624	0632	0725	...	0740	0833	0932	1032	1132	1232	1332	1432	1532	1632	1732	1832	1932	2032	2132	2232	2332		0957	until	2157
180	**Stuttgart** Hbf .... ★a.	0642	0653r	0743	...	0758	0853r	0956r	1053r	1156r	1253r	1351r	1453r	1552r	1653r	1756r	1853r	1951r	2053r	2151r	2256r	2352		1015		2215

	Ⓐ	Ⓐ	Ⓒ																⚒	†	⚒	†				
Stuttgart Hbf.......... ★d.	0453	0546r	0602	0707r	0808	0908r	1012r	1108r	1211r	1306r	1408r	1506r	1611r	1711r	1809r	1909r	2008r	2043	2108r	2108r	2211r	2211r		0743		1943
Bietigheim-Bissingen ★d.	0512	0603	0622	0729	0829	0929	1029	1129	1229	1329	1429	1529	1629	1729	1829	1929	2029	2100	2129	2129	2229	2229		0800	and	2000
Lauffen (Neckar)...... ★d.	|	0617	0637	|	|	|	|	|	|	|	|	|	|	|	|	|	|	2116	|	2145	|	2245	A	0816		2016
Heilbronn Hbf........ ★d.	0530	0629	0648	0748	0848	0948	1048	1148	1248	1348	1448	1548	1648	1748	1848	1948	2048	2128	2148	2156	2246	2255	L	0828	hourly	2028
Bad Friedrichshall Hbf d.	0543	0642	0658	0758	0858	0958	1058	1157	1258	1358	1458	1558	1658	1758	1858	1958	2058	2141	2200	2208	2256	2305	S	0843		2043
Möckmühl .... d.	0601	0705	0715	0815	0915	1015	1115	1215	1314	1415	1515	1615	1715	1815	1915	2015	2115	2202	2217	2225	2315	2322	O	0905	until	2105
Osterburken............... d.	0614	0727	0727	0827	0927	1027	1127	1227	1327	1427	1527	1627	1727	1827	1927	2027	2127	2218	2228	2236	2327	2336		0921		2121
Lauda .... d.	0639	0750	0750	0850	0950	1050	1150	1250	1350	1450	1550	1650	1750	1850	1950	2050	2150	...	2250	2259	2356	0005		...		...
Würzburg Hbf........... a.	0721	0820	0820	0921	1020	1120	1221	1321	1420	1521	1619	1721	1821	1920	2020	2120	2221	...	2325‡	2329	...	...		...		...

	⑥⑦		⑥⑦		Ⓐ	Ⓐ	Ⓒ		Ⓐ	Ⓒ		Ⓐ	Ⓐ¶	¶	Ⓐ	¶					⚒	⚒		Ⓐ		Ⓐ
Heilbronn Hbf........... d.	0111	...	0311	...	0429	0452	0455	...	0533	0557	0630	0637	0653	0730	0757	0830	0857	and	1857	1957	2057	2157	2230	2257	2330	2357
Lauffen (Neckar)........ d.	0121	...	0321	...	0439	0502	0505	...	0542	0607	0640	0647	0703	0740	0807	0840	0907	hourly	1907	2007	2107	2207	2240	2307	2340	0007
Bietigheim-Bissingen.. d.	0138	...	0337	...	0457	0519	0522	...	0559	0624	0657	0703	0719	0757	0825	0857	0925	until	1925	2025	2125	2225	2257	2325	2357	0027
Stuttgart Hbf............ a.	0156	...	0355	...	0515	0539r	0540	...	0617	0642r	0715	0722	0742	0815	0842	0915	0942		1942	2044	2142	2244	2315	2342	0015	0044

			⑥⑦		⑥⑦	Ⓐ	Ⓐ	Ⓐ		Ⓐ	Ⓐ				¶	¶	¶			⚒	⚒		⚒	†	⚒	⚒
Stuttgart Hbf............ d.	0019	...	0210	...	0410	0443	0510	0612	0643	0719	0816	0919	and	1519	1619	1719	1819	1919	2016	2120	2219	2243	2306	2306	2319	2342
Bietigheim-Bissingen.. d.	0036	...	0227	...	0427	0501	0527	0630	0700	0737	0836	0936	hourly	1536	1636	1736	1836	1936	2036	2136	2236	2300	2329	2329	2336	0000
Lauffen (Neckar)......... d.	0051	...	0242	...	0442	0516	0542	0645	0716	0752	0851	0951	until	1551	1651	1751	1851	1951	2051	2151	2251	2316	|	2344	2351	0016
Heilbronn Hbf........... a.	0101	...	0252	...	0452	0526	0552	0655	0726	0801	0901	1001		1601	1701	1801	1901	2001	2101	2201	2301	2326	2347	2355	0001	0026

r – Not July 26 - Sept. 5. See also note △.

t – Ⓐ only.

‡ – ⑥ (⚒ to July 26 and from Sept. 8).

¶ – From/to stations in Table **924** on Ⓐ.

★ – See also panel below main table.

△ – S-Bahn connections Bietigheim-Bissingen - Stuttgart and v.v. July 26 - Sept. 5 (journey 27 – 28 minutes). From Bietigheim-Bissingen at 0537 ①–⑥, 0607, 0637 ①–⑥, 0707, 0737 and every 30 minutes until 2337. From Stuttgart Hbf at 0527, 0557 ①–⑥, 0627, 0657 ①–⑥, 0727, 0757 and every 30 minutes until 2357.

S-Bahn MANNHEIM - EBERBACH - OSTERBURKEN 923

On June 19 services run as on ⑦.

km		Ⓒ		Ⓐ		Ⓐ	Ⓒ	Ⓐ	Ⓐ		Ⓐ													
0	**Mannheim** Hbf ....**924** ▷ d.	0211	...	0418	0535	...	0628	0634	*0646*	0738	0807	0837	0907	0938	and at	1907	1938	2007	2038	2107	2137	2207	2304	0021
17	**Heidelberg** Hbf........**924** ▷ d.	0240	...	0442	0555	...	0655	0655	0727	0754	0825	0854	0925	0955		1925	1955	2026	2055	2127	2201	2235	2329	0038
28	Neckargemünd............. **924** d.	0255	...	0456	0609	...	0709	0709	0741	0809	0839	0909	0939	1009	the same	1939	2009	2040	2109	2141	2216	2249	2343	0053
34	Neckarsteinach ....d.	0301	...	0502	0616	...	0715	0715	0747	0815	0845	0915	0945	1015		1945	2015	2046	2115	2147	2222	2255	2349	0059
41	Hirschhorn (Neckar)............d.	0308	...	0509	0622	...	0722	0722	0754	0822	0852	0922	0952	1022	minutes	1952	2022	2053	2122	2154	2229	2302	2356	0106
50	Eberbach .... **924** d.	0315	...	0516	0629	...	0729	0729	0801	0829	0859	0929	0959	1029	past each	1959	2029	2100	2129	2201	2235	2309	0002	0113
69	Mosbach-Neckarelz...... **924** d.	0333	...	0535	0648	0712	0748	0748	0820	0848	0918	0948	1018	1048	hour until	2018	2048	2118	2148	2219	2255	2329	0021	0132
72	Mosbach (Baden) ....d.	0338	...	0540	0653	0717	0753	0753	0824	0853	0923	0953	1023	1053		2023	2053	2123	2153	...	2300	2333	0026	0137
101	**Osterburken** ....a.	...	...	0610	0723	0751	0823	0823	...	0923	...	1023	...	1123		...	2123	...	2223	...	2332	...	0056	...

	Ⓐ	Ⓒ	Ⓐ	Ⓐ	Ⓐ	Ⓒ	Ⓐ	Ⓐ	Ⓒ		Ⓐ	Ⓐ	⚒											
Osterburken .... d.	...	...	...	0508	0534	0536	0557	...	0636	...	0640	...	0702t	0733	...	0836		...	1836	...	1938	2038	2138	2238
Mosbach (Baden) .... d.	0432	0454	0508	0537	0603	0605	0628	...	0705	0705	0718	...	0731t	0802	0835	0905	and at	1835	1905	1935	2007	2107	2207	2307
Mosbach-Neckarelz ...... **924** d.	0437	0459	0521v	0546	0608	0610	0633	0638	0710	0710	0724	0728	0740	0810	0840	0910	the same	1840	1910	1940	2012	2112	2212	2312
Eberbach .... **924** d.	0456	0518	0541	0605	0627	0629	0647	0656	0729	0729	...	0742	0759	0829	0859	0929		1859	1929	1959	2031	2131	2231	2331
Hirschhorn (Neckar) .... d.	0503	0525	0548	0612	0634	0636	|	0703	0736	0736	...	|	0806	0836	0906	0936	minutes	1906	1936	2006	2038	2138	2238	2338
Neckarsteinach .... d.	0509	0532	0555	0618	0640	0642	0659	0711	0742	0742	...	|	0812	0842	0912	0942	past each	1912	1942	2012	2045	2144	2244	2344
Neckargemünd .... **924** d.	0516	0538	0601	0625	0647	0649	0704	0717	0749	0749	...	0758	0819	0849	0919	0949	hour until	1919	1949	2019	2051	2151	2251	2351
Heidelberg Hbf ....**924** ▷ a.	0530	0551	0614	0639	0701	0702	0716	0733	0802	0802	...	0810	0832	0902	0932	1002		1932	2002	2032	2105	2205	2305	0005
Mannheim Hbf ....**924** ▷ a.	0552	0609	0634	0700	0719	0720	*0746*	0753	0819	0819	...	0824	0851	0920	0951	1019		1950	2019	2051	2129	2230	2330	0030

t – Ⓐ only.

v – Arrives 0512.

▷ – See also Tables **913**, **918**, **919**.

MANNHEIM - HEIDELBERG - HEILBRONN 924

Additional S-Bahn trains run Heidelberg - Sinsheim and Mosbach-Neckarelz / Sinsheim - Heilbronn.
Mannheim - Heilbronn operated by SWEG Bahn. S-Bahn Heidelberg - Sinsheim operated by DB. S-Bahn Mosbach-Neckarelz / Sinsheim - Heilbronn operated by Albtal-Verkehrs-Gesellschaft.

km		Ⓒ 2	Ⓐ 2	Ⓐ	Ⓐ	Ⓒ 2	Ⓐ	Ⓒ	Ⓒ 2	Ⓐ 2	Ⓒ 2	Ⓐ	Ⓐ	2	2									
0	**Mannheim** Hbf..........**923** ▷ d.	...	...	...	...	...	0629	0634	*0707*	0719	...	...	0734	*0738*	...	0834	0935	1035	1135	1235	1335	1435	1535	1635
17	**Heidelberg** Hbf ....**923** ▷ d.	...	...	...	...	...	0645	0649	0731	0731	...	...	0749	0804	...	0849	0949	1049	1149	1249	1349	1449	1549	1649
28	Neckargemünd ....**923** d.	...	...	...	...	...	0655	0659	0745	0745	...	...	0800	0818	...	0859	0959	1059	1159	1259	1359	1459	1559	1659
50	Eberbach........................**923** d.	...	...	...	...	...	|	|	|	|	...	...	0815	|	...	|	1015	|	1215	|	1415	|	1615	|
69	Mosbach-Neckarelz ....**923** d.	...	...	0619	0652	0650	|	|	|	|	0750	0752	0829	|	0850	|	1029	|	1229	|	1429	|	1629	|
	Sinsheim (Elsenz) Hbf ....d.	0542	0540	|	|	|	0710	0714	0808	0808	|	|	|	0838	|	0914	|	1114	|	1314	|	1514	|	1714
	Bad Rappenau ....d.	0600	0603	|	|	|	0727	0727	...	...	|	|	|	...	|	0927	|	1127	|	1327	|	1527	|	1727
	Bad Wimpfen ....d.	0608	0612	|	|	|	0732	0732	...	...	|	|	|	...	|	0932	|	1132	|	1332	|	1532	|	1732
87	Bad Friedrichshall Hbf.... **922** d.	0614	0619	0637	0710	0708	0741	0738	...	...	0808	0811	0843	...	0908	0938	1042	1138	1242	1338	1442	1538	1642	1738
98	**Heilbronn** Hbf ....**922** a.	0643	0648	0649	0723	0737	0753	0749	...	...	0837	0822	0853	...	0937	0949	1051	1149	1251	1349	1451	1549	1651	1749
	Stuttgart Hbf **922** ....a.	...	...	0742	0815	...	...	...	...	...	...	0915	...	...	...	...	...	...	...	...	...	...	...	...

								2
Mannheim Hbf .... **923** ▷ d.	1734	1835	1935	2035	2143	2240	0010	*0021*
Heidelberg Hbf .... **923** ▷ d.	1749	1849	1949	2050	2157	2259	0024	0045
Neckargemünd .... **923** d.	1759	1859	1959	2100	2207	2309	0035	0059
Eberbach .... **923** d.	1815	|	2015	|	2224	|	0050	|
Mosbach-Neckarelz .... **923** d.	1829	|	2029	|	2238	|	0104	|
Sinsheim (Elsenz) Hbf ....d.	|	1914	|	2114	|	2325	|	0120
Bad Rappenau ....d.	|	1927	|	2127	|	2339	|	...
Bad Wimpfen ....d.	|	1932	|	2132	|	2344	|	...
Bad Friedrichshall Hbf..... **922** d.	1842	1938	2042	2138	2251	2350	0116	...
Heilbronn Hbf .... **922** a.	1851	1949	2051	2149	2300	2359	0125	...
Stuttgart Hbf **922** ....a.	...	...	...	...	...	...	...	...

km		Ⓐ 2		Ⓐ	Ⓒ 2	Ⓒ 2	Ⓒ 2	Ⓐ	Ⓐ	Ⓒ	2
	Stuttgart Hbf **922** ....d.	...	...	...	...	...	...	...	...	...	...
	Heilbronn Hbf .... **922** d.	...	0455	0542	0543	...	0618	0636	0700	0706	...
0	Bad Friedrichshall Hbf ..... **922** d.	...	0504	0553	0614	...	0648	0647	0710	0716	...
3	Bad Wimpfen ....d.	...	|	0556	0620	...	|	|	|	|	...
9	Bad Rappenau ....d.	...	|	0604	0628	...	|	|	|	|	...
26	Sinsheim (Elsenz) Hbf ....d.	0449	|	0620	0645	0649	|	|	|	|	0749
	Mosbach-Neckarelz .... **923** d.	|	0517	|	...	|	0707	0706	0728	0729	|
	Eberbach .... **923** d.	|	0531	|	...	|	...	...	0742	0742	|
47	Neckargemünd .... **923** d.	0510	0547	0637	...	0712	...	...	0758	0758	0812
58	**Heidelberg** Hbf .... **923** ▷ a.	0526	0558	0648	...	0728	...	...	0810	0809	0828
75	**Mannheim** Hbf .... **923** ▷ a.	*0552*	0615	0706	...	*0753*	...	...	0824	0824	*0851*

	2											Ⓐ		Ⓐ		Ⓐ				2	2	2	2	2
Stuttgart Hbf **922** ....d.	...	...	...	...	...	...	...	...	...	...	...	1619	...	1719	...	1819	...	...	...	...	...	...	...	...
Heilbronn Hbf .... **922** d.	0703	0806	0906	1006	1106	1206	1306	1406	1504	1607	1704	1709	1807	1812	1906	1912	2006	2106	2206	2218	2256	2318	2350	0018
Bad Friedrichshall Hbf ...... **922** d.	0737	0819	0916	1019	1116	1219	1316	1419	1516	1619	1716	1724	1819	1824	1916	1924	2019	2116	2219	2248	2326	2348	0019	0048
Bad Wimpfen ....d.	0742	0822	|	1022	|	1222	|	1422	|	1622	|	|	1822	|	|	|	2022	|	2223	|	2330	|	0023	|
Bad Rappenau ....d.	0749	0827	|	1027	|	1227	|	1427	|	1627	|	|	1827	|	|	|	2027	|	2230	|	2341	|	0031	|
Sinsheim (Elsenz) Hbf ....d.	0810	0843	|	1043	|	1243	|	1443	|	1643	|	|	1843	|	|	|	2043	|	2245	|	2359	|	0048	|
Mosbach-Neckarelz .... **923** d.	...	|	0929	|	1129	|	1329	|	1529	|	1729	1743	|	1843	1929	1943	|	2129	|	2307	...	0007	...	0107
Eberbach .... **923** d.	...	|	0942	|	1142	|	1342	|	1542	|	1742	...	|	...	1942	...	|	2142	|	...	...	...	...	...
Neckargemünd .... **923** d.	...	0858	0958	1058	1158	1258	1358	1458	1558	1658	1758	...	1858	...	1958	...	2058	2158	2259	...	...	...	...	...
Heidelberg Hbf .... **923** ▷ a.	...	0909	1009	1109	1209	1309	1409	1509	1609	1709	1809	...	1909	...	2009	...	2109	2209	2308	...	...	...	...	...
Mannheim Hbf .... **923** ▷ a.	...	0924	1024	1124	1224	1323	1424	1524	1624	1724	1824	...	1924	...	2024	...	2124	2224	2324	...	...	...	...	...

▷ – See also Tables **913**, **918** and **919**.

925 STUTTGART - CRAILSHEIM - NÜRNBERG

Via Aalen

km		◇ Ⓐ t	IC 2061 ①–⑥ 🍷	◇	◇ Ⓐ t	◇	IC 2065 🍷	◇	◇	◇	IC 2067 🍷	◇	◇	◇	IC 2069 🍷	◇	◇	◇	IC 2161 🍷	◇	◇	◇	IC 2163 🍷	◇	◇	◇
	Karlsruhe Hbf **931** .. d.	...	...	...	0602	...	0707	...	0806	...	0906	...	1006	...	1106	...	1206	...	1306	...	1406	...	1506	...	1605	...
0	**Stuttgart** Hbf .... ‡ d.	0447	0605	0618	0708	0720	0808	0820	0908	0920	1009	1020	1108	1118	1209	1220	1308	1321	1409	1420	1508	1520	1609	1620	1708	1720
51	Schwäbisch Gmünd ‡ d.	0532	0642	0702	0741	0802	0842	0902	0941	1002	1041	1102	1141	1202	1241	1302	1341	1402	1441	1502	1541	1602	1641	1702	1741	1802
76	**Aalen** Hbf .... ‡ a.	0549	0657	0720	0756	0820	0858	0920	0956	1020	1057	1120	1156	1220	1257	1320	1356	1420	1457	1520	1556	1620	1657	1720	1756	1820
76	**Aalen** Hbf .... d.	0601	0659	0728	...	0828	0859	0928	...	1028	1058	1128	...	1228	1258	1328	...	1428	1458	1528	...	1628	1658	1728	...	1828
92	Ellwangen .... d.	0618	0710	0748	...	0845	0910	0948	...	1045	1109	1148	...	1245	1309	1348	...	1445	1509	1548	...	1645	1709	1748	...	1845
113	Crailsheim................ d.	...	0726	0812	...	...	0926	1012	...	...	1126	1212	...	...	1326	1412	...	...	1525	1612	...	...	1726	1812	...	...
159	Ansbach.................... d.	...	0750	...	...	...	0950	...	...	...	1150	...	...	...	1350	...	...	...	1550	...	...	...	1750	...	...	...
203	**Nürnberg** Hbf.......... a.	...	0818	...	...	...	1018	...	...	...	1218	...	...	...	1417	...	...	...	1616	...	...	...	1818	...	...	...
	Leipzig Hbf **849a** ... a.	...	...	...	...	...	1409	...	...	...	1609	...	...	...	...	...	...	...	2009	...	...	...	2209	...	...	...

	IC 2165 🍷	◇	◇	◇ ⊕	IC 2167 🍷	◇	◇	◇	◇	◇	◇
Karlsruhe Hbf **931** .. d.	1706	...	1806	...	1906	...	2006	...	...	2132	...
Stuttgart Hbf..........‡ d.	1809	1820	1908	1918	2009	2020	2108	2120	2220	2236	2320
Schwäbisch Gmünd .‡ d.	1841	1902	1941	2002	2041	2102	2141	2202	2302	2311	0002
Aalen Hbf...............‡ a.	1857	1920	1956	2022	2057	2120	2156	2220	2320	2326	0020
Aalen Hbf................. d.	1858	1928	...	2028	2058	2128	...	2228	2335	...	...
Ellwangen................. d.	1909	1948	...	2045	2109	2148	...	2245	2352	...	...
Crailsheim .... d.	1925	2012	...	...	2125	2212	...	...	0009	...	...
Ansbach .... d.	1950	...	...	...	2150	...	...	...	...	...	...
Nürnberg Hbf........... a.	2018	...	...	...	2218	...	...	...	...	...	...
Leipzig Hbf **849a** .... a.	...	...	...	...	...	...	...	...	...	...	...

	◇	Ⓐ t	IC 2168 Ⓐ t 🍷	◇	◇	◇	IC 2166 🍷	◇	◇	◇
Leipzig Hbf **849a** .... d.	...	...	...	...	...	...	...	...	...	...
Nürnberg Hbf................. d.	...	...	0538	...	...	...	0738	...	...	...
Ansbach .... d.	...	...	0603	...	...	...	0807	...	...	...
Crailsheim....................... d.	...	*0509*	0631	0648	...	*0752*	0835	...	...	0952
Ellwangen .... d.	...	*0527*	0647	0711	...	*0811*	0850	0911	...	1011
Aalen Hbf........................ a.	...	*0544*	0658	0728	...	*0828*	0900	0928	...	1028
Aalen Hbf................... ‡ d.	0535	0600	0700	0735	0802	0837	0902	0937	1002	1037
Schwäbisch Gmünd ...... ‡ d.	0554	0615	0718	0754	0817	0856	0918	0956	1017	1056
Stuttgart Hbf .... ‡ a.	0639	0650	0753	0841	0850	0939	0953	1039	1050	1139
Karlsruhe Hbf **931**......... a.	...	0752	0853	...	0952	...	1053	...	1152	...

	IC 2164 🍷	◇	◇	◇	IC 2162 🍷	◇	◇	◇	IC 2160 🍷	◇	◇	◇	IC 2068 🍷	◇		◇	IC 2066 🍷	◇	◇	◇	IC 2064 🍷	◇	◇	◇	IC 2166 ⑤ f	◇ a
Leipzig Hbf **849a** .... d.	...	...	...	...	0749	...	...	...	0949	...	...	...	...	...	...	...	1349	...	...	...	1549	...	...	...	...	...
Nürnberg Hbf........... d.	0942	...	...	...	1142	...	...	...	1341	...	...	...	1542	...	...	...	1741	...	...	...	1942	...	...	...	2107	...
Ansbach .... d.	1007	...	...	...	1207	...	...	...	1407	...	...	...	1607	...	...	...	1807	...	...	...	2007	...	...	...	2132	...
Crailsheim .... d.	1035	...	...	1152	1235	...	...	1352	1435	...	...	1552	1635	...	...	1752	1835	...	...	1952	2035	...	...	2152	2158	...
Ellwangen................. d.	1050	1111	...	1211	1250	1311	...	1411	1450	1511	...	1611	1650	1711	...	1811	1850	1911	...	2011	2050	2113	...	2211	2221	2311
Aalen Hbf................. a.	1100	1128	...	1230	1300	1328	...	1428	1500	1528	...	1628	1700	1728	...	1828	1900	1928	...	2028	2100	2130	...	2228	2231	2329
Aalen Hbf..............‡ d.	1102	1137	1202	1237	1302	1337	1402	1437	1502	1537	1602	1637	1702	1737	1802	1837	1902	1937	2002	2037	2102	2137	2202	2237	2233	2337
Schwäbisch Gmünd .‡ d.	1118	1156	1217	1256	1318	1356	1417	1456	1518	1556	1617	1656	1718	1756	1817	1856	1918	1956	2017	2056	2118	2156	2217	2256	2249	2356
Stuttgart Hbf..........‡ a.	1153	1239	1250	1339	1352	1439	1450	1539	1552	1639	1650	1739	1753	1839	1850	1939	1953	2039	2050	2139	2153	2239	2250	2339	2327	0039
Karlsruhe Hbf **931** .. a.	1253	...	1352	...	1453	...	1552	...	1652	...	1752	...	1853	...	1952	...	2053	...	2152	...	2300	...	0011	...	...	...

Via Schwäbisch Hall-Hessental

km				◇	◇	Ⓐ t ◇	◇		◇		◇		◇		◇		◇				◇		◇	◇		◇
0	**Stuttgart** Hbf .... d.	0034	...	0423	0513	0555	0653	0752	0857	0955	1057	1155	1300	1356	1456	1555**c**	1657	1726**c**	1755	1826	1854	1953	2057	2153	2255	2327
31	Backnang.................. d.	0058	...	0451	0541	0622	0724	0821**v**	0924	1021	1124	1221	1324	1421	1524	1621	1724	1754	1821	1854	1924	2024	2124	2224	2323	2351
73	Schwäbisch H-H ⊡ ... a.	0131	...	0536	0623	0658	0758	0856	0958	1054	1158	1254	1358	1454	1558	1654	1758	1835	1854	1935	1958	2055	2158	2258	2357	0029
73	Schwäbisch H-H ⊡ ... d.	0133**t**	...	0537	0624	0658	0800	*0900*	0959	*1100*	1200	*1300*	1400	*1501*	1600	*1700*	1759	1836	*1900*	1936**t**	2000	*2100*	2200	*2301*	2358	0030
100	Crailsheim................ d.	0150**t**	...	0610**h**	0641	0715	0820	*0920*	1020	*1120*	1220	*1320*	1420	*1521*	1620	*1720*	1820	1852	*1920*	1953**t**	2020	*2120*	2220	*2321*	0016	0047
146	Ansbach.................... d.	...	...	0641	...	...	0850	...	1050	...	1250	...	1450	...	1650	...	1850	...	...	...	2050	...	2250	...	...	...
190	**Nürnberg** Hbf........... a.	...	...	0717	...	...	0920	...	1121	...	1320	...	1520	...	1720	...	1921	...	...	...	2120	...	2320	...	...	...

	Ⓐ t ◇	◇	Ⓐ t	Ⓐ t	◇	Ⓐ t	◇	Ⓒ z		Ⓒ z	◇		◇		◇		◇		◇	Ⓐ t		◇		◇	◇	◇
Nürnberg Hbf............ d.	...	...	...	...	...	...	0637	...	...	...	0837	...	1038	...	1234	...	1438	...	1638	...	...	1838	...	2036	...	2238
Ansbach .... d.	...	...	...	...	...	...	0705	...	...	...	0907	...	1107	...	1310	...	1507	...	1707	...	...	1907	...	2107	...	2307
Crailsheim .... d.	0411	0456	0540	0605	0635	...	0742**k**	...	*0838*	...	0942	*1038*	1142	*1238*	1342	*1438*	1542	*1638*	1742	...	*1838*	1942	*2038*	2142	*2240*	2342
Schwäbisch H-H ⊡ .... a.	0428	0512	0556	0621	0652	...	0758	...	*0859*	...	0958	*1059*	1158	*1259*	1359	*1459*	1558	*1659*	1758	...	*1859*	1958	*2059*	2159	*2259*	2358
Schwäbisch H-H ⊡ .... d.	0431	0519	0559	0624	0659	0725	0800	0823	0903	0923	1000	1103	1200	1303	1400	1503	1600	1703	1800	1815	1903	1959	2103	2200	2312	0000
Backnang .... d.	0504	0605	0637	0706	0737	0807	0838	0907	0937	1007	1038	1137	1238	1337	1437	1537	1638	1737	1838	1907	1937	2038	2137	2237	2353	0039
Stuttgart Hbf............ a.	0531	0630	0701	0732	0804	0835	0905	0932	1002	1032**c**	1105	1202	1306	1402	1505	1602	1702	1802	1905	1932	2002	2106	2202	2303	0023	0109

a – Change trains at Aalen on ✝ (also June 19, Nov. 1).
c – Not July 26 - Sept. 5.
f – Also Oct. 2; not Oct. 3.
h – Arrives 0555.
k – Arrives 0735.
r – Not June 19, Nov. 1.
t – Ⓐ (not June 19).
v – 0824 on Ⓐ (not June 19).
z – Also June 19.

⊕ – Change trains at Aalen on Ⓐ (not June 19).
⊡ – Schwäbisch Hall-Hessental.
◇ – Operated by Arverio Baden-Württemberg.
‡ – Other regional services (◇) Stuttgart - Schwäbisch Gmünd - Aalen and v.v. (journey 60–66 minutes). **From Stuttgart** Hbf at 0020, 0120 Ⓒ **z**, 0320 Ⓒ **z**, 0519 Ⓐ **t**, 0549 Ⓐ **t**, 0647 Ⓐ **t**, 0747 Ⓐ **t**, 0847 Ⓐ **t**, 0947, 1047, 1147, 1247, 1347, 1446, 1547, 1647, 1747, 1846, 1947, 2047 ⚒ **r**, 2147 ⚒ **r**, 2247 ⚒ **r** and 2347 ⚒ **r**. **From Aalen** at 0037, 0237 Ⓒ **z**, 0435 Ⓐ **t**, 0505 Ⓐ **t**, 0605 Ⓐ **t**, 0635, 0705 Ⓐ **t**, 0806 Ⓐ **t**, 0907, 1007 and hourly until 1907; then 2007 ⚒ **r**, 2107 ⚒ **r**, 2207 ⚒ **r** and 2307 ⚒ **r**.

926 AALEN - ULM and HEILBRONN / ASCHAFFENBURG - CRAILSHEIM

RE / *RB* services

AALEN - ULM ⊖

km		Ⓐ t	Ⓒ z 2	Ⓐ t	2	2		2	2		2	2		2	2		2	2		2	2		2	2		2	2
0	**Aalen** Hbf....... d.	0553	0630	0703	0734	0834	0907	0934	1034	1107	1134	1234	1307	1334	1434	1507	1534	1634	1706	1734	1834	1907	1934	2034	2107	2134	2236
23	Heidenheim..... d.	0612	0654	0726	0800	0900	0924	1000	1100	1124	1200	1300	1324	1400	1500	1524	1600	1700	1724	1800	1900	1924	2000	2100	2124	2200	2300
73	**Ulm** Hbf.......... a.	0658	0742	0758	0847	0947	0956	1047	1147	1156	1247	1347	1356	1447	1547	1556	1647	1747	1756	1847	1947	1956	2047	2147	2156	2254	2354

	Ⓐ t	Ⓐ t	2	Ⓐ t 2	Ⓒ z 2		2	2		2	2		2	2		2	2		2	2		2	2		2	2	2
Ulm Hbf............d.	0425	0538	0555**c**	0644	0705	0804	0811	0911	1002	1011	1111	1202	1211	1311	1402	1411	1511	1602	1611	1711	1802	1811	1911	2002	2011	2111	2211
Heidenheim ......d.	0516	0626	0658	0800	0800	0834	0900	1000	1034	1100	1200	1234	1300	1400	1434	1500	1600	1634	1700	1800	1834	1900	2000	2034	2100	2200	2300
Aalen Hbf.........a.	0545	0652	0724	0824	0824	0852	0924	1024	1052	1124	1224	1252	1324	1424	1452	1524	1624	1652	1724	1824	1852	1924	2024	2052	2124	2224	2324

ASCHAFFENBURG - LAUDA - CRAILSHEIM ⊠

2nd class only

km		Ⓒ z	Ⓐ t	Ⓐ t							
0	**Aschaffenburg** Hbf .. d.	...	...	0541	0719**k**	0926	1126	1326	1526	1726	1926
38	Miltenberg................ d.	...	0551	0653**f**	0753**k**	1000	1200	1400	1600	1800	2000**j**
69	Wertheim .... d.	0626	0640**n**	0734	0834	1034	1234	1434	1634	1834	2034**j**
93	Tauberbischofsheim .. d.	0652	0705	0800	0900	1100	1300	1500	1700	1900	2104
100	**Lauda**...................... a.	0700	0712	0806	0906	1106	1306	1506	1706	1906	2112
100	**Lauda**...................... d.	0714	0716	0814	0914	1114	1314	1514	1714	1914	2116
110	Bad Mergentheim...... d.	0726**e**	0727	0831	0931**r**	1131**r**	1331**r**	1531**r**	1731**r**	1931**r**	2137**n**
169	**Crailsheim** .... a.	0826	0826	0926	1026	1226	1426	1626	1826	2026	2238

	Ⓐ t	Ⓒ z	Ⓐ t						Ⓒ z	Ⓐ t	
Crailsheim .... d.	...	...	0626	0731	0933	1133	1333	1533	1733	1733	1933
Bad Mergentheim... d.	0545	0629	0735**n**	0832	1032	1232	1432	1632	1832	1832	2036
Lauda.................... a.	0555	0639	0746	0842	1042	1242	1442	1642	1842	1842	2046
Lauda.................... d.	0600	0640	0752	0852	1052	1252	1452	1652	1852	1852	2052
Tauberbischofsheim d.	0610	0700**n**	0800	0900	1100	1300	1500	1700	1900	1900	2106**v**
Wertheim .... d.	0700**b**	0726	0827	0926	1126	1326	1526	1726	1926	1935**n**	2135
Miltenberg............. d.	0740**v**	0800	0900	1000	1200	1359	1600	1800	2000	2017**n**	2215**v**
Aschaffenburg Hbf. a.	0835	0835	0935	1032	1232	1435	1632	1832	2032	2104	2259

b – Arrives 0637.
c – 0606 on Ⓒ (also June 19).
e – 0731 on ⑥ (not Nov. 1).
f – Arrives 0635.
j – On Ⓐ (not June 19) Miltenberg a. 1958, d. 2008, Wertheim d. 2041.
k – On Ⓒ (also June 19) Aschaffenburg d. 0718, Miltenberg d. 0800.

n – Arrives 10–12 minutes earlier.
r – 5 minutes **earlier** on ✝ (also June 19).
t – Not June 19.
v – Arrives 6–8 minutes earlier.
z – Also June 19.

⊖ – Operated by Südwestdeutsche Landesverkehrs (trains shown as 2nd class only) or DB.
⊠ – Service from June 14.

☛ For Heilbronn - Crailsheim, see next page.

RE / *RB* services — AALEN - ULM and HEILBRONN / ASCHAFFENBURG - CRAILSHEIM — 926

HEILBRONN - CRAILSHEIM

2nd class only

km																							
		Ⓒz		Ⓐt	Ⓒz	Ⓐt				Ⓐt								⚒r					w
0	**Heilbronn** Hbf d.	0006	...	0513	0600	0702	0806	0906	1006	1106	1206	1306	1406	1506	1606	1706	1806	1906	2006	2106	2206	2306	2306
27	Öhringen d.	0028	...	0535	0623	0726	0828	0926	1028	1126	1228	1326	1428	1526	1628	1726	1828	1926	2028	2126	2228	2326	2326
54	Schwäbisch Hall d.	0051	...	0557	0646	0749	0851	0949	1051	1149	1251	1349	1451	1549	1651	1749	1851	1949	2051	2149	2251	2349	2349
61	Schwäbisch Hall-Hessental 925 a.	0058	...	0603	0653	0756	0858	0956	1058	1156	1258	1356	1458	1556	1658	1756	1858	1956	2058	2156	2258	2356	2356
88	**Crailsheim** 925 a.	0120	...	*0641*	...	*0817*	0920	*1017*	1120	*1217*	1320	*1417*	1521	*1617*	1720	*1817*	1920	*2017*	2120	*2217*	2321	...	0022

		Ⓒz		Ⓐt		Ⓐt	Ⓒz			Ⓐt								⚒r				
Crailsheim 925 d.	2342	...	...	0520	...	*0635*	*0635*	*0742*	0838	*0942*	1038	*1142*	1238	*1342*	1438	*1542*	1638	*1742*	1838	*1942*	2038	*2142*	2240
Schwäbisch Hall-Hessental 925 d.	2358	0001	...	0540	...	0655	0701	0803	0901	1003	1101	1203	1301	1403	1501	1603	1701	1803	1901	2003	2101	2203	2302
Schwäbisch Hall d.	...	0007	...	0546	...	0701	0707	0809	0907	1009	1107	1209	1307	1409	1507	1609	1707	1809	1907	2009	2107	2209	2308
Öhringen d.	...	0029	...	0610	...	0731	0731	0832	0931	1032	1131	1232	1331	1432	1531	1632	1731	1832	1931	2032	2131	2232	2332
Heilbronn Hbf a.	...	0052	...	0635	...	0752	0752	0852	0952	1052	1152	1252	1352	1452	1552	1652	1752	1852	1952	2052	2152	2252	2353

t – Not June 19. **r** – Not June 19, Nov. 1. **w** – ⑦–④ (not June 18, Oct. 2). **z** – Also June 19.

FLIXTRAIN service summary — 927

Special fares (**DB tickets not valid**). Engineering work may affect timings; **subject to alteration on and around public holidays** (please check when booking). Website: www.flixtrain.de

Route *FLX* 10	**1355**		**1240**		**1242**		**1244**	**1244**		**1248**	
	F				⑤–①		②–④	⑤–①		④–①	
Stuttgart Hbf d.	...	...	0717	...	...	...	...	1115	...	1516	...
Basel Bad Bf d.	...	...	|	...	0709	...	0927	|	...	|	...
Freiburg (Brsg) Hbf d.	...	...	|	...	0758	...	1000	|	...	|	...
Offenburg d.	...	...	|	...	0831	...	1036	|	...	|	...
Baden Baden d.	...	...	|	...	0856	...	1103	|	...	|	...
Karlsruhe Hbf d.	...	...	|	...	0930	...	1123	|	...	|	...
Mannheim Hbf d.	...	...	|	...	1012	...	|	|	...	|	...
Heidelberg Hbf d.	...	...	0807	...	|	...	1206	1206	...	1607	...
Weinheim (Bergstr) d.	...	...	|	...	|	...	|	|	...	1621	...
Darmstadt Hbf d.	...	...	0853	...	|	...	1253	1253	...	1652	...
Mainz Hbf d.	0543	...	|	...	|	...	|	|	...	|	...
Frankfurt (M) Flug ✈¶ d.	0601	...	|	...	|	...	|	|	...	|	...
Frankfurt (Main) Süd a.	0616•	...	0909	...	1107	...	1308	1308	...	1708	...
Frankfurt (Main) Süd d.	0618•	...	0912	...	1112	...	1312	1312	...	1712	...
Hanau Hbf d.	|	...	|	...	|	...	|	|	...	|	...
Fulda d.	|	...	1008	...	1208	...	1407	1407	...	1808	...
Bad Hersfeld d.	|	...	|	...	|	...	1432	1432	...	|	...
Eisenach d.	⊡	...	|	...	|	...	|	|	...	1858	...
Gotha d.	|	...	1107	...	|	...	|	|	...	|	...
Erfurt Hbf d.	|	...	1122	...	1321	...	1522	1522	...	1923	...
Halle (Saale) Hbf d.	|	...	1201	...	1401	...	1601	1601	...	2001	...
Kassel Wilhelmshöhe d.	0814	...	|	...	|	...	|	|	...	|	...
Göttingen d.	0834	...	|	...	|	...	|	|	...	|	...
Hannover Messe ◧ d.	0909	...	|	...	|	...	|	|	...	|	...
Wolfsburg Hbf d.	0954	...	|	...	|	...	|	|	...	|	...
Berlin Spandau a.	1105	...	|	...	|	...	|	|	...	|	...
Berlin Südkreuz a.	|	...	|	...	|	...	1710	1710	...	2106	...
Berlin Hbf a.	1116	...	1312	...	1516	...	1722	1722	...	2115	...

Route *FLX* 10	**1241**		**1245**	**1245**		**1247**		**1249**		**1354**
	④–①		①–③	④–⑦		④–⑦				E
Berlin Hbf d.	0726	...	1128	1128	...	1323	...	1528	...	1729
Berlin Südkreuz d.	0737	...	1137	1137	...	|	...	|	...	|
Berlin Spandau d.	|	...	|	|	...	|	...	|	...	1741
Wolfsburg Hbf d.	|	...	|	|	...	|	...	|	...	1850
Hannover Messe ◧ d.	|	...	|	|	...	|	...	|	...	1933
Göttingen d.	|	...	|	|	...	|	...	|	...	2008
Kassel Wilhelmshöhe d.	|	...	|	|	...	|	...	|	...	2029
Halle (Saale) Hbf d.	0844	...	1244	1244	...	1444	...	1644	...	|
Erfurt Hbf d.	0920	...	1321	1321	...	1520	...	1720	...	|
Gotha d.	|	...	|	|	...	|	...	1737	...	|
Eisenach d.	0951	...	|	|	...	|	...	|	...	⊙
Bad Hersfeld d.	|	...	1417	1417	...	|	...	|	...	|
Fulda d.	1041	...	1443	1443	...	1643	...	1843	...	|
Hanau Hbf d.	|	...	|	|	...	|	...	|	...	|
Frankfurt (Main) Süd a.	1133	...	1533	1533	...	1731	...	1933	...	2229•
Frankfurt (Main) Süd d.	1136	...	1537	1537	...	1734	...	1936	...	2231•
Frankfurt (M) Flug ✈¶ a.	|	...	|	|	...	|	...	|	...	2256
Mainz Hbf a.	|	...	|	|	...	|	...	|	...	2315
Darmstadt Hbf d.	1154	...	1557	1557	...	|	...	1954	...	...
Weinheim (Bergstr) d.	1218	...	|	|	...	|	...	|	...	...
Heidelberg Hbf d.	1236	...	1638	1638	...	|	...	2035	...	...
Mannheim Hbf d.	|	...	|	|	...	1838	...	|	...	...
Karlsruhe Hbf d.	|	...	1725e	|	...	1910	...	|	...	...
Baden Baden d.	|	...	|	|	...	|	...	|	...	...
Offenburg d.	|	...	1802	|	...	1954	...	|	...	...
Freiburg (Brsg) Hbf d.	|	...	1836	|	...	2039	...	|	...	...
Basel Bad Bf a.	|	...	1914	|	...	2118	...	|	...	...
Stuttgart Hbf a.	1323	...	...	1730	...	...	...	2119	...	...

Routes *FLX* 30/35 **SERVICE TO AUG. 9**	**1360**		**1230**	**1230**		**1232**	**1232**	**1364**	**1236**	**1366**	
	④–①					⑤	⑦	⑤–⑦			
	U		N	L				U		U	
Leipzig Hbf d.	0641	...	...	...	...	...	...	...	...	1641	...
Dresden Hbf d.	|	...	0623	...	...	...	0903	...	...	|	...
Dresden Neustadt d.	|	...	0630	...	...	...	0909	...	...	|	...
Elsterwerda d.	|	...	0659	...	...	...	|	...	...	|	...
Berlin Südkreuz a.	0753	...	0808	...	...	...	|	...	...	1752	...
Berlin Südkreuz d.	0756	...	0814	0814	...	...	|	1155	1617	1756	...
Berlin Ostbahnhof d.	|	...	|	|	...	1117	1117	|	|	|	...
Berlin Hbf a.	0801	...	0819	0819	...	1124	1124	1200	1622	1801	...
Berlin Hbf d.	0809	...	0828	0828	...	1129	1129	1208	1641	1808	...
Berlin Spandau d.	|	...	0840r	0840r	...	1146	1146	|	1651	|	...
Hamburg Hbf a.	1010	...	|	|	...	|	|	1411	|	2010	...
Stendal Hbf d.	...	...	|	|	...	|	|	...	|	...	...
Hannover Hbf d.	...	...	1023	1023	...	1340	1340	...	1823	...	...
Bielefeld Hbf d.	...	...	1125	1125	...	1453	1453	...	|	...	...
Gütersloh Hbf d.	...	...	1144	1144	...	1504	1504	...	|	...	...
Hamm (Westf) d.	...	...	1208	1208	...	1525	1525	...	|	...	...
Dortmund Hbf d.	...	...	1226	1226	...	1556	1556	...	2127	...	...
Bochum Hbf d.	...	...	1239	1239	...	1608	1608	...	2140	...	...
Essen Hbf d.	...	...	1250	1250	...	1624	1624	...	2152	...	...
Duisburg Hbf d.	...	...	1303	1303	...	1704	1704	...	2207	...	...
Düsseldorf Hbf d.	...	...	1318	1318	...	1718	1718	...	2228	...	...
Köln Hbf a.	...	...	1345	1345	...	1746	1746	...	2303	...	...
Aachen Hbf a.	...	...	...	...	...	...	...	...	...	...	...

Routes *FLX* 30/35 **SERVICE TO AUG. 9**	**1361**	**1231**	**1231**	**1233**	**1363**	**1235**	**1235**	**1367**	**1239**	**1239**
	⑤–①	④⑥	④⑥			⑥	⑥	④–⑦		
	U	U	V	R	U	Ud	Vd	U	P	S
Aachen Hbf d.	...	...	...	...	...	...	...	...	...	...
Köln Hbf d.	...	0613	0613	0814	...	1014	1014	...	1515	1515
Düsseldorf Hbf d.	...	0637	0637	0838	...	1037	1037	...	1559	1559
Duisburg Hbf d.	...	0651	0651	0851	...	1051	1051	...	|	|
Essen Hbf d.	...	0703	0703	0904	...	1104	1104	...	1626	1626
Bochum Hbf d.	...	0714	0714	0915	...	1115	1115	...	1637	1637
Dortmund Hbf d.	...	0731	0731	0931	...	1131	1131	...	1652	1652
Hamm (Westf) d.	...	0752	0752	0952	...	1152	1152	...	|	|
Gütersloh Hbf d.	...	0822	0822	1022	...	1222	1222	...	|	|
Bielefeld Hbf d.	...	0840	0840	1040	...	1240	1240	...	|	|
Hannover Hbf d.	...	0944	0944	1144	...	1344	1344	...	1944	1944
Stendal Hbf d.	...	|	|	|	...	|	|	...	|	|
Hamburg Hbf d.	0746	|	|	|	1148	|	|	1738	|	|
Berlin Spandau d.	|	|	|	|	|	|	|	|	|	|
Berlin Hbf a.	0948	1120z	1142	1333	1348	1517	1531	1950	2128	2128
Berlin Hbf d.	0958g	1125z	1148	1338	1354	1530	1549	1955	2135	2135
Berlin Ostbahnhof a.	|	1140	|	|	|	|	|	|	|	|
Berlin Südkreuz a.	1003g	...	1153	1345	1359	1535	1554	2000	2139	2139
Berlin Südkreuz d.	1006g	...	...	...	1404	1539	1559	2004	2142	...
Elsterwerda a.	|	...	...	...	|	1654	1714	|	2253	...
Dresden Neustadt a.	|	...	...	...	|	1721	1742	|	2321	...
Dresden Hbf a.	|	...	...	...	|	1729	1748	|	2329	...
Leipzig Hbf a.	1116g	...	...	...	1515	...	...	2116	...	...

Route *FLX* 20		**1353**		**1345**		**1347**	**1347**				
		N		⑦			④–①				
						△	▽				
Hamburg Hbf d.	...	0849	...	1050	...	1450	1450	...	...	...	...
Hamburg Harburg d.	...	0901	...	1101	...	1501	1501	...	...	...	...
Bremen Hbf d.	...	0949	...	1149	...	1549	1549	...	...	...	...
Osnabrück Hbf d.	...	1044	...	1244	...	1644	1644	...	...	...	...
Münster (Westf) Hbf d.	...	1109	...	1309	...	1709	1709	...	...	...	...
Gelsenkirchen Hbf d.	...	1148	...	1348	...	1748	1748	...	...	...	...
Essen Hbf d.	...	1203	...	1403	...	1803	1803	...	...	...	...
Duisburg Hbf d.	...	1219	...	1419	...	1819	1819	...	...	...	...
Düsseldorf Hbf d.	...	1232	...	1433	...	1833	1833	...	...	...	...
Köln Hbf a.	...	1258	...	1457	...	1856	1856	...	...	...	...

Route *FLX* 20	**1340**	**1340**		**1342**		**1348**		**1350**		
	①–⑥	K		⑦		④–⑥		⑦		
	△	▽								
Köln Hbf d.	0659	0659	...	0828	...	1500	...	1901	...	...
Düsseldorf Hbf d.	0726	0726	...	0900	...	1527	...	1926	...	...
Duisburg Hbf d.	0741	0741	...	0917	...	1541	...	1941	...	...
Essen Hbf d.	0755	0755	...	0930	...	1554	...	|	...	...
Gelsenkirchen Hbf d.	0806	0806	...	0944	...	1606	...	|	...	...
Münster (Westf) Hbf d.	0848	0848	...	1050	...	1648	...	2048	...	...
Osnabrück Hbf d.	0915	0915	...	|	...	1715	...	2115	...	...
Bremen Hbf d.	1010	1010	...	1212	...	1810	...	2210	...	...
Hamburg Harburg a.	1055	1055	...	|	...	1854	...	2255	...	...
Hamburg Hbf a.	1108	1108	...	1306	...	1907	...	2310	...	...

E – ⑤⑥ until Aug. 16.
F – ①⑥ until Aug. 18.
K – ①④⑤⑥.
L – ②③④⑦.
N – ①⑤⑥.
P – ④⑤⑦.
R – ①②③⑤⑦.
S – ①②③⑥.
U – Until Aug. 1
V – From Aug. 2.

d – Also runs on ④ Köln - Berlin Hbf.
e – Arrives 9 – 11 minutes earlier.

g – ① only.
r – Until Aug. 1.
z – Berlin **Zoo**.

⊙ – Via Marburg (d. 2133), Gießen (d. 2151) and Friedberg (d. 2210).
⊡ – Via Friedberg (d. 0636), Gießen (d. 0657) and Marburg (d. 0715).
△ – Until Sept. 5.
▽ – From Sept. 6.
• – Frankfurt (Main) **West**.
¶ – Frankfurt Flughafen Fernbahnhof ✈.
◧ – Hannover Messe/Laatzen.

928 MÜNCHEN - BAYRISCHZELL, LENGGRIES and TEGERNSEE

Bayerische Regiobahn

Most trains run with multiple portions from München (make sure you join the correct portion for your journey). On June 19, Aug. 15, Nov. 1 services run as on ⑦.

km																										
			Ⓐ		Ⓐ	Ⓐ	Ⓐ	Ⓐ		Ⓐ	Ⓐ	Ⓐ	Ⓐ	Ⓐ		Ⓒ		†	Ⓒ	⊡⊙	Ⓒ	Ⓒ	Ⓒ	†	Ⓒ	Ⓒ	Ⓒ
0	**München** Hbf . d.	Ⓐ	0010	...	0629	0702	0802	0902	and	1903	2002	2102	2202	2309	Ⓒ	0010	...	0529	0629	and	1829	1929	2002	2029	2102	2202	2310
37	Holzkirchen ..... d.		0037	...	0701	0732	0832	0932	hourly	1932	2032	2132	2232	2337		0037	...	0600	0700	hourly	1900	2000	2030	2100	2130	2232	2337
61	Schliersee .... d.		0106	...	0727	0802	0902	1001	until	2002	2102	2202	2301	0006		0106	...	0632	0732	until	1932	2025	2101	2125	2201	2301	0006
78	**Bayrischzell** ... a.		0130	...	...	0825	0925	1025		2025	2125	2225	2325	0030		0130	...	0656	0756		1956	...	2125	...	2225	2325	0030

km																									
			Ⓐ		Ⓐ	Ⓐ	Ⓐ	Ⓐ	⊖	Ⓐ	Ⓐ		Ⓒ		Ⓒ	Ⓒ	Ⓒ	◇⊡	Ⓒ	Ⓒ	Ⓒ	†	Ⓒ	Ⓒ	Ⓒ
0	**München** Hbf . d.	Ⓐ	0010	...	0603	0629	0702	0802	and hourly until	2202	2309	Ⓒ	0010	...	0602	0702	0729	and at the same minutes past each hour until	1902	1929	2002	2029	2102	2202	2310
37	Holzkirchen ..... d.		0040	...	0635	0705	0735	0835		2235	2340		0040	...	0635	0735	0802		1935	2002	2035	2102	2135	2235	2340
47	Schaftlach .... d.		0053	...	0648	0718	0748	0848		2248	2353		0053	...	0648	0748	0818		1948	2018	2048	2118	2148	2248	2353
57	Bad Tölz .... d.		0105	...	0700	0730	0800	0900		2300	0005		0105	...	0700	0800	0830		2000	2030	2100	2130	2200	2300	0005
67	**Lenggries** ...... a.		0116	...	0711	0741	0811	0911		2311	0016		0116	...	0711	0811	0841		2011	2041	2111	2141	2211	2311	0016

km																									
			Ⓐ		Ⓐ	Ⓐ	Ⓐ	Ⓐ	⊖	Ⓐ	Ⓐ		Ⓒ		Ⓒ	Ⓒ	Ⓒ	◇⊡	Ⓒ	Ⓒ	Ⓒ	†	Ⓒ	Ⓒ	Ⓒ
	München Hbf. d.	Ⓐ	0010	...	0603	0629	0702	0802	and	2202	2309	Ⓒ	0010	..	0602	0702	0729	and at the same	1902	1929	2002	2029	2102	2202	2310
0	Schaftlach .... d.		0053	...	0648	0718	0748	0848	hourly	2248	2353		0053	...	0648	0748	0818	minutes past	1948	2018	2048	2118	2148	2248	2353
12	**Tegernsee** ...... a.		0113	...	0709	0739	0809	0909	until	2309	0013		0113	...	0709	0809	0839	each hour until	2009	2039	2109	2139	2209	2309	0013

		Ⓐ	Ⓐ	Ⓐ	Ⓐ	Ⓐ	Ⓐ		Ⓐ	Ⓐ	Ⓐ	Ⓐ	Ⓐ	Ⓐ	Ⓐ	Ⓐ	Ⓐ		Ⓐ		Ⓒ	Ⓒ		Ⓒ	Ⓒ	Ⓒ	Ⓒ
Bayrischzell.....d.	Ⓐ	0449	0532	0607	0634	0705	0732	and	1132	1232	...	1432	1532	1632	1732	1832	1932	and	2232	Ⓒ	0503	0603	and	2003	2032	2132	2232
Schliersee.........d.		0516	0559	0635	0702	0734	0759	hourly	1159	1304	1359	1459	1559	1704	1759	1859	1959	hourly	2259		0530	0630	hourly	2030	2101	2201	2259
Holzkirchen.......d.		0544	0629	0705	0732	0803	0831	until	1231	1332	1431	1531	1631	1732	1831	1931	2029	until	2329		0604	0704	until	2104	2131	2231	2329
München Hbf...a.		0612	0655	0735	0759	0832	0857		1257	1359	1457	1557	1657	1758	1857	1957	2055		2355		0632	0732		2132	2157	2257	2355

		Ⓐ	Ⓐ	Ⓐ	Ⓐ	Ⓐ	Ⓐ	Ⓐ	Ⓐ	Ⓐ	Ⓐ	△	Ⓐ		⑥	Ⓒ	Ⓒ	Ⓒ	⊗	Ⓒ	Ⓒ	Ⓒ	Ⓒ	Ⓒ	Ⓒ
Lenggries ....d.	Ⓐ	0431	0506	0547	0617	0647	0717	0747	0817	0847	0947	and hourly until	2247	Ⓒ	0447	0517	0617	0647	and at the same minutes past each hour until	1917	1947	2017	2047	2147	2247
Bad Tölz...........d.		0443	0518	0600	0630	0700	0730	0800	0830	0900	1000		2300		0500	0530	0630	0700		1930	2000	2030	2100	2200	2300
Schaftlach.........d.		0454	0531	0617	0647	0717	0747	0817	0847	0917	1017		2317		0517	0549	0649	0717		1949	2017	2049	2117	2217	2317
Holzkirchen.......d.		0510	0544	0629	0701	0732	0803	0831	0903	0931	1031		2329		0531	0604	0704	0729		2004	2029	2104	2131	2231	2329
München Hbf...a.		0535	0612	0655	0730	0759	0832	0857	0931	0957	1057		2355		0557	0632	0732	0755		2032	2055	2132	2157	2257	2355

			Ⓐ	Ⓐ	Ⓐ	Ⓐ	Ⓐ	Ⓐ	Ⓐ	Ⓐ	Ⓐ	△	Ⓐ		⑥	Ⓒ	Ⓒ	Ⓒ	⊗	Ⓒ	Ⓒ	Ⓒ	Ⓒ	Ⓒ	Ⓒ
Tegernsee ....d.	Ⓐ	...	0505	0552	0622	0652	0722	0752	0822	0852	0952	and	2252	Ⓒ	0452	0522	0622	0652	and at the same	1922	1952	2022	2052	2152	2252
Schaftlach.........a.		...	0525	0613	0643	0713	0743	0813	0842	0913	1013	hourly	2313		0513	0543	0643	0713	minutes past	1943	2013	2043	2113	2213	2313
München Hbf.a.		...	0612	0655	0730	0759	0832	0857	0931	0957	1057	until	2355		0557	0632	0732	0755	each hour until	2032	2055	2132	2157	2257	2355

⊡ – München Hbf d. 1528, 1628, 1728 (not 1529, 1629, 1729).
⊙ – Holzkirchen d. 1558, 1658, 1758 (not 1600, 1700, 1800).
△ – Holzkirchen and München timings may vary by 1 – 2 minutes.
Extra trains on Ⓐ: from Lenggries to München at 1217, 1317, 1517, 1617 and 1817; from Tegernsee to München at 1222, 1322, 1522, 1622 and 1822.
◇ – No service from München (to Lenggries / Tegernsee) at 1229 or 1329.
⊖ – Extra trains on Ⓐ from München (to Lenggries / Tegernsee) at 0926, 1029, 1229, 1526, 1626, 1726, 1826 and 1926.
⊗ – Timings may vary by 1 – 2 minutes. No service from Tegernsee (to München) at 1322 or 1422. No service from Lenggries (to München) at 1417.

929 PLATTLING - BAYERISCH EISENSTEIN - PLZEŇ

Waldbahn ⊠; ČD; 2nd class only

km		753	755		757	759					761			763			767			771				775	
		◇¶	◇	Ⓐ	◇	◇	Ⓐt	Ⓐt	Ⓐt	Ⓒz	◇			◇			◇			◇		B		◇	
0	**Plattling** ....d.	...	...	...	...	...	0519	0629	0659	0706	...	0806	0906	...	1006	1106	...	1206	1306	...	1406	...	1506	...	1606
9	Deggendorf Hbf..........d.	...	...	...	...	...	0531	0638	0711	0715	...	0815	0915	...	1015	1115	...	1215	1315	...	1415	...	1515	...	1615
33	Gotteszell..............d.	...	...	...	...	...	0554	0657	0732	0734	...	0834	0934	...	1035	1134	...	1234	1334	...	1434	...	1534	...	1634
48	Regen...................d.	...	...	...	...	...	0609	0711	0747	0747	...	0847	0947	...	1048	1147	...	1247	1347	...	1447	...	1547	...	1647
58	Zwiesel (Bay)...........d.	...	...	...	...	...	0622	0724	0759	0759	...	0900	0959	...	1059	1159	...	1259	1359	...	1459	...	1559	...	1659
72	**Bayerisch Eisenstein** ☆🏛 a.	...	...	...	...	...	0635	0737	0812	0812	...	0913	1012	...	1112	1212	...	1312	1412	...	1512	...	1612	...	1712
72	**Železná Ruda-Alžbětín** ☆🏛 d.	...	...	0517	...	*0617*	▬	...	...	...	*0816*	▬	...	1017	▬	...	*1217*	▬	...	*1416*	▬	1553	...	1617	▬
75	Železná Ruda centrum.....d.	...	...	0521	...	*0621*	...	...	...	...	*0820*	...	...	1021	...	...	*1221*	...	...	*1420*	...	1557	...	1621	...
79	Špičák..................d.	...	...	0529	...	*0629*	...	...	...	...	*0827*	...	...	1029	**765**	...	*1229*	**769**	...	*1427*	**773**	1606	...	1629	**777**
131	**Klatovy** ....a.	...	...	0617	...	*0717*	◇	...	...	...	*0914*	◇	...	1116	◇	...	*1316*	◇	...	*1516*	◇	1704	...	1716	◇
131	**Klatovy** ....d.	0426	0526	...	0630	0730	0828	...	...	...	0930	1028	...	1130	1228	...	1330	1428	...	1530	1628	1708	...	1730	1828
141	Švihov u Klatov..........d.	0435	0535	...	0639	0740	0837	...	...	...	0940	1037	...	1140	1237	...	1340	1437	...	1540	1637	|	...	1740	1837
170	**Plzeň** hl.n. ....a.	0517	0617	...	0719	0819	0919	...	...	...	1019	1119	...	1219	1319	...	1419	1519	...	1619	1719	1758	...	1819	1919
	Praha hl.n. **1120** ....a.	0652	0752	...	0852	0952	...	...	...	...	1152	...	...	1352	1452	...	1552	1652	...	1752	1852	...	...	1952	2052

			779							
	E		◇							
Plattling ....d.	...	1706	...	1806	...	1906	2006	2106	2206	2306
Deggendorf Hbf ....d.	...	1715	...	1815	...	1915	2015	2115	2215	2317
Gotteszell ....d.	...	1734	...	1834	...	1934	2034	2134	2234	2336
Regen...................d.	...	1747	...	1847	...	1947	2047	2147	2247	2349
Zwiesel (Bay) ....d.	...	1759	...	1859	...	1959	2059	2157	2257	2359
Bayerisch Eisenstein ☆🏛. a.	...	1812	...	1912	...	2012	2112	...	...	...
Železná Ruda-Alžbětín ☆🏛. d.	1740	...	*1817*	...	1953	...	...	...	...	...
Železná Ruda centrum.....d.	1744	...	*1821*	...	1957	...	...	...	...	...
Špičák ....d.	1752	...	*1829*	...	2005	...	...	...	...	...
Klatovy ....a.	1835	...	*1917*	...	2057	...	...	...	...	...
Klatovy ....d.	1845	...	1930	...	2058	...	...	...	...	...
Švihov u Klatov..........d.	|	...	1940	...	2109	...	...	...	...	...
Plzeň hl.n. ....a.	1935	...	2019	...	2154	...	...	...	...	...
Praha hl.n. **1120** ....a.	...	...	2152	...	...	...	...	...	...	...

								778	778
	Ⓐt	Ⓐt	Ⓒz	Ⓐt	Ⓒz	Ⓐt		◇	Ⓐ◇
Praha hl.n. **1120** ....d.	...	...	...	...	...	...	...	...	0505
Plzeň hl.n. ....d.	...	...	...	...	...	...	0538	0640	0640
Švihov u Klatov..........d.	...	...	...	...	...	...	0618	0720	0720
Klatovy ....a.	...	...	...	...	...	...	0627	0729	0729
Klatovy ....d.	...	...	...	...	...	...	*0640*	▬	▬
Špičák ....d.	...	...	...	...	...	...	*0727*	...	...
Železná Ruda centrum.....d.	...	...	...	...	...	...	*0734*	...	...
Železná Ruda-Alžbětín ☆🏛.....a.	...	...	...	...	...	...	*0738*	Ⓐt	...
Bayerisch Eisenstein ☆🏛 ......d.	...	...	...	...	...	0708	...	0742	...
Zwiesel (Bay) ....d.	0414	0529	0603	0621	0658	0722	...	0758	0758
Regen...................d.	0424	0539	0613	0631	0708	0732	...	0808	0808
Gotteszell..............d.	0438	0555	0625	0644	0721	0751	...	0821	0821
Deggendorf Hbf...........d.	0459	0614	0645	0709	0744	0815	...	0844	0844
Plattling ....a.	0508	0623	0654	0718	0754	0825	...	0854	0854

			776		774	772			770			768	766			764		762	760		758	756		750	
		C	◇		◇	◇		◇	◇		◇	◇	◇	Ⓐ		◇		◇	◇		◇	◇		◇	
Praha hl.n. **1120** ....d.	...	...	0605	...	0705	0805	...	...	1005	...	...	1205	1305	...	...	1405	...	1505	1605	...	1705	1805	...	2105	...
Plzeň hl.n. ....d.	...	0700	0740	...	0840	0940	...	1040	1140	...	1240	1340	1440	...	...	1540	...	1640	1740	...	1840	1940	2110	2240	...
Švihov u Klatov..........d.	...	|	0818	...	0920	1018	...	1120	1218	...	1320	1418	1520	...	...	1618	...	1719	1818	...	1920	2020	2156	2320	...
Klatovy ....a.	...	0750	0827	...	0929	1027	...	1129	1227	...	1329	1427	1529	...	...	1627	...	1729	1827	...	1929	2029	2207	2329	...
Klatovy ....d.	...	0800	0840	...	▬	*1040*	...	▬	*1240*	...	▬	1440	▬	1535	...	*1640*	...	▬	*1840*	...	▬	*2040*	▬	▬	...
Špičák ....d.	...	0849	0929	...	...	*1128*	...	...	*1328*	...	...	1529	...	1629	...	*1728*	...	...	*1928*	...	...	*2126*	...	...	...
Železná Ruda centrum.....d.	...	0856	0936	...	...	*1134*	...	...	*1334*	...	...	1536	...	1635	...	*1734*	...	...	*1934*	...	...	*2132*	...	...	...
Železná Ruda-Alžbětín ☆🏛. a.	...	0900	0940	...	...	*1138*	...	...	*1338*	...	...	1540	...	1639	...	*1738*	...	...	*1938*	...	...	*2136*	...	...	...
Bayerisch Eisenstein ☆🏛. d.	0840	...	...	0944	1042	...	1142	1242	...	1342	1442	...	1544	...	1642	...	1742	1840	...	1942	2042	...	2140	...	...
Zwiesel (Bay) ....d.	0858	...	...	0959	1058	...	1158	1258	...	1358	1458	...	1558	...	1658	...	1758	1858	...	1958	2058	...	2158j	...	...
Regen...................d.	0908	...	...	1009	1108	...	1208	1308	...	1408	1508	...	1608	...	1708	...	1808	1908	...	2008	2108	...	2208	...	...
Gotteszell ....d.	0921	...	...	1022	1121	...	1221	1321	...	1421	1521	...	1621	...	1721	...	1821	1921	...	2021	2121	...	2221	...	...
Deggendorf Hbf ....d.	0944	...	...	1045	1144	...	1244	1344	...	1444	1544	...	1644	...	1744	...	1844	1944	...	2044	2144	...	2244	2329	0038
Plattling ....a.	0954	...	...	1054	1154	...	1254	1354	...	1454	1554	...	1654	...	1754	...	1854	1954	...	2054	2154	...	2254	2339	0048

BRANCH LINE SERVICES ⊠

ZWIESEL - GRAFENAU *32 km.* Journey time: 46 – 47 minutes.
From Zwiesel (Bay) at 0622 Ⓐ **t**, 0800, 0900 and hourly until 2100.
From Grafenau at 0628 Ⓐ **t**, 0808, 0908 and hourly until 2108.

ZWIESEL - BODENMAIS *15 km.* Journey time: 20 – 21 minutes.
From Zwiesel at 0627 Ⓐ **t**, 0802 Ⓐ **t**, 0902, 1002 and hourly until 2002; then 2202.
From Bodenmais at 0558 Ⓐ **t**, 0658 Ⓐ **t**, 0829, 0929 and hourly until 2029.

GOTTESZELL - VIECHTACH *25 km.* Journey time: 39 – 43 minutes.
From Gotteszell at 0459 Ⓐ **t**, 0602 Ⓐ **t**, 0659 Ⓐ **t**, 0738 ⑥ **k**, 0750 Ⓐ, 0938, 1038 ⚒ **r**, 1138, 1238 ⚒ **r**, 1336 Ⓐ **t**, 1338 Ⓒ **z**, 1438, 1538, 1638, 1738, 1838, 1938, 2038 and 2245.
From Viechtach at 0351 Ⓐ **t**, 0457 Ⓐ **t**, 0600 Ⓐ **t**, 0635 ⑥ **k**, 0657 Ⓐ **t**, 0837, 0936 ⚒ **r**, 1036, 1136 ⚒ **r**, 1236, 1334 Ⓐ **t**, 1336 Ⓒ **z**, 1436, 1536, 1636, 1736, 1836, 1936 and 2136.

B – Ⓒ from Oct. 26.
C – Daily until Aug. 31; Ⓒ from Sept. 6.
E – Daily until Aug. 31; Ⓒ Sept. 6 - Oct. 25.
j – Arrives 2153.
k – Not Nov. 1.
r – Not June 19, Aug. 15, Nov. 1.
t – Not June 19, Aug. 15.
z – Also June 19, Aug. 15.
◇ – Also conveys 🚲.
¶ – Train number **743** on Ⓒ.
⊠ – *Waldbahn* services are operated by Die Länderbahn.
☆ – Bayerisch Eisenstein (German) / Železná Ruda-Alžbětín (Czech) is the same station.

Regional trains ULM - AUGSBURG - MÜNCHEN and AUGSBURG - INGOLSTADT 930

ULM - MÜNCHEN. Operated by Arverio Bayern. See Table **910** for long-distance *ICE*, *IC* and *EC* services. On June 19, Aug. 15, Nov. 1 services run as on ⑦.

	Ⓐ	Ⓒ	Ⓐ		Ⓐ		Ⓐ										Ⓐ	Ⓒ							
Ulm Hbf ..... **945** d.	...	...	0447	0518	0546	0611	0646	0719	0819	0916	1018	1119	1219	1319	1419	1519	1617f	1625	1718	1818	1919	2018	2119	2219	2324
Günzburg ..... **945** d.	...	...	0507	0538	0607	0630	0706	0737	0839	0937	1038	1137	1239	1337	1438	1537	1641f	1648	1737	1839	1937	2041	2139	2241	2342
Augsburg Hbf ..... a.	...	...	0604	0635	0704	0723	0805	0833	0933	1033	1133	1233	1333	1434	1533	1637	1734	1738	1834	1933	2034	2133	2232	2336	...
Augsburg Hbf ..... **905** d.	0501	0531	0608	0638	0708	0737	0808	0838	0938	1038	1137	1238	1337	1438	1538	1638	1738	1808	1838	1938	2035	2139	2237	2349	...
München Pasing ... **905** a.	0541	0611	0648	0712	0749	0811	0845	0914	1012	1112	1212	1312	1412	1513	1612	1712	1812	1845	1913	2012	2112	2223	2311	0029	...
München Hbf ..... **905** a.	0551	0620	0657	0720	0758	0819	0854	0923	1020	1121	1220	1320	1420	1521	1620	1721	1821	1854	1921	2020	2120	2231	2320	0037	...

		Ⓒ					⊖									⑥	Ⓐ		⊖			Ⓒ			
München Hbf ..... **905** d.	0005	0005	...	...	...	0633	0736	0834	0935	1035	1057	1235	1335	1435	1457	1602	1602	1635	1735	1835	1935	2022	2057	2159	2258
München Pasing ... **905** d.	0014	0014	...	...	...	0641	0744	0843	0943	1043	1105	1243	1343	1443	1505	1610	1610	1643	1743	1843	1943	2030	2105	2207	2305
Augsburg Hbf ..... **905** a.	0053	0053	...	...	...	0719	0818	0918	1019	1118	1146	1317	1419	1518	1546	1646	1646	1718	1819	1918	2020	2115	2146	2246	2346
Augsburg Hbf ..... d.	...	0054	...	0520	0622	0725	0825	0924	1025	1122	1222	1322	1424	1522	1622	...	1649	1722	1825	1923	2025	2125	2149	2248	2351
Günzburg ..... **945** d.	...	0149	...	0622	0721	0820	0920	1022	1121	1222	1321	1422	1521	1622	1719	...	1755	1836	1921	2022	2121	2220	2257k	2350	0047
Ulm Hbf ..... **945** a.	...	0208	...	0641	0740	0840	0939	1041	1140	1241	1340	1441	1540	1641	1739	...	1814	1855	1940	2041	2140	2240	2316	0011	0105

AUGSBURG - INGOLSTADT. **SERVICE UNTIL SEPTEMBER 14**. See below for service from Sept. 15. Operated by Bayerische Regiobahn. 2nd class only.

km																									
				Ⓒ	Ⓐ																				
0	**Augsburg** Hbf ..... d.	0537	0645	0745	0747	0843	0945	1046	1145	1246	1345	1442	1545	1646	1745	1838	1946	2046	2145	2245	...	2359	...	...	...
41	Schrobenhausen ..... d.	0628	0728	0828	0828	0928	1028	1128	1228	1328	1428	1528	1628	1728	1828	1928	2028	2128	2228	2328	...	0036	...	...	...
67	**Ingolstadt** Hbf ..... a.	0646	0746	0846	0846	0946	1046	1146	1246	1346	1446	1546	1647	1747	1848	1948	2048	2146	2246	2346	...	0059	...	...	...

	Ⓐ	Ⓒ			Ⓒ	Ⓐ																	
Ingolstadt Hbf ..... d.	0452	0502	...	0606	0708	0709	0806	0908	1008	1108	1208	1308	1408	1508	1608	1710	1810	1908	2009	2108	2208	2308	...	...
Schrobenhausen ..... d.	0521h	0521	...	0626	0728	0728	0827	0927	1027	1127	1227	1327	1427	1527	1627	1727	1827	1927	2027	2127	2227	2327	...	...
Augsburg Hbf ..... a.	0600	0600	...	0709	0808	0809	0908	1008	1108	1208	1308	1408	1508	1608	1708	1808	1908	2008	2108	2208	2308	0008	...	...

SERVICE SEPTEMBER 15 - DECEMBER 13

km																							
			Ⓐ	†	⚒	†		⚒	†		⚒	†	⚒	†	⚒	†							
0	**Augsburg** Hbf ..... d.	0535	0624	0645	0728	0745	0843	0928	0945	and at the same	1728	1745	1828	1838	1928	1946	2045	2145	2245	...	2359	...	...
41	Schrobenhausen ..... d.	0628	0712	0728	0812	0828	0928	1012	1028	minutes past	1812	1828	1912	1928	2012	2028	2128	2228	2328	...	0036	...	...
67	**Ingolstadt** Hbf ..... a.	0646	0732	0746	0832	0846	0946	1033	1046	each hour until	1832	1848	1934	1946	2032	2046	2146	2246	2346	...	0059	...	...

	Ⓐ	Ⓒ			†	†	†	⚒		†	⚒		†	⚒	†	⚒	†	⚒				
Ingolstadt Hbf ..... d.	0452	0502	...	0606	0708	0708	0806	0806	0908	1008	1008	and at the same	1708	1708	1810	1810	1908	1908	2008	2108	2208	2308
Schrobenhausen ..... d.	0518	0521	...	0626	0728	0730	0827	0830	0927	1027	1030	minutes past	1727	1730	1827	1830	1927	1930	2027	2127	2227	2327
Augsburg Hbf ..... a.	0600	0600	...	0709	0808	0809	0907	0907	1008	1108	1108	each hour until	1808	1808	1908	1908	2008	2008	2107	2208	2308	0008

f – Aug. 1 - Sept. 15 departs Ulm 1604, Günzburg 1639.
h – Arrives 0511.
k – Arrives 2244.
⊖ – Change trains at Augsburg on Ⓒ.

KARLSRUHE - STUTTGART 931

km ◧																									
			ICE					*ICE*	*IC*				*ICE*			*IC*			*ICE*		*IC*		*ICE*		
		◇	**561**	◇	◇	⊙	◇	**1065**	**2065**		⊙	◇	**267**	◇	◇	**2067**	◇	◇	**1067**	◇	**2069**	◇	**565**	◇	◇
		Ⓐ	①–⑤	Ⓒ	Ⓐ	Ⓐ	Ⓐ	Ⓐ																	
		t	✕	z	t	t	t	✕	L🍷				B✕			L🍷			B✕		🍷		✕		
0	**Karlsruhe** Hbf ..... d.	0532	0600	0600	0602	...	0632	0659	0707	...	...	0732	0805	0806	0832	0906	0932	1006	1027	1032	1106	1132	1205	1206	1232
	Pforzheim ..... d.	0554	|	0622	0624	...	0654	|	0726	...	...	0754	|	0828	0854	0926	0954	1028	|	1054	1126	1154	|	1228	1254
21	Bruchsal ..... ▽ d.	|	0616	|	|	0619	|	0719	|	...	0715	|	0817	|	|	|	|	|	|	|	|	|	1217	|	|
	Mühlacker ..... ▽ d.	0602	|	0630	0633	0656	0702	|	0737	...	0753	0802	|	0836	0902	0937	1002	1036	|	1102	1137	1202	|	1236	1302
58	Vaihingen (Enz) ..... d.	0608	|	0637	0639	0710	0712	|	0744	...	...	0808	|	0844	0910	|	1010	1042	|	1108	1144	1208	|	1242	1310
87	**Stuttgart** Hbf ..... a.	0625	0644	0653	0655	0744	0733	0748	0802	...	...	0826	0845	0859	0928	1002	1027	1059	1103	1125	1203	1225	1245	1259	1328
	Aalen Hbf **925** ..... a.	...	|	...	0756	...	...	...	0858	...	...	...	|	0956	...	1057	...	1156	...	...	1257	...	|	1356	...
	Nürnberg Hbf **925** ..... a.	...	|	...	...	...	...	...	1018	...	...	...	|	...	...	1218	...	...	...	...	1417	...	|	...	...
	München Hbf **910** a.	...	0849	...	...	...	...	...	...	...	...	...	1049	...	...	...	...	...	...	...	...	...	1449	...	...

	IC		*ICE*			*IC*		*ICE*			*IC*		*ICE*			*IC*				*IC*					
	2161	◇	**567**	◇	◇	**2163**	◇	**569**	◇	◇	**2165**	◇	**1069**	◇	◇	**2167**	◇	◇	◇	**2167**	◇	◇	◇		◇
	L🍷		✕			L🍷		✕			🍷		✕			🍷				🍷					
Karlsruhe Hbf ..... d.	1306	1332	1405	1406	1432	1506	1532	1605	1605	1632	1706	1732	1805	1806	1832	1906	1932	2006	2032	2106	2132	2206	2232	...	2312
Pforzheim ..... d.	1326	1354	|	1428	1454	1526	1554	|	1628	1654	1726	1754	|	1828	1854	1926	1954	2028	2054	2126	2154	2228	2254	...	2338
Bruchsal ..... ▽ d.	|	|	1417	|	|	|	|	1617	|	|	|	|	1817	|	|	|	|	|	|	|	|	|	|	...	|
Mühlacker ..... ▽ d.	1337	1402	|	1436	1502	1537	1602	|	1636	1702	1737	1802	|	1836	1902	1937	2002	2036	2102	2137	2202	2236	2302	...	2346
Vaihingen (Enz) ..... d.	|	1408	|	1442	1511	1544	1609	|	1642	1709	1745	1808	|	1842	1908	1945	2010	2042	2108	2145	2210	2243	2308	...	2352
Stuttgart Hbf ..... a.	1358	1425	1445	1459	1528	1602	1625	1645	1659	1727	1803	1824	1851	1859	1925	2003	2027	2059	2125	2202	2226	2259	2325	...	0021
Aalen Hbf **925** ..... a.	1457	...	|	1556	...	1657	...	|	1756	...	1857	...	|	1956	...	2057	...	2156	...	...	2326	...	...	...	...
Nürnberg Hbf **925** ..... a.	1616	...	|	...	...	1818	...	|	...	...	2018	...	|	...	...	2218	...	...	...	...	...	...	...	...	...
München Hbf **910** . a.	...	...	1649	...	...	...	...	1849	...	...	...	...	2056	...	...	...	...	...	...	...	...	...	...	...	...

km ◐																									
		IC							*ICE*		*IC*	*IC*				*IC*			*ICE*		*IC*			*ICE*	
		2326		◇	◇	◇	⊙	◇	**1068**	◇	**2168**	**2168**	◇	◇	◇	**2166**	◇	◇	**568**	◇	**2164**	◇	◇	**566**	◇
		Ⓐ		Ⓐ	Ⓒ	Ⓐ	Ⓐ		①–⑥			Ⓐ													
		D		t	z	t	t		✕		🍷	t🍷				🍷			✕		🍷			✕	
	München Hbf **910** d.	...	...	...	...	...	...	...	0459	...	...	...	...	...	...	...	...	...	0902	...	...	...	...	1102	...
	Nürnberg Hbf **925** ..... d.	...	...	...	...	...	...	...	|	...	...	0538	...	...	...	0738	...	...	|	...	0942	...	...	|	...
	Aalen Hbf **925** ..... d.	...	...	...	...	...	...	0600t	|	...	...	0700	...	0802	...	0902	...	1002	|	...	1102	...	1202	|	...
0	**Stuttgart** Hbf ..... d.	0226	...	0532	0559	0632	...	0659	0710	0732	0759	0759	0832	0900	0932	0959	1032	1059	1112	1132	1159	1232	1259	1309	1332
39	Vaihingen (Enz) ..... d.	|	...	0548	0616	0648	...	0716	|	0748	0816	0816	0848	0916	0948	1016	1048	1116	|	1148	1216	1248	1316	|	1348
47	Mühlacker ..... d.	|	...	0554	0622	0654	0701	0723	|	0754	0824	0824	0854	0923	0954	1023	1054	1123	|	1154	1223	1254	1323	|	1354
79	Bruchsal ..... d.	|	...	|	|	|	0728	|	0739	|	|	|	|	|	|	|	|	|	1138	|	|	|	|	1337	|
60	Pforzheim ..... d.	0306	...	0603	0631	0703	...	0731	|	0803	0833	0833	0903	0931	1003	1032	1103	1131	|	1203	1232	1303	1331	|	1403
86	**Karlsruhe** Hbf ..... a.	0327	...	0625	0653	0725	...	0752	0753	0825	0853	0853	0925	0952	1025	1053	1125	1152	1152	1225	1253	1325	1352	1352	1425

	IC			*ICE*		*IC*			*ICE*		*ICE*	*IC*			*ICE*		*IC*			*ICE*		*IC*			
	2162	◇	◇	**564**	◇	**2160**	◇	◇	**1066**	◇	**1064**	**2068**	◇	◇	**266**	◇	**2066**	◇	◇	**560**	◇	**2064**	◇	◇	◇
									①–④											Ⓑ					
	L🍷			✕		L🍷			m✕		B✕	🍷			B✕		L🍷			✕		L🍷			
München Hbf **910** . d.	...	...	...	1302	...	...	...	...	...	...	...	...	...	...	1658	...	...	...	...	1900	...	...	...	...	...
Nürnberg Hbf **925** ..... d.	1142	...	...	|	...	1341	...	...	...	...	...	1542	...	...	|	...	1741	...	...	|	...	1942	...	...	...
Aalen Hbf **925** ..... d.	1302	...	1402	|	...	1502	...	1602	...	...	...	1702	...	1802	|	...	1902	...	2002	|	...	2102	...	2202	...
Stuttgart Hbf ..... d.	1358	1431	1459	1509	1533	1558	1632	1658	1701	1727	1734	1759	1832	1859	1912	1932	1959	2032	2059	2111	2132	2159	2232	2313	0016
Vaihingen (Enz) ..... d.	1416	1447	1516	|	1548	1616	1648	1716	|	1748	|	1817	1848	1916	|	1948	2016	2048	2116	|	2148	2216	2248	2331	0043
Mühlacker ..... d.	1423	1454	1523	|	1554	1623	1654	1723	|	1754	|	1824	1854	1923	|	1954	2023	2054	2123	|	2154	2224	2254	2340	0049
Bruchsal ..... d.	|	|	|	1537	|	|	|	|	1739	|	1802	|	|	|	1940	|	|	|	|	2139	|	|	|	|	|
Pforzheim ..... d.	1432	1503	1531	|	1603	1632	1703	1731	|	1803	|	1833	1903	1931	|	2003	2032	2103	2131	|	2203	2233	2303	2348	0057
Karlsruhe Hbf ..... a.	1453	1525	1552	1552	1625	1652	1725	1752	1752	1825	1820	1853	1925	1952	1952	2025	2053	2125	2152	2152	2225	2300	2325	0011	0119

Regional trains **HEIDELBERG - BRUCHSAL - MÜHLACKER** ⊙

Heidelberg Hbf .... **913** d.	0833	1033	1233	1433	1633	1829	2038	2233	...	...
Bruchsal ..... **913** a.	0900	1055	1259	1458	1655	1858	2058	2257	...	...
Bruchsal ..... d.	0900	1059	1300	1500	1658	1900	2100	2259	...	...
Mühlacker ..... a.	0925	1125	1325	1525	1725	1925	2125	2325	...	...

	Ⓒz									
Mühlacker ..... d.	0731	0931	1131	1331	1531	1731	1930	2131	...	...
Bruchsal ..... a.	0757	0957	1157	1357	1557	1756	1957	2157	...	...
Bruchsal ..... **913** d.	0758	0958	1158	1358	1558	1757	1958	2158	...	...
Heidelberg Hbf ..... **913** a.	0819	1019	1219	1419	1619	1819	2019	2219	...	...

B – To/from Basel (Table **910**).
D – To Dortmund via Frankfurt and Siegen (Tables **808** and **910**).
L – To/from Leipzig via Saalfeld (Table **849a**).
m – Not June 18, Oct. 2.
t – Ⓐ (not June 19).
z – Also June 19.
◧ – Distance via high-speed line.
▽ – See also panel below main table.
◇ – Regional train operated by Arverio Baden-Württemberg.
◐ – Distance via classic route.
⊙ – Operated by SWEG Bahn.

933 STUTTGART - ULM - FRIEDRICHSHAFEN - LINDAU

IRE / RE services (except where shown)

See Table **910** for other long-distance services Stuttgart - Ulm and v.v. On June 19 services run as on ⑦.

km		Ⓐ	Ⓒ	Ⓐ	Ⓐ	Ⓒ	Ⓒ	Ⓐ		●		Ⓐ	●			*RJ* **897** G✕	⊡						Ⓐ	Ⓒ		
0	**Stuttgart** Hbf ..... **936** d.	...	...	...	...	...	...	0539	...	0534	...	0639	0630	...	0736	0744	...	0839	...	0937	...	1039	...	...	1139	...
22	Plochingen .... **936** d.	...	...	...	...	...	...	0556	...	0600	...	0656	0647	...	0756	|	...	0856	...	0956	...	1056	...	...	1156	...
42	Göppingen .... d.	...	...	...	...	...	...	0607	...	0619	...	0707	0710j	...	0807	|	...	0907	...	1007	...	1107	...	...	1207	...
61	Geislingen (Steige) .... d.	...	...	...	...	...	...	0619	...	0649j	...	0719	0740j	...	0819	|	...	0919	...	1019	...	1119	...	...	1219	...
94	**Ulm** Hbf .... a.	...	...	...	...	...	...	0643	...	0720	...	0743	0811	...	0843	0900	...	0943	...	1043	...	1143	...	...	1243	...
94	**Ulm** Hbf .... d.	0500	0507	0543	0610	0610	0647	0644	0717	...	0747	0747	...	0819	0847	0902	0919	0947	1019	1047	1119	1147	1218	1219	1247	1319
131	Biberach (Riß) .... d.	0525	0531	0605	0632	0633	0708	0710	0740	...	0808	0808	...	0841	0908	0924	0941	1008	1041	1108	1141	1208	1240	1241	1308	1341
156	Aulendorf .... d.	0545	0549	0621	0650	0651	0724	0728	0759	...	0824	0824	...	0859	0924	0939	0959	1024	1059	1124	1159	1224	1259	1259	1324	1359
178	Ravensburg .... d.	0559	0602	0633	0702	0704	0737	0741	0812	...	0837	0837	...	0912	0937	0952	1012	1037	1112	1137	1212	1237	1312	1312	1337	1412
189	Meckenbeuren .... d.	0606	0609	0640	0709	0711	0744	0748	|	...	0844	0844	...	|	0944	|	|	1044	|	1144	|	1244	|	|	1344	|
197	Friedrichshafen Stadt . a.	0614	0617	0647	0717	0719	0752	0755	0825	...	0852	0852	...	0925	0952	1003	1025	1052	1124	1152	1225	1252	1325	1325	1352	1425
197	Friedrichshafen Stadt . d.	*0627*	*0658*	*0655*	0728	...	*0810*	*0810*	0832	...	*0907*	*0907*	...	0931	*0957*	1010	1031	*1107*	1131	*1206*	1231	*1307*	1331	1331	*1407*	1431
	Lindau Insel .... a.	|	*0730*	*0729*	|	...	*0843*	*0843*	|	...	*0941*	*0941*	...	|	*1026*	|	|	*1141*	|	*1241*	|	*1341*	|	|	*1441*	|
221	**Lindau** Reutin .... a.	*0655*	...	...	0755	...	...	...	0855	...	...	...	...	0955	...	1028	1055	...	1155	...	1255	...	1355	1355	...	1455

		ICE **119** A✕				*IC* **2013** D			Ⓐ	Ⓒ					⊡											
Stuttgart Hbf .... **936** d.	1237	1257	1339	...	1439	1459	...	1537	...	...	1639	...	1739	...	1839	...	1939	...	2039	...	2139	...	...	2239	...	2339
Plochingen .... **936** d.	1256	|	1356	...	1456	1519	...	1556	...	...	1656	...	1756	...	1856	...	1956	...	2056	...	2156	...	...	2256	...	2356
Göppingen .... d.	1307	|	1407	...	1507	1533	...	1607	...	...	1707	...	1807	...	1907	...	2007	...	2107	...	2207	...	...	2307	...	0007
Geislingen (Steige) ..... d.	1319	|	1419	...	1519	|	...	1619	...	...	1719	...	1819	...	1919	...	2019	...	2119	...	2218	...	...	2319	...	0019
Ulm Hbf .... a.	1343	1404	1443	...	1543	1614	...	1643	...	...	1743	...	1843	...	1943	...	2043	...	2143	...	2243	...	...	2343	...	0043
Ulm Hbf .... d.	1347	1412	1447	1519	1547	...	1618	1647	1718	1719	1747	1819	1847	1919	1947	2019	2047	2119	2145	2219	...	2247	2329	...	0018	...
Biberach (Riß) .... d.	1408	1436	1508	1541	1608	...	1640	1708	1740	1741	1808	1841	1908	1941	2008	2041	2108	2141	2208	2241	...	2308	2352	...	0042	...
Aulendorf .... d.	1424	|	1524	1559	1624	...	1659	1724	1759	1759	1824	1859	1924	1959	2024	2059	2124	2201	2224	2259	...	2324	0010	...	0100	...
Ravensburg .... d.	1437	1505	1537	1612	1637	...	1712	1737	1812	1812	1837	1912	1937	2012	2037	2112	2137	2214	2237	2312	...	2337	0023	...	0113	...
Meckenbeuren .... d.	1444	|	1544	|	1644	...	|	1744	|	|	1844	|	1944	|	2044	|	2144	|	2244	|	...	2344	0031	...	0120	...
Friedrichshafen Stadt .. a.	1452	1516	1552	1625	1652	...	1725	1752	1825	1825	1852	1925	1952	2025	2052	2125	2152	2225	2251	2325	...	2352	0039	...	0128	...
Friedrichshafen Stadt .. d.	*1507*	1532	*1607*	1631	*1700*	...	1731	*1806*	*1831*	1831	*1907*	1931	*2007*	2031	*2107*	2131	*2207*	2231	2258	2332	...	...	...	...	...	...
Lindau Insel .... a.	*1541*	|	*1641*	|	*1733*	...	|	*1841*	|	|	*1941*	|	*2041*	|	*2141*	|	*2241*	|	|	2354	...	...	...	...	...	...
Lindau Reutin .... a.	...	1556	...	1655	...	...	1755	...	*1855*	1855	...	1955	...	2055	...	2155	...	2257	2325	0007	...	...	...	...	...	...

	Ⓐ	Ⓐ	Ⓐ			Ⓐ	Ⓒ	●	Ⓐ		Ⓒ	Ⓐ		Ⓐ								Ⓐ	Ⓒ	*ICE* **118** B✕		
Lindau Reutin .... d.	...	...	...	...	0530t	...	*0542*	...	...	...	0655	0702	...	...	0806	...	0905	...	*1003*	...	1105	...	...	1200	...	1305
Lindau Insel .... d.	...	...	0452	...	|	...	*0604*	...	0615	...	0706	|	...	0736	|	*0822*	|	*0920*	|	*1031*	|	*1120*	*1120*	|	*1220*	|
Friedrichshafen Stadt . a.	...	...	0519	...	0557t	...	*0627*	...	0643	...	0727	0726	...	0805	0828	*0854*	0927	*0950*	1027	*1058*	1127	*1150*	*1150*	1220	*1257*	1327
Friedrichshafen Stadt . d.	...	0449	...	0527	0603	0630	0634	...	...	0704	0734	0732	0806	...	0835	0905	0934	1005	1034	1103	1134	1203	1203	1235	1303	1334
Meckenbeuren .... d.	...	0455	...	0534	0610	0637	|	...	...	0711	|	|	0812	...	|	0912	|	1012	|	1112	|	1210	1212	|	1312	|
Ravensburg .... d.	...	0502	...	0542	0616	0644	0646	...	...	0718	0746	0745	0819	...	0846	0919	0946	1019	1046	1119	1146	1217	1219	1249	1319	1346
Aulendorf .... d.	...	0516	...	0556	0630	0659	0701	...	...	0732	0801	0759	0833	...	0901	0932	1001	1032	1101	1132	1201	1230	1232	|	1332	1401
Biberach (Riß) .... d.	...	0532	...	0614	0646	0718	0718	...	...	0748	0818	0818	0848	...	0918	0948	1018	1048	1118	1148	1218	1248	1248	1321	1348	1418
Ulm Hbf .... a.	...	0558	...	0640	0710	0740	0740	...	...	0811	0840	0840	0911	...	0940	1011	1040	1111	1140	1211	1240	1311	1311	1346	1410	1440
Ulm Hbf .... d.	0503	0602	...	...	0714	...	...	0745	...	0815	...	...	0915	...	...	1015	...	1115	...	1215	...	1315	1315	1354	1415	...
Geislingen (Steige) .... d.	0533	0629	...	...	0738	...	...	0814	...	0838	...	...	0938	...	...	1038	...	1138	...	1238	...	1338	1338	|	1438	...
Göppingen .... d.	0548	0647	...	...	0750	...	...	0840	...	0851	...	...	0951	...	...	1051	...	1151	...	1251	...	1351	1351	|	1451	...
Plochingen .... **936** d.	0602	0703	...	...	0803	...	...	0858	...	0903	...	...	1003	...	...	1103	...	1203	...	1303	...	1403	1403	|	1503	...
Stuttgart Hbf .... **936** a.	0620	0720	...	...	0820	...	...	0916	...	0920	...	...	1020	...	...	1120	...	1220	...	1320	...	1422	1422	1459	1520	...

							Ⓐ	Ⓒ			*RJ* **890** G✕								⊙			●		● Ⓒ		
Lindau Reutin .... d.	...	1405	...	1505	...	1605	...	...	1703	...	1731	...	*1805*	...	1905	...	2005	...	2105	...	2205	...	...	...	...	*2337*
Lindau Insel .... d.	*1320*	|	*1420*	|	*1520*	|	*1620*	*1620*	|	1722	|	...	|	*1820*	|	*1920*	|	*2020*	|	*2120*	|	...	*2220*	...	...	|
Friedrichshafen Stadt . a.	*1350*	1427	*1450*	1527	*1550*	1627	*1650*	*1650*	1727	1749	1754	...	*1827*	*1850*	1927	*1950*	2027	*2050*	2127	*2150*	2227	...	*2253*	...	...	*0014*
Friedrichshafen Stadt . d.	1403	1434	1503	1534	1605	1634	1703	1705	1734	...	1802	1809	1835	1905	1934	2003	2034	2103	2134	2204	2234	...	2304	...	2337	0019
Meckenbeuren .... d.	1412	|	1512	|	1612	|	1712	1712	|	...	|	1815	|	1912	|	2012	|	2112	|	2212	|	...	2311	...	2343	0031
Ravensburg .... d.	1419	1446	1519	1546	1619	1647	1719	1719	1746	...	1816	1822	1847	1919	1946	2019	2046	2119	2146	2219	2246	...	2318	...	2351	0042
Aulendorf .... d.	1432	1501	1532	1601	1632	1701	1732	1732	1801	...	1830	1835	1901	1932	2001	2032	2101	2132	2201	2232	2301	...	2332	...	0008	0103
Biberach (Riß) .... d.	1448	1518	1548	1618	1648	1718	1748	1748	1818	...	1845	1851	1918	1948	2018	2048	2118	2148	2218	2248	2318	...	2348	...	0024	...
Ulm Hbf .... a.	1511	1540	1611	1640	1711	1740	1811	1811	1840	...	1907	1913	1940	2011	2040	2111	2140	2211	2240	2311	2340	...	0014	...	0052	...
Ulm Hbf .... d.	1515	...	1615	...	1715	...	1815	1815	...	...	1910	1915	...	2015	...	2115	...	2215	...	2315	...	2346	...	0036	...	...
Geislingen (Steige) .... d.	1538	...	1638	...	1738	...	1838	1838	...	...	|	1938	...	2038	...	2138	...	2238	...	2338	...	0016	...	0113j	...	...
Göppingen .... d.	1551	...	1651	...	1751	...	1851	1851	...	...	|	1951	...	2051	...	2151	...	2251	...	2351	...	0038	...	0134	...	...
Plochingen .... **936** d.	1603	...	1703	...	1803	...	1903	1903	...	...	|	2005	...	2103	...	2203	...	2303	...	0003	...	0057	...	0153	...	...
Stuttgart Hbf .... **936** a.	1622	...	1720	...	1820	...	1921	1920	...	...	2005	2023	...	2120	...	2220	...	2320	...	0020	...	0116	...	0211	...	...

A – BODENSEE – (12) ✕ Dortmund - Köln - Wiesbaden - Stuttgart - Lindau - Bregenz - Innsbruck.
B – BODENSEE – (12) ✕ Innsbruck - Bregenz - Lindau - Stuttgart - Wiesbaden - Köln - Münster.
D – ALLGÄU – (12) Dortmund - Köln - Koblenz - Stuttgart - Ulm - Oberstdorf.
G – BREGENZERWALD – (12) ✕ Wien - Innsbruck - Bregenz - Stuttgart - Frankfurt and v.v.

j – Arrives 6–9 minutes earlier.
t – Ⓐ only.

● – Stopping service operated by Arverio Baden-Württemberg.
⊡ – Change trains at Friedrichshafen on Ⓒ.
⊙ – Change trains at Friedrichshafen on Ⓐ.

934 MÜNCHEN and AUGSBURG - MEMMINGEN - LINDAU

RE / RB services except where shown

See Table **935** for services via Kempten (also for connecting services from / to Augsburg). On June 9, Aug. 15, Nov. 1 services run as on ⑦.

km		⊖ Ⓐ	Ⓐ	⑥	Ⓐ	⊖ Ⓐ	†	Ⓐ	Ⓒ	⊖	⊖	Ⓐ	*ECE* **198** ✕				⊖	⊖	*ECE* **196** ✕				⊖	⊖	*ECE* **194** ✕	
0	**München** Hbf .... ⊡ d.	...	...	...	0439	...	...	...	...	...	0620	...	0654	0720	...	...	0753	0820	0853	0920	...	...	0952	1020	1054	1120
7	München Pasing .... d.	...	...	...	0447	...	...	...	...	...	0626	...	|	0727	...	...	0800	0827	|	0927	...	...	0959	1027	|	1127
42	Geltendorf .... d.	...	...	...	0507	...	...	...	...	...	0648	...	|	0747	...	...	|	0850	|	0947	...	...	|	1048	|	1147
56	Kaufering .... d.	...	...	...	0515	...	...	...	...	...	0657	...	|	0756	...	...	|	0858	|	0956	...	...	|	1057	|	1156
	Augsburg Hbf .... d.	...	...	...	|	...	...	0520	0532	...	|	*0646*	|	|	0735k	0735k	|	|	|	|	0941	0941	|	|	|	|
68	Buchloe .... a.	...	...	...	0522	...	...	0553	0603	...	0703	*0722*	0733	0803	0804	0804	0832	0904	0933	1005	1004	1004	1032	1104	1133	1205
68	Buchloe .... d.	...	0428	0502	▬	0543	0542	0558	0606	...	0712	0732	0736	▬	0806	0806	0833	0912	0936	▬	1008	1008	1033	1112	1135	▬
76	Türkheim (Bay) ...... ♠ d.	...	0435	0510	...	0549	0549	0615b	0615	...	0718	0746f	|	...	0817f	0820f	0839	0920	|	...	1016	1020f	1039	1120	|	...
81	Bad Wörishofen . ♠ a.	...	0442	0517	...	|	0556	|	|	...	|	0753	|	...	0823	|	|	|	|	...	1023	|	|	|	|	...
87	Mindelheim .... d.	...	▬	...	⊖	0559	...	0630f	0630f	...	0727	...	|	⊖	...	0831	0845	0929	|	⊖	...	1031	1045	1129	|	⊖
114	**Memmingen** .... a.	...	...	...	Ⓒ	0621	...	0657	0652	...	0745	...	0758		...	0851	0859	0948	0958		...	1050	1059	1147	1156	
114	**Memmingen** .... d.	0455	...	...	0606	0624	...	...	...	0706	...	...	0801	0806	...	...	0901	...	1001	1006	...	...	1101	...	1201	1206
146	Leutkirch .... **937** d.	0523	⊖	...	0636f	0702f	...	...	...	0744e	...	...	|	0836f	...	...	0923	...	|	1036f	...	...	1123	...	|	1236
157	Kißlegg .... **937** a.	0530	Ⓒ	...	0643	0711	...	...	...	0752	...	...	|	0843	...	...	0931	...	|	1043	...	...	1131	...	|	1243
157	Kißlegg .... **937** d.	0537	0542	...	0644	0717	...	...	...	0753	...	...	|	0844	...	...	0939	...	|	1044	...	...	1139j	...	|	1244
170	Wangen (Allgäu) . **937** d.	0546	0553	...	0653	0731f	...	...	...	0808f	...	...	|	0853	...	...	0951	...	|	1053	...	...	1151	...	|	1253
176	Hergatz .... d.	0551	0559	...	0659	0736	...	...	...	0814	...	...	|	0859	...	...	0958	...	|	1059	...	...	1158	...	|	1259
199	**Lindau** Insel .... a.	0608	0615	...	0715	0752	...	...	...	0830	...	...	|	0915	...	...	1015	...	|	1115	...	...	1215	...	|	1315
	Lindau Reutin .... a.	0619	0629	...	0725	*0759*	...	...	...	0841	...	...	0850	0925	...	...	*1024*	...	1050	1125	...	...	*1226*	...	1250	*1328*
	Zürich HB **75** .... a.	...	...	...	...	...	...	...	...	...	...	...	1027	...	...	...	...	...	1227	...	...	...	...	...	1427	...

FOR NOTES, SEE NEXT PAGE →

RE / RB services except where shown — MÜNCHEN and AUGSBURG - MEMMINGEN - LINDAU — 934

See Table **935** for services via Kempten (also for connecting services from / to Augsburg). On June 9, Aug. 15, Nov. 1 services run as on ⑦.

			⊖	⊖	*ECE* **192** ✕				⊖	⊖	*ECE* **190** ✕				⊖	⊖	*ECE* **98** ✕				⊖	⊖	*ECE* **96** ✕			
München Hbf ⊡ d.	...	...	1151	1220	1254	1320	...	...	1352	1420	1454	1520	...	...	1552	1620	1653	1720	...	...	1752	1820	1851	1920	...	...
München Pasing d.	...	...	1159	1227	|	1327	...	...	1359	1427	|	1527	...	...	1559	1627	|	1727	...	...	1759	1827	|	1927	...	...
Geltendorf d.	...	...	|	1248	|	1347	...	...	|	1448	|	1547z	...	...	|	1648	|	1747z	...	...	|	1848	|	1947	...	...
Kaufering d.	...	...	|	1257	|	1356	...	...	|	1457	|	1556	...	...	|	1657	|	1756	...	...	|	1857	|	1956	...	...
Augsburg Hbf d.	1140	1140	|	|	|	|	1326r	1326r	|	|	|	|	1541	1541	|	|	|	|	1741	1741	|	|	|	|	1942	1942
Buchloe a.	1204	1204	1232	1304	1333	1405	1404	1404	1432	1504	1533	1605	1604	1604	1632	1704	1733	1805	1804	1804	1832	1904	1933	2005	2004	2004
Buchloe d.	1208	1208	1233	1312	1336	▬	1408	1408	1433	1512	1536	▬	1608	1608	1633	1712	1736	▬	1808	1808	1833	1912	1936	▬	2008	2008
Türkheim (Bay) ♠ d.	1216	1220f	1239	1320	|	...	1416	1420f	1439	1520	|	...	1616	1620f	1639	1720	|	...	1816	1820f	1839	1920	|	...	2016	2020f
Bad Wörishofen ♠ a.	1223	|	|	|	|	...	1423	|	|	|	|	...	1623	|	|	|	|	...	1823	|	|	|	|	...	2023	|
Mindelheim d.	...	1231	1245	1329	|	⊖	...	1431	1445	1529	|	⊖	...	1631	1645	1729	|	⊖	...	1831	1845	1929	|	⊖	...	2031
Memmingen a.	...	1252	1259	1348	1358		...	1450	1459	1548	1558		...	1650	1659	1748	1758		...	1850	1859	1948	1958		...	2050
Memmingen d.	...	...	1301	...	1401	1406	...	...	1501	...	1601	1606	...	...	1701	...	1801	1806	...	...	1901	...	2001	2006	...	...
Leutkirch 937 d.	...	...	1323	...	|	1436f	...	...	1523	...	|	1636f	...	...	1723	...	|	1836f	...	...	1923	...	|	2036f	...	...
Kißlegg 937 a.	...	...	1331	...	|	1443	...	...	1531	...	|	1643	...	...	1731	...	|	1843	...	...	1931	...	|	2043	...	...
Kißlegg 937 d.	...	...	1339	...	|	1444	...	...	1539	...	|	1644	...	...	1739	...	|	1844	...	...	1939	...	|	2044	...	...
Wangen (Allgäu) 937 d.	...	...	1351	...	|	1453	...	...	1551	...	|	1653	...	...	1748	...	|	1853	...	...	1951	...	|	2053	...	...
Hergatz d.	...	...	1358	...	|	1459	...	...	1558	...	|	1659	...	...	1758	...	|	1859	...	...	1958	...	|	2059	...	...
Lindau Insel a.	...	...	1415	...	|	1515	...	...	1615	...	|	1715	...	...	1815	...	|	1915	...	...	2015	...	|	2115	...	...
Lindau Reutin a.	...	...	*1426*	...	1450	*1524*	...	...	*1626*	...	1650	*1725*	...	...	*1826*	...	1850	*1928*	...	...	*2032*	...	2050	*2126*	...	...
Zürich HB 75 a.	...	...	...	...	1627	...	...	...	...	...	1827	...	...	...	...	...	2027	...	...	...	...	...	2227	...	...	...

	⊖	⊖	*ECE* **296** Ⓑ v	⊖			⊖	⊖		
München Hbf ⊡ d.	1952	2020	2055	...	2120	...	...	2220	2320	...
München Pasing d.	2000	2026	|	...	2127	...	...	2227	2327	...
Geltendorf d.	|	2048	|	...	2147	...	...	2249	2347	...
Kaufering d.	|	2057	|	...	2156	...	...	2257	2356	...
Augsburg Hbf d.	|	|	|	...	|	2133	...	|	|	2333
Buchloe a.	2032	2104	2133	...	2204	2204	...	2304	0004	0004
Buchloe d.	2033	2112	2136	...	...	2207	...	2312	...	0008
Türkheim (Bay) ♠ d.	2039	2120	|	...	...	2219f	...	2320	...	0020f
Bad Wörishofen ♠ a.	|	|	|	...	...	|	...	|	...	|
Mindelheim d.	2045	2129	|	...	...	2230	...	2329	...	0031
Memmingen a.	2059	2148	2158	...	...	2250	...	2348	...	0053
Memmingen d.	2101	...	2201	2206	...	...	2306	...	...	...
Leutkirch 937 d.	2123	...	|	2236f	...	...	2329	...	...	...
Kißlegg 937 a.	2131	...	|	2243	...	...	2336	...	...	...
Kißlegg 937 d.	2139	...	|	2245	...	...	2339	...	...	...
Wangen (Allgäu) 937 d.	2151	...	|	2255	...	...	2348	...	...	...
Hergatz d.	2158	...	|	...	...	...	2359f	...	...	...
Lindau Insel a.	2215	...	|	...	...	...	0015	...	...	...
Lindau Reutin a.	2228	...	2249	...	...	...	0038	...	...	...
Zürich HB 75 a.	...	...	0027	...	...	...	...	...	...	...

	⊖ Ⓐ	⚒	⊖ Ⓐ	⊖ Ⓒ	⊖ Ⓐ	⊖ Ⓐ	⊖ Ⓐ	⊖ Ⓒ			
Zürich HB 75 d.	...	...	...	...	...	...	...	...	...	...	...
Lindau Reutin d.	...	...	...	...	...	...	0534	...	...	...	...
Lindau Insel d.	...	...	...	...	...	...	0545	...	...	...	...
Hergatz d.	...	...	...	...	...	...	0602	...	...	...	...
Wangen (Allgäu) 937 d.	...	...	...	...	0525	...	0611	0608	...	...	...
Kißlegg 937 a.	...	...	...	...	0534	...	0620	0618	...	...	...
Kißlegg 937 d.	...	...	0501	...	0535	...	0622	0628	...	...	...
Leutkirch 937 d.	...	...	0508	...	0542	...	0629	0635	...	...	...
Memmingen a.	...	...	0536	...	0607	...	0657	0657	...	...	...
Memmingen d.	0450	0503	0540	0611	0611	0640	...	...	0707	...	...
Mindelheim d.	0508	0524	0558	0630	0630	0658	...	...	0729	...	...
Bad Wörishofen ♠ d.	|	|	|	|	|	|	...	...	|	0735	...
Türkheim (Bay) ♠ d.	0515	0535	0605	0641	0642	0706	...	...	0744f	0744	...
Buchloe a.	0520	0541	0611	0647	0648	0712	...	...	0752	0752	...
Buchloe d.	0522	0552	0616	0656	0656	0716	...	...	0755	0755	0755
Augsburg Hbf a.	|	0624	|	|	|	|	...	...	0818	0818	|
Kaufering d.	0529	...	0623	0703	0703	0723	...	...	...	...	0803
Geltendorf d.	0538	...	0631	0711	0711	0731	...	...	...	...	0811z
München Pasing a.	0558	...	0653	0733	0736	0759	...	...	...	...	0833
München Hbf ⊡ a.	0606	...	0700	0741	0743	0806	...	...	...	...	0840

	⊖ Ⓐ	⊖ Ⓐ	*ECE* **297** ★✕	⊖ Ⓐ	⊖ Ⓒ	⊖			⊖	*ECE* **97** ✕	⊖	⊖			⊖	*ECE* **99** ✕	⊖	⊖			⊖	*ECE* **191** ✕	⊖	⊖		
Zürich HB 75 d.	...	...	0535	...	...	...	...	...	...	0733	...	...	...	...	...	0933	...	...	...	...	...	1133	...	...	...	...
Lindau Reutin d.	...	0644	0710	...	0634	0734	...	...	0823	0910	...	*0930*	...	...	1021	1110	...	*1130*	...	...	1222	1310	...	*1330*	...	...
Lindau Insel d.	...	|	|	...	0645	0745	...	...	0835	|	...	0945	...	...	1035	|	...	1145	...	...	1235	|	...	1345	...	...
Hergatz d.	...	0701	|	...	0703	0801	...	...	0859f	|	...	1002	...	...	1059f	|	...	1202	...	...	1259f	|	...	1402	...	...
Wangen (Allgäu) 937 d.	...	0706	|	...	0708	0808	...	...	0904	|	...	1008	...	...	1104	|	...	1208	...	...	1304	|	...	1408	...	...
Kißlegg 937 a.	...	0716	|	...	0717	0819	...	...	0913	|	...	1019	...	...	1113	|	...	1219	...	...	1313	|	...	1419	...	...
Kißlegg 937 d.	...	0723	|	...	0723	0828	...	...	0914	|	...	1028	...	...	1114	|	...	1228	...	...	1314	|	...	1428	...	...
Leutkirch 937 d.	...	0730	|	...	0730	0835	...	...	0928f	|	...	1035	...	...	1128f	|	...	1235	...	...	1328f	|	...	1435	...	...
Memmingen a.	...	0752	0758	...	0753	0858	...	...	0954	0958	...	1058	...	...	1152	1158	...	1258	...	...	1354	1358	...	1458	...	...
Memmingen d.	0746	▬	0802	0811	0808	0900	0907	...	▬	1001	1011	1100	1107	...	▬	1201	1207	1300	1307	...	▬	1401	1411	1500	1507	...
Mindelheim d.	0806	...	|	0830	0830	0913	0929	...	...	|	1030	1113	1129	...	...	|	1230	1313	1329	...	...	|	1430	1513	1529	...
Bad Wörishofen ♠ d.	|	...	|	|	|	|	|	0935	...	|	|	|	|	1135	...	|	|	|	|	1335	...	|	|	|	|	1535
Türkheim (Bay) ♠ d.	0813	...	|	0841	0841	0920	0944f	0944	...	|	1041	1120	1144f	1144	...	|	1241	1320	1344f	1344	...	|	1441	1520	1544f	1544
Buchloe a.	0819	...	0823	0847	0847	0926	0952	0952	...	1023	1047	1125	1152	1152	...	1223	1247	1326	1352	1352	...	1423	1447	1526	1552	1552
Buchloe d.	0820	0838	0825	0856	0856	0927	0955	0955	0955	1025	1056	1127	1155	1155	1155	1225	1256	1327	1355	1355	1355	1425	1456	1527	1555	1555
Augsburg Hbf a.	|	0909	|	|	|	|	1020	1020	|	|	|	|	1219	1219	|	|	|	|	1419	1419	|	|	|	|	1618	1618
Kaufering d.	|	...	|	0903	0903	|	...	...	1003	|	1103	|	...	...	1203	|	1303	|	...	...	1403	|	1503	|	...	...
Geltendorf d.	0833	...	|	0911	0911	|	...	...	1011	|	1111	|	...	...	1211	|	1311	|	...	...	1411	|	1511	|	...	...
München Pasing a.	|	...	|	0933	0933	0957	...	...	1033	|	1133	1157	...	...	1233	|	1333	1357	...	...	1433	|	1533	1558	...	...
München Hbf ⊡ a.	0859	...	0905	0940	0940	1005	...	...	1042	1104	1142	1204	...	...	1242	1304	1340	1405	...	...	1442	1504	1541	1605	...	...

	⊖	*ECE* **193** ✕	⊖	⊖			⊖	*ECE* **195** ✕	⊖	⊖			⊖	*ECE* **197** ✕	⊖	⊖	⊖ †		⊖	*ECE* **199** w✕	⊖	⊖				⊖ Ⓒ
Zürich HB 75 d.	...	1333	...	...	...	...	...	1533	...	...	...	...	...	1733	...	...	...	...	...	1933	...	...	...	...	...	...
Lindau Reutin d.	1422	1510	...	*1530*	...	...	1622	1710	...	*1725*	...	...	1822	1910	...	*1930*	*1930*	...	2022	2110	...	*2131*	...	...	...	2221
Lindau Insel d.	1435	|	...	1545	...	...	1635	|	...	1745	...	...	1835	|	...	1945	1945	...	2035	|	...	2145	...	...	...	2240
Hergatz d.	1459f	|	...	1602	...	...	1659f	|	...	1803	...	...	1859f	|	...	2002	2002	...	2059f	|	...	2202	...	...	...	2257
Wangen (Allgäu) 937 d.	1504	|	...	1608	...	...	1704	|	...	1808	...	...	1904	|	...	2008	2008	...	2104	|	...	2208	...	...	...	2306
Kißlegg 937 a.	1513	|	...	1619	...	...	1713	|	...	1819	...	...	1913	|	...	2019	2019	...	2113	|	...	2219	...	...	...	2315
Kißlegg 937 d.	1514	|	...	1628	...	...	1714	|	...	1828	...	...	1914	|	...	2028	2028	...	2114	|	...	2228	...	...	...	2319
Leutkirch 937 d.	1528h	|	...	1635	...	...	1728f	|	...	1835	...	...	1928f	|	...	2035	2035	...	2128f	|	...	2235	...	...	...	2331
Memmingen a.	1554	1558	...	1658	...	...	1754	1758	...	1858	...	...	1954	1958	...	2058	2058	...	2154	2158	...	2257	...	...	...	2355
Memmingen d.	▬	1601	1611	1700	1707	...	▬	1801	1811	1900	1906	...	▬	2001	2011	...	2100	2107	▬	2201	2211	...	2307	...	...	...
Mindelheim d.	...	|	1630	1713	1729	...	...	|	1830	1913	1929	...	...	|	2030	...	2113	2129	...	|	2230	...	2329	...	...	...
Bad Wörishofen ♠ d.	...	|	|	|	|	1735	...	|	|	|	|	1935	...	|	|	...	|	|	...	|	|	...	|	...	0031	...
Türkheim (Bay) ♠ d.	...	|	1641	1720	1744f	1744	...	|	1841	1920	1944f	1944	...	|	2041	...	2120	2144f	...	|	2240	...	2344f	...	0038	...
Buchloe a.	...	1623	1647	1726	1752	1752	...	1823	1847	1926	1952	1952	...	2022	2047	...	2126	2150	...	2223	2246	...	2350	...	0044	...
Buchloe d.	1555	1625	1656	1727	1755	1755	1755	1825	1856	1927	1955	1955	1955	2025	2056	...	2127	2158	2156	2225	2256	...	0010	2355	...	...
Augsburg Hbf a.	|	|	|	|	1818	1818	|	|	|	|	2020	2020	|	|	|	...	|	2226	|	|	|	...	0046	|	...	...
Kaufering d.	1603	|	1703	|	...	...	1803	|	1903	|	...	...	2003	|	2103	...	|	...	2203	|	2303	...	...	0003	...	...
Geltendorf d.	1611	|	1711	|	...	...	1811	|	1911	|	...	...	2011	|	2111	...	|	...	2211	|	2311	...	...	0011	...	...
München Pasing a.	1633	|	1733	1757	...	...	1833	|	1934	1958	...	...	2033	|	2133	...	2157	...	2233	|	2333	...	...	0033	...	...
München Hbf ⊡ a.	1642	1704	1741	1805	...	...	1842	1904	1942	2006	...	...	2042	2105	2141	...	2204	...	2242	2304	2342	...	...	0042	...	...

b – Arrives 0605.
e – Arrives 0729.
f – Arrives 5–8 minutes earlier.
g – 1137 Oct. 6 - Nov. 3.
h – Arrives 1522; departs 1526 Oct. 6 - Nov. 3.
k – 0741 on Ⓒ.
r – 1341 on Ⓒ.
v – Not June 8.
z – Ⓒ only.

★ – ①–⑥ (not June 9).
⊖ – Operated by Arverio Bayern.
⊡ – Most trains in Table **934** use platforms 27–36 at München Hbf (minimum connecting time with other services is 10 minutes).
♠ – Other journeys Türkheim - Bad Wörishofen and v.v. (journey time: 6–7 minutes).
From Türkheim at 0510 Ⓐ, 0541 ⚒, 0617, 0643, 0722, 0843, 0922, 1043, 1122, 1243, 1322, 1443, 1522, 1643, 1722, 1843, 1922, 2043, 2122, 2216, 2243, 2322 and 0018.
From Bad Wörishofen at 0448 Ⓐ, 0524 ⚒, 0554 Ⓐ, 0602 Ⓒ, 0630, 0656 Ⓐ, 0702 Ⓒ, 0805 Ⓐ, 0829, 0907, 1029, 1107, 1229, 1307, 1429, 1507, 1629, 1707, 1829, 1907, 2029, 2107, 2135, 2229, 2301 and 2335.

935 MÜNCHEN, AUGSBURG and ULM - KEMPTEN - LINDAU

RE / RB services except where shown.

See Table **934** for other services München - Buchloe - Memmingen - Lindau. On June 9, Aug. 15, Nov. 1 services run as on ⑦.

km		Ⓐ	Ⓐ	⚒	Ⓐ	Ⓐ	◇ Ⓐ	Ⓐ	Ⓒ	Ⓒ	⚒	⑥	◇ Ⓒ			Ⓐ	Ⓒ	◇ Ⓐ	⊖			◇ Ⓒ	◇ Ⓐ		Ⓐ	Ⓒ	
0	**München** Hbf ⊡ d.	...	...	...	0439	...	...	...	...	...	0520	0520	...	0539	...	...	...	...	0620	...	...	...	...	0639	...	...	...
7	München Pasing d.	...	...	...	0447	...	...	...	...	...	0527	0527	...	0547	...	...	...	...	0626	...	...	...	...	0647	...	...	...
42	Geltendorf d.	...	...	...	0507	...	...	...	...	...	0547	0547	...	0607	...	...	...	...	0648	...	...	...	...	0707	...	...	...
56	Kaufering d.	...	...	...	0515	...	...	...	...	...	0556	0556	...	0615	...	...	...	...	0657	...	...	...	...	0715	...	...	...
	Nürnberg Hbf **905** d.	...	...	...	|	...	...	...	...	...	|	|	...	|	...	...	...	...	|	...	...	...	...	|	...	...	...
	Augsburg Hbf d.	...	...	...	|	0450	*0520*	...	...	0532	|	|	...	|	0609**t**	...	...	0618	|	0632	0632	...	...	|	0707	...	0735**k**
68	Buchloe a.	...	...	...	0522	0523	*0553*	...	...	0603	0603	0603	...	0624	0638**t**	...	...	0651	0703	0700**e**	0700**e**	...	...	0723	0738	...	0804
68	Buchloe d.	...	...	...	▬	0529	0557	...	...	▬	0606	0606	...	▬	0639	...	...	0655	...	0707**e**	0707**e**	...	←	▬	0739	0739	▬
88	Kaufbeuren d.	...	...	...	...	0546	0611	...	...	...	0616	0616	0621	...	0651	...	...	0708	...	0718**e**	0718**e**	0721	0728	...	0751	0751	...
94	Biessenhofen d.	...	...	...	...	0550	0617	...	...	...	|	|	0626	...	0656	...	...	→	...	|	|	0726	0734	...	0758	0758	...
100	Marktoberdorf d.	...	...	...	...	|	0639**k**	...	...	...	|	|	0635	...	|	...	...	...	...	|	|	0735	0745	...	|	|	...
131	**Füssen** a.	...	...	...	...	|	0721	...	...	...	|	|	0715	...	|	...	...	...	...	|	|	0815	0837	Ⓒ	|	|	Ⓐ
	Ulm Hbf d.	...	...	...	...	|	...	...	0510	...	|	|	▬	...	|	0548	0614	...	...	|	|	...	...	0719	|	|	0713
	Memmingen a.	...	...	...	...	|	...	...	0553	...	|	|	...	...	|	0641	0701	...	...	|	|	...	...	0753	|	|	0801
	Memmingen d.	...	...	...	...	|	...	0554	0600	...	|	|	...	...	|	0642	0702	...	...	|	|	...	...	0758	|	|	0803
131	**Kempten** Hbf a.	...	...	...	⚒	0616	...	0623	0626	...	0640	0640	Ⓒ	...	0722	0709	0727	...	...	0741	0741	...	...	0820	0823	0823	0827
131	**Kempten** Hbf d.	0452	...	0540	0540	...	...	0628	...	0641	0641	0641	0641	...	...	0727	0729	...	...	0742	0742	...	...	0820	...	0830	0830
152	Immenstadt a.	0508	...	0553	0553	...	...	0645	...	0655	0655	0655	0655	Ⓐ	...	0742	0745	...	...	0755	0755	...	...	0834	...	0845	0846
152	Immenstadt d.	0510	0519	0555	0612	...	...	0651	...	0657	0657	0705	0705	0715	...	0751	0751	...	...	0757	0812	...	...	0840	...	0851	0851
	Sonthofen d.	|	0528	|	0621	...	...	0703	...	|	|	0714	0714	0726	...	0800	0800	...	...	|	0821	...	...	0850	...	0901	0900
	Oberstdorf a.	|	0557	|	0646	...	...	0725	...	|	|	0734	0734	0752	...	0821	0821	...	...	|	0849	...	...	0909	...	0928	0920
197	Hergatz d.	0545	...	0626	...	...	...	...	...	0728	0728	...	...	...	...	...	...	...	...	0828	...	...	...	...	...	...	...
220	**Lindau** Reutin a.	|	...	0643	...	...	...	...	...	0745	0745	...	...	...	...	...	...	...	...	0845	...	...	...	...	...	...	...
	Lindau Insel a.	*0608*	...	0654	...	...	...	...	...	0755	0755	...	...	...	...	...	...	...	...	0855	...	...	...	...	...	...	...

				◇ Ⓐ	◇ Ⓒ			◇ Ⓒ	⊖		Ⓒ	Ⓐ		◇					◇	◇		⊖				◇	
München Hbf ⊡ d.	0720	0720	0739	...	...	...	...	0807	0820	...	...	...	0839	...	...	...	0920	0920	...	0941	...	1020	...	...	1039	...	...
München Pasing d.	0727	0727	0745	...	...	...	...	0815	0827	...	...	...	0847	...	...	...	0927	0927	...	0947	...	1027	...	...	1047	...	...
Geltendorf d.	0747	0747	0807	...	...	...	...	|	0850	...	...	...	0907	...	...	...	0947	0947	...	1007	...	1048	...	...	1107	...	...
Kaufering d.	0756	0756	0815	...	...	...	...	|	0858	...	...	...	0915	...	...	...	0956	0956	...	1016	...	1057	...	...	1115	...	...
Nürnberg Hbf **905** d.	|	|	|	...	...	...	...	|	|	0719**x**	0719**x**	0719**x**	|	...	...	...	|	|	...	|	...	|	...	...	|	...	...
Augsburg Hbf d.	|	|	|	0745	0747	0809	...	|	|	0842	0842	0842	|	0846	0909**t**	0941	|	|	0948	|	1009	|	1042	1042	|	1046	1109
Buchloe a.	0803	0803	0824	0818	0819	0838	...	0848	0904	0905	0905	0905	0924	0922	0938**t**	1004	1005	1005	1020	1024	1038	1104	1105	1105	1124	1118	1138
Buchloe d.	0807	0807	...	0830	0831	0839	...	0858	...	0907	0907	0907	...	0930	0939	▬	1007	1007	...	1030	1039	▬	1107	1107	...	1128	1140
Kaufbeuren d.	0817	0817	...	0845	0845	0851	...	0911	...	0919	0919	0919	...	0945	0951	...	1019	1019	...	1045	1051	...	1119	1119	...	1145	1151
Biessenhofen d.	|	|	...	0850	0850	0856	...	|	...	|	|	|	...	0950	0956	...	|	|	...	1050	1056	...	|	|	...	1150	1156
Marktoberdorf d.	|	|	...	0901	0859	|	...	0926	...	|	|	|	...	1001	|	...	|	|	...	1101	|	...	|	|	...	1201	|
Füssen a.	|	|	...	0942	0939	|	...	1012	...	|	|	|	...	1042	|	...	|	|	...	1142	|	...	|	|	...	1242	|
Ulm Hbf d.	|	|	...	...	...	|	0817	...	...	|	|	|	...	...	|	0917	|	|	...	...	|	1017	|	|	...	...	|
Memmingen a.	|	|	...	...	...	|	0855	...	...	|	|	|	...	...	|	0954	|	|	...	...	|	1054	|	|	...	...	|
Memmingen d.	|	|	...	...	...	|	0904	...	...	|	|	|	...	...	|	1000	|	|	...	...	|	1102	|	|	...	...	|
Kempten Hbf a.	0841	0841	...	...	...	0922	0926	...	...	0941	0941	0941	...	...	1022	1026	1041	1041	...	...	1122	1125	1141	1141	...	...	1222
Kempten Hbf d.	0842	0842	...	...	...	...	0930	...	...	0942	0942	0942	...	...	...	1030	1042	1042	...	...	...	1130	1142	1142	...	...	...
Immenstadt a.	0855	0855	...	...	...	...	0945	...	...	0955	0955	0955	...	...	...	1045	1055	1055	...	...	...	1145	1155	1155	...	...	...
Immenstadt d.	0857	0912	...	...	...	...	0951	...	...	0957	1012	1021	...	...	...	1051	1057	1112	...	...	...	1151	1157	1212	...	...	...
Sonthofen d.	|	0921	...	...	...	...	1000	...	...	|	1030	1030	...	...	...	1100	|	1121	...	...	...	1201	|	1221	...	...	...
Oberstdorf a.	|	0947	...	...	...	...	1025	...	...	|	1053	1054	...	...	...	1120	|	1154**j**	...	...	...	1221	|	1251	...	...	...
Hergatz d.	0928	...	...	...	...	...	...	...	...	1028	...	...	...	...	...	...	1128	...	...	...	...	...	1228	...	...	...	...
Lindau Reutin a.	0945	...	...	...	...	...	...	...	...	1045	...	...	...	...	...	...	1145	...	...	...	...	...	1245	...	...	...	...
Lindau Insel a.	0955	...	...	...	...	...	...	...	...	1055	...	...	...	...	...	...	1156	...	...	...	...	...	1255	...	...	...	...

	Ⓐ			Ⓒ	Ⓐ		◇ Y	◇ Ⓐ **d**		⊖				◇		Ⓐ	Ⓒ				◇	*IC* **2085** **H**		⊖			◇
München Hbf ⊡ d.	...	...	1120	1120	1120	1139	...	...	...	1220	...	...	1239	...	...	...	...	1320	1320	1339	...	...	...	1420	...	...	...
München Pasing d.	...	...	1127	1127	1127	1147	...	...	...	1227	...	...	1247	...	...	...	...	1327	1327	1347	...	...	...	1427	...	...	...
Geltendorf d.	...	...	1147	1147	1147	1207	...	...	...	1248	...	...	1307	...	...	...	...	1347	1347	1407	...	...	...	1448	...	...	...
Kaufering d.	...	...	1156	1156	1156	1215	...	...	...	1257	...	...	1315	...	...	...	...	1356	1356	1415	...	...	...	1457	...	...	...
Nürnberg Hbf **905** d.	...	...	|	|	|	|	...	...	...	|	...	...	|	...	...	...	...	|	|	|	...	...	...	|	...	...	...
Augsburg Hbf d.	...	1140	|	|	|	|	1148	1148	1209	|	1241	1241	|	1246	...	1326	1341	|	|	|	1346	1355	1409	|	1442	1442	1452
Buchloe a.	...	1204	1205	1205	1205	1224	1220	1220	1238	1304	1304	1304	1324	1322	...	1404	1404	1405	1405	1424	1430	1423	1438	1504	1505	1505	1524
Buchloe d.	...	▬	1207	1207	1207	...	1230	1230	1239	▬	1307	1307	...	1330	1339	▬	▬	1407	1407	...	1431	1424	1439	▬	1507	1507	...
Kaufbeuren d.	...	...	1219	1219	1219	...	1245	1245	1251	...	1319	1319	...	1345	1351	...	...	1419	1419	...	1445	1439	1451	...	1519	1519	...
Biessenhofen d.	...	...	|	|	|	...	1250	1250	1256	...	|	|	...	1350	1356	...	...	|	|	...	1450	|	1456	...	|	|	...
Marktoberdorf d.	...	...	|	|	|	...	1301	1311**k**	|	...	|	|	...	1401	|	...	...	|	|	...	1501	|	|	...	|	|	...
Füssen a.	...	Ⓒ	|	|	|	...	1342	1356	|	...	|	|	...	1442	|	...	Ⓐ	|	|	...	1542	|	|	...	|	|	...
Ulm Hbf d.	1113	1117	|	|	|	...	...	...	|	1217	|	|	...	...	|	1317	1317	|	|	...	...	|	|	1417	|	|	...
Memmingen a.	1200	1200	|	|	|	...	...	...	|	1255	|	|	...	...	|	1354	1354	|	|	...	...	|	|	1455	|	|	...
Memmingen d.	1201	1201	|	|	|	...	...	...	|	1302	|	|	...	...	|	1401	1401	|	|	...	...	|	|	1504	|	|	...
Kempten Hbf a.	1227	1227	1241	1241	1241	...	...	...	1322	1326	1341	1341	...	...	1422	1428	1428	1441	1441	...	...	1510	1522	1526	1541	1541	...
Kempten Hbf d.	1230	...	1242	1242	1242	...	...	...	...	1327	1342	1342	...	...	...	...	1429	1442	1442	...	...	1511	...	1529	1542	1542	...
Immenstadt a.	1245	...	1255	1255	1255	...	...	...	...	1345	1355	1355	...	...	...	...	1445	1455	1455	...	...	1527	...	1545	1555	1555	...
Immenstadt d.	1251	...	1257	1312	1314	...	...	...	...	1351	1357	1412	...	...	...	...	1452	1457	1512	...	...	1542	...	1551	1557	1612	...
Sonthofen d.	1300	...	|	1321	1322	...	...	...	...	1400	|	1421	...	...	...	...	1501	|	1521	...	...	1551	...	1601	|	1621	...
Oberstdorf a.	1321	...	|	1351	1351	...	...	...	...	1420	|	1451	...	...	...	...	1521	|	1551	...	...	1612	...	1622	|	1650	...
Hergatz d.	...	...	1328	...	...	...	...	...	...	...	1428	...	...	...	...	...	...	1528	...	...	...	...	...	...	1628	...	...
Lindau Reutin a.	...	...	1345	...	...	...	...	...	...	...	1445	...	...	...	...	...	...	1545	...	...	...	...	...	...	1645	...	...
Lindau Insel a.	...	...	1355	...	...	...	...	...	...	...	1455	...	...	...	...	...	...	1555	...	...	...	...	...	...	1655	...	...

	◇		Ⓐ				Ⓐ	Ⓒ	◇	*IC* **2013** **A**		⊖				◇					Ⓐ	Ⓒ	◇		⊖		
München Hbf ⊡ d.	1440	...	...	...	1520	1520	1535	1539	...	...	...	1620	...	...	1639	...	...	...	1720	1720	1734	1736	...	...	1820	...	...
München Pasing d.	1448	...	...	...	1527	1527	1542	1547	...	...	...	1627	...	...	1646	...	...	...	1727	1727	1740	1747	...	...	1827	...	...
Geltendorf d.	1507	...	...	...	1547**z**	1547**z**	1607	1607	...	...	...	1648	...	...	1707	...	...	...	1747**z**	1747**z**	1807	1807	...	...	1848	...	...
Kaufering d.	1515	...	...	...	1556	1556	1615	1615	...	...	...	1657	...	...	1715	...	...	...	1756	1756	1815	1815	...	...	1857	...	...
Nürnberg Hbf **905** d.	|	...	...	...	|	|	|	|	...	...	...	|	...	...	|	...	...	...	|	|	|	|	...	...	|	1713**y**	1713**y**
Augsburg Hbf d.	|	...	...	1541	|	|	|	|	1547	...	1609	|	1642	1642	|	1651	1709**t**	1741	|	|	|	|	1746	1809	|	1842	1842
Buchloe a.	1523	...	...	1604	1605	1605	1624	1624	1620	...	1638	1704	1705	1705	1722	1722	1738**t**	1804	1805	1805	1824	1824	1820	1838	1904	1905	1905
Buchloe d.	1531	1539	...	▬	1607	1607	...	...	1630	...	1639	▬	1707	1707	▬	1731	1739	▬	1807	1807	▬	...	1830	1839	▬	1907	1907
Kaufbeuren d.	1545	1551	...	...	1619	1619	...	...	1645	...	1651	...	1719	1719	...	1745	1751	...	1819	1819	...	...	1845	1851	...	1919	1919
Biessenhofen d.	1551	1556	...	...	|	|	...	...	1650	...	1656	...	|	|	...	1750	1756	...	|	|	...	...	1850	1856	...	|	|
Marktoberdorf d.	1601	|	...	...	|	|	...	...	1701	...	|	...	|	|	...	1801	|	...	|	|	...	...	1901	|	...	|	|
Füssen a.	1642	|	...	Ⓒ	|	|	...	...	1742	...	|	Ⓒ	|	|	Ⓐ	1842	|	...	|	|	...	...	1942	|	...	|	|
Ulm Hbf d.	...	|	1517	1517	|	|	...	...	...	1616	|	1620	|	|	1620	...	|	1717	|	|	...	...	...	|	1817	|	|
Memmingen a.	...	|	1554	1554	|	|	...	...	...	1644	|	1704	|	|	1726	...	|	1755	|	|	...	...	...	|	1855	|	|
Memmingen d.	...	|	1600	1600	|	|	...	...	...	1645	|	1705	|	|	1736	...	|	1801	|	|	...	...	...	|	1904	|	|
Kempten Hbf a.	...	1622	1627	1627	1641	1641	...	...	...	1708	1722	1731	1741	1741	1808	...	1822	1827	1841	1841	Ⓐ	...	...	1922	1926	1941	1941
Kempten Hbf d.	...	...	1629	1629	1642	1642	...	...	...	1709	1730**t**	1731	1742	1742	...	...	...	1829	1842	1842	1907	...	...	...	1929	1942	1942
Immenstadt a.	...	...	1645	1645	1655	1655	...	...	...	1724	1745**t**	1746	1755	1755	...	...	...	1845	1855	1855	1923	...	...	...	1945	1955	1955
Immenstadt d.	...	...	1651	1653	1657	1712	...	...	...	1742	1751**t**	1752	1757	1812	...	...	...	1851	1857	1912	1924	...	...	...	1952	1957	2012
Sonthofen d.	...	...	1701	1702	|	1721	...	...	...	1751	1801**t**	1801	|	1821	...	...	...	1901	|	1921	|	...	...	...	2001	|	2021
Oberstdorf a.	...	...	1726	1727	|	1749	...	...	...	1812	1822**t**	1822	|	1849	...	...	...	1921**g**	|	1946	|	...	...	...	2021	|	2045
Hergatz d.	...	...	...	...	1728	...	...	...	...	...	...	...	1828	...	...	...	...	...	1928	...	2008	...	...	...	...	2028	...
Lindau Reutin a.	...	...	...	...	1745	...	...	...	...	...	...	...	1845	...	...	...	...	...	1945	...	|	...	...	...	...	2045	...
Lindau Insel a.	...	...	...	...	1755	...	...	...	...	...	...	...	1855	...	...	...	...	...	1955	...	2028	...	...	...	...	2055	...

FOR NOTES, SEE NEXT PAGE →

RE / RB services except where shown — MÜNCHEN, AUGSBURG and ULM - KEMPTEN - LINDAU — 935

See Table **934** for other services Lindau - Memmingen - Buchloe - München. On June 9, Aug. 15, Nov. 1 services run as on ⑦.

		◇ Ⓐ	◇ Ⓐ	◇ Ⓒ					◇	◇ Ⓑ	◇ ⑥	⊖		⊖		⊗	◇				◇	⊖		◇			
München Hbf ⊡ d.	1836	...	...	...	...	...	1920	1920	...	1939	1939	1952	...	2020	...	...	...	2039	...	2120	...	2220	...	...	...	2320	0020
München Pasing d.	1847	...	...	...	...	...	1927	1927	...	1947	1947	2000	...	2026	...	...	...	2047	...	2127	...	2227	...	...	...	2327	0027
Geltendorf d.	1907	...	...	...	...	...	1947	1947	...	2007	2007	|	...	2048	...	...	...	2107	...	2147	...	2249	...	...	...	2347	0048
Kaufering d.	1915	...	...	...	...	...	1956	1956	...	2016	2016	|	...	2057	...	...	...	2115	...	2156	...	2257	...	...	...	2356	0057
Nürnberg Hbf **905** d.	|	...	...	...	...	...	|	|	...	|	|	|	...	|	...	...	...	|	...	|	...	|	...	...	...	|	|
Augsburg Hbf d.	|	1846	...	1846	1909**t**	1942	|	|	1946	|	|	|	...	|	2032	2032	...	|	2133	|	...	|	2232	...	2333	|	|
Buchloe a.	1924	1922	...	1922	1938**t**	2004	2005	2005	2018	2024	2024	2032	...	2104	2105	2105	...	2122	2204	2204	...	2304	2305	...	0004	0004	0104
Buchloe d.	...	1927	...	1930	1939	▬	2007	2007	...	2027	2027	...	2039	▬	2107	2107	...	...	▬	2207	...	▬	2308	...	▬	0007	...
Kaufbeuren d.	...	1938	1945	1945	1951	...	2019	2019	...	2046**f**	2045**f**	...	2051	...	2118	2118	2123	...	...	2218	2226	...	2319	2336	...	0018	...
Biessenhofen d.	...	...	1950	1950	1956	...	|	|	...	2051	2050	...	2056	...	2122	2122	2128	...	...	2222	2231	...	2323	2345	...	0022	...
Marktoberdorf d.	...	...	2001	2001	|	...	|	|	...	2101	2106**f**	...	|	...	|	|	2137	...	...	|	2240	...	|	0005**f**	...	|	...
Füssen a.	...	...	2042	2042	|	...	|	|	...	2144	2147	...	|	...	|	|	2220	...	...	|	2321	...	|	0045	...	|	...
Ulm Hbf d.	...	...	...	...	|	1917	|	|	...	...	...	...	|	2017	|	|	...	...	2117	|	▬	2217	|	▬	2317	|	...
Memmingen a.	...	...	...	...	|	1954	|	|	...	...	...	...	|	2055	|	|	...	...	2154	|	...	2257	|	...	2359	|	...
Memmingen d.	...	...	...	...	|	2004	|	|	...	...	...	...	|	2059	|	|	...	...	2203	|	...	2302	|	...	0006	|	...
Kempten Hbf a.	...	...	...	...	2022	2030	2041	2041	...	...	...	...	2122	2126	2143	2143	...	...	2229	2243	...	2328	2344	...	0032	0044	...
Kempten Hbf d.	...	...	...	...	...	...	2042	2042	...	...	...	...	...	...	2145	2145	...	...	...	2245	...	...	2345	...	...	...	...
Immenstadt a.	...	...	...	...	...	...	2056	2056	...	...	...	...	...	...	2201	2201	...	...	...	2300	...	...	2400	...	...	...	...
Immenstadt d.	...	...	...	...	...	...	2058	2112	...	...	...	...	...	...	2203	2212	...	...	...	2302	2312	...	0002	0012	...	...	...
Sonthofen d.	...	...	...	...	...	...	|	2121	...	...	...	...	...	...	|	2221	...	...	...	|	2321	...	|	0021	...	...	...
Oberstdorf a.	...	...	...	...	...	...	|	2145	...	...	...	...	...	...	|	2244	...	...	...	|	2344	...	|	0042	...	...	...
Hergatz d.	...	...	...	...	...	...	2128	...	...	...	...	...	...	...	2238	...	...	...	...	2333	...	...	0035	...	...	...	...
Lindau Reutin a.	...	...	...	...	...	...	2145	...	...	...	...	...	...	...	2253	...	...	...	...	2350	...	...	0052	...	...	...	...
Lindau Insel a.	...	...	...	...	...	...	2155	...	...	...	...	...	...	...	2302	...	...	...	...	2400	...	...	0102	...	...	...	...

km		Ⓐ	⊖ Ⓐ	Ⓐ	Ⓐ	Ⓒ	Ⓒ	Ⓐ		Ⓐ	◇		Ⓒ	Ⓐ	Ⓐ	⊖	◇ Ⓐ	Ⓒ	Ⓐ	Ⓐ	⊖ Ⓐ	◇ Ⓒ	Ⓒ			Ⓒ	Ⓐ
	Lindau Insel d.	...	...	...	...	...	...	...	0411**t**	...	...	...	...	...	0454	...	...	...	...	...	...	...	...	...	0551	...	...
	Lindau Reutin d.	...	...	...	...	...	...	...	|	...	...	...	...	...	0504	...	...	...	...	...	...	...	...	...	0604	...	...
	Hergatz d.	...	...	...	...	...	...	...	0427**t**	...	...	...	...	...	0518	...	...	...	...	...	...	...	...	...	0620	...	...
0	**Oberstdorf** d.	...	...	...	...	...	...	0433	|	...	...	...	...	0520	|	...	...	...	0534	...	...	...	...	0612	|	...	0628
13	Sonthofen d.	...	...	...	...	...	...	0454	|	...	...	...	...	0539	|	...	...	...	0554	...	...	...	...	0632	|	...	0652
21	Immenstadt a.	...	...	...	...	...	...	0505	0505**t**	...	...	...	...	0548	0554	...	...	...	0604	...	...	...	...	0642	0656	...	0704
21	Immenstadt d.	...	...	...	...	...	...	▬	0508**t**	...	...	...	...	0557	0557	...	...	...	0610	...	...	...	...	0659	0659	...	0713
42	**Kempten** Hbf a.	...	...	...	...	...	...	...	0523**t**	...	...	...	...	0611	0611	...	...	...	0626	...	...	...	...	0713	0713	...	0728
42	**Kempten** Hbf d.	0433	...	0506	...	0512**v**	...	...	0528	0533	...	...	0616	0616	0616	...	...	0629	0629	0633	...	...	...	0718	0718	0731	0731
77	Memmingen a.	|	...	|	...	|	...	...	0553	|	...	...	|	|	|	...	...	0655	0702	|	...	...	...	|	|	0757	0757
77	Memmingen d.	|	...	|	...	|	...	◇	0554	|	...	...	|	|	|	...	...	0703	0704	|	...	...	...	|	|	0805	0805
129	**Ulm** Hbf a.	|	...	|	...	|	...	Ⓐ	0642	|	...	...	|	|	|	...	...	0743	0743	|	...	...	...	|	|	0837	0838
——	**Füssen** d.	|	...	|	...	|	...	0450	▬	|	0519**z**	...	|	|	|	...	0550	...	...	|	...	0625	...	|	|	▬	...
	Marktoberdorf d.	|	...	|	...	|	...	0532	...	|	0600	...	|	|	|	...	0632	...	...	|	...	0706	...	|	|	...	...
	Biessenhofen d.	0457	...	0530	...	0534**v**	...	0540	...	0557	0607	...	|	|	|	...	0640	...	...	0657	...	0713	...	|	|	...	...
	Kaufbeuren d.	0502	...	0537	...	0540**v**	...	0548	⊖	0602	0618	...	0640	0640	0640	...	0648	...	...	0702	...	0718	...	0742	0742	...	...
	Buchloe a.	0513	...	0548	...	0551**v**	...	0601	Ⓐ	0613**c**	0630	...	0650	0650	0650	...	0701	...	...	0713	...	0729	...	0752	0752	...	...
0	Buchloe d.	0523	0522	0555	0552	0555	0554	0608	0616	0619	0640	0636	0651	0651	0651	0656	0708	...	...	0719	0716	0738	0736	0755	0755	0755	...
40	**Augsburg** Hbf a.	0557	|	|	0624	|	0624	0640	|	0649	0712	|	0715	0718	0718	|	0742	...	...	0751	|	0809	|	|	|	0818	...
	Nürnberg Hbf **905** a.	...	|	|	...	|	...	...	|	...	...	|	...	...	...	|	...	...	...	...	|	...	|	|	|	...	...
	Kaufering d.	...	0529	0603	...	0603	...	...	0623	...	...	0644	...	...	...	0703	...	...	...	...	0723	...	0744	0803	0803	...	...
	Geltendorf d.	...	0538	|	...	0611	...	...	0631	...	...	0651	...	...	...	0711	...	...	...	...	0731	...	0751	0811**z**	0811**z**	...	...
	München Pasing a.	...	0558	0633	...	0633	...	...	0653	...	...	0711	...	...	...	0736**r**	...	...	...	...	0759	...	0810	0833	0833	...	...
	München Hbf ⊡ a.	...	0606	0641	...	0641	...	...	0700	...	...	0719	...	...	...	0743**r**	...	...	...	...	0806	...	0819	0840	0840	...	...

	◇ Ⓐ		◇ Ⓐ	◇ Ⓒ	◇	Ⓐ	Ⓒ				◇		Ⓐ	Ⓒ				◇						*IC* **2084** **N**	◇		*IC* **2012** **D**
Lindau Insel d.	...	...	...	...	...	...	...	0703	...	...	...	...	...	...	0804	...	...	...	...	...	0904	...	...	...	...	...	...
Lindau Reutin d.	...	...	...	...	...	...	...	0714	...	...	...	...	...	...	0814	...	...	...	...	...	0914	...	...	...	...	...	...
Hergatz d.	...	...	...	...	...	...	...	0729	...	...	...	...	...	...	0829	...	...	...	...	...	0929	...	...	...	...	...	...
Oberstdorf d.	...	...	...	...	...	0707	0717	|	0735**q**	...	...	...	0824	0824	|	0833	...	...	...	0923**p**	|	...	...	0931	...	...	0950
Sonthofen d.	...	...	...	...	...	0736	0740	|	0801	...	...	...	0841	0848	|	0901	...	...	...	0941	|	...	...	1001	...	...	1011
Immenstadt a.	...	...	...	...	...	0746	0750	0803	0811	...	...	...	0850	0900	0903	0911	...	...	...	0950	1003	...	...	1011	...	...	1020
Immenstadt d.	...	...	...	...	...	0806	0806	0806	0817	...	...	...	0906	0906	0906	0917	...	...	...	1006	1006	...	...	1027	...	...	1038
Kempten Hbf a.	...	...	...	...	...	0818	0818	0818	0832	...	...	...	0918	0918	0918	0932	...	...	...	1018	1018	...	...	1043	...	...	1052
Kempten Hbf d.	...	0735	...	...	...	0819	0819	0819	0833	0837	...	...	0919	0919	0919	0933	0937	...	...	1019	1019	1031	1037	1044	...	...	1054
Memmingen a.	...	|	...	...	...	|	|	|	0856	|	...	...	|	|	|	0959	|	...	...	|	|	1055	|	|	...	...	1122
Memmingen d.	...	|	...	...	...	|	|	|	0904	|	...	...	|	|	|	1004	|	...	...	|	|	1102	|	|	...	...	1123
Ulm Hbf a.	...	|	...	...	...	|	|	|	0938	|	...	...	|	|	|	1037	|	...	...	|	|	1141	|	|	...	...	1155
Füssen d.	0659	|	...	0725	...	|	|	|	▬	|	0815	...	|	|	|	▬	|	0920	...	|	|	▬	|	|	1020	...	...
Marktoberdorf d.	0743	|	...	0806	...	|	|	|	...	|	0903	...	|	|	|	...	|	1003	...	|	|	...	|	|	1103	...	...
Biessenhofen d.	0751	0759	←	0813	...	|	|	|	...	0901	0911	...	|	|	|	...	1001	1011	...	|	|	...	1101	|	1113	...	...
Kaufbeuren d.	0757	0804	0818	0818	...	0842	0842	0842	⊖	0906	0918	...	0942	0942	0942	...	1006	1018	...	1042	1042	⊖	1106	1114	1121	...	...
Buchloe a.	→	0816	0830	0830	...	0853	0853	0853		0918	0930	...	0952	0952	0952	...	1018	1030	...	1053	1053		1118	1127	1131	...	...
Buchloe d.	...	0818**t**	0835	0835	0838	0855	0855	0855	0856	0919	0938	0936	0955	0955	0955	0955	1019**t**	1038	1036	1055	1055	1056	1119	1134	1142	1136	...
Augsburg Hbf a.	...	0851**t**	|	|	0909	0915	0915	0915	|	0947	1009	|	|	|	|	1020	1048**t**	1109	|	1117	1117	|	1153	1200	1213	|	...
Nürnberg Hbf **905** a.	...	...	|	|	...	1045**y**	1045**y**	1045**y**	|	...	...	|	|	|	|	...	...	...	|	...	...	|	...	...	...	|	...
Kaufering d.	...	...	0844	0844	...	...	...	...	0903	...	...	0944	1003	1003	1003	...	...	...	1044	...	...	1103	...	...	...	1144	...
Geltendorf d.	...	...	0852	0852	...	...	...	...	0911	...	...	0951	1011	1011	1011	...	...	...	1051	...	...	1111	...	...	...	1151	...
München Pasing a.	...	...	0912	0912	...	...	...	...	0933	...	...	1011	1033	1033	1033	...	...	...	1111	...	...	1133	...	...	...	1212	...
München Hbf ⊡ a.	...	...	0919	0919	...	...	...	...	0940	...	...	1019	1042	1042	1042	...	...	...	1119	...	...	1142	...	...	...	1219	...

NOTES for pages 450 and 451.

A – ALLGÄU – 🚃12 Dortmund - Köln - Ulm - Oberstdorf.
D – ALLGÄU – 🚃12 Oberstdorf - Ulm - Stuttgart - Köln - Dortmund.
H – Until Oct. 8. 🚃12 Hamburg (**2083**) - Augsburg (**2085**) - Oberstdorf.
N – Until Oct. 9. 🚃12 Oberstdorf - Augsburg (**2082**) - Hamburg.
Y – Ⓒ (daily June 7–22, Aug. 1 - Sept. 14).

c – Connects with train in preceding column.
d – Not June 9–20, Aug. 1 - Sept. 12.
e – On Ⓒ Buchloe a. 0704, d. 0706, Kaufbeuren d. 0716.
f – Arrives 6–10 minutes earlier.
g – 1932 on Ⓒ.
h – 0741 on Ⓒ.
j – 1150 on Ⓒ.
k – Arrives 12–14 minutes earlier.
p – 0912 on Ⓒ.
q – 0739 on Ⓒ.
r – On Ⓒ München Pasing a. 0733, München Hbf a. 0741.
t – Ⓐ only.
v – ⑥ only.
x – From Aug. 2. Departs 0716 from Oct. 10.
y – ⑥⑦ to July 27 (also June 9, 19); daily from Aug. 1.
z – Ⓒ only.

⊗ – Change trains at Immenstadt on Ⓒ.
◇ – Operated by Bayerische Regiobahn.
⊖ – Operated by Arverio Bayern.
⊡ – Most trains in Table **935** use platforms 27–36 at München Hbf (minimum connecting time with other services is 10 minutes).

935 LINDAU and OBERSTDORF - ULM, AUGSBURG and MÜNCHEN *RE / RB services except where shown*

See Table **934** for other services Lindau - Memmingen - Buchloe - München. On June 9, Aug. 15, Nov. 1 services run as on ⑦.

					◇						◇ Ⓐ	◇ Ⓒ	◇				Ⓐ		◇ Ⓐ **d**	◇ **Y**						◇	
Lindau Insel d.	...	1003	...	...	...	...	...	1104	...	...	...	...	...	...	1204	...	...	...	...	...	...	...	1304	...	...	...	...
Lindau Reutin d.	...	1013	...	...	...	...	...	1113	...	...	...	...	...	...	1214	...	...	...	...	...	...	...	1314	...	...	...	...
Hergatz d.	...	1029	...	...	...	...	...	1129	...	...	...	...	...	...	1229	...	...	...	...	...	...	...	1329	...	...	...	...
Oberstdorf d.	1007	|	1036	...	...	...	1123	|	1137**e**	...	...	...	...	1224	|	...	1234	...	...	...	...	1324**r**	|	1334	...	...	...
Sonthofen d.	1040	|	1100	...	...	...	1141	|	1201	...	...	...	...	1241	|	...	1301	...	...	...	...	1342	|	1401	...	...	...
Immenstadt a.	1050	1103	1111	...	...	...	1150	1203	1211	...	...	...	...	1252	1303	...	1311	...	...	...	...	1350	1403	1411	...	...	...
Immenstadt d.	1106	1106	1117	...	...	...	1206	1206	1217	...	...	...	...	1306	1306	...	1317	...	...	...	...	1406	1406	1417	...	...	...
Kempten Hbf a.	1118	1118	1131	...	...	...	1218	1218	1232	...	...	...	...	1318	1318	...	1332	...	...	...	...	1418	1418	1432	...	...	...
Kempten Hbf d.	1119	1119	1132	1137	...	...	1219	1219	1233	1237	...	...	...	1319	1319	1334	1334	1337	...	...	...	1419	1419	1433	1437	...	...
Memmingen a.	|	|	1157	|	...	...	|	|	1256	|	...	...	...	|	|	1400	1400	|	...	...	...	|	|	1455	|	...	...
Memmingen d.	|	|	1204	|	...	...	|	|	1303	|	...	...	...	|	|	1404	1404	|	...	...	...	|	|	1504	|	...	...
Ulm Hbf a.	|	|	1238	|	...	...	|	|	1339	|	...	...	...	|	|	1438	1438	|	...	...	...	|	|	1538	|	...	...
Füssen d.	|	|	▬	|	1120	...	|	|	▬	|	1220	1219	...	|	|	▬	...	|	1305	1320	...	|	|	▬	|	1420	...
Marktoberdorf d.	|	|	...	|	1203	...	|	|	...	|	1303	1305**f**	...	|	|	...	...	|	1403**b**	1403	...	|	|	...	|	1503	...
Biessenhofen d.	|	|	...	1201	1211	...	|	|	...	1301	1311	1312	...	|	|	...	...	1401	1411	1411	...	|	|	...	1501	1511	...
Kaufbeuren d.	1142	1142	...	1206	1218	...	1242	1242	⊖	1306	1318	1320	...	1342	1342	...	...	1406	1418	1418	...	1442	1442	⊖	1506	1518	...
Buchloe a.	1152	1152	...	1218	1230	...	1253	1253		1318	1330	1331	...	1352	1352	...	...	1418	1430	1430	...	1453	1453		1518	1530	...
Buchloe d.	1155	1155	1155	...	1238	1236	1254	1254	1256	1319	1334	1335	1338	1355	1355	1355	...	...	1438	1438	1436	1455	1455	1456	1524	1538	1536
Augsburg Hbf a.	|	|	1219	...	1309	|	1314	1314	|	1352	|	|	1409	|	|	1419	...	...	1509	1509	|	1515	1515	|	1553	1609**j**	|
Nürnberg Hbf **905** a.	|	|	...	...	...	|	...	...	|	...	|	|	...	|	|	...	...	...	...	...	|	...	...	|	...	...	|
Kaufering d.	1203	1203	...	...	...	1244	...	...	1303	...	1342	1343	...	1403	1403	...	...	...	...	...	1444	...	...	1503	...	...	1544
Geltendorf d.	1211	1211	...	...	...	1251	...	...	1311	...	1350	1351	...	1411	1411	...	...	...	...	...	1451	...	...	1511	...	...	1551
München Pasing a.	1233	1233	...	...	...	1311	...	...	1333	...	1411	1413	...	1433	1433	...	...	...	...	...	1510	...	...	1533	...	...	1611
München Hbf ⊡ a.	1242	1242	...	...	...	1319	...	...	1340	...	1419	1420	...	1442	1442	...	...	...	...	...	1519	...	...	1541	...	...	1619

					◇						◇					Ⓐ		◇	◇					◇			
Lindau Insel d.	...	1403	...	...	...	...	...	1504	...	...	...	...	...	1604	...	...	...	...	...	...	1704	...	...	...	...	...	1804
Lindau Reutin d.	...	1413	...	...	...	...	...	1514	...	...	...	...	...	1614	...	...	...	...	...	...	1714	...	...	...	...	...	1814
Hergatz d.	...	1429	...	...	...	...	...	1529	...	...	...	...	...	1629	...	...	...	...	...	...	1729	...	...	...	...	...	1829
Oberstdorf d.	1423	|	1434	...	...	...	1504**n**	|	1534	...	...	...	1625	|	...	1634	...	...	...	1705	|	1733	...	...	...	1825	|
Sonthofen d.	1441	|	1501	...	...	...	1531	|	1601	...	...	...	1642	|	...	1701	...	...	...	1730	|	1801	...	...	...	1842	|
Immenstadt a.	1451	1502	1511	...	...	...	1541	1603	1611	...	...	...	1652	1703	...	1711	...	...	...	1740	1803	1811	...	...	...	1851	1903
Immenstadt d.	1505	1505	1517	...	...	...	1606	1606	1617	...	...	...	1706	1706	...	1717	...	...	...	1806	1806	1817	...	...	...	1906	1906
Kempten Hbf a.	1517	1517	1532	...	...	...	1618	1618	1632	...	...	...	1718	1718	...	1732	...	...	...	1818	1818	1832	...	...	...	1918	1918
Kempten Hbf d.	1518	1518	1533	1537	...	...	1619	1619	1635	1637	...	...	1719	1719	1733	1733	1737	...	...	1819	1819	1833	1837	...	...	1919	1919
Memmingen a.	|	|	1559	|	...	...	|	|	1705	|	...	...	|	|	1800	1800	|	...	...	|	|	1856	|	...	...	|	|
Memmingen d.	|	|	1604	|	...	...	|	|	1707	|	...	...	|	|	1804	1804	|	...	...	|	|	1904	|	...	...	|	|
Ulm Hbf a.	|	|	1644	|	...	...	|	|	1739	|	...	...	|	|	1838	1838	|	...	...	|	|	1938	|	...	...	|	|
Füssen d.	|	|	▬	|	1520	...	|	|	▬	|	1620	...	|	|	▬	...	|	1720	...	|	|	▬	|	1820	...	|	|
Marktoberdorf d.	|	|	...	|	1603	...	|	|	...	|	1703	...	|	|	...	...	|	1803	...	|	|	...	|	1903	...	|	|
Biessenhofen d.	|	|	...	1601	1611	...	|	|	...	1701	1711	...	|	|	...	...	1801	1811	...	|	|	...	1901	1911	...	|	|
Kaufbeuren d.	1541	1541	...	1606	1618	...	1642	1642	⊖	1706	1718	...	1742	1742	...	...	1806	1818	...	1842	1842	⊖	1906	1918	...	1942	1942
Buchloe a.	1552	1552	...	1618	1630	...	1653	1653		1718	1731	...	1752	1752	...	...	1818	1830	...	1853	1853		1918	1930	...	1952	1952
Buchloe d.	1555	1555	1555	1619**t**	1638	1636	1655	1655	1656	1723	1738	1736	1755	1755	1755	...	1819**t**	1835	1838	1855	1855	1856	1919	1938	1936	1955	1955
Augsburg Hbf a.	|	|	1618	1649**t**	1709	|	1716	1716	|	1751	1809	|	|	|	1818	...	1849**t**	|	1909	1914	1914	|	1949	2009	|	|	|
Nürnberg Hbf **905** a.	|	|	...	...	...	|	...	...	|	...	...	|	|	|	...	...	...	|	...	2035**g**	2035**g**	|	...	...	|	|	|
Kaufering d.	1603	1603	...	...	...	1644	...	...	1703	...	...	1744	1803	1803	...	...	...	1842	...	...	...	1903	...	...	1944	2003	2003
Geltendorf d.	1611	1611	...	...	...	1651	...	...	1711	...	...	1751	1811	1811	...	...	...	1850	...	...	...	1911	...	...	1951	2011	2011
München Pasing a.	1633	1633	...	...	...	1711	...	...	1733	...	...	1811	1833	1833	...	...	...	1910	...	...	...	1934	...	...	2011	2033	2033
München Hbf ⊡ a.	1642	1642	...	...	...	1719	...	...	1741	...	...	1819	1842	1842	...	...	...	1919	...	...	...	1942	...	...	2019	2042	2042

		◇ Ⓒ	Ⓐ	Ⓒ		Ⓒ	◇ Ⓐ	◇ Ⓒ	Ⓒ	Ⓒ	Ⓐ				◇				◇ Ⓒ					⑤ **v**			
Lindau Insel d.	...	...	...	...	...	...	...	...	...	...	...	1904	...	...	...	...	2004	...	...	...	2104	...	...	...	2201	...	2308
Lindau Reutin d.	...	...	...	...	...	...	...	...	...	...	...	1914	...	...	...	...	2014	...	...	...	2114	...	...	...	2211	...	2317
Hergatz d.	...	...	...	...	...	...	...	...	...	...	...	1929	...	...	...	...	2029	...	...	...	2129	...	...	...	2225	...	2332
Oberstdorf d.	...	...	1833	1833	...	...	...	...	1852	1915	1924	|	...	...	...	2024	|	...	...	2122	|	...	2222	2222	|	2322	|
Sonthofen d.	...	...	1901	1901	...	...	...	...	1910	1941	1943	|	...	...	...	2043	|	...	...	2141	|	...	2241	2241	|	2341	|
Immenstadt a.	...	...	1911	1911	...	...	...	...	1922	1951	1951	2003	...	...	...	2052	2103	...	...	2151	2203	...	2251	2251	2259	2351	0006
Immenstadt d.	...	...	1917	1917	...	...	...	...	1928	...	2006	2006	...	...	...	2106	2106	...	...	▬	2204	...	▬	2302	2302	▬	0007
Kempten Hbf a.	...	...	1932	1932	...	...	...	...	1941	...	2018	2018	...	...	...	2120	2120	...	...	...	2217	...	...	2316	2316	...	0021
Kempten Hbf d.	...	...	1933	1937	1937	...	...	...	1942	...	2019	2019	2033	2037	...	2121	2121	2132	...	...	2218	2234	...	2317	2317	2335	...
Memmingen a.	...	...	2000	|	|	...	...	...	2003	...	|	|	2058	|	...	|	|	2158	...	...	|	2301	...	|	|	0002	...
Memmingen d.	...	...	2004	|	|	...	...	...	2004	...	|	|	2104	|	...	|	|	2204	...	◇	|	2304	◇	|	|	0004	...
Ulm Hbf a.	...	...	2038	|	|	...	...	...	2038	...	|	|	2140	|	...	|	|	2248	...	Ⓐ	|	2349		|	|	0047	...
Füssen d.	...	1852	▬	|	|	...	1920	1920	▬	...	|	|	▬	|	2020	|	|	▬	2123	2123	|	▬	2228	|	|	▬	...
Marktoberdorf d.	...	1936**f**	...	|	|	...	2003	2003	...	...	|	|	...	|	2103	|	|	...	2208	2208	|	...	2311	|	|	...	...
Biessenhofen d.	...	|	...	2001	2001	...	2011	2011	...	...	|	|	...	2101	2111	2140	2140	...	2215	2215	|	...	2319	2337	2337	...	...
Kaufbeuren d.	...	1948	...	2006	2006	...	2018	2018	◇	...	2042	2042	⊖	2106	2118	2145	2145	...	2221	2222	2241	⊖	2324	2342	2342	...	...
Buchloe a.	...	1959	...	2018	2018	...	2030	2030		...	2053	2053		2118	2130	2155	2155	...	...	2235	2253		...	2353	2353	...	...
Buchloe d.	1955	2001	...	...	...	2036	2036	2038	2038	...	2054	2054	2056	...	2138	2156	2156	2158	...	2238	2255	2256	...	2355	2355	0010	...
Augsburg Hbf a.	2020	|	...	...	...	|	|	2109	2109	...	2120	2120	|	...	2209	|	|	2226	...	2309	2325	|	...	|	|	0046	...
Nürnberg Hbf **905** a.	...	|	...	...	...	|	|	...	...	...	...	...	|	...	...	|	|	...	...	...	...	|	...	|	|	...	...
Kaufering d.	...	|	...	...	...	2044	2044	...	...	...	...	...	2103	...	...	2203	2203	...	...	...	...	2303	...	0003	0003	...	...
Geltendorf d.	...	|	...	...	...	2051	2053	...	...	...	...	...	2111	...	...	2211	2211	...	...	...	...	2311	...	0011	0011	...	...
München Pasing a.	...	2038	...	...	...	2112	2112	...	...	...	...	...	2133	...	...	2233	2233	...	...	...	...	2333	...	0033	0033	...	...
München Hbf ⊡ a.	...	2046	...	...	...	2119	2119	...	...	...	...	...	2141	...	...	2242	2242	...	...	...	...	2342	...	0042	0042	...	...

Y – Ⓒ (daily June 7 – 22, Aug. 1 - Sept. 14).

b – Arrives 1347.
d – Not June 9 – 20, Aug. 1 - Sept. 12.
e – 1134 on Ⓒ.
f – Arrives 6 – 7 minutes earlier.

g – From Aug. 1.
j – 1606 on Ⓐ.
n – 1513 on Ⓒ.
r – 1322 on Ⓒ.
t – Ⓐ only.
v – Not Oct. 3.

◇ – Operated by Bayerische Regiobahn.
⊖ – Operated by Arverio Bayern.
⊡ – Most trains in Table **935** use platforms 27 – 36 at München Hbf (minimum connecting time with other services is 10 minutes).

European Rail Timetable Subscription

Keep up to date with the latest changes to European rail schedules with a subscription.

See page 12 for details of our various subscription options

Order on-line at **www.europeanrailtimetable.eu**

✆ +44 (0) 1832 270198 (Monday to Friday 1000 – 1600)

IRE / *RB* services — STUTTGART - TÜBINGEN - AULENDORF — 936

On June 19 services run as on ⑦.

km		Ⓐ	2		2	⊖2		2	⊖2		2	⊖2		2	⊖2		2	⊖2		2	⊖2		2	⊖2			
0	**Stuttgart** Hbf ☆ d.	...	...	0607j	...	...	0815j	...	...	1015j	...	...	1215j	...	...	1415j	...	...	1615j	...	...	1815j	...	...	2015j	...	2215j
57	Reutlingen ☆ d.	...	...	0645j	...	...	0850j	...	...	1050j	...	...	1250j	...	...	1450j	...	...	1650j	...	...	1850j	...	...	2050j	...	2252j
71	**Tübingen** Hbf ☆ a.	...	...	0654j	...	...	0858j	...	...	1058j	...	...	1258j	...	...	1458j	...	...	1658j	...	...	1858j	...	...	2058j	...	2303j
71	**Tübingen** Hbf d.	...	...	0658	...	0729	0900	...	0929	1100	...	1129	1300	...	1329	1500	...	1529	1700	...	1729	1900	...	1929	2100	...	2310
96	Hechingen d.	...	...	0719	...	0801	0920	...	1000	1120	...	1200	1320	...	1400	1520	...	1600	1720	...	1800	1920	...	2000	2120	...	2330
113	Balingen (Württ) d.	...	...	0734	...	0823	0936	...	1023f	1136	...	1223f	1336	...	1423f	1536	...	1623f	1736	...	1823f	1936	...	2023f	2136	...	2342
131	Albstadt-Ebingen d.	...	0625r	0747	...	0845	0948	...	1045	1148	...	1245	1348	...	1445	1548	...	1645	1748	...	1845	1948	...	2045	2148	...	2355
158	**Sigmaringen** a.	...	0654	0811	...	0914	1011	...	1114	1211	...	1314	1411	...	1514	1611	...	1714	1811	...	1914	2011	...	2114	2211	...	0017
158	**Sigmaringen 938** d.	0557	0655	0813	0906	...	1013	1106	...	1213	1306	...	1413	1506	...	1613	1706	...	1813	1906	...	2013	2106	...	2213	2311	...
175	Herbertingen **938** d.	0617	0714	0831	0931	...	1031	1131	...	1231	1331	...	1431	1531	...	1631	1731	...	1831	1931	...	2031	2131	...	2231	2335	...
184	Bad Saulgau d.	0627	0730f	0840	0940	...	1040	1140	...	1240	1340	...	1440	1540	...	1640	1740	...	1840	1940	...	2040	2140	...	2240	2344	...
203	**Aulendorf** a.	0643	0745	0856	0956	...	1056	1156	...	1256	1356	...	1456	1556	...	1656	1756	...	1856	1956	...	2056	2156	...	2256	2400	...

	Ⓐ	Ⓒ	Ⓐ2		⊖2	2		⊖2	2		⊖2	2		⊖2	2		⊖2	2		⊖2	2		⊖2	2	2	2	2
Aulendorf d.	...	...	0541	0703	...	0806	0906	...	1006	1106	...	1206	1306	...	1406	1506	...	1606	1706	...	1806	1906	...	2006	2106	2206	2306
Bad Saulgau d.	...	...	0557	0723	...	0821	0921	...	1021	1121	...	1221	1321	...	1421	1521	...	1621	1721	...	1821	1921	...	2021	2121	2221	2321
Herbertingen **938** d.	...	...	0605	0732	...	0829	0929	...	1029	1129	...	1229	1329	...	1429	1529	...	1629	1729	...	1829	1929	...	2029	2129	2231	2332
Sigmaringen 938 a.	...	...	0621	0746	...	0850	0948	...	1050	1148	...	1250	1348	...	1450	1548	...	1650	1748	...	1850	1948	...	2051	2148	2250	2348
Sigmaringen d.	0538	0544	...	0750	0847	...	0950	1047	...	1150	1247	...	1350	1447	...	1550	1647	...	1750	1847	...	1950	2047	...	2149	2251	...
Albstadt-Ebingen d.	0601	0612	...	0811	0915	...	1010	1115	...	1210	1315	...	1410	1515	...	1610	1715	...	1810	1915	...	2010	2115	...	2213	2315	...
Balingen (Württ) d.	0615	0625	...	0825	0943f	...	1025	1143f	...	1225	1343f	...	1425	1543f	...	1625	1743f	...	1825	1943f	...	2025	2143f	...	2232	...	...
Hechingen d.	0631	0639	...	0839	1001	...	1039	1201	...	1239	1401	...	1439	1601	...	1639	1801	...	1839	2001	...	2039	2201	...	2244	...	...
Tübingen Hbf a.	0652	0657	...	0857	1028	...	1057	1228	...	1257	1428	...	1457	1628	...	1657	1828	...	1857	2028	...	2057	2227	...	2302	...	...
Tübingen Hbf ☆ d.	0658j	0700j	...	0900j	...	...	1100j	...	...	1300j	...	...	1500j	...	...	1700j	...	...	1900j	...	...	2100j	...	...	...	...	...
Reutlingen ☆ d.	0709j	0709j	...	0909j	...	...	1109j	...	...	1309j	...	...	1509j	...	...	1709j	...	...	1909j	...	...	2109j	...	...	...	...	...
Stuttgart Hbf ☆ a.	0742j	0742j	...	0942j	...	...	1142j	...	...	1342j	...	...	1542j	...	...	1743j	...	...	1942j	...	...	2143j	...	...	...	...	...

OTHER SERVICES STUTTGART - TÜBINGEN ⊖

km		Ⓐ	Ⓐ	Ⓒ	Ⓐ					Ⓐ				⊠				♥					♣			
0	**Stuttgart** Hbf **933** d.	0524	0546	0547	0622	0656	0723	0752	0823	0854	0911	0923	0952	and at	1923	1952	2023	2032	2054	2123	2152	2223	2232	2252	2323	0048
22	Plochingen **933** d.	0545	0605	0606	0644	0714	0745	0812	0845	0912	|	0945	1012	the same	1945	2012	2045	2050	2112	2145	2212	2245	2248	2312	2345	0107
29	Wendlingen d.	0551	0612	0612	0650	0719	0751	0818	0851	0918	|	0951	1018	minutes	1951	2018	2051	|	2118	2151	2218	2251	|	2318	2351	0115
35	Nürtingen d.	0557	0620	0620	0655	0725	0757	0824	0856	0924	0932	0956	1024	past each	1956	2024	2056	2101	2124	2156	2224	2256	2302	2324	2358	0121
57	Reutlingen Hbf d.	0614	0638	0638	0710	0742	0814	0842	0912	0942	0948	1012	1042	hour until	2012	2042	2112	2121	2142	2213	2242	2312	2321	2342	0015	0138
71	**Tübingen** Hbf a.	0624	0650	0650	0723	0753	0824	0853	0922	0952	0958	1022	1053		2022	2053	2122	2130	2153	2222	2253	2322	2330	2353	0025	0150

	Ⓐ	j				Ⓐ			Ⓐ	♠							✣									
Tübingen Hbf d.	0414	0456	0532	0551	0633	0703	0733	0758	0805	0826	0833	0905	0933	0958	1005	1033	and at	2005	2033	2105	2133	2158	2205	2233	2305	2333
Reutlingen Hbf d.	0426	0508	0543	0601	0643	0717	0743	0809	0816	0837	0845	0916	0943	1009	1016	1043	the same	2016	2043	2116	2143	2209	2216	2243	2316	2343
Nürtingen d.	0445	|	0559	0617	0700	0734	0759	0825	0833	0856	0902	0933	0958	1025	1033	1058	minutes	2033	2058	2133	2158	2225	2233	2259	2333	2359
Wendlingen d.	0451	|	0606	|	0707	0741	0806	|	0841	|	0910	0941	1005	|	1041	1105	past each	2040	2105	2140	2205	|	2241	2306	2341	0006
Plochingen **933** d.	0501	|	0616	0628	0717	0750	0813	|	0848	0911	0919	0949	1012	|	1048	1112	hour until	2048	2112	2148	2212	|	2248	2314	2349	0014
Stuttgart Hbf **933** a.	0519	0543	0635	0643	0736	0808	0828	0857	0908	0928	0936	1006	1028	1056	1108	1129		2108	2128	2205	2228	2257	2306	2332	0007	0032

REGIONAL *IRE 200* TRAINS WENDLINGEN - ULM (via high-speed line)

km		⑥⑦v	⑥⑦v		Ⓐ						
0	**Wendlingen** d.	0024	0124	...	0624	0724	0824	and	2324	...	...
35	Merklingen d.	0039	0139	...	0701k	0739	0839	hourly	2339	...	...
60	**Ulm** Hbf a.	0051	0151	...	0713	0751	0851	until	2351	...	...

	⑥⑦v		Ⓐ						⑤⑥s
Ulm Hbf d.	0029	...	0529	0629	0729	and	2229	...	2329	2329
Merklingen d.	0040	...	0540	0640	0740	hourly	2240	...	2340	2340
Wendlingen a.	0059	...	0559	0700	0759	until	2259	...	...	2359

f – Arrives 8 minutes earlier.
j – Not July 26 - Sept. 5.
k – Arrives 0638.
r – 0630 on Ⓒ.
s – Also June 18, Oct. 2; not Oct. 3, Nov. 1.
v – Also June 19, Oct. 3; not Oct. 4, Nov. 2.

♥ – Until Aug. 8. *IC* **2048**. See also Tables **800** and **910**.
♣ – From Aug. 9. *IC* **2440**. See also Tables **800** and **910**.
♠ – *IC* **2047**. See also Tables **800** and **910**.
⊠ – Timings may vary by 1–2 minutes.
✣ – Timings may vary by up to 3 minutes.
⊖ – Operated by Südwestdeutsche Landesverkehrs.
☆ – See panel below main table for other services.

S-Bahn 2/3 — STUTTGART - STUTTGART FLUGHAFEN / MESSE ✈ — 936a

20 km. Journey time: 27 minutes. On June 19, Nov. 1 services run as on ⑦.

SERVICE TO JULY 25 AND FROM SEPTEMBER 6

From Stuttgart Hbf: On Ⓐ at 0025, 0055, 0430, 0455, 0515, 0525, 0540, 0555, 0610, 0625, 0640, 0655 and every 15 minutes until 2010, 2025, 2040, 2055; then 2115, 2125, 2145, 2155, 2215, 2225, 2245, 2255, 2315, 2325 and 2355. On ⑥ at 0025, 0055, 0125, 0225, 0325, 0345, 0425, 0525, 0555, 0625, 0655, 0725, 0740, 0755, 0810, 0825, 0840, 0855 and every 15 minutes until 2010, 2025, 2040, 2055; then 2125, 2155, 2225, 2255, 2325 and 2355. On † at 0025, 0055, 0125, 0225, 0325, 0345, 0425, 0525, 0545, 0625, 0645, 0725, 0745, 0755, 0815, 0825, 0845, 0855 and at 15, 25, 45 and 55 minutes past each hour until 1815, 1825, 1845, 1855; then 1925, 1955 and every 30 minutes until 2325, 2355.

From Stuttgart Flughafen ✈: On Ⓐ at 0008, 0038, 0508, 0518, 0538, 0548, 0608, 0623, 0638, 0653 and every 15 minutes until 1908, 1923, 1938, 1953; then 2008, 2023, 2038, 2048, 2108, 2118, 2138, 2148, 2208, 2218, 2238, 2248, 2308, 2318, 2338, 2348. On ⑥ at 0008, 0038, 0108, 0208, 0308, 0408, 0508, 0538, 0608, 0638, 0708, 0738, 0808, 0823, 0838, 0853 and every 15 minutes until 1908, 1923, 1938, 1953; then 2008, 2023, 2038, 2108, 2138, 2208, 2238, 2308 and 2338. On † at 0008, 0038, 0108, 0208, 0308, 0408, 0508, 0548, 0608, 0648, 0708, 0748, 0808, 0818, 0838, 0848 and at 08, 18, 38 and 48 minutes past each hour until 1808, 1818, 1838, 1848; then 1908, 1918, 1938, 2008, 2038 and every 30 minutes until 2308, 2338.

AMENDED SERVICE JULY 26 - SEPTEMBER 5

By replacement 🚌 Stuttgart Hbf (Arnulf Klett Platz) - Vaihingen and v.v. Journey time to airport: 57–62 minutes

From Stuttgart Hbf: 0020, 0050⑥⑦, 0150 ⑥⑦, 0250 ⑥⑦, 0350 ⑥⑦, 0420⑥⑦, 0435 ①–⑤, 0450, 0450Ⓐ**b**, 0520, 0550, 0625, 0655 and every 30 minutes until 1925, then 1950, 2020, 2050, 2120, 2150, 2220, 2250, 2320, 2350.

From Stuttgart Flughafen ✈: 0008, 0038, 0108⑥⑦, 0208 ⑥⑦, 0308 ⑥⑦, 0408 ⑥⑦, 0508, 0538 and every 30 minutes until 2308, 2338.

b – Through 🚌 to airport (journey 28 minutes).

RB services; 2nd class only — AULENDORF - KISSLEGG - LEUTKIRCH and WANGEN — 937

On June 19 services run as on ⑦.

km		Ⓐ	Ⓒ	Ⓐ																				
0	**Aulendorf** d.	0500	0540	0546	0651	...	0803	0907	1003	1107	1203	1307	1403	1507	1603	1707	1803	1907	2003	2107	2203	...	2310	...
10	Bad Waldsee d.	0508	0548	0556	0658	...	0811	0915	1011	1115	1211	1315	1411	1515	1611	1715	1811	1915	2011	2115	2211	...	2318	...
30	Kißlegg a.	0530	0605	0613	0714	...	0825	0933	1025	1133	1225	1333	1425	1533	1625	1733	1825	1933	2025	2133	2225	...	2335	...
	Kißlegg **934** d.	...	...	0622t	...	...	...	0943	...	1143	1232	1343	...	1543	...	1743	...	1943	...	2143	...	...	2337	...
	Wangen (Allgäu) **934** a.	...	...	0632t	...	...	...	|	...	|	1242	|	...	|	...	|	...	|	...	|	...	...	|	...
	Leutkirch 934 a.	...	...	...	...	...	...	0951	...	1151	...	1351	...	1551	...	1751	...	1951	...	2151	...	...	2345	...

	Ⓐ	Ⓐ	Ⓐ		Ⓒ		Ⓐ																	
Leutkirch 934 d.	0453	...	...	...	0714	...	0806	...	1006	...	1206	...	1406	...	1606	...	1806	...	2006	...	2206	...	...	...
Wangen (Allgäu) **934** d.	|	...	...	...	|	...	|	...	|	...	|	1315	|	...	|	...	|	...	|	...	|	...	...	...
Kißlegg **934** a.	0500	...	...	...	0722	...	0814	...	1014	...	1214	1325	1414	...	1614	...	1814	...	2014	...	2214	...	...	...
Kißlegg d.	0506	0539	0624	0725	0725	0827	0827	0934	1027	1134	1227	1334	1427	1534	1627	1734	1827	1934	2027	2134	2228	...	2341	...
Bad Waldsee d.	0528	0556	0641	0741	0741	0846	0846	0948	1046	1148	1246	1348	1446	1548	1646	1748	1846	1948	2046	2149	2245	...	2357	...
Aulendorf a.	0535	0604	0651	0749	0749	0854	0854	0956	1054	1156	1254	1356	1454	1556	1654	1756	1854	1956	2054	2157	2253	...	0005	...

t – Not Aug. 15.

☛ See Table **934** for other connecting services Kißlegg - Wangen and Leutkirch.

938 ULM and ROTTWEIL - DONAUESCHINGEN - NEUSTADT - FREIBURG

DB (*RE* / *S-Bahn* services)

ULM - DONAUESCHINGEN - VILLINGEN. On June 19, Nov. 1 services run as on ⑦.

km																									
		Ⓐ	Ⓒ	Ⓒ	Ⓐ			Ⓐ					Ⓐ			Ⓐ						2			
0	**Ulm** Hbf ... d.	0602	0602	0644	0702	0817	0917	0917	1017	1117	1217	1317	1317	1417	1517	1517	1617	1717	1817	1917	2017	2034	2117	2217	2326
16	Blaubeuren ... d.	0614	0618	0702	0714	0829	0929	0929	1029	1129	1229	1329	1329	1429	1529	1529	1629	1729	1829	1929	2029	2053	2130	2231	2344
34	Ehingen (Donau) ... d.	0636	0636	0725	0739	0842	0942	0942	1042	1142	1242	1342	1342	1442	1542	1542	1642	1742	1842	1942	2042	2111	2143	2243	0001
76	Herbertingen ... **937** d.	0712	0713	0758	0814	0915	1015	1015	1115	1215	1316	1415	1415	1515	1615	1615	1716	1815	1916	2015	2116	2146	2218	2320	0032
93	**Sigmaringen** ... **937** d.	0730	0728	0812	0829	0932	1029	1032	1132	1229	1332	1429	1432	1532	1629	1632	1732	1832	1932	2030	2134	2200	2232	2335	0046
135	Tuttlingen ... d.	0813	0813	...	...	1013	...	1113	1213	...	1413	...	1513	1613	...	1713	1813	1913	2013	...	2216	...	...	...	...
145	Immendingen ... **916** d.	0821	0821	...	...	1021	...	1121	1221	...	1421	...	1521	1621	...	1721	1821	1921	2021	...	2224	...	...	...	...
164	**Donaueschingen** ... **916** a.	0835	0835	...	...	1035	...	1135	1235	...	1435	...	1535	1635	...	1735	1835	1935	2035	...	2237	...	...	...	...
178	**Villingen** (Schwarzw) ... **916** a.	...	...	...	...	...	...	...	...	...	...	...	...	...	...	...	...	1945	2045	...	2305	...	...	...	...

	Ⓐ	Ⓐ	Ⓒ	Ⓐ			Ⓐ	Ⓒ								Ⓐ			Ⓐ			Ⓐ			
Villingen (Schwarzw) ... **916** d.	...	...	...	0504	...	...	0705	0711	0812	...	...	...	...	...	...	...	...	...	...	...	...	...	...	...	2059
Donaueschingen ... **916** d.	...	...	...	0514	...	...	0717	0721	0821	0921	...	1121	...	1321	...	1421	1521	...	1604	1721	...	1821	1921	...	2121j
Immendingen ... **916** d.	...	...	...	0528	...	...	0733	0735	0835	0935	...	1135	...	1335	...	1435	1535	...	1621	1735	...	1835	1935	...	2135
Tuttlingen ... d.	...	...	...	0536	...	...	0750j	0746	0844	0944	...	1144	...	1344	...	1444	1544	...	1637f	1744	...	1844	1944	...	2147
Sigmaringen ... **937** d.	0432	0520	0521	0619	0626	0727	0830	0830f	0931	1030	1131	1230	1331	1430	1531	1531	1630	1731	1731	1830	1931	1931	2031	2131	2233
Herbertingen ... **937** d.	0444	0534	0536	...	0639	0742	0843	0843	0944	1043	1144	1243	1344	1443	1544	1544	1643	1744	1744	1843	1944	1944	2045	2143	2246
Ehingen (Donau) ... d.	0520	0606	0605	...	0712	0814	0913	0913	1013	1113	1213	1313	1413	1513	1613	1613	1713	1813	1813	1913	2013	2013	2114	2217	2317
Blaubeuren ... d.	0534	0625	0621	...	0729	0827	0927	0927	1027	1127	1227	1327	1427	1527	1627	1627	1727	1827	1827	1927	2027	2027	2131	2230	2332
Ulm Hbf ... a.	0549	0637	0639	...	0741	0841	0941	0941	1041	1141	1241	1341	1441	1541	1641	1641	1741	1841	1841	1941	2041	2041	2143	2242	2351

VILLINGEN / SEEBRUGG - FREIBURG (BREISGAU). On June 19, Nov. 1 services run as on ⑦.

km																									
		⚒	Ⓐ	Ⓐ		⚒		⚒		⚒												🚌		🚌	
	Villingen (Schwarzw) d.	...	...	0424	...	...	...	0521	...	...	...	0618	...	...	0737	and at the same minutes past each hour until	...	...	1937	...	2037	...	2137	...	2237
	Donaueschingen ... d.	...	...	0435	...	...	...	0540	...	...	...	0639	...	...	0748		...	...	1948	...	2048	...	2148	...	2248
0	**Neustadt** (Schwarzw) d.	0447	...	0515	0515	0550	...	0623	0623	0656	...	0728	0802	...	0828		2002	...	2028	...	2128	...	2228	...	2328
	Seebrugg ... d.	|	0459	|	|	|	0600	|	|	|	0701	|	|	0801	|		|	2001	|	2101	|	2158	|	2258	|
5	Titisee ... a.	0453	0525	0521	0521	0556	0626	0629	0629	0702	0727	0734	0808	0827	0834		2008	2027	2034	2127	2134	2228	2234	2328	2334
	Titisee ... d.	0454	...	0528	0528	0600	0633	0633	0633	0705	0737	0737	0809	0838	0838		2009	2038	2038	...	2138	...	2238	...	2338
36	**Freiburg** (Brsg) Hbf .. a.	0529	...	0607	0607	0638	0715	0715	0715	0743	0818	0818	0848	0918	0918		2048	2118	2118	...	2218	...	2318	...	0018

km																									
				Ⓐ			Ⓐ			⚒										🚌		🚌		🚌		🚌
0	**Freiburg** (Brsg) Hbf ... d.	0536	0536	0608	0642	0642	0713	0740	0740	0810	0840	0840	0910	and at the same minutes past each hour until	1940	1940	2010	2040	...	2140	...	2240	...	2340	...
31	Titisee ... a.	0610	0610	0643	0715	0715	0746	0819	0819	0848	0919	0919	0948		2019	2019	2048	2119	...	2219	...	2319	...	0019	...
	Titisee ... ⊡ d.	0613	0629	0644	0717	0729	0747	0820	0829	0849	0920	0929	0949		2020	2029	2049	2120	2128	2220	2228	2320	2328	0020	0028
50	**Seebrugg** ... ⊡ a.	|	0655	|	|	0755	|	|	0855	|	|	0955	|		|	2055	|	|	2158	|	2258	|	2358	|	0058
	Neustadt (Schwarzw) d.	0623	...	0650	0730f	...	0753	0830	...	0855	0930	...	0955		2030	...	2055	2130	...	2230	...	2330	...	0026	...
	Donaueschingen ... d.	0703	...	...	0810	...	...	0910	...	...	1010	...	...		2110	...	...	2210	...	2310	...	0010	...	...	...
	Villingen (Schwarzw) a.	0718	...	...	0820	...	...	0920	...	...	1020	...	...		2120	...	...	2220	...	2320	...	0020	...	...	...

ROTTWEIL - DONAUESCHINGEN. ◇ On June 19, Nov. 1 services run as on ⑦.

km										
		Ⓐ			⊠					
0	**Rottweil** ... d.	0514	0643	0749		1949	2049	2149	2249	2359
12	Trossingen Bf ▲ ... d.	0529	0655	0800	and	2000	2100	2200	2300	0010
27	Villingen (Schwarzw) .. a.	0548	0713	0818	hourly	2018	2118	2218	2318	0028
27	Villingen (Schwarzw) .. d.	*0605*	0720	0823	until	2023	2123	2223	*2323*	...
41	**Donaueschingen** ... a.	*0623*	0738	0840		2040	2140	2240	*2340*	...

		Ⓐ		Ⓐ	Ⓐ	Ⓒ				k	
Donaueschingen ... d.	0502	0537	*0624*	*0703*	...	0714	0816		2016	2116	*2319*
Villingen (Schwarzw) ... a.	0520	0555	*0634*	*0718*	...	0731	0834	and	2034	2134	*2328*
Villingen (Schwarzw) ... d.	0525	0606	0638	0722	...	0735	0840	hourly	2040	2140	2333
Trossingen Bf ▲ ... d.	0547	0625	0656	0739	0801	0801	0901	until	2101	2201	2346
Rottweil ... a.	0558	0635	0707	...	0811	0811	0911		2111	2212	2355

f – Arrives 7–8 minutes earlier.
j – Arrives 10–12 minutes earlier.
k – Not Nov. 1. Change trains at Villingen on Ⓑ.

⊠ – On Ⓒ the 1449 from Rottweil departs Villingen 1522, arrives Donaueschingen 1537.
◇ – Operated by Südwestdeutsche Landesverkehrs (SWEG). 2nd class only.
▲ – Connecting services run to / from Trossingen Stadt (operated by SWEG ◇). Journey time: 5 minutes.

939 FRIEDRICHSHAFEN - SINGEN - BASEL

IRE / *RB* services

km																										
		Ⓐ	Ⓐt	Ⓐt	Ⓒz	Ⓐt	Ⓒz	Ⓐt	Ⓒz	Ⓐt													⊙			
0	**Friedrichshafen** Stadt d.	0416t	0523	0618	0644	0651	0705	0733	0800	0800	0845	0902	1045	1105	1245	1305	1445	1502	1645	1702	1845	1902	2045	2102	2202	2305
34	Überlingen ... d.	0458t	0555	0653	0710	0730	0742	0809	0842	0842	0910	0942	1110	1142	1310	1342	1510	1542	1710	1742	1910	1942	2110	2142	2242	2342
59	Radolfzell ... a.	0526t	0629	0719	0731	0756	0809	0839	0909	0909	0930	1009	1130	1209	1330	1409	1530	1609	1730	1809	1930	2009	2130	2209	2309	0007
59	Radolfzell ... **916** d.	0527t	*0632*	0722	0732	*0816*	*0816*	*0846*	*0914*	*0916*	0932	*1016*	1132	*1216*	1332	*1416*	1532	*1616*	1732	*1816*	1932	*2016*	2132	*2222*	*2346*	...
69	**Singen** ... **916** a.	0535t	*0642*	0730	0740	*0826*	*0826*	*0856*	*0923*	*0926*	0940	*1026*	1140	*1226*	1340	*1426*	1540	*1626*	1740	*1826*	1940	*2026*	2140	*2233*	*2356*	...
		|	d	|	|		d	d			|		|		|		|		|		|		|			
69	**Singen** 🏛 ... **940** d.	0541	0645	0745	0745	...	0845	0906	...	...	0945	1045	1145	1245	1345	1445	1545	1645	1745	1845	1945	2045	2145	2236	0006	...
88	**Schaffhausen** 🏛 **940** d.	0556	0700	0800	0800	...	0900	0924	...	...	1000	1100	1200	1300	1400	1500	1600	1700	1800	1900	2000	2100	2200	2254	0024	...
107	Erzingen (Baden) 🏛 .. d.	0609	0714	0815	0815	...	0915	...	...	...	1015	1115	1215	1314	1415	1515	1615	1715	1815	1915	2015	2115	2215	...	...	...
127	Waldshut ... d.	0632f	0731	0834f	0834f	...	0934f	...	...	...	1034f	1134f	1234f	1334f	1434f	1534f	1634f	1734f	1834f	1934f	2034f	2131	2231	...	...	...
150	Bad Säckingen ... d.	0649	0750	0849	0849	...	0949	...	...	...	1049	1149	1249	1349	1449	1549	1649	1749	1849	1949	2049	2153	2254	...	...	...
167	Rheinfelden (Baden) .. d.	0701	0801	0901	0901	...	1001	...	...	...	1101	1201	1301	1401	1501	1601	1701	1801	1901	2001	2101	2209	2304	...	...	...
182	**Basel** Bad Bf ... a.	0711	0812	0912	0912	...	1012	...	...	...	1112	1212	1312	1412	1512	1612	1712	1812	1912	2012	2112	2224	2317	...	...	...

					Ⓐ		Ⓐ	Ⓒ	Ⓐ																	
Basel Bad Bf ... d.	...	...	...	...	0447	...	0532	0633	0638	0749	0849	0949	1049	1149	1249	1349	1449	1549	1649	1749	1849	1949	2049	...	2152	2253
Rheinfelden (Baden) ... d.	...	...	...	...	0502	...	0547	0648	0649	0759	0859	0959	1059	1159	1259	1359	1459	1559	1659	1759	1859	1959	2059	...	2206	2307
Bad Säckingen ... d.	...	...	...	...	0518	...	0603	0704	0701	0809	0909	1010	1109	1209	1309	1409	1511	1609	1709	1809	1909	2009	2109	...	2223	2324
Waldshut ... d.	...	...	...	...	0542	...	0626	0729	0729	0829	0929	1029	1129	1229	1329	1429	1529	1629	1729	1829	1929	2029	2129	...	2246	2346
Erzingen (Baden) 🏛 ... d.	...	...	...	...	0601	...	0644	0744	0744	0844	0944	1044	1144	1244	1344	1444	1544	1644	1744	1844	1944	2044	2144	...	2303	▬
Schaffhausen 🏛 **940** d.	...	...	...	0521	0616	0632	0700	0800	0800	0900	1000	1100	1200	1300	1400	1500	1600	1700	1800	1900	2000	2100	2200	...	2318	...
Singen 🏛 ... **940** a.	...	...	...	0539	0630	0651	0718	0814	0814	0914	1014	1114	1214	1314	1414	1514	1614	1714	1814	1914	2014	2114	2214	...	2333	...
	Ⓐt	Ⓐt	Ⓒz	Ⓐt	Ⓐt	Ⓒz	|		d	|		|		|		|		|		|		|		Ⓑh	
Singen ... **916** d.	0411	0527	0539	*0557*	*0654*	0716	0721	...	*0832*	0916	*1032*	1116	*1232*	1316	*1432*	1516	*1632*	1716	*1832*	1916	*2032*	2116	*2232*	2335	2352	...
Radolfzell ... **916** a.	0418	0534	0546	*0606*	*0704*	0723	0729	...	*0841*	0923	*1041*	1123	*1241*	1323	*1441*	1523	*1641*	1723	*1841*	1923	*2041*	2123	*2241*	2344	2359	...
Radolfzell ... d.	0419	0535	0547	0637	0708	0725	0730	...	0847	0925	1047	1125	1247	1325	1447	1525	1647	1725	1847	1925	2047	2125	2247	...	...	0004
Überlingen ... d.	0442	0604	0615	0701	0735	0747	0756	...	0915	0948	1115	1148	1316	1348	1515	1548	1715	1748	1915	1948	2115	2148	2315	...	...	0029
Friedrichshafen Stadt. a.	0522	0644	0655	0745	0813	0813	0828	...	0955	1013	1152	1213	1355	1413	1555	1613	1755	1813	1952	2013	2152	2213	2352	...	...	0106

d – Daily.
f – Arrives 6–8 minutes earlier.
h – Also Nov. 1.
t – Ⓐ (not June 19).
z – Also June 19.
⊙ – Change trains at Singen on Ⓒ (also June 19).

STUTTGART - SINGEN - ZÜRICH and KONSTANZ 940

Regional tickets are valid Stuttgart - Singen and v.v. (also between Singen and Konstanz) on *IC* trains. German holiday dates apply.

km			*IC* 1181				*IC* 181			*IC* 481						*IC* 183	*IC* 483			*IC* 185		*IC* 485			*IC* 187	*IC* 487
		⑥–① c	①–⑤	Ⓐ t	Ⓐ t⊙	Ⓐ t△	①–⑥ e🍷		⑥⑦ w	①–⑤ vF🍷		⑦K ⊡	† z	† z	⚒ s	🍷	🍷			🍷	⑦ G	🍷			🍷	🍷
0	**Stuttgart** Hbf d.	0018	...	0458	...	*0535*●	0616	...	0715	0717**x**	...	0801	0818*	...	0818**r**	0828**x**	0917	...	1018**r**	1027**x**	1018**r**	1117	...	1217*	1228**b**	1317
26	Böblingen d.	0039	...	0522	...	*0559*	0638	...	0738	0738**r**	...	0822	0838	...	0839	0850	0938**r**	...	1039	1050	1039	1138**r**	...	1239	1250	1338**r**
42	Herrenberg d.	0048	...	0535	...	0620	0647	...	0747	0747	...	|	0847	...	0848	|	0947	...	1048	|	1048	1147	...	1248	|	1347
51	Bondorf d.	0056	...	0542	...	0627	0655	...	0755	0755	0802	|	0854	...	0856	|	0955	1002	1056	|	1056	1155	1202	1256	|	1355
57	Eutingen im Gäu d.	|	...	0549	...	0636	0700	0708	|	|	0809	|	0900	0908	0908	|	|	1009	1108	|	1112	|	1209	1308	|	|
62	Hochdorf (b. Horb) d.	|	...	|	...	0642	|	0713	|	|	0814	|	|	0913	0913	|	|	1014	1113	|	|	|	1214	1313	|	|
87	**Freudenstadt** Hbf d.	|	...	|	...	0710	|	0744	|	|	0843	|	|	0944	0944	|	|	1043	1144	|	|	|	1243	1344	|	|
67	Horb d.	0108	...	0557	...	▬	0708	▬	0806	0807	...	0848	0920**j**	...	...	0914	1007	...	...	1114	1120	1207	...	...	1314	1407
110	Rottweil d.	...	...	0639**h**	...	...	0742	...	0843	0842	...	0923	0956	...	...	0943	1042	...	...	1143	1158	1242	...	...	1343	1442
138	Tuttlingen d.	...	...	0719	0726	...	0801	*IC*	0900	0900	...	0945	...	...	...	1001	1100	...	...	1201	1221	1300	...	...	1401	1500
157	Engen **916** d.	...	...	...	0740	...	|	**181**	0914	0914	...	1002	...	...	...	|	1114	...	...	|	|	1314	...	...	|	1514
172	**Singen** **916** a.	...	...	...	0751	...	0826		0923	0926	...	1011	...	...	...	1026	1126	...	...	1226	1242	1326	...	...	1426	1526
172	**Singen** **916 939** d.	...	0732	...	...	0806	0832	0832	0925	0932	...	1016	...	...	...	1032	1132	...	...	1232	1244	1332	...	...	1432	1532
	Radolfzell **916** d.	...	|	...	...	|	|	|	0933	|	...	1029	...	...	...	|	|	...	...	|	1252	|	...	...	|	|
	Konstanz **916** a.	...	|	...	...	|	|	|	0949	|	...	1100	...	...	...	|	|	...	...	|	1309	|	...	...	|	|
191	**Schaffhausen** 🏛 **939** a.	...	0745	...	...	0824	0845	0845	...	0945	...	...	...	...	...	1045	1145	...	...	1245	...	1345	...	...	1445	1545
239	**Zürich** HB a.	...	0823	...	...	...	0923	0923	...	1023	...	...	...	...	...	1123	1223	...	...	1323	...	1423	...	...	1523	1623

			IC 2383	*IC* 1089	*IC* 189	*IC* 489			*IC* 281		*IC* 381				*IC* 283	*IC* 389			*IC* 285	*IC* 2385				*IC* 2387		
			Ⓐ 🍷	⑥⑦	①–⑤	🍷			🍷	Ⓐ t△	🍷		Ⓐ rt		🍷	🍷			🍷	🍷				⑦–④ m	⑤ f	⑥
Stuttgart Hbf d.	...	1418*	1428**b**	1429**b**	...	1517	...	1616**r**	1624**x**	1647	1716	...	1748	1816*	1828**b**	1917	...	2018*	2026**b**	2117	...	2217	...	2325	2326‡	2326
Böblingen d.	...	1439	1450	1450	...	1538**r**	...	1639	1650	1709	1738**r**	...	1809	1839	1850	1938**r**	...	2039	2048	2138**r**	...	2239	...	2347	2347	2347
Herrenberg d.	...	1448	|	|	...	1547	...	1648	|	1719	1747	...	1818	1848	|	1947	...	2048	|	2147	...	2248	...	2356	2356	2356
Bondorf d.	1402	1456	|	|	...	1555	1602	1656	|	1726	1755	1802	1826	1856	|	1955	2002	2056	|	2155	2202	2256	...	0004	0004	0004
Eutingen im Gäu d.	1409	1508	|	|	...	|	1609	1708	|	1733	|	1809	1839**h**	1908	|	|	2009	2108	|	|	2209	2304	2309	0011	0013	0013
Hochdorf (b. Horb) d.	1414	1513	|	|	...	|	1614	1713	|	|	|	1814	|	1913	|	|	2014	2114	|	|	2214	|	2315	|	|	|
Freudenstadt Hbf a.	1443	1542	|	|	...	|	1644	1744	|	|	|	1843	|	1944	|	|	2043	2146	|	|	2243	|	2343	|	|	|
Horb d.	...	...	1514	1514	...	1607	...	...	1714	1742	1807	...	1848	...	1914	2007	...	...	2113	2207	...	2318**h**	...	0023	0023	0023
Rottweil d.	...	...	1543	1543	...	1642	...	...	1743	...	1842	...	...	...	1943	2042	...	...	2145	2242	...	2349	...	0056	0055	0102**h**
Tuttlingen d.	...	...	1601	1601	...	1700	...	...	1801	...	1900	...	...	...	2001	2100	...	...	2203	2300	...	...	...	...	...	0126
Engen **916** d.	...	...	|	|	...	1714	...	...	|	...	1914	...	...	...	|	2114	...	...	|	2314	...	...	...	...	...	0139
Singen **916** a.	...	...	1625	1626	...	1726	...	...	1826	...	1926	...	...	...	2026	2126	...	...	2226	2326	...	...	...	...	...	0148
Singen **916 939** d.	...	...	1627	1632	1632	1732	...	...	1832	...	1932	...	...	...	2032	2132	...	...	2232	2328	...	...	...	...	...	0149
Radolfzell **916** d.	...	...	1636	|	|	|	...	...	|	...	|	...	...	...	|	|	...	...	|	2335	...	...	...	...	...	0155
Konstanz **916** a.	...	...	1648	|	|	|	...	...	|	...	|	...	...	...	|	|	...	...	|	2347	...	...	...	...	...	0208
Schaffhausen 🏛 **939** a.	...	...	...	1645	1645	1745	...	...	1845	...	1945	...	...	...	2045	2145	...	...	2245	...	...	...	...	...	...	...
Zürich HB a.	...	...	...	1723	1723	1823	...	...	1923	...	2023	...	...	...	2123	2223	...	...	2323	...	...	...	...	...	...	...

				IC 2388						*IC* 1184		*IC* 2386			*IC* 284				*IC* 388	*IC* 282			*IC* 380		*IC* 280	
	Ⓐ t	Ⓐ t	△	Ⓐ F△	⚒ s	⚒ s	① g	† z	† z	①–⑤ v🍷		①–⑥ e🍷	⑦		🍷		⊕△		◇🍷	🍷			🍷	⑦ G	⊗ 🍷	⑦ G
Zürich HB d.	...	...	...	...	...	...	...	...	...	...	...	...	...	...	0637	...	...	...	0737	0837	...	...	0937	...	1037	...
Schaffhausen 🏛 **939** d.	...	...	...	...	...	...	...	...	...	0530	...	...	...	...	0716	...	...	...	0816	0916	...	...	1016	...	1116	...
Konstanz **916** d.	...	...	...	...	...	...	0430	...	...	|	...	0604	0603	...	|	...	...	...	|	|	...	...	|	1047	|	...
Radolfzell **916** d.	...	...	...	...	...	...	0454	...	...	|	...	0620	0620	...	|	...	...	...	|	|	...	...	|	1105	|	...
Singen **916 939** a.	...	...	...	...	...	...	0500	...	...	0544	...	0627	0627	...	0730	...	...	...	0830	0930	...	...	1029	1111	1130	...
Singen **916** d.	...	...	...	...	...	...	0506	...	...	0550	...	0629	0629	...	0736	...	...	...	0835	0936	...	...	1035	1112	1136	...
Engen **916** d.	...	...	...	...	...	...	0515	...	...	0600	...	0638	0638	...	|	...	...	...	0844	|	...	...	1044	1121	|	...
Tuttlingen d.	...	...	...	...	...	...	0530	...	...	0615	...	0652	0652	...	0800	...	...	...	0859	1000	...	...	1059	1136	1200	...
Rottweil d.	...	...	0511**t**	0536	...	0604	0604	...	0614	0638	...	0711	0711	0802	0817	...	...	...	0917	1017	...	...	1117	1202	1217	...
Horb d.	0447	...	0547	0610	...	0640	0640	...	0644	0711	...	0751	0752	0837	0845	...	...	...	0951	1045	...	...	1151	1237	1245	...
Freudenstadt Hbf d.	|	0511	|	|	0611	|	|	0611	|	|	0715	|	|	|	|	...	0811	0915	|	|	1013	1115	|	|	|	...
Hochdorf (b. Horb) d.	|	0541	|	|	0643	|	|	0645**h**	|	|	0745	|	|	|	|	←	0845	0945	|	|	1045	1145	|	|	|	←
Eutingen im Gäu d.	0456	0548	0556	0622	0656**h**	0656	0656	0650	0656	|	0751	|	|	0848	|	0856	0856	0951	|	|	1056	1151	|	1248	|	1257
Bondorf d.	0503	0556	0602	0630	0702	0702	0702	...	0702	|	0757	0802	0804	→	|	0902	0902	0957	1003	|	1103	1157	1203	→	|	1303
Herrenberg d.	0511	0604	0611	0640	0711*	0711*	0711*	...	0711	0726	...	0811	0812	...	|	0911	0911	...	1011	|	1111	...	1211	...	|	1311
Böblingen d.	0521	...	0621	0650	0721*	0721*	0721*	...	0721	0736	...	0821**r**	0823	...	0911	0921	0921	...	1022**r**	1111	1121	...	1222**r**	...	1311	1321
Stuttgart Hbf a.	0544	...	0642	0711	0741	0741	0741	...	0742	0759	...	0843	0843**r**	...	0932**k**	0942**r**	0942	...	1043	1132**u**	1142	...	1243	...	1332**u**	1342

			IC 488	*IC* 188			*IC* 486	*IC* 186			*IC* 484			*IC* 184		*IC* 482	*IC* 1082	*IC* 2382	*IC* 182			*IC* 480				*IC* 180
			🍷	🍷			🍷	🍷			🍷	⑥⑦ w	Q	🍷	⊕§	①–⑤	⑥⑦	Ⓐ 🍷	🍷	§		🍷		⊙		
Zürich HB d.	...	...	1137	1237	...	...	1337	1437	...	...	1537	...	...	1637	...	1737	1737	...	1837	...	...	1937	...	...	...	2037
Schaffhausen 🏛 **939** d.	...	...	1216	1316	...	...	1416	1516	...	...	1616	...	...	1716	...	1816	1816	...	1916	...	...	2016	...	*2107*	...	2116
Konstanz **916** d.	...	...	|	|	...	...	|	|	...	...	|	1648	...	|	...	|	|	1807	|	...	...	|	...	|	...	|
Radolfzell **916** d.	...	...	|	|	...	...	|	|	...	...	|	1704	...	|	...	|	|	1824	|	...	...	|	...	|	...	|
Singen **916 939** a.	...	...	1229	1330	...	...	1429	1530	...	...	1629	1710	...	1730	...	1829	1829	1833	1930	...	...	2029	...	*2125*	...	2130
Singen **916** d.	...	...	1235	1336	...	...	1435	1536	...	...	1635	1712	...	1736	...	▬	1835	1835	1936	...	...	2035	...	2129	...	▬
Engen **916** d.	...	...	1244	|	...	...	1444	|	...	...	1644	|	...	|	...	...	1844	1844	|	...	...	2044	...	2139	...	...
Tuttlingen d.	...	...	1259	1400	...	...	1459	1600	...	...	1659	1735	...	1800	...	...	1859	1859	2000	...	...	2059	...	2153	...	...
Rottweil d.	...	...	1317	1417	...	...	1517	1617	...	...	1717	1756	1802	1817	...	...	1917	1917	2017	...	...	2117	...	2214	2217	...
Horb d.	...	...	1351	1445	...	...	1551	1645	...	...	1751	1828	1837	1845	...	...	1951	1951	2045	...	...	2151	...	...	2247	...
Freudenstadt Hbf d.	1213	1315	|	|	1413	1515	|	|	1617	1715	|	|	|	|	1813	1915	|	|	|	2013	2115	|	2215	...	|	...
Hochdorf (b. Horb) d.	1245	1345	|	|	1445	1545	|	|	1645	1745	|	|	|	|	1845	1945	|	|	|	2045	2145	|	2245	...	|	...
Eutingen im Gäu d.	1257	1351	|	|	1456**h**	1551	|	|	1656**h**	1751	|	|	1856	|	1856	1951	|	|	|	2056	2151	|	2250	...	2256	...
Bondorf d.	1303	1357	1403	|	1503	1557	1603	|	1703	1757	1803	|	1903	|	1903	1957	2003	2003	|	2103	2157	2203	...	...	2303	...
Herrenberg d.	1311	...	1411	|	1511	...	1611	|	1711	...	1811	1843	1910	|	1911	...	2011	2011	|	2111	...	2211	...	...	2311	2316
Böblingen d.	1321	...	1422**r**	1511	1521	...	1622**r**	1711	1721	...	1822**r**	1853	1920	1911	1921	...	2022**r**	2022**r**	2111	2121	...	2222	...	...	2320**n**	2330
Stuttgart Hbf a.	1342**d**	...	1443	1532**k**	1542	...	1643	1732**u**	1742**d**	...	1843	1916	1945	1932**u**	1942	...	2043	2043	2132	2142	...	2243	...	...	2340**n**	2355

SCHAFFHAUSEN - ZÜRICH (operated by SBB)

km									
0	**Schaffhausen** d.	0547	0617	and at the same	2117	2147	2157	2247	2327
28	Bülach d.	|	0637	minutes past	2137	|	2228	|	2358
48	**Zürich** HB a.	0623	0655	each hour until	2155	2223	2253	2323	0023

Zürich HB d.	0507	0605	0637	and at the same	2037	2105	2205	2305	0005
Bülach d.	0532	0623	|	minutes past	|	2123	2223	2323	0023
Schaffhausen a.	0604	0643	0713	each hour until	2113	2143	2243	2343	0043

F – From / to Frankfurt (Table **910**) except July 26 - Sept. 5.
G – ⑦ until Oct. 19 (also June 9, Oct. 3). Runs daily Stuttgart - Rottweil and v.v.
K – ⑦ until Nov. 2 (also June 9, 19, Oct. 3, Nov. 1).
Q – July 26 - Sept. 5.

b – 13–15 minutes earlier July 26 - Sept. 5 (change trains at Böblingen).
c – Also June 20; not June 9, Nov. 1.
d – 8 minutes later July 26 - Sept. 5.
e – Not June 9, Oct. 4.
f – Also June 18, Oct. 2.
g – Also June 10, 20; not June 9.
h – Arrives 6–9 minutes earlier.
j – Arrives 0908.
k – Arrives 28 minutes later July 26 - Sept. 5 (by 🚌 Vaihingen - Stuttgart).
m – Not June 18, 30, Oct. 2.
n – ⑥ only.
r – Not July 26 - Sept. 5.
s – Not June 19, Nov. 1.
t – Ⓐ (not June 19).
u – Arrives 14–18 minutes later July 26 - Sept. 5 (change trains at Böblingen).
v – Not June 9, Oct. 3.
w – Also June 9, Oct. 3; not July 26 - Sept. 5.
x – 24–32 minutes earlier July 26 - Sept. 5 (by 🚌 Stuttgart Hbf Arnulf Klett Platz - Vaihingen).
z – Also June 19, Nov. 1.

● – Underground platforms.
◇ – On ①–⑤ (not June 9, Oct. 3) change trains at Singen (train **1180** Zürich - Singen).
⊕ – Change trains at Eutingen im Gäu on †.
⊗ – Change at Singen June 7–14.
⊙ – Operated by *SWEG*.
⊡ – Operated by *SVG*.
△ – Subject to alteration July 26 - Sept. 5 (with partial 🚌 substitution).
§ – Change trains at Eutingen im Gäu July 26 - Sept. 5.
‡ – 2313 on ⑤ Aug. 1 - Sept. 5.
* – Timings vary up to 5 minutes earlier July 26 - Sept. 5.

941 TÜBINGEN - HORB - PFORZHEIM

2nd class only

On June 19, Nov. 1 services run as on ⑦.

km		Ⓐ	Ⓐ	⑥	Ⓐ		Ⓒ	Ⓐ				Ⓐ				Ⓐ				Ⓒ	Ⓐ					
	Tübingen Hbf ★ d.	...	...	...	...	...	0723	...	0806b	0929	...	...	1129	...	...	1329	...	...	...	...	...	...	...	1929	...	2129
0	**Horb** ★ d.	0424	...	0557	0616	0649	0756	0804	0853	1004	1056	1125	1204	1256	1404	1404	1456	1604	...	1656	1725	1804	1856	2004	...	2204
15	Hochdorf (b. Horb) a.	0436	...	0609	0627	0701	0809	0819	0906	1019	1108	1137	1219	1307	1419	1419	1507	1619	...	1707	1737	1819	1907	2019	...	2219
15	Hochdorf (b. Horb) d.	0437	0602	0610	0627	0701	0820	0820	0917	1020	1117	1149	1220	1317	1420	1420	1517	1620	1717	1717	1749	1820	1917	2020	...	2220
25	Nagold d.	0455c	0614	0621	0638	0712	0831	0831	0931	1031	1131	1201	1231	1331	1431	1431	1531	1631	1731	1731	1801	1831	1931	2031	...	2231
34	Wildberg (Württ) d.	0503	0621	0629	0646	0720	0839	0839	0939	1039	1139	1209	1239	1339	1439	1439	1539	1639	1739	1739	1809	1839	1939	2039	...	2239
45	Calw d.	0518	0631	0639	0657	0730	0850	0850	0950	1050	1150	1220	1250	1350	1450	1450	1550	1650	1750	1750	1820	1850	1950	2050	...	2250
52	Bad Liebenzell d.	0526	0639	0647	0705	0738	0901	0901	1001	1101	1201	1231	1301	1401	1501	1501	1601	1701	1801	1801	1831	1901	2001	2101	...	2308e
71	**Pforzheim** Hbf a.	0548	0659	0708	0727	0759	0923	0923	1023	1122	1223	1253	1322	1423	1522	1522	1623	1722	1823	1823	1853	1922	2023	2122	...	2329

	Ⓐ	Ⓐ	Ⓒ	Ⓐ	⚒						Ⓒ				Ⓐ		Ⓐ			Ⓐ					⑤⑥d
Pforzheim Hbf d.	0439	0617	0638	0641	0741	0836	0936	1036	1136	1236	1236	1336	1436	1536	1606	1636	1706	1736	1836	1906	1936	2036	...	2246	2352
Bad Liebenzell d.	0459	0640	0702	0710	0805	0900	1000	1100	1200	1300	1300	1400	1500	1600	1630	1700	1730	1800	1900	1930	2000	2100	...	2307	0012
Calw d.	0506	0647	0709	0716	0812	0907	1007	1107	1207	1307	1307	1407	1507	1607	1637	1707	1737	1807	1907	1937	2007	2107	...	2314	0019
Wildberg (Württ) d.	0516	0702	0721	0731	0822	0921	1021	1121	1221	1321	1321	1421	1521	1621	1651	1721	1751	1821	1921	1951	2021	2121	...	2324	0029
Nagold d.	0523	0716c	0728	0739	0834c	0929	1032	1129	1232	1329	1329	1432	1529	1632	1701	1729	1801	1832	1929	2001	2032	2129	...	2332	0035
Hochdorf (b. Horb) a.	0535	0727	0739	0749	0843	0939	1042	1140	1242	1339	1339	1442	1539	1642	1712	1739	1811	1842	1939	2011	2042	2140	...	2343	...
Hochdorf (b. Horb) d.	...	0728	0740	0750	0851	0940	1052	1140	1252	1340	1340	1452	1540	1652	...	1740	1821	1850	1940	2021	2052	2140	...	2344	...
Horb ★ a.	...	0741	0756	0801	0904	0956	1106	1156	1305	1356	1356	1505	1553	1705	...	1756	1834	1903	1953	2033	2105	2154	...	2358	...
Tübingen Hbf ★ a.	...	...	0830	...	...	1029	...	1229	...	...	1429	...	...	...	...	...	1923	1952b	2030	...	...	2229	...	...	...

Full service **TÜBINGEN - HORB**

km		Ⓐ	Ⓐ	Ⓐ	Ⓒ	Ⓐ	†b						Ⓐ					Ⓐ								⑤⑥d
0	**Tübingen** Hbf d.	0524	0600	0628	0723	0725	0806	0834	0929	1034	1129	1234	1303	1329	1434	1529	1634	1703	1729	1834	1929	2034	2129	...	2234	2333
32	**Horb** a.	0553	0633	0705	0752	0756	0838	0910	0958	1110	1158	1310	1337	1358	1510	1558	1710	1737	1758	1910	1958	2110	2158	...	2310	0011

		Ⓐ	Ⓐ	Ⓒ	Ⓐ	Ⓐ	Ⓒ	Ⓒ						Ⓐ				Ⓐ		Ⓐ		†b				
Horb d.	0452	0613	0644	0652	0725	0759	0800	0852	0959	1052	1159	1252	1359	1415	1452	1559	1652	1716	1759	1820	1852	1918	1959	2052	2159	2252
Tübingen Hbf a.	0522	0651	0724	0723	0801	0830	0830	0924	1029	1124	1229	1324	1429	1454	1523	1629	1723	1752	1829	1854	1923	1952	2030	2124	2229	2326

b – † until Oct. 19.
c – Arrives 6–7 minutes earlier.
d – Also June 8, 18, Oct. 2.
e – Arrives 2257.
★ – See panel below main table for full service Tübingen - Horb and v.v.

941a PFORZHEIM - BAD WILDBAD

S-Bahn 6 (2nd class only)

On June 19, Nov. 1 services run as on ⑦.

km		Ⓐ	⑥	Ⓐ	Ⓐ	Ⓒ	Ⓐ	Ⓐ				Ⓒ	Ⓐ				Ⓐ			Ⓐ				
0	**Pforzheim** Hbf d.	0507	0557	0607	0645	0657	0717	0747	0817	and	1117	1217	1224	1317	1417	1517	1547	and at the same	1817	1847	1917	and	2317	2357
23	**Bad Wildbad** Bf a.	0537	0628	0638	0718	0728	0748	0818	0848	hourly	1148	1248	1255	1348	1448	1548	1618	minutes past	1848	1918	1948	hourly	2348	0028
24	**Bad Wildbad** Kurpark a.	0540	0632	0642	0722	0732h	0752	0822	0852	until	1152	1252	1259	1352	1452	1552	1622	each hour until	1852	1922	1952	until	2352	0032

	Ⓐ	Ⓐ	Ⓐ	⑥	Ⓐ	Ⓐ	†	⚒				Ⓒ	Ⓐ		Ⓐ					Ⓐ		Ⓐ				
Bad Wildbad Kurpark d.	0459	0559	0635	0647	0705	0735	0747	0805a	0905	1005	1105	1205	1216	1305	1335	1405	1505	1535	1605	1635	1705	1735	1805	and	2305	0015
Bad Wildbad Bf d.	0502	0602	0639	0651	0709	0739	0751	0809	0909	1009	1109	1209	1219	1309	1339	1409	1509	1539	1609	1639	1709	1739	1809	hourly	2309	0019
Pforzheim Hbf a.	0533	0633	0710	0722	0740	0810	0822	0840	0940	1040	1140	1240	1250	1340	1410	1440	1540	1610	1640	1710	1740	1810	1840	until	2340	0049

a – Ⓐ only.
h – † only.

942 FREUDENSTADT - OFFENBURG

Operated by Südwestdeutsche Landesverkehrs. 2nd class only. On June 19, Nov. 1 services run as on ⑦.

km		Ⓐ	Ⓒ	Ⓐ				❖			
0	**Freudenstadt** Hbf d.	0529	0610	0633	0716	0820	0901	and	2101	2201	2301
16	Alpirsbach d.	0547	0627	0655	0733	0838	0917	hourly	2117	2217	2318
25	Schiltach d.	0559	0641	0708	0750	0850	0929	until	2129	2229	2330
35	Wolfach d.	0610	0653	0720	0802	0902	0941		2141	2241	2342
39	Hausach **916** a.	0615	0658	0725	0807	0907	0946		2146	2246	2347
72	**Offenburg** **916** a.	*0645*	0725	0753	0835	0935	1014		2214	2314j	0014j

	Ⓐ	Ⓒ	Ⓐ						
Offenburg **916** d.	0450	0546	0554	0701k	0741	0841	and	2141	2241
Hausach **916** d.	0518	0622	0622	0729	0809	0910	hourly	2210	2310
Wolfach d.	0523	0627	0627	0734	0814	0915	until	2215	2315
Schiltach d.	0535	0639	0639	0746	0825	0929		2229	2331
Alpirsbach d.	0547	0652	0652	0757	0838	0939		2239	2342
Freudenstadt Hbf a.	0605	0709	0709	0814	0855	0955		2255	2358

j – Does not run Hausach - Offenburg on ⑦.
k – *0656* on Ⓒ (change trains at Hausach).
❖ – The 1200 from Freudenstadt runs on Ⓒ only. On Ⓐ service is retimed as follows: Freudenstadt d. 1220, Alpirsbach d. 1240, Schiltach d. 1253, Wolfach d. 1304, Hausach a. 1309, Offenburg a. 1340.

943 KARLSRUHE - FREUDENSTADT

S-Bahn (2nd class only)

On June 19, Nov. 1 services run as on ⑦.

km		Ⓐ	⑥	Ⓐ	Ⓐ	Ⓒ	Ⓐ	Ⓒ	Ⓐ	†		†M	Ⓒ	Ⓐ		Ⓒ	Ⓐ								
	Karlsruhe Bahnhofsvorplatz d.	0505	0511	0535	...	0611	...	0711	...	...	0811	...	0911	0911	...	1011	1011	1111	...	1211	1311	...	1411	1511	...
0	**Karlsruhe** Hbf. **910a 916** d.	|	|	|	0610	|	0707	|	0745	0807	|	0906	|	|	1010	|	|	|	1210	|	|	1410	|	|	1610
24	Rastatt **910a 916** d.	0533	0538	0608	0633	0638	0738	0738	0807	0829	0838	0922	0938	0938	1030	1038	1038	1138	1229	1238	1338	1429	1438	1538	1629
40	Gernsbach Bf d.	0556	0600	0630	0656	0700	0800	0800	0830	0844	0900	0941	1000	1000	1044	1100	1100	1200	1244	1300	1400	1444	1500	1600	1644
51	Forbach (Schwarzw) d.	0613	0618	0648	0717	0717	0817	0817	0850	0900	0917	0958	1017	1017	1100	1117	1117	1217	1300	1317	1417	1500	1517	1617	1700
61	Schönmünzach d.	0624	0631	0659	0729	0729	0829	0829	0901	0911	0929	1010	1029	1029	1111	1129	1129	1229	1311	1329	1429	1511	1529	1629	1711
74	Baiersbronn Bf d.	0642	0649	0716	0750	0749	0849	0849	0923	0922	0949	1023	1049	1049	1122	1149	1149	1249	1322	1349	1449	1522	1549	1649	1722
79	**Freudenstadt** Stadt a.	0650	0657	0724	0758	0757	0857	0857	0931	0930	0957	1029	1057	1057	1130	1157	1157	1257	1330	1357	1457	1530	1557	1657	1730
	Freudenstadt Stadt d.	0700	0702	0727	0802	0802	0902	0902	0932	0932	1002	1032	1102	1107	1132	1202	1205	1302	1332	1402	1502	1532	1602	1702	1732
82	**Freudenstadt** Hbf a.	0705	0707	0732	0807	0807	0907	0907	0937	0937	1007	1037	1107	1112	1137	1207	1210	1307	1337	1407	1507	1537	1607	1707	1737

										⑤⑥f
Karlsruhe Bahnhofsvorplatz d.	1611	1711	...	1811	1911	...	2011	2111	2211	2311
Karlsruhe Hbf... **910a 916** d.	|	|	1810	|	|	2007	|	|	|	|
Rastatt **910a 916** d.	1638	1738	1829	1838	1938	2029	2038	2138	2238	2338
Gernsbach Bf d.	1700	1800	1844	1900	2000	2044	2100	2200	2300	0000
Forbach (Schwarzw) d.	1717	1817	1900	1917	2017	2100	2117	2217	2317	0017
Schönmünzach d.	1729	1829	1911	1929	2029	2111	2129	2229	2329	0029
Baiersbronn Bf d.	1750	1849	1922	1949	2049	2122	2149	2249	2346	0046
Freudenstadt Stadt a.	1758	1857	1930	1957	2057	2130	2157	2257	2354	0054
Freudenstadt Stadt d.	1802	1902	1932	2002	2102	2132	2202	2302	2355	0055
Freudenstadt Hbf a.	1807	1907	1937	2007	2107	2137	2207	2307	2400	0100

	Ⓒ		Ⓐ	Ⓐ	⑥	Ⓐ	⑥	Ⓐ	Ⓒ	Ⓐ
Freudenstadt Hbf d.	0015	...	0436	0524	0555	0614	0620	0648	0653	0720
Freudenstadt Stadt a.	0019	...	0442	0529	0600	0619	0626	0653	0658	0725
Freudenstadt Stadt d.	0025	...	0443	0530	0607	0620	0630	0654	0703	0730
Baiersbronn Bf d.	0032	...	0453	0539	0616	0628	0638	0702	0711	0738
Schönmünzach d.	0049	...	0508	0556	0631	0645	0649	0728e	0728	0749
Forbach (Schwarzw) d.	0100	...	0525	0613e	0643	0701	0701	0742	0742	0801
Gernsbach Bf d.	0117	...	0541	0631	0659	0728	0715	0800	0800	0815
Rastatt **910a 916** d.	0140	...	0557	0706v	0722	0754	0738e	0822	0822	0830
Karlsruhe Hbf **910a 916** a.	|	...	0614	0728	|	0816	0750	|	|	0843
Karlsruhe Bahnhofsvorplatz a.	0204	...	...	...	0746	...	...	0846	0846	...

		⚒	†					Ⓒ	Ⓐ									†M		Ⓒ					
Freudenstadt Hbf d.	0748r	0822	0823	0853	0953	1021	1053	1153	1157	1223	1257	1353	1423	1453	1553	1623	1653	1722	1753	1823	1853	1953	2053	2153	2253
Freudenstadt Stadt a.	0753r	0828	0828	0858	0958	1026	1058	1158	1202	1228	1302	1358	1428	1458	1558	1628	1658	1728	1758	1828	1858	1958	2058	2158	2258
Freudenstadt Stadt d.	0803	0830	0830	0903	1003	1030	1103	1203	1203	1230	1303	1403	1430	1503	1603	1630	1703	1730	1803	1830	1903	2003	2103	2203	2303
Baiersbronn Bf d.	0811	0838	0838	0911	1011	1038	1111	1211	1211	1238	1311	1411	1438	1511	1611	1638	1711	1738	1811	1838	1911	2011	2111	2211	2311
Schönmünzach d.	0828	0849	0849	0928	1028	1049	1128	1228	1228	1249	1328	1428	1449	1528	1628	1649	1728	1754	1828	1849	1928	2028	2128	2228	2328
Forbach (Schwarzw) d.	0842	0901	0901	0942	1042	1101	1142	1242	1242	1301	1342	1442	1501	1542	1642	1701	1742	1808	1842	1901	1942	2042	2153v	2254v	2341
Gernsbach Bf d.	0900	0915	0915	1000	1100	1115	1200	1300	1300	1315	1400	1500	1515	1600	1700	1715	1800	1825	1900	1915	2000	2100	2211	2311	0000
Rastatt **910a 916** d.	0922	0931	0933	1022	1122	1132	1222	1322	1322	1331	1422	1522	1531	1622	1722	1731	1822	1849	1922	1931	2022	2122	2232	2332	0022
Karlsruhe Hbf... **910a 916** a.	|	0949	0946	|	|	1149	|	|	|	1347	|	|	1547	|	|	1747	|	1904	|	1947	|	|	|	|	|
Karlsruhe Bahnhofsvorplatz a.	0946	...	...	1046	1146	...	1246	1346	1346	...	1446	1546	...	1646	1746	...	1846	...	1946	...	2046	2146	2256	2356	0046

M – From/to Mannheim (Table **913**).
e – Arrives 7–9 minutes earlier.
f – Also June 8, 18, Oct. 2.
r – 5 minutes later on Ⓒ.
v – Arrives 13–15 minutes earlier.

RE services MÜNCHEN - PASSAU 944

On June 19, Aug. 15, Nov. 1 services run as on ⑦.

km			Ⓐ	⑥	Ⓐ	Ⓐ	Ⓒ																	
0	**München** Hbf .... **878** d.	0444	...	...	0524	0604	0624	0724	0824	0924	1024	1124	1224	1324	1424	1524	1623	1724	1824	1924	2024	2124	2224	2324
42	Freising .... **878** d.	0508	...	...	0549	0630	0649	0749	0849	0949	1049	1149	1249	1349	1449	1549	1649	1749	1849	1949	2049	2149	2249	2349
76	Landshut (Bay) Hbf .... **878** a.	0527	...	...	0611	0651	0712	0812	0912	1012	1112	1212	1312	1413	1512	1612	1712	1812	1912	2012	2112	2212	2312	0011
76	Landshut (Bay) Hbf .... d.	▬	0534	0614	0614	0701	0715	0815	0915	1015	1115	1215	1315	1416	1515	1615	1715	1815	1915	2015	2115	2215	2315	0012
121	Landau (Isar) .... d.	...	0610	0649	0701**f**	0737	0748	0848	0948	1048	1148	1249	1348	1448	1548	1648	1748	1848	1948	2048	2148	2248	2348	0047
139	Plattling .... a.	Ⓐ	0623	0700	0714	0750	0800	0900	1000	1100	1200	1300	1400	1500	1600	1700	1800	1900	2000	2100	2200	2300	0004	0100
139	Plattling .... **920** d.	0559	0642	0702	0725	0800	0802	0902	1004	1102	1204	1302	1404	1504	1604	1702	1804	1904	2004	2102	2202	2302	0006	0102
191	**Passau** Hbf .... **920** a.	0634	0716	0737	0800	0835	0837	0937	1039	1137	1239	1337	1439	1539	1639	1737	1839	1939	2039	2137	2237	2337	0041	0137

	⚒	Ⓐ	Ⓒ	Ⓐ	Ⓒ	Ⓐ																		h
Passau Hbf .... **920** d.	0439	0519	0519	0600	0626	0646	0726	0819	0919	1026	1119	1219	1319	1426	1519	1626	1719	1826	1919	2026	2126	2226	2313	...
Plattling .... **920** a.	0513	0553	0553	0636	0700	0720	0800	0853	0953	1100	1153	1253	1353	1500	1553	1700	1753	1900	1953	2100	2200	2300	2347	...
Plattling .... d.	0517	0558	0600	0640	0702	0723	0802	0902	1002	1102	1202	1302	1402	1502	1602	1702	1802	1902	2002	2102	2202	2302	2350	...
Landau (Isar) .... d.	0529	0610	0612	0653	0714	0736	0814	0914	1014	1114	1214	1314	1414	1514	1614	1714	1814	1914	2014	2114	2214	2314	0002	...
Landshut (Bay) Hbf .... a.	0600	0640	0641	0725	0743	0804	0843	0943	1043	1143	1243	1343	1443	1543	1643	1743	1843	1943	2043	2143	2243	2343	0031**h**	...
Landshut (Bay) Hbf .... **878** d.	0608	0647	0647	0728	0749	0806	0849	0949	1049	1149	1249	1349	1449	1549	1649	1749	1849	1949	2049	2149	2249	2349	...	0035
Freising .... **878** d.	0629	0710	0710	0748	0810	0829	0910	1010	1110	1210	1310	1410	1510	1610	1710	1810	1910	2010	2110	2210	2310	0010	...	0054
München Hbf .... **878** a.	0656	0736	0736	0817	0837	0856	0937	1037	1137	1237	1337	1437	1537	1636	1737	1837	1937	2036	2137	2236	2337	0037	...	0119

f – Arrives 0649.

h – 3 minutes later on mornings July 5 - Sept. 3.

agilis REGENSBURG - INGOLSTADT - DONAUWÖRTH - ULM 945

On June 19, Aug. 15, Nov. 1 services run as on ⑦. **WARNING!** Journeys from / to Regensburg (and Plattling) are subject to alteration July 5 - Sept. 1 (see notes ❦ and ◐).

km						Ⓐ	Ⓐ		Ⓐ	Ⓐ	Ⓐ	Ⓐ	Ⓐ	Ⓐ	Ⓐ	Ⓐ	Ⓐ	Ⓐ		Ⓐ	Ⓐ	Ⓐ		Ⓐ		Ⓐ
	Plattling **921** .... ❦ d.		...	...	...	...	...	...	...	0606	...	0808	...	1008	...	1208	...	1408	...	...	...	1608	...	...	...	1808
0	**Regensburg** Hbf .. ❦ d.	Ⓐ	...	...	...	0418	0514	...	0554	0651	0742	0853	0945	1053	1145	1253	1342	1453	...	1545	1614	1653	...	1745	...	1853
46	Neustadt (Donau) .. ❦ d.		...	...	...	0457	0553	...	0651	0732	0829	0930	1029	1130	1229	1332	1427	1530	...	1627	1703	1734	...	1823	...	1930
74	**Ingolstadt** Hbf ...... ❦ a.		...	...	...	0518	0618	...	0719	0755	0853	0953	1053	1153	1253	1353	1453	1553	...	1654	1730	1754	...	1845	...	1953
			Ⓐ	Ⓐ	Ⓐ	Ⓐ	Ⓐ	Ⓐ		Ⓐ	Ⓐ	Ⓐ	Ⓐ	Ⓐ	Ⓐ	Ⓐ	Ⓐ	Ⓐ	Ⓐ	Ⓐ	|	Ⓐ	Ⓐ	Ⓐ	Ⓐ	Ⓐ
74	**Ingolstadt** Hbf .... d.		...	0505	...	0556	0627	0701	...	0810	0905	1011	1111	1211	1311	1411	1511	1611	1634	1706	1736	1806	1838	1911	...	2011
95	Neuburg (Donau) .... d.		...	0527	...	0619	0653	0719	...	0829	0928	1029	1129	1229	1329	1429	1529	1629	1659	1728	1759	1828	1859	1935**j**	...	2029
127	**Donauwörth** .... a.		...	0552	...	0650	0725	0752	...	0853	0954	1053	1153	1253	1353	1453	1553	1653	1736	1753	1837	1853	1936	1959	...	2053
127	**Donauwörth** .... d.		0447	0555	0623	0702	0734	0818	...	0902	1016	1102	1216	1302	1416	1502	1616	1708	1738	1816	...	1902	...	2001	2016	2102
153	Dillingen (Donau) .... d.		0508	0616	0649	0730	0755	0839	...	0928	1037	1128	1237	1328	1437	1528	1637	1733	1801	1837	...	1928	...	2023	2037	2123
176	Günzburg ...... **910 930** a.		0528	0638	0710	0749	0812	0855	...	0945	1054	1145	1254	1345	1453	1545	1654	1751	1825	1855	...	1945	...	2040	2054	2141
200	**Ulm** Hbf ...... **910 930** a.		0546	0657	*0740*	0811	0832	0915	...	1008	1115	1209	1315	1408	1515	1608	1715	1810	*1855*	1915	...	2008	...	...	2115	2208

	Ⓐ	Ⓐ	Ⓐ						Ⓒ	Ⓒ	Ⓒ	Ⓒ	Ⓒ	Ⓒ	Ⓒ	Ⓒ	Ⓒ	Ⓒ	Ⓒ	Ⓒ	Ⓒ	Ⓒ	Ⓒ	Ⓒ	Ⓒ	
Plattling **921** .... ❦ d.	...	2008	...	2208		...	...	...	...	...	...	0808	...	1008	...	1208	...	1408	...	1608	...	1808	...	2008	...	2208
Regensburg Hbf ... ❦ d.	1945	2053	2146	2253	Ⓒ	...	...	...	0543	0653	0758	0853	0958	1053	1158	1253	1358	1453	1558	1653	1758	1853	1958	2053	2158	2253
Neustadt (Donau) ... ❦ d.	2029	2130	2229	2330		...	...	...	0623	0733	0837	0933	1037	1133	1237	1333	1437	1533	1637	1733	1837	1933	2037	2133	2237	2330
Ingolstadt Hbf .... ❦ a.	2050	2153	2254	2353		...	...	...	0645	0755	0854	0954	1054	1154	1254	1354	1454	1554	1654	1754	1854	1954	2054	2153	2254	2353
	Ⓐ	Ⓐ	Ⓐ			Ⓒ	⑥	Ⓒ	|	|	|	|	|	|	|	|	|	|	|	|	|	|	|	|	|	|
Ingolstadt Hbf .... d.	2111	2211	2311	0038		...	...	0612	0710	0810	0911	1011	1111	1211	1311	1411	1511	1611	1711	1808	1911	2011	2111	2211	2311	0038
Neuburg (Donau) .... d.	2129	2229	2329	0054		...	...	0630	0729	0829	0929	1029	1129	1229	1329	1429	1529	1629	1729	1828	1929	2029	2129	2229	2329	0054
Donauwörth .... a.	2153	2253	2355	0120		...	...	0654	0753	0853	0954	1053	1153	1253	1353	1454	1553	1653	1753	1853	1953	2053	2153	2253	2355	0120
Donauwörth .... d.	2216	...	0001	...		0513	0616	0702	0816	0902	1016	1102	1216	1302	1416	1502	1616	1702	1816	1902	2016	2102	2216	2302	0001	...
Dillingen (Donau) .... d.	2237	...	0022	...		0534	0637	0730	0837	0928	1037	1128	1237	1328	1437	1528	1637	1728	1837	1928	2037	2123	2237	2323	0022	...
Günzburg ...... **910 930** a.	2253	...	0038	...		0550	0653	0749	0854	0945	1054	1145	1254	1345	1453	1545	1654	1745	1854	1945	2054	2141	2253	2339	0038	...
Ulm Hbf .... **910 930** a.	2312	...	0057	...		0609	0712	0811	0915	1008	1115	1209	1315	1408	1515	1608	1715	1808	1915	2008	2116	2208	2312	0005	0057	...

			Ⓐ		Ⓐ	Ⓐ	Ⓐ	Ⓐ	Ⓐ	Ⓐ	Ⓐ	Ⓐ	Ⓐ	Ⓐ	Ⓐ	Ⓐ	Ⓐ		Ⓐ		Ⓐ	Ⓐ	Ⓐ	Ⓐ	Ⓐ	Ⓐ
Ulm Hbf .... **910 930** d.	Ⓐ	...	...	...	...	0453	0531	0552	0626	*0719*	0747	0847	0947	1047	1147	1247	1347	...	1447	...	1547	1647	1726	1747	1847	1947
Günzburg ...... **910 930** d.		...	...	...	...	0511	0555	0611	0644	0740	0806	0905	1006	1105	1206	1305	1406	...	1505	...	1606	1705	1744	1806	1905	2006
Dillingen (Donau) .... d.		...	...	...	...	0528	0616	0633	0701	0803	0823	0923	1023	1123	1223	1328	1423	...	1523	...	1623	1722	1801	1823	1923	2023
Donauwörth .... a.		...	...	...	...	0549	0637	0700	0726	0829	0850	0944	1048	1144	1248	1349	1448	...	1544	...	1648	1749	1827	1848	1944	2048
Donauwörth .... d.		...	0433	...	0529	0555	0640	0702	0728	0831	0901	1002	1102	1202	1302	1402	1502	...	1601	...	1702	1802	...	1903	2001	2102
Neuburg (Donau) .... d.		...	0457	...	0600	0630	0706	0731	0758	0900	0926	1031	1131	1231	1331	1431	1530	...	1631	...	1728	1828	...	1931	2031	2131
Ingolstadt Hbf .... a.		...	0514	...	0617	0650	0727	0748	0817	0923	0942	1049	1147	1247	1349	1447	1548	...	1648	...	1748	1849	...	1948	2047	2147
		Ⓐ	Ⓐ	Ⓐ	Ⓐ	Ⓐ		Ⓐ	Ⓐ		Ⓐ	Ⓐ	Ⓐ	Ⓐ	Ⓐ	Ⓐ	Ⓐ	Ⓐ	Ⓐ	Ⓐ	Ⓐ	Ⓐ		Ⓐ	Ⓐ	Ⓐ
Ingolstadt Hbf .... ◐ d.		0452	0520	0606	0625	0705	...	0807	0905	...	1005	1105	1205	1318	1405	1505	1605	1640	1718	1740	1810	1905	...	2006	2105	2205
Neustadt (Donau) .... ◐ d.		0518	0555	0627	0652	0730	...	0827	0930	...	1027	1130	1227	1343	1427	1530	1627	1702	1746	1807	1835	1930	...	2027	2130	2227
Regensburg Hbf .... ◐ a.		0610	0644	0707	0740	0809	...	0908	1013	...	1108	1213	1308	1421	1508	1613	1708	1740	1834	1856	1919	2013	...	2108	2213	2308
Plattling **921** .... ◐ a.		...	...	...	...	...	...	0952	...	...	1152	...	1352	...	1552	...	...	...	...	...	...	...	...	2152	...	2352

	Ⓐ	Ⓐ	Ⓐ	Ⓐ		Ⓒ	⑥	Ⓒ	Ⓒ	Ⓒ	Ⓒ	Ⓒ	Ⓒ	Ⓒ	Ⓒ	Ⓒ	Ⓒ	Ⓒ	Ⓒ	Ⓒ	Ⓒ	Ⓒ	Ⓒ	Ⓒ	Ⓒ	Ⓒ
Ulm Hbf .... **910 930** d.	2047	2147	2246	*2324*	Ⓒ	...	...	...	0547	0642	0747	0847	0947	1047	1147	1247	1347	1447	1547	1647	1747	1847	1947	2047	2147	2246
Günzburg ...... **910 930** d.	2105	2206	2305	2347		...	...	...	0606	0702	0806	0905	1006	1105	1206	1305	1406	1505	1606	1705	1806	1905	2006	2105	2206	2305
Dillingen (Donau) .... d.	2123	2223	2323	0003		...	...	...	0623	0724	0823	0923	1023	1123	1223	1323	1423	1523	1623	1723	1823	1923	2023	2123	2223	2323
Donauwörth .... a.	2144	2248	2345	0034		...	...	...	0648	0745	0850	0944	1048	1144	1248	1344	1448	1544	1648	1744	1848	1944	2048	2144	2248	2345
Donauwörth .... d.	2202	2302	...	...		...	0507	0553	0702	0802	0901	1002	1102	1202	1302	1402	1502	1601	1702	1802	1901	2001	2102	2202	2302	...
Neuburg (Donau) .... d.	2231	2331	...	...		...	0532	0617	0731	0831	0931	1031	1131	1231	1331	1431	1531	1631	1731	1828	1931	2031	2131	2231	2331	...
Ingolstadt Hbf .... a.	2251	2348	...	...		...	0547	0640	0748	0847	0947	1047	1147	1248	1347	1447	1547	1648	1747	1849	1948	2047	2147	2250	2348	...
	Ⓐ						|	|	|	|	|	|	|	|	|	|	|	|	|	|	|	|	|	|		
Ingolstadt Hbf .... ◐ d.	2305	...	...	...		0602	0602	0705	0805	0905	1005	1105	1205	1305	1405	1505	1605	1705	1804	1905	2005	2105	2205	2305	...	...
Neustadt (Donau) .... ◐ d.	2331	...	...	...		0625	0625	0722	0827	0922	1027	1122	1227	1322	1427	1522	1627	1722	1827	1922	2027	2122	2227	2331	...	...
Regensburg Hbf .... ◐ a.	0010	...	...	...		0707	0707	0757	0908	0958	1108	1157	1308	1357	1508	1558	1708	1758	1908	1957	2108	2158	2308	0010	...	...
Plattling **921** .... ◐ a.	...	...	...	...		0756	0756	...	0952	...	1152	...	1352	...	1552	...	1752	...	1952	...	2152	...	2352	...	...	...

j – Arrives 1928.

❦ – Regensburg - Ingolstadt journeys depart approx. 23 minutes earlier July 5 - Sept. 1 (by 🚌 Regensburg - Sinzing), with no connection from Plattling.

◐ – Ingolstadt - Regensburg journeys are by 🚌 July 5 - Sept. 1 between Sinzing and Regensburg. Arrival in Regensburg is approx. 15 minutes later (no onward connection to Plattling).

European Rail Timetable Subscription

Keep up to date with the latest changes to European rail schedules with a subscription.

See page 12 for details of our various subscription options

Order on-line at **www.europeanrailtimetable.eu**

✆ +44 (0) 1832 270198 (Monday to Friday 1000 – 1600)

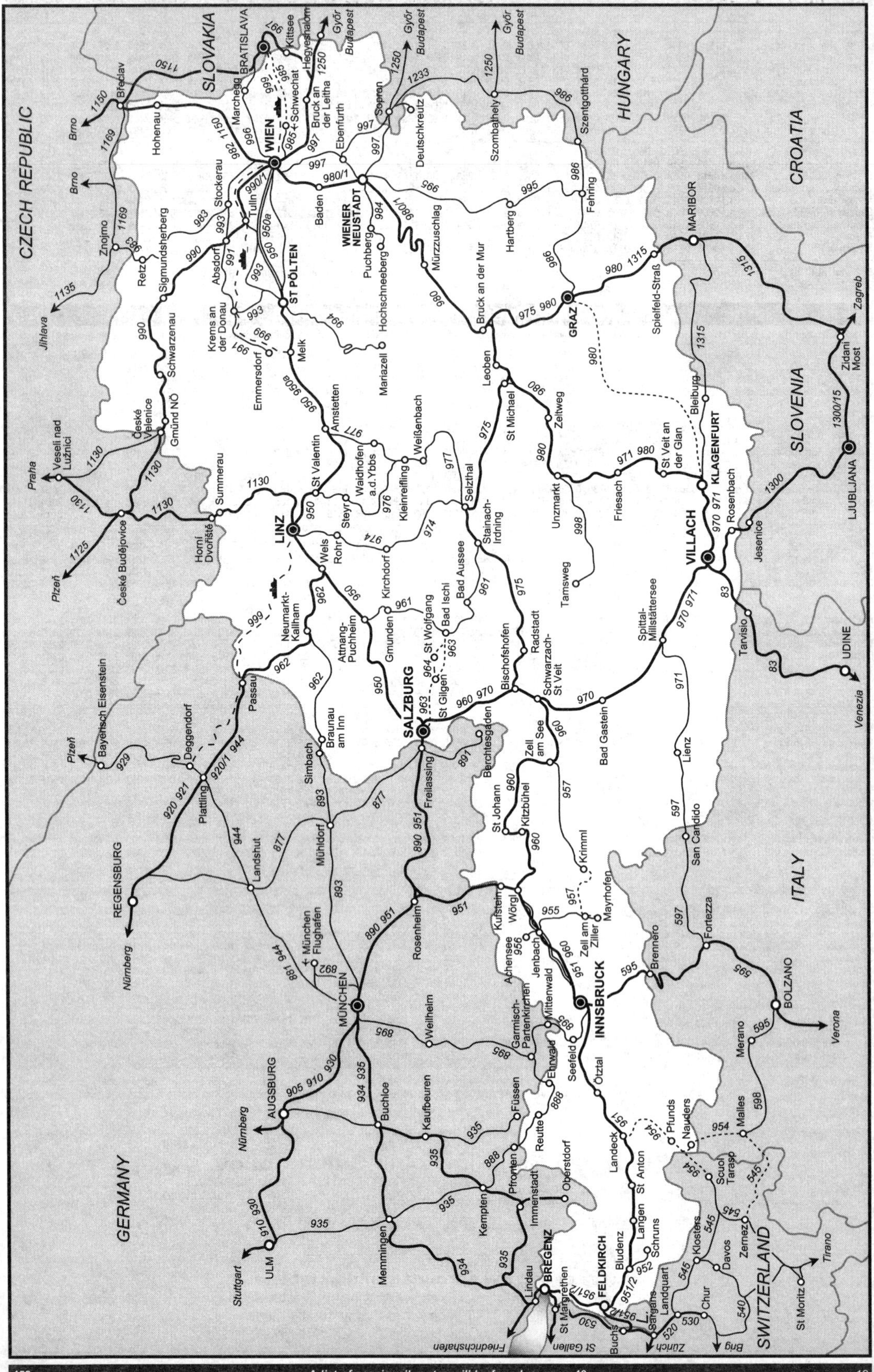
CZECH REPUBLIC
SLOVAKIA
HUNGARY
CROATIA
SLOVENIA
ITALY
SWITZERLAND
GERMANY
BRATISLAVA
Břeclav
Brno
Znojmo
Jihlava
Praha
Plzeň
Veselí nad Lužnicí
České Velenice
České Budějovice
Horní Dvořiště
Summerau
Gmünd NÖ
Schwarzenau
Sigmundsherberg
Retz
Hohenau
Marchegg
Kittsee
Hegyeshalom
Győr
Budapest
WIEN
Schwechat
Bruck an der Leitha
Ebenfurth
Sopron
Deutschkreutz
Szombathely
Szentgotthárd
Stockerau
Tullin
Absdorf
Krems an der Donau
Emmersdorf
ST PÖLTEN
Melk
Baden
WIENER NEUSTADT
Puchberg
Hochschneeberg
Mariazell
Mürzzuschlag
Bruck an der Mur
Hartberg
Fehring
GRAZ
Spielfeld-Straß
MARIBOR
Zagreb
Zidani Most
LJUBLJANA
Jesenice
Leoben
St Michael
Zeltweg
Unzmarkt
Tamsweg
Friesach
St Veit an der Glan
KLAGENFURT
Bleiburg
VILLACH
Rosenbach
Tarvisio
UDINE
Venezia
Amstetten
St Valentin
Waidhofen a.d.Ybbs
Weißenbach
Kleinreifling
Selzthal
Steyr
LINZ
Wels
Rohr
Kirchdorf
Stainach-Irdning
Bad Aussee
Bad Ischl
Gmunden
Attnang-Puchheim
Neumarkt-Kallham
Passau
St Wolfgang
St Gilgen
SALZBURG
Bischofshofen
Radstadt
Schwarzach-St Veit
Bad Gastein
Spittal-Millstättersee
Lienz
San Candido
Fortezza
Brennero
BOLZANO
Verona
Merano
Malles
Braunau am Inn
Simbach
Berchtesgaden
Freilassing
Zell am See
St Johann
Kitzbühel
Krimml
Mayrhofen
Zell am Ziller
Wörgl
Kufstein
Jenbach
Achensee
INNSBRUCK
Mittenwald
Garmisch-Partenkirchen
Seefeld
Ehrwald
Ötztal
Landeck
St Anton
Langen
Bludenz
Schruns
FELDKIRCH
BREGENZ
Lindau
Friedrichshafen
St Margrethen
St Gallen
Buchs
Sargans
Zürich
Landquart
Chur
Klosters
Davos
Zernez
Scuol Tarasp
Pfunds
Nauders
St Moritz
Tirano
Brig
Bayerisch Eisenstein
Deggendorf
Plattling
REGENSBURG
Nürnberg
Landshut
Mühldorf
München Flughafen
Rosenheim
MÜNCHEN
Weilheim
AUGSBURG
Buchloe
Kaufbeuren
Füssen
Reutte
Pfronten
Kempten
Immenstadt
Oberstdorf
Memmingen
ULM
Stuttgart

AUSTRIA

Operator: Except where otherwise stated, rail services are operated by Österreichische Bundesbahnen (**ÖBB**) www.oebb.at

Timings: Valid **December 15**, 2024 - **December 15**, 2025 (unless stated otherwise in individual tables). See page 4 for public holiday dates.

Services: Trains convey both first and second class seating unless footnotes show otherwise or there is a '2' in the train column. Overnight sleeping car (🛏) or couchette (▬) trains do not necessarily convey seating accommodation - refer to individual footnotes for details. Descriptions of sleeping and couchette cars appear on page 10.

Train categories:

RJX or *RJ*	**Railjet Xpress** **Railjet**	Austrian high-speed train. Conveys first and economy (2nd) class. *Business class* also available to first class ticket holders (supplement payable).
ICE	**InterCity Express**	German high-speed train.
EC	**EuroCity**	International express train.
IC	**InterCity**	Internal or international express train.
D	**Schnellzug**	Ordinary fast train.
NJ	**ÖBB nightjet**	Quality overnight express train - see page 10.
EN	**EuroNight**	Other international overnight express train - see page 10.
WB	**Westbahn**	Wien - Salzburg private operator (special fares payable).
REX	**Regional Express**	Semi-fast regional train (train number not usually shown).
CJX	**Cityjet Xpress**	Similar to *REX* but using dedicated modern rolling stock.
	Regional / S-Bahn	Local stopping trains – no category or train number shown.

Reservations: Seats may be reserved on all long-distance express trains (*RJX, RJ, ICE, EC, IC, NJ, D*).

Catering: Three types of catering are indicated in the tables: ✕ – Restaurant car; ⊗ – Bordbistro; 🍷 – At seat trolley service.

WIEN - LINZ - SALZBURG 950

km		*RJ*	*RJ*	*RJ*	*RJX*	*WB*	*RJ*	*WB*	*ICE*	*RJX*	*RJX*	*WB*	*WB*	*RJ*	*ICE*	*RJX*	*RJX*	*WB*	*RJ*	*RJX*	*RJX*	*WB*	*D*	*RJ*	*WB*
		668	**848**	**848**	**368**	**900**	**540**	**960**	**94**	**660**	**260**	**902**	**970**	**542**	**228**	**160**	**560**	**962**	**544**	**662**	**262**	**906**	**1018**	**546**	**972**
		Ⓐ	Ⓐ														⚒								
		✕	✕	✕	✕	🍷	✕	🍷	P✕	✕	✕	🍷	T🍷	✕	R✕	L✕	F✕	C🍷	✕	✕	✕	🍷	S🍷	✕	🍷
0	**Flughafen Wien** ✈ . d.	...	...	...	...	...	...	...	...	...	...	...	...	...	...	...	0702	...	0733	0802	...	...	...	0833	...
17	**Wien** Hbf d.	...	0455	...	0528	...	0555	...	0613	0628	0628	...	...	0655	0713	0728	0728	...	0755	0828	0828	...	...	0855	...
21	**Wien** Meidling d.	...	0502	...	0535	...	0602	...	0620	0635	0635	...	...	0702	0720	0735	0735	...	0802	0835	0835	...	...	0902	...
	Wien Westbahnhof d.	...	│	...	│	0538	│	0608	│	│	│	0638	0708	│	│	│	│	0808	│	│	│	0838	0845	│	0908
	Wien Hütteldorf d.	...	│	...	│	0545	│	0615	│	│	│	0645	0715	│	│	│	│	0815	│	│	│	0845	0852	│	0915
52	Tullnerfeld **993** d.	...	0516	...	│	│	0616	│	│	│	│	│	│	0716	│	│	│	│	0816	│	│	│	│	0916	│
82	**St Pölten** Hbf **993** d.	...	0530	...	0559	0606	0630	0636	0646	0659	0659	0706	0736	0730	0746	0759	0759	0836	0830	0859	0859	0906	0913	0930	0936
142	Amstetten d.	...	0600**p**	...	│	0630	0655	0700	│	│	│	0730	0800	0755	│	│	│	0900	0855	│	│	0930	│	0955	1000
179	St Valentin **976** d.	...	0615	...	│	│	0715**r**	│	│	│	│	│	│	0815**r**	│	│	│	│	0915**r**	│	│	│	│	1015**r**	│
204	**Linz** Hbf **976** a.	...	0628	...	0643	0654	0728	0724	0732	0743	0743	0754	0824	0828	0832	0843	0843	0924	0928	0943	0943	0954	1000	1028	1024
204	**Linz** Hbf **962** d.	0530	0630	0630	0645	0656	0730	0726	0734	0745	0745	0756	0826	0830	0834	0845	0845	0926	0930	0945	0945	0956	1004	1030	1026
229	**Wels** Hbf **962** d.	0546	0646	0646	│	0711	0746	0741	0751	│	│	0811	0841	0846	│	│	│	0941	0946	│	│	1011	│	1046	1041
	Passau Hbf **962** ▦ a.	│	│	│	│	│	│	│	0834	│	│	│	│	│	0931	│	│	│	│	│	│	│	│	│	│
259	Attnang-Puchheim d.	0600	0700	0700	│	0724	0800	0754	...	│	│	0824	0854	0900	...	│	│	0954	1000	│	│	1024	1035	1100	1054
264	Vöcklabruck d.	0606	0706	0706	│	0729	0806	0759	...	│	│	0829	0859	0906	...	│	│	0959	1006	│	│	1029	...	1106	1059
329	**Salzburg** Hbf a.	0649	0749	0749	0753	0808	0849	0838	...	0853	0853	0908	0938	0949	...	0953	0953	1038	1049	1053	1053	1108	...	1149	1138
	München Hbf **890** a.	│	...	...	│	...	...	1014	...	│	1033	...	│	...	...	│	│	1214	...	│	1232	...	...	...	│
	Innsbruck Hbf **951** a.	0844	...	...	0944	...	...	...	...	1044	...	...	1134	...	...	1144	1144	...	...	1244	...	...	...	...	1334
	Zürich HB **520** a.	│	...	...	1320	...	...	...	...	│	...	...	│	...	...	1520	...	...	...	│	...	...	...	...	...
	Bregenz **951** a.	1117	...	...	...	...	...	...	...	1317	...	...	1418	...	...	...	...	...	...	1517	...	...	...	...	...

	ICE	*RJX*	*RJX*	*WB*	*WB*	*RJ*	*ICE*	*RJX*	*RJX*	*WB*	*WB*	*RJ*	*ICE*	*RJX*	*WB*	*WB*	*RJ*	*RJX*	*RJX*	*WB*	*RJ*	*ICE*	*RJX*	*RJX*
	28	**162**	**562**	**908**	**964**	**548**	**92**	**60**	**860**	**910**	**974**	**640**	**26**	**766**	**912**	**950**	**642**	**62**	**862**	**914**	**644**	**90**	**166**	**566**
									V															
	R✕	B✕	F✕	🍷	🍷	✕	P✕	B✕	Q✕	🍷	🍷	✕	R✕	✕	🍷	🍷	✕	B✕	✕	🍷	✕	E✕	✕	F✕
Flughafen Wien ✈ d.	...	...	0902	...	...	...	...	...	1002	...	...	1033	...	1102	...	...	...	...	1202	...	1233	...	...	1302
Wien Hbf d.	0913	0928	0928	...	...	0955	1013	1028	1028	...	...	1055	1113	1128	...	...	1155	1228	1228	...	1255	1313	1328	1328
Wien Meidling d.	0920	0935	0935	...	...	1002	1020	1035	1035	...	...	1102	1120	1135	...	...	1202	1235	1235	...	1302	1320	1335	1335
Wien Westbahnhof d.	│	│	│	0938	1008	│	│	│	│	1038	1108	│	│	│	1138	1208	│	│	│	1238	│	│	│	│
Wien Hütteldorf d.	│	│	│	0945	1015	│	│	│	│	1045	1115	│	│	│	1145	1215	│	│	│	1245	│	│	│	│
Tullnerfeld **993** d.	│	│	│	│	│	1016	│	│	│	│	│	1116	│	│	│	│	1216	│	│	│	1316	│	│	│
St Pölten Hbf **993** d.	0946	0959	0959	1006	1036	1030	1046	1059	1059	1106	1136	1130	1146	1159	1206	1236	1230	1259	1259	1306	1330	1346	1359	1359
Amstetten d.	│	│	│	1030	1100	1055	│	│	│	1130	1200	1155	│	│	1230	1300	1255	│	│	1330	1400**p**	│	│	│
St Valentin **976** d.	│	│	│	│	│	1115**r**	│	│	│	│	│	1215**r**	│	│	│	│	1315**r**	│	│	│	1415	│	│	│
Linz Hbf **976** a.	1032	1043	1043	1054	1124	1128	1132	1143	1143	1154	1224	1228	1232	1243	1254	1324	1328	1343	1343	1354	1428	1432	1443	1443
Linz Hbf **962** d.	1034	1045	1045	1056	1126	1130	1134	1145	1145	1156	1226	1230	1234	1245	1256	...	1330	1345	1345	1356	1430	1434	1445	1445
Wels Hbf **962** d.	│	│	│	1111	1141	1146	│	│	│	1211	1241	1246	│	│	1311	...	1346	│	│	1411	1446	│	│	│
Passau Hbf **962** ▦ a.	1131	│	│	│	│	│	1231	│	│	│	│	│	1331	│	│	...	│	│	│	│	│	1531	│	│
Attnang-Puchheim d.	...	│	│	1124	1154	1200	...	│	│	1224	1254	1300	...	│	1324	...	1400	│	│	1424	1500	...	│	│
Vöcklabruck d.	...	│	│	1129	1159	1206	...	│	│	1229	1259	1306	...	│	1329	...	1406	│	│	1429	1506	...	│	│
Salzburg Hbf a.	...	1153	1153	1208	1238	1249	...	1253	1253	1308	1338	1349	...	1353	1408	...	1449	1453	1453	1508	1549	...	1553	1553
München Hbf **890** a.	...	│	│	...	1412	...	...	1432	│	...	│	...	...	│	...	...	...	1634	│	...	...	...	│	│
Innsbruck Hbf **951** a.	...	1344	1344	...	...	...	...	...	1444	...	1530	...	...	1544	...	...	...	...	1644	...	...	...	1744	1744
Zürich HB **520** a.	...	1720	...	...	...	...	...	...	│	...	...	...	...	...	...	...	...	...	│	...	...	...	2120	...
Bregenz **951** a.	...	...	...	...	...	...	...	...	1717	...	...	...	...	...	...	...	...	...	1917	...	...	...	...	...

	WB	*WB*	*RJ*	*RJX*	*RJX*	*WB*	*IC*	*WB*	*RJ*	*ICE*	*RJX*	*WB*	*WB*	*RJ*	*RJX*	*RJX*	*WB*	*D*	*WB*	*RJ*	*ICE*	*RJX*	*WB*	*WB*
	916	**952**	**646**	**64**	**864**	**918**	**1060**	**976**	**268**	**22**	**168**	**920**	**966**	**740**	**66**	**866**	**922**	**722**	**978**	**742**	**20**	**760**	**924**	**968**
							⑤ **b**											Ⓐ **a**						
	🍷	🍷	✕	B✕	✕	🍷	G🍷	🍷	✕	R✕	Y✕	🍷	C🍷	✕	B✕	✕	🍷	2	🍷	✕	Q✕	✕	Z🍷	🍷
Flughafen Wien ✈ d.	...	...	...	...	1402	...	...	...	1433	...	1502	...	...	1533	...	1602	...	...	...	1633	...	1702	...	...
Wien Hbf d.	...	...	1355	1428	1428	...	1440	...	1455	1513	1528	...	...	1555	1628	1628	...	1640	...	1655	1713	1728	...	...
Wien Meidling d.	...	...	1402	1435	1435	...	1447	...	1502	1520	1535	...	...	1602	1635	1635	...	1647	...	1702	1720	1735	...	...
Wien Westbahnhof d.	1338	1408	│	│	│	1438	│	1508	│	│	│	1538	1608	│	│	│	1638	│	1708	│	│	│	1738	1808
Wien Hütteldorf d.	1345	1415	│	│	│	1445	│	1515	│	│	│	1545	1615	│	│	│	1645	│	1715	│	│	│	1745	1815
Tullnerfeld **993** d.	│	│	1416	│	│	│	│	│	1516	│	│	│	│	1616	│	│	│	1702	│	1716	│	│	│	│
St Pölten Hbf **993** d.	1406	1436	1430	1459	1459	1506	1513	1536	1530	1546	1559	1606	1636	1630	1659	1659	1706	1716	1736	1730	1746	1759	1806	1836
Amstetten d.	1430	1500	1455	│	│	1530	│	1600	1555	│	│	1630	1700	1655	│	│	1730	1741	1800	1755	│	│	1830	1900
St Valentin **976** d.	│	│	1515**r**	│	│	│	│	│	1615**r**	│	│	│	│	1715**r**	│	│	│	│	│	1815**r**	│	│	│	│
Linz Hbf **976** a.	1454	1524	1528	1543	1543	1554	1600	1624	1628	1632	1643	1654	1724	1728	1743	1743	1754	1808	1824	1828	1832	1843	1854	1924
Linz Hbf **962** d.	1456	...	1530	1545	1545	1556	1604	1626	1630	1634	1645	1656	1726	1730	1745	1745	1756	1810**e**	1826	1830	1834	1845	1856	1926
Wels Hbf **962** d.	1511	...	1546	│	│	1611	│	1641	1646	│	│	1711	1741	1746	│	│	1811	1829**e**	1841	1846	1851	│	1911	1941
Passau Hbf **962** ▦ a.	│	...	│	│	│	│	│	│	│	1731	│	│	│	│	│	│	│	...	│	│	1934	│	│	│
Attnang-Puchheim d.	1524	...	1600	│	│	1624	│	1654	1700	...	│	1724	1754	1800	│	│	1824	...	1854	1900	...	│	1924	1954
Vöcklabruck d.	1529	...	1606	│	│	1629	│	1659	1706	...	│	1729	1759	1806	│	│	1829	...	1859	1906	...	│	1929	1959
Salzburg Hbf a.	1608	...	1649	1653	1653	1708	1730	1738	1749	...	1753	1808	1838	1849	1853	1853	1908	...	1938	1949	...	1953	2008	2038
München Hbf **890** a.	...	...	...	1831	│	...	...	│	1938	...	│	...	2016	...	2031	│	...	...	│	...	...	│	...	2213
Innsbruck Hbf **951** a.	...	...	...	...	1844	...	...	1930	...	...	1944	...	...	...	...	2044	...	...	2134	...	...	2144	...	...
Zürich HB **520** a.	...	...	...	...	│	...	...	│	...	...	2323	...	...	...	...	│	...	...	...	...	...	│	...	...
Bregenz **951** a.	...	...	...	...	2117	...	...	2218	...	...	...	...	...	...	...	2317	...	...	...	...	...	0017	...	...

A – 🛏 1,2 cl., ▬ 2 cl. and [2] Wien - Zürich and v.v.; conveys from July 14 🛏 1,2 cl., ▬ 2 cl. and [2] (*NJ* **40466** / *NJ* **40236**) Wien - Salzburg - Villach - Tarvisio ▦ - Venezia and v.v.
B – From/ to Budapest (Table **1250**).
C – To/from Stuttgart (Table **910**).
D – KÁLMÁN IMRE – 🛏 1,2 cl., ▬ 2 cl. and [2] Budapest - Wien - München - Stuttgart and v.v.
E – [12] and ✕ Hamburg - Hannover - Nürnberg - Regensburg - Passau - Wien and v.v.
F – To / from Feldkirch on dates in Table **951**.
G – To/from Wörgl via Zell am See (Table **960**).
H – 🛏 1,2 cl., ▬ 2 cl. and [2] Wien - Hannover - Hamburg and v.v.; 🛏 1,2 cl., ▬ 2 cl. and [2] (**40490** / **40421**) Wien - Nürnberg - Amsterdam and v.v. (see Table **53**).
L – From/to Bratislava (Table **86**).
M – 🛏 1,2 cl., ▬ 2 cl. and [2] Wien - Paris and v.v.; 🛏 1,2 cl., ▬ 2 cl. and [2] (**40468** / **40425**) Wien - Köln - Brussels and v.v. (see Table **53**).
N – 🛏 1,2 cl., ▬ 2 cl. and [2] Wien - Klagenfurt - Villach - Tarvisio ▦ - Venezia and v.v.
P – [12] and ✕ Hamburg (until Aug. 1) - Berlin - Erfurt - Nürnberg - Regensburg - Passau ▦ - Wien and v.v.
Q – [12] and ✕ Frankfurt - Nürnberg - Regensburg - Passau ▦ - Wien and v.v.
R – [12] and ✕ Dortmund - Frankfurt - Nürnberg - Regensburg - Passau ▦ - Wien and v.v.
S – SALZKAMMERGUT – [2] Wien - Attnang-Puchheim - Stainach-Irdning (Table **961**).
T – To Lindau-Insel (Table **951**).
U – [12] Wien - Nürnberg - Leipzig - Berlin - Rostock and v.v.
V – Conveys [12] Wien - Bregenz (**890**) - Ulm - Stuttgart - Frankfurt (Tables **910** and **933**).
W – Conveys [12] Frankfurt (**897**) - Ulm - Stuttgart - Bregenz (**867**) - Wien (Tables **910**/**933**).
X – Conveys [12] (*RJX* **184**) Bolzano - Innsbruck - Wien Hbf and v.v. (Tables **86**/**595**).
Y – Conveys [12] (*RJX* **185**) Wien Hbf - Innsbruck - Bolzano and v.v. (Tables **86**/**595**).
Z – To/from St Johann im Pongau (Table **960**).

NOTES CONTINUE ON NEXT PAGE → → →

950 WIEN - LINZ - SALZBURG

	RJ	NJ	RJX	RJX	WB	RJ	IC	RJX	WB	WB	RJ	NJ	RJX	RJX	WB	WB	RJ	RJX	NJ	NJ	IC	RJX	NJ	EN	EN	RJ
	744	**468**	**68**	**868**	**954**	**746**	**494**	**762**	**928**	**956**	**748**	**490**	**664**	**264**	**930**	**958**	**840**	**764**	**466**	**1237**	**460**	**768**	**446**	**50462**	**40462**	**820**
		②④⑦										k		h						c		✕				
	✕	M	B✕	✕	🍷	✕	U🍷	✕	🍷	🍷	✕	H♣	✕♠	B✕	🍷	🍷	✕	✕	A	N		2202	♥	D♣	⊙	✕
Flughafen Wien ✈ . ❋ d.	...	...	...	1802	...	1833	...	1902	...	...	1933	...	2002	...	...	...	2033	2102	...	...	...	2228	...	...	...	0002
Wien Hbf d.	1755	1813	1828	1828	...	1855	1913	1928	...	...	1955	2010	2028	2028	...	...	2055	2128	2139	2149	2155	2235	2244	2328	2328	0028
Wien Meidling d.	1802	1820	1835	1835	...	1902	1920	1935	...	...	2002	2017	2035	2035	...	...	2102	2135	2147	2156	2202	|	2251	2335	2335	0035
Wien Westbahnhof d.	|	|	|	|	1908	|	|	|	1938	2008	|	|	|	|	2038	2108	|	|	|	|	|	|	|	|	|	|
Wien Hütteldorf d.	|	|	|	|	1915	|	|	|	1945	2015	|	|	|	|	2045	2115	|	|	|	|	|	|	|	|	|	|
Tullnerfeld **993** d.	1816	|	|	|	|	1916	|	|	|	|	2016	|	|	|	|	|	2116	|	|	|	2216	|	|	|	|	0049
St Pölten Hbf **993** d.	1830	1848	1859	1859	1936	1930	1946	1959	2006	2036	2030	2044	2059	2059	2106	2136	2130	2159	2214**u**	2224**u**	2230	2259	2323	0001	0001	0103
Amstetten d.	1855	|	|	|	2000	1955	|	|	2030	2100	2055	|	|	|	2130	2200	2155	|	2241**u**	2249**u**	2300**p**	|	2353	|	|	0127
St Valentin **976** d.	1915**r**	|	|	|	|	2015**r**	|	|	|	|	2115**r**	|	|	|	|	|	2215**r**	|	|	|	2315	|	|	|	|	0143
Linz Hbf **976** a.	1928	1936	1943	1943	2024	2028	2032	2043	2054	2124	2128	2132	2143	2143	2154	2224	2228	2243	|	2318	2328	2343	0023	0048	0048	0157
Linz Hbf **962** d.	1930	1938	1945	1945	2026	2030	2034	2045	2056	2126	2130	2134	2145	2145	2156	...	2230	2245	2310**u**	...	2330	2345	0026	0051	0051	0159
Wels Hbf **962** d.	1946	|	|	|	2041	2046	2051	|	2111	2140	2146	2151	2202	2202	2211	...	2246	2302	2327**u**	...	2346	0002	0043	|	|	0215
Passau Hbf **962** 🏛 a.	|	|	|	|	|	|	2137	|	|	|	|	2234	|	|	|	...	|	|	|	...	|	|	|	|	|	...
Attnang-Puchheim d.	2000	|	|	|	2054	2100	...	|	2124	2153	2200	...	2217	2217	2224	...	2300	2317	2345**u**	...	0000	0017	0101	|	|	...
Vöcklabruck d.	2006	|	|	|	2059	2106	...	|	2129	...	2206	...	|	|	2229	...	2306	|	|	...	0006	|	0107	|	|	...
Salzburg Hbf a.	2049	2112	2053	2053	2138	2149	...	2153	2208	...	2249	...	2259	2259	2312	...	2349	2359	0230**u**	...	0049	0059	0149	0207	0207	...
München Hbf **890** a.	...	2313	2232	|	...	...	...	|	...	...	...	...	...	...	...	...	...	...	|	...	...	...	|	0550**d**	|	...
Innsbruck Hbf **951** a.	...	...	...	2248	...	...	...	2348	...	...	...	...	...	...	...	...	...	...	0423	...	...	...	0515	...	0423	...
Zürich HB **520** a.	...	...	...	...	...	...	...	...	...	...	...	...	...	...	...	...	...	...	0820	...	...	...	|	...	0820	...
Bregenz **951** a.	...	...	...	...	...	...	...	...	...	...	...	...	...	...	...	...	...	...	...	...	...	...	0829	...	...	...

	RJ	RJ	IC	NJ	EN	EN	RJ	WB	RJX	RJX	NJ	NJ	D	RJ	WB	WB	RJX	RJ	WB	NJ	WB	RJX	RJX	RJ	WB	NJ
	821	**821**	**461**	**447**	**40467**	**50237**	**823**	**901**	**769**	**769**	**467**	**1236**	**525**	**541**	**951**	**903**	**761**	**543**	**953**	**491**	**905**	**669**	**269**	**545**	**955**	**469**
	Ⓐ	⑥							Ⓐ	Ⓒ		c	Ⓐ										⚒			②④⑥
	✕	✕		♥	⊖	D	✕	🍷	✕	✕	A	N	2	✕	🍷	🍷	✕	✕	🍷	H♣	🍷	✕	B✕	✕	🍷	M
Bregenz **951** d.	...	...	...	2140	...	...	...	...	...	...	...	...	...	...	...	...	...	...	...	...	...	...	...	...	...	...
Zürich HB **520** d.	...	...	...	|	2140	...	...	...	...	...	2140	...	...	...	...	...	...	...	...	...	...	...	...	...	...	...
Innsbruck Hbf **951** d.	...	...	...	0044	0128	...	...	...	...	...	0128	...	...	...	...	...	...	...	...	...	...	0510	...	...	...	...
München Hbf **890** d.	...	...	...	|	|	2354**d**	...	...	...	...	|	...	...	...	...	...	...	...	...	...	...	|	...	...	...	0543
Salzburg Hbf d.	...	...	0311	0255**s**	0353	0353	...	...	0501	...	0433	...	...	0511	...	0552	0601	0611	0622	...	0652	0707	0707	0711	0722	0730
Vöcklabruck d.	...	...	0355	0359**s**	|	|	...	...	|	...	|	...	...	0555	...	0632	|	0655	0702	...	0732	|	|	0755	0802	|
Attnang-Puchheim d.	...	...	0401	0405**s**	|	|	...	...	0546	...	0521	...	...	0601	0607	0637	0646	0701	0707	...	0737	|	|	0801	0807	|
Passau Hbf **962** 🏛 d.	...	...	|	|	|	|	...	...	|	...	|	...	...	|	|	|	|	|	|	0615	|	|	|	|	|	|
Wels Hbf **962** d.	0354	...	0416	0424**s**	|	|	...	...	0601	...	0541	...	0608	0616	0620	0650	0701	0716	0720	0723	0750	|	|	0816	0820	|
Linz Hbf **962** a.	0408	...	0430	0443**s**	0504	0504	...	...	0615	...	0558**s**	...	0624	0630	0634	0704	0715	0730	0734	0743	0804	0815	0815	0830	0834	0846
Linz Hbf **976** d.	0410	0410	0432	|	0510	0510	0532	0606	0617	0617	|	...	0625	0632	0636	0706	0717	0732	0736	0747	0806	0817	0817	0832	0836	0848
St Valentin **976** d.	|	|	0445	0502**s**	|	|	0545	|	|	|	|	...	|	0650**r**	|	|	|	0750**r**	|	|	|	|	|	0850**r**	|	|
Amstetten d.	0437	0437	0507**p**	0524**s**	|	|	0607**p**	0631	|	|	0637**s**	0626	0651	0707	0701	0731	|	0807	0801	|	0831	|	|	0907	0901	|
St Pölten Hbf **993** d.	0502	0502	0532	0610**s**	0600	0600	0632	0655	0703	0703	0710**s**	0739	0715	0732	0725	0755	0803	0832	0825	0840	0855	0903	0903	0932	0925	0938
Tullnerfeld **993** d.	0515	0515	0545	|	|	|	0645	|	|	|	|	|	0729	0745	|	|	|	0845	|	|	|	|	|	0945	|	|
Wien Hütteldorf a.	|	|	|	|	|	|	|	0714	|	|	|	|	|	|	0744	0814	|	|	0844	|	0914	|	|	|	0944	|
Wien Westbahnhof a.	|	|	|	|	|	|	|	0722	|	|	|	|	|	|	0752	0822	|	|	0852	|	0922	|	|	|	0952	|
Wien Meidling a.	0528	0528	0558	0648	0624	0624	0658	...	0725	0725	0751	0810	0745	0758	...	...	0825	0858	...	0908	...	0925	0925	0958	...	1005
Wien Hbf a.	0535	0535	0605	0658	0632	0632	0705	...	0732	0732	0758	0819	0752	0805	...	...	0832	0905	...	0917	...	0932	0932	1005	...	1013
Flughafen Wien ✈ . ❋ a.	0557	0557	...	...	...	...	0727	...	0757	0757	...	...	...	0827	...	...	0857	0927	...	...	...	0957	...	...	...	...

	WB	RJX	RJX	IC	RJ	WB	WB	RJX	RJX	RJX	RJ		WB	WB	RJX	ICE	RJ	WB	RJX	RJX	RJ	WB	WB	RJX	ICE	RJ
	907	**763**	**265**	**495**	**547**	**971**	**909**	**861**	**861**	**61**	**549**		**961**	**911**	**765**	**21**	**641**	**973**	**863**	**63**	**643**	**963**	**915**	**161**	**23**	**645**
								Ⓐ																		
	Z🍷	✕	✕	U🍷	✕	🍷	🍷	✕	✕	B✕	✕		🍷	🍷	✕	Q✕	✕	🍷	✕	B✕	✕	C🍷	🍷	X✕	R✕	✕
Bregenz **951** d.	...	...	...	...	...	...	...	0440	...	...	...	...	...	...	0537	...	...	0540	0639	...	...	...	...	...	...	...
Zürich HB **520** d.	...	...	...	...	...	...	...	|	...	...	...	...	...	...	|	...	...	|	|	...	...	...	...	0640	...	...
Innsbruck Hbf **951** d.	...	0610	...	...	...	0626	...	0714	0714	...	...	...	...	...	0817	...	...	0830	0914	...	...	...	...	1016	...	...
München Hbf **890** d.	...	|	0621	...	...	|	...	|	|	0722	...	...	0749	...	|	...	...	|	|	0928	...	0947	...	|	...	...
Salzburg Hbf d.	0752	0807	0807	...	0811	0822	0852	0907	0907	0907	0911	...	0922	0952	1007	...	1011	1022	1107	1107	1111	1122	1152	1207	...	1211
Vöcklabruck d.	0832	|	|	...	0855	0902	0932	|	|	|	0955	...	1002	1032	|	...	1055	1102	|	|	1155	1202	1232	|	...	1255
Attnang-Puchheim d.	0837	|	|	...	0901	0907	0937	|	|	|	1001	...	1007	1037	|	...	1101	1107	|	|	1201	1207	1237	|	...	1301
Passau Hbf **962** 🏛 d.	|	|	|	0824	|	|	|	|	|	|	|	...	|	|	|	1026	|	|	|	|	|	|	|	|	1229	|
Wels Hbf **962** d.	0850	|	|	0911	0916	0920	0950	|	|	|	1016	...	1020	1050	|	1111	1116	1120	|	|	1216	1220	1250	|	|	1316
Linz Hbf **962** a.	0904	0915	0915	0926	0930	0934	1004	1015	1015	1015	1030	...	1034	1104	1115	1126	1130	1134	1215	1215	1230	1234	1304	1315	1326	1330
Linz Hbf **976** d.	0906	0917	0917	0928	0932	0936	1006	1017	1017	1017	1032	...	1036	1106	1117	1128	1132	1136	1217	1217	1232	1236	1306	1317	1328	1332
St Valentin **976** d.	|	|	|	|	0950**r**	|	|	|	|	|	1050**r**	...	|	|	|	|	1150**r**	|	|	|	1250**r**	|	|	|	|	1350**r**
Amstetten d.	0931	|	|	|	1007	1001	1031	|	|	|	1107	...	1101	1131	|	|	1207	1201	|	|	1307	1301	1331	|	|	1407
St Pölten Hbf **993** d.	0955	1003	1003	1016	1032	1025	1055	1103	1103	1103	1132	...	1125	1155	1203	1216	1232	1225	1303	1303	1332	1325	1355	1403	1416	1432
Tullnerfeld **993** d.	|	|	|	|	1045	|	|	|	|	|	1145	...	|	|	|	|	1245	|	|	|	1345	|	|	|	|	1445
Wien Hütteldorf a.	1014	|	|	|	|	1044	1114	|	|	|	|	...	1144	1214	|	|	|	1244	|	|	|	1344	1414	|	|	|
Wien Westbahnhof a.	1022	|	|	|	|	1052	1122	|	|	|	|	...	1152	1222	|	|	|	1252	|	|	|	1352	1422	|	|	|
Wien Meidling a.	...	1025	1025	1040	1058	...	...	1125	1125	1125	1158	...	...	...	1225	1240	1258	...	1325	1325	1358	...	...	1425	1440	1458
Wien Hbf a.	...	1032	1032	1047	1105	...	...	1132	1132	1132	1205	...	...	...	1232	1247	1305	...	1332	1332	1405	...	...	1432	1447	1505
Flughafen Wien ✈ . ❋ a.	...	1057	...	...	1127	...	...	1157	1157	...	...	...	...	...	1257	...	1327	...	1357	...	1427	...	...	1457	...	1527

	WB	WB	RJX	RJX	RJ	WB	IC	WB	RJX	ICE	RJ	WB	RJX	RJX	ICE	RJ		WB	RJX	RJX	ICE	RJ	WB	WB	RJX	RJX
	957	**917**	**65**	**865**	**647**	**965**	**1061**	**919**	**767**	**91**	**649**	**921**	**867**	**67**	**93**	**741**		**923**	**565**	**165**	**27**	**743**	**975**	**925**	**869**	**69**
							n																			
	🍷	🍷	B✕	✕	✕	🍷	G🍷	🍷	✕	E✕	✕	🍷	W✕	B✕	P✕	✕		🍷	F✕	B✕	R✕	✕	🍷	🍷	✕	✕
Bregenz **951** d.	...	...	...	0840	...	...	...	...	...	...	...	...	1040	...	...	...	...	...	...	...	...	...	...	...	1240	...
Zürich HB **520** d.	...	...	...	|	...	...	...	...	...	...	...	...	|	...	...	...	...	...	...	1040	...	...	...	...	|	...
Innsbruck Hbf **951** d.	...	...	...	1114	...	...	...	...	1216	...	...	...	1314	...	...	...	...	...	1416	1416	...	...	1426	...	1514	...
München Hbf **890** d.	...	...	1127	|	...	1145	...	...	|	...	...	...	|	1328	...	...	...	...	|	|	...	...	|	...	|	1528
Salzburg Hbf d.	...	1252	1307	1307	1311	1322	1330	1352	1407	...	1411	1452	1507	1507	...	1511	...	1552	1607	1607	...	1611	1622	1652	1707	1707
Vöcklabruck d.	...	1337	|	|	1355	1402	|	1432	|	...	1455	1532	|	|	...	1555	...	1632	|	|	...	1655	1702	1732	|	|
Attnang-Puchheim d.	...	1336	|	|	1401	1407	|	1437	|	...	1501	1537	|	|	...	1601	...	1637	|	|	...	1701	1707	1737	|	|
Passau Hbf **962** 🏛 d.	...	|	|	|	|	|	|	|	|	1429	|	|	|	|	1529	|	...	|	|	|	1629	|	|	|	|	|
Wels Hbf **962** d.	...	1350	|	|	1416	1420	|	1450	|	|	1516	1550	|	|	|	1616	...	1650	|	|	|	1716	1720	1750	|	|
Linz Hbf **962** a.	...	1404	1415	1415	1430	1434	1446	1504	1515	1526	1530	1604	1615	1615	1626	1630	...	1704	1715	1715	1726	1730	1734	1804	1815	1815
Linz Hbf **976** d.	1336	1406	1417	1417	1432	1436	1448	1506	1517	1528	1532	1606	1617	1617	1628	1632	...	1706	1717	1717	1728	1732	1736	1806	1817	1817
St Valentin **976** d.	|	|	|	|	1450**r**	|	|	|	|	|	1550**r**	|	|	|	|	1645	...	|	|	|	|	1750**r**	|	|	|	|
Amstetten d.	1401	1431	|	|	1507	1501	|	1531	|	|	1607	1631	|	|	|	1707**p**	...	1731	|	|	|	1807	1801	1831	|	|
St Pölten Hbf **993** d.	1425	1455	1503	1503	1532	1525	1538	1555	1603	1616	1632	1655	1703	1703	1716	1732	...	1755	1803	1803	1816	1832	1825	1855	1903	1903
Tullnerfeld **993** d.	|	|	|	|	1545	|	|	|	|	|	1645	|	|	|	|	1745	...	|	|	|	|	1845	|	|	|	|
Wien Hütteldorf a.	1444	1514	|	|	|	1544	|	1614	|	|	|	1714	|	|	|	|	...	1814	|	|	|	|	1844	1914	|	|
Wien Westbahnhof a.	1452	1522	|	|	|	1552	|	1622	|	|	|	1722	|	|	|	|	...	1822	|	|	|	|	1852	1922	|	|
Wien Meidling a.	...	...	1525	1525	1558	...	1603	...	1625	1640	1658	...	1725	1725	1740	1758	...	...	1825	1825	1840	1858	...	...	1925	1925
Wien Hbf a.	...	...	1532	1532	1605	...	1610	...	1632	1647	1705	...	1732	1732	1747	1805	...	...	1832	1832	1847	1905	...	...	1932	1932
Flughafen Wien ✈ . ❋ a.	...	...	...	1557	...	...	...	...	1657	...	1727	...	1757	...	...	...	...	...	1857	...	...	1927	...	...	1957	...

← ← ← **NOTES** (continued from previous page)

a – Ⓐ (not May 30, June 20).
b – ⑤ (also Apr. 17, 30, May 28, June 18, Aug. 14).
c – Until July 13.
d – München **Ost**.
e – ①–④ (not public holidays).
h – Ⓑ (not Jan. 5, Apr. 20, June 8, Aug. 15, Dec. 7).
k – Not Jan. 10, May 11–31, June 1–6.
n – ⑥ (also May 1, 29, June 19, Aug. 15).
p – Arrives 7 minutes earlier.

r – Arrives 5 minutes earlier.
s – Stops to set down only.
u – Calls to pick up only.

⊙ – 🛏 1, 2 cl., 🛌 2 cl. and [2] Budapest (**462**) - Salzburg (**466**) - Zürich.
⊖ – 🛏 1, 2 cl., 🛌 2 cl. and [2] Zürich (**467**) - Salzburg (**463**) - Budapest.
♥ – Conveys 🛏 1, 2 cl., 🛌 2 cl. (1, 4 berth) and [2] (*ÖBB nightjet* new generation).
❋ – See Table **985** for full service from / to Wien Flughafen ✈.
♣ – Ⓡ for journeys to / from Germany.
♠ – Runs as *RJX* **1164** on ⑥ (also Jan. 5, Apr. 20, June 8, Aug. 15, Dec. 7).

SALZBURG - LINZ - WIEN 950

	RJ	WB	WB	RJX	RJX	ICE	RJ	WB	IC	WB	RJX	RJX	ICE	RJ	WB	WB	RJX	RJ	WB	ICE	RJX	RJ	RJX	RJ	RJ
	745	**967**	**927**	**167**	**567**	**29**	**747**	**977**	**1019**	**929**	**661**	**261**	**95**	**749**	**969**	**931**	**169**	**841**	**979**	**229**	**663**	**843**	**367**	**845**	**263**
					z																				**v**
	✕	🍷	🍷	**L** ✕	**F** ✕	**R** ✕	✕	🍷	**S**	🍷	✕	**B** ✕	**P** ✕	✕	**C** 🍷	🍷	✕	✕	**T** 🍷	**R** ✕	✕	✕	✕	✕	✕
Bregenz **951** d.	...	...	...	...	...	...	...	...	...	...	1440	...	...	...	...	...	...	...	1540	...	1640	...	...	...	...
Zürich HB **520** d.	...	...	...	1240	...	...	...	...	...	...	|	...	...	...	...	...	1440	...	|	...	|	...	1640	...	...
Innsbruck Hbf **951** d.	...	...	...	1616	1616	...	...	1626	...	...	1714	...	...	...	...	...	1816	...	1826	...	1914	...	2016	...	...
München Hbf **890** d.	...	1548	...	|	|	...	...	|	...	...	|	1729	...	...	1749	...	|	...	|	...	|	...	|	...	2116
Salzburg Hbf d.	1711	1722	1752	1807	1807	...	1811	1822	...	1852	1907	1907	...	1911	1922	1952	2007	2011	2022	...	2107	2111	2207	2211	2311
Vöcklabruck d.	1755	1802	1832	|	|	...	1855	1902	...	1932	|	|	...	1955	2002	2032	|	2055	2102	...	|	2155	|	2255	2355
Attnang-Puchheim d.	1801	1807	1837	|	|	...	1901	1907	1925	1937	|	|	...	2001	2007	2037	|	2101	2107	...	|	2201	|	2301	0001
Passau Hbf **962** 🏛 d.	|	|	|	|	|	1829	|	|	|	|	|	|	1926	|	|	|	|	|	|	2031	|	|	|	|	|
Wels Hbf **962** d.	1816	1820	1850	|	|	|	1916	1920	|	1950	|	|	2011	2016	2020	2050	|	2116	2120	2123	|	2216	2303	2316	0016
Linz Hbf **962** a.	1830	1834	1904	1915	1915	1926	1930	1934	1956	2004	2015	2015	2026	2030	2034	2104	2115	2130	2134	2138	2215	2230	2318	2330	0030
Linz Hbf **976** d.	1832	1836	1906	1917	1917	1928	1932	1936	2001	2006	2017	2017	2028	2032	2036	2106	2117	...	2136	2141	2217	2232	2320	...	0032
St Valentin **976** d.	1850**r**	|	|	|	|	|	1950**r**	|	|	|	|	|	|	2050**r**	|	|	|	...	|	|	|	2245	|	...	0045
Amstetten d.	1907	1901	1931	|	|	|	2007	2001	|	2031	|	|	|	2107	2101	2131	|	...	2201	2207	|	2307**p**	|	...	0102
St Pölten Hbf **993** d.	1932	1925	1955	2003	2003	2016	2032	2025	2048	2055	2103	2103	2116	2132	2125	2155	2203	...	2225	2232	2303	2332	0006	...	0126
Tullnerfeld **993** d.	1945	|	|	|	|	|	2045	|	|	|	|	|	|	2145	|	|	|	...	|	2245	|	2345	|	...	|
Wien Hütteldorf a.	|	1944	2014	|	|	|	|	2044	2108	2114	|	|	|	|	2144	2214	|	...	2244	|	|	|	|	...	|
Wien Westbahnhof a.	|	1952	2022	|	|	|	|	2052	2115	2122	|	|	|	|	2152	2222	|	...	2252	|	|	|	|	...	|
Wien Meidling a.	1958	...	...	2025	2025	2040	2058	...	...	...	2125	2125	2140	2158	...	...	2225	...	...	2258	2325	2358	0028	...	0213
Wien Hbf a.	2005	...	...	2032	2032	2047	2105	...	...	...	2132	2132	2147	2205	...	...	2232	...	...	2305	2332	0005	0035	...	0220
Flughafen Wien ✈ ... ≋ a.	...	...	...	...	2057	...	2127	...	...	...	2157	...	...	...	...	...	...	...	...	...	...	...	...	...	...

B – To Budapest (Table **1250**).
C – from Stuttgart (Table **910**).
F – From Feldkirch on dates in Table **951**.
L – To Bratislava (Table **86**).
P – [12] and ✕ Hamburg (until Aug. 1) - Berlin - Erfurt - Nürnberg - Regensburg - Passau 🏛 - Wien.
R – [12] and ✕ Dortmund - Frankfurt - Nürnberg - Regensburg - Passau 🏛 - Wien.
S – SALZKAMMERGUT [2] Stainach-Irdning - Attnang-Puchheim - Wien (Table **961**).

T – From Lindau-Insel (Table **951**).

p – Arrives 2300.
r – Arrives 5 minutes earlier.
v – ⑤⑥⑦ (also Apr. 21, 30, May 1, 28, 29, June 9, 18, 19, Aug. 14, Dec. 8).
z – Ⓑ (also Aug. 14, Dec. 8; not Apr. 20, June 8, Aug. 15, Dec. 7).

≋ – See Table **985** for full service from/to Wien Flughafen ✈.

2nd class only * Regional trains WIEN - ST PÖLTEN - ST VALENTIN 950a

km		Ⓒ**h**	⚒		Ⓐ								⑤**g**		Ⓐ		Ⓐ		Ⓐ		Ⓐ		Ⓐ						
0	**Wien** Westbahnhof d.	0053	...	0518	0549	0618	0648	0718	0748**a**	0818		1418	1448	1518	1548	1618	1648	1718	1748	1818	1848	1918	1948	2018	2118	2218	2318	0018
6	**Wien** Hütteldorf d.	0100	...	0526	0556	0626	0656	0726	0756**a**	0826		1426	1456	1526	1556	1626	1656	1726	1756	1826	1856	1926	1956	2026	2126	2226	2326	0026
30	Tullnerfeld d.	|	...	0540	0609	0640	0710	0740	0810**a**	0840	and	1440	1510	1540	1610	1640	1710	1740	1810	1840	1910	1940	2010	2040	2140	2240	2340	0040
60	**St Pölten** Hbf a.	0154	...	0554	0623	0654	0724	0754	0824**a**	0854		1454	1524	1554	1624	1654	1724	1754	1824	1854	1924	1954	2024	2054	2154	2254	2354	0054
60	**St Pölten** Hbf d.	0156	0447	0603	0624	0703	0725**c**	0803	0839	0903	hourly	1503	1525	1603	1625	1703	1725	1803	1825	1903	1925	2003	2025	2103	2205	2305	0005	0106
84	Melk d.	0213	0506	0621	0644	0721	0740**c**	0821	0858	0921		1521	1540	1621	1640	1721	1740	1821	1840	1921	1940	2021	2040	2121	2221	2321	0021	0122
93	Pöchlarn d.	0219	0512	0628	0656**f**	0728	|	0828	0905	0928	until	1528	1547	1628	1647	1728	1747	1828	1847	1928	1947	2028	2047	2128	2228	2328	0028	0128
106	Ybbs an der Donau d.	0229	0523	0637	0707	0737	0753**c**	0837	...	0937		1537	1556	1637	1656	1737	1756	1837	1856	1937	1956	2037	2056	2137	2237	2337	0037	0137
123	Amstetten a.	0243	0536	0650	0720	0750	0803**c**	0850	...	0950		1550	1809	1650	1709	1750	1809	1850	1909	1950	2013	2050	2113	2150	2250	2350	0050	0150
123	Amstetten d.	*0431*	0537	*0708*	...	*0808*	*0808*	*0908*	...	*1008*		*1608*	...	*1708*	...	*1808*	...	1908	...	*2008*	...	*2108*	...	*2208*	2308	*0008*	...	*0431*
162	**St Valentin** a.	*0500*	0606	*0737*	...	*0837*	*0837*	*0937*	...	*1037*		*1637*	...	*1737*	...	*1837*	...	1937	...	*2037*	...	*2137*	...	*2237*	2337	*0037*	...	*0500*

		Ⓐ		Ⓐ	Ⓐ	Ⓐ			Ⓐ		Ⓐ							Ⓐ		**k**	Ⓒ						
St Valentin d.	...	0400	*0430***a**	0430	*0454*	0454	...	*0523*	...	...	0559	*0623*	...	*0723*	*0823*		*1623*	...	*1723*	1751	*1823*	*1823*	...	*1923*	*2023*	*2123*	2223	*2323*
Amstetten a.	...	0429	*0459***a**	0459	*0523*	0523	...	*0552*	...	...	0628	*0652*	...	*0752*	*0852*		*1652*	...	*1752*	1822	*1852*	*1852*	...	*1953*	*2052*	*2153*	2252	*2352*
Amstetten d.	0407	0442	0503	0517	0531	0547	...	0604	0617	0631	0646	0710	0730**a**	0810	0910	and	1710	1746	1810	...	1858	1910	...	2010	2110	2210	2310	0010
Ybbs an der Donau d.	0420	0455	0516	0527	0544	0557	...	0617	0627	0644	0657	0723	0743**a**	0823	0923		1723	1759	1823	...	1907	1923	...	2023	2123	2223	2323	0023
Pöchlarn d.	0431	0504	0528	0535	0556	0605	...	0628	0635	0656	0705	0734	0755	0834	0934	hourly	1734	1811	1834	...	|	1934	...	2034	2134	2234	2334	0034
Melk d.	0437	0510	0533	0541	0602	0611	...	0634	0641	0702	0711	0740	0801	0840	0940		1740	1817	1840	...	1920	1940	...	2040	2140	2240	2340	0040
St Pölten Hbf a.	0457	0527	0554	0557	0624	0627	...	0653	0658	0724	0727	0758	0821	0858	0958	until	1758	1833	1858	...	1934	1958	...	2058	2158	2258	2358	0058
St Pölten Hbf d.	0506	0536	0606	0606	0636	0636	...	0706	0706	0736**a**	0736	0806	0836**a**	0906	1006		1806	1836	1906	...	1936	2006	...	2106	2206	2306	0009	0106**n**
Tullnerfeld d.	0520	0550	0620	0620	0650	0650	...	0720	0720	0750**a**	0750	0820	0850**a**	0920	1020		1820	1850	1920	...	1950	2020	...	2120	2220	2320	0023	|
Wien Hütteldorf a.	0534	0604	0634	0634	0704	0704	...	0734	0734	0804**a**	0804	0834	0904**a**	0934	1034		1834	1904	1934	...	2004	2034	...	2134	2234	2334	0036	0140**n**
Wien Westbahnhof a.	0541	0612	0641	0641	0712	0712	...	0741	0741	0812**a**	0812	0842	0912**a**	0942	1042		1842	1912	1942	...	2012	2042	...	2142	2242	2342	0043	0147**n**

a – Ⓐ only.
c – Ⓒ only.
f – Arrives 0650.
g – Not Aug. 15.
h – From Sept. 6 runs 38 minutes later from St Pölten.
k – ①–④ (not Apr. 21, May, 1, 29, June 9, 19, Dec. 8).
n – From Sept. 1.
* – Most trains from/to Wien are classified *CJX*.

SALZBURG and MÜNCHEN - INNSBRUCK - FELDKIRCH - BREGENZ - LINDAU 951

km		*NJ*	*EN*		*NJ*		*NJ*		*D*		*RJX*	*ICE*		*RJ*	*ICE*	*NJ*	*EC*		*RJX*			*RJX*	*RJ*		*WB*	*RJX*		
		466	**40462**		**1464**		**446**		**666**		**366**	**1203**		**668**	**118**	**421**	**81**		**368**			**660**	**83**		**970**	**160**		
												⑥**b**				Ⓡ										**D**		
		N	⊙	2	♦	2	**N**	2	2	2	✕	✕	2	✕	🍷♦	♦	**A** 🍷	2	✕	2	2	✕	**A** ✕	2	🍷	**R** ✕	2	2
	Wien Hbf **950** d.	2139	2328	...	...	...	2244	...	...	...	...	...	...	...	...	...	...	...	0528	...	...	0628	...	...	...	0728	...	...
	Wien Westbahnhof **950** d.	|	|	...	...	...	|	...	...	...	...	...	...	...	...	...	...	...	|	...	...	|	...	...	0708	|	...	...
	Linz Hbf **950** d.	2310	0051	...	...	...	0026	...	...	...	...	...	...	0530**f**	...	...	...	...	0645	...	...	0745	...	...	0826	0845	...	...
0	**Salzburg** Hbf d.	0230	0230	...	...	...	0212	...	...	...	0556	...	...	0656	...	...	...	...	0756	...	...	0856	...	...	0939	0956	...	...
	München Hbf **890** ‡ d.	|	|	...	...	...	|	...	...	...	|	0626	...	|	...	0728	0732	...	|	...	...	|	0933	...	|	|	...	...
	München Ost **890** ‡ d.	|	|	...	...	...	|	...	...	...	|	0638	...	|	...	|	0744	...	|	...	...	|	0944	...	|	|	...	...
	Rosenheim **890** ‡ d.	|	|	...	...	...	|	...	...	...	|	0705	...	|	...	0806	0813	...	|	...	...	|	1013	...	|	|	...	...
120	Kufstein 🏛 ‡ d.	|	|	...	...	...	|	0542	...	0631	0709	0728	...	|	...	0828	0836	...	0909	0931	...	|	1036	...	1051	1109	1112	...
134	Wörgl Hbf **960** d.	|	|	...	...	...	|	0554	...	0645**c**	0719	0739	...	0815	...	0839	0846	...	0919	0945**c**	...	1015	1046	...	1101	1119	1124	...
159	Jenbach **960** d.	|	|	...	...	...	|	0615	...	0659	|	0755	...	0829	...	0855	0900	...	|	0959	...	1029	1100	...	1117	|	1145	...
193	**Innsbruck** Hbf **960** a.	0423	0423	...	...	...	0515	0640	...	0718	0744	0814	...	0844	...	0914	0918	...	0944	1018	...	1044	1118	...	1134	1144	1210	...
193	**Innsbruck** Hbf d.	0431	0431	...	0453	...	0520	▬	0644	...	0747	0817	0822	0847	0852	...	...	0922	0947	▬	1022	1047	...	1120	1140	1147	▬	1222
239	Ötztal d.	|	|	...	|	...	0546	...	|	...	0812	0848	0859	|	0917	...	...	0959	1012	...	1059	|	...	1157	|	1212	...	1259
248	Imst-Pitztal d.	|	|	...	|	...	0557	...	0716	...	|	0901	0909	0919	|	...	...	1009	|	...	1109	1119	...	1208	1214	|	...	1310
265	Landeck-Zams d.	0520	0520	...	0545	...	0622	...	0730	...	0833	0925**e**	0924	0933	0954**c**	...	...	1024	1033	...	1124	1133	...	1222	1227	1233	...	1324
293	St Anton am Arlberg d.	|	|	...	0611	...	0648	...	0754	...	0857	0948	▬	|	1022	...	...	...	1057	...	...	|	...	...	1249	1257	...	...
304	Langen am Arlberg d.	|	|	...	0621	...	0659	2	0804	...	|	...	...	1004	1032	...	...	...	|	...	...	1204	...	...	|	|	...	...
329	Bludenz **952** d.	0625	0625	0630	0706	0730	0735**e**	0800	0831	...	0931	...	...	1031	1102	...	...	...	1131	...	...	1231	...	...	1323	1331	...	...
350	**Feldkirch** **952** a.	0637	0637	0645	0721	0745	0748	0815	0842	...	0942	...	2	1042	1113	...	...	...	1142	2	...	1242	...	...	1336	1342	2	...
350	**Feldkirch** **952** d.	0640	0640	0647	0739	0747	0753	0817	0847	...	0944	...	0947	1047	1116	...	...	...	1148	1147	...	1247	...	...	1337	1348	1347	...
369	**Buchs** 🏛 **952** a.	0656	0656	|	0754	|	|	|	|	...	0959	...	|	|	|	...	...	...	1206	|	...	|	...	...	|	1406	|	...
	Zürich HB **520** a.	0820	0820	|	0920	|	|	|	|	...	1120	...	|	|	|	...	...	...	1320	|	...	|	...	...	|	1520	|	...
375	Dornbirn **952** d.	...	...	0709	...	0809	0821	0839	0909	...	...	...	1009	1109	1139	...	...	...	...	1209	...	1309	...	...	1406	...	1412	...
387	**Bregenz** 🏛 **952** a.	...	...	0718	...	0818	0829	0848	0917	...	...	...	1018	1117	1149	...	...	...	...	1218	...	1317	...	...	1418	...	1422	...
	Lindau Reutin 🏛 **952** a.	...	...	0728	...	0828	...	0858	...	...	...	...	1028	...	1158	...	...	...	...	1228	...	...	...	...	1426	...	1432	...
397	**Lindau**-Insel 🏛 **952** a.	...	...	0733	...	0832	...	0903	...	...	...	...	1032	...	...	...	...	...	...	1232	...	...	...	...	1431	...	1436	...

♦ – **NOTES** (LISTED BY TRAIN NUMBER)

18 – BODENSEE – [12] Innsbruck - Lindau - Stuttgart - Köln - Münster. Apr. 17 - June 6 runs Innsbruck - Lindau - Stuttgart - Berlin.

21 – 🛏 1, 2 cl., ━ 2 cl. and [2] Amsterdam / Düsseldorf - Innsbruck; 🛏 1, 2 cl., ━ 2 cl. and [2] (**40491**) Hamburg - Innsbruck.

464 – 🛏 1, 2 cl., ━ 2 cl. and [2] Graz - Schwarzach - Zürich; 🛏 1, 2 cl., ━ 2 cl. and [2] (*EN* **40414**) Zagreb - Ljubljana - Villach - Schwarzach - Zürich. Runs as *NJ* **464** from July 14.

A – To Verona, Bologna, Rimini or Venezia via Brennero (Table **70**).

D – ⚒ (not Apr. 21, June 9, Aug. 16, Dec. 8) conveys [12] (*RJX* **560**) Flughafen Wien - Wien Hbf - Innsbruck (- Feldkirch ⑤⑥ **v**).

N – Conveys 🛏 1, 2 cl., ━ 2 cl. (1, 4 berth) and [2] (*ÖBB nightjet* new generation).

R – From Bratislava (Table **86**).

b – ⑥ Dec. 21 - Apr. 5; ⑥ June 21 - Oct. 4.
c – Arrives 5 minutes earlier.
e – Arrives 10 minutes earlier.
f – Ⓐ only.
r – Ⓒ only.
t – Arrives 10–12 minutes earlier.
v – Also Apr. 30, May 1, 28, 29, June 18, 19, Aug. 14, 15; not May 2, 30, June 20, Aug. 16.

⊙ – 🛏 1, 2 cl., ━ 2 cl. and [2] Budapest (**462**) - Salzburg (**466**) - Zürich and v.v.
‡ – See note ‡ on page 463 for other regional services Kufstein - München and v.v.

951 SALZBURG and MÜNCHEN - INNSBRUCK - FELDKIRCH - BREGENZ - LINDAU

	RJX 662 F✕	*RJ* 85 A✕	2	*WB* 972 🍷	*RJX* 162 U B✕	2	*ICE* 1201 ⑥d D✕	2	2	*RJX* 860 M F✕	*RJ* 87 A✕	2	*WB* 974 🍷	*EC* 164 ✕♦	*RJX* 766 F✕	*RJ* 1287 ⑥E ✕	2	2	*RJX* 862 F✕	*RJ* 1287 ⑥E ✕	*RJ* 89 A✕	2	*RJX* 166 V ✕	2	*RJX* 864 F✕	*RJ* 287 ✕	2
Wien Hbf **950** d.	0828	...	...	...	0928	...	...	...	...	1028	...	...	...	...	1128	...	...	...	1228	...	...	...	1328	...	1428	...	...
Wien Westbahnhof **950** d.	│	...	...	0908	│	...	...	...	...	│	...	...	1108	...	│	...	...	...	│	...	...	...	│	...	│	...	...
Linz Hbf **950** d.	0945	...	...	1026	1045	...	...	...	...	1145	...	...	1226	...	1245	...	...	...	1345	...	...	...	1445	...	1545	...	...
Salzburg Hbf d.	1056	...	...	1139	1156	...	...	...	...	1256	...	...	1339	...	1356	...	...	...	1456	...	...	...	1556	...	1656	...	...
München Hbf **890** ‡ d.	│	1132	...	│	│	...	1224a	...	...	│	1333	...	│	...	│	1426	...	...	│	...	1533	...	│	...	│	1733	...
München Ost **890** ‡ d.	│	1144	...	│	│	...	1236	...	...	│	1344	...	│	...	│	1437	...	...	│	...	1544	...	│	...	│	1744	...
Rosenheim **890** ‡ d.	│	1213	...	│	│	...	1305	...	...	│	1413	...	│	...	│	1506	...	...	│	...	1613	...	│	...	│	1813	...
Kufstein 🏛 ‡ d.	│	1236	...	1251	1309	...	1328	1331	...	│	1436	...	1451	...	1509	1528	1531	...	│	...	1636	...	1709	1731	│	1836	...
Wörgl Hbf **960** d.	1215	1246	...	1301	1319	...	1339	1345e	...	1415	1446	...	1500	1504	1519	1539	1545e	...	1615	...	1646	...	1719	1745e	1815	1846	...
Jenbach **960** d.	1229	1300	...	1317	│	...	1355	1359	...	1429	1500	...	1514	1518	│	1555	1559	...	1629	...	1700	...	│	1759	1829	1900	...
Innsbruck Hbf **960** a.	1244	1318	...	1334	1344	...	1414	1418	...	1444	1518	...	1530	1540	1544	1614	1618	...	1644	...	1718	...	1744	1818	1844	1918	...
Innsbruck Hbf d.	1247	...	1322	...	1347	...	1417	...	1422	1447	...	1522	...	1547	▬	1617	...	1622	1647	...	...	1722	1747	1822	1847	...	1920
Ötztal d.	│	...	1359	...	1412	...	1448	...	1459	│	...	1559	...	1612	...	1648	...	1659	│	...	...	1759	1812	1859	│	...	1957
Imst-Pitztal d.	1319	...	1409	...	│	...	1501	...	1509	1519	...	1609	...	│	...	1702	...	1709	1719	...	...	1809	│	1909	1919	...	2008
Landeck - Zams d.	1333	...	1424	...	1433	...	1537c	...	1524	1533	...	1624	...	1633	...	1738c	...	1724	1733	←	...	1824	1833	1924	1933	...	2022
St Anton am Arlberg d.	│	...	...	...	1457	...	1600	...	...	│	...	...	...	1657	...	1804	...	...	│	1806	...	...	1857	▬	│	...	...
Langen am Arlberg d.	1404	...	...	...	│	...	...	...	...	1604	...	...	...	│	...	→	...	...	1804	1816	...	...	│	...	2004	...	...
Bludenz **952** d.	1431	...	...	...	1531	...	...	...	...	1631	...	...	...	1731	...	...	...	...	1831	1854	...	...	1931	...	2031	...	...
Feldkirch **952** a.	1442	...	...	...	1542	2	...	...	...	1642	...	...	...	1742	2	...	...	...	1842	1905	...	...	1942	2	2042	...	...
Feldkirch **952** d.	1447	...	...	...	1548	1547	...	...	...	1647	...	...	...	1744	1747	...	...	...	1847	...	...	...	1948	1947	2047	...	...
Buchs 🏛 **952** a.	│	...	...	...	1606	│	...	...	...	│	...	...	...	1759	│	...	...	...	│	...	...	...	2006	│	│	...	...
Zürich HB **520** a.	│	...	...	...	1720	│	...	...	...	│	...	...	...	1920	│	...	...	...	│	...	...	...	2120	│	│	...	...
Dornbirn **952** d.	1509	...	...	...	...	1609	...	...	...	1709	...	...	...	...	1809	...	...	...	1909	...	...	...	...	2009	2109	...	...
Bregenz 🏛 **952** a.	1517	...	...	...	...	1618	...	...	...	1717	...	...	...	...	1818	...	...	...	1917	...	...	...	...	2018	2117	...	...
Lindau Reutin 🏛 **952** a.	...	...	...	...	...	1628	...	...	...	1728	...	...	...	...	1828	...	...	...	...	...	...	...	...	2028	...	...	...
Lindau-Insel 🏛 **952** a.	...	...	...	...	...	1632	...	...	...	...	...	...	...	...	1832	...	...	...	...	...	...	...	...	2032	...	...	...

	WB 976 🍷	*RJX* 168 Y F✕	2	2	*RJX* 866 F✕	*ICE* 1219 D T✕	*WB* 978 🍷	*RJX* 760 F✕	2	*RJX* 868 F✕	2	*RJX* 762 F✕
Wien Hbf **950** d.	...	1528	...	...	1628	...	...	1728	...	1828	...	1928
Wien Westbahnhof **950** d.	1508	│	...	...	│	...	1708	│	...	│	...	│
Linz Hbf **950** d.	1626	1645	...	...	1745	...	1826	1845	...	1945	...	2045
Salzburg Hbf d.	1739	1756	...	...	1856	...	1939	1956	...	2056	...	2156
München Hbf **890** ‡ d.	│	│	...	...	│	1933	│	│	...	│	...	│
München Ost **890** ‡ d.	│	│	...	...	│	1944	│	│	...	│	...	│
Rosenheim **890** ‡ d.	│	│	...	...	│	2013	│	│	...	│	...	│
Kufstein 🏛 ‡ d.	1851	1909	1931	...	│	2036	2051	2109	2131	2209	...	2309
Wörgl Hbf **960** d.	1900	1919	1945e	...	2015	2046	2101	2119	2145e	2219	...	2319
Jenbach **960** d.	1914	│	1959	...	2029	2100	2117	│	2159	2233	...	2333
Innsbruck Hbf **960** a.	1930	1944	2018	...	2044	2118	2134	2144	2218	2248	...	2348
Innsbruck Hbf d.	1940	1947	▬	2022	2047	...	...	2147	...	...	2252	*0005*
Ötztal d.	│	2012	...	2059	│	...	...	2212	...	...	2329	*0055*
Imst-Pitztal d.	2014	2022	...	2109	2119	...	...	2222	...	...	2339	*0106*
Landeck - Zams d.	2027	2033	...	2124	2133	...	...	2236	...	...	2354	*0120*
St Anton am Arlberg d.	2049	2057	...	...	│	...	...	2300	...	...	...	...
Langen am Arlberg d.	│	│	...	...	2204	...	...	2310	...	...	...	...
Bludenz **952** d.	2123	2131	...	...	2231	...	...	2337	...	...	...	...
Feldkirch **952** a.	2136	2142	2	...	2242	...	...	2348	...	...	...	...
Feldkirch **952** d.	2137	2148	2147	...	2247	...	...	2350	...	...	...	...
Buchs 🏛 **952** a.	│	2203	│	...	│	...	...	│	...	...	...	...
Zürich HB **520** a.	│	2320	│	...	│	...	...	│	...	...	...	...
Dornbirn **952** d.	2206	...	2212	...	2309	...	...	0009	...	...	...	...
Bregenz 🏛 **952** a.	2218	...	2222	...	2317	...	...	0017	...	...	...	...
Lindau Reutin 🏛 **952** a.	...	...	2232	...	...	...	...	...	...	...	...	...
Lindau-Insel 🏛 **952** a.	...	...	2235	...	...	...	...	...	...	...	...	...

	RJX 669 F✕	*RJX* 763 F✕	2	*WB* 971 🍷	*RJ* 288 ✕	*RJX* 861 Ⓐ F✕	*RJX* 861 F✕	*RJX* 765 F✕	*WB* 973 🍷	*ICE* 1218 D P✕
Lindau-Insel 🏛 **952** d.	...	...	...	...	...	...	...	...	...	...
Lindau Reutin 🏛 **952** d.	...	...	...	...	...	...	...	...	...	...
Bregenz 🏛 **952** d.	...	...	...	...	...	0440	...	0537	0540	...
Dornbirn **952** d.	...	...	...	...	...	0451	...	0548	0553	...
Zürich HB **520** d.	...	...	...	...	...	│	...	│	│	...
Buchs 🏛 **952** d.	...	...	...	...	...	│	...	│	│	...
Feldkirch **952** a.	...	...	...	...	...	0511	...	0608	0617	...
Feldkirch **952** d.	...	...	...	...	...	0513	...	0613	0618	...
Bludenz **952** d.	...	...	...	...	...	0526	...	0626	0633	...
Langen am Arlberg d.	...	...	...	...	...	│	...	0652	│	...
St Anton am Arlberg d.	...	...	...	...	...	0559	...	0703	0707	...
Landeck - Zams d.	...	*0504*	...	...	*0528*	0623	...	0727	0731	...
Imst-Pitztal d.	...	*0519*	...	...	*0544*	0636	...	│	0745	...
Ötztal d.	...	*0529*	...	...	*0559*	0647	...	0748	│	...
Innsbruck Hbf a.	...	*0606*	...	...	*0636*	0711	...	0811	0820	...
Innsbruck Hbf **960** d.	0510	0610	0620	0626	0642	0714	0714	0817	0830	0842
Jenbach **960** d.	0527	0627	0645	0642	0702	0731	0731	│	0847	0902
Wörgl Hbf **960** d.	0541	0641	0705	0701	0716	0745	0745	0843	0901	0916
Kufstein 🏛 ‡ d.	0551	0651	0717f	0710	0726	│	│	0853	0910	0926
Rosenheim **890** ‡ a.	│	│	...	│	0745	│	│	│	│	0947
München Ost **890** ‡ a.	│	│	...	│	0816	│	│	│	│	1017
München Hbf **890** ‡ a.	│	│	...	│	0826	│	│	│	│	1029
Salzburg Hbf a.	0702	0802	...	0821	...	0902	0902	1003	1021	...
Linz Hbf **950** a.	0815	0915	...	0934	...	1015	1015	1115	1134	...
Wien Westbahnhof **950** a.	│	│	...	1052	...	│	│	│	1252	...
Wien Hbf **950** a.	0932	1032	...	...	...	1132	1132	1232	...	...

	RJX 863 F✕	2	2	*RJX* 161 X F✕	2	*RJ* 286 ✕	*RJ* 1286 ⑥E ✕	*RJX* 865 F✕	2	2	*RJ* 1286 ⑥E ✕	2	*EC* 163 ✕♦	2	*RJ* 88 A✕	*RJX* 897 Z F✕	2	*ICE* 1200 ⑥E D✕	2	*RJX* 165 W B✕	*WB* 975 🍷	2	*RJ* 86 A✕	*RJX* 869 F✕	2	2	*RJX* 167 C R✕
Lindau-Insel 🏛 **952** d.	...	0725	...	...	...	...	...	...	...	...	...	0925	...	...	...	...	...	...	1125	...	...	...	...	...	...	1325	...
Lindau Reutin 🏛 **952** d.	...	0729	...	...	...	...	...	...	...	...	...	0929	...	...	...	1031	...	...	1129	...	...	...	...	...	...	1329	...
Bregenz 🏛 **952** d.	0639	0741	...	...	...	...	...	0840	...	...	...	0941	...	...	...	1040	...	...	1141	...	...	...	...	1240	...	1341	...
Dornbirn **952** d.	0652	0752	...	...	...	...	...	0851	...	...	...	0952	...	...	...	1051	...	...	1152	...	...	...	...	1251	...	1352	...
Zürich HB **520** d.	│	│	...	0640	...	...	...	│	...	...	...	│	0840	...	...	│	...	...	│	1040	...	...	...	│	...	│	1240
Buchs 🏛 **952** d.	│	│	...	0757	...	...	...	│	...	...	...	│	1000	...	...	│	...	...	│	1154	...	...	...	│	...	│	1354
Feldkirch **952** a.	0712	0812	...	0812	...	...	...	0912	...	...	...	1012	1015	...	...	1112	...	...	1212	1209	...	...	...	1312	...	1412	1409
Feldkirch **952** d.	0717	▬	...	0817	...	...	0850	0917	...	...	...	▬	1017	...	...	1117	...	...	...	1217	...	...	...	1317	...	▬	1417
Bludenz **952** d.	0730	...	...	0830	...	...	0905	0930	...	...	...	...	1030	...	...	1130	...	...	...	1230	...	...	...	1330	...	...	1430
Langen am Arlberg d.	0756	...	...	│	...	...	0937	0956	...	...	...	...	│	...	...	1156	...	...	...	│	...	...	...	1356	...	...	│
St Anton am Arlberg d.	│	2	...	0903	...	...	0948	│	...	...	←	...	1103	...	...	│	...	1213	...	1303	...	...	...	│	...	...	1503
Landeck - Zams d.	0827	0834	...	0927	0934	...	1015	1027	...	1034	1040	*RJX*	1127	1132	...	1227	*1234*	1246	...	1327	...	1334	...	1427	1434	...	1527
Imst-Pitztal d.	0840	0849	...	│	0949	...	→	1040	...	1049	1055	**767**	│	1147	...	1240	*1249*	1300	...	│	...	1349	...	1440	1449	...	│
Ötztal d.	│	0859	...	0948	0959	...	...	│	...	1059	1111		1148	1159	...	│	*1259*	1311	...	1348	...	1359	...	│	1459	...	1548
Innsbruck Hbf a.	0911	0936	...	1011	1036	...	...	1111	...	1136	1142	F✕	1211j	1236	...	1311	*1336*	1342	...	1411	...	1436	...	1511	1536	2	1611
Innsbruck Hbf **960** d.	0914	...	0942	1016	...	1042	...	1114	1142	...	1146	1216	1221	...	1242	1314	1342	1346	...	1416	1426	...	1442	1514	...	1542	1616
Jenbach **960** d.	0931	...	1002	│	...	1102	...	1131	1202	...	1207	│	1243	...	1302	1331	1402	1407	...	│	1442	...	1502	1531	...	1602	│
Wörgl Hbf **960** d.	0945	...	1020e	1043	...	1116	...	1145	1220e	...	1223	1243	1256	...	1316	1345	1420e	1423	...	1443	1501	...	1516	1545	...	1620e	1643
Kufstein 🏛 ‡ d.	│	...	1029	1053	...	1126	...	│	1229	...	1233	1253	...	...	1326	│	1429	1433	...	1453	1510	...	1526	│	...	1629	1653
Rosenheim **890** ‡ a.	│	...	...	│	...	1145	...	│	...	...	1251	│	...	...	1345	│	...	1458	...	│	│	...	1545	│	...	...	│
München Ost **890** ‡ a.	│	...	...	│	...	1217	...	│	...	...	1322	│	...	...	1416	│	...	1528	...	│	│	...	1616	│	...	...	│
München Hbf **890** ‡ a.	│	...	...	│	...	1226	...	│	...	...	1333	│	...	...	1426	│	...	1548a	...	│	│	...	1626	│	...	...	│
Salzburg Hbf a.	1102	...	...	1203	...	...	...	1302	...	...	...	1403	...	...	...	1502	...	...	...	1603	1621	...	...	1702	...	...	1803
Linz Hbf **950** a.	1215	...	...	1315	...	...	...	1415	...	...	...	1515	...	...	...	1615	...	...	...	1715	1734	...	...	1815	...	...	1915
Wien Westbahnhof **950** a.	│	...	...	│	...	...	...	│	...	...	...	│	...	...	...	│	...	...	...	│	1852	...	...	│	...	...	│
Wien Hbf **950** a.	1332	...	...	1432	...	...	...	1532	...	...	...	1632	...	...	...	1732	...	...	...	1832	...	...	...	1932	...	...	2032

♦ – **NOTES** (LISTED BY TRAIN NUMBER)

163/4 – TRANSALPIN – 🚃12 and ✕ Zürich - Kitzbühel - Schwarzach - Graz and v.v.

A – To/from Verona, Bologna or Venezia via Brennero (Table **70**).
B – To/from Budapest (Table **1250**).
C – On Ⓑ (not Apr. 20, June 8, Aug. 15, Dec. 7) conveys 🚃12 (*RJX* **567**) (Feldkirch ⑤⑦ **t** -) Innsbruck - Wien Hbf - Flughafen Wien.
D – Through service from Wiesbaden, Berlin or Hamburg - see Table **910**.
E – ⑥ Dec. 21 - Apr. 26; ⑥ June 21 - Oct. 4.
F – From/to Flughafen Wien ✈ (Table **950**).
M – Conveys 🚃12 Wien - Bregenz (*RJX* **890**) - Ulm - Stuttgart - Frankfurt (Tables **910** and **933**).
P – Apr. 17 - June 6 runs as *ICE* **1188** Innsbruck - München only.
R – To Bratislava (Table **86**).
T – Apr. 17 - June 6 runs as *RJ* **1189** München - Innsbruck only.
U – Conveys 🚃12 (*RJX* **562**) Flughafen Wien - Wien Hbf - Innsbruck (- Feldkirch ⑤–⑦ **v**).
V – Conveys 🚃12 (*RJX* **566**) Flughafen Wien - Wien Hbf - Innsbruck (- Feldkirch Ⓑ **n**).
W – Conveys 🚃12 (*RJX* **565**) (Feldkirch ⑥⑦ **r** -) Innsbruck - Wien Hbf - Flughafen Wien.
X – Conveys 🚃12 (*RJX* **184**) Bolzano - Innsbruck - Wien Hbf (Tables **86** and **595**).
Y – Conveys 🚃12 (*RJX* **185**) Wien Hbf - Innsbruck - Bolzano (Tables **86** and **595**).
Z – Conveys 🚃12 Frankfurt - Stuttgart - Ulm - Bregenz (*RJ* **867**) - Wien (Tables **910** and **933**).

a – Not Dec. 21 - Apr. 5.
c – Arrives 22–23 minutes earlier.
e – Arrives 5 minutes earlier.
f – Ⓐ only.
j – Connects with train in previous column.
n – Not Apr. 20, June 8, Aug. 15, Dec. 7.
r – Also Apr. 21, May 1, 29, June 9, 19, Aug. 15, Dec. 8; not Apr. 20, June 8, Dec. 7.
t – Also Apr. 21, 30, May 28, June 9, 18, Aug. 14, Dec. 8; not Apr. 20, May 2, 30, June 8, 20, Aug. 15, Nov. 1.
v – Also Apr. 21, 30, May 1, 28, 29, June 9, 18, 19, Aug. 14, 15, Dec. 8; not May 2, 30, June 20.

⊙ – 🛏 1, 2 cl., 🛌 2 cl. and 🚃2 Zürich (**467**) - Salzburg (**463**) - Budapest. Also conveys through cars to Praha (see Table **52**).
‡ – See note ‡ on page 463 for other regional services Kufstein - München and v.v.

LINDAU - BREGENZ - FELDKIRCH - INNSBRUCK - MÜNCHEN and SALZBURG 951

	WB 977		*RJ* 84	*RJX* 661		*RJX* 169	*WB* 979		*RJ* 82	*ICE* 119	*RJX* 663		*ICE* 1202 E	*RJX* 367		*EC* 80		*D* 665		*RJX* 369			*NJ* 447	*NJ* 1465		*EN* 40467	*NJ* 467
	🍷	2	A✕	✕	2	✕	🍷	2	A✕	✕♦	✕	2	✕	✕	2	A🍷	2	2	2	✕	2	2	N	♦	2	⊙	N
Lindau-Insel 🏛 .... **952** d.	...	...	...	...	1521	...	1527	...	...	...	...	1722	...	...	...	...	1755	...	1925	...	...	...	...	...	2225	...	...
Lindau Reutin 🏛....... **952** d.	...	...	...	...	1525	...	1532	...	...	1558	...	1729	...	...	...	...	1759	...	1929	...	...	...	...	...	2229	...	...
Bregenz 🏛............... **952** d.	...	...	...	1440	1537	...	1540	...	...	1606	1640	1741	...	...	...	...	1811	1840	1941	...	...	...	2140	...	2241	...	...
Dornbirn .... **952** d.	...	...	...	1451	1552	...	1556	...	...	1617	1651	1752	...	...	...	...	1822	1851	1952	...	...	...	2151	...	2252	...	...
Zürich HB **520** .... d.	...	...	...	|	|	1440	|	...	...	|	|	|	...	1640	...	...	|	|	|	1840	...	...	|	2040	|	2140	2140
Buchs 🏛 .... **952** d.	...	...	...	|	|	1554	|	...	...	|	|	|	...	1800	...	...	|	|	|	1954	...	...	|	2204	|	2305	2305
Feldkirch .... **952** a.	...	...	...	1512	1612	1609	1620	...	...	1634	1712	1812	...	1815	...	...	1842	1912	2012	2009	...	...	2216	2220	2312	2321	2321
Feldkirch .... **952** d.	...	...	...	1517	▬	1617	1621	...	...	1637	1717	▬	...	1817	...	...	1844	1917	▬	2017	...	...	2227	2245	2314	2324	2324
Bludenz .... **952** d.	...	...	...	1530	...	1630	1636	...	...	1656	1730	...	...	1830	...	...	1859	1930	...	2030	...	...	2242	2301	2329	2340	2340
Langen am Arlberg .... d.	...	...	...	1556	...	|	|	...	...	1727	1756	...	...	|	...	...	▬	1956	...	|	...	...	2310	2336	...	|	|
St Anton am Arlberg .... d.	...	...	...	|	2	1703	1708	...	...	1737	|	2	1808	1903	...	...	...	|	...	2103	...	...	2320	2346	...	|	|
Landeck - Zams................ d.	...	1534	...	1627	*1634*	1727	1731	1734	...	1808**f**	1827	1834	1839**j**	1927	1932	...	*NJ*	2027	...	2127	...	2155	2349	0011	...	0036	0036
Imst-Pitztal...................... d.	...	1549	...	1640	*1649*	|	1745	1749	...	|	1840	1849	1859	|	1947	...	**420**	2040	...	2140	...	2210	0003	|	...	|	|
Ötztal................................ d.	...	1559	...	|	*1659*	1748	|	1759	...	1843	|	1859	1911	1948	1959	...	R	2051	...	2151	...	2229	0014	|	...	|	|
Innsbruck Hbf.................. a.	...	1636	...	1711	*1736*	1811	1820	1836	...	1907	1911	1936	1942	2011	2036	...	♦	2114	2	2214	...	2306	0039	0054	...	0120	0120
Innsbruck Hbf........... **960** d.	1626	...	1642	1714	1742	1816	1826	...	1842	...	1914	...	1946	2016	...	2042	2046	...	2142	2216	2220	...	0044	...	...	0128	0128
Jenbach.................... **960** d.	1642	...	1702	1731	1802	|	1842	...	1902	...	1931	...	2007	|	...	2102	2106	...	2202	|	2245	...	|	...	...	|	|
Wörgl Hbf .... **960** d.	1701	...	1716	1745	1820**f**	1843	1901	...	1916	...	1945	...	2023	2043	...	2116	2123	...	2220**f**	2243	2305	...	|	...	...	|	|
Kufstein 🏛...................... ‡ d.	1710	...	1724	|	1829	1853	1910	...	1926	...	|	...	2033	2053	...	2126	2135	...	2229	2253	2317	...	|	...	...	|	|
Rosenheim........... **890** ‡ a.	|	...	1745	|	...	|	|	...	1945	...	|	...	2056	|	...	2145	2157	...	...	|	...	...	|	...	...	|	|
München Ost........ **890** ‡ a.	|	...	1816	|	...	|	|	...	2014	...	|	...	2125	|	...	2217	|	...	...	|	...	...	|	...	...	|	|
München Hbf........ **890** ‡ a.	|	...	1828	|	...	|	|	...	2026	...	|	...	2137	|	...	2228	2236	...	...	|	...	...	|	...	...	|	|
Salzburg Hbf..................... a.	1821	...	...	1902	...	2003	2021	...	...	...	2104	...	...	2205	...	...	...	...	...	0003	...	...	0255	...	...	0322	0322
Linz Hbf **950**.................. a.	1934	...	...	2015	...	2115	2134	...	...	...	2215	...	...	2318	...	...	...	...	...	...	...	...	0443	...	...	0504	0558
Wien Westbahnhof **950** . a.	2052	...	...	|	...	|	2252	...	...	...	|	...	...	|	...	...	...	...	...	...	...	...	|	...	...	|	|
Wien Hbf **950** .... a.	...	...	...	2132	...	2232	...	...	...	...	2332	...	...	0035	...	...	...	...	...	...	...	...	0658	...	...	0632	0758

♦ – **NOTES** (LISTED BY TRAIN NUMBER)

119 – BODENSEE – 🚃12 Dortmund - Köln - Stuttgart - Lindau - Innsbruck. Apr. 17 - June 6 runs Berlin - Stuttgart - Lindau - Innsbruck.

420 – 🛏 1, 2 cl., 🛌 2 cl. and 🚃2 Innsbruck - Frankfurt - Düsseldorf - Amsterdam; 🛏 1, 2 cl., 🛌 2 cl. and 🚃2 (**40420**) Innsbruck - Hamburg.

1465 – 🛏 1, 2 cl., 🛌 2 cl. and 🚃2 Zürich - Schwarzach - Graz; 🛏 1, 2 cl., 🛌 2 cl. and 🚃2 (*EN* **40465**) Zürich - Schwarzach - Villach - Ljubljana - Zagreb. Runs as *NJ* **465** from July 14.

A – From Verona, Bologna or Venezia via Brennero (Table **70**).

E – ⑥ Dec. 21 - Apr. 26; ⑥ June 21 - Oct. 4.

N – Conveys 🛏 1, 2 cl., 🛌 2 cl. (1, 4 berth) and 🚃2 (*ÖBB nightjet* new generation).

f – Arrives 6 minutes earlier.

j – Arrives 1831.

⊙ – 🛏 1, 2 cl., 🛌 2 cl. and 🚃2 Zürich - Salzburg - Budapest.

‡ – Additional local services run München - Rosenheim - Kufstein and v.v. (branded *Meridian*, operated by Bayerische Oberlandbahn). Journey 73 – 80 minutes. **From München** at 0506, 0641, 0738, 0841 and hourly until 2044 (also Rosenheim to Kufstein at 0039, 2235 and 2335). **From Kufstein** at 0600, 0702, 0802 and hourly until 1902 (also Kufstein to Rosenheim at 1959, 2059, 2159 and 2259).

VORARLBERG LOCAL SERVICES 952

2nd class only (except where shown)

BLUDENZ - BREGENZ - LINDAU ⊖ △

Bludenz ....d.	0439	0600	0630	0730	0800	0809	0900	1000	...	1200	1209	1300	1400	1409	1500	1600	1609	1700	1800	1809	1900	2000	2100	2139	2209	2309	0039
Feldkirch ....d.	0500	0617	0647	0747	0817	0830	0917	1017	1147	1217	1230	1317	1417	1430	1517	1617	1630	1717	1817	1830	1917	2017	2117	2200	2230	2330	0100
Dornbirn ....d.	0529	0639	0709	0809	0839	0859	0939	1039	1209	1239	1259	1339	1439	1459	1539	1639	1659	1739	1839	1859	1939	2039	2139	2229	2259	2359	0129
Bregenz 🏛.......d.	0545	0649	0719	0819	0849	0920**c**	0949	1049	1219	1249	1320**c**	1349	1449	1520**c**	1549	1649	1715	1749	1849	1920**c**	1949	2049	2149	2249**c**	2320**c**	0014	0144
Lindau Reutin 🏛 a.	0554	0658	0728	0828	0858	0929	0958	1058	1228	1258	1329	1358	1458	1529	1558	1658	1724	1758	1858	1929	1958	2058	2158	2258	2329	...	...
Lindau Insel 🏛 a.	0559	0703	0733	0832	0903	0934	1002	1103	1232	1303	1334	1403	1503	1534	1604	1703	1729	1803	1903	1934	2003	2103	2203	2307	2335	...	...

Lindau Insel 🏛 d.	0555	0621	0655	0756	0823	0855	0955	1021	1055	1155	1223	1255	1355	1423	1455	1557	1623	1655	1755	1823	1855	1955	2029	2123	2225	2256	2359
Lindau Reutin 🏛 d.	0559	0626	0659	0800	0827	0859	0959	1024	1059	1159	1227	1259	1359	1427	1459	1602	1627	1659	1759	1827	1859	1959	2033	2127	2229	2303	0003
Bregenz 🏛.......d.	0611	0644**e**	0711	0811	0844**e**	0911	1011	1044**f**	1111	1211	1244**e**	1311	1411	1444**e**	1511	1614	1644**e**	1711	1811	1844**e**	1911	2011	2044	2144**e**	2241	2314	0014
Dornbirn ....d.	0622	0700	0722	0822	0900	0922	1022	1100	1122	1222	1300	1322	1422	1500	1522	1630	1700	1722	1822	1900	1922	2022	2100	2200	2252	2330	0030
Feldkirch ....d.	0644	0731	0744	0844	0931	0944	1044	1131	1144	1244	1331	1344	1444	1531	1544	1701	1731	1744	1844	1931	1944	2044	2131	2231	2314	0001	0101
Bludenz ....a.	0659	0751	0759	0859	0951	0959	1059	1151	1159	1259	1351	1359	1459	1551	1559	1721	1751	1803	1859	1951	1959	2059	2151	2251	2329	0021	0121

ST MARGRETHEN - BREGENZ - LINDAU △

km								*EC* 97			*EC* 99					*EC* 191				*EC* 193				*EC* 195				
					⚒	Ⓒ		♥	⚒		♥		⚒	Ⓒ		♥	⚒	Ⓒ	⚒	♥	⚒		⚒	♥	⚒			⚒
0	St Margrethen 🏛 d.	0555	0625	0655	0725	0751	0755	0851	0925	0951	1051	1055	1125	1151	1155	1251	1325	1351	1425	1451	1525	1551	1625	1651	1725	1751	1755	1825
12	**Bregenz** 🏛 .... a.	0610	0640	0710	0740	0801	0810	0900	0940	1000	1100	1110	1140	1200	1210	1300	1340	1400	1440	1500	1540	1600	1640	1700	1740	1800	1810	1840
20	Lindau Reutin 🏛. a.	*0629*	*0658*	*0728*	*0759*	0808	*0828*	0908	*0958*	1008	1108	*1129*	*1208*	1208	*1228*	1308	*1358*	1408	*1458*	1508	*1558*	1612	*1658*	1708	*1758*	1808	*1828*	*1858*
22	**Lindau** Insel 🏛 .. a.	*0633*	*0703*	*0733*	*0803*	0813	*0832*	*0934*	*1002*	1013	*1134*	*1134*	*1213*	1213	*1232*	*1334*	*1403*	1413	*1503*	*1534*	*1604*	1615	*1703*	*1729*	*1803*	1812	*1832*	*1903*

	EC 197					*EC* 199					
	♥		⚒	C		♥	Ⓒ				
St Margrethen 🏛 . d.	...	1855	1925	1951	1955	2051	2151	2155	2255	2355	0025
Bregenz 🏛.......... a.	1902	1910	1940	2000	2010	2100	2200	2210	2310	0010	0040
Lindau Reutin 🏛 .. a.	1908	*1929*	*1958*	2008	*2028*	2108	2208	*2232*	*2329*	...	...
Lindau Insel 🏛 ... a.	*1934*	*1934*	*2003*	2013	*2032*	*2135*	2213	*2235*	*2335*	...	...

						EC 290					*EC* 198		
			Ⓐ			♥⚒	⚒		Ⓒ	⚒	♥		Ⓒ
Lindau Insel 🏛 .... d.	...	*0519*	0547	*0555*	*0621*	*0621*	*0655*	*0725*	0747	*0756*	*0823*	*0925*	0947
Lindau Reutin 🏛 ... d.	...	*0524*	0551	*0559*	*0626*	0652	*0659*	*0729*	0751	*0800*	0852	*0929*	0951
Bregenz 🏛 .... d.	0517	0547	0600	0617	0647	0700	0717	0747	0800	0817	0900	0947	1000
St Margrethen 🏛 .. a.	0534	0604	0609	0634	0704	0709	0734	0804	0809	0834	0909	1004	1009

		EC 196				*EC* 194					*EC* 192				*EC* 190					*EC* 98					*EC* 96			
	⚒	♥	⚒		⚒	♥	⚒		Ⓒ	⚒	♥		Ⓒ	⚒	♥	⚒			⚒	♥	⚒		C		♥			
Lindau Insel 🏛 ... d.	*0955*	*1021*	*1055*	1147	*1155*	*1223*	*1255*	*1325*	1347	*1355*	*1423*	*1521*	1547	*1557*	*1623*	*1655*	*1722*	1747	*1755*	*1823*	*1855*	*1925*	1947	*2029*	*2029*	*2123*	*2225*	*2327*
Lindau Reutin 🏛 .. d.	*0959*	1052	*1059*	1151	*1159*	1252	*1259*	*1329*	1351	*1359*	1452	*1525*	1551	*1602*	1652	*1659*	*1729*	1751	*1759*	1852	*1859*	*1929*	1951	*2033*	2052	*2127*	*2229*	*2333*
Bregenz 🏛.......... d.	1017	1100	1117	1200	1217	1300	1317	1347	1400	1417	1500	1547	1600	1617	1700	1717	1747	1800	1817	1900	1917	1947	2000	2047	2100	2147	2247	2347
St Margrethen 🏛 . a.	1034	1109	1134	1209	1234	1309	1334	1404	1409	1434	1509	1604	1609	1634	1709	1734	1804	1809	1834	1909	1934	2004	2009	2104	2109	2204	2304	0004

FELDKIRCH - BUCHS ⊖

km		Ⓐ	Ⓐ	Ⓐ B	Ⓐ	Ⓐ	Ⓐ	Ⓐ	Ⓐ	Ⓐ	Ⓐ	Ⓐ
0	**Feldkirch**........ d.	0535	0648	0709	0747	0847	1520	1615	1645	1715	1815	1845
16	Schaan-Vaduz d.	0554	0707	0731	0809	0906	1539	1634	1704	1734	1834	1904
19	**Buchs** 🏛........ a.	0557	0710	0734	0812	0909	1542	1637	1707	1737	1837	1907

	Ⓐ	Ⓐ	Ⓐ	Ⓐ	Ⓐ	Ⓐ	Ⓐ	Ⓐ	Ⓐ	Ⓐ	Ⓐ
Buchs 🏛............... d.	0617	0716	0819	0919	1233	1619	1649	1719	1819	1849	1919
Schaan-Vaduz .... d.	0620	0719	0822	0922	1236	1622	1652	1722	1822	1852	1922
Feldkirch.............. a.	0639	0739	0841	0941	1255	1641	1711	1741	1841	1911	1941

BLUDENZ - SCHRUNS ⊡

Operated by Montafonerbahn.

km		Ⓒ		Ⓒ		Ⓐ															
0	**Bludenz** ....d.	0053	...	0224	...	0532	0602	0632	0702	0735	0805	and at the same	1805	1835	1905	1935	2005	2035	2135	2245	2353
6	St. Anton im Montafon ....d.	0102	...	0233	...	0541	0611	0641	0711	0744	0814	minutes past	1814	1844	1914	1944	2014	2044	2144	2254	0002
12	**Schruns**..............................a.	0112	...	0243	...	0551	0621	0651	0721	0754	0824	each hour until	1824	1854	1924	1954	2024	2054	2154	2304	0012

	Ⓒ		Ⓒ		Ⓐ																
Schruns.............................d.	0018	...	0118	...	0501	0531	0601	0631	0701	0734	0804	and at the same	1834	1904	1934	2004	2104	...	2204	...	2312
St. Anton im Montafon ....d.	0028	...	0128	...	0511	0541	0611	0641	0711	0744	0814	minutes past	1844	1914	1944	2014	2114	...	2214	...	2322
Bludenz ....a.	0037	...	0137	...	0520	0550	0620	0650	0720	0753	0823	each hour until	1853	1923	1953	2023	2123	...	2223	...	2331

B – From Bludenz (d. 0646).

C – ⑤–⑦ (also Apr. 21, May 29, June 9).

c – Arrives 5 – 6 minutes earlier.

e – Arrives 7 minutes earlier.

f – Arrives 1034.

♥ – 🚃12 and ✕ Zürich - München and v.v. See Table **75**.

⊖ – Selected local trains. See also Table **951**.

△ – Austrian holiday dates apply.

⊡ – Certain services run as through trains from / to Bregenz or Lindau.

954 🚌 LANDECK / SCUOL TARASP - PFUNDS - NAUDERS - MALLES

Routes 273 / 921	273	273	921	273		921	273		273		
Landeck - Zams Bahnhof d.	0630	0745	...	0845	⊠	...	1845	...	1945	...	...
Ried im Oberinntal (Gemeindeamt) d.	0654	|	...	|		...	|	...	|	...	...
Pfunds Dorf d.	0712	|	...	|	and at	...	|	...	|	...	...
Scuol Tarasp Staziun d.	|	|	0830	|	the same	1830	|	...	|	...	...
Martina cunfin 🏛 d.	|	|	0900	|	minutes	1858	|	...	|	...	...
Pfunds Kajetansbrücke d.	0717	0817	0910	0917	past each	1910	1917	...	2017	...	...
Nauders Mühle d.	0746	0846	...	0946	hour until	...	1946	...	2046	...	...
Reschenpass / Passo di Resia 🏛 d.	0749	0849	...	0949		...	1949	...	2049	...	...
Resia / Reschen, Zentrum d.	0751	0851	...	0951		...	1951	...	2051	...	...
Malles Stazione **598** a.	0820	0920	...	1020		...	2020	...	2120	...	...

	273	273	921	273		273	921	273	273	273	
Malles Stazione **598** a.	0640	0740	...	0840	✣	1640	...	1740	1840	1940	...
Resia / Reschen, Zentrum d.	0708	0808	...	0908		1708	...	1808	1908	2008	...
Reschenpass / Passo di Resia 🏛 d.	0711	0811	...	0911	and at	1711	...	1811	1911	2011	...
Nauders Mühle d.	0716	0816	...	0916	the same	1716	...	1816	1916	2016	...
Pfunds Kajetansbrücke d.	0745	0845	0840	0945	minutes	1745	1740	1845	1945	2045	...
Martina cunfin 🏛 d.	|	|	0900	|	past each	|	1800	|	|	|	...
Scuol Tarasp Staziun a.	|	|	0927	|	hour until	|	1827	|	|	|	...
Pfunds Dorf d.	|	|	...	|		|	...	|	|	|	...
Ried im Oberinntal (Gemeindeamt) d.	|	|	...	|		|	...	|	|	|	...
Landeck - Zams Bahnhof a.	0818	0918	...	1018		1818	...	1918	2018	2118	...

⊠ – No route **921** 🚌 at 1230.
✣ – No route **921** 🚌 at 1440.

Operators
Landeck - Malles: Tioler Linien Bus GmbH, Nauders. ✆ +43 (0)664 384 1360.

Scuol Tarasp - Pfunds: Auto Da Posta, Svizra. CH-7550 Scuol. ✆ +41 (0)58 453 28 28.

955 JENBACH - MAYRHOFEN

2nd class only   Narrow gauge   Zillertalbahn *

km																	🚂 A
0	**Jenbach** Zillertalbahnhof § d.	0630	0652	0748	0811	0841	0911	0941	and at	1711	1741	1811	1841	1911	2007		1044
11	Fügen-Hart d.	0646	0709	0806	0826	0856	0926	0956	the same	1726	1756	1826	1856	1926	2022		1114
17	Kaltenbach-Stumm d.	0656	0720	0817	0837	0907	0937	1007	minutes	1737	1807	1837	1907	1937	2033	also	1131
21	Aschau im Zillertal d.	0703	0727	0823	0843	0913	0943	1013	past each	1743	1813	1843	1913	1943	2039		1146
25	**Zell am Ziller** d.	0710	0735	0830	0850	0920	0950	1020	hour until	1750	1820	1850	1920	1950	2046		1157
32	**Mayrhofen** a.	0722	0747	0841	0901	0931	1001	1031		1801	1831	1901	1931	2001	2057		1216

																	🚂 A
Mayrhofen d.	0546	...	0610	0635	0734	0819	0849	and at	1619	1649	1719	1749	1819	1912	1949		1335
Zell am Ziller d.	0557	...	0621	0647	0744	0831	0901	the same	1631	1701	1731	1801	1831	1924	2001		1352
Aschau im Zillertal d.	0603	...	0627	0653	0750	0837	0907	minutes	1637	1707	1737	1807	1837	1929	2006	also	1409
Kaltenbach-Stumm d.	0610	...	0634	0659	0757	0843	0913	past each	1643	1713	1743	1813	1843	1936	2013		1419
Fügen-Hart d.	0620	...	0646	0710	0807	0854	0925	hour until	1654	1725	1754	1825	1854	1947	2023		1441
Jenbach Zillertalbahnhof § a.	0637	...	0704	0727	0823	0910	0940		1710	1740	1810	1840	1910	2002	2038		1504

A – ②-④ June 3 - Sept. 18.

x – Trains call on request.

🚂 – Steam train. Special fares apply.
§ – Adjacent to ÖBB station.
* – Zillertaler Vehrkehrsbetriebe, Austraße 1, A-6200 Jenbach. ✆ +43 (0) 5244 606 0.

956 JENBACH - ACHENSEE

2nd class only   *Achenseebahn*

Narrow gauge rack railway operated by steam locomotives (special fares apply). *7 km*. Journey time 42 – 50 minutes.
Operator: Achenseebahn AG, A-6200 Jenbach: ✆ +43 (0) 5244 62243, Fax +43 (0) 5244 622435. Jenbach Achensee Bf is adjacent to the ÖBB station.

Until July 4 and September 1 – 28: **From Jenbach Achensee Bf** at 1100, 1315. **From Achensee Seespitz Bahnstation** at 1210, 1635.
July 5 - August 31: **From Jenbach Achensee Bf** at 0950, 1045, 1205, 1325. **From Achensee Seespitz Bahnstation** at 1105, 1225, 1420, 1635.
September 5 - October 25: **From Jenbach Achensee Bf** at 1100 and 1302. **From Achensee Seespitz Bahnstation** at 1205 and 1557.

957 ZELL AM SEE - KRIMML and 🚌 KRIMML - MAYRHOFEN

2nd class only

ZELL AM SEE - KRIMML ⊡

							Ⓐ								S 🚂		S 🚂
0	**Zell am See** Lokalbahn d.	0502	0632	0802		1602	1651	1702	1802	1902	2002	2102	2202		0920	...	1420
15	Niedernsill d.	0530	0700	0830	and	1630	1715	1730	1830	1930	2030	2130	2230		0954	...	1453
29	Mittersill d.	0549	0725	0850	hourly	1650	1730	1750	1850	1950	2049	2149	2249	also	1023	...	...
39	Bramberg d.	...	0739	0906	until	1706	1741	1806	1906	2006	2106r	2206t	...		...	...	...
53	**Krimml** a.	...	0758	0925		1725	1757	1825	1925	2025	2125r	2225t	...		...	...	...

		Ⓐ	Ⓐ												S 🚂		S 🚂
Krimml d.	0535	0605	0629	0635	0735		1535	1635	1735	1835	1935	...	...		...	...	...
Bramberg d.	0554	0624	0645	0654	0754	and	1554	1654	1754	1854	1954	...	...		...	...	...
Mittersill d.	0610	0640	0657	0710	0810	hourly	1610	1710	1810	1910	2010	2110	2210	also	1137	...	...
Niedernsill d.	0630	0700	0714	0730	0830	until	1630	1730	1830	1930	2030	2130	2230		1204	...	1504
Zell am See Lokalbahn a.	0657	0727	0738	0757	0857		1657	1757	1857	1957	2057	2157	2257		1238	...	1538

🚌 Krimml Bahnhof - Krimml Wasserfälle and v.v. Route **670**. *3 km*. Journey time: 6 – 9 minutes.

From Krimml Bahnhof at 0753, 0829Ⓐ, 0921, 0944Ⓐ, 1021, 1044, 1121, 1144Ⓐ, 1221, 1244Ⓐ, 1321, 1444, 1521, 1621, 1644Ⓐ, 1721, 1744Ⓐ, 1755Ⓐ, 1821, 1844, 1939Ⓐ, 2202Ⓐ.

From Krimml Wasserfälle at 0434Ⓐ, 0537Ⓐ, 0650Ⓐ, 0828, 0900 Ⓐ, 1028, 1100, 1128, 1155Ⓐ, 1228, 1300Ⓐ, 1328, 1428, 1528, 1500, 1555Ⓐ, 1628, 1700Ⓐ, 1728, 1828, 1928Ⓐ.

Additional buses also run at irregular intervals.

🚌 routes **673** and **4094**: KRIMML - KÖNIGSLEITEN - MAYRHOFEN

km		A	A	C	A		A	C	D	A		B	D	C	A	D	A	C		A	B	D	A
0	**Krimml** Bahnhof d.	...	...	0834	...	...	...	1024	...	...	...	...	...	1354	...	...	...	1524	...	...	...	...	...
3	Krimml Wasserfälle d.	...	...	0840	...	...	...	1030	...	...	...	...	...	1400	...	...	...	1530	...	...	...	1630	...
16	Almdorf (Königsleiten) d.	...	...	0905	0925	...	1025	1055	1125	1225	...	...	1325	1425	1425	1455	1525	1555	...	1625	...	1655	...
25	**Gerlos** Gasthaus Oberwirt d.	0701	0841	...	0941	...	1041	...	1141	1241	...	1341	1341	...	1441	1511	1541	...	...	1641	1711	1711	1841
45	Zell am Ziller Bahnhof **955** a.	0735	0915	...	1015	...	1115	...	1215	1310	...	1415	1415	...	1515	1545	1615	...	...	1715	1745	1745	1915
53	**Mayrhofen** Bahnhof **955** a.	0745	...	...	...	...	...	...	...	...	...	...	...	...	...	...	...	...	...	1725	...	1755	1925

	A	A	D	C			A	D	C	A		B	D	D	A	C	A		A	C	A		A	A
Mayrhofen Bahnhof **955** d.	0730	0820	0850	...	...	...	0950	...	...	...	...	...	...	...	...	...	...	...	...	...	...	...	1840
Zell am Ziller Bahnhof **955** d.	0745	0835	0905	...	...	0935	1005	...	1035	...	1135	1135	1235	1335	...	1435	...	1535	...	1635	...	1745	1855
Gerlos Gasthaus Oberwirt d.	0818	0908	0938	...	...	1008	1038	...	1108	...	1208	1208	1308	1406	...	1508	...	1608	...	1708	...	1818	1926
Königsleiten Almdorf d.	...	0925	0955	0940	...	1025	1055	1055	1125	...	...	1225	1325	1425	1430	1525	...	1625	1650	...	...	...	...
Krimml Wasserfälle a.	...	...	1017	1005	...	...	...	1120	...	...	...	...	...	...	1455	...	...	...	1715	...	...	...	...
Krimml Bahnhof a.	...	...	...	1016	...	...	...	1131	...	...	...	...	...	...	1501	...	...	...	1726	...	...	...	...

A – Until Oct. 26.
B – Until July 5 and Sept. 6 - Oct. 26.
C – July 5 - Sept. 28.
D – July 6 - Sept. 5.
S – ④ until Sept. 25.
r – Ⓐ only.
t – Ⓒ only.

SALZBURG - SCHWARZACH - INNSBRUCK 960

km		NJ 464 c A	NJ 1464 b A	2	2	2	2	2	Ⓒ 2	Ⓒ 2	Ⓐ 2	2	IC 894 🍷⊖	2	2	ICE 1282 P ✕	2	2	IC 898 🍷⊖	2	2	ICE 1284 L ✕	2	RJ 111 ✕⊖	2	2
	Wien Hbf **950** d.	...	...	...	...	...	...	...	...	...	...	...	...	...	...	...	...	...	...	...	...	...	...	...	...	...
0	**Salzburg** Hbf **951 970 975** ‡ d.	...	...	...	...	...	...	...	0421	...	0421	0507	0612	...	...	...	0708	...	0812	...	...	...	0908	1012	...	...
29	Golling-Abtenau **970** ‡ d.	...	...	...	...	...	...	...	0459	...	0459	0545	0633	...	...	...	0734	...	0833	...	...	...	0934	1033	...	...
53	**Bischofshofen** **970 975** ‡ d.	0158	0217	...	...	...	...	...	0524	...	0524	0610	0654	...	...	...	0756	...	0854	...	...	...	0956	1054	...	...
61	St Johann im Pongau **970** ‡ d.	|	|	...	...	...	...	...	0534	...	0534	0620	0704	...	...	...	0804	...	0904	...	...	...	1004	1104	...	...
67	**Schwarzach - St Veit** **970** ‡ a.	0211	0230	...	...	...	...	...	0539	...	0539	0625	0709	...	...	...	0810	...	0909	...	...	...	1010	1109	...	...
67	**Schwarzach - St Veit** d.	0232	0232	...	...	...	...	...	0541	...	0541	▬	▬	0712	...	...	0812	...	...	0912	...	...	1012	▬	1112	...
	Zell am See a.	|	|	...	...	...	...	...	0616	...	0615	...	2	0744	...	0800	0844	...	...	0944	...	1000	1044	2	1144	...
99	**Zell am See** d.	|	|	...	...	...	...	0603	0617	...	0616	...	0703	0745	0803	0831	0845	0903	...	0945	1003	1031	1045	1103	1145	1203
113	Saalfelden d.	|	|	0402	0502	0514	0555	0614	0629	0644	0644j	...	0714	0756	0814	0842	0856	0914	...	0956	1014	1042	1056	1114	1156	1214
131	Hochfilzen d.	|	|	0419	0519	0531	0613	0631	...	0701	0701	...	0731	0813	0831	0858	0913	0931	...	1013	1031	1058	1113	1131	1213	1231
148	St Johann in Tirol d.	|	|	0434	0534	0549	0627	0650	...	0719	0719	...	0749	0827	0849	0916	0927	0949	...	1027	1049	1116	1127	1149	1227	1249
157	**Kitzbühel** d.	|	|	0442	0542	0558	0635	0659	...	0728	0728	...	0758	0835	0858	0925	0935	0958	...	1035	1058	1125	1135	1158	1235	1258
166	Kirchberg in Tirol d.	|	|	0451	0551	0609	0643	0709	...	0739	0739	...	0809	0843	0909	0937	0943	1009	...	1043	1109	1137	1143	1209	1243	1309
192	Wörgl Hbf a.	|	|	0518	0616	0638	0709	0738	...	0808	0808	2	0838	0909	0938	1002	1009	1038	...	1109	1138	1202	1209	1238	1309	1338
192	Wörgl Hbf **951** d.	|	|	*0524*	*0624*	0645	*0719*	0745	...	*0815*	*0815*	0824	*0846*	*0919*	*0945*	1027	*1015*	*1046*	...	*1119*	*1145*	1223	*1215*	*1246*	*1319*	*1345*
	München Hbf **951** a.	|	|	|	|	|	|	|	...	|	|	|	|	|	|	1134	|	|	...	|	|	1348	|	|	|	|
217	Jenbach **951** a.	|	|	*0544*	*0644*	0658	|	0758	...	*0827*	*0827*	0844	*0858*	|	*0958*	...	*1027*	*1058*	...	|	*1158*	...	*1227*	*1258*	|	*1358*
251	**Innsbruck** Hbf **951** a.	0449	0449	*0610*	*0710*	0718	*0744*	0818	...	*0844*	*0844*	0910	*0918*	*0944*	*1018*	...	*1044*	*1118*	...	*1144*	*1218*	...	*1244*	*1318*	*1344*	*1418*

	2	IC 596 ✕⊖	EC 164 Z ✕	2	2	EC 113 🍷⊖	2	2	2	ICE 115 🍷⊖	IC 518 G 🍷	Ⓐ 2	2	2	IC 1060 ⑤g 🍷	Ⓐ 2	IC 698 ✕⊖	2	2	2	ICE 117 🍷⊖	2	WB 924 🍷	IC 794 🍷⊖	2	2
Wien Hbf **950** d.	...	...	...	...	...	...	...	...	...	...	...	...	...	...	1440	...	...	...	...	...	...	...	1738f	...	...	...
alzburg Hbf.. **951 970 975** ‡ d.	1108	1212	...	...	1308	1412	...	...	1508	1612	...	1643	1708	...	1740	1743	1812	...	...	1908	2012	...	2019	2112	...	2215
olling-Abtenau **970** ‡ d.	1134	1233	...	...	1334	1433	...	...	1534	1633	...	1712	1734	...	1804	1812	1833	...	...	1934	2033	...	2045	2138	...	2242
ischofshofen **970 975** ‡ d.	1156	1254	1250	...	1356	1454	...	...	1556	1654	1650	1737	1756	...	1828	1837	1854	...	...	1956	2054	...	2107	2200	...	2305
t Johann im Pongau .. **970** ‡ d.	1204	1304	1259	...	1404	1504	...	...	1604	1704	1659	1746	1804	...	1840	1846	1904	...	...	2004	2104	...	2114	2209	...	2314
chwarzach - St Veit ... **970** ‡ a.	1210	1309	1305	...	1410	1509	...	...	1610	1709	1705	1752	1810	...	1846	1852	1909	...	...	2010	2109	...	▬	2214	...	2319
chwarzach - St Veit d.	1212	▬	1313	...	1412	▬	1512	...	1612	▬	1713	▬	1812	...	1848	1853	...	1912	...	2012	...	2112	...	*2219*	...	2321
ell am See a.	1244	2	1342	...	1444	2	1544	...	1644	2	1742	2	1844	...	1917	1926	...	1945	...	2045	...	2145	2	*2254*	...	2355
ell am See d.	1245	1303	1344	1403	1445	1503	1545	1603	1645	1703	1744	1803	1845	1903	1919	1927	...	1946	2003	2046	...	2146	2203	*2255*	2303	2356
aalfelden d.	1256	1314	1354	1414	1456	1514	1556	1614	1656	1714	1754	1814	1856	1914	1930	1939	...	1956	2014	2057	...	2156	2214	*2307*	2314	0007
ochfilzen d.	1313	1331	|	1431	1513	1531	1613	1631	1713	1731	|	1831	1912	1931	|	...	...	2013	2033	2113	...	2213	2231	...	2331	...
t Johann in Tirol d.	1327	1349	1423	1449	1527	1549	1627	1649	1727	1749	1823	1849	1927	1949	2001	...	...	2027	2049	2127	...	2227	2249	...	2349	...
itzbühel d.	1335	1358	1431	1458	1535	1558	1635	1658	1735	1758	1831	1858	1934	1958	2010	...	...	2035	2058	2134	...	2235	2258	...	2358	...
irchberg in Tirol d.	1343	1409	1440	1509	1543	1609	1643	1709	1743	1809	1840	1909	1944	2009	2019	...	...	2043	2109	2144	...	2243	2309	...	0009	...
Vörgl Hbf a.	1409	1438	1502	1538	1609	1638	1709	1738	1809	1838	1902	1938	2009	2038	2044	...	...	2109	2138	2209	...	2309	2338	...	0038	...
Vörgl Hbf **951** d.	*1415*	*1446*	1504	1545	*1615*	*1646*	*1719*	1745	*1815*	*1846*	1904	*1945*	*2015*	*2046*	*2054*	...	...	*2119*	*2145*	*2219*	...	*2319*	*2359*	...	...	...
München Hbf **951** a.	|	|	|	|	|	|	|	|	|	|	|	|	|	|	|	...	...	|	|	|	...	|	|	...	...	...
enbach **951** a.	*1427*	*1458*	1516	1558	*1627*	*1658*	|	1758	*1827*	*1858*	1916	*1958*	*2027*	*2058*	*2114*	...	...	|	*2158*	*2231*	...	*2331*	*0019*	...	...	...
nnsbruck Hbf **951** a.	*1444*	*1518*	1540	1618	*1644*	*1718*	*1744*	1818	*1844*	*1918*	1940	*2018*	*2044*	*2118*	*2140*	...	...	*2144*	*2218*	*2248*	...	*2348*	*0055*	...	...	...

	NJ 465 c A	NJ 1465 b A	⚒ 2	WB 907 🍷	2	2	Ⓐ 2	2	2	IC 691 🍷⊖	2	2	2	IC 515 G 🍷	ICE 114 ✕⊖	2	IC 1061 ⑥n 🍷	2	2	EC 112 🍷⊖	2	2	2	EC 163 Z ✕	IC 793 🍷⊖	2
nnsbruck Hbf **951** d.	0059	0059	...	...	...	*0510*	*0520*	...	*0610*	...	*0642*	*0714*	0742	0821	...	*0914*	*0920*	*0942*	*1016*	...	*1042*	*1114*	*1142*	1221	...	*1242*
enbach **951** d.	|	|	...	...	...	*0527*	*0545*	...	*0627*	...	*0702*	*0731*	0802	0843	...	*0931*	*0945*	*1002*	|	...	*1102*	*1131*	*1202*	1243	...	*1302*
München Hbf **951** d.	|	|	...	...	...	|	|	...	|	...	|	|	|	|	...	|	|	|	|	...	|	|	|	|	...	|
Vörgl Hbf **951** a.	|	|	...	...	...	*0539*	*0604*	...	*0639*	...	*0714*	*0743*	0814	0856	...	*0943*	*1004*	*1014*	*1041*	...	*1114*	*1143*	*1214*	1256	...	*1314*
Vörgl Hbf d.	|	|	...	...	...	0551	0608	...	0651	...	0722	0751	0822	0858	...	0951	1016	1022	1051	...	1122	1151	1222	1258	...	1322
irchberg in Tirol d.	|	|	...	...	...	0616	0636	...	0716	...	0750	0816	0850	0920	...	1016	1042	1050	1116	...	1150	1216	1250	1320	...	1350
itzbühel d.	|	|	...	...	...	0625	0646	...	0725	...	0800	0825	0900	0929	...	1025	1051	1100	1125	...	1200	1225	1300	1329	...	1400
t Johann in Tirol d.	|	|	...	...	...	0633	0655	...	0733	...	0809	0833	0909	0937	...	1033	1100	1109	1133	...	1209	1233	1309	1337	...	1409
ochfilzen d.	|	|	...	...	...	0648	0713	...	0748	...	0828	0848	0928	|	...	1048	|	1128	1148	...	1228	1248	1328	|	...	1428
aalfelden d.	|	|	0451	...	0551	0705	0731	0734r	0805	...	0846	0905	0946	1005	...	1105	1132	1146	1205	...	1246	1305	1346	1405	...	1446
ell am See a.	|	|	0502	...	0602	0714	...	0746r	0814	...	0857	0914	0957	1014	...	1114	1142	1157	1214	...	1257	1314	1357	1414	...	1457
ell am See d.	|	|	0503	...	0603	0715	...	0747r	0815	...	...	0915	...	1016	...	1115	1144	...	1215	...	...	1315	...	1416	...	...
chwarzach - St Veit a.	0317	0317	0538	...	0638	0748	...	0822r	0848	...	...	0948	...	1046	...	1148	1214	...	1248	...	...	1348	...	1446	...	...
chwarzach - St Veit ... **970** ‡ d.	0324	...	0540	...	0640	0749	...	0824	...	0852	...	0949	...	1056	1052	1149	1216	...	...	1252	...	1349	...	1456	1452	...
t Johann im Pongau .. **970** ‡ d.	|	...	0547	0643	0647	0755	...	0829	...	0858	...	0955	...	1102	1058	1155	1223	...	...	1258	...	1355	...	1502	1458	...
ischofshofen **970 975** ‡ d.	0336	...	0557	0651	0656	0804	...	0840	...	0908	...	1004	...	1110	1108	1204	1233	...	...	1308	...	1404	...	1510	1508	...
olling-Abtenau **970** ‡ d.	...	...	0619	0712	0719	0825	...	0904	...	0928	...	1025	...	...	1128	1225	1254	...	...	1328	...	1425	...	...	1528	...
alzburg Hbf.. **951 970 975** ‡ a.	...	...	0646	0743	0746	0851	...	0940	...	0948	...	1051	...	...	1148	1251	1315	...	...	1348	...	1451	...	...	1544	...
Wien Hbf **950** a.	...	...	...	1022f	...	...	...	...	...	...	...	...	...	...	...	...	1610	...	...	...	...	...	...	...	...	...

	2	2	2	RJ 797 🍷⊖	2	2	2	ICE 1283 B ✕	2	RJ 110 ✕⊖	2	2	2	2	IC 895 🍷⊖	2	2	2	ICE 1285 D ✕	2	2	ICE 899 ✕⊖	2	2	2	2
nnsbruck Hbf **951** d.	*1314*	*1342*	*1416*	...	*1442*	*1514*	1542	...	*1616*	...	*1642*	*1714*	1742	*1816*	...	...	*1842*	*1914*	...	1942	*2016*	...	*2142*	*2216*	*2220*	*2320*
enbach **951** d.	*1331*	*1402*	|	...	*1502*	*1531*	1602	...	|	...	*1702*	*1731*	1802	|	...	...	*1902*	*1931*	...	2002	|	...	*2202*	|	*2245*	*2345*
München Hbf **951** d.	|	|	|	...	|	|	|	1520	|	...	|	|	|	|	...	...	|	|	1826	|	|	...	|	|	|	|
Vörgl Hbf **951** a.	*1343*	*1414*	*1441*	...	*1514*	*1543*	1614	1631	*1641*	...	*1714*	*1743*	1814	*1841*	...	...	*1914*	*1943*	1950	2014	*2041*	...	*2214*	*2241*	*2304*	*0004*
Vörgl Hbf d.	1351	1422	1451	...	1522	1551	1622	1639	1651	...	1722	1751	1822	1851	...	...	1922	1951	1958	2022	2051	...	2222	2251	2322	0022
rchberg in Tirol d.	1416	1450	1516	...	1550	1616	1650	1705	1716	...	1750	1816	1850	1916	...	...	1950	2016	2024	2050	2116	...	2250	2316	2350	0050
itzbühel d.	1425	1500	1525	...	1600	1625	1700	1717	1725	...	1800	1825	1900	1925	...	...	2000	2025	2036	2100	2125	...	2300	2325	0000	0100
t Johann in Tirol d.	1433	1509	1533	...	1609	1633	1709	1726	1733	...	1809	1833	1909	1933	...	...	2009	2033	2045	2109	2133	...	2309	2333	0009	0109
ochfilzen d.	1448	1528	1548	...	1628	1648	1728	1744	1748	...	1828	1848	1928	1948	...	...	2028	2048	2103	2128	2148	...	2328	2348	0028	0128
aalfelden d.	1505	1546	1605	...	1646	1705	1746	1801	1805	...	1846	1905	1946	2005	...	2034r	2046	2104	2120	2146	2205	...	2346	0005	0045	0145
ell am See a.	1414	1557	1614	...	1657	1714	1757	1809	1814	...	1857	1914	1957	2014	...	2046r	2057	...	2128	2157	2214	...	2357	...	...	...
ell am See d.	1515	...	1615	...	...	1715	...	1811	1815	...	...	1915	...	2015	...	2047r	...	...	2130	▬	2215	...	...	...	...	...
chwarzach - St Veit a.	1548	...	1648	...	...	1748	...	1841	1848	...	...	1948	...	2048	...	2122r	...	...	2200	2	2248	...	...	...	...	...
chwarzach - St Veit ... **970** ‡ d.	1549	...	...	1652	...	1749	...	...	...	1852	...	1949	...	...	2052	2124	...	...	...	2224	...	2252	...	...	...	...
t Johann im Pongau .. **970** ‡ d.	1555	...	...	1658	...	1755	...	...	...	1858	...	1955	...	...	2058	2129	...	...	...	2229	...	2258	...	...	...	...
ischofshofen **970 975** ‡ d.	1604	...	...	1708	...	1804	...	...	...	1908	...	2004	...	...	2108	2140	...	...	...	2240	...	2308	...	...	...	...
olling-Abtenau **970** ‡ d.	1625	...	...	1728	...	1825	...	...	...	1928	...	2025	...	...	2128	2204	...	...	...	2304	...	2331	...	...	...	...
alzburg Hbf.. **951 970 975** ‡ a.	1651	...	...	1748	...	1851	...	...	...	1948	...	2051	...	...	2148	2240	...	...	...	2340	...	2355	...	...	...	...
Wien Hbf **950** a.	...	...	...	...	...	...	...	...	...	...	...	...	...	...	...	...	...	...	...	...	...	...	...	...	...	...

– 🛏 1, 2 cl., 🛌 2 cl. and (2) Graz - Feldkirch - Buchs 🏛 - Zürich and v.v. Conveys from / to Schwarzach 🛏 1, 2 cl., 🛌 2 cl. and (2) (*EN* **40414/40465**) Zagreb - Ljubljana - Villach - Zürich and v.v.
– ⑥ Dec. 21 - Apr. 26 (also Apr. 18, 20; not Apr. 19); ⑥ June 21 - Oct. 4.
– ⑤ Dec. 20 - Apr. 25 (also Apr. 17; not Apr. 18); ⑤ June 20 - Oct. 3. From Hamburg (Table **900**).
– From / to Graz (Table **975**).
– ⑦ Dec. 22 - Apr. 27 (also Apr. 21; not Apr. 20); ⑦ June 22 - Oct. 5. To Hamburg (Table **900**).
– ⑥ Dec. 21 - Apr. 26 (also Apr. 18); ⑥ June 21 - Oct. 4.
– TRANSALPIN – (12) and ✕ Graz - Bischofshofen - Innsbruck - Buchs 🏛 - Zürich and v.v.

a – Ⓐ only.
b – Until July 13.
c – From July 14.
f – Wien Westbanhof.
g – ⑤ (also Apr. 17, 30, May 28, June 18, Aug. 14).
j – Arrives 0629.
n – ⑥ (also May 1, 29, June 19, Aug. 15).
r – ⚒ only.

⊖ – See Table **970** for further details.
‡ – See panel below main table for additional S-Bahn services (calling at all stations).

Freilassing **890** d.	0607		2307
Salzburg Hbf **890** d.	0621	and	2321
Golling-Abtenau d.	0659	hourly	2359
Bischofshofen d.	0724	until	0024
St Johann im Pongau d.	0734		0034
Schwarzach - St Veit a.	0739		0039

Schwarzach - St Veit d.	0424		2224
St Johann im Pongau d.	0429	and	2229
Bischofshofen d.	0540	hourly	2240
Golling-Abtenau d.	0504	until	2304
Salzburg Hbf **890** a.	0540		2340
Freilassing **890** a.	0553		2354

961 ATTNANG-PUCHHEIM - STAINACH-IRDNING

2nd class only (except trains **A** and **B**)

km		Ⓐ		Ⓒ	Ⓐ			Ⓒ			A			Ⓒ					Ⓒ						⚒	
	Wien Westbhf **950** d.	...	...	...	...	...	...	...	...	...	0845	...	...	...	...	...	...	...	...	...	...	...	...	...	...	...
0	**Attnang-Puchheim** d.	0440	...	0604	0604	0716	0808	0837	0908	1008	1037	1108	1208	1237	1308	1408	1508	1608	1637	1708	1808	1908	2008	2108	2208	2308
12	**Gmunden** d.	0456	...	0621	0621	0736	0824	0852	0924	1024	1052	1124	1224	1252	1324	1424	1524	1624	1652	1724	1824	1924	2024	2124	2224	2324
17	Altmünster am Traunsee d.	0502	...	0626	0626	0742	0830	0859	0930	1030	1059	1130	1230	1259	1330	1430	1530	1630	1659	1730	1830	1930	2030	2130	2230	2330
22	Traunkirchen d.	0509	...	0633	0633	0748	0836	|	0937	1036	|	1137	1236	|	1337	1436	1537	1636	|	1737	1836	1937	2036	2137	2237	2337
27	Ebensee Landungsplatz d.	0517	...	0640	0640	0756	0843	|	0944	1043	|	1144	1243	|	1344	1443	1544	1643	|	1744	1843	1944	2043	2144	2244	2344
28	Ebensee d.	0519	...	0643	0643	0759	0846	0912	0947	1046	1112	1147	1246	1312	1347	1446	1547	1646	1712	1747	1846	1947	2046	2147	2247	2347
44	**Bad Ischl** d.	0536	...	0704	0705	0819	0904	0928	1010t	1104	1128	1210t	1304	1328	1410t	1504	1610t	1704	1728	1810t	1904	2010t	2104	2205	2305	0004
54	Bad Goisern d.	▬	...	0713	0717	0832	0913	0942	1025	1113	1142	1225	1313	1342	1425	1513	1625	1713	1742	1825	1913	2025	2113	2218	2318	...
64	Hallstatt ⊡ d.	...	...	0725	0730	0848	0925	0956	1048	1125	1156	1248	1325	1356	1448	1525	1648	1725	1756	1848	|	|	|	|	|	...
67	Obertraun-Dachsteinhöhlen d.	⚒	...	0728	0734	0851	0928	1001	1051	1128	1201	1251	1328	1401	1451	1528	1651	1728	1801	1851	1928	2051	2128	2233	2333	...
78	**Bad Aussee** d.	0502	0630	0742	0749	...	0942	1016	...	1142	1216	...	1342	1416	...	1542	...	1742	1816	...	1942	...	2142	2246	2346	...
93	Bad Mitterndorf d.	0520	0648	0759	0804	...	0959	1035	...	1159	1235	...	1359	1435	...	1559	...	1759	1835	...	1959	...	2159	...	...	...
108	**Stainach-Irdning** a.	0537	0705	0815	0818	...	1015	1051	...	1215	1251	...	1415	1451	...	1615	...	1815	1851	...	2015	...	2215	...	...	...

			Ⓐ		⚒	Ⓐ	Ⓒ		Ⓒ					Ⓒ			Ⓒ			B						
Stainach-Irdning d.	...	...	...	...	0609j	0713	0740	...	0904	0940	...	1140	...	1304	1340	...	1504	1540	...	1704	1740	...	1940	...	2140	2345
Bad Mitterndorf d.	...	...	...	...	0627j	0730	0759	...	0921	0959	...	1159	...	1321	1359	...	1521	1559	...	1721	1759	...	1959	...	2159	0003
Bad Aussee d.	...	0459	...	0612	0651t	0810f	0816	...	0942	1016	...	1216	...	1342	1416	...	1542	1616	...	1742	1816	...	2016	...	2215	0019
Obertraun-Dachsteinhöhlen d.	...	0511	...	0624	0703	0823	0828	0903	0959	1028	1103	1228	1303	1359	1428	1503	1559	1628	1703	1759t	1828	1903	2028	2103	...	...
Hallstatt ⊡ d.	...	|	...	|	0707	0828	0832	0907	1004	1032	1107	1232	1307	1404	1432	1507	1604	1632	1707	1803	1832	|	|	|	...	...
Bad Goisern d.	...	0526	...	0639	0725	0843	0843	0934	1016	1043	1134	1243	1334	1416	1443	1534	1617	1643	1734	1816	1843	1934	2043	2134	...	...
Bad Ischl d.	0440	0540	0554	0652	0740	0853	0853	0953	1031	1053	1153	1253	1353	1431	1453	1553	1631	1653	1753	1831	1853	1953	2053	2153	...	...
Ebensee d.	0459	0559	0611	0712	0800	0912	0912	1013	1047	1112	1213	1312	1413	1447	1512	1613	1647	1712	1813	1847	1912	2013	2112	2213	...	...
Ebensee Landungsplatz d.	0501	0601	0613	0714	0802	0914	0914	1015	|	1114	1215	1314	1415	|	1514	1615	|	1714	1815	|	1914	2015	2114	2215	...	...
Traunkirchen d.	0509	0609	0620	0722	0810	0922	0922	1023	|	1122	1223	1322	1423	|	1522	1623	|	1722	1823	|	1922	2023	2122	2223	...	...
Altmünster am Traunsee d.	0514	0614	0630	0727	0816	0930	0930	1030	1059	1130	1230	1330	1430	1459	1530	1630	1659	1730	1830	1859	1930	2030	2130	2230	...	...
Gmunden d.	0521	0621	0636	0736	0836r	0936	0936	1036	1106	1136	1236	1336	1436	1506	1536	1636	1706	1736	1836	1906	1936	2036	2136	2236	...	...
Attnang-Puchheim a.	0538	0638	0652	0752	0852	0951	0951	1052	1123	1151	1252	1351	1452	1523	1551	1652	1723	1751	1852	1923	1951	2052	2151	2252	...	...
Wien Westbhf **950** a.	...	...	...	...	...	...	...	...	...	...	...	...	...	...	...	...	...	...	...	2125	...	...	...	...	...	...

A – *D* **1018**. SALZKAMMERGUT – (2) Wien - Attnang-Puchheim - Stainach-Irdning.
B – *D* **1019**. SALZKAMMERGUT – (2) Stainach-Irdning - Attnang-Puchheim - Wien.

f – Arrives 0748.
j – ⚒ only.
r – Arrives 0822.
t – Arrives 5 minutes earlier.

⊡ – ⛴ services operate Hallstatt Bahnhof - Hallstatt Markt. Journey: 8 minutes. **Operator**: Hallstättersee-Schifffahrt Hemetsberger KG ✆ +43 (0) 6134 8228. **From Hallstatt Bahnhof** at 0707 Ⓐ, 0730 Ⓐ, 0900, 0930, 1030, 1100, 1130, 1300, 1330, 1430, 1500, 1530, 1630, 1700, 1730 and 1850. **From Hallstatt Markt** at 0650 ⚒, 0715 Ⓐ, 0845, 0915, 1015, 1045, 1115, 1145, 1245, 1315 Ⓒ, 1415, 1445, 1515 Ⓒ, 1615, 1645, 1715 Ⓒ and 1815.

962 LINZ - PASSAU and SIMBACH

km											*ICE* **94**			*ICE* **228**					*ICE* **28**			*ICE* **92**			*ICE* **26**			
		Ⓐ		⚒	Ⓐ	⚒							Ⓐ					Ⓐ						⚒				
		2	2	2	2	2	**G** 2	2	2	2	**B** ✕	2	2	**D** ✕	2	2	2	2	**D** ✕	2	2	**B** ✕	2	2	**D** ✕	2	2	2
	Wien Hbf **950** d.	...	...	...	...	...	...	...	...	...	0613	...	...	0713	...	...	...	...	0913	...	...	1013	...	...	1113	...	...	...
0	**Linz** Hbf **950** d.	...	...	0452	...	...	0540	0556	0650	...	0734	0750	...	0834	0850	...	0950	...	1034	1050	...	1134	1150	...	1234	1250	...	1350
25	**Wels** Hbf **950** d.	0444	...	0516	...	...	0613j	0620	0709	...	0751	0809	...	|	0909	...	1009	...	|	1109	...	|	1209	...	|	1309	...	1409
54	Neumarkt-Kallham d.	0508	...	0543	0553	0620	0641	0646	0736	0740	|	0832	0840	|	0936	0940	1032	1040	|	1140t	1140	|	1232	1240	|	1336	1340	1432
	Ried im Innkreis d.	0529	...	|	0614	0643	|	0710	|	0801	|	|	0901	|	|	1001	|	1101	|	1201	|	|	|	1301	|	|	1401	|
	Braunau am Inn a.	0604	0642	|	...	0718	|	0740	|	0841	|	|	0941	|	|	1041	|	1141	|	1241	|	|	|	1341	|	|	1441	|
	Simbach (Inn) 🏛 .. **893** a.	...	0645	|	...	...	|	0745	|	0845	|	|	0945	|	|	1045	|	1145	|	1245	|	|	|	1345	|	|	1445	|
92	Schärding d.	...	...	0615	...	...	0714	...	0809	...	|	0857	...	|	1009	...	1057	...	|	...	1211	|	1257	...	|	1409	...	1457
106	**Passau** Hbf a.	...	...	0628	...	...	0727	...	0822	...	0836	0912	...	0931	1022	...	1112	...	1131	...	1224	1231	1312	...	1331	1422	...	1512
	Nürnberg Hbf **920** a.	...	...	...	...	...	...	...	...	...	1030	...	...	1127	...	...	...	...	1327	...	...	1430	...	...	1528	...	...	...
	Frankfurt (Main) Hbf **920** a.	...	...	...	...	...	...	...	...	...	...	...	...	1336	...	...	...	...	1536	...	...	...	...	...	1736	...	...	...

		ICE **90**								*ICE* **22**						*ICE* **20**					*IC* **494**			*NJ* **490**	*RJX* **664**			
	⚒				Ⓐ	Ⓐ			Ⓐ		Ⓐ				Ⓐ								Ⓐ					
	2	**H** ✕	2	2	2	2	2	2	2	**D** ✕	2	2	2	2	2	✕	2	2	2	2	**W** 🍷	2	2	⊡	✕	2	2	2
Wien Hbf **950** d.	...	1313	...	...	...	...	...	...	...	1513	...	...	...	...	...	1713	...	...	...	...	1913	...	...	2010	2028	...	...	...
Linz Hbf **950** d.	...	1434	1450	...	1534	...	1550	...	1614	1634	1640	1650	...	1750	1814	1834	1850	...	1950	...	2034	2050	...	2134	2145	...	...	*2250*
Wels Hbf **950** d.	...	|	1509	...	1551	...	1609	...	1631	|	1655	1709	...	1809	1831	1851	1909	...	2009	...	2051	2109	...	2151	2200	2209	...	*2307*
Neumarkt-Kallham d.	1440	|	1540t	1540	1617	1620	1632	1640d	1652	|	1720	1736	1740	1840t	1852	|	1936	1940a	2036	2040	|	2136	2140	|	...	2236	2240	2340
Ried im Innkreis d.	1501	|	1601	|	|	1637	|	1701d	|	|	1737	|	1801	1901	|	|	|	2001a	|	2101	|	|	2201	|	...	|	2301	2400
Braunau am Inn a.	1541	|	1641	|	|	1707	|	1741	|	|	1808	|	1841	1941	|	|	|	2041	|	2141	|	|	2236	|	...	|	2336	0032
Simbach (Inn) 🏛 ... **893** a.	1545	|	1645	|	|	1711	|	1745	|	|	...	|	1845c	1945	|	|	|	2045	|	2145	|	|	...	|	...	|	...	...
Schärding d.	...	|	...	1611	1650	...	1657	...	1717	|	...	1809	...	...	1918	|	2009	...	2109	...	2126	2209	...	|	...	2309	...	...
Passau Hbf a.	...	1531	...	1624	1702	...	1712	...	...	1731	...	1822	...	...	1930	1934	2022	...	2122	...	2137	2222	...	2234	...	2322	...	...
Nürnberg Hbf **920** a.	...	1729	...	...	...	...	...	...	...	1928	...	...	...	...	...	2129	...	...	...	...	2400	...	...	0057	...	...	...	...
Frankfurt (Main) Hbf **920** a.	...	...	...	...	...	...	...	...	...	2138	...	...	...	...	...	2337	...	...	...	...	...	...	...	...	...	...	...	...

km											*NJ* **491**							*IC* **495**				*ICE* **21**						*ICE* **23**
		⚒	Ⓐ		Ⓐ	Ⓐ	⚒	†		⚒		Ⓐ	Ⓐ											Ⓐ				
		2	2	2	2	2	2	2	2	2	⊡	2	2	2	2	2	2	**W** 🍷	2	2	2	✕	2	2	2	2	2	**D** ✕
	Frankfurt (Main) Hbf **920** d.	...	...	...	...	...	...	...	...	...	...	...	...	...	...	...	...	...	...	...	...	0619	...	...	...	...	...	0822
	Nürnberg Hbf **920** d.	...	...	...	...	...	...	...	...	...	0408	...	...	...	...	...	...	0600	...	...	...	0831	...	...	...	...	...	1031
	Passau Hbf d.	...	0411	0420c	...	...	...	...	0539	0604	0615	...	0625	...	0650	0752	...	0824	...	0840	...	1026	...	...	1048	...	1140	1229
	Schärding d.	0358	0423	0432	0509	0541	...	...	0552	0616	|	...	0637	...	0703	0804	...	0835	...	0852	...	|	...	...	1102	...	1152	|
0	**Simbach** (Inn) 🏛 .. **893** d.	|	|	|	|	|	...	...	|	|	|	...	|	...	|	|	0718	|	...	|	0918	|	1018	1018	|	1118	|	|
2	**Braunau** am Inn d.	|	|	|	|	|	0514	0526	|	|	|	0610	|	0629	|	|	0723	|	0824	|	0924	|	1021	1024	|	1124	|	|
39	Ried im Innkreis d.	|	|	*0442*a	|	|	0552	0601	|	|	|	0643	|	0710	|	|	0801	|	0901	|	1001	|	...	1101	|	1201	|	|
61	Neumarkt-Kallham d.	0429	0451	0504	0540	0608	0613	0619	0624	0642	|	0709r	0706	0728	0736	0838	0824t	|	0919	0924	1024t	|	...	1119	1128	1219	1224	|
90	**Wels** Hbf **950** d.	0456	0515	0531	0607	0628	0637	...	0653	0711t	0723v	0736	0730	...	0806	0907	0853	0911	...	0953	1053	1111	...	...	1153	...	1253	|
115	**Linz** Hbf **950** a.	0519	0532	0554	...	...	0652	...	0709	0740e	0743	...	0747	...	0824	0922	0910	0926	...	1010	1110	1126	...	...	1210	...	1310	1326
	Wien Hbf **950** a.	...	...	...	...	...	...	...	...	...	0917	...	...	...	...	...	...	1047	...	...	...	1247	...	...	...	...	...	1447

					ICE **91**				*ICE* **93**		*ICE* **27**					*ICE* **29**				*ICE* **229**						*RJX* **367**		
	⚒					⚒						⚒										Ⓐ						Ⓐ
	2	2	2	2	**H** ✕	2	2	2	**B** ✕	2	**D** ✕	2	2	2	2	**D** ✕	2	2	2	**D** ✕	2	2	2	2	2	✕	2	2
Frankfurt (Main) Hbf **920** d.	...	...	...	...	...	...	...	...	...	...	1222	...	...	...	...	1421	...	...	...	1621	...	...	...	...	...	...	...	...
Nürnberg Hbf **920** d.	...	...	...	...	1231	...	...	...	1332	...	1431	...	...	...	...	1631	...	...	...	1831	...	...	...	...	...	...	...	...
Passau Hbf d.	...	1248	1336	...	1429	...	1448	...	1529	1540	1629	...	1648	1736	...	1829	...	1840	...	2031	...	...	2040	...	2140	...	...	...
Schärding d.	...	1302	1349	...	|	...	1502	...	|	1552	|	...	1702	1749	...	|	...	1852	...	2043	...	...	2052	...	2152	...	...	...
Simbach (Inn) 🏛 ... **893** d.	1218a	|	|	1318	|	1418	|	1518	|	|	|	1618	|	|	1718	|	1818	|	1918	|	2018	...	|	2118	|	...	2224	...
Braunau am Inn d.	1224	|	|	1324	|	1424	|	1524	|	|	|	1624	|	|	1724	|	1824	|	1924	|	2021	2024	|	2124	|	...	2227	2246
Ried im Innkreis d.	1301	|	|	1401	|	1501	|	1601	|	|	|	1701	|	|	1801	|	1901	|	2001	|	...	2101	|	2201	|	...	...	2324
Neumarkt-Kallham d.	1319	1328	1420	1424t	|	1519	1528	1619	|	1624	|	1719	1728	1820	1824t	|	1919	1924	2024t	|	...	2119	2124	2219	2224	...	...	...
Wels Hbf **950** d.	...	1353	...	1453	|	...	1553	...	|	1653	|	...	1753	1841b	1853	|	...	1953	2053	2123t	...	...	2153	...	2251	2303	...	...
Linz Hbf **950** a.	...	1410	...	1510	1526	...	1610	...	1626	1710	1726	...	1810	...	1910	1926	...	2010c	2110	2138	...	...	2210	...	...	2318	...	...
Wien Hbf **950** a.	...	...	...	...	1647	...	...	...	1747	...	1847	...	...	...	...	2047	...	...	...	2305	...	...	...	...	...	0035	...	...

B – To / from Berlin and Hamburg (Table **850**).
D – To / from Dortmund (Table **800**).
G – From Garsten (Table **976**).
H – To / from Hamburg (Table **900**).
W – To / from Rostock via Berlin (Tables **835** and **849a**).

a – Ⓐ only.
b – † only
c – Ⓒ only.
d – ⚒ only.
e – ⑥ only (not Nov. 1).
j – Arrives 0603.
r – Arrives 0702.
t – Arrives 5 minutes earlier.
v – Arrives 0714.

⊡ – 🛏 1, 2 cl., 🛌 2 cl. and (2) Wien - Nürnberg - Hamburg and v.v.; 🛏 1, 2 cl., 🛌 2 cl. and (2) (**40490/40421**) Wien - Frankfurt - Köln - Amsterdam and v.v. Ⓡ for journeys to / from Germany.

Routes 150, 546 — SALZBURG and ST WOLFGANG - STROBL - BAD ISCHL — 963

km	Route 150	⚒	Ⓐ	Ⓒ		Ⓐ																	⚒	
0	**Salzburg** Hbf △ d.	0526	0556	0615	...	0615	0645	0715	0745	and every	1615	1645	1715	1745	...	1815	1845	1915	...	1945	2015	...	2115	2215	2315
32	St Gilgen (Busbahnhof) d.	0610	0645	0659	...	0704	0738	0808	0838	30 minutes	1708	1738	1808	1834	...	1904	1934	2004	...	2029	2059	...	2159	2259	2359
45	Strobl (Busbahnhof) d.	0624	0702	0713	...	0721	0756	0826	0856	until	1726	1756	1826	1851	...	1921	1951	2021	...	2043	2113	...	2213	2313	0013
57	**Bad Ischl** Bahnhof a.	0640	0719	0729	...	0738	0815	0845	0915		1745	1815	1845	1908	...	1938	2008	2038	...	2059	2129	...	2229	2329	0029

Route 150	⚒	Ⓐ	⚒	Ⓐ	Ⓐ	Ⓒ	Ⓐ		⑥	Ⓑ	⚒	Ⓑ												Ⓒ		⑥
Bad Ischl Bahnhof d.	0457	0525	0541	0557	0611	0624	0646	...	0654	0724	0754	0824	0854	0924	and every	1724	1754	1824	1854	1924	1954	2024	2054	2124	2224
Strobl (Busbahnhof) d.	0513	0542	0557	0616	0630	0640	0705	...	0715	0745	0815	0845	0915	0945	30 minutes	1745	1811	1841	1911	1941	2010	2040	2110	2140	2240
St Gilgen (Busbahnhof) d.	0528	0558	0612	0631	0645	0655	0721	...	0734	0804	0834	0904	0934	1004	until	1804	1827	1857	1927	1957	2025	2055	2125	2155	2255
Salzburg Hbf △ a.	0612	0645	0700	0723	0730	0739	0812	...	0826	0856	0926	0956	1026	1056		1856	1914	1944	2014	2044	2109	2139	2209	2239	2339

km	Route 546	Ⓐ	⚒	⚒	Ⓒ	Ⓐ	Ⓐ	Ⓐ			Ⓐ	Ⓒ		Ⓒ	Ⓐ		Ⓒ	Ⓐ		Ⓒ	Ⓐ		Ⓒ			Ⓐ
0	**St Wolfgang** ⊡ ‡ d.	0500	0600	0649	0732	0740	0813	0900	0913	1013	1100	1113	1213	1313	1323	1413	1513	1513	1613	1713	1713	1813	1828	1908	1956	2058
7	Strobl (Busbahnhof) d.	0512	0613	0702	0745	|	0824	|	0924	1026	|	1124	1226	1324	1336	1426	1524	1526	1626	1724	1726	1826	1839	1919	2007	2109
19	**Bad Ischl** Bahnhof a.	0531	0639	0728	0811	0811	...	0931	...	1047	1131	...	1247	...	1402	1447	...	1547	1647	...	1747	1847	...	...	...	...

Route 546	Ⓐ	⚒	Ⓐ				Ⓒ	Ⓐ		†	⚒	Ⓒ	Ⓐ	Ⓒ	Ⓐ			Ⓒ	Ⓐ			Ⓒ	Ⓐ			
Bad Ischl Bahnhof d.	0606	0642	...	0823	0913	...	...	1023	1113	...	1223	1323	1336	...	1423	...	1513	...	1623	1713	...	...	1823	...	1913	...
Strobl (Busbahnhof) d.	0630	0706	0825	0845	0935	...	1045	1045	1135	1245	1245	1345	1358	1445	1445	...	1535	1645	1645	1735	...	1845	1850	1925	|	2045
St Wolfgang ⊡ ‡ a.	0642	0718	0837	0857	0947	...	1057	1057	1147	1257	1257	1357	1410	1457	1457	...	1547	1657	1657	1747	...	1857	1902	1937	1940	2057

△ – All services also call at Mirabellplatz.

⊡ – St Wolfgang Schafbergbahnhof. All services also call at St Wolfgang Markt.

‡ – **Schafbergbahn** narrow-gauge steam rack railway operates St Wolfgang - Schafbergspitze (*6 km*). Services operate subject to demand and weather conditions Apr. 26 - Nov. 2. 2nd class only. Special fares payable. Journey time: 35 minutes each way. ✆ +43 (0) 6138 2232 0.

STROBL - ST GILGEN (WOLFGANGSEE) — 964

	b	b	a		b	e	b	a	b	e	b	a	b	e		b	d	a	b	c
Strobl Schiffstation ⊡ d.	...	0840	...	...	0925	1025	1125	1155	1225	1325	1425	1455	1525	1625	...	1725	1725	1750	1820	1920
St Wolfgang Markt d.	...	|	...	...	|	|	1200	1230	1300	1400	1500	1530	1600	1700	...	1800	1750s	1815s	1832s	1932s
St Wolfgang Schafbergbahnhof ‡ d.	0830	0905	0925	...	0955	1055	1208	1238	1308	1408	1508	1538	1608	1708	...	1808	1758	1823	1840	1940
St Wolfgang Markt d.	|	0913	0932	...	1005	1105	|	|	|	|	|	|	|	|	...	|	...	...	...	...
St Gilgen Schiffstation ● a.	0855	0950	1005	...	1045	1145	1245	1315	1345	1445	1545	1615	1645	1745	...	1845	...	...	...	...

	b	b	b	a	b	a	b	a	b	b	a	b	a	b	b	a	b	c	e	c
St Gilgen Schiffstation ● d.	...	...	0900	0920	1000	1020	1100	1200	1200	1300	1330	1400	1500	1500	1600	1630	1700	1800	1800	1850
St Wolfgang Markt d.	...	...	|	|	|	|	|	|	|	|	|	|	|	|	|	|	|	|	|	1920
St Wolfgang Schafbergbahnhof ‡ d.	0820	0855	0937	0952	1037	1100	1137	1235	1237	1337	1405	1437	1535	1537	1637	1705	1737	1837	1837s	1928
St Wolfgang Markt d.	|	0905	0950	1000	1050	1115	1150	1245	1250	1350	1415	1450	1545	1550	1650	1715	1750	1850	1845	...
Strobl Schiffstation ⊡ a.	0835	0920	1015	1015	1115	1140	1215	1310	1315	1415	1440	1515	1610	1615	1715	1740	1815	1915	...	...

a – ①–⑤ until June 13; ①–⑤ Sept. 8 - Oct. 26; daily Oct. 27 - Nov. 2.
b – ⑥⑦ until June 13; daily June 14 - Sept. 7; ⑥⑦ Sept. 8 - Oct. 26.
c – June 14 - Sept. 7.
d – ⑥⑦ until June 13; ⑥⑦ Sept. 8 - Oct. 26.
e – Until Nov. 2.
s – Disembarkation only.

‡ – See note ‡ under Table **963**. ⊡ – Approximately 400 metres from Strobl Busbahnhof. ● – Approximately 500 metres from St Gilgen Busbahnhof.

SERVICE SUSPENDED UNTIL JULY 4, 2025 — TAUERN TUNNEL CAR-CARRYING TRAINS — 969

BÖCKSTEIN - MALLNITZ-OBERVELLACH *11 km.* Transit time: 11 minutes. Passengers without cars are also conveyed. ✆ 05-1717. E-mail: autoschleuse.tauernbahn@pv.oebb.at

From Böckstein at 0620, 0720 and hourly until 2320. **From Mallnitz-Obervellach** at 0550, 0650 and hourly until 2250.

SALZBURG - VILLACH - KLAGENFURT — 970

SERVICE FROM JULY 14. See page 609 for amended service until July 13.

km		NJ 40237 R ♦	NJ 237 R ♦	NJ 40466 R ♦	a 2	NJ 40237 R ♦	EN 40465 R ♦	IC 730 A 🍷	⚒ 2	2	IC 894 ✕	IC 898 🍷	EC 111 🍷	IC 596 🍷	EC 113 🍷♦	ICE 115 ✕♦	Ⓐ 2	2	D 696 Ⓐ 2	IC 698 🍷	ICE 117 ✕♦	IC 794	NJ 295 R ♦
	Wien Hbf **950** d.	...	...	2139	...	...	...	...	...	...	...	...	...	...	...	...	...	...	...	...	...	...	...
	München Hbf **890** d.	2354t	2354t	|	...	...	...	...	...	...	...	...	0816r	...	1217r	1417r	...	...	...	...	1817r	...	2008
0	**Salzburg** Hbf **960 975** d.	0210	0214	0214	...	...	...	...	...	...	0612	0812	1012	1212	1412	1612	...	...	1716	1812	2012	2112	2202
29	Golling-Abtenau **960** d.	|	|	|	...	...	...	...	...	...	0633	0833	1033	1233	1433	1633	...	...	|	1833	2033	2138	|
53	**Bischofshofen** **960 975** d.	|	0255	0255	...	...	...	...	...	...	0654	0854	1054	1254	1454	1654	...	...	1800	1854	2054	2200	|
61	St Johann im Pongau **960** d.	|	|	|	...	←	...	...	...	...	0704	0904	1104	1304	1504	1704	...	...	1810	1904	2104	2209	|
67	**Schwarzach - St Veit** **960** d.	0300	|	|	...	0415	0415	...	...	...	0711	0911	1111	1311	1511	1711	...	...	1817	1911	2111	2216	2254
86	Bad Hofgastein d.	→	|	|	...	0432	0432	...	...	...	0730	0930	1130	1330	1530	1730	...	...	1836	1930	2130	2233	|
97	Bad Gastein d.	...	|	|	...	0446	0446	...	...	...	0743	0943	1143	1343	1543	1743	...	...	1849	1943	2143	2245	|
113	Mallnitz-Obervellach d.	...	|	|	...	0501	0501	...	0650	...	0757	0957	1157	1357	1557	1757	1800	...	1902	1957	2157	2259	|
146	Spittal-Millstättersee **971** d.	...	|	|	...	0526	0526	...	0717	0732	0821	1021	1221	1421	1621	1821	1827	1832	...	2021	2221	2322	|
182	**Villach** Hbf **971** a.	...	0426	0426	...	0551	0551	...	...	0804	0844	1044	1244	1444	1644	1844	...	1904	...	2044	2244	2344	0019
182	**Villach** Hbf **971** d.	...	...	...	0450	...	...	0613	...	0820	0847	1047	1247	1447	1647	1847	...	1920	...	2047	2247	2347	...
198	Velden am Wörthersee **971** d.	...	...	...	0504	...	...	0624	...	0834	0859	1059	1259	1459	1659	1859	...	1934	...	2059	2259	2359	...
207	Pörtschach am Wörthersee **971** d.	...	...	...	0512	...	...	0630	...	0842	0906	1106	1306	1506	1706	1906	...	1942	...	2106	2306	0006	...
220	**Klagenfurt** Hbf **971** a.	...	...	...	0526	...	...	0638	...	0856	0915	1115	1319	1515	1719	1919	...	1956	...	2119	2319	0015	...

	2	EN 40414 R ♦	EN 414 R ♦	NJ 236 R ♦	NJ 40236 R ♦		D 595 Ⓐ 2	NJ 294 R ♦	IC 597 🍷	Ⓐ 2	IC 691 🍷	EC 1214 ⑥b 🍷	ICE 114 ✕♦	EC 112 🍷♦	IC 793 🍷		RJ 797 🍷	Ⓐ 2	Ⓐ 2	RJ 110 ✕		IC 895 🍷	ICE 899 ✕
Klagenfurt Hbf **971** d.	2232	...	...	...	...	...	...	...	0442	...	0645	...	0842	1042	1245	...	1445	1532	...	1642	...	1845	2045
Pörtschach am Wörthersee **971** d.	2247	...	...	...	...	...	...	...	0454	...	0655	...	0854	1054	1255	...	1455	1547	...	1654	...	1855	2055
Velden am Wörthersee **971** d.	2254	...	...	...	...	...	...	...	0502	...	0702	...	0902	1102	1302	...	1502	1554	...	1702	...	1902	2102
Villach Hbf **971** a.	2309	...	...	...	...	...	...	...	0513	...	0713	...	0913	1113	1313	...	1513	1609	...	1713	...	1913	2113
Villach Hbf **971** d.	...	0013	0013	0045	0045	...	...	0426	0516	0529	0716	0807	0916	1116	1316	...	1516	1610	...	1716	...	1916	2116
Spittal-Millstättersee **971** d.	...	0038	0038	|	|	...	...	|	0540	0605	0740	0831	0940	1140	1340	...	1540	1634	1644	1740	...	1940	2140
Mallnitz-Obervellach d.	...	0102	0102	|	|	...	0432	|	0604	0633	0804	0855	1004	1204	1404	...	1604	...	1712	1804	...	2004	2204
Bad Gastein d.	...	0117	0117	|	|	...	0446	|	0619	...	0819	0910	1019	1219	1419	...	1619	...	...	1819	...	2019	2219
Bad Hofgastein d.	...	0129	0129	|	|	...	0459	|	0632	...	0832	0923	1032	1232	1432	...	1632	...	...	1832	...	2032	2232
Schwarzach - St Veit **960** d.	...	0145	0157j	|	|	...	0519	0550	0652	...	0852	0943	1052	1252	1452	...	1652	...	...	1852	...	2052	2252
St Johann im Pongau **960** d.	...	...	|	|	|	...	0526	|	0658	...	0858	0949	1058	1258	1458	...	1658	...	...	1858	...	2058	2258
Bischofshofen **960 975** a.	...	...	|	0217	0217	...	0535	|	0706	...	0906	0959	1106	1306	1506	...	1706	...	...	1906	...	2106	2306
Golling-Abtenau **960** a.	...	...	|	|	|	...	0556	|	|	...	0927	1020	1127	1327	1527	...	1727	...	...	1927	...	2127	2330
Salzburg Hbf **960 975** a.	...	...	0245	0300	0300	...	0619	0649	0749	...	0948	1045	1148	1348	1548	...	1748	...	...	1948	...	2148	2355
München Hbf **890** a.	...	...	0550t	0550t	|	...	...	0921r	...	...	...	1239	1341r	1541r	...	...	...	...	...	2141r	...	...	...
Wien Hbf **950** a.	...	...	...	...	0758	...	...	...	...	...	...	...	...	...	...	...	...	...	...	...	...	...	...

♦ – **NOTES** (LISTED BY TRAIN NUMBER)

112 – BLAUER ENZIAN – (12) and 🍷 Klagenfurt - München (- Stuttgart - Frankfurt ●).
113 – BLAUER ENZIAN – (12) and 🍷 (Frankfurt - Stuttgart - München ● -) Salzburg - Klagenfurt.
114 – WÖRTHERSEE – (12) and ✕ Klagenfurt - München (- Stuttgart - Köln - Dortmund ●).
115 – WÖRTHERSEE – (12) and ✕ (Münster - Köln - Stuttgart ● -) München - Klagenfurt.
117 – SALZACH – (12) and ✕ (Frankfurt - Stuttgart- München ● -) Salzburg - Klagenfurt.
236/7 – 🛏 1, 2 cl., ▬ 2 cl. and (2) Venezia - Tarvisio 🏛 - Villach - Salzburg - München - Stuttgart and v.v.
294/5 – 🛏 1, 2 cl., ▬ 2 cl. and (2) Roma - Firenze - Bologna - München and v.v.;
🛏 1, 2 cl., ▬ 2 cl. and (2) (**40235/40295**) La Spezia - Milano - Verona - München and v.v.
414 – LISINSKI 🛏 1, 2 cl., ▬ 2 cl. and (2) Zagreb - Ljubljana - Villach - Schwarzach - Salzburg - München - Stuttgart.
40236 – 🛏 1, 2 cl., ▬ 2 cl. and (2) Venezia - Tarvisio 🏛 - Villach - Salzburg - Wien.
40237 – LISINSKI 🛏 1, 2 cl., ▬ 2 cl. and (2) Stuttgart - München - Villach - Jesenice 🏛 - Ljubljana - Zagreb.
40414 – 🛏 1, 2 cl., ▬ 2 cl. and (2) Zagreb - Ljubljana - Villach - Schwarzach - Innsbruck - Feldkirch - Zürich.
40465 – 🛏 1, 2 cl., ▬ 2 cl. and (2) Zürich - Feldkirch - Innsbruck - Schwarzach - Villach - Ljubljana - Zagreb.
40466 – 🛏 1, 2 cl., ▬ 2 cl. and (2) Wien - Salzburg - Villach - Tarvisio 🏛 - Venezia.

A – To Wien (Table **890**).
R – Ⓡ for international journeys.

a – ⚒ (daily from Sept. 14).
b – ⑥ Aug. 16 - Oct. 4.
j – Arrives 0145.
r – Not July 14 - Aug. 2.
t – München **Ost**.
v – Arrives 1646.

● – From Aug. 3.

971 LIENZ - VILLACH - KLAGENFURT - FRIESACH (- WIEN)

km		NJ 235 ★ 2	⚒j 2	RJ 530 ✗	U 2	2	IC 730 M🍷	2	2	RJ 532 ✗	2	2	2	IC 894 d ◐🍷	IC 534 🍷	2	2	IC 898 d ◐🍷	RJ 536 ✗	2	IC 736 M🍷	2	EC 111 d ◐✗	RJ 132 V✗	2	D 738 ⑦w 2
0	**Lienz** d.	...	...	...	...	...	...	...	0524	...	...	0629	...	...	0753	0719	*0824*	...	...	0924	...	1024	...	...	1124	1253
68	Spittal-Millstättersee a.	...	...	...	...	...	...	...	0627	...	...	0726	...	...	0842	0822	*0922*	...	...	1022	...	1122	...	...	1222	1343
68	Spittal-Millstättersee **970** d.	...	...	...	0448j	0530a	0546b	...	0630	...	0635a	0729	0732	0821	0846	0832	0932	1021	1046b	1032	1146b	1132	1221	...	1232	1346
104	**Villach** Hbf **970** a.	...	...	...	0520j	0558a	0609b	...	0656	...	0708a	0753	0804	0844	0909	0904f	1004	1044	1109b	1104f	1209b	1204f	1244	...	1304f	1409
104	**Villach** Hbf **970** d.	0417	0450	0525	0529	0604	0613	0620	0659a	0714	0720	0756	0820	0847	0914	0920	1020	1047	1114	1120	1213	1220	1247	1315	1320	1413
120	Velden am Wörthersee **970** d.	|	0504	|	0543	|	0624	0634	0710a	0725	0734	0806	0834	0859	|	0934	1034	1059	1125	1134	1224	1234	1259	|	1334	1424
129	Pörtschach am Wörthersee **970** d.	|	0512	|	0551	|	0630	0642	|	|	0742	|	0842	0906	0929	0942	1042	1106	|	1142	1230	1242	1306	|	1342	1430
135	Krumpendorf d.	|	0518	|	0557	|	|	0648	|	|	0748	|	0848	|	|	0948	1048	|	|	1148	|	1248	1313	|	1348	|
142	**Klagenfurt** Hbf **970** a.	0438	0526	0546	0605	0625	0638	0656	0727a	0737	0756	0822	0856	0915	0937	0956	1056	1115	1137	1156	1238	1256	1319	1337	1356	1438
142	**Klagenfurt** Hbf **980** d.	0440	...	0548	0607	0626	0639	0704	...	0739	0804	0824	0904	...	0939	1004	1104	...	1139	1204	1239	1304	...	1339	1404	1439
162	St Veit an der Glan **980** d.	|	...	0600	0627	0639	0653	0724	...	0753	0824	0838	0924	...	0953	1024	1124	...	1153	1224	1253	1324	...	1353	1424	1453
195	**Friesach** **980** a.	|	...	|	0658	0703	0717	0756	...	|	0856	...	0956	...	1015	1056	1156	...	|	1256	1317	1356	...	1415	1456	1517
	Wien Hbf **980** a.	0904	...	0936	...	...	1036	...	...	1136	...	...	...	...	1336	...	...	...	1536	...	1636	...	...	1736	...	1836

	2	IC 596 d ◐✗	Ⓐ 2	RJ 630 ✗	2	Ⓐ 2	IC 830 M🍷	2	EC 113 d ◐🍷	Ⓐ 2	IC 632 🍷	2	Ⓐ 2	D 832 ⑦t 2	2	ICE 115 d ◐✗	RJ 130 V✗	2	IC 834 ⑦w 🍷	2	IC 698 d ◐🍷	2	2	ICE 117 d ◐✗	IC 794 d ◐🍷	2
Lienz d.	1224	...	...	...	1324	...	...	1424	...	...	1553	1524	...	...	1624	...	...	1724	1853	1824	...	1924	2024	...	...	...
Spittal-Millstättersee a.	1322	...	...	...	1422	...	...	1522	...	...	1642	1622	...	...	1722	...	...	1822	1942	1922	...	2022	2122	...	...	...
Spittal-Millstättersee **970** d.	1332	1421	*1407*	...	1432	*1507*	1546b	1532	1621	*1607*	1646	1632	*1707*	...	1732	1821	...	1832	1946	1932	2021	2032	2132	2221	2322	...
Villach Hbf **970** a.	1404f	1444	*1439*f	...	1504f	*1539*f	1609b	1604f	1644	*1639*f	1709	1704f	*1739*f	...	1804f	1844	...	1904f	2009	2004f	2044	2104	2204	2244	2344	...
Villach Hbf **970** d.	1420	1447	1450	1514	1520	1550	1613	1620	1647	1650	1714	1720	1750	1813	1820	1847	1915	1920	2013	2020	2047	2120	2220	2247	2347	2354
Velden am Wörthersee **970** d.	1434	1459	1504	1525	1534	1604	1624	1634	1659	1704	|	1734	1804	1824	1834	1859	|	1934	2024	2034	2059	2134	2234	2259	2359	0008
Pörtschach am Wörthersee **970** d.	1442	1506	1512	|	1542	1612	1630	1642	1706	1712	1729	1742	1812	1830	1842	1906	|	1942	2030	2042	2106	2142	2242	2306	0006	0016
Krumpendorf d.	1448	|	1518	|	1548	1618	|	1648	1713	1718	|	1748	1818	|	1848	1913	|	1948	|	2048	2113	2148	2248	2313	|	0022
Klagenfurt Hbf **970** a.	1456	1515	1526	1537	1556	1626	1638	1656	1719	1726	1737	1756	1826	1838	1856	1919	1937	1956	2038	2056	2119	2156	2256	2319	0015	0030
Klagenfurt Hbf **980** d.	1504	...	1528	1539	1604	1628	1639	1704	...	1728	1739	1804	1828	1839	1904	...	1939	2004	2039	2104	...	2204	2304	...	...	0032
St Veit an der Glan **980** d.	1524	...	1547	1553	1624	1647	1653	1724	...	1747	1753	1824	1847	1853	1924	...	1953	2024	2053	2124	...	2224	2324	...	...	0051
Friesach **980** a.	1556	...	...	|	1656	...	1717	1756	...	...	1815	1856	...	1917	1956	...	|	2056	2117	2156	...	2256	2356	...	...	...
Wien Hbf **980** a.	...	...	...	1936	...	...	2036	...	...	...	2136	...	...	2236	...	...	2336	...	0036	...	...	...	...	...	...	...

	IC 597 d ◐🍷	⚒ 2	2	⚒ 2	IC 691 d ◐🍷	2	⚒ 2	⚒⊕ U2	⊡ 2	RJ 639 M G✗	ICE 114 d ◐✗	2	2	RJ 131 V✗	EC 112 d ◐🍷	2	IC 733 M🍷	2	IC 533 🍷	Ⓐ 2	IC 793 d ◐🍷	2	Ⓐ 2	2	RJ 535 ✗	Ⓐ 2
Wien Hbf **980** d.	...	...	...	...	...	...	...	...	...	...	...	...	...	0624	...	...	0724	...	0824	...	...	...	...	...	1024	...
Friesach **980** d.	...	...	0502	0540	...	0608	...	0646	0708	0741	...	0808	0908	|	...	1008	1042	1108	1144	...	...	1208	...	1308	|	...
St Veit an der Glan **980** d.	...	0512j	0536	0611	...	0642	...	0718	0742	0808	...	0842	0942	1008	...	1042	1108	1142	1208	1212	...	1242	1312	1342	1408	1412
Klagenfurt Hbf **980** a.	...	0530j	0554	0625	...	0700	...	0738	0800	0820	...	0900	1000	1019	...	1100	1119	1200	1219	1230	...	1300	1330	1400	1419	1430
Klagenfurt Hbf **970** d.	0442	0532	0602	0633	0645	0702	0732	0744	0802	0822	0842	0902	1002	1021	1042	1102	1121	1202	1221	1232	1245	1302	1332	1402	1421	1432
Krumpendorf d.	0448	0540	0610	0642	|	0710	0740	0752	0810	|	0848	0910	1010	|	1048	1110	|	1210	|	1240	|	1310	1340	1410	|	1440
Pörtschach am Wörthersee **970** d.	0455	0547	0617	0647	0655	0717	0747	0757	0817	0832	0854	0917	1017	|	1054	1117	1131	1217	1232	1247	1255	1317	1347	1417	|	1447
Velden am Wörthersee **970** d.	0502	0554	0624	0654	0702	0724	0754	0803	0824	|	0902	0924	1024	|	1102	1124	1138	1224	|	1254	1302	1324	1354	1424	1436	1454
Villach Hbf **970** a.	0513	0609	0639	0710	0713	0739	0809	0819	0839	0846f	0913	0939	1039	1044f	1113	1139	1148f	1239	1246f	1309	1313	1339	1409	1439	1446f	1509
Villach Hbf **970** d.	0516	0619a	0654	...	0716	0754	...	...	0854	0850b	0916	0954	1054	...	1116	1154	1150b	1254	1250	...	1316	1354	*1424*	1454	...	...
Spittal-Millstättersee **970** a.	0538	0652a	0726	...	0738	0826	...	...	0926	0912b	0938	1026	1126	...	1138	1226	1212b	1326	1312	...	1338	1426	*1456*	1526	...	...
Spittal-Millstättersee d.	*0632*r	...	0737	...	...	0837	...	...	0937	...	...	1037	1137	...	...	1237	...	1337	1316	...	...	1437	...	1537	...	...
Lienz a.	*0732*r	...	0837	...	...	0937	...	...	1037	...	...	1137	1237	...	...	1337	...	1437	1406	...	...	1537	...	1637	...	...

	IC 797 d ◐✗	2	Ⓐ 2	2	RJ 133 V✗	Ⓐ 2	RJ 110 d ◐✗	2	IC 739 ⑤y 🍷	Ⓐ 2	2	IC 539 z ✗	IC 895 d ◐✗	2	D 831 ⑤y 2	Ⓐ 2	⊖ 2	RJ 631 ✗	ICE 899 d ◐✗	2	IC 833 M🍷	2	RJ 633 ✗	2	NJ 233 ★ 2	2
Wien Hbf **980** d.	...	...	...	...	1224	...	...	...	1324	...	...	1424	...	...	1524	...	...	1624	...	...	1724	...	1824	...	1918	...
Friesach **980** d.	...	1408	...	1508	1544	...	...	1608	1642	...	1708	|	...	1808	1842	...	1908	1944	...	2008	2042	2108	|	...	|	...
St Veit an der Glan **980** d.	...	1442	1512	1542	1608	1612	...	1642	1708	1712	1742	1808	...	1842	1908	1912	1942	2008	...	2042	2108	2142	2208	...	2324	...
Klagenfurt Hbf **980** a.	...	1500	1530	1600	1619	1630	...	1700	1719	1730	1800	1819	...	1900	1919	1930	2000	2019	...	2100	2119	2200	2219	←	2336	...
Klagenfurt Hbf **970** d.	1445	1502	1532	1602	1621	1632	1642	1702	1721	1732	1802	1821	1845	1902	1921	1932	2002	2021	2045	2102	2121	2232	2221	2232	2338	2341
Krumpendorf d.	|	1510	1540	1610	|	1640	1648	1710	|	1740	1810	|	|	1910	|	1940	2010	|	|	2110	|	→	|	2240	|	2349
Pörtschach am Wörthersee **970** d.	1455	1517	1547	1617	|	1647	1654	1717	1731	1747	1817	|	1855	1917	1931	1947	2017	2032	2055	2117	2131	...	|	2247	|	2355
Velden am Wörthersee **970** d.	1502	1524	1554	1624	|	1654	1702	1724	1738	1754	1824	1836	1902	1924	1938	1954	2024	|	2102	2124	2138	...	2236	2254	|	0002
Villach Hbf **970** a.	1513	1539	1609	1639	1644f	1709	1713	1739	1748	1809	1839	1846	1913	1939	1948	2009	2039	2046f	2113	2139	2148	...	2246	2309	0001	0018
Villach Hbf **970** d.	1516	1554	1610	1654	...	1710	1716	1754	1750	1810	1854	1850	1916	1954	1950	...	2054	2050b	2116	2154	2150b	...	*2254*	...	*0013*	...
Spittal-Millstättersee **970** a.	1538	1626	1634	1726	...	1733	1738	1826	1812	1834	1926	1912	1938	2026	2012	...	2126	2112b	2138	2226	2212b	...	*2326*	...	*0036*	...
Spittal-Millstättersee d.	...	*1637*	1637	1737	...	...	...	1837	1816	...	1937	1916	...	*2037*	2016	...	2143	...	*2143*	...	...	...	...	...	...	...
Lienz a.	...	*1737*	1737	1837	...	...	...	1937	1906	...	2037	2006	...	*2136*	2106	...	2241	...	*2241*	...	...	...	...	...	...	...

G – From Graz (Table **980**).
M – To / from Mallnitz until July 13 (see Table **970** on page 580).
U – To / from Unzmarkt (Table **980**).
V – From / to Venezia (Table 88).

a – Ⓐ only.
b – Until July 13.

d – From July 14.
f – Connects with train in previous column.
j – ⚒ (daily from Sept. 14).
r – ⚒ only.
t – ⑦ (also Apr. 17, 21, June 9, Dec. 8; not Apr. 20, June 8, Dec. 7).
w – ⑦ (also Apr. 21, June 9, Dec. 8; not Apr. 20, June 8, Dec. 7).
y – ⑤ (also Apr. 17, 30, May 28, June 18, Aug. 14; not May 2, 30, June 20, Aug. 15).
z – Runs as *IC* **839** on ⑦ (also Apr. 21, June 9, Dec. 8; not Apr. 20, June 8, Dec. 7).

⊕ – A change of trains may be required at Klagenfurt.
⊖ – Change trains at Spittal-Millstättersee on Ⓑ.
★ – See Table **980** for through cars to / from Roma and Milano.
◐ – See Table **970** for further details.
⊡ – Change trains at Spittal-Millstättersee on Ⓐ.

974 LINZ - SELZTHAL

2nd class only (except *IC* trains)

km		⚒	Ⓐ		IC 501 ⚒f			IC 503 🍷				IC 507 🍷		Ⓐ	Ⓐ			IC 601 🍷			IC 603 🍷		Ⓐ				
0	**Linz** Hbf d.	0455	0506	0536	0555	0655	0736	0755	0855	1055	1136	1155	1255	1355	1406	1455	1536	1555	1655	1736	1755	1855	1955	2055	2136	2236	2336
28	Rohr - Bad Hall d.	0519	0540	0610	0619	0719	0810	0819	0919	1119	1210	1219	1319	1419	1440	1519	1610	1619	1719	1810	1819	1919	2019	2119	2210	2310	0010
32	Kremsmünster d.	0524	0546	0616	0624	0724	0816	0824	0924	1124	1216	1224	1324	1424	1446	1524	1616	1624	1724	1816	1824	1924	2024	2124	2216	2316	0016
51	Kirchdorf a. d. Krems d.	0537	0603	0633	0639	0739	0833	0839	0939	1139	1233	1239	1339	1437	1503	1539	1633	1637	1739	1833	1839	1939	2037	2139	2233	2334	0033
68	Hinterstoder d.	0601	...	...	0700	0801	...	0900	1001	1201	...	1300	1401	1501	...	1601	...	1657	1801	...	1900	2001	2100	2201	...	2355	...
82	Windischgarsten d.	0615	...	...	0713	0815	...	0913	1015	1215	...	1313	1415	1515	...	1615	...	1712	1815	...	1913	2015	2114	2215	...	0010	...
87	Spital am Pyhrn d.	0621	...	...	|	0821	...	|	1021	1221	...	|	1421	1520	...	1621	...	1718	1821	...	|	2021	2119	2221	...	0016	...
104	**Selzthal** a.	0639	...	...	0733	0840	...	0933	1040	1240	...	1333	1440	...	...	1640	...	1733	1840	...	1933	2040	2134	2240	...	0032	...
	Liezen **975** a.	0700	...	...	|	0851a	...	|	...	1251a	...	|	1451a	...	...	1648a	...	|	...	...	|	...	...	...	...	...	...
	Graz Hbf **975** a.	...	...	...	0903	...	...	1103	...	...	...	1503	...	...	...	...	...	1903	...	...	2103	...	...	...	...	...	...

		Ⓐ	⚒	⚒	Ⓐ	Ⓐ	Ⓒ			IC 500 🍷			IC 502 🍷				IC 506 🍷			Ⓐ			IC 600 🍷		IC 602 Ⓑ🍷t		
Graz Hbf **975** d.	...	...	...	...	...	...	...	...	...	0656	...	...	0856	...	...	...	1256	...	...	...	...	...	1656	...	1856	...	...
Liezen **975** d.	...	...	...	...	...	...	...	0706r	...	|	...	0906a	|	...	...	1306a	|	1506a	...	...	1706a	...	|	...	|	...	...
Selzthal d.	...	0420	...	0520	...	0613	0613	0720	...	0826	...	0920	1026	1120	...	1320	1426	1520	...	...	1720	...	1826	1920	2026	...	2120
Spital am Pyhrn d.	...	0438	...	0538	...	0638	0638	0738	...	|	...	0938	|	1138	...	1338	|	1538	1634	...	1738	...	|	1938	|	...	2138
Windischgarsten d.	...	0444	...	0544	...	0644	0644	0744	...	0846	...	0944	1046	1144	...	1344	1446	1544	1640	...	1744	...	1846	1944	2046	...	2144
Hinterstoder d.	...	0500	...	0600	...	0700	0700	0800	...	0900	...	1000	1100	1200	...	1400	1500	1600	1657	...	1800	...	1900	2000	2100	...	2200
Kirchdorf a. d. Krems d.	0425	0521	0555	0621	0648	0721	0725	0821	0825	0918	0925	1021	1118	1221	1325	1421	1518	1621	1718	1655	1821	1825	1918	2021	2118	2125	2221
Kremsmünster d.	0445	0535	0615	0635	0703	0735	0745	0835	0845	0935	0945	1035	1135	1235	1345	1435	1535	1635	1735	1715	1835	1845	1935	2035	2135	2145	2235
Rohr - Bad Hall d.	0449	0540	0619	0640	0709	0740	0749	0840	0849	0940	0949	1040	1140	1240	1349	1440	1540	1640	1740	1719	1840	1849	1940	2040	2140	2149	2240
Linz Hbf a.	0524	0605	0654	0705	0738	0806	0824	0905	0924	1005	1024	1105	1205	1305	1424	1505	1605	1705	1805	1754	1905	1924	2005	2105	2205	2224	2305

a – Ⓐ only.
f – Not Apr. 21, June 9, Aug. 16, Dec. 8.

r – ⚒ only.
t – Not Apr. 20, June 8, Aug. 15, Dec. 7.

☛ Additional trains run Linz - Kirchdorf and v.v.:
From Linz at 0036, 0636, 0836, 0936, 1036, 1236, 1336, 1436, 1636, 1836, 1936, 2036.
From Kirchdorf at 0455 Ⓐ, 0625, 1025, 1125, 1225, 1425, 1525, 1625, 1725, 1925, 2025.

SALZBURG - BISCHOFSHOFEN - SELZTHAL - GRAZ 975

km			NJ 465	NJ 1465		D 619	IC 501				IC 511		IC 503			IC 513	RJ 111	IC 515		IC 507		EC 217		EC 113	EC 163		IC 601
		⚒	a	b	⚒		⚒g	⚒	Ⓐ			Ⓐ		†	⚒				Ⓐ				Ⓐ			Ⓐ	
		2	A🍷	A🍷	2	2		2L	2	2	🍷	2L	🍷	2	2	🍷		🍷	2L	🍷	2	G🍷	2L		Z✕	2L	🍷
0	**Salzburg** Hbf ..... **960 970** d.	...	...	...	...	...	...	...	...	...	0616	...	...	...	*0621*	0816	1012	...	...	...	...	1216	...	1412	...	...	...
	Innsbruck Hbf **960** d.	...	0059	0059	...	...	...	...	...	...	|	...	...	...	|	|	|	0821	...	...	...	|	...	|	1221	...	...
	Schwarzach ⊖ **960 970** d.	...	0324	0324	...	0446	...	...	...	...	|	...	...	...	|	|	|	1056	...	...	...	|	...	|	1456	...	...
53	**Bischofshofen** ... **960 970** a.	...	0336	|	...	0500	...	...	...	...	0702	...	...	...	*0722*	0902	1052	1110	...	...	...	1302	...	1452	1510	...	...
53	**Bischofshofen** d.	...	0338	|	...	0502	...	...	...	...	0712	...	...	...	0741	0912	▬	1112	...	...	...	1312	...	▬	1512	...	...
77	Radstadt d.	...	|	|	...	0527	...	...	...	0603	0735	...	...	0809	0809	0935	2	1135	...	...	...	1335	...	2	1535	...	...
94	Schladming d.	...	0416	|	0459	0544	...	...	...	0626	0752	...	...	0831	0831	0952	1031	1152	...	...	1231	1352	...	1431	1552	...	...
133	**Stainach-Irdning** d.	0415	0446	|	0540	0619	...	...	...	0708	0822	...	...	0912	0912	1022	1112	1222	...	...	1312	1422	...	1512	1622	...	...
145	Liezen d.	0427	0457	|	0552	0629	...	0706	...	0726f	0832	0906	...	0926	0926	1032	1126	1232	1306	...	1326	1432	1506	1526	1632	1706	...
	Linz Hbf **974** d.	|	|	|	|	|	0555	|	...	|	|	|	0755	|	|	|	|	|	|	1155	|	|	|	|	|	|	1555
152	**Selzthal** a.	0433	0504	0453	0558	0636	0733	0712	...	0732	0839	0912	0933	0932c	0932c	1039	1132	1239	1312	1333	1332c	1439	1512	1532	1639	1712	1733
152	**Selzthal** d.	0440	0513	0513	0606	0643	0735	...	0716	0739	0848	...	0935	0939	0939	1048	1139	1248	...	1335	1339	1448	...	1539	1648	...	1735
158	Stadt Rottenmann d.	0447	|	|	0613	0650	0742	...	0722	0745	|	...	0942	0945	0945	|	1145	|	...	1342	1345	|	...	1545	|	...	1742
169	Trieben d.	0455	|	|	0621	0657	|	...	0729	0753	|	...	|	0953	0953	|	1153	|	...	|	1353	|	...	1553	|	...	|
215	St Michael **980** a.	0530	0550	0550	0655j	0721	|	...	0802	0828	0921	...	|	1028	1028	1121	1228	1321	...	|	1428	1521	...	1628	1721	...	|
225	Leoben Hbf **980** a.	0538	0557	0557	0708	0728	0817	...	0811	*0840*	0928	...	1017	*1040*	*1040*	1128	*1240*	1328	...	1417	*1440*	1528	...	*1640*	1728	...	1817
	Bruck a. d. Mur **980** a.	|	0609	0609	|	|	|	...	0826	*0854*	|	...	|	*1054*	*1054*	|	*1254*	|	...	|	*1454*	|	...	*1654*	|	...	|
293	**Graz** Hbf **980** a.	0635	0658	0658	0801	0817	0903	...	*0925*	...	1014	...	1103	...	...	1214	...	1414	...	1503	...	1614	...	...	1814	...	1903

		IC 611	IC 603			EC 219	IC 615		
					Ⓐ				
	2	🍷	🍷	2	2	F🍷	🍷	2	2
Salzburg Hbf...... **960 970** d.	...	1616	...	...	*1643*	1816	2016	...	...
Innsbruck Hbf **960** d.	...	|	...	...	|	|	|	...	...
Schwarzach ⊖ **960 970** d.	...	|	...	...	|	|	|	...	2258
Bischofshofen... **960 970** a.	...	1702	...	...	*1735*	1902	2102	...	2312
Bischofshofen d.	...	1712	...	...	1740	1912	2112	2213	2313
Radstadt d.	...	1735	...	...	1809	1935	2135	2243	2343
Schladming d.	1631	1752	...	1833	1828	1952	2152	2301	2400
Stainach-Irdning d.	1712	1822	...	1912	...	2022	2222	2340r	...
Liezen d.	1726	1832	...	1926	...	2032	2232	...	...
Linz Hbf **974** d.	|	|	1755	|	...	|	|	...	...
Selzthal a.	1732c	1839	1933	1932c	...	2039	2239	...	...
Selzthal d.	1739	1848	1935	1939	...	2048	2246	...	...
Stadt Rottenmann d.	1745	|	1942	1945	...	|	2253	...	...
Trieben d.	1753	|	|	1953	...	|	|	...	...
St Michael **980** a.	1828	1921	|	2028	...	2121	2321	...	...
Leoben Hbf **980** a.	*1840*	1928	2017	*2040*	...	2128	2328	...	...
Bruck a. d. Mur **980** a.	*1854*	|	|	*2054*	...	|	|	...	...
Graz Hbf **980** a.	...	2014	2103	...	...	2214	0014	...	...

			D 618				EC 218		IC 500		IC 512	
	⚒	⚒		⚒	Ⓐ	⚒				Ⓐ		
	2	2	2🍷	2	2	2L	F✕	2	🍷	2L	🍷	2
Graz Hbf **980** d.	...	...	...	*0445*t	...	...	0545	...	0656	...	0745	...
Bruck a. d. Mur **980** d.	...	...	...	0536	...	...	|	*0706*	|	...	|	*0906*
Leoben Hbf **980** d.	...	...	...	0550	...	...	0630	*0721*	0741	...	0830	*0921*
St Michael **980** d.	...	...	...	0557	0600	...	0638	0731	|	...	0838	0931
Trieben d.	...	...	...	▬	0636	...	|	0805	|	...	|	1005
Stadt Rottenmann d.	...	...	...	⚒	0644	...	0708	0812	0818	...	|	1012
Selzthal a.	...	...	...	2	0650	...	0713	0818	0823c	...	0911	1018
Selzthal d.	...	...	...	0543	▬	0653	0719	0826	0826	0844	0919	1026
Linz Hbf **974** a.	...	...	...	|	...	|	|	|	1005	|	|	|
Liezen d.	...	...	...	0551	†	0700	0727	0832	▬	0851	0927	1032
Stainach-Irdning d.	...	...	...	0603	2	...	0738	0845	2	...	0938	1045
Schladming d.	0506	...	0545	0645	0702	...	0810	...	0902	...	1010	1128
Radstadt d.	0526	...	0602	0704	0720	...	0826	...	0920	...	1026	...
Bischofshofen a.	0554	...	0628	0736	0750	...	0848	...	0950	...	1048	...
Bischofshofen **960 970** d.	0557	0557	0635	*0740*	*0804*	...	0857	...	*1004*	...	1057	...
Schwarzach ⊖ **960 970** a.	0612	|	|	|	|	...	|	...	|	...	|	...
Innsbruck Hbf **960** a.	...	|	|	|	|	...	|	...	|	...	|	...
Salzburg Hbf **960 970** a.	...	0646	0719	*0840*	*0851*	...	0944	...	*1051*	...	1144	...

	IC 602	EC 161	EC 112			EC 216		IC 606		IC 618	RJ 707				IC 610			IC 600		IC 612		IC 602	D 614		D 616	NJ 464	NJ 1464
					Ⓐ				Ⓐ				Ⓐ	⚒		Ⓐ			⚒			Ⓑh				b	a
	2	Z✕	✕	2	2L	G🍷	2	🍷	2L	🍷	✕	2	2L	2	🍷	2	2	🍷	2	✕	2	🍷	2🍷	2	2🍷	A	A
Graz Hbf **980** d.	0856	0945	...	...	...	1145	...	1256	...	1345	...	...	...	1501	1545	...	...	1656	1701	1745	...	1856	1945	...	2145	2225	2226
Bruck a. d. Mur **980** d.	|	|	...	*1106*	...	|	*1306*	|	...	|	...	*1506*	...	|	|	...	*1706*	|	|	|	*1906*	|	|	2206	|	2317	2317
Leoben Hbf **980** d.	0941	1030	...	*1121*	...	1230	*1321*	1341	...	1430	...	*1521*	...	1557	1630	...	*1721*	1741	1801	1830	*1921*	1941	2030	2219	2230	2330	2330
St Michael **980** d.	|	1038	...	1131	...	1238	1331	|	...	1438	...	1531	...	1608	1638	...	1731	|	1810	1838	1931	|	2038	▬	2238	2340	2340
Trieben d.	|	|	...	1205	...	|	1405	|	...	|	...	1605	...	1644t	|	...	1805	|	1846	|	2005	|	|	...	|	|	|
Stadt Rottenmann d.	1018	|	...	1212	...	|	1412	1418	...	|	...	1612	...	1652t	|	...	1812	1818	1854	|	2012	2018	2108	...	2310	|	|
Selzthal a.	1023c	1111	...	1218	...	1311	1418	1423c	...	1511	...	1618	...	1658t	1711	...	1818	1823c	1900	1911	2018	2023	2113	...	2315	0017	0017
Selzthal d.	1026	1119	...	1226	1244	1319	1426	1426	1444	1519	...	1626	1641	...	1719	1746	1826	1826	...	1919	2026	2026	2120	...	2321	0028	0047
Linz Hbf **974** a.	1205	|	...	|	|	|	|	1605	|	|	...	|	|	...	|	|	|	2005	...	|	|	2205	|	...	|	|	|
Liezen d.	...	1127	...	1232	1251	1327	1432	...	1451	1527	...	1632	1648	...	1727	1753	1832	...	...	1927	2032	...	2127	...	2329	0036	0055
Stainach-Irdning d.	...	1138	...	1245	...	1338	1445	...	...	1538	...	1645	...	...	1738	1806	1845	...	...	1938	2045	...	2137	...	2341	0046	0105
Schladming d.	...	1210	...	1328	...	1410	1528	...	...	1610	...	1728	...	...	1810	1849	1929	...	...	2010	2126	...	2210	*ICE*	0024	0118	0137
Radstadt d.	...	1226	...	...	...	1426	...	...	...	1626	...	...	...	...	1826	*1920*	1952	...	...	2026	...	...	2226	**899**	...	|	|
Bischofshofen a.	...	1248	...	...	...	1448	...	...	...	1648	...	...	...	...	1848	*1950*	...	...	...	2048	...	...	2251	✕	...	0156	0215
Bischofshofen... **960 970** d.	...	1250	1308	...	...	1457	...	...	...	1650	1708	...	...	...	1857	...	...	...	...	2057	...	...	2253	2308	...	0158	0217
Schwarzach ⊖ **960 970** a.	...	1305	|	...	...	|	...	...	...	1705	|	...	...	...	|	...	...	...	...	|	...	...	2308	|	...	0211	0230
Innsbruck Hbf **960** a.	...	1540	|	...	...	|	...	...	...	1940	|	...	...	...	|	...	...	...	...	|	...	...	...	|	...	0449	0449
Salzburg Hbf...... **960 970** a.	...	...	1348	...	...	1544	...	...	...	...	1748	...	...	...	1944	...	...	...	...	2144	..	...	...	2355	...	...	...

A – 🛏 1, 2 cl., 🛌 2 cl. and (2) Graz - Innsbruck - Buchs 🏛 - Zürich and v.v.
F – CHIEMGAU – (12) and ⊗ Graz - Salzburg (- München - Stuttgart - Frankfurt ●) and v.v.
G – DACHSTEIN – (12) Graz - Salzburg (- München - Stuttgart - Saarbrücken ●) and v.v.
L – To / from Linz (Table **974**).
Z – TRANSALPIN – (12) and ✕ Zürich - Graz and v.v.

a – From July 14.
b – Until July 13.
c – Connects with train in previous column.
f – Arrives 0720.
g – Not Apr. 21, June 9, Aug. 16, Dec. 8.
h – Not Apr. 20, June 8, Aug. 15, Dec. 7.

j – Departs 0701.
r – Ⓑ only.
t – Ⓐ only.
⊖ – Schwarzach-St Veit.
● – See Table **890** for running dates beyond Salzburg.

LINZ - STEYR - KLEINREIFLING - WEISSENBACH 976

2nd class only

km																										
		⚒	⚒		Ⓐ	Ⓒ	Ⓐ	Ⓒ	Ⓐ		Ⓐ	Ⓒ	Ⓐ		Ⓐ	Ⓒ	Ⓐ	Ⓒ	Ⓐ	Ⓐ	Ⓒ	Ⓐ		Ⓐ	Ⓐ	Ⓒ
0	**Linz** Hbf ...... **950 992** d.	0425	0514	0621	0649	0649	0753	0753	0823	0853	0953	0953	*1032*	1053	1153	1153	1223	1253	1253	1353	1353	1423	1453	1523	1553	1553
17	Enns **992** d.	0442	0532	0638	0707	0707	0811	0811	0841	0911	1011	1011	|	1111	1211	1211	1241	1311	1311	1411	1411	1441	1511	1541	1611	1611
25	St Valentin **950** d.	0509v	0540	0650	0721t	0721t	0821	0821	0851	0921	1021	1021	1051	1121	1221	1221	1251	1321	1321	1421	1421	1451	1521	1551	1621	1621
45	**Steyr** d.	0532	0604	0714	0754t	0754t	0846	0846	0912	0946	1046	1046	1112	1146	1246	1246	1312	1346	1346	1446	1446	1512	1546	1612	1646	1646
47	Garsten d.	0536	0607	0717	0758	0758	0849	0850	0916	0949	1049	1050	1116	1149	1249	1250	1316	1349	1350	1449	1450	1516	1549	1616	1649	1650
67	Losenstein d.	0601	...	...	0822	0822	...	0917	0937	...	...	1117	1137	...	...	1317	1337	...	1423	...	1517	1537	...	1640	...	1717
89	Kastenreith **977** a.	0628	...	...	0848	0852	...	0941	1004	...	...	1141	1204	...	...	1341	1404	...	1447	...	1541	1604	...	1704	...	1741
92	**Kleinreifling** **977** a.	0633	...	...	0852	0856	...	0946	1008	...	...	1146	1208	...	...	1346	1408	...	1451	...	1546	1608	...	1708	...	1746
106	Weißenbach ⊡ .. **977** a.	0648a	...	...	0907	*0916*	...	...	...	...	...	*1216*	...	...	...	*1416*	...	...	...	...	...	1623	...	1723	...	*1816*k

	Ⓐ		Ⓐ	Ⓐ	Ⓒ	Ⓐ					
Linz Hbf .... **950 992** d.	1623	1653	1723	1753	1753	1823	*1853*	1953	*2053*	2153	2253
Enns **992** d.	1641	1711	1741	1811	1811	1841	*1911*	2011	*2111*	2211	2311
St Valentin **950** d.	1651	1721	1751	1821	1821	1851	1921	2021	2121	2221	2321
Steyr d.	1712	1746	1812	1846	1846	1912	1946	2045	2146	2246	2346
Garsten d.	1716	1749	1816	1849	1850	1916	1949	2048	2149	2250	2349
Losenstein d.	1737	...	1840	...	1917	1937	...	2111	...	2313	...
Kastenreith **977** a.	1804	...	1904	...	1941	2005	...	2135	...	2337	...
Kleinreifling **977** a.	1808	...	1908	...	1946	2009	...	2139	...	2341	...
Weißenbach ⊡ **977** a.	1823	...	1923	...	...	...	...	...	...	...	...

	P	Ⓐ	⚒		⚒			Ⓐ	Ⓐ	Ⓐ	Ⓒ
Weißenbach ⊡ .**977** d.	...	...	...	...	...	0603a	...	0706	...	...	...
Kleinreifling **977** d.	...	0437	0512	0520f	0546	0618	...	0721	0754	...	0812
Kastenreith **977** d.	...	0441	0516	0524f	0550	0622	...	0724	0758	...	0816
Losenstein d.	...	0505	0539	0549f	0615	0647	...	...	0822	...	0843
Garsten d.	0442	0527	0600	0612	0637	0709	0809	...	0843	0909	0909
Steyr d.	0446	0532	0604	0616	0642	0714	0814	...	0847	0914	0914
St Valentin **950** d.	0511	0556	0621	0641	0712	0741	0841	...	0907	0941	0941
Enns **992** d.	0518	0602	0627	0646	0719	0748	0848	...	|	0948	0948
Linz Hbf ... **950 992** a.	0534	0617	0639	0701	0735	0804	0904	...	*0928*	1004	1004

		Ⓐ	Ⓐ	Ⓒ		Ⓐ	Ⓐ	Ⓒ		Ⓐ	Ⓐ	Ⓒ	Ⓐ		Ⓐ	Ⓐ	Ⓒ	Ⓐ	Ⓒ	Ⓐ	Ⓐ	Ⓐ	Ⓒ			
Weißenbach ⊡ **977** d.	...	0940	...	...	...	...	...	*1144*	...	1338	...	*1341*	...	...	...	...	*1541*	...	...	1639	1738	...	*1744*	...	*1941*	...
Kleinreifling **977** d.	...	0954	...	1015	...	1154	...	1215	...	1354	...	1415	...	...	1554	...	1615	...	...	1654	1753	...	1815	...	2021	...
Kastenreith **977** d.	...	0958	...	1019	...	1158	...	1219	...	1358	...	1419	...	...	1558	...	1619	...	...	1658	1757	...	1819	...	2025	...
Losenstein d.	...	1022	...	1044	...	1222	...	1244	...	1422	...	1444	...	...	1621	...	1644	...	...	1744v	1821	...	1844	...	2050	...
Garsten d.	1009	1043	1109	1109	1209	1243	1309	1309	1409	1443	1509	1509	1543	1609	1643	1709	1709	1743	1809	1809	1843	1909	1909	2009	2113	2209
Steyr d.	1014	1047	1114	1114	1214	1247	1314	1314	1414	1447	1514	1514	1547	1614	1647	1714	1714	1747	1814	1814	1847	1914	1914	2014	2116	2214
St Valentin **950** d.	1041	1111	1141	1141	1241	1311	1341	1341	1441	1511	1541	1541	1607	1641	1711	1741	1741	1807	1841	1841	1907	1941	1941	2041	2141	2241
Enns **992** d.	1048	1118	1148	1148	1248	1318	1348	1348	1448	1518	1548	1548	|	1648	1718	1748	1748	|	1848	1848	|	1948	1948	2048	2148	2248
Linz Hbf **950 992** a.	1104	1139	1204	1204	1304	1339	1404	1404	1504	1539	1604	1604	*1628*	1704	1739	1804	1804	*1828*	1904	1904	*1928*	2004	2004	2104	2204	2304

P – To Passau (Table **962**). **a** – Ⓐ only. **f** – † only. **k** – ⑥ only. **t** – Arrives 8–9 minutes earlier. **v** – Arrives 19 minutes earlier. ⊡ – Weißenbach-St Gallen.

977 AMSTETTEN - KLEINREIFLING - SELZTHAL

2nd class only

km																									
		⚒	⚒		†		©	©	Ⓐ		©	Ⓐ		Ⓐ	©	Ⓐ	Ⓐ		©	©	Ⓐ		Ⓐ	†	⑥
	Wien Westbahnhof **950** d.	...	0448**k**	...	...	...	0648	...	...	...	...	...	...	...	1118	...	...	...	1218	...	...	...	...	1518	...
0	**Amstetten** d.	0451	0622	0705	0705	0805	0805	0905	0905	1005	1105	1105	1205	1205	1305	1305	1323	1405	1405	1505	1505	1605	1605	1705	1705
23	Waidhofen a. d. Ybbs d.	0548**h**	0710**j**	0729	0730	0829	0830	0930	0930	1029	1130	1130	1229	1230	1330	1330	1351	1430	1430	1530	1530	1629	1630	1730	1730
41	Weyer d.	0607	0729	...	0748	...	0852	0948	0948	...	1148	1148	...	1248	1348	1348	...	1448	1448	1548	1548	...	1648	1748	1748
44	Kastenreith **976** d.	0611	0733	...	0752	...	0856	0952	0951	...	1152	1151	...	1252	1352	1351	...	1452	1452	1551	1551	...	1651	1752	1752
47	**Kleinreifling** **976** a.	0615	0737	...	0756	...	0859	0956	*1008*	...	1156	*1208*	...	1256	1356	*1408*	...	1456	1456	1556	*1608*	...	*1708*	1756	1756
61	Weißenbach-St Gallen **976** a.	*0648***a**	...	...	...	...	0916	...	...	...	1216	...	...	...	1416	...	...	...	1516	...	*1623*	...	*1723*	...	1816
119	**Selzthal** a.	...	...	...	...	...	1015	...	...	...	...	...	...	...	...	...	...	...	1615	...	...	...	...	...	...

	Ⓐ		Ⓐ	†			e				
Wien Westbahnhof **950** d.	...	...	...	...	...	...	...	1918**v**	...	...	...
Amstetten d.	1705	1805	1805	1805	1905	2005	2005	2105	2205	2305	0005
Waidhofen a. d. Ybbs d.	1730	1829	1830	1830	1930	2029	2033	2129	2229	2329	0029
Weyer d.	1748	...	1848	1848	1948	...	2051	...	...	...	...
Kastenreith **976** d.	1751	...	1852	1852	1952	...	2056	...	...	...	...
Kleinreifling **976** a.	*1808*	...	1856	1856	1956	...	2059	...	...	...	...
Weißenbach-St Gallen **976** a.	*1823*	...	...	1911	...	...	...	...	...	...	...
Selzthal a.	...	...	...	...	...	...	...	...	...	...	...

	⚒	Ⓐ		Ⓐ	Ⓐ		⚒		Ⓐ
Selzthal d.	...	...	...	...	...	...	...	...	...
Weißenbach-St Gallen **976** d.	...	...	...	...	...	...	*0603***a**	...	0706
Kleinreifling **976** d.	...	...	...	0504	...	0600	0623	...	0721
Kastenreith **976** d.	...	...	...	0508	...	0604	0632	...	0725
Weyer d.	...	...	...	0511	...	0609	0635	...	0728
Waidhofen a. d. Ybbs d.	0430	0459	0530	0530	0550	0628	0654	0734	...
Amstetten a.	0455	0526	0555	0555	0615	0655	0720	0755	...
Wien Westbahnhof **950** a.	0641**a**	0712	0741	0741	0812	...	...	0942	...

			Ⓐ	©		Ⓐ	©	©		Ⓐ	©		Ⓐ	Ⓐ	©		Ⓐ	Ⓐ	©		†				
Selzthal d.	...	...	...	...	...	...	1045	...	...	...	...	...	...	...	...	...	...	...	1645	...	...	...	...	...	...
Weißenbach-St Gallen **976** d.	...	...	*0940*	...	...	...	1144	...	...	*1338*	1341	...	...	...	*1541*	...	*1639*	*1738*	1744	...	...	1941	...	...	...
Kleinreifling **976** d.	0804	...	*0954*	1004	...	*1154*	1204	...	1304**a**	*1354*	1404	...	1504	*1554*	1604	...	*1654*	*1753*	1804	...	1904	1955	2000	...	...
Kastenreith **976** d.	0808	...	1008	1008	...	1208	1208	...	1308**a**	1408	1408	...	1508	1608	1608	...	1708	1808	1808	...	1908	...	2008	...	...
Weyer d.	0811	...	1011	1011	...	1211	1211	...	1311**a**	1411	1411	...	1511	1611	1611	...	1711	1811	1811	...	1911	...	2011	...	...
Waidhofen a. d. Ybbs d.	0830	0930	1030	1030	1130	1230	1230	1330	1330	1430	1430	1530	1530	1630	1630	1730	1730	1830	1830	1930	1930	...	2030	2130	2230
Amstetten a.	0855	0955	1055	1055	1155	1255	1255	1355	1355	1455	1455	1555	1555	1655	1655	1755	1755	1855	1855	1955	1955	...	2055	2155	2255
Wien Westbahnhof **950** a.	...	...	...	...	...	...	1442	1542	...	...	...	...	...	...	...	...	...	...	2012	...	...	...	2242**v**	...	...

a – Ⓐ only.
e – ⑦–④ (also Nov. 1; not Apr. 30, May 28, June 18, Aug. 14).
h – Arrives 0525.
j – Arrives 0652.
k – Ⓐ only. 0423 on ①.
v – † only.

980 WIEN - GRAZ and KLAGENFURT

km																												
				RJ 639		*RJ* 72				*RJ* 551		*RJ* 131		*RJ* 553		*IC* 733		*EC* 151		*IC* 533		*RJ* 71		*RJ* 559		*RJ* 535	*RJ* 73	
		Ⓐ			Ⓐ			⚒																				
		2	2	D✕	2	✕	2	2	2	✕	2	V✕	2	✕	2	C🍷	2	E✕	2	L🍷	2	K✕	2	✕	2	✕	P✕	2
	Flughafen Wien ✈ **985** d.	...	...	...	...	...	...	...	...	...	...	...	...	0633	...	...	...	...	...	...	...	...	...	0933	...	...	...	...
0	**Wien** Hbf **981 985** d.	...	...	...	...	...	...	...	...	0558	...	0624	...	0658	...	0724	...	0758	...	0824	...	0858	...	0958	...	1024	1058	...
4	**Wien** Meidling **981** d.	...	...	...	...	...	...	...	...	0605	...	0631	...	0705	...	0731	...	0805	...	0831	...	0905	...	1005	...	1031	1105	...
49	**Wiener Neustadt** Hbf **981** a.	...	...	...	...	...	...	...	...	0630	...	0654	...	0730	...	0754	...	0830	...	0854	...	0930	...	1030	...	1054	1130	...
	Wiener Neustadt Hbf **981** d.	...	...	...	...	...	...	...	...	0632	...	0656	...	0732	...	0756	...	0832	...	0856	...	0932	...	1032	...	1056	1132	...
104	Semmering **981** d.	...	...	...	...	...	...	...	...	|	...	|	...	0814	...	|	...	0914	...	|	...	1014	...	1114	...	|	1214	...
118	Mürzzuschlag **981** d.	...	0520**r**	...	...	...	0620**k**	0620	...	0728	...	|	...	0828	...	|	...	0928	...	|	...	1028	...	1128	...	|	1228	...
	Graz Hbf **975** ▷ d.	...	|	0519	...	0626	|	|	...	|	*0726*	|	...	|	*0826*	|	...	|	*0926*	|	...	|	*1026*	|	*1126*	|	|	*1226*
158	**Bruck** an der Mur a.	...	0600**r**	0557	...	0701	0701**k**	0701	...	0756	*0801*	0813	...	0856	*0901*	0913	...	0956	*1001*	1013	...	1056	*1101*	1156	*1201*	1213	1256	*1301*
158	**Bruck** an der Mur **975** ⊙ d.	0436	0608	0609	0636	...	0708	0706	0706	0758	0806	0815	...	0858	0906	0915	...	0958	1006	1015	...	1058	1106	1158	1206	1215	1258	1306
212	**Graz** Hbf ⊙ a.	|	0655	|	|	...	0755	|	|	0833	|	|	...	0933	|	|	...	1033	|	|	...	1133	|	1233	|	|	1333	|
174	Leoben Hbf **975** d.	0451	▬	0622	0650	...	...	0721	0721	▬	0821	0826	...	...	0921	0926	...	▬	1021	1026	...	...	1121	▬	1221	1226	...	1321
◧	St Michael **975** a.	0458	...	|	0657	...	...	0728	0728	...	0828	|	←	...	0928	|	←	...	1028	|	←	...	1128	...	1228	|	...	1328
◧	St Michael d.	0507	...	|	0702	...	...	0734	0734	...	0834	|	0834	...	0934	|	0934	...	1034	|	1034	...	1134	...	1234	|	...	1334
205	Knittelfeld d.	0525	...	0641	0720	...	...	0752	0752	...	→	0847	0852	...	→	0947	0952	...	→	1047	1052	...	1152	...	1252	1247	...	1352
213	Zeltweg d.	0531	⚒	|	0726	...	...	0758	0758	...	...	|	0858	...	...	|	0958	...	...	|	1058	...	1158	...	1258	|	...	1358
220	Judenburg d.	0539	2	0655	0734	...	...	0806	0806	...	...	0859	0906	...	...	0959	1006	...	...	1059	1106	...	1206	...	1306	1259	...	1406
239	Unzmarkt d.	0554	0612	0709	0750	...	...	0822	0822	2**L**	...	0913	0921	...	...	|	1022	2**L**	...	1113	1121	...	1222	2**L**	1321	1313	...	1422
276	Friesach **971** a.	...	0645	0739	...	...	...	0855	0855	0908	...	|	...	...	...	1042	1055	1108	...	1143	...	...	1255	1308	...	|	...	1455
309	St Veit an der Glan **971** a.	...	*0740*	0806	...	...	...	...	...	0940	...	1006	...	...	...	1107	...	1140	...	1206	...	...	...	1340	...	1406	...	...
329	**Klagenfurt** Hbf **971** ▷ a.	...	*0800*	0820	...	...	...	...	...	1000	...	1019	...	...	...	1119	...	1200	...	1219	...	...	...	1400	...	1419	...	...
	Villach Hbf **971** a.	...	*0839*	0846	...	...	...	...	...	1039	...	1044	...	...	...	1148	...	1239	...	1246	...	...	...	1439	...	1446	...	...

	IC 737	*RJ* 653		*RJ* 133		*RJ* 75		*IC* 739		*RJ* 657		*IC* 539		*RJ* 257		*D* 831		*IC* 359		*RJ* 631		*RJ* 79		*IC* 833		*RJ* 755		*RJ* 633
								⑤f			Ⓐ	d	Ⓐ			⑤f	⚒											
	C🍷	✕	2	V✕	2	P✕	2	L🍷	2	✕	2	L✕	2	N✕	2	L2	2	✕	2	D✕	2	P✕	2	C🍷	2	✕	2	✕
Flughafen Wien ✈ **985** d.	...	1133	...	...	...	...	...	...	...	1333	...	...	...	...	...	...	...	...	...	...	...	...	...	...	...	1733	...	...
Wien Hbf **981 985** d.	1124	1158	...	1224	...	1258	...	1324	...	1358	...	1424	...	1458	...	1524	...	1558	...	1624	...	1658	...	1724	...	1758	...	1824
Wien Meidling **981** d.	1131	1205	...	1231	...	1305	...	1331	...	1405	...	1431	...	1505	...	1531	...	1605	...	1631	...	1705	...	1731	...	1805	...	1831
Wiener Neustadt Hbf **981** a.	1154	1230	...	1254	...	1330	...	1354	...	1430	...	1454	...	1530	...	1554	...	1630	...	1654	...	1730	...	1754	...	1830	...	1854
Wiener Neustadt Hbf **981** d.	1156	1232	...	1256	...	1332	...	1356	...	1432	...	1456	...	1532	...	1556	...	1632	...	1656	...	1732	...	1756	...	1832	...	1856
Semmering **981** d.	|	1314	...	|	...	|	...	|	...	1514	...	|	...	|	...	|	...	|	...	|	...	|	...	|	...	1914	...	|
Mürzzuschlag **981** d.	|	1328	...	|	...	1428	...	|	...	1528	...	|	...	1628	...	|	...	1728	...	|	...	1828	...	|	...	1928	...	|
Graz Hbf **975** ▷ d.	|	|	*1326*	|	...	|	*1426*	|	...	|	*1526*	|	1601	|	*1626*	|	1701	|	*1726*	|	...	|	*1826*	|	...	|	*1926*	|
Bruck an der Mur a.	1313	1356	*1401*	1413	...	1456	*1501*	1513	...	1556	*1601*	1613	|	1656	*1701*	1713	|	1756	*1801*	1813	...	1856	*1901*	1913	...	1956	*2001*	2013
Bruck an der Mur **975** ⊙ d.	1315	1358	1406	1415	...	1458	1506	1515	...	1558	1606	1615	|	1658	1706	1715	|	1758	1806	1815	...	1858	1906	1915	...	1958	2006	2015
Graz Hbf ⊙ a.	|	1433	|	|	...	1533	|	|	...	1633	|	|	|	1733	|	|	|	1833	|	|	...	1933	|	|	...	2033	|	|
Leoben Hbf **975** d.	1326	▬	1421	1426	...	...	1521	1526	...	▬	1621	1626	1656	...	1721	1726	1758	▬	1821	1826	...	...	1921	1926	...	...	2021	2026
St Michael **975** a.	|	...	1428	|	←	...	1528	|	←	...	1628	|	1703	...	1728	|	|	...	1828	|	←	...	1928	|	←	...	2028	|
St Michael d.	|	...	1434	|	1434	...	1534	|	1534	...	1634	|	1709	...	1734	|	|	...	1834	|	1834	...	1934	|	1934	...	2034	|
Knittelfeld d.	1347	...	→	1447	1452	...	→	1547	1552	...	1652	1647	1728	...	1752	1747	1820	...	→	1847	1852	...	→	1947	1952	...	→	2047
Zeltweg d.	|	...	...	|	1458	...	...	|	1558	...	1658	|	1734	...	1758	|	1826	...	...	|	1858	...	...	|	1958	...	...	|
Judenburg d.	1359	...	...	1459	1506	...	...	1559	1606	...	1706	1659	1742	...	1806	1759	1834	...	...	1859	1906	...	...	1959	2006	...	...	2059
Unzmarkt d.	|	2**L**	...	1513	1521	...	...	|	1622	2**L**	1721	1713	1757	...	1822	|	1849	2**L**	...	1913	1921	...	...	|	2021	...	...	2113
Friesach **971** a.	1441	1508	...	1543	...	...	...	1641	1655	1708	...	|	...	...	1855	1841	...	1908	...	1943	...	...	...	2041	...	...	...	|
St Veit an der Glan **971** a.	1507	1540	...	1606	...	...	...	1707	...	1740	...	1806	...	...	...	1907	...	1940	...	2006	...	...	...	2107	...	...	...	2206
Klagenfurt Hbf **971** ▷ a.	1519	1600	...	1619	...	...	...	1719	...	1800	...	1819	...	...	...	1919	...	2000	...	2019	...	...	...	2119	...	...	...	2219
Villach Hbf **971** a.	1548	1639	...	1644	...	...	...	1748	...	1839	...	1846	...	...	...	1948	...	2039	...	2046	...	...	...	2148	...	...	...	2246

A – 🛏 1, 2 cl., ▬ 2 cl. and (2) La Spezia - Milano - Wien and v.v.;
🛏 1, 2 cl., ▬ 2 cl. and (2) (**40294/40233**) Roma - Bologna - Venezia - Wien and v.v.
B – 🛏 1, 2 cl., ▬ 2 cl. and (2) Graz - Wien - Brno - Dresden - Berlin (Table **60**).
C – Until July 13 to/from Mallnitz-Obervellach (Table **970** on page 580).
D – Until July 13 to/from Spittal-Millstättersee (Table **970** on page 580).
E – EMONA – (12) and ✕ Wien - Graz - Spielfeld-Straß 🛃 - Maribor - Ljubljana - Trieste and v.v. (Table **89**).
J – To/from Lienz on dates in Table **971**.
K – (12) and ✕ Graz - Wien - Břeclav 🛃 - Brno (- Praha ◻) and v.v. (Table **60**).
L – To/from Lienz (Table **971**).
N – (12) and ✕ Decin - Praha - Břeclav 🛃 - Wien - Graz and v.v. (Table **60**).
P – (12) and ✕ Graz - Wien - Břeclav 🛃 - Brno - Praha and v.v. (Table **60**).
Q – PORTA MORAVICA – (12) and ✕ Przemyśl - Kraków - Katowice - Wien - Graz and v.v. (Table **99**).
R – 🅁 for journeys from/to Italy.
S – (12) and ✕ Graz - Wien - Břeclav 🛃 - Brno (Table **60**).
T – Runs as *RJ* **1255** ((12) and ✕) on ⑤ (also Apr. 30, May 28, June 18, Aug. 14).
U – Runs as *RJ* **1252** ((12) and ✕) on ⑤ (also Apr. 30, May 28, June 18, Aug. 14).
V – (12) and ✕ Wien - Tarvisio 🛃 - Udine - Venezia and v.v. (Table **83**).

NOTES CONTINUE ON THE NEXT PAGE → → →

WIEN - GRAZ and KLAGENFURT — 980

		RJ 371		NJ 233	EC 107		RJ 373	RJ 853	IC 855 ⚒T
	2	P✕	2	AR	Q✕	2	P✕	✕	b2🍷
Flughafen Wien ✈ ..... 985 d.	...	...	...	...	...	...	...	2133	2302**a**
Wien Hbf ..... 981 985 d.	...	1858	...	1918	1958	...	2058	2158	2324
Wien Meidling ..... 981 d.	...	1905	...	1925	2005	...	2105	2205	2332
Wiener Neustadt Hbf .. 981 a.	...	1930	...	|	2030	...	2130	2230	2359
Wiener Neustadt Hbf .. 981 d.	...	1932	...	2002	2032	...	2132	2232	0002
Semmering ..... 981 d.	...	|	...	|	|	...	2214	|	|
Mürzzuschlag ..... 981 d.	...	2028	...	|	2128	...	2228	2328	0059
Graz Hbf ..... 975 ▷ d.	...	|	*2026*	|	|	*2126*	|	|	|
Bruck an der Mur ..... a.	...	2056	*2101*	|	2156	*2201*	2256	2356	0126
Bruck an der Mur ... 975 ⊙ d.	...	2058	2106	2126	2158	2206	2258	2358	0128
Graz Hbf ..... ⊙ a.	...	2133	|	|	2233	|	2333	0033	0203
Leoben Hbf ..... 975 d.	...	...	2121	2140	...	2220	...	...	...
St Michael ..... 975 a.	←	...	2128	|	...	|	...	...	...
St Michael ..... d.	2034	...	2134	|	...	|	...	...	...
Knittelfeld ..... d.	2052	...	2152	2205	...	2243	...	...	...
Zeltweg ..... d.	2058	...	2158	|	...	2249	...	...	...
Judenburg ..... d.	2106	...	2206	|	...	2256	...	...	...
Unzmarkt ..... d.	2121	...	2221	|	...	2311	...	...	...
Friesach ..... 971 a.	...	...	...	|	...	...	...	...	...
St Veit an der Glan ..... 971 a.	...	...	...	2322	...	...	...	...	...
Klagenfurt Hbf ..... 971 ▷ a.	...	...	...	2336	...	...	...	...	...
Villach Hbf 971 ..... a.	...	...	...	0001	...	...	...	...	...

		IC 854				EC 106		NJ 235				
	⚒ 2	Ⓐ 2🍷	⚒ 2	⚒ 2	⚒ 2	Q✕	⚒ 2	AR	⚒ 2	⚒ 2	Ⓐ 2	⚒ 2
Villach Hbf 971 ..... d.	...	...	...	...	...	...	...	0417	...	...	...	...
Klagenfurt Hbf ... 971 ▷ d.	...	...	...	...	...	...	...	0440	...	...	...	...
St Veit an der Glan .. 971 d.	...	...	...	...	...	...	...	|	...	...	...	...
Friesach ..... 971 d.	...	...	...	...	...	...	...	|	...	0527	...	...
Unzmarkt ..... d.	0332	...	...	0438	...	...	0528	|	0548	0601	0608	...
Judenburg ..... d.	0349	...	...	0454	...	...	0544	|	0605	▬	0624	...
Zeltweg ..... d.	0356	...	...	0502	...	...	0552	|	0612	...	0632	...
Knittelfeld ..... d.	0403	...	...	0508	...	...	0559	|	0619	*RJ*	0638	...
St Michael ..... a.	0421	...	...	0525	...	...	|	|	|	**72**	0655	...
St Michael ..... 975 d.	0426	...	...	0535	0531	...	|	|	|		0705	0701
Leoben Hbf ..... 975 d.	0434	...	...	0543	0539	...	0623	0627	0641	P✕	0713	0709
Graz Hbf ..... ⊙ d.	|	0414	0422	|	|	0526	|	|	|	0626	|	|
Bruck an der Mur 975 ⊙ a.	0448	0452	0508	0557	|	0601	|	0639	0655	0701	0727	|
Bruck an der Mur ..... d.	*0457*	0454	0512	*0608*	|	0603	|	|	*0708*	0703	*0730*	|
Graz Hbf ..... 975 ▷ a.	*0544*	|	|	*0655*	0635	|	0716	|	*0755*	|	*0814*	0801
Mürzzuschlag ..... 981 d.	...	0524	0552	...	...	0633	...	|	...	0733	...	...
Semmering ..... 981 d.	...	0537	...	...	...	|	...	|	...	0747	...	...
Wiener Neustadt Hbf 981 a.	...	0626	...	...	...	0726	...	0815	...	0828	...	...
Wiener Neustadt Hbf 981 d.	...	0628	...	...	...	0728	...	|	...	0830	...	...
Wien Meidling ..... 981 a.	...	0657	...	...	...	0757	...	0857	...	0855	...	...
Wien Hbf ..... 981 985 a.	...	0703	...	...	...	0803	...	0904	...	0902	...	...
Flughafen Wien ✈ .. 985 a.	...	...	...	...	...	...	...	...	...	...	...	...

		D 619	RJ 530	RJ 551		IC 730		RJ 74	RJ 532				RJ 256	IC 534				RJ 78	RJ 536				IC 736	RJ 370	RJ 132	
	2	2🍷	✕	✕	2	C🍷	2	P✕	✕	2	2	2	N✕	L✕	2	2L	2	P✕	D✕	2	2L	2	C🍷	P✕	V✕	2
Villach Hbf 971 ..... d.	...	...	0525	...	0529	0613	...	...	0714	...	0720	...	...	0914	...	0920	...	...	1114	...	1120	...	1213	...	1315	...
Klagenfurt Hbf ..... 971 ▷ d.	...	...	0548	...	0607	0639	...	...	0739	...	0804	...	...	0939	...	1004	...	...	1139	...	1204	...	1239	...	1339	...
St Veit an der Glan ..... 971 d.	...	...	0600	...	0627	0653	...	...	0753	...	0824	...	...	0953	...	1024	...	...	1153	...	1224	...	1253	...	1353	...
Friesach ..... 971 d.	...	...	|	...	0659	0718	...	...	|	...	0856	0904	...	1016	...	1056	1104	...	|	...	1256	1304	1318	...	1416	...
Unzmarkt ..... d.	0632	...	|	...	0733	|	0738	...	0848	0838	▬	0938	...	1048	1038	▬	1138	...	1248	1238	▬	1338	|	...	1448	1438
Judenburg ..... d.	0649	...	|	...	▬	0802	0754	...	0902	0854	...	0954	...	1102	1054	...	1154	...	1302	1254	...	1354	1402	...	1502	1454
Zeltweg ..... d.	0656	...	|	...	...	|	0802	...	|	0902	...	1002	...	|	1102	...	1202	...	|	1302	...	1402	|	...	|	1502
Knittelfeld ..... d.	0703	...	|	...	*RJ*	0814	0808	...	0914	0908	*RJ*	1008	...	1114	1108	*EC*	1208	...	1314	1308	*RJ*	1405	1414	...	1514	1508
St Michael ..... a.	|	...	|	...	**554**	|	0825	...	|	0925	**558**	1025	...	|	1125	**158**	1225	...	|	1325	**656**	1425	|	...	|	1525
St Michael ..... 975 d.	|	0722	|	...		|	0832	...	|	0932		1032	...	|	1132		1232	...	|	1332		1432	|	...	|	1532
Leoben Hbf ..... 975 d.	0725	0729	0733	...	✕	0833	0841	...	0933	0941	✕	1041	...	1133	1141	✕	1241	...	1333	1341	✕	1441	1433	...	1533	1541
Graz Hbf ..... ⊙ d.	|	|	|	...	0726	|	|	0826	|	|	0926	|	1026	|	|	1126	|	1226	|	|	1326	|	|	1426	|	|
Bruck an der Mur ... 975 ⊙ a.	0735	|	0743	...	0801	0843	0854	0901	0943	0954	1001	1054	1101	1143	1154	1201	1254	1301	1343	1354	1401	1454	1443	1501	1543	1554
Bruck an der Mur ..... d.	...	|	0745	0758	0803	0845	*0858*	0903	0945	*0958*	1003	*1058*	1103	1145	*1158*	1203	*1258*	1303	1345	*1358*	1403	*1458*	1445	1503	1545	*1558*
Graz Hbf ..... 975 ▷ a.	...	0817	|	0833	|	|	*0933*	|	|	*1033*	|	*1133*	|	|	*1233*	|	*1333*	|	|	*1433*	|	*1533*	|	|	|	*1633*
Mürzzuschlag ..... 981 d.	...	...	|	...	0833	|	...	0933	|	...	1033	...	1133	|	...	1233	...	1333	|	...	1433	...	|	1533	|	...
Semmering ..... 981 d.	...	...	|	...	0847	|	...	0947	|	...	|	...	1147	|	...	|	...	1347	|	...	|	...	|	1547	|	...
Wiener Neustadt Hbf .. 981 a.	...	...	0903	...	0928	1003	...	1028	1103	...	1128	...	1228	1303	...	1328	...	1428	1503	...	1528	...	1603	1628	1703	...
Wiener Neustadt Hbf .. 981 d.	...	...	0905	...	0930	1005	...	1030	1105	...	1130	...	1230	1305	...	1330	...	1430	1505	...	1530	...	1605	1630	1705	...
Wien Meidling ..... 981 a.	...	...	0929	...	0955	1029	...	1055	1129	...	1155	...	1255	1329	...	1355	...	1455	1529	...	1555	...	1629	1655	1729	...
Wien Hbf ..... 981 985 a.	...	...	0936	...	1002	1036	...	1102	1136	...	1202	...	1302	1336	...	1402	...	1502	1536	...	1602	...	1636	1702	1736	...
Flughafen Wien ✈ ..... 985 a.	...	...	...	...	1027	...	...	...	...	...	1227	...	...	...	...	...	...	...	...	...	1627	...	...	...	...	...

			D 738 ⑦w	RJ 372		RJ 630			IC 830	RJ 374		IC 632		⑦w	NJ 456			D 832 ⑦t	RJ 850	RJ 130	EC 107	D 852	IC 834 ⑦t			
	2L	2	2L	P✕	2	✕	2L	2	C🍷	S✕	2	L✕	2	2	B	2L	2	2	✕	V✕	✕	2U	L	2	2	2
Villach Hbf 971 ..... d.	1320	...	1413	...	...	1514	1520	...	1613	...	...	1714	...	...	...	1720	...	1813	...	1915	...	...	2013	...	...	...
Klagenfurt Hbf ..... 971 ▷ d.	1404	...	1439	...	...	1539	1604	...	1639	...	...	1739	...	...	...	1804	...	1839	...	1939	...	...	2039	...	...	...
St Veit an der Glan ..... 971 d.	1424	...	1553	...	...	1553	1624	...	1652	...	...	1753	...	...	...	1824	...	1852	...	1953	...	...	2053	...	...	...
Friesach ..... 971 d.	1456	1504	1518	...	...	|	1656	1704	1718	...	...	1816	...	...	...	1856	1904	1918	...	|	...	...	2118	...	...	...
Unzmarkt ..... d.	▬	1538	|	...	1638	1648	▬	1738	|	...	1838	1848	...	1906	...	▬	1938	|	...	2048	...	...	|	2138	...	...
Judenburg ..... d.	...	1554	1602	...	1654	1702	...	1754	1802	...	1854	1902	...	1919	...	...	1954	2002	...	2102	...	...	2118	2154	...	...
Zeltweg ..... d.	...	1602	|	...	1702	|	...	1802	|	...	1902	|	...	1927	...	...	2002	|	...	|	...	...	|	2202	...	...
Knittelfeld ..... d.	*RJ*	1608	1614	...	1708	1714	*RJ*	1808	1814	...	1908	1914	...	1933	...	*EC*	2008	2014	...	2114	...	...	2214	2208	...	...
St Michael ..... a.	**750**	1625	|	...	1725	|	**754**	1825	|	...	1925	|	←	|	...	**150**	2025	|	...	|	...	...	|	2225	...	...
St Michael ..... 975 d.		1632	|	...	1732	|		1832	|	...	1932	|	1932	|	...		2032	|	...	|	...	...	|	2232	...	...
Leoben Hbf ..... 975 d.	✕	1641	1633	...	1741	1733	✕	1841	1833	...	→	1933	1941	1954	...	E✕	2041	2033	...	2133	...	...	2233	2241	...	...
Graz Hbf ..... ⊙ d.	1526	|	|	1626	|	|	1726	|	|	1826	...	|	|	|	1920	1926	|	|	2026	|	...	2126	|	|	2205	0005
Bruck an der Mur ... 975 ⊙ a.	1601	1654	1643	1701	1754	1743	1801	1854	1843	1901	...	1943	1954	|	1957	2001	2054	2043	2101	2143	...	2201	2243	2254	2251	0051
Bruck an der Mur ..... d.	1603	*1658*	1645	1703	*1758*	1745	1803	*1858*	1845	1903	...	1945	*1958*	|	1959	2003	*2058*	2045	2103	2145	2158	2203	2245	*2258*	2308**r**	0054**p**
Graz Hbf ..... 975 ▷ a.	|	*1733*	|	|	*1833*	|	|	*1933*	|	|	...	|	*2033*	2038	|	|	*2133*	|	|	|	2233	|	|	*2333*	|	|
Mürzzuschlag ..... 981 d.	1633	...	|	1733	...	|	1833	...	|	1933	...	|	...	...	2026	2033	...	|	2133	|	...	2233	|	...	2350**r**	0135**p**
Semmering ..... 981 d.	|	...	|	1747	...	|	1847	...	|	|	...	|	...	...	|	|	...	|	|	|	...	2247	|	...	...	...
Wiener Neustadt Hbf .. 981 a.	1728	...	1803	1828	...	1903	1928	...	2003	2028	...	2103	...	...	2130	2128	...	2203	2228	2303	...	2328	0003	...	...	...
Wiener Neustadt Hbf .. 981 d.	1730	...	1805	1830	...	1905	1930	...	2005	2030	...	2105	...	...	2132	2130	...	2205	2230	2305	...	2330	0005	...	...	...
Wien Meidling ..... 981 a.	1755	...	1829	1855	...	1929	1955	...	2029	2055	...	2129	...	...	|	2155	...	2229	2255	2329	...	2355	0029	...	...	...
Wien Hbf ..... 981 985 a.	1802	...	1836	1902	...	1936	2002	...	2036	2102	...	2136	...	...	2207	2202	...	2236	2302	2336	...	0002	0036	...	...	...
Flughafen Wien ✈ ..... 985 a.	1827	...	...	...	...	...	2027	...	...	...	...	...	...	...	...	...	...	...	...	...	...	...	...	...	...	...

Local stopping trains **BRUCK AN DER MUR - GRAZ - SPIELFELD-STRASS** (for international services Graz - Spielfeld Straß - Maribor - Ljubljana / Zagreb see Table **1315**).

km				Ⓐ	⊖						
	Bruck a. d. Mur ..... d.	*0457*	*0608*	*0649*	*0708*	and	*1908*	*2008*	*2108*	*2208*	*2308*
	Graz Hbf ..... a.	*0544*	*0655*	*0728*	*0755*		*1955*	*2055*	*2155*	*2255*	*2355*
0	**Graz** Hbf ..... 1315 d.	0610	0710	0740	0810	hourly	2010	2110	2210	2310	0010
9	Flughafen Graz ✈ ..... d.	0621	0721	0751	0821		2021	2121	2221	2321	0021
35	Leibnitz ..... d.	0649	0749	0819	0849	until	2049	2149	2249	2349	0049
47	**Spielfeld-Straß 1315** a.	0659	0759	0829	0859		2059	2205	2259	2359	0059

	Ⓐ			⚒			✣				
Spielfeld-Straß 1315 d.	0400	0430	0500	0525	0600	0700	and	1854	2000	2100	2151
Leibnitz ..... d.	0410	0440	0510	0535	0610	0710		1910**c**	2010	2110	2210**e**
Flughafen Graz ✈ .. d.	0438	0508	0538	0603	0638	0738	hourly	1938	2038	2138	2238
Graz Hbf ..... 1315 a.	0450	0520	0550	0615	0652	0750		1950	2050	2150	2250
Graz Hbf ..... d.	...	...	*0609*	*0640***n**	*0700*	*0805*	until	*2005*	*2105*	*2205*	*2305*
Bruck a. d. Mur ..... a.	...	...	*0655*	*0729***n**	*0746*	*0851*		*2051*	*2151*	*2251*	*2351*

ÖBB *Intercitybus* services **GRAZ - KLAGENFURT**. Rail tickets valid. 1st and 2nd class. 🍷 in 1st class. Number of seats limited so reservation is recommended.

	🚌	🚌	🚌		🚌	🚌	🚌	🚌	🚌	
Graz Hbf ..... d.	0545	0745	0945	...	1145	1345	1545	1745	1945	...
Klagenfurt Hbf ..... a.	0745	0945	1145	...	1345	1545	1745	1945	2145	...

	🚌	🚌	🚌		🚌	🚌	🚌		🚌	🚌	
Klagenfurt Hbf ..... d.	0615	0815	1015	...	1215	1415	1615	...	1815	2015	...
Graz Hbf ..... a.	0815	1015	1215	...	1415	1615	1815	...	2015	2215	...

← ← ← **NOTES** (continued from previous page).

- **a** – ⑤ (also Apr. 30, May 28, June 18, Aug. 14).
- **b** – ⚒ (not Apr. 21, June 9, Dec. 8). Also calls at Baden (d. 2347).
- **c** – Arrives 1903.
- **d** – Runs as *IC* **839** on ⑦ (also Apr. 21, June 9, Dec. 8; not Apr. 20, June 8).
- **e** – Arrives 2202.
- **f** – ⑤ (also Apr. 17, 30, May 28, June 18, Aug. 14; not May 2, 30, June 20, Aug. 15).
- **k** – ✝ only.
- **n** – Ⓐ only.
- **p** – Ⓒ only.
- **r** – ⚒ only.
- **t** – ⑦ (also Apr. 17, 21, June 9, Dec. 8; not Apr. 20, June 8, Dec. 7).
- **w** – ⑦ (also Apr. 21, June 9, Dec. 8; not Apr. 20, June 8, Dec. 7).
- **y** – Runs on Feb. 3, 10, Mar. 23, 30, May 9, 18, 30, June 29, Oct. 26.
- ● – Praha - Berlin from Mar. 20.
- ✣ – Spielfeld-Straß departs 1053 (not 1100) and arrives Leibnitz 1103; the 0800 from Spielfeld-Straß runs on Ⓑ only.
- ⊙ – For other local journeys see panel below main table.
- ▷ – For fast **ÖBB** *Intercitybus* services Graz - Klagenfurt and v.v., see panel below main table.
- ⊖ – The 0908 from Bruck departs Graz 1005, Flughafen Graz 1016, Leibnitz 1048 and arrives Spielfeld-Straß 1107.
- ⊡ – Brno - Praha and v.v. on ⚒ (not Apr. 19, 21, Nov. 17).
- ◧ – Leoben - St Michael is *10 km*. St Michael - Knittelfeld is *22 km*.

981 Local trains WIEN - WIENER NEUSTADT - MÜRZZUSCHLAG

2nd class only

WIEN - WIENER NEUSTADT ⊡

km			Ⓐ							
0	**Wien** Floridsdorf d.	0409	0449	0509	0539		2309	2339	0009c	0052
5	**Wien** Praterstern d.	0418	0457	0518	0548	and at	2318	2348	0018	0100
7	**Wien** Mitte d.	0422	0501	0522	0552	the same	2322	2352	0022	0105
10	**Wien** Hbf d.	0429	0508	0529	0559	minutes	2329	2359	0029	0112
14	**Wien** Meidling d.	0437	0515	0537	0607	past each	2337	0007	0037	0120
26	Mödling d.	0449	0529	0549	0619	hour until	2349	0019	0049	0137
37	Baden d.	0457	0536	0557	0627		2358	0027	0057	0149
59	**Wiener Neustadt** Hbf a.	0521	0551	0621	0648		0022	0048	0121	0216

Wiener Neustadt Hbf d.	0503		0733	0811	0838		2211	2238	2311	0011
Baden d.	0523		0753	0833	0903	and at	2233	2303	2333	0033
Mödling d.	0530	and every	0800	0840	0910	the same	2240	2310	2340	0040
Wien Meidling a.	0542	30 minutes	0812	0853	0923	minutes	2253	2323	2353	0053
Wien Hbf a.	0549	until	0819	0900	0930	past each	2300	2330	0000	0100
Wien Mitte a.	0556		0826	0907	0937	hour until	2307	2337	0007	0104
Wien Praterstern a.	0600		0830	0911	0941		2311	2341	0011	0111
Wien Floridsdorf a.	0609		0839	0919	0949		2319	2349	0019	0119

(WIEN -) WIENER NEUSTADT - PAYERBACH-REICHENAU - MÜRZZUSCHLAG ⊡

km		⚒				©B				⊖	◇	⊖		⊖	⊖	◇	Ⓐ				Ⓐ						
	Wien Hbf d.	0523a	0553	0623	...	0727	0753	0823	...	0953	...	1053	and	1453	1553	...	1623	...	1653	1753	1823	...	1853	1953	2053	2253	2353
	Wien Meidling d.	0535a	0602	0635	...	0735	0802	0835	...	1002	...	1102	hourly	1502	1602	...	1635	...	1702	1802	1835	...	1902	2002	2102	2302	0002
	Baden d.	0547a	0614	0647a	...	0747	0814	0847a	...	1014	...	1114	(⊖)	1514	1614	...	1647	...	1714	1814	1847	...	1914	2014	2114	2314	0014
	Wiener Neustadt Hbf a.	0600a	0627	0700	...	0800	0827	0900	...	1027	...	1127	or	1527	1627	...	1700	...	1727	1827	1900	...	1927	2027	2127	2327	0027
0	**Wiener Neustadt** Hbf d.	0605	0635	0705a	0705c	0802	0835	0905a	0905c	1035	...	1135	every	1535	1635	...	1705	1705c	1735	1835	1905	1905c	1935	2035	2135	2335	0035
14	Neunkirchen NÖ d.	0615	0645	0715a	0715c	0811	0845	0915a	0915c	1045	...	1145	**two**	1545	1645	...	1715	1715c	1745	1845	1915	1915c	1945	2045	2145	2345	0045
27	Gloggnitz d.	0626	0656	0726a	0726c	0819	0856	0926a	0926c	1056	...	1156	hours	1556	1656	...	1726	1726c	1756	1856	1926	1926c	1956	2056	2156	2356	0056
34	Payerbach-Reichenau d.	0635	0705	0735a	0739	0827	0905	0935a	0939	1105	1139	1205	(◇)	1605	1705	1739	1735	1739	1805	1905	1935	1939	2005	2105	2205	0006	0105
55	Semmering a.	...	...	...	0807	0856	...	...	1007	...	1207	...	until	...	...	1707	...	1807	...	...	...	2007	...	...	*2238*	0032	...
69	**Mürzzuschlag** a.	...	...	...	0823	0912	...	...	1023	...	1223	...		...	...	1723	...	1823	...	...	...	2023	...	...	*2254*	0049	...

	Ⓐ		GⒶ	©	Ⓐ		©	Ⓐ		⊖	◇	⊖		◇	⊖	⊖		❖	Ⓐ	©B			❖	©			
Mürzzuschlag d.	0342	...	0524	0525	0606	...	0637	...	...	...	0837	...	and	1437	...	...	...	1637	...	1650	...	...	1837	1850	...	2101	...
Semmering d.	0358	...	0537	0540	0621	...	0652	...	...	...	0852	...	hourly	1452	...	...	...	1652	...	1707	...	...	1852	1907	...	2116	...
Payerbach-Reichenau d.	0425	0525	0602	0607	0650	0653	0725	0725	0755	0855	0921	0955	(⊖)	1521	1455	1555	1655	1725	1725	1735	1755	1855	1925	1935	1955	2151	2155
Gloggnitz d.	0434	0534	0611	0615	...	0702	0734	0734	0804	0904	...	1004	or	...	1504	1604	1704	1734	1734	1743	1804	1904	1934	1943	2004	...	2204
Neunkirchen NÖ d.	0444	0544	|	|	...	0712	0744	0744	0814	0914	...	1014	every	...	1514	1614	1714	1744	1744	1750	1814	1914	1944	1950	2014	...	2214
Wiener Neustadt Hbf a.	0454	0554	0626	0628	...	0723	0754	0754	0825	0925	...	1025	**two**	...	1525	1625	1725	1754	1754	1758	1825	1925	1954	1958	2025	...	2225
Wiener Neustadt Hbf d.	0500	0600	0628	0630	...	0730	*0800*	0800	0833	0933	...	1033	hours	...	1533	1633	1733	...	1800	1800	1833	1933	...	2000	2033	...	2233
Baden d.	0512	0612	|	0642	...	0742	*0812*	0812	0845	0945	...	1045	(◇)	...	1545	1645	1745	...	1812	1812	1845	1945	...	2012	2045	...	2245
Wien Meidling a.	0527	0629	0657	0659	...	0759	*0829*	0829	0858	0958	...	1058	until	...	1558	1658	1758	...	1826	1825	1858	1958	...	2026	2058	...	2258
Wien Hbf a.	0532	0635	0703	0706	...	0806	*0835*	0835	0904	1004	...	1104		...	1604	1704	1804	...	1832	...	1904	2004	...	2033	2104	...	2304

B – From / to Bratislava-Petržalka (Table **997**).
G – From Graz (Table **980**).

a – Ⓐ only.
c – © only.

⊖ – Train runs hourly.
◇ – Train runs every two hours.
❖ – Change at Payerbach-Reichenau on Ⓐ.
⊡ – Only selected services are shown Wien Floridsdorf - Wiener Neustadt - Payerbach-Reichenau and v.v. Some services may only run on certain dates - check locally for details. Additional journeys Wien Floridsdorf - Wiener Neustadt are shown in Tables **982** and **983**. See Table **980** for long-distance services.

982 Local trains WIEN - BŘECLAV

2nd class only — Austrian Holiday dates apply

See Table **1150** for other fast international services

km				Ⓐ		E		E		E			E				E				E				
	Wiener Neustadt Hbf . 980/1 d.	...	0448a	0615	0715a	0811	0911	1011	1111	1211	1238	1311	1411	1438	1511	1538	1611	1638	1711	1738	1811	1911	2011	2111	2211
	Baden 981 d.	...	0515a	0638	0738a	0833	0933	1033	1133	1233	1303	1333	1433	1503	1533	1603	1633	1703	1733	1803	1833	1933	2033	2133	2233
0	**Wien** Meidling 980/1 d.	0454	0557	0657	0757	0854	0954	1054	1154	1254	1324	1354	1454	1524	1554	1624	1654	1724	1754	1824	1854	1954	2054	2154	2254
4	**Wien** Hbf 980/1 d.	0500	0603	0703	0803	0900	1000	1100	1200	1300	1330	1400	1500	1530	1600	1630	1700	1730	1800	1830	1900	2000	2100	2200	2300
7	**Wien** Mitte 981 d.	0507	0610	0710	0810	0907	1007	1107	1207	1307	1337	1407	1507	1537	1607	1637	1707	1737	1807	1837	1907	2007	2107	2207	2307
9	**Wien** Praterstern 981 d.	0511	0614	0714	0814	0911	1011	1111	1211	1311	1341	1411	1511	1541	1611	1641	1711	1741	1811	1841	1911	2011	2111	2211	2311
14	**Wien** Floridsdorf 981 d.	0520	0623	0723	0823	0920	1020	1120	1220	1320	1350	1420	1520	1550	1620	1650	1720	1750	1820	1850	1920	2020	2120	2220	2320
40	Gänserndorf d.	0543	0646	0746	0846	0943	1043	1143	1243	1343	1413a	1443	1543	1612a	1643	1713a	1743	1814a	1843	1913a	1943	2043	2143	2243	2343
74	Hohenau 🏛 a.	0613	0716	0816	0916	1013	1113	1213	1313	1413	1443a	1513	1613	1643a	1713	1736a	1813	1837a	1913	1936a	2013	2113	2213	2313	0013
92	**Břeclav** 🏛 a.	0629	0732	0832	0932	1029	1129	1229	1329	1429	...	1529	1629	...	1729	...	1829	...	1929	...	2029	2129	...	2329	...

									D		D		D			D				D		D			
Břeclav 🏛 d.	0427	...	...	0557a	0627c	0657a	0727	0827	0927	1027	1127	1227	1327	1427	...	1527	...	1627	...	1727	1827	1927	2027	2127a	2227
Hohenau 🏛 d.	0443	0513a	0543	0613a	0643	0713a	0743	0843	0943	1043	1143	1243	1343	1443	1513a	1543	1616a	1643	1717a	1743	1843	1943	2043	2143a	2242
Gänserndorf d.	0514	0544a	0614	0644a	0714	0744a	0814	0914	1014	1114	1214	1314	1414	1514	1544a	1614	1641a	1714	1741a	1814	1914	2014	2114	2214a	2315
Wien Floridsdorf 981 d.	0539	0609	0639	0709	0739	0809	0839	0939	1039	1139	1239	1339	1439	1539	1609	1639	1709	1739	1809	1839	1939	2039	2139	2239	2339
Wien Praterstern 981 a.	0546	0616	0646	0716	0746	0816	0846	0946	1046	1146	1246	1346	1446	1546	1616	1646	1716	1746	1816	1846	1946	2046	2146	2246	2346
Wien Mitte 981 a.	0551	0621	0651	0721	0751	0821	0851	0951	1051	1151	1251	1351	1451	1551	1621	1651	1721	1751	1821	1851	1951	2051	2151	2251	2350
Wien Hbf 980/1 a.	0558	0628	0658	0728	0758	0828	0858	0958	1058	1158	1258	1358	1458	1558	1628	1658	1728	1758	1828	1858	1958	2058	2158	2258	2358
Wien Meidling 980/1 a.	0604	0634	0704	0734	0804	0834	0904	1004	1104	1204	1304	1404	1504	1604	1634	1704	1734	1804	1834	1904	2004	2104	2204	2304	0004
Baden 981 a.	0626	0656	0726	0756	0826	0856	0926	1026	1126	1226	1326	1426	1526	1626	1656	1726	1756	1829	1856	1926	2026	2126	2226	2326	0026
Wiener Neustadt Hbf 980/1 a.	0648	0721	0748	0821	0848	0921	0948	1048	1148	1248	1348	1448	1548	1648	1721	1748	1821	1848	1921	1948	2048	2148	2248	2348	0048

D – Břeclav - Gänserndorf on Ⓐ only; Gänserndorf - Wiener Neustadt daily.
E – Wiener Neustadt - Gänserndorf daily; Gänserndorf - Břeclav on Ⓐ only.

a – Ⓐ only.
c – © only.

983 WIEN - RETZ - ZNOJMO

2nd class only — Austrian holiday dates apply

km		⚒											Ⓐ		Ⓐ		Ⓐ		Ⓐ						
	Wiener Neustadt Hbf 980/1 d.	...	0503	0603	0703	0808r	0908a	...	...	...	...	...	...	1508a	1535	1608a	1635	1708a	1735	1808a	1908a	2008a	...	...	...
	Baden 981 d.	...	0523	0623	0723	0823r	0923a	...	...	...	...	...	...	1523a	1553	1623a	1653	1723a	1753	1823a	1923a	2023a	...	...	...
0	**Wien** Meidling 980/1 d.	...	0544	0644	0744	0844	0944	1044	1144	1244	1344	1444	1514	1544	1614	1644	1714	1744	1814	1844	1944	2044	2144	2244	2344
4	**Wien** Hbf 980/1 d.	...	0550	0650	0750	0850	0950	1050	1150	1250	1350	1450	1520	1550	1620	1650	1720	1750	1820	1850	1950	2050	2150	2250	2350
7	**Wien** Mitte 981 d.	...	0557	0657	0757	0857	0957	1057	1157	1257	1357	1457	1527	1557	1627	1657	1727	1757	1827	1857	1957	2057	2157	2257	2357
9	**Wien** Praterstern 981 d.	...	0601	0701	0801	0901	1001	1101	1201	1301	1401	1501	1531	1601	1631	1701	1731	1801	1831	1901	2001	2101	2201	2301	0001
14	**Wien** Floridsdorf 981 d.	...	0611	0711	0811	0911	1011	1111	1211	1311	1411	1511	1541	1611	1641	1711	1741	1811	1841	1911	2011	2111	2211	2311	0011
34	Stockerau d.	...	0628	0728	0828	0928	1028	1128	1228	1328	1428	1528	1601	1628	1701	1728	1801	1828	1901	1928	2028	2128	2228	2328	0028
60	Hollabrunn d.	...	0645	0745	0845	0945	1045	1145	1245	1345	1445	1545	1623	1645	1723	1745	1823	1845	1923	1945	2045	2145	2245	2345	0045
90	**Retz** a.	...	0712	0812	0912	1012	1112	1212	1312	1412	1512	1612	1652	1712	1752	1812	1852	1912	1952	2012	2112	2212	2312	0012	0121
90	**Retz** 🏛 d.	0620	...	0817	...	1017	...	1217	...	1417	1517a	1617	...	...	...	1817	...	...	...	2017	...	...	...	...	...
96	Šatov 🏛 d.	0628	...	0825	...	1025	...	1225	...	1425	1525a	1625	...	...	...	1825	...	...	...	2025	...	...	...	...	...
107	**Znojmo** a.	0638	...	0836	...	1036	...	1236	...	1436	1536a	1636	...	...	...	1836	...	...	...	2036	...	...	...	...	...

		Ⓐ		Ⓐ	Ⓐ		Ⓐ		⚒									Ⓐ	©						
Znojmo d.	...	...	...	...	...	0555a	...	...	0655	...	0857	...	1057	...	1257	...	1457	1557	...	1657	...	1857	...	2057	...
Šatov 🏛 d.	...	...	...	...	...	0606a	...	...	0706	...	0906	...	1106	...	1306	...	1506	1606	...	1706	...	1906	...	2106	...
Retz 🏛 a.	...	...	...	...	...	0614a	...	...	0714	...	0914	...	1114	...	1314	...	1514	1614	...	1714	...	1914	...	2114	...
Retz d.	0404	0434	0510	0530	0552	0616	0636	0716	0716	0816	0916	1016	1116	1216	1316	1416	1516	1616	1616	1716	1816	1916	2016	2116	2216
Hollabrunn d.	0430	0502	0539	0558	0620	0645	0706	0745	0745	0845	0945	1045	1145	1245	1345	1445	1545	1645	1645	1745	1845	1945	2045	2145	2245
Stockerau d.	0447	0527	0556	0625	0640	0702	0728	0802	0802	0902	1002	1102	1202	1302	1402	1502	1602	1702	1702	1802	1902	2002	2102	2202	2302
Wien Floridsdorf 981 d.	0503	0549	0619	0649	0700	0719	0749	0819	0819	0919	1019	1119	1219	1319	1419	1519	1619	1719	1719	1819	1919	2019	2119	2219	2319
Wien Praterstern 981 a.	0510	0556	0626	0656	0707	0726	0756	0826	0826	0926	1026	1126	1226	1326	1426	1526	1626	1726	1726	1826	1926	2026	2126	2226	2326
Wien Mitte 981 a.	0515	0600	0630	0700	0712	0730	0800	0830	0830	0930	1030	1130	1230	1330	1430	1530	1630	1730	1730	1830	1930	2030	2130	2230	2330
Wien Hbf 980/1 a.	0522	0608	0638	0708	0719	0738	0808	0838	0838	0938	1038	1138	1238	1338	1438	1538	1638	1738	1738	1838	1938	2038	2138	2238	2338
Wien Meidling 980/1 a.	0528	0614	0644	0714	0725	0744	0814	0844	0844	0944	1044	1144	1244	1344	1444	1544	1644	1744	1744	1844	1944	2044	2144	2244	2344
Baden 981 a.	0547a	0635	0705a	0735	...	0805r	0835	...	...	...	...	...	...	...	1505a	1605a	1705a	1805	...	1905a	2005a	...	...	...	...
Wiener Neustadt Hbf 980/1 a.	0600a	0651	0724a	0751	...	0824r	0851	...	...	...	...	...	...	...	1524a	1624a	1724a	1824	...	1924a	2024a	...	...	...	...

a – Ⓐ only.
r – ⚒ only.

2nd class only — WIENER NEUSTADT - PUCHBERG am Schneeberg - HOCHSCHNEEBERG — 984

WIENER NEUSTADT - **PUCHBERG** am Schneeberg *28 km.* Journey time: 45 – 48 minutes.
From Wiener Neustadt at 0037 Ⓒ, 0609 Ⓐ, 0637 Ⓒ, 0737 and hourly until 2237, 2337.
From Puchberg at 0406 Ⓐ, 0452 Ⓐ, 0522 Ⓐ, 0536 Ⓒ, 0552 Ⓐ, 0622 Ⓐ, 0636 Ⓒ, 0645 Ⓐ, 0736, 0836 and hourly until 2136, 2236 ⑤⑥.

PUCHBERG am Schneeberg - **HOCHSCHNEEBERG** *Schneebergbahn* (narrow-gauge rack railway). *9 km.* Journey time: ± 40 minutes.
Services operate April 26 - Nov. 23, **subject to demand and weather conditions**. Operator: **NÖ Schneebergbahn GmbH, Bahnhofplatz 1, A-2734 Puchberg.** ✆ +43 (0) 2636 3661 20.
From Puchberg at 0900, 1030, 1200, 1430, 1600. **From Hochschneeberg** at 0945, 1115, 1345, 1515, 1645. Additional trains operate during June, July and August, also at other times when there is sufficient demand. A steam service operates on † June 1, 15, 29, July 13, 27, Aug. 10, 24, Sept. 7, 21. Departs Puchberg 1050, departs Hochschneeberg 1547 (extended journey time; special fares apply).

CAT ★; S-Bahn (2nd class only) — FLUGHAFEN WIEN ✈ Schwechat — 985

km																						
						★		★		★			★		★		★					
0	**Wien** Floridsdorf ... d.	0406	0436	...	0506	...	0536	...	0606	...	0636	and at the same	...	2206	...	2236	...	2306	...	2336	0006	...	0036
5	**Wien** Praterstern ... d.	0415	0445	...	0515	...	0545	...	0615	...	0645	minutes past	...	2215	...	2245	...	2315	...	2345	0015	...	0045
7	**Wien** Mitte ... d.	0419	0449	...	0519	0537	0549	0607	0619	0637	0649	each hour until	2207	2219	2237	2249	2307	2319	...	2349	0019	...	0049
26	**Flughafen Wien** ✈ ... a.	0441	0511	...	0541	0553	0611	0623	0641	0653	0711		2223	2241	2253	2311	2323	2341	...	0011	0041	...	0111

				★		★		★		★		★		★			★		★			
Flughafen Wien ✈ ... d.	0449	0519	0549	0607	0619	0637	0649	0707	0719	0737	0749	0807	0819	0837	0849	and at the same	2307	2319	2337	2349	0019	0049	0119
Wien Mitte ... d.	0513	0543	0613	0624	0643	0654	0713	0724	0743	0754	0813	0824	0843	0854	0913	minutes past	2324	2343	2354	0013	0043	0113	0142
Wien Praterstern ... d.	0517	0547	0617	...	0647	...	0717	...	0747	...	0817	...	0847	...	0917	each hour until	...	2347	...	0017	0047	0117	0146
Wien Floridsdorf ... a.	0525	0555	0625	...	0655	...	0725	...	0755	...	0825	...	0855	...	0925		...	2355	...	0025	0055	0125	0155

★ – *City Airport Train (CAT).* Non-stop service with special fares.

RJ trains **Wien Hbf** - **Flughafen Wien** ✈ and v.v. Journey time: 15 – 17 minutes. Most trains run from / to Salzburg, Linz and St Pölten (Table **950**) or Graz (Table **980**).
From Wien Hbf at 0542, 0612, 0642, 0712, 0742, 0812, 0840, 0912, 0942, 1012, 1040, 1112, 1142, 1212, 1240, 1312, 1342, 1412, 1440, 1512, 1542, 1612, 1640, 1712, 1742, 1812, 1840, 1912, 1940, 2012, 2040, 2112, 2142, 2212 and 2242. **From Flughafen Wien** ✈ at 0002, 0633, 0702, 0733 and at the same times past each hour until 2202, 2233, 2302.

🚌 *Vienna Airport Lines*: Wien Westbahnhof (Europaplatz) – Flughafen Wien ✈ and v.v. Journey time: 40 minutes.
🚌 From **Wien Westbahnhof**: 0030, 0130, 0230, 0300, 0330 and every 30 minutes until 2330, 0000.
🚌 From **Flughafen Wien** ✈ 0030, 0130, 0230, 0330, 0430, 0530 and every 30 minutes until 2330, 0000.

🚌 Slovak Lines: **Bratislava**, AS Mlynské nivy (bus station) – **Flughafen Wien** ✈ and v.v. Journey time: 60 – 65 minutes.
Reservation recommended ✆ +43 (0) 810 222333-6 or +421 2 55422734. Please note that a much reduced service operates on Dec. 24, 25, 26, 31, Jan. 1.
🚌 From **Bratislava** AS Mlynské nivy at 0830, 0915, 1015, 1205, 1330, 1430, 1645, 2230.
🚌 From **Flughafen Wien** ✈ at 0950, 1055, 1150, 1320, 1445, 1550, 1815, 2359.

ÖBB, GySEV •; 2nd class only — GRAZ - SZENTGOTTHÁRD - SZOMBATHELY — 986

km																											
					A							⊖		Ⓐ		Ⓐ		Ⓐ				Ⓐ					
0	**Graz** Hbf ... d.	0607	0707	0807	0837	0907	1008	1107	1207	1307	1407	1437	1507	1537	1607	1637	1707	1737	1807	1837	1907	1937	2007	2107	2207	2307	0007
29	Gleisdorf ... d.	0650	0749	0850	0914	0950	1050	1150	1250	1350	1450	1513	1550	1613	1650	1713	1750	1813	1850	1913	1950	2013	2050	2150	2249	2345	0045
53	Feldbach ... d.	0714	0814	0914	0929	1014	1114	1214	1314	1414	1514	1530	1614	1630	1714	1730	1814	1830	1914	1930	2014	2033	2114	2214	2310	0006	0106
62	Fehring ... d.	0727	0822	0924	0938	1022	1124	1227**v**	1326	1431**j**	1524	1538	1622	1637	1724	1737	1822	1837	1924	1942**v**	2022	2042	2130**t**	2222	2318	0015	0115
82	**Szentgotthárd** 🏛 a.	0748	...	0945	0956	...	1145	1248	1347	1452**a**	1545**c**	1556	...	*1703*	1745**c**	*1803*	...	...	1945**c**	2003**a**	...	2103	2151	...	...	...	...

		Ⓐ		Ⓐ	Ⓐ	⑥	†	Ⓐ	⚒	Ⓐ H						⊖		Ⓐ	Ⓒ						B		
Szentgotthárd 🏛 .. d.	...	*0450*	0518**k**	*0534*	...	...	0618	*0620*	0642**k**	...	...	0818	...	1018	...	1206	1304	1409	1418	*1509***a**	1618	1718**a**	1818	...	2006	...	2108
Fehring ... d.	0406	0514	0541	0558	0616	0618	0641	0644	0704	0733	0741	0841	0941	1041	1141	1225	1326**z**	1432	1441	1541	1641	1741	1841	1941	2025	2041	2141**h**
Feldbach ... d.	0416	0523	0550	0606	0626	0627	0650	0654	0715	0741	0750	0850	0950	1050	1150	1234	1350**z**	1450**t**	1450	1550	1650	1750	1850	1950	2034	2050	2153
Gleisdorf ... d.	0439	0542	0613	0626	0650	0655	0713	0714	0738	0802	0813	0914	1013	1113	1213	1250	1413	1513	1513	1613	1713	1813	1913	2013	2050	2113	2213
Graz Hbf ... a.	0515	0615	0653	0704	0724	0734	0753	0748	0816	0836	0853	0953	1053	1153	1253	1320	1453	1553	1553	1653	1753	1853	1953	2053	2120	2153	2253

SZENTGOTTHÁRD - SZOMBATHELY •

km																										
				⊖		⚒			A				Ⓐ		⚒		Ⓐ	⊖	Ⓐ							
0	**Szentgotthárd** 🏛 ... d.	0401	0431	0501	0606	0636	0706	0806	1006	1206	...	1306	1336	1406	1436	1506	1536	1606	1636	1706	1806	1906	...	2006	2106	2236
28	Körmend ... d.	0425	0455	0525	0630	0700	0730	0830	1030	1230	...	1330	1400	1430	1500	1530	1600	1630	1700	1730	1830	1930	...	2030	2130	2300
64	**Szombathely** ... a.	0448	0518	0547	0653	0723	0753	0853	1053	1253	...	1353	1423	1453	1523	1553	1623	1653	1723	1753	1853	1953	...	2053	2153	2323
	Sopron **1233** ... a.	0556	...	...	*0750*	...	0851	0951	*1151*	1351	...	1451	*1531*	1551	...	1651	...	*1751*	...	1851	1951	2051	...	2151	*2327*	...

				⚒				⊖	⚒		Ⓐ		Ⓐ		Ⓐ			Ⓐ				B			⊖	
Sopron **1233** ... d.	...	0408	0452	...	0556	...	0808	*1008*	...	1208	...	1308	...	1408	*1428*	...	1508	...	1606	1706	...	*1806*	1906	...	*2108*	*2245*
Szombathely ... d.	0431	0501	0606	0636	0706	...	0906	1106	1236	1306	1336	1406	1436	1506	1536	...	1606	1636	1706	1806	1836	1906	2006	2036	2106	2236
Körmend ... d.	0455	0525	0630	0700	0730	...	0930	1130	1300	1330	1400	1430	1500	1530	1600	...	1630	1700	1730	1830	1900	1930	2030	2100	2130	2300
Szentgotthárd 🏛 ... a.	0519	0549	0654	0724	0754	...	0954	1154	1324	1354	1424	1454	1524	1554	1624	...	1654	1724	1754	1854	1924	1954	2054	2124	2154	2324

A – 12 and 🍷 Ljubljana (*IC* **251**) - Graz - Szentgotthárd - Budapest.
B – 12 and 🍷 Budapest (*IC* **250**) - Szentgotthárd - Graz - Ljubljana.
H – From Hartberg (Table **995**).

a – Ⓐ only.
c – Ⓒ only.
h – Arrives 2129.
j – Arrives 1422.
k – ⑥ only.
t – Arrives 8 minutes earlier.
v – Arrives 5 minutes earlier.
z – Fehring d. 1341 on Ⓒ; Feldbach a. 1335 on Ⓐ.
⊖ – *IC* train to / from Budapest (Table **1250**). 🄁 and supplement payable.
• – Szentgotthárd - Szombathely operated by Gysev Raaberbahn.

2nd class only — WIEN - GMÜND - ČESKÉ VELENICE — 990

km																										
					Av							Av		Ⓐ		Ⓐ		Ⓐ	Ⓐ		Ⓐ					
0	**Wien** Franz-Josefs-Bf .. **991/3** d.	0628	0732	0828	0856	0928	1028	1128	1228	1328	1428	1456	1528	1616	1628	1659	1728	1759	1816	1828	1859	1928	2028	2128	2228	2328
1	Wien Spittelau ... ● **991/3** d.	0631	0735	0831	0859	0931	1031	1131	1231	1331	1431	1459	1531	1619	1631	1702	1731	1802	1819	1831	1902	1931	2031	2131	2231	2331
3	Wien Heiligenstadt ... △ **991/3** d.	0634	0738	0834	0902	0934	1034	1134	1234	1334	1434	1502	1534	1622	1634	1705	1734	1805	1822	1834	1905	1934	2034	2134	2234	2334
33	Tulln a. d. Donau ... **991/3** d.	0656	0800	0856	0925	0956	1056	1156	1256	1356	1456	1525	1556	|	1656	1727	1756	1827	1845	1856	1927	1956	2056	2156	2256	2356
44	Absdorf-Hippersdorf ... **991** d.	0704	0809	0904	|	1004	1104	1204	1304	1404	1504	|	1604	|	1704	1735	1804	1835	|	1904	1935	2004	2104	2204	2304	0004
79	Eggenburg ... d.	0734	0837	0934	1003	1037	1134	1237	1334	1437	1534	1603	1638	1714	1734	1806	1838	1905	1914	1934	2005	2038	2134	2232	2332	0033
89	Sigmundsherberg ... d.	0742	0846	0942	1014	1045	1142	1245	1342	1445	1542	1614	1646	1722	1742	1815	1846	1913	1922	1942	2014	2046	2142	2241	2342	0041
121	Göpfritz an der Wild ... d.	0807	0907**c**	1007	1036	...	1207	...	1407	...	1607	1636	1712**a**	1748	1807**c**	1838	1912**a**	...	1948	2007**c**	2038**f**	2112**a**	2207	2306**j**	0007**g**	...
138	Schwarzenau ... d.	0821	0919**c**	1021	1049	...	1221	...	1421	...	1621	1649	1729**a**	1802	1821**c**	1850	1933**a**	...	2002	2021**c**	2050**f**	2127**a**	2221	2320**j**	0021**g**	...
162	**Gmünd** NÖ ... a.	0842	0938**c**	1042	1107	...	1242	...	1442	...	1642	1707	1750**a**	1823	1842**c**	1911	1954**a**	...	2023	2042**c**	2111**f**	2148**a**	2242	2342**j**	0042**g**	...
162	**Gmünd** NÖ 🏛 ... ⊡ d.	0845	...	1045	1112	...	1245	...	1445	...	1645	1712	...	1826	1845**c**	...	...	...	2026	2045**c**	...	...	...	...	...	...
164	**České Velenice** 🏛 ... ⊡ a.	0849	...	1049	1115	...	1249	...	1449	...	1649	1715	...	1830	1849**c**	...	...	...	2030	2049**c**	...	...	...	...	...	...

	Ⓐ	⚒		Ⓐ	Ⓐ	Ⓐ		Ⓐ						A							Ⓐ	Ⓒ	Ⓒ			A
České Velenice 🏛 ... ⊡ d.	...	n	...	...	...	...	...	...	0602	0707	...	0907	...	1039	1107	...	1307	...	1507	...	1701	1707	...	...	1905	2039
Gmünd NÖ 🏛 ... ⊡ a.	...	...	...	...	...	...	...	...	0606	0711	...	0911	...	1042	1111	...	1311	...	1511	...	1705	1711	...	...	1911	2042
Gmünd NÖ ... d.	...	0350	...	0429	...	0455	0511	0546	0609	0714	...	0914	...	1046	1114	...	1314	...	1514	...	1708	1714	1802	...	1912	2046
Schwarzenau ... d.	...	0411	...	0448	...	0516	0534	0605	0631	0735	...	0935	...	1106	1135	...	1335	...	1535	...	1735**t**	1735	1821	...	1935	2110
Göpfritz an der Wild ... d.	...	0425	...	0500	...	0530	0548	0617	0645	0749	...	0949	...	1120	1149	...	1349	...	1549	...	1749	1749	1834	...	1949	2123
Sigmundsherberg ... d.	0409	0449	0509	0521	0539	0554	0614	0639	0709	0814	0909	1014	1109	1143	1214	1309	1414	1509	1613	1655**p**	1814	1814	1855	1855**p**	2014	2144
Eggenburg ... d.	0417	0458	0517	0528	0548	0603	0622	0647	0718	0822	0917	1022	1117	1154	1222	1317	1422	1517	1622	1717**b**	1822	1822	1903	1917**b**	2022	2153
Absdorf-Hippersdorf ... **991** d.	0448	|	0546	|	0616	|	0650	0717	0748	0851	0951	1050	1150	|	1250	1350	1458	1550	1651	1750	1850	1850	|	1950	2050	|
Tulln a. d. Donau ... **991/3** d.	0457	0528	0554	0558	0624	0558	0659	0725	0757	0859	0959	1059	1159	1226	1259	1359	1507	1559	1659	1759	1859	1859	|	1959	2059	2226
Wien Heiligenstadt ... △ **991/3** d.	0518	0551	0619	0622	0647	0622	0720	0746	0818	0921	1021	1121	1221	1248	1321	1421	1527	1621	1721	1821	1921	1921	1957	2021	2121	2248
Wien Spittelau ... ● **991/3** d.	0522	0554	0622	0625	0650	0625	0724	0750	0821	0925	1023	1124	1224	1252	1324	1424	1531	1624	1724	1824	1924	1924	2001	2024	2124	2252
Wien Franz-Josefs-Bf ... **991/3** a.	0524	0557	0624	0627	0654	0627	0726	0752	0824	0927	1026	1127	1227	1254	1327	1427	1532	1627	1726	1827	1927	1927	2003	2027	2127	2254

A – To / from Praha (Table **1130**).

a – Ⓐ only.
b – Arrives 13 minutes earlier on Ⓐ.
c – Ⓒ only.
f – Not ⑤.
g – Mornings of ⑥⑦ only.
j – ①–④ †.
n – Runs 4 – 5 minutes later on Ⓐ.
p – Departs 14 minutes later on Ⓒ.
r – Ⓐ only. Arrives 2126.
t – Arrives 1728.
v – Departures Wien Franz-Josefs - Tulln are 3 – 4 minutes later on Ⓐ.

⊡ – Additional trains Gmünd - České Velenice: **From Gmünd** at 0522 and 0622.
△ – S-Bahn (Line **S45**) trains run every 10 – 15 minutes from / to Wien Hütteldorf (journey: 21 – 23 minutes).
● – Direct U-Bahn links: Line **U4** – Wien Mitte - Spittelau. Line **U6** – Wien Meidling - Westbahnhof - Spittelau - Floridsdorf.

991 WIEN - KREMS an der Donau - EMMERSDORF

2nd class only

km																						
0	**Wien** Franz-Josefs-Bf .... **990/3** d.	0432	0503	0532	0603	0632	0703	0729	0803	0832	0903	1003	1032	1103	1203	1232	and at	2032	2103	2200	2300	0000
1	Wien Spittelau .... ● **990/3** d.	0435	0506	0535	0606	0635	0706	0732	0806	0835	0906	1006	1035	1106	1206	1235	the same	2035	2106	2203	2303	0003
3	Wien Heiligenstadt .... △ **990/3** d.	0438	0509	0538	0609	0638	0709	0735	0809	0838	0909	1009	1038	1109	1209	1238	minutes	2038	2109	2206	2306	0006
33	Tulln a. d. Donau .... **990/3** d.	0500	0532	0600	0632	0700	0732	0757	0832	0900	0932	1032	1000	1132	1232	1200	past each	2100	2132	2228	2328	0028
44	Absdorf-Hippersdorf .... **990** d.	|	0540	|	0640	|	0740	0806	0840	|	0940	1040	|	1140	1240	|	hour until	|	2140	2237	2337	0037
76	**Krems** a. d. Donau .... a.	0538	0608	0638	0709	0738	0808	0838	0908	0938	1008	1108	1138	1208	1308	1338		2138	2208	2308	0008	0108

																⊡				
Krems a. d. Donau .... d.	0422	0452	0522	0552	0614	0652	0722	and at	0922	0952	1052	1122	...	1152	1252	1322	and at	2022	2052	2152	2252
Absdorf-Hippersdorf .... **990** d.	0454	0520	0554	0620	|	0722	0754	the same	0954	1022	1122	1154	...	1222	1322	1354	the same	2054	2122	2224	2324
Tulln a. d. Donau .... **990/3** d.	0503	0529	0603	0629	|	0730	0803	minutes	1003	1030	1130	1103	...	1230	1330	1403	minutes	2103	2130	2232	2332
Wien Heiligenstadt .... △ **990/3** d.	0524	0551	0624	0651	0711	0751	0824	past each	1024	1051	1151	1124	...	1251	1351	1424	past each	2124	2151	2254	2354
Wien Spittelau .... ● **990/3** d.	0528	0554	0628	0655	0714	0755	0828	hour until	1028	1055	1155	1128	...	1255	1355	1428	hour until	2128	2155	2257	2357
Wien Franz-Josefs-Bf .... **990/3** a.	0530	0557	0630	0657	0716	0757	0830		1030	1057	1157	1130	...	1257	1357	1430		2130	2157	2300	2400

KREMS - EMMERSDORF ⊠

km		R		R	R	S	S	R		S
0	**Krems** an der Donau .... d.	0918	...	1118	1318	1418	1618	1618	...	1818
18	**Spitz** an der Donau .... d.	0946	...	1146	1346	1445	1645	1646	...	1845
34	**Emmersdorf** an der Donau .. a.	1005	...	1205	1405	...	...	1705	...	...

	R		R	R	S	S		R	S
Emmersdorf an der Donau d.	1015	...	1215	1455	...	...	...	1755	...
Spitz an der Donau .... d.	1035	...	1235	1515	1515	1715	...	1815	1915
Krems an der Donau .... a.	1102	...	1302	1542	1542	1742	...	1842	1942

R – Ⓒ Mar. 15 - Apr. 27; daily May 2 - Oct. 31; Ⓒ Nov. 1 – 30.
Special fares apply. A modified timetable operates on Sept. 17.
S – ⑥⑦ Dec. 6 - Dec. 21 (also Dec. 8). Special fares apply.

⊡ – Krems d. 1348 (not 1352).
● – Direct U-bahn links: Line **U4** – Wien Mitte - Spittelau.
Line **U6** – Wien Meidling - Westbahnhof - Spittelau - Floridsdorf.
△ – S-Bahn trains run every 10 – 15 minutes from / to Wien Hütteldorf (journey: 21 – 23 minutes).
⊠ – Operated by NÖVOG (Wachaubahn). ✆ +43 (0) 2742 360 990-99. www.wachaubahn.at

993 ST PÖLTEN - KREMS and TULLN

2nd class only

ST PÖLTEN - KREMS

km				Ⓐ			Ⓐ				Ⓐ		Ⓐ				Ⓐ					
0	**St Pölten** Hbf .... d.	0009	0506	0539	...	0606	0639	0706	and	1206	1239	1306	1339	1406	and at the same	1906	1939	2006	2106	...	2206	2306
10	Herzogenburg .... d.	0017	0514	0548	...	0614	0648	0714	hourly	1214	1248	1314	1348	1414	minutes past	1914	1947	2014	2114	...	2214	2314
30	**Krems** a. d. Donau .... a.	0044	0541	0618	...	0641	0727	0741	until	1241	1316	1341	1415	1451	each hour until	1941	2013	2041	2140	...	2240	2341

	Ⓒ	Ⓐ	Ⓐ		⚒		Ⓐ	Ⓐ		Ⓐ		Ⓐ						Ⓐ						
Krems a. d. Donau .... d.	0022	0419	0446	0519	0546	0619	0646	0707	0719	0746	0819	0846	0919	1019	1119	1219	1319	1342	1419	and	2019	2119	2219	2319
Herzogenburg .... d.	0049	0446	0513	0546	0613	0646	0714	0733	0746	0814	0846	0914	0946	1046	1146	1246	1346	1414	1446	hourly	2046	2146	2246	2346
St Pölten Hbf .... a.	0057	0454	0522	0554	0622	0654	0723	0741	0754	0823	0854	0923	0954	1054	1154	1254	1354	1422	1454	until	2054	2154	2254	2354

ST PÖLTEN - TULLN - WIEN

km		⚒	Ⓐ	⚒		⚒			⚒																	
0	**St Pölten** Hbf .... **950** d.	0404	...	0445a	0512	0545a	...	0612	0656a	...	0712	0812	0912		1412	1512	...	1612	...	1712	...	1812	1912	2012	2112	2212
10	Herzogenburg .... d.	0418	...	0503a	0528	0603a	...	0631	0708a	...	0731	0831	0931		1431	1531	...	1631	...	1731	...	1831	1931	2031	2131	2231
40	Tullnerfeld .... **950** a.	0449	...	0538a	0608	0638a	...	0708	0737a	...	0808	0908	1008	and	1508	1608	...	1708	...	1808	...	1908	2008	2108	2208	2308
40	Tullnerfeld .... d.	0450	0524	0554	0624	0654	0648	0724	0754	0748	0824	0924	1024		1524	1624	1648	1724	1748	1824	1848	1924	2024	2124	2224	2324
46	**Tulln** Stadt .... d.	0456	0530	0600	0630	0700	0653	0730	0800	0753	0830	0930	1030	hourly	1530	1630	1653	1730	1753	1830	1853	1930	2030	2130	2230	2330
	Absdorf-Hippersdorf ▷ a.	|	|	|	|	|	0700	|	|	0801	|	|	|		|	|	1701	|	1801	|	1901	|	|	|	|	|
	Stockerau .... ▷ a.	|	|	|	|	|	0724	|	|	0826	|	|	|	until	|	|	1726	|	1826	|	1926	|	|	|	|	|
47	**Tulln** a. d. Donau .. **990/1** a.	0458	0532	0602	0632	0702	...	0732	0802	...	0832	0932	1032		1532	1632	...	1732	...	1832	...	1932	2032	2132	2232	2332
77	Wien Heiligenstadt **990/1** a.	0542	0612	0642	0717f	0742	...	0812	0842	...	0912	1012	1112		1612	1712	...	1812	...	1912	...	2015	2112	2212	2312	0012

	Ⓐ			⚒			⚒																			
Wien Heiligenstadt . **990/1** d.	...	...	...	0512	0542	...	0612	0642	...	0742	0842	0942	1042		1442	1542	...	1642	...	1742	1842	1942	2042	2142	2242	2342
Tulln a. d. Donau ... **990/1** d.	0441	0527	...	0556	0627	...	0656	0727	...	0827	0927	1027	1127		1527	1627	...	1727	...	1827	1927	2027	2127	2227	2327	0023
Stockerau .... ▷ d.	|	|	0531	|	|	0631	|	|	0731	|	|	|	|	and	|	|	1631	|	1731	|	|	|	|	|	|	|
Absdorf-Hippersdorf. ▷ d.	|	|	0558	|	|	0658	|	|	0758	|	|	|	|		|	|	1700	|	1800	|	|	|	|	|	|	|
Tulln Stadt .... d.	0445	0529	0606	0600	0629	0706	0700	0729	0806	0829	0929	1029	1129	hourly	1529	1629	1708	1729	1808	1829	1929	2029	2129	2229	2329	0025
Tullnerfeld .... a.	0450	0535	0611	0605	0635	0711	0705	0735	0811	0835	0935	1035	1135		1535	1635	1713	1735	1813	1835	1935	2035	2135	2235	2335	...
Tullnerfeld .... **950** d.	0451	0548	...	0618	0648	...	0718	0748	...	0848	0948	1048	1148	until	1548	1648	...	1748	...	1848	1948	2048	2148	2248	...	...
Herzogenburg .... d.	0525	0631	...	0653	0735r	...	0753	0830	...	0930	1030	1130	1230		1630	1732	...	1830	...	1930	2030	2130	2230	2330	...	...
St Pölten Hbf .... **950** a.	0538	0649	...	0704	0750	...	0804	0845	...	0945	1045	1145	1249		1649	1749	...	1849	...	1949	2045	2145	2245	2345	...	...

a – Ⓐ only. **f** – Arrives 0712 on Ⓒ. **r** – Arrives 0729. ▷ – Additional local trains run Absdorf-Hippersdorf - Stockerau and v.v.

994 ST PÖLTEN - MARIAZELL

2nd class only · Narrow gauge

km				Ⓒj¶	R	C🅁	S🅁						
0	**St Pölten** Hbf .... d.	0635	0735	0805	0837	0842	0902	0937	1037	1137	1237	1437	1637
12	Ober Grafendorf . d.	0654	0754	0819	0854	0904	0922	0954	1054	1154	1254	1454	1654
31	Kirchberg .... d.	0723	0823	0843	0923	0938	1003	1023	1123	1223	1323	1523	1723
43	Frankenfels .... ⊗ d.	0741	0841	|	0941	0959	|	1041	1141	1241	1341	1541	1741
48	Laubenbachmühle d.	0751	0851	0909	0951	1011	1056f	1051	1151	1251	1351	1551	1751
67	Gösing .... ⊗ d.	0820	0920t	|	1020	1045	|	1120z	1220	1320z	1420	1620	1820
80	Mitterbach ...... ⊗ d.	0845	0945t	0958	1045	1115	1215	1145z	1245	1345z	1445	1645	1845
84	**Mariazell** .... a.	0854	0954t	1004	1054	1124	1224	1154z	1254	1354z	1454	1654	1854

							C🅁	S🅁	n	ⒸR¶			
Mariazell .... d.	0905	1105	1205z	1305	1405z	1505	1520	1535	1605v	1605	1705	1805z	1905
Mitterbach ..... ⊗ d.	0912	1112	1212z	1312	1412z	1512	1527	1542	1612v	1612	1712	1812z	1912
Gösing .... ⊗ d.	0937	1137	1237z	1337	1437z	1537	1557	|	1637v	1637	1737	1837z	1937
Laubenbachmühle d.	1009	1209	1309	1409	1509	1609	1634	1714r	1709	1709	1809	1909	2009
Frankenfels ... ⊗ d.	1017	1217	1317	1417	1517	1617	1642	|	1717	1717	1817	1917	2017
Kirchberg .... d.	1035	1235	1335	1435	1535	1635	1702	1752	1735	1735	1835	1935	2035
Ober Grafendorf .. d.	1104	1304	1404	1504	1604	1704	1734	1834	1804	1804	1904	2004	2104
St Pölten Hbf...... a.	1122	1322	1422	1522	1622	1722	1757	1857	1822	1822	1922	2022	2122

C – Ⓒ May 3 - Nov. 2 (also Nov. 22, 29, Dec, 6, 13; not May 11, June 8, July 13, Aug. 10, Sept. 14, Oct. 12). ÖTSCHERBÄR – Traditional loco-hauled electric train. Conveys (2) and ✕.
R – On Ⓒ May 3 - Nov. 2, Nov. 22 - Dec. 13 conveys (12) and ✕.
S – Runs on May 11, June 8, July 13, Aug. 10, Sept. 14, Oct. 12, Nov. 23, 30, Dec. 7, 8. Steam train with special fares. Conveys (12) and ✕.
f – Arrives 1041.
j – Ⓒ May 3 - Nov. 2 (not Sept. 27, 28).

n – Does not run on dates in note **R**.
r – Arrives 1657.
t – May 1 - Nov. 2 and from Nov. 22.
v – Not Jan 1 - Apr. 30, Nov. 3 – 21.
z – Ⓒ May 3 - Nov. 2 and from Nov. 22.
¶ – Conveys first class panorama cars (🅁 and special fares payable for travel in the panorama car which includes drinks and meals served at your seat).

⊗ – Trains call on request only.

Operator: NÖVOG.
✆ +43 (0) 2742 360 990 99
www.noevog.at/mariazellerbahn

☛ Additional trains run between St Pölten and Laubenbachmühle.

995 (WIEN -) WIENER NEUSTADT - FEHRING

2nd class only

km		⚒	Ⓐ	Ⓒ	Ⓐ		Ⓐ	⚒		B	Ⓐ		Ⓐ	Ⓐ	Ⓐ		Ⓑ			
	Wien Hbf .... **980/1** d.	...	...	...	...	...	...	...	...	...	1550	...	1650	1707	1750	...	...	...	...	...
0	**Wien** Meidling .... **980/1** d.	...	...	0835	...	...	...	...	...	...	1557	...	1657	1714	1757	...	...	...	...	...
44	**Wiener Neustadt** Hbf **980/1** d.	...	0639	0903	0903	1103	...	1303	1503	1503	1633	1703	1733t	1801r	1833t	1903	2003	2103	2139	2239
99	Friedberg .... d.	...	0802	1002	1002	1202	...	1402	1602	1602	1738	1802	1837	1856	1932	2003	2058	2158	2245	2345
126	Hartberg .... d.	0621	0836	1036	1036	1235	1328	1436	1635	1636	1814	1836	...	1929	...	2037	2132a	2232	...	...
157	Fürstenfeld .... d.	0654	0909	1109	1109	...	1359	1509	...	1709	...	1909	...	...	...	2109	...	...	...	...
177	**Fehring** .... a.	0722	0937	*1140*	1137	...	1426	1537a	...	1737	...	1937	...	...	...	2137	...	...	...	...
	Graz Hbf **986** .... a.	0836a	*1053*	*1253*	*1253*	...	*1553*	*1653*a	...	*1853*	...	*2053*	...	...	...	*2253*	...	...	...	...

	Ⓐ	Ⓐ	Ⓐ	Ⓒ	Ⓐ	Ⓐ						Ⓐ	Ⓒ	Ⓒ	Ⓐ		Ⓒ	Ⓒ	⑤b	
Graz Hbf **986** .... d.	...	...	...	...	...	...	...	...	*0707*	*0907*	...	*1107*	1307	...	*1307*	...	1507	...	*1507*	*1707*
Fehring .... d.	...	...	...	...	...	0501	...	0627	0827	1027	...	1227	1424	...	1427	...	1624	...	1627	1827
Fürstenfeld .... d.	...	...	...	...	...	0528	...	0654	0854	1054	...	1254	1451	1454	1454	...	1651	1654	1654	1854
Hartberg .... d.	...	...	0435	0524	0533	0600	...	0726	0926	1126	1326	1326	...	1526	1526	1726	...	1726	1726	1929
Friedberg .... d.	0348	0428	0509	0558	0608	0636	0700	0802	1002	1202	1402	1402	...	1602	1602	1802	...	1802	1802	2004
Wiener Neustadt Hbf . **980/1** a.	0453	0529	0611	0655	0711	0735	0757	0857	1057	1257	1457	1457	...	1657	1657	1857	...	1857	1857	2057
Wien Meidling .... **980/1** a.	...	0559	0643	...	0743	...	...	...	...	...	...	...	...	1726	...	...	...	1926	...	...
Wien Hbf .... **980/1** a.	...	0606	0651	...	...	...	...	...	...	...	...	...	...	1732	...	...	...	1932	...	...

B – ⑤⑥† (also Apr. 30, May 28, June 18, Aug. 16).
a – Ⓐ only.
b – ⑤ (also Apr. 30, May 28, June 18; not May 2, 30, June 20, Aug. 15).
r – Arrives 1746.
t – Arrives 6 minutes earlier.

WIEN - BRATISLAVA via Marchegg — 996

Austrian holiday dates apply

km		2	🚌	2	🚌	2	Ⓐ	2	🚌	E a	2	🚌	C	F a
0	**Wien** Hbf ◧ d.	0614	...	0814	...	1414	🚌	1614	...	1642	1814	...	2042	2142
4	**Wien** Simmering ⊖ ◧ d.	0618	...	0818	...	1418	...	1618	...	|	1818	...	|	|
47	Marchegg 🏛 ◧ d.	0647	0705	0847	0905	1447	1505	1647	1705	|	1647	1905	⊠	|
53	Devínska Nová Ves 🏛 d.	...	|	...	|	...	|	...	|	|	...	|	|	|
66	**Bratislava** hl. st. a.	...	0745	...	0945	...	1545	...	1745	1729	...	1945	2151	2229

	D	🚌	2	🚌	2	E a	Ⓐ 🚌	2	🚌	2	🚌	2	F a
Bratislava hl. st. d.	0608	0620	...	0815	...	1431	1415	...	1615	...	1815	...	1831
Devínska Nová Ves 🏛 d.	|	|	...	|	...	|	|	...	|	...	|	...	|
Marchegg 🏛 ◧ d.	⊠	0700	0712	0855	0912	|	1455	1512	1655	1712	1855	1912	|
Wien Simmering ⊖ ◧ d.	|	...	0742	...	0942	|	...	1542	...	1742	...	1942	|
Wien Hbf ◧ a.	0718	...	0746	...	0946	1518	...	1546	...	1746	...	1946	1918

C – *RJX* **167** – (12) ✕ Zürich - Bratislava.
D – *RJX* **160** – (12) ✕ Bratislava - Zürich.
E – *D* **46**/**47** – (2) Wien - Bratislava and v.v.
F – *D* **48**/**49** – (2) Wien - Bratislava and v.v.

a – From Oct. 10.

⊠ – Via Bratislava - Petržalka.
⊖ – For U-Bahn connections (line U3) from/to Wien Mitte and Wien Westbahnhof.
◧ – Additional trains run between Wien Hbf and Marchegg.

☛ **Note**: From Oct. 10 hourly through services will recommence Wien Hbf - Bratislava hl. st. and v.v. (timings will be shown in the October edition).

BRATISLAVA - WIEN - SOPRON - DEUTSCHKREUTZ — 997

2nd class only; Austrian holiday dates apply

km	△		Ⓐ		Ⓐ	©M	Ⓐ	©	P	Ⓐ						Ⓐ		Ⓐ		Ⓐ		Ⓐ				
0	**Bratislava**-Petržalka 🏛 ☆ d.	0416	0446	0516	0546	0611	0611	...	0632	0646	0716	0816		1316	...	1416	...	1516	...	1616	...	1716		2216	2316
5	Kittsee 🏛 d.	0421	0451	0521	0551	0617	0617	...	|	0651	0721	0821		1321	...	1421	...	1521	...	1621	...	1721		2221	2321
33	Bruck an der Leitha d.	0447	0517	0547	0617	0647	0647	...	|	0717	0747	0847	and	1347	...	1447	...	1547	...	1647	...	1747	and	2247	2347
74	**Wien** Hbf a.	0515	0553	0615	0651	0715	0715	...	0718	0751	0815	0915		1415	...	1515	...	1615	...	1715	...	1815		2315	0015
74	**Wien** Hbf d.	0523a	...	0623	...	0727	0723	0723	...	...	0823	0923	hourly	1423	1459	1523	1559	1623	1659	1723	1759	1823	hourly	2323	0026f
78	**Wien** Meidling d.	0531a	...	0631	...	0731	0731	0731	...	...	0831	0931		1431	1506	1531	1606	1631	1706	1731	1806	1831		2331	0034f
116	Ebenfurth d.	0601a	...	0701	...	...	0801	0801	...	...	0901	1002	until	1502	1537	1602	1637	1702	1737	1802	1837	1902	until	0001	0103f
148	**Sopron** 🏛 a.	0637a	...	0737	...	...	0837	0837	...	...	0937	1037		1537	1610	1637	1710	1737	1810	1837	1910	1937		0037	0138f
157	**Deutschkreutz** a.	0658a	...	0759	...	...	0847	0847	...	...	0947	1047		1547	1622	1647	1722	1747	1822	1847	1922	1947		0047	0148f

△				Ⓐ		Ⓐ		Ⓐ		Ⓐ				Ⓐ		Ⓐ		Ⓐ	©	©M		Q			
Deutschkreutz d.	...	...	0413	0435	0513	0535	0613	0635	0713	0735	0813		1413	...	1513	...	1613	1713	1713	...	1813	...	1913		2213
Sopron 🏛 d.	...	...	0423	0446	0523	0546	0623	0646	0723	0746	0823		1423	...	1523	...	1623	1723	1723	...	1823	...	1923		2223
Ebenfurth d.	...	...	0505	0527	0605	0627	0705	0727	0805	0827	0905	and	1505	...	1605	...	1705	1805	1805	...	1905	...	2005	and	2305
Wien Meidling a.	...	...	0529	0553	0629	0653	0729	0753	0829	0853	0929		1529	...	1629	...	1729	1829	1829	1827	1929	...	2029		2329
Wien Hbf a.	...	...	0537	0600	0637	0700	0737	0800	0837	0900	0937	hourly	1537	...	1637	...	1737	1837	1837	1832	1937	...	2037	hourly	2337
Wien Hbf d.	0054	0441	0538	...	0645	...	0745	...	0845	...	0945		1545	1615	1645	1715	1745	1845	...	1845	1945	2042	2045		2345
Bruck an der Leitha d.	0133	0509	0607	...	0713	...	0813	...	0913	...	1013	until	1613	1643	1713	1743	1813	1913	...	1913	2013	|	2113	until	0013
Kittsee 🏛 d.	0156	0539	0637	...	0739	...	0839	...	0939	...	1039		1639	1709	1739	1809	1839	1939	...	1939	2039	|	2139		0039
Bratislava-Petržalka 🏛 ☆ a.	0201	0544	0641	...	0744	...	0844	...	0944	...	1044		1644	1714	1744	1814	1844	1944	...	1944	2044	2126	2144		0044

km	▽	Ⓐ							Ⓐ	Ⓐ		Ⓐ	Ⓐ		Ⓐ	Ⓐ		Ⓐ	Ⓐ		Ⓐ	Ⓐ		Ⓐ	Ⓐ
	Wien Meidling **980 981** d.	...	...	...	...	...		...	...	...	...	...	...	...	...	...	...	...	1557	...	...	1657	...	...	1757
0	**Wiener Neustadt** Hbf d.	0503	0603	0703	0739	0837	and	1237	1301	1331	1337	1401	1431	1437	1501	1531	1537	1601	1631	1637	1701	1731	1737	1801	1831
16	Mattersburg d.	0525	0625	0725	0802	0901	hourly	1301	1319	1344	1401	1421	1444	1501	1521	1544	1601	1621	1644	17012	1721	1744	1801	1821	1844
33	**Sopron** 🏛 a.	0541	0641	0741	0818	0917	until	1317	1336	1400	1417t	1436	1500	1517	1536	1600	1617t	1636	1700	1717t	1736	1800	1817t	1836	1900
42	**Deutschkreutz** a.	...	...	...	...	...		...	...	1410	...	...	1510	...	...	1610	...	...	1710	...	...	1810	...	...	1910

▽		Ⓐ	Ⓐ					
Wien Meidling **980 981** d.	...	...	...	...	...	...	...	...
Wiener Neustadt Hbf d.	1837	1901	1931	1937	2037	2137	2237	2337
Mattersburg d.	1901	1921	1944	2002	2102	2202	2302	0002
Sopron 🏛 a.	1917t	1936	2000	2017	2117	2217	2317	0017
Deutschkreutz a.	...	...	2010	...	...	...	...	...

▽	Ⓐ	⚒	Ⓐ		Ⓐ		⑥	Ⓐ				
Deutschkreutz d.	...	...	0459	...	0559	...	0635	0659	...	...		...
Sopron 🏛 d.	0417	0447	0509	0547	0609	0647	0647	0709	0747	0844	and	2244
Mattersburg d.	0433	0503	0526	0603	0626	0703	0703	0726	0803	0901	hourly	2301
Wiener Neustadt Hbf a.	0453	0525	0539	0625	0639	0725	0725	0739	0825	0925	until	2325
Wien Meidling **980 981** a.	...	...	0613	...	0713	...	...	0813	...	...		...

M – To/from Mürzzuschlag (Table **981**).
P – *RJX* **160** – (12) ✕ Bratislava - Zürich.
Q – *RJX* **167** – (12) ✕ Zürich - Bratislava.

a – Ⓐ only.
f – ①⑥⑦ mornings only.
t – © only.

▽ – Operated by ÖBB.
☆ – Bus 93 links Petržalka station with Bratislava hlavná every 5–10 minutes (journey time ±12 minutes).
△ – Operated by GySEV Györ - Sopron - Ebenfurti Vasút (in Germany Raab - Oedenburg - Ebenfurter Eisenbahn – ROeEE).

UNZMARKT - TAMSWEG — 998

2nd class only; narrow gauge

km		Ⓐ	Ⓐ	Ⓐ 🚌	© 🚌	© D			A 🚂	Ⓐ	©						🚌		🚌
0	**Unzmarkt** d.	...	0720	...	0722	0827	...	0922	...	1122	...	...	1322	1522	...	1722	...	1917	2125
27	Murau-Stolzalpe d.	0623	0800	0805	0801	0910	...	1000	1035	1200	1200	...	1400	1600	...	1758	1805	1951	2200
34	St Lorenzen d.	0636	0812r	0817	0812	0923	...	1012	1055	1212	1212	...	1412	1612	...	...	1816	2000	2209s
44	Stadl an der Mur d.	0653	0827r	0831	0825	0940	...	1027	1135	1227	1227	...	1427	1627	...	...	1827	2013	2222
65	**Tamsweg** a.	0727	0857r	0858	0853	1012	...	1057	1225	1257	1257	...	1457	1657	...	...	1855	2039	2245

	Ⓐ	© D	© D	Ⓐ	© E		Ⓐ	© 🚌	© D				A 🚂				Ⓐ 🚌	© 🚌	Ⓐ 🚌
Tamsweg d.	*0535**	...	0643	0650	0703	...	0903	0910	1020	1103	...	1303	1410	1503	...	1703	1820	1910	2020
Stadl an der Mur d.	*0555**	...	0711	0721	0731	...	0931	0929	1052	1131	...	1331	1500	1531	...	1731	1839	1929	2039
St Lorenzen d.	*0610**	...	0725	0738	0745	...	0945	0945	1106	1145	...	1345	1520	1545	...	1745	1855	1945	2055
Murau-Stolzalpe d.	0630	0658	0740	0800	0800	...	1000	1000	1116	1200	...	1400	1535	1600	...	1800	1907	2000	2107
Unzmarkt a.	0710	0734	0816	0836	0836	...	1036	1038	...	1236	...	1436	...	1636	...	1836	*2038*	2038	...

A – July 22, 24, 31, Aug. 5, 7, 10, 12, 14, Sept. 2, 4, 9, 11, 14, 16, 18.
D – © May 1 - Oct. 31.
E – © (not May 1 - Oct. 31).

r – Ⓐ Apr. 14–18, July 7 - Sept. 5, Oct. 27–31.
s – Stops to set down only.

* – By 🚌.
🚂 – Steam train. Special fares payable.

Operator: Steiermärkische Landesbahnen.

Danube shipping — 999

Catamaran services. 🍷	W Ⓡ ♠	Z Ⓡ ♠		Y Ⓡ ♠		W Ⓡ ♠		W Ⓡ ♠	
Wien Schwedenplatz ▲ d.	0830	0900	...	1030	...	1230	...	1630	...
Bratislava a.	0945	1015	...	1145	...	1345	...	1745	...

Catamaran services. 🍷	W Ⓡ ♠		W Ⓡ ♠		Z Ⓡ ♠		Y Ⓡ ♠		W Ⓡ ♠
Bratislava d.	1030	...	1430	...	1600	...	1630	...	1830
Wien Schwedenplatz ▲ a.	1200	...	1600	...	1730	...	1800	...	2000

All sailings convey ✕	B ◐	B ◐		K ◐	J ◐ Ⓡ		K ◐	K ◐	
Wien Reichsbrücke ▲ d.	...	...	...	...	0830	...	...	...	...
Tulln d.	...	...	...	...	1120	...	...	...	...
Krems an der Donau d.	1015	1100	...	1310	1400	...	1545	...	...
Dürnstein d.	1045	1130	...	1340	1430	...	1620	...	...
Spitz an der Donau d.	1145	1230	...	1445§	...	...	1720	1730	...
Emmersdorf d.	|	|	...	1555	...	...	...	1840	...
Melk a.	1320	1405	...	1605	...	...	...	1850	...

All sailings convey ✕	K ◐		B ◐		B ◐	J ◐ Ⓡ		K ◐	K ◐
Melk d.	1100	...	'1350	...	1435	...	...	1625	...
Emmersdorf d.	1110	...	|	...	|	...	...	|	...
Spitz an der Donau d.	1200‡	...	1440	...	1525	...	...	1710	1725
Dürnstein d.	1230	...	1510	...	1555	1640	...	...	1750
Krems an der Donau d.	1250	...	1530	...	1615	1700	...	...	1810
Tulln d.	...	...	...	...	...	1900	...	...	...
Wien Reichsbrücke ▲ a.	...	...	...	...	...	2115	...	...	...

All sailings convey ✕	⊖ A		
Linz Lentos d.	...	...	...
Schlögen d.	...	...	...
Engelhartszell d.	1400	...	...
Passau Liegestelle 11 🏛 d.	1630	...	...
Deggendorf a.	...	...	...

All sailings convey ✕	⊖ F	⊖ A	
Deggendorf d.	...	...	...
Passau Liegestelle 11 🏛 d.	0900	1230	...
Engelhartszell d.	1030	1400	...
Schlögen a.	1110	...	...
Linz Lentos a.	1410	...	...

A – June 7 - Oct. 10.
B – Mar. 29 - Nov. 2.
C – Apr. 13 - Oct. 27, 2025.
F – ⑤⑥ Aug. 15 - Sept. 9; ⑥ Sept. 13 - Oct. 4 (also July 26, Aug. 8).
J – ⑦ May 4 - Oct. 12 (also ⑤ July 5 - Sept. 27).
K – Apr. 26 - Oct. 5.
W – ⑤–⑦ Mar. 21 - May 4 (also Apr. 1); daily May 5 - Sept. 28; ⑤–⑦ Sept. 29 - Nov. 2.
Y – ⑥⑦ Feb. 2 Mar. 16; ⑤–⑦ Nov. 28 - Dec. 12.
Z – ①–④ Mar. 21 - May 4; ①–④ Sept. 29 - Nov. 2.

b – Apr. 26 - Oct. 5.

‡ – Arrives 1140.
§ – Arrives 1435.

▲ – DDSG operates Wien sightseeing cruises Schwedenplatz - Reichsbrücke and v.v. Daily Mar. 29 - Nov. 2.
From Schwedenplatz (duration 1 h 55 m via Schleuse Freudenau) at 1030, 1400, 1730**b**.
From Reichsbrücke (duration 1 h 20 m via Schleuse Nussdorf) at 1230, 1600.
Also shorter *City Cruise* available daily throughout the year from Schwedenplatz at 1100, 1300, 1430, 1600 (duration 1 h 15 m).

Operators:
◐ – DDSG Blue Danube Schifffahrt, Handelskai 265, A-1020 Wien. ✆ +43 (0)1 588 80. www.ddsg-blue-danube.at
⊖ – Wurm und Noé, Höllgasse 26, D-94032 Passau. ✆ +49 (0) 851 92 92 92. www.donauschifffahrt.eu
♠ – *Twin City Liner*. DDSG Blue Danube, Handelskai 265, A-1020 Wien. Check-in 30 minutes before departure. Austrian holiday dates apply. ✆ +43 (0)1 904 88 80. Internet booking: www.twincityliner.com

POLAND

Operators: Express services are operated by PKP INTERCITY www.intercity.pl. Most regional services are operated by POLREGIO www.polregio.pl. Other regional services are operated by companies owned by local government, such as Koleje Dolnośląskie, Koleje Małopolskie, Koleje Mazowieckie, Koleje Śląskie and Koleje Wielkopolskie.

Services: **PKP INTERCITY**: Reservations are compulsory (Ⓡ) on all services operated by PKP INTERCITY (*EC, EIC, EIP, EN, IC, TLK*).
EC, EIC and *EIP* trains are fast premium-rate trains on long-distance routes (*EC* trains run on international routes) which convey first and second class seating; higher fares apply and a supplement is payable for pass holders; catering (✕ or 🍸) is usually available for at least part of the route.
IC and *TLK* trains are lower-cost long distance trains with first and second class seats (also sleeping cars and couchettes on night trains as indicated in the tables). *TLK* is short for *Twoje Linie Kolejowe* (Your Railway Lines). Certain *IC* and *TLK* trains may also convey 🍸 or ✕. *TLK* fares apply within Poland.
Overnight *EN* (*EuroNight*) services offer all-inclusive fares which include overnight accommodation. Descriptions of sleeping (🛏) and couchette (▬) cars appear on page 10.
POLREGIO runs semi-fast trains mainly on longer distance routes, with second class seats. Fares are cheaper than *TLK* services, but slightly higher than the other regional operators (whose services are also normally second class only). No train category is shown in our tables for these trains. Specific operators are normally shown in each table heading, or in the table notes section.

Timings: **Valid June 15 - August 30, 2025** (unless otherwise shown). **Readers are strongly advised to confirm timings before travelling as alterations are possible at short notice (particularly on and around public holidays)**. Engineering work can often affect schedules; major changes are shown in the tables where possible, but other changes may occur at short notice. Note that PKP trains with 4 or 5 figure numbers often reverse the first two digits for example 38xxx to 83xxx, sometimes trains may also change number en route by one or two digits. In station names, Gł. is short for Główna, Główne or Główny, meaning main railway station.

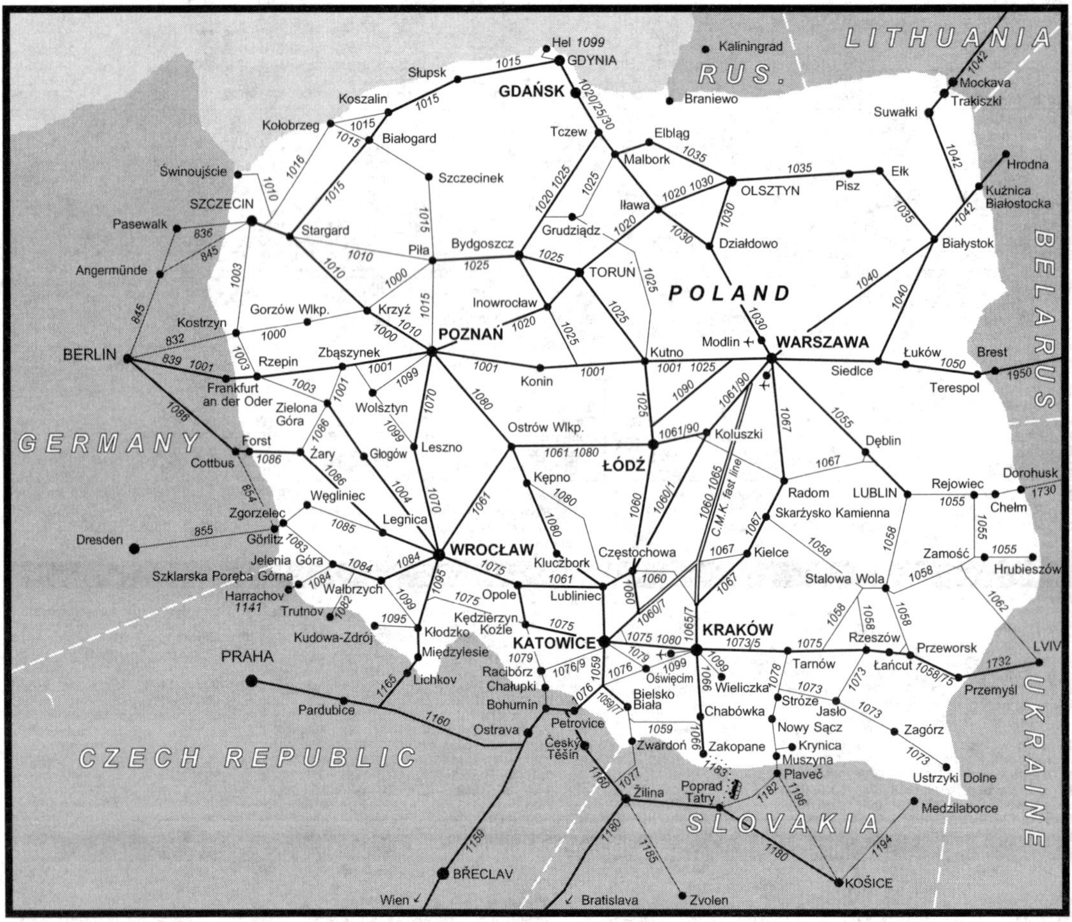

1000 KOSTRZYN - KRZYŻ - POZNAŃ and PIŁA

PKP, Polrail

km			IC 80102				⚒	Ⓐ	Ⓐ c	Ⓑ	Ⓐ					TLK 85110 G					n	Ⓐ	Ⓑ	
0	**Kostrzyn** d.	...	0546	...	0649	...	0852	...	1003	...	...	1202	...	1252	...	1503	1521	1606	...	1702	1809	...	2102	...	2209
43	Gorzów Wlkp d.	...	0631	0715	0732	...	0939	...	1044	...	...	1242	...	1333	...	1545	1600	1649	...	1742	1851	...	2143	...	2251
103	Krzyż **1010** a.	...	0726	0808	0825	...	1034	...	1137	...	...	1335	...	1426	...	1637	1654	1744	...	1835	1944	...	2236	...	2344
103	Krzyż **1010** d.	0624	0736	0809	...	0831	1042	1045	...	1157	1243	...	1353	...	1503	...	1655	1748	1757	...	...	2007	...	2241	...
186	**Poznań** Gł. **1010** a.	|	0851	|	...	|	1157	|	...	1301	|	...	|	...	|	...	|	1903	|	...	...	2113	...	|	...
163	Piła Gł. a.	0713	...	0857	...	0920	...	1134	...	...	1332	...	1442	...	1551	...	1742	...	1847	...	...	...	...	2330	...

		⚒							Ⓐ	TLK 58110 G		⚒	Ⓐ			Ⓐ	Ⓑ				IC 88103	Ⓐ		
Piła Gł. d.	...	0515	...	0724	...	0917	...	1044	...	1145	...	1333	...	1444	...	...	1606	...	1731	...	1859	...	2025	...
Poznań Gł. **1010** d.	...	|	...	|	...	|	0903	|	...	|	1211	|	...	|	...	...	|	...	|	...	|	...	|	2001
Krzyż **1010** a.	...	0606	...	0816	...	1008	1016	1135	...	1235	1335	1424	...	1536	...	...	1657	...	1822	...	1950	...	2116	2127
Krzyż **1010** d.	0520	...	0621	...	0859	...	1017	...	1208	1237	1340	...	1429	...	1542	1618	...	1727	...	1910	1951	...	...	2129
Gorzów Wlkp. d.	0613	...	0716	...	0952	...	1114	...	1304	1349	1443	...	1524	...	1636	1712	...	1821	...	2004	2043	2048	...	2228
Kostrzyn a.	0652	...	0755	...	1032	...	1155	...	1343	1427	1524	...	1604	...	1715	1751	...	1859	...	2043	...	2128	...	2309

G – To/from Gdynia (Table **1025**).
c – Also ⑥⑦ June 28 - Aug. 30.
n – Not June 28 - Aug. 30.

PKP — BERLIN - POZNAŃ - WARSZAWA — 1001

km		IC 81170		IC 72100	EIC 6112	EIC 8100	IC 71100	EC 41 ①–⑥	IC 71102	EIC 8102		IC 75104	IC 8110	EC 59	EC 45	IC 77108	IC 8108	EC 47	IC 83100	EC 57	EC 49	EC 231	EIC 8104
		R		L	W	S		A		S		M	S	G	A		SY	A	LU	E	A	B	S
0	**Berlin** Hbf ⊖ d.	...	...	...	...	...	...	0549**b**	...	...	...	...	...	0849**b**	0948**b**		...	1149**b**	...	1249**b**	1349**b**	1449**b**	...
5	**Berlin** Ostbahnhof ⊖ d.	...	...	...	...	...	...	|	...	...	...	...	...	|	|	...	...	|	...	|	|	|	...
87	Frankfurt (Oder) 🏛 ⊖ d.	...	...	...	...	...	...	0650	...	...	...	...	...	0950	1050	...	...	1250	...	1350	1450	1550	...
108	Rzepin 🏛 ◐ ▷ d.	0124	...	...	...	...	...	0708	...	...	...	...	...	1012	1108	...	...	1308	...	1412	1508	1608	...
•58	**Zielona Góra** Gł. ▷ d.	|	...	...	...	...	0523	|	0728	...	...	0955	...	1055	|	1137	...	|	...	1455	|	|	...
185	Zbąszynek ▷ d.	0213	...	...	...	...	0625	0745	0810	...	...	1034	...	...	1145	1222	...	1345	...	...	1545	1645	...
264	**Poznań** Gł. ▷ a.	0311	...	...	...	...	0715	0832	0858	...	...	1122	...	...	1232	1315	...	1432	...	...	1632	1732	...
264	**Poznań** Gł. d.	0316	...	0546	0635	0740	0745	0835	0910	0940	...	...	1137	...	1235	...	1337	1435	1537	...	1635	...	1741
364	Konin d.	0424	...	0645	0721	|	0844	0921	|	|	...	...	1244	...	1321	...	1444	1521	1644	...	1721	...	|
443	Kutno **1025** d.	0511	...	0723	0756	|	0923	0957	1120	|	...	...	1323	...	1357	...	1523	1557	1723	...	1756	...	|
565	**Warszawa** Zachodnia **1025** a.	0625	...	0825	0854	0954	1024	1054	1224	1153	...	...	1424	...	1454	...	1624	1654	1824	...	1854	...	1955
568	**Warszawa** Centralna **1025** a.	0630	...	0830	0900	0959	1030	1100	1230	1159	...	...	1430	...	1500	...	1630	1700	1830	...	1900	...	2000
572	**Warszawa** Wschodnia **1025** a.	0701	...	0846	0916	1016	1046	1116	1246	1216	...	...	1451	...	1516	...	1701	1716	1846	...	1916	...	2016

	IC 7102 7202	EC 247	IC 75108	EC 55	IC 8106 Ⓑ	IC 8156	EC 249 Ⓑ
	n	A	M	C	Sg	Uh	A
Berlin Hbf ⊖ d.	...	1549**b**	...	1649**b**	...	...	1748**b**
Berlin Ostbahnhof ⊖ d.	...	|	...	|	...	...	|
Frankfurt (Oder) 🏛 ⊖ d.	...	1650	...	1750	...	...	1850
Rzepin 🏛 ◐ ▷ d.	...	1708	...	1812	...	...	1908
Zielona Góra Gł. ▷ d.	1543	|	1740	1855	...	...	|
Zbąszynek ▷ d.	1638	1745	1822	...	...	...	1945
Poznań Gł. ▷ a.	1725	1832	1916	...	...	...	2032
Poznań Gł. d.	1745	1835	...	...	1937	1937	2035
Konin d.	1844	1921	...	...	2044	2044	2121
Kutno **1025** d.	1923	1957	...	...	2123	2123	2157
Warszawa Zachodnia a.	2024	2054	...	...	2224	2224	2254
Warszawa Centralna **1025** a.	2030	2100	...	...	2230	2230	2300
Warszawa Wschodnia **1025** a.	2046	2116	...	...	2246	2246	2316

	EC 248 ⚒	IC 54	IC 1806	IC 1856	IC 57108	EC 246	IC 1702 2702	EIC 1804	EC 230
	A	C	S	Uh	M	C	m	S	B
Warszawa Wschodnia **1025** d.	0444	...	0514	0514	...	0644	0709	0744	...
Warszawa Centralna **1025** d.	0500	...	0530	0530	...	0700	0730	0800	...
Warszawa Zachodnia d.	0505	...	0535	0535	...	0705	0735	0805	...
Kutno **1025** d.	0602	...	0637	0637	...	0802	0837	|	...
Konin d.	0639	...	0715	0715	...	0839	0916	|	...
Poznań Gł. a.	0724	...	0821	0821	...	0924	1013	1019	...
Poznań Gł. ▷ d.	0730	...	...	...	0831	0930	1035	...	1030
Zbąszynek ▷ d.	0819	...	...	...	0925	1019	1141	...	1119
Zielona Góra Gł ▷ d.	|	0904	...	...	1005	|	1217	...	|
Rzepin 🏛 ◐ ▷ d.	0857	0949	...	...	...	1057	...	...	1157
Frankfurt (Oder) 🏛 ⊖ d.	0912	1012	...	...	...	1112	...	...	1212
Berlin Ostbahnhof ⊖ a.	|	|	...	...	...	|	...	...	|
Berlin Hbf ⊖ a.	1013**b**	1113**b**	...	...	...	1213**b**	...	...	1314**b**

	EC 48	EC 56	IC 38100		EC 46	IC 1808	IC 70108	EC 44	EC 58	IC 1810	IC 57104		EIC 1612	IC 17102	EIC 1800	EC 40 Ⓑ	IC 17100	EIC 1802		IC 27100		IC 18170
	A	E	LU		A	SY		A	G	S	M				S	A		S		L		R
Warszawa Wschodnia **1025** d.	0844	...	0914	...	1044	1059	...	1244	...	1304	...	...	1500	1509	1544	1644	1714	1744	...	1914	...	2239
Warszawa Centralna **1025** d.	0900	...	0930	...	1100	1130	...	1300	...	1330	...	...	1505	1530	1600	1700	1730	1800	...	1930	...	2250
Warszawa Zachodnia d.	0905	...	0935	...	1105	1135	...	1305	...	1334	...	...	1602	1536	1605	1705	1735	1805	...	1935	...	2255
Kutno **1025** d.	1002	...	1037	...	1202	1237	...	1402	...	1437	...	...	1639	1638	|	1802	1837	|	...	2037	...	0010
Konin d.	1039	...	1116	...	1239	1316	...	1439	...	1516	...	...	1724	|	|	1839	1916	|	...	2116	...	0056
Poznań Gł. a.	1124	...	1221	...	1324	1421	...	1524	...	1621	...	...	...	1847	1818	1924	2013	2019	...	2213	...	0203
Poznań Gł. ▷ d.	1130	...	...	...	1330	...	1441	1530	...	...	1639	...	...	1859	...	1930	2025	...	...	...	...	0212
Zbąszynek ▷ d.	1210	...	...	...	1410	...	1537	1610	...	...	1736	...	...	1040	...	2010	2120	...	...	...	...	0300
Zielona Góra Gł. ▷ a.	|	1304	...	...	|	...	1620	|	1704	...	1818	...	...	2025	...	|	2205	...	...	...	...	|
Rzepin 🏛 ◐ ▷ d.	1257	1349	...	...	1457	...	...	1657	1749	...	...	...	...	...	...	2057	...	...	...	...	...	0352
Frankfurt (Oder) 🏛 ⊖ d.	1312	1412	...	...	1512	...	...	1712	1812	...	...	...	...	...	...	2112	...	...	...	...	...	...
Berlin Ostbahnhof ⊖ a.	|	|	...	...	|	...	...	|	|	...	...	...	...	...	...	|	...	...	...	...	...	...
Berlin Hbf ⊖ a.	1412**b**	1513**b**	...	...	1613**b**	...	...	1812**b**	1915**b**	...	...	...	...	...	...	2217**b**	...	...	...	...	...	...

SELECTED LOCAL TRAINS RZEPIN - ZBASZYNEK / ZIELONA GORA - POZNAŃ

		Ⓐ			Ⓐ						Ⓐ
Rzepin d.	0554	0651	...	0856	1047	...	1330	...	1620	2007	...
Zielona Góra Gł. d.	|	|	0754	|	|	1110	|	1441	|	|	2047
Zbąszynek d.	0650	0757	0836	0952	1143	1159	1426	1528	1716	2103	2127
Poznań Gł. a.	...	...	0945	...	...	1307	...	1647	...	...	2236

			Ⓐ			Ⓐ		Ⓐ			
Poznań Gł. d.	...	0608	...	...	1045	...	...	...	1710	...	1843
Zbąszynek d.	0700	0721	0905	1116	1201	1345	1510	1626	1826	1825	2013
Zielona Góra Gł. a.	|	0807	|	|	1245	|	|	|	1910	|	2052
Rzepin a.	0757	...	1002	1213	...	1442	1607	1723	...	1922	...

A – BERLIN WARSZAWA EXPRESS – (12) ✕ 🅁 Berlin - Poznań - Warszawa and v.v. See Table **56**.
B – BERLIN GDANSK EXPRESS / GEDANIA – (12) ✕ 🅁 Berlin - Poznań - Gdansk - Gdynia and v.v. (Tables **57**, **1020**).
C – ODER / ODRA – (12) ✕ 🅁 Berlin - Zielona Góra - Kraków and v.v.
E – WAWEL – (12) ✕ Berlin - Zielona Góra - Kraków - Przemyśl and v.v. See Table **77**.
G – GALICJA – (12) ✕ Berlin - Zielona Góra - Kraków - Przemyśl and v.v. See Table **77**.
L – To / from Lublin or Rzeszow (Table **1055**).
M – To / from Gdynia (Table **1020**).
R – To / from Świnoujście (Table **1003**).
S – To / from Szczecin (Table **1010**).
U – To / from Świnoujście (Table **1010**).
W – To / from Wrocław (Table **1070**).
Y – To / from Suwałki (Table **1042**).

b – Berlin Gesundbrunnen. Depart / arrive Berlin Hbf and Berlin Ostbahnhof on certain dates.
g – June 15 – 18, 23 – 27 only.
h – June 19 – 22 and June 28 - Aug. 30.
m – Starts from Lublin (Table **1055**) on ①⑥ (also June 19, Aug. 15, Nov. 12; not June 21, Aug. 16).
n – Extended to Lublin (Table **1055**) on ⑤⑦ (also June 20, Aug. 15; not June 18, Aug. 14).

◐ – Ticketing point is Kunowice.
• – Distance from Zbąszynek.
▷ – For local trains see panel below main table.
⊖ – Berlin - Frankfurt an der Oder: see also Table **838**. Frankfurt an der Oder - Rzepin: see also Table **1003**.

PKP, Polregio — SZCZECIN and FRANKFURT ODER - RZEPIN - ZIELONA GÓRA — 1003

km		IC 82160	⚒	⑦	IC 8314 8354		EC 59		IC 8308 8358		EC 57		IC 8302		Ⓑ		EC 55		IC 86102 86152	⑥⑦	IC 81170
		Lt			Km		G		Ps		E		KR				C		Jp		RW
0	**Szczecin** Gł. d.	0418	0530	...	0644	...	...	0830	1049	...	...	1230	1456	...	1530	1630	...	...	1816	...	2356
104	Kostrzyn d.	0526	0657	0657	0753	...	...	0958	1158	...	...	1402	1610	...	1700	1803	...	...	1924	2105	0107
	Frankfurt (Oder) 🏛 d.	|	|	|	|	0812	0950	|	|	1212	1350	|	|	1610	|	|	1750	2015	|	|	|
	Kunowice d.	|	|	|	|	0825	|	|	|	1225	|	|	|	1624	|	|	|	2028	|	|	|
136	Rzepin 🏛 ◐ d.	0559	0742	0742	0817	0850	1012	1029	1223	1236	1412	1432	1634	1650	1729	1833	1812	2046	1955	2129	0129
207	**Zielona Góra** Gł. a.	0642	0838	0838	0900	0949	1055	1125	1306	1342	1455	1528	1717	1749	...	1935	1854	2145	2040	2216	...

	IC 18170				IC 68102 68152	⚒	EC 54			IC 3802		EC 56		IC 3808 3858		EC 58		IC 3814		IC 28160
	RW				Jn		C			KR		E		Pr		G		K		Lq
Zielona Góra Gł d.	...	...	0453	0637	0719	...	0904	0913	1005	1042	1222	1304	1430	1454	1633	1704	1829	1859	...	2134
Rzepin 🏛 ◐ d.	0353	...	0551	0737	0802	0828	0949	1013	1111	1126	1319	1349	1535	1538	1731	1749	1936	1948	...	2218
Kunowice d.	|	...	|	0746	|	|	|	|	1121	|	|	|	1546	|	|	|	1946	|	...	|
Frankfurt (Oder) 🏛 a.	|	...	|	0801	|	|	1009	|	1136	|	|	1409	1603	|	|	1809	2001	|	...	|
Kostrzyn d.	0416	...	0628	...	0824	0858	...	1045	...	1149	1353	...	...	1600	1801	...	...	2011	...	2241
Szczecin Gł. a.	0533	...	0754	...	0933	1024	...	1211	...	1254	1524	...	...	1709	1927	...	...	2119	...	2354

C – ODER / ODRA – (12) ✕ Berlin - Zielona Góra - Kraków and v.v.
E – WAWEL – (12) ✕ Berlin - Zielona Góra - Przemyśl and v.v.
G – GALICJA – (12) ✕ Berlin - Zielona Góra - Przemyśl and v.v.
J – To / from Wrocław Gł (Table **1004**).
K – To / from Kraków (Table **1075**).
L – To / from Lublin (Table **1061** / **1067**).
P – To / from Przemyśl (Table **1075**).
R – To / from Świnoujście (Table **1010**).
W – To / from Warszawa (Table **1001**).

m – Extended to Przemyśl on ⑤⑦ (also June 18, Aug. 14; not June 20).
n – Extended to Świnoujście June 19 – 22 and June 28 - Aug. 30.
p – Starts from Świnoujście June 19 – 22 and June 28 - Aug. 30.
q – ⑤⑦ (also June 18, Aug. 14; not June 20, Aug. 15).
r – Extended to Świnoujście on ⑤⑥ (also June 18, Aug. 14, Nov. 10).
s – Starts from Świnoujście on ⑥⑦ (also June 19, Aug. 15, Nov. 11).
t – ①⑥ (also June 19, Aug. 15, Nov. 12; not June 21, Aug. 16).

◐ – Ticketing point is Kunowice.

☛ For additional trains Frankfurt Oder - Rzepin see Table **1001**. Additional services operate **Szczecin - Kostrzyn** and v.v.

1004 ZIELONA GÓRA - WROCŁAW

Koleje Dolnośląskie, PKP

km			IC 73104 P		IC 82160 t LS		IC 8314 Sm			EC 59 G		IC 8308 Ⓐ PS	IC 8358 s PR		EC 57 E		IC 8302 R		EC 55 C		IC 86102 86152 Sp		
0	**Zielona Góra** Gł	d.	0529	0640	0652	0703	0801	0902	0919	1007	1057	1208	1308	1308	1406	1457	1535	1719	1758	1856	1905	2042	2059	2150
23	Nowa Sól	d.	0548	0655	0711	0723	0820	0917	0937	1023	|	1227	1322	1322	1424	|	1554	1733	1817	|	1924	2057	2118	2208
54	Glogów	d.	0620	0720	0739	0751	0846	0945	1006	1044	1133	1258	1346	1346	1452	1533	1628	1757	1844	1929	1953	2122	2155	2236
154	**Wrocław** Gł	a.	0802	0844	0913	0917	1014	1100	1137	1228	1252	1431	1506	1506	1628	1653	1806	1912	2024	2047	2147	2241	2324	0008
	Kraków **1075**	a.	...	1223	...	...	...	1422	...	...	1606	...	1815	1815	...	2006	...	2205	...	2347	...	...	...	...

			IC 68102 68152 Sn			EC 54 C		IC 3802 R			EC 56 E	IC 3808 Ⓐ PS	IC 3858 r PR			EC 58 G		IC 3814 S		IC 37104 P		IC 28160 q LS	
	Kraków **1075**	d.	...	...	...	...	0420	...	0555	...	...	0759	0944	0944	...	...	1156	...	1333	...	1543	...	...	...
	Wrocław Gł	d.	...	0520	...	0552	0713	0740	0847	0854	1037	1109	1251	1251	1257	1450	1510	1552	1657	1715	1900	1907	1844	2054
	Glogów	d.	0532	0638	0646	0721	0830	0909	1005	1028	1208	1229	1412	1412	1429	1636	1629	1728	1819	1843	2015	2035	2055	2226
	Nowa Sól	d.	0600	0702	0711	0747	|	0936	1026	1049	1235	|	1433	1433	1456	1703	|	1756	1840	1906	2037	2102	2117	2254
	Zielona Góra Gł	a.	0618	0717	0730	0806	0902	0955	1040	1104	1255	1302	1446	1446	1515	1722	1702	1815	1855	1920	2052	2121	2132	2312

C – ODER / ODRA – (12) ✕ Berlin - Zielona Góra - Kraków and v.v.
E – WAWEL – (12) ✕ Berlin - Zielona Góra - Kraków - Przemyśl and v.v.
G – GALICJA – (12) ✕ Berlin - Zielona Góra - Kraków - Przemyśl and v.v.
L – To / from Lublin (Table **1061** / **1067**).
P – To / from Przemyśl (Table **1075**).
R – To / from Świnoujście (Table **1010**).
S – To / from Szczecin (Table **1003**).

m – Extended to Przemyśl on ⑤⑦ (also June 18, Aug. 14; not June 20).
n – Extended to Świnoujście June 19 – 22 and June 28 - Aug. 30.
p – Starts from Świnoujście June 19 – 22 and June 28 - Aug. 30.
q – ⑤⑦ (also June 18, Aug.14; not June 20, Aug. 15).
r – ⑤⑥ (also June 18, Aug. 14).
s – ⑥⑦ (also June 19, Aug. 15).
t – ①⑥ (also June 19, Aug. 15; not June 21, Aug. 16).

1010 SZCZECIN - POZNAŃ

Koleje Wielkopolskie, Polregio, PKP

km				EIC 8100	IC 83106 Z	Ⓐ	EIP 8102	IC 8322 n	IC 8352 Zh	IC 8110	IC 8108 Y		IC 83100 E	IC 8320	EIC 8104 n	EIC 8154 h	IC 8120 L		IC 8106 g	IC 8156 k		IC 83196 Z	IC 83172 A	IC 81170 ◧ B
	Świnoujście	d.	...	...	...	...	...	...	...	...	...	...	1155	...	...	1423	...	...	...	1554	1649	1823	1915	2209
0	**Szczecin** Gł. **1015**	d.	...	0541	0603	0606	0745	0827	0827	0928	1120	1210	1326	1430	1540	1540	1626	1633	1727	1727	1824	2014	2039	2356
15	Szczecin Dąbie **1015**	d.	...	0553	0616	0621	0758	0840	0840	0940	1132	1223	1338	1443	1552	1552	1638	1647	1739	1739	1837	2027	2052	|
40	Stargard **1015**	d.	...	0608	0635	0640	0813	0854	0854	0955	1146	1241	1353	1457	1608	1608	1653	1706	1754	1754	1856	2044	2107	|
130	Krzyż **1000**	d.	0506	0649	0731	0749	0853	0939	0702	1039	1233	1350	1439	1543	1649	1649	1739	1813	1839	1839	2007	2140	2155	|
213	**Poznań** Gł. **1000**	a.	0618	0728	0823	0856	0932	1023	0800	1123	1317	1454	1523	1627	1729	1729	1823	1916	1923	1923	2113	2234	2241	0311
	Warszawa Cent. **1001**	a.	...	0959	|	...	1159	|	|	1430	1630	...	1830	|	2000	2000	...	...	2230	2230	...	|	|	0630
	Katowice **1075 1080**	a.	...	...	1258	...	...	|	|	...	...	...	...	|	...	...	...	...	...	...	...	0452	|	...
	Kraków Gł **1075 1080**	a.	...	...	1401	...	...	1653	1653	...	...	...	...	2217	...	...	...	...	...	...	...	...	0525	...

			IC 18170 ◧ B	IC 38172 A		IC 1806 g	IC 1856 m	IC 1820 L	EIC 1804 j	EIC 1854		IC 3820	IC 38100 E		IC 1808 Y	IC 1810		IC 3822 j	IC 3852 Z	EIP 1800	IC 38107 Z	EIC 1802		
	Kraków Gł. **1075 1080**	d.	...	2229	...	...	...	...	...	...	...	0534	...	...	...	...	...	1202	1202	...	1403	...	...	...
	Katowice **1075 1080**	d.	...	|	...	...	...	...	...	...	...	|	...	...	...	...	...	|	|	...	1516	...	...	...
	Warszawa Cent. **1001**	d.	2250	|	...	0530	0530	...	0800	0800	...	|	0930	...	1130	1330	...	|	|	1600	|	1800	...	...
	Poznań Gł. **1000**	d.	0212	0515**a**	0633	0836	0836	0936	1031	1031	1037	1136	1236	1336	1436	1636	1642	1743	1743	1826	1936	2031	2157	2257
	Krzyż **1000**	d.	|	0602	0738	0921	0921	1020	1111	1111	1142	1221	1324	1442	1521	1721	1749	1827	1827	1906	2028	2111	2307	0006
	Stargard **1015**	d.	|	0649	0845	1005	1005	1105	1151	1151	1250	1307	1415	1550	1607	1806	1855	1912	1912	1946	2121	2151	...	...
	Szczecin Dąbie **1015**	d.	|	0703	0906	1019	1019	1120	1205	1205	1312	1321	1430	1615	1622	1820	1919	1926	1926	2000	2138	2205	...	...
	Szczecin Gł. **1015**	a.	0533	0717	0920	1031	1031	1132	1217	1217	1326	1334	1442	1630	1635	1833	1933	1939	1939	2014	2151	2217	...	...
	Świnoujście	a.	0715	0841	1057	...	1201	...	...	1334	...	...	1620	1827	...	...	2133	...	...	...	...	...	...	...

km			Ⓐ	Ⓒ	Ⓐ		Ⓐ		Ⓐp	k		
0	**Świnoujście**	d.	0419	0516	0622	0728	0828	0956	1347	1539	1741	1951
99	Szczecin Dąbie	d.	0542	0640	0746	0852	0958	1127	1512	1704	1907	2114
111	**Szczecin** Gł.	a.	0556	0653	0800	0906	1011	1142	1526	1718	1921	2129

		Ⓐp		Ⓐp			Ⓐp				
Szczecin Gł.	d.	0404	0526	0633	0806	1145	1348	1520	1742	...	...
Szczecin Dąbie	d.	0418	0540	0648	0820	1159	1403	1535	1756	...	...
Świnoujście	a.	0544	0704	0811	0946	1319	1524	1701	1922	...	...

km			⚒q					IC 80100			e	
0	**Szczecin** Gł.	d.	...	...	0712	...	1059	1403	1514	1737	1905	...
12	Szczecin Dąbie	d.	...	...	0726	...	1114	1418	1529	1752	1920	...
37	Stargard	d.	0437	...	0747	...	1133	1439	1553	1818	1947	...
102	Kalisz Pomorski	d.	0531	...	0903	...	1236	1540	1713	1925	2056	...
146	Wałcz	d.	0624	...	0947	...	1320	1629	1755	2012	2140	...
176	**Piła** Główna	a.	0653	...	1016	...	1349	1700	1823	2040	2210	...

		f		⚒			IC 88100				
Piła Główna	d.	...	...	0546	0725	...	1057	1419	1558	1942	...
Wałcz	d.	0356	...	0617	0755	...	1131	1448	1628	2011	...
Kalisz Pomorski	d.	0440	...	0700	0840	...	1214	1541	1712	2055	...
Stargard	d.	0555	...	0805	0947	...	1323	1654	1817	2201	...
Szczecin Dąbie	d.	0613	...	0831	1005	...	1344	1713	1843	2227	...
Szczecin Gł.	a.	0627	...	0846	1020	...	1359	1728	1858	2242	...

A – PRZEMYŚLANIN – 🛏 1, 2 cl., ▬ 2 cl., (12) ✕ Świnoujście - Kraków - Przemyśl and v.v.
B – 🛏 1, 2 cl., ▬ 2 cl., (12) Świnoujście - Szczecin - Kostrzyn - Poznan - Warszawa and v.v.
E – To / from Lublin or Rzeszow (Table **1055**).
L – To / From Łódź (Table **1080**).
Y – To / from Suwałki (Table **1042**).
Z – To / from Zakopane (Table **1066**).

a – Arrives at Poznań Główny 0445.
e – ⑤⑦ (also June 18, Aug. 14).
f – ①⑥ (also June 19, Aug. 15).

g – June 15 – 18, 23 – 27.
h – June 28 - Aug. 30.
j – June 15 – 27.
k – June 19 – 22, June 28 - Aug. 30.
m – Not June 23 – 27.
n – Not June 28 - Aug. 30.
p – Not June 19, 20.
q – Not June 19, Aug. 15.

◧ – Via Kostrzyn (Table **1003**).

KOŁOBRZEG - SZCZECIN / KOSZALIN - GDYNIA - GDAŃSK 1015

PKP, Polregio

km		IC 85108 O	EIP 8300 K	IC 68150 ⑤⑥ Wd	IC 38150 Eg	TLK 83108 Z	TLK 38190 Dm	IC 78172 P	IC 85106 O	IC 81114 L	IC 68101 ⚒ W	IC 48100 S	IC 18100 T	IC 81104 B	IC 68105 ⑦ Wr	IC 3804 D	IC 85104 O		IC 3806 P	IC 85102 O	TLK 38110 K	IC 85100	TLK 83170 K	n	IC 3812 P	IC 38102 R	
0	**Szczecin** Gł. 1010 d.	0400	...	...	...	...	...	...	0658	...	...	...	...	1110	...	...	1317	...	...	1505	...	1754	...	...	...	...	1938
15	Szczecin Dąbie 1010 d.	0413	...	...	...	...	...	...	0711	...	...	...	...	1123	...	...	1330	...	...	1518	...	1808	...	...	...	...	1953
40	Stargard 1010 d.	0430	...	...	...	...	...	...	0728	...	...	...	...	1141	...	...	1346	...	...	1537	...	1827	...	...	...	...	2017
*231	**Poznań** Gł. d.	|	...	0145	0303	...	...	0532	|	...	0745	0942	...	|	1024	1142	|	1230	1342	|	1542	|	...	1650	1737	...	|
*135	Piła Gł. d.	|	...	0253	0411	...	0523	0639	|	...	0905	1049	1110	|	1201	1251	|	1412	1449	|	1706	|	...	1828	1851	1902	|
64	Szczecinek d.	|	...	0349	0516	...	0621	0738	|	...	1000	1143	1203	|	1304	1342	|	1518	1545	|	1812	|	...	1930	1945	2000	|
151	Białogard d.	0545	...	0432	0606	...	0709	0829	0854	...	1044	1237	1248	1257	1406	1423	1505	1618	1641	1703	1905	1950	...	2020	2043	2055	2140
187	Kołobrzeg ◧ d.	|	0608	|	0635	0649	0747	|	|	1031	1114	|	1323	|	1435	1452	|	1659	|	|	1940	|	2028	2056	|	2123	|
175	**Koszalin** d.	0603	0643	0452	...	0730	...	0848	0911	1112	...	1253	...	1316	...	...	1524	...	1658	1719	...	2006	2119	...	2100	...	2158
242	Słupsk d.	0648	0724	0545	...	0818	...	0937	0955	1205	...	1335	...	1406	...	...	1605	...	1738	1814	...	2051	2212	...	2155	...	...
294	Lębork d.	0722	0755	...	...	0851	...	...	1032	1235	...	...	...	1439	...	...	1637	...	...	1846	...	2127	2245	...	...	...	...
353	**Gdynia** Gł. a.	0809	0830	...	...	0932	...	...	1115	1317	...	...	...	1521	...	...	1726	...	...	1930	...	2208	2329	...	...	...	...
353	**Gdynia** Gł. ▷ d.	0811	0833	...	...	0935	...	...	1118	1320	...	...	...	1538	...	...	1740	...	...	1933	...	2210	2334	...	...	...	...
362	Sopot ▷ d.	0819	0842	...	...	0944	...	...	1127	1329	...	...	...	1549	...	...	1749	...	...	1942	...	2218	2345	...	...	...	...
374	**Gdańsk** Gł. ▷ a.	0833	0856	...	...	0957	...	...	1140	1342	...	...	...	1602	...	...	1803	...	...	1956	...	2232	2400	...	...	...	...
	Warszawa C. 1025/30 a.	...	1130	...	...	1305	...	...	...	1700	...	...	...	...	...	...	...	...	...	...	...	...	0345	...	...	...	...

	p	Ⓐ q	IC 83102 R	IC 8312 P	IC 58100 n	TLK 83110 K	IC 38170 K	IC 8306 P	IC 58102 O	IC 83150 Ef	EIC 1850 h	IC 58104 O	IC 8304 D	IC 86150 ⑥⑦ We	IC 86104 ⑥ W	IC 18104 B	IC 81100 T	IC 84100 S	IC 86100 Ⓑ Wj	IC 18114 L	IC 58106 O	IC 87172 P	TLK 38108 Z	EIP 3800 K	IC 58108 O
Warszawa C. 1025/30 d.	...	...	...	...	...	...	0202	...	...	...	0645	...	...	...	...	...	...	...	...	1100	...	...	1500	1630	...
Gdańsk Gł. ▷ d.	...	...	...	...	0515	...	0604	...	0836	...	0934	1017	...	...	...	1220	...	...	...	1420	1607	...	1819	1857	1924
Sopot ▷ d.	...	...	...	...	0529	...	0621	...	0850	...	0949	1031	...	...	...	1235	...	...	...	1435	1621	...	1834	1912	1938
Gdynia Gł. ▷ a.	...	...	...	...	0538	...	0631	...	0859	...	0958	1039	...	...	...	1244	...	...	...	1444	1630	...	1843	1921	1947
Gdynia Gł. d.	...	...	...	...	0541	...	0636	...	0903	...	1001	1042	...	...	...	1247	...	...	...	1449	1648	...	1847	1926	1950
Lębork d.	...	...	...	...	0637	...	0757	...	0949	...	1048	1132	...	...	...	1332	...	...	...	1532	1738	...	1935	2004	2034
Słupsk d.	...	0504	...	0609	0725	...	0836	1013	1026	...	1127	1206	...	1219	...	1405	...	1415	...	1607	1812	1829	2008	2035	2119
Koszalin d.	...	0603	...	0711	0812	...	0930	1102	1112	...	1210	1254	...	1323	...	1448	...	1502	...	1703	1853	1911	2057	2118	2201
Kołobrzeg d.	0435	|	0656	|	|	0908	1009	|	|	1117	1249	|	1300	|	1350	|	1454	|	1633	1752	|	|	2136	2152	|
Białogard d.	0511	0621	0728	0739	0828	0938	...	1118	1127	1147	...	1314	1329	1341	1424	1505	1522	1533	1706	...	1909	1926	...	...	2217
Szczecinek d.	0607	|	0807	0821	|	1019	...	1203	|	1302	...	|	1419	|	1503	|	1601	1617	1750	...	|	2019	...	...	|
Piła Gł. d.	0720	|	0858	0913	|	1118	...	1308	|	1415	...	|	1516	1543	1607	|	1722	1711	1859	...	|	2115	...	...	|
Poznań Gł. a.	0906	|	...	1016	|	1230	...	1416	|	1530	...	|	1620	1655	1715	|	...	1816	2015	...	|	2226	...	...	|
Stargard 1010 d.	...	0745	...	...	0939	...	...	...	1241	...	...	1431	...	...	...	1623	...	...	...	...	2030	...	...	...	2330
Szczecin Dąbie 1010 d.	...	0807	...	...	0955	...	...	...	1257	...	...	1447	...	...	...	1639	...	...	...	...	2046	...	...	...	2346
Szczecin Gł. 1010 a.	...	0821	...	...	1008	...	...	...	1310	...	...	1500	...	...	...	1653	...	...	...	...	2059	...	...	...	2359

B – To / from Białystok (Table **1035**).
D – To / from Kraków (Table **1025**, **1060**, **1075**).
E – To / from Kraków (Table **1070**, **1075**).
K – To / from Kraków (Tables **1065**, **1067**, **1080**).
L – To / from Łódź (Table **1090**).
O – To / from Olsztyn (Table **1035**).
P – To / from Przemyśl (Table **1075**).
R – To / from Rzeszów (Table **1058**).
S – To / from Katowice (Tables **1070**, **1075**).
T – To / from Warszawa (Table **1025**).
W – To / from Wrocław (Table **1070**).
Z – To / from Zakopane (Table **1066**).

d – Also Aug. 14.
e – Also Aug. 15.
f – ⑥⑦ June 28 - Aug. 30.
g – ⑤⑥ June 27 - Aug. 30.
h – June 28 - Aug. 30.
j – Also June 21.
m – June 27 - Aug. 30.
n – Not June 21.
p – Not June 15, 22.
q – Not June 19, Aug. 15.
r – Not June. 15.

* – Distance from Białogard.
◧ – Distance from Koszalin to Kołobrzeg 43km.
▷ – Frequent local trains run between Gdynia and Gdansk.

SZCZECIN - KOŁOBRZEG 1016

Polregio

km		Ⓐ						Ⓐ m	n		
0	**Szczecin** Gł. d.	0506	0617	0901	1028	1246	1442	1549	1702	1848	2056
35	Goleniów ✈ d.	0556	0657	0934	1101	1328	1522	1629	1746	1927	2134
141	Kołobrzeg a.	0740	0857	1106	1301	1513	1701	1816	1924	2115	2259

	⚒ p			Ⓐ	q			k		Ⓑ
Kołobrzeg d.	0404	0500	0605	0757	0936	1126	1339	1557	1716	1937
Goleniów ✈ d.	0553	0651	0758	0956	1126	1327	1522	1808	1909	2115
Szczecin Gł. a.	0632	0730	0840	1030	1201	1404	1601	1837	1946	2156

k – June 19 - Aug. 30. **m** – Also June 15; not Aug. 15. **n** – Not June 19, 20. **p** – Not June 19, Aug. 15. **q** – Not June 19, 22.

GDYNIA / GDAŃSK and OLSZTYN - BYDGOSZCZ - TORUŃ - POZNAŃ 1020

PKP

km		IC 261 B	IC 57108 G	IC 57100	IC 56100 J	EC 230 D	IC 56102	IC 263 B		IC 54104 E		IC 57102	IC 265 B	IC 57104 G	IC 54100 E		IC 5602	IC 5604	IC 57112	IC 5600	IC 5700		IC 461 B§
0	**Gdynia** Gł. ▷ d.	0403	0430	...	0547	0706	...	0803	...	0957	...	...	1203	1257	1359	...	...	1558	...	1753	1856	...	2323
9	Sopot ▷ d.	0412	0440	...	0557	0716	...	0812	...	1007	...	...	1212	1305	1409	...	...	1608	...	1803	1906	...	2333
21	**Gdańsk** Gł. ▷ d.	0429	0456	...	0614	0733	...	0829	...	1023	...	...	1229	1321	1425	...	...	1625	...	1821	1921	...	2350
53	Tczew ▷ d.	0445	0518	...	0632	0749	...	0845	...	1040	...	...	1245	1339	1441	...	...	1642	...	1839	1940	...	0007
181	**Bydgoszcz** Gł. d.	0555	0639	...	0746	0856	...	0955	...	1153	...	...	1355	1447	1553	...	...	1754	...	1951	2053	...	0120
	Olsztyn Gł. d.	|	|	0549	|	|	0750	|	...	|	...	1150	|	|	|	...	1546	|	1745	|	|	...	|
	Iława Gł. d.	|	|	0639	|	|	0839	|	...	|	...	1239	|	|	|	...	1634	|	1834	|	|	...	|
	Toruń Gł. d.	|	|	0749	|	|	0949	|	...	|	...	1349	|	|	|	...	1754	|	1944	|	|	...	|
227	Inowrocław d.	0623	0709	0811	0819	0924	1011	1023	...	1221	...	1411	1423	1515	1621	...	1816	1823	2006	2020	2121	...	0149
283	Gniezno d.	0654	0746	0848	0853	0954	1048	1054	...	1254	...	1448	1454	1553	1654	...	1848	1854	2049	2054	2154	...	0223
334	**Poznań** Gł. a.	0720	0816	0916	0920	1020	1116	1120	...	1320	...	1516	1520	1620	1720	...	1914	1920	2116	2120	2220	...	0249
	Wrocław 1070 a.	0849	...	...	1113	...	1317	1249	...	1511	...	...	1649	...	1908	...	2107	2050	...	2307	...	...	0425

km		IC 7500	IC 6500	IC 75112		IC 6504	IC 6502	IC 45100 E	IC 75104 G	IC 264 B	IC 75102		IC 45104 E		IC 262 B	IC 65102	EC 231 D	IC 65100 J	IC 75100	IC 75108 G	IC 260 B		IC 460 B‡
	Wrocław 1070 d.	...	0456	...	...	0710	0650	0851	...	1110	...	...	1250	...	1510	1438	...	1647	...	...	1910	...	2350
	Poznań Gł. d.	0520	0640	0644	...	0840	0846	1040	1140	1240	1244	...	1440	...	1640	1644	1740	1840	1844	1940	2040	...	0141
	Gniezno d.	0546	0707	0717	...	0907	0913	1107	1209	1307	1318	...	1506	...	1707	1718	1806	1907	1917	2010	2107	...	0208
0	Inowrocław d.	0618	0739	0748	...	0937	0944	1138	1241	1336	1348	...	1538	...	1736	1748	1835	1941	1948	2046	2136	...	0241
35	**Toruń** Gł. d.	|	|	0814	...	|	1008	|	|	|	1414	...	|	...	|	1814	|	|	2014	|	|	...	|
129	Iława Gł. d.	|	|	0923	...	|	1117	|	|	|	1524	...	|	...	|	1923	|	|	2123	|	|	...	|
198	**Olsztyn** Gł. a.	|	|	1009	...	|	1203	|	|	|	1609	...	|	...	|	2009	|	|	2208	|	|	...	|
	Bydgoszcz Gł. ▷ d.	0647	0810	...	...	1006	...	1207	1311	1406	...	...	1608	...	1806	...	1904	2012	...	2117	2206	...	0327
	Tczew ▷ d.	0759	0921	...	...	1113	...	1317	1418	1512	...	...	1715	...	1912	...	2009	2124	...	2235	2312	...	0437
	Gdańsk Gł. ▷ a.	0816	0936	...	...	1128	...	1332	1435	1527	...	...	1731	...	1927	...	2024	2141	...	2256	2327	...	0453
	Sopot ▷ a.	0831	0953	...	...	1147	...	1348	1450	1543	...	...	1747	...	1943	...	2040	2157	...	2312	2343	...	0509
	Gdynia Gł. ▷ a.	0841	1003	...	...	1158	...	1359	1501	1554	...	...	1757	...	1954	...	2051	2208	...	2323	2354	...	0520

B – BALTIC EXPRESS To / from Praha (Table **1010** / **1095**).
D – GEDANIA – (12) ✕ Ⓡ Berlin - Poznań - Gdynia and v.v. (Table **56**).
E – To / from Bielsko-Biała (Tables **1075** / **1076** / **1079**).
G – To / from Zielona Góra (Table **1001**).
J – To / from Jelenia Góra (Table **1084**).

§ – Also conveys 🛏 (1, 2, 3 berth) until Aug. 30.
‡ – Also conveys 🛏 (1, 2, 3 berth) until Aug. 31.
▷ – See also Table **1025**. Frequent local services run between Gdynia and Gdansk (see Table **1035**).

1025 GDYNIA - GDAŃSK - BYDGOSZCZ - WARSZAWA / ŁODŹ

Arriva RP, PKP, Polregio

Warning! Timings may vary by several minutes on certain dates. Readers are strongly advised to confirm timings locally before travelling.

km		*IC* 5224	*IC* 5334		*IC* 83104	*IC* 52100		*IC* 5422	*IC* 83102	*IC* 5222	*TLK* 54102	*IC* 5360			*IC* 5124		*IC* 5220		*IC* 5420	*IC* 81100	*IC* 5128		
		L		Ⓑ	**R**	**C**			**KR**	**L**		**Z**	Ⓐ				**L**		**B**	**K**			Ⓐ
0	**Gdynia** Gł.... **1020 1030 1035** d.	...	...	...	...	...	...	0707	...	...	0855	1052	...	...	...	...	...	...	1452	...	1651	...	...
9	Sopot .... **1020 1030 1035** d.	...	...	...	...	...	...	0717	...	...	0904	1102	...	...	...	...	...	...	1502	...	1701	...	...
21	**Gdańsk** Gł... **1020 1030 1035** d.	...	...	...	...	...	...	0733	...	...	0921	1118	...	...	...	...	...	...	1517	...	1716	...	...
53	Tczew .... **1020 1030 1035** d.	...	...	...	...	...	...	0752	...	...	0944	1137	...	...	...	...	...	...	1537	...	1735	...	...
	Malbork.............**1030 1035** d.	...	...	...	...	...	...	|	...	...	0959	|	...	...	...	...	...	...	|	...	|	...	...
	Piła Gł. .... d.	...	...	...	0517	...	...	|	0927	...	|	|	...	...	...	...	...	...	|	1722	|	...	...
181	**Bydgoszcz** Gł. .... **1020** a.	...	...	...	0624	...	...	0902	1037	...	|	1250	...	...	...	...	...	...	1650	1830	1844	...	...
181	**Bydgoszcz** Gł. .... d.	0438	0552	0602	0628	0831	0851	0916	1040	1240	|	1300	1327	...	1440	1445	1638	1645	1700	1838	1854	2029	2145
232	**Toruń** Gł. .... d.	0516	0630	|	0719	0911	|	0954	1118	1318	|	1338	|	...	1518	|	1716	|	1738	1918	1932	|	|
287	Włocławek .... d.	0549	0703	|	0751	0944	|	1030	1151	1351	|	1410	|	...	1551	|	1749	|	1810	1951	2005	|	|
	Grudziądz .... d.	|	|	0715	|	|	1016	|	|	|	1120**a**	|	1447	...	|	1558	|	1804	|	|	|	2142	2255
342	Kutno .... **1001** d.	0620	0738	...	0823	1022	...	1101	1222	1422	1505	1441	...	...	1622	...	1822	...	1841	2022	2045	...	...
469	**Warszawa** Centralna..... **1001** a.	0730	|	...	0930	1130	...	|	1330	1530	|	|	...	...	1730	...	1930	...	|	2130	|	...	...
474	**Warszawa** Wschodnia... **1001** a.	0746	|	...	0946	1146	...	|	1346	1546	|	|	...	...	1746	...	1946	...	|	2146	|	...	...
413	**Łódź** Widzew..................... a.	...	0853	...	...	...	...	1217	...	...	1622	1607	...	...	...	...	...	...	1937	...	2208	...	...
	Katowice **1060**................ a.	...	|	...	...	...	...	1505	...	...	1940	|	...	...	...	...	...	...	2212	...	...	...	...
	Kraków **1065** .... a.	...	1138	...	...	...	...	...	...	...	...	1915	...	...	...	...	...	...	...	...	...	...	...

km					*IC* 1528	*IC* 18100	*IC* 4520	*IC* 2520		*IC* 1524	*IC* 3560	*TLK* 45102	*IC* 2522		*IC* 38102		*IC* 4522	*IC* 25100		*IC* 38104	*IC* 3534	*IC* 1508	*IC* 2524
				Ⓐ		**K**	**B**	**L**			**Z**		**L**	Ⓑ	**KR**			**C**		**R**			**L**
	Kraków **1065**. .... d.	...	...	...	...	...	...	...	...	...	0922	...	...	...	...	...	...	...	...	...	1608	...	...
	Katowice **1060**................ d.	...	...	...	...	...	0520	...	...	...	|	0841	...	...	...	...	1319	...	...	...	|	...	...
	Łódź Widzew..................... d.	...	...	...	0550	...	0752	...	...	...	1200	1146	...	...	...	...	1613	...	...	...	1856	...	...
	Warszawa Wschodnia... **1001** d.	...	...	...	|	0614	|	0814	...	1014	|	|	1214	...	1414	...	|	1614	...	1814	|	1904	2014
	Warszawa Centralna..... **1001** d.	...	...	...	|	0630	|	0830	...	1030	|	|	1230	...	1430	...	|	1630	...	1830	|	1940	2030
	Kutno .... **1001** d.	...	...	...	0718	0737	0912	0941	...	1136	1318	1302	1336	...	1536	...	1734	1739	...	1936	2016	|	2138
	Grudziądz .... d.	0412	0600	0722	|	|	|	|	1108	|	|	1703**b**	|	1501	|	1738	|	|	...	|	|	|	|
	Włocławek............................ d.	|	|	|	0749	0807	0943	1011	|	1207	1349	|	1407	|	1607	|	1805	1809	...	2007	2046	2114	2208
	Toruń Gł. .... d.	|	|	|	0823	0842	1018	1046	|	1247	1424	|	1442	|	1642	|	1841	1845	...	2042	2121	2148	2243
	Bydgoszcz Gł. .... a.	0533	0712	0834	0900	0919	1055	1123	1221	1319	1501	|	1519	1613	1719	1902	1917	1922	...	2118	2158	2222	2320
0	**Bydgoszcz** Gł. .... **1020** d.	...	...	...	0908	0926	1105	...	...	...	1512	|	...	...	1723	...	1926	...	...	2121	...	...	...
85	Piła Gł. .... a.	...	...	...	|	1034	|	...	...	...	|	|	...	...	1830	...	|	...	...	2226	...	...	...
	Malbork.............**1030 1035** d.	...	...	...	|	...	|	...	...	...	|	1804	...	...	...	...	|	...	...	...	...	...	...
	Tczew .... **1020 1030 1035** d.	...	...	...	1022	...	1221	...	...	...	1622	1819	...	...	...	...	2047	...	...	...	...	...	...
	Gdańsk Gł... **1020 1030 1035** a.	...	...	...	1039	...	1238	...	...	...	1639	1841	...	...	...	...	2104	...	...	...	...	...	...
	Sopot .... **1020 1030 1035** a.	...	...	...	1100	...	1255	...	...	...	1654	1857	...	...	...	...	2119	...	...	...	...	...	...
	Gdynia Gł.... **1020 1030 1035** a.	...	...	...	1111	...	1304	...	...	...	1704	1908	...	...	...	...	2128	...	...	...	...	...	...

LOCAL TRAINS PIŁA - BYDGOSZCZ

		⚒n				Ⓑ		
Piła Gł. .... d.	0551	0742	1018	1152	1452	1612	1852	2116
Bydgoszcz Gł.................................. a.	0714	0907	1144	1314	1621	1741	2015	2237

	⚒n				Ⓑ			
Bydgoszcz Gł.................................. d.	0546	0740	1200	1253	1434	1546	1745	2027
Piła Gł. .... a.	0709	0900	1327	1417	1600	1707	1905	2147

B – To / from Bielsko-Biała (Tables **1059**).
C – To / from Chełm (Table **1055**).
K – To / from Kołobrzeg (Table **1015**).
L – To / from Lublin (Table **1055**).
R – To / from Rzeszów (Table **1058**).
Z – To / from Zakopane (Table **1066**).

a – Arrives 1100.
b – Arrives 1641.
n – Not June 19, Aug. 15, 16.

1030 GDYNIA - GDAŃSK and OLSZTYN - WARSZAWA

km		*TLK* 51108	*TLK* 53104	*EIP* 5300	*EIP* 5302	*IC* 51106	*EIP* 5400	*EIP* 8300	*EIP* 5402	*TLK* 83108	*EIP* 5304	*TLK* 51104	*EIP* 5306	*IC* 81114	*EIP* 5404	*EIP* 5308	*EIP* 5406	*IC* 51102	*EIP* 5104	*IC* 51100	*EIP* 5310	*EIP* 5102	*EIC* 5100	*TLK* 53170	*IC* 83170
			Z				**G**		**B**	**Z**					**G**	**R**	**B**			Ⓐ				**Z**	
	Kołobrzeg **1015** .... d.	...	...	...	...	...	...	0608	...	0649	...	...	...	1031	...	...	...	...	...	...	...	...	...	...	2028
0	**Gdynia** Gł. .... ▶ d.	0358	0515	0526	0633	0713	0726	0833	0926	0935	1026	1126	1226	1320	1326	1426	1526	1532	1626	1720	1733	1826	1926	1944	2334
9	Sopot...................... ▶ d.	0406	0525	0535	0642	0723	0735	0842	0935	0944	1035	1136	1235	1329	1335	1435	1535	1541	1635	1729	1742	1835	1935	1954	2345
21	**Gdańsk** Gł. .... ▶ d.	0422	0542	0552	0659	0741	0752	0859	0952	1000	1052	1152	1252	1345	1352	1452	1552	1557	1652	1744	1759	1852	1952	2012	0003
53	Tczew.................... ▶ d.	0440	0559	0606	|	0759	0806	|	1006	1017	1106	1210	1306	1410	1406	1506	1606	1614	1706	1803	|	1906	2006	2038	0024
72	Malbork .... ▶ d.	0451	0611	0617	|	0811	0817	|	1017	1029	1117	1223	1317	1422	1417	1517	1617	1625	1717	1815	|	1917	2017	2051	0038
141	Iława Gł. .... d.	0528	0657	0651	|	0858	0851	|	1051	1108	1151	1300	1351	1500	1451	1551	1651	1703	1751	1900	|	1951	2051	2130	0125
201	Działdowo.................... d.	0559	0730	|	|	0931	|	|	|	1140	|	1332	|	1531	|	|	|	1735	|	1932	|	|	|	2203	0201
251	Ciechanów.................... d.	0625	0758	|	|	1000	|	|	|	1206	|	1400	|	1557	|	|	|	1801	|	1959	|	|	|	2230	0233
345	**Warszawa** Wsch. .... a.	0722	0851	0822	0922	1051	1022	1122	1222	1256	1322	1451	1522	1651	1622	1722	1822	1851	1922	2051	2022	2122	2222	2326	0335
350	**Warszawa** Cent........... a.	0730	0859	0830	0930	1100	1030	1130	1230	1305	1330	1500	1530	1700	1630	1730	1830	1900	1930	2100	2030	2130	2230	2335	0345
	Kraków Gł. **1065** ..... a.	|	1156	1105	1205	|	...	1409	...	1659	1607	|	1810	|	...	2004	...	|	...	|	2305	...	...	0325	0757
	Łódź Fabr **1090** ... a.	0851	...	...	...	1231	...	...	...	...	...	1634	...	1837	...	...	...	2032	...	2229	...	...	...	...	...

	EIP 1500	*IC* 15100	*IC* 18154	*EIP* 1502	*EIP* 3510	*IC* 15102	*EIP* 4508	*EIP* 3508	*IC* 18114	*EIP* 4506	*EIP* 3506	*TLK* 15104	*TLK* 38108	*EIP* 3504	*EIP* 4505	*EIP* 3800	*IC* 15106	*EIP* 4502	*EIP* 3502	*TLK* 35104	*EIP* 3500	*EIP* 4500	*TLK* 15108	*IC* 38170	*TLK* 35170
		Ⓐ	⑥				**G**	**R**		**B**			**Z**		**B**			**G**		**Z**		**B**			**Z**
Łódź Fabr **1090** .... d.	...	0521	0521	...	...	0730	...	...	0928	...	...	1131	...	...	...	...	1524	...	...	...	...	...	1921		...
Kraków Gł. **1065**............... d.	...	|	|	...	0553	|	...	0756	|	...	0956	|	1051	1155	...	1356	|	...	1552	1603	1656	...	|	2150	0048
Warszawa Cent.................. d.	0550	0700	0700	0730	0830	0900	0930	1030	1100	1130	1230	1300	1500	1430	1530	1630	1645	1730	1830	1855	1930	2030	2100	0202	0420
Warszawa Wsch................. d.	0558	0709	0709	0738	0837	0909	0938	1038	1109	1138	1238	1309	1509	1438	1538	1637	1709	1738	1837	1908	1938	2038	2108	0230	0438
Ciechanów.......................... d.	|	0759	0759	|	|	0959	|	|	1202	|	|	1401	1600	|	|	|	1800	|	|	1958	|	|	2206	0331	0533
Działdowo........................... d.	|	0826	0826	|	|	1025	|	|	1229	|	|	1428	1626	|	|	|	1826	|	|	2025	|	|	2232	0403	0606
Iława Gł. .... d.	0725	0858	0858	0905	|	1058	1105	1205	1308	1305	1405	1501	1658	1605	1705	|	1858	1905	|	2058	2105	2205	2305	0440	0641
Malbork .... ▶ d.	0758	0949	0949	0938	|	1144	1138	1238	1348	1338	1438	1539	1744	1638	1738	|	1944	1938	|	2145	2138	2238	2343	0525	0720
Tczew.............................. ▶ d.	0809	1003	1003	0951	|	1156	1149	1249	1401	1349	1449	1553	1759	1649	1749	|	1957	1949	|	2158	2149	2249	2355	0541	0741
Gdańsk Gł. .... ▶ a.	0823	1020	1020	1005	1057	1212	1203	1303	1417	1403	1503	1609	1816	1703	1803	1855	2012	2003	2057	2214	2203	2303	0011	0601	0758
Sopot............................. ▶ a.	0839	1036	1036	1022	1113	1227	1219	1319	1433	1419	1519	1626	1832	1719	1819	1911	2028	2019	2113	2230	2219	2319	0026	0619	0820
Gdynia Gł. .... ▶ a.	0849	1047	1047	1032	1123	1238	1229	1329	1444	1429	1529	1635	1843	1729	1829	1921	2039	2029	2123	2241	2229	2329	0036	0631	0830
Kołobrzeg **1015** .... a.	...	...	...	...	...	...	...	...	1752	...	...	...	2136	...	...	2152	...	...	...	...	...	...	...	1012	...

km		*IC* 5332	*IC* 5330	*IC* 5328	*IC* 5326	*IC* 5324	*IC* 5424	*IC* 5122	*IC* 5320	
							K	**L**		
0	**Olsztyn** Gł.......................... d.	0533	0733	0933	1133	1319	1533	1733	1916	...
	Iława Gł. .... d.	|	|	|	|	|	|	|	2003	...
84	Działdowo.............................. d.	0634	0836	1036	1236	1422	1636	1836	2034	...
134	Ciechanów.............................. d.	0659	0901	1101	1301	1448	1701	1901	2059	...
228	**Warszawa** Wsch. .... a.	0752	0952	1152	1352	1541	1752	1952	2152	...
233	**Warszawa** Cent.................... a.	0800	1000	1200	1400	1600	1800	2000	2200	...
	Kraków Gł. **1067** .... a.	1150	1350	1550	1804	1952	...	...	0040	...

	IC 1520	*IC* 1522	*IC* 4524	*IC* 3524	*IC* 3526	*IC* 3528	*IC* 3530	*IC* 3532	
		L	**K**						
Kraków Gł. **1067**............ d.	...	...	...	0802	1008	1208	1406	1558	...
Warszawa Cent.................. d.	0600	0750	1000	1200	1400	1600	1800	2000	...
Warszawa Wsch.................. d.	0608	0808	1008	1209	1408	1608	1808	2008	...
Ciechanów........................... d.	0659	0858	1058	1300	1458	1701	1859	2100	...
Działdowo............................ d.	0724	0924	1124	1326	1524	1727	1925	2128	...
Iława Gł. .... d.	0756	|	|	|	|	|	|	|	...
Olsztyn Gł........................... a.	0843	1022	1222	1423	1622	1824	2023	2226	...

B – To / from Bielsko Biała (Table **1059**).
G – To / from Gliwice (Table **1059**).
K – To / from Racibórz (Table **1060**, **1075**).
L – To / from Łódź (Table **1090**).
R – To / from Rzeszów (Table **1075**).
Z – To / from Zakopane (Table **1066**).
▶ – For additional trains Gdynia - Gdańsk (- Olsztyn) see Table **1035**.
SKM operates frequent local trains Gdynia - Gdańsk and v.v.

PKP, Polregio — GDYNIA - GDAŃSK - EŁBLAG - OLSZTYN - BIAŁYSTOK — 1035

km			TLK 51110		IC 85108	IC 85106		IC 81104	IC 85104	IC 85102	
			A								
	Szczecin Gł. **1015** d.	...	...	...	0400	0658	...	1110	1317	1505	...
0	**Gdynia** Gł. ▶ d.	0536	0620	0626	0811	1118	1445	1538	1740	1933	2152
9	Sopot ▶ d.	0545	0629	0635	0819	1127	1454	1549	1749	1942	2201
21	**Gdańsk** Gł. ▶ d.	0600	0645	0649	0836	1143	1509	1605	1806	2000	2216
53	Tczew ▶ d.	0639	0705	0721	0855	1203	1551	1625	1825	2021	2248
72	Malbork ▶ d.	0659	0726	0741	0908	1216	1610	1638	1839	2034	2307
101	**Ełblag** d.	0724	0748	0807	0930	1237	1636	1659	1900	2056	2332
200	**Olsztyn** Gł a.	...	0920	...	1100	1407	...	1828	2030	2219	...
200	**Olsztyn** Gł d.	...	0945	...	...	...	...	1903	...	...	...
245	Szczytno d.	...	1020	...	...	...	...	1956	...	...	...
302	Pisz d.	...	1100	...	...	...	...	2037	...	...	...
366	Ełk a.	...	1148	...	...	...	...	2126	...	...	...
366	Ełk d.	...	1213	...	...	...	...	2150	...	...	...
470	**Białystok** a.	...	1331	...	...	...	...	2309	...	...	...

			IC 58102	IC 58104	IC 18104		IC 58106	IC 58108	TLK 15110	
									A	
Białystok d.	...	...	...	...	0524	...	...	...	1404	...
Ełk a.	...	...	...	...	0645	...	...	...	1522	...
Ełk d.	...	...	...	...	0710	...	...	...	1554	...
Pisz d.	...	...	...	...	0758	...	...	...	1650	...
Szczytno	...	...	...	...	0841	...	...	...	1731	...
Olsztyn Gł a.	...	...	...	...	0917	...	...	...	1806	...
Olsztyn Gł d.	...	...	0600	0745	0942	...	1345	1700	1836	...
Ełblag d.	0419	0612	0730	0920	1112	1440	1509	1829	2006	2026
Malbork ▶ d.	0446	0640	0751	0942	1133	1507	1531	1850	2027	2057
Tczew ▶ d.	0506	0704	0815	0957	1159	1526	1545	1903	2050	2117
Gdańsk Gł. ▶ d.	0538	0743	0836	1016	1220	1557	1607	1924	2112	2150
Sopot ▶ d.	0551	0757	0850	1030	1235	1610	1621	1938	2127	2204
Gdynia Gł. ▶ a.	0602	0807	0859	1039	1244	1620	1630	1947	2136	2214
Szczecin Gł. **1015** a.	...	...	1310	1500	1653	...	2059	2359	...	...

OTHER SERVICES OLSZTYN - EŁK - BIAŁYSTOK

km		⚒	IC 5620	Ⓑ					Ⓑ		
			B								
0	**Olsztyn** d.	...	...	...	...	1002	...	1425	...	...	1820
45	Szczytno d.	...	...	...	...	1043	...	1505	...	...	1900
102	Pisz d.	...	...	...	...	1134	...	1556	...	...	1951
157	Ełk d.	0531	0648	0735	...	1232	1446	1655	1726	...	2049
261	**Białystok** a.	0708	0804	0907	...	...	1623	...	1859	...	...

		Ⓐ				Ⓑ				IC 6520
										W
Białystok d.	...	0540	...	1022	...	1456	...	...	1801	2004
Ełk d.	0431	0722	...	1153	1244	1634	1710	...	1935	2122
Pisz d.	0526	...	...	...	1340	...	1806	...	...	...
Szczytno d.	0617	...	...	...	1431	...	1901	...	...	...
Olsztyn a.	0700	...	...	...	1517	...	1943	...	...	...

A – To / from Warszawa via Siedlce (Table **1050**).
W – To / from Wrocław (Table **1061**).

▶ – For additional trains Gdynia - Gdansk - Malbork (- Warszawa) see Table **1030**.
Frequent local trains run between Gdynia, Sopot and Gdańsk operated by *Szybka Kolej Miejska* (every 10 – 30 minutes).

PKP — WARSZAWA - BIAŁYSTOK — 1040

km		IC 1000		IC 144		IC 1002		IC 61106		IC 61104		IC 6128		IC 6126		IC 8108		IC 6520		IC 1006		IC 6124	
		L		H		L		W		W		W		L		S T		E W		L		W	
0	**Warszawa** Centralna d.	0555	...	0755	...	0920	...	0950	...	1155	...	1355	...	1555	...	1655	...	1755	...	1850	...	1955	...
5	**Warszawa** Wschodnia d.	0604	...	0804	...	0927	...	1004	...	1205	...	1404	...	1604	...	1704	...	1804	...	1857	...	2003	...
94	Małkinia d.	0659	...	0858	...	|	...	1058	...	1259	...	1459	...	1659	...	1759	...	1859	...	|	...	2057	...
183	**Białystok** a.	0749	...	0948	...	1050	...	1448	...	1349	...	1549	...	1749	...	1849	...	1949	...	2020	...	2147	...

	IC 1420		IC 1624		IC 1106		IC 5620		IC 1808		IC 1626		IC 1628		IC 16104		IC 16106		IC 1102		IC 143	IC 1100
	B		W		L		E W		S T		L		W		W		W		L		H	L
Białystok d.	0514	...	0614	...	0740	...	0815	...	0914	...	1014	...	1214	...	1414	...	1614	...	1710	...	1814	2014
Małkinia d.	0605	...	0705	...	|	...	0904	...	1005	...	1105	...	1305	...	1503	...	1703	...	|	...	1905	2105
Warszawa Wschodnia a.	0657	...	0757	...	0903	...	0956	...	1057	...	1157	...	1357	...	1556	...	1756	...	1833	...	1957	2157
Warszawa Centralna a.	0705	...	0805	...	0910	...	1005	...	1105	...	1205	...	1405	...	1605	...	1810	...	1840	...	2005	2205

B – To / from Bielsko-Biała (Table **1059**).
E – To / from Ełk (Table **1035**).
H – HAŃCZA – 12 ✕ 🅁 Kraków - Warszawa - Białystok - Mockava and v.v.
L – To / from Łódź (Table **1090**).
S – To / from Szczecin (Table **1042**).
T – To / from Suwałki (Table **1042**).
W – To / from Wrocław (Table **1061**).

PKP, Polregio, BCh, LG — BIAŁYSTOK - VILNIUS and HRODNA — 1042

km				IC 144	24				IC 8108
				H		⚒		Ⓐ	S
0	*Warszawa Centralna* **1040** d.	...	...	0755	...	...	...	...	1655
5	*Warszawa Wschodnia* **1040** d.	...	...	0804	...	...	...	...	1704
183	**Białystok** a.	...	...	0948	...	...	...	...	1849
183	**Białystok** d.	0506	0603	1030	...	1254	1450	1839	1914
224	Sokółka d.	0545	0640	1059	...	1338	1529	1924	1943
323	**Suwałki** a.	0721	|	1210	...	|	1709	|	2056
348	Trakiszki 🏛 a.	...	|	1313	...	|	...	|	...
366	Mockava 🏛 ◐ § a.	...	|	1435	1515	|	...	|	...
467	**Kaunas** **1809** § a.	...	|	...	1626	|	...	|	...
570	**Vilnius** **1809** § a.	...	|	...	1729	|	...	|	...
240	Kuźnica Białostocka 🏛 a.	...	0657	...	...	1354	...	1941	...
240	Kuźnica Białostocka 🏛 ▶ d.	...	...	...	...	...	...	...	...
266	**Hrodna** 🏛 ▶ ‡ a.	...	...	...	...	...	...	...	...

			IC 1808			23	IC 143	
			S		⚒		H	
Hrodna 🏛 ▶ ‡ d.	...	...	...	...	...	...	...	...
Kuźnica Białostocka 🏛 ▶ a.	...	...	...	...	...	...	...	...
Kuźnica Białostocka 🏛 d.	...	0714	...	...	1440	...	...	1903
Vilnius **1809** § d.	...	|	...	...	|	1235	...	|
Kaunas **1809** § d.	...	|	...	...	|	1339	...	|
Mockava 🏛 ◐ § d.	...	|	...	...	|	1452	1525	|
Trakiszki 🏛 d.	...	|	...	...	|	...	1445	|
Suwałki d.	0449	|	0705	1111	|	...	1547	|
Sokółka d.	0623	0730	0819	1257	1456	...	1700	1927
Białystok a.	0709	0808	0848	1336	1541	...	1727	2013
Białystok d.	...	...	0914	...	...	...	1814	...
Warszawa Wschodnia **1040** a.	...	...	1057	...	...	...	1957	...
Warszawa Centralna **1040** a.	...	...	1105	...	...	...	2005	...

H – HAŃCZA – 12 ✕ 🅁 Kraków - Warszawa - Mockava and v.v.
S – From / to Szczecin (Table **1010**).
§ – Lithuanian time.
‡ – Belarus time.
🏛 = Trakiszki (Poland) / Mockava (Lithuania).
◐ – Ticketing point is Mockava.
▶ – There are no trains running between Kuźnica Białostocka and Hrodna (Belarus) until further notice.

PKP, Polregio — WARSZAWA - TERESPOL - BREST — 1050

km			IC 1026		IC 1020			IC 1022	IC 10102		IC 1024
		Ⓐ n		Ⓐ n		⚒				⚒	
0	**Warszawa** Zach d.	...	...	...	...	...	...	1511	1711	...	2111
2	**Warszawa** Cent. d.	...	...	...	...	...	...	1520	1720	...	2120
5	**Warszawa** Wsch. d.	...	0727	...	1127	...	...	1527	1727	...	2127
93	Siedlce d.	...	0815	0910	1215	1237	...	1615	1817	1838	2215
121	Łuków d.	0639	0829	0943	1229	1325	1558	1629	1831	1910	2229
173	Biała Podlaska d.	0723	0857	1026	1257	1410	1642	1657	1858	1954	2257
210	Terespol 🏛 ▶ a.	0755	0920	1058	1320	1442	1714	1721	1922	2026	2320
217	**Brest** Tsentralny 🏛 ▶ a.	...	...	...	...	...	...	...	...	...	...

	IC 1124		IC 11102		IC 1122	IC 1120			IC 1126	
							Ⓐ n			⚒
Brest Tsentralny 🏛 ▶ ‡ d.	...	...	...	...	...	...	...	...	...	...
Terespol 🏛 ▶ d.	0432	0554	0636	0842	1037	1437	1457	1623	1837	1915
Biała Podlaska d.	0457	0623	0701	0914	1101	1501	1529	1654	1901	1948
Łuków d.	0527	0710	0728	0958	1128	1528	1622	1738	1928	2032
Siedlce d.	0542	0737	0742	1025	1142	1542	1649	...	1942	...
Warszawa Wsch. a.	0632	...	0832	...	1232	1632	...	...	2032	...
Warszawa Cent. a.	0639	...	0840	...	1240	...	...	...	2040	...
Warszawa Zach a.	0648	...	0848	...	1248	...	...	...	2056	...

n – Not June 20.
▶ – There are no trains running between Terespol and Brest Tsentralny (Belarus) until further notice.

1055 WARSZAWA - LUBLIN - CHEŁM - DOROHUSK

PKP, Polregio

km		Ⓐ n	Ⓐ n	IC 13108 R	IC 12100	IC 32100 C	IC 5224 B	IC 72100 P	Ⓐ n	IC 62102 W	IC 83104 PR	IC 32110 E	IC 32106 C	IC 52100 B			Ⓐ n	IC 82160 ①⑥ Dg	IC 83102 KR	IC 32102 C		IC 5222 B		IC 1220	IC 32112 E
0	**Warszawa** Centralna d.	...	...	0540	0640	...	0740	0840	...	...	0940	...	...	1140	...	...	...	...	1340	...	...	1540	...	1640	...
5	**Warszawa** Wschodnia d.	...	...	0549	0649	...	0749	0849	...	...	0949	...	...	1149	...	...	...	...	1349	...	...	1549	...	1649	...
104	Dęblin d.	0502	0601	0644	0747	...	0847	0947	...	...	1047	...	...	1247	...	...	...	...	1447	...	...	1647	...	1747	...
125	Puławy Miasto d.	0523	0621	0656	0759	0841	0859	0959	...	1038	1059	...	1233	1259	...	...	...	1445	1459	1641	...	1659	...	1759	...
175	**Lublin** a.	0610	0710	0726	0829	0910	0929	1029	...	1107	1129	...	1305	1329	...	...	...	1520	1529	1708	...	1729	...	1829	...
175	**Lublin** d.	0620	0727	...	0832	...	...	...	1040	...	...	...	...	1333	1340	1440	1510	...	...	...	1640	...	1740	...	...
228	Rejowiec d.	0711	0818	...	0908	...	...	...	1131	...	...	...	...	1410	1437	1531	1600	...	...	...	1738	...	1831	...	...
	Zamość Wschod a.	|	|	...	|	...	...	...	|	...	...	1321	...	|	1604	|	|	...	...	...	1856	...	|	...	2107
	Hrubieszów Miasto a.	|	|	...	|	...	...	...	|	...	...	1405	...	|	...	|	|	...	...	...	...	...	|	...	2150
249	Chełm a.	0726	0834	...	0923	...	...	...	1147	...	...	...	...	1425	...	1547	1616	...	...	...	...	...	1847	...	...
270	**Dorohusk** 🏛 a.	...	...	...	...	...	...	...	...	...	...	...	...	...	...	...	...	...	...	...	...	...	...	...	...

	Ⓑ	IC 7220 P	IC 12010 D20 A	IC 83100 RS	IC 20101	Ⓐ n	IC 32104 C	IC 5220 B	IC 62104 W
Warszawa Centralna d.	...	...	...	1840	...	...	...	1940	...
Warszawa Wschodnia d.	...	...	1749	1849	...	...	...	1949	...
Dęblin d.	...	...	1858	1949	...	2000	...	2049	...
Puławy Miasto d.	...	1902	1912	2002	...	2017	2041	2101	2243
Lublin a.	...	1930	1951	2031	...	2103	2110	2130	2312
Lublin d.	1920	...	2000	...	2118	2140	...	...	...
Rejowiec d.	|	...	2044	...	|	2231	...	...	...
Zamość Wschod a.	2118	...	|	...	2323	|	...	...	...
Hrubieszów Miasto a.	...	...	|	...	0005	|	...	...	...
Chełm a.	...	...	2102	...	...	2247	...	...	...
Dorohusk 🏛 a.	...	...	2131	...	...	...	...	...	...

km		IC 26104 W	IC 2702 ①⑥ Zg	Ⓑ	IC 2520 B	IC 22100	IC 23104 C		IC 38100 RS	⚒
	Dorohusk 🏛 d.	...	...	...	...	...	...	...	...	...
	Chełm d.	...	...	...	...	...	...	0604	...	...
0	Hrubieszów Miasto d.	...	...	...	...	0356	...	|	...	...
49	Zamość Wschod d.	...	...	...	...	0439	...	|	...	0522
114	Rejowiec d.	...	...	...	...	|	...	0619	...	0647
	Lublin a.	...	...	...	...	0647	...	0710	...	0739
	Lublin d.	0452	0533	0619	0633	...	0655	...	0733	...
	Puławy Miasto d.	0520	0604	0712	0704	...	0723	...	0804	...
	Dęblin d.	...	0616	0733	0716	...	...	...	0816	...
	Warszawa Wschodnia a.	...	0712	...	0812	...	...	...	0911	...
	Warszawa Centralna a.	...	0720	...	0820	...	...	...	0920	...

	IC 23112 E	IC D19 21010 A	Ⓐ n	IC 2720 T	IC 2120 ①⑥ g		IC 2522 B	⚒	IC 38102 KR	IC 26100 Wh	Ⓐ n	IC 25100 B	IC 23106 C		⑦ d	IC 23110 E	IC 38104 PR	IC 26102 W		IC 27100 P	IC 2524 B	IC 23100 C	IC 21100	IC 31108 R	Ⓐ n
Dorohusk 🏛 d.	...	0637	...	...	...	...	...	...	...	...	...	...	...	...	...	...	...	...	...	...	...	...	...	...	...
Chełm d.	...	0659	0803	...	...	...	...	1103	...	...	1203	1336	...	1419	...	...	...	...	1611	...	...	...	1837	...	2128
Hrubieszów Miasto d.	0630	|	|	...	...	...	...	|	...	...	|	|	...	|	...	1426	...	...	|	...	...	...	|	...	|
Zamość Wschod d.	0713	|	|	...	...	0800	...	|	...	...	|	|	...	|	1359	1508	...	...	|	...	...	...	|	...	|
Rejowiec d.	...	0718	0819	...	...	0931	...	1119	...	...	1219	1353	...	1434	1529	...	...	...	1627	...	...	...	1853	...	2144
Lublin a.	...	0801	0910	...	...	1023	...	1210	...	...	1310	1430	...	1526	1620	...	...	...	1718	...	...	...	1930	...	2235
Lublin d.	...	0808	...	0832	0933	...	1033	...	1233	1240	1340	1433	1456	1540	...	...	1633	1655	...	1733	1833	1852	1933	2033	2240
Puławy Miasto d.	...	0849	...	0902	1004	...	1104	...	1304	1315	1426	1504	1529	1626	...	...	1704	1722	...	1804	1904	1919	2004	2104	2326
Dęblin d.	...	0904	...	...	1016	...	1116	...	1316	...	1448	1516	...	1646	...	...	1716	...	...	1816	1916	...	2016	2116	2344
Warszawa Wschodnia a.	...	1014	...	...	1112	...	1212	...	1411	...	...	1611	...	...	...	...	1811	...	...	1911	2012	...	2111	2211	...
Warszawa Centralna a.	...	...	...	...	1120	...	1220	...	1420	...	...	1620	...	...	...	...	1820	...	...	1920	2020	...	2120	2220	...

A – KYIV EKSPRES / KIEV EXPRESS – 🛏 1, 2 cl. Kyiv - Warszawa and v.v. (Table **1730**). International journeys only.
B – To / from Bydgoszcz (Table **1025**).
C – To / from Krakow (Table **1067**).
D – To / from Szczecin (Table **1003** / **1075** / **1067**).
E – To / from Krakow (Table **1058** / **1075**).
K – To / from Kołobrzeg (Table **1015**).
P – To / from Piła or Poznań (Table **1001** / **1025**).
R – To / from Rzeszów (Table **1058**).
S – To / from Świnoujście (Table **1010**).
T – To / from Poznań (Table **1067** / **1080**).
W – To / from Wrocław (Table **1067**).
Z – To / from Zielona Góra (Table **1001**).

d – Daily June 28 - Aug. 30.
h – ①②③④⑥ (also June 20, Aug. 15; not June 18, Aug. 14).
g – Also June 19, Aug. 15; not June 21, Aug. 16.
n – Not June 20.

1058 LUBLIN - RZESZÓW

PKP

km		IC 13108	IC 13104 ◧ L	IC 23112 E	IC 83104 P	IC 23110 E	IC 83102 K		IC 13106 ◧ LP	IC 83100 S
	Warszawa Wschodnia d.	...	0654	...	...	...	...	...	1659	...
	Warszawa Centralna d.	0540	0710	...	0940	...	1340	...	1710	1840
	Warszawa Zachodnia d.	|	1715	...	|	...	|	...	1715	|
0	**Lublin** d.	0757	|	...	1200	...	1602	...	|	2056
103	Stalowa Wola Rozwadów d.	0907	|	0912	1308	1701	1713	...	|	2205
132	Tarnobrzeg d.	|	1027	0940	|	1730	|	...	2026	|
204	**Rzeszów** Gł. a.	1035	1123	...	1438	...	1848	...	2145	2332

	IC 38100 S		IC 31106 ◧ L	IC 38102 K	IC 32110 E	IC 38104 P	IC 31104 ◧ L	IC 32112 E	IC 31108
Rzeszów Gł. d.	0429	...	0628	0920	...	1325	1622	...	1735
Tarnobrzeg d.	|	...	0719	|	1103	|	1719	1832	|
Stalowa Wola Rozwadów d.	0601	...	|	1053	1130	1502	|	1900	1906
Lublin d.	0733	...	|	1233	...	1633	|	...	2033
Warszawa Zachodnia a.	|	...	1045	|	...	|	|	...	|
Warszawa Centralna a.	0920	...	1050	1420	...	1820	2051	...	2220
Warszawa Wschodnia a.	...	...	1101	...	...	...	2101	...	...

E – To / from Krakow (Table **1075**).
K – To / from Kołobrzeg (Table **1015**).
L – To / from Przemyśl.
P – To / from Piła (Table **1025**).
S – To / from Świnoujście (Table **1010**).
◧ – Via Radom (Table **1067**).

1059 KATOWICE - RACIBÓRZ - BIELSKO BIAŁA - ZYWIEC and ZAKOPANE

Koleje Śląskie, PKP

km		IC 83192 Hk	EC 101 M◧		TLK 402 DG	IC 116 R	EC 105 P		EIP 1401 A	IC 1420 B	IC 131 J		Ⓐ n	IC 1422 A	EIP 5402 G	EC 112 R	Ⓐ n	EC 109 1277 S	EIC 1410 p A	IC 1428 A	IC 110 R		IC 5406 G	IC 5424 C◧	IC 5420 G
0	**Katowice** **1075** d.	0457	0459	0622	0537	0818	0852	0931	1016	1045	1145	1215	1314	1442	1506	1624	1639	1701	1807	1959	2022	2033	2107	2145	2241
17	Tychy d.	0521	|	0652	0620	0836	0912	0953	1037	1106	1206	1235	1333	1503	1523	1643	1705	1720	1825	2019	2039	2054	2128	|	2257
45	Rybnik a.	|	|	|	0702	0903	0939	|	|	|	...	|	|	|	|	1709	|	1748	|	|	2106	|	|	|	|
	Racibórz **1075** a.	|	0608	|	0742	...	1008	|	|	|	...	|	|	|	|	...	|	...	|	|	...	|	|	2314	|
55	**Bielsko Biała** Gł. a.	0555	...	0742	...	...	...	1035	1110	1139	...	1324	1407	1537	1559	...	1748	...	1900	2052	...	2139	2202	...	2334
55	**Bielsko Biała** Gł. d.	0610	...	0744	...	...	...	1039	...	...	...	1327	1413	...	...	...	1752	...	...	2107	...	2143	...	...	...
76	**Zywiec** a.	|	...	0814	...	...	...	1108	...	...	...	1402	1439	...	...	...	1821	...	...	2131	...	2213	...	...	...
	Zakopane a.	0943	...	...	...	...	...	...	...	...	...	...	...	...	...	...	...	...	...	...	...	...	...	...	...

km		IC 4520 G	EIC 4110 ⚒ m	IC 4524 C◧		EC 111 R	IC 4128 A	EIC 4506 G		EC 108 1276 S	EC 113 R		EIP 4505 G	IC 4122 A			IC 130 J	IC 4120 B	EIP 4500 G	Ⓐ n	EC 104 P	IC 117 R	Ⓐ n	EC 100 M◧	IC 38192 He
	Zakopane d.	...	...	...	...	...	...	...	...	...	...	...	...	...	...	...	...	...	...	...	...	...	...	...	1853
0	**Zywiec** d.	...	...	...	0557	...	0643	...	0854	...	...	1046	...	...	1202	1343	...	...	...	1704	...	...	1904	...	|
	Bielsko Biała Gł. a.	...	...	...	0625	...	0709	...	0924	...	...	1121	...	...	1230	1411	...	...	...	1732	...	...	1932	...	2221
21	**Bielsko Biała** Gł. d.	0421	0445	...	0629	...	0730	0758	0932	...	...	1138	1159	1228	1234	1418	...	1630	1657	1735	...	...	1935	...	2238
	Racibórz **1075** d.	|	|	0450	|	...	|	|	|	...	...	|	|	|	|	|	...	|	|	|	1751	...	|	2149	|
	Rybnik d.	|	|	|	|	0653	|	|	|	1014	1052	|	|	|	|	|	...	|	|	|	1817	1900	|	|	|
55	Tychy d.	0501	0524	|	0716	0729	0808	0835	1017	1044	1125	1225	1237	1306	1317	1502	1612	1711	1734	1821	1847	1931	2019	|	2318
72	**Katowice** **1075** a.	0515	0539	0620	0736	0746	0822	0850	1037	1108	1143	1245	1251	1320	1338	1521	1629	1725	1749	1842	1904	1950	2038	2302	2333

A – To / from Warswawa (Tables **1060**).
B – To / from Białystok (Table **1040**).
C – To / from Olsztyn (Table **1030**).
D – To / from Bohumin (Tables **1030**).
G – To / from Gdynia (Tables **1030**).
H – To / from Świnoujście (Table **1010**).
J – BATORY – [12] ✕ Warszawa - Budapest and v.v.
M – MORAVIA – [12] ✕ Katowice - Wien and v.v.
P – POLONIA – [12] ✕ Warszawa - Wien and v.v.
R – SILESIA – [12] ✕ Warszawa - Bohumin / Praha and v.v.
S – SOBIESKI – [12] ✕ Warszawa - Wien and v.v. Also conveys on ②④⑤⑦ June 27 - Aug. 29 [2] 🛏 2 cl (**1277**) Warszawa - Wien - Rijeka / on ①③⑤⑦ June 29 - Aug. 31 [2] 🛏 2 cl (**1276**) Rijeka - Wien - Warszawa (Table **99**).
h – Train **38196** from June 27.
k – Train **83196** from June 28.
m – On ⑥ (also June 19) runs with train number **4550** and is extended to Gdynia (Table **1030**).
n – Not June 20.
p – ①-④ (not 18, 19, Aug. 10).
◧ – Via Gliwice (Table **1075**).

PKP, Polregio — WARSAWA and ŁÓDŹ - KRAKÓW and KATOWICE — 1060

Warning! Timings may vary by a few minutes on certain dates.

km			IC 116 A		EC 105 B		IC 1424 M	IC 1420 C	EIP 1401 D	IC 5334 R	IC 131 E		EIP 5400 F	IC 1422 D	IC 5422 P	EIP 5402 G	IC 112 A	IC 8322 S	EC 109 1277 B	EIC 1410 ①–④ Dn		IC 5360 T	TLK 54102 P	IC 1428 H	EIP 5404 F
0	**Warszawa** Wschodnia d.	...	0509	...	0559	...	...	0659	0734	...	0839	...	1024	1109	...	1224	1314	...	1344	1514	...	...	...	1604	1624
5	**Warszawa** Centralna d.	...	0522	...	0609	...	...	0718	0744	...	0905	...	1035	1118	...	1235	1335	...	1405	1535	...	...	...	1614	1635
7	**Warszawa** Zachodnia d.	...	0528	...	0614	...	...	0727	0749	...	0910	...	1040	1123	...	1240	1340	...	1411	1540	...	...	...	1619	1640
	Łódź Kaliska d.	...	│	0437	│	...	0720	│	│	0838	│	...	│	│	1143	│	│	1318	│	│	...	1541	1605	│	│
	Łódź Widzew d.	...	│	0505	│	...	0740	│	│	0900	│	...	│	│	1208	│	│	1401	│	│	...	1612	1626	│	│
	Łódź Fabryczna d.	0446	│	0526	│	0602	│	│	│	│	│	1050	│	│	│	│	│	│	│	│	1534	│	│	│	│
	Koluszki d.	0527	│	0609	│	0647	│	0819	│	│	│	1131	│	1215	│	│	│	│	│	│	1618	│	│	1713	│
	Piotrków Trybunalski d.	0600	│	0659	│	0725	0816	0842	│	│	│	1205	│	1238	1242	│	│	│	│	│	1705	│	1702	1736	│
	Częstochowa d.	0713	│	0811	│	0853	0912	0935	│	│	│	1319	│	1330	1336	│	│	│	│	│	1818	│	1759	1829	│
	Kraków Gł. a.	...	│	...	│	...	│	│	│	1138	│	...	│	│	│	│	│	1653	│	│	...	1902	│	│	│
258	Zawiercie **1067** d.	...	0726	...	0801	...	0943	1002	0937	...	1101	...	1225	1357	1403	1425	1539	...	1607	1726	...	...	│	1905	1825
293	Sosnowiec Gł. **1067** d.	...	0754	...	0835	...	1010	1031	1001	...	1129	...	1251	1427	1432	1450	1606	...	1642	1750	...	...	│	1938	1852
301	**Katowice** **1067** a.	...	0815	...	0849	...	1027	1042	1013	...	1143	...	1306	1439	1452	1503	1621	...	1657	1804	...	...	1940	1954	1903

		IC 110 J	IC 5424 K	EIP 5406 G		IC 8320 S	IC 5420 G	EIC 5450 ⑦ G	IC 14100 L
Warszawa Wschodnia d.	...	1709	1754	1824	...	...	...	2009	2029
Warszawa Centralna d.	...	1735	1814	1835	...	...	...	2018	2044
Warszawa Zachodnia d.	...	1740	1819	1840	...	...	...	2023	2049
Łódź Kaliska d.	...	│	│	│	...	1927	1947	│	│
Łódź Widzew d.	...	│	│	│	...	1945	2005	│	│
Łódź Fabryczna d.	1645	│	│	│	1840	│	│	│	│
Koluszki d.	1728	│	1911	│	1921	│	│	│	│
Piotrków Trybunalski d.	1801	│	1935	│	1954	│	2039	│	│
Częstochowa d.	1914	│	2032	│	2106	│	2131	│	│
Kraków Gł. a.	...	│	│	│	...	2217	│	│	│
Zawiercie **1067** d.	...	1938	2054	2028	...	...	2158	2210	2249
Sosnowiec Gł. **1067** d.	...	2004	2127	2052	...	...	2227	2236	2320
Katowice **1067** a.	...	2019	2142	2104	...	...	2238	2248	2332

		IC 41100 L		IC 4520 G	IC 3820 S		EIC 4110 Ⓐ D	EIC 4550 ⑥ G	IC 4524 K
Katowice **1067** d.	...	0410	...	0520	...	...	0542	0542	0623
Sosnowiec Gł. **1067** d.	...	0432	...	0532	...	...	0559	0559	0634
Zawiercie **1067** d.	...	0501	...	0604	...	...	0632	0632	0709
Kraków Gł. d.	...	│	...	│	0534	...	│	│	│
Częstochowa d.	0445	│	0546	0633	│	0645	│	│	0736
Piotrków Trybunalski d.	0557	│	0659	0724	│	0807	│	│	0826
Koluszki d.	0639	│	0744	│	│	0854	│	│	0849
Łódź Fabryczna a.	0712	│	0814	│	│	0927	│	│	│
Łódź Widzew a.	0729	│	0830	0756	0815	0944	│	│	│
Łódź Kaliska a.	0808	│	0859	0813	0833	1018	│	│	│
Warszawa Zachodnia a.	...	0655	...	...	...	...	0819	0819	0940
Warszawa Centralna a.	...	0700	...	...	...	...	0825	0825	0946
Warszawa Wschodnia a.	...	0716	...	...	...	...	0851	0851	1006

km		EIP 4508 F	IC 111 J	IC 4128 H	TLK 45102 P	IC 3560 T	EIP 4506 G	IC 108 1276 B	EC 113 A	IC 3822 S	EIP 4505 G		IC 4522 P	IC 4122 D	EIP 4502 F		IC 130 E	IC 3534 R		IC 4124 M	IC 4120 C		EIP 4500 G	EC 104 B	IC 117 A
	Katowice **1067** d.	0649	0749	0825	0841	...	0853	1111	1146	...	1254	...	1308	1323	1454	...	1632	...	...	1711	1728	...	1752	1907	1953
	Sosnowiec Gł. **1067** d.	0706	0804	0837	│	...	0907	1130	1201	...	1309	...	│	1335	1509	...	1650	...	...	1726	1741	...	1807	1923	2013
0	Zawiercie **1067** d.	0734	0839	0905	│	...	0932	1158	1230	...	1334	...	1359	1406	1534	...	1719	...	...	1759	1820	...	1832	1959	2043
	Kraków Gł. d.	│	│	│	│	0922	│	│	│	1202	│	...	│	│	│	...	│	1608	...	│	│	...	│	│	│
44	**Częstochowa** d.	│	│	0936	1019	│	│	│	│	│	│	1245	1430	1436	│	1551	│	│	1645	1831	1849	1858	│	│	│
129	Piotrków Trybunalski d.	│	│	1026	1110	│	│	│	│	│	│	1358	1523	1528	│	1706	│	│	1758	1922	1939	2011	│	│	│
169	Koluszki d.	│	│	1049	│	│	│	│	│	│	│	1445	│	1550	│	1747	│	│	1845	│	2002	2053	│	│	│
	Łódź Fabryczna a.	│	│	│	│	│	│	│	│	│	│	1517	│	│	│	1818	│	│	1916	│	│	2124	│	│	│
	Łódź Widzew a.	│	│	│	1144	1151	│	│	│	1432	│	...	1558	│	│	...	│	1854	...	1954	│	2140	│	│	│
	Łódź Kaliska a.	│	│	│	1200	1215	│	│	│	1447	│	...	1616	│	│	...	│	1911	...	2018	│	2212	│	│	│
271	**Warszawa** Zachodnia a.	0919	1030	1141	...	...	1119	1349	1421	...	1520	...	...	1641	1719	...	1910	...	...	...	2058	...	2019	2146	2242
273	**Warszawa** Centralna a.	0925	1038	1146	...	...	1125	1355	1426	...	1525	...	...	1646	1725	...	1916	...	...	...	2109	...	2025	2151	2248
278	**Warszawa** Wschodnia a.	0936	1051	1156	...	...	1136	1416	1446	...	1536	...	...	1706	1736	...	1926	...	...	...	2131	...	2036	2201	2256

A – [12] Warszawa - Praha and v.v.
B – [12] Warszawa - Wien and v.v. Also conveys on ②④⑤⑦ June 27 - Aug. 29 [2] 🛏 (**1277**) Warszawa - Rijeka / on ①③⑤⑦ June 30 - Sept. 1 [2] 🛏 (**1276**) Rijeka - Warszawa.
C – [12] Białystok - Bielsko Biała and v.v.
D – [12] Warszawa - Bielsko Biała and v.v.
E – [12] Warszawa - Budapest and v.v.
F – [12] Gdynia - Gliwice and v.v.
G – [12] Gdynia - Bielsko Biała and v.v.
H – [12] Warszawa - Zywiec and v.v.
J – [12] Warszawa - Bohumín and v.v.
K – [12] Olsztyn - Racibórz and v.v.
L – [12] Warszawa - Gliwice and v.v.
M – [12] Płock - Katowice and v.v.
P – [12] Gdynia - Katowice and v.v.
R – [12] Bydgoszcz - Kraków and v.v.
S – [12] Szczecin - Kraków and v.v.
T – [12] Gdynia - Zakopane and v.v.
n – Not June 18, 19, Aug. 14.

PKP — WARSZAWA - ŁÓDŹ and CZESTOCHOWA - WROCŁAW — 1061

km		IC 1620	IC 16108 ①	IC 16110 Ⓐ	IC 16150 Ⓒ Hk	IC 1622	EIC 1600	IC 1624 B	IC 16100 Gf	IC 16152 ④–⑦ H	IC 5620 C	EIC 1602	IC 1626 B	IC 1630	IC 1628 B	IC 16102	IC 16104 B	EIP 1604	IC 1632 D	IC 16106 B		IC 1634	IC 16170 Ag	IC 16190 Eh
0	**Warszawa** Wschodnia d.	0404	0434	0524	0524	0604	0639	0759	0909	0909	0959	1134	1159	1309	1359	1459	1559	1609	1704	1804	...	2039	2324	2324
5	**Warszawa** Centralna d.	0414	0447	0534	0522	0614	0648	0814	0922	0922	1014	1144	1214	1322	1414	1510	1622	1618	1722	1822	...	2048	2340	2340
7	**Warszawa** Zachodnia d.	0419	0452	0539	0527	0619	0653	0819	0927	0927	1019	1149	1219	1327	1419	1516	1630	1623	1727	1830	...	2053	2345	2345
122	Koluszki d.	0510	0556	0631	0630	0710	│	0910	1030	1030	1110	│	1310	1419	1510	1610	1733	│	1819	1930	...	2145	0046	0046
160	Piotrków Trybunalski d.	│	│	0654	0657	│	│	│	1054	1054	│	│	│	1442	│	1633	│	│	1842	│	...	2209	│	│
•	Częstochowa d.	│	│	0751	0748	│	│	│	1147	1147	│	│	│	1534	│	1724	│	│	1934	│	...	2301	│	│
	Częstochowa Stradom d.	│	│	0756	0754	│	0849	│	1152	1152	│	1345	│	1539	│	1730	│	1817	1939	│	...	2306	│	│
130	**Łódź** Widzew ▷ d.	0528	0609	│	│	0728	│	0928	│	│	1128	│	1345	│	1523	│	1755	│	│	1945	...	│	0103	0103
257	Kalisz ▷ d.	0658	0810	│	│	0855	│	1055	│	│	1254	│	1522	│	1655	│	1924	│	│	2114	...	│	0232	0232
281	Ostrów Wlkp ▷ d.	0716	0834	│	│	0912	│	1112	│	│	1311	│	1539	│	1712	│	1941	│	│	2132	...	│	0249	0249
	Opole Gł. d.	│	│	0854	0900	│	0945	│	1259	1259	│	1438	│	1637	│	1822	│	1910	2034	│	...	0002	│	│
	Brzeg d.	│	│	0914	0920	│	│	│	1323	1323	│	│	│	1655	│	1842	│	│	2054	│	...	0021	│	│
382*	**Wrocław** Gł. ▷ a.	0834	1017	0940	0948	1031	1024	1244	1351	1351	1434	1517	1710	1724	1846	1909	2101	1951	2118	2251	...	0045	0420	0420

	IC 61170 Af	IC 61190 Ee		IC 6134	IC 61106 B	EIP 6104	IC 6132 D	IC 61104 B	IC 61102	IC 6128 B	IC 6130	IC 6126 B	EIC 6102	IC 6520 C	IC 61100 Gf	IC 61152 He	IC 6124 B	EIC 6100	IC 6122	IC 61108 ⑥	IC 61110 Ⓐ	IC 61150 ⑥⑦ Hk	IC 6120
Wrocław Gł. ▷ d.	0002	0002	...	0355	0501	0640	0659	0655	0855	0911	1042	1103	1239	1323	1433	1433	1505	1631	1729	1834	1835	1835	1920
Brzeg d.	│	│	...	0420	│	│	0724	│	0918	│	1107	│	│	│	1502	1502	│	│	│	│	1905	1905	│
Opole Gł. d.	│	│	...	0440	│	0722	0744	│	0937	│	1128	│	1319	│	1527	1527	│	1710	│	│	1927	1927	│
Ostrów Wlkp ▷ d.	0136	0136	...	│	0633	│	│	0828	│	1049	│	1223	│	1448	│	│	1649	│	1848	2017	│	│	2049
Kalisz ▷ d.	0152	0152	...	│	0649	│	│	0845	│	1105	│	1239	│	1505	│	│	1706	│	1905	2033	│	│	2106
Łódź Widzew ▷ d.	0324	0324	...	│	0823	│	│	1019	│	1237	│	1436	│	1635	│	│	1836	│	2037	2208	│	│	2237
Częstochowa Stradom d.	│	│	...	0534	│	0815	0837	│	1031	│	1220	│	1412	│	1624	1624	│	1806	│	│	2023	2023	│
Częstochowa d.	│	│	...	0542	│	│	0844	│	1047	│	1227	│	│	│	1631	1631	│	│	│	│	2031	2031	│
Piotrków Trybunalski d.	│	│	...	0633	│	│	0935	│	1138	│	1318	│	│	│	1724	1724	│	│	│	│	2122	2122	│
Koluszki d.	0338	0338	...	0656	0838	│	0959	1035	1202	1250	1341	1450	│	1650	1758	1758	1849	│	2049	2223	2146	2146	2249
Warszawa Zachodnia a.	0438	0438	...	0748	0932	1010	1049	1131	1253	1340	1432	1540	1606	1741	1900	1900	1940	2001	2140	2324	2237	2237	2340
Warszawa Centralna a.	0444	0444	...	0754	0938	1016	1055	1138	1258	1346	1438	1546	1612	1746	1908	1908	1946	2008	2146	2330	2242	2242	2346
Warszawa Wschodnia a.	0456	0456	...	0821	0956	1026	1121	1201	1316	1401	1456	1601	1620	1801	1921	1921	2001	2021	2156	2346	2306	2306	2356

A – 🛏 [2] Warszawa - Jelenia Gora and v.v.
B – [12] Białystok - Wrocław and v.v.
C – [12] Ełk - Wrocław and v.v.
D – [12] Warszawa - Zgorzelec and v.v.
E – 🛏 [2] Warszawa - Szklarska Poreba Gorna and v.v.
F – [12] Wrocław - Gdynia.
G – To / from Jelenia Gora
H – To / from Szklarska Poreba Gorna.
e – June 19 - Aug. 30.
f – June 15 – 18.
g – June 15 – 17.
h – June 18 - Aug. 30.
k – Also June 19, Aug. 15.
▷ – For local trains see Table **1080**.
* – *406 km* via CMK.
• – Częstochowa - Opole Gł: *91 km*.

1062 WARSZAWA - LVIV

PKP, UZ

km		863		766 ◧	865		768 ◧	867		
	Warszawa Centralna d.	...	...	0540	...	...	...	...	...	...
	Warszawa Wschodnia d.	...	...	0549	...	...	1248	...	...	...
0	Lublin d.	...	...	0811	...	...	1502	...	...	...
196	Rava Ruska 🛃 a.	...	...	1342	...	...	2004	...	...	...
196	Rava Ruska 🛃 d.	0615	...	...	1432	...	...	2114	...	...
263	**Lviv** a.	0747	...	...	1600	...	...	2305	...	...

	863		866	765 ◧		867	767 ◧		
Lviv d.	0913	...	1329	...	...	2025	...	...	...
Rava Ruska 🛃 a.	1043	...	1519	...	...	2203	...	...	...
Rava Ruska 🛃 d.	...	...	...	1556	...	...	2247	...	...
Lublin a.	...	...	...	1959	...	...	0245	...	...
Warszawa Wschodnia a.	...	...	...	2211	...	...	0510	...	...
Warszawa Centralna a.	...	...	...	2220	...	...	...	...	...

◧ – International journeys only.

1065 WARSZAWA - KRAKÓW

PKP

For slower trains Warszawa - Kraków via Radom see Table **1067**.

km		IC 13100 ⑤–①	EIP 1302	EIC 1350		EIP 5300	TLK 53104	EIP 5302		EIP 1304	EIP 8300	EIP 1306	EIP 5304		EIP 5306	IC 13102	EIP 1310	EIP 5308	EIP 1312		IC 60407	EIC 5310		IC 5320
		H		**H**		**K**	**L**	**K**			**M**		**K**		**K**			**P**			**C**	**K**		**J**
0	**Warszawa** Wschodnia d.	0529	0629	0729	...	0824	0853	0924	...	1029	1124	1229	1324	...	1524	1529	1629	1724	1829	...	1939	2024	...	2154
5	**Warszawa** Centralna d.	0539	0640	0740	...	0840	0914	0940	...	1040	1140	1240	1340	...	1540	1552	1640	1740	1840	...	1952	2040	...	2204
7	**Warszawa** Zachodnia d.	0544	0645	0745	...	0845	0919	0945	...	1045	1145	1245	1345	...	1545	1558	1645	1745	1845	...	1958	2045	...	2209
246	**Kraków** Gł. a.	0814	0912	1007	...	1105	1156	1205	...	1313	1409	1505	1607	...	1810	1840	1908	2004	2103	...	2229	2305	...	0040

	EIP 3510	IC 60406	EIP 3112		EIP 3508	IC 31102		EIP 3506		EIP 3504	EIP 3108	EIP 3800		EIP 3106	EIC 3502	TLK 35104		EIP 3500	EIC 3150	EIP 3102	EIC 3100		IC 3124
	K	**C**			**P**			**K**		**K**		**M**			**K**	**L**		**K**	**H**				
Kraków Gł. d.	0553	0640	0655	...	0756	0821	...	0956	...	1155	1255	1356	...	1456	1552	1603	...	1656	1755	1854	1956	...	2110
Warszawa Zachodnia a.	0814	0911	0914	...	1014	1102	...	1214	...	1414	1514	1614	...	1714	1814	1835	...	1914	2014	2114	2214	...	2349
Warszawa Centralna a.	0820	0917	0920	...	1020	1108	...	1220	...	1420	1520	1620	...	1720	1820	1841	...	1920	2020	2120	2220	...	2355
Warszawa Wschodnia a.	0836	0931	0931	...	1036	1126	...	1236	...	1436	1531	1636	...	1731	1836	1901	...	1936	2031	2136	2231	...	0005

C – CHOPIN – Warszawa - Munchen and v.v.
H – Warszawa - Zakopane and v.v.
J – Kraków - Olsztyn and v.v
K – Gdynia - Kraków and v.v.
L – Gdynia - Zakopane and v.v.
M – Kołobrzeg - Kraków and v.v.
P – Gdynia - Rzeszów and v.v.

1066 KRAKÓW - ZAKOPANE

PKP, Polregio, Koleje Małopolskie

Warning! Timings may vary by a few minutes on certain dates.

km		TLK 53170		Ⓐ	Ⓒ	IC 30107 Ⓐ	IC 83192	IC 83196		IC 13100 ⑤–①		EIC 1350		IC 73150	TLK 53104		IC 83107		IC 8352	TLK 83108			IC 5360	
		L		**q**	**n**	**q**	**Kf**	**Ke**		**m**				**S**	**L**		**N**		**Ne**	**N**			**L**	
	Warszawa Cent. **1065** d.	2345	...	...	...	...	...	...	...	0529	...	0740	...	...	0914	...	...	...	...	1310	...	...	...	...
0	**Kraków** Gł. d.	0400	...	0530	0628	0630	...	...	0721	0835	0920	1014	...	...	1228	1251	1416	...	1715	1730	1734	...	1914	1952
62	Sucha Beskidzka Zamek d.	0459	...	|	0731	0731	0756	0756	|	0954	|	|	...	1251	|	|	1553	...	1823	|	|	...	2010	|
	Sucha Beskidzka d.	|	...	0659	|	|	|	|	0853	|	1054	|	...	|	|	1417	|	...	|	|	1910	...	|	|
	Sucha Beskidzka d.	|	...	0709	|	|	|	|	0904	|	1115	|	...	|	|	1426	|	...	|	|	1917	...	|	|
	Chabówka a.	|	...	|	|	|	|	|	|	|	1206	|	...	|	|	1511	|	...	|	|	1959	...	|	|
	Chabówka d.	|	...	|	|	|	|	|	|	|	1222	|	...	|	|	1522	|	...	|	|	2008	...	|	|
95	Chabówka Stadion d.	0543	...	0756	0826	0827	0836	0836	0951	1034	1224	|	...	1323	1401	1525	1644	...	1902	1930	2011	...	2040	2220
116	Nowy Targ d.	0610	...	0837	0906	0905	0918	0918	1025	1058	1259	1158	...	1347	1431	1554	1718	...	1926	2003	2044	...	2108	2258
136	**Zakopane** a.	0637	...	0906	0922	0923	0943	0943	1050	1125	1324	1214	...	1406	1454	1627	1741	...	1943	2028	2114	...	2126	2323

			IC 3560		TLK 38108	IC 3852		IC 38107	Ⓐ	TLK 35104	IC 37150		EIC 3150		IC 31100		IC 38192	IC 38196	IC 30108 Ⓐ	Ⓒ	IC 30108 ⑥⑦		IC 35170
			L		**N**	**Ne**		**N**	**n**	**L**	**S**							**Kg**	**q**	**n**	**n**		**L**
Zakopane d.	0422	...	0650	0711	0829	0840	0925	1100	1220	1326	1429	1456	1550	...	1725	1745	1853	1853	1904	1905	1949	...	2205
Nowy Targ d.	0447	...	0710	0739	0847	0904	0951	1118	1245	1349	1449	1520	1606	...	1745	1810	1911	1911	1929	1929	2013	...	2225
Chabówka Stadion d.	0514	...	0739	0810	0911	0933	1019	1147	1311	1413	1512	1553	|	...	1809	1844	1942	1942	2001	2000	2052	...	2249
Chabówka a.	0517	...	|	|	|	|	|	|	1314	|	|	1556	|	...	|	|	|	|	|	|	|	...	|
Chabówka d.	0527	...	|	|	|	|	|	|	1334	|	|	1604	|	...	|	|	|	|	|	|	|	...	|
Sucha Beskidzka a.	0606	...	|	0851	|	|	1058	|	1420	|	|	1651	|	...	|	1935	|	|	|	|	|	...	|
Sucha Beskidzka d.	0615	...	|	0900	|	|	1109	|	1427	|	|	1711	|	...	|	1942	|	|	|	|	|	...	|
Sucha Beskidzka Zamek d.	|	...	0812	|	|	1024	|	1216	|	|	1540	|	|	...	1838	|	2025	2025	2039	2040	2122	...	2320
Kraków Gł. a.	0757	...	0910	1037	1043	1155	1238	1314	1620	1538	...	1854	1752	...	1943	2120	...	...	2146	2146	2237	...	0016
Warszawa Cent. **1065** a.	...	...	...	...	1450	...	...	...	...	1841	...	...	2020	...	2246	...	...	...	...	...	...	...	0420

K – Świnoujście - Zakopane and v.v.
L – Gdynia - Zakopane and v.v.
N – Kołobrzeg / Szczecin - Zakopane and v.v.
S – Poznań - Zakopane and v.v.
e – June 28 - Aug. 30.
f – June 18 – 27.
g – June 27 - Aug. 30.
m – Also June 18, 19, Aug. 14.
n – Also June 19, 20, Aug. 15.
p – June 15 – 20.
q – Not June 20.

1067 WARSZAWA and LUBLIN - RADOM - KRAKÓW

PKP

For trains Warszawa - Kraków via the CMK fast line see Table **1065**. **Warning!** Timings may vary by a few minutes on certain dates.

km		IC 83170	IC 83170	IC 26104	IC 1320	IC 23104	IC 13104	IC 5332	IC 2720	IC 5330	IC 23102	IC 5328	IC 26100	IC 28160 ⑤⑦	TLK 83108	IC 5326	IC 23106	IC 5324	IC 26102	IC 13106		IC 1322	IC 23100	IC 143 🅁
		Af	**Ag**	**F**			**B**	**C**	**G**	**C**		**C**	**Fd**	**He**	**D**	**C**		**C**	**F**	**B**		Ⓐ		**E**
0	**Warszawa** Wschodnia d.	0339	0350	...	0459	...	0654	0754	...	0954	...	1154	...	...	1259	1354	...	1554	...	1659	...	1759	...	1959
5	**Warszawa** Centralna d.	0352	0400	...	0510	...	0710	0810	...	1010	...	1210	...	...	1310	1410	...	1610	...	1710	...	1810	...	2010
7	**Warszawa** Zachodnia d.	0357	0405	...	0515	...	0715	0815	...	1015	...	1215	...	...	1316	1415	...	1615	...	1715	...	1815	...	2016
	Lublin d.	|	|	0452	|	0655	|	|	0832	|	1052	|	1240	1240	|	|	1456	|	1655	|	...	|	1852	|
107	Radom Gł. ⊡ d.	0509	0511	0606	0614	0808	0817	0914	0944	1114	1205	1314	1403	1403	1415	1514	1615	1714	1808	1817	...	1914	2005	2111
148	Skarżysko Kamienna d.	0536	0538	0631	0639	0834	...	0939	...	1139	1232	1339	1430	1430	1440	1539	1641	1739	1834	...	...	1939	2031	2140
192	Kielce Gł. d.	0614	0616	0703	0717	0920	...	1017	...	1217	1317	1417	1504	1504	1517	1617	1717	1817	1906	...	...	2017	2117	2215
324	**Kraków** Gł. a.	0757	0757	...	0906	1059	...	1150	...	1350	1455	1550	...	...	1659	1804	1914	1958	...	...	...	2155	2250	2352

km		IC 144 🅁	IC 32100	IC 3122 Ⓐ	IC 31106	IC 62102	IC 3524	IC 32106	IC 3526	TLK 38108	IC 62100	IC 82160 ①⑥	IC 3528	IC 32102	IC 3530	IC 7220	IC 3532	IC 31104	IC 32104	IC 3120	IC 4160 ⑥⑦	IC 31100	IC 62104	IC 38170
		E			**B**	**F**	**C**		**C**	**D**	**Fh**	**Hj**	**C**		**C**	**G**	**C**	**B**			**j**		**F**	**A**
0	**Kraków** Gł. d.	0348	0507	0601	...	...	0802	0907	1008	1051	...	...	1208	1302	1406	...	1558	...	1702	1905	1913	2014	...	2150
132	Kielce Gł. d.	0540	0654	0743	...	0852	0943	1042	1143	1245	1254	1254	1343	1453	1543	...	1743	...	1854	2043	|	|	2055	2339
176	Skarżysko Kamienna d.	0615	0729	0820	...	0927	1020	1118	1220	1319	1330	1330	1420	1529	1620	...	1820	...	1929	2120	|	|	2131	0016
217	Radom Gł. ⊡ d.	0648	0756	0845	0942	0953	1045	1145	1245	1344	1356	1356	1445	1557	1645	1817	1845	1942	1956	2145	|	|	2158	0043
338	**Lublin** a.	|	0910	|	|	1107	|	1305	|	|	1520	1520	|	1708	|	1930	|	|	2110	|	|	|	2312	|
	Warszawa Zachodnia a.	0742	...	0944	1045	...	1144	...	1344	1443	...	...	1546	...	1744	...	1944	2045	...	2244	2154	2241	...	0150
	Warszawa Centralna a.	0750	...	0950	1050	...	1150	...	1350	1450	...	...	1550	...	1750	...	1950	2051	...	2250	2200	2246	...	0157
	Warszawa Wschodnia a.	0801	...	1001	1101	...	1206	...	1406	1506	...	...	1606	...	1806	...	2006	2101	...	2301	2216	2256	...	0208

A – Kołobrzeg - Kraków and v.v.
B – Warszawa - Przemyśl and v.v.
C – Olsztyn - Kraków and v.v.
D – Kołobrzeg - Zakopane and v.v.
E – Kraków - Mockava and v.v.
F – Lublin - Wrocław and v.v.
G – Lublin - Poznań and v.v.
H – Lublin - Szczecin and v.v.

d – ①②③④⑥ (also June 20, Aug. 15; not June 18, Aug. 14).
e – ⑤⑦ (also June 18, Aug. 14; not June 20, Aug. 15).
f – June 15 – 27.
g – June 28 - Aug. 30.
h – ②③④⑤⑦ (also June 21, Aug. 16; June 19, Aug. 15).
j – Also June 19, Aug. 15.

⊡ – Local trains Dęblin - Radom Gł. and v.v. (journey 49 – 51 minutes).
From Dęblin at 0507 Ⓐ, 0610, 0707, 0806, 0951, 1151, 1302, 1408 Ⓐ, 1504, 1610 Ⓐ, 1705, 1803 Ⓐ, 1902, 2105.
From Radom Gł. at 0518 Ⓐ, 0617 Ⓑ, 0712 Ⓐ, 0851, 1020, 1216, 1405 Ⓐ, 1458, 1606 Ⓐ, 1651, 1758 Ⓐ, 1853 Ⓒ, 2006 Ⓐ, 2051, 2255.

☛ For *IC* trains Lublin - Katowice via Radom see next page.

PKP, Koleje Małopolskie

WARSZAWA and LUBLIN - RADOM - KRAKÓW 1067

LUBLIN - RADOM - KATOWICE

km		IC 23104 24105		IC 23102 24103		IC 23100 24101 J				
0	**Lublin** d.	0655	...	1052	...	1852	...	...	...	...
	Radom Gł. ⊡ d.	0808	...	1205	...	2005	...	...	...	...
	Skarżysko Kamienna d.	0834	...	1231	...	2031	...	...	...	...
	Kielce Gł. d.	0930	...	1338	...	2119	...	...	...	...
	Zawiercie d.	1039	...	1444	...	2225	...	...	...	...
	Sosnowiec Gł. d.	|	...	1516	...	2257	...	...	...	...
	Katowice a.	1131	...	1527	...	2309	...	...	...	...

	IC 42100 32100 J		IC 42102 32102		IC 42104 32104				
Katowice d.	0431	...	1229	...	1642	...	...	...	...
Sosnowiec Gł. d.	0444	...	1243	...	1655	...	...	...	...
Zawiercie d.	0524	...	1315	...	1723	...	...	...	...
Kielce Gł. d.	0654	...	1453	...	1854	...	...	...	...
Skarżysko Kamienna d.	0729	...	1529	...	1929	...	...	...	...
Radom Gł. ⊡ d.	0756	...	1557	...	1956	...	...	...	...
Lublin a.	0910	...	1708	...	2110	...	...	...	...

J – (12) Lublin - Gliwice and v.v.

PKP

POZNAŃ - WROCŁAW 1070

km		IC 461 C§	IC 73150 A	IC 73102 B	76108 P🍷	IC 261 C	IC 73106 B	IC 56100 D	IC 8312 E	IC 263 C	IC 56102 F	TLK 83110 G	IC 54104 54154 H	IC 8306 E	IC 265 C	IC 83150 ⑥⑦ Gf	IC 8304 G	IC 86150 ⑥⑦ Sd	EIC 1612 K	IC 54100 H	IC 84100 L	IC 5604 M	IC 5602 F	IC 86100 Ⓑ b	IC 5600 M	IC 83172 N
0	**Poznań** Gł d.	0254	0538	0638	0653	0731	0838	0938	1038	1131	1138	1238	1338	1438	1531	1535	1638	1701	1731	1738	1838	1931	1938	2038	2138	2311
69	Leszno d.	0331	0623	0715	0747	0805	0916	1016	1114	1205	1220	1316	1414	1516	1605	1611	1715	1744	1805	1814	1920	2005	2014	2123	2214	2356
165	**Wrocław** Gł a.	0424	0725	0810	0904	0849	1012	1113	1206	1249	1317	1412	1511	1609	1649	1721	1808	1857	1850	1908	2025	2050	2107	2226	2307	0102

	IC 38150 ⑤⑥ Ge	IC 38172 N	IC 6500 M	EIC 6112 K	IC 68101 ⚒ J	IC 6502 F	IC 6504 M	IC 48100 L	IC 45100 H	IC 3804 G	IC 264 C	IC 3806 E	IC 45104 45154 H	TLK 38110 G	IC 65102 F	IC 262 C	IC 3812 E	IC 65100 D	67900 P🍷	IC 37106 B	IC 260 C	IC 37102 B	IC 37150 A	IC 460 C‡	IC 68150 ⑤⑥ Sc
Wrocław Gł d.	0127	0254	0456	0512	0524	0650	0710	0735	0851	0950	1110	1150	1250	1350	1438	1510	1550	1647	1652	1746	1910	1950	2051	2350	2355
Leszno d.	0222	0400	0550	0557	0628	0746	0756	0840	0946	1045	1156	1245	1346	1444	1540	1556	1646	1744	1828	1845	1956	2045	2155	0046	0058
Poznań Gł a.	0258	0445	0626	0630	0728	0822	0830	0922	1022	1122	1229	1322	1422	1522	1622	1629	1722	1822	1948	1929	2029	2122	2237	0123	0140

A – (12) Poznań - Zakopane and v.v.
B – (12) Poznań - Przemyśl and v.v.
C – (12) Gdynia - Praha and v.v.
D – (12) Gdynia - Jelenia Góra and v.v.
E – (12) Słupsk - Przemyśl and v.v.
F – (12) Olsztyn - Wrocław and v.v.
G – (12) Kołobrzeg - Kraków and v.v.
H – (12) Gdynia - Bielsko Biała and v.v.
J – (12) Kołobrzeg - Wrocław and v.v.
K – (12) Warszawa - Wrocław and v.v.
L – (12) Słupsk - Katowice and v.v.
M – (12) Gdynia - Wrocław and v.v.
N – 🛏 ▬ (12) Świnoujście - Przemyśl and v.v.
P – Poznań - Szklarska Poreba Gorna and v.v.
S – (12) Wrocław - Słupsk and v.v.
b – Also June 21.
c – Also Aug. 14.
d – Also Aug. 15.
e – June 27 - Aug. 30.
f – June 28 - Aug. 30.
§ – Also conveys 🛏 (1, 2, 3 berth) until Aug. 30.
‡ – Also conveys 🛏 (1, 2, 3 berth) until Aug. 31.

PKP, Polregio

RZESZÓW - KROSNO - ZAGÓRZ - UZTRYKI DOLNE 1073

km		Ⓐ	⑥⑦ k		IC 30112 Ⓐ h	Ⓐ	⚒ q	p	Ⓐ p	IC 30110 p	
0	**Rzeszów** Gł d.	0457	0516	0737	...	1159	1444	1539	1627	...	1936
9	Boguchwała d.	0512	0525	0751	...	1220	1458	1553	1642	...	1950
31	Strzyzów d.	0546	0547	0819	...	1250	1531	1621	1710	...	2024
52	Przybówka d.	0614	|	0842	...	1315	1554	1643	1741	...	2046
	Kraków Gł d.	|	|	|	0910	|	|	|	|	1833	|
70	Jasło d.	0642	0630	0901	1141	1345	1613	1703	1800	2105	2106
92	**Krosno** d.	0711	0655	...	1207	1415	...	...	...	2131	...
132	Sanok a.	0809	0741	...	1257	1533	...	...	...	2221	...
138	Zagórz a.	0818	0750	...	1306	1542	...	...	...	2230	...
174	**Ustrzyki Dolne** a.	0917	0845	...	...	1641	...	...	...	...	...

	Ⓐ	Ⓐ p	IC 33110			Ⓐ	Ⓐ	IC 33112 Ⓐ h	⑥⑦ m	Ⓐ
Ustrzyki Dolne d.	...	...	...	...	...	...	1413	...	1600	1654
Zagórz d.	...	...	0458	...	...	...	1507	1512	1655	1754
Sanok d.	...	...	0508	...	...	...	...	1521	1704	1804
Krosno d.	...	...	0600	...	...	...	...	1612	1750	1858
Jasło d.	0435	0545	0632	0733	0916	1430	...	1639	1825	1937
Kraków Gł a.	|	|	0912	|	|	|	...	1916	|	|
Przybówka d.	0453	0604	...	0752	0934	1449	...	...	|	1956
Strzyzów d.	0516	0627	...	0821	0957	1513	...	...	1857	2021
Boguchwała d.	0543	0654	...	0854	1025	1557	...	...	1923	2050
Rzeszów Gł a.	0558	0709	...	0909	1040	1612	...	...	1933	2105

h – Also June 15, 21. Aug. 16.
k – Also June 19, Aug. 15.
m – Also June 19, Aug. 15; not June 22.
p – Not June 18, 27.
q – Not June 22.

PKP

WROCŁAW - KATOWICE - KRAKÓW - PRZEMYŚL 1075

Warning! Timings may vary by a few minutes on certain dates.

km		IC 83172 N	IC 30166	IC 43100	IC 4524 O	IC 63172	IC 32110 E	IC 62102 V	IC 6300	IC 63100	IC 73150 F	IC 73102 B	IC 63102 D	IC 73104 P	IC 82160 ①⑥ Wf	IC 73106 B	EC 106 X	IC 8314 Am	IC 8354 ⑤⑦ Qd	IC 8312 E	EC 59 R	IC 32112 E	IC 115 Y	TLK 83110 G	IC 8308 ①–⑤ Q	IC 8358 ⑥⑦ Se
0	**Wrocław** Gł 1061 d.	0117	...	...	...	0509	...	0545	0609	0715	0730	0815	...	0915	0920	1015	...	1115	1115	1215	1315	...	...	1415	1515	1515
41	Brzeg 1061 d.	0142	...	...	...	0534	...	0608	0635	|	0757	0840	...	|	0948	1040	...	|	|	1238	|	...	...	1442	|	|
81	Opole Gł. 1061 d.	0216	...	...	...	0556	...	0630	0658	0756	0822	0902	...	0957	1013	1102	...	1157	1157	1259	1356	...	...	1504	1557	1557
123	Kędzierzyn Koźle d.	0243	...	...	0529	0625	...	|	|	|	0851	|	0940	1019	|	|	...	1220	1220	|	1418	...	...	|	|	|
160	Gliwice ⊡ 1060 d.	|	...	0551	0558	0700	...	|	0751	0901	...	1004	1011	1055	|	1157	...	1300	1300	1355	1447	...	...	1556	1656	1656
190	**Katowice** 1060 a.	0411	...	0613	0620	0724	...	|	0829	0923	...	1026	1034	1117	|	1219	...	1324	1324	1422	1509	...	...	1617	1718	1718
190	**Katowice** d.	0417	...	0616	...	0731	...	|	0830	0928	...	1029	1037	1120	|	1222	...	1330	1330	1426	1512	...	...	1621	1721	1721
	Częstochowa Stradom a.	|	...	|	...	|	...	0722	|	|	...	|	|	|	1109	|	...	|	|	|	|	...	...	|	|	|
268	**Kraków** Gł. a.	0525	...	0713	...	0830	...	...	0922	1015	...	1126	1143	1208	...	1326	...	1422	1422	1520	1603	...	...	1727	1815	1815
268	**Kraków** Gł. 1078 d.	0530	0630	0730	...	0835	0845	...	0930	1020	...	1130	...	1220	...	1330	1425	...	1430	1525	1618	1623	1720	...	1820	1820
273	**Kraków** Płaszów 1078 d.	0536	0636	0736	...	0841	0850	...	0936	1027	...	1135	...	1225	...	1336	1430	...	1436	1530	1623	1628	1725	...	1826	1826
346	Tarnów 1078 d.	0628	0717	0822	...	0922	0933	...	1018	1106	...	1216	...	1304	...	1419	1507	...	1515	1611	1701	1706	1805	...	1904	1904
379	Dębica d.	0650	0734	0840	...	0939	0951	...	1036	1123	...	1233	...	1322	...	1437	1523	...	1550	1628	1718	1725	1821	...	1920	1920
426	**Rzeszów** Gł. 1058 d.	0720	0807	0912	...	1011	...	...	1109	1149	...	1305	...	1348	...	1508	1548	...	1621	1658	1745	...	1852	...	1948	1948
463	Przeworsk 1058 d.	0749	0832	0938	...	1037	...	...	1135	1215	...	1330	...	1414	...	1534	1626	...	1648	1723	1820	...	1917	...	2014	2014
478	Jarosław 1058 d.	0801	0843	0949	...	1048	...	...	1146	1225	...	1341	...	1424	...	1545	1636	...	1659	1733	1830	...	1928	...	2024	2024
513	**Przemyśl** Gł. 1058 a.	0826	0910	1017	...	1116	...	...	1214	1251	...	1409	...	1450	...	1613	1702	...	1726	1800	1855	...	1955	...	2049	2049

	IC 8306 C	EIP 5308 Z	EC 57 R	IC 62104 V	IC 63106 D	IC 8304 G	IC 8302 T	IC 84100 L	EC 55 U	EC 100 M
Wrocław Gł 1061 d.	1615	...	1715	1745	...	1815	1915	2030	2100	...
Brzeg 1061 d.	1641	...	|	1813	...	1839	|	2058	|	...
Opole Gł. 1061 d.	1702	...	1755	1832	...	1900	1956	2123	2140	...
Kędzierzyn Koźle d.	|	...	1817	|	1859	|	|	|	2202	...
Gliwice 1060 d.	1757	...	1845	|	1929	1957	2050	2222	2232	2241
Katowice 1060 a.	1819	...	1908	|	1953	2019	2112	2246	2253	2302
Katowice d.	1822	...	1912	|	1956	2024	2115	...	2257	...
Częstochowa Stradom a.	|	...	|	1930	|	|	|	...	|	...
Kraków Gł. a.	1923	...	2001	...	2101	2121	2205	...	2349	...
Kraków Gł. 1078 d.	1930	2007	2021	...	...	...	...	...	...	...
Kraków Płaszów 1078 d.	1935	2013	2026	...	...	...	...	...	...	...
Tarnów 1078 d.	2017	2048	2104	...	...	...	...	...	...	...
Dębica d.	2034	2105	2120	...	...	...	...	...	...	...
Rzeszów Gł. 1058 d.	2106	2128	2146	...	...	...	...	...	...	...
Przeworsk 1058 d.	2131	...	2213	...	...	...	...	...	...	...
Jarosław 1058 d.	2141	...	2223	...	...	...	...	...	...	...
Przemyśl Gł. 1058 a.	2208	...	2248	...	...	...	...	...	...	...

	EC 101 M	IC 48100 L	EC 54 U	IC 3802 T	IC 3804 G	IC 38106 D	IC 26104 V	EC 56 R	EIP 3508 Z
Przemyśl Gł. 1058 d.	...	...	...	...	...	...	...	0505	...
Jarosław 1058 d.	...	...	...	...	...	...	...	0530	...
Przeworsk 1058 d.	...	...	...	...	...	...	...	0541	...
Rzeszów Gł. 1058 d.	...	...	...	...	...	...	...	0610	0633
Dębica d.	...	...	...	...	...	...	...	0638	0655
Tarnów 1078 d.	...	...	...	...	...	...	...	0655	0712
Kraków Płaszów 1078 d.	...	...	...	...	...	...	...	0730	0748
Kraków Gł. 1078 a.	...	...	...	...	...	...	...	0735	0753
Kraków Gł. d.	...	...	0418	0555	0631	0643	...	0759	...
Częstochowa Stradom d.	...	...	|	|	|	|	0831	|	...
Katowice a.	...	...	0507	0647	0736	0757	|	0857	...
Katowice 1060 d.	0459	0506	0510	0650	0742	0803	|	0900	...
Gliwice 1060 d.	0519	0535	0540	0716	0810	0831	|	0926	...
Kędzierzyn Koźle d.	...	|	0608	|	|	0857	|	0953	...
Opole Gł. 1061 d.	...	0634	0631	0804	0902	...	0924	1016	...
Brzeg 1061 d.	...	0657	|	|	0921	...	0943	|	...
Wrocław Gł. 1061 a.	...	0725	0709	0844	0945	...	1007	1055	...

FOR ADDITIONAL SERVICES AND FOOTNOTES SEE NEXT PAGE →

1075 WROCŁAW - KATOWICE - KRAKÓW - PRZEMYŚL

Warning! Timings may vary by a few minutes on certain dates.

	IC 3806	*IC* 3808 ⑦–④	*IC* 3858 ⑤⑥	*TLK* 38110	*IC* 114	*IC* 23112	*EC* 58	*IC* 3812	*EC* 107	*IC* 3814	*IC* 37106	*IC* 36102	*IC* 26100	*IC* 28160 ⑤⑦	*IC* 37104	*IC* 37102	*IC* 36101	*IC* 3600	*IC* 26102	*IC* 23110	*IC* 36172	*IC* 5424	*IC* 34100	*IC* 3350 ⑤⑦	*IC* 38172	*IC* 33166
	E	Qc	Sg	G	Y	E	R	C	X	A	B	D	Vm	Wd	P	B			V	E		O		d	N	
Przemyśl Gł. 1058 d.	0541	0707	0707	...	0815	...	0918	1002	1117	...	1146	...	...	...	1255	1345	1522	1606	...	...	1711	...	1814	1906	1934	2120
Jarosław 1058 d.	0609	0732	0732	...	0842	...	0944	1029	1142	...	1214	...	...	...	1320	1413	1548	1633	...	...	1739	...	1841	1934	1958	2147
Przeworsk 1058 d.	0619	0742	0742	...	0853	...	0954	1040	1153	...	1224	...	...	...	1330	1424	1559	1645	...	...	1749	...	1851	1945	2010	2158
Rzeszów Gł. 1058 d.	0648	0809	0809	...	0921	...	1022	1107	1221	...	1252	...	...	...	1358	1452	1626	1713	...	...	1817	...	1920	2013	2038	2225
Dębica d.	0719	0834	0834	...	0950	1038	1045	1135	1244	...	1322	...	...	...	1422	1522	1649	1743	...	1831	1846	...	1948	2043	2107	2254
Tarnów 1078 d.	0737	0852	0852	...	1006	1059	1106	1152	1302	...	1340	...	...	...	1442	1540	1707	1802	...	1852	1904	...	2005	2103	2129	2312
Kraków Płaszów 1078 d.	0820	0930	0930	...	1044	1137	1142	1230	1339	...	1421	...	...	...	1521	1621	1745	1843	...	1930	1944	...	2044	2144	2217	2352
Kraków Gł. 1078 a.	0825	0935	0935	...	1049	1142	1147	1235	1344	...	1426	...	...	...	1526	1626	1750	1849	...	1935	1949	...	2050	2149	2223	2357
Kraków Gł. d.	0833	0944	0944	1025	...	...	1157	1239	...	1333	1437	1503	...	...	1543	1631	1754	1857	...	...	1953	...	2054	...	2229	...
Częstochowa Stradom d.	|	|	|	|	...	...	|	|	...	|	|	|	1643	1643	|	|	|	|	2035	...	|	...	|	...	|	...
Katowice a.	0933	1034	1034	1125	...	...	1250	1335	...	1431	1541	1610	|	|	1647	1733	1842	2001	|	...	2057	...	2156	...	2341	...
Katowice 1060 d.	0936	1037	1037	1128	...	...	1253	1338	...	1434	1544	1613	|	|	1650	1736	1845	2004	|	...	2102	2145	2159	...	2348	...
Gliwice 1060 d.	1009	1116	1116	1201	...	...	1316	1412	...	1512	1609	1640	|	|	1717	1811	1918	2035	|	...	2135	2212	2227	...	|	...
Kędzierzyn Kozle d.	|	|	|	|	...	...	1342	|	...	1537	|	1704	|	|	1742	|	|	|	|	...	2200	2236	...	...	0113	...
Opole Gł. 1061 d.	1100	1205	1205	1255	...	...	1406	1504	...	1605	1658	...	1749	1749	1806	1902	2006	2127	2134	...	2229	...	...	...	0149	...
Brzeg 1061 d.	1121	|	|	1318	...	...	|	1523	...	|	1719	...	1813	1813	|	1922	|	2147	2155	...	2249	...	...	...	0214	...
Wrocław Gł. 1061 a.	1145	1245	1245	1345	...	...	1445	1545	...	1645	1743	...	1840	1840	1845	1946	2046	2214	2219	...	2313	...	...	...	0239	...

Polregio, Koleje Śląskie — **ADDITIONAL SERVICES KATOWICE - KRAKÓW** — 2nd class only

km																								
0	**Katowice** d.	0445	0535	0656	0752	0901	...	0953	1044	1148	1244	1352	...	1447	1552	1656	1745	...	1850	2003	2052	2200	...	...
78	**Kraków** Gł. a.	0555	0652	0755	0915	1000	...	1111	1150	1306	1345	1508	...	1551	1711	1811	1903	...	1952	2131	2215	2315	...	...
	Kraków Gł d.	0357	0522	0608	0725	0808	...	0918	0951	1117	1209	1323	...	1409	1510	1606	1718	...	1822	1920	2027	2146	...	...
	Katowice a.	0525	0628	0723	0830	0926	...	1020	1118	1218	1328	1424	...	1534	1626	1726	1827	...	1943	2036	2127	2302	...	...

A – [12] Kraków - Szczecin and v.v.
B – [12] Poznań - Przemyśl and v.v.
C – [12] Słupsk - Przemyśl and v.v.
D – [12] Jelenia Góra - Kraków and v.v.
E – [12] Hrubieszów Miasto - Kraków and v.v.
F – [12] Poznań - Zakopane and v.v.
G – [12] Kołobrzeg - Kraków and v.v.
L – [12] Słupsk - Katowice and v.v.
M – [12] ✕ Katowice - Wien and v.v.
N – 🛏 ▬ [12] Świnoujście - Przemyśl and v.v.
O – [12] Olsztyn - Racibórz and v.v.

P – [12] Zielona Góra - Przemyśl and v.v.
Q – [12] Szczecin - Przemyśl and v.v.
R – [12] Berlin - Przemyśl and v.v.
S – [12] Świnoujście - Przemyśl and v.v.
T – [12] Świnoujście - Kraków and v.v.
U – [12] Berlin - Kraków and v.v.
V – [12] Lublin - Wrocław and v.v.
W – [12] Lublin - Szczecin and v.v.
X – [12] Graz - Przemyśl and v.v.
Y – [12] Praha - Przemyśl and v.v.
Z – [12] Gdynia - Rzeszów and v.v.

c – ⑦–④ June 15–27 (not June 18).
d – Also June 18, Aug. 14; not June 20.
e – Also June 19, Aug. 15.
f – Also June 19, Aug. 15; not June 21, Aug. 16.
g – Also June 18, Aug. 14.
m – ①②③④⑥ (also June 20, Aug.15; not June 18, Aug. 14).

⊡ – Wrocław Gł to Gliwice via Strzelce Opolskie is *152 km*.

1076 KRAKÓW - KATOWICE - BOHUMÍN - OSTRAVA

PKP, Koleje Śląskie

Most *IC* trains are classified *EC* in the Czech Republic. For night trains including Leo Express services see Table **99**.

km		*EC* 101	*EC* 203	*EC* 103			*IC* 116	*EC* 105		*IC* 114	*IC* 131			*EC* 107	Ⓐ	*TLK* 212	*IC* 112	*EC* 109 1277	Ⓐ		*IC* 110		
										A				B	p			S	p			m	n
	Warszawa Cen 1060 d.	...	...	...	...	...	0522	0609	...	...	0905	...	...	...	...	...	1335	1405	...	...	1735	...	...
	Kraków Gł. 1077 1099 d.	...	...	0627	...	...	|	|	...	1110	|	...	...	1359	...	1537	|	|	...	...	|	...	...
0	**Katowice** d.	0459	...	|	0627	0830	0818	0852	1029	|	1146	1228	1424	|	1553	|	1624	1701	1725	1827	2022	2027	2027
	Oświęcim 1079 1099 d.	|	...	|	|	|	|	|	|	1155	|	|	|	1451	|	1626	|	|	|	|	|	|	|
74	Zebrzydowice 🏛 d.	|	...	0809	|	|	|	|	|	1252	1302	|	|	|	|	1719	|	|	|	|	|	|	|
45	Rybnik 1079 1099 d.	|	...	|	0737	0931	0904	0943	1137	|	|	1336	1528	1551	1646	|	1710	1750	1827	1941	2109	2134	2142
	Wrocław Gł. d.	|	0629	|	|	|	|	|	|	|	|	|	|	|	|	|	|	|	|	|	|	|	|
82	Racibórz 1079 1099 d.	0609	0802	|	|	|	|	1009	|	|	|	|	|	|	|	|	|	|	|	|	|	|	|
102	Chałupki 🏛 1079 1099 d.	0624	0816	|	0827	1033	0937	1023	1218	|	|	1416	1609	1624	1728	|	1742	1823	1908	2022	2143	2215	2223
∆94	Bohumín 🏛 a.	0630	0822	0830	0833	1039	0943	1030	1224	1313	1322	1424	...	1630	...	1740	1748	1830	1914	...	2149	...	...
94	Bohumín 🏛 1160 d.	0642	0842	0842	...	...	1004	1042	...	1404	1342	...	...	1642	...	1804	1804	1842	...	...	...	...	...
102	**Ostrava** hlavní nádraži 1160 a.	0649	0851	0851	...	...	1011	1049	...	1411	1349	...	...	1649	...	1811	1811	1849	...	...	...	...	...
	Praha hlavní nádraži 1160 a.	|	|	|	...	...	1336	|	...	1736	|	...	...	|	...	2136	2136	|	...	...	...	...	...
	Wien Hbf 1150 a.	0949	1149	1149	...	...	...	1349	...	...	|	...	...	1949	...	...	...	2149	...	...	...	...	...
	Budapest Nyugati a.	...	...	...	...	...	...	...	...	...	1949	...	...	...	...	...	...	...	...	...	...	...	...

km		Ⓐ		*IC* 111			*EC* 108 1276	*IC* 113	*TLK* 213		*EC* 106			*IC* 130	*IC* 115	Ⓐ	*EC* 104	*IC* 117		*EC* 102	*EC* 202		*EC* 100
		p					S				B				A	n							
	Budapest Nyugati d.	...	...	...	...	...	...	...	...	...	...	...	...	0812	...	...	...	...	...	...	...	...	...
	Wien Hbf 1150 d.	...	...	...	...	...	0610	...	...	...	0810	...	...	|	...	...	1410	...	...	1610	1610	...	1810
	Praha hlavní nádraži 1160 d.	...	...	...	...	...	|	0622	...	...	|	...	...	|	1022	...	|	1422	...	|	|	...	|
	Ostrava hlavní nádraži 1160 d.	...	...	...	...	...	0905	0950	...	...	1105	...	...	1405	1350	...	1705	1750	...	1905	1905	...	2105
	Bohumín 🏛 1160 a.	...	...	...	...	...	0912	0956	...	...	1112	...	...	1412	1356	...	1712	1756	...	1912	1912	...	2112
	Bohumín 🏛 d.	...	...	0613	...	0844	0927	1009	1017	1049	1127	1243	1435	1438	1445	...	1727	1809	...	1927	1935	2041	2127
	Chałupki 🏛 1079 1099 d.	0527	...	0620	0651	0851	0937	1017	|	1056	1134	1250	1442	|	|	1637	1735	1824	1848	|	1942	2048	2134
	Racibórz 1079 1099 d.	|	...	|	|	|	|	|	|	|	|	|	|	|	|	|	1751	|	|	|	1956	|	2149
	Wrocław Gł. a.	|	...	|	|	|	|	|	|	|	|	|	|	|	|	|	|	|	|	|	2124	|	|
	Rybnik 1079 1099 d.	0612	...	0653	0736	0940	1014	1052	|	1140	1206	1334	1524	|	|	1740	1817	1900	1938	|	...	2134	|
0	Zebrzydowice 🏛 d.	|	...	|	|	|	|	|	1037	|	|	|	|	1458	1518	|	|	|	|	1949	...	|	|
51	Oświęcim 1079 1099 d.	|	...	|	|	|	|	|	1130	|	1316	|	|	|	1615	|	|	|	|	2040	...	|	|
	Katowice a.	0701	...	0746	0833	1050	1108	1143	|	1239	|	1435	1638	1629	|	1848	1904	1950	2045	|	...	2234	2302
116	**Kraków** Gł. 1077 1099 a.	...	...	|	...	...	|	|	1216	...	1417	...	...	|	1700	...	|	|	...	2125	...	...	...
	Warszawa Cen 1060 a.	...	...	1038	...	...	1355	1426	...	...	...	...	...	1916	...	...	2151	2248	...	...	...	...	...

A – [12] Przemyśl - Praha and v.v.
B – [12] Przemyśl - Graz and v.v.
S – SOBIESKI – [12] ✕ Warszawa - Wien and v.v. Also conveys on ②④⑤⑦ June 27 - Aug. 29 [2] ▬ 2 cl (**1277**) Warszawa - Wien - Rijeka / on ①③⑤⑦ June 29 - Aug. 31 [2] ▬ 2 cl (**1276**) Rijeka - Wien - Warszawa (Table **99**).

m – June 15–26.
n – June 27 - Aug. 30.
p – Not June 20.
∆ – *106 km* via Chałupki.

KATOWICE - BIELSKO BIAŁA - ZWARDOŃ - ŽILINA 1077

Koleje Śląskie

km																									
km				Ⓐn	Ⓒm	Ⓐn					Ⓐn			Ⓐn	Ⓐn	Ⓐn	Ⓐn	Ⓐn							
0	**Katowice** **1060** d.	0528	...	0711	0746	0824	...	0931	0958	1215	1314	...	1333	1405	1418	1527	1610	1639	...	1731	1839	1934	2033	2116	...
17	Tychy d.	0549	...	0732	0808	0845	...	0953	1020	1235	1333	...	1353	1423	1438	1547	1629	1705	...	1754	1902	1954	2054	2137	...
44	Czechowice-Dziedzice d.	0619	0624	0801	0832	0923	1003	1022	1049	1311	1358	1436	1423	1452	1509	1618	1658	1735	1751	1825	1934	2024	2125	2208	2210
	Zebrzydowice d.	|	0706	|	|	|	1045	|	|	|	|	1525	|	|	|	|	|	|	1832	|	|	|	|	|	2252
	Cieszyn ★ a.	|	0729	|	|	|	1108	|	|	|	|	1548	|	|	|	|	|	|	1855	|	|	|	|	|	2315
55	**Bielsko Biała** Gł. **1060** d.	0635	...	0820	0845	0941	...	1039	1108	1327	1413	...	1440	1507	1526	1634	1711	1752	...	1849	1948	2044	2143	2226	...
76	Zywiec a.	0703	...	0849	0914	1022	...	1108	1138	1402	1439	...	1514	1532	1555	1702	1736	1821	...	1923	2031	2119	2213	2257	...
113	**Zwardoń** a.	0804	...	0948	1014	...	...	1206	...	1512	...	...	1617	1632	1703	1803	...	1933	...	2027	...	2218	...	2358	...

km																									
km		Ⓐn			Ⓐn	Ⓐn										Ⓐn	Ⓐn		Ⓐ	Ⓐn	Ⓐn	Ⓐn	Ⓒm		
	Zwardoń d.	...	0457	...	0603	0629	...	...	0836	...	...	1209	...	1241	...	1421	...	...	1526	1634	1805	...	1851	...	1956
	Zywiec d.	0531	0557	0630	0706	0734	...	0854	0946	1046	1202	1309	...	1343	1454	1534	1625	...	1704	1738	1904	2010	2011	...	2100
	Bielsko Biała Gł. **1060** d.	0603	0629	0657	0738	0808	...	0932	1020	1138	1234	1338	...	1418	1536	1612	1652	...	1735	1817	1935	2043	2043	...	2131
0	Cieszyn ★ d.	|	|	|	|	|	0758	|	|	|	|	|	1309	|	|	|	|	1558	|	|	|	|	|	1945	|
16	Zebrzydowice d.	|	|	|	|	|	0830	|	|	|	|	|	1342	|	|	|	|	1631	|	|	|	|	|	2018	|
46	Czechowice-Dziedzice d.	0613	0643	0707	0753	0818	0903	0947	1035	1153	1248	1352	1415	1433	1556	1627	1702	1704	1750	1831	1949	2057	2057	2051	2145
	Tychy d.	0637	0716	0733	0824	0842	...	1017	1105	1225	1317	1422	...	1502	1631	1658	1726	...	1821	1907	2019	2127	2127	...	2221
	Katowice **1060** a.	0655	0736	0750	0844	0858	...	1037	1125	1245	1338	1441	...	1521	1653	1719	1742	...	1842	1927	2038	2146	2146	...	2240

km																									
km			Ⓐ			Ⓐ			Ⓐ		Ⓐ			Ⓐ			Ⓐ			Ⓐ			Ⓐ		
0	**Zwardoń** 🏛 d.	*0616*	...	...	*0816*	...	*1016*	...	...	*1216*	...	...	*1416*	...	*1616*	...	...	*1816*	...	...	*2016*	...	...	...	*2216*
8	Skalité d.	0635	0734	...	0834	0934	1034	...	1134	1234	1334	...	1434	1534	1634	...	1734	1834	...	1934	2034	...	2134	...	2234
22	Čadca **1160** d.	0704	0804	...	0904	1004	1104	...	1204	1304	1404	...	1504	1604	1704	...	1804	1904	...	2004	2104	...	2204	...	2304
52	**Žilina** **1160** a.	0742	0843	...	0942	1042	1142	...	1242	1342	1442	...	1542	1642	1742	...	1842	1942	...	2043	2142	...	2242	...	2342

		Ⓐ			Ⓐ			Ⓐ		Ⓐ			Ⓐ				Ⓐ			Ⓐ			Ⓐ		
Žilina **1160** d.	0617	0717	...	0817	0917	1017	...	1117	1217	1317	...	1417	1517	...	1617	...	1717	...	1817	1917	...	2017	2117	...	2217
Čadca **1160** d.	0705	0805	...	0908	1008	1108	...	1205	1308	1405	...	1508	1605	...	1708	...	1805	...	1908	2005	...	2108	2205	...	2308
Skalité a.	0726	0825	...	0928	1027	1128	...	1225	1328	1425	...	1528	1625	...	1728	...	1825	...	1928	2025	...	2128	2225	...	2328
Zwardoń 🏛 a.	*0748*	...	...	*0948*	...	*1148*	...	...	*1348*	...	...	*1548*	...	...	*1748*	...	...	...	*1948*	...	...	*2148*	...	...	*2348*

m – Also June 19, 20, Aug 15. **n** – Not June 20. ★ – Cieszyn station (Poland) is situated ± 1500 metres from Český Těšín station (Czech Republic).

KRAKÓW - NOWY SĄCZ - KRYNICA ZDRÓJ 1078

PKP, Polregio, Koleje Małopolskie

See Table **1182** for connections Muszyna - Poprad Tatry and v.v.

Engineering work may affect services between Nowy Sącz and Krynica Zdrój until June 14 – please check before travelling.

km		*TLK* **30170**			*IC* **30100** ⑤–①	*TLK* **30104**	Ⓑ			
0	**Kraków** Gł. **1075** d.	0404	0543	0748	0833	1230	...	1552	1654	2027
5	**Kraków** Płaszów **1075** d.	|	0551	0755	|	|	...	1559	1700	2034
78	Tarnów **1075** d.	0511	0650	0845	0945	1334	1552	1651	1758	2144
136	Stróze d.	0624	0747	0945	1039	1436	1711	1814	1917	2256
167	**Nowy Sącz** d.	0703	0822	1023	1113	1511	1750	1852	1953	2334
217	Muszyna d.	0821	0944	1135	1246	1629	1901	...	2111	...
228	**Krynica Zdrój** a.	0835	0959	1149	1308	1643	...	...	2125	...

	①⑥	⚒		*TLK* **33104**		*IC* **33100** ⑤–①		Ⓐ	*TLK* **33170**
Krynica Zdrój d.	0500	...	...	1110	1416	1500	1728	...	2010
Muszyna d.	0521	0621	0915	1147	1437	1533	1749	...	2043
Nowy Sącz d.	0630	0747	1021	1247	1549	1641	1855	1955	2143
Stróze d.	0702	0825	1059	1320	1626	1714	1927	2033	2216
Tarnów **1075** d.	0810	0932	1206	1419	1730	1818	2039	2144	2317
Kraków Płaszów **1075** d.	0900	...	...	|	1821	|	2140	2301	|
Kraków Gł. **1075** a.	0907	...	...	1521	1828	1921	2150	2308	0019

LOCAL SERVICES IN SILESIA 1079

Koleje Małopolskie, Polregio

KRAKÓW - OŚWIĘCIM (for Auschwitz-Birkenau Memorial and Museum).

Warning! Timings may vary by a few minutes on certain dates.

km													
0	Kraków Gł d.	0600	0743	0853	0928	1043	1122	1246	1443	1549	1843	2039	2243
65	Oświęcim a.	0703	0846	0956	1035	1146	1225	1349	1549	1649	1954	2149	2347

Oświęcim d.	0630	0733	0934	1022	1139	1228	1323	1444	1640	1733	1826	2135
Kraków Gł. d.	0733	0843	1044	1125	1239	1337	1433	1546	1743	1836	1933	2244

WROCŁAW - BRZEG - OPOLE - KEDZIERZYN KOŹLE - RACIBÓRZ

km		Ⓒ		Ⓐ	Ⓐ	Ⓐ	Ⓐ	Ⓐ		Ⓐ		Ⓐ	Ⓐ
0	Wrocław Gł d.	0515	0735	0825	1121	1220	1320	1355	1421	1525	1655	1840	1959
41	Brzeg d.	0551	0811	0900	1156	1301	1353	1428	1504	1601	1737	1917	2042
81	Opole Gł. d.	0625	0844	0934	1229	1335	1424	1459	1538	1634	1809	1950	2114
123	Kedzierzyn K.. d.	0701	0921	1011	1306	1412	1459	1533	1615	1711	1854	2027	2150
155	Racibórz a.	0734	0954	...	...	1445	1531	...	1648	1744	1927	2100	...

	Ⓐ	Ⓐ		Ⓐ	Ⓐ		Ⓒm	Ⓐ	Ⓐ	Ⓐ		
Racibórz d.	...	...	0600	0703	...	1110	1333	1423	1529	1659	1815	1936
Kedzierzyn K d.	0512	0617	0654	0737	0922	1145	1408	1459	1603	1749	1849	2015
Opole Gł. d.	0550	0710	0748	0813	0959	1223	1446	1537	1642	1826	1927	2101
Brzeg d.	0623	0741	0830	0844	1041	1255	1525	1607	1722	1858	1959	2133
Wrocław Gł. a.	0658	0817	0908	0918	1113	1331	1600	1640	1758	1934	2035	2209

m – Also June 19, Aug. 15.

1080 POZNAŃ - OSTRÓW - KATOWICE - KRAKÓW
Koleje Wielkopolskie, PKP, Polregio

For other trains Poznań - Katowice - Kraków (via Wrocław) see Table **1075**

km		IC 7324		IC 83107		TLK 73100		IC 7322		TLK 74100	
				S Z							
0	**Poznań** Gł. d.	0550	...	0840	...	1250	...	1550		1740	...
67	Jarocin d.	0632	...	0923	...	1333	...	1633	...	1823	...
114	Ostrów Wielkopolski. d.	0703	...	0954	...	1403	...	1704	...	1854	...
160	Kępno d.	0733	...	1025	...	1436	...	1734	...	1924	...
201	Kluczbork d.	0801	...	1054	...	|	...	1802	...	1952	...
252	Lubliniec d.	0834	...	1135	...	|	...	1835	...	2026	...
	Gliwice d.	|	...	1229	...	|	...	|	...	2113	...
	Częstochowa Stradom d.	0901	...	|	...	1617	...	1900	...	|	...
320	**Katowice** a.	|	...	1258	...	|	...	|	...	2135	...
398	**Kraków** Gł. a.	1033	...	1401	...	1746	...	2030	...	...	...

	TLK 47101		IC 3722		TLK 37100		IC 38107		IC 3724	
							S Z			
Kraków Gł. d.	...	...	0717	...	1011	...	1421	...	1728	...
Katowice d.	0617	...	|	...	|	...	1516	...	|	...
Częstochowa Stradom d.	|	...	0903	...	1145	...	|	...	1904	...
Gliwice d.	0653	...	|	...	|	...	1545	...	|	...
Lubliniec d.	0734	...	0925	...	|	...	1629	...	1925	...
Kluczbork d.	0809	...	0959	...	|	...	1706	...	1959	...
Kępno d.	0836	...	1027	...	1324	...	1736	...	2028	...
Ostrów Wielkopolski. d.	0907	...	1058	...	1357	...	1807	...	2059	...
Jarocin d.	0938	...	1127	...	1428	...	1838	...	2129	...
Poznań Gł. a.	1020	...	1210	...	1510	...	1920	...	2210	...

2nd class — SELECTED REGIONAL TRAINS POZNAŃ - OSTRÓW WIELKOPOLSKI - ŁÓDŹ

	Ⓐn		Ⓐn							
Poznań Gł. d.	0457	0557	0757	1021	1222	1442	1630	1914	...	2218
Jarocin d.	0602	0653	0854	1107	1319	1538	1726	2015	...	2317
Ostrów Wlkp. **1061** d.	0640	0739	0931	1154	1411	1625	1818	2052	2140	0008
Kalisz **1061** d.	...	0800	...	1211	1432	1647	1840	...	2202	0029
Łódź Kaliska **1061** a.	...	0935	...	1327	1607	1838	2014	...	2337	...

		Ⓐ							Ⓐ	
Łódź Kaliska **1061** d.	0510	...	0705	1021	1220	1422	1511	1610	1816	...
Kalisz **1061** d.	0646	...	0840	1154	1356	1558	1629	1750	1954	...
Ostrów Wlkp. **1061** d.	0708	0729	0921	1226	1428	1619	1659	1822	2018	2028
Jarocin d.	...	0806	0957	1302	1505	...	1730	1902	...	2104
Poznań Gł. a.	...	0903	1054	1400	1601	...	1813	1958	...	2202

S – To/from Szczecin (Table **1010**). **Z** – To/from Zakopane (Table **1066**). **n** – Not June 20.

1082 JELENIA GÓRA - TRUTNOV
Koleje Dolnośląskie, Polregio,

Engineering work may affect this route from June 16 – please check with operator before travelling.

km													
0	**Jelenia Góra** d.	0612	...	0923	...	1129	...	...	1629	...	...	1734	...
27	Sędzisław d.	0639	0647	0951	1006	1155	1206	...	1655	1700	...	1801	1910
43	Lubawka 🏛 d.	...	0707	▬	1027	...	1227	...	...	1720	...	...	1931
48	Královec d.	...	0714	0825	1034	...	1234	1235	...	1727	1938	...	1937
65	**Trutnov** Hlavní a.	...	...	0850	...	...	...	1300	...	...	2003	...	...

Trutnov Hlavní d.	0537	...	...	0853	...	...	1337	...	...	...	1802
Královec d.	0604	0607	...	0920	...	...	1405	...	1620	...	1830
Lubawka 🏛 d.	...	0613	...	0926	...	...	1411	...	1626	...	1836
Sędzisław d.	...	0634	0639	0947	0952	...	1432	1448	1647	1652	1857
Jelenia Góra a.	...	...	0711	...	1022	...	...	1516	...	1720	...

☛ Operated in the Czech Republic by GW Train Regio.

1083 GÖRLITZ - JELENIA GÓRA
Koleje Dolnośląskie

km											
0	**Görlitz** **855** d.	0539	0739	0939	...	1139	1339	1539	1739	1939	...
2	Zgorzelec **855** d.	0544	0744	0944	...	1144	1344	1544	1744	1944	...
25	Lubań Śląski d.	0613	0813	1013	...	1213	1413	1613	1813	2013	...
39	Gryfow Śląski d.	0632	0832	1032	1038	1232	1432	1632	1832	2032	2038
76	**Jelenia Góra** a.	0715	0915	...	1121	1315	1515	1715	1921	...	2121

Jelenia Góra d.	0545	0745	0945	1145	...	1340	1545	1745	...	1945
Gryfow Śląski d.	0634	0834	1034	1228	1233	1434	1634	1828	1834	2034
Lubań Śląski d.	0653	0853	1053	...	1252	1453	1653	...	1853	2053
Zgorzelec **855** d.	0723	0923	1123	...	1323	1523	1723	...	1923	2123
Görlitz **855** a.	0727	0927	1127	...	1327	1527	1727	...	1927	2127

☛ 🚌 services also run Görlitz Bahnhof - Zgorzelec Miasto and v.v. every 30 minutes (journey 22 minutes).

1084 SZKLARSKA POREBA - JELENIA GÓRA - WROCŁAW
Koleje Dolnośląskie, Polregio, PKP

Subject to alteration from June 16 – please check with operator before travelling.

km		IC 66100			IC 61100 Wc	IC 61152 Wd	67900 P🍷	IC 65100 G			IC 61170 Wc	IC 61190 Wd
0	**Sz. Poreba** ◧ d.	...	0632	0832	...	1126	1317	...	1640	1837	...	2051
32	Jelenia Góra d.	0643	0723	0930	1220	1220	1408	1442	1730	1941	2138	2138
59	Sedzisław d.	0705	0750	0956	1243	1243	1439	1523	1801	2008	2201	2201
78	Wałbrzych Gł. d.	0724	0812	1018	1302	1302	1503	1523	1824	2032	2220	2220
109	Jaworzyna Śląska d.	0757	0847	1053	1336	1336	1541	1555	1902	2113	2253	2253
158	**Wrocław** Gł. a.	0828	0932	1135	1409	1409	1622	1627	1943	2156	2325	2325

	IC 16170 Wc	IC 16190 Wd			76108 P🍷		IC 56100 G	IC 16100 Wc	IC 16152 Wd		IC 60101
Wrocław Gł. d.	0445	0445	0450	0659	0921	1101	1138	1417	1417	1733	1925
Jaworzyna Śląska d.	0517	0517	0534	0744	1004	1146	1211	1452	1452	1808	1958
Wałbrzych Gł. d.	0553	0553	0620	0821	1042	1227	1257	1543	1543	1846	2038
Sedzisław d.	0611	0611	0643	0844	1102	1250	1316	1602	1602	1906	2056
Jelenia Góra a.	0636	0650	0711	0912	1129	1320	1340	1626	1626	1933	2121
Sz. Poreba ◧ a.	...	0733	0814	1015	1216	1415	...	...	1732	2018	...

G – To/from Gdynia (Table **1020**). **W** – To/from Warszawa (Table **1061**). **c** – Until June 18. **d** – June 19 - Aug. 30. ◧ – Szklarska Poreba Gorna.
P – To/from Poznań (Table **1070**).

1085 ZGORZELEC - WROCŁAW
Koleje Dolnośląskie, Polregio

Subject to alteration from June 16 – please check with operator before travelling. For services from/to Görlitz and Dresden see Table **855** and **1083**.

km			Ⓐ	Ⓐ								
0	**Zgorzelec** d.	0616	0700	...	0809	1010	1259	...	1417	1614	1835	2018
2	Zgorzelec Miasto d.	0619	0703	...	0812	1012	1302	...	1420	1617	1838	2021
26	Węgliniec d.	0640	0720	...	0826	1027	1319	1332	1437	1633	1854	2034
52	Bolesławiec d.	0658	0737	...	0841	1041	...	1349	1455	1650	1912	2049
97	Legnica **1086** d.	0738	0810	0824	0906	1108	...	1422	1537	1724	1949	2115
162	**Wrocław** Gł. **1086** a.	0833	...	0908	0943	1146	...	1501	1633	1818	2044	2152

										c	
Wrocław Gł. **1086** d.	0605	0820	1020	1143	...	1229	1445	1651	1820	1944	2158
Legnica **1086** d.	0644	0859	1100	1241	...	1340	1541	1745	1859	2041	2255
Bolesławiec d.	0716	|	|	1314	...	1413	1616	1818	1923	2115	2328
Węgliniec d.	0732	0937	1138	1332	1337	1431	1634	1836	1938	2144	2347
Zgorzelec Miasto d.	0748	0951	1152	...	1355	1448	1652	1852	1952	2204	0004
Zgorzelec a.	0750	0954	1155	...	1358	1451	1654	1856	1955	2207	0007

c – Change of trains at Węgliniec (arrives at 2133).

1086 COTTBUS and ZIELONA GÓRA - FORST - WROCŁAW
Koleje Dolnośląskie, Polregio, PKP

Subject to alteration from June 16 – please check with operator before travelling.

km			IC 76106	Ⓐn	Ⓐ	Ⓐn	Ⓐn		Ⓐm	g	Ⓐ	Ⓐ
0	**Cottbus** **854** d.	...	...	0609	...	0907	1207	...	1507	...	1807	...
	Zielona Góra d.	...	0452	|	...	|	|	...	|	...	|	...
22	Forst 🏛 **854** d.	...	|	0632	...	0930	1230	...	1530	...	1835	...
36	Tuplice d.	0510	|	0647	...	0945	1245	...	1544	1629	1850	...
57	Żary d.	0531	0621	0708	0822	1006	1306	...	1605	1651	1921	1935
70	Żagań d.	0551	0635	0720	0835	1018	1318	...	1618	1703	1933	1950
144	Legnica **1085** d.	0707	0758	...	0942	...	...	...	...	1814	...	2103
210	**Wrocław** Gł. **1085** a.	0752	0849	...	...	...	...	...	...	...	...	...

	Ⓒh	Ⓐn	Ⓐn			Ⓐn	Ⓐm	Ⓒ	Ⓐm	IC 67104	g
Wrocław Gł. **1085** d.	0515	...	...	0916	...	...	...	1535	...	1915	...
Legnica **1085** d.	0609	...	...	0955	1000	...	...	1620	...	2006	2100
Żagań d.	0724	0738	1034	...	1113	1340	1625	1725	1940	2124	2206
Żary d.	0735	0751	1051	...	1124	1351	1648	1738	1951	2143	2218
Tuplice d.	0755	0812	1112	...	...	1412	1709	1759	2012	|	2239
Forst 🏛 **854** a.	0810	0830	1127	...	...	1427	1730	1814	2027	|	...
Zielona Góra a.	...	|	|	...	...	|	|	...	|	2239	...
Cottbus **854** a.	...	0849	1149	...	...	1449	1749	...	2049	...	...

g – ①②③④⑥. **h** – Also June 19, Aug. 15. **m** – Not July 14–17. **n** – Not July 14–18.

PKP — WARSZAWA - ŁÓDŹ — 1090

Additional regional trains run on Ⓐ operated Polregio, and on Ⓒ operated by Łódźka Kolej Aglomeracyjna (ŁKA).

km		*IC* 1620	*IC* 16108	*IC* 1622	*TLK* 51108	*IC* 1624	*IC* 1106	*IC* 5620	*IC* 51106	*IC* 1626	*IC* 1628	*IC* 1902	*TLK* 51104	*IC* 19132	*IC* 16104	*IC* 19130	*IC* 81114	*IC* 1904	*IC* 16106	*IC* 1102	*IC* 51102	*IC* 5122	*IC* 51100	*IC* 1100	*IC* 1900	*IC* 16170	
			①④								Ⓐ			Ⓐ		⚒		Ⓐ					Ⓐ		Ⓑ	16190	
		W	Wc	W	G	BW	B	EW	G	BW	BW		G		BW		K		BW	B	G	O	G	B		S	
0	**Warszawa** Wsch .... d.	0357	0439	0604	0724	0759	0904	0959	1054	1159	1359	1439	1454	1534	1559	1639	1654	1739	1804	1834	1854	1954	2054	2159	2309	2324	...
4	**Warszawa** Cent........ d.	0414	0448	0614	0748	0814	0914	1014	1114	1214	1414	1448	1522	1546	1614	1648	1714	1748	1822	1848	1914	2014	2114	2214	|	2336	...
70	Skierniewice .... d.	0451	0533	0651	0824	0851	|	1052	1151	1251	1450	1525	1606	1634	1651	1734	1752	1828	1859	|	1951	2051	2151	2253	2356	0018	...
109	Koluszki........ d.	0511	0556	0711	0844	0910	|	1113	1210	1311	1510	1547	1627	1658	1712	1755	1814	1848	1918	|	2012	2110	2211	2313	0016	0041	...
130	**Łódź** Widzew .... d.	0521	0608	0722	0856	0923	1015	1124	1222	1322	1521	1602	1641	1713	1722	1808	1829	1902	1932	1949	2025	2125	2224	2325	0028	0054	...
135	**Łódź** Fabryczna .... a.	...	...	...	0902	...	1019	...	1228	...	...	1607	1646	1719	...	1813	1835	1908	...	1953	2030	2130	2230	2330	0034	...	...

	IC 61170	*IC* 1000	*IC* 9100	*IC* 15100	*IC* 91130	*IC* 1522	*IC* 91132	*IC* 15102	*IC* 1002	*IC* 61106	*IC* 18114	*IC* 61104	*TLK* 15104	*IC* 6128	*IC* 9102	*IC* 6126	*IC* 15106	*IC* 6520	*IC* 1006	*IC* 6124	*TLK* 15108	*IC* 6122	*IC* 6120		
	61190		⚒	Ⓐ	⚒		Ⓐ								Ⓐ										
	S	B		G		O		G	B	BW	K	BW	G	BW		BW	G	EW	B	BW	G	W	W		
Łódź Fabryczna........ d.	...	0420	0458	0523	0552	0627	0641	0736	0806	...	0928	...	1131	...	1331	...	1524	...	1740	...	1925	...	...	...	...
Łódź Widzew........ d.	0326	0427	0505	0532	0601	0635	0650	0743	0812	0836	0935	1039	1138	1238	1338	1438	1531	1637	1745	1837	1931	2100	2257	...	...
Koluszki........ d.	0340	0439	0518	0544	0616	0648	0704	0755	|	0849	0948	1052	1150	1250	1350	1450	1544	1651	|	1849	1943	2113	2309	...	...
Skierniewice........ d.	0403	0459	0538	0605	0638	0708	0727	0816	|	0909	1008	1111	1210	1309	1409	1510	1603	1710	|	1909	2003	2133	2330	...	...
Warszawa Cent........ a.	0446	0538	0616	0642	0722	0745	0812	0852	0912	0944	1046	1146	1246	1346	1445	1546	1638	1746	1846	1946	2038	2212	0006	...	...
Warszawa Wsch........ a.	0456	0601	0626	0706	0731	0756	0826	0906	0926	1001	1106	1201	1306	1401	1501	1601	1706	1801	1856	2001	2106	2220	0026	...	...

B – To / from Białystok (Table **1040**).
E – To / from Ełk (Table **1035**).
G – To / from Gdynia (Table **1030**).
K – Kołobrzeg (Table **1015**).
O – To / from Olsztyn (Table **1030**).
S – To / from Jelenia Góra (Table **1084**).
W – To / from Wrocław (Table **1061**).
c – June 16 – 23.

Koleje Dolnośląskie, PKP — WROCŁAW - KŁODZKO - LICHKOV / KUDOWA ZDRÓJ — 1095

km			*IC* 461			⑥⑦	⑥⑦	Ⓐ	*IC* 261	*IC* 60151	⑥⑦	Ⓐ		*IC* 263			Ⓐ	*IC* 265	Ⓐ						
			B§			b	b		B	Kb	b	n		B				B		m					
0	**Wrocław** Gł. .... d.	...	0515	0612	...	0806	...	0820	0915	1027	...	1208	1237	1315	1518	1554	1640	1715	1733	...	1850	2053	2155	2300	...
37	Strzelin .... d.	...	0539	0638	...	0830	...	0852	0939	1058	...	|	1311	1339	1549	1626	1711	1739	1806	...	1923	2125	2227	2332	...
72	Kamieniec Ząbkowicki. d.	...	0600	0709	...	0854	0947	0919	1000	1130	...	|	1344	1400	1615	1652	1740	1800	1842	1851	1948	2154	2255	2359	...
93	**Kłodzko** Główne .... d.	...	|	0734	...	0910	1007	0938	|	1149	...	1431	1404	|	1634	1710	1759	|	1901	1911	2006	2216	2315	0018	...
95	**Kłodzko** Miasto. .... d.	0517	0619	0737	0753	0913	1013	0943	1019	1200	1234	1435	1439**c**	1419	1637	1713	1802	1819	1905	1916	2009	2219	2318	...	...
	Kudowa Zdrój .... a.	0612	|	|	0847	1003	1107	|	|	1304	1329	1530	|	|	|	...	|	|	...	2011	|	|	...	...	...
129	Międzylesie 🏛 (PL)..... a.	...	0645	0807	...	...	...	1014	1043	...	...	...	1509	1443	1713	...	1834	1843	...	...	2039	2252	...	...	...
138	**Lichkov** 🏛 (CZ) **1165** a.	...	0657	0818	...	...	...	...	1057	...	...	...	1518	1457	1722	...	...	1857	...	...	...	...	...	...	...

km		Ⓐ	Ⓐ	Ⓐ						*IC* 264	⑥⑦	⑥⑦	*IC* 262	⑥⑦	*IC* 66150	⑥⑦	Ⓐ	⑥⑦	*IC* 260		⑥⑦				*IC* 460
										B	b	b	B	b	Kb	b	q	p	B		b				B‡
	Lichkov 🏛 (CZ) **1165** d.								0852	0902			1302	1336		1552			1702	1736					2102
	Międzylesie 🏛 (PL)..... d.	...	0456	...	0558**f**	...	0704	0811**f**	0925	0917	...	1220	1317	1345	...	1606	...	...	1717	1749	...	1858	...	2101	2117
0	**Kudowa Zdrój** .... d.	...	|	...	|	0631	|	|	|	|	1109	|	|	|	1435	|	1542	...	|	|	1748	|	2025	|	|
42	**Kłodzko** Miasto. .... d.	0437	0528	0607	0639	0727	0737	0843	1001	0943	1159	1253	1343	1438	1613	1652	1647**a**	1658	1743	1824	1838	1929	2120	2132	2143
	Kłodzko Główne .... d.	0440	0542	0610	0643	...	0741	0846	1005	|	1202	1256	|	1441	1618	1655	1700	1701	|	1828	1841	1932	2122	2135	|
	Kamieniec Ząbkowicki. d.	0459	0601	0629	0706	...	0801	0906	1024	1002	1218	1313	1402	1505	1637	1718	...	|	1802	1847	1858	1952	...	2153	2202
	Strzelin .... d.	0527	0629	0702	0733	...	0829	0938	1050	1024	1242	1340	1424	1534	1725	1751	...	|	1824	1910	1922	2019	...	2215	2224
	Wrocław Gł. .... a.	0557	0702	0733	0803	...	0902	1008	1121	1047	1305	1406	1447	1604	1754	1822	...	1926	1847	1936	1945	2049	...	2238	2247

B – BALTIC EXPRESS – ✕ (12) Gdynia - Wrocław - Praha and v.v.
K – ⑥⑦. (12) Warszawa (**16150/1**) - Wrocław - Kudowa-Zdrój and v.v.
a – Arrival time.
b – Also June 19, Aug. 15.
c – Arrives 1407.
f – Ⓐ only.
m – Not July 7 – 10.
n – Not July 14 – 25, Aug. 14 – 18.
p – Not July 19 – 27, Aug. 16 – 23.
q – Not June 19, July 14 – 31, Aug. 1, 15.
§ – Also conveys 🛏 (1, 2, 3 berth) until Aug. 30.
‡ – Also conveys 🛏 (1, 2, 3 berth) until Aug. 31.

2nd class only — OTHER LOCAL SERVICES — 1099

76 km, journey 1 hr 25 mins - 1 hr 55 mins — GDYNIA - HEL

Gdynia Główna depart: 0520, 0700, 0911, 1033, 1228, 1328, 1530, 1630, 1839, 2034, 2234.
Hel depart: 0526, 0714, 0852, 1144, 1251, 1346, 1421, 1455, 1603, 1700, 1805, 1845, 2041.
Operator: Polregio. Timings may vary by 5 - 10 minutes until June 29. Please confirm locally.

12 km, journey 18 mins — KRAKÓW - JOHN PAUL II Airport ✈

Kraków Główny depart: 0046, 0436, 0536, 0606, 0636 and at the same minutes past each hour until 2106, 2136, 2236, 2336.
Kraków Airport depart: 0007, 0057, 0417, 0517, 0617, 0647 and at the same minutes past each hour until 2117, 2147, 2217, 2317.
Operator: Koleje Małopolskie.

62 km, journey 1 hr 25 mins - 1 hr 56 mins — KRAKÓW - WADOWICE

Kraków Główny depart: 0415, 0649, 0842, 1049, 1355, 1422, 1614, 1823, 2047.
Wadowice depart: 0433, 0745, 1022, 1223, 1355, 1605, 1813, 2030, 2200.
Operator: Polregio (Wadowice is the birthplace of Pope John Paul II).

14 km, journey 22 – 23 mins — KRAKÓW - WIELICZKA (for Salt Mine)

Kraków Główny depart: 0538, 0638, 0708, 0738, 0808, 0838 and at the same minutes past each hour until 2008, 2038, 2108, 2138, 2238, 2338.
Wieliczka Rynek-Kopalnia depart: 0411, 0511, 0541 and at the same minutes past each hour until 2111, 2141, 2211, 2311.
Operator: Koleje Małopolskie.

LESZNO - WOLSZTYN - ZBĄSZYNEK

		Ⓐn	Ⓐn		Ⓐn	Ⓐ 🚂	Ⓐn				Ⓑ
Leszno .... d.	0508	0543	0854	1040	1244	...	1428	1529	1705	1907	2112
Wolsztyn .... d.	0612	0654	0954	1137	1344	1415	1522	1629	1803	2001	2211
Zbąszyń .... d.	0640	0729	...	1203	...	1456	...	1655	1831	...	...
Zbąszynek........ a.	0647	0737	...	1210	...	1503	...	1701	1839	...	...

	Ⓐn	Ⓐn		Ⓐn	Ⓐn		Ⓐn	Ⓐ 🚂			
Zbąszynek........ d.	...	...	0705	0844	...	1236	...	1535	1726	1926	...
Zbąszyń .... d.	...	...	0711	0851	...	1243	...	1545	1733	1932	...
Wolsztyn .... d.	0533	0614	0740	0919	1058	1310	1554	1621	1801	2003	2137
Leszno .... a.	0627	0708	0834	1013	1200	1404	1649	...	1853	2055	2231

Operator: Koleje Wielkopolskie.

80 km, journey 1 hr 25 mins - 1 hr 43 mins — POZNAN - WOLSZTYN

Poznan Główny depart: 0531Ⓐ **n**, 0619Ⓐ, 0735, 0831, 0954Ⓐ **n**, 1148, 1344, 1450, 1544⑥ 🚂, 1627Ⓐ **n**, 1711, 1856, 2006Ⓐ **n**, 2045, 2200, 2304⚒.
Wolsztyn depart: 0419Ⓐ **n**, 0449, 0529, 0552⑥ , 0629, 0804, 0831Ⓐ **n**, 0941, 1039⑥ 🚂, 1146Ⓐ, 1338, 1413Ⓐ **n**, 1545, 1652Ⓑ, 1804, 1925**d,** 2108.
Operator: Koleje Wielkopolskie.

51 km, journey 1 hr 10 - 1 hr 17 mins — WAŁBRZYCH - KŁODZKO

Wałbrzych Główny depart: 0622, 0849⑥⑦ **c**, 1048⑥⑦ **e**, 1638.
Kłodzko Miasto depart: 1445, 1658Ⓐ.
Operator: Koleje Dolnośląskie.

13 km, journey 29 – 32 mins — WARSZAWA - CHOPIN AIRPORT ✈

Warszawa Wschodnia depart: 0401, 0431Ⓐ, 0501Ⓐ, 0519, 0531, 0601, 0619, 0631, and at the same minutes past each hour until 2201, 2219, 2231. 2301
Warszawa Chopin ✈ depart: 0455, 0525, 0555, 0610, 0625, 0655, 0710, 0725, 0755 and at the same minutes past each hour until 2210, 2225, 2255Ⓐ, 2310Ⓐ, 2325Ⓐ, 2355.
Operator: Szybka Kolej Miejska.

40 km, journey 51 – 65 mins — WARSZAWA - MODLIN AIRPORT ✈

Warszawa Wschodnia depart: 0337Ⓐ, 0414, 0514, 0613, 0714, and at the same minutes past each hour until 2114, 2214, 2314.
🚌 connects at Modlin rail station to / from the airport terminal, journey time 10 minutes. Modlin depart: 0514, 0614, and at the same minutes past each hour until 2314, 2325, 0025.
☛ Most trains to / from Modlin start from / continue to Warszawa Chopin Airport via central Warszawa.
Operator: Koleje Mazowieckie.

NOTES FOR TABLE 1099 (ALL ROUTES):

c – Also June 19.
d – ①-④ (not June 19).
e – Also June 19, Aug. 15; not July 19, 20.
n – Not June 20.
🚂 Normally operated with a steam locomotive.

CZECH REPUBLIC

Services: Operator: České Dráhy (ČD), www.cd.cz. Railway infrastructure and timetables are the responsibility of Správa Železnic, www.spravazeleznic.cz.
All daytime trains convey first and second classes of travel unless otherwise shown by '2' at the top of the column or by a note (which may be in the table heading).

Timings: Valid **until December 13, 2025** with amendments as received. Certain trains are cancelled during the Christmas / New Year period, particularly the evening of Dec. 24, 31 and the morning of Dec. 25, 26, Jan. 1; passengers travelling during this period are advised to confirm train times before travel.

Tickets: It is possible to reserve seats on most Express trains. SuperCity (*SC*) tilting trains have a compulsory reservation fee. *Business* class on Railjet (*RJ*) trains requires a first class ticket and a supplement. Note that ČD tickets, including day passes and Interrail / Eurail passes, are not valid on trains operated by Arriva or GW Train Regio.

Station names: hlavní nádraží (hl. n.) = main station; západ = west; východ = east; horní = upper; dolní = lower; střed = centre, starý = old; město = town; předměstí = outskirts.

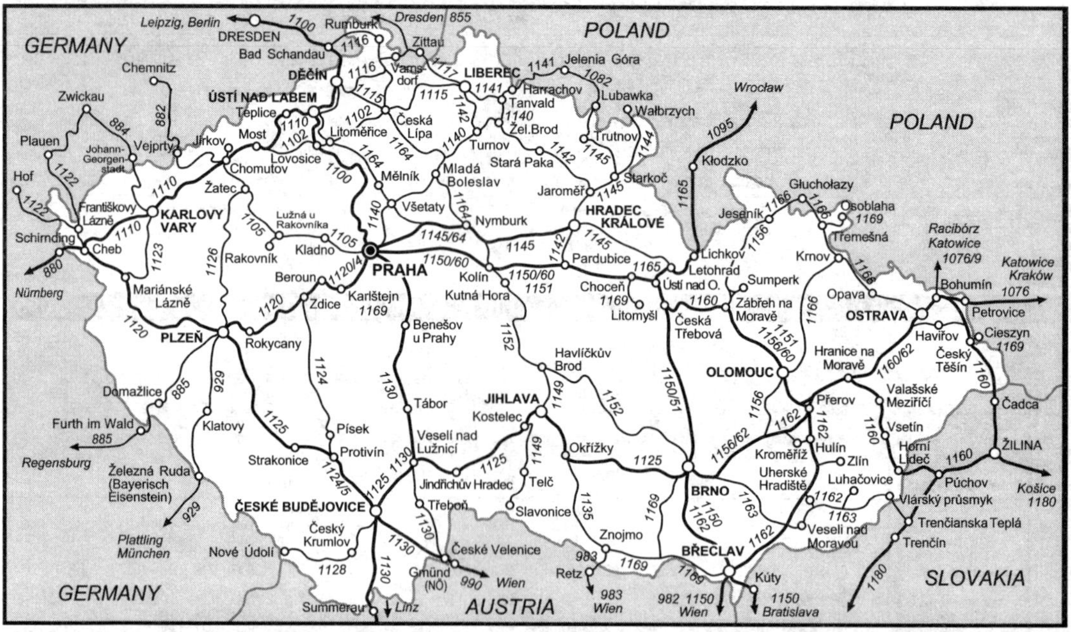

1100 PRAHA - ÚSTÍ NAD LABEM - DĚČÍN - DRESDEN

Warning! 🅁 required for international journeys June 15 - August 31.
For European Sleeper services Praha - Bruxelles and v.v. see Table **78**. The routeing point for international tickets is Schöna.

km		*NJ* 456 A	618 d	698	*EC* 178 B	696	*EC* 176 B	692	*EC* 174 B	690	*EC* 378 B	688	*EC* 172 C	684	*EC* 170 B	680	*RJ* 256 D	*EC* 458 E	676	*EC* 258 B e	672	602 d	600 Ⓑ f	670
0	**Praha** hlavní nádraží ... **1110** d.	0308	0521	0545	0628	0645	0828	0845	1028	1045	1233	1245	1433	1445	1628	1645	1728	1828	1845	2028	2045	2128	2233	2335
3	**Praha** Holešovice .... **1110** d.	0319	0531	0555	0639	0655	0839	0855	1039	1055	1243	1255	1443	1455	1639	1655	1740	1839	1855	2039	2055	2139	2243	2345
27	Kralupy nad Vltavou..... **1110** d.	|	0550	0618	|	0718	|	0918	|	1118	|	1318	|	1518	|	1718	|	|	1918	|	2118	|	|	0006
66	Roudnice nad Labem... **1110** d.	|	0614	0643	|	0743	|	0943	|	1143	|	1343	|	1543	|	1743	|	|	1943	|	2143	2218	2321	0031
84	Lovosice...................... **1110** d.	|	0627	0659	|	0759	|	0959	|	1159	|	1359	|	1559	|	1759	|	|	1959	|	2159	2227	2330	0045
106	**Ústí nad Labem** hl. n. . **1110** a.	0418	0642	0715	0742	0815	0942	1015	1142	1215	1342	1415	1542	1615	1742	1815	1840	1941	2015	2142	2215	2243	2346	0101
106	**Ústí nad Labem** hl. n. . **1110** d.	0420	...	0717	0745	0817	0945	1017	1145	1217	1345	1417	1545	1617	1745	1817	1842	1943	2017	2145	2217	...	...	0101
129	**Děčín** .... **1110** a.	0435	...	0733	0800	0833	1000	1033	1200	1233	1400	1433	1600	1633	1800	1833	1857	1958	2033	2200	2233	...	...	0119
129	**Děčín** 🏛..................... **1116** d.	0507	...	...	0807	...	1007	...	1207	...	1407	...	1607	...	1807	...	1907	2001	...	2207	...	...	...	...
151	Bad Schandau 🏛 . **857 1116** a.	0524	...	...	0824	...	1024	...	1224	...	1424	...	1624	...	1824	...	1924	2019	...	2224	...	...	...	...
191	**Dresden** Hbf .... **857** a.	0550	...	...	0850	...	1050	...	1250	...	1450	...	1650	...	1850	...	1950	2059	...	2250	...	...	...	...

	EC 259 e	601 d	673	675 Ⓐ	677	*EC* 459 E	*RJ* 257 D	681	*EC* 171 B	683	*EC* 173 C		685	*EC* 379 B	689	*EC* 175 B	691 Ⓐ	693	*EC* 177 B	697	*EC* 179 B	699	*NJ* 457 A
Dresden Hbf .... **857** d.	0241	...	...	...	...	0708	0810	...	0910	...	1110	...	...	1310	...	1510	...	...	1710	...	1910	...	2210
Bad Schandau 🏛 .... **857 1116** d.	0307	...	...	...	...	0734	0836	...	0935	...	1135	...	...	1335	...	1535	...	...	1735	...	1935	...	2236
Děčín 🏛.............................. **1116** a.	0324	...	...	...	...	0751	0853	...	0952	...	1152	...	...	1352	...	1552	...	...	1752	...	1952	...	2253
Děčín .... **1110** d.	0350	...	0525	0625	0725	0757	0900	0925	0957	1125	1157	...	1325	1357	1525	1557	1625	1725	1757	1925	1957	2147	2259
Ústí nad Labem hl. n............. **1110** a.	0404	...	0540	0640	0740	0811	0914	0940	1011	1140	1211	...	1340	1411	1540	1611	1640	1740	1811	1940	2011	2202	2313
Ústí nad Labem hl. n............. **1110** d.	0406	0513	0542	0642	0742	0813	0916	0942	1013	1142	1213	...	1342	1413	1542	1613	1642	1742	1813	1942	2013	2204	2314
Lovosice .... **1110** d.	|	0530	0558	0659	0759	|	|	0959	|	1159	|	...	1359	|	1559	|	1659	1759	|	1959	|	2221	|
Roudnice nad Labem.............. **1110** d.	|	0540	0613	0713	0813	|	|	1013	|	1213	|	...	1413	|	1613	|	1713	1813	|	2013	|	2236	|
Kralupy nad Vltavou................ **1110** d.	|	|	0639	0740	0840	|	|	1040	|	1240	|	...	1440	|	1640	|	1740	1840	|	2040	|	2304	|
Praha Holešovice .... **1110** a.	0513	0616	0700	0801	0901	0913	1016	1101	1116	1301	1313	...	1501	1513	1701	1713	1801	1901	1913	2101	2113	2325	0014
Praha hlavní nádraží .... **1110** a.	0523	0627	0712	0812	0912	0923	1026	1112	1127	1312	1324	...	1512	1523	1712	1723	1812	1912	1923	2112	2123	2336	0025

A – *ÖBB nightjet* – 🛏 1, 2 cl., 🛌 2 cl., 🚃 2 Berlin - Graz and v.v.; 🛏 1, 2 cl., 🛌 2 cl., 🚃 2 Berlin - (**457/476**) - Břeclav (**477/456**) - Budapest and v.v.
B – BERLINER – 🚃 12 ✕ Praha - Berlin, Hamburg, Flensburg or Kiel and v.v.
C – HUNGARIA – 🚃 12 ✕ Budapest - Hamburg and v.v.
D – VINDOBONA – 🚃 12 ✕ Graz - Děčín (- Berlin until June 30) and v.v.
E – CANOPUS – 🚃 12 ✕ Praha - Leipzig and v.v.; 🛏 1, 2 cl., 🛌 2 cl. 🚃 2 Praha - Zürich and v.v.

d – To / from destinations on Table **1110**.
e – Until Sept. 14.
f – Ⓑ (not Nov. 16).

1102 MOST - ČESKÁ LIPA

2nd class

Operators: AŽD Praha (Most - Litoměřice horní); ČD (Lovosice - Česká Lípa).

km										
0	**Most** ....d.	...	0627	...	0827	then each	...	2027	...	2233
44	Lovosice ....a.	...	0725	...	0925	train runs	...	2122	...	2328
44	Lovosice ....d.	0602	0732	0802	0932	every **two**	2002	2132	2202	*2340*
52	Litoměřice horní.........d.	0613	0742	0813	0942	hours until	2013	2142	2213	*2351*
94	**Česká Lípa** ....a.	0716	...	0916	...		2116	...	...	...

	Ⓐ									
Česká Lípa ....d.	0434	...	0634	...	0834	then each	...	2034	...
Litoměřice horní.........d.	0542	0614	0736	0814	0942	train runs	2014	2142	2159
Lovosice.....................a.	0555	0625	0755	0825	0955	every **two**	2025	2155	2213
Lovosice.....................d.	...	0632	...	0832	...	hours until	2032	...	2237
Most ....a.	...	0727	...	0927	...		2127	...	2333

2nd class PRAHA - RAKOVNIK - CHOMUTOV - JIRKOV 1105

Additional journeys Praha - Rakovnik and v.v. are possible by changing at Kladno. Operators: Arriva / ČD (Praha - Rakovnik); Die Länderbahn CZ (Rakovnika - Jirkov).

km				Ⓒ			Ⓐ			⑦ e	
0	**Praha** Dejvice d.	0712	0912	1112	1312	1512	1628	1712	1912	2112	...
25	Kladno d.	0743	0943	1143	1343	1543	1707	1743	1943	2143	...
58	Lužná u Rakovnika a.	0820	1020	1220	1420	1620	1750	1820	2020	2220	...
67	**Rakovník** a.	0828	1028	1228	1428	1628	1759	1828	2028	2228	...

			Ⓒ				⑦ e	⑦ e	g	
Rakovník d.	0722	0922	1122	1322	1522	1722	1922	2209	2222	...
Lužná u Rakovnika d.	0731	0931	1131	1331	1531	1731	1931	2220	2232	...
Kladno d.	0814	1014	1214	1414	1614	1814	2014	2317	2317	...
Praha Dejvice a.	0842	1042	1242	1442	1642	1842	2042	2349	2349	...

km		Ⓐ	Ⓒ	Ⓐ		Ⓒ	Ⓒ	Ⓐ			⑦ h
0	**Rakovnik** d.	0646	0800	1000	...	...	...	1429	...	...	2008
9	Lužná u Rakovnika a.	0655	0809	1009	...	...	...	1438	...	...	2017
9	Lužná u Rakovnika d.	0659	0822	1022	1022	1222	1422	1440	1622	1822	2022
50	Žatec a.	0742	0906	1106	1106	1306	1506	1521	1706	1906	2106
50	Žatec 1126 d.	0743	0921	1121	1121	1321	1521	1521	1721	1921	2121
75	**Chomutov** 1126 a.	0809	0947	1147	1147	1347	1457	1547	1747	1947	2147
81	**Jirkov** a.	0819	0956	1156	1156	1356	1556	1556	1756	1956	2156

	Ⓐ	⑥ j	Ⓒ	Ⓒ		Ⓐ	Ⓒ		Ⓒ	Ⓐ
Jirkov d.	0552	0552	0802	1002	1201	1201	1402	1602	1802	2002
Chomutov 1126 d.	0600	0600	0810	1010	1210	1210	1410	1610	1810	2010
Žatec 1126 a.	0624	0635	0836	1036	1236	1236	1436	1636	1836	2036
Žatec d.	0625	0636	0839	1039	1239	1239	1439	1639	1839	2039
Lužná u Rakovnika a.	0710	0719	0924	1124	1324	1324	1524	1724	1924	2124
Lužná u Rakovnika d.	0712	0731	...	...	...	1331	...	...	1937	2126
Rakovnik a.	0721	0741	...	...	...	1340	...	...	1947	2136

e – ⑦ (also Oct. 28, Nov. 17; not Nov. 16).
g – ①–⑥ (also Nov. 16; not Nov. 17).
h – ⑦ (also Oct. 28, Nov. 17; not Nov. 16).
j – ⑥ (also Nov. 16).

PRAHA - ÚSTI NAD LABEM - KARLOVY VARY - CHEB 1110

km		620 Ⓐ	618 ◧	616	614	612	610	608	606	604	602 ◧
0	**Praha** hlavní d.	...	0521	0728	0928	1128	1328	1528	1733	1928	2128
3	**Praha** Holešovice d.	...	0531	0739	0939	1139	1339	1539	1743	1939	2139
106	**Ústí nad Labem** hl. n. a.	...	0642	0842	1042	1242	1442	1642	1842	2042	2243
106	**Ústí nad Labem** hl. n. d.	0440	0648	0848	1048	1248	1448	1648	1848	2048	2258
123	Teplice v Čechách d.	0501	0705	0905	1105	1305	1505	1705	1905	2105	2313
152	Most d.	0528	0730	0930	1130	1330	1530	1730	1930	2130	...
177	Chomutov d.	0552	0754	0954	1154	1354	1554	1754	1954	2152	...
190	Kadaň-Prunéřov d.	0602	0804	1004	1204	1404	1604	1804	2004	*2206*	...
236	**Karlovy Vary** a.	0645	0847	1047	1247	1447	1647	1847	2047	*2255*	...
236	**Karlovy Vary** 1120 d.	0647	0849	1049	1249	1449	1649	1849	2049	...	...
262	Sokolov 1120 d.	0709	0911	1111	1311	1511	1711	1911	2111	...	...
290	**Cheb** 1120 a.	0732	0934	1134	1334	1534	1734	1934	2134	...	...

	601 ◧	603 A	605 B	607	609	611	613	615	617	619
Cheb 1120 d.	...	...	0424	0624	0824	1024	1224	1424	1624	1826
Sokolov 1120 d.	...	...	0448	0648	0848	1048	1248	1448	1648	1850
Karlovy Vary 1120 a.	...	...	0508	0708	0908	1108	1308	1508	1708	1910
Karlovy Vary d.	...	...	0510	0710	0910	1110	1310	1510	1710	1911
Kadaň-Prunéřov d.	...	0452	0552	0752	0952	1152	1352	1552	1752	1953
Chomutov d.	...	0503	0603	0803	1003	1203	1403	1603	1803	2003
Most d.	...	0526	0626	0826	1026	1226	1426	1626	1826	2026
Teplice v Čechách d.	0451	0551	0651	0851	1051	1251	1451	1651	1851	2051
Ústí nad Labem hl. n. a.	0507	0607	0707	0907	1107	1307	1507	1707	1907	2107
Ústí nad Labem hl. n. d.	0513	0613	0713	0913	1113	1313	1513	1713	1913	2113
Praha Holešovice a.	0616	0713	0813	1013	1213	1413	1613	1813	2013	2213
Praha hlavní a.	0627	0723	0823	1023	1223	1424	1623	1823	2023	2223

LOCAL TRAINS **DĚČÍN - ÚSTI NAD LABEM - CHOMUTOV - KADAŇ-PRUNÉŘOV** 2nd class

km			C			C		C		
0	**Děčín** § d.	0530	0630	0730	each	1630	1730	1830	1930	2030
23	**Ú n Labem** hl. n. § a.	0556	0656	0756	train	1656	1756	1856	1956	2056
23	**Ústí nad Labem** hl. n. d.	0558	0658	0758	runs	1658	1758	1858	1958	2120
40	Teplice v Čechách d.	0619	0719	0819	every	1719	1819	1919	2019	2140
69	Most a.	0650	0750	0850	**two**	1750	1850	1950	2050	2207
69	Most d.	0701	0801	0901	hours	1801	1901	2001	2101	2209
94	**Chomutov** a.	0723	0823	0923	until	1823	1923	2023	2123	2231
107	**Kadaň-Prunéřov** a.	0735	0836	0936	⊡	1836	1936	2045	2136	2243

	C	D	C				C		C
Kadaň-Prunéřov d.	0522	0622	0722	0822	each	1822	1922	2022	2122
Chomutov d.	0535	0635	0735	0835	train	1835	1935	2035	2135
Most a.	0556	0656	0756	0856	runs	1856	1956	2056	2156
Most d.	0605	0705	0805	0905	every	1905	2005	2105	2200
Teplice v Čechách d.	0637	0737	0837	0937	**two**	1937	2037	2137	2231
Ústí nad Labem hl. n. a.	0657	0757	0857	0957	hours	1957	2057	2157	2251
Ústí nad Labem hl. n d.	0658	0758	0858	0958	until	1958	2058	*2217*	*2255*
Děčín a.	0724	0824	0924	1024	⊡	2024	2124	*2233*	*2323*

A – Ⓐ Kadaň-Prunéřov - Ústí nad Labem; ①–⑥ **f** Ústí nad Labem - Praha.
B – Ⓐ Cheb - Chomutov; daily Chomutov - Praha.
C – Daily Chomutov - Děčín and v.v.; Ⓐ Chomutov - Kadaň-Prunéřov and v.v.
D – Ⓒ Kadaň-Prunéřov - Most; daily Most - Děčín.
f – ①–⑥ (not Nov. 17).
◧ – For additional station calls see Table **1100**.
⊡ – For other trains Děčín - Ústí nad Labem see Tables **1100** and **1115**.

Arriva 2nd class ÚSTÍ NAD LABEM - DĚČÍN - LIBEREC 1115

km		●								
0	**Ústí nad Labem** hl. ‡ d.	...	0727	0927	1127	1327	1527	1727	1927	2123
23	**Děčín** ‡ d.	0645	0745	0945	1145	1345	1545	1745	1945	2141
54	Česká Lipa d.	0734	0822	1022	1222	1422	1622	1822	2022	2223
113	**Liberec** a.	0852	0926	1126	1326	1526	1726	1926	2126	2331

	●								
Liberec d.	0501	0628	0828	1028	1228	1428	1628	1828	2028
Česká Lipa d.	0632	0737	0937	1137	1337	1537	1737	1937	2134
Děčín ‡ d.	0712	0812	1012	1212	1412	1612	1812	2012	2209
Ústí nad Labem hl. ‡ a.	...	0828	1028	1228	1428	1628	1828	2028	2225

● – Also from Děčín at 0845 and every two hours until 2043; also from Liberec at 0702 and every two hours until 2102. Timings may vary by 3 minutes. Operated by Die Länderbahn CZ.
‡ – See also Tables **1100** and **1110**.

DĚČÍN - RUMBURK 1116

Operators: ČD (trains via Rybniště); Arriva (trains via Sebnitz). Subject to alteration on and around Czech and German holiday dates (see page 4).

km										
0	**Děčín** d.	0636	0836	1036	1236	1436	1636	1836	2036	2236
25	Česká Kamenice d.	0706	0906	1106	1306	1506	1706	1906	2106	2306
50	Rybniště d.	0736	0936	1136	1336	1536	1736	1936	2136	2336
61	**Rumburk** a.	0750	0950	1150	1350	1550	1750	1951	2151	2350

Rumburk d.	0605	0805	1005	1205	1405	1605	1805	2005	2205
Rybniště d.	0617	0817	1017	1217	1417	1617	1817	2017	2217
Česká Kamenice d.	0646	0846	1046	1246	1446	1646	1846	2046	2246
Děčín a.	0719	0919	1119	1319	1519	1719	1920	2120	2319

km										
0	**Děčín** d.	0641	0841	1041	1241	1441	1641	1841	2041	...
22	Bad Schandau 🏛 d.	0718	0918	1118	1318	1518	1718	1918	2118	...
37	Sebnitz d.	0742	0942	1142	1342	1542	1742	1942	2142	...
38	Dolní Poustevna 🏛 d.	0746	0946	1146	1346	1546	1746	1946	2146	...
65	**Rumburk** a.	0828	1028	1228	1428	1628	1828	2028	2224	...

Rumburk d.	0530	0730	0930	1130	1330	1530	1730	1930	...
Dolní Poustevna 🏛 d.	0612	0812	1012	1212	1412	1612	1812	2012	...
Sebnitz d.	0618	0818	1018	1218	1418	1618	1818	2018	...
Bad Schandau 🏛 d.	0648	0843	1048	1248	1448	1648	1848	2048	...
Děčín a.	0716	0911	1116	1316	1516	1716	1916	2116	...

ČD 2nd class DĚČÍN - VARNSDORF - ZITTAU - LIBEREC 1117

Additional trains operate Rybniště - Varnsdorf and v.v. on Ⓒ until November 2. For Varnsdorf - Liberec see next page.

km		Ⓐ	Ⓐ	Ⓐ	Ⓐ					
0	**Děčín** d.	0536	1136	1336	1536	...	...	...	...	...
25	Česká Kamenice d.	0606	1206	1406	1606	...	...	...	...	...
50	Rybniště d.	0638	1238	1438	1638	...	...	...	...	...
61	**Varnsdorf** a.	0652	1253	1453	1553	...	...	...	...	...

	Ⓐ	Ⓐ	Ⓐ	Ⓐ					
Varnsdorf d.	0701	1301	1501	1701	...	...	...	...	...
Rybniště d.	0715	1315	1515	1715	...	...	...	...	...
Česká Kamenice d.	0746	1346	1546	1746	...	...	...	...	...
Děčín a.	0819	1419	1619	1819	...	...	...	...	...

1117 DĚČÍN - VARNSDORF - ZITTAU - LIBEREC
2nd class Die Länderbahn

WARNING! Service until September 30. Due to engineering work services are operated by 🚌 Zittau - Liberec and v.v.
For Děčín - Varnsdorf see previous page. Subject to alteration on and around Czech and German holiday dates (see page 4).

km			Ⓐ	Ⓐ	Ⓐ	Ⓐ	Ⓐ		Ⓐ	Ⓐ	Ⓐ	Ⓐ			Ⓒ	Ⓒ	Ⓒ	Ⓒ	Ⓒ	Ⓒ	Ⓒ	Ⓒ	
0	**Varnsdorf** 🏛 d.	Ⓐ	0637	0737	0937	1045	1245	and	1745	1835	1945	2115	...	Ⓒ	0724	0924	1124	1328	1524	1728	1924	2131	...
18	**Zittau** 🏛 a.		0654	0754	0954	1102	1302	hourly	1802	1852	2002	2132	...		0741	0941	1141	1345	1541	1745	1941	2148	...
18	**Zittau** d.		0710	0810	1010	1110	1310	until	1810	1910	2010	2140	...		0805	1005	1205	1405	1605	1805	2005	2205	...
45	**Liberec** a.		0804	0904	1104	1204	1404		1904	2004	2114	2244	...		0854	1054	1254	1454	1654	1854	2104	2304	...
			Ⓐ	Ⓐ	Ⓐ	Ⓐ	Ⓐ		Ⓐ	Ⓐ	Ⓐ	Ⓐ			Ⓒ	Ⓒ	Ⓒ	Ⓒ	Ⓒ	Ⓒ	Ⓒ	Ⓒ	
	Liberec d.	Ⓐ	0605	0705	0905	1105	1205	and	1705	1805	1905	2126	...	Ⓒ	0705	0905	1105	1305	1505	1705	1856	2105	...
	Zittau a.		0656	0755	0955	1155	1256	hourly	1756	1855	1956	2226	...		0754	0954	1154	1354	1554	1754	1954	2203	...
	Zittau 🏛 d.		0704	0800	1000	1200	1308	until	1808	1900	2010	2230	...		0810	1014	1211	1414	1610	1818	2010	2230	...
	Varnsdorf 🏛 a.		0720	0816	1016	1216	1325		1825	1916	2027	2247	...		0828	1031	1228	1431	1627	1836	2027	2247	...

1120 PRAHA - PLZEŇ - CHEB - KARLOVY VARY
🍷 on most *EC* and *IC* trains

Service from July 1.

km		2 d	2 Ⓐ	*IC* 568 d	778 Ⓐ	2 ⑦h	2 Ⓒ	2	*EC* 362 A	776 k	*IC* 566	774	2 Ⓒ	*EC* 360 A	772	*IC* 564	*EC* 358 A	2 Ⓐ	770	*IC* 512 B	*EC* 356 A	2	768 k	*IC* 562
0	**Praha** hlavní n. 1124 d.	...	...	...	0505	...	...	...	0535	0605	0635	0705	...	0735	0805	0835	0935	...	1005	1035	1135	...	1205	1235
4	**Praha** Smíchov 1124 d.	...	...	...	0515	...	...	...	|	0615	|	0715	...	|	0815	|	|	...	1015	|	|	...	1215	|
43	Beroun 1124 d.	...	...	...	0552	...	...	...	|	0652	|	0752	...	|	0852	|	|	...	1052	|	|	...	1252	|
52	Zdice 1124 d.	...	...	...	0600	...	...	...	|	0700	|	0800	...	|	0900	|	|	...	1100	|	|	...	1300	|
90	Rokycany d.	...	...	...	0627	...	...	...	|	0727	|	0827	...	|	0927	|	|	...	1127	|	|	...	1327	|
107	**Plzeň** hlavní n. a.	...	...	...	0637	...	...	...	0658	0737	0758	0837	...	0858	0937	0958	1058	...	1137	1158	1258	...	1337	1358
107	**Plzeň** hlavní n. d.	...	...	0605	0640	...	...	0707	...	0740	0805	0840	0907	━	0940	1005	...	1107	1140	1205	...	1307	1340	1405
	Klatovy 929 a.	...	...	|	0729	...	...	|	...	0827	|	0929	|	...	1027	|	...	|	1227	|	...	|	1427	|
140	Stříbro d.	...	...	0631	...	...	...	0737	...	...	0831	...	0937	2	...	1031	...	1137	...	1231	...	1337	...	1431
171	Planá u Mariánských Lázní d.	0545	0545	0654	...	0654	...	0804	...	...	0854	...	1004	Ⓐ	...	1054	...	1204	...	1254	...	1404	...	1454
183	Mariánské Lázně ◧ d.	0556	0556	0707	...	0706	...	0815	...	...	0907	...	1015	1039	...	1107	...	1215	...	1307	...	1415	...	1507
213	**Cheb** ◧ a.	0622	0622	0728	...	0733	...	0838	...	...	0927	...	1038	1108	...	1127	...	1238	...	1327	...	1438	...	1527
213	**Cheb** 1110 d.	...	0634	...	...	0737	0737	0840	...	...	...	...	1040	1110	...	...	...	1240	...	|	...	1440	...	...
241	Sokolov 1110 d.	...	0704	...	...	0807	0807	0908	...	...	...	...	1108	1140	...	...	...	1307	...	f	...	1507	...	...
267	**Karlovy Vary** 1110 a.	...	0728	...	...	0831	0831	0932	...	...	...	...	1132	1204	...	...	...	1331	...	...	...	1531	...	...

	766	2	*EC* 354 A	764	*IC* 560	762	*EC* 352 A	2 D	760	*IC* 558	758	*EC* 364 A	2 Ⓑe	2 ⑥g	756	*IC*• 504 C	754	*IC* 556	752	*IC* 554	750	*IC* 550 Ⓑe	748
Praha hlavní n. 1124 d.	1305	...	1335	1405	1435	1505	1535	...	1605	1635	1705	1735	...	...	1805	1835	1905	1935	2005	2035	2105	2205	*2350**
Praha Smíchov 1124 d.	1315	...	|	1415	|	1515	|	...	1615	|	1715	|	...	...	1815	|	1915	|	2015	|	2115	2215	*0000**
Beroun 1124 d.	1352	...	|	1452	|	1552	|	...	1652	|	1752	|	...	...	1852	|	1952	|	2052	|	2152	|	0035
Zdice 1124 d.	1400	...	|	1500	|	1600	|	...	1700	|	1800	|	...	...	1900	|	2000	|	2100	|	2200	|	0043
Rokycany d.	1427	...	|	1527	|	1627	|	...	1727	|	1827	|	...	...	1927	|	2027	|	2127	|	2227	2322	0110
Plzeň hlavní n. a.	1437	...	1458	1537	1558	1637	1658	...	1737	1758	1837	1858	...	...	1937	1958	2037	2058	2137	2158	2238	2332	0120
Plzeň hlavní n. d.	1440	1507	...	1540	1605	1640	...	1707	1740	1805	1840	...	1907	...	1940	2005	...	...	...	2205	2240	...	...
Klatovy 929 a.	1529	|	...	1627	|	1729	...	|	1827	|	1929	...	|	...	2029	|	...	...	...	|	2329	...	...
Stříbro d.	...	1537	...	...	1631	...	...	1737	...	1831	...	...	1937	...	...	2031	...	...	...	2231	...	...	...
Planá u Mariánských Lázní d.	...	1604	...	...	1654	...	...	1804	...	1854	...	...	2004	...	...	2054	...	...	...	2254	...	...	...
Mariánské Lázně ◧ d.	...	1615	...	...	1707	...	...	1815	...	1907	...	...	2015	2015	...	2107	...	...	...	2303	...	...	...
Cheb ◧ a.	...	1638	...	...	1727	...	...	1838	...	1927	...	...	2038	2043	...	2127	...	...	...	2324	...	...	...
Cheb 1110 d.	...	1640	...	...	...	...	...	1840	...	...	...	...	2040	2044	...	2131	...	...	...	...	...	...	...
Sokolov 1110 d.	...	1707	...	...	...	...	...	1908	...	...	...	...	2108	2113	...	2154	...	...	...	...	...	...	...
Karlovy Vary 1110 a.	...	1731	...	...	...	...	...	1932	...	...	...	...	2132	2138	...	2211	...	...	...	...	...	...	...

	751 Ⓐ	*IC* 551 d	743 753	*IC* 553	*IC* 553 d	755	2 d	*IC* 555	757	*IC*• 503 C	759	2	2 Ⓐ	*EC* 365 A	*IC* 557	761	*EC* 353 A	618	*IC* 559	763 k	2	*EC* 355 A	765
Karlovy Vary 1110 d.	...	...	...	...	...	...	0424	...	...	0550	...	...	0624	...	...	...	...	0849	...	...	1024	...	...
Sokolov 1110 d.	...	...	...	...	...	...	0449	...	...	0608	...	...	0649	...	...	...	...	0911	...	...	1049	...	...
Cheb 1110 a.	...	...	...	...	...	...	0517	...	...	0630	...	...	0717	...	...	...	...	0934	...	...	1117	...	...
Cheb ◧ d.	...	...	...	...	0432	...	0519	...	...	0634	...	0719	0719	...	0833	...	...	...	1033	...	1119	...	...
Mariánské Lázně ◧ d.	...	...	...	...	0455	...	0544	...	...	0655	...	0744	0744	...	0854	...	...	...	1054	...	1144	...	...
Planá u Mariánských Lázní d.	...	...	...	...	0505	...	0555	...	...	0705	...	0755	0755	...	0905	...	...	...	1105	...	1155	...	...
Stříbro d.	...	...	...	...	0527	...	0622	...	...	0727	...	0822	0822	...	0927	...	...	...	1127	...	1222	...	...
Klatovy 929 d.	...	...	0426	...	|	0526	|	...	0630	|	0730	|	|	...	|	0930	...	...	|	1130	|	...	1228
Plzeň hlavní n. a.	...	...	0517	...	0552	0617	0649	...	0719	0752	0819	0849	0849	...	0952	1019	...	...	1152	1219	1249	...	1319
Plzeň hlavní n. d.	0421	0500	0521	0600	0600	0621	...	0700	0721	0800	0821	...	...	0900	1000	1021	1100	...	1200	1221	...	1300	1321
Rokycany d.	0432	0511	0532	|	|	0632	...	|	0732	|	0832	...	...	|	|	1032	|	...	|	1232	...	|	1332
Zdice 1124 d.	0459	|	0559	|	|	0659	...	|	0759	|	0859	...	...	|	|	1059	|	...	|	1259	...	|	1359
Beroun 1124 d.	0508	|	0608	|	|	0708	...	|	0808	|	0908	...	...	|	|	1108	|	...	|	1308	...	|	1408
Praha Smíchov 1124 a.	0543	|	0643	|	|	0743	...	|	0843	|	0943	...	...	|	|	1143	|	...	|	1343	...	|	1443
Praha hlavní n. 1124 a.	0552	0623	0652	0722	0722	0752	...	0822	0852	0922	0952	...	...	1022	1122	1152	1222	...	1322	1352	...	1422	1452

	IC 561	767	2	*EC* 357 A	769	*IC* 515 B	771	2	*EC* 359 A	773	*IC* 563	775 k	2	*EC* 361 A	777	*IC* 565	779	608	2	2 Ⓒ	*EC* 363 A	2 k	*IC* 567
Karlovy Vary 1110 d.	...	...	1225	...	...	...	...	1425	...	...	...	...	1625	...	...	...	...	1849	...	1910	...	...	...
Sokolov 1110 d.	...	...	1250	...	...	j	...	1450	...	...	...	...	1650	...	...	...	...	1911	...	1934	...	...	...
Cheb 1110 a.	...	...	1317	...	...	|	...	1517	...	...	...	...	1717	...	...	...	...	1934	...	2002	...	...	...
Cheb ◧ d.	1233	...	1319	...	...	1433	...	1519	...	...	1633	...	1719	...	...	1833	...	...	2009	2009	...	...	2033
Mariánské Lázně ◧ d.	1254	...	1344	...	...	1454	...	1544	...	...	1654	...	1744	...	...	1854	...	...	2039	2039	...	...	2054
Planá u Mariánských Lázní d.	1305	...	1355	...	...	1505	...	1555	...	...	1705	...	1755	...	...	1905	...	...	2049	2049	...	...	2105
Stříbro d.	1327	...	1422	...	...	1527	...	1622	...	...	1727	...	1822	...	...	1927	...	...	...	...	...	...	2127
Klatovy 929 d.	|	1330	|	...	1428	|	1530	|	...	1628	|	1730	|	...	1828	|	1930	...	...	...	...	2058	|
Plzeň hlavní n. a.	1352	1419	1449	...	1519	1552	1619	1649	...	1719	1752	1819	1849	...	1919	1952	2019	...	...	...	...	2154	2152
Plzeň hlavní n. d.	1400	1421	...	1500	1521	1600	1621	...	1700	1721	1800	1821	...	1900	1921	2000	2021	...	...	...	2100	...	2200
Rokycany d.	|	1432	...	|	1532	|	1632	...	|	1732	|	1832	...	|	1932	|	2032	...	...	...	|	...	2210
Zdice 1124 d.	|	1459	...	|	1559	|	1659	...	|	1759	|	1859	...	|	1959	|	2058	...	...	...	|	...	|
Beroun 1124 d.	|	1508	...	|	1608	|	1708	...	|	1808	|	1908	...	|	2008	|	2108	...	...	...	2145	...	|
Praha Smíchov 1124 a.	|	1543	...	|	1643	|	1743	...	|	1843	|	1943	...	|	2043	|	2143	...	...	...	*2215**	...	2313
Praha hlavní n. 1124 a.	1522	1552	...	1622	1652	1722	1752	...	1822	1852	1922	1952	...	2022	2052	2122	2152	...	...	...	*2224**	...	2322

A – BAVORSKÝ EXPRES – 🚃12 🍷 Praha - Plzeň - München and v.v.
B – OSTRAVAN – 🚃12 🍷 Bohumín - Praha - Františkovy Lázně and v.v.
C – PENDOLINO – 🚃12 🍷 Ostrava - Praha - Karlovy Vary and v.v.
D – Daily Plzeň - Cheb; Ⓒ Cheb - Karlovy Vary.

d – ①-⑥ (not Nov. 17).
e – Ⓑ (not Nov. 16).
f – To Františkovy Lázně (a. 1336).
g – ⑥ (also Nov. 16).
h – ⑦ (also Nov. 17).
j – From Františkovy Lázně (d. 1424).

k – To/from Železná Ruda (Table **929**).
m – Daily until Sept. 28; Ⓐ from Sept. 29.
n – Until Sept. 28.

• – PENDOLINO – classified *SC* (with 🅁) Ostrava - Praha and v.v.
* – Connection by 🚌.

◧ – Additional local trains Mariánské Lázně - Cheb and v.v.:
From **Mariánské Lázně** at 0647 Ⓐ, 0919 **m**, 1239 Ⓒ, 1519 **m**, 1719 **m**.
From **Cheb** at 0545 Ⓐ, 0648 Ⓐ, 0759 Ⓒ **n**, 0959, 1409 **m**, 1600 **m**, 1809, 2255 Ⓐ.

2nd class — MARKTREDWITZ - CHEB - FRANTIŠKOVY LÁZNĚ - HOF and ZWICKAU — 1122

Subject to alteration on Czech and German public holiday dates (see page 4).

km																				
0	**Marktredwitz** 880 d.	0703	0903	1103	1302	1502	1702	1902	2102	...	**Hof** d.	0714	0912	1112	1312	1512	1712	1912	...	...
27	Cheb 880 d.	0740	0940	1140	1339	1539	1740	1940	2140	2256	Aš 🏛 d.	0751	0951	1151	1351	1551	1751	1951	2045	2219
34	Františkovy Lázně d.	0748	0948	1148	1348	1548	1748	1948	2145	2303	Františkovy Lázně d.	0813	1013	1213	1413	1613	1813	2013	2108	2241
55	Aš 🏛 d.	0813	1013	1213	1413	1613	1813	2013	2207	2325	Cheb 880 a.	0820	1020	1220	1420	1620	1820	2020	2115	2248
89	**Hof** a.	0855	1055	1255	1455	1655	1855	2055	...	...	**Marktredwitz** 880 a.	0858	1058	1257	1457	1657	1857	2057	...	...

km		①–⑤ d	⑥⑦ e																	
0	**Cheb** d.	0547	0805	1005	1205	1605	1805	...	...	...	**Zwickau** Zentrum d.	0735	0935	1335	1535	1735	...	...	...	...
7	Františkovy Lázně d.	0554	0814	1014	1214	1614	1814	...	...	...	**Zwickau** Stadthalle d.	0739	0939	1339	1539	1739	...	...	...	...
24	Bad Brambach 🏛 a.	0621	0835	1035	1235	1635	1835	...	...	...	**Zwickau** Hbf d.	0743	0943	1343	1543	1743	...	...	...	...
73	Plauen Oberer Bf a.	0726	0926	1126	1326	1726	1926	...	...	...	Plauen Oberer Bf d.	0832	1032	1432	1632	1832	...	...	...	...
121	**Zwickau** Hbf a.	0815	1015	1215	1415	1815	2015	...	...	...	Bad Brambach 🏛 d.	0925	1125	1525	1725	1925	...	...	...	...
123	**Zwickau** Stadthalle a.	0820	1020	1220	1420	1820	2020	...	...	...	Františkovy Lázně d.	0949	1149	1549	1749	1949	...	...	...	...
	Zwickau Zentrum a.	0824	1024	1224	1424	1824	2024	...	...	...	**Cheb** a.	0956	1156	1556	1756	1956	...	...	...	...

d – ①–⑤ (not Oct. 3, 31, Nov. 19).

e – ⑥⑦ (also Oct. 3, 31, Nov. 19).

GW Train Regio 2nd class — KARLOVY VARY - MARIÁNSKÉ LÁZNĚ — 1123

km																				
0	**Karlovy Vary** dolní d.	0620	0858	1058	1256	1458	1658	1928	2128	2234	**Mariánské Lázně** d.	0604	0840	1040	1238	1440	1640	1910	2110	2305
33	Bečov nad Teplou d.	0651	0927	1127	1325	1527	1727	1957	2157	2302	Bečov nad Teplou d.	0651	0927	1127	1325	1527	1727	1957	2157	2350
53	**Mariánské Lázně** a.	0736	1011	1211	1409	1611	1811	2041	2241	...	**Karlovy Vary** dolní a.	0719	0955	1155	1353	1555	1755	2025	2225	...

Arriva 2nd class — PRAHA - PŘÍBRAM - ČESKÉ BUDĚJOVICE — 1124

ČD operates additional services Beroun - Březnice, Březnice - Protivín and Protivín - České Budějovice. For direct trains Praha - České Budějovice see Table **1130**.

km					Ⓒ	Ⓐ				⑦ f		Ⓐ	Ⓒ	Ⓐ						⑦ f
0	**Praha** hlavní n. 1120 d.	...	0722	0922	0922	...	1322	1522	1722	1722	**České Budějovice** ◧ d.	...	...	0712	0912	1311	1511	1712	1912	2207
4	**Praha** Smichov 1120 d.	...	0731	0931	0931	...	1331	1531	1731	1731	Protivín ◧ d.	...	...	0744	0944	1343	1544	1744	1944	2238
43	Beroun 1120 d.	...	0813	1013	1013	...	1413	1513	1813	1813	Pisek d.	0558	0756	0757	0959	1357	1559	1800	1957	2252
52	Zdice 1120 d.	...	0822	1022	1022	...	1422	1622	1822	1822	Březnice d.	0640	0838	...	1041	1438	1640	1842	...	...
82	**Přibram** d.	...	0853	1053	1053	...	1453	1653	1853	1853	**Přibram** d.	0702	0902	...	1102	1502	1702	1902	...	...
100	Březnice d.	...	0916	1119	1119	...	1516	1718	1920	1920	Zdice 1120 d.	0733	0933	...	1133	1533	1733	1933	...	...
142	Pisek d.	0802	1002	1201	1202	1402	1602	1802	2001	2002	Beroun 1120 d.	0744	0944	...	1144	1544	1744	1944	...	...
155	Protivín ◧ d.	0815	1015	...	1215	1415	1615	1815	...	2015	**Praha** Smichov 1120 a.	0827	1027	...	1227	1627	1827	2027	...	...
192	**České Budějovice** ◧ a.	0846	1046	...	1246	1446	1646	1845	...	2045	**Praha** hlavní n. 1120 a.	0835	1035	...	1235	1635	1835	2035	...	...

f – ⑦ (also Nov. 17; not Nov. 16).

◧ – See also Table **1125**.

🍷 on most trains — PLZEŇ - ČESKÉ BUDĚJOVICE - JIHLAVA - BRNO — 1125

km		651 B	653	661	663	665	667	669	655	657	659		658	656 C	654	668	666	664	662	660	652	650
0	**Plzeň** hlavní n. d.	...	...	0604	0804	1004	1204	1404	1604	1804	2004	**Brno** hlavní n. d.	...	...	0541	0742	0944	1144	1344	1544	1744	1944
34	Nepomuk d.	...	...	0631	0831	1031	1231	1431	1631	1831	2031	Náměšť nad Oslavou d.	...	...	0628	0828	1028	1228	1428	1628	1828	2028
59	Horaždovice předměstí d.	...	...	0651	0851	1051	1251	1451	1651	1851	2051	Trebič d.	...	...	0650	0850	1050	1250	1450	1650	1850	2050
76	Strakonice d.	...	...	0706	0906	1106	1306	1506	1706	1906	2106	Okříšky d.	...	...	0707	0907	1107	1307	1507	1707	1907	2107
99	Protivín d.	...	...	0726	0926	1126	1326	1526	1726	1928	2126	**Jihlava** a.	...	...	0733	0933	1133	1333	1533	1733	1933	2133
136	**České Budějovice** a.	...	...	0754	0954	1154	1354	1554	1754	1957	2154	**Jihlava** d.	...	0540	0740	0940	1140	1340	1540	1740	1940	...
136	**České Budějovice** d.	0402	0602	0802	1002	1202	1402	1602	1802	...	...	Jindřichův Hradec d.	...	0659	0859	1059	1259	1459	1659	1859	2059	...
175	Veselí nad Lužnicí d.	0430	0630	0830	1030	1230	1430	1630	1830	...	...	Veselí nad Lužnicí d.	...	0728	0928	1128	1328	1528	1728	1928	2128	...
201	Jindřichův Hradec d.	0500	0700	0900	1100	1300	1500	1700	1900	...	...	**České Budějovice** a.	...	0755	0955	1155	1355	1555	1755	1955	2155	...
268	**Jihlava** a.	0618	0818	1018	1218	1418	1618	1818	2018	...	...	**České Budějovice** d.	0604	0804	1004	1204	1404	1604	1804	2004	...	...
268	**Jihlava** d.	0626	0826	1026	1226	1426	1626	1826	2026	...	...	Protivín d.	0632	0832	1032	1232	1432	1632	1832	2034	...	...
297	Okříšky d.	0653	0853	1053	1253	1453	1653	1853	2053	...	...	Strakonice d.	0653	0853	1053	1253	1453	1653	1853	2053	...	...
309	Trebič d.	0708	0908	1108	1308	1508	1708	1908	2108	...	...	Horaždovice předměstí d.	0710	0910	1110	1310	1510	1710	1910	2110	...	...
329	Náměšť nad Oslavou d.	0728	0928	1128	1328	1528	1728	1928	2128	...	...	Nepomuk d.	0730	0930	1130	1330	1530	1730	1930	2130	...	...
372	**Brno** hlavní n. a.	0814	1014	1214	1414	1614	1814	2014	2214	...	...	**Plzeň** hlavní n. a.	0756	0956	1156	1356	1556	1756	1956	2156	...	...

B – From České Budějovice on ①–⑥ **g**; from Jihlava daily.

C – From Jihlava on ①–⑥ **g**; from České Budějovice daily.

g – ①–⑥ (not Nov. 17).

GW Train Regio 2nd class — PLZEŇ - CHOMUTOV - MOST — 1126

km		Ⓐ								⑦ h		①–⑥ g							Ⓐ	⑦ h
0	**Plzeň** hlavní n. d.	...	0606	0806	1006	1206	1406	1606	1806	2006	**Most** 1110 d.	0511	0711	0911	1111	1311	1511	1711	1911	1911
59	Blatno u Jesenice d.	0509	0710	0910	1110	1310	1510	1710	1910	2110	Chomutov 1110 d.	0536	0736	0936	1136	1336	1536	1735	1936	1936
107	Žatec a.	0559	0758	0958	1158	1358	1558	1758	1958	2158	Žatec d.	0600	0800	1000	1200	1400	1600	1800	2000	2000
130	Chomutov 1110 a.	0635	0822	1022	1222	1422	1622	1822	2022	2222	Blatno u Jesenice d.	0649	0849	1049	1249	1449	1649	1849	2049	2049
155	**Most** 1110 a.	0701	0847	1047	1247	1447	1647	1847	2047	2247	**Plzeň** hlavní n. a.	0753	0953	1153	1353	1553	1753	1953	...	2153

g – ①–⑥ (not Nov. 17).

h – ⑦ (also Oct. 29, Nov. 17; not Nov. 16).

GW Train Regio 2nd class — ČESKÉ BUDĚJOVICE - NOVÉ ÚDOLÍ — 1128

km			j	k	k	j					Ⓒ m											Ⓒ m
0	**České Budějovice** d.	0513	0742	0810	1012	1012	1209	1400	1611	1811	2010	**Nové Údolí** d.	...	...	...	...	1112	1314	1518	...	1712	1914
31	Český Krumlov d.	0605	0833	0900	1100	1100	1300	1453	1700	1900	2058	Černý Kříž d.	0443	0649	...	0913	1128	1330	1536	...	1729	1930
68	Horní Planá d.	0658	0940	0956	1156	1205	1358	1547	1756	1957	2147	Horní Planá d.	0509	0717	...	0940	1157	1358	1604	...	1758	1958
88	Černý Kříž a.	0726	1013	1022	1222	1236	1423	1615	1821	2023	2211	Český Krumlov d.	0602	0813	...	1039	1256	1455	1659	...	1857	2058
96	**Nové Údolí** a.	0744	1042	1040	1239	1254	1441	1635	1838**k**	...	...	**České Budějovice** a.	0648	0900	...	1131	1343	1542	1746	...	1945	2144

j – May 1 - Sept. 30.

k – Not May 1 - Sept. 30.

m – Ⓒ (daily May 1 - Sept. 30).

1130 PRAHA - TÁBOR - ČESKÉ VELENICE and ČESKÉ BUDĚJOVICE

🍷 on most *EC* and *IC* trains

km								*EC*				*IC*				*IC*			*EC*			*IC*			
		2	2	**701**	2	**703**	2	**331**	**705**	2	**321**	**531**	2	**709**	2	**533**	**711**	2	**333**	**713**	**715**	**535**	2	**717**	2
			Ⓐ	Ⓐ	h	d	j			Ⓒ	A	◧		f	Ⓐ		B					◧		Ⓐ	Ⓐ
0	**Praha** hlavní nádrazi d.	...	...	...	...	...	...	0620	0646	...	0746	0820	...	0846	...	0920	0946	...	1020	1046	1146	1220	...	1246	...
49	Benešov u Prahy d.	...	...	...	...	...	...	|	0729	...	0829	|	...	0929	...	|	1029	...	|	1129	1229	|	...	1329	...
103	**Tábor** d.	...	...	0600	...	0700	...	0723	0800	...	0900	0923	...	1000	...	1023	1100	...	1123	1200	1300	1323	...	1400	...
130	Veselí nad Lužnicí a.	...	...	0622	...	0719	...	|	0819	...	0920	|	...	1019	...	|	1119	...	|	1219	1319	|	...	1419	...
130	Veselí nad Lužnicí ⊡ d.	...	0602	0623	0706	0721	0740	|	0821	0845	0932	|	...	1021	1026	|	1121	1141	|	1221	1332	|	...	1421	1432
151	Třeboň d.	...	0643	|	0735	|	0808	|	|	0911	0952	|	...	|	1052	|	|	1209	|	|	1352	|	...	|	1459
185	**České Velenice** 🏛 a.	...	0722	|	0821	|	0849	|	|	0951	1029	|	...	|	1131	|	|	1249	|	|	1429	|	...	|	1537
169	**České Budějovice** ⊡ a.	...	...	0653	...	0749	...	0759	0849	...	...	0959	...	1049	...	1059	1149	...	1159	1249	...	1359	...	1449	...
169	**České Budějovice** d.	0600	...	...	...	...	...	0805	...	...	...	...	1005	...	...	1112	...	...	1205	...	...	...	1405	...	...
	Český Krumlov a.	|	...	...	...	...	...	|	...	...	...	...	|	...	...	1149	...	...	|	...	...	...	|	...	...
219	Rybnik d.	0653	...	...	...	...	...	0853	...	...	...	...	1052	...	...	...	...	...	1251	...	...	...	1452	...	...
233	Summerau 🏛 a.	0707	...	...	...	...	...	0906	...	...	...	...	1107	...	...	...	...	...	1306	...	...	...	1507	...	...
242	Freistadt a.	0720	...	...	...	...	...	0916	...	...	...	...	1120	...	...	...	...	...	1316	...	...	...	1520	...	...
295	**Linz** Hbf a.	0824	...	...	...	...	...	1006	...	...	...	...	1224	...	...	...	...	...	1406	...	...	...	1624	...	...

				EC				*IC*		*IC*				*IC*		*EC*			*IC*	*IC*				
	719	2	2	**335**	2	**721**	2	**537**	**723**	**539**	2	**725**	2	**541**	**323**	**337**	**729**	2	**543**	**545**	2	**733**	2	**735**
	C	d	⑦k				n	Ⓐ		◧				Ⓑf	A				⑦g ◧			◧	⑤p	
Praha hlavní nádrazi d.	1346	...	...	1420	...	1446	...	1520	1546	1620	...	1646	...	1720	1746	1820	1846	...	1920	2020	...	2046	...	2216
Benešov u Prahy d.	1429	...	...	|	...	1529	...	|	1629	|	...	1729	...	|	1829	|	1929	...	|	|	...	2129	...	2259
Tábor d.	1500	...	...	1523	...	1600	...	1623	1700	1723	...	1800	...	1823	1900	1923	2000	...	2023	2123	...	2200	...	2330
Veselí nad Lužnicí a.	1519	...	...	|	...	1619	...	|	1719	|	...	1819	...	|	1919	|	2019	...	|	2135	...	2219	...	2349
Veselí nad Lužnicí ⊡ d.	1521	1535	1540	|	...	1621	1645	|	1742	|	...	1821	1845	|	1932	|	2021	2040	|	2136	2145	2221	2245	2351
Třeboň d.	|	1603	1610	|	...	|	1710	|	1803	|	...	|	1911	|	1952	|	|	2105	|	|	2211	|	2313	|
České Velenice 🏛 a.	|	1643	1649	|	...	|	1801	|	1839	|	...	|	1950	|	2029	|	|	2145	|	|	2250	|	2350	|
České Budějovice ⊡ a.	1549	...	...	1559	...	1649	...	1659	...	1759	...	1849	...	1859	...	1959	2049	...	2059	2202	...	2249	...	0017
České Budějovice d.	...	...	...	...	1605	...	...	...	...	...	1805	...	...	...	...	2005	...	...	...	...	...	...	...	...
Rybnik d.	...	...	...	...	1651	...	...	...	...	...	1852	...	...	...	...	2054	...	...	...	...	...	...	...	...
Summerau 🏛 a.	...	...	...	...	1707	...	...	...	...	...	1907	...	...	...	...	2107	...	...	...	...	...	...	...	...
Freistadt a.	...	...	...	...	1716	...	...	...	...	...	1920	...	...	...	...	2116	...	...	...	...	...	...	...	...
Linz Hbf a.	...	...	...	...	1806	...	...	...	...	...	2024	...	...	...	...	2206	...	...	...	...	...	...	...	...

		IC			*IC*			*IC*		*IC*			*EC*								*IC*	**322**		
	734	**544**	2	**732**	**542**	**730**	2	**540**	**728**	**538**	2	**726**	**330**	2	**724**	2	2	**722**	2	**720**	**536**	**326**	2	**716**
	D	Ⓐ				E		f						Ⓐ	f				Ⓒ	Ⓐ		A		
Linz Hbf d.	...	...	...	...	...	...	...	...	...	...	...	...	0652	...	...	...	0735	...	...	...	...	...	0935	...
Freistadt d.	...	...	...	...	...	...	...	...	...	...	...	...	0742	...	...	...	0839	...	...	...	...	...	1039	...
Summerau 🏛 d.	...	...	...	...	...	...	...	...	...	...	...	...	0753	...	...	...	0852	...	...	...	...	...	1051	...
Rybnik d.	...	...	...	...	...	...	...	...	...	...	...	...	0806	...	...	...	0909	...	...	...	...	...	1107	...
České Budějovice a.	...	...	...	...	...	...	...	...	...	...	...	...	0852	...	...	...	0957	...	...	...	...	...	1157	...
České Budějovice ⊡ d.	0410	0458	...	0510	0558	...	...	0658	0710	0758	...	...	0858	...	0910	...	...	1010	...	1110	1158	...	...	1310
České Velenice 🏛 d.	|	|	0405	|	|	0531	0541	|	|	|	0631	0734	|	0808	|	0911	...	|	1016	|	|	1134	...	|
Třeboň d.	|	|	0445	|	|	0606	0619	|	|	|	0709	0808	|	0848	|	0953	...	|	1057	|	|	1208	...	|
Veselí nad Lužnicí ⊡ a.	0436	|	0509	0536	|	0626	0644	|	0736	|	0733	0827	|	0912	0936	1017	...	1036	1122	1136	|	1227	...	1336
Veselí nad Lužnicí d.	0438	|	...	0538	|	0638	...	|	0738	|	...	0838	|	...	0938	...	...	1038	...	1138	|	1238	...	1338
Tábor d.	0501	0537	...	0600	0637	0700	...	0737	0800	0837	...	0900	0937	...	1000	...	...	1100	...	1200	1237	1300	...	1400
Benešov u Prahy d.	0531	0601	...	0631	|	0731	...	|	0831	|	...	0931	|	...	1031	...	...	1131	...	1231	|	1331	...	1431
Praha hlavní nádrazi a.	0610	0640	...	0710	0739	0810	...	0839	0910	0939	...	1010	1039	...	1110	...	...	1210	...	1310	1339	1410	...	1510

	EC			*IC*			*IC*						*IC*		*EC*		**320**					*EC*		
	332	2	**714**	**534**	2	**712**	**532**	2	2	2	**710**	**708**	**530**	**706**	**334**	2	**324**	**702**	2	2	**700**	**336**	2	2
			F		n			⑦k	d		⑦k	G	⑦g				A							Ⓐ
Linz Hbf d.	1154	...	...	...	...	...	...	...	...	1335	...	...	...	...	1554	...	...	...	...	1735	...	1854	...	...
Freistadt d.	1242	...	...	...	...	...	...	...	...	1439	...	...	...	...	1644	...	...	...	...	1839	...	1944	...	...
Summerau 🏛 d.	1252	...	...	...	...	...	...	...	...	1451	...	...	...	...	1653	...	...	...	...	1851	...	1953	...	...
Rybnik d.	1306	...	...	...	...	...	...	...	...	1508	...	...	...	...	1706	...	...	...	...	1907	...	2006	...	...
Český Krumlov d.	|	...	...	1408	...	...	...	...	...	|	...	...	...	...	|	...	...	...	...	|	...	|	...	...
České Budějovice a.	1352	...	...	1443	...	...	...	...	...	1556	...	...	...	...	1752	...	...	...	...	1959	...	2052	...	...
České Budějovice ⊡ d.	1358	...	1410	1458	...	1510	1558	...	...	...	...	1610	1658	1710	1758	...	...	1910	...	...	2010	2058	...	...
České Velenice 🏛 d.	|	1310	|	|	1416	|	|	1503	1524	...	1536	|	|	|	|	1700	1726	|	1911	...	|	|	2106	2209
Třeboň d.	|	1352	|	|	1459	|	|	1543	1603	...	1609	|	|	|	|	1738	1806	|	1953	...	|	|	2145	2249
Veselí nad Lužnicí ⊡ a.	|	1419	1436	|	1524	1536	|	1608	1627	...	1628	1636	|	1736	|	1806	1825	1936	2017	...	2036	2124	2212	2313
Veselí nad Lužnicí d.	|	...	1438	|	...	1538	|	...	...	...	1638	1638	|	1738	|	...	1838	1938	...	...	2038	2125	...	...
Tábor d.	1437	...	1500	1537	...	1600	1637	...	...	...	1700	1700	1737	1800	1837	...	1900	2000	...	...	2100	2139	...	...
Benešov u Prahy d.	|	...	1531	|	...	1631	|	...	...	...	1731	1731	|	1831	|	...	1931	2031	...	...	2131	2202	...	...
Praha hlavní nádrazi a.	1539	...	1610	1639	...	1710	1739	...	...	...	1810	1810	1839	1910	1939	...	2010	2110	...	...	2210	2239	...	...

ČESKÉ VELENICE - ČESKÉ BUDĚJOVICE. *50 km.* Journey 50 minutes.
From **České Velenice** at 0601 ⑥ **q**, 0615 Ⓐ, 0633 Ⓐ, 0703 ⑥⑦ **j**, 0717 ①–⑤ **h**, 0903, 1103, 1303, 1403 Ⓐ, 1503, 1603 Ⓐ **n**, 1703, 1803, 1903, 2003 ⑤ **p**, 2103.
From **České Budějovice** at 0609 ⑥⑦ **j**, 0624 ①–⑤ **h**, 0810, 1010, 1210, 1310 Ⓐ, 1410, 1510 Ⓐ **n**, 1610, 1710 Ⓐ, 1810, 1910 Ⓐ, 2010, 2110 Ⓑ **f**, 2256.

RYBNIK - LIPNO NAD VLTAVOU. *22 km.* Journey 41 – 52 minutes.
From **Rybnik** at 0623, 0729, 0906, 1005, 1104, 1205 **m**, 1304, 1401 **n**, 1504, 1604, 1703, 1801, 1911, 2058.
From **Lipno nad Vltavou** at 0711, 0818, 1010, 1106, 1210, 1307 **m**, 1410, 1510 **n**, 1610, 1707, 1808, 1914, 2008.

A – SILVA NORTICA – 🚃12 Praha - Wien and v.v.
B – Daily Praha - Veselí nad Lužnicí; Ⓐ Veselí nad Lužnicí - České Budějovice.
C – Daily Praha - Veselí nad Lužnicí; Ⓑ **e** Veselí nad Lužnicí - České Budějovice.
D – From České Budějovice on Ⓐ; from Tábor on ①–⑥ **f**.
E – From České Velenice on ①–⑥ **f**; from Veselí nad Lužnicí daily.
F – From České Budějovice on Ⓐ; from Veselí nad Lužnicí daily.
G – From České Budějovice on Ⓐ; from Veselí nad Lužnicí on ①–⑥ **f**.

d – ①–⑥ (not Nov. 17).
e – Ⓑ (not Oct. 28).
f – Ⓑ (not Nov. 16).
g – ⑦ (also Oct. 28, Nov. 17; not Oct. 26, Nov. 16).
h – ①–⑤ (not June 30 - Aug. 29, Oct. 27 – 29, Nov. 11).
j – ⑥⑦ (daily June 30 - Aug. 31; also Oct. 27 – 29, Nov. 17).
k – ⑦ (also Nov. 17).
m – May 17 - Oct. 12.
n – Ⓐ (daily May 12 - Oct. 12).
p – ⑤ (also Oct. 27).
q – ⑥ (also Oct. 28, Nov. 16).
⊡ – See Table **1125** for other services.

1135 OKŘÍŠKY - ZNOJMO

Service from July 19.

km										
								Ⓐ	⑤⑥	†
					r	r				
0	**Jihlava** **1125** d.	...	...	...	...	...	...	1734	...	1934
29	**Okříšky** **1125** d.	0702	0902	1102	1302	1502	1702	1759	1912	|
61	Moravské Budějovice a.	0737	0937	1137	1350	1550	1737	1828	1947	2029
99	**Znojmo** a.	0830	1022	1222	1439	1639	1822	1906	2043	2104

	Ⓐ					†		Ⓒ	
		s		t					
Znojmo d.	0536	0738	0938	1138	1338	1458	1538	1738	1914
Moravské Budějovice d.	0622	0822	1022	1222	1422	1533	1622	1822	2012
Okříšky a.	0658	0858	1058	1258	1458	|	1658	1858	2048
Jihlava a.	...	...	...	...	...	1625	...	...	...

r – On ⚒: Moravské Budějovice a. 1350, 1550; Znojmo a. 1422, 1622.
s – Daily until Aug. 31; Ⓒ from Sept. 6.
t – On ⑥: Znojmo d. 1120, Moravské Budějovice d. 1207.

Arriva 2nd class PRAHA - MLADÁ BOLESLAV - TURNOV - TANVALD 1140

km										
									Ⓑ	
			A	B		C			f	
0	**Praha** hlavní nádrazi d.	0722	0922	1122	1322	1522	1722	1922	2122	...
34	Neratovice d.	0757	0957	1157	1357	1557	1757	1957	2157	...
40	Všetaty d.	0804	1004	1204	1404	1604	1804	2004	2204	...
72	**Mladá Boleslav** a.	0831	1031	1231	1431	1631	1831	2031	2231	...
72	**Mladá Boleslav** d.	0841	1041	1241	1441	1641	1841	2041	...	...
88	Mnichovo Hradiště d.	0858	1058	1258	1458	1658	1858	2058	...	...
102	**Turnov** a.	0910	1110	1310	1510	1710	1910	2110	...	...
102	**Turnov** **1142** d.	0917	1117	1317	1517	1717	1917	...	...	...
116	Železný Brod **1142** a.	0933	1132	1332	1532	1732	1932	...	...	...
116	Železný Brod △ d.	0933	1133	1333	1533	1733	1933	...	...	...
133	**Tanvald** △ a.	1002	1157	1357	1557	1757	1957	...	...	...

						Ⓒ		Ⓒ	
	D		d	j	e	k	m	k	m
Tanvald ▽ d.	0558	0758	1158	1346	1358	1543	1558	1743	1758
Železný Brod ▽ a.	0620	0820	1220	1409	1420	1610	1620	1810	1820
Železný Brod **1142** d.	0621	0821	1221	1412	1421	1621	1621	1814	1821
Turnov **1142** a.	0636	0836	1238	1427	1436	1636	1636	1832	1836
Turnov ◧ d.	0644	0844	1244	1444	1444	1644	1644	1844	1844
Mnichovo Hradiště ◧ d.	0659	0859	1259	1459	1459	1659	1659	1859	1859
Mladá Boleslav ◧ a.	0719	0919	1319	1519	1519	1719	1719	1919	1919
Mladá Boleslav ◧ d.	0723	0923	1323	1523	1523	1723	1723	1923	1923
Všetaty ◧ d.	0750	0950	1350	1550	1550	1750	1750	1950	1950
Neratovice ◧ d.	0758	0958	1358	1558	1558	1758	1758	1958	1958
Praha hlavní nádrazi ◧ a.	0831	1031	1431	1631	1631	1831	1831	2031	2031

A – Daily Praha - Turnov; ⑥⑦ **d** Turnov - Tanvald.
B – Daily Praha - Železný Brod; Ⓒ **e** Železný Brod - Tanvald.
C – Daily Praha - Turnov; Ⓑ **f** Turnov - Tanvald.
D – From Tanvald on ⑥ **h**; from Turnov daily.

d – Daily until Sept. 28; ⑥⑦ from Sept. 30 (also Oct. 27 – 29, Nov. 17).

e – Ⓒ (daily June 30 - Aug. 31).
f – Ⓑ (not Nov. 16).
g – Ⓐ (daily Apr. 22 - Sept. 28).
h – ⑥ (not Nov. 17).
j – Ⓐ (not June 30 - Aug. 29).

k – Ⓒ Mar. 29 - Oct. 28.
m – Ⓐ (also ⑥⑦ from Nov. 1).

◧ – Also from Turnov at 1044.
△ – Also at 0700 and every two hours until 2100, 2300 **g**.
▽ – Also at 0627 and every two hours until 2027, 2227 **g**.

2nd class LIBEREC - TANVALD - SZKLARSKA POREBA 1141

Service until September 26. Additional services are available Liberec - Tanvald and v.v. on Ⓐ.

km																								
																								⑤⑥
												E		E										
0	**Liberec** d.	0535	0635	0735	0835	...	0935	1035	1135	1235	...	1335	1435	1535	1635	...	1735	1835	1935	2035	...	2135	2235	2335
12	Jablonec nad Nisou d.	0556	0656	0756	0856	...	0956	1056	1156	1256	...	1356	1456	1556	1656	...	1756	1856	1956	2056	...	2156	2256	2353
16	Jablonecké Paseky a.	0602	0702	0802	0902	...	1002	1102	1202	1302	...	1402	1502	1602	1702	...	1802	1902	2002	2102	...	2202	2302	2358
27	**Tanvald** a.	*0624**	*0724**	*0824**	*0924**	...	*1024**	*1124**	*1224**	*1324**	...	*1424**	*1524**	*1624**	*1724**	...	*1824**	*1924**	*2024**	*2124**	...	*2224**	*2324**	*0024**
39	Harrachov a.	...	*0756**	*0856**	*0956**	...	*1056**	*1156**	*1256**	*1356**	...	*1456**	*1556**	*1656**	*1756**	...	*1856**	*1956**	...	...	...	...	...	...
55	**Szklarska Poreba** Górna ‡ a.	...	*0822**	*0922**	*1022**	...	*1122**	*1222**	...	*1422**	...	*1522**	*1622**	*1722**	*1822**	...	...	*2022**	...	...	...	...	...	...

						Ⓒ																	
																E		E					
Szklarska Poreba Górna ‡ d.	...	...	...	...	...	...	*0830**	*0930**	*1030**	...	*1130**	*1230**	...	*1430**	...	*1530**	*1630**	*1730**	*1830**	...	...	*2030**	...
Harrachov d.	...	...	...	...	...	*0756**	*0856**	*0956**	*1056**	...	*1156**	*1256**	*1356**	*1456**	...	*1556**	*1656**	*1756**	*1856**	...	*1956**	*2056**	...
Tanvald d.	*0525**	*0625**	*0725**	*0825**	...	*0825**	*0925**	*1025**	*1125**	...	*1225**	*1325**	*1425**	*1525**	...	*1625**	*1725**	*1825**	*1925**	...	*2025**	*2125**	*2225**
Jablonecké Paseky d.	0547	0647	0747	0847	...	0847	0947	1047	1147	...	1247	1347	1447	1547	...	1647	1747	1847	1947	...	2047	2147	2247
Jablonec nad Nisou d.	0557	0657	0757	0857	...	0857	0957	1057	1157	...	1257	1357	1457	1557	...	1657	1757	1857	1957	...	2057	2157	2257
Liberec a.	0618	0718	0817	0917	...	0917	1017	1117	1217	...	1318	1418	1518	1618	...	1718	1818	1917	2017	...	2117	2217	2317

E – To / from Harrachov daily; to / from Szklarska Poreba Górna on ⑥⑦ (also June 19, 20, Aug. 15).

* – Connection by 🚌.
‡ – 🏛 Czech Republic / Poland = Jakuszyce.

Arriva 2nd class LIBEREC - HRADEC KRÁLOVÉ - PARDUBICE 1142

km										
0	**Liberec** d.	0402	0605	0805	1003	1203	1405	1605	1805	2005
38	Turnov a.	0435	0639	0839	1035	1235	1439	1639	1839	2038
38	Turnov **1140** d.	0440	0640	0840	1040	1240	1440	1640	1840	2040
52	Železný Brod **1140** a.	0456	0656	0856	1056	1256	1456	1656	1856	2056
52	Železný Brod d.	0457	0657	0857	1057	1257	1457	1657	1857	2057
76	Stará Paka d.	0527	0731	0931	1131	1331	1531	1731	1931	2130
107	Dvůr Králové nad Labem d.	0601	0802	1002	1202	1402	1602	1802	2002	2157
122	Jaroměř d.	0618	0818	1018	1218	1418	1618	1818	2018	2209
139	**Hradec Králové** a.	0631	0831	1031	1231	1430	1631	1831	2031	2224
139	**Hradec Králové** d.	0633	0833	1033	1233	1433	1633	1833	2033	2228
161	**Pardubice** a.	0650	0850	1050	1250	1450	1650	1850	2050	2249

Pardubice d.	0505	0707	0907	1107	1307	1507	1707	1907	2107
Hradec Králové a.	0523	0725	0925	1125	1325	1525	1725	1925	2125
Hradec Králové d.	0526	0727	0927	1127	1327	1527	1727	1926	2127
Jaroměř d.	0542	0743	0943	1143	1343	1543	1743	1943	2144
Dvůr Králové nad Labem d.	0558	0758	0958	1158	1358	1558	1758	1958	2157
Stará Paka d.	0630	0830	1030	1230	1430	1630	1830	2030	2235
Železný Brod a.	0655	0855	1055	1255	1455	1655	1855	2055	2258
Železný Brod **1140** d.	0657	0857	1057	1257	1457	1657	1857	2057	2259
Turnov **1140** a.	0715	0916	1116	1316	1516	1716	1916	2116	2316
Turnov d.	0720	0920	1120	1320	1520	1720	1920	2119	2323
Liberec a.	0753	0953	1153	1355	1553	1755	1953	2151	2358

2nd class STARKOČ - WAŁBRZYCH 1144

Starkoč - Meziměsti is operated by ČD. Meziměsti - Wroclaw is operated by GW Train Regio (ČD tickets and passes not valid).

km											
			⑥⑦		⑥⑦						
			B		B						
0	**Starkoč** ⊡ d.	0942	...	1742	...	...	...	...	...	...	...
9	Náchod ⊡ d.	1000	...	1800	...	...	...	...	...	...	...
40	Meziměsti 🏛 ⊡ d.	1038	1112	1838	1912	...	...	...	...	...	...
62	**Walbrzych** Gl. a.	...	1142	...	1940	...	...	...	...	...	...
	Wroclaw Gl. **1084** a.	...	1303	...	2103	...	...	...	...	...	...

	⑥⑦		⑥⑦							
	B		B							
Wroclaw Gl. **1084** d.	0800	...	1550	...	...	...	...	...	...	...
Walbrzych Gl. d.	0913	...	1709	...	...	...	...	...	...	...
Meziměsti 🏛 ⊡ d.	0946	1019	1746	1819	...	...	...	...	...	...
Náchod ⊡ a.	...	1103	...	1903	...	...	...	...	...	...
Starkoč ⊡ a.	...	1117	...	1917	...	...	...	...	...	...

B – Until Sept. 28 (also Aug. 15).

⊡ – Also: Starkoč - Meziměsti at 0642 and hourly until 2042; also Meziměsti - Starkoč at 0619 and hourly until 2019.

🍷 on most **9xx** trains PRAHA - HRADEC KRÁLOVÉ - TRUTNOV and LETOHRAD 1145

km		939	941		921	943		923	945		925		927	947		929	949		931	951		933	953		955		957
			Ⓐ	2Ⓒ			2			2		2			2			2			2			2		2	
0	**Praha** hlavní n. d.	...	0510	...	0610	0710	...	0810	0910	...	1010	...	1210	1310	...	1410	1510	...	1610	1710	...	1810	1910	...	2010	...	2210
55	Nymburk **1157** d.	...	0555	...	0655	0755	...	0855	0955	...	1055	...	1255	1355	...	1455	1555	...	1655	1755	...	1855	1955	...	2055	...	2255
66	Poděbrady **1157** d.	...	0602	...	0702	0802	...	0902	1002	...	1102	...	1302	1402	...	1502	1602	...	1702	1802	...	1902	2002	...	2102	...	2302
125	**Hradec Králové** a.	...	0650	...	0750	0850	...	0950	1050	...	1150	...	1350	1450	...	1550	1650	...	1750	1850	...	1950	2050	...	2150	...	2350
125	**Hradec Králové** d.	0604	...	0702	0804	...	0904	1004	...	1104	1204	1304	1404	...	1504	1604	...	1704	1804	...	1904	2004	...	2104	...	2204	...
142	Jaroměř d.	0619	...	0718	0819	...	0918	1019	...	1118	1219	1318	1419	...	1518	1619	...	1718	1819	...	1918	2019	...	2119	...	2224	...
160	Starkoč d.	0639	...	0739	0840	...	0939	1040	...	1139	1240	1339	1440	...	1539	1640	...	1739	1840	...	1939	2040	...	2136	...	2245	...
194	**Trutnov** hlavní n. a.	0720	...	0819	0920	...	1019	1120	...	1219	1320	1419	1520	...	1619	1720	...	1819	1920	...	2019	2120	...	2216	...	2321	...

	954	952	934		950	932		948	930		928		946		926		944	924		942	922		940	920		
	Ⓐ			2			2			2		2				2			2			2			2	2
Trutnov hlavní n. d.	...	...	0441	0543	...	0642	0743	...	0842	0943	1042	1143	...	...	1242	1343	...	1442	1543	...	1642	1743	...	1842	1943	2043
Starkoč d.	...	...	0520	0625	...	0721	0825	...	0921	1025	1121	1225	...	...	1321	1425	...	1521	1625	...	1721	1825	...	1921	2025	2121
Jaroměř d.	...	...	0540	0643	...	0741	0843	...	0941	1043	1141	1243	...	...	1341	1444	...	1541	1643	...	1741	1843	...	1941	2043	2141
Hradec Králové a.	...	...	0555	0657	...	0755	0856	...	0955	1056	1155	1256	...	...	1355	1457	...	1555	1656	...	1755	1856	...	1955	2058	2157
Hradec Králové d.	0408	0508	0608	...	0708	0808	...	0908	1008	...	1208	...	1308	...	1408	...	1508	1608	...	1708	1808	...	1908	2008	...	...
Poděbrady **1157** a.	0452	0552	0652	...	0752	0852	...	0952	1052	...	1252	...	1352	...	1452	...	1552	1652	...	1752	1852	...	1952	2052	...	...
Nymburk **1157** a.	0500	0600	0700	...	0800	0900	...	1000	1100	...	1300	...	1400	...	1500	...	1600	1700	...	1800	1900	...	2000	2100	...	...
Praha hlavní n. a.	0542	0644	0744	...	0844	0944	...	1044	1144	...	1344	...	1444	...	1544	...	1644	1744	...	1844	1944	...	2044	2144	...	...

km		Ⓐ					Ⓐ		Ⓐ			Ⓐ
0	**Hradec Králové** d.	0605	0705	0905	1105	1305	1404	1505	1605	1705	1905	2105
21	Týniště nad Orlicí d.	0631	0731	0931	1131	1331	1429	1531	1631	1731	1931	2131
29	Častolovicě d.	0642	0741	0941	1141	1341	1439	1542	1641	1741	1941	2141
62	**Letohrad** a.	0727	0830	1030	1230	1429	1526	1630	1726	1830	2030	2227

		Ⓐ					Ⓐ		Ⓐ		
Letohrad a.	0530	0633	0733	0933	1133	1332	1435	1533	1635	1733	1933
Častolovicě d.	0620	0720	0819	1019	1220	1419	1519	1620	1719	1820	2020
Týniště nad Orlicí d.	0632	0732	0832	1032	1232	1433	1533	1633	1733	1832	2032
Hradec Králové d.	0654	0756	0853	1052	1253	1455	1555	1655	1755	1853	2053

1149 HAVLÍČKŮV BROD - JIHLAVA - TELČ - SLAVONICE

2nd class

km										
					⊡	⊡	⊡		⊡	
0	**Havlíčkův Brod** △ d.	0602	0803	1003	1203	1403	1603	1803	2003	2208
27	**Jihlava** △ d.	0622	0823	1023	1223	1423	1623	1823	2023	2237
42	Kostelec u Jihlavy △ d.	0646	0846	1046	1246	1446	1646	1846	2046	2300
65	**Telč** △ a.	0729	0929	1129	1329	1529	1729	1929	2129	2337
65	**Telč** d.	0734	0934	1134	1334	1534	1734	1934	2134	...
95	**Slavonice** a.	0827	1027	1227	1427	1627	1827	2027	2227	...

	⊡	⊡			⊡	Ⓐ	⊡	⊡	
Slavonice d.	0538	0726	0926	1126	1326	...	1526	1726	1926
Telč a.	0629	0827	1027	1227	1427	...	1627	1827	2027
Telč △ d.	0635	0835	1035	1235	1435	1535	1635	1835	2035
Kostelec u Jihlavy △ d.	0712	0912	1112	1312	1512	1612	1712	1912	2112
Jihlava △ d.	0736	0936	1136	1336	1536	1636	1736	1936	2136
Havlíčkův Brod △ a.	0757	0957	1157	1357	1557	1657	1757	1957	2203

△ – Additional trains are available Havlíčkův Brod - Jihlava and v.v., and Havlíčkův Brod - Telč and v.v.

⊡ – Daily Havlíčkův Brod - Telč and v.v.; Ⓒ Telč - Slavonice and v.v.

1150 PRAHA - PARDUBICE - BRNO - BŘECLAV - WIEN and BRATISLAVA

FAST TRAINS. For semi-fast trains Praha - Brno see Table **1151**. Most *EC* and *RJ* trains convey ✕. Regiojet trains (♥) convey 🍸.

km		*IC* 579	*EN* 477		*NJ* 457	*EC* 271		*RJ* 71 ①–⑥	*EC* 273		♥ 1031	*RJ* 73		♥ 1041	*EC* 275		*RJ* 75	♥ 1033		*EC* 277	*RJ* 257		♥ 1043	*EC* 279
		⊖	A		B			d													C			
0	**Praha** hlavní nádrazi 1160 d.	0001	0036	...	0036	...	...	0439	0542	...	0616	0642	...	0716	0742	...	0840	0916	...	0942	1035	...	1116	1142
62	Kolín 1160 d.	0041	|	...	|	...	...	0518	0618	...	|	|	...	|	0818	...	|	|	...	1018	|	...	|	1218
104	**Pardubice** 1160 d.	0103	0140	...	0140	...	...	0540	0640	...	0713	0740	...	0813	0840	...	0940	1013	...	1040	1140	...	1213	1240
164	Česká Třebová 1160 d.	0141	|	...	|	...	...	0614	0714	...	|	0814	...	|	|	...	1014	|	...	|	1214	...	|	|
255	**Brno** hlavní nádrazí d.	0243	0314	...	0314	0622	...	0722	0822	...	0848	0922	...	0948	1022	...	1122	1148	...	1222	1322	...	1348	1422
314	Břeclav a.	...	0345	...	0345	0652	...	0752	0852	...	0918	0952	...	1018	1052	...	1152	1218	...	1252	1352	...	1418	1452
314	Břeclav 982 d.	...	0455	...	0549	0655	...	0755	0855	...	0920	0955	...	1020	1055	...	1155	1220	...	1255	1355	...	1420	1455
402	**Wien** Hbf 982 a.	...	|	...	0700	|	...	0849	|	...	1021	1049	...	|	|	...	1249	1318	...	|	1449	...	|	|
	Graz 980 a.	...	|	...	0959	|	...	1133	|	...	|	1333	...	|	|	...	1533	|	...	|	1733	...	|	|
332	Kúty 🛃 a.	...	0511	...	...	0711	...	...	0911	...	|	...	...	|	1111	...	...	|	...	1311	...	...	|	1511
396	**Bratislava** hl. st. a.	...	0602	...	...	0802	...	...	1002	...	|	...	...	1126	1202	...	...	|	...	1402	...	...	1526	1602
	Budapest Nyugati 1175 a.	...	0829	...	...	1028	...	...	1228	...	|	...	...	...	1428	...	...	|	...	1628	...	...	...	1828
	Budapest Déli 1250 a.	...	...	...	...	...	...	...	...	...	1314	...	...	...	...	...	...	1614	...	...	...	...	...	...

	RJ 79	*EC* 131		♥ 1035	*EC* 173		*RJ* 371	♥ 1045		*EC* 281	♥ 1037		*RJ* 373	♥ 1047		*EC* 283	♥ 1049		*RJ* 375	*RJ* 285		♥ 1051	*IC* 577
		D			E			F								G	⊖					⊖	⊖
Praha hlavní nádrazi 1160 d.	1242	...	...	1316	1342	...	1442	1516	...	1542	1616	...	1642	1716	...	1742	1816	...	1842	1942	...	2047	2201
Kolín 1160 d.	|	...	...	|	1418	...	|	|	...	1618	|	...	|	|	...	1818	|	...	|	2018	...	|	2242
Pardubice 1160 d.	1340	...	...	1413	1440	...	1540	1613	...	1640	1713	...	1740	1813	...	1840	1913	...	1940	2040	...	2144	2304
Česká Třebová 1160 d.	1414	...	...	|	|	...	1614	|	...	|	|	...	1814	|	...	|	|	...	2014	2114	...	|	2343
Brno hlavní nádrazí d.	1522	...	...	1548	1622	...	1722	1748	...	1822	1848	...	1922	1948	...	2022	2047	...	2122	2222	...	2322	0048
Břeclav a.	1552	...	...	1618	1652	...	1752	1818	...	1852	1918	...	1952	2018	...	2052	...	...	2152	2252	...	...	0118
Břeclav 982 d.	1555	1555	...	1620	1655	...	1755	1820	...	1855	1920	...	1955	2020	...	2055	...	...	2155	2255	...	...	...
Wien Hbf 982 a.	1649	|	...	1721	|	...	1849	|	...	|	2018	...	2049	|	...	|	...	...	2249	|	...	...	...
Graz 980 a.	1933	|	...	|	|	...	2133	|	...	|	...	...	2333	|	...	|	...	...	...	|	...	...	...
Kúty 🛃 a.	...	1611	...	|	1711	...	...	|	...	1911	...	...	...	|	...	2111	...	...	...	|	...	...	...
Bratislava hl. st. a.	...	1705	...	|	1802	...	...	1926	...	2002	...	...	...	2126	...	2203	...	...	...	2359	...	...	...
Budapest Nyugati 1175 a.	...	1949	...	|	2028	...	...	...	...	2230	...	...	...	...	...	...	...	...	...	...	...	...	...
Budapest Déli 1250 a.	...	...	...	2014	...	...	...	...	...	...	...	...	...	...	...	...	...	...	...	...	...	...	...

	RJ 578 ①–⑥	♥ 1040		*IC* 576	♥ 1042		*RJ* 284	♥ 1044		*EC* 282	♥ 1030		*RJ* 70	*EC* 280		♥ 1046	*RJ* 72		*EC* 172	♥ 1032		*EC* 130	*RJ* 74
	d ⊖	⊖			⊖					G						F			E			D	
Budapest Déli 1250 d.	...	...	...	...	...	...	...	...	...	...	...	...	...	...	...	...	...	...	...	0745	...	...	...
Budapest Nyugati 1175 d.	...	...	...	...	...	...	...	...	...	...	...	...	...	0530	...	...	...	...	0730	|	...	0812	...
Bratislava hl. st. d.	...	...	...	...	...	...	0455	0500	...	0558	...	...	...	0758	...	0826	...	...	0958	|	...	1055	...
Kúty 🛃 d.	...	...	...	...	...	...	0549	|	...	0649	...	...	...	0849	...	|	...	...	1049	|	...	1149	...
Graz 980 d.	...	...	...	...	...	...	|	|	...	|	...	...	...	|	...	|	0626	...	|	|	...	|	0826
Wien Hbf 982 d.	...	...	...	...	...	...	|	|	...	|	0639	...	0710	|	...	|	0910	...	|	1039	...	|	1110
Břeclav 982 a.	...	...	...	...	...	...	0604	0625	...	0704	0736	...	0804	0904	...	0936	1004	...	1104	1136	...	1204	1204
Břeclav d.	...	...	...	0507	...	...	0607	0638	...	0707	0738	...	0807	0907	...	0938	1007	...	1107	1138	...	...	1207
Brno hlavní nádrazí d.	0426	0503	...	0539	0609	...	0639	0709	...	0739	0809	...	0839	0939	...	1009	1039	...	1139	1209	...	...	1239
Česká Třebová 1160 d.	0536	|	...	0638	|	...	0738	|	...	|	|	...	0938	|	...	|	1138	...	|	|	...	...	1338
Pardubice 1160 a.	0615	0642	...	0711	0742	...	0811	0842	...	0911	0942	...	1011	1111	...	1142	1211	...	1311	1342	...	...	1411
Kolín 1160 a.	|	|	...	0733	|	...	|	|	...	0933	|	...	|	1133	...	|	|	...	1333	|	...	...	|
Praha hlavní nádrazi 1160 a.	0715	0739	...	0815	0839	...	0915	0939	...	1015	1039	...	1115	1215	...	1239	1315	...	1415	1439	...	...	1515

	EC 278	♥ 1048		*RJ* 256	*EC* 276		♥ 1034	*RJ* 78		*EC* 274	♥ 1050		*RJ* 370	♥ 1036		*EC* 272	*RJ* 372		*EC* 270	*RJ* 374		*NJ* 456	*EN* 476
				C													⊖		⊖			B	A
Budapest Déli 1250 d.	...	...	...	...	...	...	1145	...	...	...	...	...	...	1445	...	...	...	...	...	...	...	...	...
Budapest Nyugati 1175 d.	0930	...	...	...	1130	...	|	...	...	1330	...	...	...	|	...	1530	...	...	1730	...	...	...	1930
Bratislava hl. st. d.	1158	1226	...	...	1358	...	|	...	...	1558	1626	...	...	|	...	1758	...	...	1958	...	...	...	2158
Kúty 🛃 d.	1249	|	...	...	1449	...	|	...	...	1649	|	...	...	|	...	1849	...	...	2049	...	...	...	2249
Graz 980 d.	|	|	...	1026	|	...	|	1226	...	|	|	...	1426	|	...	|	1626	...	|	1826	...	1920	|
Wien Hbf 982 d.	|	|	...	1310	|	...	1439	1510	...	|	|	...	1710	1736	...	|	1910	...	|	2110	...	2210	|
Břeclav 982 a.	1304	1336	...	1404	1504	...	1536	1604	...	1704	1736	...	1804	1836	...	1904	2004	...	2104	2204	...	2304	2304
Břeclav d.	1307	1338	...	1407	1507	...	1538	1607	...	1707	1738	...	1807	1838	...	1907	2007	...	2107	2207	...	2357	2357
Brno hlavní nádrazí d.	1339	1409	...	1439	1539	...	1609	1639	...	1739	1809	...	1839	1909	...	1939	2039	...	2139	2236	...	0029	0029
Česká Třebová 1160 d.	|	|	...	1538	|	...	|	1738	...	|	|	...	1938	|	...	2038	2148	...	2242	...	...	|	|
Pardubice 1160 a.	1511	1542	...	1611	1711	...	1742	1811	...	1911	1942	...	2011	2042	...	2111	2219	...	2316	...	...	0158	0158
Kolín 1160 a.	1533	|	...	|	1733	...	|	|	...	1933	|	...	|	|	...	2133	2240	...	2340	...	...	|	|
Praha hlavní nádrazi 1160 a.	1615	1639	...	1720	1815	...	1839	1915	...	2015	2039	...	2115	2139	...	2215	2319	...	0018	...	...	0301	0301

A – METROPOL – 🛏 1, 2 cl., ▬ 2 cl., (2) Berlin (**457/476**) - Břeclav (**477/456**) - Budapest and v.v; 🛏 1, 2 cl., ▬ 2 cl., (2) Warszawa (**407/6**) - Břeclav (**477/456**) - Budapest and v.v.

B – *ÖBB nightjet* – 🛏 1, 2 cl., ▬ 2 cl., (2) Berlin - Graz and v.v.

C – VINDOBONA – (12) ✕ Graz - Děčín (- Berlin until June 30) and v.v.

D – BATHORY – (12) ✕ Budapest - Warszawa and v.v.

E – HUNGARIA - (12) ✕ Budapest - Berlin (- Hamburg until July 31) and v.v.

F – (12) 🍸 Praha - Žilina and v.v.

G – METROPOLITAN SLOVENSKÁ STRELA (12) 🍸 Praha - Nové Zámky and v.v.

d – ①–⑥ (not Nov. 17).

♥ – Operated by REGIOJET. Separate fares apply.

⊖ – For other station calls see Table **1151**.

RJ – Railjet train (operated by ÖBB and ČD). Conveys Business, First and Economy class.

PRAHA - OLOMOUC and BRNO — 1151

🍷 on most trains

SEMI-FAST TRAINS. For faster trains see Tables **1150** and **1160**. Most Přerov trains continue to/from destinations on Table **1162**.

km		579	861	883	863	885	865	887	867	889	869	891	871	893	873	895	875	1049	897	877	1051	879	899	577	999
			Ⓐ	①–⑥																					
		◧		d														♥			♥			◧	
0	**Praha** hlavní nádrazi d.	0001	...	0501	0601	0701	0801	0901	1001	1101	1201	1301	1401	1501	1601	1701	1801	1816	1901	2001	2047	2101	2131	2201	2301
62	Kolín d.	0041	...	0542	0642	0742	0842	0942	1042	1142	1242	1342	1442	1542	1642	1742	1842	|	1942	2042	|	2142	2210	2242	2342
104	Pardubice d.	0103	...	0606	0706	0806	0906	1006	1106	1206	1306	1406	1506	1606	1706	1806	1906	1913	2006	2106	2144	2206	2232	2304	0006
139	Choceň d.	0119	...	0623	0725	0823	0925	1023	1125	1223	1325	1423	1525	1623	1725	1823	1925	|	2023	2123	|	2223	|	2321	...
154	Ústí nad Orlicí d.	0131	...	0635	0737	0835	0937	1035	1137	1235	1337	1435	1537	1635	1737	1835	1937	|	2035	2137	|	2235	|	2333	...
164	Česká Třebová d.	0141	0548	0645	0750	0845	0950	1045	1150	1245	1350	1445	1550	1645	1750	1845	1950	|	2045	2146	|	2245	2307	2343	...
252	Olomouc d.	|	|	0731	|	0931	|	1131	|	1331	|	1531	|	1731	|	1931	|	|	2134	...	|	|	2352	|	...
274	**Přerov** a.	|	|	0743	|	0943	|	1143	|	1343	|	1543	|	1743	|	1943	|	|	2147	...	|	|	0005	|	...
181	Svitavy d.	0151	0559	...	0802	...	1002	...	1202	...	1402	...	1602	...	1802	...	2002	1955	...	...	2225	2256	...	|	...
208	Letovice d.	|	0622	...	0822	...	1022	...	1222	...	1422	...	1622	...	1822	...	2022	|	...	...	2243	2314	...	|	...
233	Blansko d.	0224	0642	...	0842	...	1042	...	1242	...	1442	...	1642	...	1842	...	2042	|	...	...	2302	2331	...	|	...
255	**Brno** hlavní nádrazí a.	0243	0702	...	0903	...	1102	...	1302	...	1502	...	1702	...	1902	...	2102	2047	...	...	2322	2351	...	0045	...

	876	898	578	896	1040	874	874	1042	894	872	892	870	890	868	888	866	886	864	884	862	882	860	372	270
			①–⑥	①–⑥			Ⓐ																	
			d ◧	d	♥			♥															◧	◧
Brno hlavní nádrazi d.	0310	...	0426	...	0503	...	0500	0609	...	0656	...	0856	...	1056	...	1256	...	1456	...	1656	...	1856	2039	2139
Blansko d.	0329	...	0446	...	0524	...	0519	|	...	0716	...	0916	...	1116	...	1316	...	1516	...	1716	...	1916	2059	|
Letovice d.	|	...	0504	...	0542	...	0537	|	...	0737	...	0937	...	1137	...	1337	...	1537	...	1737	...	1937	2117	|
Svitavy d.	0403	...	0523	...	0600	...	0603	0700	...	0803	...	1003	...	1203	...	1403	...	1603	...	1803	...	2003	2135	2230
Přerov d.	|	0352	|	0448	|	...	|	|	0616	|	0816	|	1016	|	1216	|	1416	|	1616	|	1816	|	|	|
Olomouc d.	|	0407	|	0502	|	...	|	|	0631	|	0831	|	1031	|	1231	|	1431	|	1631	|	1831	|	|	|
Česká Třebová d.	0415	0453	0536	0602	|	0615	0615	|	0715	0815	0915	1015	1115	1215	1315	1415	1515	1615	1715	1815	1915	2015	2148	2242
Ústí nad Orlicí d.	0424	0502	|	0611	|	0624	0624	|	0724	0824	0924	1024	1124	1224	1324	1424	1524	1624	1724	1824	1924	2024	|	|
Choceň d.	0436	0515	|	|	|	0636	0636	|	0736	0836	0936	1036	1136	1236	1336	1436	1536	1636	1736	1836	1936	2036	|	|
Pardubice a.	0454	0534	0615	0637	0642	0655	0655	0742	0757	0855	0957	1055	1157	1255	1357	1455	1557	1655	1757	1855	1957	2055	2219	2316
Kolín a.	0519	0557	|	0657	|	0719	0719	|	0819	0919	1019	1119	1219	1319	1419	1519	1619	1719	1819	1919	2019	2119	2240	2340
Praha hlavní nádrazi a.	0606	0636	0715	0736	0739	0806	0806	0839	0902	1006	1106	1206	1306	1406	1506	1606	1706	1806	1906	2006	2102	2203	2319	0018

d – ①–⑥ (not Nov. 17).

◧ – *EC*, *IC* or *RJ* train (see Table **1150**).

♥ – Operated by REGIOJET. Seperate fares apply.

PRAHA - HAVLIČKŮV BROD - BRNO — 1152

🍷 on most trains

km		971	971	973		975	975	977		979	981	983		985	987	989		989	991	963		965	967	
		Ⓐ	①–⑥				①–⑥							Ⓐ		Ⓑ		⑦		Ⓑ				
			d				d									e		f		e				
0	**Praha** hlavní nádrazi ⊡ d.	...	...	...	...	...	0608	0808	...	1008	1208	1408	...	1508	1608	1708	...	1708	1808	1908	...	2008	2208	...
62	Kolín ⊡ d.	...	...	...	...	0648	0648	0848	...	1048	1248	1448	...	1548	1648	1748	...	1748	1848	1948	...	2048	2249	...
73	Kutná Hora d.	...	...	...	...	0659	0659	0859	...	1059	1259	1459	...	1559	1659	1759	...	1759	1859	1959	...	2059	2259	...
82	Čáslav d.	...	...	...	...	0708	0708	0908	...	1108	1308	1508	...	1608	1708	1808	...	1808	1908	2008	...	2108	2307	...
136	**Havlíčkův Brod** a.	...	...	...	...	0757	0757	0957	...	1157	1357	1557	...	1657	1757	1857	...	1857	1957	2057	...	2157	...	...
136	**Havlíčkův Brod** d.	0501	...	0601	...	0801	0801	1001	...	1201	1401	1601	...	1701	1801	1901	...	1901	2001	2101	...	...	...	...
169	Žďár nad Sázavou d.	0533	0533	0633	...	0833	0833	1033	...	1233	1433	1633	...	1733	1833	1931	...	1933	2033	2131	...	...	...	...
246	**Brno** hlavní nádrazi a.	0640	0640	0740	...	0940	0940	1140	...	1340	1540	1740	...	1840	1940	...	...	2040	2140	...	...	...	...	...

	964	962	962		990	990	990		988	986	984		982	960	980		978	976	974		972	970	
	①–⑥		①–⑥		①–⑥	Ⓐ	①							⑦			Ⓑ		Ⓐ				
	d		d		d		g							f			e						
Brno hlavní nádrazi d.	...	...	...	...	...	...	0520	...	0620	0820	1020	...	1220	...	1420	...	1520	1620	1720	...	1820	2020	...
Žďár nad Sázavou d.	...	...	0527	...	...	0627	0627	...	0727	0927	1127	...	1327	...	1527	...	1627	1727	1827	...	1927	2127	...
Havlíčkův Brod a.	...	...	0557	...	...	0657	0657	...	0757	0957	1157	...	1357	...	1557	...	1657	1757	1857	...	1957	2157	...
Havlíčkův Brod d.	0501	0601	0601	...	...	0701	0701	...	0801	1001	1201	...	1401	1501	1601	...	1701	1810	...	...	2001	...	...
Čáslav d.	0552	0652	0652	...	0752	0752	0752	...	0852	1052	1252	...	1452	1552	1652	...	1752	1852	...	...	2052	...	...
Kutná Hora d.	0601	0701	0701	...	0801	0801	0801	...	0901	1101	1301	...	1501	1601	1701	...	1801	1901	...	...	2101	...	...
Kolín ⊡ d.	0612	0712	0712	...	0812	0812	0812	...	0912	1112	1312	...	1512	1612	1712	...	1812	1912	...	...	2112	...	...
Praha hlavní nádrazi ⊡ a.	0654	0755	0755	...	0855	0855	0855	...	0955	1155	1355	...	1555	1655	1755	...	1854	1955	...	...	2154	...	...

d – ①–⑥ (not Nov. 17).
e – Ⓑ (not Nov. 16).
f – ⑦ (also Oct. 28, Nov. 17; not Nov. 16).
g – ① (also Oct. 29, Nov. 18; not Nov. 17).

⊡ – For other trains Praha - Kolín see Tables **1150**, **1151** and **1160**.

BRNO - OLOMOUC - ŠUMPERK and JESENÍK — 1156

Trains without numbers convey 2nd class only

km		901			903		905			907			909			911					913		915	917
				Ⓐ								Ⓐ							Ⓐ					⑦
		A	A																				B	h
0	**Brno** hlavní nádrazi d.	0522	0522	...	0718	0718	0921	0921	...	1121	1121	...	1321	1321	...	1521	...	1521	...	...	1721	...	1921	2121
45	Vyškov na Moravé d.	0601	0601	...	0801	0801	1001	1001	...	1201	1201	...	1401	1401	...	1601	...	1601	...	...	1801	...	2001	2201
61	Nezamyslice d.	0622	0622	...	0822	0822	1022	1022	...	1222	1222	...	1422	1422	...	1622	...	1622	...	...	1822	...	2022	2222
80	Prostějov d.	0637	0637	...	0837	0837	1037	1037	...	1237	1237	...	1437	1437	...	1637	...	1637	...	...	1837	...	2037	2237
100	**Olomouc** d.	0656	0656	...	0856	0856	1056	1056	...	1256	1256	...	1456	1456	...	1656	...	1656	...	...	1856	...	2056	2253
146	Zábřeh na Moravé a.	0722	0722	...	0922	0922	1122	1122	...	1322	1322	...	1522	1522	..	1722	...	1722	...	...	1924	...	2124	...
146	Zábřeh na Moravé d.	0726	0731	...	0926	0931	1126	1131	...	1326	1331	...	1526	1531	...	1726	...	1731	...	...	1926	...	2126	...
159	**Šumperk** d.	0741	|	0827	0941	|	1141	|	...	1341	|	1413	1541	|	1613	1741	...	|	1832	1931	1944	2113	2141	...
	Hanušovice d.	...	0802	0915	...	1002	...	1202	...	...	1402	1458	...	1602	1658	...	...	1802	1922	2002	...	2202	...	...
	Lipová Lázně d.	...	0851	1010	...	1051	...	1251	...	...	1451	1554	...	1651	1754	...	...	1851	2011	2052	...	2251	...	...
	Jeseník a.	...	0858	1017	...	1058	...	1258	...	...	1458	1602	...	1658	1802	...	...	1858	2019	2059	...	2259	...	...

	916	914		912			910		908		906			904			902					900	
	Ⓐ		①–⑥													Ⓐ			Ⓐ	Ⓒ	⑦	⑤⑦	
			d																	j	k	m	
Jeseník d.	...	...	0531	...	0700	0745	...	0901	...	1101	...	...	1301	...	1501	1545	...	1701	1745	1745	1901	...	2106
Lipová Lázně d.	...	...	0543	...	0708	0753	...	0908	...	1108	...	...	1308	...	1508	1553	...	1708	1753	1753	1909	...	2114
Hanušovice d.	...	...	0643	...	0800	0849	...	1000	...	1200	...	...	1400	...	1600	1655	...	1800	1848	1844	2001	...	2208
Šumperk d.	...	0608	0720	0808	|	0931	1008	|	1208	|	1408	...	|	1608	|	1746	1808	|	1950	|	|	2014	2235
Zábřeh na Moravé a.	...	0628	...	0822	0825	...	1022	1025	1222	1225	1422	...	1425	1622	1625	...	1822	1825	...	1909	2026	2031	...
Zábřeh na Moravé d.	...	0630	...	0834	0834	...	1034	1034	1234	1234	1434	...	1434	1634	1634	...	1834	1834	...	...	...	2034	...
Olomouc d.	0558	0705	...	0905	0905	...	1105	1105	1305	1305	1505	...	1505	1705	1705	...	1905	1905	...	...	...	2105	...
Prostějov d.	0616	0724	...	0924	0924	...	1124	1124	1324	1324	1524	...	1524	1724	1724	...	1924	1924	...	...	...	2124	...
Nezamyslice a.	0638	0738	...	0938	0938	...	1138	1138	1338	1338	1538	...	1538	1738	1738	...	1938	1938	...	...	...	2138	...
Vyškov na Moravé a.	0657	0757	...	0957	0957	...	1157	1157	1357	1357	1557	...	1557	1757	1757	...	1957	1957	...	...	...	2157	...
Brno hlavní nádrazi a.	0743	0842	...	1041	1041	...	1241	1241	1443	1443	1643	...	1643	1843	1843	...	2038	2038	...	...	...	2236	...

A – From Brno on ①–⑥ **d**; from Oloumoc daily.
B – Daily Brno - Olomouc; Ⓑ Olomouc - Šumperk. Change trains at Olomouc on Ⓐ.
d – ①–⑥ (not Nov. 17).
h – ⑦ (also Oct. 28, Nov. 17; not Oct. 26, Nov. 16).
j – Ⓒ Apr. 5 - Oct. 28.
k – ⑦ (also Oct. 28, nov. 17; not Oct. 26, Nov. 16).
m – ⑤⑦ (also Oct. 27, 28, Nov. 17; not Oct. 26, Nov. 16).

1160 PRAHA - PÚCHOV, OSTRAVA, BOHUMÍN and ŽILINA

For additional fast trains Praha - Česká Třebová and v.v. see Table **1150**. For semi-fast trains Praha - Olomouc and v.v. see Table **1151**.
SC and *IC* trains are not available for local travel Ostravá - Bohumín or v.v.

km				*EC*	♥	*EC*	*EC*	*EC*		*EC*	*EC*	♥	*LE*♠	*EC*	*LE*♠	*EC*	*SC*•	♥	*EC*	*EC*		*EC*	*LE*♠
		341	**343**	**121**	**1001**	**241**	**113**	**213**	**345**	**264**	**123**	**1003**	**1251**	**141**	**1253**	**125**	**503**	**1005**	**130**	**115**	**347**	**262**	**1255**
		🍷	✕	🍷	🍷 ①–⑥	🍷 R	🍷	🍷	🍷		🍷	🍷	🍷 R	🍷	🍷 R	🍷	🍷 R	🍷	🍷	🍷	🍷		🍷 R
				●	d		A ◧	A ◧		B	●					●	C		D ◧	D ◧		B	
0	**Praha** hlavní nádraží d.	...	...	0522	0547	0558	0622	0622	...	0651	0722	0747	0758	0822	0858	0922	0931	0947	1022	1022	...	1051	1058
62	Kolín d.	...	...	0601	|	0636	0701	0701	...	0732	0801	|	0836	0901	0936	1001	|	|	1101	1101	...	1132	1136
104	**Pardubice** d.	...	...	0622	0643	0658	0722	0722	...	0754	0822	0843	0859	0922	0959	1022	1029	1043	1122	1122	...	1154	1159
139	Choceň d.	...	...	|	|	|	|	|	...	|	|	|	|	|	|	|	|	|	|	|	...	|	|
154	Ústí nad Orlici d.	...	...	|	|	|	|	|	...	0827	|	|	0927	|	1027	|	|	|	|	|	...	1227	1227
155	Ústí nad Orlici městó d.	...	...	|	|	|	|	|	...	...	|	|	|	|	|	|	|	|	|	|	...	...	|
164	Česká Třebová d.	...	...	0656	0716	0733	0759	0759	...	...	0856	0916	|	0959	|	1056	|	1116	1159	1159	...	...	|
206	Zábřeh na Moravé d.	...	...	0720	0739	|	0822	0822	...	...	0920	0939	0955	1022	1055	1121	|	1139	1222	1222	...	...	1255
252	**Olomouc** d.	...	...	0751	0801	0814	0844	0844	...	...	0951	1001	1017	1044	1117	1151	1141	1201	1244	1244	...	...	1317
	Přerov d.	...	...	|	|	|	|	|	...	...	|	|	1034	|	1134	|	|	|	|	|	...	...	1334
303	Hranice na Moravě d.	...	...	0825	0835	|	0915	0915	...	...	1025	1035	1055	1115	1155	1225	|	1235	1315	1315	...	...	1355
329	Valašské Meziříčí d.	...	...	0925	|	|	|	|	...	...	1125	|	|	|	|	1325	|	|	|	|	...	...	|
348	Vsetín d.	...	...	0941	|	|	|	|	...	...	1141	|	|	|	|	1341	|	|	|	|	...	...	|
366	Horní Lideč 🏛 **1180** d.	...	...	1004	|	|	|	|	...	...	1204	|	|	|	|	1404	|	|	|	|	...	...	|
394	**Púchov** **1180** a.	...	...	1027	|	|	|	|	...	...	1227	|	|	|	|	1427	|	|	|	|	...	...	|
353	**Ostrava** Svinov d.	0542	0746	...	0902	0907	0942	0942	0946	...	...	1102	1125	1142	1225	...	1234	1302	1342	1342	1346	...	1425
381	**Opava** východ a.	|	|	...	|	|	|	|	|	...	...	|	|	|	|	...	|	|	|	|	|	...	|
358	**Ostrava** hl. n. d.	0550	0754	...	0911	0914	0950	0950	0954	...	...	1111	1131	1150	1231	...	1244	1311	1350	1350	1354	...	1431
376	Havířov d.	|	|	...	0931	|	|	|	|	...	...	1133	|	|	|	...	...	1331	|	|	|	...	|
366	**Bohumín** a.	0556	0800	...	...	|	0956	0956	1000	...	...	|	1138	1156	1238	...	...	...	1356	1356	1400	...	1438
366	**Bohumín** d.	0601	0801	...	...	|	1009	1017	1001	...	...	|	...	1201	...	...	...	...	1438	1445	1401	...	...
	Katowice **1076** a.	|	|	...	...	|	1143	|	|	...	...	|	...	|	...	...	...	...	1632	|	|	...	...
	Kraków Glowny **1076** a.	|	|	...	...	|	|	1216	|	...	...	|	...	|	...	...	...	...	|	1700	|	...	...
	Warszawa Centralna **1060** a.	|	|	...	...	|	1426	...	|	...	...	|	...	|	...	...	...	...	1916	...	|	...	...
381	Karviná hl. n. d.	0611	0811	...	...	|	...	...	1011	...	...	|	...	1211	...	...	...	...	...	...	1411	...	...
397	**Český Těšín** d.	0626	0826	...	...	0939	...	...	1026	...	...	1154	...	1226	...	...	...	...	...	...	1426	...	...
405	Trinec centrum d.	0633	0833	...	...	|	...	...	1033	...	...	1202	...	1233	...	...	...	...	...	...	1433	...	...
417	Návsi d.	0640	0840	...	...	|	...	...	1040	...	...	|	...	1240	...	...	...	...	...	...	1440	...	...
435	Čadca 🏛 a.	0658	0858	...	...	1005	...	...	1058	...	...	1225	...	1258	...	...	...	...	...	...	1458	...	...
△466	**Žilina** a.	0726	0926	...	...	1033	...	...	1126	...	...	1249	...	1326	...	...	...	...	...	...	1526	...	...
	Poprad Tatry **1180** a.	...	...	...	...	1240	...	...	...	...	...	1451	...	...	...	...	...	...	...	...	...	...	...
	Prešov **1196** a.	...	...	...	...	|	...	...	...	...	...	|	...	...	...	...	...	...	...	...	...	...	...
	Košice **1180** a.	...	...	...	...	1412	...	...	...	...	...	1612	...	...	...	...	...	...	...	...	...	...	...

	EC	*SC*•	♥	*EC*	*LE*♠	*EC*	*SC*•	♥	*LE*♠	*EC*		♥	*EC*	*EC*	*SC*•	♥	*LE*♠	*EC*	*SC*•	♥	*LE*♠	*LE*♠
	127	**505**	**1007**	**143**	**1257**	**129**	**507**	**1009**	**1259**	**117**	**349**	**1011**	**260**	**221**	**511**	**1013**	**1261**	**145**	**513**	**1015**	**411**	**411**
	🍷	🍷 R	🍷	✕	🍷 R	🍷	🍷 R	🍷	🍷 R	🍷	🍷	🍷		🍷	🍷 R	🍷	🍷 R	🍷	🍷 R ④–⑥	🍷	🍷 R	🍷 R ③–⑦
	●					●				E ◧			B	●					e			
Praha hlavní nádraží d.	1122	1131	1147	1222	1258	1322	1331	1347	1358	1422	...	1447	1450	1522	1531	1547	1558	1622	1631	1647	1658	1658
Kolín d.	1201	|	|	1301	1336	1401	|	|	1436	1501	...	|	1532	1601	|	|	1636	1701	|	|	1736	1736
Pardubice d.	1222	1229	1243	1322	1359	1422	1429	1443	1459	1522	...	1543	1554	1622	1629	1643	1659	1722	1729	1743	1759	1759
Choceň d.	|	|	|	|	|	|	|	|	|	|	...	|	|	|	|	|	|	|	|	|	|	|
Ústí nad Orlici d.	|	|	|	|	1427	|	|	|	1527	|	...	|	1627	|	|	|	1727	|	|	|	1827	1827
Ústí nad Orlici městó d.	|	|	|	|	|	|	|	|	|	|	...	|	...	|	|	|	|	1750	|	|	|	|
Česká Třebová d.	1256	|	1316	1359	|	1456	|	1516	|	1559	...	1616	...	1656	|	1716	|	1759	|	1816	|	|
Zábřeh na Moravé d.	1321	|	1339	1422	1455	1521	|	1539	1555	1622	...	1640	...	1721	|	1739	1755	1823	|	1840	1855	1855
Olomouc d.	1351	1341	1401	1444	1517	1551	1541	1601	1617	1644	...	1704	...	1751	1741	1801	1817	1847	1844	1904	1917	1917
Přerov d.	|	|	|	|	1534	|	|	|	1634	|	...	|	...	|	|	|	1834	|	|	|	1934	1934
Hranice na Moravě d.	1425	|	1435	1515	1555	1625	|	1635	1655	1715	...	1736	...	1825	|	1835	1855	1918	|	1936	1955	1955
Valašské Meziříčí d.	1525	|	|	|	|	1725	|	|	|	|	...	|	...	1925	|	|	|	|	|	|	|	|
Vsetín d.	1541	|	|	|	|	1741	|	|	|	|	...	|	...	1941	|	|	|	|	|	|	|	|
Horní Lideč 🏛 **1180** d.	1604	|	|	|	|	1804	|	|	|	|	...	|	...	2004	|	|	|	|	|	|	|	|
Púchov **1180** a.	1627	|	|	|	|	1827	|	|	|	|	...	|	...	2027	|	|	|	|	|	|	|	|
Ostrava Svinov d.	...	1434	1502	1542	1625	...	1634	1702	1725	1742	1746	1803	...	|	1834	1901	1925	1945	1937	2003	2025	2025
Opava východ a.	...	|	|	|	|	...	|	|	|	|	|	|	...	|	|	1928	|	|	1958	|	|	|
Ostrava hl. n. d.	...	1444	1511	1550	1632	...	1644	1711	1732	1750	1754	1811	...	|	1842	...	1931	1953	...	2011	2032	2032
Havířov d.	...	...	1531	|	|	...	...	1731	|	|	|	1833	...	|	|	...	|	|	...	2033	|	|
Bohumín a.	...	...	...	1556	1638	...	...	...	1738	1756	1800	|	...	|	1850	...	1938	1959	...	|	2038	2038
Bohumín d.	...	...	...	1601	...	...	...	...	1740	1809	1801	|	...	|	...	...	...	2001	...	|	...	2041
Katowice **1076** a.	...	...	...	|	...	...	...	...	|	1950	|	|	...	|	...	...	...	|	...	|	...	|
Kraków Glowny **1076** a.	...	...	...	|	...	...	...	...	|	|	|	|	...	|	...	...	...	|	...	|	...	2256
Warszawa Centralna **1060** a.	...	...	...	|	...	...	...	...	|	2248	|	|	...	|	...	...	...	|	...	|	...	...
Karviná hl. n. d.	...	...	...	1611	...	...	...	...	1750	...	1811	|	...	|	...	...	...	2011	...	|	...	...
Český Těšín d.	...	...	...	1626	...	...	...	...	1805	...	1826	1854	...	|	...	...	...	2026	...	2054	...	...
Trinec centrum d.	...	...	...	1633	...	...	...	...	1812	...	1833	1902	...	|	...	...	...	2033	...	2102	...	...
Návsi d.	...	...	...	1640	...	...	...	...	|	...	1840	|	...	|	...	...	...	2040	...	2113	...	...
Čadca 🏛 a.	...	...	...	1658	...	...	...	...	1834	...	1858	1925	...	|	...	...	...	2058	...	...	...	...
Žilina a.	...	...	...	1726	...	...	...	...	1904	...	1926	1950	...	2101	...	...	...	2126	...	...	...	...
Poprad Tatry **1180** a.	...	...	...	...	...	...	...	...	2058	...	...	2151	...	...	...	...	...	...	...	...	...	...
Prešov **1196** a.	...	...	...	...	...	...	...	...	|	...	...	|	...	...	...	...	...	...	...	...	...	...
Košice **1180** a.	...	...	...	...	...	...	...	...	2249	...	...	2312	...	...	...	...	...	...	...	...	...	...

A – SILESIA – (12) 🍷 Praha - Warszawa and v.v.; (2) Praha - Bohumín (**213/212**) - Kraków and v.v.
B – BALTIC EXPRESS – (12) Praha - Gdynia and v.v. Classified *IC* in Poland.
C – PENDOLINO – (12) 🍷 Ostrava - Praha - Karlovy Vary and v.v.
D – CRACOVIA – (12) 🍷 Praha - Przemyśl and v.v.; (2) Praha - Bohumín (**130/131**) - Warszawa and v.v.
E – SILESIA – (12) 🍷 Praha - Warszawa and v.v.
F – OSTRAVAN – (12) 🍷 Bohumín - Praha - Františkovy Lázně and v.v.
G – 🛏 (1, 2, 3, 4 berth), 🛏 (6 berth), (12) 🍷 Praha - Košice (**1222/1223**) - Chop and v.v.
H – 🛏 (4 berth), (2) 🍷 Praha - Kraków - Przemyśl and v.v.
J – SLOVAKIA – 🛏 1, 2 cl., 🛏 2 cl., (2) Praha - Humenné and v.v.
K – CHOPIN – 🛏 1, 2 cl., (2) München - Praha (**443/442**) - Bohumín - Warszawa and v.v.
L – Also conveys 🛏 1, 2 cl. (1, 2, 3 berth) as follows: Train **461** Apr. 14 - Aug. 30; train **460** Apr. 15 - Aug. 31.

d – ①–⑥ (not Nov. 17).
e – ④–⑥ (also Oct. 26, 27, Nov. 16).
f – ⑧ (not Nov. 16).
g – ⑦ (also Oct. 28, Nov. 17; not Oct. 26, Nov. 16).
h – ⑦ (also Nov. 17).
j – ①⑤⑥ (also Oct. 26, 29, Nov. 16, 15; not Nov. 17).

◧ – R for international journeys. Uses a different classification in Poland.
♠ – Operated by LEO EXPRESS. Separate fare tariff applies.
♥ – Operated by REGIOJET. Separate fare tariff applies.
• – *SUPERCITY PENDOLINO* train, R with fee.
● – Operated by 🚌 Hranice na Morave - Valašské Meziříčí and v.v.
△ – *439 km* via Vsetín.
* – Connection by 🚌.

*Table **1160** continues on pages 499 and 500.*
*For local trains Ostrava - Český Těšín and v.v. see Table **1160a**.*

PRAHA - PÚCHOV, OSTRAVA, BOHUMÍN and ŽILINA — 1160

For additional fast trains Praha - Česká Třebová and v.v. see Table **1150**. For semi-fast trains Praha - Olomouc and v.v. see Table **1151**.
SC and *IC* trains are not available for local travel Ostravá - Bohumín or v.v.

	EC 223	*IC* 515	♥ 1017	*IC* 547	*IC* 547		*EC* 460	*LE*♠ 1263	*IC* 521	*IC* 517	♥ 1019		*IC* 549	*LE*♠ 413	*LE*♠ 413	*SC*• 519		899	♥ 1021	♥ 1023	*EN* 443	*EN* 406
	🍷	🍷 R	🍷	✕	✕			🍷 R	🍷	✕ R	🍷		🍷 R	🍷 R	🍷 R	🍷 R		🍷	🍷	🍷		
					⑧								⑧		⑤⑦	⑦						
		F			f		B L						f			g			G	H	J	K
Praha hlavní nádraží d.	1722	1731	1747	1822	1822	...	1851	1858	1922	1931	1947	...	2022	2058	2058	2128	...	2131	2144	2147	2216	2216
Kolín d.	1801	|	|	1901	1901	...	1932	1936	2001	|	|	...	2101	2136	2136	|	...	2210	|	|	2258	2258
Pardubice d.	1822	1829	1843	1922	1922	...	1954	1959	2022	2029	2043	...	2122	2201	2201	2225	...	2232	2246	2250	2327	2327
Choceň d.	|	|	|	|	|	...	|	|	|	|	|	...	|	|	|	|	...	|	|	|	|	|
Ústí nad Orlici d.	|	|	|	|	|	...	2027	2027	|	|	|	...	|	2239	2239	|	...	|	|	|	|	|
Ústí nad Orlici městó d.	|	|	|	1950	1950	...	...	|	|	|	|	...	|	|	|	|	...	|	|	|	|	|
Česká Třebová d.	1856	|	1916	1959	1959	...	...	|	2056	|	2116	...	2159	|	|	|	...	2307	|	|	0007	0007
Zábřeh na Moravé d.	1921	|	1939	2022	2022	...	...	2055	2121	|	2139	...	2222	2307	2307	|	...	2330	2342	|	|	|
Olomouc d.	1953	1941	2001	2044	2044	...	...	2117	2151	2141	2201	...	2244	2331	2331	2338	...	2352	0004	0008	0059	0059
Přerov d.	|	|	|	|	|	...	...	2134	|	|	|	...	|	2348	2348	|	...	0005	|	|	|	|
Hranice na Moravě d.	2033	|	2035	2115	2115	...	...	2155	2223	|	2235	...	2315	0009	0009	|	...	...	|	|	|	|
Valašské Meziříčí d.	|	|	|	|	|	...	...	|	*2247**	|	|	...	|	|	|	|	...	...	|	|	|	|
Vsetín d.	|	|	|	|	|	...	...	|	*2303**	|	|	...	|	|	|	|	...	...	|	|	|	|
Horní Lideč 🏛 **1180** d.	|	|	|	|	|	...	...	|	...	|	|	...	|	|	|	|	...	...	|	|	|	|
Púchov **1180** a.	|	|	|	|	|	...	...	|	...	|	|	...	|	|	|	|	...	...	|	|	|	|
Ostrava Svinov d.	2058	2034	2102	2147	2147	...	...	2225	...	2234	2302	...	2342	0039	0039	0031	...	...	0100	0105	0202	0202
Opava východ a.	|	|	|	|	|	...	...	|	...	|	|	...	|	|	|	0052	...	...	|	|	|	|
Ostrava hl. n. d.	|	2042	2111	2155	2155	...	...	2232	...	2242	2308	...	2348	0046	0046	...	...	...	0108	0113	0210	0210
Havířov d.	|	|	2133	|	|	...	...	|	...	|	|	...	|	|	|	...	...	...	0127	|	|	|
Bohumín a.	2114	2050	|	2201	2201	...	...	2238	...	2250	2316	...	2356	0052	0052	...	...	...	|	|	0218	0218
Bohumín d.	2114	...	|	...	2203	...	...	2240	...	...	...	...	...	...	0143	...	...	...	|	|	0259	0405
Katowice **1076** a.	|	...	|	...	|	...	...	|	...	...	...	...	...	...	|	...	...	...	|	|	|	|
Kraków Glowny **1076** a.	|	...	|	...	|	...	...	|	...	...	...	...	...	...	0346	...	...	...	|	0446	|	0628
Warszawa Centralna **1060** a.	|	...	|	...	|	...	...	|	...	...	...	...	...	...	...	...	...	...	|	...	|	0917
Karviná hl. n. d.	|	...	|	...	2213	...	...	2250	...	...	...	...	...	...	...	...	...	...	|	...	|	...
Český Těšín d.	|	...	2154	...	2228	...	...	2305	...	...	...	...	...	...	...	...	...	...	|	...	|	...
Trinec centrum d.	|	...	2202	...	2237	...	...	2313	...	...	...	...	...	...	...	...	...	...	|	...	|	...
Návsi d.	|	...	2213	...	2245	...	...	|	...	...	...	...	...	...	...	...	...	...	|	...	|	...
Čadca 🏛 a.	2213	...	...	...	...	...	...	2336	...	...	...	...	...	...	...	...	...	...	0212	...	0351	...
Žilina a.	2245	...	...	...	...	...	...	0001	...	...	...	...	...	...	...	...	...	...	0238	...	0417	...
Poprad Tatry **1180** a.	...	...	...	...	...	...	...	0151	...	...	...	...	...	...	...	...	...	...	0432	...	0614	...
Prešov **1196** a.	...	...	...	...	...	...	...	|	...	...	...	...	...	...	...	...	...	...	|	...	|	...
Košice **1180** a.	...	...	...	...	...	...	...	0307	...	...	...	...	...	...	...	...	...	...	0608	...	0812	...

	♥ 1020	♥ 1022	*EN* 407	*EN* 442	*LE*♠ 410	*LE*♠ 410	*IC* 518	♥ 1000	*IC* 520	*LE*♠ 1250	*SC*• 516	*EC* 461	♥ 1002	*SC*• 514	*IC* 546	*IC* 546	♥ 1004	♥ 1024	*EC* 222	*LE*♠ 412	*LE*♠ 412	*IC* 512
	🍷	🍷	R	R	🍷 R	🍷 R	🍷 R	🍷	🍷	🍷 R	🍷 R		🍷	🍷 R	🍷	🍷	🍷	🍷	🍷	🍷 R	🍷 R	🍷 R
						④–①	①–⑥	①–⑥						①⑤⑥		①–⑥	①–⑥	⑦			①⑥	
	G	H	J	J			d	d				B L		j		d	d	h				F
Košice **1180** d.	2142	...	...	2207	...	...	...	...	...	2319	...	...	...	...	...	...	...	...	...	...	...	...
Prešov **1196** d.	|	...	...	|	...	...	...	...	...	0001	...	...	...	...	...	...	...	...	...	...	...	...
Poprad Tatry **1180** d.	2259	...	...	2342	...	...	...	...	...	0133	...	...	...	...	...	...	...	...	...	...	...	...
Žilina d.	0049	...	...	0146	...	...	...	...	...	0321	...	...	...	...	...	...	...	...	0521	...	...	...
Čadca 🏛 d.	0115	...	...	0213	...	...	...	...	...	0353	...	...	...	...	...	...	...	...	0550	...	...	...
Návsi d.	|	...	...	|	...	...	...	...	...	|	...	...	...	...	...	0508	0543	...	|	...	...	...
Trinec centrum d.	|	...	...	|	...	...	...	...	...	0417	...	...	...	...	...	0516	0554	...	|	...	...	...
Český Těšín d.	|	...	...	|	...	...	...	...	...	0424	...	...	...	...	...	0526	0603	...	|	...	...	...
Karviná hl. n. d.	|	...	...	|	...	...	...	...	...	0439	...	...	...	...	...	0540	|	...	|	...	...	...
Warszawa Centralna **1060** a.	|	...	2000	|	...	...	...	...	...	|	...	...	...	...	...	|	|	...	|	...	...	...
Kraków Glowny **1076** d.	|	0058	2243	|	...	0011	...	...	...	|	...	...	...	...	...	|	|	...	|	...	0409	...
Katowice **1076** d.	|	|	|	|	...	|	...	...	...	|	...	...	...	...	...	|	|	...	|	...	|	...
Bohumín a.	|	|	0102	0309	...	0233	...	...	...	0448	...	...	...	...	...	0550	|	...	0643	...	0624	...
Bohumín d.	|	|	0327	0327	0349	0349	0353	0437	...	0451	0501	...	...	...	0553	0553	|	0637	0645	0649	0649	0701
Havířov d.	0208	|	|	|	|	|	|	|	...	|	|	...	...	...	|	|	0623	|	|	|	|	|
Ostrava hl. n. d.	0227	0326	0336	0336	0356	0356	0402	0445	...	0458	0510	...	...	...	0602	0602	0645	0645	|	0658	0658	0710
Opava východ d.	|	|	|	|	|	|	|	|	...	|	|	...	0520	0555	|	|	|	|	|	|	|	|
Ostrava Svinov d.	0235	0334	|	|	0403	0403	0410	0453	...	0505	0518	...	0553	0618	0609	0609	0653	0653	0701	0705	0705	0718
Púchov **1180** d.	|	|	|	|	|	|	|	|	...	|	|	...	|	|	|	|	|	|	|	|	|	|
Horní Lideč 🏛 **1180** d.	|	|	|	|	|	|	|	|	...	|	|	...	|	|	|	|	|	|	|	|	|	|
Vsetín d.	|	|	|	|	|	|	|	|	*0446**	|	|	...	|	|	|	|	|	|	|	|	|	|
Valašské Meziříčí d.	|	|	|	|	|	|	|	|	*0504**	|	|	...	|	|	|	|	|	|	|	|	|	|
Hranice na Moravě d.	|	|	|	|	0433	0433	0437	0520	0524	0535	|	...	0620	|	0643	0643	0720	0720	0730	0735	0735	|
Přerov d.	|	|	|	|	0457	0457	|	|	|	0559	|	...	|	|	|	|	|	|	|	0759	0759	|
Olomouc d.	0328	0428	0440	0440	0511	0511	0508	0550	0603	0613	0611	...	0650	0711	0716	0716	0750	0750	0803	0813	0813	0811
Zábřeh na Moravé d.	0349	|	|	|	0533	0533	0530	0613	0640	0634	|	...	0713	|	0739	0739	0813	0813	0840	0834	0834	|
Česká Třebová d.	|	|	0531	0531	|	|	|	0635	0702	|	|	...	0735	|	0802	0802	0835	0835	0902	|	|	|
Ústí nad Orlicí město d.	|	|	|	|	|	|	|	|	|	|	|	...	|	|	0809	0809	|	|	|	|	|	|
Ústí nad Orlicí d.	|	|	|	|	0602	0602	|	|	|	0702	|	0734	|	|	|	|	|	|	|	0902	0902	|
Choceň d.	|	|	|	|	|	|	|	|	|	|	|	|	|	|	|	|	|	|	|	|	|	|
Pardubice d.	0444	0543	0610	0610	0627	0627	0623	0708	0737	0727	0723	0803	0808	0825	0837	0837	0908	0908	0937	0927	0927	0923
Kolín d.	|	|	|	|	0646	0646	|	|	0758	0746	|	0824	|	|	0858	0858	|	|	0958	0946	0946	|
Praha hlavní nádraží a.	0540	0639	0751	0751	0727	0727	0724	0809	0836	0827	0824	0906	0909	0927	0936	0936	1009	1009	1036	1027	1027	1024

CONTINUED FROM PREVIOUS PAGE. FOR FOOTNOTES SEE PAGE 498. TABLE CONTINUES ON NEXT PAGE.

OSTRAVA - ČESKÝ TĚŠÍN LOCAL TRAINS — 1160a

Opava východ d.	...	0642	...	...	0742	...	...	0842	...	0942		...	1942	...	2042	...	...	*2142*	...	...	*2246*
Ostrava Svinov a.	...	0716	...	...	0814	...	...	0913	...	1014		...	2016	...	2113	...	...	*2212*	...	...	*2315*
Ostrava Svinov d.	0634	0719	...	0734	0819	...	0834	0921	0934	1019		1934	2020	2039	2120	...	2130	2220	...	2239	2350
Ostrava hl. n. a.	0640	|	...	0740	|	...	0840	|	0940	|	and	1940	|	2046	|	...	2136	|	...	2246	|
Ostrava hl. n. d.	0641	|	...	0741	|	...	0841	|	0941	|	hourly	1941	|	2047	|	...	2137	|	...	2247	|
Havířov d.	|	0746	...	|	0846	...	|	0946	|	1046	until	|	2046	|	2146	...	|	2246	...	|	0016
Bohumín d.	0648	|	...	0748	|	...	0848	|	0948	|		1948	|	2055	|	...	2144	|	...	2255	...
Karviná hl. n. d.	0701	|	...	0801	|	...	0901	|	1001	|		2001	|	2108	|	...	2157	|	...	2308	...
Český Těšín d.	0718	0809	...	0818	0909	...	0927	1009	1018	1109		2018	2109	2125	2209	...	2214	2309	...	2325	...
Trinec centrum d.	0730	...	...	0830	...	...	0930	...	1030	...		2030	...	2136	...	...	2225	...	...	2336	...
Návsi a.	0746	...	...	0846	...	...	0942	...	1046	...		2046	...	2150	...	...	2238	...	...	2349	...

1160 ŽILINA, BOHUMÍN, OSTRAVA and PÚCHOV - PRAHA

For additional fast trains Praha - Česká Třebová and v.v. see Table **1150**. For semi-fast trains Praha - Olomouc and v.v. see Table **1151**.
SC and *IC* trains are not available for local travel Ostravá - Bohumín or v.v.

	♥ 1006 🍷	*EC* 144 🍷	♥ 1008 🍷	*EC* 220 🍷 ●	*LE*♠ 1252 🍷 [R]	*IC* 510 🍷 [R]	*EC* 261 B	*LE*♠ 1254 🍷 [R]	348 🍷	*EC* 116 🍷 E◧	♥ 1010 🍷	♥ 1010 🍷 ⑦ h	*EC* 128 🍷 ●	*LE*♠ 1256 🍷 [R]	*EC* 142 🍷	♥ 1012 🍷	*EC* 126 🍷 ●	*LE*♠ 1258 🍷 [R]	*SC*• 506 🍷 [R]	*EC* 263 B	346 🍷	*EC* 114 🍷 D◧
Košice **1180** d.	...	...	0350	...	...	...	...	0342	...	...	...	...	...	...	...	0748	...	...	...	...	...	...
Prešov **1196** d.	...	...	|	...	...	...	...	0415	...	...	...	...	...	...	...	|	...	...	...	...	...	...
Poprad Tatry **1180** d.	...	...	0442	...	...	...	...	0540	...	...	...	...	...	...	...	0912	...	...	...	...	...	...
Žilina d.	...	0634	0703	...	...	...	...	0743	0834	...	...	...	...	...	1034	1103	...	...	...	...	1234	...
Čadca 🏛 d.	...	0701	0730	...	...	...	...	0825	0901	...	...	...	...	...	1101	1130	...	...	...	...	1301	...
Návsi d.	0641	0720	|	...	...	...	...	|	0920	...	...	0942	...	...	1120	|	...	...	...	...	1320	...
Třinec centrum d.	0652	0727	0755	...	...	...	...	0849	0927	...	...	0953	...	...	1127	1155	...	...	...	...	1327	...
Český Těšín d.	0701	0735	0803	...	...	...	...	0856	0935	...	...	1001	...	...	1135	1203	...	...	...	...	1335	...
Karviná hl. n. d.	|	0750	|	...	...	...	...	0911	0950	...	...	|	...	...	1150	|	...	...	...	...	1350	...
Warszawa Centralna **1060** a.	|	|	|	...	...	...	...	|	|	0522	...	|	...	...	|	|	...	...	...	...	|	...
Kraków Glowny **1076** d.	|	|	|	...	...	...	...	|	|	|	...	|	...	...	|	|	...	...	...	...	|	1110
Katowice **1076** d.	|	|	|	...	...	...	...	|	|	0816	...	|	...	...	|	|	...	...	...	...	|	|
Bohumín a.	|	0800	|	...	...	...	...	0920	1000	0943	...	|	...	...	1200	|	...	...	...	...	1400	1313
Bohumín d.	|	0804	|	...	0851	0901	...	0951	1001	1004	...	|	...	1151	1204	|	...	1251	...	...	1401	1404
Havířov d.	0723	|	0823	...	|	|	...	|	|	|	1023	1023	...	|	|	1223	...	|	...	...	|	|
Ostrava hl. n. d.	0745	0813	0845	...	0858	0910	...	0958	1007	1013	1045	1045	...	1158	1213	1245	...	1258	1310	...	1407	1413
Opava východ d.	|	|	|	...	|	|	...	|	|	|	|	|	...	|	|	|	...	|	|	...	|	|
Ostrava Svinov d.	0753	0821	0853	...	0905	0918	...	1005	1015	1021	1053	1053	...	1205	1221	1253	...	1305	1318	...	1415	1421
Púchov **1180** d.	|	|	|	0808	|	|	...	|	...	|	|	|	1008	|	|	|	1208	|	|	...	...	|
Horní Lideč 🏛 **1180** d.	|	|	|	0833	|	|	...	|	...	|	|	|	1033	|	|	|	1233	|	|	...	...	|
Vsetín d.	|	|	|	0852	|	|	...	|	...	|	|	|	1052	|	|	|	1252	|	|	...	...	|
Valašské Meziříčí d.	|	|	|	0910	|	|	...	|	...	|	|	|	1110	|	|	|	1310	|	|	...	...	|
Hranice na Moravě d.	0820	0846	0920	0930	0935	|	...	1035	...	1046	1120	1120	1130	1235	1246	1320	1330	1335	|	...	...	1446
Přerov d.	|	|	|	|	0959	|	...	1059	...	|	|	|	|	1259	|	|	|	1359	|	...	...	|
Olomouc d.	0850	0916	0950	1003	1013	1011	...	1113	...	1116	1150	1150	1203	1313	1316	1351	1403	1413	1411	...	...	1516
Zábřeh na Moravé d.	0913	0939	1013	1040	1034	|	...	1134	...	1139	1213	1213	1240	1334	1339	1413	1440	1434	|	...	...	1539
Česká Třebová d.	0935	1002	1035	1102	|	|	...	|	...	1202	1235	1235	1302	|	1402	1435	1502	|	|	...	...	1602
Ústí nad Orlicí město d.	|	1009	|	|	|	|	...	|	...	|	|	|	|	|	|	|	|	|	|	...	...	|
Ústí nad Orlicí d.	|	|	|	|	1102	|	1134	1202	...	|	|	|	|	1402	|	|	|	1502	|	1534	...	|
Choceň d.	|	|	|	|	|	|	|	|	...	|	|	|	|	|	|	|	|	|	|	|	...	|
Pardubice d.	1008	1037	1108	1137	1127	1123	1203	1227	...	1237	1308	1308	1337	1427	1437	1508	1537	1527	1523	1603	...	1637
Kolín d.	|	1058	|	1158	1146	|	1227	1246	...	1258	|	|	1358	1446	1458	|	1558	1546	|	1627	...	1658
Praha hlavní nádraží a.	1109	1136	1209	1236	1227	1219	1312	1327	...	1336	1409	1409	1436	1527	1536	1609	1636	1627	1624	1712	...	1736

	EC 131 🍷 D◧	♥ 1014 🍷	*EC* 124 🍷 ●	*LE*♠ 1260 🍷 [R]	*SC*• 504 🍷 [R] C	*SC*• 502 🍷 [R] ⑦ g	*EC* 140 🍷	♥ 1016 🍷	*LE*♠ 1262 🍷 [R]	*SC*• 500 🍷 [R]	*EC* 122 🍷 ●		*EC* 265 B	344 🍷	*EC* 212 🍷 A◧	*EC* 112 🍷 A◧		♥ 1018 🍷	*SC*• 240 🍷 [R]	*EC* 120 🍷 ●	342 🍷	340 🍷
Košice **1180** d.	...	...	...	...	...	...	...	...	...	...	...	...	...	...	...	...	...	...	1448	...	...	...
Prešov **1196** d.	...	...	...	...	...	...	...	...	...	...	...	...	...	...	...	...	...	...	|	...	...	...
Poprad Tatry **1180** d.	...	...	...	...	...	...	...	...	...	...	...	...	...	...	...	...	...	...	1610	...	...	...
Žilina d.	...	...	...	...	...	...	1434	...	...	...	...	...	...	1634	...	...	...	...	1803	...	1834	2034
Čadca 🏛 d.	...	...	...	...	...	...	1501	...	...	...	...	...	...	1701	...	...	...	...	1835	...	1901	2101
Návsi d.	...	...	...	...	...	...	1520	...	...	...	...	...	...	1720	...	...	...	...	|	...	1920	2120
Třinec centrum d.	...	...	...	...	...	...	1527	...	...	...	...	...	...	1727	...	...	...	...	|	...	1927	2127
Český Těšín d.	...	...	...	...	...	...	1535	...	...	...	...	...	...	1735	...	...	...	...	1904	...	1935	2135
Karviná hl. n. d.	...	...	...	...	...	...	1550	...	...	...	...	...	...	1750	...	...	...	...	|	...	1950	2150
Warszawa Centralna **1060** a.	0905	...	...	...	...	...	|	...	...	...	...	...	...	|	...	1334	...	...	|	...	|	|
Kraków Glowny **1076** d.	|	...	...	...	...	...	|	...	...	...	...	...	...	|	1537	|	...	...	|	...	|	|
Katowice **1076** d.	1146	...	...	...	...	...	|	...	...	...	...	...	...	|	|	1621	...	...	|	...	|	|
Bohumín a.	1322	...	...	...	...	...	1600	...	...	...	...	...	...	1800	1740	1748	...	...	|	...	2000	2200
Bohumín d.	1404	...	...	1451	...	...	1604	...	1659	...	...	...	...	1801	1804	1804	...	...	|	...	2001	2201
Havířov d.	|	1423	...	|	...	...	|	1623	|	...	...	...	...	|	|	|	...	1823	|	...	|	|
Ostrava hl. n. d.	1413	1445	...	1458	1510	...	1613	1645	1706	1710	...	...	...	1807	1813	1813	...	1846	1934	...	2007	2207
Opava východ d.	|	|	...	|	|	1555	|	|	|	|	...	...	...	|	|	|	...	|	|	...	|	|
Ostrava Svinov d.	1421	1453	...	1505	1518	1619	1621	1653	1713	1718	...	...	...	1815	1821	1821	...	1854	1942	...	2015	2215
Púchov **1180** d.	|	|	1408	|	|	|	|	|	|	|	1608	...	...	...	|	|	...	|	|	1808	...	...
Horní Lideč 🏛 **1180** d.	|	|	1433	|	|	|	|	|	|	|	1633	...	...	...	|	|	...	|	|	1833	...	...
Vsetín d.	|	|	1452	|	|	|	|	|	|	|	1652	...	...	...	|	|	...	|	|	1852	...	...
Valašské Meziříčí d.	|	|	1510	|	|	|	|	|	|	|	1710	...	...	...	|	|	...	|	|	1910	...	...
Hranice na Moravě d.	1446	1520	1530	1535	|	|	1646	1720	|	|	1730	...	...	...	1846	1846	...	1920	|	1948	...	...
Přerov d.	|	|	|	1559	|	|	|	|	1759	|	|	...	...	...	|	|	...	|	|	|	...	...
Olomouc d.	1516	1550	1603	1613	1611	1711	1716	1751	1813	1811	1803	...	...	...	1916	1916	...	1951	2035	2026	...	...
Zábřeh na Moravé d.	1539	1613	1640	1634	|	|	1739	1813	1834	|	1840	...	...	...	1939	1939	...	2013	|	2100	...	...
Česká Třebová d.	1602	1635	1702	|	|	|	1802	1835	|	|	1902	...	...	...	2002	2002	...	2035	2115	2122	...	...
Ústí nad Orlicí město d.	|	|	|	|	|	|	|	|	|	|	|	...	...	...	|	|	...	|	|	|	...	...
Ústí nad Orlicí d.	|	|	|	1702	|	|	|	|	1902	|	|	...	1934	...	|	|	...	|	|	2131	...	...
Choceň d.	|	|	|	|	|	|	|	|	|	|	|	...	|	...	|	|	...	|	|	2143	...	...
Pardubice d.	1637	1708	1737	1727	1723	1823	1837	1908	1927	1923	1937	...	2003	...	2037	2037	...	2108	2148	2202	...	...
Kolín d.	1658	|	1758	1746	|	|	1858	|	1946	|	1958	...	2027	...	2058	2058	...	|	2210	2225	...	...
Praha hlavní nádraží a.	1736	1809	1836	1827	1824	1921	1936	2009	2027	2021	2036	...	2110	...	2136	2136	...	2209	2247	2303	...	...

CONTINUED FROM PREVIOUS PAGES. FOR FOOTNOTES SEE PAGE 498.

1160a ČESKÝ TĚŠÍN - OSTRAVA LOCAL TRAINS

Návsi d.	0616	...	...	0714	...	...	0818	...	0914	...		1914	...	2018	...	...	2114	...	...	2218	...
Třinec centrum d.	0629	...	...	0731	...	...	0831	...	0931	...		1931	...	2031	...	...	2131	...	...	2231	...
Český Těšín d.	0646	0647	...	0746	0747	...	0846	0847	0946	0947		1946	1947	2046	2047	...	2146	2147	...	2246	2247
Karviná hl. n. d.	0703	|	...	0803	|	...	0903	|	1003	|	and	2003	|	2103	|	...	2203	|	...	2303	|
Bohumín d.	0718	|	...	0818	|	...	0918	|	1018	|	hourly	2018	|	2118	|	...	2218	|	...	2318	|
Havířov d.	|	0714	...	|	0814	...	|	0914	|	1014	until	|	2014	|	2114	...	|	2214	...	|	2314
Ostrava hl. n. a.	0724	|	...	0824	|	...	0924	|	1024	|		2024	|	2124	|	...	2224	|	...	2324	|
Ostrava hl. n. d.	0725	|	...	0825	|	...	0925	|	1025	|		2025	|	2125	|	...	2225	|	...	2325	|
Ostrava Svinov a.	0731	0739	...	0830	0839	...	0930	0939	1030	1039		2030	2039	2130	2139	...	2230	2239	...	2330	2339
Ostrava Svinov d.	...	0742	...	...	0842	...	...	0942	...	1042		...	2042	...	2156	...	...	*2259*	...	...	2348
Opava východ a.	...	0815	...	...	0914	...	...	1015	...	1114		...	2114	...	2229	...	...	*2329*	...	...	0017

BOHUMÍN - OSTRAVA - UHERSKÉ HRADIŠTĚ - BŘECLAV - BRNO and WIEN 1162

For faster trains Praha - Bratislava and v.v. see Table **1150**. For other local trains Bohumín - Brno see next page.

km		*EN* 407	828		826 834		824	824	881	814	*EC* 101	883	883		812	*EC* 103	885		810	*EC* 105	887			808
			🍷				🍷	🍷	🍷	🍷		🍷	🍷		🍷		🍷		🍷		🍷			🍷
		A	Ⓐ	Ⓐ			f	Ⓐ	f		B§	f				C§				D§			Ⓐ	
0	**Bohumín** 1160 d.	0145	...	...	...	...	...	...	...	...	0642	...	...	...	...	0842	...	...	...	1042	...	...	...	...
8	**Ostrava** hl. n. 1160 d.	0154	...	...	...	...	...	...	...	...	0651	...	...	...	...	0851	...	...	...	1051	...	...	...	...
13	**Ostrava** Svinov 1160 d.	|	...	...	...	...	...	...	...	...	0659	...	...	...	...	0859	...	...	...	1059	...	...	...	...
50	Hranice na Moravě 1160 d.	|	...	...	...	...	...	...	...	...	0726	...	...	...	...	0926	...	...	...	1126	...	...	...	...
	Praha hl. n. **1151 1160** d.	|	...	...	...	...	...	...	...	...	|	0501	...	...	...	|	0701	...	...	|	0901	...	...	...
101	**Olomouć** 1160 d.	|	...	...	...	...	...	...	0557	0705	|	0731	0731	...	0905	|	0931	...	1105	|	1131	...	...	1305
123	Přerov 1160 d.	|	...	0443	...	0542	...	...	0612	0720	0749	0746	0746	0739	0920	0949	0946	0939	1120	1149	1146	1139	1243	1320
138	Hulín d.	|	...	0458	...	0600	...	...	0622	0731	|	0756	0756	0801	0931	|	0956	1001	1131	|	1156	1201	1301	1331
151	Otrokovice ▷ d.	|	...	0510	...	0612	...	...	0632	0742	0808	0805	0805	0814	0942	1008	1005	1014	1142	1208	1205	1214	1314	1342
169	Staré Město U.H. ⊖ a.	|	...	0526	...	0628	...	...	0644	0753	0820	0817	0817	0830	0953	1020	1017	1030	1153	1220	1217	1230	1330	1353
169	Staré Město U.H. ⊖ 1163 d.	|	...	0537	...	0637	...	0704	0658	0757	0821	0833	0833	0837	0957	1021	1033	1037	1157	1221	1233	1237	1337	1357
174	Uherské Hradiště 1163 a.	|	...	|	...	|	...	|	0704	|	|	0839	0839	|	|	|	1039	|	|	|	1239	|	|	|
191	Uherský Brod 1163 a.	|	...	|	...	|	...	|	0722	|	|	0856	0856	|	|	|	1056	|	|	|	1256	|	|	|
205	**Luhačovice** 1163 a.	|	...	|	...	|	...	|	0741	|	|	0920	0920	|	|	|	1120	|	|	|	1320	|	|	|
203	Hodonin d.	|	0522	0608	0619	0708	0724	0724	...	0823	0838	...	...	0908	1023	1038	...	1108	1223	1238	...	1308	1408	1423
223	Břeclav a.	0338	0536	0625	0634	0725	0736	0736	...	0835	0849	...	...	0925	1035	1049	...	1125	1235	1249	...	1325	1425	1435
223	Břeclav 1150 d.	0422	0542	...	0641	...	0742	0742	...	0844	0855	...	...	...	1044	1055	...	...	1244	1255	...	...	...	1444
282	**Brno** hlavní nádrazi 1150 a.	|	0622	...	0722	...	0822	0822	...	0922	|	...	...	...	1122	|	...	...	1322	|	...	...	...	1522
311	**Wien** Hbf 1150 a.	0525	...	...	...	...	...	...	...	...	0949	...	...	...	...	1149	...	...	...	1349	...	...	...	...

	889		822	*EC* 131		806	891		820	804	*EC* 107		893			802	895	*EC* 109		800	897		2
	🍷		🍷			🍷	🍷		🍷	🍷			🍷			🍷	🍷				🍷		
			Ⓐ	E§	Ⓐ				Ⓐ		F§							G§		Ⓑg			
Bohumín 1160 d.	...	...	...	1342	...	...	...	...	...	...	1642	...	...	...	...	...	...	1842	...	...	...	...	...
Ostrava hl. n. 1160 d.	...	...	...	1351	...	...	...	...	...	...	1651	...	...	...	...	...	...	1851	...	...	...	...	...
Ostrava Svinov 1160 d.	...	...	...	1359	...	...	...	...	...	...	1659	...	...	...	...	...	...	1859	...	...	...	...	...
Hranice na Moravě 1160 d.	...	...	...	1426	...	...	...	...	...	...	1726	...	...	...	...	...	...	1926	...	...	...	...	...
Praha hl. n. **1151 1160** d.	1101	...	...	|	...	...	1301	...	...	...	|	...	1501	...	...	...	1701	|	...	...	1901	...	...
Olomouć 1160 d.	1331	...	...	|	...	1505	1531	...	...	1708	|	...	1731	...	...	1908	1931	|	...	2105	2134	...	...
Přerov 1160 d.	1346	1339	...	1449	1439	1520	1546	1539	...	1722	1749	...	1746	1739	1910	1922	1946	1949	...	2120	2149	...	2243
Hulín d.	1356	1401	...	|	1501	1531	1556	1601	...	1732	|	...	1756	1801	1928	1932	1956	|	←	2131	2159	...	2259
Otrokovice ▷ d.	1405	1414	...	1508	1514	1542	1605	1614	...	1742	1808	...	1805	1814	1939	1942	2006	2008	2014	2142	2206	2213	2323
Staré Město U.H. ⊖ a.	1417	1430	...	1520	1530	1553	1617	1630	...	1753	1820	...	1817	1830	→	1953	2017	2020	2030	2153	|	2230	2342
Staré Město U.H. ⊖ 1163 d.	1433	1437	1504	1521	1537	1557	1633	1637	1704	1757	1821	...	1833	1837	...	1957	2034	2021	2037	2157	j	...	...
Uherské Hradiště 1163 a.	1439	|	|	|	|	|	1639	|	|	|	|	...	1839	|	...	|	2040	|	|	|	...	...	...
Uherský Brod 1163 a.	1456	|	|	|	|	|	1656	|	|	|	|	...	1901	|	...	|	|	|	|	|	...	...	...
Luhačovice 1163 a.	1520	|	|	|	|	|	1720	|	|	|	|	...	1922	|	...	|	h	|	|	|	...	...	...
Hodonin d.	...	1508	1524	1538	1608	1623	...	1708	1724	1823	1838	...	...	1908	...	2023	...	2038	2108	2217	...	...	...
Břeclav a.	...	1525	1536	1549	1625	1635	...	1725	1736	1835	1849	...	...	1925	...	2035	...	2049	2125	2229	...	...	...
Břeclav 1150 d.	...	...	1542	...	...	1644	...	...	1742	1844	1855	...	...	...	...	2044	...	2055	...	...	...	...	...
Brno hlavní nádrazi 1150 a.	...	...	1622	...	...	1722	...	...	1822	1922	|	...	...	...	...	2122	...	|	...	...	...	...	...
Wien Hbf 1150 a.	...	...	...	...	...	...	...	...	...	...	1949	...	...	...	...	...	...	2149	...	...	...	...	...

	EN 406	896	894	801			*EC* 108	892		803	*EC* 106	890	890		805	888		807	*EC* 130	886		809	
				🍷						🍷		🍷	🍷		🍷	🍷		🍷		🍷		🍷	
	A	f		f		Ⓐ	G§				F§		f						E§				Ⓐ
Wien Hbf 1150 d.	2319	...	...	...	...	...	0610	...	...	...	0810	...	...	...	...	...	...	...	...	...	...	...	...
Brno hlavní nádrazi 1150 d.	|	...	...	...	...	...	|	...	...	0636	|	...	...	...	0836	...	...	1036	...	...	...	1236	...
Břeclav 1150 a.	0034	...	...	...	...	...	0704	...	...	0715	0904	...	...	...	0915	...	...	1115	...	...	...	1315	...
Břeclav d.	0100	...	...	0525	...	0535	0709	...	0635	0721	0909	...	...	0835	0921	...	1035	1121	1209	...	1235	1321	1335
Hodonin d.	|	...	...	0538	...	0554	0721	...	0654	0738	0921	...	...	0854	0938	...	1054	1138	1221	...	1254	1338	1354
Luhačovice 1163 d.	|	...	...	|	...	|	|	h	|	|	|	...	0831	|	|	1031	|	|	|	1231	|	|	|
Uherský Brod 1163 d.	|	...	...	|	...	|	|	|	|	|	|	...	0857	|	|	1057	|	|	|	1257	|	|	|
Uherské Hradiště 1163 d.	|	...	...	|	...	|	|	0714	|	|	|	...	0914	|	|	1114	|	|	|	1314	|	|	|
Staré Město U.H. ⊖ 1163 a.	|	...	k	0556	...	0624	0737	0720	0724	0756	0937	...	0920	0924	0956	1120	1124	1156	1237	1320	1324	1356	1424
Staré Město U.H. ⊖ d.	|	0412	|	0601	0627	0627	0739	0741	0729	0801	0939	0941	0941	0928	1001	1141	1128	1201	1239	1341	1327	1401	1427
Otrokovice ▷ d.	|	0426	0555	0614	0644	0644	0751	0756	0746	0814	0951	0956	0956	0945	1014	1156	1145	1214	1251	1356	1345	1414	1445
Hulín d.	|	0437	0605	0628	0659	0659	|	0805	0808	0828	|	1005	1005	1008	1028	1205	1208	1228	|	1405	1408	1428	1500
Přerov 1160 d.	|	0448	0616	0639	0713	0713	0808	0816	0822	0839	1009	1016	1016	1022	1039	1216	1222	1239	1309	1416	1422	1439	1514
Olomouć 1160 d.	|	0502	0631	0652	...	...	|	0831	...	0852	|	1031	1031	...	1052	1231	...	1252	|	1431	...	1452	...
Praha hl. n. **1151 1160** a.	|	0736	0902	...	...	...	|	1106	...	...	|	1306	1306	...	...	1506	...	...	|	1706	...	...	...
Hranice na Moravě 1160 d.	|	...	...	...	...	...	0830	...	...	...	1030	...	...	...	...	...	...	...	1330	...	...	...	...
Ostrava Svinov 1160 a.	|	...	...	...	...	...	0855	...	...	...	1055	...	...	...	...	...	...	...	1355	...	...	...	...
Ostrava hl. n. 1160 a.	0240	...	...	...	...	...	0903	...	...	...	1103	...	...	...	...	...	...	...	1403	...	...	...	...
Bohumín 1160 a.	0248	...	...	...	...	...	0912	...	...	...	1112	...	...	...	...	...	...	...	1412	...	...	...	...

	823	*EC* 104	884		811		825	*EC* 102	882		813	880	827		*EC* 100	815	858	829		2	831 833	2	835
	🍷		🍷		🍷		🍷		🍷		🍷	🍷				🍷		🍷					
	Ⓐ	D§				Ⓐ	Ⓐ	C§					Ⓐ		B§			Ⓑg					
Wien Hbf 1150 d.	...	1410	...	...	...	...	...	1610	...	...	...	...	...	...	1810	...	...	...	...	...	...	...	...
Brno hlavní nádrazi 1150 d.	1336	|	...	...	1436	...	1534	|	...	...	1636	...	1736	...	|	1836	...	1935	...	...	2036	...	2236
Břeclav 1150 a.	1415	1504	...	...	1515	...	1615	1704	...	...	1715	...	1815	...	1904	1915	...	2014	...	...	2117	...	2315
Břeclav d.	1421	1509	...	1435	1521	1535	1621	1709	...	1635	1721	...	1821	1835	1909	1921	...	2021	2035	...	2125	...	2321
Hodonin d.	1434	1521	...	1454	1538	1554	1634	1721	...	1654	1738	...	1834	1854	1921	1938	...	2034	2054	...	2140	2145	2335
Luhačovice 1163 d.	|	|	1431	|	|	|	|	|	1631	|	|	1803	...	|	|	|	1942	...	|	...	...	|	...
Uherský Brod 1163 d.	|	|	1457	|	|	|	|	|	1657	|	|	1827	...	|	|	|	2001	...	|	...	...	|	...
Uherské Hradiště 1163 d.	|	|	1514	|	|	|	|	|	1714	|	|	1845	...	|	|	|	2019	...	|	...	...	|	...
Staré Město U.H. ⊖ 1163 a.	1452	1537	1520	1524	1556	1624	1652	1737	1720	1724	1756	1852	...	1924	1937	1956	2025	...	2124	...	...	2213	...
Staré Město U.H. ⊖ d.	...	1539	1541	1528	1601	1627	...	1739	1741	1728	1801	1906	...	1927	1939	2001	...	...	2128	...	...	2214	...
Otrokovice ▷ d.	...	1551	1556	1545	1614	1645	...	1751	1756	1745	1814	1920	...	1945	1951	2014	...	...	2143	2147	...	2233	...
Hulín d.	...	|	1605	1608	1628	1700	...	|	1805	1808	1828	1933	...	2002	|	2028	...	...	...	2203	...	2245	...
Přerov 1160 d.	...	1609	1616	1622	1639	1714	...	1809	1816	1822	1839	1944	...	2016	2009	2039	...	...	...	2220	...	2300	...
Olomouć 1160 a.	...	|	1631	...	1652	...	...	|	1831	...	1852	1957	...	...	|	2052	...	...	...	2252	...	...	...
Praha hl. n. **1151 1160** a.	...	|	1906	...	...	...	...	|	2102	...	...	...	...	...	|	...	...	...	...	...	...	...	...
Hranice na Moravě 1160 d.	...	1630	...	...	...	...	...	1830	...	...	...	...	...	...	2030	...	...	...	...	...	...	...	...
Ostrava Svinov 1160 a.	...	1655	...	...	...	...	...	1855	...	...	...	...	...	...	2055	...	...	...	...	...	...	...	...
Ostrava hl. n. 1160 a.	...	1703	...	...	...	...	...	1903	...	...	...	...	...	...	2103	...	...	...	...	...	...	...	...
Bohumín 1160 a.	...	1712	...	...	...	...	...	1912	...	...	...	...	...	...	2112	...	...	...	...	...	...	...	...

A – CHOPIN – 🛏 1, 2 cl., 🛏 2 cl., (2) Warszawa - München and v.v.
B – MORAVIA – (12) 🍷 Katowice - Wien and v.v.
C – DANUBIUS – (12) 🍷 Kraków - Wien and v.v.
D – POLONIA – (12) 🍷 Warszawa - Wien and v.v.
E – BATHORY – (12) ✕ Warszawa - Budapest and v.v.
F – PORTA MORAVICA – (12) Przemyśl - Graz and v.v. ✕ Bohumín - Graz and v.v.
G – SOBIESKI – (12) ✕ Warszawa - Wien and v.v. See note ◧.

d – ①–⑥ (not July 5, Nov. 17).
e – ④⑤⑦ (Also Oct. 28, Nov. 17; not Nov. 16).
f – ①–⑥ (not Nov. 17).

g – Ⓑ (not Nov. 16).
h – To/from Veseli nad Moravou (a. 2058/d. 0700).
j – To Zlín střed (Otrokovice d. 2216, Zlín střed a. 2232).
k – From Zlín střed (d. 0528).

⊖ – Full name: Staré Město u Uherské Hradiště.
▷ – Local trains Otrokovice - Zlín: 1–2 per hour (trolleybus every 10 mins).
§ – Ⓡ for international journeys to/from Poland.
● – Timings may vary by up to 5 minutes.
◧ – Conveys on ②④⑤⑦ June 27 - Aug. 29 from Bohumín and ①②④⑥ June 30 - Sept. 1 from Wien: *EN* **1277/1276** – 🛏 (2) Warszawa - Rijeka and v.v. (Tables **89** and **99**).

1162 BRNO - PŘEROV - OSTRAVA - BOHUMÍN *Regiojet*

km		①–⑥ d					④⑤⑦ e		
0	**Brno** hlavní nádrazi ..... **1156** d.	0502	0602	0702		1902	2002	2102	...
45	Vyškov na Moravě .... **1156** d.	0538	0640	0740	and at	1940	2040	2139	...
71	Kojetin ..... d.	0558	0700	0800	the same	2000	2100	2200	...
88	Přerov ..... **1160** d.	0618	0718	0818	minutes	2018	2118	2218	...
117	Hranice na Moravě ...... **1160** d.	0640	0740	0839	past each	2039	2140	2240	...
167	**Ostrava** Svinov .... **1160** a.	0710	0810	0912	hour until	2112	2210	2310	...
172	**Ostrava** hl. n. ..... **1160** a.	0718	0818	0918	●	2118	2217	2318	...
180	**Bohumín** ..... **1160** a.	0727	0827	0927		2127	2227	2327	...

	①–⑥ d					④⑤⑦ e		
Bohumín ..... **1160** d.	0428	0528	0628		1828	1929	2028	...
Ostrava hl. n. ..... **1160** d.	0436	0536	0636	and at	1836	1937	2036	...
Ostrava Svinov .... **1160** d.	0444	0544	0644	the same	1844	1945	2044	...
Hranice na Moravě .... **1160** d.	0515	0615	0715	minutes	1915	2016	2115	...
Přerov ..... **1160** d.	0540	0640	0740	past each	1940	2040	2140	...
Kojetin ..... d.	0559	0700	0800	hour until	2000	2100	2200	...
Vyškov na Moravě .... **1156** d.	0622	0721	0821	●	2021	2122	2222	...
Brno hlavní nádrazi .. **1156** a.	0659	0759	0859		2059	2157	2256	...

FOR FOOTNOTES SEE PREVIOUS PAGE.

1163 BRNO - UHERSKÉ HRADIŠTĚ - LUHAČOVICE and BYLNICE *2nd class*

Local trains. For long distance train see Table **1162**. Operators: ČD Brno - Uherské Hradiště; Arriva Uherské Hradiště - Luhačovice, Bylnice and Vlárský průsmyk.

km		⚒	†		Ⓐ																B			
0	**Brno** hlavní nádrazi ..... d.	0512	...	...	0612	0735	...	0812	0928	...	1015	1128	...	1215	1328	...	1414	1528	...	1614	1728	...	1814	1928
67	Kyjov ..... d.	0632	...	...	0738	0834	...	0938	1032	...	1138	1232	...	1338	1432	...	1538	1632	...	1738	1832	...	1938	2032
90	Veselí nad Moravou ..... d.	0706	0706	...	0806	0900	...	1006	1100	...	1206	1300	...	1406	1500	...	1606	1700	...	1806	1900	...	2006	2100
104	Kunovice zastávka ..... d.	0721	0721	...	0822	0914	...	1022	1114	...	1222	1314	...	1422	1514	...	1622	1714	...	1822	1913	...	2022	2114
106	**Uherské Hradiště** .... **1162** a.	0724	0724	...	0827	0918	...	1027	1118	...	1227	1318	...	1427	1518	...	1627	1718	...	1827	...	...	2027	2118
111	**Staré Město u Uh. H** ⊖ **1162** a.	0758	0758	...	...	0926	...	...	1126	...	...	1326	...	...	1526	...	...	1726	...	1846	...	...	...	2126

		B		Ⓐ																	Cg	
Staré Město u Uh. H ⊖ .... **1162** d.	...	...	...	0726	0827	...	...	1027	...	...	1227	...	...	1427	...	...	1627	...	...	1827	...	...	...
Uherské Hradiště ..... **1162** d.	0534	...	...	0735	0836	...	0935	1036	...	1135	1236	...	1335	1436	...	1535	1636	...	1735	1836	...	...	2036
Kunovice zastávka ..... d.	0546	0639	...	0739	0840	...	0939	1040	...	1139	1240	...	1339	1440	...	1539	1640	...	1739	1840	...	2005	2040
Veselí nad Moravou ..... d.	0601	0701	...	0757	0901	...	0957	1101	...	1157	1301	...	1357	1501	...	1557	1701	...	1757	1901	...	2023	2101
Kyjov ..... d.	0628	0728	...	0825	0928	...	1025	1128	...	1225	1328	...	1425	1528	...	1625	1728	...	1825	1928	...	2048	2128
Brno hlavní nádrazi ..... a.	0733	0833	...	0948	1033	...	1148	1233	...	1348	1433	...	1548	1633	...	1748	1833	...	1948	2033	...	2145	2233

km			⑥	⑦									f	⑤ h	⑦ g	jt				B	Ⓑ			
0	**Staré Město u Uh. H** ⊖ **1162** d.	0632	0800	0800	0935	1000	1135	1200	1338	1400	1409	1539	1600	...	1600	...	1609	1739	1800	...	2000	2028	2129	2200
5	**Uherské Hradiště** .... **1162** d.	0639	0807	0829	0942	1029	1142	1229	1346	1410	1429	1546	1609	...	1609	...	1629	1746	1809	...	2009	2039	2136	2207
7	Kunovice ..... d.	0642	|	0832	0945	1032	1145	1232	1349	|	1432	1550	|	...	|	...	1632	1750	|	1920	|	2042	2140	2210
22	Uherský Brod ..... **1162** d.	0700	0822	0853	1004	1053	1204	1253	1410	1425	1454	1610	1625	...	1625	...	1654	1810	1825	1937	2030	2105	2200	2228
26	Újezdec u Luhačovic ..... a.	0703	|	0856	1007	1056	1207	1256	1413	|	1457	1614	|	...	|	...	1657	1813	1828	1940	2034	2108	2203	2231
26	Újezdec u Luhačovic ..... d.	0704	|	0905	1007	1105	1208	1305	1414	|	1505	1615	|	...	|	...	1705	1813	1828	1941	2036	2110	2204	2231
35	Bojkovice ..... a.	0717	0836	0917	1020	1117	1220	1317	1426	1437	1516	1628	1637	...	1637	...	1716	1827	1838	1956	2046	2122	2216	2243
63	**Bylnice** ..... a.	0754	0911	0952	...	1152	...	1352	...	1513	1552	...	1713	...	1713	...	1752	...	1915	...	...	...	2251	...
63	**Bylnice** ..... d.	...	0912	...	...	...	...	...	...	...	...	...	1715	...	1830	...	...	...	...	...	...	...	...	...
68	Vlárský průsmyk ..... a.	...	0918	...	...	...	...	...	...	...	...	...	1721	1736	1836	1844	...	...	...	...	...	...	...	...
80	**Trenčianska Teplá** ..... a.	...	...	...	...	...	...	...	...	...	...	...	...	1755	...	1955	...	...	...	...	...	...	...	...

	B	A	Ⓐ				⑥					Ⓒ					⑤ h	n	⑦ j	Cg	⑦ g		
Trenčianska Teplá ..... d.	...	...	...	...	...	...	...	...	...	...	...	...	...	...	...	...	1705	...	1805	...	...	...	...
Vlárský průsmyk ..... d.	...	...	...	...	...	...	0924	...	...	...	...	...	...	...	...	...	1724	1730	1824	1850	...	...	...
Bylnice ..... a.	...	...	...	...	...	...	0930	...	...	...	...	...	...	...	...	...	...	1736	...	1857	...	...	...
Bylnice ..... d.	...	0558	0643	...	0800	...	...	1000	...	1200	1400	1440	...	1640	...	1805	...	1805	...	1900	...	...	2013
Bojkovice ..... d.	0556	0640	0719	0731	0835	0931	...	1035	1131	1237	1437	1517	1535	1718	1731	1842	...	1842	...	1933	...	2023	2056
Újezdec u Luhačovic ..... d.	0610	0656	|	0743	0849	0943	...	1049	1143	1249	1449	|	1548	|	1744	1856	...	1856	...	1943	...	2036	2110
Uherský Brod ..... a.	0615	0659	0731	0746	0852	0946	...	1052	1146	1253	1453	1530	1552	1730	1748	1859	...	1859	...	1947	...	2039	2113
Uherský Brod ..... **1162** d.	0617	0708	0732	0750	0903	0947	...	1103	1147	1303	1503	1531	1554	1731	1754	1902	...	1902	...	1948	...	2046	2120
Kunovice ..... d.	0635	0726	|	0810	0922	1006	...	1122	1206	1322	1522	|	1612	|	1813	1921	...	1921	...	2001	2004	2104	2139
Uherské Hradiště ..... **1162** a.	...	0728	0746	0813	0925	1009	...	1125	1209	1325	1525	1545	1615	1745	1816	1924	...	1924	...	...	2007	2107	2142
Staré Město u Uh. H ⊖ .... **1162** a.	...	0738	0753	0822	0951	1017	...	1151	1217	1351	1533	1552	1622	1752	1824	1932	...	1932	...	...	2015	2114	2151

km			Ⓐ k											①–⑥ f	⑦ g									
0	**Újezdec u Luhačovic** ..... d.	0613	0710	...	0816	1012	...	1212	1416	...	1616	1746	...	1926	2003	...	2037	2112	...	2223	...	...	...	...
10	**Luhačovice** ..... a.	0627	0724	...	0830	1026	...	1226	1430	...	1630	1800	...	1940	2017	...	2051	2126	...	2247	...	...	...	...

				Ⓐ k									①–⑥ f	⑦ g									
Luhačovice ..... d.	0554	0636	...	0754	0927	...	1127	1330	...	1532	1728	...	1840	1924	...	2020	2054	...	2146	...	...	...	...
Újezdec u Luhačovic ..... a.	0608	0650	...	0838	0941	...	1141	1344	...	1546	1742	...	1854	1938	...	2034	2108	...	2200	...	...	...	...

A – From Bylnice on Ⓒ; from Bojkovice daily.
B – (2) Brno - Bojkovice and v.v. Operated by ČD.
C – (2) Vlárský průsmyk - Brno. Operated by ČD.
f – ①–⑥ (daily June 30 - Aug. 31).
g – ⑦ (not June 29 - Aug. 24).
h – ⑤ (not July 4 - Aug. 29).
j – ⑦ (also Nov. 17; not June 29 - Aug. 24, Nov. 16).
k – Not June 30 - Aug. 29.
n – ⑤⑥ (⑤⑥† July 4 - Aug. 31).
t – Change at Horné Srnie (a. 1851 / d. 1945).

⊖ – Full name is Staré Město u Uherské Hradiště.

1164 DĚČÍN - ÚSTÍ NAD LABEM - MĚLNÍK - KOLÍN and RUMBURK - KOLÍN *Arriva, Regiojet*

Operators: Regiojet Děčín - Ústí nad Labem - Kolín; Arriva Rumburk - Kolín.

km						
0	**Ústí n. L** hlavní n. d.	0441	0641		1641	1841
1	**Ústí n. L** západ ... d.	0448	0648		1648	1848
3	**Ústí n. L** Střekov d.	0453	0653	and	1653	1853
28	Litoměřice město d.	0513	0713	every	1713	1913
64	**Mělník** ..... d.	0540	0740	**two**	1740	1940
74	Všetaty ..... d.	0549	0748	hours	1748	1949
86	Stará Boleslav .... d.	0558	0758	until	1758	1958
97	Lysá n. Labem ▷ d.	0606	0806		1806	2006
112	Nymburk ..... ▷ d.	0618	0818		1818	2018
119	Poděbrady ...... ▷ d.	0625	0825		1825	2025
135	**Kolín** ..... a.	0640	0840		1840	2040

Kolín ..... d.	0714	0914		1914	2114
Poděbrady .... ▷ d.	0729	0929		1929	2129
Nymburk ..... ▷ d.	0737	0937	and	1937	2137
Lysá n. Labem. ▷ d.	0748	0948	every	1948	2148
Stará Boleslav ..... d.	0755	0955	**two**	1955	2155
Všetaty ..... d.	0806	1006	hours	2006	2206
Mělník ..... d.	0816	1016	until	2016	2216
Litoměřice město . d.	0845	1045		2045	2244
Ústí n. L Střekov . a.	0902	1102		2102	2301
Ústí n. L západ.... a.	0907	1107		2107	2306
Ústí n. L hlavní n. a.	0914	1114		2114	2313

km					
0	**Děčín** hl. n. ..... d.	0600	and every	1800	...
28	**Ústí n. L** Střekov a.	0638	**two** hours until	1838	...

Ústí n. L Střekov. d.	0517	and every	1917	...
Děčín hl. n. ..... a.	0553	**two** hours until	1953	...

	D						
Rumburk ..... d.	0518	0712	*0838*	*1038*	1312	1511**r**	1712
Česka Lipá ..... d.	0624	0824	1024	1224	1424	1624	1824
Mladá Boleslav d.	0722	0922	1122	1322	1522	1722	1922
Nymburk..... ▷ d.	0749	0949	1149	1349	1549	1749	1949
Poděbrady... ▷ d.	0757	0957	1157	1357	1557	1757	1957
Kolín ..... a.	0810	1010	1210	1410	1610	1810	2010

Kolín ..... d.	0745	0945	1145	1345	1545	1745	1945
Poděbrady... ▷ d.	0758	0958	1158	1358	1558	1758	1958
Nymburk..... ▷ d.	0808	1008	1208	1408	1608	1808	2008
Mladá Boleslav d.	0837	1037	1237	1437	1637	1837	2037
Česka Lipá ..... a.	0931	1131	1331	1531	1731	1931	2131
Rumburk ..... a.	1037	*1324*	1437	1637**r**	1837	2037	*2317*

D – From Rumburk on Ⓐ; from Česka Lipá daily.

r – ⑤⑥†.

▷ – See also Table **1145**.

2nd class ÚSTI NAD ORLICI - LICHKOV - KLODZKO (- WROCŁAW) 1165

Local trains (those without numbers) convey 2 only and are operated by Leo Express (Koleje Dolnośląskie in Poland). Subject to alteration on Czech and Polish holiday dates (see page 4).

km				EC 264 A			EC 262 A	Ⓐ		C		Ⓑf			EC 260 A						EC 460 AB		Ⓒ	Ⓐ
	Praha hlavní nádraží **1160**	d.	...	...	0651	...	...	1051	...	...	...	...	...	...	...	1450	...	...	...	...	...	1851	...	...	...
0	**Ústi nad Orlici**	d.	0742	...	0827	0942	1142	1227	1242	...	...	1342	1442	...	1542	1627	1642	...	...	1742	1842	2027	2043	2148	*2148*
12	Letohrad	d.	0802	...	0838	1002	1202	1238	1302	...	...	1402	1501	...	1602	1638	1702	...	...	1802	1901	2038	2112	2208	2230
35	**Lichkov**	d.	0828	0852	0902	1028	1228	1302	1328	...	1336	1428	1528	1552	1628	1702	1728	...	1736	1828	1928	2102	2138	2234	2256
44	Miedzylesie 🏛	d.	...	0924	0915	...	...	1311	...	...	1345	...	...	1601	...	1711	...	...	1749	...	...	2115	...	...	...
	Klodzko Miasto	a.	...	1000	0942	...	...	1342	...	...	1418	...	...	1637	...	1742	...	...	1818	...	...	2142	...	...	...
80	**Klodzko** Gl.	a.	...	1004	|	...	...	|	...	...	1440	...	...	1654	...	|	...	...	1826	...	...	|	...	...	...
	Wroclaw Gl. **1095**	a.	...	1121	1047	...	...	1447	...	...	1604	...	...	1824	...	1847	...	...	1937	...	...	2247	...	...	...

			EC 461 AB					EC 261 A			C		Ⓐ			EC 263 A		Ⓑf			Ⓒ	EC 265 A		
	Wroclaw Gl. **1095**	d.	...	0515	...	0612	...	...	0915	...	...	1017	...	...	1237	...	1315	...	...	1518	...	...	1715	...	...
	Klodzko Gl.	d.	...	|	...	0732	...	...	|	...	...	1136	...	...	1404	...	|	...	...	1634	...	...	|	...	...
	Klodzko Miasto	d.	...	0619	...	0737	...	...	1019	...	...	1139	...	...	1435	...	1419	...	...	1637	...	...	1819	...	...
	Miedzylesie 🏛	d.	...	0649	...	0810	...	...	1049	...	...	1210	...	...	1510	...	1449	...	...	1714	...	...	1849	...	...
	Lichkov	d.	0633	0700	0733	0818	0830	0930	1100	...	1130	1218	1330	1430	1518	1530	1500	...	1630	1722	1730	1830	1900	1930	2044
	Letohrad	d.	0703	0720	0803	...	0903	1003	1120	...	1203	...	1403	1503	...	1603	1520	...	1703	...	1803	1903	1920	2003	2114
	Ústí nad Orlicí	a.	0720	0732	0820	...	0920	1020	1132	...	1220	...	1420	1520	...	1602	1532	...	1720	...	1820	1920	1932	2020	2131
	Praha hlavní nádraží **1160**	a.	...	0906	...	...	...	...	1312	...	...	...	...	...	...	...	1712	...	...	...	...	...	2110	...	...

A – BALTIC EXPRESS 12 Praha - Gdynia and v.v. Classified *IC* in Poland.
B – Conveys 🛏 1, 2 cl. (1, 2, 3 berth) as follows: Train **461** Apr. 14 - Aug. 30; train **460** Apr. 15 - Aug. 31.
C – Subject to confirmation until Aug. 30.
f – Ⓑ (not Nov. 16).

2nd class OLOMOUC - KRNOV - OPAVA - OSTRAVA 1166

Warning! Services may be operated by 🚌 Bruntál - Kurnov and v.v. until December 4 with extended journey times.

km			839 Ⓐ	841	843 D	845	847	849	851	853	855
0	**Olomouc**	d.	...	...	0706	0906	1106	1306	1506	1706	1906
64	Bruntál	d.	...	...	0826	1026	1226	1426	1626	1826	2026
87	Krnov	a.	...	...	0852	1052	1252	1452	1652	1852	2052
87	Krnov	d.	0502	0706	0906	1106	1306	1506	1706	1906	...
116	**Opava** východ	a.	0529	0732	0932	1132	1332	1532	1732	1932	...
116	**Opava** východ **1160a**	d.	0533	0737	0937	1137	1337	1537	1737	1937	...
144	**Ostrava** Svinov **1160a**	a.	0553	0757	0957	1157	1357	1557	1757	1959	...

		856 d	852/4	850	848	846	844	842	840	838 Ⓐ
Ostrava Svinov **1160a**	d.	...	0556	0800	1000	1200	1400	1600	1800	2000
Opava východ **1160a**	a.	...	0623	0822	1022	1222	1422	1622	1822	2024
Opava východ	d.	...	0628	0828	1028	1228	1428	1628	1828	...
Krnov	a.	...	0656	0856	1056	1256	1456	1656	1856	...
Krnov	d.	0505	0705	0905	1105	1305	1505	1705	...	...
Bruntál	d.	0534	0733	0934	1134	1334	1534	1734	...	...
Olomouc	a.	0652	0852	1052	1252	1452	1652	1852	...	...

km			g		g			g		g	
0	**Jesenik**	d.	0515	...	0910	...	...	1310	...	1710	...
22	Glucholazy (Poland)	d.	0609	...	1009	...	...	1409	...	1809	...
43	Tremešná ve Slezsku	d.	0637	0835	1037	1235	...	1437	1635	1837	2034
60	**Krnov**	a.	0656	0856	1056	1256	...	1456	1702	1856	2056

		g			g			g		g
Krnov	d.	0705	0748	0905	1105	...	1305	1505	1705	1905
Tremešná ve Slezsku	d.	0726	0808	0924	1126	...	1324	1526	1732	1926
Glucholazy (Poland)	d.	0759	...	...	1159	...	...	1559	...	1959
Jesenik	a.	0850	...	...	1250	...	...	1650	...	2050

D – From Olomouc on ①–⑥ **d**; from Krnov daily.
d – ①–⑥ (not Nov. 17).
g – By 🚌 Jesenik - Mikulovice (not shown) and v.v.

2nd class May vary on and around public holiday dates OTHER LOCAL SERVICES 1169

BRECLAV - ZNOJMO — Additional trains run on Ⓒ Mar. 29 - Oct. 28 — Arriva

km			Ⓐ	Ⓒ		Ⓐ			Ⓐ				Ⓐ			Ⓐ			Ⓐ			Ⓑ			
0	**Břeclav**	d.	0552	0604	...	0643	0742	...	0844	0942	...	1142	1244	...	1342	1441	...	1542	1644	...	1742	1844	...	1942	2142
43	Hrušovany ◧	d.	0651	0651	...	0727	0827	...	0927	1027	...	1227	1327	...	1427	1527	...	1627	1727	...	1827	1938	...	2027	2232
69	**Znojmo**	a.	0717	0717	...	0754	0854	...	0954	1054	...	1254	1354	...	1454	1554	...	1654	1754	...	1854	2005	...	2054	2259

		Ⓒ	Ⓐ			Ⓐ					Ⓐ			Ⓐ			Ⓐ			Ⓐ	Ⓒ		Ⓐ	
Znojmo	d.	0534	0556	...	0656	0758	...	0858	1058	...	1158	1258	...	1358	1458	...	1558	1658	...	1758	1858	...	1910	2106
Hrušovany ◧	d.	0602	0627	...	0728	0828	...	0928	1128	...	1228	1328	...	1428	1528	...	1628	1728	...	1828	1928	...	1940	2133
Břeclav	a.	0650	0715	...	0816	0915	...	1016	1216	...	1315	1416	...	1515	1616	...	1715	1816	...	1915	2016	...	2027	2217

BRNO - HRUŠOVANY *63 km* Journey 80 minutes

From Brno at 1529 Ⓐ, 1729 Ⓐ, 1955 Ⓑ, 2055 ⑦.
From Hrušovany nad Jevišovkou – Šanov at 0509 Ⓐ, 0537 ⑥, 0609 Ⓐ, 0713 Ⓐ, 2037 ⑤.

ČESKÝ TĚŠÍN - CIESZYN (Poland) *3 km* Journey 5 minutes

From Český Těšín at 0522 Ⓐ, 0552 Ⓒ, 0722 Ⓐ, 0752 Ⓒ, 0952, 1152, 1352, 1552, 1752, 1952, 2152.
From Cieszyn at 0535 Ⓐ, 0605 Ⓒ, 0805, 1005, 1205, 1405, 1605, 1805, 2005, 2205.

CHOCEŇ - LITOMYŠL *24 km* Journey 55 minutes

From Choceň at 0502 Ⓐ, 0629 Ⓐ, 0639 Ⓒ, 0839, 1039, 1339 Ⓒ, 1426 Ⓐ, 1639 Ⓒ, 1739 Ⓐ, 1839 Ⓒ, 2236 Ⓑ, 2326 ⑥.
From Litomyšl at 0535 Ⓒ, 0610 Ⓐ, 0715 Ⓐ **e**, 0935, 1235, 1535, 1735 Ⓒ, 1835 Ⓐ, 1933 Ⓒ.

KOJETIN - KROMĚŘÍŽ *9 km* Journey 12 minutes

From Kojetin at 0603 and hourly until 2003, 2103 ④⑤⑦, 2203, 2313 Ⓐ.
From Kroměříž at 0542 and hourly until 1943, 2042 ④⑤⑦, 2142, 2242 Ⓐ.

KROMĚŘÍŽ - HULIN *8 km* Journey 8 minutes

From Hulin: 1-2 trains per hour connecting with trains in Table **1162**.
From Kroměříž: 1-2 trains per hour connecting with trains in Table **1162**.

PRAHA - KARLŠTEJN *33 km* Journey 42 minutes

From Praha hl. n. at 0615, 0645, 0715, 0745 ⚒, 0815, 0845, 0915, 0945 Ⓒ, 1015, 1045 Ⓒ, 1115, 1145 Ⓒ, 1215, 1245, 1315, 1345, 1415, 1445, 1515, 1545, 1615, 1645, 1715, 1745, 1815, 1845, 1915, 1945 Ⓐ, 2015, 2115, 2215, 2315.
From Karlštejn at 0626 Ⓐ, 0656, 0726, 0756, 0826 ⚒, 0856, 0926, 0956, 1026 Ⓒ, 1056, 1126 Ⓒ, 1156, 1226 Ⓒ, 1256, 1326, 1356, 1426, 1456, 1526, 1556, 1626, 1656, 1726, 1756, 1826, 1856, 1926, 1956, 2026 Ⓐ, 2056, 2156, 2306.
Trains continue to/from Beroun (journey 10 mins).

TŘEMEŠNÁ VE SLEZSKU - OSOBLAHA *20 km* Narrow gauge, 45 minutes

From Třemešná at 0727 ①–⑥ **d**, 1045 **E**, 1127, 1527, 1927.
From Osoblaha at 0546 ①–⑥ **d**, 0946, 1346, 1510 **E**, 1746.

D – ⑥ June 7 - Sept. 20 (also ⑦ July 6 - Aug. 24). Steam hauled train. Special fares. Journey 80–90 minutes.
d – ①–⑥ (not Nov. 17).
e – Until June 27.
◧ – Full name is Hrušovany nad Jevišovkou – Šanov.

SLOVAKIA

Operator: National railway operator is Železničná spoločnosť Slovensko (ŽSSK), www.slovakrail.sk, which runs on the network of Železnice Slovenskej Republiky (ŽSR), www.zsr.sk.

Services: All trains convey first and second class seating, **except** where shown otherwise in footnotes or by '2' in the train column, or where the footnote shows sleeping and/or couchette cars only. Reservation of 1st class seats is compulsary on domestic trains. Descriptions of sleeping (🛏) and couchette (▬) cars appear on page 10.
Note: hl. st. = hlavná stanica = main station.

Timings: Valid **until December 13, 2025** with amendments as received. Certain trains may be cancelled during the period December 23 - January 6.

Supplements: A higher level of fares applies to travel by *EC* and *IC* trains. It is possible to reserve seats on most Express trains.

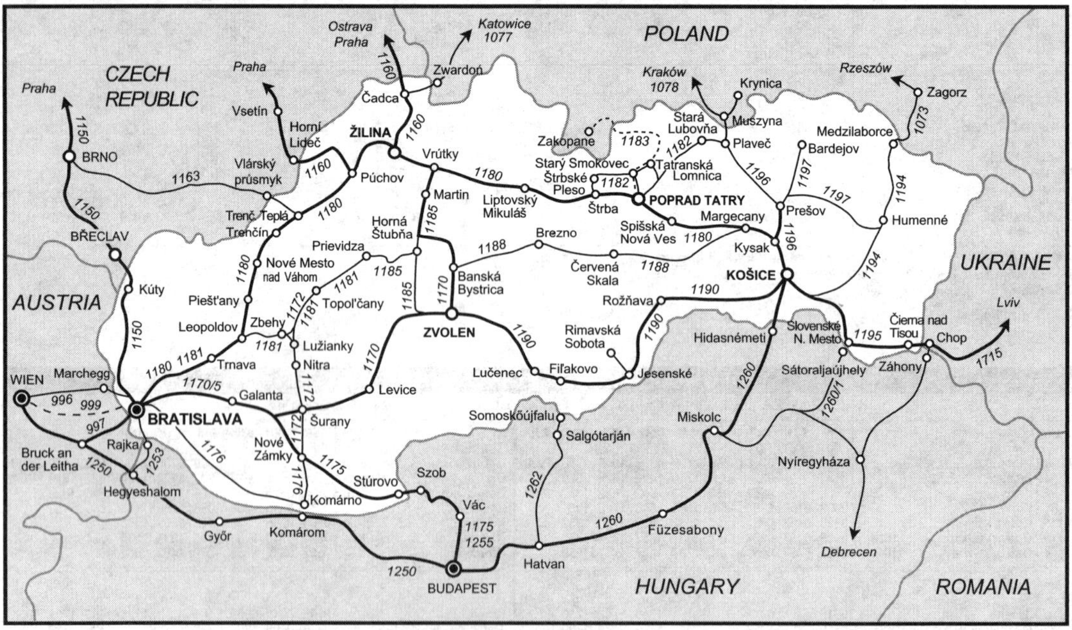

1170 BRATISLAVA - ŠURANY - ZVOLEN - BANSKÁ BYSTRICA

Warning! Services are operated by 🚌 Kozárovce - Nová Baňa and v.v. Different train numbers are used Kozárovce - Zvolen and v.v.

km		13831 ① d	12861 ②–⑥ e	2	11831	2	11833	2	11835	2	11837	2	11839	2	11841	2	853 ①–④ f	15845 ⑤ g	2	2 Ⓐ	11845	2	855 Ⓑ h
0	**Bratislava** hl. st. ... **1175** d.	0352	...	...	0552	...	0752	...	0952	...	1152	...	1352	...	1552	...	1651	1651	...	...	1752	...	1952
49	Galanta ... **1175** d.	0426	...	...	0626	...	0826	...	1026	...	1226	...	1426	...	1626	...	1724	1724	...	...	1826	...	2026
60	Šal'a ... **1175** d.	0434	...	...	0634	...	0834	...	1034	...	1234	...	1434	...	1634	...	1734	1734	...	...	1834	...	2034
	Nové Zámky ... d.	|	...	0628	|	0828	|	1028	|	1228	|	1428	|	1628	|	1728	|	|	...	1828	|	1928	|
89	**Šurany** ... a.	0455	...	0640	0655	0840	0855	1040	1055	1240	1255	1440	1455	1640	1655	1740	1755	1755	...	1840	1855	1940	2055
89	**Šurany** ... d.	0456	...	...	0657	...	0857	...	1057	...	1257	...	1457	...	1657	...	1757	1757	...	...	1857	1950	2057
132	Levice ... d.	0540	0540	...	0738	...	0938	...	1138	...	1338	...	1538	...	1738	...	1839	1842	...	...	1938	2056	2136
187	Žiar nad Hronom ... d.	0700	0700	...	0900	...	1100	...	1300	...	1500	...	1700	...	1900	...	...	1958	...	...	2100	...	...
209	**Zvolen** osob. ... a.	0719	0719	...	0919	...	1119	...	1319	...	1519	...	1719	...	1919	...	...	2021	...	...	2119	...	...
209	**Zvolen** osob. ... **1185** d.	0725	0725	...	0925	...	1125	...	1325	...	1525	...	1725	...	1925	...	...	...	2041	...	2125	...	...
230	**Banská Bystrica** ... **1185** a.	0745	0745	...	0945	...	1145	...	1345	...	1545	...	1745	...	1945	...	...	...	2110	...	2145	...	...

	850 Ⓐ	2	11830 ①–⑥ j	2 Ⓐ	11832	2	11834	2	11836	2 Ⓐ	11838	2	11840	2	2 Ⓐ	2	17842 ⑦ k	11842	2	11844	2	860
Banská Bystrica ... **1185** d.	...	...	0405	...	0615	...	0815	...	1015	...	1215	...	1415	...	...	1445	...	1615	...	1815	...	2015
Zvolen osob. ... **1185** d.	...	...	0434	...	0637	...	0837	...	1037	...	1237	...	1437	...	...	1519	...	1637	...	1837	...	2037
Zvolen osob. ... d.	...	...	0439	...	0639	...	0839	...	1039	...	1239	...	1439	...	...	...	1535	1639	...	1839	...	...
Žiar nad Hronom ... d.	...	...	0503	...	0659	...	0859	...	1059	...	1259	...	1459	...	...	...	1559	1659	...	1859	...	...
Levice ... d.	0503	0523	0612	0619	0812	...	1012	...	1212	...	1412	...	1612	...	...	...	1714	1812	...	2012	...	...
Šurany ... a.	0546	0622	0651	0717	0851	...	1051	...	1251	...	1451	...	1651	...	...	...	1758	1851	...	2051	...	...
Šurany ... d.	0547	0627	0704	0727	0904	0854	1104	1054	1304	1254	1504	1454	1704	1654	1748	...	1804	1904	1854	2104	2054	...
Nové Zámky ... a.	|	0642	|	0742	|	0906	|	1106	|	1306	|	1506	|	1706	1800	...	|	|	1906	|	2106	...
Šal'a ... **1175** d.	0612	...	0726	...	0926	...	1126	...	1326	...	1526	...	1726	...	...	...	1826	1926	...	2126	...	...
Galanta ... **1175** d.	0622	...	0735	...	0935	...	1135	...	1335	...	1535	...	1735	...	...	...	1835	1935	...	2135	...	...
Bratislava hl. st. ... **1175** a.	0659	...	0808	...	1008	...	1208	...	1408	...	1608	...	1808	...	...	...	1908	2008	...	2208	...	...

d – Also Sept. 16, Nov. 18; not Sept. 15, Nov. 17.
e – Not Aug. 30, Sept. 16, Nov. 18.
f – Not Aug. 28, Sept. 15, Nov. 17.
g – Also Aug. 28; not Aug. 29.
h – Not Aug. 29, Sept. 14, Nov. 16.
j – Not Aug. 30, Sept. 15, Nov. 17.
k – Also Sept. 15, Nov. 17; not Sept. 14, Nov. 16.

1172 NOVÉ ZAMKY - NITRA - TOPOL'ČANY

2nd class

km																				
0	**Nové Zamky** ... ⊡ d.	0706	0906	1106	1306	1506	1706	1906	2106	2316	**Nitra** ... ⊡ d.	0610	0810	1010	1210	1410	1610	1810	2010	2210
10	Šurany ... ⊡ d.	0718	0918	1118	1318	1518	1718	1918	2118	2328	Šurany ... ⊡ d.	0642	0842	1042	1242	1442	1642	1842	2042	2242
36	**Nitra** ... ⊡ a.	0749	0949	1149	1349	1549	1749	1949	2149	2359	**Nové Zamky** ... ⊡ a.	0654	0854	1054	1254	1454	1654	1854	2054	2254

km																				
0	**Nitra** ... **1181** ⊖ d.	0618	0818	1018	1218	1418	1618	1818	2018	2218	**Topol'čany** ... ⊖ d.	0649	0849	1049	1249	1449	1649	1849	2049	2249
4	Lužianky ... **1181** ⊖ d.	0632	0832	1032	1232	1432	1632	1832	2032	2232	Lužianky ... **1181** ⊖ d.	0731	0931	1131	1331	1531	1731	1931	2131	2331
33	**Topol'čany** ... ⊖ a.	0709	0909	1109	1309	1509	1709	1909	2109	2309	**Nitra** ... **1181** ⊖ a.	0743	0943	1143	1343	1543	1743	1943	2143	2343

⊡ – Also from Nové Zamky at 0356 Ⓐ, 0506, 0606 Ⓐ, 0806 Ⓐ, 1406 Ⓐ, 1606 Ⓐ, 1806 Ⓐ; also from Nitra at 0357, 0502 Ⓐ, 0702 Ⓐ, 1302 Ⓐ, 1502 Ⓐ, 1702 Ⓐ, 1902 Ⓐ.
⊖ – Also from Nitra at 0418, 0518 Ⓐ, 0718 Ⓐ, 1518 Ⓐ, 1718 Ⓐ; also from Topol'čany at 0449, 0549 Ⓐ, 0749 Ⓐ, 1549 Ⓐ, 1749 Ⓐ.

BRATISLAVA - ŠTÚROVO - BUDAPEST 1175

All *EC* trains convey ✕. For additional trains Bratislava - Šal'a see Table **1170**. For local trains Szob - Budapest and v.v. see Table **1255**.

km																								
		2	2	*EN* **477**	2	2	2	2		*EC* **271**	2	2	2	*EC* **273**	2	2		2	*EC* **275**	2	2	2	*EC* **277**	2
			Ⓐ	🄡		Ⓐ		Ⓐ					Ⓐ					Ⓐ				Ⓐ		
		◧		**A**			◧					◧				◧					◧			
	Praha hlavní **1150** d.	...	...	0036	...	...	...	...	...	...	...	...	...	0542	...	...	...	...	0742	...	...	...	0942	...
	Brno hlavní n. **1150** d.	...	...	0314	...	...	...	...	...	0622	...	...	...	0822	...	...	...	...	1022	...	...	...	1222	...
	Břeclav **1150** d.	...	...	0455	...	...	...	...	...	0655	...	...	...	0855	...	...	...	...	1055	...	...	...	1255	...
0	**Bratislava** hl. st. **1170** d.	0509	0533	0605	0609	0633	0709	0733	...	0805	0809	0909	0933	1005	1009	1109	...	1133	1205	1209	1309	1333	1405	1409
49	Galanta **1170** a.	0556	0605	|	0656	0705	0756	0805	...	|	0856	0956	1005	|	1056	1156	...	1205	|	1256	1356	1405	|	1456
49	Galanta **1170** d.	0607	0607	|	...	0707	0807	0807	...	|	...	1007	1007	|	...	1207	...	1207	|	...	1407	1407	|	...
60	Šal'a **1170** d.	0617	0617	|	...	0717	0817	0817	...	|	...	1017	1017	|	...	1217	...	1217	|	...	1417	1417	|	...
91	Nové Zámky d.	0645	0645	0659	...	0745	0845	0845	...	0859	...	1045	1045	1059	...	1245	...	1245	1259	...	1445	1445	1459	...
135	Štúrovo 🏛 d.	...	...	0727	...	...	...	...	...	0927	...	...	...	1127	...	...	...	...	1327	...	...	...	1527	...
150	Szob 🏛 d.	...	...	|	...	...	...	...	...	0938	...	...	...	1138	...	...	...	...	1338	...	...	...	1538	...
163	Nagymaros-Visegrád ¶ d.	...	...	|	...	...	...	...	...	0948	...	...	...	1148	...	...	...	...	1348	...	...	...	1548	...
180	Vác d.	...	...	0800	...	...	...	...	...	1002	...	...	...	1202	...	...	...	...	1402	...	...	...	1602	...
214	**Budapest** Nyugati a.	...	...	0829	...	...	...	...	...	1028	...	...	...	1228	...	...	...	...	1428	...	...	...	1628	...

	2	2	2	2	*EC* **279**	2	2		*EC* **131**	2	2	*EC* **173**	2	2	2		2	*EC* **281**	2	2	*EC* **283**	2	2
	Ⓐ	Ⓐ		Ⓐ			Ⓐ				Ⓐ			Ⓐ			Ⓐ						
			◧						**B**	◧		**C**			◧								
Praha hlavní **1150** d.	...	...	...	...	1142	...	...	...	...	...	...	1342	...	...	...	...	...	1542	...	...	1742	...	...
Brno hlavní n. **1150** d.	...	...	...	...	1422	...	...	...	...	...	...	1622	...	...	...	...	...	1822	...	...	2022	...	...
Břeclav **1150** d.	...	...	...	...	1455	...	...	...	1555	...	...	1655	...	...	...	...	...	1855	...	...	2055	...	...
Bratislava hl. st. **1170** d.	1433	1504	1509	1533	1605	1609	1633	...	1713	1704	1733	1805	1809	1833	1909	...	1933	2005	2009	2109	2205	2209	2309
Galanta **1170** a.	1505	1538	1556	1605	|	1656	1705	...	|	1756	1805	|	1856	1905	1956	...	2005	|	2056	2156	2236	2256	2356
Galanta **1170** d.	1517	1539	1607	1607	|	...	1707	...	|	1807	1807	|	...	1907	2007	...	2007	|	...	2207	2237	...	2357
Šal'a **1170** d.	1527	1547	1617	1617	|	...	1717	...	|	1817	1817	|	...	1917	2017	...	2017	|	...	2217	2245	...	0007
Nové Zámky d.	1545	1606	1645	1645	1659	...	1745	...	1808	1845	1845	1859	...	1945	2045	...	2045	2101	...	2245	2304	...	0035
Štúrovo 🏛 d.	...	...	...	...	1727	...	...	...	1840	...	...	1927	...	...	...	...	...	2129	...	...	...	...	...
Szob 🏛 d.	...	...	...	...	1738	...	...	...	1851	...	...	1938	...	...	...	...	...	2140	...	...	...	...	...
Nagymaros-Visegrád ¶ d.	...	...	...	...	1748	...	...	...	1902	...	...	1948	...	...	...	...	...	2150	...	...	...	...	...
Vác d.	...	...	...	...	1802	...	...	...	1923	...	...	2002	...	...	...	...	...	2204	...	...	...	...	...
Budapest Nyugati a.	...	...	...	...	1828	...	...	...	1949	...	...	2028	...	...	...	...	...	2230	...	...	...	...	...

	2	2	*EC* **282**	2	2	2	2		2	*EC* **280**	2	2	2	*EC* **172**	2		2	*EC* **130**	2	*EC* **278**	2	2	2
	Ⓐ			Ⓐ		Ⓐ	Ⓐ				Ⓐ				Ⓐ						Ⓐ		
					◧							◧		**C**			◧	**B**				◧	
Budapest Nyugati d.	...	...	...	...	...	...	...	...	...	0530	...	...	...	0730	...	...	...	0812	...	0930	...	...	...
Vác d.	...	...	...	...	...	...	...	...	...	0557	...	...	...	0757	...	...	...	0844	...	0957	...	...	...
Nagymaros-Visegrád ¶ d.	...	...	...	...	...	...	...	...	...	0610	...	...	...	0810	...	...	...	0857	...	1010	...	...	...
Szob 🏛 d.	...	...	...	...	...	...	...	...	...	0623	...	...	...	0823	...	...	...	0909	...	1023	...	...	...
Štúrovo 🏛 d.	...	...	...	...	...	...	...	...	...	0636	...	...	...	0836	...	...	...	0923	...	1036	...	...	...
Nové Zámky d.	0411	...	0452	0511	0511	0603	0611	...	...	0703	0711	0711	...	0903	0911	...	0911	0951	...	1103	1111	1111	...
Šal'a **1170** d.	0441	...	0512	0541	0541	0624	0641	...	...	|	0741	0741	...	|	0941	...	0941	|	...	|	1141	1141	...
Galanta **1170** a.	0450	...	0519	0550	0550	0631	0650	...	...	|	0750	0750	...	|	0950	...	0950	|	...	|	1150	1150	...
Galanta **1170** d.	0452	0504	0521	0552	0604	0633	0652	...	0704	|	0752	0804	0904	|	0952	...	1004	|	1104	|	1152	1204	1304
Bratislava hl. st. **1170** a.	0526	0550	0555	0626	0651	0710	0726	...	0751	0755	0826	0851	0951	0955	1026	...	1056	1044	1151	1155	1226	1251	1351
Břeclav **1150** a.	...	...	0704	...	...	...	...	...	...	0904	...	...	...	1104	...	...	...	1204	...	1304	...	...	...
Brno hlavní n. **1150** a.	...	...	0736	...	...	...	...	...	...	0936	...	...	...	1136	...	...	...	...	...	1336	...	...	...
Praha hlavní **1150** a.	...	...	1015	...	...	...	...	...	...	1215	...	...	...	1415	...	...	...	...	...	1615	...	...	...

	EC **276**	2	2	2	2	*EC* **274**	2		2	2	2		*EC* **272**	2	2		2	2	*EC* **270**	2	2	*EN* **476**	2
		Ⓐ		Ⓐ			Ⓐ			Ⓐ				Ⓐ			Ⓐ					🄡	
			◧						◧						◧							**A**	
Budapest Nyugati d.	1130	...	...	...	...	1330	...	...	...	...	...	...	1530	...	...	...	...	...	1730	...	...	1930	...
Vác d.	1157	...	...	...	...	1357	...	...	...	...	...	...	1557	...	...	...	...	...	1757	...	...	1957	...
Nagymaros-Visegrád ¶ d.	1210	...	...	...	...	1410	...	...	...	...	...	...	1610	...	...	...	...	...	1810	...	...	|	...
Szob 🏛 d.	1223	...	...	...	...	1423	...	...	...	...	...	...	1623	...	...	...	...	...	1823	...	...	|	...
Štúrovo 🏛 d.	1236	...	...	...	...	1436	...	...	...	...	...	...	1636	...	...	...	...	...	1836	...	...	2036	...
Nové Zámky d.	1303	1311	1311	1411	...	1503	1511	...	1511	1611	...	...	1703	1711	1711	...	1811	...	1903	1911	...	2103	2111
Šal'a **1170** d.	|	1341	1341	1441		|	1541	...	1541	1641		...	|	1741	1741	...	1841	...	|	1941	...	|	2141
Galanta **1170** a.	|	1350	1350	1450	...	|	1550	...	1550	1650	...	...	|	1750	1750	...	1850	...	|	1950	...	|	2150
Galanta **1170** d.	|	1352	1404	1452	1504	|	1552	...	1604	1652	1704	...	|	1752	1804	...	1852	1904	|	2004	2104	|	2204
Bratislava hl. st. **1170** a.	1355	1426	1451	1526	1551	1555	1626	...	1650	1726	1751	...	1755	1826	1851	...	1926	1951	1955	2051	2151	2155	2251
Břeclav **1150** a.	1504	...	...	...	...	1704	...	...	...	...	...	...	1904	...	...	...	...	...	2104	...	...	2304	...
Brno hlavní n. **1150** a.	1536	...	...	...	...	1736	...	...	...	...	...	...	1936	...	...	...	...	...	2136	...	...	0026	...
Praha hlavní **1150** a.	1815	...	...	...	...	2015	...	...	...	...	...	...	2215	...	...	...	...	...	0018	...	...	0301	...

LOCAL TRAINS NOVÉ ZÁMKY - STÚROVO

From Nové Zámky at 0512, 0612 Ⓐ, 0712, 0912, 1112, 1312, 1512, 1612 Ⓐ, 1712, 1912, 2112. Journey 40 minutes.
From Štúrovo at 0512 Ⓐ, 0612, 0702 Ⓐ, 0812, 1012, 1412, 1612, 1712 Ⓐ, 1812, 2012 Ⓒ. Journey 40 minutes.

A – METROPOL – 🛏 1, 2 cl., ▬ 2 cl., 🚃2 Berlin (**457/456**) - Břeclav (**477/476**) - Budapest and v.v.;
🛏 1, 2 cl., ▬ 2 cl., 🚃2 Warszawa (**407/406**) - Bohumín (**457/456**) - Břeclav (**477/476**) - Budapest and v.v.
B – BATHORY – 🚃12 ✕ Budapest - Warszawa and v.v.; 🚃2 Budapest - Bohumín (**115/131**) - Przemysl and v.v.
C – HUNGARIA – 🚃12 ✕ Budapest - Berlin (- Hamburg until July 31) and v.v.

◧ – Daily Bratislava - Galanta and v.v.;
Ⓒ Galanta - Nové Zámky and v.v.
¶ – A ferry operates across the river to Visegrád.

2nd class BRATISLAVA - KOMÁRNO - NOVÉ ZÁMKY 1176

Bratislava - Komarno is operated by LEO Express.

km																								
		Ⓐ	Ⓒ				Ⓐ		Ⓐ		Ⓐ						Ⓒ							
0	**Bratislava** hl. st. d.	0604	0613	0810	1010	1210	1310	1410	1503	1610	1710	1810	2010	2134	...	**A**	0534	0634	0734	and	2034	2134	2303	
46	Dunajská Streda a.	0706	0706	0906	1106	1306	1406	1506	1606	1706	1806	1906	2106	2238	...	**L**	0638	0738	0838	hourly	2138	2238	0006	
46	Dunajská Streda d.	0710	0710	0910	1110	1310	*1423*	1510	*1623*	1710	*1823*	1910	2110	*2242*	...	**S**	...	...	...	until	...	...	...	
94	**Komárno** a.	0816	0816	1016	1216	1416	*1529*	1616	*1728*	1816	*1928*	2016	2216	*2347*	...	**O**	...	...	...		...	...	...	

		Ⓐ					Ⓐ		Ⓐ		Ⓒ	Ⓐ									Ⓒ	
Komárno d.	0545	*0633*	0745	0945	1145	1345	1439	1545	1633	1745	1945	1945	2103	...	**A**	...	...	...	and	...	...	...
Dunajská Streda a.	0649	*0737*	0849	1049	1249	1449	1539	1649	1737	1849	2049	2049	2206	...	**L**	...	...	...	hourly	...	...	...
Dunajská Streda d.	0652	0752	0852	1052	1252	1452	*1552*	1652	*1820*	1852	2052	*2120*	...	...	**S**	0621	0720	0820	until	1920	2020	2120
Bratislava hl. st. a.	0750	0850	0950	1150	1350	1553	*1650*	1750	*1925*	1950	2155	*2225*	...	...	**O**	0725	0825	0925		2025	2125	2225

km																								
			Ⓐ			Ⓐ						Ⓐ			Ⓐ			Ⓐ						
0	**Komárno** d.	0420	0533	...	0633	0733	...	0833	1033	...	1233	1333	...	1433	1533	...	1633	1733	...	1833	2033	...	...	...
29	**Nové Zámky** a.	0445	0558	...	0658	0758	...	0858	1058	...	1258	1358	...	1458	1558	...	1658	1758	...	1858	2058	...	...	...

		Ⓐ			Ⓐ						Ⓐ			Ⓐ			Ⓐ					
Nové Zámky d.	0502	0602	...	0702	0802	...	0902	1102	...	1302	1402	...	1502	1602	...	1702	1802	...	1902	2102	...	...	...
Komárno a.	0527	0627	...	0727	0827	...	0927	1127	...	1327	1427	...	1527	1627	...	1727	1827	...	1927	2127	...	...	...

1180 BRATISLAVA - ŽILINA - POPRAD TATRY - KOŠICE

km		1263	681	1761	1021	1763	443	641		443	601	701	603	703	505		705	607	707	609	709	611	241
		♠ 🍷	E	Ⓐ	♥ 🍷 A		EN [R] B	Ex 🍷		EN [R] B	Ex ✕		Ex ✕		Ex ✕			Ex 🍷		Ex ✕		Ex 🍷	EC ✕ C
0	**Bratislava** hl. st. d.	...	2255	...	...	...	...	...	...	...	0327	...	0427	0455	0527	...	0555	0627	0655	0727	0755	0827	...
46	Trnava **1181** d.	...	2328	...	...	...	...	...	...	...	0401	...	0501	0530	0601	...	0630	0701	0730	0801	0830	0901	...
63	Leopoldov **1181** d.	...	2341	...	...	...	...	...	...	...	|	...	|	0542	|	...	0642	|	0742	|	0842	|	...
81	Piešťany d.	...	2354	...	...	...	...	...	...	...	|	...	|	0554	|	...	0654	|	0754	|	0854	|	...
99	Nové Mesto nad Váhom d.	...	0007	...	...	...	...	...	...	...	|	...	|	0606	|	...	0706	|	0806	|	0906	|	...
124	**Trenčín** d.	...	0024	...	...	...	...	...	...	...	0438	0519	0538	0621	0638	...	0721	0738	0821	0838	0921	0938	...
132	Trenčianska Teplá d.	...	0030	...	...	...	...	...	...	...	|	0525	|	0627	|	...	0727	|	0827	|	0927	|	...
	Praha hl. n. **1160** d.	1858	|	...	2144	...	2216	...	...	...	|	|	|	|	|	...	|	|	|	|	|	|	0558
159	**Púchov** **1161** d.	|	0048	...	|	...	|	...	...	...	0457	0549	0557	0648	|	...	0750	0757	0848	0857	0950	0957	|
171	Považská Bystrica **1161** d.	|	0057	...	|	...	|	...	...	...	0507	0558	0607	...	|	...	0759	0807	...	0907	0958	1007	|
203	**Žilina** **1161** a.	0001	0124	...	0238	...	0417	...	...	...	0530	0624	0630	...	0722	...	0824	0830	...	0930	→	1030	1033
203	**Žilina** **1185** d.	0003	0129	...	0240	...	0419	0433	...	...	0533	...	0633	...	0723	...	...	0831	...	0933	...	1033	1038
224	Vrútky **1185** d.	0024	0152	...	0304	...	0443	0456	...	...	0556	...	0656	...	|	...	...	0856	...	0956	...	1056	1103
242	Kraľovany d.	|	0206	...	|	...	0456	0510	...	...	0610	...	0710	...	|	...	...	0910	...	1010	...	1110	1120
260	Ružomberok d.	0050	0222	...	0330	...	0511	0525	...	...	0625	...	0725	...	|	...	...	0925	...	1025	...	1125	1137
286	Liptovský Mikuláš d.	0110	0243	...	0351	...	0532	0547	...	...	0647	...	0747	...	0827	...	...	0947	...	1047	...	1147	1158
325	Štrba d.	0139	|	...	0419	...	0600	0616	...	...	0716	...	0816	...	|	...	...	1016	...	1116	...	1216	1226
344	**Poprad-Tatry** d.	0153	0328	0419	0434	0531	0621	0633	...	...	0733	...	0833	...	0910	...	...	1033	...	1133	...	1233	1246
370	Spišská Nová Ves d.	0218	0346	0454	0458	0557	0640	0658	...	←	0758	...	0858	...	0935	...	...	1058	...	1158	...	1258	1316
410	Margecany d.	|	0414	0525	0541	0627	→	0726	...	0742	0826	...	0926	...	|	...	...	1126	...	1226	...	1326	|
429	Kysak **1196** d.	0256	0428	0540	0554	0641	...	0740	...	0800	0850	...	0940	...	1014	...	...	1140	...	1240	...	1340	1355
445	**Košice** **1196** a.	0307	0441	0553	0608	0653	...	0753	...	0812	0917	...	0953	...	1026	...	...	1153	...	1253	...	1353	1412
	Humenné **1194** a.	...	0655*	...	...	...	...	...	...	1105*	...	...	...	...	...	...	...	...	...	...	...	...	...

	709	711	613	713	615	1003	715		617	717	619	719	621	721		623	723	525	725	627	1259	727
			Ex 🍷		Ex ✕	♥ 🍷			Ex ✕		Ex ✕		Ex ✕			Ex ✕		Ex ✕		Ex ✕	♠ 🍷	
Bratislava hl. st. d.	...	0855	0927	0955	1027	...	1055	...	1127	1155	1227	1255	1327	1355	...	1427	1455	1527	1555	1627	...	1655
Trnava **1181** d.	...	0930	1001	1030	1101	...	1130	...	1201	1230	1301	1330	1401	1430	...	1501	1530	1601	1630	1701	...	1730
Leopoldov **1181** d.	...	0942	|	1042	|	...	1142	...	|	1242	|	1342	|	1442	...	|	1542	|	1642	|	...	1742
Piešťany d.	...	0954	|	1054	|	...	1154	...	|	1254	|	1354	|	1454	...	|	1554	|	1654	|	...	1754
Nové Mesto nad Váhom d.	...	1006	|	1106	|	...	1206	...	|	1306	|	1406	|	1506	...	|	1606	|	1706	|	...	1806
Trenčín d.	...	1021	1038	1121	1138	...	1221	...	1238	1321	1338	1421	1438	1521	...	1538	1621	1638	1721	1738	...	1821
Trenčianska Teplá d.	...	1027	|	1127	|	...	1227	...	|	1327	|	1427	|	1527	...	|	1627	|	1727	|	...	1827
Praha hl. n. **1160** d.	...	|	|	|	|	0747	|	...	|	|	|	|	|	|	...	|	|	|	|	|	1358	|
Púchov **1161** d.	←	1048	1057	1150	1157	|	1248	...	1257	1350	1357	1448	1457	1550	...	1557	1648	|	1750	1757	|	1848
Považská Bystrica **1161** d.	1027	...	1107	1159	1207	|	...	...	1307	1359	1407	...	1507	1559	...	1607	...	|	1759	1807	|	...
Žilina **1161** a.	1052	...	1130	1224	1230	1249	...	...	1330	1424	1430	...	1530	1624	...	1630	...	1722	1824	1830	1904	...
Žilina **1185** d.	...	...	1133	...	1233	1253	...	...	1333	...	1433	...	1533	...	...	1633	...	1723	...	1833	1906	...
Vrútky **1185** d.	...	...	1156	...	1256	1320	...	...	1356	...	1456	...	1556	...	...	1656	...	|	...	1856	1930	...
Kraľovany d.	...	...	1210	...	1310	|	...	...	1410	...	1510	...	1610	...	...	1710	...	|	...	1910	|	...
Ružomberok d.	...	...	1225	...	1325	1349	...	...	1425	...	1525	...	1625	...	...	1725	...	|	...	1925	1958	...
Liptovský Mikuláš d.	...	...	1247	...	1347	1409	...	...	1447	...	1547	...	1647	...	...	1747	...	1829	...	1947	2018	...
Štrba d.	...	...	1316	...	1416	1438	...	...	1516	...	1616	...	1716	...	...	1816	...	|	...	2026	2045	...
Poprad-Tatry d.	...	...	1333	...	1433	1453	...	...	1533	...	1633	...	1733	...	...	1833	...	1910	...	2033	2125	...
Spišská Nová Ves d.	...	...	1358	...	1458	1516	...	...	1558	...	1658	...	1758	...	...	1858	...	1935	...	2058	2151	...
Margecany d.	...	...	1426	...	1526	|	...	...	1626	...	1726	...	1826	...	...	1926	...	|	...	2126	|	...
Kysak **1196** d.	...	...	1440	...	1540	1556	...	...	1640	...	1740	...	1840	...	...	1940	...	2014	...	2140	2235	...
Košice **1196** a.	...	...	1453	...	1553	1612	...	...	1653	...	1753	...	1853	...	...	1953	...	2026	...	2153	2249	...
Humenné **1194** a.	...	...	...	...	...	...	...	...	...	...	...	...	...	...	...	...	...	...	...	...	...	...

	629	1011	729	631		221	2	731	2		2	651	1045	2		733	653	735	655		737	739
	Ex ✕	♥ 🍷		Ex ✕		EC ✕			Ⓐ			Ex 🍷 Ⓑ d	♥ 🍷 D				Ex ✕		Ex 🍷			
Bratislava hl. st. d.	1727	...	1755	1827	...	...	...	1855	...	...	...	1927	1935	...	...	1955	2027	2055	2127	...	2155	2227
Trnava **1181** d.	1801	...	1830	1901	...	...	...	1930	...	...	...	2001	2005	...	...	2030	2101	2130	2201	...	2230	2302
Leopoldov **1181** d.	|	...	1842	|	...	...	...	1942	...	...	...	|	|	...	...	2042	|	2142	|	...	2242	2314
Piešťany d.	|	...	1854	|	...	...	...	1954	...	...	...	|	2024	...	...	2054	|	2154	|	...	2254	2326
Nové Mesto nad Váhom d.	|	...	1906	|	...	...	...	2006	...	...	...	|	2035	...	...	2106	|	2206	|	...	2306	2338
Trenčín d.	1838	...	1921	1938	...	...	...	2021	...	...	...	2038	2048	...	...	2121	2138	2219	2238	...	2319	2351
Trenčianska Teplá d.	|	...	1927	|	...	...	...	2027	...	...	...	|	2054	...	...	2127	|	...	|	...	...	...
Praha hl. n. **1160** d.	|	1447	|	|	...	1522	...	2048	...	...	...	|	|	...	...	2148	|	...	|	...	...	...
Púchov **1161** d.	1857	|	1950	1957	...	2029	...	...	...	...	...	2057	2107	...	...	...	2157	...	2257	...	...	...
Považská Bystrica **1161** d.	1907	|	1959	2007	...	2038	...	...	...	...	...	2107	2115	...	...	...	2207	...	2307	...	...	...
Žilina **1161** a.	1930	1950	2024	2030	...	2101	...	...	...	...	...	2130	2138	...	...	...	2230	...	2330	...	...	...
Žilina **1185** d.	1933	1953	...	2031	...	...	...	...	...	...	...	2133	...	2144	...	...	...	...	2333	...	...	...
Vrútky **1185** d.	1956	2020	...	2056	...	...	...	...	2110	...	...	2154	...	2210	...	...	...	...	2354	...	...	...
Kraľovany d.	2010	|	...	2110	...	...	...	...	2131	...	...	...	...	2231	...	...	...	...	...	...	...	...
Ružomberok d.	2025	2049	...	2125	...	...	...	...	2156	...	...	...	...	2256	...	...	...	...	...	...	...	...
Liptovský Mikuláš d.	2047	2110	...	2147	...	...	...	...	2219	...	2226	...	...	2319	...	...	...	...	...	...	...	...
Štrba d.	2116	2137	...	2216	...	...	...	...	...	...	2306	...	...	...	...	...	...	...	...	...	...	...
Poprad-Tatry d.	2133	2153	...	2233	...	...	2258	...	...	...	2326	...	...	...	...	...	...	...	...	...	...	...
Spišská Nová Ves d.	2158	2216	...	2258	...	...	2326	...	...	...	...	...	...	...	...	...	...	...	...	...	...	...
Margecany d.	2226	|	...	2326	...	...	0008	...	...	...	...	...	...	...	...	...	...	...	...	...	...	...
Kysak **1196** d.	2240	2256	...	2340	...	...	...	...	...	...	...	...	...	...	...	...	...	...	...	...	...	...
Košice **1196** a.	2253	2312	...	2353	...	...	...	...	...	...	...	...	...	...	...	...	...	...	...	...	...	...
Humenné **1194** a.	...	...	...	...	...	...	...	...	...	...	...	...	...	...	...	...	...	...	...	...	...	...

LOCAL TRAINS PÚCHOV - HORNÍ LIDEČ

km										
0	**Púchov** **1160** d.	0428	...	1132	...	1432	...	1832	...	2232	...
28	**Horní Lideč** **1160** a.	0505	...	1209	...	1509	...	1909	...	2309	...
	Horní Lideč **1160** d.	0512	...	1250	...	1550	...	2112	...	2333	...
	Púchov **1160** a.	0546	...	1324	...	1624	...	2146	...	0007	...

A – 🛏 (1, 2, 3, 4 berth), ▬ (6 berth), [12] 🍷 Praha - Košice (**1222/1223**) - Chop and v.v.
B – SLOVAKIA – 🛏 1, 2 cl., ▬ 2 cl., [2] Praha - Humenné and v.v.
C – PENDOLINO KOŠIČAN – [12] ✕ Praha - Košice and v.v.
D – [12] 🍷 Praha - Žilina and v.v. (Table **1150**).
E – ZEMPLÍN – 🛏 1, 2 cl., ▬ 2 cl., [2] Bratislava - Humenné and v.v.
F – From Martin (**652** d. 0447, **654** d. 0547).

d – Not Aug. 29, Sept. 14, Nov. 16.
e – Not Apr. Aug. 30, Sept. 15, Nov. 17.

* – By 🚌 Bánovce nad Ondavou - Humenné and v.v.

♥ – Operated by REGIOJET. Separate fares.
♠ – Operated by LEO EXPRESS. Separate fares.

TABLE CONTINUES ON NEXT PAGE →

KOŠICE - POPRAD TATRY - ŽILINA - BRATISLAVA 1180

		700	680 E	♠ 1250 🍷	702	Ex 650 🍴	704	Ex 652 🍴 ①–⑥ 🍷F e		706	♥ 1046 🍷 D	Ex 654 🍷 F		708	♥ 1008 🍷	Ex 600 🍴		710	♠ 1254 🍷	Ex 502 🍴		712	Ex 604 🍴
Humenné **1194**	d.	...	2120*	...	...	...	...	...	...	...	...	...	...	...	...	...	...	...	...	...	...	...	...
Košice **1196**	d.	...	2345	2319	...	...	...	...	...	...	...	...	...	...	0350	0407	...	...	0342	0535	...	...	0610
Kysak **1196**	d.	...	0000	0030	...	...	...	...	...	...	...	...	...	...	0403	0421	...	...	0436	0549	...	...	0623
Margecany	d.	...	0015	|	...	...	...	...	...	...	...	...	...	...	|	0437	...	...	|	|	...	...	0638
Spišska Nová Ves	d.	...	0042	0108	...	...	...	...	...	...	...	...	...	...	0442	0504	...	...	0514	0628	...	...	0704
Poprad-Tatry	d.	...	0106	0133	...	...	...	...	...	...	...	...	...	...	0510	0530	...	...	0540	0654	...	...	0730
Štrba	d.	...	|	0146	...	...	...	...	...	...	...	...	...	...	0524	0545	...	...	0553	|	...	...	0745
Liptovský Mikuláš	d.	...	0148	0213	...	...	...	...	...	...	...	...	...	...	0552	0614	...	...	0631	0734	...	...	0814
Ružomberok	d.	...	0207	0231	...	...	...	...	...	...	...	...	...	...	0609	0633	...	...	0649	|	...	...	0833
Kraľovany	d.	...	0223	|	...	...	...	...	...	...	...	...	...	...	|	0649	...	...	|	|	...	...	0849
Vrútky **1185**	d.	...	0238	0257	...	...	...	0504	...	...	...	0604	...	...	0637	0704	...	...	0719	|	...	...	0904
Žilina **1185**	a.	...	0259	0319	...	...	...	0527	...	...	...	0627	...	...	0659	0729	...	...	0741	0837	...	...	0927
Žilina **1161**	d.	...	0303	0321	...	0431	...	0531	...	...	0603	0631	...	...	0703	0731	...	0737	0743	0838	...	...	0931
Považská Bystrica **1161**	d.	...	0329	|	...	0454	...	0554	...	...	0633	0654	...	...	|	0754	...	0802	|	|	...	...	0954
Púchov **1161**	d.	...	0339	|	...	0504	...	0604	...	0612	0642	0704	...	0712	|	0804	...	0812	|	|	...	0912	1004
Praha hl. n. **1160**	a.	...	|	0827	...	|	...	|	...	|	|	|	...	|	1209	|	...	|	1327	|	...	|	|
Trenčianska Teplá	d.	...	0356	...	...	|	...	|	...	0632	0656	|	...	0732	...	|	...	0832	...	|	...	0932	|
Trenčín	d.	0341	0404	...	0441	0524	0541	0624	...	0641	0702	0724	...	0741	...	0824	...	0841	...	0924	...	0941	1024
Nové Mesto nad Váhom	d.	0354	0421	...	0454	|	0554	|	...	0654	0715	|	...	0754	...	|	...	0854	...	|	...	0954	|
Piešťany	d.	0405	0433	...	0505	|	0605	|	...	0705	0724	|	...	0805	...	|	...	0905	...	|	...	1005	|
Leopoldov **1181**	d.	0419	0447	...	0519	|	0619	|	...	0719	|	|	...	0819	...	|	...	0919	...	|	...	1019	|
Trnava **1181**	d.	0433	0501	...	0533	0601	0633	0701	...	0732	0746	0801	...	0833	...	0901	...	0933	...	1002	...	1033	1101
Bratislava hl. st.	a.	0505	0533	...	0605	0633	0705	0733	...	0805	0812	0833	...	0905	...	0933	...	1005	...	1033	...	1105	1133

		714	Ex 606 🍷	♥ 1012 🍷	716		Ex 608 🍴	718	Ex 610 🍴	720		Ex 612 🍴	722		Ex 614 🍴	724	Ex 616 🍴	726		Ex 618 🍷	728	Ex 620 🍴	730
Humenné **1194**	d.	...	...	...	...	...	...	...	...	...	...	...	...	...	...	...	...	...	...	...	...	...	...
Košice **1196**	d.	...	0707	0748	...	...	0807	...	0907	...	...	1007	...	...	1107	...	1207	...	...	1307	...	1407	...
Kysak **1196**	d.	...	0721	0804	...	...	0821	...	0921	...	...	1021	...	...	1121	...	1221	...	...	1321	...	1421	...
Margecany	d.	...	0737	|	...	...	0837	...	0937	...	...	1037	...	...	1137	...	1237	...	...	1337	...	1437	...
Spišska Nová Ves	d.	...	0804	0846	...	...	0904	...	1004	...	...	1104	...	...	1204	...	1304	...	...	1404	...	1504	...
Poprad-Tatry	d.	...	0830	0912	...	...	0930	...	1030	...	...	1130	...	...	1230	...	1330	...	...	1430	...	1530	...
Štrba	d.	...	0845	0925	...	...	0945	...	1045	...	...	1145	...	...	1245	...	1345	...	...	1445	...	1545	...
Liptovský Mikuláš	d.	...	0914	0953	...	...	1014	...	1114	...	...	1214	...	...	1314	...	1414	...	...	1514	...	1614	...
Ružomberok	d.	...	0933	1011	...	...	1033	...	1133	...	...	1233	...	...	1333	...	1433	...	...	1533	...	1633	...
Kraľovany	d.	...	0949	|	...	...	1049	...	1149	...	...	1249	...	...	1349	...	1449	...	...	1549	...	1649	...
Vrútky **1185**	d.	...	1004	1039	...	...	1104	...	1204	...	...	1304	...	...	1404	...	1504	...	...	1604	...	1704	...
Žilina **1185**	a.	...	1027	1101	...	...	1127	...	1227	...	...	1327	...	...	1427	...	1527	...	...	1627	...	1729	...
Žilina **1161**	d.	0937	1031	1103	...	...	1131	1137	1231	...	...	1331	1337	...	1431	...	1531	1537	...	1631	...	1731	1737
Považská Bystrica **1161**	d.	1002	1054	|	...	...	1154	1202	1254	...	...	1354	1402	...	1454	...	1554	1602	...	1654	...	1754	1802
Púchov **1161**	d.	1012	1104	|	1112	...	1204	1212	1304	1312	...	1404	1412	...	1504	1512	1604	1612	...	1704	1712	1804	1812
Praha hl. n. **1160**	a.	|	|	1609	|	...	|	|	|	|	...	|	|	...	|	|	|	|	...	|	|	|	|
Trenčianska Teplá	d.	1032	|	...	1132	...	|	1232	|	1332	...	|	1432	...	|	1532	|	1632	...	|	1732	|	1832
Trenčín	d.	1041	1124	...	1141	...	1224	1241	1324	1341	...	1424	1441	...	1524	1541	1624	1641	...	1724	1741	1824	1841
Nové Mesto nad Váhom	d.	1054	|	...	1154	...	|	1254	|	1354	...	|	1454	...	|	1554	|	1654	...	|	1754	|	1854
Piešťany	d.	1105	|	...	1205	...	|	1305	|	1405	...	|	1505	...	|	1605	|	1705	...	|	1805	|	1905
Leopoldov **1181**	d.	1119	|	...	1219	...	|	1319	|	1419	...	|	1519	...	|	1619	|	1719	...	|	1819	|	1919
Trnava **1181**	d.	1133	1201	...	1233	...	1301	1333	1401	1433	...	1501	1533	...	1601	1633	1701	1733	...	1801	1833	1901	1933
Bratislava hl. st.	a.	1205	1233	...	1305	...	1333	1405	1433	1505	...	1533	1605	...	1633	1705	1733	1805	...	1833	1905	1933	2005

		EC 240 🍴 C	Ex 622 🍷	732		Ex 624 🍷	734		Ex 526 🍴	736		738	Ex 628 🍴		738	Ex 630 🍴		Ex 640 🍷	1764		2	♥ 1020 🍷 A	EN 442 🅁 B
Humenné **1194**	d.	...	...	...	...	...	...	...	...	...	...	...	...	...	...	...	...	...	...	...	...	...	1855*
Košice **1196**	d.	1448	1507	...	...	1607	...	...	1735	...	...	...	1807	...	...	1907	...	2007	2107	...	...	2142	2207
Kysak **1196**	d.	1502	1521	...	...	1621	...	...	1749	...	...	...	1821	...	...	1921	...	2021	2119	...	...	2156	2220
Margecany	d.	|	1537	...	...	1637	...	...	|	...	...	...	1837	...	...	1937	...	2037	2135	...	...	2212	2235
Spišska Nová Ves	d.	1545	1604	...	...	1704	...	...	1828	...	...	...	1904	...	...	2004	...	2104	2211	...	...	2239	2302
Poprad-Tatry	d.	1610	1630	...	...	1730	...	...	1854	...	...	...	1930	...	...	2035	...	2130	2236	...	2241	2259	2342
Štrba	d.	1623	1645	...	...	1745	...	...	|	...	...	...	1945	...	...	2049	...	2145	...	...	2258	2313	|
Liptovský Mikuláš	d.	1652	1714	...	...	1814	...	...	1934	...	...	...	2014	...	...	2117	...	2214	...	...	2334	2341	0022
Ružomberok	d.	1709	1733	...	...	1833	...	...	|	...	...	...	2033	...	...	2135	...	2233	...	...	...	2358	0040
Kraľovany	d.	1725	1749	...	...	1849	...	...	|	...	...	...	2049	...	...	2150	...	2249	...	...	...	|	|
Vrútky **1185**	d.	1739	1804	...	...	1904	...	...	|	...	...	...	2104	...	...	2204	...	2304	...	...	...	0025	0122
Žilina **1185**	a.	1800	1827	...	...	1927	...	...	2037	...	...	...	2127	...	...	2227	...	2327	...	...	...	0047	0145
Žilina **1161**	d.	1803	1831	...	...	1931	1937	...	2038	...	...	2119	2131	...	←	2231	...	...	...	...	...	0049	0146
Považská Bystrica **1161**	d.	|	1854	...	...	1954	2002	...	|	...	...	2141	2154	...	2200	2254	...	...	...	...	...	|	|
Púchov **1161**	d.	|	1904	1912	...	2004	2012	...	|	2112	...	→	2204	...	2212	2303	...	...	...	...	...	|	|
Praha hl. n. **1160**	a.	2247	|	|	...	|	|	...	|	|	...	...	|	...	|	|	...	...	...	...	...	0540	0751
Trenčianska Teplá	d.	...	|	1932	...	|	2032	...	|	2132	...	...	|	...	2232	|	...	...	...	...	...	...	...
Trenčín	d.	...	1924	1941	...	2024	2041	...	2124	2141	...	...	2224	...	2238	2321	...	...	...	...	...	...	...
Nové Mesto nad Váhom	d.	...	|	1954	...	|	2054	...	|	2154	...	...	|	...	...	|	...	...	...	...	...	...	...
Piešťany	d.	...	|	2005	...	|	2105	...	|	2205	...	...	|	...	...	|	...	...	...	...	...	...	...
Leopoldov **1181**	d.	...	|	2019	...	|	2119	...	|	2219	...	...	|	...	...	|	...	...	...	...	...	...	...
Trnava **1181**	d.	...	2001	2033	...	2101	2133	...	2202	2233	...	...	2301	...	...	2356	...	...	...	...	...	...	...
Bratislava hl. st.	a.	...	2033	2105	...	2133	2205	...	2233	2305	...	...	2333	...	...	0024	...	...	...	...	...	...	...

FOR RETURN SERVICE AND FOOTNOTES SEE PREVIOUS PAGE.

1181 BRATISLAVA - PRIEVIDZA and TRNAVA - NITRA — 2nd class

km		741	743	745	747	749	751	753	755	
0	**Bratislava** Nové Mesto d.	0501	0701	0901	1101	1301	1501	1701	1901	...
46	Trnava 1180 d.	0539	0739	0939	1139	1339	1539	1739	1939	...
63	Leopoldov 1180 d.	0555	0755	0955	1155	1355	1555	1755	1955	...
87	Zbehy d.	0622	0822	1022	1222	1422	1622	1822	2022	...
114	Topoľčany ◧ d.	0646	0846	1046	1246	1446	1646	1846	2046	...
131	Partizánske ◧ d.	0718	0918	1118	1318	1518	1718	1918	2114	...
158	**Prievidza** ◧ a.	0750	0950	1150	1350	1550	1750	1950	2152	...

	740	742	744	746	748	750	752	754	
Prievidza ◧ d.	0410	0616	0816	1016	1216	1416	1616	1816	...
Partizánske ◧ d.	0448	0649	0849	1049	1249	1449	1649	1849	...
Topoľčany ◧ d.	0515	0715	0915	1115	1315	1515	1715	1915	...
Zbehy d.	0541	0741	0941	1141	1341	1541	1741	1941	...
Leopoldov 1180 d.	0611	0811	1011	1211	1411	1611	1811	2011	...
Trnava 1180 d.	0626	0826	1026	1226	1426	1626	1826	2026	...
Bratislava Nové Mesto a.	0700	0900	1100	1300	1500	1700	1900	2100	...

km																									
0	**Bratislava** Nové Mesto d.	...	0431	...	0631	...	...	0831	...	1031	...	...	1231	...	1431	...	...	1631	...	1831	...	...	2031	...
46	Trnava 1180 d.	...	0506	0606	0706	...	0806	0906	1006	1106	...	1206	1306	1406	1506	...	1606	1706	1806	1906	...	2018	2106	2206
63	Leopoldov 1180 d.	0421	0521	0621	0721	...	0821	0921	1021	1121	...	1221	1321	1421	1521	...	1621	1721	1821	1921	...	2037	2121	2221
87	Zbehy d.	|	0554	|	0754	...	|	0954	|	1154	...	|	1354	|	1554	...	|	1754	|	1954	...	2110	2154	|
91	Lužianky 1172 d.	0501	0601	0701	0801	...	0901	1001	1101	1201	...	1301	1401	1501	1601	...	1701	1801	1901	2001	...	2119	2201	2301
98	**Nitra** 1172 a.	0513	0608	0708	0808	...	0913	1008	1113	1208	...	1313	1408	1513	1608	...	1713	1808	1913	2008	...	2130	2208	2313

Nitra 1172 d.	0351	0448	0551	0648	...	0751	0848	0951	1048	...	1151	1248	1351	1448	...	1551	1648	1751	1848	...	1951	2048	2151
Lužianky 1172 d.	0401	0502	0601	0702	...	0801	0902	1001	1102	...	1201	1302	1401	1502	...	1601	1702	1801	1902	...	2001	2102	2201
Zbehy d.	0406	|	0606	|	...	0806	|	1006	|	...	1206	|	1406	|	...	1606	|	1806	|	...	2006	|	2206
Leopoldov 1180 d.	0438	0538	0638	0738	...	0838	0938	1038	1138	...	1238	1338	1438	1538	...	1638	1738	1838	1938	...	2038	2138	2238
Trnava 1180 d.	0454	0552	0654	0752	...	0854	0952	1054	1152	...	1254	1352	1454	1552	...	1654	1752	1854	1952	...	2054	2152	2252
Bratislava Nové Mesto a.	0536	...	0736	...	...	0936	...	1136	...	...	1336	...	1536	...	...	1736	...	1936	...	...	2136	...	...

◧ – Slower local trains are available from Topoľčany at 0535 and every two hours until 2135; from Prievidza at 0521, 0714 and every two hours until 2114, 2225 Ⓐ.

1182 LOCAL LINES IN POPRAD TATRY AREA — 2nd class

km										
0	Poprad Tatry d.	0436	...	...	and	2136	...	...	2236	...
13	Starý Smokovec d.	0505	0506	...	hourly	2205	2206	...	2305	2306
19	Tatranská Lomnica a.	|	0520	...	until	|	2220	...	|	2320
29	Štrbské Pleso a.	0545	...	0547	⊡	2245	...	2247	2345	...
34	Štrba a.	...	...	0603		...	...	2303	...	...

Štrba d.	...	0426	...	...		2126	...	...	2226
Štrbské Pleso d.	0416	0439	...	0516	and	2139	...	2216	2239
Tatranská Lomnica d.	|	...	0542	|	hourly	...	2242	|	...
Starý Smokovec d.	0502	...	0556	0602	until	...	2256	2302	...
Poprad Tatry a.	0525	...	...	0625		...	...	2325	...

km			Ⓐ	d		e	d		d		d		Ⓐ		d		⑤f	e	⑦g	d		d		d		
0	Poprad Tatry d.	0445	0545	0616	0645	0729	0816	0845	1016	1045	1216	1245	1345	...	1416	1445	...	1529	...	1616	1645	1816	1845	2016	2045	2300
8	Studený Potok d.	0502	0602	0627	0702	0741	0827	0902	1027	1102	1227	1302	1402	...	1427	1502	...	1541	...	1627	1702	1827	1902	2027	2102	2317
17	Tatranská Lomnica a.	|	|	0639	|	|	0839	|	1039	|	1239	|	|	...	1439	|	...	|	...	1639	|	1839	|	2039	|	|
14	Kežmarok d.	0515	0615	...	0715	0751	...	0915	...	1115	...	1315	1415	...	...	1515	...	1551	...	...	1715	...	1915	...	2115	2330
44	Stará Lubovňa 1196 a.	0558	0657	...	0758	0835	...	0958	...	1158	...	1358	1457	...	...	1558	1605	1634	1705	...	1758	...	1958	...	2158	0013
60	Plaveč 🏛 1196 a.	...	...	...	...	0851	...	...	...	...	...	...	...	...	...	...	1623	1651	1723	...	...	...	...	...	...	...
75	Muszyna a.	...	...	...	...	0910	...	...	...	...	...	...	...	...	...	...	...	1709	...	...	...	...	...	...	...	...

			d	Ⓐ		d		e	d		d			d	Ⓐ		d	⑤f	⑦g		e	d		d	
Muszyna d.	...	...	...	...	...	...	...	1000	...	...	...	...	...	...	...	...	...	...	...	...	1800	...	...	...	...
Plaveč 🏛 1196 d.	...	...	...	...	...	...	...	1019	...	...	...	...	...	...	...	...	...	1637	1737	...	1819	...	...	...	...
Stará Lubovňa 1196 d.	0402	0602	...	0700	0802	...	1002	1033	...	1202	...	1402	...	...	1500	1602	...	1656	1756	1802	1833	...	2002	...	2217
Kežmarok d.	0449	0649	...	0749	0849	...	1049	1117	...	1249	...	1449	...	...	1549	1649	...	...	...	1849	1917	...	2049	...	2304
Tatranská Lomnica d.	|	|	0726	|	|	0926	|	|	1126	|	1326	|	...	1526	|	|	1726	...	...	|	|	1926	|	2126	|
Studený Potok d.	0501	0701	0742	0801	0901	0942	1101	1128	1142	1301	1342	1501	...	1542	1601	1701	1742	...	...	1901	1928	1942	2101	2142	2316
Poprad Tatry a.	0515	0715	0804	0815	0915	0954	1115	1140	1154	1315	1404	1515	...	1604	1615	1715	1804	...	...	1915	1940	1954	2115	2154	2330

d – Ⓒ (daily June 28 - Aug. 31).
e – ⑥⑦ June 14 - Sept. 14.
f – Also Oct. 29; not July 4 - Aug. 29, Oct. 31.
g – Also Sept. 15, Nov. 17; not June 29 - Aug. 30, Sept. 14, Nov. 16.

⊡ – 2036 Poprad Tatry - Štrbské Pleso requires a change of trains at Starý Smokovec. The 21xx Starý Smokovec - Tatranská Lomnica departs at 2116. Some trains are retimed June 28 - Aug. 31.

1183 🚌 POPRAD TATRY - ZAKOPANE - KRAKÓW 🚌 — Flixbus

Poprad Tatry (Bus Station)* d.	0518	1650	1540	1935	...
Starý Smokovec (Bus Station) d.	0530	1702	1555	1950	...
Tatranská Lomnica (Bus Station) d.	0538	1710	1607	2005	...
Zakopane (Bus Station)* a.	|	|	1730	2135	...
Zakopane (Bus Station)* d.	|	|	1740	2145	...
Kraków (MDA Terminal) ⊖ a.	0825	1945	2005	2400	...

Kraków (MDA Terminal) ⊖ d.	0630	1025	1010	2150	...
Zakopane (Bus Station)* a.	0840	|	1215	|	...
Zakopane (Bus Station)* d.	0850	|	1225	|	...
Tatranská Lomnica (Bus Station) d.	1022	1310	1420	0017	...
Starý Smokovec (Bus Station) d.	1035	1320	1432	0027	...
Poprad Tatry (Bus Station)* a.	1055	1335	1450	0045	...

RAIL TICKETS NOT VALID.
* – Adjacent to railway station
⊖ – adjacent to Kraków Gowny.
🏛 = Lysa Polana.

1185 ZVOLEN, BANSKÁ BYSTRICA and PRIEVIDZA - VRÚTKY — 2nd class

km			930			932			934		936		938				940			942			944		946	
		Ⓐ		Ⓒ	Ⓐ		Ⓐ								Ⓐ			Ⓐ			Ⓐ					
0	**Zvolen** osob. 1170 d.	...	0513	...	...	0606	...	...	0806	...	1006	...	1206	...	...	...	1406	...	...	1606	...	...	1806	...	2006	...
21	**Banská Bystrica** 1170 a.	...	0535	...	...	0634	...	...	0834	...	1034	...	1234	...	...	...	1434	...	...	1634	...	...	1834	...	2034	...
21	**Banská Bystrica** d.	...	0537	...	...	0636	...	...	0836	...	1036	...	1236	...	...	...	1436	...	...	1636	...	...	1836	...	2036	...
	Prievidza d.	0439	|	0544	...	|	...	0744	|	0944	|	1144	|	...	...	1344	|	...	1544	|	...	1744	|	1937	|	2214
	Handlová d.	0524	|	0616	...	|	...	0816	|	1016	|	1216	|	...	...	1416	|	...	1616	|	...	1816	|	2021	|	2246
	Horná Štubňa d.	0554	|	0647	...	|	...	0847	|	1047	|	1247	|	...	...	1447	|	...	1647	|	...	1847	|	2050	|	2310
66	Turčianske Teplice d.	0603	0620	0657	0707	0720	0809	0857	0918	1057	1118	1257	1318	...	1409	1457	1518	1609	1657	1718	1809	1857	1918	2058	2118	...
89	Martin d.	0635	0642	0727	0734	0742	0837	0927	0936	1127	1136	1327	1336	...	1437	1527	1536	1637	1727	1736	1837	1927	1936	2128	2136	...
96	**Vrútky** a.	0643	0651	0735	0741	0751	0844	0935	0943	1135	1143	1335	1343	...	1444	1535	1543	1644	1735	1743	1844	1935	1943	2136	2143	...

		931				933		935		937				939			941			943		945		947	
	Ⓐ		Ⓐ	Ⓒ	Ⓐ							Ⓐ				Ⓐ			Ⓐ						
Vrútky d.	0514	0605	0614	0619	0714	0811	0819	1011	1019	1211	1219	1314	...	1411	1419	1514	1611	1619	1714	1811	1819	2011	2019	2113	2224
Martin d.	0522	0613	0622	0627	0722	0819	0827	1019	1027	1218	1227	1322	...	1419	1427	1522	1619	1627	1722	1819	1827	2019	2027	2121	2232
Turčianske Teplice d.	0551	0634	0648	0656	0749	0836	0856	1036	1056	1236	1256	1349	...	1436	1456	1549	1636	1656	1749	1836	1856	2036	2056	2138	2301
Horná Štubňa d.	0611	|	...	0711	...	|	0911	|	1111	|	1311	...	...	|	1511	...	|	1711	...	|	1911	|	2111	|	2311
Handlová d.	0636	|	...	0736	...	|	0936	|	1136	|	1336	...	...	|	1536	...	|	1736	...	|	1936	|	2136	|	...
Prievidza a.	0709	|	...	0812	...	|	1012	|	1212	|	1412	...	...	|	1612	...	|	1812	...	|	2009	|	2208	|	...
Banská Bystrica a.	...	0725	...	...	...	0925	...	1125	...	1325	...	...	...	1525	...	...	1725	...	...	1925	...	2125	...	2223	...
Banská Bystrica 1170 d.	...	0726	...	...	...	0926	...	1126	...	1326	...	...	...	1526	...	...	1726	...	...	1926	...	2126	...	2231	...
Zvolen osob. 1170 a.	...	0754	...	...	...	0954	...	1154	...	1354	...	...	...	1554	...	...	1754	...	...	1954	...	2154	...	2254	...

km		Ⓐ	Ⓒ	Ⓐ	Ⓒ	Ⓒ	Ⓐ				
0	**Horná Štubňa** d.	0349	0519	0604	0909	1319	1519	1719	...	...	...
20	Kremnica d.	0414	0545	0629	0935	1345	1545	1745	...	...	...
46	Hronská Dúbrava a.	0446	0619	0701	1007	1419	1619	1819	...	...	...
57	**Zvolen** osob. a.	0504	0630	0713	1018	1430	1630	1830	...	...	...

	Ⓐ	Ⓒ	Ⓒ		Ⓐ					
Zvolen osob d.	0432	0533	1130	1330	1530	1730	...	...	...	...
Hronská Dúbrava d.	0454	0545	1145	1345	1545	1745	...	...	...	...
Kremnica d.	0527	0618	1218	1418	1618	1818	...	...	...	...
Horná Štubňa a.	0551	0643	1243	1443	1643	1843	...	...	...	...

2nd class — BANSKÁ BYSTRICA - MARGECANY — 1188

Warning! Services are operated by 🚌 Červená Skala - Telgárt and v.v.

km		Ⓐ	Ⓐ	d			Ⓐ		Ⓐ	d
0	**Banská Bystrica** ⊡ d.	...	...	0613	...	1017	...	1417	...	1817
43	Brezno ⊡ d.	...	...	0713	...	1113	...	1513	...	1913
86	Červená Skala d.	...	...	0806	...	1206	...	1606	...	2006
94	Telgárt d.	...	...	0816	...	1216	...	1616	...	2016
106	Dobšinká L'adová Jaskyňa d.	0420	0610	0829	...	1229	1410	1629	1810	2029
114	Dedinky d.	0430	0620	0839	...	1239	1420	1639	1820	2039
139	Nálepkovo a.	0503	0653	0906	...	1306	1453	1706	1853	2106
		◧	◧	|	...	|	◧	|	◧	|
139	Nálepkovo ⊡ d.	0506	0706	0906	1106	1306	1506	1706	1906	2106
171	Gelnica ⊡ d.	0542	0742	0942	1142	1342	1542	1742	1942	2142
179	**Margecany** ⊡ a.	0553	0753	0953	1153	1353	1553	1753	1953	2153

			d				d	Ⓐe	
Margecany ⊡ d.	0607	0807	1007	1207	1407	1607	1807	1807	2007
Gelnica ⊡ d.	0617	0817	1017	1217	1417	1617	1817	1817	2017
Nálepkovo ⊡ a.	0658	0856	1058	1256	1458	1656	1858	1858	2054
	|		|	Ⓐ	|	Ⓐ	|		Ⓐ
Nálepkovo d.	0658	...	1058	1309	1458	1709	1858	...	2109
Dedinky d.	0728	...	1126	1342	1526	1742	1926	...	2142
Dobšinká L'adová Jaskyňa d.	0739	...	1136	1352	1536	1752	1936	...	2152
Telgárt d.	0755	...	1152	...	1552	...	1952	...	...
Červená Skala d.	0814	...	1214	...	1614	...	2014	...	...
Brezno ⊡ d.	0914	...	1314	...	1714	...	2114	...	...
Banská Bystrica ⊡ a.	1012	...	1412	...	1812	...	2212	...	...

– Ⓒ (daily June 14 - Sept. 15).
– Not June 14 - Sept. 15.
⊡ – Local trains run Banská Bystrica - Brezno and Nálepkovo - Margecany every two hours. Some Brezno trains extend to / from Červená Skala.
◧ – Daily.

ZVOLEN - KOŠICE — 1190

km		927 f	911	913	915	917	919	921	923	925 Ⓑg
0	**Zvolen** osob. ⊖ d.	...	0511	0711	0911	1111	1311	1511	1711	1911
54	Lučenec ⊖ d.	...	0600	0800	1000	1200	1400	1600	1800	2000
69	Fil'akovo ⊖ d.	...	0626	0826	1026	1226	1426	1626	1826	2026
98	Jesenské ● d.	...	0654	0854	1054	1254	1454	1654	1854	2054
162	Rožňava d.	0546	0748	0948	1148	1348	1548	1748	1948	2148
202	Moldava nad Bodvou d.	0619	0819	1019	1219	1419	1619	1819	2019	2219
233	**Košice** a.	0644	0844	1044	1244	1444	1644	1905	2044	2244

	910 f	912	914	916	918	920	922	924	926 Ⓑg
Košice d.	0522	0722	0922	1100	1322	1522	1722	1900	2257
Moldava nad Bodvou d.	0546	0746	0946	1146	1346	1546	1746	1946	2322
Rožňava d.	0616	0816	1016	1216	1416	1616	1816	2016	2355
Jesenské ● d.	0707	0907	1107	1307	1507	1707	1907	2107	...
Fil'akovo zastávka ⊖ d.	0737	0937	1137	1337	1537	1737	1937	2137	...
Lučenec ⊖ d.	0804	1004	1204	1404	1604	1804	2004	2204	...
Zvolen osob. ⊖ a.	0849	1049	1249	1449	1649	1849	2049	2249	...

– ①–⑥ (not Aug. 30, Sept. 15, Nov. 17).
– Not Aug. 29, Sept. 14, Nov. 16.
⊖ – Local trains run Zvolen - Lučenec and Lučenec - Jesenské every two hours.
● – Jesenske - Rimavská Sobota and v.v. (*11 km.* Journey 12 minutes):
From Jesenske at 0509, 0609 Ⓐ, 0709 and every two hours until 2109.
From Rimavská Sobota at 0535 Ⓐ, 0635 and every two hours until 2035.

2nd class — KOŠICE - HUMENNÉ - MEDZILABORCE — 1194

Except where otherwise noted, Košice - Humenné and v.v. services are operated by 🚌 Bánovce nad Ondavou - Humenné and v.v.

km		681 A		443 B							Ⓑg
0	**Košice** d.	0501	0701	0901	1101	1301	1501	1701	1901	2101	2301
53	Trebišov d.	0547	0753	0948	1153	1353	1553	1753	1953	2153	2353
64	Bánovce nad Ondavou d.	0605	0815	1015	1215	1415	1615	1815	2015	2205	0005
73	Michalovce d.	0627	0837	1037	1237	1437	1637	1837	2037	2227	0027
88	Strážske d.	0645	0855	1055	1255	1455	1655	1855	2055	2245	0045
97	**Humenné** a.	0655	0905	1105	1305	1505	1705	1905	2105	2255	0055

		Ⓐ							442 B	680 A
Humenné d.	0500	0555	0655	0855	1055	1255	1455	1655	1855	2120
Strážske d.	0510	0605	0705	0905	1105	1305	1505	1705	1905	2130
Michalovce d.	0530	0625	0725	0925	1125	1325	1525	1725	1925	2150
Bánovce nad Ondavou d.	0558	0658	0758	0958	1158	1358	1558	1758	1958	2228
Trebišov d.	0608	0708	0808	1008	1208	1408	1608	1808	2008	2238
Košice a.	0659	0759	0859	1059	1259	1459	1659	1859	2059	2325

km					⑦h	j	⑦h	j	⑦h	j	
0	**Humenné** ⊙ d.	0836	1036	1236	1356	1436	1556	1636	1756	1836	2110
41	**Medzilaborce** ⊙ a.	0946	1146	1346	1506	1546	1706	1746	1906	1946	2207

				⑦h	j	⑦h	j	⑦h	j	
Medzilaborce ⊙ d.	0827	1027	1227	1349	1427	1549	1627	1749	1827	2007
Humenné ⊙ a.	0924	1124	1324	1445	1524	1645	1724	1845	1924	2104

A – ZEMPLÍN – see Table **1180.**
B – SLOVAKIA – see Table **1180**.
– Not Aug. 29, Sept. 14, Nov. 16.
h – Also Sept. 15, Nov. 17; not Sept, 14, Nov. 16.
j – ①–⑥ (also Sept. 14, Nov. 16; not Sept. 15, Nov. 17).
⊙ – Also from Humenné at 0636, 2312; also from Medzilaborce at 0627, 2211.

2nd class — KOŠICE - ČIERNA NAD TISOU - CHOP - MUKACHEVO — 1195

km		960 [R]	1222 ♥	962 [R]	964 [R]					
0	**Košice** d.	0546	0638	1046	1746	...		0706	and	2306
62	Slovenské N. Mesto d.	|	|	|	|	...	**A**	0812	every	0012
95	**Čierna nad Tisou** a.	0710	|	1213	|	...	**L**	0850	**two**	0050
95	**Čierna nad Tisou** 🏛 d.	0737	|	1311	|	...	**S**	...	hours	...
105	Chop 🏛 a.	0750	0938	1335	2041	...	**O**	...	until	...
105	Chop **1715** d.	0847	...	1422	...	...		...		...
146	**Mukachevo** ⊕ **1715** a.	1105	...	1653	...	...		...		...

	961 [R]	963 [R]	1223 ♥	965 [R]					
Mukachevo ⊕ **1715** d.	...	1154	...	1857	...		...	and	...
Chop **1715** a.	...	1204	...	1915	...	**A**	...	every	...
Chop 🏛 d.	0859	1248	1635	2006	...	**L**	...	**two**	...
Čierna nad Tisou 🏛 a.	|	1306	|	2024	...	**S**	...	hours	...
Čierna nad Tisou d.	|	1358	|	2128	...	**O**	0702	until	1902
Slovenské N. Mesto d.	|	|	|	|	...		0745	⊖	1945
Košice a.	1218	1520	2018	2250	...		0850		2050

♥ – To / from Praha (Table **1180**). Operated by Regiojet. Seperate fares apply.
⊕ – Ukraine time (one hour ahead of Slovakia).
⊖ – Changes to Čierna nad Tisou departure times: 1442, 1642 (**not** 1502, 1702).

2nd class — KOŠICE - PREŠOV - PLAVEČ — 1196

km														⑤j		⑦k								
0	**Košice** **1180** d.	0443	0543	0643	0743	0843	0943	1043	...	1143	1243	1343	1443	1443	1543	1543	...	1643	1743	1843	1943	2043	2137	2243
16	Kysak **1180** d.	0459	0559	0659	0759	0859	0959	1059	...	1159	1259	1359	1459	1459	1559	1559	...	1659	1759	1859	1959	2059	2159	2259
33	**Prešov** **1180** a.	0514	0614	0714	0814	0914	1014	1114	...	1214	1314	1414	1514	1514	1614	1614	...	1714	1814	1914	2014	2114	2214	2314
33	**Prešov** d.	0517	0617	0717	0817	0917	1017	1117	...	1217	1317	1417	1517	1517	1617	1617	...	1717	1817	1917	2017	2117	2217	2317
65	Lipany a.	0555	0659	0755	0855	0955	1055	1155	...	1255	1355	1455	1555	1555	1655	1655	...	1755	1855	1955	2055	2155	2255	2355
88	**Plaveč** a.	...	...	...	...	...	...	...	...	...	...	...	...	1627	...	1723	...	...	...	...	...	...	...	...

																	⑤j		⑦k				
Plaveč d.	...	...	...	...	...	...	...	...	...	...	...	...	...	...	...	...	1635	...	1731	...	...	...	...
Lipany d.	0402	0502	0602	0702	0802	0902	1002	...	1102	1202	1302	1402	1502	1602	1702	...	1702	1802	1802	1902	2002	2102	2202
Prešov a.	0439	0539	0639	0739	0839	0939	1039	...	1139	1239	1339	1439	1539	1639	1739	...	1739	1839	1839	1939	2039	2139	2239
Prešov **1180** d.	0442	0542	0642	0742	0842	0942	1042	...	1142	1242	1342	1442	1542	1642	1742	...	1742	1842	1842	1942	2042	2142	2242
Kysak **1180** a.	0500	0604	0700	0804	0900	1000	1100	...	1200	1300	1404	1500	1604	1700	1800	...	1800	1900	1900	2000	2100	2200	2304
Košice **1180** a.	0512	0617	0712	0817	0912	1012	1112	...	1212	1312	1417	1512	1617	1712	1812	...	1812	1912	1912	2012	2112	2212	2317

– Also Oct. 29; not July 4 - Aug. 29, Oct. 31.
k – Also Sept. 15, Nov. 17; not June 29 - Aug. 30, Sept. 14, Nov. 16.

2nd class — PREŠOV - BARDEJOV and HUMENNÉ — 1197

km				Ⓐ	Ⓐ	Ⓒ								Ⓐ			Ⓐ								
0	**Prešov** d.	0418	0448	0548	0618	0625	0648	0825	0848	1025	1048	1225	1248	1348	1425	1448	1548	1625	1648	1825	1848	2025	2048	2225	2248
10	Kapušany pri Prešove d.	0429	0502	0602	0629	0636	0702	0836	0902	1036	1102	1236	1302	1402	1436	1502	1602	1636	1702	1836	1902	2036	2102	2236	2302
45	**Bardejov** a.	0523	|	|	0723	0730	|	0930	|	1130	|	1330	|	|	1530	|	|	1730	|	1930	|	2130	|	2330	|
46	Vranov nad Toplou d.	...	0546	0646	...	...	0746	...	0946	...	1146	...	1346	1446	...	1546	1646	...	1746	...	1946	...	2146	...	2346
70	**Humenné** a.	...	0620	0720	...	...	0820	...	1020	...	1220	...	1420	1520	...	1620	1720	...	1820	...	2020	...	2220	...	...

			Ⓐ		Ⓐ	Ⓒ	Ⓐ										Ⓐ							
Humenné d.	...	...	0439	0539	...	...	0637	0739	...	0939	...	1139	...	1339	...	1439	1539	...	1739	...	1939	...	2139	...
Vranov nad Toplou d.	0415	...	0508	0608	...	...	0708	0808	...	1008	...	1208	...	1408	...	1508	1608	...	1808	...	2008	...	2208	...
Bardejov d.	|	0423	|	|	0623	0630	|	|	0830	|	1030	|	1230	|	1430	|	|	1630	|	1830	|	2030	|	2230
Kapušany pri Prešove d.	0502	0514	0602	0702	0714	0722	0802	0902	0922	1102	1122	1302	1322	1502	1522	1602	1702	1722	1902	1922	2102	2122	2302	2322
Prešov a.	0513	0525	0613	0713	0725	0733	0813	0913	0933	1113	1133	1313	1333	1513	1533	1613	1713	1733	1913	1933	2113	2133	2313	2333

HUNGARY

Operators: MÁV Személyszállítási (www.mavcsoport.hu) running the network of MÁV. Certain western services are operated by Györ-Sopron-Ebenfurthi Vasút (GySEV - www.gysev.hu).

Services: All trains convey first and second class seating, except where shown otherwise in table headers, footnotes or train columns, or where the footnote shows sleeping or couchette cars only. Descriptions of sleeping (🛏) and couchette (▬) cars appear on page 10. Certain international services cannot be used for internal journeys. Readers are advised to ensure they have a valid ticket before boarding trains as tickets purchased on board are subject to high surcharges (25000 HUF in the Budapest suburban area).

Timings: Valid **December 15, 2024 - December 13, 2025** with amendments as received. Engineering work may affect travel - it is not always possible to show short-term changes.

Reservations: Most InterCity (*IC*) and Expressvonat (*Ex*) trains have **compulsory seat reservation**, as shown by 🄁 in the tables. Seat reservation is also compulsory for domestic journeys on international EuroCity (*EC*), RailJet Express (*RJX*) and EuroNight (*EN*) services. Note that the former distance-related *IC* supplement no longer applies. Seat reservation fees: Expressvonat (*Ex*): 300 HUF. InterCity (*IC*), EuroCity (*EC*), RailJet Express (*RJX*) and EuroNight (*EN*): In second-class bought at least one day in advance 650 HUF, or on the day of travel 990 HUF; in first-class 1990 HUF (the same price if bought in advance or at the day of travel); in first-class premium (available only on some domestic InterCitytrains) 2990 HUF this includes a free hot drink from the buffet carriage. If the reservation is not paid in advance a higher fee is payable on the train 1000 HUF or 10 EURO.

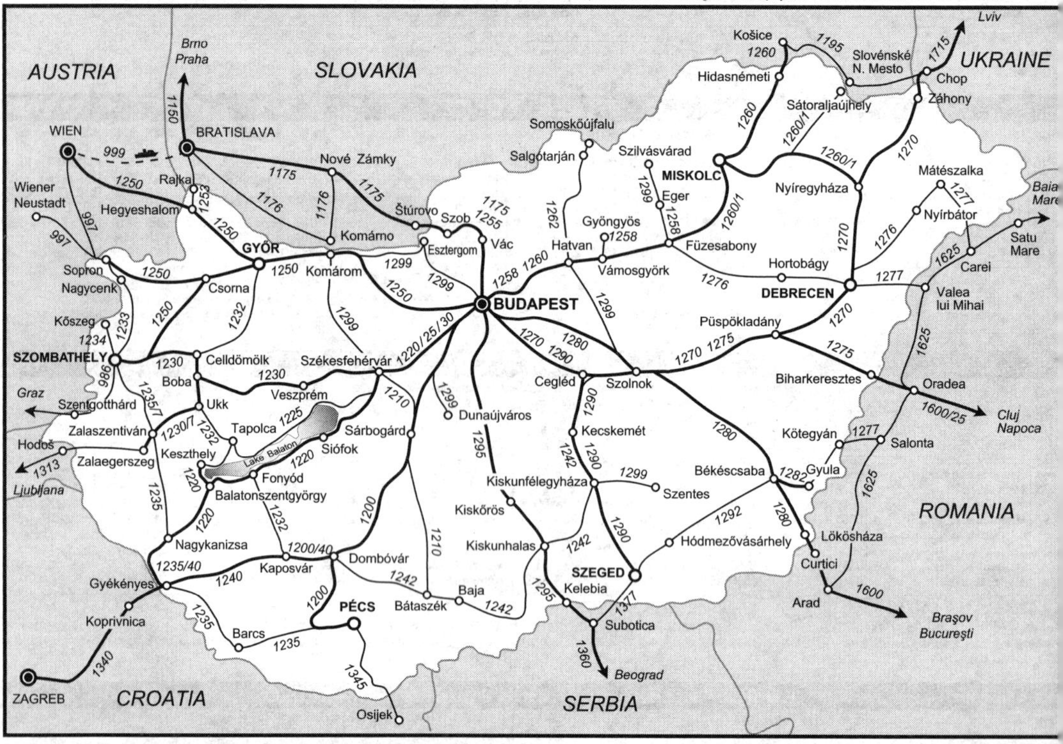

1200 BUDAPEST - DOMBÓVÁR - KAPOSVÁR and PÉCS

km		2 Ⓐ	2	2	2	*IC* **800** 🄁	2	*IC* **822** 🄁	2	*IC* **802** 🄁	2	2	*IC* **812** 🄁	2	2 ⑦	*IC* **804** 🄁	2	*IC* **824** 🄁	2	*IC* **814** 🄁	2	2	*IC* **806** 🄁	2 Ⓐ	2
0	**Budapest** Keleti d.	...	...	...	...	0553	...	0630	...	0753	...	...	0953	...	...	1153	...	1230	...	1353	...	...	1553	...	...
	Budapest Déli d.	...	...	...	0450	|	...	|	0650	|	...	0850	|	...	1050	|	...	|	1250	|	...	1450	|	1550	...
13	Kelenföld d.	...	...	...	0457	0612**u**	...	0652**u**	0657	0812**u**	...	0857	1012**u**	...	1057	1212**u**	...	1252**u**	1257	1412**u**	...	1457	1612**u**	1557	...
62	Pusztaszabolcs a.	...	...	...	0549	|	...	|	0749	|	...	0949	|	...	1149	|	...	|	1349	|	...	1549	|	1649	...
62	Pusztaszabolcs d.	...	...	...	0559	|	...	|	0759	|	...	0959	|	...	1159	|	...	|	1359	|	...	1559	|	1656	...
93	Sárbogárd d.	...	0441	...	0629	0700	...	|	0829	0900	...	1029	1100	...	1219	1300	...	|	1429	1500	...	1629	1659	1724	...
173	Dombóvár a.	...	0557	...	0746	0752	...	0858	0946	0952	...	1146	1152	...	...	1352	...	1458	1546	1552	...	1746	1752	...	...
173	Dombóvár **1240** d.	0511	...	0600	...	0753	0800	0859	...	0953	1000	...	1153	1200	...	1353	1400	1459	...	1553	1600	...	1753	...	1800
204	**Kaposvár** **1240** a.	|	...	|	...	|	|	0925	...	|	|	...	|	|	...	|	|	1525	...	|	|	...	|	...	|
218	Szentlőrinc **1232** d.	0601	...	0647	...	0824	0846	...	...	1024	1046	...	1224	1246	...	1424	1446	...	...	1624	1646	...	1824	...	1846
237	**Pécs** **1232** a.	0617	...	0707	...	0838	0909	...	...	1038	1109	...	1238	1309	...	1438	1509	...	...	1638	1709	...	1838	...	1909

	IC **826** 🄁	2	*IC* **808** 🄁	2 Ⓐ	2	2	*IC* **818** 🄁	2	
Budapest Keleti d.	1630	...	1753	...	...	...	1953	...	...
Budapest Déli d.	|	1650	|	1750	...	1850	|	2050	...
Kelenföld d.	1652**u**	1657	1812**u**	1757	...	1857	2012**u**	2057	...
Pusztaszabolcs a.	|	1749	|	1849	...	1949	|	2149	...
Pusztaszabolcs d.	|	1804	|	1904	...	2004	|	2159	...
Sárbogárd d.	|	1829	1900	1941	...	2029	2100	2227	...
Dombóvár a.	1858	1946	1952	...	...	2146	2152	...	...
Dombóvár **1240** d.	1859	...	1953	...	2007	...	2153	...	...
Kaposvár **1240** a.	1925	...	|	...	|	...	|	...	...
Szentlőrinc **1232** d.	**d**	...	2024	...	2052	...	2226	...	...
Pécs **1232** a.	...	...	2038	...	2117	...	2240	...	...

	2 Ⓐ	2 Ⓒ	2	2 Ⓐ	*IC* **809** 🄁	2 Ⓐ	*IC* **829** 🄁	2	*IC* **807** 🄁
Pécs **1232** d.	...	...	0435	...	0514	...	...	0633	0714
Szentlőrinc **1232** d.	...	...	0459	...	0529	...	**d**	0702	0729
Kaposvár **1240** d.	...	...	|	...	|	...	0605	|	|
Dombóvár **1240** a.	...	...	0549	...	0605	...	0631	0747	0805
Dombóvár d.	0344	0409	...	...	0606	0609	0632	...	0806
Sárbogárd d.	0457	0527	...	0623	0701	0727	|	...	0900
Pusztaszabolcs a.	0521	0552	...	0652	|	0752	|	...	|
Pusztaszabolcs d.	0526	0608	...	0658	|	0757	|	...	|
Kelenföld a.	0606	0701	...	0737	0749**s**	0836	0839**s**	...	0946**s**
Budapest Déli a.	0614	0709	...	0744	|	0844	|	...	|
Budapest Keleti a.	...	...	...	...	0805	...	0859	...	1005

	2	2	*IC* **817** 🄁	2	2	*IC* **805** 🄁	2 ⑦	*IC* **825** 🄁	2	*IC* **815** 🄁	2	2	*IC* **803** 🄁	2	*IC* **823** 🄁	2	*IC* **801** 🄁	2	2	*IC* **811** 🄁	2	2	2 Ⓑ	2 Ⓑ
Pécs **1232** d.	...	0843	0914	...	1043	1114	...	...	1243	1314	...	1443	1514	...	...	1643	1714	...	1843	1914	...	2045	2148	2245
Szentlőrinc **1232** d.	...	0902	0929	...	1102	1129	...	...	1302	1329	...	1502	1529	...	...	1702	1729	...	1902	1929	...	2108	2204	2300
Kaposvár **1240** d.	...	|	|	...	|	|	...	1200	|	|	...	|	|	...	1600	|	|	...	|	|	...	|	...	|
Dombóvár **1240** a.	...	0947	1005	...	1147	1205	...	1231	1347	1405	...	1547	1605	...	1631	1747	1805	...	1947	2005	...	2153	...	2352**e**
Dombóvár d.	0809	...	1006	1009	...	1206	...	1232	...	1406	1409	...	1606	1609	1632	...	1806	1809	...	2006	2009	...	...	...
Sárbogárd d.	0927	...	1100	1127	...	1300	1327	|	...	1500	1527	...	1659	1727	|	...	1859	1927	...	2059	2127	...	...	...
Pusztaszabolcs a.	0952	...	|	1152	...	|	1352	|	...	|	1552	...	|	1752	|	...	|	1952	...	|	2152	...	...	...
Pusztaszabolcs d.	0957	...	|	1208	...	|	1408	|	...	|	1608	...	|	1808	|	...	|	2008	...	|	2208	...	...	...
Kelenföld a.	1101	...	1146**s**	1301	...	1346**s**	1501	1439**s**	...	1546**s**	1701	...	1746**s**	1901	1839**s**	...	1946**s**	2101	...	2146**s**	2301	...	...	...
Budapest Déli a.	1109	...	|	1309	...	|	1509	|	...	|	1709	...	|	1909	|	...	|	2109	...	|	2309	...	...	...
Budapest Keleti a.	...	...	1205	...	...	1405	...	1459	...	1605	...	...	1805	...	1859	...	2005	...	...	2205	...	...	...	...

d – To/from Gyékényes (Table **1240**).
e – Ⓑ only.
s – Calls to set down only.
u – Calls to pick up only.

2nd class SZÉKESFEHÉRVÁR - SZEKSZÁRD - BAJA 1210

km		2	IR 8302 Ⓐ	IR 18302 Ⓐ	IR 8392 ⑥	IR 8304	IR 8394	IR 8306	IR 8396	IR 8308	IR 8398
0	**Székesfehérvár** d.	...	*0523*	0558	0758	0958	1158	1358	1558	1758	1958
39	Sárbogárd ◧ a.	...	*0619*	0654	0854	1054	1254	1454	1654	1854	2054
39	Sárbogárd ◧ d.	0407	0702	0702	0902	1102	1302	1502	1702	1902	2102
104	Szekszárd d.	0512	0800	0800	1000	1200	1400	1600	1800	2000	2200
123	Bátaszék **1242** a.	0530	0818	0818	1018	1218	1418	1618	1818	2018	2218
143	**Baja** **1242** a.	0555	0839	0839	1039	1239	1439	1639	1839	2039	...

	2 Ⓒ	2 Ⓐ	IR 8309	IR 8307	IR 8397 ⚒	IR 8305	IR 8395	IR 8303	IR 8393	IR 8301
Baja **1242** d.	...	...	0514	0714	0914	1114	1314	1514	1714	1914
Bátaszék **1242** d.	0353	...	0534	0734	0934	1134	1334	1534	1734	1934
Szekszárd d.	0415	...	0559	0759	0959	1159	1359	1559	1759	1959
Sárbogárd ◧ a.	0519	...	0655	0855	1055	1255	1455	1655	1855	2055
Sárbogárd ◧ d.	...	0620	0701	0901	1101	1301	1501	1701	1901	2101
Székesfehérvár a.	...	0716	0757	0957	1157	1357	1557	1757	1957	2157

◧ – For connections from/to Budapest see Table **1200**.

2nd class BUDAPEST - SIÓFOK - FONYÓD - KESZTHELY and NAGYKANIZSA 1220

SERVICE TO MAY 11 AND FROM SEPTEMBER 22. The summer service will be found on pages 519 – 522.
Additional slower trains and connections are available Budapest - Székesfehérvár - Siófok and v.v. Carriages without 🅁 are available on *IC* trains.
TRAIN NAMES: Budapest - Nagykanizsa *IC* trains are named TOPART. Budapest - Keszthely *IC* trains are named BALATON.

km		Ⓐ		Ⓐ		IC 850 🅁	IC 860 🅁	IC 842 🅁	IC 862 🅁	IC 852 🅁	IC 864 🅁	IC 844 🅁	IC 874 🅁	IC 854 🅁	IC 866 🅁	IC 204 🅁 A	IC 876 🅁	IC 856 🅁	IC 868 🅁	IC 848 🅁		IC 878 🅁	
0	**Budapest** Déli 1225 1230 d.	...	...	0405	...	0530	0635	0735	0835	0935	1035	1135	1235	1335	1435	1535	1635	1735	1835	1935	...	2035	...
4	Kelenföld 1225 1230 d.	...	...	0412	...	0537	0642	0742	0842	0942	1042	1142	1242	1342	1442	1542	1642	1742	1842	1942	...	2042	*2207*
67	**Székesfehérvár** 1225 1230 a.	...	...	0509	...	0615	0720	0820	0920	1020	1120	1220	1320	1420	1520	1620	1720	1820	1920	2020	...	2120	*2239*
67	**Székesfehérvár** d.	...	...	0511	...	0616	0721	0821	0921	1021	1121	1221	1321	1421	1521	1621	1721	1821	1921	2021	...	2121	2251
95	Lepsény d.	...	...	0535	...	0640	0740	0840	|	1040	|	1240	|	1440	|	1640	|	1840	|	2040	...	2142	2315
115	**Siófok** a.	...	...	0555	...	0655	0755	0855	0955	1055	1155	1255	1355	1455	1555	1655	1755	1855	1955	2055	...	2159	2334
115	**Siófok** d.	...	...	...	...	0657	0757	0857	0957	1057	1157	1257	1357	1457	1557	1657	1757	1857	1957	2057	...	2201	...
124	Zamárdi d.	...	...	...	...	0704	0804	0904	1004	1104	1204	1304	1404	1504	1604	1704	1804	1904	2004	2104	...	2208	...
130	Balatonföldvár d.	...	...	...	...	0709	0809	0909	1009	1109	1209	1309	1409	1509	1609	1709	1809	1909	2009	2109	...	2213	...
139	Balatonszemes d.	...	...	...	...	0718	0818	0918	1018	1118	1218	1318	1418	1518	1618	1718	1818	1918	2018	2118	...	2222	...
146	Balatonlelle d.	...	...	...	...	0724	0824	0924	1024	1124	1224	1324	1424	1524	1624	1724	1824	1924	2024	2124	...	2228	...
149	Balatonboglár d.	...	...	...	...	0730	0830	0930	1030	1130	1230	1330	1430	1530	1630	1730	1830	1930	2030	2130	...	2233	...
157	**Fonyód** a.	...	...	...	...	0735	0835	0935	1035	1135	1235	1335	1435	1535	1635	1735	1835	1935	2035	2135	...	2239	...
157	**Fonyód** 1232 d.	...	...	...	0632	0737	0837	0937	1037	1137	1237	1337	1437	1537	1637	1737	1837	1937	2037	2137	...	...	...
165	Balatonfenyves 1232 d.	...	...	...	0641	0743	0843	0943	1043	1143	1243	1343	1443	1543	1643	1743	1843	1943	2043	2143	...	...	...
181	Balatonszentgyörgy 1232 a.	...	...	...	0659	0756	0857	0956	1057	1156	1257	1356	1457	1556	1657	1756	1857	1956	2057	2156	...	...	...
181	Balatonszentgyörgy 1232 d.	0442	0601	...	0700	0801	0900	1001	1100	1201	1300	1401	1500	1601	1700	1801	1900	2001	2100	2201	2208	...	...
221	**Keszthely** 1232 a.	|	|	...	0711	|	0911	|	1111	|	1311	|	1511	|	1711	|	1911	|	2111	|	2219	...	...
221	**Nagykanizsa** a.	0529	0644	...	...	0844	...	1044	...	1244	...	1444	...	1644	...	1844	...	2044	...	2244	...	...	...
352	*Zagreb* 1340 a.	...	...	...	...	...	...	...	...	...	...	...	...	...	...	2200	...	...	...	...	...	...	...

				IC 849 🅁	Ⓐ	Ⓐ	IC 867 🅁	IC 847 🅁	IC 877 🅁	IC 857 🅁	IC 865 🅁	IC 845 🅁	IC 875 🅁	IC 855 🅁	IC 863 🅁	IC 843 🅁	IC 873 🅁	IC 853 🅁	IC 861 🅁	IC 201 🅁 A	IC 871 🅁	
Zagreb 1340 d.	...	...	...	...	...	...	...	...	...	...	...	...	...	...	...	...	...	...	...	1630	...	...
Nagykanizsa d.	...	0350	...	0514	0610	...	...	0714	...	0914	...	1114	...	1314	...	1514	...	1714	...	1914	...	...
Keszthely 1232 d.	...	|	0428	|	|	...	0648	|	0848	|	1048	|	1248	|	1448	|	1648	|	1848	|	2048	...
Balatonszentgyörgy 1232 a.	...	0433	0439	0557	0656	...	0659	0757	0859	0957	1059	1157	1259	1357	1459	1557	1659	1757	1859	1957	2059	...
Balatonszentgyörgy 1232 d.	...	...	0440	0603	...	...	0702	0803	0902	1003	1102	1203	1302	1403	1502	1603	1702	1803	1902	2003	2102	...
Balatonfenyves 1232 d.	...	...	0458	0617	...	...	0717	0817	0917	1017	1117	1217	1317	1417	1517	1617	1717	1817	1917	2017	2118	...
Fonyód 1232 a.	...	...	0506	0622	...	...	0722	0822	0922	1022	1122	1222	1322	1422	1522	1622	1722	1822	1922	2022	2123	...
Fonyód d.	...	...	0507	0624	...	0645	0724	0824	0924	1024	1124	1224	1324	1424	1524	1624	1724	1824	1924	2024	2124	...
Balatonboglár d.	...	...	0516	0630	...	0652	0730	0830	0930	1030	1130	1230	1330	1430	1530	1630	1730	1830	1930	2030	2130	...
Balatonlelle d.	...	...	0520	0634	...	0657	0734	0834	0934	1034	1134	1234	1334	1434	1534	1634	1734	1834	1934	2034	2134	...
Balatonszemes d.	...	...	0527	0640	...	0705	0740	0840	0940	1040	1140	1240	1340	1440	1540	1640	1740	1840	1940	2040	2140	...
Balatonföldvár d.	...	...	0535	0649	...	0718	0749	0849	0949	1049	1149	1249	1349	1449	1549	1649	1749	1849	1949	2049	2149	...
Zamárdi d.	...	...	0541	0654	...	0725	0754	0854	0954	1054	1154	1254	1354	1454	1554	1654	1754	1854	1954	2054	2154	...
Siófok a.	...	...	0551	0701	...	0735	0801	0901	1001	1101	1201	1301	1401	1501	1601	1701	1801	1901	2001	2101	2201	...
Siófok d.	0428	...	0552	0703	...	...	0803	0903	1003	1103	1203	1303	1403	1503	1603	1703	1803	1903	2003	2103	2203	2205
Lepsény d.	0449	...	0612	0717	...	...	|	0917	|	1117	|	1317	|	1517	|	1717	|	1917	|	2117	|	2224
Székesfehérvár a.	0513	...	0636	0736	...	...	0836	0936	1036	1136	1236	1336	1436	1536	1636	1736	1836	1936	2036	2136	2236	2247
Székesfehérvár 1225 1230 d.	0527	...	0637	0737	...	...	0837	0937	1037	1137	1237	1337	1437	1537	1637	1737	1837	1937	2037	2137	2237	2248
Kelenföld 1225 1230 a.	0611	...	0721	0816	...	...	0916	1016	1116	1216	1316	1416	1516	1616	1716	1816	1916	2016	2116	2216	2316	2345
Budapest Déli 1225 1230 a.	0619	...	0729	0824	...	...	0924	1024	1124	1224	1324	1424	1524	1624	1724	1824	1924	2024	2124	2224	2324	2354

A – AGRAM-TOPART – 2 Budapest - Zagreb and v.v.

2nd class BUDAPEST - SZÉKESFEHÉRVÁR - BALATONFÜRED - TAPOLCA 1225

SERVICE TO MAY 11 AND FROM SEPTEMBER 22. The summer service will be found on pages 519 – 522.
Connecting trains Budapest - Székesfehérvár and v.v. may require 🅁.

km		Ⓐ				Ⓐ											Ⓒ d							
0	**Budapest** Déli 1220 1230 d.	...	...	...	...	0405	...	*0530*	0705	*0735*	0905	*0935*	1105	*1135*	1305	*1335*	...	1505	*1535*	1705	*1735*	1905	*1935*	...
4	Kelenföld 1220 1230 d.	...	...	...	...	0412	...	*0537*	0712	*0742*	0912	*0942*	1112	*1142*	1312	*1342*	...	1512	*1542*	1712	*1742*	1912	*1942*	*2145*
67	**Székesfehérvár** 1220 1230 a.	...	...	...	...	0509	...	*0615*	0750	*0820*	0950	*1020*	1150	*1220*	1350	*1420*	...	1550	*1620*	1750	*1820*	1950	*2020*	*2239*
67	**Székesfehérvár** d.	...	...	0421	...	...	0526	0626	0751	0829	0951	1029	1151	1229	1351	1429	...	1551	1629	1751	1829	1951	2029	2256
105	Balatonkenese d.	...	...	0505	...	...	0620	0711	0825	0910	1025	1110	1225	1310	1425	1510	...	1625	1710	1825	1910	2025	2110	2337
117	Balalatonalmádi d.	...	...	0521	...	...	0633	0732	0838	0932	1038	1132	1238	1332	1438	1532	...	1638	1732	1838	1932	2038	2129	2350
123	Alsóörs d.	...	...	0528	...	...	0640	0739	0845	0939	1045	1139	1245	1339	1445	1539	...	1645	1739	1845	1939	2045	2136	2357
132	**Balatonfüred** a.	...	...	0538	...	...	0651	0750	0855	0950	1055	1150	1255	1350	1455	1550	...	1655	1750	1855	1950	2055	2147	0008
132	**Balatonfüred** d.	0408	0508	...	0602	...	0705	...	0905	...	1105	...	1305	...	1505	...	1600	1705	...	1905	...	2105	...	...
157	Révfülöp d.	0442	0551	...	0640	...	0742	...	0942	...	1142	...	1342	...	1542	...	1636	1742	...	1942	...	2142	...	...
168	Badacsonytomaj d.	0500	0609	...	0654	...	0759	...	0959	...	1159	...	1359	...	1559	...	1650	1759	...	1959	...	2159	...	...
170	Badacsony d.	0503	0612	...	0657	...	0803	...	1003	...	1203	...	1403	...	1603	...	1653	1803	...	2003	...	2203	...	...
184	**Tapolca** a.	0522	0631	...	0715	...	0822	...	1022	...	1222	...	1422	...	1622	...	1709	1822	...	2022	...	2222	...	...

			Ⓐ						Ⓒ d														
Tapolca d.	...	...	...	0441	...	0551	...	0734	0844	...	0934	...	1134	...	1334	...	1534	...	1734	...	1934	2134	...
Badacsony d.	...	...	...	0457	...	0606	...	0753	0859	...	0953	...	1153	...	1353	...	1553	...	1753	...	1953	2153	...
Badacsonytomaj d.	...	...	...	0500	...	0609	...	0759	0903	...	0959	...	1159	...	1359	...	1559	...	1759	...	1959	2159	...
Révfülöp d.	...	...	...	0514	...	0621	...	0815	0917	...	1015	...	1215	...	1415	...	1615	...	1815	...	2015	2215	...
Balatonfüred a.	...	...	...	0547	...	0652	...	0852	0956	...	1052	...	1252	...	1452	...	1652	...	1852	...	2052	2252	...
Balatonfüred d.	0351	0451	...	...	0551	0702	0805	0902	...	1005	1102	1205	1302	1405	1502	1605	1702	1805	1902	2005	2111	...	...
Alsóörs d.	0401	0501	...	...	0601	0711	0815	0911	...	1015	1111	1215	1311	1415	1511	1615	1711	1815	1911	2015	2122	...	...
Balalatonalmádi d.	0408	0508	...	...	0608	0718	0822	0918	...	1022	1118	1222	1318	1422	1518	1622	1718	1822	1918	2022	2129	...	...
Balatonkenese d.	0420	0520	...	...	0620	0731	0844	0931	...	1044	1131	1244	1331	1444	1531	1644	1731	1844	1931	2044	2144	...	...
Székesfehérvár a.	0503	0603	...	...	0703	0806	0930	1006	...	1130	1206	1330	1406	1530	1606	1730	1806	1930	2006	2130	2226	...	...
Székesfehérvár 1220 1230 d.	*0514*	...	0607	...	0706	0807	*0937*	1007	...	*1137*	1207	*1337*	1407	*1537*	1607	*1737*	1807	*1937*	2007	*2137*	*2237*	...	...
Kelenföld 1220 1230 a.	*0612*	...	0651	...	0746	0846	*1016*	1046	...	*1216*	1246	*1416*	1446	*1616*	1646	*1816*	1846	*2016*	2046	*2216*	*2316*	...	...
Budapest Déli 1220 1230 a.	...	...	0659	...	0754	0854	*1024*	1054	...	*1224*	1254	*1424*	1454	*1624*	1654	*1824*	1854	*2024*	2054	*2224*	*2324*	...	...

d – Mar. 15 - May 12 and Sept. 22 - Nov. 2.

1230 BUDAPEST - ZALAEGERSZEG and SZOMBATHELY — 2nd class

Trains numbered **9xx** are classified *IC* (Ⓡ is required for certain carriages). For local trains Zalaegerszeg - Celldömölk / Szombathely see Table **1237**.

km			950	900	952	902	246	904		954	914	964	906	956	916		966	908	958	918			
			⚒				A															n	
0	**Budapest** Déli ... 1220 1225 d.	...	0500	0600	0700	0800	0900	1000	...	1100	1200	1300	1400	1500	1600	...	1700	1800	1900	2000	...	2100	2240
4	Kelenföld ... 1220 1225 d.	...	0507	0607	0707	0807	0907	1007	...	1107	1207	1307	1407	1507	1607	...	1707	1807	1907	2007	...	2107	2247
67	Székesfehérvár ... 1220 1225 d.	...	0546	0646	0746	0846	0946	1046	...	1146	1246	1346	1446	1546	1646	...	1746	1846	1946	2046	...	2146	2340
90	Várpalota ... d.	...	0606	0706	0806	0906	1006	1106	...	1206	1306	1406	1506	1606	1706	...	1806	1906	2006	2106	...	2206	2400
112	Veszprém ... d.	0558	0629	0734	0829	0934	1029	1134	...	1229	1334	1429	1534	1629	1734	...	1829	1934	2029	2134	...	2229	0023
148	Ajka ... d.	0633	0701	0806	0901	1006	1101	1206	...	1301	1406	1501	1606	1701	1806	...	1901	2006	2101	2206	2233	2300	...
181	Boba ... d.	0713	|	0831	|	1031	|	1231	...	|	1431	|	1631	|	1831	...	|	2031	|	2231	2307	...	...
199	Ukk ... d.	|	0735	|	0935	|	1135	|	...	1335	|	1535	|	1735	|	...	1935	|	2135	|	|	...	...
230	Zalaszentiván ... 1235 a.	|	0759	|	0959	|	1159	|	...	1359	|	1559	|	1759	|	...	1959	|	2159	|	|	...	...
239	**Zalaegerszeg** ... 1235 a.	|	0808	|	1008	|	1208	|	...	1408	|	1608	|	1808	|	...	2008	|	2208	|	|	...	...
191	Celldömölk ... a.	0723	...	0840	...	1040	...	1240	...	...	1440	...	1640	...	1840	...	...	2040	...	2240	2317	...	...
236	**Szombathely** ... a.	...	...	0917	...	1117	...	1317	...	...	1517	...	1717	...	1917	...	...	2117	...	2317	...	...	...

				919	959	909	957		907	967	905	955	915	247	903	953	913	963	901	951		
		Ⓐ												A						Ⓑ		
Szombathely ... d.	...	...	...	0441	...	0641	...	...	0841	...	1041	...	1241	...	1441	...	1641	...	1841	...	...	...
Celldömölk ... d.	...	...	0433	0516	...	0716	...	...	0916	...	1116	...	1316	...	1516	...	1716	...	1916	...	2038	...
Zalaegerszeg ... 1325 d.	...	...	|	|	0549	|	0749	...	|	0949	|	1149	|	1349	|	1549	|	1749	|	1949	|	...
Zalaszentiván ... 1235 d.	...	...	|	|	0600	|	0800	...	|	1000	|	1200	|	1400	|	1600	|	1800	|	2000	|	...
Ukk ... d.	...	...	|	|	0623	|	0823	...	|	1023	|	1223	|	1423	|	1623	|	1823	|	2023	|	...
Boba ... d.	...	...	0442	0525	|	0725	|	...	0925	|	1125	|	1325	|	1525	|	1725	|	1925	|	2048	...
Ajka ... d.	0427	...	0519	0552	0700	0751	0900	...	0951	1100	1151	1300	1351	1500	1551	1700	1751	1900	1951	2100	2124	...
Veszprém ... d.	0458	0518	0553	0632	0732	0832	0932	...	1032	1132	1232	1332	1432	1532	1632	1732	1832	1932	2032	2132	...	...
Várpalota ... d.	0520	0540	0616	0654	0754	0854	0954	...	1054	1154	1254	1354	1454	1554	1654	1754	1854	1954	2054	2154	...	...
Székesfehérvár ... 1220 1225 d.	0538	0607	0633	0712	0812	0912	1012	...	1112	1212	1312	1412	1512	1612	1712	1812	1912	2012	2112	2212	...	...
Kelenföld ... 1220 1225 a.	0622	0652	0717	0752	0852	0952	1052	...	1152	1252	1352	1452	1552	1652	1752	1852	1952	2052	2152	2252	...	...
Budapest Déli ... 1220 1225 a.	0629	0659	0724	0759	0859	0959	1059	...	1159	1259	1359	1459	1559	1659	1759	1859	1959	2059	2159	2259	...	...

LOCAL TRAINS CELLDÖMÖLK - SZOMBATHELY

km																							
							Ⓐ		Ⓐ				Ⓐ		Ⓐ			Ⓐ					
0	**Celldömölk** ... d.	0415	0450	0540	0610	...	0640	0740	0805	0940	...	1140	1205	1340	1425	...	1540	1605	1740	1940	...	2144	...
45	**Szombathely** ... a.	0454	0534	0619	0649	...	0719	0819	0855	1019	...	1219	1244	1419	1501	...	1619	1645	1819	2019	...	2222	...

			Ⓐ						Ⓐ		Ⓐ		Ⓐ			Ⓐ						
Szombathely ... d.	0454	0539	0624	0739	...	0939	1139	1339	1421	...	1502	1539	1621	1739	...	1809	1939	2103	...	2239	...	...
Celldömölk ... a.	0534	0624	0705	0820	...	1020	1220	1420	1505	...	1539	1620	1705	1825	...	1855	2025	2143	...	2320	...	...

A – CITADELLA – (12) Budapest - Ljubljana and v.v.; conveys June 21 - Aug. 31 (12) Budapest - Ljubljana (**509/508**) - Koper and v.v., returning June 18 - Aug. 25.

n – Not June 20 - Aug. 30.

1232 GYÖR - CELLDÖMÖLK - TAPOLCA - KESZTHELY - FONYÓD - KAPOSVÁR — 2nd class

Trains with numbers are classified *IR*. Some trains use different numbers on ⑤⑦. Additional trains are available Tapolca - Keszthely and v.v.

km			9609		9697			9607		9605		9695			9603			9693			9601			
0	**Győr** ... d.	0505	...	0610	0711	0807	...	0911	1007	1111	1207	1311	1407	...	1511	1607	...	1711	1807	...	1911	2007	2109	2241
47	Pápa ... d.	0559	...	0702	0802	0902	...	1002	1102	1202	1302	1402	1502	...	1602	1702	...	1802	1902	...	2002	2102	2227**g**	2329
72	**Celldömölk** ... a.	0628	...	0732	0825	0932	...	1025	1132	1225	1332	1425	1532	...	1625	1732	...	1825	1932	...	2025	2132	2256	2358
72	**Celldömölk** ... d.	...	0633	...	0833	...	...	1033	...	1233	...	1433	...	...	1633	...	...	1833	...	...	2033	...	...	...
108	Sümeg ... d.	...	0701	...	0901	...	...	1101	...	1301	...	1501	...	...	1701	...	...	1901	...	...	2101	...	...	...
128	**Tapolca** ... d.	...	0719	...	0919	...	...	1119	...	1319	...	1519	...	...	1719	...	...	1919	...	...	2119	...	...	...
153	**Keszthely** ... 1220 d.	...	0748	...	0948	...	...	1148	...	1348	...	1548	...	...	1748	...	...	1948	...	...	2148	...	...	...
163	Balatonszentgyörgy ... 1220 a.	...	0759	...	0959	...	...	1159	...	1359	...	1559	...	...	1759	...	...	1959	...	...	2159	...	...	...
163	Balatonszentgyörgy ... 1220 d.	...	0806	...	1006	...	...	1206	...	1406	...	1606	...	...	1806	...	...	2006	...	...	...	...	...	...
179	Balatonfenyves ... 1220 d.	...	0825	...	1025	...	...	1225	...	1425	...	1625	...	...	1825	...	...	2025	...	...	...	...	...	...
187	**Fonyód** ... 1220 a.	...	0836	...	1036	...	...	1236	...	1436	...	1636	...	...	1836	...	...	2036	...	...	...	...	...	...
187	**Fonyód** ... d.	...	0849	...	1049	...	...	1249	...	1449	...	1649	...	...	1844	...	...	2046	...	...	...	...	...	...
240	**Kaposvár** ... a.	...	0945	...	1145	...	...	1345	...	1545	...	1745	...	...	1940	...	...	2140	...	...	...	...	...	...

					9600		9690		9602			9604		9694		9606			9696	9608			
																					Ⓐ		
Kaposvár ... d.	...	...	...	...	...	...	0614	...	0815	...	...	1015	...	1215	...	1415	...	...	1615	1810	1951	...	2237
Fonyód ... a.	...	...	...	...	...	...	0714	...	0914	...	...	1114	...	1314	...	1514	...	...	1714	1909	2045	...	2333
Fonyód ... 1220 d.	...	...	...	...	...	...	0723	...	0923	...	...	1123	...	1323	...	1523	...	...	1723	1923	...	...	...
Balatonfenyves ... 1220 d.	...	...	...	...	...	...	0733	...	0933	...	...	1133	...	1333	...	1533	...	...	1733	1933	...	...	...
Balatonszentgyörgy ... 1220 a.	...	...	...	...	...	...	0753	...	0953	...	...	1153	...	1353	...	1553	...	...	1753	1953	...	...	...
Balatonszentgyörgy ... 1220 d.	...	...	...	...	0600	...	0800	...	1000	...	...	1200	...	1400	...	1600	...	...	1800	2000	...	...	...
Keszthely ... 1220 d.	...	...	...	...	0612	...	0812	...	1012	...	...	1212	...	1412	...	1612	...	...	1812	2012	...	...	...
Tapolca ... d.	...	...	...	...	0641	...	0841	...	1041	...	...	1241	...	1441	...	1641	...	...	1841	2041	...	...	...
Sümeg ... d.	...	...	...	...	0701	...	0901	...	1101	...	...	1301	...	1501	...	1701	...	...	1901	2101	...	...	...
Celldömölk ... a.	...	...	...	...	0729	...	0929	...	1129	...	...	1329	...	1529	...	1729	...	...	1929	2129	...	...	...
Celldömölk ... d.	0339	0444	0542	0630	0737	0830	0937	1030	1137	...	1230	1337	1430	1537	1630	1737	...	1830	1937	...	...	2155	...
Pápa ... d.	0410	0515	0615	0701	0801	0901	1001	1101	1201	...	1301	1401	1501	1601	1701	1801	...	1901	2001	...	...	2226	...
Győr ... a.	0458	0603	0708	0749	0846	0949	1046	1149	1246	...	1349	1446	1549	1646	1749	1846	...	1949	2046	...	...	2318	...

LOCAL TRAINS UKK - TAPOLCA

km							h			
28	**Ukk** ... d.	0510	0940	1140	1340	1426	1540	1747	1947	...
36	Sümeg ... d.	0521	0951	1151	1351	1437	1551	1800	2000	...
56	**Tapolca** ... a.	0541	...	...	...	...	1612	1820	2020	...

		h							
Tapolca ... d.	0430	0550	0740	...	...	...	...	1740	...
Sümeg ... d.	0449	0609	0758	0957	1207	1407	1607	1800	...
Ukk ... a.	0459	0620	0808	1008	1218	1418	1618	1812	...

d – Not May 12 - Sept. 22.

g – Arrives 2200.

h – To / from Celldömölk (Table **1237**).

1233 SOPRON - SZOMBATHELY — 2nd class GySEV

km																								
															Ⓐ									
0	**Sopron** ... d.	0408	0452	0556	0644	0808	1008	...	1108	1208	1308	...	1408	1428	1508	...	1606	1706	1806	...	1906	2008	2108	2245
12	Nagycenk ... d.	0419	0503	0607	0655	0819	1019	...	1119	1219	1319	...	1419	1439	1519	...	1619	1719	1812	...	1919	2019	2119	2256
38	Bük ... d.	0440	0524	0628	0717	0840	1040	...	1140	1240	1340	...	1440	1500	1540	...	1640	1740	1840	...	1940	2040	2140	2317
62	**Szombathely** ... a.	0458	0542	0650	0735	0858	1058	...	1158	1258	1358	...	1458	1520	1558	...	1658	1758	1858	...	1958	2058	2158	2334
	Szentgotthárd 🚌 **986** ... a.	0549	0654	0754	...	0954	...	...	...	1354	1454	...	1554	...	1654	...	1754	1854	...	...	2054	...	...	...

													Ⓐ										
Szentgotthárd 🚌 **986** ... d.	...	0401	...	...	0706	0806	...	...	...	1206	1306	...	...	1406	1506	...	...	1706	1806	...	1906	2006	...
Szombathely ... d.	0423	0506	0630	0700	0800	0900	...	1100	1200	1300	1400	...	1437	1500	1600	...	1700	1800	1900	...	2000	2100	2237
Bük ... d.	0441	0524	0652	0718	0818	0918	...	1118	1218	1318	1418	...	1459	1518	1618	...	1718	1818	1918	...	2018	2118	2255
Nagycenk ... d.	0502	0545	0715	0739	0839	0939	...	1139	1239	1339	1439	...	1520	1539	1639	...	1739	1839	1939	...	2039	2139	2316
Sopron ... a.	0513	0556	0727	0750	0851	0951	...	1151	1251	1351	1451	...	1531	1551	1651	...	1751	1851	1951	...	2051	2151	2327

GySEV 2nd class — SZOMBATHELY - KÖSZEG — 1234

km																								
				Ⓐ				Ⓐ			Ⓐ			Ⓐ					Ⓐ					
0	**Szombathely** d.	0458	0606	0706	...	0806	0906	1006	...	1106	1206	1306	...	1406	1506	1606	...	1706	1806	1906	...	2106	2257	...
18	**Köszeg** a.	0521	0629	0729	...	0829	0929	1029	...	1129	1229	1329	...	1429	1529	1629	...	1729	1829	1929	...	2129	2320	...

					Ⓐ		Ⓐ			Ⓐ			Ⓐ					Ⓐ					
Köszeg d.	0432	0524	0632	...	0732	0832	0932	...	1032	1132	1232	...	1332	1432	1532	...	1632	1732	1832	...	2032	2202	...
Szombathely a.	0455	0547	0655	...	0755	0855	0955	...	1055	1155	1255	...	1355	1455	1555	...	1655	1755	1855	...	2055	2225	...

2nd class — SZOMBATHELY - NAGYKANIZSA - PÉCS — 1235

km			*IR* 8900	*IR* 8902	*IR* 8992	*IR* 8904	*IR* 8994	*IR* 8906	*IR* 8996	*IR* 9808
0	**Szombathely** 1237 d.	...	0508	0703	0912	1103	1310	1512	1710	1903
24	Vasvár 1237 d.	...	0528	0726	0933	1126	1333	1533	1733	1926
49	Zalaszentiván 1237 a.	...	0549	0754	0954	1154	1354	1554	1754	1954
49	Zalaszentiván d.	...	0550	0802	1002	1202	1402	1602	1802	2002
101	**Nagykanizsa** a.	...	0641	0853	1048	1253	1448	1653	1848	2053
101	**Nagykanizsa** 1240 d.	0412	0648	0855	1050	1255	1450	1655	1850	...
130	Gyékényes 1240 a.	0442	0717	0921	1119	1321	1519	1721	1919	...
130	Gyékényes d.	0443	0720	0922	1120	1322	1520	1722	1920	...
185	Barcs d.	0548	0826	1026	1226	1426	1626	1826	2026	...
215	Szigetvár d.	0623	0858	1058	1258	1458	1658	1858	2101	...
230	Szentlörinc d.	0644	0916	1116	1316	1516	1716	1916	2118	...
249	**Pécs** a.	0700	0938	1138	1338	1538	1738	1938	2138	...

		IR 9807	*IR* 8907	*IR* 8997	*IR* 8905	*IR* 8995	*IR* 8903	*IR* 8993	*IR* 8901
Pécs d.	...	...	0622	0813	1013	1213	1413	1613	1813
Szentlörinc d.	...	...	0642	0835	1035	1235	1435	1635	1835
Szigetvár d.	...	...	0659	0858	1058	1258	1458	1658	1858
Barcs d.	0515	...	0730	0930	1130	1330	1530	1730	1930
Gyékényes a.	0615	...	0825	1028	1225	1428	1625	1828	2028
Gyékényes 1240 d.	0628	...	0837	1030	1237	1430	1637	1830	2029
Nagykanizsa 1240 a.	0702	...	0908	1103	1308	1503	1708	1903	2058
Nagykanizsa d.	...	0705	0910	1105	1310	1505	1710	1905	2105
Zalaszentiván a.	...	0757	0957	1157	1357	1557	1757	1957	2157
Zalaszentiván 1237 d.	...	0802	1002	1202	1402	1602	1802	2002	2202
Vasvár 1237 d.	...	0827	1022	1227	1425	1627	1822	2027	2222
Szombathely 1237 a.	...	0852	1043	1252	1455	1652	1843	2052	2248

2nd Class — CELLDÖMÖLK and SZOMBATHELY - ZALAEGERSZEG — 1237

km																								
						d					Ⓐ			e			Ⓐ					⑤–⑦		
0	**Celldömölk** 1232 d.	0348	0437	0553	...	...	0753	...	1153	...	...	1353	...	1448	1553	...	...	...	1753	...	1958	...	2206	...
10	Boba 1232 d.	0357	0446	0603	...	...	0803	...	1203	...	...	1403	...	1458	1603	...	...	...	1803	...	2010	...	2216	...
28	Ukk 1232 a.	0412	0504	0621	...	...	0821	...	1221	...	...	1421	...	1520	1621	...	...	...	1821	...	2034	...	2234	...
28	Ukk d.	0413	0515	0625	...	...	0825	...	1225	...	...	1425	...	...	1625	...	...	...	1825	...	2035	...	2235	...
	Szombathely 1235 d.	|	|	|	0614	...	|	...	|	1208	1403	|	1437	...	|	1605	1628	...	|	1808	|	2108	|	2230
	Vasvár 1235 d.	|	|	|	0637	...	|	...	|	1236	1426	|	1500	...	|	1628	1656	...	|	1832	|	2132	|	2253
59	Zalaszentiván 1235 a.	0447	0546	0656	0658	...	0856	...	1256	1302	1448	1456	1522	...	1656	1650	1721	...	1856	1853	2105	2155	2305	2314
59	Zalaszentiván 1230 d.	0448	0600	0700	...	0706	0900	...	1300	1306	...	1500	1525	...	1700	1706	1725	...	1900	1906	2106	2205	2306	2320
68	**Zalaegerszeg** 1230 a.	0456	0608	0709	...	0715	0909	...	1309	1315	...	1509	1533	...	1709	1715	1733	...	1909	1915	2115	2214	2315	2328

					e																		
Zalaegerszeg 1230 d.	0349	0425	0439	...	...	0540	0651	...	1045	1051	...	1251	...	1451	...	1645	1651	...	1845	1851	...	2040	2149
Zalaszentiván 1230 a.	0357	0432	0447	...	...	0548	0659	...	1053	1059	...	1259	...	1459	...	1653	1659	...	1853	1859	...	2048	2157
Zalaszentiván 1235 d.	0400	0433	0456	...	...	0602	0700	0702	1100	1100	...	1300	...	1500	...	1706	1700	...	1002	1000	...	2049	2201
Vasvár 1235 d.	0424	|	0517	...	...	0625	|	0726	1125	|	...	|	...	|	...	1732	|	...	1925	|	...	|	|
Szombathely 1235 a.	0447	|	0541	...	...	0649	|	0748	1149	|	...	|	...	|	...	1754	|	...	1947	|	...	|	|
Ukk a.	...	0504	...	...	...	...	0731	...	...	1131	...	1331	...	1531	...	...	1731	...	...	1931	...	2121	2234
Ukk 1232 d.	...	0505	...	...	0638	...	0735	...	...	1135	...	1335	...	1535	...	...	1735	...	...	1935	...	2122	2235
Boba 1232 a.	...	0524	...	...	0701	...	0753	...	...	1153	...	1353	...	1553	...	...	1753	...	...	1953	...	2142	2251
Celldömölk 1232 a.	...	0533	...	...	0712	...	0803	...	...	1203	...	1403	...	1603	...	...	1803	...	...	2003	...	2153	2301

d – From Nagykanizsa (d. 0602).

e – To / from Tapolca (Table **1232**).

2nd class — DOMBÓVAR - KAPOSVÁR - NAGYKANIZSA — 1240

km																								
		⚒	⑦												Ⓐ					*IC* **826** ® **A**				Ⓑ
0	**Dombóvár** 1200 d.	0415	...	...	0623	...	0759	...	0959	...	1159	...	1359	...	...	...	1559	1759	...	1859	1959	...	2159	2159
31	**Kaposvár** 1200 a.	0445	...	...	0655	...	0829	...	1029	...	1229	...	1429	...	...	...	1629	1831	...	1925	2031	...	2231	2231
31	**Kaposvár** d.	0446	0446	...	0709	...	0845	...	1045	...	1245	...	1445	...	1551	...	1649	1837	...	1926	2108	...	...	2251
71	Somogyszob a.	0539	0539	...	0759	...	0939	...	1139	...	1339	...	1539	...	1645	...	1739	1927	...	2012	2158	...	...	2341
71	Somogyszob d.	0546	0546	...	0800	...	0940	...	1140	...	1340	...	1556	...	1646	...	1740	1928	...	2013	2202	...	...	2342
101	Gyékényes a.	0621	0621	...	0831	...	1011	...	1211	...	1411	...	1627	...	1717	...	1811	2004	...	2042	2233	...	...	0013
101	Gyékényes 1235 d.	...	...	...	...	...	...	...	...	...	...	...	1641	...	...	...	...	...	...	...	...	2236	...	...
130	**Nagykanizsa** 1235 a.	...	...	...	...	...	...	...	...	...	...	...	1725	...	...	...	...	...	...	...	...	2305	...	...

	⚒		Ⓐ		*IC* **829** ® **A**																	⑥	Ⓑ
Nagykanizsa 1235 d.	...	...	...	0412	...	...	0501	...	...	...	...	...	...	...	...	...	...	...	1714	...	...	2100	2100
Gyékényes 1235 a.	...	...	...	0442	...	...	0529	...	...	...	...	...	...	...	...	...	...	...	1744	...	...	2129	2129
Gyékényes d.	0344	...	0409	...	0448	...	0537	...	0724	...	0945	...	1145	...	1345	...	1524	...	1745	1939	...	2130	2130
Somogyszob a.	0416	...	0441	...	0517	...	0609	...	0755	...	1020	...	1220	...	1420	...	1555	...	1820	2010	...	2201	2201
Somogyszob d.	0417	...	0447	...	0518	...	0611	...	0821	...	1021	...	1221	...	1421	...	1557	...	1826	2013	...	2202	2202
Kaposvár a.	0510	...	0541	...	0604	...	0705	...	0911	...	1111	...	1311	...	1511	...	1647	...	1919	2103	...	2249	2249
Kaposvár 1200 d.	0520	0520	...	...	0605	...	0727	...	0927	...	1127	...	1327	...	1527	...	1727	...	1927	2115	...	...	2250
Dombóvár 1200 a.	0550	0550	...	...	0631	...	0757	...	0957	...	1157	...	1357	...	1557	...	1757	...	1957	2145	...	...	2320

A – (12) Budapest - Kaposvár - Gyékényes and v.v.

2nd class — DOMBÓVAR - BAJA - KISKUNFÉLEGYHÁZA - KECSKEMÉT — 1242

Engineering work is affecting journeys Baja - Kecskemét and v.v until July 6.

km				B						
0	**Dombóvár** d.	0613	...	1017	...	1413	...	1613	...	1813
60	Bátaszék a.	0727	...	1127	...	1527	...	1727	...	1927
60	Bátaszék 1210 d.	0734	...	1134	...	1534	...	1734	...	1934
80	**Baja** 1210 a.	0755	...	1155	...	1555	...	1755	...	1955

	Ⓐ	Ⓐ	Ⓒ	B					
Baja 1210 d.	0615	...	0615	0815	...	1415	1615	...	1815
Bátaszék 1210 a.	0636	...	0636	0839	...	1439	1639	...	1839
Bátaszék d.	...	0641	0641	0841	...	1441	1641	...	1841
Dombóvár a.	...	0752	0752	0952	...	1552	1752	...	1952

km			Ⓐ							
0	**Baja** d.	0344	0426	0535	0740	0940	1140	1340	1540	1740
76	Kiskunhalas a.	0509	0551	0704	0909	1109	1309	1509	1709	1909
76	Kiskunhalas d.	0510	0610	0710	0910	1110	1310	1510	1710	1910
122	Kiskunfélegyháza 1290 d.	0615	0714	0815	1015	1215	1415	1615	1815	2014
147	**Kecskemét** 1290 a.	0637	...	0837	1037	1237	1437	1637	1837	...

		Ⓐ							
Kecskemét 1290 d.	...	...	0721	0921	1121	1321	1521	1721	1921
Kiskunfélegyháza 1290 d.	0544	0644	0744	0944	1144	1344	1544	1744	1944
Kiskunhalas a.	0644	0744	0844	1044	1244	1444	1644	1844	2044
Kiskunhalas d.	0650	0803	0850	1050	1250	1450	1650	1850	2050
Baja a.	0815	0928	1015	1215	1415	1615	1815	2021	2215

B – Ⓒ (daily June 23 - Aug. 31).

1250 BUDAPEST - GYÖR - WIEN

For additional services Budapest - Kelenföld and v.v. see Tables **1200**, **1220**, **1225**, **1230**. 🅁 **not** required for local journeys Gyor - Sopron / Szombathely / Szentgottárd and v.v.

km		EC 346	IC 922	RJX 162	IC 982	RJX 60	♥ 1032	IC 254	EC 140	IC 992	RJX 62	IC 924	EC 142	IC 984	RJX 64	♥ 1034	IC 934	EC 144	IC 994	RJX 66	IC 926	EC 146	♥ 1036	IC 986	RJX 68
		🅁✕	🅁	✕⊖	🅁	✕⊖	🍷🅁	🅁	⊖	🅁	✕⊖	🅁	⊖	🅁	✕🅁	🍷⊖	🅁	⊖	🅁	✕⊖	🅁	✕⊖	🍷🅁	🅁	✕⊖
		A		B		C	D	E	F		C				C	D				C		G	D		C
0	**Budapest** Keleti d.	0540	0613	0640	0713	0740	...	0813	0840	0913	0940	1013	1040	1113	1140	...	1213	1240	1313	1340	1413	1440	...	1513	1540
	Budapest Déli d.	|	|	|	|	|	0745	|	|	|	|	|	|	|	|	1145	|	|	|	|	|	|	1445	|	|
13	Kelenföld d.	0555	0629	0655	0729	0755	0758	0829	0855	0929	0955	1029	1055	1129	1155	1158	1229	1255	1329	1355	1429	1455	1458	1529	1555
75	Tatabánya d.	0626	0700	0726	0800	0826	|	0900	0926	1000	1026	1100	1126	1200	1226	|	1300	1326	1400	1426	1500	1526	|	1600	1626
83	Tata d.	|	0707	|	0807	|	|	0907	|	1007	|	1107	|	1207	|	|	1307	|	1407	|	1507	|	|	1607	|
103	Komárom d.	|	0719	|	0819	|	|	0919	|	1019	|	1119	|	1219	|	|	1319	|	1419	|	1519	|	|	1619	|
140	**Györ** a.	0700	0737	0800	0837	0900	0905	0937	1000	1037	1100	1137	1200	1237	1300	1305	1337	1400	1437	1500	1537	1600	1605	1637	1700
140	**Györ** d.	0702	0739	0802	0839	0902	0907	0939	1002	1039	1102	1139	1202	1239	1302	1307	1339	1402	1439	1502	1539	1602	1607	1639	1702
171	Csorna d.	|	0759	|	0859	|	|	0959	|	1059	|	1159	|	1259	|	|	1359	|	1459	|	1559	|	|	1659	|
225	**Sopron** a.	|	|	|	0938	|	|	|	|	1138	|	|	|	1338	|	|	|	|	1538	|	|	|	|	1738	|
243	**Szombathely** a.	|	0849	|	...	|	|	1049	|	...	|	1249	|	...	|	|	1449	|	...	|	1649	|	|	...	|
176	Mosonmagyaróvár d.	0720	...	0820	...	0920	0925	...	1020	...	1120	...	1220	...	1320	1325	...	1420	...	1520	...	1620	1625	...	1720
187	Hegyeshalom 🛃 a.	0729	...	0829	...	0929	0934	...	1029	...	1129	...	1229	...	1329	1334	...	1429	...	1529	...	1629	1634	...	1729
256	**Wien** Hbf a.	0820	...	0918	...	1020	1032	...	1120	...	1220	...	1320	...	1420	1432	...	1520	...	1620	...	1720	1732	...	1820

	IC 250	EC 148	IC 996	RJX 264	♥ 1068	IC 928	EC 340	IC 988	RJX 266	IC 938	EN 462 40466		2	2	2	2		2	2	2		
	⊖	⊖	🅁	✕⊖	🍷🅁	🅁	⊖	🅁	✕⊖	🅁	🅁											
	H			J		K					L											
Budapest Keleti d.	1613	1640	1713	1740	...	1813	1840	1913	1940	2013	2040	L	...	...	...	...	and	...	...	...	...	...
Budapest Déli d.	|	|	|	|	1745	|	|	|	|	|	|	O	0525	0625	0725	0825	at	2025	2225	2325	...	...
Kelenföld d.	1629	1655	1729	1755	1758	1829	1855	1929	1955	2029	2055	C	0532	0632	0732	0832	the	2032	2232	2332	...	...
Tatabánya d.	1700	1726	1800	1826	|	1900	1926	2000	2026	2100	2126	A	0617	0717	0817	0917	same	2117	2317	0017	...	...
Tata d.	1707	|	1807	|	|	1907	|	2007	|	2107	|	L	0626	0726	0826	0926	minutes	2126	2326	0026	...	...
Komárom d.	1719	|	1819	|	|	1919	|	2019	|	2119	|		0653	0753	0853	0953	past	2153	2347	0047	...	...
Györ a.	1737	1800	1837	1900	1905	1937	2000	2037	2100	2137	2200	T	0719	0819	0919	1019	each	2219	0013	0113	...	...
Györ d.	1739	1802	1839	1902	1907	1939	2002	2039	2102	2139	2202	R	...	...	...	...	hour	...	...	...	...	...
Csorna d.	1759	|	1859	|	|	1959	|	2059	|	2159	|	A	...	...	...	...	until	...	...	...	...	...
Sopron a.	|	|	1938	|	|	|	|	2138	|	|	|	I	...	...	...	...		...	...	...	...	...
Szombathely a.	1849	|	...	|	|	2049	|	...	|	2249	|	N	...	...	...	...		...	...	...	...	...
Mosonmagyaróvár d.	...	1820	...	1924	1925	...	2020	...	2120	...	2220	S	...	...	...	...	◧	...	...	...	...	...
Hegyeshalom 🛃 a.	...	1829	...	|	1934	...	2029	...	2129	...	2229		...	...	...	...		...	...	...	...	...
Wien Hbf a.	...	1920	...	2020	2027	...	2120	...	2220	...	2320		...	...	...	...		...	...	...	...	...

	IC 989	IC 929	IC 987	EN 463 40467	IC 927	♥ 1065	RJX 267	IC 997	EC 141	IC 937	RJX 269	IC 985	♥ 1031	EC 143	IC 251	RJX 61	IC 995	EC 145	IC 925	♥ 1067	RJX 63	IC 983	EC 147	IC 923
	🅁	🅁	🅁		🅁	🍷🅁	✕⊖	🅁	⊖	🅁	✕⊖	🅁	🍷🅁	✕⊖	⊖	✕⊖	🅁	⊖	🅁	🍷🅁	✕⊖	🅁	⊖	🅁
		K		L							J		D	G	H	C				D	C			
Wien Hbf d.	...	...	...	0640	...	0734	0740	...	0842	...	0940	...	1027	1042	...	1140	...	1242	...	1327	1340	...	1442	...
Hegyeshalom 🛃 d.	...	...	...	0728	...	0822	0828	...	0928	...	1028	...	1122	1128	...	1228	...	1328	...	1422	1428	...	1528	...
Mosonmagyaróvár d.	...	...	...	0736	...	0831	0836	...	0936	...	1036	...	1131	1136	...	1236	...	1336	...	1431	1436	...	1536	...
Szombathely d.	...	0552	...	|	0710	|	|	...	|	0910	|	...	|	|	1110	|	...	|	1310	|	|	...	|	1510
Sopron d.	...	|	0622	|	|	|	|	0821	|	|	|	1021	|	|	|	|	1221	|	|	|	|	1421	|	|
Csorna d.	...	0640	0702	|	0759	|	|	0859	|	0959	|	1059	|	|	1159	|	1259	|	1359	|	|	1459	|	1559
Györ a.	...	0701	0722	0754	0819	0849	0853	0919	0954	1019	1054	1119	1149	1154	1219	1254	1319	1354	1419	1449	1454	1519	1554	1619
Györ d.	0621	0703	0726	0756	0821	0850	0856	0921	0956	1021	1056	1121	1150	1156	1221	1256	1321	1356	1421	1450	1456	1521	1556	1621
Komárom d.	0638	|	0743	|	0838	|	|	0938	|	1038	|	1138	|	|	1238	|	1338	|	1438	|	|	1538	|	1638
Tata d.	0650	|	0755	|	0850	|	|	0950	|	1050	|	1150	|	|	1250	|	1350	|	1450	|	|	1550	|	1650
Tatabánya d.	0657	|	0802	0830	0857	|	0930	0957	1030	1057	1130	1157	|	1230	1257	1330	1357	1430	1457	|	1530	1557	1630	1657
Kelenföld a.	0728	0807	0833	0902	0928	0958	1002	1028	1102	1128	1202	1228	1258	1302	1328	1402	1428	1502	1528	1558	1602	1628	1702	1728
Budapest Déli a.	|	|	|	|	|	1014	|	|	|	|	|	|	1314	|	|	|	|	|	|	1614	|	|	|	|
Budapest Keleti a.	0744	0823	0849	0919	0944	...	1019	1044	1119	1144	1219	1244	...	1319	1344	1419	1444	1519	1544	...	1619	1644	1719	1744

	RJX 65	IC 993	EC 149	IC 255	♥ 1035	RJX 67	IC 981	RJX 165	IC 921	EC 347	EC 341	RJX 261		2	2	2	2	2		2	2	2
	✕⊖	🅁	⊖	🅁	🍷🅁	✕⊖	🅁	✕⊖	🅁	✕🅁	⊖	✕⊖		Ⓐ	Ⓒ	Ⓐ	Ⓒ					
	C		F	E	D	C		B		A		C										
Wien Hbf d.	1540	...	1642	...	1727	1740	...	1842	...	1942	2037	2140	L	...	...	...	...	...	and	...	...	...
Hegyeshalom 🛃 d.	1628	...	1728	...	1822	1828	...	1928	...	2028	2128	2228	O	...	...	...	...	...	at	...	...	...
Mosonmagyaróvár d.	1636	...	1736	...	1831	1836	...	1936	...	2036	2136	2236	C	...	...	...	...	...	the	...	...	...
Szombathely d.	|	...	|	1710	|	|	...	|	1910	|	|	|	A	...	...	...	...	...	same	...	...	...
Sopron d.	|	1621	|	|	|	|	1821	|	|	|	|	|	L	...	...	...	...	...	minutes	...	...	...
Csorna d.	|	1659	|	1759	|	|	1859	|	1959	|	|	|		...	...	...	...	...	past	...	...	...
Györ a.	1654	1719	1754	1819	1849	1854	1919	1954	2019	2053	2154	2254	T	...	...	...	...	...	each	...	...	...
Györ d.	1656	1721	1756	1821	1850	1856	1921	1956	2021	2056	2156	2256	R	0506	0536	0559	0636	0738	hour	2038	2138	2238
Komárom d.	|	1738	|	1838	|	|	1938	|	2038	|	|	|	A	0531	0601	0624	0701	0803	until	2103	2203	2303
Tata d.	|	1750	|	1850	|	|	1950	|	2050	|	|	|	I	0549	0619	0643	0719	0827		2127	2227	2327
Tatabánya d.	1730	1757	1830	1857	|	1930	1957	2030	2057	2130	2230	2330	N	0608	0638	0708	0738	0838	◧	2138	2238	2338
Kelenföld a.	1802	1828	1902	1928	1958	2002	2028	2102	2128	2202	2302	0002	S	0657	0724	0754	0824	0924		2224	2324	0024
Budapest Déli a.	|	|	|	|	2014	|	|	|	|	|	|	|		0704	0734	0804	0834	0934		2234	2334	0034
Budapest Keleti a.	1819	1844	1919	1944	...	2019	2044	2119	2144	2219	2319	0019		...	...	...	...	...		...	...	...

LOCAL TRAINS **GYÖR - SOPRON** (SEE NOTE ⊡) GySEV

km												
			Ⓐ									
0	**Györ** d.	0643	0751	0851	1051	1251	1451	1651	1851	1951	2051	2251
31	Csorna d.	0716	0821	0921	1121	1321	1521	1721	1921	2021	2120	2317
85	**Sopron** a.	0804	0906	1006	1206	1413	1614	1814	2014	2110	2209	2400

		Ⓐ									
Sopron d.	0550	0645	0742	0945	1145	1345	1545	1745	1847	1945	2230
Csorna d.	0646	0734	0834	1034	1234	1434	1634	1834	1935	2034	2317
Györ a.	0715	0806	0906	1106	1306	1506	1706	1906	2006	2106	2345

A – DACIA – 🛏 1, 2 cl., ▬ 1, 2 cl. Bucureşti - Wien and v.v.; ✕ Bucureşti - Arad and v.v.
B – 🚃 ✕ Budapest - Wien - Salzburg - Innsbruck - Zürich and v.v.
C – 🚃 ✕ Budapest - Wien - Salzburg - München and v.v.
D – 🚃 🍷 Praha - Wien - Budapest and v.v.
E – MURA – 🚃 Budapest - Szombathely - Graz and v.v.
F – HORTOBÁGY – 🚃 ✕ Chop - Záhony - Nyiregyháza - Debrecen - Budapest - Wien and v.v.; conveys 🛏 1, 2 cl. Kyiv - Lviv - Chop - Záhony - Budapest - Wien and v.v.
G – TISZA-SZAMOS – 🚃 Chop - Záhony - Nyiregyháza - Debrecen - Budapest - Wien and v.v.; 🚃 ✕ Baia Mare (**686/687**) - Satu Mare - Debrecen - Budapest - Wien and v.v.
H – DRÁVA – 🚃 Budapest - Szombathely - Ljubljana and v.v.
J – 🚃 ✕ Budapest - Wien - Salzburg and v.v.
K – 🚃 Budapest - Szombathely - Szentgotthárd and v.v.

L – KÁLMÁN IMRE – 🛏 1,2 cl., ▬ 2 cl., 🚃 Budapest - Wien - Salzburg - München - Stuttgart and v.v.; 🛏 1, 2 cl., 🚃 Budapest - Wien - Salzburg - Zurich and v.v.

♥ – Operated by REGIOJET. Separate fare tariff applies.
⊖ – Reservation compulsory for domestic journeys in Hungary.
◧ – For local trains Györ - Hegyeshalom - Bruck an der Leitha see Table **1254**.
⊡ – Also from Györ at 0402, 0514 Ⓐ, 0552, 1351 Ⓐ, 1551, 1751, 2151.
Also from Sopron at 0345, 0448, 1447, 1647, 2117.

RJX – Railjet Express. Conveys Business, 1st and economy class.

1253 HEGYESHALOM - BRATISLAVA

2nd class

km											
		Ⓐ	Ⓐ	Ⓐ			Ⓐ	Ⓐ			
0	**Hegyeshalom** 1250 d.	0633	0733	...	0933	1133	1333	1510	1733	1933	2133
13	Rajka 🛃 a.	0645	0745	0749	0945	1145	1345	1522	1745	1945	2145
30	**Bratislava** Petržalka ☆ a.	0707	...	0807	1007	1207	1407	1544	1807	2007	2207

	e	e				Ⓐ	Ⓐ	Ⓐ	Ⓐ	
Bratislava Petržalka ☆ d.	0726	...	0849	1049	1249	1430	1649	1849	2049	...
Rajka 🛃 d.	0744	0752	0910	1110	1310	1451	1710	1910	2110	...
Hegyeshalom a.	...	0804	0925	1125	1325	1503	1725	1925	2125	...

e – ①–⑤ (subject to alteration on and around Slovak and Hungarian public holiday dates).

☆ – Bus 93 links Petržalka station with Bratislava hlavná stanica (main station) every 5 – 12 minutes; journey approx 10 minutes.

2nd class GYÖR - BRUCK AN DER LEITHA 1254

Engineering work is affecting services until October 5 (please check locally before travelling). Also subject to alteration on and around Hungarian and Austrian holiday dates.

km		①–⑤	①–⑤	①–⑤		①–⑤	①–⑤	①–⑤		
0	**Györ** ◇ d.	0446	0536	0746	0946	1146	1336	1546	1746	1946
36	Mosonmagyaróvár ◇ d.	0512	0602	0812	1012	1212	1402	1612	1812	2012
47	Hegyeshalom 🏛 ◇ a.	0522	0612	0822	1022	1222	1412	1622	1822	2022
47	Hegyeshalom 🏛 d.	0531	0615	0845	1045	1245	1415	1645	1845	2045
79	**Bruck an der Leitha** a.	0555	0639	0909	1109	1309	1439	1709	1909	2109

	①–⑤	①–⑤			①–⑤	①–⑤	①–⑤		
Bruck an der Leitha d.	0739	0951	1150	1350	1451	1751	1851	...	2150
Hegyeshalom 🏛 a.	0804	1016	1215	1415	1516	1816	1916	...	2215
Hegyeshalom 🏛 ◇ d.	0835	1035	1235	1435	1535	1835	1935	...	2221
Mosonmagyaróvár ◇ d.	0844	1044	1244	1444	1544	1844	1944	...	2243
Györ ◇ a.	0911	1111	1311	1511	1611	1911	2011	...	2311

◇ – Györ - Hegyeshalom runs hourly 0446 - 2246; Hegyeshalom - Györ runs hourly 0535 - 2235.

2nd class BUDAPEST - VÁC - SZOB 1255

Local trains. For *EC* trains every two hours (to / from Praha) see Table **1175**.

km			Ⓒ							
0	**Budapest** Nyugati d.	0050	0250	0450	0608	and	2108	2208	2250	2350
34	Vác d.	0133	0333	0533	0633	hourly	2133	2233	2333	0033
51	Nagymaros-Visegrád ¶ d.	0148	0348	0548	0648	until	2148	2248	2348	0048
64	**Szob** a.	0204	0404	0604	0704		2204	2304	0004	0104

		Ⓐ	⚒						
Szob d.	0456	0502	0526	0556	and	1956	2059	2159	2259
Nagymaros-Visegrád ¶ d.	0511	0517	0541	0611	hourly	2011	2114	2214	2314
Vác d.	0528	0534	0558	0628	until	2028	2134	2234	2334
Budapest Nyugati a.	0554	0614	0634	0654		2054	2214	2314	0014

¶ – A ferry operates across the river to Visegrád.

2nd class BUDAPEST - GYÖNGYÖS, FÜZESABONY and EGER 1258

km										
0	**Budapest** Keleti d.	0500	0530	0600		1930	2000	2030	2100	2130
67	Hatvan d.	0555	0622	0652		2022	2052	2122	2152	2222
87	Vámosgyörk d.	0608	0636	0706	and	2036	2106	2136	2206	2236
100	**Gyöngyös** a.	|	0654	|	hourly	2054	|	2154	|	2254
126	**Füzesabony** a.	0643	...	0733	until	...	2138	...	2233	...
126	**Füzesabony** d.	0652	...	0734	●	...	2139	...	2239	...
143	**Eger** a.	0710	...	0752		...	2157	...	2257	...

Eger d.	0500	0600	0703	...		1908	...	2008	...
Füzesabony a.	0521	0621	0726	...		1926	...	2026	...
Füzesabony d.	0522	0622	0727	...	and	1927	...	2027	...
Gyöngyös d.	|	|	|	0808	hourly	|	2008	|	2108
Vámosgyörk d.	0556	0656	0756	0825	until	1956	2025	2056	2125
Hatvan d.	0611	0711	0811	0840	●	2011	2040	2111	2140
Budapest Keleti a.	0705	0805	0905	0935		2105	2135	2205	2235

● – Timings may vary slightly. Other trains: Budapest - Gyöngyös at 2230; Gyöngyös - Budapest at 0508, 0608, 0708.

BUDAPEST - MISKOLC - KOŠICE, SÁTORALJAÚJHELY and NYÍREGYHÁZA 1260

Fast trains. For slower connecting trains via Füzesabony see Tables **1258** and **1261**.

km		*IC* 580 [R]	*IC* 582 [R]	*IC** 182 ⊖	*IC* 520 [R]	*IC* 560 [R]	*IC** 184 ⊖	*IC* 522 [R]	*IC* 562 [R]	*IC** 186 ⊖	*IC* 504 [R]	*IC* 564 [R]	*IC** 188 ⊖	*IC* 524 [R]	*IC* 566 [R]	*IC** 190 ⊖	*IC* 506 [R]	*IC* 568 [R]	*IC** 192 ⊖	*IC* 526 [R]	*IC* 586 [R]	*IC** 194 ⊖	*IC* 528 [R]	*IC* 508 [R]	*IC* 518 [R]
0	**Budapest** Keleti d.	...	0525	0625	0625	0725	0825	0825	0925	1025	1025	1125	1225	1225	1325	1425	1425	1525	1625	1625	1725	1825	1825	1925	2025
67	Hatvan d.	...	0610	0710	0710	0810	0910	0910	1010	1110	1110	1210	1310	1310	1410	1510	1510	1610	1710	1710	1810	1910	1910	2010	2110
126	Füzesabony d.	...	0650	|	|	0850	|	|	1050	|	|	1250	|	|	1450	|	|	1650	|	|	1850	|	|	2050	2150
139	Mezökövesd d.	...	|	0759	0759	|	0959	0959	|	1159	1159	|	1359	1359	|	1559	1559	|	1759	1759	|	1959	1959	2100	2200
183	**Miskolc - Tiszai** a.	...	0727	0827	0827	0927	1027	1027	1127	1227	1227	1327	1427	1427	1527	1627	1627	1727	1827	1827	1927	2027	2027	2129	2231
183	**Miskolc - Tiszai** d.	0626	0730	0831	0840	0930	1031	1040	1130	1231	1240	1330	1431	1440	1530	1631	1640	1730	1831	1840	1930	2031	2040	2130	...
244	Hidasnémeti 🏛 a.	|	|	0934	|	|	1134	|	|	1334	|	|	1534	|	|	1734	|	|	1934	|	|	2134	|	|	...
270	**Košice** a.	|	|	1014	|	|	1214	|	|	1414	|	|	1614	|	|	1814	|	|	2014	|	|	2214	|	|	...
221	Szerencs d.	0653	0756	...	0906	0956	...	1106	1156	...	1306	1356		1506	1556	...	1706	1756	...	1906	1956	...	2106	2156	...
257	Sárospatak d.	|	|	...	0941	|	...	1141	|	...	1341	|	...	1541	|	...	1741	|	...	1941	|	...	2141	|	...
267	**Sátoraljaújhely** a.	|	|	...	0950	|	...	1150	|	...	1350	|	...	1550	|	...	1750	|	...	1950	|	...	2150	|	...
239	Tokaj d.	0706	0809	...	...	1009	...	...	1209	...	...	1409	...	...	1609	...	...	1809	...	...	2009	...	...	2216	...
271	**Nyíregyháza** a.	0728	0829	...	...	1029	...	...	1229	...	...	1429	...	...	1629	...	...	1829	...	...	2029	...	...	2238	...
	Debrecen **1270** a.	0802	0902	...	...	1102	...	...	1302	...	...	1502	...	...	1702	...	...	1902	...	...	2102	...	...	...	...

	IR 5019	*IC* 519 [R]	*IC* 507 [R]	*IC** 181 ⊖	*IC* 682 [R]	*IC* 527 [R]	*IC** 183 ⊖	*IC* 650 [R]	*IC* 525 [R]	*IC** 185 ⊖	*IC* 652 [R]	*IC* 523 [R]	*IC** 187 ⊖	*IC* 654 [R]	*IC* 503 [R]	*IC** 189 ⊖	*IC* 684 [R]	*IC* 521 [R]	*IC** 191 ⊖	*IC* 656 [R]	*IC* 501 [R]	*IC** 193 ⊖	*IC* 658 [R]	*IC* 688 [R]
Debrecen **1270** d.	...	...	...	...	0657	...	...	0857	...	...	1057	...	...	1257	...	...	1457	...	...	1657	...	...	1857	2057
Nyíregyháza d.	...	0524	...	...	0729	...	...	0929	...	...	1129	...	...	1329	...	...	1529	...	...	1729	...	...	1929	2129
Tokaj d.	...	0548	...	...	0750	...	...	0950	...	...	1150	...	...	1350	...	...	1550	...	...	1750	...	...	1950	2153
Sátoraljaújhely d.	...	|	0604	...	|	0804	...	|	1004	...	|	1204	...	|	1404	...	|	1604	...	|	1804	...	|	|
Sárospatak d.	...	|	0614	...	|	0814	...	|	1014	...	|	1214	...	|	1414	...	|	1614	...	|	1814	...	|	|
Szerencs d.	...	0602	0653	...	0804	0852	...	1004	1052	...	1204	1252	...	1404	1452	...	1604	1652	...	1804	1852	...	2004	2210
Košice d.	...	|	|	0542	|	|	0742	|	|	0842	|	|	1142	|	|	1342	|	|	1542	|	|	1742	|	|
Hidasnémeti 🏛 d.	...	|	|	0617	|	|	0817	|	|	1017	|	|	1217	|	|	1417	|	|	1617	|	|	1817	|	|
Miskolc - Tiszai a.	...	0628	0717	0710	0829	0917	0913	1029	1117	1113	1229	1317	1313	1429	1517	1513	1629	1717	1713	1829	1917	1913	2029	2235
Miskolc - Tiszai d.	0520	0635	0735	0735	0835	0935	0935	1035	1135	1135	1235	1335	1335	1435	1535	1535	1635	1735	1735	1835	1935	1935	2035	...
Mezökövesd d.	0550	|	0804	0804	|	1004	1004	|	1204	1204	|	1404	1404	|	1604	1604	|	1804	1804	|	2004	2004	|	...
Füzesabony d.	0604	0714	|	|	0914	|	|	1114	|	|	1314	|	|	1514	|	|	1714	|	|	1914	|	|	2114	...
Hatvan d.	0650	0755	0855	0855	0955	1055	1055	1155	1255	1255	1355	1455	1455	1555	1655	1655	1755	1855	1855	1955	2055	2055	2155	...
Budapest Keleti a.	0745	0847	0947	0947	1047	1147	1147	1247	1347	1347	1447	1547	1547	1647	1747	1747	1847	1947	1947	2047	2147	2147	2247	...

⊖ – [R] for domestic journeys.

* – Classified *EC* in Slovakia.

2nd class FÜZESABONY - MISKOLC - SÁTORALJAÚJHELY and NYÍREGYHÁZA 1261

For fast trains Budapest - Miskolc - Sátoraljaújhely / Nyiregyháza see Table **1260**.

km		c			Ⓐ				Ⓐ		Ⓐ													
0	**Füzesabony** d.	...	...	0357	0429	...	...	0459	...	...	0529	...	...	0625	...	0736	0836	0936	...	1036	1136	...	1236	1336
13	Mezökövesd d.	...	...	0408	0440	...	...	0510	...	...	0540	...	...	0636	...	0747	0847	0947	...	1047	1147	...	1247	1347
57	**Miskolc - Tiszai** a.	...	...	0445	0517	...	...	0549	...	...	0617	...	...	0713	...	0824	0924	1024	...	1124	1224	...	1322	1424
57	**Miskolc - Tiszai** d.	...	0412	...	...	0523	...	...	0605	...	...	0637	...	...	0737	0837	0937	1037	...	1137	1237	...	1337	1437
95	Szerencs a.	...	0449	...	...	0600	...	...	0643	...	...	0715	...	...	0815	0915	1015	1115	...	1215	1315	...	1415	1516
95	Szerencs d.	0410	0450	...	...	0609	0604	...	...	0702	...	0718	0804	...	0816	...	1016	...	1204	1216	1316	1404	1416	1516
131	Sárospatak d.	|	0530	...	...	|	0642	...	...	0740	...	|	0842	...	|	...	|	...	1242	|	|	1442	|	|
141	**Sátoraljaújhely** a.	|	0539	...	...	|	0651	...	...	0749	...	|	0851	...	|	...	|	...	1251	|	|	1451	|	|
113	Tokaj d.	0430	...	...	...	0636	...	...	...	...	...	0735	...	...	0835	...	1035	...	...	1235	1335	...	1435	1535
145	**Nyíregyháza** a.	0505	...	...	...	0715	...	...	...	...	...	0815	...	...	0915	...	1115	...	...	1315	1415	...	1515	1615

Füzesabony d.	...	1436	1536	...	1636	1736	...	1836	1936	...	...	2114	...	2259	...	...	...	...	...	...	...	...	...
Mezökövesd d.	...	1447	1547	...	1647	1747	...	1847	1947	...	...	2125	...	2312	...	...	...	...	...	...	...	...	...
Miskolc - Tiszai a.	...	1524	1624	...	1724	1824	...	1924	2024	...	...	2202	...	2355	...	...	...	...	...	...	...	...	...
Miskolc - Tiszai d.	...	1537	1637	...	1737	1837	...	1937	2037	2137	...	...	2310	...	...	...	...	...	...	...	...	...	...
Szerencs a.	...	1615	1715	...	1815	1915	...	2015	2116	2215	...	...	2347	...	...	...	...	...	...	...	...	...	...
Szerencs d.	1604	1616	1716	1804	1816	1916	2004	2016	2117	2216	2223	...	2353	...	...	...	...	...	...	...	...	...	...
Sárospatak d.	1642	|	|	1842	|	|	2042	|	|	|	2301	...	|	...	...	...	...	...	...	...	...	...	...
Sátoraljaújhely a.	1651	|	|	1851	|	|	2051	|	|	|	2310	...	|	...	...	...	...	...	...	...	...	...	...
Tokaj d.	...	1635	1735	...	1835	1935	...	2035	2135	2235	...	...	0010	...	...	...	...	...	...	...	...	...	...
Nyíregyháza a.	...	1715	1815	...	1915	2015	...	2116	2215	2315	...	...	0043	...	...	...	...	...	...	...	...	...	...

c – ①–⑤ June 22 - Aug. 31 (not Aug. 21).

FOR RETURN SERVICE SEE NEXT PAGE →

1261 NYÍREGYHÁZA and SÁTORALJAÚJHELY - MISKOLC - FÜZESABONY

2nd class

For fast trains Nyiregyháza / Sátoraljaújhely - Miskolc - Budapest see Table **1260**.

					Ⓐ	Ⓒ														Ⓐ			
Nyíregyháza d.	0300	...	0343	...	...	...	...	...	0440	...	0539	0639	...	...	0839	...	1038	...	1139	...	1239	...	1339
Tokaj d.	0333	...	0417	...	...	...	...	...	0518	...	0617	0719	...	...	0922	...	1122	...	1222	...	1322	...	1422
Sátoraljaújhely d.	|	...	|	0352	...	...	...	0456	|	...	|	|	0704	...	|	...	|	1104	|	...	|	1304	|
Sárospatak d.	|	...	|	0402	...	...	...	0506	|	...	|	|	0714	...	|	...	|	1114	|	...	|	1314	|
Szerencs a.	0350	...	0435	0438	...	...	...	0542	0536	...	0635	0740	0752	...	0940	...	1140	1152	1240	...	1340	1352	1440
Szerencs d.	0351	...	...	0439	0508	...	...	...	0544	0615	0638	0741	...	0841	0941	1041	1141	...	1241	...	1341	...	1441
Miskolc - Tiszai a.	0427	...	...	0515	0545	...	...	...	0620	0652	0715	0818	...	0918	1018	1118	1218	...	1318	...	1418	...	1518
Miskolc - Tiszai d.	...	0500	...	0525	0550	0550	0620	...	...	...	0720	0820	...	0920	1020	1120	1220	...	1320	1359	1420	...	1520
Mezőkövesd d.	...	0536	...	0601	0626	0626	0656	...	...	...	0756	0856	...	0956	1056	1156	1256	...	1356	1435	1456	...	1556
Füzesabony a.	...	0548	...	0613	0639	0638	0708	...	...	...	0808	0908	...	1008	1108	1208	1308	...	1408	1447	1508	...	1608

Nyíregyháza d.	1439	...	1539	1639	...	1739	1839	...	...	1939	...	...	2039	...	...	...	...	...	...	...	...	...	...
Tokaj d.	1522	...	1622	1722	...	1822	1922	...	...	2022	...	...	2122	...	...	...	...	...	...	...	...	...	...
Sátoraljaújhely d.	|	1504	|	|	1704	|	|	...	1904	|	2006	2129	|	...	...	...	...	...	...	...	...	...	...
Sárospatak d.	|	1514	|	|	1714	|	|	...	1914	|	2016	2141	|	...	...	...	...	...	...	...	...	...	...
Szerencs a.	1540	1552	1640	1740	1752	1840	1940	...	1952	2040	2054	2217	2140	...	...	...	...	...	...	...	...	...	...
Szerencs d.	1541	...	1641	1741	...	1841	1941	...	...	...	2059	...	2222	...	...	...	...	...	...	...	...	...	...
Miskolc - Tiszai a.	1618	...	1718	1818	...	1918	2018	...	...	...	2135	...	2258	...	...	...	...	...	...	...	...	...	...
Miskolc - Tiszai d.	1620	...	1720	1820	...	1920	...	2020	...	...	...	...	...	2310	...	...	...	...	...	...	...	...	...
Mezőkövesd d.	1656	...	1756	1856	...	1956	...	2056	...	...	...	...	...	2355	...	...	...	...	...	...	...	...	...
Füzesabony a.	1708	...	1808	1908	...	2008	...	2108	...	...	...	...	...	0008	...	...	...	...	...	...	...	...	...

FOR RETURN SERVICE AND FOOTNOTES SEE PREVIOUS PAGE.

1262 HATVAN - SALGÓTARJÁN - SOMOSKÖÚJFALU

2nd class

km																								
			Ⓐ			Ⓐ						Ⓐ			Ⓐ			Ⓐ			Ⓐ			
0	**Hatvan** d.	0414	0514	...	0614	0714	...	0814	1014	...	1214	1314	...	1414	1514	...	1614	1714	...	1814	1914	...	2014	2230
59	Salgótarján d.	0536	0636	...	0736	0836	...	0936	1136	...	1336	1436	...	1536	1636	...	1736	1836	...	1936	2036	...	2136	2352
65	**Somosköújfalu** a.	0547	0647	...	0747	0847	...	0947	1147	...	1347	1447	...	1547	1647	...	1747	1847	...	1947	2047	...	2144	0003

				Ⓐ			Ⓐ						Ⓐ			Ⓐ			Ⓐ				
Somosköújfalu d.	0304	0416	...	0514	0614	...	0714	0814	...	1014	1214	...	1314	1414	...	1514	1614	...	1714	1814	...	2014	2214
Salgótarján d.	0316	0425	...	0525	0625	...	0725	0825	...	1025	1225	...	1325	1425	...	1525	1625	...	1725	1825	...	2025	2225
Hatvan a.	0435	0546	...	0646	0746	...	0846	0946	...	1146	1346	...	1446	1546	...	1646	1746	...	1846	1946	...	2146	2346

1270 BUDAPEST - DEBRECEN - NYÍREGYHÁZA - ZÁHONY - CHOP

Ferihegy ✈ is served by 5–6 trains per hour. For other trains Budapest Nyugati - Szolnok and v.v. see Tables **1280** and **1290**.
All times in Ukraine are subject to confirmation. The minimum connection time to / from Chop local trains at Záhony is 15 minutes.

km		*IC* 682	*IC* 600	*IC* 650	*IC* 367	*IC* 34	*IC* 652	*IC* 612	*IC* 654	*IC* 604	*IC* 656	*IC* 614	*EC* 143	*IC* 656	*IC* 606	*IC* 658	*IC* 626	*IC* 407	*IC* 688	*IC* 618	*EC* 149	*IC* 628	*IR* 6088	*IR* 6098		D10
		R	R	R	R H	L ⊖	R	R	R	R	R	R	R G	R	R K	R	R	C	R	R	J ⊖	R				R T
0	**Budapest** Nyugati d.	0350	0520	0620	0640k	0720	0820	0920	1020	1120	1220	1320	1340k	1420	1520	1620	1720	1740k	1820	1920	1940k	2020	2125	2225	...	2240k
11	Köbánya Kispest d.	0406	0536	0636	|	0736	0836	0936	1036	1136	1236	1336	|	1436	1536	1636	1736	|	1836	1936	|	2036	2141	2241	...	|
18	Ferihegy ✈ d.	0412	0542	0642	|	0742	0842	0942	1042	1142	1242	1342	|	1442	1542	1642	1742	|	1842	1942	|	2042	2147	2248	...	|
73	Cegléd d.	0448	0617	0717	|	0817	0917	1017	1117	1217	1317	1417	|	1517	1617	1717	1817	|	1917	2017	|	2117	2222	2329	...	|
100	**Szolnok** d.	0519	0639	0739	0802	0839	0939	1039	1139	1239	1339	1439	1502	1539	1639	1739	1839	1902	1939	2039	2104	2139	2249	2353	...	0018
177	Püspökladány d.	0619	0728	0828	0858	0928	1028	1128	1228	1328	1428	1528	1558	1628	1728	1828	1928	1958	2028	2128	2155	2222	2349	0053	...	|
201	Hajdúszoboszló d.	0638	0747	0843	|	0943	1043	1143	1243	1343	1443	1543	1615	1643	1743	1843	1943	|	2043	2143	2210	2243	0008	0112	...	|
221	**Debrecen** a.	0653	0802	0855	0927	0955	1055	1155	1255	1355	1455	1555	1629	1655	1755	1855	1955	2025	2055	2155	2222	2255	0023	0127	...	0157
221	**Debrecen** d.	0657	0804	0857	...	0957	1057	1157	1257	1357	1457	1557	1634	1657	1800	1857	1957	...	2057	2157	2224	2257	...	...	...	0159
270	Nyíregyháza a.	0728	0835	0928	...	1028	1128	1228	1328	1428	1528	1628	1710	1728	1831	1928	2028	...	2128	2228	2300	2328	...	...	...	0239
	Miskolc **1260** a.	0829	...	1029	...	|	1229	|	1429	...	1629	|	|	1829	|	2029	|	...	2235	...	|	...	...	...	...	|
335	**Záhony** a.	...	...	...	...	1121	...	1321	...	...	...	1721	1820	...	1922	...	2121	...	...	...	2353	...	...	...	...	0340

	IR 6029	*EC* 140	*IR* 6129	*IC* 609	*IC* 619	*IC* 406	*IC* 580	*IC* 582	*IC* 617	*IC* 560	*EC* 146	*IC* 605	*IC* 562	*IC* 33	*IC* 564	*IC* 615	*IC* 566	*IC* 603	*IC* 603	*IR* 6001	*IC* 568	*IC* 31	*IC* 366	*IC* 586	D9
		J ⊖		R	R K	R C	R	R	R	R	R G	R	R	L ⊖	R	R	R	R	⑦ R		R	R L	R H	R	R T
Záhony d.	...	0405	...	...	0528	...	...	...	0837	...	0935	...	...	1237	...	1437	...	...	1624	...	...	1837	...	...	0012
Miskolc **1260** d.	...	|	...	...	|	...	0622	0730	|	0930	|	...	1130	|	1330	|	1530	...	|	...	1730	|	...	1930	|
Nyíregyháza d.	...	0458	...	0530	0620	...	0730	0830	0930	1030	1034	1130	1230	1330	1430	1530	1630	1730	1730	...	1830	1930	...	2030	0110
Debrecen a.	...	0529	...	0602	0652	...	0802	0902	1002	1102	1106	1202	1302	1402	1502	1602	1702	1802	1802	...	1902	2002	...	2102	0125
Debrecen d.	0430	0531	0537	0604	0704	0707	0804	0904	1004	1104	1131	1204	1304	1404	1504	1604	1704	1804	1804	1837	1904	2004	2015	2104	0206
Hajdúszoboszló d.	0446	0546	0553	0617	0717	|	0817	0917	1017	1117	1146	1217	1317	1417	1517	1617	1717	1817	1817	1853	1917	2017	|	2117	0208
Püspökladány d.	0506	0602	0612	0632	0732	0737	0832	0932	1032	1132	1202	1232	1332	1432	1532	1632	1732	1832	1832	1912	1932	2032	2045	2132	|
Szolnok d.	0610	0659	0715	0721	0821	0834	0921	1021	1121	1221	1259	1321	1421	1521	1621	1721	1821	1921	1921	2015	2021	2121	2139	2221	0406
Cegléd d.	0633	|	0738	0743	0843	|	0943	1043	1143	1243	|	1343	1443	1543	1643	1743	1843	1943	1943	2038	2043	2143	|	2243	|
Ferihegy ✈ d.	0711	|	0811	0816	0916	|	1016	1116	1216	1316	|	1416	1516	1616	1716	1816	1916	2016	2016	2111	2116	2216	|	2316	|
Köbánya Kispest d.	0717	|	0817	0822	0922	|	1022	1122	1222	1322	|	1422	1522	1622	1722	1822	1922	2022	2022	2117	2122	2222	|	2322	|
Budapest Nyugati a.	0734	0820k	0834	0839	0939	0955k	1039	1139	1239	1337	1420k	1439	1539	1639	1739	1839	1939	2039	2039	2134	2139	2239	2300k	2339	0600k

km			642						*IC* 34								*IC* 614		*IC* 143			*IC* 606			*IC* 626	*EC* 149
									L ⊖		Ⓐ		⚒	Ⓐ	Ⓐ	Ⓐ	R	Ⓐ	R G	Ⓐ	⑥	R	⑥–④	⑥–④	R	J ⊖
0	*Budapest Nyugati* d.	...	...	...	...	...	...	...	0720	...	...	...	...	...	...	...	1320	...	1340k	...	...	1520	...	...	1720	1940k
221	**Debrecen** d.	...	...	...	0603	0703	...	...	0957	0938	1038	1138	1238	1338	1403	1503	1557	1603	1634	1638	1638	1800	1738	1838	1957	2225
270	Nyíregyháza a.	...	...	...	0645	0745	...	...	1028	1020	1120	1220	1320	1420	1445	1545	1628	1645	1710	1720	1720	1831	1820	1920	2028	2255
270	Nyíregyháza d.	...	0432	0546	0646	0746	0846	0946	1031	1046	1146	1246	1346	1423	1446	1546	1631	1646	1715	1721	1746	1832	1846	1946	2031	2257
313	Kisvárda d.	...	0517	0631	0731	0831	0931	1031	1102	1131	1231	1331	1431	1508	1531	1631	1702	1731	1751	1806	1831	1903	1931	2031	2102	2330
335	**Záhony** a.	...	0545	0657	0757	0857	0957	1057	1121	1157	1257	1357	1457	1534	1557	1657	1721	1757	1820	1832	1857	1922	1957	2057	2121	2353
		640	|			**644**			|						**646**				|					**690**	|
335	**Záhony** 🏛 d.	0340	0635	...	...	0940	...	...	1240	...	...	...	...	...	1640	...	...	...	1940	...	...	...	...	...	2140	0108
341	Chop 🏛 ⊡ a.	0458	0753	...	...	1058	...	...	1358	...	...	...	...	...	1758	...	...	...	2059	...	...	...	...	...	2258	0227
382	**Mukachevo** ⊡ a.	...	0932	...	...	...	...	...	1540	...	...	...	...	...	...	...	...	...	...	...	...	...	...	...	...	0616

	EC 140		641	*IC* 619					*IC* 617	*EC* 146				*IC* 33			*IC* 615	647	*IC* 603			*IC* 31		649	D9
	J ⊖	Ⓐ		R K		Ⓐ			R	R G		⚒	⚒	R L	Ⓐ		R		⑦ R			R L	Ⓐ		R T
Mukachevo ⊡ d.	2359	...	...	...	...	...	...	...	...	...	...	...	...	1030	...	...	...	...	...	...	...	1630	...	...	1937
Chop 🏛 ⊡ d.	0329	...	0602	...	...	...	...	...	...	0901	...	...	...	1202	...	...	...	1602	...	...	...	1832	...	2132	2332
Záhony 🏛 a.	0248	...	0520	...	...	...	...	...	...	0820	...	...	...	1120	...	...	...	1520	...	...	...	1750	...	2050	2250
	|									|				|								|		|
Záhony d.	0405	0355	0520	0528	0553	0613	0703	0803	0837	0935	1003	1103	1203	1237	1303	1403	1437	...	1624	1703	1803	1837	1929	2003	0012
Kisvárda d.	0423	0421	0546	0547	0619	0639	0729	0829	0856	0954	1029	1129	1229	1256	1329	1429	1456	...	1643	1729	1829	1856	1955	2029	|
Nyíregyháza a.	0456	0506	0633	0618	0704	0724	0814	0914	0927	1025	1114	1214	1314	1327	1414	1514	1527	...	1714	1814	1914	1927	2040	2114	0110
Nyíregyháza d.	0458	0510	0640	0620	0707	0737	0837	0937	0930	1034	1137	1237	1337	1330	1415	1515	1530	...	1730	...	1937	1930	2047	2137	0125
Debrecen a.	0529	0554	0723	0652	0751	0821	0921	1021	1002	1106	1221	1321	1421	1402	1459	1559	1602	...	1802	...	2021	2002	2131	2221	0206
Budapest Nyugati a.	0820k	...	...	0939	...	...	...	...	1239	1420k	...	...	...	1639	...	...	1839	...	2039	...	...	2239	...	...	0600k

C – CORONA – 🛏 1, 2 cl., ▬ 2 cl., [2] Braşov - Dej - Jibou - Debrecen - Budapest and v.v. (Table **1277**).
G – TISZA-SZAMOS – [12] ✕ Chop - Záhony - Nyiregyháza - Debrecen - Budapest - Wien and v.v.; [2] Baia Mare (**686/687**) - Satu Mare - Debrecen - Budapest - Wien and v.v. (Table **1277**).
H – HARGHITA – [12] Braşov - Dej - Jibou - Debrecen - Budapest and v.v.
J – HORTOBÁGY – [12] Wien - Budapest - Debrecen - Záhony - Chop and v.v.; conveys 🛏 1, 2 cl. Wien - Budapest - Chop - Lviv - Kyiv and v.v.
K – NYSIREG-KRASZNA – Also conveys [2] Budapest Nyugati - Debrecen (**638/639**) - Mátészalka and v.v. (Table **1276**).
L – LATORCA – [12] Budapest - Záhony and v.v.; [2] Budapest - Mukachevo and v.v.; [2] Záhony - Chop and v.v. (Table **1715**).

T – TRANSCARPATHIA – 🛏 1, 2 cl., [2] Budapest - Chop - Lviv - Kyiv and v.v.
k – Budapest **Keleti**.
⊖ – R for domestic journeys within Hungary.
⊡ – Ukrainian (East European) time, one hour ahead of Hungarian time.
● – Timings may vary by up to 5 minutes.

MAV CFR — BUDAPEST - BIHARKERESZTES - ORADEA (and BRASOV) — 1275

Engineering work is affecting services until July 10 with bus a replacement between Biharkeresztes and Episcopia Bihor and v.v. Please check timings locally before travelling.

	359	367	361		363		365	407	369
		⊠ H [R]						⊠ C [R]	
Budapest Keleti 1270 d.	...	0640	...	...	...	...	...	1740	...
Szolnok 1270 a.	...	0801	...	...	...	...	...	1901	...
Szolnok 1270 d.	...	0802	...	...	...	...	...	1902	...
Püspökladány 1270 a.	...	0857	...	...	...	...	...	1957	...
Püspökladány d.	0730	0858	1030	...	1330	...	1630	1958	2030
Biharkeresztes a.	0815	|	1115	...	1415	...	1715	|	2115
Biharkeresztes ▦ d.	0835	|	1135	...	1435	...	1735	|	2135
Episcopia Bihor ⊙ a.	0951	|	1251	...	1551	...	1851	|	2251
Oradea ⊙ a.	1017	|	1321	...	1602	...	1902	|	2329
Brasov 1600 ⊙ a.	...	2306	...	...	...	...	...	1000	...

	358	406	360		362		364	366	368
		⊠ C [R]						⊠ H [R]	
Brasov 1600 ⊙ d.	...	1905	...	...	...	...	...	0805	...
Oradea ⊙ d.	0625	|	1035	...	1435	...	1735	|	2040
Episcopia Bihor ▦ ⊙ d.	0654	|	1104	...	1504	...	1804	|	2109
Biharkeresztes ▦ a.	0610	|	1020	...	1420	...	1720	|	2025
Biharkeresztes d.	0633	|	1041	...	1441	...	1741	|	2041
Püspökladány a.	0719	0736	1127	...	1527	...	1827	2044	2127
Püspökladány 1270 d.	...	0737	...	...	...	...	...	2045	...
Szolnok 1270 a.	...	0833	...	...	...	...	...	2133	...
Szolnok 1270 d.	...	0834	...	...	...	...	...	2139	...
Budapest Keleti 1270 a.	...	0955	...	...	...	...	...	2300	...

C – CORONA – 🛏 1,2 cl., ▬ 2 cl., (2) ✕ Budapest - Debrecen - Jibou - Dej - Miercurea Ciuc - Brasov and v.v. (Table **1277** and **1610**).
H – HARGITA – (12) Budapest - Debrecen - Jibou - Dej - Miercurea Ciuc - Brasov and v.v.
⊙ – Romanian (East European) time, one hour ahead of Hungary.
⊠ – *IC* in Hungary; *IR* in Romania.

2nd class — DEBRECEN - MÁTÉSZALKA and FÜZESABONY — 1276

km								⑦	E		⑥	d
0	**Debrecen** d.	0507	0711	0913	1113	1313	1513	1709	1812	1905	2009	2245
58	Nyírbátor d.	0636	0836	1036	1236	1436	1636	1836	1921	2026	2139	0004
78	**Mátészalka** a.	0659	0859	1059	1259	1459	1659	1859	1940	2049	2202	0027

	⚒	E	⚒						⚒		
Mátészalka d.	0415	0506	0613	0705	0905	1105	1305	1505	1705	1916	2115
Nyírbátor d.	0438	0526	0639	0728	0928	1128	1328	1528	1728	1942	2138
Debrecen a.	0557	0645	0759	0847	1047	1247	1454	1654	1858	2059	2251

km										⑥		
0	**Debrecen** d.	0421	0707	0911	1111	1311	1511	1711	1911	2100	2245	...
42	Hortobágy d.	0521	0759	1001	1159	1359	1559	1759	1959	2155	2336	...
73	Tiszafüred d.	0611	0850	1050	1250	1450	1650	1850	2050	2244	0020	...
103	**Füzesabony** a.	0642	0921	1121	1321	1521	1721	1921	2121	...	...	...

	⚒			Ⓐ							
Füzesabony d.	...	0459	0738	...	0938	1138	1338	1538	1738	1938	...
Tiszafüred d.	0432	0531	0810	0913	1010	1210	1410	1610	1810	2010	...
Hortobágy d.	0536	0615	0854	1001	1054	1254	1454	1654	1854	2054	...
Debrecen a.	0625	0704	0946	1050	1146	1346	1546	1746	1946	2140	...

E – KRASZNA (2) [R] Budapest Nyugati (**606/619**) - Debrecen (**638/639**) - Mátészalka.
d – Runs 16 minutes later on ⑤.

MAV CFR — DEBRECEN - NYIRÁBRÁNY - BAIA MARE and BÉKÉSCSABA - SALONTA — 1277

km		367 H	686 F	407 C
0	**Debrecen** d.	0940	1705	2040
30	Nyirábrány a.	1013	1751	2113
30	Nyirábrány ▦ d.	1049	1752	2114
39	Valea lui Mihai ▦ ⊙ a.	1204	1907	2229
39	Valea lui Mihai ⊙ d.	1229	1947	2321
70	Carei 1625 ⊙ d.	1256	2010	2345
106	Satu Mare 1625 ⊙ a.	...	2042	...
165	**Baia Mare** 1625 ⊙ a.	...	2200	...

	406 C	687 F	366 H
Baia Mare 1625 ⊙ d.	...	0800	...
Satu Mare 1625 ⊙ d.	...	0925	...
Carei 1625 ⊙ d.	0514	0958	1840
Valea lui Mihai ⊙ a.	0541	1023	1909
Valea lui Mihai ▦ ⊙ d.	0608	1054	1945
Nyirábrány ▦ a.	0523	1009	1900
Nyirábrány d.	0600	1019	1920
Debrecen a.	0640	1059	2000

km				
0	**Békéscsaba** 1280 d.	0642	1244	1644
16	Gyula 1280 d.	0700	1300	1700
36	Kötegyán a.	0726	1326	1726
36	Kötegyán ▦ d.	0730	1330	1730
50	**Salonta** ▦ ⊙ 1625 a.	0850	1450	1850

Salonta ▦ ⊙ 1625 d.	1000	1600	1800
Kötegyán ▦ a.	0920	1520	1720
Kötegyán d.	0931	1531	1731
Gyula 1280 d.	1000	1600	1800
Békéscsaba 1280 a.	1015	1615	1815

km	*Currently closed*		
0	**Mátészalka** d.	...	...
18	Tiborszállás a.	...	...
18	Tiborszállás ▦ d.	...	...
33	**Carei** ⊙ a.	...	...

Currently closed		
Carei ⊙ d.	...	...
Tiborszállás ▦ a.	...	...
Tiborszállás d.	...	...
Mátészalka a.	...	...

C – CORONA – 🛏 1,2 cl., ▬ 2 cl., (2) ✕ Budapest - Debrecen - Jibou - Dej - Miercurea Ciuc - Brasov and v.v.
F – SZAMOS – (2) Wien (**143/146**) - Debrecen (**686/687**) - Baia Mare and v.v.
H – HARGITA – (12) Budapest - Debrecen - Jibou - Dej - Miercurea Ciuc - Brasov and v.v.
⊙ – Romanian (East European) time, one hour ahead of Hungary. For other trains within Romania see Table **1625**.

2nd class (except where noted) — BUDAPEST - BÉKÉSCSABA - LÖKÖSHÁZA - ARAD — 1280

Carriages without [R] are available on *IC* trains.

km					*IC** 371 ⊖	*IC* 7400 [R]	*IC** 73 T ⊖	*IC* 7402 [R]	*IC** 75/76 C ⊖	*IC* 742 [R]	*IC** 375 ⊖	*IC* 7404 [R]	*IC** 377 ⊖	*IC* 746 [R]	*IC** 79 M ⊖	*IC* 7406 [R]	*IC** 379 ⊖	*IC* 748 [R]	*IC** 473 [R] H	7408 [R]			347 [R] D
0	**Budapest** Keleti 1270 d.	...	...	...	0510	0610	0710	0810	0910	1010	1110	1210	1310	1410	1510	1610	1710	1810	1910	2010	...	...	2305
100	Szolnok 1270 d.	...	0444	0544	0644	0732	0832	0932	1032	1132	1232	1332	1432	1532	1632	1732	1832	1932	2032	2132	...	...	0032
141	Mezötúr d.	0429	0531	0631	0720	0800	0900	1000	1100	1200	1300	1400	1500	1600	1700	1800	1900	2000	2100	2200	...	...	|
159	Gyoma d.	0445	0547	0647	0732	0812	0911	1012	1111	1212	1311	1412	1512	1611	1711	1812	1911	2012	2111	2213	...	...	|
196	**Békéscsaba** a.	0515	0617	0717	0759	0839	0939	1039	1139	1239	1339	1439	1539	1639	1739	1839	1939	2039	2139	2239	...	...	0132
196	**Békéscsaba** d.	0538	0635	...	0818	...	0944	...	1144	...	1344	...	1544	...	1744	...	1944	...	2144	...	...	...	0135
225	Lökösháza a.	0607	0715	...	0847	...	1013	...	1213	...	1413	...	1613	...	1813	...	2013	...	2213	...	...	...	0159
225	Lökösháza ▦ d.	...	...	...	0915	...	1045	...	1245	...	1445	...	1645	...	1845	...	2045	...	2245	...	...	...	0239
236	Curtici ▦ ⊙ a.	...	...	...	1025	...	1155	...	1355	...	1555	...	1755	...	1955	...	2155	...	2355	...	...	...	0349
236	Curtici ⊙ d.	...	...	...	1045	...	1220	...	1420	...	1615	...	1815	...	2020	...	2215	...	0030	...	...	...	0419
253	**Arad** ⊙ a.	...	...	...	1057	...	1232	...	1434	...	1627	...	1829	...	2032	...	2227	...	0041	...	...	...	0431
	Timisoara Nord 1630 ⊙ a.	...	...	...	...	...	1354	...	|	...	...	...	1956	...	2217	...	...	...	|	...	...	...	|
	Brasov 1600 ⊙ a.	...	...	...	...	...	...	...	2254	...	...	...	...	...	|	...	...	...	0848	...	...	...	1249
	Bucuresti Nord 1600 ⊙ a.	...	...	...	...	...	...	...	...	...	...	...	...	...	0936	...	...	...	1135	...	...	...	1526

	346 [R] D		7509 2	*IC** 472 [R] H	*IC* 759 [R]	*IC** 378 ⊖	*IC* 7407 [R]	*IC** 78 M ⊖	*IC* 747 [R]	*IC** 376 ⊖	*IC* 745 [R]	*IC** 374 ⊖	*IC* 743 [R]	*IC** 74/77 C ⊖	*IC* 741 [R]	*IC** 72 T ⊖	*IC* 7401 [R]	*IC** 370 ⊖				
Bucuresti Nord 1600 ⊙ d.	1507	...	...	1758	...	...	...	1945	...	...	...	...	...	...	...	...	...	...	...	...	...	...
Brasov 1600 ⊙ d.	1746	...	...	2036	...	...	...	|	...	...	...	...	...	0700	...	...	...	...	...	...	...	...
Timisoara Nord 1630 ⊙ d.	|	...	...	|	...	0533	...	0721	...	...	...	...	...	|	...	1539	...	...	...	...	...	...
Arad ⊙ d.	0128	...	...	0443	...	0700	...	0857	...	1100	...	1300	...	1501	...	1657	...	1900	...	...	...	...
Curtici ⊙ a.	0140	...	...	0456	...	0714	...	0909	...	1113	...	1313	...	1514	...	1709	...	1913	...	...	...	...
Curtici ▦ ⊙ d.	0210	...	...	0534	...	0734	...	0934	...	1134	...	1334	...	1534	...	1734	...	1934	...	...	...	...
Lökösháza ▦ a.	0120	...	...	0444	...	0644	...	0844	...	1044	...	1244	...	1444	...	1644	...	1844	...	...	...	...
Lökösháza d.	0200	...	0446	0537	0641	0742	...	0942	...	1142	...	1342	...	1542	...	1742	...	1942	2048	...	...	...
Békéscsaba a.	0225	...	0515	0610	0712	0811	...	1015	...	1215	...	1415	...	1615	...	1815	...	2015	2117	...	...	...
Békéscsaba d.	0229	...	0530	0620	0720	0820	0920	1020	1120	1220	1320	1420	1520	1620	1720	1820	1920	2020	...	2120	2240	...
Gyoma d.	|	...	0557	0647	0747	0847	0947	1047	1147	1247	1347	1447	1547	1647	1747	1847	1947	2047	...	2151	2311	...
Mezötúr d.	|	...	0612	0700	0800	0900	1000	1100	1200	1300	1400	1500	1600	1700	1800	1900	2000	2100	...	2207	2326	...
Szolnok 1270 d.	0332	...	0650	0729	0829	0929	1029	1129	1229	1329	1429	1529	1629	1729	1829	1929	2029	2129	...	2243	...	...
Budapest Keleti 1270 a.	0500	...	0815	0850	0950	1050	1150	1250	1350	1450	1550	1650	1750	1850	1950	2050	2150	2250	...	...	...	...

C – CLAUDIOPOLIS - FOGARAS – (12) Cluj Napoca - Simeria - Arad - Budapest and v.v.; (2) Braşov - Sibiu - Simeria - Arad - Budapest and v.v.
D – DACIA - CORVIN – 🛏 1,2 cl., ▬ 1,2 cl., (2) Wien - Budapest - Arad - Brasov - Bucuresti and v.v.; ▬ 1,2 cl., (2) Wien - Budapest - Szolnok (**405/4**) - Cluj Napoca and v.v.
H – ISTER – 🛏 1,2 cl., ▬ 2 cl., (2) ✕ Budapest - Arad - Sibiu - Brasov - Bucuresti and v.v.
M – MUNTENIA – ▬ 2 cl., (2) Budapest - Arad - Timisoara - Craiova - Bucuresti and v.v.
T – TRAIANUS – (2) Craiova - Timişoara - Arad - Budapest and v.v.
* – Classified *IR* in Romania
⊙ – Romanian (East European) time, one hour ahead of Hungary.
⊖ – Reservation compulsory for domestic journeys in Hungary ([R] in Romania).

1282 BÉKÉSCSABA - GYULA *2nd class*

km																							
											Ⓐ												
0	**Békéscsaba** d.	0527	0642	0742	...	0944	1144	1244	...	1344	1403	1444	...	1544	1644	1744	...	1844	1944	2044	...	2244	...
16	**Gyula** a.	0543	0659	0759	...	0959	1159	1259	...	1359	1418	1459	...	1559	1659	1759	...	1859	1959	2059	...	2259	...

			Ⓐ																			
Gyula d.	0500	0546	0623	...	0700	0800	0900	...	1000	1100	1300	...	1500	1600	1700	...	1800	1900	2000	...	2100	...
Békéscsaba a.	0515	0604	0641	...	0715	0815	0915	...	1015	1115	1315	...	1515	1615	1718	...	1815	1915	2015	...	2118	...

1290 BUDAPEST - KECSKEMÉT - SZEGED

Carriages without 🅁 are available on *IC* trains.

km																								
		IC		*IC*	*IC*	*IC*	*IC*	*IC*		*IC*	*IC*	*IC*		*IC*	*IC*	*IC*		*IC*	*IC*	*IC*		*IC*	*IC*	
		720		**700**	**702**	**712**	**722**	**732**		**704**	**714**	**724**		**734**	**706**	**716**		**726**	**736**	**708**		**718**	**728**	2
		🅁		🅁	🅁	🅁	🅁	🅁		🅁	🅁	🅁		🅁	🅁	🅁		🅁	🅁	🅁		🅁	🅁	
0	**Budapest** Nyugati **1270** d.	0430	...	0550	0650	0750	0850	0950	...	1050	1150	1250	...	1350	1450	1550	...	1650	1750	1850	...	1950	2050	2200
11	Kőbánya Kispest **1270** d.	0446	...	0606	0706	0806	0906	1006	...	1106	1206	1306	...	1406	1506	1606	...	1706	1806	1906	...	2006	2106	2217
18	Ferihegy ✈ **1270** d.	0453	...	0612	0712	0812	0912	1012	...	1112	1212	1312	...	1412	1512	1612	...	1712	1812	1912	...	2012	2112	2223
73	Cegléd **1270** a.	0533	...	0646	0746	0846	0946	1046	...	1146	1246	1346	...	1446	1546	1646	...	1746	1846	1946	...	2046	2146	2312
73	Cegléd d.	0534	...	0648	0748	0848	0948	1048	...	1148	1248	1348	...	1448	1548	1648	...	1748	1848	1948	...	2048	2148	2313
106	**Kecskemét** d.	0605	...	0711	0811	0911	1011	1111	...	1211	1311	1411	...	1511	1611	1711	...	1811	1911	2011	...	2111	2211	2343
131	Kiskunfélegyháza a.	0627	...	0727	0827	0927	1027	1127	...	1227	1327	1427	...	1527	1627	1727	...	1827	1927	2027	...	2127	2227	2400
131	Kiskunfélegyháza d.	0630	...	0730	0830	0930	1030	1130	...	1230	1330	1430	...	1530	1630	1730	...	1830	1930	2030	...	2130	2230	0001
191	**Szeged** a.	0716	...	0816	0916	1016	1116	1216	...	1316	1416	1516	...	1616	1716	1816	...	1916	2016	2116	...	2216	2316	0047

		IC	*IC*		*IC*	*IC*	*IC*		*IC*	*IC*	*IC*		*IC*	*IC*	*IC*		*IC*	*IC*	*IC*		*IC*	*IC*	*IC*
	2	**719**	**709**		**707**	**717**	**727**		**737**	**705**	**715**		**725**	**735**	**703**		**713**	**723**	**733**		**701**	**711**	**721**
			🅁		🅁	🅁	🅁		🅁	🅁	🅁		🅁	🅁	🅁		🅁	🅁	🅁		🅁	🅁	🅁
Szeged d.	0325	0430	0546	...	0644	0744	0844	...	0944	1044	1144	...	1244	1344	1444	...	1544	1644	1744	...	1844	1944	2044
Kiskunfélegyháza a.	0409	0517	0630	...	0730	0830	0930	...	1030	1130	1230	...	1330	1430	1530	...	1630	1730	1830	...	1930	2030	2130
Kiskunfélegyháza d.	0410	0518	0631	...	0731	0831	0931	...	1031	1131	1231	...	1331	1431	1531	...	1631	1731	1831	...	1931	2031	2131
Kecskemét d.	0432	0537	0648	...	0748	0848	0948	...	1048	1148	1248	...	1348	1448	1548	...	1648	1748	1848	...	1948	2048	2148
Cegléd a.	0500	0602	0712	...	0812	0912	1012	...	1112	1212	1312	...	1412	1512	1612	...	1712	1812	1912	...	2012	2112	2212
Cegléd **1270** d.	0502	0603	0713	...	0813	0913	1013	...	1113	1213	1313	...	1413	1513	1613	...	1713	1813	1913	...	2013	2113	2214
Ferihegy ✈ **1270** a.	0539	0640	0745	...	0845	0945	1045	...	1145	1245	1345	...	1445	1545	1645	...	1745	1845	1945	...	2045	2145	2249
Kőbánya Kispest **1270** a.	0546	0647	0751	...	0851	0951	1051	...	1151	1251	1351	...	1451	1551	1651	...	1751	1851	1951	...	2051	2151	2256
Budapest Nyugati **1270** a.	0604	0704	0809	...	0909	1009	1109	...	1209	1309	1409	...	1509	1609	1709	...	1809	1909	2009	...	2109	2209	2314

1292 SZEGED - BÉKÉSCSABA *2nd class*

km																								
												Ⓐ												
0	**Szeged** d.	...	...	0528	0628	0728	...	0828	0928	1028	1128	1228	...	1328	1428	1528	1628	1728	...	1828	1928	2028	2128	2228
31	Hódmezővásárhely d.	...	...	0601	0705	0801	...	0905	1001	1105	1201	1305	...	1401	1505	1601	1705	1801	...	1905	2001	2105	2201	2259
62	Orosháza d.	0430	0531	0631	0731	0831	...	0931	1031	1131	1231	1331	...	1431	1531	1631	1731	1831	...	1931	2031	2131	2229	2327
97	**Békéscsaba** a.	0509	0612	0712	0810	0910	...	1010	1110	1210	1310	1410	...	1510	1610	1710	1810	1910	...	2010	2110	2210	...	...

											Ⓐ												
Békéscsaba d.	...	...	0547	0647	0747	...	0847	0947	1047	1147	1247	...	1347	1445	1547	1645	1747	...	1847	1947	2047	2147	2245
Orosháza d.	0432	0528	0632	0732	0832	...	0932	1032	1132	1232	1332	...	1432	1532	1632	1732	1832	...	1932	2032	2132	2226	2329
Hódmezővásárhely d.	0502	0602	0702	0802	0902	...	1002	1102	1202	1300	1402	...	1502	1602	1702	1802	1902	...	2002	2102	2202	...	...
Szeged a.	0533	0633	0733	0833	0933	...	1033	1133	1233	1333	1433	...	1533	1633	1733	1833	1933	...	2033	2133	2233	...	...

1295 BUDAPEST - KELEBIA - SUBOTICA *2nd class*

Warning! Rail services Budapest - Kelebia are suspended due to engineering work. No rail replacement 🚌 service is available.

km										
0	**Budapest** Nyugati **1290** d.	...	...	...	...	...	...	...	...	...
	Szeged **1290** d.	...	...	...	...	...	...	...	...	...
	Kunszentmiklós-Tass d.	...	...	...	...	...	...	...	...	...
	Kiskőrös d.	...	...	...	...	...	...	...	...	...
	Kiskunhalas d.	...	...	...	...	...	...	...	...	...
	Kelebia 🏛 d.	...	...	...	...	...	...	...	...	...
	Subotica 🏛 a.	...	...	...	...	...	...	...	...	...

Subotica 🏛 d.	...	...	...	...	...	...	...	...	...
Kelebia 🏛 d.	...	...	...	...	...	...	...	...	...
Kiskunhalas d.	...	...	...	...	...	...	...	...	...
Kiskőrös d.	...	...	...	...	...	...	...	...	...
Kunszentmiklós-Tass d.	...	...	...	...	...	...	...	...	...
Szeged **1290** d.	...	...	...	...	...	...	...	...	...
Budapest Nyugati **1290** a.	...	...	...	...	...	...	...	...	...

1299 OTHER LOCAL SERVICES

BUDAPEST - DUNAÚJVÁROS — *80* km, journey 65 – 95 minutes

From **Budapest** Déli: 0450, 0550 Ⓒ, 0615 Ⓐ, 0650, 0750 Ⓐ, 0850, 1050, 1250, 1350 Ⓒ, 1415 Ⓐ, 1450 Ⓒ, 1515 Ⓐ, 1550 Ⓒ, 1615 Ⓐ, 1650 Ⓒ, 1715 Ⓐ, 1850Ⓒ, 1915Ⓐ, 2050, 2250.

From **Dunaújváros**: 0432, 0532, 0632, 0732, 0832 Ⓐ, 0932, 1132, 1332, 1432, 1532, 1632, 1732, 1832, 1932 Ⓐ, 2032, 2242.

BUDAPEST - ESZTERGOM — *53 km*, journey 65 – 74 minutes

From **Budapest** Nyugati: 0025, 0225 Ⓒ, 0414, 0451, 0521, 0551, 0621, 0651 and every 30 minutes until 2121, 2151, 2221, 2315.

From **Esztergom**: 0356, 0435, 0505, 0535, 0605, 0635 and every 30 minutes until 2105, 2135, 2235, 2335.

BUDAPEST - SZENTENDRE — *21 km*, journey 40 minutes

HÉV suburban trains (line H5) from Budapest Batthyány tér (on metro M2), every 12 – 30 mins.

EGER - SZILVÁSVÁRAD — *34 km*, journey 65 minutes

Trains call at Szilvásvárad-Szalajkavölgy (for the forest railway), 58 minutes after Eger and 6 minutes after Szilvásvárad.

From **Eger**: 0737 **A**, 1009, 1305, 1605 **A**.

From **Szilvásvárad**: 0852 **A**, 1149, 1449, 1749 **A**.

A – Daily Mar. 15 - Oct. 31; Ⓒ Nov. 1 - Dec. 7.

ESTERGOM - KOMÁROM — *53 km*, journey 90 minutes

From **Esztergom**: 0742 Ⓐ, 0812 Ⓒ *, 1212 Ⓒ *, 1442 Ⓐ, 1612 Ⓒ *, 1642 Ⓐ, 1842 Ⓐ, 1942 Ⓐ, 2012Ⓒkiskun.

From **Komárom**: 0446 Ⓐ, 0546, 1003 Ⓒ* 1246 Ⓐ, 1403 Ⓒ *, 1444 Ⓐ, 1644 Ⓐ, 1803 Ⓒ *.

* – Change trains at Almásfüzitö (total journey time 100 minutes).

KOMÁROM - SZÉKESFEHÉRVÁR — *82 km*, journey 81 minutes

From **Komárom**: 0605, 0805 and every **two** hours until 2005.

From **Székesfehérvár**: 0608, 0826 and every **two** hours until 2026.

HATVAN - SZOLNOK — *68 km*, journey 71 – 73 minutes

From **Hatvan**: 0406, 0508 Ⓐ, 0601, 0701 Ⓐ, 0801, 1001, 1201, 1301 Ⓐ, 1401, 1501 Ⓐ, 1601, 1701 Ⓐ, 1801, 1901 Ⓐ, 2001, 2101 Ⓐ, 2225.

From **Szolnok**: 0314, 0432, 0516 Ⓐ, 0619, 0721 Ⓐ, 0821, 1021, 1221, 1321 Ⓐ, 1421, 1521 Ⓐ, 1621, 1721 Ⓐ, 1821, 1921 Ⓐ, 2021, 2121.

KISKUNFÉLEGYHÁZA - SZENTES — *39 km*, journey 51 minutes

Trains call at **Csongrád** 36 minutes after Kiskunfélegyháza / 17 minutes after Szentes.

From **Kiskunfélegyháza**: 0548 Ⓐ, 0748, 0948, 1148, 1338, 1538, 1738, 1938, 2138.

From **Szentes**: 0410 Ⓐ, 0621, 0821, 1021, 1221, 1406, 1606, 1806, 2006.

2nd class BUDAPEST - SIÓFOK - FONYÓD - KESZTHELY and NAGYKANIZSA 1220

SUMMER SERVICE MAY 12 - JUNE 20 and SEPTEMBER 1 – 21.

Carriages without 🅁 are available on *IC* trains. **Train names:** Budapest - Nagykanizsa *IC* trains are named TOPART. Budapest - Keszthely *IC* trains are named BALATON.

km						*IC* 850 🅁		*IC* 860 ✕🅁	*IC* 842 🅁	*IR* 18502	*IC* 862 ✕🅁	*IR* 18702		*IC* 852 🅁	*IC* 864 ✕🅁	*IR* 18404	*IR* 18494		*IC* 844 🅁	*IR* 18504	*IC* 874 ✕🅁	*IC* 854 🅁	*IC* 866 ✕🅁
		Ⓐ		Ⓐ								Ⓒ d				Ⓐ	Ⓒ						
0	**Budapest** Déli 1225 1230 d.	...	...	0405	...	0530	...	0635	0735	0805	0835	...	...	0935	1035	1005	1005	...	1135	1205	1235	1335	1435
4	Kelenföld 1225 1230 d.	...	...	0412	...	0537	...	0642	0742	0812	0842	0901	...	0942	1042	1012	1012	...	1142	1212	1242	1342	1442
67	**Székesfehérvár** 1225 1230 a.	...	...	0509	...	0615	...	0720	0820	0851	0920	0942	...	1020	1120	1051	1051	...	1220	1251	1320	1420	1520
67	**Székesfehérvár** d.	...	...	0511	...	0616	...	0721	0821	0852	0921	0944	...	1021	1121	1052	1052	...	1221	1252	1321	1421	1521
95	Lepsény d.	...	...	0535	...	0640	...	0740	0840	0920	|	|	...	1040	|	1120	1120	...	1240	1320	|	1440	|
115	**Siófok** a.	...	...	0555	...	0655	...	0755	0855	0945	0955	1028	...	1055	1155	1145	1145	...	1255	1345	1355	1455	1555
115	**Siófok** d.	...	0436	...	...	0657	...	0757	0857	1004	0957	1031	...	1057	1157	...	1204	...	1257	1404	1357	1457	1557
124	Zamárdi d.	...	0448	...	...	0704	...	0804	0904	1016	1004	1042	...	1104	1204	...	1216	...	1304	1416	1404	1504	1604
130	Balatonföldvár d.	...	0456	...	...	0709	...	0809	0909	1024	1009	1054	...	1109	1209	...	1224	...	1309	1424	1409	1509	1609
139	Balatonszemes d.	...	0505	...	...	0718	...	0818	0918	1034	1018	1101	...	1118	1218	...	1234	...	1318	1434	1418	1518	1618
146	Balatonlelle d.	...	0512	...	...	0724	...	0824	0924	1042	1024	1108	...	1124	1224	...	1242	...	1324	1442	1424	1524	1624
149	Balatonboglár d.	...	0516	...	...	0730	...	0830	0930	1047	1030	1113	...	1130	1230	...	1247	...	1330	1447	1430	1530	1630
157	**Fonyód** a.	...	0524	...	...	0735	...	0835	0935	1056	1035	1123	...	1135	1235	...	1256	...	1335	1456	1435	1535	1635
157	**Fonyód** 1232 d.	...	0528	...	0632	0737	...	0837	0937	1103	1037	...	...	1137	1237	...	...	...	1337	1500	1437	1537	1637
165	Balatonfenyves 1232 d.	...	0538	...	0641	0743	...	0843	0943	1122	1043	...	...	1143	1243	...	...	...	1343	1522	1443	1543	1643
181	Balatonszentgyörgy 1232 a.	...	0557	...	0659	0756	...	0857	0956	1142	1057	...	...	1156	1257	...	...	...	1356	1542	1457	1556	1657
181	Balatonszentgyörgy 1232 d.	0442	0601	...	0700	0801	...	0900	1001	...	1100	...	...	1201	1300	...	...	...	1401	...	1500	1601	1700
221	**Keszthely** 1232 a.	|	|	...	0711	|	...	0911	|	...	1111	...	...	|	1311	...	...	...	|	...	1511	|	1711
221	**Nagykanizsa** a.	0529	0644	...	...	0844	...	...	1044	...	...	...	...	1244	...	...	...	...	1444	...	...	1644	...
352	*Zagreb* **1340** a.	...	...	...	...	...	...	...	...	...	...	...	...	...	...	...	...	...	...	...	...	...	...

	IR 18406	*IR* 18496	*IC* 204 🅁	*IR* 18506	*IR* 18596	*IC* 876 ✕🅁		*IC* 856 🅁	*IR* 18408	*IC* 868 ✕🅁			*IC* 848 🅁		*IR* 18598	*IC* 1878 ✕🅁						
	Ⓐ	Ⓒ	A	④	⑤–⑦										⑤⑥					⑤⑥		
Budapest Déli 1225 1230 d.	1405	1405	1535	1605	1605	1635	...	1735	1805	1835	...	...	1935	...	2005	2135	...	2205	...	2300	...	...
Kelenföld 1225 1230 d.	1412	1412	1542	1612	1612	1642	...	1742	1812	1842	...	...	1942	...	2012	2142	...	2212	...	2307	...	...
Székesfehérvár 1225 1230 a.	1451	1451	1620	1651	1651	1720	...	1820	1851	1920	...	...	2020	...	2051	2220	...	2250	...	2346	...	...
Székesfehérvár d.	1452	1452	1621	1652	1652	1721	...	1821	1852	1921	...	...	2021	...	2052	2221	...	2251	...	2352	...	...
Lepsény d.	1520	1520	1640	1720	1720	|	...	1840	1920	|	...	...	2040	...	2120	|	...	2315	...	0013	...	...
Siófok a.	1545	1545	1655	1745	1745	1755	...	1855	1945	1955	...	...	2055	...	2145	2255	...	2334	...	0033	...	...
Siófok d.	...	1604	1657	...	1804	1757	...	1857	2004	1957	...	...	2057	...	2150	2257	...	2336	...	0036	...	...
Zamárdi d.	...	1616	1704	...	1816	1804	...	1904	2016	2004	...	...	2104	...	2202	2304	...	2348	...	0048	...	...
Balatonföldvár d.	...	1624	1709	...	1824	1809	...	1909	2024	2009	...	...	2109	...	2212	2309	...	2356	...	0056	...	...
Balatonszemes d.	...	1634	1718	...	1834	1818	...	1918	2034	2018	...	...	2118	...	2222	2318	...	0006	...	0106	...	...
Balatonlelle d.	...	1642	1724	...	1842	1824	...	1924	2042	2024	...	...	2124	...	2230	2324	...	0013	...	0113	...	...
Balatonboglár d.	...	1647	1730	...	1847	1830	...	1930	2047	2030	...	...	2130	...	2240	2330	...	0017	...	0117	...	...
Fonyód a.	...	1656	1735	...	1856	1835	...	1935	2056	2035	...	...	2135	...	2248	2335	...	0025	...	0125	...	...
Fonyód 1232 d.	...	...	1737	...	1900	1837	...	1937	2103	2037	...	...	2137	...	...	2337	...	...	...	0128	...	...
Balatonfenyves 1232 d.	...	...	1743	...	1922	1843	...	1943	2122	2043	...	...	2143	...	...	2343	...	...	...	0138	...	...
Balatonszentgyörgy 1232 a.	...	...	1756	...	1942	1857	...	1956	2142	2057	...	...	2156	...	...	2357	...	...	...	0157	...	...
Balatonszentgyörgy 1232 d.	...	...	1801	...	...	1900	...	2001	...	2100	...	...	2201	2208	...	0000	...	...	...	0200	...	...
Keszthely 1232 a.	...	...	|	...	...	1911	...	|	...	2111	...	...	|	2219	...	0011	...	...	...	0211	...	...
Nagykanizsa a.	...	...	1844	...	...	...	...	2044	...	...	...	...	2244	...	...	...	...	...	...	...	...	...
Zagreb **1340** a.	...	...	2200	...	...	...	...	...	...	...	...	...	...	...	...	...	...	...	...	...	...	...

					IC 919 🅁		*IC* 849 🅁		*IR* 18509		*IC* 867 ✕🅁		*IC* 847 🅁	*IR* 18407	*IC* 877 ✕🅁	*IC* 857 🅁	*IR* 18495	*IC* 865 ✕🅁	*IR* 18405	*IC* 845 🅁	*IC* 875 ✕🅁
	h	j			Ⓐ				Ⓐ								Ⓒ		Ⓐ		
Zagreb **1340** d.	...	...	...	...	...	...	...	...	...	...	...	...	...	...	...	...	...	...	...	...	...	...
Nagykanizsa d.	...	...	0350	...	...	...	...	0514	...	0536	...	...	...	0714	...	...	0914	...	...	...	1114	...
Keszthely 1232 d.	...	...	|	0428	...	...	0541	|	...	|	...	0648	...	|	...	0848	|	...	1048	...	|	1248
Balatonszentgyörgy 1232 a.	...	...	0433	0439	...	...	0552	0557	...	0620	...	0659	...	0757	...	0859	0957	...	1059	...	1157	1259
Balatonszentgyörgy 1232 d.	...	...	...	0440	...	...	...	0603	...	0621	...	0702	...	0803	0815	0902	1003	...	1102	...	1203	1302
Balatonfenyves 1232 d.	...	...	...	0458	...	...	...	0617	...	0643	...	0717	...	0817	0846	0917	1017	...	1117	...	1217	1317
Fonyód 1232 a.	...	...	...	0506	...	...	...	0622	...	0653	...	0722	...	0822	0856	0922	1022	...	1122	...	1222	1322
Fonyód d.	0333	...	...	0507	...	...	...	0624	0645	0655	...	0724	...	0824	0902	0924	1024	1102	1124	...	1224	1324
Balatonboglár d.	0341	...	...	0516	...	...	...	0630	0652	0703	...	0730	...	0830	0913	0930	1030	1113	1130	...	1230	1330
Balatonlelle d.	0345	...	...	0520	...	...	...	0634	0657	0707	...	0734	...	0834	0917	0934	1034	1117	1134	...	1234	1334
Balatonszemes d.	0353	...	...	0527	...	...	...	0640	0705	0725	...	0740	...	0840	0925	0940	1040	1125	1140	...	1240	1340
Balatonföldvár d.	0406	...	...	0535	...	...	...	0649	0718	0735	...	0749	...	0849	0935	0949	1049	1135	1149	...	1249	1349
Zamárdi d.	0413	...	...	0541	...	...	...	0654	0725	0743	...	0754	...	0854	0943	0954	1054	1143	1154	...	1254	1354
Siófok a.	0425	...	...	0551	...	...	...	0701	0735	0756	...	0801	...	0901	0956	1001	1101	1156	1201	...	1301	1401
Siófok d.	0428	0428	...	0552	0615	...	...	0703	...	0815	...	0803	...	0903	1015	1003	1103	1215	1203	1215	1303	1403
Lepsény d.	0449	0449	...	0612	0642	...	...	0717	...	0840	...	|	...	0917	1043	|	1117	1240	|	1240	1317	|
Székesfehérvár a.	0513	0513	...	0636	0708	...	...	0736	...	0905	...	0836	...	0936	1105	1036	1136	1305	1236	1305	1336	1436
Székesfehérvár 1225 1230 d.	0527	0527	...	0637	...	0712	...	0737	...	0906	...	0837	...	0937	1106	1037	1137	1306	1237	1306	1337	1437
Kelenföld 1225 1230 a.	0611	0611	...	0721	...	0751	...	0816	...	0946	...	0916	...	1016	1146	1116	1216	1346	1316	1346	1416	1516
Budapest Déli 1225 1230 a.	0619	0619	...	0729	...	0759	...	0824	...	0954	...	0924	...	1024	1154	1124	1224	1354	1324	1354	1424	1524

	IR 18505	*IC* 855 🅁	*IC* 863 ✕🅁	*IR* 18403	*IR* 18493	*IC* 843 🅁	*Ex* 18703		*IC* 873 ✕🅁	*IR* 18503	*IC* 853 🅁	*IC* 861 ✕🅁	*IR* 18401	*IR* 18491		*IC* 201 🅁	*IR* 18511	*IC* 871 ✕🅁				
				Ⓐ	Ⓒ		Ⓒ d						Ⓐ	Ⓒ		A	⑤–⑦					⑤⑥
Zagreb **1340** d.	...	...	...	...	...	...	...	...	...	...	...	...	...	...	...	1630	...	...	...	...	...	...
Nagykanizsa d.	...	1314	...	...	...	1514	...	...	...	...	1714	...	...	...	...	1914	...	...	...	2114	...	...
Keszthely 1232 d.	...	|	1448	...	...	|	...	...	1648	...	|	1848	...	...	...	|	...	2048	...	|	...	2348
Balatonszentgyörgy 1232 a.	...	1357	1459	...	...	1557	...	...	1659	...	1757	1859	...	...	...	1957	...	2059	...	2158	...	2359
Balatonszentgyörgy 1232 d.	1215	1403	1502	...	...	1603	...	...	1702	1615	1803	1902	...	...	...	2003	2015	2102	...	2202	...	0002
Balatonfenyves 1232 d.	1246	1417	1517	...	...	1617	...	...	1717	1646	1817	1917	...	...	...	2017	2046	2118	...	2221	...	0021
Fonyód 1232 a.	1256	1422	1522	...	...	1622	...	...	1722	1656	1822	1922	...	...	...	2022	2056	2123	...	2231	...	0031
Fonyód d.	1302	1424	1524	...	1502	1624	1636	...	1724	1702	1824	1924	...	1902	...	2024	2102	2124	...	2233	2321	0033
Balatonboglár d.	1313	1430	1530	...	1513	1630	1646	...	1730	1713	1830	1930	...	1913	...	2030	2113	2130	...	2241	2341	0041
Balatonlelle d.	1317	1434	1534	...	1517	1634	1650	...	1734	1717	1834	1934	...	1917	...	2034	2117	2134	...	2245	2345	0045
Balatonszemes d.	1325	1440	1540	...	1525	1640	1656	...	1740	1725	1840	1940	...	1925	...	2040	2125	2140	...	2253	2353	0053
Balatonföldvár d.	1335	1449	1549	...	1535	1649	1703	...	1749	1735	1849	1949	...	1935	...	2049	2135	2149	...	2301	0006	0106
Zamárdi d.	1343	1454	1554	...	1543	1654	1713	...	1754	1743	1854	1954	...	1943	...	2054	2143	2154	...	2313	0013	0113
Siófok a.	1356	1501	1601	...	1556	1701	1726	...	1801	1756	1901	2001	...	1956	...	2101	2156	2201	...	2325	0025	0125
Siófok d.	1415	1503	1603	1615	1615	1703	1730	...	1803	1815	1903	2003	2015	2015	...	2103	2205	2203	...	...	0028	0128
Lepsény d.	1440	1517	|	1640	1640	1717	|	...	|	1840	1917	|	2040	2040	...	2117	2224	|	...	...	0049	0148
Székesfehérvár a.	1505	1536	1636	1705	1705	1736	1812	...	1836	1905	1936	2036	2105	2105	...	2136	2247	2236	...	...	0109	0209
Székesfehérvár 1225 1230 d.	1506	1537	1637	1706	1706	1737	1814	...	1837	1906	1937	2037	2106	2106	...	2137	2248	2237	...	...	...	0212
Kelenföld 1225 1230 a.	1546	1616	1716	1746	1746	1816	1855	...	1916	1946	2016	2116	2146	2146	...	2216	2345	2316	...	...	...	0301
Budapest Déli 1225 1230 a.	1554	1624	1724	1754	1754	1824	...	...	1924	1954	2024	2124	2154	2154	...	2224	2354	2324	...	...	...	0309

A – AGRAM-TOPART – (2) Budapest - Zagreb and v.v.

d – From / to Szob.
h – Sept. 1 only.
j – Not Sept. 1.
k – Budapest **Keleti**.

1225 BUDAPEST - SZÉKESFEHÉRVÁR - BALATONFÜRED - TAPOLCA

2nd class

SUMMER SERVICE MAY 12 - JUNE 20 and September 1 – 21.
IC trains Budapest - Székesfehérvár and v.v. may require [R].

km									*IR* **19740** Ⓒ	*IC* **860** ✕[R]	Ⓐ	*Ex* **19702** [R]	**19712**	*IR* **19742** Ⓒ	*IC* **862** ✕[R]	Ⓐ	*Ex* **19792** [R]	**19722**	*IR* **19734** Ⓒ	*IC* **864** ✕[R]	Ⓐ	*Ex* **19704** [R]	**19714**	*IR* **19744** Ⓒ
		Ⓐ																						
0	**Budapest** Déli ..... **1220 1230** d.	...	...	...	...	0405	...	...	0630	0635	...	0705	0730	0830	0835	...	0905	0930	1030	1035	...	1105	1130	1230
4	Kelenföld .... **1220 1230** d.	...	...	...	...	0412	...	...	0638	0642	...	0712	0738	0838	0842	...	0912	0938	1038	1042	...	1112	1138	1238
67	**Székesfehérvár** .. **1220 1230** a.	...	...	...	...	0509	...	...	0716	0720	...	0750	0816	0916	0920	...	0950	1016	1116	1120	...	1150	1216	1316
67	**Székesfehérvár** .... d.	...	...	0421	...	...	0526	...	0726	...	0726	0751	0817	0926	...	0926	0951	1017	1126	...	1126	1151	1217	1326
105	Balatonkenese .... d.	...	...	0505	...	...	0620	...	0810	...	0810	|	0852	1010	...	1010	|	1052	1210	...	1210	|	1252	1410
117	Balalatonalmádi .... d.	...	...	0521	...	...	0633	...	0823	...	0823	0837	0906	1023	...	1023	1037	1106	1223	...	1223	1237	1306	1423
123	Alsóörs .... d.	...	...	0528	...	...	0640	...	0835	...	0835	|	0922	1035	...	1035	|	1122	1235	...	1235	|	1322	1435
132	**Balatonfüred** .... a.	...	...	0538	...	...	0651	...	0847	...	0847	0851	0934	1047	...	1047	1051	1134	1247	...	1247	1251	1334	1447
132	**Balatonfüred** .... d.	0408	0508	...	0602	...	0705	0702	...	...	...	0902	...	...	...	...	1102	...	...	...	...	1302	...	...
157	Révfülöp .... d.	0442	0551	...	0640	...	...	0740	...	...	...	0940	...	...	...	...	1140	...	...	...	...	1340	...	...
168	Badacsonytomaj .... d.	0500	0609	...	0654	...	...	0759	...	...	...	0959	...	...	...	...	1159	...	...	...	...	1359	...	...
170	Badacsony .... d.	0503	0612	...	0657	...	...	0803	...	...	...	1003	...	...	...	...	1203	...	...	...	...	1403	...	...
184	**Tapolca** .... a.	0522	0631	...	0715	...	...	0822	...	...	...	1022	...	...	...	...	1222	...	...	...	...	1422	...	...

	IC **874** ✕[R]	Ⓐ	*Ex* **19794** [R]	**19724**	*IR* **19736** Ⓒ	*IC* **866** ✕[R]	Ⓐ	*Ex* **19706** [R]	**19716**	Ⓒ	*IR* **19746** Ⓒ	*IC* **876** ✕[R]	Ⓐ	*Ex* **19796** [R]	**19726**	*IR* **19738** Ⓒ	*IC* **868** ✕[R]	Ⓐ	*Ex* **19708** [R] Ⓐ	**19718**			
Budapest Déli .... **1220 1230** d.	1235	...	1305	1330	1430	1435	...	1505	1530	...	1630	1635	...	1705	1730	1830	1835	...	1905	1930	2010	...	...
Kelenföld .... **1220 1230** d.	1242	...	1312	1338	1438	1442	...	1512	1538	...	1638	1642	...	1712	1738	1838	1842	...	1912	1938	2017	...	...
Székesfehérvár .... **1220 1230** a.	1320	...	1350	1416	1516	1520	...	1550	1616	...	1716	1720	...	1750	1816	1916	1920	...	1950	2016	2109	...	...
Székesfehérvár .... d.	...	1326	1351	1417	1526	...	1526	1551	1617	...	1726	...	1726	1751	1817	1926	...	1926	1951	2017	...	2126	2256
Balatonkenese .... d.	...	1410	|	1452	1610	...	1610	|	1652	...	1810	...	1810	|	1852	2010	...	2010	|	2052	...	2210	2337
Balalatonalmádi .... d.	...	1423	1437	1506	1623	...	1623	1637	1706	...	1823	...	1823	1837	1906	2023	...	2023	2037	2106	...	2223	2350
Alsóörs .... d.	...	1435	|	1522	1635	...	1635	|	1722	...	1835	...	1835	|	1922	2035	...	2035	|	2122	...	2231	2357
Balatonfüred .... a.	...	1447	1451	1534	1647	...	1647	1651	1734	...	1847	...	1847	1851	1934	2047	...	2047	2051	2134	...	2242	0008
Balatonfüred .... d.	...	...	1502	...	...	...	...	1702	...	...	...	...	...	1902	...	...	...	...	2102	...	...	...	...
Révfülöp .... d.	...	...	1540	...	...	...	...	1740	...	1836	...	...	...	1940	...	...	...	...	2140	...	...	...	...
Badacsonytomaj .... d.	...	...	1559	...	...	...	...	1759	...	1850	...	...	...	1959	...	...	...	...	2159	...	...	...	...
Badacsony .... d.	...	...	1603	...	...	...	...	1803	...	1853	...	...	...	2003	...	...	...	...	2203	...	...	...	...
Tapolca .... a.	...	...	1622	...	...	...	...	1822	...	1909	...	...	...	2022	...	...	...	...	2222	...	...	...	...

		Ⓐ			**9709**		*IC* **867** ✕[R]	**19727**	*Ex* **19707** [R] Ⓐ	Ⓐ	*IC* **877** ✕[R]	*IR* **19747** Ⓒ	**19715**	*Ex* **19797** [R]	Ⓐ	*IC* **865** ✕[R]	*IR* **19735** Ⓒ	Ⓒ	**19725**	*Ex* **19705** [R]	Ⓐ	*IC* **875** ✕[R]	*IR* **19745** Ⓒ
Tapolca .... d.	...	...	0441	...	0551	...	...	...	0736	...	...	...	...	0938	...	...	...	1044	...	1136	...	...	...
Badacsony .... d.	...	...	0457	...	0606	...	...	...	0755	...	...	...	...	0955	...	...	...	1059	...	1155	...	...	...
Badacsonytomaj .... d.	...	...	0500	...	0609	...	...	...	0759	...	...	...	...	0959	...	...	...	1103	...	1159	...	...	...
Révfülöp .... d.	...	...	0514	...	0621	...	...	...	0815	...	...	...	...	1015	...	...	...	1116	...	1215	...	...	...
Balatonfüred .... a.	...	...	0547	...	0652	...	...	...	0855	...	...	...	...	1055	...	...	...	...	...	1255	...	...	...
Balatonfüred .... d.	0351	0451	...	0551	0702	0711	...	0823	0908	0911	...	0911	1023	1108	1111	...	1111	...	1223	1308	1311	...	1311
Alsóörs .... d.	0401	0501	...	0601	0711	0722	...	0843	|	0922	...	0922	1043	|	1122	...	1122	...	1243	|	1322	...	1322
Balalatonalmádi .... d.	0408	0508	...	0608	0718	0729	...	0851	0921	0929	...	0929	1051	1121	1129	...	1129	...	1251	1321	1329	...	1329
Balatonkenese .... d.	0420	0520	...	0620	0731	0744	...	0906	|	0944	...	0944	1106	|	1144	...	1144	...	1306	|	1344	...	1344
Székesfehérvár .... a.	0503	0603	...	0703	0806	0831	...	0941	1006	1031	...	1031	1141	1206	1231	...	1231	...	1341	1406	1431	...	1431
Székesfehérvár .... **1220 1230** d.	*0514*	*0607*	...	0706	0807	...	0837	0942	1007	...	1037	1040	1142	1207	...	1237	1240	...	1342	1407	...	1437	1440
Kelenföld .... **1220 1230** a.	*0612*	*0651*	...	0746	0846	...	0916	1021	1046	...	1116	1120	1221	1246	...	1316	1320	...	1421	1446	...	1516	1520
Budapest Déli .... **1220 1230** a.	...	*0659*	...	0754	0854	...	0924	1029	1054	...	1124	1129	1229	1254	...	1324	1329	...	1429	1454	...	1524	1529

	19713	*Ex* **19795** [R] Ⓐ	Ⓐ	*IC* **863** ✕[R]	*IR* **19733** Ⓒ	Ⓒ	**19723**	*Ex* **19703** [R] Ⓐ	Ⓐ	*IC* **873** ✕[R]	*IR* **19743** Ⓒ	**19711**	*Ex* **19793** [R] Ⓐ	Ⓐ	*IC* **861** ✕[R]	*IR* **19731** Ⓒ	**19721**		Ⓒ	Ⓐ	*IC* **871** ✕[R]	*IR* **19741** Ⓒ	
Tapolca .... d.	...	1336	...	...	...	1430	...	1536	...	...	...	...	1736	...	...	...	...	1936	...	...	...	...	2136
Badacsony .... d.	...	1355	...	...	...	1445	...	1555	...	...	...	...	1755	...	...	...	...	1955	...	...	...	...	2155
Badacsonytomaj .... d.	...	1359	...	...	...	1449	...	1559	...	...	...	...	1759	...	...	...	...	1959	...	...	...	...	2159
Révfülöp .... d.	...	1415	...	...	...	1503	...	1615	...	...	...	...	1815	...	...	...	...	2015	...	...	...	...	2215
Balatonfüred .... a.	...	1455	...	...	...	1540	...	1655	...	...	...	...	1855	...	...	...	...	2055	...	...	...	...	2252
Balatonfüred .... d.	1423	1508	1511	...	1511	...	1623	1708	1711	...	1711	1823	1908	1911	...	1911	2023	...	2108	2111	...	2111	...
Alsóörs .... d.	1443	|	1522	...	1522	...	1643	|	1722	...	1722	1843	|	1922	...	1922	2043	...	|	2122	...	2122	...
Balalatonalmádi .... d.	1451	1521	1529	...	1529	...	1651	1721	1729	...	1729	1851	1921	1929	...	1929	2051	...	2121	2129	...	2129	...
Balatonkenese .... d.	1506	|	1544	...	1544	...	1706	|	1744	...	1744	1906	|	1944	...	1944	2106	...	|	2144	...	2144	...
Székesfehérvár .... a.	1541	1606	1631	...	1631	...	1741	1806	1831	...	1831	1941	2006	2031	...	2031	2141	...	2206	2231	...	2231	...
Székesfehérvár .... **1220 1230** d.	1542	1607	...	1637	1640	...	1742	1807	...	1837	1840	1942	2007	...	2037	2040	2142	...	2207	...	2237	2240	...
Kelenföld .... **1220 1230** a.	1621	1646	...	1716	1720	...	1821	1846	...	1916	1920	2021	2046	...	2116	2120	2221	...	2246	...	2316	2320	...
Budapest Déli .... **1220 1230** a.	1629	1654	...	1724	1729	...	1829	1854	...	1924	1929	2029	2054	...	2124	2129	2229	...	2304	...	2324	2329	...

European Rail Timetable Subscription

Keep up to date with the latest changes to European rail schedules with a subscription.

See page 12 for details of our various subscription options

Order on-line at **www.europeanrailtimetable.eu**

✆ +44 (0) 1832 270198 (Monday to Friday 1000 – 1600)

2nd class BUDAPEST - SIÓFOK - FONYÓD - KESZTHELY and NAGYKANIZSA 1220

SUMMER SERVICE JUNE 21 - AUGUST 31.

Carriages without Ⓡ are available on *IC* trains. **Train names**: Budapest - Nagykanizsa *IC* trains are named TOPART. Budapest - Keszthely *IC* trains are named BALATON.

km										*IR*	*IC*	*IR*	*IC*	*IR*	*IC*	*IR*	*IR*	*IC*	*Ex*	*IC*	*Ex*	*IR*	*IC*	*Ex*
										9690	**850**	**18500**	**860**	**9602**	**842**	**18700**	**18502 18592**	**862**	**18702**	**852**	**15607**	**18404**	**864**	**1787**
											Ⓡ		✕Ⓡ		Ⓡ	Ⓡ		✕Ⓡ	Ⓡ	Ⓡ	Ⓡ		✕Ⓡ	Ⓡ
			ⓒ	⑤–⑦		①–④	⑤–⑦	Ⓐ								ⓒ d			A e		f			g
0	**Budapest** Déli.....**1225 1230** d.	0100	...	0140	...	0240	...	...	0405	...	0530	0605	0635	...	0735	...	0805	0835	...	0935	...	1005	1035	...
4	Kelenföld............**1225 1230** d.	0107	...	0147	...	0247	...	...	0412	...	0537	0612	0642	...	0742	0747	0812	0842	0901	0942	0941	1012	1042	1041
67	**Székesfehérvár**..**1225 1230** a.	0146	...	0244	...	0344	...	...	0509	...	0615	0651	0720	...	0820	0827	0851	0920	0942	1020	1024	1051	1120	1127
67	**Székesfehérvár**..................d.	0152	...	...	0252	0352	...	...	0511	...	0616	0652	0721	...	0821	0830	0852	0921	0944	1021	1025	1052	1121	1130
95	Lepsény..............................d.	0213	...	...	0313	0413	...	...	0535	...	0640	0720	0740	...	|	|	0920	|	|	|	|	1120	|	|
115	**Siófok**..............................a.	0233	...	...	0333	0433	...	...	0555	...	0655	0745	0755	...	0855	0914	0945	0955	1028	1055	1102	1145	1155	1205
115	**Siófok**..............................d.	0236	...	...	0336	0436	...	0536	...	...	0657	0804	0757	...	0857	0918	1004	0957	1031	1057	1104	1204	1157	1206
124	Zamárdi...............................d.	0248	...	...	0348	0448	...	0548	...	...	0704	0816	0804	...	0904	0928	1016	1004	1042	1104	1113	1216	1204	1213
130	Balatonföldvár......................d.	0256	...	...	0356	0456	...	0556	...	...	0709	0824	0809	...	0909	0939	1024	1009	1054	1109	1122	1224	1209	1219
139	Balatonszemes.....................d.	0306	...	...	0406	0505	...	0605	...	...	0718	0834	0818	...	0918	0949	1034	1018	1101	1118	1140	1234	1218	1229
146	Balatonlelle.........................d.	0313	...	...	0413	0512	...	0611	...	...	0724	0842	0824	...	0924	0955	1042	1024	1108	1124	1148	1242	1224	1239
149	Balatonboglár.......................d.	0317	...	...	0417	0516	...	0615	...	...	0730	0847	0830	...	0930	1000	1047	1030	1113	1130	1155	1247	1230	1243
157	**Fonyód**..............................a.	0325	...	...	0425	0524	...	0622	...	...	0735	0856	0835	...	0935	1008	1056	1035	1123	1135	1202	1256	1235	1250
157	**Fonyód**.......................**1232** d.	0328	...	...	0426	0528	0632	0632	...	0723	0737	...	0837	0923	0937	...	1103	1037	...	1137	...	...	1237	1257
165	Balatonfenyves............**1232** d.	0338	...	...	0435	0538	0641	0641	...	0733	0743	...	0843	0933	0943	...	1122	1043	...	1143	...	...	1243	|
181	Balatonszentgyörgy......**1232** a.	0357	...	...	0455	0557	0659	0659	...	0753	0756	...	0857	0953	0956	...	1142	1057	...	1156	...	...	1257	1322
181	Balatonszentgyörgy......**1232** d.	0400	0442	...	0500	0601	0700	0700	...	0800	0801	...	0900	1000	1001	...	...	1100	...	1201	...	...	1300	...
221	**Keszthely**...............**1232** a.	0411	|	...	0511	|	0711	0711	...	0811	|	...	0911	1011	|	...	...	1111	...	|	...	...	1311	...
221	**Nagykanizsa**.......................a.	...	0529	...	...	0644	...	...	...	...	0844	...	...	...	1044	...	...	...	...	1244	...	...	...	...
352	*Zagreb* **1340**.......................a.	...	...	...	...	...	...	...	...	...	...	...	...	...	...	...	...	...	...	...	...	...	...	...

	Ex	*IC*	*IR*	*IC*	*IC*	*IR*	*IC*	*IC*	*IR*	*IC*		*IR*	*IC*	*IR*	*IC*	*EN*	*IC*		*IR*	*IC*			
	16707	**844**	**18504**	**874**	**854**	**18406**	**866**	**204**	**18506**	**876**		**9608**	**856**	**18408**	**868**	**1204**	**848**		**18608**	**1878**			
	Ⓡ	Ⓡ		✕Ⓡ	Ⓡ		✕Ⓡ	Ⓡ		✕Ⓡ			Ⓡ		✕Ⓡ	✕Ⓡ				✕Ⓡ			
	h							B								C							
Budapest Déli...............**1225 1230** d.	...	1135	1205	1235	1335	1405	1435	1535	1605	1635	...	...	1735	1805	1835	1845**k**	1935	...	2005	2135	2205	...	2300
Kelenföld.......................**1225 1230** d.	1101	1142	1212	1242	1342	1412	1442	1542	1612	1642	...	...	1742	1812	1842	1901	1942	...	2012	2142	2212	...	2307
Székesfehérvár............**1225 1230** a.	1142	1220	1251	1320	1420	1451	1520	1620	1651	1720	...	...	1820	1851	1920	1941	2020	...	2051	2220	2250	...	2346
Székesfehérvár.........................d.	1144	1221	1252	1321	1421	1452	1521	1621	1652	1721	...	...	1821	1852	1921	1942	2021	...	2052	2221	2252	...	2352
Lepsény.....................................d.	|	|	1320	|	|	1520	|	|	1720	|	...	...	|	1920	|	|	|	...	2119	|	2315	...	0013
Siófok.....................................a.	1228	1255	1345	1355	1455	1545	1555	1655	1745	1755	...	...	1855	1945	1955	2026	2055	...	2145	2255	2334	...	0033
Siófok.....................................d.	1230	1257	1404	1357	1457	1604	1557	1657	1804	1757	...	...	1857	2004	1957	2028	2057	...	2150	2257	2336	...	0036
Zamárdi......................................d.	1242	1304	1416	1404	1504	1616	1604	1704	1816	1804	...	...	1904	2016	2004	|	2104	...	2202	2304	2348	...	0048
Balatonföldvár.............................d.	1254	1309	1424	1409	1509	1624	1609	1709	1824	1809	...	...	1909	2024	2009	|	2109	...	2212	2309	2356	...	0056
Balatonszemes............................d.	1301	1318	1434	1418	1518	1634	1618	1718	1834	1818	...	...	1918	2034	2018	|	2118	...	2222	2318	0006	...	0106
Balatonlelle................................d.	1308	1324	1442	1424	1524	1642	1624	1724	1842	1824	...	...	1924	2042	2024	|	2124	...	2230	2324	0013	...	0113
Balatonboglár..............................d.	1313	1330	1447	1430	1530	1647	1630	1730	1847	1830	...	...	1930	2047	2030	|	2130	...	2240	2330	0017	...	0117
Fonyód.....................................a.	1323	1335	1456	1435	1535	1656	1635	1735	1856	1835	...	...	1935	2056	2035	2058	2135	...	2248	2335	0025	...	0125
Fonyód..............................**1232** d.	...	1337	1500	1437	1537	...	1637	1737	1900	1837	...	1923	1937	...	2037	2100	2137	...	2250	2337	...	...	0128
Balatonfenyves.....................**1232** d.	...	1343	1522	1443	1543	...	1643	1743	1922	1843	...	1933	1943	...	2043	|	2143	...	2300	2343	...	...	0138
Balatonszentgyörgy...............**1232** a.	...	1356	1542	1457	1556	...	1657	1756	1942	1857	...	1953	1956	...	2057	2115	2156	...	2319	2357	...	...	0157
Balatonszentgyörgy...............**1232** d.	...	1401	...	1500	1601	...	1700	1801	...	1900	...	2000	2001	...	2100	2117	2201	2208	2320	2400	...	...	0200
Keszthely..........................**1232** a.	...	|	...	1511	|	...	1711	|	...	1911	...	2011	|	...	2111	|	|	2219	2331	0011	...	...	0211
Nagykanizsa................................a.	...	1444	...	...	1644	...	...	1844	...	...	...	...	2044	...	...	2159	2244	...	...	...	...	...	...
Zagreb **1340**..................................a.	...	...	...	...	...	...	...	2200	...	...	...	...	...	...	...	...	...	...	...	...	...	...	...

				EN			*IC*		*IC*	*IR*	*IC*	*IC*	*IR*	*IR*	*IC*	*IC*	*IR*	*IC*	*IC*	*IR*	*IR*	*IC*	*IC*
				1205			**919**		**849**	**18509**	**867**	**847**	**9609**	**18407**	**877**	**857**	**18405**	**865**	**845**	**9607**	**18505**	**875**	**855**
				✕Ⓡ			Ⓡ		Ⓡ		✕Ⓡ	Ⓡ			✕Ⓡ	Ⓡ		✕Ⓡ	Ⓡ			✕Ⓡ	
	⑤–⑦			D		Ⓐ																	
Zagreb **1340**..................................d.	...	...	...	...	...	...	...	...	...	...	...	...	...	...	...	...	...	...	...	...	...	...	...
Nagykanizsa................................d.	...	...	...	0556	...	...	...	...	0514	0536	...	0714	...	...	...	0914	...	...	1114	...	...	...	1314
Keszthely..........................**1232** d.	...	0148	...	|	0428	...	...	0541	|	|	0648	|	0748	...	0848	|	...	1048	|	1148	...	1248	|
Balatonszentgyörgy...............**1232** a.	...	0159	...	0642	0439	...	...	0552	0557	0621	0659	0757	0759	...	0859	0957	...	1059	1157	1159	...	1259	1357
Balatonszentgyörgy...............**1232** d.	...	0202	...	0643	0440	...	...	...	0603	0622	0702	0803	0806	0815	0902	1003	...	1102	1203	1206	1215	1302	1403
Balatonfenyves.....................**1232** d.	...	0221	...	|	0458	...	...	...	0617	0643	0717	0817	0825	0846	0917	1017	...	1117	1217	1225	1246	1317	1417
Fonyód..............................**1232** a.	...	0231	...	0709	0506	...	...	...	0622	0653	0722	0822	0836	0856	0922	1022	...	1122	1222	1236	1256	1322	1422
Fonyód.....................................d.	0133	0233	0333	0710	0507	...	...	...	0624	0655	0724	0824	...	0902	0924	1024	1102	1124	1224	...	1302	1324	1424
Balatonboglár..............................d.	0141	0241	0341	|	0516	...	...	...	0630	0703	0730	0830	...	0913	0930	1030	1113	1130	1230	...	1313	1330	1430
Balatonlelle................................d.	0145	0245	0345	|	0520	...	...	...	0634	0707	0734	0834	...	0917	0934	1034	1117	1134	1234	...	1317	1334	1434
Balatonszemes............................d.	0153	0253	0353	|	0527	...	...	...	0640	0725	0740	0840	...	0925	0940	1040	1125	1140	1240	...	1325	1340	1440
Balatonföldvár.............................d.	0206	0306	0406	|	0535	...	...	...	0649	0735	0749	0849	...	0935	0949	1049	1135	1149	1249	...	1335	1349	1449
Zamárdi......................................d.	0213	0313	0413	|	0541	...	...	...	0654	0743	0754	0854	...	0943	0954	1054	1143	1154	1254	...	1343	1354	1454
Siófok.....................................a.	0225	0325	0425	0739	0551	...	...	...	0701	0756	0801	0901	...	0956	1001	1101	1156	1201	1301	...	1356	1401	1501
Siófok.....................................d.	0228	0328	0428	0740	0552	0615	...	...	0703	0815	0803	0903	...	1015	1003	1103	1215	1203	1303	...	1415	1403	1503
Lepsény.....................................d.	0248	0348	0449	|	0612	0642	...	...	0717	0840	|	|	...	1043	|	|	1240	|	|	...	1440	|	|
Székesfehérvár.........................a.	0309	0409	0513	0827	0636	0708	...	...	0736	0905	0836	0936	...	1105	1036	1136	1305	1236	1336	...	1505	1436	1536
Székesfehérvár............**1225 1230** d.	0314	0412	0527	0828	0637	...	0712	...	0737	0906	0837	0937	...	1106	1037	1137	1306	1237	1337	...	1506	1437	1537
Kelenföld.......................**1225 1230** a.	0411	0451	0611	0916	0721	...	0751	...	0816	0946	0916	1016	...	1146	1116	1216	1346	1316	1416	...	1546	1516	1616
Budapest Déli...............**1225 1230** a.	0419	0459	0619	0935**k**	0729	...	0759	...	0824	0954	0924	1024	...	1154	1124	1224	1354	1324	1424	...	1554	1524	1624

	Ex	*Ex*	*IR*	*IC*	*Ex*	*IC*	*Ex*	*IR*	*Ex*	*Ex*	*IC*	*IC*	*Ex*	*IR*	*IC*	*IC*	*IR*	*IC*					
	16706	**1843**	**18403**	**863**	**15606**	**843**	**18703**	**18503**	**1786**	**18803**	**873**	**853**	**18701**	**18401**	**861**	**201**	**18511**	**871**					
	Ⓡ	Ⓡ	⚒	✕Ⓡ	Ⓡ	Ⓡ	Ⓡ		Ⓡ	Ⓡ	✕Ⓡ	Ⓡ	Ⓡ		✕Ⓡ	Ⓡ		✕Ⓡ					
	h	⑦			f		A e	Ⓐ	Ⓐ g	Ⓐ			ⓒ d			B			④–⑥		④–⑥	⑤–⑦	
Zagreb **1340**..................................d.	...	...	...	...	...	...	...	...	...	...	...	...	...	...	...	1630	...	...	...	...	...	...	...
Nagykanizsa................................d.	...	...	...	...	...	1514	...	...	...	...	...	1714	...	...	...	1914	...	...	...	2114	...	...	...
Keszthely..........................**1232** d.	...	...	...	1448	...	|	...	...	...	1625	1648	|	...	...	1848	|	...	2048	...	|	...	...	2348
Balatonszentgyörgy...............**1232** a.	...	...	...	1459	...	1557	...	...	...	1636	1659	1757	...	...	1859	1957	...	2059	...	2158	...	...	2359
Balatonszentgyörgy...............**1232** d.	...	...	...	1502	...	1603	...	1615	1622	1637	1702	1803	...	...	1902	2003	2015	2102	...	2202	...	...	0002
Balatonfenyves.....................**1232** d.	...	...	...	1517	...	1617	...	1646	|	1709	1717	1817	...	...	1917	2017	2046	2118	...	2221	...	...	0021
Fonyód..............................**1232** a.	...	...	...	1522	...	1622	...	1656	1659	1719	1722	1822	...	...	1922	2022	2056	2123	...	2231	...	...	0031
Fonyód.....................................d.	1436	1502	1502	1524	1555	1624	1636	1702	1700	...	1724	1824	1836	1902	1924	2024	2102	2124	2155	2233	2321	...	0033
Balatonboglár..............................d.	1446	1513	1513	1530	1603	1630	1646	1713	1706	...	1730	1830	1846	1913	1930	2030	2113	2130	2205	2241	2341	...	0041
Balatonlelle................................d.	1450	1517	1517	1534	1607	1634	1650	1717	1710	...	1734	1834	1850	1917	1934	2034	2117	2134	2209	2245	2345	...	0045
Balatonszemes............................d.	1456	1525	1525	1540	1618	1640	1656	1725	1718	...	1740	1840	1856	1925	1940	2040	2125	2140	2222	2253	2353	...	0053
Balatonföldvár.............................d.	1503	1535	1535	1549	1634	1649	1703	1735	1728	...	1749	1849	1903	1935	1949	2049	2135	2149	2232	2301	0006	...	0106
Zamárdi......................................d.	1513	1543	1543	1554	1644	1654	1713	1743	1734	...	1754	1854	1913	1943	1954	2054	2143	2154	2238	2313	0013	...	0113
Siófok.....................................a.	1526	1556	1556	1601	1652	1701	1726	1756	1740	...	1801	1901	1926	1956	2001	2101	2156	2201	2250	2325	0025	...	0125
Siófok.....................................d.	1530	1558	1615	1603	1653	1703	1730	1815	1742	...	1803	1903	1930	2015	2003	2103	2205	2203	...	2328	0028	...	0128
Lepsény.....................................d.	|	|	1640	|	|	|	|	1840	|	...	|	|	|	2040	|	|	2224	|	...	2349	0048	...	0148
Székesfehérvár.........................a.	1612	|	1705	1636	1731	1736	1812	1905	1826	...	1836	1936	2011	2105	2036	2136	2247	2236	...	0009	0109	...	0209
Székesfehérvár............**1225 1230** d.	1614	|	1706	1637	1732	1737	1814	1906	1831	...	1837	1937	2014	2106	2037	2137	2248	2237	...	0012	...	0112	0212
Kelenföld.......................**1225 1230** a.	1655	1711	1746	1716	1816	1816	1855	1946	1916	...	1916	2016	2055	2146	2116	2216	2345	2316	...	0101	...	0201	0301
Budapest Déli...............**1225 1230** a.	...	1719	1754	1724	...	1824	...	1954	...	...	1924	2024	...	2154	2124	2224	2354	2324	...	0109	...	0209	0309

FOR NOTES, SEE NEXT PAGE →

1225 BUDAPEST - SZÉKESFEHÉRVÁR - BALATONFÜRED - TAPOLCA

2nd class

SUMMER SERVICE JUNE 21 to AUGUST 31.
Connecting trains Budapest - Székesfehérvár and v.v. may require [R].

km													IR 19740	IC 19702 ✕[R]			Ex 1972 [R] c ⑥⑦	IR 19742	IC 19792 ✕[R]	19722		Ex 16907 [R] h	IR 19734	IC 19704 ✕[R]	19714
			©	©	©																				
0	**Budapest** Déli .. **1220 1230** d.	...	...	...	0140	...	...	0240	...	0405	...	...	0630	0705	0730	...	...	0830	0905	0930	...	...	1030	1105	1130
	Köbánya-Kispest d.	...	...	...	|	...	...	|	...	|	...	...	|	|	|	...	0746	|	|	|	...	0947	|	|	|
4	Kelenföld **1220 1230** d.	...	...	...	0147	...	...	0247	...	0412	...	...	0638	0712	0738	...	0801	0838	0912	0938	...	1001	1038	1112	1138
67	**Székesfehérvár 1220 1230** a.	...	...	...	0244	...	...	0344	...	0509	...	...	0716	0750	0816	...	0842	0916	0950	1016	...	1042	1116	1150	1216
67	**Székesfehérvár** d.	...	0048	...	0247	...	...	...	0421	...	0526	...	0726	0751	0817	...	0845	0926	0951	1017	...	1045	1126	1151	1217
105	Balatonkenese d.	...	0122	...	0322	...	...	...	0505	...	0620	...	0810	|	0852	...	0932	1010	|	1052	...	1132	1210	|	1252
117	Balalatonalmádi d.	...	0134	...	0334	...	...	...	0521	...	0633	...	0823	0837	0906	...	0945	1023	1037	1106	...	1145	1223	1237	1306
123	Alsóörs d.	...	0141	...	0341	...	...	...	0528	...	0640	...	0835	|	0922	...	0952	1035	|	1122	...	1152	1235	|	1322
132	**Balatonfüred** a.	...	0150	...	0350	...	...	...	0538	...	0651	...	0847	0851	0934	...	1003	1047	1051	1134	...	1203	1247	1251	1334
132	**Balatonfüred** d.	0015	...	0205	...	0408	0508	...	...	...	...	0704	...	0902	...	0955	1016	...	1102	...	1155	...	...	1302	...
157	Révfülöp d.	0050	...	0241	...	0442	0551	...	...	...	...	0742	...	0943	...	1036	1050	...	1143	...	1236	...	...	1343	...
168	Badacsonytomaj d.	0108	...	0258	...	0500	0609	...	...	...	...	0801	...	1001	...	1051	1109	...	1201	...	1251	...	...	1401	...
170	Badacsony d.	0111	...	0301	...	0503	0612	...	...	...	...	0805	...	1005	...	1054	1113	...	1205	...	1254	...	...	1405	...
184	**Tapolca** a.	0129	...	0319	...	0522	0631	...	...	...	...	0824	...	1024	...	1112	1129	...	1224	...	1312	...	...	1424	...

		IR 19744	IC 19794 [R]	19724		IR 19736	IC 19706 [R]	19716		IR 19746	IC 19796 ✕[R] ⑦–④	IC 19796 ✕[R] ⑤⑥	19726		IR 19738	IC 19708 ✕[R]	19718	⑤⑥		IR 19748	④⑦	IC 19798 ✕[R] ⑤⑥		
Budapest Déli **1220 1230** d.	...	1230	1305	1330	...	1430	1505	1530	...	1630	1705	1705	1730	...	1830	1905	1930	...	...	2030	...	2105	2205	...
Köbánya-Kispest d.	...	|	|	|	...	|	|	|	...	|	|	|	|	...	|	|	|	...	...	|	...	|	|	...
Kelenföld **1220 1230** d.	...	1238	1312	1338	...	1438	1512	1538	...	1638	1712	1712	1738	...	1838	1912	1938	...	...	2038	...	2112	2212	...
Székesfehérvár 1220 1230 a.	...	1316	1350	1416	...	1516	1550	1616	...	1716	1750	1750	1816	...	1916	1950	2016	...	...	2116	...	2150	2250	...
Székesfehérvár d.	...	1326	1351	1417	...	1526	1551	1617	...	1726	1751	1751	1817	...	1926	1951	2017	...	...	2126	...	2151	...	2256
Balatonkenese d.	...	1410	|	1452	...	1610	|	1652	...	1810	|	|	1852	...	2010	|	2052	...	...	2210	...	|	...	2341
Balalatonalmádi d.	...	1423	1437	1506	...	1623	1637	1706	...	1823	1837	1837	1906	...	2023	2037	2106	...	...	2228	...	2241	...	2354
Alsóörs d.	...	1435	|	1522	...	1635	|	1722	...	1835	|	|	1922	...	2035	|	2122	...	...	2235	...	|	...	0002
Balatonfüred a.	...	1447	1451	1534	...	1647	1651	1734	...	1847	1851	1851	1934	...	2047	2051	2134	...	...	2247	...	2255	...	0013
Balatonfüred d.	1355	...	1502	...	1555	...	1702	...	1755	...	1902	1902	...	1955	...	2102	...	2155	...	...	2306	2306	...	...
Révfülöp d.	1436	...	1543	...	1636	...	1743	...	1836	...	1943	1943	...	2036	...	2145	...	2236	...	...	2343	2343	...	...
Badacsonytomaj d.	1451	...	1601	...	1651	...	1801	...	1851	...	2001	2001	...	2051	...	2201	...	2251	...	...	0001	0001	...	...
Badacsony d.	1454	...	1605	...	1654	...	1805	...	1854	...	2005	2005	...	2054	...	2205	...	2254	...	...	0005	0005	...	...
Tapolca a.	1512	...	1624	...	1712	...	1824	...	1912	...	2024	2024	...	2112	...	2224	...	2313	...	...	0024	0024	...	...
Boba **1237** d.	...	...	...	...	...	...	1909	...	...	...	...	2109	...	...	...	...	...	...	...	...	...	...	...	...
Celldömölk **1237** d.	...	...	...	...	...	...	1920	...	...	...	...	2120	...	...	...	...	...	...	...	...	...	...	...	...
Szombathely a.	...	...	...	...	...	...	1956	...	...	...	...	2156	...	...	...	...	...	...	...	...	...	...	...	...

	©	©	©					IC 19709 ✕[R]	IR 19737		19727	IC 19707 ✕[R]	IR 19747		19715	IC 19797 ✕[R]	IR 19735		19725	IC 19705 ✕[R] Ⓐ	IC 19705 ✕[R] ⑥⑦	IR 19745	Ex 16906 [R] h	
Szombathely d.	...	...	...	...	...	...	...	...	...	...	...	...	...	...	...	0802	...	...	...	...	1002	...	...	...
Celldömölk **1237** d.	...	...	...	...	...	...	...	...	...	...	...	...	...	...	...	0841	...	...	...	...	1041	...	...	...
Boba **1237** d.	...	...	...	...	...	...	...	...	...	...	...	...	...	...	...	0850	...	...	...	...	1050	...	...	...
Tapolca d.	0049	...	0235	...	...	0441	...	0551	...	0645	...	0738	...	0847	...	0938	...	1047	...	1138	1138	...	...	1247
Badacsony d.	0105	...	0251	...	...	0457	...	0606	...	0701	...	0757	...	0906	...	0957	...	1106	...	1157	1157	...	...	1306
Badacsonytomaj d.	0108	...	0258	...	...	0500	...	0609	...	0704	...	0801	...	0909	...	1001	...	1109	...	1201	1201	...	...	1309
Révfülöp d.	0123	...	0313	...	...	0514	...	0621	...	0719	...	0816	...	0924	...	1016	...	1124	...	1216	1216	...	...	1324
Balatonfüred a.	0156	...	0345	...	...	0547	...	0652	...	0759	...	0855	...	1008	...	1055	...	1208	...	1255	1255	...	...	1408
Balatonfüred d.	...	0158	...	0351	0451	▬	0551	0708	0711	...	0823	0908	0911	...	1023	1108	1111	...	1223	1308	1308	1311	1350	...
Alsóörs d.	...	0208	...	0401	0501	...	0601	|	0722	...	0843	|	0922	...	1043	|	1122	...	1243	|	|	1322	1400	...
Balalatonalmádi d.	...	0215	...	0408	0508	...	0608	0721	0729	...	0851	0921	0929	...	1051	1121	1129	...	1251	1321	1321	1329	1407	...
Balatonkenese d.	...	0227	...	0420	0520	...	0620	|	0744	...	0906	|	0944	...	1106	|	1144	...	1306	|	|	1344	1427	...
Székesfehérvár a.	...	0305	...	0503	0603	Ⓐ	0703	0806	0831	...	0941	1006	1031	...	1141	1206	1231	...	1341	1406	1406	1431	1510	...
Székesfehérvár **1220 1230** d.	...	...	...	*0514*	...	0607	0706	0807	0840	...	0942	1007	1040	...	1142	1207	1240	...	1342	1407	1407	1440	1514	...
Kelenföld **1220 1230** a.	...	...	...	*0612*	...	0651	0746	0846	0920	...	1021	1046	1120	...	1221	1246	1320	...	1421	1446	1446	1520	1555	...
Köbánya-Kispest a.	...	...	...	*0631*	...	|	|	|	|	...	|	|	|	...	|	|	|	...	|	|	|	|	1611	...
Budapest Déli **1220 1230** a.	...	...	...	...	...	0659	0754	0854	0929	...	1029	1054	1129	...	1229	1254	1329	...	1429	1454	1454	1529	...	...

	19713	IC 19795 ✕[R]	IR 19733		19723	IC 19703 ✕[R]	IR 19743	Ex 1973 [R] c ⑥⑦		19711	IC 19793 ✕[R]	IR 19731		19721	Ⓐ	IC 19701 ✕[R] ⑥⑦	IR 19741		Ⓐ	19791 ©			①–④	⑤–⑦
Tapolca d.	...	1338	...	1447	...	1538	...	1629	1647	...	1738	...	1847	...	1938	1938	...	2047	...	...	2136	2229	...	...
Badacsony d.	...	1357	...	1506	...	1557	...	1644	1706	...	1757	...	1906	...	1957	1957	...	2107	...	...	2155	2246	...	...
Badacsonytomaj d.	...	1401	...	1509	...	1601	...	1650	1709	...	1801	...	1909	...	2001	2001	...	2110	...	...	2201	2251	...	...
Révfülöp d.	...	1416	...	1524	...	1616	...	1703	1724	...	1816	...	1924	...	2016	2016	...	2125	...	...	2216	2306	...	...
Balatonfüred a.	...	1455	...	1608	...	1655	...	1736	1808	...	1855	...	2008	...	2055	2055	...	2208	...	...	2252	2345	...	...
Balatonfüred d.	1423	1508	1511	...	1623	1708	1711	1750	...	1823	1908	1911	...	2023	...	2108	2111	...	2210	2210	...	...	2349	2349
Alsóörs d.	1443	|	1522	...	1643	|	1722	1800	...	1843	|	1922	...	2043	...	|	2122	...	2221	2221	...	...	0002	0002
Balalatonalmádi d.	1451	1521	1529	...	1651	1721	1729	1807	...	1851	1921	1929	...	2051	...	2121	2129	...	2228	2228	...	...	0009	0009
Balatonkenese d.	1506	|	1544	...	1706	|	1744	1827	...	1906	|	1944	...	2106	...	|	2144	...	2241	2241	...	...	0022	0022
Székesfehérvár a.	1541	1606	1631	...	1741	1806	1831	1913	...	1941	2006	2031	...	2141	...	2206	2231	...	2316	2316	...	...	0101	0101
Székesfehérvár **1220 1230** d.	1542	1607	1640	...	1742	1807	1840	1914	...	1942	2007	2040	...	2142	...	2207	2240	...	...	2317	...	...	...	0112
Kelenföld **1220 1230** a.	1621	1646	1720	...	1821	1846	1920	1955	...	2021	2046	2120	...	2221	...	2246	2320	...	...	2356	...	...	...	0201
Köbánya-Kispest a.	|	|	|	...	|	|	|	2012	...	|	|	|	...	|	...	|	|	...	...	|	...	...	...	|
Budapest Déli **1220 1230** a.	1629	1654	1729	...	1829	1854	1929	...	...	2029	2054	2129	...	2229	...	2304	2329	...	...	0004	...	...	...	0209

NOTES FOR TABLES 1220 AND 1225 VALID JUNE 21 - AUGUST 31:

A – © until July 6; daily July 7 - Aug. 22; © from Aug. 23.
B – AGRAM-TOPART – (2) Budapest - Zagreb and v.v.
C – June 19, 21, 26, 28, July **and** Aug. 2, 4, 6, 8, 10, 12, 14, 16, 18, 20, 22, 24, 26, 28, 30, Sept. 2, 4, 6, 11, 13.
ADRIA – 1, 2 cl., 2 cl., (2) ✕ Budapest - Knin - Split.
D – June 20, 22, 27, 29, July **and** Aug. 3, 5, 7, 9, 11, 13, 15, 17, 19, 21, 23, 25, 27, 29, 31, Sept. 3, 5, 7, 12, 14.
ADRIA – 1, 2 cl., 2 cl., (2) ✕ Split - Knin - Budapest.

c – From/to Békéscsaba.
d – From/to Szolnok.
e – From/to Szob.
f – From/to Miskolc.
g – From/to Szeged.
h – From/to Zahóny.
k – Budapest Keleti.

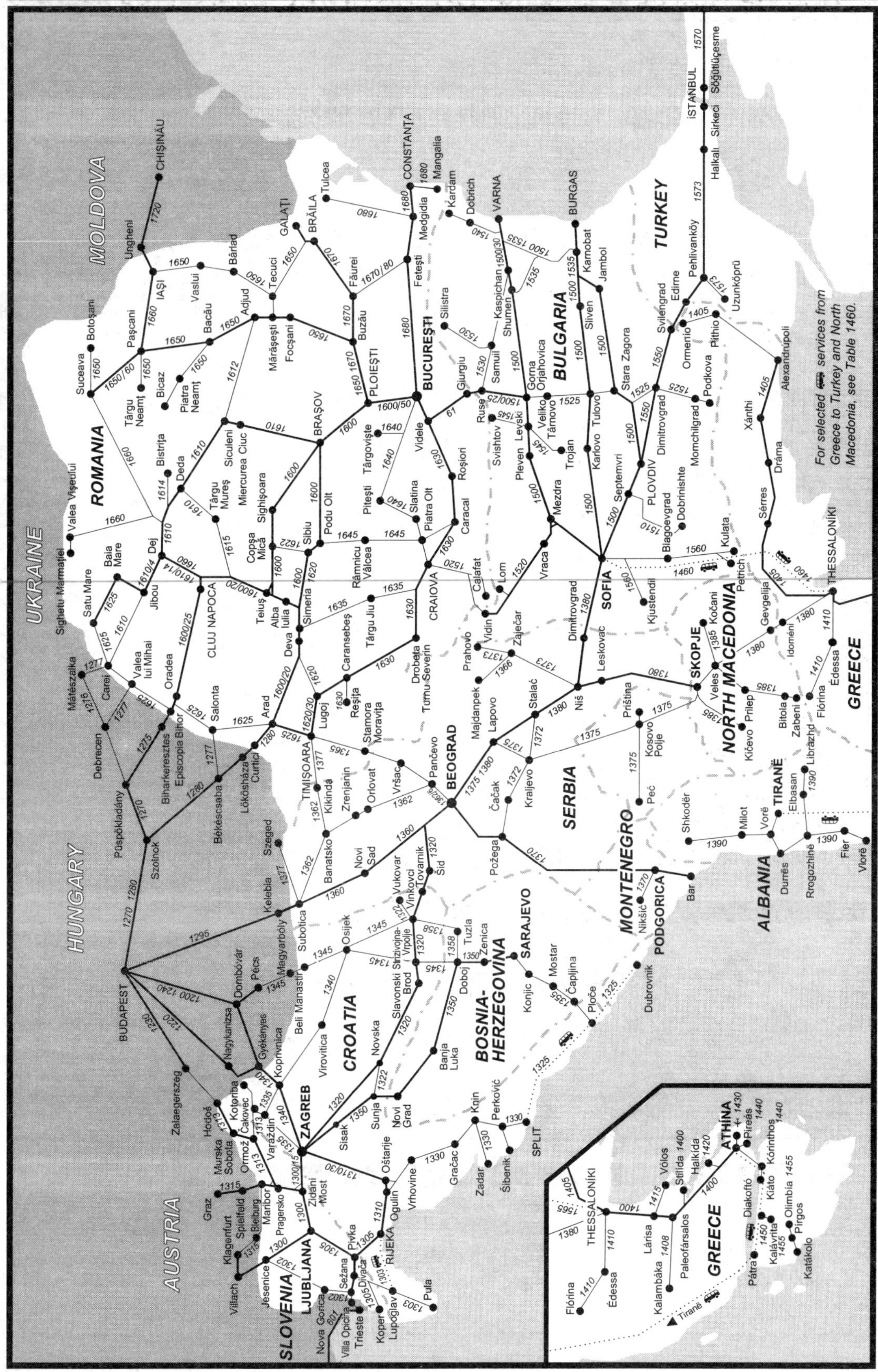
MOLDOVA
UKRAINE
ROMANIA
HUNGARY
AUSTRIA
SLOVENIA
CROATIA
BOSNIA-HERZEGOVINA
SERBIA
MONTENEGRO
ALBANIA
NORTH MACEDONIA
BULGARIA
TURKEY
GREECE
CHIŞINĂU
Ungheni
IAŞI
Vaslui
Bârlad
Suceava
Botoşani
Paşcani
Târgu Neamţ
Bicaz
Piatra Neamţ
Bacău
Adjud
Mărăşeşti
Focşani
Tecuci
GALAŢI
BRĂILA
Tulcea
Făurei
Buzău
PLOIEŞTI
BUCUREŞTI
Feteşti
Medgidia
CONSTANŢA
Mangalia
BRAŞOV
Siculeni
Miercurea Ciuc
Târgu Mureş
Deda
Bistriţa
Valea Vişeului
Sighetu Marmaţiei
Baia Mare
Dej
Jibou
Satu Mare
Carei
Valea lui Mihai
Mátészalka
Debrecen
Oradea
CLUJ NAPOCA
Teiuş
Alba Iulia
Copşa Mică
Sighişoara
Sibiu
Podu Olt
Râmnicu Vâlcea
Piteşti
Târgovişte
Slatina
Piatra Olt
Caracal
Roşiori
Videle
Giurgiu
CRAIOVA
Calafat
Vidin
Lom
Târgu Jiu
Simeria
Deva
Arad
Salonta
Curtici
Lőkösháza
Békéscsaba
Biharkeresztes
Episcopia Bihor
Püspökladány
Szolnok
Szeged
Kelebia
BUDAPEST
TIMIŞOARA
Lugoj
Caransebeş
Reşiţa
Stamora Moravita
Drobeta Turnu Severin
Kikinda
Zrenjanin
Orlovat
Vršac
Pančevo
BEOGRAD
Novi Sad
Subotica
Banatsko
Vukovar
Vinkovci
Tovarnik
Šid
Osijek
Strizivojna-Vrpolje
Slavonski Brod
Tuzla
Doboj
Zenica
SARAJEVO
Konjic
Mostar
Čapljina
Ploče
Dubrovnik
Banja Luka
Novska
Sisak
Sunja
Novi Grad
ZAGREB
Koprivnica
Gyékényes
Nagykanizsa
Dombóvár
Pécs
Magyarboly
Beli Manastir
Virovitica
Zalaegerszeg
Hodoš
Murska Sobota
Kotoriba
Čakovec
Ormož
Varaždin
Pragersko
Maribor
Graz
Spielfeld
Bleiburg
Klagenfurt
Villach
Jesenice
LJUBLJANA
Zidani Most
Pivka
Sežana
Divača
Nova Gorica
Villa Opicina
Trieste
Koper
Lupoglav
Pula
RIJEKA
Ogulin
Oštarije
Vrhovine
Gračac
Knin
Perković
Zadar
Šibenik
SPLIT
Požega
Čačak
Kraljevo
Lapovo
Stalać
Niš
Majdanpek
Prahovo
Zaječar
Leskovac
Priština
Kosovo Polje
Peć
Bar
PODGORICA
Nikšić
Shkodër
Milot
Vorë
TIRANË
Durrës
Elbasan
Librazhd
Rrogozhinë
Fier
Vlorë
SKOPJE
Veles
Kočani
Prilep
Kičevo
Bitola
Gevgelija
Idomeni
Flórina
Édessa
THESSALONÍKI
SOFIA
Dimitrovgrad
Kjustendil
Blagoevgrad
Kulata
Petrich
Pernik
Mezdra
Vraca
Pleven
Levski
Svishtov
Ruse
Gorna Orjahovica
Veliko Târnovo
Trojan
Karlovo
Tulovo
Stara Zagora
Septemvri
PLOVDIV
Dimitrovgrad
Momchilgrad
Podkova
Dobrinishte
Svilengrad
Ormenio
Pithio
Edirne
Pehlivanköy
Uzunköprü
Alexandrúpoli
Xánthi
Dráma
Sérres
Kaspichan
Shumen
Samuil
Silistra
VARNA
Dobrich
Kardam
BURGAS
Karnobat
Jambol
Sliven
İSTANBUL
Halkalı
Sirkeci
Söğütlüçeşme
ATHÍNA
Piréas
Kórinthos
Kiáto
Pátra
Diakoftó
Kalávrita
Olimbía
Pírgos
Katákolo
Lárisa
Vólos
Stilída
Halkída
Paleofársalos
Kalambáka
Tiranë
For selected services from Greece to Turkey and North Macedonia, see Table 1460.

SLOVENIA, CROATIA and BOSNIA-HERZEGOVINA

Operators: Slovenske Železnice (SŽ): www.slo-zeleznice.si; Hrvatske Željeznice (HŽ): www.hzpp.hr; Željeznice Federacije Bosne i Hercegovine (ŽFBH): www.zfbh.ba
Services: Descriptions of sleeping (🛏) and couchette (🛏) cars appear on page 10.
In Slovenia, travel by *ICS* train requires reservation and payment of a special fare.
Timings: **Valid until December 13, 2025** unless otherwise shown.
Tickets: A supplement is payable for travel by internal express trains. Reservation of seats is possible on most express trains.

1300 VILLACH - JESENICE - LJUBLJANA - ZAGREB — SŽ, HŽ, ÖBB

km										*EN*	*EN*									*EC*							
										40237	**40237**					**315**				**211**						**317**	
										R f	R g									R							
		Ⓐ			Ⓐ			Ⓐ	Ⓐ	♦	♦		Ⓒ		Ⓐ		Ⓐ		Ⓐ	♦	Ⓐ		Ⓐ		Ⓑ		Ⓐ
	München Hbf **890** d.	...	...	...	...	...	...	...	...	2354c	2354c	...	...	...	...	...	...	...	...	...	...	...	...	...	...	...	...
	Salzburg Hbf **970** d.	...	...	...	...	...	...	...	...	0146	0146	...	...	...	...	...	...	...	...	...	...	...	...	...	...	...	...
0	**Villach** Hbf d.	...	...	...	...	...	...	...	...	0614	|	...	...	...	...	0853	...	...	...	1253	...	...	...	...	...	1453	...
38	**Jesenice** d.	...	0424	...	0501	0533	...	0611	0632	0703	|	...	0739	...	...	0935	...	1122	1237	1335	...	1422	...	...	...	1535	...
51	Lesce-Bled d.	...	0437	...	0514	0546	...	0624	0645	0716	|	...	0752	...	...	0947	...	1135	1250	1347	...	1435	...	...	...	1548	...
74	Kranj d.	...	0459	...	0536	0612	...	0646	0707	0749	|	...	0814	...	...	1014	...	1159	1321	1409	...	1501	...	...	...	1628	...
102	**Ljubljana** a.	...	0531	...	0608	0644	...	0719	0744	0809	|	...	0848	...	...	1050	...	1230	1354	1432	...	1533	...	...	...	1700	...
102	**Ljubljana** 1315 d.	0445	...	0550	...	...	0650	...	...	0830	|	...	...	0850	0950	...	1150	...	...	1445	1450	...	1535	1545	1650	...	1720
166	Zidani Most 1315 d.	0606	...	0701	...	...	0805	...	...	0919	|	...	...	1000	1100	...	1305	...	...	1547	1608	...	1636	1702	1805	...	1831
182	Sevnica 1315 d.	0624	...	0719	...	...	0823	...	...	0935	1027	...	...	1018	1118	...	1323	...	...	1603	1626	...	1652	1721	1823	...	1849
215	Dobova 1315 a.	0657	...	0752	...	...	0856	...	...	1000	1054	...	...	1051	1151	...	1356	...	...	1630	1659	...	1721	1754	1856	...	1922
245	**Zagreb Glavni** 1315 a.	...	...	...	...	...	...	...	...	1039	1133	...	...	...	...	...	...	...	...	1710	...	...	...	...	...	...	...

		EC									
		213					**215**			**319**	
		R					R				
	Ⓐ	♦			Ⓐ	Ⓒ N			Ⓐ		
München Hbf **890** d.	...	...	...	...	...	...	...	...	...	...	...
Salzburg Hbf **970** d.	...	...	...	...	...	...	...	...	...	...	...
Villach Hbf. d.	...	1653	...	...	...	...	1853	...	...	2053	...
Jesenice d.	1628	1735	...	1806	...	1926	1935	2043	...	2135	...
Lesce-Bled d.	1651	1747	...	1823	...	1941	1951	2056	...	2146	...
Kranj d.	1718	1810	...	1846	...	2004	2012	2121	...	2204	...
Ljubljana a.	1748s	1833	...	1919	...	2043	2035	2153	...	2230	...
Ljubljana 1315 d.	...	1845	1850	...	1955	...	2105	...	2225	...	...
Zidani Most 1315 d.	...	1943	2002	...	2106	...	2205	...	2333	...	...
Sevnica 1315 d.	...	1958	2020	...	2124	...	2221	...	2351	...	...
Dobova 1315 a.	...	2024	2051	...	2154	...	2249	...	0022	...	...
Zagreb Glavni 1315 a.	...	2045	...	...	...	...	...	...	...	...	...

											EC
		318					**214**				**212**
							R				R
	Ⓐ		Ⓐ		Ⓐ	Ⓒ N			Ⓐ		♦
Zagreb Glavni 1315 d.	...	...	...	...	...	...	...	...	...	...	0705
Dobova 1315 d.	...	...	...	0422	0445	...	0535	0558	...	0706	0745
Sevnica 1315 d.	...	...	...	0455	0519	...	0604	0632	...	0739	0812
Zidani Most 1315 d.	...	...	...	0518	0539	...	0620	0700	...	0808	0828
Ljubljana 1315 a.	...	...	...	0625	0640	...	0721	0807	...	0915	0924
Ljubljana d.	0440	0524	0610	...	...	0650	0725	...	0825	...	0930
Kranj d.	0515	0551	0646	...	...	0722	0749	...	0900	...	0954
Lesce-Bled d.	0546	0611	0712	...	...	0752	0817	...	0922	...	1015
Jesenice a.	0559	0627	0726	...	...	0805	0827	...	0934	...	1025
Villach Hbf. a.	...	0707	...	...	...	...	0907	...	...	...	1107
Salzburg Hbf **970** a.	...	...	...	...	...	...	...	...	...	...	...
München Hbf **890** a.	...	...	...	...	...	...	...	...	...	...	...

										EC														*EN*	*EN*		
		316								**210**						**314**								**414**	**414**		
										R														R	R		
			Ⓐ			Ⓐ	Ⓐ			♦		Ⓐ	Ⓐ	Ⓐ			Ⓒ		Ⓑ	Ⓐ			Ⓑ	♦ g	♦ f	r	
Zagreb Glavni 1315 d.	...	...	...	...	...	...	...	...	...	1250	...	...	...	...	...	...	...	...	...	...	...	...	...	1840	1938	...	...
Dobova 1315 d.	0906	...	1005	...	1105	...	1206	...	1306	1330	...	...	1406	...	1515	...	...	1608	...	1707	1808	...	1905	1921	2018	...	2110
Sevnica 1315 d.	0940	...	1039	...	1139	...	1240	...	1340	1400	...	...	1440	...	1549	...	...	1642	...	1741	1842	...	1939	1948	2045	...	2144
Zidani Most 1315 d.	1001	...	1058	...	1158	...	1307	...	1359	1416	...	...	1500	...	1617	...	...	1701	...	1804	1901	...	1958	|	2101	...	2203
Ljubljana 1315 a.	1108	...	1205	...	1305	...	1414	...	1506	1513	...	...	1607	...	1724	...	...	1808	...	1909	2006	...	2103	|	2157	...	2308
Ljubljana d.	...	1135	...	1250	...	1331	...	1445	...	1527	1535	1552	...	1624	...	1715	1750	...	1843	...	...	2047	...	|	2213	2222	...
Kranj d.	...	1159	...	1321	...	1409	...	1519	...	1555	1609	1628	...	1700	...	1751	1825	...	1918	...	...	2121	...	|	2237	2258	...
Lesce-Bled d.	...	1217	...	1346	...	1435	...	1548	...	1615	1631	1651	...	1722	...	1813	1851	...	1941	...	...	2146	...	|	2256	2321	...
Jesenice a.	...	1227	...	1359	...	1448	...	1601	...	1625	1646	1703	...	1734	...	1826	1903	...	1954	...	...	2159	...	|	2307	2333	...
Villach Hbf. a.	...	1307	...	...	...	...	...	...	...	1707	...	...	...	...	...	1908	...	...	...	...	...	...	...	|	2348	...	...
Salzburg Hbf **970** a.	...	...	...	...	...	...	...	...	...	...	...	...	...	...	...	...	...	...	...	...	...	...	...	0258	0245	...	...
München Hbf **890** a.	...	...	...	...	...	...	...	...	...	...	...	...	...	...	...	...	...	...	...	...	...	...	...	0550c	0550c	...	...

♦ – **NOTES** (LISTED BY TRAIN NUMBER)

210/1 – SAVA – [12] Vinkovci - Zagreb - Ljubljana - Villach and v.v.
212/3 – MIMARA – [2] Zagreb - Ljubljana - Villach and v.v.
414 – LISINSKI – 🛏, couchette and [2] Zagreb - Maribor - Graz - Salzburg - München - Stuttgart;
conveys 🛏, couchette and [2] (**40414**) Zagreb - Maribor - Graz - Innsbruck - Zurich;
also conveys July 14 - Dec. 13 🛏, couchette and [2] Rijeka (**480**) - Ljubljana - Salzburg - München - Stuttgart.
40237 – LISINSKI – 🛏, couchette and [2] Stuttgart - München - Salzburg - Graz - Maribor - Zagreb;
conveys 🛏, couchette and [2] (**40465**) Zurich - Innsbruck - Graz - Maribor - Zagreb;
also conveys July 14 - Dec. 13 🛏, couchette and [2] Stuttgart - München - Salzburg - Ljubljana (**481**) - Rijeka.

N – Conveys on Ⓒ: [2] Ljubljana - Jesenice - Nova Gorica and v.v.
c – München Ost until further notice.
f – July 14 - Dec. 13.
g – Dec. 15 - July 13.
r – Runs 30 – 35 minutes later Apr. 24 - Sept. 28.
s – Ljubljana **Šiška** (approx. 1.5km from Ljubljana main station).

1302 JESENICE - NOVA GORICA - SEŽANA — 2nd class only SŽ

km		Ⓐ	Ⓐ e	Ⓒ d	Ⓐ	N	Ⓐ			Ⓐ			
0	**Jesenice** d.	...	0410	0410	0607	0813	0852	1119	...	1427	1651	...	1922
10	Bled Jezero d.	...	0427	0427	0624	0828	0915	1135	...	1443	1706	...	1939
28	Bohinjska Bistrica 🚗 d.	...	0448	0448	0652	0855	0935	1155	...	1504	1726	...	1959
56	Most na Soči 🚗 d.	...	0529	0529	0732	0943	1021	1236	...	1551	1806	...	2046
89	Nova Gorica ♣ a.	...	0608	0608	0811	1021	1100	1315	...	1633	1845	...	2126
89	Nova Gorica ♣ d.	0455	0612	...	0849	...	...	...	1441	...	...	1908	...
130	**Sežana** a.	0551	0711	...	0945	...	...	...	1547a	...	...	2004	...

	Ⓐ		Ⓐ e	Ⓒ d	b		Ⓐ	Ⓐ		Ⓒ	N	Ⓐ	
Sežana d.	...	...	0630	...	0743	1010	...	1428	...	1628	...	1643	...
Nova Gorica ♣ a.	...	...	0723	...	0843	1103	...	1520	...	1720	...	1735	...
Nova Gorica ♣ d.	0321	0525	0728	0728	0900	1126	1445	...	1553	...	1723	...	2003
Most na Soči 🚗 d.	0402	0609	0812	0812	0955	1207	1526	...	1634	...	1807	...	2045
Bohinjska Bistrica 🚗 d.	0449	0650	0853	0853	1036	1255	1606	...	1727	...	1846	...	2126
Bled Jezero d.	0510	0711	0913	0913	1056	1315	1626	...	1747	...	1906	...	2146
Jesenice a.	0526	0725	0928	0928	1111	1330	1641	...	1802	...	1921	...	2201

N – Conveys on Ⓒ: [2] Ljubljana - Jesenice - Nova Gorica and v.v.

a – On Ⓒ arrives 1538.
b – June 25 - Aug. 24.
d – Not June 25 - Aug. 24.
e – Daily June 25 - Aug. 24.

♣ – Line **1** 🚌 service operates between Nova Gorica (bus stop 100 metres from station on Italian side) and Gorizia Centrale (Italy) stations. Total journey time ±20 minutes.
🚗 – Car-carrying service runs between Bohinjska Bistrica and Most na Soči. Depart Bohinjska Bistrica 0910, 1330, 1648. Depart Most na Soči 0746, 1042, 1441.

1303 DIVAČA - PULA — 2nd class only HŽ, SŽ

km			Ⓐ			Ⓐ n		Ⓐ	🚌		
	Ljubljana **1305** d.	...	...	...	...	...	...	...	...	...	...
0	**Divača** d.	...	...	...	...	...	...	...	1612	...	...
12	Hrpelje-Kozina d.	...	...	...	...	...	...	...	1626	...	...
30	Rakitovec d.	...	...	...	...	...	...	...	|	...	...
36	Buzet d.	0448n	0654	...	1052	1340	...	...	1705	1716	...
43	Lupoglav ▲ d.	0509	0715	...	1113	1401	...	1520	...	1737	2027
117	**Pula** a.	0706	0905	...	1258	1545	...	1711	...	1922	2212

	Ⓐ	Ⓐ n			Ⓐ		🚌	Ⓐ	Ⓐ	
Pula d.	0437	0629	0831	...	1319	1422	...	1550	1730	1945
Lupoglav ▲ d.	0623	0823	1019	...	1508	1632	...	1733	1916	2138
Buzet d.	0643	0843	1039	...	...	1652	1707	...	...	2158n
Rakitovec d.	...	...	...	...	...	...	|	...	...	...
Hrpelje-Kozina d.	...	...	...	...	...	...	1747	...	...	...
Divača a.	...	...	...	...	...	...	1800	...	...	...
Ljubljana **1305** a.	...	...	...	...	...	...	...	...	...	...

n – Not June 16 - Sept. 5.

▲ – 🚌 service **Lupoglav - Rijeka** and v.v. Journey 40 minutes.
From Lupoglav at 0622Ⓐ, 1040, 1631, 2137.
From Rijeka at 0538Ⓐ, 0955, 1435Ⓐ, 1545Ⓒ, 1930.

SŽ, HŽ — LJUBLJANA - RIJEKA, KOPER, SEŽANA and TRIESTE — 1305

Warning! Due to engineering work, some journeys from / to **Ljubljana** are by 🚌 to / from **Brezovica** station (approximately 10km). Please check locally before travelling.

km						EN					IC					EC						IC				
				1605	**1281**	**1277**	**1246**			**481**	**503**					**134**	**483**					**509**				
		Ⓐ	u	♦	Ⓡ	♦Ⓡ	♦			♦Ⓡ	♦		Ⓐ	Ⓐ		♦Ⓡ	Ⓡ	b	Ⓑ	Ⓐ		♦		Ⓐ	Ⓒc	
0	**Ljubljana** d.	0409	0550	0602	0625	0645	0648	0643	0800	0840	0910	...	1015	1200	1325	1425	1520	1545	1618	1705	...	1756	1847	1915	...	2111
67	Postojna d.	0534	0654	0708	0729	0750	0805	0807	0909	0944	1014	...	1139	1325	1434	1529	1632	1655	1727	1832	...	1904	1956	2039	...	2219
80	Pivka ▲ d.	0548	0707	0721	0742	0837	|	0821	0923	0956	1026	...	1152	1339	1448	1542	1646	1709	1741	1846	...	1917	2010	2053	...	2233
	Ilirska Bistrica 🏛 ▲ d.	|	|	|	0757	0853	|	|	|	1012	|	...	|	|	|	|	1702	|	|	|	...	|	|	|	...	|
	Šapjane 🏛 d.	|	|	|	0825	0907	|	|	|	1040	|	...	|	|	|	|	1730	|	|	|	...	|	|	|	...	|
	Rijeka a.	|	|	|	0906	1003	|	|	|	1121	|	...	|	|	|	|	1811	|	|	|	...	|	|	|	...	|
104	Divača d.	0614	0728	0748	...	...	0842	0842	0944	...	1048	1052	1215	1401	1509	1605	...	1735	1805	1907	...	1938	2032	2115	2115	2255
116	Hrpelje-Kozina ⊡ d.	|	|	0801	...	...	|	|	|	...	1102	|	|	|	|	|	...	1754	|	|	...	1951	|	|	|	|
153	**Koper** ⊡ a.	|	|	0834	...	...	0931	|	|	...	1135	|	|	|	|	|	...	1814	|	|	...	2024	|	|	|	|
113	**Sežana** 🏛 a.	0624	0738	...	...	...	...	0852	0955	...	...	1102	1225	1411	1520	1614	...	...	1815	1917	...	...	2042	2125	2125	2305
113	**Sežana** 🏛 d.	...	0739	...	...	...	...	...	...	...	...	...	...	...	...	1616	...	...	...	...	1928	...	2043	...	...	...
120	Villa Opicina ¶ a.	...	0750	...	...	...	...	...	...	...	...	...	...	...	...	1627	...	...	...	...	1939	...	2054	...	...	...
144	**Trieste** Centrale ¶ a.	...	0833	...	...	...	...	...	...	...	...	...	...	...	...	1716	...	...	...	...	...	...	2132	...	...	...

km				IC										EC		IC						EN				
				508								**482**		**135**		**502**					**1247**	**1276**	**480**		**1604**	
		Ⓐ	Ⓐ	♦	Ⓐ		Ⓐ			Ⓒb	Ⓐb	Ⓡ	Ⓐ	♦Ⓡ	Ⓐ	♦	Ⓐ	Ⓒ	Ⓐ	Ⓑ	♦	♦Ⓡ	♦Ⓡ	u	♦	
	Trieste Centrale ¶ d.	...	...	...	...	...	...	0903	...	...	...	...	...	1252	...	...	...	...	...	...	...	...	...	1907	...	...
	Villa Opicina ¶ d.	...	...	...	...	...	...	0946	...	...	...	...	...	1338	...	...	...	...	...	...	...	...	...	1945	...	2128
	Sežana 🏛 a.	...	...	...	...	...	...	0957	...	...	...	...	...	1349	...	...	...	...	...	...	...	...	...	1956	...	2139
	Sežana 🏛 d.	0428	0454	...	...	0715	0846	0959	1032	...	...	...	1332	1350	1435	...	1650	1752	1752	1858	...	...	...	2010	...	...
	Koper ⊡ d.	|	|	0525	...	|	|	|	|	1005	1005	...	|	|	|	1515	|	|	|	|	1852	...	...	|	2002	...
	Hrpelje-Kozina ⊡ d.	|	|	0559	...	|	|	|	|	1025	1025	...	|	|	|	1549	|	|	|	|	|	...	...	|	2042	...
	Divača d.	0439	0505	0616	...	0726	0856	1010	1042	1049	1049	...	1343	1401	1446	1609	1701	1803	1803	1909	1940	...	...	2020	2057	...
0	**Rijeka** d.	|	|	|	...	|	|	|	...	|	|	1150	|	|	|	|	|	|	|	|	|	1815	1857	|	|	...
28	Šapjane 🏛 d.	|	|	|	...	|	|	|	...	|	|	1248	|	|	|	|	|	|	|	|	|	1913	1955	|	|	...
40	Ilirska Bistrica 🏛 ▲ d.	|	|	|	0634	|	|	|	...	|	|	1303	|	|	|	|	|	|	|	|	|	1930	2010	|	|	...
56	Pivka ▲ d.	0502	0528	0639	0651	0748	0919	1031	...	1110	1110	1320	1405	1422	1509	1630	1723	1824	1824	1931	|	1946	2025	2041	2118	...
	Postojna d.	0516	0542	0653	0705	0802	0933	1043	...	1124	1124	1333	1419	1435	1523	1643	1737	1838	1838	1945	2106	2106	2041	2054	2131	...
	Ljubljana a.	0624	0651	0755	0813	0910	1058	1146	...	1230	1247	1436	1544	1537	1647	1745	1845	1945	2001	2109	2207	2220	2144	2158	2233	...

♦ – **NOTES** (LISTED BY TRAIN NUMBER)

134 – EMONA – [12] ✕ Wien (**151**) - Graz - Ljubljana (**134**) - Trieste.
135 – EMONA – [12] ✕ Trieste - Ljubljana (**150**) - Graz - Wien.
480 – OPATIJA – [12] Rijeka - Ljubljana. Also conveys July 14 - Dec. 13 🛏, 🛏 and [2] Rijeka - Ljubljana - Salzburg - München - Stuttgart.
481 – OPATIJA – [12] Ljubljana - Rijeka. Also conveys July 14 - Dec. 13 🛏, 🛏 and [2] Stuttgart - München - Salzburg - Ljubljana - Rijeka.
502/3 – POHORJE – [12] Hodoš - Ljubljana - Koper and v.v.
508/9 – KOPER – [12] Ljubljana - Koper and v.v. Conveys [12] (**246/7**) Budapest - Ljubljana - Koper and v.v.
1246 – June 27 - Aug. 30. ISTRA 🛏, 🛏 and [2] Budapest - Maribor - Ljubljana - Koper.
1247 – June 28 - Aug. 31. ISTRA 🛏, 🛏 and [2] Koper - Ljubljana - Maribor - Budapest.
1276 – ①③⑤⑦ June 29 - Aug. 31. [2] 🛏 Rijeka - Ljubljana - Graz - Wien (**108**) - Warszawa (Table **99**).
1277 – ②④⑤⑦ June 27 - Aug. 29. [2] 🛏 Warszawa (**109**) - Wien - Graz - Ljubljana - Rijeka (Table **99**).
1604 – Apr. 26 - Sept. 28. [2] Koper - Ljubljana - Maribor.
1605 – Apr. 26 - Sept. 28. [2] Maribor - Ljubljana - Koper.

b – By 🚌 Divaca - Koper and v.v.
c – Apr. 26 - Sept. 28.
u – From / to Udine (Table **601**).

¶ – For frequent tram connections Villa Opicina - Trieste and v.v., see panel in Table **601**.

▲ – Local services **Pivka - Ilirska Bistrica** and v.v.: Journey 16 minutes.
From Pivka at 0553Ⓐ, 0925Ⓐ, 1200Ⓐ, 1341Ⓐ, 1455Ⓐ, 1545Ⓐ, 1727Ⓑ, 1850Ⓑ.
From Ilirska Bistrica at 0507Ⓐ, 0748Ⓐ, 1050Ⓐ, 1319Ⓐ, 1426Ⓐ, 1519Ⓐ, 1609Ⓐ, 1803Ⓑ.

⊡ – 🚌 service **Koper - Trieste** and v.v.: Journey 40 minutes.
From Koper at 0600⚒, 0700Ⓐ, 0730⚒, 1030⚒, 1115Ⓐ, 1215Ⓐ, 1400⚒, 1730⚒.
From Trieste at 0645⑥, 0700Ⓐ, 0900⚒, 1000Ⓐ, 1115Ⓐ, 1230Ⓐ, 1300⚒, 1400Ⓐ, 1530⚒, 1830⑥, 1900Ⓐ.
Service is subject to alteration. No service on ⑦, Slovenian and Italian holidays.
Operator: Arriva Slovenija, Meljska cesta 97, 2000 Maribor.

HŽ — RIJEKA - OGULIN - ZAGREB — 1310

km													
			⚒					⚒	Ⓐn		Ⓐ		
0	**Rijeka** d.	...	...	0526	0738	...	...	...	1125	1408	1532	...	1930
61	Delnice d.	...	...	0641	0855	...	...	...	1244	1524	1652	...	2047
90	Moravice d.	...	...	0721	0930	...	...	...	1317	1557	1724	...	2120
120	Ogulin 1330 d.	0400	0623	0755	1002	1027	...	1210	1354	1633	1758	2011	2150
126	Oštarije 1330 d.	0405	0628	|	...	1036	...	1215	...	1639	...	2016	...
176	Karlovac 1330 d.	0509	0742	0903	...	1145	...	1320	...	1749	...	2120	...
229	**Zagreb Gl** 1330 a.	0615	0857	1007	...	1249	...	1426	...	1855	...	2229	...

		Ⓐ			Ⓐn			Ⓐ			⚒	
Zagreb Gl 1330 d.	...	...	0626	0825	...	1306	...	1433	1513	1536	1823	2143
Karlovac 1330 d.	...	...	0741	0930	...	1415	...	1541	1613	1646	1932	2251
Oštarije 1330 d.	...	...	0900	1035	...	1522	...	1653	|	1803	2044	2356
Ogulin 1330 d.	0414	0552	0905	1042	1412	1526	1546	1658	1715	1807	2048	2400
Moravice d.	0445	0629	...	1114	1448	...	1617	...	1744	...	...	...
Delnice d.	0519	0712	...	1148	1525	...	1651	...	1813	...	...	...
Rijeka a.	0638	0830	...	1304	1644	...	1807	...	1921	...	...	...

n – Not June 16 - Sept. 5.

SŽ, MÁV — MARIBOR - ČAKOVEC, MURSKA SOBOTA and ZALAEGERSZEG — 1313

km										IC 247														IC 502				1247
		Ⓐ		Ⓐ	Ⓐ	Ⓐ		Ⓐ		♦		⚒	⑦g	Ⓐ	Ⓐ		Ⓐ				Ⓐ		Ⓐ	♦		Ⓐ	Ⓐ	♦k
	Ljubljana 1315 d.	...	...	...	...	...	...	...	...	0915	...	...	...	...	...	...	...	...	...	...	...	...	...	1750	...	...	...	2220
0	**Maribor** 1315 d.	...	...	...	...	...	0711	...	0935	|	...	...	...	...	...	1440	...	1538	...	1615	...	...	1710	|	...	1910	2210	|
19	Pragersko 1315 d.	...	...	...	...	0605	|	...	0958	1123	...	1330	1330	1423	...	1507	...	|	...	|	1701	...	|	1954	...	|	|	0030
37	Ptuj d.	...	...	...	...	0629	0749	...	1010	1135	...	1351	1351	1446	...	1524	...	1616	...	1653	1713	...	1750	2007	...	1950	2248	0044
59	Ormož d.	...	...	0452	0555	0650	0807	0811	1022	1149	1208	1411	1411	1503	1506	1542	1600	1636	1645	1713	1726	1733	1810	2019	...	2025a	2307	|
	Središče 🏛 a.	...	...	0503	|	...	|	0822	|	|	1219	|	|	...	1517	|	1611	|	1656	...	|	1744	...	|	...	|	...	|
	Čakovec a.	...	...	...	|	...	|	0841	|	|	...	|	|	...	...	|	...	|	...	...	|	1803	...	|	...	|	...	|
98	**Murska Sobota** d.	0332	...	...	0639	...	0843	...	1047	1220	...	1446	1446	...	...	1618	...	1717	...	...	1756	...	...	2044	...	2103	...	0125
127	Hodoš a.	0357	...	...	...	...	0905	...	...	1240	...	...	...	...	...	...	...	...	...	...	1818	...	...	2100	...	2125	...	0143
127	Hodoš 🏛 d.	...	0623	...	...	...	...	...	...	1253	...	...	...	...	...	...	...	...	...	...	...	...	...	...	2102	...	...	0250
174	**Zalaegerszeg** a.	...	0713	...	...	...	...	...	...	1337	...	...	...	...	...	...	...	...	...	...	...	...	...	...	2146	...	...	0337
	Budapest Déli 1230 a.	...	...	...	...	...	...	...	...	1659	...	...	...	...	...	...	...	...	...	...	...	...	...	...	...	...	...	0906

km								IC 503							IC 246													1246
				Ⓐ	Ⓐ	Ⓐ		♦	Ⓐ	Ⓒ	Ⓐ				♦	Ⓐ	⚒	g	Ⓐ		Ⓐ	g	g			Ⓐ		♦k
	Budapest Déli 1230 d.	...	...	...	...	...	...	...	...	...	...	...	...	...	0900	...	...	...	...	...	...	...	...	...	...	...	...	2117
	Zalaegerszeg d.	...	...	...	...	...	0455	...	...	...	...	...	...	...	1222	...	...	...	...	...	...	...	...	...	...	...	2013	0149
	Hodoš 🏛 a.	...	...	...	...	...	0546	...	...	...	...	...	...	...	1307	...	...	...	...	...	...	...	...	...	...	...	2057	0238
	Hodoš d.	...	...	0430	...	...	...	0553	0618	...	...	0923	...	...	1320	...	...	...	...	...	1600	1622	...	...	...	1918	...	0257
	Murska Sobota d.	...	...	0453	...	...	...	0612	0642	...	...	0945	1232	...	1341	...	1505	1506	...	...	1621	1646	1830	...	1855	1942	...	0316
0	**Čakovec** d.	...	...	|	...	...	...	|	|	...	0930	|	|	...	|	...	|	|	...	...	|	|	|	1811	|	...	...	|
12	Središče 🏛 d.	0433	...	|	0531	...	...	|	|	...	0949	|	|	1349	|	1527	|	|	1620	1710	|	|	|	1830	|	...	...	|
22	Ormož d.	0444	0450	0523	0542	0547	...	0639	0716	0847	1000	1022	1308	1400	1410	1538	1543	1543	1631	1721	1700	1726	1900	1841	1931	...	...	|
	Ptuj d.	...	0508	0535	...	0605	...	0652	0735	0902	...	1040	1328	...	1425	...	1602	1602	...	...	1724	1745	1913	...	1951	...	...	0356
	Pragersko 1315 d.	...	0531	0545	...	|	...	0704	|	|	...	1057	|	...	1437	...	1630	1630	...	...	1745	1809	1927	...	2020	...	...	0435
	Maribor 1315 a.	...	0549	...	...	0640	...	|	0813	0929	...	...	1405	...	|	...	1647	1647	...	...	...	|	|	...	2037	...	...	|
	Ljubljana 1315 a.	...	...	...	...	...	...	0902	...	...	...	...	...	...	1642	...	...	...	...	...	...	2010	2119	...	...	...	...	0645

♦ – **NOTES** (LISTED BY TRAIN NUMBER)

246/7 – CITADELLA – [12] Budapest - Ljubljana and v.v.; [12] Budapest - Ljubljana (**508/9**) - Koper and v.v.
502/3 – POHORJE – [12] Hodoš - Ljubljana - Koper and v.v.
1246 – June 27 - Aug. 30. ISTRA – 🛏 1, 2 cl. and [2] Budapest - Zalaegerszeg - Hodoš - Ljubljana - Koper.
1247 – June 28 - Aug. 31. ISTRA – 🛏 1, 2 cl. and [2] Koper - Ljubljana - Hodoš - Zalaegerszeg - Budapest.

a – Arrives at 2008.
g – ⑦ Dec. 15 - June 22, Aug. 31 - Dec. 7.
k – From / to Budapest Keleti.

1315 LJUBLJANA and ZAGREB - MARIBOR - GRAZ

SŽ, HŽ, ÖBB

km				EN	IC	IC	ICS		EC	IC				IC			ICS		EC	IC		IC		EN		
		1247		1152	251	512	30	354	158	247	156		154	518		152	20		150	502	352	526		1276	1604	604
		R		R	R		R		✕ R	R							R		R							
		♦	h	♦ s	♦		Ⓑ		♦	♦ n									♦	♦				♦	♦	♦
0	**Ljubljana** ... 1300 d.	0025	0050	...	0500	...	...	...	...	0915	1015	1050	...	1310	1250	...	1515	...	1605	1750	...	...	2050	2220	2250	2250
*	**Zagreb Glavni** .. 1300 d.	|	|	0151z	|	...	...	...	0705	|	|	|	...	|	|	...	|	...	|	|	...	...	|	|	|	|
	Dobova 🏛 ... 1300 d.	|	|	0212	|	...	...	...	0810	|	|	|	...	|	|	...	|	...	|	|	...	...	|	|	|	|
	Sevnica ... 1300 d.	|	|	|	|	...	...	...	0839	|	|	|	...	|	|	...	|	...	|	|	...	...	|	|	|	|
64	Zidani Most ... 1300 d.	0124	0148	|	0600	...	...	...	|	1016	1110	1200	...	1405	1408	...	1605	...	1701	1850	...	...	2206	2317	2352	2356
89	Celje ... d.	0150	0211	0337	0624	0650	...	...	0919	1042	1132	1224	...	1426	1432	...	1624	...	1725	1914	...	2102	2231	2332	0016	0020
137	Pragersko ... 1313 d.	0228	0250	|	0702	0725	...	...	0959	1121	1206	1307	...	1459	1515	...	1657	...	1800	1950	2003	2136	2313	2343	0053	0057
156	**Maribor** ... ▲ 1313 a.	...	0302	0427	0716	0737	...	...	1013	...	1217	1324	...	1510	1532	...	1710	...	1811	...	2019	2148	2330	0059	0105	0109
156	**Maribor** ... d.	...	...	0447	0719	...	0740	0827	1020	...	1227	...	1427	...	...	1627	...	...	1821	...	2027	...	...	0102	...	...
172	Spielfeld-Straß 🏛 ... a.	...	...	0502	0734	...	0754	0841	1035	...	1241	...	1441	...	...	1641	...	...	1836	...	2041	...	...	|	...	...
172	Spielfeld-Straß 🏛 ... 980 d.	...	...	0514	0746	...	...	0846	1048	...	1246	...	1446	...	...	1646	...	...	1848	...	2046	...	...	|	...	...
219	**Graz** Hbf ... 980 a.	...	...	0552	0822	...	...	0922	1122	...	1322	...	1522	...	...	1722	...	...	1922	...	2122	...	...	0158	...	...
	Wien Hbf **980** ... a.	...	...	0854	...	...	...	...	...	...	...	...	...	...	...	...	...	...	2202	...	...	...	...	0605	...	...

				EN		ICS	IC	ICS	ICS		ICS	EC		IC								EC	IC		IC	EN
	1605	605	1246	1277	Ⓐ	11	503	31	35	353	17	151	153	246	155		157		1615	355	1643	159	523	1613	250	1153
						R		R	R		R	R		R								✕ R			R	R
	♦	♦	♦	♦			♦	Ⓑ	⑥			♦		♦ n		⑦ g		⑦ g	⑦ g		⑦ g	♦		⑦ g	♦	♦
Wien Hbf **980** ... d.	...	...	...	2155	...	...	...	...	...	...	...	0758	...	...	...	...	...	...	...	...	...	...	...	...	...	1905
Graz Hbf ... 980 d.	...	...	...	0338	...	...	...	...	...	0838	...	1038	1238	...	1438	...	1638	...	...	1738	...	1838	...	...	2138	2202
Spielfeld-Straß 🏛 ... 980 a.	...	...	...	|	...	...	...	...	...	0912	...	1113	1312	...	1512	...	1714	...	...	1814	...	1913	...	...	2211	2233
Spielfeld-Straß 🏛 ... d.	...	...	...	|	...	...	...	0804	...	0917	...	1125	1317	...	1517	...	1719	...	...	1824	...	1925	...	...	2225	2245
Maribor ... a.	...	...	...	0331	...	...	...	0817	...	0931	...	1140	1331	...	1531	...	1733	...	...	1842	...	1940	...	...	2240	2301
Maribor ... ▲ 1313 d.	0333	0333	...	0338	0450	0550	...	0820	0820	...	1050	1145	...	...	1535	1625	1740	...	1810	...	...	1945	2010	2020	2245	2304
Pragersko ... 1313 d.	0345	0345	0435	0352	0502	0602	0704	|	|	...	1102	1200	...	1437	1547	1639	1752	1809	1822	...	1927	2000	2022	2032	2259	|
Celje ... d.	0422	0422	0520	0518	0540	0634	0741	0900	0904	...	1132	1239	...	1516	1622	1718	1827	1848	1901	...	2002	2040	2057	2111	2338	2355
Zidani Most ... 1300 d.	0445	0445	0545	0543	0605	0654	0804	..	...	...	1156	1305	...	1542	1643	1739	1848	1912	1926	...	2024	|	...	2134	0002	|
Sevnica ... 1300 d.	|	|	|	|	|	|	|	...	...	...	...	|	...	|	|	|	|	|	|	...	|	2118	...	|	|	|
Dobova 🏛 ... 1300 d.	|	|	|	|	|	|	|	...	...	...	...	|	...	|	|	|	|	|	|	...	|	2201	...	|	|	0110
Zagreb Glavni ... 1300 a.	|	|	|	|	|	|	|	...	...	...	...	|	...	|	|	|	|	|	|	...	|	2226	...	|	|	0133z
Ljubljana ... 1300 a.	0545	0545	0645	0645	0706	0744	0902	...	...	...	...	1400	...	1642	1737	1834	1942	2010	2023	...	2119	...	...	2228	0101	...

ADDITIONAL SERVICES MARIBOR - ZIDANI MOST and v.v.: 2nd class only

		Ⓐ	Ⓐ			Ⓐ	Ⓐ				Ⓐ		
Maribor ... ▲ d.	0520	0620	0725	0825	1020	1125	1225	1428	1523	1720	1825	2025	2120
Pragersko ... d.	0538	0639	0744	0844	1039	1144	1244	1447	1552	1739	1844	2044	2139
Celje ... d.	0622	0726	0828	0928	1125	1228	1328	1531	1636	1832	1929	2128	2223
Zidani Most ... a.	0645	0749	0851	0950	1146	1250	1351	1554	1659	1855	1952	2151	2246

			Ⓐ	Ⓐ		Ⓐ	Ⓐ			Ⓐ			Ⓐ
Zidani Most . d.	0453	0705	0805	0929	1004	1114	1314	1610	1708	1803	1905	2006	2105
Celje ... d.	0519	0729	0830	0952	1028	1138	1338	1634	1733	1828	1929	2031	2128
Pragersko ... d.	0602	0812	0912	1035	1110	1222	1420	1717	1816	1910	2012	2113	2212
Maribor .. ▲ a.	0619	0829	0929	1052	1128	1240	1437	1734	1833	1928	2029	2130	2229

♦ – **NOTES** (LISTED BY TRAIN NUMBER)

150/1 – EMONA – (12) ✕ Wien - Graz - Ljubljana (**135/134**) - Trieste and v.v.
158/9 – CROATIA – (2) Zagreb - Maribor - Graz and v.v.
246/7 – CITADELLA – (12) Budapest - Zalaegerszeg - Hodoš - Ljubljana and v.v.
250/1 – DRAVA – (12) Budapest - Györ - Graz - Ljubljana and v.v.
502/3 – POHORJE – (12) Hodoš - Ljubljana - Koper and v.v.
604 – Not Apr. 26 - Sept. 28. (2) Ljubljana - Maribor.
605 – Not Apr. 26 - Sept. 28. (2) Maribor - Ljubljana.
1152 – ①④⑥ May 2 - Oct. 14 (from Split; following morning from Zagreb). 🛏 1, 2 cl., ▬ 2 cl., (2) Split - Zagreb - Maribor - Graz - Wien - Bratislava.
1153 – ③⑤⑦ Apr. 30 - Oct. 12. 🛏 1, 2 cl., ▬ 2 cl., (2) Bratislava - Wien - Graz - Maribor - Zagreb - Split.
1246 – June 27 - Aug. 30. ISTRA – 🛏 1, 2 cl. and (2) Budapest - Zalaegerszeg - Hodoš - Ljubljana - Koper.
1247 – June 28 - Aug. 31. ISTRA – 🛏 1, 2 cl. and (2) Koper - Ljubljana - Hodoš - Zalaegerszeg - Budapest.
1276 – ①③⑤⑦ June 29 - Aug. 31. (2) ▬ Rijeka - Ljubljana - Graz - Wien - Warszawa (Table **99**).
1277 – ②④⑤⑦ June 27 - Aug. 29. (2) ▬ Warszawa - Wien - Graz - Ljubljana - Rijeka (Table **99**).
1604 – Apr. 26 - Sept. 28. (2) Koper - Ljubljana - Maribor.
1605 – Apr. 26 - Sept. 28. (2) Maribor - Ljubljana - Koper.

g – ⑦ (also June 29 - Aug. 24).
h – June 8 - Sept. 28.
n – Not June 21 - Aug. 31.
s – Set down only from Zagreb Zapadni.
z – Zagreb **Zapadni**.

* – Zagreb - Celje: *104 km*.
▲ – For Maribor - Bleiburg (- Klagenfurt) services see seperate panel.

MARIBOR - BLEIBURG (- KLAGENFURT)

km		Ⓐ	Ⓐ
0	Maribor ... d.	0520	1120
87	Bleiburg 🏛 ... a.	0730	1323
126	*Klagenfurt* ... a.	*0811*	*1356*

	Ⓐ	Ⓐ
Klagenfurt ... d.	*0801*	*1301*
Bleiburg 🏛 ... d.	0833	1410
Maribor ... a.	1034	1613

Other services are available Maribor - Bleiburg - Klagenfurt and v.v.

1320 ZAGREB - VINKOVCI - VUKOVAR

HŽ

km		741	1841			743		745	211	747
		R	R ✕			R		R	R	R
		j	♦	2	2	Ⓐ	2		♦	Ⓐ d
	Ljubljana **1300** ... d.	...	...	...	...	...	...	...	1445	...
0	**Zagreb Glavni** ... d.	0616	0616	0808	...	1250	1406	1511	1731	2133
105	Novska ... d.	0842	0842	1055	...	1512	1701	1746	2003	2358
191	Slavonski Brod ... d.	1010	1010	1230	...	1641	1837	1915	2130	0131
224	Strizivojna-Vrpolje ... **1345** d.	1033	1033	1259	...	1707	1906	1938	2153	0158
253	**Vinkovci** ... a.	1054	1054	1322	1530	1731	1929	1958	2214	0222
271	Vukovar ... a.	...	1136	...	1607	...	|	2040	...	...
285	Tovarnik 🏛 ... a.	...	...	...	...	...	2018f	...	...	...
292	Šid 🏛 ... a.	...	...	...	...	...	...	...	...	...
407	**Beograd** Centar ... a.	...	...	...	...	...	...	...	...	...

	740	742		210	744		746	1840	
	R	R		R	R		R	R ✕	
	Ⓐ	Ⓐ	2	♦	Ⓑ	2	k	♦	2
Beograd Centar ... d.	...	...	...	...	...	...	...	...	...
Šid 🏛 ... d.	...	...	...	...	...	...	...	...	...
Tovarnik 🏛 ... d.	...	...	0547f	...	...	1420f	...	...	...
Vukovar ... d.	...	0435	|	...	...	|	...	1623	2055
Vinkovci ... d.	0153	0518	0620	0803	1104	1524	1706	1706	2134
Strizivojna-Vrpolje ... **1345** d.	0218	0543	0644	0824	1125	1548	1733	1733	...
Slavonski Brod ... d.	0245	0607	0722	0848	1149	1618	1802	1802	...
Novska ... d.	0417	0736	0856	1014	1316	1752	1935	1935	...
Zagreb Glavni ... a.	0643	1004	1136	1235	1550	2101	2205	2205	...
Ljubljana **1300** ... a.	...	...	...	1513	...	...	...	...	...

♦ – **NOTES** (LISTED BY TRAIN NUMBER)

210/1 – SAVA – (12) Vinkovci - Zagreb - Ljubljana - Villach and v.v.
1840 – June 28 - Aug. 29. 🛏, ▬ and (2) Vukovar - Vinkovci - Zagreb - Knin - Split.
1841 – June 30 - Aug. 31. 🛏, ▬ and (2) Split - Knin - Zagreb - Vinkovci - Vukovar.

d – Also Dec. 6, 7, 13.
f – Ⓐ only.

j – Not June 30 - Aug. 31.
k – Not June 28 - Aug. 29.

1322 LOCAL SERVICES in Croatia

2nd class only HŽ

ZAGREB - SISAK CAPRAG: Journey 60 – 75 minutes. All services call at Sisak (5 minutes from Sisak Caprag).
From Zagreb at 0540⚒, 0631, 0732Ⓐ, 0903, 1113, 1216Ⓐ, 1344, 1446Ⓐ, 1529Ⓐ, 1758Ⓐ, 1916, 2033, 2137Ⓐ, 2250.
From Sisak Caprag at 0521, 0559Ⓐ, 0616, 0703Ⓐ, 0755⚒, 1105⚒, 1214, 1405Ⓐ, 1504, 1606Ⓐ, 1805Ⓐ, 2015, 2135.

SISAK CAPRAG - SUNJA: Journey 30 minutes.
From Sisak Caprag at 0740, 0832Ⓐ, 1005, 1215, 1442, 1648, 1856Ⓐ, 2014, 2348.
From Sunja at 0458⚒, 0553, 0640Ⓐ, 0901Ⓐ, 1151, 1252, 1622, 1948, 2109.

SUNJA - NOVSKA: Journey 70 minutes.
From Sunja at 0802, 1237, 1514Ⓐ **m**, 2046Ⓑ.
From Novska at 0502, 0549Ⓐ, 1100, 1840Ⓑ.

m – Not June 16 - Sept. 5.

1325 🚌 SPLIT - PLOČE - DUBROVNIK

Subject to confirmation

🚌 SPLIT - DUBROVNIK: Journey 4 hrs - 5 hrs 10 mins.
🚌 SPLIT - PLOČE: Journey 2 hrs - 2 hrs 50 mins.
🚌 PLOČE - DUBROVNIK: Journey 2 hrs - 2 hrs 20 mins.

Note: various operators run on these routes; tickets are not interchangeable.
Split and Ploče bus stations are situated adjacent to the railway stations.
Buses pass through Bosnia between Ploče and Dubrovnik (passports required).

HŽ Most trains are 2nd class only — ZAGREB - KNIN - ZADAR, ŠIBENIK and SPLIT — 1330

km	km				Ⓐn	g	EN 1204 R ♦	EN 1153 R ♦	Ⓐ		Ⓐr	IC 521 R ✕ h	Ⓐp	h	j	k		IC 523 R ♦		Ⓐ		1821 R ♦	1840 R ♦	1880 R ♦
		Budapest Keleti **89** d.	...	...	...	...	1845	...	...	...	...	...	...	...	...	...	...	...	...	...	...	...	...	...
0		**Zagreb Glavni** **1310** d.	...	...	...	...	|	0133z	...	...	...	0702	...	...	...	...	...	1358	...	...	...	2230	2230	0057
53		Karlovac **1310** d.	...	...	...	...	|	|	...	...	...	0808	...	...	...	...	...	1457	...	...	...	2325	2325	0157
103		Oštarije **1310** d.	...	...	...	...	|	0327	...	...	...	0915	...	...	...	...	...	1552	...	...	...	|	0026	|
109		Ogulin **1310** d.	...	...	...	...	|	|	...	...	...	|	...	...	...	...	...	|	...	...	...	0034	|	|
225		Gospić d.	...	...	...	...	|	|	...	...	...	1055	...	...	...	...	...	1753	...	...	...	0242	0233	0458
269		Gračac d.	...	...	...	...	|	|	...	...	...	1129	...	...	...	...	...	1842	...	...	...	0321	0312	0536
333		**Knin** a.	...	...	...	...	|	0730	...	...	...	1220	...	...	...	...	...	1945	...	...	...	0425	0416	0640
333	0	**Knin** ‡ d.	0412	...	...	...	0709	0731	0809	...	...	1231	...	...	...	1537	...	1947	2002b	...	...	0436	0427	0641
	95	**Zadar** ‡ a.	|	...	...	...	|	|	|	...	...	|	...	...	...	|	...	|	|	...	...	|	|	|
387	—	Perković a.	0510	...	...	...	0852	0824	0907	...	...	1316	...	...	...	1635	...	2040	2100b	...	...	0533	0523	0736
387	0	Perković d.	0542	0519	0705	0742	0857	0837	0908	0918	1230	1317	1306	1323	1518	1642	1645	2042	2106	2112	...	0538	0534	0737
	22	**Šibenik** a.	0612	|	0735	0812	|	|	0938	|	|	|	1336	1353	1547	1712	|	|	2136	|	...	|	|	|
435		**Split** a.	...	0627	...	...	0944	1006	...	1026	1338	1415	...	...	...	...	1753	2154	...	2222	...	0658	0650	0856

	Ⓐ	Ⓐn	g			IC 520 R ♦		k	Ⓐr		j	IC 522 R ✕ E		Ⓐ	EN 1152 R ♦	EN 1205 R ♦	Ⓐ			1820 R ♦	1841 R ♦	1881 R ♦
Split d.	...	...	...	0718	...	0801	...	...	1039	...	...	1406	1529	...	1722	1743	1950	...	...	2111	2111	2223
Šibenik d.	0448	0618	0701	|	0835	|	...	1109	|	...	1427	|	|	1604	|	|	|	2033	...	|	|	|
Perković a.	0517	0647	0730	0831	0904	0912	←	1138	1148	...	1456	1505	1638	1633	1834	1858	2105	2102	...	2237	2242	2337
Perković d.	0525	...	...	...	→	0914	0930	...	...	...	...	1507	...	1641	1835	1859	...	2107	...	2239	2244	2338
Zadar ‡ d.	|	...	...	...	...	|	|	...	...	...	...	|	...	|	|	|	...	|	...	|	|	|
Knin ‡ a.	0627	...	...	...	...	1010	1032	...	...	...	...	1551	...	1743	1939	2028	...	2209	...	2336	2340	0034
Knin d.	...	...	...	...	...	1012	...	...	...	...	...	1552	...	...	1952	2030	...	...	...	2338	2342	0035
Gračac d.	...	...	...	...	...	1136	...	...	...	...	...	1645	...	...	|	|	...	...	...	0052	0056	0149
Gospić d.	...	...	...	...	...	1214	...	...	...	...	...	1720	...	...	|	|	...	...	...	0141	0135	0227
Ogulin **1310** d.	...	...	...	...	...	|	...	...	...	...	...	|	...	...	|	|	...	...	...	0353	|	|
Oštarije **1310** d.	...	...	...	...	...	1409	...	...	...	...	...	1915	...	...	2355	|	...	...	...	|	0357	|
Karlovac **1310** d.	...	...	...	...	...	1518	...	...	...	...	...	2022	...	...	|	|	...	...	...	0453	0453	0527
Zagreb Glavni **1310** a.	...	...	...	...	...	1620	...	...	...	...	...	2124	...	...	0151z	|	...	...	...	0550	0550	0623
Budapest Keleti **89** a.	...	...	...	...	...	...	...	...	...	...	...	...	...	...	...	0935	...	...	...	...	...	...

♦ – **NOTES** (LISTED BY TRAIN NUMBER):

520/3 – ⚒ to June 28; daily June 29 - Aug 31; ⚒ from Sept. 1. MARJAN – [2] ✕ Zagreb - Knin - Split and v.v.
1152 – ①④⑥ May 1 - Oct. 13. [sleeper] 1, 2 cl., [couchette] 2 cl., [2] Split - Zagreb - Graz - Wien - Bratislava.
1153 – ③⑤⑦ Apr. 30 - Oct. 12. [sleeper] 1, 2 cl., [couchette] 2 cl., [2] Bratislava - Wien - Graz - Zagreb - Split.
1204 – June 19, 21, 26, 28, July **and** Aug. 2, 4, 6, 8, 10, 12, 14, 16, 18, 20, 22, 24, 26, 28, 30, Sept. 2, 4, 6, 11, 13. ADRIA – [sleeper] 1, 2 cl., [couchette] 2 cl., [2] ✕ Budapest - Knin - Split.
1205 – June 20, 22, 27, 29, July **and** Aug. 3, 5, 7, 9, 11, 13, 15, 17, 19, 21, 23, 25, 27, 29, 31, Sept. 3, 5, 7, 12, 14. ADRIA – [sleeper] 1, 2 cl., [couchette] 2 cl., [2] ✕ Split - Knin - Budapest.
1820 – ⑦ to June 22 and from Oct. 5 (also Nov. 18; not Nov. 16); [sleeper], [couchette] and [2] Split - Knin - Zagreb.
1821 – ⑤ to June 13 and from Oct. 3 (also June 18); [sleeper], [couchette] and [2] Zagreb - Knin - Split.
1840 – June 28 - Aug. 29. [sleeper], and [2] Vukovar - Vinkovci - Zagreb - Knin - Split.
1841 – June 30 - Aug. 31. [sleeper], and [2] Split - Knin - Zagreb - Vinkovci - Vukovar.
1880 – June 29 - Aug. 30. DALMACIJA – [sleeper] and [2] Osijek - Zagreb - Knin - Split.
1881 – June 30 - Aug. 31. DALMACIJA – [sleeper] and [2] Split - Knin - Zagreb - Osijek.

E – † to June 22; daily June 27 - Aug. 31; † from Sept. 7 (not Nov. 1).

b – Ⓐ.
g – June 29 - Aug. 30.
h – June 27 - Aug. 31.
j – Ⓑ to June 27; daily June 28 - Aug. 31; Ⓑ from Sept. 1
k – Ⓐ to June 27; daily June 28 - Aug. 31; Ⓐ from Sept. 1.
n – Not June 30 - Aug. 29.
p – Not June 27 - Aug. 31.
r – Not June 16 - Sept. 5.
z – Zagreb **Zapadni** station, 2km from Zabreb **Glavni** (Main station).

‡ – Services Knin - Zadar and v.v are suspended until further notice.

HŽ 2nd class only — ZAGREB - VARAŽDIN - KOTORIBA and KOPRIVNICA — 1335

km		⚒		Ⓐ	Ⓐ	Ⓐ	Ⓐr		⚒	⚒			Ⓐ	⚒	Ⓐ		⊕	772 Ⓐ♦	Ⓐ				Ⓐ	⚒	Ⓐ				⊙
0	**Zagreb Gl** d.	...	...	...	0543	...	0654	...	...	*0955*	...	1137	...	...	*1321*	1430	...	...	*1540*	...	1652	...	...	...	1925	2016	...	2210	2243
38	Zabok d.	...	...	0605	0631	0703	0744	0842	...	1046	...	1221	1228	...	1416	1516	1528	...	1627	...	1736	1747	...	1925	2011	2100	2112	2252	2330
104	**Varaždin** d.	0524	0700	0749	...	0838	...	1019	1023	1219	1306	...	1405	1432	1601	...	1707t	1748	1808	1920	...	1948	2024	2107	...	...	2245	...	0103
115	Čakovec d.	0537	0713	0802	...	0849	...	...	1036	...	1319	...	...	1445	1612	...	1725	1759	1819	1933	...	...	2037	2118	...	...	...	...	0114
145	**Kotoriba** a.	0615	0748	0842	...	...	...	...	1115	...	1353	...	...	1525	...	...	1800	...	...	2008	...	...	2112	...	...	...	...	...	...

	⊙		773 Ⓐ♦	⚒	⚒			⚒	Ⓐ		⚒		Ⓐ	Ⓐ	Ⓐr	⚒	⚒	⚒	⚒			†		Ⓑ				
Kotoriba d.	...	...	...	...	...	0543	...	0633	...	0810	...	...	...	...	...	1156	...	...	1452	...	...	1614	1647	...	1822	...	...	2120
Čakovec d.	...	0414r	0454	0510	...	0619	...	0714	*0822*	0852	...	...	...	...	...	1232	...	...	1529	...	...	1650	1727	...	1859	...	...	2154
Varaždin d.	0300	*0433*r	0509	0527	...	0651j	...	0725	*0839*	0903	1035	...	1223	...	...	1243	1414	...	1603j	1603	...	1701	1738	1756	1910	1918	...	2205
Zabok d.	0445	0606	...	0648	0704	0829	0844	...	1047	...	1212	1230	1356	1415	1527	...	1554	1612	1736	1736	1748	...	...	1918	...	2055	2111	...
Zagreb Gl a.	0531	0658	...	...	0748	...	0927	...	1130	...	...	1314	...	1459	1614	...	...	1704	...	...	1832	...	...	...	...	...	2154	...

VARAŽDIN - KOPRIVNICA

km		Ⓐ	773 Ⓐ		Ⓐ	⚒	⚒		Ⓐ	†	Ⓐ		Ⓐ
0	Varaždin d.	0402	0506	0638	0750	1022	1245	1447	1600	1708	1800	1921	2218
42	Koprivnica a.	0457	0549	0728	0840	1111	1336	1538	1651	1756	1854	2011	2308

	Ⓐ	⚒	Ⓐr	Ⓐ		⚒	Ⓐ	⚒		772 Ⓐ	Ⓑv	Ⓐ	
Koprivnica d.	0410	0525	0638	0813	0922	1144	1309	1448	1601	1704	1807	1922	2039
Varaždin a.	0501	0624	0733	0911	1013	1235	1408	1543	1655	1746	1858	2016	2130

♦ – **NOTES** (LISTED BY TRAIN NUMBER):

772 – [2] Zagreb (**771**) - Koprivnica (**772**) - Varaždin - Čakovec.
773 – [2] Čakovec - Varaždin (**773**) - Koprivnica (**770**) - Zagreb.

j – Arrives 21 – 23 minutes earlier.
k – Via Koprivnica.
r – Not June 16 - Sept. 5.

t – Arrives 1658.
v – Also Nov. 1.

⊕ – Change trains at Varaždin on †.
⊙ – Change trains at Zabok on †.

HŽ, MÁV — ZAGREB - KOPRIVNICA - NAGYKANIZSA and OSIJEK — 1340

km		1881 R ♦		781 R ♦n		771 R Ⓐt		201 R ♦		581 R ♦	
	Split **1330** d.	2223	...	...	...	...	...	...	...	...	...
0	**Zagreb Glavni** d.	0640	...	0640	...	1533	...	1630	...	1630	...
57	Križevci d.	|	...	0737	...	1629	...	1729	...	1729	...
88	Koprivnica d.	|	...	0812	...	1654	...	1804	...	1804	...
103	Gyékényes 🏛 d.	|	...	|	...	...	...	1823	...	|	...
132	**Nagykanizsa** a.	|	...	|	...	...	...	1848	...	|	...
	Budapest Déli **1220** a.	|	...	|	...	...	...	2224	...	|	...
153	Virovitica d.	0925	...	0927	...	...	...	...	...	1923	...
225	Našice d.	1112	...	1113	...	...	...	...	...	2108	...
275	**Osijek** a.	1218	...	1219	...	...	...	...	...	2214	...

	770 R Ⓐt		580 R ♦		204 R ♦		780 R m		1880 R ♦
Osijek d.	...	...	0510	...	...	...	1618	...	1923
Našice d.	...	...	0616	...	...	...	1725	...	2029
Virovitica d.	...	...	0804	...	...	...	1922	...	2228
Budapest Déli **1220** d.	...	...	|	...	1535	...	|	...	|
Nagykanizsa d.	...	...	|	...	1908	...	|	...	|
Gyékényes 🏛 d.	...	...	|	...	1951	...	|	...	|
Koprivnica d.	0558	...	0924	...	2015	...	2043	...	|
Križevci d.	0625	...	0951	...	2051	...	2110	...	|
Zagreb Glavni a.	0719	...	1050	...	2200	...	2210	...	0051
Split **1330** a.	...	...	...	...	...	...	...	...	0856

♦ – **NOTES** (LISTED BY TRAIN NUMBER):

201/4 – AGRAM – [12] Budapest - Gyékényes - Koprivnica - Zagreb and v.v.
580/1 – PODRAVKA – [12] Zagreb - Koprivnica - Osijek and v.v.
780/1 – DRAVA – [12] Zagreb - Koprivnica - Osijek and v.v.
1880 – June 29 - Aug. 30. DALMACIJA – [sleeper], [couchette] and [2] Osijek - Zagreb - Knin - Split.
1881 – June 30 - Aug. 31. DALMACIJA – [sleeper], [couchette] and [2] Split - Knin - Zagreb - Osijek.

m – Not June 28 - Aug. 29.
n – Not June 30 - Aug. 31.
t – To / from Čakovec via Varaždin (Table **1335**).

CROATIA and BOSNIA-HERZEGOVINA

1345 PÉCS - OSIJEK - DOBOJ

2nd class only except where shown HŽ, MÁV, ŽRS

There are currently no trains running Slavonski Šamac (Croatia) - Šamac (Bosnia-Herzegovina) - Doboj and v.v.

km		⚒	Ⓐ						⚒	Ⓐ	⚒	Ⓐ			⑦	⚒			Ⓑ							Ⓑ		Ⓑ
	Budapest Déli **1200** ... d.	...	...	...	...	...	...	...	...	...	...	...	...	...	...	...	...	...	...	...	...	...	...	...	...	...	...	...
0	**Pécs** ... d.	...	...	0508	...	...	...	0650	...	...	...	...	0850	...	...	...	1250	...	...	1450	...	...	1650	...	...	...	1850	...
36	Villány ... d.	...	...	0555	...	...	...	0734	...	...	...	...	0934	...	...	...	1334	...	...	1534	...	...	1734	...	...	...	1934	...
43	Magyarbóly 🛃 ... d.	...	...	0603	...	...	...	0742	...	...	...	...	0942	...	...	...	1342	...	...	1542	...	...	1742	...	...	...	1942	...
54	Beli Manastir 🛃 ... d.	...	0533	0614	...	0653	...	0753	0814	...	...	...	0953	1048	...	...	1353	1425	...	1553	1622	...	1753	1847	...	...	1953	2009
82	**Osijek** ... a.	...	0604	...	...	0724	...	...	0845	...	...	...	...	1119	...	...	...	1456	...	...	1653	...	...	1918	...	...	...	2040
82	**Osijek** ... d.	0416	...	...	0712	...	0727	...	...	0925	1014	1130	...	...	1310	1324	...	...	1530	...	...	1837	...	...	2035	2043	...	...
	Vinkovci ... a.	│	...	...	0759	...	│	...	...	1011	1101	│	...	...	1356	1411	...	...	│	...	...	1924	...	...	│	2130	...	...
130	Strizivojna-Vrpolje ... d.	0507	...	...	...	...	0819	...	...	...	...	1221	...	...	...	...	...	...	1622	...	...	...	...	...	2127	...	...	...
150	Slavonski Šamac 🛃 ... d.	...	...	...	...	...	...	...	...	...	...	...	...	...	...	...	...	...	...	...	...	...	...	...	...	...	...	...
154	Šamac 🛃 ... d.	...	...	...	...	...	...	...	...	...	...	...	...	...	...	...	...	...	...	...	...	...	...	...	...	...	...	...
226	**Doboj** ... a.	...	...	...	...	...	...	...	...	...	...	...	...	...	...	...	...	...	...	...	...	...	...	...	...	...	...	...

km			Ⓐ	⚒			⚒	⚒	⚒			Ⓐ	Ⓐ		Ⓐ					Ⓐ			Ⓑ		Ⓑ			Ⓑ
	Doboj ... d.	...	...	...	...	...	...	...	...	...	...	...	...	...	...	...	...	...	...	...	...	...	...	...	...	...	...	...
	Šamac 🛃 ... d.	...	...	...	...	...	...	...	...	...	...	...	...	...	...	...	...	...	...	...	...	...	...	...	...	...	...	...
	Slavonski Šamac 🛃 ... d.	...	...	...	...	...	...	...	...	...	...	...	...	...	...	...	...	...	...	...	...	...	...	...	...	...	...	...
	Strizivojna-Vrpolje ... d.	...	0523	...	...	...	...	0626	...	...	...	1035	...	...	1226	...	...	...	...	1710	...	...	...	...	1940	...	2156	...
0	Vinkovci ... d.	...	│	0527	...	...	0619	│	...	...	0837	│	...	1138	│	...	...	...	...	│	1742	...	...	...	│	1949	│	2218
35	**Osijek** ... a.	...	0613	0615	...	...	0704	0717	...	...	0922	1125	...	1223	1317	...	...	...	...	1801	1827	...	...	...	2030	2034	2246	2303
	Osijek ... d.	...	...	...	0617	...	...	...	0729	...	...	...	1147	...	...	1328	...	1527	...	...	...	...	1928	...	...	...	...	...
	Beli Manastir 🛃 ... d.	0528	...	...	0648	0802	...	...	0800	0958	...	...	1218	...	...	1359	1402	1559	1602	...	...	1758	1959	2002	...	...	...	...
	Magyarbóly 🛃 ... d.	0540	...	...	...	0814	...	...	...	1014	...	...	...	...	...	...	1414	...	1614	...	...	1814	...	2014	...	...	...	...
	Villány ... d.	0554	...	...	...	0822	...	...	...	1022	...	...	...	...	...	...	1422	...	1622	...	...	1822	...	2022	...	...	...	...
	Pécs ... a.	0635	...	...	...	0907	...	...	...	1107	...	...	...	...	...	...	1507	...	1707	...	...	1907	...	2107	...	...	...	...
	Budapest Déli **1200** ... a.	...	...	...	...	...	...	...	...	...	...	...	...	...	...	...	...	...	...	...	...	...	...	...	...	...	...	...

1350 ZAGREB - DOBOJ - ZENICA - SARAJEVO

2nd class only HŽ, ŽFBH, ŽRS

There are currently no trains running Volinja (Croatia) - Novi Grad (Bosnia-Herzegovina) and v.v.

km					711 🅁		Ⓐ					Ⓐ				Ⓐ			n					⑤–⑦ d	
0	**Zagreb Glavni** ... d.	...	...	...	...	...	...	...	...	...	...	...	...	0903	...	...	...	1344	...	1550	...	...	1916	...	2250
72	Sunja ... d.	...	...	...	...	...	...	...	...	...	...	...	...	1027	...	...	...	1442	...	1648	...	...	2035	...	0009
92	Volinja 🛃 ... d.	...	...	...	...	...	...	...	...	...	...	...	...	1055	...	...	...	1532	...	1738	...	...	2104**a**	...	0038**e**
98	Dobrljin 🛃 ... d.	...	...	...	...	...	...	...	...	...	...	...	...	...	...	...	...	...	...	...	...	...	...	...	...
112	Novi Grad ... d.	...	...	...	...	...	...	0432	...	...	0703	...	...	...	...	...	1515	...	...	...	...	1900	...	...	...
214	Banja Luka ... d.	...	...	...	...	0439	...	0633	0726	...	0914	...	...	...	1526	...	1720	...	...	...	1930	2114	...	...	...
324	**Doboj** ... a.	...	...	...	...	0638	...	...	0921	...	...	...	...	...	1721	...	...	...	...	...	2138	...	...	...	...
324	**Doboj** ... d.	...	...	...	...	...	...	...	...	...	...	...	...	...	...	...	...	...	...	...	...	...	...	...	...
347	Maglaj ... d.	...	...	0448	0607	...	...	...	...	...	...	...	...	...	...	...	...	...	...	...	...	...	...	...	...
370	Zavidovici ... d.	...	...	0520	0624	...	...	...	...	...	...	...	...	...	...	...	...	...	...	...	...	...	...	...	...
419	**Zenica** ... d.	0459	...	0621	0720	...	...	...	...	...	...	...	1532	...	...	...	...	...	...	...	...	...	...	...	...
447	Kakanj ... d.	0531	...	...	0749	...	...	...	...	...	...	...	1605	...	...	...	...	...	...	...	...	...	...	...	...
465	Visoko ... d.	0553	0648	...	0806	...	0929	...	...	1129	...	1432	1627	...	...	1836	...	...	2027	...	...	...	...	2306	...
472	Podlugovi ... d.	0602	0655	...	0814	...	0938	...	...	1136	...	1441	1658	...	...	1845	...	...	2036	...	...	...	...	2315	...
496	**Sarajevo** ... a.	0639	0732	...	0847	...	1013	...	...	1213	...	1516	1742	...	...	1920	...	...	2111	...	...	...	...	2350	...

		⚒							Ⓐ							Ⓐ				710 🅁		n		⑤–⑦ d	
	Sarajevo ... d.	...	...	...	...	0444	...	0524	0817	...	...	...	...	...	1030	1329	...	1541	...	1628	...	1932	...	2202	...
	Podlugovi ... d.	...	...	...	...	0518	...	0604	0854	...	...	...	...	...	1104	1403	...	1615	...	1656	...	2006	...	2236	...
	Visoko ... d.	...	...	...	...	0527	...	0612	0904	...	...	...	...	...	1114	1413	...	1629	...	1704	...	2016	...	2246	...
	Kakanj ... d.	...	...	...	...	0553	...	...	...	...	...	...	...	...	...	...	...	1651	...	1721	...	...	...	...	...
	Zenica ... d.	...	...	...	...	0628	...	...	...	...	...	...	...	...	...	...	1536	1725	...	1750	...	...	...	...	...
	Zavidovici ... d.	...	...	...	...	...	...	...	...	...	...	...	...	...	...	...	1634	...	...	1839	...	...	...	...	...
	Maglaj ... d.	...	...	...	...	...	...	...	...	...	...	...	...	...	...	...	1708	...	...	1901	...	...	...	...	...
	Doboj ... a.	...	...	...	...	...	...	...	...	...	...	...	...	...	...	...	...	...	...	...	...	...	...	...	...
	Doboj ... d.	...	...	0426	...	...	0727	...	...	...	...	...	...	1528	...	...	...	...	...	...	1925	...	...	...	...
	Banja Luka ... d.	...	0358	0622	0724	...	0935	...	...	...	...	1529	...	1735	...	...	...	...	1920	...	2124	...	...	...	...
	Novi Grad ... d.	...	0604	...	0925	...	...	...	...	...	...	1740	...	...	...	...	...	...	2122	...	...	...	...	...	...
	Dobrljin 🛃 ... d.	...	...	...	...	...	...	...	...	...	...	...	...	...	...	...	...	...	...	...	...	...	...	...	...
	Volinja 🛃 ... d.	0430	...	...	...	...	...	...	...	1113	1554	...	1920	...	...	...	...	...	...	...	...	...	...	...	...
	Sunja ... d.	0458	...	...	...	...	...	...	...	1140	1622	...	1948	...	...	...	...	...	...	...	...	...	...	...	...
	Zagreb Glavni ... a.	0617	...	...	...	...	...	...	...	...	1750	...	2111	...	...	...	...	...	...	...	...	...	...	...	...

a – Ⓐ only. **d** – June 27 - Aug. 31. **e** – ⚒ only. **n** – Does not run on ⑤⑥⑦ June 27 - Aug. 31.

1355 SARAJEVO - PLOČE

Most services 2nd class only HŽ, ŽFBH

km		723			721						
0	**Sarajevo** ... d.	0715	...	...	1646	...	...	...	...	...	...
69	Konjic ... d.	0825	...	...	1800	...	...	...	...	...	...
129	Mostar ... d.	0915	...	...	1850	...	...	...	...	...	...
145	Žitomislići ... d.	0928	...	...	1903	...	...	...	...	...	...
163	Čapljina 🛃 d.	0940	...	...	1915	...	...	...	...	...	...
173	Metković ... d.	...	...	...	...	...	...	...	...	...	...
195	**Ploče** ... a.	...	...	...	...	...	...	...	...	...	...

	720			722						
Ploče ... d.	...	...	...	...	...	...	...	...	...	...
Metković ... d.	...	...	...	...	...	...	...	...	...	...
Čapljina 🛃 d.	0606	...	...	1642	...	...	...	...	...	...
Žitomislići ... d.	0618	...	...	1655	...	...	...	...	...	...
Mostar ... d.	0633	...	...	1709	...	...	...	...	...	...
Konjic ... d.	0722	...	...	1758	...	...	...	...	...	...
Sarajevo ... a.	0835	...	...	1907	...	...	...	...	...	...

☛ Alternative 🚌 services are available Sarajevo - Mostar - Metković - Dubrovnik and v.v.

1358 OTHER LOCAL SERVICES

2nd class only HŽ, ŽRS

VINKOVCI - TUZLA

km		Ⓐ		⚒				Ⓐ
0	Vinkovci ... d.	0300	...	0855	...	1454	...	2001
49	Gunja ... d.	0359	...	0954	...	1553	...	2100
53	Brčko 🛃 d.	...	...	...	...	...	...	...
127	Tuzla ... a.	...	...	...	...	...	...	...

	Ⓐ		⚒				Ⓐ
Tuzla ... d.	...	...	...	...	...	...	...
Brčko 🛃 d.	...	...	...	...	...	...	...
Gunja ... d.	0407	...	1002	...	1603	...	2108
Vinkovci ... a.	0506	...	1101	...	1709	...	2207

TUZLA - DOBOJ

km					Ⓐ			
0	Tuzla ... d.	...	...	...	...	...	...	...
32	Petrovo Novo ... d.	0536	1054	...	1412	...	1753	2044
60	Doboj ... a.	0631	1149	...	1505	...	1846	2135

				Ⓐ			
Doboj ... d.	0420	0730	...	1310	1526	...	1932
Petrovo Novo ... d.	0515	0825	...	1405	1620	...	2025
Tuzla ... a.	...	...	...	...	...	...	...

SERBIA, MONTENEGRO and NORTH MACEDONIA

MAP PAGE 523

Operators: Železnice Srbije (ŽS): www.srbvoz.rs; Železnice Crne Gore (ŽPCG): www.zcg-prevoz.me; Makedonski Železnici (MŽ): www.mztransport.mk; Trainkos (HK): www.trainkos.com

Services: All trains convey first- and second-class seating, except where shown otherwise in footnotes, by a '2' in the train column, or where the footnote shows that the train conveys sleeping- (🛏) and / or couchette (🛏) cars only. Descriptions of sleeping- and couchette cars are given on page 10.

Timings: **Valid until December 13, 2025.**
Services may be amended or cancelled at short notice and passengers are strongly advised to check locally before travelling.

Tickets: A supplement is payable for travel by internal express trains. Reservation of seats is possible on most express trains.

Visas: Most nationals do not require a visa to enter Serbia and Montenegro, but must obtain an entry stamp in their passport, sight of which will be required by officials on leaving the country. These must be obtained at a border crossing recognised by the authorities - this excludes Kosovo's external borders with Montenegro, North Macedonia and Albania. Note also that Serbia should not be entered from Kosovo unless initial travel into Kosovo was via Serbia. Visas are not required for entry into North Macedonia for most nationals.

Currency: Visitors must declare large amounts of foreign currency upon arrival; currently 2,000 EUR in Montenegro, and 10,000 EUR in Serbia and North Macedonia. It is reported, however, that North Macedonia may now be operating on a threshold of 2,000 EUR. A certificate issued by the customs officer must be presented on departure, otherwise any funds held may be confiscated.

Security: Following the declaration of independence by Kosovo (which has not been recognised by Serbia) caution should be exercised when travelling in southern Serbia and northern Kosovo. Caution is also advised in the northern and western border regions of North Macedonia.

ŽS (BUDAPEST -) KELEBIA - SUBOTICA - NOVI SAD - BEOGRAD 1360

Rail services between Novi Sad and Subotica are suspended until further notice.

Selected bus services between Novi Sad and Subotica and v.v, run by **Auto Kodeks** and **Niš Ekspres** are shown in this table.
Note that bus services operate to / from Novi Sad and Subotica central bus stations (not the rail station). **Rail tickets are not valid on bus services.**

km		IR 641 Ⓐ	IC 541 Ⓐ	IR 643	IC 543	IR 615 C	IR 1131 A	IR 645	🚌	IC 545	IR 647	IC 547	🚌	IR 649	IC 549	IR 651	IC 551	IR 653	IC 553	🚌	IR 655	IC 555	🚌	IR 657	IC 557
	Budapest Nyugati **1295** d.	...	...	...	...	...	...	...	...	...	...	...	...	...	...	...	...	...	...	...	...	...	...	...	...
0	**Kelebia** 🏛 d.	...	...	...	...	...	...	...	...	...	...	...	...	...	...	...	...	...	...	...	...	...	...	...	...
10	**Subotica** 🏛 a.	...	...	...	...	...	...	...	...	...	...	...	...	...	...	...	...	...	...	...	...	...	...	...	...
10	**Subotica** d.	...	...	...	...	...	...	...	0840	...	...	...	1115	...	...	...	...	...	...	1700	...	...	1900	...	...
108	**Novi Sad** a.	...	...	...	...	...	...	...	1015	...	...	...	1300	...	...	...	...	...	...	1830	...	...	2030	...	...
108	**Novi Sad** **1370** d.	0555	0643	0755	0843	0858	0858	0955	...	1043	1155	1243	...	1355	1443	1555	1643	1755	1843	...	1955	2043	...	2155	2243
181	Novi Beograd **1370** d.	0635	0716	0835	0916	0937	1015	1035	...	1116	1235	1316	...	1435	1516	1635	1716	1835	1916	...	2035	2116	...	2235	2316
184	**Beograd** Centar **1370** a.	0638	0719	0838	0919	0940	1019	1038	...	1119	1238	1319	...	1438	1519	1638	1719	1838	1919	...	2038	2119	...	2238	2319

	IR 640 Ⓐ	IC 540 Ⓐ	🚌	IR 642	IC 542	IR 644	🚌	IC 544	IR 646	IC 546	🚌	IR 550	IC 548	IR 650	IC 550	🚌	IR 652	IC 552	IR 654	IC 554	🚌	IR 616 D	IR 1130 B	IR 656	IC 556
Beograd Centar **1370** d.	0500	0600	...	0700	0800	0900	...	1000	1100	1200	...	1300	1400	1500	1600	...	1700	1800	1900	2000	...	2020	2020	2100	2200
Novi Beograd **1370** d.	0504	0604	...	0704	0804	0904	...	1004	1104	1204	...	1304	1404	1504	1604	...	1704	1804	1904	2004	...	2024	2024	2104	2204
Novi Sad **1370** a.	0543	0636	...	0743	0836	0943	...	1036	1143	1236	...	1343	1436	1543	1636	...	1743	1836	1943	2036	...	2101	2101	2143	2236
Novi Sad d.	...	...	0720	...	...	...	1035	...	...	...	1350	...	...	...	...	1805	...	...	...	...	2115	...	...	...	...
Subotica a.	...	...	0855	...	...	...	1210	...	...	...	1525	...	...	...	...	1940	...	...	...	...	2300	...	...	...	...
Subotica 🏛 d.	...	...	...	...	...	...	...	...	...	...	...	...	...	...	...	...	...	...	...	...	...	...	...	...	...
Kelebia 🏛 a.	...	...	...	...	...	...	...	...	...	...	...	...	...	...	...	...	...	...	...	...	...	...	...	...	...
Budapest Nyugati **1295** a.	...	...	...	...	...	...	...	...	...	...	...	...	...	...	...	...	...	...	...	...	...	...	...	...	...

A – June 13 - Sept. 14. TARA – (12) Novi Sad - Beograd - Podgorica - Bar.
B – June 14 - Sept. 15. TARA – (12) Bar - Podgorica - Beograd - Novi Sad.
C – To June 12 / from Sept. 15. (12) Novi Sad - Beograd - Užice.
D – To June 13 / from Sept. 16. (12) Užice - Beograd - Novi Sad.

☛ *IC* and *IR* high-speed services Beograd - Novi Sad and v.v. are branded *Soko (Falcon)* and require compulsory reservation (Ⓡ); other slower services are available with a journey time of approximately one hour.

ŽS 2nd class only SUBOTICA and KIKINDA - ZRENJANIN - PANČEVO - BEOGRAD 1362

Services on the Zrenjanin - Pančevo - Beograd route are suspended until further notice.

km		⚒			Ⓐ				Ⓐ		Ⓑ
	Subotica d.	...	0705	...	...	...	...	1505	1705	...	1902
	Senta d.	...	0803	...	...	...	...	1603	1748	...	2000
	Banatsko Miloševo d.	...	0855	...	...	...	...	1709	...	...	2106
0	**Kikinda** d.	0455	|	...	1125	...	1745	1729	...	...	2126
19	Banatsko Miloševo d.	0516	|	...	1210	...	1806	...	...	...	...
71	**Zrenjanin** d.	0639	1018	...	1333	...	1929	...	...	...	...
96	Orlovat Stajalište d.	...	...	...	...	...	...	...	...	...	...
145	**Pančevo** Glavna **1365** d.	...	...	...	...	...	...	...	...	...	...
159	Pančevački Most **1365/6** d.	...	...	...	...	...	...	...	...	...	...
163	**Beograd** Centar **1365/6** a.	...	...	...	...	...	...	...	...	...	...

	⚒	Ⓐ					Ⓐ			Ⓑ
Beograd Centar **1365/6** d.	...	...	...	...	...	...	...	...	...	...
Pančevački Most **1365/6** d.	...	...	...	...	...	...	...	...	...	...
Pančevo Glavna **1365** d.	...	...	...	...	...	...	...	...	...	...
Orlovat Stajalište d.	...	...	...	...	...	...	...	...	...	...
Zrenjanin d.	...	0720	...	1033	...	1430	...	...	...	2010
Banatsko Miloševo d.	...	0905	...	|	...	1554	...	...	...	2134
Kikinda d.	0400	0925	...	|	...	1614	...	1810	...	2154
Banatsko Miloševo d.	0435	...	...	1157	...	...	...	1845	...	...
Senta d.	0541	...	...	1302	...	...	1804	1951	...	...
Subotica a.	0624	...	...	1347	...	...	1847	2034	...	...

ŽS, CFR 2nd class only BEOGRAD - VRŠAC - TIMIŞOARA 1365

There are currently no trains running between Vršac (Serbia) and Stamora Moraviţa (Romania).

km										
0	Novi Beograd **1366** d.	0655	...	1000	...	1140	1455	1630	...	2055
3	**Beograd** Centar **1362/6** d.	0700	...	1004	...	1144	1500	1634	...	2059
7	Pančevački Most **1362/6** d.	0713	...	1016	...	1156	1513	1646	...	2111
21	Pančevo Glavna **1362** d.	0731	...	1034	...	1214	1531	1704	...	2129
86	Vršac a.	0845	...	1148	...	1328	1645	1818	...	2243
86	Vršac 🏛 d.	...	...	...	...	...	....	...	...	...
106	Stamora Moraviţa 🏛 § a.	...	...	...	...	...	...	...	...	...
106	Stamora Moraviţa § d.	...	0508	...	1147	...	...	...	2040	...
162	**Timişoara** Nord § a.	...	0626	...	1302	...	...	...	2155	...

Timişoara Nord § d.	...	0755	...	...	...	...	1603	...	1907
Stamora Moraviţa § a.	...	0913	...	...	...	...	1716	...	2025
Stamora Moraviţa 🏛 § d.	...	...	...	...	...	...	...	...	...
Vršac 🏛 a.	...	...	...	...	...	...	...	...	...
Vršac d.	0608	...	0910	1217	1409	...	...	1840	...
Pančevo Glavna **1362** d.	0723	...	1026	1339	1524	...	...	1955	...
Pančevački Most **1362/6** d.	0741	...	1044	1358	1542	...	...	2013	...
Beograd Centar **1362/6** d.	0752	...	1055	1409	1553	...	...	2024	...
Novi Beograd **1366** a.	0756	...	1059	1413	1557	...	...	2028	...

§ – Romanian (East European) time.

ŽS 2nd class only OVČA - BEOGRAD - BATAJNICA 1366

Ovča d.	0610	0710	0815	0950	1050	1210	1310	1350	1510	1710	1910
Pančevački Most **1362/5** d.	0626	0726	0831	1006	1106	1226	1326	1406	1526	1726	1926
Beograd Centar **1362/5** d.	0636	0736	0841	1016	1116	1236	1336	1416	1536	1736	1936
Novi Beograd **1365** d.	0640	0740	0845	1020	1120	1240	1340	1420	1540	1740	1940
Batajnica a.	0658	0758	0903	1038	1138	1258	1358	1438	1558	1758	1958

Batajnica d.	0600	0710	0800	1010	1110	1200	1310	1400	1600	1710	2000
Novi Beograd **1365** d.	0619	0729	0819	1029	1129	1219	1329	1416	1619	1729	2019
Beograd Centar **1362/5** d.	0623	0733	0823	1033	1133	1223	1333	1423	1623	1733	2023
Pančevački Most **1362/5** d.	0635	0745	0835	1045	1145	1235	1345	1435	1635	1745	2035
Ovča a.	0648	0758	0848	1058	1158	1248	1358	1448	1648	1758	2048

☛ Additional trains run on Ⓐ between 0540 and 2020.

1370 NOVI SAD - BEOGRAD and NIKŠIĆ - PODGORICA - BAR

ŽPCG, ŽS

km																								
																615	1131					611		433
																C	A							L
																R	R					R		R ✕
0	**Novi Sad** .... 1360 d.	...	...	...	...	...	...	...	...	...	...	...	...	...	...	0858	0858	...	...	...	...	...	...	...
72	Novi Beograd .... 1360 d.	...	...	...	...	...	...	...	...	...	...	...	0643	...	...	0937	0937	1230	...	...	1521	1653	...	...
75	**Beograd** Centar .... 1360 d.	...	...	...	...	...	...	...	...	...	...	...	0709	...	...	0945	0945	1238	...	...	1527	1700	1929	2000
164	Valjevo .... d.	...	...	...	...	...	...	...	...	...	...	...	0836	...	...	1101	1101	1400	...	...	1652	1813	2055	2116
227	Požega .... d.	...	...	...	...	...	...	...	...	...	...	...	1022	...	...	1237	1237	1540	...	...	1833	1938	2224	2242
250	Užice .... d.	...	...	...	...	...	...	...	...	...	0750	...	1050	...	...	1257	1305	1623	...	...	1910	1958	2252	2312
312	Priboj .... d.	...	...	...	...	...	...	...	...	...	0954	...	1239**b**	...	...	...	1457	1825	...	...	2107	...	...	0057
342	Prijepolje Teretna .... d.	...	...	...	...	...	...	...	...	...	1103	...	...	...	...	...	1610	1935	...	...	2216	...	...	0207
384	Bijelo Polje 🏛 .... d.	...	...	...	0626	...	0909	...	...	...	...	...	...	...	...	...	1745**c**	...	...	1949	...	...	...	0340
	Nikšić .... d.	...	0620	...	|	1015	|	...	1415	...	...	...	...	1704	...	...	|	...	2000	|	...	...	...	|
492	**Podgorica** .... a.	...	0727	...	0851	1121	1128	...	1521	...	...	...	...	1810	...	...	1956	...	2107	2222	...	...	...	0540
492	**Podgorica** .... d.	0510	...	0755	0912	...	1135	1255	...	1530	...	1636	...	...	1936	...	2010	...	...	2227	...	...	...	0548
533	Sutomore .... d.	0555	...	0841	1007	...	1221	1341	...	1616	...	1721	...	...	2025	...	2056	...	...	2312	...	...	...	0640
542	**Bar** .... a.	0609	...	0855	1021	...	1235	1355	...	1630	...	1735	...	...	2039	...	2110	...	...	2326	...	...	...	0654

km																								
		610									616	1130											432	
											D	B											L	
		R									R	R											R ✕	
	Bar .... d.	...	...	...	...	...	0511	0624	...	...	...	0900	0923	...	1136	...	1413	...	1530	1703	...	1805	2010	...
	Sutomore .... d.	...	...	...	...	...	0526	0639	...	...	...	0917	0938	...	1151	...	1428	...	1545	1722	...	1821	2029	...
	Podgorica .... a.	...	...	...	...	...	0614	0723	...	...	...	0954	1022	...	1239	...	1512	...	1634	1806	...	1905	2109	...
0	**Podgorica** .... d.	...	...	...	...	...	0619	...	0800	...	...	1000	...	...	...	1250	...	1535	1706	...	1830	1917	2120	2145
61	**Nikšić** .... a.	...	...	...	...	...	|	...	0907	...	...	|	...	...	...	1356	...	1641	|	...	1936	|	|	2252
	Bijelo Polje 🏛 .... d.	...	...	...	...	...	0839	...	...	...	...	1252**c**	...	...	...	...	...	...	1922	...	...	2137	0006	...
	Prijepolje Teretna .... d.	...	...	0320	...	0625	...	...	...	1140	...	1358	...	...	...	...	...	...	...	...	...	...	0059	...
	Priboj .... d.	...	...	0430	...	0737	...	...	...	1244	...	1458	...	1612**b**	...	...	...	...	...	...	...	...	0211	...
	Užice .... d.	0500	...	0634	...	0952	...	...	...	1503	1706	1706	...	1835	...	...	...	...	...	...	...	...	0406	...
	Požega .... d.	0523	...	0700	...	1021	...	...	...	1543	1728	1728	...	1906	...	...	...	...	...	...	...	...	0428	...
	Valjevo .... d.	0648	...	0841	...	1203	...	...	...	1723	1903	1903	...	2035	...	...	...	...	...	...	...	...	0551	...
	Beograd Centar .... 1360 a.	0756	...	1010	...	1338	...	...	...	1853	2017	2017	...	2215	...	...	...	...	...	...	...	...	0709	...
	Novi Beograd .... 1360 a.	0816	...	1016	...	1346	...	...	...	...	2023	2023	...	2221	...	...	...	...	...	...	...	...	...	...
	Novi Sad .... 1360 a.	...	...	...	...	...	...	...	...	...	2101	2101	...	...	...	...	...	...	...	...	...	...	...	...

A – June 13 - Sept. 14. TARA – 12 Novi Sad - Beograd - Podgorica - Bar.
B – June 14 - Sept. 15. TARA – 12 Bar - Podgorica - Beograd - Novi Sad.
C – To June 12 / from Sept. 15. 12 Novi Sad - Beograd - Užice.
D – To June 13 / from Sept. 16. 12 - Užice - Beograd - Novi Sad.

L – LOVĆEN – 1, 2 cl., 2 cl., 2 Beograd - Podgorica - Bar and v.v.
b – ⑦.
c – A change of trains is necessary at Bijelo Polje (also border / customs checks between Serbia and Montenegro).

1372 POŽEGA - KRALJEVO - KRUŠEVAC - JAGODINA

2nd class only ŽS

km										
0	**Požega** .... d.	...	...	...	...	...	...	...	...	...
41	Čačak .... d.	...	...	...	...	...	...	...	...	...
75	**Kraljevo** .... d.	0500	...	...	...	1520	...	...	...	...
132	**Kruševac** .... d.	0713	...	...	...	1733	...	...	...	...
147	Stalać .... 1380 d.	0744	...	...	...	1804	...	...	...	...
168	Paraćin .... 1380 d.	0823	...	...	...	1843	...	...	...	...
188	**Jagodina** .... 1380 a.	0840	...	...	...	1900	...	...	...	...

Jagodina .... 1380 d.	0855	...	...	...	1915	...	...	...	...
Paraćin .... 1380 d.	0915	...	...	...	1935	...	...	...	...
Stalać .... 1380 d.	1003	...	...	...	2023	...	...	...	...
Kruševac .... d.	1034	...	...	...	2054	...	...	...	...
Kraljevo .... d.	1246	...	...	...	2306	...	...	...	...
Čačak .... d.	...	...	...	...	...	...	...	...	...
Požega .... a.	...	...	...	...	...	...	...	...	...

1373 MAJDANPEK and PRAHOVO - ZAJEČAR - NIŠ

2nd class only ŽS

km										
0	**Majdanpek** .... d.	...	...	...	0930	...	...	...	1740	...
50	Bor Teretna .... d.	...	...	...	1059	...	...	...	1909	...
★	Prahovo Pristanište .... d.	...	...	0920	|	...	...	1740	|	...
	Negotin .... d.	...	...	0940	|	...	...	1800	|	...
87	**Zaječar** .... d.	0630	...	1130	1205	1420	...	1950	2015	...
130	Knjaževac .... d.	0801	...	...	...	1551	...	...	...	...
195	**Niš** .... a.	0941	...	...	...	1731	...	...	...	...

Niš .... d.	...	...	...	1025	...	...	...	1520	...
Knjaževac .... d.	...	...	...	1202	...	...	...	1717	...
Zaječar .... d.	0620	0640	...	1334	1430	1500	...	1849	...
Negotin .... d.	|	0836	...	...	|	1656	...	...	...
Prahovo Pristanište .... a.	|	0855	...	...	|	1715	...	...	...
Bor Teretna .... d.	0726	...	...	...	1536		...	...	...
Majdanpek .... a.	0858	...	...	...	1708	...	...	...	...

★ – Prahovo - Zaječar: *81 km*.

1375 LAPOVO and MITROVICA - PRISHTINË - SKOPJE

2nd class only ŽS, HK, MŽ

km										
		891							*IC* 761	
		h ❋								Ⓐ
	Beograd **1380** .... d.	...	...	...	...	...	...	...	...	...
0	**Lapovo** .... d.	...	...	...	...	0700	...	...	...	1607
30	Kragujevac .... d.	...	...	...	...	0736	...	...	...	1643
85	Kraljevo .... d.	...	...	0650	...	0935	...	1450	...	1842
162	Rudnica .... d.	...	...	0850	...	...	...	1650	...	...
173	Lešak .... ♣ d.	...	...	...	...	...	...	...	...	...
211	Zvečan .... ♣ d.	...	...	...	...	...	...	...	...	...
214	Kosovska Mitrovica Sever .... ♣ a.	...	...	...	...	...	...	...	...	...
—										
0	Mitrovicë .... ♣ d.	...	...	...	...	...	...	...	...	...
*	**Prishtinë** .... d.	0710	0750	...	...	...	...	...	1630	...
34	Fushë Kosovë .... d.	0722	0804	...	...	...	...	...	1641	...
	Pejë .... a.	|	0953	...	...	...	...	...	1829	...
67	Ferizaj .... d.	0802	...	...	...	...	...	...	...	...
97	Deneral Janković / Hani I Elezit .... 🏛 a.	0900	...	...	...	...	...	...	...	...
130	**Skopje** .... a.	0952	...	...	...	...	...	...	...	...

	IC 760				892				
					h ❋			Ⓐ	
Skopje .... d.	...	...	...	...	1630	...	...	...	...
Deneral Janković / Hani I Elezit . 🏛 d.	...	...	...	...	1735	...	...	...	...
Ferizaj .... d.	...	...	...	...	1816	...	...	...	...
Pejë .... d.	0532	...	1210	...	|	...	...	...	...
Fushë Kosovë .... d.	0723	...	1359	...	1900	...	...	...	...
Prishtinë .... a.	0732	...	1410	...	1910	...	...	...	...
Mitrovicë .... ♣ a.	...	...	...	...	...	...	...	...	...
Kosovska Mitrovica Sever .... ♣ d.	...	...	...	...	...	...	...	...	...
Zvečan .... ♣ d.	...	...	...	...	...	...	...	...	...
Lešak .... ♣ d.	...	...	...	...	...	...	...	...	...
Rudnica .... d.	...	...	...	1232	...	...	1710	...	...
Kraljevo .... d.	...	1125	...	1432	...	...	1910	1935	...
Kragujevac .... d.	...	1324	...	...	...	...	...	2134	...
Lapovo .... a.	...	1359	...	...	...	...	...	2209	...
Beograd **1380** .... a.	...	...	...	...	...	...	...	...	...

h – A change of train maybe necessary at Deneral Janković / Hani I Elezit.

♣ – Currently no Železnice Srbije (ŽS) service between Rudnica - Kosovska Mitrovica Sever and v.v. No Trainkos (HK) service between Mitrovicë - Fushë Kosovë and v.v.

❋ – Currently suspended due to engineering works.

* – Prishtinë to Fushë Kosovë 7 km; Prishtinë to Pejë 88 km.

1377 MINOR BORDER CROSSINGS

2nd class only ŽS, MÁV

SUBOTICA - SZEGED

km										
0	Subotica ... d.	0603	0737	1337	1637	Szeged ...... d.	0858	1458	1758	2143
24	Horgoš 🏛 d.	0630	0804	1404	1704	Röszke . 🏛 d.	0949	1549	1849	2242
31	Röszke 🏛 d.	0657	0844	1444	1744	Horgoš .. 🏛 d.	0959	1559	1859	2252
44	Szeged .... a.	0715	0902	1502	1802	Subotica .... a.	1024	1624	1924	2317

KIKINDA - JIMBOLIA - TIMISOARA

Operated by Regio Călători

km												
0	Kikinda .... d.	...	...	...	...	...	Timisoara .... § d.	0650	0742	1400	1638	1935
19	Jimbolia .... a.	...	...	...	...	...	Jimbolia .. 🏛 § a.	0753	0846	1500	1738	2038
19	Jimbolia ... 🏛 § d.	0529	0900	1240	1510	1748	Jimbolia .... d.	...	...	...	...	...
58	Timisoara ..... § a.	0632	1003	1343	1610	1849	Kikinda .... a.	...	...	...	...	...

§ – East European time, one hour ahead of Central European time.

BEOGRAD - NIŠ - SOFIA, SKOPJE and THESSALONÍKI — 1380

ŽS, MŽ, BDŽ

No service currently running Niš - Skopje/Sofia, and also between Gevgelija and Thessaloniki and v.v. Due to long term engineering work.

km		611		641		601					643		631			1491		645			691		1335
		2			⚒	2			2⚒		2		2 🅁			B ✤		🅁		2⚒	🅁		H ✤
0	**Novi Beograd** 1360/70 d.	...	...	...	...	...	0318	...	...	...	...	...	...	...	...	...	...	...	...	...	1500	...	...
3	**Beograd** Centar 1360/70 d.	...	...	...	...	...	0323	...	...	...	...	...	...	0730	...	0915	...	...	1330	...	1510	...	1825
113	Lapovo d.	...	...	...	0225	...	0613	...	...	...	...	...	...	1023	...	1101	...	...	1610	...	1723	...	2028
138	Jagodina **1372** d.	...	...	...	0323	...	0712	...	...	...	...	...	...	1122	...	1141	...	...	1709	...	1816	...	2108
158	Paraćin **1372** d.	...	...	...	0342	...	0730	...	...	...	...	...	...	1140	...	1157	...	...	1728	...	1837	...	2124
179	Stalać **1372** d.	...	...	...	0426	...	0814	...	...	...	...	...	...	1225	...	1232	...	...	1810	...	1918	...	2159
247	**Niš** a.	...	...	...	0612	...	1013	...	...	...	...	...	...	1413	...	1341	...	...	1957	...	2035	...	2308
247	**Niš** d.	...	...	...	...	...	...	...	...	...	...	...	...	...	...	1407	...	...	...	...	...	...	2318
	Dimitrovgrad 🏛 d.	...	...	...	...	...	...	...	...	...	...	...	...	...	...	1718	...	...	...	...	...	...	|
	Dragoman 🏛 § d.	...	...	...	...	...	...	...	...	...	...	...	...	...	...	1949	...	...	...	...	...	...	|
	Sofia § a.	...	...	...	...	...	...	...	...	...	...	...	...	...	...	2037	...	...	...	...	...	...	|
291	Leskovac d.	...	...	...	...	...	...	...	...	...	...	...	...	...	...	...	...	...	...	...	...	...	0003
395	Preševo 🏛 d.	...	...	...	...	...	...	...	...	...	...	...	...	...	...	...	...	...	...	...	...	...	0307
404	Tabanovci 🏛 d.	...	...	...	...	...	...	...	...	...	...	...	...	...	...	...	...	...	...	...	...	...	0345
452	**Skopje** a.	...	...	...	...	...	...	...	...	...	...	...	...	...	...	...	...	...	...	...	...	...	0425
452	**Skopje** **1385** d.	0620	...	0706	...	0800	...	...	1320	...	1430	...	1655	...	...	...	...	2005	...	2240	...	...	0445
516	Veles **1385** d.	0722	...	0759	...	0852	...	...	1412	...	1522	...	1747	...	...	...	...	2057	...	2332	...	...	0526
629	Gevgelija a.	0859	...	...	...	...	...	...	...	...	...	...	1928	...	...	...	...	...	...	...	...	...	0650
629	Gevgelija 🏛 d.	...	...	...	...	...	...	...	...	...	...	...	...	...	...	...	...	...	...	...	...	...	0723
632	Idoméni 🏛 § a.	...	...	...	...	...	...	...	...	...	...	...	...	...	...	...	...	...	...	...	...	...	0828
632	Idoméni § d.	...	...	...	...	...	...	...	...	...	...	...	...	...	...	...	...	...	...	...	...	...	0856
708	**Thessaloníki** § a.	...	...	...	...	...	...	...	...	...	...	...	...	...	...	...	...	...	...	...	...	...	1033

km				690			600	640		630			1490					642		632		644	1334
		⚒		🅁			2	2		2			B ✤		2		2⚒	2		2	2	2	H ✤
	Thessaloníki § d.	...	...	...	...	...	...	...	...	...	...	...	...	...	...	...	...	...	...	...	...	...	1851
	Idoméni § a.	...	...	...	...	...	...	...	...	...	...	...	...	...	...	...	...	...	...	...	...	...	1936
	Idoméni 🏛 § d.	...	...	...	...	...	...	...	...	...	...	...	...	...	...	...	...	...	...	...	...	...	2011
	Gevgelija 🏛 a.	...	...	...	...	...	...	...	...	...	...	...	...	...	...	...	...	...	...	...	...	...	1916
	Gevgelija d.	...	...	...	...	...	...	...	...	0430	...	...	...	...	...	...	...	...	...	1702	...	...	1948
	Veles **1385** d.	...	...	...	...	...	0500	0543	...	0609	...	...	...	...	1210	...	1424	1524	...	1840	...	2057	2113
	Skopje **1385** a.	...	...	...	...	...	0552	0634	...	0701	...	...	...	...	1302	...	1520	1615	...	1932	...	2148	2154
	Skopje d.	...	...	...	...	...	...	...	...	...	...	...	...	...	...	...	...	...	...	...	...	...	2219
	Tabanovci 🏛 d.	...	...	...	...	...	...	...	...	...	...	...	...	...	...	...	...	...	...	...	...	...	2329
	Preševo 🏛 d.	...	...	...	...	...	...	...	...	...	...	...	...	...	...	...	...	...	...	...	...	...	0018
	Leskovac d.	...	...	...	...	...	...	...	...	...	...	...	...	...	...	...	...	...	...	...	...	...	0239
0	**Sofia** § d.	...	...	...	...	...	...	...	...	...	...	...	0915	...	...	...	...	...	...	...	...	...	|
42	Dragoman 🏛 § d.	...	...	...	...	...	...	...	...	...	...	...	1005	...	...	...	...	...	...	...	...	...	|
63	Dimitrovgrad 🏛 d.	...	...	...	...	...	...	...	...	...	...	...	1100	...	...	...	...	...	...	...	...	...	|
161	**Niš** a.	...	...	...	...	...	...	...	...	...	...	...	1336	...	...	...	...	...	...	...	...	...	0323
	Niš d.	...	...	0500	...	0705	...	...	...	...	1240	...	1410	...	...	1558	...	...	...	...	...	...	0337
	Stalać **1372** d.	...	...	0616	...	0845	...	...	...	...	1417	...	1520	...	...	1745	...	...	...	...	...	...	0447
	Paraćin **1372** d.	...	...	0648	...	0920	...	...	...	...	1453	...	1541	...	...	1821	...	...	...	...	...	...	0508
	Jagodina **1372** d.	...	...	0706	...	0937	...	...	...	...	1510	...	1557	...	...	1838	...	...	...	...	...	...	0524
	Lapovo d.	0420	...	0744	...	1020	...	...	...	...	1604	...	1634	...	...	1923	...	...	...	...	...	...	0606
	Beograd Centar 1360/70 a.	0705	...	1005	...	1310	...	...	...	...	1903	...	1829	...	...	2210	...	...	...	...	...	...	0813
	Novi Beograd 1360/70 a.	...	...	1011	...	...	...	...	...	...	1915	...	...	...	...	2215	...	...	...	...	...	...	...

B – BALKAN – 🚃2 Beograd - Niš - Sofia and v.v.
H – HELLAS – 🛏 2 cl., 🚃2 Beograd - Skopje - Gevgelija - Thessaloniki and v.v.

§ – East European time.
✤ – Service currently suspended.

BRANCH LINES in North Macedonia — 1385

MŽ 2nd class only

SKOPJE - KOČANI and ZABENI

km		641		643	651		645
					✤		
0	**Skopje** **1380** d.	0706	...	1430	1523	...	2005
64	Veles **1380** d.	0759	...	1525	1621	...	2058
★	Kočani a.	|	...	|	1813	...	|
134	Prilep d.	0944	...	1709	...	...	2242
178	Bitola a.	1031	...	1756	...	...	2329
189	**Zabeni** a.	1054	...	...	...	...	...

	640	650		642		644
		✤				
Zabeni d.	...	...	...	1115	...	...
Bitola d.	0310	...	...	1246	...	1822
Prilep d.	0359	...	...	1335	...	1911
Kočani d.	|	0500	...	|	...	|
Veles **1380** d.	0543	0657	...	1524	...	2057
Skopje **1380** a.	0634	0756	...	1615	...	2148

★ – Veles - Kočani : *110 km.*
✤ – Service currently suspended.

SKOPJE - KIČEVO

km				660
				✤
0	**Skopje** d.	...	...	1645
56	Tetovo d.	...	...	1748
79	Gostivar d.	...	...	1810
116	**Kičevo** a.	...	...	1849

	661		
	✤		
Kičevo d.	0530	...	...
Gostivar d.	0607	...	...
Tetovo d.	0630	...	...
Skopje a.	0732	...	...

ALBANIA

SEE MAP PAGE 523

Operator: Hekurudha Shqiptarë (HSH). www.hsh.com.al
Services: Trains convey one class of accommodation only. Tickets are not sold in advance, only for the next available departure.
Timings: **Timings have been compiled from the latest information received.**
Readers should be aware that timetable amendments usually come into effect at short notice.
Trains can also be cancelled at short notice; readers are advised to check information locally before travelling.
Security: Most visits to Albania are reported to be trouble free.

ALBANIAN RAILWAYS — 1390

HSH One class only

km	km		c	d							
	0	**Shkodër** d.	0600	...	...	...	...	...	...	...	...
	53	Laç d.	0832	...	...	...	...	...	...	...	...
	55	Gjormë a.	0840	...	...	...	...	...	...	...	...
	82	Vorë d.	...	...	...	...	...	...	...	...	...
0	98	**Tiranë** d.	...	...	...	...	...	...	...	...	...
16		Vorë d.	...	...	...	...	...	...	...	...	...
36		**Durrës** a.	...	...	...	...	...	...	...	...	...
—	0	**Durrës** d.	...	...	...	...	...	...	...	...	...
	4	Plazh d.	...	1500	...	...	...	...	...	...	...
0	36	Rrogozhinë d.	...	1620	...	...	...	...	...	...	...
	44	Peqin a.	...	1637	...	...	...	...	...	...	...
	77	Elbasan a.	...	...	...	...	...	...	...	...	...
	98	**Librazhd** a.	...	...	...	...	...	...	...	...	...
17		Lushnjë a.	...	...	...	...	...	...	...	...	...
49		Fier a.	...	...	...	...	...	...	...	...	...
83		**Vlorë** a.	...	...	...	...	...	...	...	...	...

	c	d							
Vlorë d.	...	...	...	...	...	...	...	...	...
Fier d.	...	...	...	...	...	...	...	...	...
Lushnjë d.	...	...	...	...	...	...	...	...	...
Librazhd d.	...	...	...	...	...	...	...	...	...
Elbasan d.	...	...	...	...	...	...	...	...	...
Peqin d.	...	0730	...	...	...	...	...	...	...
Rrogozhinë d.	...	0748	...	...	...	...	...	...	...
Plazh a.	...	0907	...	...	...	...	...	...	...
Durrës a.	...	...	...	...	...	...	...	...	...
Durrës d.	...	...	...	...	...	...	...	...	...
Vorë d.	...	...	...	...	...	...	...	...	...
Tiranë a.	...	...	...	...	...	...	...	...	...
Vorë d.	...	...	...	...	...	...	...	...	...
Gjormë d.	1230	...	...	...	...	...	...	...	...
Laç d.	1300	...	...	...	...	...	...	...	...
Shkodër a.	1530	...	...	...	...	...	...	...	...

c – ② Mar. 18 - June 13.
d – ①⑤⑥⑦ from June 6.

GREECE

SEE MAP PAGE 523

Operator: Hellenic Train S.A.: www.hellenictrain.gr

Services: All trains convey first and second class seating except where shown otherwise in footnotes or by '2' in the train column, or where the footnote shows sleeping and/or couchette cars only. Descriptions of sleeping (🛏) and couchette (🛌) cars appear on page 10. Services that convey catering may vary from day to day.

Timings: Timings have been compiled from the latest available information (**valid from January 13, 2025**). Readers should be aware that timetable amendments may come into effect at short notice, and are advised to check information locally before travelling.

Tickets: Reservation of seats is possible (and recommended) on most express trains. *IC* trains carry a supplement which varies depending upon distance travelled. Break of journey is only permitted when tickets are so endorsed before travel with the station quoted.

1400 ATHÍNA - LÁRISA - THESSALONÍKI HT

km			*IC* 50				*IC* 882		*IC* 52				*IC* 60		*IC* 54				*IC* 56				
		🚌	✕↗	🚌	🚌		🍷 ≋		✕↗	🚌	🚌		✕↗ ≋		✕↗	🚌		🚌	✕↗	🚌	🚌		
0	**Athína** Lárisa **1420** d.	...	0758	...	...	...	0828	...	1058	...	...	...	1259	...	1458	...	...	...	1758	...	...	...	...
61	Inói **1420** d.	...	0846	...	...	...	0920	...	1146	...	...	...	1347	...	1546	...	...	...	1846	...	...	...	...
89	Thíva d.	...	0901	...	...	...	0939	...	1201	...	...	...	1403	...	1601	...	...	...	1901	...	...	...	...
129	Levadiá d.	...	0921	...	...	...	1004	...	1221	...	...	...	1426	...	1621	...	...	...	1921	...	...	...	...
154	Tithoréa d.	...	0934	...	...	...	1020	...	1234	...	...	...	1441	...	1634	...	...	...	1934	...	...	...	...
210	Lianokládi d.	0808	1001	1015	...	...	1052	...	1301	1315	...	...	1507	...	1701	1715	...	...	2001	2015	...	...	...
	Lamia d.	0819	|	1026	...	...	|	...	|	1326	...	...	|	...	|	1726	...	...	|	2026	...	...	...
	Stilída a.	0855	|	1102	...	...	|	...	|	1402	...	...	|	...	|	1802	...	...	|	2102	...	...	...
276	Domokos d.	...	|	...	...	...	1132	...	|	...	...	...	|	...	|	...	...	...	|	...	...	...	...
291	Paleofársalos d.	...	1046	...	1100	...	1142	...	1346	...	1400	...	1540	...	1746	...	...	1800	2046	...	2100	...	...
	Kalambáka **1408** a.	...	|	...	1300	...	1249	...	|	...	1600	...	|	...	|	...	...	2000	|	...	2300	...	...
333	**Lárisa** ▲ d.	...	1121	...	...	...	...	...	1421	...	...	...	1602	...	1821	...	...	...	2121	...	...	...	...
417	Kateríni ▲ d.	...	1207	...	...	...	...	...	1507	...	...	...	1647	...	1907	...	...	...	2207	...	...	...	...
465	Platí **1410** ▲ d.	...	1229	...	...	...	...	...	1529	...	...	...	1709	...	1929	...	...	...	2229	...	...	...	...
502	**Thessaloníki** **1410** ▲ a.	...	1251	...	...	...	...	...	1551	...	...	...	1732	...	1951	...	...	...	2251	...	...	...	...

km					*IC* 51				*IC* 53			*IC* 61				*IC* 55			*IC* 887		*IC* 57		
			🚌	🚌	🍷↗		🚌	🚌	✕↗		🚌	✕↗ ≋		🚌	🚌	✕↗		🚌	🍷 ≋	🚌	✕↗		
	Thessaloníki **1410** ▲ d.	...	...	...	0704	...	...	...	1004	...	...	1325	...	...	...	1404	...	...	...	...	1710	...	...
	Platí **1410** ▲ d.	...	...	...	0727	...	...	...	1027	...	...	1349	...	...	...	1427	...	...	...	...	1733	...	...
	Kateríni ▲ d.	...	...	...	0749	...	...	...	1049	...	...	1411	...	...	...	1449	...	...	...	...	1755	...	...
	Lárisa ▲ d.	...	...	...	0834	...	...	...	1134	...	...	1454	...	...	...	1534	...	...	...	...	1840	...	...
	Kalambáka **1408** d.	...	0700	...	|	...	1000	...	|	...	...	|	...	1400	...	|	...	1705	1735	...	|	...	...
	Paleofársalos d.	...	0900	...	0908	...	1200	...	1208	...	...	1515	...	1600	...	1608	...	1905	1842	...	1914	...	...
	Domokos d.	...	...	...	|	...	...	...	|	...	...	|	...	...	...	|	...	...	1852	...	|	...	...
0	Stilída d.	0500	...	0855	|	...	...	1140	|	...	1440	|	...	...	1555	|	...	...	|	1900	|	...	...
17	Lamia d.	0536	...	0931	|	...	...	1216	|	...	1516	|	...	...	1631	|	...	...	|	1936	|	...	...
23	Lianokládi d.	0546	...	0941	0953	...	...	1227	1253	...	1527	1548	...	...	1641	1653	...	...	1933	1946	1959	...	...
	Tithoréa d.	...	...	...	1020	...	...	...	1320	...	...	1614	...	...	...	1720	...	...	2006	...	2026	...	...
	Levadiá d.	...	...	...	1034	...	...	...	1334	...	...	1629	...	...	...	1734	...	...	2021	...	2040	...	...
	Thíva d.	...	...	...	1055	...	...	...	1355	...	...	1651	...	...	...	1755	...	...	2047	...	2101	...	...
	Inói **1420** d.	...	...	...	1110	...	...	...	1410	...	...	1708	...	...	...	1810	...	...	2105	...	2116	...	...
	Athína Lárisa **1420** a.	...	...	...	1158	...	...	...	1457	...	...	1805	...	...	...	1857	...	...	2157	...	2204	...	...

▲ – Local service Thessaloníki - Litóhoro - Lárisa and v.v.

Thessaloníki d.	0500	0730	1030	1225	1510	1645	1945	2150	...
Platí d.	0528	0758	1058	1253	1538	1713	2013	2218	...
Kateríni d.	0553	0823	1123	1318	1603	1738	2038	2243	...
Litóhoro △ d.	0603	0833	1133	1328	1613	1748	2048	2253	...
Lárisa a.	0643	0913	1213	1408	1653	1828	2128	2333	...

Lárisa d.	0515	0710	1000	1245	1440	1725	1935	2200	...
Litóhoro △ d.	0558	0753	1043	1328	1523	1808	2018	2243	...
Kateríni d.	0608	0803	1053	1338	1533	1818	2028	2253	...
Platí d.	0633	0828	1118	1403	1558	1843	2053	2318	...
Thessaloníki a.	0700	0855	1145	1430	1625	1910	2120	2345	...

↗ – 🅁 with supplement payable. △ – Station for Mount Ólimbos. ≋ – Service currently suspended.

1405 THESSALONÍKI - ALEXANDRÚPOLI - ORMENÍO HT

km				🚌	🚌	🚌		🚌		🚌
		3632	**1680**	**C670**	**C672**	**C674**	**1682**	**C676**	**1634**	**C602**
0	**Thessaloníki** d.	0535	...	...	...	...	...	...	1500	...
42	Kilkís d.	0608	...	...	...	...	...	...	1533	...
97	Rodópolis d.	0703	...	...	...	...	...	...	1628	...
130	Strimón d.	0806	...	...	...	...	...	...	1731	...
162	Sérres d.	0839	...	...	...	...	...	...	1804	...
232	Dráma d.	...	...	0540	...	...	...	...	1927	1930
327	Xánthi d.	...	...	0752	0805	1230	...	1710	...	2130
374	Komotiní d.	...	...	...	0906	1331	...	1806	...	2215
443	**Alexandrúpoli Port** a.	...	...	...	1025	1450	...	1925	...	2305
443	**Alexandrúpoli Port** d.	...	0500	...	...	...	1520	...	...	...
556	Píthio d.	...	0641	...	...	...	1656	...	...	...
573	Orestiáda d.	...	0653	...	...	...	1714	...	...	...
610	Díkaia d.	...	...	...	...	...	1745	...	...	...
618	**Ormenío** a.	...	...	...	...	...	1751	...	...	...

		🚌	🚌		🚌		🚌		
	3633	**C671**	**C679**	**1681**	**C673**	**1635**	**C675**		**1683**
Ormenío d.	...	...	...	...	...	...	...	...	1810
Díkaia d.	...	...	...	...	...	...	...	...	1818
Orestiáda d.	...	...	...	0710	...	...	...	...	1849
Píthio d.	...	...	...	0728	...	...	...	...	1906
Alexandrúpoli Port d.	...	...	...	0911	...	...	...	...	2041
Alexandrúpoli Port d.	...	0555	...	...	1020	...	1500	...	...
Komotiní d.	...	0714	...	...	1139	...	1619	...	...
Xánthi d.	...	0800	0830	...	1225	...	1705	...	...
Dráma d.	...	...	1019	...	...	1707	...	...	...
Sérres d.	0910	...	...	...	...	1830	...	...	...
Strimón d.	0943	...	...	...	...	1903	...	...	...
Rodópolis d.	1046	...	...	...	...	2006	...	...	...
Kilkís d.	1142	...	...	...	...	2102	...	...	...
Thessaloníki a.	1214	...	...	...	...	2134	...	...	...

1408 LÁRISA - PALEOFÁRSALOS - KALAMBÁKA HT

km			*IC* 882						
		🚌	🍷 ≋		🚌		🚌		🚌
	Thessaloníki **1400** d.	...	...	...	...	...	...	...	...
	Athína **1400** d.	...	0828	...	...	...	...	...	...
	Lárisa **1400** d.	...	|	...	...	...	...	...	...
0	Paleofársalos **1400** d.	1100	1142	...	1400	...	1800	...	2100
31	Kardítsa d.	1150	1205	...	1450	...	1850	...	2150
60	Tríkala d.	1220	1229	...	1520	...	1920	...	2220
82	**Kalambáka** ⊡ a.	1300	1249	...	1600	...	2000	...	2300

								IC 887
	🚌		🚌		🚌		🚌	🍷 ≋
Kalambáka ⊡ d.	0700	...	1000	...	1400	...	1705	1735
Tríkala d.	0725	...	1025	...	1425	...	1730	1755
Kardítsa d.	0755	...	1055	...	1455	...	1800	1819
Paleofársalos **1400** a.	0900	...	1200	...	1600	...	1905	1842
Lárisa **1400** a.	...	...	...	...	...	...	...	|
Athína **1400** a.	...	...	...	...	...	...	...	2157
Thessaloníki **1400** a.	...	...	...	...	...	...	...	...

⊡ – An infrequent bus service operates Kalambáka - Igumenítsa and v.v. (approximately *250 km*). ≋ – Service currently suspended.

HT THESSALONÍKI - ÉDESSA - FLÓRINA 1410

km		1731			1733			1735			
0	**Thessaloníki** 1400 d.	0510	...	...	1215	...	...	1910	...	...	...
38	Platí 1400 d.	0538	...	...	1243	...	...	1938	...	...	...
69	Véria d.	0610	...	...	1315	...	...	2010	...	...	...
97	Skídra d.	0637	...	...	1342	...	...	2037	...	...	...
112	**Édessa** d.	0711	...	...	1356	...	...	2051	...	...	...
162	Amíndeo d.	0811	...	...	1456	...	...	...	...	...	...
196	**Flórina** a.	0846	...	...	1531	...	...	...	...	...	...

	1732			1734			1736			
Flórina d.	0530	...	...	1420	...	...	...	...	...	...
Amíndeo d.	0605	...	...	1455	...	...	...	...	...	...
Édessa d.	0705	...	...	1555	...	...	2130	...	...	...
Skídra d.	0719	...	...	1609	...	...	2144	...	...	...
Véria d.	0746	...	...	1636	...	...	2211	...	...	...
Platí 1400 d.	0818	...	...	1707	...	...	2243	...	...	...
Thessaloníki 1400 a.	0846	...	...	1736	...	...	2311	...	...	...

HT LÁRISA - VÓLOS 1415

km		🚌	🚌	🚌	🚌	🚌		🚌		🚌	
0	Lárisa d.	0650	0830	0950	1240	1445	...	1655	...	2130	...
61	Vólos a.	0750	0930	1050	1340	1545	...	1755	...	2230	...

	🚌	🚌	🚌	🚌	🚌		🚌		🚌	
Vólos d.	0525	0700	0850	1320	1550	...	1800	...	2110	...
Lárisa a.	0630	0805	0955	1425	1655	...	1905	...	2215	...

HT PIREÁS - ATHÍNA - HALKÍDA 1420

km			Ⓐ				❖			❖	Ⓐ												
0	**Pireás** 1430 d.	...	...	0444	...	0644	...	and at	1444	...	...	1644	...	1744	...	1844	1944	...	2044	...	...	...	...
10	**Athína** Lárisa ▲ 1400/30/40 d.	...	0428	0505	0524	0705	0728	the same	1505	1528	1628	1705	1728	1805	1828	1905	2005	2028	2105	2228	...	...	...
17	SKA (Acharnon) d.	...	0439	...	0535	...	0739	minutes	...	1539	1639	...	1739	...	1839	...	...	2039	...	2239	...	...	...
71	Inói 1400 d.	0440	0526	...	0626	...	0826	every two	...	1626	1726	...	1826	...	1926	...	...	2126	...	2326	...	...	...
94	**Halkída** a.	0500	0547	...	0647	...	0847	hours until	...	1647	1747	...	1847	...	1947	...	...	2147	...	2347	...	...	...

			Ⓐ				❖		❖				Ⓐ										
Halkída d.	0503	...	0603	...	0711	...	0904	and at	1504	...	1703	...	1803	...	1903	...	2004	...	2204	...	2355	...	...
Inói 1400 d.	0527	...	0627	...	0734	...	0927	the same	1527	...	1727	...	1827	...	1927	...	2027	...	2227	...	0016	...	...
SKA (Acharnon) d.	0613	...	0713	...	0820	...	1013	minutes	1613	...	1813	...	1913	...	2013	...	2113	...	2313	...	...	...	...
Athína Lárisa . ▲ 1400/30/40 d.	0626	0652	0726	0752	0833	0852	1025	every two	1625	1652	1825	1852	1925	1952	2025	2052	2125	2152	2236	2252	...	...	...
Pireás 1430 a.	...	0710	...	0812	...	0912	...	hours until	...	1712	...	1912	...	2012	...	2112	...	2212	...	2312	...	...	...

❖ – Every two hours.

▲ – See below Table **1440** for summary of Metro services.

HT PIREÁS - ATHÍNA - ATHÍNA AIRPORT ✈ 1430

km									
0	**Pireás** 1420/1440 d.	...	0444	0544	0644	and at	2044	...	...
10	**Athína** Lárisa ▲ 1400/20/40 d.	0415	0505	0605	0705	the same	2105	...	...
15	Káto Acharnai 1440 d.	0427	0515	0616	0716	minutes	2116	...	...
21	Neratziótissa ▲ d.	0436	0524	0625	0725	past each	2125	...	...
46	**Athína Airport** ✈ ▲ a.	0500	0548	0649	0749	hour until	2149	...	...

Athína Airport ✈ ▲ d.	0607	0707	and at	2207	2308	...	...	...
Neratziótissa ▲ d.	0632	0732	the same	2232	2332	...	...	...
Káto Acharnai 1440 d.	0640	0740	minutes	2240	2340	...	...	...
Athína Lárisa ▲ 1400/20/40 d.	0652	0752	past each	2252	2352	...	...	...
Pireás 1420 1440 a.	0712	0812	hour until	2312	...	...	...	...

▲ – See below Table **1440** for summary of Metro services.

HT PIREÁS - ATHÍNA - KÓRINTHOS - KIÁTO 1440

km									
0	**Pireás** 1420/1430 d.	...	0614	and at	2214				
10	**Athína** Lárisa ▲ 1400/20/30 d.	0530	0635	the same	2235	...	...	...	...
15	Káto Acharnai 1430 d.	0541	0645	minutes	2245	...	...	...	...
95	**Kórinthos** d.	0637	0741	every hour	2341	...	...	...	...
116	**Kiáto 1450** a.	0652	0755	until	2355	...	...	...	...

Kiáto 1450 d.	0456	0556	0656	0759	and at	2059	2159	...
Kórinthos d.	0512	0612	0712	0814	the same	2114	2214	...
Káto Acharnai 1430 d.	0609	0709	0809	0909	minutes	2209	2309	...
Athína Lárisa ▲ 1400/20/30 a.	0622	0722	0822	0921	past each	2221	2321	...
Pireás 1420/1430 d.	0642	0742	0842	0941	hour until	2241	...	...

▲ – Frequent Metro services operate as follows:
Line 1 (green): Pireás - Monastiraki - Omónia - Attiki - Neratziótissa - Kifissia.
Line 2 (red): Elliniko - Syntagma - Omónia - Athína Lárisa (for **Athína** mainline station) - Attiki - Anthoupoli.
Line 3 (blue): Agia Marina - Monastiraki - Syntagma - Athína Airport ✈.
Operators: ISAP Line 1; Attiko Metro Lines 2 and 3.

HT KIÁTO - PÁTRA 🚌 services 1450

	🚌	🚌	🚌	🚌	🚌	🚌	🚌	🚌	🚌	🚌
Kiáto 1440 d.	0805	0903	1005	1103	1205	1405	1605	1805	2005	2105
Diakoftó **1455** a.	|	0944	|	1144	|	|	1650	1850	|	|
Pátra a.	0930	...	1130	...	1330	1530	1740	1940	2130	2230

	🚌	🚌	🚌	🚌	🚌	🚌	🚌	🚌	🚌	🚌
Pátra d.	0625	...	0810	1225	1425	...	1625	...	1825	1925
Diakoftó **1455** d.	|	0710	0905	|	|	1510	|	1810	|	|
Kiáto 1440 a.	0750	0752	0950	1350	1550	1552	1750	1852	1950	2050

HT PELOPÓNNISOS narrow-gauge branches 1455

DIAKOFTÓ – KALÁVRITA *Rack railway*

km						
0	Diakoftó d.	0952	...	1217	...	1507
23	Kalávrita a.	1059	...	1324	...	1618

Kalávrita d.	1104	...	1337	...	1625
Diakoftó a.	1211	...	1448	...	1738

KATÁKOLO – PÍRGOS – OLIMBÍA

km		⚒		⚒		⚒		⚒			
0	**Katákolo** d.	...	...	0840	...	...	...	1410	...	...	...
12	Pírgos d.	0700	...	0903	...	1235	...	1432	...	...	...
33	**Olimbía** a.	0729	...	0932	...	1303	...	...	...	...	...

	⚒		⚒		⚒					
Olimbía d.	0735	...	0940	...	1310	...	...	...	...	...
Pírgos d.	0805	...	1009	...	1340	...	...	...	...	...
Katákolo a.	0827	...	...	...	1402	...	...	...	...	...

🚌 INTERNATIONAL BUS SERVICES 1460

A number of operators run long-distance 🚌 services to and from Greece, and selected services are listed below. Details should be checked with the relevant operator before travel. Rail tickets and passes are not valid. Further details about travelling to Greece by bus can be found on www.europebyrail.eu

ATHÍNA - ISTANBUL: Depart Athína 1700. Depart Istanbul 1800. Journey 16 hours. Operator: Metro www.metroturizm.com.tr

THESSALONIKI - ISTANBUL: Depart Thessaloniki 1000. Depart Istanbul (Esenler Otogari) 0530. Journey 10 hours. Operator: Ozikizler Turizm www.ozikizlerturizm.com
Depart Thessaloniki 1000, 2200, 2330. Depart Istanbul 1000, 1800, 2200. Journey 10 - 11 hours. Operator: Metro www.metroturizm.com.tr

THESSALONIKI - SKOPJE: Depart Thessaloniki 0830 or 1530. Depart Skopje 1530. Journey 3½ - 5½ hours. Not daily, Operator: Simeonidis Tours www.simeonidistours.gr

THESSALONIKI - SOFIA: Bus services are operated by Union Ivkoni (www.union-ivkoni.com) as follows:

Thessaloniki railway station 0115 → Sofia central bus station 0700.
Thessaloniki railway station 0900 → Sofia central bus station 1415.
Thessaloniki railway station 1615 → Sofia central bus station 2200.

Sofia central bus station 0730 → Thessaloniki railway station 1300.
Sofia central bus station 1630 → Thessaloniki railway station 2230.
Sofia central bus station 2030 → Thessaloniki railway station 0145.

BULGARIA

SEE MAP PAGE 523

Operators: Bâlgarski Dârzhavni Zheleznitsi (BDZ Passenger Services) www.bdz.bg

Services: Trains convey first- and second-class seating, except where shown otherwise in footnotes or by '2' in the train column, or where the footnote shows sleeping and / or couchette cars only. Descriptions of sleeping (🛏) and couchette (▬) cars appear on page 10. Seat reservation is possible on most long-distance trains (compulsory on express trains).

Timings: **Valid until December 13, 2025**. Subject to alteration on and around public holiday dates. **Note that from May 13, 2024, for approximately 15 months, engineering work will affect many trains from / to Sofia Central station. During this period trains will be either retimed to start earlier / arrive later (and diverted), or will start from / terminate at Sofia Sever (North), Ilijanci or Kurilo suburban stations with a connecting rail shuttle service operating from / to Central station. Arrangements may vary for individual trains during the work so please check before travelling.** Other timetable amendments are possible at short notice and so we strongly advise readers to confirm timings locally before travelling.

1500 SOFIA - RUSE, BURGAS and VARNA — BDŽ

km	km		2655	8631	3621	8611	2611	460	462	2613	8651		8613	2615	3623	4660	4610		2641	4632	3625	493	9647	8657	8627	2627	3637
				R	R	R	R	R	R	R	R		R	R	R						R	R					
						🍷		A	E											2		B	S	Z	Z	Z	D
0	0	**Sofia** Central .. **1520** d.	...	...	0615	0635	0650	0650	0650	1009	0955	...	1250	1305	1315	...	1525	...	1630	...	1640	1845	2010	2055	2225	2300	2305
	103	Septemvri d.	...	...	│	0843	│	│	│	│	1214	...	1520	│	│	...	│	...	│	...	│	2100	│	2310	0039	│	│
	119	Pazardzhik d.	...	...	│	0853	│	│	│	│	1225	...	1530	│	│	...	│	...	│	...	│	2110	│	2321	0050	│	│
	156	**Plovdiv** a.	...	...	│	0913	│	│	│	│	1248	...	1556	│	│	...	│	...	│	...	│	2134	│	2344	0114	│	│
	156	**Plovdiv** d.	...	...	│	0918	│	│	│	│	1255	...	1602	│	│	...	│	...	│	1600	│	...	│	2349	0117	│	│
	262	Stara Zagora d.	...	0855	│	1141	│	│	│	│	1525	...	1844	│	│	1610	│	...	│	│	│	...	│	0210	0340	│	│
	340	Jambol d.	...	0949	│	1232	│	│	│	│	1617	...	1938	│	│	│	│	...	│	│	│	...	│	0301	0432	│	│
		Karlovo d.	...	│	0825	│	│	│	│	│	│	...	│	│	1534	│	│	...	│	1717	1853	...	│	│	│	│	0125
		Kazanlak d.	...	│	0918	│	│	│	│	│	│	...	│	│	1632	│	│	...	│	1822	1954	...	│	│	│	│	0218
		Tulovo d.	...	│	│	│	│	│	│	│	│	...	│	│	1647	1638	│	...	│	1842	2008	...	│	│	│	│	0240
		Sliven d.	...	│	1043	│	│	│	│	│	│	...	│	│	1810	│	│	...	│	│	2121	...	│	│	│	│	0349
	389	Karnobat ..... **1535** d.	...	1028	1124	1312	│	│	│	│	1657	...	2026	│	1853	│	│	...	│	│	2202	...	│	0337	0506	│	0434
	450	**Burgas** ..... **1535** a.	...	│	1205	1356	│	│	│	│	│	...	2110	│	1936	│	│	...	│	│	2245	...	│	│	0550	│	│
33		Svoge d.	...	│	...	...	0738	0738	0738	1052	│	...	...	1353	...	│	1610	...	│	│	...	...	2058	│	...	2358	│
88		Mezdra ..... **1520** d.	0537	│	...	...	0836	0836	0836	1147	│	...	...	1447	...	│	1704	...	1804	│	...	...	2159	│	...	0038	│
194		Pleven d.	0705	│	...	...	0953	0953	0953	1303	│	...	...	1605	...	│	1826	...	1920	│	...	...	2314	│	...	0152	│
239		Levski d.	0736	│	...	...	1022	1022	1022	1333	│	...	...	1635	...	│	1856	...	1949	│	...	...	2342	│	...	0222	│
294		Gorna Orjahovica a.	0816	│	...	...	1100	1100	1100	1412	│	...	...	1714	...	1929	1936	...	2034	2056	...	...	0019	│	...	0304	│
294		Gorna Orjahovica d.	0830	│	...	...	1120	1135	1135	1421	│	...	...	1727	...	1944	1946	...	...	2101	...	...	0029	│	...	0315	│
405		**Ruse** 🏛 a.	│	│	...	...	│	1331	1331	│	│	...	...	│	...	│	2155	...	...	2300	...	...	0227	│	...	│	│
435		Shumen ..... **1530/5** d.	1015	│	...	...	1306	...	...	1608	│	...	...	1912	...	2131	...	...	...	...	...	...	...	│	...	0507	│
459		Kaspichan .... **1530/5** d.	1035	│	...	...	1325	...	...	1626	│	...	...	1930	...	2149	...	...	...	...	...	...	...	│	...	0526	│
518		Poveljanovo . **1530/5** d.	1135	1235	...	...	1426	...	...	1728	│	...	...	2031	...	2251	...	...	...	...	...	...	...	│	...	0628	0646
543	546	**Varna** ..... **1530/5** a.	1159	1300	...	...	1450	...	...	1752	1934	...	...	2055	...	2315	...	...	...	...	...	...	...	0600	...	0652	0709

km		2640	3620	4631	4611	8610	3622	4661		2612		8650	2614		461	463	2616	8612	3624	2654	8632		8626	9646	2626	8656
			R			R	R			R		R	R		R	R	R	R	R		R					
				2											A	E		🍷					Z	S	D	Z
	Varna ..... **1530/5** d.	...	...	...	...	...	...	0500	...	0745	...	0900	1045	...	...	...	1400	...	...	1635	1655	...	...	...	2155	2330
	Poveljanovo ..... **1530/5** d.	...	...	...	...	...	...	│	...	0810	...	│	1110	...	...	...	1425	...	...	1700	1719	...	...	...	2221	│
	Kaspichan ..... **1530/5** d.	...	...	...	...	...	...	0623	...	0908	...	│	1206	...	...	...	1521	...	...	1758	│	...	...	...	2317	│
	Shumen ..... **1530/5** d.	...	...	...	...	...	...	0646	...	0928	...	│	1225	...	...	...	1540	...	...	1820	│	...	...	...	2337	│
	Ruse 🏛 d.	...	...	0450	0620	...	...	│	...	│	...	│	│	...	1425	1425	│	...	...	│	│	...	...	2311	│	│
	Gorna Orjahovica a.	...	...	0652	0815	...	...	0829	...	1112	...	│	1409	...	1626	1626	1723	...	...	2008	│	...	...	0115	0121	│
	Gorna Orjahovica d.	0520	...	0702	0841	...	...	0838	...	1122	...	│	1418	...	1648	1648	1730	...	...	2019	│	...	...	0143	0143	│
	Levski d.	0556	...	│	0919	...	...	│	...	1202	...	│	1457	...	1725	1725	1811	...	...	2058	│	...	...	0224	0224	│
	Pleven d.	0624	...	│	0947	...	...	│	...	1232	...	│	1527	...	1754	1754	1841	...	...	2128	│	...	...	0255	0255	│
	Mezdra ..... **1520** d.	0744	...	│	1055	...	...	│	...	1346	...	│	1645	...	1910	1910	1959	...	...	2243	│	...	...	0412	0412	│
	Svoge d.	0844	...	│	1150	...	...	│	...	1440	...	│	1739	...	│	│	2054	...	...	...	│	...	...	0508	0508	│
0	**Burgas** ..... **1535** d.	│	0520	│	│	0655	0820	│	...	│	...	│	│	...	│	│	│	1455	1555	...	│	...	2145	│	│	│
61	Karnobat ..... **1535** d.	│	0602	│	│	0736	0901	│	...	│	...	1127	│	...	│	│	│	1536	1633	...	1914	...	2227	│	│	0157
119	Sliven d.	│	0649	│	│	│	0945	│	...	│	...	│	│	...	│	│	│	│	1716	...	│	...	│	│	│	│
195	Tulovo d.	│	0800	0932	│	│	1119	1110	...	│	...	│	│	...	│	│	│	│	1826	...	│	...	│	│	│	│
210	Kazanlak d.	│	0815	0946	│	│	1133	│	...	│	...	│	│	...	│	│	│	│	1841	...	│	│	│	│	│	│
269	Karlovo d.	│	0923	1048	│	│	1231	│	...	│	...	│	│	...	│	│	│	│	1937	...	│	...	│	│	│	│
	Jambol d.	│	│	│	│	0815	│	│	...	│	...	1207	│	...	│	│	│	1616	│	...	1951	...	2308	│	│	0237
	Stara Zagora d.	│	│	│	│	0902	│	1136	...	│	...	1256	│	...	│	│	│	1706	│	...	2044	...	2356	│	│	0329
	Plovdiv a.	│	│	1200	│	1127	│	...	...	│	...	1520	│	...	│	│	│	1952	│	...	2240	...	│	│	│	0559
	Plovdiv d.	│	│	...	│	1137	│	...	...	│	...	1524	│	...	│	│	│	1956	│	...	...	...	│	│	│	0604
	Pazardzhik d.	│	│	...	│	1204	│	...	...	│	...	1548	│	...	│	│	│	2023	│	...	...	...	│	│	│	0635
	Septemvri d.	│	│	...	│	1218	│	...	...	│	...	1558	│	...	│	│	│	2034	│	...	...	...	│	│	│	0645
418	**Sofia** Central ..... **1520** a.	0930	1135	...	1235	1427	1459	...	...	1521	...	1817	1820	...	2035	2035	2136	2242	2152	...	...	...	0520	0546	0546	0900

Other fast trains **SOFIA - PLOVDIV**

	1621					
Sofia Central d.	1622	...	...	...	...	...
Septemvri d.	1840	...	...	...	...	...
Pazardzhik d.	1850	...	...	...	...	...
Plovdiv a.	1913	...	...	...	...	...

	1620		1622			
	B					
Plovdiv d.	0655	...	1325	...	...	...
Pazardzhik d.	0720	...	1350	...	...	...
Septemvri d.	0731	...	1401	...	...	...
Sofia Central .. a.	0948	...	1611	...	...	...

Other local trains **GORNA ORJAHOVICA - RUSE**

	2	2		2	2
Gorna Orjahovica d.	0440	0840	...	1440	1735
Ruse a.	0708	1104	...	1705	1954
	2		2		2
Ruse d.	0740	...	1134	...	1745
Gorna Orjahovica a.	1006	...	1359	...	2012

A – June 13 - Oct. 13. From / to București (Table **61**).
B – SOFYA EXPRESS – [12] Sofia - Svilengrad and v.v.; 🛏 and ▬ Sofia - Halkalı and v.v. (Tables **1550** and **1573**).
D – Conveys 🛏 and [2] Sofia - Poveljanovo - Dobrich and v.v. (Table **1540**).
E – To June 12 and from Oct. 14.
S – ▬ and [2] Sofia - Ruse - Silistra and v.v (Table **1530**).
Z – Conveys 🛏 and [12].

1510 SEPTEMVRI - VELINGRAD - DOBRINISHTE — Narrow gauge; 2nd class only

km										
						R				
0	**Septemvri** d.	0330	...	...	...	0855	...	1240	...	1620
39	Velingrad d.	0502	...	...	...	1019	...	1409	...	1804
69	Avramovo d.	0617	...	...	...	1122	...	1518	...	1908
115	Razlog d.	0759	...	0940	...	1255	...	1703	...	2044
119	Bansko d.	0810	...	0953	...	1310	...	1721	...	2059
125	**Dobrinishte** a.	0822	...	1005	...	1321	...	1733	...	2110

								R		
Dobrinishte d.	...	...	0625	0840	...	1025	...	1425	...	1805
Bansko d.	...	...	0638	0853	...	1039	...	1439	...	1821
Razlog d.	...	...	0648	0901	...	1050	...	1452	...	1833
Avramovo d.	...	...	0841	...	...	1235	...	1631	...	2020
Velingrad d.	0655	...	0948	...	...	1339	...	1735	...	2138
Septemvri a.	0825	...	1123	...	...	1508	...	1902	...	2258

1520 SOFIA - LOM / VIDIN and VIDIN / CALAFAT - CRAIOVA — BDŽ

km				7620		7622				7624		7630
		2	2				2	Ⓑ	2		2	Ⓑ
0	**Sofia** C. **1500** d.	...	...	...	...	1155	...	...	...	1710	...	1917
88	Mezdra.. **1500** d.	0440	0705	0900	...	1353	...	1720	...	1913	...	2127
106	Vraca d.	0458	0723	0916	...	1409	...	1737	...	1931	...	2142
145	Bojchinovci d.	0539	0817	0954	...	1453	...	1831	...	2011	...	2222
182	Brusarci ..... ⊖ d.	0628	0905	1036	1040	1533	1545	1924	1930	2053	2100	2303
204	**Lom** ..... ⊖ a.	│	0928	│	1103	│	1608	│	1953	│	2123	2331
269	**Vidin** a.	0821	...	1215	...	1712	...	2109	...	2230	...	...

	7631		7621					7623		7625			
	⚒	2		2	2	2⚒	2		Ⓑ2		2	Ⓑ2	
Vidin d.	...	...	0450	...	0605	...	...	1230	...	1600	...	1740	...
Lom ..... ⊖ d.	0445	0540	│	0715	│	1120	1340	│	1715	│	1840	│	...
Brusarci ... ⊖ d.	0516	0605	0629	0738	0748	1144	1403	1411	1738	1750	1903	1925	...
Bojchinovci .. d.	0556	...	0710	...	0831	1223	...	1453	...	1831	...	2012	...
Vraca d.	0639	...	0755	...	0919	1313	...	1535	...	1912	...	2055	...
Mezdra **1500** a.	0655	...	0809	...	0935	1330	...	│	...	1928	...	2111	...
Sofia C **1500** a.	...	...	1005	...	...	...	...	1725	...	...	...	...	...

km			⚒		
	Vidin 🏛 d.	...	...	...	1300
0	**Calafat** d.	0307	0538	...	│
107	**Craiova** a.	0600	0909	...	1630

km					Ⓑ
0	**Craiova** d.	0655	...	1638	1925
	Calafat a.	│	...	2004	2249
119	**Vidin** 🏛 a.	1028	...	...	...

⊖ – Other services Brusarci - Lom and v.v:
From Brusarci at 0633, 0755, 1220 Ⓑ, 1420, 1755 Ⓑ.
From Lom at 0840, 0948, 1500 and 2020.

BDŽ RUSE - STARA ZAGORA - DIMITROVGRAD 1525

km		8656 V	2	4631 2P	4661 T	2	2	2	465 B2	
0	**Ruse** 1500 d.	...	...	0450	...	...	...	...	...	...
111	**Gorna Orjahovica** 1500 d.	...	0515	0702	0838	...	1135	1425	1735	2040
125	Veliko Târnovo d.	...	0534	0723	0855	...	1154	1444	1751	2103
226	Tulovo a.	...	0749	0924	1108	...	1409	1655	2005	...
226	Tulovo d.	...	0803	...	1110	...	1410	1656	2012	...
253	Stara Zagora d.	0329	0832	...	1136	1300	1438	1723	2100	...
310	**Dimitrovgrad** a.	0437	...	...	...	1431	...	...	2215	...

	8657 V		2	464 B2	2		2	4660 T	4632 2P
Dimitrovgrad d.	0100	...	...	0710	...	...	...	...	...
Stara Zagora d.	0209	...	0720	0840	1041	...	1317	1610	...
Tulovo a.	...	...	0748	0906	1109	...	1345	1637	...
Tulovo d.	...	...	0750	0907	1110	...	1346	1638	1842
Veliko Târnovo d.	...	0700	1023	1056	1322	...	1610	1915	2041
Gorna Orjahovica 1500 a.	...	0719	1041	1110	1340	...	1629	1929	2056
Ruse 1500 a.	...	...	...	...	...	...	...	...	2300

B – [2] Gorna Orjahovica - Dimitrovgrad and v.v. See Table **61** for seasonal through cars, Bucureşti - Ruse - Svilengrad - Kapıkule - Halkalı and v.v.
P – Ruse - Gornja Orjahovica - Karlovo - Plovdiv and v.v. Table **1500**.
T – Varna - Gornja Orjahovica - Stara Zagora and v.v. (see tables **1500**/**1530**).
V – Conveys 🛌 and [12] Varna - Stara Zagora - Dimitrovgrad - Plovdiv - Sofia and v.v. (see Tables **1500** and **1550**).

BDŽ *2nd class only* RUSE - SILISTRA and VARNA 1530

km		9647 S			9621		9623			
0	**Ruse** d.	0232	...	...	0555	...	1550	...	1845	...
5	Ruse Razpredelitelna d.	0253	...	...	0604	...	1559	...	1853	...
71	Razgrad d.	0405	...	...	0716	...	1712	...	2014	...
93	Samuil d.	0440f	0505	...	0737	0755	1736	...	2033	2105
	Silistra a.	0720	|	...	|	1045	|	...	...	2350
142	Kaspichan 1500 d.	...	0556	0604	0832	...	1830	...	...	...
	Shumen 1500 a.	...	...	|	|	...	|	...	...	...
201	Poveljanovo 1500 d.	...	...	0714	|	...	|	...	...	...
226	**Varna** 1500 a.	...	...	0747	0951	...	1950	...	...	...

km					9620 c					9622	9646 D
	Varna 1500 d.	...	...	...	0930	...	...	1415	...	1815	...
	Poveljanovo 1500 d.	...	...	...	0955	...	...	1449	...	1840	...
	Shumen 1500 d.	...	...	...	|	...	...	|	...	|	...
	Kaspichan 1500 d.	...	0635	...	1056	...	...	1558	1635	1942	...
0	**Silistra** d.	0435	|	...	|	...	1440	...	|	|	1820
113	Samuil d.	0720	0738	...	1148	...	1725	...	1737	2036	2120f
	Razgrad d.	...	0801	...	1208	...	...	...	1759	2058	2142
	Ruse Razpredelitelna d.	...	0926	...	1317	...	...	...	1917	2209	2258
	Ruse a.	...	0935	...	1325	...	...	...	1925	2217	2306

D – 🛏 and [2] Silistra - Ruse - Gorna Orjahovica (**2626**) - Sofia.
S – 🛏 and [2] Sofia - Gorna Orjahovica - Ruse - Silistra.
c – Engineering work may affect this train, please check before travel.
f – Arrives 20–25 minutes earlier.

BDŽ *Most trains 2nd class only* VARNA and SHUMEN - BURGAS - SLIVEN 1535

km			8650 [R]	8611 [R]						8632 [R]	8613 [R]		8656 [R]
	Varna 1500 d.	0655	0900	...	1115	...	...	1250	...	1655	...	1855	2330
	Poveljanovo 1500 d.	0725	|	...	1147	...	...	1323	...	1719	...	1929	|
0	**Shumen** d.	|	|	...	|	...	1310	|	...	|	...	|	|
50	Komunari d.	0816	1002	...	1240	...	1410	1418	...	1758	...	2020	0036
	Sliven 1500 d.	|	|	...	|	1330	...	|	1520	|	...	|	|
133	Karnobat 1500 d.	1032	1126	1250	1414	1421	...	1557	1632	1918	1925	2152	0155
194	**Burgas** 1500 a.	1137	...	1335	...	1525	...	...	1735	...	2010	...	...

	8657 [R]				8631 [R]			8612 [R]	8651 [R]	3624 [R]	
Burgas 1500 d.	...	...	0625	0905	...	1330	...	1520	...	1600	...
Karnobat 1500 d.	0337	...	0746	1018	1028	1430	1440	1601	1657	1637	1735
Sliven 1500 a.	|	...	|	1120	|	1513	|	...	|	1716	|
Komunari d.	0452	0600	0931	...	1154	...	1608	...	1825	...	1917
Shumen a.	|	0700	|	...	|	...	|	...	|	...	|
Poveljanovo 1500 d.	|	...	1023	...	1235	...	1658	...	|	...	2015
Varna 1500 a.	0600	...	1053	...	1300	...	1726	...	1934	...	2046

BDŽ *Most trains 2nd class only* VARNA - DOBRICH - KARDAM 1540

km		D	2637								
0	**Varna** 1500 d.	...	0600	0655	...	...	1205	1555	...	...	2025
	Sofia 1500 d.	2305	|	|	...	...	|	|	...	...	|
25	Poveljanovo 1500 d.	0655	0655	0724	0740	...	1239	1628	...	...	2100
93	**Dobrich** a.	0816	0816	...	0857	0905	1402	1750	1755	...	2225
131	Kardam a.	...	...	...	...	1010	...	...	1900	...	...

									E	2636
Kardam d.	...	...	...	1030	...	...	...	1920	...	...
Dobrich d.	0505	...	0940	1135	1145	...	1505	2025	2035	2035
Poveljanovo 1500 d.	0621	0736	1057	...	1303	...	1622	...	2221	2226
Sofia 1500 a.	...	|	|	...	|	...	|	...	0546	|
Varna 1500 a.	...	0808	1130	...	1335	...	1655	...	...	2250

D – 🛌 and [2] Sofia (**2627**) - Poveljanovo (**2637**) - Dobrich.
E – 🛌 and [2] Dobrich (**2636**) - Poveljanovo (**2626**) - Sofia.

BDŽ *2nd class only* SVISHTOV - LEVSKI - TROJAN 1545

km											
0	**Svishtov** d.	0445	...	0750	...	...	1200	...	1520	...	1825
48	**Levski** a.	0539	...	0844	...	...	1254	...	1614	...	1919
48	**Levski** d.	...	0600	...	1210	...	...	...	...	...	...
96	Lovech d.	...	0657	...	1307	...	...	...	...	...	...
131	**Trojan** a.	...	0755	...	1405	...	...	...	...	...	...

Trojan d.	...	...	0820	...	...	...	1420	...	...	...
Lovech d.	...	...	0918	...	...	...	1518	...	...	...
Levski a.	...	...	1015	...	...	...	1615	...	...	...
Levski d.	0610	...	...	1035	...	1345	...	1650	...	2000
Svishtov a.	0704	...	...	1129	...	1439	...	1744	...	2054

Most trains 2nd class only (SOFIA -) PLOVDIV - DIMITROVGRAD - SVILENGRAD and PODKOVA 1550

km						1611 [R]			1613 [R]		493 A [R]	8657 V [R]
0	*Sofia* 1500 d.	...	...	...	...	0822	...	...	1500	...	1845	2055
156	**Plovdiv** ◧ d.	...	0530	0705	0930	1119	1305	1435	1821	1925	2142	2349
202	Parvomaj ◧ d.	...	0623	0754	1018	1200	1355	1529	1905	2013	2223	0025
234	**Dimitrovgrad** ◧ a.	...	0654	0825	1049	1217	1423	1557	1924	2041	2241	0042
234	**Dimitrovgrad** d.	0445	0656	...	1054	1219	1425	1558	1925	...	2303	...
257	Haskovo d.	0511	|	...	|	|	1453	|	|	...	|	...
321	Kârdzhali d.	0656	|	...	|	|	1645	|	|	...	|	...
335	**Momchilgrad** d.	0716	|	...	|	|	1708	|	|	...	|	...
353	Podkova a.	0740	|	...	|	|	1730	|	|	...	|	...
299	**Svilengrad** ⊞ a.	...	0753	...	1150	1306	...	1700	2010	...	2350	...
	Kapıkule 1573 ⊞ a.	...	...	...	...	...	...	...	...	...	0105	...
	Halkalı 1573 a.	...	...	...	...	...	...	...	...	...	0956	...

	8656 V [R]		1612 [R]					1614 [R]			492* A [R]
Halkalı 1573 d.	...	...	...	...	...	...	...	...	...	...	2000
Kapıkule 1573 ⊞ d.	...	...	...	...	...	...	...	...	...	...	0320
Svilengrad ⊞ d.	...	...	0605	...	0815	...	1155	1620	...	...	0425
Podkova d.	...	...	|	...	|	0745	|	|	1735	...	|
Momchilgrad d.	...	...	|	...	|	0808	|	|	1800	...	|
Kârdzhali d.	...	...	|	...	|	0828	|	|	1821	...	|
Haskovo d.	...	...	|	...	|	1014	|	|	2009	...	|
Dimitrovgrad a.	...	...	0654	...	0910	1042	1257	1707	2035	...	0507
Dimitrovgrad ◧ d.	0455	0610	0655	0740	0921	...	1259	1712	...	2045	0527
Parvomaj ◧ d.	0515	0639	0713	0809	0954	...	1331	1730	...	2113	0449
Plovdiv ◧ a.	0559	0725	0753	0900	1043	...	1425	1812	...	2202	0622
Sofia 1500 a.	0900	...	1050	...	...	...	...	2112	...	...	0948

A – SOFYA EXPRESS – [2] Sofia - Svilengrad and v.v.; 🛌 and 🛏 Sofia - Halkalı and v.v. Seasonal through cars run Bucureşti - Halkalı and v.v June 13 - October 13 (see Table **61**).
V – Conveys 🛌 and [12] Varna - Stara Zagora - Dimitrovgrad - Plovdiv - Sofia and v.v. (see Tables **1500** and **1525**).
* – Between Dimitrovgrad and Sofia this train is attached to train **1620**.
◧ – Additional trains: From Plovdiv to Dimitrovgrad at 1730. From Dimitrovgrad to Plovdiv at 1125, 1500, 1725.

BDŽ SOFIA - KJUSTENDIL, PETRICH and KULATA 1560

km		2	2	5611	2	6621	2	5613	2	5615	2	5617	5621
0	**Sofia** d.	...	0525	0730	...	0830	1020	1235	1440	1630	1725	1810	1930
9	Gorna Banja ⊡ d.		0540	0746	...	0847	1034	1250	1458	1644	1740	1826	1944
33	Pernik d.	...	0628	0829	...	0927	1111	1317	1534	1713	1820	1905	2020
48	Radomir d.	...	0646	0846	...	0943	1131	1333	1557	1728	1841	1924	2036
102	**Kjustendil** a.	...	|	|	...	1111	|	|	|	|	|	|	|
91	Dupnitsa d.	0625	0742	0931	...	...	1227	1417	1700	1807	1937	2012	2115
123	**Blagoevgrad** a.	0705	0826	0959	...	...	1310	1447	▬	1835	...	2047	2145
123	**Blagoevgrad** d.	0710	...	1005	...	...	...	1450	...	1840	...	...	...
186	Sandanski d.	0827	...	1117	...	...	...	1607	...	1956	...	...	...
197	General Todorov. a.	0838	...	1129	...	...	...	1619	...	2007	...	...	...
197	General Todorov. d.	0857	...	1142	1145	...	...	1632	1635	2018	...	...	...
207	**Petrich** a.	0910	...	1155	|	...	...	1645	|	2031	...	...	...
210	**Kulata** a.	...	...	...	1158	...	...	...	1648	...	...	...	...

	2	5620	2	5610	2	5612	2	5614	2	6622	5616
Kulata d.	...	...	0605		...	1105	1335	...	...	...	...
Petrich d.	...	...	|	0605	...	|	|	1340	...	...	1730
General Todorov a.	...	...	0618	0619	...	1118	1348	1354	...	...	1744
General Todorov d.	...	...	...	0630	...	1135	▬	1405	...	...	1755
Sandanski d.	...	...	...	0642	...	1146	...	1418	...	...	1808
Blagoevgrad a.	...	...	...	0752	...	1244	...	1530	...	...	1924
Blagoevgrad d.	...	0505	...	0800	0930	1245	1420	1540	...	...	1926
Dupnitsa d.	0430	0542	...	0830	1018	1316	1503	1615	1720	...	2012
Kjustendil d.	|	|	...	|	|	|	|	|	|	1830	|
Radomir d.	0527	0625	...	0908	1111	1356	1554	1656	1824	2004	2058
Pernik d.	0552	0651	...	0925	1135	1413	1612	1714	1849	2020	2114
Gorna Banja ⊡ a.	0630	0729	...	0953	1214	1440	1650	1748	1950	2052	2148
Sofia a.	0645	0744	...	1006	1230	1455	1704	1803	2005	2107	2203

⊡ – Gorna Banja Metro station, change for Sofia Metro Line 3.

☛ Additional journeys Radomir - Kjustendil and v.v.: **From Radomir** at 0717, 1135, 1400, 1600, 1845 and 2023. **From Kjustendil** at 0425, 0700, 0925, 1210, 1355 and 1545.

☛ For 🚌 services between Sofia and Thessaloniki (Greece) see Table **1460**.

TURKEY

Operator: Türkiye Cumhuryeti Devlet Demiryolları Taşımacılık (TCDDT). Services are operated by tcddtasimacilik.gov.tr

Services: YHT (high-speed) trains convey business and second class seating. Long distance trains convey a single class of seating known locally as 'Pullman' (shown as [1] in footnotes) which are gender specific and may also convey sleeping and/or couchette cars. Local trains convey 2nd class seating, shown as '2' in the train column. Descriptions of sleeping (🛏) and couchette (▬) cars appear on page 10. Reservation of seats (free of charge) is required for high-speed (*YHT*) and express trains.

Timings: Valid from **May 19, 2025**. Timetable amendments are possible at short notice, please confirm timings locally before travelling.

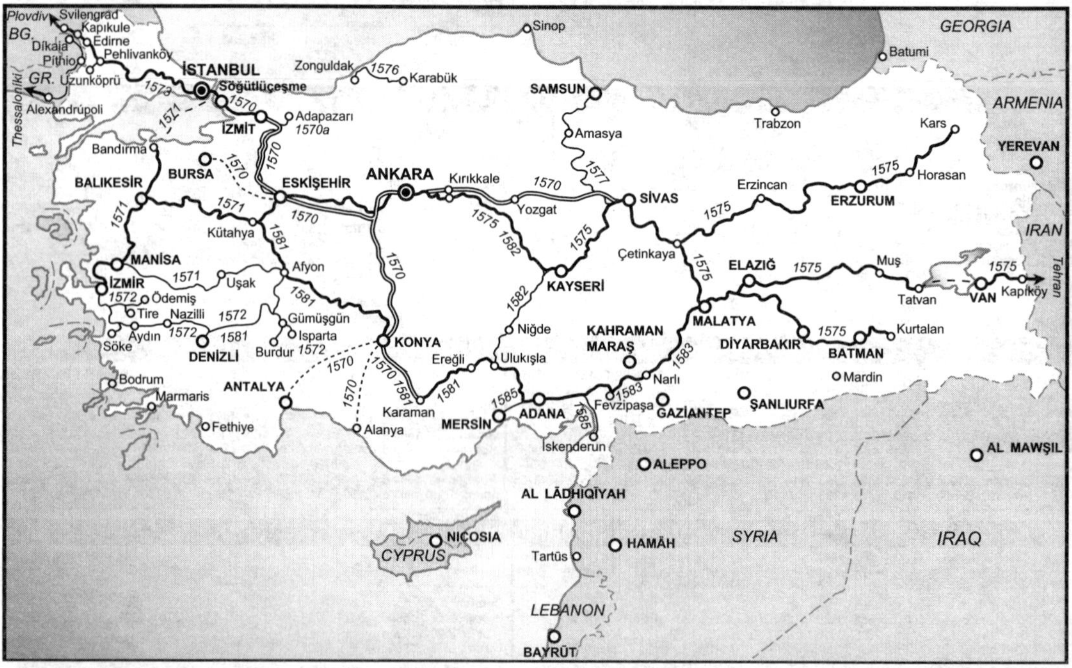

1570 İSTANBUL and KONYA - ANKARA - SIVAS; İSTANBUL - KONYA - KARAMAN

TCDDT

km	*YHT* trains: 🅁 and 🍷	*YHT* 81100 ⚒	*YHT* 81102 ⑦	*YHT* 81002	*YHT* 81302	*YHT* 81004	*YHT* 81030	*YHT* 81340	*YHT* 81458 ◇	*YHT* 81032	*YHT* 81006	*YHT* 81008	*YHT* 81304	*YHT* 81010	*YHT* 81012	*YHT* 81014	*YHT* 81016	*YHT* 81306	*YHT* 81018	*YHT* 81020	*YHT* 81022	*YHT* 81308	*YHT* 81024	*YHT* 81502	12002 ● 🅁
0	**Halkalı** **1550** d.	...	...	...	...	...	0705	0735	...	0835	...	...	...	...	...	...	...	...	...	...	...	...	...	...	2200
33	**İstanbul** Söğütluçesme d.	...	...	0600	0630	0720	0754	0824	0900	0924	1040	1110	1150	1220	1255	1410	1510	1545	1630	1730	1820	1900	1930	2040	2255
41	**İstanbul** Bostancı d.	...	...	0611	0641	|	0805	0835	|	0934	1052	1122	1201	1231	1307	1421	1522	1600	1641	1741	1831	1911	|	2051	2306
56	Pendik d.	...	...	0630	0700	0748	0824	0854	0928	0959	1111	1143	1220	1251	1326	1440	1546	1619	1706	1805	1850	1930	2003	2112	2333
75	Gebze **1570a** d.	...	...	0650	0720	|	0844	0918	|	1019	|	1203	1243	|	1346	|	1606	1639	|	1825	1918	1950	|	2137	2354
122	Izmit YHT **1570a** d.	...	...	0723	0753	|	0917	0951	1023	1052	1203	1236	1316	1343	1419	1532	1639	1712	1758	1858	1951	2023	2058	2210	0027
162	Arifiye **1570a** d.	...	...	0745	0815	|	0939	1013	1045	1115	|	1259	|	|	1442	|	1701	1735	|	1920	2014	2045	|	2232	0056
247	Bilecik YHT d.	...	...	0819	0849	|	1013	1048	|	1151	|	1334	|	|	1517	|	1735	1812	|	1955	2050	2119	|	2314	0224
279	Bozüyük YHT d.	...	...	0844	0913	|	1037	1112	|	1215	|	1358	|	|	1541	|	1755	1836	|	2019	2115	2143	|	2338	0255
322	**Eskişehir** ⊡ d.	0635	0730	0904	0931	1011	1057	1132	1158	1234	1335	1418	1448	1515	1601	1707	1819	1856	1930	2039	2135	2203	2230	2353	0338
677	Konya Selçuklu ⊙ .. **1581** a.	|	|	|	1110	|	|	1311	|	|	|	|	1627	|	|	|	|	2035	|	|	|	2342	|	...	|
721	Çumra **1581** d.	|	|	|	...	|	|	...	|	|	|	|	...	|	|	|	|	...	|	|	|	...	|	...	|
779	**Karaman** **1581** d.	|	|	|	...	|	|	...	|	|	|	|	...	|	|	|	|	...	|	|	|	...	|	...	|
	Polatli YHT d.	0723	0818	0952	...	|	1145	...	|	1322	|	1506	...	|	1649	1755	1907	...	|	2127	2223	...	|	...	0545‡
	Eryaman d.	0747	0842	1016	...	1120	1209	...	|	1346	1444	1530	...	1624	1713	1819	1931	...	2039	2151	2247	...	2339	...	|
	Ankara YHT a.	0759	0854	1028	...	1132	1221	...	1317	1358	1456	1542	...	1636	1725	1831	1943	...	2051	2203	2259	...	2351	...	0651

km	*YHT* trains: 🅁 and 🍷	*YHT* 81501	*YHT* 81001	*YHT* 81301	*YHT* 81003	*YHT* 81005	*YHT* 81007	*YHT* 81303	*YHT* 81009	*YHT* 81011	*YHT* 81013	*YHT* 81305	*YHT* 81015	*YHT* 81017	*YHT* 81019	*YHT* 81459 ◇	*YHT* 81031	*YHT* 81033	*YHT* 81341	*YHT* 81103	*YHT* 81021	*YHT* 81307	*YHT* 81023		22001 ● 🅁
0	**Ankara** YHT d.	...	0600	...	0650	0735	0840	...	1000	1055	1145	...	1310	1415	1510	1546	1650	1720	...	1750	1830	...	1930	...	2200
20	Eryaman d.	...	0614	...	0704	0749	0854	...	1014	1109	1159	...	1324	1429	1524	|	1704	1734	...	1804	1844	...	1944	...	|
84	Polatllı YHT d.	...	|	...	0726	|	0916	...	|	1131	|	...	1346	|	1546	|	|	1756	...	1826	1906	...	|	...	2308‡
	Karaman **1581** d.	...	|	...	|	|	|	...	|	|	|	...	|	|	|	|	|	|	...	|	|	...	|	...	|
	Çumra **1581** d.	...	|	...	|	|	|	...	|	|	|	...	|	|	|	|	|	|	...	|	|	...	|	...	|
	Konya Selçuklu ⊙ .. **1581** d.	...	|	0608	|	|	|	0903	|	|	|	1223	|	|	|	|	|	|	1717	|	|	1843	|	...	|
245	**Eskişehir** ⊡ d.	0640	0723	0750	0816	0858	1006	1044	1125	1221	1308	1405	1436	1539	1636	1707	1813	1846	1858	1911	1956	2024	2053	...	0124
287	Bozüyük YHT d.	0656	|	0807	0832	|	1023	|	|	1238	|	1421	1452	|	1654	|	|	1902	1914	...	2013	|	|	...	0204
320	Bilecik YHT d.	0718	|	0829	0854	|	1045	|	|	1301	|	1444	1514	|	1716	|	|	1924	1937	...	2036	|	|	...	0243
405	Arifiye **1570a** d.	0751	|	0903	0927	|	1118	|	|	1335	|	1518	1547	|	1749	1813	|	1957	2011	...	2109	2131	|	...	0414
445	Izmit YHT **1570a** d.	0815	|	0925	0950	1026	1141	1213	1253	1358	1436	1545	1611	1707	1812	1835	1943	2020	2034	...	2132	2155	|	...	0440
491	Gebze **1570a** d.	0848	|	0957	1022	|	1213	1246	|	1430	|	1617	1643	|	1844	|	|	2052	2107	...	2204	2227	|	...	0513
511	Pendik d.	0909	0942	1022	1043	1124	1234	1314	1349	1453	1530	1642	1705	1759	1905	1929	2035	2113	2128	...	2225	2248	2310	...	0535
526	**İstanbul** Bostancı d.	0919	|	1039	1109	1148	1255	1340	1407	1510	1549	1700	1725	1817	1928	|	2055	2131	2146	...	2243	2311	|	...	0554
533	**İstanbul** Söğütlüçesme a.	0948	1007	1052	1122	1201	1307	1349	1421	1522	1558	1709	1741	1831	1941	1954	2104	2140	2155	...	2252	2320	2335	...	0611
567	**Halkalı** **1550** a.	...	...	...	...	...	...	...	...	...	...	...	...	...	...	...	2154	2232	2247	...	...	...	...	...	0702

KARAMAN - KONYA - ANKARA

Service until June 10. Due to engineering work there are no services between Karaman and Konya. 🚌 buses connect Konya with Konya Selçuklu.

km	*YHT* trains: 🅁 and 🍷	*YHT* 81200	*YHT* 81202	*YHT* 81270	*YHT* 81204	*YHT* 81206	YHT 81272	*YHT* 81208 ⑤–⑦		
0	**Karaman** **1581** d.	...	...	...	...	...	...	...	...	...
58	Çumra **1581** d.	...	...	...	...	...	...	...	...	...
102	**Konya** **1581** a.	...	...	...	...	...	...	...	...	...
	Konya ⊙ **1581** d.	...	...	...	...	...	...	...	...	...
106	Konya Selçuklu d.	0633	0933	1157	1533	1743	2112	2143	...	...
327	Polatli YHT d.	0734	1034	1258	1634	1844	2213	2239	...	...
397	Eryaman d.	0758	1058	1322	1658	1908	2237	2303	...	...
417	**Ankara** YHT a.	0810	1110	1334	1710	1920	2249	2315	...	...

YHT trains: 🅁 and 🍷	*YHT* 81271	*YHT* 81201	*YHT* 81203	*YHT* 81273	*YHT* 81205	*YHT* 81207 ⑤–⑦	*YHT* 81209		
Ankara YHT d.	0630	0900	1225	1630	1810	2030	2110	...	...
Eryaman d.	0644	0914	1239	1644	1824	2044	2124	...	...
Polatllı YHT d.	0706	0936	1301	1706	1846	2106	2146	...	...
Konya Selçuklu a.	0809	1039	1404	1809	1949	2209	2249	...	...
Konya ⊙ **1581** a.	...	...	...	...	...	...	...	...	...
Konya **1581** d.	...	...	...	...	...	...	...	...	...
Çumra **1581** d.	...	...	...	...	...	...	...	...	...
Karaman **1581** a.	...	...	...	...	...	...	...	...	...

FOR ANKARA - SIVAS AND FOOTNOTES SEE NEXT PAGE →

TCDDT İSTANBUL and KONYA - ANKARA - SIVAS; İSTANBUL - KONYA - KARAMAN 1570

ANKARA - SIVAS

km	YHT trains: 🅁 and 🍷	YHT 81402		YHT 81458		YHT 81404				
	İstanbul Söğütlüçesme d.	...	...	0900	...	...	...	...	...	...
0	**Ankara** YHT d.	0700	...	1322	...	1840	...	...	...	...
75	Kırıkkale YHT d.	0737	...	1354	...	1917	...	...	...	...
168	Yerköy YHT d.	0815	...	|	...	1955	...	...	...	...
203	Yozgat YHT d.	0837	...	1449	...	2017	...	...	...	...
232	Sorgun YHT d.	0853	...	|	...	2033	...	...	...	...
359	Yildizeli YHT ⊗ d.	0945	...	1547	...	2125	...	...	...	...
405	**Sivas** a.	1020	...	1622	...	2200	...	...	...	...

YHT trains: 🅁 and 🍷	YHT 81401		YHT 81459		YHT 81403				
Sivas d.	0710	...	1255	...	1750	...	...	...	...
Yildizeli YHT ⊗ d.	0733	...	1318	...	1813	...	...	...	...
Sorgun YHT d.	0819	...	|	...	1859	...	...	...	...
Yozgat YHT d.	0835	...	1410	...	1915	...	...	...	...
Yerköy YHT d.	0852	...	|	...	1932	...	...	...	...
Kırıkkale YHT d.	0930	...	1458	...	2010	...	...	...	...
Ankara YHT a.	1020	...	1541	...	2100	...	...	...	...
İstanbul Söğütlüçesme a.	...	...	1954	...	...	...	...	...	...

⊡ – 🚌 connections Eskişehir - Bursa and v.v (journey time 2 hrs 10 mins).
From Eskişehir at 0901, 1115, 1445 and 1920. **From Bursa** at 0830, 1145, 1530 and 1755.
⊙ – 🚌 connections Konya - Alanya and v.v (journey time 4 hrs 30 mins - 5 hrs).
From Konya at 0850, 1420 and 2020. **From Alanya** at 1000 and 1200.
🚌 connections Konya - Antalya and v.v (journey time 5 hrs 15 mins - 6 hrs).
From Konya at 1130 and 1720. **From Antalya** 0100, 1300, 1500 and 2359.
⊗ – 🚌 connections Yildizeli - Tokat and v.v (journey time 1 hr).
From Yildizeli at 1159, 1549 and 2224. **From Tokat** 0606, 1156 and 1636.

◇ – To / from Sivas.
● – ANKARA EKSPRESİ – Conveys 🛏, [1] and ✕
‡ – Departs from Polatli town station.

Suburban services run Halkalı - İstanbul - Gebze via the 1.4 km Marmaray Tunnel at least every 15 minutes 0600 - 2230. Route (with journey time): Halkalı (0) - Yenikapi (32) - Sirkeci (35) - Söğütlüçesme (46) - Pendik (80) - Gebze (108).

TCDDT GEBZE - IZMIT - ADAPAZARI 1570a

km		12602		12604		12606		12608		12610		12612
0	**Gebze** d.	0730	...	1100	...	1315	...	1504	...	1730	...	2050
30	Yarımca d.	0755	...	1124	...	1339	...	1528	...	1754	...	2114
47	**Izmit** YHT d.	0808	...	1138	...	1352	...	1541	...	1807	...	2127
80	Sapanca d.	0836	...	1207	...	1420	...	1609	...	1832	...	2152
88	Arifiye d.	0844	...	1216	...	1428	...	1617	...	1841	...	2201
95	**Adapazarı** a.	0858	...	1229	...	1442	...	1631	...	1854	...	2214

	12601		12603		12605		12607		12609		12611
Adapazarı d.	0625	...	0955	...	1325	...	1510	...	1740	...	2100
Arifiye d.	0639	...	1008	...	1340	...	1524	...	1753	...	2113
Sapanca d.	0646	...	1015	...	1347	...	1531	...	1800	...	2120
Izmit YHT d.	0714	...	1043	...	1417	...	1602	...	1828	...	2147
Yarımca d.	0727	...	1056	...	1430	...	1615	...	1841	...	2200
Gebze a.	0749	...	1118	...	1452	...	1637	...	1903	...	2222

☛ Suburban Marmaray services run central İstanbul - Gebze via the 1.4 km Marmaray Tunnel at least every 15 minutes 0600 - 2230.

TCDDT ESKIŞEHIR, BANDIRMA and AFYON - IZMIR 1571

km		32008 A	22006 B	32604	32606	32004 D	72018 E	32610	32002 C	72610	72606
	Ankara **1570** d.	...	2000	...	...	...	...	...	...	...	...
0	**Eskişehir** 1581 d.	...	2338	...	...	...	0905	...	...	...	2000
77	Kütahya 1581 d.	...	0052	...	...	...	1021	...	...	1630	2115
127	Tavşanlı d.	...	0137	...	...	...	1105	...	...	1722	2204
‡	**Bandirma** Şehir d.	...	|	...	...	0800	|	...	1640	|	...
331	Balikesir d.	...	0518	...	...	0943	1445	...	1823	2100	...
386	Savaştepe d.	...	0607	...	...	1038	1542	...	1920	...	...
413	Soma d.	...	0633	...	...	1106	1607	...	1945	...	...
454	Akhisar d.	...	0709	...	...	1145	1646	...	2020	...	...
◇	**Afyon** 1581 d.	2332	|	...	...	|	|	...	|	...	...
◇	Uşak d.	0205	|	...	0620	|	|	1630	|	...	...
◇	Alaşehir d.	0426	|	0710	0837	|	|	1845	|	...	...
506	Manisa d.	0608	0756	0905	1032	1235	1739	2039	2107	...	...
572	**Izmir** Basmane a.	0740	0927	1037	1201	1404	1916	2213	2240	...	...

	72601	72609	32011 E	32601	32001 C	32605	32607	32003 D	22005 B	32007 A
Izmir Basmane d.	...	...	0655	0730	0855	1305	1515	1605	1905	2005
Manisa d.	...	...	0831	0906	1025	1437	1651	1738	2037	2140
Alaşehir d.	...	...	|	1057	|	1625	1844	|	|	2322
Uşak d.	...	...	|	1307	|	...	2054	|	|	0214
Afyon 1581 a.	...	...	|	...	|	...	...	|	|	0437
Akhisar d.	...	...	0927	...	1109	...	...	1822	2123	...
Soma d.	...	...	1011	...	1146	...	...	1857	2200	...
Savaştepe d.	...	...	1037	...	1209	...	...	1921	2224	...
Balikesir d.	...	0645	1150	...	1304	...	...	2018	2326	...
Bandirma Şehir a.	...	|	|	...	1444	...	...	2158	|	...
Tavşanlı d.	0600	1021	1525	...	...	...	...	...	0257	...
Kütahya 1581 d.	0650	1124	1611	...	...	...	...	...	0345	...
Eskişehir 1581 a.	0804	...	1721	...	...	...	...	...	0454	...
Ankara **1570** a.	...	...	...	...	...	...	...	...	0846	...

⛴ Istanbul - Bandirma

İstanbul Deniz Otobüsleri *

	Ⓐ		⑥⑦							
İstanbul Kadiköy ⊖ d.	1130	...	1200	...	1900	...	...	...	...	...
İstanbul Yenikapı ⊖ d.	1200	...	1230	...	1930	...	...	...	...	...
Bandirma Şehir a.	1435	...	1505	...	2205	...	...	...	...	...

	Ⓐ		⑥⑦							
Bandirma Şehir d.	0745	...	0830	...	1530	...	...	...	...	...
İstanbul Yenikapı ⊖ a.	1025	...	1110	...	1810	...	...	...	...	...
İstanbul Kadiköy ⊖ a.	1035	...	1120	...	1820	...	...	...	...	...

A – KONYA MAVI TRENİ – 🛏 [1] and ✕ Izmir - Konya and v.v.
B – IZMIR MAVI TRENİ – 🛏 [1] and ✕ Izmir - Ankara and v.v.
C – 6 EYLÜL EKSPRESİ – [1] Izmir - Balikesir - Bandirma and v.v.
D – 17 EYLÜL EKSPRESİ – [1] Izmir - Balikesir - Bandirma and v.v.
E – EGE EKSPRESİ – [1] Izmir - Eskişehir and v.v.
‡ – Bandirma Şehir - Balıkesir *100 km*.
◇ – Afyon - Manisa : *355 km*. Uşak - Manisa : *220 km*. Alaşehir - Manisa : *103 km*.
⊖ – **Kadiköy** is on the Asian side of İstanbul; **Yenikapı** is on the European side.
* – İstanbul Deniz Otobüsleri. ✆ +90 (212) 455 6900. www.ido.com.tr

TCDDT IZMIR - TIRE, ÖDEMIŞ, SÖKE, DENIZLI and ISPARTA 1572

km		32743	32721	32701	32703	32723	32751	32013 H	32725	32707	32739	32753	32709	32745	32727	32755	32711	32729	32713	32757		32731		32015 G
0	**Izmir** Basmane ⊡ d.	...	0635	0700	0835	0900	1035	1000	1220	1235	1300	1400	1410	...	1435	1620	1645	1730	1755	1910	...	2120	...	2310
18	Adnan Menderes ✈ ⊡ d.	...	0700	0723	0858	0923	1100	1024	1247	1258	1324	1423	1435	...	1458	1647	1711	1759	1824	1936	...	2147	...	2336
48	Torbalı ⊡ d.	...	0726	0753	0923	0950	1126	1054	1317	1323	1352	1454	1500	...	1528	1719	1742	1836	1857	2010	...	2215	...	0006
86	Çatal d.	...	0822	|	|	1044	1223	|	1413	|	|	1542	|	...	1623	1807	|	1934	|	2056	...	2304	...	|
96	**Tire** a.	...	|	|	|	|	1239	|	|	|	|	1557	|	...	|	1823	|	|	|	2111	...	|	...	|
111	**Ödemiş** Gar a.	...	0857	|	|	1114	...	|	1446	|	|	...	|	...	1653	...	|	2009	|	...	...	2334	...	|
112	**Ödemiş** Şehir a.	...	0903	|	|	1120	...	|	1453	|	|	...	|	...	1659	...	|	2015	|	...	...	2340	...	|
77	Selçuk d.	...	...	0831	0956	...	...	1131	...	1354	1429	...	1531	...	...	...	1813	...	1936	...	...	...	...	0038
	Söke d.	0630	...	|	|	...	...	|	...	|	|	...	|	1640	...	...	|	...	|	...	...	...	...	|
99	Ortaklar d.	0659	...	0905	1027	...	...	1207	...	1425	1503	...	1603	1709	...	...	1844	...	2007	...	...	...	...	0112
130	Aydin d.	0732	...	0939	1058	...	...	1241	...	1456	1538	...	1634	1742	...	...	1919	...	2039	...	...	...	...	0144
175	Nazilli d.	0825	...	1033	1154	...	...	1336	...	1546	1631	...	1734	1836	...	...	2014	...	2131	...	...	...	...	0231
260	**Denizli** d.	0952	...	1202	1340	...	...	1519	...	1719	...	...	1907	2004	...	...	2141	...	2258	...	...	...	...	0412
376	Dinar d.	...	...	...	...	...	...	1727	...	...	...	...	...	...	...	...	...	...	...	...	...	...	...	0617
390	Karakuyu d.	...	...	...	...	...	...	1745	...	...	...	...	...	...	...	...	...	...	...	...	...	...	...	0635
423	Gümüşgün d.	...	...	...	...	...	...	1818	...	...	...	...	...	...	...	...	...	...	...	...	...	...	...	0710
447	Burdur a.	...	...	...	...	...	...	1832	...	...	...	...	...	...	...	...	...	...	...	...	...	...	...	|
452	**Isparta** a.	...	...	...	...	...	...	1937	...	...	...	...	...	...	...	...	...	...	...	...	...	...	...	0735

km		32722	32752	32702	32724	32754	32704	32744	32726	32706	32728	32708	32756	32730	32710	32758	72012 H	32732	32746	32714		32716		72016 G
	Isparta d.	...	...	...	...	...	...	...	...	...	...	...	...	...	...	...	0950	...	...	...	...	...	...	2205
	Burdur d.	...	...	...	...	...	...	...	...	...	...	...	...	...	...	...	1050	...	...	...	...	...	...	|
	Gümüşgün d.	...	...	...	...	...	...	...	...	...	...	...	...	...	...	...	1021	...	...	...	...	...	...	2233
	Karakuyu d.	...	...	...	...	...	...	...	...	...	...	...	...	...	...	...	1153	...	...	...	...	...	...	2306
	Dinar d.	...	...	...	...	...	...	...	...	...	...	...	...	...	...	...	1218	...	...	...	...	...	...	2325
	Denizli d.	...	...	0425	...	...	0535	0630	...	0830	...	1015	...	...	1220	...	1437	...	...	1600	...	1840	...	0244
	Nazilli d.	...	...	0556	...	...	0706	0801	...	1006	...	1149	...	...	1404	...	1609	...	1705	1736	...	2015	...	0314
	Aydin d.	...	...	0648	...	...	0758	0854	...	1057	...	1240	...	...	1455	...	1701	...	1810	1831	...	2105	...	0403
0	Ortaklar d.	...	...	0719	...	...	0828	0927	...	1135	...	1310	...	...	1525	...	1735	...	1845	1904	...	2136	...	0436
22	**Söke** a.	...	...	|	...	...	|	0955	...	|	...	|	...	...	|	...	|	...	1912	|	...	|	...	|
	Selçuk d.	...	...	0750	...	...	0901	...	...	1158	...	1341	...	...	1557	...	1810	...	...	1935	...	2209	...	0511
	Ödemiş Şehir d.	0505	...	|	0715	...	|	...	0940	|	1145	|	...	1520	|	...	|	1820	...	|	...	|	...	|
	Ödemiş Gar d.	0509	...	|	0719	...	|	...	0945	|	1150	|	...	1525	|	...	|	1825	...	|	...	|	...	|
	Tire d.	|	0625	|	|	0800	|	...	|	|	|	|	1330	|	|	1605	|	|	...	|	...	|	...	|
	Çatal d.	0545	0640	|	0751	0821	|	...	1018	|	1224	|	1346	1558	|	1624	|	1905	...	|	...	|	...	|
	Torbalı ⊡ d.	0641	0729	0829	0852	0917	0932	...	1114	1230	1320	1415	1434	1653	1630	1720	1842	2013	...	2008	...	2240	...	0544
	Adnan Menderes ✈ ⊡ d.	0710	0758	0858	0922	0946	0958	...	1145	1259	1346	1446	1500	1722	1658	1746	1910	2047	...	2034	...	2306	...	0610
	Izmir Basmane ⊡ a.	0733	0824	0924	0948	1012	1024	...	1212	1324	1409	1512	1524	1748	1724	1812	1936	2112	...	2100	...	2328	...	0634

G – GÖLLER EKSPRESİ – Conveys [1].
H – GÜLLER EKSPRESİ – Conveys [1].
⊡ – IZBAN suburban trains operate Izmir - (Alsancak) - Torbalı and v.v. 0545 - 2359.

1573 KAPIKULE - EDIRNE - HALKALI (İSTANBUL) TCDDT BDŽ

km		493 12504		12710		12734		12712	
		A							
		R		R		R		R	
	Sofia **1500** d.	1845	...	...	...	...	...	...	...
	Plovdiv **1550** d.	2142	...	...	...	...	...	...	...
0	**Kapıkule** 🏛 d.	0400	...	...	...	...	...	...	...
20	**Edirne** d.	|	...	0850	...	...	...	1715	...
	Uzunköprü ● d.	|	...	|	...	1700	...	|	...
76	Pehlivanköy d.	|	...	0955	...	1718	...	1823	...
147	Muratlı d.	|	...	1134	...	1852	...	1959	...
173	Çorlu d.	|	...	1208	...	1926	...	2035	...
197	Çerkezköy d.	0813	...	1248	...	2007	...	2116	...
250	Çatalca d.	|	...	1351	...	2117	...	2222	...
274	Ispartakule d.	|	...	1413	...	2139	...	2245	...
284	**Halkalı** ⊡ a.	0956	...	1427	...	2153	...	2259	...

km		12711		12733		12713		12503 492		
								A§		
		R		R		R		R		
	Halkalı ⊡ d.	0840	...	1055	...	1805	...	2000	...	...
	Ispartakule d.	0856	...	1110	...	1821	...	|	...	...
	Çatalca d.	0921	...	1136	...	1848	...	|	...	...
	Çerkezköy d.	1028	...	1246	...	2003	...	2200	...	...
	Çorlu d.	1101	...	1321	...	2036	...	|	...	...
	Muratlı d.	1137	...	1355	...	2111	...	|	...	...
0	Pehlivanköy d.	1310	...	1530	...	2247	...	|	...	...
20	Uzunköprü ● a.	|	...	1546	...	|	...	|	...	...
	Edirne d.	1413	...	...	...	2350	...	|	...	...
	Kapıkule 🏛 a.	...	...	...	...	...	...	0209	...	...
	Plovdiv **1550** a.	...	...	...	...	...	...	0615	...	...
	Sofia **1500** a.	...	...	...	...	...	...	0948	...	...

A – SOFYA EXPRESS – 🛏 and 🛏 Sofia - Halkalı and v.v. Seasonal through cars run Bucureşti - Halkalı and v.v June 13 to October 13 (see Table **61**).

§ – Attached to train **1620** between Plovdiv and Sofia (see Table **1550**).

● – Uzunköprü rail station is in the village of Demirtaş approximately 5 km from Uzunköpru town.

⊡ – Frequent Maramary suburban services (at least every 15 minutes) operate Halkalı - İstanbul - Gebze and v.v. See shaded panel below Table **1570**.

1575 ANKARA - SIVAS, KARS, KURTALAN, TATVAN and TEHRAN TCDDT

km				52602	22012	22014	22010	22018		42044	
				②⑤⑦	②⑦	△		④⑥		R	
					B	A	D	E		c	
0	**Ankara 1570 1582** d.	...	...	...	1120	1120	1800	1910	...	...	...
43	Elmadağ **1582** d.	...	...	...	1213	1213	1853	2004	...	...	...
92	Kırıkkale **1582** d.	...	...	...	1313	1313	1953	2104	...	...	...
203	Yerköy **1582** d.	...	...	...	1509	1509	2145	2256	...	...	...
379	Kayseri d.	...	...	...	1920	1920	0106	0231	...	...	...
602	**Sivas** **1570** a.	...	...	...	2251	2251	0440	0557	...	...	...
602	**Sivas** d.	...	...	...	2311	2311	0456	0618	0725	1655	1745
710	Çetinkaya d.	...	...	...	0050	0050	0644	0758	0857	1818	1927
779	Divriği d.	0535	1545	...	|	|	0818	|	1014	|	2044
935	Erzincan d.	0835	1847	...	|	|	1140	|	▬	|	...
1150	Erzurum d.	▬	▬	...	|	|	1609	|	...	|	...
1235	Horasan d.	...	...	...	|	|	1735	|	...	|	...
1307	Sarkamiş d.	...	...	...	|	|	1907	|	...	|	...
1365	**Kars** a.	...	...	...	|	|	2010	|	...	|	...
854	**Malatya** a.	...	...	...	0331	0331	...	1034	...	2052	...
854	**Malatya** d.	...	...	...	0356	0356	...	...	...	...	...
1107	Diyarbakir d.	0840	1800	...	|	1026	...	...	...	...	...
1198	Batman d.	1103	2023	...	|	1238	...	...	...	...	...
1267	**Kurtalan** a.	...	...	...	|	1419	...	...	...	...	...
973	**Elazığ** a.	...	...	...	0635	...	...	...	...	...	...
973	**Elazığ** d.	...	...	0705	0705	...	...	...	...	...	...
1043	Palu d.	...	...	0834	0835	...	...	...	...	...	...
1062	Beyhan d.	...	...	0855	0856	...	...	...	...	...	...
1106	Genç d.	...	...	0949	0948	...	...	...	...	...	...
1201	Muş d.	...	...	1204	1159	...	...	...	...	...	...
1295	**Tatvan** Gar a.	...	...	1355	1344	...	...	...	**52502**	...	...
1300	**Tatvan** Iskele a.	...	...	...	...	...	...	...	**427** *	...	...
0	**Van** Iskele d.	...	...	...	...	...	...	...	①④	...	...
3	**Van** Gar d.	...	...	...	...	...	...	...	2000	...	...
114	Kapiköy 🏛 d.	...	...	...	...	...	...	...	2351	...	...
120	Razi 🏛 d.	...	...	...	...	...	...	...	0250	...	...
342	Tabriz **4630** a.	...	...	...	...	...	...	...	0617	...	...
1078	**Tehran** **4630** a.	...	...	...	...	...	...	...	1830	...	...

		52043				52501	52019	92009	52013	52011	52601
		R				426 *	⑤⑦		▽	②④	①③⑥
		c				③⑦	E	D	A	B	
Tehran **4630** d.	...	...	...	...	...	1235	...	...	...	...	...
Tabriz **4630** d.	...	...	...	...	...	0135	...	...	...	...	...
Razi 🏛 d.	...	...	...	...	...	0730	...	...	...	...	...
Kapiköy 🏛 d.	...	...	...	...	...	0900	...	...	...	...	...
Van Gar a.	...	...	...	...	...	1100	...	...	...	...	...
Van Iskele a.	...	...	...	...	...	...	...	...	...	...	...
Tatvan Iskele d.	...	...	...	...	...	...	...	...	...	...	...
Tatvan Gar d.	...	...	...	...	...	...	...	...	...	1025	1030
Muş d.	...	...	...	...	...	...	...	...	...	1202	1207
Genç d.	...	...	...	...	...	...	...	...	...	1354	1404
Beyhan d.	...	...	...	...	...	...	...	...	...	1441	1456
Palu d.	...	...	...	...	...	...	...	...	...	1502	1519
Elazığ a.	...	...	...	...	...	...	...	...	...	1634	1651
Elazığ d.	...	...	...	...	...	...	...	...	...	1651	...
Kurtalan d.	...	...	...	...	...	...	...	...	0920	|	...
Batman d.	...	...	0530	1500	...	...	...	...	1105	|	...
Diyarbakir d.	...	...	0753	1723	...	...	...	...	1325	|	...
Malatya a.	...	...	▬	▬	...	...	...	...	1929	1929	...
Malatya d.	...	0810	...	...	...	...	1530	...	1949	1949	...
Kars d.	...	|	...	...	...	...	|	0800	|	|	...
Sarkamiş d.	...	|	...	...	...	...	|	0906	|	|	...
Horasan d.	...	|	...	...	...	...	|	1033	|	|	...
Erzurum d.	...	|	...	...	...	...	|	1214	|	|	...
Erzincan d.	...	|	0615	1400	...	...	|	1625	|	|	...
Divriği d.	0600	|	0920	1700	1730	...	|	1933	|	|	...
Çetinkaya d.	0718	1040	...	...	1853	...	1817	2108	2232	2232	...
Sivas a.	0846	1200	...	...	2021	...	1955	2241	0005	0005	...
Sivas **1570** d.	...	...	...	...	...	...	2018	2304	0028	0028	...
Kayseri d.	...	...	...	...	...	...	0010	0250	0428	0428	...
Yerköy **1582** d.	...	...	...	...	...	...	0345	0621	0805	0805	...
Kırıkkale **1582** d.	...	...	...	...	...	...	0540	0819	1003	1003	...
Elmadağ **1582** d.	...	...	...	...	...	...	0640	0920	1111	1111	...
Ankara.. **1570 1582** a.	...	...	...	...	...	...	0736	1013	1159	1159	...

A – GÜNEY EKSPRESİ – 🛏 🛏 (4 berth) 🚃 and ✕ Ankara - Sivas - Malatya - Diyarbakir - Kurtalan and v.v.

B – VANGÖLÜ EKSPRESİ – 🛏 🛏 (4 berth) 🚃 and ✕ Ankara - Sivas - Malatya - Elazığ - Tatvan and v.v.

D – DOĞU EKSPRESİ – 🛏 (4 berth) and ✕ Ankara - Sivas - Erzincan - Erzurum - Kars and v.v.

E – 4 EYLÜL MAVI TRENİ – 🛏 (4 berth) and 🚃 ✕ Ankara - Sivas - Malatya and v.v.

F – 🛏 (4 berth) 🚃 and ✕ Van - Tabriz - Tehra. and v.v.

c – Connects at Sivas to YHT high speed services to / from Ankara and Istanbul see table **1570**.

△ – ①③④⑤⑥ from Ankara.

▽ – ①③⑤⑥⑦ from Kurtalan.

* – Iranian Railways train number.

1576 KARABÜK - ZONGULDAK TCDDT

km		22641	22643	22645	22647		22642	22644	22646	22648
0	**Karabük** d.	0705	1300	1605	1810	**Zonguldak** d.	0730	1130	1330	1835
59	Gökçebey d.	0825	1420	1727	1930	Filyos d.	0812	1213	1412	1924
75	Çaycuma d.	0846	1443	1748	1955	Çaykuma d.	0845	1246	1444	1956
96	Filyos d.	0918	1515	1823	2027	Gökçebey d.	0906	1308	1505	2017
120	**Zonguldak** a.	1000	1556	1910	2110	**Karabük** a.	1025	1435	1626	2136

Additional local trains run Zonguldak - Gökçebey and v.v.:
From Zonguldak at 0925, 1635, 1735, 2035.
From Gökçebey at 0540, 0630, 1225, 1830.

1577 SIVAS - AMASYA - SAMSUN TCDDT

km		42631		42621		42622		42632
				①④⑥		②⑤⑦		
0	**Sivas** d.	...	...	0845	**Samsun** d.	0835	...	1730
53	Yildizeli d.	...	...	0935	Havza d.	1039	...	1933
186	Zile d.	...	...	1205	Suluova ✈ d.	1109	...	2006
205	Turhal d.	...	...	1224	**Amasya** d.	1145	...	2039
268	**Amasya** d.	0620	...	1346	Turhal d.	1300	...	...
295	Suluova ✈ d.	0654	...	1418	Zile d.	1322	...	...
315	Havza d.	0723	...	1443	Yildizeli d.	1549	...	...
401	**Samsun** a.	0927	...	1644	**Sivas** a.	1641	...	...

1581 ESKIŞEHIR - AFYON - DENIZLI & KONYA - ADANA TCDDT

For YHT (high-speed) services between Eskişehir, Konya and Karaman, see Table **1570**.

km			72007	72018	72602	72014	62006	72604	72608		72606	72006
							❦					
			A	E		P	T				t	C
0	**Eskişehir** **1571** d.	...	...	0905	1000	1110	...	1500	1745	...	2000	2338
77	Kütahya **1571** d.	...	...	1016	1113	1230	...	1610	1903	...	2110	0045
180	**Afyon** d.	...	0447	...	...	1445	...	...	2053	...	...	...
292	Karakuyu **1572** d.	...	|	...	...	1656	...	...	...	...	...	...
	Dinar **1572** d.	...	|	...	...	1723	...	...	...	...	...	...
	Denizli **1572** d.	...	|	...	...	1944	...	...	...	...	...	...
278	Akşehir d.	...	0618	...	...	...	...	...	...	...	...	...
452	**Konya** **1570** d.	0645	0910	...	...	...	1520	...	...	2025	...	...
496	Çumra **1570** d.	0725	...	...	...	...	1601	...	...	2105	...	...
554	Karaman **1570** d.	0801	...	...	...	...	1644	...	...	2141	...	...
641	Ereğli d.	...	...	...	...	...	1821	...	...	...	...	...
689	Ulukışla **1582** d.	...	...	...	...	...	1931	...	...	...	...	...
733	Pozantı **1582** d.	...	...	...	...	...	2022	...	...	...	...	...
796	Yenice **1582** d.	...	...	...	...	...	2137	...	...	...	...	...
822	**Adana** **1582** a.	...	...	...	...	...	2206	...	...	...	...	...

	72005		72601	72607	72603	72011	72013	72605	62005	72008	
									❦		
	C		t			E	P		T	A	
Adana **1582** d.	...	...	...	...	...	...	...	...	0730	...	...
Yenice **1582** d.	...	...	...	...	...	...	...	...	0804	...	...
Pozantı **1582** d.	...	...	...	...	...	...	...	...	0929	...	...
Ulukışla **1582** d.	...	...	...	...	...	...	...	...	1042	...	...
Ereğli d.	...	...	...	...	...	...	...	...	1133	...	...
Karaman **1570** d.	...	0650	...	...	...	...	...	...	1316	...	1745
Çumra **1570** d.	...	0728	...	...	...	...	...	...	1358	...	1823
Konya **1570** d.	...	0807	...	...	...	...	...	...	1436	1900	1902
Akşehir d.	...	...	...	...	...	...	...	...	...	2150	...
Denizli **1572** d.	...	...	...	...	...	...	0955	...	...	|	...
Dinar **1572** d.	...	...	...	...	...	...	1223	...	...	|	...
Karakuyu **1572** d.	...	...	...	...	...	...	1243	...	...	|	...
Afyon d.	...	...	...	0730	...	...	1459	...	...	2321	...
Kütahya **1571** d.	0345	...	0646	0920	1200	1611	1658	1800	...	...	...
Eskişehir **1571** a.	0454	...	0758	1030	1313	1721	1815	1913	...	...	...

A – KONYA MAVI TRENİ – 🛏 🚃 and ✕ Konya - Afyon - Izmir and v.v.

C – IZMIR MAVI TRENİ – 🛏 🚃 and ✕ Izmir - Balikesir - Eskişehir - Ankara and v.v.

E – EGE EKSPRESİ – 🚃 Izmir - Balikesir - Eskişehir and v.v.

P – PAMUKKALE EKSPRESİ – 🚃 Eskişehir - Afyon - Denizli and v.v.

T – TOROS EKSPRESİ – 🚃 Adana - Konya and v.v.

t – To / from Tavşanlı (Table **1581**).

❦ – Currently suspended.

TCDDT — ANKARA - KAYSERI - ADANA — 1582

km		22002 G		22012 B △	22014 C ▽	62006 T ❦		22010 D	22018 E ④⑥	
0	**Ankara** 1575 d.	...	...	1120	1120	...	...	1800	1910	...
43	Elmadağ 1575 d.	...	...	1213	1213	...	...	1853	2004	...
92	Kırıkkale 1575 d.	...	...	1313	1313	...	...	1953	2104	...
203	Yerköy 1575 d.	...	...	1509	1509	...	...	2145	2256	...
379	**Kayseri** 1575 a.	...	...	1845	1845	...	...	0051	0214	...
	Kayseri 1575 d.	0730	...	...	...	...	...	...	...	...
479	Niğde d.	0947	...	...	...	...	...	...	...	...
542	Ulukışla 1581 d.	1100	...	...	...	1931	...	...	...	...
590	Pozantı 1581 d.	1147	...	...	...	2022	...	...	...	...
651	Yenice 1581 d.	1309	...	...	...	2137	...	...	...	...
674	**Adana** 1581 d.	1338	...	...	...	2206	...	...	...	...

	62005 T ❦		62001 G	22019 E ①⑥		92009 D	22011 B △	22013 C ▽	
Adana 1581 d.	0730	...	1630	...	...	...	...	...	...
Yenice 1581 d.	0804	...	1700	...	...	...	...	...	...
Pozantı 1581 d.	0929	...	1809	...	...	...	...	...	...
Ulukışla 1581 d.	1042	...	1858	...	...	...	...	...	...
Niğde d.	...	...	2009	...	...	...	...	...	...
Kayseri a.	...	...	2227	...	...	...	...	...	...
Kayseri 1575 d.	...	...	...	0010	...	0250	0428	0428	...
Yerköy 1575 d.	...	...	...	0345	...	0621	0805	0805	...
Kırıkkale 1575 d.	...	...	...	0540	...	0819	1003	1003	...
Elmadağ 1575 d.	...	...	...	0648	...	0926	1111	1111	...
Ankara 1575 a.	...	...	...	0736	...	1013	1159	1159	...

B – VANGÖLÜ EKSPRESİ – 🛏 ▬ and [1] ✕ Ankara - Tatvan and v.v.
C – GÜNEY EKSPRESİ – 🛏 ▬ and [1] ✕ Ankara - Kurtalan and v.v.
D – DOĞU EKSPRESİ – 🛏 ▬ and [1] ✕ Ankara - Kars and v.v.
E – 4 EYLÜL MAVI TRENİ – ▬ and [1] ✕ Ankara - Malatya and v.v.
G – ERCIYES EKSPRESİ – [1] Kayseri - Adana and v.v.
T – TOROS EKSPRESİ – [1] Adana - Konya and v.v.

△ – Runs on ②⑦ from Ankara. Runs on ②④ from Tatvan.
▽ – Runs on ①③④⑤⑥ from Ankara.
Runs on ①③⑤⑥⑦ from Kurtalan.
❦ – Currently suspended.

TCDDT — ADANA - MALATYA - ELAZIĞ — 1583

km		62004 F			52003 F	
0	**Adana** 1585 d.	0900	...	**Elazığ** d.	0830	...
47	Ceyhan 1585 d.	0959	...	**Malatya** d.	1127	...
78	Toprakkale 1585 d.	1031	...	Doğanşehir d.	1248	...
141	Fevzipaşa d.	1212	...	Narlı d.	1532	...
210	Narlı d.	1316	...	Fevzipaşa d.	1652	...
335	Doğanşehir d.	1600	...	Toprakkale 1585 d.	1809	...
392	**Malatya** d.	1733	...	Ceyhan 1585 d.	1842	...
511	**Elazığ** a.	2012	...	**Adana** 1585 a.	1938	...

F – FIRAT EKSPRESİ – [1] Adana - Malatya - Elazığ and v.v.
SERVICE CURRENTLY SUSPENDED.

TCDDT — MERSIN - ADANA - ISKENDERUN — 1585

Service is currently suspended between Adana and Mersin due to engineering works.

km		62780			62782																				
0	**Mersin** d.	...	...	...	...	...	...	...	...	...	...	...	...	...	...	...	...	...	...	...	...	...	...	...	...
26	Tarsus d.	...	...	...	...	...	...	...	...	...	...	...	...	...	...	...	...	...	...	...	...	...	...	...	...
43	Yenice d.	...	...	...	...	...	...	...	...	...	...	...	...	...	...	...	...	...	...	...	...	...	...	...	...
68	**Adana** a.	...	...	...	...	...	...	...	...	...	...	...	...	...	...	...	...	...	...	...	...	...	...	...	...
	Adana d.	0733	...	...	1738	...	...	...	...	...	...	...	...	...	...	...	...	...	...	...	...	...	...	...	...
115	Ceyhan d.	0827	...	...	1832	...	...	...	...	...	...	...	...	...	...	...	...	...	...	...	...	...	...	...	...
146	Toprakkale d.	0909	...	...	1914	...	...	...	...	...	...	...	...	...	...	...	...	...	...	...	...	...	...	...	...
204	**Iskenderun** a.	1007	...	...	2012	...	...	...	...	...	...	...	...	...	...	...	...	...	...	...	...	...	...	...	...
		62781			62783																				
	Iskenderun d.	0730	...	...	1735	...	...	...	...	...	...	...	...	...	...	...	...	...	...	...	...	...	...	...	...
	Toprakkale d.	0830	...	...	1835	...	...	...	...	...	...	...	...	...	...	...	...	...	...	...	...	...	...	...	...
	Ceyhan d.	0914	...	...	1919	...	...	...	...	...	...	...	...	...	...	...	...	...	...	...	...	...	...	...	...
	Adana a.	1004	...	...	2010	...	...	...	...	...	...	...	...	...	...	...	...	...	...	...	...	...	...	...	...
	Adana d.	...	...	...	...	...	...	...	...	...	...	...	...	...	...	...	...	...	...	...	...	...	...	...	...
	Yenice d.	...	...	...	...	...	...	...	...	...	...	...	...	...	...	...	...	...	...	...	...	...	...	...	...
	Tarsus d.	...	...	...	...	...	...	...	...	...	...	...	...	...	...	...	...	...	...	...	...	...	...	...	...
	Mersin a.	...	...	...	...	...	...	...	...	...	...	...	...	...	...	...	...	...	...	...	...	...	...	...	...

GEORGIA and ARMENIA

Operators: **Georgian Railways (GR) / South Caucasus Railways (SCR).**

Services: Overnight trains convey sleeping and couchette cars and may not convey seating accommodation. Prior reservation is necessary except for travel by purely local trains. Higher fares are payable on Stadler services, indicated by note ⊠.

Timings: Schedules are the latest available June 1st, 2025. **Timetable amendments are possible at short notice, please confirm timings locally before travelling.**

GR South Caucasus Railway" SCR — YEREVAN - TBILISI - BATUMI — 1590

km		684		100 ⑤–⑦		202 C		686		682		372 A
0	**Yerevan** AR d.	0755	...	0915	...	1400	...	1425	...	1825	...	2130
154	Gyumri d.	1103	...	1125	...	1645	...	1730	...	2146	...	0013
216	Vanadzor d.	...	...	...	...	1809	...	...	...	...	...	0138
295	Ayrum 🏛 AR d.	...	...	...	...	2055	...	...	...	...	...	0415
299	Sadakhlo 🏛 GE d.	...	...	...	...	2220	...	...	...	...	...	0540
374	**Tbilisi** a.	...	...	...	...	0011	...	...	...	...	...	0735

	681		687		685		101 ⑤–⑦		371 B		201 D
Tbilisi d.	...	...	...	...	...	...	...	...	2020	...	2240
Sadakhlo 🏛 GE d.	...	...	...	...	...	...	...	...	2315	...	0138
Ayrum 🏛 AR d.	...	...	...	...	...	...	...	...	0040	...	0312
Vanadzor d.	...	...	...	...	...	...	...	...	0225	...	0447
Gyumri d.	0745	...	1155	...	1815	...	1940	...	0410	...	0625
Yerevan AR a.	1057	...	1505	...	2123	...	2150	...	0655	...	0859

km		614	806 J ⊠	802 ⊠	870	854			804 ⊠	874	812 K ⊠	202 C
0	**Tbilisi** d.	...	0630	0800	0820	0900	...	...	1710	1730	0030	0045
76	Gori d.	...	│	│	0922	1008	...	...	│	1832	│	│
120	Khashuri d.	...	│	│	1003	1049	...	...	│	1913	│	0255
183	Zestafoni d.	...	│	│	1155	1238	...	...	│	2105	│	0453
213	Rioni d.	...	│	│	1233	1319	1325	...	│	2138	│	│
221	Kutaisi 1 a.	...	│	│	│	│	1345	...	│	│	│	│
231	Kutaisi Airport ✈ d.	...	0951	1145	1250	1334	...	...	2055	2155	0415	│
244	Samtredia 1 d.	...	│	│	1308	1433	...	...	│	2213	│	0556
312	Poti a.	...	│	│	│	│	...	...	│	2337	│	│
316	Zugdidi a.	...	│	│	1508	│	...	...	│	...	│	│
326	Kobuleti d.	...	1118	1314	...	│	...	...	2224	...	0518	0732
328	Ozurgeti a.	0715	│	│	...	1618	...	...	│	...	│	│
343	**Batumi** a.	0933	1138	1335	...	...	...	...	2245	...	0605	0757

	811 K ⊠	873	803 ⊠	853		805 J ⊠	201 D	801 ⊠	869		613
Batumi d.	0045	...	0800	...	...	1420	1445	1655	...	...	2040
Ozurgeti d.	│	...	│	0840	...	│	│	│	...	...	2259
Kobuleti d.	0107	...	0828	│	...	1447	1522	1723	...	...	...
Zugdidi d.	│	...	│	│	...	│	│	│	1655	...	...
Poti d.	│	0700	│	│	...	│	│	│	│	...	...
Samtredia 1 d.	│	0830	│	1109	...	│	1658	│	1901	...	...
Kutaisi Airport ✈ d.	0239	0845	0954	1125	...	1618	│	1849	1916	...	...
Kutaisi 1 d.	│	│	│	│	1155	│	│	│	│	...	...
Rioni d.	│	0900	│	1140	1215	│	│	│	1931	...	...
Zestafoni d.	│	0928	│	1315	...	│	1813	│	2004	...	...
Khashuri d.	│	1113	│	1515	...	│	1953	│	2149	...	...
Gori d.	│	1153	│	1601	...	│	│	│	2228	...	...
Tbilisi a.	0602	1302	1317	1600	...	1928	2147	2217	2337	...	...

A – Even dates from Oct. 2. - June 10. 🛏 1, 2 cl. ▬ 3 cl. Yerevan - Tbilisi.
B – Uneven dates from Oct. 3 - June 11. 🛏 1, 2 cl. ▬ 3 cl. Tbilisi - Yerevan.
C – Even dates June 13 - Sept. 30. 🛏 1, 2 cl. ▬ 3 cl. Yerevan - Tbilisi - Batumi.
D – Uneven dates June 14 - Sept. 30. 🛏 1, 2 cl. ▬ 3 cl. Batumi - Tbilisi - Yerevan.
J – July 1–31.
K – ①⑥⑦.

⊠ – Stadler train. Higher fares.

AR – Armenia (UTC + 4).
GE – Georgia (UTC + 4).

TBILISI - TBILISI AIRPORT
Journey: 40 minutes.
From Tbilisi at 0755 and 1655.
From Tbilisi Airport at 0835 and 1740.

ROMANIA

SEE MAP PAGE 523

Operator: Societatea Natională de Transport Feroviar de Călători (CFR Călători): www.cfrcalatori.ro. Certain services are operated by private companies as shown in relevant tables.

Services: Trains convey 1st- and 2nd-class seating accommodation unless otherwise indicated. Sleeping- (🛏) and couchette (▬) cars are described on page 10. Faster long-distance trains are classified *IC* (Intercity), *IR* (Interregio), or *R-E* (Regional Express) shown in our tables with just the train number.

Timings: Valid **until December 13, 2025**. Note that holiday variations during the Christmas / New Year and Easter periods are not shown in our tables (please confirm timings locally if travelling during holiday periods). Alterations to schedules are possible at any time.
Warning! Cluj Napoca - Huedin - Oradea is closed for engineering works until further notice; rail replacement bus services operate (please check before travelling).

Tickets: Reservation is obligatory for travel by all CFR Călători services for which a train number is shown in the tables, and passengers boarding without a prior reservation are surcharged. CFR trains shown without numbers are slower stopping-services calling at all, or most stations.

1600 BUCUREŞTI - BRAŞOV - CLUJ NAPOCA / ORADEA / SIBIU / ARAD (- BUDAPEST)

km		360		74	77	72	366	1735 4004	1621		1645	531	521	346	406	1635 2105	1936	472	78	1942	1920	1641	1643	1914	1821
		S		C	C	T	H				c	🍷	🍷	D	B	en	t	R	M	⊕t	⊕t	⊗2	⊗2	⊕t	⊕
	Constanţa **1680** d.	...	...	...	...	...	...	...	...	...	...	...	...	...	...	1330	1400	...	...	1713	1800	...	...	2010	...
0	**Bucureşti** Nord ▷ d.	...	...	...	...	...	...	0611	1000	...	1300	1310	1310	1507	...	1647	1647	1758	1945	2002**b**	2102	2124	2124	2319	2345
59	Ploieşti Vest ▷ d.	...	...	...	...	...	...	0649	1046	...	1340	1349	1349	1546	...	1727	1727	1836	|	2049	|	2207	2207	|	|
121	Sinaia ▷ d.	...	...	...	...	...	...	0743	1140	...	1437	|	|	1637	...	1818	1818	1924	|	2139	|	2259	2259	|	|
140	Predeal ▷ d.	...	...	...	...	...	...	0808	1207	...	1505	|	|	1703	...	1845	1845	1950	|	2205	|	2324	2324	|	|
166	**Braşov** ▷ a.	...	...	...	...	...	...	0841	1241	...	1542	1529	1529	1737	...	1919	1919	2024	|	2240	|	2358	2358	|	|
166	**Braşov** d.	...	...	...	0700	...	0805	0854	1256	...	...	1534	1534	1746	1905	1937	...	2036	|	2309	|	0012	0013	|	|
294	**Sighişoara** **1622** d.	...	...	...	|	...	|	1231	|	...	...	|	|	2112	|	|	...	|	|	|	|	|	0346	|	|
333	Mediaş **1622** d.	...	...	...	|	...	|	1259	|	...	...	|	|	2137	|	|	...	|	|	|	|	|	0413	|	|
344	Copşa Mică **1622** d.	...	...	...	|	...	|	1308	|	...	...	|	|	|	|	|	...	|	|	|	|	|	0421	|	|
374	Blaj d.	...	...	...	|	...	◐	1329	|	...	...	|	|	2200	◐	|	...	|	◧	◐	▽	◐	0441	△	▽
395	Teiuş **1620** d.	...	...	...	|	...	|	1353	|	...	...	2009	2035	|	|	|	...	|	|	|	|	|	0502	|	|
408	Aiud **1620** d.	...	...	...	|	...	|	1415	|	...	...	|	|	|	|	|	...	|	|	|	|	|	0526	|	|
429	Războieni **1620** d.	...	...	...	|	...	|	1446	|	...	...	|	|	|	|	|	...	|	|	|	|	|	0555	|	|
446	Câmpia Turzii **1620** d.	...	...	...	|	...	|	1502	|	...	...	|	|	|	|	|	...	|	|	|	|	|	0612	|	|
497	**Cluj Napoca** **1620** a.	...	...	...	|	...	|	1557	|	...	...	2214	|	|	|	|	...	|	|	|	|	|	0711	|	|
497	**Cluj Napoca** d.	...	...	0836	|	...	|	1614	|	...	...	...	|	|	|	|	...	|	|	|	|	|	...	|	|
547	Huedin d.	...	...	|	|	...	|	|	|	...	...	...	|	|	|	|	...	|	|	|	|	|	...	|	|
649	**Oradea** **1625** d.	1035	...	|	|	...	|	|	|	...	...	...	|	|	|	|	...	|	|	|	|	|	...	|	|
	Baia Mare **1610/14** a.	|	...	|	|	...	|	2020	|	...	...	...	|	|	|	|	...	|	|	0850	|	0924	...	|	|
	Satu Mare **1610/25** a.	|	...	|	|	...	|	...	|	...	...	...	|	|	|	|	...	|	|	...	|	1056	...	|	|
§65	Făgăraş d.	|	...	|	0823	...	|	...	1416	...	...	...	|	|	|	2137	...	2201	|	...	|	...	...	|	|
§127	Podu Olt **1645** d.	|	...	|	|	...	|	...	1516	...	...	...	|	|	|	|	...	|	|	...	|	...	...	0702	|
§149	**Sibiu** **1645** d.	|	...	|	0953	...	|	...	1550	...	...	...	|	|	|	2315	...	2329	|	...	|	...	...	0753	|
§223	Sebeş Alba d.	|	...	|	1118	...	|	...	...	...	...	...	|	|	|	...	...	0055	|	...	|	...	...	...	|
	Alba Iulia d.	|	...	1108	|	...	|	...	...	...	...	...	2056	2221	|	...	...	|	|	...	|	...	...	...	|
§232	Vinţu de Jos **1620** d.	|	...	1117	1130	...	|	...	...	...	...	...	|	|	|	...	...	0107	|	...	|	...	...	...	|
§276	Simeria **1620** d.	|	...	1220	1220	...	|	...	...	...	...	...	|	2302	|	...	...	0149	|	...	0700	...	...	...	0955
§285	Deva **1620** d.	|	...	1230	1230	◧	|	...	...	...	...	...	2137	2311	|	...	...	0158	|	...	0709	...	...	...	1008
§433	**Arad** **1620** a.	|	...	1500	1500	1657	|	...	...	...	...	...	2356	0114	|	...	...	0409	0841	...	0932	...	...	...	1239
	Oradea **1625** a.	|	...	|	|	|	|	...	...	...	...	...	...	|	|	...	...	0806**g**	1153**h**	...	1230	...	...	...	...
	Budapest Keleti **1280** a.	1350**v**	...	1850	1850	2050	2300	...	...	...	...	...	...	0500	0955	...	...	0850	1250	...	...	...	...	...	...

	367	73	1912	75	76	1941		365	1822	1922	1642	1644	79	2100 1630	1930	407	473		347	522	532	4006 1734		1622	1646
	H	T	⊕s	C	C	⊕s		S	⊕n	⊕s	⊗	⊗	M	fn	t	B	R		D	🍷	🍷				c
Budapest Keleti **1280** d.	0640	0710	...	0910	0910	...	...	1340	...	...	...	...	1510	...	...	1740	1910	...	2305	...	...	...	...	...	...
Oradea **1625** d.	|	|	...	|	|	...	...	|	...	1430	...	...	1804**k**	...	...	|	|	...	|	...	...	...	...	...	...
Arad **1620** d.	|	1232	...	1430	1430	...	...	|	1710	1724	...	...	2057	...	...	|	0043	...	0436	0659	...	...	...	...	...
Deva **1620** d.	|	◧	...	1700	1700	...	...	|	1939	2019	...	...	|	...	...	|	0301	...	0650	0915	...	...	...	...	...
Simeria **1620** d.	|	...	...	1715	1732	...	...	|	1952	2037	...	...	|	...	...	|	0339	...	0725	|	...	...	...	...	...
Vinţu de Jos **1620** d.	|	...	...	1754	1809	...	...	|	|	|	...	...	|	...	...	|	0411	...	|	|	...	...	...	...	...
Alba Iulia d.	|	...	...	1806	|	...	...	|	|	|	...	...	|	...	...	|	|	...	0801	0955	...	...	...	...	...
Sebeş Alba d.	|	...	...	|	1822	...	...	|	|	|	...	...	|	...	...	|	0423	...	|	|	...	...	...	...	...
Sibiu **1645** d.	|	...	1838	|	1952	...	...	|	|	|	...	...	|	0342	...	|	0552	...	|	|	...	...	...	1635	...
Podu Olt **1645** d.	|	...	1916	|	|	...	...	|	|	|	...	...	|	|	...	|	|	...	|	|	...	...	...	1714	...
Făgăraş d.	|	...	|	|	2117	...	...	|	|	|	...	...	|	0528	...	|	0720	...	|	|	...	...	...	1816	...
Satu Mare **1610/25** d.	|	...	|	|	|	1320	...	|	|	|	1620	...	|	|	...	|	|	...	|	|	...	...	...	|	...
Baia Mare **1610/14** d.	|	...	|	|	|	1501	...	|	|	|	1750	...	|	|	...	|	|	...	|	|	...	0610	...	|	...
Oradea **1625** d.	|	...	|	|	|	|	...	1926**v**	|	|	|	...	|	|	...	|	|	...	|	|	...	|	...	|	...
Huedin d.	|	...	|	|	|	|	...	...	|	|	|	...	|	|	...	|	|	...	|	|	...	|	...	|	...
Cluj Napoca a.	|	...	|	2045	|	|	...	...	|	|	|	...	|	|	...	|	|	...	|	|	...	1005	...	|	...
Cluj Napoca **1620** d.	|	...	|	...	|	|	...	...	|	|	|	1944	|	|	...	|	|	...	|	|	0815	1022	...	|	...
Câmpia Turzii **1620** d.	|	...	|	...	|	|	...	...	|	|	|	2043	|	|	...	|	|	...	|	|	|	1124	...	|	...
Războieni **1620** d.	|	...	|	...	|	|	...	...	|	|	|	2102	|	|	...	|	|	...	|	|	|	1142	...	|	...
Aiud **1620** d.	|	...	|	...	|	|	...	...	|	|	|	2138	|	|	...	|	|	...	|	|	|	1217	...	|	...
Teiuş **1620** d.	|	...	|	...	|	|	...	...	|	|	|	2204	|	|	...	|	|	...	|	1044	1044	1237	...	|	...
Blaj d.	◐	...	△	...	|	◐	...	...	▽	▽	◐	2224	◧	|	...	◐	|	...	0826	|	|	1304	...	|	...
Copşa Mică **1622** d.	|	...	|	...	|	|	...	...	|	|	|	2243	|	|	...	|	|	...	|	|	|	1324	...	|	...
Mediaş **1622** d.	|	...	|	...	|	|	...	...	|	|	|	2252	|	|	...	|	|	...	0853	|	|	1335	...	|	...
Sighişoara **1622** d.	|	...	|	...	|	|	...	...	|	|	|	2322	|	|	...	|	|	...	0917	|	|	1405	...	|	...
Braşov a.	2306	...	|	...	2242	0105	...	...	|	|	0317	0254	|	0716	...	1000	0848	...	1249	1505	1505	1738	...	1934	...
Braşov ▷ d.	...	...	|	...	...	0117	...	...	|	|	0329	0329	|	0738	0738	...	0904	...	1254	1511	1511	1758	...	1955	1955
Predeal ▷ d.	...	...	|	...	...	0202	...	...	|	|	0413	0413	|	0815	0815	...	0941	...	1332	|	|	1843	...	2032	2032
Sinaia ▷ d.	...	...	|	...	...	0230	...	...	|	|	0438	0438	|	0841	0841	...	1008	...	1358	|	|	1910	...	2058	2058
Ploieşti Vest ▷ d.	...	...	|	...	...	0320	...	...	|	|	0537	0537	|	0935	0935	...	1057	...	1449	1652	1652	2004	...	2150	2150
Bucureşti Nord ▷ a.	...	...	0256	...	...	0406**b**	...	...	0532	0532	0617	0617	0936	1012	1012	...	1135	...	1526	1728	1728	2042	...	2230	2230
Constanţa **1680** a.	...	...	0611	...	...	0646	...	...	...	0843	...	...	...	1257	1257	...	...	...	...	...	...	...	...	...	...

SELECTED ADDITIONAL TRAINS BUCUREŞTI - BRAŞOV

	1631	1680	1732	1633	3003			536	3031	
						⊠	⊠	U✕		⊠
Constanţa **1680** d.	...	0530	...	...	...	...	...	1730	...	...
Bucureşti Nord d.	0715	0824	**p**	1221	1514	1540	1813	1954	2025	2044
Ploieşti Vest d.	0754	0902	1026	1301	1601	1619	1923	2033	2131	2152
Sinaia d.	0846	0951	1116	1354	1655	1707	2038	|	2228	2250
Predeal d.	0912	1016	1143	1421	1721	1734	2104	|	2257	2316
Braşov a.	0946	1050	1218	1457	1755	1807	2138	2210	2337	2350

	1628	538	1632	3002	3004	1634	1730	1636	3032	1638
		U✕			m			⑦		
Braşov d.	0442	0658	0915	1110	1317	1408	1730	1747	1854	2035
Predeal d.	0519	|	0952	1147	1355	1446	1807	1825	1936	2111
Sinaia d.	0545	|	1019	1214	1422	1515	1834	1851	2006	2137
Ploieşti Vest d.	0643	0836	1115	1313	1515	1614	1924	1947	2118	2230
Bucureşti Nord a.	0721	0914	1152	1359	1600	1658	**p**	2026	2220	2307
Constanţa **1680** a.	...	1136	...	...	1901	...	...	...	...	...

B – CORONA – 🛏 1, 2 cl., ▬ 2 cl., [2] Braşov - Dej - Carei - Debrecen - Budapest and v.v.
C – CLAUDIOPOLIS – FĂGĂRAS [12] Cluj Napoca - Simeria - Arad - Budapest and v.v.; also [2] Braşov - Sibiu - Simeria - Arad - Budapest and v.v.
D – DACIA - CORVIN – 🛏 1, 2 cl., ▬ 1, 2 cl., [2] Bucureşti - Arad - Budapest - Wien and v.v.
H – HARGHITA – [12] Braşov - Dej - Jibou - Carei - Debrecen - Budapest and v.v.
M – MUNTENIA – 🛏 1, 2 cl., ▬ 2 cl., [12] Bucureşti - Timişoara - Budapest and v.v.
R – ISTER – 🛏 1, 2 cl., ▬ 2 cl., [2] Bucureşti - Sibiu - Arad - Oradea / Budapest and v.v.
S – TRANSILVANIA – [12] Oradea - Biharkeresztes - Püspökladány and v.v.
T – TRAIANUS – [2] Craiova - Timişoara - Arad - Budapest and v.v.
U – TOMIS EXPRES – [12] Brasov - Bucureşti - Constanţa and v.v.

b – Bucureşti **Băneasa**.
c – Bucureşti - Braşov - Târgu Mureş and v.v. (Table **1610**).

e – Train **1584** Constanţa - Bucureşti.
f – Train **1585** Bucureşti - Constanţa.
g – Train **1743** Arad - Oradea (Table **1625**).
h – Train **1741** Arad - Oradea (Table **1625**).
k – Train **1744** Oradea - Arad (Table **1625**).
m – Train **1589** Bucureşti - Constanţa.
n – Not June 13 / 14 to Sept. 6 / 7.
p – From / to Galaţi via Ploieşti Sud (Table **1670**).
s – June 13 - Sept. 6.
t – June 14 - Sept. 7.
v – Change of trains at Püspökladány for Budapest.

◐ – Via Miercurea Ciuc (Table **1610**).
◧ – Via Timişoara (Table **1630**).
▷ – For additional trains Bucureşti - Braşov and v.v. see panel below main table.
△ – Via Râmnicu Vâlcea (Table **1645**).
▽ – Via Craiova and Târgu Jiu (Tables **1630** and **1635**).
⊠ – Operated by Regio Călători.
⊕ – 🛏 1, 2 cl., ▬ 2 cl., [12]
⊗ – 🛏 1, 2 cl., ▬ 2 cl., [2]
§ – Distance from Braşov.

BRAŞOV - TÂRGU MUREŞ / CLUJ NAPOCA / BAIA MARE 1610

For other trains from Bucureşti and Braşov to Cluj Napoca and Baia Mare / Satu Mare see Table **1600**.

km			366	1543			1645		406	1942	1641
		2	H✕	c 2	2	2		2	C✕	J🍷	D
	Bucureşti N **1600** d.	...	...	...	...	...	1300	...	...	2002**b**	2124
0	**Braşov** d.	0600	0805	1202	1237	...	1554	1604	1905	2309	0012
32	Sfântu Gheorghe d.	0647	0830	1233	1317	...	1623	1646	1936	2340	0053
95	Miercurea Ciuc d.	0822	0938	1332	1445	1555	1722	1918**d**	2039	0048	0151
103	Siculeni d.	0830	0947	1340	1456	1606	1735	1930	2050	0058	0202
150	Gheorghieni d.	...	1045	...	1614	1739	1832	2047	2145	0201	0259
228	Deda a.	...	1223	...	...	1953	2022	...	2321	0336	0436
228	Deda ▷ d.	...	1248	...	...	...	2042	...	2322	0348	0439
250	Reghin ▷ d.	...	|	...	...	...	2100	...	|	0428*	|
282	**Târgu Mureş** ▷ a.	...	|	...	...	...	2133	...	|	0501*	|
275	Sărăţel d.	...	1340	...	...	...	...	...	0014	0449	0541
286	Bistriţa Nord a.	...	|	...	...	...	...	...	|	|	0602*
300	Beclean pe Someş d.	...	1402	...	...	...	...	...	0036	0511	0611
324	Dej Călători **1614** d.	...	1449	...	...	...	...	...	0121	0555	0653
383	**Cluj Napoca** a.	...	|	...	...	...	...	...	|	0812*	|
401	Jibou **1614** d.	...	1626	...	...	...	...	...	0259	0741	0831
512	Carei d.	...	1840	...	...	...	...	...	0514	|	|
458	**Baia Mare** **1614** a.	...	|	...	...	...	...	...	|	0850	0924
	Satu Mare **1625** a.	...	|	...	...	...	...	...	|	1056	1056
	Budapest Kel. **1275** a.	...	2300	...	...	...	...	...	0955	...	...

		407	1541			1646		367	1941	1642
					Ⓐ					
	2	C✕	c 2	2	2	f		H✕	K🍷	D
Budapest Kel. **1275** d.		1740		...				0640	...	...
Satu Mare **1625** d.	...	|	...	...	...	...	...	|	1320	1620
Baia Mare **1614** d.	...	|	...	...	...	...	...	|	1501	1750
Carei **1614** d.	...	2316	...	...	...	...	...	1257	|	|
Jibou **1614** d.	...	0118	...	...	...	...	...	1458	1622	1849
Cluj Napoca d.	...	|	...	...	...	...	...	|	1614*	|
Dej Călători **1614** d.	...	0304	...	...	...	...	...	1640	1814	2026
Beclean pe Someş d.	...	0336	...	...	...	...	...	1712	1846	2116
Bistriţa Nord d.	...	|	...	...	...	...	...	|	|	2110*
Sărăţel d.	...	0400	...	...	...	...	...	1734	1908	2157
Târgu Mureş ▷ d.	...	|	...	...	...	1347	1525	|	1908*	|
Reghin ▷ d.	...	|	...	...	...	1431	1607	|	1951*	|
Deda ▷ a.	...	0504	...	...	...	1447	1629	1826	1959	2249
Deda d.	...	0508	...	...	1241	1459	...	1850	2032	2253
Gheorghieni d.	0501	0648	...	1250	1439	1637	...	2026	2222	0038
Siculeni d.	0629	0750	1222	1415	1604	1738	...	2128	2328	0139
Miercurea Ciuc d.	0734**a**	0804	1233	1425	1615	1748	...	2138	2338	0152
Sfântu Gheorghe d.	0855	0916	1340	1624**e**	1736	1849	...	2236	0035	0248
Braşov a.	0939	0946	1410	1715	1824	1928	...	2306	0105	0317
Bucureşti N **1600** a.	...	...	...	...	...	2230	...	...	0406**b**	0617

C – CORONA – 1,2 cl., 2 cl., [2] Braşov - Jibou - Carei - Debrecen - Budapest and v.v.
D – 1,2 cl., 2 cl., [2] Bucureşti - Dej Călători - Baia Mare - Satu Mare and v.v.;
1,2 cl., 2 cl., [2] Bucureşti - Sărăţel (**4007/8**) - Bistriţa Nord and v.v.;
1,2 cl., 2 cl., [2] Bucureşti - Beclean pe Someş (**4112/6**) - Sighetu Marmaţiei and v.v.
H – HARGHITA – [12] Braşov - Jibou - Carei - Debrecen - Budapest and v.v.
J – June 14 - Sept. 7. 1,2 cl., 2 cl., [12] Mangalia - Constanţa - Bucureşti Băneasa - Satu Mare / Târgu Mureş / Cluj Napoca.
K – June 13 - Sept. 6. 1,2 cl., 2 cl., [12] Satu Mare / Târgu Mureş / Cluj Napoca. Bucureşti Băneasa - Constanţa - Mangalia.

a – Arrives at 0638.
b – Bucureşti **Băneasa**.
c – Braşov - Iaşi and v.v. (Tables **1612** and **1650**).
d – Arrives at 1816.
e – Arrives at 1537.
f – Train **1622** between Braşov and Bucureşti.
▷ – Additional trains: Deda - Târgu Mureş at 0509, 0609, 0901, 1228, 1714, 1844. Târgu Mureş - Deda at 0735, 1019, 1128, 1425, 1932, 2245. Journey 1hr 20m.
* – Seperate portion of train.

MĂRĂŞEŞTI - ADJUD - COMĂNEŞTI - MIERCUREA CIUC 1612

2nd class

km					1541	Ⓐ					
					c						
0	**Mărăşeşti** d.	...	0400	0602	...	1236	1433	1723	...	2128	...
25	Adjud d.	...	0507	0637	0930	1312	1509	1757	2000	2203	...
63	Oneşti d.	...	0557	0731	1010	1407	1600	1847	2050	2318	...
100	Comăneşti d.	0432	0657	0829	1055	1511	1658	1944	2146	0012	...
135	Ghimeş d.	0519	0745	0916	1133	1557	1745	2029	...	...	...
176	Siculeni a.	0614	0851	1013	1217	...	1840	2122	...	...	...
184	**Miercuria Ciuc** a.	0630	0906	1028	1230	...	1848	...	...	...	...

						1543		Ⓐ		
						c				
Miercuria Ciuc d.	...	...	0725	...	1242	1332	...	...	1612	1932
Siculeni d.	...	0435	0733	...	1252	1344	...	...	1624	1946
Ghimeş d.	...	0545	0834	...	1353	1432	...	1621	1725	2055
Comăneşti d.	0426	0632	0927	1300	1441	1510	...	1715	1826	2148
Oneşti d.	0521	0732	...	1409	1537	1554	1558	1811	1929	2320
Adjud a.	0616	0826	...	1503	...	1633	1649	1905	2023	0014
Mărăşeşti a.	0648	0859	...	1535	...	...	1738	1937	2055	0046

c – Braşov - Iasi and v.v (Tables **1610** and **1650**).

CLUJ NAPOCA - DEJ - BAIA MARE / BISTRIŢA 1614

2nd class

km								4004			
								b			
0	**Cluj Napoca** ▷ d.	...	0540	0627	1145	1407	1531	1614	1643	1725	1930
59	Dej Călători **1610** d.	0458	0711	0741	1259	1511	1648	1727	1756	1844	2043
135	Jibou **1610** d.	|	0905	...	|	1708	|	1910	...	|	...
193	**Baia Mare** **1610** a.	|	...	...	|	1825	|	2020	...	|	...
84	Beclean pe Someş ▷ d.	0540	...	...	1338	...	1744	...	...	1924	...
109	Sărăţel d.	0617	...	...	1416	...	1814	...	...	1959	...
119	**Bistriţa** Nord a.	0632	...	...	1430	...	1828	...	...	2014	...

				4006						
				b						
Bistriţa Nord d.	...	0410	...	...	0740	...	...	1540	...	...
Sărăţel d.	...	0422	...	...	0756	...	...	1557	...	...
Beclean pe Someş ▷ d.	...	0517	...	...	0826	...	...	1626	...	...
Baia Mare **1610** d.	...	|	...	0610	|	0720	...	|	1525	1945
Jibou **1610** d.	...	|	...	0715	|	0841	...	|	1639	2100
Dej Călători **1610** d.	0518	0556	0700	0848	0914	1030	1450	1721	1837	...
Cluj Napoca ▷ a.	0657	0717	0812	1005	1042	1137	1613	1847	2006	...

b – Also conveys [12] from / to Bucureşti Nord (Table **1600**).
▷ – For additional trains Cluj Napoca - Dej Călători - Beclean pe Someş and v.v, see Table **1660**.

RĂZBOIENI - TÂRGU MUREŞ 1615

2nd class

km									1746		
				⚒							
0	**Războieni** **1620** d.	0413	0510	0550	...	1215	...	1709	1759	...	1952
19	Luduş d.	0440	0536	0612	...	1241	...	1735	1818	...	2026
58	**Târgu Mures** a.	0540	0635	0724	...	1339	...	1834	1904	...	2125

				1745						
						Ⓐ				Ⓐ
Târgu Mures d.	0250	...	0734	1148	...	1428	1523	...	1923	2240
Luduş d.	0345	...	0840	1242	...	1527	1622	...	2027	2350
Râzboieni **1620** a.	0411	...	0904	1300	...	1552	1647	...	2051	0018

CLUJ NAPOCA - SIMERIA - ARAD and TIMIŞOARA 1620

km				532	74	1836	1734		1833		1644		1763
			2		C	D			2	2	⊗2	2	⊗e
	Iaşi **1660** d.	...	...	...	...	...	...	...	0557	...	...	...	1540
	Suceava **1660** d.	...	...	...	...	...	...	...	0804	...	...	...	1748
0	**Cluj Napoca** d.	0453	0752	0815	0836	0933	1022	1108	1510	1650	1940	1945	0055
51	Câmpia Turzii d.	0609	0904	|	0936	1034	1124	1222	1609	1802	2043	2102	0155
69	Războieni **1615** d.	0631	0937	|	0953	1052	1142	1249	1626	1824	2102	2132	0212
89	Aiud d.	0710	1016	|	1023	1123	1217	1329	1708	1912	2138	2211	0243
102	Teiuş d.	0758	1037	1019	1048	1150	1237	1350	1733	1937	2159	2232	0309
121	Alba Iulia d.	0840	...	**b**	1108	1211	**b**	...	1754	...	**b**	...	0330
131	Vinţu de Jos **1600** d.	0851	...	...	1117	1220	...	...	1803	...	...	...	0339
175	**Simeria** a.	0952	...	...	1148	1253	...	...	1838	...	...	...	0412
175	**Simeria** **1600** ▷ d.	...	...	...	1220	...	...	...	1904	...	...	...	0418
184	Deva **1600** ▷ d.	...	...	...	1230	...	...	...	1920	...	...	...	0427
333	**Arad** **1600** ▷ a.	...	...	...	1500	...	...	...	|	...	...	...	0704
290	Lugoj d.	...	...	...	...	...	...	...	2139	...	...	...	|
349	**Timişoara** Nord a.	...	...	...	...	...	...	...	2305	...	...	...	0905

	1835		1643			1831	1735			75	531	1767
	D	2	⊗2	2	2	2		2		C		⊗e
Timişoara Nord a.	...	...	...	...	...	0642	...	...	...	...	...	1451
Lugoj d.	...	...	...	...	...	0809	...	...	...	...	...	|
Arad **1600** ▷ d.	...	...	...	...	...	|	...	...	...	1434	...	1650
Deva **1600** ▷ d.	...	...	...	...	...	1009	...	...	...	1702	...	1919
Simeria **1600** ▷ a.	...	...	...	...	...	1018	...	...	...	1711	...	1928
Simeria d.	0247	...	...	...	...	1043	...	...	1400	1729	...	1933
Vinţu de Jos **1600** d.	0323	...	...	...	...	1121	...	...	1511	1804	...	2006
Alba Iulia d.	0331	...	**b**	...	...	1130	**b**	...	1522	1813	**b**	2014
Teiuş d.	0354	0400	0502	0748	1058	1154	1353	1400	1556	1841	2009	2037
Aiud d.	0415	0422	0526	0810	1124	1216	1415	1422	1617	1905	|	2058
Războieni **1615** d.	0453	0501	0555	0849	1219	1248	1446	1503	1708	1936	|	2133
Câmpia Turzii d.	0509	0524	0612	0909	1238	1304	1502	1521	1726	1954	|	2149
Cluj Napoca a.	0611	0652	0711	1021	1350	1401	1557	1632	1840	2052	2214	2247
Suceava **1660** a.	...	...	...	...	...	2054	...	...	...	...	...	0540
Iaşi **1660** a.	...	...	...	...	...	2253	...	...	...	...	...	0752

C – CLAUDIOPOLIS – [12] Cluj Napoca - Arad - Budapest and v.v.
D – Cluj Napoca - Simeria - Craiova - Bucureşti and v.v (via Târgu Jiu, Table **1635**).

b – To / from Bucureşti (via Sighişoara, Table **1600**).
e – Conveys [2] Botosani - Suceava - Timişoara and v.v. (Table **1660**).

▷ – Additional local trains run Arad - Deva - Simeria and v.v.
⊗ – 1,2 cl., 2 cl., [2]

SIGHIŞOARA - SIBIU 1622

2nd class

km			⚒				Ⓐ			
0	**Sighişoara** **1600** d.	...	0515	0701	1009	...	...	1544	1850	...
39	Mediaş **1600** d.	0419	0558	0747	1052	1249	...	1629	1940	1956
50	Copşa Mică **1600** d.	0432	0612	0800	...	1302	1557	1646	...	2012
95	**Sibiu** a.	0544	0715	0911	...	1414	1719	1801	...	2126

				Ⓐ					Ⓑ
Sibiu d.	0720	...	1222	1441	1527	1732	...	1935	2335
Copşa Mică **1600** d.	0834	...	1345	1552	1645	1849	...	2055	0052
Mediaş **1600** d.	0846	...	1401	...	1701	1907	...	2115	0106
Sighişoara **1600** a.	...	...	1444	...	...	1946	...	2156	...

1625 TIMIŞOARA - ARAD - ORADEA - SATU MARE - BAIA MARE (- DEBRECEN)

For Timişoara - Cluj Napoca via Simeria and Teiuş, see Table **1620**.

km		⚒ 2	⚒ 2	2	1743 N	2	2	6822 2	1941 b⊕	378 B	367 H	2	78 M	1741 ⊕e	Ⓑ 2	1642 D	2	Ⓐ 2	686 S	Ⓑ 2	72 T	Ⓐ 2	1531 ⑤–⑦	1533 ①–④	1537	2	407 C✕
0	**Timişoara** Nord ▷ d.	...	...	...	...	...	0359	...	...	0533	...	...	0721	...	...	...	...	...	...	1244	1539	...	1545	1545	1707	1802	...
57	**Arad** ▷ a.	...	...	...	...	...	0540	...	...	0658	...	...	0841	...	...	...	...	...	...	1422	1655	...	1711	1711	1830	2007	...
57	**Arad** d.	...	0310	...	0505	...	0550	...	...	...	...	...	...	0923	...	...	...	...	...	1451	...	...	1719	1719	1842	2012	...
139	Salonta d.	...	0517	...	0708	...	0752	...	...	...	...	...	...	1100	...	...	...	...	...	1705	...	...	1857	1857	2023	2155	...
178	**Oradea** a.	...	0629	...	0805	...	0854	...	...	...	...	...	...	1153	...	...	...	...	...	1802	...	...	1952	1952	2120	2259	...
178	**Oradea** d.	0235	...	0735	...	...	...	...	...	...	...	...	...	...	...	...	1521	1631	...	...	...	1928	1957	1957	...	...	...
282	*Debrecen* **1277** d.	|	...	|	...	...	...	0816	...	...	0940	...	...	...	...	...	|	|	1705	...	...	|	|	|	...	...	2040
243	Valea lui Mihai 🏛 d.	0432	...	0857	...	...	...	1056	...	...	1229	1250	...	...	...	...	1706	1759	1947	...	...	2138	2059	2059	...	...	2321
275	Carei d.	0512	...	...	...	...	...	1130	...	...	1256	1328	...	...	...	...	1739	...	2010	...	...	2210	2124	2124	...	...	2345
311	**Satu Mare** a.	0557	...	...	...	...	...	1215	...	...	...	1413	...	...	...	...	1824	...	2042	...	...	2253	2158	2158	...	...	...
311	**Satu Mare** d.	...	...	...	...	0745	...	...	1320	...	...	...	...	...	1541	1620	...	...	2044	...	...	...	2202	...	...	...	...
371	**Baia Mare** a.	...	...	...	...	0920	...	...	1446	...	...	...	...	...	1715	1735	...	...	2200	...	...	...	2318	...	...	...	...

	1530 ⑥–①	1532 ②–⑤		⚒ 2	406 C✕	Ⓐ 2	⚒ 2	1539	73 T	2	2	687 S	2	1641 Dc		6813 2	377 B		1744 ⊕d	79 M	2	2	Ⓐ 2	366 H	Ⓐ 2	2Ⓑ
Baia Mare d.	0035	...	...	...	...	...	...	...	...	...	...	0800	...	0939	...	...	...	...	...	...	...	1541	...	...	...	2035
Satu Mare a.	0148	...	...	...	...	...	...	...	...	...	...	0922	...	1056	...	...	...	...	...	...	...	1725	...	...	...	2219
Satu Mare d.	0150	0150	...	0325	...	...	...	...	...	0740	...	0925	...	...	...	1240	...	...	...	...	1545	...	...	...	1918	...
Carei d.	0222	0222	...	0356	0514	...	...	...	...	0839	...	0958	...	...	...	1327	...	...	...	...	1628	...	...	1840	2052	...
Valea lui Mihai 🏛 d.	0247	0247	...	0445	0608f	0600	...	...	...	0928	...	1023	...	...	...	1420	...	...	...	...	1703	...	...	1945	2156	...
Debrecen **1277** a.	|	|	...	|	0645	|	...	...	...	|	...	1109	...	...	...	1434	...	...	...	...	|	...	...	2000	|	...
Oradea a.	0355	0355	...	0620	...	0724	...	...	...	1056	...	...	...	...	...	...	...	...	...	...	1836	...	...	...	2317	...
Oradea d.	0400	0400	0417	...	...	...	0649	0840	...	...	...	...	...	...	...	...	...	1608	1804	...	...	...	1954	...	...	...
Salonta d.	0454	0454	0518	...	...	...	0753	0934	...	...	...	...	...	...	...	...	...	1717	1856	...	...	...	2110	...	...	...
Arad a.	0620	0620	0713	...	...	...	1000	1057	...	...	...	...	...	...	...	...	...	1932	2021	...	...	...	2322	...	...	...
Arad ▷ d.	0635	0635	0802	...	...	...	...	1102	1234	...	1301	...	1554	...	...	...	1831	1940	...	2057	...	...	2337	...	...	...
Timişoara Nord ▷ a.	0807	0807	0956	...	...	...	...	1223	1354	...	1450	...	1801	...	...	...	1956	2127	...	2217	...	...	0117	...	...	...

B – BEGA – 🚃2 Timişoara - Arad - Budapest and v.v.
C – CORONA – 🛏 1, 2 cl., ▬ 2 cl., 🚃2 Braşov - Dej - Jibou - Carei- Debrecen - Budapest and v.v.
D – 🛏 1, 2 cl., ▬ 2 cl., 🚃2 Bucureşti - Dej - Jibou - Baia Mare - Satu Mare and v.v.
H – HARGHITA – 🚃12 Braşov - Dej - Jibou - Carei - Debrecen - Budapest and v.v.
M – MUNTENIA – 🛏 1, 2 cl., ▬ 2 cl., 🚃12 Bucureşti - Timişoara - Arad - (**1741/4**) Oradea / Budapest. and v.v.
N – ISTER – 🛏 1, 2 cl., ▬ 2 cl., 🚃2 Bucureşti - Sibiu - Arad - Budapest and v.v.; also 🛏 1, 2 cl., 🚃2 Bucureşti - Arad (**1743**) - Oradea.
S – SOMES – 🚃2 Baia Mare - Satu Mare - Debrecen - (**143/146**) - Budapest - Wien and v.v.
T – TRAIANUS – 🚃12 Craiova - Timişoara - Arad - Budapest and v.v (Table **1630**).

b – June 13 - Sept. 6 to Constanţa / Mangalia.
c – June 14 - Sept. 8 runs as train **1942** from Constanţa / Mangalia.
d – June 13 - Sept. 6 runs as train **1922** to Constanţa / Mangalia.
e – June 15 - Sept. 8 runs as train **1920** from Constanţa / Mangalia.
f – Arrives at 0541, connection to Oradea at 0600.

▷ – Additional local trains run Timişoara - Arad and v.v.
⊕ – 🛏 1, 2 cl., ▬ 2 cl., 🚃12

1630 BUCUREŞTI - CRAIOVA - TIMIŞOARA

km		2	2		72 T🍷	2	1599	2	1591	1823	1691		9907	1835	1593 n	1996 g	9911		78 M	11501 ◇m	11502 ◇f	1920 ⊕g	1821 ⊕n	1990 ⊕g
	Constanţa **1680** d.	...	...	...	...	...	...	...	...	...	...	...	...	...	...	1434	...	...	...	...	1736	1800	...	2150
0	**Bucureşti** Nord d.	...	...	...	...	...	0502	...	0749	0857	1043	...	1434	1618	1732	1732	1846	...	1945	2030	2030	2102	2345	0038b
51	Videle d.	...	...	...	...	...	0609	...	0910	1005	1146	...	1555	1726	1836	1836	1950	...	2046	2135	2135	2208	0046	0138
100	Roşiori Nord d.	...	...	...	...	...	0721	...	1010	1105	1241	...	1658	1826	1933	1933	2054	...	2143	2229	2229	2304	0141	0233
155	Caracal d.	...	...	...	...	...	0857	...	1142	1237	1413	...	1832	1956	2103	2103	2223	...	2313	2356	2356	0033	0318	0401
209	**Craiova** a.	...	...	...	...	...	0944	...	1230	1325	1500	...	1921	2043	2150	2150	2310	...	2400	0043	0043	0120	0403	0448
209	**Craiova** **1635** d.	...	...	...	0820	...	0955	...	...	1328	1506	...	...	2051	...	...	...	...	0008	0052	0052	0127	0411	0457
245	Filiaşi **1635** d.	...	...	...	0850	...	1026	...	...	1358	1536	...	...	2121	...	...	...	...	0037	0123	0123	0157	0441	0534
323	Drobeta Turnu Severin d.	...	...	...	1040	...	1219	...	...	e	1733	...	...	c	...	...	...	...	0228	0330	0330	|	|	0726
347	Orşova d.	...	...	...	1117	...	...	1317	...	...	1807	...	...	...	...	...	...	...	0310	0404	0404	|	|	0758
364	Băile Herculane d.	...	...	...	1147	...	...	1347	...	...	1833	...	...	...	...	...	...	...	0337	0431	0431	◐	◐	0825
435	Caransebeş ⊡ d.	0406	0706	...	1318	1322	...	1542	...	...	1959	...	...	...	...	...	...	...	0503	0557	0557	|	|	1009
474	Lugoj d.	0511	0815	...	1411	1427	...	1653	...	...	2052	...	...	...	...	...	...	...	0558	0651	0651	|	|	1103
533	**Timişoara** Nord a.	0649	1006	...	1536	1604	...	1829	...	...	2219	...	...	...	...	...	...	...	0716	0812	0812	|	|	1223
	Arad **1625** a.	...	...	...	1655	...	...	...	...	...	...	...	...	...	...	...	...	...	0841	0939	0939	0932	1225	...

	9900	1594 n	1994 g		9910	9922 9902	Ⓐ 2	1824	1692	2	9918	1590	1836	⚒ 2	73 T🍷	2	Ⓑ 2	1992 ⊕h	1822 ⊕p	1922 ⊕h	11500 ◇m	11504 ◇k	79 M
Arad **1625** d.	...	...	...	...	...	...	...	...	...	...	...	...	...	...	1234	...	...	...	1724	1724	1948	1948	2057
Timişoara Nord d.	...	...	...	...	...	...	...	...	0606	0754	...	...	...	1323	1359	1610	...	1709	|	|	2111	2113	2232
Lugoj d.	...	...	...	...	...	...	...	...	0740	0948	...	...	...	1506	1521	1748	...	1844	|	|	2233	2227	2355
Caransebeş ⊡ d.	...	...	...	...	...	...	...	...	0831	1054	...	...	...	1619	1615	1852	1931	2002	|	|	2325	2314	0047
Băile Herculane d.	...	...	...	...	...	...	...	...	0955	...	...	...	...	1815	1741	...	2146	2131	◐	◐	0051	0040	0212
Orşova d.	...	...	...	...	...	...	...	...	1021	...	...	...	...	...	1808	...	2215	2159	|	|	0117	0106	0237
Drobeta Turnu Severin d.	...	...	...	...	...	e	0725	e	1059	...	...	1531	c	...	1842	...	...	2234	|	|	0151	0140	0311
Filiaşi **1635** d.	...	...	...	...	...	0700	0947	1116	1251	...	...	1722	1838	...	2033	...	...	0027	0049	0049	0342	0328	0502
Craiova **1635** a.	...	...	...	...	...	0721	...	1144	1320	...	...	1750	1908	...	2101	...	...	0055	0119	0119	0410	0354	0530
Craiova d.	0155	0332	0332	...	0615	0735	...	1152	1350	...	1550	1757	1913	...	...	...	...	0105	0126	0126	0416	0416	0537
Caracal d.	0248	0422	0422	...	0705	0826	...	1244	1441	...	1640	1847	2002	...	...	...	...	0200	0216	0216	0504	0504	0627
Roşiori Nord d.	0410	0531	0531	...	0817	0937	...	1353	1550	...	1752	1956	2109	...	...	...	...	0305	0325	0325	0612	0612	0732
Videle d.	0527	0640	0640	...	0926	1053	...	1454	1650	...	1909	2055	2217	...	...	...	...	0405	0425	0425	0713	0713	0833
Bucureşti Nord a.	0647	0749	0749	...	1043	1217	...	1559	1757	...	2024	2215	2320	...	...	...	...	0509b	0532	0532	0816	0816	0936
Constanţa **1680** a.	...	...	1040	...	...	...	...	...	...	...	...	...	...	...	...	...	...	0744	...	0843	...	1058	...

M – MUNTENIA – 🛏 1, 2 cl., ▬ 2 cl., 🚃12 Bucureşti - Timişoara - Arad - Budapest and v.v.; also Arad (**1741/4**) - Oradea and v.v.
T – TRAIANUS – 🚃12 Craiova - Timişoara - Arad - Budapest and v.v. (✕ from Timişoara).

b – Bucureşti **Băneasa**.
c – To / from Teiuş / Cluj Napoca via Târgu Jiu (Table **1635**).
e – To / from Deva or Târgu Jiu (Table **1635**).
f – June 13 - Sept. 8.
g – June 14 - Sept. 7.
h – June 13 - Sept. 6.
k – June 12 - Sept. 7.

m – Not Dec. 25, 26, 31, Jan 1, Apr. 19, 20, June 13 - Sept. 8.
n – Not June 14 - Sept. 7.
p – Not June 13 - Sept. 6.

⊕ – 🛏 1, 2 cl., ▬ 2 cl., 🚃12
⊗ – 🛏 1, 2 cl., ▬ 2 cl., 🚃2
◇ – 🛏 Lux, Standard, ▬ (4 berth)., 🚃2 Operated by Astra TC.
◐ – Via Simeria and Târgu Jiu (Table **1635**).

⊡ – **CARANSEBES - REŞIŢA SUD** (journey 66 – 72 minutes):
From Caransebeş at 0349Ⓐ, 0700, 1301Ⓐ, 1628, and 2055.
From Reşiţa Sud at 0535Ⓐ, 0853Ⓐ, 1344, 1451Ⓐ and 2300.

1635 CRAIOVA - TÂRGU JIU - DEVA

km			2	2	2Ⓑ	1823	2	Ⓑ		1835	1821 ⊕s
	Bucureşti N **1630** d.	...	...	...	...	0857	...	...	...	1618	2345
0	**Craiova** **1630** d.	0253	...	...	0517	1328	...	1438	1642	2051	0411
36	Filiaşi **1630** d.	0407	...	...	0610	1358	...	1554	1737	2121	0441
107	**Târgu Jiu** a.	0603	...	...	0805	1543	...	1805	1940	2248	0608
107	**Târgu Jiu** d.	0615	...	...	0820	1545	...	1810	1942	2251	0611
157	Petroşani a.	0805	...	...	1017	1712	...	1958	2128	0023	0735
157	Petroşani d.	...	0820	...	...	1715	1942	...	...	0028	0741
237	Simeria **1620** d.	...	1055	1113	...	1911	2218	...	...	0247	0955
246	**Deva** **1620** a.	...	...	1124	...	1918	...	...	...	|	1008
	Cluj Napoca **1620** a.	...	...	|	...	...	...	...	...	0611	|
	Arad **1600** a.	...	...	1445	...	...	...	...	...	...	1239

	9922		1824		2n	Ⓑ	1836	2	2	1822 ⊕s
Arad **1600** d.	...	...	...	...	0754	...	...	...	...	1710
Cluj Napoca **1620** d.	...	...	...	...	|	...	0933	...	...	|
Deva **1620** d.	...	...	0551	...	1125	...	|	...	...	1939
Simeria **1620** d.	...	...	0602	...	1137	...	1313	1619	...	1952
Petroşani a.	...	...	0817	...	...	...	1523	1904	...	2152
Petroşani d.	...	0402	0822	0851	...	1450	1528	...	...	2156
Târgu Jiu a.	...	0554	0948	1042	...	1645	1701	...	...	2321
Târgu Jiu d.	0518	0609	0950	1050	...	1648	1703	...	1941	2323
Filiaşi **1630** d.	0700	0825	1116	1255	...	1851	1838	...	2138	0049
Craiova **1630** a.	0728	0916	1144	1348	...	1944	1908	...	2231	0119
Bucureşti N **1630** a.	1217	...	1559	...	...	...	2320	...	...	0532

s – Extended from / to Constanţa / Mangalia on dates in Table **1630** (numbered **1920/2**).

n – Not Apr. 20.

⊕ – 🛏 1, 2 cl., ▬ 2 cl. and 🚃12

BUCUREŞTI - TÂRGOVIŞTE - PITEŞTI and CRAIOVA 1640

km			9251	9201	9205	9207	9253		9209		9257		9217
		2	Ⓑc	2	2	2	c	2		2	c	2	2
0	**Bucureşti** Nord	d.	0505	0600	0728	1131	1228	1343	1406	1452	1624f	1732	1939	2104
48	Titu	d.	0615	0739	0826	1224	1322	1436	1518	1545	1733	1832	2056	2143
80	**Târgovişte**	a.	0700	|	|	|	|	|	1603	|	1818	|	2141	|
108	**Piteşti**	d.	...	0830	0932	1327	1427	1552	...	1650	...	1953	...	2252
189	Slatina	d.	...	1010	...	...	...	1725	...	...	...	2125	...	...
206	Piatra Olt .. **1645**	a.	...	1028	...	...	...	1750	...	...	...	2143	...	...
250	**Craiova** **1645**	a.	...	1115	...	...	...	1908	...	...	...	2230	...	...

		9200		9202	9204	9264		9210	9266		9214		9268
			2	⚒2	2	c	2	2	Ⓑc	2	2	2	c
Craiova **1645**	d.	...	...	...	...	0642	...	...	1200	...	...	...	1645
Piatra Olt **1645**	d.	...	...	...	...	0746	...	...	1256	...	...	...	1708
Slatina	d.	...	...	...	...	0806	...	...	1316	...	...	...	1749
Piteşti	d.	0446	...	0552	0815	1007	...	1400	1458	...	1705	...	1945
Târgovişte	d.	|	0503	|	|	|	1150	|	|	1632	|	1945	|
Titu	d.	0553	0602	0654	0925	1117	1235	1500	1558	1716	1817	2029	2052
Bucureşti Nord	a.	0639	0703f	0730	1006	1158	1333	1540	1638	1816f	1900	2124	2124

c – Change of train numbers at Piteşti.

f – Bucureşti Basarab station, 1km north of Bucureşti Nord.

SIBIU - RÂMNICU VÂLCEA - CRAIOVA / BUCUREŞTI 1645

km			2010		2012		Ⓑ		⚒	2014		1912
				2	Ⓑ	2	2		2		2	J
0	**Sibiu** **1600**	d.	0200	0235	0646	0754	...	1157	...	1512	1618	1838
22	Podu Olt **1600**	d.	|	0320	0724	0839	...	1241	1420	1552	1707	1916
83	Călimăneşti	d.	0413	0510	0912	1032	...	...	1614	1745	1909	2100
99	**Râmnicu Vâlcea**	d.	0438	0550	0952	1100	1421	...	1643	1810	1940	2122
186	Piatra Olt **1640**	d.	0620	0815	1138	...	1700	...	1905	1940	2209	2307
230	**Craiova** **1640**	a.	|	...	1235	...	...	...	...	...	...	|
•32	Caracal **1630**	a.	0700	...	...	...	...	...	...	...	...	|
•17	Slatina	d.	...	...	...	...	...	...	...	...	...	2327
•98	Piteşti	d.	...	...	...	...	...	...	...	...	...	0120
•206	**Bucureşti** Nord . **1630**	a.	...	...	...	...	...	...	...	...	...	0256
	Constanţa **1680**	a.	...	...	...	...	...	...	...	...	...	0611

		⚒	1914	⚒			2016		2018	2011	
		2	K	2	2	2		2	Ⓑ		
Constanţa **1680**	d.	...	2010	...	...	...	...	...	...	...	...
Bucureşti N ... **1630**	d.	...	2319	...	...	...	...	...	...	...	...
Piteşti	d.	...	0130	...	...	...	...	...	...	...	...
Slatina	d.	...	0302	...	...	...	...	...	...	...	...
Caracal **1630**	d.	...	|	...	...	...	...	...	...	1908	...
Craiova ... **1640**	d.	...	|	...	...	...	0743	...	1505	|	...
Piatra Olt **1640**	d.	...	0342	0403	...	0638	0855	...	1610	2000	...
Râmnicu Vâlcea	d.	0240	0512	0641	...	0925	1024	1618	1751	2140	...
Călimăneşti	d.	0308	0532	0709	...	0954	1047	1646	1814	2203	...
Podu Olt **1600**	d.	0538	0714	0912	0930	1150	1227	1845	1954	2343	...
Sibiu **1600**	a.	0619	0753	...	1010	1236	1301	1937	2029	0017	...

J – June 13 - Sept. 6.

K – June 14 - Sept. 7.

• – Distance from Piatra Olt.

BUCUREŞTI - BUZĂU - BACĂU - IAŞI and SUCEAVA 1650

km ☆					1830	1655	1661			1751	1663	1543	1866	1753	1657	1665	551	562	402	5003	1653	1667	1862	1960	1954
									Ⓐ								✕	✕	🍸	Ⓑ					
				2	2c				2			b2	2				S	S	P2	2	⊕	⊕	2n	⊙g	⊙g
0	**Bucureşti** Nord .. **1600/70**	d.	...	0445	...	0624	0650	...	0925	1110	1200	...	...	1400	1500	1610	1725	1725	1910	1947	2236	2254	...	...	...
59	Ploieşti Sud **1600/70**	d.	...	0550	...	0704	0730	...	1039	1149	1239	...	...	1439	1538	1651	1804	1804	1959	2038	2318	2333	...	...	...
	Constanţa **1680**	d.	...	|	...	|	|	...	|	|	|	...	...	|	|	|	|	|	|	|	|	|	2059	2230	2330
	Făurei **1670**	d.	...	|	...	|	|	...	|	|	|	...	...	|	|	|	|	|	|	|	|	|	2332	|	0200
128	**Buzău** **1670**	d.	...	0805	...	0816	0841	...	1211	1300	1349	...	...	1550	1649	1802	1913	1913	2109	2154	0029	0059	0059	|	0248
161	Râmnicu Sărat	d.	...	0848	...	0844	0910	...	...	1329	1418	...	...	1619	1718	1831	|	|	2138	2223	0058	0128	0128	|	0318
199	Focşani	d.	...	1016	...	0924	0951	...	...	1410	1459	...	...	1700	1759	1911	2017	2017	2219	2302	0139	0208	0208	△	0359
219	Mărăşeşti	d.	0445	1040	...	0943	|	...	...	1429	|	...	...	1719	1819	1945	|	|	2238	2321	0158	|	|	|	0419
244	Adjud	d.	0520	...	...	1007	|	...	...	1453	|	1654	...	1743	1843	|	|	|	2303	...	0223	|	|	|	0443
302	**Bacău**	d.	0638	...	...	1045	|	...	...	1531	|	1732	...	1827	1947	|	2134	2134	2356	...	0301	|	|	|	0521
362	Piatra Neamţ	a.	|	...	...	|	|	...	...	|	|	|	...	2036y	2058	|	|	|	|	...	|	|	|	|	|
346	Roman	d.	0728	...	...	1116	|	...	...	1604	|	1805	...	1901	...	|	2207	2207	0034	...	0334	|	|	|	0555
386	Paşcani **1660**	d.	0811	...	...	1143	|	...	...	1630	|	|	...	1928	...	|	2240	2250	|	...	0402	|	|	|	0622
238	**Galaţi**	d.	...	...	0615	|	|	...	...	|	|	|	1555	|	...	|	|	|	|	...	|	|	|	|	|
288	Tecuci	d.	...	...	0754	|	1055	...	...	|	1552	|	1738	|	...	2008t	|	|	|	...	|	0300	0300	0352	|
340	Bârlad	d.	...	...	0856	|	1135	...	...	|	1646	|	1833	|	...	2047	|	|	|	...	|	0339	0339	0432	|
408	Vaslui	d.	...	...	0943	|	1216	...	...	|	1731	|	1917	|	...	2132	|	|	|	...	|	0424	0424	0517	|
538	**Iaşi**	a.	...	...	1051	|	1321	...	...	|	1839	1932	2025	|	...	2241	|	2349	0207	...	|	0532	0532	0627	|
	Chişinău **1720** .MD	a.	...	...	...	|	...	...	...	|	...	...	...	|	...	...	|	...	0844	...	|	...	...	...	|
432	Vereşti **1660**	d.	...	...	...	1214	...	...	...	1711	...	...	...	2002	...	...	|	...	...	...	0442	...	...	...	0657
476	Botoşani	a.	...	...	...	|	...	...	...	1838v	...	...	...	|	...	...	|	...	...	...	0622v	...	...	...	|
447	**Suceava** **1660**	a.	...	...	...	1225	...	...	...	1722	...	...	...	2013	...	...	2319	...	...	...	0453	...	...	...	0708
450	**Suceava** Nord	a.	...	...	...	...	...	...	...	...	...	...	...	2020	...	...	...	...	...	...	d	...	...	...	0716

		5002	1658	552	561	1660	1541		1752	1864		1754		1662	1656	1664		1832	1952	1962	1668	1861	1654	401
				✕	✕																			🍸
		2		S	S		b2			2	2							2c	⊙h	⊙h	⊕	2n	⊕	P2
Suceava Nord	d.	...	...	...	...	...	...	...	0900	...	...	...	...	...	...	...	...	...	2015	...	...	...	d	...
Suceava **1660**	d.	...	...	0552	...	...	...	...	0907	...	...	1240	...	...	1617	...	...	...	2024	...	...	...	2300	...
Botoşani	d.	...	...	|	...	...	...	...	|	...	...	1117v	...	...	|	...	...	...	|	...	...	...	2133v	...
Vereşti **1660**	d.	...	...	|	...	...	...	...	0919	...	...	1303	...	...	1629	...	...	...	2036	...	...	...	2325	...
Chişinău **1720**	MD d.	...	...	|	...	...	...	...	|	...	...	|	...	...	|	...	...	...	|	...	...	...	|	1705
Iaşi	d.	...	...	|	0516	0609	0630	...	|	0807	0907	|	1250	1420	|	1607	1635	1846	|	2118	2230	2230	|	2333
Vaslui	d.	...	...	|	|	0717	|	...	|	0917	|	|	|	1528	|	1715	|	2001	|	2222	2339	2339	|	|
Bârlad	d.	...	...	|	|	0808	|	...	|	1006	|	|	|	1619	|	1807	|	2052	|	2334	0031	0031	|	|
Tecuci	d.	...	...	|	|	0901	|	...	|	1103	|	|	|	1712	|	1844t	|	2134	|	0013	0124	0124	|	|
Galaţi	a.	...	...	|	|	|	|	...	|	1237	|	|	|	|	|	|	|	2305	|	|	|	|	|	|
Paşcani **1660**	d.	...	...	0639	0639	|	|	...	0958	...	1055	1341	1445	|	1704	|	1851	...	2115	|	|	|	0004	|
Roman	d.	...	...	0708	0708	|	0805	...	1027	...	1144	1410	1537	|	1733	|	1942	...	2145	|	|	|	0033	0116
Piatra Neamţ	d.	...	...	|	|	|	|	...	0928y	...	|	|	|	|	|	|	|	...	|	|	|	|	2315y	|
Bacău	d.	...	0428	0738	0738	|	0834	...	1107	...	1232	1444	1637	|	1803	|	2044	...	2215	|	|	|	0113	0156
Adjud	d.	...	0506	|	|	|	0910	...	1145	...	...	1521	1744	|	1840	|	2149	...	2252	|	|	|	0150	0240
Mărăşeşti	d.	0350	0532	|	|	|	...	...	1211	...	...	1547	1815	|	1923	1923	2220	...	2319	△	|	|	0216	0306
Focşani	d.	0415	0556	0901	0901	0945	...	...	1236	...	...	1612	...	1757	1949	1949	...	...	2344	|	0209	0209	0241	0330
Râmnicu Sărat	d.	0500	0639	|	|	1027	...	...	1320	...	...	1654	...	1840	2032	2032	...	...	0028	|	0252	0252	0324	0413
Buzău **1670**	d.	0531	0710	1011	1011	1107	...	...	1350	...	...	1724	...	1909	2102	2102	...	...	0116	|	0330	0407	0355	0442
Făurei **1670**	d.	|	|	|	|	|	...	...	|	...	...	|	...	|	|	|	...	...	0146	|	|	0436	|	|
Constanţa **1680**	a.	|	|	|	|	|	...	...	|	...	...	|	...	|	|	|	...	...	0358	0503	|	0654	|	|
Ploieşti Sud **1600/70**	d.	0649	0829	1126	1126	1227	...	...	1508	...	...	1842	...	2025	2219	2219	...	...	...	...	0447	...	0516	0559
Bucureşti Nord **1600/70**	a.	0736	0908	1204	1204	1307	...	...	1546	...	...	1925	...	2103	2257	2257	...	...	...	...	0525	...	0557	0647

BACĂU - PIATRA NEAMŢ - BICAZ

km			Ⓐ						Ⓐ	a	a
0	**Bacău**	d.	0352	0539	...	0751	...	1447	1648	1859	1947
60	Piatra Neamţ	a.	0529	0710	...	0922	...	1616	1824	2036	2051
60	Piatra Neamţ	d.	0650	...	...	...	...	...	...	2037	...
86	**Bicaz**	a.	0741	...	...	...	...	...	...	2128	...

				Ⓐ	Ⓐ	a			Ⓐ		a
Bicaz	d.	...	...	...	0806	...	...	...	...	2150	
Piatra Neamţ	a.	...	...	...	0855	...	...	...	...	2239	...
Piatra Neamţ	d.	0443	...	0731	...	0928	1426	1637	1847	...	2315
Bacău	a.	0620	...	0907		1041	1602	1806	2025	...	0045

P – PRIETENIA – [sleeper] 1, 2 cl., [2] Bucureşti - Ungheni (**106/5**) - Chişinău and v.v.
S – STEFAN CEL MARE EXPRES [12] Bucureşti - Bacau - Paşcani - Suceava and v.v.; [12] Paşcani (**561/2**) - Iaşi and v.v.

a – Through coaches from / to Bucureşti, see also main table above.
b – From / to Braşov via Comăneşti (Table **1610/1612**).
c – From / to Cluj Napoca via Suceava (Table **1660**).
d – From / to Vatra Dornei Băi (Table **1660**).
f – Departs at 0710 June 14 - Sept. 7.
g – June 14 - Sept. 7.
h – June 13 - Sept. 6.
n – Not June 14 - Sept. 7.
t – Tecuci **Nord**.
v – Portion attached / detached to the main train at Vereşti.
y – Portion attached / detached to the main train at Bacau.

⊕ – [sleeper] 1, 2 cl., [couchette] 2 cl., [12]
⊗ – [sleeper] 1, 2 cl., [couchette] 2 cl., [2]
⊙ – [couchette] 2 cl., [12]
△ – Via Brăila.
☆ – Tecuci - Galaţi 85 km.

PAŞCANI - TÂRGU NEAMŢ *31 km*, ± 45 mins
From Paşcani: 0415Ⓐ, 0720, 1651, 1910Ⓐ.
From Târgu Neamţ: 0524Ⓐ, 1047, 1801, 2021Ⓐ.

VEREŞTI - BOTOŞANI *44 km*, ± 75 mins
From Vereşti: 0513, 0630**f**, 0901, 1316, 1730, 1836.
From Botoşani: 0650, 0921, 1117, 1454, 1906, 2133.

1660 IAŞI - SUCEAVA - DEJ - CLUJ NAPOCA

km		1653	1833	1830	4116	4113	1763	4118	1837
		⊕	2	2g	2¶	2	⊕B	2Ⓐ	⊗2
0	**Iaşi** d.	c	0557	1115	...	...	1540	...	2122
76	Paşcani **1650** d.	0402	0704	1222	...	...	1647	...	2228
122	Vereşti **1650** d.	0442	0737	1255	...	...	1721	...	2301
137	**Suceava** **1650** a.	0453	0749	1307	...	...	1733	...	2313
137	**Suceava** d.	0507	0804	1310	...	...	1748	...	2323
184	Gura Humorului Oraş d.	0553	0850	1356	...	...	1836	...	0010
216	Câmpulung Moldovenesc d.	0638	0937	1447	...	...	1923	...	0059
254	Vatra Dornei Băi d.	0741	1041	1553	...	...	2036	...	0213
348	Năsăud d.	...	1235	1750	...	...	2230	...	0420
0	**Sighetu Marmaţiei** d.	...	|	|	1600	...	|	2330	|
25	Valea Vişeului d.	...	|	|	1701	...	|	0033	|
57	Vişeu de Jos d.	...	|	|	1804	...	|	0133	|
354	Salva d.	...	1244	1800	2005	...	2238	0313	0428
376	Beclean pe Someş **1610/4** d.	...	1313	1824	2046	2101	2301	0356*	0452
400	Dej Călători **1610/4** d.	...	1348	1853	...	2140	2338	0443	0530
459	**Cluj Napoca** **1610/4** a.	...	1455	2012	...	2255	0043	0620	0646
	Simeria **1620** a.	...	1838	...	...	...	0412	...	...
	Timişoara N **1620/5** a.	...	2305	...	...	...	0905	...	...

km		4110	4112	1832	1831	4114	4115	1654	1838	1767
		2	2¶	2g	2	2⚒	2	⊕	⊗2	⊕B
	Timişoara N **1620/5** d.	...	...	...	0642	...	...	...	...	1451
	Simeria **1620** d.	...	...	...	1043	...	...	...	...	1933
	Cluj Napoca **1610/4** d.	0400	...	0940	1420	1446	...	...	2125	2304
	Dej Câlâtori **1610/4** d.	0507	...	1040	1516	1619	...	...	2223	0002
	Beclean pe Someş **1610/4** d.	0552	0610	1113	1547	1657	...	...	2302	0035
0	Salva d.	...	0644	1135	1608	1750	...	...	2324	0057
61	Vişeu de Jos d.	...	0820	|	|	1930	1945	...	|	|
93	Valea Vişeului d.	...	0950	|	|	...	2104	...	|	|
118	**Sighetu Marmaţiei** a.	...	1036	|	|	...	2150	...	|	|
	Năsăud d.	...		1144	1616	...	...	...	2332	0105
	Vatra Dornei Băi d.	...	...	1343	1816	...	...	2011	0132	0300
	Câmpulung Moldovenesc d.	...	...	1446	1924	...	...	2116	0235	0403
	Gura Humorului Oraş d.	...	...	1530	2010	...	...	2201	0319	0449
	Suceava a.	...	...	1614	2054	...	...	2245	0403	0540
	Suceava **1650** d.	...	...	1629	2059	...	...	2301	0405	0555
	Vereşti **1650** d.	...	...	1641	2111	...	...	2325	0416	0608
	Paşcani **1650** d.	...	...	1719	2151	...	...	0004	0451	0649
	Iaşi a.	...	...	1821	2253	...	...	c	0553	0752

B – Conveys 🛏 1, 2 cl., 🛌 2 cl., [2] Botoşani - Suceava - Timişoara and v.v.

c – From / to Bucureşti, also conveys from / to Botoşani and Piatra Neamţ (Table **1650**).

g – From / to Galaţi (Table **1650**).buzau

⊕ – 🛏 1, 2 cl., 🛌 2 cl., [12]

⊗ – 🛌 2 cl., [2]

¶ – Conveys 🛏 1, 2 cl., [2] to / from Bucureşti.

* – Train **4101** between Beclean pe Someş and Cluj Napoca.

1670 BUCUREŞTI - GALAŢI

km		1571		1573		1575		571		1730	
								🍷		b	
0	**Bucureşti** Nord **1650** d.	0530	...	0815	...	1316	...	1750	...	...	...
59	Ploieşti Sud **1650** d.	0611	...	0857	...	1356	...	1828	...	1936	...
128	Buzău **1650** d.	0722	...	1009	...	1507	...	1937	...	2047	...
168	Făurei d.	0750	...	1047	...	1535	...	|	...	2117	...
228	Brăila d.	0844	...	1141	...	1629	...	2054	...	2211	...
259	**Galaţi** a.	0920	...	1217	...	1705	...	2127	...	2247	...

	572		1732		1572		1574		1576	
	🍷		b							
Galaţi d.	0441	...	0701	...	0827	...	1405	...	1743	...
Brăila d.	0518	...	0739	...	0905	...	1442	...	1821	...
Făurei d.	|	...	0830	...	0956	...	1534	...	1912	...
Buzău **1650** d.	0632	...	0900	...	1025	...	1604	...	1949	...
Ploieşti Sud **1650** d.	0746	...	1026	...	1143	...	1720	...	2105	...
Bucureşti Nord **1650** a.	0824	...	...	...	1223	...	1800	...	2145	...

b – From / to Braşov (Table **1600**).

1680 BUCUREŞTI - CONSTANŢA - MANGALIA

km		1952	1962		1912	1861	1941	1992		1922			1970	1581		1981	1994	1583	11504	538		1585	1930	
		⊙	⊙	2		2	⊕🍷	⊕	2	⊕	2	2			2				⊕					2
		F•	F•	N	F•	Nd•	F•	F•	N	F•	D	N	D	N	N	D	F	N	Ga	A🍷		N	D	D
	From:	*Suc*	*Iasi*		*Ram*	*Ia/S*	*Sat*	*Tim*		*Ora*			*Gal*				*Cra*		*Ara*	*Bra*		*Bra*	*Bra*	
0	**Bucureşti** Nord d.	|	|	...	0315	|	0411b	0514b	...	0600	...	...	|	0700	...	0700	0811	0820	0835	0929	...	1030	1030	...
146	Feteşti d.	0258	0403	...	0458	0447	0535	0635	...	0733	...	...	0810	0830	...	0830	0941	0941	|	|	...	1158	1158	...
334	**Tulcea** Oraş d.	|	|	...	|	|	|	|	...	|	0514	0527	|	|	...	|	|	|	|	|	...	|	|	...
190	Medgidia d.	0335	0432	...	0537	0647	0612	0710	...	0810	0827	0827	0847	0905	...	0905	1017	1017	|	|	...	1234	1234	...
225	**Constanţa** a.	0359	0503	...	0611	0713	0646	0744	...	0843	...	...	0912	0928	...	0928	1040	1040	1058	1136	...	1257	1257	...
225	**Constanţa** d.	0416	0518	0625	0630	...	0705	0759	0827	0901	...	...	...	...	0945	0946	1057	...	...	...	...	...	...	1335
251	Costineşti d.	0504	0607	0708	0722	...	0801	0854	0917	0950	...	...	...	...	1025	1042	1235	...	...	...	...	...	...	1450
260	Neptun halta d.	0523	0627	0721	0747	...	0820	0916	0932	1008	...	...	...	...	1038	1101	1200	...	...	...	...	...	...	1509
268	**Mangalia** a.	0532	0636	0731	0759	...	0832	0927	0942	1017	...	...	...	...	1047	1110	1219	...	...	...	...	...	...	1519

	1881		1883	1983		1587		1885				1589		581			1887			1681			
		2			2		2		2	2	2		2		2	2		2					
		N		D	D	N	N		N	D	D			🍷	N	D		ⓑN	D				
From:												*Bra*								*Bra*			
Bucureşti Nord d.	1130	...	1230	1330	...	1420	...	1525	...	...	...	1633	...	1730	...	...	1830	...	...	2105	...	...	...
Feteşti d.	1304	...	1404	1501	...	1550	...	1659	...	...	...	1802	...	|	...	...	2005	...	...	2235	...	...	...
Tulcea Oraş d.	|	...	|	|	...	|	...	|	...	...	1418	|	1530	|	...	...	|	...	...	|	...	...	...
Medgidia d.	1340	...	1440	1537	...	1626	...	1735	...	...	1726	1838	1845	|	...	...	2041	...	...	2311	...	...	...
Constanţa a.	1403	...	1503	1600	...	1649	...	1758	...	...	1825	1901	1929	1937	...	...	2104	...	...	2334	...	...	...
Constanţa d.	...	1422	...	...	1617	...	1705	...	1813	1826	...	...	...	...	2013	2015	...	2121	2130	...	...	...	...
Costineşti d.	...	1502	...	...	1719	...	1745	...	1856	1937	...	...	...	...	2108	2107	...	2201	2230	...	...	...	...
Neptun halta d.	...	1517	...	...	1741	...	1758	...	1910	2000	...	...	...	...	2124	2123	...	2214	2251	...	...	...	...
Mangalia a.	...	1526	...	...	1753	...	1808	...	1920	2010	...	...	...	...	2134	2133	...	2223	2301	...	...	...	...

		1680				1580			1582				582	1882			1584	1936	1586	1996		1588	
	2			2	2		2	2		2	2	2			2	2		2			2		
	D		D	D	N		⚒N	N			N	D	🍷		P	C	N	D	N	D			
Mangalia d.	...	...	0432	0538	0540	...	0637	0644	...	...	0756	0910	...	...	1203	1203	...	...	...	1243	1243	...	...
Neptun halta d.	...	...	0442	0548	0550	...	0647	0656	...	...	0806	0929	...	...	1213	1213	...	...	...	1303	1303	...	...
Costineşti d.	...	...	0507	0610	0605	...	0711	0724	...	...	0821	0953	...	...	1226	1226	...	...	...	1321	1321	...	...
Constanţa a.	...	...	0610	0657	0650	...	0752	0815	...	...	0904	1037	...	...	1306	1313	...	...	...	1411	1411	...	...
Constanţa d.	0517	0530	...	...	...	0730	...	...	0820	...	...	...	1040	1130	...	...	1330	1400	1420	1434	...	1526	...
Medgidia d.	0621	0554	...	...	...	0754	...	...	0844	0919	...	...	|	1154	...	...	1354	1424	1444	1458	...	1549	...
Tulcea Oraş a.	0922	|	...	...	...	|	...	...	|	1220	...	...	|	|	...	...	|	|	|	|	...	|	...
Feteşti d.	...	0631	...	...	...	0831	...	...	0920	...	...	...	|	1230	...	...	1431	1500	1521	1535	...	1626	...
Bucureşti Nord a.	...	0802	...	...	...	1000	...	...	1050	...	...	...	1247	1403	...	...	1600	1629	1653	1704	...	1756	...
To:		*Bra*															*Sib*	*Bra*		*Cra*			

			1682	1942		536	11502	1920	1982	1684	1972	1984		1884	1914		1990	1862	1960	1954			
	2	2		⊕	2		⊕	⊕					2			2	⊕	2	⊙	⊙			
		N		D🍷	N	A🍷	Ha	D	D	N	D	D	N	N	D	N	D	Nc	D	D			
Mangalia d.	...	1433	...	1531	1553	...	...	1558	...	...	...	1734	1827	...	1829	1945	1953	...	2033	2157	...	...	...
Neptun halta d.	...	1443	...	1541	1602	...	...	1609	...	...	...	1755	1837	...	1839	1954	2015	...	2044	2208	...	...	...
Costineşti d.	...	1505	...	1558	1616	...	...	1635	...	...	...	1814	1859	...	1859	2007	2036	...	2110	2227	...	...	...
Constanţa a.	...	1546	...	1652	1657	...	...	1735	...	...	...	1904	1843	...	1943	2048	2125	...	2204	2312	...	...	...
Constanţa d.	1540	...	1630	1713	...	1730	1736	1800	1836	1836	1850	1927	...	2000	2010	...	2150	2059	2230	2330	...	...	...
Medgidia d.	1639	...	1654	1739	...	|	|	1826	1900	1900	1917	1951	...	2024	2039	...	2218	2125	2257	2356	...	...	...
Tulcea Oraş a.	1943	...	|	|	...	|	|	|	|	|	|	|	...	|	|	...	|	|	|	|	...	...	...
Feteşti d.	...	...	1731	1823	...	|	|	1844	1936	1936	1954	2028	...	2101	2117	...	2256	2200	2335	0032	...	...	...
Bucureşti Nord a.	...	...	1900	1947b	...	1937	2001	2046	2101	2101	|	2154	...	2233	2259	...	0027b	|	|	|	...	...	...
To:				*Sat*		*Bra*	*Ara*	*Ora*			*Gal*				*Ram*		*Tim*	*Ia/S*	*Iasi*	*Suc*			

To / From:

Ara – Arad via Craiova (Table **1630**).
Bra – Braşov (Table **1600**).
Cra – Craiova (Table **1630**).
Gal – Galaţi (Table **1670**).
Iasi – Iaşi (Table **1650**).
Ia/S – Iaşi and Suceava (Table **1650**).
Ora – Oradea via Târgu Jiu (Table **1625/35**).
Ram – Sibiu via Râmnicu Vâlcea (Table **1645**).
Sat – Satu Mare (Tables **1600/10**).
Sib – Sibiu via Braşov (Table **1600**).
Suc – Suceava (Table **1650**).
Tim – Timişoara via Craiova (Table **1630**).

A – TOMIS EXPRES – [12] Braşov - Bucureşti - Constanţa and v.v.
C – Apr. 26 - Sept. 14.
D – June 14 - Sept. 7.
F – June 13 - Sept. 6.
G – June 12 - Sept. 7.
H – June 13 - Sept. 8.
N – Not June 14 - Sept. 7.
P – Not Apr. 26 - Sept. 14.

a – Astra Trains Carpatic service, special fares apply.
b – Bucureşti **Băneasa**.

c – Attached to train **1667** at Buzău (Table **1650**).
d – Detached from train **1668** at Buzău (Table **1650**).

⊕ – 🛏 1, 2 cl., 🛌 2 cl., [12]
⊙ – 🛌 2 cl., [12]
• – Previous day from point of origin.
☛ – Long distance trains to / from Mangalia change train numbers between Constanţa and Mangailia.

BALTIC STATES, BELARUS, MOLDOVA, RUSSIA and UKRAINE

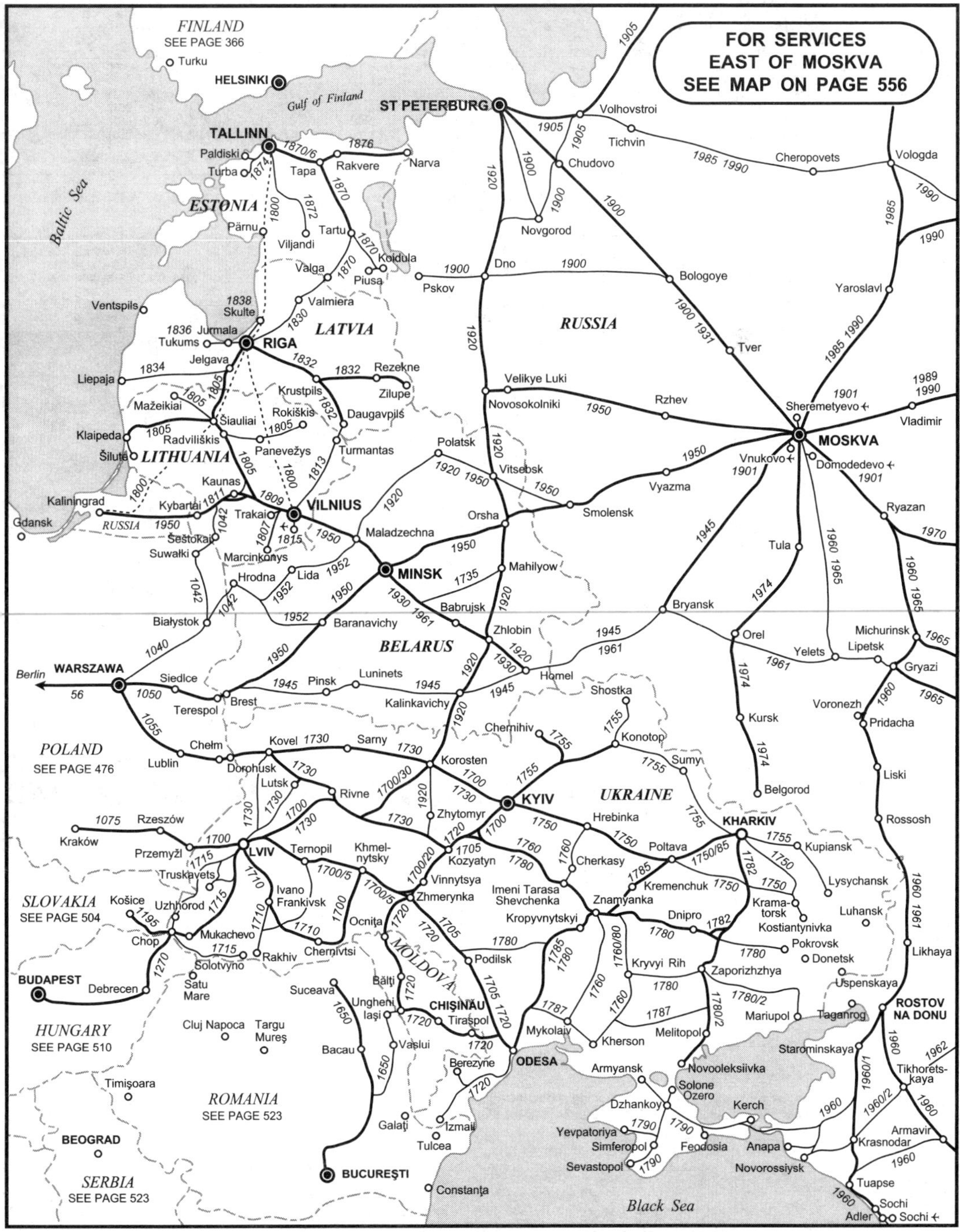

UKRAINE and MOLDOVA

Operators: **UZ**: Ukrzaliznytsya, www.uz.gov.ua **CFM**: Calea Ferată din Moldova, www.railway.md Other operators as indicated in the table headings and notes.

Services: Overnight trains convey sleeping and couchette cars and may not convey seating accommodation. Prior reservation is necessary except for travel by purely local trains. See also the panel on page 555. Trains shown as *IC* are fast day trains classified *Interciti* or *Interciti+* at premium fares.

Timings: **Timings are valid from June 15, 2025** Unless otherwise shown and are subject to alteration at any time.
Readers should consult the latest government advice regarding travel in this region.

Time zones: Local time is used throughout: East European Time for Ukraine and Moldova (UTC+2 winter, UTC+3 summer). Times within European Russia are in the Moskva time zone (UTC+3 all year) unless otherwise shown. As Russia and Belarus do not put their clocks forward in summer (daylight saving time), trains running between Ukraine or Moldova and Russia or Belarus change their timings by approximately one hour when clocks change (last Sunday in March and October) as shown in the tables.

1700 KYIV - LVIV - PRZEMYŚL and IVANO-FRANKIVSK — UZ

km				1	21		*IC*	*IC*		55			*IC*					15	43					
		142	**143**	**123**	**104**	**32**	**715**	**749**	**771**	**137**	**13**	**81**	**705**	**95**	**7**	**59**	**51**	**145**	**49**	**91**	**89**	**73**		
		■	■	■						■	●							●			●	■		
		A	**B**	**X**	**C**	**D**		**E**		**FO**	**N**	**G**		**F**	**J**	**H**		**L**	**KR**					
	Kharkiv **1750 1755** d.	...	...	1845	1935	...	...	...	...	...	...	...	...	...	...	...	...	1401	...	...	...	1440	...	...
0	**Kyiv** d.	0106	0106	0151	0256	...	1136	1319	1404	1657	1657	1830	1918	1957	2013	2037	2109	2117	2133	2236	2252	2252	...	...
159	Kozyatyn 1 **1780** d.	0321	0321	|	|	...	|	|	1628	1853	1853	2044	2108	|	|	2242	|	|	|	|	0058	0058	...	...
221	Vinnytsya **1780** d.	0420	0420	|	0539	...	1400	|	1727	1946	1946	2156	2151	|	|	2338	|	|	|	|	0159	0159	...	...
367	Khmelnytsky **1780** d.	0635	0635	|	0735	...	1540	|	2028	2143	2143	0008	2331	|	|	0139	|	|	|	|	0431	0431	...	...
486	Ternopil **1780** d.	0836	0836	|	0933	...	1717	|	...	2344	2344	0242	0109	|	|	0351	|	|	|	|	0632	0632	...	...
627	**Lviv** **1780** a.	1037	1037	0835	1121	...	1845	1943	...	0144	0144	0436	0240	0256	0307	0559	0333	0419	0445	0640	0828	0828	...	...
627	**Lviv** **1710** d.	1057	1057	0859	...	1305	1900	...	...	0210	...	...	0245	0348	0327	...	0413	0439	...	...	0851	0851	...	...
725	**Przemyśl** Glowny ⊖ PL a.	|	|	|	...	1517	2020	...	...	|	...	...	0400	|	|	...	0629	|	...	...	1112	1112	...	...
768	**Ivano-Frankivsk** **1710** a.	1314	1314	1120	...	...	...	...	...	0437	...	...	...	0559	0539	...	...	0700	...	...	...	...	...	...

	IC		*IC*	16			22			2		43					56				*IC*		
	749	**772**	**706**	**146**	**141**	**144**	**104**	**90**	**74**	**123**	**92**	**50**	**8**	**60**	**31**	**81**	**137**	**13**	**52**	**96**	**716**		
				■	●	●		■	●	●							●						
	E			**LT**	**A**	**B**	**C**			**X**		**KR**	**J**	**H**	**D**	**G**	**FO**	**N**		**F**			
Ivano-Frankivsk **1710** d.	...	...	...	1623	1441	1441	...	...	...	1847	...	...	2132	...	...	...	2100	...	...	2346	...	...	...
Przemyśl Glowny ⊖ PL d.	...	...	0949	|	|	|	...	1349	1349	|	...	...	|	...	1811	...	|	...	2032	|	2355	...	...
Lviv **1710** a.	...	...	1226	1845	1708	1708	...	1726	1726	2109	...	...	2350	...	2200	...	2318	...	0021	0206	0239	...	...
Lviv **1780** d.	1019	...	1241	1905	1738	1738	1852	1746	1746	2129	2309	2334	0011	2135	...	2252	2350	2350	0043	0335	0254	...	...
Ternopil **1780** d.	|	...	1414	|	1952	1952	2048	2010	2010	|	|	|	|	0033	...	0049	0154	0154	|	|	0428	...	...
Khmelnytsky **1780** d.	|	1105	1543	|	2156	2156	2233	2238	2238	|	|	|	|	0224	...	0313	0336	0336	|	|	0600	...	...
Vinnytsya **1780** d.	|	1411	1724	|	2355	2355	0026	0129	0129	|	|	|	|	0421	...	0515	0529	0529	|	|	0745	...	...
Kozyatyn 1 **1780** d.	|	1507	1808	|	0053	0053	|	0234	0234	|	|	|	|	0514	...	0628	0623	0623	|	|	|	...	...
Kyiv a.	1641	1722	2010	0221	0306	0306	0316	0505	0505	0413	0628	0635	0702	0738	...	0904	0838	0838	0744	1001	1008	...	...
Kharkiv **1750 1755** a.	...	...	...	0928	...	...	1025	...	1342	1119	...	...	...	...	...	...	...	...	...	...	...	...	...

km		*IC*	63							126	
		743	**112**	**113**	**9**	**29**	**27**	**43**	**17**	**129**	**45**
		④–⑦							■	●	●
			U	**S**	**Y**	**G**	**W**	**R**	**Z**	**PQ**	**M**
	Kharkiv **1750 1755** d.	...	2245	2136	...	...	...	...	1430	...	1412
0	**Kyiv** d.	0619	0635	0739	1016	1926	1957	2133	2141	2141	2341
156	Korosten d.	0806	|	1240	|	|	|	2345	|	|	0159
	Shepetivka d.	|	|	|	|	|	|	|	|	|	0450
572	**Lviv** a.	1159	1326	2232	1636	0200	0256	0445	0403	0403	0925
572	**Lviv** **1710** d.	...	...	...	...	...	...	0530	...	...	...
713	**Ivano-Frankivsk** **1710** a.	...	...	...	...	...	...	0920	...	...	...

				64	*IC*			125		
	29	**28**	**10**	**112**	**744**	**45**	**17**	**129**	**114**	**43**
			■		④–⑦	■	●	■		
	G	**W**	**Y**	**U**		**M**	**Z**	**PQ**	**S**	**R**
Ivano-Frankivsk **1710** d.	...	...	...	...	...	...	...	...	...	2009
Lviv **1710** a.	...	...	...	...	...	...	...	...	...	0027
Lviv d.	0024	0335	1248	1556	1630	1725	1920	1920	1807	0051
Shepetivka d.	|	|	|	|	|	2228	|	|	|	0445
Korosten d.	|	0813	|	|	2041	0102	|	|	0426	0654
Kyiv a.	0708	1001	1911	2246	2228	0259	0155	0155	0937	0911
Kharkiv **1750 1755** a.	...	...	...	0618	...	1212	0846	...	1930	...

A – Chernihiv - Kyiv - Lviv - Ivano-Frankivsk and v.v.
B – Sumy - Kyiv - Lviv - Ivano-Frankivsk - Rakhiv and v.v.
C – Kharkiv (**21**) and Kramatorsk (**104**) - Kyiv - Lviv and v.v.
D – Zaporizhzhya - Lviv - Przemyśl and v.v.
E – Kyiv - Lviv - Chop - Uzhhorod and v.v.; conveys 🛏 1, 2 cl. Kyiv (**749**) - Lviv - Chop (**140/149**) - Wien and v.v.
F – Kyiv - Lviv - Ivano-Frankivsk - Rakhiv and v.v.
G – Kyiv - Lviv - Mukachevo - Uzhhorod and v.v.
H – Kyiv - Lviv - Uzhhorod - Chop and v.v.
J – Kyiv - Lviv - Ivano-Frankivsk - Chernivtsi and v.v.
K – Kyiv - Lviv - Truskavets and v.v.
L – Kharkiv - Kyiv - Lviv - Ivano Frankivsk - Chernivtsi (**15/16**) Kharkiv - Kyiv - Lviv - Yasynya and v.v.
M – Kyiv - Lviv - Uzhhorod and v.v.
N – Kyiv - Lviv - Mukachevo - Solotvyno and v.v.
O – Kyiv (**137**) - Lviv - Ivano-Frankivsk and v.v.
P – Poltava - Kyiv - Lviv - Uzhhorod and v.v.
Q – Kremenchuk - Kyiv - Lviv - Uzhhorod and v.v.
R – Cherkasy - Kyiv - Lviv - Ivano Frankivsk and v.v.
S – Kharkiv - Sumy - Kyiv - Zhytomyr - Kovel - Lviv and v.v.
T – Dnipro - Kyiv - Zhytomyr - Kovel - Lviv and v.v.
U – Lviv - Kyiv - Kharkiv - (**112**) - Izyum and v.v.
W – Kyiv - Lviv - Chop and v.v.
X – Kharkiv - Kyiv - Lviv - Ivano Frankivsk (**1**) - Vorokhta and v.v.
Y – Kyiv - Lviv - Chop - Debrecen - Budapest and v.v.
Z – Kharkiv - Kyiv - Lviv - Mukachevo and v.v.

● – Even dates Dec. 2024, Feb, Mar, June, July, Sep, Oct. 2025, Uneven dates Jan, Apr, May, Aug, Nov, Dec. 2025 (see page 555).
■ – Uneven dates Dec. 2024, Feb, Mar, June, July, Sep, Oct. 2025, Even dates Jan, Apr, May, Aug, Nov, Dec. 2025 (see page 555).
⊖ – 🏛 = Medyka / Mostiska II.
PL – Poland (UTC + 1 winter, UTC + 2 summer).

1705 ODESA - LVIV — UZ

km		**36**	**38**	**26**	**136**	**12**	**78**			
							●			
							S			
0	**Odesa** Holovna d.	1441	1441	1818	1818	1942	2001	...	...	...
186	Podilsk d.	1715	1715	2058	2058	|	2239	...	...	...
	Rudnytsia d.	1833	1833	2216	2216	|	0003	...	...	...
387	Zhmerynka d.	2030	2030	0021	0021	0059	0216	...	...	...
	Vinnytsya d.	|	|	|	|	|	0302	...	...	...
498	Kozyatyn 1 a.	|	|	|	|	|	0359	...	...	...
486	Khmelnytsky d.	2208	2208	0156	0156	0228	...	...	...	...
605	Ternopil d.	0024	0024	0401	0401	0421	...	...	...	...
746	**Lviv** a.	0224	0224	0609	0609	0616	...	...	...	...
	Lviv d.	0413	...	0631	0631	...	...	...	...	...
844	**Przemyśl** Glowny ⊖ PL a.	0629	...	|	|	...	...	...	...	...
	Yasynya **1710** a.	...	...	1213	|	...	...	...	...	...
	Chernivtsi **1710** a.	...	...	...	1124	...	...	...	...	...

	12	**26**	**136**	**78**	**37**	**35**			
				■					
				S					
Chernivtsi **1710** d.	...	...	1520	...	...	...	...	...	...
Yasynya **1710** d.	...	1438	|	...	...	...	...	...	...
Przemyśl Glowny ⊖ PL d.	...	|	|	...	...	2032	...	...	...
Lviv a.	...	2043	2043	...	...	0012	...	...	...
Lviv d.	1946	2103	2103	...	0115	0115	...	...	...
Ternopil d.	2148	2315	2315	...	0332	0332	...	...	...
Khmelnytsky d.	2335	0111	0111	...	0536	0536	...	...	...
Kozyatyn 1 d.	|	|	|	0123	|	|	...	...	...
Vinnytsya d.	|	|	|	0225	|	|	...	...	...
Zhmerynka d.	0116	0257	0257	0322	0727	0727	...	...	...
Rudnytsia d.	|	0442	0442	0520	0905	0905	...	...	...
Podilsk d.	|	0552	0552	0633	1016	1016	...	...	...
Odesa Holovna a.	0607	0850	0850	0908	1251	1251	...	...	...

S – Odesa - Kozyatyn - Kovel and v.v.
● – Even dates (see page 555).
■ – Uneven dates (see page 555).
⊖ – 🏛 = Medyka / Mostiska II.
PL – Poland (UTC + 1 winter, UTC + 2 summer).

1710 LVIV - RAKHIV and CHERNIVTSI — UZ

km		**55**	**95**	**7**	**15**	**145**	**6**	**116**	**136**	**26**	**1**
		137									**123**
		■			●	●					■
		FO	**F**		**L**	**K**	**T**	**Z**			**V**
	Kyiv **1700** d.	1657	1957	2013	2117	2117	...	...	...	...	0151
	Odesa **1705** d.	|	|	|	|	|	...	...	1818	1818	|
0	**Lviv** **1700** d.	0210	0348	0327	0439	0439	0516	0516	0631	0631	0859
145	Ivano-Frankivsk **1700** a.	0437	0559	0539	0700	0700	0733	0733	0854	0854	1120
145	Ivano-Frankivsk d.	0507	0619	0552	0721	0805	0753	0805	0906	0924	1140
	Vorokhta a.	0720	0829	|	0930	|	1004	...	|	1135	1359
	Yasynya a.	0811	0908	|	1010	|	1043	...	|	1213	...
	Rakhiv a.	0857	0950	|	...	|	...	...	|	...	...
196	Kolomyia a.	...	...	0650	...	0911	...	0911	1002	...	...
267	**Chernivtsi** a.	...	...	0759	...	1025	...	1025	1124	...	...
km											
0	Rakhiv d.	1245	...	...	...	...	...	...	...	...	...
13	Dilove a.	1325	...	...	...	...	...	...	...	...	...

	6	**116**	**146**	**16**	**136**	**26**	**2**	**56**	**8**	**96**
							123	**137**		
			■	■			●	●		
	T	**Z**	**K**	**L**			**V**	**FO**		**F**
Chernivtsi d.	...	1306	1306	...	1520	...	...	...	1912	...
Kolomyia d.	1217	1419	1419	...	1640	...	...	...	2024	...
Rakhiv d.	1303	|	|	...	|	...	...	1635	|	1943
Yasynya d.	1459	|	|	1319	|	1438	...	1729	|	2038
Vorokhta d.	1540	|	|	1403	|	1524	1627	1821	|	2122
Ivano-Frankivsk a.	1806	1507	1507	1555	1733	1723	1819	2032	2117	2318
Ivano-Frankivsk **1700** d.	...	1540	1540	1623	1801	1801	1847	2100	2132	2346
Lviv **1700** a.	...	1806	1806	1845	2043	2043	2129	2318	2350	0206
Odesa **1705** a.	...	...	|	|	0831	0831	|	|	|	|
Kyiv **1700** a.	...	...	0221	0221	...	...	0413	0838	0702	1001
Dilove d.	1418	...	...	...	...	...	...	...	...	...
Rakhiv a.	1500	...	...	...	...	...	...	...	...	...

F – Kyiv - Lviv - Ivano-Frankivsk - Rakhiv and v.v.
K – Kharkiv - Kyiv - Lviv - Chernivtsi and v.v.
L – Kharkiv - Kyiv - Lviv - Vorokhta - Yasynya and v.v.
O – Kyiv (**137**) - Lviv - Ivano-Frankivsk and v.v.
T – Zaporizhzhia - Lviv - Yasynya and v.v.
V – Kharkiv - Kyiv - Lviv - Ivano Frankivsk (**1/2**) - Vorokhta and v.v.
Z – Zaporizhzhya - Lviv - Chernivtsi and v.v.

● – Even dates (see page 555).
■ – Uneven dates (see page 555).

UZ — LVIV - TRUSKAVETS, CHOP, UZHHOROD and SOLOTVYNO — 1715

Revised service from March 31 to July 31.

km		29	13 ■	38 A	17 ■ Z	126/9 ● PQ	81	49	33 L	59	41 ■ D	48 ● M	40 ■ S	4 E	45 ● B	31 L	9	829 ④–⑦	IC 749	749 J	368 K	83 ■	
	Kyiv **1700** d.	1926	1657	...	2141	2141	1830	2133	...	2037	...	...	...	...	2341	...	1016	...	1319	1319	...	1521	...
0	**Lviv** d.	0225	0210	0251	0429	0429	0502	0510	...	0627	0812	0840	0840	0908	0950	...	1701	1710	2008	2008	2231	2317	...
74	Styri d.	|	0332	0403	0530	0530	0605	|	...	|	|	0943	0943	|	|	...	|	1814	2110	2110	2354	0017	...
78	Sambir d.	0332	|	|	|	|	|	|	...	0745	|	|	|	1015	1056	...	|	|	|	|	0204	|	...
133	**Truskavets** a.	|	|	|	|	|	|	0719	...	|	1029	|	|	|	|	...	|	|	|	|	|	|	...
225	Mukachevo **1195** d.	|	0647	0744	0818	0818	0933	...	1022	|	...	1238	1243	|	|	1630	2028	2118	2359	2359	|	0317	...
	Chop ◧ **1195** a.	|	|	...	...	...	1026	...	1132	|	...	...	|	|	|	1744	2113	2213	0048	0048	|	|	...
288	**Uzhhorod** a.	0752	|	...	...	...	...	...	|	1226	...	...	|	1437	1536	|	|	...	0134	|	0645	|	...
	Solotvyno 1 a.	...	1133	...	...	...	...	...	|	...	...	...	1720	...	...	|	|	...	...	|	...	0808	...
	Budapest Keleti **1270** a.	...	...	...	...	...	...	...	|	...	...	...	...	...	...	|	0600	...	...	0820	...	...	...
	Budapest Nyugati **1270** a.	...	...	...	...	...	...	...	1639	...	...	...	...	...	...	2239	...	...	...	...	...	...	...

	749 J	IC 749	829 ⑤–①	10	42 ● D	45 ■ B	48 ■ M	39 ● S	125/9 ■ PQ	17 ● Z	34 L	60	3 E	81	50	13	29	37 A	367 K	83 ●		
Budapest Nyugati **1270** d.	...	...	...	...	...	...	...	...	...	...	0720	...	...	...	...	...	...	...	...	...	...	...
Budapest Keleti **1270** d.	1940	...	...	2240	...	...	...	...	...	...	|	...	...	...	...	...	...	...	...	...	...	...
Solotvyno 1 d.	|	...	...	|	...	...	...	0930	...	...	|	...	...	...	...	1340	...	...	...	1952	...	...
Uzhhorod d.	|	...	...	|	...	1035	...	|	...	...	|	1502	1612	...	...	|	1833	...	2126	|	...	...
Chop ◧ **1195** d.	0521	0521	0541	|	...	|	...	|	...	...	1428	|	|	1709	...	|	|	...	|	|	...	...
Mukachevo **1195** d.	0621	0621	0643	0808	...	|	1438	1438	1512	1512	1538	|	|	1812	...	1859	|	2057	|	0058	...	...
Truskavets d.	|	|	|	|	1303	|	|	|	|	|	...	|	|	|	2054	|	|	|	|	|	...	...
Sambir d.	|	|	|	|	|	1553	|	|	|	|	...	1957	2032	|	|	|	2257	|	0258	|	...	...
Styri d.	0858	0858	0942	|	|	|	1722	1722	1753	1753	...	|	|	2126	|	2212	|	2352	0505	0352	...	...
Lviv a.	0959	0959	1048	1228	1521	1700	1822	1822	1855	1855	...	2105	2135	2230	2302	2318	0004	0053	0610	0500	...	...
Kyiv **1700** a.	1641	1641	...	1911	...	0529	...	...	0155	0155	...	0738	...	0904	0635	0838	0710	...	...	1312	...	...

A – Odesa - Lviv - Mukachevo and v.v.
D – Dnipro - Lviv - Truskavets and v.v.
E – Zaporizhzhya - Lviv - Uzhhorod and v.v.
J – 🛏 1, 2 cl. Kyiv (**749**) - Lviv - Chop (**140/149**) - Záhony - Wien and v.v.
K – Uzhhorod - Lviv - Kovel and v.v.
L – LATORCA – (2) Budapest - Mukachevo and v.v.
M – Zaporizhzhya - Lviv - Mukachevo and v.v.
P – Poltava - Kyiv - Lviv - Uzhhorod and v.v.
Q – Kremenchuk - Kyiv - Lviv - Uzhhorod and v.v.
S – Zaporizhzhya - Lviv - Solotvino and v.v.
Z – Kharkiv - Kyiv - Lviv - Mukachevo and v.v.

● – Even dates (see page 555).
■ – Uneven dates (see page 555).
◧ – 🏛 for trains to / from Hungary, Slovakia.

UZ, CFM — KYIV - ODESA - BEREZYNE / IZMAIL and TIRASPOL - CHISINĂU - IAŞI / OCNITA — 1720

Tiraspol and Bender (formerly Tighina) are located in the *de facto* autonomous region of Transnistria.

km		763 ③⑤⑦		351 ■ K		105				
0	**Kyiv** **1700** d.	1429	...	1705	...	2244	...	...	...	...
157	Kozyatyn 1 **1700** d.	1620	...	1909	...	0042	...	...	...	...
221	Vinnytsya **1700** d.	1707	...	2001	...	0133	...	...	...	...
268	Zhmerynka **1700 1705** d.	1752	...	2117	...	0214	...	...	...	...
	Mohyliv-Podil'sk'yi 🏛 a.	|	...	2352	...	|	...	...	...	...
	Rudnitsya d.	|	...	...	...	0347	...	...	...	...
469	Podilsk **1705** d.	2007	...	...	...	0500	...	...	...	...
655	**Odesa** Holovna **1705** a.	2218	...	...	...	0720	...	...	...	...
655	**Odesa** Holovna d.	...	...	...	...	...	...	...	...	...
740	Bilhorod-Dnistrovsky d.	...	...	...	...	...	...	...	...	...
830	Artsyz a.	...	...	...	...	...	...	...	...	...
865	**Berezyne** a.	...	...	...	...	...	...	...	...	...
937	**Izmail** a.	...	...	...	...	...	...	...	...	...

	106		352 ● K		764 ①④⑥				
Izmail d.	...	...	...	...	...	...	...	...	...
Berezyne d.	...	...	...	...	...	...	...	...	...
Artsyz d.	...	...	...	...	...	...	...	...	...
Bilhorod-Dnistrovsky d.	...	...	...	...	...	...	...	...	...
Odesa Holovna a.	...	...	...	...	...	...	...	...	...
Odesa Holovna **1705** d.	2100	...	...	...	0610	...	...	...	...
Podilsk **1705** d.	2323	...	...	...	0818	...	...	...	...
Rudnitsya d.	0034	...	...	...	|	...	...	...	...
Mohyliv-Podil'sk'yi 🏛 d.	|	...	0517	...	|	...	...	...	...
Zhmerynka **1700 1705** d.	0208	...	0816	...	1052	...	...	...	...
Vinnytsya **1700** d.	0251	...	0903	...	1133	...	...	...	...
Kozyatyn 1 **1700** d.	0343	...	1000	...	1222	...	...	...	...
Kyiv **1700** a.	0547	...	1220	...	1418	...	...	...	...

km		1061		821b 1051		352 ● K	105b 401 B			
0	**Tiraspol** MD d.	...	...	...	...	...	...	...	...	...
13	Bender 3 d.	...	...	...	...	...	...	...	...	...
71	**Chisinău** a.	...	...	...	...	...	...	...	...	...
71	**Chisinău** d.	...	...	0627	...	1705	1705	...	1807	...
178	Ungheni a.	...	...	0915	...	1958	1958	...	2127	...
178	Ungheni 🏛 MD d.	0710	...	0951	...	2029	2135	...	...	...
179	Ungheni Prut 🏛 RO d.	0808	...	1038	...	|	2235	...	...	...
194	**Iaşi** Socola a.	0836	...	1113	...	|	|	...	...	...
199	**Iaşi** a.	0846	...	...	...	|	2308	...	...	...
256	Bălti Oraş d.	...	...	...	...	2232	...	...	...	...
354	**Ocnita** d.	...	...	...	...	0202	...	...	...	...
	Vălcineţ 🏛 MD d.	...	...	...	...	0334	...	...	...	...
	Mohyliv-Podil'sk'yi 🏛 a.	...	...	...	...	0347	...	...	...	...

			402 106b B		351 ■ K		1054 824b	1062	
Mohyliv-Podil'sk'yi 🏛 d.	...	...	...	...	0122	...	...	...	...
Vălcineţ 🏛 MD d.	...	...	...	...	0225	...	...	...	...
Ocnita d.	...	...	...	...	0345	...	...	...	...
Bălti Oraş d.	...	...	...	...	0652	...	...	...	...
Iaşi d.	...	...	0232	...	|	...	...	1906	...
Iaşi Socola d.	...	...	|	...	|	...	1740	1918	...
Ungheni Prut 🏛 RO d.	...	...	0402	...	|	...	1849	2025	...
Ungheni 🏛 MD a.	...	...	0408	...	0850	...	1856	2031	...
Ungheni d.	0356	...	0603	...	0920	...	1936	...	...
Chisinău a.	0711	...	0844	...	1153	...	2216	...	...
Chisinău d.	...	...	...	...	...	...	...	...	...
Bender 3 d.	...	...	...	...	...	...	...	...	...
Tiraspol MD a.	...	...	...	...	...	...	...	...	...

B – PRETENIA 🛏 1, 2 cl, 🍷 Chisinău (**105b / 106b**) - Ungheni (**401 / 402**) - Iaşi - Bucuresti and v.v.
K – Kyiv - Ocnita - Ungheni - Chisinău and v.v.

● – Even dates (see page 555).
■ – Uneven dates (see page 555).

MD – Moldova (UTC + 2 in winter, UTC + 3 in summer).
RO – Romania (UTC + 2 in winter, UTC + 3 in summer).

UZ — KYIV and KOZYATYN - RIVNE - LVIV, KOVEL and CHELM — 1730

km		19	67 [R] L	97	23	93 ■ M	78 ■ N	88 ● P	367 K	119 D	113 T
0	**Kyiv** d.	2021	2021	2149	2308	2308	...	...	...	0627	0739
156	Korosten d.	|	|	0014	|	|	...	...	...	|	1240
311	Sarny d.	|	|	|	|	|	...	...	...	|	1549
*234	**Kozyatyn** 1 d.	|	|	|	|	|	0419	0419	...	|	|
	Shepetivka d.	|	|	0234	0250	0250	0634	0634	...	|	|
*207	**Lviv** d.	|	|	|	|	|	|	|	0642	|	|
383	**Rivne** a.	|	|	0438	0420	0420	0812	0812	0952	1112	|
383	**Rivne** d.	|	|	0448	0430	0430	0817	0817	0957	1114	|
461	Lutsk d.	|	|	0633	|	|	0931	0931	1145	|	|
545	**Kovel** a.	0213	0213	0828	0643	0643	1132	1132	1332	1258	1813
545	**Kovel** d.	0233	0233	...	0705	0705	...	...	...	1320	1833
744	**Lviv** a.	|	|	...	|	|	...	...	...	|	2232
	Yahodyn 🏛 ⊡ d.	0330	0330	...	0807	0807	...	...	...	1422	...
634	**Chelm** a.	0544	0654	...	1116	1116	...	...	...	1649	...
	Lublin **1055** a.	*0758*	0758	...	*1431*	*1431*	...	...	...	*1931*	...
	Warszawa W **1055** a.	*1011*	1011	...	*1611*	*1611*	...	...	...	*2111*	...

	68 [R] L	20	120 D	368 K	78 ● N	88 ■ P	94 ● M	24	98	114 T
Warszawa W **1055** d.	1749	*1749*	*0648*	...	...	...	*1148*	*1148*	...	...
Lublin **1055** d.	2010	*2010*	*0832*	...	...	...	*1333*	*1333*	...	...
Chelm d.	2123	2303	1037	...	...	...	1607	1607	...	...
Yahodyn 🏛 ⊡ d.	0252	0252	1432	...	...	...	2019	2019	...	...
Lviv d.	|	|	|	...	...	...	|	|	...	1807
Kovel a.	0401	0401	1531	...	...	...	2119	2119	...	2228
Kovel d.	0421	0421	1552	1519	1740	1740	2139	2139	1911	2248
Lutsk d.	|	|	|	1721	1949	1949	|	|	2119	|
Rivne a.	|	|	1739	1831	2107	2107	2325	2325	2233	|
Rivne d.	|	|	1741	1834	2112	2112	2327	2327	2238	|
Lviv a.	|	|	|	2154	|	|	|	|	|	|
Shepetivka d.	|	|	|	...	2247	2247	0057	0057	0032	|
Kozyatyn 1 a.	|	|	|	...	0101	0101	|	|	|	|
Sarny d.	|	|	|	...	...	...	|	|	|	0110
Korosten d.	|	|	|	...	...	...	|	|	0334	0426
Kyiv a.	1045	1045	2239	...	...	...	0512	0512	0600	0937

D – Chelm - Kyiv - Dnipro and v.v.
K – Uzhhorod - Lviv - Kovel and v.v.
L – KYIV EKSPRES / KIEV EXPRESS – 🛏 1, 2 cl. Kyiv - Warszawa and v.v.
M – Kharkiv - Kyiv - Kovel - Chelm and v.v.
N – Odesa - Kozyatyn - Kovel and v.v.
P – Zaporizhzhya - Kozyatyn - Kovel and v.v.
T – Kharkiv - Kyiv - Zhytomyr - Kovel - Lviv and v.v.

⊡ – 🏛 = Yahodyn (Ukraine) and Dorohusk (Poland). Ukraine is one hour ahead of Poland.
● – Even dates (see page 555).
■ – Uneven dates (see page 555).
* – Distance from Rivne.

1750 KYIV - KHARKIV - DONETSK UZ

km		17 ● B	125 ■ P	129 ■ Q	16 ■ A	146 ■ T	22	104	92 ● G	2/123 ● X	74 ● H	94 ● F	IC712	IC722	IC724	101 ■(1) K	64	112
	Ivano-Frankivsk **1700** d.	...	...	...	1623	1623	...	...	...	1847	...	...	...	...	...	...	...	...
	Lviv **1700** d.	1920	1920	1920	1905	1905	1852	1852	...	2129	1746	...	...	...	...	...	1556	1556
0	**Kyiv** d.	0215	0215	0215	0241	0241	0336	0336	...	0433	0552	0552	0644	0652	1525	2109	2306	2306
150	Hrebinka d.	|	0355	0355	|	|	|	|	...	|	0753	0753	0809	|	|	2303	0056	0056
	Kremenchuk a.	|	|	0748	|	|	|	|	...	|	|	|	|	|	|	|	|	|
335	Poltava Kyivska a.	0616	0723	...	0656	0656	0748	0748	...	0841	1101	1101	1002	1014	1841	0222	0330	0330
335	Poltava Kyivska **1785** d.	0636	...	...	0716	0716	0811	0831	...	0905	1121	1121	1004	1016	1843	0227	0400	0400
493	**Kharkiv** **1785** a.	0846	...	...	0928	0928	1025	|	...	1119	1342	1342	|	1152	2020	|	0618	0619
493	**Kharkiv** d.	...	...	...	...	...	...	|	...	...	...	...	|	...	...	|	...	0755
	Bakhmut a.	...	...	...	...	...	...	|	...	...	...	...	|	...	...	|	...	|
	Izyum a.	...	...	...	...	...	...	|	...	...	...	...	|	...	...	|	...	1115
	Dnipro Hol. d.	...	...	...	...	...	...	|	1050	...	...	...	|	...	...	|	...	...
635	Slovyansk d.	...	...	...	...	...	...	1456	1625	...	...	...	1324	...	...	0805	...	...
649	Kramatorsk a.	...	...	...	...	...	...	1514	1643	...	...	...	1338	...	...	0823	...	...
679	Kostiantynivka a.	...	...	...	...	...	...	...	...	...	...	...	...	...	...	...	...	...
744	**Donetsk** a.	...	...	...	...	...	...	...	...	...	...	...	...	...	...	...	...	...

	IC725	102 ● L	IC723	15 ● A	145 ● T	129 ● P	126 ● Q	17 ■ B	IC712	73 ■ H	93 ■ F	92 ■ G	1/123 ■ X	104	21	63	112
Donetsk d.	...	...	...	...	...	...	...	...	...	...	...	...	...	...	...	...	...
Kostiantynivka d.	...	...	...	...	...	...	...	...	...	...	...	...	...	...	...	...	...
Kramatorsk d.	...	0915	...	...	...	...	...	...	1430	...	...	1732	...	1603	...	...	...
Slovyansk d.	...	0942	...	...	...	...	...	...	1443	...	...	1752	...	1620	...	...	...
Dnipro Hol. a.	...	|	...	...	...	...	...	...	|	...	...	0004	...	|	...	...	...
Izyum d.	...	|	...	...	...	...	...	...	|	...	...	...	...	|	...	...	1829
Bakhmut d.	...	|	...	...	...	...	...	...	|	...	...	...	...	|	...	...	|
Kharkiv a.	...	|	...	...	...	...	...	...	|	...	...	...	...	|	...	...	2140
Kharkiv **1785** d.	0721	|	1356	1401	1401	...	...	1430	|	1440	1440	...	1845	|	1935	2245	2245
Poltava Kyivska **1785** a.	0903	1458	1542	1616	1616	...	...	1642	1750	1705	1705	...	2100	2134	2150	0105	0105
Poltava Kyivska d.	0905	1503	1546	1636	1636	1603	...	1702	1752	1725	1725	...	2120	2220	2220	0127	0127
Kremenchuk d.	|	|	|	|	|	|	1515	|	|	|	|	...	|	|	|	|	|
Hrebinka d.	|	1807	|	|	|	1926	1926	|	1944	2016	2016	...	|	|	|	0401	0401
Kyiv a.	1229	2010	1918	2053	2053	2121	2121	2112	2100	2205	2205	...	0131	0236	0236	0604	0604
Lviv **1700** a.	...	...	...	0419	0419	0403	0403	0403	...	0828	...	...	0840	1121	1121	1326	1326
Ivano-Frankivsk **1700** a.	...	...	...	0654	0654	...	...	...	...	...	...	...	1128	...	...	...	...

A – Kharkiv (**15**/**16**) - Kyiv - Lviv - Ivano Frankivsk - Yasynya and v.v.
B – Kharkiv - Kyiv - Lviv - Uzhhorod and v.v.
F – Kharkiv - Kyiv - Kovel - Chelm and v.v.
G – Odesa - Dnipro - Kramatorsk and v.v.
H – Kharkiv - Kyiv - Lviv - Przemyśl and v.v.
K – From Kherson (Table **1760**).
L – To Kherson (Table **1760**).
P – Poltava - Kyiv - Lviv - Uzhhorod and v.v.
Q – Kremenchuk - Kyiv - Lviv - Uzhhorod and v.v.
T – Kharkiv (**145**/**146**) - Kyiv - Lviv - Ivano Frankivsk - Chernivsti and v.v.
X – Kharkiv - Kyiv - Lviv - Ivano Frankivsk (**1/2**) - Vorokhta and v.v.
● – Even dates (see page 555).
■ – Uneven dates (see page 555).

1755 KYIV - CHERNIHIV, SHOSTKA, KHARKIV and LYSYCHANSK UZ

km		45 ■ B	144 ● H	141 ● J	786	116	114 S	774	780	788
	Lviv **1700** d.	1725	1738	1738	...	...	1807	...	...	...
0	**Kyiv** d.	0319	0326	0326	0716	0733	0957	1037	1640	1805
209	**Chernihiv** a.	|	|	0720	|	|	|	|	|	|
197	Bakhmach Pas. d.	0555	0651	...	1002	1027	1255	1335	1903	2102
221	Konotop d.	0637	0735	...	1025	1109	1339	1411	1942	2135
302	**Shostka** a.	|	|	...	1135	|	|	1525	|	2256
350	Sumy d.	0852	0952	...	...	1322	1608	...	2141	...
552	**Kharkiv** a.	1212	...	...	...	...	1930	...	...	...
552	**Kharkiv** d.	...	...	...	...	...	...	...	...	...
681	Kupiansk-Vuslov d.	...	...	...	...	...	...	...	...	...
806	**Lysychansk** a.	...	...	...	...	...	...	...	...	...
934	**Luhansk** a.	...	...	...	...	...	...	...	...	...

	788	779	786	115	774	45 ● B	142 ■ J	143 ■ H	113 S
Luhansk d.	...	...	...	...	...	...	...	...	...
Lysychansk d.	...	...	...	...	...	...	...	...	...
Kupiansk-Vuslov d.	...	...	...	...	...	...	...	...	...
Kharkiv a.	...	...	...	...	...	...	...	...	...
Kharkiv d.	...	...	...	...	...	1444	...	...	2150
Sumy d.	...	0643	...	1450	...	1834	...	1901	0138
Shostka d.	0526	|	1220	|	1714	|	...	|	|
Konotop d.	0655	0905	1331	1727	1844	2101	...	2134	0407
Bakhmach Pas. d.	0723	0926	1354	1751	1907	2124	...	2158	0431
Chernihiv d.	|	|	|	|	|	|	2118	|	|
Kyiv a.	0952	1142	1636	2034	2157	2342	0054	0054	0717
Lviv **1700** a.	...	...	...	...	...	0920	1030	1030	2246

B – Kharkiv - Kyiv - Lviv - Uzhhorod and v.v.
H – Sumy - Kyiv - Lviv - Ivano-Frankivsk - Rakhiv and v.v.
J – Chernihiv - Kyiv - Lviv - Ivano-Frankivsk and v.v.
S – Kharkiv - Kyiv - Zhytomyr - Kovel - Lviv and v.v. Does not run every 3rd day.
● – Even dates (see page 555).
■ – Uneven dates (see page 555).

1760 LVIV and KYIV- MYKOLAIV and KHERSON UZ

km		794 ③–①		102 ● K	122 ■(3)		110 ●	165 ● N	43 R	
	Lviv d.	...	...	...	...	...	1604	...	2334	...
	Ternopil d.	...	...	...	...	...	1819	...	|	...
	Khmelnytsky d.	...	...	...	...	...	2030	...	|	...
	Zhmerynka d.	...	...	...	...	...	2214	...	|	...
	Vinnytsya d.	...	...	...	...	...	2302	...	|	...
	Kozyatyn 1 d.	...	...	...	...	...	2359	...	|	...
0	**Kyiv** d.	1655	...	2057	2057	...	|	...	0724	...
216	Im. T. Shevchenka d.	2013	...	0023	0023	...	0428	0457	1050	...
240	Cherkasy d.	2053	...	|	|	...	|	0540	1131	...
308	Znamyanka d.	...	...	|	|	...	|	...	...	...
448	Kryvyi Rih Hol. d.	...	...	|	|	...	|	...	...	...
651	**Mykolaiv** a.	...	...	0551	0551	...	0957	...	...	...
706	**Kherson** a.	...	...	0818**t**	0818**z**	...	1224**t**	...	...	...

	793 ④–②		101 ■(1) K	43 R		109 ■(1)	165 ■ N	121 ●	
Kherson d.	...	...	0903	...	...	1309**u**	...	1844	...
Mykolaiv d.	...	...	1122	...	...	1554	...	2146	...
Kryvyi Rih Hol. d.	...	...	|	...	...	|	...	|	...
Znamyanka d.	...	...	|	...	...	|	...	|	...
Cherkasy d.	0625	...	|	1655	...	|	2120	|	...
Im. T. Shevchenka d.	0732	...	1705	1759	...	2153	2200	0403	...
Kyiv a.	1031	...	2027	2105	...	|	...	0727	...
Kozyatyn 1 d.	...	...	...	|	...	0205	...	...	...
Vinnytsya d.	...	...	...	|	...	0300	...	...	...
Zhmerynka d.	...	...	...	|	...	0402	...	...	...
Khmelnytsky d.	...	...	...	|	...	0541	...	...	...
Ternopil d.	...	...	...	|	...	0746	...	...	...
Lviv a.	...	...	...	0445	...	0955	...	...	...

K – From/to Kramatorsk (Table **1750**).
N – Cherkasy - Dnipro - Kharkiv and v.v.
R – Ivano Frankivsk - Lviv - Kyiv - Cherkasy and v.v.
t – Not July 30, Aug. 30, Oct. 30.
u – Not Aug. 1, Sept. 1, Nov. 1.
z – Not July 31, Aug. 31, Oct. 31.
● – Even dates (see page 555).
■ – Uneven dates (see page 555).

UZ LVIV and KYIV - DNIPRO - ZAPORIZHZHYA 1780

km		86	86	75	38	80	120	128	42	39	48	6	116	60	92	254	54	52	88	3	31	IC732	IC734	
									●	●	■			●	●	●	●	■	■					
							D		E	S	M	F	Z	B	C				A	G	H			
	Lviv 1705 d.	1105	1105	...	...	1450	...	1500	1542	1842	1842	1827	1827	...	...	...	...	...	...	2155	2222	...	...	...
	Ternopil 1705 d.	1317	1317	...	...	|	...	1711	1756	|	|	|	|	...	...	...	...	...	...	|	|	...	...	...
	Khmelnytsky 1705 d.	1512	1512	...	...	|	...	1910	2015	|	|	|	|	...	...	...	...	...	...	|	|	...	...	...
	Vinnytsya 1705 d.	1755	1755	...	...	|	...	|	2217	|	|	|	|	...	...	...	...	...	...	|	|	...	...	...
◐	Kozyatyn 1 1705 d.	1848	1848	...	...	|	...	|	2314	|	|	|	|	...	...	...	...	...	0121	|	|	...	...	...
0	**Kyiv** d.	|	|	2005	2201	2209	2259	|	|	|	|	|	|	...	...	...	...	...	|	|	|	0632	1614	...
216	Im. Tar. Shevchenka d.	2342	2342	0003	0041	0049	0148	|	0356	0342	0342	0420	0420	...	...	...	...	...	0610	0640	0728	0851	1829	...
	Odesa Holovna d.	|	|	|	|	|	|	|	|	|	|	|	|	2110	2110	2318	2318	2318	|	|	|	|	|	...
	Kropyvnytskyi d.	|	|	|	|	|	|	0452	|	|	|	|	|	0436	0436	0504	0504	0504	|	|	|	|	|	...
308	Znamyanka d.	0107	0107	0133	0204	0212	0308	0608	0524	0502	0502	0540	0540	0553	0553	0622	0622	0622	0737	0800	0848	1002	1942	...
353	Oleksandria d.	0149	0149	0220	|	0253	|	0654	0606	0543	0843	|	|	0637	0637	0709	0709	0709	0821	|	0929	1037	2018	...
490	**Kryvyi Rih** Hol. a.	|	|	0538	|	|	|	1011	|	|	|	|	|	|	|	1114	|	|	|	|	|	|	|	...
496	Kamianske d.	0419	0419	...	0458	0515	0642	1324	0845	0804	0804	0901	0901	0935	0935	...	1033	1033	1106	1050	1156	1216	2156	...
534	**Dnipro** Hol. a.	0450	0450	...	0528	0550	0728	1400	0915	0834	0834	0931	0931	1015	1015	...	1111	1111	1137	1119	1229	1241	2222	...
534	**Dnipro** Hol. d.	0510	...	...	0543	0718	...	1420	...	0854	0854	0951	0951	...	...	...	...	1143	1157	1134	1257	1249	...	...
658	**Zaporizhzhya** 1 a.	0701	...	...	0723	...	...	1632	...	1035	1035	1126	1126	...	...	...	...	1330	1344	1308	1500	1411	...	...
770	Melitopol 1782 a.	...	...	...	...	...	...	...	...	...	...	...	...	...	...	...	...	...	...	...	...	...	...	...
861	Novooleksiivka 1782 a.	...	...	...	...	...	...	...	...	...	...	...	...	...	...	...	...	...	...	...	...	...	...	...
1033	**Mariupol** 1782 a.	...	...	...	...	...	...	...	...	...	...	...	...	...	...	...	...	...	...	...	...	...	...	...

	IC733	41	6	116	IC732	128	88	40	48	254	53	52	4	76	86	79	38	119	32	59	92		
		■					●	■	●	■	■	●								■	■		
		E	F	Z			A	S	M				G					D	H	B	C		
Mariupol 1782 d.	...	...	...	...	...	...	...	...	...	...	...	...	...	...	...	...	...	...	...	...	...	...	...
Novooleksiivka 1782 d.	...	...	...	...	...	...	...	...	...	...	...	...	...	...	...	...	...	...	...	...	...	...	...
Melitopol 1782 d.	...	...	...	...	...	...	...	...	...	...	...	...	...	...	...	...	...	...	...	...	...	...	...
Zaporizhzhya 1 d.	...	...	1242	1242	1449	0950	1508	1617	1617	...	...	1600	1753	...	1905	...	2029	...	2103	...	...	...	...
Dnipro Hol. a.	...	...	1419	1419	1607	1207	1703	1757	1757	...	...	1747	1927	...	2053	...	2222	...	2244	...	...	...	...
Dnipro Hol. d.	0652	1412	1434	1434	1615	1231	1723	1817	1817	...	1807	1807	1942	...	2113	2152	2226	2239	2304	0024	0024	...	...
Kamianske d.	0718	1445	1507	1507	1642	1311	1841	1850	1850	...	1840	1840	2013	...	2146	2228	2259	2300	2337	0059	0059	...	...
Kryvyi Rih Hol. d.	|	|	|	|	|	1630	|	|	|	1803	|	|	|	2045	|	|	|	|	|	|	|	...	...
Oleksandria d.	0851	1724	|	|	1816	1948	2050	2115	2115	2145	2145	2145	|	2352	0013	0055	|	|	0200	0336	0336	...	...
Znamyanka d.	0926	1818	1837	1837	1851	2059	2143	2200	2200	2249	2249	2249	2258	0040	0059	0137	0152	0200	0242	0440	0440	...	...
Kropyvnytskyi d.	|	|	|	|	|	2148	|	|	|	2335	2335	2335	|	|	|	|	|	|	|	0527	0527	...	...
Odesa Holovna a.	|	|	|	|	|	|	|	|	|	0525	0525	0525	|	|	|	|	|	|	|	1300	1300	...	...
Im. Tar. Shevchenka d.	1031	2011	2003	2003	1954	|	2321	2313	2313	...	...	...	0011	0205	0232	0254	0304	0325	0355	...	...	...	...
Kyiv a.	1246	|	|	|	2213	|	|	|	|	...	...	...	|	0624	|	0539	0546	0555	|	...	...	...	...
Kozyatyn 1 1705 d.	...	0020	|	|	...	|	0338	|	|	...	...	...	|	...	0656	|	...	...	|	...	...	...	...
Vinnytsya 1705 d.	...	0121	|	|	...	|	...	|	|	...	...	...	|	...	0807	|	...	...	|	...	...	...	...
Khmelnytsky 1705 d.	...	0331	|	|	...	0748	...	|	|	...	...	...	|	...	1110	|	...	...	|	...	...	...	...
Ternopil 1705 d.	...	0536	|	|	...	1003	...	|	|	...	...	...	|	...	1326	|	...	...	|	...	...	...	...
Lviv 1705 a.	...	0747	0456	0456	...	1217	...	0815	0815	...	...	...	0842	...	1540	1301	...	...	1517	...	...	...	...

A – Zaporizhzhya - Kozyatyn - Kovel and v.v.
D – Odesa - Dnipro - Kharkiv and v.v.
C – Odesa - Dnipro - Kramatorsk and v.v.
D – Chelm - Kyiv - Dnipro and v.v.
E – Dnipro - Lviv - Truskavets and v.v.
F – Zaporizhzhya - Lviv - Yasynya and v.v.
G – Zaporizhzhya - Lviv - Uzhhorod and v.v.
H – Zaporizhzhya - Lviv - Przemyśl and v.v.
M – Zaporizhzhya - Lviv - Mukachevo and v.v.
S – Zaporizhzhya - Lviv - Solotvyno and v.v.
V – Kryvyi Rih - Kyiv - Lviv - Vorokhta - Yasynya and v.v.
Z – Zaporizhzhya - Lviv - Chernivtsi and v.v.
● – Even dates (see page 555).
■ – Uneven dates (see page 555).
◐ – Kozyatyn - Im. Tarasa Shevchenka *304 km*.

UZ KHARKIV - ZAPORIZHZHYA - MELITOPOL and MARIUPOL 1782

km		823		165	59					
		⑤–③		●	■					
				N	B					
0	**Kharkiv** d.	0933	...	1850	1902	...	...	...	...	...
**	**Dnipro** Hol. a.	1322	...	2314	0004	...	...	...	...	...
	Dnipro Hol. d.	...	...	...	...	...	...	...	...	...
327	**Zaporizhzhya** 1 a.	...	...	...	...	...	...	...	...	...
327	**Zaporizhzhya** 1 1780 d.	...	...	...	...	...	...	...	...	...
	Kamianske d.	...	...	...	...	...	...	...	...	...
512	**Kryvyi Rih** Hol. a.	...	...	...	...	...	...	...	...	...
439	Melitopol 1780 a.	...	...	...	...	...	...	...	...	...
530	Novooleksiivka 1780 a.	...	...	...	...	...	...	...	...	...
702	**Mariupol** 1780 a.	...	...	...	...	...	...	...	...	...

	165		60	824					
	■		●	④–②					
	N		B						
Mariupol 1780 d.	...	...	...	...	...	...	...	...	...
Novooleksiivka 1780 d.	...	...	...	...	...	...	...	...	...
Melitopol 1780 d.	...	...	...	...	...	...	...	...	...
Kryvyi Rih Hol. d.	...	...	...	...	...	...	...	...	...
Kamianske d.	...	...	...	...	...	...	...	...	...
Zaporizhzhya 1 1780 a.	...	...	...	...	...	...	...	...	...
Zaporizhzhya 1 d.	...	...	...	...	...	...	...	...	...
Dnipro Hol. a.	...	...	...	...	...	...	...	...	...
Dnipro Hol. d.	0440	...	1050	1609	...	...	...	...	...
Kharkiv a.	0905	...	1640	2003	...	...	...	...	...

B – Odesa - Dnipro - Kharkiv and v.v.
N – Cherkasy - Dnipro - Kharkiv and v.v.
● – Even dates (also see table **1785**).
■ – Uneven dates (also see table **1785**).
** – Kharkiv - Dnipro Hol.: *300 km*.

UZ KHARKIV - KREMENCHUK - ODESA 1785

km		7	59
		●	■
0	**Kharkiv** d.	1951	1902
140	Poltava Pivdenna d.	2201	|
259	**Kremenchuk** d.	0004	|
353	Znamyanka d.	0120	0440
407	Kropyvnytskyi d.	0204	0527
765	**Odesa** Holovna a.	0642	1300

	8	60
	■	●
Odesa Holovna d.	2229	2110
Kropyvnytskyi d.	0316	0436
Znamyanka d.	0408	0553
Kremenchuk d.	0548	|
Poltava Pivdenna d.	0723	|
Kharkiv a.	0921	1640

UZ ODESA - MARIUPOL 1787

km			
0	**Odesa** Hol. d.	...	...
232	Mykolaiv d.	...	...
287	Kherson d.	...	...
643	**Zaporizhzhya** 1 a.	...	...
643	**Zaporizhzhya** 1 d.	...	...
1018	**Mariupol** a.	...	...

Mariupol d.	...	...
Zaporizhzhya 1 a.	...	...
Zaporizhzhya 1 d.	...	...
Kherson d.	...	...
Mykolaiv d.	...	...
Odesa Hol. a.	...	...

Crimean Railway UTC+3 CRIMEAN PENINSULA 1790

Due to the ongoing conflict there are no updates in Crimea until further notice

km						
0	Simferopol d.	...	...	...	...	...
78	Sevastopol a.	...	...	...	...	...

Sevastopol d.	...	...	...	...	...
Simferopol a.	...	...	...	...	...

km						
0	Simferopol d.	...	...	...	...	...
79	Yevpatoria a.	...	...	...	...	...

Yevpatoriya d.	...	...	...	...	...
Simferopol a.	...	...	...	...	...

km													
0	Armyansk d.	...	...	...	...	...	...	...	...	...	...	...	...
78	Dzhankoy ● d.	...	...	...	...	...	...	...	...	...	...	...	...
	Feodosia ● d.	...	...	...	...	...	...	...	...	...	...	...	...
179	Vladyslavivka ● d.	...	...	...	...	...	...	...	...	...	...	...	...
196	Feodosia ● a.	...	...	...	...	...	...	...	...	...	...	...	...
270	Kerch a.	...	...	...	...	...	...	...	...	...	...	...	...

Kerch d.	...	...	...	...	...	...	...	...	...	...	...	...
Feodosia ● d.	...	...	...	...	...	...	...	...	...	...	...	...
Vladyslavivka ● d.	...	...	...	...	...	...	...	...	...	...	...	...
Feodosia ● a.	...	...	...	...	...	...	...	...	...	...	...	...
Dzhankoy ● d.	...	...	...	...	...	...	...	...	...	...	...	...
Armyansk a.	...	...	...	...	...	...	...	...	...	...	...	...

km													
	Feodosia ● d.	...	...	...	...	...	...	...	...	...	...	...	...
	Vladyslavivka ● d.	...	...	...	...	...	...	...	...	...	...	...	...
0	Solone Ozero d.	...	...	...	...	...	...	...	...	...	...	...	...
20	Dzhankoy ● d.	...	...	...	...	...	...	...	...	...	...	...	...
111	Simferopol a.	...	...	...	...	...	...	...	...	...	...	...	...

Simferopol d.	...	...	...	...	...	...	...	...	...	...	...	...
Dzhankoy ● d.	...	...	...	...	...	...	...	...	...	...	...	...
Solone Ozero a.	...	...	...	...	...	...	...	...	...	...	...	...
Vladyslavivka ● d.	...	...	...	...	...	...	...	...	...	...	...	...
Feodosia ● a.	...	...	...	...	...	...	...	...	...	...	...	...

LITHUANIA, LATVIA and ESTONIA

SEE MAP PAGE 545

Operators: Lithuania: **LTG Link** (www.ltglink.lt) Latvia: **Vivi / Pasažieru vilciens** (www.vivi.lv or www.pv.lv) Estonia: **Elron** (www.elron.ee).
Services: Trains convey first- and second-class seating unless indicated otherwise. For Lithuania - Poland trains see Tables **59a** and **1042**.
Timings: Schedules are the latest available and may be subject to alteration at any time. Timings are expressed in local time at the station concerned (time comparison chart: page 4).

1800 RIGA - TALLINN, ST PETERBURG, VILNIUS and KALININGRAD 🚌

Riga and Vilnius coach stations are close to the railway stations. Tallinn coach station is *3 km* from the railway station by tram.

🚌 **RIGA - PÄRNU - TALLINN** Lux Express (www.luxexpress.eu) Journey 4½ hours:
From **Riga**: 0700, 0800, 0900, 1000, 1100, 1230, 1400, 1500, 1640, 1800, 1930.
From **Tallinn**: 0700, 0800, 0900, 1000, 1100, 1230, 1400, 1500, 1600, 1700, 1800, 2230.

🚌 **TALLINN - ST PETERBURG** Lux Express (www.luxexpress.eu) Journey 7 – 11 hours:
From **Tallinn** and **St Peterburg**: A number of journeys are possible with most requiring a change of vehicles at the Narva-Ivangorod border. Please check with operator as times vary.

🚌 **RIGA - VILNIUS** Lux Express (www.luxexpress.eu) Journey 4 - 4½ hours:
From **Riga**: 0700, 0930, 1200, 1440, 1630, 1720.
From **Vilnius**: 0645, 0900, 1020, 1200, 1500, 1730, 2230.

🚌 **RIGA - KALININGRAD** Ecolines (www.ecolines.net). Journey 10 hours:
From **Riga**: 1030 ②⑤⑦.
From **Kaliningrad**: 1140 ②⑤⑦.

1805 VILNIUS and KAUNAS - ŠIAULIAI - RIGA and KLAIPEDA (LTG Link)

Warning! Due to engineering work timings are subject to alteration. For connecting services Tallinn - Riga - Vilnius and v.v. see Table **49**.

km																								
			Ⓐ	①	⚒		Ⓒ			⑥								⑤–⑦						
		3	3		3		3	A		2			3	3			3	2	3		3		3	
0	**Vilnius** 1809 d.	...	...	0534	...	...	...	0705	0743	0851	...	1105	...	...	...	1259	...	1440	...	...	...	1718	...	1836
67	Kaišiadorys 1809 d.	...	...	0516	...	...	...	0745	|	0936	...	|	...	...	...	1345	...	1524	...	...	...	|	...	1917
	Kaunas 1809 d.	...	...	|	...	...	...	|	|	|	...	|	...	1140	...	|	...	|	...	...	1705	|	...	|
	Jonava d.	...	...	0635	...	...	...	0803	0849	0955	...	|	...	1217	...	1405	...	1543	...	...	1739	|	...	1936
	Kėdainiai d.	...	...	0656	...	...	...	0823	0911	1016	...	|	...	1238	...	1427	...	1606	...	...	1800	|	...	1957
	Rokiškis d.	...	...	|	...	...	...	|	|	|	...	|	...	|	...	|	...	|	...	...	|	|	...	|
	Panevežys d.	...	...	|	0655	...	...	|	|	|	...	|	1142	|	...	|	1410	|	...	...	|	|	1859	|
192	Radviliškis d.	0557	0651	0736	0744	...	0815	0901	0952	1059	...	|	1229	1325	...	1508	1512	1646	1647	...	1841	|	1847	2037
212	**Šiauliai** d.	0627	0723	0753	0816	...	0847	0916	1009	1117	...	1312	1318	1347	...	1525	1544	1704	1718	...	1903	1925	1930	2054
290	**Mažeikiai** a.	|	...	|	0925	...	...	|	|	...	...	|	1427	...	...	|	1653	...	|	...	...	|	2039	|
	Joniškis 🏛 LT d.	|	...	|	...	...	...	0953	|	...	...	|	...	...	...	|	...	...	|	...	...	|	...	|
	Jelgava 🏛 LV d.	|	...	|	...	...	...	1030	|	...	...	|	...	...	...	|	...	...	|	...	...	|	...	|
	Riga a.	|	...	|	...	...	...	1104	|	...	...	|	...	...	...	|	...	...	|	...	...	|	...	|
	Telšiai d.	0728	...	0841	...	...	...	...	1053	...	...	1355	...	...	...	1609	...	...	1838	...	...	2010	...	2138
	Plunge d.	0758	...	0901	...	...	...	...	1117	...	...	|	...	...	...	1629	...	...	1910	...	...	|	...	2258
376	**Klaipeda** ⊡ a.	0907	...	0949	...	...	...	...	1205	...	...	1457	...	...	...	1719	...	...	2008	...	...	2112	...	2246

	Ⓐ	①	Ⓐ		⑥		Ⓒ	⑥⑦								⑤⑥							
	3		3		3		3	2	3		3		3		3	2	3			A	3	3	
Klaipeda ⊡ d.	...	0546	...	0652	...	...	...	...	0917	1033	...	...	...	1253	...	...	1530	...	1647	...	...	...	1816
Plunge d.	...	0634	...	0740	...	...	...	...	1018	|	...	...	...	1344	...	...	1627	...	|	...	...	...	1907
Telšiai d.	...	0654	...	0800	...	...	...	...	1050	1135	...	...	...	1404	...	...	1655	...	1749	...	...	...	1927
Riga d.	...	|	...	|	...	...	...	...	|	|	...	...	...	|	...	...	|	...	|	1655	...	...	|
Jelgava 🏛 LV d.	...	|	...	|	...	...	...	...	|	|	...	...	...	|	...	...	|	...	|	1732	...	...	|
Joniškis 🏛 LT d.	...	|	...	|	...	...	...	...	|	|	...	...	...	|	...	...	|	...	|	1808	...	...	|
Mažeikiai d.	0600	|	...	|	0727	...	...	...	|	|	1101	...	...	|	1445	...	|	...	|	|	1715	...	|
Šiauliai d.	0709	0739	0750	0845	0855	...	0925	1140	1153	1220	1225	...	1413	1452	1554	1740	1804	...	1834	1845	1853	1945	2015
Radviliškis d.	0741	0755	0812	0901	0927	...	0947	1200	1222	|	1257	...	1438	1510	1626	1800	1837	...	|	1901	1925	2016	2033
Panevežys a.	0833	|	|	|	1021	...	|	|	...	|	1349	...	|	|	1720	|	...	...	|	|	2017	...	|
Rokiškis a.	...	|	|	|	...	...	|	|	...	|	...	...	|	|	...	|	...	...	|	|	...	...	|
Kėdainiai d.	...	0836	0856	0942	...	...	1028	1244	...	|	...	...	1527	1551	...	1841	...	...	|	1942	...	...	2114
Jonava d.	...	0859	0919	1005	...	...	1051	1307	...	|	...	...	1550	1614	...	1904	...	...	|	2004	...	...	2137
Kaunas 1809 a.	...	|	0953	|	...	...	1123	|	...	|	...	...	1622	|	...	|	...	...	|	|	...	...	|
Kaišiadorys 1809 d.	...	0920	...	|	...	...	...	1329	...	|	...	...	...	1636	...	1926	...	...	|	2023	...	...	2159
Vilnius 1809 a.	...	1002	...	1113	...	...	...	1411	...	1430	...	...	...	1722	...	2008	...	...	2044	2103	...	...	2241

A – 🚆2 Vilnius - Riga - Valga and v.v. (Table **1830**).
B – Daily until Sept. 28; ⑤–⑦ from Oct. 3.
⊡ – **Klaipeda - Šilute** (2nd class. *46 km*. Journey 65 minutes). From **Klaipeda** at 0800, 1220 **B**, 1520, 1800. From **Šilute** at 0623 Ⓐ, 0920, 1340 **B**, 1640, 1920.
LT – Lithuania.
LV – Latvia.

1807 VILNIUS - TRAKAI and MARCINKONYS (LTG Link)

Vilnius - Trakai and v.v. *27 km*. Journey 37 minutes.
From Vilnius (trains call at **Lentvaris** 15 – 20 minutes later) at 0613 Ⓐ, 0711, 0904, 1000 ⑥⑦, 1053, 1200 ⑤–⑦, 1248, 1431, 1530 ⑥⑦, 1625, 1732, 1928.
From Trakai (trains call at **Lentvaris** 15 minutes later) at 0700 Ⓐ, 0803, 0954, 1105 ⑤–⑦, 1157, 1300 ⑤–⑦, 1407, 1530, 1622 ⑥⑦, 1730, 1825, 2042.

Vilnius - Marcinkonys and v.v. 3rd class only. *108 km*. Journey 2 hours.
From Vilnius (trains call at **Lentvaris** 16 – 19 minutes, and **Varena** 80 – 85 minutes later) at 0600 ①–⑥, 1030, 1445, 1810 ⑤.
From Marcinkonys (trains call at **Varena** 23 – 26 minutes, and **Lentvaris** 90 – 95 minutes later) at 0800 ①–⑥, 1344, 1650.

1809 VILNIUS - KAUNAS (LTG Link)

km																								
		Ⓐ		Ⓐ																				⑤⑥
0	**Vilnius** 1805 d.	0514	0555	0628	0720	0810	0924	1015	...	1115	1208	1330	1422	1540	1615	1645	...	1722	1745	1847	1944	2025	2125	2215
	Lentvaris d.	|	0610	0643	0737	0827	0939	1032	...	1130	1223	1347	1437	1555	1630	1704	...	1739	1802	1902	2001	2042	2142	2230
	Vievis d.	|	0627	0658	0757	0842	|	1047	...	1153	1238	1407	|	1610	1645	1724	...	1755	1820	1920	2016	2100	2157	2245
67	Kaišiadorys 1805 d.	0557	0644	0715	0817	0858	1010	1103	...	1210	1256	1425	1507	1628	1701	1742	...	1811	1840	1938	2035	2118	2213	2301
104	**Kaunas** 1805 a.	0626	0716	0741	0847	0921	1040	1131	...	1240	1324	1457	1530	1657	1727	1808	...	1836	1910	2006	2057	2146	2236	2327

	Ⓐ					Ⓐ																⑥
Kaunas 1805 d.	0505	0537	0632	0700	0750	0830	0925	...	1016	1110	1225	1325	1435	1540	1644	...	1715	1746	1840	1915	2050	2120	2215
Kaišiadorys 1805 d.	0529	0605	0658	0730	0818	0854	0953	...	1047	1135	1255	1355	1459	1610	1714	...	1739	1815	1911	1945	2108	2146	2239
Vievis d.	0547	0623	0715	0752	0836	0910	1011	...	1107	|	1312	1413	|	1628	1732	...	1756	1833	1929	|	2125	|	2256
Lentvaris d.	0607	0645	0731	0812	0855	0925	1031	...	1127	1206	1327	1436	1529	1643	1754	...	1811	1853	1947	2020	2140	2217	2311
Vilnius 1805 a.	0624	0705	0745	0830	0909	0939	1045	...	1146	1220	1344	1454	1543	1702	1811	...	1825	1909	2001	2036	2154	2231	2325

1811 KAUNAS - MARIJAMPOLE and KYBARTAI (3rd class, LTG Link)

Kaunas - Marijampole and v.v. *53 km*. Journey 55 – 65 minutes.
From Kaunas (trains call at **Kazlu Ruda** 30 – 35 minutes later) at 0637 Ⓐ, 0752, 1047, 1425 Ⓑ, 1635, 1750, 2025.
From Marijampole (trains call at **Kazlu Ruda** 23 – 27 minutes later) at 0620, 0748, 0950, 1255, 1620 Ⓑ, 1755.

Kaunas - Kybartai and v.v. *87 km*. Journey 80 – 85 minutes.
From Kaunas (trains call at **Kazlu Ruda** 30 – 35 minutes and **Vilkaviškis** 65 – 70 minutes later) at 0823 ①–⑥, 1140, 1508, 1845.
From Kybratai (trains call at **Vilkaviškis** 17 minutes and **Kazlu Ruda** 48 minutes later) at 0610 ①–⑥, 1000, 1357, 1705.

1813 VILNIUS - TURMANTAS (3rd class, LTG Link)

km										
0	**Vilnius** d.	0528	0737	1112	1433	1630	1747	1948	...	...
	Naujoji Vilina d.	0542	0753	1128	1447	1644	1803	2002	...	...
	Pabrade d.	0622	0839	1214	1533	1730	1845	2042	...	...
101	Ignalina d.	0715	0923	1258	1606	1806	1934	2116	...	...
	Visaginas d.	0743	0957	1333	1641	...	2004	2144	...	...
147	**Turmantas** 🏛 a.	0751	1005	1341	1649	...	2012	2152	...	...
174	Daugavpils a.	...	...	...	...	...	...	...	...	...

Daugavpils d.	...	...	...	...	...	...	...	...	...
Turmantas 🏛 d.	...	0508	0546	0919	1254	1602	1812	...	...
Visaginas d.	...	0519	0557	0930	1305	1613	1823	...	...
Ignalina d.	0500	0545	0627	1005	1339	1647	1849	...	...
Pabrade d.	0533	0622	0715	1048	1415	1730	1939	...	...
Naujoji Vilina d.	0612	0705	0801	1131	1457	1815	2021	...	...
Vilnius a.	0626	0716	0815	1145	1511	1829	2032	...	...

VILNIUS - VILNIUS AIRPORT - JAŠIUNAI — 1815

LTG Link 3rd class

km		Ⓐ							Ⓐ	
0	**Vilnius** ⊖ d.	0800	1011	1052	1200	1253	1355	1502	1635	1830
4	**Vilnius** Airport ✈ ⊖ d.	0808	1018	1100	1207	1300	1402	1510	1643	1838
	Jašiunai a.	0838	...	...	...	...	...	...	1714	...

	Ⓐ	Ⓐ							Ⓐ
Jašiunai d.	0638	0855	...	...	...	...	...	...	1735
Vilnius Airport ✈ ⊖ d.	0710	0924	1027	1139	1215	1308	1410	1551	1807
Vilnius ⊖ a.	0718	0933	1035	1147	1223	1316	1418	1559	1815

⊖ – Also from Vilnius at 0655 Ⓒ, 0800, 0900 Ⓒ, 1610 Ⓒ, 1715 Ⓒ, 1753 Ⓒ; also from Vilnius Airport ✈ at 0710 Ⓒ, 0815 Ⓒ, 0950 Ⓒ, 1625 Ⓒ, 1730 Ⓒ, 1808 Ⓒ, 1920.

RIGA - VALMIERA - VALGA — 1830

Vivi / Pasažieru vilciens

For connecting services Tallinn - Riga - Vilnius and v.v. see Table **49**.

km			⑤–⑦	A		Ⓐ				⑦
0	**Riga** ◧ d.	0630	0926	1120	1526	1726	1826	1926	2126	2126
53	Sigulda ◧ d.	0739	1034	1213	1632	1817	1920	2033	2235	2235
93	Cesis d.	0821	1113	1245	1710	1846	1953	2114	2307	2317
121	**Valmiera** a.	0850	1141	1311	...	1913	2019	2142	...	2343
164	Lugaži 🏛 LV a.	...	1215	1345	...	...	2053	...	...	...
168	**Valga** 🏛 EE a.	...	1221	1351	...	...	2059	...	...	...

		①–⑥					A		⑤–⑦
Valga 🏛 EE d.	...	...	0543	...	...	...	1411	...	1737
Lugaži 🏛 LV d.	...	...	0551	...	...	...	1418	...	1744
Valmiera d.	0449	0543	0624	...	...	0920	1449	...	1817
Cesis d.	0519	0611	0650	0726	...	0952	1514	1726	1846
Sigulda ◧ d.	0600	0643	0718	0800	...	1032	1544	1805	1917
Riga ◧ a.	0706	0736	0806	0906	...	1136	1637	1906	2017

A – (2) Vilnius - Riga - Valga and v.v. (Table **1805**).

◧ – Additional trains Riga - Sigulda at 0756, 0926, 1056 ⑤–⑦, 1226, 1426, 1756, 2026 Ⓐ, 2226.
Additional trains Sigulda - Riga at 0729, 0929, 1229, 1359, 1726, 1929 Ⓐ, 2159.

EE – Estonia.
LV – Latvia.

RIGA - GULBENE, DAUGAVPILS, REZEKNE and ZILUPE — 1832

Vivi / Pasažieru vilciens

km			⑥		⑦						⑤
0	**Riga** ⊡ d.	0808	0831	0938	1131	1138	1338	1538	1638	1901	1901
	Ogre ⊡ d.	0849	0905	1018	1205	1218	1419	1619	1719	1935	1935
51	Lielvarde ⊡ d.	0904	0919	1031	1219	1231	1434	1634	1734	1949	1949
	Aizkraukle ⊡ d.	0930	0942	1057	1242	1257	1500	1700	1800	2012	2012
	Madona d.	...	1054	...	1356	...	...	...	...	2125	2136
179	**Gulbene** a.	...	1141	...	1443	...	...	...	...	...	2213

	Ⓐ	⑥	⑦					⑦	⑥	
Gulbene d.	...	0647	...	...	...	...	...	1548	1820	...
Madona d.	0503	0738	0738	...	...	...	...	1639	1911	...
Aizkraukle ⊡ d.	0616	0851	0851	0859	1026	1126	1226	1751	2021	2029
Lielvarde ⊡ d.	0640	0915	0915	0925	1052	1152	1252	1815	2045	2055
Ogre ⊡ d.	0653	0928	0928	0941	1108	1208	1308	1828	2058	2111
Riga ⊡ a.	0729	0959	0959	1021	1151	1251	1351	1859	2129	2151

km							C	A			C
0	**Riga** ⊡ d.	0731	0931	1001	1201	1301	1438	1629	1701	1801	2108
	Ogre ⊡ d.	0805	1005	1032	1232	1335	1514	1701	1735	1835	2144
51	Lielvarde ⊡ d.	0819	1019	|	|	1349	1527	|	1749	1849	2157
	Aizkraukle ⊡ d.	0842	1042	1105	1305	1414	1600	1734	1812	1912	2229
129	Krustpils ⊖ d.	0928	1128	1143	1343	1500	1646	1813	1855	1958	2300
218	**Daugavpils** a.	1046	|	1246	|	1618	1808	1920	|	2116	0030
224	**Rezekne** 2 d.	...	1257	...	1448	...	...	...	2024	...	...
279	**Zilupe** a.	...	1359	...	...	...	...	...	2126	...	...

			B			C				C
Zilupe d.	...	0329	...	...	...	...	...	1511	...	...
Rezekne 2 d.	...	0434	...	...	...	...	1515	1616	...	...
Daugavpils d.	0347	|	0618	0746	1140	1322	|	|	1740	1948
Krustpils ⊖ d.	0503	0601	0722	0906	1309	1427	1622	1743	1904	2108
Aizkraukle ⊡ d.	0558	0643	0800	0951	1351	1536	1700	1821	1950	2201
Lielvarde ⊡ d.	0615	0710	|	1015	1415	1559	|	1845	2014	2226
Ogre ⊡ d.	0628	0723	0832	1028	1428	1612	1732	1858	2028	2242
Riga ⊡ a.	0659	0759	0859	1059	1459	1651	1759	1929	2059	2321

A – To **Kraslava** (a. 1950) and **Indra** (④⑤ only, a. 2010).
B – From **Indra** (⑤⑥ only, d. 0524) and **Kraslava** (d. 0544).
C – Passengers must change from electric to diesel train at Aizkraukle.

⊖ – For Jekabpils.
⊡ – Additional trains Riga - Aizkraukle at 0508, 0608, 0708, 1038, 1738, 1838, 1938, 2238.
Additional trains Aizkraukle - Riga at 0459, 0559, 0659, 0807, 1326, 1629, 1726, 1829, 1929.

RIGA - JELGAVA - LIEPAJA — 1834

Vivi / Pasažieru vilciens

km							⑦		
0	**Riga** d.	0535	and	2335	...	A	1355	1825	...
43	**Jelgava** a.	0621	hourly	0021	...	L	1433	1905	...
	Dobele	...	until	...	...	S	1455	1927	...
125	Saldus a.	...		...	...	O	1542	2014	...
223	**Liepaja** a.	...		...	...		1705	2137	...

						⑦		
Liepaja d.	...	and	...	...	A	0455	1755	...
Saldus d.	...	hourly	...	...	L	0619	1919	...
Dobele d.	...	until	...	...	S	0704	2004	...
Jelgava d.	0538		2238	...	O	0728	2028	...
Riga a.	0625		2325	...		0804	2104	...

RIGA - SLOKA - TUKUMS — 1836

Vivi / Pasažieru vilciens

Jurmala's *33 km* coastline has several stations; the principal stations are Majori and Sloka. There is no station called Jurmala.

km												Ⓒ	Ⓐ	Ⓒ	Ⓐ	Ⓒ	Ⓐ							
0	**Riga** ● d.	0530	0630	0730	0830	0930	1130	1230	1330	1430	1530	1630	1645	1730	1745	1830	1845	1930	2030	2130	2200	2230	2300	2345
22	Majori ● d.	0601	0659	0802	0902	1002	1202	1302	1402	1502	1602	1701	1711	1801	1811	1901	1911	2002	2102	2201	2232	2301	2332	0016
	Dubulti ● d.	0604	0702	0805	0905	1005	1205	1305	1405	1505	1605	1704	1714	1804	1814	1904	1914	2005	2105	2204	2235	2304	2335	0019
32	**Sloka** ● d.	0620	0718	0821	0920	1021	1221	1320	1421	1525	1621	1724	1724	1824	1824	1924	1924	2021	2121	2220	2251	2320	2351	0035
	Ķemeri d.	0629	0728	0830	...	1030	1230	...	1430	1530	1630	1731	1731	1833	1833	1931	1931	2030	2130	2230	2258	2328	2358	0043
65	**Tukums** 1 a.	0646	0745	0847	...	1047	1247	...	1447	1547	1647	1748	1748	1850	1850	1948	1948	2047	2147	2247	...	2345	...	0100
	Tukums 2 a.	0650	0749	0851	...	1051	1251	...	1451	1551	1651	1755	1752	1854	1854	1952	1952	2051	2151	2251	...	2349	...	0104

					Ⓐ		Ⓒ																
Tukums 2 d.	0440	...	0539	0607	0705	...	0705	0807	0907	...	1107	...	...	1307	...	1507	1607	1708	1810	1909	2007	2107	2207
Tukums 1 d.	0445	...	0544	0612	0710	...	0710	0812	0912	...	1112	...	...	1312	...	1512	1612	1713	1815	1914	2012	2112	2212
Ķemeri d.	0501	0530	0600	0630	0727	...	0727	0830	0930	...	1130	...	...	1330	...	1530	1630	1732	1833	1932	2030	2130	2230
Sloka ● d.	0510	0540	0609	0639	0736	0740	0740	0839	0939	1039	1139	...	1239	1339	1439	1539	1639	1741	1841	1941	2039	2139	2239
Dubulti ● d.	0525	0555	0624	0654	0745	0755	0755	0854	0954	1054	1154	...	1254	1354	1454	1554	1654	1756	1856	1956	2054	2154	2254
Majori ● d.	0528	0558	0627	0657	0748	0758	0758	0857	0957	1057	1157	...	1257	1357	1457	1557	1657	1758	1858	1958	2057	2157	2257
Riga ● a.	0559	0629	0659	0729	0814	0829	0829	0929	1029	1129	1229	...	1329	1429	1529	1629	1729	1829	1929	2029	2129	2229	2329

● – Additional trains: Riga - Sloka at 0600 and hourly until 2100 (also 1630 Ⓐ, 1730 Ⓐ, 1830 Ⓐ); Sloka - Riga at 0709 and hourly until 2209 (also 1734 Ⓐ, 1834 Ⓐ, 1935 Ⓐ).

RIGA - SAULKRASTI - SKULTE — 1838

Vivi / Pasažieru vilciens

km																								
0	**Riga** d.	0538	0638	0738	0838	0938	...	1038	1138	1238	1338	1438	...	1538	1638	1738	1838	1938	...	2038	2138	2238	2338	...
	Carnikava d.	0618	0718	0818	0918	1018	...	1118	1218	1318	1418	1518	...	1618	1718	1818	1918	2018	...	2118	2218	2318	0018	...
48	**Saulkrasti** d.	0639	0739	0839	0939	1038	...	1139	1238	1339	1438	1539	...	1638	1739	1839	1939	2039	...	2139	2239	2339	0039	...
	Skulte a.	0647	0747	0847	0947	...	...	1147	...	1347	...	1547	...	...	1747	1847	1947	2047	...	2147	2247	2347	0047	...

Skulte d.	0446	...	0616	0716	0816	...	0916	1016	...	1216	...	...	1416	...	1616	...	1816	...	1916	2016	2116	2216	...
Saulkrasti d.	0456	0556	0626	0726	0826	...	0926	1026	1126	1226	1326	...	1426	1526	1626	1726	1826	...	1926	2026	2126	2226	...
Carnikava d.	0517	0617	0647	0747	0847	...	0947	1047	1147	1247	1347	...	1447	1547	1647	1747	1847	...	1947	2047	2147	2247	...
Riga a.	0555	0655	0725	0825	0925	...	1025	1125	1225	1325	1425	...	1525	1625	1725	1825	1925	...	2025	2125	2225	2325	...

TALLINN - TARTU - VALGA and KOIDULA — 1870

Elron

For connecting services Tallinn - Riga - Vilnius and v.v. see Table **49**.

km		🚌										Ⓒ			Ⓐ						Ⓒ		⊡	⊡
0	**Tallinn** **1876** d.	...	0625	...	0753	0753	...	1002	1122	...	1238	1238	...	1402	1402	...	1532	1652	...	1811	1811	...	2027	2208
77	Tapa **1876** d.	...	0732	...	0850	0850	...	1100	1221	...	1342	1342	...	1502	1502	...	1629	1757	...	1911	1911	...	2136	2306
	Tamsalu d.	...	0749	...	0909	0909	...	1118	1238	...	1401	1401	...	1521	1521	...	1645	1814	...	1927	1927	...	2157	2325
142	Jõgeva d.	0635	0841	...	0955	0955	...	1203	1324	...	1453	1453	...	1608	1608	...	1735	1905	...	2012	2012	...	2304	0013
190	**Tartu** a.	0730	0927	...	1043	1043	...	1246	1409	...	1545	1545	...	1651	1651	...	1819	1953	...	2055	2055	...	0004	0102
190	**Tartu** d.	...	...	...	1046	1053	...	1249	1414	...	...	1555	...	1714	1719	...	...	...	...	2058	2103	...	...	...
215	Elva d.	...	...	...	1116	|	...	1312	1448	...	...	|	...	1746	|	...	...	...	...	2128	|	...	...	...
273	**Valga** a.	...	...	...	1202	|	...	1349	1534	...	...	|	...	1832	|	...	...	...	...	2214	|	...	...	...
233	Põlva d.	...	...	...	...	1137	...	...	...	...	...	1639	...	...	1803	...	...	...	...	...	2147	...	...	...
262	Orava d.	...	...	...	...	1201	...	...	...	...	...	1703	...	...	1827	...	...	...	...	...	2211	...	...	...
275	**Koidula** a.	...	...	...	...	1218	...	...	...	...	...	1720	...	...	1837	...	...	...	...	...	2221	...	...	...
282	**Piusa** a.	...	...	...	...	1226	...	...	...	...	...	1728	...	...	...	...	...	...	...	...	...	...	...	...

⊡ – By 🚌 Tamsalu - Tartu and v.v.

FOR RETURN SERVICE SEE NEXT PAGE →

1870 TALLINN - TARTU - VALGA and KOIDULA — Elron

For connecting services Tallinn - Riga - Vilnius and v.v. see Table **49**.

	⊡	Ⓐ				Ⓒ								Ⓒ				Ⓐ				⊡	Ⓒ⊡
Piusa d.	...	...	...	...	...	...	...	...	...	...	...	...	...	1326	...	...	...	1446	...	...	...	...	1826
Koidula d.	...	0611	...	...	...	0734	...	...	...	...	...	...	...	1341	...	...	...	1501	...	...	...	...	1841
Orava d.	...	0621	...	...	...	0744	...	...	...	...	...	...	...	1351	...	...	...	1511	...	...	...	...	1851
Pölva d.	...	0645	...	...	...	0808	...	...	...	...	...	...	...	1415	...	...	...	1535	...	...	...	...	1915
Valga d.	...	|	0623	...	0738	|	...	...	...	...	...	...	1224	|	1410	...	...	|	1622	...	...	...	|
Elva d.	...	|	0710	...	0825	|	...	...	...	...	...	...	1313	|	1447	...	...	|	1709	...	...	...	|
Tartu a.	...	0730	0738	...	0853	0853	...	...	...	...	...	...	1341	1500	1507	...	...	1620	1737	...	...	...	2000
Tartu d.	0437	0741	0741	...	...	...	0942	...	0942	1101	1209	...	1347	1510	1510	...	1630	1630	1743	...	1840	2011	2011
Jõgeva d.	0538	0824	0824	...	...	...	1025	...	1025	1144	1302	...	1430	1553	1553	...	1719	1719	1832	...	1934	2112	2112
Tamsalu d.	0700	0909	0909	...	...	...	1117	...	1117	1238	1401	...	1421	1646	1646	...	1814	1814	1928	...	2034	2234	2234
Tapa **1876** d.	0718	0929	0929	...	...	...	1135	...	1135	1256	1419	...	1542	1704	1704	...	1832	1832	1946	...	2052	2252	2252
Tallinn **1876** a.	0834	1028	1028	...	...	...	1234	...	1234	1355	1527	...	1649	1805	1805	...	1932	1932	2059	...	2200	0008	0008

FOR RETURN SERVICE AND FOOTNOTES SEE PREVIOUS PAGE.

1872 TALLINN - VILJANDI — Elron

km																								
		Ⓐ																						
0	**Tallinn** d.	0631	0738	0842	1034	...	1201	1259	1356	1452	...	1551	1640	1718	1844	...	1815	1922	2022	2120	...	2225	...	...
	Saku d.	0654	0758	0904	1055	...	1220	1321	1418	1511	...	1613	1702	1740	1803	...	1838	1944	2042	2142	...	2248	...	...
	Kohila d.	0714	0816	0923	1113	...	1234	1341	1437	1525	...	1631	1720	1759	1818	...	1856	2002	2054	2201	...	2306	...	...
54	Rapla d.	0732	0832	0941	1132	...	1250	1359	1455	1541	...	1649	1739	1817	1834	...	1914	2021	2110	2219	...	2325	...	...
98	Türi d.	...	0911	...	1207	...	1326	...	...	1616	...	...	1813	...	1910	...	...	2055	2142	...	...	2359	...	...
	Võhma d.	...	0929	...	...	...	1344	...	...	1634	...	...	...	...	1928	...	...	...	2155	...	...	...	...	...
151	**Viljandi** a.	...	0952	...	...	...	1408	...	...	1657	...	...	...	...	1951	...	...	...	2215	...	...	...	...	...

		Ⓐ	Ⓐ	Ⓒ																			
Viljandi d.	...	...	...	...	...	0624	...	...	0837	...	...	1047	...	...	...	...	1455	...	...	...	1827	...	...
Võhma d.	...	...	...	...	...	0647	...	...	0856	...	...	1110	...	...	...	...	1518	...	...	...	1850	...	...
Türi d.	...	0604	...	0620	...	0706	...	0829	0911	...	...	1129	1247	...	...	...	1537	...	...	...	1910	2104	...
Rapla d.	0548	0639	0655	0655	...	0741	0757	0904	0945	...	1034	1203	1322	1418	...	1506	1613	1740	1837	...	1945	2142	...
Kohila d.	0606	0655	0713	0713	...	0757	0815	0922	1002	...	1052	1219	1340	1436	...	1525	1631	1759	1856	...	2002	2200	...
Saku d.	0623	0708	0730	0730	...	0811	0832	0939	1014	...	1110	1233	1357	1453	...	1542	1644	1817	1913	...	2015	2217	...
Tallinn a.	0645	0727	0752	0752	...	0830	0855	1001	1033	...	1131	1252	1420	15196	...	1605	1704	1839	1936	...	2035	2239	...

1874 TALLINN - PALDISKI and TURBA — Elron

Tallinn - Paldiski and v.v. *48 km.* Journey 65 minutes.
From Tallinn (trains call at **Keila** 45 minutes later) at 0545 and hourly until 1545, 1616 Ⓐ, 1645, 1716 Ⓐ, 1745, 1845, 1945, 2045, 2145.
From Paldiski (trains call at **Keila** 25 minutes later) at 0600, 0638 Ⓐ, 0700, 0738 Ⓐ, 0800, 0900, 1000, 1100, 1200 and hourly until 2200.

Tallinn - Turba and v.v. *58 km.* Journey 70 minutes.
From Tallinn (trains call at **Keila** 45 minutes, and **Riisipere** 65 minutes later) at 0615 Ⓐ, 0705, 0805 and hourly until 1905, 2015, 2115.
From Turba (trains call at **Riisipere** 5 minutes, and **Keila** 35 minutes later) at 0612, 0647 Ⓐ, 0732 and hourly until 1932, 2022, 2123.

1876 TALLINN - NARVA — Elron

km										
0	**Tallinn** **1870** d.	0625	1122	...	1410	1606	...	1840	2320	...
77	Tapa **1870** d.	0741	1229	...	1522	1716	...	1958	0026	...
104	Rakvere d.	0802	1249	...	1543	1736	...	2019	0046	...
	Kiviõli d.	0831	1311	...	1612	1758	...	2045	...	...
165	Jõhvi d.	0822	1327	...	1633	1814	...	2107	...	...
209	**Narva** a.	0923	1354	...	1704	1841	...	2138	...	...

Narva d.	...	0658	...	0936	1439	...	1729	2013	...
Jõhvi d.	...	0728	...	1002	1509	...	1759	2039	...
Kiviõli d.	...	0749	...	1008	1530	...	1822	2055	...
Rakvere d.	0542	0816	...	1039	1557	...	1849	2116	...
Tapa **1870** d.	0603	0837	...	1108	1618	...	1913	2144	...
Tallinn **1870** a.	0711	0957	...	1209	1752	...	2020	2245	...

KAZAKHSTAN

SEE MAP PAGE 556

Operators: The services shown are operated by Kazakhstan Temir Joly (www.railways.kz). Several private operators also run passenger services.

Services: Trains convey first- and second-class seating unless indicated otherwise. Trains which run overnight generally convey sleeping accommodation.

Timings: Schedules are the latest available and may be subject to alteration at any time. Timings are expressed in railway time which is one hour later than times at stations with note ♡.

1880 KAZAKHSTAN

Time zone UTC + 6 (♡ + 5) — Kazakhstan Temir Joly

ALMATY - OSKEMEN, SEMEY, PAVLODAR and ASTANA

km		22	139	31	301	351	45	353	37	67
		A	D◧		◧			◧	B◧	
	Almaty 2 d.	...	...	...	1455	1620	...	...	...	...
0	**Almaty** 1 d.	1150	...	1520	1553	1715	...	...	...	...
71	Qapshaghay d.	1308	...	1638	1720	1841	...	...	...	...
303	Ush Tobe d.	1756	...	2115	2211	2353	...	...	...	...
557	Aktogay d.	2324	...	0236	0343	0605	...	...	...	...
799	Zharma d.	0403	...	0718	0827	1153	...	...	...	...
	Oskemen 1 a.	|	...	|	|	1845	...	...	...	1200
1025	**Semey** d.	0832	...	1205	1352	...	...	1240	1240	1733
1416	**Pavlodar** d.	...	1339	1802	...	...	1806	2029	2029	2310
1548	Ekibastuz 1 d.	...	1617	...	...	...	2110	2306	2306	0106
1854	**Astana** 1 a.	...	2136	...	...	...	0352	|	0527	|
1868	**Astana** Nurly Zhol a.	...	...	...	...	...	...	0505	...	0548

	301	354	68	38	46	139	21	31	351
	◧	◧		B◧		D◧	A		
Astana Nurly Zhol d.	...	1645	1710	...	...	...	...	...	...
Astana 1 d.	...	|	|	1805	2250	0104	...	...	...
Ekibastuz 1 d.	...	2241	2124	0011	0503	0621	...	...	...
Pavlodar d.	...	0157	2329	0326	0757	0849	...	0900	...
Semey d.	0748	0853	0458	0956	...	...	1112	1551	...
Oskemen 1 d.	|	...	1000	...	...	...	|	|	2115
Zharma d.	1301	...	...	...	...	...	1605	2014	0441
Aktogay d.	1818	...	...	...	...	...	2055	0057	1050
Ush Tobe d.	2355	...	...	...	...	...	0217	0603	1652
Qapshaghay d.	0437	...	...	...	...	...	0658	1023	2237
Almaty 1 a.	0606	...	...	...	...	...	0819	1144	0030
Almaty 2 a.	0700	...	...	...	...	...	...	...	0148

ALMATY and NUR-SULTAN - ZHEZKAZGAN

km		73		66		108				
		◧		◧						
0	**Almaty** 2 d.	0100	...	...	...	...	...	...	...	...
9	**Almaty** 1 d.	0134	...	...	...	...	...	...	...	...
314	Shu d.	0630	...	...	...	...	...	...	...	...
758	Moyynty d.	1235	...	...	...	...	...	...	...	...
	Astana Nurly Zhol d.	|	...	2120	...	1553	...	...	...	...
	Karagandy d.	|	...	0057	...	1924	...	...	...	...
1235	Kyzl Dzhar d.	2002	...	0733	...	0428	...	...	...	...
1399	**Zhezkazgan** a.	2258	...	0952	...	0725	...	...	...	...

	73		65		107				
	◧		◧						
Zhezkazgan d.	0136	...	1133	...	2005	...	...	...	...
Kyzl Dzhar d.	0419	...	1358	...	2302	...	...	...	...
Karagandy d.	|	...	1938	...	0700	...	...	...	...
Astana Nurly Zhol a.	|	...	2308	...	1114	...	...	...	...
Moyynty d.	1140	...	...	...	...	...	...	...	...
Shu d.	1842	...	...	...	...	...	...	...	...
Almaty 1 a.	2340	...	...	...	...	...	...	...	...
Almaty 2 a.	0028	...	...	...	...	...	...	...	...

FOR FOOTNOTES SEE NEXT PAGE. FOR ADDITIONAL SERVICES SEE NEXT TWO PAGES →

Kazakhstan Temir Joly   Time zone UTC+6 (♡+5)

KAZAKHSTAN 1880

ALMATY and DOSTYK - ASTANA - PETROPAVL and PRESNOGORKOVSKAYA

km		15	3	9	83	113	54	145	139	623
						①	③⑥			
		T◧			◧			g	D◧	◧
0	**Almaty** 2 d.	0750	1522	1610	...	1845	...	...	...	...
9	**Almaty** 1 d.	0833	|	|	...	1917	...	...	...	...
314	Shu d.	1344	2003	2047	...	0132	...	...	...	...
	Dostyk d.	|	|	|	...	|	1820	...	...	...
	Aktogay d.	|	|	|	...	|	0040	...	...	...
	Balkhash 2 d.	|	|	|	...	|	0605	...	...	...
	Balkhash 1 d.	|	|	|	...	|	0633	...	...	...
758	Moyynty d.	2023	|	|	...	0848	0924	...	...	...
1094	Karagandy d.	0135	0434	0514	0625	1407	1431	1458	...	...
	Astana Nurly Zhol a.	|	0747	|	1036	1822	1832	1909	...	...
	Astana Nurly Zhol d.	|	...	|	1115	1910	...	1957	...	2235
1335	**Astana** 1 a.	0606	...	0835	|	|	...	|	...	|
1335	**Astana** 1 d.	0636	...	...	|	|	...	|	2205	|
1631	Kokshetau 1 d.	1152	...	...	1650	0032	...	0105	0320	0535
1826	**Petropavl** a.	1325	...	...	1805	0200	...	0200	|	0806
	Presnogorkovskaya a.	...	...	...	...	...	...	...	1026	...

	84	140	16	624	146	114	54	4	10
						④	②⑤		
	◧	D◧	T◧	◧	h				
Presnogorkovskaya d.	...	1150	...	...	...	...	...	...	...
Petropavl d.	0650	|	1550	1647	1825	2059	...	...	...
Kokshetau 1 d.	1207	1937	2112	0025	2345	0246	...	...	...
Astana 1 a.	|	0034	0159	|	|	|	...	...	...
Astana 1 d.	|	...	0240	|	|	|	...	...	2057
Astana Nurly Zhol a.	1717	...	|	0645	0442	0756	...	...	|
Astana Nurly Zhol d.	1805	...	|	...	0530	0826	1523	2020	|
Karagandy d.	2206	...	0711	...	0940	1252	1939	2333	0014
Moyynty d.	...	...	1155	...	...	1758	0115	|	|
Balkhash 1 d.	...	...	|	...	...	|	0319	|	|
Balkhash 2 d.	...	...	|	...	...	|	0342	|	|
Aktogay d.	...	...	|	...	...	|	1000	|	|
Dostyk a.	...	...	|	...	...	|	1547	|	|
Shu d.	...	...	1920	...	...	0202	...	0908	0949
Almaty 1 a.	...	...	0013	...	...	0755	...	|	|
Almaty 2 a.	...	...	0058	...	...	0843	...	1325	1403

ALMATY - ASTANA - ORAL, ATYRAU and MANGISTAU

km		37		81		47				
		B◧		◧		◧				
0	**Almaty** 2 d.	...	...	...	...	...	...	...	...	...
241	Karagandy d.	...	...	...	...	...	...	...	...	...
	Astana Nurly Zhol d.	...	...	0955	...	2015	...	...	...	...
0	**Astana** 1 a.	...	...	|	...	|	...	...	...	...
0	**Astana** 1 d.	0605	...	|	...	|	...	...	...	...
	Kokshetau 1 d.	|	...	|	...	0130	...	...	...	...
229	Atbasar d.	0952	...	1310	...	|	...	...	...	...
376	Esil d.	1228	...	1507	...	|	...	...	...	...
	Kostanai d.	2213	...	|	...	0949	...	...	...	...
684	Tobol d.	|	...	1951	...	1206	...	...	...	...
	Kostanai a.	|	...	2218	...	|	...	...	...	...
	Khromtau d.	0126	...	0725	...	2007	...	...	...	...
1337	Kandyagash d.	0628	...	|	...	2343	...	...	...	...
1431	Aktobe 1 ♡ d.	|	...	1213	...	|	...	...	...	...
	Kazakhstan ♡ d.	|	...	1746	...	|	...	...	...	...
	Oral ♡ a.	|	...	1943	...	|	...	...	...	...
1727	Makat ♡ d.	1505	...	...	...	0711	...	...	...	...
1857	**Atyrau** ♡ a.	|	...	...	...	0913	...	...	...	...
2027	Beineu ♡ d.	0333	...	...	...	...	...	...	...	...
2431	**Mangistau** ♡ a.	0420	...	...	...	...	...	...	...	...

	48		82		37				
	◧		◧		B◧				
Mangistau ♡ d.	...	...	...	...	1856	...	...	...	...
Beineu ♡ d.	...	...	...	...	0241	...	...	...	...
Atyrau ♡ d.	2226	...	...	...	|	...	...	...	...
Makat ♡ d.	0055	...	...	...	0858	...	...	...	...
Oral ♡ d.	|	...	0500	...	|	...	...	...	...
Kazakhstan ♡ d.	|	...	0702	...	|	...	...	...	...
Aktobe 1 ♡ d.	|	...	1240	...	|	...	...	...	...
Kandyagash d.	0845	...	|	...	1748	...	...	...	...
Khromtau d.	1212	...	1716	...	2115	...	...	...	...
Kostanai d.	|	...	0400	...	|	...	...	...	...
Tobol d.	2041	...	0650	...	|	...	...	...	...
Kostanai d.	2314	...	|	...	|	...	...	...	...
Esil d.	|	...	1040	...	1123	...	...	...	...
Atbasar d.	|	...	1226	...	1405	...	...	...	...
Kokshetau 1 d.	0741	...	|	...	|	...	...	...	...
Astana 1 a.	|	...	|	...	1730	...	...	...	...
Astana 1 d.	|	...	|	...	...	...	...	...	...
Astana Nurly Zhol a.	1236	...	1512	...	...	...	...	...	...
Karagandy a.	...	...	...	...	...	...	...	...	...
Almaty 2 a.	...	...	...	...	...	...	...	...	...

ALMATY and ASTANA - TOSHKENT, ATYRAU, ORAL and MANGISTAU

km		86	72		21	56		23		45	87	11	1	305	107	27	41	33	25	29	77		
					A	N		◧		C	◧		m	②④	◧⊖	◧⊖	◧			◧			
0	**Almaty** 2 d.	...	...	...	...	...	...	...	...	...	1730	1820	1930	...	2000	2055	2055	...	2329	...	2340	...	...
9	**Almaty** 1 d.	...	...	...	0855	...	...	1445	...	...	1802	|	|	...	2045	|	|	2140	|	...	0023	...	...
	Astana Nurly Zhol d.	2000	2040	...	|	2159t	...	|	...	0433t	|	|	|	...	|	|	|	|	|	...	|	...	...
	Karagandy d.	2313	2353	...	|	0240	...	|	...	0941	|	|	|	...	|	|	|	|	|	...	|	...	...
314	Shu d.	0828	0920	...	1352	1457	...	1939	...	2251	0025	2245	2351	...	0229	0117	0117	0252	0417	...	0542	...	...
547	Taraz d.	1128	1230	...	1737	1859	...	2329	...	0324	0445	0145	0254	...	0619	0424	0424	0655	0748	...	0944	...	...
748	Shymkent d.	1500	1601	...	2138	2317	...	0339	...	0837	0934	0523	0639	...	1024	0757	0757	1118	1133	1250	1411	...	...
827	Arys 1 d.	...	...	...	|	|	...	|	...	|	1111	...	|	...	|	|	|	|	...	|	|	...	...
955	Saryagash 🏛 a.	...	...	...	|	|	...	|	...	|	1323	...	1038	...	|	|	|	|	...	|	|	...	...
982	**Toshkent** Shimolly a.	...	...	...	|	|	...	|	...	|	...	...	1243	2350	|	|	|	|	...	|	|	...	...
824	Arys 2 d.	...	...	...	2305	0046	...	0508	...	1012	...	...	...	0645s	1158	0921	0921	1249	...	1421	1542	...	...
932	Turkestan d.	...	...	...	0104	0255	...	0734	...	1210	...	...	...	0926	1408	1116	1116	1452	...	1626	1759	...	...
1216	Kyzylorda ♡ d.	...	...	...	0555	0845	...	1320	...	...	...	...	...	1641	2026	1601	1601	2135	...	2317	0045	...	...
1363	Zhosaly ♡ d.	...	...	...	...	...	...	1535	...	...	...	...	...	1905	2229	1751	1751	2356	...	0135	0303	...	...
1536	Kazaly ♡ d.	...	...	...	...	...	...	1820	...	...	...	...	...	2212	0126	2021	2021	0301	...	0439	0559	...	...
1664	Aral ♡ d.	...	...	...	...	...	...	2025	...	...	...	...	...	0025	0315	2201	2201	0510	...	0704	0830	...	...
1881	Shalkar ♡ d.	...	...	...	...	...	...	0044	...	...	...	...	...	0426	0719	0123	0123	0940	...	1108	1331	...	...
2147	Kandyagash ♡ d.	...	...	...	...	...	...	0612	...	...	...	...	...	0853	1219	0516	0539	1513	...	1632	|	...	...
2545	Makat ♡ d.	...	...	...	...	...	...	|	...	...	...	...	...	|	|	|	|	|	...	|	|	...	...
2675	**Atyrau** ♡ a.	...	...	...	...	...	...	|	...	...	...	...	...	|	|	|	1335	|	...	0318	|	...	...
2241	Aktobe 1 ♡ d.	...	...	...	...	...	...	0734	...	...	...	...	...	1015	1413	0705	...	1642	...	...	|	...	...
2699	**Oral** ♡ a.	...	...	...	...	...	...	...	...	...	...	...	...	...	0003	1415	...	...	...	...	|	...	...
2380	Beineu ♡ d.	...	...	...	...	...	...	...	...	...	...	...	...	...	...	...	...	...	...	...	2208	...	...
2778	**Mangistau** ♡ a.	...	...	...	...	...	...	...	...	...	...	...	...	...	...	...	...	...	...	...	0609	...	...

	56	72	86		12	26	88	112	46		2	22	41	28	29	8	24	305	77	34		
	N						◧	k	C		k	A	◧	◧	◧		◧	②④				
Mangistau ♡ d.	...	...	...	...	...	...	...	...	...	...	...	...	...	...	...	...	...	...	0830	...	...	...
Beineu ♡ d.	...	...	...	...	...	...	...	...	...	...	...	...	...	...	...	...	...	...	1642	...	...	...
Oral ♡ d.	...	...	...	...	...	...	...	...	...	...	...	...	...	1735	...	0241	...	...	|	...	...	...
Aktobe 1 ♡ d.	...	...	...	...	...	...	...	...	...	...	...	...	...	0109	...	1326	1553	2104	|	2359	...	...
Atyrau ♡ d.	...	...	...	...	...	...	...	...	...	...	...	...	1830	|	1950	|	|	|	|	|	...	...
Makat ♡ d.	...	...	...	...	...	...	...	...	...	...	...	...	|	|	2218	|	|	|	|	|	...	...
Kandyagash ♡ d.	...	...	...	...	...	...	...	...	...	...	...	...	0303	0323	0706	1459	1730	2237	|	0147	...	...
Shalkar ♡ d.	...	...	...	...	...	...	...	...	...	...	...	...	0705	0705	1215	2009	2301	0335	0133	0742	...	...
Aral ♡ d.	...	...	...	...	...	...	...	...	...	...	...	...	1023	1023	1605	2355	0316	0721	0606	1155	...	...
Kazaly ♡ d.	...	...	...	...	...	...	...	...	...	...	...	...	1212	1212	1839	0210	0542	0926	0847	1416	...	...
Zhosaly ♡ d.	...	...	...	...	...	...	...	...	...	...	...	...	1426	1426	2124	0442	0814	1158	1127	1652	...	...
Kyzylorda ♡ d.	2210	...	...	...	...	...	...	...	...	...	...	1325	1622	1622	0016	0701	1047	1417	1405	1923	...	...
Turkestan d.	0331	...	...	...	...	...	...	...	1612	...	...	1840	2140	2140	2240	1157	1708	1934	2022	0115	...	...
Arys 2 d.	0550	...	...	...	...	...	...	...	1832	...	...	2055	2350	2350	0611	1415	1938	2155s	2247	0335	...	...
Toshkent Shimolly d.	|	...	...	...	...	...	...	...	|	...	1615	|	|	|	|	|	|	0359	|	|	...	...
Saryagash 🏛 d.	|	...	...	...	...	...	1440	...	|	...	1911	|	|	|	|	|	|	...	|	|	...	...
Arys 1 d.	|	...	...	...	...	...	1706	...	|	...	|	|	|	|	|	|	|	...	|	|	...	...
Shymkent d.	0721	1310	1405	...	1720	1825	1855	1930	2015	...	2232	2242	0120	0120	1000	1546	2124	...	0022	0509	...	...
Taraz d.	1155	1718	1805	...	2115	2240	0008	2324	0057	...	0232	0301	0508	0508	...	2028	0211	...	0600	0946	...	...
Shu d.	1547	2026	2107	...	0025	0146	0401	0224	0453	...	0533	0639	0808	0808	...	0034	0649	...	1003	1335	...	...
Karagandy d.	0317	0454	0535	...	|	|	|	1052	1730	...	|	|	|	|	...	|	|	...	|	|	...	...
Astana Nurly Zhol a.	0716t	0811	0849	...	|	|	|	1405	2211t	...	|	|	|	|	...	|	|	...	|	|	...	...
Almaty 1 a.	...	...	...	...	|	|	0905	...	...	...	|	1115	|	|	...	0523	1145	...	1525	1821	...	...
Almaty 2 a.	...	...	...	...	0445	0605	0938	...	...	...	0955	...	1220	1220	...	0616	...	...	1608	...	...	...

A – Semey - Almaty - Kyzlorda and v.v.
B – Semey - Astana - Mangistau and v.v.
C – Pavlodar - Astana - Turkestan and v.v.
D – Pavlodar - Astana - Presnogorkovskaya and v.v.
O – Operated by Otpan Logistik.
T – Operated by Turksib Astana LLP.
N – Operated by Nomadas.

g – ②⑤⑦.
h – ①③⑥.
k – ①③⑤⑦.
m – ②④⑥.
s – Arys 1.
t – Astana 1.

◧ – Runs on alternate days - please check locally for departure dates.
⊖ – Train traverses Russian territory (transit visa may be required).
♡ – Time zone UTC+5.

FOR ADDITIONAL SERVICES SEE PAGES 552 AND 554.

1880 KAZAKHSTAN

Time zone UTC+6 (♡+5) Kazakhstan Temir Joly

ORAL - ATYRAU - MANGISTAU

km		692		110		313		614		
				O				◧		
0	**Oral** ♡ d.	...	...	...	...	...	...	1910	...	...
118	Kazakhstan ♡ d.	...	...	...	...	...	...	2231	...	...
—	Aktobe 1 ♡ d.	1515	...	1917	...	...	...	0837	...	...
	Atyrau ♡ d.	|	...	|	...	1140	...	|	...	...
0	Makat ♡ d.	0425	...	0535	...	1535	...	1859	...	...
130	**Atyrau** ♡ a.	0755	...	|	...	|	...	|	...	...
300	Beineu ♡ d.	...	...	1143	...	2334	...	0142	...	...
704	**Mangistau** ♡ a.	...	...	1855	...	0902	...	0933	...	...

	109		313		613		691		
	O				◧				
Mangistau ♡ d.	1615	...	1400	...	1856	...	...	...	...
Beineu ♡ d.	2352	...	2310	...	0224	...	...	...	...
Atyrau ♡ d.	|	...	|	...	|	...	1430	...	...
Makat ♡ d.	0608	...	0806	...	0858	...	1823	...	...
Atyrau ♡ a.	|	...	1129	...	|	...	|	...	...
Aktobe 1 ♡ d.	1552	...	...	...	1946	...	0721	...	...
Kazakhstan ♡ d.	...	...	...	...	0523	...	...	...	...
Oral ♡ a.	...	...	...	...	0836	...	...	...	...

FOR FOOTNOTES SEE PAGE 553. FOR ADDITIONAL SERVICES SEE PREVIOUS TWO PAGES.

UZBEKISTAN

SEE MAP PAGE 556

Operators: The services shown are operated by O'zbekiston Temir Yo'llari (www.railway.uz).

Services: Trains convey first- and second-class seating unless indicated otherwise. Trains which run overnight generally convey sleeping accommodation.

Timings: Schedules are the latest available and may be subject to alteration at any time. Timings are expressed in local time.

1890 ANDIJAN - TOSHKENT - SAMARQAND - BUKHARA - KHIVA and KUNGRAD

O'zbekiston Temir Yo'llari

Toshkent stations: Toshkent Shimolly = Central; Toshkent Janubiy = South.

km		764	766	768	770	710	716	733		54	302	772	712	80	82	56	58	729	72	76	125	129	127	91
		①–⑥						①③			②						①②⑤			②			②③⑥	②
							◧				T					B			◧		A	C		
480	**Andijon** 1 d.	...	...	...	...	...	...	0530	...	...	...	...	...	...	...	...	...	1509	...	...	1538	1633	1720	1816
435	Namagan d.	...	...	...	...	...	...	0740	...	...	...	...	...	...	...	...	...	|	...	...	|	|	1930	2026
344	Kokand 1 d.	...	...	...	...	...	...	|	...	...	...	...	...	...	...	...	...	1653	...	...	1724	1817	|	|
	Pap d.	...	...	...	...	...	...	0833	...	...	...	...	...	...	...	...	...	1728	...	...	1803	1856	2026	2121
0	**Toshkent** Shimolly a.	...	...	...	...	...	...	1238	...	...	...	...	...	...	...	...	...	2117	...	...	|	|	|	0123
0	**Toshkent** Shimolly d.	0630	0721	0804	0829	0840	0912	...	...	...	1450	1941	2013	...	...	...	...	...	...	...	|	|	|	...
	Toshkent Janubiy a.	|	|	|	|	|	|	...	...	...	|	|	|	...	...	...	...	...	...	...	2154	2247	0027	...
	Toshkent Janubiy d.	|	|	|	|	|	|	...	...	1315	|	|	|	2049	2049	2124	2124	...	2248	2248	2248	2332	0110	...
240	Djizakh d.	|	0900	|	|	1052	1124	...	...	1542	1739	|	2232	2327	2327	0005	0005	...	0120	0120	0120	0159	0341	...
354	**Samarqand** d.	0858	0951	1032	1103	1215	1247	...	...	1738	1931	2220	2400	0110	0110	0147	0147	...	0259	0259	0259	0340	0534	...
511	Karshi d.	1009	...	|	|	|	1415	...	...	|	2140	|	|	0333	0333	|	|	...	|	|	|	0601	|	...
	Darband d.	...	...	|	|	|	...	...	...	|	|	|	|	0742	0742	|	|	...	|	|	|	1009	|	...
	Kumkurgan d.	...	...	|	|	|	...	...	...	|	0424	|	|	0957	1031	|	|	...	|	|	|	1157	|	...
844	**Termez** a.	...	...	|	|	|	...	...	...	|	|	|	|	1055	|	|	|	...	|	|	|	1255	|	...
	Saryasia a.	...	...	|	|	|	...	...	...	|	0533	|	|	...	1147	|	|	...	|	|	|	...	|	...
510	Navoiy d.	...	...	1148	1205	1338	...	...	...	1936	...	2322	0137	...	...	0357	0357	...	0517	0517	0517	...	0724	...
602	**Bukhara** 1 d.	...	...	1215	1246	1438	...	...	...	2103	...	0003	0237	...	...	0529	0529	...	0732	0712	0712	...	0902	...
	Alat a.	...	...	...	...	...	...	...	...	|	...	...	...	...	...	|	|	...	0859	|	|	...	|	...
1111	Miskin d.	...	...	...	...	...	...	...	...	0239	...	...	...	...	...	|	|	...	...	|	|	...	1425	...
	Urgench d.	...	...	...	...	...	...	...	...	|	...	...	...	...	...	1132	1132	...	...	1308	1308	...	|	...
	Khiva a.	...	...	...	...	...	...	...	...	|	...	...	...	...	...	1202	|	...	...	1338	1338	...	|	...
	Shavat a.	...	...	...	...	...	...	...	...	|	...	...	...	...	...	...	1201	...	...	...	...	...	|	...
1041	Turtgul d.	...	...	...	...	...	...	...	...	0312	...	...	...	...	...	...	...	...	...	...	...	...	1508	...
1207	Nukus d.	...	...	...	...	...	...	...	...	0614	...	...	...	...	...	...	...	...	...	...	...	...	1817	...
1354	**Kungrad** a.	...	...	...	...	...	...	...	...	0822	...	...	...	...	...	...	...	...	...	...	...	...	2019	...

	771	730	711	703	301	732	769	765	767	763	715	709	76	126	126	128	130	71	54	56	58	80	82
					①					①–⑥			②		②⑤⑥	②⑤⑥					②③⑥		
					T	G					◧			F			D	◧		F			
Kungrad d.	...	...	...	...	...	...	...	...	...	...	...	...	...	...	...	0945	...	...	1104	...	...	...	...
Nukus d.	...	...	...	...	...	...	...	...	...	...	...	...	...	...	...	1204	...	...	1325	...	...	...	...
Turtgul d.	...	...	...	...	...	...	...	...	...	...	...	...	...	...	...	1455	...	...	1621	...	...	...	...
Shavat d.	...	...	...	...	...	...	...	...	...	...	...	...	...	...	...	|	...	...	|	...	1621	...	...
Khiva d.	...	...	...	...	...	...	...	...	...	...	...	...	1423	1424	...	|	...	...	|	1620	|	...	...
Urgench d.	...	...	...	...	...	...	...	...	...	...	...	...	1514	1514	1400	|	...	...	|	1720	1720	...	...
Miskin d.	...	...	...	...	...	...	...	...	...	...	...	...	|	|	1609	1609	...	...	1714	|	|	...	...
Alat d.	...	...	...	...	...	...	...	...	...	...	...	...	|	|	|	|	...	2007	|	|	|	...	...
Bukhara 1 d.	0315	...	0515	...	...	...	1458	...	1617	...	...	1646	2135	2135	2135	2135	...	2202	2258	2345	2345	...	...
Navoiy d.	0359	...	0619	...	...	...	1542	...	1701	...	...	1750	2241	2241	2241	2241	...	2321	0022	0102	0102	...	...
Saryasia d.	|	...	|	...	2309	...	|	...	|	...	...	|	|	|	|	|	...	|	|	|	|	...	1648
Termez d.	|	...	|	...	|	...	|	...	|	...	...	|	|	|	|	|	1549	|	|	|	|	1740	|
Kumkurgan d.	|	...	|	...	0041	...	|	...	|	...	...	|	|	|	|	|	1658	|	|	|	|	1909	1909
Darband d.	|	...	|	...	|	...	|	...	|	...	...	|	|	|	|	|	1842	|	|	|	|	2057	2057
Karshi d.	|	...	|	0542	0718	...	|	...	|	1729	1737	|	|	|	|	|	2305	|	|	|	|	0135	0135
Samarqand d.	0508	...	0807	0807	0922	...	1651	1735	1810	1850	1923	1935	0058	0058	0058	0058	0116	0156	0235	0311	0311	0355	0355
Djizakh d.	|	...	0936	0936	1103	...	|	1828	|	|	2056	2122	0239	0239	0239	0239	0304	0341	0410	0438	0438	0526	0526
Toshkent Janubiy a.	|	...	|	|	|	...	|	|	|	|	|	|	0510	0510	0510	0510	0540	0618	0651	0719	0719	0819	0819
Toshkent Janubiy d.	|	...	|	|	|	...	|	|	|	|	|	|	...	0550	0550	0615	0655	...	...	...	...	...	...
Toshkent Shimolly a.	0735	...	1214	1214	1351	...	1917	2008	2031	2110	2331	2348	...	|	|	|	|	...	...	...	...	...	...
Toshkent Shimolly d.	...	0810	...	...	...	1755	...	...	...	...	...	...	...	|	|	|	|	...	...	...	...	...	...
Pap d.	...	1156	...	...	...	2201	...	...	...	...	...	...	...	0946	0946	|	1108	...	...	...	...	...	...
Kokand 1 d.	...	1233	...	...	...	2236	...	...	...	...	...	...	...	1023	1023	|	1145	...	...	...	...	...	...
Namagan d.	...	|	...	...	...	|	...	...	...	...	...	...	...	|	|	1128	|	...	...	...	...	...	...
Andijon 1 a.	...	1414	...	...	...	0017	...	...	...	...	...	...	...	1206	1206	1332	1336	...	...	...	...	...	...

A – ①②⑤⑥.
B – ②③⑤⑥.
C – ①②③⑤⑦.
D – ②③④⑤⑦.
E – ③④⑥⑦.
F – ②③⑥⑦.
G – ③④⑤⑥.
T – Operates from / to Dushanbe (Tajikistan).

◧ – Runs on alternate days, please enquire locally for exact dates.

RUSSIA and BELARUS

SEE MAPS PAGES 545 and 556

Operators : **RZhD** : Rossiskiye Zheleznye Dorogi, www.rzd.ru **BCh** : Belaruskaya Chyhunka, www.rw.by

Timings : **Due to the ongoing conflict in the region, we will not be updating the Russian and Belarusian section until further notice**. All times are now shown in LOCAL time (time zone is UTC+3 all year unless otherwise shown in the notes or by a shaded column).

Tickets : Except for travel by purely local trains, prior reservation is necessary and passports and visas must be presented when purchasing tickets. Most nationalities require visas.

RAIL TRAVEL IN RUSSIA, BELARUS, UKRAINE and MOLDOVA

CARRIAGE TYPES

As trains generally operate over long distances, most accommodation is designed for overnight as well as day use. Carriage types (with their Russian names) are:

Spálny vagón SV – 2-berth sleeping compartments (9 per carriage), found only in the best trains. Sometimes referred to as 1st class. A small number of named trains also have *de luxe* carriages (also known as *VIP*) with ensuite facilities.

Kupéiny K – 4-berth compartments (9 per carriage) found in almost all long-distance trains. Sometimes referred to as 2nd class.

Platskártny – open-plan dormitory-style carriage with 54 bunks, found in all except the best trains. Sometimes referred to as 3rd class.

Óbshchi – open-plan carriages with hard seating, found in some slow trains. Sometimes referred to as 4th class and not recommended for long-distance travel.

TRAIN TYPES

The top grade of fast long-distance train is classified *Firménny* (shown as *Fir* in the tables). These are composed of higher-quality carriages dedicated to a particular service (often named) and higher fares apply. Normal long-distance express trains are classified *Skóry* (shown as *Sko* in the tables). The lowest class of long-distance train is classified *Passazhírsky* (*Pas* in the tables) which call at many stations en-route.

Trains are identified by a number, followed by a cyrillic character, or a two-letter transliteration which is shown in some tables to assist in making bookings.

High-speed train types with 1st and 2nd class seating are *Sapsan* (Peregrine Falcon) running between Moskva and St Peterburg, and the Talgo-built *Strizh* (Swift) running between Moskva and Nizhny Novgorod (also with 1st class sleeping compartments for daytime use). Fast *Lastochka* (Swallow) trains with 2nd class seats run on several routes.

INTERNATIONAL SERVICES

International services to, from and via Poland, Slovakia, Hungary and Romania convey through sleeping cars of the normal European ('RIC') types, with single and double compartments in first class, and 3- or 4-berth compartments in second class. The railways of the former Soviet Union being of broad gauge (1520mm), the bogies (trucks) of these through cars are changed at the frontier with these countries.

DAYS OF RUNNING

Many trains run on alternate days only, on even or uneven numbered dates. The examples below illustrate the system used to indicate exceptions to the pattern of even or uneven dates at the end of a month with 31 days and at the beginning of the month following:

e.g. "Uneven dates [... *29, 1* ...]" means that the train does not run on the 31st of a month with 31 days.

e.g. "Even dates [... *30, 1, 4* ...]" means that the train, **following a month with 31 days**, runs exceptionally on the 1st, but not the 2nd, of the month.

In these cases, the following symbols are used in the tables to indicate days of running:

■ – Uneven dates.	● – Even dates.
■(1) – Uneven dates [.. *29, 1* ..]	●(1) – Even dates [.. *28, 2* ..]
■(2) – Uneven dates [.. *31, 2, 3* ..]	●(2) – Even dates [.. *30, 2* ..]
■(3) – Uneven dates [.. *31, 3* ..]	●(3) – Even dates [.. *30, 1, 3, 8* ..]
■(4) – Uneven dates [.. *29, 3* ..]	●(4) – Even dates [.. *30, 1, 4* ..]
■(5) – Uneven dates [.. *31, 2, 5* ..]	●(5) – Even dates [.. *30, 1, 3, 4* ..]
■(6) – Uneven dates [.. *31, 2, 7* ..]	●(6) – Even dates [.. *30, 1, 3, 6* ..]
■(7) – Uneven dates [.. *31, 2, 4, 7* ..]	●(7) – Even dates [.. *30, 1, 6* ..]
■(8) – Uneven dates [.. *31, 2, 4, 6, 8, 10, 11* ..]	●(8) – Even dates [.. *30, 1, 3, 5, 8* ..]
■(9) – Uneven dates [.. *31, 2, 4, 6, 9* ..]	●(9) – Even dates [.. *30, 1, 3, 5, 7, 10* ..]

ST PETERBURG - MOSKVA 1900

km																			
0	**Moskva** Oktyabrskaya §	d.	...	...	...	...	...	...	...	...	**St Peterburg** Glavny ‡	d.	...	...	...	...	...	...	...	...
167	Tver	d.	...	...	...	...	...	...	...	...	Chudovo Mos.	d.	...	...	...	...	...	...	...	...
331	Bologoye	d.	...	...	...	...	...	...	...	...	Bologoye	d.	...	...	...	...	...	...	...	...
532	Chudovo Mos.	d.	...	...	...	...	...	...	...	...	Tver	d.	...	...	...	...	...	...	...	...
650	**St Peterburg** Glavny ‡	a.	...	...	...	...	...	...	...	...	**Moskva** Oktyabrskaya §	a.	...	...	...	...	...	...	...	...

km																			
0	**Moskva** Oktyabrskaya §	d.	...	...	...	...	...	...	...	...	**Pskov**	d.	...	...	...	...	...	...	...	...
167	Tver	d.	...	...	...	...	...	...	...	...	Dno	d.	...	...	...	...	...	...	...	...
331	Bologoye	d.	...	...	...	...	...	...	...	...	**Veliky Novgorod** ⊖	d.	...	...	...	...	...	...	...	...
	St Peterburg Glavny	d.	...	...	...	...	...	...	...	...	Chudovo Mos.	d.	...	...	...	...	...	...	...	...
532	Chudovo Mos.	d.	...	...	...	...	...	...	...	...	**St Peterburg** Glavny	a.	...	...	...	...	...	...	...	...
	Veliky Novgorod ⊖	a.	...	...	...	...	...	...	...	...	Bologoye	d.	...	...	...	...	...	...	...	...
588	Dno	a.	...	...	...	...	...	...	...	...	Tver	d.	...	...	...	...	...	...	...	...
687	**Pskov**	a.	...	...	...	...	...	...	...	...	**Moskva** Oktyabrskaya §	a.	...	...	...	...	...	...	...	...

§ – Also known as *Leningradski vokzal*. ‡ – Also known as *Moskovski vokzal*. ⊖ – Station is named **Novgorod na Volkhove**.

MOSKVA AIRPORTS ✈ 1901

MOSKVA DOMODEDOVO AIRPORT ✈
Aeroexpress rail service Moskva Paveletskaya - Moskva Domodedovo ✈. *35 km* Journey time 45 minutes.

MOSKVA SHEREMETYEVO AIRPORT ✈
Aeroexpress rail service Moskva Belorusskaya - Moskva Sheremetyevo ✈. *35 km* Journey time 50 minutes.

MOSKVA VNUKOVO AIRPORT ✈
Aeroexpress rail service Moskva Kiyevskaya - Moskva Vnukovo ✈. *28 km* Journey time 35-40 minutes.

RZhD (MOSKVA -) ST PETERBURG - PETROZAVODSK - MURMANSK 1905

km																			
	Moskva Oktyabrskaya **1900**	d.	...	...	...	...	...	...	...	...	**Murmansk**	d.	...	...	...	...	...	...	...	...
0	**St Peterburg** Ladozhski	d.	...	...	...	...	...	...	...	...	Kandalaksha	d.	...	...	...	...	...	...	...	...
**114*	Volkhovstroi 1	d.	...	...	...	...	...	...	...	...	Belomorsk	d.	...	...	...	...	...	...	...	...
394	**Petrozavodsk**	d.	...	...	...	...	...	...	...	...	**Petrozavodsk**	d.	...	...	...	...	...	...	...	...
773	Belomorsk	d.	...	...	...	...	...	...	...	...	Volkhovstroi 1	d.	...	...	...	...	...	...	...	...
1161	Kandalaksha	d.	...	...	...	...	...	...	...	...	**St Peterburg** Ladozhski	a.	...	...	...	...	...	...	...	...
1438	**Murmansk**	a.	...	...	...	...	...	...	...	...	*Moskva Oktyabrskaya* **1900**	a.	...	...	...	...	...	...	...	...

* – Moskva - Vokhovstroi : *641 km*.

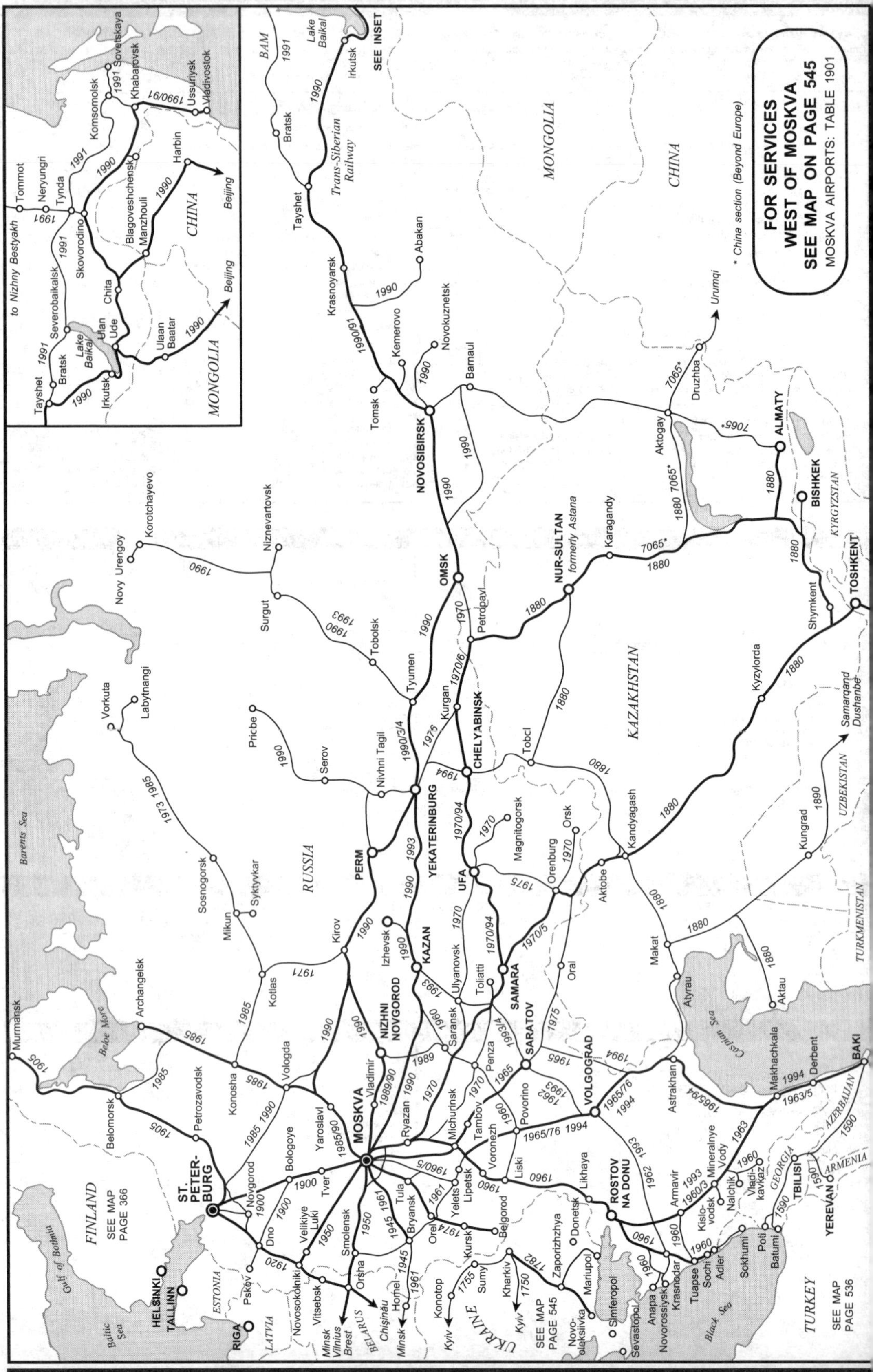

See also the map on page 545

ST PETERBURG - HOMEL and KOZYATYN — 1920

RZhD, BCh, UZ

km									
0	**St Peterburg** Vitebski ... d.	...	...	...	...	...	...	...	...
	St Peterburg Glavny ... d.	...	...	...	...	...	...	...	...
245	Dno ... d.	...	...	...	...	...	...	...	...
421	Novosokolniki ... RU d.	...	...	...	...	...	...	...	...
568	Vitsebsk ... ⊖ BY d.	...	...	...	...	...	...	...	...
670	Polatsk ... d.	...	...	...	...	...	...	...	...
868	Maladzechnia ... a.	...	...	...	...	...	...	...	...
	Moskva Bel. **1950** ... d.	...	...	...	...	...	...	...	...
652	**Orsha** Tsentralnaya ... a.	...	...	...	...	...	...	...	...
652	**Orsha** Tsentralnaya ... **1950** d.	...	...	...	...	...	...	...	...
	Minsk ... **1950** a.	...	...	...	...	...	...	...	...
	Hrodna **1952** ... a.	...	...	...	...	...	...	...	...
	Brest Tsent. **1950** ... a.	...	...	...	...	...	...	...	...
726	Mahilyow 1 ... d.	...	...	...	...	...	...	...	...
853	Zhlobin ... **1930** d.	...	...	...	...	...	...	...	...
	Homel ... **1930** a.	...	...	...	...	...	...	...	...
	Kyiv **1930** ... a.	...	...	...	...	...	...	...	...
954	Kalinkavichy ... BY d.	...	...	...	...	...	...	...	...
1109	Korosten ... ⊡ UA d.	...	...	...	...	...	...	...	...
1191	Zhytomyr ... d.	...	...	...	...	...	...	...	...
1267	**Kozyatyn** 1 ... a.	...	...	...	...	...	...	...	...
	Chisinău **1720** ... a.	...	...	...	...	...	...	...	...

Chisinău **1720** ... d.	...	...	...	...	...	...	...	...
Kozyatyn 1 ... d.	...	...	...	...	...	...	...	...
Zhytomyr ... d.	...	...	...	...	...	...	...	...
Korosten ... UA d.	...	...	...	...	...	...	...	...
Kalinkavichy ... ⊡ BY d.	...	...	...	...	...	...	...	...
Kyiv **1930** ... d.	...	...	...	...	...	...	...	...
Homel ... **1930** d.	...	...	...	...	...	...	...	...
Zhlobin ... **1930** d.	...	...	...	...	...	...	...	...
Mahilyow 1 ... d.	...	...	...	...	...	...	...	...
Brest Tsent. **1950** ... d.	...	...	...	...	...	...	...	...
Hrodna **1952** ... d.	...	...	...	...	...	...	...	...
Minsk ... **1950** d.	...	...	...	...	...	...	...	...
Orsha Tsentralnaya ... **1950** a.	...	...	...	...	...	...	...	...
Orsha Tsentralnaya ... d.	...	...	...	...	...	...	...	...
Moskva Bel. **1950** ... a.	...	...	...	...	...	...	...	...
Maladzechnia ... d.	...	...	...	...	...	...	...	...
Polatsk ... d.	...	...	...	...	...	...	...	...
Vitsebsk ... BY d.	...	...	...	...	...	...	...	...
Novosokolniki ... ⊖ RU d.	...	...	...	...	...	...	...	...
Dno ... d.	...	...	...	...	...	...	...	...
St Peterburg Glavny ... a.	...	...	...	...	...	...	...	...
St Peterburg Vitebski ... a.	...	...	...	...	...	...	...	...

⊖ – 🏛 : Yezyaryshcha (BY) / Zaverezhye (RU).
⊡ – 🏛 : Slovechno (BY) / Berezhest (UA).

BY – Belarus (UTC + 3)
RU – Russia (Moskva Time UTC + 3).
UA – Ukraine (UTC + 2 winter, UTC + 3 summer).

MINSK - HOMEL - KYIV — 1930

BCh, UZ

km									
	St P'burg Vit. **1920** ... d.	...	...	...	...	...	...	...	...
0	**Minsk** ... d.	...	...	...	...	...	...	...	...
149	Babruysk ... d.	...	...	...	...	...	...	...	...
214	Zhlobin ... **1920** d.	...	...	...	...	...	...	...	...
304	**Homel** ... **1920** a.	...	...	...	...	...	...	...	...
304	**Homel** ... BY d.	...	...	...	...	...	...	...	...
415	Chernihiv ... § UA d.	...	...	...	...	...	...	...	...
624	**Kyiv** ... a.	...	...	...	...	...	...	...	...
	Kharkiv ... a.	...	...	...	...	...	...	...	...
	Odesa ... a.	...	...	...	...	...	...	...	...

Odesa ... d.	...	...	...	...	...	...	...	...
Kharkiv ... d.	...	...	...	...	...	...	...	...
Kyiv ... d.	...	...	...	...	...	...	...	...
Chernihiv ... § UA d.	...	...	...	...	...	...	...	...
Homel ... BY a.	...	...	...	...	...	...	...	...
Homel ... **1920** d.	...	...	...	...	...	...	...	...
Zhlobin ... **1920** d.	...	...	...	...	...	...	...	...
Babruysk ... d.	...	...	...	...	...	...	...	...
Minsk ... a.	...	...	...	...	...	...	...	...
St P'burg Vit. **1920** ... a.	...	...	...	...	...	...	...	...

§ – 🏛 : Teryukha (BY) / Hornostayivka (UA).
BY – Belarus (UTC + 3).
UA – Ukraine (UTC + 2 / + 3).

MOSKVA - BRYANSK - HOMEL - BREST — 1945

RZhD, BCh

km									
0	**Moskva** Belorusskaya ... d.	...	...	...	...	...	...	...	...
485	**Bryansk** Orlovski ... d.	...	...	...	...	...	...	...	...
713	Zlynka ... RU d.	...	...	...	...	...	...	...	...
739	Dobrush ... BY d.	...	...	...	...	...	...	...	...
764	**Homel** ... d.	...	...	...	...	...	...	...	...
892	Kalinkavichy ... d.	...	...	...	...	...	...	...	...
1069	Luninets ... d.	...	...	...	...	...	...	...	...
1297	**Brest** Tsentralny ... a.	...	...	...	...	...	...	...	...

Brest Tsentralny ... d.	...	...	...	...	...	...	...	...
Luninets ... d.	...	...	...	...	...	...	...	...
Kalinkavichy ... d.	...	...	...	...	...	...	...	...
Homel ... a.	...	...	...	...	...	...	...	...
Dobrush ... BY d.	...	...	...	...	...	...	...	...
Zlynka ... RU d.	...	...	...	...	...	...	...	...
Bryansk Orlovski ... d.	...	...	...	...	...	...	...	...
Moskva Belorusskaya ... a.	...	...	...	...	...	...	...	...

BY – Belarus (UTC + 3).
RU – Russia (UTC + 3).

MOSKVA - MINSK - VILNIUS, KALININGRAD and BREST — 1950

RZhD, BCh

km									
0	**Moskva** Belorusskaya ... d.	...	...	...	...	...	...	...	...
243	Vyazma ... d.	...	...	...	...	...	...	...	...
419	**Smolensk** ... RU d.	...	...	...	...	...	...	...	...
560	Vitsebsk ... RU d.	...	...	...	...	...	...	...	...
662	**Polatsk** ... BY a.	...	...	...	...	...	...	...	...
	St Peterburg Glavny **1920** ... d.	...	...	...	...	...	...	...	...
538	Orsha Tsentralnaya ... BY d.	...	...	...	...	...	...	...	...
750	**Minsk** ... d.	...	...	...	...	...	...	...	...
827	Maladzechnia ... BY d.	...	...	...	...	...	...	...	...
943	**Vilnius** ... LT a.	...	...	...	...	...	...	...	...
1285	**Kaliningrad** ... KA a.	...	...	...	...	...	...	...	...
892	Baranavichy Tsentral'nyye ... d.	...	...	...	...	...	...	...	...
1094	**Brest** Tsentralny ... a.	...	...	...	...	...	...	...	...
	Warszawa Wschodnia **1050** ... a.	...	...	...	...	...	...	...	...

Warszawa Wschodnia **1050** ... d.	...	...	...	...	...	...	...	...
Brest Tsentralny ... d.	...	...	...	...	...	...	...	...
Baranavichy Tsentral'nyye ... d.	...	...	...	...	...	...	...	...
Kaliningrad ... KA d.	...	...	...	...	...	...	...	...
Vilnius ... LT d.	...	...	...	...	...	...	...	...
Maladzechna ... d.	...	...	...	...	...	...	...	...
Minsk ... d.	...	...	...	...	...	...	...	...
Orsha Tsentralnaya ... BY d.	...	...	...	...	...	...	...	...
St Peterburg Glavny **1920** ... a.	...	...	...	...	...	...	...	...
Polatsk ... BY d.	...	...	...	...	...	...	...	...
Vitsebsk ... RU d.	...	...	...	...	...	...	...	...
Smolensk ... RU d.	...	...	...	...	...	...	...	...
Vyazma ... d.	...	...	...	...	...	...	...	...
Moskva Belorusskaya ... a.	...	...	...	...	...	...	...	...

km									
0	**Sebezh** ... d.	...	...	...	...	...	...	...	...
111	Novosokolniki ... d.	...	...	...	...	...	...	...	...
140	Velikiye Luki ... d.	...	...	...	...	...	...	...	...
381	Rzhev ... d.	...	...	...	...	...	...	...	...
616	**Moskva** Belorusskaya ... a.	...	...	...	...	...	...	...	...

Moskva Belorusskaya ... d.	...	...	...	...	...	...	...	...
Rzhev ... d.	...	...	...	...	...	...	...	...
Velikiye Luki ... d.	...	...	...	...	...	...	...	...
Novosokolniki ... d.	...	...	...	...	...	...	...	...
Sebezh ... a.	...	...	...	...	...	...	...	...

BY – Belarus (UTC + 3).
KA – Kaliningrad region of Russia (UTC + 2). Local time.
LT – Lithuania (UTC + 2 in winter, UTC + 3 in summer).
RU – Russia (Moskva Time UTC + 3).

BORDER CROSSINGS:
Between Smolensk and Polatsk: Rudnya (RU) / Zavolsha (BY).
Between Smolensk and Orsha: Krasnoye (RU) / Osinovka (BY).
Between Maladzechna and Vilnius: Hudahai (BY) / Kena (LT).
Between Vilnius and Kaliningrad: Kybartai (LT) / Nesterov (KA).

1952 VITSEBSK - MINSK - HRODNA BCh

km										
0	**Vitsebsk**	d.	...	...	...	...	...	...	...	...
84	Orsha Tsentralnaya	a.	...	...	...	...	...	...	...	...
84	Orsha Tsentralnaya	d.	...	...	...	...	...	...	...	...
296	**Minsk**	a.	...	...	...	...	...	...	...	...
296	**Minsk**	d.	...	...	...	...	...	...	...	...
373	Maladzechna	d.	...	...	...	...	...	...	...	...
501	Lida	d.	...	...	...	...	...	...	...	...
437	Baranavichy Pol.	d.	...	...	...	...	...	...	...	...
**633*	**Hrodna**	a.	...	...	...	...	...	...	...	...

Hrodna	d.	...	...	...	...	...	...	...	...
Baranavichy Pol.	d.	...	...	...	...	...	...	...	...
Lida	d.	...	...	...	...	...	...	...	...
Maladzechna	d.	...	...	...	...	...	...	...	...
Minsk	a.	...	...	...	...	...	...	...	...
Minsk	d.	...	...	...	...	...	...	...	...
Orsha Tsentralnaya	a.	...	...	...	...	...	...	...	...
Orsha Tsentralnaya	d.	...	...	...	...	...	...	...	...
Vitsebsk	a.	...	...	...	...	...	...	...	...

* – *657 km* via Baranavichy.

1960 MOSKVA - ROSTOV - SEVASTOPOL, NOVOROSSIYSK, KISLOVODSK, SOCHI and ADLER

km	*Time zone: UTC+3*								
	St Peterburg Glavny	d.	+3	...	...	...	...	...	...
	Bologoye	d.	+3	...	...	...	...	...	...
	Tver	d.	+3	...	...	...	...	...	...
0	**Moskva** Kazanskaya	d.	+3	...	...	...	...	...	...
198	Ryazan 2	d.	+3	...	...	...	...	...	...
412	Michurinsk Voronezhski	d.	+3	...	...	...	...	...	...
469	Gryazi Voronezhski	d.	+3	...	...	...	...	...	...
426	Yelets	d.	+3	...	...	...	...	...	...
504	Lipetsk	d.	+3	...	...	...	...	...	...
591	Voronezh Pridacha	d.	+3	...	...	...	...	...	...
	Tomsk 2	d.	+7	...	...	...	...	...	...
	Tomsk 1	d.	+7	...	...	...	...	...	...
	Tayga	d.	+7	...	...	...	...	...	...
	Barnaul	d.	+7	...	...	...	...	...	...
	Novosibirsk	d.	+7	...	...	...	...	...	...
	Omsk	d.	+6	...	...	...	...	...	...
	Tyumen	d.	+5	...	...	...	...	...	...
	Yekaterinburg	d.	+5	...	...	...	...	...	...
	Sarapul	d.	+4	...	...	...	...	...	...
	Kazan 2 ◧	d.	+3	...	...	...	...	...	...
	Saransk	d.	+3	...	...	...	...	...	...
	Penza 1	d.	+3	...	...	...	...	...	...
	Povorino	d.	+3	...	...	...	...	...	...
667	Liski	d.	+3	...	...	...	...	...	...
786	Rossosh	d.	+3	...	...	...	...	...	...
1062	Likhaya	d.	+3	...	...	...	...	...	...
1226	**Rostov na Donu**	d.	+3	...	...	...	...	...	...
	Vladyslavivka	d.	+3	...	...	...	...	...	...
	Dzhankoy	d.	+3	...	...	...	...	...	...
	Simferopol	a.	+3	...	...	...	...	...	...
	Sevastopol	a.	+3	...	...	...	...	...	...
1405	Tikhoretskaya	d.	+3	...	...	...	...	...	...
1332	Starominskaya Tim.	d.	+3	...	...	...	...	...	...
1510	Krasnodar 1	d.	+3	...	...	...	...	...	...
1645	**Novorossiysk**	a.	+3	...	...	...	...	...	...
1636	**Anapa**	a.	+3	...	...	...	...	...	...
1533	Armavir Rostovski	d.	+3	...	...	...	...	...	...
1721	Mineralnye Vody	d.	+3	...	...	...	...	...	...
1747	Pyatigorsk	d.	+3	...	...	...	...	...	...
1785	**Kislovodsk**	a	+3						
1658	Tuapse	d.	+3	...	...	...	...	...	...
1738	**Sochi**	a.	+3	...	...	...	...	...	...
1761	**Adler**	a.	+3	...	...	...	...	...	...
1800	Gagra ◐	a.	+3	...	...	...	...	...	...
1873	**Sukhumi** ◐	a.	+3	...	...	...	...	...	...

Time zone: UTC+3								
Sukhumi ◐	d.	+3	...	...	...	...	...	...
Gagra ◐	d.	+3	...	...	...	...	...	...
Adler	d.	+3	...	...	...	...	...	...
Sochi	d.	+3	...	...	...	...	...	...
Tuapse	d.	+3	...	...	...	...	...	...
Kislovodsk	d.	+3	...	...	...	...	...	...
Pyatigorsk	d.	+3	...	...	...	...	...	...
Mineralnye Vody	d.	+3	...	...	...	...	...	...
Armavir Rostovski	d.	+3	...	...	...	...	...	...
Anapa	d.	+3	...	...	...	...	...	...
Novorossiysk	d.	+3	...	...	...	...	...	...
Krasnodar 1	d.	+3	...	...	...	...	...	...
Starominskaya Tim.	d.	+3	...	...	...	...	...	...
Tikhoretskaya	d.	+3	...	...	...	...	...	...
Sevastopol	d.	+3	...	...	...	...	...	...
Simferopol	d.	+3	...	...	...	...	...	...
Dzhankoy	d.	+3	...	...	...	...	...	...
Vladyslavivka	d.	+3	...	...	...	...	...	...
Rostov na Donu	d.	+3	...	...	...	...	...	...
Likhaya	d.	+3	...	...	...	...	...	...
Rossosh	d.	+3	...	...	...	...	...	...
Liski	d.	+3	...	...	...	...	...	...
Povorino	d.	+3	...	...	...	...	...	...
Penza 1	d.	+3	...	...	...	...	...	...
Saransk	d.	+3	...	...	...	...	...	...
Kazan 2 ◧	d.	+3	...	...	...	...	...	...
Sarapaul	d.	+4	...	...	...	...	...	...
Yekaterinburg	d.	+5	...	...	...	...	...	...
Tyumen	d.	+5	...	...	...	...	...	...
Omsk	d.	+6	...	...	...	...	...	...
Novosibirsk	d.	+7	...	...	...	...	...	...
Barnaul	a.	+7	...	...	...	...	...	...
Tayga	d.	+7	...	...	...	...	...	...
Tomsk 1	a.	+7	...	...	...	...	...	...
Tomsk 2	a.	+7	...	...	...	...	...	...
Voronezh Pridacha	d.	+3	...	...	...	...	...	...
Lipetsk	d.	+3	...	...	...	...	...	...
Yelets	d.	+3	...	...	...	...	...	...
Gryazi Voronezhski	d.	+3	...	...	...	...	...	...
Michurinsk Voronezhski	d	+3						
Ryazan 2	d.	+3	...	...	...	...	...	...
Moskva Kazanskaya	a.	+3	...	...	...	...	...	...
Tver	d.	+3	...	...	...	...	...	...
Bologoye	d.	+3	...	...	...	...	...	...
St Peterburg Glavny	a.	+3	...	...	...	...	...	...

◧ – Also known as Vosstanie Passazhirskaja.

◐ – Abkhazia Autonomous Region (🚉 = Veseloe / Tsandryphsh).

1961 KALININGRAD - MINSK - ADLER

For other trains Kaliningrad - Minsk - Smolensk see Table **1950**.

km	*UTC+3*				
0	**Kaliningrad**	KA d.	...	...
342	Maladzechna	BY d.	...	...
535	**Minsk**	d.	...	...
684	Babruysk	d.	...	...
749	Zhlobin	d.	...	...
839	Homel	d.	...	...
890	Zlynka	d.	...	...
747	Orsha Tsent.	BY d.	...	...
866	**Smolensk**	RU d.	...	...
1112	Bryansk O.	d.	...	...
	Kursk	d.	...	...
1443	Yelets	d.	...	...
1521	Lipetsk	d.	...	...
1684	Voronezh 1	d.	...	...
1763	Liski	d.	...	...
1882	Rossosh	d.	...	...
2158	Likhaya	d.	...	...
2322	**Rostov na Donu** ◧	d.	...	...
2428	Starominskaya Tim.	d.	...	...
2533	Krasnodar 1	d.	...	...
2753	Tuapse	d.	...	...
2833	**Sochi**	a.	...	...
2856	**Adler**	a.	...	...

UTC+3			
Adler	d.	...	...
Sochi	d.	...	...
Tuapse	d.	...	...
Krasnodar 1	d.	...	...
Starominskaya Tim.	d.	...	...
Rostov na Donu ◧	d.	...	...
Likhaya	d.	...	...
Rossosh	d.	...	...
Liski	d.	...	...
Voronezh 1	d.	...	...
Lipetsk	d.	...	...
Yelets	d.	...	...
Kursk	d.	...	...
Bryansk O.	d.	...	...
Smolensk	RU d.	...	...
Orsha Tsent.	BY d.	...	...
Zlynka	d.	...	...
Homel	d.	...	...
Zhlobin	d.	...	...
Babruysk	d.	...	...
Minsk	d.	...	...
Maladzechna	BY d.	...	...
Kaliningrad	KA a.	...	...

1962 SARATOV - ADLER

km	*UTC+3*			
0	**Saratov** 1 (UTC +4)	d.	...	...
429	Volgograd 1	d.	...	...
964	Tikhoretskaya	d.	...	...
1100	Krasnodar 1	d.	...	...
1248	Tuapse	d.	...	...
1328	Sochi	a.	...	...
1351	**Adler**	a.	...	...

UTC+3			
Adler	d.	...	...
Sochi	d.	...	...
Tuapse	d.	...	...
Krasnodar 1	d.	...	...
Tikhoretskaya	d.	...	...
Volgograd 1	d.	...	...
Saratov 1 (UTC +4)	a.	...	...

1963 ROSTOV - BAKI

km	*UTC+3*			
0	**Rostov na Donu**	d.	...	...
307	Armavir Rost.	d.	...	...
495	Mineralnye Vody	d.	...	...
896	Makhachkala	d.	...	...
1025	Derbent	d.	...	...
1286	**Baki**	AZ a.	...	...

UTC+3			
Baki	AZ d.	...	...
Derbent	d.	...	...
Makhachkala	d.	...	...
Mineralnye Vody	d.	...	...
Armavir Rost.	d.	...	...
Rostov na Donu	a.	...	...

◧ – Rostov na Donu **Pervomajskaya**.

AZ – Azerbaijan (UTC+4). 🚉 = Yalama.

KA – Kaliningrad region of Russia (UTC+2). Local time.

BY – Belarus.

RU – Russia.

MOSKVA - SARATOV, VOLGOGRAD and BAKI 1965

km	Times are local time		time zone UTC+						
0	**Moskva** Pavelets	d.	+3	...	...	...	...	...	...
198	Ryazan 2	d.	+3	...	...	...	...	...	...
408	Michurinsk Uralski	d.	+3	...	...	...	...	...	...
541	Gryazi Voronezhski	d.	+3	...	...	...	...	...	...
778	Povorino	d.	+3	...	...	...	...	...	...
481	Tambov 1	d.	+3	...	...	...	...	...	...
861	**Saratov** 1	a.	+4	...	...	...	...	...	...
861	**Saratov** 1	d.	+4	...	...	...	...	...	...
1145	**Volgograd** 1	a.	+3	...	...	...	...	...	...
1595	Astrakhan 1	a.	+4	...	...	...	...	...	...
⊡	Makhachkala	a.	+3	...	...	...	...	...	...
2212	Derbent	a.	+3	...	...	...	...	...	...
2473	**Baki**	AZ a.	+4	...	...	...	...	...	...

Times are local time		time zone UTC+						
Baki	AZ d.	+4	...	...	...	...	...	...
Derbent	d.	+3	...	...	...	...	...	...
Makhachkala	d.	+3	...	...	...	...	...	...
Astrakhan 1	d.	+4	...	...	...	...	...	...
Volgograd 1	d.	+3	...	...	...	...	...	...
Saratov 1	a.	+4	...	...	...	...	...	...
Saratov 1	d.	+4	...	...	...	...	...	...
Tambov 1	d.	+3	...	...	...	...	...	...
Povorino	d.	+3	...	...	...	...	...	...
Gryazi Voronezhski	d.	+3	...	...	...	...	...	...
Michurinsk Uralski	d.	+3	...	...	...	...	...	...
Ryazan 2	d.	+3	...	...	...	...	...	...
Moskva Pavelets.	a.	+3	...	...	...	...	...	...

⊡ – *1537 km (2083 km* via Volgograd).

AZ – Azerbaijan (UTC+4).

MOSKVA - SAMARA - UFA - CHELYABINSK 1970

km	Times are local time		time zone UTC+						
0	**Moskva** Kazanskaya	d.	+3	...	...	...	...	...	...
197	Ryazan 1	d.	+3	...	...	...	...	...	...
601	Ruzayevka	d.	+3	...	...	...	...	...	...
627	**Saransk**	a.	+3	...	...	...	...	...	...
710	**Penza** 1	d.	+3	...	...	...	...	...	...
712	Inza	d.	+4	...	...	...	...	...	...
873	**Ulyanovsk**	d.	+4	...	...	...	...	...	...
908	Syzran 1	d.	+4	...	...	...	...	...	...
	Toliatti	a.	+4	...	...	...	...	...	...
1044	**Samara**	a.	+4	...	...	...	...	...	...
1044	**Samara**	d.	+4	...	...	...	...	...	...
1216	Buzuluk'	d.	+5	...	...	...	...	...	...
1462	Orenburg	a.	+5	...	...	...	...	...	...
	Orsk	a.	+5	...	...	...	...	...	...
1567	Ufa	d.	+5	...	...	...	...	...	...
1933	**Magnitogorsk**	a.	+5	...	...	...	...	...	...
2048	**Chelyabinsk**	a.	+5	...	...	...	...	...	...

Times are local time		time zone UTC+						
Chelyabinsk	d.	+5	...	...	...	...	...	...
Magnitogorsk	d.	+5	...	...	...	...	...	...
Ufa	d.	+5	...	...	...	...	...	...
Orsk	d.	+5	...	...	...	...	...	...
Orenburg	d.	+5	...	...	...	...	...	...
Buzuluk'	d.	+5	...	...	...	...	...	...
Samara	a.	+4	...	...	...	...	...	...
Samara	d.	+4	...	...	...	...	...	...
Toliatti	d.	+4	...	...	...	...	...	...
Syzran 1	d.	+4	...	...	...	...	...	...
Ulyanovsk	d.	+4	...	...	...	...	...	...
Inza	d.	+4	...	...	...	...	...	...
Penza 1	d.	+3	...	...	...	...	...	...
Saransk	d.	+3	...	...	...	...	...	...
Ruzayevka	d.	+3	...	...	...	...	...	...
Ryazan 1	d.	+3	...	...	...	...	...	...
Moskva Kazanskaya	a.	+3	...	...	...	...	...	...

BELGOROD - NOVOSIBIRSK 1971

Times are local time		time zone UTC+	
Belgorod	d.	+3	...
Voronezh 1	d.	+3	...
Gryazi Voronezhski	d.	+3	...
Michurinsk Uralski	d.	+3	...
Tambov 1	d.	+3	...
Penza 1	d.	+3	...
Syzran 1	d.	+4	...
Samara	a.	+4	...
Samara	d.	+4	...
Ufa	a.	+5	...
Ufa	d.	+5	...
Chelyabinsk	a.	+5	...
Chelyabinsk	d.	+5	...
Kurgan	d.	+5	...
Omsk	a.	+6	...
Omsk	d.	+6	...
Novosibirsk	a.	+7	...

Times are local time		time zone UTC+	
Novosibirsk	d.	+7	...
Omsk	a.	+6	...
Omsk	d.	+6	...
Kurgan	d.	+5	...
Chelyabinsk	a.	+5	...
Chelyabinsk	d.	+5	...
Ufa	a.	+5	...
Ufa	d.	+5	...
Samara	a.	+4	...
Samara	d.	+4	...
Syzran 1	d.	+4	...
Penza 1	d.	+3	...
Tambov 1	d.	+3	...
Michurinsk Uralski	d.	+3	...
Gryazi Voronezhski	d.	+3	...
Voronezh 1	d.	+3	...
Belgorod	a.	+3	...

NIZHNI NOVGOROD - VORKUTA 1973

Times are local time		time zone UTC+	
Nizhni Novgorod	d.	+3	...
Kirov	d.	+3	...
Kotlas Yuzhny	d.	+3	...
Mikun	d.	+3	...
Sosnogorsk	d.	+3	...
Vorkuta	a.	+3	...

Times are local time		time zone UTC+	
Vorkuta	d.	+3	...
Sosnogorsk	d.	+3	...
Mikun	d.	+3	...
Kotlas Yuzhny	d.	+3	...
Kirov	d.	+3	...
Nizhni Novgorod	a.	+3	...

MOSKVA - OREL - BELGOROD 1974

km										
	St Peterburg Gl. **1900**	d.	...	...	...	...	...	...	...	...
0	**Moskva** Kurskaya	d.	...	...	...	...	...	...	...	...
194	Tula I	d.	...	...	...	...	...	...	...	...
383	Orel	d.	...	...	...	...	...	...	...	...
537	Kursk	d.	...	...	...	...	...	...	...	...
697	**Belgorod**	a.	...	...	...	...	...	...	...	...

Belgorod	d.	...	...	...	...	...	...	...	...
Kursk	d.	...	...	...	...	...	...	...	...
Orel	d.	...	...	...	...	...	...	...	...
Tula I	d.	...	...	...	...	...	...	...	...
Moskva Kurskaya	a.	...	...	...	...	...	...	...	...
St Peterburg Gl. **1900**	a.	...	...	...	...	...	...	...	...

SAMARA and SARATOV - AKTOBE - TOSHKENT, BISHKEK and ALMATY 1975

km	Times are local time		time zone UTC+						
0	*Moskva Kaz* **1970**	d.	+3	...	...	...	...	...	...
1044	**Samara**	d.	+4	...	...	...	...	...	...
•681	Ufa	d.	+5	...	...	...	...	...	...
1462	Orenburg	d.	+5	...	...	...	...	...	...
•894	**Saratov** 1	d.	+4	...	...	...	...	...	...
•459	Oral / Uralsk	KA d.	+5	...	...	...	...	...	...
1734	Aktobe 1	KA a.	+5	...	...	...	...	...	...
1734	Aktobe 1	KA d.	+5	...	...	...	...	...	...
1828	Kandyagash	KA d.	+5	...	...	...	...	...	...
2924	Mangystau ⊙	KA a.	+5	...	...	...	...	...	...
2767	Kyzylorda	KA d.	+5	...	...	...	...	...	...
3315	**Toshkent**	UZ a.	+5	...	...	...	...	...	...
3738	Andijon	UZ a.	+5	...	...	...	...	...	...
3240	Shymkent	KA d.	+6	...	...	...	...	...	...
3729	**Bishkek** 2	KY a.	+6	...	...	...	...	...	...
4001	**Almaty** 1	KA a.	+6	...	...	...	...	...	...
4010	**Almaty** 2	KA a.	+6	...	...	...	...	...	...

Times are local time		time zone UTC+						
Almaty 2	KA d.	+6	...	...	...	...	...	...
Almaty 1	KA d.	+6	...	...	...	...	...	...
Bishkek 2	KY d.	+6	...	...	...	...	...	...
Shymkent	KA d.	+6	...	...	...	...	...	...
Andijon	UZ d.	+5	...	...	...	...	...	...
Toshkent	UZ d.	+5	...	...	...	...	...	...
Kyzylorda	KA d.	+5	...	...	...	...	...	...
Mangystau ⊙	KA d.	+5	...	...	...	...	...	...
Kandyagash	KA d.	+5	...	...	...	...	...	...
Aktobe 1	KA a.	+5	...	...	...	...	...	...
Aktobe 1	KA d.	+5	...	...	...	...	...	...
Oral / Uralsk	KA a.	+5	...	...	...	...	...	...
Saratov 1	a.	+4	...	...	...	...	...	...
Orenburg	d.	+5	...	...	...	...	...	...
Ufa	a.	+5	...	...	...	...	...	...
Samara	a.	+4	...	...	...	...	...	...
Moskva Kaz **1970**	a.	+3	...	...	...	...	...	...

⊙ – Station for Aktau (*15 km*).
• – Distance from Aktobe.

KA – Kazakhstan (Almaty = UTC+6, western zone = UTC+5).
KY – Kyrgyzstan (UTC+6).
UZ – Uzbekistan (UTC+5).

1976 SAMARA and KAZAN - ASTANA - ALMATY and TOSHKENT

km	*Times are local time*	*time zone UTC+*							
0	*Moskva Kaz* **1970** ....d.	+3	...	...	...	...	...	...	...
1044	**Samara**..........................d.	+4	...	...	...	...	...	...	...
2048	Chelyabinsk.....................d.	+5	...	...	...	...	...	...	...
	Kazan................**1990** d.	+3	...	...	...	...	...	...	...
	Yekaterinburg....**1990** d.	+5	...	...	...	...	...	...	...
2306	Kurgan ....d.	+5	...	...	...	...	...	...	...
2573	Petropavl.................. KA d.	+6	...	...	...	...	...	...	...
3064	**Astana** 1.................. KA a.	+6	...	...	...	...	...	...	...
3064	**Astana** 1.................. KA d.	+6	...	...	...	...	...	...	...
3305	Karagandy................ KA d.	+6	...	...	...	...	...	...	...
	Almaty 1 .... KA a.	+6	...	...	...	...	...	...	...
4407	**Almaty** 2 .... KA a.	+6	...	...	...	...	...	...	...
4356	Bishkek 2.............. KY a.	+6	...	...	...	...	...	...	...
4522	Shymkent.................. KA a.	+6	...	...	...	...	...	...	...
4755	**Toshkent**.................. UZ a.	+5	...	...	...	...	...	...	...

Times are local time	*time zone UTC+*							
Toshkent.................UZ d.	+5	...	...	...	...	...	...	...
Shymkent.................KA d.	+6	...	...	...	...	...	...	...
Bishkek 2..............KY d.	+6	...	...	...	...	...	...	...
Almaty 2 ....KA d.	+6	...	...	...	...	...	...	...
Almaty 1 ....KA d.	+6	...	...	...	...	...	...	...
Karagandy................KA d.	+6	...	...	...	...	...	...	...
Astana 1..................KA a.	+6	...	...	...	...	...	...	...
Astana 1..................KA d.	+6	...	...	...	...	...	...	...
Petropavl..................KA d.	+6	...	...	...	...	...	...	...
Kurgan .... d.	+5	...	...	...	...	...	...	...
Yekaterinburg... **1990** a.	+5	...	...	...	...	...	...	...
Kazan............... **1990** a.	+3	...	...	...	...	...	...	...
Chelyabinsk................... d.	+5	...	...	...	...	...	...	...
Samara......................... a.	+4	...	...	...	...	...	...	...
Moskva Kaz **1970** .... a.	+3	...	...	...	...	...	...	...

MOSKVA - MAKAT - TOSHKENT and DUSHANBE

km	*Times are local*	*zone UTC+*		*Times are local*	*zone UTC+*	
0	**Moskva** Kazan. ....d.	+3	...	**Dushanbe** 1.... TA d.	+5	...
198	Ryazan 2.............d.	+3	...	Termez.......... UZ d.	+5	...
411	Michurinsk Vor......d.	+3	...	Karshi............ UZ d.	+5	...
1075	**Volgograd**............d.	+4	...	**Toshkent**.... UZ d.	+5	...
1804	Atyrau.............KA d.	+5	...	Samarqand.. UZ d.	+5	...
1934	Makat..............KA d.	+5	...	Navoiy .... UZ d.	+5	...
2641	Kungrad..........UZ d.	+5	...	Bukhara.......... UZ d.	+5	...
3048	Urgench..........UZ d.	+5	...	Urgench......... UZ d.	+5	...
3465	Bukhara..........UZ a.	+5	...	Kungrad.......... UZ d.	+5	...
3558	Navoiy ....UZ a.	+5	...	Makat .... KA d.	+5	...
3714	Samarqand...UZ a.	+5	...	Atyrau............ KA d.	+5	...
4057	**Toshkent**.....UZ a.	+5	...	**Volgograd**.......... d.	+4	...
3714	Karshi.............UZ a.	+5	...	Michurinsk Vor..... d.	+3	...
4046	Termez............UZ a.	+5	...	Ryazan 2............ d.	+3	...
4271	**Dushanbe** 1.....TA a.	+5	...	**Moskva** Kazan. ... a.	+3	...

NOVOSIBIRSK - ALMATY and TOSHKENT

km	*Times are local*	*zone UTC+*		*Times are local*	*zone UTC+*	
0	**Novosibirsk**.........d.	+7	...	**Toshkent**....... UZ d.	+7	...
228	Barnaul.................d.	+7	...	Shymkent...... KA d.	+7	...
1121	Aktogay ....KA d.	+6	...	**Almaty** 2 .... KA d.	+6	...
	Almaty 2......KA d.	+6	...	**Almaty** 1........ KA a.	+6	...
1678	**Almaty** 1 ....KA a.	+6	...	**Almaty** 1........ KA d.	+6	...
1678	**Almaty** 1 ....KA d.	+6	...	**Almaty** 2 .... KA a.	+6	...
1687	**Almaty** 2......KA a.	+6	...	Aktogay.......... KA d.	+6	...
2424	Shymkent ....KA d.	+6	...	Barnaul .... d.	+6	...
2657	**Toshkent** ....UZ a.	+5	...	**Novosibirsk**........ a.	+5	...

KA – Kazakhstan (Almaty zone = UTC+6).
TA – Tajikistan (UTC+5).
UZ – Uzbekistan (UTC+5).

1985 MOSKVA - ARCHANGELSK, LABYTNANGI and VORKUTA

km	*Local time (UTC+3)*								
0	**Moskva** Yaroslavskaya...................d.	...	...	...	...	...	...	...	...
282	Yaroslavl ....d.	...	...	...	...	...	...	...	...
	St Peterburg Ladozhski.............d.	...	...	...	...	...	...	...	...
496	Vologda 1...d.	...	...	...	...	...	...	...	...
707	Konosha 1..d.	...	...	...	...	...	...	...	...
1134	**Archangelsk**..................................d.	...	...	...	...	...	...	...	...
1620	Belomorsk..d.	...	...	...	...	...	...	...	...
2008	Kandalaksha ....d.	...	...	...	...	...	...	...	...
2285	**Murmansk**.....................................a.	...	...	...	...	...	...	...	...
825	Velsk ....d.	...	...	...	...	...	...	...	...
1084	**Kotlas** Yuzhny..................................d.	...	...	...	...	...	...	...	...
1325	Mikun ....d.	...	...	...	...	...	...	...	...
1412	**Syktyvkar**.......................................a.	...	...	...	...	...	...	...	...
1571	Sosnogorsk ....a.	...	...	...	...	...	...	...	...
2406	**Labytnangi** (*UTC+5*).................a.	...	...	...	...	...	...	...	...
2277	**Vorkuta**..a.	...	...	...	...	...	...	...	...

Local time (UTC+3)								
Vorkuta.......................................d.	...	...	...	...	...	...	...	...
Labytnangi (*UTC+5*)................d.	...	...	...	...	...	...	...	...
Sosnogorsk.....................................d.	...	...	...	...	...	...	...	...
Syktyvkar d								
Mikun...d.	...	...	...	...	...	...	...	...
Kotlas Yuzhny.............................d.	...	...	...	...	...	...	...	...
Velsk ....d.	...	...	...	...	...	...	...	...
Murmansk ....d.	...	...	...	...	...	...	...	...
Kandalaksha...................................d.	...	...	...	...	...	...	...	...
Belomorsk ....d.	...	...	...	...	...	...	...	...
Archangelsk................................d.	...	...	...	...	...	...	...	...
Konosha 1 ....d.	...	...	...	...	...	...	...	...
Vologda 1 ....d.	...	...	...	...	...	...	...	...
St Peterburg Ladozhski ....a.	...	...	...	...	...	...	...	...
Yaroslavl..d.	...	...	...	...	...	...	...	...
Moskva Yaroslavskaya ....a.	...	...	...	...	...	...	...	...

1989 MOSKVA - NIZHNI NOVGOROD - SAMARA

km	*Local time (UTC+3)*								
	St Peterburg Glavny.......................d.	...	...	...	...	...	...	...	...
0	**Moskva** Vostochny...........................d.	...	...	...	...	...	...	...	...
186	Vladimir...d.	...	...	...	...	...	...	...	...
437	**Nizhni Novgorod**..............................d.	...	...	...	...	...	...	...	...
	Nizhni Novgorod Strigino ✈..........d.	...	...	...	...	...	...	...	...
	Arzamas 1...d.	...	...	...	...	...	...	...	...
	Saransk...d.	...	...	...	...	...	...	...	...
	Syzran 1..d.	...	...	...	...	...	...	...	...
	Samara...a.	...	...	...	...	...	...	...	...

Local time (UTC+3)								
Samara ....d.	...	...	...	...	...	...	...	...
Syzran 1..d.	...	...	...	...	...	...	...	...
Saransk...d.	...	...	...	...	...	...	...	...
Arzamas 1...d.	...	...	...	...	...	...	...	...
Nizhni Novgorod Strigino ✈........d.	...	...	...	...	...	...	...	...
Nizhni Novgorod ....d.	...	...	...	...	...	...	...	...
Vladimir..d.	...	...	...	...	...	...	...	...
Moskva Vostochny........................a.	...	...	...	...	...	...	...	...
St Peterburg Glavny ....a.	...	...	...	...	...	...	...	...

MOSKVA - YEKATERINBURG - NOVOSIBIRSK - IRKUTSK - VLADIVOSTOK 1990

km			time zone UTC +						
0	**Moskva** Yaroslavskaya	d.	+3	...	...	...	...	...	...
	Moskva Kazanskaya	d.	+3	...	...	...	...	...	...
282	Yaroslavl	d.	+3	...	...	...	...	...	...
	Murom 1	d.	+3	...	...	...	...	...	...
	Kazan 1	d.	+3	...	...	...	...	...	...
	Kazan 2 ◧	d.	+3	...	...	...	...	...	...
	Sarapul	d.	+4	...	...	...	...	...	...
210	Vladimir	d.	+3	...	...	...	...	...	...
461	**Nizhni Novgorod**	d.	+3	...	...	...	...	...	...
917	Kirov	d.	+3	...	...	...	...	...	...
1397	Perm 2	d.	+5	...	...	...	...	...	...
	Perm Sortirovochnaya	d.	+5	...	...	...	...	...	...
	Nivhni Tagil	d.	+5	...	...	...	...	...	...
	Serov	d.	+5	...	...	...	...	...	...
	Priobe	a.	+5	...	...	...	...	...	...
1778	**Yekaterinburg**	a.	+5	...	...	...	...	...	...
1778	**Yekaterinburg**	d.	+5	...	...	...	...	...	...
2104	Tyumen	d.	+5	...	...	...	...	...	...
	Tobolsk	d.	+5	...	...	...	...	...	...
	Surgut	d.	+5	...	...	...	...	...	...
	Niznevartovsk	a.	+5	...	...	...	...	...	...
	Korotchayevo	d.	+5	...	...	...	...	...	...
	Novy Urengoy	a.	+5	...	...	...	...	...	...
2676	Omsk	a.	+6	...	...	...	...	...	...
2676	Omsk	d.	+6	...	...	...	...	...	...
3303	**Novosibirsk**	a.	+7	...	...	...	...	...	...
3303	**Novosibirsk**	d.	+7	...	...	...	...	...	...
	Barnaul	a.	+7	...	...	...	...	...	...
	Novokuznetsk	a.	+7	...	...	...	...	...	...
	Kemerovo	a.	+7	...	...	...	...	...	...
3534	Tayga	d.	+7	...	...	...	...	...	...
3621	**Tomsk** 2	a.	+7	...	...	...	...	...	...
	Abakan	a.	+7	...	...	...	...	...	...
4065	Krasnoyarsk	a.	+7	...	...	...	...	...	...
4065	Krasnoyarsk	d.	+7	...	...	...	...	...	...
4483	Tayshet	d.	+8	...	...	...	...	...	...
	Bratsk Padunskie Porogi	d.	+8	...	...	...	...	...	...
	Severobaikalsk	d.	+8	...	...	...	...	...	...
5152	**Irkutsk**	a.	+8	...	...	...	...	...	...
5152	**Irkutsk**	d.	+8	...	...	...	...	...	...
5608	Ulan Ude	d.	+8	...	...	...	...	...	...
6165	Chita 2	d.	+9	...	...	...	...	...	...
7274	Skovorodino	d.	+9	...	...	...	...	...	...
8492	Khabarovsk	d.	+10	...	...	...	...	...	...
9147	Ussuriysk	d.	+10	...	...	...	...	...	...
9258	**Vladivostok**	a.	+10	...	...	...	...	...	...

		time zone UTC +						
Vladivostok	d.	+10	...	...	...	...	...	...
Ussuriysk	d.	+10	...	...	...	...	...	...
Khabarovsk	d.	+10	...	...	...	...	...	...
Skovorodino	d.	+9	...	...	...	...	...	...
Chita 2	d.	+9	...	...	...	...	...	...
Ulan Ude	d.	+8	...	...	...	...	...	...
Irkutsk	a.	+8	...	...	...	...	...	...
Irkutsk	d.	+8	...	...	...	...	...	...
Severobaikalsk	d.	+8	...	...	...	...	...	...
Bratsk Padunskie Porogi	d.	+8	...	...	...	...	...	...
Tayshet	d.	+8	...	...	...	...	...	...
Krasnoyarsk	a.	+7	...	...	...	...	...	...
Krasnoyarsk	d.	+7	...	...	...	...	...	...
Abakan	d.	+7	...	...	...	...	...	...
Tomsk 2	d.	+7	...	...	...	...	...	...
Tayga	d.	+7	...	...	...	...	...	...
Kemerovo	d.	+7	...	...	...	...	...	...
Novokuznetsk	d.	+7	...	...	...	...	...	...
Barnaul	d.	+7	...	...	...	...	...	...
Novosibirsk	a.	+7	...	...	...	...	...	...
Novosibirsk	d.	+7	...	...	...	...	...	...
Omsk	a.	+6	...	...	...	...	...	...
Omsk	d.	+6	...	...	...	...	...	...
Novy Urengoy	d.	+5	...	...	...	...	...	...
Korotchayevo	d.	+5	...	...	...	...	...	...
Niznevartovsk	d.	+5	...	...	...	...	...	...
Surgut	d.	+5	...	...	...	...	...	...
Tobolsk	d.	+5	...	...	...	...	...	...
Tyumen	d.	+5	...	...	...	...	...	...
Yekaterinburg	a.	+5	...	...	...	...	...	...
Yekaterinburg	d.	+5	...	...	...	...	...	...
Priobe	d.	+5	...	...	...	...	...	...
Serov	d.	+5	...	...	...	...	...	...
Nivhni Tagil	d.	+5	...	...	...	...	...	...
Perm Sortirovochnaya	d.	+5	...	...	...	...	...	...
Perm 2	d.	+5	...	...	...	...	...	...
Kirov	d.	+3	...	...	...	...	...	...
Nizhni Novgorod	d.	+3	...	...	...	...	...	...
Vladimir	d.	+3	...	...	...	...	...	...
Sarapul	d.	+4	...	...	...	...	...	...
Kazan 2 ◧	d.	+3	...	...	...	...	...	...
Kazan 1	d.	+3	...	...	...	...	...	...
Murom 1	d.	+3	...	...	...	...	...	...
Yaroslavl	d.	+3	...	...	...	...	...	...
Moskva Kazanskaya	a.	+3	...	...	...	...	...	...
Moskva Yaroslavskaya	a.	+3	...	...	...	...	...	...

MOSKVA and ST PETERBURG - IZHEVSK, YEKATERINBURG, CHELYABINSK and PETROPAVL

			time zone UTC+						
0	**Moskva** Kazanskaya	d.	+3	...	...	...	...	...	...
	St Peterburg Ladozhski	d.	+3	...	...	...	...	...	...
	Vologda 1	d.	+3	...	...	...	...	...	...
	Kirov	d.	+3	...	...	...	...	...	...
	Perm 2	d.	+5	...	...	...	...	...	...
	Murom 1	d.	+3	...	...	...	...	...	...
	Kazan 1	d.	+3	...	...	...	...	...	...
	Kazan 2 ◧	d.	+3	...	...	...	...	...	...
	Izhevsk	a.	+4	...	...	...	...	...	...
	Sarapul	d.	+4	...	...	...	...	...	...
	Yekaterinburg	a.	+5	...	...	...	...	...	...
	Yekaterinburg	d.	+5	...	...	...	...	...	...
	Kurgan	a.	+5	...	...	...	...	...	...
	Chelyabinsk	a.	+5	...	...	...	...	...	...
	Petropavl KA	a.	+6	...	...	...	...	...	...

		time zone UTC+						
Petropavl KA	d.	+6	...	...	...	...	...	...
Chelyabinsk	d.	+5	...	...	...	...	...	...
Kurgan	d.	+5	...	...	...	...	...	...
Yekaterinburg	a.	+5	...	...	...	...	...	...
Yekaterinburg	d.	+5	...	...	...	...	...	...
Sarapul	d.	+4	...	...	...	...	...	...
Izhevsk	d.	+4	...	...	...	...	...	...
Kazan 2 ◧	d.	+3	...	...	...	...	...	...
Kazan 1	d.	+3	...	...	...	...	...	...
Murom 1	d.	+3	...	...	...	...	...	...
Perm 2	d.	+5	...	...	...	...	...	...
Kirov	d.	+3	...	...	...	...	...	...
Vologda 1	d.	+3	...	...	...	...	...	...
St Peterburg Ladozhski	a.	+3	...	...	...	...	...	...
Moskva Kazanskaya	a.	+3	...	...	...	...	...	...

MOSKVA - ULAAN BAATAR - BEIJING

km	*Trans-Mongolian route*		time zone UTC+						
0	*Moskva Yar. (above)*	d.	+3	...	...	...	...	...	...
3303	*Novosibirsk (above)*	d.	+7	...	...	...	...	...	...
5152	**Irkutsk**	d.	+8	...	...	...	...	...	...
5608	Ulan Ude	d.	+8	...	...	...	...	...	...
5863	Naushki 🛃	d.	+8	...	...	...	...	...	...
5886	Suche Bator 🛃 MO	d.	+8	...	...	...	...	...	...
6265	**Ulaan Baatar** MO	a.	+8	...	...	...	...	...	...
6265	**Ulaan Baatar** MO	d.	+8	...	...	...	...	...	...
6770	Dzamin Uud 🛃 MO	d.	+8	...	...	...	...	...	...
6780	Erlan 🛃 CH	a.	+8	...	...	...	...	...	...
7622	**Beijing** CH	a.	+8	...	...	...	...	...	...

Trans-Mongolian route		time zone UTC+						
Beijing CH	d.	+8	...	...	...	...	...	...
Erlan 🛃 CH	d.	+8	...	...	...	...	...	...
Dzamin Uud 🛃 MO	d.	+8	...	...	...	...	...	...
Ulaan Baatar MO	a.	+8	...	...	...	...	...	...
Ulaan Baatar MO	d.	+8	...	...	...	...	...	...
Suche Bator 🛃 MO	d.	+8	...	...	...	...	...	...
Naushki 🛃	d.	+8	...	...	...	...	...	...
Ulan Ude	d.	+8	...	...	...	...	...	...
Irkutsk	a.	+8	...	...	...	...	...	...
Novosibirsk (above)	a.	+7	...	...	...	...	...	...
Moskva Yar. (above)	a.	+3	...	...	...	...	...	...

MOSKVA - HARBIN - BEIJING

km	*Trans-Manchurian route*		time zone UTC+						
0	*Moskva Yar. (above)*	d.	+3	...	...	...	...	...	...
1778	*Yekaterinburg (above)*	d.	+5	...	...	...	...	...	...
3303	*Novosibirsk (above)*	d.	+7	...	...	...	...	...	...
5152	**Irkutsk**	d.	+8	...	...	...	...	...	...
6165	Chita 2	d.	+9	...	...	...	...	...	...
6626	Zabaikalsk 🛃	d.	+9	...	...	...	...	...	...
6638	Manzhouli 🛃 CH	d.	+8	...	...	...	...	...	...
7573	Harbin CH	a.	+8	...	...	...	...	...	...
8122	Shenyang CH	a.	+8	...	...	...	...	...	...
8849	Tianjin CH	a.	+8	...	...	...	...	...	...
8986	**Beijing** CH	a.	+8	...	...	...	...	...	...

Trans-Manchurian route		time zone UTC+						
Beijing CH	d.	+8	...	...	...	...	...	...
Tianjin CH	d.	+8	...	...	...	...	...	...
Shenyang CH	d.	+8	...	...	...	...	...	...
Harbin CH	d.	+8	...	...	...	...	...	...
Manzhouli 🛃 CH	d.	+8	...	...	...	...	...	...
Zabaikalsk 🛃	d.	+9	...	...	...	...	...	...
Chita 2	d.	+9	...	...	...	...	...	...
Irkutsk	a.	+8	...	...	...	...	...	...
Novosibirsk (above)	a.	+7	...	...	...	...	...	...
Yekaterinburg (above)	a.	+5	...	...	...	...	...	...
Moskva Yar. (above)	a.	+3	...	...	...	...	...	...

◧ – Also known as Vosstanie Passazhirskaja. CH – China (UTC+8). MO – Mongolia (UTC+8).

1991 NOVOSIBIRSK - SEVEROBAIKALSK - TYNDA - NERYUNGRI - NIZHNY BESTYAKH

Baikal-Amur Magistrale (BAM) line. For other trains Moskva - Severobaikalsk see Table **1990**.

km	*Times are local times*	*time zone UTC+*								*Times are local times*	*time zone UTC+*							
	Moskva Kaz. **1990** d.	+3	...	...	...	...	...	...	...	**Nizhny Bestyakh** ⊕ d.	+9	...	...	...	...	...	...	...
0	**Novosibirsk** d.	+7	...	...	...	...	...	...	...	Tommot a.	+9	...	...	...	...	...	...	...
762	Krasnoyarsk d.	+7	...	...	...	...	...	...	...	Tommot d.	+9	...	...	...	...	...	...	...
	Irkutsk d.	+8	...	...	...	...	...	...	...	Neryungri a.	+9	...	...	...	...	...	...	...
1180	**Tayshet** a.	+8	...	...	...	...	...	...	...	Neryungri d.	+9	...	...	...	...	...	...	...
1180	**Tayshet** d.	+8	...	...	...	...	...	...	...	**Tynda** a.	+9	...	...	...	...	...	...	...
1473	Bratsk Padunskie Porogi d.	+8	...	...	...	...	...	...	...	**Tynda** d.	+9	...	...	...	...	...	...	...
2243	**Severobaikalsk** a.	+8	...	...	...	...	...	...	...	**Severobaikalsk** a.	+8	...	...	...	...	...	...	...
2243	**Severobaikalsk** d.	+8	...	...	...	...	...	...	...	**Severobaikalsk** d.	+8	...	...	...	...	...	...	...
3528	**Tynda** a.	+9	...	...	...	...	...	...	...	Bratsk Padunskie Porogi d.	+8	...	...	...	...	...	...	...
3528	**Tynda** d.	+9	...	...	...	...	...	...	...	**Tayshet** a.	+8	...	...	...	...	...	...	...
3757	Neryungri a.	+9	...	...	...	...	...	...	...	**Tayshet** d.	+8	...	...	...	...	...	...	...
3757	Neryungri d.	+9	...	...	...	...	...	...	...	Irkutsk a.	+8	...	...	...	...	...	...	...
4125	Tommot a.	+9	...	...	...	...	...	...	...	Krasnoyarsk a.	+7	...	...	...	...	...	...	...
4125	Tommot d.	+9	...	...	...	...	...	...	...	**Novosibirsk** a.	+7	...	...	...	...	...	...	...
4563	**Nizhny Bestyakh** ⊕ a.	+9	...	...	...	...	...	...	...	*Moskva Kaz.* **1990** a.	+3	...	...	...	...	...	...	...

	Times are local	*UTC+*		*Times are local*	*UTC+*			*Times are local*	*UTC+*			*Times are local*	*UTC+*		
0	**Tynda** d.	+9	...	**Komsomolsk** d.	+10	...	*0*	**Vladivostok** **1990** d.	+10	...	...	**Sovetskaya Gavan** d.	+10	...	...
669	Fevralsk d.	+9	...	Novy Urgal a.	+10	...	*111*	Ussuriysk **1990** d.	+10	...	...	Komsomolsk d.	+10	...	...
951	Novy Urgal a.	+10	...	Novy Urgal d.	+10	...	*766*	**Khabarovsk** **1990** d.	+10	...	...	**Khabarovsk** **1990** a.	+10	...	...
951	Novy Urgal d.	+10	...	Fevralsk d.	+9	...	*1155*	Komsomolsk a.	+10	...	...	Ussuriysk **1990** a.	+10	...	...
1469	**Komsomolsk** a.	+10	...	**Tynda** a.	+9	...	*1618*	**Sovetskaya Gavan** a.	+10	...	...	**Vladivostok** **1990** a.	+10	...	...

⊕ – In summer a ferry (15 km from station) runs to Yakutsk. Connection by 🚌 in winter (no service in Spring or Autumn).

1993 YEKATERINBURG - KAZAN - SARATOV - VOLGOGRAD

km	*Local times*	*time zone UTC+*			*Local times*	*time zone UTC+*			km	*Local times*	*time zone UTC+*			*Local times*	*time zone UTC+*		
0	**Yekaterinburg** d.	+5	...	...	**Kislovodsk** d.	+3	...	...	*0*	**Niznevartovsk** d.	+5	...	...	**Volgograd** 1 d.	+3	...	...
515	Sarapul d.	+4	...	...	Pyatigorsk d.	+3	...	...	*216*	Surgut d.	+5	...	...	**Saratov** 1 d.	+4	...	...
875	**Kazan** 1 d.	+3	...	...	Mineralnye Vody d.	+3	...	...	*692*	Tobolsk d.	+5	...	...	**Samara** d.	+4	...	...
1121	Ulyanovsk d.	+4	...	...	Armavir Ros. d.	+3	...	...	*921*	Tyumen d.	+5	...	...	Ulyanovsk d.	+4	...	...
1407	**Samara** a.	+4	...	...	Volgograd 1 d.	+3	...	...	*1247*	**Yekaterinburg** d.	+5	...	...	**Kazan** 1 d.	+3	...	...
1576	**Saratov** 1 d.	+4	...	...	**Saratov** 1 d.	+4	...	...	*1762*	Sarapul d.	+4	...	...	Sarapul d.	+4	...	...
2005	Volgograd 1 d.	+3	...	...	**Samara** d.	+4	...	...	*2122*	**Kazan** 1 d.	+3	...	...	**Yekaterinburg** d.	+5	...	...
2665	Armavir Ros. d.	+3	...	...	Ulyanovsk d.	+4	...	...	*2368*	Ulyanovsk d.	+4	...	...	Tyumen d.	+5	...	...
2853	Mineralnye Vody d.	+3	...	...	**Kazan** 1 d.	+3	...	...	*2654*	**Samara** a.	+4	...	...	Tobolsk a.	+5	...	...
2879	Pyatigorsk d.	+3	...	...	Sarapul d.	+4	...	...	*2823*	**Saratov** 1 d.	+4	...	...	Surgut a.	+5	...	...
2917	**Kislovodsk** a.	+3	...	...	**Yekaterinburg** a.	+5	...	...	*3252*	**Volgograd** 1 d.	+3	...	...	**Niznevartovsk** a.	+5	...	...

1994 YEKATERINBURG - SAMARA - SARATOV and KYIV - BAKI

km	*Local times*	*time zone UTC+*			*Local times*	*time zone UTC+*			km	*Local times*	*time zone UTC+*		*Local times*	*time zone UTC+*	
0	**Tyumen** d.	+5	...	...	**Makhachkala** d.	+3	...	...	*0*	**Kyiv** UA d.	◧	...	**Baki** AZ d.	+4	...
326	**Yekaterinburg** d.	+5	...	...	Astrakhan 1 d.	+4	...	...	*335*	Poltava K UA d.	◧	...	Derbent d.	+3	...
578	Chelyabinsk d.	+5	...	...	**Saratov** 1 a.	+4	...	...	*493*	**Kharkiv** UA d.	◧	...	Makhachkala d.	+3	...
1059	Ufa d.	+5	...	...	**Saratov** 1 d.	+4	...	...	*861*	Liski d.	+3	...	Astrakhan 1 d.	+4	...
1582	**Samara** d.	+4	...	...	**Samara** d.	+4	...	...	*1453*	Volgograd d.	+4	...	Volgograd d.	+4	...
2019	**Saratov** 1 a.	+4	...	...	Ufa d.	+5	...	...	*1903*	Astrakhan 1 d.	+4	...	Liski d.	+3	...
2019	**Saratov** 1 d.	+4	...	...	Chelyabinsk d.	+5	...	...	*2391*	Makhachkala d.	+3	...	**Kharkiv** UA a.	◧	...
2695	Astrakhan 1 d.	+4	...	...	**Yekaterinburg** a.	+5	...	...	*2520*	Derbent d.	+3	...	Poltava K UA a.	◧	...
3183	**Makhachkala** a.	+3	...	...	**Tyumen** a.	+5	...	...	*2765*	**Baki** AZ a.	+4	...	**Kyiv** UA a.	◧	...

◧ – UTC+2 winter, UTC+3 summer. AZ – Azerbaijan (UTC+4). UA – Ukraine (UTC+2 winter, UTC+3 summer).

European Rail Timetable Subscription

Keep up to date with the latest changes to European rail schedules with a subscription.

See page 12 for details of our various subscription options

Order on-line at **www.europeanrailtimetable.eu**

✆ +44 (0) 1832 270198 (Monday to Friday 1000 – 1600)

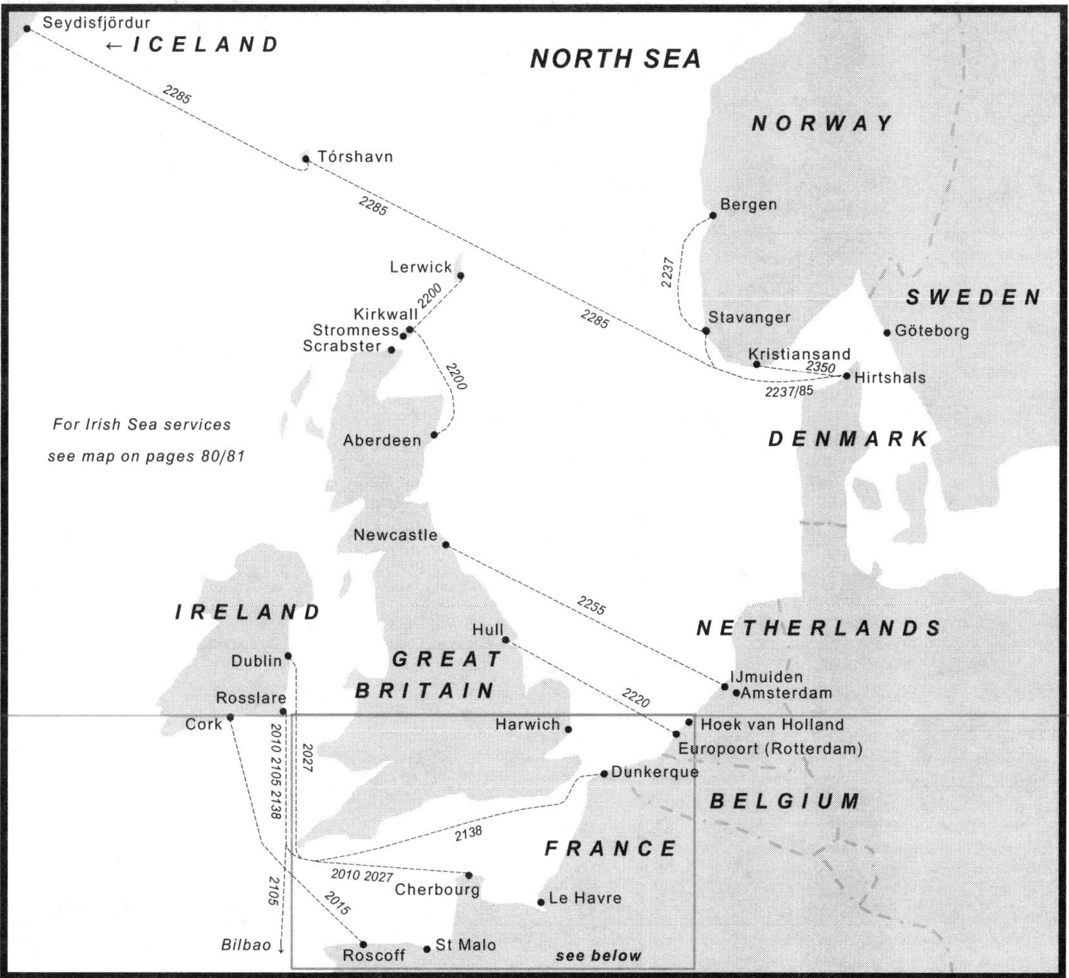
Seydisfjördur
← ICELAND
NORTH SEA
2285
Tórshavn
NORWAY
2285
Bergen
Lerwick
2237
SWEDEN
2200
2285
Kirkwall
Stromness
Scrabster
Stavanger
Göteborg
Kristiansand
2350
Hirtshals
2200
2237/85
For Irish Sea services
see map on pages 80/81
Aberdeen
DENMARK
Newcastle
2255
IRELAND
NETHERLANDS
Hull
Dublin
GREAT
BRITAIN
IJmuiden
Amsterdam
2220
Rosslare
Cork
Harwich
Hoek van Holland
Europoort (Rotterdam)
2010 2105 2138
2027
Dunkerque
BELGIUM
2138
FRANCE
2010 2027
Cherbourg
2105
2015
Le Havre
Bilbao ↓
Roscoff
St Malo
see below

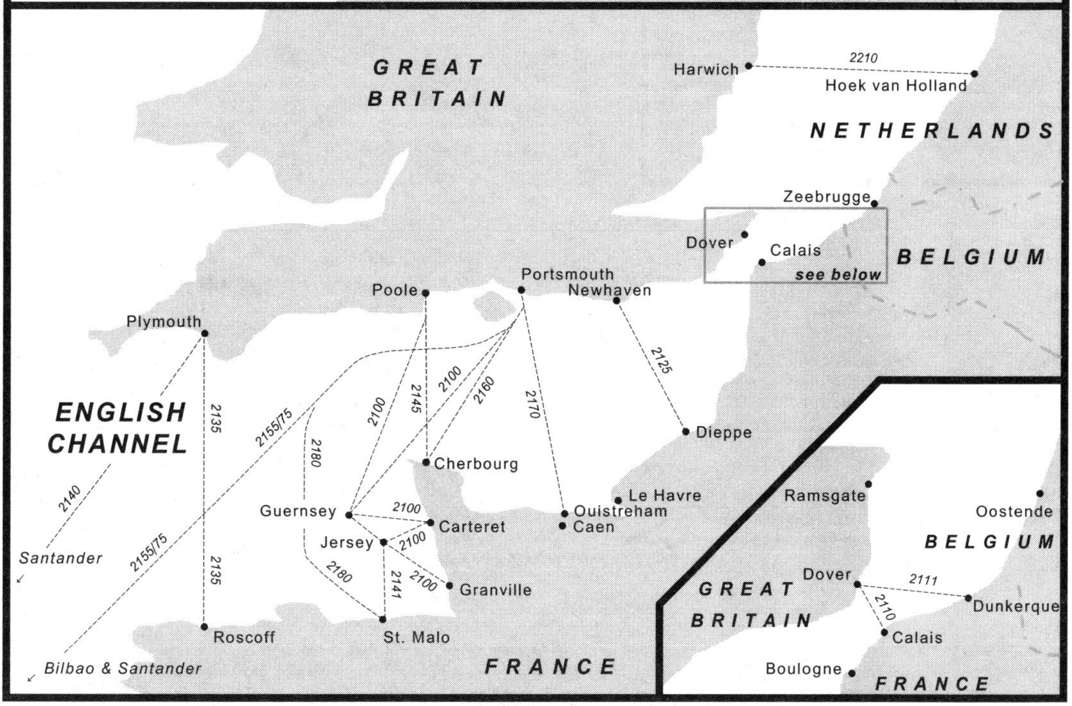
GREAT
BRITAIN
Harwich
2210
Hoek van Holland
NETHERLANDS
Zeebrugge
Dover
Calais
see below
BELGIUM
Portsmouth
Newhaven
Poole
Plymouth
2125
2100
2160
2145
2170
ENGLISH
CHANNEL
2135
2155/75
2100
2180
Dieppe
Cherbourg
2140
Le Havre
Guernsey
2100
Ouistreham
Carteret
Caen
Jersey
2100
Santander ↙
2155/75
2180
2141
2100
Granville
2135
Roscoff
St. Malo
↙ Bilbao & Santander
FRANCE
Ramsgate
Oostende
BELGIUM
Dover
2111
GREAT
BRITAIN
2110
Dunkerque
Calais
Boulogne
FRANCE

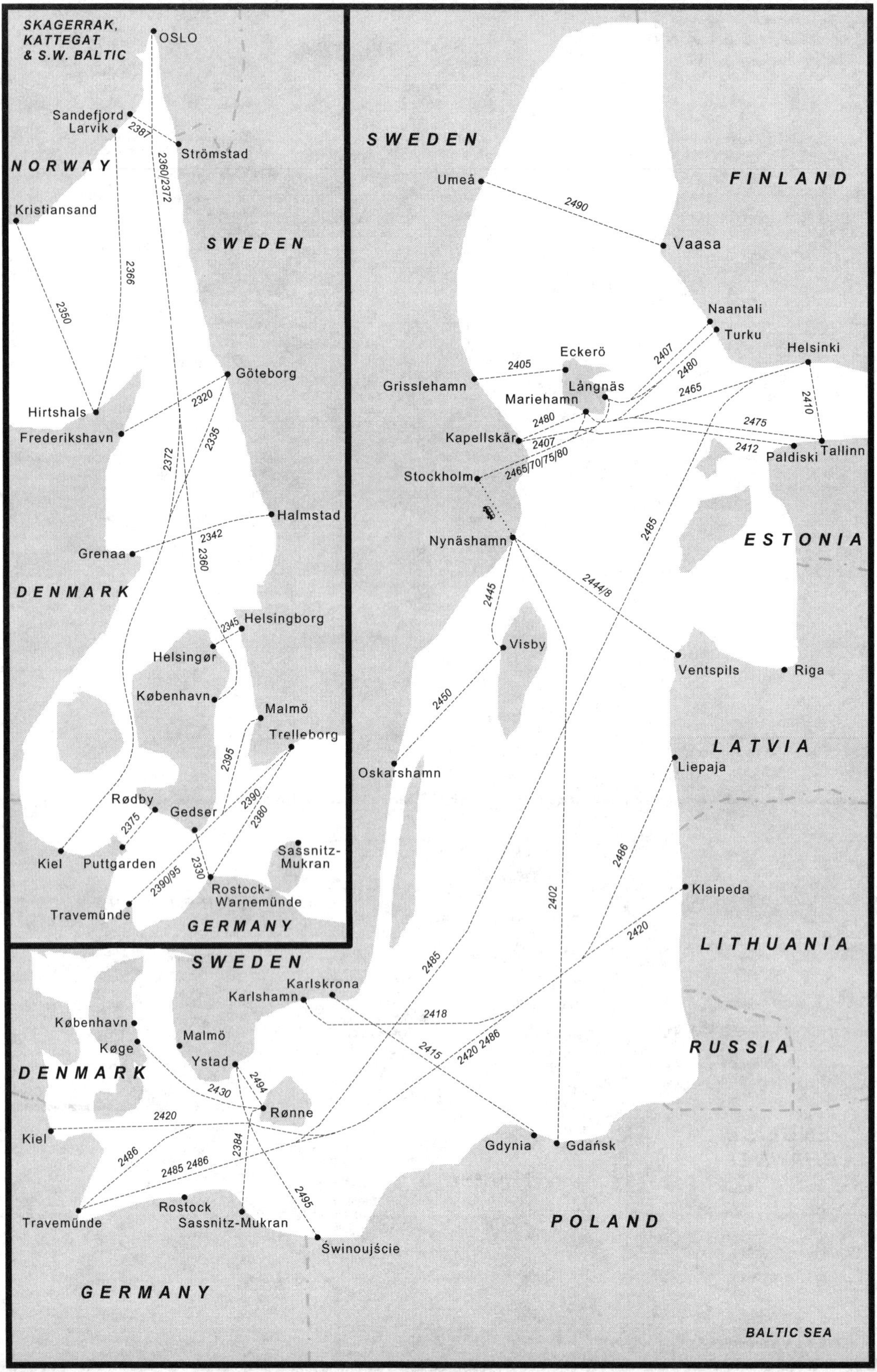
SKAGERRAK, KATTEGAT & S.W. BALTIC
OSLO
Sandefjord
Larvik
2387
Strömstad
2360/2372
NORWAY
Kristiansand
SWEDEN
2366
2350
Göteborg
2320
Hirtshals
Frederikshavn
2335
2372
Halmstad
2342
Grenaa
2360
DENMARK
2345
Helsingborg
Helsingør
København
Malmö
Trelleborg
2395
Rødby
2390
Gedser
2375
2380
Kiel
Puttgarden
Sassnitz-Mukran
2330
2390/95
Rostock-Warnemünde
Travemünde
GERMANY
SWEDEN
FINLAND
Umeå
2490
Vaasa
Naantali
Turku
Eckerö
2405
2407
Helsinki
Grisslehamn
2480
Långnäs
2465
Mariehamn
2410
2480
2475
Kapellskär
2407
2412
Paldiski
Tallinn
Stockholm
2465/70/75/80
2485
Nynäshamn
ESTONIA
2445
2444/8
Visby
Ventspils
Riga
2450
LATVIA
Oskarshamn
Liepaja
2486
2402
Klaipeda
2420
LITHUANIA
2485
SWEDEN
Karlskrona
Karlshamn
2418
København
2415
Malmö
2420 2486
Køge
RUSSIA
Ystad
DENMARK
2494
2430
Rønne
2420
Kiel
Gdynia
Gdańsk
2384
2486
2485 2486
2495
Rostock
Sassnitz-Mukran
Travemünde
POLAND
Świnoujście
GERMANY
BALTIC SEA

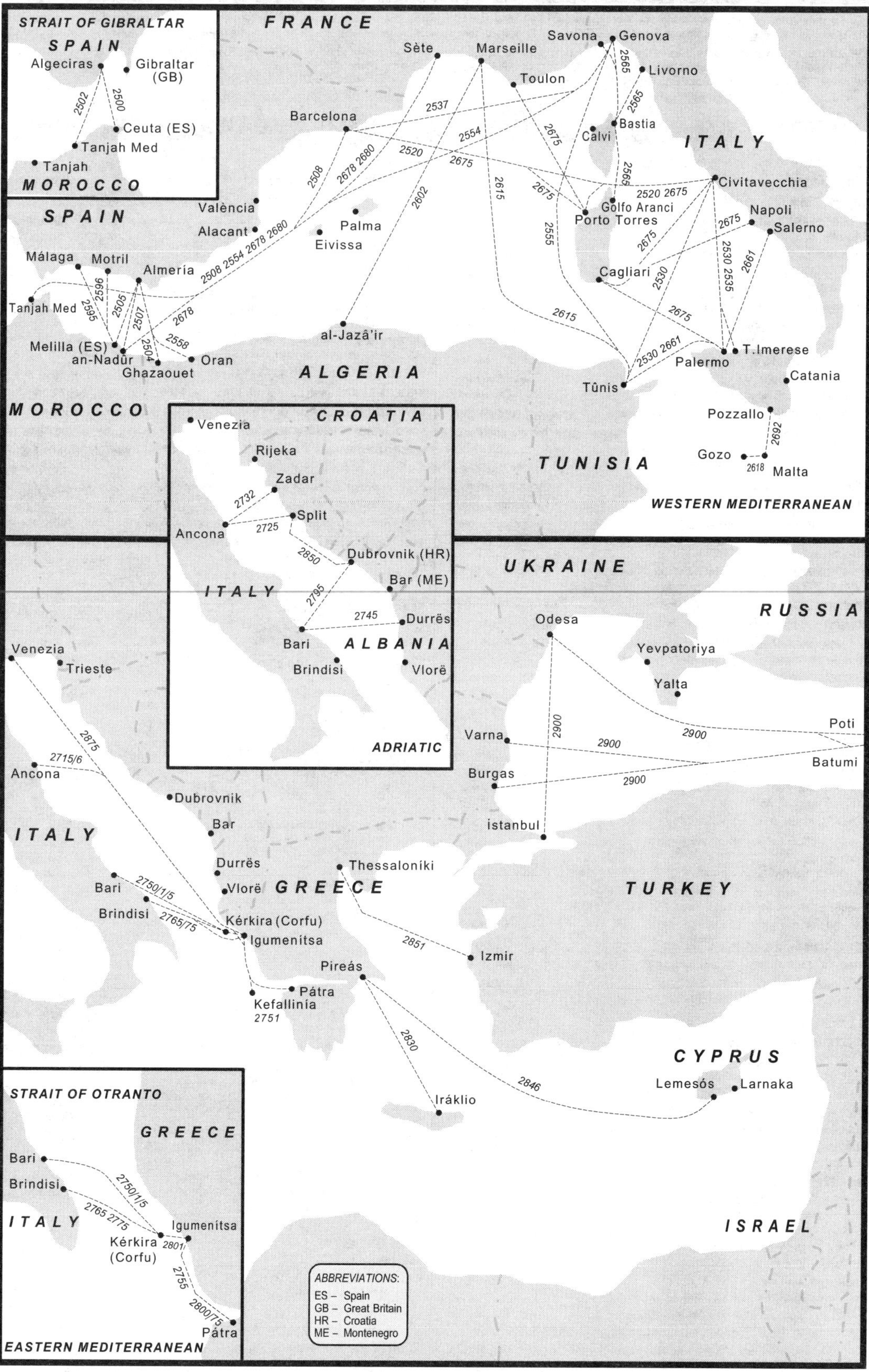
STRAIT OF GIBRALTAR
SPAIN
Algeciras
Gibraltar (GB)
2502
2500
Ceuta (ES)
Tanjah Med
Tanjah
MOROCCO
FRANCE
Sète
Marseille
Savona
Genova
2565
Livorno
Toulon
2537
Barcelona
2554
2565
Bastia
Calvi
ITALY
2508
2678 2680
2520
2675
2615
2675
2675
2566
2520 2675
Civitavecchia
València
Alacant
2602
Palma
Eivissa
Golfo Aranci
Porto Torres
2555
Napoli
2675
Salerno
SPAIN
2508 2554 2678 2680
2675
Málaga
Motril
Almería
Cagliari
2530
2530 2535
2661
Tanjah Med
2596
2505
2595
2678
2507
2615
2675
Melilla (ES)
an-Nadûr
2504
2558
Ghazaouet
Oran
al-Jazâ'ir
ALGERIA
2530 2661
Palermo
T.Imerese
Tûnis
Catania
MOROCCO
Pozzallo
2692
Gozo
2618
Malta
TUNISIA
WESTERN MEDITERRANEAN
CROATIA
Venezia
Rijeka
Zadar
2732
Split
2725
Ancona
2850
Dubrovnik (HR)
Bar (ME)
ITALY
2795
2745
Durrës
Bari
ALBANIA
Brindisi
Vlorë
ADRIATIC
UKRAINE
RUSSIA
Odesa
Yevpatoriya
Yalta
Venezia
Trieste
2875
2900
2900
Poti
Varna
2900
Batumi
2715/6
Ancona
Burgas
2900
Dubrovnik
Istanbul
Bar
ITALY
Durrës
Thessaloníki
Bari
Vlorë
GREECE
TURKEY
2750/1/5
Brindisi
2765/75
Kérkira (Corfu)
Igumenítsa
2851
Izmir
Pireás
Pátra
Kefallinía
2751
2830
CYPRUS
Lemesós
Larnaka
2846
Iráklio
STRAIT OF OTRANTO
GREECE
Bari
2750/1/5
Brindisi
2765 2775
ITALY
Igumenítsa
Kérkira (Corfu)
2801
2755
2800/75
Pátra
EASTERN MEDITERRANEAN
ISRAEL
ABBREVIATIONS:
ES – Spain
GB – Great Britain
HR – Croatia
ME – Montenegro

FERRY SERVICES

Sailing times are shown as a guide and readers are recommended to check latest schedules with the operator before travel. Sailings can be affected by holidays (especially Christmas and New Year), tidal variations, ship maintenance periods, and weather. Certain domestic ferry services are shown alongside rail services in the relevent country sections (see maps and Index).

TIME ZONES: for time zones and the dates of Daylight Saving Time (Summer Time) see the Time Comparison chart on page 4. West European Time (UTC / GMT in Winter, UTC + 1 in Summer) also applies to Algeria, Faeroe Islands, Morocco and Tunisia. Central European Time (UTC + 1 in Winter, UTC + 2 in Summer) also applies in Israel. East European Time (UTC + 2 in Winter, UTC + 3 in Summer) also applies in Cyprus.

FERRY OPERATORS

ADRIA FERRIES Durrës ✆ +39 07150 211 621 www.adriaferries.com

AFRICA MOROCCO LINK Tanger ✆ +212 539 322253 www.aml.ma

A G EMS Emden ✆ +49 (0)1805 180 182 www.ag-ems.de

ALGERIE FERRIES (E N T M V) www.algerieferries.dz
Marseille ✆ +33 (0)4 91 90 64 70

ALILAURO Napoli ✆ +39 081 497 2222 www.alilauro.it

ALSLINJEN For contact details see Molslinjen www.faergen.dk

ANEK LINES Pireás ✆ +30 210 4197 470 www.anek.gr
U.K. agent: Viamare Ltd. ✆ 020 8206 3420 www.viamare.com

BALEÀRIA (EUROLÍNIES MARÍTIMES) www.balearia.com
Dénia, Spain ✆ +34 902 160 180

BLUE STAR FERRIES Athína ✆ +30 210 891 9800 www.bluestarferries.com

BLUFERRIES and **BLU JET** www.bluferries.it
Villa San Giovanni, Italy ✆ +39 340 98 48 540 www.blujetlines.it

BORNHOLMSLINJEN For contact details see Molslinjen www.bornholmslinjen.com

BRITTANY FERRIES Plymouth ✆ 0330 159 7000 www.brittany-ferries.co.uk
France: ✆ +33 825 828 828

CAREMAR Napoli ✆ +39 081 1896 6690 www.caremar.it

CARONTE & TOURIST Messina ✆ +39 090 5737 www.carontetourist.it

CATAMARAN LINE Split ✆ +385 (0)21 352 527 www.catamaran-line.hr

COLOR LINE Oslo ✆ +47 22 94 42 00 www.colorline.com
Customer service (Denmark): ✆ +45 99 56 19 00
Enquiries within Sweden: ✆ 0526 62000

COMPAGNIE TUNISIENNE DE NAVIGATION Tûnis www.ctn.com.tn
✆ +33 (1) 4742 1755. U.K. agent: www.southernferries.co.uk

CONDOR FERRIES Poole ✆ 0845 609 1024 www.condorferries.co.uk

CORSICA SARDINIA FERRIES Bastia ✆ +33 4 9532 9595 www.corsica-ferries.fr

CORSICA LINEA Marseille ✆ +33 (0)825 88 80 88 www.corsicalinea.com
U.K. agent: Southern Ferries www.southernferries.co.uk

DESTINATION GOTLAND Visby ✆ +46 (0)498 20 18 00 www.destinationgotland.se

DFDS SEAWAYS Harwich www.dfdsseaways.co.uk
Bookings from UK: Dover - France route: ✆ 0871 574 7235
Newhaven - Dieppe route: ✆ 0800 917 1201
Newcastle - Amsterdam, also Baltic and Scandinavian routes: ✆ 0871 522 9955
Sweden: ✆ +46 (0)42 26 60 00 www.dfdsseaways.se
Norway: ✆ +47 2162 1340 www.dfdsseaways.no

ECKERÖ LINE Helsinki: ✆ +358 9 228 8544 www.eckeroline.com
Within Finland: ✆ 06000 4300 www.eckeroline.fi

ECKERÖ LINJEN Åland ✆ +358 (0)18 28 000 www.eckerolinjen.se

FANØLINJEN For contact details see Molslinjen www.faergen.dk

FERRYSPED www.navbul.com
Navigation Maritime Bulgare (Navibulgar) ✆ +359 526 83409

FINNLINES Finland call centre: ✆ +358 9 231 43 100 www.finnlines.com
Germany: ✆ +49 451 1507 443. Sweden ✆ +46 771 340 900

FJORD LINE Bergen ✆ +47 51 46 40 99 www.fjordline.com

FORSEA Helsingborg ✆ +46 42 186 000 www.forsea.se

FRED. OLSEN S.A. Santa Cruz de Tenerife ✆ +34 902 100 107 www.fredolsen.e

F R S Tarifa - Cádiz ✆ +34 956 68 18 30 www.frs.es

F R S HELGOLINE Flensburg ✆ +49 (0)461 86444 www.helgoline.de

G & V Line Zadar ✆ +385 23 250 733 www.gv-zadar.com

GOZO CHANNEL Mgarr, Gozo ✆ +356 2210 9000 www.gozochannel.com

GRANDI NAVI VELOCI Genova ✆ +39 010 2094 591 www.gnv.it
U.K. agent: Viamare Ltd (see Anek Lines)

GRIMALDI LINES Napoli ✆ +39 081 496 444 www.grimaldi-lines.com
U.K. agent: Viamare Ltd (see Anek Lines)

HOLLAND NORWAY LINES ✆ +31 85 40 15 252 www.hollandnorwaylines.com

HURTIGRUTEN (NORWEGIAN COASTAL VOYAGE) www.hurtigruten.no
Norway ✆ +47 7759 7201. U.K. bookings ✆ 02035 532 516 www.hurtigruten.com

IRISH FERRIES Dublin ✆ +353 818 300 400 www.irishferries.com
U.K.: ✆ 08717 300 400. France: ✆ +33 1 70 72 03 26

ISLE OF MAN STEAM PACKET ✆ (Isle of Man) 661 661 www.steam-packet.com
U.K.: ✆ 08722 992 992. Ireland: ✆ +44 8722 992 992

ISLES OF SCILLY STEAMSHIP www.islesofscilly-travel.co.uk
Penzance ✆ +44 (0)1736 334220

JADROLINIJA Rijeka ✆ +385 51 666 111 www.jadrolinija.hr
U.K. agent: Viamare (see Anek Lines)

KAPETAN LUKA Jesenice ✆ +385 21 645 476 www.krilo.hr

KERKYRA LINES Kérkira ✆ +30 26610 20520 www.kerkyralines.com

LA MÉRIDIONALE Marseille ✆ +33 970 832 020 www.lameridionale.fr

LEVANTE FERRIES Thessaloníki ✆ +30 21 0949 9400 www.levanteferries.com

LIBERTY LINES Trapani ✆ +39 0923 022022 www.libertylines.it

MANCHE ÎLES EXPRESS Jersey ✆ 01534 880 756 www.manche-iles.com
Guernsey: ✆ 01481 701 316. France: ✆ 0825 131 050

MEDMAR Napoli ✆ +39 (0)81 333 44 11 www.medmargroup.it

MINOAN LINES Heraklion, Crete ✆ +30 2810 399899 www.minoan.gr
U.K. agent: Viamare (see Anek Lines)

MOBY LINES Within Italy: ✆ 199 30 30 40 www.mobylines.com
Call centre: ✆ +49 (0)611 14020.
U.K. agent: Viamare (see Anek Lines)

MOLSLINJEN Aarhus ✆ +45 70 10 14 18 www.molslinjen.dk

NAVIERA ARMAS Gran Canaria ✆ +34 902 456 500 www.navieraarmas.com

NAVIGAZIONE LIBERA del GOLFO Napoli ✆ +39 081 552 07 63 www.navlib.it

NORDLANDEKSPRESSEN Bodø ✆ +47 9100 9600 www.reisnordland.no

NORTHLINK FERRIES Orkney ✆ 0845 6000 449 www.northlinkferries.co.uk

P B M Burgas, Bulgaria ✆ +359 56 871 628 www.pbm.bg

P & O FERRIES Dover ✆ +44 (0)1304 44 88 88 www.poferries.com
Republic of Ireland: ✆ +353 1 686 9467

POLFERRIES Polish Baltic Shipping Co. ✆ +48 94 35 52 102 www.polferries.com

REEDEREI CASSEN EILS Cuxhaven ✆ +49 (0)4721 667 600 www.cassen-eils.de

ST PETER LINE (MOBY LINE) St Peterburg www.stpeterline.com
✆ +7 (812) 507 89 92. Helsinki: ✆ +358 9 6187 2000
Tallinn: ✆ +372 6660 800

SAMSØLINJEN For contact details see Molslinjen www.faergen.dk

SCANDLINES Rostock: ✆ +49 (0)381 7788 7766 www.scandlines.com
Denmark (Odense): ✆ +45 33 15 15 15

SCANDRO HOLDING LTD Cyprus ✆ +357 9664 6450 www.scandroholding.com

SMYRIL LINE Tórshavn, Faroe Islands ✆ +298 34 59 00 www.smyrilline.com
Iceland: ✆ +354 570 8600. Denmark: ✆ +45 96 55 85 00 www.smyrilline.fo

SNAV Napoli ✆ +39 081 428 55 55 www.snav.it
U.K. agent: Viamare (see Anek Lines)

STENA LINE (U.K.) Holyhead ✆ 08447 70 70 70 www.stenaline.co.uk
Belfast: ✆ +44 (0)8447 70 70 70
Rosslare: ✆ +353 (0)1 907 5555

STENA LINE Göteborg ✆ +46 (0)770 57 57 00 www.stenaline.com
Denmark: ✆ +45 96 200 200
Germany: ✆ +49 (0)180 602 0100.
Netherlands: ✆ +31 (0)174 389 333
Norway: ✆ +47 02010. Poland: ✆ +48 58 660 92 00

SUPERFAST FERRIES Athína www.superfast.com
Ancona route: +30 210 8919 700
Bari route: +30 210 8919 130
U.K. Agent: Viamare (see Anek Lines).

TALLINK SILJA Helsinki ✆ +358 9 180 41 www.tallinksilja.com
International call centre (Hamburg): ✆ +49 (0)40 547 541 222
Tallinn Sales Centre: ✆ +372 640 9808

TIRRENIA Napoli ✆ (within Italy) 199 30 30 40 www.tirrenia.it
Reservation Centre for Europe: +49 611 14020

TOREMAR ✆ (within Italy) 199 11 77 33 www.toremar.it
Reservation Centre for Europe: +49 611 14020

TORGHATTEN NORD Tromsø ✆ +47 906 20 700 www.torghatten-nord.no

TRASMEDITERRANEA Madrid ✆ +34(0) 902 454 645 www.trasmediterranea.es
Calls from Morocco: ✆ 0801 00 35 36.
U.K. agent: Southern Ferries www.southernferries.co.uk

TT-LINE Lübeck-Travemünde ✆ +49 (0)4502 801 81 www.ttline.com

UKR FERRY Varna 9000, Bulgaria ✆ +359 52 602012 www.ukrferry.com

UNITY LINE Świnoujście ✆ +48 801 989 771 www.unityline.eu

VENEZIA LINES Poreč, Croatia ✆ +385 52 422 896 www.venezialines.com

VENTOURIS FERRIES Pireás ✆ +30 210 482 8001 www.ventourisferries.com
UK agent: Viamare (see Anek Lines)

VIKING LINE Finland ✆ +358 (0)600 41577 www.vikingline.com

VIRTU FERRIES LTD Malta ✆ +356 2206 9022 www.virtuferries.com
Catania: ✆ +39 095 7031211

WASALINE Vaasa, Finland: ✆ +358 (0)207 716 810 www.wasaline.com
Sweden: ✆ +46 (0)90 185 200

CONTENTS

IRISH SEA

BELFAST - CAIRNRYAN 2002

Stena Line

Belfast		Cairnryan		Cairnryan		Belfast	
0330§	→	0552	②–⑥	0330§	→	0545	②–⑥
0730	→	0952		0700	→	0915	⑦
1130	→	1352		0730	→	0945	①–⑥
1530	→	1752		1130	→	1345	
1930	→	2152		1530	→	1745	
2330§	→	0152		1930	→	2145	
				2300§	→	0145	⑦
				2330§	→	0145	①–⑥

§ – No foot passengers conveyed.

CAIRNRYAN - LARNE 2005

P & O Ferries Journey 2 hours

Until July 3 and from Sept. 1
Depart Cairnryan and Larne: 0400①–⑥, 0800, 1200, 1600, 2000, 2359 ①–⑤.

July 4 - Aug. 31
Depart Cairnryan and Larne: 0400①–⑥, 0800, 1100, 1400, 1700, 2000, 2359①–⑤.

☛ Fewer sailings Dec. 24–31 (no sailings on Dec. 25).

CHERBOURG - ROSSLARE 2010

Stena Line **Valid until Dec. 18**

Cherbourg		Rosslare		Rosslare		Cherbourg	
1830	→	1330	⑤	1800	→	1430	④
1900	→	1400	①	1800	→	1500	⑥
2030	→	1400	③	2100	→	1600	②

Brittany Ferries **Valid until Oct. 26**

Cherbourg		Rosslare		Rosslare		Cherbourg	
1500	→	0600	②	1800	→	1200	①
1900	→	1200	④⑥	1800	→	1300	⑤
2000	→	1500	⑤	1800	→	1400	⑦
2030	→	1330	②	2000	→	1400	③
				2100	→	1900	⑥

CORK - ROSCOFF 2015

Brittany Ferries **Valid Apr. 2 - Nov. 1**

Sailings from Cork (Ringaskiddy) and Roscoff

Cork		Roscoff		Roscoff		Cork
1600③⑥	→	0800④⑦	⊕	1930②	→	0930③
				2300⑤	→	1100⑥

⊕ – Arrives Roscoff 0700 on ⑦.

☛ **No winter service Nov. 2, 2025 - Mar. 31, 2026**

DOUGLAS - BELFAST 2020

Isle Of Man Steam Packet Co. Journey 2 hours 45 minutes **Apr. 3 to Aug. 30**

Infrequent sailings (5–8 sailings per month). No winter service.

DOUGLAS - DUBLIN 2025

Isle Of Man Steam Packet Co. Journey 2 hours 55 minutes **Apr. 9 to Aug. 27**

Infrequent sailings (2–5 sailings per month). No winter service.

DUBLIN - CHERBOURG 2027

Irish Ferries Journey 18–20 hourrs **Valid Feb. 2 - Sept. 30**

Sailings Dublin to Cherbourg at 1600 or 1830; Cherbourg to Dublin at 1630 or 1830.

Dublin → Cherbourg
February - June: ②④⑥ (also June 23, 25, 27, 29; not June 24, 26, 28).
July: Odd dates only.
August: Even dates only.
September: ②④⑥ (also Sept. 1, 3, 5, 7; not Sept. 2, 4, 6).

Cherbourg → Dublin
February - June: ③⑤⑦ (also June 24, 26, 28, 30; not June 25, 27, 29).
July: Even dates only.
August: Odd dates only.
September: ③⑤⑦ (also Sept. 2, 4, 6, 8; not Sept. 3, 5, 7).

FISHGUARD - ROSSLARE 2030

Stena Line by ship

Fishguard		Rosslare	Rosslare		Fishguard
0130	→	0530	0815	→	1145
1400	→	1730	1930	→	2300

This is the regular service for most days; please confirm timings with operator.

HEYSHAM - DOUGLAS 2035

Isle Of Man Steam Packet Co.

Heysham		Douglas	Douglas		Heysham
0215	→	0600	0830	→	1215
1415	→	1800	1945	→	2330

Timings may vary; sailings may be cancelled on certain dates

HOLYHEAD - DUBLIN 2040

Irish Ferries by ship

Sailings from Holyhead and Dublin Ferryport. Up to 4 sailings daily.

Holyhead		Dublin		Dublin		Holyhead	
0240	→	0555		0200§	→	0525	
0815§	→	1145		0730	→	0945	⊕
1110	→	1325	⊕	0805	→	1130	
1410	→	1725		1350	→	1605	⊕
1715	→	1930	⊕	1430§	→	1800	
2015§	→	2330		2055	→	0020	

§ – Foot passengers are not normally conveyed.
⊕ – Service by *Dublin Swift* fast ferry.

Sailing times may vary owing to tidal conditions.

🚌 Dublin Ferryport - Dublin Talbot Street via Connolly Rail Station

Stena Line by ship **Daily until June 30**

Holyhead		Dublin		Dublin		Holyhead	
0400	→	0730	②–⑥❖	0400	→	0730	②–⑥❖
0930	→	1305		1010	→	1335	
1550	→	1920		1630	→	2000	
2215	→	0140		2235	→	0200	

Daily from July 1

Holyhead		Dublin		Dublin		Holyhead	
0215	→	0530	⊠	0215	→	0545	⊠
0900	→	1215		0815	→	1150	
1445	→	1800		1445	→	1820	
2030	→	2345		2030	→	0001	

❖ – Also June 29, 30. ⊠ – ②–⑥ from Sept. 7.

Sailing times may vary owing to tidal conditions.

🚌 Dublin Ferryport - Dublin Talbot Street via Connolly Rail Station

BIRKENHEAD (LIVERPOOL) - BELFAST 2050

Stena Line

Sailings from Birkenhead Twelve Quays Terminal and Belfast Victoria Terminal 2.

Birkenhead		Belfast	Belfast		Birkenhead
1030	→	1830	1030	→	1830
2230	→	0630	2230	→	0630

LIVERPOOL - DOUGLAS 2053

Isle Of Man Steam Packet Co. High-speed car ferry

Sailings from Liverpool Landing Stage and Douglas

Liverpool→Douglas Mar. 22 - Oct. 31 a minimum of one sailing a day, two during July / Aug. Most regular timings d. 1115, a. 1400; d. 1915, a. 2215.

Douglas→Liverpool Mar. 22 - Oct. 31 a minimum of one sailing a day, two during July / Aug. Most regular timings d. 0715, a. 1000; d. 1500, a. 1745.

Times may vary by several hours on certain dates - please check with operator.

PEMBROKE - ROSSLARE 2055

Irish Ferries **Valid until Sept. 14**

Pembroke		Rosslare	Rosslare		Pembroke
0245	→	0646	0845	→	1246
1445	→	1846	2045	→	0046

Sailing times may vary owing to tidal conditions

ENGLISH CHANNEL
AND BAY OF BISCAY

CHANNEL ISLAND SERVICES 2100

Condor Ferries

POOLE - GUERNSEY by fast ferry
PORTSMOUTH - GUERNSEY
ST MALO - GUERNSEY by fast ferry
GUERNSEY - JERSEY by fast ferry

Services operate all year round. Departure times vary - contact operator for details

DFDS

PORTSMOUTH - JERSEY
POOLE - JERSEY

Services operate all year round. Departure times vary - contact operator for details

OTHER SERVICES:

Manche îles Express operate catamaran services in summer from Jersey to Carteret, Granville, Sark and Guernsey, and from Guernsey to Alderney and Diélette, and from Alderney to Diélette.

ROSSLARE - BILBAO 2105

Brittany Ferries **Until Nov. 2**

Rosslare		Bilbao		Bilbao		Rosslare
0900③	→	1330④		1100⑦	→	1430①
2359⑤	→	0800⑥	See note **B**.	1800④	→	2030⑤

B – On Oct. 31 departs Rosslare 2330.

☛ A free shuttle bus operates between Bilbao ferry terminal and Bilbao City (16 km).

2110 DOVER - CALAIS

DFDS Seaways

Sailings from Dover Eastern Docks and Calais Maritime. Journey 90 minutes
Conveys passengers with vehicles only (includes bicyles). Some sailing times vary.

Until July 17 and from Sept. 2.

Depart Dover: 0035②–⑦, 0440①–⑥, 0740, 0910, 1040, 1255, 1425, 1555, 1810, 1940, 2110⑧.

Depart Calais: 0230①–⑥, 0605, 0735, 0905, 1120, 1250, 1420, 1635, 1805, 1935⑧, 2300.

July 18 - Sept. 1.

Depart Dover: 0015⑤⑥§, 0035②–④, 0220⑤⑥§, 0340*, 0440‡, 0505*, 0710*, 0740‡, 0830*, 0910‡, 0955*, 1040‡, 1155*, 1255‡, 1315*, 1425‡, 1440*, 1555‡, 1640*, 1805*, 1810‡, 1930*, 1940‡, 2110‡, 2130*, 2250⑤⑥¶.

Depart Calais: 0050⑤⑥§, 0210*, 0230‡, 0335*, 0540*, 0605‡, 0700*, 0735‡, 0825*, 0905‡, 1030*, 1120‡, 1150*, 1250‡ 1315*, 1420‡, 1515*, 1635, 1801, 1935‡, 2001*, 2120⑤⑥¶, 2245*, 2300‡.

* – ⑤–⑦ (also Aug. 25, Sept. 1; not Aug. 29). § – Not Aug. 29.
‡ – ①–④ (also Aug. 29; not Aug. 25, Sept. 1). ¶ – Also Aug. 31, Sept. 1: not Aug. 29.

P & O Ferries

Sailings from Dover Eastern Docks and Calais Maritime. Journey 90 minutes
Some sailing times vary.

Until July 17 and from Aug. 24.

Depart Dover: 0330, 0615①–⑥, 0815, 0945, 1130, 1340, 1505, 1640, 1850, 2045, 2355.

Depart Calais: 0100, 0430①–⑥, 0545⑦, 0615①–⑥, 0800, 0950, 1200, 1320, 1500, 1715, 1900, 2225.

July 18 - Aug. 23.

Depart Dover: 0225*, 0330‡, 0615§, 0630*, 0715*, 0815‡, 0900*, 0945‡, 1115*, 1130‡, 1200*, 1340‡, 1345*, 1505‡, 1605*, 1640‡, 1645*, 1835*, 1850‡, 2045‡, 2050*, 2320*, 2355‡.

Depart Calais: 0055*, 0100‡, 0430‡, 0500*, 0545¶, 0615§, 0730*, 0800‡, 0950, 1035*, 1200‡, 1220*, 1320‡, 1435*, 1500‡, 1520*, 1705*, 1715‡, 1900‡, 1920*, 2150*, 2225‡,

Foot passengers may only travel on the following sailings: From Dover at 0945, 1115, 1340, 1345, 1640 and 1645; from Calais at 0950, 1500, 1520, 1900 and 1920. All other sailings convey passengers with vehicles only. Subject to variation, especially Jan. to Mar. and Christmas.

* – ⑤⑥. ‡ – ⑦–④. § – ①–④. ¶ – ⑤–⑦.

2111 DOVER - DUNKERQUE

DFDS Seaways

Sailings from Dover Eastern Docks and Dunkerque. Journey 2 hours
Conveys passengers with vehicles only (includes bicyles). Timings vary (those shown below are based on sailings during August 11 – 17).

Depart Dover: 0200②–⑤, 0600①–⑥, 0800, 1000①–⑥, 1200, 1400, 1600, 1800, 2000, 2200.

Depart Dunkerque: 0400①–⑥, 0600, 0800①–⑥, 1000, 1200, 1400, 1600, 1800⑧, 2000, 2359①–④

2125 NEWHAVEN - DIEPPE

DFDS Seaways

The basic sailing pattern is two per day on ①–⑥, one per day on ⑦.
During high season (May to mid-Sept.) three per day on ①–⑤, up to four per day on ⑥⑦.
Sample timings show sailings for Aug. 25 – 31. Please check with operator for actual timings.

Newhaven		Dieppe		Dieppe		Newhaven	
0530	→	1030	⑥⑦				
0930	→	1445	①②⑤	0630	→	0930	⑥⑦
1000	→	1500	③④	1200	→	1500	
1100	→	1600	⑥⑦	1700	→	2000	④
1700	→	2230	①–⑥	1800	→	2130	①②⑤⑥⑦
2300	→	0600	①②⑤⑥⑦	1830	→	2200	③
2359	→	0600	③④	2359	→	0500	

Newhaven ferry terminal is adjacent to Newhaven Town rail station (Table **102**).

2130 PENZANCE - ST. MARY'S

Isles Of Scilly Steamship Co. **Mar. 17 - Oct. 31 (no winter service)**

Sailings from Penzance Lighthouse Pier (South Pier) and St Mary's.
From Penzance and St Mary's: sailings on ①③⑤⑥ Mar. 17 – 31; ①–⑥ Apr. 1 - June 30; daily July 1 - Oct. 11 (not Sept. 21, 28); ①③⑤⑥ Oct. 13 – 31.

Departure times vary owing to tidal conditions
(most sailings Penzance depart 0915, St Mary's depart 1630).

2135 PLYMOUTH - ROSCOFF

Brittany Ferries **Valid Mar. 31 to Nov. 2**

Sailings from Plymouth Millbay and Roscoff. **No winter service**

From Plymouth: ①②④⑤⑥⑦ Mar. 31 - Nov. 2.
From Roscoff: ①③④⑤⑥⑦ Mar. 31 - Nov. 2.
Departure times vary (up to 8 sailings a week). Journey time approx. 6 – 9 hours.

2138 ROSSLARE - DUNKERQUE

DFDS **Valid until Dec. 13**

Sailings from Rosslare and Dunkirk
Conveys passengers with vehicles only (includes bicycles).

Rosslare		Dunkerque		Dunkerque		Rosslare	
0400	→	0400‡	④	0055	→	0055‡	③
2000	→	2000‡	①	0500	→	0500‡	④⑦
2245	→	2245‡	⑤	2100	→	2100‡	①⑤
2355	→	2355‡	②⑥				

‡ – Arrives following day.

2140 PLYMOUTH - SANTANDER

Brittany Ferries **Valid until Nov. 2**

Sailings from Plymouth Millbay and Santander **No winter service**

April - November, 2025

Plymouth		Santander		Santander		Plymouth	
1545③	→	1300④§	Apr. 2 - Oct. 29.	1600④‡	→	1115⑤	Apr. 3 - Oct. 30.
1645⑦	→	1400①	Apr. 6 - Nov. 2.	1700①	→	1400②	Apr. 7 - Oct. 27.

§ – Arrives 1315 Oct. 29. ‡ – On Oct. 30 departs 1545, arrives 1045.

2141 JERSEY - ST MALO

DFDS Seaways **Valid until Sept. 29**

Sailings from Jersey and St. Malo Terminal Ferry du Naye

From Jersey
May - Aug.: Daily
Sept.: Daily except ②③.

From St Malo
May - Aug.: Daily
Sept.: Daily except ②③.

Timings vary. Check with operator for confirmed timings.

2145 POOLE - CHERBOURG

Brittany Ferries **Mar. 25 - Nov. 2, (no winter service)**

Poole		Cherbourg	Cherbourg		Poole	
0830	→	1415	1700	→	2030	See note **N**.
			1815	→	2145	See note **P**.
			2130	→	0700	See note **R**.

N – ⑥ until Aug. 30.
P – ①④⑤⑥⑦ until June 30; ⑧ July 1 - Sept. 1; ①④⑤⑥⑦ Sept. 4 - Nov. 2.
R – ②③ until June 25; ②③ Sept. 2 - Oct. 29.

*See Table **2160** for high-speed service Portsmouth to Cherbourg*

2155 PORTSMOUTH - BILBAO

Brittany Ferries **Valid until Nov. 2**

Portsmouth		Bilbao	
2130⑦	→	0800②	Nov. 2.
2200⑦	→	0800②	Mar. 30 - Oct. 26.
1900④	→	0800⑥	Mar. 27 - Oct. 30.
Bilbao		**Portsmouth**	
1300⑥	→	1730⑦	Mar. 29 - Nov. 1 (also Dec. 12, Mar. 29).
1300②	→	2045③	Mar. 25 - Oct. 28.

☛ – A free shuttle bus operates between Bilbao ferry terminal and Bilbao City (16 km).

2160 PORTSMOUTH - CHERBOURG

Brittany Ferries **Until Nov. 2 (no wnter service)**

Sailings from Portsmouth Continental Ferry Port and Cherbourg.

Portsmouth		Cherbourg	
1130⑤	→	1900⑤	Apr. 4 - Oct. 31.
2300④	→	0800⑤	Apr. 3 - Oct. 30.
2315③	→	0800④	Apr. 9 - Oct. 29.
Cherbourg		**Portsmouth**	
1200④	→	1600④	Apr. 10 - Oct. 30.
1200⑤	→	1645⑤	Oct. 31.
1215⑤	→	1645⑤	Apr. 4. - Oct. 24.
2145⑦	→	0700①	Apr. 6 - Oct. 26
2330⑦	→	0700①	Nov. 2.

Free 🚌 runs Cherbourg Port - Cherbourg town centre.

2170 PORTSMOUTH - OUISTREHAM (CAEN)

Brittany Ferries **Valid until Nov. 2.**

Sailings from Portsmouth Continental Ferry Port and Ouistreham

Portsmouth Ouistreham

Apr. 1 - Nov. 2

0800	→	1500	Daily (not Apr. 19, 23, 30, ③ May 7 - Oct. 29).
1400	→	2200	May 14, June 11.
1500	→	2200	Daily.
2245	→	0645	③.
2300	→	0645	Daily except ②③.
2300	→	0730	②.

Ouistreham Portsmouth

Apr. 1 - Nov. 2.

0830	→	1330	Daily except ③.
1630	→	2115	③.
1630	→	2130	Daily except ③.
2330	→	0615	Daily except ②⑥.
2330	→	0645	②⑥.

Some departure and arrival times are subject to alteration.

Local 🚌 service operated by Twisto links Caen with Ouistreham (500m from ferry terminal, not contactless). Does not connect with evening ferry arrivals or departures.

2175 PORTSMOUTH - SANTANDER

Brittany Ferries **Valid until Nov. 2**

Sailings from Portsmouth Continental Ferry Port and Santander

Portsmouth		Santander	Santander		Portsmouth
2130①⑤	→	0800③⑦	1400⑦	→	1730①
			1400③	→	2000④

2180 PORTSMOUTH - ST MALO

Brittany Ferries **Valid until Nov. 2**

Sailings from Portsmouth Continental Ferry Port and St. Malo Terminal Ferry du Naye

From Portsmouth:
Apr. - June: Daily except ②.
July - Aug.: Daily.
Sept. - Nov.: Daily except ②.

From St. Malo:
Apr. - June: Daily except ③.
July - Aug.: Daily.
Sept. - Nov.: Daily except ③.

Timings vary. Check with operator for confirmed timings.

NORTH SEA

ABERDEEN - KIRKWALL - LERWICK 2200

NorthLink Ferries **Valid until Oct. 31 (Sailings all year)**

Aberdeen		Kirkwall		Kirkwall		Lerwick
			Until March 31			
1700④⑥⑦	→	2300④⑥⑦	→	2345④⑥⑦	→	0730⑤⑦①
1900①②③⑤	→	→	→	→	→	0730②③④⑥
			April 1 - Oct. 31			
1700②④⑥⑦	→	2300②④⑥⑦	→	2345②④⑥⑦	→	0730③⑤⑦①
1900①③⑤	→	→	→	→	→	0730②④⑥

Lerwick		Kirkwall		Kirkwall		Aberdeen
			Until March 31			
1730③⑤	→	2300③⑤	→	2345③⑤	→	0700④⑥
1900①②④⑥⑦	→	→	→	→	→	0700②③⑤⑦①
			April 1 - Oct. 31			
1730①③⑤	→	2300①③⑤	→	2345①③⑤	→	0700②④⑥
1900②④⑥⑦	→	→	→	→	→	0700②③⑤⑦①

Subject to alteration during ship maintenance (January to March)

A 🚌 transfer service is available Kirkwall - Stromness and v.v. in conjunction with evening sailings.

HARWICH - HOEK VAN HOLLAND 2210

Stena Line

Sailings from Harwich International Port and Hoek van Holland.

Harwich		Hoek	Hoek		Harwich
0900	→	1715	1345	→	1945
2300	→	0800	2200	→	0630

See Table **15** for connecting rail services London - Harwich and v.v.
Connection Hoek van Holland - Schiedam - Rotterdam is by RET metro line B (Table **497**).

HULL - ROTTERDAM 2220

P & O Ferries

Sailings from Hull King George Dock and Rotterdam Europoort.

Hull		Rotterdam		Rotterdam		Hull	
2000	→	0900	⑥⑦	2030	→	0800	⑥⑦
2030	→	0845	①–⑤	2100	→	0700	①–⑤

Arrival times may vary. Sailings do not operate everyday during January

🚌 connections (reservation recommended):

Hull (Paragon Interchange, regular departures until 1700) - King George Dock and v.v.
Rotterdam (Centraal Station, depart 1700) - Europoort and v.v.

HIRTSHALS - STAVANGER - BERGEN 2237

Fjord Line

Hirtshals*		Stavanger		Bergen		Stavanger		Hirtshals*
1915 **A k**	→	0700/0730	→	1300				
2000 **B**	→	0700/0730	→	1300				
				1400 **C**	→	1930/2030	→	0800

A – Daily until May 27 and from Sept. 1 (not Dec. 24, 25).
B – Daily May 28 - Aug. 31.
C – Daily (not Dec. 24, 25).
k – Sails via Kristiansand (d. 2330).

* – Shuttle 🚌 operates to/from Hirtshals station; alternatively it is a 2500 m signposted walk from Lilleheden station (a request stop on the Hjørring - Hirtshals line, approx. 3 minutes from Hirtshals – see Table **728**).

☛ Stavanger ferry terminal is located at Risavik havn, approx 15 km from Stavanger: Fjord Line 🚌 service departs Stavanger bus station (stop 6) at 0550 and 1815.

Fjord Line

Stavanger		Bergen	Bergen		Stavenger
0730	→	1300 **A**	1400	→	1930 **A**

A – Not Jan. 10, 12, 14, 16, 18, 20, 22, 24, 26, Dec. 24, 25).

HELGOLAND (Germany) services 2238

BREMERHAVEN - HELGOLAND May - Sept. Operator: Reederei Cassen Eils
BÜSUM - HELGOLAND Apr. - Oct. Operator: Adler & Eils
CUXHAVEN - HELGOLAND All year (Reederei Cassen Eils); Mar. - Oct. (FRS Helgoline)
HAMBURG - HELGOLAND Mar. - Oct. Operator: FRS Helgoline

LOFOTEN ISLANDS 2239

Map page 342

Reis Nordland **fast ferry**

Bodø		Svolvær		Svolvær		Bodø	
1800	→	2125	①–⑥	0600	→	0920	①–⑤
1900	→	2225	⑦	0755	→	1115	⑥
				1245	→	1600	⑦

Torghatten Nord Most sailings 3 hours 15 mins

BODØ - MOSKENES 1–2 sailings daily (up to 6 sailings daily June to August).

NORWEGIAN COASTAL SERVICES 2240

Map page 342

Hurtigruten **BERGEN - TRONDHEIM - TROMSØ - KIRKENES**

Daily	NORTHBOUND WINTER ◇ arrive	depart	SUMMER ☆ arrive	depart	day	SOUTHBOUND ALL YEAR	arrive	depart	day
Bergen ♣	...	2030	...	2030	A	**Kirkenes**	...	1230	A
Florø	0245	0300	0245	0300	B	Vadsø	|	|	
Måløy	0515	0530	0515	0530	B	Vardø	1605	1700	A
Torvik	0820	0830	0820	0830	B	Båtsfjord	2000	2030	A
Ålesund	0945	2000	0945	1000	B	Berlevåg	2225	2235	A
Hjørundfjord ▲	|	|	1215	1545		Mehamn	0120	0130	B
Ålesund	0945	2000	1800	2000	B	Kjøllefjord	0325	0335	B
Molde	2235	2305	2235	2305	B	**Honningsvåg**	0545	0600	B
Kristiansund	0245	0300	0245	0300	C	Havøysund	0800	0815	B
Trondheim	0945	1245	0945	1245	C	**Hammerfest**	1100	1245	B
Rørvik	2140	2200	2140	2200	C	Øksfjord	1550	1605	B
Brønnøysund	0135	0145	0135	0145	D	Skjervøy	1930	1945	B
Sandnessjøen	0435	0450	0435	0450	D	**Tromsø**	2345	0130	B/C
Nesna	0600	0610	0600	0610	D	Finnsnes	0420	0440	C
Ørnes	1000	1010	1000	1010	D	**Harstad**	0800	0830	C
Bodø	1305	1520	1305	1520	D	Risøyhamn	1045	1100	C
Stamsund	1915	1940	1915	1940	D	Sortland	1230	1300	C
Svolvaer	2120	2215	2120	2215	D	Stokmarknes	1415	1515	C
Stokmarknes	0130	0140	0130	0140	E	**Svolvaer**	1830	2030	C
Sortland	0255	0310	0255	0310	E	Stamsund	2215	2230	C
Risøyhamn	0435	0450	0435	0450	E	**Bodø**	0230	0330	D
Harstad	0710	0745	0710	0745	E	Ørnes	0625	0635	D
Finnsnes	1100	1130	1100	1130	E	Nesna	1025	1035	D
Tromsø	1415	1815	1415	1815	E	Sandnessjøen	1145	1215	D
Skjervøy	2210	2225	2210	2225	E	Brønnøysund	1500	1725	D
Øksfjord	0150	0200	0150	0200	F	Rørvik	2100	2130	D
Hammerfest	0505	0545	0505	0545	F	**Trondheim**	0630	0930	E
Havøysund	0830	0845	0830	0845	F	Kristiansund	1630	1730	E
Honningsvåg	1055	1430	1055	1430	F	Molde	2115	2145	E
Kjøllefjord	1640	1700	1640	1700	F	Ålesund	0030	0120	F
Mehamn	1855	1915	1855	1915	F	Geiranger	|	|	
Berlevåg	2200	2210	2200	2210	F	Ålesund	0030	0120	F
Båtsfjord	2400	0030	2400	0030	F/G	Torvik	0235	0245	F
Vardø	0330	0345	0330	0345	G	Måløy	0545	0600	F
Vadsø	0655	0710	0655	0710	G	Florø	0815	0830	F
Kirkenes	0900	...	0900	...	G	**Bergen ♣**	1445	...	F

A – 1st day G – 7th day.

▲ – Apr. 1 - Oct. 31 sailings will anchor by the secluded hamlet of Urke in Hjørundford at 1215, where a tender boat will transfer guests ashore.
♣ – Sailings from Bergen Nøstegaten.
☆ – Nov. 1 - Mar. 31.
◇ – Apr. 1 - Oct. 31

Havila Voyage

Havila Voyages also operate a tour sequence the same as Hurtigruten. Departing Bergen **A** 2030, arriving Kirkenes **G** 0900. Departing Kirkenes **G** 1230, arriving Bergen **F** 1445. Please refer to notes above.

NEWCASTLE - IJMUIDEN (for Amsterdam) 2255

DFDS Seaways

Sailings from Newcastle International Passenger Terminal (Royal Quays, North Shields) and IJmuiden Felison Terminal.

Newcastle		IJmuiden	IJmuiden		Newcastle
1700	→	0945	1730	→	0915

Sailings alternate days Jan. 3–30, then daily from Feb. 1

DFDS 🚌 connections:

Newcastle rail station (Bewick St, depart 1500) - Ferry Terminal, return after ship arrives.

Amsterdam (behind Centraal station, De Ruijterkade 153) - IJmuiden and v.v. (reservation recommended, depart Amsterdam approx. 1530; depart ferry terminal approx. 1040, arriving Centraal station approx. 1135).

STROMNESS - SCRABSTER 2280

NorthLink Ferries Journey 90 minutes Sailings all year

Peak timetable May 1 - Sept. 30:
From Stromness 0630 ①–⑥ (also Aug. 10), 0900 ⑦ (not Aug. 10), 1100 ①–⑥ (also Aug. 10), 1645 daily.
From Scrabster 0845 ①–⑥ (also Aug. 10), 1200 ⑦ (not Aug. 10), 1315 ①–⑥ (also Aug. 10), 1900 daily.

Off-peak timetable **Jan 3 - Apr. 30 and Oct. 1 - Dec. 31 (please confirm sailing times on Apr. 5, 12, 19, 26 and Oct. 4, 11, 18, 25).**
From Stromness at 0630 ①–⑤, 0900 ⑥⑦, 1645.
From Scrabster at 0845 ①–⑤, 1200 ⑥⑦, 1900.

ICELAND and the FAEROE ISLANDS 2285

Smyril Line

Hirtshals		Tórshavn		Seydisfjördur		Tórshavn		Hirtshals
				January 3 - March 15				
1500⑦	→	0730②	→	→	→	2000⑤	→	1100⑦
				March 16 - May 31				
1500⑦	→	0730②/1300②	→	0900③/2000④	→	1600⑤/2000⑤	→	1100⑦
				June 1 - September 6				
1530⑥	→	2230⑦/2330⑦	→	→	→	...	→	0930②
1130②	→	1730③/1800③	→	0830④/1030④	→	0300⑤/0330⑤	→	1230⑥
				November 23 - December 31				
1500⑦	→	0730②	→	→	→	2000⑤	→	1100⑦

In poor weather conditions sailings may dock at Frederikshavn or Hanstholm (for Hirtshals) and Klaksvík or Kollafjørdur (for Tórshavn). In winter season (November - March) sailings between Tórshavn and Seydisfjördur may be advanced, delayed or (in rare cases) cancelled at short notice due to adverse weather conditions.

☛ See note * in Table **2237** for information regarding rail connections from/to Hirtshals.

SKAGERRAK, KATTEGAT & SOUTH WEST BALTIC

2301 AARHUS / EBELTOFT - SJÆLLANDS ODDE

MolsLinjen

From Aarhus / Ebeltoft and Sjællands Odde: up to 32 sailings daily. Journey 55 – 75 minutes.

2304 BØJDEN - FYNSHAV

Als-Linjen (Molslinjen) Journey 50 minutes

From Bøjden and Fynshav: approximately every two hours (additional sailings in summer).

2312 ESBJERG - FANØ

FanøLinjen (Molslinjen) Journey 12 minutes

From Esbjerg and Fanø: Frequent service (up to 3 departures hourly).

2320 FREDERIKSHAVN - GÖTEBORG

Stena Line Journey approximately 3 hours 30 minutes

From Frederikshavn (Færgehavnsvej) and Göteborg (Danmarksterminalen): High season (June - Sept.) 37 sailings a week. Low season (Oct. - May) 17 sailings a week.

2330 GEDSER - ROSTOCK

Scandlines Journey 2 hours

From Gedser and Rostock International Port: up to 10 sailings daily.

2335 GÖTEBORG - KIEL

Stena Line Journey 14½ – 15½ hours

Sailings from Kiel (Schwedenkai) and Göteborg (Elof Lindälvs Gata)

Göteborg		Kiel	Kiel		Göteborg
1845	→	0915 ①–⑤	1845	→	0915 ①–⑤
1745	→	0915 ⑥⑦	1745	→	0915 ⑥⑦

2342 GRENAA - HALMSTAD

Stena Line Journey 4½ hours

From Grenaa and Halmstad: 1 - 2 sailings per day. Timings vary.
Foot passengers are **not** pemitted.

Grenaa port is located approximately 3 km from Grenaa railway station, which is linked with Aarhus by route L1 of the *Letbanan* light rail line, running every 30 mins (hourly on ⑦).

2345 HELSINGØR - HELSINGBORG

ForSea Journey 20 minutes

From Helsingør and Helsingborg: sailings approximately every 20 minutes (every 40 minutes at night).

2350 HIRTSHALS - KRISTIANSAND

Color Line by ferry Journey 3 hours 15 minutes

From Hirtshals and Kristiansand: 2 sailings daily (normally 1215 and 2045 from Hirtshals; 0800 and 1630 from Kristiansand; timings may vary, particularly in January). From the terminal, it is a 500m signposted walk to Hirtshals station (see Table **728**).

Fjord Line by Ferry

Hirtshals*		Kristiansand	Kristiansand		Hirtshals*
Until Apr. 10 and Sept. 22 - Dec. 28					
0930 **a**	→	1325	1430 **a**	→	1815
1915 **a**	→	2300			
Apr. 11 - May 27 and Sept. 1 – 21					
0930	→	1325	1430	→	1815
1915	→	2300			
May 28 - June 19 and Aug. 11 – 31					
0930	→	1325	1420	→	1815
June 20 - Aug. 10					
0930	→	1325	1430	→	1825

a – Not Jan. 11, 13, 15, 17, 19, 23, 25, Dec. 24, 25.

Fjord Line by catamaran

Hirtshals*		Kristiansand	Kristiansand		Hirtshals*
Apr. 11 - May 27 and Sept. 1 – 21					
1500	→	1725	0900	→	1125
May 28 - June 19 and Aug. 11 – 31					
1210	→	1435	0900	→	1125
2030	→	2255	1730	→	1955
June 20 - Aug. 10					
0945 **b**	→	1210	0630 **b**	→	0855
1615	→	1840	1300	→	1525
2250	→	0115	1945	→	2210

b – Not ②.

* – Shuttle 🚌 operates from to Hirtshals station; alternatively it is a 2500 m signposted walk from Lilleheden station (a request stop on the Hjørring - Hirtshals line, approx. 3 minutes from Hirtshals – see Table **728**).

2355 KALUNDBORG - SAMSØ

SamsøLinjen

From Kalundborg and Ballen (Samsø): 3 – 5 sailings daily in summer; 2 – 3 sailings daily in winter. Journey 80 – 90 minutes.

☛ **Due to the reconstruction of Ballen harbour, all sailings are to / from Kolby Kås (on the West of the island) until further notice.**

2360 KØBENHAVN - OSLO

DFDS Seaways / Go Nordic Cruise Lines

This route is now operated by Go Nordic Cruise Lines, under the DFDS brand f.t.b.

Sailings from København Dampfærgevej and Oslo Vippetangen (Akershusstranda 31).

København		Oslo	Oslo		København
1630	→	1000 **A**	1500	→	1000 **B**

A – Alternate days Jan. 3 – 21; daily Jan. 23 - Mar. 15; alternate days Mar. 17 – Apr. 2; daily Apr. 4 – Dec. 13. Departure times may vary; check with operator.

B – Alternate days Jan. 4 – 22, 2025; daily 24 - Mar. 16; alternate days Mar. 18 – Apr. 3; daily Apr. 5 – Dec. 13. Departure times may vary; check with operator.

☛ DFDS shuttle bus links København port with the city centre.

2366 LARVIK - HIRTSHALS

Color Line Journey 3 hours 45 minutes

From Larvik and Hirtshals: 1 - 2 sailings daily. Departure times vary.
From the terminal it is a 500m signposted walk to Hirtshals station (see Table **728**).

2372 OSLO - KIEL

Color Line

Sailings from Oslo Color Line Terminalen (Filipstadveien 25) and Kiel Norwegenkai.

Oslo		Kiel	Kiel		Oslo
1400	→	1000	1400	→	1000

2375 PUTTGARDEN - RØDBY

Scandlines Journey 45 minutes

Departures every 30 minutes (at 15 and 45 minutes past each hour). Sailing times between 2215 and 0415 may vary.

2380 ROSTOCK - TRELLEBORG

Stena Line

Sailings from Rostock (Überseehafen) and Trelleborg (Kontinentplan).

Rostock		Trelleborg		Trelleborg		Rostock	
0730	→	1330	①–⑥	0730	→	1330	①–⑥
1145	→	1800	⑦	1100	→	1715	⑦
1510	→	2110	①–⑥	1500	→	2100	①–⑥
2200	→	0540	⑦	2145	→	0540	⑦
2230	→	0540	①–⑥	2255	→	0610	①–⑥

Timings may vary. An additional night sailing operates on certain dates.

TT Line Journey 6 – 6½ hours

Sailings from Rostock Überseehafen and Trelleborg: 1 – 3 sailings per day. Timings vary.

2384 SASSNITZ-MUKRAN - RØNNE

Bornholmslinjen Journey 3 hours 20 minutes

From Sassnitz :
Sailing at 1150 ④⑥⑦ Apr. 10 - June 8, ④–① June 9 – 29, daily except ② June 30 - Aug. 31, ④–① Sept. 1 – 22, ④⑥⑦ Sept. 25 - Oct. 19 (also Oct. 25, 26), ⑥ Nov. 1 - Dec. 27.
Sailing at 1430 ⑥ May 24 - June 21, ⑥⑦ June 28 - Aug. 24, ⑥ Aug. 30 - Oct. 18.

From Rønne :
Sailing at 0800 ④⑥⑦ Apr. 10 - June 8, ④–① June 9 – 29, daily except ② June 30 - Sept. 22, ④⑥⑦ Sept. 25 - Oct. 19 (also Oct. 25, 26), ⑥ Nov. 1 - Dec. 27.
Sailing at 1000 ⑥ May 24 - June 21, ⑥⑦ June 28 - Aug. 24, ⑥ Aug. 30 - Oct. 18.

Sailing dates may vary; please check locally.

2387 STRÖMSTAD - SANDEFJORD

Color Line Journey 2½ hours

From Strømstad: 1330, 2000.
From Sandefjord: 1000, 1700.

2390 TRAVEMÜNDE - TRELLEBORG

TT Line Journey 7½ - 9 hours

Sailings from Travemünde Skandinavienkai and Trelleborg: 2 – 3 sailings per day.

Local 🚌 services are available from Travemünde Skandinavienkai railway station (Table **825**) to the ferry terminal or direct 🚌 from Lübeck ZOB.

2395 TRAVEMÜNDE - MALMÖ

Finnlines

Up to three sailings every day - journey time 9 hours

Travemünde		Malmö	Malmö		Travemünde
0100⑦	→	1030①	1000②③④	→	1900③④⑤
0230②–⑤	→	1115②–⑤	1000⑤⑥	→	1915⑤⑥
0300①	→	1145①	1330⑥	→	2300⑦
0300⑥	→	1200⑥	1600①–⑤	→	0045②–⑥
1000②–⑤	→	1915②–⑤	1600⑦	→	0115①
1100⑥	→	2000⑥	2200①②⑤	→	0700②③⑥
2145②③	→	0715③④	2200③⑦	→	0715④①
2200①④⑤	→	0715②⑤⑥	2230⑥	→	0830⑦
2200⑥⑦	→	0730⑦①			

BALTIC SEA

GDAŃSK - NYNÄSHAMN 2402

Polferries **Valid until Dec. 22**

Gdańsk		Nynäshamn		Nynäshamn		Gdańsk	
1800	→	1200	See note **A**.	1800	→	1200	See note **A**.

A – ①–⑥ (daily June 9 - Aug. 23).

Suburban rail service operates every 30 minutes (60 minutes on ©) Nynäshamn - Stockholm

GRISSLEHAMN - ECKERÖ 2405

Eckerö Linjen **Valid until Jan. 6, 2026**

Grisslehamn		Eckerö		Eckerö		Grisslehamn	
1000	→	1300	**A**	0800	→	0900	**A C**
1500	→	1800		1330	→	1430	
2000	→	2300	**B**	1830	→	1930	

A – Not Jan. 1. **B** – Not June 20. **C** – Not June 21.

☛ No sailings Jan. 7 - 9, Dec. 24, 25.

🚌 connections available Stockholm and Uppsala - Grisslehamn and v.v.

NAANTALI - KAPELLSKÄR via Långnäs 2407

Finnlines

Naantali		Långnäs		Kapellskär		Kapellskär		Långnäs		Naantali	
1000	→	1500	→	1745	③–⑦	1030	→	1515	→	1955	①②
1045	→	1600	→	1830	①②	1045	→	1530	→	2010	③–⑦
2245	→	0355	→	0615	①② ‡	2145	→	0210	→	0715	Daily
2300	→	0355	→	0615	③–⑦ ‡						

‡ – Arrival next day.

HELSINKI - TALLINN 2410

Eckerö Line

Sailings from Helsinki Länsiterminaali 2 (West Terminal T2) and Tallinn A-terminal.

Helsinki		Tallinn		Tallinn		Helsinki	
0900	→	1115		0600	→	0815	Not ⑦
1515	→	1730		1200	→	1415	
2140	→	0010 ‡	Not ⑥	1830	→	2100	

‡ – Arrival next day.

Tram routes 7 and 6T link Helsinki railway station with the Länsiterminaali

Tallink Silja

Sailings from Helsinki Länsiterminaali 1 / 2 and Tallinn D-terminal. Journey 2 hours.

Depart Tallinn: 0730 1030, 1330, 1630, 1930, 2230.

Depart Helsinki: 0730 1030, 1330, 1630, 1930 2230.

Additional services operate at other peak periods throughout the year.

Distance between Länsiterminaali terminals approximately 700 metres

Tram routes 7 and 6T link Helsinki railway station with the Länsiterminaali

Viking Line Journey 2½ hours

Sailings from Helsinki Katajanokka terminal and Tallinn Reisisdam:
2 sailings ①②③④⑥, 3 on ⑤⑦. Departure times vary.

KAPELLSKÄR - PALDISKI 2412

DFDS Journey 10 hours

Sailings from Kapellskär and Paldiski Northern Port:
6 sailing per week (not ⑥ from Kapellskär, ③ from Paldiski). Departure times vary.

KARLSKRONA - GDYNIA 2415

Stena Line Journey 10½ – 12 hours

From Karlskrona and Gdynia: up to 3 sailings daily. Departure times vary.

KARLSHAMN - KLAIPEDA 2418

DFDS Seaways Journey 14 hours

Sailings from Karlshamn Ferry Terminal and Klaipeda International Ferry Port:
daily evening departures. Timings vary.

KIEL - KLAIPEDA 2420

DFDS Seaways Journey 21 hours

Sailings from Kiel Ostuferhafen and Klaipeda International Ferry Port:
overnight crossings six days a week, Monday to Saturday, timings vary.

KØGE - RØNNE 2430

Bornholmslinjen

Køge		Rønne	Rønne		Køge
0030	→	0600	1700	→	2230

NYNÄSHAMN - VISBY 2445

Destination Gotland **Valid until Aug. 31**

Sailings Nynäshamn - Visby and v.v.: 1 – 2 sailings daily (3 – 6 sailings in high summer).
Departure times vary. Journey 3 hours 15 minutes to 3 hours 30 minutes.
Foot passengers not accepted unless travelling with a bicycle / moped / motocycle.

All sailings have 🚌 connection Stockholm City Terminal - Nynäshamn and v.v.

Suburban rail service operates every 30 minutes (60 minutes on ©) Nynäshamn - Stockholm.

NYNÄSHAMN - VENTSPILS 2448

Stena Line Journey 8½ hours

From Nynäshamn and Ventspils: Up to 2 sailings daily. Departure times vary.

Suburban rail service operates every 30 minutes (60 minutes on ©) Nynäshamn - Stockholm.

OSKARSHAMN - VISBY 2450

Destination Gotland

From Oskarshamn and Visby: 1 – 2 sailings daily (January - March runs 6 days per week).
Departure times vary. Foot passengers not accepted unless travelling with a bicycle / moped / motocycle.

STOCKHOLM - MARIEHAMN - HELSINKI 2465

Tallink Silja

Sailings from Stockholm Värtahamnen terminal and Helsinki Olympiaterminaali.

Stockholm		Mariehamn		Helsinki	Helsinki		Mariehamn		Stockholm
1645	→	2355	→	1030	1700	→	0420	→	1000

Tallink Silja 🚌 transfer links Stockholm Värtahamnen with city centre.
Alternatively Stockholm Värtahamnen is 500 metres from Gärdet metro station.

Viking Line

Sailings from Stockholm Stadsgården and Helsinki Katajanokka.

Jan. 1 - June 17 and Aug. 11 - Dec. 31

Stockholm		Mariehamn		Helsinki	Helsinki		Mariehamn		Stockholm
1630	→	2325	→	1010	1715	→	0430	→	1000

June 18 - Aug. 10

Stockholm		Mariehamn		Helsinki	Helsinki		Mariehamn		Stockholm
1600	→	2255	→	0915	1810	→	0430	→	1000

The above sailings are by way of an example, please check locally with the shippiing company.

Viking Line 🚌: Stockholm Cityterminalen (near Central station) - Viking Line terminal.

STOCKHOLM - MARIEHAMN / LÅNGNÄS 2470

Viking Line Journey 5½ - 6½ hours

Sailings from:
Stockholm to Mariehamn: One sailing per day at 1730.
Mariehamn to Stockholm: One sailing per day at 0730.
No sailings Stockholm/Långnäs/Stockholm.

STOCKHOLM - MARIEHAMN - TALLINN 2475

Tallink Silja

Sailings from Stockholm Värtahamnen terminal and Tallinn D-terminal.

Stockholm		Mariehamn		Tallinn	Tallinn		Mariehamn		Stockholm
1730	→	0100 **A**	→	1045	1800 **A**	→	0500	→	1015

A – Alternate days.

STOCKHOLM - MARIEHAMN / LÅNGNÄS - TURKU 2480

Tallink Silja

This is an indicative sailing pattern; please confirm when booking.
Sailings from Stockholm Värtahamnen and Turku Harbour.

Stockholm		Mariehamn		Mariehamn		Turku
0710 ①④⑤	→	1335	→	1345 ①④⑤	→	1915
0710 ⑥⑦	→	1415	→	...	→	...
Stockholm		**Mariehamn**		**Mariehamn**		**Stockholm**
0710 ⑥⑦	→	1415	→	0045 ①④-⑦	→	0610
1645	→	2345	→	0045 ②	→	0930
1730 ①④⑤⑦	→	0050 ②⑤⑥①	→	0420	→	1000
1900 ②	→	0510 ③	→	0500 ①③⑤⑦	→	1030
Turku		**Långnäs §**		**Långnäs §**		**Stockholm**
1930 ⑥	→	0040 ⑦	→	0515 ③	→	1015
2015 ①③④⑤⑦	→	0040 ②④⑤⑥①	→	1420 ⑥⑦	→	1830

§ – Långnäs is 28km from Mariehamn (🚌 connection available).

Service is suspended on certain dates for ship maintenance.

Tallink Silja 🚌 transfer links Stockholm Värtahamnen with city centre.

Alternatively Stockholm Värtahamnen is 500 metres from Gärdet metro station.

Viking Line

Sailings from Stockholm Stadsgården and Turku Linnansatama.

Stockholm		Mariehamn		Långnäs §		Turku
0745	→	1425	→	→	→	1950
2000	→	→	→	0320	→	0735
Turku		**Långnäs §**		**Mariehamn**		**Stockholm**
0845	→	→	→	1425	→	1855
2055	→	0110	→	→	→	0630

§ – Långnäs is 28km from Mariehamn (🚌 connection available).

Båtbussarna 🚌 links Stockholm Cityterminalen (near Central station) with ferry terminal.

In Turku 🚌 number 1 runs between city centre and the harbour.

Service is suspended on certain dates for ship maintenance

TRAVEMÜNDE - HELSINKI 2485

Finnlines Journey 30 hours

Sailings from Travemünde Skandinavienkai and Helsinki Vuosaaren satama.

Travemünde		Helsinki	Helsinki		Travemünde
0200	→	1000	1500	→	2100

Note Vuosaari harbour (Vuosaaren satama) is located approx 18 km east of Helsinki - can be reached by metro to Vuosaari then 🚌 route 90.

TRAVEMÜNDE - LIEPAJA 2486

Stena Line Journey 21 – 26 hours

From Travemünde and Liepaja: 1 crossing per day. Departure times vary.

VAASA - UMEÅ (HOLMSUND) 2490

Wasaline Journey 4½ hours

From Vaasa and Umeå: 1 – 2 sailings daily. Departure times vary.

2494 YSTAD - RØNNE

Bornholmslinjen **by fast ferry**

2–9 sailings daily, departure times vary, journey 80 minutes.

2495 YSTAD - ŚWINOUJŚCIE

Polferries

Ystad		Świnoujście		Świnoujście		Ystad	
1340	→	1945	Daily	1230	→	1900	Daily
2245	→	0615	Daily	2230	→	0615	Daily

These are the most regularly service days, confirm with operator

Free connecting 🚌 866 operates København - Ystad ferry terminal and v.v. (1 hr 15 min).

Unity Line

Ystad		Świnoujście	Świnoujście		Ystad
1330	→	2000	1300	→	2015
2255	→	0730	2300	→	0630

Services depart on various days, check with operator

WESTERN MEDITERRANEAN

2500 ALGECIRAS - CEUTA

Baleària (Eurolínies Marítimes) Journey 1¼–1½ hours

From Algeciras and Ceuta: Up to 10 sailings per day ①–⑥; up to 9 sailings per day on ⑦.

Trasmediterranea (Armas) Journey 60 minutes

From Algeciras and Ceuta: 5 sailings per day.

DFDS (FRS) Journey 60 minutes

From Algeciras and Ceuta: 5 sailings per day.

2502 ALGECIRAS - TANJAH (TANGIERS) MED

Africa Morocco Link (AML) Journey 1½ hours

From Algeciras and Tanjah Med: 8 sailings daily; departure times vary.

DFDS (FRS) Journey 1½ hours

From Algeciras and Tanjah Med: 8 sailings daily; departure times vary.

Baleària (Eurolínies Marítimes) Journey 1½ hours

From Algeciras and Tanjah Med: 8 sailings daily; departure times vary.

Trasmediterranea (Armas) Journey 1½ hours

From Algeciras and Tanjah Med: 6 sailings daily; departure times vary.

2504 ALMERÍA - GHAZAOUET

Trasmediterranea / Naviera Armas Journey 8–13 hours **Valid until Sept. 6**

Almería		Ghazaouet	Ghazaouet		Almería
2359⑤	→	0830⑥	2000⑥	→	0800⑦

2505 ALMERÍA - MELILLA

Baleària (Eurolínies Marítimes) Journey 6½ hours **Valid until Oct. 30**

Timings are an indictive example, please confirm with operator

Almería		Melilla	Melilla		Almería
1500	→	2300 daily except ⑥.	2359	→	0715 daily except ⑥.

Trasmediterranea / Naviera Armas Journey 7 hours **Valid until Oct. 30**

Almería		Melilla	Melilla		Almería
2330	→	0630 ①②③.	1530	→	2100 ①②③.

2507 ALMERÍA - AN-NADÛR (NADOR)

Baleària (Eurolínies Marítimes) Journey 6–9 hours **Valid until Oct. 31**

1 daily sailing in each direction. Usually departs Almeria at 1130, Nador at 2300.

2508 BARCELONA - TANJAH (TANGIERS) MED

Grandi Navi Veloci Journey 29–38 hours **Valid until Sept. 29**

From Barcelona and Tanjah Med (departures times vary):
Up to 4 sailings per week May - Sept.
Tanjah (Tangiers) Med port is located approximately 45 km east of Tanjah.
A connecting 🚌 operates between Tanjah Med and Tanjah.

2510 BALEARIC ISLANDS

Map page 315

Baleària (Eurolínies Marítimes)

BARCELONA - CIUTADELLA (MENORCA) Journey 3½–9½ hours. 1–3 sailings per day.

BARCELONA - EIVISSA (IBIZA) Journey 9 hours. 1 sailing per day (not ⑥ from Baracelona, not ⑦ from Eivissa). Most sailings depart Barcelona at 2200 and Eivissa at 1000.

BARCELONA - PALMA / ALCUDIA Journey 3½ - 6 hours. 1–2 sailing per day. Most sailings depart Barcelona at 2130 or 1545 and Palma at 0945 or 1300.

DÉNIA - EIVISSA (IBIZA) - PALMA Additional sailings in summer

This is an indicative sailing pattern; please confirm when booking.

Dénia		Eivissa		Palma	Palma		Eivissa		Dénia
1700	→	1915 / 2000	→	2215	0800	→	1015 / 1100	→	1315

VALENCIA - PALMA Journey 7–9 hours Additional sailings run via Eivissa

Indicative timings (please confirm with operator).
From Valencia at 1700 and 2230.
From Palma at 0800 and 1131.
* arrives next day.

Grimaldi Lines **Valid until Oct. 31**

Departure times may vary. All routes subject to alteration on and around holidays.

BARCELONA - EIVISSA (IBIZA) Journey 8–9 hrs

Depart Barcelona:
2145 ①③⑤.
2200 ②④.
Depart Ibiza:
1045 ②④.
1100 ③⑤.
2200 ⑦.

BARCELONA - MAÓ-MAHÓN (MENORCA) Journey 8–9 hrs

Depart Barcelona: 2145 ②④, 2230 ①③⑤ **A**, 0800 ⑦ **B**, 2359 ⑦ **B**.
Depart Maó-Mahón: 1100 ②③④⑤, 1930 ⑦ **C**, 0700 ⑦ **B**, 2359 ⑦ **B**.
A – During Nov. and Dec. may depart at 2230.
B – July 26 - Sept. 7.
C – During Nov. and Dec. may depart at 1800.

BARCELONA - PALMA (MALLORCA) Journey 7½–8 hrs **Until July 31**

Depart Barcelona: 2230 ①–⑤.
Depart Palma: 1100 ②③④⑤⑦.
Times vary, please confirm locally. Weekend sailings commence July 26.

PALMA (MALLORCA) - MAÓ-MAHÓN (MENORCA) Journey 6 hrs

Depart Palma: 0800 ⑦. Depart Maó-Mahón: 1700 ⑦. Please confirm sailing times.

VALÈNCIA - MAÓ-MAHÓN (MENORCA) via Palma Journey 16 hrs **Until Oct. 25**

Depart València: 2200 ⑥. Depart Maó-Mahón: 1700 ⑦.

VALÈNCIA - PALMA (MALLORCA) Journey 8–10 hrs **Until Oct 31**

Depart València: 2030 ①②③④⑤⑦, 2200 ⑥.
Depart Palma: 1000 ①, 1100 ②–⑥, 2358 ⑦.
Times vary, please confirm locally.

2512 CANARY ISLANDS

Fred. Olsen Express **Inter-Island services**

Playa Blanca (Lanzarote) - Corralejo (Fuerteventura), journey 25/35 minutes;
Morro del Jable (Fuerteventura) - Las Palmas de Gran Canaria (Gran Canaria), journey 120 minutes;
Agaete (Gran Canaria) - Santa Cruz de Tenerife (Tenerife), journey 80 minutes;
Los Cristianos (Tenerife) - San Sebastián de la Gomera (La Gomera), journey 50 minutes;
Santa Cruz de La Palma (La Palma) - Los Cristianos (Tenerife), journey 150 minutes;
Huelva - Las Palmas de Gran Canaria (Gran Canaria), journey 30/40 minutes;
Santa Cruz de La Palma (La Palma) - San Sebastián de la Gomera (La Gomera), journey 230 minutes.

Trasmediterranea

Huelva - Arrecife (Lanzarote)* - Las Palmas (Gran Canaria) - Santa Cruz (Tenerife): twice a week. * Once a week.
Inter-Island services link all the main islands - most services run daily.

Naviera Armas / Trasmediterranea

Cádiz		Lanzarote (Arrecife)		Gran Canaria (Las Palmas)		Tenerife (Santa Cruz)		Palma (Santa Cruz)
1230⑥	→	1500⑦/1130①	→	1800①/1100③	→	1240③/1400④	→	2100④
Palma (Santa Cruz)		**Tenerife (Santa Cruz)**		**Gran Canaria (Las Palmas)**		**Lanzarote (Arrecife)**		**Cádiz**
1600⑤	→	2200⑤/1520⑦	→	1700⑦/2315①	→	0515②/1530④	→	2130⑤

This a representative example timetable, various options are available

2520 CIVITAVECCHIA - BARCELONA

Grimaldi Lines

Up to six sailings a week in each direction – timings vary.
The following are sample sailings for the period July 14–20

Civitavecchia		Barcelona	Barcelona		Civitavecchia
2100①	→	1900②	2100①	→	1900②
2230②	→	1800③	2230②	→	1800③
2130③	→	1700④	2130③	→	1700④
2030④	→	1915⑤	2030④	→	1845⑤
2230⑤	→	2045⑥	2245⑤	→	2045⑥
0030⑦	→	2245⑦	0030⑦	→	2245⑦

2530 CIVITAVECCHIA - SICILY - TÛNIS

Grandi Navi Veloci

Civitavecchia		Palermo		Tûnis		Palermo		Civitavecchia
0900④	→	1115⑤/1230⑥	→	1230⑥/1159⑥	→	1445⑦/1800⑦	→	0800①

Timings vary (sample timings shown departing Aug. 14, returning Sept. 13).
Please check with operator for confirmed sailing times.

Grimaldi Lines

Civitavecchia		Tûnis	Tûnis		Civitavecchia
1930③	→	1400④ **B**	1930②	→	1400③ **F**
2030③	→	1400④ **D**	1930②	→	1430④ **G**

B – Oct. 27 - Dec. 21.
D – June 1 - Oct. 26.
F – Oct. 27 - Dec. 21.
G – June 1 - Oct. 26.

CIVITAVECCHIA - TERMINI IMERESE 2535

Grandi Navi Veloci Departure times vary. Journey 14 hours

From Civitavecchia and Termini Imerese (for Palermo): up to 5 sailings per week.

GENOVA - BARCELONA 2537

Grandi Navi Veloci Departure times vary. Journey 20–22 hours

From Genova and Barcelona: up to 3 sailings per week.

GENOVA - PALERMO 2547

Grandi Navi Veloci Departure times vary. Journey 20½ hours

From Genova and Palermo: up to 7 sailings per week.

GENOVA / BARCELONA - TANJAH (TANGIERS) MED 2554

Grandi Navi Veloci Departure times vary. Journey 49–58 hours

From Genova and Tanjah Med: up to 3 sailings per week.

Tanjah (Tangiers) Med port is located approximately 45 km east of Tanjah.
A connecting 🚌 operates between Tanjah Med and Tanjah.
Other sailings from sailings from Barcelona (see Table **2508**)

GENOVA - TÛNIS 2555

Grandi Navi Veloci Departure times vary. Journey 25½ hours

From Genova and Tûnis: 2–3 sailings per week.

ALMERIA - ORAN 2558

Trasmediterranea Journey 8–9 hours **Valid until Sept. 14**

From Almeria: Up to 2 sailings a week. From Oran: Up to 2 sailings a week.

GULF OF NAPOLI 2560

Including Gulf of Salerno and Ponziane Islands

Alilauro

Napoli Beverello - Forio: up to 5 sailings daily (summer only). Sailings via Ischia in winter.
Napoli Beverello - Ischia: up to 14 sailings daily.
Napoli Beverello - Sorrento: 5 sailings daily.
Salerno - Capri: daily sailing.

Additional infrequent services to Capri operate (summer only) from Ischia, Castellammare di Stábia, Positano and Amalfi.

Caremar

Napoli - Capri: 3 sailings daily by catamaran, 3 sailings by ship (4 / 3 in summer).
Napoli - Ischia: 6 sailings daily by catamaran, 7 sailings by ship (6 / 7 in summer).
Napoli - Procida: 7 sailings daily by catamaran, 7 sailings by ship (8 / 7 in summer).
Pozzuoli - Procida: 1 sailing by catamaran, 3 sailings by ship (1 / 3 in summer).
Procida - Ischia: 6 sailings daily by catamaran, 9 sailings by ship.
Sorrento - Capri: 4 sailings daily by catamaran.

Medmar

Ischia - Pozzuoli: up to 10 sailings daily.
Additional infrequent services operate between Pozzuoli, Procida, Casamicciola, and Ischia.

Navigazione Libera del Golfo (NLG) by catamaran

Napoli (Molo Beverello) - Capri: up to 10 sailings daily (more in summer). Journey 40 minutes.
Sorrento - Capri: 2 sailings daily (more in summer). Journey 25 minutes.
Additional services operate (summer only) between Castellammare di Stábia and Capri.

SNAV

NAPOLI - CAPRI By hydrofoil, journey 40 minutes

From Napoli (Beverello): 0700, 0805, 0910, 1015, 1110, 1400, 1600, 1810, 2000.
From Capri: 0650, 0805, 0905, 1010, 1210, 1450, 1710, 1810, 1910.

NAPOLI - PROCIDA By hydrofoil, journey 40 minutes

From Napoli (Beverello): 0830, 1130**b**, 1230, 1620, 1710**b**, 1900.
From Procida: 0735, 1010, 1425, 1805, 1900**a**.

ISCHIA - PROCIDA By hydrofoil, journey 10 - 20 minutes

From Ischia (Casamicciola): 0710, 0945, 1400, 1740, 1830**a**.
From Procida: 0910, 1215**b**, 1315, 1705, 1755**a**, 1945.
a – ⑤⑥⑦ June 1- Sept. 28 **b** – ⑤⑦ May 2 - 30, daily from June 1.

CORSICA 2565

MAINLAND FRANCE TO CORSICA (map page 161)

Corsica Linea *Departure times vary*

MARSEILLE - AJACCIO Journey 12 hours. Most sailings overnight.
MARSEILLE - BASTIA Journey 11–13 hours. Most sailings overnight.
MARSEILLE - L'ÎLE ROUSSE Journey 12–13 hours. Most sailings overnight ◇.
MARSEILLE - PROPRIANO Journey 12½ hours. 3 night sailings a week operated by La Méridionale.

◇ – Most sailings ①③⑤ from Marseille, returning ②④⑥. Additional sailings in summer.

Corsica Ferries *Departure times vary*

NICE - AJACCIO Journey 4½–9 hours. Irregular sailings. Most sailings by day.
NICE - BASTIA Journey 7½ hours. 3–5 sailings per week. Most sailings by day.
NICE - L'ÎLE ROUSSE Journey 5–5½ hours. Irregular sailings. Most sailings by day.
NICE - PORTO VECCHIO Journey 13 hours. Irregular sailings. Sailings by night.

TOULON - AJACCIO Journey 6–10 hours. 1–2 sailings daily (daily night sailing).
TOULON - BASTIA Journey 9–10 hours. 1–2 sailings daily (daily night sailing).
TOULON - L'ÎLE ROUSSE Journey 6–7 hours. Irregular sailings. Most sailings by day.
TOULON - PORTO VECCHIO Journey 17 hours (calls at Porto Torres). Irregular sailings. Sailings by night.

ITALY TO CORSICA

Corsica Ferries *Departure times vary*

LIVORNO - BASTIA Journey 4–7½ hours. 1–2 sailings per day. Most sailings by day.
SAVONA - BASTIA Journey 6–10 hours. 1–2 sailings per day (irregular in winter).
Other (irregular) sailings Savona to L'île Rousse

Moby Lines *Departure times vary* **Summer 2025**

GENOVA - BASTIA Journey 5–10 hours. Summer only, day and night sailings.
LIVORNO - BASTIA Journey 4½ hours. Summer only, 1–2 sailings per day (not daily).

CORSICA TO SARDINIA

Corsica Ferries / Sardinia Ferries **2024 Service**

PORTO VECCHIO - GOLFO ARANCI July - September, up to 1–3 sailings per week.
BONIFACIO - SANTA TERESA DI GALLURA Journey 50 minutes. 3–4 sailings daily.

Moby Lines

BONIFACIO - SANTA TERESA DI GALLURA Journey 50 minutes. Several sailings daily.

ITALIAN ISLAND SERVICES 2570

Egadi, Eolie, Pantelleria, Pelagie and Ustica Islands (map page 283)

SNAV **May 31 - Sept. 15. Summer only**

Napoli Mergellina - Stromboli - Panarea - Salina - Vulcano - Lipari and v.v.:
Daily sailings late May to early September. Additional sailing on ⑤⑥⑦ July / August (not serving Salina and Vulcano).

Liberty Lines by hydrofoil

EGADI & EOLIAN ISLANDS and USTICA

The Sicilian ports of Messina, Milazzo, Palermo and Trapani are linked by island-hopping services serving Alicudi, Favignana, Filicudi, Levanzo, Lipari, Marettimo, Panarea, Rinella, Salina, Stromboli, Ustica and Vulcano.
Services operate to differing frequencies (additional sailings in summer).

MILAZZO - PALERMO Journey 5 hours

Milazzo		Palermo		Milazzo	
0630	→	1135 / 1330	→	1830	**A**

A – ①⑤ until May 30; daily June 1 - Sept. 30; ①⑤ Oct. 3–31.

MILAZZO - VULCANO by hydrofoil Journey 50 minutes

From Milazzo and Vulcano: 10–14 departures daily.

OTHER SERVICES:
Inter-island sailings operate, also from mainland Sicily to the islands. Services operate to differing frequencies (additional sailings in summer).

MÁLAGA - MELILLA 2595

Baleària (Eurolínies Marítimes) Journey 7 hours.

From Málaga: 1500 ①–⑤, 1700 ⑦.
From Melilla: 0100 ①, 2359 ①–⑤.

MOTRIL - MELILLA 2596

Trasmediterranea Journey 7 hours. **Service to Oct. 31.**

From Motril: 2330 ④⑤⑦.
From Melilla: 1530 ③⑤, 1630⑦.

MARSEILLE - AL-JAZÂ'IR (ALGIERS) 2602

Corsica Linea

One sailing a week in each direction (Marseille departs on ②, al-Jazâ'ir on ④), increases to two or three trips per week during July and August.

MARSEILLE - TÛNIS 2615

Compagnie Tunisienne de Navigation / Corsica Linea

The service is currently operated by two ferry companies.
The **Corsica Linea** low season 1 sailing a week, July and August 2–3 sailings a week. Journey time approx. 20½ hours.

Compagnie Tunisienne de Navigation (CTN):
Up to three sailings a week from Marseille usually on ②④⑥ until Oct.
Up to three sailings a week from Tûnis on ①③⑤ until Oct..
Then generally one sailing a week in each direction until Dec. 27.
Please confirm locally. Journey time approx. 24 hours.

CIRKEWWA (Malta) - MGARR (Gozo) 2618

Gozo Channel Co.

Sailings Cirkewwa (Malta) - Mgarr (Gozo) and v.v.: every 45 minutes (approx every 90 mins early morning and late evening). Journey 25 minutes.
Frequent 🚌 services serve both ferry terminals.

2625 NAPOLI - PALERMO

Grandi Navi Veloci Journey 11½ hours

From Napoli and Palermo: up to 8 sailings per week. Departure times vary.

Tirrenia Journey 11½ hours

Napoli		Palermo	Palermo		Napoli
2015	→	0645	2015	→	0645

2661 SALERNO - PALERMO - TÛNIS

Grimaldi Lines

Salerno		Palermo		Tûnis
0100⑥ **A**	→	1015⑥ / 0230② **B**	→	1400②
1315①	→	2330① / 1030⑥ **C**	→	2230⑥
2000⑤ **F**	→	0700⑥ /1145⑥ **E**	→	2300⑥
2345⑤	→	0900⑥ / 1230⑥ **A**	→	2400⑥
Tûnis		**Palermo**		**Salerno**
0330⑦	→	1630⑦ / 2000⑦	→	0700①
1700④ **E**	→	0600⑤ / 0915⑤ **E**	→	1900⑤
1930④ **A**	→	0730⑤ / 1030⑤ **A**	→	2000⑤
		1045⑤ **D**	→	2000⑤

A – Until Jan. 31, Mar. 31 - Apr. 30, June 1 - Oct. 26, Dec. 8–21.
B – Until Feb. 28, Mar. 31 - Dec. 21.
C – Feb. 1–28, May 1–31.
D – Mar. 31 - Apr. 30, June 1 - Oct. 26.
E – Mar. 1–30.
F – Feb. 1–28, May 1–31, Oct. 27 - Dec. 7.

2675 SARDINIA

FRANCE TO SARDINIA

Corsica Ferries

TOULON - PORTO TORRES Journey 10–16 hours. Weekly in winter; up to 2 sailings per week in summer.

MAINLAND ITALY TO SARDINIA (map page 283)

Corsica Ferries

LIVORNO / PIOMBINO - GOLFO ARANCI Journey 8½. Overnight sailings (also by day May - September).

Tirrenia

CIVITAVECCHIA - OLBIA Journey 5½–7 hours. Night sailing every day. 1–2 additional day sailings June - August.
GENOA - PORTO TORRES Journey 10½ hours. Night sailings every day.

Grimaldi Lines **CIVITAVECCHIA - OLBIA** **June 1 - Sept. 30**

Civitavecchia		Olbia	Olbia		Civitavecchia
2245	→	0615	1230	→	1900

CIVITAVECCHIA - CAGLIARI

Civitavecchia	Cagliari	Cagliari	Civitavecchia
2000②④⑥	1100③⑤⑦	2000①③⑤	1100②③⑤

NAPOLI - CAGLIARI

Napoli		Cagliari	Cagliari		Napoli
1900 ①③⑤	→	1000 ②④⑥	1900 ②④	→	1000 ⑤⑥
...		...	2359 ⑦	→	1430 ①

CIVITAVECCHIA - PORTO TORRES Journey 7–12 hours. 1 sailing per week.

CIVITAVECCHIA - ARBATAX Journey 9–10 hours. 2 sailings per week until Aug. 3 and from Sept. 9; 3 sailings per week Aug. 4–31.

LIVORNO - OLBIA Journey 9–10 hours. 11–14 sailings per week.

Moby Lines **Valid until Oct. 31**

GENOVA - OLBIA Journey 11–12 hours. Up to 4 sailings per week Apr. 16 - May 26 (daily sailings May 28 - Oct. 31).

LIVORNO - OLBIA Journey 6½–9 hours. Daily sailings.

PIOMBINO - OLBIA Journey 5–5¼ hours. 4–6 sailings per week during Aug. only.

Grandi Navi Veloci **Operates May - Oct.**

GENOVA - OLBIA Journey 12¼ hours. Daily June - Sept. 27.

GENOVA - PORTO TORRES Journey 11½ hours. Daily June - Sept. 27.

SICILY TO SARDINIA (map page 283)

Grimaldi Lines

PALERMO - CAGLIARI Journey 13 hours. 1 weekly departure a week.
Departs Palemo 0900⑦, arrives 2100⑦; from Cagliari 1700⑥, arrives 0500⑦

SPAIN TO SARDINIA

Grimaldi Lines **Valid until Dec. 10**

BARCELONA - PORTO TORRES Journey 12¼ – 14¼ hours

Sailing times and days vary check locally. Journey timings vary.

Barcelona to Porto Torres: 1 sailing per week Jan. 2 - May 21 (on ③or④); also on June 29, 30, July 2, 12, 13, Sept. 18, 19, 25, 26; 1 sailing per week Sept. 1 - Dec. 10 (on ③); 3 sailings per week June 19 - July 13 and Sept. 11–14 (on ④⑤⑦); 4 sailings per week July 14 - Sept. 7 (on ①④⑤⑦).

Porto Torres to Barcelona: 1 sailing per week Jan. 7 - May 22 (on ②or④); also on June 13, 14, Sept. 19, 20; 1 sailing per week Oct. 2 - Dec. 11; 3 sailings per week June 20 - July 13 and Sept. 12–14 (on ⑤⑥⑦); 4 sailings per week July 15 - Sept. 7 (on ②⑤⑥⑦).

2678 SÈTE - AN-NADÛR (NADOR)

Grandi Navi Veloci **Journey 38–44 hours** **Valid until Sept. 26**

From Sète and an-Nadûr: up to 2 sailings per week. Departure times vary.

2680 SÈTE - TANJAH (TANGIERS) MED

Grandi Navi Veloci Departure times vary. Journey ±49 hours **Valid until Sept. 28**

From Sète and Tanjah Med: up to 3 sailings per week.

Tanjah (Tangiers) Med port is located approximately 45 km east of Tanjah (connecting 🚌).

2692 VALLETTA - POZZALLO

Virtu Ferries **by catamaran** Journey 1 hr 45 min

From Valletta and Pozzallo: between 11 and 16 sailings per week, departure times vary.

2695 STRETTO DI MESSINA

MESSINA - REGGIO DI CALABRIA

Liberty Lines **by hydrofoil** Journey 30 minutes

From Messina:
①–⑤: 0530, 0615, 0700, 0740, 0815, 0840, 1000, 1130, 1245, 1300, 1430, 1530, 1630, 1730, 1830. 1930, 2030, 2230.
⑥⑦: 0620, 0720, 0815, 1000, 1130, 1245, 1420, 1730, 2230.
From Reggio di Calabria:
①–⑤: 0620, 0700, 0745, 0830, 0850, 0925, 1050, 1220, 1345, 1420, 1520, 1620, 1720,1820, 1920, 2020, 2120, 2320.
⑥⑦: 0710, 0810, 0850, 1050, 1220, 1510, 1820, 2320.

MESSINA - VILLA SAN GIOVANNI

Caronte & Tourist Journey 20 minutes **Valid until Sept. 8**

From Messina: every 40 minutes 0640 - 0040.
From Villa San Giovanni: every 40 minutes 0640 - 0000.

Bluferries Journey 30 minutes

Foot passengers not conveyed.
From Messina and Villa San Giovanni: approx every 30 - 40 minutes.

Blu Jet **by hydrofoil** Journey 20 minutes

From Messina: 0520, 0610, 0740, 0830, 0930, 1150, 1310, 1440, 1540, 1640, 1730, 1830, 1930, 2100, 2220, 2135.

From Villa San Giovanni: 0545, 0715, 0805, 0900, 1000, 1240, 1410, 1510, 1610, 1705, 1800, 1900, 2025, 2145, 2305, 0020.

2699 OTHER SERVICES

Corsica Ferries

From Piombino to Portoferraio (Elba): May 25 - Sept. 29: up to 7 sailings daily by fast ferry; journey time 40 minutes.
From Bastia to Portoferraio (Elba): June - Sept: ④⑤ depart 0700, return 1830. Journey time 90 minutes.

Moby Lines / Toremar

Piombino - Portoferraio (Elba): up to 30 sailings daily in high-summer, less frequent at other times; journey time 1 hour.

Toremar

Services operate from Piombino to Cavo, Pianosa, Portoferraio and Rio Marina; from Livorno to Capraia and Gorgona; from Porto Santo Stefano to Isola del Giglio and Giannutri.

ADRIATIC / EASTERN MEDITERRANEAN

2715 ANCONA - IGUMENÍTSA

Anek Lines / Superfast Ferries **Valid until October 31, 2025**

Ancona		Igumenítsa	Igumenítsa		Ancona
1330②④⑤ **Y**	→	0800③⑤⑥	0045②④⑥ ⊖	→	1600②④⑥
1330② **B**	→	0900③	0130①② ●	→	1800①②
1330④⑤ **M**	→	0800⑤⑥	0300③ **A**	→	1930③
1400⑤ **C**	→	0830⑥	1700④ **J**	→	1100⑤
1430⑥ **U**	→	0800⑦	1730⑤♠	→	1130⑥
1430② **P**	→	1230③	1730①☆	→	1130②
1530③ **L**	→	1100④	1930③④★	→	1330④⑤‡
1600①⑤ **T**	→	0930②⑥	2015① ◧	→	1130②
1630④ **R**	→	1430⑤	2030⑤ **C**	→	1400⑥
1730⑦ **W**	→	1100⑦	2030⑦ **H**	→	1430①
1730⑥⑦ **K**	→	1100①⑦	2100⑦♣	→	1330①
1730② **N**	→	1100③	2145⑦❖	→	1300①
1730③ **Q**	→	1100④	2200② **O**	→	1600③
1730④ **S**	→	1100⑤	2315②⑥♥	→	1430③⑦
1730① **D**	→	1530②	2315⑤⑥ ⊕	→	1430⑥⑦
1730③ **V**	→	1530④	2330⑥ **F**	→	1700⑦
1900③ **E**	→	1500④	2359②③ **Z**	→	1630③§④
1930⑥ **X**	→	1500⑦	2359① **D**	→	2000②
1930⑥ **F**	→	1730⑦			
1930⑦ **G**	→	1500⑦			
2000④ **J**	→	1800⑤			

A – June 2 only.
B – May 6 - June 17, Sept. 25 - Oct. 30.
C – May 2–30.
D – May 5–26.
E – May 7–28.
F – May 3–24, Aug. 16–31, Sept. 6 arrives 1500.
G – May 4–25 (also May 31) arrives 1300.
H – May 4–25.
J – May 1–29.
K – June 1 - Aug. 10, Sept. 13 - Oct. 26.
L – June 4–25, Sept. 10–17, Oct. 8–22.
M – June 5–27, Sept. 9.
O – May 6–27.
N – July 1 - Aug. 5.
P – July 1 - Sept. 2.
Q – July 2–9.
R – July 3 - Sept. 4.
S – July 3 - Aug. 7.
T – July 4 - Sept. 5.
U – July 5 - Aug. 30.
V – July 9 - Sept. 3.
W – Aug. 17 - Sept. 7.
Y – June 24, Sept. 9 - Oct. 31 (not Sept. 25, Oct. 2, 9, 16, 23, 30).
Z – June 2–25, Sept. 9 - Oct. 29. (also Sept. 8).
⊕ – June 6–28 (also May 31), Sept. 12 - Oct. 31.
● – June 9–30, Sept. 15 - Oct. 28.
◧ – June 30 - Aug. 11.
★ – July 2 - Sept. 4.
♠ – July 4 - Sept. 5.
❖ – July 6 - Aug. 31.
♥ – July 1 - Sept. 6.
‡ – On ⑤ arrives 1300.
⊖ – Aug. 12 - Sept. 6.
☆ – Aug. 25 - Sept. 1.
♣ – Sept. 7 only.
§ – On ③ Sept. 24 - Oct. 28 arrives 1730.

Grimaldi Lines / Minoan Lines

Ancona		Igumenítsa	Igumenítsa		Ancona
1930 **A**	→	1800	2130 **B**	→	1700

A – ①②④⑤⑥ Mar. 31 - June 22; ①–⑥ June 23 - Sept. 14; ①②③⑤⑥ Sept. 15 - Dec. 28.
B – ①②③⑤⑥ Mar. 31 - June 22; ①–⑥ June 23 - Sept. 14; ①②③⑤⑥ Sept. 15 - Dec. 28.

ANCONA - PÁTRA 2716

Anek Lines / Superfast Ferries — **Valid until Oct. 31**

Ancona	→	Pátra	Pátra	→	Ancona
1330② **R**	→	1430③	1430① ⊠	→	1130②
1330⑤ **T**	→	1430⑥	1430⑦♣	→	1330①
1330④⑤ **J**	→	1430⑤⑥	1600⑦ ⊕	→	1300①
1330④ **S**	→	1530⑤	1700⑥ **D**	→	1630⑦
1330② **B**	→	1530③	1730⑤⑥ **X**	→	1430⑥⑦
1400⑤ **A**	→	1500⑥	1730②⑥ ◧	→	1430③⑦
1430⑥ **M**	→	1330⑦	1730③ ☆	→	1630④
1530③ **E**	→	1730④	1730②③ **Z**	→	1630③④
1530③ **C**	→	1830④	1730② ⊡	>	1730③
1600①⑤ **L**	→	1500②⑥	1730① **U**	→	1930②
1630⑥ **D**	→	1800⑦	1730⑤ **W**	→	1630⑥
1730⑥⑦ **H**	→	1630⑦①	1800⑤ **A**	→	1700⑥
1730⑦ **Q**	→	1630①	1800②③⑤ **V**	→	1700③④⑥
1730②④ **K**	→	1630③⑤	1900①③⑤●	→	1430②④⑥
1900②④ **N**	→	1630③⑤	1900①③⑤★	→	1600②④⑥
1930⑥ **F**	→	1830⑦	1900⑦① ❖	→	1800①②
1930⑥ **P**	→	2130⑦	2000⑦ **G**	→	1900①
1930⑦ **G**	→	2130①	2030⑦ **Y**	→	1930①

A – May 2–30.
B – May 6–27, June 10–17 (also May 1).
C – May 7–28.
D – May 3–24.
E – June 4–25, Sept. 17 - Oct. 29.
F – May 31 only.
G – May 4–25.
H – June 1 - Aug. 10, Sept. 13 - Oct. 26.
J – May 8, 15, 22, 29, June 5–27, Sept. 11–26.
K – July 1 - Aug. 21.
L – July 4 - Sept. 5.
M – July 5 - Sept. 6.
N – Aug. 26 - Sept. 4.
P – Sept. 6 only.
Q Aug. 17 - Sept. 7.
R – June 3, 24, Sept. 9 - Oct. 28.
S – Oct. 2–30.
T – Oct. 3–31.
U – May 5–26.
V – May 6–28.
W – May 30 only.
X – May 31 - June 28, Sept. 12 - Oct. 31.
Y – June 1 only.
Z – June 3–25, Sept. 9–17 (also June 2).
❖ – June 8–29, Sept. 14 - Oct. 27.
⊠ – June 30 - Aug. 11.
● – June 30 - Aug. 8.
◧ – July 1 - Sept. 6.
⊕ – July 6 - Aug. 31.
★ – Aug. 11 - Sept. 5.
♣ – Sept. 7 only.
☆ – Sept. 24 - Oct. 20 (also Sept. 0).
⊡ – Sept. 23 - Oct. 28.

🚌 connection Pátra - Pireás - Athína and v.v. operates most days durimg the summer.

ANCONA - SPLIT 2725

SNAV — **No winter service**

Ancona		Split	Split		Ancona
1930①③⑤ **A**	→	0700②④⑥	1930②④⑦ **C**	→	0700
			1930②④⑥ **D**	→	0700
1000⑦ **B**	→	1930	2130⑦ **B**	→	0730①

A – May 1 - Oct. 3.
B – July 20 - Aug. 31.
C – May 1 - July 17, Sept. 1 - Oct. 5.
D – July 19 - Aug. 30.

Jadrolinija

Ancona		Split	Split		Ancona
		Nov. 11 - Dec. 31			
1945 ②⑤	→	0830 ③⑥	2000 ⑦③	→	07000 ①④
		May 9 - June 25 and Sept. 7 - Nov. 7			
1945 ①③⑤	→	0700 ②④⑥	2000 ②④⑦	→	0700 ③⑤①
		June 26 - July 27 and Sept 1–5			
1945 ①③⑤	→	0700 ②④⑥	1000 ④⑥	→	1900 ④⑥
2200 ⑥	→	0900 ⑦	2000 ⑦②	→	0700 ①③
		July 29 - Aug. 21			
1000 ②	→	1900 ②	1000 ④⑥	→	1900 ④⑥
1945 ③⑤	→	0700 ④⑥	2000 ⑦	→	0700 ①
2200 ⑥	→	0900 ⑦	2200 ②	→	0900 ③
		Aug. 23–31			
1000 ②	→	1900 ②	2000 ④	→	0700 ⑤
1000 ⑥⑦	→	1800 ⑥⑦	2100 ⑥⑦	→	0700 ⑦①
1945 ③	→	0700 ④	2200 ②	→	0900 ③

ANCONA - ZADAR 2732

Jadrolinija — **No winter service**

Ancona		Zadar	Zadar		Ancona
		June 26 - July 25 and Sept. 4–5			
2200 ④	→	0700 ⑤	1000 ⑤	→	1700 ⑤
		July 28 - Aug. 21			
1000 ①	→	1800 ①	1000 ⑤	→	1700 ⑥
2200 ④	→	0700 ⑤	2200 ①	→	0700 ②
		Aug. 22–29			
1000 ①⑤	→	1800 ①	2200 ①⑤	→	0700 ②⑥

ANCONA - KORFU 2733

Anek Lines / Superfast Ferries — **No winter service**

Ancona		Kerkira (Corfu)	Kerkira (Corfu)		Ancona
		July 1 - September 5			
1430② **A**	→	1115③	1845⑤ **C**	→	1130⑥
1630④ **B**	→	1315⑤	1845① **E**	→	1130②
			2045③ **D**	→	1330④

A – July 1 - Sept. 2.
B – July 3 - Sept. 4.
C – July 4 - Sept. 5.
D – July 2 - Sept. 3.
E – Aug. 18 - Sept. 1.

BARI - DURRËS 2745

Adria Ferries

Journey 9–11 hours.

From Bari: One sailing a day generally departs at 2300, with some additional sailings during high summer departing 1200 or 1300.

From Durrës: One sailing a day generally departs at 2200, with some additional sailings during high summer departing departing 1130.

Adria Ferries also operates from Ancona to Durrës.

Ventouris Ferries

From Bari and Durrës: 1 sailings per day, Journey 9–10 hours.

BARI - IGUMENÍTSA via Kérkira (Corfu) 2750

Ventouris Ferries — **July 1 - Sept. 13 (no winter sailings)**

Bari		Kérkira (Corfu)		Igumenítsa	
1000	→	→	→	2200	Aug. 17, 24, 31.
2000	→	0700 / 0730	→	0845	July 1–31 (not July 14, 19–21, 26, –28). Aug. 1–6, 7, 8, 12–16, 19, 20, 21, 22, 26–29. Sept. 2–8, 10, 12.
2200	→	0900 / 0930	→	1045	July 20, 27, Aug. 3, 10.
2359	→	1100 / 1130	→	1245	July 19, 26, Aug. 1, 9.
Igumenítsa		**Kérkira (Corfu)**		**Bari**	
1000	→	→	→	2000	July 19, 26, 20, 27. Aug. 3, 10.
2130	→	2230 / 2300	→	0815	July 1–31 (not July 15, 19, 22, 26, 29). Aug. 1, 3, 4, 6–8, 10, 11, 13–16, 18, 20, 23, 27–30, Sept. 3–9, 11, 13.
2359	→	0100/0130	→	1045	Aug. 17, 22, 29, Sept. 1.

BARI - IGUMENÍTSA - KÉRKIRA - SAMI (Kefallinia) 2751

Ventouris Ferries

Bari		Kérkira (Corfu)		Igumenítsa		Sami (Krfallina)
2000	→	0700/0730	→	0845/0930	→	1415

Departs Bari July 14, 21, 28, Aug. 4, 11, 18, 25, Sept. 1 (arrives Sami the following day).

Sami (Krfallina)		Igumenítsa		Kérkira (Corfu)		Bari
1500	→	1930/2130	→	2230/2300	→	0815

Departs Sami July 15, 22, 29, Aug. 5, 12, 19, 26, Sept. 2 (arrives Bari the following day).

BARI - PÁTRA via Kérkira and Igumenítsa 2755

Anek Lines / Superfast Ferries — **Valid until Dec. 31, 2025**

	Bari		Kérkira (Corfu)		Igumenítsa		Pátra
				Until May 31 and Oct. 1 - Dec. 31			
	1330 ⑦	→	→	→	2300 ⑦	→	0700 ①
C	1930 ①–⑥	→	→	→	0530 ①–⑥	→	1300 ①–⑥
				June 1 - July 13 and Sept. 1–30			
	1330 ⑦	→	→	→	2300 ⑦	→	0700 ①
	1930 ①②③⑤⑥	→	→	→	0530 ②③④⑥⑦	→	1300 ②③④⑥⑦
	1930 ④	→	0430 ⑤	→	0600 ⑤	→	1300 ⑤
				July 14 - Aug. 17			
	1330 ⑦	→	→	→	2300 ①	→	0700①
	1200 ⑤⑥	→	2100⑤⑥	→	2230 ⑤⑥		...
	1930 ①②③⑥	→	→	→	0530 ②③④⑦	→	1300 ②③④⑦
	1930 ④	→	0430 ⑤	→	0600 ⑤	→	1300 ⑤
				Aug. 18–31			
	1330⑦	→	→	→	2300①	→	0700①
	1930 ①②③⑤⑥	→	→	→	0530 ②③④⑥⑦	→	1300 ②③④⑥⑦
	1930 ④	→	0430 ⑤	→	0600 ⑤	→	1300 ⑤

	Pátra		Igumenítsa		Kérkira (Corfu)		Bari
				Until May 31 and Oct. 1 - Dec. 31			
C	1730	→	2359	→	→	→	0900
				June 1 - July 13 and Sept. 1–30			
	1730 not ③	→	2359 not ③	→	→	→	0900 not ④
	1730③	→	2359③	→	0130④	→	0930④
				July 14 - Aug. 17			
	1730 ①②④⑦	→	2359 ①②④⑦	→	→	→	0900 ①②③⑤
	1730 ③	→	2359 ③	→	0130 ④	→	0930 ④
	1730⑤	→	→	→	→	→	0730⑥
	...		2359⑤⑥	→	0130⑥⑦	→	0830⑥⑦
				Aug. 18–31			
	1730 ①②④⑤	→	2359 ①②④⑤	→	→	→	0900 ②③⑤⑥
	1730 ③⑥⑦	→	2359 ③⑥⑦	→	0130 ④⑦①	→	0930 ④⑦①

C – Not Dec. 25, 31.

Subject to alteration during ship maintenance periods

🚌 connection Pátra - Pireás - Athína and v.v.

2765 BRINDISI - IGUMENÍTSA

Grimaldi Lines

		Until Aug. 23 and Sept. 15 - Dec. 28			
Brindisi		Igumenítsa	Igumenítsa		Brindisi
1300	→	2200	0100	→	0900
2230 **A**	→	0900*	1400 **A**	→	2100
		Aug. 23 - Sept. 14			
Brindisi		Igumenítsa	Igumenítsa		Brindisi
1300	→	2200	0100	→	0900
2230	→	0700 * **b**	1400	→	2100 **c**

A – ⑤⑥ until Mar. 30; ①②③⑤⑥⑦ Mar. 31; daily from June 23.
b – Arrives two hour earlier on ④⑤⑥.
c – Arrives 2030 ①②③④.
* – Following morning.

2775 BRINDISI - KÉRKIRA (CORFU)

Grimaldi Lines — **June 26 - Sept. 14 (no winter service)**

Brindisi		Kérkira	Kérkira		Brindisi
2230 ④⑤⑥	→	0530 ⑤⑥⑦	1530 ⑤⑥⑦	→	2100 ⑤⑥⑦

Grimaldi Lines also operate between Ancona and Kérkira June 26 - Sept. 14 on ④⑤ departing 1930, arriving 1600 on ⑤⑥.

2795 DUBROVNIK - BARI

Jadrolinija — **Valid May 14 - Nov. 6**

Bari		Dubrovnik	Dubrovnik		Bari
		May 14 - June 21 and Sept. 22 - Oct. 18			
1100 ②④⑥ **a**	→	1930	1100 ①③⑤	→	1900
		June 22 - July 20 and			
1100 ④⑥ **b**	→	1930	1100 ①⑤⑦	→	1900
2200 ⑦	→	0700 ①	2200 ② **c**	→	0800 ③
		July 21 - Aug. 17			
1100 ④⑤⑥	→	1900	1100 ①⑦	→	1900
2200 ⑦	→	0700 ①	2200 ④⑥	→	0800 ⑤⑦
		Aug. 18 – 31			
1100 ④	→	1930	1100 ①⑤⑥⑦	→	1900
2200 ⑤⑥⑦	→	0800 ⑥⑦①	2200 ⑤⑥⑦	→	0800
		Sept. 1 – 21			
1100 ②④⑥	→	1900	1100 ①③⑤⑦	→	1900
2200 ⑦	→	0800 ①			
		Oct. 20 - Nov. 6			
1100 ②④ **d**	→	1930	1100 ①③	→	1900

a – On June 12 departs 1300, arrives 2100; on Oct. 6 departs 2200, arrives 0800.
b – Also June 24.
c – July 7 only.
d – Also Oct. 24; not Oct. 23.

2800 GREEK ISLANDS

Summary table of regular services to the Greek Islands

Routes are operated by various ferry companies to differing schedules.
Additional inter-island routes are operated at less regular intervals.

Pireás to Égina, Póros, Ídra, Spétses, Kíthira, Andikíthira.
Pireás to Sérifos, Sífnos, Mílos, Folégandros.
Pireás to Páros, Íos, Thíra (Santorini), Iráklio.
Pireás to Náxos, Amorgós, Astipálea.
Pireás to Pátmos, Léros, Kálimnos, Kos, Nísiros, Tílos, Sími, Ródos, Kárpathos, Kásos.
Pireás to Ikaría, Sámos, Híos, Lésvos.
Pireás and **Rafína** to Síros, Dílos, Míkonos, Tínos, Ándros.
Pátra to Zákinthos (Zante), Kefallinía, Itháki, Kérkira (Corfu), Igumenítsa.
Kyllini to Zákinthos (Zante), Kefallinía, Itháki.
Vólos, Ágios Konstantínos and **Kimi** to Skíathos, Skópelos, Alónissos, Skíros.
Kavála to Thásos, Samothráki, Límnos.

2801 IGUMENÍTSA - KÉRKIRA (CORFU)

Kerkyra Lines — Journey 70 – 80 minutes

9 – 13 sailings per day in each direction.

2830 PIREÁS - IRÁKLIO

Minoan Lines — **Valid until Oct. 29**

Pireás		Iráklio		Iráklio		Pireás	
0930	→	1845	**A**	0930	→	1845	**A**
2100	→	0630		2100	→	0630	

A – July 9, 13, 15, 17, 20, 22, 25 – 27, 29, 31, Aug. 1 – 3, 5, 7 – 10, 12 – 14, 16, 17, 19, 21 – 24, 26, 28, 30, 31, Sept. 7.

Anek Lines / Blue Star Ferries

Pireás		Iráklio	Iráklio		Pireás
2100	→	0615	2100	→	0615

2846 PIREÁS - LEMESÓS (LIMASSOL)

Scandro Holding Ltd — **(no winter sailings)**

Pireás		Lemesós	Lemesós		Pireás
0100 ② **A**	→	0800 ③	1200 ⑦ **C**	→	1900 ①
0400 ⑤ **B**	→	1100 ⑥	1300 ③ **D**	→	2000 ④

A – June 3 - Sept. 2.
B – June 13, July 4 - Aug. 8, Aug 22, 29.
C – June 6 – 20, Aug. 3 – 31.
D – June 11, July 2 - Aug. 6, Aug. 20, 27 (also May 31).

2850 SPLIT - DUBROVNIK

Jadrolinija — **June 6 - Sept. 21 (no winter sailings)**

Split		Bol		Hvar		Korčula		Dubrovnik
1530	→	1645	→	1755	→	1925	→	2125
Dubrovnik		**Korčula**		**Hvar**		**Bol**		**Split**
0745	→	0940	→	1110	→	1210	→	1305

No service Split - Dubrovnik on Sept. 21. No services Dubrovnik - Split on June 6.

Kapetan Luka — **Apr. 1 - Oct. 31, (no winter sailings)**

Split		Brač		Hvar		Korčula		Mljet		Dubrovnik
0800	→	0830	→	0910	→	1030	→	1110	→	1235
Dubrovnik		**Mljet**		**Korčula**		**Hvar**		**Brač**		**Split**
1500	→	1625	→	1710	→	1840	→	1920	→	1945

2851 THESSALONIKI - IZMIR

Levante Ferries — **This service is currently suspended**

Thessaloniki		Izmir	Izmir		Thessaloniki
1900 ①③⑤	→	0900 ②④⑥	1900 ②④⑦	→	0900 ③⑤①

2875 VENEZIA - IGUMENÍTSA - PÁTRA

Anek Lines / Superfast Ferries

Venezia		Igumenítsa		Pátra	Pátra		Igumenítsa		Venezia
				Until June 7					
1400③ **e**	→	1630④*	→	2330④	2359① **c**	→	0745②	→	0900③
1230⑦	→	1500①*	→	2200①	2300④ **d**	→	0645⑤	→	0800⑥
1300⑥ **a**	→	1600⑦*	→	2300⑦	2200⑤	→	0545⑥	→	0700⑦
				June 8 – 30 and Sept. 10 – 30					
1230⑦ **f**	→	1530①*	→	2200①	2359④	→	0745⑤	→	0900⑥
1400⑥	→	1630⑦*	→	2330⑦	2300⑤ **h**	→	0530⑥	→	0630⑦
1230③	→	1500④*	→	2200④	2200①	→	0545②	→	0700③
				July 1 - September 9					
1230③	→	1530④* **b**	→	2200④	2200①	→	0545②	→	0700③
1400⑥	→	1630⑦*	→	2330⑦	2359④	→	0745⑤	→	0900⑥
				October 1 - December 31					
1230⑦	→	1530①*	→	2200①	2359④	→	0745⑤	→	0900⑥
1300③	→	1600④*	→	2300④	2300⑤	→	0530⑥	→	0600⑦
1300⑥	→	1530⑦*	→	2200⑦	2200①	→	0545②	→	0700③

No sailings on Dec. 26, 28.

a – On June 7 Venezia d. 1400, Igumenítsa a. 1630, Pátra a. 2330.
b – On July 3 a. 1500.
c – On June 2 Pátra d. 2200, Igumenítsa d. 0545, Venezia a. 0700.
d – On June 5 Pátra d. 2359, Igumenítsa d. 0745, Venezia a. 0900.
e – On June 4 Venezia d. 1230, Igumenítsa a. 1500, Pátra a. 2200.
f – Sails via Kérkira (Corfu), arriving 1415.
h – Sails via Kérkira (Corfu), departing 0645.
* – Arrival times.

2899 CROATIAN COASTAL SERVICES

Catamaran Line

Runs Pula - Unije - Susak - Mali Lošinj - Ilovik - Silba - Zadar and Split - Split (Resnik) airport.

G & V Line

Services operate from Rijeka and Zadar to the islands.

Jadrolinija

Local services operate from Rijeka, Zadar, Šibenik and Dubrovnik to the Islands.

Venezia Lines

Services run May to September linking Venezia with destinations on Croatia's Istrian Peninsula (Poreč, Pula, Rovinj), also with Piran in Slovenia.

Journey time 2 hours 30 minutes to 4 hours.

2900 BLACK SEA services

Irregular services operate on the following routes (freight services; also carry passengers).
Services subject to disruption and cancellation at short notice owing to the ongoing conflict in Ukraine.

Istanbul - Odesa	**Ukrferry**	
Burgas - Batumi	**PBM**	Certain sailings call at Novorossiysk
Varna - Batumi	**Ukrferry**	
Odesa - Batumi	**Ukrferry**	Certain sailings call at Samsun
Odesa - Poti	**Ukrferry**	

Odesa's ferry terminal is at Chornomorsk, 20km from Odesa, and is **currently closed**. Please confirm locally for dates and times.

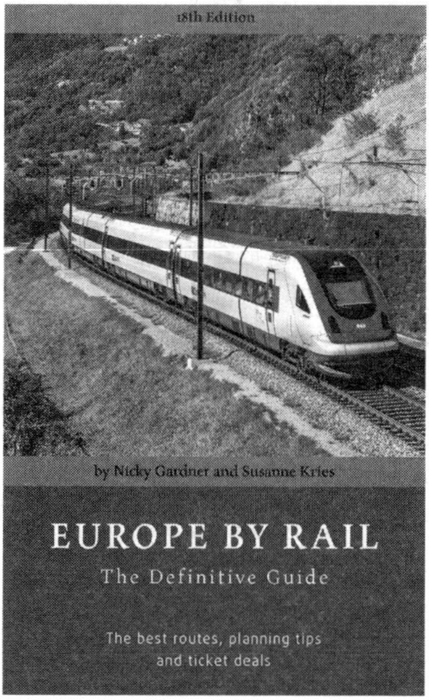

Exploring Europe by rail has never been easier. Written by Nicky Gardner and Susanne Kries, two highly experienced travellers, this guidebook contains all you need for planning your journey.

- ★ 50 routes
- ★ 544 pages
- ★ over 40,000 km of journeys
- ★ over 30 countries
- ★ tips on fares and ticketing
- ★ detailed route descriptions
- ★ sketch maps for each route
- ★ index maps which show all routes
- ★ suggestions for overnight stays

... and a very fine read!

The 18th edition of *Europe by Rail,* published in October 2024, has better coverage of France, Spain and Poland, improved ferry and bus connections, and a new section on travel apps. It is available directly from European Rail Timetable Ltd, all good bookshops and online retailers.

www.EuropeByRail.eu

Liège Guillemins station (photo © Erzsi Molnár / dreamstime.com)

71 (Summer) STUTTGART, MÜNCHEN and WIEN - VENEZIA, LA SPEZIA and ROMA

SERVICE JULY 14 - DECEMBER 13. For services until July 13 see page 72

train type	*RJ*	*RJ*	*NJ*	*NJ*	*NJ*	*NJ*	*NJ*	*NJ*
train number	**131**	**133**	**295**	**40233**	**295**	**40233**	**237**	**40466**
notes								
notes	✕	✕	**EQ**	**AP**	**DP**	**CR**	**G**	**B**
Stuttgart Hbf d.	...	...	...	...	...	...	2029	...
München Hbf d.	...	...	2009	...	2008	...	│	...
München Ost d.	...	...	2019	...	2020	...	2354	...
Wien Hbf d.	0624	1224	│	1918	│	1918	│	2139
Wien Meidling d.	0631	1231	│	1925	│	1925	│	2147
Bruck an der Mur d.	0815	1415	│	2126	│	2126	│	│
Linz Hbf d.	│	│	│	│	│	│	│	2310
Salzburg Hbf d.	│	│	│	│	2202	│	0214	0214
Klagenfurt Hbf d.	1021	1621	2202	2338	│	2338	│	│
Villach Hbf d.	1049	1649	0055	0055	0101	0134	0500	0500
Tarvisio ▦ a.	1111	1711	0119	0119	0125	0157	0523	0523
Udine a.	1216	1816	│	│	│	│	0623	0623
Venezia Mestre a.	1402	1952	│	│	│	│	0822	0822
Venezia Santa Lucia a.	1414	2004	│	│	│	│	0834	0834
Padova a.	...	...	0457	│	│	0457	...	...
Verona Porta Nuova a.	...	...	0551	│	│	0551	...	...
Milano Rogoredo a.	...	...	0742	│	│	0742	...	...
Genova Piazza Principe a.	...	...	...	│	│	...	...	...
La Spezia Centrale a.	...	...	...	│	│	...	...	...
Bologna Centrale a.	...	...	...	0536	0515	...	...	...
Rimini a.	...	...	...	│	│	...	...	...
Ancona a.	...	...	...	│	│	...	...	...
Firenze Campo di Marte a.	...	...	...	0642	0648	...	...	...
Pisa Centrale a.	...	...	...	│	│	...	...	...
Livorno Centrale a.	...	...	...	│	│	...	...	...
Roma Tiburtina a.	...	...	...	1105	1005	...	...	...

train type	*RJ*	*RJ*	*NJ*	*NJ*	*NJ*	*NJ*	*NJ*	*NJ*
train number	**132**	**130**	**236**	**40236**	**40294**	**40294**	**294**	**294**
notes								
notes	✕	✕	**G**	**B**	**CR**	**AP**	**EQ**	**DP**
Roma Tiburtina d.	...	...	...	...	...	1730	...	2017
Livorno Centrale d.	...	...	...	...	...	│	...	│
Pisa Centrale d.	...	...	...	...	...	│	...	│
Firenze Campo di Marte d.	...	...	...	...	...	2148	...	2231
Ancona d.	...	...	...	...	...	│	...	│
Rimini d.	...	...	...	...	...	│	...	│
Bologna Centrale d.	...	...	...	...	...	2254	...	2345
La Spezia Centrale d.	...	...	...	...	...	│	...	│
Genova Piazza Principe d.	...	...	...	...	...	│	...	│
Milano Rogoredo d.	...	...	...	...	2126	│	2126	│
Verona Porta Nuova d.	...	...	...	...	2258	│	2258	│
Padova d.	...	...	...	...	2343	│	2343	│
Venezia Santa Lucia d.	0956	1552	2105	2105	│	│	│	│
Venezia Mestre d.	1008	1604	2117	2117	│	│	│	│
Udine d.	1028	1744	2247	2247	│	│	│	│
Tarvisio ▦ d.	1249	1849	0005	0005	0300	0335	0300	0335
Villach Hbf a.	1311	1911	0027	0027	0323	0357	0323	0358
Klagenfurt Hbf a.	1337	1937	│	│	0438	0438	0649	0649
Salzburg Hbf a.	│	│	0300	0300	│	│	│	│
Linz Hbf a.	│	│	│	0558	│	│	│	│
Bruck an der Mur a.	1543	2143	│	│	0639	0639	│	│
Wien Meidling a.	1729	2329	│	0751	0857	0857	│	│
Wien Hbf a.	1736	2336	│	0758	0904	0904	│	│
München Ost a.	...	...	0550	...	...	...	│	│
München Hbf a.	...	...	│	...	...	...	0920	0920
Stuttgart Hbf a.	...	...	0838	...	...	...	...	...

A – *ÖBB nightjet* – 🛏 1, 2 cl., ▬ 2 cl. (4, 6 berth), [2] 🍷 Wien - Roma and v.v.
B – *ÖBB nightjet* – 🛏 1, 2 cl., ▬ 2 cl. (4, 6 berth), [2] 🍷 Wien - Venezia and v.v.
C – *ÖBB nightjet* – 🛏 1, 2 cl., ▬ 2 cl. (4, 6 berth), [2] 🍷 Wien - Milano and v.v.
D – *ÖBB nightjet* – 🛏 1, 2 cl., ▬ 2 cl. (4, 6 berth), [2] 🍷 München - Roma and v.v.
E – *ÖBB nightjet* – 🛏 1, 2 cl., ▬ 2 cl. (4, 6 berth), [2] 🍷 München - Milano and v.v.
G – *ÖBB nightjet* – 🛏 1, 2 cl., ▬ 2 cl. (4, 6 berth), [2] 🍷 Stuttgart - Wien and v.v.

P – July 14 - Sept. 28.
Q – Sept. 29 - Dec. 13.
R – July 14 - Dec. 13.

2025 European Rail Timetable Price List

Printed seasonal edition (published two times a year in January and June): £24.99

Monthly digital edition: £14.99. Beyond Europe digital edition: £4.99.

Annual subscription for 12 digital editions: £135.00

Annual subscription for 12 digital editions, together with two printed copies: £179.99

Two year printed subscription (four consecutive printed editions): £94.99

Special bundle deal which includes an annual subscription for 12 digital editions and two printed timetables, together with the latest Rail Map Europe and the 18th edition of the Europe by Rail guide book: £199.99

Note: Prices quoted do not include postage and packaging.

For details of other products and to order on-line visit **www.europeanrailtimetable.eu**

By post to: 28 Monson Way, Oundle, Northamptonshire, PE8 4QG (cheques payable to European Rail Timetable Limited)

✆ +44 (0) 1832 270198 (Monday to Friday 1000 – 1600)

AW 2nd class CARDIFF - SWANSEA - SOUTH WEST WALES 136

Amended service on ⑦ August 3 - September 14

	⑦	⑦🍷	⑦🍷	⑦	⑦	⑦	⑦	⑦	⑦	⑦	⑦	⑦A	⑦S	⑦	⑦🍷	⑦	⑦A	⑦	⑦	⑦🍷	⑦	⑦A	⑦🍷	⑦
Manchester Piccadilly **149** d.	...	...	...	...	...	...	...	...	...	...	...	...	🍷	...	0930	...	...	...	...	1128	...	...	1231	...
ardiff Central **133** d.	...	...	...	...	0824	0859	...	...	0950	1048	...	1130	1137	...	1256	...	1335	...	...	1450	...	1540	1556	...
ridgend **133** d.	...	...	...	...	0844	0922	...	...	1009	1106	...	1150	1156	...	1314	...	1355	...	...	1509	...	1601	1618	...
ort Talbot **133** d.	...	...	...	...	0859	0937	...	...	1023	1121	...	1202	1211	...	1329	...	1409	...	...	1523	...	1613	1632	...
eath **133** d.	...	...	...	...	0907	0945	...	...	1030	1128	...	1210	1219	...	1336	...	1416	...	...	1530	...	1621	1639	...
wansea **133** a.	...	...	...	...	0921	0959	...	...	1045	1142	...	1221	1234	...	1350	...	1428	...	...	1545	...	1632	1652	...
wansea **145** d.	...	...	...	...	0944	1001	1027	1050	1057	1145	...	1232	1241	1307	1352	...	1435	...	1458	1551	...	1640	1658	1717
lanelli **145** d.	...	...	...	...	1003	1017	1043	1106	1115	1204	...	1249	1259	1323	1409	...	1452	...	1515	1608	...	1657	1715	1733
armarthen **145** a.	...	...	...	...	1035	1043	1111	1132	1148	1235	...	1316	1331	1349	1441	...	1519	...	1541	1640	...	1724	1749	1757
armarthen d.	0748	0755	0930	1003	1035	1044	...	1136	1149	1237	1249	...	1336	1355	1442	1451	...	1533	1545	1641	1658	...	1750	1801
/hitland d.	0804	0811	0946	1019	1052	1100	...	1159f	1205	1252	1306	...	1351	1411	1457	1513g	...	1548	1609h	1656	1715	...	1805	1817
Tenby a.	0833	|	|	1049	|	1124	...	1232	|	|	1330	...	|	1440	|	1536	...	|	1639	|	1739	...	|	1847
Pembroke Dock a.	0905	|	|	1121	|	...	...	1304	|	|	...	...	|	1512	|	...	...	|	1711	|	...	...	|	1919
larbeston Road ⊗ d.	...	0826	1001	...	1107	...	...	...	1219	1306	...	...	1406	...	1511	...	...	1602	...	1710	...	...	1819	...
averfordwest d.	...	0835	1010	...	1116	...	...	...	|	1315	...	...	1415	...	1521	...	...	|	...	1719	...	...	1828	...
ilford Haven a.	...	0853	1028	...	1134	...	...	...	|	1331	...	...	1438	...	1543	...	...	|	...	1741	...	...	1851	...
Fishguard Harbour a.	...	...	...	...	...	...	...	...	1242	...	...	...	...	...	...	...	...	1624	...	...	...	...	...	...

	⑦🍷	⑦🍷	⑦	⑦🍷	⑦🍷	⑦	⑦🍷	⑦	⑦
Manchester Piccadilly **149** d.	1330	1430	...	1530	1630	...	1730	1830	1930
ardiff Central **133** d.	1647	1753	...	1851	1955	...	2054	2150	2251
ridgend **133** d.	1706	1811	...	1909	2014	...	2112	2209	2310
ort Talbot **133** d.	1720	1826	...	1924	2030	...	2127	2225	2324
eath **133** d.	1727	1833	...	1933	2038	...	2134	2232	2332
wansea **133** a.	1740	1847	...	1948	2052	...	2148	2247	2347
wansea **145** d.	1744	1849	1934	1951	...	2101	2200	2252	2349
lanelli **145** d.	1801	1907	1951	2010	...	2121	2218	2310	0007
armarthen **145** a.	1828	1939	2017	2043	...	2155	2250	2339	0036
armarthen d.	...	1940	2026	2043	...	2156	2252	...	...
/hitland d.	...	1955	2042	2059	...	2211	2307	...	...
Tenby a.	...	|	2111	|	...	|	|	...	...
Pembroke Dock a.	...	|	2143	|	...	|	|	...	...
larbeston Road ⊗ d.	...	2009	...	2113	...	2226	2321	...	...
averfordwest d.	...	2018	...	|	...	2234	2334j	...	...
ilford Haven a.	...	2040	...	|	...	2250	2356	...	...
Fishguard Harbour a.	...	...	...	2135	...	...	...	...	...

	⑦🍷	⑦🍷	⑦🍷	⑦🍷	⑦	⑦	⑦A	⑦🍷	⑦
Fishguard Harbour d.	...	...	...	...	...	...	...	...	...
Milford Haven d.	...	...	...	0901	...	...	...	1100	...
Haverfordwest d.	...	...	...	0916	...	...	...	1116	...
Clarbeston Road ⊗ d.	...	...	...	0924	...	...	...	1124	...
Pembroke Dock d.	...	...	...	|	...	0913	...	|	...
Tenby d.	...	...	...	|	...	0944	...	|	1130
Whitland d.	...	...	...	0938	...	1013	...	1140	1155
Carmarthen a.	...	...	...	0953	...	1029	...	1157	1212
Carmarthen **145** d.	...	0853	...	0957	1024	1048	1125	1201	...
Llanelli **145** d.	...	0922	...	1025	1048	1117	1153	1229	...
Swansea **145** a.	...	0942	...	1043	1105	1137	1211	1247	...
Swansea **133** d.	0841	...	0950	1047	...	...	1223	1253	...
Neath **133** d.	0852	...	1001	1059	...	...	1235	1305	...
Port Talbot **133** d.	0859	...	1008	1106	...	...	1242	1313	...
Bridgend **133** d.	0915	...	1025	1122	...	...	1255	1329	...
Cardiff Central **133** a.	0935	...	1048	1143	...	...	1316	1349	...
Manchester Piccadilly **149** a.	1311	...	1415	1515	...	...	...	1715	...

	⑦🍷	⑦	⑦🍷	⑦A	⑦	⑦🍷	⑦	⑦🍷	⑦A	⑦🍷	⑦	⑦🍷	⑦	⑦	⑦A	⑦T	⑦	⑦🍷	⑦	⑦	⑦	⑦🍷	⑦	⑦	⑦
Fishguard Harbour d.	...	...	1303	...	...	...	...	...	...	...	...	1639	...	...	...	...	...	...	...	...	...	2146	...	...	...
ilford Haven d.	1154	...	|	...	...	1341	...	1504	...	1600	...	|	...	1741	...	...	...	1900	...	...	2040	|	...	2255	2355
averfordwest d.	1209	...	|	...	...	1356	...	1521	...	1615	...	|	...	1756	...	...	...	1915	...	...	2056	|	...	2311	0011
larbeston Road ⊗ d.	1217	...	1325	...	...	1404	...	1529	...	1623	...	1701	...	1804	...	...	...	1923	...	...	2104	2208	...	2319	0019
Pembroke Dock d.	|	1157	|	...	...	|	1409	|	...	|	1607	|	...	|	...	...	1816	|	1936	...	|	|	2201	|	|
Tenby d.	|	1228	|	...	1335	|	1440	|	*1540*	|	1639	|	1745	|	...	...	1850	|	2007	...	|	|	2232	|	|
/hitland d.	1231	1257	1338	...	1400	1418	1511	1543	*1605*	1637	1709	1721g	1810	1820	...	...	1920	1937	2037	...	2119	2221	2301	2334	0034
armarthen a.	1247	1315	1355	...	1417	1433	1530	1558	*1622*	1652	1727	1738	1827	1837	...	...	1938	1952	2054	...	2136	2238	2319	2351	0051
armarthen **145** d.	1251	1321	1358	1415	...	1441	1532	1602	1630	1656	1730	1739	...	1839	1920	...	1946	2001	2056	2115	2138	2240	...	...	...
lanelli **145** d.	1319	1350	1427	1446	...	1509	1603	1630	1657	1724	1755	1809	...	1903	1954	2005	2015	2029	2122	2139	2207	2309	...	...	...
wansea **145** a.	1337	1407	1446	1504	...	1529	1620	1648	1713	1742	1812	1829	...	1919	2012	2028	2032c	2047	2143	2201	2226	2328	...	...	...
wansea **133** d.	1341	...	1453	1523	...	1532	...	1653	1721	1751	...	1837	...	1939	2020	2040	...	2055	...	2208	2230	2332	...	...	...
eath **133** d.	1353	...	1505	1535	...	1544	...	1705	1734	1803	...	1850	...	|	2032	2051	...	2108	...	2220	2242	2344	...	...	...
ort Talbot **133** d.	1401	...	1513	1542	...	1551	...	1712	1742	1810	...	1858	...	|	2039	2100	...	2116	...	2228	2249	2351	...	...	...
ridgend **133** d.	1417	...	1529	1554	...	1607	...	1728	1754	1826	...	1914	...	|	2052	2115	...	2133	...	2244	2305	0006	...	...	...
ardiff Central **133** a.	1436	...	1549	1615	...	1628	...	1749	1816	1846	...	1937	...	2022	2114	2139	...	2153	...	2305	2326	0026	...	...	...
Manchester Piccadilly **149** a.	1814	...	1914	...	...	2015	...	2115	...	2214	...	...	...	...	...	...	...	...	...	...	...	...	...	...	...

A – To/from London Paddington (operated by GW, see Table **133**). Conveys (12) and 🍷.
S – From Shrewsbury (Table **149**).

T – From Shrewsbury (Table **145**).
c – Connects with train in previous column.
f – Arrives 1152.

g – Arrives 6 minutes earlier.
h – Arrives 1601.
j – Arrives 2329.

AW CARDIFF - HEREFORD - CREWE - MANCHESTER 149

Amended service on ⑦ August 3 - September 14

	⑦ 2	⑦ 2🍷	⑦ 2	⑦ 2🍷	⑦2 Sa	⑦ 2	⑦2 S🍷	⑦ 2a	⑦2 M🍷	⑦ 2	⑦2 S🍷	⑦ 2🍷	⑦2 M🍷	⑦ 2	⑦2 M🍷	⑦ 2🍷	⑦2 F🍷	⑦ 2	⑦2 M🍷	⑦ 2🍷	⑦ M2	⑦ 2	⑦2 M🍷	⑦ 2	⑦ 2	⑦ M2
ardiff Central .. **133** § d.	...	...	...	0842	0939	...	1053	1114	1150	...	1253	1323	1351	...	1453	1522	1556	...	1641	1716	1753	...	1853	1939	2108	2330
lewport **133** § d.	...	...	...	0901	0958	...	1107	1128	1204	...	1306	1337	1404	...	1506	1535	1610	...	1655	1730	1808	...	1907	1952	2121	2344
wmbrân d.	...	...	...	0912	1009	...	1117	1138	1214	...	1318	1348	1415	...	1517	1545	1620	...	1706	1741	1818	...	1922	2003	2132	2354
ontypool & New Inn d.	...	...	...	0917	1015	...	|	1144	|	...	|	1354	|	...	|	1551	1625	...	1712	1747	1823	...	|	2008	2137	0002
bergavenny d.	...	...	...	0927	1025	...	1131	1153	1226	...	1332	1405	1428	...	1531	1600	1635	...	1722	1757	1833	...	1935	2018	2147	0010
ereford d.	...	...	...	0953	1050	...	1157	1220	1252	...	1401	1434	1453	...	1605j	1629	1701	...	1748	1823	1858	...	2002	2045	2212	0034
eominster d.	...	...	...	1006	1104	...	1210	|	1305	...	1415	|	1506	...	1619	|	1714	...	1802	|	1912	...	2015	2058	2225	—
udlow d.	...	...	...	1017	1115	...	1221	1240	1315	...	1427	1455	1517	...	1629	1650	1725	...	1813	1844	1923	...	2026	2109	2236	...
raven Arms **145** d.	...	...	...	1025	1123	...	|	1249	1324	...	|	1503	1525	...	|	1659	1733	...	1822	|	1932	...	|	2118	2245	...
hurch Stretton **145** d.	...	...	...	1034	1132	...	|	1258	1332	...	|	1512	1534	...	|	1707	1742	...	1831	|	1942	...	|	2127	2254	⑦
hrewsbury **145** a.	...	...	...	1051	1150	...	1250	1313	1349	...	1454	1527	1550	...	1657	1722	1757	...	1846	1911	1958	...	2053	2145	2310	K2
hrewsbury d.	0825	0938	1020	1054	1150	1220	1255	1326	1352	1420	1455	1529	1550	1620	1658	1731	1758	1820	1857	1926	1959	2020	2055	2146	2313	2348
Vhitchurch d.	0852	1004	1047	|	1207	1247	|	|	1408	1447	|	|	1607	1647	|	|	1815	1847	|	|	2015	2047	|	|	2339	|
rewe a.	0917	1026	1113	1126	1227	1312	1328	|	1430	1512	1528	|	1627	1712	1730	|	1835	1912	1927	|	2035	2112	2128	|	0002	0021
Chester **146 150** a.	...	|	...	|	|	...	|	1420	|	...	|	1624	|	...	|	1825	|	...	|	2026	|	...	|	2240	0024	0044
Holyhead **150** a.	...	|	...	|	|	...	|	...	|	...	|	...	|	...	|	2018	|	...	|	2220	|	...	|	...	...	...
tockport a.	...	1059	...	|	1259	...	1401	...	1502	...	1602	...	1702	...	1802	...	1903	...	2001	...	2102	...	2203	...	...	...
anchester Piccadilly a.	...	1114	...	1214	1311	...	1415	...	1515	...	1615	...	1715	...	1814	...	1914	...	2015	...	2115	...	2214	...	...	...

	⑦ 2	⑦2 M🍷	⑦2 M🍷	⑦ 2🍷	⑦ 2	⑦2 M🍷	⑦ 2🍷	⑦2 M🍷	⑦ 2	⑦2 C🍷	⑦ 2🍷	⑦2 M🍷	⑦ 2	⑦ F🍷	⑦ 2🍷	⑦2 S🍷	⑦ 2	⑦2 M🍷	⑦ 2🍷	⑦ C2	⑦ 2	⑦ C2	⑦ 2	⑦ 2	⑦ 2	⑦ 2
anchester Piccadilly d.	...	...	0930	1030	...	1128	...	1231	...	1330	...	1430	...	1530	...	1630	...	1730	...	1830	...	1930	2030	...	2135	...
tockport d.	...	...	0941	1040	...	1139	...	1241	...	1340	...	1440	...	1540	...	1640	...	1740	...	1840	...	1940	2040	...	2146	...
Holyhead **150** d.	...	...	|	|	...	|	1019	|	...	|	...	|	...	|	...	|	...	|	1625	|	...	|	|	...	|	...
Chester **146 150** d.	...	...	|	|	...	|	1229	|	...	|	1430	|	...	|	1630	|	...	|	1826	|	...	|	|	...	|	2302
rewe d.	...	...	1010	1110	1125	1210	|	1310	1320	1410	|	1510	1520	1610	|	1710	1720	1810	|	1910	1920	2010	2110	2145	2214	2330
Vhitchurch d.	...	...	1028	|	1148	1227	|	|	1342	1427	|	|	1542	1627	|	|	1742	1827	|	|	1942	2027	2130	2207	2234	2352
hrewsbury a.	...	...	1049	1142	1216	1246	1321	1344	1411	1447	1522	1539	1611	1645	1722	1741	1811	1848	1920	1942	2011	2045	2159	2236	2302	0020
hrewsbury **145** d.	*0750**	0930	1050	1143	...	1247	1325	1344	...	1447	1523	1543	...	1646	1723	1743	...	1848	1922	1947	...	2046	2205	...	...	...
hurch Stretton **145** d.	*0820**	0945	1104	|	...	1301	1340	|	...	1502	1537	|	...	1701	1737	|	...	1903	1936	|	...	2101	2219	...	...	...
raven Arms **145** d.	*0840**	0953	1112	|	...	1309	1349	|	...	1510	1545	|	...	1710	1745	|	...	1911	1944	|	...	2109	2227	...	...	...
udlow d.	*0855**	1002	1121	1211	...	1318	1359	1410	...	1518	1554	1609	...	1718	1754	1808	...	1919	1953	2013	...	2117	2236	...	...	...
eominster d.	*0920**	1013	1131	1222	...	1328	|	1423	...	1529	|	1620	...	1729	|	1819	...	1930	|	2025	...	2128	2246	...	...	...
ereford d.	1005	1029	1147	1240	...	1344	1424	1440	...	1545	1617	1639	...	1745	1817	1837	...	1946	2017	2042	...	2144	2305	...	...	...
bergavenny d.	1027	1052	1209	1304	...	1406	1446	1503	...	1607	1639	1702	...	1807	1839	1900	...	2008	2039	2105	...	2206	2327	...	...	...
ontypool & New Inn d.	1038	1102	1219	|	...	|	1456	|	...	|	1649	|	...	1817	1849	|	...	2018	|	|	...	2216	2337	...	...	...
wmbrân d.	1043	1107	1224	1317	...	1406	1501	1516	...	1619	1654	1716	...	1822	1854	1913	...	2023	2051	2118	...	2221	2342	...	...	...
lewport **133** § a.	1056	1120	1239	1331	...	1432	1513	1529	...	1631	1706	1730	...	1834	1906	1928	...	2035	2105	2130	...	2233	2356	...	...	...
ardiff Central .. **133** § a.	1111	1134	1254	1350	...	1448	1527	1555	...	1647	1722	1746	...	1851	1922	1943	...	2049	2123	2145	...	2250	0017	...	...	...

C – From/to Carmarthen (Table **136**).
F – From/to Fishguard Harbour(Table **136**).
M – From/to Milford Haven (Table **136**).

S – From/to Swansea (Table **136**).
a – Conveys 🍷 from Shrewsbury.
j – Arrives 1558.

§ – See also Tables **115** and **117**.
* – Connection by 🚌.

Products for sale from European Rail Timetable Limited

3rd Edition 3rd Revision of the
Rail Map Europe.
£12.99 + p&p

European Rail Timetable
Two seasonal editions.
£49.98 + p&p

18th Edition of the
Europe by Rail guidebook.
£20.99 + p&p

Autumn 2024 digital edition of the
Beyond Europe Timetable.
£4.99

Order on-line at **www.europeanrailtimetable.eu**
Telephone **01832 270198**

2025 European Rail Timetable Price List

Printed seasonal edition (published two times a year in January and June): £24.99

Monthly digital edition: £14.99. Beyond Europe digital edition: £4.99.

Annual subscription for 12 digital editions: £135.00

Annual subscription for 12 digital editions, together with two printed copies: £179.99

Two year printed subscription (four consecutive printed editions): £94.99

Special bundle deal which includes an annual subscription for 12 digital editions and two printed timetables, together with the latest Rail Map Europe and the 18th edition of the Europe by Rail guide book: £199.99

Note: Prices quoted do not include postage and packaging.

For details of other products and to order on-line visit **www.europeanrailtimetable.eu**

By post to: 28 Monson Way, Oundle, Northamptonshire, PE8 4QG (cheques payable to European Rail Timetable Limited)

✆ +44 (0) 1832 270198 (Monday to Friday 1000 – 1600)

EUROPEAN RAIL PASSES

Rail passes represent excellent value for train travellers who are touring around Europe (or parts of it) or making a number of journeys within a short period. They can offer substantial savings over point-to-point tickets, as well as greater flexibility.

The principal pass schemes for Europe are **Interrail** for residents of Europe, and **Eurail** for those resident outside Europe. Both schemes have a choice of **Global** passes covering 33 countries, or **One Country Passes** for individual countries. Note, however, that you cannot use the pass in your country of residence. Passes are available in either a mobile (for use on your smart phone) or the more traditional paper format.

Passes either cover a specified number of consecutive days, or are of the *flexi* type where you get so many 'travel days' within a specified period (you record your travel dates on each type of pass). Free travel requires the use of a travel day, whereas discounted travel does not.

Passes generally cover the ordinary services of the national rail companies, but supplements often have to be paid for travel on high-speed services, night trains, and 'global price' trains. Independent rail operators may not accept passes but may give discounts to passholders.

Interrail and Eurail

Europe-wide or single-country passes website: www.interrail.eu www.eurail.com

Anyone of any age can buy a pass, either for pretty much the whole of Europe, or for an individual country. **Global** passes cover 33 countries of Europe and can either be *Continuous* passes for a set number of consecutive days or months, or *Flexi* passes for a certain number of travel days within a period of one or two months (you choose the travel days as you go along, writing the date on the pass). **One Country Passes** are all flexi passes for a certain number of days within one month (sometimes there is more than one country, as with the Benelux pass).

The two pass schemes (Interrail and Eurail) are now very similar, but Interrail passes are for **residents of Europe**, whilst Eurail passes are for those resident **outside Europe**. Turkey, Russia and the CIS countries count as Europe for this purpose. You may need proof of residence.

Passes can be purchased up to eleven months before travel begins. It's best to buy the pass online or in your own country before travelling, although most passes can also be purchased at major stations in Europe. Note, however, that the 4 day Global pass cannot be purchased from stations. Recommended retail prices are now the same for both Interrail and Eurail and are in Euros as shown below, but prices may vary between different outlets. At certain times of year special offer prices may be available. All passes are either for second class or first class travel (of course first class passes can also be used to travel in second class).

Passes come with a travel diary which has to be filled in with each journey. You cannot use the pass in your own country of residence. However, with an Interrail Global Pass you can make one outbound and one inbound journey in your country of residence (see next page).

INTERRAIL / EURAIL GLOBAL PASS - valid in 33 countries:

Austria, Belgium, Bosnia-Herzegovina, Bulgaria, Croatia, Czech Republic, Denmark, Estonia, Finland, France, Germany, Great Britain, Greece, Hungary, Ireland (including Northern Ireland), Italy, Latvia, Lithuania, Luxembourg, Montenegro, Netherlands, North Macedonia, Norway, Poland, Portugal, Romania, Serbia, Slovakia, Slovenia, Spain, Sweden, Switzerland and Turkey.

NOT VALID in the passholder's country of residence.

PRICES - INTERRAIL / EURAIL GLOBAL PASS - FIRST CLASS

Current prices	Adult (28-59) 1st cl.	Senior (60+) 1st cl.	Youth (12-27) 1st cl.	Child * (under 12) 1st cl.
FLEXI PASSES:				
4 days within 1 month	€359	€323	€269	€0
5 days within 1 month	€404	€364	€303	€0
7 days within 1 month	€484	€436	€363	€0
10 days within 2 months	€568	€511	€426	€0
15 days within 2 months	€702	€632	€527	€0
CONTINUOUS DAYS:				
15 days	€605	€545	€454	€0
22 days	€744	€670	€558	€0
1 month	€884	€796	€663	€0
2 months	€1049	€944	€787	€0
3 months	€1214	€1093	€911	€0

PRICES - INTERRAIL / EURAIL GLOBAL PASS - SECOND CLASS

Current prices	Adult (28-59) 2nd cl.	Senior (60+) 2nd cl.	Youth (12-27) 2nd cl.	Child * (under 12) 2nd cl.
FLEXI PASSES:				
4 days within 1 month	€283	€255	€212	€0
5 days within 1 month	€318	€286	€239	€0
7 days within 1 month	€381	€343	€286	€0
10 days within 2 months	€447	€402	€335	€0
15 days within 2 months	€553	€498	€415	€0
CONTINUOUS DAYS:				
15 days	€476	€428	€357	€0
22 days	€586	€527	€440	€0
1 month	€696	€626	€522	€0
2 months	€826	€743	€620	€0
3 months	€956	€860	€717	€0

* Child : two children per fare paying Adult (not Senior) travel free.

INTERRAIL / EURAIL ONE COUNTRY PASS

Covers any one of the participating countries below. **NOT** available for the passholder's country of residence. Note that Benelux passes (also the Eurail Scandinavia pass) actually cover more than one country. As with the Global pass, two children per fare paying Adult travel free.

Bosnia-Herzegovina and Montenegro do not have One Country Passes. There are some variations between Eurail and Interrail as shown below, for example Germany, Great Britain and Switzerland participate in the Interrail OCP scheme but not the Eurail OCP scheme as they have their own passes for overseas visitors (for Great Britain see under Britrail). The Scandinavia Pass only applies to Eurail, not Interrail.

Interrail: Germany. See page 585 for prices of the German Rail Pass

Interrail: Great Britain.
Eurail: Scandinavia (Norway, Sweden, Denmark, Finland combined).

	Adult 1st cl.	Senior 1st cl.	Youth 1st cl.	Adult 2nd cl.	Senior 2nd cl.	Youth 2nd cl.
3 days within 1 month	€276	€248	€207	€218	€196	€164
4 days within 1 month	€314	€283	€236	€247	€222	€185
5 days within 1 month	€346	€312	€260	€273	€246	€205
6 days within 1 month	€377	€339	€283	€297	€268	€223
8 days within 1 month	€427	€384	€320	€337	€302	€253

Norway, Spain, Sweden or Switzerland
Norway only available for 2nd class

	Adult 1st cl.	Senior 1st cl.	Youth 1st cl.	Adult 2nd cl.	Senior 2nd cl.	Youth 2nd cl.
3 days within 1 month	€245	€220	€184	€193	€174	€145
4 days within 1 month	€284	€256	€213	€223	€201	€167
5 days within 1 month	€317	€286	€238	€250	€226	€188
6 days within 1 month	€349	€314	€262	€274	€247	€208
8 days within 1 month	€404	€364	€303	€318	€287	€239

Austria, France or Italy.
Eurail France Pass: 1, 2 and 7 day passes also for sale outside Europe

	Adult 1st cl.	Senior 1st cl.	Youth 1st cl.	Adult 2nd cl.	Senior 2nd cl.	Youth 2nd cl.
3 days within 1 month	€210	€190	€158	€165	€149	€124
4 days within 1 month	€248	€223	€186	€196	€177	€147
5 days within 1 month	€283	€255	€212	€223	€201	€167
6 days within 1 month	€314	€283	€236	€247	€222	€185
8 days within 1 month	€371	€334	€278	€292	€263	€219

Benelux, Denmark, Finland, Ireland.
Benelux is Belgium, Netherlands and Luxembourg combined
Ireland includes Northern Ireland

	Adult 1st cl.	> Senior 1st cl.	Youth 1st cl.	Adult 2nd cl.	Senior 2nd cl.	Youth 2nd cl.
3 days within 1 month	€174	€156	€131	€137	€123	€103
4 days within 1 month	€209	€189	€157	€165	€149	€124
5 days within 1 month	€243	€219	€182	€191	€173	€143
6 days within 1 month	€273	€246	€205	€216	€194	€162
8 days within 1 month	€329	€297	€247	€259	€233	€194

Czech Republic, Estonia, Greece, Hungary, Portugal or Romania

	Adult 1st cl.	Senior 1st cl.	Youth 1st cl.	Adult 2nd cl.	Senior 2nd cl.	Youth 2nd cl.
3 days within 1 month	€133	€120	€100	€105	€94	€79
4 days within 1 month	€164	€148	€123	€129	€117	€97
5 days within 1 month	€193	€174	€145	€152	€137	€114
6 days within 1 month	€221	€200	€166	€175	€158	€131
8 days within 1 month	€273	€246	€205	€216	€194	€162

Bulgaria, Croatia, Latvia, Lithuania, North Macedonia, Poland, Serbia, Slovakia, Slovenia or Turkey

	Adult 1st cl.	Senior 1st cl.	Youth 1st cl.	Adult 2nd cl.	Senior 2nd cl.	Youth 2nd cl.
3 days within 1 month	€84	€76	€63	€67	€60	€50
4 days within 1 month	€107	€96	€80	€84	€76	€63
5 days within 1 month	€128	€115	€96	€100	€91	€75
6 days within 1 month	€150	€135	€113	€118	€107	€89
8 days within 1 month	€190	€170	€143	€150	€135	€113

Interrail and Eurail - continued

GREEK ISLANDS PASS

This is a special ferry pass available in both the Interrail and Eurail schemes. It is valid on ferries operated by the Attica Group, which includes Superfast Ferries, Blue Star Ferries and Hellenic Seaways. The 4 day pass is valid for five domestic trips on ferries within Greece. The 6 day pass is valid for two international trips between Italy and Greece plus four domestic trips in Greece. The 6 day pass includes accommodation in either 1st or 2nd class, also rail / bus transfers between Patras and Piraeus. Both passes give 30% discount on additional ferry trips.

	Adult 1st cl.	Senior 1st cl.	Youth 1st cl.	Adult 2nd cl.	Senior 2nd cl.	Youth 2nd cl.
4 days within 1 month	N/A	N/A	N/A	€1110	€99	€82
6 days within 1 month	€260	€233	€196	€235	€211	€176

OVERNIGHT TRAVEL

Passes do not include supplements for travel in sleeping car or couchette accommodation and these have to be purchased separately. Many overnight trains have a *global* price where the ticket price includes the sleeping accommodation - in these cases pass holders pay a specified supplement or passholder fare (see below for further details).

Holders of flexi passes travelling overnight and leaving before midnight need to record the date of departure in the travel diary, and of course the pass can be used for the whole of that day. Pass holders will not need to activate a second day on their pass for the day of arrival unless they board a second train (but the day of arrival does need to be within the overall validity of the pass). The rule can also be used for late evening trains arriving after midnight. If you need to use a connecting train having arrived overnight it may be worth buying a regular ticket to avoid having to use a travel day.

FREE TRAVEL TO THE BORDER, AIRPORT OR SEAPORT

Although it is not possible to purchase an Interrail pass for the holder's own country of residence, a Global pass entitles the holder to two free journeys (one outbound, one inbound) between any station in their country of residence and its border, an airport or seaport. Each journey must be completed in one day (no overnight stops allowed), at any time within the overall validity of the pass, or include a travel day if using a flexi pass. Details must be entered in the travel diary.

SUPPLEMENTS AND RESERVATION FEES

Required for certain types of high-speed or 'global price' train.

International day train examples, 2nd class (subject to change): France - Italy *TGV* €31; *Berlin - Warszawa Express* €5; *EC Switzerland - Italy* €11; *Eurostar* €30 - 35 (€38 - 43 in standard premier with 1st class pass); *TGV / ICE* France - Germany from €17; *TGV Lyria* (France - Switzerland) from €25; *ECB* Germany - Italy €13; *X2000* Stockholm - København €5.50. Note that from June 1 to September 1 reservation is compulsory for most international journeys from / to Germany on long-distance trains (€5.20) - the only exceptions are journeys services to / from Switzerland via Basel or Singen.

Higher fares apply if pass not valid in both countries.

Domestic examples (approximate; subject to alteration): **Croatia** *IC / ICN* €3.60. **Czech Republic** *SC* up to €2.90. **Finland** *Pendolino* €2.70. **France** *TGV* €10 limited allocation (otherwise €20), *Intercités* with compulsory reservation €10 / 20. **Hungary** *IC* €1.70 to 2.60. **Italy** *FA*, *FB* and *FR* €10 / €13, *IC* €3. **Netherlands** Intercity Direct between Schiphol and Rotterdam €2.90. **Norway** long-distance trains €4.40. **Poland** *EIP* €10, *EIC / TLK* €0.70. **Portugal** *AP / IC* €5. **Romania** *IC/IR* €1 - 3.60. **Serbia** €1.00. **Slovakia** *IC/EC* €5 - 1 **Slovenia** *IC / Pendolino* €4. **Spain** *AVE* €10, most other long-distanc trains €6.50, *Euromed* €6.50. **Sweden** *Snabbtåg* €5.70, *Snälltåget* I and regional services €3.10. **Switzerland** *IC* domestic 5 CHF, Berni Express observation car 28 - 36 CHF, Glacier Express 37 - 53 CH Golden Pass 5 - 25 CHF, Gotthard Panoramic Express 15 CHF, Choco late Train 59 CHF. **Turkey** no fees but mandatory on long distanc services.

Night trains: sleeping accommodation is typically €20 to €75 for couchette, and €35 to €175 for a berth in a sleeping car. Some trair also include reclining seats. Many night trains are globally priced an fares for passholders vary widely.

As some of the supplements / passholder fares can be rather high, it worth checking whether a regular advance purchase ticket might be better option, particularly if booked a month or two ahead. Supplement can often be avoided altogether by taking slower regional trains.

VALIDITY ON PRIVATE RAILWAYS

Passes are valid on the national railway companies in each country, plu many privately run railways (some give discounts). For details se www.interrail.eu, www.eurail.com, or the Traveller's Guide that come with your pass.

Selected details are as follows (subject to change): **Austria**: free trave on WESTbahn, GYSEV, RegioJet and ROeEE. **Czech Republic**: vali on Leo Express and RegioJet. **Denmark**: free travel on Go Collective DSB-Øresund / S-Tog, Nordjyske Jernbaner and Lokaltog. **France** SNCF bus services included. **Germany**: free on most regional service and many private companies. **Hungary**: GySEV/Raaberbahn service are included. **Italy**: free travel on Trenord and Leonardo Express (1s class only). **Netherlands**: privately run regional lines are includec **Norway**: Flåmsbana (Myrdal - Flåm) gives 30% discount. **Poland**: vali on Koleje Dolnośląskie, Przewozy Regionaine. **Spain**: FEVE is includec **Sweden**: most private operators are included. **Switzerland**: free trave on AB, ASM, AVA, BDWM, BLS, BLT, BOB, CJ, FART, FW, LEB, MBC MGB, MOB/MVR, NStCM, RA, RBS, RhB, SOB, SSIF, THURBO, TMF TPC, TPF, TRAVYS, TRN, WAB, and ZB. Others offer 25 - 50% discoun including ASM, BET, EB, G3AG, Jungfrau, LSMS, LSS, PB, RB, SMF Ism, SthB. Discounted fare on Gothard Panorama Express (rail and boa tour).

VALIDITY ON FERRY AND BUS SERVICES

Global passes includes free deck passage between Italy and Greece o SuperFast Ferries / Anek Lines (you pay port taxes and possibly a fue surcharge); free air-type seatsor dormitories for 1st class pass holders 30% discount if pass only valid in Italy or Greece. Many other ferr companies offer discounts (not usually on cabins), for example: Blue Sta Ferries 30%, Fjord Line 30%, Grimaldi 20%, Irish Ferries 30%, Minoa Ferries 20%, Polferries 20%, SNAV 20%, Tallink Silja 20% (high-season) up to 50% (low-season).

Most Swiss lakes give 50%. The following bus services in Scandinavi between Sweden and Finland are included; Luleå - Haparand (Länstrafiken Norrbotten), Haparanda - Tornio - Kemi (Net-matkat).

Other benefits are often available, such as hotel discounts, bike hir discounts, free entry to railway museums, and access to railway statio lounges.

Where to Buy your Pass

ACP Rail www.acprail.com

All Aboard www.allaboard.eu

Deutsche Bahn UK (German Railways) www.bahn.com
UK Booking Centre ✆ 08718 80 80 66

Eurail – buy at www.eurail.com or see www.eurailgroup.org for a list of sales partners. All participating European railway companies sell passes.

Ffestiniog Travel www.ffestiniogtravel.com
Former St Mary's Church, Tremadog, Porthmadog, Gwynedd LL49 9RA
✆ 01766 512400

French Railways www.sncf.com

International Rail www.internationalrail.com
PO Box 153, Alresford, Hampshire SO24 4AQ ✆ 0871 231 0790

Interrail www.interrail.eu.
All participating railway companies sell passes.

Interrail by National Rail www.myinterrail.co.uk

Rail Europe www.raileurope.co.uk
Also raileurope.de, raileurope.it, raileurope.es

RailTourGuide www.railtourguide.com
Suite 42, 7 - 15 Pink Lane, Newcastle upon Tyne, NE1 5DW
✆ 0191 246 0708

Switzerland Travel Centre www.stc.co.uk
2nd Floor, Techspace Whitechapel, 38 - 40 Commercial Road, London, E1 1LN ✆ 0207 420 4900
Visits by appointment only.

Trainseurope www.trainseurope.co.uk
4th Floor, Silverstream House, 45 Fitzroy Street, Fitzrovia, London, W1T 6EB ✆ 01354 660222 / 01354 707098
email: sales@trainseurope.co.uk.
Visits by appointment only.

Other useful websites:

www.seat61.com
www.ricksteves.com

BritRail

BritRail is a pass for overseas visitors to Great Britain, allowing unlimited travel on the national rail network in England, Scotland and Wales. It is not available to residents of Great Britain, Northern Ireland, the Isle of Man or the Channel Islands. Passes must be purchased before arriving in Britain. Youth prices apply to ages 16 to 25, senior applies to 60+. All passes are available for First or Standard class. For further details see www.britrail.com or www.acprail.com.

BRITRAIL CONSECUTIVE PASS

(USD prices)	Adult 1st cl.	Youth 1st cl.	Senior 1st cl.	Adult Std cl.	Youth Std cl.	Senior Std cl.
2 days	226	136	192	149	90	128
3 days	338	203	287	224	134	190
4 days	420	252	357	277	166	236
8 days	598	339	509	402	217	342
15 days	884	531	751	598	359	509
22 days	1123	674	955	748	449	636
1 month	1330	798	1131	884	531	751

BRITRAIL FLEXIPASS

(USD prices)	Adult 1st cl.	Youth 1st cl.	Senior 1st cl.	Adult Std cl.	Youth Std cl.	Senior Std cl.
2 days within 1 month	282	169	239	190	115	162
3 days within 1 month	420	252	357	284	171	242
4 days within 1 month	516	310	439	356	214	302
8 days within 1 month	759	456	645	509	306	433
15 days within 2 months	1134	680	964	766	460	651

BRITRAIL ENGLAND PASSES

The Britrail England Pass excludes Wales and Scotland, giving a saving of approximately 20%. Britrail South West and North of England Rover passes are also available. All three are available in consecutive and flexi versions (no 2-day passes).

BRITRAIL LONDON PLUS PASS

This 'flexi' pass allows unlimited rail travel in London and the surrounding area. You can visit such places as Canterbury, Salisbury, Bristol, Bath, Oxford, Cambridge, Stratford-Upon-Avon, Worcester, Ely, Kings Lynn, and anywhere on the coast between Harwich to Weymouth.

(USD prices)	Adult 1st cl.	Youth 1st cl.	Senior 1st cl.	Adult Std cl.	Youth Std cl.	Senior Std cl.
3 days within 1 month	244	159	208	174	113	148
4 days within 1 month	282	184	240	212	138	181
8 days within 1 month	400	260	340	295	192	251

BRITRAIL SCOTLAND PASSES

Three different passes are available, all standard class adult passes: Spirit of Scotland covers the whole country; available as 4 days within 8 days, or 8 days within 15 days. The other areas are Central Scotland (3 days consecutive), and Highlands (4 days within 8 days).

M-PASS

All Britrail Passes are available as a mobile ticket on your mobile phone (saving shipping cost) - see www.acprail.com.

DISCOUNTS

Saver Discount: groups of 3 to 9 people receive a discount of up to 20%. Passes must be of the same type (BritRail, BritRail England and BritRail SouthWest passes only) and duration and the party must travel together at all times. Cannot be combined with the family discount.

Family Discount: if any adult or senior pass is purchased, one accompanying child (aged 5 - 15) may receive a free pass of the same type and duration. Any further children travelling receive a 50% discount. All children under 5 travel free.

Other International Passes

BAYERN-BÖHMEN TICKET

One day's unlimited travel on regional trains in the German state of Bavaria together with trains operated by Czech Railways (categories R, Ex, Sp and Os) in the entire border area of the Czech Republic with Germany. Validity in the Czech Republic encompasses the border region from Liberec (near the Polish border) to České Budějovice (near the Austrian border) via Karlovy Vary and Plzeň. Valid from 0900 Mondays to Fridays and all day at weekends and on public holidays. Price €35 (€37 from staffed ticket offices in Germany); for groups of 2–5 people add €10.60 per extra person; up to three children (up to the age of 15) travel free of charge. Available on-line or from DB sales points and ticket machines within the area of validity.

EUREGIO TICKET MAAS-RHEIN

One days unlimited travel in border region Belgium / Netherlands / Germany by rail and bus (covers Liège, Hasselt, Maastricht, Roermond, Aachen, Düren). In Germany and Belgium covers only local trains and buses. Price €22.90, bike €4.60. At weekends / public holidays valid as a family ticket (2 adults plus 3 children under 12).

PASSBASK

One day's travel in the area between Bayonne in France and San Sebastian in Spain on SNCF trains (includes *TGV* but not night trains) and EuskoTren services. A barrier pass for EuskoTren should be obtained at Hendaye station. Price €14.30, child aged 4 - 11 €9.50. Avaiable at all stations between Lasarte - Oria and Hendaye, ticket offices or ticket vending machines.

SAAR-LOR-LUX TICKET

One day's unlimited 2nd class travel on Saturday or Sunday throughout Saarland (i.e. Saarbrücken area of Germany, local trains only), Lorraine (i.e. Metz, Nancy, Épinal area of France) and all CFL trains in Luxembourg. Price €27 (€29 over the counter in Germany); for groups of 2 - 5 people add €11 per extra person. Not valid on *TGV* or *ICE* trains. Available at DB sales points and ticket machines in the area of validity.

BODENSEE TICKET

Unlimited travel by rail, bus and ferry in the border region of Austria / Germany / Switzerland surrounding the Bodensee (Lake Constance). One day 47 CHF / €42, 3 days 74 CHF / €65. Discounts for children and families. Not valid on ICE / IC / EC / RJX / RJ trains In Germany or on Friederikshafen - Konstanz catamarans. Valid on Friedrichshafen - Romanshorn and Konstanz - Meersburg ferries and 25% discount on VSU cruises. Zonal versions also available for smaller areas, One day Zone Ost 29 CHF / €25, Zone West 29 CHF / €25, and Zone Ost + West 34 CHF / €29.50, 3 days 55 CHF / €48.

EURO-NEISSE-TICKET+

Unlimited travel in the border region on trains, buses and trams of Germany (Saxony districts of Görlitz and the eastern part of Bautzen), Czech Republic (Liberec region) and Poland (Upper Lusatia and Lower Silesia) for 1 to 5 adults for 1 or 3 days (known as EURO-NYSA-Ticket+ in Poland and EURO-NISA-Ticket+ in the Czech Republic). 1 day €17.50, 24.00, 28.50, 33.00, 37.50 (1–5 adults respectively); 3 days €29.00, 53.00, 58.00, 63.00, 68.00. No discounts for Seniors. Children free as follows: Germany under school age, Czech Republic under six, Poland one child free with each paying adult. Regardless of the number of travellers three additional children up to 15 travel free. Bikes and dogs an additional €5 each on 1 day tickets only. Note that prices are lower in Poland and the Czech Republic (with Poland being the cheapest).

PASS ALSACE - RHEIN-NECKAR

A day ticket valid on Saturdays, Sundays and French public holidays covering local trains (2nd class), buses and trams in the Rhein-Neckar area (VRN) centered on Mannheim and Heidelberg, the Karlsruhe area (KVV), plus local trains in the Bas Rhin area of France centered on Strasbourg. Price: from France to Germany €19 for one person or €31.50 for a group of 2 - 5 people, from Germany to France daily tickets €6 for one person or €12 for a group of 2 - 5 people, Available at TER Alsace and Bas-Rhin stations except Wissembourg, ticket offices or ticket vending machines.

Passes for Domestic Travel

Most cities offer day tickets valid on public transport (some include local trains). Larger cities often have Visitor Cards (some are shown below) which include tourist attractions as well as public transport; these are available from airports and tourist information offices, often also from hotels and online.

AUSTRIA

See separate sections for Interrail / Eurail Global and One Country passes (page 581), Bodensee Ticket (page 583).

KlimaTicket Ö: a single ticket providing a 365 days travel on all public transport throughout Austria (not valid on tourist railways).

KlimaTicket Ö Youth - 25 and under, €884.20 (€975.00 from Aug. 1)
KlimaTicket Ö Classic - 26 to 64 €1179.30 (€1300.00 from Aug. 1)
KlimaTicket Ö Senior - 65 and over €884.20 (€975.00 from Aug. 1)
KlimaTicket Ö Special - for disabied travellers €884.20 (€975.00 from Aug. 1)
Up to 4 children between 6 and 15 (children 5 and under travel free) can be added for an additional €118.50 to each category of ticket.

Regional versions and 1st class upgrades available.

Einfach-Raus-Ticket: one day's 2nd class travel (until 0300 hrs the following day) on regional and local trains in Austria (except Vorarlberg) for groups of 2 to 5 people, €37-49. On Mon to Fri not valid before 0900 hrs. Add €9 to include bicycles.

Vorteilscard annual discount card gives 50% discount; Classic (€71). There are cheaper cards for families, and those under 26.

Wien all public transport (not airport): 24 / 48 / 72 hours €8 / 14.10 / 17.10; weekly ticket €19.70; 31 days €51.00.

Vienna City Card: unlimited travel on local transport (excludes airport) plus discounted museum entry, 24 / 48 / 72 hours, 7 days, €17 / 25 / 29 / 35. Similar **Easy City Pass Vienna** also available.

Other visitor cards giving local travel plus museum / sights discounts for 24 / 48 / 72 hours: **Salzburg Card** €31/ 40 / 46 (reduced by €3-5 low season Nov. to Apr.); **Innsbruck Card** €69/ 79 / 90. Children half price.

BELGIUM

See separate sections for Interrail / Eurail Global and Benelux passes (page 581), Euregio Ticket Maas-Rhein (page 583).

Netabonnement / Abonnement Réseau : unlimited travel on rail network; 1 month €402/619 (2nd / 1st class), 3 months €1125/ 1733, 1 year €4019 / 6189. Add-ons for city transport also available.

Tickets available on NMBS/SNCB rail network include: **Standard Multi** (age 26+) allows 10 single journeys within Belgium for €105 2nd class, €161 1st class (€3 cheaper on App), valid 6 mths. **Youth Multi** is under 26 version, €64 2nd class (€2 cheaper on App). **Weekend Ticket**: gives 50% discount, from Friday 1900 hrs. **Senior Ticket** (65+), flat fare of €8.50 return 2nd class, €18.00 return 1st class, from 0900 Mon-Fri.

Brussels: **Brupass** covers all transport in greater Brussels (De Lijn, NMBS/SNCB, MIVB/STIB and TEC) Day pass €9.50 . Personal Mobib or Mobib Basic card required (€6). STIB (Bus, Tram & Metro) also has a contactless day ticket for €8.90, no card required.

De Lijn has 24 or 72 hour system passes (€9 / 18) for its trams and buses; includes coastal tram. Buy in advance. A 24h smartphone ticket is also available costs €9.

BULGARIA

See separate sections for Interrail / Eurail Global and One Country passes (page 581).

Sofia: metro, tram and bus: 1 day 4 BGN, 24hrs 6 BGN, 72hrs 15 BGN (the 24 & 72hr requires an electronic card, cost 2 BGN).

CROATIA

See separate section for Interrail / Eurail Global and One Country passes (page 581).

Zagreb: day ticket (dnevna karta) all ZET tram / bus (zone 1): €4, available as paper ticket. Also multi-day tickets (višednevne karte): 3 / 7 / 15 / 30 days, €10 / 20 / 27 / 53, requires stored value card €2.

Zagreb Card adds museums, discounts, 24 hrs €31, 72 hrs €37.

CZECH REPUBLIC

See separate sections for Interrail / Eurail Global and One Country passes (page 581).

See also under *Other International Passes* for a range of passes covering border areas (page 583).

Day ticket (Celodenní Jízdenka): 2nd class travel on whole rail network 799 CZK (reservation payable on *SC* trains, up to 250 CZK). 8 regional areas also available, 179-319 CZK. Certain regions also have day tickets plus Poland, 259-319 CZK.

Other day tickets cover specific cross-border areas: EgroNet 200 CZK, Labe-Elbe 410 CZK. Note that day tickets (also Interrail / Eurail passes) are not valid on services operated by GW Train Regio.

OneTicket (Jedna Jízdenka) valid on all ČD and private carriers acros the entire country except those detailed at www.oneticket.cz/exceptions The Network ticket best suited for vistors is valid for 1/7/30 days 997/ 2200/6600 CZK. 90, 180 day and yearly tickets are also available. Ticket are available as paper or digital.

Group Weekend ticket (Skupinová víkendová jízdenka): 2nd class travel on whole network on Sat. or Sun. for 2 adults and up to 3 childrer 999 CZK (1179 CZK including local transport in Praha). Reservation fee payable on *SC* trains. Valid cross-border to first station on local trains (except Austria). Regional areas also available, 289-479 CZK.

Summer Ticket (2024 prices; available for purchase from June 15) Jízdenka na leto: unlimited rail travel for 7 or 14 days during July and August, 7 days 1390 CZK, 14 days 1990 CZK.

Praha: all public transport: 24 hrs 120 CZK, 3 days (72 hrs) 330 CZK, 3 days 550 CZK. Wider areas available. **COOLPASS**: (formerly Prague Card) 1-10 day admission card, includes public transport, €64-144 (child/student €48-100). Most cities have day tickets for city transport

DENMARK

See separate sections for Interrail / Eurail Global and One Country passes, Eurail Scandinavia pass (page 381).

Fares based on national zonal system; 30-day **Pendlerkort** is availabl (photocard required) including all-zones version. **Rejsekortet** is a pre-pay travel card aimed at Danish residents, but a **Rejsekort Anonymt** may be purchased by anyone (card costs 80 DKK, plus an initial amour for travel purposes).

København: **City Pass Small** zones 1-4 (includes airport) on bus, metro and train 24-120 hrs 100-340 DKK (child half price); **City Pass Large** 200-680 DKK, zones 1-99 includes Helsingør, Roskilde etc.

Copenhagen Card - Discover: public transport (whole region), free entry to over 80+ attractions, 24 / 48 / 72 / 96 / 120 hrs €67 / 107/ 130 / 151 / 174 (two children up to 11 years old free). **Copenhagen Card - Hop**: Stromma Hop On-Hop Off buses, free entry to over 40 attractions 24 / 48 / 72 €74 / 109 / 132 (two children up to 11 years old free).

ESTONIA

See separate section for Interrail / Eurail Global and One Country passe (page 581).

Estonian Railways: a zonal system operates; there is no network pass

Tallinn: tram / bus / trolley-bus **Ühiskaart** pre-pay travel card (deposit €3) available for 1 / 3 / 5 / 30 days: €5.50 / 9 / 11 / 30.

Tallinn Card: public transport plus over 50 museums and attractions, 2 hrs €45, 48 hrs €65, 72 hrs €78, under 18s €27 / 34 /41.

FINLAND

See separate sections for Interrail / Eurail Global and One Country passes, also Eurail Scandinavia pass (page 581).

Helsinki: single-charge electronic cards for all public transport includin local trains: 1 / 2 / 3 days €10 / 15 / 20; 7 days €40 (1-13 days available)

Helsinki Card CITY: public transport zones AB plus free entry to 25+ attractions and bus & boat tours, 24 / 48 / 72 hrs €62 / 77 / 93, child 7-16 half price; REGION version includes zones ABC and airport for €4 extra

FRANCE

See separate sections for Interrail / Eurail Global and One Country passes (page 581), Pass Alsace - Rhein-Neckar, Passbask, Saar-Lor-Lu Ticket (page 583).

Annual discount cards: **Carte Avantage Jeune** (ages 12-27), **Carte Avantage Senior** (over 60), **Avantage Weekend** (ages 27-59) and **Avantage Famille** (ages 27-59) all cost €49 and give 30% discount of normal rail fares for one year including certain international journeys. They also give discounts on Prem's and last minute tickets, and 60% discount for up to three accompanying children.

Regional Tickets: several regions offer day tickets on TER (local) train at weekends and holidays. Conditions vary and some only valid in summer. Details generally available on TER website www.ter.sncf.com.

Alsa + 24h: a zonal day pass (24 hours) for the Alsace region, which includes Strasbourg, Colmar and Mulhouse. Valid on train (not TGV), bus and tram. €37.40 for the whole region. Smaller areas are also available

Paris Visite: public transport within Paris including metro, RER, SNCF suburban trains, bus and tram. Available for 1 / 2 / 3 / 4 / 5 days covering zones 1-5, includes trains to Versailles and Disneyland. Prices €30 / 45 / 63 / 77. Child 4-11: half price.

Mobilis : Paris one-day public transport ticket (excludes airport services) €9 (zones 2-3) to €21 (zones 1-5).

Navigo daily, weekly and monthly passes also available; all zones 1 day €12, 7 day (Mon to Sun) ticket costs €32.00; monthly €89; photocard required at extra cost. Navigo Easy pass also available for smart phones.

Lille City Pass: local public transport (metro, tram, bus) plus museums and attractions, 24/48/72 hrs, €25/35/45. The 72-hour pass includes TER trains in regional area for 24 hours (includes Dunkerque) and additional attractions in the wider area.

Most cities have day tickets for urban bus and tram services, e.g. **Lyon**: 24/48/72 hrs €7/13/18; **Lille** 1 to 7 days, €6 to €18.

GERMANY

See separate sections for Bodensee Ticket, Euregio Ticket Mass-Rhein, Saar-Lor-Lux Ticket (page 583). Note that Eurail/Interrail effectively issue German Railways (DB) passes as shown below.

German Rail Pass is available only to non-European residents and gives unlimited travel on DB trains in Germany, also to certain destinations in Switzerland, Austria, Belgium and Italy. Includes IC Bus. Available in flexi and consecutive versions as shown below. No supplements on *ICE*, *EC*. Youth passes apply to those aged 12 to 27. Accompanied children aged 6-11 get a free pass (two with an adult pass).

	Adult 1st cl.	Adult 2nd cl.	Youth 1st cl.	Youth 2nd cl.
FLEXI PASSES:				
3 days within 1 month	€299	€223	€239	€178
4 days within 1 month	€339	€254	€271	€203
5 days within 1 month	€375	€281	€300	€225
7 days within 1 month	€436	€326	€349	€261
10 days within 1 month	€509	€407	€407	€326
15 days within 1 month	€649	€507	€519	€406
CONSECUTIVE DAYS:				
3 days	€277	€206	€222	€165
4 days	€314	€235	€251	€188
5 days	€347	€260	€278	€208
7 days	€403	€302	€322	€242
10 days	€471	€376	€377	€301
15 days	€681	€166	€138	€312

Quer-durchs-Land-Ticket: one day's unlimited travel (not before 0900 Mon. - Fri., but valid until 0300 following day) on local trains (IRE/RE/RB/S-Bahn), 2nd class. Valid for up to 5 people. €49 for one person (€89 for a group of five).

Das Deutschland-Ticket: €58 unlimited travel for a month throughout Germany on regional trains and buses (not valid on ICE, IC/EC).

Regional tickets (Länder-Tickets): one day's unlimited 2nd class travel for up to 5 people on DB local trains (not before 0900 on Mon.-Fri., valid to 0300 the following day). Buy on the day. First class versions also available for some regions. Some tickets include other public transport. Regions available:
Baden-Württemberg: 1 person €27 (add €8 per additional person).
Bayern: 1 person €32 (add €10 for each additional person).
Brandenburg-Berlin: €35 (up to 5 passengers).
Hessen (2024): €38 (up to 5 passengers).
Mecklenburg-Vorpommern: 1 person €24 (add €5 per person).
Niedersachsen: 1 person €28 (add €7 for each additional person).
Nordrhein-Westfalen (SchönerTag Ticket NRW): 1 person €34, 2-5 people €52.20.
Rheinland-Pfalz: 1 person €29 (add €9 for each additional person).
Saarland: 1 person €29 (add €9 for each additional person).
Sachsen: 1 person €33 (add €8 for each additional person).
Sachsen-Anhalt: 1 person €33 (add €8 for each additional person).
Schleswig-Holstein: 1 person €30 (add €6 for each additional person). Includes public transport in Hamburg.
Thüringen: 1 person €33 (add €8 for each additional person).

Annual Railcards: **Bahncard 25/50**: gives discounts of 25% or 50% on all national DB trains for €63/244 in 2nd class (1st class €125/492). A Jugend (Youth) Bahncard 25 is available for those aged 6 to 18, price €8 (valid for 1st and 2nd class). **Bahncard 100** gives unlimited travel for one year, €4,899 in 2nd class, €7,999 in 1st class, passport photo required. 3 month trail cards available.

Harz: HSB narrow gauge railway, 3/5 days €114/171; children aged 6-14 pay €69/103. Deutschlandticket valid expect to Brocken.

Tageskarte (day ticket): most urban areas offer 24/48/72 hour tickets valid on most public transport; generally a zonal system operates.

Welcome Tickets: most public transport in selected cities, also includes free or reduced entry to many museums and visitor attractions. Buy from Tourist Information, main stations, some airports and hotels. Examples:

Berlin Welcome Card: one adult and up to 3 children aged 3-14; all public transport plus up to 50% off at 180 attractions: 48 hrs €33, 72 hrs €43, 4 days €54, 5 days €56, 6 days €60. Covers zones A, B, C (includes Potsdam and Schönefeld Airport); €3-7 less for zones A, B only. Also available 72 hrs + Museum Island (free entry) €63.

Dresden City Card: 1 day €18, 2 day €25, 3 day €35 valid for 2 adults and up to 4 children under 15. **Frankfurt Card**: 1 day €12, 2 days €19; basic group ticket (up to 5 people) €13 per person.

Hamburg Card: Day Ticket €11.90, also 2-5 days €21.90 - 48.90; group version (up to 5 people) €20.90 one day, €37.90-86.90 for 2-5 days. **Hannover Card**: 1 day €13, 2 days €20, 3 days €26, group ticket (up to 5 people) €22/32/46. **Köln Card**: 24/48 hrs €9/18, group ticket (up to 5 people) €19/38. **Leipzig Card**: 1 day €10, 3 days €25, 3 day group ticket (2 adults and up to 3 children under 14) €50. **Nürnberg Card**: 2 days €38 (children aged 6-11 €12).

GREAT BRITAIN

See separate sections for Interrail/Eurail Global pass, Interrail One Country pass (page 581), Britrail (page 583).

Railcards: annual cards giving 33.4% discount on most rail fares; 16-25 Railcard, 26-30 Railcard, Two Together Railcard, Family & Friends Railcard, Senior Railcard (60+), Veterans: all £35; HM Forces Railcard £21; Disabled Persons, £20. Some have 3-year versions (£54-£80 online). Network Railcard gives off-peak discount in south-east England, £35. There is also a 16-17 Saver card giving a 50% discount (£35).

All-Line Rail Rover: covers whole National Rail network. 1st/standard class £949/625 (7 days), £1450/949 (14 days), children 5-15 half price. 33.4% discount for holders of Senior/Disabled/Two Together railcard, and (standard class only) 16-25, 26-30 and Family & Friends railcards. Some restrictions before 1000 Mon.-Fri. Not valid on Eurostar, Heathrow Express, London Underground, DLR, London Trams. Valid on Ffestiniog Railway and Welsh Highland Railway but not other private railways.

Spirit of Scotland Travelpass: all rail services in Scotland (includes Carlisle and Berwick) plus some coaches. Standard class only. Valid 4 out of 8 days £155, or 8 out of 15 days £196; not before 0915 Mon. to Fri. (except on Glasgow - Oban/Mallaig/Stranraer services and north of Inverness). 33.4% discount with most annual railcards. 50% discount for children (5-15). 20% discount on Northlink Ferries to Orkney and Shetland. Smaller areas also available: **Highland Rover**, 4 out of 8 days £99; **Central Scotland Rover** 3 days (consecutive) £57; **Strathclyde Roundabout** 1 day ranger £7.70; 50% discount for children (5-15).

Explore Wales Pass: standard class rail travel on any 4 days out of 8 (not valid before 0930 Mon.-Fri.), plus most buses on all 8 days, price £149, children half price, railcard discounts apply. Tickets available from staffed stations and on the train. Other areas available: **South Wales** £119, **North and Mid Wales** £119, **South West Wales** £119.

A range of **Rover** tickets is available covering various areas, typically for 7 days, 3 in 7 days, 4 in 8 days, or 8 in 15 days. Most not valid until after the morning peak on Mon. to Fri. Examples: Anglia Plus, Coast and Peaks, East Midlands, Freedom of Devon & Cornwall, Freedom of North East, Freedom of Severn & Solent, North West Rover, Freedom of South West, Heart of England, Kent, North Country, North Wales, Thames Rover. Details: www.nationalrail.co.uk or www.railrover.org.

Ranger day tickets also available: e.g. Cheshire, Cotswolds, Cumbria, Cumbian Coast, Devon, East Midlands, Isle of Wight, Lakes, Lancashire, Lincolnshire, North Downs, Oxfordshire, South Pennines, Thames Branches, Tyne & Tees, West Midlands, West Yorkshire, Yorkshire Coast. Details: www.nationalrail.co.uk or www.railrover.org.

London: Day Travelcards cover almost all transport (Underground, bus and rail) in the London area; peak version from £16.60 (central London, zones 1-4) to £23.60 (zones 1-6), off-peak version (not before 0930 Mon.-Fri.) £16.60 (zones 1-6). 7-day tickets from £44.70 (zones 1-2) to £81.60 (zones 1-6), no off-peak version. Wider zones also available. For single journeys contactless debit and credit cards, or stored-value Oyster cards offer the best value as prices are capped. Visitor Oyster cards are available preloaded from £15 - £50 (plus £5 fee, non-refundable). Children under 11 travel free on buses and trams (also on Tube, DLR and some rail services) when accompanied by a fare paying adult.

All-day tickets (some off-peak) covering local rail and most buses are available in Bristol, Derbyshire, Glasgow, Greater Manchester, Merseyside, South Yorkshire, West Yorkshire, Tyneside and West Midlands.

Isle of Man: Go Explore card: all buses and trains, Douglas horse trams (includes Groudle Glen Railway, Great Laxey Mine Railway), 1/3/5/7 days, £21/42/49/59, children aged 5-15 half price. Family card: 2 adults and up to 3 children, £48/92/105/129. Prices include card fee.

GREECE

See separate sections for Interrail/Eurail Global, One Country and Greek Islands passes (pages 581 and 582).

ATH.ENA ticket: 24-hour ticket valid on metro, tram and bus (excludes airport) €5, 5 days €9 (airport is €9 single). 3-day tourist ticket including metro or bus to/from airport (one journey each way) €20.

HUNGARY

See separate sections for Interrail/Eurail Global and One Country passes (page 581).

2nd class travel by rail and local transport is free for over-65s with an EU passport or ID card; rail tickets need to be obtained but are free of charge.

Passes for Domestic Travel

START Klub Card: gives 50% discount on 2nd class travel. Valid for either 6 months or one year: HUF 19900 / 34900 (HUF 14900 / 24900 under 26 years). Requires passport style photograph. On Saturdays cardholders may obtain 50% discount for a second person.

Budapest: tram / metro / bus / rail, 24 hr travelcard HUF 2.500, 72 hrs HUF 5,500.

Budapest Card also includes museums, walking tour and discounts: 24 hrs HUF 16000, 48 hrs HUF 22000, 72 hrs HUF 28,000, 96 hrs HUF35,000, 120hrs HUF 39,000.

Balaton 24: Includes tourist attractions and entertainment venues along the lakeside settlements of Lake Balaton. 2nd class only with the option to upgrade to 1st class. Tickets available from railway stations and the MAV App. Valid for 24hrs from first validation, costs HUF 1090 (a 5% discount when purchased using the MAV App). Available for use daily May 11 - Sept. 21, otherwise weekends and holidays only.

Hungary Pass: valid throughout the country for 30 days in 2nd class on MÀV-START, MÀV-HEV and GYSEV trains and interurban buses (note that seat reservation is compulsory on most InterCity and Express trains). Can also be used on local transport (metros/trams/buses) in the following cities: Budapest, Csongràd, Esztergom Èrd, and on TramTrain (lines 1 and 1A) in the Szeged area. Price: HUF 18900. **Hungary 24** also available, valid for 24 hours and costs HUF 4999.

County Pass: individual passes for each of the 19 counties of Hungary. Same conditions apply as for Hungary Pass. Price: HUF 9450. **County 24** also available, valid for 24 hours and costs HUF 999.

IRELAND

See separate sections for Interrail / Eurail Global and One Country passes (page 581). Interrail and Eurail passes valid in the Republic of Ireland are also valid in Northern Ireland.

REPUBLIC OF IRELAND ONLY:

Irish Explorer: any 5 days in 15 on IÉ rail services, €128 (child €64), standard class. **Trekker** gives 4 consecutive days on Irish Rail for €110.

Dublin area: **Leap Visitor Card**: smartcard 24 hrs €8, 72 hrs €16.00, 7 days (168 hrs) €32. Includes rail in Short Hop zone, Luas tram and bus (also Airlink); purchase at airport or tourist offices (not railway stations). Can top up with additional periods. Luas **Flexi** ticket (tram only): 1 day €5.80, zonal tickets available for 7 days. **Leap** cards are also available for the bus network in Cork and most other cities.

NORTHERN IRELAND ONLY:

iLink Travel Card: unlimited bus and rail travel on Translink services (Northern Ireland Railways, Ulsterbus and Belfast Citybus). Zone 4 covers the whole of Northern Ireland: 1 day £19, 7 days £66, 1 month £230. Zone 1 covers Belfast city (£6 / 21 / 75). Children half price. North West zone: £15 / 55 / 195. Initial £1 fee for card.

Belfast Visitor Pass: local public transport (includes rail to Cultra; not bus to Belfast International Airport) plus visitor discounts: 1 / 2 / 3 days, adult £7 / 13 / 17, child £4 / 7 / 9.

ITALY

See separate sections for Interrail / Eurail Global and One Country passes (page 581). Prices quoted are indicative, please check locally.

Mobilcard Südtirol: regional trains, buses, funiculars and cable cars in Bolzano, Malles, Brennero area: 1 / 3 / 7 days; €20 / 30 / 45 (child under 14 €10 / 15 / 23).

Roma: Roma Tourist Ticket covers rail/metro/bus in urban area (but not Fiumicino Airport), 24 / 48 / 72 hrs, €7 / 13 / 18; 7-day ticket (CIS) €24.

Roma Pass: 48 / 72 hr transport pass (€37 / 58) with museum discounts.

Milano: Milan Pass Light access to all public transport without any restrictions 24 / 48 / 72 hrs, €14 / 21 / 23.

Napoli: 'Campania artecard' is a 3-day transport and museum visitors card, allowing free entry or disounts. Two areas available, Napoli (€28 adult, €17 for ages 18 - 25) and wider Campania area (€42 / 31).

Venezia: Travel cards for ACTV buses and boats: 1 / 2 / 3 / 7 days €25 / 35 / 45 / 65. Each card is also available with airport transfer add-on (€7 single or €13 return).

LATVIA

See separate section for Interrail / Eurail Global and One Country passes (page 581).

Latvian Railways: tickets are available for 1 / 3 / 4 / 5 days for unlimited travel between specified stations, but there are no network passes.

Riga: trams and buses 24 hrs €5, 3 / 5 days €8 / 10.

LITHUANIA

See separate section for Interrail / Eurail Global and One Country passes (page 581).

Vilnius: 1 / 3 day tickets available on local VVT buses / trolleybuses; €5 / 8. **Vilnius Pass**: free entry to museums and various discounts, 24 / 48 / 72 hrs, €37 / 47 /56.

LUXEMBOURG

See separate sections for Interrail / Eurail Global and Benelux passes (page 581), Sar-Lor-Lux Ticket (page 583).

All public transport is free of charge throughout the country. On the railways this applies only in 2nd class.

Dagesbilljee / Billet longue durée: unlimited 1st class travel on all publi transport throughout the country for one day (until 0400 hrs following morning), not valid to border points €6 (not for sale on the train).

Monatsabo: 1st class network season ticket, valid one month: €75.

Luxembourg Pass: Discounted and free entry to 73 attractions. 1 day €21, 2 days €31, 3 days €36. Group pass for 3 - 5 people for 1 / 2 / 3 days: €51 / 61 / 66.

MONTENEGRO

See separate sections for Interrail / Eurail Global pass (page 581).

NETHERLANDS

See separate sections for Interrail / Eurail Global and Benelux passes (page 581), Euregio Ticket Maas-Rhein (page 583).

A national stored-value OV-chipkaart is used for public transport, initial cost €7.50, which can be loaded with day tickets. A single-use chipcar or e-ticket may be used by less frequent travellers. A 24 hour-ticket is als available. Supplements payable on IC Direct trains.

Railrunner: Children aged 4 - 11 travel for a flat rate of €2.50 each, vali all day.

Day ticket: unlimited rail travel (NS and other carriers) for one day; 1st class €107, 2nd class €63.

Holland Travel Ticket: valid one day on all public transport (not Thalys) includes 2nd class on all NS and private operators' trains, tram, bus an metro, €74 all day, or Off-Peak version (not 0630 - 0900 Mon-Fri) €51

Amsterdam: GVB tram / bus / metro 24 / 48 / 72 / 96 / 120 / 144 / 168 hrs €9.50 / 15.50 / 21.50 / 27.50 / 34 / 38.50 / 42.50.

Amsterdam Travel Ticket: adds local NS trains (includes Schiphol airport): 1 / 2 / 3 days €18 / 24 / 30, valid to 0400 next day.

Amsterdam & Region Travel Ticket: covers wider area (e.g. Haarlem Almere, Hilversum) and regional buses, 1 / 2 / 3 days €21 / 32 / 41.

I Amsterdam Card: GVB tram / bus / metro, canal tour, plus discounted or free entry to 70+ attractions; 24 / 48 / 72 / 96 / 120 hrs, €65 / 90 / 108, 123 / 135.

South Holland: **Tourist Day Ticket** gives tram / bus / metro / waterbus throughout Rotterdam and Den Haag area, €17.00. Excludes NS trains

NORTH MACEDONIA

See separate sections for Interrail / Eurail Global and One Country passes (page 581).

NORWAY

See separate section for Interrail / Eurail Global and One Country passes Eurail Scandinavia pass (page 581).

Oslo: 24 hour ticket for all 'Ruter' public transport in zone 1 day, 132 NOK, 7 days 366 NOK; all zones (includes airport) 1 day 303 NOK, 7 days 887 NOK. Children, youth (18 - 19) and seniors (67+) half price.

Oslo Pass: all public transport including Vy local trains (zones 1 - 2, excludes airport), free entry to 30 attractions, discounts on sightseeing buses / boats: 24 / 48 / 72 hours 550 / 800 / 945 NOK (senior approx 80%, child approx 50%).

Bergen Card: local bus and tram travel plus free or discounted entry to various attractions; 24 / 48 / 72 / 96 hrs, 420 / 540 / 660 / 780 NOK (child 3 - 15 pay 35%).

POLAND

See separate section for Interrail / Eurail Global and One Country passes (page 581).

Intercity Card: available in both 1st and 2nd class; unlimited domestic trips on PKP Intercity and other carriers (cards are sold as either 'named' or 'bearer'). Monthly named 1st 2810 PLN, 2nd 2060 PLN; bearer 3940 / 2810 PLN. Discounts for Seniors and children of up to 50%. Applications are made in writing at PKP customer service centres.

Polregio operates REGIO and IR trains: **Bilety Sieciowe** (network tickets) are monthly tickets with a 33 - 93% discount. **REGIOpass / REGIOkarnet**: valid for any 3 days out of 2 months, 93 PLN (Polregio plus most other regional operators) or 80 PLN for a **miniREGIOpass**

alid on Polregio REGIO trains only; validate ticket before travel.

ilet Turystyczny (tourist ticket): valid 1800 Friday or public holiday to 300 first working day, 59 PLN (Polregio plus most other regional perators); or 48 PLN for Mini version (Polregio REGIO trains only). olders of these tickets can travel on selected lines in the Czech epublic and Germany.

oleje Mazowieckie (KM) trains: wide area around Warsaw, 24 hr and 3 ay passes are available (Sieciowy Imienny KM).

arsaw ZTM tram / bus / metro / rail, Zone 1 (includes Chopin airport): 1 ay 15 PLN, 3 days 36 PLN. Zones 1 + 2, 1 day 26 PLN, 3 days 57 PLN, eekend ticket valid 1900 Fri. - 0800 Mon. 24 PLN, group weekend ticket r up to 5 people, 40 PLN.

PORTUGAL

ee separate section for Interrail / Eurail Global and One Country passes Page 581).

reen Rail Pass: Allows passengers to travel on nearly all urban, egional, inter-regional and inter city services operated by Comboios de ortugal (CP), 30 / 60 / 90 days, € 20 / 40 / 60. Not valid on Alfa Pendular ain, urban trains in Lisbon and Porto or on metros and light rail systems.

tra-Rail: for ages 12 - 30, rail travel with free nights at youth hostels; *Cape* version valid 3 days € 58 (€ 64 without youth card). *XPlore* ersion valid 7 days € 127 (€ 146 without youth card). Not valid on *AP* ains. Buy at main stations, show Card and ID for ticket.

isboa: Carris tram / bus / metro - one-day ticket (bilhete diário 24 h) € 7; ith Transtejo (Cacilhas) included € 10. Carris, metro and local CP trains 11. Includes the funiculars and lift.

isboa Card: public transport plus free / discounted attractions: 24 / 48 / 2 hrs, € 27 / 44 / 54 (children aged 4 - 15: € 18 / 25 / 31).

orto: *Andante Tour Card* gives metro + STCP bus + local rail, all zones, 4 hrs € 8, 72 hrs € 16. **Porto Card** also includes free / discounted entry museums etc, 1 day € 15, 2 days € 27, 3 days € 32, 4 days € 41.50.

oimbra: 1 / 3 / 7 day ticket on SMTUC local buses € 4 /9 / 15.

ROMANIA

ee separate section for Interrail / Eurail Global and One Country passes page 581).

ucureşti: STB tram, bus, trolleybus and metro network (not express uses): 1/3/7 days, 14/35/50 RON, fares are loaded onto an 'Activ' martcard. The metro also has a day ticket.

SERBIA

ee separate sections for Interrail / Eurail Global and One Country asses (page 581).

SLOVAKIA

ee separate sections for Interrail / Eurail Global and One Country asses (page 581).

ero fare rail tickets for most trains can be obtained by EU citizens under 5 and over 62. Supplements on *EC* and *SC*.

ratislava: urban trams, buses and local trains, 24 hrs € 5, 3 days € 11, days € 15. **Bratislava Card** includes many discounts, 24 hrs € 30, 48 rs € 36, 72 hrs € 39, available online or from tourist offices.

SLOVENIA

ee separate section for Interrail / Eurail Global and One Country passes page 581).

jubljana Card: city buses, castle funicular, tourist boat and museums, alid for 24, 48 or 72 hours, € 41 / 49 / 54, child 6 - 14 years € 26 / 31 / 35.

SPAIN

ee separate sections for Interrail / Eurail Global and One Country asses (page 581), Passbask (page 583).

RENFE Spain Pass: for people resident outside Spain giving 4, 6, 8 or 0 individual journeys. Tickets must be obtained in advance using the ass; reservations are compulsory but free. Valid 1 month from first ourney. Can be purchased and printed online (www.renfe.com).

Madrid: **Abono Turístico** (Tourist Ticket) gives all public transport in one A, 1 / 2 / 3 / 4 / 5 / 7 days € 10 / 17 / 23 / 27 / 33 / 42, children under 11 ears 50%. Available for wider area (zone T) at 50% of the price. Various museum passes are available but these exclude public transport.

Barcelona T-Dia ticket: valid 1 day on metro / TMB bus / tram / local rail, € 12 (zone 1, includes airport), wider areas available.

Hola Barcelona: zone 1 travelcard available for 2 / 3 / 4 / 5 days, approx € 18 / 26 / 34 / 41.

Barcelona Card: adds free or discounted museums, 3 to 5 days approx € 57 / 67 / 79 (children 4 - 12 years € 35 / 44 / 49).

SWEDEN

See separate sections for Interrail / Eurail Global and One Country passes, Eurail Scandinavia pass (page 581).

Stockholm: Travelcards give all SL public transport in Greater Stockholm, 24 / 72 hours 175 / 350 SEK, 7 days 455 SEK; SL Access smartcard required (20 SEK). Discount for under 20s / 65 +.

Go Stockholm Pass gives bus / boat tour plus free museums, 1 / 2 / 3 / 4 / 5 days (899 - 1879 SEK).

SWITZERLAND

See separate sections for Interrail / Eurail Global pass, Interrail One Country pass (page 581), Bodensee Ticket (Page 583).

Swiss Travel Pass: available to all non-Swiss residents. Consecutive days on Swiss Railways, boats and most alpine postbuses and city buses. Valid for 3, 4, 6, 8 or 15 days; 1st class 389 / 469 / 602 / 665 / 723 CHF, 2nd class 244 / 295 / 379 / 419 / 459 CHF. Youth Pass (16 - 25 years) gives approximately 15% reduction. All versions give up to 50% reduction on most funicular and mountain railways. Includes free admission to over 500 tourist sites. Children aged 6 - 15 travel free with a Family Card if accompanied by a parent (not other relatives), otherwise half fare.

Swiss Travel Pass Flex: as above but for 3 / 4 / 6 / 8 / 15 days within 1 month. 1st class: 445 / 539 / 644 / 697 / 755 CHF, 2nd class 279 / 339 / 405 / 439 / 479 CHF. Youth version (16 - 25 years) gives approximately 15% reduction.

Swiss Half Fare Card: discount card offering up to 50% off most public transport, valid for 1 month, 120 CHF. For non-Swiss residents.

Holders of the Swiss Half Fare Card can purchase a **1-day Travelpass** for 78 CHF 2nd class or 128 CHF 1st class, valid on most trains and public transport. A **Saver Day Pass** is also available but is more restrictive, from 29 CHF (or from 59 CHF without a Half Fare Card); prices vary according to when it is purchased, passes may sell out.

Berner Oberland Pass: Available for 3, 4, 6, 8 or 10 days unlimited travel in the area; 1st class: 288 / 336 / 420 / 474 / 522 CHF. 2nd class: 240 / 280 / 350 / 395 / 435 CHF. Flat fare of 30 CHF for children under 16.

Regional Passes: other areas available include Lake Geneva - Alps and Tell-Pass (Central Switzerland).

Jungfrau Travel Pass: 3 / 4 / 5 / 6 / 7 / 8 days travel, 210 / 235 / 270 / 290 / 310 / 330 CHF. Covers most routes in area; connecting ticket for Jungfraujoch € 63 (or € 75 June to August). Includes boats on Lakes Brienz and Thun. Reduced fare for holders of Travel Pass or Half Fare Card.

Bern: LIBERO day ticket for city area (2 zone) 11 CHF. **Bern Ticket** is issued to overnight guests offering free LIBERO bus and tram travel within city zones 100/101. Also includes Gurten and Marzilibahn funiculars.

Genève: Day ticket (Carte 24 Heures) includes buses, trams, trains and boats: 10 CHF. **Carte 9 h** is valid from 0900 hrs, 8 CHF. **Lèman Day Pass** cover the wider Genève area from 16 CHF. The **Geneva Transport Card** is given to those staying at a hotel or youth hostel in the city and allows unrestricted travel on all public transport for the duration of the stay.

Zürich: ZVV Tageskarte gives 24 hours on all transport including SBB trains, 16 / 10 CHF 1st / 2nd class (zones 1 - 2 only); all zones in Canton 59 / 36 CHF. Off-peak version is 9-UhrPass, all zones, not before 0900 Mon. - Fri., 45 / 27 CHF. **Zürich Card** includes most museums and other discounts: 24 hours 29 CHF, 72 hours 56 CHF (children 19 / 37 CHF), includes airport.

Ticino: **Ticino Ticket** is given to those staying at a hotel, hostel or campsite in the Canton and allows free public transport and discounts on tourist attractions including mountain railways and boat trips.

TURKEY

See separate sections for Interrail / Eurail Global and One Country passes (page 581).

Istanbul City Card unlimited access on all public transport for 1 / 3 / 5 / 7 / 15 days: Tourist prices €40 / 60 / 95 / 110 / 150.
Pre-order on line (can be delivered to your hotel).

IstanbulKart is a prepaid, rechargeable card which costs 130 TL and can be shared with up to 5 other people; it becomes unusable once a total of 500 TL has been loaded and used and so a new card will need to be purchased. It generally offers better value than the Istanbul City Card.

UKRAINE

Note: This section has not been updated

Kyïv: With either an e-ticket, Kyïv Smart Card, Kyïv Card or QR-code paper ticket travel on all modes of public transport, the more trips the cheaper the fare. **Kyïv Pass** gives metro trips and various museums, 24 / 48 / 72 hours, € 15 / 25 / 35.

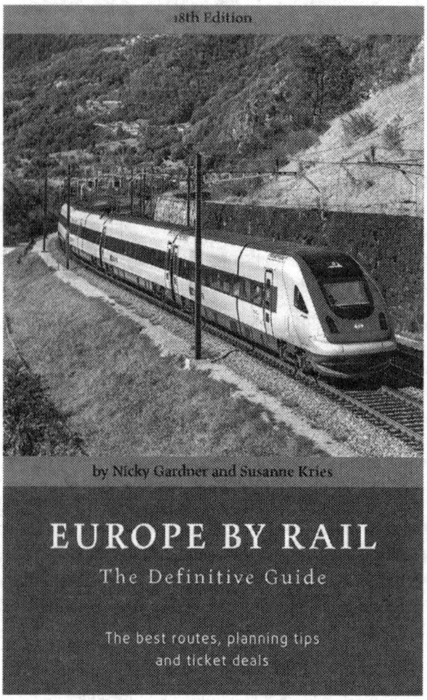

Exploring Europe by rail has never been easier. Written by Nicky Gardner and Susanne Kries, two highly experienced travellers, this guidebook contains all you need for planning your journey.

★ 50 routes
★ 544 pages
★ over 40,000 km of journeys
★ over 30 countries
★ tips on fares and ticketing
★ detailed route descriptions
★ sketch maps for each route
★ index maps which show all routes
★ suggestions for overnight stays

... and a very fine read!

The 18th edition of *Europe by Rail*, published in October 2024, has better coverage of France, Spain and Poland, improved ferry and bus connections, and a new section on travel apps. It is available directly from European Rail Timetable Ltd, all good bookshops and online retailers.

www.EuropeByRail.eu

Liège Guillemins station (photo © Erzsi Molnár / dreamstime.com)

RAIL *EXTRA*

RAIL EXTRA enables the editorial team an opportunity to include further information on rail travel throughout Europe to supplement our timetables. In particular we have selected a number of tourist and heritage lines from the many hundreds on offer, with timetable details where possible (though it's always best to check before travel in case of late changes). We would also encourage readers to seek out the many museum and heritage lines which we cannot show for space reasons, many of which include steam operation.

AUSTRIA

RAIL TRAVEL

See Tables **950 - 999**. Most trains are operated by Österreichische Bundesbahnen (ÖBB) www.oebb.at. For train types see page 459. Scenic highlights include the Semmeringbahn (Table **980**), the Arlberg route (**951**) and the Salzburg to Villach Tauern line. Many minor routes are also scenic.

Opening of the Wien to St Pölten high-speed line in 2012, together with ongoing infrastructure upgrades elsewhere, has led to significant journey time reductions on the key east to west 'Westbahn' route between Wien and Salzburg. ÖBB's high-speed *Railjet* trains take advantage of this, running at up to 230 km/h. Private operator *Westbahn* competes with ÖBB on the route. ÖBB also operate the *Nightjet* brand for overnight trains, with an extensive network of international and domestic routes. A new high-speed line between Graz and Klagenfurt, known as the *Koralmbahn*, is currently under construction which, when opened in 2026, will significantly speed up journeys between Wien, Graz and Klagenfurt.

Services around Wien (Vienna) were revolutionised following the opening of the impressive Hauptbahnhof (central station) in 2015. A notable feature of the station is the diamond shaped roof employing 25,000 square metres of translucent glass and steel. Westbahnhof is now only used by *Westbahn* and ÖBB regional services.

Note that several local lines are run by private operators.

MARIAZELLERBAHN

Niederösterreichische Verkehrsorganisationsgesellschaft (NÖVOG) run several local lines including the 84 km narrow gauge Mariazellerbahn from St Pölten Hbf to Mariazell. Full details are shown in Table **994**.

The electrified Mariazellerbahn is widely recognised as one of the most attractive Alpine railway journeys and an excursion is highly recommended. There are 21 tunnels and 75 bridges or viaducts along the route with the highest point (892m) situated in the 2368m Gösing Tunnel. Between Kirchberg and Laubenbachmühle the line passes through the spectacular gorge of the River Pielach and at Winterbach there are some particularly fine views. On Ⓒ May 3 - November 2 a heritage electric train runs one trip each way, whilst a steam hauled journey also operates on several dates.

STEYRTAL-MUSEUMSBAHN

A 10 minute walk from Steyr station (Table **976**) takes you to the Lokalbahn station from where the 17 km line operated by ÖGEG www.oegeg.at takes you to Grünburg. Opened in 1889, the Steyrtalbahn is the oldest narrow gauge (760mm) line in Austria. Passing through the scenic Steyr valley, it has been operating as a heritage line since 1986 using steam traction.

Operates ⑦ during June and July; ⑥⑦ during Aug. and Sept. (also on May 1, Oct. 26). Two services operate in each direction. Journey time is 60 minutes each way.

NIEDERÖSTERREICHISCHE SCHNEEBERGBAHN

This 9.8 km narrow gauge rack railway runs from Puchberg am Schneeberg to Hochschneeberg. Timings, which include a steam service on Sundays and public holidays in high summer, can be found in Table **984**.

Construction was completed in 1897. The journey to the summit provides wonderful views of the Schneeberg mountain range, with Hochschneeberg station being the highest in Austria at 1795m above sea-level.

WALDVIERTLER SCHMALSPURBAHNEN

A narrow gauge (760mm) network based on Gmünd NÖ (**Table 990**) close to the Czech border, running through enchanting, densely wooded landscapes. The line runs for 68 km Groß Gerungs - Gmünd - Alt Nagelberg - Litschau. Operated by NÖVOG www.noevog.at.

Services run May 1 – Oct. 26.

Gmünd to Groß Gerungs Operated by railcars except on ③⑥ when trains are hauled by heritage diesel (steam on 1st / 3rd ⑥ of the month until Oct. 19).

	B†	A	BJ	†	C		B†	A	BJ	C	†
Gmünd NÖ . d.	0900	1115	1300	1330	1400	G. Gerungs d.	1130	1345	1615	1630	1630
Weitra......... d.	0925	1140	1328	1355	1425	Weitra........ d.	1228	1443	1714	1728	1728
G. Gerungs . a.	1025	1240	1450	1455	1525	Gmünd NÖ a.	1250	1505	1740	1750	1750

Gmünd to Litschau Operated by railcars except on ③⑥ when trains are hauled by heritage diesel (steam on 1st / 3rd ⑦ of the month).

	A	C	B	Ⓒ	Ⓒ	B	A	E
Gmünd NÖ .... d.	0900	1000	1000	1000	1430	1430	1530	1700
Alt Nagelberg............... ▷ d.	0920	1030	1030	1030	1500	1500	1550	1730*
Litschau............................ a.	0945	1055	1055	1055	1525	1525	1525	1755

	A	B	C	Ⓒ	Ⓒ	B	A	E
Litschau............................ d.	1000	1130	1245	1300	1600	1600	1700	2200
Alt Nagelberg............... ▷ d.	1030	1200	1315	1330	1630	1630	1730	2230
Gmünd NÖ .... a.	1050	1220	1335	1350	1650	1650	1750	2250

A – ⑤ July 4 - Aug. 29.
B – ③ June 4 - Sept. 24.
C – ①②④ June 30 - Aug. 28.
D – ③ until Aug. 30.
E – Aug. 13 only.
G – ①②⑥ until Aug. 30.
J – ⑥ 2nd, 4th, 5th of the month until Oct. 25.
* – Arrives 1718.
▷ – Heritage trains also run Alt Nagelberg - Heidenreichstein on ③Ⓒ July 16 - Aug.27. From Alt Nagelberg 1030, 1500, 1700 ; from Heidenreichstein 0945, 1245†, 1345③, 1545. Journey 40 minutes. www.wackelsteinexpress.at

ACHENSEEBAHN

This short (6.8 km) narrow gauge steam-operated rack railway runs from Jenbach, adjacent to the ÖBB station, to Seespitz-Bahnstation. The timetable is shown in Table **956**. The line climbs from Jenbach (532m) to the southern tip of the Achensee (931m), the departure point for Achensee boat excursions.

RAILWAY MUSEUMS

One of Austria's principal railway museums is the Eisenbahnmuseum Strasshof, also known as *Das Heizhaus*, situated adjacent to Silberwald station on the Wien to Břeclav line and served by local trains. Open ②–⑦ Apr. 1 - Oct. 27. Steam is in operation within the large site on the following dates: May 18, June 1, Aug. 3, Sept. 21, Oct. 26.

Another large railway museum is the Lokpark Ampflwang, operated by ÖGEG. Steam / diesel trips run on most ⑦ June - Sept. and ⑥ Aug. - Sept. (confirm locally) on the 11 km line which links the museum with Timelkam, which is served by local trains from Linz.

Austrian Railways *CityJet* suburban service, Wien

BELGIUM

RAIL TRAVEL

See Tables **400 - 449**. Operated by NMBS (in Dutch) / SNCB (in French) www.belgiantrain.be. With over 3,500 km of lines, Belgium is well served by frequent rail services, mostly running to regular-interval timetables at the same minutes past each hour (with some peak hour extras). Note, however, that timetables and the route network can vary on Saturdays and Sundays, as shown in our tables. The most scenic lines are those in the Ardennes region, for example Liège to Gouvy and on to Luxembourg.

The two principal stations in Brussels, Midi/Zuid (south) and Nord, were long ago linked by a cross-city line, including the uninspiring Central station with its underground platforms, and most trains run through Brussels by way of this line, many also serving Brussels Airport. However, a further line serves Luxembourg and Schuman stations in the European quarter of Brussels, and this too has a link to the airport via a recently opened tunnel.

Journeys between Brussels and Liège (Table **400**), as well as international journeys to Germany, were considerably speeded up by the opening of the high-speed line in 2002, and from Liège to Aachen in 2009. Other high-speed lines are used by *Eurostar* trains to London and by trains to the Netherlands.

Belgium's coastal resorts are linked with each other not by the national rail system but by a frequent coastal tramway (the *Kusttram*) operated by De Lijn. For details see Table **406**.

Heritage lines include Stoomtrein Dendermonde-Puurs www.stoomtrein.be, Stoomcentrum Maldegem, which links Eeklo (Table **413**) with Maldegem www.stoomtreinmaldegem.be, and the historic Tramway Vicinal des Grottes de Han. However, the most significant heritage operation is the 'Three Valleys' CFV3V, detailed below.

Brussels also has a recently opened railway museum close to Schaerbeek station. See www.trainworld.be for further details. Closed on Mondays.

CHEMIN DE FER À VAPEUR DES TROIS VALLÉES (CFV3V)

This 14 km line runs from Mariembourg (800m from the SNCB/NMBS station in Table **421**) to Treignes, where there is a railway museum on the site of the old international station building. See www.cfv3v.eu for details.

Trains run Ⓒ Apr. 1 - Nov. 2 (also ②④ July 3 - Aug. 28). There are three return services departing Mariembourg 1130, 1420 and 1730 returning from Treignes 1310, 1620 and 1810 (1830 certain dates). Many dates include steam-hauled journeys but check the website for details. Journey time is 30 minutes each way by diesel railcar or by steam train. A steam festival takes place Sept. 27 – 28 and special timetables run on a handful of other dates.

BULGARIA

RAIL TRAVEL

See Tables **1500 - 1560**. Bulgarian State Railways (BDZ) www.bdz.bg run on a network of a little over 4,000 km, the principal lines of which link the capital Sofia with the Black Sea resorts of Burgas and Varna. Trains are often crowded and reservations are recommended for long-distance travel (and are obligatory for certain express trains). Signs at stations are in Cyrillic, although the website does have an English version.

BDZ has one narrow gauge line, running 125 km from Septemvri to Dobrinishte, serving en route the winter resort town of Bansko. Timings for this (very slow) line are in Table **1510**.

The Museum of Transport is in a former railway station in the outskirts of Ruse (see link foot of http://fan.bdz.bg). There is little else in the form of heritage lines, although there are occasional steam specials, and Plovdiv has a 600mm gauge Children's Railway (formerly Pioneer Railway).

CROATIA

RAIL TRAVEL

See Tables **1300 - 1358**. National railway company is Hrvatske Željeznice (HŽ) www.hzpp.hr. The network is centred on the capital Zagreb, but services are generally infrequent, even on the main lines to Rijeka and Split. The Zagreb to Split line (Table **1330**) is particularly scenic; the day trains on this line are operated by modern diesel units, with compulsory reservation. Sadly, connections from Knin to Zadar are no longer by train but provided by bus, although the route is still considered part of the rail network for ticketing purposes. Buses along the coast from Split to Ploče and Dubrovnik are, however, privately operated - brief details are given in Table **1325**.

The Croatian Railway Museum consists of an outdoor collection of exhibits in Zagreb, accessed from Ulica grada Vukovara 47, with limited opening hours (see http://muzej.hzinfra.hr). Currently open ③–⑥ at varying times.

CZECH REPUBLIC

RAIL TRAVEL

See Tables **1100 - 1169**. National rail company is České Dráhy (ČD) (www.cd.cz), whilst the railway infrastructure is administered by Správa Železnic (www.spravazeleznic.cz). An extensive network of over 9,000 km is operated, with many branch lines serving towns and villages away from the main lines, making it possible to visit almost anywhere by rail. If you like to explore on slow, winding, country branch lines, this is definitely a country to visit. With a rail pass or day ticket you can hop on and off trains at will, since the only trains requiring advance reservation are the handful of *SC* (*SuperCity*) Pendolino trains, which run mainly on the Praha - Ostrava route (reservation fee varies up to a maximum of CZK 250).

Other high-quality trains are classified *IC*, *EC* or *Ex*, whilst *Railjet RJ* trains also run on the Praha - Wien axis (whilst *Railjet* is an Austrian train type, there are also some in the colours of Czech Railways). Regular fast trains are classified *R* (for rychlík) or *Rx* and are shown in our tables with just the train number. Seats can be reserved on all of these train types (recommended at busy times), and many convey buffet cars. Semi-fast trains are *Sp* or spešný. Local trains, which can be very slow, are *Os* or osobný.

Other operators compete with ČD on several major routes, principally Regiojet from Praha to Ostrava, Bratislava, Košice and Wien, and Leo Express to Ostrava and Bohumín. Tickets are not interchangeable with those of ČD. Some lines are now franchised to private companies.

In Praha, most services are concentrated on Praha hlavní nádraží (which means main station) though some services of a more local nature leave from the nearby Masarykovo station (10 minute walk). Holešovice station is of less importance with a line enabling all through trains to serve hlavní nádraži.

Chomutov depository: Czech loco 498.106 built by Škoda in 1955

As with many countries in this listing, it is possible to book tickets online (with an account) and to print tickets at home. Although Praha airport is not rail connected, the Airport Express (AE) bus between the airport and Praha hlavní is included in ČD's ticket system so it is possible to print your own ticket from the airport to rail stations in the Czech Republic - very handy for a quick getaway and avoiding ticket office queues!

HERITAGE LINES

Heritage operations mainly consist of special trains on parts of the Czech rail system, and these are shown in ČD's online timetable (some in a special section listed on their website as ZVL). Many of these trains are run by KŽC (www.kzc.cz) with heritage diesel railcars or locos, mainly on summer weekends.

Recommended is a short 30 minute trip from Praha hlavní nádraží over the scenic so-called *Prague Semmering* line to Praha-Zličín. Operated by KŽC and known as *Pražský motoráček*, it is included in the Prague public transport tariff. Departures are on © at 0824, 1038, 1238 and 1438, returning at 0947, 1147, 1347 and1607 (or by tram from adjacent terminus).

Posázavsky motoráček line from Praha to Týnec nad Sázavou via Vrané nad Vltavou. As well as ČD local trains, KŽC runs heritage journeys in summer (Mar. 23 to Oct 26.) from Praha to Týnec nad Sázavou at 1455 ⑦, returning at 1738 ⑦.

ČD's only narrow gauge line is also worth a mention, running to the village of Osoblaha close to the Polish border - see Table **1169** for brief details.

The principal railway museum is at Lužna u Rakovnika, 64 km from Praha (Table **1105**), open © Apr. - Oct.; (also ②–⑦ June to Aug.). Steam trips operate on certain summer weekends to and from Lužna (for example from Praha or Chomutov). The museum's website is www.cdnostalgie.cz - click on the AKCE link for a document listing the many heritage events and trips.

The National Technical Museum also has a large railway depository in Chomutov, open ⑤–⑦ Apr. 11 - Oct. 28 (also ②–⑦ June 3 - Sept. 28). www.muzeum-chomutov.cz. Approx 1.4 km on foot from Chomutov station via Globus car park.

DENMARK

RAIL TRAVEL

See Tables **700 - 728**. Operator is Danske Statsbaner (DSB) www.dsb.dk. There are also some independent lines, and certain former DSB services in Jutland are now operated by private company ArrivaTog www.arriva.dk. See page 343 for further information.

Principal trains linking København with the rest of Denmark are classified InterCity (*IC*) and InterCityLyn (*Lyn*), travelling at up to 200 km/h. Reservations are recommended but not compulsory, and can be made by telephone ✆ 70 13 14 15 as well as online and on the DSB app.

Travel from Sjælland (the island on which København sits) to the rest of the country (Fyn and Jylland) is by way of the impressive 18 km Great Belt Fixed Link (Storebælt), consisting of a bridge and a tunnel, with an island in between. Prior to 1997 trains were conveyed on board ferries to make the crossing. On the other side of København, the equally impressive 16 km Øresund Bridge, opened in 2000, links the city with Malmø in Sweden, with a frequent rail service which also serves København's Kastrup Airport en route. The airport is also linked to the city by metro.

There are also plans for a Fehmarn Belt fixed link between Denmark and Germany (an undersea tunnel between Rødby and Puttgarden), although it's several years away. The process of loading trains to Germany on ferries has now ceased with trains to Hamburg now routed via Padborg.

Denmark's railway museum is situated in Odense, adjacent to the railway station and is open daily all year. www.jernbanemuseet.dk

MUSEUMSBANEN MARIBO-BANDHOLM

Starting at Maribo on the privately operated Nykøbing to Nakskov line (see footnote in Table **720**), this short museum line in the south of Denmark heads 8 km north to Bandholm. After pausing for 20 minutes at Bandholm station, where the railway is based, the train continues for a further 400 metres to a platform adjacent to the harbour. www.museumsbanen.dk

		A	C	A	C	B	C
Maribo	d.	1015	1015	1245	1315	1445	1515
Bandholm	a.	1042	1042	1312	1342	1512	1532
Bandholm havn	a.	...	1113	1343	1413	1543	1613

		A	C	A	C	B	C
Bandholm havn	d.	...	1123	1353	1423	1553	1623
Bandholm	d.	1105	1135	1405	1435	1605	1635
Maribo	a.	1133	1203	1433	1503	1633	1703

A – ③ July 2–30, Aug. 20, 27.
B – ③ July 2–30.
C – ⑦ June 15 - Aug. 17; ④ July 4 - Aug. 8, Oct. 17. Trains are steam hauled.

ESTONIA

RAIL TRAVEL

See Tables **1870 - 1876**. Local services are run by the state owned railway company under the name Elron www.elron.ee using modern diesel multiple units on broad gauge tracks. The most important route links Tallinn with the country's second largest city, Tartu (Table **1870**).

In January 2025, the operators of passenger services in Estonia, Latvia and Lithuania introduced co-ordinated connecting services on the Vilnius - Riga - Tallinn corridor (Table **49**). There are good bus links to Latvia's capital, Riga, and also to St Peterburg (Table **1800**), although journeys to the latter currently require a change of bus at the Russian border. Note that Tallinn's bus station is located three kilometres from the rail station, with a tram service linking the two. A new standard gauge rail project, known as *Rail Baltica*, will eventually offer a direct link between Tallinn and Poland via Latvia and Lithuania (expected to be operating partially by 2028 and fully open by 2030).

Tallinn's proximity to Helsinki means that many tourists combine a trip to both cities. The various ferry routes linking the two cities are shown in our Ferry section (Table **2410**).

There is a railway museum in the impressive former station at Haapsalu, which can no longer be reached by rail (1h 45m by bus). Open ③–⑦ 1100 - 1700 see the Raudtee ja Sidemuuseum link on www.salm.ee. There is also a narrow gauge railway museum at Lavassaare, 17 km from Pärnu. www.museumrailway.ee. Open ⑦ June to September (also ① June to August and ⑥ in September).

FINLAND

RAIL TRAVEL

See Tables **790 - 799**. Trains are run by national rail company VR www.vr.fi. Long distance day trains are generally high-speed tilting Pendolinos (up to 220 km/h) or modern double-deck trains. Trains are spacious, helped by the wider 'Russian' track gauge of 1524mm. Fares depend on train type - for further information on train types and ticketing see the introduction to the Finland section on page 366.

Focal point of the rail system is Helsinki's iconic 19-platform central rail station, designed by Eliel Saarinen in *Art Nouveau* style and incorporating four giant granite figures on the frontage. No fewer than 10 tracks head north for 3 km to Pasila, where lines start to divide.

Helsinki's Vantaa airport was added to the rail network in 2015 and can be reached either way around a loop, the anti-clockwise service (lettered 'I') being slightly quicker than the clockwise service ('P').

JOKIOINEN MUSEUM RAILWAY

Finland's only 750mm gauge railway (www.jokioistenmuseorautatie.fi) starts from Humppila on the Turku to Tampere line (Table **795**) and runs for 14 km to Jokioinen. The line also features a collection of preserved Finnish narrow gauge engines and rolling stock at Minkiö station, where the museum is open June – August.

Operates ⑦ June 15 - July 27; ⑥ Aug. 2–23 (also Sept. 13).

Humppila	d.	1030	1305	1550	Jokioinen	d.	...	1145	1435
Minkiö	a.	1053	1328	1613	Minkiö	a.	...	1204	1454
Minkiö	d.	1110	1400	...	Minkiö	d.	0950	1225	1515
Jokioinen	a.	1129	1419	...	Humppila	a.	1013	1248	1538

FINNISH RAILWAY MUSEUM

Rail enthusiasts will find the 59 km trip from Helsinki to Hyvinkää worthwhile, served by half-hourly regional trains (Table **790**). A short walk from the station is the excellent Finnish Railway Museum, open most days (but not Mondays Sept. to May). The museum is closed on Bank Holidays, including the Midsummer holiday June 21, 23. www.rautatiemuseo.fi

Finnish Railway Museum

FRANCE

RAIL TRAVEL

See Tables **250 - 398**. The national operator is SNCF - Société Nationale des Chemins de fer Français. www.sncf.com

Within France, the premium rate customer service line is ✆ 36 35.

Since opening its first section of high-speed line in 1981, French Railways has constructed an extensive network of dedicated high-speed lines, fanning out in all directions from Paris. The longest is that to Marseille, with the 750 km being covered in around 3h 20m. The line to the north is of international significance, with *Eurostar* trains from London and Paris to Brussels, Amsterdam and Köln. Other international *TGV* services run to Germany, Switzerland and Spain. Speeds of up to 320 km/h (200 mph) are attained, with many trains continuing on conventional track to serve most parts of France. Future high-speed line extensions to Nice, Perpignan and Toulouse are planned.

The high-speed *TGV* trains (*TGV* stands for Train à Grande Vitesse) are branded *TGV inOui*, whilst *Ouigo* is a name used for a network of special low-cost high-speed services which are available on most long-distance routes. *Ouigo* also operate some low-cost classic loco-hauled trains on certain routes, known as *Ouigo Classique*. Note that *Ouigo* services can only be booked on-line using its website. *TGV* trains require compulsory reservation, but there are exceptions for some local journeys between Lille and the coast (Calais, Boulogne, Dunkerque). See Table **250** on pages 162 and 163, for details. Although reservations can often be made at the last minute (space permitting) it does make it difficult to make spontaneous travel decisions. It also increases the cost for rail pass holders, who need to take into account the cost of reservation fees (for normal tickets the reservation fee is included in the ticket price). Light refreshments are available on *TGV* trains, except on short routes such as Paris to Lille.

On other lines, most local and regional trains (outside Paris) are branded *TER* (Transport Express Régional), organised in conjunction with regional authorities. Off-peak services are often infrequent. Some departures may be provided by bus - if the bus uses the *TER* branding and is running on a route normally provided by train then rail tickets and passes are valid.

With France being western Europe's largest country, with much long-distance travel, there are huge peaks in travel demand, notably on Friday afternoons and Sunday evenings, also on and around public holidays. Fares are generally higher at these times (known as *périodes blanche*), as well as during the normal Monday to Friday peaks. Note that when engineering work affects schedules, it is not uncommon for trains to leave earlier than normal, or for services to be partially or wholly replaced by bus, so a last-minute check of timings is recommended.

There has been a recent revival in overnight rail travel with government support being provided for strategically important routes between Paris and the south of France. Domestic overnight services convey couchettes and reclining seats using recently refurbished rolling stock.

Terminal stations in Paris are scattered around the periphery of the city centre (see page 33), linked by metro lines, or in some cases by *RER* services which are cross-city outer suburban routes. Beware of pickpockets operating on these lines, which can be very crowded.

CHEMIN DE FER TOURISTIQUE DU VERMANDOIS

On June 15*, July 6*, 13, Aug. 17, 24, Sept. 14*, Oct. 5*, 19 heritage trains run from the SNCF station at St Quentin (Tables **255/6/8**) on a 90 minute round trip to Mézières-sur-Oise. www.cftv.fr. Departures from St Quentin are at 1345, 1545 and 1745.

On dates showing an * a luxurious dining car experience can also be had on the *Restaurant Art-Deco Express* which operates with an authentic restaurant car built in 1928.

Contact www.cftv.fr direct for timings.

CHEMIN DE FER DE LA BAIE DE SOMME

As the name suggests, the line runs around the Somme Bay, an area north of Abbeville on the Picardy coast noted for its varied flora and fauna. Operated by historic narrow gauge, the line runs for 27 km on the route Le Crotoy - Noyelles - St.Valery - Cayeux. At Noyelles-sur-Mer connections can be made with SNCF trains (Table **261**). www.cfbs.eu

Services operate daily Apr. 5 - Sept. 21, ②③④⑥⑦ Sept. 23–Oct. 31 (also Nov. 1, 8, 9, 10) with a mixture of steam and diesel traction.

A connecting diesel service from St. Valery to Cayeux on the south side of the bay operates on certain dates in the summer taking 35 minutes.

TRAIN THUR DOLLER ALSACE

Situated west of Mulhouse, this 14 km standard-gauge line runs from Cernay St André to Sentheim. The station at Cernay is approximately 2 km from the SNCF station, which is served by trains on the Mulhouse - Thann line. Certain journeys are steam hauled. www.train-doller.org

Splendid scenery and varied wildlife are features of the trip along this line. Some of the railway's rolling stock dates back to 1892 and includes traditional wooden-bodied coaches.

Services commence from June 1: On ⑦ June to September trains depart Cernay at 1030 and 1500 (journey 90 mins) returning from Sentheim at 1330 and 1730 (journey 60 mins). On ③ in July and August trains depart Cernay at 1000 and 1500 (journey 80 mins) returning from Sentheim at 1330 and 1730 (journey 50 mins).

CHEMIN DE FER DE LA VENDÉE

Situated in the Pays de la Loire region, Mortagne-sur-Sèvre is 10 km from Cholet (Table **299**). This tourist line, normally steam hauled, runs for 22 km on the route Mortagne-sur-Sèvre - Les Épesses - Les Herbiers, noted for its three spectacular viaducts. Les Herbiers station features a 1930s period style bar.

The train runs ⑦ June 1 - Sept. 28 (not Sept. 21), ③⑤ July 6 - Aug. 31 (not July 11) departing Mortagne at 1530 for the one hour journey to Les Herbiers. Arrival back at Mortagne is at 1800. www.vendeetrain.fr

Special *Grands Express* restaurant car services also operate most ④–⑦ Apr. 3 - Nov. 2, departing Mortagne at 1200 for a three-hour dining experience. Bookings can be made online.

LE PETIT TRAIN DE LA RHUNE

This vintage rack railway with panoramic views takes passengers to the summit of La Rhune, a mountain in the Basque country close to the Spanish border. The electrified metre-gauge line is 4.2 km long and climbs to a height of 905 metres. www.rhune.com

The start point is Col de St Ignace (11 km from St Jean de Luz, Table **305**) which can be reached by bus. Operating until Nov. 11, departures from Col de St Ignace are at 0930, 1050, 1210, 1410, 1530; from July 7 to August 31 services operate from 0850 and then approximately every 40 minutes until 1730.

Opened in 1924, the line uses traditional wooden-bodied coaches. The journey to the summit takes 35 minutes at a leisurely speed of 8 km/h. The wonderful scenery of the western Pyrenees can be enjoyed during the journey and the views at the summit are spectacular. A return journey takes approx two and a half hours. There are a number of scenic walking routes from the summit station including a signed route back to Col de St Ignace.

LIGNE DE CERDAGNE (SNCF)

Also known as *Le Petit Train Jaune* (the little yellow train), this narrow gauge line is part of the SNCF (French Railways) system and runs for 63 km from Latour de Carol to Villefranche. Timings are shown in Table **354**.

Construction of this steeply graded line was completed as late as 1929 and it provides some fine views of the Pyrenees. The bright yellow trains are electrically powered using a third rail system and during the summer most trains include open sightseeing carriages. Rail or bus connections are available at both ends of the line - at Latour de Carol for Toulouse (Table **312**) and at Villefranche for Perpignan (Table **354**).

TRAIN À VAPEUR DES CÉVENNES

Based at Anduze in the foothills of the Cévennes mountains in southern France, this standard gauge line runs for 14 km to St Jean du Gard. The nearest SNCF station is Alès (Table **333**), about 15 km from Anduze.

The 40 minute journey includes some fine panoramas as the line crosses a number of spectacular viaducts. A notable nearby attraction is the *Bambouseraie* botanical gardens, originally created in 1855.

The high-season timetable runs from July 15 to Aug. 28 with departures from Anduze at 0930, 1130, 1430 and 1630, returning from St Jean du Gard at 1030, 1330, 1530 and 1730. Trains are steam hauled except for the 0930 from Anduze and 1730 from St Jean du Gard.

There is also a low-season service on most days Apr. 6 - July 14 and Aug. 30 - Oct. 31, but note that the line is closed on certain dates. Departures from Anduze are at 1130, 1500 and 1700 (one way), returning at 1030, 1400, 1600 with the last journey in each direction being diesel hauled. www.trainavapeur.com

CITÉ DU TRAIN - MULHOUSE RAILWAY MUSEUM

One of the largest railway museums in the world, Cité du Train (the French National Railway Museum) is situated in Mulhouse in eastern France. It is open every day except Christmas day and is served by the *Musées* stop on tram line 3 from Mulhouse railway station. www.citedutrain.com

Thalys TGV trains at Paris Nord

GERMANY

RAIL TRAVEL

See Tables **800 - 945**. National operator is Deutsche Bahn (DB) www.bahn.de. Telephone enquiries: ✆ 030 2970 (24 hrs).

The vast rail network of over 33,000 km covers all parts of Germany, with dedicated high-speed lines in various parts of the country helping to speed up long distance journeys, whether they be north to south or east to west. The sleek white *ICE* trains (InterCity Express) provide the fastest service, and whilst they have higher fares, reservation is not compulsory, and therefore there is no extra charge for pass holders. Several other train categories are in use, and these are explained at the start of the German section on page 372. Independent operator FlixTrain offers an expanding network of domestic German routes using refurbished rolling stock.

In addition to DB, there are a large number of private operators running local lines. Also, services are increasingly being franchised out to other operators, including certain *S-Bahn* networks, which are suburban services in large cities. Most urban areas have integrated ticketing, with day and period tickets being valid on all modes of public transport.

A common abbreviation in timetables is Hbf. which refers to the main station (Hauptbahnhof), whilst a smaller station is simply Bf. In most cities, principal rail services are concentrated on a single main station. This includes Berlin, with its impressive Hauptbahnhof, with east to west and north to south lines on two different levels.

Several major airports are rail connected; the important airport station at Frankfurt has direct long-distance trains to various parts of the country, as well as regional and local S-Bahn services.

Readers interested in the many museum and heritage lines in Germany may find the following website useful: www.vdmt.de.

DB has its own museum in Nürnberg (closed Mondays), 750m west of the main station: www.dbmuseum.de.

HARZER SCHMALSPURBAHNEN

With a total length of 140 km this system of narrow gauge lines is one of the most extensive in Europe with scheduled steam and diesel services running throughout the year. It has the added advantage of being easily accessible with no less than three interchanges with the DB network. The journey to the 1125m summit at Brocken, the highest point in northern Germany, is particularly impressive (weather permitting) passing through the scenic Hochharz National Park. Three and five day tickets are available for unlimited travel over the whole network. www.hsb-wr.de

Timings are shown in Table **867**. Connections with DB services are made at Nordhausen (Tables **865/8/9**), Wernigerode (Table **860**) and Quedlinburg (Table **862**).

SÄCHSISCH-OBERLAUSITZER EISENBAHNGESELLSCHAFT

A narrow gauge steam operated line situated close to the Polish and Czech border with services running throughout the year. The line, which is 16 km in total, runs from Zittau to a junction at Bertsdorf, from where trains continue to Kurort Oybin or Kurort Jonsdorf. The timetable features simultaneous steam departures from Bertsdorf to Oybin and Jonsdorf which create an impressive sight! www.zittauer-schmalspurbahn.de

Timings are shown in Table **853**, and Zittau can be reached by means of Tables **854**, **855** and **1117**.

LÖSSNITZGRUNDBAHN

Operated by Sächsische Dampfeisenbahngesellschaft mbH, this steam-operated narrow gauge line starts in the unlikely setting of the Dresden suburbs at Radebeul Ost, running for 16.6 km via Moritzburg to Radeburg. Radebeul Ost can be reached by train (Tables **842** and **857**) and the narrow gauge service runs daily throughout the year (see Table **853** for timings). The main tourist attraction in the area is the impressive Moritzburg Castle. www.loessnitzgrundbahn.de

DAMPFBAHN FRÄNKISCHE SCHWEIZ

From Forchheim in the area known as Upper Franconia (Oberfranken) in northern Bavaria, an hourly train service (VGN route R22) brings you 20 minutes later to Ebermannstadt. From there the steam railway (sometimes diesel) runs 16 km to Behringersmühle.

Trains run on ⑦ and public holidays from May 11 to October 26. Departures from Ebermannstadt are at 1005, 1405, 1605, returning from Behringersmühle at 1105, 1505, 1705. For steam operation days please check locally. Journey time is 45 minutes each way. There are also Christmas specials in December. Steam trains convey a buffet car. www.dfs.ebermannstadt.de

BROHLTAL EISENBAHN

The Brohltalbahn (also known as the 'Vulkan-Express') is a charming narrow gauge railway located a few kilometres north-west of Andernach. Services run on many dates from April 27 to October 27 (daily except Mondays from June 1 to September 30). Steam locomotives haul trains on selected dates. The 17½ km route between Brohl and Engeln is located in the ancient volcanic region of Laacher See. The journey takes 85 minutes, climbing 400 metres from the Rhein river to the summit through attractive Eifel countryside. Brohl can be reached using hourly Mittelrheinbahn stopping services between Köln and Koblenz. www.vulkan-express.de

RÜGENSCHE BÄDERBAHN

This well-known 26.7 km narrow gauge (750 mm) line nicknamed *Rasender Roland* runs on the route Lauterbach (Mole) - Putbus - Binz - Göhren on the island of Rügen in north-eastern Germany. Timings are shown in Table **844a**. Connections with DB trains are made at Putbus where there is a service from Bergen auf Rügen (also in Table **844a**). The Lokalbahn station in Binz, however, is over 2 km from DB's Ostseebad Binz station. www.ruegensche-baederbahn.de

Services operate throughout the year with steam traction. However, the Putbus to Lauterbach narrow gauge section is seasonal.

ÖCHSLE MUSEUMS-SCHMALSPURBAHN

A 19 km narrow gauge steam railway running from Warthausen to Ochsenhausen. Warthausen is located 34 km south of Ulm and 3 km north of Biberach (Table **933**) and is served by the adjacent Warthausen station. Note, however, that most trains in Table **933** do not call at Warthausen (suggested DB connections are shown below). www.oechsle-bahn.de.

Trains run on ⑦ May 1 - Oct. 13 and first ⑥ of the month May 4 - Oct. 5; also on ④ July 11 - Sept. 5.

Ulm Hbf (DB)	d.	*0947*	*1347*	Ochsenhausen	d.	1200	1615
Biberach (DB)	d.	*1007*	*1407*	Warthausen	a.	1310	1725
Warthausen	d.	1030	1445	*Biberach* (DB)	a.	*1321*	*1748*
Ochsenhausen	a.	1140	1555	*Ulm Hbf* (DB)	a.	*1346*	*1811*

Completed in 1899, the Öchsle Museums-Schmalspurbahn was one of five narrow gauge railways built by the old *Königlich Württembergischen Staats-Eisenbahnen*. Passenger traffic ceased in 1964, although freight traffic continued to use the line for a further 19 years. Tourist trains have been running since 1985.

BUCKOWER KLEINBAHN

This short standard gauge electric railway is situated in the picturesque *Märkische Schweiz* region, approximately 50 km east of Berlin. The railway's museum at Buckow station has a number of exhibits charting the region's railway heritage. The line runs 5 km from its base at Buckow to Müncheberg. Connecting trains from Berlin Ostkreuz or Lichtenberg to Müncheberg run hourly, as shown in Table **832**. The 2023 season commences on Apr. 29 although schedules are not yet confirmed.

The Kleinbahn runs on © Apr. 27 - Oct. 6 with departures
from Buckow at 0955, 1055, 1155, 1425, 1525, 1625 and 1725;
from Müncheberg at 1020, 1120, 1220, 1450, 1550, 1650 and 1750.
Journey time is 12 – 13 minutes each way. www.buckower-kleinbahn.de

GREAT BRITAIN

RAIL TRAVEL

See Tables **100 - 229**. Rail services in Great Britain are currently franchised out to a number of different train operating companies - a list is provided in the introduction to the Great Britain section on page 79, and codes are used in our tables to show the operator. Collectively the railway companies work together as National Rail (www.nationalrail.co.uk) which means that timetable enquiries are available irrespective of operator, as are full price tickets, which are available between any two stations. A 24-hour national telephone enquiry line is available ✆ 03457 48 49 50.

The railway infrastructure is in the hands of publicly owned Network Rail (www.networkrail.co.uk), which also runs major stations.

Best value advance purchase tickets are usually only valid on a specified train, and some other tickets may be restricted to a particular operator. Many ticket types have complex time restrictions, and there can be vast differences in the price of tickets (travelling to or from London in the peak period, between 0600 – 0930, can be particularly expensive).

The network of over 15,000 km of lines covers most parts of Britain, although closures in the 1960s and 1970s have left some gaps in coverage. Services are particularly dense in the south-east, where outer suburban lines from London stretch right to the coast. Kent has also benefitted from high-speed services on the line (known as HS1) to the Channel Tunnel. A dense network also operates around the northern conurbations, notably Manchester and Liverpool. Key long distance routes are the East Coast Main Line from London King's Cross to Leeds, Newcastle and Edinburgh, and the West Coast Main Line from London Euston to Birmingham, Manchester, Liverpool and Glasgow. A new high-speed line (HS2) from London to Birmingham is under construction (with a planned opening of between 2029 and 2033).

All major airports have good rail links (see Table **100** for London airports). London's stations are mostly terminals linked by London Underground lines, but there are also north-south through services known as Thameslink (Tables **103** / **185**). The Elizabeth Line opened in 2022 and stretches more than 100km from Reading and Heathrow airport in the west through central London in tunnels via Paddington, the West End and Docklands to Shenfield and Abbey Wood in the east. This has revolutionised travel across central London.

Major engineering work usually takes place at weekends and at other times when commuting is at its lowest (for example during the Christmas and Easter periods). Buses may replace trains on affected routes.

HERITAGE AND TOURIST RAILWAYS

There are numerous heritage railway operations up and down Great Britain, many with steam locomotives, and only a small number can be described below. In addition, contact details for the following will be found in our Great Britain section: Bodmin Railway, Table **110**, Isle of Wight Steam Railway, Table **106**; Dartmouth Steam Railway, Table **110, 112**; Dean Forest Railway, Table **117**; South Devon Railway, Table **110**, Talyllyn Railway, Table **148**, Ravenglass and Eskdale Railway, Table **157**; Ecclesbourne Valley and Peak Rail, Table **172**; North Norfolk Railway and Bure Valley Railway, Table **203**. A useful independent website is www.heritage-railways.com.

Several organisations run occasional heritage trains on the main line network - see www.railadvent.co.uk for further details.

The National Railway Museum at York is a major tourist attraction and is free of charge (www.railwaymuseum.org.uk). There is also an offshoot at Shildon (Table **212**), known as *Locomotion* (www.locomotion.org.uk). Many of the heritage railways also have their own small museums.

WEST SOMERSET RAILWAY

Based in Minehead, the West Somerset Railway runs for 32 km to Bishops Lydeard, with no fewer than eight intermediate stations. This former Great Western Railway country branch line is now one of the largest tourist attractions in south-west England. From Minehead the line runs close to the coastline through Dunster, Blue Anchor and Watchet before turning inland at Williton. The railway continues alongside the Quantock Hills before arriving at Bishops Lydeard. Most services are steam-hauled and a buffet car is conveyed on most trains. www.west-somerset-railway.co.uk

The heritage railway runs ②③④⑥⑦ June - Sept. (also most days in Apr., May, and Oct. and specials in Dec.), with between four and five journeys each way. The journey takes approximately 80 minutes. Bishops Lydeard can be reached in around 30 minutes by First Bus route 28 from Taunton bus station, also calling at Taunton railway station (Tables **110**, **115**, **132**).

SEVERN VALLEY RAILWAY

Connected to the National Rail network at Kidderminster (Table **122**), the long-established Severn Valley Railway is within easy reach of Birmingham and the West Midlands. The line runs for 25 km to the attractive Shropshire town of Bridgnorth, serving four beautifully restored intermediate stations en route, which are ideal starting points for walks around the surrounding area. The railway is based at the first of these stations, Bewdley. Refreshments are available at most stations and on most trains, and a full dining car service operates most weekends, for which advance booking is required. Currently trains are only running between Kidderminster and Hampton Loade due to a landslip. www.svr.co.uk

Days of operation: ③④⑥⑦ May - July 21, Sept. 1 – 28, ②③④⑥⑦ July 22 - Aug. 31 (and on various other dates). Trains are hauled by a steam or heritage diesel locomotive, with the journey taking 70 – 80 minutes each way. As with most heritage lines, there are also 'Santa Specials' in Dec.

BLUEBELL RAILWAY

Making a connection with National Rail services at the West Sussex town of East Grinstead (48 km south of London, Table **102**) the well known Bluebell Railway runs for 17.7 km via Horsted Keynes to Sheffield Park, where the railway has its main base. Stations have been restored to show how they would have been at various points in history, that at Sheffield Park having a Victorian ambience. The line has featured in many films and TV programmes including Downton Abbey. Most trains are steam hauled.

The timetable features between two and five journeys each way (depending on the date). During the peak-summer season in August, trains depart Sheffield Park at 1030, 1145, 1300, 1415, 1530 returning one hour later from East Grinstead. The journey takes 40 – 50 minutes each way. www.bluebell-railway.com

KEIGHLEY & WORTH VALLEY RAILWAY

Starting at Keighley, where it shares the station on the scenic Leeds - Settle - Carlisle rail line (Tables **173/4**), this attractive heritage railway runs to Haworth and Oxenhope in 'Brontë Country'. Along the way is the *Rail Story* museum at Ingrow. Trains operate Mar. 1 - Sept. 26 (daily in August and on most days in June and July). Special events take place on selected dates. Timetables vary according to the date, with between four and nine return trips. Trains are steam or diesel hauled. www.kwvr.co.uk

Another popular line is the Great Central Railway, a double track main line heritage railway from Loughborough to Leicester. A *Standard 5* built at Doncaster in 1956.

NORTH YORKSHIRE MOORS RAILWAY

Running through the North Yorkshire Moors National Park, this 29 km standard gauge line runs from Pickering to Grosmont, passing through the villages of Levisham and Goathland along the way. Grosmont is a station on the National Rail line between Middlesbrough and Whitby (Table **211**). Indeed some of the heritage line's steam trains continue on this line to the popular resort of Whitby, with the through journey taking up to two hours.

Most trains are steam hauled and convey refreshment facilities. Trains run daily from April to October, with a limited winter timetable on certain dates outside this period. www.nymr.co.uk

Details of the summer timings can be found in Table **211**. Pickering can be reached by *Yorkshire Coastliner* bus from Leeds and York.

FFESTINIOG RAILWAY

The Ffestiniog Railway, a former industrial narrow gauge line, starts on the Cambrian coast at Porthmadog, before heading inland for 22 km through the magnificent scenery of the Snowdonia National Park. The 75 minute journey ends at Blaenau Ffestiniog by which time the line has climbed over 200m. The huge slate mines clearly visible at Blaenau Ffestiniog provide a reminder of this line's original purpose when built back in 1832. Indeed, the railway can claim to be the oldest railway company in the world still operating trains. Most trains are steam-hauled, with some locomotives being over 150 years old. www.festrail.co.uk

Trains run from Mar. 29 to Oct. 31. Timings can be found in Table **150b**. Porthmadog station is a short walk from the town's station on the Welsh Coast line to Pwllheli (Table **148**), and interchange is also possible at Minffordd. At Blaenau Ffestiniog there are connections with the National Rail service to Llandudno (Table **150a**).

WELSH HIGHLAND RAILWAY

Also running from Porthmadog (Table **148**), and operated by the same company as the Ffestiniog Railway, the Welsh Highland Railway is the UK's longest heritage line, running for 39 km across stunning landscape to Caernarfon. The journey across Snowdonia takes a little over two hours. At Porthmadog the railway shares a newly rebuilt station with the Ffestiniog Railway, whilst Caernarfon can be reached on bus **5C** from Bangor on the Chester - Holyhead line (Table **150**).

Trains run Mar. 29 to Oct. 31. Timings can be found in Table **150b**. www.festrail.co.uk

SNOWDON MOUNTAIN RAILWAY

Yet another line in Wales, this narrow gauge (800mm) railway to the summit of Snowdon dates back to the 1890s and is Britain's only public rack and pinion railway. Starting from Llanberis, Summit station is reached after an arduous 7.5 km climb with the steepest gradient being 1 in 5.5. A return trip takes two and a half hours, which includes approximately 30 minutes at the summit (single tickets are also available for those who wish to walk down). www.snowdonrailway.co.uk

Trains, which may be steam or diesel operated, run from Mar. 29 to Oct. 26 at regular intervals, subject to demand. Advance reservation is recommended during the summer months and during school holiday periods.

The nearest railhead is Bangor on the Chester to Holyhead line (Table **150**). Bus number 85 operated by Gwynfor Coaches runs every two hours or so from Bangor to Llanberis taking 55 minutes.

VALE OF RHEIDOL RAILWAY

The final Welsh line in our listing is the 19 km narrow gauge steam line from Aberystwyth (adjacent to the mainline station in Table **147**) to Devil's Bridge. Opened in 1902, it has operated continuously since then, and unusually remained part of the nationalised British Rail network until being privatised in 1989.

The journey through the spectacular Rheidol Valley to Devil's Bridge takes 60 minutes. From there it is possible to walk to the Mynach Falls, Jacob's Ladder, and Devil's Punch Bowl. www.rheidolrailway.co.uk.

Trains run daily Apr. 5 - Nov. 2 with departures from Aberystwyth at 1030 and 1400, taking one hour to Devil's Bridge and returning at 1230 and 1600. Additional journeys run on certain dates, mostly midweek at 1215 and 1545 and returning at 1415 and 1715.

STRATHSPEY RAILWAY

Representing Scotland in our listing, the Strathspey Railway runs from Aviemore, where connections can be made with trains on the Edinburgh to Inverness line (Table **223**), to Broomhill via Boat of Garten. The 14 km standard gauge line is mainly steam operated.

Trains run ③④⑥⑦ Apr. 5 - Nov. 2 (③–⑦ in June and September; ②–⑦ in July and August). A round trip takes 1h 40m, with trains leaving Aviemore at 1015, 1245, 1500. Returning from Broomhill 1121, 1351, 1606. Light lunches are served on the 1245 departure, and afternoon tea on 1500 departure. www.strathspeyrailway.co.uk.

ISLE OF MAN RAILWAYS

Situated in the Irish Sea some two or three hours by ferry from Heysham or Liverpool, the Isle of Man is a self-governing British dependency which is synonymous with heritage transport, and a mecca for enthusiasts and tourists alike. The main transport attractions consist of:

Isle of Man Steam Railway: Douglas - Port Erin (25 km)

Manx Electric Railway: Douglas (Derby Castle) - Laxey - Ramsey (29 km)

Snaefell Mountain Railway: Laxey - Snaefell Summit (8 km)

In Douglas, the famous horse-drawn trams (dating from 1876) run along the promenade between Derby Castle and Broadway.

The Manx Electric Railway serves Laxey station en route where there is interchange with the Snaefell Mountain Railway. The original electric trains, dating back to 1895, are used for the journey to Snaefell Summit from where it is possible to see England, Wales, Scotland and Ireland on a clear day.

Go Explore travelcards give unlimited travel on all scheduled rail and bus services for 1/3/5/7 days. **Go Explore Heritage** additionally provides admission to Heritage sites. Further details: see Table **229**. www.iom-ssp.unicard-uk.com.

The Electric Railway has a small museum in Douglas open on Sundays, whilst the Steam Railway has a museum in Port Erin. Further attractions on the island (included on the Go Explore tickets) are the steam operated Groudle Glen Railway (www.ggr.org.uk) and the miniscule Great Laxey Mine Railway (www.laxeyminerailway.im). The annual heritage transport festival takes place July 22 - 27 in 2025.

NORTHERN IRELAND

In Northern Ireland, trains are operated by Northern Ireland Railways (NIR), part of Translink, and are not administered by National Rail.

Apart from the line across the border to Dublin, the principal line runs from Belfast to Londonderry, with a branch to Portrush (Table **233**). Local lines run from Belfast to Bangor and Larne.

✆ +44 (0)28 90 66 66 30 www.translink.co.uk

Tourist railways in Northern Ireland include the 914mm gauge (3 foot) Giant's Causeway and Bushmills Railway, which is a great way to visit the famous Giant's Causeway on the County Antrim coast, with its thousands of interlocking basalt columns, a major tourist attraction. Normally running at weekends Easter to October, the 3.2 km line starts from Bushmills, which can be reached by bus from Portrush. Trains normally leave Giant's Causeway at 1100, 1300, 1500, and from Bushmills 30 minutes later.

Located adjacent to Cultra Halt on the Belfast - Bangor line (Table **231**), the Ulster Folk and Transport Museum houses one of Europe's largest transport collections. Closed Mondays. www.nmni.com

Snaefell Mountain Railway, Isle of Man. This car was built in 1895.

GREECE

RAIL TRAVEL

See Tables **1400 - 1460**. Trains in Greece are operated by Hellenic Train, a subsidiary of Italian Railways (having previously been state owned until 2017) www.hellenictrain.gr. Call centre for reservations and information: ✆ 14 511; international line +30 2106241945.

The network of a little over 2,200 km is centered on the 500 km main line between Athína (Athens) and Thessaloníki (Table **1400**). Daytime services on the route are operated by modern InterCity trains, on which reservation is compulsory and a supplement is payable. The line has recently been electrified and upgraded with daytime trains now taking around 4 hours and 20 minutes.

There are currently no international rail services to or from Greece. Many travellers arrive by sea from one of several ports in Italy, arriving at Pátra (Patras) in the northern Peloponnese; for schedules see our ferry section. Patras, Greece's third largest city, is a destination in itself, but for those continuing to Athens there is a frequent bus service. Alternatively there are OSE buses to Kiáto (Table **1450**), connecting with trains to Athens (Table **1440**). Athens airport is also rail connected.

Tickets can be purchased at major stations (principally Athens, Thessaloniki, Larissa and Volos), and also online.

DIAKOFTÓ - KALÁVRITA RAILWAY (OSE)

Also known as the Odontotos Rack Railway, this historic 750mm gauge rack line runs for 22 km through spectacular Peloponnese scenery. Starting at Diakoftó, its climb to Kalávrita involves numerous bridges and tunnels and a height difference of 700m. Shortly after departure the line turns inland and enters the dramatic canyon of the Vouraikos river.

The line runs daily throughout the year. Timings are shown in Table **1455**. www.hellenictrain.gr

Diakoftó can be reached by OSE bus from Patra or Kiáto as shown in Table **1450**; rail services operate between Athína and Kiáto (Table **1440**).

THE PELION RAILWAY

The 16 km narrow gauge (600 mm) mountainous line from Ano Lehonia to Milies closed in 1971 but was resurrected as a museum line in 1996, operated by OSE. The scenic route, with two tunnels and nine bridges, affords spectacular views over Pagasitikos Bay. The nearest OSE station is Vólos (Table **1415**). See www.hellenictrain.gr.

2025 service: Trains run on ⑥⑦ leaving Ano Lehonia at 1000 for the 90 minute journey. Return from Milies is at 1500. A 15 minute stop is made at Ano Gatzea in both directions.

Services are operated using a diesel locomotive disguised to look somewhat like a steam loco, with historic wooden carriages.

HUNGARY

AIL TRAVEL

See Tables **1200 - 1299**. A comprehensive network of over 7,000 km is operated by Hungarian State Railways (MÁV Személyszállítási) www.mav.hu. Principal cities are connected by *IC* trains, with compulsory reservation. See the introduction to the Hungary section on page 510 for further information about reservations and supplements.

The main holiday area is around Lake Balaton, and services in the area have different schedules from mid June to late August. Northern Hungary around Eger and Miskolc is another popular area for tourism, and some of the forest railways that we have selected below are situated in this region.

The three main stations in Budapest are named after points of the compass: Keleti (East), Nyugati (West) and Déli (South). However, don't take this as an indication of the direction of travel; trains from Nyugati can go north and east, and as some international trains serve Keleti your train from the 'East' station might well be heading west! Note, however, that the day trains to Bratislava, Praha and beyond have switched from Keleti to Nyugati giving a shorter route.

A curiosity is that hourly *IC* trains leave Budapest Keleti, circumnativate Eastern Hungary via Miskolc and Debrecen, ending up back in Budapest at Nyugati station (Tables **1260** and **1270**). Main stations are connected by metro as shown on the city plan, page 31.

Apart from the metro and MÁV lines, suburban rail services in Budapest include several unconnected lines known as the HÉV, which have only recently become the responsibility of MÁV, through a subsidiary company. Day tickets for Budapest are, however, valid on almost all transport, including some MÁV lines.

BUDAPEST CHILDREN'S RAILWAY (GYERMEKVASÚT)

Running through the Buda hills on the outskirts of Budapest, this charming and popular diesel operated narrow gauge line, formerly known as the Pioneer Railway, runs for 12 km from Hüvösvölgy to Széchenyihegy. Apart from the engine drivers, it is operated mainly by children, who stand and salute as the train leaves the station.

The intermediate station of Jánoshegy is close to the highest point of Budapest where there is a look-out tower, and is only a short walk from the chair lift (Libegö) which offers excellent views of Budapest on the way down to Zugliget (connected by bus 291 to/from Nyugati station).

The Hüvösvölgy end of the line can be reached by taking metro line M2 to Széll Kálmán tér, then tram 61 to Hüvösvölgy terminus.

To reach the southern end of the line at Széchenyihegy take tram 59 or 61 two stops from Széll Kálmán tér to Városmajor, then the rack railway (route 60) which terminates 250m from the Children's Railway.

Trains run throughout the year (except winter Mondays), up to 8 services in each direction in winter, and 13 during summer. Journey time is 40–50 minutes each way. Diesel trains are the norm, but there are steam hauled journeys on certain weekends. Full timings are available from www.gyermekvasut.hu.

NAGYCENK MUSEUM RAILWAY

Nagycenki Széchenyi Múzeumvasút is a 3.6 km narrow gauge tourist railway situated in the north-western corner of Hungary on the GySEV operated Sopron to Györ line (Table **1250**). The museum line starts from Fertöboz which is 11 km from Sopron (certain Sopron trains call there).

The route is Fertöboz - Barátság - Kastély (Nagycenk), so named because Kastély (Castle) station is located close to Nagycenk village and is about 25 minutes walk from Nagycenk station on the Sopron - Szombathely line (12 km from Sopron, most trains in Table **1233** call there). The Kastély terminus of this 760mm gauge light railway is adjacent to the Schloss Széchenyi, a major tourist attraction in this area. The station also features an outdoor display of plinthed narrow gauge steam locomotives.

The museum line is operated by GySEV. As the line is currently being reconstructed, trains may only be running between Kastély and Barátság and details should be verified from the GySEV website www.gysev.hu

ÁLLAMI ERDEI VASUTAK *HUNGARIAN FOREST RAILWAYS*

There are a number of narrow gauge forest railways in Hungary, mostly operated by ÁEV using diminutive diesel locomotives. Timings are available on www.kisvasut.hu. For this feature we have selected the following lines in the scenic Matra mountains area in north-eastern Hungary, which are of particular interest to tourists:

ÁEV SZILVÁSVÁRAD *Forest Railway - see above*

Route: Szalajka Fatelep - Szalajka Fátyolvizesés (5 km). Szalajka-Fatelep is situated 2 km from Szilvásvárad-Szalajkavölgy station, on the Eger - Szilvásvárad line (one stop from Szilvásvárad, Table **1299**).
Typical timetable: May 1 - Oct. 31: from Szalajka-Fatelep 0930, 1030, 1130, 1300, 1400, 1500 (also 1600 May - Sept.; 1700 June - Aug.). Trains return from Szalajka-Fátyolvizesés 1000, 1100, 1200, 1330, 1430, 1530 (also 1630 May - Sept.; 1730 June - Aug.). Journey 16 minutes. Limited winter service. Check timings locally www.szilvasvarad.hu.

ÁEV MÁTRAVASÚT *Forest Railway - see above*

Route: Gyöngyös -Szalajkaház (13 km). Connections with MÁV are made at Gyöngyös (Table **1258**); from the station approach road turn right, then about 400 metres to the ÁEV station. Journey time is 22 minutes.

Typical timetable:
Depart Gyöngyös: 1008 **E**, 1308 **E**, 1508 **E**.
Depart Szalajkaház: 1110 **E**, 1410 **E**,1610 **E**.
E – Ⓒ Mar. 15 - Oct. 31 (also ④⑤ June 24 - Aug. 31).

ÁEV LILLAFÜRED *Forest Railway - see above*

Route: Miskolc (Dorottya utca) - Papírgyár - Lillafüred - Garadna (13 km). From Miskolc station (Tables **1260/1**) take tram number 1 towards Felsö-Majláth and alight at Dorottya utca (approx. 8 km).

The 13 km journey takes approximately one hour. Timings can be found on www.laev.hu.

HUNGARIAN RAILWAY MUSEUM

Based at a 34-track roundhouse built in 1911, this extensive railway museum opened in the year 2000. www.vasuttortenetipark.hu

Located at Tatai út 95 in the northern suburbs of Budapest, it is open Mar. 29 to Dec. 1 daily except Mondays. During opening times, certain trains on the Budapest - Esztergom line make a special stop at *Vasútmúzeum* - see Table **1299** for timings. Otherwise, access is by bus or tram to the Rokolya utca stop. The urban transport museum at Szentendre also has some railway exhibits (21 km from Budapest by HÉV train).

Budapest's impressive Keleti (East) station

IRELAND

RAIL TRAVEL

See Tables **230 - 245**. Rail services are operated by Iarnród Éireann (IÉ) www.irishrail.ie. Telephone enquiries can be made 0700 - 1900 Ⓐ, 0800 - 1900 Ⓒ ✆ +353 (0)1 8366 222.

Running on a network of nearly 2,000 km based on Dublin, many services are operated by modern diesel multiple units, with loco-hauled trains on the Dublin - Cork and Dublin - Belfast routes. The trains to Belfast, branded *Enterprise*, are operated jointly with Northern Ireland Railways (for NIR see separate section under Great Britain). The local IÉ north-south electric line in Dublin is called DART (Dublin Area Rapid Transit). Tracks in Ireland are built to the 'Irish gauge' of 1600mm (5ft 3in), not found elsewhere in Europe.

A scenic highlight of the Irish rail system is the Dublin to Wexford line, particularly the section between Dun Loaghaire (pronounced Dun Leery) and Greystones where the line hugs the coast.

The two railway stations in Dublin are named Connolly and Heuston. Both gained their current names in 1966 on the 50th anniversary of the Easter Rising and are named after James Connolly and Sean Heuston, both of whom were executed following the Rising. The two stations are linked by the frequent red line service of Dublin's LUAS tram system.

WATERFORD & SUIR VALLEY RAILWAY

Part of the abandoned Waterford to Dungarvan track bed was used to build this 8.5 km narrow gauge heritage railway, which runs mostly along the picturesque banks of the River Suir. A restored Simplex locomotive pulls two partially open carriages travelling at 15 km/h on a 40 - 50 minute round trip. www.wsvrailway.ie

Situated 12 km from Waterford, and sadly not accessible by public transport, trains run daily Apr. 1 to Sept. 30 leaving Kilmeaden hourly 1100 - 1500 (1600 May - August). On ⑦ 1200 - 1600 (1700 May - August)

Other short heritage lines in Ireland include the Fintown Railway, the Cavan & Leitrim Railway, and the West Clare Railway.

ITALY

RAIL TRAVEL

See Tables **580 - 645**. The national operator is Trenitalia, a division of Ferrovie dello Stato (FS) www.trenitalia.com. A 24-hour telephone line is available for information and reservation changes: ✆ 89 20 21 (calls from abroad can be made 0700-2359 daily on ✆ +39 06 6847 5475).

The network exceeds 16,000 km, most of which is electrified.

Dedicated high-speed lines have been a major feature of the Italian rail network since the Roma - Firenze *Direttissima* was opened in 1977. The backbone of the system is the high-speed line stretching for nearly a thousand kilometres from Torino in the north via Milano, Bologna, Firenze, Roma and Napoli to Salerno in the south (Table **600**). Headline journey time for the Milano - Roma journey is just 2h 59m. High-speed trains are branded *Frecciarossa* (Red Arrow), whilst those which divert off the line to other desinations are *Frecciargento* (Silver Arrow). The best trains on the traditional network are another colour of arrow, this time white, being branded *Frecciabianca*. Reservation is required on all high-speed trains. For other train categories see the start of the Italian section on page 284.

Whilst several countries these days have competing operators on both their main and high-speed lines (thanks to EU rules which favour liberalisation), Italy was the first to have an 'open access' competitor running high-speed trains. NTV (Nuovo Trasporto Viaggiatori) runs trains branded *.italo* over the entire length of the core high-speed line; timings can be found in Table **600**. Private operators are also found on a multitude of local lines across the country, whilst local services in Lombardy (the Milano region) are handled by *Trenord*, jointly owned by Trenitalia and FNM (Ferrovie Nord Milano).

Italy's vast coastline, along with its Appennine mountain range stretching for over 1,000 km along the spine of the country, means that there is no shortage of scenic railway lines. For example, much of the line from the French border at Ventimiglia to La Spezia follows the coast, although a newly opened route has taken part of the line inland. Bear in mind that the most scenic routes across the mountains are by the slower conventional routes, as the high-speed line is constantly in and out of tunnels.

TRENINO VERDE DELLA SARDEGNA

As well as the Trenitalia services in Table **629**, Sardinia is blessed with a network of scenic narrow gauge tourist railways (the 'green' trains) running on five different routes during the summer. Services have been cut back over the years and now run on just a few days per week on the following routes: Tempio to Palau (59 km), Mandas to Laconi (37 km), Mandas to Sadali (58 km), Arbatax to Gairo (62 km) and Sindai to Bosa (33 km). Services are diesel hauled or use diesel railcars. Details can be found on www.treninoverde.com.

PIETRARSA RAILWAY MUSEUM

Italy's principal railway museum is located in the suburbs of Naples in the old works adjacent to Pietrarsa station. Managed by Fondazione FS Italiane, the museum has recently re-opened following redevelopment work. The museum is open Thursday to Sunday. Fondazione FS Italiane also operates a number of excursion trains using heritage locomotives and rolling stock. www.fondazionefs.it

LATVIA

RAIL TRAVEL

See Tables **1800** and **1830 - 1870**. Trains in Latvia are operated by Pasažieru vilciens under the brand name *Vivi* (www.vivi.lv) using the 'Russian' track gauge of 1520mm. The hub of the network is Riga's centrally located station. Services to other Latvian cities, such as Daugavpils, are not particularly frequent, however, good local services run from Riga to the nearby coastal resorts.

In January 2025, the operators of passenger services in Latvia, Lithuania and Estonia introduced co-ordinated connecting services on the Vilnius - Riga - Tallinn corridor (Table **49**). A new standard gauge rail project, known as *Rail Baltica*, will eventually offer a direct link between the Baltic States and Poland (expected to be operating partially by 2028 and fully open by 2030). Express bus services operate from Riga's busy bus station located a few hundred metres from the rail station (Table **1800**).

Riga has an interesting railway museum open on Tuesdays to Saturdays, a short tram ride from the city centre on the other side of the river (alight at Nacionala biblioteka). www.railwaymuseum.lv.

GULBENE - ALUKSNE

Catering for both locals and tourists this 33 km narrow gauge (750 mm) line is situated in the north east of the country. Gulbene is no longer linked to the rest of the rail network (except by special trains) but there is a bus service from Riga. From Gulbene at 1300 (steam hauled on some ⑥), 1800Ⓑ and 1830⑥, returning at 1525Ⓑ, 1630⑥ (1600 when steam trains are running), 1955Ⓑ and 2010⑥. The journey takes 1.5 hours in each direction. www.banitis.lv

LITHUANIA

RAIL TRAVEL

See Tables **1805 - 1815**. Services are operated by Lithuanian Railways (www.ltglink.lt) using the 'Russian' track gauge of 1520mm. ✆ +370 700 55111, 0700 - 2100. A frequent service is run from Vilnius to Kaunas, Lithuania's second city - fans of old funicular railways will enjoy a visit there. Vilnius Airport is rail connected.

In January 2025 the operators of passenger services in Latvia, Lithuania and Estonia introduced co-ordinated connecting services on the Vilnius - Riga - Tallinn corridor (Table **49**). A new standard gauge rail project known as *Rail Baltica* will eventually link the Baltic States and Poland (expected to be operating partially by 2028 and fully open by 2030). Bus services are also available between Lithuania and its northern neighbours (Table **1800**).

A small indoor railway museum is located within the station building at Vilnius, and some outdoor exhibits are stabled in an adjacent siding.

A train from Vilnius having arrived at Kaunas

LUXEMBOURG

RAIL TRAVEL

See Tables **445/6/9** (also **384**, **379**, **390**, **915**). Operator is Société Nationale des Chemins de fer Luxembourgeois (CFL) www.cfl.lu. Telephone enquiry line: ✆ +352 2489 2489.

This small country has a rail network of only 275 km, but services are fairly frequent, and there are good international links, including *TGV* services to Paris and hourly trains to Brussels and Koblenz.

The country is heavily forested, with some attractive scenery, particularly on the main line to the north. One of the attractions of exploring the country by rail is that 2nd class travel has been free since 2020. Most rail stations are small with few facilities.

AMTF TRAIN 1900

Luxembourg's only preserved steam railway is situated close to the French and Belgian borders, operated by Assoc. des Musée et Tourisme Ferroviaires (AMTF). The line runs from Pétange to Bois-de-Rodange, pausing at Fond-de-Gras where the railway is based. www.train1900.lu

Pétange can be reached by regular CFL local train (Table **449**) whilst Rodange CFL station is approximately 2 km from Bois-de-Rodange.

Trains run on ⑦ and holidays May to September, and most ⑥ in July and August. Services marked 🚂 are hauled by an historic steam locomotive. Other services are operated by a diesel railcar.

		🚂		🚂		🚂		
Pétange .... d.	1315	1415	1515	1615	1715	1815	1848	...
Fuussbësch .... d.	1334	1430	1527	1630	1727	1833	|	...
Fond-de-Gras .... a.	1344	1442	1537	1642	1737	1845	1906	...
		🚂		🚂		🚂		
Fond-de-Gras .... d.	1245	1320	1445	1540	1645	1740	1820	...
Fuussbësch .... d.	1259	1334	1456	1552	1656	1752	1833	...
Pétange .... a.	1309	1345	1506	1603	1706	1803	1843	...

Service Fond-de-Gras - Bois-de-Rodange (journey 5 – 6 minutes):
From Fond-de-Gras at 1420, 1520 🚂, 1620, 1720 🚂 and 1800.
From Bois-de-Rodange at 1430, 1530 🚂, 1630, 1730 🚂 and 1810.

NETHERLANDS

RAIL TRAVEL

See Tables **450 - 499**. National rail company is Nederlandse Spoorwegen (NS) www.ns.nl ✆ +31 30 751 5155.

A comprehensive network of over 3,000 km provides frequent regular-interval services linking most towns and cities. Most services are provided by NS, although other operators, notably Arriva, are contracted to run local train services in some parts of the north and east.

Fast domestic trains, calling only at principal stations, are classified *Intercity*, whilst local stopping trains are known as *Sprinter* services. A further category is *Intercity direct* for which a supplement is payable - these use the *HSL-Zuid* high-speed line linking Amsterdam and Schiphol Airport with the Belgian border and on to Antwerpen. Through services to Paris via Brussels are provided by *Eurostar* (formerly *Thalys*) trains. *Eurostar* trains link London with Amsterdam. Schiphol airport is well served by rail services, not only to Amsterdam but also to many other towns and cities across the country.

Through tickets can be purchased between all stations in the Netherlands, regardless of operator. A national stored-value smartcard scheme operates throughout the country known as OV-chipkaart, used for all public transport (for further information see the introduction to the Netherlands section on page 242). Cycle hire and cycle and baggage storage are usually available at larger stations. Smaller stations are usually unstaffed, but all stations have ticket vending machines. Seat reservations are not available for domestic journeys.

A recent development (2019) is the conversion of the Hoek van Holland to Rotterdam line, once traversed by many long distance trains connecting with ferries, into a metro line, now part of Rotterdam's metro system.

MUSEUMSPOORLIJN S.T.A.R.

Located in the north-eastern corner of the Netherlands, this former NS line runs from Veendam to Stadskanaal, where the railway is based. Veendam can be reached by local train from Groningen (Table **498**). Trains can be steam or diesel hauled. www.stadskanaalrail.nl

The timetable below operates on ③⑦ July 14 - Aug. 28. Trains also run on numerous other dates between March 31 and December 20.

Stadskanaal .... d.	1050	1405	...	Veendam .... d.	1205	1520	...
Veendam .... a.	1135	1450	...	Stadskanaal .... a.	1250	1605	...

VELUWSCHE STOOMTREIN MAATSCHAPPIJ (VSM)

Running on the route Apeldoorn - Eerbeek - Dieren (22 km), this line connects with NS services at both ends: Apeldoorn (Tables **463/498**) and Dieren (Table **475**). It runs through the Veluwe nature area and, on certain dates, a ride on the train can be combined with a boat trip along the River IJssel between Dieren and Zutphen (boats are scheduled to connect with the trains). The journey back to Apeldoorn can be completed by train from Zutphen (Table **498**). Special tickets are available for this interesting day trip known as *De Veluwe-IJssel-Boemel*. www.stoomtrein.org.

Steam services operate on ⑦ Apr. 7 - Oct. 26 between Apeldoorn and Eerbeek. From July 13 to Aug. 31 steam services operate daily except ⑥ either between Apeldoom and Erbeek or, on certain dates, between Beekbergen and Dieren (via Eerbeek). Please check the website for full details. During both operating periods services call at the museum and allow 45 minutes to visit the steam depot.

MUSEUMSTOOMTRAM HOORN - MEDEMBLIK

This long-established standard gauge line runs for 20 km between Hoorn and Medemblik and is easily accessible from Amsterdam (Table **461/470**). All trains are operated by steam traction. A popular triangular journey (known locally as *De Historische Driehoek*) uses the boat between Medemblik and Enkhuizen (see below), returning to Hoorn or Amsterdam by rail. A day ticket valid on steam tram and boat services is available. The station at Hoorn includes a steam tram museum. www.stoomtram.nl

		A				**A**	
Hoorn .... d.	...	1040	...	Enkhuizen .... d.	...	1040	...
Medemblik .... a.	...	1320	...	Medemblik .... a.	...	1155	...
		A				**A**	
Medemblik .... d.	...	1320	...	Medemblik .... d.	...	1320	...
Enkhuizen................ a.	...	1450	...	Hoorn .... a.	...	1440	...

A – ②–⑦ Mar. 29 - July 30; daily Aug. 1 – 24; ②–⑦ Aug. 26 - Sept. 30 (also Apr. 21, 28, June 9, 23, July 21, 28; not June 23, July 19, 26).

NARROW GAUGE

Fans of narrow gauge trains will enjoy the Stoomtrein Katwijk Leiden along the shore of Lake Valkenburg, along with the associated museum. Open weekends Apr. to Sept. (also ②④ July 15 - Aug. 28). Reach by bus from Den Haag or Leiden. Currently the train is not running along Lake Valkenburg due to a landslip - please see the website for more details. www.stoomtreinkatwijkleiden.nl

A further narrow gauge line and museum is the RTM Ouddorp situated in Zeeland and reached by bus from Rotterdam's Spikenisse metro station to Port Zelande, which is part way along this short line. Service operates on ⑥⑦ Apr. 6 - June 29, Sept. 13 – 29; ③④⑥⑦ July 2 - Sept. 7. Other events take place throughout the year; please check the website www.rtm-ouddorp.nl for further details.

MUSEUM STOOMTREIN GOES - BORSELE

Evoking railways of the 1930's, this standard gauge line runs for 16 km across the beautiful landscape of the province of Zeeland. Starting from Goes (a short walk from the NS station, Table **450**) steam trains run for 40 minutes to the scenic village of Hoedekenskerke calling at Kwadendamme. Departures from Goes ⑦ Apr. 6 - Oct. 26 at 1045 and 1415, returning at 1240 and 1610. Main operating days are ②③④⑦ July 6 - Aug. 28, also occassional services on ⑥ May - Oct. www.destoomtrein.nl

UTRECHT RAILWAY MUSEUM

The National Railway Museum is located in the former Maliebaan railway station in Utrecht, open ②–⑦ (also ① in school holidays). The museum has a dedicated hourly railway service from Utrecht Centraal (or 1.6 km on foot). www.spoorwegmuseum.nl

A London to Amsterdam *Eurostar* train at Rotterdam

NORWAY

RAIL TRAVEL

See Tables **770 - 787**. Many trains are operated by the Vy Group (using the name Vy), owned by the Norwegian government. www.vy.no. Services between Oslo and Stavanger are now operated by GoAhead Nordic while services Oslo – Trondheim / Åndalsnes, Hamar – Røros – Trondheim and Trondheim – Steinkjer - Bodø are mostly operated by SJ Nord.

As you might expect, a high proportion of the country's 4,000 km rail network can be regarded as scenic. For those touring the country by rail, a circular route can often be arranged by including buses or boats in the itinerary. Trips to the far north can also be extended by catching the bus from Bodø to Narvik (Table **787**) and returning through Sweden.

Trains convey 2nd-class seating, whilst most medium- and long-distance trains also convey *Komfort* accommodation, a dedicated area with complimentary tea/coffee and newspapers (supplement payable). Sleeping cars have one- and two-berth compartments; a sleeper supplement is payable per compartment (for two people travelling together, or sole use for single travellers). Long-distance trains convey a bistro car serving hot and cold meals, drinks and snacks. Reservation is possible (and recommended) on all long-distance trains. Reserved seats may not be marked, but your confirmation specifies carriage and seat/berth numbers.

FLÅMSBANA

Branching off the Olso to Bergen line (Table **781**), this is undoubtedly one of Europe's most spectacular railway journeys. Trains descend from an altitude of 865m at Myrdal to sea-level at Flåm in just 20 km. In between the 20 tunnels there is some breathtaking scenery and, to reassure passengers, the trains have no less than five sets of brakes, each of which can stop the train on the extremely steep inclines! Timings are shown in Table **781**. This journey can be included as part of various circular excursions, such as the *Norway in a Nutshell* tour (see Table **781a** for boat and bus connections). For further details see www.visitflam.com

KRØDERBANEN

This former NSB line closed to passengers in 1958 but was resurrected as a museum line in the 1980s. Operated by the Norwegian Railway Club, it is Norway's longest museum railway at 26 km and makes an ideal day trip from Oslo. It runs from the railway's base at Krøderen to Vikersund, which is situated between Drammen and Hønefoss (Table **780**). Its 150th anniversary was celebrated in 2022. Trains are not currently running. See the website for more details. www.njk.no.

GAMLE VOSSEBANEN

Also operated by the Norsk Jernbaneklubb, the 18 km 'Old Voss Steam Railway' runs from Garnes to Haukeland, crossing the Bergen to Voss line (Table **781**) at Arna, where the station is 300m from the old station on the steam railway. Both ends of the line can also be reached by bus from Bergen bus station.

Services are hauled by one of the original steam locomotives built for the Bergen Railway in 1913 and the restored teak coaches are from the same period. Until 1964 the line was actually part of the main Oslo - Bergen railway. www.njk.no. Trains run on ⑦ June 15 - Sept. 14 as follows:

Garnes .... d.	1100	1415	...	Midttun.................. d.	1210	1525	...
Arna (old station) ...... d.	1110	1425	...	Haukeland .... d.	1230	1545	...
Haukeland .... d.	1130	1445	...	Arna (old station) .. d.	1250	1605	...
Midttun .... a.	1150	1505	...	Garnes.................. a.	1300	1615	...

Connecting trains: Bergen - Arna at 1035, 1317; Arna - Bergen at 1407, 1647.

On Sept. 14 an enhanced service will operate.

NORWEGIAN RAILWAY MUSEUM

The museum is located 3 km from the centre of Hamar, on the Oslo - Lillehammer - Trondheim line (Table **785**), and is open daily except Mondays (daily June / August). Bus number B25 runs from the railway station. www.jernbanemuseet.no.

POLAND

RAIL TRAVEL

See Tables **1000 - 1099**. Long-distance trains are operated by PKP Intercity (www.intercity.pl). The best trains on the principal routes are classified *EIP* (Express InterCity Premium), which are operated with the latest sleek *Pendolino* type trains. Other fast trains are *EIC* or *IC* (along with international *EC* trains), plus the cheaper *TLK* trains which make more stops. Reservation is compulsory on all trains operated by PKP Intercity, whose trains are shown in red on PKP timetables and station departure sheets. See page 476 for further details of train classifications.

Trains on the Warszawa - Berlin route are operated jointly with German Railways and are branded *Berlin-Warszawa Express*. The Russian Railways services to or through Warszawa (including the Berlin - Moscow *Talgo* train) are currently suspended.

Things get more complicated when it comes to local trains. Przewozy Regionalne is the main operator, using the name PolRegio (polregio.pl), with train categories *RE* or *R* (local trains are shown without numbers in our tables). However, several local authorities have set up their own railway organisations, such as Koleje Wielkopolskie and Koleje Ślaskie. Outer suburban services in the Warsaw area come under Koleje Mazowieckie, whilst local electric services in the Tricity area (Gdansk, Sopot, Gdynia) have long been the preserve of PKP subsidiary SKM Trojmiasto. Ticket inter-availability between operators is complex.

Poland is a large country with many scenic rail routes, notably in the more hilly areas in the south of the country. In addition to the standard gauge network, the country used to be covered with hundreds of kilometres of narrow gauge lines, and some of these survived in PKP ownership as late as 2001. Since closure, many sections have resurfaced as museum lines, some with regular summer operation, others with only occasional trains. Further information can be found on www.narrowrail.net, and two of the lines are included below.

WOLSZTYN ROUNDHOUSE

Wolsztyn (Table **1099**) is located some 80 km south-west of Poznań and is famous for its steam depot running the last regularly timetabled steam hauled passenger services on a main line in Europe between Wolsztyn and Poznań or Zbaszynek. See Table **1099** for timings.

The atmospheric steam depot is a short walk from the station and can be visited every day between 0700 and 1800 (summer) / 1600 (winter) for a small fee and has a collection of 30 steam locomotives and 19 historical wagons.

A Parade of Steam is held yearly (in 2025 on May 3) between 1000 and 2000. Further information can be found at www.parowozowniawolsztyn.pl.

WARSAW RAILWAY MUSEUM

Warsaw's railway museum is located in the former Warszawa Glówna terminus in the city centre, between Centralna and Zachodnia stations in ul.Towarowa. There is an extensive outdoor display of rolling stock as well as indoor exhibits. Open daily. www.stacjamuzeum.pl

SOCHACZEW MUSEUM RAILWAY

A short walk from Sochaczew station (local trains approximately hourly from Warszawa Wschodnia) is the narrow gauge station which has been made into a museum with a large collection of narrow gauge rolling stock, open daily. See www.stacjamuzeum.pl (link top right).

The season operates Apr. 27 - Oct. 26 mainly on ⑥⑦. On ⑤⑥⑦ July 5 - Aug. 31 a steam hauled 'Retro' train leaves the museum at 1030 for a trip to Wilcze Tułowskie in the Kampinos Forest. The itinerary includes a guided forest walk, and arrival back at Sochaczew is at 1520.

ZNINSKA KOLEJ WASKOTOROWA

The 12 km Znin - Gasawa railway is the last remaining section of a much larger narrow gauge (600mm) network in this area which, by 1913, had reached 79 km in length. Regular passenger services were withdrawn in 1962 but since 1976 tourist trains have been running regularly between Znin and Gasawa. Znin can be reached by bus from Bydgoszcz.

A varied collection of narrow gauge rolling stock is situated adjacent to Wenecja Muzeum station, where trains arrive 10 - 15 minutes before the time shown. www.muzeumznin.pl

Trains run May 1 - Sept. 1, also during the Archaeological Festival September 14 – 19. Confirm Festival dates and timings locally.

				R	**S**				**S**	**R**	**R**
Znin .... d.	0900	1030	1205	1350	1440	Gasawa ... d.	1030	1205	1345	1400	1530
Wenecja § d.	0940	1110	1255	1435	1525	Wenecja § d.	1110	1250	1435	1520**f**	1620
Gasawa ... a.	1015	1150	1340	1515	1610	Znin .... a.	1140	1320	1505	1550	1745

Other services: from Zinin 1535 ⑥⑦ July / Aug.
from Gasawa 1625 **R**, 1705 ⑥⑦ July / Aug.

R – ①–⑤ May / June, ⑥⑦ July / Aug.
S – ⑥⑦ May / June, ①–⑤ July / Aug.
f – Arrives 1445.
§ – Wenecja Muzeum.

CHABÓWKA AND JAWORZYNA ŚLĄSKA

The 'Skansen' at Chabówka is an extensive open air railway museum, located on the scenic Kraków - Zakopane line (Table **1066**). Steam trips normally run on several summer dates in July and August from Skansen to Nowy Targ. www.parowozy.pl

Another railway museum is located at Jaworzyna Śląska on the Wroclaw - Jelenia Góra line (Table **1084**), open daily 1000 - 1600 Oct. - Apr. 1000 - 1800 May - Sept.. www.muzeumtechniki.pl

Polish EIP (Express InterCity Premium) *Pendolino* train

Photos in this Rail Extra feature are by
Brendan Fox - pages 653 - 655, 657, 658, 660 - 662
Graham Benbow - pages 656, 659, 663, 664

PORTUGAL

RAIL TRAVEL

See Tables **690 - 699**. Operator is Comboios de Portugal (CP) www.cp.pt
Telephone enquiries (24 hours): ✆ 808 109 110.

The network is approximately 2,500 km, and as with Spain, trains run on tracks of 'Iberian' gauge, 1668 mm. Backbone of the network is the 337 km line between Lisboa and Porto, with the longest distance trains running all the way from Faro in the south to Porto in the north. The best trains are the modern *AP* (Alfa Pendular) trains, which along with *IC* and international trains require advance reservation. Lines in the north of the country are particularly scenic, especially the Douro Valley line to Régua and Pocinho (see Table **694** and the tourist train below).

Lisboa's traditional terminus at Santa Apolónia was joined by an impressive through station in 1998 called Oriente, located 6 km north of the centre. Noted for its metal and glass roof, it is part of a major transport hub including metro and bus links. Trains to Cascais, however, leave from Cais do Sodre station, whilst Rossio is the city centre terminus for trains to Sintra (see city plan on page 32).

Another impressive feature of Lisbon's transport network is the *25 de Abril* bridge across the Tagus, to which railway tracks were added under the road in 1999, and which is sometimes compared to San Francisco's Golden Gate Bridge. As well as CP trains to the south, it carries local trains of private operator *Fertagus*.

The national railway museum is located at Entroncamento, open on ②–⑦ 1030 to 1730. www.fmnf.pt Access is from Rua Ferreira de Mesquita on the north side of the tracks across the footbridge. There are also several small regional railway museums.

COMBOIO HISTÓRICO

This steam hauled tourist train runs in summer on the scenic Douro line between Régua and Tua. Details of dates and timings can be found in Table **694**. The train is operated by CP at special fares.

ROMANIA

RAIL TRAVEL

See Tables **1600 - 1680**. State railway Căile Ferate Române (CFR) operates an extensive network of over 10,000 km, and trains of its passenger subsidiary CFR Călători link all major towns. www.cfrcalatori.ro Telephone information is available on ✆ 021 9521 for domestic traffic or ✆ 021 314 5528 for international services.

Most main lines are electrified and quite fast, but branch line services are very slow. Trains are fairly punctual and very cheap. Except for local trains, reserve and pay a speed supplement in advance (tickets issued abroad include the supplement). Cheapest are *regio* (very slow), then *Interregio*, and finally *IC* trains, whose prices approach Western levels. Food and drink is normally available only on *IC* and some *IR* trains. Couchette (*cuşeta*) or sleeper (*vagon de dormit*) accommodation is inexpensive. An increasing number of services are now operated by private operators, such as Regio Călători, Transferoviar Grup SA, and Softrans S.R.L.

VIŞEU DE SUS / MURAMUREŞ FOREST RAILWAY

Situated in the north of Romania, the Vaser Valley forest railway has been transporting wood to a processing plant in Vişeu de Sus since its opening in 1932, and claims to be the last European forestry railway. The 22 km narrow gauge railway also started running steam-hauled tourist trains in the year 2000. Visitors can enjoy the remote mountain scenery during the very leisurely two hour journey from Vişeu de Sus along the winding valley to Paltin, where there is a break before the return journey.

Vişeu de Sus is situated 7 km from the CFR station at Vişeu de Jos (Table **1660**) and it can also be reached by bus from Baia Mare or Sighetu Marmatiei. The train runs on ④–⑦ all year (daily April - Oct.) leaving Vişeu de Sus at either 0900 or 1000 (check timings when purchasing tickets) arriving back at approximately 1500. www.mocanita-maramures.com

SERBIA

RAIL TRAVEL

See Tables **1360 - 1380**. The 3,300 km network is operated by Železnice Srbije www.srbvoz.rs which is the passenger arm of the state railway company.

Both daytime and nightime international services link Beograd with Ljubljana, Zagreb and Budapest, whilst Sofia has one daytime train. There is also a night train on the lengthy run to Thessaloniki via Skopje, whilst travel to Timisoara in Romania involves trains of a more local nature, changing at Vršac. **All these services are currently suspended**

Scenic highlight, however, is the line from Beograd to neighbouring Montenegro, passing through its capital Podgorica before continuing to the coast at Bar. Opened as late as 1976, this winding 524 km line (Table **1370**) involves no fewer than 435 bridges and 254 tunnels!

There is an indoor railway museum in Beograd at 6 Nemanjina Street, open on Mondays to Fridays 0900-1500 hrs., and a narrow gauge section near Pozega station. For details see the *Museum* link: www.zeleznicesrbije.com

ŠARGANSKA OSMICA *(ŠARGAN EIGHT)*

Threading its way through the scenic Mokra Gora mountain region, close to the border with Bosnia, this line was originally part of a narrow gauge route between Beograd and Sarajevo which was closed in 1974. Between 1999 and 2003 the line was rebuilt as a tourist railway using diesel or steam traction. See *Museum trains* link: www.zeleznicesrbije.com

The 15.4 km narrow gauge (760 mm) line runs from Mokra Gora to Šargan Vitasi, passing through 22 tunnels and over five bridges. The nearest mainline ŽS station is Užice on the Beograd - Bar main line (Table **1370**). The 40 km journey from Užice to Mokra Gora can be made by bus or taxi.Trains run daily Mar. - Oct., departing Mokra Gora at 1030 and 1330. Total journey time for a return trip is approximately 2½ hours.

SLOVAKIA

RAIL TRAVEL

See Tables **1170 - 1197**. The national rail operator is Železničná spoločnost' (ŽSSK) www.slovakrail.sk. Track and infrastructure is managed by ŽSR www.zsr.sk. Call centre (24h) is ✆ 18 188, or from abroad ✆ +421 24 48 58 188.

An efficient network of 3,600 km is operated, with the fastest trains being the handful of *IC* trains on the principal route between Bratislava and Košice (Table **1180**). On the international Praha (Prague) to Košice route, the state railways compete for passengers with two other companies, Regiojet and Leo Express.

Trains are cheap, but often crowded. In fact most resident children, seniors and students qualify for free travel (except on *IC* trains or cross-border services) in a recently introduced scheme. Qualifying EU citizens may also be entitled to register for the scheme (especially children under 15 and seniors of 62 or over).

Apart from the small number of *EC* and *IC* trains, for which higher fares apply, the fastest trains are *expresný* (*Ex*) and *Rýchlik* (*R*, usually those with three-digit train numbers). Cheaper are *zrýchlený* (semi-fast) and *osobný* (very slow). Sleeping cars and couchettes are provided on most overnight trains (reserve at all main stations, well in advance in summer). Seat reservations may be made at station counters marked R, and are recommended for express trains.

The most scenic areas are close to the Tatra mountains, particularly the High Tatras (Vysoké Tatry) where a network of electrified narrow gauge lines is run by ŽSR subsidiary TEŽ (Table **1182**). Most lines in the centre of the country, radiating from Banská Bystrica, are also scenic, particularly the line following the River Hron (Table **1188**).

ČIERNOHRONSKÁ ŽELEZNICA

After closure in 1982, enthusiasts eventually managed to save this narrow gauge (760 mm) forestry railway and transform it into a tourist railway. It is the last remaining section of a once extensive system in central Slovakia.

The line starts at Chvatimech, which is served by all trains between Banská Bystrica and Brezno (Table **1188**, eight minutes before Brezno). The first 7 km to Šánske is, however, currently being rebuilt. 5 km further on is Čierny Balog, the railway's headquarters, where the line continues 4 km to Dobroč, and there is also a 4 km branch to Vydrovo. The section of line to Dobroč is notable as it passes through a local Football stadium! www.chz.sk.

A variety of trips are available. Diesel-hauled trains run on Ⓑ from Mar. 1 - Sept. 15, whilst steam-hauled trains run on ⑥ (daily June 29 to Aug. 31).

DETSKÁ ŽELEZNICA KOŠICE

This short railway in Košice was completed in 1956 as one of the Pioneer Railways in the former Czechoslovakia. The line was built to allow children to learn how railways operate, so most of the railway's functions were performed by children. Some of the railway's rolling stock dates from as far back as 1884. www.detskazeleznica.sk

The 4.2 km narrow gauge line runs from Čermel' to Alpinka. Čermel' can be reached from the main station by tram 2 to Havlíčkova then bus 14.

Trains run on ③–⑦ May to September (daily in June, July and August); with the number of journeys offered varying. There are also limited services on weekends in October and ⑥ in November.

NATIONAL RAILWAY MUSEUM

This is located at Bratislava Vychod depot and is open daily April 15 to October 15 (1000-1700) with only the outdoor exhibits accessible to visitors. Guided tours of the museum's indoor exhibits are possible by booking at least 3 days in advance (Telephone 02 2029 7296). The nearest station is Bratislava Rača, served by local trains on the line to Trnava, and 1.6 km from the museum. The website (www.mdc.sk) also has a list of special heritage trains running on the Slovak network on various dates throughout the year. A special annual *Rendez* event takes place at the museum in June.

There is also an indoor transport museum near Bratislava hlavná station at Šancová 1/A, closed on Mondays. www.muzeumdopravy.com.

A long-distance train at Bratislava Hlavná Stanica (main station)

SLOVENIA

RAIL TRAVEL

See Tables **1300 - 1320**. Slovenia's relatively small network of 1,200 km is operated by Slovenske Železnice (SŽ) www.slo-zeleznice.si. Telephone information is available from within Slovenia on ✆ 080 81 11.

Hub of the network is the capital Ljubljana. The best trains are the *IC* trains on the Maribor route, and the *EC* trains which continue beyond Maribor into Austria. Other international links include those to München, Budapest and Beograd, all with a choice of daytime or overnight timings, except that the night train to Budapest runs only in high summer.

LJUBLJANA RAILWAY MUSEUM

Ljubljana has a railway museum in a former roundhouse at Parmova 35, open daily except Mondays from 1000 to 1800.

Steam-hauled heritage trains normally run between Jesenice and Nova Gorica on the scenic Bohinj line, which could also be booked as part of a guided tour. Operating two to four times per month from May to October (but not running during 2025). www.soca-valley.com.

SPAIN

RAIL TRAVEL

See Tables **650 - 689**. National rail company is Red Nacional de los Ferrocarriles Españoles (RENFE) www.renfe.es. ✆ 912 320 320.

The opening of the Madrid - Sevilla high-speed line in 1992 was just the start of what is now Europe's largest high-speed network. Particularly important is the 621 km Madrid - Barcelona line, which also continues northwards into France, and which has taken a large market share away from the airlines. Another principal route runs from Madrid to València and Alicant, and in fact travel to just about any area of Spain can benefit from a high-speed train for at least part of the way. Trains which run purely on these lines are classified *AVE* (Alta Velocidad Española). For other train categories see the introduction to the Spanish section on page 318.

The traditional network is built to the 'Iberian' track gauge of 1668 mm, whereas the new high-speed network is standard gauge (1435 mm). Trains which switch between the two networks, such as the *Alvia* train, therefore have to have gauge changing equipment.

Spain also has around 1,200 km of narrow gauge lines, built to metre gauge, and in the main these are in the hands of a separate division of RENFE known as FEVE. These are largely in coastal areas, and particularly interesting is the long and scenic narrow gauge line along the north coast of Spain (Table **687**), along with the associated Bilbao to León line (Table **683**). Several narrow gauge lines are run by other operators, such as Euskotren, FGC, and FGV.

Reservation is compulsory on all services for which a train category (*AVE*, *IC* etc) is shown in the timing columns of this timetable. RENFE attaches a high degree of importance to punctuality and has a comprehensive scheme of refunds if trains run late.

VALL DE NÚRIA

A 12.5 km rack railway operated by Ferrocarrils de la Generalitat de Catalunya (FGC) runs from Ribes Enllaç to Núria. The train climbs from 905m at Ribes to 1967m at Nuria and passes through some fine scenery. At one point the train is travelling above the narrow gorge of the River Nuria. Table **658** has the timings. www.valldenuria.cat

Ribes Enllaç station is adjacent to RENFE's Ribes de Freser station on the Barcelona to Latour de Carol line (Table **656**).

CERCEDILLA - COTOS MOUNTAIN RAILWAY

This line is currently closed (until mid 2025) for extensive modernisation; a rail replacement bus service is in operation.

Apart from the FEVE network, RENFE has a narrow gauge line of its own. It runs from Cercedilla to Cotos and is actually part of Madrid's suburban network, allocated route number **C9**. The 18 km journey through the scenic *Sierra de Guadarrama* region takes around 45 minutes (25 minutes Cercedilla to Puerto de Navacerrada). This is excellent walking country and a number of marked routes are available at stations en-route.

Regular services (at least hourly) operate between central Madrid and Cercedilla (line **C8** - journey 80 minutes from Atocha or 70 mins from Chamartín). See www.renfe.com under the heading 'Cercanias' (suburban) then 'Madrid'.

FERROCARRIL DE SÓLLER

Opened in 1912, the line from Mallorca's capital Palma to the northern town of Sóller is operated by historic electric traction and runs through the scenic *Sierra de Tramuntana* region. The 28 km line is built to the unusual gauge of 914mm (one yard).

From Sóller a narrow gauge tramway runs for 5 km to Port de Sóller. Further details of both lines are in Table **674**. www.trendesoller.com

A modern RENFE suburban train at Bilbao Abando station, previously known as Estación del Norte

SWEDEN

RAIL TRAVEL

See Tables **730 - 768**. National rail company is SJ AB www.sj.se. The company was formed when Statens Järnvägar (SJ) was split into different companies. Telephone enquiries: ✆ +46 771 75 75 75 (daily 0600-2200, but ticket purchase only available Mon-Fri 0800-1700).

Travellers must ensure they are in possession of a valid ticket before joining a train; a penalty fare will be charged if you do not have a valid ticket. There are no staffed ticket offices or auomatic ticket machines at Swedish stations. Readers are therefore advised to purchase tickets on-line at www.sj.se before travelling. However, it is possible to purchase and collect SJ tickets at all Pressbyrån shops and certain 7-Eleven stores (some of which are located at rail stations). The highest ranked services are operated by high-speed trains (*Snabbtåg*, shown as *Sn* in our tables) running at up to 200 km/h and using either X2000 trains or the newer SJ 3000 units. Supplements are required on *Snabbtåg*. Some local lines are run by regional authorities or private companies such as Norrtåg www.norrtag.se; see page 350 for other operators.

Sleeping-cars have one or two berths in 2nd class, couchettes have six berths; female-only compartments are available. 1st-class sleeping-cars with en-suite shower and WC run on many overnight services; 2nd-class compartments have washbasins, while a shower and WC are at the end of the carriage. Long-distance trains have a refreshment service. Many trains have a family coach with a playroom, and facilities for the disabled. Seat reservations are compulsory on *Sn*, *IC* and overnight trains, also on services operated by independent operators *Snälltåget*, and *MTR Express*. *Sn* services also operate between Sweden and Copenhagen via the Öresund bridge and tunnel but it is better to use the frequent local trains for short journeys.

'C' (for Central) in timetables etc. means the town's main station.

Journeys north from Stockhom along the coast to Umeå and beyond have been revolutionised by the *Botniabanan* which opened in 2010. An interesting alternative route to the far north of Sweden, albeit much slower, is the privately operated *Inlandsbanan*, with a single train each way in summer taking all day for the 746 km journey between Östersund and Gälllivare (Table **766**).

UPPSALA - LENNA JERNVÄG

Starting at Uppsala (Tables **760 / 761**), head for tracks 9/10 at the Central station from where this narrow gauge heritage line runs for 33 km east to Faringe. The focal point of the railway is Marielund station, where trains often pass and steam trains refill their water tanks. A popular station café is also located there. The railway's collection of rollling stock is based at the Faringe engine sheds. Track gauge is 891mm (Swedish 'three foot'), unique to Sweden.

Trains run on ⑤⑥ May 30 - Sept. 27 (also ②③June 24 - Aug. 6). There are up to six departures from Uppsala depending on the date, with some journeys steam-hauled. A round trip takes three to four hours. For timings see www.lennakatten.se.

ÖSTRA SÖDERMANSLAND JÄRNVÄG

Mariefred - Läggesta - Taxinge is the route of this 11 km narrow gauge (600mm) museum line. Läggesta nedre station is a 500m walk from the SJ station in Table **732**, located west of Stockholm on the line to Eskilstuna. The narrow gauge line offers some great views of Lake Mälaren. Starting on the north side of the lake at Mariefred, trains reverse at Läggesta nedre with several services continuing along the south shore to Taxinge.

On summer weekends it is possible to cross the lake by steamer between Mariefred and Taxinge (round trip fares are available), giving an ideal day out from Stockholm.

Trains run on ⑥⑦ June - August (also June 20; not June 21) with some additional midweek operating dates in July. Timings, including historic steamboat connections from Stockholm, can be found at www.oslj.nu

SMALSPÅRSJÄRNVÄGEN (SMALSPÅRET)

A 71km 891mm narrow gauge railway operating by rail bus between Hultsfred and Västervik (Table **738**) in southern Sweden with a network of 22 stations and operated and maintained entirely by volunteers.

Trains run June 17, 19, 24, 26, 28; daily June 30 - Aug. 16; ⑥ Aug. 23 - Sept. 27.

Trains marked * run July 7 - Aug. 3 only, ** not July 7 - Aug. 3.

From Västervik at 0812, 1212*, 1512** and 1612*.

From Hultsfred at 1010, 1410*, 1710** and 1810*.

SWITZERLAND

RAIL TRAVEL

See Tables **500 - 578**. The principal rail carrier is Swiss Federal Railways (SBB / CFF / FFS) www.sbb.ch. A 24 hour premium rate helpline is available on ✆ 0848 44 66 88 (German, French, Italian, English spoken).

As might be expected, there are a large number of scenic routes and mountain lines, with endless possibilities for exciting days out. Rail travel can often be combined with other modes such as lake steamers, buses, funicular railways and even cable cars to complete a round trip. Several examples are given on the official tourism site www.myswitzerland.com.

The Swiss rail system is characterised by the large number of rail operators other than SBB. Many of these are narrow gauge, notably the Rhätische Bahn (RhB), which has a large network in the south-east, and the Matterhorn-Gotthard-Bahn (MGB) in the south-west. Together these two railways provide the famous *Glacier Express* running for 290 km from St Moritz to Zermatt (Table **575**). This requires a supplement and advance reservation, but of course the exact same lines can also be traversed with a series of local trains (Tables **576** and **545**).

Other services very popular with tourists include the *Bernina Express* from Chur to Tirano, just across the border in Italy (Table **545**), MOB's *Golden Pass* trains from Montreux to Zweizimmen, some of which have panorama cars (Table **566**), and Zentralbahn's Luzern to Interlaken route with its many lakeside views (Table **561**). Some other highlights are mentioned below, but there are many more. The Swiss rail network is, of course, synonymous with punctuality and spotlessly clean trains.

CHEMIN DE FER - MUSÉE BLONAY - CHAMBY (BC)

Situated in the south-west corner of Switzerland close to Lake Geneva, this narrow gauge railway museum has an extensive collection of rolling stock. Trains run from Blonay to Chamby (3 km) before changing direction to reach the nearby Chaulin museum. Trains leaving the museum return to Blonay. Both steam and electric trains are operated. Passengers are treated to fine views over Lake Geneva during the short journey. Rail connections are available at both Blonay (regular trains from Vevey) and Chamby (Table **566**). www.blonay-chamby.ch

Trains run on ⑥⑦ May 3 - Oct. 26 (also May 20). An enhanced service operates June 7 – 9 for the Swiss Steam Festival (see website for timings).

		b	**a**		🚂		🚂		**a**	**a**	🚂	**a**
Blonay .... d.	1010	1110	1125	1210	1405	1440	1525	1610	1655	1710	1710	1720
Chamby .... d.	1026	1126	1143	1226	1420	1455	1543	1626	|	1726	1726	|
Chaulin-Musée a.	1030	1130	1147	1230	1427	1502	1549	1630	1710	1730	1730	1733
	b		🚂			🚂	**a**			🚂	**a**	
Chaulin-Musée d.	1040	1140	1335	...	1420	1455	1505	1540	...	1640	1640	1750
Blonay .... a.	1055	1155	1350	...	1435	1510	1520	1555	...	1655	1655	1805

a – Last Sunday of the month May - Sept. **b** – 🚂 on ⑦. 🚂 – Steam train.

BRIENZ ROTHORN BAHN (BRB)

Within easy reach of Interlaken by rail (Table **561**) or boat (Table **508**), this narrow gauge (800mm) mountain rack railway from Brienz can claim the unusual fact that its lowest and highest stations have the greatest height difference of any railway in Switzerland. With stunning views, the distance to the summit at Rothorn (2244m) is 7.6 km, and the journey takes about one hour. Built in 1892, an added attraction is that most trips are steam operated, since it is one of the very few non-electrified routes in Switzerland. Trains run from June to October and timings are shown in Table **553**. www.brienz-rothorn-bahn.ch

DAMPFBAHN FURKA-BERGSTRECKE (DFB)

This tortuous narrow gauge mountain route is the original main line over the Furkapass which was closed in 1982 following the opening of the Furka base tunnel. Since 1992 the line has reopened in stages as a spectacular tourist route, the final section between Gletsch and Oberwald being completed in 2010. Steam-hauled journeys over the full 18 km route from Realp to Oberwald via Furka take over two hours (reservation is compulsory), whilst shorter diesel-hauled journeys are available between Oberwald and Gletsch taking 25 minutes. Itineraries are also available using both steam and diesel services with a break of journey at Gletsch, near to the Rhone Glacier.

Trains run ④–⑦ June 19 - Sept. 28. For timings and reservations see www.dfb.ch. Both ends of the route can be reached by means of the hourly MGB trains between Brig and Andermatt in Table **576**. In Realp the DFB station is a 10 minute walk from the MGB station.

RIGI-BAHNEN (RB)

There are two electrified rack railways to the Rigi-Kulm summit (1750m), an 8.5 km line from Arth Goldau on the Gotthard main line, and a 7 km line from Vitznau by the lake. Opening in 1871, the latter was Europe's first rack railway, and is the more scenic of the two routes. The lines are also notable for being the highest standard gauge railway in Europe. At the summit, one of the finest Swiss panoramas, overlooking the *Vierwald-stättersee*, awaits the visitor. Website: www.rigi.ch

Trains run hourly all year on both routes, but evening services run only in summer; timings are shown in Table **553**.

Arth-Goldau, where the RB station is adjacent to the main line station, can be reached by means of rail services in Tables **525** and **550**. In Vitznau the station is by the quayside (lake steamer services: Table **507**).

PILATUS BAHN (PB)

The world's steepest rack railway runs from Alpnachstad, south-west of Lake Luzern, to the mountain's summit at Pilatus Kulm, a distance of 4.6 km, reaching a height of 2070m. The 800mm gauge line was first opened in 1889 and uses an unusual rack system with teeth on either side of a horizontal rail. The line has been electrified since the 1930s.

Alpnachstad is 13 km from Luzern on the line to Interlaken (Table **561**). A popular excursion from Luzern is to take the train or boat to Alpnachstad, rack railway to Pilatus Kulm, cable-car and gondolas down to Kriens, then trolleybus route **1** back to central Luzern.

The Pilatus Bahn runs early-May to mid-November; there is no winter service - see Table **553** for timings. www.pilatus.ch

JUNGFRAUBAHNEN (JB)

Reached from Interlaken by two different routes (Table **564**), Kleine Scheidegg is the start point for the Jungfraubahn, which burrows through the Mönch and the Eiger to reach Europe's highest station at Jungfraujoch (3454m). The 9.3 km electrified narrow gauge rack railway is mostly in tunnel but stops twice on the way up at Eigerwand and Eismeer from where there are spectacular views through windows incorporated into the mountain side. On a clear day the views from the summit are breathtaking. Visitors are strongly advised to check weather conditions at the summit before travelling. The Eiger Express was launched in December 2020 enabling a 47 minute quicker trip to the summit. www.jungfrau.ch

The line runs all year, every 30 minutes, but may sometimes be affected by snowfall in winter. The journey takes 35 minutes. See Table **564** for timings.

GORNERGRATBAHN (GGB)

Starting from Zermatt, western terminus of the famous *Glacier Express* (Table **575**, also local services in Table **576**), the Gornergratbahn runs for 9.4 km to the summit at 3089m. Gornergrat is the highest open-air station in Europe, since the higher Jungfraujoch station described above is actually situated inside the mountain! www.gornergratbahn.ch

The journey on this electrified narrow gauge rack railway takes 33 minutes (44 downhill) and initially provides a birds-eye view of Zermatt followed by fine views of the Matterhorn. From Zermatt sit on the right-hand side for the best views. The GGB station at Zermatt is close to the MGB station, at right angles to it. The service runs all year; see Table **578** for timings.

SWISS MUSEUM OF TRANSPORT

Known as the Verkehrshaus, the museum is located eight minutes by local train from Luzern station (route S3 to the Verkehrshaus stop), and can also be reached by bus or boat. It is open daily. www.verkehrshaus.ch

TURKEY

RAIL TRAVEL

See Tables **1570 - 1585** (**1573** for European Turkey). Operator is TCDD (Turkish State Railways) www.tcdd.gov.tr. Istanbul and Ankara are linked by a dedicated high-speed line via Eskişehir, with a further high-speed section extending south to Konya and Karaman. Turkey's high-speed network expanded further in May 2023 with the opening of a brand new line between Ankara and Sivas; journey time between the two cities has been dramatically cut from over ten hours to just 2½ hours via the more direct high-speed route. Other traditional routes are rather tortuous and slow, but long-distance coaching stock is generally very comfortable.

Journeys between European and Asian Turkey were revolutionised with the opening of the 1.4 kilometre long Marmaray Tunnel in 2013. Frequent local services operate between Halkali and Gebze via central Istanbul. High-speed trains from Istanbul use the centrally located Söğütlüçeşme station, with certain services extended via the tunnel to serve Halkali (Table **1570**). The neoclassical pseudo-castle Haydarpasa station building on the Asian side of the Bosphorus is now out of use but is being restored.

UKRAINE

RAIL TRAVEL

See Tables **1700 - 1790**, which also include neighbouring Moldova. Ukrainian Railways goes under the initials UZ. www.uz.gov.ua

This vast 1520mm gauge railway network links all major towns and many small ones, and the introduction of modern diesel multiple units in recent years has seen a new *InterCity* category of train, giving fast links on key routes. The most scenic routes are in the south west of the country.

Determined railfans may find the remaining narrow gauge lines of interest, although services are sparse, time consuming to access, and information scarse. One of the lines, that between Rudnytsia and Holovanivs'k, is actually Europe's longest 750mm gauge line at 130 km, but its future is far from certain.

Owing to the ongoing conflict in Ukraine, all rail services are subject to change at short notice. Readers are advised to consult the latest official advice regarding travel to Ukraine.

380 PARIS - TROYES - BELFORT - MULHOUSE

AMENDED SERVICE JUNE 30 - AUGUST 31 ⊡. During this period services are operated by 🚌 Nogent - Troyes and v.v. (shaded timings).

km	🅁 for journeys from Paris	Ⓐ	⑥	Ⓐ	①–⑥ k	Ⓐ L	Ⓐ 🚌	⑥	Ⓐ	Ⓐ	Ⓐ	⑥	① a	②–⑤ b	Ⓒ	Ⓐ 🚌		Ⓐ 🚌	Ⓒ	Ⓐ	Ⓐ	⑥	†	Ⓒ
0	**Paris** Est d.	...	...	...	...	...	...	...	0622	0542	0618	0642	0730	0825	0811	...	0742	...	0842	0942	...	1042	...	1142
110	Nogent sur Seine a.	...	...	...	...	...	...	...	|	0642	0713	0738	|	|	|	...	0838	...	0939	1038	...	1139	...	1238
	Nogent sur Seine 🚌 d.	...	...	...	...	...	...	...	|	0652	0723	0748	|	|	|	...	0848	...	0949	1048	...	1149	...	1248
129	Romilly sur Seine 🚌 d.	...	...	...	...	...	...	...	|	0722	0753	0818	|	|	|	...	0918	...	1019	1118	...	1219	...	1318
166	**Troyes** 🚌 a.	...	...	...	...	...	...	...	|	0812	0843*	0908	|	|	|	...	1008*	...	1109*	1208	...	1309	...	1408*
	Troyes d.	0507	0639	...	...	...	0645	0808	|	0822	...	0919	|	|	|	0920	...	1020	▬	▬	1311	1319	1319	...
221	Bar sur Aube d.	0538	0709	...	...	...	|	0839	|	0854	...	0950	|	|	|	1025	...	1125	...	...	1342	1348	1350	...
262	Chaumont 381 d.	0600	0731	...	...	...	0815	0900	0908	0916	...	1011	1022	1103	1108	1105	...	1205	...	...	1404	1410	1411	...
296	Langres 381 d.	0623	0752	...	...	...	▬	0921	0928	0936	...	1032	1042	1123	1128	...	...	...	...	...	1424	1430	1432	...
307	Culmont Chalindrey **379a 381** d.	0637	0800	...	...	...	Ⓐ	0929	0937	0944	...	1040	1059	1137	1146	...	...	...	Ⓐ	...	1434	1440	1440	...
	Dijon Ville **379a 381** a.	0741	...	...	...	...		...	|	...	...	...	|	|	|	...	...	...	...	...	1533	1528	...	...
380	Vesoul d.	...	...	0638	0738	0808	0838	...	1015	...	...	...	1137	1215	1224	...	...	...	1238	1338	...	...	...	...
410	Lure 382 d.	...	...	0656	0756	0826	0856	...	1032	...	...	...	1154	1232	1241	...	...	...	1256	1356	...	...	...	...
442	**Belfort** Ville 382 ▷ d.	...	...	0724	0824	0854	0924	...	1052	...	...	...	1212	1250	1301	...	...	...	1324	1424	...	...	...	...
474	Altkirch ▷ d.	...	...	...	...	...	...	...	1108	...	...	...	...	...	1318	...	...	...	...	...	...	...	...	...
490	**Mulhouse** ▷ a.	...	...	...	...	...	...	...	1118	...	...	...	...	...	1328	...	...	...	...	...	...	...	...	...

🅁 for journeys from Paris	A	Ⓐ		⑥	†	Ⓐ c	Ⓒ	Ⓐ 🚌		Ⓐ	⑥	†	Ⓑ	Ⓐ	Ⓒ	Ⓐ ⊙	⑥ △	⚒	†	Ⓐ	†	⚒	Ⓑ	
Paris Est d.	1225	...	1240v	1323	1323	1325	...	...	1512	...	1536	1635	1642	...	...	...	1736	1742	1812	1812	1821	1842	1942	2042
Nogent sur Seine a.	|	...	1338	|	|	|	...	...	1608	...	|	|	1738	...	...	...	|	1838	1908	1912	|	1939	2037	2138
Nogent sur Seine 🚌 d.	|	...	1348	|	|	|	...	...	1618	...	|	|	1749	...	...	...	|	1848	1918	1922	|	1949	2048	2148
Romilly sur Seine 🚌 d.	|	...	1418	|	|	|	...	...	1648	...	|	|	1819	...	...	...	|	1918	1948	1952	|	2019	2118	2218
Troyes 🚌 a.	|	...	1508*	|	|	|	...	...	1738*	...	|	|	1909*	...	...	...	|	2008*	2038*	2042*	|	2109	2208*	2308*
Troyes d.	|	...	...	|	|	|	1641	1700	▬	1801	|	|	...	1920	1951	1952	|	...	...	...	|	...	...	...
Bar sur Aube d.	|	...	...	|	|	|	1712	|	...	1831	|	|	...	1949	2022	2022	|	...	...	...	|	...	...	...
Chaumont 381 d.	1500	...	...	1557	1556	1604	1734	1830	...	1853	1905	1916	...	2010	2043	2042	2059	...	...	...	2102	...	...	...
Langres 381 d.	1520	...	...	1618	1616	1625	1754	▬	...	1913	1925	1936	...	2030	2104	2105	2123	...	...	...	2122	...	...	...
Culmont Chalindrey **379a 381** d.	1538	...	...	1628	1633	1638	1802	...	Ⓑ	1938	1939	1953	...	2040	2112	2113	2131	...	...	...	2131	...	...	...
Dijon Ville **379a 381** a.	|	...	...	|	|	|	...	...	h	|	|	|	...	...	...	|	|	...	...	...	|	...	...	...
Vesoul d.	1618	1638	...	1708	1710	1716	...	1738	1838	2029	2018	2031	...	...	...	2151	2211	...	...	...	2209	...	...	...
Lure 382 d.	1636	1656	...	1726	1727	1733	...	1756	1856	2047	2035	2048	...	...	...	2208	2228	...	...	...	2226	...	...	...
Belfort Ville 382 ▷ d.	1655	1724	...	1745	1747	1751	...	1824	1924	2107	2055	2108	...	...	...	2226	2247	...	...	...	2245	...	...	...
Altkirch ▷ d.	...	...	...	...	...	...	...	...	...	2124	2111	2126	...	...	...	2244	2304	...	...	...	2302	...	...	...
Mulhouse ▷ a.	...	...	...	...	...	...	...	...	...	2143	2120	2140	...	...	...	2300	2314	...	...	...	2313	...	...	...

🅁 for journeys to Paris	Ⓐ	⚒	Ⓐ	⚒	⑥	Ⓐ	Ⓐ e	⑥	⊖	† ◇	Ⓐ	⑥	Ⓐ	Ⓐ L	①–⑥ k	Ⓐ		Ⓐ 🚌	Ⓒ	Ⓐ 🚌	Ⓐ	Ⓒ	Ⓒ	Ⓐ
Mulhouse ▷ d.	...	...	...	...	...	...	...	...	...	0531	0530	...	...	...	...	...	0742	...	...	...	...	...	...	...
Altkirch ▷ d.	...	...	...	...	...	...	...	...	...	0542	0545	...	...	...	...	...	0752	...	...	...	...	...	...	...
Belfort Ville 382 ▷ d.	...	...	...	...	...	...	...	...	...	0601	0606	...	0636	0706	0736	...	0811	...	...	...	0936	...	...	...
Lure 382 d.	...	...	...	...	...	...	...	...	...	0619	0624	...	0705	0734	0805	...	0829	...	...	...	1005	...	...	...
Vesoul d.	...	...	...	...	...	...	...	...	...	0636	0641	...	0722	0751	0822	...	0846	...	...	...	1022	...	...	...
Dijon Ville **379a 381** d.	...	...	...	...	...	...	...	...	...	|	|	...	...	...	▬	0819	|	...	...	...	▬	...	...	...
Culmont Chalindrey **379a 381** d.	...	...	...	...	...	0520	...	0610	...	0715	0720	0725	...	...	...	0908	0925	...	...	...	...	1125	...	1225
Langres 381 d.	...	...	...	...	...	0530	...	0619	...	0724	0728	0734	...	...	...	0918	0934	...	...	...	...	1134	...	1234
Chaumont 381 d.	...	...	...	...	...	0551	...	0640	...	0744	0749	0755	...	...	...	0938	0955	1005	...	1055	...	1155	...	1255
Bar sur Aube d.	...	...	...	...	...	0612	...	0701	...	|	0811	0816	...	...	Ⓒ	0958	|	|	...	1135	Ⓐ	1216	...	1316
Troyes a.	...	...	...	...	...	0640	...	0732	...	|	0840	0845	...	...		1028	|	1135	...	1240		1245	...	1345
Troyes 🚌 d.	0420	0450	0516•	0550	0649	0650•	0720	...	0750	|	...	0850•	...	...	1050	1050•	|	...	1149•	...	1250•	...	1349•	...
Romilly sur Seine 🚌 d.	0510	0540	0606	0640	0739	0740	0810	...	0840	|	...	0940	...	...	1140	1140	|	...	1239	...	1340	...	1439	...
Nogent sur Seine 🚌 a.	0540	0610	0636	0710	0809	0810	0840	...	0910	|	...	1010	...	...	1210	1210	|	...	1309	...	1410	...	1509	...
Nogent sur Seine d.	0550	0620	0646	0720	0819	0820	0850	...	0920	|	...	1020	...	...	1220	1220	|	...	1319	...	1420	...	1519	...
Paris Est a.	0646	0716	0746	0816	0916	0916	0946	...	1016	1023	...	1116	...	...	1316	1320	1236z	...	1416	...	1516	...	1616	...

🅁 for journeys to Paris	Ⓒ	†	Ⓑ h	Ⓐ	⑥	①–⑥ k	Ⓐ	Ⓐ 🚌	Ⓑ	Ⓒ	Ⓑ ⊕	⑦	⑥	⑥	H	B	Ⓐ	Ⓐ	Ⓐ		Ⓐ	Ⓒ ♡	Ⓑ h	⑦ d
Mulhouse ▷ d.	...	1150	...	...	...	...	...	...	...	...	...	1531	1533	...	...	1533	1535	...	...	...	...	...	...	...
Altkirch ▷ d.	...	1200	...	...	...	...	...	...	...	...	...	1543	1544	...	...	1543	1546	...	...	...	...	...	...	...
Belfort Ville 382 ▷ d.	...	1219	1236	1305	...	1336	...	...	...	...	...	1602	1602	...	...	1602	1605	...	1636	1736	1814	1824	1836	...
Lure 382 d.	...	1238	1305	1323	...	1405	...	...	...	...	...	1620	1620	...	...	1620	1623	...	1705	1805	1832	1843	1905	...
Vesoul d.	...	1255	1322	1340	...	1422	...	...	...	...	...	1638	1638	...	...	1638	1640	...	1722	1822	1849	1901	1922	...
Dijon Ville **379a 381** d.	...	|	...	|	...	▬	...	...	...	...	...	|	|	1613	...	|	|	1705	▬	▬	|	|	...	...
Culmont Chalindrey **379a 381** d.	1326	1335	...	1420	1426	...	...	...	...	...	1640	1727	1726	1726	...	1726	1720	1807	...	...	1933	1945	...	2108
Langres 381 d.	1335	1344	...	1429	1435	...	...	...	...	...	1649	1736	1735	1735	...	1735	1728	1816	...	...	1942	1954	...	2117
Chaumont 381 d.	1355	1404	...	1449	1455	...	...	1455	...	...	1709	1755	1755	1755	...	1755	1748	1836	...	...	2003	2014	...	2138
Bar sur Aube d.	1416	|	...	|	1516	Ⓒ	...	1535	...	...	1730	|	|	|	...	|	|	1857	...	⑦	2024	|	...	2158
Troyes a.	1445	|	...	|	1546	...	...	1640	...	...	1800	|	|	|	...	|	|	1926	J	f	2054	|	...	2228
Troyes 🚌 d.	...	|	...	|	...	1549•	1549•	...	1650•	1749•	...	|	|	|	1850•	|	|	...	1938•	1938•	...	|	...	...
Romilly sur Seine 🚌 d.	...	|	...	|	...	1639	1639	...	1740	1839	...	|	|	|	1940	|	|	...	2028	2028	...	|	...	...
Nogent sur Seine 🚌 a.	...	|	...	|	...	1709	1709	...	1810	1909	...	|	|	|	2010	|	|	...	2058	2058	...	|	...	...
Nogent sur Seine d.	...	|	...	|	...	1720	1719	...	1820	1919	...	|	|	|	2020	|	|	...	2108	2119	...	|	...	...
Paris Est a.	...	1645	...	1722	...	1816	1824	...	1916	2019	...	2036	2054	2054	2116	2118	2120	...	2216	2216	...	2317	...	...

Other trains **BELFORT - MULHOUSE**

	⚒	Ⓐ M	⚒	Ⓐ	Ⓒ	Ⓐ M	Ⓐ	Ⓒ	Ⓐ M	Ⓐ	Ⓒ	Ⓐ	Ⓒ	Ⓐ M	Ⓐ	P	Ⓐ	†	Ⓐ	Q	†	Ⓐ	Ⓐ M	⑥	†	Ⓐ 🚌
Belfort Ville d.	0555	0631	0701	0734	0736	0806	0906	1005	1006	1202	1210	1304	1404	1506	1606	1706	1736	1800	1806	1848	1900	1907	2006	2016	2057	2102
Altkirch d.	0619	0653	0723	0755	0758	0826	0926	1025	1026	1222	1231	1326	1426	1525	1626	1726	1758	1822	1828	1910	1922	1928	2026	2036	2119	2148
Mulhouse a.	0637	0710	0740	0811	0815	0839	0939	1040	1039	1234	1245	1339	1439	1539	1639	1740	1810	1839	1840	1922	1939	1940	2040	2050	2134	2213

	Ⓐ	⚒	Ⓐ M	Ⓐ		Ⓐ M	Ⓐ M	Ⓒ	Ⓐ	Ⓐ M	Ⓒ		Ⓐ		†	⚒	Ⓐ M	Ⓐ	P	Ⓐ	Ⓐ M		Ⓐ M			Ⓐ 🚌
Mulhouse d.	0620	0650	0723	0802	0823	0923	1023	1122	1220	1310	1315	...	1423	...	1559	1619	1650	1719	1751	1823	1901	1929	2020	2056	...	2230
Altkirch d.	0632	0704	0735	0816	0835	0935	1035	1136	1235	1322	1332	...	1435	...	1616	1636	1707	1736	1808	1838	1915	1946	2037	2110	...	2254
Belfort Ville a.	0654	0727	0758	0840	0857	0956	1056	1159	1256	1343	1355	...	1456	...	1640	1659	1730	1800	1831	1901	1939	2010	2100	2132	...	2345

A – Aug. 5, 12 only.
B – July 14, Aug. 15 only.
H – Ⓐ to July 25; ①②⑤ July 28 - Aug. 29 (not Aug. 15).
J – ③④ July 30 - Aug. 28.
L – Until July 4.
M – From Aug. 18.
P – Ⓒ (daily from Aug. 15).
Q – ⑥ (⚒ from Aug. 16).

a – Also July 25; not July 14.
b – Not July 25, Aug. 15.
c – Not Aug. 5, 12.
d – Also July 14.
e – Not July 18, 30, 31.
f – Also Aug. 15.
h – Not Aug. 15.

k – Not July 14.
v – 1242 on Ⓒ.
z – 1234 on ⑥. 1235 on †. 1306 on Aug. 12.

* – A direct 🚌 Nogent - Troyes also operates (arriving Troyes 10 minutes earlier).
• – A direct 🚌 Troyes - Nogent also operates (departing Troyes 10 minutes later).
⊙ – On July 4 Lure d. 2231, Belfort d. 2251, Altkirch d. 2315, Mulhouse a. 2326. Does not run Vesoul - Mulhouse on June 30, Aug. 18 – 22.
△ – Does not run Vesoul - Mulhouse on July 5.
⊖ – Runs 60 – 64 minutes later July 7 – 11.
◇ – On July 14, Aug. 15 departs Lure 0620, Vesoul 0638, Culmont 0718, Langres 0727, Chaumont 0750, arrives Paris 1050 (other timings as shown).
♡ – On July 14, Aug. 15 departs Belfort 1816, Lure 1834, Vesoul 1851, Culmont 1930, Langres 1938, Chaumont 1958 (arrives Paris 2317).
⊕ – Runs 11 – 12 minutes later on Ⓐ.
⊡ – Early morning services on June 30 and services from mid-afternoon on Aug. 31 may vary.

PARIS - STRASBOURG, NANCY, METZ and LUXEMBOURG 390

SERVICE JULY 5 - AUGUST 31. See pages 227 and 228 for service until July 4 and from September 1.
See Tables **30** and **32** for full details of international *TGV*/*ICE* services between Paris and Germany (including services via Forbach and Saarbrücken).
See Table **391** for *TGV* services from/to Marne la Vallée and Paris Charles de Gaulle ✈. Timings may vary by a few minutes – please check your reservation for confirmed timings.
Warning! Journeys to/from Luxembourg are subject to alteration during this period – please check before travelling.

km		*ICE* **9571**	*TGV* **2501**	*TGV* **9561**	*TGV* **2363**	*TGV* **2801**	*TGV* **2807**	*TGV* **2807**	*TGV* **2503**	*TGV* **2407**	*TGV* **2407**	*TGV* **2807**	*TGV* **2587**	*TGV* **2571**	*TGV* **2365**	*TGV* **2409**	*TGV* **2429**	*ICE* **9591**	*TGV* **2507**	*TGV* **2507**	*Ouigo* **7691**	*TGV* **2409**	*TGV* **2815**	*ICE* **9573**
			Ⓐ	①–⑥	①–⑥	①		②–⑥	⑥	Ⓐ		①	⑦	⑥		①	⑦		Ⓐ			⑥		
		♧		⊡	**b**	**g**	**S**	**z**	**t**		**L**	**g**	**e**	**t**	**M**	**g**	**w**	♡		**J**	⊠	§		♧◐
0	**Paris** Est d.	0654	0707	0718**r**	0718**r**	0719	0727	0739	0746	0758	0805	0822	0909	0920	0925	0925	0925	0955	0958	1004	1008	1025	1040	1054
136	Champagne-Ardenne TGV ★ a.	│	0746	│	│	0802	0810	0819	0827	0838	0845	│	0949	│	│	│	│	│	1042	│	│	│	│	│
136	Champagne-Ardenne TGV ★ d.	│	0749	│	│	0805	0813	0822	0830	0841	0848	│	0952	│	│	│	│	│	1048	│	│	│	│	│
236	Meuse TGV d.	│	│	│	│	│	│	│	0858	0908	│	│	1019	│	│	│	│	│	│	│	│	│	│	│
330	**Nancy** 386 387 a.	│	0844	│	│	│	│	│	0936	│	│	│	1053	1057	│	│	│	│	1144**c**	1136	│	│	│	│
	St Dié 387 a.	│	...	│	│	│	│	│	...	│	│	│	│	│	│	│	│	│	...	...	│	│	│	│
	Épinal 386 a.	│	...	│	│	│	│	│	...	│	│	│	│	1144	│	│	│	│	...	...	│	│	│	│
	Remiremont 386 a.	│	...	│	│	│	│	│	...	│	│	│	│	1208	│	│	│	│	...	...	│	│	│	│
315	**Metz** 384 a.	│	...	│	│	0851	0907	0910	...	│	│	0944	▽	...	│	│	│	│	...	...	│	│	1204	│
345	Thionville 384 a.	│	...	│	│	0916	0935	0935	...	│	│	1008	│	...	│	│	│	│	...	...	│	│	1228**j**	│
379	**Luxembourg** 384 a.	│	...	│	│	...	...	...	...	│	│	...	│	...	│	│	│	│	...	...	│	│	...	│
304	Lorraine TGV d.	│	...	│	│	...	...	...	...	│	│	...	│	...	│	│	│	│	...	...	│	│	...	│
439	**Strasbourg** 385 a.	0839	...	0902	0902	...	...	...	...	0959	0959	...	1224	...	1111	1111	1112	1140	...	...	1154	1211	...	1239
482	Sélestat 385 a.	...	...	...	│	...	...	...	...	...	...	...	...	...	...	...	...	...	...	...	...	...	...	...
504	**Colmar** 385 a.	...	...	...	0943	...	...	...	...	...	...	...	...	...	...	...	...	...	...	...	...	...	...	...

	TGV **2507**	*TGV* **2507**	*TGV* **2571**	*TGV* **2591**	*TGV* **2421**	*TGV* **2421**	*TGV* **2817**	*TGV* **2421**	*TGV* **2817**	*TGV* **2817**	*TGV* **9575**	*TGV* **2369**	*TGV* **2509**	*TGV* **2509**	*TGV* **2817**	*ICE* **9563**	*TGV* **2613**	*TGV* **9577**	*TGV* **2513**	*Ouigo* **7693**	*TGV* **2515**	*TGV* **2833**	*TGV* **9531**	*TGV* **2833**
			⑦	⑦		⑤	⑦	⑦	⑤	①–④		Ⓑ	Ⓐ	⑥	⑥		⑤	Ⓑ			①⑤	⑦	Ⓑ	①–⑥
	H	**G**	**e**	**e**	■	**f**	**e**	**w**	**f**	**m**	♧	**h**		**t**	**t**	⊡	**f**	⊙	**T**	⊠	**a**	**e**	⊖	**b**
Paris Est d.	1104	1124	1242	1242	1246	1255	1255	1258	1306	1340	1354	1354	1358	1358	1410	1521	1524	1554	1607	1616	1713	1719	1725	1740
Champagne-Ardenne TGV ★ a.	│	│	│	│	1326	│	│	1338	│	│	│	│	1438	1438	│	│	│	│	1646	│	│	1800	│	│
Champagne-Ardenne TGV ★ d.	│	│	│	│	1329	│	│	1341	│	│	│	│	1441	1441	│	│	│	│	1649	│	│	1805	│	│
Meuse TGV d.	│	│	1345	1345	│	│	│	│	│	│	│	│	1509	1510	│	│	│	│	│	│	│	│	│	│
Nancy 386 387 a.	1236	1255	1421	1421	│	│	│	│	│	│	│	│	1544	1547	│	│	│	│	1744	│	1844	│	│	│
St Dié 387 a.	...	...	│	1526	│	│	│	│	│	│	│	│	...	...	│	│	│	│	...	│	...	│	│	│
Épinal 386 a.	...	...	1514	...	│	│	│	│	│	│	│	│	...	...	│	│	│	│	...	│	...	│	│	│
Remiremont 386 a.	...	...	1538	...	│	│	│	│	│	│	│	│	...	...	│	│	│	│	...	│	...	│	│	│
Metz 384 a.	...	...	...	...	│	│	1419	│	1432	1504	│	│	...	...	1534	│	1648	│	...	1741	...	1854	│	1904
Thionville 384 a.	...	...	...	...	│	│	...	│	...	...	│	│	...	...	...	│	...	│	...	│	...	...	│	1927
Luxembourg 384 a.	...	...	...	...	│	│	...	│	...	...	│	│	...	...	...	│	...	│	...	│	...	...	│	...
Lorraine TGV d.	...	...	...	...	1410	│	...	│	...	...	│	│	...	...	...	│	...	│	...	│	...	...	│	...
Strasbourg 385 a.	...	...	...	...	1447	1440	...	1451	...	...	1539	1539	...	...	...	1707	...	1741	...	1900	...	...	1911	...
Sélestat 385 a.	...	...	...	...	...	...	...	...	...	...	...	│	...	...	...	...	...	...	...	...	...	...	...	...
Colmar 385 a.	...	...	...	...	...	...	...	...	...	...	...	1627	...	...	...	...	...	...	...	...	...	...	...	...

	TGV **9579**	*TGV* **9531**	*TGV* **2573**	*TGV* **2593**	*TGV* **2625**	*TGV* **2377**	*TGV* **2785**	*TGV* **2595**	*TGV* **2785**	*TGV* **2839**	*TGV* **2685**	*TGV* **2583**	*TGV* **2519**	*TGV* **2527**	*TGV* **2465**	*TGV* **2465**	*TGV* **2843**	*TGV* **2647**	*TGV* **2647**	*TGV* **2527**	*TGV* **2647**		*TGV* **2471**	*TGV* **2471**
		⑥		Ⓐ	①–④		⑦	⑦	Ⓐ	Ⓒ	Ⓑ	Ⓐ	⑥		Ⓒ	Ⓐ	⑥			⑤⑦	⑦			⑦
	⊕	⊖			**m**		**w B**	**w**	**B**	**y**	**v**		**t**	**F**		✥		**X**	**Y**	**s**	**e**		**K**	**w**
Paris Est d.	1754	1754	1807	1807	1840	1854	1913	1913	1928	1940	1940	1943	2007	2010	2025	2025	2040	2042	2109	2113	2128	...	2155	2205
Champagne-Ardenne TGV ★ a.	│	│	│	│	1919	│	1953	1953	2008	│	│	│	│	│	│	│	│	│	│	│	2207	...	│	│
Champagne-Ardenne TGV ★ d.	│	│	│	│	1922	│	...	1959	...	│	│	│	│	│	│	│	│	│	│	│	2210	...	│	│
Meuse TGV d.	│	│	1909	1909	│	│	...	2026	...	│	│	│	2109	│	│	2127	│	│	│	│	│	...	│	│
Nancy 386 387 a.	│	│	1944	1944	│	│	...	2101	...	│	│	2114	2144	2142	│	│	│	│	│	2244	│	...	│	│
St Dié 387 a.	│	│	│	2047	│	│	...	2158	...	│	│	│	...	...	│	│	│	│	│	...	│	...	│	│
Épinal 386 a.	│	│	2039	...	│	│	...	...	...	│	│	│	...	...	│	│	│	│	│	...	│	...	│	│
Remiremont 386 a.	│	│	2104	...	│	│	...	...	...	│	│	│	...	...	│	│	│	│	│	...	│	...	│	│
Metz 384 a.	│	│	...	...	2010	│	...	...	...	2104	2104	▽	...	...	│	│	2204	2209	2233	...	2258	...	│	│
Thionville 384 a.	│	│	...	...	2039	│	...	...	...	2127	...	│	...	...	│	│	...	│	│	...	...	...	│	│
Luxembourg 384 a.	│	│	...	...	...	│	...	...	...	...	...	│	...	...	│	│	...	│	│	...	...	...	│	│
Lorraine TGV d.	│	│	...	...	...	│	...	...	...	...	...	│	...	...	│	2148	...	│	│	...	...	...	│	│
Strasbourg 385 a.	1939	1939	...	...	...	2040	...	...	...	...	...	2242	...	...	2211	2225	...	2340	2337	...	...	...	2341	2351
Sélestat 385 a.	...	...	...	...	...	2106	...	...	...	...	...	...	...	...	...	...	...	...	...	...	...	...	...	...
Colmar 385 a.	...	...	...	...	...	2120	...	...	...	...	...	...	...	...	...	...	...	...	...	...	...	...	...	...

	TGV **2530**	*TGV* **2650**	*TGV* **2778**	*TGV* **2852**	*TGV* **2404**	*TGV* **2404**	*TGV* **2574**	*TGV* **2350**	*TGV* **2654**	*TGV* **2654**	*TGV* **2654**	*TGV* **2350**	*TGV* **2350**	*TGV* **9530**	*TGV* **2534**	*TGV* **2596**		*TGV* **9578**	*TGV* **9532/4**	*TGV* **2860**	*TGV* **2860**	*TGV* **2860**	*ICE* **9568**	*TGV* **9534**
	①	①	①–⑥	②–⑤	②–④	①	⚒	⑤	①–④	⑥	⑤	①–④	⑥	⚒	⑦	①–⑥		①–⑥		⑦	⑥	①	Ⓑ	⑦
	◇	**g**	★**B**	¶	**o**	**g**		**f**	**m**	**u**	**f**	**q**		⊖	**e**	★		♧	**D** ⊖			**g**	⊡	⊖
Colmar 385 d.	...	...	...	...	...	...	...	0614	...	...	...	0638	0647	...	...	...	...	...	...	...	...	...	...	...
Sélestat 385 d.	...	...	...	...	...	...	...	0627	...	...	...	0652	0701	...	...	...	...	...	...	...	...	...	...	...
Strasbourg 385 d.	...	...	...	...	0642	0642	...	0659	0525•	0533	0525‡	0719	0749	0749	...	...	...	0821	0821	...	...	...	0852	0908
Lorraine TGV d.	...	...	...	...	│	│	...	0737	│	│	│	0759	│	│	...	...	...	│	│	...	...	...	│	│
Luxembourg 384 d.	...	...	...	...	│	│	...	│	▽	▽	▽	│	│	│	...	...	...	│	│	...	...	...	│	│
Thionville 384 d.	...	...	...	0620	│	│	...	│	│	│	│	│	│	│	...	...	...	│	│	...	0823	0824	│	│
Metz 384 d.	...	0623	...	0650	│	│	...	│	0725	0726	0735	│	│	│	...	...	...	│	│	0849	0850	0853	│	│
Remiremont 386 d.	...	│	...	│	│	│	0559	│	│	│	│	│	│	│	...	...	...	│	│	│	│	│	│	│
Épinal 386 d.	...	│	...	│	│	│	0624	│	│	│	│	│	│	│	...	...	...	│	│	│	│	│	│	│
St Dié 387 d.	...	│	...	│	│	│	│	│	│	│	│	│	│	│	...	0714	...	│	│	│	│	│	│	│
Nancy 386 387 d.	0612	│	...	│	│	│	0716	│	│	│	│	│	│	│	0811	0816	...	│	│	│	│	│	│	│
Meuse TGV d.	│	│	...	0720	│	0734	│	│	│	│	│	│	│	│	0848	│	...	│	│	│	0920	0924	│	│
Champagne-Ardenne TGV ★ a.	│	│	...	│	│	│	│	│	│	│	│	│	│	│	│	│	...	│	│	│	│	│	│	│
Champagne-Ardenne TGV ★ d.	│	│	0718	│	│	│	│	│	│	│	│	│	│	│	│	│	...	│	│	│	│	│	│	│
Paris Est a.	0746	0750	0801	0820	0836	0836	0846	0850	0851	0850	0909	0916	0935	0935	0948	0946	...	1006	1006	1013	1021	1024	1038	1052

A – ①⑤⑥ (also July 9, 10, 15, Aug. 14; not July 14).
B – To/from Bar le Duc (Table **381**).
D – July 14, Aug. 15 only.
E – ⑤ (also July 7 – 10, Aug. 14; not Aug. 15)
F – July 18 only.
G – July 14 only.
H – July 6 only.
J – July 5 only.
K – July 11 only.
L – July 12 only.
M – July 8 – 10; ④⑤ July 17 - Aug. 29 (not Aug. 15).
N – July 6, 14 only.
P – July 6, 14, 20, Aug. 31 only.
Q – ⑦ July 27 - Aug. 24.
R – July 7 only.
S – July 17, 24, 31 only.
T – ②③④⑦ (also July 7, 14; not July 15, Aug. 14). Arrives Nancy 1749 on ②–④ July 16 - Aug. 7.
X – July 18, 25 only. On July 25 Paris d. 2052, Metz a. 2218, Strasbourg a. 2340.
Y – July 11, Aug. 1, 8, 14, 22, 29 only.
a – Also July 8, 9, 10, 15, Aug. 14; not July 14, Aug. 15.

b – Not July 14.
c – 1150 on ⑤.
d – Not July 13, Aug. 14.
e – Also July 14.
f – Also Aug. 14; not Aug. 15.
g – Also July 15; not July 14.
h – Not Aug. 15.
j – Not July 7 – 11.
m – Not July 14, Aug. 14.
n – Also July 13; not July 14.
o – Not July 15, Aug. 14.
q – Also Aug. 15; not July 14, Aug. 14.
r – 0715 on ① (also July 15; not July 14).
s – Also July 14, Aug. 14; not July 18, Aug. 15.
t – Also Aug. 15.
u – Also Aug. 15; not Aug. 16.
v – Not July 11, Aug. 15.
w – Also July 14; not July 13.
y – Also July 11.
z – Not July 15, 17, 24, 31.

TGV – High-speed train. [R]. 🍸.
ICE – German high-speed train. [R]. ✕.

• – 0520 on ②–④ July 8 – 24; 0541 on July 7, 21.
‡ – 0520 on July 11, 18, 25.
¶ – Not July 15, Aug. 15.
★ – Not July 14, Aug. 16.
♠ – Also July 14, Aug. 14.
♣ – Also July 14, Aug. 14; not Aug. 15.
◇ – Also July 8 – 10, 15; not July 14.
♥ – ①②③④⑥ (also Aug. 15; not July 14, Aug. 14).
▲ – Aug. 14 – 16, 18 – 22, 25 – 29 does not call at Metz and arrives Paris 2143.
■ – ①–④ to Aug. 28 (not July 14, Aug. 14). Runs 9 – 14 minutes later on July 7.
§ – Also July 11, Aug. 15. On July 11 Paris d. 1021, Strasbourg a. 1206.
◐ – Runs as *TGV* **9593** on July 19.
◧ – Runs as *TGV* **9592** on July 19.
✥ – Runs up to 12 minutes earlier Aug. 25 – 29.
⊕ – [12] Paris - Stuttgart (- München ⑥). See Table **32**.
⊙ – To/from München via Stuttgart (Table **32**).
⊡ – To/from Frankfurt (Table **30**).
♧ – To/from Stuttgart (Table **32**).
♡ – To/from Berlin via Frankfurt (Table **30**).
⊖ – From/to Freiburg (Brsg) Hbf (Table **32**).
⊠ – OUIGO low-cost TGV. Internet bookings only: www.ouigo.com

390 PARIS - STRASBOURG, NANCY, METZ and LUXEMBOURG

SERVICE JULY 5 - AUGUST 31. See pages 227 and 228 for service until July 4 and from September 1.
See Tables **30** and **32** for full details of international *TGV / ICE* services between Germany and Paris (including services via Forbach and Saarbrücken).
See Table **391** for *TGV* services to Marne la Vallée and Paris Charles de Gaulle ✈. Timings may vary by a few minutes – please check your reservation for confirmed timings.
Warning! Journeys to / from Luxembourg are subject to alteration during this period – please check before travelling.

	TGV **2536** ⚒	*TGV* **2578** †	*TGV* **2406** **R**	*TGV* **2864** Ⓑ **h**	*TGV* **2864** ⑥ **t**	*TGV* **2356** ⑦ **e**	*TGV* **2356** ①–⑥ **b**	*TGV* **9576** ⊙	*ICE* **9566** ⑥ ⊡		*ICE* **9574** ♧		*Ouigo* **7692** ⊠	*TGV* **2540** Ⓐ	*TGV* **2580** ⑥ **t**	*TGV* **2588** ⑦ **e**	*TGV* **2870** ⑥	*TGV* **2870** ⑤⑦ ♠	*TGV* **2430** **A**	*TGV* **2440** ⑤ **f**	*TGV* **2870** ①–④ **m**	*TGV* **2440** ⑦–④ **d**	*TGV* **2542** Ⓐ	*ICE* **9572** ◧♧
Colmar 385 d.	...	...	...	...	...	0958	1000	...	...	...	...	...	...	...	...	...	...	...	...	...	...	...	...	...
Sélestat 385 d.	...	...	...	...	...	1012	|	...	...	...	...	...	...	...	...	...	...	...	...	...	...	...	...	...
Strasbourg 385 d.	...	...	1031	...	...	1046	1046	1046	1052	...	1222	...	1250	...	...	1242	...	...	1449	1531	...	1544	...	1620
Lorraine TGV d.	...	...	|	...	...	|	|	|	|	...	|	...	|	...	...	|	...	...	|	|	...	|	...	|
Luxembourg 384 d.	...	...	|	...	...	|	|	|	|	...	|	...	|	...	...	|	...	...	|	|	...	|	...	|
Thionville 384 d.	...	...	|	1034	1034	|	|	|	|	...	|	...	|	...	...	|	...	...	|	|	...	|	...	|
Metz 384 d.	...	...	|	1057	1059	|	|	|	|	...	|	...	1352	...	...	▽	1459	1505	|	|	1551	|	...	|
Remiremont 386 d.	...	0859	|	|	|	|	|	|	|	...	|	...	|	...	1255	|	|	|	|	|	|	|	...	|
Épinal 386 d.	...	0923	|	|	|	|	|	|	|	...	|	...	|	...	1319	|	|	|	|	|	|	|	...	|
St Dié 387 d.	...	|	|	|	|	|	|	|	|	...	|	...	|	...	|	|	|	|	|	|	|	|	...	|
Nancy 386 387 d.	1011	1011	|	|	|	|	|	|	|	...	|	...	|	1338	1414	1414	|	|	|	|	|	|	1624	|
Meuse TGV d.	|	|	|	|	|	|	|	|	|	...	|	...	|	1421	|	1451	1530	|	|	|	|	|	|	|
Champagne-Ardenne TGV ★ a.	1104	1104	|	|	|	|	|	|	|	...	|	...	|	1444	|	1515	|	|	|	|	|	|	1717	|
Champagne-Ardenne TGV ★ d.	1107	1107	|	|	|	|	|	|	|	...	|	...	|	1447	|	1518	|	|	|	|	|	|	1720	|
Paris Est a.	1148	1148	1216	1220	1222	1231	1231	1231	1238	...	1406	...	1517	1531	1547	1606	1630	1631	1635	1717	1721	1735	1801	1805

	TGV **2872** ⑤⑦ ♣	*TGV* **2872** ♥	*TGV* **2442** **N**	*TGV* **2544** ⑥ **t**	*TGV* **2680** ⑤ **f**	*TGV* **2580** ⑦ **e**	*TGV* **2598** ⑦ **e**	*TGV* **2362** Ⓑ **bh**	*TGV* **2548** ⑤ **E**	*ICE* **9590** ♡	*TGV* **2454** ①–⑤ ◇	*TGV* **9560** ⊡	*TGV* **2550** ⑥ **k**	*TGV* **2886**	*TGV* **2552** ⑤⑦ ♣	*TGV* **2552** ①–④ **m**	*TGV* **9570** ①–⑥ **n**♧	*TGV* **9570** ⑦ **w**♧	*TGV* **9532** ⑦ **w**⊖	*Ouigo* **7694** ▲⊠	*TGV* **2554** ⑦ **e**		*TGV* **2474** **P**	*TGV* **2474** ⑦ **Q**
Colmar 385 d.	...	...	...	...	...	...	...	1645	...	...	...	...	...	...	...	...	...	...	...	...	...	...	...	...
Sélestat 385 d.	...	...	...	...	...	...	...	|	...	...	...	...	...	...	...	...	...	...	...	...	...	...	...	...
Strasbourg 385 d.	...	...	1652	...	...	...	...	1719	...	1801	1819	1857	...	...	...	...	2025	2030	2030	1958	...	...	2119	2152
Lorraine TGV d.	...	...	|	...	...	...	...	|	...	|	|	|	...	...	...	...	|	|	|	|	...	...	|	|
Luxembourg 384 d.	...	...	|	...	...	...	...	|	...	|	|	|	...	...	...	...	|	|	|	|	...	...	|	|
Thionville 384 d.	1634	1633	|	...	...	...	...	|	...	|	|	|	...	...	...	...	|	|	|	|	...	...	|	|
Metz 384 d.	1657	1657	|	...	1728	...	...	|	...	|	|	|	...	1942	...	...	|	|	|	2101	...	...	|	|
Remiremont 386 d.	|	|	|	...	|	1555	...	|	...	|	|	|	...	|	...	...	|	|	|	|	...	...	|	|
Épinal 386 d.	|	|	|	...	|	1619	...	|	...	|	|	|	...	|	...	...	|	|	|	|	...	...	|	|
St Dié 387 d.	|	|	|	...	|	|	1615	|	...	|	|	|	...	|	...	...	|	|	|	|	...	...	|	|
Nancy 386 387 d.	|	|	|	1718	|	1717	1717	|	1811	|	|	|	1920	|	1943	1943	|	|	|	|	2116	...	|	|
Meuse TGV d.	|	|	|	|	|	1754	1754	|	1847	|	|	|	1957	|	|	2021	|	|	|	|	|	...	|	|
Champagne-Ardenne TGV ★ a.	|	1746	|	|	1816	1817	1717	|	|	|	1928	|	2020	2029	2037	2045	|	|	|	|	|	...	|	|
Champagne-Ardenne TGV ★ d.	|	1749	|	|	1819	1820	1820	|	|	|	1931	|	2023	2032	2040	2048	|	|	|	|	|	...	|	|
Paris Est a.	1821	1830	1844	1848	1901	1901	1901	1905	1948	1959	2012	2041	2105	2113	2120	2131	2213	2217	2217	2224	2246	...	2305	2338

← **FOR NOTES, SEE PREVIOUS PAGE.**

310 PARIS - LIMOGES - TOULOUSE

Intercités services are valid **August 4 – 31**. For *Intercités* service July 6 - August 3 see page 187.
Timings of *Intercités* services may vary by a few minutes - please check your reservation. For *TGV* services Paris - Toulouse see Table **300**.

km		■ **3751** ⑥⑦ 🅁	■ **3751** ①–⑤ 🅁	★ **3605** ①–⑤	★ **3605** ⑥	★ **3615** ①–⑤ **C**	★ **3615** ⑦	★ **3615** ①–⑤ **B**	★ **3619** **A**	★ **3619** ①–⑤ **B**	★ **3625** ©	★ **3629** ⑦	★ **3635** ⑥⑦	★ **3645** ⑥⑦	★ **3655** ⑥	★ **3655** ⑦	★ **3655** ①–⑤	★ **3665** ①–⑤	★ **3665** ⑥⑦	★ **3675** ①–⑤ **C**	★ **3675** ①–⑤ **B**	★ **3685** ⑥⑦	★ **3685** ①–⑤ **C**	★ **3685** ①–⑤ **B**
0	**Paris** Austerlitz 294 315 d.	2207	2213	0622	0624	0712	0715	0724	0814	0824	1023	1128	1223	1428	1615	1615	1651	1713	1728	1812	1837	1921	1928	1928
119	Les Aubrais-Orléans 294 315 d.	2322	2330	0731	0734	|	|	|	0931	0932	|	1240	|	1537	|	|	|	|	|	|	|	|	|	|
200	Vierzon Ville 315 d.	|	|	0813	0813	0908	0908	0908	1011	1013	1207	1315	1408	1613	1800	1809	|	1908	1913	2006	2017	2110	2122	2124
236	Issoudun d.	|	|	|	|	0927	|	0927	|	|	1228	|	|	|	1819	1830	1909	|	|	2028	2037	|	|	|
263	Châteauroux d.	|	|	0843	0843	0943	0940	0943	1042	1044	1245	1347	1440	1643	1835	1846	1926	1940	1944	2044	2054	2141	2153	2156
294	Argenton sur Creuse d.	|	|	|	|	|	0957	|	1059	1101	|	|	1457	|	|	|	|	1957	2001	|	|	2157	2209	2212
341	La Souterraine d.	|	|	0921	0921	1023	1023	1023	1124	1126	1323	1425	1523	1722	1912	1924	|	2023	2027	2123	2136	2223	2235	2238
400	**Limoges** Benedictins a.	|	|	0953	0953	1055	1055	1055	1156	1158	1355	1457	1555	1755	1944	1957	2033	2055	2058	2155	2208	2255	2307	2310
400	**Limoges** Benedictins d.	|	|	0956	0956	1058	1058	1058	1159	1201	1358	1500	1558	1758	1947	2000	2036	2058	2101	2158	2211	2258	2310	2313
459	Uzerche d.	|	|	|	|	1138	1137	1138	|	|	1437	|	|	|	2025	2038	2124	|	|	2238	2250	|	|	|
499	**Brive la Gaillarde** a.	|	|	1100	1100	1203	1203	1203	1300	1301	1504	1601	1701	1901	2051	2104	2150	2200	2201	2303	2315	0001	0011	0014
499	**Brive la Gaillarde** d.	|	|	1103	1103	...	...	...	1303	1304	...	...	1704	1904	...	...	...	2203	2204	...	...	...	...	...
536	Souillac d.	0440	0440	1128	1128	...	...	...	1330	1329	...	...	1730	1930	...	...	...	2230	2230	...	...	...	...	...
559	Gourdon d.	0457	0457	1145	1145	...	...	...	1347	1346	...	...	1748	1946	...	...	...	2247	2247	...	...	...	...	...
600	**Cahors** d.	0527	0527	1213	1213	...	...	...	1414	1413	...	...	1815	2014	...	...	...	2314	2314	...	...	...	...	...
639	Caussade d.	0557	0557	1240	1240	...	...	...	1441	1441	...	...	...	2041	...	...	...	...	...	...	...	...	...	...
662	Montauban 355 355a d.	0615	0615	1255	1255	...	...	...	1456	1456	...	...	...	2056	...	...	...	...	...	...	...	...	...	...
713	**Toulouse** Matabiau 355 355a a.	0700	0700	1332	1332	...	...	...	1532	1532	...	...	...	2132	...	...	...	...	...	...	...	...	...	...

	■ **3750** 🅁	★ **3604** ①–⑤	★ **3614** ①–⑤ **B**	★ **3614** **A**	★ **3624** ①–⑤ **B**	★ **3624** ①–⑤ **C**	★ **3624** ⑥	★ **3628** ⑦	★ **3634** ⑥	★ **3638** ⑦	★ **3644** ⑥	★ **3648** ⑦	★ **3650** ⑥⑦	★ **3654** ①–⑤ **C**	★ **3654** ①–⑤ **B**	★ **3654** ⑥⑦	★ **3664** ⑦	★ **3674**	★ **3684** ⑥	★ **3684** Ⓑ	★ **3694** ①–⑤	★ **3694** ⑦	★ **3694** ⑥
Toulouse Matabiau 355 355a d.	2216	...	...	...	...	...	...	...	...	...	0718	...	1027	1027	1027	...	...	...	...	...	1600	1607	1607
Montauban 355 355a d.	2255	...	...	...	...	...	...	...	...	...	0800	...	1105	1106	1106	...	...	...	...	...	1638	1644	1644
Caussade d.	2312	...	...	...	...	...	...	...	...	...	0816	...	1120	1133	1133	...	...	...	...	...	1654	1659	1659
Cahors d.	2342	...	...	...	0407	0407	...	...	0644	0754	0843	...	1146	1228	1228	1242	...	...	...	...	1726	1726	1726
Gourdon d.	0013	...	...	...	0437	0435	...	...	0712	0822	0911	...	1214	1302	1302	1310	...	...	...	...	1753	1753	1753
Souillac d.	0031	...	...	...	0454	0452	...	...	0728	0838	0928	...	1231	1322	1322	1326	...	...	...	...	1810	1810	1810
Brive la Gaillarde a.	|	...	...	...	0517	0516	...	...	0754	0903	0954	...	1255	1354	1354	1352	...	...	...	...	1835	1835	1835
Brive la Gaillarde d.	|	0358	0456	0458	0520	0519	0558	0705	0757	0906	0957	1102	1258	1357	1357	1355	1558	1658	1756	1757	1838	1838	1838
Uzerche d.	|	|	0523	0525	|	|	|	|	0824	0933	|	1129	|	1424	1424	1421	|	|	1823	1824	|	|	|
Limoges Benedictins a.	|	0459	0559	0601	0620	0620	0659	0807	0901	1010	1101	1206	1400	1501	1501	1458	1659	1759	1900	1901	1939	1939	1939
Limoges Benedictins d.	|	0502	0602	0604	0623	0623	0702	0810	0904	1013	1104	1209	1403	1504	1504	1501	1702	1802	1903	1904	1942	1942	1942
La Souterraine d.	|	0534	0634	0636	0654	0655	0735	0843	0937	1045	1136	|	1435	1538	1538	1536	1734	1834	1935	1936	2016	2016	2016
Argenton sur Creuse d.	|	|	0659	0701	|	|	|	0908	1002	|	|	1301	1459	|	|	|	1759	1859	1959	|	|	|	|
Châteauroux d.	|	0611	0717	0719	0732	0733	0815	0926	1020	1123	1214	1321	1516	1619	1619	1615	1817	1918	2017	2014	2057	2057	2057
Issoudun d.	|	0628	|	|	0749	0753	0831	|	|	1140	|	1338	|	|	|	1631	|	|	|	2030	|	|	|
Vierzon Ville 315 d.	|	0650	0754	0754	0811	0822	0854	|	1055	1202	1248	1359	1550	1653	1653	1653	1855	1955	2051	2052	2131	2131	2131
Les Aubrais-Orléans 294 315 a.	0554	|	|	|	0844	0907	|	1032	|	|	1329	|	1628	|	|	|	|	|	|	|	2205	2205	2205
Paris Austerlitz 294 315 a.	0703	0838	0931	0931	0955	1008	1031	1134	1231	1332	1431	1531	1734	1831	1838	1831	2030	2131	2231	2231	2310	2309	2310

A – Daily until Aug. 17; ⑥⑦ from Aug. 23.
B – From Aug. 18.
C – Until Aug. 14.

★ – *INTERCITÉS*. 🅁.
■ – *INTERCITÉS DE NUIT*. Conveys 🛏 1, 2 cl. and 2nd class seats. Overnight journeys only. **Timings and running days may vary**. For confirmed days of running and timings please consult the SNCF journey planner: www.sncf-connect.com.

SBB BIEL/BIENNE and PORRENTRUY - BASEL 500a

AMENDED SERVICE UNTIL SEPTEMBER 28. All services are operated by 🚌 Laufen - Aesch and v.v. (shaded timings). **Note**: Train numbers only apply Biel/Bienne - Laufen and v.v.

km					*IC* 1607						*IC* 1609		*IC* 1611			*IC* 1637		*IC* 1639		*IC* 1641				*IC* 1545
		⚒			✗		⑥	Ⓐ	†		✗		✗	✣										L
0	**Biel / Bienne** 515 d.	...	...	...	0548	...	...	...	...	...	0649	...	0749	and at	...	2048	...	2148	...	2248	...	2319	...	0019
13	Grenchen Nord 515 d.	...	...	...	0559	...	...	...	...	...	0659	...	0759	the same	...	2059	...	2159	...	2259	...	2329	...	0029
24	Moutier 515 d.	...	...	...	0608	...	...	...	...	...	0708	...	0808	minutes	...	2108	...	2208	...	2308	...	2338	...	0038
	Porrentruy 515 d.	0508	0508	...	|	...	0610	0610	0610	...	|	0710	|	past each	2010	|	2110	|	2210	|	2310	|	...	|
	Glovelier 515 d.	0525	0525	...	|	...	0625	0625	0625	...	|	0725	|	hour until	2025	|	2125	|	2225	|	2325	|	...	|
35	Delémont 515 a.	0539	0539	...	0618	...	0639	0639	0639	...	0718	0739	0818		2039	2118	2139	2218	2239	2318	2339	2348	...	0048
	Delémont d.	0543	0543	...	0623	...	0643	0643	0643	...	0723	0743	0823		2043	2123	2143	2223	2243	2323	2343	...	...	...
	Laufen a.	0555	0555	...	0635	...	0655	0655	0655	...	0735	0755	0835		2055	2135	2155	2235	2255	2335	2355	...	...	...
	Laufen 🚌 d.	0600	...	...	0638t	...	0700	0700	0708	...	0738	0800	0845		2100	2145	2200	2238	2308	2338	0008	...	...	...
	Aesch 🚌 a.	0619	...	...	0702t	...	0719	0724	0729	...	0804	0819	0904		2119	2204	2219	2259	2329	2359	0029	...	...	...
	Aesch d.	0622	...	...	0707	...	0722	0737	0737	...	0807	0822	0907		2122	2207	2222	2307	2337	0007	0037	...	...	...
74	**Basel** SBB a.	0636	...	...	0721	...	0736	0751	0751	...	0821	0836	0921		2136	2221	2236	2321	2351	0021	0051	...	...	...

		IC 1606			*IC* 1608		*IC* 1610		*IC* 1612		*IC* 1614			*IC* 1638		*IC* 1640								
		L		△	⊙ ✗	△	⊙ ✗	△	⊙ ✗		✗													
Basel SBB d.	...	...	0442	0517	0532	0617	0632	0717	0732	0817	0832	0917	and at	2032	2117	2132	2217	2312	...	...	...	...	...	...
Aesch a.	...	...	0455	0533	0548	0633	0648	0733	0748	0833	0848	0933	the same	2048	2133	2148	2233	2325	...	...	...	...	...	...
Aesch 🚌 d.	...	...	0500	0537	0552	0637	0652	0737	0752	0837	0852	0937	minutes	2052	2137	2152	2237	2330	...	...	...	...	...	...
Laufen 🚌 a.	...	...	0521	0556	0611	0656	0711	0756	0811	0856z	0911	0956	past each	2111	2156	2211	2256	2351	...	...	...	...	...	...
Laufen d.	...	...	0529	0606	0621	0706	0721	0806	0821	0906	0921	1006	hour until	2121	2206	2221	2306	0008	...	...	...	...	...	...
Delémont a.	...	...	0543	0619	0637	0719	0737	0819	0837	0919	0937	1019		2137	2219	2237	2319	0022	...	...	...	...	...	...
Delémont 515 d.	0510	0542	*0551*	0621	0642	0721	0742	0821	0842	0921	0942	1021		2142	2221	2242	2321	0023	...	...	...	...	...	...
Glovelier 515 d.	|	|	*0603*	0633	|	0733	|	0833	|	0933	|	1033		|	2233	|	2333	0035	...	...	...	...	...	...
Porrentruy 515 a.	|	|	*0620*	0650	|	0750	|	0850	|	0950	|	1050		|	2250	|	2350	0052	...	...	...	...	...	...
Moutier 515 d.	0520	0552	...	...	0652	...	0752	...	0852	...	0952	...		2152	...	2252	...	...	...	...	...	...	...	...
Grenchen Nord 515 d.	0530	0601	...	...	0701	...	0801	...	0901	...	1001	...		2201	...	2301	...	...	...	...	...	...	...	...
Biel / Bienne 515 d.	0541	0611	...	...	0711	...	0811	...	0911	...	1011	...		2211	...	2311	...	...	...	...	...	...	...	...

– From / to Lausanne (Table **500**).

– On ⑥ Laufen d. 0645, Aesch a. 0704.

– 0903 on †.

✣ – *IC* services may depart Biel/Bienne at xx48 (not xx49).

△ – On † Basel d. xx12, Aesch a. xx25, d. xx30, Laufen a. xx51 and then as shown.

⊙ – On † Basel d. xx42, Aesch a. xx55, d. xx00, Laufen a. xx19 and then as shown.

☞ See Table **515** for other servicesBiel/Bienne - Delémont - Porrentruy and v.v.

BLS BERN - LUZERN 514

AMENDED SERVICE UNTIL JULY 31. All services are operated by 🚌 Langnau - Schüpfheim and v.v. (shaded timings).

km		Ⓐ			Ⓐ	★					★						★					★			
0	**Bern** d.	...	...	...	0536	0600	...	...	0612	0636	0700	...	and at	...	2112	2136	2200	...	...	2212	2236	2300	...	2312	2342
21	Konolfingen d.	...	...	...	0552	|	...	...	0634	0652	|	...	the same	...	2134	2152	|	...	...	2234	2252	|	...	2334	0005
38	Langnau a.	...	...	...	0605	|	...	...	0652	0705	|	...	minutes	...	2152	2205	|	...	...	2252	2305	|	...	2352	0023
	Langnau 🚌 d.	0451	0522a	0551	...	|	0622	0651	...	...	|	0722	past each	2151	...	...	|	2222	2251	...	...	|	2309	...	...
	Schüpfheim 🚌 a.	0524	0555a	0624	...	|	0654	0724	...	...	|	0754	hour until	2224	...	...	|	2254	2324	...	...	|	2341	...	...
	Schüpfheim d.	0528	0559	0629	...	|	0659	0729	...	...	|	0759		2229	...	...	|	2259	2329	...	...	|	2344	...	...
75	Wolhusen d.	0545	0620	0645	...	|	0720	0745	...	...	|	0820		2245	...	...	|	2320	2345	...	...	|	2359	...	...
96	**Luzern** a.	0603	0643	0703	...	0701	0743	0803	...	...	0801	0843		2303	...	...	2301	2343	0010	...	...	0001	0019	...	...

		Ⓐ	Ⓐ		★					★						★						★			
Luzern d.	...	...	0450	...	0600	...	...	0557	0616	0700	...	...	and at	2057	2116	2200	...	...	2157	2216	2257	2300	...	2316	0016
Wolhusen d.	...	...	0514	...	|	...	...	0615	0644	|	...	...	the same	2115	2144	|	...	...	2215	2244	2315	|	...	2344	0041
Schüpfheim a.	...	...	0528	...	|	...	...	0628	0659	|	...	...	minutes	2128	2159	|	...	...	2228	2259	2328	|	...	2359	0056
Schüpfheim 🚌 d.	...	...	0531	...	|	...	...	0631	0702	|	...	...	past each	2131	2202	|	...	...	2231	2302	2331	|	...	0002	0105
Langnau 🚌 a.	...	...	0603	...	|	...	...	0703	0734	|	...	...	hour until	2203	2234	|	...	...	2303	2334	0003	|	...	0035	0138
Langnau d.	0507	0554	...	0607	|	0637	0654	0707	...	|	0737	0754		2207	...	|	2237	2254	2307	...	...	|	0007	...	...
Konolfingen d.	0526	0607	...	0626	|	0656	0707	0726	...	|	0756	0807		2226	...	|	2256	2307	2326	...	...	|	0026	...	...
Bern a.	0548	0627	...	0648	0700	0719	0727	0748	...	0800	0819	0827		2248	...	2300	2319	2327	2348	...	...	2400	0048	...	...

– Ⓐ only.

★ – Fast *IR* service via Zofingen (see Table **565**).

Operator: *Västtågen* (2nd class only) ÖREBRO - HALLSBERG - MARIESTAD - GÖTEBORG 736

SERVICE JULY 14 - AUGUST 17

km		Ⓐ	Ⓐ	⑥	Ⓐ	Ⓐ d	Ⓒ	Ⓐ	Ⓐ e	Ⓐ	⑦	⑥	Ⓐ	⑦	⑦	Ⓐ	⑥	Ⓐ	⑦	①–④	⑤	⑥	⑦	⚒	
	Örebro C 755 756 d.	...	...	...	...	...	...	0755	0755	...	...	...	...	...	...	...	...	...	...	1635	1634	...	...	...	...
0	**Hallsberg** 755 756 d.	...	...	...	...	...	...	0816	0816	...	...	1128	...	1246	...	...	...	...	...	1656	1656	1724	1906	...	...
30	Laxå 756 d.	...	...	...	...	...	...	0833	0833	...	...	1145	1238	1303	...	...	...	...	...	1713	1713	1742	1923	...	...
92	Mariestad a.	...	...	...	...	...	...	0920	0920	...	...	1232	1324	1353	...	...	...	...	...	1759	1800	1827	2008	...	...
92	Mariestad d.	...	0554	...	0653	0653	0811	0924	0924	1026	...	1233	1331	...	1413	1437	1442	1627	1707	1812	1815	1829	2010	...	...
146	Lidköping a.	...	0637	...	0742	0742	0855	1011	1011	1119	...	1319	1423	...	1455	1524	1529	1714	1754	1859	1904	1916	2057	...	...
146	Lidköping d.	0540	0640	0732	0753	0753	0857	1023	1023	1122	1129	1338	1427	...	1457	1536	1533	1727	1757	1918	1917	1922	...	2140	...
201	**Herrljunga** 740 756 a.	0626	0727	0821	|	0849	|	|	1116	1209	|	|	1513	...	|	1622	1621	1813	|	2007	2007	2008	...	2227	...
	Göteborg C 740 756 a.	...	...	...	0940	...	1045	1210	...	...	1325	1525	...	...	1650	...	...	...	1950	...	...	...	...	...	...

	Ⓐ	Ⓐ	Ⓐ	⑥	Ⓐ	⑥	⑦	Ⓐ	⑦	⑥	Ⓐ	Ⓐ	Ⓐ f	⑦	⑦	⑥	Ⓐ	⑦	⑥	Ⓐ	Ⓐ	Ⓐ	⑥	⑦	⚒
Göteborg C 740 756 d.	...	...	...	...	...	...	...	1030	1145	1145	...	1345	...	1400	...	...	...	1730	1730	...	...	...	...	2015	...
Herrljunga 740 756 d.	...	...	0658	...	0933	0933	...	|	|	|	1235	|	1427	|	...	1634	1632	|	|	1834	1928	2033	2035	|	2234
Lidköping a.	...	...	0747	...	1019	1022	...	1223	1328	1328	1320	1527	1527	1557	...	1721	1719	1917	1919	1915	2019	2121	2121	2206	2321
Lidköping d.	...	0545	0756	0802	1025	1025	1043	1225	1328	1332	1328	1530	1530	1600	...	1725	1722	1920	1923	1920	...	...	...	...	...
Mariestad a.	...	0635	0844	0857	1112	1112	1130	1312	1406	1413	1417	1618	1618	1647	...	1814	1809	2002	2005	2006	...	...	...	...	...
Mariestad d.	0537	...	...	0858	1124	...	1132	...	...	1415	1454	...	...	...	1705	...	...	...	...	...	...	...	...	...	...
Laxå 756 d.	0627	...	...	0950	1211	...	1220	...	...	1507	1542	...	...	...	1756	...	...	...	...	...	...	...	...	...	...
Hallsberg 755 756 a.	0644	...	...	1007	...	...	1236	...	...	1526	1559	...	...	...	1812	...	...	...	...	...	...	...	...	...	...
Örebro C 755 756 a.	0716	...	...	...	...	...	...	...	...	...	1621	...	...	...	...	...	...	...	...	...	...	...	...	...	...

d – Change at Håkantorp (arrives 0819 / departs 0827).

e – Change at Håkantorp (arrives 1049 / departs 1056).

f – Change at Håkantorp (arrives 1448 / departs 1500).

804 HAGEN and DORTMUND - WARBURG and BRILON *RE services*

AMENDED SERVICE JUNE 22 - SEPTEMBER 21. See page 383 for service outside this period.

km		Ⓐ	Ⓐ	Ⓐ	⚒		Ⓐ	Ⓒ		Ⓐ																
0	**Hagen** Hbf **802** d.	...	0502	...	0602	...	...	0700	...	0717	...	0817	...	...	0917	...	...	1017	...	...	1117	...	...	1215	...	...
	Dortmund Hbf **802** d.	...	|	...	|	...	0641	|	...	|	0741	|	...	0841	|	...	0941	|	...	1041	|	...	1141	|	...	124
14	Schwerte (Ruhr) . **802** d.	...	0512	...	0612	...	|	0712	...	0728	|	0828	...	|	0928	...	|	1028	...	|	1128	...	|	1228	...	|
57	Arnsberg (Westf) d.	...	0541	...	0641	...	0725	0741	...	0758	0825	0858	...	0925	0958	...	1025	1058	...	1125	1158	...	1225	1258	...	132
77	Meschede d.	...	0559	...	0658	...	0742	0759	...	0816	0842	0916	...	0942	1016	...	1042	1116	...	1142	1216	...	1242	1316	...	134
85	Bestwig a.	...	0605	...	0704	...	0748	0805	...	0822	0848	0922	...	0948	1022	...	1048	1122	...	1148	1222	...	1248	1322	...	134
	Bestwig d.	0442*	0615*	...	0732*	...	0750	0832*	...	0832*	0850	0932*	...	0950	1032*	...	1050	1132*	...	1150	1232*	...	1250	1332*	...	135
	Brilon Stadt d.	|	|	0706	|	0806	|	|	0906	|	|	|	1006	|	|	1106	|	|	1206	|	|	1306	|	|	1406	|
100	Brilon Wald a.	0521*	0654*	0714	0811*	0814	0834r	0911*	0914	0911*	0934r	1011*	1014	1034r	1111*	1114	1134r	1211*	1214	1234r	1311*	1314	1334r	1411*	1414	1434
	Brilon Wald d.	0528	...	0722	...	0819	...	...	0919	...	...	...	1019	...	...	1119	...	...	1219	...	...	1319	...	...	1419	...
126	Marsberg d.	0553	...	0747	...	0845	...	...	0945	...	...	...	1045	...	...	1145	...	...	1245	...	...	1345	...	...	1445	...
151	**Warburg** (Westf) d.	0614	...	0808	...	0907	...	...	1007	...	...	...	1107	...	...	1207	...	...	1307	...	...	1407	...	...	1507	...

																									¶	¶
Hagen Hbf **802** d.	1317	...	...	1417	...	...	1517	...	...	1615	...	...	1717	...	...	1817	...	...	1917	...	...	2017	...	...	...	...
Dortmund Hbf **802** d.	|	...	1341	|	...	1441	|	...	1541	|	...	1641	|	...	1741	|	...	1841	|	...	1941	|	2041	2123	2223	232
Schwerte (Ruhr) **802** d.	1328	...	|	1428	...	|	1528	...	|	1628	...	|	1728	...	|	1828	...	|	1928	...	|	2028	|	2149	2249	234
Arnsberg (Westf) d.	1358	...	1425	1458	...	1525	1558	...	1625	1658	...	1725	1758	...	1825	1858	...	1925	1958	...	2025	2058	2125	2221	2321	002
Meschede d.	1416	...	1442	1516	...	1542	1616	...	1642	1716	...	1742	1816	...	1842	1916	...	1942	2016	...	2042	2116	2142	2239	2339	003
Bestwig a.	1422	...	1448	1522	...	1548	1622	...	1648	1722	...	1748	1822	...	1848	1922	...	1948	2022	...	2048	2122	2148	2245	2345	004
Bestwig d.	1432*	...	1450	1532*	...	1550	1632*	...	1650	1732*	...	1750	1832*	...	1850	1932*	...	1950	2032*	...	2050	2132*	2150	2246	...	...
Brilon Stadt d.	|	1506	|	|	1606	|	|	1706	|	|	1806	|	|	1906	|	|	2006	|	|	2106	|	|	|	|	...	...
Brilon Wald a.	1511*	1514	1534r	1611*	1614	1634r	1711*	1714	1734r	1811*	1814	1834r	1911*	1914	1934r	2011*	2014	2034r	2111*	2114	2134r	2211*	2234r	2320r	...	...
Brilon Wald d.	...	1519	...	...	1619	...	...	1718	...	...	1819	...	...	1919	...	...	2019	...	...	2119	...	...	...	...	...	...
Marsberg d.	...	1545	...	...	1645	...	...	1745	...	...	1845	...	...	1945	...	...	2045	...	...	2145	...	...	...	...	...	...
Warburg (Westf) d.	...	1607	...	...	1707	...	...	1807	...	...	1907	...	...	2007	...	...	2107	...	...	2207	...	...	...	...	...	...

km		⚒	Ⓐ	⚒	Ⓐ		⚒		⚒v	⚒																
	Warburg (Westf) d.	...	...	...	...	...	0535	...	0631	...	...	...	...	0752	...	...	0852	...	...	0952	...	...	1052	...	...	115
	Marsberg d.	...	...	...	...	...	0555	...	0650	...	...	...	...	0812	...	...	0912	...	...	1012	...	...	1112	...	...	121
0	Brilon Wald a.	...	...	...	...	...	0619	...	0716	...	...	...	...	0839	...	...	0939	...	...	1039	...	...	1139	...	...	123
4	Brilon Wald d.	...	...	...	0519*	...	0629*	...	0726	0726*	...	...	0835r	0844	0849*	0935r	0944	0949*	1035r	1044	1049*	1135r	1144	1149*	1235r	124
	Brilon Stadt a.	...	...	...	|	...	|	...	0734	|	...	...	|	0852	|	|	0952	|	|	1052	|	|	1152	|	|	125
98	Bestwig a.	...	...	...	0558*	...	0708*	...	...	0805*	...	...	0907	...	0928*	1007	...	1028*	1107	...	1128*	1207	...	1228*	1307	...
—	Bestwig d.	0434	0505	0534	0610	0634	0710	0734	...	0810	0810	0834	0910	...	0934	1010	...	1034	1110	...	1134	1210	...	1234	1310	...
	Meschede d.	0441	0511	0541	0616	0641	0717	0741	...	0817	0817	0841	0917	...	0941	1017	...	1041	1117	...	1141	1217	...	1241	1317	...
0	Arnsberg (Westf) d.	0459	0528	0559	0633	0659	0734	0759	...	0834	0834	0859	0934	...	0959	1034	...	1059	1134	...	1159	1234	...	1259	1334	...
	Schwerte (Ruhr) **802** a.	0528	|	0628	|	0728	|	0828	...	|	|	0928	|	...	1028	|	...	1128	|	...	1228	|	...	1328	|	...
59	**Dortmund** Hbf **802** a.	|	0616	|	0717	|	0817	|	...	0917	0917	|	1017	...	|	1117	...	|	1217	...	|	1317	...	|	1417	...
	Hagen Hbf **802** a.	0542	...	0642	...	0742	...	0842	...	...	...	0942	...	...	1042	...	...	1142	...	...	1242	...	...	1342	...	...

Warburg (Westf) d.	...	...	1252	...	...	1352	...	...	1452	...	...	1552	...	...	1652	...	...	1752	...	...	1852	...	1952	...	2052	215
Marsberg d.	...	...	1312	...	...	1412	...	...	1512	...	...	1612	...	...	1712	...	...	1812	...	...	1912	...	2012	...	2112	221
Brilon Wald a.	...	...	1339	...	...	1439	...	...	1539	...	...	1639	...	...	1739	...	...	1839	...	...	1939	...	2039	...	2139	223
Brilon Wald d.	1249*	1335r	1344	1349*	1435r	1444	1449*	1535r	1544	1549*	1635r	1644	1649*	1735r	1744	1749*	1835r	1844	1849*	1935r	1944	1949*	2049*	2135r	2149*	2249
Brilon Stadt a.	|	|	1352	|	|	1452	|	|	1552	|	|	1652	|	|	1752	|	|	1852	|	|	1952	|	|	|	|	|
Bestwig a.	1328*	1407	...	1428*	1507	...	1528*	1607	...	1628*	1707	...	1728*	1807	...	1828*	1907	...	1928*	2007	...	2028*	2128*	2207	2228*	2328
Bestwig d.	1334	1410	...	1434	1510	...	1534	1610	...	1634	1710	...	1734	1810	...	1834	1910	...	1934	2010	...	2034	...	2210	...	...
Meschede d.	1341	1417	...	1441	1517	...	1541	1617	...	1641	1717	...	1741	1817	...	1841	1917	...	1941	2017	...	2041	...	2217	...	...
Arnsberg (Westf) d.	1359	1434	...	1459	1534	...	1559	1634	...	1659	1734	...	1759	1834	...	1859	1934	...	1959	2034	...	2059	...	2234	...	...
Schwerte (Ruhr) **802** a.	1428	|	...	1528	|	...	1628	|	...	1728	|	...	1828	|	...	1928	|	...	2028	|	...	2128	...	|	...	...
Dortmund Hbf **802** a.	|	1517	...	|	1617	...	|	1717	...	|	1817	...	|	1917	...	|	2017	...	|	2117	...	|	...	2326	...	...
Hagen Hbf **802** a.	1442	...	...	1542	...	...	1642	...	...	1742	...	...	1842	...	...	1942	...	...	2042	...	...	2142	...	...	...	...

BRILON STADT - MARBURG SERVICE JUNE 22 - SEPTEMBER 21

	Ⓐ				Ⓐ					
Marburg (Lahn) d.	0629	0829	1029	1229	1329	1429	1529	1629	1829	1929
Brilon Wald a.	0841	1041	1241	1441	1540	1641	1741	1841	2041	2141
Brilon Wald d.	0844	1044	1244	1444	...	1644	1817	1844	2044	2144
Brilon Stadt a.	0852	1052	1252	1452	...	1652	1825	1852	2052	2152

	Ⓐ										
Brilon Stadt d.	0706	0806	0906	1106	1306	1406	1506	1606	1706	1806	1906
Brilon Wald a.	0714	0814	0914	1114	1314	1414	1514	1614	1714	1814	1914
Brilon Wald d.	0727	0822	0922	1122	1322	1422	1522	1622	1722	1822	1922
Marburg (Lahn) a.	0923	1023	1123	1323	1523	1623	1723	1823	1923	2023	212

r – By 🚌 Bigge - Brilon Wald and v.v. (rail tickets valid).

v – Runs 3–4 minutes later Warburg - Brilon Wald on ⑥.

* – Service is by rail-replacement 🚌 (rail tickets valid).

¶ – By 🚌 Arnsberg - Bestwig from July 1 (arrives 33 minutes later).

841 MAGDEBURG - STENDAL - UELZEN and WITTENBERGE *RE / S-Bahn services*

AMENDED SERVICE AUGUST 2 - DECEMBER 13 A partially amended service also operates on August 1. See page 400 for service to August 1.

km		⚒	Ⓐ			⚒																						
0	**Magdeburg** Hbf . d.	0347	...	0447	0510	0541	0610	0641	0710	0741	0810	0841	0910	0941	1010	1041	1110	1141	1210	1241	1310	1341	1410	1441	1510	1541	1610	1641
58	Stendal Hbf a.	0430	...	0530	0558	0625	0658	0725	0758	0825	0858	0925	0958	1025	1058	1125	1158	1225	1258	1325	1358	1425	1458	1525	1558	1625	1658	1725
58	Stendal Hbf ◇ d.	0432	0500	0534	0600	▬	0700	0734	0800	▬	0900	0934	1000	▬	1100	1134	1200	▬	1300	1334	1400	▬	1500	1534	1600	▬	1700	1734
	Osterburg a.	|	0524	|	0624	...	0724	|	0824	...	0924	|	1024	...	1124	|	1224	...	1324	|	1424	...	1524	|	1624	...	1724	|
	Osterburg d.	|	0534*	|	0634*	...	0734*	|	0834*	...	0934*	|	1034*	...	1134*	|	1234*	...	1334*	|	1434*	...	1534*	|	1634*	...	1734*	|
113	**Wittenberge** a.	|	0624*	|	0724*	...	0824*	|	0924*	...	1024*	|	1124*	...	1224*	|	1324*	...	1424*	|	1524*	...	1624*	|	1724*	...	1824*	|
116	Salzwedel ◇ a.	0507	...	0610	...	...	...	0810	...	...	...	1010	...	...	...	1210	...	...	...	1410	...	...	...	1610	...	...	...	1810
116	Salzwedel ◇ d.	0517*	...	0620*	...	0737*	...	0820*	...	0930*	...	1020*	...	1137*	...	1220*	...	1330*	...	1420*	...	1537*	...	1620*	...	1737*	...	1820*
167	**Uelzen** ◇ a.	0634*	...	0737*	...	0854*	...	0915*	...	1047*	...	1115*	...	1254*	...	1315*	...	1447*	...	1515*	...	1654*	...	1715*	...	1854	...	1915*

Magdeburg Hbf d.	1710	1741	1810	1841	1910	1941	2010	2041	2110	2141	2210	2310
Stendal Hbf a.	1758	1825	1858	1925	1958	2025	2058	2125	2158	2225	2258	2358
Stendal Hbf ◇ d.	1800	▬	1900	1934	2000	...	2100	2134	2200	2236	...	...
Osterburg a.	1824	...	1924	|	2024	...	2124	|	2224	|	...	...
Osterburg d.	1834*	...	1934*	|	2034*	...	2134*	|	2234*	|	...	...
Wittenberge a.	1924*	...	2024*	|	2124*	...	2224*	|	2324*	|	...	...
Salzwedel ◇ a.	...	...	...	2010	...	...	...	2207	...	2316	...	...
Salzwedel ◇ d.	...	1930*	...	2020*	...	...	...	2208	...	...	...	...
Uelzen ◇ a.	...	2047*	...	2115*	...	...	...	2247	...	...	...	...

	Ⓐ		⚒	Ⓐd		Ⓐd						
Uelzen ◇ d.	...	...	...	...	...	...	0506*	...	0623*	...	0654*	...
Salzwedel ◇ a.	...	...	...	...	...	...	0623*	...	0740*	...	0811*	...
Salzwedel ◇ d.	...	...	0435	...	0550	...	▬	...	0750	...	▬	...
Wittenberge d.	...	...	|	0432*	|	0532*	...	0632*	|	0732*	...	0832*
Osterburg a.	...	...	|	0522*	|	0622*	...	0722*	|	0822*	...	0922*
Osterburg d.	...	...	|	0532	|	0632	...	0732	|	0832	...	0932
Stendal Hbf ◇ a.	...	...	0511	0555	0628	0655	...	0755	0827	0855	...	0955
Stendal Hbf d.	0357	0457	0532	0557	0632	0657	0732	0757	0832	0857	0932	0957
Magdeburg Hbf a.	0445	0545	0615	0645	0715	0745	0815	0845	0915	0945	1015	1045

Uelzen ◇ d.	0845*	...	0906*	...	1045*	...	1054*	...	1240*	...	1306*	...	1445*	...	1506*	...	1638*	...	1654*	...	1840*	...	1902*	...	2030*	...	...	2302
Salzwedel ◇ a.	0940*	...	1023*	...	1140*	...	1211*	...	1335*	...	1423*	...	1540*	...	1623*	...	1733*	...	1811*	...	1935*	...	2019*	...	2125*	...	...	2334
Salzwedel ◇ d.	0950	...	▬	...	1150	...	▬	...	1345	...	▬	...	1550	...	▬	...	1743	...	▬	...	1945	...	▬	...	2135	...	...	2335
Wittenberge d.	|	0932*	...	1032*	|	1132*	...	1232*	|	1332*	...	1432*	|	1532*	...	1632*	|	1732*	...	1832*	|	1932*	...	2032*	|	2132*	2225*	|
Osterburg a.	|	1022*	...	1122*	|	1222*	...	1322*	|	1422*	...	1522*	|	1622*	...	1722*	|	1822*	...	1922*	|	2022*	...	2122*	|	2222*	2315*	|
Osterburg d.	|	1032	...	1132	|	1232	...	1332	|	1432	...	1532	|	1632	...	1732	|	1832	...	1932	|	2032	...	2132	|	2232	2325	|
Stendal Hbf ◇ a.	1027	1055	...	1155	1227	1255	...	1355	1422	1455	...	1555	1627	1655	...	1755	1820	1855	...	1955	2022	2055	...	2155	2212	2255	2348	0005
Stendal Hbf d.	1032	1057	1132	1157	1232	1257	1332	1357	1432	1457	1532	1557	1632	1657	1732	1757	1832	1857	1932	1957	2032	2057	2132	2157	2223	2257	...	0007
Magdeburg Hbf a.	1115	1145	1215	1245	1315	1345	1415	1445	1515	1545	1615	1645	1715	1745	1815	1845	1915	1945	2015	2045	2115	2145	2212	2244	2302	2345	...	0047

d – Runs daily Stendal - Magdeburg.

* – Service is by rail-replacement 🚌 (rail tickets valid).

◇ – See amended Table **840** on page 608 for fast *ICE* services Stendal - Salzwedel - Uelzen and v.v. Aug. 2 - Dec. 13.

HAMBURG - ROSTOCK - STRALSUND 830

RE services except where shown

AMENDED SERVICE AUGUST 2 - DECEMBER 13. For alternative rail connections Hamburg - Bad Kleinen and v.v. see Tables **825** and **836** (via Lübeck).

km				Ⓐ				◇	*IC* **2260**					◇	*IC* **2262**			Ⓐ			◇	*IC* **2264** G				
0	**Hamburg** Hbf d.	...	...	...	...	...	...	...	0838	...	...	...	...	...	1230	...	...	...	...	...	...	1633	...	...	...	...
	Lübeck Hbf d.	...	...	...	...	...	...	...	0936	...	...	...	...	...	1333	...	...	...	...	...	...	1736	...	...	...	...
123	**Schwerin** Hbf **837** d.	0448	*0543*	0626	*0743*	*0843*	*0943*	1013	|	*1043*	*1143*	*1243*	*1343*	1413	|	*1443*	*1543*	1626	*1643*	*1743*	1813	|	*1843*	*1943*	*2143*	*2343*
140	Bad Kleinen **837** a.	0458	*0555*	0636	*0755*	*0855*	*0956*	1024	1032	*1056*	*1155*	*1255*	*1355*	1424	1432	*1455*	*1555*	1636	*1655*	*1756*	1824	1832	*1855*	*1955*	*2155*	*2355*
140	Bad Kleinen **836** d.	0503	0603	0638	0803	0903	1003	...	1034	1103	1203	1303	1403	...	1434	1503	1603	1638	1703	1803	...	1834	1903	2003	2203	0006
181	Bützow **836** d.	0529	0629	0702	0829	0929	1029	...	1100	1129	1229	1329	1429	...	1500	1529	1629	1702	1729	1829	...	1900	1929	2029	2229	0032
211	**Rostock** Hbf a.	0550	0650	0724	0850	0950	1050	...	1126	1150	1252	1350	1450	...	1526	1550	1650	1724	1750	1850	...	1926	1950	2050	2250	0053
	Stralsund Hbf ◧ a.	...	...	...	...	...	...	...	1230**z**	...	...	...	...	...	1627**z**	...	...	...	...	...	...	2028**v**	...	...	...	...
	Ostseebad Binz ◧ a.	...	...	...	...	...	...	...	1329**z**	...	...	...	...	...	1720**z**	...	...	...	...	...	...	...	...	...	...	...

			Ⓐ			*IC* **2261** G					*IC* **2263**					Ⓐ	*IC* **2265**									
Ostseebad Binz ◧ d.	...	...	...	...	...	...	...	...	...	...	1043**z**	...	...	...	...	...	1427**z**	...	...	...	...	...	...	...	...	...
Stralsund Hbf ◧ d.	...	...	...	...	...	0727**x**	...	...	...	...	1138**z**	...	...	...	...	...	1524**z**	...	...	...	...	...	...	...	...	...
Rostock Hbf d.	0508	0608	0634	0708	0808	0854	0908	1008	1108	1208	1254	1308	1408	1508	1608	1634	1655	1708	1808	1908	2008	2108	2208	2313	...	...
Bützow **836** d.	0529	0629	0655	0729	0829	0919	0929	1029	1129	1229	1319	1329	1429	1529	1629	1655	1720	1729	1829	1929	2029	2129	2229	2334	...	...
Bad Kleinen **836** a.	0554	0654	0718	0754	0854	0947	0954	1054	1154	1254	1347	1354	1454	1554	1654	1718	1748	1754	1854	1954	2054	2154	2254	2359	...	...
Bad Kleinen **837** d.	*0559*	*0659*	0720	*0759*	*0859*	0951	*0959*	*1059*	*1159*	*1259*	1351	*1359*	*1459*	*1559*	*1659*	1720	1751	*1759*	*1859*	*1959*	*2059*	*2159*	2255	*0003*	...	...
Schwerin Hbf **837** a.	*0609*	*0709*	0732	*0809*	*0909*	|	*1009*	*1109*	*1209*	*1309*	|	*1409*	*1509*	*1609*	*1709*	1732	|	*1809*	*1909*	*2009*	*2109*	*2209*	2306	*0016*	...	...
Lübeck Hbf a.	...	...	...	...	...	1041	...	...	...	...	1442	...	...	...	...	...	1841	...	...	...	...	...	...	...	...	...
Hamburg Hbf a.	...	...	...	...	...	1130	...	...	...	...	1532	...	...	...	...	...	1936	...	...	...	...	...	...	...	...	...

ROSTOCK - STRALSUND AMENDED SERVICE AUGUST 2 - DECEMBER 13

km		◇ S	◇ Ⓐ S	◇ S	◇ Ⓐ D		◇ S	*ICE* **1974** ⑥L H	◇ S	*IC* **2260** D	◇ S		*IC* **2474** ⑥⑦ JD	◇ S	*IC* **2262** D	◇ Ⓐd D		◇ S	◇ S	*IC* **2264** B G		◇ S	◇			
0	*Hamburg Hbf* ◐ d.	...	...	...	...	...	...	...	...	0838	...	...	...	...	1230	...	...	...	...	1633	...	...	...	...	...	...
211	**Rostock** Hbf d.	0454**r**	0553**r**	0700**r**	0811	...	0900**r**	1049	1100**r**	1138	1300**r**	...	1445	1500**r**	1538	1610	...	1700**r**	1900**r**	1938	...	2100**r**	2300**r**	...	...	...
	Gelbensande d.	0510	0609	0718	0834	...	0915	|	1115	|	1315	...	|	1515	|	1635	...	1715	1915	|	...	2115	2315	...	...	...
240	Ribnitz-D'garten West d.	0517	0616	0725	0849	...	0922	1109	1122	1200	1322	...	1512	1522	1600	1650	...	1722	1922	2000	...	2122	2322	...	...	...
265	Velgast d.	0539	0638	0742	0903	...	0940	1123	1140	1215	1340	...	1524	1540	1614	1711	...	1740	1940	2015	...	2140	2340	...	...	...
283	**Stralsund** Hbf a.	0555	0655	0758	0917	...	0957	1136	1157	1230	1357	...	1538	1557	1627	1724	...	1757	1957	2028	...	2157	2357	...	...	...
	Ostseebad Binz **844** a.	...	...	...	...	...	...	1232	...	1329	...	...	1631	...	1720	...	...	...	...	...	...	...	...	...	...	...

	◇ Ⓐ S	◇ S	◇ Ⓐ	*IC* **2261** ①–⑤ DG	*IC* **2261** ⑥⑦ DG	◇ S	◇ S		*IC* **2263** D	◇ S	*IC* **2479** 🍷 CK		◇ S	*ICE* **1971** ⑥L H	Ⓐ D	Ⓐ E	*IC* **2265** D	◇ S	◇ D	◇ E		◇ S		◇ S	◇ S	
Ostseebad Binz **844** d.	...	...	...	...	...	...	...	...	1043	...	1114	...	...	1318	...	...	1427	...	1602	1602	...	...	...	...	...	...
Stralsund Hbf d.	0449	0558	0637	0727	0741	0759	0959	...	1138	1159	1213	...	1359	1415	1451	1451	1524	1559	1659	1659	...	1759	...	1959	2200	...
Velgast d.	0505	0014	0051	0741	0756	0015	1015	...	1166	1216	1220	...	1116	1127	1606	1606	1640	1615	1712	1712	...	1815	...	2015	2215	...
Ribnitz-Damgarten West d.	0524	0632	0706	0757	0813	0833	1033	...	1215	1233	1242	...	1433	1442	1522	1522	1558	1633	1737	1731	...	1833	...	2033	2233	...
Gelbensande a.	0531	0638	0712	|	|	0839	1039	...	|	1239	|	...	1439	|	|	1528	|	1639	|	1738	...	1839	...	2039	2239	...
Rostock Hbf a.	0547**t**	0654**t**	0746**t**	0840	0840	0855**t**	1055**t**	...	1240	1255**t**	1314	...	1455**t**	1514	1547	*1611***e**	1627	1655**t**	1801	*1822***e**	...	1855**t**	...	2055**t**	2255**t**	...
Hamburg Hbf ◐ a.	...	...	...	1130	1130	...	...	...	1532	...	...	...	...	...	...	...	1936	...	...	...	...	...	...	...	...	...

B – Not Sept. 5 - Nov. 7.
C – Not Sept. 6 - Nov. 8.
D – Not Sept. 6 - Nov. 7.
E – Sept. 6 - Nov. 7.
G – To / from Greifswald (Table **846**).
H – (12) Berlin (Table **835**) - Rostock - Stralsund - Ostseebad Binz (Table **844**) and v.v.
J – (12) Magdeburg - Berlin - Rostock - Stralsund - Ostseebad Binz (Table **844**).
K – (12) Ostseebad Binz - Stralsund - Rostock - Berlin - Magdeburg - Leipzig.

L – ⑥ Aug. 2 - 30.
S – To / from Sassnitz (Table **844**).

d – Ⓐ (daily June 23 - Sept. 5).
e – By 🚌.
r – Departs 27 minutes earlier Sept. 6 - Nov. 7 (by 🚌 Rostock - Gelbensande §) .
t – Arrives approx. 27 minutes later Sept. 6 - Nov. 7 (by 🚌 Gelbensande - Rostock §).
v – Not Sept. 5 - Nov. 7.
x – Not Sept. 6 - Nov. 8. Departs 0741 on ⑥⑦.

z – Not Sept. 6 - Nov. 7.

◧ – See lower section of table.
◐ – See upper section of table.
◇ – Operated by Ostdeutsche Eisenbahn.
§ – 🚌 dep./arr. Rostock Hbf Süd (Albrecht Kossel Platz). Note that 0746 Rostock arrival is 0752 by 🚌.

SEE NEXT PAGE FOR AMENDED TABLES 837, 839 AND 840

LEIPZIG - DRESDEN 842

AMENDED SERVICE AUGUST 10 - DECEMBER 13. See page 400 for service until August 9.

	EN **40459** 🅁 A	*EC* **459** B		*IC* **2249** ①–⑤ 🍷	*IC* **2449** M 🍷	*ICE* **1553** ①–⑥ E ✕	*IC* **2447** H 🍷		*ICE* **1555** ✕	*IC* **2445** K 🍷	*ICE* **1557** ✕	*IC* **2443** K 🍷	*ICE* **1559** ✕		*IC* **2441** K 🍷	*ICE* **1651** ✕	*IC* **2049** K 🍷	*ICE* **1653** ✕	*IC* **2047** K 🍷	*ICE* **1655** ✕	*IC* **2045** Ⓑ K ✕	*ICE* **1657**		
Wiesbaden Hbf **911** d.	...	...	...	...	...	...	...	...	0627	...	0826	...	1026	...	...	1226	...	1426	...	1626	...	1826	...	...
Frankfurt (Main) Hbf **850** d.	0027•	0027•	...	...	...	...	...	...	0718	...	0918	...	1118	...	...	1318	...	1518	...	1718	...	1918	...	...
Leipzig Hbf d.	0545	0545	...	0631	0731	0831	0931	...	1031	1131	1231	1331	1431	...	1531	1631	1731	1831	1931	2031	2131	2231	...	...
Riesa d.	0623	0623	...	0701	0801	0901	1002	...	1101	1201	1301	1401	1501	...	1601	1701	1801	1901	2002	2101	2201	2301	...	...
Dresden Neustadt a.	0659	0659	...	0732	0832	0933	1032	...	1133	1232	1333	1432	1533	...	1632	1733	1832	1933	2032	2133	2232	2335	...	...
Dresden Hbf a.	0706	0706	...	0740	0840	0940	1040	...	1140	1240	1340	1439	1540	...	1639	1740	1840	1940	2040	2140	2240	2343	...	...

	IC **2044** K ✕	*ICE* **1654** ✕	*IC* **2046** ①–⑥ K 🍷		*ICE* **1652** ✕	*IC* **2048** K 🍷	*ICE* **1650** ✕		*IC* **2440** K 🍷	*ICE* **1558** ✕	*IC* **2442** K 🍷	*ICE* **1556** ✕	*IC* **2444** K 🍷	*ICE* **1554** ✕		*IC* **2446** H	*ICE* **1552** ✕	*IC* **2448** H 🍷		*EN* **40458** 🅁 A	*EC* **458** B			
Dresden Hbf d.	0509	0610	0709	...	0810	0909	1010	...	1109	1210	1309	1410	1509	1610	...	1709	1810	1909	...	2102	2102	...	...	...
Dresden Neustadt d.	0516	0616	0716	...	0816	0916	1016	...	1116	1216	1316	1416	1516	1619	...	1716	1816	1916	...	2109	2109	...	...	...
Riesa d.	0547	0649	0747	...	0849	0947	1049	...	1147	1249	1347	1449	1547	1649	...	1747	1849	1947	...	2143	2143	...	...	...
Leipzig Hbf a.	0621	0726	0821	...	0926	1021	1126	...	1221	1326	1421	1526	1621	1726	...	1821	1926	2021	...	2218	2218	...	...	...
Frankfurt (Main) Hbf **850** a.	...	1036	...	...	1236	...	1436	...	...	1636	...	1836	...	2036	...	...	2236	...	...	0335•	0335•	...	...	...
Wiesbaden Hbf **911** a.	...	1133	...	...	1333	...	1533	...	...	1733	...	1933	...	2133	...	...	...	...	...	...	...	...	...	...

RE services August 10 - December 13

km		⚒		⚒				
0	**Leipzig** Hbf d.	0400	0500	0600	0700		2200	2308
26	Wurzen d.	0418	0518	0618	0718	and	2218	2326
53	Oschatz d.	0436	0536	0636	0736		2236	2344
66	Riesa d.	0445	0545	0645	0745	hourly	2245	2354
102	Coswig **843 856 857** d.	0515	0615	0715	0815		2315	0027
110	Radebeul Ost **857** d.	0520	0620	0720	0820	until	2320	0033
116	**Dresden** Neustadt **856/7** a.	0526	0626	0726	0826		2326	0038
120	**Dresden** Hbf **843 856 857** a.	0533	0633	0733	0833		2333	0045

	⚒		⚒		⊡				
Dresden Hbf. **843 856 857** d.	0417	0515	0615	0715		2115	2215	2315	...
Dresden Neustadt ... **856/7** d.	0424	0523	0623	0723	and	2123	2223	2323	...
Radebeul Ost **857** d.	0430	0529	0629	0729		2129	2229	2329	...
Coswig **843 856 857** d.	0437	0537	0637	0737	hourly	2137	2237	2337	...
Riesa d.	0506	0606	0706	0806		2206	2306	0006	...
Oschatz d.	0514	0614	0714	0814	until	2214	2314	0014	...
Wurzen d.	0532	0632	0732	0832		2232	2332	0032	...
Leipzig Hbf a.	0550	0650	0750	0850		2250	2350	0050	...

A – CANOPUS – 🛏 1, 2 cl. and ▬ 2 cl. Zürich - Basel - Leipzig - Dresden - Praha and v.v.
B – (2) Zürich - Basel - Leipzig - Dresden - Praha and v.v.; also conveys (1) and ✕ Leipzig - Dresden - Praha and v.v.
E – From Erfurt on ⑥ (Table **850**).

H – To / from Hannover (Table **866**).
K – To / from Köln via Hannover (Tables **800**, **810** and **866**). Certain services also run beyond Köln to / from stations in Table **800**.
M – From Magdeburg (Table **866**).

• – Frankfurt (Main) **Süd** (not Hbf).
⊡ – 1715 departure is 2 minutes earlier on ⑥ to Nov. 1.

837 SCHWERIN and WISMAR - BERLIN - COTTBUS

AMENDED SERVICE AUGUST 2 - DECEMBER 13 Schwerin - Berlin trains are diverted via Güstrow due to closure of the Hamburg - Berlin line Operator: ◇

Schwerin Hbf d.	0613	0813	1013	1213	1413	1613	1813	2013	2213
Bad Kleinen a.	0624	0824	1024	1224	1424	1624	1824	2024	2224
Bad Kleinen d.	0626	0826	1026	1226	1426	1626	1826	2026	2226
Güstrow **835** d.	0657	0857	1057	1257	1457	1657	1857	2057	2257
Waren (Müritz) **835** d.	0726	0926	1126	1326	1526	1726	1926	2126	2326
Neustrelitz Hbf **835** d.	|	|	|	|	|	|	|	|	|
Oranienburg **835** d.	0815	1015	1215	1415	1615	1815	2015	2215	0015
Berlin Gesundbrunnen **835** a.	0838	1038	1238	1438	1638	1838	2038	2238	0038
Berlin Hbf **835** a.	0844	1044	1244	1444	1645	1843	2044	2244	0047
Berlin Südkreuz **835** a.	0854	1054	1254	1454	1654	1853	2053	2253	0055

Berlin Südkreuz **835** d.	0501	0701	0901	1101	1301	1501	1703	1901	210
Berlin Hbf **835** d.	0511	0709	0911	1111	1310	1511	1711	1911	211
Berlin Gesundbrunnen **835** d.	0517	0717	0917	1117	1316	1517	1717	1917	211
Oranienburg **835** d.	0539	0739	0939	1139	1339	1539	1739	1939	213
Neustrelitz Hbf **835** d.	0612	0812	1012	1212	1412	1612	1812	2012	221
Waren (Müritz) **835** d.	0630	0830	1030	1230	1430	1630	1830	2030	223
Güstrow **835** d.	0702	0902	1102	1302	1502	1702	1902	2102	230
Bad Kleinen a.	0732	0932	1132	1332	1532	1732	1932	2132	233
Bad Kleinen d.	0734	0934	1134	1334	1534	1734	1934	2134	233
Schwerin Hbf a.	0747	0947	1147	1347	1547	1747	1947	2148	234

SCHWERIN - BAD KLEINEN - WISMAR **AMENDED SERVICE AUGUST 2 - DECEMBER 13** Operator: ◇

Schwerin Hbf **830** d.	0443	0543	0643	0743	and hourly until	2143	2243	2343
Bad Kleinen **830** a.	0455	0555	0655	0755		2155	2255	2355
Bad Kleinen d.	0500	0600	0700	0800		2200	2300	0000
Wismar a.	0515	0615	0715	0815		2215	2315	0015

Wismar d.	0442	0542	0642	0742	and hourly until	2142	2242	234
Bad Kleinen a.	0457	0557	0657	0757		2157	2258	235
Bad Kleinen **830** d.	0459	0559	0659	0759		2159	2259	235
Schwerin Hbf **830** a.	0509	0609	0710	0809		2209	2309	000

◇ – Operated by Ostdeutsche Eisenbahn.

839 BERLIN - DRESDEN

AMENDED SERVICE SEPTEMBER 24 - DECEMBER 13. See page 399 for service until September 23.

km	*For night trains see Table* **60**	*EC* **171** ✕		*IC* **2173** 🍷	*EC* **173** B✕		*IC* **2175** 🍷	*EC* **379** ✕		*IC* **2177** 🍷	*EC* **175** ✕		*IC* **2179** 🍷	*EC* **177** ✕		*IC* **2271** C🍷	*EC* **179** ✕		*IC* **2273** C🍷	*RJ* **2079** ✕		*IC* **2275** Ⓑ 🍷		
	Hamburg Hbf **840** d.	...	...	...	...	...	...	...	...	...	...	...	...	...	...	...	...	...	...	...	...	...	...	...
	Rostock Hbf **835** d.	...	...	0621	...	...	0821	...	...	1021	...	...	1221	...	...	1421	...	...	1621	...	...	1821	...	...
0	**Berlin** Hbf **835** d.	0653	...	|	0856	...	|	1055	...	|	1256	...	|	1456	...	|	1656	...	|	1856	...	|	...	...
	Berlin Ostbahnhof **835** d.	|	...	|	0906	...	|	1104	...	|	1304	...	|	1504	...	|	1704	...	|	1904	...	|	...	...
	Berlin Ostkreuz △ d.	|	...	0832	|	...	1033	|	...	1233	|	...	1433	|	...	1633	|	...	1833	|	...	2033	...	...
6	**Berlin** Südkreuz **835** d.	|	...	|	|	...	|	|	...	|	|	...	|	|	...	|	|	...	|	|	...	|	...	...
120	Doberlug-Kirchhain **835** d.	|	...	0926	|	...	1126	|	...	1326	|	...	1526	|	...	1726	|	...	1926	|	...	2126	...	...
140	Elsterwerda **843 835** d.	|	...	0937	|	...	1137	|	...	1337	|	...	1537	|	...	1737	|	...	1937	|	...	2137	...	...
193	**Dresden** Neustadt a.	0900	...	1021	1100	...	1221	1300	...	1421	1500	...	1621	1700	...	1821	1900	...	2021	2100	...	2221	...	...
197	**Dresden** Hbf **843** a.	0906	...	1027	1106	...	1227	1306	...	1427	1506	...	1627	1706	...	1827	1906	...	2027	2107	...	2227	...	...
	Praha hl.n. **1100** a.	1127	...	...	1323	...	...	1523	...	...	1723	...	...	1923	...	...	2123	...	...	...	...	...	...	...

km	*For night trains see Table* **60**	*IC* **2274** ①–⑥ 🍷n		*RJ* **2078** ✕	*IC* **2272** C🍷	*IC* **2472** N 🍷		*EC* **178** ✕	*IC* **2270** C🍷		*EC* **176** ✕	*IC* **2178** 🍷		*EC* **174** ✕	*IC* **2176** 🍷		*EC* **378** ✕	*IC* **2174** 🍷		*EC* **172** B✕	*IC* **2172** 🍷		*EC* **170** ✕	
	Praha hl.n. **1100** d.	...	...	...	...	...	...	0628	...	...	0828	...	...	1028	...	...	1233	...	...	1433	...	...	1628	...
0	**Dresden** Hbf **843** d.	0530	...	0700	0730	0805	...	0855	0930	...	1055	1130	...	1255	1330	...	1455	1530	...	1655	1730	...	1855	...
4	**Dresden** Neustadt d.	0537	...	0707	0737	0820	...	0902	0937	...	1102	1137	...	1302	1337	...	1502	1537	...	1702	1737	...	1902	...
57	Elsterwerda **843 835** d.	0624	...	|	0824	0900	...	|	1024	...	|	1224	...	|	1424	...	|	1624	...	|	1824	...	|	...
77	Doberlug-Kirchhain **835** d.	0634	...	|	0835	|	...	|	1034	...	|	1234	...	|	1434	...	|	1634	...	|	1834	...	|	...
205	**Berlin** Südkreuz **835** a.	0728	...	|	|	|	...	|	|	...	|	|	...	|	|	...	|	|	...	|	|	...	|	...
	Berlin Ostkreuz ▽ a.	|	...	|	0929	|	...	|	1128	...	|	1328	...	|	1528	...	|	1728	...	|	1928	...	|	...
	Berlin Ostbahnhof **835** a.	|	...	0853	|	1043**g**	...	1112	|	...	1312	|	...	1512	|	...	1712	|	...	1912	|	...	2112	...
211	**Berlin** Hbf **835** a.	0733	...	0904	|	|	...	1124	|	...	1324	|	...	1524	|	...	1724	|	...	1924	|	...	2124	...
	Rostock Hbf **835** a.	0936	...	...	1138	1236	...	...	1337	...	...	1537	...	...	1737	...	...	1936	...	...	2136	...	...	...
	Hamburg Hbf **840** a.	...	...	...	...	...	...	...	...	...	...	...	...	...	...	...	...	...	...	...	...	...	...	...

B – To/from Budapest (Table **60**).
C – To/from Chemnitz (Table **880**).
N – ⑥ until Nov. 1 (also Oct. 3).

g – Berlin **Gesundbrunnen**.
n – Not Oct. 4.

△ – Trains also call at Gesundbrunnen 11 minutes earlier.
▽ – Trains also call at Gesundbrunnen 11 minutes later.

840 HAMBURG - BERLIN

AMENDED SERVICE AUGUST 2 - DECEMBER 13. See pages 399/400 for service until August 1.
All services are diverted via Salzwedel during this period (trains do not call at Büchen, Ludwigslust or Wittenberge so these stations have been temporarily removed from this table).
Note that there are no through trains from Hamburg to Dresden and Praha during this period – see Table **839** for connecting trains Berlin - Dresden - Praha.

km		*ICE* **701** ①–⑤ M✕	*ICE* **505** ①–⑥ M✕	*ICE* **703** M✕	*ICE* **507** M✕	*ICE* **705** M✕	*ICE* **509** M✕	*ICE* **707** M✕	*ICE* **1601** M✕	*ICE* **709** M✕	*ICE* **603** M✕	*ICE* **801** M✕		*ICE* **1605** M✕	*ICE* **1705** Ⓑh J✕		*ICE* **803** N✕	*ICE* **1607** D✕	*ICE* **699** F✕	*ICE* **609** ✕	*ICE* **807** ✕	*ICE* **907** z ✕		*ICE* **809** ⑤⑦ ✕f z
	Kiel Hbf **820** d.	...	...	...	...	0742	...	...	...	...	...	...	...	...	...	...	...	...	...	...	...	...	...	
0	**Hamburg** Altona d.	0432	0533	0634	0719	|	0922	1020	1134	1219	1334	1421	...	1538	1538	...	1616	1735	1836	1937	2035	2121	...	2236
7	**Hamburg** Hbf d.	0449	0550	0648	0737	0852	0937	1040	1149	1240	1348	1440	...	1552	1552	...	1638	1748	1849	1950	2049	2137	...	2249
92	Uelzen d.	0536	0632	0736	0830	|	1030	1135	1230	|	1431	1537	...	1631	1631	...	1736	1833	|	2031	|	2226	...	2334
143	Salzwedel d.	0610	0658	0810	0857	1010	1057	1210	|	1410	1458	1610	...	|	|	...	1810	|	2010	2057	2157	2253	...	0010
201	Stendal Hbf d.	0637	0727	0837	0927	1037	1127	1237	1327	1437	1527	1637	...	1727	1727	...	1837	1927	2037	|	2226	2321	...	0039
293	**Berlin** Spandau a.	0711	0808	0911	1011	1110	1207	1311	1407	1511	1610	1710	...	1810	1810	...	1911	2006	2111	2157	2304	2356	...	0116
306	**Berlin** Hbf a.	0722	0820	0922	1022	1123	1220	1322	1420	1522	1622	1722	...	1821	1821	...	1922	2019	2121	2209	2316	0007	...	0126
312	**Berlin** Südkreuz a.	0739	0833	0939	1033	1139	1233	1339	1434	1539	1633	1739	...	1834	1834	...	1936	2034**b**	2131	2217	2325	0016	...	0134
	Dresden Hbf **839** a.	...	...	...	...	...	...	...	...	...	...	...	...	...	...	...	...	...	...	...	...	...	...	...
	Praha hl.n. **60** a.	...	...	...	...	...	...	...	...	...	...	...	...	...	...	...	...	...	...	...	...	...	...	...

	ICE **908** ①–⑤ ✕	*ICE* **1608** ⑦ ✕	*ICE* **608** ①–⑤ ✕		*ICE* **808** ✕	*ICE* **1606** L✕	*ICE* **806** E✕	*ICE* **1604** N✕	*ICE* **1704** ①–⑥ dJ ✕	*ICE* **804** M✕	*ICE* **602** M✕	*ICE* **802** M✕	*ICE* **1600** M✕	*ICE* **800** M✕	*ICE* **508** M✕	*ICE* **708** M✕	*ICE* **506** M✕	*ICE* **706** M✕	*ICE* **504** M✕	*ICE* **704** z M✕	*ICE* **502** z M✕	*ICE* **700** z ✕	*ICE* **906** ⑦ ✕	
Praha hl.n. **60** d.	...	...	...	...	...	...	...	...	...	...	...	...	...	...	...	...	...	...	...	...	...	...	...	...
Dresden Hbf **839** d.	...	...	...	...	...	...	...	...	...	...	...	...	...	...	...	...	...	...	...	...	...	...	...	...
Berlin Südkreuz d.	0430	0534	0533	...	0629	0724	0828	0924	0924	1017	1124	1217	1324	1417	1524	1617	1725	1817	1925	2017	2125	2227	2332	...
Berlin Hbf d.	0438	0544	0544	...	0639	0738	0838	0938	0938	1037	1137	1237	1338	1437	1538	1637	1738	1837	1938	2038	2137	2238	2341	...
Berlin Spandau d.	0450	0559	0558	...	0649	0749	0849	0949	0949	1049	1148	1249	1351	1449	1548	1649	1748	1849	1949	2049	2147	2249	2352	...
Stendal Hbf d.	0523	0633	0633	...	0722	0831	0922	1031	1031	1122	1231	1322	1431	1522	1630	1722	1831	1922	2030	2123	2232	2322	0036	...
Salzwedel d.	0549**r**	0702	0702	...	0749	|	0949	|	|	1149	1302	1349	|	1549	1702	1749	1902	1949	2102	2159	2312	2349	0105	...
Uelzen d.	0621	0730	0730	...	|	0930	1017	1130	1130	|	1330	|	1530	1617	1730	|	1930	|	2130	|	2343	0017	0131	...
Hamburg Hbf a.	0712	0814	0814	...	0908	1011	1104	1211	1211	1306	1411	1506	1611	1717	1823	1911	2011	2109	2209	2310	0031	0100	0216	...
Hamburg Altona a.	0726	...	...	...	0921	1025	1120	1225	1225	1320	1425	1521	1625	1736	1838	|	2025	2123	2225	2324	0047	0116	0229	...
Kiel Hbf **820** a.	...	...	...	...	...	...	...	...	...	...	...	...	...	...	...	2022	...	...	...	...	...	...	...	...

D – [12] Hamburg - Berlin (- Leipzig - Erfurt Ⓑ**b**) (- München ⑤**f**).
E – [12] (Eisenach ①–⑤ -) Leipzig - Berlin - Hamburg.
F – [12] Hamburg - Berlin - Leipzig - Erfurt - Frankfurt - Stuttgart - München.
J – To/from Jena (Table **849a**).
L – [12] (Erfurt ①–⑤ -) Leipzig - Berlin - Hamburg.
M – To/from München via Erfurt (Table **850**).
N – To/from Nürnberg via Erfurt (Table **850**).

b – Not ⑥.
d – Not Oct. 4.
f – Also Oct. 2; not Oct. 3.
h – Not Oct. 3.
r – Not ①.
z – Also runs on Aug. 1.

Replacement 🚌 service Aug. 2 - Oct. 31.
Hamburg - Ludwigslust - Wittenberge:
From Hamburg Hbf (ZOB): 1000, 1400, 1615.
From Wittenberge: 0530, 0830, 1400.
Journey 1h 35m Hamburg - Ludwigslust, 2h 35m Hamburg - Wittenberge.

970 SALZBURG - VILLACH - KLAGENFURT

AMENDED SERVICE UNTIL JULY 13, 2025. See page 467 for service from July 14.
During this period the Tauern Tunnel (between Bad Gastein and Mallnitz-Obervellach) is closed for modernisation work.

km		IC 730	IC 770	IC 894				IC 772	IC 898			RJ 536		IC 736	RJ 111	IC 15111			D 874		IC 776	IC 596			D 876		IC 830	EC 113
					n	a	a			n	a		a			c	n	a		a			n	a		a		
		A 🍷	🍷	🍷	🚌	🚌	🚌	🍷	🍷	🚌	🚌	A ✕	🚌	A 🍷	✕	🍷	🚌	🚌	2	🚌	🍷	🍷	🚌	🚌	2	🚌	A 🍷	B 🍷
	Wien Hbf **950** d.	...	...	...	...	...	...	...	...	...	...	...	...	...	...	...	...	...	...	...	...	...	...	...	...	...	...	...
	München Hbf **890** d.	...	...	...	...	...	...	...	...	...	...	...	...	...	0816r	...	...	...	...	...	...	...	...	...	...	...	...	1217r
0	**Salzburg** Hbf **960 975** d.	...	...	0612	...	...	...	...	0812	...	...	...	...	...	1012	...	...	...	...	...	...	1212	...	...	...	...	...	1412
29	Golling-Abtenau **960** d.	...	...	0633	...	...	...	...	0833	...	...	...	...	...	1033	...	...	...	...	...	...	1233	...	...	...	...	...	1433
53	**Bischofshofen** **960 975** d.	...	...	0654	...	0715	0815	...	0854	...	0915	...	1015	...	1054	...	...	1115	...	1215	...	1254	...	1315	...	1415	...	1454
61	St Johann im Pongau **960** d.	...	...	0704	...	|	|	...	0904	...	|	...	|	...	1104	...	...	|	...	|	...	1304	...	|	...	|	...	1504
67	**Schwarzach - St Veit 960** d.	...	...	0711	0715	|	|	...	0911	0915	|	...	|	...	1109	1114	1115	|	...	|	...	1311	1315	|	...	|	...	1511
86	Bad Hofgastein d.	...	...	0730c	0738	|	|	...	0930c	0938	|	...	|	...	...	1133	1138	|	...	|	...	1330c	1338	|	...	|	...	1530c
97	Bad Gastein d.	...	...	0741c	0755	|	|	...	0941c	0955	|	...	|	...	...	1144	1155	|	...	|	...	1341c	1355	|	...	|	...	1541c
113	Mallnitz-Obervellach d.	0517	0717	...	...	|	|	0917	...	...	|	...	|	1117	...	...	...	|	...	|	1317	...	...	|	...	|	1517	...
146	Spittal-Millstättersee **971** d.	0546	0746	...	...	0835	0935	0946	...	...	1035	1046	1135	1146	...	...	...	1235	1246	1335	1350f	...	...	1435	1446	1535	1546	...
182	**Villach** Hbf **971** a.	0609	0809	...	...	...	...	1009	...	...	...	1109	...	1209	...	...	...	...	1309	...	1413	...	...	...	1509	...	1609	...
182	**Villach** Hbf **971** d.	0613	0812	...	...	...	...	1012	...	...	...	1114	...	1213	...	...	...	...	...	...	1416	...	...	...	...	...	1613	...
198	Velden am Wörthersee **971** d.	0624	0823	...	...	...	...	1023	...	...	...	1125	...	1224	...	...	...	...	...	...	1428	...	...	...	...	...	1624	...
207	Pörtschach ⊙ **971** d.	0630	0830	...	...	...	...	1030	...	...	...	|	...	1230	...	...	...	...	...	...	1435	...	...	...	...	...	1630	...
220	**Klagenfurt** Hbf **971** a.	0638	0842	...	...	...	...	1042	...	...	...	1137	...	1238	...	...	...	...	...	...	1446	...	...	...	...	...	1638	...

				IC 780	ICE 115	RJ 15115				D 880	D 696			IC 782	IC 698			D 882		IC 784	ICE 117			RJ 884	IC 794			IC 786
	n	a	a			c	n	Ⓐ	a		e	gn	a			n	a		a			cn	a			n	a	
	🚌	🚌	🚌	🍷	C	✕	🚌	🚌	🚌	2	2	🚌	🚌	🍷	🍷	🚌	🚌	2	🚌	🍷	D	🚌	🚌	✕	🍷	🚌	🚌	🍷
Wien Hbf **950** d.	...	...	...	...	...	...	...	...	...	...	...	...	...	...	...	...	...	...	...	...	...	...	...	...	...	...	...	...
München Hbf **890** d.	...	...	...	...	1417t	...	...	...	...	...	...	...	...	...	...	...	...	...	...	...	1817	...	...	...	...	...	...	...
Salzburg Hbf **960 975** d.	...	...	...	...	1612	...	...	...	...	...	1716	...	...	...	1812	...	...	...	...	...	2012	...	...	...	2112	...	...	...
Golling-Abtenau **960** d.	...	...	...	...	1633	...	...	...	...	...	|	...	...	...	1833	...	...	...	...	...	2033	...	...	...	2138	...	...	...
Bischofshofen **960 975** d.	...	1515	1615	...	1654	...	...	...	1715	...	1800	...	1815	...	1854	...	1915	...	2015	...	2054	...	2115	...	2200	...	2215	...
St Johann im Pongau **960** d.	...	|	|	...	1704	...	...	...	|	...	1810	...	|	...	1904	...	|	...	|	...	2104	...	|	...	2209	...	|	...
Schwarzach - St Veit. **960** d.	1515	|	|	...	1709	1714	1715	...	|	...	1815	1825	|	...	1911	1915	|	...	|	...	2111	2115	|	...	2216	2220	|	...
Bad Hofgastein d.	1538	|	|	...	...	1733	1738	...	|	...	...	1848	|	...	1930c	1938	|	...	|	...	2128	2138	|	...	2233c	2243	|	...
Bad Gastein d.	1555	|	|	...	...	1744	1755	...	|	...	...	1905	|	...	1941c	1955	|	...	|	...	...	2155	|	...	2244c	2300	|	...
Mallnitz-Obervellach d.	...	|	|	1717	...	...	...	1800	|	...	...	...	|	1917	...	...	|	...	|	2117	...	...	|	...	...	...	|	2317
Spittal-Millstättersee **971** d.	...	1635	1735	1750f	...	...	...	1827	1835	1846	...	...	1935	1950f	...	...	2035	2046	2135	2146	...	...	2235	2246	...	...	2335	2346
Villach Hbf **971** a.	...	...	...	1813	...	...	...	...	...	1909	...	...	...	2013	...	...	...	2109	...	2209	...	...	...	2309	...	...	...	0009
Villach Hbf **971** d.	...	...	...	1816	...	...	...	...	...	...	...	...	...	2016	...	...	...	2112	...	2212	...	...	...	2312	...	...	...	0012
Velden am Wörthersee **971** d.	...	...	...	1828	...	...	...	...	...	...	...	...	...	2028	...	...	...	2123	...	2223	...	...	...	2323	...	...	...	0023
Pörtschach ⊙ **971** d.	...	...	...	1835	...	...	...	...	...	...	...	...	...	2035	...	...	...	2130	...	2230	...	...	...	2330	...	...	...	0030
Klagenfurt Hbf **971** a.	...	...	...	1846	...	...	...	...	...	...	...	...	...	2046	...	...	...	2142	...	2242	...	...	...	2342	...	...	...	0042

	IC 889				IC 771	IC 597		D 871			IC 691	IC 773		RJ 639			IC 15114	ICE 114	IC 775		D 875			EC 112	IC 733			
		a	Ⓐ	n			a		a	n			a		a	n	c			a		a	n			a	a	n
	🍷	🚌	2	🚌	🍷	🍷	🚌	2	🚌	🚌	🍷	🍷	🚌	F ✕	🚌	🚌	🍷	E 🍷	🍷	🚌	2	🚌	🚌	B 🍷	A 🍷	🚌	🚌	🚌
Klagenfurt Hbf **971** d.	0416	...	...	...	0516	...	...	0616	...	...	...	0716	...	0822	...	...	...	...	0916	...	...	...	...	...	1121	...	...	...
Pörtschach ⊙ **971** d.	0429	...	...	...	0529	...	...	0629	...	...	...	0729	...	0832	...	...	...	...	0929	...	...	...	...	...	1131	...	...	...
Velden am Wörthersee **971** d.	0436	...	...	...	0536	...	...	0636	...	...	...	0736	...	|	...	...	...	...	0936	...	...	...	...	...	1138	...	...	...
Villach Hbf **971** a.	0447	...	...	...	0547	...	...	0647	...	...	...	0747	...	0846	...	...	...	...	0947	...	...	...	...	...	1148	...	...	...
Villach Hbf **971** d.	0450	...	0529	...	0550	...	...	0650	...	...	...	0750	...	0850	...	...	...	...	0950	...	1050	...	...	...	1150	...	...	...
Spittal-Millstättersee **971** d.	0512	0520	0605	...	0642	...	0620	0712	0720	...	...	0819h	0820	0912	0920	...	...	...	1019h	1020	1112	1120	...	...	1219h	1220	1320	...
Mallnitz-Obervellach d.	▬	|	0633	...	▬	...	|	▬	|	...	...	0842	|	▬	|	...	...	...	1042	|	▬	|	...	...	1242	|	|	...
Bad Gastein d.	*D* **595**	|	...	0600	n 🚌	0619c	|	n 🚌	|	0800	0819c	...	|	n 🚌	|	1000	1016	...	...	|	n 🚌	|	1200	1219c	...	|	|	...
Bad Hofgastein d.	**e** 2	|	...	|	0618	0632c	|	0818	|	|	0832c	...	|	1018	|	|	1029	...	...	|	1218	|	|	1232c	...	|	|	1418
Schwarzach - St Veit. **960** d.	0519	|	...	0640	0640	0652	|	0840	|	0840	0852	...	|	1040	|	1040	1047	1052	...	|	1240	|	1240	1252	...	|	|	1440
St Johann im Pongau **960** d.	0526	|	...	...	...	0658	|	...	|	...	0858	...	|	...	|	...	...	1058	...	|	...	|	...	1258	...	|	|	...
Bischofshofen **960 975** a.	0535	0640	...	...	...	0708	0740	...	0840	...	0908	...	0940	...	1040	...	...	1108	...	1140	...	1240	...	1308	...	1340	1440	...
Golling-Abtenau **960** a.	0556	...	...	...	...	|	...	...	...	...	0928	...	...	...	...	...	...	1128	...	...	...	...	...	1328	...	...	...	...
Salzburg Hbf **960 975** a.	0619	...	...	...	...	0749	...	...	...	...	0948	...	...	...	...	...	...	1148	...	...	...	...	...	1348	...	...	...	...
München Hbf **890** a.	...	...	...	...	...	...	...	...	...	...	...	...	...	...	...	...	...	1341t	...	...	...	...	...	1541r	...	...	...	...
Wien Hbf **950** a.	...	...	...	...	...	...	...	...	...	...	...	...	...	...	...	...	...	...	...	...	...	...	...	...	...	...	...	...

		IC 793	IC 779		D 879			IC 797	IC 737		D 881			RJ 110	IC 783		IC 539			IC 895	IC 785		RJ 631		IC 833			IC 789
	n			a		a	n			a		a	n			a	⚒	a	n			a		a		n		
	🚌	🍷	🍷	🚌	2	🚌	🚌	🍷	A 🍷	🚌	2	🚌	🚌	✕	🍷	🚌	🍷	🚌	🚌	🍷	🍷	🚌	A ✕	🚌	A 🍷	🚌	2	🍷
Klagenfurt Hbf **971** d.	...	...	1316	...	...	...	...	...	1521	...	...	...	...	...	1716	...	1821	...	...	...	1912	...	2021	...	2121	...	2338	...
Pörtschach ⊙ **971** d.	...	...	1329	...	...	...	...	...	1531	...	...	...	...	...	1725	...	|	...	...	...	1925	...	2032	...	2131	...	|	...
Velden am Wörthersee **971** d.	...	...	1336	...	...	...	...	...	1538	...	...	...	...	...	1732	...	1836	...	...	...	1932	...	|	...	2138	...	|	...
Villach Hbf **971** a.	...	...	1347	...	...	...	...	...	1548	...	...	...	...	...	1743	...	1846	...	...	...	1943	...	2046	...	2148	...	0001	...
Villach Hbf **971** d.	...	...	1350	...	1450	...	...	...	1550	...	1650	...	...	...	1746	...	1850	...	...	...	1946	...	2050	...	2150	...	▬	0013
Spittal-Millstättersee **971** d.	...	...	1419h	1420	1512	1520	...	...	1619h	1620	1712	1720	...	...	1819f	1820	1912	1920	...	...	2019f	2015	2112	2120	2219h	...	*ICE*	0037
Mallnitz-Obervellach d.	...	...	1442	|	▬	|	...	...	1642	|	▬	|	...	...	1842	|	▬	|	...	...	2042	|	▬	|	2242	...	**899**	0100
Bad Gastein d.	1400	1419c	...	|	n 🚌	|	1600	1619c	...	|	n 🚌	|	1800	1819c	...	|	n 🚌	|	2000	2019c	...	|	n 🚌	|	...	2200		...
Bad Hofgastein d.	|	1432c	...	|	1618	|	|	1632c	...	|	1818	|	|	1832c	...	|	2018	|	|	2032c	...	|	2218	|	...	|	✕	...
Schwarzach - St Veit. **960** d.	1440	1452	...	|	1640	|	1640	1652	...	|	1840	|	1840	1852	...	|	2040	|	2040	2052	...	|	2240	|	...	2240	2252	...
St Johann im Pongau **960** d.	...	1458	...	|	...	|	...	1658	...	|	...	|	...	1858	...	|	...	|	...	2058	...	|	...	|	...	...	2258	...
Bischofshofen **960 975** a.	...	1508	...	1540	...	1640	...	1708	...	1740	...	1840	...	1908	...	1940	...	2040	...	2108	...	2135	...	2240	...	...	2308	...
Golling-Abtenau **960** a.	...	1528	...	...	...	...	...	1728	...	...	...	...	...	1928	...	...	...	...	...	2128	...	...	...	...	...	...	2331	...
Salzburg Hbf **960 975** a.	...	1548	...	...	...	...	...	1748	...	...	...	...	...	1948	...	...	...	...	...	2148	...	...	...	...	...	...	2355	...
München Hbf **890** a.	...	...	...	...	...	...	...	...	...	...	...	...	...	2141r	...	...	...	...	...	...	...	...	...	...	...	...	...	...
Wien Hbf **950** a.	...	...	...	...	...	...	...	...	...	...	...	...	...	...	...	...	...	...	...	...	...	...	...	...	...	...	...	...

A – To/from Wien via Leoben (Table **980**).
B – (12) and 🍷 Frankfurt - München - Salzburg - Bad Gastein and v.v.
C – (12) and ✕ Münster - Köln - Stuttgart - München - Salzburg - Schwarzach - St Veit.
D – (12) and ✕ Frankfurt - München - Bad Hofgastein.
E – (12) and ✕ Schwarzach - St Veit - Salzburg - München - Stuttgart - Köln - Dortmund.
F – To/from Graz (Table **980**).

a – Until June 27.
b – Until July 13.
c – Until Mar. 2.
d – Until Apr. 15.
e – Ⓐ (not Dec. 25, 26, Jan. 1, 6, Apr. 21, May 29, June 9, 19).
f – Arrives 11 minutes earlier.
g – ①②③④⑦ until Mar. 2 (not Dec. 24, 31).
h – Arrives 7 minutes earlier.
n – Mar. 3 - July 13.
r – Not May 31 - July 13.
t – Not Apr. 16 - July 13.

⊙ – Pörtschach am Wörthersee.

NEWSLINES (continued from page 5)

ITALY

Due to late availability of timetable data combined with a large amount of engineering work taking place this summer, the Italian section has proved particularly difficult to update for this edition. Long-distance and high-speed trains (those shown with train numbers) have been checked and updated where possible and are generally valid from June 16 to September 14. All other services should be regarded as subject to confirmation – we hope to have them fully updated in time for the July digital edition. A summary of engineering work affecting principal tables can be found on page 284.

IC **608** Lecce – Bologna is extended to Milano Centrale (Table **615**).

Trains *IC* **558** and **562** Bari – Reggio di Calabria have been extended to and from Villa S. Giovanni (Tables **637** and **640**).

Due to engineering work, services between Napoli and Baiano are operated by bus until September 30 (Table **639**).

SPAIN

On May 22 Spanish Railways introduced an additional service in each direction between Madrid and Barcelona on Thursdays (Table **650**). The new trains depart Madrid at 1357 and Barcelona at 1425.

Two additional daily *Ouigo* services have been introduced in each direction between Madrid and Málaga, doubling the previous service level (Table **660**).

After nearly two years of closure for engineering work, rail services between Huesca and Canfranc resumed from June 9 (Table **670**).

Additional platforms are being constructed at València Joaquín Sorolla, temporarily reducing station capacity. Therefore, all *Euromed* services between Barcelona and València will use València Nord station until June 2026 (Table **672**).

A third *Alvia* service has been introduced in each direction between Madrid and Badajoz. The new *Alvia* services **194** (from Madrid) and **291**/**297** (to Madrid) are routed via Plasencia, where the trains reverse direction, but do not call at Monfragüe-Plasencia or Mérida (Table **677**).

Services between Madrid and the Spanish region of Galicia were recast from June 9 (Tables **680**, **681** and **682**). Two additional *AVE* services operate between Madrid and A Coruña on Mondays to Fridays with extra services also running on Saturdays and Sundays.

Through *Alvia* services **4064** and **4175** between Ferrol and Madrid have been withdrawn (Table **681**), but alternative connections are available via A Coruña (shown on Table **682**).

PORTUGAL

Until October 5 an additional pair of daily *InterRegional* trains will run between Porto São Bento and Pochino (Table **694**). Train **865** will start at Porto Campanhã rather than São Bento and an additional service will run between Régua and Pinhão by extending existing trains. The *Comboio Historico* excursion train from Régua to Tua returns this summer but, due to gauge clearance issues following modernisation works, it will be hauled by an historic diesel locomotive until the necessary safety checks have been made to allow a steam locomotive to be used once again.

SWEDEN

Services operated by SJ (Swedish Railways) are valid until August 31, although the large amount of engineering work taking place across the network, along with complex summer variations, means that it has not been possible to show full details. Passengers are advised to recheck timings when reserving or before travel.

Notable areas where bus substitution is in place this summer include the Borlänge – Ludvika – Mora line which is closed between July 14 and August 10 (Tables **755**, **758** and **766**), whilst there is no rail service between Mjölby and Hallsberg from July 7 to August 10 (Table **755**).

A new through service between Malmö and Oslo, operated by *Vy*, will be introduced from July 14 with two journeys each way, although it will only run for a four week period until early August (Table **735**). Another innovation aimed at summer holidaymakers is *Snälltåget*'s twice-weekly Malmö – Stockholm – Storlien train, details for which will be found in Table **767**. Note that on certain dates the train will run via Göteborg rather than the Malmö to Stockholm main line.

GERMANY

Line closures and other trackwork continue to have a large impact on the German rail network. The most significant change will be in the north with the complete closure of the Hamburg to Berlin line from August 2, requiring special versions of Table **840** and other associated tables which will be found on pages 606 to 608. Many trains are diverted via Salzwedel, whilst others are cancelled between Hamburg and Berlin, including trains to and from Praha via Dresden. Services on the Hamburg – Rostock – Stralsund route (Table **830**) are also affected with only a limited number of through *IC* trains (which are diverted via Lübeck). Note that Wittenberge will be left without trains during this period, the journey to Stendal being partly by bus (Table **841**).

Another significant period of engineering work affects most of the Köln - Hannover – Leipzig – Dresden *IC* trains, which are split to run in two sections from June 7 to August 8, no longer running between Bielefeld and Hannover (Tables **810** and **866**). From July 26 to September 5 it is the turn of certain services in the Stuttgart area to be retimed, with some bus substitution involved, notably affecting S-Bahn services to the airport (Table **936a**) and some Stuttgart – Zürich trains (Table **940**). These changes are in connection with the major *Stuttgart 21* project which involves the complete rebuilding of Stuttgart's main station with underground through platforms replacing the existing terminus.

Later in the year, Essen to Dortmund via Bochum will once again be affected, this time between September 6 and October 31, with many trains retimed and others rerouted via Wuppertal. Bochum will only be served by local trains. Where possible, details are shown in our tables.

Those wishing to sample the excellent Harz narrow gauge network (Table **867**) should note that there are no trains serving the Harzgerode branch (with no bus substitution) during the current summer timetable which runs until November 11.

Just under four years since the line between Köln and Trier via Gerolstein was severely damaged by flooding, the middle section between Kall and Gerolstein is the final part of the route to be fully restored allowing the long-awaited return of through trains between Köln and Gerolstein from June 16 (Table **915a**). Work to electrify the entire route is continuing which means the section between Gerolstein and Trier will be closed to rail traffic until September 29. The full service between Köln and Trier will resume for a short period until October 12. This will be followed by further service alterations between Euskirchen and Gerolstein as electrification work continues.

Another line with an improved service is Table **849** where the hourly Halle – Naumburg trains are extended to Erfurt which, when combined with the Leipzig – Erfurt – Eisenach trains, gives a half-hourly service between Naumburg and Erfurt.

AUSTRIA

Readers are reminded that major engineering work on the Tauern Tunnel route continues until July 13 after which normal services are expected to resume. A special version of Table **970** will be found on page 609 with details of the amended service until July 13.

Table **956** has been updated with the full service between Jenbach and Achensee until October 25. Table **957** has been expanded and updated for the summer season, showing the full bus service between Krimml and Mayrhofen as well as updated steam train schedules between Zell am See and Mittersill.

Work to electrify the Wien – Marchegg – Bratislava route is taking longer than expected and it is now hoped the full service will resume on October 10 (Table **996**).

CZECH REPUBLIC

Due to engineering work, services between Zittau and Liberec are operated by bus until September 30 (Table **1117**).

FERRIES

DFDS has introduced a new direct ferry service between Rosslare and Dunkerque which operates five days per week with a sailing time of between 23 and 25 hours (Table **2138**). It should be noted that it is only available for passengers with vehicles (including bicycles).

DFDS is also operating a service between Kapellskär (Sweden) and Paldiski (Estonia), timings for which will be found in Table **2412**.

Table **2502** has been expanded to include additional sailings between Algeciras and Tanjah (Tangiers) operated by Baleària and Trasmediterranea.